WHO'S WHO
1978

WHO *WAS* WHO

Six volumes containing the biographies removed from WHO'S WHO each year on account of death, with final details and date of death added.

VOL.   I.   1897-1915

VOL.   II.   1916-1928

VOL.   III.   1929-1940

VOL.   IV.   1941-1950

VOL.   V.   1951-1960

VOL.   VI.   1961-1970

ADAM & CHARLES BLACK : LONDON

WHO'S WHO
1978

AN
ANNUAL BIOGRAPHICAL DICTIONARY

ONE HUNDRED AND THIRTIETH
YEAR OF ISSUE

ADAM AND CHARLES BLACK
LONDON

PUBLISHED BY A. & C. BLACK LIMITED
35 BEDFORD ROW LONDON WC1

———

COPYRIGHT © 1978 A. & C. BLACK LTD

"WHO'S WHO" IS A REGISTERED TRADE MARK
IN THE UNITED KINGDOM

ISBN 0 7136 1794 2

The United States
ST MARTIN'S PRESS, NEW YORK

Europe
JOHN A. KEEP, BEDFORD ROW, LONDON

Australia
EDWARD ARNOLD (AUSTRALIA) LTD, PORT MELBOURNE

New Zealand
BOOK REPS (NEW ZEALAND) LTD, AUCKLAND

Canada
THOMAS NELSON & SONS LTD, DON MILLS

Southern Africa
BOOK PROMOTION (PTY) LTD, WYNBERG

West Indies
C. B. C. (TRINIDAD) LTD

Far East
BOOKS FOR ASIA LTD, SINGAPORE, KUALA LUMPUR,
HONG KONG, TOKYO, BANGKOK

DATA COMPUTED BY COMPUTER DATA PROCESSING (CDP) LIMITED
AND COMPUTER TYPESET BY COMPUTAPRINT LIMITED

PRINTED IN GREAT BRITAIN BY BUTLER & TANNER LTD, FROME & LONDON

PREFACE

Some occurrences of a date later than November 1977, when this edition had to go to press, could not be recorded in the relevant entries; a number of these, of the most general interest, are listed in a supplement preceding the first page of the biographies. The names in the second part of the supplement of those who received titles gazetted in the New Year Honours List, 1978, include some who have as yet no entry in the body of the book. The obituary, on pages 26–30, includes the deaths reported up to mid-November 1977.

A proof of each entry is posted to its subject every year for personal revision, but this cannot be sent unless an address is given. It should be pointed out that the numbers given of the children of a marriage are, unless otherwise indicated, those of the sons and daughters now living; also, that it is the practice to print the names of London clubs unaccompanied by the word London. Forenames printed within brackets are those which the subject of the entry does not commonly use. While every care is taken to ensure accuracy, neither the publishers nor the printers can admit liability for any loss incurred through misprint or other circumstances.

It cannot be stated too emphatically that inclusion in *Who's Who* has never at any time been a matter for payment or of obligation to purchase the volume.

CONTENTS

ABBREVIATIONS USED IN THIS BOOK

Some of the designatory letters in this list are used merely for economy of
space and do not necessarily imply any professional or other qualification

A

AA	Anti-Aircraft; Automobile Association; Architectural Association; Augustinians of the Assumption
AAA.	Amateur Athletic Association; American Accountancy Association
AAAL	American Academy of Arts and Letters
AA&QMG	Assistant Adjutant and Quartermaster-General
AAAS	American Association for Advancement of Science
AACCA	Associate of the Association of Certified and Corporate Accountants; now see ACCA
AAF	Auxiliary Air Force (now RAuxAF)
AAG.	Assistant Adjutant-General
AAI	Associate of Chartered Auctioneers' and Estate Agents' Institute; now (after amalgamation) see ARICS
AAMC	Australian Army Medical Corps
A&AEE	Aeroplane and Armament Experimental Establishment
AASA	Associate of Australian Society of Accountants
AAUQ	Associate in Accountancy, University of Queensland
AB	Bachelor of Arts (US); able-bodied seaman
ABA	Amateur Boxing Association; Antiquarian Booksellers' Association; American Bar Association
ABC	Australian Broadcasting Commission
ABCA	Army Bureau of Current Affairs
ABCC	Association of British Chambers of Commerce
ABCFM	American Board of Commissioners for Foreign Missions
Abp	Archbishop
ABPsS	Associate, British Psychological Society
ABRC	Advisory Board for the Research Councils
ABSI	Associate, Boot and Shoe Institution
ABSM	Associate, Birmingham and Midland Institute School of Music
ABTAPL	Association of British Theological and Philosophical Libraries
AC	Companion of the Order of Australia; Ante Christum (before Christ)
ACA	Associate of the Institute of Chartered Accountants
Acad.	Academy
ACAS	Assistant Chief of the Air Staff
ACC	Association of County Councils
ACCA	Associate of the Association of Certified Accountants
ACCM	Advisory Council for the Church's Ministry (formerly CACTM)
ACCS	Associate of Corporation of Secretaries (formerly of Certified Secretaries)
ACDS	Assistant Chief of Defence Staff
ACF	Army Cadet Force
ACG.	Assistant Chaplain-General
ACGI	Associate of City and Guilds of London Institute
ACII	Associate of the Chartered Insurance Institute
ACIS	Associate of the Institute of Chartered Secretaries and Administrators (formerly Chartered Institute of Secretaries)
ACIT	Associate, Chartered Institute of Transport
ACLS	American Council of Learned Societies
ACMA	Associate, Institute of Cost and Management Accountants
ACommA.	Associate, Society of Commercial Accountants; now see ASCA
ACOS	Assistant Chief of Staff
ACP.	Association of Clinical Pathologists
ACS	American Chemical Society; Additional Curates Society
ACSEA	Allied Command SE Asia
ACSM	Associate of the Camborne School of Mines
ACT.	Australian Capital Territory; Australian College of Theology; Associate of the College of Technology
ACTT	Association of Cinematograph, Television and Allied Technicians
ACU.	Association of Commonwealth Universities
ACWA	Associate of the Institute of Cost and Works Accountants; now see ACMA
AD	Anno Domini
ADB.	Asian Development Bank
ADC.	Aide-de-camp

ADCM	Archbishop of Canterbury's Diploma in Church Music
AD Corps	Army Dental Corps, now RADC
ADC (P)	Personal Aide-de-camp to HM The Queen
Ad eund.	Ad eundem gradum; and see under a e g
ADFW	Assistant Director of Fortifications and Works
ADGB	Air Defence of Great Britain
ADGMS	Assistant Director-General of Medical Services
ADH	Assistant Director of Hygiene
Adjt.	Adjutant
ADJAG	Assistant Deputy Judge Advocate General
Adm.	Admiral
ADMS	Assistant Director of Medical Services
ADOS	Assistant Director of Ordnance Services
ADPR	Assistant Director of Public Relations
ADS&T	Assistant Director of Supplies and Transport
Adv.	Advisory; Advocate
ADVS	Assistant Director of Veterinary Services
ADWE&M	Assistant Director of Works, Electrical and Mechanical
AE	Air Efficiency Award (changed 1975)
AEA.	Atomic Energy Authority; Air Efficiency Award (now see AE)
AEAF	Allied Expeditionary Air Force
AEC.	Agriculture Executive Council; Army Educational Corps (now RAEC)
AEF	Amalgamated Union of Engineering and Foundry Workers; American Expeditionary Forces
a e g	ad eundem gradum (to the same degree—of the admission of a graduate of one university to the same degree at another without examination)
AEGIS	Aid for the Elderly in Government Institutions
AEI	Associated Electrical Industries
AEM	Air Efficiency Medal
AER	Army Emergency Reserve
AERE	Atomic Energy Research Establishment (Harwell)
AEt., AEtat.	AEtatis (aged)
AEU.	Amalgamated Engineering Union
AFA.	Amateur Football Alliance
AFAIAA	Associate Fellow of American Institute of Aeronautics and Astronautics (and see under AFIAS)
AFC.	Air Force Cross; Association Football Club
AFCAI	Associate Fellow of the Canadian Aeronautical Institute
AFD.	Doctor of Fine Arts (US)
AFHQ	Allied Force Headquarters
AFIA	Associate of Federal Institute of Accountants (Australia)
AFIAS	(now see under AFAIAA) (formerly) Associate Fellow Institute of Aeronautical Sciences (US)
AFICD	Associate Fellow Institute of Civil Defence
AFM	Air Force Medal
AFRAeS	Associate Fellow Royal Aeronautical Society
AFV	Armoured Fighting Vehicles
AG	Attorney-General
AGARD	Advisory Group for Aerospace Research and Development
AGH	Australian General Hospital
AGI	Artistes Graphiques Internationales; Associate of the Institute of Certificated Grocers
AGRA	Army Group Royal Artillery
AGSM	Associate of Guildhall School of Music
AHA.	Area Health Authority
AHA(T)	Area Health Authority (Teaching)
AHQ	Army Headquarters
AH-WC	Associate of Heriot-Watt College, Edinburgh
ai	ad interim
AIA	Associate of the Institute of Actuaries; American Institute of Architects
AIAL	Associate Member of the International Institute of Arts and Letters
AIArb	Associate, Institute of Arbitrators
AIAS	Associate Surveyor Member, Incorporated Association of Architects and Surveyors
AIB	Associate of the Institute of Bankers
AIBD	Associate of the Institute of British Decorators

7

AIBP	.	Associate of the Institute of British Photographers
AIC	. .	Agricultural Improvement Council; also formerly Associate of the Institute of Chemistry (see ARIC)
AICA	.	Associate Member Commonwealth Institute of Accountants; Association Internationale des Critiques d'Art
AICC	.	All-India Congress Committee
AICE	.	Associate of the Institution of Civil Engineers
AICTA	.	Associate of the Imperial College of Tropical Agriculture
AIEE	.	Associate of the Institution of Electrical Engineers
AIF	. .	Australian Imperial Forces
AIG	. .	Adjutant-Inspector-General
AIIA	.	Associate Insurance Institute of America
AIInfSc	.	Associate, Institute of Information Scientists
AIL	. .	Associate of the Institute of Linguists
AILA	.	Associate of the Institute of Landscape Architects
AILocoE	.	Associate of Institution of Locomotive Engineers
AIM	. .	Associate, Institution of Metallurgists (now see MIM)
AIME	.	American Institute of Mechanical Engineers
AIMarE	.	Associate of the Institute of Marine Engineers
AInstM	.	Associate Member, Institute of Marketing
AInstP	.	Associate of Institute of Physics
AInstPI	.	Associate of the Institute of Patentees and Inventors
AIProdE	.	Associate, Institution of Production Engineers
AIS	. .	Associate of Institute of Statisticians; now see MIS
AISA	.	Associate of the Incorporated Secretaries' Association
AIStructE	.	Associate, Institution of Structural Engineers
AJAG	.	Assistant Judge Advocate General
AK	. .	Knight of the Order of Australia
AKC	. .	Associate of King's College (London)
ALA	. .	Associate of the Library Association
Ala	. .	Alabama (US)
ALAA	.	Associate, Library Association of Australia
ALAM	.	Associate, London Academy of Music and Dramatic Art
ALCD	.	Associate of London College of Divinity
ALCM	.	Associate of London College of Music
ALFSEA	.	Allied Land Forces South-East Asia
ALI	. .	Argyll Light Infantry
ALLC	.	Association for Literary and Linguistic Computing
ALP	. .	Australian Labor Party
ALS	. .	Associate of the Linnaean Society
Alta	. .	Alberta
AM	. .	Albert Medal; Member of the Order of Australia; Master of Arts (US); Alpes Maritimes
AMA	.	Association of Metropolitan Authorities; Assistant Masters Association; Associate of the Museums Association; Australian Medical Association
Amb.	.	Ambulance; Ambassador
AMBIM	.	Associate Member, British Institute of Management
AMBritIRE	.	(now see under AMIERE) (formerly) Associate Member of British Institution of Radio Engineers
AMC	.	Association of Municipal Corporations
AMet	.	Associate of Metallurgy (Sheffield University)
AMF	.	Australian Military Forces
AMGOT	.	Allied Military Government of Occupied Territory
AMIAE	.	Associate Member, Institution of Automobile Engineers
AMIAgrE	.	Associate Member of Institution of Agricultural Engineers
AMICE	.	Associate Member of Institution of Civil Engineers (formerly lower rank of corporate membership of Instn. now see under MICE; change dated July 1968)
AMIChemE	.	Associate Member of Institution of Chemical Engineers
AMIEA	.	Associate Member of Institute of Engineers, Australia
AMIED	.	Associate Member of Institution of Engineering Designers
AMIEE	.	Associate Member of Institution of Electrical Engineers (formerly lower rank of corporate membership of Instn, now see under MIEE; change dated Dec. 1966)
AMIE(Ind)	.	Associate Member, Institution of Engineers, India
AMIERE	.	Associate Member of Institution of Electronic and Radio Engineers (and see under AMBritIRE)
AMIMechE	.	Associate Member of Institution of Mechanical Engineers (formerly lower rank of corporate membership of Instn, now see under MIMechE, change dated April 1968)
AMIMinE	.	Associate Member of Institution of Mining Engineers
AMIMM	.	Associate Member of Institution of Mining and Metallurgy
AMInstBE	.	Associate Member of Institution of British Engineers
AMInstCE	.	Associate Member of Institution of Civil Engineers (changed 1946 to AMICE)
AmInstEE	.	American Institute of Electrical Engineers
AMInstR	.	Associate Member of Institute of Refrigeration
AMInstT	.	Associate Member of the Institute of Transport; now see ACIT
AMIStructE	.	Associate Member of the Institution of Structural Engineers
AMP	.	Advanced Management Program
AMRINA	.	Associate Member of Royal Institution of Naval Architects
AMS	. .	Assistant Military Secretary; Army Medical Service
AMTE	.	Admiralty Marine Technology Establishment
ANA	. .	Associate National Academician (America)
ANAF	.	Arab Non-Arab Friendship
Anat.	.	Anatomy; Anatomical
ANECInst	.	Associate of NE Coast Institution of Engineers and Shipbuilders
ANGAU	.	Australia New Guinea Administrative Unit
Anon.	.	Anonymously
ANU	.	Australian National University
ANZAAS	.	Australian and New Zealand Association for the Advancement of Science
AO	. .	Officer of the Order of Australia; Air Officer
AOA	. .	Air Officer in charge of Administration
AOC	. .	Air Officer Commanding
AOC-in-C	.	Air Officer Commanding-in-Chief
AOD	.	Army Ordnance Department
AOER	.	Army Officers Emergency Reserve
APA	. .	American Psychiatric Association
APD	. .	Army Pay Department
APEX	.	Association of Professional, Executive, Clerical and Computer Staffs
APHA	.	American Public Health Association
APS	. .	Aborigines Protection Society
APsSI	.	Associate, Psychological Society of Ireland
APSW	.	Association of Psychiatric Social Workers
APT&C	.	Administrative, Professional, Technical and Clerical
APTC	.	Army Physical Training Corps
AQ	. .	Administration and Quartering
AQMG	.	Assistant Quartermaster-General
AR	. .	Associated Rediffusion (Television)
ARA	. .	Associate of the Royal Academy
ARACI	.	Associate, Royal Australian Chemical Institute
ARAD	.	Associate of the Royal Academy of Dancing
ARAeS	.	Associate of the Royal Aeronautical Society
ARAM	.	Associate of the Royal Academy of Music
ARAS	.	Associate of the Royal Astronomical Society
ARBA	.	Associate of the Royal Society of British Artists
ARBC	.	Associate Royal British Colonial Society of Artists
ARBS	.	Associate Royal Society of British Sculptors
ARC	. .	Architects' Registration Council; Agricultural Research Council; Aeronautical Research Council
ARCA	.	Associate Royal College of Art; Associate Royal Canadian Academy
ARCamA	.	Associate Royal Cambrian Academy (formerly ARCA)
ARCE	.	Academical Rank of Civil Engineers
Archt	.	Architect
ARCM	.	Associate Royal College of Music
ARCO	.	Associate Royal College of Organists
ARCO(CHM)	.	Associate Royal College of Organists with Diploma in Choir Training
ARCPsych	.	Associate Member, Royal College of Psychiatrists
ARCS	.	Associate Royal College of Science
ARCST	.	Associate Royal College of Science and Technology (Glasgow)
ARCUK	.	Architects' Registration Council of the United Kingdom
ARCVS	.	Associate of Royal College of Veterinary Surgeons
ARE	. .	Associate of Royal Society of Painter-Etchers and Engravers; Arab Republic of Egypt
ARIAS	.	Associate, Royal Incorporation of Architects in Scotland
ARIBA	.	Associate of the Royal Institute of British Architects; and see RIBA
ARIC	.	Associate of the Royal Institute of Chemistry (now see MRIC)
ARICS	.	Professional Associate of the Royal Institution of Chartered Surveyors
Ark	. .	Arkansas (US)
ARLT	.	Association for the Reform of Latin Teaching
ARMS	.	Associate of the Royal Society of Miniature Painters
ARP	. .	Air Raid Precautions
ARPS	.	Associate of the Royal Photographic Society
ARRC	.	Associate of the Royal Red Cross
ARSA	.	Associate Royal Scottish Academy
ARSCM	.	Associate, Royal School of Church Music
ARSM	.	Associate Royal School of Mines
ARTC	.	Associate Royal Technical College (Glasgow) (name changed) see under ARCST
ARVIA	.	Associate Royal Victoria Institute of Architects
ARWA	.	Associate Royal West of England Academy
ARWS	.	Associate Royal Society of Painters in Water-Colours
AS	. .	Anglo-Saxon
ASA	. .	Associate Member, Society of Actuaries
ASAA	.	Associate of the Society of Incorporated Accountants and Auditors
ASAM	.	Associate of the Society of Art Masters
AS&TS of SA	.	Associated Scientific and Technical Societies of South Africa

ASBAH	. .	Association for Spina Bifida and Hydrocephalus
ASC	. .	Administrative Staff College, Henley
ASCA	. .	Associate, Society of Company and Commercial Accountants
AScW	. .	Association of Scientific Workers
ASE	. .	Amalgamated Society of Engineers
ASIA(Ed)	.	Associate, Society of Industrial Artists (Education)
ASLE	. .	American Society of Lubrication Engineers
ASLEF	. .	Associated Society of Locomotive Engineers and Firemen
ASLIB	.	Association of Special Libraries and Information Bureaux
ASME	. .	American Society of Mechanical Engineers; Association for the Study of Medical Education
ASO	. .	Air Staff Officer
ASSC	. .	Accounting Standards Steering Committee
ASSET	.	Association of Supervisory Staffs, Executives and Technicians
AssocISI	.	Associate of Iron and Steel Institute
AssocMCT	.	Associateship of Manchester College of Technology
AssocMIAeE	.	Associate Member Institution of Aeronautical Engineers
AssocRINA	.	Associate of the Royal Institution of Naval Architects
AssocSc	.	Associate in Science
Asst	.	Assistant
ASTMS	.	Association of Scientific, Technical and Managerial Staffs
Astr.	. .	Astronomy
ASW	. .	Association of Scientific Workers
ATA	. .	Air Transport Auxiliary
ATAF	. .	Association of Tutors in Adult Education
ATC	. .	Air Training Corps
ATCDE	.	Association of Teachers in Colleges and Departments of Education (now see NATFHE)
ATCL	. .	Associate of Trinity College of Music, London
ATD	. .	Art Teacher's Diploma
ATI	. .	Associate of Textile Institute
ATII	. .	Associate Member of the Institute of Taxation
ato	. .	Ammunition Technical Officer
ATS	. .	Auxiliary Territorial Service
ATTI	. .	Association of Teachers in Technical Institutions (now see NATFHE)
ATV	. .	Associated TeleVision
AUA	. .	American Urological Association
AUCAS	. .	Association of University Clinical Academic Staff
AUEW	. .	Amalgamated Union of Engineering Workers
AUEW(TASS)	.	Amalgamated Union of Engineering Workers (Technical and Supervisory Section)
AUS	. .	Army of the United States
AUT	. .	Association of University Teachers
AVD	. .	Army Veterinary Department
AVLA	. .	Audio Visual Language Association
AVR	. .	Army Volunteer Reserve
AWA	. .	Anglian Water Authority
AWRE	. .	Atomic Weapons Research Establishment

B

b	. . .	born; brother
BA	. .	Bachelor of Arts
BAAB	. .	British Amateur Athletic Board
BAAL	. .	British Association for Applied Linguistics
BAAS	. .	British Association for the Advancement of Science
BAB	. .	British Airways Board
BAC	. .	British Aircraft Corporation
BACM	. .	British Association of Colliery Management
BAe	. .	British Aerospace
B&FBS	. .	British and Foreign Bible Society
BAFO	. .	British Air Forces of Occupation
BAFTA	.	British Academy of Film and Television Arts (formerly SFTA)
BAI	.	Bachelor of Engineering (Baccalarius in Arte Ingeniaria)
BAIE	. .	British Association of Industrial Editors
BALPA	. .	British Air Line Pilots' Association
BAO	. .	Bachelor of Art of Obstetrics
BAOR	. .	British Army of the Rhine (formerly on the Rhine)
BAOS	. .	British Association of Oral Surgeons
BAppSc(MT)	.	Bachelor of Applied Science (Medical Technology)
BARC	. .	British Automobile Racing Club
Bart or Bt	.	Baronet
BAS	. .	Bachelor in Agricultural Science
BASc	. .	Bachelor of Applied Science
BASW	. .	British Association of Social Workers
Batt.	. .	Battery
BBA	. .	British Bankers' Association
BB&CIRly	.	Bombay, Baroda and Central India Railway
BBB of C	.	British Boxing Board of Control
BBC	. .	British Broadcasting Corporation
BBM	. .	Bintang Bakti Masharakat (Public Service Star) (Singapore)
BC	. .	Before Christ; British Columbia
BCC	. . .	British Council of Churches

BCE (Melb)	.	Bachelor of Civil Engineering (Melbourne Univ.)
BCh or BChir	.	Bachelor of Surgery
BCL	. .	Bachelor of Civil Law
BCMS	. .	Bible Churchmen's Missionary Society
BCOF	. .	British Commonwealth Occupation Force
BCom	. .	Bachelor of Commerce
BComSc	. .	Bachelor of Commercial Science
BCS	. .	Bengal Civil Service
BCURA	. .	British Coal Utilization Research Association
BCYC	. .	British Corinthian Yacht Club
BD	. .	Bachelor of Divinity
Bd	. .	Board
BDA	. .	British Dental Association
Bde	. .	Brigade
BDS	. .	Bachelor of Dental Surgery
BDSc	. .	Bachelor of Dental Science
BE	. .	Bachelor of Engineering; British Element
BEA	. .	British East Africa; British European Airways; British Epilepsy Association
BEAMA	.	British Electrical and Allied Manufacturers' Association
BE&A	. .	Bachelor of Engineering and Architecture (Malta)
BEAS	. .	British Educational Administration Society
BEC	. .	Business Education Council
BEc	. .	Bachelor of Economics (Australian)
BEd	. .	Bachelor of Education
Beds	. .	Bedfordshire
BEE	. .	Bachelor of Electrical Engineering
BEF	. .	British Expeditionary Force
BEM	. .	British Empire Medal
BEO	. .	Base Engineer Officer
Berks	. .	Berkshire
BFI	. .	British Film Institute
BFPO	. .	British Forces Post Office
BGS	. .	Brigadier General Staff
Bhd	. .	Berhad
BHS	. .	British Horse Society
BICC	. .	British Insulated Callender's Cables
BICERA	.	British Internal Combustion Engine Research Association
BIF	. .	British Industries Fair
BIM	. .	British Institute of Management
BIR	. .	British Institute of Radiology
BIS	. .	Bank for International Settlements
BISF	. .	British Iron and Steel Federation
BISFA	. .	British Industrial and Scientific Film Association
BISRA	. .	British Iron and Steel Research Association
BJ	. .	Bachelor of Journalism
BJSM	. .	British Joint Services Mission
BKSTS	.	British Kinematograph, Sound and Television Society
BL	. .	Bachelor of Law
BLA	. .	British Liberation Army
BLE	. .	Brotherhood of Locomotive Engineers
BLESMA	.	British Limbless Ex-Servicemen's Association
BLitt	. .	Bachelor of Letters
BM	. .	British Museum; Bachelor of Medicine; Brigade Major; British Monomark
BMA	. .	British Medical Association
BMEO	. .	British Middle East Office
BMEWS	.	Ballistic Missile Early Warning System
BMH	. .	British Military Hospital
BMJ	. .	British Medical Journal
Bn	. .	Battalion
BNAF	. .	British North Africa Force
BNC	. .	Brasenose College
BNEC	. .	British National Export Council
BNOC	. .	British National Opera Company
BOAC	. .	British Overseas Airways Corporation
BomCS	. .	Bombay Civil Service
BomSC	. .	Bombay Staff Corps
BoT	. .	Board of Trade
Bot.	. .	Botany; Botanical
BOTB	. .	British Overseas Trade Board
Bp	. .	Bishop
BPharm	. .	Bachelor of Pharmacy
BPIF	. .	British Printing Industries Federation
BPsS	. .	British Psychological Society
BR	. .	British Rail
Br.	. .	Branch
BRA	. .	Brigadier Royal Artillery
BRCS	. .	British Red Cross Society
Brig.	. .	Brigadier
BritIRE	.	British Institution of Radio Engineers (now see IERE)
BRNC	. .	Britannia Royal Naval College
BRS	. .	British Road Services
BS	. .	Bachelor of Surgery; Bachelor of Science
BSA	. .	Bachelor of Scientific Agriculture; Birmingham Small Arms
BSAA	. .	British South American Airways
BSAP	. .	British South Africa Police
BSC	. .	British Steel Corporation; Bengal Staff Corps
BSc	. .	Bachelor of Science
BSc (Dent)	.	Bachelor of Science in Dentistry
BSE	. .	Bachelor of Science in Engineering (US)

BSF		British Salonica Force
BSI		British Standards Institution
BSJA		British Show Jumping Association
BSocSc		Bachelor of Social Science
BT		Bachelor of Teaching
Bt		Baronet; Brevet
BTA		British Tourist Authority (*formerly* British Travel Association)
BTC		British Transport Commission
BTh		Bachelor of Theology
Btss		Baroness
BUAS		British Universities Association of Slavists
BUPA		British United Provident Association
BVA		British Veterinary Association
BVM		Blessed Virgin Mary
Bucks		Buckinghamshire
BWI		British West Indies (now WI: West Indies)
BWM		British War Medal

C

(C)		Conservative; 100
c		Child; cousin
CA		Central America; County Alderman; Chartered Accountant (Scotland, and Canada)
CAA		Civil Aviation Authority
CAB		Citizens' Advice Bureau
CACTM		Central Advisory Council of Training for the Ministry (*now see* ACCM)
CALE		Canadian Army Liaison Executive
Cambs		Cambridgeshire
CAMC		Canadian Army Medical Corps
CAMRA		Campaign for Real Ale
CAMW		Central Association for Mental Welfare
Cantab		Of Cambridge University
CARIFTA		Caribbean Free Trade Area
CAS		Chief of the Air Staff
CASI		Canadian Aeronautics and Space Institute
Cav.		Cavalry
CAWU		Clerical and Administrative Workers' Union
CB		Companion of the Bath
CBE		Commander Order of the British Empire
CBI		Confederation of British Industry (and *see under* FBI)
CBSA		Clay Bird Shooting Association
CC		Companion of the Order of Canada; City Council; County Council; Cricket Club; Cycling Club; County Court
CCAHC		Central Council for Agricultural and Horticultural Cooperation
CCC		Corpus Christi College; Central Criminal Court; County Cricket Club
CCF		Combined Cadet Force
CCFM		Combined Cadet Forces Medal
CCG		Control Commission Germany
CChem		Chartered Chemist
CCPR		Central Council of Physical Recreation
CCRA		Commander Corps Royal Artillery
CCS		Casualty Clearing Station; Ceylon Civil Service
CCTA		Commission de Cooperation Technique pour l'Afrique
CD		Canadian Forces Decoration; Commander of the Order of Distinction (Jamaica)
CDEE		Chemical Defence Experimental Establishment
Cdre		Commodore
CDS		Chief of the Defence Staff
CDU		Christliche Demokratische Union
CE		Civil Engineer
CEE		Communauté Economique Europeenne
CEF		Canadian Expeditionary Force
CEGB		Central Electricity Generating Board
CEI		Council of Engineering Institutions
CEIR		Corporation for Economic and Industrial Research
CEMA		Council for the Encouragement of Music and the Arts
CEMS		Church of England Men's Society
CEN		Comité Européen de Normalisation
CEng		Chartered Engineer
Cento		Central Treaty Organisation
CERL		Central Electricity Research Laboratories
CERN		Conseil (now Organisation) Européenne pour la Recherche Nucleaire
CETS		Church of England Temperance Society
CF		Chaplain to the Forces
CFA		Canadian Field Artillery
CFE		Central Fighter Establishment
CFR		Commander of Federal Republic of Nigeria
CFS		Central Flying School
CGA		Community of the Glorious Ascension
CGH		Order of the Golden Heart of Kenya (1st class)
CGIA		City and Guilds of London Insignia Award
CGLI		City and Guilds of London Institute
CGM		Conspicuous Gallantry Medal
CGRM		Commandant-General Royal Marines
CGS		Chief of the General Staff

CH		Companion of Honour
Chanc.		Chancellor; Chancery
Chap.		Chaplain
ChapStJ		Chaplain of Order of St John of Jerusalem (now ChStJ)
ChB		Bachelor of Surgery
Ch. Ch.		Christ Church
Ch. Coll.		Christ's College
CHM		Chevalier of Honour and Merit (Haiti)
(CHM)		*See under* ARCO(CHM), FRCO(CHM)
ChM.		Master of Surgery
Chm.		Chairman
ChStJ		Chaplain of Order of St John of Jerusalem
CI		Imperial Order of the Crown of India; Channel Islands
CIAD		Central Institute of Art and Design
CIAgrE		Companion, Institution of Agricultural Engineers
CIAL		Corresponding Member of the International Institute of Arts and Letters
CIBS		Chartered Institution of Building Services (formerly IHVE)
CID		Criminal Investigation Department
CIDEC		Conseil International pour le Développement du Cuivre
CIE		Companion of the Order of the Indian Empire; 'Confederation Internationale des Etudiants
CIGRE		Conference Internationale des Grands Réseaux Electriques
CIGS		(formerly) Chief of the Imperial General Staff (now CGS)
CIMarE		Companion of the Institute of Marine Engineers
CIMechE.		Companion of the Institution of Mechanical Engineers
CIMGTechE		Companion, Institution of Mechanical and General Technician Engineers
C-in-C		Commander-in-Chief
CINCHAN		Allied Commander-in-Chief Channel
CIPFA		Chartered Institute of Public Finance and Accountancy (formerly IMTA)
CIPM		Companion, Institute of Personnel Management
CIR		Commission on Industrial Relations
CIRIA		Construction Industry Research and Information Association
CISAC		Confederation Internationale des Sociétés d'Auteurs et Compositeurs
CIT		Chartered Institute of Transport
CIV		City Imperial Volunteers
CJ		Chief Justice
CJM.		Congregation of Jesus and Mary (Eudist Fathers)
CL		Commander of Order of Leopold
c.l.		*cum laude*
Cl.		Class
CLA		Country Landowners' Association
CLit		Companion of Literature (Royal Society of Literature Award)
CLJ		Commander, St Lazarus of Jerusalem
CLRAE		Conference of Local and Regional Authorities of Europe
CM		Member of the Order of Canada; Congregation of the Mission (Vincentians); Master in Surgery; Certificated Master; Canadian Militia
CMA		Canadian Medical Association
CMAC		Catholic Marriage Advisory Council
CMB		Central Midwives' Board
CMF		Commonwealth Military Forces Central Mediterranean Force
CMG		Companion of St Michael and St George
CMM		Commander, Order of Military Merit (Canada)
CMO		Chief Medical Officer
CMP		Corps of Military Police
CMS		Church Missionary Society
CMT		Chaconia Medal of Trinidad
CNAA		Council for National Academic Awards
CNR.		Canadian National Railways
CNRS		Centre National du Recherche Scientifique
CO		Commanding Officer; Commonwealth Office (from Aug. 1966) (*see also* FCO); Colonial Office (before Aug. 1966); Conscientious Objector
Co.		County; Company
C of E		Church of England
C of S		Chief of Staff
COI		Central Office of Information
CoID		Council of Industrial Design (now Design Council)
Co.L or Coal.L		Coalition Liberal
Col		Colonel
Coll.		College; Collegiate
Colo		Colorado (US)
Col.-Sergt.		Colour-Sergeant
Com		Communist
Comd		Command
Comdg		Commanding
Comdr		Commander
Comdt		Commandant
COMEC		Council of the Military Education Committees of the Universities of the UK

Commn	Commission
Commnd	Commissioned
ComplEE.	Companion of the Institution of Electrical Engineers
ComplERE	Companion of the Institution of Electronic and Radio Engineers
CompTI	Companion of the Textile Institute
Comr	Commissioner
Comy-Gen.	Commissary-General
CON	Cross of Order of the Niger
Conn.	Connecticut (US)
Const.	Constitutional
COPA	Comite des Organisationels Agricoles de la CEE
COPEC	Conference of Politics, Economics and Christianity
Corp.	Corporation; Corporal
Corr. Mem. or Fell.	Corresponding Member or Fellow
COS	Chief of Staff; Charity Organization Society
COSA	Colliery Officials and Staffs Association
COSIRA	Council for Small Industries in Rural Areas
COSSAC	Chief of Staff to Supreme Allied Commander
COTC	Canadian Officers' Training Corps
Co.U or Coal.U	Coalition Unionist
CP	Central Provinces; Cape Province
CPA	Commonwealth Parliamentary Association; Chartered Patent Agent; also (formerly) Certified Public Accountant (Canada) (now merged with CA)
CPAS	Church Pastoral Aid Society
CPC	Conservative Political Centre
CPM	Colonial Police Medal
CPR	Canadian Pacific Railway
CPRE	Council for the Protection of Rural England
CPSA	Civil and Public Services Association (formerly CSCA)
CPSU	Communist Party of the Soviet Union
CPU	Commonwealth Press Union
CQSW	Certificate of Qualification in Social Work
CR	Community of the Resurrection
cr	created or creation
CRA	Commander, Royal Artillery
CRASC	Commander, Royal Army Service Corps
CRCP(C).	Certificate, Royal College of Physicians of Canada
CRE.	Commander, Royal Engineers; Commission for Racial Equality; Commercial Relations and Exports
Cres.	Crescent
CRMP	Corps of Royal Military Police
CRO.	Commonwealth Relations Office (before Aug. 1966; *now see* CO and FCO)
CS	Civil Service; Clerk to the Signet
CSB	Bachelor of Christian Science
CSC	Conspicuous Service Cross
CSCA	Civil Service Clerical Association (*now see* CPSA)
CSD.	Civil Service Department; Cooperative Secretaries Diploma
CSEU	Confederation of Shipbuilding and Engineering Unions
CSG.	Companion of the Order of the Star of Ghana
CSI	Companion of the Order of the Star of India
CSIR	Commonwealth Council for Scientific and Industrial Research (re-named: Commonwealth Scientific and Industrial Research Organization; *see* below)
CSIRO	Commonwealth Scientific and Industrial Research Organization (and *see* above)
CSO.	Chief Scientific Officer; Chief Signal Officer; Chief Staff Officer
CSP	Chartered Society of Physiotherapists; Civil Service of Pakistan
CSSp	Holy Ghost Father
CSSR	Congregation of the Most Holy Redeemer (Redemptorist Order)
CStJ.	Commander of the Order of St John of Jerusalem
CTA	Chaplain Territorial Army
CTB.	College of Teachers of the Blind
CTC.	Cyclists' Touring Club
CTR (Harwell)	Controlled Thermonuclear Research
CU	Cambridge University
CUAC	Cambridge University Athletic Club
CUAFC	Cambridge University Association Football Club
CUBC	Cambridge University Boat Club
CUCC	Cambridge University Cricket Club
CUF.	Common University Fund
CUHC	Cambridge University Hockey Club
CUP.	Cambridge University Press
CURUFC	Cambridge University Rugby Union Football Club
CV	Cross of Valour (Canada)
CVO.	Commander of the Royal Victorian Order
CWS.	Co-operative Wholesale Society

D

D	Duke
d	Died; daughter

DA	Diploma in Anaesthesia; Diploma in Art
DAA&QMG	Deputy Assistant Adjutant and Quartermaster-General
DAAG	Deputy Assistant Adjutant-General
DA&QMG	Deputy Adjutant and Quartermaster-General
DACG	Deputy Assistant Chaplain-General
DAD	Deputy Assistant Director
DADMS	Deputy Assistant Director of Medical Services
DADOS	Deputy Assistant Director of Ordnance Services
DADQ	Deputy Assistant Director of Quartering
DADST	Deputy Assistant Director of Supplies and Transport
DAG	Deputy Adjutant-General
DAMS	Deputy Assistant Military Secretary
DAQMG	Deputy Assistant Quartermaster-General
DASc	Doctor in Agricultural Sciences
DATA	Draughtsmen's and Allied Technicians' Association
DBA.	Doctor of Business Administration
DBE.	Dame Commander Order of the British Empire
DC	District Council; District of Columbia (US)
DCAe	Diploma of College of Aeronautics
DCAS	Deputy Chief of the Air Staff
DCB.	Dame Commander of the Bath
DCG	Deputy Chaplain-General
DCGRM.	Department of the Commandant General Royal Marines
DCGS	Deputy Chief of the General Staff
DCh.	Doctor of Surgery
DCH	Diploma in Child Health
DCIGS	(formerly) Deputy Chief of the Imperial General Staff (now DCGS)
DCL.	Doctor of Civil Law
DCLI	Duke of Cornwall's Light Infantry
DCM	Distinguished Conduct Medal
DCMG	Dame Commander of St Michael and St George
DCnL	Doctor of Canon Law
DCP.	Diploma in Clinical Pathology
DCS.	Deputy Chief of Staff; Doctor of Commercial Sciences
DCSO	Deputy Chief Scientific Officer
DCT.	Doctor of Christian Theology
DCVO	Dame Commander of Royal Victorian Order
DD	Doctor of Divinity
DDL	Deputy Director of Labour
DDME	Deputy Director of Mechanical Engineering
DDMI	Deputy Director of Military Intelligence
DDMS	Deputy Director of Medical Services
DDMT	Deputy Director of Military Training
DDNI	Deputy Director of Naval Intelligence
DDO	Diploma in Dental Orthopaedics
DDPR	Deputy Director of Public Relations
DDPS	Deputy Director of Personal Services
DDR	Deutsche Demokratische Republik
DDRA	Deputy Director Royal Artillery
DDS.	Doctor of Dental Surgery; Director of Dental Services
DDSc	Doctor of Dental Science
DDSD	Deputy Director Staff Duties
DDST	Deputy Director of Supplies and Transport
DDWE&M	Deputy Director of Works, Electrical and Mechanical
DE	Doctor of Engineering
DEA.	Department of Economic Affairs
Decd.	Deceased
DEconSc.	Doctor of Economic Science
DEd	Doctor of Education
Del	Delaware (US)
Deleg.	Delegate
DEng	Doctor of Engineering
DenM	Docteur en Médicine
DEOVR	Duke of Edinburgh's Own Volunteer Rifles
DEP.	Department of Employment and Productivity
Dep.	Deputy
DES.	Department of Education and Science
DesL	Docteur ès lettres
DesS.	Docteur ès sciences
DesRCA	Designer of the Royal College of Art
DFA.	Doctor of Fine Arts
DFC.	Distinguished Flying Cross
DFH	Diploma of Faraday House
DFLS	Day Fighter Leaders' School
DFM	Distinguished Flying Medal (Canada)
DG	Dragoon Guards
DGAMS	Director-General Army Medical Services
DGMS	Director-General of Medical Services
DGMT	Director-General of Military Training
DGMW	Director-General of Military Works
DGNPS	Director-General of Naval Personal Services
DGP	Director-General of Personnel
DGS.	Director of Graduate Studies
DGStJ	(formerly) Dame of Grace, Order of St John of Jerusalem (now DStJ)
DGU	Doctor of Griffith University
Dhc	Doctor *honoris causa*
DHL	Doctor of Humane Letters; Doctor of Hebrew Literature
DHM	Dean Hole Medal

DHMSA	. .	Diploma in the History of Medicine (Society of Apothecaries)
DHQ	. .	District Headquarters
DHSS	. .	Department of Health and Social Security
DIAS	. .	Dublin Institute of Advanced Sciences
DIC	. .	Diploma of the Imperial College
DIG	. .	Deputy Inspector-General
DIH	. .	Diploma in Industrial Health
Dio.	. .	Diocese
DipCAM	. .	Diploma in Communications, Advertising and Marketing
DipCD	. .	Diploma in Civic Design
DipEd	. .	Diploma in Education
DipM	. .	Diploma in Marketing
DipPA	. .	Diploma of Practitioners in Advertising (*now see* DipCAM)
DipTP	. .	Diploma in Town Planning
DipTPT	. .	Diploma in Theory and Practice of Teaching
DisTP	. .	Distinction Town Planning
Div.	. .	Division; divorced
DJAG	. .	Deputy Judge Advocate General
DJStJ	. .	formerly Dame of Justice of St John of Jerusalem (now DStJ)
D.Jur.	. .	Doctor Juris
DK	. .	Most Esteemed Family Order (Brunei)
DL	. .	Deputy Lieutenant
DLC	. .	Diploma Loughborough College
DLES	. .	Doctor of Letters in Economic Studies
DLI	. .	Durham Light Infantry
DLitt or DLit	. .	Doctor of Literature; Doctor of Letters
DLO	. .	Diploma in Laryngology and Otology
DM	. .	Doctor of Medicine
DMD	. .	Doctor of Medical Dentistry (Australia)
DME	. .	Director of Mechanical Engineering
DMet	. .	Doctor of Metallurgy
DMI	. .	Director of Military Intelligence
DMJ	. .	Diploma in Medical Jurisprudence
DMR	. .	Diploma in Medical Radiology
DMRD	. .	Diploma in Medical Radiological Diagnosis
DMRE	. .	Diploma in Medical Radiology and Electrology
DMRT	. .	Diploma in Medical Radio-Therapy
DMS	. .	Director of Medical Services; Decoration for Meritorious Service (South Africa)
DMus	. .	Doctor of Music
DMT	. .	Director of Military Training
DNB	. .	Dictionary of National Biography
DNE	. .	Director of Naval Equipment
DNI	. .	Director of Naval Intelligence
DO	. .	Diploma in Ophthalmology
DObstRCOG	. .	Diploma Royal College of Obstetricians and Gynaecologists
DOC	. .	District Officer Commanding
DocEng	. .	Doctor of Engineering
DoE	. .	Department of the Environment
DoI	. .	Department of Industry
DOL	. .	Doctor of Oriental Learning
Dom.	. .	*Dominus*
DOMS	. .	Diploma in Ophthalmic Medicine and Surgery
DOR	. .	Director of Operational Requirements
DOS	. .	Director of Ordnance Services
Dow.	. .	Dowager
DPed	. .	Doctor of Pedagogy
DPA	. .	Diploma in Public Administration; Discharged Prisoners' Aid
DPEc	. .	Doctor of Political Economy
DPH	. .	Diploma in Public Health
DPh or DPhil.	. .	Doctor of Philosophy
DPLG	. .	Diplômé par le Gouvernement
DPM	. .	Diploma in Psychological Medicine
DPR	. .	Director of Public Relations
DPS	. .	Director of Postal Services; also (formerly) Director of Personal Services
DQMG	. .	Deputy Quartermaster-General
Dr	. .	Doctor
DRAC	. .	Director Royal Armoured Corps
DrIng	. .	Doctor of Engineering (Germany)
DrOEcPol	. .	Doctor OEconomicæ Politicæ
DS	. .	Directing Staff
DSA	. .	Diploma in Social Administration
DSAO	. .	Diplomatic Service Administration Office
DSC	. .	Distinguished Service Cross
DSc	. .	Doctor of Science
DScA	. .	Docteur en sciences agricoles
DScMil	. .	Doctor of Military Science
DSD	. .	Director Staff Duties
DSIR	. .	Department of Scientific and Industrial Research (now *see under* SRC)
DSLJ	. .	Dato Seri Laila Jasa Brunei
DSM	. .	Distinguished Service Medal
DSNB	. .	Dato Setia Negara Brunei
DSO	. .	Companion of the Distinguished Service Order
DSocSc	. .	Doctor of Social Science
DSP	. .	Director of Selection of Personnel; Docteur en sciences politiques (Montreal)
d.s.p.	. .	*decessit sine prole* (died without issue)

DSS	. .	Doctor of Sacred Scripture
DSSc	. .	Doctor of Social Science (USA)
DST	. .	Director of Supplies and Transport
DStJ	. .	Dame of Grace, Order of St John of Jerusalem; Dame of Justice, Order of St John of Jerusalem; and *see* GCStJ
DTD-	. .	Dekoratie voor Trouwe Dienst (Decoration for Devoted Service)
DTech	. .	Doctor of Technology
DTH	. .	Diploma in Tropical Hygiene
DTheol	. .	Doctor of Theology
DThPT	. .	Diploma in Theory and Practice of Teaching (Durham University)
DTI	. .	Department of Trade and Industry
DTM&H	. .	Diploma in Tropical Medicine and Hygiene
DU	. .	Doctor of the University
DUniv	. .	Doctor of the University
DUP	. .	Docteur de l'Université de Paris
DVH	. .	Diploma in Veterinary Hygiene
DVM	. .	Doctor of Veterinary Medicine
DVR	. .	Diploma in Veterinary Radiology
DVSM	. .	Diploma in Veterinary State Medicine

E

E	. .	East; Earl
e	. .	eldest
EAHY	. .	European Architectural Heritage Year
EAP	. .	East Africa Protectorate
EAW	. .	Electrical Association for Women
Ebor	. .	(*Eboracensis*) of York
EBU	. .	European Broadcasting Union
EC	. .	Etoile du Courage (Canada); East Central (postal district); Emergency Commission
ECA	. .	Economic Co-operation Administration
ECAFE	. .	Economic Commission for Asia and the Far East (*now see* ESCAP)
ECE	. .	Economic Commission for Europe
ECGD	. .	Export Credits Guarantee Department
ECLA	. .	Economic Commission for Latin America
ECSC	. .	European Coal and Steel Community
ECU	. .	English Church Union
ED	. .	Efficiency Decoration; Doctor of Engineering (US)
EdB	. .	Bachelor of Education
EDC	. .	Economic Development Committee
EdD	. .	Doctor of Education
Edin.	. .	Edinburgh
Edn	. .	Edition
EDP	. .	Executive Development Programme
Educ	. .	Educated
Educn	. .	Education
EEC	. .	European Economic Community; Commission of the European Communities
EEF	. .	Engineering Employers' Federation; Egyptian Expeditionary Force
EETS	. .	Early English Text Society
EFTA	. .	European Free Trade Association
e.h.	. .	*ehrenhalber*; see under h.c.
EI	. .	East Indian; East Indies
EICS	. .	East India Company's Service
E-in-C	. .	Engineer-in-Chief
EIU	. .	Economist Intelligence Unit
EM	. .	Earl Marshal
EMS	. .	Emergency Medical Service
Ency. Brit.	. .	Encyclopaedia Britannica
Eng.	. .	England
Engr	. .	Engineer
ENSA	. .	Entertainments National Service Association
ENT	. .	Ear, Nose and Throat
EOPH	. .	Examined Officer of Public Health
EORTC	. .	European Organisation for Research on Treatment of Cancer
er	. .	elder
ER	. .	Eastern Region (BR)
ERC	. .	Electronics Research Council
ERD	. .	Emergency Reserve Decoration (Army)
ESCAP	. .	Economic and Social Commission for Asia and the Pacific
ESRO	. .	European Space Research Organization
E-SU	. .	English-Speaking Union
ETH	. .	Eidgenössische Technische Hochschule
EUDISED	. .	European Documentation and Information Service for Education
Euratom	. .	European Atomic Energy Commission
Ext	. .	Extinct

F

FA	. .	Football Association
FAA	. .	Fellow of the Australian Academy of Science; also (formerly) Fleet Air Arm

FAAAS . .	Fellow of the American Association for the Advancement of Science
FACC . .	Fellow of the American College of Cardiology
FACCA .	Fellow of the Association of Certified and Corporate Accountants; *now see* FCCA
FACCP .	Fellow of American College of Chest Physicians
FACD .	Fellow of the American College of Dentistry
FACDS .	Fellow, Australian College of Dental Surgeons; *now see* FRACDS
FACE .	Fellow of the Australian College of Education
FACI .	*now see* FRACI
FACMA .	Fellow, Australian College of Medical Administrators
FACOG .	Fellow, Australian College of Gynæcologists
FACP .	Fellow of American College of Physicians
FACR .	Fellow of American College of Radiology
FACS .	Fellow of American College of Surgeons
FACVT .	Fellow, American College of Veterinary Toxicology
FAGS .	Fellow American Geographical Society
FAHA .	Fellow, Australian Academy of the Humanities
FAI .	Fellow of Chartered Auctioneers' and Estate Agents' Institute; *now* (after amalgamation) *see* FRICS; Fédération Aéronautique Internationale
FAIA .	Fellow of American Institute of Architects
FAIAA .	Fellow of American Institute of Aeronautics and Astronautics (and *see under* FIAS)
FAIAS .	Fellow of Australian Institute of Agricultural Science
FAIM .	Fellow of the Australian Institute of Management
FAIP .	Fellow of Australian Institute of Physics
FAMS .	Fellow of the Ancient Monuments Society
FAmSCE .	Fellow of the American Society of Civil Engineers
FANY .	First Aid Nursing Yeomanry
FAO .	Food and Agriculture Organization
FAPHA .	Fellow American Public Health Association
FAPI .	*now see* FRAPI
FARELF .	Far East Land Forces
FAS .	Fellow of the Antiquarian Society
FASA .	Fellow of Australian Society of Accountants
FASc .	Fellow, Indian Academy of Sciences
FASCE .	Fellow of the American Society of Civil Engineers
FASSA .	Fellow, Academy of the Social Sciences in Australia
FBA .	Fellow of the British Academy; Federation of British Artists
FBCS .	Fellow of the British Computer Society
FBHI .	Fellow of the British Horological Institute
FBI .	Federation of British Industries (*see under* CBI, in which now merged)
FBIA .	Fellow, Bankers' Institute of Australasia
FBIM .	Fellow of the British Institute of Management (formerly FIIA)
FBKS .	Fellow, British Kinematograph, Sound and Television Society
FBOA .	Fellow of British Optical Association
FBOU .	Fellow British Ornithologists' Union
FBritIRE .	(formerly) Fellow of British Institution of Radio Engineers
FBPsS .	Fellow of British Psychological Society
FBS .	Fellow Building Societies Institute
FBSI .	Fellow of Boot and Shoe Institution
FBSM .	Fellow of the Birmingham School of Music
FC .	Football Club
FCA .	Fellow of the Institute of Chartered Accountants (formerly FCAI) Fellow of the Canadian Aeronautics and Space Institute
FCCA .	Fellow, Association of Certified Accountants
FCCP .	Fellow, American College of Chest Physicians
FCCS .	Fellow of Corporation of Secretaries (formerly of Certified Secretaries)
FCEC .	Federation of Civil Engineering Contractors
FCGI .	Fellow of City and Guilds of London Institute
FCGP .	Fellow of the College of General Practitioners; *now see* FRCGP
FCH .	Fellow of Coopers Hill College
FChS .	Fellow of the Society of Chiropodists
FCI .	Fellow of the Institute of Commerce
FCIB .	Fellow, Corporation of Insurance Brokers
FCIBS .	Fellow, Chartered Institution of Building Services (formerly FIHVE)
FCIC .	Fellow Chemical Institute of Canada (formerly Canadian Institute of Chemistry)
FCII .	Fellow of the Chartered Insurance Institute
FCIPA .	(formerly used for) Fellow of the Chartered Institute of Patent Agents (*now see* CPA)
FCIS .	Fellow of the Institute of Chartered Secretaries and Administrators (formerly Chartered Institute of Secretaries)
FCIT .	Fellow of Chartered Institute of Transport
FCMA .	Fellow, Institute of Cost and Management Accountants
FCO .	Foreign and Commonwealth Office (departments merged Oct. 1968)
FCommA .	Fellow, Society of Commercial Accountants; *now see* FSCA
FCP . . .	Fellow College of Preceptors

FCPath . .	Fellow of the College of Pathologists (*now see* FRCPath)
FCP(SoAf) .	Fellow of the College of Physicians, South Africa
FCPSO(SoAf)	(and *see* FCP(SoAf) and FCS(SoAf) Fellow of the College of Physicians and Surgeons and Obstetricians, South Africa
FCRA .	Fellow of the College of Radiologists of Australia
FCS .	Federation of Conservative Students
FCS or FChemSoc	Fellow of the Chemical Society
FCSP	Fellow of the Chartered Society of Physiotherapy
FCS(SoAf)	Fellow of the College of Surgeons, South Africa
FCST	Fellow of the College of Speech Therapists
FCT	Federal Capital Territory (now ACT)
FCTB	Fellow of the College of Teachers of the Blind
FCU .	Fighter Control Unit
FCWA	Fellow of the Institute of Cost and Works Accountants; *now see* FCMA
FDS .	Fellow in Dental Surgery
FDSRCPS Glas	Fellow in Dental Surgery, Royal College of Physicians and Surgeons of Glasgow
FDSRCS .	Fellow in Dental Surgery, Royal College of Surgeons of England
FDSRCSE .	Fellow in Dental Surgery, Royal College of Surgeons of Edinburgh
FEAF .	Far East Air Force
FEIS .	Fellow of the Educational Institute of Scotland
FES .	Fellow of the Entomological Society; Fellow of the Ethnological Society
FF .	Field Force
FFA .	Fellow of Faculty of Actuaries (in Scotland)
FFARACS .	Fellow of Faculty of Anaesthetists, Royal Australian College of Surgeons
FFARCS .	Fellow of Faculty of Anaesthetists, Royal College of Surgeons of England
FFARCSI	Fellow of Faculty of Anaesthetists, Royal College of Surgeons in Ireland
FFAS	Fellow of Faculty of Architects and Surveyors, London
FFB .	Fellow, Faculty of Building
FFCM	Fellow, Faculty of Community Medicine
FFDRCSI	Fellow of Faculty of Dentistry, Royal College of Surgeons in Ireland
FFF .	Free French Forces
FFHom .	Fellow of Faculty of Homœopathy
FFI .	French Forces of the Interior; Finance for Industry
FFR .	Fellow of Faculty of Radiologists (*now see* FRCR)
FGA .	Fellow of Gemmological Association
FGI .	Fellow of the Institute of Certificated Grocers
FGS .	Fellow of Geological Society
FGSM	Fellow of Guildhall School of Music
FGSMT .	Fellow, Guildhall School of Music (Music Therapy)
FHA .	Fellow of the Institute of Health Service Administrators (formerly Hospital Administrators)
FHAS	Fellow of Highland and Agricultural Society of Scotland
FHCIMA	Fellow, Hotel Catering and Institutional Management Association
FH-WC .	Fellow of Heriot-Watt College (now University), Edinburgh
FIA . . .	Fellow of Institute of Actuaries
FIAAS	Fellow of the Institute of Australian Agricultural Science
FIAA&S .	Fellow of the Incorporated Association of Architects and Surveyors
FIAgrE	Fellow of the Institution of Agricultural Engineers
FIAI .	Fellow of the Institute of Industrial and Commercial Accountants
FIAL	Fellow of the International Institute of Arts and Letters
FIAM	Fellow, International Academy of Management
FIArb	Fellow of Institute of Arbitrators
FIAS .	(*now see under* FAIAA) (formerly) Fellow Institute of Aeronautical Sciences (US)
FIAWS	Fellow, International Academy of Wood Sciences
FIB .	Fellow of Institute of Bankers
FIBD	Fellow of the Institute of British Decorators
FIBP	Fellow of the Institute of British Photographers
FIBiol	Fellow of Institute of Biology
FIC .	*See* FRIC
FICA	Fellow of the Commonwealth Institute of Accountancy; Fellow of the Institute of Chartered Accountants in England and Wales (but *see* FCA)
FICAI	Fellow, Institute of Chartered Accountants in Ireland
FICD	Fellow of the Institute of Civil Defence; Fellow of the Indian College of Dentists
FICE	Fellow of the Institution of Civil Engineers (*see also* MICE)
FICeram .	Fellow of the Institute of Ceramics
FIChemE.	Fellow of Institution of Chemical Engineers
FICI .	Fellow of the Institute of Chemistry of Ireland; Fellow of the International Colonial Institute
FICS	Fellow of Institute of Chartered Shipbrokers; Fellow of the International College of Surgeons
FIDE	Fédération Internationale des Echecs

FIE . . Fellow of Institute of Engineers

FIEE . . Fellow of the Institution of Electrical Engineers (see also MIEE)

FIEEE . . Fellow of Institute of Electrical and Electronics Engineers (NY)

FIEI . . Fellow of the Institution of Engineering Inspection; now see FIQA

FIERE . . Fellow of Institution of Electronic and Radio Engineers

FIES. . . Fellow of Illuminating Engineering Society; now see FIllumES

FIFM . . Fellow, Institute of Fisheries Management

FIFor . . Fellow, Institute of Forestry

FIFST . . Fellow of Institute of Food Science and Technology

FIGasE . . Fellow of Institution of Gas Engineers

FIGCM . . Fellow Incorporated Guild of Church Musicians

FIGD . . Fellow, Institute of Grocery Distribution

FIHsg . . (formerly) Fellow of Institute of Housing (now see under FIHM)

FIHE . . Fellow of Institute of Health Education

FIHM . . Fellow of Institute of Housing Managers

FIHospE . . Fellow, Institute of Hospital Engineering

FIHVE . . Fellow, Institution of Heating & Ventilating Engineers (now see FCIBS and MCIBS)

FIIA . . Fellow of Institute of Industrial Administration (now see FBIM)

FIInfSc . . Fellow, Institute of Information Scientists

FIInst . . Fellow of the Imperial Institute

FIIP . . Fellow, Institute of Incorporated Photographers

FIL . . Fellow of the Institute of Linguists

FILA . . Fellow of the Institute of Landscape Architects.

FILLM . . Fédération Internationale des Langues et Littératures Modernes

FIllumES. . Fellow of Illuminating Engineering Society

FIM . . Fellow of the Institution of Metallurgists

FIMA . . Fellow of the Institute of Mathematics and its Applications

FIMarE . . Fellow, Institute of Marine Engineers

FIMC . . Fellow, Institute of Management Consultants

FIMechE. . Fellow of the Institution of Mechanical Engineers (see also MIMechE)

FIMGTechE . Fellow, Institution of Mechanical and General Technician Engineers

FIMI . . Fellow of the Institute of the Motor Industry (formerly FIMT: Fellow, Institute of Motor Trade)

FIMinE . . Fellow of the Institution of Mining Engineers

FIMIT . . Fellow, Institute of Musical Instrument Technology

FIMLT . . Fellow, Institute of Medical Laboratory Technology

FIMM . . Fellow, Institute of Mining and Metallurgy

FIMS . . Fellow, Institute of Mathematical Statistics

FIMTA . . Fellow of the Institute of Municipal Treasurers and Accountants (now see IPFA)

FIMunE . . Fellow of Institution of Municipal Engineers

FIN . . Fellow of the Institute of Navigation (now see FRIN)

FInstAM . . Fellow, Institute of Administrative Management

FInstB . . Fellow, Institution of Buyers

FInstBiol . . Fellow of Institute of Biology (now see FIBiol)

FInstD . . Fellow of Institute of Directors

FInstF . . Fellow of Institute of Fuel

FInstFF . . Fellow, Institute of Freight Forwarders Ltd

FInstHE . . Fellow, Institution of Highway Engineers

FInstM . . Fellow of the Institute of Meat; Fellow of the Institute of Marketing

FInstMC . . Fellow, Institute of Measurement and Control

FInstMSM . . Fellow of the Institute of Marketing and Sales Management (formerly FSMA; now see FInstM)

FInstMet . . (formerly) Fellow of Institute of Metals (now part of Metals Society)

FInstP . . Fellow of Institute of Physics

FInstPet . . Fellow of the Institute of Petroleum

FInstPI . . Fellow of the Institute of Patentees and Inventors

FInstPS . . Fellow of Institute of Purchasing and Supply

FInstSM . . Fellow, Institute of Sales Management

FInstW . . Fellow of the Institute of Welding

FInstWPC . . Fellow, Institute of Water Pollution Control

FINucE . . Fellow of the Institution of Nuclear Engineers

FIOA . . Fellow, Institute of Acoustics

FIOB . . Fellow of Institute of Building

FIPA . . Fellow of the Institute of Practitioners in Advertising

FIPHE . . Fellow of the Institution of Public Health Engineers

FIPM . . Fellow of the Institute of Personnel Management

FIPR . . Fellow of Institute of Public Relations

FIProdE . . Fellow, Institution of Production Engineers

FIQA . . Fellow, Institute of Quality Assurance

FIRA(Ind) . . Fellow of Institute of Railway Auditors and Accountants (India)

FIRE(Aust) . Fellow, Institution of Radio Engineers (Australia) (now see FIREE (Aust))

FIREE(Aust) . Fellow of the Institution of Radio and Electronics Engineers (Australia)

FIRI . . Fellow of the Institution of the Rubber Industry (now see FPRI)

FIRTE . . Fellow, Institute of Road Transport Engineers

FIS . . Fellow of the Institute of Statisticians (formerly Assoc. of Incorporated Statisticians)

FISA . . Fellow of the Incorporated Secretaries' Association

FISE . . Fellow, Institution of Sales Engineers; Fellow, Institution of Sanitary Engineers

FIST. . . Fellow of the Institute of Science Technology

FIStructE. . Fellow of Institution of Structural Engineers

FITE . . Fellow, Institution of Electrical and Electronics Technician Engineers

FIW . . Fellow of the Welding Institute

FIWE . . Fellow, Institution of Water Engineers (now see FIWES)

FIWES . . Fellow, Institution of Water Engineers and Scientists

FIWM . . Fellow of the Institution of Works Managers

FIWPC . . Fellow, Institution of Water Pollution Control

FIWSc . . Fellow of the Institute of Wood Science

FIWSP . . Fellow, Institute of Work Study Practitioners (now see FWSOM)

FJI . . Fellow of Institute of Journalists

FJIE. . Fellow, Junior Institution of Engineers (now see CIMGTechE)

FKC. . . Fellow of King's College (London)

FLA . . Fellow of Library Association

Fla . . Florida (US)

FLAS . . Fellow of the Chartered Land Agents' Society (now (after amalgamation) see FRICS)

FLCM . . Fellow of the London College of Music

FLHS . . Fellow of the London Historical Society

FLS . . Fellow of the Linnaean Society

Flt . . Flight

FM . . Field-Marshal

FMA . . Fellow of the Museums Association

FMANZ . . Fellow, Medical Association of New Zealand

FMF. . Fiji Military Forces

FMS. . Federated Malay States

FMSA . . Fellow of the Mineralogical Society of America

FNA. . Fellow of Indian National Science Academy

FNECInst . . Fellow, North East Coast Institution of Engineers and Shipbuilders

FNI . . . Fellow, Nautical Institute; Fellow of National Institute of Sciences in India (now see FNA)

FNZIA . . Fellow of the New Zealand Institute of Architects

FNZIAS . . Fellow of the New Zealand Institute of Agricultural Science

FNZIC . . Fellow of the New Zealand Institute of Chemistry

FNZIE . . Fellow of the New Zealand Institution of Engineers

FO . . . Foreign Office (see also FCO); Field Officer; Flying Officer

FOIC . . Flag Officer in charge

FPA . . Family Planning Association

FPEA . . Fellow, Physical Education Association

FPhS . . Fellow of the Philosophical Society of England

FPI . . Fellow, Plastics Institute (now see FPRI)

FPRI . . Fellow, Plastics and Rubber Institute

FPS . . Fellow of the Pharmaceutical Society

FPhysS . . Fellow of the Physical Society

FRACDS. . Fellow, Royal Australian College of Dental Surgeons

FRACI . . Fellow of the Royal Australian Chemical Institute (formerly FACI)

FRACP . . Fellow of the Royal Australasian College of Physicians

FRACS . . Fellow of the Royal Australasian College of Surgeons

FRAD . . Fellow of the Royal Academy of Dancing

FRAeS . . Fellow of the Royal Aeronautical Society

FRAgS . . Fellow of the Royal Agricultural Societies (ie of England, Scotland and Wales)

FRAHS . . Fellow of Royal Australian Historical Society

FRAI . . Fellow of the Royal Anthropological Institute

FRAIA . . Fellow of the Royal Australian Institute of Architects

FRAIB . . Fellow, Royal Australian Institute of Building

FRAIC . . Fellow of the Royal Architectural Institute of Canada

FRAM . . Fellow of the Royal Academy of Music

FRAPI . . Fellow, Royal Australian Planning Institute

FRAS . . Fellow of the Royal Astronomical Society; Fellow of the Royal Asiatic Society

FRASB . . Fellow of Royal Asiatic Society of Bengal

FRASE . . Fellow of the Royal Agricultural Society of England

FRBS . . Fellow of Royal Society of British Sculptors; Fellow of the Royal Botanic Society

FRCGP . . Fellow of the Royal College of General Practitioners

FRCM . . Fellow of the Royal College of Music

FRCN . . Fellow, Royal College of Nursing

FRCO . . Fellow of the Royal College of Organists

FRCO(CHM). . Fellow of the Royal College of Organists with Diploma in Choir Training

FRCOG . . Fellow of the Royal College of Obstetricians and Gynaecologists

FRCP . . Fellow of the Royal College of Physicians, London

FRCP&S. (Canada) . Fellow, Royal College of Physicians and Surgeons of Canada

FRCPath . . Fellow of the Royal College of Pathologists

FRCP(C). . Fellow of the Royal College of Physicians of Canada

FRCPE and FRCPEd . Fellow of the Royal College of Physicians of Edinburgh

FRCPGlas . Fellow of the Royal College (formerly Faculty) of Physicians and Surgeons, Glasgow (and see under FRFPSG)

FRCPI	.	Fellow of the Royal College of Physicians in Ireland
FRCPS(Hon)	.	Hon. Fellow of Royal College Physicians and Surgeons (Glasgow)
FRCPsych	.	Fellow of the Royal College of Psychiatrists
FRCR	.	Fellow, Royal College of Radiologists
FRCS	.	Fellow of the Royal College of Surgeons of England
FRCSE and FRCSEd	.	Fellow of the Royal College of Surgeons of Edinburgh
FRCSGlas	.	Fellow of the Royal College of Surgeons of Glasgow
FRCSI	.	Fellow of the Royal College of Surgeons in Ireland
FRCSoc	.	Fellow of the Royal Commonwealth Society
FRCUS	.	Fellow of the Royal College of University Surgeons (Denmark)
FRCVS	.	Fellow of the Royal College of Veterinary Surgeons
FREconS	.	Fellow of Royal Economic Society
FREI	.	Fellow of the Real Estate Institute (Australia)
FRES	.	Fellow of Royal Entomological Society of London
FRFPSG	.	(formerly) Fellow of Royal Faculty of Physicians and Surgeons, Glasgow (now Royal College of Physicians and Surgeons, Glasgow) (and see under FRCPGlas)
FRGS	.	Fellow of the Royal Geographical Society
FRHistS	.	Fellow of Royal Historical Society
FRHS	.	Fellow of the Royal Horticultural Society
FRIAS	.	Fellow of the Royal Incorporation of Architects of Scotland
FRIBA	.	Fellow of the Royal Institute of British Architects (and see RIBA)
FRIC		(formerly FIC) Fellow of Royal Institute of Chemistry
FRICS	.	Fellow of the Royal Institution of Chartered Surveyors
FRIH	.	Fellow of Royal Institute of Horticulture (NZ)
FRIN	.	Fellow, Royal Institute of Navigation
FRINA	.	Fellow of Royal Institution of Naval Architects
FRIPA	.	Fellow, Royal Institute of Public Administration
FRIPHH	.	Fellow of the Royal Institute of Public Health and Hygiene
FRMCM	.	Fellow of Royal Manchester College of Music
FRMedSoc	.	Fellow of Royal Medical Society
FRMetS	.	Fellow of the Royal Meteorological Society
FRMS	.	Fellow of the Royal Microscopical Society
FRNCM	.	Fellow, Royal Northern College of Music
FRNS	.	Fellow of Royal Numismatic Society
FRPS	.	Fellow of the Royal Photographic Society
FRPSL	.	Fellow of the Royal Philatelic Society, London
FRS	.	Fellow of the Royal Society
FRSA	.	Fellow of Royal Society of Arts
FRSAI	.	Fellow of the Royal Society of Antiquaries of Ireland
FRSAMD	.	Fellow, Royal Scottish Academy of Music and Drama
FRSanI	.	Fellow of Royal Sanitary Institute (now see FRSH)
FRSC	.	Fellow of the Royal Society of Canada
FRSCM	.	Fellow of the Royal School of Church Music
FRSE	.	Fellow of the Royal Society of Edinburgh
FRSGS	.	Fellow of the Royal Scottish Geographical Society
FRSH	.	Fellow of the Royal Society for the Promotion of Health (formerly FRSanI)
FRSL	.	Fellow of the Royal Society of Literature
FRSM or FRSocMed	.	Fellow of Royal Society of Medicine
FRSNZ	.	Fellow of Royal Society of New Zealand
FRSSAf	.	Fellow of Royal Society of South Africa
FRST	.	Fellow of the Royal Society of Teachers
FRSTM&H	.	Fellow of Royal Society of Tropical Medicine and Hygiene
FRTPI	.	Fellow, Royal Town Planning Institute
FRVA	.	Fellow, Rating and Valuation Association
FRVC	.	Fellow, Royal Veterinary College
FRVIA	.	Fellow Royal Victorian Institute of Architects
FRZSScot	.	Fellow of the Royal Zoological Society of Scotland
FS	.	Field Security
fs	.	Graduate of Royal Air Force Staff College
FSA	.	Fellow of the Society of Antiquaries
FSAA	.	Fellow of the Society of Incorporated Accountants and Auditors
FSAE	.	Fellow, Society of Automotive Engineers
FSAIEE	.	Fellow, South African Institute of Electrical Engineers
FSAM	.	Fellow of the Society of Art Masters
FSArc	.	Fellow of Society of Architects (merged with the RIBA 1952)
FSAScot	.	Fellow of the Society of Antiquaries of Scotland
FSASM	.	Fellow of the South Australian School of Mines
FSBI	.	Fellow, Savings Banks Institute
fsc	.	Foreign Staff College
FSCA	.	Fellow, Society of Company and Commercial Accountants
FSDC	.	Fellow of Society of Dyers and Colourists
FSE	.	Fellow of the Society of Engineers
FSG	.	Fellow of the Society of Genealogists
FSGT	.	Fellow of Society of Glass Technology
FSI	.	Fellow of Royal Institution of Chartered Surveyors (changed Aug. 1947 to FRICS)
FSIAD	.	Fellow of Society of Industrial Artists and Designers

FSLAET	.	Fellow, Society of Licensed Aircraft Engineers and Technologists
FSMA	.	Fellow of Incorporated Sales Managers' Association (now see FInstMSM, FIM)
FSMC	.	Freeman of the Spectacle-Makers' Company
FSS	.	Fellow of the Royal Statistical Society
FSVA	.	Fellow, Society of Valuers and Auctioneers
FTCD	.	Fellow of Trinity College, Dublin
FTCL	.	Fellow of Trinity College of Music, London
FTI	.	Fellow of the Textile Institute
FTII	.	Fellow of the Institute of Taxation
FTP	.	Fellow, Thames Polytechnic
FTS	.	Fellow, Australian Academy of Technological Sciences; Flying Training School
FUCUA	.	Federation of University Conservative and Unionist Associations (now see FCS)
FUMIST	.	Fellow of University of Manchester Institute of Science and Technology
FWA	.	Fellow of the World Academy of Arts and Sciences
FWeldI	.	Fellow, Welding Institute
FWSOM	.	Fellow, Institute of Practitioners in Work Study, Organisation and Method
FZS	.	Fellow of the Zoological Society
FZSScot	.	Fellow, Zoological Society of Scotland (now see FRZSScot)

G

Ga	.	Georgia (US)
G&MWU	.	General and Municipal Workers' Union
GAPAN	.	Guild of Air Pilots and Air Navigators
GATT	.	General Agreement on Tariffs and Trade
GB	.	Great Britain
GBA	.	Governing Bodies Association
GBE	.	Knight or Dame Grand Cross Order of the British Empire
GBGSA	.	Association of Governing Bodies of Girls' Public Schools
GBSM	.	Graduate of Birmingham and Midland Institute School of Music
GC	.	George Cross
GCB	.	Knight Grand Cross of the Bath
GCH	.	Knight Grand Cross of Hanover
GCIE	.	Knight Grand Commander of the Indian Empire
GCKLJ	.	Grand Cross, St Lazarus of Jerusalem
GCMG	.	Knight or Dame Grand Cross of St Michael and St George
GCON	.	Grand Cross, Order of the Niger
GCSG	.	Knight Grand Cross of the Order of St Gregory the Great
GCSI	.	Knight Grand Commander of the Star of India
GCStJ	.	Bailiff or Dame Grand Cross of the Order of St John of Jerusalem
GCVO	.	Knight or Dame Grand Cross of Royal Victorian Order
GDC	.	General Dental Council
Gdns	.	Gardens
GDR	.	German Democratic Republic
Gen.	.	General
Ges.	.	Gesellschaft
GFS	.	Girls' Friendly Society
ggs	.	great grandson
GHQ	.	General Headquarters
Gib.	.	Gibraltar
GIMechE	.	Graduate Institution of Mechanical Engineers
GL	.	Grand Lodge
GLC	.	Greater London Council
Glos.	.	Gloucestershire
GM	.	George Medal; Grand Medal (Ghana)
GMC	.	General Medical Council; Guild of Memorial Craftsmen
GMIE	.	Grand Master of Indian Empire
GMSI	.	Grand Master of Star of India
GNC	.	General Nursing Council
GOC	.	General Officer Commanding
GOC-in-C	.	General Officer Commanding-in-Chief
GOE	.	General Ordination Examination
Gov.	.	Governor
Govt	.	Government
GP	.	General Practitioner; Grand Prix
GPDST	.	Girls' Public Day School Trust
GPO	.	General Post Office
GQG	.	Grand Quartier General (French GHQ)
Gr.	.	Greek
GRSM	.	Graduate of the Royal Schools of Music
GS	.	General Staff
gs	.	Grandson
GSM	.	General Service Medal; Guildhall School of Music
GSO	.	General Staff Officer
GTCL	.	Graduate, Trinity College of Music

GTS.	. .	General Theological Seminary (New York)
GUI.	. .	Golfing Union of Ireland
GWR	. .	Great Western Railway

H

HA	. .	Historical Association
HAA.	. .	Heavy Anti-Aircraft
HAC.	. .	Honourable Artillery Company
Hants	. .	Hampshire
HARCVS.	. .	Honorary Associate of the Royal College of Veterinary Surgeons
Harv.	. .	Harvard
HBM	. .	His (or Her) Britannic Majesty (Majesty's); Humming Bird Gold Medal (Trinidad)
hc	. .	honoris causa
HCEG	. .	Honourable Company of Edinburgh Golfers
HCF.	. .	Hon. Chaplain to the Forces
HCIMA	. .	Hotel, Catering and Institutional Management Association
HDA	. .	Hawkesbury Diploma in Agriculture (Australian)
HDD	. .	Higher Dental Diploma
HE	. .	His Excellency; His Eminence
HEH	. .	His Exalted Highness
HEIC	. .	Honourable East India Company
HEICS	. .	Honourable East India Company's Service
Heir-pres..	. .	Heir-presumptive
Herts	. .	Hertfordshire
HFARA	. .	Honorary Foreign Associate of the Royal Academy
HFRA	. .	Honorary Foreign Member of the Royal Academy
HG	. .	Home Guard
HH	. .	His (or Her) Highness; His Holiness
HHD	. .	Doctor of Humanities (US)
HIH	. .	His (or Her) Imperial Highness
HIM	. .	His (or Her) Imperial Majesty
HJ	. .	Hilal-e-Jurat (Pakistan)
HLD	. .	Doctor of Humane Letters
HLI	. .	Highland Light Infantry
HM	. .	His (or Her) Majesty, or Majesty's
HMAS	. .	His (or Her) Majesty's Australian Ship
HMC	. .	Headmasters' Conference; Hospital Management Committee
HMHS	. .	His (or Her) Majesty's Hospital Ship
HMI.	. .	His (or Her) Majesty's Inspector
HMOCS	. .	His (or Her) Majesty's Overseas Civil Service
HMS	. .	His (or Her) Majesty's Ship
HMSO	. .	His (or Her) Majesty's Stationery Office
HNC	. .	Higher National Certificate
HND	. .	Higher National Diploma
H of C	. .	House of Commons
Hon..	. .	Honourable; Honorary
HP	. .	House Physician
HPk.	. .	Hilal-e-Pakistan
HQ.	. .	Headquarters
HQA	. .	Hilal-i-Quaid-i-Azam
(HR).	. .	Home Rule
HRCA	. .	Honorary Royal Cambrian Academician
HRH	. .	His (or Her) Royal Highness
HRHA	. .	Honorary Member of Royal Hibernian Academy
HRI.	. .	Honorary Member of Royal Institute of Painters in Water Colours
HROI	. .	Honorary Member of Royal Institute of Oil Painters
HRSA	. .	Honorary Member of Royal Scottish Academy
HRSW	. .	Honorary Member of Royal Scottish Water Colour Society
HS	. .	House Surgeon
HSH.	. .	His (or Her) Serene Highness
Hum.	. .	Humanity, Humanities (Classics)
Hunts	. .	Huntingdonshire
Hy	. .	Heavy

I

I	. .	Island
Ia	. .	Iowa (US)
IA	. .	Indian Army
IAEA	. .	International Atomic Energy Agency
IAF	. .	Indian Air Force; Indian Auxiliary Force
IAHM	. .	Incorporated Association of Headmasters
IAMC	. .	Indian Army Medical Corps
IAMTACT	. .	Institute of Advanced Machine Tool and Control Technology
IAOC	. .	Indian Army Ordnance Control
IAPS	. .	Incorporated Association of Preparatory Schools
IARO	. .	Indian Army Reserve of Officers
IAS	. .	Indian Administrative Service
IASS.	. .	International Association for Scandinavian Studies
IATA	. .	International Air Transport Association

IATUL	. .	International Association of Technical University Libraries
Ib. or Ibid.	. .	Ibidem (in the same place)
IBA	. .	Independent Broadcasting Authority; International Bar Association
IBG	. .	Institute of British Geographers
IBRD	. .	International Bank for Reconstruction and Development (World Bank)
i/c	. .	In charge
ICA	. .	Institute of Contemporary Arts
ICAA	. .	Invalid Children's Aid Association
ICAI.	. .	Institute of Chartered Accountants in Ireland
ICAO	. .	International Civil Aviation Organization
ICD	. .	Iuris Canonici Doctor
ICE	. .	Institution of Civil Engineers
Icel.	. .	Icelandic
ICF	. .	International Federation of Chemical and General Workers' Unions
ICFC	. .	Industrial and Commercial Finance Corporation
ICFTU	. .	International Confederation of Free Trade Unions
IChemE	. .	Institution of Chemical Engineers
ICI	. .	Imperial Chemical Industries
ICMA	. .	Institute of Cost and Management Accountants
ICOM	. .	International Council of Museums
ICOMOS	. .	International Council of Monuments and Sites
ICRC	. .	International Committee of the Red Cross
ICS	. .	Indian Civil Service
ICSS.	. .	International Committee for the Sociology of Sport
ICSU	. .	International Council of Scientific Unions
ICT	. .	International Computers and Tabulators Ltd
Id	. .	Idaho (US)
IDA	. .	International Development Association
IDB	. .	Internal Drainage Board
IDC	. .	Imperial Defence College (now see RCDS)
idc	. .	Completed a Course at, or served for a year on the Staff of, the Imperial Defence College (now see rcds)
IDS	. .	Institute of Development Studies
IEE	. .	Institution of Electrical Engineers
IEEE	. .	Institute of Electrical and Electronics Engineers (NY)
IERE	. .	Institution of Electronic and Radio Engineers (and see under BritIRE)
IES	. .	Indian Educational Service; Institution of Engineers and Shipbuilders in Scotland
IFIP	. .	International Federation for Information Processing
IFLA	. .	International Federation of Library Associations
IFS	. .	Irish Free State; Indian Forest Service
IG	. .	Instructor in Gunnery
IGasE	. .	Institution of Gas Engineers
IGU	. .	International Geographical Union; International Gas Union
IHA	. .	Institute of Health Service Administrators
IHVE	. .	Institution of Heating and Ventilating Engineers
IIS	. .	International Institute of Sociology
IISS.	. .	International Institute of Strategic Studies
ILEA	. .	Inner London Education Authority
ILEC	. .	Inner London Education Committee
Ill	. .	Illinois (US)
ILO	. .	International Labour Office
ILP	. .	Independent Labour Party
ILR	. .	International Labour Review
IM	. .	Individual Merit
IMA.	. .	International Music Association
IMCO	. .	Inter-Governmental Maritime Consultative Organization
IMEA	. .	Incorporated Municipal Electrical Association
IMechE	. .	Institution of Mechanical Engineers
IMEDE	. .	Institut pour l'Etude des Méthodes de Direction de l'Entreprise
IMF	. .	International Monetary Fund
IMGTechE	. .	Institution of Mechanical and General Technician Engineers
IMinE	. .	Institution of Mining Engineers
IMMTS	. .	Indian Mercantile Marine Training Ship
Imp..	. .	Imperial
IMS.	. .	Indian Medical Service
IMTA	. .	Institute of Municipal Treasurers and Accountants; now see CIPFA
IMunE	. .	Institution of Municipal Engineers
IN	. .	Indian Navy
Inc.	. .	Incorporated
Incog.	. .	Incognito (in secret)
Ind.	. .	Independent; Indiana (US)
INSEA	. .	International Society for Education through Art
INSEAD	. .	Institut Européen d'Administration des Affaires
Insp..	. .	Inspector
Inst..	. .	Institute
Instn	. .	Institution
InstnMM.	. .	Institution of Mining and Metallurgy
InstT	. .	Institute of Transport
IODE	. .	Imperial Order of the Daughters of the Empire
I of M	. .	Isle of Man
IOGT	. .	International Order of Good Templars
IOM.	. .	Isle of Man; Indian Order of Merit
IOOF	. .	Independent Order of Odd-fellows
IOP	. .	Institute of Painters in Oil Colours

IoW	. .	Isle of Wight
IPCS	. .	Institution of Professional Civil Servants
IPFA	. .	Member, Chartered Institute of Public Finance and Accountancy
IPI	. .	International Press Institute
IPM	. .	Institute of Personnel Management
IPPF	. .	International Planned Parenthood Federation
IPPS	. .	Institute of Physics and The Physical Society
IPS	. .	Indian Police Service; Indian Political Service
IPU	. .	Inter-Parliamentary Union
IRA	. .	Irish Republican Army
IRAD	. .	Institute for Research on Animal Diseases
IRC	. .	Industrial Reorganization Corporation
IREE(Aust)	. .	Institution of Radio and Electronics Engineers (Australia)
IRI	. .	Institution of the Rubber Industry (now see PRI)
IRO	. .	International Refugee Organization
IRTE	. .	Institute of Road Transport Engineers
Is	. .	Island(s)
IS	. .	International Society of Sculptors, Painters and Gravers
ISC	. .	Imperial Service College, Haileybury; Indian Staff Corps
ISE	. .	Indian Service of Engineers
ISI	. .	International Statistical Institute
ISIS	. .	Independent Schools Information Service
ISM	. .	Incorporated Society of Musicians
ISMRC	. .	Inter-Services Metallurgical Research Council
ISO	. .	Imperial Service Order; International Standards Organization
IStructE	. .	Institution of Structural Engineers
IT	. .	Indian Territory (US)
ITA	. .	Independent Television Authority; now see IBA
Ital. or It..	. .	Italian
ITB	. .	Industry Training Board
ITF	. .	International Transport Workers' Federation
ITO	. .	International Trade Organization
ITV	. .	Independent Television
IUA	. .	International Union of Architects
IUB	. .	International Union of Biochemistry
IUC	. .	Inter-University Council for Higher Education Overseas
IUCN	. .	International Union for the Conservation of Nature and Natural Resources
IUCW	. .	International Union for Child Welfare
IUP	. .	Association of Independent Unionist Peers
IUPAC	. .	International Union of Pure and Applied Chemistry
IUPAP	. .	International Union of Pure and Applied Physics
IVS	. .	International Voluntary Service
IW	. .	Isle of Wight
IWES	. .	Institution of Water Engineers and Scientists
IWGC	. .	Imperial War Graves Commission
IWM	. .	Institution of Works Managers
IWSOM	. .	Institute of Practitioners in Work Study Organisation and Methods
IWSP	. .	Institute of Work Study Practitioners; now see IWSOM
IY	. .	Imperial Yeomanry
IZ	. .	I Zingari

J

JA	. .	Judge Advocate
JACT	. .	Joint Association of Classical Teachers
JAG	. .	Judge Advocate General
Jas	. .	James
JCB	. .	Juris Canonici Bachelor (Bachelor of Canon Law)
JCS	. .	Journal of the Chemical Society
JCD	. .	Juris Canonici Doctor (Doctor of Canon Law)
JCL	. .	Licentiate of Canon Law
JCO	. .	Joint Consultative Organisation (of ARC, MAFF, and Department of Agriculture and Fisheries for Scotland)
JD	. .	Doctor of Jurisprudence
JDipMA	. .	Joint Diploma in Management Accounting Services
JG	. .	Junior Grade
JInstE	. .	Junior Institution of Engineers; now see IMGTechE
jls	. .	Journals
JMN	. .	Johan Mangku Negara (Malaysian Honour)
Joh. or Jno.	. .	John
JP	. .	Justice of the Peace
Jr	. .	Junior
jsc	. .	Qualified at a Junior Staff Course, or the equivalent, 1942–46
JSD	. .	Doctor of Juristic Science
JSLS	. .	Joint Services Liaison Staff
JSM	. .	Johan Sedia Mahkota (Malaysia)
jssc	. .	Joint Services Staff Course
jt, jtly	. .	joint, jointly
JWS or jws	. .	Joint Warfare Staff
JUD	. .	Juris Utriusque Doctor, Doctor of Both Laws (Canon and Civil)
Jun.	. .	Junior
Jun. Opt.	. .	Junior Optime

K

Kans	. .	Kansas (US)
KAR	. .	King's African Rifles
KBE	. .	Knight Commander Order of the British Empire
KC	. .	King's Counsel
KCB	. .	Knight Commander of the Bath
KCC	. .	Commander of Order of Crown, Belgian and Congo Free State
KCH	. .	King's College Hospital; Knight Commander of Hanover
KCIE	. .	Knight Commander of the Indian Empire
KCL	. .	King's College, London
KCMG	. .	Knight Commander of St Michael and St George
KCSG	. .	Knight Commander of St Gregory
KCSI	. .	Knight Commander of the Star of India
KCSS	. .	Knight Commander of St Silvester
KCVO	. .	Knight Commander of the Royal Victorian Order
KDG	. .	King's Dragoon Guards
KEH	. .	King Edward's Horse
KG	. .	Knight of the Order of the Garter
KGStJ	. .	formerly Knight of Grace, Order of St John of Jerusalem (now KStJ)
KH	. .	Knight of Hanover
KHC	. .	Hon. Chaplain to the King
KHDS	. .	Hon. Dental Surgeon to the King
KHNS	. .	Hon. Nursing Sister to the King
KHP	. .	Hon. Physician to the King
KHS	. .	Hon. Surgeon to the King; Knight of the Holy Sepulchre
K-i-H	. .	Kaisar-i-Hind
KJStJ	. .	formerly Knight of Justice, Order of St John of Jerusalem (now KStJ)
KLJ	. .	Knight, St Lazarus of Jerusalem
KORR	. .	King's Own Royal Regiment
KOSB	. .	King's Own Scottish Borderers
KOYLI	. .	King's Own Yorkshire Light Infantry
KP	. .	Knight of the Order of St Patrick
KPM	. .	King's Police Medal
KRRC	. .	King's Royal Rifle Corps
KStJ	. .	Knight of Order of St John of Jerusalem; and see GCStJ
KS	. .	King's Scholar
KSC	. .	Knight of St Columba
KSG	. .	Knight of St Gregory the Great
KSLI	. .	King's Shropshire Light Infantry
KSLJ	. .	Knight of St Lazarus of Jerusalem
KSS	. .	Knight of St Silvester
KT	. .	Knight of the Order of the Thistle
Kt or Knt	. .	Knight
Ky	. .	Kentucky (US)

L

(L)	. .	Liberal
LA	. .	Los Angeles; Literate in Arts; Liverpool Academy
La	. .	Louisiana (US)
(Lab)	. .	Labour
LAC	. .	London Athletic Club
LAMDA	. .	London Academy of Music and Dramatic Art
LAMSAC	. .	Local Authorities' Management Services and Computer Committee
L-Corp. or Lance-Corp.	. .	Lance-Corporal
Lancs	. .	Lancashire
LCC	. .	London County Council (now see under GLC)
LCh	. .	Licentiate in Surgery
LCJ	. .	Lord Chief Justice
LCL	. .	Licentiate of Canon Law
LCP	. .	Licentiate of the College of Preceptors
LDiv	. .	Licentiate in Divinity
LDS	. .	Licentiate in Dental Surgery
LDV	. .	Local Defence Volunteers
LEA	. .	Local Education Authority
LEPRA	. .	British Leprosy Relief Association
LèsL	. .	Licencié ès lettres
LH	. .	Light Horse
LHD	. .	(Literarum Humaniorum Doctor) Doctor of Literature
LI	. .	Light Infantry; Long Island
LicMed	. .	Licentiate in Medicine
Lieut	. .	Lieutenant
Lincs	. .	Lincolnshire
LIOB	. .	Licentiate of Institute of Building
Lit.	. .	Literature; Literary
LitD	. .	Doctor of Literature; Doctor of Letters
Lit. Hum.	. .	Literae Humaniores (Classics)
LittD	. .	Doctor of Literature; Doctor of Letters
LJ	. .	Lord Justice
LLA	. .	Lady Literate in Arts
LLB	. .	Bachelor of Laws
LLCM	. .	Licentiate London College of Music
LLD	. .	Doctor of Laws
LLL	. .	Licentiate in Laws

LLM	. .	Master of Laws
LM	. .	Licentiate in Midwifery
LMBC	.	Lady Margaret Boat Club
LMCC	.	Licentiate of Medical Council of Canada
LMR	.	London Midland Region (BR)
LMS.	.	London, Midland and Scottish Railway; London Missionary Society
LMSSA	.	Licentiate in Medicine and Surgery, Society of Apothecaries
LMRTPI.	.	Legal Member, Royal Town Planning Institute
(LNat)	.	Liberal National
LNER	.	London and North Eastern Railway
LOB.	.	Location of Offices Bureau
L of C	.	Lines of Communication
LPTB	.	London Passenger Transport Board
LRAD	.	Licentiate of the Royal Academy of Dancing
LRAM	.	Licentiate of the Royal Academy of Music
LRCP	.	Licentiate of the Royal College of Physicians, London
LRCPE	.	Licentiate Royal College of Physicians, Edinburgh
LRCS	.	Licentiate of the Royal College of Surgeons of England
LRCSE	.	Licentiate of the Royal College of Surgeons, Edinburgh
LRFPS(G)	.	(formerly Licentiate of the Royal Faculty of Physicians and Surgeons, Glasgow (now Royal College of Physicians and Surgeons, Glasgow)
LRIBA	.	Licentiate Royal Institute British Architects
LSA.	.	Licentiate of the Society of Apothecaries
Lt	. .	Light (eg Light Infantry)
Lt or Lieut	.	Lieutenant
LT	. .	Licentiate in Teaching
LTB.	.	London Transport Board
LTCL	.	Licentiate of Trinity College of Music London
Lt-Col	.	Lieutenant-Colonel
LTE.	.	London Transport Executive
Lt-Gen.	.	Lieutenant-General
LTh.	.	Licentiate in Theology
(LU)	.	Liberal Unionist
LUOTC	.	London University Officers' Training Corps
LWT	.	London Weekend Television
LXX.	.	Septuagint

M

M	. .	Marquess; Member; Monsieur
m	. .	married
MA	. .	Master of Arts
MAA	.	Manufacturers' Agents' Association of Great Britain
MAAF	.	Mediterranean Allied Air Forces
MACE	.	Member of the Australian College of Education
MACI	.	Member of the American Concrete Institute
MACS	.	Member of the American Chemical Society
MAEE	.	Marine Aircraft Experimental Establishment
MAFF	.	Ministry of Agriculture, Fisheries and Food
MAI.	.	Master of Engineering (*Magister in Arte Ingeniaria*)
MAIAA	.	Member of American Institute of Aeronautics and Astronautics (and *see under* MIAS)
MAICE	.	Member of American Institute of Consulting Engineers
MAIChE	.	Member of the American Institute of Chemical Engineers
Maj.-Gen.	.	Major-General
Man.	.	Manitoba (Canada)
MAO	.	Master of Obstetric Art
MAOU	.	Member American Ornithologists' Union
MAP	.	Ministry of Aircraft Production
MArch	.	Master of Architecture
Marq.	.	Marquess
MASAE	.	Member American Society of Agricultural Engineers
MASCE	.	Member American Society of Civil Engineers
MASME	.	Member American Society of Mechanical Engineers
Mass.	.	Massachusetts (US)
Math.	.	Mathematics; Mathematical
MB	. .	Medal of Bravery (Canada); Bachelor of Medicine
MBA	.	Master of Business Administration
MBASW	.	Member, British Association of Social Workers
MBCS	.	Member, British Computer Society
MBE	.	Member of the Order of the British Empire
MBFR	.	Mutual and Balanced Force Reductions (negotiations)
MBIM	.	Member of the British Institute of Management (formerly MIIA)
MBKS	.	Member, British Kinematograph, Sound and Television Society
MBOU	.	Member British Ornithologists' Union
MBritIRE	.	(now *see under* MIERE) (formerly) Member of British Institution of Radio Engineers
MC	. .	Military Cross
M CAM	.	Member, CAM Society
MCB	.	Master in Clinical Biochemistry
MCC	.	Marylebone Cricket Club; Metropolitan County Council
MCD	.	Master of Civic Design

MCE(Melb)	.	Master of Civil Engineering (Melbourne University)
MCFP	.	Member, College of Family Physicians (Canada)
MCh or MChir	.	Master in Surgery
MChOrth.	.	Master of Orthopaedic Surgery
MChemA.	.	Master in Chemical Analysis
MCIBS	.	Member, Chartered Institution of Building Services (formerly FIHVE or MIHVE)
MCL	.	Master in Civil Law
MCMES	.	Member of Civil and Mechanical Engineers' Society
MCom	. .	Master of Commerce
MConsE	.	Member of Association of Consulting Engineers
MCP	.	Member of Colonial Parliament; Master of City Planning (US)
MCPA	.	Member of the College of Pathologists of Australia (*now see* MRCPA)
MCPath	.	Member of College of Pathologists (*now see* MRCPath)
MCPS	.	Member College of Physicians and Surgeons
MCS.	.	Madras Civil Service; Malayan Civil Service
MCSEE	.	Member, Canadian Society of Electrical Engineers
MCSP	.	Member, Chartered Society of Physiotherapy
MD	. .	Doctor of Medicine; Military District
Md	. .	Maryland (US)
MDC	.	Metropolitan District Council
MDS	.	Master of Dental Surgery
Me	. .	Maine (US)
ME	. .	Mining Engineer; Middle East
MEAF	.	Middle East Air Force
MEC	.	Member of Executive Council
MEc.	.	Master of Economics
MECAS	.	Middle East Centre for Arab Studies
Mech.	.	Mechanics; Mechanical
Med..	.	Medical
MEd.	.	Master of Education
MEF	.	Middle East Force
MEIC	.	Member Engineering Institute of Canada
MELF	.	Middle East Land Forces
MEng	.	Master of Engineering
MetR	.	Metropolitan Railway
MetSoc	.	Metals Society (formed by amalgamation of Institute of Metals and Iron and Steel Institute)
MEXE	.	Military Engineering Experimental Establishment
MFCM	.	Member, Faculty of Community Medicine
MFGB	.	Miners' Federation of Great Britain
MFH	.	Master of Foxhounds
MGA	.	Maj.-Gen. i c Administration
MGC	.	Machine Gun Corps
MGGS	.	Major-General, General Staff
MGI.	.	Member of the Institute of Certificated Grocers
Mgr.	.	Monsignor
MHA	.	Member of House of Assembly
MHK	.	Member of the House of Keys
MHR	.	Member House of Representatives
MHRA	.	Modern Humanities Research Association
MHRF	.	Mental Health Research Fund
MI	. .	Military Intelligence
MIAeE	.	Member Institute of Aeronautical Engineers
MIAgrE	.	Member of Institution of Agricultural Engineers
MIAS	.	(now *see under* MAIAA) (formerly) Member Institute of Aeronautical Science (US)
MIBF	.	Member Institute of British Foundrymen
MIBritE	.	Member, Institution of British Engineers
MIBS	.	Member, Institute of Bankers in Scotland
MICE	.	Member of Institution of Civil Engineers (formerly the higher rank of corporate membership of the Institution, now the lower rank; *see also* FICE; change dated July 1968)
MICEI	.	Member of Institution of Civil Engineers of Ireland
Mich.	.	Michigan (US)
MIChemE	.	Member of the Institution of Chemical Engineers
MIEAust	.	Member Institution of Engineers, Australia
MIED	.	Member, Institute of Engineering Designers
MIEE	.	Member of Institution of Electrical Engineers (formerly the higher rank of corporate membership of the Institution, now the lower rank; *see also* FIEE; change dated Dec. 1966)
MIEEE	.	Member of Institute of Electrical and Electronics Engineers (NY)
MIEI	.	Member of Institution of Engineering Inspection
MIE(Ind)	.	Member of Institution of Engineers, India
MIERE	.	Member of Institution of Electronic and Radio Engineers (and *see under* MBritIRE)
MIES	.	Member Institution of Engineers and Shipbuilders, Scotland
MIEx	.	Member Institute of Export
MIGasE	.	Member, Institution of Gas Engineers
MIH.	.	Member Institute of Hygiene
MIHVE	.	Member Institution of Heating and Ventilating Engineers (*now see* MCIBS)
MIIA	.	Member of the Institute of Industrial Administration (now *see under* MBIM)
Mil.	. .	Military
MILocoE.	.	Member of Institution of Locomotive Engineers
MIM	.	Member, Institution of Metallurgists
MIMarE	.	Member of the Institute of Marine Engineers

MIMC	.	Member, Institute of Management Consultants
MIMechE	.	Member of Institution of Mechanical Engineers (formerly the higher rank of corporate membership of the Institution, now the lower rank; *see also* FIMechE; change dated April 1968)
MIMGTechE	.	Member, Institution of Mechanical and General Technician Engineers
MIMI	.	Member of Institute of Motor Trade Industry
MIMinE	.	Member of the Institution of Mining Engineers
MIMM	.	Member Institution of Mining and Metallurgy
MIMunE	.	Member Institution of Municipal Engineers
Min.	. .	Ministry
MIN.	.	Member of the Institute of Navigation (*now see* MRIN)
Minn.	.	Minnesota (US)
MInstAM	.	Member, Institute of Administrative Management
MInstBE	.	Member, Institution of British Engineers
MInstCE	.	Member of Institution of Civil Engineers (changed Feb. 1940 to MICE)
MInstD	.	Member, Institute of Directors
MInstF	.	Member of Institute of Fuel
MInstGasE	.	Member Institution of Gas Engineers
MInstHE	.	Member of the Institution of Highway Engineers
MInstMC	.	Member, Institute of Measurement and Control
MInstME	.	Member of Institution of Mining Engineers
MInstMet	.	(formerly) Member of the Institute of Metals (now part of Metals Society)
MInstP	.	Member, Institute of Physics
MInstPet	.	Member of the Institute of Petroleum
MInstPI	.	Member of the Institute of Patentees and Inventors
MInstPS	.	Member, Institute of Purchasing and Supply
MInstR	.	Member of the Institute of Refrigeration
MInstRA	.	Member of the Institute of Registered Architects
MInstT	.	Member of the Institute of Transport
MInstW	.	Member Institute of Welding
MINucE	.	Member of Institution of Nuclear Engineers
MIOB	.	Member of the Institute of Building
MIPA	.	Member of the Institute of Practitioners in Advertising
MIPlantE	.	Member of the Institution of Plant Engineers
MIPM	.	Member of the Institute of Personnel Management
MIPR	.	Member of the Institute of Public Relations
MIProdE	.	(formerly MIPE) Member of the Institution of Production Engineers
MIQ.	.	Member, Institute of Quarrying
MIRE	.	(now *see under* MIERE) (formerly) Member of the Institution of Radio Engineers
MIREE(Aust)	.	Member of the Institution of Radio and Electronics Engineers (Australia)
MIRTE	.	Member of Institute of Road Transport Engineers
MIS	.	Member, Institute of Statisticians
MIS(India)	.	Member of the Institution of Surveyors of India
MISI	.	(formerly) Member of Iron and Steel Institute (now part of Metals Society)
Miss.	.	Mississippi (US)
MIStructE	.	Member of the Institution of Structural Engineers
MIT	.	Massachusetts Institute of Technology
MITA	.	Member, Industrial Transport Association
MITE	.	Member, Institution of Electrical and Electronics Technician Engineers
MIWE	.	Member of the Institution of Water Engineers (*now see* MIWES)
MIWES	.	Member, Institution of Water Engineers and Scientists
MIWPC	.	Member, Institute of Water Pollution Control
MIWSP	.	Member, Institute of Work Study Practitioners (*now see* MWSOM)
MJI	.	Member of Institute of Journalists
MJIE	.	Member of the Junior Institution of Engineers (*now see* MIGTechE)
MJS	.	Member of the Japan Society
ML	. .	Licentiate in Medicine; Master of Laws
MLA	.	Member of Legislative Assembly; Modern Language Association; Master in Landscape Architecture
MLC	.	Member of Legislative Council
MLitt	.	Master of Letters
Mlle	.	*Mademoiselle* (Miss)
MLO	.	Military Liaison Officer
MM	.	Military Medal
MME	.	Master of Mining Engineering
Mme.	.	Madame
MMechE	.	Master of Mechanical Engineering
MMet	.	Master of Metallurgy
MMGI	.	Member of the Mining, Geological and Metallurgical Institute of India
MMM	.	Member, Order of Military Merit (Canada)
MMSA	.	Master of Midwifery, Society of Apothecaries
MN	.	Merchant Navy
MNAS	.	Member of the National Academy of Sciences (US)
MNI	.	Member, Nautical Institute
MNSE	.	Member, Nigerian Society of Engineers
MO	. .	Medical Officer; Military Operations
Mo	. .	Missouri (US)
MoD	.	Ministry of Defence
Mods	.	Moderations (Oxford)

MOH	.	Medical Officer(s) of Health
MOI.	.	Ministry of Information
Mon	.	Monmouthshire
Mont	.	Montana (US); Montgomeryshire
MOP	.	Ministry of Power
Most Rev.	.	Most Reverend
MoT	.	Ministry of Transport
MP	.	Member of Parliament
MPBW	.	Ministry of Public Building and Works
MPP	.	Member Provincial Parliament
MPS	.	Member of Pharmaceutical Society
MR	.	Master of the Rolls; Municipal Reform
MRAC	.	Member, Royal Agricultural College
MRACP	.	Member, Royal Australasian College of Physicians
MRAeS	.	Member, Royal Aeronautical Society
MRAIC	.	Member Royal Architectural Institute of Canada
MRAS	.	Member of Royal Asiatic Society
MRC	.	Medical Research Council
MRCA	.	Multi-Role Combat Aircraft
MRCGP	.	Member, Royal College of General Practitioners
MRCOG	.	Member of Royal College of Obstetricians and Gynaecologists
MRCP	.	Member of the Royal College of Physicians, London
MRCPA	.	Member of Royal College of Pathologists of Australia
MRCPE	.	Member of the Royal College of Physicians, Edinburgh
MRCPGlas	.	Member of the Royal College (formerly Faculty) of Physicians and Surgeons, Glasgow
MRCS	.	Member Royal College of Surgeons of England
MRCSE	.	Member of the Royal College of Surgeons, Edinburgh
MRCVS	.	Member of the Royal College of Veterinary Surgeons
MREmpS	.	Member of the Royal Empire Society
MRI	.	Member Royal Institution
MRIA	.	Member Royal Irish Academy
MRIAI	.	Member, Royal Institute of the Architects of Ireland
MRIC	.	Member, Royal Institute of Chemistry
MRIN	.	Member, Royal Institute of Navigation
MRINA	.	Member of Royal Institution of Naval Architects
MRSanI	.	Member of Royal Sanitary Institute (*see* MRSH)
MRSH	.	Member of the Royal Society for the Promotion of Health (formerly MRSanI)
MRST	.	Member of Royal Society of Teachers
MRTPI	.	Member of Royal Town Planning Institute
MRUSI	.	Member of the Royal United Service Institution
MRVA	.	Member, Rating and Valuation Association
MS	. .	Master of Surgery; Master of Science (US)
MS, MSS.	.	Manuscript, Manuscripts
MSA	.	Master of Science, Agriculture (US); Mineralogical Society of America
MSAE	.	Member of the Society of Automotive Engineers (US)
MSAICE	.	Member of South African Institution of Civil Engineers
MSAInstMM	.	Member of South African Institute of Mining and Metallurgy
MS&R	.	Merchant Shipbuilding and Repairs
MSAutE	.	Member of the Society of Automobile Engineers
MSC	.	Madras Staff Corps
MSc.	.	Master of Science
MScD	.	Master of Dental Science
MSE.	.	Master of Science in Engineering (US)
MSH	.	Master of Stag Hounds
MSIA	.	Member Society of Industrial Artists
MSIAD	.	Member Society of Industrial Artists and Designers
MSINZ	.	Member Surveyors' Institute New Zealand
MSIT	.	Member Society of Instrument Technology (*now see* MInstMC)
MSM	.	Meritorious Service Medal; Madras Sappers and Miners
MSocSc	.	Master of Social Sciences
MSR.	.	Member Society of Radiographers
Mt	.	Mount, Mountain
MT	.	Mechanical Transport
MTA	.	Music Trades Association
MTAI	.	Member of Institute of Travel Agents
MTCA	.	Ministry of Transport and Civil Aviation
MTh.	.	Master of Theology
MTPI	.	Member of Town Planning Institute (*now see* MRTPI)
MusB	.	Bachelor of Music
MusD	.	Doctor of Music
MusM	.	Master of Music
MV	.	Merchant Vessel, Motor Vessel (naval)
MVO	.	Member of the Royal Victorian Order
MWSOM	.	Member, Institute of Practitioners in Work Study Organisation and Methods

N

(N)	.	Nationalist; Navigating Duties
N	. .	North
n	. .	Nephew
NA	.	National Academician (America)
NAACP	.	National Association for the Advancement of Colored People

NAAFI	Navy, Army and Air Force Institutes
NABC	National Association of Boys' Clubs
NALGO (Nalgo)	National and Local Government Officers' Association
NAMCW.	National Association for Maternal and Child Welfare
NAMH	National Association for Mental Health
NAPT	National Association for the Prevention of Tuberculosis
NASA	National Aeronautics and Space Administration (US)
NAS/UWT	National Association of Schoolmasters/Union of Women Teachers
NATCS	National Air Traffic Control Services
NATFHE	National Association of Teachers in Further and Higher Education (combining ATCDE and ATTI)
NATO	North Atlantic Treaty Organisation
Nat.Sci.	Natural Sciences
NB	New Brunswick
NBA.	North British Academy
NBC.	National Book Council (now National Book League); National Broadcasting Company (of America)
NBL.	National Book League (formerly National Book Council)
NBPI	National Board for Prices and Incomes
NC	National Certificate; North Carolina (US)
NCA.	National Certificate of Agriculture
NCB.	National Coal Board
NCCL	National Council for Civil Liberties
NCDAD	National Council for Diplomas in Art and Design
NCLC	National Council of Labour Colleges
NCU	National Cyclists' Union
NDA	National Diploma in Agriculture
NDak	North Dakota (US)
ndc	National Defence College (Canada)
NDD	National Diploma in Dairying; National Diploma in Design
NDH	National Diploma in Horticulture
NE	North-east
NEAC	New English Art Club
NEAF	Near East Air Force
Neb	Nebraska (US)
NEBSS	National Examinations Board for Supervisory Studies
NEC.	National Executive Committee
NECCTA	National Educational Closed Circuit Television Association
NECInst	North-East Coast Institution of Engineers and Shipbuilders
NEDC	National Economic Development Council; North East Development Council
NEDO	National Economic Development Office
NEL.	National Engineering Laboratory
NERC	Natural Environment Research Council
Nev	Nevada (US)
New M	New Mexico (US)
NFC.	National Freight Corporation
NFER	National Foundation for Educational Research
NFS.	National Fire Service
NFU	National Farmers' Union
NFWI	National Federation of Women's Institutes
NGO	Non-Governmental Organisation(s)
NH	New Hampshire (US)
NHS.	National Health Service
NI	Northern Ireland; Native Infantry
NIAB	National Institute of Agricultural Botany
NIAE	National Institute of Agricultural Engineering
NICS	Northern Ireland Civil Service
NID.	Naval Intelligence Division; National Institute for the Deaf; Northern Ireland District
NIESR	National Institute of Economic and Social Research
NIH.	National Institutes of Health (US)
NILP	Northern Ireland Labour Party
NJ	New Jersey (US)
NL	National Liberal
NLF.	National Liberal Federation
Northants.	Northamptonshire
Notts	Nottinghamshire
NP	Notary Public
NPFA	National Playing Fields Association
NPk.	Nishan-e-Pakistan
NPL.	National Physical Laboratory
NRA.	National Rifle Association; National Recovery Administration
NRD	National Registered Designer
NRDC	National Research Development Corporation
NRR.	Northern Rhodesia Regiment
NS	Nova Scotia; New Style in the Calendar (in Great Britain since 1752); National Society; National Service
ns	Graduate of Royal Naval Staff College, Greenwich
NSA.	National Skating Association
NSAIV	Distinguished Order of Shaheed Ali (Maldives)
NSPCC	National Society for Prevention of Cruelty to Children

NSRA	National Small-bore Rifle Association
N/SSF	Novice, Society of St Francis
NSTC	Nova Scotia Technical College
NSW	New South Wales
NT	New Testament; Northern Territory of South Australia
NTDA	National Trade Development Association
NT	New Testament; Northern Territory (Australia)
NUBE	National Union of Bank Employees
NUGMW	National Union of General and Municipal Workers; *now see* G&MWU
NUHKW.	National Union of Hosiery and Knitwear Workers
NUI	National University of Ireland
NUJ.	National Union of Journalists
NUM	National Union of Mineworkers
NUPE	National Union of Public Employees
NUR	National Union of Railwaymen
NUT	National Union of Teachers
NUTG	National Union of Townswomen's Guilds
NUTN	National Union of Trained Nurses
NUU	New University of Ulster
NW	North-west
NWFP	North-West Frontier Province
NWP	North-Western Provinces
NWT	North-Western Territories
NY	New York
NYC.	New York City
NZ	New Zealand
NZEF	New Zealand Expeditionary Force
NZIA	New Zealand Institute of Architects

O

O	Ohio (US)
o	only
OA	Officier d'Académie
O & E	Operations and Engineering (US)
O & M	organisation and method
O & O	Oriental and Occidental Steamship Co.
OAS.	Organisation of American States; On Active Service
OAU	Organisation for African Unity
ob	died
OBE.	Officer Order of the British Empire
OBI	Order of British India
OC	Officer of the Order of Canada (equivalent to former award SM)
o c	only child
OC and o/c	Officer Commanding
OCA	Old Comrades Association
OCF.	Officiating Chaplain to the Forces
OCTU	Officer Cadet Training Unit
ODA	Overseas Development Administration
ODI	Overseas Development Institute
ODM	Ministry of Overseas Development
OE	Order of Excellence (Guyana)
OECD	Organization for Economic Co-operation and Development (formerly OEEC)
OEEC	Organization for European Economic Co-operation; *see* OECD
OFM	Order of Friars Minor (Franciscans)
OFS	Orange Free State
OHMS	On His (or Her) Majesty's Service
OJ.	Order of Jamaica
OL	Officer of the Order of Leopold
OM	Order of Merit
OMI.	Oblate of Mary Immaculate
OMM	Officer, Order of Military Merit (Canada)
Ont	Ontario
OON	Officer of the Order of Niger
OP	*Ordinis Praedicatorum* of the Order of Preachers (Dominican Ecclesiastical Title); Observation Post
OPCS	Office of Population Censuses and Surveys
OR	Order of Rorima (Guyana); Operational Research
ORC.	Orange River Colony
Ore	Oregon (US)
ORS	Operational Research Society
ORSL	Order of the Republic of Sierra Leone
ORT.	Organization for Rehabilitation by Training
ORTF	Office de la Radiodiffusion et Télévision Française
os	only son
OSA	Order of St Augustine (Augustinian); Ontario Society of Artists
OSB.	Order of St Benedict (Benedictine)
OSFC	Franciscan (Capuchin) Order
O/Sig	Ordinary Signalman
OSNC	Orient Steam Navigation Co.
OSRD	Office of Scientific Research and Development
OStJ.	Officer of Order of St John of Jerusalem
OSUK	Ophthalmological Society of the United Kingdom
OT	Old Testament
OTC.	Officers' Training Corps
OTL.	Officer of the Order of Toussaint L'Ouverture (Haiti)
OU	Oxford University

OUAC	. .	Oxford University Athletic Club
OUAFC	. .	Oxford University Association Football Club
OUBC	.	Oxford University Boat Club
OUCC	.	Oxford University Cricket Club
OUDS˙	.	Oxford University Dramatic Society
OUP	.	Oxford University Press
OURC	.	Oxford University Rifle Club
OURFC	. .	Oxford University Rugby Football Club
Oxon	.	Oxfordshire; of Oxford

P

PA	. .	Pakistan Army; Personal Assistant
Pa	.	Pennsylvania (US)
pac	.	passed the final examination of the Advanced Class. The Military College of Science
P&O	.	Peninsular and Oriental Steamship Co.
P&OSNCo.		Peninsular and Oriental Steam Navigation Co.
PASI	.	Professional Associate Chartered Surveyors' Institution (changed August 1947 to ARICS)
PC	.	Privy Councillor; Police Constable; Perpetual Curate; Peace Commissioner (Ireland)
pc	.	*per centum* (by the hundred)
PCMO		Principal Colonial Medical Officer
PdD	.	Doctor of Pedagogy (US)
PDSA	.	People's Dispensary for Sick Animals
PE	.	Procurement Executive
PEI	.	Prince Edward Island
PEN	.	(Name of Club: Poets, Playwrights, Editors, Essayists. Novelists)
PEng	.	Registered Professional Engineer (Canada)
PEP	.	Political and Economic Planning
PER	.	Professional and Executive Register
PEST	.	Pressure for Economic and Social Toryism
PF	.	Procurator-Fiscal
pfc	.	Graduate of RAF Flying College
PFE	.	Program for Executives
PGA	.	Professional Golfers' Association
PGCE	.	Post Graduate Certificate of Education
PH	.	Presidential Order of Honour (Botswana)
PhB	.	Bachelor of Philosophy
PhC	.	Pharmaceutical Chemist
PhD	.	Doctor of Philosophy
Phil.	. .	Philology, Philological; Philosophy, Philosophical
PhL	.	Licentiate of Philosophy
PhM	.	Master of Philosophy (USA)
PhmB		Bachelor of Pharmacy
Phys.	.	Physical
PIARC	.	Permanent International Association of Road Congresses
PIB	.	Prices and Incomes Board (*see* NBPI)
PICAO		Provisional International Civil Aviation Organization (*now* ICAO)
pinx.	. .	(He) painted it
PIRA	.	Paper Industries Research Association
Pl	.	Place; Plural
PLA	.	Port of London Authority
Plen.	.	Plenipotentiary
PLP	.	Parliamentary Labour Party
PMG	.	Postmaster-General
PMN	.	*Panglima Mangku Negara* (Malaysian Honour)
PMO	·	Principal Medical Officer
PMRAFNS	.	Princess Mary's Royal Air Force Nursing Service
PMS	.	Presidential Order of Meritorious Service (Botswana); President Miniature Society
PNBS	.	*Panglima Negara Bintang Sarawak*
PNEU	.	Parents' National Educational Union
PNG	.	Papua New Guinea
PO	.	Post Office
POB	.	Presidential Order of Botswana
POMEF	.	Political Office Middle East Force
Pop.	. .	Population
POW	.	Prisoner of War; Prince of Wales's
PP	.	Parish Priest; Past President
Pp	.	Pages
PPCLI	.	Princess Patricia's Canadian Light Infantry
PPE	.	Philosophy, Politics and Economics (Oxford Univ.)
PPInstHE	.	Past President, Institution of Highway Engineers
PPIStructE	.	Past President, Institution of Structural Engineers
PPRA	.	Past President of the Royal Academy
PPRBA	.	Past President of the Royal Society of British Artists
PPRBS	.	Past President, Royal Society of British Sculptors
PPRE	.	Past President of the Royal Society of Painter-Etchers and Engravers
PPS	.	Parliamentary Private Secretary
PPSIA	.	Past President of the Society of Industrial Artists
PPTPI	.	Past President Town Planning Institute
PQ	.	Province of Quebec
PRA	.	President of the Royal Academy
PRBS	.	President, Royal Society of British Sculptors
PRCS	.	President of the Royal College of Surgeons
PRE	.	President of the Royal Society of Painter-Etchers and Engravers

Preb.	. .	Prebendary
PrEng.	.	Professional Engineer
Pres.	. .	President
PRHA	.	President of the Royal Hibernian Academy
PRI	.	President of the Royal Institute of Painters in Water Colours; Plastics and Rubber Institute
PRIA	.	President of the Royal Irish Academy
Prin.	. .	Principal
PRO	.	Public Relations Officer; Public Records Office
Proc.	.	Proctor; Proceedings
Prof.	. .	Professor
PROI	.	President of the Royal Institute of Oil Painters
Pro tem	.	*Pro tempore* (for the time being)
Prov.	.	Provost; Provincial
Prox.	.	*Proximo* (next)
Prox. acc.	. .	*Proxime accessit* (next in order of merit to the winner, or a very close second)
PRS	.	President of the Royal Society; Performing Right Society Ltd.
PRSA	.	President of the Royal Scottish Academy
PRSE	.	President of the Royal Society of Edinburgh
PRSH	.	President of the Royal Society for the Promotion of Health
PRSW	.	President of the Royal Scottish Water Colour Society
PRUAA	.	President of the Royal Ulster Academy of Arts
PRWS	.	President of the Royal Society of Painters in Water Colours; Plastics and Rubber Institute
PS	.	Pastel Society
ps	.	passed School of Instruction (of Officers)
PSA	.	Property Services Agency
psa	.	Graduate of RAF Staff College
psc	.	Graduate of Staff College (†indicated Graduate of Senior Wing Staff College)
PSD	.	Petty Sessional Division
PSIA	.	President of the Society of Industrial Artists
PSM	.	*Panglima Setia Mahkota*
psm	.	Certificate of Royal Military School of Music
PSMA	.	President of Society of Marine Artists
PSNC	.	Pacific Steam Navigation Co.
PTE	.	Passenger Transport Executive
Pte	.	Private (soldier)
ptsc	.	passed Technical Staff College
Pty	.	Proprietary
PUP	.	People's United Party
PVSM	.	Param Vishishc Seva Medal (India)
PWD	.	Public Works Department
PWO	.	Prince of Wales's Own

Q

Q	. .	Queen
QAIMNS	.	Queen Alexandra's Imperial Military Nursing Service
QALAS	.	Qualified Associate Chartered Land Agents' Society *now* (after amalgamation) *see* ARICS
QARANC	.	Queen Alexandra's Royal Army Nursing Corps
QARNNS	.	Queen Alexandra's Royal Naval Nursing Service˙
QC	. .	Queen's Counsel
QFSM	.	Queen's Fire Service Medal for Distinguished Service
QGM	.	Queen's Gallantry Medal
QHC	.	Queen's Honorary Chaplain
QHDS	.	Queen's Honorary Dental Surgeon
QHNS	.	Queen's Honorary Nursing Sister
QHP	.	Queen's Honorary Physician
QHS	.	Queen's Honorary Surgeon
Qld	. .	Queensland
Qly	. .	Quarterly
QMAAC	.	Queen Mary's Army Auxiliary Corps
QMC	.	Queen Mary College (London)
QMG	.	Quartermaster-General
Q(ops)	.	Quartering (operations)
QPM	.	Queen's Police Medal
Qr	.	Quarter
QRV	.	Qualified Valuer, Real Estate Institute of New South Wales
QS	.	Quarter Sessions
qs	.	RAF graduates of the Military or Naval Staff College (symbol omitted if subsequently qualified psa)
QSM	.	Queen's Service Medal (NZ)
QSO	.	Queen's Service Order (NZ)
QUB	.	Queen's University, Belfast
qv	.	*quod vide* (which see)

R

(R)	. .	Reserve
RA	.	Royal Academician; Royal Artillery
RAAF	.	Royal Australian Air Force
RAAMC	.	Royal Australian Army Medical Corps
RAC	.	Royal Automobile Club; Royal Agricultural College; Royal Armoured Corps
RACGP	.	Royal Australian College of General Practitioners

RAChD	. .	Royal Army Chaplains' Department
RACP	. .	Royal Australasian College of Physicians
RACS	. .	Royal Australasian College of Surgeons; Royal Arsenal Co-operative Society
RADA	. .	Royal Academy of Dramatic Art
RADC	. .	Royal Army Dental Corps.
RAE	. .	Royal Australian Engineers; Royal Aircraft Establishment
RAEC	. .	Royal Army Educational Corps
RAeS	. .	Royal Aeronautical Society
RAF	. .	Royal Air Force
RAFA	. .	Royal Air Force Association
RAFO	. .	Reserve of Air Force Officers (now Royal Air Force Reserve of Officers)
RAFRO	. .	Royal Air Force Reserve of Officers
RAFVR	. .	Royal Air Force Volunteer Reserve
RAI	. .	Royal Anthropological Institute
RAIA	. .	Royal Australian Institute of Architects
RAIC	. .	Royal Architectural Institute of Canada
RAM	. .	(Member of) Royal Academy of Music
RAMC	. .	Royal Army Medical Corps
RAN	. .	Royal Australian Navy
R&D	. .	Research and Development
RANR	. .	Royal Australian Naval Reserve
RANVR	. .	Royal Australian Naval Volunteer Reserve
RAOC	. .	Royal Army Ordnance Corps
RAPC	. .	Royal Army Pay Corps
RARO	. .	Regular Army Reserve of Officers
RAS	. .	Royal Astronomical Society; Royal Asiatic Society
RASC	. .	(formerly) Royal Army Service Corps (now see under RCT)
RASE	. .	Royal Agricultural Society of England
RAuxAF	. .	Royal Auxiliary Air Force
RAVC	. .	Royal Army Veterinary Corps
RB	. .	Rifle Brigade
RBA	. .	Member Royal Society of British Artists
RBC	. .	Royal British Colonial Society of Artists
RBK&C	. .	Royal Borough of Kensington and Chelsea
RBS	. .	Royal Society of British Sculptors
RBSA	. .	Royal Birmingham Society of Artists
RC	. .	Roman Catholic
RCA	. .	Member Royal Canadian Academy of Arts; Royal College of Art
RCAC	. .	Royal Canadian Armoured Corps
RCAF	. .	Royal Canadian Air Force
RCamA	. .	Member Royal Cambrian Academy (formerly RCA)
RCAS	. .	Royal Central Asian Society; now see RSAA
RCDS	. .	Royal College of Defence Studies
rcds	. .	Completed a Course at, or served for a year on the Staff of, the Royal College of Defence Studies
RCGP	. .	Royal College of General Practitioners
RCHA	. .	Royal Canadian Horse Artillery
RCHM	. .	Royal Commission on Historical Monuments
RCM	. .	Royal College of Music
RCN	. .	Royal Canadian Navy
RCNC	. .	Royal Corps of Naval Constructors
RCNR	. .	Royal Canadian Naval Reserve
RCNVR	. .	Royal Canadian Naval Volunteer Reserve
RCO	. .	Royal College of Organists
RCOG	. .	Royal College of Obstetricians and Gynaecologists
RCP	. .	Royal College of Physicians, London
RCPath	. .	Royal College of Pathologists
RCPE and RCPEd	. .	Royal College of Physicians of Edinburgh
RCPGlas	. .	Royal College of Physicians and Surgeons, Glasgow
RCR	. .	Royal College of Radiologists
RCS	. .	Royal College of Surgeons of England; Royal Corps of Signals; Royal College of Science
RCSE and RCSEd	. .	Royal College of Surgeons of Edinburgh
RCSI	. .	Royal College of Surgeons in Ireland
RCT	. .	Royal Corps of Transport
RCVS	. .	Royal College of Veterinary Surgeons
RD	. .	Rural Dean; Royal Navy Reserve Decoration
Rd	. .	Road
RDA	. .	Royal Defence Academy
RDC	. .	Rural District Council
RDF	. .	Royal Dublin Fusiliers
RDI	. .	Royal Designer for Industry (Royal Society of Arts)
RDS	. .	Royal Dublin Society
RE	. .	Royal Engineers; Fellow of Royal Society of Painter-Etchers and Engravers
Rear-Adm.	. .	Rear Admiral
REconS	. .	Royal Economic Society
Reg. Prof.	. .	Regius Professor
Regt	. .	Regiment
REME	. .	Royal Electrical and Mechanical Engineers
RERO	. .	Royal Engineers Reserve of Officers
RES	. .	Royal Empire Society (now Royal Commonwealth Society)
Res.	. .	Resigned; Reserve; Resident; Research
Rev.	. .	Reverend; Review
RFA	. .	Royal Field Artillery
RFC	. .	Royal Flying Corps (now RAF); Rugby Football Club

RFPS(G)	. .	see under FRFPSG (formerly)
RFR	. .	Rassemblement des Français pour la République
RFU	. .	Rugby Football Union
RGA	. .	Royal Garrison Artillery
RGN	. .	Registered General Nurse
RGS	. .	Royal Geographical Society
RHA	. .	Royal Hibernian Academy; Royal Horse Artillery; Regional Health Authority
RHB	. .	Regional Hospitals Board
RHF	. .	Royal Highland Fusiliers
RHG	. .	Royal Horse Guards
RHistS	. .	Royal Historical Society
RHR	. .	Royal Highland Regiment
RHS	. .	Royal Horticultural Society; Royal Humane Society
RI	. .	Member Royal Institute of Painters in Water Colours; Rhode Island
RIA	. .	Royal Irish Academy
RIAM	. .	Royal Irish Academy of Music
RIAS	. .	Royal Incorporation of Architects in Scotland
RIASC	. .	Royal Indian Army Service Corps
RIBA	. .	Royal Institute of British Architects; also Member of the Institute
RIBI	. .	Rotary International in Great Britain and Ireland
RIC	. .	Royal Irish Constabulary; Royal Institute of Chemistry
RICS	. .	Royal Institution of Chartered Surveyors
RIE	. .	Royal Indian Engineering (College)
RIF	. .	Royal Irish Fusiliers
RIIA	. .	Royal Institute of International Affairs
RIM	. .	Royal Indian Marine
RIN	. .	Royal Indian Navy
RINA	. .	Royal Institution of Naval Architects
RIPA	. .	Royal Institute of Public Administration
RIPH&H	. .	Royal Institute of Public Health and Hygiene
RIrF	. .	Royal Irish Fusiliers
RM	. .	Royal Marines; Resident Magistrate
RMA	. .	Royal Marine Artillery; Royal Military Academy Sandhurst (now incorporating Royal Military Academy, Woolwich)
RMB	. .	Rural Mail Base
RMC	. .	Royal Military College Sandhurst (now Royal Military Academy)
RMCS	. .	Royal Military College of Science
RMedSoc	. .	Royal Medical Society, Edinburgh
RMetS	. .	Royal Meteorological Society
RMFVR	. .	Royal Marine Forces Volunteer Reserve
RMIT	. .	Royal Melbourne Institute of Technology
RMLI	. .	Royal Marine Light Infantry
RMO	. .	Resident Medical Officer(s)
RMPA	. .	Royal Medico-Psychological Association
RMS	. .	Royal Microscopical Society; Royal Mail Steamer; Royal Society of Miniature Painters
RN	. .	Royal Navy; Royal Naval
RNAS	. .	Royal Naval Air Service
RNAY	. .	Royal Naval Aircraft Yard
RNC	. .	Royal Naval College
RNCM	. .	Royal Northern College of Music
RNEC	. .	Royal Naval Engineering College
RNIB	. .	Royal National Institute for the Blind
RNID	. .	Royal National Institute for the Deaf
RNLI	. .	Royal National Life-boat Institution
RNR	. .	Royal Naval Reserve
RNS	. .	Royal Numismatic Society
RNT	. .	Registered Nurse Tutor
RNUR	. .	Régie Nationale des Usines Renault
RNVR	. .	Royal Naval Volunteer Reserve
RNVSR	. .	Royal Naval Volunteer Supplementary Reserve
RNZN	. .	Royal New Zealand Navy
RNZNVR	. .	Royal New Zealand Naval Volunteer Reserve
ROC	. .	Royal Observer Corps
ROF	. .	Royal Ordnance Factories
R of O	. .	Reserve of Officers
ROI	. .	Royal Institute of Oil Painters
RoSPA	. .	Royal Society for the Prevention of Accidents
(Rot.)	. .	Rotunda Hospital, Dublin (after degree)
RP	. .	Member Royal Society of Portrait Painters
RPC	. .	Royal Pioneer Corps
RPMS	. .	Royal Postgraduate Medical School
RPO	. .	Royal Philharmonic Orchestra
RPS	. .	Royal Photographic Society
RRC	. .	Royal Red Cross
RRE	. .	Royal Radar Establishment (formerly TRE)
RRS	. .	Royal Research Ship
RSA	. .	Royal Scottish Academician; Royal Society of Arts
RSAA	. .	Royal Society for Asian Affairs (formerly RCAS)
RSAI	. .	Royal Society of Antiquaries of Ireland
RSAMD	. .	Royal Scottish Academy of Music and Drama
RSanI	. .	Royal Sanitary Institute (now see RSH)
RSC	. .	Royal Society of Canada; Royal Shakespeare Company
RSCM	. .	Royal School of Church Music
RSCN	. .	Registered Sick Children's Nurse
RSE	. .	Royal Society of Edinburgh
RSF	. .	Royal Scots Fusiliers
RSFSR	. .	Russian Socialist Federated Soviet Republic

RSGS	Royal Scottish Geographical Society
RSH	Royal Society for the Promotion of Health (formerly Royal Sanitary Institute)
RSL	Royal Society of Literature; Returned Services League of Australia
RSM	Royal School of Mines
RSM. or RSocMed	Royal Society of Medicine
RSMA	(formerly SMA) Royal Society of Marine Artists
RSO	Rural Sub-Office; Railway Sub-Office; Resident Surgical Officer
RSPB	Royal Society for Protection of Birds
RSPCA	Royal Society for Prevention of Cruelty to Animals
RSSAILA	Returned Sailors, Soldiers and Airmen's Imperial League of Australia; *now see* RSL
RSSPCC	Royal Scottish Society for Prevention of Cruelty to Children
RSW	Member Royal Scottish Water Colour Society
Rt Hon.	Right Honourable
RTO	Railway Transport Officer
RTPI	Royal Town Planning Institute
RTR	Royal Tank Regiment
Rt Rev.	Right Reverend
RTS	Religious Tract Society; Royal Toxophilite Society
RTYC	Royal Thames Yacht Club
RU	Rugby Union
RUI	Royal University of Ireland
RUKBA	Royal United Kingdom Beneficent Association
RUR	Royal Ulster Regiment
RUSI	Royal United Services Institute for Defence Studies (formerly Royal United Service Institution)
RVC	Royal Veterinary College
RWA (RWEA)	Member of Royal West of England Academy
RWAFF	Royal West African Frontier Force
RWF	Royal Welch Fusiliers
RWS	Member Royal Society of Painters in Water Colours
RYA	Royal Yachting Association
RYS	Royal Yacht Squadron
RZS	Royal Zoological Society

S

(S)	(in Navy) Paymaster
S	Succeeded; South; Saint
s	Son
SA	South Australia; South Africa; Société Anonyme
SAAF	South African Air Force
SACEUR	Supreme Allied Commander (Europe)
SACLANT	Supreme Allied Commander Atlantic
SACSEA	Supreme Allied Command, SE Asia
SADF	Sudanese Auxiliary Defence Force
SADG	Société des Architectes Diplômés par le Gouvernement
Salop	(formerly) Shropshire
SAMC	South African Medical Corps
Sarum	Salisbury
SAS	Special Air Service
SASO	Senior Air Staff Officer
SB	Bachelor of Science (US)
SBAC	Society of British Aerospace Companies (formerly Society of British Aircraft Constructors)
SBStJ	Serving Brother, Order of St John of Jerusalem
SC	Star of Courage (Canada); Senior Counsel (Eire and Guyana); South Carolina (US)
sc	Student at the Staff College
SCAO	Senior Civil Affairs Officer
SCAPA	Society for Checking the Abuses of Public Advertising
ScD	Doctor of Science
SCF	Senior Chaplain to the Forces
Sch.	School
SCL	Student in Civil Law
SCM	State Certified Midwife; Student Christian Movement
SCONUL	Standing Conference of National and University Libraries
Sculpt.	Sculptor
SDak	South Dakota (US)
SDB	Salesian of Don Bosco
SDF	Sudan Defence Force; Social Democratic Federation
SDLP	Social Democratic and Labour Party
SE	South-east
SEAC	South-East Asia Command
SEALF	South-East Asia Land Forces
SEATO	South-East Asia Treaty Organization
Sec.	Secretary
SEN	State Enrolled Nurse
SESO	Senior Equipment Staff Officer
SFInstF	Senior Fellow, Institute of Fuel
SFTA	Society of Film and Television Arts; *now see* BAFTA
SG	Solicitor-General
SGA	Member Society of Graphic Art
Sgt	Sergeant

SHAEF	Supreme Headquarters, Allied Expeditionary Force
SHAPE	Supreme Headquarters, Allied Powers, Europe
SHHD	Scottish Home and Health Department
SIAD	Society of Industrial Artists and Designers
SIB	Shipbuilding Industry Board
SIMG	*Societas Internationalis Medicinae Generalis*
SinDrs	Doctor of Chinese
SITA	Société Internationale de Télécommunications Aéronautiques
SITPRO	Simplification of International Trade Procedures
SJ	Society of Jesus (Jesuits)
SJAB	St John Ambulance Brigade
SJD	Doctor of Juristic Science
SL	Serjeant-at-Law
SLA	Special Libraries Association
SLAET	Society of Licensed Aircraft Engineers and Technologists
SLAS	Society for Latin-American Studies
SLP	Scottish Labour Party
SM	Medal of Service (Canada) (*now see* OC); Master of Science; Officer qualified for Submarine Duties
SMA	Society of Marine Artists (now *see under* RSMA)
SME	School of Military Engineering
SMIEEE	Senior Member of Institution of Electrical and Electronic Engineering (US)
SMIRE	Senior Member Institution of Radio Engineers (New York)
SMMT	Society of Motor Manufacturers and Traders Ltd
SMO	Senior Medical Officer; Sovereign Military Order
SMPTE	Society of Motion Picture and Television Engineers (US)
SNAME	Society of Naval Architects and Marine Engineers (US)
SNCF	Société Nationale des Chemins de Fer Français
SNP	Scottish National Party
SNTS	Society for New Testament Studies
SO	Staff Officer
SOAS	School of Oriental and African Studies
Soc.	Society
SODEPAX	Committee on Society, Development and Peace
SOE	Special Operations Executive
SOGAT	Society of Graphical and Allied Trades
sowc	Senior Officers' War Course
s.p.	*sine prole* (without issue)
SP	Self-Propelled (Anti-Tank Regt)
SPAB	Society for the Protection of Ancient Buildings
SPCK	Society for Promoting Christian Knowledge
SPD	Salisbury Plain District
SPG	Society for the Propagation of the Gospel (now USPG)
SPk	Sitara-e-Pakistan
SPMO	Senior Principal Medical Officer
SPRC	Society for Prevention and Relief of Cancer
sprl	société de personnes à responsabilité limitée
SPTL	Society of Public Teachers of Law
Sq.	Square
Sqdn	Squadron
SR	Special Reserve; Southern Railway; Southern Region (BR)
SRC	Science Research Council (formerly DSIR)
SRCN	State Registered Sick Children's Nurse
SRHE	Society for Research into Higher Education
SRN	State Registered Nurse
SRO	Supplementary Reserve of Officers
SRP	State Registered Physiotherapist
SRY	Sherwood Rangers Yeomanry
SS	Saints; Straits Settlements; Steamship
SSA	Society of Scottish Artists
SS&AFA	Soldiers', Sailors', and Airmen's Families Association
SSC	Solicitor before Supreme Court (Scotland); Sculptors Society of Canada
SSEES	School of Slavonic and East European Studies
SSJE	Society of St John the Evangelist
SSM	Society of the Sacred Mission
SSO	Senior Supply Officer
SSRC	Social Science Research Council
SSStJ	Serving Sister, Order of St John of Jerusalem
St	Street; Saint
STB	*Sacrae Theologiae Bachelor* (Bachelor of Sacred Theology)
STC	Senior Training Corps
STD	*Sacrae Theologiae Doctor* (Doctor of Sacred Theology)
STh	Scholar in Theology
Stip.	Stipend; Stipendiary
STL	*Sacrae Theologiae Lector* (Reader or a Professor of Sacred Theology)
STM	*Sacrae Theologiae Magister*
STP	*Sacrae Theologiae Professor* (Professor of Divinity, old form of DD)
STRIVE	Society for Preservation of Rural Industries and Village Enterprises
STSO	Senior Technical Staff Officer
Supp. Res.	Supplementary Reserve (of Officers)
Supt	Superintendent

Surg..	. .	Surgeon
Surv..	. .	Surviving
SW	. .	South-west
SWPA	. .	South West Pacific Area
Syd. .	. .	Sydney

T

′T	. .	Telephone; Territorial
TA	. .	Telegraphic Address; Territorial Army
TAA.	. .	Territorial Army Association
TAF.	. .	Tactical Air Force
T&AFA	. .	Territorial and Auxiliary Forces Association
TANS	. .	Territorial Army Nursing Service
TANU	. .	Tanganyika African National Union
TARO	. .	Territorial Army Reserve of Officers
T&AVR	. .	Territorial and Army Volunteer Reserve
TA&VRA	. .	Territorial Auxiliary and Volunteer Reserve Association
TC	. .	Order of the Trinity Cross (Trinidad and Tobago)
TCD.	. .	Trinity College, Dublin (University of Dublin, Trinity College)
TCF.	. .	Temporary Chaplain to the Forces
TCPA	. .	Town and Country Planning Association
TD	. .	Territorial Efficiency Decoration; Efficiency Decoration (T&AVR) (since April 1967); (Teachta Dala) Member of the Dail, Eire
TEC.	. .	Technician Education Council
Tech (CEI)	. .	Technician
TEM	. .	Territorial Efficiency Medal
TEMA	. .	Telecommunications Engineering Manufacturers' Association
Temp.	. .	Temperature; Temporary
TEng (CEI)	. .	Technician Engineer
Tenn.	. .	Tennessee (US)
TeolD	. .	Doctor of Theology
Tex	. .	Texas (US)
TF	. .	Territorial Force
TFR.	. .	Territorial Force Reserve
TGO	. .	Timber Growers' Organisation
TGWU	. .	Transport and General Workers' Union
ThL	. .	Theological Licentiate
TIMS	. .	The Institute of Management Sciences
TLS	. .	Times Literary Supplement
TOSD	. .	Tertiary Order of St Dominic
TP	. .	Transvaal Province
TPI	. .	Town Planning Institute (now see RTPI)
Trans.	. .	Translation. Translated
Transf.	. .	Transferred
TRC.	. .	Thames Rowing Club
TRE.	. .	Telecommunications Research Establishment (now see RRE)
TRH.	. .	Their Royal Highnesses
Trin..	. .	Trinity
TRRL	. .	Transport and Road Research Laboratory
TSB .	. .	Trustee Savings Bank
tsc	. .	passed a Territorial Army Course in Staff Duties
TSD.	. .	Tertiary of St Dominick
TUC.	. .	Trades Union Congress
TV	. .	Television
TYC.	. .	Thames Yacht Club (now see RTYC)

U

(U)	. .	Unionist
u	. .	Uncle
UAR.	. .	United Arab Republic
UAU	. .	Universities Athletic Union
UC	. .	University College
UCCA	. .	Universities Central Council on Admissions
UCET	. .	Universities Council for Education of Teachers
UCH	. .	University College Hospital (London)
UCL	. .	University College London
UCLA	. .	University of California at Los Angeles
UCNW	. .	University College of North Wales
UCW	. .	University College of Wales
UDC	. .	Urban District Council
UDF	. .	Union Defence Force; Ulster Defence Force
UDR	. .	Ulster Defence Regiment; Union des Democrates pour la Veme Republique (now see RFR)
UEA.	. .	University of East Anglia
UEFA	. .	Union of European Football Associations
UF	. .	United Free Church
UGC	. .	University Grants Committee
UJD.	. .	Utriusque Juris Doctor, Doctor of both Laws (Doctor of Canon and Civil Law)
UK	. .	United Kingdom
UKAC	. .	United Kingdom Automation Council
UKAEA	. .	United Kingdom Atomic Energy Authority
UKLF	. .	United Kingdom Land Forces

UMIST	.	University of Manchester Institute of Science and Technology
UN	. .	United Nations
UNA	. .	United Nations Association
UNCIO	.	United Nations Conference on International Organisation
UNCSAT	.	United Nations Conference on the Application of Science and Technology
UNCTAD (Unctad)	.	United Nations Commission for Trade and Development
UNDP	.	United Nations Development Programme
UNESCO (Unesco)	.	United Nations Educational, Scientific and Cultural Organisation
UNFAO	. -.	United Nations Food and Agriculture Organisation
UNHCR	.	United Nations High Commissioner for Refugees
UNICEF (Unicef)	.	United Nations Children's Fund (formerly United Nations International Children's Emergency Fund)
UNIDO	.	United Nations Industrial Development Organisation
UNIPEDE	.	Union Internationale des Producteurs et Distributeurs d'Energie Electrique
UNISIST	.	Universal System for Information in Science and Technology
UNITAR	.	United Nations Institute of Training and Research
Univ..	.	University
UNRRA	.	United Nations Relief and Rehabilitation Administration
UNRWA	.	United Nations Relief Works Agency
UNSCOB	.	United Nations Special Commission on the Balkans
UP	. .	United Provinces; Uttar Pradesh; United Presbyterian
UPNI	.	Unionist Party of Northern Ireland
URC.	.	United Reformed Church
URSI	.	Union Radio-Scientifique Internationale
US	. .	United States
USA	. .	United States of America
USAAF	.	United States Army Air Forces
USAF	.	United States Air Force
USAID	.	United States Agency for International Development
USAR	.	United States Army Reserve
USDAW	.	Union of Shop Distributive and Allied Workers
USMA	.	United States Military Academy
USN.	.	United States Navy
USNR	.	United States Naval Reserve
USPG	.	United Society for the Propagation of the Gospel (formerly SPG)
USS .	.	United States Ship
USSR	.	Union of Soviet Socialist Republics
UTC.	.	University Training Corps
(UU)	.	Ulster Unionist
(UUUC)	.	United Ulster Unionist Coalition
(UUUP)	.	United Ulster Unionist Party
UWIST	.	University of Wales Institute of Science and Technology
UWT	.	Union of Women Teachers

V

V	. .	Five (Roman numerals); Version; Vicar; Viscount; Vice
v	. .	Versus (against)
v or vid.	. .	Vide (see)
Va	. .	Virginia (US)
VAD.	. .	Voluntary Aid Detachment
V&A.	. .	Victoria and Albert
VAT.	. .	Value Added Tax
VC	. .	Victoria Cross
VCAS	. .	Vice-Chief of the Air Staff
VD	. .	Royal Naval Volunteer Reserve Officers' Decoration (now VRD); Volunteer Officers' Decoration; Victorian Decoration
VDC.	. .	Volunteer Defence Corps
Ven.	. .	Venerable (of an Archdeacon)
Very Rev..	. .	Very Reverend (of a Dean)
Vet.	. .	Veterinary
VG	. .	Vicar-General
VHS.	. .	Hon. Surgeon to Viceroy of India
VIC	. .	Victoria Institute of Colleges
Vice-Adm.	. .	Vice-Admiral
Visc.	. .	Viscount
VM	. .	Victory Medal
VMH	. .	Victoria Medal of Honour (Royal Horticultural Society)
Vol.	. .	Volume; Volunteers
VP	. .	Vice-President
VPP.	. .	Volunteer Political Party
VQMG	. .	Vice-Quartermaster-General
VR	. .	Victoria Regina (Queen Victoria)
VRD.	. .	Royal Naval Volunteer Reserve Officers' Decoration

VSO.	. .	Voluntary Service Overseas
Vt	. .	Vermont (US)
(VUP)	. .	Vanguard Unionist Party

W

W	. .	West
WA	. .	Western Australia
WAAF	. .	Women's Auxiliary Air Force (now WRAF)
Wash	. .	Washington State (US)
WCC	. .	World Council of Churches
W/Cdr	. .	Wing Commander
WEA	. .	Workers' Educational Association; Royal West of England Academy
WEU	. .	Western European Union
WFTU	. .	World Federation of Trade Unions
WHO	. .	World Health Organization
WhSch	. .	Whitworth Scholar
WI	. .	West Indies (formerly BWI: British West Indies); Women's Institute
Wilts.	. .	Wiltshire
Wis	. .	Wisconsin (US)
Wits	. .	Witwatersrand
WJEC	. .	Welsh Joint Education Committee
WLA	. .	Women's Land Army
WLF	. .	Women's Liberal Federation
Wm	. .	William
WNO	. .	Welsh National Opera
WO	. .	War Office
Worcs	. .	Worcestershire
WOSB	. .	War Office Selection Board

WR	. .	West Riding; Western Region (BR)
WRAC	. .	Women's Royal Army Corps
WRAF	. .	Women's Royal Air Force (formerly WAAF)
WRNS	. .	Women's Royal Naval Service
WRVS	. .	Women's Royal Voluntary Service (previously WVS)
WS	. .	Writer to the Signet
WSPU	. .	Women's Social and Political Union
WUS	. .	World University Service
WVa.	. .	West Virginia (US)
WVS.	. .	Women's Voluntary Services (now see WRVS)
Wyo.	. .	Wyoming (US)

X

X	. . .	Ten (Roman numerals)

Y

y	. . .	youngest
YC	. .	Young Conservative
YCNAC	. .	Young Conservatives National Advisory Committee
Yeo.	. .	Yeomanry
YHA.	. .	Youth Hostels Association
YMCA	. .	Young Men's Christian Association
Yorks	. .	Yorkshire
yr	. . .	younger
yrs	. .	years
YWCA	. .	Young Women's Christian Association

OBITUARY

Deaths notified from mid-November 1976 to mid-November 1977

Acton, Maj.-Gen. Thomas Heward, CBE, 22 Jan. 1977.
Adamson, Sir Kenneth Thomas, CMG   [*Deceased.*
Addinsell, Richard Stewart, 14 Nov. 1977.
Adie, Edward Percival, MC, 18 May 1977.
Adrian, 1st Baron; Edgar Douglas Adrian, OM, FRS, 4 Aug. 1977.
Ahmed, Fakhruddin Ali, Tamra Patra, 11 Feb. 1977.
Ainsley, John William   [*Deceased.*
Alexander, Maj.-Gen. Henry Templer, CB, CBE, DSO, 16 March 1977.
Allen, Charles Peter Selwyn, CMG, MVO, OBE, 18 March 1977.
Allerton, Air Cdre Ord Denny, CB, CBE, 22 Sept. 1977.
Allison, James Anthony, CMG, OBE, PH   [*Deceased.*
Ames, Sir Cecil Geraint, 17 Aug. 1977.
Amies, Sir Arthur Barton Pilgrim, CMG, 4 Dec. 1976.
Angas, Sir (John) Keith, 13 April 1977.
Ansorge, Sir Eric Cecil, CSI, CIE, 3 Jan. 1977.
Anstey, Vera, 26 Nov. 1976.
Antrim, 13th Earl of; Randal John Somerled McDonnell, KBE, 26 Sept. 1977.
Armagh, Cardinal Archbishop of; His Eminence Cardinal William Conway, 17 April 1977.
Armstrong, Hon. John Ignatius, AC, 10 March 1977.
Ashdown, Baron (Life Peer); Arnold Silverstone, 23 July 1977.
Asher, Florence May, 22 Jan. 1977.
Ashworth, Air Comdt Dame Veronica Margaret, DBE, RRC, 12 Jan. 1977.
Avon, 1st Earl of; Robert Anthony Eden, KG, PC, MC, 14 Jan. 1977.
Aylmer, 11th Baron; Basil Udolphus Aylmer, 13 March 1977.

Baden-Powell, Olave, Lady; (Olave St Clair), GBE, 25 June 1977.
Bahadur Shamsher Jang Bahadur Rana, Commanding-Gen., Hon. GBE, Hon. KCB, 19 May 1977.
Baird, William George, CMG   [*Deceased.*
Baker, Col Thomas McDonald, CBE, TD, 31 Dec. 1976.
Balcon, Sir Michael, 17 Oct. 1977.
Balfour, Lt.-Gen. Sir Philip Maxwell, KBE, CB, MC, 4 Feb. 1977.
Ball, Air Vice-Marshal Sir Ben, KBE, CB, 24 Jan. 1977.
Balmforth, Rev. Canon Henry, 9 Feb. 1977.
Balsdon, John Percy Vyvian Dacre, FBA, 18 Sept. 1977.
Barberton, Ivan Graham Mitford-   [*Deceased.*
Barff, Stafford Edward Douglas, OBE, 28 Nov. 1976.
Barker, Air Vice-Marshal Clifford Cockcroft, CBE, AFC, 10 April 1977.
Barlow, Ralph Mitford Marriott, 1 Feb. 1977.
Barnes, Harry Cheetham   [*Deceased.*
Barrett, Col John Cridlan, VC, TD, 7 March 1977.
Barry, Sir Rupert Rodney Francis Tress, 4th Bt, MBE, 9 March 1977.
Bartlett, Rt Rev. David Daniel, DD, 10 April 1977.
Barton, Guy Trayton, CMG, OBE, 22 April 1977.
Barton, Rt Rev. Mgr Canon John Mackintosh Tilney, DD, 16 April 1977.
Baynes, Keith Stuart, 17 April 1977.
Bean, Sir Edgar Layton, CMG, 28 July 1977.
Beauman, Brig.-Gen. Archibald Bentley, CBE, DSO, 22 March 1977.
Beaumont, Air Rank Edward Blackett, CBE, TD, 18 Sept. 1977.
Belisario, Dr John Colquhoun, CMG, CBE, ED   [*Deceased.*
Bellerby, Major John Rotherford, MC, 1 April 1977.
Bennet, Dr Edward Armstrong, MC, 7 March 1977.
Bentley, Phyllis Eleanor, OBE, 27 June 1977.
Bernard, Hon. Charles Brodrick Amyas, CBE, 28 Feb. 1977.
Berry, Very Rev. Hugh Frederick   [*Deceased.*
Bevir, Sir Anthony, KCVO, CBE, 17 Jan. 1977.
Bewley, William Fleming, CBE, 11 Dec. 1976.
Bickerton, John Myles, 13 March 1977.
Bickley, Francis Lawrance, 29 Dec. 1976.
Bing, Geoffrey Henry Cecil, CMG, QC, 24 April 1977.
Bingham, Lt-Col Ralph Charles, CVO, DSO, 4 Nov. 1977.
Binyon, Basil, OBE, 4 April 1977.
Birkbeck, Harold Edward, 24 Sept. 1977.
Birkinshaw, Air Cdre George William, CB, 22 Oct. 1977.
Birtwistle, Ivor Treharne, OBE   [*Deceased.*
Black, Sir Misha, OBE, 11 Aug. 1977.
Blackford, 3rd Baron; Keith Alexander Henry Mason, DFC, 21 April 1977.
Bligh, Sir Edward Clare, 27 Dec. 1976.
Bliven, Bruce, 27 May 1977.
Blyth, 3rd Baron; Ian Audley James Blyth, 29 Oct. 1977.
Bolton, Lt-Col Ralph Edward Frederick, DSO, 3 March 1977.
Bonsor, Sir Bryan Cosmo, 3rd Bt, MC, TD, 5 March 1977.
Borschette, Albert, 8 Dec. 1976.
Borthwick, Brig.-Gen. Francis Henry, CMG, DSO, 12 Feb. 1977.
Bostock, John, CBE, 26 Oct. 1977.
Bourne, Sir Frederick Chalmers, KCSI, CIE, 3 Nov. 1977.

Bovenschen, Sir Frederick Carl, KCB, KBE, 9 Nov. 1977.
Braddock, Thomas, 9 Dec. 1976.
Bradley, Sir Kenneth Granville, CMG, 6 Feb. 1977.
Brain, Sir Hugh Gerner, CBE, 31 Dec. 1976.
Brander, George Maconachie, CIE, 11 Feb. 1977.
Brayley, Baron (Life Peer); (John) Desmond Brayley, MC, 16 March 1977.
Brennan, Maj.-Gen. William Brian Francis, CB, 1 July 1977.
Briggs, Sir (Alfred) George (Ernest), 30 Nov. 1976.
Briggs, Martin Shaw, 13 Oct. 1977.
Brillant, Jules-André, CBE, ED   [*Deceased.*
Brittain, William James, 12 July 1977.
Britten, Baron (Life Peer); (Edward) Benjamin Britten, OM, CH, 4 Dec. 1976.
Britten, Forester Richard John, CBE, 7 July 1977.
Broadmead, Sir Philip Mainwaring, KCMG, MC, 23 May 1977.
Brockman, Edward Phillimore, 27 Jan. 1977.
Brodeur, Rear-Adm. Victor Gabriel, CB, CBE   [*Deceased.*
Brogan, Colm, 28 Jan. 1977.
Brook, Cdre James Kenneth, CBE, DSO, RD, RNR, 16 Dec. 1976.
Brown, Frank Leslie, CMG, OBE, MC, 11 Sept. 1977.
Brown, Rear-Adm. George Herbert Hempson, CBE, 3 June 1977.
Brown, John, CBE, MC, 24 Aug. 1977.
Brown, John Stirling, CB, 22 Oct. 1977.
Brunton, John Stirling, CB, 22 Oct. 1977.
Budge, Rev. Ronald Henderson Gunn, MVO, 22 Nov. 1976.
Bunt, Rev. Frederick Darrell, CB, OBE, 31 Oct. 1977.
Burgess, His Honour Sir Thomas Arthur Collier, 19 June 1977.
Burrough, Adm. Sir Harold Martin, GCB, KBE, DSO, DSM (USA), 22 Oct. 1977.
Bustamante, Rt Hon. and Exc. Sir (William) Alexander, PC, GBE, 6 Aug. 1977.
Butler, Prof. John Alfred Valentine, FRS, 16 July 1977.
Byers, Joseph Austen, 18 May 1977.

Callas, Maria, 16 Sept. 1977.
Calvert-Jones, Maj.-Gen. Percy George, CB, CBE, DSO, MC, 1 Jan. 1977.
Campbell, Sybil, OBE, 29 Aug. 1977.
Cannan, Maj.-Gen. James Harold, CB, CMG, DSO, VD   [*Deceased.*
Cantlie, Sir Keith, CIE, 29 April 1977.
Capper, Sir (William) Derrick, QPM, 21 March 1977.
Carden Roe, Brig. William, CB, CBE, MC, 22 March 1977.
Carpentier, Général d'Armée Marcel Maurice, 14 Sept. 1977.
Carr, John Dickson, 27 Feb. 1977.
Carr, Sir William Emsley, 14 Nov. 1977.
Carroll, Sir Alfred Thomas (Sir Turi Carroll), KBE   [*Deceased.*
Carter, Francis Edward, OBE, 16 July 1977.
Carus-Wilson, Prof. Eleanora Mary, FBA, 1 Feb. 1977.
Cecil, Rev. Canon Philip Henry, 11 March 1977.
Chalmers, Archibald MacDonald, MC, 9 Aug. 1977.
Chapman, Fitzroy Tozer, CBE, 21 Dec. 1976.
Chapman, Mrs Murray, (Olive), 11 June 1977.
Charles, Robert Lonsdale, MC, 8 March 1977.
Charley, Sir Philip Belmont   [*Deceased.*
Charrington, Sir John, 16 July 1977.
Chiang, Yee, 17 Oct. 1977.
Chick, Dame Harriette, DBE, 9 July 1977.
Chisholm, Alexander Hugh, OBE, 10 July 1977.
Clarabut, Maj.-Gen. Reginald Blaxland, CB, 18 March 1977.
Clark, Brig. George Philip, CBE, DSO, 24 Aug. 1977.
Clark, Sir Thomas, 3rd Bt, 21 April 1977.
Clark, Thomas Campbell, (Tom C. Clark), 13 June 1977.
Clarkson, (George Wensley) Anthony, 17 April 1977.
Clarkson, Rt Rev. George William, 15 Aug. 1977.
Claye, Sir Andrew Moynihan, 25 Feb. 1977.
Clutton-Brock, Prof. Alan Francis, 18 Dec. 1976.
Coates, Sir Albert Ernest, OBE, 8 Oct. 1977.
Cobb, Hon. Sir John Francis Scott; Hon. Mr Justice Cobb, 7 Feb. 1977.
Cobb, John Leslie, 14 Jan. 1977.
Cobham, 10th Viscount; Charles John Lyttelton, KG, PC, GCMG, GCVO, TD, 20 March 1977.
Cohen of Birkenhead, 1st Baron; Henry Cohen, CH, 7 Aug. 1977 (*ext*).
Cole, Edward Nicholas, 2 May 1977.
Colebrook, Edward Hilder, CIE, MC, KPM, 4 Jan. 1977.
Collishaw, Air Vice-Marshal Raymond, CB, DSO, OBE, DSC, DFC   [*Deceased.*
Colquhoun, (Cecil) Brian (Hugh), 26 Sept. 1977.
Compton, Edward Robert Francis, 8 Feb. 1977.
Conacher, Mungo, OBE, 15 Sept. 1977.
Conway, Brig. Albert Edward, CB, OBE   [*Deceased.*

Cooke, Maj.-Gen. Sidney Arthur, CB, OBE, 25 March 1977.
Cools-Lartigue, Alexander Raphael, QC (Windward Islands)
[Deceased.
Cooper, Malcolm Edward, CBE, 17 Feb. 1977.
Cordingley, Air Vice-Marshal Sir John Walter, KCB, KCVO, CBE, 5 Jan. 1977.
Cot, Pierre Donatien Alphonse, 21 Aug. 1977.
Cox, Euan Hillhouse Methven, 26 March 1977.
Craddock, Lt.-Gen. Sir Richard Walter, KBE, CB, DSO, 14 Feb. 1977.
Craig, Prof. John, 19 April 1977.
Craig, Sir John Herbert McCutcheon, KCVO, CB, 8 April 1977.
Crathorne, 1st Baron; Thomas Lionel Dugdale, PC, TD, 26 March 1977.
Crawford, Joan, 10 May 1977.
Cripps, Hon. Frederick Heyworth; see under Parmoor, 3rd Baron.
Cronin, Henry Francis, CBE, MC, 11 Jan. 1977.
Crosby, Harry Lillis, (Bing), 14 Oct. 1977.
Crosland, Rt Hon. (Charles) Anthony (Raven), PC, MP, 19 Feb. 1977.
Crousaz, Engineer Rear-Adm. Augustus George, CB, 25 Aug. 1977.
Crowe, Hon. Philip Kingsland   [Deceased.
Cunningham, Ebenezer, 12 Feb. 1977.
Cunningham-Reid, Captain Alec Stratford, DFC, 26 March 1977.
Currie, Lt-Col George Selkirk, CMG, DSO, MC   [Deceased.
Curtis, Air Marshal Wilfred Austin, OC, CB, CBE, DSC, ED, 7 Aug. 1977.

Dalton, Thomas Wilson Fox, CB, 9 Jan. 1977.
Daly, Ashley Skeffington, 15 Sept. 1977.
Dannreuther, Rear-Adm. Hubert Edward, DSO, 12 Aug. 1977.
D'Arcy, Very Rev. Martin Cyril, SJ, 20 Nov. 1976.
Darke, Harold Edwin, CBE, 28 Nov. 1976.
Darlington, Prof. Reginald Ralph, FBA, 30 May 1977.
Daubney, Robert, CMG, OBE, 16 April 1977.
Davidson, Very Rev. (Andrew) Nevile, DD, 20 Dec. 1976.
Davies, (Arthur Edward) Miles, CB, 16 Jan. 1977.
d'Avigdor-Goldsmid, Major Sir Henry Joseph, 2nd Bt, DSO, MC, TD, 11 Dec. 1976.
Dawson, Maj.-Gen. Robert Boyd, CB, CBE, DSO, 24 July 1977.
Dean, Comdr Brian, DSO, RN   [Deceased.
Deanesly, Prof. Margaret, 9 Oct. 1977.
De Butts, Brig. Frederick Cromie, CB, DSO, MC, 7 Jan. 1977.
Deeves, Thomas William, CMG, CBE, MC, 11 Sept. 1977.
de Haan, Edward Peter Nayler, CMG, OBE, 26 July 1977.
Deller, Captain Harold Arthur, 26 Dec. 1976.
Dening, Sir (Maberly) Esler, GCMG, OBE, 29 Jan. 1977.
Dent, George Irving, 22 Dec. 1976.
Deutsch, Dr John James, CC   [Deceased.
Dible, James Kenneth Victor, 13 Dec. 1976.
Dickey, Edward Montgomery O'Rorke, CBE, 12 Aug. 1977.
Dill-Russell, Patrick Wimberley, CBE, 5 Aug. 1977.
Dillon, Prof. Thomas   [Deceased.
Dimsdale, Mrs Helen Easdale, 20 April 1977.
Dodds, George Elliott, CBE, 20 Feb. 1977.
Dodson, John Michael, 18 May 1977.
Doll, William Alfred Millner, CMG, 17 June 1977.
Donald, Air Marshal Sir Grahame, KCB, DFC, AFC, 23 Dec. 1976.
Dorman-Smith, Col Rt Hon. Sir Reginald Hugh, PC, GBE, 20 March 1977.
Douglas, Lt-Col Archibald Vivian Campbell, 28 Oct. 1977.
Drayson, Rear-Adm. Edwin Howard, CB, CBE, 28 Oct. 1977.
Duffield, Anne, 11 Nov. 1976.
Dukes, Dr Cuthbert Esquire, OBE, 3 Feb. 1977.
Dumas, Sir Russell John, KBE, CMG   [Deceased.
Dunbar of Mochrum, Sir Adrian Ivor, 12th Bt, 14 June 1977.

Eastham, Prof. Leonard Ernest Sydney, 19 July 1977.
Edman, Prof. Pehr Victor, FRS, 19 March 1977.
Edwards, Lt-Col Sir Bartle Mordaunt Marsham, CVO, MC, 28 May 1977.
Egerton, Lady Alice, CVO, 7 Oct. 1977.
Eliott Lockhart, Sir Allan Robert, CIE, 9 April 1977.
Elliott, Rt Rev. Robert Cyril Hamilton, DD, 3 April 1977.
Ellis, Very Rev. Vorley Spencer, 2 Aug. 1977.
Elphick, Ronald, OBE, 13 June 1977.
Emslie, Rosalie, 28 Sept. 1977.
Ensor, Arthur Hinton, 5 Oct. 1977.
Erhard, Prof. Ludwig, 5 May 1977.
Erskine, Sir Derek Quicke, 6 Sept. 1977.
Erskine-Wyse, Marjorie Anne, 7 Dec. 1976.
Evans, Dame Joan, DBE, 14 July 1977.
Ezard, Bernard John Bycroft, CBE, 24 Nov. 1976.

Fage, Arthur, CBE, FRS, 7 Nov. 1977.
Falconer, Murray Alexander, 11 Aug. 1977.
Faringdon, 2nd Baron; Alexander Gavin Henderson, 29 Jan. 1977.
Farrer, Hon. Dame Frances Margaret, DBE, 27 Jan. 1977.
Faulkner of Downpatrick, Baron (Life Peer); Arthur Brian Deane Faulkner, PC (NI), 3 March 1977.
Fedden, (Henry) Robin Romilly, CBE, 20 March 1977.
Feiling, Sir Keith Grahame, CBE, 16 Sept. 1977.
Fell, Vice-Adm. Sir Michael Frampton, KCB, DSO, DSC, 3 Dec. 1976.
Ferguson, Prof. Thomas, CBE, 1 May 1977.
Fethers, Hon. Col Wilfrid Kent, DSO, VD   [Deceased.
Finch, Peter, 14 Jan. 1977.
Finley, David Edward, 1 Feb. 1977.
Fischer, Harry Robert, 12 April 1977.
Fishenden, Margaret White, 21 Oct. 1977.

Fisher, Vardis   [Deceased.
Fitzgerald, Walter, (Walter Fitzgerald Bond), 20 Dec. 1976.
Fleming, Richard Evelyn, MC, TD, 14 Aug. 1977.
Fletcher, Prof. Frank Thomas Herbert, 29 May 1977.
Ford, Ven. Frank Edward, 26 Nov. 1976.
Fordham, Lt-Col Reginald Sydney Walter, ED, QC, 17 Nov. 1976.
Forester, 7th Baron; Col Cecil George Wilfrid Weld-Forester, 4 Jan. 1977.
Forman, John Calder   [Deceased.
Forrest, Gilbert Alexander; His Honour Judge Forrest, 24 Sept. 1977.
Forrest, Richard Haddow, QC; His Honour Judge Haddow Forrest, 29 Oct. 1977.
Fortescue, 6th Earl; Denzil George Fortescue, MC, TD, 1 June 1977.
Fox, Rev. Canon Adam, DD, 17 Jan. 1977.
Fox, Captain Charles, CBE, 15 Oct. 1977.
Fraser, Very Rev. Dr Duncan, 16 Sept. 1977.
Frend, Charles Herbert, 8 Jan. 1977.
Fullerton, Brig. John Parke, DSO, 19 March 1977.

Galbraith, Prof. Vivian Hunter, FBA, 25 Nov. 1976.
Galloway, Lt-Gen. Sir Alexander, KBE, CB, DSO, MC, 28 Jan. 1977.
Galway, 10th Viscount; William Arundell Monckton-Arundell, 15 Aug. 1977.
Garner, Sir Harry Mason, KBE, CB, 7 Aug. 1977.
Garnett, Bernard John, CMG, OBE, 4 April 1977.
Garrett, Sir William Herbert, MBE, 20 Aug. 1977.
Gascoyne-Cecil, Victor Alexander, 17 Jan. 1977.
Gasson, Sir Lionel Bell, 16 March 1977.
Gault, Brig. Sir James Frederick, KCMG, MVO, OBE, 14 Jan. 1977.
George, Ven. Christopher Owen, 8 Sept. 1977.
Geraghty, Sir William, KCB, 7 May 1977.
Gerhardie, William Alexander, OBE, 15 July 1977.
Gerrard, Major Frederick Wernham, CIE   [Deceased.
Gilkes, Antony Newcombe, 14 Jan. 1977.
Gillies, Prof. Alexander, 25 Oct. 1977.
Gilmour, Sir John Little, 2nd Bt, 13 Feb. 1977.
Gilroy, His Eminence Sir Norman Thomas, Cardinal, KBE, DD, 21 Oct. 1977.
Goitein, Hugh, 20 Dec. 1976.
Goldsmith, Sir Allen John Bridson, KCVO, 13 Dec. 1976.
Goodfellow, Keith Frank, QC, 4 Sept. 1977.
Gordon, Seton, CBE, 19 March 1977.
Goschen, 3rd Viscount; John Alexander Goschen, KBE, 22 March 1977.
Götz, Hon. Sir Frank Léon Aroha, KCVO   [Deceased.
Gough, Sir (Arthur) Ernest
Gough, Col (Charles) Frederick (Howard), MC, TD, 19 Sept. 1977.
Grace, Sir Raymond Eustace, 6th Bt, 16 April 1977 (ext).
Graham, Captain Lord Alastair Mungo, RN, 26 Nov. 1976.
Graham, Sir Montrose Stuart, 12th Bt   [Deceased.
Greaves, Sir John Bewley, CMG, OBE, 28 June 1977.
Green, Ernest, CBE, 12 Nov. 1977.
Green, Dr Francis Henry Knethell, CBE, 30 April 1977.
Greenslade, David Rex Willman, CBE, 16 Jan. 1977.
Greenwood, Ranolf Nelson, MC, 15 April 1977.
Grew, Major Benjamin Dixon, OBE, 23 June 1977.
Griffith, (Llewelyn) Wyn, CBE, 27 Sept. 1977.
Griffiths, David, 13 Jan. 1977.
Gropper, William, 6 Jan. 1977.
Guest, Air Marshal Sir Charles Edward Neville, KBE, CB, 23 June 1977.
Gunter, Rt Hon. Raymond Jones, PC, 12 April 1977.
Guppy, Ronald James, CB, 27 Jan. 1977.

Hale, Lionel Ramsay, 14 May 1977.
Halmos, Prof. Paul, 18 Oct. 1977.
Hamilton, Arthur Plumptre Faunce, CIE, OBE, MC, 17 Jan. 1977.
Hamilton, Rev. Herbert Alfred, 13 Nov. 1977.
Hamilton, Brig. James Melvill, DSO   [Deceased.
Hanlon, Air Vice-Marshal Thomas James, CB, CBE, 6 Jan. 1977.
Hanmer, Lt-Col Sir (Griffin Wyndham) Edward, 7th Bt, 1 Jan. 1977.
Hansen, Harry, 2 Jan. 1977.
Hardwick, Donald Ross, CIE, KPM, 6 Jan. 1977.
Hardy, Francis, 29 April 1977.
Harland, Ven. Lawrence Winston, MBE, 10 March 1977.
Harmsworth, Sir Hildebrand Alfred Beresford, 2nd Bt, 15 Nov. 1977.
Harries, Victor Percy, CB, 17 Feb. 1977.
Harsant, Maj.-Gen. Arnold Guy, CB, OBE, 8 April 1977.
Hart, Sir William Ogden, CMG, 29 April 1977.
Hartley, Percival Hubert Graham Horton-Smith, OBE, 3 Jan. 1977.
Harty, Maj.-Gen. Arthur Henry, CIE, 19 Oct. 1977.
Hasted, Maj.-Gen. William Freke, CB, CIE, CBE, DSO, MC, 29 Oct. 1977.
Haston, Dougal, 17 Jan. 1977.
Havers, Sir Cecil Robert, QC, 5 May 1977.
Hawkins, Sir Michael Babington Charles, KCVO, MBE, 26 May 1977.
Haworth, James, 16 Dec. 1976.
Hayes, Prof. Michael, 11 July 1976.
Hayward, Dr Graham William, 26 Nov. 1976.
Henderson, Philip Prichard, 13 Sept. 1977.
Herbert, Prof. Desmond Andrew, CMG   [Deceased.
Heslop, Air Vice-Marshal Herbert William, CB, OBE, 27 Dec. 1976.
Heywood, Wilfred Lanceley, CBE, 8 Oct. 1977.
Hibbert, Denys Heseltine, CBE, 15 May 1977.
Hickling, Charles Frederick, CMG, 14 June 1977.
Hill, Adrian Keith Graham, 22 June 1977.
Hill, Prof. Archibald Vivian, CH, OBE, FRS, 3 June 1977.
Hill, Charles Loraine, 14 Dec. 1976.

Hill, Captain Duncan C., DSO, RN, 2 May 1977.
Hill, Reginald John James, CIE, 24 Jan. 1977.
Hilton of Upton, Baron (Life Peer); Albert Victor Hilton, 3 May 1977.
Hinton, Prof. Howard Everest, FRS, 2 Aug. 1977.
Hislop, Prof. Joseph, 6 May 1977.
Hoare, Col Robert Rawdon, DSO, MC, 11 Aug. 1977.
Hobbs, Maj.-Gen. Reginald Geoffrey Stirling, CB, DSO, OBE, 7 Nov. 1977.
Hobson, Prof. Alfred Dennis   [Deceased.
Hodges, Captain Michael, CB, OBE, RN, 19 June 1977.
Holden, Sir George, 3rd Bt, 2 Dec. 1976.
Holden, Harold Henry, 19 April 1977.
Holden, Sir James Robert, 21 Sept. 1977.
Holder, Prof. Douglas William, FRS, 18 April 1977.
Holland, Edgar William, CIE   [Deceased.
Holland-Martin, Adm. Sir Deric, (Douglas Eric), GCB, DSO, DSC, 6 Jan. 1977.
Hollenden, 2nd Baron; Geoffrey Hope Hope-Morley, 19 Oct. 1977.
Hollis, (Maurice) Christopher, 5 May 1977.
Holmes, Air Vice-Marshal Peter Hamilton, CB, OBE, 27 April 1977.
Hornibrook, Sir Manuel Richard, OBE   [Deceased.
Howard, Frederick Richard, CB, CMG, 20 Oct. 1977.
Howard, Maj.-Gen. Gordon Byron, CBE, 26 Dec. 1976.
Howard, Lt-Col Hon. Henry Anthony Camillo, CMG, 19 Oct. 1977.
Howe, Sir Ronald Martin, CVO, MC, 30 Aug. 1977.
Hughes, John Turnbull, OBE, 25 April 1977.
Humphrey, Marshal of the Royal Air Force Sir Andrew Henry, GCB, OBE, DFC, AFC, 24 Jan. 1977.
Humphreys, Humphrey Francis, CBE, MC, TD, 21 March 1977.
Hutchins, Ven. George Francis, 3 Feb. 1977.
Hutchins, Robert Maynard, 14 May 1977.
Hynes, Sir Lincoln Carruthers, OBE, 7 Aug. 1977.

Iggulden, Sir Douglas Percy, CBE, DSO, TD, 30 May 1977.
Ilyushin, Sergei Vladimirovich, 9 Feb. 1977.
Irwin, Prof. Raymond, 13 Dec. 1976.
Isles, Prof. Keith Sydney, CMG, 18 June 1977.

Jacks, Graham Vernon, 10 Aug. 1977.
Jackson, Harry, 30 Nov. 1976.
James, William Garnet, OBE, 10 March 1977.
Janes, Sir Herbert Charles, 21 June 1977.
Jeffrey, Maj.-Gen. Hugh Crozier, CBE, 27 Nov. 1976.
Jellicoe, Rear-Adm. Christopher Theodore, CB, DSO, DSC, 15 April 1977.
Jerrard, Brig. Charles Ian, CB, CBE, 18 Jan. 1977.
Jessel, Sir George, 2nd Bt, MC, 18 Aug. 1977.
Johnson, Prof. Harry Gordon, FBA, 8 May 1977.
Johnson, Most Rev. Martin Michael, DD   [Deceased.
Jolly, Gen. Sir Alan, GCB, CBE, DSO, 15 Sept. 1977.
Jones, Sir (David) Fletcher, OBE, 22 Feb. 1977.
Jones, James, 9 May 1977.
Jones, Prof. John Kenyon Netherton, FRS, 13 April 1977.
Jones, Judge Marvin   [Deceased.
Joules, Dr Horace, 25 Jan. 1977.

Katenga, Bridger Winston   [Deceased.
Kay, Prof. Herbert Davenport, CBE, FRS, 24 Nov. 1976.
Kaye, Ven. Martin, 16 June 1977.
Keene, Prof. Mary Frances Lucas, 9 May 1977.
Kenyon, Sir Bernard, 26 Aug. 1977.
Ker, Frederick Innes, CBE, 24 Sept. 1977.
Kerr, Captain Frank Robison, DSO, 3 May 1977.
Kerr, Lt-Col Sir Howard, KCVO, CMG, OBE, 11 July 1977.
Kilmorey, 5th Earl of; Francis Jack Richard Patrick Needham, 12 April 1977.
Kimpton, Lawrence Alpheus, 31 Oct. 1977.
King, Sir Anthony Highmore, CBE, 28 March 1977.
King, Colin Henry Harmsworth, 18 Jan. 1977.
Kirk, Sir Peter Michael, MP, 17 April 1977.
Kirkconnell, Watson, OC, 26 Feb. 1977.
Kirkpatrick, Air Vice-Marshal Herbert James, CB, CBE, DFC, 28 Aug. 1977.
Kitson, Captain James Buller, DSO, RN, 7 Dec. 1976.
Kleinwort, Ernest Greverus, 3 Nov. 1977.
Klijnstra, Gerrit Dirk Ale, Hon. KBE, 18 Dec. 1976.
Klyne, Prof. William, 13 Nov. 1977.
Knowles, Rt Rev. Donald Rowland, OBE, 26 Sept. 1977.
Knowles, Air Vice-Marshal Edgar, CB, CBE, 8 Feb. 1977.
Knowles, John, March 1977.
Knox, Collie, 3 May 1977.
Kothavala, Tehmasp Tehmul, CIE, 20 Aug. 1977.

Lakin, John Edmund Douglas, 13 Oct. 1977.
Lamb, Lynton Harold, 4 Sept. 1977.
Lancaster, Col Claude Granville, 25 July 1977.
Lane, Ernest Olaf, CBE, DFC, AFC, 29 Dec. 1976.
Lang, Air Vice-Marshal Albert Frank, CB, MBE, AFC, 20 June 1977.
Lawley, Edgar Ernest, CBE, 3 Sept. 1977.
Lawson, John, CB, 1 Feb. 1977.
Laybourne, Rear-Adm. Alan Watson, CB, CBE, 6 Feb. 1977.
Leake, Hugh Martin-, 29 April 1977.
Leech, Prof. Clifford, 26 July 1977.
Legge, Maj.-Gen. Stanley Ferguson, CBE, 25 July 1977.
Lever, Baron (Life Peer); Leslie Maurice Lever, 26 July 1977.

Levy, Aaron Harold, 31 March 1977.
Lewis, Edward Daly; His Honour Judge Daly Lewis, 3 April 1977.
Lewis, Ivor Evan Gerwyn, 25 April 1977.
Lewis, Sir John Todd, OBE, 10 Aug. 1977.
Lindsay, Sir (Ernest) Daryl, 25 Dec. 1976.
Little, Sir (Rudolf) Alexander, KCB, 27 Feb. 1977.
Littlewood, Prof. John Edensor, FRS, 6 Sept. 1977.
Lloyd, Huw Ifor, OBE, MC, 10 June 1977.
Lloyd-Williams, Dorothy Sylvia, 13 April 1977.
Lloyd-Williams, Comdr Hugh, DSO, VRD, 22 Feb. 1977.
Longworth, Rt Rev. Tom, DD, 15 Oct. 1977.
Lonsdale, Allister; His Honour Judge Lonsdale, 29 July 1977.
Lowell, Robert Traill Spence, Jr, 12 Sept. 1977.
Loweth, Sidney Harold, 1 May 1977.
Lowther, Col John George, CBE, DSO, MC, TD, 19 March 1977.
Luce, Rev. Arthur Aston, MC, DD, 27 June 1977.
Luce, Sir William Henry Tucker, GBE, KCMG, 7 July 1977.
Lucker, Sydney Charles, 27 Aug. 1977.
Ludbrook, Dr Samuel Lawrence, CMG   [Deceased.
Lunt, Alfred, 3 Aug. 1977.
Lynes, Rear-Adm. Charles Edward, CMG, 30 Jan. 1977.

McCoy, William Frederick, QC, 4 Dec. 1976.
McCrie, John Gibb, OBE, TD, 24 Jan. 1977.
McCrindle, Major John Ronald, CMG, OBE, MC, 12 March 1977.
McDonald, Hon. Sir John Gladstone Black, 23 April 1977.
McGarvey, Sir Daniel, CBE, 26 April 1977.
Macgregor, Lewis Richard, CBE   [Deceased.
MacInnes, Rt Rev. Angus Campbell, CMG, 29 April 1977.
MacInnes, Prof. William Alexander, MC, 21 Oct. 1977.
MacKeith, Dr Ronald Charles, 30 Oct. 1977.
Macklin, Sir (Albert) Sortain (Romer), 28 Dec. 1976.
MacLennan, Sir Robert Laing, CIE, 30 June 1977.
McMahon, Sir (William) Patrick, 7th Bt, 5 Jan. 1977.
McMillan, James Athole, CBE, 9 Sept. 1977.
McMillan, William, CVO, RA, 25 Sept. 1977.
McVeigh, Rt Hon. Sir Herbert Andrew, PC (NI), 3 Oct. 1977.
Magowan, Joseph Irvine, CB, 31 May 1977.
Maitland, Comdr Sir John Francis Whitaker, 17 Nov. 1977.
Makarios III, Archbishop, 3 Aug. 1977.
Malraux, André, 23 Nov. 1976.
Maltby, Sir Thomas Karran   [Deceased.
Manktelow, Sir (Arthur) Richard, KBE, CB, 14 Jan. 1977.
Mannering, Rev. Ernest, 24 Oct. 1977.
Manning, Dame (Elizabeth) Leah, DBE, 15 Sept. 1977.
Manning, Hon. Sir (James) Kenneth   [Deceased.
Marling, Lt-Col Sir John Stanley Vincent, 4th Bt, CBE, 20 Sept. 1977.
Marriott, Cyril Herbert Alfred, CBE, 8 Sept. 1977.
Marshall, Sheina Macalister, OBE, FRS, 7 April 1977.
Marshall-Reynolds, Clyde Albert, QC, 15 Aug. 1977.
Martin, Rt Rev. Clifford Arthur, DD, 11 Aug. 1977.
Martin, Sir David Christie, CBE, 16 Dec. 1976.
Mason, Dr (Richard) Michael, 30 June 1977.
Massiah, Sir (Hallam) Grey, KBE   [Deceased.
Masterman, Sir John Cecil, OBE, 6 June 1977.
Mathys, Sir (Herbert) Reginald, TD, 11 June 1977.
Mawby, Sir Maurice Alan Edgar, CBE, 4 Aug. 1977.
Mbanefo, Sir Louis Nwachukwu, 28 March 1977.
Meech, Sir John Valentine, KCVO   [Deceased.
Mekie, Eoin Cameron, CBE, 4 Aug. 1977.
Meredith, Air Vice-Marshal Sir Charles Warburton, KBE, CB, AFC, 19 April 1977.
Merthyr, 3rd Baron; William Brereton Couchman Lewis, PC, KBE, TD, 5 April 1977.
Merz, Charles, 31 Aug. 1977.
Metcalfe, Sir Ralph Ismay, 2 Nov. 1977.
Micklem, Rev. Nathaniel, CH, 26 Dec. 1976.
Micklem, Brig. Ralph, CMG, CBE, 21 March 1977.
Micklethwait, Rear-Adm. St John Aldrich, CB, DSO, 31 July 1977.
Miles, Maj.-Gen. Eric Grant, CB, DSO, MC, 3 Nov. 1977.
Miller, Sir James, GBE, 20 March 1977.
Miller, Bt Col Sir James MacBride, MC, TD, 9 Nov. 1977.
Miller, John Duncan, CMG, 20 May 1977.
Miller, Mrs Millie, MP, 29 Oct. 1977.
Miller, Prof. William Christopher, 17 Dec. 1976.
Mockett, Sir Vere, MBE, 13 Jan. 1977.
Moody, Arthur Seymour, 12 Dec. 1976.
Moore, Sir Harold John de Courcy, 6 Dec. 1976.
Moore, Henry Ian, CBE   [Deceased.
Moran, 1st Baron; Charles McMoran Wilson, MC, 12 April 1977.
Moran, Prof. Frances Elizabeth, 7 Oct. 1977.
Morgan, James Conwy, CMG, 24 June 1977.
Morgan, Gen. Sir William Duthie, GCB, DSO, MC, 13 May 1977.
Morris, Rt Rev. Arthur Harold, DD, 15 Oct. 1977.
Morshead, Sir Owen Frederick, GCVO, KCB, DSO, MC, 1 June 1977.
Morton, Prof. Richard Alan, FRS, 21 Jan. 1977.
Mountain, Lt-Col Sir Brian Edward Stanley, 2nd Bt, 17 Feb. 1977.
Mowrer, Edgar Ansel, 2 March 1977.
Murdock, Kenneth Ballard   [Deceased.
Mure, William, OBE, 26 April 1977.
Murphy, Sir Alexander Paterson, MC   [Deceased.
Murray, Sir Andrew Hunter Arbuthnot, OBE, 21 March 1977.
Murray, Sir William Patrick Keith, 11th Bt, 2 Nov. 1977.
Musto, Sir Arnold Albert, CIE, 29 May 1977.
Myles, Captain Edgar Kinghorn, VC, DSO, 31 Jan. 1977.

Nabokov, Vladimir, 2 July 1977.
Naish, Lt-Comdr George Prideaux Brabant, VRD, RNR, 30 July 1977.
Nan Kivell, Sir Rex de Charambac, CMG, 7 June 1977.
Napier, Ian Patrick Robert, MC, 9 May 1977.
Nash, John Northcote, CBE, RA, 23 Sept. 1977.
Neilson-Terry, Phyllis, 25 Sept. 1977.
Newburgh, Countess of (10th in line); Donna Maria Sofia Giuseppina Giustiniani Bandini, 30 April 1977.
Newton, Bernard St John, CIE, 5 July 1977.
Nicholl, Rear-Adm. Angus Dacres, CB, CBE, DSO, 12 April 1977.
Nightingale, Sir Charles Athelstan, 16th Bt, 7 March 1977.
Niles, Emory Hamilton   [Deceased.
Nimptsch, Uli, RA, 2 Jan. 1977.
Norman, Sir Charles, CBE, 9 Dec. 1976.
Norrie, 1st Baron; Lt-Gen. Charles Willoughby Moke Norrie, GCMG, GCVO, CB, DSO, MC, 25 May 1977.
Nott-Bower, Sir (William) Guy, KBE, CB, 19 July 1977.

Oakley, Rev. Austin, 2 April 1977.
O'Donoghue, Geoffrey Charles Patrick Randal (The O'Donoghue of the Glens)   [Deceased.
Ogilvy-Wedderburn, Comdr Sir (John) Peter, 12th and 6th Bt, RN, 13 Aug. 1977.
Oldham, James Bagot, CBE, VRD, 1 March 1977.
Olson, Sven Olof; His Honour Judge Olson, 22 April 1977.
O'Neill, Sir (Matthew) John   [Deceased.
Opie, Air Vice-Marshal William Alfred, CB, CBE, 14 Oct. 1977.
Orde, Brig. Reginald John, CBE, QC (Canada)   [Deceased.
Ortcheson, Sir John, CBE, 5 Sept. 1977.
Orton-Jones, Harry, CBE   [Deceased.
Owen, Sir (Arthur) Douglas, KBE, CB, 26 April 1977.
Owen, John Glendwr, CB, 14 Feb. 1977.

Packer, Joy, (Lady Packer), 6 Sept. 1977.
Parmoor, 2nd Baron; Alfred Henry Seddon Cripps, 12 May 1977.
Parmoor, 3rd Baron; Frederick Heyworth Cripps, DSO, TD, 5 Oct. 1977.
Parry, Rear-Adm. Cecil Ramsden Langworthy, CB, DSO, 31 March 1977.
Paterson, Aylmer John Noel, CBE, 4 Oct. 1977.
Patey, David Howard, 27 March 1977.
Paton, Florence Beatrice, 12 Oct. 1976.
Paton, John, 14 Dec. 1976.
Pavlides, Sir Paul George, CBE, 14 Oct. 1977.
Pearson, Hon. Sir Glen Gardner, 30 Nov. 1976.
Pearson, Prof. William   [Deceased.
Pelletier, Hector Rooney   [Deceased.
Perkins, Alan Hubert Banbury, MVO, MBE, 15 June 1977.
Perkins, Sir (Albert) Edward, KCVO, 20 May 1977.
Peshall, Samuel Frederick, CBE, MC, 25 Aug. 1977.
Peto, Gladys Emma, 21 May 1977.
Phillips, John Henry Hood, 17 Jan. 1977.
Phillips Brocklehurst, Charles Douglas Fergusson, 31 July 1977.
Phillipson, Prof. Andrew Tindal, 10 10 Jan. 1977.
Piggott, Col Joseph Clive, CBE, MC   [Deceased.
Pilkington, Captain Sir Richard Antony, KBE, MC, 9 Dec. 1976.
Pilling, Tom Sharpley, 9 Jan. 1977.
Pink, Ven. Hubert Arthur Stanley, 22 Dec. 1976.
Pinnock, Frank Frewin, CMG, 2 Feb. 1977.
Polson, Milson George, QC; His Honour Judge Polson, 5 Oct. 1977.
Pool, Bernard Frank, CB, CBE, 3 March 1977.
Poole, Prof. John Hewitt Jellett   [Deceased.
Popplewell, Baron (Life Peer); Ernest Popplewell, CBE, 11 Aug. 1977.
Portland, 7th Duke of; William Arthur Henry Cavendish-Bentinck, KG, 21 March 1977.
Preston, Sir Thomas Hildebrand, 6th Bt, OBE, 30 Dec. 1976.
Price, Herbert Spencer, CBE   [Deceased.
Prior-Palmer, Maj.-Gen. George Erroll, CB, DSO, 18 Aug. 1977.
Pritchard, Leslie Francis Gordon, MBE, TD, 9 Sept. 1977.
Proud, Sir George   [Deceased.
Prynne, Maj.-Gen. Michael Whitworth, CB, CBE, 27 Sept. 1977.
Pudney, John Sleigh, 10 Nov. 1977.
Purchas, Rev. Canon Alban Charles Theodore   [Deceased.
Pyke, Air Cdre Alan, CB, OBE, 11 March 1977.
Pyke, Cyril John, CMG, 11 Dec. 1976.

Radcliffe, 1st Viscount; Cyril John Radcliffe, PC, GBE, FBA, 1 April 1977 (ext).
Radley, Oswald Alfred, CBE, MC, 23 July 1977.
Raeburn, Sir Edward Alfred, 3rd Bt, 21 April 1977.
Railton, Reid Antony, 1 Sept. 1977.
Ralfs, Maj.-Gen. Bertram George, CB, 16 April 1977.
Ramsay, Maj.-Gen. Sir Alan Hollick, CB, CBE, DSO   [Deceased.
Randall, Sir Alec Walter George, KCMG, OBE, 4 Aug. 1977.
Ranger, James   [Deceased.
Rawlins, His Honour Percy Lionel Edwin, 27 April 1977.
Ray, Ted, 8 Nov. 1977.
Raybould, Prof. Sidney Griffith, 1 Oct. 1977.
Rayner, Brig. Sir Ralph, 17 July 1977.
Read, Col Alfred Howard, CB, OBE, TD, 14 Jan. 1977.
Rees, Thomas Ifor, CMG, 11 Feb. 1977.
Reid, Prof. Donald Darnley, 26 March 1977.
Richmond, Prof. Oliffe Legh, 27 May 1977.
Ride, Sir Lindsay Tasman, CBE, ED, 17 Oct. 1977.
Ridley, Frederick Thomas, 2 Feb. 1977.
Rifaat, Kamai Eldin Mahmoud, 13 July 1977.

Ripon, Bishop of; Rt Rev. Stuart Hetley Price, 15 March 1977.
Ritchie, Sir John Neish, CB, 28 Sept. 1977.
Rivington, Gerald Chippindale, 2 March 1977.
Roach, Air Vice-Marshal Harold Jace, CB, CBE, AFC, 21 June 1977.
Robb, Leonard Arthur, CMG, MVO   [Deceased.
Robb, Ven. Percy Douglas, 28 Nov. 1976.
Roberts, Rev. Prof. Bleddyn Jones, DD, 11 Aug. 1977.
Roberts, Cecil Edric Mornington, 20 Dec. 1976.
Roberts, John Reginald, CBE   [Deceased.
Roberts, Brig. Michael Rookherst, DSO, 30 Aug. 1977.
Robertson, Prof. Andrew, FRS, 22 Oct. 1977.
Robertson, Col John Richard Hugh, CBE, 20 Feb. 1977.
Robieson, Sir William, 19 July 1977.
Robinson, David Morrant, CBE, 3 March 1977.
Robinson, Air Cdre Maurice Wilbraham Sandford, CBE, 2 April 1977.
Robinson, Rev. William Gordon, 1 Feb. 1977.
Roche, Sir Standish O'Grady, 4th Bt, DSO, 2 April 1977.
Ropner, Col Sir Leonard, 1st Bt, MC, TD, 12 Oct. 1977.
Ropner, Sir Robert Desmond, 31 Aug. 1977.
Rosa, John Nogueira, OBE, 14 Aug. 1977.
Ross, William Alexander, CBE, 1 July 1977.
Rostand, Jean, 3 Sept. 1977.
Rowlands, Sir (Richard) Alun, KBE, 1 March 1977.
Ruck Keene, Vice-Adm. Philip, CB, CBE, DSO, 28 May 1977.
Rudd, Surgeon Rear-Adm. Eric Thomas Sutherland, CB, CBE, 21 May 1977.
Rusholme, 1st Baron; Robert Alexander Palmer, 18 Aug. 1977 (ext).
Russell, Adm. Hon. Sir Guy Herbrand Edward, GBE, KCB, DSO, 25 Sept. 1977.
Russell, Brig. Nelson, CB, DSO, MC   [Deceased.
Russell, Rosalind, (Mrs F. Brisson), 28 Nov. 1976.

Sackett, Alfred Barrett, MC, 24 Sept. 1977.
Sangster, John Young, 26 March 1977.
Saugman, Christian Ditlev Trappaud, Hon. KBE   [Deceased.
Sayers, Sir Frederick, CIE, KPM, 7 April 1977.
Scamp, Sir (Athelstan) Jack, 30 Oct. 1977.
Scarsdale, 2nd Viscount; Richard Nathaniel Curzon, TD, 19 Oct. 1977.
Schumacher, Ernst Friedrich, CBE, 4 Sept. 1977.
Schuschnigg, Dr Kurt von, 18 Nov. 1977.
Scott, His Honour Henry Cooper, QC, 11 Nov. 1977.
Scott, Dr Peter Duncan, CBE, 6 Aug. 1977.
Shannon, Howard Huntley, CMG   [Deceased.
Sharp, Gen. Sir John Aubrey Taylor, KCB, MC, 15 Jan. 1977.
Shaw, Air Cdre Gerald Stanley, CB, 14 Nov. 1976.
Shaw, Dr Maurice Elgie, 31 Oct. 1977.
Sheehy, Hon. Sir Joseph Aloysius, KBE   [Deceased.
Sheffield, Edmund Charles Reginald, 6 March 1977.
Sheffield, Sir Robert Arthur, 7th Bt, 2 June 1977.
Shipton, Eric Earle, CBE, 28 March 1977.
Silsoe, 1st Baron; Arthur Malcolm Trustram Eve, GBE, MC, TD, QC, 3 Dec. 1976.
Simmonds, Sidney, CBE, 30 Jan. 1977.
Simpson, John Alexander, CIE, 5 June 1977.
Simpson, Sir John Roughton, CB, 14 Dec. 1976.
Simpson, Rev. Robert, 15 Feb. 1977.
Sims, Sir Alfred John, KCB, OBE, 25 Aug. 1977.
Sims, Arthur Mitford, CIE, 2 March 1977.
Sinclair, Maj.-Gen. Sir John Alexander, KCMG, CB, OBE, 22 March 1977.
Sinclair, Sir William, CBE   [Deceased.
Sinha, Rajandhari, CIE, 30 Dec. 1976.
Sinker, Sir (Algernon) Paul, KCMG, CB, 26 Feb. 1977.
Slater, Baron (Life Peer); Joseph Slater, BEM, 21 April 1977.
Smallwood, Maj.-Gen. Gerald Russell, CB, DSO, MC, 3 Feb. 1977.
Smart, Leslie Masson, CBE   [Deceased.
Smith, Lt-Gen. Sir Arthur Francis, KCB, KBE, DSO, MC, 8 Aug. 1977.
Smith, Hon. David John, CBE, 26 Nov. 1976.
Smith, Brig. Ernest Thomas Cobley, CB, 25 Jan. 1977.
Smith, Brig. Henry Gilbertson, CB, OBE, MC, TD, 23 July 1977.
Smith, Herbert Alexander, CBE   [Deceased.
Smith, Captain Norman Wesley, CBE, 14 Jan. 1977.
Smith-Gordon, Sir Lionel Eldred Pottinger, 4th Bt, 6 Dec. 1976.
Snow, Rt Rev. George D'Oyly, 17 Nov. 1977.
Sowerby, Amy Millicent   [Deceased.
Spearman, Sir Alexander Bowyer, 4th Bt, 27 May 1977.
Spooner, Edgar Clynton Ross   [Deceased.
Stannard, Captain Richard Been, VC, DSO, RD, RNR, 22 July 1977.
Stapleton, Major Sir Miles Talbot, 9th Bt, 4 April 1977.
Starkey, Lt-Col Sir William Randle, 2nd Bt, 10 July 1977.
Starr, Sir Kenneth William, CMG, OBE, ED   [Deceased.
Steele, Norman James, 1 Sept. 1977.
Stephens, Sir (Leon) Edgar, CBE, 24 Jan. 1977.
Stephenson, Basil Ernest, CBE, 7 May 1977.
Stevens, Maj.-Gen. William George, CB, CBE   [Deceased.
Stevenson, Sir Ralph Clarmont Skrine, GCMG, 23 June 1977.
Steward, Sir Harold Macdonald, 3 March 1977.
Stewart, Donald, CIE, OBE   [Deceased.
Stewart, Major Oliver, MC, AFC, 22 Dec. 1976.
Steyn, Hon. Lucas Cornelius   [Deceased.
Stokes, Sir Harold Frederick, CBE, 4 Aug. 1977.
Stokowski, Leopold Boleslawowicz Stanislaw Antoni, 13 Sept. 1977.
Storrs, Rt Rev. Christopher E., 19 Feb. 1977.
Stott, May, Lady; (May B. Lee), 2 Jan. 1977.
Strangman, James Gonville, QC, 3 June 1977.

Strickland, Lady; (Barbara), DBE, 20 March 1977.
Stronge, Brig. Humphrey Cecil Travell, CBE, DSO, MC, 27 March 1977.
Studd, Sir (Robert) Kynaston, 3rd Bt, 27 May 1977.
Sugden, Maj.-Gen. Sir Henry Haskins Clapham, KBE, CB, DSO, 11 March 1977.
Sugerman, Hon. Sir Bernard   [*Deceased.*
Sullivan, Sir Richard Benjamin Magniac, 8th Bt, 22 Aug. 1977.
Summers, Sir Richard Felix, 6 Feb. 1977.
Surplice, Reginald Alwyn, 21 April 1977.
Sutton, Sir (Oliver) Graham, CBE, FRS, 26 May 1977.
Sutton, Stanley Cecil, CBE, 6 May 1977.
Swindells, Rev. Bernard Guy, SJ, 2 July 1977.
Swinfen, 2nd Baron; Charles Swinfen Eady, 19 March 1977.
Symons, Ronald Stuart, CMG, CIE, 5 Aug. 1977.
Synge, Prof. Victor Millington   [*Deceased.*

Tapp, Norman Charles, QC, 9 Aug. 1977.
Tarbat, Sir John Allan, 7 Oct. 1977.
Taylor, Sir Eric Stuart, 2nd Bt, OBE, 25 Oct. 1977.
Taylor, William, CB, 12 Feb. 1977.
Templeton, James Stanley, 24 March 1977.
Tennyson, Sir Charles Bruce Locker, CMG, 22 June 1977.
Thomas, Sir Ben Bowen, 26 July 1977.
Thomas, Meirion, FRS, 5 April 1977.
Thomas, Richard, 2 Feb. 1977.
Thomas, Ronald Hamilton Eliot, OBE, 4 Feb. 1977.
Thompson, Prof. Frank Charles, 12 Aug. 1977.
Thompson, Prof. John McLean, 17 April 1977.
Thomson, Adam Bruce, OBE, 4 Dec. 1976.
Thomson, Sir (Arthur) Landsborough, CB, OBE, 9 June 1977.
Thomson, Sir Arthur Peregrine, MC, 15 July 1977.
Thornton, Sir (Henry) Gerard, FRS, 6 Feb. 1977.
Thornton-Kemsley, Col Sir Colin Norman, OBE, TD, 17 July 1977.
Thorpe, Prof. Harry, OBE, 14 Feb. 1977.
Thorpe, Prof. Lewis Guy Melville, 10 Oct. 1977.
Thumboo Chetty, Amatyasiromani Sir Bernard T., OBE   [*Deceased.*
Topp, Brig.-Gen. Charles Beresford, CBE, DSO, MC   [*Deceased.*
Tottenham, Sir (George) Richard (Frederick), KCIE, CSI, 11 Jan. 1977.
Touche, Sir Norman George, 2nd Bt, 18 May 1977.
Towers, Graham Ford, CC, CMG   [*Deceased.*
Towner, Major Edgar Thomas, VC, MC   [*Deceased.*
Townley, Rt Rev. George Frederick, 9 March 1977.
Trafford, Rt Rev. Ralph Sigebert, OSB, 22 Nov. 1976.
Tredgold, Rt Hon. Sir Robert Clarkson, PC, KCMG, QC (Rhodesia), 8 April 1977.
Trueta, Prof. Joseph, 19 Jan. 1977.
Turner, Douglas William, 2 Sept. 1977.
Turner, Vice-Adm. Sir Robert Ross, KBE, CB, DSO, 26 June 1977.
Turquet, Prof. Gladys, 17 Jan. 1977.
Tweedsmuir, Susan, Lady, 21 March 1977.

Uganda, Rwanda, Burundi and Boga Zaire, Archbishop of; Most Rev. Janani Luwum, 17 Feb. 1977.
Uhr, Sir Clive Wentworth, CBE   [*Deceased.*
Upton, James Bryan, MBE, TD, 15 Dec. 1976.

Vaughan, (John) Keith, CBE, 4 Nov. 1977.
Vaux of Harrowden, 9th Baron; Rev. Peter Hubert Gordon Gilbey, OSB, 1 Nov. 1977.
Venter, Gen. Christoffel Johannes, CB, DFC, 20 Feb. 1977.
Vinden, Brig. Frederick Hubert, CIE, 2 Feb. 1977.
von Braun, Wernher, 16 June 1977.

Wace, Ernest William Cornish, CSI, CIE, 5 Nov. 1977.
Walmsley, Kenneth Maurice, CMG, OBE, 26 Feb. 1977.
Walsh, Prof. Arthur Donald, FRS, 23 April 1977.
Walsh, Henry Francis Chester, OBE, 16 Sept. 1977.
Walter, William Grey, 6 May 1977.
Walton, Brig. Sir George Hands, KBE, CB, TD, 25 Nov. 1976.
Wand, Rt Rev. and Rt Hon. (John) William (Charles), PC, KCVO, 16 Aug. 1977.
Warren, Rev. Dr Max Alexander Cunningham, 23 Aug. 1977.
Waterhouse, Prof. Gilbert, 25 July 1977.
Watherston, Sir David Charles, KBE, CMG, Hon. PMN, 16 Jan. 1977.
Watkins, Brig. Bernard Springett, CBE, 11 June 1977.
Watson, Prof. Benjamin Philp   [*Deceased.*
Watson, Dennis George, CIE, KPM, 24 Jan. 1977.
Watson, Robert, CMG, OBE, 11 Sept. 1977.
Wedgwood, Dame Ivy Evelyn, DBE   [*Deceased.*
Welby, Sir Oliver Charles Earle, 6th Bt, TD, 6 Oct. 1977.
Were, Cecil Allan Walter, CMG, 5 Aug. 1977.
Weston, Rev. Arthur Ernest, MM   [*Deceased.*
Weston, Maj.-Gen. Gerald Patrick Linton, CB, CBE, DSO, 26 Oct. 1977.
Wheatcroft, Harry, 8 Jan. 1977.
Wheatley, Dennis Yates, 11 Nov. 1977.
Wheeler, Dr Denis Edward, CBE, 24 Jan. 1977.
Wheeler, Brig. Ralph Pung, CBE, 23 June 1977.
Wiggin, Sir Charles Douglas, KCMG, DFC, AFC, 8 March 1977.
Wilcocks, Charles, CMG, 6 March 1977.
Wilcox, Herbert, CBE, 15 May 1977.
Wilkinson, Brig. John Shann, CB, DSO, MC, 27 Feb. 1977.
Williams, Alfred Cecil, CB   [*Deceased.*
Williams, Maj.-Gen. Aubrey Ellis, CBE, DSO, MC, 25 March 1977.
Williams, Brig. Edward Stephen Bruce, CBE, 20 Jan. 1977.
Williams, Prof. Sir Frederic Calland, CBE, FRS, 11 Aug. 1977.
Williams, Prof. Mary, 17 Oct. 1977.
Williams, Neville John, 29 Jan. 1977.
Williams, Sir Robert Ernest, 9th Bt   [*Deceased.*
Williams, Lt-Col. Stanley Price, CIE, 29 Oct. 1977.
Williams, Sir William Emrys, CBE, 30 March 1977.
Williamson, Mrs Catherine Ellis, 25 April 1977.
Williamson, Henry, 13 Aug. 1977.
Willmott, Sir Maurice Gordon, MC, 14 Oct. 1977.
Willoughby, Prof. Leonard Ashley, 5 Oct. 1977.
Wills, Brig. Sir Kenneth Agnew, KBE, MC, ED, 13 May 1977.
Wilson, Sir Arton, KBE, CB, 19 Sept. 1977.
Wilson, Prof. Graham Malcolm, 15 April 1977.
Wilson, Rev. Richard Mercer, 26 Nov. 1976.
Windham, William Evan, 28 Sept. 1977.
Wombwell, Sir (Frederick) Philip (Alfred William), 6th Bt, MBE, 4 April 1977.
Wood, Eric Rawlinson, CIE, MC, 17 Aug. 1977.
Woodham-Smith, Cecil, CBE, 16 March 1977.
Woolmer, Rt Rev. Laurence Henry, 5 Aug. 1977.
Wright, Adm. Sir Royston Hollis, GBE, KCB, DSC, 18 July 1977.
Wrigley, Sir John Crompton, KBE, CB, 7 June 1977.
Wrottesley, 5th Baron; Richard John Wrottesley, MC, 23 Oct. 1977.
Wynn, Hon. Rowland Tempest Beresford, CBE, 24 April 1977.

Yeaman, Sir Ian David, 28 Feb. 1977.
Young, Arthur Primrose, OBE, 1 Feb. 1977.
Young, Rev. Canon Charles Edgar, AFC, 25 Sept. 1977.
Young, Stephen   [*Deceased.*
Young, Thomas, CBE, TD, 8 March 1977.

WHO'S WHO 1978

THE ROYAL FAMILY

THE SOVEREIGN

Born

Her Majesty Queen Elizabeth II . . . . 21 Apr. 1926

    Succeeded her father, King George VI, 6 February 1952.

    Married 20 Nov. 1947, H R H The Duke of Edinburgh (*now* H R H The Prince Philip, Duke of Edinburgh), *b* 10 June 1921; *s* of H R H Prince Andrew of Greece (*d* 1944) and of H R H Princess Andrew of Greece (*d* 1969), *g g-d* of Queen Victoria.

    Residences: Buckingham Palace, London, SW1; Windsor Castle, Berkshire; Sandringham House, Norfolk; Balmoral Castle, Aberdeenshire.

SONS AND DAUGHTER OF HER MAJESTY

H R H The Prince of Wales (Prince Charles Philip Arthur George) . . . . 14 Nov. 1948

    Office: Buckingham Palace, London, SW1.

H R H The Prince Andrew (Albert Christian Edward) . . . . 19 Feb. 1960

H R H The Prince Edward (Antony Richard Louis) . . . . 10 Mar. 1964

H R H The Princess Anne (Elizabeth Alice Louise), Mrs Mark Phillips . . . . 15 Aug. 1950

    Married 14 Nov. 1973, Mark Anthony Peter Phillips, *qv*, and has issue—

        PETER MARK ANDREW PHILLIPS . . . . 15 Nov. 1977

    Office: Buckingham Palace, London, SW1; Gatcombe Park, Minchinhampton, Stroud, Gloucestershire.

SISTER OF HER MAJESTY

H R H The Princess Margaret, Countess of Snowdon . . . . 21 Aug. 1930

    Married 6 May 1960, Antony Charles Robert Armstrong-Jones (*now* 1st Earl of Snowdon, *qv*) and has issue—

        DAVID ALBERT CHARLES ARMSTRONG-JONES (VISCOUNT LINLEY, *qv*) . . . . . . 3 Nov. 1961

        SARAH FRANCES ELIZABETH ARMSTRONG-JONES (LADY SARAH ARMSTRONG-JONES) . . . . 1 May 1964

    Residence: Kensington Palace, W8 4PU.

MOTHER OF HER MAJESTY

Her Majesty Queen Elizabeth The Queen Mother . . . . 4 Aug. 1900

    Married 26 April 1923 (as Lady Elizabeth Bowes-Lyon, *d* of 14th Earl of Strathmore), H R H The Duke of York (Prince ALBERT), who succeeded as KING GEORGE VI, 11 Dec. 1936; he died 6 Feb. 1952.

    Residences: Clarence House, St James's, SW1; Royal Lodge, Windsor Great Park, Berkshire; Castle of Mey, Caithness-shire.

WIDOWS OF UNCLES OF HER MAJESTY

H R H Princess Alice, Duchess of Gloucester, 3rd *d* of 7th Duke of Buccleuch . . . . 25 Dec. 1901

    Married 6 Nov. 1935, H R H The Duke of Gloucester (Prince Henry William Frederick Albert), *b* 31 March 1900; he died 10 June 1974. They had issue—

        H R H PRINCE WILLIAM HENRY ANDREW FREDERICK, *b* 18 Dec. 1941; *d* 28 Aug. 1972.

        H R H THE DUKE OF GLOUCESTER (PRINCE RICHARD ALEXANDER WALTER GEORGE) (*see below*).

    Residences: Kensington Palace, W8 4PU; Barnwell Manor, Peterborough, PE8 5PJ.

The Duchess of Windsor (Wallis Warfield), *d* of Teakle Wallis Warfield, Baltimore, Maryland . . . . 19 June 1896

    Married 3 June 1937, H R H The Duke of Windsor (Prince Albert Edward Christian George Andrew Patrick David), *b* 23 June 1894; he died 28 May 1972.

    Residence: 4 Route du Champ d'Entraînement, 75016 Paris.

COUSINS OF HER MAJESTY

Child of H R H The Duke of Gloucester and of H R H Princess Alice Duchess of Gloucester (*see above*).

H R H The Duke of Gloucester (Prince Richard Alexander Walter George) . . . . . . 26 Aug. 1944

Married 8 July 1972, Birgitte van Deurs, *d* of Asger Preben Wissing Henriksen, and has issue—

ALEXANDER PATRICK GREGERS RICHARD (EARL OF ULSTER, *qv*) . . . . 24 Oct. 1974

DAVINA ELIZABETH ALICE BENEDIKTE (LADY DAVINA WINDSOR) . . . . 19 Nov. 1977

Residences: Kensington Palace, W8 4PU; Barnwell Manor, Peterborough, PE8 5PJ.

Children of H R H The Duke of Kent (Prince George Edward Alexander Edmund, *b* 20 Dec. 1902, *d* 25 Aug. 1942) and H R H Princess Marina, Duchess of Kent (*b* 13 Dec. 1906, *d* 27 Aug. 1968), *y d* of late Prince Nicolas of Greece.

H R H The Duke of Kent (Prince Edward George Nicholas Patrick) . . . . 9 Oct. 1935

Married 8 June 1961, Katharine, *b* 22 Feb. 1933, *o d* of Sir William Worsley, 4th Bt, and has issue—

GEORGE PHILIP NICHOLAS (EARL OF ST ANDREWS, *qv*) . . . . 26 June 1962

NICHOLAS CHARLES EDWARD JONATHAN (LORD NICHOLAS WINDSOR) . . . . . 25 July 1970

HELEN MARINA LUCY (LADY HELEN WINDSOR) . . . . 28 Apr. 1964

Residences: York House, St James's Palace, SW1; Anmer Hall, King's Lynn, Norfolk, PE31 6RW.

H R H Prince Michael George Charles Franklin . . . . 4 July 1942

Residence: Kensington Palace, W8 4PU.

H R H Princess Alexandra, the Hon. Mrs Angus Ogilvy . . . . 25 Dec. 1936

Married 24 April 1963, Hon. Angus James Bruce Ogilvy, *qv*, and has issue—

JAMES ROBERT BRUCE OGILVY . . . . 29 Feb. 1964

MARINA VICTORIA ALEXANDRA OGILVY . . . . 31 July 1966

Residence: Thatched House Lodge, Richmond, Surrey; *office:* Kensington Palace, W8 4PU.

SUPPLEMENT

TO WHO'S WHO 1978

Part I of this Supplement contains a selection of the alterations and additions too late for inclusion in the body of the book, noted up to late December 1977.

Part II of the Supplement contains a selection of names included in the New Year Honours List, 1978.

SUPPLEMENT: PART I

ABEL-SMITH, Prof. Brian. Adviser to Commissioner for Social Affairs, European Commission, since 1977.

ABERDEEN and ORKNEY, Bishop of. *See infra* Darwent.

ADAMS, Air Vice-Marshal Alexander Annan. Director, Mental Health Foundation, 1970-77.

AIKEN, Air Chief Marshal Sir John (Alexander Carlisle). Air Member for Personnel, 1976-78.

ALLINSON, Walter Leonard. Minister, New Delhi, 1975-78.

ANDERSON, Prof. Ephraim Saul. Director, Enteric Reference Laboratory, Public Health Laboratory Service, 1954-77; Visiting Professor, School of Biological Sciences, Brunel University, 1973-77.

ANYAOKU, Eleazar Chukwuemeka, (Emeka). A Deputy Secretary-General of the Commonwealth, since 1978.

ARCHER, Lt-Gen. Sir (Arthur) John. C-in-C UK Land Forces from April 1978, in the rank of General.

ARUNDEL and BRIGHTON, Bishop of, (RC). *See infra* Murphy-O'Connor.

ASHTON, Sir Frederick (William Mallandaine). OM 1977.

ASHTON, Joseph William. An Assistant Government Whip, 1976-77.

ASTWOOD, Lt-Col Sir Jeffrey (Carlton). Chief Justice of Bermuda, since 1977.

ATHABASCA, Bishop of; Rt. Rev. Frederick Hugh Wright Crabb. Now Archbishop of Athabasca and Metropolitan of Rupert's Land.

***ATKINSON, David Anthony.** MP (C) Bournemouth East, since Nov. 1977.

AYER, Sir Alfred (Jules). Wykeham Professor of Logic in the University of Oxford, 1959-Sept. 1978.

BAIN, John Taylor. Lay Observer in Scotland, since 1977.

BAKER, John Randal. *Address:* Laura Cottage, Bank, near Lyndhurst, Hants SO4 2EG.

BALL, Air Marshal Sir Alfred (Henry Wynne). Deputy Commander-in-Chief, RAF Strike Command, since 1977.

BANCROFT, Sir Ian Powell. Head of the Home Civil Service and Permanent Secretary, Civil Service Department, since 1978.

BARBACK, Ronald Henry. Deputy Director (Economics) and Head, Economic Research, Confederation of British Industry, since 1977.

BARNES, Clive Alexander. Associate Editor and Chief Drama and Dance Critic, New York Post, since 1977.

BARNES, Michael Cecil John. Chairman, Electricity Consumers' Council, since 1977.

BARR, Rev. Prof. James. Regius Professor of Hebrew, Oxford University, from Sept. 1978.

BARRON, Rt. Rev. Patrick Harold Falkiner. Bishop of George, 1966-77.

BASS, Harry Godfrey Mitchell. Chapter Clerk, St. George's Chapel, Windsor, 1974-Dec. 1977.

BEAUCHAMP, Charles Edward. Acting Board Member for Finance and Corporate Planning, Post Office Corporation, 1977-78.

BELL DAVIES, Vice-Adm. Sir Lancelot (Richard). Commandant, NATO Defence College, Rome, from 28 July 1978. *Address:* NATO Defence College, Viale della Civiltà del Lavorno 38, Roma 00144, Italy.

BENTON, Gordon William. *Address:* 21 Lodge Gardens, Alverstoke, Hants PO12 3PY.

BERTHON, Vice-Adm. Stephen Ferrier. Deputy Chief of Defence Staff (Operational Requirements), since 1978.

BINNY, John Anthony Francis. Chairman, Associated Portland Cement Manufacturers, 1975-May 1978.

BIRKS, Dr Jack. A Managing Director, British Petroleum, since 1978.

BLAKE, Alfred (Lapthorn). Director, The Duke of Edinburgh's Award Scheme, 1967-June 1978.

BLUNDELL, Sir (Edward) Denis. QSO 1977.

BLYTH, 3rd Baron, *See* Obituary and *p* 237 for heir.

BOARDMAN, John. Lincoln Professor of Classical Archaeology and Art, University of Oxford, from Oct. 1978.

BODEN, Edward Arthur. Agent-General for Saskatchewan, 1973-77. *Address:* 289 Coldwell Road, Regina, Saskatchewan S4R 4L4, Canada.

BOOTH, Charles Leonard. Ambassador in Rangoon, since 1978.

BOWRING, Edgar Rennie Harvey. Chairman, The Bowring Group of Companies, 1973-May 1978.

BRADBURY, Rear-Adm. Thomas Henry. Chief Naval Supply and Secretariat Officer, since 1978.

BRAIN, Albert Edward Arnold. Regional Director (East Midlands), Department of the Environment, and Chairman of Regional Economic Planning Board, 1972-77.

* The current edition contains no entry under this name.

BRAMALL, Gen. Sir Edwin (Noel Westby). Vice Chief of the Defence Staff, since 1978.

BRANDT, Willy. Chairman, Commission on Development Issues, since 1977.

BRANSON, Rear Adm. Cecil Robert Peter Charles. *Address:* The Old Parsonage, West End, Swanland, North Humberside.

BRANT, Colin Trevor. Ambassador to Qatar, since 1978. *Address:* c/o Foreign and Commonwealth Office, SW1.

BRASH, Rev. Alan Anderson. Moderator, Presbyterian Church of New Zealand, from Nov. 1978. *Address:* Presbyterian Church of New Zealand, Dalmuir House, 114 The Terrace, Wellington 1, NZ.

BRITTAN, Leon. *Address:* 14 Ponsonby Terrace, SW1P 4QA. *T:* 01-821 7290.

BROKE, Major George Robin Straton. MVO 1977.

BROWN, Rt. Rev. Laurence Ambrose. Priest-in-Charge of Odstock with Nunton and Bodenham, dio. of Salisbury, since 1978.

BROWN, Ven. Michael René Warneford. Now Archdeacon Emeritus. *Address:* Faygate, Liverpool Road, Walmer, Deal, Kent. *T:* unchanged.

BRUCE, Prof. Frederick Fyvie. Rylands Professor of Biblical Criticism and Exegesis, University of Manchester, 1959-Sept. 1978.

BULLER, Prof. Arthur John. Chief Scientist, Department of Health and Social Security (on secondment), since 1978 (part-time, Jan.-July 1978).

BURNS, Arthur F. Chairman, Board of Governors of the Federal Reserve System in the United States, 1970-78.

BUTLER, Keith Stephenson. *Address:* Easter Cottage, Westbrook, Boxford, near Newbury, Berks.

CADBURY, Kenneth Hotham. Deputy Managing Director, Telecommunications, Post Office, since 1978.

CAMBRIDGE, Sydney John Guy. Ambassador to Kuwait, since 1977.

CAMERON, Prof. Alan Douglas Edward. *Address:* 454 Riverside Drive, New York, NY 10027, USA. *T:* 662 9319.

CAMPBELL, Robin Francis. Director of Art, Arts Council of Great Britain, 1969-78.

CAVENDISH-BENTINCK, Victor Frederick William. Now Cavendish-Bentinck, Lord (Victor Frederick) William; granted, 1977, the same title and precedence that would have been due to him if his father had succeeded to the dukedom of Portland.

CHAMPERNOWNE, David Gawen. *Address:* 25 Worts Causeway, Cambridge CB1 4RJ.

CHESTER, Dean of. *See infra* Cleasby.

CHESTERFIELD, Archdeacon of (1963-77). *See infra* Cleasby.

CHESWORTH, Donald Piers. Director, Notting Hill Social Council, 1967-77. *Address:* Toynbee Hall, Universities' Settlement in East London, 28 Commercial Street, E1 6LS. *T:* 01-247 3633.

CHRISTIE, Charles Henry. Director of Studies, Britannia Royal Naval College, Dartmouth, from Sept. 1978. *Address:* Britannia Royal Naval College, Dartmouth, Devon TQ6 0HJ.

CHRISTIE, John Rankin. Deputy Master and Comptroller of the Royal Mint, 1974-77.

CLARKSON, Derek Joshua. *T:* Harrogate 504673.

CLEASBY, Very Rev. Thomas Wood Ingram. Dean of Chester since 1977.

CLORE, Sir Charles. President, Sears Holdings Ltd, since 1978.

CLUTTERBUCK, Edmund Harry Michael. Deputy Chairman, Scottish & Newcastle Breweries Ltd, 1973-77.

COCKERILL, Geoffrey Fairfax. Secretary, University Grants Committee, since 1978.

COLE, Ven. Ronald Berkeley. Also Residentiary Canon of Leicester Cathedral, since 1977.

COMYN, James. Judge of the High Court of Justice, Family Division, since 1978.

COPLAND, Very Rev. Charles McAlester. Dean of the Diocese of Argyll and the Isles since 1977.

COSTELLO, Gordon John. Chief Accountant of the Bank of England, 1975-78.

COUNSELL, Hazel Rosemary. A Circuit Judge, since 1978.

COUPER, Sir (Robert) Nicholas (Oliver), 6th Bt. *Heir: s, b* 27 Oct. 1977.

COWDRAY, Viscount. Chairman, S. Pearson & Son Ltd, 1954-77.

COWEN, Sir Zelman. GCMG 1977.

CRAIGIE, Dr Hugh Brechin. *Address:* Saviskaill, Westerdunes Park, North Berwick.

CRANE, Prof. Francis Roger. Professor of Law, Queen Mary College, University of London, 1965-Sept. 1978.

CRAWFORD, David Gordon. Ambassador to Qatar, 1974-78.

CRICHTON, David George. *Address:* Church House, Medstead, Alton, Hampshire. *T:* Alton 62632.

CRICHTON, Sir (John) Robertson (Dunn). Judge of the High Court of Justice, Queen's Bench Division, 1967-77.

CUNNINGHAM, Lt.-Gen. Sir Hugh (Patrick). Deputy Chief of Defence Staff (Operational Requirements), 1976-78.

CURRIE, (Joseph) Austin. Research Fellow, Faculty of Economic and Social Studies, Trinity College, Dublin, 1977-78.

CURRIE, Piers William Edward. Deputy Master, Court of Protection, 1971-77.

DANN, Most Rev. Robert William. Archbishop of Melbourne, since 1977. *Address:* Bishopscourt, Clarendon Street, Melbourne, Vic 3002, Australia.

DARWENT, Rt. Rev. Frederick Charles. Bishop of Aberdeen and Orkney since 1978.

DAVIES, Air Marshal Alan Cyril. Director International Military Staff, NATO, Brussels, since 1978.

DAVIS, William. *Address:* Headway Publications, 4 Golden Square, W1.

DENBIGH, Kenneth George. Emeritus Professor in the University of London, 1977; Director, Council for Science and Society, since 1977.

DENHAM, Baron. Opposition Chief Whip, House of Lords, since 1978.

de TRAFFORD, Dermot Humphrey. Director, Low & Bonar Group, since 1977.

DHENIN, Air Marshal Sir Geoffrey (Howard). Director-General, Medical Services (RAF), 1974-78.

DICKSON, Ian Anderson. Sheriff of South Strathclyde, Dumfries and Galloway, at Hamilton, 1961-77.

DOBSON, Sir Richard (Portway). Chairman, British Leyland Ltd, 1976-77.

DONALD, Alan Ewen. Ambassador to the Republic of Zaire and concurrently Ambassador (non-resident) to the Republic of Burundi and to the Republic of Rwanda, since 1977.

DONALDSON, David Abercrombie. Her Majesty's Painter and Limner in Scotland, since 1977.

DOUGLAS, Gavin Stuart. *Address:* Parliament House, Parliament Square, Edinburgh 1.

DUNBAR-NASMITH, James Duncan. Professor and Head of Department of Architecture, Heriot-Watt University, since 1978.

DUNDAS, Group Captain Hugh Spencer Lisle. Chairman: Humphries Holdings Ltd, 1975-77; Redifon, 1970-78.

EDWARDES, Michael Owen. Chairman, British Leyland, since 1977; non-executive Deputy Chairman, Chloride Group, since 1977 (formerly Chairman and Chief Executive). *Address:* Nuffield House, 41-46 Piccadilly, W1V 0BD. *T:* 01-734 6080.

EDWARDS, John Braham Scott. A Circuit Judge, since 1977.

EHRMAN, John Patrick William. Hon. Treasurer, Friends of the National Libraries, 1960-77.

ELDERFIELD, Maurice. Finance Director, British Shipbuilders, since 1977.

ELDRIDGE, John Barron. Chairman, Matthews Wrightson Holdings Ltd, 1971-77.

ELTON, (Peter) John. Deputy Chairman and Chief Executive, Hill Samuel & Co. Ltd, since 1978.

EMERY, Joyce Margaret. Secretary of the Post Office, 1975-77.

EWANS, Martin Kenneth. Minister, New Delhi, since 1978.

EWART, Sir (William) Ivan (Cecil). East Africa Regional Representative, Royal Commonwealth Society for the Blind, since 1977. *Address:* PO Box 46656, Nairobi, Kenya.

FABER, Richard Stanley. Ambassador to Algeria, since 1977.

FAIRHAVEN, Baron. Vice Lord-Lieutenant, Cambridgeshire, since 1977.

FARNHAM, Baron. Chairman, Avon Rubber Co., since 1978.

FATEH, A. F. M. Abul. Ambassador of Bangladesh at Algiers, since 1977. *Address:* Bangladesh Embassy, 141 Boulevard Salah Bouakouir, 5th Floor, Algiers, Algeria.

FAULKS, Sir Neville (Major Ginner). Judge of the High Court of Justice, Family Division, 1963-77.

FEILDEN, Geoffrey Bertram Robert. President, European Committee for Standardisation, since 1977.

FIDDES, James Raffan. Sheriff of South Strathclyde, Dumfries and Galloway at Hamilton, since 1977.

FINDLAY, Ian Herbert Fyfe. Chairman of Lloyd's, 1978.

FitzCLARENCE, Viscount. *Address:* 1 Lessar Avenue, SW4. *T:* 01-673 1489.

FRANKEL, Prof. Joseph. Professor of Politics, University of Southampton, 1963-Aug. 1978.

FRANKS, Baron. OM 1977.

FROST, Albert Edward. Director, British Leyland Ltd, since 1977.

GARLICK, Sir John. Permanent Secretary, Department of the Environment, since 1978.

GEDLING, Raymond. Deputy Secretary, Department of Health and Social Security, 1971-77.

GEORGE, Bishop of. *See supra* Barron.

GIBSON, Baron. Chairman: Financial Times Ltd, 1975-77; S. Pearson & Son Ltd, since 1978.

GIBSON, Sir Christopher (Herbert). *Address:* 1603 1-A Street S, Cranbrook, BC V1C 1B9, Canada.

GINGELL, Air Marshal John. Air Member for Personnel, since Feb. 1978.

GODFREY, Derrick Edward Reid. Director, Thames Polytechnic, 1970-78.

GOLDMANN, Dr Nahum. President of the World Jewish Congress, 1951-77.

GOPALLAWA, William. President of Sri Lanka, 1972-77. *Address:* 128 Dharmapala Mawatha, Matale, Sri Lanka.

GORDON, Gerald Henry. Sheriff of Glasgow and Strathkelvin at Glasgow, since 1978.

GRAHAM, Maj.-Gen. John David Carew. General Officer Commanding Wales, 1976-78; Secretary, The Chevening Trust, since 1978. *Address:* The Lodge, Chevening, Sevenoaks, Kent TN14 6HG.

GRANDY, Marshal of the Royal Air Force Sir John. Governor and Commander-in-Chief, Gibraltar, 1973-78. *Address:* 7 Vale House, De Vere Gardens, W8 5AQ.

GRAY, Prof. Edward George. Head of the Laboratory of Ultrastructure, National Institute for Medical Research, Mill Hill, since 1977.

GREENHILL OF HARROW, Baron. Director, British Leyland Ltd, 1975-77.

GREY, Col Geoffrey Bridgman. Chairman, West Midlands TA & VRA, 1970-77.

GRIST, John Frank. United States Representative, BBC, since 1978. *Address:* 630 5th Avenue, New York, NY 10020, USA.

HADDOW, Prof. Alexander John. Administrative Dean, Faculty of Medicine, 1970-78, and Professor of Administrative Medicine, 1971-78, University of Glasgow.

HAITINK, Bernard. Hon. KBE 1977.

HALSEY, Dr Albert Henry. Professor of Social and Administrative Studies, Oxford University, since 1978.

HAMYLTON JONES, Keith. *Address:* Morval House, Morval, near Looe, Cornwall.

HARE, Hon. Alan Victor. Chairman, Financial Times Ltd, since 1978.

HARGREAVES, Prof. John Desmond. *Address:* Balcluain, Raemoir Road, Banchory, Kincardine AB3 3UJ. *T:* Banchory 2655.

HARLECH, Baron. Chairman, Royal Institute of International Affairs, since 1978.

HARMSWORTH, Sir Hildebrand Alfred Beresford, 2nd Bt. *See* Obituary and *p* 1062 for heir.

HARPER, John Mansfield. Assistant Managing Director, Post Office Telecommunications, since 1978.

HARRISON, Denis Byrne. *Address:* Doucegrove Farm, Northiam, near Rye, East Sussex; London address unchanged.

HAYWARD, Sir Richard (Arthur). Chairman, New Towns Staff Commission, 1976-77.

HEINZ, Henry John, II. Hon KBE 1977.

HENDERSON, Julie Juanita. Secretary-General, International Planned Parenthood Federation, 1971-77.

HENDERSON, Robert Alistair. Chairman, Kleinwort, Benson, Lonsdale Ltd, since 1978.

HENLEY, 7th Baron. Died 20 Dec. 1977. *See p* 1114 for heir.

HENNINGS, John Dunn. High Commissioner in Singapore, since 1978.

HERBERT, Robin Arthur Elidyr. Chairman, Leopold Joseph Holdings Ltd, from July 1978.

HEWITT, Rev. Canon George Henry Gordon. Residentiary Canon, Chelmsford Cathedral, 1964-April 1978; Canon Emeritus from 1978.

HODGSON, Maurice Arthur Eric. Chairman, ICI Ltd, since 1978.

HOLDSWORTH, Albert Edward. *Address:* Sutton Gate, Sutton, Pulborough, West Sussex RH20 1PN.

HOLLAND, Rt. Rev. Alfred Charles. Bishop of Newcastle, NSW, since Feb. 1978.

HOLLENDEN, 2nd Baron. *see* Obituary and *infra* Hope-Morley.

HOLLINGSWORTH, Dorothy Frances. Director-General, British Nutrition Foundation, 1970-77.

HOLT, Prof. James Clarke. Professorial Fellow, Emanuel College, Cambridge, from Oct. 1978.

HOPE, Sir Archibald (Philip). Chairman, Airline Users' Committee, since 1977.
HOPE-MORLEY, Gordon Hope. Succeeded uncle as 3rd Baron Hollenden, 1977.
HUNTER JOHNSTON, David Alan. Chairman, Association of Investment Trust Companies, 1975-77.
HURFORD, Peter John. Master of the Music, Cathedral and Abbey Church of St. Alban, 1958-Aug. 1978.
HUTTON, Gabriel Bruce. A Circuit Judge, since 1978.

ILLINGWORTH, Raymond. Captain, Leicestershire County Cricket Club, 1969-Sept. 1978.

JACKSON, Glenda. *Address:* c/o Crouch-Salmon Associates, Suite 7, 3-5 Bateman Street, W1.
JACKSON, Gen. Sir William (Godfrey Fothergill). Governor and Commander-in-Chief, Gibraltar, since 1978. *Address:* The Convent, Gibraltar.
JACOBS, Sir Wilfred (Ebenezer). KCVO 1977.
JAMES, John Richings. Professor of Town and Regional Planning, University of Sheffield, 1967-Sept. 1978.
JOHNSTONE, Mrs Dorothy (Christian Liddle). European Affairs Adviser, BAT Industries Ltd, 1976-77.

KEARTON, Baron. Chairman, Electricity Supply Research Council, 1960-77 (Member, 1954-77).
KENNEDY, William Quarrier. *Address:* 2 Stone Rings Lane, Harrogate, N Yorks.
KINGSTON-UPON-THAMES, Bishop Suffragan of. *See infra* Sutton.
KLEINWORT, Sir Alexander Santiago, 2nd Bt. Heir now *nephew* Kenneth Drake Kleinwort.
KLEINWORT, Sir Cyril (Hugh). Chairman, Kleinwort, Benson, Lonsdale Ltd, 1968-77.
KNIGHT, Edmund Alan. European Affairs Adviser, British-American Tobacco Company Ltd, since 1978.
KOEPPLER, Sir Henry, (Sir Heinz), Educational Consultant, Shell International Petroleum Company, since 1977.

LAMB, Albert Thomas. Ambassador to Norway, since 1978.
LANGDON, Alfred Gordon. *Address:* 1763 Main Street, Apt 171 K, Dunedin, Fla 33528, USA.
LAWSON, Nigel An Opposition Whip, 1976-77; an Opposition Spokesman on Treasury and Economic Affairs, since 1977.
LEACH, Prof. Sir Edmund Ronald. Provost of King's College, Cambridge, 1966-Jan 1979; Professor of Social Anthropology, 1972-Sept. 1978.
LECHMERE, Sir Berwick (Hungerford). Vice Lord-Lieutenant, Hereford and Worcester, since 1977.
LENNARD, Sir (Thomas) Richard (Fiennes) Barrett-, 5th Bt. Died 28 Dec. 1977. *See p* 1441 for heir.
LLOYD, Anthony (John Leslie). Judge of the High Court of Justice, Queen's Bench Division, since 1978.
LLOYD, Richard Ernest Butler. Deputy Chairman, Hill Samuel & Co. Ltd, and Director, Hill Samuel Group Ltd, since 1978.
LORD, Cyril. *Address:* c/o Coutts & Co., 16 Cavendish Square, W1.
LOUGHBOROUGH, Lord. Succeeded father as 7th Earl of Rosslyn, 1977.
LOWRY, John Patrick. Director of Personnel and Administration, British Leyland Ltd, since 1977.
LOWTHIAN, George Henry. Part-time Member, British Transport Docks Board, 1963-77.
LYGO, Adm. Sir Raymond Derek. Vice-Chief of Naval Staff, 1975-78.
LYNCH, Rt. Hon Phillip Reginald. Minister for Industry and Commerce, Australia, since 1977.
LYONS, Sir Rudolph. Honorary Recorder of Manchester, since 1977.

MACDONALD, Ian Wilson. Deputy Chairman, National and Commercial Banking Group Ltd, 1969-78.
McGIRR, Prof. Edward McCombie. Professor of Administrative Medicine, and Administrative Dean of the Faculty of Medicine, University of Glasgow, since 1978.
McHARDY, Prof. William Duff. Regius Professor of Hebrew, Oxford University, 1960-Sept. 1978.
MacKINNON, Prof. Donald MacKenzie. Norris-Hulse Professor of Divinity, Cambridge University, 1960-Sept. 1978.
MACLEOD OF BORVE, Baroness. Chairman, National Gas Consumers' Council, 1972-77.
MACPHERSON, Colin. Chairman, Commission for the New Towns, since 1978.
MANCHESTER, 10th Duke of. Died 23 Nov. 1977. *See infra* Mandeville.
MANDEVILLE, Viscount. Succeeded father as 11th Duke of Manchester, 1977.
MARDER, Prof. Arthur Jacob. *Address:* 730 Woodland Drive, Santa Barbara, Calif 93108, USA. *T:* (805) 969-4491.
MARSABIT, Bishop of, (RC); Rt. Rev. Charles Cavallera. *Address:* PO Box 6, Marsabit, Kenya.
MARSHALL, James. An Assistant Government Whip, since 1977.
MASON, Prof. Ronald. Chief Scientific Adviser, Ministry of Defence, since 1977. *Additional address:* Ministry of Defence, Main Building, Whitehall, SW1A 2HB.
MAURITIUS, Bishop of. Rt. Rev. Trevor Huddleston, Bishop of Stepney, *qv,* will become Bishop of Mauritius in May 1978.
MAXWELL, Sir Robert Hugh. *Address:* Le Colomby, 01170 Gex, France.
MENDIS, Vernon Lorraine Benjamin. Ambassador for the Republic of Sri Lanka in France, since 1977. *Address:* Embassy of the Republic of Sri Lanka, 61 quai d'Orsay, 75007 Paris, France.
MEREDITH, Richard Alban Creed. Head master of Monkton Combe School from Aug. 1978. *Address:* Head Master's House, Monkton Combe School, Bath.
MEYJES, Sir Richard Anthony. Chairman, Coates Brothers and Co. Ltd, since 1977.
MILES, Frank Stephen. High Commissioner in Bangladesh, since 1978.
MILLS, Peter William. Manager, Toronto Office, Currie, Coopers & Lybrand Ltd, since 1977. *Address:* Currie, Coopers & Lybrand Ltd, 145 King Street West, Toronto, Ont M5H 1J8, Canada; 390 Glencairn Avenue, Toronto, Ont M5N 1V1.
MITCHELL, Alec Burton. Director, Admiralty Marine Technology Establishment, since 1977.
MONCREIFFE of that Ilk, Sir (Rupert) Iain (Kay). Chairman, Debrett's Peerage, since 1977.
MORTIMER, Penelope (Ruth). *Address:* 113 Broadhurst Gardens, NW6.
MORTON, Vice-Adm. Sir Anthony Storrs. Vice Chief of Naval Staff, since 1978.
MOWBRAY, SEGRAVE and STOURTON, Baron. Deputy Opposition Whip, House of Lords, since 1978.
MUIR, (Isabella) Helen (Mary). Also Director, Kennedy Institute of Rheumatology, since 1977.
MUNRO, Alan Gordon. Head of East African Department, Foreign and Commonwealth Office, since 1977.
MURPHY-O'CONNOR, Rt. Rev. Mgr. Cormac. Bishop of Arundel and Brighton, (RC), since 1978.

NEDEN, Sir Wilfred John. *Address:* Courtneys, 36 Forest Drive, Keston Park, Keston, Kent BR2 6EF. *T:* Farnborough 51936.
NEWBY, (Percy) Howard. Managing Director, BBC Radio, 1975-78.
NEWCASTLE, NSW, Bishop of. *See supra* Holland.
NEWTON-CLARE, Herbert Mitchell. Director, FMC Ltd, 1976-77; Managing Director, FMC Harris Products Division, 1976-77.
NODDER, Timothy Edward. Deputy Secretary, Department of Health and Social Security, since 1978.

OATES, Sir Thomas. *Address:* Tristan, Trevone, Padstow, Cornwall.
O'BRIEN, Conor Cruise. Editor-in-Chief, The Observer, since 1978.
O'BRIEN, Terence John. Ambassador in Jakarta, since 1978.
O'CONNOR, Prof. Daniel John. Professor of Philosophy, University of Exeter, since 1957. *Address:* University of Exeter, Queen's Building, The Queen's Drive, Exeter EX4 4QH.
OGILVIE, Sir Alec (Drummond). Chairman, Powell Duffryn Ltd, 1969-July 1978.

PARKINSON, Desmond John. *Address:* Bourton Orchard, Penselwood, Wincanton, Somerset. *T:* Bourton (Dorset) 423.
PAZ, Octavio. *Address:* c/o Revista Vuelta, Fresas Núm. 13, Col. del Valle, México 12, DF, México.
PEARSON, Sir Neville. President of St. Dunstan's, 1947-77.
PERKINS, Dexter. *Address:* The Brightonian, 1919 Elmwood Avenue, Rochester, NY 14620, USA.
PEROWNE, Rear-Adm. Benjamin Cubitt. Director, Management and Support Intelligence, since 1976, also Chief Naval Supply and Secretariat Officer, 1977-78.
PETRIE, Sir Charles (Alexander), 3rd Bt. Died 13 Dec. 1977. *See p* 1923 for heir.
PHILIPS, Prof. Sir Cyril Henry. Chairman, Royal Commission on Criminal Procedure, since 1978.
PIGOT, Maj.-Gen. Sir Robert Anthony, 7th Bt. Succeeded to baronetcy of uncle, Brig.-Gen. Sir Robert Pigot, 6th Bt, who died 27 Dec. 1977.
PILCHER, Sir (Charlie) Dennis. Chairman, Commission for the New Towns, 1971-78.
POSNETT, Richard Neil. United Kingdom Commissioner, British Phosphate Commissioners, since 1978.
PRICE, Very Rev. Hilary Martin Connop. Provost Emeritus since 1977.
PUGH, John Stanley. Editor, Liverpool Echo, since 1978.

RAMSEY, Sir Alfred (Ernest). Consultant, Birmingham City Football Club, since 1977.
RANGER, Douglas. *Address:* The Tile House, The Street, Chipperfield, King's Langley, Herts WD4 9BH. *T:* King's Langley 68910.
RATTER, John. Consultant. *Address:* Old Timbers, Poole Street, Great Yeldham, Essex.
REES, Sir (Charles William) Stanley. Judge of the High Court of Justice, Family Division, 1962-77.
REMNANT, Baron. Chairman, Association of Investment Trust Companies, since 1977.
RICHARDSON, Gen. Sir Charles (Leslie). Chief Royal Engineer, 1972-77.
ROBERTS, Eirlys Rhiwen Cadwaladr. Chief Executive, Bureau of European Consumer Organisations, 1973-77.
ROBERTSON, Ronald Foote. Physician to the Queen in Scotland, since 1977.
ROGERS, Hugh Charles Innes. Chairman, Avon Rubber Co., 1968-78.
ROSSLYN, 6th Earl of. Died 22 Nov. 1977. *See supra* Loughborough.
ROWALLAN, 2nd Baron. Died 30 Nov. 1977. *See p* 2130 for heir.
ROZHDESTVENSKY, Gennadi Nikolaevich. Chief Conductor, Stockholm Philharmonic Orchestra, 1974-77.

ST. ALDWYN, Earl. Opposition Chief Whip, House of Lords, 1974-77.
SCHWEITZER, Pierre-Paul. Chairman, Bank of America International, Luxembourg, 1974-77.
SCOTT, Sir (Charles) Peter. Ambassador to Norway, 1975-78.
SELBY, Bishop Suffragan of. *Address:* Greenriggs, 8 Bankside Close, Upper Poppleton, York YO2 6LH. *T:* York 795342.
SIMON, William Edward. Member of the Board of Directors: Citibank and Citicorp; INA Corporation; Senior Advisor, Booz Allen & Hamilton; President, John M. Olin Foundation; Senior Consultant, Blyth Eastman Dillon & Co. Inc. *Address:* Sand Spring Road, New Vernon, NJ 07976, USA.
SINGER, Aubrey Edward. Managing Director, BBC Radio, since 1978.
SMALLMAN, Barry Granger. High Commissioner in Bangladesh, 1975-78.
SNAITH, George Robert. Director of Research, British Shipbuilders, since 1977.
SNAPE, Peter Charles. A Lord Commissioner, HM Treasury, since 1977.
SOUTAR, Air Marshal John Williamson. Director-General, Medical Services (RAF), since 1978.
STARK, Sir Andrew (Alexander Steel). Deputy Under-Secretary of State, Foreign and Commonwealth Office, 1976-77.
STODDART, David Leonard. A Lord Commissioner, HM Treasury, 1976-77.
STOKER, Prof. Michael George Parke. *Address:* 16 Storey's Way, Cambridge CB3 0DT.
SUMMERFIELD, Hon. Sir John (Crampton). Chief Justice of Bermuda, 1972-77. *Address:* c/o The Grand Court, Grand Cayman, Cayman Islands, West Indies.
SUTTON, Rt. Rev. Keith Norman. Bishop Suffragan of Kingston-upon-Thames since 1978.
SUTTON, Thomas Francis. General Manager, J. Walter Thompson Co. Japan, Tokyo, since 1972. *Address:* 1401 Azabu Towers, 2-1-3 Azabudai, Minuto-Ku, Tokyo 106, Japan.
SWEETMAN, Seamus George. Vice-Chairman, Unilever Ltd, 1974-May 1978.
SYMINGTON, Professor Sir Thomas. Director, Institute of Cancer Research, 1970-77.

TEMPLE, Ernest Sanderson. Honorary Recorder of Liverpool, since 1977.
THORNTON, Jack Edward Clive. Chief Education Adviser and Under Secretary, Ministry of Overseas Development, 1970-77.
TITFORD, Rear-Adm. Donald George. Deputy Controller of Aircraft, Ministry of Defence, 1976-78.
TREVELYAN, Dennis John. Deputy Under-Secretary of State, Home Office, and Director-General, Prison Service, since 1978.
TREVOR, William, (William Trevor Cox). CBE (Hon.) 1977.
TRIPP, John Peter. High Commissioner in Singapore, 1974-78.
TRYPANIS, Constantine Athanasius. Minister of Culture and Science, Government of Greece, 1974-77.

TURNER, Eric Gardner. Professor of Papyrology, University College London, 1950-78.
TURNER, Sir (Ronald) Mark (Cunliffe). Deputy Chairman, Kleinwort, Benson, Lonsdale Ltd, 1969-77.

VINE, Philip Mesban. Chairman, New Towns Staff Commission, since 1977.

WADDELL, Sir Alexander (Nicol Anton). United Kingdom Commissioner, British Phosphate Commissioners, 1965-77.
WADE, Air Chief Marshal Sir Ruthven (Lowry). Chief of Personnel and Logistics, Ministry of Defence, 1976-78.
WATERHOUSE, Ronald Gough. Judge of the High Court of Justice, Family Division, since 1978.
WEEKS, Sir Hugh (Thomas). Chairman, Leopold Joseph Holdings Ltd, 1966-July 1978.
WENGER, Marjorie Lawson. *Address:* 6 Concord Close, Paddock Wood, Tonbridge, Kent TN12 6UJ. *T:* Paddock Wood 2699.
WHITEHORN, John Roland Malcolm. A Deputy Director-General, Confederation of British Industry, 1966-78.
WHITLAM, Hon. (Edward) Gough. Leader of the Opposition, Australia, 1976-77.
WHITTET, Dr Thomas Douglas. Chief Pharmacist, Department of Health and Social Security, 1967-78.
WILLIAMS, Arthur Vivian. *Address:* Monks, Lindsey, Ipswich. *T:* Boxford 210039.
WILLISON, Lt-Gen. Sir David (John). Chief Royal Engineer, since 1977.
WINSTANLEY, Baron. Chairman, Countryside Commission, since 1978.
WORTH, Irene. *Address:* c/o ICM Sixth Floor, Milton Goldman, 40 West 57th Street, New York, NY 10019, USA.
WRIGHT, Claud William. Research Fellow, Wolfson College, Oxford, since 1977.
WRIGHT, Eric David. Deputy Under-Secretary of State, Home Office, and Director-General, Prison Service, 1973-77. *Address:* 32 Valley Road, Rickmansworth, Herts. WD3 4DS.
WRIGHT, Sir Rowland (Sydney). Chairman, ICI Ltd, 1975-78; Chairman, Associated Portland Cement Manufacturers, from May 1978. *Address:* Portland House, Stag Place, SW1E 5BJ.

YOUNG, Sir Stephen Stewart Templeton. Advocate, since 1977. *Address:* 18 Moray Place, Edinburgh EH3 6DT.

SUPPLEMENT: PART II

A SELECTION OF NAMES IN THE NEW YEAR HONOURS LIST: 31 DEC. 1977

ADAMS, Ernest Victor. CB 1978.
AKERS-JONES, David. CMG 1978.
ALLEN, Sir Douglas Albert Vivian. Baron (Life Peer), cr 1978.
ALVINGHAM, Baron. CBE 1978.
ATTLEE, Air Vice-Marshal Donald Laurence. CB 1978.
AUTY, Richard Mossop. CBE 1978.

BAGNALL, Maj.-Gen. Nigel Thomas. CVO 1978.
BAILLIE, Dame Isobel. DBE 1978.
BANWELL, Derick Frank. CBE 1978.
*BARKER, Sir Harry Heaton. KBE 1978. For services to city of Gisborne, New Zealand.
BARRACLOUGH, Sir Kenneth James Priestley. Kt 1978.
BATE, Sir David Lindsay. KBE 1978.
BATES, Sir David Robert. Kt 1978.
BAYLISS, Sir Richard Ian Samuel. KCVO 1978.
BECKETT, William Cartwright. CB 1978.
BEETHAM, Air Chief Marshal Sir Michael (James). GCB 1978.
BLUNT, Maj.-Gen. Peter. CB 1978.
BOND, Maurice Francis. CB 1978.
BRIERLEY, John David. CB 1978.
BROWN, Joseph Lawler. CBE 1978.
BUNCH, Austin Wyeth. CBE 1978.
BUTTERFIELD, Sir William John Hughes. Kt 1978.

CAMPBELL, Douglas Mason. CBE 1978.
CAMPBELL, Robin Francis. CBE 1978.
*CARMODY, Sir Alan Thomas. Kt 1978. For distinguished public service, Australia.
CARTER, Sir Charles Frederick. Kt 1978.
*CASS, Sir John Patrick. Kt 1978. Chairman, Australian Wheat Board
CECIL, Rear-Adm. Oswald Nigel Amherst. CB 1978.
CHARTERIS, Rt. Hon. Sir Martin Michael Charles. Baron (Life Peer), cr 1978.
CHEETHAM, John Frederick Thomas. CB 1978.
CHRISTOPHERSON, Harald Fairbairn. CMG 1978.
*CHUNG, Sir Sze-yuen. Kt 1978. For public services in Hong Kong.
CLAYTON, Vice-Adm. Sir Richard Pilkington. KCB 1978.
COBB, Richard Charles. CBE 1978.
COHEN, Prof. Sydney. CBE 1978.
CONCANNON, Rt. Hon. John Dennis. PC 1978.
COPE, James Francis. CMG 1978.
*COTTON, Hon. Sir Robert Carrington. KCMG 1978. For distinguished public and parliamentary service, Australia.
*COVACEVICH, Sir Anthony Thomas. Kt 1978. For services to the welfare of the people of North Queensland.
CREASEY, Lt.-Gen. Sir Timothy May. KCB 1978.
CROCKER, Sir Walter Russell. KBE 1978.
CROOK, Kenneth Roy. CMG 1978.

DAVEY, William. CBE 1978.
DAVIES, Rt. Hon. (David John) Denzil. PC 1978.
DAVIS, Sir (Ernest) Howard. Kt 1978.

DEXTER, Dr Keith. CB 1978.
DICK, Air Vice-Marshal Alan David. CB 1978.
* DURACK, Dame Mary. DBE 1978. For distinguished service to literature, Australia.

EDE, Jeffery Raymond. CB 1978.
EGERTON, Stephen Loftus. CMG 1978.
ELLIS, Sir Ronald. Kt 1978.
ERSKINE, Ralph. CBE 1978.
EVANS, Richard Mark. CMG 1978.

FARVIS, Prof. William Ewart John. CBE 1978.
FINNEY, Prof. David John. CBE 1978.
*FOLEY, Sir Thomas John Noel. Kt 1978. For distinguished service to industry, Australia.
FRASER, Sir (James) Campbell. Kt 1978.
FRASER, (William) Kerr. CB 1978.
FREEDMAN, Louis. CBE 1978.
FREETH, Hon. Sir Gordon. KBE 1978.
FRODSHAM, Anthony Freer. CBE 1978.

GALLOWAY, Maj.-Gen. Kenneth Gardiner. CB 1978.
*GANDELL, Sir Alan Thomas. Kt 1978. For services to the Order of St. John, New Zealand.
*GARRIOCH, Sir William Henry. Kt 1978. Chief Justice, Mauritius.
GILBERT, Rt. Hon. John William. PC 1978.
GILCHRIST, Sir James Finlay Elder. Kt 1978.
GORDON-CUMMING, Alexander Roualeyn. CMG 1978.
GOULD, Patricia. CBE 1978.
GRAHAM, Maj.-Gen. John David Carew. CB 1978.
GREENHAM, Peter George. CBE 1978.
GRIFFIN, Air Vice-Marshal Charles Robert. CB 1978.

HALL, George Edmund. CMG 1978.
HAMILTON, Sir James Arnot. KCB 1978.
HARMAN, Gen. Sir Jack (Wentworth). GCB 1978.
*HASSETT, Maj.-Gen. Ronald Douglas Patrick. CB 1978. Chief of General Staff, New Zealand Army.
HAZELL, Quinton. CBE 1978.
HEDGELAND, Air Vice-Marshal Philip Michael Sweatman. CB 1978.
*HENARE, Sir James Clendon Tau. KBE 1978. For service to the community, especially Maori affairs, New Zealand.
HOCKADAY, Sir Arthur Patrick. KCB 1978.
HOMAN, Rear-Adm. Thomas Buckhurst. CB 1978.
HOPKINSON, Sir (Henry) Thomas. Kt 1978.

JACKSON, Frederick Hume. CMG 1978.
JAFFRAY, Alistair Robert Morton. CB 1978.
JOHNSTON, Sir John (Baines). GCMG 1978.
JONES, Gwyn Owain. CBE 1978.
JONES, James Larkin, (Jack). CH 1978.
JONES, Thomas Philip. CB 1978.
JONES, Sir William Elwyn Edwards. Kt 1978.

KELLY, Charles Henry. QPM 1978.

* The current edition contains no entry under this name.

LACEY, (William) Daniel. CB 1978.
LAING, Sir Hector. Kt 1978.
LANCASTER, Joan Cadogan. CBE 1978.
LEAVIS, Frank Raymond. CH 1978.
LE BRETON, David Francis Battye. CBE 1978.
*LEE-STEERE, Sir Ernest Henry. KBE 1978. Lord Mayor of Perth, Western Australia.
LENNOX, Robert Smith. CBE 1978.
LIDDIARD, Richard England. CBE 1978.
LIPMAN, Vivian David. CVO 1978.
LOCK, Air Vice-Marshal Basil Goodhand. CB 1978.
LOCK, Lt-Comdr Sir (John) Duncan. Kt 1978.
*LOCKWOOD, Betty. Baroness (Life Peer), cr 1978.
LOEWENTHAL, Prof. Sir John. Kt 1978. For distinguished service to health, Australia.
LOWRY, John Patrick. CBE 1978.

*McCRAY, Sir Lionel Joseph. Kt 1978. For services to the business community and people of Queensland.
MacDONALD, Gen. Sir Arthur Leslie. KBE 1978.
MACDONALD, Vice-Adm. Sir Roderick Douglas. KBE 1978.
McENTEE, Peter Donovan. CMG 1978.
McGIRR, Prof. Edward McCombie. CBE 1978.
McGREGOR, Prof. Oliver Ross. Baron (Life Peer), cr 1978.
*McINERNEY, Sir Murray Vincent. Kt 1978. Judge of the Supreme Court of Victoria.
MACMILLAN, Iain Alexander. CBE 1978.
McNEE, Sir David Blackstock. Kt 1978.
*McNEILL, Sir James Charles. Kt 1978. For services to the State through industry.
MANGHAM, Maj.-Gen. William Desmond. CB 1978.
MARKING, Sir Henry Ernest. KCVO 1978.
MASON, Vice-Adm. Dennis Howard. CVO 1978.
MATTHEWS, Peter Jack. CVO 1978.
METHVEN, Sir (Malcolm) John. Kt 1978.
MILLS, Laurence John. CBE 1978.
MOBERLY, Patrick Hamilton. CMG 1978.
MORETON, Sir John (Oscar). KCMG 1978.
MORRIS, Rt. Hon. Charles Richard. PC 1978.
MORTON, Vice-Adm. Sir Anthony Storrs. KCB 1978.
MURPHY, Sir Leslie Frederick. Kt 1978.
MURRAY, Sir Jack Keith. KBE 1978.
MURRAY, Sir James. KCMG 1978.

NESBITT, Cathleen. CBE 1978.
NEW ZEALAND, Primate and Archbishop of; Most Rev. Allen Howard Johnston. CMG 1978.
NEWMAN, Sir Kenneth Leslie. Kt 1978.

OTTON, Geoffrey John. CB 1978.

PACK, Prof. Donald Cecil. CBE 1978.
PAGE, Charles James. CBE 1978.
PAIGE, Victor Grellier. CBE 1978.
*PARBO, Sir Arvi Hillar. Kt 1978. For service to industry, Australia.
PARKER, James Roland Walter. CMG 1978.
PATTERSON, (Constance) Marie. CBE 1978.
PEARS, Sir Peter. Kt 1978.
PENRICE, Geoffrey. CB 1978.
PEROWNE, Rear-Adm. Benjamin Cubitt. CB 1978.
PERRY, Sir Thomas Wilfred. Kt 1978.
PILE, Sir William (Dennis). GCB 1978.
POTTER, Sir (Joseph) Raymond (Lynden). Kt 1978.
POUT, Harry Wilfred. CB 1978.
PRESTON, Sir Peter Sansome. KCB 1978.

RAMSBOTHAM, Hon. Sir Peter (Edward). GCMG 1978.
RAWLINSON, Sir Anthony Keith. KCB 1978.
* READER, Dame Audrey Tattie Hinchliffe. DBE 1978. For distinguished service to women's affairs and to politics, Australia.
REES, William Linford Llewelyn. CBE 1978.
REID, Harold Martin Smith. CMG 1978.
RHYS, Jean. CBE 1978.
RIDLEY, Philip Waller. CB 1978.
*ROBERTS, Sir Edward Fergus Sidney. Kt 1978. For distinguished service to primary industry, Australia.
ROBERTS, Geoffrey Frank Ingleson. CBE 1978.
ROBERTS, Lewis Edward John. CBE 1978.
ROBERTSON, Prof. Noel Farnie. CBE 1978.
ROWLEY, Frederick Allan. CMG 1978.

SAYER, Guy Mowbray. CBE 1978.
SCOTT, Sir (Charles) Peter. KBE 1978.
SELIGMAN, Sir Peter Wendel. Kt 1978.
SHIMELD, Kenneth Reeve. CB 1978.
SHONFIELD, Sir Andrew (Akiba). Kt 1978.
SMART, Prof. Sir George Algernon. Kt 1978.
SMEDLEY, Sir Harold. KCMG 1978.
SMITH, Sir George Fenwick. Kt 1978.
SNEDDEN, Rt. Hon. Sir Billy Mackie. KCMG 1978.
SOWREY, Air Marshal Sir Frederick Beresford. KCB 1978.
SPINKS, Alfred. CBE 1978.
SPRINGETT, Jack Allan. CBE 1978.
STAIR, Earl of. KCVO 1978.
STEER, Kenneth Arthur. CBE 1978.
STONE, Sir (John) Richard (Nicholas). Kt 1978.
STOPPARD. Thomas. CBE 1978.
STURGE, Maj.-Gen. Henry Arthur John. CB 1978.
SUGDEN, Sir Arthur. Kt 1978.
SYMINGTON, Prof. Sir Thomas. Kt 1978.

TERRY, Air Marshal Sir Peter David George. KCB 1978.
THOMPSON, Charles Norman. CBE 1978.
THOMSON, Sir John Adam. KCMG 1978.
THORNTON, Jack Edward Clive. CB 1978.
TOMBS, Sir Francis Leonard. Kt 1978.
TWISS, Adm. Sir Frank (Roddam). KCVO 1978.
TYERMAN, Donald. CBE 1978.

* UATIOA, Dame Meere. DBE 1978. For services to the community in the Gilbert Islands.
URWICK, Alan Bedford. CMG 1978.
UVAROV, Olga. CBE 1978.

VERNON, Kenneth Robert. CBE 1978.

WADDILOVE, Lewis Edgar. CBE 1978.
WALKER, John Riddell Bromhead. CVO 1978.
WALL, Maj.-Gen. Robert Percival Walter. CB 1978.
WALTER, Kenneth Burwood. CVO 1978.
WATTS, Roy. CBE 1978.
WILDE, Derek Edward. CBE 1978.
WILSON, Prof. Robert. CBE 1978.
WINTERBOTTOM, Sir Walter. Kt 1978.
WINTOUR, Charles Vere. CBE 1978.
WOOD, Maj.-Gen. Denys Broomfield. CB 1978.
WOOD, Joseph Neville. CBE 1978.
WRIGHT, Patrick Richard Henry. CMG 1978.

YOUNG, Michael. Baron (Life Peer), cr 1978.

* The current edition contains no entry under this name.

A

AARON, Richard Ithamar, MA, DPhil; FBA 1955; Professor of Philosophy, University College of Wales, Aberystwyth, 1932-69; *b* 6 Nov. 1901; *s* of William and Margaret Aaron, Ynystawe, Swansea; *m* Rhiannon, *d* of Dr M. J. Morgan, Aberystwyth; two *s* three *d. Educ:* Ystalyfera Grammar School; Cardiff University College; Oriel College, Oxford. Fellow, Univ. of Wales, 1923; Lectr at Swansea, 1926; Chm., Central Adv. Coun. for Educn (Wales), 1946-52; Mem., Coun. for Wales, 1956-63 (Chm., 1960-63); Chm. Library Advisory Council (Wales), 1965-72; Mem. Gen. Advisory Council, BBC, 1962-73, and TV Research Council, 1963-69; Mem. Council, National Library of Wales, 1953-73; Vice-Chm., Coleg Harlech Residential Coll.; Chm., Pembroke and Cardigan Agricultural Wages Cttee, 1962-73. Vis. Prof. in Philosophy, Yale Univ., US, 1952-53 (Fell. of Pierson Coll.). Pres., Mind Assoc., 1955-56; Pres., Aristotelian Society, London, 1957-58. Hon. DLitt Wales, 1973. *Publications:* The Nature of Knowing, 1930; Hanes Athroniaeth, 1932; An Early Draft of Locke's Essay (with Jocelyn Gibb), 1936; John Locke, 1937, 3rd rev. edn 1971; The Limitations of Locke's Rationalism, in Seventeenth Century Studies, 1938; Our Knowledge of Universals, Annual Philosophical Lecture to British Academy, 1945; The Theory of Universals, 1952, 2nd rev. edn 1967; The True and the Valid, Friends of Dr Williams's Library Lecture, 1954; Knowing and the Function of Reason, 1971; Editor, Efrydiau Athronyddol, 1938-68; contributor to Mind, Proc. Arist. Soc., Philosophy, Mod. Lang. Rev., Llenor, etc. *Recreation:* finding oneself again first in Who's Who. *Address:* Garth Celyn, Aberystwyth, Dyfed. *T:* 3535.

AARONS, Sir Daniel (Sidney), Kt 1970; OBE 1966; MC 1917 and Bar, 1918; retired; *b* 1 Aug. 1885; *s* of Solomon Aarons and Hannah Hart; *m* 1925, Jessie Chaddock Stronach; no *c. Educ:* North Broken Hill Public School. Joined Vacuum Oil Co. Australia in West Australia, 1903; enlisted AIF, 1915, 16th Infantry Battalion; returned 1920 and joined Head Office of Company, Melbourne; transf. to Sydney as Gen. Man. NSW, 1935; retd 1947. Foundn Mem., Liberal Party of Australia, 1945; subseq. Chm. of Finance Cttee; Treas. 1969. Past Pres., Legacy Club of Sydney; Mem. Federal Council, Legacy Clubs of Australia; Past Pres., Civic Reform Assoc. (local govt). *Recreations:* lawn bowls; formerly rowing (Mem. King's Cup 8-oared Crew WA 1912), lacrosse (Player Man., WA Interstate Lacrosse Team, 1912) and golf. *Address:* Australian Club, 165 Macquarie Street, Sydney, NSW 2000, Australia. *T:* 221 1533. *Club:* Australian (Sydney).

AARVOLD, His Honour Sir Carl (Douglas), Kt 1968; OBE 1945; TD 1950; DL; Recorder of London, 1964-75; *b* 7 June 1907; *s* of late O. P. Aarvold and late J. M. Aarvold, West Hartlepool, County Durham; *m* 1934, Noeline Etrenne Hill, Denton Park, Yorks; three *s. Educ:* Durham Sch.; Emmanuel College, Cambridge (Hon. Fellow, 1976). Called to the Bar, Inner Temple, 1932; North Eastern Circuit. Master of the Bench, Inner Temple, 1959. Recorder of Pontefract, 1951-54; a Judge of the Mayor's and City of London Court, 1954-59; Common Serjeant, City of London, 1959-64; Chm., City of London QS, 1969-71. Chm., Inner London Probation Cttee, 1965-75; Pres., Central Council of Probation Cttees, 1968-75. DL Surrey, 1973. Hon. LLD Dalhousie, 1962; Hon. DCL Durham, 1965. Pres., Lawn Tennis Assoc., 1962-. *Recreations:* golf, tennis, gardening. *Address:* Foxbury, Westhumble, Dorking, Surrey. *T:* Dorking 2771.

ABAYOMI, Sir Kofo Adekunle, Kt 1951; MD, ChB, DTM&H; DOMS (Eng.); FRSA; Member Privy Council, Nigeria, 1951; Chief Ona Ishokun of Oyo since 1949; Chief Baba Isale of Lagos since 1952; is an Eye Specialist; *b* 10 July 1896; *s* of Joseph N. John and Aiyelagbe Davies; *m* 1932, Oyinkan Morenikeji, MBE, *o d* of Sir Kitoyi Ajasa, OBE; five *s* one *d. Educ:* Methodist Boys' High School, Lagos; Edinburgh Univ. Served European War, 1914-17 (medals). Pharmacist, 1917-22; Edinburgh Univ., 1922; MB, ChB 1928. Demonstrator in Physiological Methods, Edinburgh Univ., 1927-30; DTM&H Edinburgh 1929; MD with speciality in Tropical Medicine, 1936; FRSA 1934; Rhodes Scholar in Ophthalmology, 1941; studied also at Moorfields Eye Hosp., 1940-41; DOMS England 1941. MLC, Nigeria, 1938-40; MEC, Nigeria, 1949-51; Member: Government and educational committees; Univ. Coll. Council, Ibadan, 1947-; Dep. Chm., Univ. Coll. Hosp., Ibadan, 1953-; Chm. Bd of Management, Univ. Teaching Hosp., Ibadan; President: Nigeria Federal Soc. for the Blind, 1953-; Assoc. of Medical Practitioners, 1946-; Nigeria Br., BMA, 1953-; Nigeria Medical Assoc., 1960; Chm., Lagos Exec. Development Board; Director: Barclays Bank, DCO (Nigeria); ICI (Nigeria); P & Z Co. Ltd; Vice-Chm., British Bata Shoe Co. (Nigeria); Chm. Bd of Trustees, Glover Memorial Hall. Hon. LLD Mount Allison Univ., Canada, 1958; Hon. LLD Univ. of Ibadan, 1963. *Recreation:* walking. *Address:* 2 Keffi Street, PO Box 300, Lagos, Nigeria. *Clubs:* Royal Commonwealth Society; Dining, Metropolitan, Ikoyi (Lagos).

ABBADO, Claudio; Principal Conductor, Vienna Philharmonic Orchestra, since 1971; Artistic Director, La Scala Orchestra, Milan, since 1977 (Permanent Conductor, 1969-76, and Music Director, 1971-76); *b* 26 June 1933. *Educ:* Conservatorio G. Verdi, Milan; Musical Academy, Vienna. Guest Conductor of principal orchestras in Europe and America: conductor at principal festivals and opera houses, 1961-. Sergei Koussewitzky Prize, Tanglewood, 1958; Dimitri Mitropoulos Prize, 1963; Mozart-Medaille, Mozart-Gemeinde, Vienna, 1973; winner of major international prizes for recordings (Diapason, Deutscher Schalplatten-Preis, Grand Prix du Disque, etc), 1965-. *Address:* via Nirone 2/A, 20123 Milan, Italy.

ABBOT, Dermot Charles Hyatt, CB 1959; Assistant Under-Secretary of State, Department of Health and Social Security, 1968-69 (Under-Secretary, Ministry of Pensions and National Insurance, 1955-66, Ministry of Social Security, 1966-68); retired 1969; *b* 8 Sept. 1908; *e s* of late Reginald Arthur Brame Abbot and late Sarah Ethel Abbot; *m* 1947, Elsie Myrtle Arnott (*see* Dame Elsie Abbot). *Educ:* High School, Newcastle-under-Lyme; High School, Southend-on-Sea; University College, London. Post Office, 1929-40 and 1945-49; transferred to Ministry of Pensions and National Insurance, 1949. *Recreations:* gardening, fishing, travel. *Address:* 4 Constable Close, NW11. *T:* 01-455 9413. *Club:* Royal Automobile.

ABBOT, Dame Elsie (Myrtle), DBE 1966 (CBE 1957); Third Secretary, HM Treasury, 1958-67; *b* 3 Sept. 1907; *d* of Leonard and Frances Tostevin, Streatham, London; *m* 1st, 1938, E. A. Arnott, *s* of R. E. Arnott, Pontypridd; one *s* one *d*; 2nd, 1947, D. C. H. Abbot, *qv. Educ:* Clapham County Secondary School; St Hugh's College, Oxford. 1st Class Hons Modern History, 1929; 1st Class Hons Philosophy, Politics and Economics, 1930. Entered Administrative Class of Home Civil Service, 1930; Post Office, 1930-47; transferred to HM Treasury, 1947. *Address:* 4 Constable Close, NW11. *T:* 01-455 9413.

ABBOTT, Arthur William, CMG 1956; CBE 1949; FRHistS; *b* 5 Feb. 1893; *s* of late William Henry Abbott, Southampton, sometime President, Hampshire Law Society; *m* 1926, Kathleen, *d* of Richard Way; one *s. Educ:* Blundell's School, Tiverton.

Entered Crown Agents' Office, 1912; served European War, 1914-18, Hampshire Regt, North Russia, 1917-19; Secretary, East African Currency Board, 1930-38; Head of Department, 1938; Establishment Officer, 1948; Secretary to the Crown Agents (for oversea governments and administrations), 1954-58. *Publications:* History of the Crown Agents (printed for private circulation, 1960); review and magazine articles. *Address:* Frithys Orchard, West Clandon, Surrey. *T:* Guildford 222565.

ABBOTT, Hon. Douglas Charles, PC (Can.) 1945; QC 1939; BCL (McGill); Hon. LLD, Hon. DCL; Justice of the Supreme Court, Canada, 1954-73; *b* Lennoxville, PQ, 29 May 1899; *s* of Lewis Duff Abbott and Mary Jane Pearce; *m* 1925, Mary Winifred Chisholm; two *s* one *d. Educ:* Bishop's College; McGill University; Dijon University, France. Elected to House of Commons, 1940; re-elected, 1945, 1949 and 1953. Minister of National Defence for Naval Services, April 1945; Minister of National Defence (Army), Aug. 1945; Min. of Finance, Canada, 1946-54. Practised law in Montreal with firm of Robertson, Abbott, Brierley and O'Connor. Chancellor, Bishop's Univ., 1958-68. *Recreations:* fishing, curling, golf. *Address:* 124 Springfield Road, Ottawa, Canada. *TA:* Ottawa Canada. *T:* 745-6250. *Clubs:* University, Royal Montreal Curling (Montreal); Rideau (Ottawa).

ABBOTT, Rev. Eric Symes, KCVO 1966; DD (Lambeth); MA Cantab and Oxon (by incorporation); Dean of Westminster, 1959-74; *b* 26 May 1906; *s* of William Henry and Mary Abbott, Nottingham. *Educ:* Nottingham High School; Jesus College, Cambridge. Curate, St John's, Smith Square, Westminster, 1930-32; Chaplain, King's College, London, 1932-36; Chaplain to Lincoln's Inn, 1935-36; Warden of the Scholae Cancellarii, Lincoln, 1936-45; Canon and Prebendary of Lincoln Cathedral, 1940-60. Dean of King's College, London, 1945-55; Warden of Keble College, Oxford, 1956-60; Chaplain to King George VI, 1948-52, and to the Queen, 1952-59; an Extra Chaplain to the Queen, 1974-. Chaplain and Sub-Prelate, Order of St John of Jerusalem, 1969-. Freeman, City of Westminster, 1973. FKC, London, 1946-; Hon. Fellow: Keble Coll., Oxford, 1960; Jesus Coll., Cambridge, 1966. Hon. DD London, 1966. *Address:* 17 Vincent Square, SW1. *Club:* Athenæum.

ABBOTT, John Sutherland, JP; Chairman, R. Wyliehill Ltd, 1971-75; formerly Director: The Bank of Scotland; Royal Exchange Assurance (Chairman Glasgow Local Board); Glenfield and Kennedy Holdings Ltd, 1952-65, and other Companies; Chairman and Managing Director, Saxone Lilley & Skinner (Holdings) Ltd, 1938-64; Hon. President, Ayrshire Chamber of Industries; Governor, Welbeck College; Member, Scottish National Committee, English-Speaking Union; Vice-Chairman, Kennel Club Cttee, 1973; *b* 24 August 1900; 2nd *s* of late George Sutherland Abbott, JP, Middleton House, Ayr, and Isabel Cathrine Cable; *m* 1928, Winifred May, 2nd *d* of George Thomas, Wolverhampton; one *s. Educ:* Bedales School; Pembroke College, Cambridge. JP Ayrshire 1942. *Recreations:* shooting, racing, breeding and exhibiting wire-haired foxterriers. *Address:* 25B Rutland Gate, SW7; Admirals Walk, West Cliff, Bournemouth, Dorset. *Clubs:* East India, Devonshire, Sports and Public Schools, Kennel; Leander; Prestwick Golf.

ABBOTT, Sir Myles (John), Kt 1964; Chief Justice of Bermuda, 1961-71; *b* 27 Feb. 1906; *s* of Edmund Rushworth Abbott, 13 Victoria Street, London, Solicitor; *m* 1st, 1932, Grace Ada Jeffery; one *d*; 2nd, 1960, Dorothy Anne Campbell, *widow* of Robert Currie Campbell. *Educ:* King's Sch., Canterbury. Admitted Solicitor, 1929; Partner, Chas Rogers Sons & Abbott, 1930. 2nd Lieut 9th Middlesex Regt. (TA), 1933. Selected for appointment to Colonial Legal Service, 1935; Lieut 9th Middx Regt and transferred to TARO, 1936; Asst Crown Solicitor, Hong Kong, 1936; called to the Bar, 1940; Official Receiver and Registrar of Trade Marks, Hong Kong, 1941. Served War of 1939-45 (prisoner); released, 1945. President, High Court of Ethiopia, Oct. 1946-Oct. 1949; Puisne Judge, Nigeria, 1950-55; Judge of High Court of Lagos, 1955-57; Federal Justice of Federal Supreme Court of Nigeria, 1957-61. *Publications:* (ed) West African Court of Appeal Reports, 1946-49; (ed) Federal Supreme Court Reports, Nigeria, Vol. 4, 1959, 1960. *Address:* High Ferry, Harbour Road, Warwick, Bermuda. *T:* Bermuda 23521. *Club:* Naval and Military.

ABBOTT, Roderick Evelyn; Chef de Division, Directorate-General of External Relations, EEC Commission, Brussels, since 1973; *b* 16 April 1938; *e s* of Stuart Evelyn Abbott, OBE; *m* 1963, Elizabeth Isobel McLean; three *d. Educ:* Rugby Sch.; Merton Coll., Oxford (BA Lit Hum). Board of Trade, 1962-68 (Private Sec. to Pres. of BoT, 1965-66; seconded to DEA, 1966-68); UK Mission to UN, Geneva, 1968-71; Foreign Office, London, 1971-73. *Recreation:* travel. *Address:* c/o EEC Delegation, 37 rue de Vermont, 1202 Geneva, Switzerland. *Club:* Royal Commonwealth Society.

ABDELA, Jack Samuel Ronald, TD 1948; QC 1966; **His Honour Judge Abdela;** a Circuit Judge, Central Criminal Court (formerly Deputy Chairman, Inner London Quarter Sessions), since 1970; *b* 9 Oct. 1913; *s* of Joseph and Dorothy Abdela, Manchester; *m* 1942, Enid Hope Russell, *y d* of Edgar Dodd Russell, London; one *s* (and one *s* decd). *Educ:* Manchester Gram. Sch.; Milton Sch., Bulawayo; Fitzwilliam House, Cambridge (MA). Called to the Bar, Gray's Inn, 1935. 2nd Lieut, Lancashire Fusiliers (TA), 1938; Lieut-Col. Comdt 55 Div. Battle School, 1943; 7th Bn Royal Welch Fusiliers, NW Europe, 1944-46; Major, Inns of Court Regt. (TA), 1946-52. *Recreations:* swimming, tennis, gardening. *Address:* 42 Lloyd Baker Street, WC1X 9AB. *T:* 01-837 5889; Central Criminal Court, EC4; Pond Cottage, Hoxne, Diss, Norfolk. *T:* Hoxne 337. *Club:* Savage.

ABDUL RAHMAN PUTRA, Tunku (Prince), CH 1961; Order of the National Crown, Malaysia; Kedah Order of Merit; Secretary General, Islamic Conference of Foreign Ministers, 1969-73; Prime Minister of Malaysia, 1963-70; Chairman, Star Publications, Penang; *b* 1903; *m* 3rd, 1939, Puan Sharifah Rodziah binti Syed Alwi Barakbah; one *s* one *d* (both by 1st wife); one *s* three *d* (all adopted). *Educ:* Alor Star; Bangkok; St Catharine's Coll., Cambridge; Inner Temple, London (Hon. Master, 1971). Joined Kedah State Civil Service, 1931, District Officer. During the occupation, when the Japanese returned Kedah to Siam, he served as Supt of Educn and Dir of Passive Defence until the reoccupation, Sept. 1945; opposed British Govt fusion of States and Colonies to form the Malayan Union and took a leading part in formation of United Malays National Organisation (UMNO); when the Malayan Union gave way to the Federation of Malaya in 1949, he became Chairman of UMNO in Kedah; after being called to Bar (Inner Temple), he returned to Kedah and was seconded to Federal Legal Dept as a Dep. Public Prosecutor, 1949; President of UMNO, 1951; resigned from CS and a year later was apptd an unofficial Mem. Federal Executive and Legislative Councils; leader of the Alliance Party (UMNO, Malayan Chinese Association, Malayan Indian Congress), 1954; Mem., Federal Legislative Council, 1955-73; became Chief Minister and Minister of Home Affairs; in reshuffle of 1956 also took portfolio of Minister for Internal Defence and Security; was also Chm. Emergency Ops Council which decides on policy in fighting Malayan Communist Party; headed Alliance deleg. to London to negotiate Independence for the Federation, Dec. 1955; after Independence on 31 Aug. 1957, became Prime Minister and Minister of External Affairs and continued to be Chm. Emergency Ops Council; resigned as Prime Minister in Feb. 1959 to prepare for general elections in Aug.; became Prime Minister for second time, Aug. 1959, and in Sept. initiated Min. of Rural Development; became also Minister of Ext. Affairs, Nov. 1960, and Minister of Information and Broadcasting, June 1961; Prime Minister, Federation of Malaya, until it became Malaysia, 1963; became Prime Minister for third time, April 1964, following Gen. Elections in States of Malaya, also Minister of External Affairs and Minister of Culture, Youth and Sports. Attended Prime Ministers' Conferences in London, May 1960 and March 1961; Head of mission to London to discuss and agree in principle proposed formation of Federation of Malaysia, Nov. 1961; Head of second mission to London on formation of Malaysia, July 1962; attended Prime Ministers' Confs, London, 1965, 1966. Apptd Chancellor, Univ. Malaya, 1962. Pres., Football Assoc. of Malaya; Pres., Asian Football Confedn; Vice-Pres. (for life), Royal Commonwealth Society. Dr of Law, Univ. of Malaya; Hon. LLD: Araneta Univ., 1958; Cambridge Univ., 1960; Univ. of Sydney, 1960; Univ. of Saigon, 1961; Aligarh Muslim Univ., 1962; Univ. Sains, Malaysia, 1975; Hon. DLitt, Seoul National Univ., 1965; Hon. DCL Oxford, 1970. Holds various foreign Orders. *Publications:* Mahsuri (imaginary play of Malaya; performed on stage in North Malaya throughout 1941; filmed in Malaya, 1958); Raja Bersiong (filmed 1966). *Relevant publication:* Prince and Premier (Biography) by Harry Miller, 1959. *Recreations:* golf, football, tennis, walking, swimming, racing, motor-boating, photography (both cine and still); collector of ancient weapons, particularly the Malay kris. *Address:* 1 Jalan Tunku, Kuala Lumpur, Malaysia; 16 Ayer Rajah Road, Penang, Malaysia.

ABDULLAH bin Ali, Datuk; High Commissioner for Malaysia in London, and concurrently Ambassador to Republic of Ireland, since Sept. 1975; *b* Johore State, 31 Aug. 1922; *m* Datin Badariah binti Haji Abdul Aziz; two *s* two *d. Educ:* Raffles Coll., Singapore; ANU, Canberra. Entered Johore Civil Service, 1949, later Malayan Civil Service; with Independence of Malaysia joined Malaysian Foreign Service; served in India,

Australia, Indonesia, Thailand, and as Head of Mission in Ethiopia, Morocco; Chief of Protocol and Dep. Sec.-Gen. (Admin and Gen Affairs), Min. of Foreign Affairs, Kuala Lumpur, 1969-71; High Comr to Singapore, 1971-74; Ambassador to Fed. Rep. of Germany, 1975. Has attended many foreign confs, incl. UNO in NY. Holds Orders: Dato Paduka Mahkota Johore (Order of Crown of Johore, Malaysia); Kesatria Mangku Negara (Order of Upholder of Realm, Malaysia); Order of Sacred Heart (Japan). *Address:* High Commission of Malaysia, 45 Belgrave Square, SW1X 8QT. *T:* 01-245 9221.

ABDY, Sir Valentine (Robert Duff), 6th Bt *cr* 1850; *b* 11 Sept. 1937; *s* of Sir Robert Henry Edward Abdy, 5th Bt, and Lady Diana Bridgeman (*d* 1967), *e d* of 5th Earl of Bradford; *S* father, 1976; *m* 1971, Mathilde Coche de la Ferté. *Educ:* Eton. *Address:* 39 rue de Turenne, 75003 Paris, France; Newton Ferrers, Callington, Cornwall. *Clubs:* Travellers', Polo (Paris).

ABEL, Arthur Lawrence, MS; MD(*hc*); FRCS; Consulting Surgeon: Princess Beatrice Hospital; Gordon Hospital (Westminster Hospital Group); Royal Marsden Hospital and Institute of Cancer Research, Royal Cancer Hospital; Hon. Consulting Surgeon: Woolwich War Memorial Hospital; Wood Green and Southgate Hospital; Hounslow Hospital; Vice-President, British Medical Association; *b* 15 Nov. 1895; *s* of Rev. A. E. Abel; *m* (wife *d* 1963); three *s* one *d. Educ:* University Coll., London; University Coll. Hospital. MB, BS 1917; MS Lond. 1921; MRCS, LRCP 1917; FRCS 1920; MD(*hc*) Bristol 1967. Jacksonian Prize 1924 and Hunterian Professor 1926, RCS; Fellowes Silver Medal in Clinical Medicine; First Prize in Clinical Surgery, UCH; Bradshaw Lectr, 1957. Member: Council RCS, 1947-63 (Vice-Pres., 1956-57); Grand Council Cancer Research Campaign; former Member, Bd of Governors: Westminster Hosp.; Royal Marsden Hosp. and Inst. of Cancer Research, Royal Cancer Hospital; Fellow Royal Society of Medicine; Fellow, Chelsea Clinical Soc.; Hon. Fellow, Member Council and Past Pres. Metropolitan Cos Br., BMA; Hon. Fellow and Auditor, Hunterian Soc. (Pres., 1963; Orator, 1962). Fellow and Past Pres., Harveian Society. Visiting Professor: Royal North Shore Hospital, Sydney; Marquette Univ., Milwaukee; Brooklyn Med. Centre, NY. Lectr, Cook County Graduate Sch. of Medicine, Chicago. Hon. Mem., Soc. of Surgeons of Madrid. Hon. Fellow: Amer. Med. Assoc.; Amer. Soc. of Colon and Rectal Surgs; Argentine Proctol. Soc. Late House Surg. and House Physician, Univ. Coll. Hosp. and Hosp. for Sick Children, Gt Ormond Street; Surg. Registrar (5 years) Cancer Hosp.; Temp. Surg. Lieut RN. Hon. Admiral, Texas Navy. *Publications:* contribs to med. jls. *Address:* 48 Harley Street, W1N 1AD. *T:* 01-580 4118.

ABEL SMITH, Sir Alexander, Kt 1968; TD; JP; retired Merchant Banker; J. Henry Schroder Wagg and Co. Ltd, 1946-67; Chairman: Pressed Steel Co., 1955-65; Provident Mutual Life Assurance Association, 1966-73; Director of other companies; *b* 18 Sept. 1904; *s* of late Lieut-Col Francis Abel Smith, DL; *m* 1st, 1936, Elizabeth (*d* 1948), *d* of David B. Morgan, Biltmore, North Carolina, USA; one *s* one *d*; 2nd, 1953, Henriette Alice (*see* Lady Abel Smith); one *s* one *d. Educ:* Eton College; Magdalen College, Oxford. Served War of 1939-45, AA Command and British Army Staff, Washington (hon. Brigadier). Mem., BNEC, 1965-69; Dep. Chm., Export Council for Europe, 1963-69. Chm., Sussex Church Campaign, 1970-; Trustee, Duke of Edinburgh Award Scheme. JP Herts 1949, JP Sussex 1955. Order of Legion of Merit, USA. Knight (1st Class) Order of Dannebrog (Denmark). *Recreations:* shooting and fishing. *Address:* Quenington Old Rectory, Cirencester, Glos. *T:* Coln St Aldwyns 231. *Clubs:* Buck's, MCC.
See also Col Sir Henry Abel Smith.

ABEL-SMITH, Prof. Brian; Professor of Social Administration, University of London, at the London School of Economics, since 1965; *b* 6 Nov. 1926; *s* of late Brig.-Gen. Lionel Abel-Smith. *Educ:* Haileybury Coll.; Clare Coll., Cambridge. MA, PhD, 1955. Served Army: Private 1945; commissioned Oxford and Bucks Light Inf., 1946; Mil. Asst to Dep. Comr, Allied Commn for Austria (Capt.), 1947-48. Res. Fellow, Nat. Inst. of Economic and Social Res., collecting economic evidence for Guillebaud Cttee (cost of NHS), 1953-55. LSE: Asst Lectr in Social Science, 1955; Lectr, 1957; Reader in Social Administration, University of London, 1961. Assoc. Prof., Yale Law Sch., Yale Univ., 1961. Consultant and Expert Adv. to WHO on costs of med. care, 1957-; Consultant: to Social Affairs Div. of UN, 1959, 1961; to ILO, 1967; Senior Adviser to Sec. of State for Health and Social Security, 1968-70, 1974-. Member: SW Metrop. Reg. Hosp. Bd, 1956-63; Cent. Health Services Coun. Sub-Cttee on Prescribing Statistics, 1960-64; Sainsbury Cttee (Relationship of Pharmaceut. Industry with NHS), 1965-

67; Long-term Study Group (to advise on long-term develt of NHS), 1965-68; Hunter Cttee (Functions of Medical Administrators,) 1970-72; Fisher Cttee (Abuse of Social Security Benefits), 1971-73. Chm., Chelsea and Kensington HMC, 1961-62; Governor: St Thomas' Hosp., 1957-68; Maudsley Hosp. and Inst. of Psychiatry, 1963-67. *Publications:* (with R. M. Titmuss) The Cost of the National Health Service in England and Wales, 1956; A History of the Nursing Profession, 1960; (with R. M. Titmuss) Social Policy and Population Growth in Mauritius, 1961; Paying for Health Services (for WHO), 1963; The Hospitals, 1800-1948, 1964; (with R. M. Titmuss *et al.*) The Health Services of Tanganyika, 1964; (with K. Gales) British Doctors at Home and Abroad, 1964; (with P. Townsend) The Poor and the Poorest, 1965; (with R. Stevens) Lawyers and the Courts, 1967; An International Study of Health Expenditure (for WHO), 1967; (with R. Stevens) In Search of Justice, 1968; (with M. Zander and R. Brooke) Legal Problems and the Citizen, 1973; People Without Choice, 1974; Value for Money in Health Services, 1976; pamphlets for Fabian Soc., 1953-; articles. *Recreations:* skiing, swimming. *Address:* London School of Economics, Houghton Street, WC2. *T:* 01-405 7686.

ABEL SMITH, Vice-Adm. Sir (Edward Michael) Conolly, GCVO 1958 (KCVO 1954; CVO 1946); CB 1951; RN retd; Extra Equerry to the Queen since 1952; *b* 3 Dec. 1899; 2nd *s* of Eustace Abel Smith, Longhills, Lincoln, and Aileen Geta, *d* of Col. John A. Conolly, VC, Coldstream Guards; *m* 1932, Lady Mary Elizabeth Carnegie, *d* of 10th Earl of Southesk; one *s* one *d. Educ:* Royal Naval Colleges, Osborne and Dartmouth. Mid. HMS Princess Royal, 1915; Qualified Pilot, 1924; Comdr 1933; Naval Equerry to the King, 1939; Capt. 1940; HMS Biter, 1942; Naval Attaché, British Embassy, Washington, DC, 1944-46; HMS Triumph, 1947; Naval ADC to the King, 1949; Rear-Adm. 1949; Vice-Controller (Air), Chief of Naval Air Equipment and Chief Naval Representative, Min. of Supply, 1950; Vice-Adm. 1952; Flag Officer, Royal Yachts, 1953-58. JP 1958. HM Lieutenant for Selkirk, 1958-74. Grand Cross of St Olav, 1955. *Recreations:* hunting, shooting. *Address:* Ashiestiel, Galashiels, Scotland. *T:* Clovenfords 214. *Clubs:* Naval and Military, Buck's.

ABEL SMITH, Henriette Alice, (Lady Abel Smith), DCVO 1977 (CVO 1964); JP; a Lady-in-Waiting to the Queen (formerly as HRH Princess Elizabeth) since 1949; *b* 6 June 1914; *d* of late Comdr Francis Charles Cadogan, RN, and late Ruth Evelyn (*née* Howard, *widow* of Captain Gardner Sebastian Bazley); *m* 1st, 1939, Sir Anthony Frederick Mark Palmer, 4th Bt (killed in action, 1941); one *s* one *d*; 2nd, 1953, Sir Alexander Abel Smith, *qv*; one *s* one *d.* JP Tunbridge Wells 1955, Gloucestershire 1971. *Address:* Quenington Old Rectory, Cirencester, Glos. *T:* Coln St Aldwyns 231.
See also Sir T. S. Bazley, Bt, Sir C. M. Palmer, Bt.

ABEL SMITH, Col Sir Henry, KCMG 1961; KCVO 1950; DSO 1945; DL; late Royal Horse Guards; Governor of Queensland, 1958-66; Administrator, Australian Commonwealth, during part of 1965; *b* 8 March 1900; *er s* of late Francis Abel Smith and Madeline St Maur, *d* of late Rev. Henry Seymour; *m* 1931, Lady May Cambridge, *o* surv. *c* of Earl of Athlone, KG, PC, GCB, GCMG, GCVO, DSO, FRS (*d* 1957), and of Princess Alice, Countess of Athlone, *qv*; one *s* two *d. Educ:* RMC, Sandhurst. Entered RHG, 1919; Capt. 1930; Major, 1934; Temp. Lieut-Col 1941; Lieut-Col 1944; Acting Colonel, Corps of Household Cavalry, 1946; retired, 1950. ADC to Earl of Athlone, Governor-General of S Africa, 1928-31. DL Berks 1953. KStJ 1958; Hon. LLD Univ. of Queensland, 1962. Hon. Air Cdre, RAAF, 1966. *Recreations:* hunting, shooting, fishing, polo. *Address:* Barton Lodge, Winkfield, Windsor, Berks. *T:* Winkfield Row 2632. *Club:* Turf.
See also Sir Alexander Abel Smith.

ABELES, Sir (Emil Herbert) Peter, Kt 1972; Deputy Chairman and Managing Director, Thomas Nationwide Transport Ltd, Australia, and associated companies, since 1967; Managing Director, Alltrans Group (Aust.) Pty Ltd; *b* 25 April 1924; *s* of late Alexander Abel and of Mrs Anna Deakin; *m* 1969, Katalin Ottilia (*née* Fischer); two *d. Educ:* Budapest. Scrap metal industry, Hungary; emigrated to Australia, Sept. 1949; formed Alltrans Pty Ltd, 1950. Director: Bulkships Ltd and associated cos; R. W. Miller (Holdings) Ltd; Seatainer Terminals Ltd; Tricontinental Corp. Ltd; Union Steam Ship Co. of NZ Ltd; Tasman Union Ltd; TNT Shipping NZ Ltd; Ansett Transport Industries Ltd. *Recreations:* swimming, bridge. *Address:* 6 Queens Avenue, Vaucluse, NSW 2030, Australia. *T:* 371 9795. *Clubs:* Carlton; Royal Automobile of Australia, Royal Motor Yacht, Tattersalls, Australian Jockey.

ABELL, Sir Anthony (Foster), KCMG 1952 (CMG 1950); part-time Member, Civil Service Commission; Gentleman Usher of the Blue Rod, in the Order of St Michael and St George, since 1972; *b* 11 Dec. 1906; 2nd *s* of late G. F. Abell, JP, Foxcote Manor, Andoversford, Glos; unmarried. *Educ*: Repton; Magdalen Coll., Oxford. Joined Colonial Admin. Service, Nigeria, 1929. Resident, Oyo Province, Nigeria, 1949; Governor and C-in-C, Sarawak, 1950-59; High Commissioner, Brunei, 1950-58. Member: Council, Royal Over-Seas League; Advisory Council, Overseas Services Resettlement Bureau. Family Order of Brunei (First Class), 1954. *Address*: Gavel House, Wherwell, Andover, Hants. *Clubs*: MCC, Royal Over-Seas League, Bath.
See also Sir George Abell.

ABELL, Charles, OBE 1948; CEng, Hon. FRAeS; Consultant, British Airways Overseas Division, 1974-77; *b* 1 Dec. 1910; *s* of late Major George Henry Abell and Muriel Abell (*née* Griesbach); *m* 1939, Beryl Anne Boyce (*d* 1973); one *s*; *m* 1976, M. A. Newbery. *Educ*: Sherborne Sch. Imperial Airways, 1934-39; BOAC 1939-74: Manager No 3 Line, 1946-51; Dep. Operations Dir (Engineering), 1951-55; Chief Engineer, 1955-68; Engineering Dir, 1968-74; Board Mem., 1972-74; Chm., British Airways Engine Overhaul Ltd, 1972-74. Hon FRAeS (Pres., 1976-77; Vice-Pres., 1972-74); Hon. FSLAET (Pres. 1973-74). British Silver Medal for Aeronautics, RAeS, 1957. *Recreation*: sailing. *Address*: Five Oaks, Woodlands Road West, Virginia Water, Surrey. *T*: Wentworth 2560. *Clubs*: Cruising Association; Royal Lymington Yacht; Royal Western Yacht.

ABELL, Sir George (Edmond Brackenbury), KCIE 1947 (CIE 1946); OBE 1943; Hon. LLD (Aberdeen), 1947; Director, Portals Holdings Ltd, 1968-76; Member Council, Reading University (President, 1969-74); *b* 22 June 1904; *s* of late G. F. Abell, JP, Foxcote Manor, Andoversford, Glos; *m* 1928, Susan Norman-Butler; two *s* one *d*. *Educ*: Marlborough; Corpus Christi Coll., Oxford (Hon. Fellow, 1971-). Joined Indian Civil Service, 1928; Private Sec. to the Viceroy, 1945-47. Advisor, 1948-52, Director, 1952-64, Bank of England; First Civil Service Comr, 1964-67. Rhodes Trustee, 1949-74 (Chm., 1969-74). Mem. Council, 1955-77, Chm., 1974-77, Marlborough Coll. *Address*: Whittonditch House, Ramsbury, Wilts. *T*: Ramsbury 449. *Clubs*: Oriental, MCC.
See also Sir Anthony Abell.

ABERCONWAY, 3rd Baron, *cr* 1911, of Bodnant; **Charles Melville McLaren**, Bt 1902; JP; Chairman: John Brown & Co. Ltd; Sheepbridge Engineering Ltd; English China Clays Ltd; Vice-Chairman, Sun Alliance & London Insurance Ltd; President, Royal Horticultural Society, since 1961; *b* 16 April 1913; *e s* of 2nd Baron Aberconway, CBE, LLD and Christabel (*d* 1974), *y d* of Sir Melville Macnaghten, CB; *S* father, 1953; *m* 1st, 1941, Deirdre Knewstub (marr. diss. 1949); one *s* two *d*; 2nd, 1949, Ann Lindsay Bullard, *o d* of Mrs A. L. Aymer, New York City; one *s*. *Educ*: Eton; New Coll., Oxford. Barrister, Middle Temple, 1937. Served War of 1939-45, 2nd Lieut RA. Director: National Westminster Bank Ltd; Westland Aircraft Ltd; Sub-Gov., London Assce. JP Denbighshire 1946; High Sheriff of Denbighshire 1950. *Recreations*: gardening, travel, motoring. *Heir*: *s* Hon. Henry Charles McLaren, *b* 26 May 1948. *Address*: 25 Egerton Terrace, SW3; Bodnant, Tal-y-cafn, North Wales.
See also K. R. M. Carlisle.

ABERCORN, 4th Duke of, *cr* 1868; **James Edward Hamilton**; Baron of Paisley, 1587; Baron Abercorn, 1603; Baron Hamilton and Earl of Abercorn, 1606; Baron of Strabane, 1617; Viscount of Strabane, 1701; Viscount Hamilton, 1786; Marquess of Abercorn, 1790; Marquess of Hamilton, 1868; Bt 1660; HM Lieutenant for County of Tyrone since 1951; Captain Grenadier Guards; Member: Tyrone County Council, 1946; of Senate, Government of Northern Ireland, 1949-62; *b* 29 Feb. 1904; *er s* of 3rd Duke of Abercorn, KG, KP, and Lady Rosalind Cecilia Caroline Bingham (*d* 1958, as Dowager Duchess of Abercorn, DBE), *o d* of 4th Earl of Lucan; *S* father, 1953; *m* 1928, Lady Mary Kathleen Crichton (Duchess of Abercorn, DCVO 1969); two *s* one *d*. *Educ*: Eton; RMC Sandhurst. High Sheriff, Co. Tyrone, 1946. Chm. Trustees, Ulster Museum, 1962; Chancellor, University of Ulster at Coleraine, 1970-. Chm., NI Br., GB-USSR Assoc.; President: Royal Forestry Soc. of England, Wales and N Ireland, 1964; Internat. Dendrological Union, 1964; N Ireland Council of YMCAs; Army Cadet Force Assoc. for N Ireland; Not Forgotten Assoc., N Ireland; RN Lifeboat Inst., N Ireland; Royal UK Beneficent Assoc.; Nat. Playing Fields Assoc., N Ireland; Western Counties NI Assoc.; TA&VR; County Pres., Scout Assoc.; Vice-Pres., N Ireland Area, British Legion. Hon. Col, 5th Bn The Royal Inniskilling Fusiliers (TA), 1963. Hon. DLitt Ulster 1970. *Heir*: *s* Marquess of Hamilton, *qv*. *Address*: Barons Court, Co. Tyrone, Northern Ireland. *Club*: Turf.
See also Earl of Erne, Lady Katharine Seymour.

ABERCROMBIE, Prof. David; Professor of Phonetics, Edinburgh University, since 1964; *b* 19 Dec. 1909; *e s* of Lascelles and Catherine Abercrombie; *m* 1944, Mary, *d* of Eugene and Mary Marble, Carmel, Calif; no *c*. *Educ*: Leeds Grammar Sch.; Leeds Univ.; University Coll., London; Sorbonne. Asst Lectr in English, LSE, 1934-38; Dir of Studies, Inst. of English Studies, Athens, 1938-40; Lectr in English: Cairo Univ., 1940-45; LSE, 1945-47; Lectr in Phonetics, Leeds Univ., 1947-48; Edinburgh Univ.: Lectr in Phonetics, 1948-51; Sen. Lectr 1951-57; Reader, 1957-63. *Publications*: Isaac Pitman: a Pioneer in the Scientific Study of Language, 1937; Problems and Principles in Language Study, 1956; English Phonetic Texts, 1964; Studies in Phonetics and Linguistics, 1965; Elements of General Phonetics, 1967. *Address*: 13 Grosvenor Crescent, Edinburgh EH12 5EL. *T*: 031-337 4864. *Clubs*: Scottish Arts, New (Edinburgh).
See also Prof. Michael Abercrombie.

ABERCROMBIE, George Francis, VRD 1940; MA, MD Cambridge; Surgeon Captain, RNVR, retired; in General Practice, 1924-66; *b* 25 June 1896; *o s* of late George Kennedy Abercrombie, Solicitor, London, and Margaret Jane (*née* Forbes); *m* 1932, Marie, *yr d* of late Frank Underhill, JP, Plympton, S Devon; one *s* two *d*. *Educ*: Charterhouse Sch.; Gonville and Caius Coll., Cambridge. MA, BCh 1922; MB 1924, MD 1935. House Surg. and Resident Midwifery Asst, St Bartholomew's Hosp.; House Phys., Hosp. for Sick Children, Gt Ormond Street. Hon. FRSocMed (first Pres., Sect. of Gen. Practice, 1950); Mem. of Management Cttee, 1963-67, and Chm., Emerg. Bed Service Cttee, King Edward's Hosp. Fund for London, 1951-67; Lectr on Gen. Practice, St Bart's Hosp. Med. Sch., 1953-66. Foundn Mem., Coll. of Gen. Practitioners (Chm. Coun., 1952-55; James Mackenzie Lectr, 1958; Pres., 1959-62). Formerly Surg. Probationer, RNVR (HMS Warwick, Zeebrugge, 1918, despatches); Surg. Lieut 1922; Surg. Comdr 1935. War of 1939-45 (VRD): HMS Birmingham; HMS Anson. Surg. Captain 1948; KHP 1950; retired, 1951. *Publications*: papers in Alpine and med. jls; Joint Editor, The Encyclopædia of General Practice, 1963. *Recreations*: country walking, chess. *Address*: 4 The Barnyard, Ebbisham Lane, Walton-on-the-Hill, Surrey. *T*: Tadworth 2656.

ABERCROMBIE, Michael, FRS 1958; MA, BSc; Director, Strangeways Research Laboratory, and Fellow of Clare Hall, Cambridge, since 1970; *b* 14 Aug. 1912; *s* of Lascelles and Catherine Abercrombie; *m* 1939, Minnie Louie Johnson; one *s*. *Educ*: Leeds Grammar Sch.; The Queen's Coll., Oxford (Hastings Scholar, 1931; Taberdar, 1935; Junior Research Fellow, 1937). Beit Memorial Fellow for Medical Research, 1940; Lecturer in Zoology, Birmingham University, 1945; Reader in Embryology, UCL, 1950-59, Professor, 1959-62, Jodrell Prof. of Zoology, 1962-70. Mem. Council, Royal Soc., 1967-69. *Publications*: Dictionary of Biology (with C. J. Hickman and M. L. Johnson), 1951; papers on embryology, tissue culture and wound healing. *Address*: Strangeways Research Laboratory, Wort's Causeway, Cambridge.
See also Prof. David Abercrombie.

ABERCROMBIE, Nigel James; free-lance writer; *b* 5 Aug. 1908; 2nd *s* of late Lieutenant-Colonel A. W. Abercrombie; *m* 1931, Elisabeth Brownlees; one *s* one *d*. *Educ*: Haileybury; Oriel College, Oxford. BA 1929; DPhil 1933; MA 1934. Lecturer in French, Magdalen College, Oxford, 1931-36; Paget Toynbee Prize, 1934; Professor of French and Head of Mod. Lang. Dept, University College, Exeter, 1936-40. Entered Secretary's Department, Admiralty, 1940; Asst Sec., 1942; Under-Secretary, 1956; Cabinet Office, 1962-63; Sec.-Gen., 1963-68, Chief Regional Advr, 1968-73, Arts Council of Great Britain. Editor, Dublin Review, 1953-55. *Publications*: The Origins of Jansenism, 1936; St Augustine and French Classical Thought, 1938; editions of Le Misanthrope and Tartuffe, 1938; Life and Work of Edmund Bishop, 1959; The Arts in the South-East, 1974; Artists and Their Public, 1975; contrib. to: Times Anthology of Detective Stories, 1972; New Stories I, 1976; Essays on the Religious History of Sussex, 1977; articles and reviews in theological, philological and literary periodicals. *Recreations*: The 3 R's. *Address*: 32 Springett Avenue, Ringmer, Lewes, E Sussex BN8 5HE. *T*: Ringmer 813029.
See also J. L. Gardner.

ABERCROMBIE, Robert James, CMG 1964; General Manager, Bank of New South Wales, 1962-64, retired; *b* 9 July 1898; *s* of P. M. Abercrombie, Whitburn, Scotland; *m* 1924, Dorothy, *d* of H. F. Oldham; two *d*. *Educ*: Sydney Grammar School; Scotch Coll., Melbourne. Chairman, Consultative Council of Export

Payments Insurance Corporation, 1958-64; Chairman, Australian Bankers' Assoc., 1964. Dir., London Australia Investment Co. Ltd. *Recreation:* golf. *Address:* 1 Hillside Avenue, Vaucluse, NSW 2030, Australia. *Clubs:* Union (Sydney); Australian, Athenæum (Melbourne).

ABERCROMBY, Sir Ian George, 10th Bt *cr* 1636, of Birkenbog; *b* 30 June 1925; *s* of Robert Ogilvie Abercromby (*g s* of 5th Bt); *S* kinsman, 1972; *m* 1st, 1950, Joyce Beryl, *d* of Leonard Griffiths; 2nd, Fanny Mary, *d* of late Dr Graham Udale-Smith; one *d*; 3rd, 1976, Diana Marjorie, *d* of H. G. Cockell, and *widow* of Captain Ian Charles Palliser Galloway. *Educ:* Lancing Coll.; Bloxham Sch. *Heir:* none. *Address:* c/o National Westminster Bank, 224 King's Road, SW3; Tynte Park, Dunlavin, Co. Wicklow, Eire; El Amador, Marbella, Spain. *Clubs:* Ski Club of Great Britain; Kandahar; Real Nautico (Tenerife).

ABERDARE, 4th Baron, *cr* 1873, of Duffryn; **Morys George Lyndhurst Bruce,** PC 1974; DL; Chairman of Committees, House of Lords, since 1976; Prior for Wales, Order of St John; *b* 16 June 1919; *s* of 3rd Baron Aberdare, GBE, and Margaret Bethune (*née* Black); *S* father 1957; *m* 1946, Maud Helen Sarah, *o d* of Sir John Dashwood, 10th Bt, CVO; four *s.* *Educ:* Winchester; New College, Oxford (MA). Welsh Guards, 1939-46. Minister of State, DHSS, 1970-74; Minister Without Portfolio, 1974. Chm., Albany Life Assurance Co. Ltd. DL Glamorgan, 1966. Bailiff Grand Cross, OStJ, 1974. *Publication:* The Story of Tennis, 1959. *Recreations:* real tennis and rackets. *Heir:* s Hon. Alastair John Lyndhurst Bruce [*b* 2 May 1947; *m* 1971, Elizabeth Mary Culbert, *d* of John Foulkes; one *s*]. *Address:* 1 St Peter's Square, W6. *T:* 01-748 1403. *Clubs:* Lansdowne, MCC.

ABERDEEN, Bishop of, (RC), since 1977; **Rt. Rev. Mario Joseph Conti;** *b* Elgin, Moray, 20 March 1934; *s* of Louis Joseph Conti and Josephine Quintilia Panicali. *Educ:* St Marie's Convent School and Springfield, Elgin; Blairs Coll., Aberdeen; Pontifical Gregorian Univ. (Scots College), Rome. PhL 1955, STL 1959. Ordained, Rome, 1958; Curate, St Mary's Cathedral, Aberdeen, 1959-62; Parish Priest, St Joachim's, Wick and St Anne's, Thurso (joint charge), 1962-77. *Recreations:* music, art, book browsing, TV, travel, swimming. *Address:* 156 King's Gate, Aberdeen AB2 6BR. *T:* Aberdeen 39154.

ABERDEEN, Provost of (St Andrew's Cathedral); *see* Hodgkinson, Very Rev. A. E.

ABERDEEN and ORKNEY, Dean of; *see* Darwent, Very Rev. F. C.

ABERDEEN AND TEMAIR, 5th Marquess of, *cr* 1916; **Archibald Victor Dudley Gordon;** Bt of Nova Scotia, 1642; Earl of Aberdeen, Viscount Formartine, Lord Haddo, Methlic, Tarves and Kellie, 1682, Peerage of Scotland; Viscount Gordon, 1814, and Earl of Haddo, 1916, Peerage of UK; writer and broadcaster; *b* 9 July 1913; *s* of 3rd Marquis cf Aberdeen and Temair, DSO, and Cécile Elizabeth (*d* 1948), *d* of George Drummond, Swaylands, Penshurst, Kent; *S* brother, 1974; unmarried. *Educ:* Harrow. An assistant secretary, Council for the Protection of Rural England, 1936-40; joined BBC Monitoring Service, April 1940; BBC Talks Dept (Radio), 1946-72; Producer of The Week in Westminster, and of party political and election broadcasts (radio), 1946-66; Editor, Radio Documentaries and Talks, 1967-72. Independent. *Heir-pres.:* b Lord Alastair Ninian John Gordon [*b* 20 July 1920; *m* 1950, Anne, *d* of late Lt-Col Gerald Barry, MC; one *s* two *d*]. *Address:* Haughley Grange, Stowmarket, Suffolk IP14 3QT.

ABERDEEN AND TEMAIR, Marchioness of; (Beatrice Mary) June Gordon, MBE 1971; DL; Musical Director and Conductor, Haddo House Choral Society, since 1945; *b* 29 Dec. 1913; *d* of Arthur Paul Boissier, MA, and Dorothy Christina Leslie Smith; *m* 1939, David George Ian Alexander Gordon (later 4th Marquess of Aberdeen and Temair, CBE, TD) (*d* 1974); two adopted *s* two adopted *d*. *Educ:* Southlands School, Harrow; Royal Coll. of Music. GRSM, ARCM. Teacher of Music, Bromley High School for Girls, 1936-39. Director of Haddo House Choral Soc. and Arts Centre, 1945-. Chairman: Scottish Children's League, 1969; Advisory Cttee (local) Internat. Festival of Youth Orchestras, 1972; NE Scotland Music School. Governor, Gordonstoun Sch., 1971-. FRCM 1967. DStJ. DL Aberdeenshire, 1971. Hon. LLD Aberdeen, 1968. *Publications:* contribs to Aberdeen Univ. Jl, RCM magazine. *Address:* Haddo House, Aberdeen AB4 0ER. *T:* Tarves 216. *Club:* Bath.

ABERDEEN, David du Rieu, FRIBA, MRTPI; Architect (Private Practice); *b* 13 Aug. 1913; *s* of David Aberdeen and Lilian du Rieu; *m* 1940, Phyllis Irene Westbrook (*née* Buller),

widow; two *step c.* *Educ:* privately; Sch. of Architecture, London Univ. (BA Hons, Arch.). RIBA Donaldson Medallist, 1934; RIBA Alfred Bossom Research Fell., 1946-47. Works include: Brabazon Hangars, Filton, for Bristol Aeroplane Co.; TUC Headquarters, London, won in open architectural competition, 1948 (RIBA London Architecture Bronze Medal, 1958); 13-storey point block flats, New Southgate; housing for Basildon and Harlow New Towns. Architect for: new headquarters in City for Swiss Bank Corp.; redevelopment of Paddington Gen. Hosp.; New Gen. Market Hall, Shrewsbury; Swiss Centre, cultural and trade Headquarters, Leicester Square; First National City Bank of NY, London Office. Lectr, Atelier of Advanced Design, Sch. of Architecture, London Univ., 1947-53. *Publications:* contrib. to architectural press. *Address:* 20 Green Moor Link, N21; 19 Bloomsbury Square, WC1A 2NS.

ABERDOUR, Lord; John Stewart Sholto Douglas; *b* 17 Jan. 1952; *s* and *heir* of 22nd Earl of Morton, *qv.*

ABERGAVENNY, 5th Marquess of, *cr* 1876; **John Henry Guy Nevill,** KG 1974; OBE 1945; JP; Baron Abergavenny, 1450; Earl of Abergavenny and Viscount Nevill, 1784; Earl of Lewes, 1876; Lt-Col late Life Guards; Lord-Lieutenant of East Sussex, since 1974 (Vice-Lieutenant of Sussex, 1970-74); Chancellor, Order of the Garter, since 1977; *b* 8 Nov. 1914; *er s* of 4th Marquess and Isabel Nellie (*d* 1953), *d* of James Walker Larnach; *S* father, 1954; *m* 1938, Patricia (CVO 1970), *d* of Major and Hon. Mrs J. F. Harrison, King's Walden Bury, Hitchin; three *d* (and one *s* one *d* decd). *Educ:* Eton; Trinity Coll., Cambridge. Joined Life Guards, 1936; served War of 1939-45 (despatches, OBE); Lt-Col, retired 1946; Hon. Col, Kent & Co. of London Yeomanry, 1948-62. Director: Massey-Ferguson Holdings Ltd; Massey-Ferguson, Toronto; Lloyds Bank Ltd; Lloyds Bank SE Regional Bd (Chm.); Whitbread Investment Co. Trustee, Ascot Authority, 1953-; HM Representative at Ascot, 1972-; President: Royal Assoc. of British Dairy Farmers, 1955 and 1963; Assoc. of Agriculture, 1961-63; Royal Agric. Soc. of England, 1967 (Dep. Pres. 1968, 1972); Hunters' Improvement Soc., 1959; British Horse Soc., 1970-71; Vice-Chm., Turf Bd, 1967-68; Mem. Nat. Hunt Cttee, 1942 (Senior Steward, 1953 and 1963); Mem. Jockey Club, 1952. Member: E Sussex CC, 1947-54 (Alderman 1954-62); E Sussex Agric. Cttee, 1948-54. JP Sussex, 1948; DL Sussex, 1955. KStJ 1976 (Pres. Council, Order of St John, Sussex, 1975). *Heir:* b Lord Rupert Charles Montacute Nevill, *qv. Address:* (seat) Eridge Park, Tunbridge Wells, East Sussex. *T:* Tunbridge Wells 27378; 19 Lowndes Square, SW1. *T:* 01-235 7486. *Club:* White's. *See also* Earl of Cottenham.

ABERNETHY, William Leslie, CBE 1972; FCA, IPFA; Consultant, Touche Ross & Co., since 1973; Managing Trustee, Municipal Mutual Insurance Ltd, since 1973; Comptroller of Financial Services, Greater London Council, 1972-73 (Treasurer, 1964-72) and Chief Financial Officer, Inner London Education Authority, 1967-73; *b* 10 June 1910; *s* of Robert and Margaret Abernethy; *m* 1937, Irene Holden; one *s.* *Educ:* Darwen Grammar Sch., Lancs. Hindle & Jepson, Chartered Accts, Darwen, 1925-31; Borough Treasurer's Dept, Darwen, 1931-37; Derbyshire CC, Treasurer's Dept, 1937-48 (Dep. Co. Treas., 1944-48); 1st Treas., Newcastle upon Tyne Regional Hosp. Bd, 1948-50. LCC: Asst Comptroller, 1950-56; Dep. Comptroller, 1956-64; Comptroller, Sept. 1964-Mar. 1965. A General Commissioner of Income Tax, 1975-. Mem. Bd of Management, Young Vic Co. Ltd, 1972-. A Vice-Pres. and Trustee, Roy. Inst. of Public Admin (Chm. Exec. Coun., 1959-60). Mem. Council, IMTA, 1966-73. *Publications:* Housing Finance and Accounts (with A. R. Holmes), 1953; Internal Audit in Local Authorities and Hospitals, 1957; Internal Audit in the Public Boards, 1957; contribs professional jls. *Address:* 6c South Cliff Tower, Bolsover Road, Eastbourne, East Sussex. *T:* Eastbourne 36996.

ABINGDON, Earl of; *see* Lindsey and Abingdon, Earl of.

ABINGER, 8th Baron, *cr* 1835; **James Richard Scarlett,** DL; Lt-Col, late Royal Artillery; farmer and company director; *b* 28 Sept. 1914; *e s* of 7th Baron and Marjorie (*d* 1965), 2nd *d* of John McPhillamy, Blair Athol, Bathurst, NSW; *S* father, 1943; *m* 1957, Isla Carolyn, *o d* of late Vice-Adm. J. W. Rivett-Carnac, CB, CBE, DSC; two *s.* *Educ:* Eton; Magdalene College, Cambridge (MA 1952). India, France, Airborne Corps, and attached RAF; RNXS, 1968. Chairman: Keats Shelley Memorial Assoc. DL Essex, 1968. CStJ. *Heir:* s Hon. James Harry Scarlett, *b* 28 May 1959. *Address:* Clees Hall, Bures, Suffolk. *T:* Bures 227. *Clubs:* Carlton, Royal Automobile. *See also* Hon. J. L. C. Scarlett.

ABNEY-HASTINGS, family name of **Countess of Loudoun.**

ABOYADE, Prof. Ojetunji, PhD; Vice-Chancellor and Professor of Economics, University of Ife, since 1975; *b* 9 Sept. 1931; *s* of Mr and Mrs Aboyade, Awe, Oyo, Nigeria; *m* 1961, Olabimpe (*née* Odubanjo); two *s* two *d*. *Educ*: The University, Hull (Groves Prize, Best Perf. Econs Dept, 1957; BSc Hons Econs 1st Cl.); Pembroke Coll., Cambridge (PhD 1960). Govt Scholar, 1953-60. Res. Asst, Nigerian National Income Accounts, Fed. Office of Statistics, Lagos 1958—59; University of Ibadan, Nigeria: Lectr, Grade II and I, 1960—64; Sen. Lectr, 1964—66; Prof. of Econs, 1966-; Head, Dept. of Econs, 1966-71; Dean of Social Sciences 1972-74. Head, National Econ. Planning, Fed. Govt of Nigeria (Econ. Develt), 1969-70. Vis. Asst Prof. and Res. Fellow, Dept of Econs, Univ. of Mich, Ann Arbor, 1963-64; Vis. Consultant (Econ.), World Bank, USA, 1971-72. Editor, Nigerian Jl of Economic and Social Studies, 1961-71. Pres., Nigerian Econ. Soc., 1973-74; Member: Bd of Trustees, Internat. Food Policy Research Inst., USA; Internat. Assoc. for Res. and Income, 1964-; Council, Assoc. of Commonwealth Univs. *Publications*: Foundations of an African Economy: a study of investment and growth in Nigeria, 1967 (USA); Issues in the Development of an African Economy, 1976 (Nigeria); chapters in and essay contribs to books, and articles in professional jls, 1961-75. *Recreations*: hobbies include farming. *Address*: Vice-Chancellor's Office, University of Ife, Ile-Ife, Nigeria. *T*: Ile-Ife 2291-2299, ext. 100.

ABOYNE, Earl of; Granville Charles Gomer Gordon; *b* 4 Feb. 1944; *s* and *heir* of 12th Marquess of Huntly, *qv*; *m* 1972, Jane Elizabeth Angela, *d* of late Col Alistair Gibb and of Lady McCorquodale of Newton; one *s* one *d*. *Educ*: Gordonstoun. *Heir*: *s* Lord Strathavon and Glenlivet, *b* 26 July 1973. *Address*: Aboyne Castle Home Farm, Aberdeenshire. *T*: Aboyne 2118. *See also Baron Cranworth.*

ABRAHALL, Rt. Rev. A. L. E. H.; *see* Hoskyns-Abrahall, Rt Rev. A. L. E.

ABRAHAM, Edward Penley, CBE 1973; FRS 1958; MA, DPhil (Oxon); Fellow of Lincoln College, Oxford, since 1948; Professor of Chemical Pathology, Oxford, since 1964; *b* 10 June 1913; *s* of Albert Penley Abraham and Mary Abraham (*née* Hearn); *m* 1939, Asbjörg Harung, Bergen, Norway; one *s*. *Educ*: King Edward VI School, Southampton; The Queen's College, Oxford (1st cl. Hons Sch. of Natural Science), Hon. Fellow 1973. Rockefeller Foundation Travelling Fellow at Universities of Stockholm (1939) and California (1948). Ciba lecturer at Rutgers University, NJ, 1957; Guest lecturer, Univ. of Sydney, 1960; Reader in Chemical Pathology, Oxford, 1960-64; Rennebohm Lecturer, Univ. of Wisconsin, 1966-67; Squibb Lectr, Rutgers Univ., 1972. Royal Medal, Royal Soc., 1973; Scheele Medal, Swedish Academy of Pharmaceut. Sciences, 1975; Chemical Soc. Award in Medicinal Chemistry, 1975. *Publications*: Biochemistry of Some Peptide and Steroid Antibiotics, 1957; Biosynthesis and Enzymic Hydrolysis of Penicillins and Cephalosporins, 1974; contribs to: Antibiotics, 1949; The Chemistry of Penicillin, 1949; General Pathology, 1957, 4th edn 1970; Cephalosporins and Penicillins, Chemistry and Biology, 1972; scientific papers on the biochemistry of natural products, incl. penicillins and cephalosporins. *Recreations*: walking, ski-ing. *Address*: Badger's Wood, Bedwells Heath, Boars Hill, Oxford. *T*: Oxford 735395. *Club*: Athenæum.

ABRAHAM, Gerald Ernest Heal, CBE 1974; MA; FBA 1972; FTCL; President, Royal Musical Association, 1970-74; *b* 9 March 1904; *s* of Ernest and Dorothy Mary Abraham; *m* 1936, Isobel Patsie Robinson; one *d*. Asst Editor, Radio Times, 1935-39; Dep. Editor, The Listener, 1939-42; Director of Gramophone Dept, BBC, 1942-47; James and Constance Alsop Prof. of Music, Liverpool Univ., 1947-62; BBC Asst Controller of Music, 1962-67; Music Critic, The Daily Telegraph, 1967-68; Ernest Bloch Prof. of Music, Univ. of Calif (Berkeley), 1968-69. Chairman, Music Section of the Critics' Circle, 1944-46. Editor, Monthly Musical Record, 1945-60; Editor, Music of the Masters (series of books); General Editor, The History of Music in Sound (gramophone records and handbooks); Chm., Editorial Bd, Grove's Dictionary of Music; Gen. Editor, New Oxford History of Music; Chm., Early English Church Music Cttee; Mem. Editorial Cttee, Musica Britannica. President, International Society for Music Education, 1958-61; Dep. Chm. Haydn Institute (Cologne), 1961-68; Mem. Directorium, Internat. Musicological Soc., 1967-77; Governor, Dolmetsch Foundn, 1970-73. Hon. RAM 1970. Hon. DMus Dunelm, 1961; Hon. Dr of Fine Arts, California (Berkeley), 1969. *Publications*: This Modern Stuff, 1933; Nietzsche, 1933; Studies in Russian Music, 1935; Tolstoy, 1935; Masters of Russian Music (with M. D.

Calvocoressi), 1936; Dostoevsky, 1936; A Hundred Years of Music, 1938; On Russian Music, 1939; Chopin's Musical Style, 1939; Beethoven's Second-Period Quartets, 1942; Eight Soviet Composers, 1943; Tchaikovsky, 1944; Rimsky-Korsakov, 1945; Design in Music, 1949; Slavonic and Romantic Music, 1968; The Tradition of Western Music, 1974; (ed, with Dom Anselm Hughes) New Oxford History of Music, Vol. III (Ars Nova and the Renaissance), 1960; (ed) New Oxford History of Music, Vol. IV (The Age of Humanism), 1968. *Recreations*: walking, languages, military history. *Address*: The Old School House, Ebernoe, near Petworth, West Sussex. *T*: North Chapel 325.

ABRAHAM, Louis Arnold, CB 1956; CBE 1950; *b* 26 Nov. 1893; *y s* of late William Abraham, MP: West Limerick, 1885-92; North East Cork, 1893-1910; Dublin (Harbour), 1910-15; *m* 1921, Irene (*d* 1974), *yr d* of late Frederick George Kerin, Ennis, County Clare. *Educ*: Owen's School, London; Peterhouse, Cambridge (Exhibr) (1st cl. Hist. Tripos, pt 2, 1920). Pres., Cambridge Union, 1920. Asst Clerk, House of Commons, 1920; called to the Bar (certif. of honour), 1928; Pres., Hardwicke Soc., 1928; Senior Clerk, House of Commons, 1932; Clerk of Private Bills, 1945-52; Examr of Petitions for Private Bills and Taxing Officer, 1946-52; Principal Clerk of Committees, 1952-58. *Publications*: (with S. C. Hawtrey) A Parliamentary Dictionary, 1956; Defamation as Contempt of Parliament, in, Wicked, Wicked Libels, 1972; (ed) Palgrave's Chairman's Handbook, 1964. *Address*: 13 Lushington Road, Eastbourne, East Sussex BN21 4LG. *T*: Eastbourne 32223.

ABRAHAM, Maj.-Gen. Sutton Martin O'Heguerty, CB 1973; MC 1942 and Bar, 1943; Secretary, Bedford College, University of London, since 1976; *b* 26 Jan. 1919; *s* of Capt. E. G. F. Abraham, CB, late Indian Civil Service, and Ruth Eostre Abraham; *m* 1950, Iona Margaret, *d* of Sir John Stirling, KT, MBE; two *s* one *d*. *Educ*: Durnford; Eton; Trinity Coll., Cambridge (BA Modern Languages). Commissioned in RA, 1939; transf. to 12th Royal Lancers, 1941; Egypt, 1941; Armoured Car Troop Leader, desert campaigns; Armoured Car Sqdn 2nd-in-Comd, Italian campaign, Sangro Valley, Rimini, Po Valley; accepted surrender of Trieste (Sqdn Ldr); Mil. Asst to C-in-C Austria, and accompanied him to BAOR, 1946; psc 1948; Mem. Chiefs of Staff Secretariat, 1949-52; Sqdn Ldr 12th Lancers, Malaya, 1953-54; Mem. Staff Coll. Directing Staff, 1955-57; 2nd-in-Comd 12th Lancers, 1957-58; CO 12th Lancers, 1958-62 (Cyprus, 1959-60); Asst Mil. Sec., Southern Comd, 1960-62; GSO1, Staff Coll. (Minley Div.), 1960-62; Comdr RAC (Brig.), 1st Brit. Corps, Germany, 1964-66; idc 1967; Dir, Combat Develt (Army), MoD, 1968-71; Chief of Jt Services Liaison Orgn, BAOR, 1971-74; Mil. Adviser to Arms Control and Disarmament Res. Unit and Western Organisations Dept, FCO, 1973-76. *Recreations*: painting, reading, sundry practical country pursuits and chores, shooting. *Address*: c/o C. Hoare & Co., 37 Fleet Street, EC4. *T*: 01-353 4522. *Club*: Cavalry and Guards.

ABRAHAM, Maj.-Gen. Sir William Ernest Victor, Kt 1977; CBE 1942; FGS; Lay Member of Restrictive Practices Court, 1961-70, retired; *b* 21 Aug. 1897; *s* of John and Frances Abraham, Enniskillen; *m* 1928, Susan Jeanette Bidwell (*d* 1965), Kinsley, Kansas, USA; one *s* two *d*; *m* 1966, Rosemary Eustace, *d* of Louis H. King, Berrow, Somerset. *Educ*: Methodist Coll., Belfast; Royal Coll. of Science, Dublin. In Burma and India as Geologist, 1920-37. Commanded Upper Burma Bn, Burma Auxiliary Force, 1932-37; rejoined army, 1940, as 2nd Lieut and rose to rank of Major-General, after service in Greece, Middle East (OBE, despatches twice), Burma, Tunisia (CBE), Sicily; Controller General of Mil. Economy, India, 1945. Formerly Managing Director of Burmah Oil Co. Ltd, retd 1955. National Chm., Burma Star Assoc., 1962-77. *Address*: Kencot Manor, Lechlade, Glos. *T*: Filkins 212. *Clubs*: East India, Devonshire, Sports and Public Schools, Royal Automobile.

ABRAHAMS, Allan Rose, CMG 1962; company director; *b* 29 Nov. 1908; *s* of late Mr and Mrs Frank Abrahams; *m* 1948, Norma Adeline Neita; one *s* two *d*. *Educ*: Jamaica College, Jamaica. Joined Civil Service, 1927; Permanent Secretary, Ministry of Communications and Works, Jamaica, 1955-64, retired. *Recreation*: gardening. *Address*: 20 Widcombe Road, Kingston 6, Jamaica. *T*: 78214. *Club*: Kingston (Kingston, Jamaica).

ABRAHAMS, Sir Charles (Myer), KCVO 1970; Deputy Chairman and Joint Managing Director, Aquascutum and associated companies; *b* 25 April 1914; *s* of late Isidor and Eva Abrahams; *m* 1940, Luisa (*née* Kramer); two *d*. *Educ*: Westminster School. Hon. President, Friends of the Duke of Edinburgh's Award Scheme, 1975-; Vice-President: Nightingale House, Home for Aged Jews, 1971-; British Paraplegic Sports

Soc., 1976-. Served War of 1939-45 in Italy, Flt-Lt RAFVR. *Recreations:* golf and sculpture. *Address:* 188 Coombe Lane West, Kingston-upon-Thames, Surrey. *T:* 01-942 3379. *Clubs:* Coombe Hill Golf (Surrey); Sunningdale Golf (Berks).

ABRAHAMS, Gerald; barrister, author, occasional lecturer; *b* 15 April 1907; *s* of Harry and Leah Abrahams; *m* 1971, Elsie Krengel. *Educ:* Liverpool Collegiate Sch.; Wadham Coll., Oxford (Schol., MA). 1st cl. hons PPE, 1928; called to Bar, Gray's Inn, 1931. WEA Lectr, 1930-33; temp. Actg Prof. of Law, Belfast, 1934; lectures to HM Forces, 1940-44. Contested (L) Hallam Div. of Sheffield, 1945. Occasional broadcasts, law, chess, etc; sometime Chess Champion of Oxford Univ., Oxfordshire, Liverpool, Manchester, Lancs, N of England; some internat. chess. *Publications:* Law Affecting Police and Public, 1938; Law Relating to Hire Purchase, 1939; Ugly Angel (fiction), 1940; Retribution, 1941; Day of Reckoning, 1943; World Turns Left, 1943; Conscience Makes Heroes (fiction), 1945; Teach Yourself Chess, 1948; The Chess Mind, 1951; Lunatics and Lawyers (fiction), 1951; The Legal Mind, 1954; La Mediocrazia Contemporanea, 1956; Lo Stato Come Societa Commerciale: e la Irresponsibilita dei Ministri, 1957; Law for Writers and Journalists, 1958; According to the Evidence, 1958; The Jewish Mind, 1961; Technique in Chess, 1961 (trans. Spanish 1965); Brains in Bridge, 1962; Test Your Chess, 1963; Police Questioning: The Judges' Rules, 1964; Pan Book of Chess, 1965; Handbook of Chess, 1965; Let's Look at Israel, 1966; Trade Unions and the Law, 1968; Morality and the Law, 1971; Not only Chess, 1974; Brilliance in Chess, 1977; contrib. Encycl. Judaica, Philosophy, Nat. Review, Courier, Jewish Chronicle, Brit. Chess Magazine, etc. *Recreations:* philosophy, languages, chess, bridge, music, Bible. *Address:* 223 Woolton Road, Liverpool L16 8NA. *T:* 051-722 7712; 21 North John Street, Liverpool L2 5QU. *T:* 051-236 0718; 3 King's Bench Walk, Temple, EC4Y 7DQ. *T:* 01-236 1184. *Club:* Authors'.

ABRAHAMS, Gerald Milton, CBE 1967; Chairman and Managing Director, Aquascutum and Associated Companies Ltd, since 1947; *b* 20 June 1917; *s* of late Isidor Abrahams; *m* 1st, 1946, Doris, *d* of Mark Cole, Brookline, Mass, USA; two *d*; 2nd, 1972, Marianne Wilson, *d* of David Kay, London. *Educ:* Westminster Sch. Served War of 1939-45, Major HAC, RHA, in Greece and W Desert. Member: Council, CBI; British Menswear Guild (Chm., 1959-61, 1964-66); Clothing Export Council (Chm., 1966-70; Vice-Pres., 1970-); Clothing Manufacturers Fedn of GB (Chm., 1965-66); BNEC Cttee for Exports to Canada, 1965-70; Econ. Develt Cttee for Clothing Industry, 1966-69. FRSA 1972; FBIM 1973. *Recreations:* swimming, golf. *Address:* Aquascutum Ltd, 100 Regent Street, W1R 6AL. *T:* 01-734 6090. *Club:* Buck's.

ABRAHAMS, Harold Maurice, CBE 1957; MA, LLB; Secretary of National Parks Commission, 1950-63; *b* 15 December 1899; *s* of late Isaac Abrahams; *m* 1936, Sybil Marjorie (*d* 1963), *er d* of late C. P. Evers; one adopted *s* one adopted *d*. *Educ:* Repton; Gonville and Caius Coll., Cambridge. Hons Law Tripos, Cambridge, 1923; called to Bar, 1924; Ministry of Economic Warfare, 1939, Head of Statistics Section, 1941-42; Temp. Asst Sec., 1942-44; Assistant Secretary, Ministry of Town and Country Planning, 1946. Pres. Cambridge Univ. Athletic Club, 1922-23; represented Cambridge against Oxford, 1920-23, winning eight events in all; represented Great Britain in the Olympic Games, 1920 and 1924, winner 100 metres 1924; Captain British Athletic Team Olympic Games, 1928; Mem., Gen. Cttee of Amateur Athletic Assoc., 1926- (Vice-Pres., 1948; Life Vice-Pres., 1958; Pres., 1976); British Amateur Athletic Board: Asst Hon. Sec., 1939-48; Hon. Treas., 1948-68; Chm., 1968-75; 1st Life Vice-Pres., 1975. Hon. Pres., World Assoc. of Track and Field Statisticians, 1950; Athletics Corresp. Sunday Times, 1925-67; first broadcast, on radio, March 1924, on television, 1939. JP Essex, 1956-63. *Publications:* Sprinting, 1925; Athletics, 1926; Training for Athletics (with late A. Abrahams and others), 1928; Oxford *v* Cambridge (with late J. Bruce Kerr), 1931; Training for Health and Athletics (with late A. Abrahams), 1936; Official Records of 1928 and 1936 Olympic Games; Track and Field Olympic Records, 1948; The Olympic Games, 1896-1952, 1956; Empire and Commonwealth Games, 1930-58, 1958; The Rome Olympiad, 1960; Athletics Sportsgraph, 1972. *Recreations:* photography, statistics. *Address:* 42 Orpington Road, N21. *T:* 01-886 6472. *Clubs:* Achilles (Chm., 1947-61), Garrick; Cambridge University Pitt.

ABRAMS, Mark Alexander, PhD; Director of Research Unit, Age Concern, since 1976; Member, Metrication Board, since 1969; *b* 27 April 1906; *s* of Abram Abrams and Anne (*née* Jackson); *m* 1st, 1931, Una Strugnell (marr. diss. 1951); one *s* one *d*; 2nd, 1951, Jean Bird; one *d*. *Educ:* Latymer Sch., Edmonton; London Sch. of Economics, Univ. of London.

Fellow, Brookings Institute, Washington, DC, 1931-33; Research Department, London Press Exchange, 1933-39; BBC Overseas Dept, 1939-41; Psychological Warfare Board and SHAEF, 1941-46; Man. Dir, then Chm., Research Services Ltd, 1946-70; Dir, Survey Res. Unit, SSRC, 1970-76. Deputy Chairman Executive Committee, PEP. Member: Exec. Council, Austrian Soc. for Social Sci. Res.; Business Educn Council. *Publications:* Condition of the British People, 1911-1946, 1947; Social Surveys and Social Action, 1951. *Recreation:* listening to music. *Address:* 12 Pelham Square, Brighton, East Sussex. *T:* Brighton 684537. *Club:* Reform.

ABRAMSON, Sidney; Under Secretary, Department of Trade, since 1972; *b* 14 Sept. 1921; *s* of Jacob and Rebecca Abramson; *m* 1st, 1946, Lerine Freedman (marr. diss. 1958); two *s*; 2nd, 1960, Violet Ellen Eatly. *Educ:* Emanuel Sch., London; Queen's Coll., Oxford (MA). Cabinet Office, 1948-50; Board of Trade, 1950-63 (including Delegns to: OEEC, 1957-60; EFTA, 1960-62); GATT Secretariat, Geneva, 1963-65; Board of Trade (later Dept of Trade and Industry then Dept of Trade), 1965-. *Recreations:* music, gardening. *Address:* 75a Holden Road, N12. *T:* 01-445 1264.

ABSE, Leo; MP (Lab) Pontypool, since Nov. 1958; *b* 22 April 1917; *s* of Rudolph and Kate Abse; *m* 1955, Marjorie (*née* Davies); one *s* one *d*. *Educ:* Howard Gardens High School; London School of Economics. Solicitor; senior partner of Cardiff law firm; Sponsor or Co-sponsor of Private Members Acts relating to divorce, homosexuality, family planning, legitimacy, widows' damages, industrial injuries and congenital disabilities; Member: Home Office Adv. Cttee on adoption, 1972; Home Office Adv. Cttee on the Penal System, 1968; Select Cttee on Abortion, 1975-76; Council of Inst. for the Study and Treatment of Delinquency; Trustee, Clinic of Psychotherapy; Chairman: Welsh Parly Party, 1976; Cardiff City Labour Party, 1952-53; Mem., Cardiff City Council, 1955-58; contested Cardiff North, 1955. *Publication:* Private Member: a psychoanalytically orientated study of contemporary politics, 1973. *Address:* Merchaviah, 396 Cyncoed Road, Cardiff. *T:* 751844 and 23252; Beulah, 13 Cavendish Avenue, NW8. *T:* 01-286 7440.

ABUBAKAR, Prof. Iya; Vice-Chancellor, Ahmadu Bello University, Zaria, Nigeria, since 1975; *b* 14 Dec. 1934; *s* of Buba Abubakar, Wali of Mubi, and Fatima Abubakar; *m* 1963, Ummu; one *s* three *d*. *Educ:* Univ. of Ibadan (BSc London (External)); Cambridge Univ. (PhD). FRAS, FIMA. Prof. and Head of Dept of Maths, Ahmadu Bello Univ., 1967-75; Dean, Faculty of Science, 1968-69, 1973-75; Visiting Professor: Univ. of Michigan, 1965-66; City Univ. of New York, 1971-72. Chm., Natural Sciences Reg. Council of Nigeria, 1972-75. Mem., Nigerian Univs Commn, 1968-73. Dir, Central Bank of Nigeria, 1972-75. *Publications:* Entebbe Modern Mathematics, 1970; several research papers on mathematics in internat. jls. *Recreations:* chess, golf, horse riding. *Address:* Office of the Vice-Chancellor, Ahmadu Bello University, Zaria, Nigeria. *T:* 0632-2691.

ABUZEID, Salah; Order of the Star of Jordan (1st class); Ambassador of Jordan to the Court of St James's, since 1976; *b* 21 April 1925; *m* 1954, Nimat Abuzeid; two *s* five *d*; *m* 1964, Fomia Batshone; two *d*. *Educ:* Syrian Univ. Law Coll., Damascus; Syracuse Univ., Syracuse, USA. Govt Official, 1950-58; Director, Amman Radio Station, 1958-59; Asst Director-Gen., Hashemite Broadcasting Service, 1959-62; Director-Gen., Hashemite Broadcasting Service, and Chief of National Guidance, 1962-64; Minister of Culture and Information, 1964-65, 1967-68 and 1969-70; Jordan Ambassador to Court of St James's, 1969; Special Advr to HM King Hussein, 1970-71; Minister of Foreign Affairs, 1971-76. Holds numerous foreign decorations. *Recreations:* reading, music, sports. *Address:* Royal Jordan Embassy, 6 Upper Phillimore Gardens, W8 7HB.

ACHEAMPONG, Gen. Ignatius Kutu, CSG 1976; General (Head of State) and Chairman of the Supreme Military Council, Ghana, since 1972; also Chairman, National Redemption Council, and Commissioner for Finance, Economic Affairs, Defence and Sports, since 1972; Army Officer, Ghana; *b* Kumasi, 23 Sept 1931; *m*; seven *c*. *Educ:* St Peter's Catholic Sch., Kumasi; Ejisu Roman Catholic Sch.; Central Coll. of Commerce, Agona Swedru (GCE); Mons Officer Cadet Sch., Great Britain; Gen. Staff College, Fort Leavenworth, USA. Has been manual worker, teacher and secretary; Principal, Western Commercial Inst., Achiase, 1951. Enlisted in Army, Ghana, 1953; commissioned in Army, Ghana, 1959; served in the Congo, 1960 and 1962-63 (despatches). Became Chm., West Region Cttee of Admin, and Bde Comdr, 1st Infty Bde Group, Accra. *Address:* The Residence of Head of State, Accra, Ghana.

ACHEBE, Prof. Chinua; author; Professor of English, University of Nigeria, Nsukka; *b* 16 Nov. 1930; *s* of Isaiah and Janet Achebe; *m* 1961, Christiana Okoli; two *s* two *d*. *Educ:* Univ. of Ibadan. Nigerian Broadcasting Corp.: Talks Producer, 1954; Controller, 1959; Dir, 1961-66. Rockefeller Fellowship, 1960; Unesco Fellowship, 1963; Prof. of English, Univ. of Massachusetts, 1972-75; Prof. of English, Univ. of Connecticut, Storrs, 1975-76. Chairman, Soc. of Nigerian Authors, 1966. Member of Council, Univ. of Lagos, 1966. Jock Campbell New Statesman Award, 1965. Neil Gunn Internat. Fellowship, Scottish Arts Council, 1975; Hon. Fellow, Modern Language Assoc. of America, 1975. Editor, Okike, 1971-. Hon. DLitt: Dartmouth Coll., 1972; Southampton, 1975; DUniv Stirling, 1975; Hon. LLD Prince Edward Island, 1976; Hon. DHL Massachusetts, 1977. Commonwealth Poetry Prize, 1972. *Publications:* Things Fall Apart, 1958; No Longer at Ease, 1960; Arrow of God, 1964; A Man of the People, 1966; Beware Soul-brother (poems), 1971; (jtly) The Insider, 1972; Girls at War, 1972; Morning Yet on Creation Day (essays), 1975; *for children:* Chike and the River, 1966; (jt) How the Leopard Got its Claws, 1971. *Recreation:* music. *Address:* University of Nigeria, Nsukka, Nigeria.

ACHESON, family name of **Earl of Gosford.**

ACHESON, Prof. Ernest Donald; Dean, Faculty of Medicine, and Professor of Clinical Epidemiology, University of Southampton, since 1968; *b* 17 Sept. 1926; *s* of Malcolm King Acheson, MC, MD, and Dorothy Josephine Rennoldson; *m* Barbara Mary Castle; one *s* five *d*. *Educ:* Merchiston Castle Sch., Edinburgh; Brasenose Coll., Oxford (MA, DM); Middlesex Hospital. FRCP; FFCM. Medical Practitioner, 1951; various clinical posts at Middlesex Hosp.; Radcliffe Trav. Fellow of University Coll., Oxford, 1957-59; Medical Tutor, Nuffield Dept of Medicine, Radcliffe Infirmary, Oxford, 1960; Dir, Oxford Record Linkage Study, 1962; May Reader in Medicine, 1965; Fellow, Brasenose Coll., Oxford, 1968. Hon. Consultant Physician, Wessex Regional Hosp. Bd, 1968-74; Hampshire AHA (Teaching) 1974-; Examiner in Community Medicine, Univ. of Aberdeen, 1971-74; Examiner in Medicine, Univ. of Newcastle upon Tyne, 1975. *Publications:* Medical Record Linkage, 1967; Multiple Sclerosis, a reappraisal, 1966; Medicine, an outline for the intending student, 1970; scientific papers on epidemiology of cancer and chronic disease, and organisation of medical care. *Recreations:* family, gardening, music, fishing. *Address:* South Block, Southampton General Hospital, Southampton SO9 4XY.
See also *R . M . Acheson*.

ACHESON, Prof. Roy Malcolm, ScD, DM; FRCP, FFCM; Professor of Community Medicine, University of Cambridge, since 1976; Fellow, Churchill College, Cambridge, since 1977; *b* 18 Aug. 1931; *s* of Malcolm King Acheson, MC, MD and Dorothy Rennoldson; *m* 1950, Fiona Marigo O'Brien; two *s* one *d*. *Educ:* Merchiston Castle Sch., Edinburgh; TCD (MA, ScD); Brasenose Coll., Oxford (MA, DM); Radcliffe Infirmary, Oxford. FRCP 1973; FFCM 1972. Clin. and res. posts, Radcliffe Infirmary and Univ. of Oxford; Rockefeller Trav. Fellow, Western Reserve and Harvard Univs, 1955-56; Radcliffe Trav. Fellow, University Coll., Oxford, 1955-57; Lectr in Social Med., Univ. of Dublin, 1955-59; FTCD, 1957-59; Sen. Lectr, then Reader in Social and Preventive Med., Guy's Hosp. Med. Sch. and London Sch. of Hygiene and Trop. Med., 1959-62; Yale University: Associate Prof. of Epidemiology, 1962; Prof. of Epidemiology, 1964-72; Fellow, Jonathan Edwards Coll., 1966-75; London Sch. of Hygiene and Tropical Medicine: Commonwealth Fund Sen. Trav. Fellow in Med., 1968-69; Dir, Centre for Extension Trng in Community Med., 1972-76. Hon. Cons. in Community Med., NE Thames RHA (formerly NE Metrop. RHB), 1972-; Prof. of Health Service Studies, Univ. of London, 1974-76. Samuel R. McLaughlin Vis. Prof. in Med., McMaster Univ., Hamilton, Ont, 1976. Member: Exec. Cttee and Council, Internat. Epidemiol Soc., 1964-75; Expert Cttee, Methods in Chronic Disease Epidemiol, WHO, 1966. Cons., Argentina, Colombia, Guatemala, Venezuela, WHO, 1965-. Mem. Bd and Sec. to Examrs, Faculty of Community Med., 1974-77. Hon. MA Yale, 1964. *Publications:* (ed) Comparability in International Epidemiology, 1965; Seminars in Community Medicine: (ed with L. Aird) I: Sociology, 1976; (ed with L. Aird and D. J. Hall) II: Health Information, Planning and Monitoring, 1971. *Recreations:* tennis, golf (when time permits); meditating in the bath. *Address:* Department of Community Medicine, New Addenbrooke's Hospital, Hills Road, Cambridge CB2 2QQ. *T:* Cambridge 45171. *Club:* Queen's.
See also *E . D . Acheson*.

ACHONRY, Bishop of, (RC), since 1977; **Most Rev. Thomas Flynn,** DD; *b* 8 July 1931; *s* of Robert and Margaret Flynn.

Educ: St Nathy's, Ballaghaderreen; Maynooth College. BD, LPh, MA. Diocesan Religious Inspector of Schools, 1957-64; teaching in St Nathy's College, Ballaghaderreen, 1964-73; President and Headmaster of St Nathy's Coll., 1973-77. DD 1977. *Recreations:* gardening, fishing, golf. *Address:* St Nathy's, Ballaghaderreen, Co. Roscommon, Eire. *T:* Ballaghaderreen 21.

ACKERMAN, Myron, CBE 1972 (Hon.); President, since 1977, formerly Chairman and Managing Director, Chester Barrie Ltd; *b* 21 Sept. 1913; *s* of late Simon Ackerman and late May Krones Ackerman; *m* 1954, Marjorie Molyneux Jacob; no *c* . *Educ:* Yale Univ. Chm. and Man. Dir, Chester Barrie Gp. Hon Freeman, Borough of Crewe, 1973. *Address:* Henhull Cottage, Acton, Nantwich, Cheshire. *T:* Nantwich 65782. *Clubs:* Royal Automobile, American; Yale (New York).

ACKERMANN, Georg K., see Kahn-Ackermann.

ACKLAND, Joss, (Sidney Edmond Jocelyn); actor; *b* 29 Feb. 1928; *s* of Major Norman Ackland, Journalist, Daily Telegraph and Morning Post, and Ruth Izod; *m* 1951, Rosemary Jean Kirkcaldy, actress; two *s* five *d*. *Educ:* Cork Grammar Sch.; Dame Alice Owens Sch.; Central Sch. of Speech Training and Dramatic Art. *Plays:* The Hasty Heart, Aldwych, 1945; The Rising Sun, Arts, 1946; Dir, Winterset, 20th Century, 1946; Shakespeare Fest., Stratford-on-Avon, 1947; various try-out plays at Irving, Q, and Watergate Theatres, and toured, with Easy Money, in Germany, 1948; acted for Anthony Hawtrey, Embassy, Buxton and Croydon; then Arts Council tour, first Pitlochry Fest.; tours, and Repertory at Windsor, Chesterfield and Coventry. Went, with family, to Malawi, Central Africa, to work as a tea planter, 1954. S Africa: acting, directing, script writing and disc-jockeying, 1955-57; returned to England and joined Oxford Playhouse Co., 1957. Old Vic Co.: (incl. tours of America, Canada, USSR, Yugoslavia and Poland) Falstaff, Toby Belch, Caliban, Pistol, etc, 1958-61; Associate Dir, Mermaid Theatre: casting, choosing plays, Dir, Plough and the Stars, and playing numerous leading rôles, 1961-63. In 1963 his house burnt down so concentrated on television and did not return to theatre until 1965. Leading rôles on London stage: The Professor, 1966; Jorrocks, 1967; Hotel in Amsterdam, 1968-69; Come As You Are, 1969-70; Captain Brassbound's Conversion, 1971; The Collaborators, 1973; Streetcar Named Desire, 1974; A Little Night Music, 1975; Madras House, 1977. *Films:* Seven Days to Noon, 1949; Crescendo, 1969; The House that Dripped Blood, Villain, 1970; The Happiness Cage, England Made Me, 1971; Penny Gold, The Little Prince, The Black Windmill, S-P-Y-S, The Three Musketeers, 1973; Great Expectations, One of our Dinosaurs is Missing, 1974; Operation Daybreak, 1975; The Silver Bears, 1976; The End of Civilisation as we know it, 1977. Numerous appearances on TV, incl. The Bankrupt, The Widower, Access to the Children, Country Matters, The Lie, Kipling, The Crezz. *Recreations:* his seven children, writing, painting. *Club:* Garrick.

ACKLAND, Rodney; Playwright; *b* 18 May 1908; *m* 1952, Mab (*d* 1972), *d* of Frederick Lonsdale. First play, Improper People, Arts, 1929; Marionella, Players, 1930; Dance With No Music, Arts and Embassy, 1931; Strange Orchestra, Embassy and St Martin's, 1932; Ballerina, adapted from Lady Eleanor Smith's novel, Gaiety, 1933; Birthday, Cambridge, 1934; The Old Ladies, adapted from Sir Hugh Walpole's novel, New and St Martin's, 1935; After October, Criterion and Aldwych, 1936; Plot Twenty-One, Embassy, 1936; The White Guard, adapted from the Russian play by Michael Bulgakov, Phœnix, 1938; Remembrance of Things Past, Globe, 1938; Sixth Floor, adapted from the French play by Alfred Gehri, St James's, 1939; The Dark River, Whitehall, 1943; Crime and Punishment, adapted from Dostoevsky, New, 1946; (with Robert G. Newton) Cupid and Mars, Arts, 1947; Diary of a Scoundrel, based on a comedy by Ostrovsky, Arts, 1949; Before the Party, adapted from Somerset Maugham's short story, St Martin's, 1949; The Pink Room, Lyric, Hammersmith, 1952; A Dead Secret, Piccadilly, 1957; adapted Farewell, Farewell, Eugene, Garrick, 1959. *Publications:* Improper People; Dance With No Music; Strange Orchestra; The Old Ladies; Birthday; After October; The Dark River; Crime and Punishment; Cupid and Mars; Diary of a Scoundrel; Before the Party; Farewell, Farewell, Eugene; The Celluloid Mistress (autobiography); The Other Palace. *Address:* c/o Eric Glass Ltd, 28 Berkeley Square, W1X 6HD.

ACKNER, Hon. Sir Desmond (James Conrad), Kt 1971; **Hon. Mr Justice Ackner;** a Judge of the High Court of Justice, Queen's Bench Division, since 1971; Presiding Judge, Western Circuit, since 1976; *b* 18 Sept. 1920; *s* of Dr Conrad and Rhoda Ackner; *m* 1946, Joan, *d* of late John Evans, JP, and widow of K. B. Spence; one *s* two *d*. *Educ:* Highgate Sch.; Clare Coll., Cambridge (MA). Served in RA, 1941-42; Admty Naval Law

Br., 1942-45. Called to Bar, Middle Temple, 1945; QC 1961; Recorder of Swindon, 1962-71; Judge of Courts of Appeal of Jersey and Guernsey, 1967-71; Mem. Gen. Council of Bar, 1957-61, 1963-70 (Hon. Treas., 1964-66; Vice-Chm., 1966-68; Chm., 1968-70); Bencher Middle Temple, 1965; Mem. Senate of the Four Inns of Court, 1966-70 (Vice-Pres., 1968-70). *Recreations:* swimming, sailing, gardening, theatre. *Address:* 7 Rivermill, 151 Grosvenor Road, SW1. *T:* 01-821 8068; Browns House, Sutton, Petworth, West Sussex. *T:* Sutton (Sussex) 206. *Clubs:* Bath; Bar Yacht, Birdham Yacht.

ACKRILL, Prof. John Lloyd; Professor of the History of Philosophy, Oxford University, since 1966; *b* 30 Dec. 1921; *s* of late Frederick William Ackrill and Jessie Anne Ackrill; *m* 1953, Margaret Walker Kerr; one *s* three *d. Educ:* Reading School; St John's Coll., Oxford (Scholar) (1940-41 and 1945-48). War service (Royal Berks Regt and GS, Capt.), 1941-45. Assistant Lecturer in Logic, Glasgow Univ., 1948-49; Univ. Lectr in Ancient Philosophy, Oxford, 1951-52; Fellow and Tutor, Brasenose Coll., 1953-66. Mem., Inst. for Adv. Study, Princeton, 1950-51, 1961-62; Fellow Coun. of Humanities, and Vis. Prof., Princeton Univ., 1955, 1964. *Publications:* Aristotle's *Categories* and *De Interpretatione* (trans. with notes), 1963; Aristotle's *Ethics*, 1973; articles in philos. and class. jls. *Address:* 22 Charlbury Road, Oxford. *T:* 56098.

ACKROYD, Dame (Dorothy) Elizabeth, DBE 1970; MA, BLitt (Oxon); Chairman, Bloodstock and Racehorse Industries Confederation Ltd, since 1977; Independent Member, Eggs Authority, since 1970; Chairman, South Eastern Electricity Consultative Council, since 1972; Member, Seeboard, since 1972; Member, Horserace Totalisator Board, since 1976; *d* of late Major Charles Harris Ackroyd, MC. *Educ:* privately; St Hugh's Coll., Oxford. Research Asst, Barnett House, Oxford, 1936-39; Min. of Supply, 1940-42, 1946-49, 1951-52 (Under-Sec., 1952); Min. of Prodn, 1942-45; BoT, 1945-46, 1955-61; Commonwealth Fund Fell., 1949-50; Dir of Steel and Power Div., Economic Commn for Europe, 1950-51; UK Delegn to High Authority of ECSC, 1952-55; MoT, 1961-63; Director: Consumer Council, 1963-71; Nat. Innovations Centre, 1971-74. Indep. Mem., Cinematograph Films Council, 1970-; Vice-Pres., Consumers' Assoc., 1970-; Member: PO Users' Nat. Council, 1970-; Bedford Coll. Council, 1970-; Steering Cttees, Metrication Bd, 1972-; Panel of inquiry into beef supplies and prices, 1973; West Roding Community Health Council, 1974-76; Governor, Birkbeck Coll., 1973-; Chief Exec., Voluntary Service Housing, 1975-76; Exec. Cttee, London Council of Soc. Service, 1975-; Council, Royal Soc. of Arts, 1975-. Pres., Patients' Assoc., 1971-; Hon. Treasurer, Pedestrians' Assoc. for Road Safety, 1971-. *Address:* 73 St James's Street, SW1A 1PH. *T:* 01-493 6686.

ACKROYD, Sir John (Robert Whyte), 2nd Bt *cr* 1956; consultant and investment adviser to Middle East countries through various UK Investment Trusts and to developing countries; International Employee Benefit Consultant, Callund and Company Ltd, since 1976; Underwriting Member of Lloyd's, since 1960; *b* 2 March 1932; *s* of Sir Cuthbert Lowell Ackroyd, 1st Bt, and of Joyce Wallace, *d* of Robert Whyte; *S* father, 1973; *m* 1956, Jennifer Eileen McLeod, *d* of H. G. S. Bishop; two *s* two *d. Educ:* Bradfield Coll.; Worcester Coll., Oxford (BA 1955, MA 1958). Commissioned RA, 1951; Sword of Honour, Mons Officer Cadet Sch., 1951; served under Sir John Glubb (Glubb Pasha) in Arab Legion, 1951-52. Oxford Univ., 1952; Steward, OUDS, 1954. Worked in Lloyd's with broking firm, 1955-66; toured Middle East alone for purposes of writing travel book, 1967; joined Engineer Planning & Resources Ltd, 1968. Hon. Secretary, The Pilgrims of Gt Britain, 1966; Mem. Gen. Council, Victoria League for Commonwealth Friendship, 1973. Church Warden, St Mary-le-Bow, Cheapside, and The Church of All Hallows. FZS 1970. Freeman of the City of London; Liveryman Carpenters' Co. *Recreations:* music, theatre, travel, sociology, history. *Heir: er s* Timothy Robert Whyte Ackroyd, *b* 7 Oct. 1958. *Address:* 43 Lansdowne Crescent, Holland Park, W11 2NN. *T:* 01-727 5465. *Clubs:* Carlton (Mem. Management Cttee); (Life Mem.) Union Society (Oxford).

ACKROYD, Rev. Prof. Peter Runham, MA, PhD Cantab, BD, MTh, DD London; Samuel Davidson Professor of Old Testament Studies, University of London, since 1961; *b* 15 Sept. 1917; *s* of Jabez Robert Ackroyd and Winifred (*née* Brown); *m* 1940, Evelyn Alice Nutt, BSc (Manch.), *d* of William Young Nutt; two *s* three *d. Educ:* Harrow County School for Boys; Downing and Trinity Colleges, Cambridge. Open Exhibition in Modern Languages, Downing Coll., Cambridge, 1935; Mod. and Med. Langs Tripos, Pt I, 1936, Pt II, 1938; BDHons London, 1940; Stanton Student, Trin. Coll., Cambridge, 1941-43; Dr Williams's Trust Exhibnr, 1941; MTh London, 1942; PhD Cambridge, 1945; DD London, 1970. Minister of: Roydon Congregational Church, Essex, 1943-47; Balham Congregational Church, London, 1947-48; Lectr in Old Testament and Biblical Hebrew, Leeds Univ., 1948-52; Cambridge University: Univ. Lectr in Divinity, 1952-61; Select Preacher, 1955; Mem. Council of Senate, 1957-61; Hulsean Lectr, 1960-62; Select Preacher, Oxford, 1962; Dean of Faculty of Theology, King's Coll., London, 1968-69; FKC 1969; Mem. Senate, London Univ., 1971-; Dean, Univ. Faculty of Theology, 1976-. Vis. Professor: Lutheran Sch. of Theology, Chicago, 1967 and 1976; Univ. of Toronto, 1972; Selwyn Lectr, NZ, 1970. External Examiner, Belfast, Bristol, Durham, Cambridge, Edinburgh, Leeds, Nottingham. Ordained Deacon, 1957; Priest, 1958. Hon. Curate, Holy Trinity, Cambridge, 1957-61. Proctor in Convocation, Cambridge Univ., 1960-64. Hon. Sec., Palestine Exploration Fund, 1962-70. Pres., Soc. for Old Testament Study, 1972. Hon. DD St Andrews, 1970. *Publications:* Freedom in Action, 1951; The People of the Old Testament, 1959; Continuity, 1962; The Old Testament Tradition, 1963; Exile and Restoration, 1968; Israel under Babylon and Persia, 1970; 1 & 2 Chronicles, Ezra, Nehemiah, Ruth, Jonah, Maccabees, 1970; 1 Samuel (Cambridge Bible Commentary), 1971; I & II Chronicles, Ezra, Nehemiah (Torch Bible Commentary), 1973; 2 Samuel, 1977; articles and reviews in various learned jls, dictionaries, etc; *Translations:* E. Würthwein's The Text of the Old Testament, 1957; L. Köhler's Hebrew Man, 1957, repr. 1973; O. Eissfeldt's The Old Testament: An Introduction, 1965; *editor:* Faith, Law, Hope, Wrath, Life and Death (Bible Key Words), 1961-64; Society for Old Testament Study Book List, 1967-73; Palestine Exploration Quarterly, 1971-; *joint editor:* SCM Press OT Library, 1960-; Cambridge Bible Commentary, 1961-; SCM Studies in Biblical Theol., 1962-; Words and Meanings: Essays presented to D. W. Thomas, 1968; Cambridge History of the Bible; vol. I, from the beginnings to Jerome, 1970. *Recreations:* reading, music. *Address:* 34 Half Moon Lane, SE24 9HU. *T:* 01-733 1898.

ACLAND, Sir Antony (Arthur), KCVO 1976; CMG 1976; HM Diplomatic Service; Ambassador to Spain, since 1977; *b* 12 March 1930; *m* 1956, Clare Anne Verdon; two *s* one *d. Educ:* Eton; Christ Church, Oxford (MA 1956). Joined Diplomatic Service, 1953; ME Centre for Arab Studies, 1954; Dubai, 1955; Kuwait, 1956; FO, 1958-62; Asst Private Sec. to Sec. of State, 1959-62; UK Mission to UN, 1962-66; Head of Chancery, UK Mission, Geneva, 1966-68; FCO, 1968, Hd of Arabian Dept, 1970-72; Principal Private Sec. to Foreign and Commonwealth Sec., 1972-75; Ambassador to Luxembourg, 1975-77. *Address:* c/o Foreign and Commonwealth Office, SW1; 17 Fife Road, SW14. *T:* 01-878 0148. *Club:* Travellers'.

ACLAND, Lieut-Gen. Arthur N. F.; *see* Floyer-Acland.

ACLAND, Captain Sir Hubert (Guy Dyke), 4th Bt *cr* 1890; DSO 1920; *b* 8 June 1890; *y s* of Sir William Alison Dyke Acland, 2nd Bt; *S* brother, 1970; *m* 1915, Lalage Mary Kathleen (*d* 1961), *e d* of Captain John Edward Acland; two *s*. Lieutenant 1910; Lieutenant Commander, 1918; Commander, 1925; Captain 1932; served European War, 1914-19 (despatches, DSO); commanded 1st Minesweeping Flotilla, 1934-35 and Fishery Protection and Minesweeping Flotilla, 1935-36; lent to Royal Australian Navy, 1937-38, and commanded HMAS Australia, 1937-38 and HMAS Albatross, 1938; Senior Officer of Reserve Fleet, Devonport, 1939; Gunnery School, Chatham, Nov. 1939; commanded HMS Vindictive, 1941-42; retired list, 1942; on staff of C-in-C Rosyth, 1943 and of Flag Officer in Charge N Ireland, 1943-45. *Heir: s* Antony Guy Acland [*b* 17 Aug. 1916; *m* 1st, 1939, Avriel Ann (*d* 1943), *o c* of late Captain Mervyn Edward John Wingfield-Stratford; one *d*; 2nd, 1944, Margaret Joan, *er d* of late Major Nelson Rooke; one *s* one *d*]. *Address:* c/o Sunny Bank, Totland Bay, Isle of Wight. *Club:* Royal Yacht Squadron.

ACLAND, Sir (Hugh) John (Dyke), KBE 1968; a Member, 1947-72, Chairman, 1960-72, New Zealand Wool Board; Vice-Chairman, International Wool Secretariat, to 1972; *b* 18 Jan. 1904; *e s* of Sir Hugh Acland, CMG, CBE, FRCS, and Lady Acland; *m* 1935, Katherine Wilder Ormond; three *s* three *d. Educ:* Christ's College, Christchurch, NZ. MHR, NZ, 1942-47. JP S Canterbury. *Address:* Mount Peel, Peel Forest, South Canterbury, New Zealand.

ACLAND, Brigadier Peter Bevil Edward, OBE 1945; MC 1941; TD; Vice-Lord-Lieutenant of Devon, since 1962; *b* 9 July 1902; *s* of late Col A. D. Acland, CBE; *m* 1927, Susan Bridget Barnett, *d* of late Canon H. Barnett; two *s. Educ:* Eton; Christ Church, Oxford. Sudan Political Service, 1924-40. Served War of 1939-45: Abyssinia, Western Desert, Ægean (wounded, despatches). Comd Royal Devon Yeomanry, 1947-51, Hon. Col, 1953; Chairman, Devon AEC, 1948-58; Member, National Parks

Commission, 1953-60; Chairman, Devon T&AFA, 1960. DL Devon, 1948; High Sheriff for Devon, 1961; JP 1962. 4th Class Order of the Nile; Greek War Cross. *Address:* Feniton Court, Honiton, Devon. *Club:* English-Speaking Union.

ACLAND, Sir Richard Thomas Dyke, 15th Bt, *cr* 1644; *b* 26 Nov. 1906; *e s* of Rt Hon. Sir Francis Acland, 14th Bt, MP; *S* father, 1939; *m* 1936, Anne Stella Alford; three *s. Educ:* Rugby; Balliol Coll., Oxford. MP Barnstaple Div. Devon, 1935-45; contested: Torquay Div., 1929; Barnstaple, 1931; Putney, 1945; MP (Lab) Gravesend Division of Kent, 1947-55. Sen. Lectr, St Luke's College of Educn, Exeter, 1959-74. Second Church Estates Commissioner, 1950-51. *Publications:* Unser Kampf, 1940; The Forward March, 1941; What it will be like, 1943; How it can be done, 1943; Public Speaking, 1946; Nothing Left to Believe?, 1949; Why So Angry?, 1958; Waging Peace, 1958; We Teach Them Wrong: religion and the young, 1963; (with others) Sexual Morality: three views, 1965; Curriculum or Life, 1966; Moves to the Integrated Curriculum, 1967; The Next Step, 1974. *Heir: s* John Dyke Acland [*b* 13 May 1939; *m* 1961, Virginia, *d* of Roland Forge; two *s* one *d*]. *Address:* Sprydon, Broadclyst, Exeter. *T:* Broadclyst 412.

A'COURT; see Holmes A'Court.

ACTON, 3rd Baron, *cr* 1869; **John Emerich Henry Lyon-Dalberg-Acton,** Bt, *cr* 1643; CMG 1963; MBE 1945; TD; Major RA, TA; Chairman, British and Continental Holdings (Insurance Brokers) Ltd; *b* 15 Dec. 1907; *s* of 2nd Baron and Dorothy (*d* 1923), *d* of late T. H. Lyon, Appleton Hall, Cheshire; *S* father, 1924; *m* 1931, Hon. Daphne Strutt, *o d* of 4th Baron Rayleigh, FRS; five *s* five *d. Educ:* Downside; Trinity Coll., Cambridge. Served War of 1939-45 (MBE). *Recreation:* horse racing. *Heir: s* Hon. Richard Gerald Acton [*b* 30 July 1941; *m* 1st, 1965, Hilary Juliet Sarah Cookson (*d* 1973); one *s* ; 2nd, 1974, Judith, *d* of Hon. R. S. Garfield Todd, *qv* .] *Address:* Ca-Na, Rosalinda, Pollensa, Mallorca. *Club:* Shrewsbury.
See also J. D. Woodruff.

ACTON, Sir Harold (Mario Mitchell), Kt 1974; CBE 1965; author; *b* 5 July 1904; *s* of Arthur Mario Acton and Hortense Mitchell, La Pietra, Florence. *Educ:* Eton Coll.; Christ Church, Oxford (BA). FRSL. Lectr in English Literature, National University of Peking and Peking Normal College, 1933-35. Lived for seven years in Peking, devoting much time to Chinese Classical Theatre. Served in RAF during War of 1939-45, chiefly in Far East. Grand Officer, Republic of Italy; Kt of the Constantinian Order. *Publications:* Aquarium, 1923; An Indian Ass, 1925; Five Saints and an Appendix, 1927; Humdrum, 1928; Cornelian, 1928; This Chaos, 1930; The Last Medici, 1932, new edn 1958; (in collab.) Modern Chinese Poetry, 1936; (in collab.) Famous Chinese Plays, 1937; Peonies and Ponies, 1941; Glue and Lacquer, 1941 (Four Cautionary Tales, 1947, reprint of former); Memoirs of an Aesthete, 1948; Prince Isidore, 1950; The Bourbons of Naples, 1956; The Last Bourbons of Naples, 1961; Florence (an essay), 1961; Old Lamps for New, 1965; More Memoirs of an Aesthete, 1970; Tit for Tat, 1972; Tuscan Villas, 1973; Nancy Mitford: a memoir, 1975; (in collab.) The Peach Blossom Fan, 1976. *Recreations:* jettatura, hunting the Philistines. *Address:* La Pietra, Florence, Italy. *T:* 496-156. *Club:* Savile.

ACTON, William Antony; *b* 8 April 1904; *o s* of late William Walter Acton, Wolverton Hall, Pershore, Worcs; *m* 1932, Joan, *o c* of late Hon. Francis Geoffrey Pearson; one *d. Educ:* Eton; Trinity College, Cambridge. HM Treasury, 1939-45. Managing Director, Lazard Bros & Co. Ltd, 1945-53; Director: The National Bank Ltd, 1945-70 (Chm., 1964-70); Bank of London and South America Ltd, 1953-70; Standard Bank Ltd, 1953-70; Ottoman Bank, 1953-58; Bank of London and Montreal Ltd., 1959-64; Bank of West Africa Ltd, 1954-70; Bank of Ireland, 1966-70; National Commercial Bank of Scotland, 1967-70; National and Commercial Banking Group Ltd, 1969-70; The Whitehall Trust, 1945-70. High Sheriff, County of London, 1955. *Recreation:* travelling. *Address:* Poste Restante, Corfu, Greece. *T:* Corfu 91-236. *Club:* White's.
See also Sir H . H . T . Dawson , Bt .

ACUTT, Sir Keith (Courtney), KBE 1962 (CBE 1957); Deputy Chairman, Anglo-American Corporation of South Africa Ltd; Director, de Beers Consolidated Mines Ltd and several other finance and mining companies; *b* 6 Oct. 1909; *s* of late Guy Courtney Acutt. *Educ:* in South Africa. Served War of 1939-45 (despatches, 1944). *Address:* 44 Main Street, Johannesburg, South Africa. *T:* 838-8111.

ADAIR, Maj.-Gen. Sir Allan (Henry Shafto), 6th Bt, *cr* 1838; GCVO 1974 (KCVO 1967; CVO 1957); CB 1945; DSO 1940;

MC; DL; JP; Lieutenant of HM Bodyguard of the Yeomen of the Guard, 1951-67; *b* 3 Nov. 1897; *o s* of Sir R. Shafto Adair, 5th Bt and Mary (*d* 1950), *d* of Henry Anstey Bosanquet; *S* father, 1949; *m* Enid, *d* of late Hon. Mrs Dudley Ward; three *d* (one *s* killed in action, 1943). *Educ:* Harrow. Grenadier Guards, 1916-41; commanded 3rd Battalion, 1940; Comdr 30 Guards Brigade, 1941; Comdr 6 Guards Brigade, 1942; Comdr Guards Armoured Division 1942-45; retired pay, 1947. Colonel of the Grenadier Guards, 1961-74. DL for Co. Antrim; JP for Suffolk. Governor of Harrow School, 1947-52. Dep. Grand Master, United Grand Lodge of Freemasons, 1969-76. *Recreations:* shooting, golf. *Address:* 55 Green Street, W1. *T:* 01-629 3860; Holy Hill, Strabane, Co. Tyrone. *Clubs:* Turf, Cavalry and Guards.
See also Brig. Sir J. L. Darell, Bt.

ADAIR, Arthur Robin, CVO 1961; MBE 1947; HM Diplomatic Service, retired Aug. 1972; State and Ministerial Visit Escorting Officer, Government Hospitality Fund, 1973-75; retired 1975; *b* 10 Feb. 1913; *s* of late Francis Robin Adair and Ethel Anne Adair, Grove House, Youghal, Eire; *m* 1952, Diana Theodora Synnott; one *s. Educ:* abroad; Emmanuel College, Cambridge. Indian Civil Service, 1937-47 (incl. 3 yrs in Army in charge of recruitment for Bihar Prov.); Dist Magistrate and Dep. Comr, 1944-47; Treasury, July 1947; transferred to CRO, Oct. 1947; First Secretary: Dacca, 1947-50; Colombo, 1952-56; British Dep. High Comr in: Dacca, 1960-64; Cyprus, 1964-68; British High Comr in Brunei, 1968-Jan. 1972. *Recreation:* flying as private pilot. *Address:* Grove House, Youghal, Co. Cork, Eire. *T:* Youghal 2930. *Club:* Naval and Military.

ADAIR, Gilbert Smithson, FRS 1939; MA; Reader in Biophysics, Physiological Laboratory, Cambridge, 1947-63; *b* 21 Sept. 1896; *s* of Harold Adair, JP; *m* 1931, Muriel Elaine Robinson (*d* 1975); no *c. Educ:* Bootham School, York; King's College, Cambridge. Scholar and Fellow of King's College, Cambridge; Hon. Fellow, 1963; engaged in research on thermodynamical properties of proteins. *Publications:* papers in scientific periodicals. *Address:* 92 Grantchester Meadows, Cambridge. *Club:* Fell and Rock Climbing.

ADAM, Hon. Sir Alexander Duncan Grant (known as Hon. Sir Alistair Adam), Kt 1970; MA, LLM; Judge, Supreme Court of Victoria, 1957-74; *b* Greenock, Scotland, 30 Nov. 1902; *s* of late Rev. Prof. Adam and of Mrs D. S. Adam; *m* 1930, Nora Laver; one *s* two *d. Educ:* Scotch Coll., Melbourne; Melbourne Univ. Associate to Mr Justice Starke, 1927-28; Victorian Bar, 1928-57; Independent Lecturer in Real Property, Melbourne Univ., 1932-51; Defence Dept, 1942-45; QC 1950; Member Council: Melbourne Univ., 1957-69; Nat. Museum of Victoria, 1962-74. *Publications:* contributor to learned jls. *Recreations:* golf, bowls. *Address:* 39 Walsh Street, Balwyn, Vic. 3103, Australia. *T:* 801524. *Clubs:* Australian (Melbourne); Royal Automobile Club of Victoria; Deepdene Bowling.

ADAM, Colin Gurdon Forbes, CSI 1924; *b* 18 Dec. 1889; *y s* of Sir Frank Forbes Adam, 1st Bt; *m* 1920, Hon. Irene Constance Lawley, *o c* of 3rd Baron Wenlock; two *s* one *d* (and one *s* decd). *Educ:* Eton; King's Coll., Cambridge (BA). Entered Indian Civil Service, 1912; Asst Collector and Magistrate, Poona, 1913-15; Under-Sec. to Government of Bombay, 1919; Private Sec. to Governor of Bombay, 1920; Dep. Sec. to Govt, 1925; retired, 1927; District Comr for Special Area of Durham and Tyneside, 1934-39; Chairman, Yorkshire Conservative Newspaper Co., 1960-65. Served Indian Army Reserve of Officers, 1915-18; Indian Expeditionary Force, Mesopotamia and Palestine, 1916-18. DL Kingston upon Hull, 1958-66. *Publication:* Life of Lord Lloyd, 1948. *Address:* The Grange, Elvington, York YO4 5AD. *T:* Elvington 493.
See also Gen. Sir R. F. Adam.

ADAM, Kenneth, CBE 1962; MA; FRSA; Overseas Visitor to Temple University, Philadelphia, since 1969; *b* 1 March 1908; *s* of Edward Percy Adam and Ethel Jane Saunders; *m* 1932, Ruth Augusta King (*d* 1977); three *s* one *d. Educ:* Nottingham High Sch.; St John's Coll., Cambridge (Senior Scholar and Prizeman). Editorial Staff, Manchester Guardian, 1930-34; Home News Editor, BBC, 1934-36; Special Corresp. of The Star, 1936-40; Press Officer, BOAC, 1940-41; Dir of BBC Publicity, 1941-50; Controller, Light Programme, BBC, 1950-55; Gen. Manager (Joint), Hulton Press, 1955-57; Controller of Television Programmes, BBC, 1957-61; Dir of BBC Television, 1961-68. Vis. Prof. of Communications, Temple Univ., Philadelphia, 1968-; Danforth Travelling Fellow, USA, 1970, 1971. Communicating Editor, Jl of Communication Studies, USA, 1974. Chm., NZ Commission on Broadcasting, 1973; Mem., Exec. Cttee, Standing Conference on Broadcasting, UK, 1973. Governor, Charing Cross Hosp., 1960-66; Governor, British

Film Inst., 1961; Member: (co-opted), Extra Mural Delegacy, Oxford, 1962; London Topographical Soc., 1962; Brit. Travel Assoc. Council, 1966; Council of Industrial Design, 1967; Council, Nat. Youth Theatre, 1967; Council, Tavistock Inst., 1968; Internat. Broadcasting Inst., 1975. Hon. Mem., Anglo-Danish Soc., 1952-. FAMS 1962. *Address:* 19 Old Court House, W8 4PD. *T:* 01-937 0369; Tomlinson Hall, Temple University, Philadelphia, Pa 19122, USA. *T:* (215) 787-8421. *Clubs:* Caledonian; Union Society (Cambridge); Diamond (Philadelphia).

ADAM, Madge Gertrude, MA, DPhil; FRAS; University Lecturer (Astronomy), Department of Astrophysics, University Observatory, Oxford; Research Fellow of St Hugh's College, since 1957; *b* 6 March 1912; 2nd *d* of late John Gill Simpson and late Gertrude Adam; unmarried. *Educ:* Municipal High School, Doncaster; St Hugh's College, Oxford (Scholar). Research Scholar, Lady Margaret Hall, 1935-37; Junior British Scholarship, 1936-37; Assistant Tutor of St Hugh's College and Research Assistant at Oxford University Observatory, 1937; lately Fellow and Tutor, St Hugh's College. *Publications:* papers in Monthly Notices of Royal Astronomical Society from 1937. *Address:* Department of Astrophysics, The University Observatory, South Parks Road, Oxford.

ADAM, Randle R.; *see* Reid-Adam.

ADAM, Robert Wilson, (Robin); a Managing Director, British Petroleum Co. Ltd, since 1975; *b* 21 May 1923; *s* of R. R. W. Adam; *m* 1957, Marion Nancy Scott. *Educ:* Fettes, Edinburgh. Royal Scots, 1942; commnd RIASC 1942; served in India and Burma (Major). Chartered Accountant 1950. Joined British Petroleum Co. Ltd, 1950; Pres., BP North America Inc. New York, 1969-72; Dir, BP Trading Ltd, 1973-75. *Recreation:* golf. *Address:* Squirrel Wood, Seven Hills Road, Cobham, Surrey. *T:* Cobham 2888. *Clubs:* Caledonian, MCC.

ADAM, General Sir Ronald Forbes, 2nd Bt, *cr* 1917; GCB 1946 (KCB 1941; CB 1939); DSO 1918; OBE 1919; RA; Hon. LLD (Aberdeen); Hon. Fellow, Worcester College, Oxford; President, United Nations Association; *b* 30 Oct. 1885; *e* *s* of Sir Frank Forbes Adam, 1st Bt, and Rose Frances (*d* 1944), *d* of C. G. Kemball, late Judge, High Court, Bombay; *S* father, 1926; *m* 1915, Anna Dorothy (*d* 1972), *d* of late F. I. Pitman; three *d*. *Educ:* Eton; RMA, Woolwich. Served European War (France and Flanders, Italy), 1914-18 (despatches, DSO, OBE); GSO1, Staff College, Camberley, 1932-35; GSO1, War Office, 1935-36; Deputy Director of Military Operations, War Office, 1936; Commander Royal Artillery, 1st Division, 1936-37; Commandant of Staff College, Camberley, 1937; Deputy Chief of Imperial General Staff, 1938-39; Commanding 3rd Army Corps, 1939-40; General Officer Commanding-in-Chief, Northern Command, 1940-41; Adjutant-General to the Forces, 1941-46; General, 1942; retired pay, 1946. Col Comdt of RA and of Army Educational Corps, 1940-50; Col Comdt Royal Army Dental Corps, 1945-51 (Representative, 1950). President: MCC, 1946-47; Library Assoc., 1949; Nat. Inst. of Adult Education, 1949-64; Chairman: Linoleum Working Party, 1946; Nat. Inst. Industrial Psychology, 1947-52; Council, Inst. of Education, London Univ., 1948-67; Mem., Miners Welfare Commn, 1946-52; Chm. and Dir-Gen., British Council, 1946-54; Executive Board UNESCO, 1950-54, Chm., 1952-54; Principal, Working Men's Coll., 1956-61. *Heir: n* Christopher Eric Forbes Adam [*b* 12 Feb 1920; *m* 1957, Patricia Ann Wreford, *y* *d* of late John Neville Wreford Brown]. *Address:* Carylls Lea, Faygate, Sussex. *Clubs:* Athenæum, Naval and Military.
See also C. G. F. Adam, Sir P. D. Proctor.

ADAM SMITH, Janet (Buchanan), (Mrs John Carleton); author and journalist; *b* 9 Dec. 1905; *d* of late Very Rev. Sir George Adam Smith, Principal of Aberdeen Univ. and late Lady Adam Smith; *m* 1st, 1935, Michael Roberts (*d* 1948); three *s* one *d*; 2nd, 1965, John Carleton (*d* 1974). *Educ:* Cheltenham Ladies' College (scholar); Somerville College, Oxford (exhibitioner). BBC, 1928-35; Asst Editor, The Listener, 1930-35; Asst Literary Editor, New Statesman and Nation, 1949-52, Literary Editor, 1952-60. Virginia Gildersleeve Vis. Prof., Barnard Coll., New York, 1961 and 1964. Trustee, National Library of Scotland, 1950-. Pres., Royal Literary Fund, 1976-. Hon. LLD Aberdeen, 1962. *Publications:* Poems of Tomorrow (ed), 1935; R. L. Stevenson, 1937; Mountain Holidays, 1946; Life Among the Scots, 1946; Henry James and Robert Louis Stevenson (ed) 1948; Collected Poems of R. L. Stevenson (ed), 1950; Faber Book of Children's Verse (ed), 1953; Collected Poems of Michael Roberts (ed), 1958; John Buchan: a Biography, 1965; (ed) The Living Stream, 1969. *Recreation:* mountaineering. *Address:* 57 Lansdowne Road, W11. *T:* 01-727 9324. *Club:* Alpine (President, Ladies' Alpine, 1962-65).
See also Baron Balerno.

ADAMS, Rt. Rev. Albert James; *see* Barking, Bishop Suffragan of.

ADAMS, Alec Cecil Stanley, CMG 1960; CBE 1952; HM Diplomatic Service, retired; *b* 25 July 1909; *e* *s* of late Stanley A. Adams. *Educ:* King's School, Canterbury; Corpus Christi Coll., Cambridge. One of HM Vice-Consuls in Siam, 1933; served in Portuguese East Africa (acting Consul at Beira, June 1936-Feb. 1937); local rank 2nd Secretary, Bangkok Legation, 1937; Acting Consul, Sourabaya, 1938; Bangkok Legation, 1939-40; Foreign Office, Ministry of Information, 1940; Consul, in Foreign Office, 1945; Bangkok, 1946, Acting Consul-General and Chargé d'Affaires, 1948; Consul, Cincinnati, 1949; HM Chargé d'Affaires in Korea, 1950; HM Consul-General at Houston, Texas, 1953-55; Counsellor and Consul-General at HM Embassy, Bangkok, 1956-62; Deputy Commissioner-General for South East Asia, 1962-63; Political Advisor to C-in-C (Far East) at Singapore, 1963-67; retired 1967. *Address:* Flat 513, 97 Southampton Row, WC1B 4HH.

ADAMS, Air Vice-Marshal Alexander Annan, CB 1957; DFC 1944; Director, Mental Health Foundation (formerly Mental Health Trust and Research Fund), since 1970; *b* 14 Nov. 1908; *s* of Capt. Norman Anderson Adams, Durham; *m* 1933, Eileen Mary O'Neill; one *s* (one *d* decd). *Educ:* Beechmont, Sevenoaks; Bellerive, Switzerland; Austria. Commnd RAF, 1930; 54 Fighter Sqdn, 1931-32; 604 Aux. Sqdn, Hendon, 1933-35; CFS, 1935; Asst Air Attaché, Berlin, Brussels, The Hague, Berne, 1938-40; Ops, Air Min., 1940; British Embassy, Washington, 1941-42; in comd 49 (Lancaster) Sqdn, 1943-44; RAF Staff Coll., 1945; Head of RAF Intelligence, Germany, 1946-48; in comd RAF Binbrook, 1948-50; NATO Standing Gp, Washington, DC, 1951-53; idc, 1954; Air Attaché, Bonn, 1955; Min. of Defence, 1956; Chief of Staff, Far East Air Force, 1957-59. Hawker Siddeley Aviation, 1961-66. Comdr Order of Orange Nassau, 1950. *Recreations:* golf, painting. *Address:* Pound Cottage, Loders, Dorset. *Club:* Royal Air Force.

ADAMS, Bernard Charles; County Architect, Somerset County Council, since 1960; *b* 29 Oct. 1915; *s* of late Charles Willoughby Adams and Emily Alice (*née* Ambrose); *m* 1942, Marjorie Barrett Weller; two *d* (and one *d* decd). *Educ:* King James I Sch., Newport, IoW. ARIBA 1948, FRIBA 1968. TA, 1938-39; served 1939-41, 57 (Wessex) HAA Regt, RA; commissioned 1941; served 1941-46, 107 HAA Regt RA, France (Normandy), Belgium, Holland, Germany; Captain RA (despatches). Sen. Architect, Derbs CC, 1951-54; Asst County Architect, Kent CC, 1954-59; Dep. County Architect, Herts CC, 1959-60. Mem. Council, RIBA, 1963-69 and 1970- (Vice-Pres., 1970-72; Chm., S-W Regional Council, 1972-74); Mem., Nat. Consultative Council for Building and Civil Engrg Industries, 1974-; Pres., County Architects' Soc., 1973-74 (Vice-Pres, 1971-73); Pres., Soc. of Ch. Architects of Local Authorities (founded 1974), 1975-76 (Sen. Vice-Pres., 1974-75); Mem., Bd of Architectural Studies, Bristol Univ., 1964-74; Founder Chm., Architects' Cttee, Consortium for Method Building, 1961-68. RIBA Architecture Award, 1970, and Commendation, 1974. Heritage Year Award (EAHY), 1975. Civic Trust Awards, 1962, 1968, 1971, and Commendation, 1965. FRSA 1972. *Publications:* contrib. Jl of RIBA and other jls. *Recreations:* arts, music, theatre, travel, languages. *Address:* Meadowside, Wild Oak Lane, Trull, Taunton, Somerset TA3 7JT. *T:* Taunton 2485.

ADAMS, Prof. Colin Wallace Maitland, MD, DSc; FRCP, FRCPath; Sir William Dunn Professor of Pathology, Guy's Hospital Medical School, since 1965; *b* 17 Feb. 1928; *s* of Sidney Ewart Adams and Gladys Alethea Fletcher Adams; *m* 1953, Anne Brownhill; one *s*. *Educ:* Oundle School; Christ's College, Cambridge. Sir Lionel Whitby Medal, Cambridge Univ., 1959-60; MD Cantab, 1960; DSc London, 1967. FRCP; FRCPath 1975. Visiting Scientist, National Institutes of Health, Bethesda, USA, 1960-61. *Publications:* Neurohistochemistry, 1965; Vascular Histochemistry, 1967; Research on Multiple Sclerosis, 1972; papers on arterial diseases, neuropathology and microscopical chemistry in medical and biological journals. *Address:* The Knoll, Westview Drive, Rayleigh, Essex. *T:* Rayleigh 6489.

ADAMS, Air Commodore Cyril Douglas, CB 1948; OBE 1942; retired; *b* 18 Sept. 1897; British; *m* 1927, D. M. Le Brocq (*d* 1957), Highfield, Jersey; one *s* one *d*; *m* 1968, Mrs K. E. Webster, NZ. *Educ:* Parkstone Grammar School. Served European War in Army, 1915-18, Egypt, Palestine; Commissioned RFC, 1918; Flying Instructor, 1918-25; Staff Duties, Iraq Command, 1925-27; Staff and Flying Duties, Halton Comd, 1928-35; CO 15 Sqdn, 1936-38; HQ Bomber Comd, 1938; CO 38 Sqdn, 1938-39; Sen. Officer i/c Administration, No 3 Group, 1939-40; Station Comdr, Kemble,

Oakington, Abingdon, 1940-44; Base Comdr, Marston Moor and North Luffenham, 1944-45; India Command, AOA, AHQ, 1945-46; Base Comdr, Bombay, 1946; AOC No 2 Indian Group, 1946-47 (despatches 6 times, OBE (immediate award for gallantry)); Air Officer Commanding No 85 Group, BAFO, 1948-49; retired, 1949. *Recreations:* represented: RAF (Rugby, cricket, athletics); Hampshire (Rugby); Dorset and minor counties (cricket); keen golfer. *Address:* 6 Solent Pines, Whitby Road, Milford-on-Sea, Lymington, Hants. *T:* Milford-on-Sea 3754.

ADAMS, Ernest Victor; Deputy Secretary and Commissioner, Inland Revenue, since 1975; *b* 17 Jan. 1920; *s* of Ernest and Amelia Adams; *m* 1943, Joan Bastin, Halesworth, Suffolk; one *s* one *d*. *Educ:* Manchester Grammar Sch.; Keble Coll., Oxford (MA). HM Forces, RA, 1940-45. Inland Revenue Dept, 1947; Sen. Inspector of Taxes, 1956; Principal Inspector of Taxes, 1961; Sen. Principal Inspector of Taxes, 1966; Dep. Chief Inspector of Taxes, 1969. *Address:* Whitehill, Reades Lane, Sonning Common, Oxon. *T:* Kidmore End 3243; 34 Sloane Court West, Chelsea, SW3. *T:* 01-730 6482.

ADAMS, Frank Alexander, CB 1964; Member, Public Health Laboratory Service Board, since 1968; *b* 9 July 1907; *m* 1928, Esther Metcalfe; two *d*. *Educ:* Selhurst Grammar Sch.; London School of Economics, Univ. of London. HM Inspector of Taxes, 1928; Assistant Secretary, Board of Inland Revenue, 1945; Counsellor (Economic and Financial), UK Delegation to OEEC, Paris, 1957-59; Director, Civil Service Pay Research Unit, 1960-63; Under-Sec. (Finance) and Accountant-General, Min. of Health, 1963-67. *Address:* The Red House, Speldhurst, Kent. *T:* Langton 2987. *Clubs:* Royal Automobile, Climbers'; Swiss Alpine, (Geneva).

ADAMS, Frederick Baldwin, Jr; Director, Pierpont Morgan Library, 1948-69, now Emeritus; *b* 28 March 1910; *s* of Frederick B. Adams and Ellen Walters Delano; *m* 1st, 1933, Ruth Potter; 2nd, 1941, Betty Abbott; four *d*; 3rd, 1969, Marie-Louise de Croy. *Educ:* St Paul's Sch.; Yale Univ. (BA). Empl. Air Reduction Co. Inc., 1933-48. President: New-York Historical Soc., 1963-71; Bd Governors, Yale University Press, 1959-71; Assoc. Internationale de Bibliophilie; Trustee, Yale Univ., 1964-71; Fellow: Amer. Acad. Arts and Sciences; Amer. Philosophical Soc.; Amer. Antiquarian Soc.; Mass. Historical Soc.; Mem., Phi Beta Kappa. Hon. degrees: LittD: Hofstra Coll., 1959; Williams Coll., 1966; DFA, Union Coll., 1959; MA, Yale Univ., 1965; LHD, New York Univ., 1966. Chevalier, Légion d'Honneur, 1950. *Publications:* Radical Literature in America, 1939; One Hundred Influential American Books (with Streeter and Wilson), 1947; To Russia with Frost, 1963; contrib. to books and jls in bibliography, printing, collecting. *Address:* Château de Villard, 1814 La Tour de Peilz, Switzerland. *Clubs:* Athenæum, Roxburghe; Century, Grolier (NY).

ADAMS, (Harold) Richard; Management Consultant, since 1938; *b* 8 Oct. 1912; *s* of late A. Adams; *m* 1938, Joyce Love (marr. diss. 1955); two *d*; *m* 1956, P. Fribbins; one *s*. *Educ:* elementary; Emanuel School; London University; Middle Temple. Member Wandsworth Borough Council before War of 1939-45. Served War of 1939-45: joined East Surrey Regt, 1940; with 25 Army Tank Bde in N Africa and Italy; later, Staff Officer Land Forces Adriatic. Experience as business consultant; one time Asst Comr for National Savings; Lectr in Economics. MP (Lab) Balham and Tooting Div. of Wandsworth, 1945-50, Central Div., 1950-55; Asst Whip (unpaid), 1947-49; a Lord Comr of the Treasury, 1949-51. FIS. Mem., Fabian Soc. *Recreations:* antiques, politics.

ADAMS, Hervey Cadwallader, RBA 1932; FRSA 1951; landscape painter; lecturer on art; *b* Kensington, 1903; *o s* of late Cadwallader Edmund Adams and Dorothy Jane, *y d* of Rev. J. W. Knight; *m* 1928, Iris Gabrielle, *y d* of late F. V. Bruce, St Fagans, Glamorgan; two *s*. *Educ:* Charterhouse. Studied languages and singing in France and Spain, 1922-26; studied painting under Bernard Adams, 1929. Art Master, Tonbridge Sch., 1940-63. *Publications:* The Student's Approach to Landscape Painting, 1938; Art and Everyman, 1945; Eighteenth Century Painting, 1949; Nineteenth Century Painting, 1949; The Adventure of Looking, 1949. *Address:* Pummel, Houndscroft, near Stroud, Glos.

ADAMS, Prof. James Whyte Leitch; Professor of Education, University of Dundee (formerly Queen's College), since 1955; *b* 7 Nov. 1909; *o s* of Charles and Helen Adams, Stirling; *m* 1939, Isobel Margaret, ARIBA, *d* of Robert Gordon, Fraserburgh; one *s* two *d*. *Educ:* Arbroath High School; St Andrews University; Oxford University. Harkness Scholar, St Andrews, 1928; Guthrie Scholar, 1931; 1st cl. hons Classics, 1932; Marshall Prizeman, Miller Prizeman, Lewis Campbell

Medallist, etc; Waugh Scholar, Exeter Coll., Oxford, 1932; 1st cl. Classical Mods, 1934; 1st cl. Lit. Hum., 1936; Craven Fellowship, 1936; Dipl. in Educn, St Andrews Univ., 1937. Teacher of Classics, Golspie Senior Secondary Sch., 1937-39; Educn Officer (Scotland), BBC, 1939-47; RAF Education Service, 1942-45; HM Inspector of Schools, 1947-50; Lecturer in Humanity, Aberdeen University, 1950-55. *Publications:* various contributions, especially on Renaissance Latin Poetry. *Recreations:* golf and "brither" Scots. *Address:* Red Cottage, 80 Forthill Road, Broughty Ferry, Dundee. *T:* Dundee 78138.

ADAMS, Dr John Bertram, CMG 1962; FRS 1963; Executive Director-General, European Organisation for Nuclear Research (CERN), since 1976; *b* 24 May 1920; *s* of John A. Adams and Emily Searles; *m* 1943, Renie Warburton; one *s* two *d*. *Educ:* Eltham College; Research Laboratory, Siemens. Telecommunications Research Establishment, Swanage and Malvern, 1940-45; Atomic Energy Research Establishment, Harwell, 1945-53; European Organisation for Nuclear Research (CERN), Geneva, 1953, Dir of Proton Synchrotron Division, 1954-60; Director-Gen., CERN, 1960-61; Director, Culham Laboratory, AEA, Oxford, 1960-67; Controller, Min. of Technology, 1965-66; Member: Council for Scientific Policy, 1965-68; Board, UKAEA, 1966-69; Adv. Council on Technology, 1966-69; Dir-Gen., 300 GeV Accelerator Project, CERN, 1969-76. Fellow, Wolfson College, Oxford, 1966 (MA). Guthrie Lecturer, Phys. Soc., 1965. DSc *hc* : Univ. of Geneva, 1960; Birmingham Univ., 1961; Univ. of Surrey, 1966. Röntgen Prize, Univ. of Giessen, 1960; Duddell Medal, Physical Soc., 1961; Leverhulme Medal, Royal Soc., 1972; Faraday Medal, IEE, 1977. *Publications:* contributions to Nature, Nuovo Cimento, etc. *Recreations:* swimming, ski-ing. *Address:* (home) Champ Rosset, 1297 Founex VD, Switzerland; (office) European Organisation for Nuclear Research (CERN), 1211 Geneva 23, Switzerland.

ADAMS, John Crawford, MD, MS, FRCS; Consultant Orthopædic Surgeon: St Mary's Hospital, London; Paddington Green Children's Hospital; Civil Consultant in Orthopædic Surgery, Royal Air Force; Productions Editor, Journal of Bone and Joint Surgery. MB, BS 1937; MRCS 1937; LRCP 1937; FRCS 1941; MD (London) 1943; MS (London) 1965. Formerly: Chief Asst, Orthopædic and Accident Dept, London Hosp.; Orthopædic Specialist, RAFVR; Resident Surgical Officer, Wingfield-Morris Orthopædic Hosp., Oxford. FRSM; Fellow, British Orthopædic Assoc. (Hon. Sec., 1959-62; Vice-Pres.). *Publications:* Outline of Orthopædics, 1956, 1958, 1967, 1971, 1977; Outline of Fractures, 1957, 1967, 1972, 1977; Ischio-femoral Arthrodesis, 1966; Arthritis and Back Pain, 1972; Standard Orthopaedic Operations, 1976; Recurrent Dislocation of Shoulder (chapter in Techniques in British Surgery, ed Maingot), 1950; Associate Editor and Contributor Operative Surgery (ed Rob and Smith); contributions to the Journal of Bone and Joint Surgery, etc. *Address:* St Mary's Hospital, W2.

ADAMS, Prof. John Frank, MA, PhD; FRS 1964; Lowndean Professor of Astronomy and Geometry, Cambridge University, since 1970; Fellow of Trinity College, Cambridge; *b* 5 Nov. 1930; *m* 1953, Grace Rhoda, BA, BD, AAPSW, MBASW; one *s* three *d*. *Educ:* Bedford School; Trinity College, Cambridge; The Institute for Advanced Study, Princeton. Junior Lecturer, Oxford, 1955-56; Research Fellow, Trinity College, Cambridge, 1955-58; Commonwealth Fund Fellow, 1957-58; Assistant Lecturer, Cambridge, and Director of Studies in Mathematics, Trinity Hall, Cambridge, 1958-61; Reader, Manchester, 1962-64; Fielden Prof. of Pure Mathematics, Manchester Univ., 1964-71. *Publications:* Stable Homotopy Theory, 1964; Lectures on Lie Groups, 1969; Algebraic Topology, 1972; Stable Homotopy and Generalised Homology, 1974; papers in mathematical jls. *Recreations:* walking, climbing. *Address:* 7 Westmeare, Hemingford Grey, Huntingdon PE18 9BZ.

ADAMS, Rear-Adm. John Harold, CB 1967; MVO 1957; Director General of British Paper and Board Industry Federation, since 1974; *b* Newcastle-on-Tyne, 19 Dec. 1918; *m* 1st, 1943, Mary Parker (marr. diss. 1961); one *s* decd; 2nd, 1961, Ione Eadie, MVO; two *s* two *d*. *Educ:* Glenalmond. Joined Navy, 1936; Home Fleet, 1937-39; Western Approaches, Channel and N Africa, 1939-42 (despatches); Staff Capt. (D), Liverpool, 1943-45; Staff Course, Greenwich, 1945; jssc 1949; Comdr, HM Yacht Britannia, 1954-57; Asst Dir, Underwater Weapons Matériel Dept, 1957-58; Capt. (SM) 3rd Submarine Sqdn, HMS Adamant, 1958-60; Captain Supt, Underwater Detection Estab., Portland, subseq. Admty Underwater Weapons Estab., 1960-62; idc 1963; comd HMS Albion, 1964-66; Asst Chief of Naval Staff (Policy), 1966-68; retd 1968. Lieut 1941; Lieut-Comdr 1949; Comdr 1951; Capt. 1957; Rear-Adm. 1966. Dir, Paper and Paper Products Industry Training Bd,

1968-71; Dir, Employers' Federation of Papermakers and Boardmakers, 1972-73. Chm. Governors, Cheam Sch, 1974-. MBIM; MIPM. *Recreations:* sailing, photography. *Address:* The Oxdrove House, Burghclere, Newbury, Berks. *T:* Burghclere 385. *Club:* Army and Navy.

ADAMS, John Kenneth; Editor of Country Life, 1958-73; Editorial Director, Country Life Ltd, 1959-73; *b* 3 June 1915; *o c* of late Thomas John Adams and late Mabel Adams (*née* Jarvis), Oxford; *m* 1944, Margaret, *o c* of late Edward Claude Fortescue, Banbury, Oxon. *Educ:* City of Oxford Sch.; Balliol Coll., Oxford. Asst Master, Stonyhurst Coll., 1939-40; served with RAFVR, 1940-41 (invalided); Asst Master, Wellington Coll., 1941-44; attached to Manchester Guardian as Leader-writer, 1942-44; Leader-writer, The Scotsman, 1944-46; joined editorial staff of Country Life, 1946; Asst Editor, 1952; Deputy Editor, 1956; Editor, 1958; Editorial Director, 1959. *Recreations:* gardening, ornithology, travel. *Address:* 95 Alleyn Park, West Dulwich, SE21. *T:* 01-693 1736. *Club:* Athenæum.

ADAMS, Rt. Hon. John Michael Geoffrey Manningham, PC 1977; MP Barbados Labour Party, since 1966; Prime Minister of Barbados, since 1976; *b* 24 Sept. 1931; *s* of late Sir Grantley Adams, CMG, QC, and Grace Adams; *m* 1963, Genevieve, *d* of Philip Turner, *qv*; two *s*. *Educ:* Harrison Coll., Barbados; Magdalen Coll., Oxford (MA, PPE). Barrister-at-Law, Gray's Inn. Producer, BBC London, 1958-62; Polit. Party Sec., Barbados Labour Party, 1965-69; Leader of Opposition, 1971-76. *Recreations:* gardening, philately; watching, reading and writing about cricket. *Address:* (home) 14 Walkers Terrace, Gun Hill, St George, Barbados; (office) Prime Minister's Office, Bridgetown, Barbados. *Club:* Union (Bridgetown).

ADAMS, John Nicholas William B.; *see* Bridges-Adams.

ADAMS, (John) Roland, QC 1949; *b* 24 July 1900; *s* of late Alfred Courthope Adams and Sabina Newberry; *m* 1st, 1924, Ruth (marr. diss. 1946), *d* of late David Schlivek, merchant, Woonsocket, RI; no *c*; 2nd, 1946, Violet, *d* of late Sir Francis Hanson, London; no *c*. *Educ:* Charterhouse; New College, Oxford. Hon. Exhibitioner of New College, 1919; BA 1922; MA 1926. Barrister, Inner Temple, 1925; Master of the Bench, Inner Temple, 1957. Essex County Council, 1930-39; Vice-Chm., Essex Rivers Catchment Bd, 1935-39. Major, The Essex Regt, 1939-45; GSO3, War Office, 1939-40; DAAG, War Office, 1940-42; specially employed, 1942-45. Member, panel of Lloyd's arbitrators in salvage cases, 1950; appeal arbitrator, 1974; a Dep. Chm., Essex QS, 1950-56, Chairman, 1956-71. *Recreation:* staying at home. *Address:* Little Gubbions, Gubbions Hall Farm, Great Leighs, Chelmsford, Essex. *T:* Great Leighs 248.

ADAMS, Mary Grace, (Mrs Vyvyan Adams), OBE 1953; *b* Hermitage, Berks; *o d* of late Catherine Elizabeth Mary and Edward Bloxham Campin; *m* 1925, S. Vyvyan T. Adams (*d* 1951), sometime MP for W Leeds; one *d*. *Educ:* Godolphin Sch.; University Coll., Cardiff (first class Hons BSc); Newnham Coll., Cambridge. 1851 Res. Scholar and Bathurst Student, Univ. of Cambridge, 1921-23; Lectr and Tutor under Cambridge Extra-Mural Board and Board of Civil Service Studies, and broadcaster, 1925-30; joined staff of BBC, 1930; Producer, BBC TV, 1936-39; Dir, Home Intelligence, Min. of Information, 1939-41; N Amer. Broadcasting, 1942-45; Head of Talks and Current Affairs, 1945-54; Asst to Controller of Television Programmes, BBC, 1954-58, retired. Member, ITA, 1965-70; Dep. Chm., Consumers' Assoc., 1958-70. Chm., Telephone Users Assoc. Vice-Chairman: Nat. Council for the Unmarried Mother and her Child; Soc. for Anglo-Chinese Understanding. Member: Women's Group on Public Welfare; Council, Nat. Assoc. for Mental Health; Design Panel, British Railways Board; BMA Planning Unit. Trustee: Res. Inst. for Consumer Affairs; Galton Foundn; Anglo-Chinese Educational Inst. *Publications:* papers on genetical cytology; Talks on Heredity; (ed) various symposia. *Recreation:* children. *Address:* 10 Regent's Park Road, NW1. *T:* 01-485 8324.

ADAMS, Sir Maurice (Edward), KBE 1958 (OBE 1943); FICE; company director; consultant to Brian Colquhoun and Partners, consulting engineers, since 1971; *b* 20 Aug. 1901; *s* of Herbert William and Minnie Adams; *m* 1924, Hilda May Williams; one *s* one *d*. *Educ:* Bristol. Served European War, Midshipman, RNR. Entered Admty as Asst Civil Engr, 1927; HM Dockyards: Devonport, 1927-30; Malta, 1930-33; Portsmouth, 1933-35; Civil Engr: Trincomalee, 1935-37; Aden, 1937-38; Portsmouth, 1938-39; Superintending CE, Lower grade, 1939, Higher grade, 1940; served War of 1939-45: Admty, 1939-41; Singapore, from' 1941 to evacuation; Simonstown, 1942-43; Asst CE-in-Chief, 1943; Eastern Theatre, 1943-45; Admty, 1945-46; Dep. CE-in-Chief, 1946; resigned to take up appt with Balfour Beatty & Co.

Ltd, Public Works Contractors, 1949; re-entered Admty service, 1954; Civil Engr-in-Chief, Admty, 1954-59. Mem. Council, Instn of Civil Engrs, 1955. *Recreation:* yachting. *Address:* 12 Melvill Lane, Willingdon, Eastbourne, East Sussex. *Clubs:* Royal Automobile, Caledonian.

ADAMS, Surg. Rear-Adm. Maurice Henry, CB 1965; MB, BCh, DOMS; *b* 16 July 1908; *s* of Henry Adams and Dorothea (*née* Whitehouse); *m* 1938, Kathleen Mary (*née* Hardy); one *s* two *d*. *Educ:* Campbell Coll.; Queen's University, Belfast. MB, BCh, 1930. RN Medical Service 1933; HMS Cornwall, 1934; HMS Barham, 1936; Central Air Medical Board, 1940; HMS Activity, 1942; RN Hospital, Haslar, 1944; Med. Dept, Admiralty, 1946; RN Hospital: Malta, 1950; Chatham, 1952; MO i/c Trincomalee, 1957; Med. Dept, Admiralty, 1958; Medical Officer-in-Charge, Royal Naval Hosp., Malta, 1963; QHS, 1963-66; retd 1966. *Recreations:* sailing, golf. *Address:* Canberra, Rock, Cornwall.

ADAMS, Norman (Edward Albert), RA 1972; ARCA 1951; artist (painter and ceramic sculptor); *b* 9 Feb. 1927; *s* of Albert Henry Adams and Winifred Elizabeth Rose Adams; *m* 1947, Anna Theresa; two *s*. *Educ:* Royal Coll. of Art. Head of Sch. of Painting, Manchester Coll. of Art and Design, 1962-70; Lectr, Leeds Univ., 1975-. Exhibitions in most European capitals, also in America (New York, Pittsburgh); Retrospective exhibns, Royal College of Art, 1969, Whitechapel Gall. Paintings in collections of: most British Provincial Art Galleries; Tate Gall., London; Nat. Galls, New Zealand; work purchased by: Arts Coun. of Gt Brit.; Contemp. Art Soc.; Chantrey Bequest; various Educn Authorities. Murals at: Broad Lane Comprehensive Sch., Coventry; St Anselm's Church, S London; Our Lady of Lourdes, Milton Keynes. Decor for ballets, Covent Garden and Sadler's Wells. ARA 1967. *Address:* Butts, Horton-in-Ribblesdale, Settle, North Yorks. *T:* Horton-in-Ribblesdale 284; Scarp, Outer Hebrides, Scotland.

ADAMS, Sir Philip (George Doyne), KCMG 1969 (CMG 1959); Director, Ditchley Foundation, since 1977; *b* 7 Dec. 1915; *s* of late George Basil Doyne Adams, MD, and of Arline Maud Adams (*née* Dodgson); *m* 1954, Hon. (Mary) Elizabeth Lawrence, *e d* of Baron Trevethin and Oaksey (3rd and 1st Baron respectively); two *s* two *d*. *Educ:* Lancing Coll.; Christ Church, Oxford. Entered Foreign Service, 1939; served at: Beirut, 1939; Cairo, 1941; Jedda, 1945; FO, 1947; First Sec., 1948; Vienna, 1951; Counsellor, Khartoum, 1954; Beirut, 1956; FO, 1959; Chicago, 1963; Ambassador to Jordan, 1966-70; Asst Under-Sec., FCO, 1970; Dep. Sec., Cabinet Office, 1971-72; Ambassador to Egypt, 1973-75. *Address:* 78 Sussex Square, W2; Ditchley Park, Enstone, Oxon. *Club:* Brooks's.

ADAMS, Richard; *see* Adams, (Harold) Richard.

ADAMS, Richard George; author; *b* 10 May 1920; *s* of Evelyn George Beadon Adams, FRCS, and Lilian Rosa Adams (*née* Button); *m* 1949, Barbara Elizabeth Acland; two *d*. *Educ:* Bradfield Coll., Berks; Worcester Coll., Oxford (MA, Mod. Hist.). Entered Home Civil Service, 1948; retd as Asst Sec., DoE, 1974. Writer-in-residence: Univ. of Florida, 1975; Hollins Univ., Virginia, 1976. Carnegie Medal, 1972; Guardian Award for Children's Literature, 1972. Hon. FRSL 1975. *Publications:* Watership Down, 1972 (numerous subseq. edns in various languages); Shardik, 1974; Nature through the Seasons, 1975; The Tyger Voyage, 1976; The Ship's Cat, 1977; The Plague Dogs, 1977; Night and Day, 1978; Grandfather Mitron, 1978. *Recreations:* folk-song, chess, country pursuits, fly-fishing, travel. *Address:* Knocksharry House, Lhergy-Dhoo, near Peel, Isle of Man. *Club:* MCC.

ADAMS, Richard John Moreton G.; *see* Goold-Adams.

ADAMS, Robert; Sculptor and Designer; works in wood, stone, bronze, steel; *b* 5 Oct. 1917; *s* of Arthur Adams; *m* 1951, Patricia Devine; one *d*. *Educ:* Northampton School of Art. Instructor, Central School of Arts and Crafts, London, 1949-60. One man exhibitions: Gimpel Fils, London, 1947-68; Galerie Jeanne Bucher, Paris, 1949; Passedoit Gall., New York, 1950; Victor Waddington Gall., Dublin, 1955; Douglas Coll., NJ, USA, 1955; Galerie Parnass, Wuppertal, Germany, 1957; Nebelung Galerie, Düsseldorf, 1957; Galerie Vertiko, Bonn, 1957; Museum am Ostwall, Dortmund, 1957; Bertha Schaefer Gall., New York, 1963. International Biennales: São Paulo, Brazil, 1950-57; Antwerp, 1951-53; Venice, 1952; Holland Park, London, 1954-57; Battersea Park, 1961; Venice, 1962; 7th Tokyo, 1963; work in British Sculpture in the 'Sixties' exhibn, Tate Gall., 1965. Various Arts Council and British Council travelling exhibns in Europe, USA and Japan. Works in permanent collections: Arts Council; British Council; Tate Gallery; Museums of Modern

Art: New York, Rome and Turin; New York Public Library; São Paulo Museum; Univ. of Michigan, Ann Arbor; and many private collections. Commissions include sculptures for: Kings Heath Sch., Northampton; Sconce Hills Secondary Sch., Newark; The State Theatre, Gelsenkirchen; LCC Comprehensive Sch., Eltham; Hull City Centre; P & O Liner Canberra; Sekers Showroom, London; BP Building, Moorgate; London Airport; Maths Building, UCL; Kings Well, NW3; Fire Services Trng Coll., Glos; Williams & Glyn's Bank, London. *Address:* Rangers Hall, Great Maplestead, Halstead, Essex. *T:* Hedingham 60142.

ADAMS, Roland; *see* Adams, J. R.

ADAMS, Sherman; President, Loon Mountain Corporation; *b* 8 Jan. 1899; *s* of Clyde H. Adams and Winnie Marion (*née* Sherman); *m* 1923, Rachel Leona White; one *s* three *d. Educ:* Dartmouth College. Graduated, 1920; Manager, timberland and lumber operations, The Parker-Young Co., Lincoln, NH, 1928-45. Mem., New Hampshire House of Representatives, 1941-44; Chm. Cttee on Labor, 1941-42; Speaker of House, 1943-44; mem. 79th Congress, 2nd New Hampshire Dist; Gov. of New Hampshire, 1949-53; Chief of White House Staff, Asst to President of US, 1953-58, resigned. Chm., Conf. of New England Govs, 1951-52. Director (life), Northeastern Lumber Mfrs Assoc., New England Council. Served with US Marine Corps, 1918. First Robert Frost Award, Plymouth State Coll., 1970. Holds several hon. degrees. *Publications:* First Hand Report, 1961 (Gt Brit. 1962); articles in Life, American Forests, Appalachia, 1958-70. *Recreations:* golf, fishing, ski-ing. *Address:* Pollard Road, Lincoln, New Hampshire 03251, USA.

ADAMS, Sydney, MA (Oxon); Headmaster, Bancroft's School, 1944-65, retired; *b* 13 Sept. 1905; *s* of A. S. and H. R. Adams; *m* 1933, Evelyn Mary Evanson; one *d. Educ:* City of Oxford School (Head of School); St John's College, Oxford (Scholar). 1st cl. Maths Mods, 1926; 2nd cl. Maths Finals, 1928; Diploma in Educn, Oxford, 1929. Sixth Form Maths Master: Aldenham, 1929-31; Sedbergh, 1931-44. *Recreations:* gardening, walking. *Address:* Walden, 28 Roman Way, Glastonbury, Somerset. *T:* Glastonbury 31549.

ADAMS, Mrs Vyvyan; *see* Adams, Mary Grace.

ADAMS, William James, CMG 1976; HM Diplomatic Service; Counsellor, UK Permanent Representation to European Communities, since 1973; *b* 30 April 1932; *s* of late William Adams and Norah (*née* Walker); *m* 1961, Donatella, *d* of late Andrea Pais-Tarsilia; two *s* one *d. Educ:* Shrewsbury Sch.; Queen's Coll., Oxford. HM Forces, 1950-51. Foreign Office, 1954; 3rd Sec., Bahrain, 1956; Asst Political Agent, Trucial States, 1957; FO, 1958; 2nd Sec., 1959; Manila, 1960; 1st Sec. and Private Sec. to Minister of State, FO, 1963; 1st Sec. (Information), Paris, 1965-69; FCO, 1969; Counsellor, 1971; Head of European Integration Dept (2), FCO, 1971-72; seconded to Economic Commn for Africa, Addis Ababa, 1972-73. *Address:* c/o Foreign and Commonwealth Office, SW1A 2AL. *Club:* Travellers'.

ADAMS-BECK, John Melliar; Clerk and Solicitor of the Worshipful Company of Ironmongers 1946-72, Hon. Freeman, 1972, Liveryman, 1973; *b* 9 April 1909; *s* of late James Francis Adams Beck and Elsie (*née* Foster-Melliar); *m* 1st, 1939, Doris Elsie Neep (*d* 1966); two *s*; 2nd, 1968, Mrs Mary Elizabeth Helen Coates, *widow* of Captain Patrick Coates and *e d* of Comdr Sir John Best-Shaw, *qv. Educ:* Shrewsbury Sch. Admitted Solicitor, 1932. Served War of 1939-45; joined Hon. Artillery Co., 1939; commissioned RA, 1940; India and Ceylon, 1942; demobilised with rank of Major 1945. Governor of the City and Diocese of London Voluntary Schs Fund, 1947-72; Trustee, City and Metropolitan Welfare Charity, 1968-76. Freeman of the City of London, 1969. *Publication:* The Ironmongers' Company: an historical note, 1954. *Recreations:* shooting, gardening. *Address:* Southfield, Charing, Kent. *T:* Charing 2252.

ADAMSON, Sir Campbell; *see* Adamson, Sir W. O. C.

ADAMSON, Prof. Colin, DSc; Rector, The Polytechnic of Central London, since 1970; *b* 23 Nov. 1922; British; *m* 1946, Janet Marjory Conyers; one *s* one *d. Educ:* Pocklington Sch., Yorks. BSc 1947, MSc(Eng.) 1952, London; DSc Manchester, 1961. REME (Capt.), 1942-46. Asst Lectr, then with A. A. Reyrolle & Co. (power system analysis), 1946-52; Sen. Lectr, then Reader, in Electrical Power Systems Engrg, UMIST, 1952-61; Chm., Dept of Electrical Engineering and Electronics, Univ. of Manchester Institute of Science and Technology, 1961-70. Mem., Conférence Internationale des Grands Réseaux

Electriques; Chairman: Consultants of Educational Overseas Services, 1975-; Panel 1 (and Mem. Council), British Calibration Service, 1969-. Vis. Professor: Univ. of Roorkee, India, 1954-55; Univs of Washington and Wisconsin, 1959; Middle East Techn. Univ., Ankara, 1967-68; Univ. of Technology, Baghdad, 1975-. Cons. Editor, Internat. Jl of Electrical Engrg Educn. *Publications:* (jtly) High Voltage Direct Current Power Transmission, 1960; High Voltage DC Power Convertors and Systems, 1963; University Perspectives, 1970; UNESCO reports: Higher Technical Education (Egypt), 1972; Alternative University Structures (UK), 1973, 3rd edn 1977; Technical Higher Education (Iraq), 1974; Post-secondary Education for Persons Gainfully-employed, 1976; contribs to Proc. IEE and other learned jls. *Recreations:* yachting, oriental science and technology. *Address:* 309 Regent Street, W1R 8AL. *Clubs:* Athenæum; Royal Mersey Yacht.

ADAMSON, Estelle Inez Ommanney, OBE 1962; Director of Nursing, St Thomas' Hospital, London, 1965-70, retired; *b* 21 May 1910; *d* of late R. O. Adamson, MA, MD, and late Evelyn Mary Ommanney. *Educ:* Benenden School, Cranbrook, Kent. Nurse training, St Thomas' Hosp., 1932-35; Sister, etc, St Thomas' Hosp., 1936-43; Asst Matron, King Edward VII Sanatorium, Midhurst, Sussex, 1943-45; Secretary, Nursing Recruitment Service, Nuffield Provincial Hospitals Trust, Scotland, 1946-51; Matron, Western General Hosp., Edinburgh, 1951-65. *Address:* 19 Millers Close, Goring-on-Thames, Oxon.

ADAMSON, Joy-Friederike Victoria; painter since 1938, research on wild animals since 1956, and author since 1958; *b* 20 Jan. 1910; *d* of Victor and Traute Gessner; *m* 1st, 1935, Victor von Klarwill (Austrian); 2nd, 1938, Peter Bally (Swiss); 3rd, 1943, George Adamson (British). *Educ:* Vienna. Staatspruefung Piano, 1927; Diploma (Gremium) in dress-making, 1928; sculpting, 1929-30; metal work at Kunstgewerbe Schule, 1931-32; graduate course to study medicine, 1933-35; living in Kenya, 1937-; painted indigenous flora, Kenya, 1938-43, about 700 exhibited Nat. Museum, Nairobi; Gold Grenfell Medal, RHS, 1947 (London exhibn); illustrated seven books; painted tribes of Kenya, 1944-52; about 600 paintings in perm. exhbn, Nat. Museum, Nairobi, and State House, Nairobi; Exhibition of water-colours and drawings, Tryon Gall., 1972. Elsa Wild Animal Appeal, UK 1961, USA 1969, Canada 1971. Award for merit (silver medal) Czechoslovakia, 1970; Joseph Wood-Krutsh Medal, Humane Soc. USA, 1971; Cross of Honour for Science and Art, Austria, 1976. *Publications:* Born Free: a lioness of two worlds, 1960, 1964, new edn 1965 (filmed 1966); Elsa, 1961; Living Free, 1961, 1964 (filmed 1971); Forever Free, 1962, 1966 (filmed 1971); Elsa and Her Cubs, 1965; The Story of Elsa, 1966; The Peoples of Kenya, 1967; The Spotted Sphinx, 1969; Pippa and her Cubs, 1970 (filmed 1970); Joy Adamson's Africa, 1972; Pippa's Challenge, 1972; articles in Jl of RGS, Field, Country Life, Blackwood-Magazine, Geographical Jl, German Anthropolog. Jl, E African Annuals, Brit. Geographical Magazine, and in several popular magazines in England, USA and Austria. *Recreations:* riding, ski-ing, tennis, mountaineering, swimming, photography, sketching, painting, playing piano. *Address:* Elsamere, PO Box 254, Naivasha, Kenya. *Clubs:* Nanyuki, Nairobi.

ADAMSON, Rt. Rev. Mgr. Canon Thomas; Canon, Liverpool Metropolitan Cathedral, since 1950; Parish Priest of St Clare's, Liverpool, since 1945; *b* 30 Sept. 1901; *s* of George and Teresa Adamson, Alston Lane, near Preston. *Educ:* St Edward's College, Liverpool; Upholland College; Oscott College, Birmingham; Gregorian University, Rome. Ordained Priest, 1926; Beda College, Rome, 1926-28; Private Secretary to Archbishop of Liverpool, 1928-45; Privy Chamberlain to Pope Pius XI, 1932; Domestic Prelate to the Pope, 1955; Vicar General to Archbishops of Liverpool, 1955-65; Protonotary Apostolic to the Pope, 1966. *Address:* St Clare's Presbytery, Arundel Avenue, Liverpool L17 2AU. *T:* 051-733 2374.

ADAMSON, Sir (William Owen) Campbell, Kt 1976; Chairman, Revertex Chemicals Ltd, since 1978; Director: Imperial Group Ltd, Renold Ltd, and Abbey National Building Society, since 1976; Lazard Bros & Co. Ltd, Lamson Industries Ltd, Doulton & Co. Ltd, since 1977; *b* 26 June 1922; *o s* of late John Adamson, CA; *m* 1945, Gilvray (*née* Allan); two *s* two *d. Educ:* Rugby Sch.; Corpus Christi Coll., Cambridge. Royal Inst. of Internat. Affairs, 1944-45; Baldwins Ltd as Management Trainee, 1945; successive managerial appts with Richard Thomas & Baldwins Ltd and Steel Co. of Wales Ltd, 1947-69; Gen. Man. i/c of construction and future operation of Spencer Steelworks, Llanwern; Dir, Richard Thomas & Baldwins Ltd, 1959-69, seconded as Dep. Under-Sec. of State, and Co-ordinator of Industrial Advisers, DEA, 1967-69; Dir-Gen., CBI, 1969-76. Member: BBC Adv. Cttee, 1964-67 and 1967-75; SSRC (on formation), 1965-69; NEDC, 1969-76; Council, Industrial Soc.; Design Council, 1971-73; Council, Iron and Steel Inst., 1960-72; Iron and Steel Industry Delegn to Russia, 1956, and to India, 1968; Vice-Chm., National Savings Cttee for England and Wales, 1975-. Vis. Fellow: Lancaster Univ., 1970; Nuffield Coll., Oxford, 1971. *Publications:* various technical articles. *Recreations:* brass rubbing, tennis, music, arguing. *Address:* Birchamp House, Newland, Glos; 19 Chester Row, SW1. *Club:* Bath.

ADCOCK, Sir Robert (Henry), Kt 1950; CBE 1941; retired as Clerk of County Council, Lancashire (1944-60), also as Clerk of the Peace for Lancashire and Clerk of the Lancashire Lieutenancy; *b* 27 Sept. 1899; *s* of late Henry Adcock, Polesworth, Warwicks; *m* Mary, *d* of late R. K. Wadsworth, Handforth Hall, Cheshire; one *s* two *d. Educ:* Atherstone, Warwicks. Asst Solicitor, Manchester, 1923; Asst Solicitor and Asst Clerk of the Peace, Notts CC, 1926; Senior Asst Solicitor, Manchester, 1929; Deputy Town Clerk, Manchester, 1931; Town Clerk, Manchester, 1938. DL Lancs, 1950-74. *Recreation:* golf. *Address:* Summer Place, Rock End, Torquay, Devon. *T:* 22775.
See also R . W . Adcock .

ADCOCK, Robert Wadsworth; Chief Executive and Clerk, Essex County Council, since 1976; *b* 29 Dec. 1932; *s* of Sir Robert Adcock, *qv*; *m* 1957, Valerie Colston Robins; one *s* one *d. Educ:* Rugby Sch. Solicitor. Asst Solicitor, Lancs CC, 1955-56; Asst Solicitor, Manchester City Council, 1956-59; Sen. Solicitor, Berks CC, 1959-63; Asst Clerk, later Dep. Clerk, Northumberland CC, 1963-70; Dep. Chief Exec., Essex CC, 1970-76. *Recreations:* gardening, ornithology. *Address:* The Christmas Cottage, Great Sampford, Saffron Walden, Essex. *T:* Great Sampford 363. *Club:* Law Society.

ADDERLEY, family name of **Baron Norton.**

ADDINGTON, family name of **Viscount Sidmouth.**

ADDINGTON, 5th Baron *cr* 1887; **James Hubbard;** *b* 3 Nov. 1930; *s* of John Francis Hubbard, OBE (*g s* of 1st Baron) (*d* 1953) and of Betty Riversdale, *d* of late Horace West; *S* kinsman, 1971; *m* 1961, Alexandra Patricia, *yr d* of late Norman Ford Millar; two *s* two *d. Educ:* Eastbourne College; Chadacre Agricultural Institute. Served British S Africa Police, S Rhodesia, 1955-58. *Heir: s* Hon. Dominic Bryce Hubbard, *b* 24 Aug. 1963.

ADDINSELL, Richard Stewart; composer; *b* London, 13 Jan. 1904. *Educ:* privately; Hertford Coll., Oxford; Royal Coll. of Music. Spent four years in Berlin and Vienna. Contributed to Charlot's Revue, 1926; composed Adam's Opera, 1928. Has since written songs and incidental music for many stage productions including: The Good Companions, Alice in Wonderland, L'Aiglon, The Happy Hypocrite, Trespass, Ring Round the Moon, Penny Plain, Lyric Revue, Globe Revue, Airs on a Shoestring, Joyce Grenfell Requests the Pleasure; Living for Pleasure. Musical scores for films include: South Riding, Goodbye Mr Chips, The Lion Has Wings, Dangerous Moonlight (Warsaw Concerto), Love on the Dole, Blithe Spirit, The Passionate Friends, Under Capricorn, Tom Brown's Schooldays, The Prince and the Showgirl, A Tale of Two Cities, The Greengage Summer, The Roman Spring of Mrs Stone, The Waltz of the Toreadors, The War Lover. During War of 1939-45 wrote music for many documentary films. Also composes for radio and TV. *Address:* 1 Carlyle Mansions, Cheyne Walk, SW3.

ADDIS, Sir John (Mansfield), KCMG 1973 (CMG 1959); HM Diplomatic Service, retired; Senior Research Fellow in contemporary Chinese Studies, Wolfson College, University of Oxford, since 1975; *b* 11 June 1914; 5th *s* and 12th *c* of late Sir Charles and Lady Addis. *Educ:* Rugby School; Christ Church, Oxford. 3rd Sec., Foreign Office, 1938; with Allied Force HQ (Mediterranean), 1942-44; Junior Private Sec. to Prime Minister (Mr Attlee), 1945-47; 1st Sec., Nanking, 1947-50; Peking, 1950; Counsellor, Peking, 1954-57; Counsellor in the Foreign Office, 1957-60; Ambassador to Laos, 1960-62; Fellow at Harvard Centre for Internat. Affairs, 1962-63; Ambassador to the Philippines, 1963-70; Senior Civilian Instructor, IDC, later Royal Coll. of Defence Studies, 1970-71; Ambassador to China, 1972-74 (Chargé d'Affaires, Jan.-March 1972). Mem. Adv. Council, V&A Museum, 1977-. *Address:* Woodside, Frant, Sussex. *T:* Frant 202; Wolfson College, Oxford. *T:* Oxford 55605. *Club:* Boodle's.
See also Sir William Addis , Sir Dallas Bernard , Bt .

ADDIS, Sir William, KBE 1955; CMG 1948; MA; *b* 5 Sept. 1901; 3rd *s* of late Sir Charles Addis, KCMG, LLD, Woodside, Frant, Sussex; *m* 1929, Rosemary (*d* 1964), *d* of late Rev. R. T. Gardner; four *s. Educ:* Rugby; Magdalene College, Cambridge. Mechanical Science Tripos, 1923. Entered Colonial Administrative Service, 1924; served in Zanzibar and Northern Rhodesia; seconded to Dominions Office during 1933; Private Sec. to Sultan of Zanzibar, 1939-45. Served in Zanzibar Naval Volunteer Force, 1939-45. Colonial Secretary, Bermuda, 1945-50; acting Governor, Bermuda, during 1945 and 1946; Deputy Commissioner-General for Colonial Affairs, South-East Asia, 1950-53; Governor and Commander-in-Chief, Seychelles, 1953-58, retired; temporary appointment in Foreign Office, 1958-66. 3rd Class Order of Brilliant Star of Zanzibar, 1945. *Address:* Woodside, Frant, Sussex. *T:* 202.
See also Sir J. M Addis.

ADDISON, family name of **Viscount Addison.**

ADDISON, 3rd Viscount *cr* 1945 of Stallingborough; **Michael Addison;** Baron Addison 1937; *b* 12 April 1914; 2nd *s* of 1st Viscount Addison, KG, PC, MD, FRCS, and Isobel McKinnon (*d* 1934), *d* of late Archibald Gray; *S* brother, 1976; *m* 1936, Kathleen Amy, *d* of Rt Rev. and Rt Hon. J. W. C. Wand, PC, KCVO, and late Amy Agnes Wiggins; one *s* two *d. Educ:* Hele's School, Exeter; Balliol Coll., Oxford. BA (PPE) 1935, MA 1965. Min. of Labour, 1935; War Damage Commission, 1940. Served RAFVR, 1941-45, FO Intell. Branch. War Damage Commn and Central Land Bd, 1945-51; Min. of Supply/Aviation, 1951-63; HM Treasury, 1963-65; Sen. Lectr, Polytechnic of Central London (School of Management Studies), 1965-76; retired, 1976. Member: Royal Inst. of Public Administration; Assoc. of Teachers of Management. *Recreation:* gardening. *Heir: s* Hon. William Matthew Wand Addison [*b* 13 June 1945; *m* 1970, Joanna Mary, *e d* of late J. I. C. Dickinson; one *s* one *d*]. *Address:* Old Stables, Maplehurst, Horsham, West Sussex. *T:* Lower Beeding 298. *Club:* Oxford Union Society.

ADDISON, Prof. Cyril Clifford, PhD, DSc (Dunelm); FRS 1970; FInstP; FRIC; Professor of Inorganic Chemistry, University of Nottingham, since 1960; Dean of Faculty of Pure Science, 1968-71; *b* 28 Nov. 1913; *s* of late Edward Thomas Addison and Olive Clifford; *m* 1939, Marjorie Whineray Thompson; one *s* one *d. Educ:* Workington and Millom Grammar Schools, Cumberland; University of Durham (Hatfield College). Scientific Officer, British Launderers' Research Assoc., 1936-38; Lectr, Harris Inst., Preston, 1938-39; Ministry of Supply, Chemical Inspection Dept, 1939-45; Chemical Defence Research Establ., 1945; Univ. of Nottingham, Lectr, 1946; Reader in Inorganic Chemistry, 1952. Corday-Morgan Lectr, E Africa, 1969; Liversidge Lectr, 1976. Member: Chemical Soc. Council, 1954-57 (Pres. 1976-77); Inst. of Chemistry Council, 1948-51 and 1962-65 (Vice-Pres., 1965-67). Hon. DSc Dundee, 1977. *Publications:* numerous papers in Jl Chemical Soc., Trans. Faraday Soc., etc. *Recreations:* mountain walking, gardening. *Address:* Department of Chemistry, The University, Nottingham. *T:* Nottingham 56101. *Club:* Athenæum.

ADDISON, Air Vice-Marshal Edward Barker, CB 1945; CBE 1942 (OBE 1938); MA; CEng, FIEE; RAF, retired; *b* 4 Oct. 1898; *m* 1926, Marie-Blanche Marguerite Rosain; one *s* one *d. Educ:* Sidney Sussex Coll., Cambridge. Served European War, 1915-18, RFC and RAF; Cambridge Univ., 1918-21; BA (Cantab), 1921; MA (Cantab), 1926; Ingénieur Diplomé de l'Ecole Supérieure d'Electricité, Paris, 1927; re-commissioned RAF, 1921; retd from RAF, 1955; Dir and Div. Manager, Redifon Ltd, 1956-63, retd; Director, Intercontinental Technical Services Ltd, 1964-75, retd; Consultant to Vocational Guidance Assoc., 1966-72. AMIEE 1933; MIEE 1941; FIEE 1966. Commander of US Legion of Merit, 1947. *Address:* 7 Hall Place Drive, Weybridge, Surrey. *T:* Weybridge 47450.

ADDISON, Dr Philip Harold, MRCS, LRCP; Hon. Consulting Secretary, The Medical Defence Union, since 1974 (Secretary, 1959-74); *b* 28 June 1909; 2nd *s* of late Dr Joseph Bartlett Addison and Mauricia Renée Addison; *m* 1934, Mary Norah Ryan; one *s* one *d. Educ:* Clifton Coll., Bristol; St Mary's Hosp. Medical Sch. MRCS, LRCP 1933; Gold Medallist, Military Medicine and Bronze Medallist Pathology, Army Medical Sch., Millbank, SW1, 1935. Permanent Commission, IMS, 1935; served Burma Campaign, 1943-45 (despatches). Chm., Ethical Cttee of Family Planning Assoc., 1956-60; Vice-Pres., Medico-Legal Soc., 1965-74. *Publications:* Professional Negligence, in Compendium of Emergencies, 1971; The Medico-Legal Aspects of General Anaesthesia, in, Clinical Practice of General Anaesthesia, 1971; contrib. Brit. Med. Jl, Irish Med. Jl, Proc. R.Soc.Med, Medico-Legal Jl, Lancet. *Recreations:* fishing, golf, bridge. *Address:* Red-Wyn-Byn, Monkmead Lane, West

Chiltington, Pulborough, West Sussex. *T:* West Chiltington 3047. *Clubs:* East India, Devonshire, Sports and Public Schools; Shark Angling Club of Gt Britain; West Sussex Golf; BMA Bridge (Founder Mem.).

ADDISON, Sir William (Wilkinson), Kt 1974; JP; DL; Chairman of Council, The Magistrates' Association, 1970-76; *b* Mitton, WR Yorks, 4 April 1905; *s* of Joseph Addison, Bashall Eaves; *m* 1929, Phoebe, *d* of Robert Dean, Rimington, WR Yorks. Verderer of Epping Forest, 1957-. Chm., Epping Petty Sessions, 1955-, combined Epping and Ongar Petty Sessions, 1968-76; Magistrates' Assoc.: Mem. Coun., 1959-76; Dep. Chm. of Coun., 1966-70; Chm., Treatment of Offenders Cttee, 1961-68; Chm. Exec. Cttee, 1968-75. Member: Hill Hall Prison Board of Visitors, 1955-70; Chelmsford Prison, 1958-77; Bullwood Hall Borstal, 1962-76; Home Sec.'s Adv. Coun. on Probation and After-Care, 1964-67; Lord Chancellor's Adv. Coun. on Trng of Magistrates, 1964-73; Magistrates' Courts Rule Cttee, 1968-74; Council, Commonwealth Magistrates Assoc., 1970-75; Assessor to Deptl Cttee on Liquor Licensing, 1971. Member: Court, Univ. of Essex, 1965-; Coun., Essex Archaeological Soc., 1949-71 (Pres., 1964-67); Adv. Council, Univ. of Cambridge Inst. of Criminology, 1972; Pres. or Chm. of several bodies connected with local history and the preservation of antiquities in Essex, inc. Victoria County History. JP 1949, DL 1973, Essex. FSA 1965; FRHistS 1965. *Publications:* Epping Forest, 1945; The English Country Parson, 1947; Essex Heyday, 1949; Suffolk, 1950; Worthy Dr Fuller, 1951; English Spas, 1951; Audley End, 1953; English Fairs and Markets, 1953; Thames Estuary, 1953; In the Steps of Charles Dickens, 1955; Wanstead Park, 1973; Essex Worthies, 1973; Portrait of Epping Forest, 1977; The Landscape of English Place-Names, 1978; contribs to Trans Essex Arch. Soc. *Recreation:* exploring the English countryside for evidence of local history. *Address:* Ravensmere, Epping, Essex. *T:* Epping 73439.

ADDLESHAW, Very Rev. George William Outram; Dean of Chester, 1963-77; *b* 1 Dec. 1906; *s* of late Canon Stanley Addleshaw and late Mrs Rose Elgood Addleshaw. *Educ:* Bromsgrove School; Trinity College, Oxford; Cuddesdon College, Oxford. 2nd cl. hons Modern History, 1928; BA 1929; MA 1932; BD 1935; FSA 1945; FRHistS 1949. Curate of Christ Church, Highfield, Southampton, 1930-36; Curate of Basingstoke, 1936-39; Vice-Principal and Fellow of St Chad's College, Durham, 1939-46; Treasurer and Canon Residentiary of York Minster, and Prebendary of Tockerington in York Minster, 1946-63. Examining Chaplain to Archbishop of York, 1942-63; Hon. Secretary Archbishops' Canon Law Commn 1943-47; Lecturer, Leeds, Parish Church, 1947-54; Proctor in Convocation of York, 1945-; a Deputy Prolocutor, Lower House of Convocation of York, 1957-66; Prolocutor, Lower House of Convocation of York, 1966-75. Hon. Treas., York Minster Appeal, 1950-63. Select Preacher: Univ. of Oxford, 1954-56; Univ. of Cambridge, 1955-; Examining Chaplain to Bp of Chester, 1955-; Chaplain to the Queen, 1957-63; Hon. Chaplain, Cheshire Regt, 1969-. *Publications:* Jocism, 1939; Dogma and Youth Work, 1941; The High Church Tradition, 1941; Divine Humanity and the Young Worker, 1942; (with Frederick Etchells) The Architectural Setting of Anglican Worship, 1948; The Beginnings of the Parochial System, 1953; The Parochial System from Charlemagne to Urban II, 1954; Rectors, Vicars and Patrons, 1956; The Early Parochial System and the Divine Office, 1957; The Pastoral Structure of the Celtic Church in Northern Britain, 1973; contrib. to: The History of Christian Thought, 1937; The Priest as Student, 1939; The Mission of the Anglican Communion, 1948; Architectural History, 1967. *Recreations:* travel, ecclesiology. *Address:* Flat 3, The New Manor House, 37 Station Road, Thames Ditton, Surrey. *Clubs:* Athenæum; Yorkshire (York); Grosvenor (Chester).

ADDLESHAW, His Honour John Lawrence; a Circuit Judge (formerly County Court Judge), 1960-75; *b* 30 Oct. 1902; *s* of Harold Pope Addleshaw, Solicitor and Mary Gertrude (*née* Shore), Manchester; unmarried. *Educ:* Shrewsbury School; University College, Oxford (BA). Called to the Bar, Inner Temple, 1925. Auxiliary Air Force, 1939-45. *Recreations:* golf, walking. *Address:* 3 College House, Southdowns Road, Bowdon, Altrincham, Cheshire WA14 3DZ. *T:* 061-928 2139. *Club:* Clarendon (Manchester).

ADEANE, family name of Baron Adeane.

ADEANE, Baron *cr* 1972 (Life Peer), of Stamfordham; **Michael Edward Adeane**, PC 1953; GCB 1968 (KCB 1955; CB 1947); GCVO 1962 (KCVO 1951; MVO 1946); Royal Victorian Chain, 1972; MA; Chairman, Royal Commission on Historical Monuments, since 1972; Member, British Library Board, since 1972; *b* 30 Sept. 1910; *s* of late Capt. H. R. A. Adeane,

Coldstream Guards (killed in action, 1914), and Hon. Victoria Eugenie Bigge (*d* 1969); *m* 1939, Helen Chetwynd-Stapylton; one *s* (one *d* decd). *Educ:* Eton; Magdalene Coll., Cambridge (1st Cl. Hons Historical Tripos Part II); Hon. Fellow 1971. 2nd Lieut Coldstream Guards, 1931; ADC to Governor-General of Canada, 1934-36; Major, 1941; Lieut-Col 1942. Served War of 1939-45: with 2nd Bn Coldstream Guards, 1940-42; on Joint Staff Mission, Washington, 1942-43; 5th Bn Coldstream Guards, 1943-45; in NW Europe from 1944 (wounded, despatches). Page of honour to King George V; Equerry and Asst Private Sec. to the Queen, 1952-53 (to King George VI, 1937-52); Private Sec. to the Queen and Keeper of HM's Archives, 1953-72. Lieut-Col (R of O) 1954. Director: Phoenix Assurance Co. Ltd, 1972-; Banque Belge Ltd, 1972-; Royal Bank of Canada, 1972-; The Diners Club Ltd, 1976-. Governor, Wellington College, 1960-. *Recreations:* shooting and fishing. *Address:* 22 Chelsea Square, SW3 6LF. *T:* 01-352 3080; Mosshead Cottage, Kildrummy, Alford, Aberdeenshire. *T:* Kildrummy 261. *Clubs:* Brooks's, Beefsteak, Pratt's.

ADEANE, Col Sir Robert (Philip Wyndham), Kt 1961; OBE (mil.) 1943; Director: Colonial Securities Trust Co. Ltd; Decca Co. Ltd; Rubercid and other companies; *b* 1905; 2nd and *o* surv. *s* of late Charles Robert Whorwood Adeane, CB, Babraham Hall, Cambridge; *m* 1st, 1929, Joyce Violet, *d* of Rev. Cyril Burnett; one *s* one *d* (and one *s* decd); 2nd, 1947, Kathleen, (*d* 1969), *d* of Sir James Dunn, Bt; one *s* one *d*; 3rd, 1971, Mrs Elizabeth Jane Cator. *Educ:* Eton; Trinity Coll., Cambridge. 2nd Lieut RA (TA). 1938; Lt-Col 1941; Temp. Col 1943. Trustee, Tate Gallery, 1955-62. *Address:* Kingston House South, Ennismore Gardens, SW7; Loudham Hall, near Wickham Market, Suffolk. *Clubs:* Brooks's, Bath, Beefsteak.

ADEBO, Simeon Olaosebikan, (Chief), The Okanlomo of Itoko, CMG 1959; Chairman, National Universities Commission of Nigeria, since 1975; United Nations Under-Secretary-General and Executive Director of United Nations Institute for Training and Research, 1968-72; *b* 5 Oct. 1913; *s* of late Chief Adebo, the Okanlomo of Itoko, Abeokuta; *m* 1941, Regina Abimbola, *d* of Chief D. A. Majekodunmi, Abeokuta; three *s* one *d*. *Educ:* St Peter's Sch., Ake, Abeokuta; Abeokuta Grammar Sch.; King's Coll., Lagos, Nigeria. BA Hons (London) 1939; LLB Hons (London) 1946. Called to Bar, Gray's Inn, 1949. Accountant in trg, Nigerian Rly, 1933; Admin. Officer Cadet, Nigerian Govt, 1942; Asst Fin. Sec. to Govt of Nigeria, 1954; Western Nigeria: Admin. Officer, Class I, 1955; Perm. Sec., Min. of Finance, 1957; Perm. Sec. to Treasury and Head of Civil Service, 1958; Head of Civil Service and Chief Secretary to Government, 1961; Permanent Representative of Nigeria at UN and Comr-Gen. for Economic Affairs, 1962-67. Member: Nigeria Soc.; Soc. for Internat. Develt. Hon. LLD: Western Michigan, 1963; Nigeria, Nsukka, 1965; Fordham, 1966; Lincoln, 1966; Beaver Coll., 1966; Ife, 1968; Ibadan, 1969; Columbia, 1971; Ahmadu Bello (Nigeria), 1973; Open Univ., 1975; Hon. DCL, Union Coll., 1965. *Publication:* (with Sir Sydney Phillipson) Report on the Nigerianisation of the Nigerian Civil Service, 1953. *Recreations:* tennis and cricket. *Address:* c/o PO Box 139, Abeokuta, Nigeria. *Clubs:* Royal Commonwealth Society; Abeokvta Sports.

ADELAIDE, Archbishop of, and Metropolitan of South Australia, since 1975; **Most Rev. Keith Rayner;** *b* 22 Nov. 1929; *s* of Sidney and Gladys Rayner, Brisbane; *m* 1963, Audrey Fletcher; one *s* two *d*. *Educ:* C of E Grammar Sch., Brisbane; Univ. of Queensland. BA 1951; PhD 1964. Deacon, 1953; Priest, 1953. Chaplain, St Francis' Theol Coll., Brisbane, 1954; Mem., Brotherhood of St John, Dalby, 1955-58; Vice-Warden, St John's Coll., Brisbane, 1958; Rotary Foundn Fellow, Harvard Univ., 1958-59; Vicar, St Barnabas', Sunnybank, 1959-63; Rector, St Peter's, Wynnum, 1963-69; Bishop of Wangaratta, 1969-75. *Recreation:* tennis. *Address:* Bishop's Court, North Adelaide, SA 5006, Australia.

ADELAIDE, Archbishop of, (RC), since 1971; **Most Rev. James William Gleeson,** CMG 1958; DD 1957; *b* 24 Dec. 1920; *s* of John Joseph and Margaret Mary Gleeson. *Educ:* St Joseph's Sch., Balaklava, SA; Sacred Heart Coll., Glenelg, SA. Priest, 1945; Inspector of Catholic Schs, 1947-52; Dir of Catholic Education for South Australia, 1952-58; Auxiliary Bishop to the Archbishop of Adelaide and Titular Bishop of Sesta, 1957-64; Coadjutor Archbishop of Adelaide and Titular Archbishop of Aurusuliana, 1964-71. Episcopal Chm. the Young Catholic Students Movement of Australia, 1958-65. FACE 1967. *Address:* Archbishop's House, 91 West Terrace, Adelaide, SA 5000, Australia. *T:* 51.3551.

ADELSTEIN, Abraham Manie, MD; FRCP; FFCM; Senior Principal Medical Officer and Chief Medical Statistician, Office of Population Censuses and Surveys, since 1975; *b* 28 March 1916; *s* of Nathan Adelstein and Rosa Cohen; *m* 1942, Cynthia Gladys Miller; one *s* one *d*. *Educ:* Univ. of Witwatersrand. MB, ChB, MD. SAMC, 1941-45; Health Officer (res. and medical statistics), SA Railways, 1947-61; Sen. Lectr, Univ. of Manchester, 1961-67; OPCS, 1967-. *Publications:* Thesis on Accident Proneness, 1950; papers in scientific jls on the distribution and aetiology of various diseases (diseases of heart, nervous system, respiratory system, cancer, accidents) and of methods of collecting, analysing and publishing national statistics. *Address:* 21 Dunstan Road, NW11 8AG. *T:* 01-455 9983.

ADEMOLA, Rt. Hon. Sir Adetokunbo (Adegboyega), GCON 1972; CFR 1963; PC 1963; KBE 1963; Kt 1957; Chancellor, University of Nigeria, since 1976; *b* 1 Feb. 1906; *e s* of late Sir Ladapo Ademola, Alake of Abeokuta, KBE, CMG; *m* 1939, Kofoworola, *yr d* of late Eric Olawolu Moore, CBE; three *s* two *d*. *Educ:* King's Coll., Lagos, Nigeria; Selwyn Coll., Cambridge. Attached to Attorney-General's Chambers, Lagos, Nigeria, 1934-35; Assistant Secretary, Secretariat, Southern Provinces, Nigeria, 1935-36; private law practice, Nigeria, 1936-39; Magistrate, Nigeria, 1939; served on commn for Revision of Courts Legislation, Nigeria, 1948; served on commn to enquire into Enugu (Nigeria) disturbances, 1949; Puisne Judge, Nigeria, 1949; Chief Justice, Western Region, Nigeria, 1955-58; Chief Justice of Nigeria, 1958-72. Deputy Chm., United Bank for Africa, 1972-74. Hon. Bencher, Middle Temple, 1959-. Chm., Commonwealth Foundn, 1978-. Hon. LLD: Nigeria; Ahmadu Bello; Hon. DSc Benin. *Recreations:* golf, horse racing. *Address:* The Close, Adetokunbo Ademola Street, Victoria Island, Lagos, Nigeria. *T:* Lagos 52219. *Clubs:* Island, Metropolitan, Yoruba Tennis (Lagos); Ibadan Recreation, Ibadan (Ibadan).

ADEREMI I; *see* Ife.

ADERMANN, Rt. Hon. Sir Charles (Frederick), PC 1966; KBE 1971; Member, House of Representatives, for Fisher, Queensland, 1949-72 (Maranoa, 1943-49); *b* 3 Aug. 1896; *s* of late Charles and Emilie Adermann; *m* 1926, Mildred, *d* of late S. T. and Mrs Turner, Wooroolin, Qld; two *s* two *d*. Chm., Peanut Marketing Bd, 1925-30, 1933-52, retd; Chm., Kingaroy Shire Council, 1936-46, retd; Chm. cttees, House of Reps, 1950-58; Dep. Speaker, periods 1950, 1955, 1956; Minister of State for Primary Industry, in Australian Cabinet, Dec. 1958-Oct. 1967. Dep. Leader, Aust. Country Party, 1964-66. Leader, Aust. Delegn to Commonwealth Parly Conf., Wellington, Nov.-Dec. 1965. *Address:* PO Box 182, Kingaroy, Qld 4610, Australia. *T:* 722112 Kingaroy.

ADIE, Jack Jesson, CMG 1962; BA (Oxon); *b* 1 May 1913; *s* of late P. J. Adie; *m* 1940, Patricia McLoughlin; one *s* two *d*. *Educ:* Shrewsbury Sch.; Magdalen Coll., Oxford. Entered Colonial Administrative Service, 1938; served in Zanzibar, 1938-48 (on military service, 1940-42 in Kenya Regt, KAR and Occupied Territory Administration), posts included: Private Sec. to The Sultan, Private Sec. to British Resident and Sen. Asst Sec.; seconded to Colonial Office, 1949-51, as Principal; Asst Sec., Kenya, 1951; Sec. for Educn and Labour, Kenya, 1952; Sec. for Educn, Labour and Lands, Kenya, 1954; acted as Minister for Educn, Labour and Lands, Kenya, Sept. 1955-Feb. 1956; Chief Sec., Barbados, 1957; Perm. Sec. for Forest Development, Game and Fisheries, Kenya, April-Dec. 1958; for Agriculture, Animal Husbandry and Water Resources, and Chm. African Land Development Bd, Dec. 1958-July 1959; for Housing, and Chm. Central Housing Bd, Nov. 1959-April 1960; for Housing, Common Services, Probation and Approved Schools, April 1960-April 1961; for Labour and Housing, 1961-62; acted as Minister for Labour and Housing, Jan.-April 1962; Perm. Sec. for Labour, 1962-63; retd from HMOCS, Jan 1964; Temp. Principal, Min. of Overseas Develt, 1964-69. Brilliant Star of Zanzibar, 4th class, 1947. *Address:* Capricorn, Qawra Road, St Paul's Bay, Malta.

ADIE, Ven. Michael Edgar; Archdeacon of Lincoln, since 1977; Vicar of Morton with Hacconby, since 1976; *b* 22 Nov. 1929; *s* of Walter Granville Adie and Kate Emily Adie (*née* Parrish); *m* 1957, Anne Devonald Roynon; one *s* three *d*. *Educ:* Westminster School; St John's Coll., Oxford (MA). Assistant Curate, St Luke, Pallion, Sunderland, 1954-57; Resident Chaplain to the Archbishop of Canterbury, 1957-60; Vicar of St Mark, Sheffield, 1960-69; Rural Dean of Hallam, 1966-69; Rector of Louth, 1969-76. *Recreations:* gardening, walking, squash. *Address:* Morton Vicarage, near Bourne, Lincs. *T:* Morton 239.

ADIE-SHEPHERD, His Honour Harold Richard Bowman, QC 1950; a Recorder of the Crown Court, 1972-73; *b* 24 July 1904;

yr s of late Richard Atkinson Shepherd, Barrister-at-law, and Mabel Shepherd, Cumberland Priory, Headingley, Leeds; *m* 1928, Margaret Rohesia Gundred Mayo, West Lodge, Pinner; two *d*; *m* 1962, Phyllis Margaret Adie. *Educ:* Uppingham Sch.; Trinity Coll., Oxford. Called to Bar, Inner Temple, 1928; joined North-Eastern Circuit; practised at 39 Park Square, Leeds. Served War of 1939-45, in Army, Aug. 1939-Aug. 1945, including North Africa, Sicily and Italy. Recorder of Pontefract, 1948-50; Recorder of York, 1950-55; Solicitor-General of the County Palatine of Durham, 1950-55; JP Herts, 1952; Dep. Chm., Herts QS, 1953-55; Chm., Cornwall QS, 1966-71 (Dep. Chm., 1955-66); a County Court Judge, 1955-62; a Comr of Assize, 1965-71. Pres., Devon and Cornwall Rent Assessment Panel, 1965-76. *Recreations:* boats, cars, gardening. *Address:* Sealand Court, Newton Ferrers, Plymouth. *T:* Newton Ferrers 872399.

ADISESHIAH, Dr Malcolm Sathianathan; Vice-Chancellor, University of Madras, 1975-78; Director, Institute of Development Studies, Madras, 1971-78; *b* 18 April 1910; *s* of Varanasi Adiseshiah and Nesammah Adiseshiah; *m* 1951, Sanchu Pothan. *Educ:* Univ. of Madras (MA); LSE, London Univ. (PhD). Lectr in Econs, St Paul's Coll., Calcutta, 1931-36; Prof. of Econs, Madras Christian Coll., 1940-46; Associate Gen. Sec., World Univ. Service, Geneva, 1946-48; Unesco, Paris: Dep. Dir, Dept of Exchange of Persons, 1948-50; Dir, Dept of Tech. Assistance, 1950-54; Asst Dir-Gen., 1954-63; Dep. Dir-Gen., 1963-76. *Publications:* Demand for Money, 1938; Agricultural Development, 1941; Rural Credit, 1943; Planning Industrial Development, 1944; Non-political UN, 1964; Economics of Indian and Industrial Natural Resources, 1966; Education and National Development, 1967; Adult Education, 1968; Let My Country Awake, 1970; It is Time to Begin, 1972; Techniques of Perspective Planning, 1973; Plan Implementation Problems and Prospects for the Fifth Plan, 1974; Science in the Battle against Poverty, 1974; Literacy Discussion, 1976; Towards a Functional Learning Society, 1976; Madras Development Seminar Series, 1971-. *Address:* 19 Cenotaph Road, Madras-600018, India. *T:* Madras 440144.

ADLER, Larry, (Lawrence Cecil Adler); mouth organist; *b* 10 Feb. 1914; *s* of Louis Adler and Sadie Hack; *m* 1st, 1938, Eileen Walser (marr. diss. 1961); one *s* two *d*; 2nd, 1969, Sally Cline (marr. diss. 1977); one *d*. *Educ:* Baltimore City Coll. Won Maryland Harmonica Championship, 1927; first stage appearance, 1928 (NY); first British appearance, 1934 (in C. B. Cochran's Streamline revue); first appearance as soloist with Symphony Orchestra, Sydney, Australia, 1939; jt recital tours with dancer Paul Draper, US, 1941-49; soloist with NY Philharmonic and other major US Orchestras, also orchestras in England, Japan and Europe; war tours for Allied Troops, 1943, 1944, 1945; Germany, 1947, 1949; Korea (Brit. Commonwealth Div.), 1951; Israel (Six Day War), 1967; (Yom Kippur War), 1973; articles and book reviews in Sunday Times, New Statesman, Spectator, New Society; numerous TV One Man Shows; soloist, Edinburgh Festival, playing first performance of unpublished Gershwin quartet (MS gift to Adler from I. Gershwin, 1963; works composed for Adler by: Dr Ralph Vaughan Williams, Malcolm Arnold, Darius Milhaud, Arthur Benjamin, Gordon Jacob and others. *Compositions:* film scores: Genevieve; King and Country; High Wind in Jamaica; The Great Chase, etc; TV scores: Midnight Men (BBC serial); various TV plays and documentaries; music for TV commercials, children's records, stage plays, etc; concert music: Theme and Variations; Camera III; One Man Show, From Hand to Mouth, Edinburgh Festival, 1965 (other festivals, 1965-). *Publications:* How I Play, 1937; Larry Adler's Own Arrangements, 1960; Jokes and How to Tell Them, 1963. *Recreations:* tennis, journalism, cycling, conversation. *Address:* c/o Michael Bakewell, 118 Tottenham Court Rd, W1.

ADLEY, Robert James; MP (C) Christchurch and Lymington, since 1974 (Bristol North East, 1970-74); Director, Commonwealth Holiday Inns of Canada Ltd; *b* 2 March 1935; *s* of Harry and Marie Adley; *m* 1961, Jane Elizabeth Pople; two *s*. *Educ:* Falconbury; Uppingham. Lived and worked in: Malaya, Singapore, Thailand; established Pearl & Dean (Thailand) Ltd, 1956; Sales Director, May Fair Hotel, 1960-64. Vice-Chm., Parly Tourism Cttee; Mem., Cons. Parly Aviation Cttee; Chm., British-Jordanian Parly Gp; Vice-Chm., British-Chinese Parly Gp; Pres., Western Area Young Conservatives, 1972; Vice-Chm., Wessex Cons. Mems Gp. Mem. Nat. Council, British Hotels, Restaurants and Caterers Assoc. Mem., Railway Correspondence and Travel Soc.; Founder and First Chm., Brunel Soc. Patron, SS Great Britain Project. *Publications:* Hotels, the Case for Aid, 1966; One Man, No Vote, 1976. *Recreations:* railway photography, railway enthusiast. *Address:* Woodend House, Lymington, Hants. *Clubs:* Carlton; Royal Lymington Yacht.

ADMANI, Dr Haji Abdul Karim, JP; Consultant Physician, Sheffield Area Health Authority (Teaching), since 1970; Hon. Clinical Lecturer in Medicine, Sheffield University Medical School, since 1972; *b* 19 Sept. 1937; *s* of late Haji Abdul Razzak Admani (Electrical Engr in India), and of Hajiani Rahima Admani; *m* 1968, Seema (*née* Robson; Nursing Dir); one *s* one *d* . *Educ:* Gujrat Univ., India (BSc 1st Cl. Hons 1956); Karachi Univ., Pakistan (MB, BS 1962). DTM&H 1963; MRCPE (Neurology), 1967. Sec. Med. Div., Northern Dist, Sheffield, 1972-75; Mem. Dist Med. Cttee, N Dist, 1975-; Area Rep. and Mem. Exec. Cttee, BMA, Sheffield, 1975-; County Med. Officer, S Yorks Br., Red Cross. President: Muslim Council of Sheffield, Rotherham and dist, 1977- (Chm., 1970-76); Sheffield and N Reg., Pakistan Med. Soc. in UK, 1972-; Anglo-Asian Soc., Sheffield, 1973-. Chm., Islamic Centre Man. Cttee, Sheffield, 1973-. Vice-Chairman: Overseas Doctors' Assoc. in UK, 1975- (Chm. Post-grad. Med. Sub-Cttee, 1975; Chm. S Yorks Div., 1976-); National Org. of Afro-Asian-Caribbean People in UK, 1977. Member: Exec. Cttee, Standing Conf. of Pakistani Orgs in UK, 1976- (Chm. Standing Conf., 1974-76); Asian Action Cttee (National), 1976; Exec. Cttee, Sheffield Community Relations Council, 1974-76; Adv. Council, IBA for Radio Hallam, Sheffield, 1975-. Member: British Geriatric Soc.; Medico-Chirurgical Soc. Sheffield; BMA; Collegiate Cttee of Edinburgh; Magistrates' Assoc. JP City of Sheffield, 1974. *Recreations:* tennis, cricket, chess, football, golf, table tennis. *Address:* 1 Derriman Glen, Silverdale Road, Sheffield S11 9LQ. *T:* Sheffield 360465.

ADORIAN, Paul; consulting engineer; Adviser, Resource Sciences Corporation, Tulsa, Oklahoma, USA, since 1970; Director: Humphries Holdings, since 1962; Williams Brothers Engineering Ltd, since 1973; *b* 29 Nov. 1905; *s* of Dr Emil Adorian; *m* 1932, Lilian A. Griffiths; two *s* one *d* . *Educ:* City and Guilds (Eng) Coll., London. Joined Rediffusion as development engineer, 1932; retd 1970, as Man. Dir; retired as director of Rediffusion Television (Man. Dir), Wembley Stadium (Dep. Chm.), British Electric Traction. Member, Bd of Governors, British Film Inst., 1964-72. Past Pres., IERE. FCGI. *Publications:* several technical papers and lectures on electronics in general, flight simulation and distribution of broadcast sound and television programmes in particular, 1933-. *Recreations:* lawn tennis (umpired Drobny-Patty match, also Drobny-Rosewall final, at Wimbledon), archæology, nature-study. *Address:* The Mill House, Gibbons Mill, near Billingshurst, West Sussex. *T:* Rudgwick 2477. *Club:* Athenæum.

ADRIAN, family name of **Baron Adrian.**

ADRIAN, 2nd Baron, *cr* 1955, of Cambridge; **Richard Hume Adrian,** FRS 1977; Reader in Experimental Biophysics, University of Cambridge, since 1968; Fellow of Churchill College, since 1961; *b* 16 Oct. 1927; *o s* of 1st Baron Adrian, OM, FRS, FRCP, and Hester Agnes, DBE 1965 (*d* 1966), *o d* of late Hume C. and Dame Ellen Pinsent, DBE, Birmingham; *S* father, 1977; *m* 1967, Lucy Caroe, MA, PhD. *Educ:* Swarthmore High Sch., USA; Westminster Sch.; Trinity Coll., Cambridge (MA). MB, BChir Cantab. UCH, 1951; National Service, RAMC, 1952-54; Univ. of Cambridge: G. H. Lewes Student, Physiol Lab., 1954; Univ. Demonstr, 1956; Fellow, Corpus Christi Coll., 1956; Univ. Lectr, 1961. Docteur *hc* Poitiers, 1975. *Publications:* articles in Jl of Physiol. *Recreations:* sailing, skiing. *Address:* 3 Adams Road, Cambridge CB3 9AD. *T:* Cambridge 52090; Umgeni, Cley, Holt, Norfolk.

ADRIEN, Sir J. F. M. L.; *see* Latour-Adrien.

ADSHEAD, Mary; *m* 1929, Stephen Bone (*d* 1958). Trained at Slade School under Prof. Henry Tonks. Mural paintings in public and private buildings; illustrations; designs for GPO stamps. Chief works: murals in: Restaurant at Luton Hoo; St Peter's Church, Vauxhall Estate, Luton; Civic Centre, Plymouth; Town Hall, Totnes; Commonwealth Inst.; Messrs Costain & Sons; The Post House, Leicester.

AFSHAR, Amir Khosrow; Order of Homayoun, third, second and first class, Order of the Crown, fourth and third class, Iran; HIM's Ambassador to the Court of St James's, 1969-74; *b* 1920; *m* ; one *s* two *d* . *Educ:* American Coll., Tehran; Faculty of Law, Paris Univ.; Univ. of Geneva. Served in various Depts of Foreign Ministry; First Sec., Imperial Iranian Embassy, Washington, 1947; First Sec., Permanent Iranian Delegn to UN, 1948-50; Head of UN Dept, Min. of Foreign Affairs, Tehran, 1950; Head of 3rd Political Dept, MFO, 1951; Head of 4th Political Dept, MFO, 1953; appointed Chargé d'Affaires in London, after resumption of diplomatic relations, 1953; Minister Plenipotentiary, London, 1954-57; Dir Gen. (Political Affairs),

MFO, 1958; Political and Parly Under-Sec., MFO, 1959; HIM's Ambassador in Germany, 1961; HIM's Ambassador in Paris, 1963; Deputy and Acting Foreign Minister, 1967. Hon. KCMG (UK), 1961; Grand Officier de la Légion d'Honneur (France); Commander's Cross of the Order of Merit (Federal Republic of Germany). *Recreations:* horse breeding, riding.

AGA KHAN (IV), His Highness Prince Karim, granted title His Highness by the Queen, 1957, granted title His Royal Highness by the Shah of Iran, 1959; *b* 13 Dec. 1936; *s* of late Prince Aly Salomon Khan, and of Princess Joan Aly Khan (marr. diss. 1949) (*née* Hon. Joan Barbara Yarde-Buller, *e d* of 3rd Baron Churston, MVO, OBE); became Aga Khan, spiritual leader and Imam of Ismaili Muslims all over the world, on the death of his grandfather, Sir Sultan Mohamed Shah, Aga Khan III, GCSI, GCIE, GCVO, 11 July 1957; *m* 1969, Sarah Frances Crichton-Stuart, *o d* of Lt-Col A. E. Croker Poole; two *s* one *d*. *Educ:* Le Rosey, Switzerland; Harvard University (BA Hons). Commander, Ordre du Mérite Mauritanien, 1960; Grand Croix de l'Ordre National de la Côte d'Ivoire, 1965; de la Haute-Volta, 1965; Malgache, 1966; Grand Croix de l'Ordre du Croissant Vert des Comores, 1966; Grand Cordon de l'Ordre du Tadj de l'Empire d'Iran, 1967; Nishan-I-Imtiaz, Pakistan, 1970; Doctor of Laws (*hc*): Peshawar Univ., Pakistan, 1967; Sind Univ., Pakistan, 1970. *Recreations:* tennis, ski-ing. *Address:* 1 rue des Ursins, Paris 75004, France.

AGA KHAN, Prince Sadruddin; United Nations High Commissioner for Refugees since Dec. 1965; *b* 17 Jan. 1933; *s* of His late Highness Sir Sultan Mohamed Shah, Aga Khan III, GCSI, GCIE, GCVO and of Andrée Joséphine Caron; *m* 1957, Nina Sheila Dyer (marr. diss., 1962); *m* 1972, Catherine Aleya Sursock. *Educ:* Harvard Univ. (BA); Harvard Grad. Sch. Arts and Sciences; Centre of Middle Eastern Studies. Unesco Consultant for Afro-Asian Projects, 1958; Head of Mission and Adviser to UN High Comr for Refugees, 1959-60; Unesco Special Consultant to Dir-Gen., 1961; Exec. Sec., Internat. Action Cttee for Preservation of Nubian Monuments, 1961; UN Dep. High Comr for Refugees, 1962-65. Grand Cross: Order of St Silvestro (Papal), 1963; Order of Homayoun (Iran), 1967; Order of the Royal Star of Great Comoro (Comoro Is), 1970; Order of the Two Niles (First Class) Sudan, 1973. *Recreations:* Islamic art, sailing, ski-ing, photography, travel. *Address:* Château de Bellerive, Collonge-Bellerive, Canton of Geneva, Switzerland. *Clubs:* Travellers' (Paris); Knickerbocker (New York).

AGAR, family name of **Earl of Normanton.**

AGAR, Herbert Sebastian; author; *b* New Rochelle, NY, 29 Sept. 1897; *s* of John Giraud Agar and Agnes Louise Macdonough; *m* 1st, 1918, Adeline Scott; one *s* one *d* ; 2nd, 1933, Eleanor Carroll Chilton (*d* 1949); 3rd, 1945, Mrs Euan Wallace, widow of Capt. Euan Wallace and *e d* of late Sir Edwyn Lutyens. *Educ:* Columbia Univ. (BA 1919); Princeton Univ. (MA 1920, PhD 1922). London Correspondent, Louisville Courier-Journal and Louisville Times, 1929-34; Literary Editor, English Review, 1930-34; Editor, Louisville Courier-Journal, 1939-42; Special Assistant to American Ambassador in London, 1942-46; Counsellor for Public Affairs, US Embassy, 1945-46; President of Freedom House, New York, 1941-43; Director: Rupert Hart-Davis Ltd, publishers, 1953-63; TWW Ltd (Independent Television, S Wales and W of England), 1957-68. Served as seaman, later Chief Quartermaster, USNR, 1917-18; Lt-Comdr USNR, 1942. *Publications:* Milton and Plato, 1928; Bread and Circuses, 1930; The Defeat of Baudelaire (trans.), 1932; American Presidents, 1933; What is America, 1936; Pursuit of Happiness, 1938; A Time for Greatness, 1943; The Price of Union, 1950 (Eng. title The United States, 1950); Declaration of Faith, 1952; Abraham Lincoln, 1952; The Unquiet Years, 1957; The Saving Remnant, 1960; The Perils of Democracy, 1965; Britain Alone, 1973. *Address:* Beechwood, Petworth, West Sussex. *T:* Graffham 213. *Clubs:* Savile; National Arts, Century (New York).

AGER, Rear-Adm. Kenneth Gordon, CB 1977; retired Royal Navy 1977; *b* 22 May 1920; *s* of Harold Stoddart Ager and Nellie Maud (*née* Tate); *m* 1944, Muriel Lydia Lanham; one *s* one *d* . *Educ:* Dulwich Central Sch. and Royal Navy. Called up for War Service, RN, 1940; Sub Lt (Special Br.) RNVR, 1943; Lieut (Electrical) RN, 1944; Weapons and Elect. Engr; Comdr (WE) 1958; Captain (E) 1966; Fleet Weapons and Elect. Engr Officer, 1969-71; Sen. Officers' War Course, 1971-72; CSO (Eng) to Flag Off. Scotland and NI, and Captain Fleet Maintenance, Rosyth, 1972-75; Rear-Adm. (E) 1975; Flag Off., Admiralty Interview Bd, 1975-77. *Recreations:* golf, sailing, reading. *Address:* 22 West Harbour Road, Charlestown, Dunfermline, Fife KY11 3ET. *Club:* Royal Naval and Royal Albert Yacht (Portsmouth).

AGHNIDES, Thanassis; Chairman Advisory Committee on Administrative and Budgetary Questions of UNO, 1946-64; *b* Nigdé, Asia Minor, 1889; *s* of Prodromos and Anastasia Aghnides. *Educ:* Superior National Greek Coll., Phanar, Istanbul; Anatolia Coll. (Asia Minor); Univ. of Istanbul; University of Paris. Directed Greek Press Bureau at Greek Legation, London, 1918-19; worked for League of Nations, 1919-42; Dir of Disarmament Section, 1930, and Under Secretary-General of the League, 1939; Secretary of Disarmament Conference, 1932-34; Secretary-General Montreux Conference concerning the Straits, May 1936; Secretary-General Conference for the suppression of Egyptian Capitulations, 1937; Secretary-General Nyon Conference for the suppression of piracy in the Mediterranean, 1937; Permanent Under-Secretary for Foreign Affairs in Greek Cabinet, 1942-43; Greek Ambassador to the Court of St James's, 1942-47; Greek Delegate to San Francisco Conference on International Organisation, 1945; Chief Delegate for Greece on Preparatory Commission of UNO; Chm. 6th Committee, on organisation of UNO Secretariat, Dec. 1945; Delegate to the 1st Assembly of UNO; Rapporteur of its 5th Cttee (on organisation), Jan. 1946; rep. Greece on Security Council when it dealt with question of presence of British troops in Greece, 1-6 Feb. 1946; Chairman Greek Deleg. to Gen. Assembly of UNO, Oct.-Dec. 1946; Chm. Cttee on Admin of UNESCO, Feb.-April 1948. Member Curatorium Acad. of Internat. Law of The Hague, 1948-68. *Recreation:* music. *Address:* 3 Avenue Bertrand, Geneva, Switzerland. *T:* 463602. *Club:* Brooks's.

AGLEN, Anthony John, CB 1957; FRSE; Joint Deputy Secretary, Department of Agriculture and Fisheries for Scotland, 1960-71, also Fisheries Secretary for Scotland, 1946-71; *b* 30 May 1911; 2nd *s* of late Sir Francis A. Aglen, GCMG, KBE, Alyth, Perthshire; *m* 1946, Audrey Louise Murray, *o d* of late Andrew E. Murray, WS, Edinburgh; one *s* one *d*. *Educ:* Marlborough; Trinity Coll., Cambridge (Scholar). First Class Mathematical Tripos, Part I, 1931, and Part II 1933, BA 1933. Entered Civil Service (Scottish Office), 1934; Private Secretary to successive Secretaries of State for Scotland, 1939-41; Assistant Secretary, Scottish Home Dept, 1942; Under-Sec., 1953; Dep. Sec., 1956-60. President, North East Atlantic Fisheries Commission, 1963-66. *Recreations:* gardening, fishing. *Address:* Birkhill, Earlston, Berwickshire. *T:* Earlston 307. *Club:* New (Edinburgh).

AGLIONBY, Francis John; A Recorder of the Crown Court, since 1975; *b* 17 May 1932; *s* of Francis Basil and Marjorie Wycliffe Aglionby; *m* 1967, Susan Victoria Mary Vaughan; one *s* one *d*. *Educ:* Charterhouse; Corpus Christi Coll., Oxford (MA). Barrister, Inner Temple, 1956, Bencher, 1976; Chancellor of Diocese of Birmingham, 1971. *Recreations:* variable. *Address:* 36 Bark Place, W2 4AT. *T:* 01-229 7303. *Club:* Brooks's.

AGNELLI, Dr Giovanni; industrialist; car manufacturer, Italy; Chairman: Fiat, since 1966; RIV-SKF, since 1943; Instituto Finanziario Industriale, since 1959; Agnelli Foundation, since 1968; Fiat-Allis, since 1974; *b* Turin, Italy, 12 March 1921; *s* of Edoardo Agnelli, and *g s* of Giovanni Agnelli, founder of Fabbrica Italiana Automobili Torino (FIAT); *m* 1953, Princess Marella Caracciolo di Castagneto; one *s* one *d*. *Educ:* Turin. DrJur, Univ. of Turin, 1943. Director: Montedison, 1966-71; Mediobanca; Credito Italiano; SKF of Sweden; Assonime. Member: Internat. Adv. Cttee, Chase Manhattan Bank, NY; Conf. Bd, Internat. Indust. Conf., San Francisco. Pres., Confindustria, 1974-76. Mayor, Villar Perosa, 1945-. *Address:* 10 Corso Marconi, Turin, Italy. *T:* 65651.

AGNEW, Sir Anthony Stuart; see Agnew, Sir J. A. S.

AGNEW of Lochnaw, Major Sir Crispin Hamlyn, 11th Bt *cr* 1629; Chief of the Name and Arms of Agnew; Royal Highland Fusiliers; *b* 13 May 1944; *s* of (Sir) Fulque Melville Gerald Noel Agnew, 10th Bt and of Swanzie, *d* of late Major Esmé Nourse Erskine, CMG, MC; *S* father, 1975. *Educ:* Uppingham; RMA, Sandhurst. Leader, Army Expedn to E Greenland, 1968 and Jt Services to Chilean Patagonia, 1972-73. Member: RN Expedn to E Greenland, 1966; Jt Services to Elephant Island, 1970-71; Army Nuptse Expedn, 1975; Jt British and Royal Nepalese Army Everest Expedn, 1976 (reached the South Col). *Recreations:* mountaineering, heraldry. *Heir:* cousin Andrew David Quentin Agnew, PhD [*b* 31 Dec. 1929; *m* 1957, Shirley, *d* of late James Arnold Smithson; three *s*]. *Address:* c/o RHQ, Royal Highland Fusiliers, 518 Sauchiehall Street, Glasgow G2 3LT; (home) 3 Lonsdale Terrace, Edinburgh EH3 9HN. *Clubs:* Army and Navy, Alpine; Puffin's (Edinburgh).

AGNEW, Sir Geoffrey (William Gerald), Kt 1973; Chairman, Thos Agnew & Sons, Ltd (Fine Art Dealers), since 1965; *b* 11 July 1908; *er s* of late Charles Gerald Agnew and Olive Mary (*née* Danks); *m* 1934, Hon. Doreen Maud Jessel, *y d* of 1st Baron Jessel, CB, CMG; two *s* one *d*. *Educ:* Eton (Hon Fellow, 1976); Trinity College, Cambridge (BA 1930; MA 1971); Munich. Joined Thos Agnew & Sons (Fine Art Dealers), 1931; Managing Director, 1937-. Assistant master (History), Eton College, 1939-45. Chairman, Evelyn (Agnew) Nursing Home, Cambridge, 1955-. A Permanent Steward, 1955- and a Vice-Pres., 1968-, Artists' General Benevolent Institution; President, Fine Art Provident Institution, 1963-66; Chairman: St George's Arts Trust, King's Lynn, 1966-73; Society of London Art Dealers, 1970-74; Friends of the Courtauld Institute, 1970-; Vice-Pres., Guildhall of St George, King's Lynn, 1975-. *Publications:* Agnew's 1817-1967, 1967; various broadcasts on art published in the Listener. *Recreations:* works of art, travel, gardening. *Address:* 11 Alexander Square, SW3. *T:* 01-589 5916; Egmere Farm House, Walsingham, Norfolk. *T:* Walsingham 247. *Clubs:* Brooks's, Garrick.

AGNEW, Sir Godfrey; see Agnew, Sir W. G.

AGNEW, Sir (John) Anthony Stuart, 4th Bt, *cr* 1895; *b* 25 July 1914; *s* of Sir John Stuart Agnew, 3rd Bt, TD, DL, and Kathleen (*d* 1971), *d* of late I. W. H. White, Leeds; *S* father, 1957. *Educ:* privately in Switzerland. *Heir: b* Major George Keith Agnew, TD [*b* 25 Nov. 1918; *m* 1948, Anne Merete Louise, *yr d* of Baron Johann Schaffalitzky de Muckadell, Fyn, Denmark; two *s*]. *Address:* c/o Blackthorpe Farm, Rougham, Bury St Edmunds, Suffolk.

AGNEW, Commander Sir Peter (Garnett), 1st Bt *cr* 1957; *b* 1900; *s* of late C. L. Agnew; *m* 1928, Enid Frances, *d* of late Henry Boan, Perth, Western Australia; one *s*. *Educ:* Repton. Entered Royal Navy, 1918; ADC to Governor of Jamaica, 1927-28; retired, 1931; returned to service at sea, Aug. 1939 (despatches). MP (C) Camborne Div. of Cornwall, 1931-50; PPS to Rt Hon. Walter Runciman, President of Board of Trade, 1935-37, and to Rt Hon. Sir Philip Sassoon, First Commissioner of Works, 1937-39; an Assistant Government Whip, May-July, 1945; a Conservative Whip, Aug. 1945-Feb. 1950; contested (C) Falmouth and Camborne Div., Feb. 1950; MP (C) South Worcs, 1955-66. Member of House of Laity Church Assembly, 1935-65; a Church Comr for England, 1948-68; Trustee, Historic Churches Preservation Trust, 1968-. Chm., Iran Society, 1966-73; Internat. Pres., European Centre of Documentation and Information, 1974-76. Order of Homayoun (Iran), 1973; Kt Grand Cross, Order of Civil Merit (Spain), 1977. *Recreation:* travelling. *Heir: s* Quentin Charles Agnew-Somerville [*b* 8 March 1929; *m* 1963, Hon. April, *y d* of 15th Baron Strange, *qv*; one *s* two *d*. *Educ:* RNC Dartmouth]. *Address:* 2 Smith Square, SW1P 3HS. *T:* 01-222 7179. *Clubs:* Carlton, Buck's.

AGNEW, Peter Graeme, MBE 1946; BA; Deputy Chairman, Bradbury Agnew & Co. Ltd (Proprietors of Punch), since 1969; *b* 7 April 1914; *s* of late Alan Graeme Agnew; *m* 1937, Mary Diana (*née* Hervey); two *s* two *d*. *Educ:* Kingsmead, Seaford; Stowe School; Trinity College, Cambridge. Student Printer, 1935-37. Joined Bradbury Agnew & Co. Ltd, 1937. RAFVR 1937. Served War of 1939-45; Demobilised, 1945, as Wing Commander. *Recreations:* sailing, gardening. *Address:* Roscaddon, Manaccan, near Helston, Cornwall TR12 6JH. *T:* Manaccan 223.

AGNEW, Spiro Theodore, (Ted); *b* Baltimore, Md, 9 Nov. 1918; *s* of Theodore S. Agnew and Margaret Akers; *m* 1942, Elinor Isabel Judefind; one *s* three *d*. *Educ:* Forest Park High Sch., Baltimore; Johns Hopkins Univ.; Law Sch., Univ. Baltimore (LLB). Served War of 1939-45 with 8th and 10th Armd Divs, 1941-46, company combat comdr in France and Germany (Bronze Star). Apptd to Zoning Bd of Appeals of Baltimore County, 1957 (Chm., 1958-61); County Executive, Baltimore County, 1962-66; Governor of Maryland, 1967-68; Vice-President of the United States, 1969-73. Republican. With Pathlite Inc., Crofton, Md, 1974-. *Publication:* The Canfield Decision, 1976. *Recreations:* golf, tennis. *Address:* Towson, Md 21212, USA.

AGNEW, Stanley Clarke, CEng, FICE; Chief Engineer, Scottish Development Department, since 1976; *b* 18 May 1926; *s* of Christopher Gerald Agnew and Margaret Eleanor Agnew (*née* Clarke); *m* 1950, Isbell Evelyn Parker (*née* Davidson); two *d*. *Educ:* Royal Belfast Academical Instn; Queen's Univ., Belfast (BSc Civil Eng., 1947). FIWE, FIPHE. Site Engr, Farrans Ltd, 1947-50; Asst Engr, Fife CC, 1950-52; Site Agent, R. J. McLeod (Contractors) Ltd, 1952-53; Sen. Asst Engr, Dumfries CC, 1953-57; Resident Engr, Blyth & Blyth, 1957-59; Engr to Dungannon and Clogher RDCs, 1959-62; Eng. Inspector, Scottish Develt Dept, 1962-68, Dep. Chief Engr, 1968-75. Hon. FIWPC 1976. *Recreations:* golf, photography, motoring, gardening. *Address:*

Duncraig, 52 Blinkbonny Road, Edinburgh EH4 3HX. *T:* 031-332 4072. *Club:* Murrayfield Golf (Edinburgh).

AGNEW, Sir (William) Godfrey, KCVO 1965 (CVO 1953); CB 1975; Chairman, Lady Clare Ltd, since 1970; Director: Sun Life Assurance Society Ltd, since 1974; Seaway Shipping Agencies Ltd, since 1971; Seaway Holdings Ltd, since 1971; Artagen Properties Ltd, since 1976; Consultant, Council of Engineering Institutions, since 1974; *b* 11 Oct. 1913; *o s* of late Lennox Edelsten Agnew and Elsie Blyth Nott, Tunbridge Wells; *m* 1st, 1939, Ruth Mary (*d* 1962), *e d* of late Charles J. H. O'H. Moore, CVO, MC, and late Lady Dorothie Moore; three *s* three *d*; 2nd, 1965, Lady (Nancy Veronica) Tyrwhitt, *widow* of Adm. Sir St John Reginald Joseph Tyrwhitt, 2nd Bt, KCB, DSO, DSC; two step *s* one step *d*. *Educ:* Tonbridge. Solicitor, 1935; entered Public Trustee Office, 1936. Served RA and Surrey and Sussex Yeomanry, 1939-46; Major, 1945. Senior Clerk, Privy Council Office, 1946-51; Clerk of the Privy Council, 1953-74 (Deputy Clerk, 1951-53); Dep. Sec., Cabinet Office, 1972-74. Chairman, Sembal Trust, 1967-73. Hon. FIMechE, 1968; Hon. FIMunE, 1974; Hon. FCIBS. *Address:* Pinehurst, South Ascot, Berks. *T:* Ascot 20036. *Clubs:* Army and Navy; Swinley Forest Golf; Littlestone-on-Sea Golf.
See also Sir J. M. H. Pollen, Bt.

AGRA, Archbishop of, (RC), since 1956; **Most Rev. Dominic Romuald Athaide,** DD; OFMCap; *b* Bandra, India, 7 Feb. 1909. *Educ:* Holland; France; Pontifical Gregorian University, Rome. Priest, 1932. Lecturer in Philosophy and Theology, Quilon, India, 1937; Missionary, Aden, 1940; subsequently Director of St Joseph's High School, and Parish Priest, Aden. Member Order of Friars Minor (Capuchins). Member: Standing Cttee, Catholic Bishops' Conf. of India; CBCI Commn for Dialogue with other faiths; a Vice-Pres., Uttar Pradesh Minorities Welfare Bd. *Address:* Cathedral House, Wazirpura Road, Agra 282003, UP, India. *T:* 7-24-07. *TA:* Cathedral.

AHERN, Most Rev. John; *see* Cloyne, Bishop of, (RC).

AHERN, Maj.-Gen. Timothy Michael Richard, CBE 1959 (OBE 1945); Director of Medical Services, British Army of the Rhine, 1966-69, retired; *b* 16 Aug. 1908; *s* of late Lieut-Col M. D. Ahern and late Mrs Ahern, formerly of Glanmire, Co. Cork, Eire; *m* 1943, Joan Aisne, *d* of late S. Blencowe, and of Mrs Blencowe, Latmus, Bishopsteignton, S Devon; two *s* one *d*. *Educ:* Ampleforth College; Trinity College, Dublin. ADMS, Eighth Army, 1944-45. Chief of Medical Plans and Ops, SHAPE, 1953-56; Comdt, RAMC Field Training Centre, 1956-59; Exchange Officer, Brooke Army Medical Center, Texas, USA, 1959-60; DDMS: 1 (British) Corps, 1960-63; Eastern Comd, 1965-66. Col Comdt, RAMC, 1969-. *Publications:* contribs to Proc. Roy. Soc. Med. and Jl of Assoc. of Military Surgeons of USA. *Address:* c/o Williams & Glyn's Bank Ltd, Kirkland House, 22 Whitehall, SW1.

AICKIN, Hon. Sir Keith Arthur, KBE 1976; **Hon. Mr Justice Aickin;** Justice of High Court of Australia, since 1976; *b* Melbourne, 1 Feb. 1916; *s* of J. L. Aickin, Belfast, Ireland; *m* 1952, Elizabeth May, *d* of S. W. Gullett; one *s* one *d*. *Educ:* Church of England Grammar Sch., Melbourne; Univ. of Melbourne (LLM). Associate to Justice Dixon, High Court of Aust., 1939-41; Third Sec., Aust. Legation, Washington, DC, 1942-44; Legal Adviser, European Regional Office, UNRRA, 1944-48; in Legal Dept, UN, NY, 1948; Melbourne Bar, 1949-76. QC Vic 1957, Tas. 1959, NSW 1967. Mem., Interim Council, La Trobe Univ., 1966, Council, 1967-73. Director: Mayne Nickless Ltd, 1958-76; P&O Aust Ltd, 1969-76; Comalco Ltd, 1970-76; BHP Co. Ltd, 1971-76. *Address:* High Court of Australia, Melbourne, Vic., Australia; 41 Marne Street, South Yarra, Vic. 3141, Australia. *Clubs:* Melbourne, Australian (Melbourne); Frankston Golf.

AIERS, David Pascoe, CMG 1971; HM Diplomatic Service; High Commissioner to Sri Lanka, and Ambassador to the Republic of Maldives, since 1976; *b* 19 Sept. 1922; *s* of late George Aiers and Sarah Adshead; *m* 1943, Pauleen Victoria Brittain-Jones; one *s* one *d*. *Educ:* Stationers' Company's Sch.; Trinity Coll., Oxford. Royal Artillery, 1942-46; Third Sec., Warsaw, 1946-48; FO, 1948; Second Sec., Copenhagen, 1951-53, Buenos Aires, 1953-55; FO, 1955; First Sec. (Commercial), Manila, 1958-62; First Sec. and Head of Chancery, Ankara, 1962-65; Counsellor and Head of Chancery, Political Adviser's Office, Singapore, 1965-68; Head of SW Pacific Dept, FCO, 1968-71; Minister, Canberra, 1971-75. *Address:* Burnside, Littleworth Road, Esher, Surrey. *T:* Esher 63861. *Clubs:* Royal Automobile, Royal Commonwealth Society.

AIKEN, Frank; Member, Dáil Eirann for County Louth, 1923-73; Tánaiste (Deputy Prime Minister) in the Government of Ireland, 1965-69; *b* Camlough, Co. Armagh, 13 Feb. 1898; *y s* of James Aiken and Mary McGeeny; *m* 1934, Maud Davin; two *s* one *d*. *Educ:* Christian Brothers' Secondary Schools, Newry. Joined Irish Volunteers, 1913; Captain, Camlough Co., IRA, 1918; Comdt, Camlough Bn, IRA, 1919; Vice-Brig., Newry Bde, IRA, 1920; Comdt, 4th Northern Div., IRA, 1921; Chief of Staff, IRA, 1923. Secretary, Camlough Br., Gaelic League, 1914; Secretary, Sinn Fein Organisation, S Armagh, 1917. Military Service Medal (with Bar). Local and CCs, 1920. Minister for: Defence, Ireland, 1932-39; Lands and Fisheries, June-Nov. 1936; Co-ordination of Defensive Measures, 1939-45; Finance, 1945-48; External Affairs, 1951-54 and 1957-69; Agriculture, March-May 1957. Leader, Irish Delegn to Council of Europe, 1969. Hon. LLD: NUI; St John's Univ., Jamaica, New York; Dublin Univ. Military Service Medal with Bar. Grand Cross: Pian Order; Order of Merit of Federal Republic of Germany; Belgian Order of Crown. Grand Officer with plaque, Order of St Charles. *Address:* Dúngaoithe, Sandyford, Co. Dublin.

AIKEN, Air Chief Marshal Sir John (Alexander Carlisle), KCB 1973 (CB 1967); Air Member for Personnel, since 1976; *b* 22 Dec. 1921; *s* of Thomas Leonard and Margaret Aiken; *m* 1948, Pamela Jane (*née* Bartlett); one *s* one *d*. *Educ:* Birkenhead School. Joined RAF, 1941; Fighter Sqdns, Europe and Far East, 1942-45; Fighter Comd, 1946-47; CFS, 1948; Staff of RAF Coll., Cranwell, 1948-50; OC Univ. of Birmingham Air Sqdn, 1950-52; Staff Coll., 1953; HQ Fighter Comd, 1954-55; OC 29 Fighter Sqdn, 1956-57; jssc 1958; Headquarters AF North, 1958-60; Air Min., 1960-63; Station Comdr, RAF Finningley, 1963-64; Air Cdre Intelligence, Min. of Defence, 1965-67; idc 1968; Dep. Comdr, RAF, Germany, 1969-71; Dir-Gen. Training, RAF, 1971-72; Head of Economy Project Team (RAF), 1972-73; AOC-in-C, NEAF, Comdr British Forces Near East, and Administrator, Sovereign Base Areas, Cyprus, 1973-76. Governor, Birkenhead Sch., 1976-. *Recreations:* ski-ing, music. *Address:* 191 Latymer Court, W6. *Club:* Royal Air Force.

AIKEN, John Elliott, CB 1973; Deputy Secretary, Ministry (later Department) of Health and Social Services for Northern Ireland, 1970-74, retired; *b* 1909; *s* of Thomas John Aiken and Mary Boyton Aiken (*née* Elliott); *m* 1939, Isabel Rosaleen (*née* Hawkesworth); two *s*. *Educ:* Dungannon Royal Sch.; Queen's Univ., Belfast (BComSc). Entered Northern Ireland Civil Service, 1926; Ministry of Finance, 1926; Exchequer and Audit Dept, 1936; Ministries of: Public Security, 1941; Home Affairs, 1944; Education, 1948; Labour and National Insurance, 1957; Health and Social Services, 1965. *Recreations:* sailing, gardening. *Address:* 8 Rosepark, Belfast BT5 7RG, Northern Ireland. *T:* Dundonald 2715. *Club:* Strangford Lough Yacht (Co. Down).

AIKMAN, Colin Campbell, PhD; New Zealand High Commissioner to India, accredited also to Bangladesh and Nepal, since 1975; *b* 24 Feb. 1919; *s* of Colin Campbell Aikman and Bertha Egmont Aikman (*née* Harwood); *m* 1952, Betty Alicia, *d* of R. Y. James; three *d* (one *s* decd). *Educ:* Palmerston North Boys' High Sch.; Victoria University Coll., Wellington, NZ (LLM); London Sch. of Economics (PhD). Law Clerk in Legal Offices, 1935-41; Barrister and Solicitor of Supreme Court of New Zealand, 1940-41; Personal Asst to Air Secretary, Air Dept (NZ), 1942-43; Prime Minister's Dept and Dept of External Affairs (Legal Adviser, 1949-55), 1943-55; Mem. NZ Delgn to San Francisco Conf., 1945; Prof. of Jurisprudence and Constitutional Law, Victoria Univ. of Wellington (Dean of Law Faculty, 1957-59, 1962-67), 1955-68; Mem., Permanent Court of Arbitration, 1955-68; Mem. Council, NZ Inst. of Internat. Affairs (Nat. Pres., 1960-63), 1955-; Advr to NZ Govt on Constitutional Develt of Cook Is, Western Samoa and Niue, 1956-68; Vice-Chancellor, The Univ. of the South Pacific, Suva, Fiji, 1968-74. Member: Council of Volunteer Service Abroad (Inc.) (Chm. 1962-65), 1962-68; NZ Nat. Commn for UNESCO, 1957-65; Univ. of Waikato Academic Cttee Council and Professorial Bd, 1963-66; (Chm.) Nat. Adv. Council on Teacher Trng, 1963-68; Law Revision Commn and Public and Administrative Law Reform Cttee, 1966-68; Council, Assoc. of Commonwealth Univs, 1972-73. *Publications:* (co-author): A Report to Members of the Legislative Assembly of the Cook Islands on Constitutional Development, 1963; New Zealand, The Development of its Laws and Constitution (ed Robson), 1967 (2nd edn); New Zealand's Record in the Pacific Islands in the Twentieth Century (ed Angus Ross), 1969. *Recreations:* golf, cricket, carpentry. *Address:* New Zealand High Commission, 39 Golf Links Road, New Delhi 110003, India. *T:* 618281; c/o Ministry of Foreign Affairs, Wellington, NZ.

AILESBURY, 8th Marquess of, cr 1821; **Michael Sydney Cedric Brudenell-Bruce**; Bt 1611; Baron Brudenell 1628; Earl of Cardigan 1661; Baron Bruce 1746; Earl of Ailesbury 1776; Earl Bruce 1821; Viscount Savernake 1821; 30th Hereditary Warden of Savernake Forest; Lt RHG, 1946; Member London Stock Exchange since 1954; *b* 31 March 1926; *e s* of 7th Marquess of Ailesbury and Joan (*d* 1937), *d* of Stephen Salter, Ryde, Isle of Wight; *S* father, 1974; *m* 1st, 1952, Edwina Sylvia de Winton (from whom he obtained a divorce, 1961), *yr d* of Lt-Col Sir (Ernest) Edward de Winton Wills, 4th Bt, *qv*; one *s* two *d*; 2nd, 1963, Juliet Adrienne (marr. diss. 1974), *d* of late Hilary Lethbridge Kingsford and of Mrs Latham Hobrow, Hove; two *d*; 3rd, 1974, Mrs Caroline Elizabeth Romilly, *d* of O. F. M. Wethered, RN retd, DL, JP. *Educ:* Eton. *Heir:* s Earl of Cardigan, *qv. Address:* Avebury Manor, near Marlborough, Wilts. *T:* Avebury 203. *Club:* Sloane.

AILSA, 7th Marquess of, cr 1831; **Archibald David Kennedy,** OBE 1968; Baron Kennedy, 1452; Earl of Cassillis, 1509; Baron Ailsa (UK), 1806; *b* 3 Dec. 1925; *s* of 6th Marquess of Ailsa and Gertrude Millicent (*d* 1957), *d* of Gervas Weir Cooper, Wordwell Hall, Bury St Edmunds; *S* father 1957; *m* 1954, Mary, 7th *c* of John Burn, Amble; two *s* one *d. Educ:* Nautical Coll., Pangbourne. Scots Guards, 1943-47; Royal Northumberland Fusiliers, 1950-52. National Trust for Scotland, 1953-56. Territorial Army, 1958-68. *Recreations:* walking, motoring, modelling, sailing. *Heir:* s Earl of Cassillis, *qv. Address:* Cassillis House, Maybole, Ayrshire. *Clubs:* Carlton; New (Edinburgh); Royal Yacht Squadron.

AILWYN, 4th Baron cr 1921; **Carol Arthur Fellowes,** TD 1946; *b* 23 Nov. 1896; 4th *s* of 1st Baron Ailwyn, PC, KCVO, KBE, 2nd *s* of 1st Baron de Ramsey, and Hon. Agatha Eleanor Augusta Jolliffe, *d* of 2nd Baron Hylton; *S* brother, 1976; *m* 1936, Caroline (Cudemore), *d* of late Maynard Cowan, Victoria, BC; one adopted step *d. Educ:* Royal Naval Colls, Osborne and Dartmouth. Lieut, 3rd and 2nd Norfolk Regt., 1916-19; served in Mesopotamia, 1917-19. Subsequently fruit farmer; Agent to Earl of Strafford, 1930-52. Formed 334 (Barnet) AA Company, RE (T), 1937; served War as Major RA (T) comdg 334 Co. and on staff of Anti-Aircraft Command, 1939-44. Asst Sec., RASE, 1952-59; Sec., Norfolk Club, Norwich, 1964-69; Trustee, Lord Wandsworth Coll., 1955-72; Governor, Felixstowe Coll., 1960-74 (Chm., 1966-72). Late JP Herts and Middlesex. *Heir:* none. *Address:* The Cottage, Gissing, Diss, Norfolk. *T:* Tivetshall 221. *Club:* (Hon. Member) Norfolk (Norwich).

AINLEY, Sir (Alfred) John, Kt 1957; MC 1940; Chief Justice, Kenya, 1963-68; retired; Chairman of Industrial Tribunals, 1972-76; *b* 10 May 1906; *o s* of late Rev. A. Ainley, Cockermouth, Cumb; *m* 1935, Mona Sybil Wood; one *s* two *d. Educ:* St Bees Sch.; Corpus Christi, Oxford. Called to Bar, 1928; Magistrate, Gold Coast, 1935; Crown Counsel (Gold Coast), 1936; Puisne Judge, Uganda, 1946-55; Chief Justice of Eastern Region, Nigeria, 1955-59; Combined Judiciary of Sarawak, N Borneo and Brunei, 1959-62. Served War of 1939-45, West African Forces, E Africa and Burma. *Address:* Horrock Wood, Watermillock, Penrith, Cumbria.

AINLEY, Eric Stephen; Under-Secretary, Department of the Environment (formerly Ministry of Transport), 1968-75; *b* 15 Sept. 1918; *s* of late Captain Eric E. Ainley and Dorothy Ainley (*née* Sharp); *m* 1946, Pamela, *d* of late Mr and Mrs Philip G. Meadows; two *s. Educ:* Giggleswick Sch.; Trinity Coll., Cambridge. BA, Classics and English; MA. Served War of 1939-45: RA, RIASC, and Civil Affairs (Malaya), 1940-46. Asst Principal, Min. of Civil Aviation, 1948; Principal, 1950; Civil Air Adviser and Attaché, Singapore and Far East, 1955-58; Asst Sec., Min. of Transport, 1960; seconded as the Traffic Manager, GLC, 1965-67. *Publication:* Mathematical Puzzles, 1977. *Recreations:* mathematics, golf. *Address:* 8 Poynder Place, Hilmarton, near Calne, Wilts. *T:* Hilmarton 650. *Club:* N Wilts Golf.

AINLEY, Sir John; *see* Ainley, Sir A. J.

AINSWORTH, Sir John (Francis), 3rd Bt cr 1916; Inspector, Irish Manuscripts Commission, since 1943; *b* 4 Jan. 1912; *s* of Sir Thomas Ainsworth, 2nd Bt, and Lady Edina Dorothy Hope (*d* 1964), *d* of 4th Marquess Conyngham; *S* father, 1971; *m* 1st, 1938, Josephine (marr. diss. 1946), *e d* of Comdr W. R. Bernard, RN; 2nd, 1946, Anita M. A., *e d* of H. A. Lett, Ballynadara, Enniscorthy, Co. Wexford; no *c. Educ:* Eton (Newcastle Medallist); Trinity College, Cambridge (Sen. Scholar, BA 1933, MA 1937). Hon. General Editor, British Record Society, 1937-40; External Lecturer in Mediaeval History, University College, Cork, 1966-69; Tutor, Archives Dept, University College, Dublin, 1969-. District Commissioner, Kildare Branch, Irish Pony Club, 1960-62; Chairman, Dublin SPCA, 1965-66 and 1976- (Vice-Chm. 1964-65 and 1967-76); 1st Whipper-in, Curragh Beagles, 1964-. *Publications:* Editor or Joint Editor: Records of the Carpenters' Company, 1936; Prerogative Court of Canterbury Wills, 1671-75, 1942; The Inchiquin MSS, 1960; Analecta Hibernica nos 20 and 25, 1958 and 1967. *Recreations:* hunting and horse trials (both at ground level). *Heir:* half-b Thomas David Ainsworth [*b* 22 Aug. 1926; *m* 1957, Sarah Mary, *d* of late Lt-Col H. C. Walford; two *s* two *d*]. *Address:* Carraphuca, Shankill, Co. Dublin. *T:* Dublin 854721.

AINSWORTH, Mrs Robert; *see* Brunskill, Muriel.

AIRD, Captain Alastair (Sturgis), CVO 1977 (MVO 1969); Comptroller to Queen Elizabeth the Queen Mother since 1974; *b* 14 Jan. 1931; *s* of Col Malcolm Aird; *m* 1963, Fiona Violet, *d* of Lt-Col Ririd Myddelton, *qv*; two *d. Educ:* Eton; RMA Sandhurst. Commnd 9th Queen's Royal Lancers, 1951; served in BAOR; Adjt 9th Lancers, 1956-59; retd from Army, 1964. Equerry to Queen Elizabeth the Queen Mother, 1960; Asst Private Sec. to the Queen Mother, 1964. *Recreations:* shooting, fishing, golf. *Address:* 31B St James's Palace, SW1A 1BA. *T:* 01-839 6700. *Club:* Cavalry and Guards.

AIRD, Sir (George) John, 4th Bt cr 1901; Chairman and Managing Director, Sir John Aird & Co Ltd, since 1969; *b* 30 Jan. 1940; *e s* of Sir John Renton Aird, 3rd Bt, MVO, MC, and of Lady Priscilla Aird, *yr d* of 2nd Earl of Ancaster; *S* father, 1973; *m* 1968, Margaret, *yr d* of Sir John Muir, Bt, *qv*; two *d. Educ:* Eton; Oxford Univ.; Harvard Business Sch. MICE. Trainee, Sir Alexander Gibb & Partners, 1961-65; Manager, John Laing & Son Ltd, 1967-69. *Recreations:* farming, hunting. *Heir: cousin* Malcolm Robin Meredith Aird, *b* 16 Dec. 1923. *Address:* Grange Farm, Evenlode, Moreton-in-Marsh, Glos GL56 0NT. *T:* Moreton-in-Marsh 50607. *Club:* White's.

AIRD, Ronald, MC 1942; TD; Secretary Marylebone Cricket Club, 1952-62, retired; *b* 4 May 1902; 2nd *s* of late Malcolm R. Aird; *m* 1925, Viola Mary (*d* 1946), 2nd *d* of late Sir Godfrey Baring, Bt; one *d. Educ:* Eton; Clare College, Cambridge. Stock Exchange, 1924-26; Assistant Secretary, MCC, 1926-52; President: MCC, 1968-69; Hampshire CCC, 1971. *Recreations:* cricket, rackets, real tennis, golf, National Hunt racing. *Address:* West Down House, Yapton, West Sussex. *T:* Yapton 551140. *Clubs:* White's, Oriental, MCC.

AIREDALE, 4th Baron, cr 1907; **Oliver James Vandeleur Kitson,** Bt, cr 1886; Deputy Chairman of Committees, House of Lords, since 1961; Deputy Speaker, House of Lords, since 1962; *b* 22 April 1915; *o s* of 3rd Baron Airedale, DSO, MC, and Sheila Grace (*d* 1935), *d* of late Frank E. Vandeleur, London; *S* father, 1958; unmarried. *Educ:* Eton; Trinity College, Cambridge. Is Major, The Green Howards. Called to the Bar, Inner Temple, 1941. *Heir:* none. *Address:* (seat) Ufford Hall, Stamford, Lincs.

AIREY, Lawrence, CB 1976; Second Permanent Secretary (Domestic Economy), HM Treasury, since 1977; *b* 10 March 1926; *s* of late Lawrence Clark Airey and Isabella Marshall Pearson; *m* 1953, Patricia Anne, *d* of late Edward George Williams and Mary Selway; two *s* one *d. Educ:* Newcastle Royal Grammar Sch.; Peterhouse, Cambridge. Entered Civil Service, 1949; General Register Office, 1949-56; Cabinet Office, 1956-58; HM Treasury, 1958-; Under-Sec., 1969-73; Dep. Sec., 1973-77. Research Fellow, Nuffield Coll., Oxford, 1961-62. Mem., Bd of British Nat. Oil Corp., 1976-77. *Recreations:* collecting books; music. *Address:* 41 Fairdene Road, Coulsdon, Surrey. *T:* Downland 54191.

AIREY, Lt-Gen. Sir Terence (Sydney), KCMG 1951; CB 1944; CBE 1943 (OBE 1941); psc; retired; *b* 9 July 1900; *s* of late Sydney Airey, Orchard Cottage, Holbrook, Suffolk; *m* 1934, Constance Hedley (marr. diss. 1947); one *s*; *m* 1947, Bridget Georgiana, *d* of late Col the Hon. Thomas Vesey. 2nd Lieutenant Durham Light Infantry, 1919; Eastern Arab Corps and HQ Sudan Defence Force, 1929-36; Capt. 1933; Major 1938; Temp. Lieut-Col 1940; War Subst. Lieut-Col; Col 1945; Temp. Maj.-Gen. 1944; Brig. Sept. 1945; Maj.-Gen. 1947; Lieut-Gen. 1952. Served War of 1939-45 (despatches, OBE, CBE, CB): Acting Deputy Supreme Allied Commander, Italy, 1946; Allied Commander and Military Gov., British-US Zone of Free Territory, Trieste, 1947-51; Assistant Chief of Staff, Supreme HQ, Allied Powers, Europe, 1951-52; Commdr, British Forces, Hong-Kong, 1952-54; representative Col Light Inf. Bde, 1954-55; retd 1954. Col The Durham Light Infantry, 1952-56. Commander, Order of Merit (US); Officer, Légion d'Honneur, and Croix de Guerre (France). *Address:* Fritton Old Rectory, Fritton, near Norwich, Norfolk. *T:* Hempnall 214.

AIRLIE, 13th Earl of, *cr* 1639 (*de facto* 10th Earl, 13th but for the Attainder); **David George Coke Patrick Ogilvy**, DL; Baron Ogilvy of Airlie, 1491; Captain late Scots Guards; Chairman: Schroders Ltd, since 1977; Westpool Investment Trust Ltd; Ashdown Investment Trust Ltd; Deputy Chairman, General Accident Fire & Life Assurance Corp. Ltd, since 1975; Director: J. Henry Schroder Wagg & Co. Ltd, since 1961 (Chairman, 1973-77); Schroder Investment Co. Ltd; The Trading Investment Co. Ltd; Scottish & Newcastle Breweries Ltd; *b* 17 May 1926; *e s* of 12th (*de facto* 9th) Earl of Airlie, KT, GCVO, MC, and of Lady Alexandra Marie Bridget Coke, *d* of 3rd Earl of Leicester, GCVO; *S* father, 1968; *m* 1952, Virginia Fortune Ryan, Moorland Farm, Newport, RI, USA; three *s* three *d*. *Educ:* Eton. Lieutenant Scots Guards, 1944; serving 2nd Battalion Germany, 1945; Captain, ADC to High Comr and C-in-C Austria, 1947-48; Malaya, 1948-49; resigned commission, 1950. Ensign, Queen's Body Guard for Scotland, Royal Company of Archers, 1975-. DL Angus, 1964. *Heir:* s Lord Ogilvy, *qv*. *Address:* Cortachy Castle, Kirriemuir, Angus, Scotland. *T:* Cortachy 231; 13 St Leonards Terrace, SW3. *T:* 01-730 8741.
See also Hon. Angus Ogilvy.

AISHER, Owen A(rthur); Chairman of Marley Tile Companies; *b* 28 May 1900; *s* of late Owen Aisher, Little Marley, Western Avenue, Branksome Park, Poole; *m* 1921, Ann Allingham; two *s* two *d*. Mem. Court of Paviors; Pres., RYA, 1970-75; has had many successes in off-shore racing; was elected Yachtsman of the Year, 1958. *Recreations:* sailing, fishing, shooting. *Address:* Faygate, South Godstone, Surrey. *Clubs:* Reform, City Livery; Royal Thames Yacht; RORC (Adm. 1969-75); Ranelagh Sailing; Little Ship (Pres.); Royal Southern Yacht (Hamble); Royal Yacht Squadron, Royal London Yacht, Island Sailing (Adm.) (Cowes); Bembridge Sailing; Royal Motor Yacht (Poole); New York YC, Seawanhaka Corinthian Yacht (USA); Royal St George Yacht (Eire).

AITCHISON, Sir Charles (Walter de Lancey), 4th Bt, *cr* 1938; *b* 27 May 1951; *er s* of Sir Stephen Charles de Lancey Aitchison, 3rd Bt, and (Elizabeth) Anne (Milburn), *er d* of late Lt-Col Edward Reed, Ghyllheugh, Longhorsley, Northumberland; *S* father 1958. Lieut, 15/19th The King's Royal Hussars, 1974; RARO 1974. *Recreations:* motor sport, shooting. *Heir:* b (Stephen) Edward Aitchison, *b* 27 March 1954. *Address:* Howden Dene, Corbridge, Northumberland. *Clubs:* Cavalry and Guards; Northern Counties.
See also R . A . Cookson.

AITHRIE, Viscount; Andrew Victor Arthur Charles Hope; *b* 22 May 1969; *s* and *heir* of Earl of Hopetoun, *qv*.

AITKEN, family name of **Beaverbrook Barony.**

AITKEN, Sir Arthur Percival Hay, (Sir Peter Aitken), Kt 1968; *b* 2 Oct. 1905; *e s* of late Canon R. A. Aitken, Great Yarmouth; *m* 1937, Ursula Wales, *d* of Herbert Wales, MB; one *s* one *d*. *Educ:* Norwich Gram. Sch.; Trinity Coll., Oxford. Formerly: Man. Dir Textile Machinery Makers Ltd, 1949, Chm. 1960; Dep. Chm., Stone-Platt Industries Ltd; Director: Norwich General Trust (Chm.); Norwich Union Insurance Group; Norwich Union Life Insurance Soc.; Norwich Union Fire Insurance Soc.; Scottish Union and National Insurance Co.; Maritime Insurance Co. Chm., BNEC's Australia Cttee, 1966-69; Bd Mem., Commonwealth Develt Corp., 1960-69. *Recreations:* golf, fishing. *Address:* Roefield, Alde Lane, Aldeburgh, Suffolk IP15 5DZ. *T:* Aldeburgh 3450. *Clubs:* Royal Thames Yacht; Aldeburgh Golf, Aldeburgh Yacht.

AITKEN, Ian Hugh, CBE 1964; Deputy Secretary, Institution of Civil Engineers, since 1974; *b* 4 Dec. 1919: *y s* of late James Maven Aitken and Annie Stevenson Aitken (*née* Lowe); *m* 1944, Sheila Agnes Hamilton, *d* of late F. A. Green, Arusha, Tanzania; one *s* one *d*. *Educ:* Greenock High Sch. Served War in 51st (Highland) Div. and 11th (E African) Div., in France, Belgium, Western Desert and E Africa, 1939-44. HMOCS, Kenya, 1944; Dep. Principal Immigration Officer, 1952; Principal Immigration Officer, 1960; retired after acting as Adviser on Immigration and related matters to independent Kenya Govt, 1964. Gen. Management, British Uralite Gp, 1964-70; Admin. Sec., Royal Soc. of Medicine, 1971-74. *Recreations:* most games, music. *Address:* 22 Pitfield Drive, Meopham, Kent. *T:* Meopham 812350. *Clubs:* Royal Commonwealth Society, MCC; Nairobi (Kenya).

AITKEN, Janet Kerr, CBE 1950; MD London; FRCP; retired; late Consulting Physician: Elizabeth Garrett Anderson Hospital; Princess Louise Kensington Hospital for Children; Mothers' (Salvation Army) Hospital; *b* Buenos Aires, 1886,

Scottish parents. *Educ:* St Leonard's School, St Andrews; London School of Medicine for Women (Royal Free Hospital). LRCP, MRCS and MB, BS, London 1922; MD London 1924; MRCP 1926; FRCP 1943; Vice-Dean London Royal Free Hospital School of Medicine for Women, 1930-34; President, Medical Women's Federation, 1942-44; late Pres., Med. Women's Internat. Assoc.; late Councillor Royal College of Physicians; late Council Mem. BMA; late Member: Central Health Services Council; General Medical Council. *Publications:* papers in medical journals. *Recreation:* music; LRAM (piano), Gold Medallist (singing). *Address:* 70 Viceroy Court, Prince Albert Road, Regent's Park, NW8. *T:* 01-722 3833.

AITKEN, Prof. John Thomas; Professor of Anatomy, University College, London, since 1965; *b* 16 May 1913; *s* of David and Helen Aitken; *m* 1941, Doreen Violet Whitaker; two *s* two *d*. *Educ:* High School, Glasgow; Grammar School, Hull; Glasgow University. MB, ChB 1936, MD 1950. University College, London, 1940-. *Publications:* Manual of Human Anatomy (in collab.); Essential Anatomy (in collab.); papers on regeneration of nerves and muscles, in various jls. *Recreation:* gardening. *Address:* c/o Department of Anatomy, University College, Gower Street, WC1E 6BT.

AITKEN, Sir (John William) Max, 2nd Bt, *cr* 1916; DSO 1942; DFC 1940; President, Beaverbrook Newspapers Ltd, since 1977 (Chairman until 1977); Director: Price Company Limited; Associated Television Ltd; *b* Montreal, 15 February 1910; *e s* of 1st Baron Beaverbrook (Bt 1916), PC, ED, CD; *S* father, 1964; disclaimed the barony, 11 June 1964; *m* 1st, 1939, Cynthia Monteith (who obtained a divorce, 1944); 2nd, 1946, Mrs Jane Lindsay (who obtained a divorce, 1950); two *d*; 3rd, 1951, Violet, *d* of Sir Humphrey de Trafford, 4th Bt, MC; one *s* one *d*. *Educ:* Westminster; Pembroke Coll., Cambridge. Joined RAuxAF, 1935. Served War of 1939-45, RAF (despatches, DSO, DFC, Czech War Cross); day fighter pilot during Battle of Britain; comd night fighter squadron, 1941-42; Group Capt. comdg Strike Mosquito Wing, Norwegian waters, 1943. MP (C) Holborn, 1945-50. President, Newspaper Press Fund, 1965-. Chancellor, Univ. of New Brunswick, Fredericton, NB, 1966-. Hon. LLD, New Brunswick, 1966. *Recreations:* Cambridge Assoc. Football Blue, 1930, 1931; golf, sailing. *Heir:* s Hon. (as heir to disclaimed barony) Maxwell William Humphrey Aitken [*b* 29 Dec. 1951; *m* 1974, Susan Angela More O'Ferrall; one *s*]. *Address:* The Garden House, Cherkley, Leatherhead, Surrey. *T:* Leatherhead 73162. *Clubs:* White's, Buck's, Royal Yacht Squadron.

AITKEN, Jonathan William Patrick; MP (C) Thanet East since Feb. 1974; *b* 30 Aug. 1942; *s* of late Sir William Aitken, KBE and of Hon. Lady Aitken, MBE, JP. *Educ:* Eton Coll.; Christ Church, Oxford. MA Hons Law. Private Sec. to Selwyn Lloyd, 1964-66; Foreign Corresp., London Evening Standard, 1966-71; Man. Dir, Slater Walker (Middle East) Ltd, 1973-75; Chm., R. H. Sanbar Consultants Ltd, 1976-. *Publications:* A Short Walk on the Campus, 1966; The Young Meteors, 1967; Land of Fortune: A Study of Australia, 1969; Officially Secret, 1970; articles in Spectator, Sunday Telegraph, Amer. Heritage, Sydney Morning Herald, etc. *Recreations:* squash, ski-ing, travel. *Address:* 47 Phillimore Gardens, W8. *T:* 01-937 0438. *Clubs:* Turf, Pratt's.

AITKEN, Sir Max; *see* Aitken, Sir J. W. M.

AITKEN, Sir Peter; *see* Aitken, Sir A. P. H.

AITKEN, Air Vice-Marshal (Robert) Stanley, CB 1945; CBE 1942 (OBE 1938); MC 1917; AFC 1918; retired; *b* 4 April 1896; *s* of late Robert Aitken, Newcastle, and late Emma Louise Townsend, Manchester; *m* 1st, 1925, Jeanie Allison (*d* 1963), *o d* of late Rev. David Tweedie, Stitchill, Roxburghshire; one *s* (and one *s* decd); 2nd, 1964, Laura Barler (*d* 1976), *widow* of Arthur Sewall. *Educ:* Highgate; Wiesbaden. Enlisted 15th London Regt, 1914; commnd 1/1st (Essex) RGA, 1915; seconded RFC, July 1916; served France with 41, 52 and 7 Sqdns; Flying Instructor, 1918-21; Comd 41(F) and 25(F) Sqdns, 1928-30; British Air Attaché, China, 1938-40; Air Staff signals duties, Air Ministry, and CSO, varying periods, Air Defence of GB and Fighter Comd, 1940-42; AOC 60 (Radar) Group, 1942-43; ASO in C, HQ, MAAF, 1944-45; retired 1946. Legion of Merit (USA). *Address:* Stone House Farm, Bath, Maine 04530, USA.

AITKEN, Sir Robert (Stevenson), Kt 1960; MD (New Zealand), DPhil (Oxford); FRCP, FRACP; DL; retired; *b* NZ; *s* of late Rev. James Aitken; *m* 1929, Margaret G. Kane; one *s* two *d*. *Educ:* Gisborne High School, Gisborne, NZ; University of Otago, Dunedin, NZ; Oxford. Medical Qualification in New

Zealand, 1922; Rhodes Scholar, Balliol College, Oxford, 1924-26; attached to Medical Unit, The London Hospital, 1926-34; Reader in Medicine, British Post-Graduate Medical School, Univ. of London, 1935-38; Regius Prof. of Medicine, Univ. of Aberdeen, 1939-48; Vice-Chancellor, Univ. of Otago, Dunedin, NZ, 1948-53; Vice-Chancellor, Univ. of Birmingham, 1953-68. Vice-Chm. Association of Univs of the British Commonwealth, 1955-58; Dep. Chm., UGC, 1968-73; Chairman: Committee of Vice-Chancellors and Principals, 1958-61; Birmingham Repertory Theatre, 1962-74. DL Co. Warwick, 1967, West Midlands, 1974. Hon. FRCPE; Hon. FDSRCS; Hon. DCL Oxford; Hon. LLD: Dalhousie, Melbourne, Panjab, McGill, Pennsylvania, Aberdeen, Newfoundland, Leicester, Birmingham, Otago; Hon. DSc: Sydney, Liverpool. *Publications:* papers in medical and scientific journals. *Address:* 6 Hintlesham Avenue, Birmingham B15 2PH. *Club:* Athenæum.

AITKEN, Air Vice-Marshal Stanley; *see* Aitken, R. S.

AITKEN, Rt. Rev. William Aubrey; *see* Lynn, Bishop Suffragan of.

AIYAR, Mrs Robert Duray; *see* Carlyle, Joan Hildred.

AJAYI, Prof. Jacob Festus Ade; Vice-Chancellor, University of Lagos, since 1972; *b* 26 May 1929; *s* of Chief E. Ade Ajayi and late Mrs C. Bolajoko Ajayi; *m* 1956, Christie Aduke Martins; one *s* four *d*. *Educ:* University College, Ibadan; University College, Leicester; Univ. of London; BA, PhD (London). Research Fellow, Inst. of Historical Research, London, 1957-58; Lectr, Univ. of Ibadan, 1958-62, Sen. Lectr, 1962-63; Prof. of History, 1963-72; Dean, Faculty of Arts, 1964-66; Asst to Vice-Chancellor, 1966-68. Fellow, Centre for Advanced Study in the Behavioural Sciences, Stanford, Calif, 1970-71. Chm., UN University Council, 1976-77; Member: Nat. Archives Cttee, Nigeria, 1961-72; Nat. Antiquities Commn, Nigeria, 1970-74; Exec. Council, Internat. African Inst. London, 1971- (Chm., 1975-); Exec. Bd, Assoc. of African Univs, 1974-; Pres., Historical Soc. of Nigeria, 1972-. Hon. LLD Leicester, 1975. *Publications:* Milestones in Nigerian History, 1962; (ed, with Ian Espie) A Thousand Years of West African History, 1964; (with R. S. Smith) Yoruba Warfare in the Nineteenth Century, 1964; Christian Missions in Nigeria: the making of a new elite, 1965; (ed, with Michael Crowder) A History of West Africa, vol. I, 1972; vol. II, 1974; contribs to Jl Historical Soc. of Nigeria, Jl of African History, etc. *Recreations:* dancing, tennis. *Address:* University of Lagos, Lagos, Nigeria. *T:* 42361 (office); 45092 (residence).

AKEHURST, Brig. John Bryan, CBE 1976; Deputy Military Secretary (A), Ministry of Defence (Army), since 1976; *b* 12 Feb. 1930; *s* of late Geoffrey and of Doris Akehurst; *m* 1955, Shirley Ann, *er d* of late Major W. G. Webb, MBE, and of Ethel Webb; one *s* one *d* decd. *Educ:* Cranbrook Sch.; RMA, Sandhurst. Commnd Northamptonshire Regt, 1949; Malay Regt (despatches), 1952-55; Adjt, 5th Northamptonshire Regt (TA), 1959-60; Staff Coll., Camberley, 1961; Brigade Major, 12 Infantry Bde Gp, 1962-64; Instructor, Staff Coll., Camberley, 1966-68; commanded 2nd Royal Anglian Regt, 1968-70; Directing Staff, IDC/RCDS, 1970-72; Comdt, Jun. Div., Staff Coll., 1972-74; Comdr, Dhofar Bde, Sultan of Oman's Armed Forces, 1974-76. Order of Oman, 3rd Class (mil.), 1976. *Recreations:* golf, trout fishing. *Address:* c/o Midland Bank Ltd, Minehead, Somerset. *Clubs:* Army and Navy; Stanmore Golf.

AKENHEAD, David, OBE 1950; MA Oxon, BSc London; *b* 23 Feb. 1894; *s* of Edmund Akenhead, sometime Prebendary of Lincoln Cathedral, and Lucy Collingwood Akenhead; *m* 1933, Beatrice Carter. *Educ:* Rugby; New College, Oxford; South Eastern Agricultural College, Wye. Served European War, 1914-18. On staff: Royal Agricultural Coll., 1922-24; Internat. Inst. of Agriculture, Rome, 1926-28; helped to start what is now known as the Commonwealth Bureau of Horticulture and Plantation Crops, East Malling, Kent, in 1929, and was Director thereof, 1945-59. *Address:* Three Roods, Offham, Maidstone, Kent ME19 5NA. *T:* West Malling 842171. *Club:* United Oxford & Cambridge University.

AKERS-DOUGLAS, family name of Viscount Chilston.

AKERS-JONES, David; Hong Kong Government Secretary for the New Territories, since 1973; *b* 14 April 1927; *s* of Walter George and Dorothy Jones; *m* 1951, Jane Spickernell; one *s* one *d*. *Educ:* Worthing High Sch.; Brasenose Coll., Oxford (MA). British India Steam Navigation Co., 1945-49. Malayan Civil Service (studied Hokkien and Malay), 1954—57; Hong Kong Civil Service, 1957-. Vice-Pres. Hong Kong Football Assoc.,

1967-; Vice-Chm. Outward Bound, Hong Kong, 1970-. *Recreations:* painting, gardening, walking, music. *Address:* Island House, Taipo, New Territories, Hong Kong. *Club:* Hong Kong (Hong Kong).

ALAM, Hon. Anthony Alexander; Member of Legislative Council, 1925-59, and since 1963; Member of the Upper House, NSW, since 1925; Director: Alam Homes Pty Ltd; Alam Stores Pty Ltd; Mala Homes Pty Ltd; Latec Ltd; *b* Wallsend, NSW, 23 Jan. 1898; parents born Republic Lebanon; *m*; no *c*. *Educ:* De La Salle College, Armidale, NSW. King George V Silver Jubilee Medal; Merit of Lebanon; Commander Nichan Iftikar; King George VI Coronation Medal; Commander Toile Noir; Chevalier, Legion of Honour; Commander Order Cedars (Liban); Queen Elizabeth Coronation Medal; Grand Cross; Order of Torsani; Order of St Mark; Grand Officer, Order of Phoenix, Greece. *Recreations:* bowls, billiards, tennis, motoring, horse-racing. *Address:* Parliament House, Sydney, Australia; 69 Bradleys Head Road, Mosman, NSW 2088, Australia. *TA:* Alam Parliament, Sydney. *Club:* Commercial Travellers' (Sydney).

ALANBROOKE, 3rd Viscount *cr* 1946; **Alan Victor Harold Brooke;** Baron Alanbrooke, 1945; *b* 24 Nov. 1932; *s* of 1st Viscount Alanbrooke, KG, GCB, OM, GCVO, DSO, and Benita Blanche (*d* 1968), *d* of Sir Harold Pelly, 4th Bt; *S* half-brother, 1972. *Educ:* Harrow. Captain RA, retired. *Heir:* none.

ALBEE, Edward; American dramatist; *b* 12 March 1928. *Publications:* plays: The Zoo Story, 1959; The Death of Bessie Smith, 1960; The Sandbox, 1961; The American Dream, 1961; Who's Afraid of Virginia Woolf?, 1962; (adapted from Carson McCullers' novella) The Ballad of the Sad Café, 1963; Tiny Alice, 1964; (adapted from the novel by James Purdy) Malcolm, 1965; A Delicate Balance, 1966 (Pulitzer Prize, 1967); (adapted from the play by Giles Cooper) Everything in the Garden, 1967; Box and Quotations from Chairman Mao Tse-Tung, 1968; All Over, 1972; Seascape, 1975 (Pulitzer Prize, 1975); Listening, 1975; Counting the Ways, 1976. *Address:* 226 Lafayette Street, New York, NY 10012, USA.

ALBEMARLE, 9th Earl of, *cr* 1696; **Walter Egerton George Lucian Keppel;** MC; Baron Ashford, 1696; Viscount Bury, 1696; *b* 28 Feb. 1882; *e s* of 8th Earl and Lady Gertrude Lucia Egerton (*d* 1943), *o c* of 1st Earl Egerton of Tatton; *S* father, 1942; *m* 1st, 1909, Lady Judith Sydney Myee Carrington (*d* 1928), 4th *d* of 1st Marquis of Lincolnshire; one *s* two *d* (and two *s* decd); 2nd, 1931, Diana Cicely (*see* Countess of Albemarle), *o c* of late John Archibald Grove; one *d*. *Educ:* Eton. Late Lieut PWO Norfolk Artillery; ADC to Gov.-Gen. of Canada, 1904-05; to Viceroy of India, 1906-07; to Governor of Orange River Colony, 1907-08; Major Special Reserve Scots Guards, 1918; late commanding PWO Civil Service Rifles; commanded Norfolk Yeo. 108th Brigade RFA until 1926; contested (U) Altrincham Division, Cheshire, 1910; Vice-Lieut County of Norfolk, 1940-44; elected LCC for Central Wandsworth, 1919; elected Norfolk CC and to Church Assembly, 1943; Alderman Norfolk CC, 1957. Formerly: President: St John Amb. Bde, Norfolk (KStJ 1963); Anglo-Netherlands Soc. (1942-65); Norwich Philharmonic Soc.; Tatton Park Gardens Soc.; Vice-Pres. Assoc. of River Authorities. Grand Cross, Order of Orange Nassau. *Heir: g s* Viscount Bury, *qv*. *Address:* Beacon Hill, Woodbridge, Suffolk. *See also Sir Hew Hamilton-Dalrymple, Bt, David McKenna, Prof. M. Postan.*

ALBEMARLE, Countess of, (Diana Cicely), DBE 1956; Chairman: Development Commission, 1948-74; The Drama Board, since 1964; *b* 6 Aug. 1909; *o c* of John Archibald Grove; *m* 1931, 9th Earl of Albemarle, *qv*; one *d*. *Educ:* Sherborne Sch. for Girls. Norfolk County Organiser, WVS, 1939-44. Chairman: Exec. Cttee, Nat. Fedn of Women's Institutes, 1946-51; Departmental Cttee on Youth Service, 1958-60; Nat. Youth Employment Council, 1962-68. Vice-Chm., British Council, 1959-74. Member: Arts Council, 1951; Royal Commn on Civil Service, 1954; Harkness Fellowship Cttee of Award, 1963-69; UGC, 1956-70; Standing Commn on Museums and Galleries, 1958-71; English Local Govt Boundary Commn, 1971-77; Youth Develt Council, 1960-68; Council, Univ. of E Anglia, 1964-72. Life Trustee, Carnegie UK Trust (Chm., 1977-); Trustee of: The Observer until 1977; Glyndebourne Arts Trust, 1968-. RD Councillor, Wayland, Norfolk, 1935-46. Hon. DLitt Reading, 1959; Hon. DCL Oxon, 1960; Hon. LLD London, 1960. *Recreations:* gardening, reading. *Address:* Beacon Hill, Martlesham, Woodbridge, Suffolk. *T:* Woodbridge 264.

ALBERT, Sir Alexis (François), Kt 1972; CMG 1967; VRD 1942; Chairman and Governing Director, J. Albert & Son Pty Ltd, Sydney, since 1962; Chairman, The Australian

Broadcasting Company Pty Ltd, Sydney; *b* 15 Oct. 1904; *s* of late M. F. and M. E. Albert, Sydney; *m* 1934, Elsa K. R. (decd), *d* of late Capt. A. E. Lundgren, Sydney; three *s*. *Educ:* Knox College, Sydney; St Paul's College, University of Sydney. BEc 1930. Director: Amalgamated Television Services Pty Ltd, 1955-; Australasian Performing Right Association Ltd, 1946-76. Underwriting Member of Lloyd's, 1944-74; President, Royal Blind Soc. of NSW, 1962-; Fellow of Council, St Paul's Coll., Univ. of Sydney, 1965-; Council, Nat. Heart Foundn of Aust., NSW Div. 1959-. RANR, 1918-49; Lt-Comdr, retd. Hon. ADC to Governors of NSW, 1937-57. OStJ 1976. *Recreations:* swimming, yachting. *Address:* 25 Coolong Road, Vaucluse, NSW 2030, Australia; (office) 139 King Street, Sydney, NSW 2000. *T:* 232 2144. *Clubs:* Naval and Military; Australian, Union (Sydney); Royal Sydney Golf, Royal Sydney Yacht Squadron (Commodore 1971-75); New York Yacht.

ALBERT, Carl (Bert); Speaker, US House of Representatives, 1970-76; Member, Third Oklahoma District, 1947-76 (Democratic Whip, 1955-62; Majority Leader, 1962-71); *b* 10 May 1908, McAlester, Oklahoma; *s* of Ernest Homer and Leona Ann (Scott) Albert; *m* 1942, Mary Sue Greene Harmon; one *s* one *d*. *Educ:* Univ. of Oklahoma (AB 1931); Oxford Univ. (Rhodes Scholar, BA 1933, BCL 1934). Served US Army, 1941-46. Admitted Oklahoma Bar, 1935; Legal Clerk, Fed. Housing Admin, 1935-37; attorney and accountant, Sayre Oil Co., 1937-38; legal dept, Ohio Oil Co., 1939-40. Practised law: Oklahoma City, 1938; Mattoon, Ill, 1938-39; McAlester, Oklahoma, 1946-47. Bronze Star, 1945. *Recreation:* reading. *Address:* 827E Osage, McAlester, Oklahoma 74501, USA.

ALBERY, Sir Donald (Arthur Rolleston), Kt 1977; Chairman and Managing Director: Wyndham Theatres Ltd; Donmar Productions Ltd and associated companies; Piccadilly Theatre Ltd; Director, Anglia Television Ltd; Chairman, Theatres' National Committee; *b* London, 19 June 1914; *s* of late Sir Bronson Albery. *Educ:* Alpine Coll., Switzerland. Gen. Man., Sadler's Wells Ballet, 1941-45; Dir and Administrator, London's Festival Ballet, 1965-68. Has presented or jtly presented plays: The Living Room, 1953; Birthday Honours, 1953; I Am a Camera, The Living Room (NY, with Gilbert Miller), 1954; The Remarkable Mr Pennypacker, Lucky Strike, Waiting for Godot, 1955; The Waltz of the Toreadors, Gigi, Grab Me a Gondola, 1956; Zuleika, Tea and Sympathy, Dinner With the Family, Paddle Your Own Canoe, 1957; The Potting Shed, George Dillon, Irma La Douce (NY, 1960), 1958; The Rose Tattoo, A Taste of Honey (NY, 1960), The Hostage (NY, 1960), The Complaisant Lover, One to Another, The Ring of Truth, The World of Suzie Wong, Make Me an Offer, 1959; Fings Ain't Wot They Used T' Be, A Passage to India, Call It Love, The Art of Living, Oliver! (NY, 1963; tour, 1965), The Tinker, 1960; The Miracle Worker, Breakfast for One, Sparrers Can't Sing, Beyond the Fringe (NY, 1962), Celebration, Bonne Soupe, 1961; Not to Worry, Blitz!, Semi-Detached, Fiorello!, 1962; Licence to Murder, The Perils of Scobie Prilt (tour), A Severed Head (NY, 1964), The Time of the Barracudas (US), 1963; The Fourth of June, The Poker Session, Who's Afraid of Virginia Woolf?, A Little Winter Love (tour), Entertaining Mr Sloane (NY, 1965), Instant Marriage, Carving a Statue, The Diplomatic Baggage, Portrait of a Queen, Jorrocks, The Prime of Miss Jean Brodie, 1966; Mrs Wilson's Diary, Spring and Port Wine, The Restoration of Arnold Middleton, 1967; The Italian Girl, Man of La Mancha, 1968; Conduct Unbecoming (NY, 1970; Australia, 1971), 1969; It's a Two Foot Six Inches Above the Ground World, Mandrake, Poor Horace, 1970; Popkiss, 1972; Very Good Eddie, The Thoughts of Chairman Alf, 1976. *Address:* Albery Theatre, St Martin's Lane, WC2. *T:* 01-240 1691, 01-836 7584. *Club:* Garrick.

ALBRECHT, Ralph Gerhart; American lawyer, barrister and international legal consultant; *b* Jersey City, NJ, 11 Aug. 1896; *s* of J. Robert Albrecht and Gertrude A. F. Richter; *m* 1936, Aillinn, *d* of late William Elderkin Leffingwell, Watkins Glen, NY; one *s*. *Educ:* Pennsylvania Univ. (AB); Harvard Univ. (JD). Admitted to Bar of NY, 1924, US Supreme Court, 1927; senior partner, Peaslee, Albrecht & McMahon, 1931-61, counsel to firm, 1961-; gen. practice, specializing in foreign causes and internat. law. Special Dep. Attorney-Gen. of New York, 1926; Special Asst to US Attorney-Gen., 1945; Mem. US War Crimes Commn and leading trial counsel in Prosecution of Major Nazi War Criminals, before Internat. Mil. Tribunal, Nuremberg, 1945-46, prosecuted Hermann Goering; counsel to German steel, coal and chem. industries in decartelization procs before Allied High Commn for Germany, 1950-53. Mem. Republican County Cttee, NY Co., 1933-35; Harvard Univ. Overseers' Visiting Cttee to Faculty of Germanic Langs and Lits, 1949-63. Apprentice Seaman, USN Res. Force, 1918; served with Sqdn A (101st Cavalry, NY Nat. Guard), 1924-30; Comdr USNR, on active duty, 1941-45; Naval Observer, American Embassy, London, 1942 (letter of commendation from Chief of Naval Ops); Asst Dir OSS (War Crimes), 1945. Member: NY City Bar Assoc.; Amer. Bar Assoc.; Amer. Soc. of Internat. Law (Chm. Manley O. Hudson Medal Cttee); Internat. Bar Assoc.; International Law Assoc.; World Peace Through Law Center (Cttee on Conciliation and Mediation of Disputes); NY, Nat. and Internat., Legal Aid Assocs, etc. Fellow: Nat. Audubon Society; Massachusetts Audubon Soc.; Amer. Geog. Soc., etc. Delegate, First Internat. Congress Comparative Law, The Hague, 1932. Republican; Mason. *Publications:* (with Prof. Walter B. Pitkin) Studies for Vocational Guidance of Recent School and College Graduates; contrib. Peter Markham's (pseud.) America Next, 1940. *Address:* 520 East 86th Street, New York, NY 10028, USA. *Clubs:* University, Harvard, Pilgrims of the US, Squadron A (all in NY).

ALBROW, Desmond; Assistant Editor, Sunday Telegraph, since 1976; *b* 22 Jan. 1925; *er s* of Frederick and Agnes Albrow; *m* 1950, Aileen Mary Jennings; one *s* three *d*. *Educ:* St Bede's Grammar Sch., Bradford; Keble Coll., Oxford (MA). On the Editorial Staff of the Yorkshire Observer, 1950-51, Manchester Guardian, 1951-56, Daily Telegraph, 1956-60; Sunday Telegraph, 1960-66: Chief Sub-Editor, News Editor, and Night Editor; Editor, Catholic Herald, 1966-71; Features Editor, Sunday Telegraph, 1971-76. *Recreations:* drinking in moderation and talking to excess; watching other people cultivate their gardens. *Address:* 54 Elmfield Avenue, Teddington, Mddx. *T:* 01-979 4220.

ALBU, Mrs Austen H.; *see* Jahoda, Marie.

ALBU, Austen Harry, BSc (Eng.); FCGI, CEng; Visiting Research Fellow, University of Sussex, since 1975; *b* London, 21 Sept. 1903; *s* of Ferdinand and Beatrice Rachel Albu; *m* 1st, 1929, Rose (*d* 1956), *d* of Simon Marks, Newcastle; two *s*; 2nd, 1958, Dr Marie Jahoda, *qv*. *Educ:* Tonbridge School; City and Guilds College (Imperial College of Science and Technology). Works Manager, Aladdin Industries, Greenford, 1930-46. Dep. Pres., Govtl Sub-Commn, CCG, 1946-47. Dep. Dir, British Institute of Management, Feb.-Nov. 1948. MP (Lab) Edmonton, 1948-Feb. 1974; Minister of State, Dept of Economic Affairs, 1965-67. Fellow, Imp. Coll. of Science and Technology. DUniv Surrey, 1966. *Address:* 17 The Crescent, Keymer, Sussex BN6 8RB.

ALBU, Sir George, 3rd Bt, *cr* (UK) 1912, of Grosvenor Place, City of Westminster, and Johannesburg, Province of Transvaal, South Africa; *b* 5 June 1944; *o s* of Major Sir George Werner Albu, 2nd Bt, and Kathleen Betty (*d* 1956), *d* of Edward Charles Dicey, Parktown, Johannesburg; *S* father, 1963; *m* 1969, Joan Valerie Millar, London; two *d*. *Heir:* none. *Address:* Glen Hamish Farm, Richmond, Natal, South Africa.

ALCOCK, Prof. Leslie; Professor of Archaeology, University of Glasgow, since 1973; *b* 24 April 1925; *o s* of Philip John Alcock and Mary Ethel (*née* Bagley); *m* 1950, Elizabeth A. Blair; one *s* one *d*. *Educ:* Manchester Grammar Sch.; Brasenose Coll., Oxford. BA 1949, MA 1950. Supt of Exploration, Dept of Archaeology, Govt of Pakistan, 1950; Curator, Abbey House Museum, Leeds, 1952; Asst Lectr, etc, UC Cardiff, 1953, Prof. of Archaeology, UC Cardiff, 1973. Member: Ancient Monuments Bd, Scotland, 1974-; Royal Commn on Ancient and Historical Monuments of Scotland, 1977-. Vice-Pres., Council for British Archaeology, 1974-. FSA 1957; FRHistS 1969; FRSE 1976; Hon. Fellow, Univ. of Mississippi, 1969; Mem., Medieval Academy of America, 1973. *Publications:* Dinas Powys, 1963; Arthur's Britain, 1971; Cadbury/Camelot, 1972; articles and reviews in British and Amer. jls. *Recreations:* mountaineering; baroque and jazz music. *Address:* 29 Hamilton Drive, Hillhead, Glasgow G12 8DN.

ALDAM, Jeffery Heaton, MC 1945; County Education Officer, Hampshire, since 1973; *b* 11 Nov. 1922; *s* of William and Clara Ellen Aldam; *m* 1950, Editha Hilary Mary (*née* Preece); two *s* two *d*. *Educ:* Chesterfield Grammar Sch.; Trinity Coll., Cambridge (MA); Harvard Univ. (AM). Served 13th/18th Royal Hussars (QMO), 1942-45. Admin. Asst, Asst Educn Officer, then Sen. Asst Educn Officer, Norfolk CC, 1949-56; Dep. County Educn Officer, NR Yorks CC, 1957-62; Chief Educn Officer, East Suffolk CC, 1962-71; County Educn Officer, (former) Hampshire CC, 1972-73. *Recreations:* reading, walking, gardening. *Address:* Derrymore, 71 Andover Road, Winchester, Hampshire SO22 6AU. *T:* Winchester 3594.

ALDENHAM, 5th Baron *cr* 1896, and **HUNSDON OF HUNSDON,** 3rd Baron *cr* 1923; **Antony Durant Gibbs;** Director, Antony Gibbs & Sons, Ltd, since 1954; *b* 18 May 1922;

s of 4th Baron and of Beatrix Elinor, *d* of Herbert Paul; *S* father, 1969; *m* 1947, Mary Elizabeth, *o d* of late Walter Parkyns Tyser; two *s* one *d* (and one *s* decd). *Educ:* Eton; Christ Church, Oxford. RNVR, 1940-46. Antony Gibbs & Sons, Ltd, 1947 (Chile, 1948-51). Master, Merchant Taylors' Co., 1977. *Recreations:* shooting, fishing, sailing. *Heir: s* Hon. Vicary Tyser Gibbs, *b* 9 June 1948. *Address:* Stanstead Lodge, Stanstead Abbots, Herts. *T:* Roydon 3101. *Clubs:* Pratt's, City University; Cannonsbrook Golf; Brickendon Grange Golf.
   See also Sir C. H. Villiers.

ALDER, Mrs Alan; *see* Aldous, Lucette.

ALDERSON, Sir Harold George, Kt 1956; MBE 1938; Patron of the Olympic Federation of Australia (formerly Chairman for 45 years); Hon. Secretary Anniversary Day Regatta since 1920; Life Member, New South Wales Olympic Council (President, 1926-73); *b* Balmain, NSW, 18 Aug. 1891; *s* of J. B. Alderson, Sydney; *m* 1st, 1915, Rose Stella (*d* 1965), *d* of W. F. Wills; one *d*; 2nd, 1966, Hilda N. Buddee, Mosman, NSW. *Educ:* Mosman Sup. Public School, NSW. Hon. Manager Australian Olympic Team, Berlin, 1936; Member Organising Council, British Empire Games, Sydney, 1938; President Australian Rowing Club, 1928, 1934, 1939-52, 1958, 1964; Chm., NSW Rowing Assoc., 1921-68, Hon. Sec., 1918-20, now Patron; Member Executive Organising Committee Olympic Games, Melbourne, 1956. Member Council National Fitness, NSW; Chm., Rothman Sports Foundn, 1966-; Hon. Treasurer St John Ambulance Assoc. (for 36 years). *Address:* 8/12 Muston Street, Mosman, NSW 2088, Australia. *Clubs:* NSW Sports (President for 45 years, now Patron), Mosman Rowing (50 years, now Patron), Union of Old Oarsmen.

ALDERSON, John Cottingham, QPM 1974; Chief Constable of Devon and Cornwall, since 1973; *b* 28 May 1922; *e s* of late Ernest Cottingham Alderson and Elsie Lavinia Rose; *m* 1948, Irené Macmillan Stirling; one *s*. *Educ:* Barnsley Elem. Schs and Techn. College. Called to Bar, Middle Temple. British Meml Foundn Fellow, Australia, 1956; Extension Certif. in Criminology, Univ. of Leeds. MBIM. Highland LI, 1938-41 (Corp.); Army Phys. Trng Corps, N Africa and Italy, 1941-46 (Warrant Officer). West Riding Constabulary as Constable, 1946; Police Coll., 1954; Inspector, 1955; Sub-Divisional Comd, 1960; Sen. Comd Course, Police Coll., 1963-64; Dep. Chief Constable, Dorset, 1964-66; Metropolitan Police, Dep. Comdr (Admin and Ops), 1966; 2nd-in-comd No 3 Police District, 1967; Dep. Asst Comr (Trng), 1968; Comdt, Police Coll., 1970; Asst Comr (Personnel and Trng), 1973. Member: BBC Gen. Adv. Council, 1971; Royal Humane Soc. Cttee, 1973; Pres., Royal Life-Saving Soc., 1974. *Publications:* (contrib.) Encyclopedia of Crime and Criminals, 1960; (ed jtly) The Police We Deserve, 1973; articles in professional jls and newspapers. *Recreation:* formerly British Police Rugby International. *Address:* Devon and Cornwall Constabulary, Middlemoor, Exeter, Devon EX2 7HQ.

ALDERTON, John; actor (stage, films, television); *b* Gainsborough, Lincs, 27 Nov. 1940; *s* of Gordon John Alderton and Ivy Handley; *m* 1st, Jill Browne (marr. diss.); 2nd, Pauline Collins, *qv*; two *s* one *d*. *Educ:* Kingston High Sch., Hull. *Stage:* 1st appearance (Rep.) Theatre Royal, York, in Badger's Green, 1961; cont. Rep.; 1st London appearance, Spring and Port Wine, Mermaid (later Apollo), 1965. Royal Shakespeare Company: Dutch Uncle, Aldwych, 1969; The Night I chased the Women with an Eel, Comedy, 1969; Punch and Judy Stories, Howff, 1973; Judies, Comedy, 1974; The Birthday Party, Shaw, 1975; Confusions (4 parts), Apollo, 1976; *films:* (1962-): incl. Duffy, Hannibal Brooks; *television:* series: Please Sir, No Honestly, My Wife Next Door, P. G. Wodehouse, The Upchat Line, and various plays. *Address:* c/o Chartwell Artists Ltd, 22 South Audley Street, W1. *Clubs:* Green Room, Lord's Taverners.

ALDINGTON, 1st Baron, *cr* 1962; **Toby (Austin Richard William) Low,** PC 1954; KCMG 1957; CBE 1945 (MBE 1944); DSO 1941; TD and clasp, 1950; DL; Chairman: Sun Alliance and London Insurance Ltd; National Nuclear Corporation; Westland Aircraft Ltd; Deputy Chairman, GEC Ltd; Director: Citicorp; Lloyds Bank Ltd; Barrister-at-Law; *b* 25 May 1914; *s* of Col Stuart Low, DSO (killed at sea by enemy action, Dec. 1942), and of late Hon. Mrs Spear; *m* 1947, Araminta Bowman, *e d* of late Sir Harold MacMichael, GCMG, DSO; one *s* two *d*. *Educ:* Winchester; New Coll., Oxford (Hon. Fellow 1976). Called to the Bar, 1939. TA; 2nd Lieut 1934; Brig. BGS 5 Corps Italy, Aug. 1944-June 1945; served Greece, Crete, Egypt, Libya, Tunisia, Sicily, Italy, Austria (DSO, MBE, CBE, Croix de guerre avec palmes, Commander of Legion of Merit, USA); Hon. Col 288 LAA Regt RA (TA), 1947-59. MP (C) Blackpool North, 1945-62; Parliamentary Secretary, Ministry of Supply,

1951-54; Minister of State, Board of Trade, 1954-57; Dep. Chm., Cons. Party Organisation, Oct. 1959-63. Chm., Grindlays Bank Ltd, 1964-76. Chairman: Port of London Authority, 1971-77; Jt Special Cttee on Ports Industry, 1972. Chm., Cttee of Management, Inst. of Neurology. Chm., BBC Gen. Adv. Council. Fellow, Winchester Coll. DL Kent, 1973. *Recreation:* golf. *Heir: s* Hon. Charles Harold Stuart Low, *b* 22 June 1948. *Address:* 21d Cadogan Gardens, SW3. *T:* 01-730 1356; Knoll Farm, Aldington, Kent. *T:* Aldington 292. *Clubs:* Beefsteak, Carlton.

ALDINGTON, Sir Geoffrey (William), KBE 1965 (OBE 1946); CMG 1958; HM Diplomatic Service, retired; *b* 1 June 1907; *s* of late Henry William Aldington; *m* 1932, Roberta Finch; two *d*. *Educ:* City of London School; Magdalen Coll., Oxford. Student Interpreter, China Consular Service, 1929; Vice-Consul (Grade II), China, 1931; Vice-Consul, Peking, 1931-33; Private Secretary to HM Minister, Peking, 1933-35; Foreign Office, 1936-37; Acting Consul, Chungking, 1937-39; Consul, Tsingtao, 1939-41; seconded to Min. of Information, 1943-45; Actg Consul-Gen., Hankow, 1945-46; Suptg Consul, Shanghai, 1946-47; Foreign Office, 1947-50; Political Adviser to Hong Kong Govt, 1950-53; Consul-Gen. Zagreb, Yugoslavia, 1954-56; Consul-General at Philadelphia, Pa, USA, 1956-61; HM Ambassador to Luxembourg, 1961-66; also Consul-General, Luxembourg, 1962-66. *Recreations:* tennis, riding, reading. *Address:* The Copse, Pound Lane, Sonning, Berks. *T:* Reading 693202. *Clubs:* Phyllis Court (Henley); Hong Kong (Hong Kong); Racquet (Philadelphia, USA).
   See also S . J . G . Semple .

ALDINGTON, John Norman, BSc, PhD; FRIC; FInstP; CEng; FIEE; Chairman, Royal Worcester Ltd, 1974-75 (Director, 1968-75); *b* 2 March 1905; *s* of Allen Aldington, Preston, Lancashire; *m* 1930, Edna, *d* of late John James Entwisle; one *s*. *Educ:* Balshaws Grammar Sch., Leyland; Harris Inst., Preston. Joined Siemens Electric Lamps and Supplies Ltd, 1923; Head of Laboratories, 1935; Dir of Research, 1948; Dir of the firm, 1948; Dir Alfred Graham & Co. Ltd, 1950; Man. Dir of Siemens Bros & Co. Ltd, 1955; former Man. Dir and Vice-Chm., AEI Ltd; former Director: LEW Ltd; Sub. Cables Ltd; Welwyn Electric Co. Ltd; Worcester Industrial Ceramics Ltd; Worcester Royal Porcelain Co. Ltd. Fellow and Past Pres., Illuminating Engrg Soc.; Mem. Amer. Illum. Engrg Soc., 1950; Chm. of Light Sources Secretariat, Internat. Commn on Illumination, 1945-54; Mem. various BSI Cttees. Part-time Lectr Harris Inst., Preston, 1928-38; Gov., Preston Grammar Sch., 1950-55; JP Duchy of Lancaster, 1953-55. MRI 1958. Leon Gaster Meml Award, IES, 1945 and 1947; Crompton Award, IEE, 1949; Gold Medal, IES, 1970. *Publications:* The High Current Density Mercury Vapour Arc, 1944 (thesis, London Univ. Library); numerous papers, particularly on light sources and kindred devices, and on high current discharges and xenon gas arc. *Recreations:* gardening and golf. *Address:* White Oaks, 39 Forest Drive, Keston, Kent. *T:* Farnborough 52904. *Club:* Athenæum.

ALDISS, Brian Wilson; writer; critic; *b* 18 Aug. 1925; *s* of Stanley and Elizabeth May Aldiss; *m* 1965, Margaret Manson; one *s* one *d*, and one *s* one *d* by previous marr. *Educ:* Framlingham Coll.; West Buckland School. Royal Signals, 1943-47; book-selling, 1947-56; writer, 1956-; Literary Editor, Oxford Mail, 1958-69. Pres., British Science Fiction Assoc., 1960-64. Editor, SF Horizons, 1964-. Chairman, Oxford Branch Conservation Soc., 1968-69; Vice Pres., The Stapledon Soc., 1975-. Observer Book Award for Science Fiction, 1956; Ditmar Award for Best Contemporary Writer of Science Fiction, 1969. *Publications:* The Brightfount Diaries, 1955; Space, Time and Nathaniel, 1957; Non-Stop, 1958; Canopy of Time, 1959; The Male Response, 1961; Hothouse, 1962 (Hugo Award, 1961); Best Fantasy Stories, 1962; The Airs of Earth, 1963; The Dark Light Years, 1964; Introducing SF, 1964; Greybeard, 1964; Best SF Stories of Brian W. Aldiss, 1965; Earthworks, 1965; The Saliva Tree, 1966 (Nebula Award, 1965); Cities and Stones: A Traveller's Jugoslavia, 1966; An Age, 1967; Report on Probability A, 1968; Farewell, Fantastic Venus!, 1968; Intangibles Inc. and other Stories, 1969; A Brian Aldiss Omnibus, 1969; Barefoot in the Head, 1969; The Hand-Reared Boy, 1970; The Shape of Further Things, 1970; The Moment of Eclipse, 1971 (BSFA Award, 1972); A Soldier Erect, 1971; Brian Aldiss Omnibus II, 1971; Billion Year Spree: a history of science fiction, 1973; Frankenstein Unbound, 1973; The Eighty-Minute Hour, 1974; (ed) Space Opera, 1974; (ed) Space Odysseys: an Anthology of Way-Back-When Futures, 1975; (ed) Hell's Cartographers, 1975; (ed) Evil Earths, 1975; Science Fiction Art: the fantasies of SF, 1975; (ed with H. Harrison) Decade: the 1940s, 1976; (ed with H. Harrison) Decade: the 1950s, 1976; The Malacia Tapestry, 1976; (ed) Galactic Empires, vols 1 and 2, 1976; (ed with H. Harrison) The Year's

Best Science Fiction No 9, 1976; Brothers of the Head, 1977; Last Orders, 1977; (ed with H. Harrison) Decade: the 1960's, 1977. *Recreations:* travel, children. *Address:* Heath House, Southmoor, near Abingdon, Oxon OX13 5BG. *T:* Longworth 820215.

ALDOUS, Alan Harold; Director of Sixth Form Studies, Longsands School, St Neots, since 1976; *b* 14 Nov. 1923; *o s of* George Arthur and Agnes Bertha Aldous; *m* 1st, 1948, Margaret Annie Flower (*d* 1964); one *s* one *d*; 2nd, 1969, Edna May Thurlwell; two step *d. Educ:* Ilford County High Sch. for Boys; Jesus Coll., Oxford (MA). Royal Signals and Royal West African Frontier Force, 1943-46. Oxford Univ., 1942 and 1946-49; Asst Master, St Dunstan's Coll., Catford, 1949-54; Asst Master, Merchant Taylors' Sch., Crosby, 1954-59; Headmaster: King's Sch., Pontefract, 1959-70; Leeds Grammar Sch., 1970-75. *Recreations:* music, walking. *Address:* Casterbridge, Madeley Court, Hemingford Grey, Huntingdon, Cambs PE18 9DF. *T:* St Ives 66153.

ALDOUS, Guy Travers, QC 1956; *b* 30 Aug 1906; *s* of H. G. Aldous, Gedding Hall, Suffolk; *m* 1932, Elizabeth Angela Paul; four *s* one *d. Educ:* Harrow; Trinity College, Cambridge. Retired Bar, 1967. Director, Showerings Ltd, 1968-. MFH Suffolk, 1958-60, Essex and Suffolk, 1967-76. *Recreation:* hunting. *Address:* 5 King's Bench Walk, Temple, EC4; Freston House, Suffolk. *T:* Woolverstone 243.
See also W. Aldous.

ALDOUS, Lucette; Prima Ballerina, The Australian Ballet, since 1971; *b* 26 Sept. 1938; *d* of Charles Fellows Aldous and Marie (*née* Rutherford); *m* 1972, Alan Alder. *Educ:* Toronto Public Sch., NSW; Brisbane Public Sch., Qld; Randwick Girls' High Sch., NSW. Awarded Frances Scully Meml Schol. (Aust.) to study at Royal Ballet Sch., London, 1955; joined Ballet Rambert, 1957, Ballerina, 1958-63; Ballerina with: London Fest. Ballet, 1963-66; Royal Ballet, 1966-71. Guest appearances: Giselle, with John Gilpin, NY, 1968; Lisbon, 1969; with Rudolf Nureyev, in Don Quixote: Aust., 1970, NY, Hamburg and Marseilles, 1971; Carmen, Johannesburg, 1970; The Sleeping Beauty: E Berlin, 1970, Teheran, 1970, 1975; partnered Edward Villela at Expo '74, Spokane, USA. *Television:* title rôle, La Sylphide, with Fleming Flindt, BBC, 1960. *Film:* as Kitri, in Don Quixote, with Rudolf Nureyev and Robert Helpmann, Aust., 1972. *Recreations:* music, reading, gardening, breeding Burmese cats. *Address:* 66 Grange Road, Toorak, Victoria 3142, Australia. *T:* 269 2198.

ALDOUS, William, QC 1976; *b* 17 March 1936; *s* of Guy Travers Aldous, *qv*; *m* 1960, Gillian Frances Henson; one *s* two *d. Educ:* Harrow; Trinity Coll., Cambridge (MA). Barrister, Inner Temple, 1960. *Recreations:* hunting, tennis. *Address:* Layham Lodge, Layham, near Ipswich, Suffolk. *T:* Hadleigh 3143.

ALDRED, Cyril; *b* 19 Feb. 1914; 3rd *s* of late Frederick Aldred and Lilian Ethel (*née* Underwood); *m* 1938, Jessie Kennedy Morton; one *d. Educ:* Sloane Sch.; King's Coll. and Courtauld Art Inst., Univ. of London (BA). Asst. Keeper, Royal Scottish Museum, 1937; Scottish Educn Dept, 1939. Served War, RAF (Signals), 1942-46. Associate Curator, Dept of Egyptian Art, Metropolitan Museum of Art, New York, 1955-56; Mem. Cttee, Egypt Exploration Soc., 1959-76; Keeper, Dept of Art and Archaeology, Royal Scottish Museum, Edinburgh, 1961-74. *Publications:* The Development of Ancient Egyptian Art, 1952; The Egyptians (Ancient Peoples and Places), 1961; Egypt to the End of the Old Kingdom, 1965; Akhenaten, a New Study, 1968; Jewels of the Pharaohs, 1971; Akhenaten and Nefertiti, 1973; scripts for BBC programmes, Tutankhamun's Egypt, 1972, etc; chapters in: History of Technology; Cambridge Ancient History (2nd edn); numerous articles on Ancient Egyptian art and archaeology in scientific periodicals. *Recreations:* composing light verse, gardening. *Address:* 4a Polwarth Terrace, Edinburgh EH11 1NE. *T:* 031-229 2845. *Club:* Scottish Arts (Edinburgh).

ALDREN TURNER, Dr J. W.; *see* Turner.

ALDRIDGE, Frederick Jesse; Under-Secretary and Controller of Supply, Department of Health and Social Security, 1968-75; *b* 13 Oct. 1915; *s* of late Jesse and Clara Amelia Aldridge; *m* 1940, Grace Hetty Palser; two *d. Educ:* Westminster City Sch. Clerical Off., Air Min., 1933; Exec. Off., Min. of Health, 1935; RAF, 1940-46; Acct-General's Div., Min. of Health: Asst Acct-Gen., 1956; Dep. Acct-Gen., 1958; Asst Sec. for Finance and Dep. Acct-Gen., 1964; Asst Sec., Food, Health and Nutrition, also Civil Defence, 1966. *Recreation:* music. *Address:* High Trees, 17 Tanglewood Close, Croydon CR0 5HX. *T:* 01-656 3623.

ALDRIDGE, (Harold Edward) James; author; *b* 10 July 1918; *s* of William Thomas Aldridge and Edith Quayle Aldridge; *m* 1942, Dina Mitchnik; two *s.* With Herald and Sun, Melbourne, 1937-38; Daily Sketch, and Sunday Dispatch, London, 1939; subsequently Australian Newspaper Service and North American Newspaper Alliance (war correspondent), Finland, Norway, Middle East, Greece, USSR, until 1945; also correspondent for Time and Life, Teheran, 1944. Rhys Meml Award, 1945; Lenin Peace Prize, 1972. *Publications:* Signed With Their Honour, 1942; The Sea Eagle, 1944; Of Many Men, 1946; The Diplomat, 1950; The Hunter, 1951; Heroes of the Empty View, 1954; Underwater Hunting for Inexperienced Englishmen, 1955; I Wish He Would Not Die, 1958; Gold and Sand (short stories), 1960; The Last Exile, 1961; A Captive in the Land, 1962; The Statesman's Game, 1966; My Brother Tom, 1966; The Flying 19, 1966; (with Paul Strand) Living Egypt, 1969; Cairo: Biography of a City, 1970; A Sporting Proposition, 1973; The Marvellous Mongolian, 1974; Mockery in Arms, 1974; The Untouchable Juli, 1975; One Last Glimpse, 1977. *Recreations:* underwater, trout fishing, hunting, etc. *Address:* 21 Kersley Street, SW11. *Club:* British Sub-Aqua.

ALDRIDGE, James; *see* Aldridge, Harold Edward James.

ALDRIDGE, John Arthur Malcolm, RA 1963 (ARA 1954); painter; Assistant at The Slade School of Fine Art, 1949-67, Lecturer (part-time), 1967-70; *b* 26 July 1905; *s* of Major John Bartelott Aldridge, DSO, RHA, and Margaret Jessica (*née* Goddard); *m* 1st, 1940, Cecilia Lucie Leeds Brown (*née* Saunders) (marr. diss. 1970); no *c*; 2nd, 1970, Margareta Anna Maria Cameron (*née* Bajardi). *Educ:* Uppingham Sch.; Corpus Christi Coll., Oxford (MA). London, 1928-33; Essex, 1933-. Served, 1941-45, Army (N Africa and Italy, 1943-45). Member of 7 and 5 Soc.; Exhibitions at Leicester Galleries, 1933, 1936, 1940, 1947; exhibited Royal Acad. 1948 onwards. Pictures acquired by: Nat. Portrait Gallery; Royal Acad. of Arts, Tate Gallery, Min. of Works, Italian Min. of Education, Aberdeen, Leeds, Manchester, Newport, Northampton, British Council, Contemporary Art Society. *Publications:* Illustrations: The Life of the Dead (text by Laura Riding), 1933; Adam was a Ploughman (text by C. Henry Warren), 1948. *Recreation:* gardening. *Address:* The Place House, Great Bardfield, Essex. *T:* Great Bardfield 275.

ALDRIN, Dr. Edwin E., Jr; President, Research and Engineering Consultants Inc., since 1972; *b* Montclair, NJ, USA, 20 Jan. 1930; *s* of late Col Edwin E. Aldrin, USAF retd, Brielle, NJ, and Marion Aldrin (*née* Moon); *m* 1975, Beverly Van Zile, Los Angeles; two *s* one *d* of previous marriage. *Educ:* Montclair High Sch., Montclair, NJ (grad.); US Mil. Academy, West Point, NY (BSc); Mass Inst. of Technology (DSc in Astronautics). Received wings (USAF), 1952. Served in Korea (66 combat missions) with 51st Fighter Interceptor Wing. Aerial Gunnery Instr, Nellis Air Force Base, Nevada; attended Sqdn Officers Sch., Air Univ., Maxwell Air Force Base, Alabama; Aide to Dean of Faculty, USAF Academy; Flt Comdr with 36th Tactical Fighter Wing, Bitburg, Germany. Subseq. assigned to Gemini Target Office of Air Force Space Systems Div., Los Angeles, Calif; later transf. to USAF Field Office, Manned Spacecraft Center. One of 3rd group of astronauts named by NASA, Oct. 1963; served as back up pilot, Gemini 9 Mission and prime pilot, Gemini 12 Mission (launched into space, with James Lovell, 11 Nov. 1966), 4 day 59 revolution flight which brought Gemini Program to successful close; he established a new record for extravehicular activity and obtained first pictures taken from space of an eclipse of the sun; also made a rendezvous with the previously launched Agena; later assigned to 2nd manned Apollo flight, as back-up command module pilot; Lunar Module Pilot, Apollo 11 rocket flight to the Moon; first lunar landing with Neil Armstrong, July 1969; left NASA to return to USAF as Commandant, Aerospace Res. Pilots Sch., Edwards Air Force Base, Calif, 1971; retired USAF 1972. Mem., Soc. of Experimental Test Pilots; FAIAA; Tau Beta Pi, Sigma Xi. Further honours include Presidential Medal of Freedom, 1969; Air Force DSM with Oak Leaf Cluster; Legion of Merit; Air Force DFC with Oak Leaf Cluster; Air Medal with 2 Oak Leaf Clusters; and NASA DSM, Exceptional Service Medal, and Group Achievement Award. Various hon. membership and hon. doctorates. *Publication:* Return to Earth (autobiography), 1973. *Recreations:* athletics, scuba diving, etc. *Address:* REC Inc., 1801 Federal Avenue, Apt 106, Los Angeles, Calif 90025, USA.

ALEC-SMITH, Rupert Alexander, TD 1950; FSA; Vice Lord-Lieutenant of Humberside, since 1975; *b* 5 Sept. 1913; *o s* of late Alexander Alec-Smith, OBE, Wawne Lodge, Hull; *m* 1952, Suzette Genevieve, *e d* of James Watson, Holyrood House, Hedon, Yorks; one *d. Educ:* Malvern. Entered Horsley, Smith &

Co. Ltd, timber importers, 1932, Dir 1945. Served War of 1939-45: temp. Lt-Col Green Howards (TA); Hon. Col 20th (N and E Ridings) Bn Mobile Defence Corps, 1956-59; Mem. E Riding TA Assoc., 1947-68 (Vice-Chm. 1961-65); Mem. Yorks TA&VRA, 1968-74. Hon. Brother, Kingston upon Hull Trinity House, 1950; Patronage Trustee, living of Holy Trinity, Kingston upon Hull, 1963; Patron, Kingston upon Hull Conservative Fedn, 1970-75; Georgian Soc. for E Yorks: Founder, 1937; Hon. Sec., 1937-74; Pres., 1975; Mem. Exec. Cttee, Georgian Group, 1953; Mem. Yorks Regional Cttee, National Trust, 1969; Mem. BBC Radio Humberside Local Broadcasting Council, 1975. Kingston upon Hull: Mem. City Council, 1947-74 (leader Conservative Gp, 1955-70); Sheriff, 1949-50; Alderman, 1968-74; Lord Mayor, 1970-71; Hon. Freeman, 1973; JP 1950; DL, ER Yorks and City and County of Kingston upon Hull, 1958; JP and DL Humberside, 1974, High Sheriff 1975. FSA 1973. Publication: A Catalogue Raisonné of the Corporation Plate and Insignia of the City and County of Kingston upon Hull, 1973. Recreation: looking at buildings. Address: Winestead, Hull HU12 0NN. T: Patrington 30297, Hull 24255.

ALEXANDER, family name of **Baron Alexander of Potterhill,** of **Earl Alexander of Tunis,** and of **Earl of Caledon.**

ALEXANDER, Viscount; Nicholas James Alexander; b 6 May 1955; s and heir of 6th Earl of Caledon, qv. Educ: Sandroyd School, Gordonstoun School (Round-Square House). Recreations: ski-ing, tennis, swimming, photography, travel. Address: Caledon Castle, Caledon, Co. Tyrone, Northern Ireland. T: Caledon 232.

ALEXANDER OF POTTERHILL, Baron cr 1974 (Life Peer), of Paisley; **William Picken Alexander,** Kt 1961; LHD, PhD, MEd, MA, BSc, FBPsS; General Secretary, Association of Education Committees (England, Wales, Northern Ireland, Isle of Man and Channel Islands), 1945-77; b 13 Dec. 1905; y s of Thomas and Joan Alexander; m 1949, Joan Mary, d of Robert and Margaret Williamson; one s (and one s decd). Educ: Paisley Grammar School; Glasgow Univ. Schoolmaster in Scotland, 1929-31; Asst Lectr in Education, Glasgow Univ., 1931-32; Rockefeller Research Fellow, 1932-33; Deputy Director of Education, Walthamstow, 1934-35; Director of Education, Margate, 1935-39, Sheffield, 1939-44. Joint Sec. to Management Panel of Burnham Committees and Associated Committees negotiating salaries of teachers, 1945-73. Hon. DLitt Leeds, 1977. Publications: Intelligence, Concrete and Abstract, 1935; The Educational Needs of Democracy, 1940; A Performance Scale for the Measurement of Technical Ability, 1947; A Parents' Guide to the Education Act, 1944, 1947; Education in England, 1953; Towards a new Education Act, 1969, etc. Recreations: golf and contract bridge. Address: Woodhey, 11 Pembroke Road, Moor Park, Herts HA6 2HP. T: Northwood 21003. Club: Moor Park Golf (Herts).

ALEXANDER OF TUNIS, 2nd Earl cr 1952; **Shane William Desmond Alexander;** Viscount, 1946; Baron Rideau, 1952; Lieutenant Irish Guards, retired, 1958; b 30 June 1935; er s of 1st Earl Alexander of Tunis, KG, PC, GCB, OM, GCMG, CSI, DSO, MC, and Lady Margaret Diana Bingham (Countess Alexander of Tunis), GBE, DStJ, DL (d 1977), yr d of 5th Earl of Lucan, PC, GCVO, KBE, CB; S father, 1969. Educ: Ashbury Coll., Ottawa, Canada; Harrow. A Lord in Waiting (Govt Whip), 1974. Liveryman, Mercers Company. Heir: b Hon. Brian James Alexander, b 31 July 1939. Address: Winkfield Lodge, Windsor Forest, Berks. T: Winkfield Row 2240.

ALEXANDER, Sir Alexander Sandor, (Sir Alex), Kt 1974; Chairman, Imperial Foods Ltd, since 1969; Director, Imperial Group Ltd (formerly Imperial Tobacco Group Ltd), since 1969; Deputy Chairman, British United Trawlers; b 21 Nov. 1916; m 1946, Margaret Irma; two s two d. Educ: Charles Univ., Prague. Dir, 1954-69, Man. Dir and Chief Exec., 1967-69, Chm. 1969, Ross Group Ltd. Director: National Westminster Bank Ltd, Eastern Region; Ransomes, Sims & Jefferies Ltd. Chm., Theatre Royal (Norwich) Trust Ltd; Trustee, Glyndebourne Arts Trust, 1975. Pres., British Food Export Council, 1973-76; Governor, British Nutrition Foundn. FBIM; FRSA. Mem. Court, UEA. High Sheriff, Norfolk, 1976. Recreations: tennis, shooting, painting. Address: Westwick Hall, Westwick, Norwich. T: Swanton Abbot 664.

ALEXANDER, Sir Charles G(undry), 2nd Bt cr 1945; MA, AIMarE; Chairman, Alexander Shipping Co. Ltd; b 5 May 1923; s of Sir Frank Alexander, 1st Bt, and Elsa Mary (d 1959), d of Sir Charles Collett, 1st Bt; S father 1959; m 1944, Mary Neale, o c of S. R. Richardson; one s one d. Educ: Bishop's Stortford College; St John's College, Cambridge. Served War as

Lieut (E), RN, 1943-46. Chm., Governors Care Ltd; Dep. Chm., Houlder Bros and Co. Ltd; Director: Ore Carriers Ltd; Furness-Houlder Insurance Ltd; Furness-Houlder (Reinsurance Services) Ltd; Bergl Australia Ltd; Ocean Gas Transport Ltd; Pacific Maritime Services Ltd; Compugraphics International Ltd; Port Glaud Development Co. Ltd; World Holidays (Africa) Ltd; Vallum Shipping Co. Ltd; Inner London Region, National Westminster Bank Ltd; formerly Dir, Hull, Blyth & Co. Ltd (Chm., 1972-75). Chm., Bd of Governors, Bishop's Stortford College. Mem. Court of Common Council, 1969; Alderman (Bridge Ward), 1970-76. Recreation: farming. Heir: s Richard Alexander [b 1 Sept. 1947; m 1971, Lesley Jane, d of Frederick William Jordan, Bishop's Stortford]. Address: 53 Leadenhall Street, EC3. T: 01-481 2020; Bells Farm, East Sutton, near Maidstone, Kent. T: Sutton Valence 2410. Club: Royal Automobile.

ALEXANDER of Ballochmyle, Sir Claud Hagart-, 3rd Bt, cr 1886 of Ballochmyle; DL; b 6 Jan. 1927; s of late Wilfred Archibald Alexander (2nd s of 2nd Bt) and Mary Prudence, d of late Guy Acheson; S grandfather, 1945; assumed additional surname of Hagart, 1949; m 1959, Hilda Etain, 2nd d of Miles Malcolm Acheson, Ganges, BC, Canada; two s two d. Educ: Sherborne; Corpus Christi Coll., Cambridge (BA 1948). DL Ayrshire, 1973. Heir: s Claud Hagart-Alexander, b 5 Nov. 1963. Address: Kingencleugh House, Mauchline, Ayrshire KA5 5JL. T: Mauchline 50217. Club: New (Edinburgh).

ALEXANDER, Sir Darnley (Arthur Raymond), Kt 1974; CBE 1963; Chief Justice of Nigeria since 1975; b Castries, St Lucia, 28 Jan. 1920; e s of Pamphile Joseph Alexander and late Lucy Alexander; m 1943, Mildred Margaret (née King); one s one d. Educ: St Mary's Coll., St Lucia; University Coll., London (LLB). Called to Bar, Middle Temple, 1942. Served in: legal service, Jamaica, WI, and Turks and Caicos Is, 1944-57; legal service, Western Nigeria, 1957-63; Solicitor-Gen. 1960; QC 1961; Judge, High Court of Lagos (later Lagos State), 1964-69; Chief Justice, South Eastern State of Nigeria, 1969-75. Chairman: Nigerian Adv. Judicial Cttee; Legal Practitioners' Privileges Cttee; Member: Nigerian Body of Benchers; Nigerian Soc. of Internat. Law; Internat. Adv. Bd African Law Reports. Publications: Report of Inquiry into Owegbe Cult, 1966; Report of Inquiry into Examination Leakages, 1969. Recreations: cricket, table-tennis, swimming. Address: Supreme Court of Nigeria, Lagos, Nigeria. Club: Lagos Amateur Cricket.

ALEXANDER, Maj.-Gen. David Crichton, CB 1976; Director-General, English-Speaking Union, since 1977; b 28 Nov. 1926; s of James Alexander and Margaret (née Craig); m 1957, Diana Joyce (Jane) (née Fisher); one s two d and one step s. Educ: Edinburgh Academy. Joined RM, 1944; East Indies Fleet; 45 Commando, Malaya, Malta, Canal Zone, 1951-54; Parade Adjt, Lympstone, 1954-57; Equerry and Acting Treasurer to Duke of Edinburgh, 1957-60; psc 1960; Directing Staff, Staff Coll., Camberley, 1962-65; 45 Commando (2IC), Aden, 1965-66; Staff of Chief of Defence Staff, incl. service with Sec. of State, 1966-69; CO 40 Commando, Singapore, 1969-70; Col GS to CGRM, 1970-73; ADC to the Queen, 1973-75; RCDS 1974; Comdr, Training Gp RM, 1975-77. Recreations: fishing, gardening, golf. Address: Hillwood, Crawley Drive, Camberley GU15 2AA. T: Camberley 63072. Club: Army and Navy.

ALEXANDER, Sir Desmond William Lionel C.; see Cable-Alexander.

ALEXANDER, Sir Douglas (Hamilton), 2nd Bt, cr 1921; b 6 June 1900; e s of Sir Douglas Alexander, 1st Bt, and Helen Hamilton (d 1923), d of George Hamilton Gillespie, Hamilton; S father, 1949. Educ: Appleby College; Phillips Exeter Academy; Princeton University. BA 1921. The Singer Manufacturing Company, 1922; Secretary of the Company, 1946; now retired. Heir: b Archibald Gillespie Alexander [b 29 March 1907; m 1932, Margery Isabel Griffith, Media, Pa, USA; two s one d]. Address: Palmers Hill, Stamford, Conn 06902, USA.

ALEXANDER, Duncan Hubert David, OBE 1959; TD; MA; DL; Senior Partner, Stephenson & Alexander, Chartered Surveyors, Chartered Auctioneers and Estate Agents, Cardiff; b 15 June 1911; e c of Hubert G. and Edith Alexander; m 1937, Dorothy Evelyn, 3rd d of late Edmund L. Hann; three d. Educ: Sherborne School, Dorset; Trinity College, Cambridge (MA). Family business of Stephenson & Alexander, 1933- (except War Service, 1939-45). Mem., 1960-, Dep. Chm., 1973-, Cwmbran New Town Corporation. National Pres. of Chartered Auctioneers' and Estate Agents' Institute, 1964-65; Member, Housing Corporation, 1964-74. Indep. Mem., Lord Nugent's MoD Lands Rev. Cttee, 1971-73. Hon. Col, Glamorgan Army Cadet Force, 1975-. DL 1958, High Sheriff 1960, Glamorgan. Recreations:

golf, gardening. *Address:* Star House, Capel Llanilterne, Glamorgan. *T:* Pentyrch 890332; (business) 5 High Street, Cardiff. *T:* Cardiff 40244. *Clubs:* MCC; Cardiff and County (Cardiff).

ALEXANDER, Henry Joachim, Dr phil, Dr jur Breslau; Vice-President, Fédération Internationale des Communautés d'Enfants, Trogen, 1967-71 (Secrétaire Général Adjoint, 1960-67; Chairman, UK Section, 1960-70); *b* 4 Jan. 1897; *s* of Bruno and Lisbeth Alexander-Katz; *m* 1st, 1925, Hilda (*née* Speyer) (*d* 1974); two *s*; 2nd, 1975, Amalia Cornelia (*née* Amato). *Educ:* Gymnasium Augustum Germany; Univs of Göttingen and Breslau. Member, Berlin Bar, 1925-37. Member, European Service of BBC, 1942-56; Vice-Chm. and Trustee, Assoc. of Broadcasting Staff, 1952-54 (Chm., Foreign Langs Panel, 1952-55). Chm., British Pestalozzi Children's Village Assoc., 1947-57; Chm. Pestalozzi Children's Village Trust, 1957-62 (Exec. Vice-Pres., 1962-63); Mem. Council, Pestalozzi Children's Village Foundation, Trogen, Switzerland, 1954-; Mem. Exec. Cttee, Lifeline, an Internat. Refugee Cttee, 1965-72; Mem. Residential Child Care Assoc., 1965-, and Chm. of its Internat. Cttee, 1965-70. *Publication:* International Trade Mark Law, 1935. *Recreations:* music, hill walking. *Address:* Hildings, Pett, Hastings, East Sussex. *T:* Pett 3055.

ALEXANDER, Sir (John) Lindsay, Kt 1975; MA; Chairman: Ocean Transport and Trading Ltd (formerly Ocean Steam Ship Co. Ltd), since 1971 (Managing Director, 1955-71); Overseas Containers Holdings Ltd, since 1976 (Director, 1971-76); *b* 12 Sept. 1920; *e s* of Ernest Daniel Alexander and Florence Mary Mainsmith; *m* 1944, Maud Lilian, 2nd *d* of Oliver Ernest and Bridget Collard; two *s* one *d. Educ:* Alleyn's Sch.; Brasenose Coll., Oxford (Thomas Wall Schol.). Royal Engineers, 1940-45 (Capt.); served Middle East and Italy. Chairman: Liverpool Port Employers' Assoc., 1964-67; Cttee, European Nat. Shipowners' Assocs, 1971-73; Vice-Chm., Nat. Assoc. of Port Employers, 1965-69; President: Chamber of Shipping of UK, 1974-75 (Vice-Pres., 1973-74);Gen. Council, British Shipping Ltd, 1974-75. Director: Lloyds Bank, 1970-; Lloyds Bank International, 1975-; British Petroleum Co. Ltd, 1975-. FCIT (MInstT 1968); FBIM 1972. JP Cheshire, 1965-75. *Recreations:* gardening, music, photography. *Address:* Baskervyle, Heswall, Merseyside. *T:* 051-342 3043. *Club:* Brooks's.

ALEXANDER, Prof. John Malcolm; Professor of Applied Mechanics, Imperial College, London University, since 1969; *b* 14 Oct. 1921; *s* of Robert Henry Alexander and Gladys Irene Lightfoot Alexander (*née* Domville); *m* 1946, Margaret, *d* of F. A. Ingram; two *s. Educ:* Ipswich Sch.; City and Guilds Coll. (Imperial Coll., London Univ.). DSc (Eng) London; PhD; FCGI; FIMechE; FIProdE; FIM; FRSA. Practical trng, Ransomes Sims & Jefferies Ltd, Ipswich, 1937-42; REME commn, 1942-47; res. in plasticity and applied mechanics, City and Guilds Coll., 1950-53; Head of Metal Deformation Section, Aluminium Labs Ltd, 1953-55; Head of Mech. Engrg Res. Labs and Nuclear Reactor Mechanical Design, English Electric, 1955-57; Reader in Plasticity, Univ. of London, 1957-63; Prof. of Engrg Plasticity, Univ. of London, 1963-69. Chm., Applied Mechanics Gp, IMechE, 1963-65; Mem., Collège Internationale Recherche et Production, 1965-; Vice-Pres., Inst. of Metals, 1968-71; Chm. Board of Studies in Civil and Mech. Engrg, Univ. of London, 1966-68; Gov., Reigate Grammar Sch., 1964-67; Engrg Adviser, Van Nostrand, 1964-; Chm., British Cold Forging Gp, 1973-; Mem. Editorial Board: Jl Strain Analysis, 1965-71; Internat. Jl Mech. Sciences, 1968-; Internat. Jl Machine Tool Design and Research, 1973-; Metals Technology, 1976-; Mem. Adv. Bd, Jl Mech. Working Tech., 1976-. Joseph Bramah Medal, IMechE, 1970. *Publications:* Advanced Mechanics of Materials, Manufacturing Properties of Materials, 1963; Hydrostatic Extrusion, 1971; papers to Royal Soc., IMechE, Iron and Steel Inst., Inst. Metals, Metals Soc. *Recreations:* music, gardening, swimming, squash. *Address:* 21 Roskeen Court, 45 Arterberry Road, SW20 8AU. *T:* 01-947 6204. *Club:* Athenæum.

ALEXANDER, Prof. Kenneth John Wilson, BSc (Econ.); Chairman, Highlands and Islands Development Board, since 1976; Professor of Economics, University of Strathclyde, since 1963, on leave of absence since 1976; *b* Edinburgh, 14 March 1922; *o s* of late William Wilson Alexander; *m* 1949, Angela-May, *d* of late Capt. G. H. Lane, RN; one *s* four *d. Educ:* George Heriot's Sch., Edinburgh; Sch. of Economics, Dundee. Research Asst, Univ. of Leeds, 1949-51; Lectr, Univ. of Sheffield, 1951-56; Lectr, Univ. of Aberdeen, 1957-62; Dean of Scottish Business Sch., 1973-75 (Chm., Acad. Exec. Cttee, 1972-73). Umpire, N Derbyshire District Conciliation Bd, 1963; Mem. Adv. Cttee on University of the Air, 1965; Director: Fairfields (Glasgow) Ltd, 1966-68; Upper Clyde Shipbuilders Ltd, 1968-71; Chm., Govan

Shipbuilders, 1974-76; Dir, Glasgow Chamber of Commerce, 1969-73; Economic Consultant to Sec. of State for Scotland, 1968-; Chm., Cttee on Adult Educn in Scotland, 1970; Member: Exec. Cttee, Scottish Council (Develt and Industry), 1968-; (part-time) Scottish Transport Gp, 1969-76; SSRC, 1975-. Governor, Newbattle Abbey Coll., 1967-73; President: Section F, British Assoc., 1974; Saltire Soc., 1975-. LLD CNAA, 1976; DUniv Stirling, 1977. *Publications:* The Economist in Business, 1967; Productivity Bargaining and the Reform of Industrial Relations, 1969; (with C. L. Jenkins) Fairfields, a study of industrial change, 1971; (ed) The Political Economy of Change, 1976; articles in Oxford Econ. Papers, Quarterly Jl of Econ., Scottish Jl of Pol. Econ., Economica, Yorkshire Bulletin Economics, and other jls. *Recreation:* Scottish antiquarianism. *Address:* Ardnacraggan, Callander, Perthshire. *T:* Callander 30307.

ALEXANDER, Sir Lindsay; *see* Alexander, Sir J. L.

ALEXANDER, Rt. Rev. Mervyn Alban Newman; *see* Clifton, Bishop of, (RC).

ALEXANDER, Michael Charles; writer; *b* 20 Nov. 1920; *s* of late Rear-Adm. Charles Otway Alexander and Antonia Geermans; *m* 1963, Sarah Wignall (marr. diss.); one *d. Educ:* Stowe; RMC, Sandhurst; Oflag IVC, Colditz. Served War: DCLI; 5 (Ski) Bn Scots Gds; 8 Commando (Layforce); HQ 13 Corps (GSO 3); Special Boat Section; (POW, 1942-44); 2nd SAS Regt; War Office (Civil Affairs). Intergovtl Cttee on Refugees, 1946; Editorial Dir, Common Ground Ltd, 1946-50. Located Firuzkoh, Central Afghanistan, 1952; Himalayan Hovercraft Expedn, 1972; Yucatan Straits Hovercraft Expedn, 1975. Director: Acorn Productions Ltd; Wildlife Publications Ltd. FZS, FRGS, FRAI. *Publications:* The Privileged Nightmare (with Giles Romilly), 1952 (republ. as Hostages at Colditz, 1975); Offbeat in Asia, 1953; The Reluctant Legionnaire, 1955; The True Blue, 1957; Mrs Fraser on the Fatal Shore, 1972; Discovering the New World, 1976; Omai: Noble Savage, 1977. *Address:* 48 Eaton Place, SW1. *T:* 01-235 2724.

ALEXANDER, Michael O'Donel Bjarne; HM Diplomatic Service; Deputy Head of Personnel Department, Foreign and Commonwealth Office, since 1977; *b* 19 June 1936; *s* of late Conel Hugh O'Donel Alexander, CMG, CBE, and of Enid Constance Crichton Neate; *m* 1960, Traute Krohn; two *s* one *d. Educ:* Foyle Coll., Londonderry; Hall Sch., Hampstead; St Paul's Sch.; King's Coll., Cambridge (Schol.); Harkness Fellow (Yale and Berkeley) 1960-62. MA (Cantab), AM (Yale). Royal Navy, 1955-57. Entered HM Foreign (later Diplomatic) Service, 1962; Moscow, 1963-65; Office of Political Adviser, Singapore, 1965-68; FCO, 1968-72; Asst Private Sec. to Secretary of State (Rt Hon. Sir Alec Douglas-Home, MP, and Rt Hon. James Callaghan, MP) 1972-74; Counsellor (CSCE) and later Head of Chancery, UK Mission, Geneva, 1974-77. Former Public Schools', British Universities' and National Junior Foil Champion; fenced for Cambridge Univ., 1957-60 (Captain, 1959-60); English Internat., 1958; Silver Medallist (Epée Team) Olympic Games, 1960; Gold Medallist, US Championships, 1961; Captained England, 1963. Represented Cambridge in Field Events Match with Oxford, 1959-60. *Recreations:* reading history; watching or participating in sport of any kind. *Address:* 19 Spencer Park, SW18. *T:* 01-870 1964. *Clubs:* Hurlingham, Epée, All England Fencing; Hawks (Cambridge).

ALEXANDER, Sir Norman (Stanley), Kt 1966; CBE 1959. Professor of Physics: Raffles Coll., Singapore, 1936-49; Univ. of Malaya, Singapore, 1949-52; University Coll., Ibadan, Nigeria, 1952-60; Vice-Chancellor, Ahmadu Bello Univ., Nigeria, 1961-66.

ALEXANDER, Rear-Adm. Robert Love, CB 1964; DSO 1943; DSC 1944; *b* 29 April 1913; *o s* of Captain R. L. Alexander, Edinburgh; *m* 1936, Margaret Elizabeth, *o d* of late George Conrad Spring, and Mrs Maurice House; one *s* four *d. Educ:* Merchiston Castle; Royal Naval College, Dartmouth. Joined RNC, 1927; Cadet HMS Repulse, 1930; Midshipman HMS Kent, 1931-33; Sub-Lieut, qualified in submarines, 1935. Served throughout War of 1939-45 in submarines; first command HMS H32, 1940; later commands: HMS Proteus, 1942; HMS Truculent, 1942-44; HMS Tuna, 1945. Second in command and in temp. command HMS Glory, Korean War, 1951-52; in command First Destroyer Squadron, 1957; Imperial Defence College, 1959; in command HMS Forth and 1st Submarine Squadron, 1960; Captain Submarines and Minesweepers, Mediterranean, and NATO Commander Submarines, Mediterranean, HMS Narvik, 1960-62. Vice Naval Deputy to the Supreme Allied Commander Europe, 1962-65. Lieut 1936; Comdr 1946; Capt. 1952; Rear-Adm. 1962; retd, 1965. *Address:*

Beeches Croft, Fyning Lane, Rogate, Petersfield, Hants. *T:* Rogate 368. *Club:* Army and Navy.

ALEXANDER, Robert Scott, QC 1973; *b* 5 Sept. 1936; *s* of Samuel James and Hannah May Alexander; *m* 1963, Frances Rosemary Heveningham Pughe (marr. diss. 1973); two *s* one *d.* *Educ:* Brighton Coll.; King's Coll., Cambridge. BA 1959, MA 1963. Called to Bar, Middle Temple, Nov. 1961. *Address:* 1 Brick Court, Temple, EC4. *T:* 01-353 0777.

ALEXANDER, Stanley Walter, MBE 1918; Proprietor and Editor, 1951-66, City Press, the City of London Newspaper; Hon. Editor, Free Trader; *b* 16 Nov. 1895; *s* of Walter Henry Alexander; *m* 1919, Doris Emily Kibble; two *s.* *Educ:* Roan School, Greenwich. Entered Lord Beaverbrook's office, 1910; Canadian War Records Office, 1915-17; Ministry of Information, 1918; Financial Editor, Daily Express, Sunday Express, Evening Standard, 1923-46; contested, as Free Trade candidate, City of London, 1945, North Ilford, 1950. One of founders with late Sir Ernest Benn of Soc. of Individualists; President: Free Trade League; Cobden Club; Hon. Treasurer, Anti-Dear Food Campaign. Liveryman, Worshipful Co. of Tallow Chandlers; Mem. Council, Kipling Soc.; a Governor, Cripplegate Foundn. *Publications:* author of the Hannibal pamphlets (on free trade, sound money, against the coercion of the people by the State, and on the economics of sea power), including The Kingdom of Bevin, The Price We Pay, Tariffs Mean War, 1933-44; Save the Pound—Save the People, 1975; Montagu Norman versus Beaverbrook, 1976. *Recreation:* watching cricket. *Address:* 44 Speed House, Barbican, EC2. *Clubs:* Reform, City Livery.

ALEXANDER, William Gemmell, MBE 1945; County Road Safety Officer, West Yorkshire Metropolitan County Council, since 1974; *b* 19 Aug. 1918; *s* of Harold Gemmell Alexander and Winifred Ada Alexander (*née* Stott); *m* 1945, Janet Rona Page Alexander (*née* Elias); four *s* one *d.* *Educ:* Tre Arddur Bay Sch.; Sedbergh Sch.; Oxford Univ. (MA). Served War of 1939-45 (despatches, war stars and clasps): Driver Mechanic, 2nd Lieut, Lieut, Capt., Maj.; served in France, S Africa, Eritrea, Egypt, Middle East, Sicily, Italy, Algeria, NW Europe. HM Overseas Civil Service, 1946-59: Gilbert and Ellice Is, 1946-51; Mauritius, 1951-55; Cyprus, 1955-59; Man., Cooperative Wholesale Soc., Agricultural Dept, 1960-63; Dir, Internat. Cooperative Alliance, 1963-68; Dir-Gen., RoSPA, 1968-74. Associate Mem., BIM, 1963. *Recreations:* all sports and walking. *Address:* 8 Woolgreaves Close, Sandal, Wakefield, West Yorks WF2 6DZ. *T:* Wakefield 55214. *Club:* Royal Commonwealth Society.

ALEXANDER-SINCLAIR, Maj.-Gen. David Boyd; GOC 1st Division, 1975-77; *b* 2 May 1927; *s* of Comdr M. B. Alexander-Sinclair, RN and Avril N. Fergusson-Buchanan; *m* 1958, Ann Ruth, *d* of Lt-Col Graeme Daglish; two *s* one *d.* *Educ:* Eton (King's Scholar). Commnd into Rifle Bde, 1946, served in Germany, Kenya, Cyprus; ADC to GOC South Malaya District and Maj.-Gen. Bde of Gurkhas, 1950-51; psc 1958; Bde Major, 6th Inf. Bde Gp, 1959-61; GSO2 (Dirg Staff) Staff Coll., 1963-65; comdg 3rd Bn Royal Green Jackets, 1967-69; MoD, 1965-67 and 1969-71; Comdr, 6th Armd Bde, 1971-73; Student, RCDS, 1974. *Address:* c/o Midland Bank Ltd, 69 Pall Mall, SW1Y 5EY.

ALEXANDER-SINCLAIR, John Alexis Clifford Cerda, SMOM, FRSA, RMS; Chairman, Human Rights Trust, since 1974 (Founder and Chairman, 1969, Vice-Chairman, 1971-73); Vice-Chairman: Anti-Slavery Society and Committee for Indigenous People, since 1971 (Committee Member, since 1965); British Institute of Human Rights, since 1971; Member Committee, League Against Cruel Sports, since 1972; Chairman, Art Registration Committee, since 1969; *b* 22 Feb. 1906; *s* of Col C. H. Alexander, Jacob's Horse, and Donna Lyta Alexander dei Marchesi della Cerda; *m* 1st, 1927, Baroness von Gottberg (decd) one *d* ; 2nd, 1933, Stella Tucker; one *s* one *d* ; 3rd, 1950, Simonne de Rougemont (*née* Vion); 4th, 1965, Maureen Dover (*née* Wood); one step *s.* *Educ:* Charterhouse; Goettingen and Munich Univs. Entered HM Foreign Service, 1928; served in China as Vice-Consul and Consul; despatches (Admiralty) 1938; Liaison Free French Headquarters, Far East, 1941 (POW Shanghai, 1942); served in Washington as 1st Sec. of Embassy, 1943; seconded to UNRRA, London and Paris, 1944; CCG as Controller (Col) Economic Plans, 1945; 1st Sec. UK Delegation, UN, NY, 1946, 1947, 1948; Vice-Chm. UNICEF, 1946, 1947; Sec. Gen. UK Delegation Geneva Red Cross Conf., 1949; served UN, NY, 1950; Dir UN Office of High Comr for refugees, Geneva, 1951-52; transf. UN High Comr for Refugees Rep. (local rank Minister), Rome, 1953-55; European Dir (Paris), International Rescue Cttee, NY, 1957-58; UN Tech. Assistance Adviser to Min. of Finance, Govt of Thailand, Jan.-

Feb. 1959, to Nat. Iranian Oil Co., Tehran, Iran, 1959-60; Head of Oil Industry Labour Re-deployment Unit, 1960; Manpower Expert, FAO (UN Special Fund) in the Rif, Morocco, 1961-62. Founder Mem., Hansard Soc. for Parliamentary Govt, 1944; Executive Sec. Liberal International, London, 1963-64; Hon. Campaign Dir, UK Cttee for Human Rights Year, 1967, 1968, 1969; Mem. Cttee, Internat. Social Service, 1972. Dir, Animal Welfare Year, 1976. Knight of Magistral Grace, British Assoc. of SMO Malta, 1957. Distinguished Service Award (Internat. Rescue Cttee), 1959. Life Member, Fellow 1965, RSA; Mem., Royal Soc. of Miniature Painters, Sculptors and Gravers, 1971; Hon. Mem. Exec. Cttee, UK Section, Association Internationale des Arts Plastiques et Graphiques, 1977. *Address:* 5 Aysgarth Road, Dulwich Village, SE21 7JR. *T:* 01-733 1666; The Clink, Goodings, Woodlands St Mary, Newbury RG16 7BD. *T:* Great Shefford 450; 56 Boulevard Richard Lenoir, 75011 Paris, France. *T:* Paris 805 3588. *Clubs:* Athenæum, Royal Automobile.

ALFORD, Ven. John Richard; Archdeacon of Halifax, since 1972; *b* 21 June 1919; *s* of Walter John and Gertrude Ellen Alford. *Educ:* Fitzwilliam House, Cambridge (History Tri. Pts 1 and 2, BA 1941, MA 1947); Cuddesdon College, Oxford. Deacon 1943, priest 1944, Wakefield; Curate, St Paul, King Cross, Halifax, 1943-47; Curate, Wakefield Cathedral, 1947-50; Tutor, Wells Theological College, 1950-56; Priest Vicar, Wells Cathedral, 1950-56; Vice-Principal, The Queen's College, Birmingham, 1956-67; Exam. Chaplain to Bp of Kimberley and Kuruman, 1961-65; Domestic Chaplain, Director of Ordinands, and Exam. Chaplain to Bp of Chester, 1967-72; Vicar of Shotwick, Chester, 1967-72; Hon. Canon of Chester Cathedral, 1969-72, Emeritus, 1972; Canon Residentiary of Wakefield Cathedral, 1972-; Examining Chaplain to Bp of Wakefield, 1972-. *Recreations:* music, walking. *Address:* 4 St John's Square, Wakefield WF1 2QX. *T:* Wakefield 78532.

ALFORD, Sir Robert (Edmund), KBE 1960; CMG 1951; *b* 10 Sept. 1904; 2nd *s* of late R. G. Alford and Maud Alford (*née* Griffiths); *m* 1st, 1934, Teresa Margaret Riddell (*d* 1964); one *s* ; 2nd, 1967, Eileen Mary Riddell. *Educ:* Winchester Coll.; University Coll., Oxford. Colonial Administrative Service, Nigeria, 1928; Sen. District Officer, 1946; Financial Sec., Zanzibar, 1947; Chief Secretary, 1952; Governor and C-in-C of St Helena, 1958-62. Served War of 1939-45 in RNVR, 1940-45. Brilliant Star of Zanzibar, 1958. *Address:* The Barn, Staple Cross, Sussex.

ALFRED, Arnold Montague; Director, British Printing Corporation, since 1969; Chairman: BPC Publishing Ltd, since 1971; Caxton Publishing Company Ltd, since 1971; *b* 21 March 1925; *s* of Reuben Alfred and Bessie Alfred (*née* Arbesfield); *m* 1947, Sheila Jacqueline Gold; three *s.* *Educ:* Central Foundation Boys' Sch.; Imperial Coll., London; London Sch. of Economics. Head of Economics Dept, Courtaulds Ltd, 1953-69; Director, CELON Div., Courtaulds Ltd, 1964-69. *Publications:* Discounted Cash Flow (jointly), 1965; Business Economics (jointly), 1968. Numerous articles in: Accountant, Textile Jl, Investment Analyst, etc. *Recreation:* active in Jewish community affairs. *Address:* 44 Great Queen Street, WC2B 5AA. *T:* 01-240 3411.

ALFVÉN, Prof. Hannes Olof Gösta, PhD; Professor of Plasma Physics, Royal Institute of Technology, Stockholm, 1963-73; *b* Sweden, 30 May 1908; *s* of Johannes Alfvén and Anna-Clara Romanus; *m* 1935, Kerstin Erikson, *d* of Rolf E. and Maria Uddenberg. *Educ:* Univ. of Uppsala (PhD 1934). Prof. of Theory of Electricity, 1940-45 and of Electronics, 1945-63, Royal Inst. of Technology, Stockholm. Prof., Univ. of California at San Diego, 1967. Pres., Pugwash Confs on Science and World Affairs. Member: Swedish Acad. of Sciences; Swedish Acad. of Eng. Sciences; Swedish Science Advisory Council; several foreign acads; Foreign Associate, US Acad. of Sciences. Hon. DSc Oxon, 1977. Awarded Gold Medal of Royal Astronomical Soc. (Gt Britain), 1967; Nobel Prize for Physics, 1970. *Publications:* Cosmical Electrodynamics, 1948; On the Origin of the Solar System, 1956; Cosmical Electrodynamics: Fundamental Principles (jointly), 1963; World-Antiworlds (Eng. trans.), 1966; (as Olof Johannesson) The Tale of the Big Computer (Eng. trans.), 1968; Atom, Man and the Universe (Eng. trans.), 1969; (with Kerstin Alfvén) M70-Living on the Third Planet, 1971; papers in physics and astrophysics. *Address:* c/o Division of Plasma Physics, Royal Institute of Technology, S-100 44 Stockholm 70, Sweden.

ALGAR, Claudius Randleson, JP; barrister-at-law; *b* 18 May 1900; *s* of Claudius G. Algar; *m* 1930, Constance, *d* of Edgar Tucker, Carmarthen; one *s.* *Educ:* Highgate School. Barrister-at-law, Inner Temple, 1925. Dep. Chm., Wilts QS, 1945-71.

Member of the Corporation of London, 1930-48. JP Wiltshire, 1941. *Address:* Rye Hill, Longbridge Deverill, Warminster, Wilts. *T:* Maiden Bradley 316.

ALGIE, Hon. Sir Ronald (Macmillan), Kt 1964; retired; Speaker, House of Representatives, New Zealand, 1961-66; MP (N) for Remuera, 1943-66; *b* 22 Oct. 1888; *s* of John Alexander Algie and Agnes Macmillan Algie; *m* 1st, 1917, Helen Adair McMaster (*d* 1944); 2nd, 1947, Mary Joan Gray Stewart (*d* 1972); one *s* one *d. Educ:* primary and secondary schools in NZ; Auckland University College. Barrister, 1913. Auckland University: Lectr in Law, 1913; Prof. of Law, 1919-37. Minister of Education, New Zealand, 1950-57. Hon. LLD Univ. of Auckland, 1968. *Publications:* articles in professional jls. *Recreation:* mountaineering (Mem. Alpine Club). *Club:* Northern (Auckland, NZ).

ALGOMA, Bishop of, since 1975; **Rt. Rev. Frank Foley Nock,** DD; *b* 27 Feb. 1916; *s* of David Nock and Esther Hambidge; *m* 1942, Elizabeth Hope Adams; one *s* one *d. Educ:* Trinity Coll., Toronto (BA, BD). Curate, St Matthew's, Toronto, 1940-42; Incumbent, Christ Church, Korah, Sault Ste Marie, 1942-45; Rector: Bracebridge, St Thomas', 1945-48; Church of the Epiphany, Sudbury, 1948-57; St Luke's Cathedral, 1957-74; Dean of Algoma, 1957-74. Hon. DD, Toronto, 1957. *Recreations:* music, golfing, cross country skiing. *Address:* 134 Simpson Street, Sault Ste Marie, Ontario P6A 3V4, Canada. *T:* 705-256-7379.

ALHEGELAN, Sheikh Faisal Abdul Aziz; Order of King Abdulaziz, Saudi Arabia; Saudi Arabian Ambassador to the Court of St James's, since 1976; *b* 7 Oct. 1929; *s* of Sheikh Abdul Aziz Alhegelan and Fatima Alhegelan; *m* 1961, Nouha Tarazi; three *s* . *Educ:* Faculty of Law, Fouad Univ., Cairo. Min. of Foreign Affairs, 1952-54; Saudi Arabian Embassy, Washington, USA, 1954-58; Chief of Protocol, Jeddah, 1958-60; Polit. Adviser to the King, 1960-61; Ambassador to: Spain, 1961-68; Venezuela and Argentina (concurrently), 1968-75; Denmark, 1975-76. Gran Cruz, Isobel la Catolica, Spain; Gran Cordon Orden del Libertador, Venezuela; Grande Official, Orden Rio Branco, Brazil. *Recreations:* bridge, golf. *Address:* Royal Embassy of Saudi Arabia, 30 Belgrave Square, SW1X 8QB. *T:* 01-235 0831.

ALI, (Chaudri) Mohamad; politician, Pakistan; *b* Jullundur, India, 15 July 1905; *m* ; four *s* one *d. Educ:* Punjab University, Lahore (MSc). Lecturer in Chemistry, Islamia College, Lahore, 1927-28; Indian Audit and Accounting Service, 1928; Accountant-Gen., Bahawalpur, 1932; Private Secretary to Finance Minister, Government of India, 1936; Under Secretary Finance Dept, 1938; Deputy Financial Adviser, 1939; Addtl Financial Adviser, Dept of Supply, 1943; Financial Adviser of War and Supply, 1945; Mem. Steering Cttee of Partition Council, 1947; Secretary-General, Govt of Pakistan, 1947; Minister of Finance, 1951. Alternate Deleg. to UN Security Council. 1948; Deleg. to Commonwealth Consultative Cttee, Colombo Plan Confs, 1951-; Head of Pakistan Delegation to Commonwealth Finance Ministers' Confs, 1952, 1953, 1954; Chairman Bd of Governors of International Monetary Fund and International Bank for Reconstruction and Development, 1953; Prime Minister, Pakistan, 1955-56, resigned, also as Minister of Defence. *Publication:* The Emergence of Pakistan, 1967. *Address:* 86-D/1, Gulberg III, Lahore, Pakistan.

ALICE, HRH Princess; *see* Athlone, Countess of.

ALISON, Michael James Hugh; MP (C) Barkston Ash since 1964; *b* 27 June 1926; *m* 1958, Sylvia Mary Haigh; two *s* one *d. Educ:* Eton; Wadham Coll., Oxford. Coldstream Guards, 1944-48; Wadham Coll., Oxford, 1948-51; Lazard Bros & Co. Ltd, 1951-53; London Municipal Soc., 1954-58; Conservative Research Dept, 1958-64. Parly Under-Sec. of State, DHSS, 1970-74. *Address:* Flat 7, Sheridan Court, Barkston Gardens, SW5.

ALKER, Thomas, CBE 1958; LLM Liverpool (Hon.); Town Clerk of Liverpool and Legal and Parliamentary Officer to the Mersey Tunnel Joint Committee, 1947-67, retired; *b* 25 Aug. 1904; *m* 1930, Marion Eckersley Dove; four *d. Educ:* Wigan Grammar School; Manchester University. Asst Solicitor, Wigan, 1928-30; Sen. Asst Solicitor and Dep. Town Clerk, Kingston-upon-Hull, 1930-37; Town Clerk and Clerk of the Peace, Oldham, 1937-47. President Society of Town Clerks, 1954-55. Hon. Solicitor for England, National and Local Government Officers Association, 1957-61. *Recreations:* music, photography. *Address:* 278 Allerton Road, Liverpool L18 6JP. *T:* 051-724 2768. *Club:* National Liberal.

ALLAM, Peter John; Architect, Principal in private practice; *b* 17 June 1927; *er s* of late Leslie Francis Allam and Annette Farquharson (*née* Lawson); *m* 1961, Pamela Mackie Haynes; two *d. Educ:* Royal High Sch., Edinburgh; Glasgow Sch. of Architecture. War service, 1944-48, Far East; commnd in Seaforth Highlanders, 1946. Architectural trng, 1948-53. Bahrain Petroleum Co., Engrg Div., 1954-55; Asst in private architectural practices, 1956-64; Principal, own practice, 1964-68. Director, Saltire Soc., 1968-70. ARIBA 1964; Associate, RIAS, 1964. *Recreations:* study and practice of conservation, both architectural and natural; music; Rugby. *Address:* The Stick House, 43 Ravelston Dykes Road, Edinburgh EH4 3PA. *T:* 031-337 4022.

ALLAN, family name of **Baron Allan of Kilmahew.**

ALLAN OF KILMAHEW, Baron *cr* 1973 (Life Peer), of Cardross, Dunbarton; **Robert Alexander Allan,** DSO 1944; OBE 1942; Chairman, Ladybird Books; Director: Pearson/Longman; Longman/Penguin; Bank of Scotland (Chairman, London Board); H. Clarkson (Holdings) Ltd, and other companies; *b* 11 July 1914; *yr s* of late Claud A. Allan, VL, JP, Kilmahew Castle, Cardross, Dunbartonshire, and of Adeline Allan, OBE; *m* 1947, Maureen, *d* of late Harold Stuart-Clark, Singapore; one *s* one *d. Educ:* Harrow (Rothschild Schol.); Clare Coll., Cambridge (Mellon Fellow; ran cross-country for Cambridge, 1935, 1936); Yale University. Served War of 1939-45, mostly in Coastal Forces in Mediterranean until 1946; Lieut RNVR July 1939, Commander, 1943; Senior Officer Inshore Squadron, 1944-45; Dep. Chief of Naval Information, Washington, 1945-46. Pres. Scottish Junior Unionists, 1948-51; contested (U) Dunbartonshire, 1945 and West Dunbartonshire, general election and bye-election, 1950; MP (C) South Paddington, 1951-66; Assistant Whip, 1953-55; PPS to the Prime Minister, 1955-58; Parly and Financial Sec., Admiralty, Jan. 1958-Jan. 1959; Parly Under-Sec., Foreign Office, 1959-60. A Treasurer, Conservative and Unionist Party Organization, 1960-65; Chm., Conservative Central Board of Finance, 1961-66. A Governor, BBC, 1971-76; a Governor of Harrow School, 1968-; a Trustee and Chm., Lord Mayor Treloar Schools. Commander Légion d'Honneur, 1943;† Croix de Guerre, 1943 (France); Officer of Legion of Merit, 1944 (USA); despatches (5 times). *Publication:* The Open Door Policy in China, 1939. *Recreation:* sailing. *Address:* 5 Campden House Terrace, W8. *T:* 01-727 9515. *Club:* Royal Yacht Squadron.

ALLAN, Sir Anthony James Allan H.; *see* Havelock-Allan.

ALLAN, (Charles) Lewis (Cuthbert), MA, CEng, FICE, FIEE, FBIM; Chairman, South of Scotland Electricity Board, 1967-73 (Deputy Chairman, 1964-67); Member, North of Scotland Hydro-Electric Board, 1967-73; *b* 22 July 1911; *s* of Charles W. Allan, Edinburgh, and Isabella H. Young; *m* 1938, Kathleen Mary Robinson, Chesterfield, Derbyshire; one *s* three *d. Educ:* Merchiston Castle School, Edinburgh; Pembroke College, Cambridge (Mechanical Sciences Tripos). Bruce Peebles & Co. Ltd, Edinburgh, 1933-35; Balfour Beatty & Co. Ltd, 1935-38; Central Electricity Board, 1938-41; Ipswich Corp. Electric Supply and Transport Dept, 1941-44; North of Scotland Hydro-Electric Board, 1944-63 (Chief Electrical and Mechanical Engineer, 1954-63). *Publications:* articles in the electrical technical press and for World Power Conference. *Recreations:* gardening, walking, fishing, piping, Church work. *Address:* Killallodar, North Connel, Argyll PA37 1RE. *Club:* Royal Scottish Automobile (Glasgow).

ALLAN, Colin Faulds, CB 1976; Chief Planning Inspector (Director of Planning Inspectorate), Department of the Environment, since 1971; *b* Newcastle upon Tyne, 1917; *s* of late Jack Stanley and Ruth Allan; *m* 1940, Aurea, 2nd *d* of Algernon Noble, Hexham; one *s* one *d. Educ:* Royal Grammar Sch., Newcastle upon Tyne; King's Coll. (Newcastle), Durham Univ. DipArch, ARIBA, DipTP (Distinction), FRTPI. Capt., RA, 1940-45; served in Iraq, India, Burma (despatches). Chief Asst to Dr Thomas Sharp, Planning Consultant, 1945-47; Area Planning Officer, Cumberland and Staffs CC, 1947-57; joined Housing and Planning Inspectorate, 1957; Chief Housing and Planning Inspector, DoE (formerly Min. of Housing and Local Govt), 1967-71. *Recreations:* walking, bird-watching, reading, eighteenth-century wineglasses. *Address:* Fieldfares, Chinthurst Lane, Shalford, Guildford, Surrey. *T:* Guildford 61528.

ALLAN, Sir Colin Hamilton, KCMG 1977 (CMG 1968); OBE 1959; Governor, Solomon Islands, and High Commissioner for Western Pacific, since 1976; *b* 23 Oct. 1921; *yr s* of late John Calder Allan, Cambridge, NZ; *m* 1955, Betty Dorothy, *e d* of late A. C. Evans, Brisbane, Australia; three *s. Educ:* Hamilton High Sch., NZ; Christchurch College, Canterbury Univ., NZ;

Magdalene College, Cambridge. Military Service, NZ, 1942-44. Cadet, Colonial Admin. Service, British Solomon Is, 1945; District Comr, Western Solomons, 1946; District Comr, Malaita, 1950; Special Lands Comr, 1953; Sen. Asst Sec., Western Pacific High Commn, 1957; Asst Resident Comr, New Hebrides, 1959, British Resident Comr, 1966-73; Governor and C-in-C, Seychelles, 1973-76, and Comr, British Indian Ocean Territory, 1973-76. Commandeur, l'Ordre Nationale du Mérite (France), 1966. *Publications:* Land Tenure in the British Solomon Islands Protectorate, 1958; papers on colonial administration. *Recreations:* malacology, reading the Financial Times. *Address:* Government House, Honiara, Solomon Islands. *Club:* Royal Commonwealth Society.

ALLAN, Prof. Donald James; Professor of Greek, University of Glasgow, 1957-71; Dean of the Faculty of Arts, 1968-70; *b* 22 Dec. 1907; *s* of J. B. Allan and Ethel Allan (*née* Bullen). *Educ:* Christ's Hospital, Horsham; Christ Church, Oxford. BA 1930, MA 1933. Fellow and Tutor in Classics, Balliol College, 1931-47; Reader in Ancient Philosophy, Edinburgh Univ., 1948-57. Held temporary post at Foreign Office, 1940-45. Fellow of British Academy, 1955. Pres., Mind Assoc., 1964-65. Hon. DLitt Edinburgh, 1977. *Publications:* Aristotle, de Caelo, 1936; Plato, Republic book I, 1940; The Philosophy of Aristotle, 1952; articles in classical and philosophical journals. *Address:* 83 Bainton Road, Oxford.

ALLAN, Gordon Buchanan, TD 1950; Chartered Accountant; *b* 11 Aug. 1914; *s* of late Alexander Buchanan Allan, MIMechE, and Irene Lilian Allan, Glasgow; *m* 1971, Gwenda Jervis Davies, *d* of late John William and Elizabeth Davies, Porthcawl, Glam. *Educ:* Glasgow Academy; High Sch. of Glasgow; Glasgow Univ. Mem. Inst. Chartered Accountants (Scot.), 1937. Commissioned into Royal Signals (TA), 1938. Served War of 1939-45: DAAG, GHQ, India, 1945, (Major). Director: George Outram & Co. Ltd, 1960-75 (Dep. Man. Dir and Financial Dir, 1970-75); Holmes McDougall Ltd, 1966-72. Mem. Press Council, 1969-74. Vice-Pres., Scottish Daily Newspaper Soc., 1970, Pres. 1971-73; Dir, Glasgow Chamber of Commerce, 1971-75. Member: UK Newsprint Users' Cttee, 1972-75; Council, CBI, 1972-74; Finance Cttee, RIIA, 1975-77; Merchants' House of Glasgow, 1975-. Governor, The Queen's College, Glasgow, 1976-. *Recreations:* music, hill-walking. *Address:* 3 Winchester Court, Glasgow G12 0JN. *T:* 041-334 2353. *Club:* Royal Scottish Automobile (Glasgow).

ALLAN, Captain Henry Samuel, RD 1929; Commodore, Royal Naval Reserve and Peninsular and Oriental Steam Navigation Co. (retired); *b* 13 Dec. 1892; *o s* of John M. and Beatrice Allan, Saltcoats, Ayrshire, Scotland; *m* 1st, 1916, Ida Mary Poole, Stourbridge, Worcs; one *s*; 2nd, 1947, Isabel M. A. Fairweather, Cust, NZ. *Educ:* Ardrossan Academy, Ayrshire, Scotland. Apprentice George Smith & Sons, City Line, Glasgow, 1908-13. Joined P & OSN Co., as Junior Officer, Dec. 1913. Served European War, in RN as Sub-Lieut RNR, 1914-19, War of 1939-45 as Comdr, Capt. and Actg Cdre, RNR, 1939-46 (despatches); Commodore of Convoys, Captain HMS Largs, Normandy and South of France landings, and HMS Artifex, British Pacific Fleet. Commander, P&OSN Co., 1946; Command P&O SS Strathaird, 1947-Dec. 1952; Commodore P&OSN Co., Dec. 1951-Dec. 1952 (retd). Order of St Stanislas, 3rd Class, 1915. *Address:* 136 North Road, Hythe, Kent. *T:* Hythe 66916.

ALLAN, Rt. Rev. Hugh James Pearson; *see* Keewatin, Bishop of.

ALLAN, James Nicholas, CBE 1976; Counsellor, Foreign and Commonwealth Office, since 1976; *b* 22 May 1932; *s* of Morris Edward Allan and Joan Bach; *m* 1961, Helena Susara Crouse; one *s* one *d*. *Educ:* Gresham's Sch.; London Sch. of Economics. HM Forces, 1950-53. Asst Principal, CRO, 1956-58; Third, later Second Sec., Cape Town/Pretoria, 1958-59; Private Sec. to Parly Under-Sec., 1959-61; First Secretary: Freetown, 1961-64; Nicosia, 1964; CRO, later FCO, 1964-68; Head of Chancery, Peking, 1969-71; Luxembourg, 1971-73; Counsellor, seconded to Northern Ireland Office, Belfast, 1973-75. *Address:* c/o Foreign and Commonwealth Office, SW1. *Club:* Athenæum.

ALLAN, Commissioner Janet Laurie; retired 1957; *b* 20 March 1892; *d* of Thomas Alexander Allan, chemist, Strathaven, Scotland. *Educ:* in Scotland. Entered Salvation Army Training Coll., 1911; commissioned as sergeant to the College, 1912; opened Salvation Army work in Castle Douglas, Scotland, 1913; returned to Training College as a Brigade Officer, 1915; Home Officer at Training Coll., 1918; with "Calypso" Party sailed to India (South Travancore, South India), 1921; returned to England, 1929, and appointed to slum and goodwill work in British Isles; returned to India; served in Travancore, Calcutta,

and Eastern India; also Madras and Telegu country as Territorial Comdr; Territorial Comdr of Western India, 1951-54; Territorial Comdr of Southern India, 1954-57, Salvation Army. Leader Salvation Army Women's Social Work, Great Britain and Ireland, 1947; Comr, 1951. *Address:* Slavanka, 42 Belle Vue Road, Southbourne, Bournemouth, Dorset BH6 3DS. *T:* Bournemouth 46256.

ALLAN, John; Sheriff of Tayside, Central and Fife (formerly of Fife and Kinross) at Kirkcaldy since 1966; *b* 14 Aug. 1927; *s* of Dr John Allan, Cathcart, Glasgow; *m* 1955, Janet Evelyne Geddes; two *s. Educ:* Glasgow Academy; Glasgow University. Admitted a Member of the Faculty of Advocates, 1953; Sheriff-Substitute of Inverness, Moray, Nairn and Ross and Cromarty at Stornoway and Lochmaddy, 1961-66. *Recreations:* sailing, fishing. *Address:* Sheriff's Chambers, Kirkcaldy, Fife.

ALLAN, John Arthur Briscoe, CMG 1965; *b* 30 Nov. 1911; Scottish; *er s* of Eng Capt. (Retd) George Allan, New Malden; *m* 1935, Dorothy Mary; one *d. Educ:* Douai School. Served with HM Forces, 1940-48 (despatches); Lt-Col. Joined HMOCS, 1948; retired 1964 as Comr of Prisons, Kenya. Prisons assignments, ODM, FCO; Adviser of Prisons, Kenya, 1964-67; Dir of Prisons, Swaziland, 1968-71; Adviser of Prisons: Mauritius, 1974; Commonwealth Caribbean Dependencies, 1976. *Recreations:* golf, bowls, bridge. *Address:* 24 Cheddington Road, Moordown, Bournemouth BH9 3NB. *T:* Bournemouth 50526. *Clubs:* Special Forces; Queens Park (Bournemouth).

ALLAN, John Clifford, RCNC, FRINA; Director, Manpower, Dockyards, since 1975; *b* 3 Feb. 1920; *s* of James Arthur and Mary Alice Allan; *m* 1947, Dorothy Mary (*née* Dossett); two *d. Educ:* Royal Naval Coll., Greenwich. Entered Royal Corps of Naval Constructors, 1945; service at HM Dockyards: Portsmouth, Chatham, Devonport, Gibraltar, Singapore, 1950-75; Chief Constructor, Chief Executive Dockyard HQ, 1967-69, Asst Dir, 1969, Dir, 1975. *Recreations:* tennis, squash. *Address:* New Morney, Lansdown Road, Bath, Avon BA1 5TD. *T:* Bath 315237.

ALLAN, John Gray, CBE 1975; Legal Adviser and Solicitor to the Crown Estate Commissioners, 1961-77; *b* 10 Nov. 1915; *s* of late John Allan, CB, FSA, FBA, LLD, and Ida Mary (*née* Law). *Educ:* Charterhouse; Oriel College, Oxford. Called to Bar, Middle Temple, 1940. War Service, 1940-46: The Black Watch, GSO2 (War Office and Allied Land Headquarters, Melbourne), 1942-46. Legal Branch, Min. of Agriculture, Fisheries and Food, 1946-57. Deputy Legal Adviser, Crown Estate Office, 1957. *Recreations:* golf, bridge. *Address:* 5 Rheidol Terrace, N1. *T:* 01-226 7616. *Club:* Boodles.

ALLAN, Captain John Steele, CBE 1956; company director; *b* 25 Dec. 1889; *s* of late Andrew Allan, JP, Chirnside, Berwickshire; *m* 1915, Margaret, *d* of late Joseph Mason, Dunbar; one *s. Educ:* Berwickshire High School, Duns. Served War of 1914-18: 1/4 KOSB, Gallipoli, Egypt, and Palestine, 1915-17; wounded in Palestine, 1917. Pres., Aberdeen Chamber of Commerce, 1937-38. Chairman: Technical Section, Paper Makers' Assoc., 1932-34; North of Scotland Bank Ltd, 1942-50 (Director, 1939-50). Dep. Chm., White Fish Authority, 1954-56 (Chm., Scottish Cttee). Director: Home Flax Production, Min. of Supply, 1941-42; Aberdeen Steam Navigation Co. Ltd, 1940-64; (Chm., 1944-64); Burns & Laird Lines Ltd, 1955-64; Clydesdale Bank Ltd, 1950-67 (Dep. Chm., 1950-56); Wiggins Teape & Co. Ltd, 1931-51; Alex. Pirie & Sons Ltd, 1931-51; Dartford Paper Mills, 1931-51; Midland Bank Ltd, 1944-67; Midland Bank Executor and Trustee Co. Ltd, 1944-67. Rector's Assessor, Univ. of Aberdeen, 1949-50. FRIC 1926. DL Aberdeenshire, 1945-70. Chevalier 1st Class Royal Order of Vasa (Sweden), 1950. *Publications:* The Young Angler, 1949; My Picture Gallery of Memory, 1970. *Recreation:* angling. *Address:* Kinord, Links Road, North Berwick. *T:* North Berwick 2868. *Club:* New (North Berwick).

ALLAN, Lewis; *see* Allan, C. L. C.

ALLAN, William Nimmo, CMG 1948; MC 1917; FICE; engineering consultant; *b* 10 Nov. 1896; *s* of late Rev. W. G. Allan, MA, BD, Callander, Perthshire; *m* 1932, Mary Helen Burnett, *o d* of late Rev. T. Burnett Peter, MA, BD, Callander, Perthshire; two *s. Educ:* George Watson's Boys' College, Edinburgh. Served European War, 1914-19, 9th (Ser.) Bn The Gordon Highlanders, Captain (MC). BSc(Eng) Glasgow Univ., 1921. AMICE 1923, MICE 1944. Engineer with Kassala Cotton Co., Sudan, 1924; Irrigation Dept of Sudan Govt, 1927; Asst Director, 1941; Director, 1944; Irrigation Consultant to Sudan Govt, 1946-69; Consultant to FAO of UNO, Rome, 1959-67. *Address:* Little Garth, Butler's Bank, Forest Row, E Sussex. *T:* Forest Row 3553.

ALLANBRIDGE, Hon. Lord; William Ian Stewart; a Senator of the College of Justice in Scotland, since 1977; *b* 8 Nov. 1925; *s* of late John Stewart, FRIBA, and Mrs Maysie Shepherd Service or Stewart, Drimfearn, Bridge of Allan; *m* 1955, Naomi Joan Douglas, *d* of late Sir James Boyd Douglas, CBE, and of Lady Douglas, Barstibly, Castle Douglas; one *s* one *d*. *Educ:* Loretto; Glasgow and Edinburgh Univs. Sub-Lt, RNVR, 1944-46. Called to the Bar, 1951; QC (Scot.) 1965; Advocate-Depute, 1959-64; Mem., Criminal Injuries Compensation Bd, 1969-70; Home Advocate-Depute, 1970-72; Solicitor-General for Scotland, 1972-74; Temp. Sheriff-Principal of Dumfries and Galloway, Apr.-Dec. 1974. Mem., Criminal Injuries Compensation Bd, 1976-77. *Address:* 60 Northumberland Street, Edinburgh EH3 6JE. *T:* 031-556 2823. *Clubs:* New (Edinburgh); RNVR (Glasgow).

ALLANSON-WINN, family name of **Baron Headley.**

ALLARD, General Jean Victor, CC (Canada) 1968; CBE 1946; DSO 1943 (Bars 1944, 1945); ED 1946; CD 1958; Chief of Canadian Defence Staff, 1966-69; Representative of the Province of Quebec in New York, Sept. 1969-June 1970; now engaged in business as a consultant in industrial promotion; *b* Nicolet, PQ, 12 June 1913; *s* of late Ernest Allard and Victorine Trudel; *m* 1939, Simone, *d* of Gustave Piche, OBE; two *d*. *Educ:* St Laurent Coll., Montreal; St Jerome Coll., Kitchener, Ont. Joined Three Rivers Regt, 1933; Capt., 1938; Major, 1939; War of 1939-45: Co. of London Yeomanry, 1940-41; Canadian Army Staff Coll., Kingston, 1941-42 (Instructor, 1942); 5th Canadian Armoured Div.; second in command: Régt de la Chaudière; Royal 22e Regt, 1943 (Italy); Lt-Col 1944; CO Royal 22e Regt; Brig. 1945; Comd 6th Canadian Infantry Brigade, 1945 (Holland); Military Attaché Canadian Embassy, Moscow, 1945-48; Comd Eastern Quebec Area, 1948-50; idc 1951; Vice Quarter-Master Gen., Canada, 1952; Comdr, 25th Canadian Infantry Brigade Group, in Korea, 1953; Comdr 3rd Canadian Infantry Brigade, 1954; Comd Eastern Quebec Area, 1956; Maj.-Gen. 1958; Vice Chief of the General Staff, Canada, 1958; Comdr 4th Division, BAOR, 1961-63 (first Canadian to command a British Div.); Maj.-Gen. Survival, Ottawa, 1963; Lt-Gen. 1964; Chief of Operational Readiness, Canada, 1964-65; Comdr, Mobile Command, Canada, Oct. 1965-June 1966; General, 1966; Col Comdt, 12 Regt Blindé du Canada. Member: Royal Canadian Military Inst.; Royal 22e Regt Assoc.; La Régie du 22e; Royal Canadian Air Force Assoc.; Royal Canadian Naval Service Assoc.; Cercle Universitaire d'Ottawa; Chm. Bd of Governors, Ottawa Univ., 1966-69, Member Bd, 1969-. Hon. DSS Laval, 1958; Hon. LLD: Ottawa, 1959; St Thomas, 1966; St Mary's, Halifax, 1969; Hon. DScMil RMC Canada, 1970. FRSA. Bronze Lion (Netherlands), 1945; Légion d'Honneur and Croix de Guerre (France), 1945; Legion of Merit (US), 1954. Kt of Magistral Grace, Sovereign and Military Order of Malta, 1967. *Recreations:* golf, music, fishing, hunting. *Address:* 3265 Boulevard du Carmel, Trois-Rivieres, Quebec, Canada. *Clubs:* Quebec Garrison, KI-8-EB Gulf.

ALLARDICE, William Arthur Llewellyn; His Honour Judge Allardice; a Circuit Judge since 1972 (Midland and Oxford Circuit); *b* 18 Dec. 1924; *s* of late W. C. Allardice, MD, FRCSEd, JP, and late Constance Winifred Allardice; *m* 1956, Jennifer Ann, *d* of G. H. Jackson, Cape Town; one *s* one *d*. *Educ:* Stonyhurst Coll.; University Coll., Oxford (MA). Open Schol., Classics, 1942; joined Rifle Bde, 1943, commnd 1944; served with 52nd LI, Europe and Palestine, 1945; Oxford, 1946-48; called to Bar, Lincoln's Inn, 1950; practised Oxford Circuit, 1950-71. *Recreations:* local history, matters equestrian. *Address:* The Toft, Dunston, Stafford, *T:* Bradley 343.

ALLASON, Lt-Col James Harry, OBE 1953; *b* 6 Sept. 1912; *s* of late Brigadier-General Walter Allason, DSO; *m* 1946, Nuala Elveen (marr. diss. 1974), *d* of late J. A. McArevey, Foxrock, Co. Dublin; two *s*. *Educ:* Haileybury; RMA, Woolwich. Commissioned RA, 1932; transferred 3rd DG, 1937; War Service India and Burma, 1939-44; retired 1953. Member Kensington Borough Council, 1956-65. Contested (C) Hackney Central, General Election, 1955; MP (C) Hemel Hempstead, 1959-Sept. 1974; PPS to Sec. of State for War, 1960-64. *Recreations:* ski-ing, sailing. *Address:* 82 Ebury Mews, SW1. *T:* 01-730 1576. *Clubs:* White's; Royal Yacht Squadron.

ALLAUN, Frank; MP (Lab), East Salford, since 1955; *b* 27 Feb. 1913; *s* of Harry and Hannah Allaun; *m* 1941, Lilian Ball; one *s* one *d*. *Educ:* Manchester Grammar Sch. BA (Com); ACA. Town Hall Correspondent, and later Industrial Correspondent, Manchester Evening News; Northern Industrial Correspondent, Daily Herald; Editor, Labour's Northern Voice, 1951-67. Mem., NUJ; formerly Mem. AEU and Shop Assistants' Union; National Chm. Labour Action for Peace; helped organise first Aldermaston march. Vice-Pres. Assoc. of Public Health Inspectors. PPS to the Secretary of State for the Colonies, Oct. 1964-March 1965, resigned. Mem., Labour Party National Executive, 1967-. *Publications:* Stop the H Bomb Race, 1959; Heartbreak Housing, 1966; Your Trade Union and You, 1950; No Place Like Home, 1972; The Wasted £30 Billions, 1975; numerous broadcasts. *Recreations:* walking, swimming. *Address:* 1 South Drive, Manchester M21 2DX. *T:* 061-881 7547.

ALLAWAY, Percy Albert, CBE 1973; Director, EMI Ltd, since 1965; Chairman, EMI Electronics Ltd, since 1968; *b* 22 Aug. 1915; *s* of Albert Edward Allaway and Frances Beatrice (*née* Rogers); *m* 1959, Margaret Lilian Petyt. *Educ:* Southall Technical College. CEng, MIProdE, FIERE, FIQA. Trained EMI Ltd, 1930-35, returned 1940: Dir, Development Co., 1954; EMI Electronics Ltd: Dir 1956; Dep. Man. Dir 1957; Man. Dir 1961; Chairman: EMI-Varian Ltd; EMI-MEC Ltd; EMIHUS Ltd; Director: Nuclear Enterprises Ltd; EMI Sound & Vision Ltd; RDL (EMI) Ltd; SE Labs (EMI) Ltd. Pres., EEA, 1969-70 (former Mem. Council). Chm., Defence Industries Quality Assurance Panel; Past Chm. and Hon. Mem., NCQR; Mem., Nat. Electronics Council; Mem., Raby Cttee, 1968-69; Pres., IERE; a Vice-Pres., and Mem. Council: Inst. of Works Managers; IQA; Mem. Exec. Cttee, CEI. Mem., Bd of Governors, Central School of Art and Design; Mem. Bd, Industrial Inst., and Mem., Court and Council, Brunel Univ. CompIEE. FRSA. DTech (hc) Brunel, 1973. *Address:* Kroller, 54 Howards Wood Drive, Gerrards Cross, Bucks. *T:* Gerrards Cross 85028.

ALLCHIN, Rev. Canon Arthur Macdonald; Residentiary Canon of Canterbury Cathedral since 1973; *b* 20 April 1930; *s* of late Dr Frank Macdonald Allchin and of Louise Maude Allchin. *Educ:* Westminster Sch.; Christ Church, Oxford (BLitt, MA); Cuddesdon Coll., Oxford. Curate, St Mary Abbots, Kensington, 1956-60; Librarian, Pusey House, Oxford, 1960-69; Vis. Lectr, General Theological Seminary, NY, 1967 and 1968; Warden, Community of Sisters of Love of God, Oxford, 1967-. Editor, Sobornost, 1960-77; Jt Editor, Christian, 1971-. Hon. DD Bucharest Theol Inst., 1977. *Publications:* The Silent Rebellion, 1958; The Spirit and the Word, 1963; (with J. Coulson) The Rediscovery of Newman, 1967; Ann Griffiths, 1976; contrib. Studia Liturgica, Irenikon, Theology, Eastern Churches Review. *Recreations:* music, poetry, walking in hill country. *Address:* 12 The Precincts, Canterbury CT1 2EH. *T:* 0227 63060.

ALLCOCK, John Gladding Major, CB 1964; *b* 20 July 1905; *o s* of Rev. William Gladding Allcock, MA (TCD), and Ada Allcock (*née* Hall); *m* 1936, Eileen, *d* of Dr Ll. A. Baiss, OBE, Swanage, Dorset; one *s* one *d*. *Educ:* St Paul's School; Jesus College, Cambridge. Classical Tripos Cl. II in Pts I and II, BA 1927; MA 1931. Asst Master: Exeter School, 1927-28; Liverpool College, 1928-35. HM Inspector of Schools, 1935. Awarded Commonwealth Fund Fellowship, 1939. War Service in Admiralty, 1939-44. Divisional Inspector (NW Div.), 1949; Chief Inspector for Educational Developments, 1959-66, retired. *Recreations:* music, theatre, foreign travel. *Address:* Russet Cottage, Corfe Castle, Dorset. *T:* Corfe Castle 574.

ALLCROFT, Sir Philip Magnus-; see Magnus-Allcroft, Sir Philip.

ALLDAY, Coningsby, CBE 1971; BSc (Hons); Managing Director, British Nuclear Fuels Ltd, since 1971; Member, UKAEA, since 1976; *b* 21 Nov. 1920; *s* of late Esca and Margaret Allday; *m* 1945, Iris Helena Adams; one *s* one *d*. *Educ:* Solihull Sch.; BSc (Hons) Chemistry, London. ICI, 1939-59; UKAEA, 1959-71: Chief Chemist, Technical Dir, Commercial Dir, Dep. Man. Dir. *Recreations:* gardening, music. *Address:* British Nuclear Fuels Ltd, Risley, Warrington, Cheshire. *Club:* East India, Devonshire, Sports and Public Schools.

ALLDIS, Air Cdre Cecil Anderson, CBE 1962; DFC 1941; AFC 1956; RAF (retd); Counsellor (Defence Supply) HM Embassy, Bonn, since 1970; *b* 28 Sept. 1918; 2nd *s* of John Henry and Margaret Wright Alldis, Birkenhead; *m* 1942, Jeanette Claire Tarrant, *d* of Albert Edward Collingwood and Aida Mary Tarrant, Johannesburg; no *c*. *Educ:* Birkenhead; Emmanuel Coll., Cambridge (MA). Served War, 1939-45 (despatches, DFC): Pilot, Wing Comdr, RAF, Bomber Command. Asst Air Attaché, Moscow, 1947-49; Flying and Staff appts, RAF, 1949-59; Dir of Administrative Planning, Air Ministry, 1959-62; Air Attaché, Bonn, 1963-66. Retd from RAF and entered Home Civil Service, 1966; MoD, 1966-69; seconded to HM Diplomatic Service, 1970. *Recreations:* golf, fishing. *Address:* Tudor Cottage, Oxshott Way, Cobham, Surrey. *T:* Cobham 4789. *Club:* Naval and Military.

ALLDRITT, Walter, JP; Regional Secretary, National Union of General and Municipal Workers, in Liverpool, North Wales, and Northern Ireland, since Oct. 1970; *b* 4 July 1918; *s* of late Henry and Bridget Alldritt; *m* 1945, Mary Teresa, *d* of W. H. McGuinness; four *s* one *d. Educ:* St Francis de Sales; Liverpool University (WEA). Served with HM Forces, 1939-46. Trade Union Officer. MP (Lab) Scotland Div. of Liverpool, June 1964-Feb. 1971. Member various public bodies. Councillor 1955, JP 1958, Liverpool. *Address:* 104 Longmeadow Road, Knowsley, Prescot, Merseyside. *T:* 051-546 5703.

ALLEGRO, John Marco; author; *b* 17 Feb. 1923; *s* of late John Marco Allegro and Mabel Jessie (*née* Perry); *m* 1948, Joan Ruby Lawrence; one *s* one *d. Educ:* Wallington County Grammar Sch.; Univ. of Manchester. Royal Navy, 1941-46; Manchester Univ. 1947-52; BA 1st cl. Hons Oriental Studies, 1951; MA 1952; Bles Hebrew Prize, 1950; Scarborough Sen. Studentship, 1951-54; Leverhulme Research Award, 1958; Oxford Univ. (Magdalen), research in Hebrew dialects, 1952-53; University of Manchester: Lectureship in Comparative Semitic Philology and in Hebrew, 1954-62; Lectr in Old Testament and Intertestamental Studies, 1962-70. Brit. rep. on Internat. editing team for Dead Sea Scrolls, Jerusalem, 1953-; Adviser to Jordanian Govt on Dead Sea Scrolls, 1961-; Trustee and Hon. Sec. of Dead Sea Scrolls Fund, 1962-70. Organiser and leader of archaeological expedns to Jordan, 1959-. Popular lectr and broadcaster on archaeological subjects. TV films include: Dead Sea Scrolls, BBC, 1957; Search in the Kidron, BBC, 1963. *Publications:* The Dead Sea Scrolls (Pelican), 1956 (revised edn 1964); The People of the Dead Sea Scrolls, 1958; The Treasure of the Copper Scroll, 1960 (revised edn 1964); Search in the Desert, 1964; The Shapira Affair, 1964; Discoveries in the Judæan Desert, V, 1968; The Sacred Mushroom and the Cross, 1970; The End of a Road, 1970; The Chosen People, 1971; Lost Gods, 1977; articles in learned jls on Semitic philology. *Recreations:* ciné and still photography; sketching. *Address:* Craigmore, Ballasalla, Isle of Man. *T:* Castletown 2345.
See also Sir Douglas A . V . Allen .

ALLEN, family name of **Barons Allen of Abbeydale** and **Allen of Fallowfield.**

ALLEN OF ABBEYDALE, Baron *cr* 1976 (Life Peer), of the City of Sheffield; **Philip Allen,** GCB 1970 (KCB 1964; CB 1954); Member, Security Commission, since 1973; *b* 8 July 1912; *yr s* of late Arthur Allen and Louie Tipper, Sheffield; *m* 1938, Marjorie Brenda Coe. *Educ:* King Edward VII Sch., Sheffield; Queens' Coll., Cambridge (Whewell Schol. in internat. Law, 1934; Hon. Fellow 1974). Entered Home Office, 1934; Offices of War Cabinet, 1943-44; Commonwealth Fellowship in USA, 1948-49; Deputy Chm. of Prison Commn for England and Wales, 1950-52; Asst Under Sec. of State, Home Office, 1952-55; Deputy Sec., Min. of Housing and Local Govt, 1955-60; Deputy Under-Sec. of State, Home Office, 1960-62; Second Sec., HM Treasury, 1963-66; Permanent Under-Sec. of State, Home Office, 1966-72. Chairman: Occupational Pensions Bd, 1973-; Nat. Council of Social Service, 1973-77; Gaming Bd for GB, 1977- (Mem., 1975). Member Royal Commissions: on Standards of Conduct in Public Life, 1974-76; on Civil Liability and Compensation for Personal Injury, 1973-. Chief Counting Officer, EEC Referendum, 1975. *Address:* Holly Lodge, Englefield Green, Surrey TW20 0JP. *T:* Egham 2291. *Club:* Brooks's.

ALLEN OF FALLOWFIELD, Baron *cr* 1974 (Life Peer), of Fallowfield; **Alfred Walter Henry Allen,** CBE 1967; General Secretary, Union of Shop Distributive & Allied Workers, since 1962; a Crown Estate Commissioner since 1965; *b* Bristol, 7 July 1914; *m* 1940, Ruby Millicent Hounsell; one *s* one *d. Educ:* East Bristol Sch. Bristol Co-operative Society, 1931-40. RAF (Sergeant), 1940-45. Apptd Area Organiser, Nat. Union Distributive & Allied Workers, 1946; Nat. Officer, Union of Shop Distributive & Allied Workers, 1951. Member: Gen. Council of TUC (Chm., 1973-74); Industrial Arbitration Bd, 1973-; Government Cttee of Inquiry into Statutory Smallholdings, 1963; Council of the Manchester Business Sch.; NEDC; CIR, 1969-70; British Airports Authority, 1976-; Equal Opportunities Commn, 1975-; Cttee to Review the Functioning of Financial Institutions, 1977-. Chairman: EDC for Chemical Industry, 1975-; TUC Economic Cttee, 1975-; Governor, BBC, 1976-. Dir Industrial Training Service; Governor, Ruskin Coll. *Recreations:* reading, theatre, gardening, cricket. *Address:* Oakley, 188 Wilmslow Road, Fallowfield, Manchester M14 6LJ. *T:* 061-224 2804; 83 Manley Road, Sale, Cheshire. *T:* 061-973 3058.

ALLEN, Hon. Alfred Ernest, CMG 1973; JP; President, Associated Trustee Savings Banks of New Zealand, since 1976 (Vice-President, 1974-76); Chairman, Blinded Servicemen's Trust Board, since 1961; *b* Onehunga, NZ, 20 May 1912; 4th *s* of Ernest Richard Allen and Harriet May Allen; *m* 1935, Nancy, 3rd *d* of Frederick Arthur Cutfield and Ethel Cutfield; one *s* three *d. Educ:* numerous primary schs; Auckland Grammar School. Farm hand, 1927; farming on own account from 1933. Served War of 1939-45, 24 Bn 2 NZEF, Middle East (Sgt-Major). MP Franklin, NZ, 1957-72; Junior Govt Whip, 1963-66; Chief Govt Whip, 1966-69; Chm. of Cttees and Deputy Speaker, 1969-71; Speaker, House of Representatives, 1972. Is a Freemason (Past Master). Mem., Auckland Electric Power Bd, 1948- (Chm., 1956, 1957 and 1958). Pres., Bd of Trustees, Auckland Savings Bank, 1973-75 (Vice-Pres., 1972-73). *Recreations:* bowls, horse racing; formerly Rugby football (Country Union Rep.), tennis. *Address:* 32 Carlton Crescent, Maraetai Beach, Auckland, New Zealand. *T:* Beachlands 6595. *Clubs:* Franklin (Pukekohe); Returned Servicemen's (Franklin); (Hon. Mem.) Bellamy's (Wellington).

ALLEN, Arnold Millman, CBE 1977; Member for Finance and Administration, UKAEA, since 1976; *b* 30 Dec. 1924; *s* of Wilfrid Millman and Edith Muriel Allen; *m* 1947, Beatrice Mary Whitaker; three *s* one *d. Educ:* Hackney Downs Sec. Sch.; Peterhouse, Cambridge (Scholar). Entered HM Treasury, 1945; Private Sec. to Financial Secretary, 1951-52; Principal, HM Treasury, 1953-55; Private Sec. to Chm. of UKAEA (Lord Plowden), 1956-57; HM Treasury, 1958; Dir of Personnel and Admin., Development and Engineering Group (subseq. Reactor Group), UKAEA, 1959-63; Gen. Manager, British Waterways Bd, 1963-68, and Mem. of Bd 1965-68; Personnel Officer, 1968-69, Personnel and Programmes Officer, 1970, Secretary and Mem. for Administration, 1971, UKAEA. *Address:* 34 Brookmans Avenue, Brookmans Park, Herts. *T:* Potters Bar 55986. *Club:* Athenæum.

ALLEN, Arthur Cecil; retired as MP (Lab) Market Bosworth Division of Leicestershire (1945-Sept. 1959), and Opposition Whip (1951); *b* 10 Jan. 1887; *s* of Charles Allen; *m* 1914, Polly Mary Bradshaw; one *s* one *d. Educ:* Elementary School; Ruskin College. Served War of 1914-18. Mem. Exec., Nat. Union of Boot and Shoe Operatives, 1933. Alderman, Northants CC, 1937-49. Parliamentary Private Sec. to Chancellor of Exchequer and to Minister of State for Economic Affairs, 1950-51, to Leader of the Opposition, 1955-59. *Recreation:* reading. *Address:* Nenehurst, Thrift Street, Higham Ferrers, Wellingborough, Northants NN9 8AU.

ALLEN, Dr Clabon Walter; Professor of Astronomy at University College, London University, 1951-72, now Emeritus Professor; *b* 28 Dec. 1904; *s* of J. B. Allen and A. H. Allen; *m* 1937, Rose M. Smellie; five *s. Educ:* Perth High School; University of Western Australia. DSc (WA), 1935. Assistant at Commonwealth Observatory, Canberra, 1926-51. Solar Eclipse Expeditions, 1936, 1940, 1954, 1955 and 1959; Hackett Research Studentship, 1935-37. *Publications:* Astrophysical Quantities, 1955, 3rd rev. edn 1973; papers in Monthly Notices of Royal Astronomical Soc., Astro-physical Jl, Memoirs of Commonwealth Observatory, etc. *Address:* Mount Stromlo Observatory, Canberra, ACT 2600, Australia.

ALLEN, Sir Denis; *see* Allen, Sir W. D.

ALLEN, Rev. Derek William; Warden, Community of St Mary the Virgin, Wantage, since 1966; Vicar of St Saviour and St Peter's, Eastbourne, since 1976; *b* 2 Nov. 1925. *Educ:* Eastbourne College; Oriel College, Oxford. Curate of Christ the Saviour, Ealing, 1952-54. Tutor, 1954-56, Chaplain, 1956-60, St Stephen's House, Oxford. Asst Chaplain, Pembroke College, Oxford, 1955-60, Sub-Warden, King's College Hostel and Lecturer in Theology, King's College, London, 1960-62; Principal, St Stephen's House, Oxford, 1962-74. *Publications:* Articles in: Theology, Church Quarterly Review, Internat. Rev. of Missions, Lambeth Essays on Unity, Sobornost. *Address:* The Vicarage, Spencer Road, Eastbourne, Sussex BN21 4PA. *T:* 22317.

ALLEN, Prof. Deryck Norman de Garrs; Professor of Applied Mathematics in the University of Sheffield since 1955; Warden of Ranmoor House, since 1968; *b* 22 April 1918; *s* of Leonard Lincoln Allen and Dorothy Allen (*née* Asplin). *Educ:* King Edward VII School, Sheffield; Christ Church, Oxford. Messrs Rolls Royce, 1940; Research Asst to Sir Richard Southwell, FRS, 1941; Lectr in Applied Mathematics at Imperial Coll., London, 1945; Visiting Prof. in Dept of Mechanical Engineering, Massachusetts Inst. of Technology, 1949; Reader in Applied Mathematics at Imperial Coll. in Univ. of London, 1950. Pro-Vice-Chancellor, Sheffield Univ., 1966-70; Chm., Jt Matriculation Bd, 1973-76. *Publications:* Relaxation Methods, 1954 (US); papers on Applied Maths and Engineering Maths in:

Proc. Royal Soc.; Philosophical Trans. of Royal Soc.; Quarterly Jl of Mechanics and Applied Maths; Jl of Instn of Civil Engineers. *Recreation:* travel. *Address:* Ranmoor House, Sheffield, S Yorkshire. *T:* Sheffield 686645.

ALLEN, Donald George; HM Diplomatic Service; Counsellor and Head of Chancery, UK Permanent Delegation to OECD, Paris, since 1974; *b* 26 June 1930; *s* of Sidney George Allen and Doris Elsie (*née* Abercombie); *m* 1955, Sheila Isobel Bebbington; three *s*. *Educ:* Southall Grammar School. Foreign Office, 1948; HM Forces, 1949-51; FO, 1951-54; The Hague, 1954-57; 2nd Sec. (Commercial), La Paz, 1957-60; FO, 1961-65: 1st Sec. 1962; Asst Private Sec. to Lord Privy Seal, 1961-63 and to Minister without Portfolio, 1963-64; 1st Sec., Head of Chancery and Consul, Panama, 1966-69; FCO, 1969-72; Counsellor on secondment to NI Office, Belfast, 1972-74. *Recreations:* squash, tennis, golf. *Address:* c/o Foreign and Commonwealth Office, SW1A 2JD; 99 Parkland Grove, Ashford, Mddx TW15 2JF. *T:* Ashford 55617. *Club:* Royal Automobile.

ALLEN, Sir Donald (Richard), Kt 1954; OBE 1944; MC and Bar 1917; Clerk to Trustees of London Parochial Charities, 1930-65; *b* 31 Aug. 1894; *s* of Thomas Allen and Elizabeth (*née* Willett); *m* 1918, Irene Dora Andrews (*d* 1965); one *s* one *d*. *Educ:* William Morris School, Walthamstow. Served European War, RFA, 1914-18; Ministry of Health, 1919-25; Assistant Clerk, London Parochial Charities, 1925: Barrister-at-Law, Inner Temple, 1928; Mem. Cttee on Charitable Trusts, 1950-52. *Publication:* History City Parochial Foundation, 1951. *Address:* Sprigg's Court, Epping, Essex. *Club:* Reform.

ALLEN, Sir Douglas (Albert Vivian), GCB 1973 (KCB 1967; CB 1963); Head of the Home Civil Service and Permanent Secretary, Civil Service Department, 1974-77; *b* 15 Dec. 1917; *s* of late Albert Allen; *m* 1941, Sybil Eileen Allegro, *d* of late John Marco Allegro; two *s* one *d*. *Educ:* Wallington County Grammar Sch.; London School of Economics. BSc (Econ.) First Class Hons, 1938. Entered Board of Trade, 1939; Royal Artillery, 1940-45; Cabinet Office, 1947; Treasury, 1948-58; Under-Secretary, Ministry of Health, 1958-60; Under-Secretary, Treasury 1960-62, Third Secretary, 1962-64; Dept of Economic Affairs: Dep. Under-Sec. of State, 1964-66; Second Permanent Under-Sec. of State, May-Oct. 1966; Permanent Under-Sec. of State, 1966-68; Permanent Sec., HM Treasury, 1968-74. FBIM 1969; FRSA 1975. Hon. Fellow, LSE, 1969; Hon DSc Southampton, 1977. *Recreations:* tennis, woodwork. *Address:* 9 Manor Way, South Croydon, Surrey. *T:* 01-688 0496. *Club:* Reform.

See also J. M. Allegro.

ALLEN, Fergus Hamilton, CB 1969; ScD, MA, MAI, FICE; First Civil Service Commissioner, Civil Service Department, since 1974; *b* 3 Sept. 1921; *s* of Charles Winckworth Allen and Marjorie Helen, *d* of F. J. S. Budge; *m* 1947, Margaret Joan, *d* of Prof. M. J. Gorman; two *d*. *Educ:* Newtown Sch., Waterford; Trinity Coll., Dublin. ScD 1966. Asst Engineer, Sir Cyril Kirkpatrick and Partners, 1943-48; Port of London Authority, 1949-52; Asst Director, Hydraulics Research Station, DSIR, 1952-58; Dir of Hydraulics Research, DSIR, 1958-65; Chief Scientific Officer, Cabinet Office, 1965-69; Civil Service Comr, 1969-74; Scientific and Technological Advr, CSD, 1969-72. Instn Civil Engrs: Telford Gold Medal, 1958; Mem. Council, 1962-67, 1968-71. *Publications:* papers in technical journals; poems. *Address:* Dundrum, Wantage Road, Streatley, Berks RG8 9LB. *T:* Goring 3234. *Club:* Athenæum.

ALLEN, Frank Graham; Clerk of the Journals, House of Commons, since 1975; *b* 13 June 1920; *s* of Percy and Gertrude Allen; *m* 1947, Barbara Caulton; one *s* one *d*. *Educ:* Shrewsbury Sch. (Schol.); Keble Coll., Oxford (Exhibr, BA). 7th Bn Worcs Regt, 1940-46, India, 1942-44. Asst Clerk, House of Commons, 1946; Clerk to House of Commons Expenditure Cttee, 1971-75; Principal Clerk, 1973. Mem. House of Laity, General Synod, Church of England, 1970. *Address:* March Mount, Haddon Road, Chorleywood, Herts. *T:* 01-260 2709.

ALLEN, Prof. Geoffrey, PhD; FRS 1976; FInstP; Professor of Chemical Technology, Imperial College of Science and Technology, since 1976; Chairman, Science Research Council, since 1977 (Member, since 1976); *b* 29 Oct. 1928; *s* of John James and Marjorie Allen; *m* 1972, Valerie Frances Duckworth; one *d*. *Educ:* Clay Cross Tupton Hall Grammar Sch.; Univ. of Leeds (BSc, PhD). FInstP 1977; FPRI 1974. Postdoctoral Fellow, Nat. Res. Council, Canada, 1952-54; Lectr, Univ. of Manchester, 1955-65, Prof. of Chemical Physics, 1965-75; Prof. of Polymer Science, Imperial Coll. of Science and Technol., 1975-76. Hon. MSc Manchester. *Publications:* papers on chemical physics of polymers in Trans Faraday Soc., Polymer.

Recreations: walking, talking and eating. *Address:* 40 Pine Grove, Lake Road, Wimbledon, SW19 7HE. *T:* 01-947 7459. *Club:* Athenæum.

ALLEN, Rt. Rev. Geoffrey Francis, DD; *b* 25 August 1902; 2nd *s* of late John Edward Taylor Allen, Holt House, Mobberley, Cheshire, and Mabel Saunders; *m* 1932, Madeline, *d* of Rev. R. J. S. Gill, Tadworth, Surrey. *Educ:* Rugby (Scholar); University College, Oxford (Scholar); Ripon Hall, Oxford (1st Class Philosophy, Politics, and Economics, 1924; 2nd Class Theology, 1926). Liverpool Intercollegiate Secretary of the Student Christian Movement, 1926; Curate of St Saviour's, Liverpool, 1927; Chaplain of Ripon Hall, Oxford, 1928; Fellow and Chaplain of Lincoln College, Oxford, 1930-35; Union Theological College, Canton, 1935; Deputy Provost, Birmingham Cathedral, 1941; Sec. National Christian Council of China and Chaplain to British Embassy, Chungking, 1942-44; Archdeacon of Birmingham, 1944-47; Bishop in Egypt, 1947-52; Principal of Ripon Hall, Oxford, 1952-59; Bishop of Derby, 1959-69. *Publications:* Tell John, 1932 (part author); He that Cometh, 1932; Christ the Victorious, 1935; The Courage to be Real, 1938; Law with Liberty, 1942; The Theology of Missions, 1943. Contributor, The Churches and Christian Unity (ed R. J. W. Bevan), 1963. *Recreations:* the company of our friends, our garden. *Address:* The Knowle, Deddington, Oxford OX5 4TB. *T:* Deddington 225. *Clubs:* Athenæum, English-Speaking Union.

ALLEN, Prof. George Cyril, CBE 1958; FBA 1965; MCom, PhD; Emeritus Professor of Political Economy in the University of London; *b* Kenilworth, Warwickshire, 28 June 1900; *s* of late George Henry and late Elizabeth Allen; *m* 1929, Eleanora, (*d* 1972), *d* of late David Shanks, JP, Moseley, Birmingham. *Educ:* King Henry VIII School, Coventry; University of Birmingham. Lecturer in Economics at the Higher Commercial College, Nagoya, Japan, 1922-25; Research Fellow and Lecturer in the Faculty of Commerce, University of Birmingham, 1925-29; Professor of Economics and Commerce, University College, Hull, 1929-33; Brunner Professor of Economic Science, University of Liverpool, 1933-47; Prof. of Political Economy, Univ. of London, 1947-67; Temp. Asst Sec., Board of Trade, 1941-44. Member of Central Price Regulation Cttee, 1944-53; Temp. Counsellor, Foreign Office, Oct. 1945-April 1946. President of Economics Section, British Association, 1950; Mem. of Monopolies (and Restrictive Practices) Commn, 1950-62; Vice-Pres., Royal Economic Soc. Hon. Fellow, SOAS, Univ. of London, 1973. Order of the Rising Sun (Third Class) (Japan). *Publications:* The Industrial Development of Birmingham and the Black Country, 1860-1927, 1929, repr. 1966; British Industries and their Organization, 1933 (rev. edn 1970); Japan: the Hungry Guest, 1938; Japanese Industry: Its Recent Development and Present Condition, 1939; (part-author) The Industrialization of Japan and Manchukuo, 1930-1940, 1940; A Short Economic History of Japan, 1946 (rev. edn 1972); (jt) Western Enterprise in Far Eastern Economic Development: China and Japan, 1954; (jt) Western Enterprise in Indonesia and Malaya, 1957; Japan's Economic Expansion, 1965; The Structure of Industry in Britain, 1961 (rev. edn 1970); Japan as a Market and Source of Supply, 1967; Monopoly and Restrictive Practices, 1968; The British Disease, 1976. *Recreations:* painting, reading. *Address:* Flat 15, Ritchie Court, 380 Banbury Road, Oxford. *T:* Oxford 50417. *Club:* Reform.

ALLEN, George Oswald Browning, CBE 1962; TD 1945; *b* 31 July 1902; *s* of late Sir Walter M. Allen, KBE. *Educ:* Eton; Trinity College, Cambridge. GSO1, War Office, 1943-45. Member of London Stock Exchange. Cricket: Eton XI, 1919-21; Cambridge Univ., 1922-23; represented England in 25 Test Matches; Captain *v* India, 1936, *v* Australia, 1936-37, *v* West Indies, 1948; Chm. Selection Cttee, 1955-61; Chm. MCC cricket sub cttee, 1956-63; President, MCC, 1963-64; Treasurer, 1964-76. Legion of Merit (USA). *Recreations:* cricket, golf. *Address:* 4 Grove End Road, NW8. *T:* 01-286 4601. *Club:* White's.

ALLEN, Godfrey; see Allen, W. G.

ALLEN, Harold Major, QC 1965; *b* 2 Oct 1911; *o s* of Arthur Major Allen, journalist, and Minnie Emily (*née* Camfield); *m* 1942, Joan Renée (*née* Boesche); one *d*. *Educ:* Merchant Taylors' School. Inland Revenue Dept, 1935-50. Called to Bar, Gray's Inn, 1949; practised at Bar, 1950-72. *Recreations:* boats, walking and conversation. *Address:* 9 Harewood Green, Keyhaven, Hants. *Club:* Royal Lymington Yacht.

ALLEN, (Harold) Norman (Gwynne), CBE 1966; retired 1977; *b* 30 April 1912; *yr s* of Harold Gwynne Allen and Hilda Margaret Allen (*née* Langley), Bedford; *m* 1938, Marjorie Ellen (*née* Brown); one *s* three *d*. *Educ:* Westminster Sch.; Trinity Coll.,

Cambridge, BA 1933, MA 1936, Cantab; FICE, FIMechE, FRINA, FIMarE, FIProdE. Engrg trng, John Samuel White & Co. Ltd, Cowes, John Brown & Co. Ltd, Clydebank, and in Merchant Navy, 1933-37; W. H. Allen Sons & Co. Ltd, Bedford: progressive staff appts, 1937-43; Dir 1943-77; Techn. Dir 1945-52; Jt Man. Dir 1952-; Dep. Chm. 1962-70; Chm. 1970-77; Amalgamated Power Engrg Ltd, Bedford: Techn. Dir 1968-70; Dep. Chm. 1970-77. Belliss & Morcom Ltd, Birmingham, 1968-. Mem. Bedfordshire CC, 1947-50. Mem. Council: British Internal Combustion Engrg Res. Assoc., 1952-60 (Chm. 1953-54); British Hydromechanics Res. Assoc., 1947-59; IMechE, 1952-70 (Vice-Pres. 1959-65, Pres. 1965); Mem. Adv. Cttee, Nat. Engrg Lab., 1971-73 (Mem. Steering Cttee 1962-68); Mem. British Transport Commn Res. Adv. Council, 1958-60; Vice-Chm. of Council, Mander Coll., Bedford, 1958-74; Governor, Coll. of Aeronautics, Cranfield, 1955-69 (Vice-Chm. 1962-69); Charter Pro-Chancellor, Cranfield Inst. of Technology, 1969-75; Mem. Bd, Council of Engrg Instns, 1964-66; Mem. Exec. Bd, BSI, 1970-76. Provost, Buffalo Hunt of Manitoba, 1960. Hon. DSc Bath, 1967; Hon. DSc Cranfield, 1977. *Publications:* papers in jls of IMarE, S African IMechE, Engrg Inst. Canada, IMechE. *Recreations:* sailing, gardening (FRHS), countryside (Mem. Nat. Trust), magic (Mem. Magic Circle). *Address:* Gwylfa, Bontddu, Dolgellau, Gwynedd. *T:* Bontddu 230. *Clubs:* United Oxford & Cambridge University; Island Sailing.

ALLEN, Prof. Harry Cranbrook, MC 1944; Professor of American Studies, since 1971, and Dean of the School of English and American Studies, since 1974, University of East Anglia; *b* 23 March 1917; *s* of Christopher Albert Allen and Margaret Enid (*née* Hebb); *m* 1947, Mary Kathleen Andrews; one *s* two *d*. *Educ:* Bedford School; Pembroke College, Oxford (Open Scholar; 1st cl. hons Modern History; MA). Elected Fellow, Commonwealth Fund of New York, 1939 (held Fellowship, Harvard Univ., Jan-Sept. 1946). Served War of 1939-45, with Hertfordshire and Dorsetshire Regts, in France and Germany (Major); comdt 43rd Division Educational Coll., June-Nov. 1945. Fellow and Tutor in Modern History, Lincoln College, Oxford, 1946-55; Commonwealth Fund Prof. of American History, University Coll., 1955-71, and Dir, Inst. of United States Studies, 1966-71, Univ. of London; Senior Research Fellow, Austr. Nat. Univ., Canberra, and Visiting Scholar, Univ. of California, Berkeley, 1953-54; Schouler Lecturer, The Johns Hopkins University, April 1956; American Studies Fellow, Commonwealth Fund of New York, 1957, at the University of Virginia; Vis. Mem., Inst. for Advanced Study, Princeton, NJ, 1959; Vis. Professor: Univ. of Rochester, New York, 1963; Univ. of Michigan, Ann Arbor, 1966. Member: Dartmouth Royal Naval College Review Cttee, 1958, Naval Education Adv. Cttee, 1960-66; Academic Planning Board, Univ. of Essex, 1962; Chm., British Assoc. for American Studies, 1974-. *Publications:* Great Britain and the United States, 1955; Bush and Backwoods, 1959; The Anglo-American Relationship since 1783, 1960; The Anglo-American Predicament, 1960; The United States of America, 1964. Joint Editor, British Essays in American History, 1957. *Recreation:* travel. *Address:* Willowbank, 13 Riverside Close, Lower Hellesdon, Norwich NR6 5AU. *T:* Norwich 49795; School of English and American Studies, University of East Anglia, University Plain, Norwich NR4 7TJ. *T:* Norwich 56161. *Club:* Athenæum.

ALLEN, Brigadier Henry Isherwood, CBE 1943; DSO 1917; Commander, Legion of Merit (USA), 1946; psc; *b* 18 Nov. 1887; *s* of late Rev. Dr George Cantrell Allen; *m* 1921, Rachel Alice Houssemayne, *d* of late Col Woodford George Du Boulay of Cheltenham and widow of Capt. William Haire Forster, Royal Irish Fusiliers; (*er s* killed in action, Normandy, 1944 and one *s* decd). *Educ:* Wellington College. Gazetted North Staffordshire Regt, 1908; served European War, France, 1915; Mesopotamia, 1916-19 (DSO, Bt Majority, despatches five times); General Staff, War Office, 1921; transferred to Royal Corps of Signals; Student Staff Coll., Camberley, 1922-23; DAA and QMG 48th Div., 1924-25; GSO2, AHQ, India, 1926-27; Brigade Major 3rd (Jhelum) Infantry Brigade, 1927-29; Bt Lieut-Col 1927; Commandant School of Signals, Catterick, 1930-32; British Military Mission, Iraq Army, 1934-35; General Staff Officer, 1st Grade, War Office, 1936-38; retired pay, 1938; War Service, General Staff, 1939-45. *Address:* Beverley, Dunsfold, Surrey. *T:* Dunsfold 259.

ALLEN, Jack, DSc, LLD; FICE; FRSE; Professor of Engineering, Aberdeen University, 1946-69; *b* 19 Sept. 1905; *s* of late John and Phoebe Annie Allen, Heywood; *m* 1933, Elizabeth, *d* of late Samuel and Frances Hall, Heaton Park, Lancs. *Educ:* Elton Council School; Bury Grammar School; Manchester University, BSc (First Class Hons in Engineering) 1926; Vulcan Research Fellow, 1928-29; Asst Lecturer, 1929-35,

Lecturer, 1935-43; DSc 1939; Senior Lecturer, 1943-46 (Manchester Univ.). Engaged on investigations of Severn Barrage Scheme, Liverpool Bay training walls, proposed Humber Bridge, improvement of rivers Mersey, Dee and Parrett, Scapa Flow causeways (all as Asst to Prof. A. H. Gibson); flood relief in river Great Ouse, harbour developments at Dundee and Aberdeen, spillways on hydro-electric schemes, etc. MICE 1946; FRSE 1951 (Vice-Pres., 1964-67). James Forrest Lecturer, Institution of Civil Engineers, 1947. Member: Hydraulics Research Bd (DSIR), 1946-53, 1957-61, 1962-65; Hydraulics Research Station Steering Cttee, 1965-68; Research Advisory Council, British Transport Commn, 1957-64; Academic Advisory Council, Univs of St Andrews and Dundee, 1964-66; Chm., Res. Adv. Gp, British Transport Docks Bd, 1968-. Hon. LLD Manchester, 1968; Hon. DSc Aberdeen, 1975. *Publications:* Scale Models in Hydraulic Engineering, 1947; many papers in Jl ICE, Phil. Mag., etc. *Address:* 4 Finches Gardens, Lindfield, Sussex RH16 2PA.

ALLEN, James Godfrey Colquhoun, CMG 1956; Secretary, Nigeria Timber Association, 1961-69, retired; re-employed as Head of Social Welfare Services, 1973-76, Adviser Field Administration since 1976, Rivers State Ministry of Rural Development and Social Welfare, Port Harcourt, Nigeria; *b* 26 May 1904; *s* of Dr J. D. C. Allen and F. D. L. Allen (*née* Beckett), Bath; unmarried. *Educ:* Blundell's Sch.; Ecole Supérieure de Commerce, Lausanne; Univ. of Munich. Asst Master, Alleyn Court School, Westcliff-on-Sea, 1926. Cadet, Nigerian Administrative Service, 1926; Asst District Officer and District Officer, 1929-45; Resident, 1947; Senior Resident, 1953. Anglo-French Cameroons Boundary Commissioner, 1937-39; Nigerian Rep. with Free French, Douala, 1940; Chief Censor and Chief of Military Intelligence, Nigeria, 1940-41; W African Liaison Officer with Free French forces in Equatorial Africa, 1942-43; Political Sec. to Resident Minister, W Africa, 1943; Dep. Commissioner of the Colony, Lagos, 1946-52; Senior Resident, Rivers Province, Nigeria, 1952-56. Director of Administration, Nigerian Broadcasting Corporation, 1957-61. Mem. Bath Preservation Trust. Coronation Medal, 1953. *Publications:* A Native Court Handbook, 1955; The Organisation and Procedure of Local Government Councils, 1956. *Recreations:* golf, music. *Address:* 50 Lyncombe Hill, Bath, Avon. *T:* Bath 27903. *Clubs:* Royal Commonwealth Society; Port Harcourt.

ALLEN, Janet Rosemary; Headmistress of Benenden School, Kent, since 1976; *b* 11 April 1936; *d* of John Algernon Allen and Edna Mary Allen (*née* Orton). *Educ:* Cheltenham Ladies' Coll.; University Coll., Leicester; Hughes Hall, Cambridge. BA London 1958; CertEd Cambridge 1959. Asst Mistress, Howell's Sch., Denbigh, North Wales, 1959: Head of History Dept, 1961; in charge of First Year Sixth Form, 1968; Housemistress, 1968 and 1973-75. *Recreations:* music, drama, outdoor pursuits. *Address:* Benenden School, Cranbrook, Kent TN17 4AA. *T:* Benenden 592.

ALLEN, Prof. John F., FRS 1949; Professor of Natural Philosophy in the School of Physical Sciences, University of St Andrews, since 1947; *b* 6 May 1908; *s* of late Prof. Frank Allen, FRSC; *m* 1933, Elfriede Hiebert (marr. diss. 1951); one *s*. *Educ:* Public schools of Winnipeg, Canada. BA (University of Manitoba, 1928), MA (University of Toronto, 1930), PhD (University of Toronto, 1933). Bursar, Student and Fellow of National Research Council of Canada, 1930-33; Fellow of National Research Council of USA, 1933-35; Research Assistant, Royal Society Mond Laboratory, Cambridge, 1935-44; MA Cantab, 1936; Lecturer in Physics, Univ. of Cambridge and Fellow and Lecturer of St John's College, Cambridge, 1944-47. *Publications:* numerous scientific papers and articles, mainly on experimental low temperature physics. *Recreation:* golf. *Address:* 2 Shorehead, St Andrews, Fife. *T:* St Andrews 72717. See also *W. A. Allen*.

ALLEN, Maj.-Gen. John Geoffrey Robyn, CB 1976; Senior Army Directing Staff, Royal College of Defence Studies, since 1976; *b* 19 Aug. 1923; *s* of R. A. Allen and Mrs Allen (*née* Youngman); *m* 1959, Ann Monica (*née* Morford); one *s* one *d*. *Educ:* Haileybury. Commissioned KRRC, 1942; trans. RTR, 1947; Bt Lt-Col, 1961; Lt-Col, CO 2 RTR, 1963; Mil. Asst (GSO1) to CGS, MoD, 1965; Brig., Comd 20 Armd Bde, 1967; IDC, 1970; Dir of Operational Requirements 3 (Army), MoD, 1971; Maj.-Gen., Dir-Gen., Fighting Vehicles and Engineer Equipment, MoD, 1973-74; Dir, RAC, 1974-76. Col Comdt, RTR, 1976-. *Recreation:* dinghy sailing. *Address:* Waney Edges, Fitzroy Road, Fleet, Hants. *T:* Fleet 4570. *Club:* Army and Navy.

ALLEN, John Piers; Principal, Central School of Speech and Drama, 1972-summer 1978; *b* 30 March 1912; *s* of Percy Allen and Marjorie Nash; *m* 1937; two *s*; *m* 1945; two *s* two *d. Educ:* Aldenham Sch. Old Vic Theatre, 1933-35; Victor Gollancz Ltd, 1936-37; London Theatre Studio, 1937-39; RNVR, 1940-45; Dir, Glyndebourne Children's Theatre, 1945-51; writer-producer, BBC, 1951-61; HM Inspector of Schs, 1961-72. Mem. Enquiry into Public Subsidy for the Theatre, Council of Europe, 1977. *Publications:* Going to the Theatre, 1949; Great Moments in the Theatre, 1949; Masters of British Drama, 1957; Masters of European Drama, 1962; (ed) Three Medieval Plays, 1956. *Recreations:* pottery, gardening. *Address:* Garden Flat, 8 Upper Park Road, NW3 2UP. *T:* 01-722 2293.

ALLEN, Prof. Joseph Stanley; (first) Professor and Head of Department of Town and Country Planning, University of Newcastle upon Tyne (formerly King's College, Durham University), 1946-63 (developing first University Degree Course in Town and Country Planning); Senior Partner, J. S. Allen, Architects & Town Planning Consultants; *b* 15 March 1898; *s* of late Harry Charles Allen and of Elizabeth S. Allen; *m* 1931, Guinevere Mary Aubrey Pugh (*d* 1974); one *s* one *d. Educ:* Liverpool Collegiate School; Liverpool University. RIBA Athens Bursar, Post-graduate Study in USA; Lecturer in Architecture, Univ. of Liverpool, 1929; Head, Leeds School of Architecture, 1933-45; founded Leeds Sch. of Town and Country Planning, 1934. Vice-Chm. RIBA Bd of Architectural Education and Chm. Recognised Schools Cttee, 1943-45; Member of Council RIBA, 1943-50; Pres. Royal Town Planning Institute, 1959-60 (Vice-Pres. 1957-59). Architect and Town Planning Consultant for hospitals, churches, neighbourhood units, university and industrial undertakings. Consultant, Snowdonia National Park, 1957-74; Member, North of England Regional Advisory Committee, Forestry Commission, 1951-74; Member Diocesan Committees for Care of Churches: Ripon, Newcastle and York Dioceses. *Publications:* (with R. H. Mattocks): Report and Plan for West Cumberland; Report and Plan for Accrington (Industry and Prudence), 1950. Founder-Editor, Planning Outlook (founded 1948); contrib. to professional journals on architecture and town and country planning. *Recreations:* motoring and walking in the countryside, music, breeding Welsh ponies. *Address:* Bleach Green Farm, Ovingham, Northumberland.

ALLEN, Sir Kenneth; see Allen, Sir William Kenneth G.

ALLEN, Prof. Kenneth William; Professor of Nuclear Structure, and Fellow of Balliol College, University of Oxford, since 1963; *b* 17 Nov. 1923; *m* 1947, Josephine E. Boreham; two *s. Educ:* Ilford County High School; London University (Drapers' Scholar); St Catharine's College, Cambridge University. PhD (Cantab) 1947. Physics Division, Atomic Energy of Canada, Chalk River, 1947-51; Leverhulme Research Fellow and Lecturer, Liverpool University, 1951-54; Superintendent, later (1958) Senior Superintendent, Nuclear Research Division, Atomic Weapons Research Establishment, 1954-63. Member: Nuclear Physics Bd, SRC, 1970-73; Atlas Computer Cttee, SRC, 1972-73. *Publications:* contribs to Proc. Physical Soc., Physical Review, Review of Scientific Instruments, Nature, etc. *Recreations:* music, chess. *Address:* Ridgeway, Lincombe Lane, Boars Hill, Oxford.

ALLEN, Mark Echalaz, CMG 1966; CVO 1961; HM Diplomatic Service, retired; Ambassador and Permanent UK Representative to Disarmament Conference, Geneva, 1974-77; *b* 19 March 1917; *s* of late Lancelot John Allen and of Eleanor Mary (*née* Carlisle); *m* 1948, Elizabeth Joan, *d* of late Richard Hope Bowdler and Elsie (*née* Bryning); two *s* one *d* (and one *d* decd). *Educ:* Charterhouse; Christ Church, Oxford (MA). Appointed Asst Principal, Dominions Office, 1939. Served War of 1939-45 in Western Desert, Sicily and Italy. Dublin, 1945; Bombay, 1948; United Nations, New York, 1953; Madras, 1960; New Delhi, 1961; Diplomatic Service Inspector, 1964; Dep. Chief of Administration, DSAO, 1966; Minister (Econ. and Social Affairs), UK Mission to UN, New York, 1968; Ambassador to Zaïre and Burundi, 1971, and to Congo Republic, 1973. *Address:* The Gate House, Stratton, Cirencester, Glos.

ALLEN, Sir Milton (Pentonville), Kt 1972; OBE 1964; Governor, St Kitts/Nevis/Anguilla, 1972-75; (Acting Governor, 1969-Aug. 1972); *b* St Kitts, WI, 22 June 1888; *m* 1937, Annie Matilda (*née* Locker), MBE; no *c. Educ:* (primary) Palmetto Point, St Kitts; then (for tailoring) studied at David Mitchell designing and cutting Academy, NY (diploma). Worked at trade of tailor until the Depression, 1929. Nominated Member, 1957, Speaker, 1962, House of Assembly, St Kitts. Patron: St Kitts Cricket Assoc.; St Kitts Net Ball Assoc.; Boy

Scouts Assoc. KStJ 1974. *Publication:* Chosen Poems (a collection), (New York) 1945. *Recreations:* reading, music, gardening; interested in Arts Festival of Basseterre (one of his chosen poems set to music for a choir, by Dr Leon Forrester, FRCO). *Address:* The Fortlands, Basseterre, St Kitts, West Indies.

ALLEN, Norman; see Allen, H. N. G.

ALLEN, Prof. Percival, FRS 1973; Professor of Geology, University of Reading, since 1952; Director, Sedimentology Research Laboratory since 1965; *b* 15 March 1917; British; *m* 1941, Frances Margaret Hepworth, BSc; three *s* one *d. Educ:* Brede Council Sch.; Rye Grammar School; University of Reading. BSc 1939, PhD 1943, Reading; MA St Catharine's College, Cambridge, 1946. Univ. Demonstrator, 1942-45, Univ. Asst Lectr, 1945-46, Reading; University Demonstrator, 1946-47, Univ. Lectr, 1947-52, Cambridge; Dean of Science Faculty, Reading, 1963-66. Vis. Prof., Univ. of Kuwait, 1970. Served War of 1939-45. In Royal Air Force, 1941-42. Sedgwick Prize, Univ. of Cambridge, 1952; Daniel Pidgeon Fund, Geological Soc. of London, 1944; Leverhulme Fellowships Research Grant, 1948, 1949. Hon. Member: American Soc. of Economic Paleontologists and Mineralogists, 1949 (Keynote Speaker, SEPM Meeting, Toronto, 1964); Bulgarian Geological Soc., 1975; Geological Soc. of London: Mem. Council, 1964-67; Lyell Medal, 1971. Member: Natural Environment Res. Council, 1971-74; Adv. Panel, UNDP Project on Nile Delta, 1972-; UNESCO/UNDP Geology Consultant, India, 1976-77. UK Editor, Sedimentology, 1961-67. Chm., Org. Cttees: VII Internat. Sedimentological Congress, 1967; first European Earth and Planetary Physics Colloquium, 1971; first Meeting European Geological Socs, 1975. Sec.-Gen., Internat. Assoc. Sedimentologists, 1967-71; Algerian Sahara Glacials Expedn, 1970. *Publications:* papers in various scientific journals. *Recreations:* chess, natural history. *Address:* 6 St Barnabas Road, Emmer Green, Reading RG4 8RA.

ALLEN, Sir Peter (Christopher), Kt 1967; MA, BSc (Oxon); Director: Bank of Montreal, 1968-75; British Insulated Callender's Cables, since 1971; Advisory Director, New Perspective Fund, since 1973; *b* Ashstead, Surrey, 8 Sept. 1905; *s* of late Sir Ernest King Allen and Florence Mary (*née* Gellatly); *m* 1st, 1931, Violet Sylvester Wingate-Saul (*d* 1951); two *d*; 2nd, 1952, Consuelo Maria Linares Rivas. *Educ:* Harrow; Trinity Coll., Oxford (Hon. Fellow 1969). Joined Brunner, Mond & Co., Ltd, 1928; Chm., Plastics Div. of ICI Ltd, 1948-51 (Man. Dir, 1942-48); Pres. and Chm., ICI of Canada Ltd, 1961-68; Chm., ICI Ltd, 1968-71 (Dir, 1951-63, a Dep. Chm., 1963-68); Dir, British Nylon Spinners Ltd, 1954-58; Pres., Canadian Industries Ltd, 1959-62, Chm., 1962-68; Dir, Royal Trust Co., Canada, 1961-64. Vice-President: Inst. of Manpower Studies, 1968-76; Manufacturing Chemists' Assoc., USA, 1961-62 (Dir, 1959-62); Mem. and Vice-Chairman: Council of Assoc. of Brit. Chem. Manufacturers, 1963-65; Bd of Dirs, Société de Chimie Industrielle, 1968; Chm., Chem. Ind. Assoc., 1966-67; President: Plastics Inst., 1950-52; Brit. Plastics Fedn, 1963-65; Univ. of Manchester Inst. of Sci. and Technology, 1968-71; Vice-Pres., British Assoc. for Commercial and Industrial Educn, 1969-; Mem. of Council, CBI, 1965-67. Chm., BNEC, 1970-71 (Mem., 1964-67); Chm., Cttee for Exports to Canada, 1964-67); Mem., British Overseas Trade Bd, 1972-75. Governor, Nat. Coll. of Rubber Technology, 1964-68; Member: Court, British Shippers' Council, 1968-70; Export Council for Europe, 1962-65; Overseas Development Inst. Council, 1963-64; Iron and Steel Holding and Realisation Agency, 1963-67; NEDC for Chemical Industry, 1964-67; Commonwealth Export Council, 1964-67; Industrial Policy Group, 1969-71. FBIM 1968-; FInstD 1969-. Hon. Member: Chemical Industries Assoc., 1968- (Pres., 1965-67; Mem. Council, 1967-68); Canadian Chemical Producers' Assoc., 1962-. Trustee, Civic Trust. Governor, Harrow School, 1969-. *Publications:* The Railways of the Isle of Wight, 1928; Locomotives of Many Lands, 1954; On the Old Lines, 1957; (with P. B. Whitehouse) Narrow Gauge Railways of Europe, 1959; (with R. A. Wheeler) Steam on the Sierra, 1960; (with P. B. Whitehouse) Round the World on the Narrow Gauge, 1966; (with Consuelo Allen) The Curve of Earth's Shoulder, 1966; (with A. B. MacLeod) Rails in the Isle of Wight, 1967; Famous Fairways, 1968; Play the Best Courses, 1973; (with P. B. Whitehouse) Narrow Gauge the World Over, 1976. *Recreations:* foreign travel, railways, golf, writing, philately. *Address:* Telham Hill House, near Battle, E Sussex. *Clubs:* Junior Carlton; Royal and Ancient; Royal Cinque Ports, Rye, Royal St George's; Oxford and Cambridge Golfing Soc.; Augusta National (Ga, USA); Pine Valley (NJ, USA).

ALLEN, Sir Richard (Hugh Sedley), KCMG 1960 (CMG 1953); retired; *b* 3 Feb. 1903; *s* of late Sir Hugh Allen, GCVO; *m* 1945,

Juliet Home Thomson; one *s* one step *s*. *Educ:* Royal Naval Colleges, Osborne and Dartmouth; New College, Oxford. Junior Asst Sec., Govt of Palestine, 1925-27. Entered Foreign Office and Diplomatic Service, 1927; Second Sec., 1932; First Sec., 1939; Counsellor, 1946; Minister, British Embassy, Buenos Aires, 1950-54; Minister to Guatemala, 1954-56; British Ambassador to Burma, 1956-62. *Publications:* Malaysia: Prospect and Retrospect, 1968; A Short Introduction to the History and Politics of Southeast Asia, 1970; Imperialism and Nationalism in the Fertile Crescent, 1974. *Recreation:* sailing. *Address:* 18 Radnor Walk, SW3. *T:* 01-352 9602. *Clubs:* Athenæum; Royal Naval Sailing Association; Bosham and Itchenor Sailing.

ALLEN, Maj.-Gen. Robert Hall, CB 1942; *b* 11 June 1886; *s* of R. Allen, LLD, Barrister-at-Law; *m* 1916, Margaret Lawrence (*d* 1974), *d* of Maj.-Gen. Sir David Mercer, KCB; one *d*. *Educ:* Charterhouse; RMA, Woolwich. Retired pay, 1942. *Recreation:* solving simple chess problems. *Address:* The Old Vicarage, St Mary Street, Chippenham, Wilts.

ALLEN, Brig. Ronald Lewis, CBE 1970 (OBE 1956); General Manager, Building Societies' Staff College, Ware, since 1971; *b* 2 April 1916; *s* of W. J. Allen and M. B. Allen (*née* Lewis); *m* 1st, 1945, Jirina Georgette (*née* Valachova) (marr. diss. 1952); one *d* ; 2nd, 1956, Christine Maude (*née* Scott); one *s* one *d*. *Educ:* privately; Univ. of South Wales and Monmouthshire. BSc Hons London 1939. Scientist, Safety in Mines Research Bd; Birmingham Univ., 1939; Imperial Chemical Industries, 1939. War of 1939-45: commissioned, RAOC, 1940; served UK, 1940-42; MEF, 1942-44 (despatches, 1943); CMF, 1944-45. Egypt, 1949-50; USA, 1951-52; Cyprus, 1960-61; BAOR, 1961-62; Principal Ammunition Technical Officer, 1962-66; Comdr Ammunition Organisation and Chief Inspector, Land Service Ammunition, 1966-67; Dep. Comdr, Base Organisation RAOC, and Head of Inventory Systems Develt, 1967-71. Mem., Acceptable Risk Working Party, Council for Sci. and Soc., 1977. Mem., E Herts DC. FRIC 1962 (ARIC 1939); MBIM 1967; Fellow Brit. Computer Soc. 1969. Queen's Commendation for Brave Conduct, 1964. *Recreations:* bridge, tennis, computers, travel. *Address:* Building Societies Training College, Fanhams Hall, Ware, Herts SG12 7PZ; Thorn Knoll, Aston, Herts.

ALLEN, Rowland Lancelot, CB 1968; Principal Assistant Treasury Solicitor, 1963-69, retired; *b* 17 Feb. 1908; *s* of Rowland Allen and Maud Annie Allen (*née* Bacon); *m* 1934, Elizabeth Ethel (*née* Lewis); two *s* one *d*. *Educ:* Eton College. Called to the Bar, Inner Temple, 1931; Public Trustee Office, 1934; Treasury Solicitor's Dept, 1940; Foreign Compensation Commission, 1950-53; Treasury Solicitor's Dept, 1953. *Recreation:* golf. *Address:* Herries, Crastock, Woking, Surrey. *T:* Brookwood 2312.

ALLEN, Sir Roy George Douglas, Kt 1966; CBE 1954 (OBE 1946); MA, DSc (Econ.); FBA 1952; Professor of Statistics, University of London, 1944-73, now Professor Emeritus; Consultant, Royal Commission on Civil Liability, since 1974; *b* 3 June 1906; *er s* of G. H. Allen, Worcester; *m* 1936; two *s* one *d*. *Educ:* Royal Grammar School, Worcester; Sidney Sussex College, Cambridge (Wrangler, 1927; Hon. Fellow, 1971); DSc (Econ.) London, 1943; Assistant and later Lecturer in Statistics, London School of Economics, 1928-39; Reader in Economic Statistics, Univ. of London, 1939-44; Statistician, HM Treasury, 1939-41; Dir of Records and Statistics, British Supply Council, Washington, 1941-42; British Dir of Research and Statistics, Combined Production and Resources Board, Washington, 1942-45; Statistical Adviser, HM Treasury, 1947-48; Consultant, UN Statistical Office, 1949-50 and 1952. Visiting Professor, Univ. of California, 1958-59. Member: Air Transport Licensing Bd, 1960-72; Civil Aviation Authority, 1972-73; Cttee of Inquiry on Decimal Currency, 1962-63; Chm., Impact of Rates Cttee, 1963-65; Mem. Research Council, DSIR, 1964-65; Mem., SSRC, 1967-70. Hon. DSc (Soc. Sci.) Southampton, 1970. *Publications:* Family Expenditure (with Sir Arthur Bowley), 1935; Mathematical Analysis for Economists, 1938; Statistics for Economists, 1949; International Trade Statistics (with J. Edward Ely), 1953; Mathematical Economics, 1956; Basic Mathematics, 1962; Macro-economic Theory, 1967; Index Numbers in Theory and Practice, 1975; articles in economic and statistical journals. *Address:* 11 The Limes, Linden Gardens, W2. *T:* 01-727 9979; Greyfriars (South), South Green, Southwold, Suffolk. *T:* Southwold 3307.

ALLEN, Thomas; singer; with Royal Opera, Covent Garden, since 1972; *b* 10 Sept. 1944; *s* of Thomas Boaz Allen and Florence Allen; *m* 1968, Margaret Holley; one *s* . *Educ:* Robert Richardson Grammar Sch., Ryhope; Royal College of Music. ARCM. Welsh Nat. Opera, 1969-72; appearances include:

Glyndebourne Fest. Opera; English Opera Group; BBC TV (The Gondoliers, The Marriage of Figaro); all major orchestras and various concert engagements abroad. Major roles include: Figaro in Barber of Seville; Figaro and the Count in Marriage of Figaro; Paolo Albiani in Simon Boccanegra; Papageno in The Magic Flute; Billy Budd; Marcello in La Bohême; Belcore in l'Elisir d'Amore; Sid in Albert Herring; Tarquinius in Rape of Lucretia; Guglielmo in Cosi fan Tutte; Demetrius in A Midsummer Night's Dream; Valentin in Faust; Dr Falke in Die Fledermaus; King Arthur; The Count in Voice of Ariadne; Silvio in Pagliacci, and many others. *Recreations:* gardening, golf, sailing, reading, ornithology. *Address:* c/o Royal Opera House, Covent Garden, WC2.

ALLEN, Prof. Thomas Palmer, MSc; CEng; FIEE; Professor of Light Electrical Engineering, The Queen's University, Belfast, 1955-65, Emeritus Professor since 1965; *b* 9 Aug. 1899; *s* of William Palmer Allen and Mary Jane Allen; *m* 1925, Dorothy Margaret Mathews; two *d*. *Educ:* Rosetta School, Belfast; Trades Preparatory School, Belfast; The Queen's University, Belfast. Apprenticeship Elect. Eng, 1914-18; Lectr in Physics and Elect. Eng, Walthamstow Technical Inst., 1922; Asst Lectr in Mathematics, College of Technology, Belfast (CTB), 1923; Asst Lectr in Elect. Eng, CTB, 1924; Extra-Mural Lectr in Wireless Telegraphy and Telephony, QUB, 1927; Lectr in Elect. Eng, CTB, and Extra-Mural Lectr in Elect. Eng, QUB, 1936; Senior Lectr in Elect. Eng, CTB, 1942; Adviser of Studies, Faculty of Applied Science, QUB, 1938-52; Director of Higher Technological Studies, CTB, 1955; Dean of Faculty of Applied Science and Technology, QUB, 1958-61. Chm., N Ireland Centre of IEE, 1946-47. Senator, The Queen's Univ., Belfast, 1964-69; Gov., City of Belfast College of Technology, 1965-. *Publications:* various contributions to technical press, and many book reviews. *Recreations:* angling, cryptanalysis, amateur radio transmission (call Sign Gi6YW). *Address:* 62 Balmoral Avenue, Belfast BT9 6NY. *T:* Belfast 665982.

ALLEN, Walter Ernest, author and literary journalist; *b* Birmingham, 23 Feb. 1911; 4th *s* of Charles Henry Allen and Annie Maria Thomas; *m* 1944, Peggy Yorke, 3rd *d* of Guy Lionel Joy and Dorothy Yorke Maundrell, Calne, Wilts; two *s* two *d*. *Educ:* King Edward's Grammar School, Aston, Birmingham; Birmingham University. Assistant Master, King Edward's Grammar School, Aston, Birmingham, 1934; Visiting Lecturer in English, State University of Iowa, USA, 1935; Features Editor, Cater's News Agency, Birmingham, 1935-37; Assistant Technical Officer, Wrought Light Alloys Development Assoc., 1943-45. Asst Literary Editor, New Statesman, 1959-60, Literary Editor, 1960-61. Margaret Pilcher Vis. Prof. of English, Coe Coll., Iowa, 1955-56; Visiting Professor of English: Vassar College, New York, 1963-64; Univ. of Kansas, 1967; Univ. of Washington, 1967; Prof. of English, New Univ. of Ulster, 1967-73; Berg Prof. of English, New York Univ., 1970-71; Vis. Prof. of English, Dalhousie Univ., Halifax, NS, 1973-74; C. P. Miles Prof. of English, Virginia Polytechnic Inst. and State Univ., 1974-75. FRSL. *Publications:* Innocence is Drowned, 1938; Blind Man's Ditch, 1939; Living Space, 1940; Rogue Elephant, 1946; The Black Country, 1946; Writers on Writing, 1948; Arnold Bennett, 1948; Reading a Novel, 1949; Dead Man Over All, 1950; The English Novel-A Short Critical History, 1954; Six Great Novelists, 1955; All in a Lifetime, 1959; Tradition and Dream, 1964; George Eliot, 1964; The Urgent West: an Introduction to the Idea of the United States, 1969; Transatlantic Crossing: American visitors to Britain and British visitors to America in the nineteenth century, 1971. *Address:* 6 Canonbury Square, N1. *T:* 01-226 7085. *Club:* Savile.

ALLEN, W(alter) Godfrey, MA; FSA, FRIBA; Hon. DLitt (Oxford), 1963; Surveyor of the Fabric of St Paul's Cathedral, 1931-56; Consulting Architect to Southwark Cathedral, 1932-55, to Exeter Cathedral, 1942-52, to Gloucester Cathedral since 1953; architect in private practice; *b* 21 Oct. 1891; *s* of Walter Allen and Frances Baker; *m* 1931, Phyllis Seyler Gill (*d* 1973). *Educ:* Berkhampstead Sch.; Slade Sch.; King's Coll., London. Articled, later Asst to Sir Mervyn Macartney; Sec. to Commn of architects and engrs apptd in 1921 to investigate and report on condition of St Paul's Cathedral, Asst Architect to the Dean and Chapter, 1925-31. Member: Royal Commn on Historical Monuments (Eng.), 1952-60; Exec. Cttee of Wren Soc., 1933-43; Advisory Panel of Specialist Architects, Historic Churches Preservation Trust (London Region); Chairman Church Roofing Committee set up by Central Council for the Care of Churches and Society for the Protection of Ancient Buildings, 1952; Commander of St Paul's Watch, 1939-45; Prime Warden Goldsmiths' Co., 1951-53; Master of Art Workers' Guild, 1953-54; Hon. Mem., City and Guilds of London Inst. A Governor, Westminster Sch., 1951-70. *Works include:* restoration of St Bride's, Fleet Street; St Giles, Cripplegate; St Mary Abchurch;

St Dunstan-in-the-West; St James, Louth; St James's Chapel, Exeter Cathedral; Chapter-House, St Paul's Cathedral; Sheldonian Theatre; Old Ashmolean Building and Radcliffe Camera, Oxford. *Publications:* The Preservation of St Paul's Cathedral, RIBA Jl; A Survey of Views of St Paul's Cathedral; numerous articles. *Recreation:* walking. *Address:* Morden College, Blackheath, SE3 0PW.

ALLEN, Walter John Gardener; Controller, Capital Taxes Office (formerly Estate Duty Office), Inland Revenue, since 1974; *b* 8 Dec. 1916; *s* of late John Gardiner Allen and late Hester Lucy Allen, Deal, Kent; *m* 1944, Irene, *d* of late John Joseph and Sarah Henderson, Lisburn, N Ireland; one *s* one *d. Educ:* Manwoods, Sandwich; London Univ. (LLB). Entered Inland Revenue, 1934. Served RAF, 1940-46 (Flying Officer). *Recreations:* amateur geologist; gardening. *Address:* 43 The Chase, Eastcote, Pinner, Mddx HA5 1SH. *T:* 01-868 7101.

ALLEN, William Alexander, RIBA; Chairman, Bickerdike Allen Bramble and Partners; *b* 29 June 1914; *s* of late Professor Frank Allen, FRSC; *m* 1938, Beatrice Mary Teresa Pearson; two *s* one *d. Educ:* public schools in Winnipeg; University of Manitoba. Royal Architectural Inst. of Canada Silver Medal, 1935. Univ. Gold Medal in Architecture, 1936. Appointed to Building Research Station, Watford, 1937; Chief Architect, Bldg Res. Stn, 1953-61; Principal of the Architectural Assoc. School of Architecture, 1961-66. Member Council RIBA, 1953-72 (Chairman various committees); ARIBA 1937; FRIBA 1965; Chm., Fire Research Adv. Cttee, 1973-; Pres., Institute of Acoustics, 1975-76. Hon. Associate NZIA, 1965. Hon. LLD Manchester, 1977. Commander, Ordem do Mérito, Portugal, 1972. *Publications:* (with R. Fitzmaurice) Sound Transmission in Buildings, 1939. Papers, etc, on scientific and technical aspects of architecture, professionalism, and modern architectural history and education. *Recreations:* writing, drawing, music. *Address:* 4 Ashley Close, Welwyn Garden City, Herts. *T:* Welwyn Garden 24178. *Club:* Athenæum.
See also Prof. J. F. Allen.

ALLEN, Sir (William) Denis, GCMG 1969 (KCMG 1958; CMG 1950); CB 1955; HM Diplomatic Service, retired; *b* 24 Dec. 1910; *s* of John Allen; *m* 1939, Elizabeth Helen (*née* Watkin Williams); one *s. Educ:* Wanganui, New Zealand; Cambridge. HM Diplomatic Service, 1934-69; Deputy Commissioner General for South East Asia, 1959-62; Ambassador to Turkey, 1963-67; Dep. Under-Sec., Foreign Office (later FCO), 1967-69. *Address:* Stockland, Honiton, Devon.

ALLEN, Sir William (Guilford), Kt 1973; CBE 1970; grazier; Senior Partner, Allen, Allen & Crawshaw, livestock and wool producers, Brisbane; Director, Radio Broadcasting Network of Queensland, etc; Member, Central Council of Australian Country Party; *b* 1898; *s* of R. C. Allen, Goondiwindi, Qld; *m* 1st, 1927, Mona Maree Nolan (*d* 1956), Hughenden, Qld; two *s* one *d*; 2nd, 1961, Josephine Agnes Peacock, Brisbane. *Educ:* Nudgee Coll., Brisbane; Hunters Hill (Christian Brothers' Coll.), Sydney. Dep. Chm., Longreach Shire Council, 1948-58. Mem., Lands Advisory Cttee, Qld Central Council of Country Party. Life Mem., National Party of Queensland (formerly Country Party), 1972. Is a breeder of Poll Shorthorns and Merino sheep. Knighted for services to the Queensland pastoral industry and the community. *Recreations:* horse racing, reading. *Address:* Bexley, Longreach, Queensland 4730, Australia. *Clubs:* Brisbane, Longreach, Flinders, Tattersall's, Huntington, Queensland Turf, Brisbane Amateur Turf (all in Qld).

ALLEN, Sir (William) Kenneth (Gwynne), Kt 1961; *b* 23 May 1907; *er s* of Harold Gwynne Allen and Hilda Allen, Bedford; *m* 1931, Eleanor Mary (*née* Eeles); one *s* one *d. Educ:* Westminster Sch.; Univ. of Neuchâtel, Switzerland. Started as engineering pupil, Harland & Wolff Ltd, Glasgow and Belfast; subsequently at W. H. Allen, Sons & Co. Ltd, Bedford; Dir, 1937-70, Man. Dir, 1946-70, Chm., 1955-70, W. H. Allen, Sons & Co. Ltd; Chm., Amalgamated Power Engineering, 1968-70; Dir, Electrolux, 1970-. Past Chairman: Brit. Internal Combustion Engine Manufacturers' Assoc. (1955-57); Pres., British Engineers' Assoc., 1957-59 (now British Mechanical Engineering Fedn); Chm., BEAMA, 1959-61; Pres., Engineering Employers' Fedn, 1962-64; Chm., Labour and Social Affairs Cttee of CBI, 1965-67. FIMarE; MRINA; MIBritishE. Freeman of City of London. Liveryman, Worshipful Company of Shipwrights. Mem. Beds CC, 1945-55; High Sheriff Beds 1958-59. *Address:* Manor Close, Aspley Guise, Milton Keynes MK17 8HZ. *T:* Woburn Sands 583161.

ALLEN, William Maurice; Executive Director, Bank of England, 1964-70; *b* 16 April 1908; *s* of David Allen. *Educ:* Dulwich College; London School of Economics. Army 1940-45. Asst Dir

of Research, International Monetary Fund, 1947-49; Adviser, Bank of England, 1950-64. Fellow of Balliol Coll., Oxford, 1931-48; Visiting Fellow Nuffield Coll., Oxford, 1954-62. Hon. Fellow, LSE, 1963. Governor, LSE, 1951. *Address:* Bank of England, EC2. *Club:* Reform.

ALLEN, Prof. William Sidney, MA, PhD (Cantab); FBA 1971; Professor of Comparative Philology in the University of Cambridge since 1955; *b* 18 March 1918; *er s* of late W. P. Allen and of Ethel (*née* Pearce); *m* 1955, Aenea, *yr d* of late Rev. D. McCallum and Mrs McCallum, Invergordon. *Educ:* Christ's Hosp.; Trinity Coll., Cambridge (Classical Scholar); Porson Scholarship, 1939. War of 1939-45: RTR and General Staff (Int) (despatches). Lecturer in Phonetics, 1948-51, and in Comparative Linguistics, 1951-55, School of Oriental and African Studies, Univ. of London. Dialect research in India, 1952; Fellow of Rockefeller Foundation, USA, 1953; Brit. Council visitor, Univ. of W Indies, 1959. Linguistic Soc. of America's Professor, 1961; Collitz Professor, Linguistic Institute, USA, 1962. Pres., Philological Soc., 1965-67. Fellow of Trinity Coll., Cambridge, 1955-. *Publications:* Phonetics in Ancient India, 1953; On the Linguistic Study of Languages (inaugural lecture), 1957; Sandhi, 1962; Vox Latina, 1965; Vox Graeca, 1968; Accent and Rhythm, 1973; articles on general and comparative linguistics, phonetics, metrics and classical, Indian and Caucasian languages. *Address:* 24 Sherlock Road, Cambridge CB3 0HR. *T:* Cambridge 56739; 65621.

ALLEN-JONES, Air Vice-Marshal John Ernest, CBE 1966; Director of RAF Legal Services, 1961-70, retired; *b* 13 Oct. 1909; *s* of Rev. John Allen-Jones, Llanyblodwel Vicarage, Oswestry; *m* 1st, 1937, Margaret Rix (*d* 1973), Sawbridgeworth; one *s* two *d*; 2nd, 1973, Diana Gibbons. *Educ:* Rugby; Worcester Coll., Oxford (MA). Solicitor (Honours), 1934; Partner with Vaudrey, Osborne & Mellor, Manchester. Joined RAF, 1939. Air Vice-Marshal, 1967. Gordon-Shepherd Memorial Prizeman, 1963. *Recreations:* tennis, bridge. *Address:* Hartfield, Duton Hill, Dunmow, Essex. *T:* Great Easton 554.

ALLENBY, family name of Viscount Allenby.

ALLENBY, 2nd Viscount, *cr* 1919, of Megiddo and of Felixstowe; **Dudley Jaffray Hynman Allenby;** late 11th Hussars; *b* 8 Jan. 1903; *e s* of late Capt. Frederick Claude Hynman Allenby, CBE, RN, JP; *S* uncle 1936; *m* 1st, 1930, Mary (marr. diss. 1949), *d* of Edward Champneys, Otterpool Manor, Kent; one *s*; 2nd, 1949, Mrs Daisy Neame, CStJ. *Educ:* Eton; RMC, Sandhurst. Joined 11th Hussars, 1923; served in India, 1923-26; Adjutant, 11th Hussars, 1926-30; Instructor, Royal Military College, Sandhurst, 1930-34; Captain, 1936; served Egypt, 1934-37; Adjutant, Army Fighting Vehicles School, 1937-40; Major, 1938; 2nd in Command Royal Gloucestershire Hussars, 1940-42; Lt-Col 2nd Derbyshire Yeomanry, 1942; retd (Lt-Col) 1946. *Heir: s* Lt-Col Hon. Michael Jaffray Hynman Allenby, 11th Hussars [*b* 20 April 1931; *m* 1965, Sara Margaret Wiggin; one *s*]. *Address:* Parsonage Farm, Westwell, Ashford, Kent. *T:* Ashford 24783. *Club:* Cavalry and Guards.

ALLENBY, Rt. Rev. (David Howard) Nicholas; Assistant Bishop, Diocese of Worcester since 1968; Chaplain, St Oswald's Almshouses, Worcester, since 1973; *b* 28 Jan. 1909; *s* of late William Allenby; unmarried. *Educ:* Kelham Theological College. MA (Lambeth), 1957. Deacon, 1934; Priest, 1935. Curate of St Jude, West Derby, Liverpool, 1934-36; Tutor, Kelham Theological College and Public Preacher, Diocese of Southwell, 1936-44; Rector of Averham with Kelham, 1944-57; Proctor in Convocation, Southwell, 1950-57; Editor of Diocesan News and Southwell Review, 1950-55; Hon. Canon of Southwell, 1953-57, Canon Emeritus, 1957-62; Personal Chaplain to Bishop of Southwell, 1954-57; Rural Dean of Newark, 1955-57; Provincial of Society of Sacred Mission in Australia, 1957-62; Commissary, Melanesia, 1958-62; Warden of Community of Holy Name, City and Diocese of Melbourne, 1961-62; Bishop of Kuching, 1962-68; Commissary, Kuching, 1969. *Publication:* Pray with the Church, 1937 (jointly). *Recreation:* reading. *Address:* Chaplain's House, St Oswald's, The Tything, Worcester WR1 1HR. *T:* Worcester 22922. *Clubs:* Royal Commonwealth Society, Royal Over-Seas League.

ALLENDALE, 3rd Viscount, *cr* 1911; **Wentworth Hubert Charles Beaumont,** DL; Baron, 1906; *b* 12 Sept. 1922; *e s* of 2nd Viscount Allendale, KG, CB, CBE, MC, and Violet, *d* of Sir Charles Seely, 2nd Bt; *S* father 1956; *m* 1948, Hon. Sarah Ismay, 2nd *d* of 1st Baron Ismay, KG, PC, GCB, CH, DSO; three *s. Educ:* Eton. RAFVR, 1940; Flight-Lieutenant 1943; ADC to Viceroy of India, 1946-47. DL Northumberland, 1961. *Heir: s* Hon. Wentworth Peter Ismay Beaumont [*b* 13 Nov. 1948; *m* 1975, Theresa Mary, *d* of F. A. More O'Ferrall]. *Address:*

Bywell Hall, Stocksfield on Tyne, Northumberland. *T:* Stocksfield 3169; Allenheads, Hexham, Northumberland. *T:* Allenheads 205. *Clubs:* Turf, White's; Northern Counties (Newcastle upon Tyne).
See also Earl of Carlisle .

ALLERTON, 3rd Baron of Chapel Allerton, *cr* 1902; **George William Lawies Jackson;** Squadron-Leader Auxiliary Air Force, retired; late Lieutenant Coldstream Guards; *b* 23 July 1903; *s* of 2nd Baron and Katherine Louisa (*d* 1956), *y d* of W. W. Wickham, JP, of Chestnut Grove, Boston Spa; *S* father, 1925; *m* 1st, 1926, Joyce (who obtained a divorce, 1934; *d* 1953), *o c* of late J. R. Hatfeild, Thorp Arch Hall, Yorks; one *s*; 2nd, 1934, Mrs Hope Aline Whitelaw; 3rd, 1947, Anne, *er d* of late James Montagu, Skippetts, nr Basingstoke; one *d. Educ:* Eton; RMC, Sandhurst. *Recreations:* shooting, golf. *Heir:* s Hon. Edward Lawies Jackson, Capt. RHG (retd) [*b* 23 March 1928; *m* 1st, 1953, Sally Moore (marr. diss. 1971), *o d* of late Ian Hezlett, Cranbourne Corner, Ascot; two *d*; 2nd, 1971, Susan, *d* of Captain D. Chaytor, Leyburn, Yorks; one *d*]. *Address:* Loddington Hall, Leicestershire. *T:* Belton 220. *Clubs:* White's, Turf, Pratt's.

ALLERTON, Reginald John, CBE 1964; FRICS, FIHM; retired 1963; *b* 20 June 1898; 3rd *s* of late Robert Sterry Allerton, Lowestoft, and Mary Maria (*née* Bailey); *m* 1924, Dorothy Rose Saunders; one *s. Educ:* Lowestoft Grammar School. Entered Local Government Service, 1915; on Active Service with RNVR, 1917-19. Various urban and borough appointments until 1926; Chief Architectural and Building Asst, Reading Borough Council, 1926-30; Estates Surveyor, City of Norwich, 1930-39; Housing Manager and Sec., City of Bristol, 1939-51; Housing Manager, City of Birmingham, 1951-54; Director of Housing to the London County Council, 1954-63. Pres., Inst. of Housing, 1949-50, 1960-61. Apptd (by Minister of Housing and Local Govt) as Vice-Pres., Surrey and Sussex Rent Assessment Panel, 1965-71. Served on Govt Cttees on Housing and Immigration, and Housing in Greater London (Sir Milner Holland Cttee); Founder Mem., Hanover Housing Assoc. *Publications:* many papers and lectures to professional societies and conferences dealing mainly with municipal housing work. *Recreations:* gardening, fishing. *Address:* 10 Mill Mead, Wendover, Bucks. *T:* Wendover 622691.

ALLEY, Ronald Edgar; Keeper of the Modern Collection, Tate Gallery, London, since 1965; *b* 12 March 1926; *s* of late Edgar Thomas Alley; *m* 1955, Anthea Oswell (now painter and sculptor, as Anthea Alley); two *d. Educ:* Bristol Grammar School; Courtauld Institute of Art, London University. Tate Gallery staff as Asst Keeper II, 1951-54; Deputy Keeper, 1954-65. Member: Museum Board, Cecil Higgins Art Gallery, Bedford, 1957-; Art Cttee, Ulster Museum, Belfast, 1962-; Art Panel of Arts Council, 1963-70. *Publications:* Tate Gallery: Foreign Paintings, Drawings and Sculpture, 1959; Gauguin, 1962; William Scott, 1963; Ben Nicholson, 1963; Francis Bacon (with Sir John Rothenstein), 1964; British Painting since 1945, 1966; Picasso's "Three Dancers" 1967; Barbara Hepworth, 1968; Recent American Art, 1969; Abstract Expressionism, 1974. *Recreation:* ornithology. *Address:* 61 Deodar Road, SW15. *T:* 01-874 2016. *Club:* Institute of Contemporary Arts.

ALLEYNE, Captain Sir John (Meynell), 4th Bt *cr* 1769; DSO 1918; DSC; RN retired; *b* 11 Aug. 1889; *s* of Reynold Alleyne, *e s* of 3rd Bt and Susanna, *d* of late John Meynell of Meynell Langley, Derbyshire; *S* grandfather, 1912; *m* 1920, Alice Violet, *d* of late James Campbell, and Mrs Campbell, 12 Cornwall Gardens, SW; one *s* two *d.* Served European War; was navigator of HMS Vindictive when sunk to block Ostend Harbour, May 1918 (severely wounded); retired list, 1936. Served War of 1939-45. *Heir:* s Rev. John Olpherts Campbell Alleyne, [*b* 18 Jan. 1928; *m* 1968, Honor Irwin; one *s* one *d*]. *Address:* South Lynch, Hursley, near Winchester. *T:* Hursley 239. *Club:* Naval and Military.

ALLHUSEN, Major Derek Swithin, DL; farmer; *b* 9 Jan. 1914; 2nd *s* of late Lt-Col F. H. Allhusen, CMG, DSO, Fulmer House, Fulmer, Bucks; *m* 1937, Hon. Claudia Violet Betterton, *yr d* of 1st and last Baron Rushcliffe, PC, GBE (*d* 1949); one *s* one *d* (and one *s* decd). *Educ:* Eton; Chillon Coll., Montreux, Switzerland; Trinity Coll., Cambridge. Lieut, 9th Queen's Royal Lancers, 1935. Served War of 1939-45: France, 1940 (wounded), North Africa, Italy (Silver Star Medal of USA, 1944); Major 1942; retired, 1949. Pres., Royal Norfolk Agricultural Assoc., 1974. One of HM's Body Guard of Hon. Corps of Gentlemen-at-Arms, 1963-. Freeman, City of London; Hon. Freeman, Worshipful Co. of Saddlers and Farriers, 1969. High Sheriff, 1958, DL 1969, Norfolk. *Recreations:* riding, shooting, skiing. Represented GB: Winter Pentathlon Olympic Games, 1948;

Equestrianism European Championships Three-Day Event, 1957, 1959, 1965, 1967, 1969 (Winners of Team Championship, 1957, 1967, 1969); Olympic Games, Mexico, 1968 (Gold Medal, Team; Silver Medal, Individual); lent his horse Laurieston to British Olympic Equestrian Team, Munich, 1972 (individual and team Gold Medals). *Address:* Manor House, Claxton, Norwich, Norfolk. *T:* Thurton 228; Flat 1, 22 St James's Square, SW1. *T:* 01-839 3390. *Club:* Cavalry and Guards.

ALLIBONE, Thomas Edward, CBE 1960; FRS 1948; DSc Sheffield; External Professor of Electrical Engineering, University of Leeds, since 1967; Visiting Professor of Physics, City University, since 1971; *b* 11 Nov. 1903; *s* of Henry J. Allibone; *m* 1931, Dorothy Margery, *d* of Frederick Boulden, BSc, MEng, MIMechE; two *d. Educ:* Central Sch., Sheffield (Birley Scholar); Sheffield Univ. (Linley Scholar); Gonville and Caius Coll., Cambridge (Wollaston Scholar). PhD Sheffield; PhD Cantab. 1851 Exhibition Sen. Student, Cavendish Laboratory, Cambridge, 1926-30; i/c High-Voltage Laboratory, Metropolitan-Vickers Electrical Co., Manchester, 1930-46; Director: Res. Laboratory, AEI, Aldermaston, 1946-63; AEI (Woolwich) Ltd, 1948-63; Scientific Adviser, AEI, 1963; Chief Scientist, Central Electricity Generating Bd, 1963-70. Mem., British Mission on Atomic Energy, Berkeley, Calif, and Oakridge, Tenn, 1944-45; Visitor: BISRA, 1949-55; ASLIB, 1955-62. Lectures: Faraday, 1946, 1956; Royal Instn Christmas, 1959; Wm Menelaus, 1959; Bernard Price, 1959; Trotter Patterson, 1963; Fison Memorial, 1963; Royal Soc. Rutherford Memorial, 1964 and 1972; Baird Memorial, 1967; Melchett, 1970. President: Section A, British Assoc., 1958; EIBA, 1958-59; Inst. of Information Scientists, 1964-67. Vice-President: Inst. of Physics, 1948-52; Royal Instn, 1955-57, 1970-72. Chm., Res. Cttee, British Electrical and Allied Industries Res. Assoc., 1955-62. Member: Council, British Inst. of Radiology, 1935-38; Council, IEE, 1937-40, 1946-49, 1950-53; Cttee, Nat. Physical Laboratory, 1950-60; Govt Cttee on Copyright, 1951; DSIR (Mem., Industrial Grants Cttee, 1950-58); Council, Physical Soc., 1953-56; Council, Southern Electricity Bd, 1953-62; Adv. Council, Science Museum; Adv. Council, RMC; Adv. Court, AEA; Nuclear Safety Adv. Council, Min. of Power, 1959-. Trustee, British Museum, 1968-74. Governor, Downe House, 1959-69; Chm. Governors, Reading Technical Coll., 1959-68. FInstP; FIEE; Fellow, Amer. Inst. of Electrical Engineers. Hon. DSc: Reading, 1960; City, 1970; Hon. DEng Sheffield, 1969. Röntgen Medal, British Inst. of Radiology; Thornton and Cooper Hill Medals, IEE; Melchett Medal, Inst. of Fuel. *Publications:* The Release and Use of Nuclear Energy, 1961; Rutherford: Father of Nuclear Energy (Rutherford Lecture 1972), 1973; The Royal Society and its Dining Clubs, 1975; papers on high voltage and transient electrical phenomena, fission and fusion. *Recreations:* photography, travel, gardening, philately. *Address:* York Cottage, Lovel Road, Winkfield, Windsor, Berks. *T:* Winkfield Row 4501.

ALLIGHAN, Garry; Journalist and Author; Principal, Premier School of Journalism, Johannesburg, 1963-73; *b* 16 Feb. 1900; *s* of George and Catherine Allighan, Wickford, Essex; *m*; one *s* one *d. Educ:* St James School, Enfield; Enfield Grammar School. Naval service in European War; joined Luton News, 1919; Assistant Editor John Bull, 1921-25; Feature Editor Toronto Evening Telegram, 1925-28; Feature Writer Daily Express, 1928-31; Radio Editor Evening Standard, 1931-39; War Correspondent Toronto Star, 1939-41; News Editor Daily Mirror, 1941-44; Industrial Editor Daily Mail, 1944-46; MP (Lab) Gravesend Div. of Kent, 1945-47. Has also acted as Press Consultant to Advertising Assoc. and Radio Manufacturers Assoc. *Publications:* Priceless Treasure (Canada), 1926; Romance of the Talkies, 1929; Reith of the BBC, 1937; De Valera Revealed (USA), 1937; The First Thirteen, 1941; Curtain-Up on South Africa, 1960; Verwoerd-The End, 1961; The Welensky Story, 1962; Four Bonnets to Golgotha, 1963; The 65th Defendant, 1963; The Moving Finger, 1964; Forward into the Past, 1976. *Recreations:* motoring and photography. *Address:* 717 The Mariston, Claim Street, Johannesburg, South Africa.

ALLINSON, Air Vice-Marshal Norman Stuart, CB 1946; DL; retired; *b* 19 April 1904; *s* of late Rev. H. C. W. Allinson, Hinxhill, Kent; *m* 1928, Florence Muriel Hall (*d* 1975); one *s* one *d. Educ:* Trent Coll.; RAF, Cranwell. Served with No 13 Sqdn, 1924-29; in HMS Hermes, 1930-32; Dept of Air Member of Personnel, 1933-35; RAF Staff Coll., 1936; comd No 269 Sqdn, 1937-38; HQ Coastal Comd, 1938-39; served War of 1939-45, Armament duties, Air Min. and MAP, 1940-41; HQ Army Co-operation Comd, 1942; served in Middle East, 1943-45, on planning duties, as AOC No 212 Group and Force 438 and as Dep. SASO, HQ Middle East; Dir of Operational Trng, Air Min., 1945-47; Imperial Defence Coll., 1948; AOC Rhodesian

Air Trng Group, Bulawayo, S Rhodesia, 1949-51; Director-General of Manning, 1951-52; Director-General of Personnel I, 1953-54; Air Officer i/c Administration, Flying Training Command, 1954-56; retired, 1956. DL Essex, 1963. *Recreation:* sailing. *Address:* Dene House, Layer de la Haye, Colchester, Essex. *Club:* Royal Air Force.

ALLINSON, Walter Leonard, CMG 1976; MVO 1961; HM Diplomatic Service; Deputy High Commissioner and Minister, New Delhi, since 1975; *b* 1 May 1926; *o s* of Walter Allinson and Alice Frances Cassidy; *m* 1951, Margaret Patricia Watts; three *d* (of whom two are twins). *Educ:* Friern Barnet Grammar Sch.; Merton Coll., Oxford. First class in History, 1947; MA. Asst Principal, Ministry of Fuel and Power (Petroleum Div.), 1947-48; Asst Principal, later Principal, Min. of Education, 1948-58 (Asst Private Sec. to Minister, 1953-54); transf. CRO, 1958; First Sec. in Lahore and Karachi, 1960-62, Madras and New Delhi, 1963-66; Counsellor and Head of Political Affairs Dept, March 1968; Dep. Head, later Head, of Permanent Under Secretary's Dept, FCO, 1968-70; Counsellor and Head of Chancery, subsequently Deputy High Comr, Nairobi, 1970-73; RCDS, 1974; Diplomatic Service Inspectorate, 1975. *Address:* c/o Foreign and Commonwealth Office, SW1. *Clubs:* Travellers'; Nairobi (Nairobi).

ALLIOTT, John Downes, QC 1973; a Recorder of the Crown Court, since 1972; *b* 9 Jan. 1932; *er s* of late Alexander Clifford Alliott and Ena Kathleen Alliott (*née* Downes); *m* 1957, Patsy Jennifer, *d* of late Gordon Beckles Willson; two *s* one *d. Educ:* Charterhouse; Peterhouse, Cambridge (Schol., BA). Coldstream Guards, 1950-51; Peterhouse, 1951-54; called to Bar, Inner Temple, 1955. Dep. Chm., E Sussex QS, 1970-71. *Recreations:* rural pursuits, France and Italy, military history. *Address:* (chambers) 1 Crown Office Row, Temple, EC4Y 7HH. *T:* 01-353 1801; (home) Park Stile, Love Hill Lane, Langley, Slough SL3 6DE. *T:* Iver 652745.

ALLISON, Charles Ralph, MA; Secretary, Lord Kitchener National Memorial Fund; Headmaster of Brentwood School, 1945-65; *b* 26 May 1903; *s* of Harry A. Allison, FCA, and Gertrude Wolfsberger; *m* 1930, Winifred Rita, *d* of A. C. Williams; two *s* one *d. Educ:* Caterham Sch.; University Coll., London; St Catharine's College, Cambridge (Exhibitioner). Assistant Master, Worksop College, 1928; Malvern College, 1929-36; English Tutor, Stowe School, 1936-38; Headmaster of Reigate Grammar School, 1938-40, and Alleyn's School, 1940-45. Formerly Mem. Cttee, Headmasters' Conf. (Vice-Chm. 1965). Governor: Sidney Perry Foundation (Chm.); Lindisfarne Coll., Ruabon; Brentwood Sch.; Stowe Sch. Vice-Chm., Commonwealth Youth Exchange Cttee, 1970-72; Vice-Pres., Eastern Region, UNA, 1965-. Mem., Nat. Commn for UNESCO, 1954-65; UK Delegate to Gen. Confs, 1958 and 1960. Member: Cttee, Governing Bodies' Assoc.; Essex Education Cttee, 1967-74. Reader in the Parish of St Mary's, Great Warley. *Address:* Barn Meadow, Great Warley, near Brentwood, Essex. *T:* Brentwood 214211. *Club:* East India, Devonshire, Sports and Public Schools.

ALLISON, James Anthony, CMG 1966; OBE 1960; PH (Botswana); *b* 31 Jan. 1915; *s* of John Schiller Allison, Edinburgh and Union of South Africa, and Anna Elizabeth Christina (*née* van Velden); *m* 1946, Dorothy Patricia Kerr; one *d. Educ:* Boys' High School, Pretoria, SA; St John's College, Johannesburg, SA; Witwatersrand University, Johannesburg, SA (BA Hons); Colonial Service Course, Cambridge. Assistant District Officer, Colonial Service, 1938-39; War of 1939-45: Military Service, 3 West African Infantry Brigade, 1939-46 (Major). Asst District Officer and District Officer, Nigeria, 1946-50; District Commissioner, Secretariat, Finance Secretary, Administration Secretary, and Sec. to Cabinet, Bechuanaland, 1950-65; Sen. Permanent Sec. and Sec. to the Cabinet, Botswana (formerly Bechuanaland), 1965-Jan. 1970, retired. *Recreations:* birds, shells, literature, music, travelling. *Address:* 11 Victory Place, Amanzimtoti, Natal, South Africa.

ALLISON, Rt. Rev. Oliver Claude, CBE 1971; Travelling Secretary, Sudan Church Association; *b* Stafford, 1908; *s* of Rev. W. S. Allison. *Educ:* Dean Close School, Cheltenham; Queens' College and Ridley Hall, Cambridge. BA 1930; MA 1934. Deacon, 1932; Priest, 1933; Curate of Fulwood, 1932-36; Curate of St John, Boscombe, and Jt Sec. Winchester Dio. Council of Youth, 1936-38; CMS Miss. at Juba, Dio. Sudan, 1938-47; Asst Bp in the Sudan, 1948-53; Bishop in the Sudan, 1953-74. *Publications:* A Pilgrim Church's Progress, 1966; Through Fire and Water, 1976. *Address:* at Inkpen Rectory, Newbury, Berks RG15 0PZ. *Club:* Royal Commonwealth Society.

ALLISON, Ralph Victor, CMG 1967; retired industrialist, Australia; *b* 20 Feb. 1900; *s* of late Albert John and Edith Victoria Allison; *m* 1923, Myrtle Ellen Birch; two *d. Educ:* public and night schools, Milang, SA. General Store, A. H. Landseer Ltd: Milang, 1916-19; Adelaide, 1919-26; R. J. Finlayson Ltd, Adelaide: Company Sec., 1926-39; Dir, 1939-64; Man. Dir, 1954-64; Chm. Dirs of subsidiaries, 1954-64. Mem. Council: Royal Agric. and Hort. Soc. of SA, 1937-72 (Exec. Mem. 8 yrs); SA Chamber of Manufactures, 1948- (Pres. 1962, 1963). Mem. SA Dairy Bd, 1957-. Pres. Aust. Chamber of Manufactures, 1964; Mem. Aust. Export Develt Council, 1964-68; Director, Australian Export Promotions Ltd and various other Australian cos until 1966. Mem., many Aust. Commonwealth Cttees. *Recreations:* formerly tennis and bowls; latterly golf. *Address:* 18 Taylor Terrace, Rosslyn Park, SA 5072, Australia. *T:* 31.2538. *Club:* Commonwealth (SA).

ALLISON, Dr Richard Sydney, VRD; MD (Belfast); FRCP; FRCPI; DPM; Hon. Archivist and Consulting Neurologist (retired) to Royal Victoria and Claremont Street Hospitals, Belfast; *b* 15 May 1899; *s* of William Lowcock and Eliza Russell Allison; *m* 1925, Elizabeth Newett Barnett Steen (*d* 1976); one *s* two *d. Educ:* Royal Belfast Academical Institution; Queen's University, Belfast. RNVR Surg.-Prob. 1918-19; Surg.-Lt 1926, retd 1930 (Surg.-Comdr). Actg Surg.-Capt. and Consultant to SW and W Approaches, 1944-45. Consultant in Medicine to Admiralty, N Ireland. Asst Physician, Ruthin Castle, 1925-30; appointed Asst Physician: Royal Victoria Hospital, 1930; Claremont Street Hospital, 1938. Clinical Examiner in Medicine, Queen's University, Belfast, 1931-64; External Examiner in Neurology, Victoria Univ., Manchester, 1959-62. Visiting Professor: Medical College of South Carolina, 1957; Dalhousie Univ., Nova Scotia, 1958; Visiting Consultant Neurologist to Thailand Govt, 1965. Pres. Ulster Neuropsych. Soc., 1950-52, 1961-63; Pres. Sect. Neurology, RSM, London, 1962-63. Mem. Assoc. of Physicians of GB and Ireland (Pres., 1967); President: Ulster Med. Soc., 1970; Sect. Neurol., Royal Acad. Medicine in Ireland, 1971; Past Pres., Assoc. Brit. Neurologists; For. corresp. Mem., French Soc. of Neurology. *Publications:* Sea Diseases: the story of a great natural experiment in preventive medicine in the Royal Navy, 1943; The Senile Brain, 1962; The Very Faculties, 1969; The Seeds of Time: a history of Belfast General (Royal) Hospital, 1850-1903, 1972; HMS Caroline: a history of the Ulster Division, RNVR, 1974; (Jt) Whitla's Dictionary of Treatment (8th edn), 1938, (ed jtly) *ibid* (9th edn), 1957; papers in scientific jls. *Recreations:* travel, fly fishing, naval history. *Address:* Waringstown, Lurgan, Co. Armagh, Northern Ireland. *T:* Waringstown 353.

ALLISON, Ronald William Paul; Press Secretary to the Queen, since 1973; *b* 26 Jan. 1932; *o s* of Percy Allison and Dorothy (*née* Doyle); *m* 1956, Maureen Angela Macdonald; two *d. Educ:* Weymouth Grammar Sch.; Taunton's Sch., Southampton. Reporter, Hampshire Chronicle, 1952-57; Reporter, BBC, 1957-67; freelance broadcaster, 1968-69; special correspondent, BBC, 1969-73. *Publications:* Look Back in Wonder, 1968; The Queen, 1973. *Recreations:* photography, painting, watching football. *Address:* 36 Ormond Drive, Hampton, Mddx. *T:* 01-979 1912. *Clubs:* Stage Golf Soc.; Old Tauntonians (Southampton).

ALLISON, Rt. Rev. Sherard Falkner, MA, DD, LLD; *b* 19 Jan. 1907; *s* of Reverend W. S. Allison; *m* 1936, Ruth Hills; one *s* two *d* (and one *s* decd). *Educ:* Dean Close School, Cheltenham; Jesus Coll., Cambridge (Scholar); Ridley Hall, Cambridge. 1st Cl. Classical Tripos, Parts I and II; 2nd Class Theological Tripos, Part I and Jeremie Septuagint Prize; Curate of St James', Tunbridge Wells, 1931-34; Chaplain of Ridley Hall, Cambridge, and Examining Chaplain to Bishop of Bradford, 1934-36; Vicar of Rodbourne Cheney, Swindon, 1936-40; Vicar of Erith, 1940-45; Principal of Ridley Hall, Cambridge, 1945-50; Bishop of Chelmsford, 1951-61; Bishop of Winchester, and Prelate of the Most Noble Order of the Garter, 1961-74. Examining Chaplain to Bishop of Rochester, 1945, and to Bishop of Ely, 1947; Select Preacher: Univ. of Cambridge, 1946, 1955, 1962; Univ. of Oxford, 1953-55, 1963; Proctor in Convocation, Diocese of Ely, 1949. Hon. Fellow, Jesus College, Cambridge, 1963. DD, Lambeth, 1951; Hon. DD: Occidental Coll., Los Angeles, 1959; Wycliffe Coll., Toronto, 1959; Hon. STD, Church Divinity Sch. of the Pacific, 1959; Hon. LLD: Sheffield, 1960; Southampton, 1974. *Publication:* The Christian Life, 1938 (Joint). *Recreations:* sailing, water-colour sketching, bird watching, gardening. *Address:* Winton Lodge, Alde Lane, Aldeburgh, Suffolk.

ALLNUTT, Ian Peter, OBE 1976; Representative of the British Council in Mexico, until 1977; *b* 26 April 1917; *s* of Col E. B. Allnutt, CBE, MC, and Joan C. Gainford; *m* 1946, Doreen Louise Lenagan; four *d. Educ:* Imperial Service Coll., Windsor; Sidney Sussex Coll., Cambridge. BA 1938, MA 1942. Served

War, 1940-45, Nigeria Regt, RWAFF. HM Colonial Service, 1939-46, Asst District Officer, Nigeria. Officer of the British Council with service in Peru, E Africa, Colombia, Argentina, Malta, London and Mexico, 1946-77. Insignia of Aztec Eagle, 1975. *Recreations:* all kinds of water sport, mountains, the arts. *Address:* Karen Cottage, Boulters Lane, Maidenhead, Berks. *T:* Maidenhead 20499. *Clubs:* Royal Automobile; Leander (Henley).

ALLOTT, Prof. Antony Nicolas, JP; Professor of African Law, in the University of London, since 1964; *b* 30 June 1924; *s* of late Reginald William Allott and Dorothy Allott (*née* Dobson); *m* 1952, Anna Joan Sargant; two *s* two *d. Educ:* Downside Sch.; New Coll., Oxford. Lieut Royal Northumberland Fusiliers and King's African Rifles, 1944-46. BA Oxon (1st class Hons Jurisprudence), 1948; PhD London 1954. Lecturer in African Law, School of Oriental and African Studies, London, 1948-60; Reader in African Law, Univ. of London, 1960-64. Hon. Director, Africa Centre, 1963-66; Pres., African Studies Assoc. of UK, 1969-70 (past Hon. Treas.); Vice-Pres., Internat. African Law Assoc., 1967. Governor, Plater Coll., Oxford. JP Middlesex 1969. *Publications:* Essays in African Law, with special reference to the Law of Ghana, 1960; (ed) Judicial and Legal Systems in Africa, 1962, 2nd edn 1970; New Essays in African Law, 1970; articles in legal and other jls. *Recreations:* music, gardening, silviculture. *Address:* 21 Windsor Road, Finchley, N3 3SN. *T:* 01-346 7245.

ALLOTT, Eric Newmarch, DM, FRCP; FRIC; Consultant Adviser in Chemical Pathology, Ministry of Health, 1963-68; Director, Group Laboratory, Lewisham Hospital, 1931-64; *b* 28 May 1899; *e s* of Henry Newmarch Allott, Stretford, Manchester; *m* 1930, Edith Mary Kydd (*d* 1974); one *d. Educ:* Manchester Grammar Sch.; Balliol Coll., Oxford (Brackenbury Scholar). St Bartholomew's Hospital, BA 1920; BM Oxford, 1925. Demonstrator in Chemistry, Univ. of Oxford, 1920-22; Beit Memorial Fellow in Medical Research, 1925-27; Asst Physiologist, Sheffield Royal Hosp., 1928; Chief Asst, Medical Professorial Unit, St Barts Hosp., 1929-31. Chm. of Council, 1957-61, and former Pres., Assoc. of Clinical Pathologists; FRSocMed (Sec., 1937-44 Pres., 1944-46, Section of Experimental Medicine); Chm., Section of Chemical Pathology, 1st Internat. Congress of Clinical Pathology, 1951; Mem., Biochemical Soc. (Cttee, 1948-52); Member Council: Royal Institute of Chemistry, 1962-65; College of Pathologists, 1963-66; Member Editorial Board, Journal of Clinical Pathology; Hon. Lecturer in Pathology, KCH and RCS. *Publications:* Richter's Organic Chemistry (3rd English edn), 1934; Section Editor, Recent Advances in Clinical Pathology; papers on medical and chemical pathological subjects. *Recreation:* gardening. *Address:* 27 Ritchie Court, 380 Banbury Road, Oxford OX2 7PW. *T:* Oxford 50496.

ALLOTT, Air Cdre Molly Greenwood, CB 1975; Director of the Women's Royal Air Force, 1973-76; *b* 28 Dec. 1918; *d* of late Gerald William Allott. *Educ:* Sheffield High Sch. for Girls (GPDST). Served War of 1939-45: joined WAAF, 1941; served in: Egypt, Singapore, Germany. Staff of AOC-in-C: RAF Germany, 1960-63; Fighter Command, 1963-66; Training Command, 1971-73. ADC 1973-76. *Recreations:* travel, decorative arts. *Address:* c/o Ministry of Defence, Adastral House, Theobald's Road, WC1. *Club:* Royal Air Force.

ALLOTT, Robin Michael; Under-Secretary, General Division, Department of Trade, since 1976; *b* 9 May 1926; *s* of Reginald William Allott and Dorothy (*née* Dobson). *Educ:* The Oratory Sch., Caversham; New Coll., Oxford; Sheffield Univ. Asst Principal, BoT, 1948; UK Delegn to OECD, Paris, 1952; Private Sec. to Sec. for Overseas Trade, 1953; Principal, Office for Scotland, Glasgow, 1954; UK Delegn to UN Conf. on Trade and Develt, Geneva, 1964; Asst Sec., BoT, 1965; Counsellor, UK Delegn to EEC, Brussels, 1971; sabbatical year, New Coll., Oxford, 1974-75; Dept of Industry (motor industry), 1975. *Publication:* The Physical Foundation of Language, 1973. *Recreations:* reading Marcus Aurelius, studying the relation of language and perception. *Address:* 29 Headland Avenue, Seaford, East Sussex. *T:* Seaford 892609.
    See also *A . N . Allott.*

ALLSOP, Peter Henry Bruce; Chairman, Associated Book Publishers, since 1976; *b* 22 Aug. 1924; *s* of late Herbert Henry Allsop and of Elsie Hilpern (*née* Whitaker); *m* 1950, Patricia Elizabeth Kingwell Bown; two *s* one *d. Educ:* Haileybury; Caius Coll., Cambridge (MA). Called to Bar, Lincoln's Inn, 1948. Temp. Asst Principal, Air Min., 1944-48; Barrister in practice, 1948-50; Sweet & Maxwell: Editor, 1950-59; Dir, 1960-64; Man. Dir, 1965-73; Chm., 1974; Dir, Associated Book Publishers, 1963, Asst Man. Dir, 1965-67, Man. Dir, 1968-76. Mem.

Council, Publishers Assoc., 1969 (Treasurer, 1973; Pres., 1975-77; Vice-Pres., 1977-; Chm., Employment Cttee, 1977-). *Publications:* (ed) Bowstead's Law of Agency, 11th edn, 1951. *Recreations:* gardening, hill walking, theatre, messing about in boats. *Address:* Manor Farm, Charlton Mackrell, Somerton, Somerset. *T:* Charlton Mackrell 650. *Club:* Garrick.

ALLSOPP, family name of **Baron Hindlip.**

ALLSOPP, Bruce; *see* Allsopp, H. B.

ALLSOPP, Prof. Cecil Benjamin, MA, PhD, DSc; FInstP; Professor of Physics Applied to Medicine, University of London at Guy's Hospital Medical School, 1953-70, now Emeritus; Consultant Physicist Emeritus to Guy's Hospital; *b* 2 Sept. 1904; *m* 1935, Ivy Kathleen Johns; one *s* one *d. Educ:* Emmanuel College, Cambridge; University of Frankfurt-am-Main. MA, Cambridge, 1930; PhD, Cambridge, 1932; DSc, London, 1951. Pres., British Institute of Radiology, 1963-64; Silvanus Thompson Memorial Lectr, 1965. *Publications:* Absorption Spectrophotometry (with F. Twyman, FRS), 1934. Papers in Proc. of the Royal Soc., Jl of the Chemical Soc., Trans of the Faraday Soc., British Journal of Radiology, British Journal of Experimental Pathology, Cancer Research, etc. *Address:* 40 Queen Edith's Way, Cambridge CB1 4PW.

ALLSOPP, (Harold) Bruce, BArch, DipCD, FSA, FRIBA, MRTPI; Chairman, Oriel Press Ltd, since 1962; Director, Routledge & Kegan Paul Books Ltd, since 1974; *b* Oxford, 4 July 1912; *s* of Henry Allsopp and Elizabeth May Allsopp (*née* Robertson); *m* 1935, Florence Cyrilla Woodroffe; two *s. Educ:* Manchester Grammar Sch.; Liverpool School of Architecture. BArch (1st Cl. Hons), Liverpool, 1933; Rome Finalist, 1934; Diploma in Civic Design 1935; ARIBA 1935; AMTPI 1936; FRIBA 1955; FSA 1968. Asst Architect in Chichester and London, 1934-35; Lecturer, Leeds Coll. of Art, 1935-40. War Service 1940-46, N Africa, Italy, Captain RE. Lecturer in Architecture, Univ. of Durham, 1946; Sen. Lecturer, 1955; Sen. Lecturer, Univ. of Newcastle upon Tyne, 1963, Dir of Architectural Studies, 1965-69; Sen. Lecturer in History of Architecture, 1969-73; Reader, 1973-77. Chairman: Soc. of Architectural Historians of GB, 1959-65; Independent Publishers Guild, 1971-73; Master, Art Workers Guild, 1970. *Publications:* Art and the Nature of Architecture, 1952; Decoration and Furniture, Vol. 1 1952, Vol. 2 1953; A General History of Architecture, 1955; Style in the Visual Arts, 1957; Possessed, 1959; The Future of the Arts, 1959; A History of Renaissance Architecture, 1959; The Naked Flame, 1962; Architecture, 1964; To Kill a King, 1965; A History of Classical Architecture, 1965; Historic Architecture of Newcastle upon Tyne, 1967; Civilization, the Next Stage, 1969; The Study of Architectural History, 1970; Modern Architecture of Northern England, 1970; Inigo Jones on Palladio, 1970; Romanesque Architecture, 1971; Ecological Morality, 1972; Towards a Humane Architecture, 1974; Return of the Pagan, 1974; Cecilia, 1975; Inigo Jones and the Lords A'Leaping, 1975; A Modern Theory of Architecture, 1977; (with Ursula Clark): Oriel Guides: Architecture of France, 1963; Architecture of Italy, 1964; Architecture of England, 1964; Photography for Tourists, 1966; Historic Architecture of Northumberland, 1969; (with U. Clark and H. W. Booton): The Great Tradition of Western Architecture, 1966; articles in Encyclopedia Americana, Jl of RSA, etc; commentator TV films, including Fancy Gothic, 1974. *Recreations:* piano and harpsichord, gardening. *Address:* Woodburn, Batt House Road, Stocksfield, Northumberland NE43 7QZ. *T:* Stocksfield 2323; Stocksfield Studio, Stocksfield, Northumberland NE43 7NA. *T:* Stocksfield 3065. *Clubs:* Athenæum, Arts.

ALMISMARI, Mohamed Younis; Ambassador of the Socialist People's Libyan Arab Jamahiriya to the Court of St James's, since 1976; *b* 3 July 1937; *m* 1959, Khadija Gargoum; three *s* two *d. Educ:* Camberley Staff Coll. Colonel in the Army till 1969. Ministry of Foreign Affairs, 1974-. *Address:* 31 Phillimore Gardens, W8. *Club:* Hurlingham.

ALPHAND, Hervé; Grand Officier, Légion d'Honneur, 1968; *b* 1907; *s* of Charles Hervé and Jeanne Alphand; *m* 1958, Nicole Merenda. *Educ:* Lycée Janson de Sailly; Ecole des Sciences Politiques. Inspector of Finances and Dir Dept of Treaties, Min. of Commerce, 1937-38; Financial Attaché to Embassy, Washington, 1940-41; Dir of Economic Affairs for French National Cttee in London, 1941-44; Director-General, Economic, Financial and Technical Affairs (Min. of Foreign Affairs), 1945; French Ambassador to OEEC; French Dep. to Atlantic Council, 1950, and Mem. NATO Perm. Council, 1952-54; Ambassador: to UN, 1955-56; to USA, 1956-65; Secretary-General, Min. of Foreign Affairs, France, 1965-73. *Address:* 122 rue de Grenelle, Paris VIIe, France.

ALPORT, family name of **Baron Alport.**

ALPORT, Baron, *cr* 1961, of Colchester (Life Peer); **Cuthbert James McCall Alport,** PC 1960; TD 1949; DL; *b* 22 March 1912; *o s* of late Prof. Arthur Cecil Alport, MD, FRCP, and of Janet, *y d* of James McCall, Dumfriesshire; *m* 1945, Rachel Cecilia, *o d* of Lt-Col R. C. Bingham, *qv*; one *s* two *d. Educ:* Haileybury; Pembroke Coll., Cambridge. MA History and Law; Pres., Cambridge Union Society, 1935. Tutor Ashridge Coll., 1935-37. Barrister-at-Law, Middle Temple. Joined Artists Rifles, 1934. Served War of 1939-45: Hon. Lieut-Col; Director Conservative Political Centre, 1945-50. MP (C) Colchester division of Essex, 1950-61; Chairman Joint East and Central African Board, 1953-55; Governor, Charing Cross Hospital, 1954-55. Asst Postmaster-General, Dec. 1955-Jan. 1957; Parliamentary Under-Secretary of State, Commonwealth Relations Office, 1957-59; Minister of State, Commonwealth Relations Office, Oct. 1959-March 1961; British High Commissioner in the Federation of Rhodesia and Nyasaland, 1961-63; Mem. of Council of Europe, 1964-65; British Govt Representative to Rhodesia, June-July 1967. A Dep. Speaker, House of Lords, 1971-. Adviser to the Home Secretary, 1974-. A Dir of Dawnay, Day Group Ltd and other companies, 1965. Governor, Haileybury Coll. Master, Skinners' Co., 1969-70. Pro-Chancellor, City Univ., 1972-. High Steward of Colchester, 1967-; DL Essex 1974. *Publications:* Kingdoms in Partnership, 1937; Hope in Africa, 1952; The Sudden Assignment, 1965. *Address:* The Cross House, Layer de la Haye, Colchester, Essex. *T:* Layer de la Haye 217. *Club:* Pratt's.

AL-RIFA'I, Zaid; Prime Minister, Minister of Defence and Foreign Minister, Jordan, 1973-76; *b* 27 Nov. 1936; *s* of late Samir al-Rifa'i, many times Prime Minister of Jordan; *m* 1965, Muna Talhouni; one *s* one *d. Educ:* Harvard (BA); Columbia (MA). Entered Jordan Foreign Service; Attaché, Cairo, 1957; 3rd Sec., Beirut, 1958; Political Sec., Jordan Mission to UN, 1959-60; Dir, Internat. Organisation Dept, Foreign Min., 1960-61; 1st Sec., London, 1962-63; Chief of Royal Protocol, 1963-64; Dir, Political Dept, For. Min., 1965; Asst Chief of Royal Court, 1966; Dir-Gen. of Royal Court, 1967; Personal Sec. to King Hussein, 1968; Chief of Royal Court, 1969-70; Ambassador to London, 1970-72; Special Political Adviser to King Hussein, 1972. Holds Grand Cordon of Al-Istiqlal of Jordan, also decorations from Lebanon, Libya, Morocco, Ethiopia, China, Spain. *Recreations:* reading, music, sports, bridge. *Address:* c/o Ministry of Foreign Affairs, Amman, Jordan. *Clubs:* Burke's, Hurlingham, Travellers', etc.

AL-SABAH, Shaikh Saud Nasir; Ambassador of Kuwait to the Court of St James's, since 1975; *b* 3 Oct. 1944; *m* 1962, Shaikha Awatif Al-Sabah; two *s* two *d . Barrister-at-law, Gray's Inn. Entered Legal Dept, Min. of Foreign Affairs, Kuwait. Representative of Kuwait: to 6th Cttee of UN Gen. Assembly, 1969-74; to Seabed Cttee of UN, 1969-73; Vice-Chm., Delegn of Kuwait to Conf. of Law of the Sea, 1974-75; Rep. of Delegn to Conf. of Law of Treaties, 1969. *Address:* 11a Belgrave Square, SW1X 8PH. *T:* 01-245 9292.

ALSTEAD, Stanley, CBE 1960; MD, FRCP; Professor Emeritus, Regius Chair of Materia Medica, University of Glasgow; formerly Senior Visiting Physician, Stobhill Hospital, Glasgow; *b* 6 June 1905; *s* of late Robert Alstead, OBE, and Anne Alstead; *m* 1932, Nora, 2nd *d* of late M. W. Sowden and late Nell Sowden; one *s. Educ:* Wigan Grammar Sch.; Liverpool Univ. Held various appts in north of England, Glasgow and Inverness. Appointed Pollok Lecturer in Pharmacology, Univ. of Glasgow, 1932, and became interested in clinical aspects of subject; Regius Prof. of Materia Medica and Therapeutics, Univ. of Glasgow, 1948-70; External Examiner in Univs of St Andrews, Glasgow, Aberdeen, London, Manchester, Liverpool, Cairo, Malta. Hon. Prof., Univ. of East Africa (Makerere University Coll.) and Hon. Physician to Kenyatta Nat. Hosp., Nairobi, Kenya, 1965-66. Served War of 1939-45, in RAMC as medical specialist to 5 CCS in Tunisia and Sicily, and in Belgium and Egypt as Officer in Charge of Med. Div. 67 Gen. Hosp. and 63 Gen. Hosp. with rank of Lt-Col (despatches). MD Liverpool (N. E. Roberts Prize); FRCP; FRCPGlas; FRCPE; FRSE. Pres. RFPSG (now RCPSGlas), 1956-58. Member: British Pharmacopœia Commn, 1953-57; Standing Jt Cttee on Classification of Proprietary Preparations; Commn. on Spiritual Healing (General Assembly of Church of Scotland). Consultant/Editor, Dilling's Clinical Pharmacology; Jt Editor, Textbook of Medical Treatment. *Publications:* papers in med. jls on results of original research in clinical pharmacology. *Recreations:* gardening, music (violin) and reading poetry. *Address:* 33 Ochlochy Park, Dunblane, Perthshire. *Clubs:* Western, RASC (Glasgow).

ALSTON, (Arthur) Rex; freelance broadcaster and journalist; BBC Commentator, 1943-61, retired; *b* 2 July 1901; *e s* of late Arthur Fawssett Alston, Suffragan Bishop of Middleton, and late Mary Isabel Alston; *m* 1932, Elspeth, *d* of late Sir Stewart Stockman and Lady Stockman; one *s* one *d. Educ:* Trent College; Clare College, Cambridge. Assistant Master, Bedford School, 1924-41. Joined BBC, Jan. 1942. *Publications:* Taking the Air, 1950; Over to Rex Alston, 1953; Test Commentary, 1956; Watching Cricket, 1962. *Recreations:* golf, gardening. *Address:* Ryders, Oakwood Hill, Dorking, Surrey RH5 5NB. *T:* Oakwood Hill 410. *Clubs:* East India, Devonshire, Sports and Public Schools, MCC.

ALSTON, Rt. Rev. Mgr. Joseph Leo; Parish Priest, Sacred Heart Church, Ainsdale, Southport, since 1972; *b* 17 Dec. 1917; *s* of Benjamin Alston and Mary Elizabeth (*née* Moss). *Educ:* St Mary's School, Chorley; Upholland College, Wigan; English Coll., Rome; Christ's College, Cambridge. Priest, 1942; Licentiate in Theology, Gregorian Univ., Rome, 1942; BA (1st Cl. Hons Classics) Cantab 1945. Classics Master, Upholland Coll., Wigan, 1945-52, Headmaster, 1952-64; Rector, Venerable English Coll., Rome, 1964-71. Chm., Liverpool RC Ecumenism Commn, 1977-. *Recreation:* music. *Address:* 483 Liverpool Road, Ainsdale, Southport, Merseyside. *T:* Southport 77527.

ALSTON, Rex; *see* Alston, A. R.

ALSTON, Dr Robin Carfrae; Consultant in Bibliography to the British Library, 1977; *b* 29 Jan. 1933; *s* of Wilfred Louis Alston; *m* 1957, Joanna Dorothy Ormiston; two *s* one *d. Educ:* Rugby Sch.; Univs of British Columbia (BA), Oxford (MA), Toronto (MA) and London (PhD). Teaching Fellow, University Coll., Toronto, 1956-58; Lectr, New Brunswick Univ., 1958-60; Lectr in English Lit., Leeds Univ., 1964-76. Jt Editor Leeds Studies in English and Leeds Texts and Monographs; Editor Studies in Early Modern English; Jt Editor, The Direction Line, 1976-. Founder, Chm. and principal Editor, Scolar Press Ltd, 1966-72; Founder, Janus Press, devoted to original art prints, 1973. Mem. Adv. Cttee, British Library, 1975-. Mem. Organising Cttee, 18th Century Short Title Catalogue, 1976-. Mem. Council, Bibliographical Soc., 1967-; Founding Mem. Council, Ilkley Literature Festival. *Publications:* An Introduction to Old English, 1961 (rev. edn 1966); A Catalogue of Books relating to the English Language (1500-1800) in Swedish Libraries, 1965; English Language and Medieval English Literature: a Select Reading-List for Students, 1966; A Bibliography of the English Language from the Invention of Printing to the Year 1800: Vol. I, 1965; Vols V and VIII, 1966; Vols VII and IV, 1967; Vol. II, 1968; Vol. VI, 1969; Vol. III, 1970; Vol. IX, 1971; Vol. X, 1972; Alexander Gil's Logonomia Anglica (1619): a translation into Modern English, 1973; (jtly) The Works of William Bullokar, Vol. I, 1966; English Studies (rev. edn of Vol. III, Cambridge Bibl. Eng. Lit.), 1968; English Linguistics 1500-1800: a Collection of Texts in Facsimile (365 vols), 1967-72; European Linguistics 1500-1700: a Collection of Texts in Facsimile (12 vols), 1968-72; A Checklist of the works of Joseph Addison, 1976; numerous articles, etc. *Recreations:* music, photography. *Address:* Farrand House, Langbar, Ilkley, W Yorks LS29 0ER. *T:* Ilkley 3181.

ALSTON ROBERTS WEST, General Sir Michael M.; *see* West.

AL-TAJIR, Mohamed Mahdi; Ambassador of the United Arab Emirates to the Court of St James's, since 1972, and France, 1972-77; *b* 26 Dec. 1931; *m* 1956, Zohra Al-Tajir; five *s* one *d. Educ:* Al Tajir Sch., Bahrain; Preston Grammar Sch., Lancs, England. Dir, Dept of Port and Customs, Govt of Bahrain, 1955-63; Dir, Dept of HH the Ruler's Affairs and Petroleum Affairs, 1963-; Director: Nat. Bank of Dubai Ltd, 1963-; Dubai Petroleum Co., 1963-; Dubai Nat. Air Travel Agency, 1966-; Qatar-Dubai Currency Bd, 1965-73; United Arab Emirates Currency Bd, 1973-; Dubai Dry Dock Co., 1973-; Chm., S Eastern Dubai Drilling Co., 1968-. Hon. Citizen of State of Texas, USA, 1963. *Address:* Embassy of the United Arab Emirates, 30 Prince's Gate, SW7. *T:* 01-581 1281.

ALTAMONT, Earl of; Jeremy Ulick Browne; *b* 4 June 1939; *s* of 10th Marquess of Sligo, *qv*; *m* 1961, Jennifer June, *d* of Major Derek Cooper, Dunlewey, Co. Donegal, and Mrs C. Heber Percy, Pophleys, Radnage; four *d. Educ:* St Columba's College, Eire; Royal Agricultural College, Cirencester. *Address:* Westport House, Co. Mayo, Eire.

ALTHORP, Viscount; Charles Edward Maurice Spencer; *b* 20 May 1964; *s* and *heir* of 8th Earl Spencer, *qv. Educ:* Maidwell Hall; Eton College. Page of Honour to HM the Queen, 1977-.

ALTON, Euan Beresford Seaton, MBE 1945; MC 1943; Under Secretary, Department of Health and Social Security, 1968-76; *b* 22 April 1919; *y s* of late William Lester St John Alton and Ellen Seaton Alton; *m* 1953, Diana Margaret Ede; one *s* one *d*. *Educ:* St Paul's Sch.; Magdalen Coll., Oxford. Served with Army, 1939-45; Major RA. Admin. Officer, Colonial Service and HM OCS, Gold Coast and Ghana, 1946-58; Admin. Officer, Class 1, 1957. Entered Civil Service as Asst Principal, Min. of Health, 1958; Principal, 1958; Asst Sec., 1961; Under Sec., 1968. *Recreations:* sailing, walking, golf. *Address:* The Old School, Church Lane, Brantham, Manningtree, Essex CO11 1QA. *T:* Manningtree 3419. *Clubs:* Royal Commonwealth Society; Stour Sailing (Manningtree).

ALTRINCHAM, Barony of, *cr* 1945, of Tormarton; title disclaimed by 2nd Baron; *see under* Grigg, John Edward Poynder.

ALTY, Thomas, DSc Liverpool; PhD Cantab; DCL Dunelm; LLD Glasgow, Toronto, Rhodes; FInstP; FRSC, FRSE; Deputy Principal, University of Birmingham, 1963-69; Life Governor, University of Birmingham; *b* 30 Sept. 1899; *s* of James Alty, Rufford, Lancashire; *m* 1925, Stella West, *d* of W. Harris, solicitor, Liverpool; no *c*. *Educ:* Univ. of Liverpool (Oliver Lodge Fellow, 1921); University of Cambridge. Lecturer in Physics, University of Durham, 1924-25; Prof. of Physics, Univ. of Saskatchewan, Canada, 1925-29; Research Physicist, Imperial Chemical Industries, Northwich, Cheshire, 1929-30; Prof. of Physics, Univ. of Saskatchewan, 1930-32; Research Prof. of Physics, Univ. of Saskatchewan, 1932-35; Cargill Prof. of Applied Physics, Univ. of Glasgow, 1935-45; Cargill Prof. of Natural Philosophy, Univ. of Glasgow, 1945-48; Master of Rhodes University Coll., 1948-51; Principal and Vice-Chancellor of Rhodes Univ., Grahamstown, S Africa, 1951-63. Chm. Assoc. of Univs of British Commonwealth, 1958-60. Mem., SA Council for Scientific and Industrial Research, 1956-63. Member, SA National Council for Social Research, 1955-63. *Publications:* scientific papers. *Address:* 105 Fitzroy Avenue, Harborne, Birmingham B17 8RG.

ALUWIHARE, Sir Richard, KCMG 1950; Kt 1948; CBE 1945; High Commissioner of Ceylon in India, 1957-63, retired; *b* 23 May 1895; *m* 1921, Lucille Moonemalle (*d* 1961); two *d*. *Educ:* Trinity Coll., Kandy. Served European War, 1914-18, Somme, France (wounded); welfare work with Indian Army (despatches). Joined Ceylon Civil Service, 1920; (appointed by Governor) Actg Police Magistrate, Dandagamuwa, 1923; HM Customs, 1926; District Judge, Kegalle, 1928, Nuwara Eliya, 1931; Class II of Civil Service; Controller of Finance and Supply, General Treasury, 1934; Asst Govt Agent, Kegalle, 1937; Dep. Collector of Customs, 1939; Actg Govt Agent, North Central Prov., 1941; Class I Civil Service; Govt Agent, Central Prov., 1946; Inspector-General of Police, Ceylon, 1947-53, retd. *Recreations:* cricket, Rugby football, swimming, riding. *Address:* Aluwihare, Matale, Sri Lanka. *Clubs:* Singhalese Sports, Orient.

ALVAREZ, Alfred; author; Advisory Editor, Penguin Modern European Poets; with The Observer, since 1956 (Poetry Editor, 1956-66); *b* London, 1929; *s* of Bertie Alvarez and Katie Alvarez (*née* Levy); *m* 1st, 1956, Ursula Barr (marr. diss. 1961); one *s*; 2nd, 1966, Anne Adams; one *s* one *d*. *Educ:* Oundle Sch.; Corpus Christi Coll., Oxford. BA (Oxon) 1952, MA 1956. Sen. Research Schol., CCC, Oxon, and Research Schol. of Goldsmiths' Company, 1952-53, 1954-55. Procter Visiting Fellowship, Princeton, 1953-54; Vis. Fellow of Rockefeller Foundn, USA, 1955-56, 1958; gave Christian Gauss Seminars in Criticism, Princeton, and was Lectr in Creative Writing, 1957-58; D. H. Lawrence Fellowship, New Mexico, 1958; Drama Critic, The New Statesman, 1958-60. Visiting Prof.: Brandeis Univ., 1960; New York State Univ., Buffalo, 1966. Vachel Lindsay Prize for Poetry (from Poetry, Chicago), 1961. *Publications:* The Shaping Spirit (US title, Stewards of Excellence), 1958; The School of Donne, 1961; The New Poetry (ed and introd), 1962; Under Pressure, 1965; Beyond All This Fiddle, 1968; Lost (poems), 1968; Penguin Modern Poets, No 18, 1970; Apparition (poems), 1971; The Savage God, 1971; Beckett, 1973; Hers, 1974. *Recreations:* rock-climbing, poker, cinema. *Address:* c/o The Observer, 8 St Andrew's Hill, EC4. *Club:* Climbers'.

ALVAREZ, Prof. Luis W.; Professor of Physics, University of California, Berkeley, since 1945; *b* 13 June, 1911; *s* of Dr Walter C. Alvarez and Harriet Smyth; *m* 1st, 1936, Geraldine Smithwick; one *s* one *d*; 2nd, 1958, Janet Landis; one *s* one *d*. *Educ:* University of Chicago. SB 1932, PhD 1936. Radiation Lab., Univ. of California, 1936-; MIT Radiation Lab., 1940-43; Metallurgical Lab., Univ. of Chicago, 1943-44; Los Alamos Sci. Lab., 1944-45; Associate Dir, Lawrence Rad. Lab., 1954-59. Pres., Amer. Physical Soc., 1969; Member: Nat. Acad. of Sciences; Nat. Acad. of Engineering; Am. Phil. Soc.; Am. Acad. of Arts and Sciences; Assoc. Mem., Institut d'Egypte. Awarded: Collier Trophy, 1946; John Scott Medal, 1953; US Medal for Merit, 1947; Einstein Medal, 1961; Pioneer Award, AIEEE, 1963; Nat. Medal of Science, 1964; Michelson Award, 1965; Nobel Prize in Physics, 1968. Hon. ScD: Chicago, 1967; Carnegie-Mellon, 1968; Kenyon, 1969. *Publications:* more than 100 contributions to Physics Literature, largely in Nuclear Physics and High Energy Physics; 22 US Patents, largely in Electronics and Optics. *Recreations:* flying, golf, music. *Address:* (business) Lawrence Radiation Laboratory, University of California, Berkeley, Calif 94720, USA. *T:* 415-843-2740; (home) 131 Southampton Avenue, Berkeley, Calif 94707, USA. *T:* 415-525-0590. *Clubs:* Bohemian (San Francisco); Faculty (Berkeley); Miravista Golf (El Cerrito).

ALVEY, John; Deputy Controller, R&D Establishments and Research C, and Chief Scientist (RAF), Ministry of Defence, since 1977; *b* 19 June 1925; *s* of George C. V. Alvey and Hilda E. Alvey (*née* Pellatt); *m* 1955, Celia Edmed Marson; three *s*. *Educ:* Reeds Sch.; London Univ.; BSc (Eng), DipNEC. CEng, FIEE. London Stock Exchange, to 1943. Royal Navy, 1943-46; Royal Naval Scientific Service, 1950; Head of Weapons Projects, Admiralty Surface Weapons Estabt, 1968-72; Dir-Gen. Electronics Radar, PE, MoD, 1972-73; Dir-Gen., Airborne Electronic Systems, PE, MoD, 1974-75; Dir, Admiralty Surface Weapons Estabt, 1976-77. *Recreations:* reading, Rugby, small-bore rifle shooting, theatre going. *Address:* 9 St Omer Road, Guildford, Surrey. *T:* Guildford 63859.

ALVIN, Madame Juliette, FGSMT; violoncellist and viola da gamba player; registered Music Therapist (USA); 2nd *d* of Jeanne and Henri Alvin, Paris; *m* William A. Robson, *qv*; two *s* one *d*. *Educ:* Lycée de Versailles; Conservatoire National de Musique, Paris (First prix d'Excellence); later studied with Pablo Casals; has played in principal musical centres of Europe, including London, Paris, Berlin, Vienna, Brussels, Prague, Buda Pesth, Belgrade, Bucarest, The Hague, Warsaw, Stockholm, etc; often with the Philharmonic Orchestra; toured USA frequently, 1932-68. Has broadcast as a soloist in BBC programmes from London and provinces; musical activities during War of 1939-45 included war factory tours and other concerts organised by the Arts Council (CEMA); also recitals in military and Red Cross hospitals and service concerts; more than 200 recitals in aid of War Charities. Recognised as a leading authority on musical education in England through special recitals for school children, and a teacher of internat. reputation. Appointed for winter session, 1950-51, in music dept of North Carolina Univ., USA. Has lectured at numerous universities and colleges in Great Britain, on the Continent, in USA, Canada, S America, and Japan, esp., in recent years, on her experiments in music therapy with handicapped children and mental patients; has televised and made films on her work in music therapy. Member American National Assoc. for Music Therapy; Hon. Member: Argentine Assoc. for Music Therapy; German Assoc. for Music Therapy; Spanish Assoc. for Music Therapy; Italian Assoc. for Music Therapy; Canadian Assoc. for Music Therapy; Hon. Adviser, Japanese Soc. for Music Therapy; Founder and Chm., British Society for Music Therapy (formerly Soc. for Music Therapy and Remedial Music), London, 1958-; Vice-Pres., Internat. Council for Music Therapy and Social Psychiatry; Head of Music Therapy Dept and Dir, Diploma Course in Music Therapy, Guildhall School of Music and Drama, London. *Publications:* The Logic of Casals' Technique; Introducing music to children; Class Teaching of Instruments; Bach and the 'Cello; Musical Theory and Instrumental Technique, 1953; Casals, a great teacher; A Musical Experiment on Backward Children, 1954; 'Cello Tutor for Beginners, 1955 (2nd volume, 1958); Music for the Handicapped Child, 1965, 2nd edn 1976; Music Therapy, 1966, 2nd edn 1975; Report on a Research Project on Music Therapy, 1970. Contrib. to American Jl of Mental Deficiency, Cerebral Palsy Bulletin, The World of Music, Musik and Medizin, British Jl of Music Therapy and other learned jls. *Recreations:* tennis and swimming. *Address:* 48 Lanchester Road, N6 4TA. *T:* 01-883 1331. *Clubs:* London Violoncello, Hospitality (LSE).

ALVINGHAM, 2nd Baron, *cr* 1929, of Woodfold; **Robert Guy Eardley Yerburgh**, OBE 1972; *b* 16 Dec. 1926; *s* of 1st Baron and Dorothea Gertrude (*d* 1927), *d* of late J. Eardley Yerburgh; *S* father 1955; *m* 1952, Beryl Elliott, *d* of late W. D. Williams; one *s* one *d*. *Educ:* Eton. Brig., late Coldstream Guards. *Heir:* s Hon. Robert Richard Guy Yerburgh, *b* 10 Dec. 1956. *Address:* Bix Hall, Henley-on-Thames, Oxfordshire.

ALWYN, William; composer; Professor of Composition, Royal Academy of Music, 1926-55; *b* Northampton, 1905. *Educ:* Northampton Sch.; Royal Acad. of Music. FRAM 1936; Collard Fellow, Worshipful Company of Musicians, 1938; Chm. of Composers' Guild of Gt Britain, 1949, 1950 and 1954; Fellow, British Film Acad., 1958. *Works:* Five Orchestral Preludes (Proms., 1927); Divertimento for Flute (Internat. Contemp. Music Festival, New York, 1940); Concerto Grosso No I (commnd by BBC, 1942); Symphony No I (Cheltenham Festival, 1950, London, 1953); Concerto Grosso No II (LSO and Proms, 1951); Festival March (commnd by Arts Council for Festival of Britain, 1951); Symphonic Prelude, The Magic Island (Hallé Concerts, 1953); Symphony No II (Hallé Concerts, Manchester, 1953, BBC, Festival Hall, 1954); Lyra Angelica, Concerto for Harp Proms, 1954; Autumn Legend, for cor anglais and strings (Cheltenham Festival and Proms, 1955); Symphony No III (commnd by BBC, 1956); Elizabethan Dances (commnd by BBC, Festival Hall, 1957); Symphony No IV (Promenade Concerts, 1959); Overture: Derby Day (commnd by BBC, Proms, 1960); Concerto Grosso No III (commnd by BBC, Proms, 1964); Sinfonietta for Strings (commnd by Cheltenham Festival, 1970); Hydriotaphia, Symphony No V (commnd by Arts Council for Norwich Triennial Festival, 1973); Miss Julie, 2-act opera, 1976; String Quartet no 2 (Aldeburgh Fest., 1976). *Film Music* since 1936 includes: Odd Man Out, The Way Ahead, The True Glory, World of Plenty, The Magic Box, etc. *Publications: orchestral:* 5 symphonies, 3 concerti grossi, Oboe Concerto, Festival March, The Magic Island, Scottish Dances, Harp Concerto (Lyra Angelica); *chamber music:* Rhapsody for Piano Quartet, String Quartet in D Minor, Sonata alla Toccata for Piano, Divertimento for Solo Flute, Fantasy-Waltzes for Piano, 12 Preludes for Piano; String Trio; Movements for Piano; Sonata for Clarinet and Piano; Mirages for baritone and piano; Naiades for flute and harp. *Publications:* Ariel to Miranda *in* Adam Internat. Review, 1968; Anthology of 20th Century French Poetry, 1969; Winter in Copenhagen, 1971; Daphne, 1972; The World in my Mind, 1975. *Address:* Lark Rise, Blythburgh, Suffolk. *T:* Blythburgh 331. *Clubs:* Savile; Island Sailing (Cowes).

AMALDI, Prof. Edoardo, PhD; Italian physicist; Professor of General Physics, University of Rome, since 1937; *b* Carpaneto, Piacenza, 5 Sept. 1908; *s* of Ugo Amaldi and Luisa Basini; *m* 1933, Ginestra Giovene; two *s* one *d. Educ:* Rome Univ. Dr of Physics, 1929. Sec.-Gen., European Org. for Nuclear Research, 1952-54; Pres., Internat. Union of Pure and Applied Physics, 1957-60; President: Istituto Nazionale di Fisica Nucleare, 1960-65; Council, CERN, 1970-71; Fellow: Acad. Naz. dei Lincei; Acad. Naz. dei XL; Foreign member: Royal Soc. of Sciences, Uppsala; Acad. of Sciences, USSR; Amer. Philos. Soc.; Amer. Acad. of Arts and Sciences; Nat. Acad. of Sciences, USA; Royal Acad., Netherlands; Acad. Leopoldina; Royal Instn of GB; Royal Society, London; Royal Acad. Sweden, 1968; Real Acad. Ciencias, Spain. Hon. DSc: Glasgow, 1973; Oxford, 1974. *Publications:* The production and slowing down of neutrons, 1959; contributor many papers on atomic, molecular and nuclear physics to learned jls. *Address:* Istituto di Fisica, Città Universitaria, Rome, Italy; (home) Viale Parioli 50, 00197 Rome.

AMAN, family name of **Baron Marley.**

AMBARTSUMIAN, Victor; Hero of Socialist Labour; Order of Lenin (twice); Order of Labour Red Banner (four times); President, Academy of Sciences of Armenian Soviet Socialist Republic, USSR, since 1947; *b* 18 Sept. 1908; *m* 1931, Vera Ambartsumian; two *s* two *d. Educ:* Univ. of Leningrad. Lecturer in Astronomy, 1931-34, Prof. of Astrophysics, 1934-44, Univ. of Leningrad; Prof. of Astrophysics, Univ. of Erevan, 1944-. Full Mem., Academy of Sciences of USSR, 1953-. Pres., Internat. Council of Scientific Unions, 1968-72. Hon. Dr of Science: Univs of Canberra, 1963; Paris, 1965; Liege, 1967; Prague, 1967; Torun, 1973; Foreign Member of Academies of Science: Washington, Paris, Rome, Vienna, Berlin, Amsterdam, Copenhagen, Stockholm, Boston, New York; Foreign Member of Royal Society, London. *Publications:* Theoretical Astrophysics, 1953 (in Russian; trans. into German, English, Chinese); about 100 papers in learned jls. Editor of jl, Astrofizika. *Address:* Academy of Sciences of Armenian SSR, Barekamutyan Street 24, Erevan, Armenia, USSR.

AMBLER, Eric; novelist and screenwriter; *b* 28 June 1909; *s* of Alfred Percy and Amy Madeleine Ambler; *m* 1st, 1939, Louise Crombie; 2nd, 1958, Joan Harrison. *Educ:* Colfe's Grammar Sch.; London Univ. Apprenticeship in engineering, 1927-28; advertisement copywriter, 1929-35; professional writer, 1936-. Served War of 1939-45: RA, 1940; commissioned, 1941; served in Italy, 1943; Lt-Col, 1944; Asst Dir of Army Kinematography,

War Office, 1944-46, when released. US Bronze Star, 1946. Wrote and produced film, The October Man, 1947 and resumed writing career. Screenplays include: The Way Ahead, 1944; The October Man, 1947; The Passionate Friends, 1948; Highly Dangerous, 1950; The Magic Box, 1951; Gigolo and Gigolette, in Encore, 1952; The Card, 1952; Rough Shoot, 1953; The Cruel Sea, 1953; Lease of Life, 1954; The Purple Plain, 1954; Yangtse Incident, 1957; A Night to Remember, 1958; Wreck of the Mary Deare, 1959; Love Hate Love, 1970. *Publications:* The Dark Frontier, 1936; Uncommon Danger, 1937; Epitaph for a Spy, 1938; Cause for Alarm, 1938; The Mask of Dimitrios, 1939; Journey into Fear, 1940; Judgment on Deltchev, 1951; The Schirmer Inheritance, 1953; The Night-comers, 1956; Passage of Arms, 1959; The Light of Day, 1962; The Ability to Kill (essays), 1963; (ed and introd) To Catch a Spy, 1964; A Kind of Anger, 1964 (Edgar Allan Poe award, 1964); Dirty Story, 1967; The Intercom Conspiracy, 1969; The Levanter, 1972 (Golden Dagger award, 1973); Doctor Frigo, 1974 (MWA Grand Master award, 1975); Send No More Roses, 1977; numerous short stories, magazine and newspaper articles. *Address:* Chemin de l'Ile de Salagnon 1, 1815 Clarens, Switzerland. *Clubs:* Garrick, Savile.

AMBLER, Air Vice-Marshal Geoffrey Hill, CB 1946; CBE 1944 (OBE 1941); AFC; DL; *b* 1904; *s* of late Fred Ambler; *m* 1940, Phoebe, *d* of Edgar Gaunt, Hawksworth Hall, Guiseley; three *d. Educ:* Cambridge University (MA). Joined Auxiliary Air Force, 1931; served in Fighter Command, 1939-42; Comdt, Royal Observer Corps, 1942-43; HQ Fighter Command, 1943-45. Air ADC to the King, 1943-44; Hon. Air Cdre No 609 (W Riding) Sqdn AAF, 1947-57. Hon. LLD Leeds, 1966. DL West Riding, Yorks, 1949.

AMBLER, Harry, OBE 1963; QPM 1955; Chief Constable, City of Bradford Police, 1957-73; *b* 27 June 1908; *m* 1934, Kathleen Freda Muriel Mitchell; one *d. Educ:* Hanson Secondary Sch., Bradford; Oulton Sch., Liverpool. Joined City of Bradford Police as a Constable, 1930; Inspector, 1940; Staff Officer to HM Inspector of Constabulary, 1941-43; Superintendent, 1943; Asst and Dep. Chief Constable, 1952; Chief Constable, 1957. Hon. MA Bradford, 1973. Police Long Service and Good Conduct Medal, 1952; Coronation Medal, 1953. *Address:* Alvor, 124 Coastal Road, Hest Bank, Lancaster LA2 6HG. *T:* Hest Bank 822408.

AMBO, Rt. Rev. George Somboba; *see* Popondetta, Bishop of.

AMBROSE, Prof. Edmund Jack, MA (Cantab), DSc (London); Professor of Cell Biology, University of London, Institute of Cancer Research, since 1967; Staff of Chester Beatty Research Institute, Institute of Cancer Research: Royal Cancer Hospital since 1952; *b* 2 March 1914; *s* of Alderman Harry Edmund Ambrose and Kate (*née* Stanley); *m* 1943, Andrée (*née* Huck), Seine, France; one *s* one *d. Educ:* Perse Sch., Cambridge; Emmanuel Coll., Cambridge. Wartime research for Admiralty on infra-red detectors, 1940-45; subseq. research on structure of proteins using infra-red radiation at Courtauld Fundamental Research Laboratory. Convener of Brit. Soc. for Cell Biology. Chm., Scientific Adv. Cttee, Tate Memorial Centre, Bombay. Research on structure of proteins, on structure of normal and cancer cells, and on characteristics of surface of cancer cells. *Publications:* Cell Electrophoresis, 1965; The Biology of Cancer, 1966, 2nd edn 1975; The Cancer Cell *in vitro.* 1967; (jtly) Cell Biology, 1970, rev. edn 1976; publications on Protein Structure and Cell Biology, in Proc. Royal Soc., biological and chemical and scientific jls. *Recreation:* sailing. *Address:* Institute of Cancer Research: Royal Cancer Hospital, Fulham Road, SW3 6BJ. *Clubs:* Royal Thames Yacht; Royal Bombay Yacht.

AMBROSE, James Walter Davy; Judge, Supreme Court Singapore, 1958-68; *b* 5 Dec. 1909; *s* of Samuel Ambrose; *m* 1945, Theresa Kamala Ambrose; no *c. Educ:* Free Sch., Penang; Oxford Univ. Asst Official Assignee, Singapore, 1936; Police Magistrate and Asst District Judge, Malacca, 1940; Registrar, Superior Court, Malacca, 1945; Dep. Public Prosecutor, 1946; Sen. Asst Registrar, Supreme Courts of Ipoh, Penang, and Kuala Lumpur, 1947-52; President, Sessions Court, Penang, 1953; Acting District Judge and First Magistrate, Singapore, 1955; Official Assignee, Public Trustee, and Comr of Estate Duties, Singapore 1957. *Address:* 4 Saraca Road, Seletar Hills, Singapore 28.

AMERS, Maj.-Gen. John Henry, OBE 1941; *b* 8 July 1904; *s* of John Amers; *m* 1933, Muriel Henrietta Ethel Haeberlin; one *d. Educ:* Christ's Hospital; Royal Military Acad., Woolwich; Cambridge Univ. Commissioned 2nd Lieut into Royal Engineers, 1925. Served War of 1939-45, E Africa, Middle East and Italy. Col 1951; Brig. 1955; Maj.-Gen. 1958. Served HQ,

BCOF, Japan, 1947-48; Chief Engineer, Salisbury Plain District, 1951-54; Deputy Director of Works, BAOR, 1955-57; Director of Fortification and Works, 1958-59; retired, 1959. *Address:* c/o Lloyds Bank Ltd, Cox's and King's Branch, 6 Pall Mall, SW1Y 5NH. *Club:* Royal Commonwealth Society.

AMERY, Rt. Hon. Julian, PC 1960; MP (C) Brighton Pavilion since 1969; *b* 27 March 1919; *s* of late Rt Hon. Leopold Amery, PC, CH; *m* 1950, Catherine, *d* of Rt Hon. Harold Macmillan, *qv*; one *s* three *d. Educ:* Summerfields; Eton; Balliol Coll., Oxford. War Corresp. in Spanish Civil War, 1938-39; Attaché HM Legation, Belgrade, and on special missions in Bulgaria, Turkey, Roumania and Middle East, 1939-40; Sergeant in RAF, 1940-41; commissioned and transferred to army, 1941; on active service, Egypt, Palestine and Adriatic, 1941-42; liaison officer to Albanian resistance movement, 1944; served on staff of Gen. Carton de Wiart, VC, Mr Churchill's personal representative with Generalissimo Chiang Kai-Shek, 1945. Contested Preston in Conservative interest, July 1945; MP (C) Preston North, 1950-66; Delegate to Consultative Assembly of Council of Europe, 1950-53 and 1956. Member Round Table Conference on Malta, 1955. Parly Under-Sec. of State and Financial Sec., War Office, 1957-58; Parly Under-Sec. of State, Colonial Office, 1958-60; Sec. of State for Air, Oct. 1960-July 1962; Minister of Aviation, 1962-64; Minister of Public Building and Works, June-Oct. 1970; Minister for Housing and Construction, DoE, 1970-72; Minister of State, FCO, 1972-74. *Publications:* Sons of the Eagle, 1948; The Life of Joseph Chamberlain: vol. IV, 1901-3: At the Height of his Power, 1951; vols V and VI, 1901-14: Joseph Chamberlain and the Tariff Reform Campaign, 1969; Approach March (autobiog.), 1973; articles in National Review, Nineteenth Century and Daily Telegraph. *Recreations:* ski-ing, mountaineering, travel. *Address:* 112 Eaton Square, SW1. *T:* 01-235 1543, 01-235 7409; Forest Farm House, Chelwood Gate, Sussex. *Clubs:* White's, Beefsteak, Carlton, Buck's.

AMES, Mrs Kenneth; *see* Gainham, S. R.

AMHERST, family name of **Earl Amherst.**

AMHERST, 5th Earl, *cr* 1826; **Jeffery John Archer Amherst,** MC 1918; Baron Amherst of Montreal, 1788; Viscount Holmesdale, 1826; Major, late Coldstream Guards; Manager, External Affairs, BEA, 1946; later Director of Associated Companies, retd. Dec. 1966; Hon. Commission as Wing Commander, RAF, 1942; *b* 13 Dec. 1896; *e s* of 4th Earl and Hon. Eleanor Clementina St Aubyn (*d* 1960), *d* of 1st Baron St Levan; *S* father, 1927. *Educ:* Eton; RMC Sandhurst. Served European War, 1914-18, with Coldstream Guards (MC); placed on RARO 1921; recalled 1940, served Middle East, 1940-44. Reportorial Staff, New York Morning World, 1923-29; Commercial Air Pilot and General Manager Air Line Company, 1929-39; Asst Air Adviser to British Railways, 1945-46. Dir, BEA associated cos, 1946-66. *Publication:* Wandering Abroad (autobiog.), 1976. *Clubs:* Cavalry and Guards, Travellers', Pratt's, Garrick.

AMHERST OF HACKNEY, 3rd Baron, *cr* 1892; **William Alexander Evering Cecil,** CBE 1963; Major late Royal Horse Guards; *b* 31 May 1912; *s* of Capt. Hon. William Amherst Cecil, MC (*d* 1914), Grenadier Guards, and Gladys (*d* 1947), *o c* of Col H. C. Baggalay, of Heatherhurst Grange, Frimley; *S* grandmother, 1919; *m* 1939, Margaret E. Clifton, *y d* of late Brig.-Gen. Howard Clifton Brown; two *s* one *d. Educ:* Eton; Trinity College, Cambridge. Royal Horse Guards, 1933; served War of 1939-45, MEF, 1940-45. CStJ. *Heir: s* Hon. William Hugh Amherst Cecil [*b* 28 Dec. 1940; *m* 1965, Elisabeth, *d* of Hugh H. Merriman; one *s* one *d*]. *Address:* Shroner Wood, Martyr Worthy, Winchester, Hants. *T:* Winchester 882073; 29 Eaton Mews South, SW1. *T:* 01-235 1421. *Clubs:* Buck's, Carlton, Royal Yacht Squadron.

AMIES, (Edwin) Hardy, CVO 1977; RDI 1964; FRSA 1965; Dressmaker by Appointment to HM The Queen; Director Hardy Amies Ltd, since 1946; Design Consultant to J. Hepworth & Son, Ltd, since 1960, and to manufacturers in USA, Canada, Australia, New Zealand, Japan and S Africa; *b* 17 July 1909; *s* of late Herbert William Amies and Mary (*née* Hardy). *Educ:* Brentwood. Studied languages in France and Germany, 1927-30; trainee at W. & T. Avery Ltd, Birmingham, 1930-34; managing designer at Lachasse, Farm Street, W1, 1934-39. War Service, 1939-45: joined Intelligence Corps, 1939, becoming Lt-Col and head of Special Forces Mission to Belgium, 1944; founded dressmaking business, 1946; opened Hardy Amies' Boutique Ltd, 1950. Chairman, Incorporated Society of London Fashion Designers, 1959-60 (Vice-Chm., 1954-56): Mem., Cttee of Management, Friends of Covent Garden. Awards: Harper's Bazaar, 1962; Caswell-Massey, 1962, 1964, 1968; Ambassador

Magazine, 1964; Sunday Times Special Award, 1965. Officier de l'Ordre de la Couronne (Belgium), 1946. *Publications:* Just So Far, 1954; ABC of Men's Fashion, 1964. *Recreations:* lawn tennis, gardening, opera. *Address:* 17b Eldon Road, W8; Hardy Amies Ltd, 14 Savile Row, W1. *T:* 01-734 2436. *Clubs:* Queen's, Buck's.

AMIS, Kingsley; author; *b* 16 April 1922; *o c* of William Robert and Rosa Amis; *m* 1st, 1948, Hilary Ann, *d* of Leonard Sidney and Margery Bardwell; two *s* one *d*; 2nd, 1965, Elizabeth Jane Howard, *qv. Educ:* City of London School; St John's, Oxford (Hon. Fellow, 1976). Served in Army, 1942-45. Lectr in English, University Coll. of Swansea, 1949-61; Fellow of Peterhouse, Cambridge, 1961-63. *Publications:* A Frame of Mind (verse), 1953; Lucky Jim (novel), 1954, filmed, 1957; That Uncertain Feeling (novel), 1955, filmed (Only Two Can Play), 1962; A Case of Samples (verse), 1956; I Like it Here (novel), 1958; Take a Girl Like You (novel), 1960; New Maps of Hell (belles-lettres), 1960; My Enemy's Enemy (short stories), 1962; One Fat Englishman (novel), 1963; The James Bond Dossier (belles-lettres), 1965; The Egyptologists (novel), with Robert Conquest, 1965; The Anti-Death League (novel), 1966; A Look Round the Estate (poems), 1967; (as Robert Markham) Colonel Sun (novel), 1968; I Want it Now (novel), 1968; The Green Man (novel), 1969; What Became of Jane Austen? (belles-lettres), 1970; Girl, 20 (novel), 1971; On Drink, 1972; The Riverside Villas Murder (novel), 1973; Ending Up (novel), 1974; (ed) G. K. Chesterton selected stories, 1972; (ed) Tennyson, 1972; Rudyard Kipling and his World, 1975; The Alteration, 1976. *Recreations:* music, thrillers, television. *Address:* c/o A. D. Peters, 10 Buckingham Street, WC2. *Club:* Garrick.

AMOORE, Rt. Rev. Frederick Andrew; *see* Bloemfontein, Bishop of.

AMOROSO, Prof. Emmanuel Ciprian, CBE 1969; FRS 1957; FRCP; FRCS; FRCOG; FRCPath; FInstBiol; DSc(London), PhD, MD, BCh, BAO; Special Professor, Department of Physiology and Environmental Studies, School of Agriculture, University of Nottingham, since 1973; Professor Emeritus, Royal Veterinary College, since 1968; *Educ:* University Coll., Dublin (Grad. in Medicine); Kaiser Wilhelm Inst. für Zellforschung, Berlin; University Coll., London. McArdle Medal in Surgery and a travelling fellowship in science at NUI, 1929; then appointed to staff of Royal Veterinary College, Prof. of Physiology, 1967-68. Privy Council Rep., Houghton Poultry Res. Station, 1966-63; Vis. Prof., Washington Univ., St Louis, 1958, 1961; Royal Soc. Leverhulme Visiting Professor: Univ. of Chile, 1968-69; Univ. of Nairobi, 1975-76; T. L. Pawlett Scholar, Univ. of Sydney, 1970-71. Treas., Soc. for Endocrinology and Jl Endocrinol. Ltd, 1955-60, Chm., 1960-65; Chm., 2nd Internat. Congress of Endocrinology, London, 1964; Trinidad and Tobago Rep., Commonwealth Scientific Cttee, 1968-; Mem., Biol Scis Cttee, IPPF, 1968-; Mem., Scientific Adv. Cttee, Brit. Egg Mkting Bd, 1963-70. Chm. Council, Jl Reprodn and Fertility Ltd, 1968-76 (Chm., Adv. Cttee, 1969-71; Chm. Exec. Cttee, 1971-76). Lectures: Goldwin Smith, Cornell, 1954; Holme, UCL, 1956; Keibel, Free Univ., Berlin, 1957; Josiah Macey, Harvard, 1958; Ingleby, Birmingham, 1958; Leo Loeb, Washington Univ., St Louis, 1958; Terry, Washington Univ., St Louis, 1961; Liebig, Univ. of Geissen, 1964; Darwin, Eugenics Soc., 1967; Sir James Mackenzie Oration, Burnley, 1970; J. Y. Simpson Oration, RCOG, 1971. Hon. ARCVS 1959; Fellow: Royal Veterinary Coll., 1969; UCL, 1970. Hon. ScD NUI, 1963; Hon. DSc: Illinois, 1967; Nottingham, 1970; West Indies, 1971; Guelph, 1976; Hon DVetMed Santiago, 1967; Hon. Member: Soc. for Endocrinology, 1965; Soc. for Study of Fertility, 1965; Phys. Soc., 1976; Anat. Soc., 1976. Mary Marshall Medalist, Soc. Study of Fertility, 1972. *Publications:* chapter on the Placenta, in 3rd edn of Marshall's Physiology of Reproduction, 1952; papers in Proc. Royal Soc., Jl of Physiol., Jl of Anat. *Address:* Agricultural Research Council Institute of Animal Physiology, Babraham, Cambridge CB2 4AT. *T:* Cambridge 832312; 29 Derwent Close, Cherry Hinton Road, Cambridge CB1 4DY. *T:* Cambridge 47825.

AMORY, 1st Viscount, *cr* 1960: **Derick Heathcoat Amory,** KG 1968; PC 1953; GCMG 1961; TD; DL; Bt *cr* 1874; Lieutenant-Colonel (hon. rank); RA (TA) retired; Chancellor of Exeter University, since 1972; *b* 26 Dec. 1899; *s* of Sir Ian Murray Heathcoat Amory, 2nd Bt, CBE; *S* brother as 4th Bt, 1972. *Educ:* Eton; Christ Church, Oxford (MA). Served war of 1939-45. Governor, Hudson's Bay Co., 1965-70; Dir, Lloyds Bank, 1948-51 and 1964-70; Pres., John Heathcoat & Co., 1973 (Chm., 1966-72); Director, ICI, 1964-70. Member Devon CC, 1932-51; MP (C) Tiverton Div. of Devon, 1945-60; Minister of Pensions, Nov. 1951-Sept. 1953; Minister of State, Board of Trade, 1953-54; Minister of Agriculture and Fisheries, July 1954; Minister of

Agriculture and Fisheries and Minister of Food, Oct. 1954; Minister of Agriculture, Fisheries and Food, April 1955-Jan. 1958; Chancellor of the Exchequer, Jan. 1958-July 1960; High Commissioner for the United Kingdom in Canada, 1961-63. Jt Pro-Chancellor, University of Exeter, 1966-72; Chancellor, University of Exeter, 1972-. Chairman: Medical Research Council, 1960-61, and 1965-69; Voluntary Service Overseas, 1964-75; President: Association of County Councils, 1974- (County Councils Assoc., 1961-74); London Federation of Boys' Clubs. Prime Warden, Goldsmiths' Co., 1971-72. High Steward Borough of South Molton, 1960-74; DL Devon, 1962. Hon. FRCS 1974. Hon. LLD: Exeter Univ., 1959; McGill Univ., 1961; Hon. DCL, Oxon, 1974. *Heir* (to baronetcy only): *b* William Heathcoat Amory, DSO [*b* 19 Aug. 1901; *m* 1933, Margaret Isabella Dorothy Evelyn, *yr d* of Sir Arthur Havelock James Doyle, 4th Bt; two *s* two *d*]. *Address:* 150 Marsham Court, SW1; The Wooden House, Chevithorne, Tiverton, Devon. *Clubs:* Carlton; Royal Yacht Squadron.

AMOS, Air Comdt Barbara Mary D.; *see* Ducat-Amos.

AMOS, Francis John Clarke, CBE 1973; BSc (Soc); DipArch, SPDip, ARIBA, PPRTPI; Chief Executive, Birmingham City Council, 1973-77; Fellow, University of Birmingham, since 1977; *b* 10 Sept. 1924; *s* of late Frank Amos, FALPA (Director, H. J. Furlong & Sons, Ltd, London), and Alice Mary Amos; *m* 1956, Geraldine Mercy Sutton, JP, BSc (Econ), MRTPI; one *s* one *d* (and one *d* decd). *Educ:* Alleyns Sch., and Dulwich Coll., London; Sch. of Architecture, The Polytechnic, London (DipArch); Sch. of Planning and Regional Research, London (SPDip); LSE and Birkbeck Coll., Univ. of London (BSc(Soc)). Served War: Royal Corps of Signals, 1942-44; RIASC, 1944-47. Harlow Develt Corp, 1951; LCC, Planning Div., 1953-58; Min. of Housing and Local Govt, 1958-59 and 1962-63; Adviser to Imperial Ethiopian Govt, 1959-62; Liverpool Corp. City Planning Dept, 1962-73, Chief Planning Officer 1966-74; Chairman: Planning Sub-Cttee, Merseyside Area Land Use/Transportation Study, 1967-73; Working Gp, Educnl Objectives in Urban and Regional Planning, Centre for Environmental Studies, 1970-72. Member: Exec. Cttee, Internat. Centre for Regional Planning and Develt, 1954-59; various Cttees, Liverpool Council of Social Services, 1965-72; Exec. Cttee, Town and Country Planning Summer Sch., 1969-70; Planning, Architecture and Bldg Studies Sub-Cttee, UGC, 1968-74; Community Work Gp of Calouste Gulbenkian Foundn, 1970-; Constitution Cttee, Liverpool Community Relations Council, 1970-73; Planning and Transport Res. Adv. Council, DoE, 1971-; Town and Country Planning Council and Exec. Cttee, 1972-74; Adv. Cttee, Bldg Res. Estabt, and Chm., Planning Cttee, 1972-77; SSRC Planning and Human Geography and Planning Cttees, 1972-76; Social Studies Sub-Cttee, UGC, 1974-76; W Midlands Economic Planning Council, 1974-; Environmental Bd, DoE, 1975-. External Examiner in Planning: Univs of: Liverpool, 1967-70; Newcastle, 1968-71; Aston (Birmingham), 1970-71; Queen's (Belfast), 1972-74; Heriot-Watt, 1972-74; Nottingham, 1973-76; UCL 1975-; Polytechnics of: Leeds, 1967-68; Central London, 1967-70; Birmingham, 1975-; Liverpool, 1977-. Mem., Court, Univ. of Nottingham, 1975-. Adviser to AMA Social Services Cttee, 1974-. Royal Town Planning Inst., 1971-72 (AMPTI, 1955; Fellow 1967); Architect RIBA, 1951. Freeman of City of London, 1968. *Publications:* Education for Planning (CES Report), 1973; various reports on Liverpool incl.: Annual Reviews of Plans, Study of Social Malaise; ATPI Report on Future of Planning; (part) City Centre Redevelopment; articles on Planning and Management in Local Govt in various professional jls. *Recreations:* travel; unsystematic philately and unskilled building. *Address:* 20 Westfield Road, Edgbaston, Birmingham B15 3QG. *T:* 021-454 5661.

AMPLEFORTH, Abbot of; *see* Griffiths, Rt. Rev. M. A.

AMPTHILL, 4th Baron *cr* 1881; **Geoffrey Denis Erskine Russell;** *b* 15 Oct. 1921; *s* of 3rd Baron Ampthill, CBE, and Christabel, Lady Ampthill (*d* 1976); *S* father, 1973; *m* 1st, 1946, Susan Mary (marr. diss. 1971), *d* of late Hon. Charles John Frederic Winn; two *s* one *d* (and one *s* decd); 2nd, 1972, Elisabeth Anne Marie, *d* of late Claude Henri Gustave Mallon. *Educ:* Stowe. Irish Guards, 1941-46; 2nd Lt 1941, Captain 1944. Gen. Manager, Fortnum and Mason, 1947-51; Chairman, New Providence Hotel Co. Ltd, 1951-64. Managing Director of theatre owning and producing companies, 1953-. *Heir:* *s* Hon. David Whitney Erskine Russell, *b* 27 May 1947. *Address:* 24 Egerton Terrace, SW3 2BT. *T:* 01-589 4652.

AMRITANAND, Rt. Rev. Joseph; *see* Calcutta, Bishop of.

AMULREE, 2nd Baron, *cr* 1929; **Basil William Sholto Mackenzie,** KBE 1977; MD; FRCP; Liberal Whip, House of Lords, 1955-77; Chairman, Attendance Allowance Board, 1970-76; *b* 25 July 1900; *o s* of 1st Baron and Lilian (*d* 1916), *e d* of late W. H. Bradbury; *S* father, 1942. *Educ:* Lancing Coll.; Gonville and Caius Coll., Cambridge (MA 1925); Paris; University Coll. Hosp. MRCS, LRCP 1925; MRCP 1928; MD Cantab 1936; FRCP 1946. Asst Pathologist: University Coll. Hosp., 1929-31; Royal Northern Hosp., 1931-36; MO, Min. of Health, 1936-50; Physician, University Coll. Hosp., 1949-66. President: London Co. Div., British Red Cross, 1945-60; Assoc. of Occupational Therapists, 1956-60; Soc. of Chiropodists, 1963; Assoc. of Welfare Officers, 1960-68; British Geriatric Soc., 1949-65. Chm., Invalid Meals for London, 1956-59 (Mem. Inner London Area Adv. Cttee, 1965-75). Chm. Bd of Governors, London Medical Gp, 1968. Vice-Chm., Chadwick Trust, 1955-56. Member: Nat. Radium Commn, 1942-48; (professional) Assoc. of Water Engineers; Royal Inst. of Health. Hon. Mem. Faculty of Radiologists; Hon. FRGCP. Star of Ethiopia (1st class), 1952. *Publications:* Adding Life to Years; Min. of Health Report on Public Health and Medical Subjects, No 89; various articles in periodicals. *Recreation:* walking. *Heir:* none. *Address:* 18 Egerton Terrace, SW3. *Club:* Reform.

AMWELL, 2nd Baron *cr* 1947, of Islington; **Frederick Norman Montague;** *b* 6 Nov. 1912; *o s* of 1st Baron Amwell, CBE, and Constance (*d* 1964), *d* of James Craig; *S* father, 1966; *m* 1939, Kathleen Elizabeth Fountain; one *s* one *d*. *Educ:* Highbury Grammar School; Northampton Coll. of Technology. Aircraft Design Engineer (Apprenticeship in 1930). AFRAeS. *Heir:* *s* Hon. Keith Norman Montague, BSc, CEng, MICE, AMInstHE, FGS [*b* 1 April 1943; *m* 1970, Mary, *d* of Frank Palfreyman, Potters Bar, Herts]. *Address:* 34 Halliford Road, Sunbury-on-Thames, Mddx. *T:* Sunbury-on-Thames 85413.

ANCASTER, 3rd Earl of, *cr* 1892; **Gilbert James Heathcote-Drummond-Willoughby,** KCVO 1971; TD; DL; Baron Willoughby de Eresby, 1313; Baron Aveland, 1856; Lord-Lieutenant of County of Lincoln, 1950-75; *b* 8 Dec. 1907; *s* of 2nd Earl of Ancaster, GCVO, and late Eloise, *e d* of W. L. Breese, New York; *S* father 1951; *m* 1933, Hon. Nancy Phyllis Louise Astor (*d* 1975), *o d* of 2nd Viscount Astor; one *d* (one *s* decd). *Educ:* Eton; Magdalene Coll., Cambridge (MA). Served War of 1939-45: Leicestershire Yeomanry and Major RA (wounded, despatches). MP (C) Rutland and Stamford, 1933-50; summoned to the Upper House of Parliament as Baron Willoughby de Eresby, 1951; Lord Great Chamberlain of England, 1950-52. Nat. Pres., BLESMA, 1956-. JP 1937, CC 1950, Alderman, 1954, Kesteven; DL 1947-50, 1977-, Co. Lincoln. KStJ 1957. *Heir:* (to Barony of Willoughby de Eresby): *d* Lady Nancy Jane Marie Heathcote-Drummond-Willoughby, *b* 1 Dec. 1934; (to Baronetcy) (Gilbert) Simon Heathcote, *qv*. *Address:* Grimsthorpe, Bourne, Lincs. *T:* Edenham 222; Drummond Castle, Crieff. *T:* Muthill 321.
See also Earl of Dalhousie.

ANCHORENA, Dr Manuel de; Argentine Ambassador to the Court of St James's, 1974-76; *b* 3 June 1933; *s* of Norberto de Anchorena and Ena Arrotea; *m* 1955, Elvira Peralta Martinez; three *s* two *d*. *Educ:* Univ. of Buenos Aires. Doctorate in Law, Buenos Aires, 1955. Landowner, politician, and historian. *Publications:* several articles contrib. to jl of Inst. of Historic Investigation, Argentina; articles on wild life and natural preservation. *Recreations:* polo, tennis, squash. *Address:* c/o Ministry of Foreign Affairs, Buenos Aires, Argentina. *Clubs:* Hurlingham, Lansdowne, Royal Automobile; Guards Polo; Jockey Club of Buenos Aires.

ANCRAM, Earl of; Michael Andrew Foster Jude Kerr; advocate; *b* 7 July 1945; *s* and *heir* of 12th Marquess of Lothian, *qv*; *m* 1975, Lady Jane Fitzalan-Howard, *y d* of 16th Duke of Norfolk, KG, PC, GCVO, GBE, TD, and of Lavinia Duchess of Norfolk, *qv*. *Educ:* Ampleforth; Christ Church, Oxford (BA); Edinburgh Univ. (LLB). Advocate, Scottish Bar, 1970. MP (C) Berwickshire and East Lothian, Feb.-Sept. 1974; Vice-Chm., Cons. Party in Scotland, 1975-. *Recreations:* ski-ing, shooting and folksinging. *Address:* 6 Ainslie Place, Edinburgh; Monteviot, Jedburgh, Scotland. *T:* 031-226 3147. *Clubs:* Turf; New (Edinburgh).

ANDERSEN, Valdemar Jens, CMG 1965; OBE 1960 (MBE 1955); VRD 1962; Resident Commissioner, Gilbert and Ellice Islands Colony, 1962-70, retired; *b* 21 March 1919; 2nd *s* of Max Andersen, Maraenui, NZ; *m* 1946, Alison Leone, 2nd *d* of G. A. Edmonds, Remuera, Auckland, NZ; one *s* one *d*. *Educ:* Napier Boys High Sch. NZ; Auckland University Coll. (BSc). Lieut, RNZNVR, 1940-46; Lieut, RANVR, 1947-62. British Solomon Islands Protectorate: Administrative Officer, 1947; Class A,

Administrative Officer, 1954; Secretary Protectorate Affairs, 1958. *Recreations:* drama, poetry, gardening. *Address:* Porchester Road, Manurewa, New Zealand.

ANDERSON, family name of **Viscount Waverley.**

ANDERSON, Mrs Ande; *see* Barstow, J.

ANDERSON, Rt. Hon. Betty H.; *see* Harvie Anderson.

ANDERSON, Carl David, PhD; Professor of Physics, California Institute of Technology, since 1939; Chairman, Division of Physics, Mathematics and Astronomy, 1962-70; *b* 3 Sept. 1905; *s* of Carl David Anderson and Emma Adolfina Ajaxson; *m* 1946, Lorraine Bergman; two *s. Educ:* California Institute of Technology. BS 1927, PhD 1930. War activities on projects, 1941-45; Presidential Certificate of Merit, 1945. Has conducted research on X-rays, gamma rays, cosmic rays, elementary particles, etc. Member: Nat. Acad. of Sciences; Amer. Philosoph. Soc.; Amer. Acad. of Arts and Sciences. Gold Medal, Amer. Inst., City of NY, 1935; Nobel prize in Physics, 1936; Elliott Cresson Medal of the Franklin Inst., 1937; John Ericsson Medal of Amer. Soc. of Swedish Engineers, 1960, etc. Holds hon. degrees. *Address:* California Institute of Technology, Pasadena, Calif 91109, USA.

ANDERSON, Rear-Adm. (Charles) Courtney, CB 1971; Flag Officer, Admiralty Interview Board, 1969-71, retired; *b* 8 Nov. 1916; *s* of late Lt-Col Charles Anderson, Australian Light Horse, and Mrs Constance Powell-Anderson, OBE, JP; *m* 1940, Pamela Ruth Miles; three *s. Educ:* RNC, Dartmouth. Joined RN, 1930. Served War of 1939-45: in command of Motor Torpedo Boats, Destroyers and Frigates. Naval Intelligence, 1946-49 and 1955-57; Commanded HMS Contest, 1949-51; Comdr, 1952; BJSM, Washington, 1953-55; Capt., 1959; Naval Attaché, Bonn, 1962-65; Director, Naval Recruiting, 1966-68; ADC to Queen, 1968; Rear-Adm., 1969. Editor, The Board Bulletin, 1971-. *Publications:* The Drum Beats Still, 1951. Numerous articles and short stories. *Recreations:* gardening, do-it-yourself. *Address:* Coomb Cottage, Charlton, near Malmesbury, Wilts.

ANDERSON, Lt-Col Charles Groves Wright, VC 1942; MC; Member House of Representatives, for Hume, New South Wales, 1949-51 and 1955-61; grazier; *b* Capetown, South Africa, 12 Feb. 1897; *s* of A. G. W. Anderson; *m* 1931, Edith M. Tout; two *s* two *d.* Served European War, 1914-18 (MC), KAR, E Africa. Served War of 1939-45 (VC, POW), 2nd AIF, Malaya. *Recreation:* motoring. *Address:* Springfield, Young, NSW 2594, Australia. *Club:* Commonwealth (Canberra).

ANDERSON, Sir Colin (Skelton), KBE 1969; Kt 1950; *b* 15 July 1904; *e s* of late Sir Alan Anderson, GBE; *m* 1932, Morna Campbell, 2nd *d* of Sir Alexander MacCormick, KCMG; two *d* (and one *d* decd). *Educ:* Eton; Trinity College, Oxford. Director: Midland Bank Ltd, 1950-74; Marine Insurance Co. Ltd, 1950-70; Orient Steam Navigation Co. Ltd, 1950-69; P&O Steam Navigation Co., 1960-69; Australia & New Zealand Bank Ltd, 1951-70; Royal Opera House, Covent Garden, Ltd, 1961-73; City Arts Trust Ltd, 1962-70; English Opera Group Ltd, 1963-73. Chairman: London Shipowners' Dock Labour Cttee, 1944-45; London Port Employers (and a Member of London Bd of Nat. Dock Labour Bd), 1945-47; Nat. Assoc. of Port Employers, 1947-48, 1950-54; General Council of British Shipping, 1949-50; British Liner Cttee, 1949-50; Internat. Chamber of Shipping, 1949-63; Min. of Transport's Advisory Cttee on Traffic Signs for Motor Roads, 1957-61; Min. of Education's Cttee on Grants to Students, 1958-60; Gray, Dawes, Westray & Co. Ltd, 1960-70; Trustees of Tate Gall., 1960-67 (Vice-Chm., 1953-59); Ocean Travel Development, 1961-68; Anderson Green & Co. Ltd, 1963-70 (Dir, 1930); HMS Victory Adv. Technical Cttee, 1964-76; Sea Transport Commn of Internat. Chamber of Commerce, 1965-71; Hampstead Heath and Old Hampstead Protection Soc., 1960-67. President: Seamen's Hospital Soc., 1962-; Chamber of Shipping of the UK, 1949-50 (Vice-Pres., 1948-49); British Employers' Confederation, 1956-58 (Vice-Pres., 1952-56); Hon. Pres., Internat. Chamber of Shipping, 1963-. Member: Min. of Transport's Cttee on the Prevention of Pollution of the Sea by Oil, 1954-64; Commonwealth Office's Oversea Migration Board, 1953-66; Court of Enquiry into National Railway Strike (with Sir J. Cameron and Mr H. Douglas), 1954; Contemporary Art Soc. (Chairman, 1956-60); Council of Royal College of Art (Chairman, 1952-56; Provost, 1967-); National Council of Design and Industries Association (President, 1950-53); Council of Industrial Design, 1951-60; Trustee, Nat. Gall. (representing Tate Gall.), 1963-67. Chm., Royal Fine Art Commn, 1968-76 (Mem., 1959-76). Prime Warden of the Fishmongers' Company, 1963-64. Corres. Mem., Bayerische Akademie der Schönen

Künste, 1969-. Hon. ARIBA 1957; Hon. Fellow, Trinity College, Oxford, 1963. Hon. LLD, Aberdeen, 1963. Hon. Designer, RCA, 1953; Hon. Dr, RCA, 1967. Jubilee Medal, RSA, 1954. Officer of the Order of Orange Nassau, 1948. *Recreations:* the home, the arts, the garden. *Address:* Le Val House, St Brelade, Jersey, Channel Islands. *Clubs:* Brooks's, City of London.

ANDERSON, Courtney; *see* Anderson, (Charles) Courtney.

ANDERSON, Rev. David; Principal Lecturer in Religious Education, Hertfordshire College of Higher Education (formerly Wall Hall College), Aldenham, Herts, since 1974 (Senior Lecturer, 1970-74); *b* 30 Oct. 1919; *s* of William and Nancy Anderson, Newcastle upon Tyne; *m* 1953, Helen Finlay Robinson, 3rd *d* of Johnson and Eleanor Robinson, Whitley Bay, Northumberland; one *s* two *d. Educ:* Royal Grammar Sch. Newcastle upon Tyne; Selwyn Coll., Cambridge. Served in RA, 1940-42, Intelligence Corps, 1942-46, Lieut. Deacon, 1949, Priest, 1950; Curate of parish of St Gabriel, Sunderland, 1949-52; Tutor of St Aidan's Coll., Birkenhead, 1952-56; Warden of Melville Hall, Ibadan, Nigeria, 1956-58; Principal of: Immanuel Coll., Ibadan, Nigeria, 1958-62; Wycliffe Hall, Oxford, 1962-69. Examining Chaplain: to Bishop of Liverpool, 1969-75; to Bishop of St Albans, 1972-. *Publications:* The Tragic Protest, 1969; Simone Weil, 1971; contrib. Religion and Modern Literature, 1975. *Recreations:* listening to music, hi-fi gramophones. *Address:* Hertfordshire College of Higher Education, Aldenham, Watford, Herts.

ANDERSON, David Colville, VRD 1947, and Clasp, 1958; QC (Scotland) 1957; *b* 8 Sept. 1916; *yr s* of late J. L. Anderson of Pittormie, Fife, solicitor and farmer, and late Etta Colville; *m* 1948, Juliet, *yr d* of late Hon. Lord Hill Watson, MC, LLD; two *s* one *d. Educ:* Trinity Coll., Glenalmond; Pembroke Coll., Oxford; Edinburgh Univ. BA (Hons) Oxford 1938; LLB (Distinction) 1946. Thow Scholar, Maclagan Prizeman, Dalgety Prizeman, Edinburgh Univ. Lecturer in Scots Law, Edinburgh Univ., 1947-60; Advocate, 1946; Standing Junior Counsel to Ministry of Works, 1954-55, and to War Office, 1955-57. Contested (C) Coatbridge and Airdrie, 1955, and East Dunbartonshire, 1959; MP (C) Dumfries, Dec. 1963-Sept. 1964. Solicitor-General for Scotland, 1960-64; Vice-Chairman, Commissioners of Northern Lighthouses, 1963-64; Hon. Sheriff-Substitute, Lothians and Peebles, 1965-; Chm., Industrial Tribunals (Scotland), 1971-72; Chief Reporter for Public Inquiries and Under Sec., Scottish Office, 1972-74. Joined RNVR, 1935. In VIII awarded Ashburton Shield, Bisley, 1933 (Trinity Coll., Glenalmond; schools event); Inter-Services XX at Bisley, 1936-38. Served War of 1939-45 in destroyers (despatches); Lieut 1940; Egerton Prizeman in Naval Gunnery, 1943; Gunnery Officer, Rosyth Escort Force, 1943-45; Norway, 1945; Lt-Comdr 1948. King Haakon VII Liberty Medal, 1946. *Address:* 8 Arboretum Road, Edinburgh EH3 5PD. *T:* 031-552 3003. *Club:* New (Edinburgh).

ANDERSON, David Dick, CBE 1951; MC 1916 (and Bar, 1918); retired as HM Chief Inspector of Schools, Scottish Education Department, 1954; *b* 26 March 1889; *m* 1930; three *s. Educ:* Glasgow High School and University. Teacher: Queen's Park Senior Secondary School, Glasgow; Madras College, St Andrews; Daniel Stewart's College, Edinburgh. Served European War; officer, 1914-19, in East Yorkshire Regiment; retired with rank of Major. *Recreations:* golf, gardening, foreign travel. *Address:* 12 Ross Road, Edinburgh EH16 5QN. *T:* 031-667 8873. *Clubs:* Royal Over-Seas League; Royal Scots (Edinburgh).

ANDERSON, David Fyfe, MD, ChB, FRCOG, FRCPGlas; Muirhead Professor of Obstetrics and Gynæcology, University of Glasgow, 1946-70; Obstetric Surgeon, Royal Maternity Hospital, Glasgow; Gynæcological Surgeon, Royal Infirmary, Glasgow; *b* 8 June 1904; *o s* of David Fyfe Anderson and Mary Ann Mackay, Viewfield, Strathaven, Lanarkshire; *m* 1945, Elizabeth Rose, 2nd *d* of W. F. McAusland, Wyndyknowe, Scotstounhill, Glasgow; three *s* one *d. Educ:* Strathaven Academy (Dux); High Sch. of Glasgow (Dux, Modern Side); Univ. of Glasgow (Gardiner Bursary); Johns Hopkins Univ. MB, ChB (Commendation), Univ. of Glasgow, 1926; McCunn Research Scholar, 1929-31; MRCOG 1932; FRFPSG 1935; MD (Hons) 1935; FRCOG 1940; Rockefeller Travelling Fellowship 1935-36; FRSM; FRCPGlas 1964; Fellow of Glasgow Obstetrical and Gynæcological Soc. and of Edinburgh Obstetrical Soc.; formerly Examiner to Central Midwives Board for Scotland; lately Professor of Midwifery and Diseases of Women at Anderson College of Medicine, Glasgow. Freeman of City of Glasgow. Member of Incorporations of: Barbers, Bonnetmakers and Dyers, and Tailors (Ex-Deacon). OStJ 1973.

Publications: Medical papers and verse. *Address:* 6 Cleveden Drive, Glasgow G12 0SE. *T:* 041-339 8345.

ANDERSON, David Heywood; Legal Counsellor, Foreign and Commonwealth Office, since 1972; Barrister-at-Law; *b* 14 Sept. 1937; *s* of late Harry Anderson; *m* 1961, Jennifer Ratcliffe; one *s* one *d. Educ:* King James' Grammar Sch., Almondbury. LLB (Leeds); LLM (London). Called to Bar, Gray's Inn, 1963. Asst Legal Adviser, FCO, 1960-69; Legal Adviser, British Embassy, Bonn, 1969-72. *Recreations:* reading, gardening. *Address:* c/o Foreign and Commonwealth Office, SW1. *T:* 01-233 5710.

ANDERSON, Prof. David Steel; Emeritus Professor of Accounting and Business Method, Edinburgh University; *b* 27 Oct. 1902; *s* of David Anderson and Jessie Marian Steel; *m* 1931, Cicely Bouskell Hockin; one *s. Educ:* Viewpark School; George Watson's College, Edinburgh. Mem. Soc. of Accountants in Edinburgh, 1925; private practice as Chartered Accountant, 1927-29; joined firm of Wallace & Somerville, Edinburgh, as partner, 1929; retired partner of Whinney Murray & Co. External Examiner in Accounting, Faculty of Law, Edinburgh Univ., 1938-41; Mem. Gen. Examining Bd, Chartered Accountants of Scotland, 1939; Mem. Council Soc. of Accountants in Edinburgh, 1942-46; Mem. Advisory Cttee, Gen. Examining Bd, Inst. of Chartered Accountants of Scotland, 1937-57; Mem. Council Inst. of Chartered Accountants of Scotland, 1955-57, Vice-Pres., 1966, President, 1967-68. Hon. MA (Edinburgh Univ.), 1957. *Recreations:* golf, tennis, fishing. *Address:* 12 Succoth Gardens, Edinburgh. *T:* 031-337 3617. *Club:* Caledonian (Edinburgh).

ANDERSON, Sir David (Stirling), Kt 1957; PhD, LLD Glasgow and Strathclyde; FRSE; FIMechE; *b* 25 Sept. 1895; *s* of Alexander Anderson and Sarah Stirling; *m* 1st, 1932, Grace Boyd (*d* 1973); 2nd, 1974, Lorna Ticehurst. *Educ:* Royal Technical College, Glasgow (Greenock Research Schol.). Engineering experience with North British Locomotive Company and Fullerton, Hodgart and Barclay; 2nd Lieut RAF 1918; Head of Dept of Mech. Engineering, Derby Tech. Coll., 1924-26, Principal, 1926-30; Principal, Coll. of Technology, Birmingham, 1930-46; Dir, Royal College of Science and Technology, Glasgow, 1946-59; part-time Mem., S of Scotland Electricity Bd, 1960-67; Mem., Cttee on Higher Education, 1961-63; Chm., Scottish Certificate of Education Examination Bd, 1964-69. Pres. Assoc. of Principals of Technical Institutions, 1937; Chm. of Council, Assoc. of Tech. Instns, 1951; Mem. Council, Inst. Mech. Engrs, 1941-42, 1948-50. Hon. LLD: Glasgow, 1961; Strathclyde, 1965; Hon. DSc Aston, 1966. *Publications:* numerous papers and contributions on technical education. *Recreation:* climbing. *Address:* Braehead, Helensburgh, Dunbartonshire. *T:* 2227. *Clubs:* Royal Automobile; Royal Scottish Automobile, Western (Glasgow); Scottish Mountaineering (Edinburgh).

ANDERSON, Brig. David William, CBE 1976 (OBE 1972); Commandant, School of Infantry, since 1976; *b* 4 Jan. 1929; *s* of David Anderson and Frances Anderson; *m* 1954, Eileen Dorothy Scott; one *s* two *d. Educ:* St Cuthbert's Grammar Sch., Newcastle on Tyne; RMA, Sandhurst. Black Watch, 1946; RMA, Sandhurst, 1947; commnd HLI, 1948; served ME and Malaya; RHF, Staff Coll., Trucial Oman Scouts, Sch. of Inf., I RHF, Germany, and HQ NORTHAG, 1959-66; Instr, Staff Coll., 1967-69; CO I RHF, Scotland, N Ireland, Singapore, 1969-72; Colonel GS: MoD, 1972-73; HQ Dir of Inf., 1974; Comdr, 3 Inf. Bde, N Ireland, 1975-76. *Recreations:* golf, walking. *Address:* c/o Williams and Glyn's Bank, Whitehall, SW1. *Club:* Army and Navy.

ANDERSON, Prof. Declan John; Professor of Oral Biology, University of Bristol, since 1966; *b* 20 June 1920; *s* of Arthur John Anderson and Katherine Mary Coffey; *m* 1947, Vivian Joy Dunkerton; four *s* three *d. Educ:* Christ's Hospital; Guy's Hospital Medical School, Univ. of London. BDS (London) 1942; LDSRCS 1943, BSc 1946, MSc 1947, PhD 1955. Prof. of Physiology, Univ. of Oregon, USA, 1957-58; Prof. of Physiology in Relation to Dentistry, Univ. of London, 1963-66. *Publications:* Physiology for Dental Students, 1952; scientific papers in professional jls. *Recreations:* silversmithing and music. *Address:* Haversham House, 12 New Street, Wells, Somerset.

ANDERSON, Donald; MP (Lab) Swansea East, since Oct. 1974; barrister-at-law; *b* 17 June 1939; *s* of David Robert Anderson and Eva (*née* Mathias); *m* 1963, Dorothy Trotman, BSc, PhD; three *s. Educ:* Swansea Grammar Sch.; University Coll. of Swansea. 1st cl. hons Modern History and Politics, Swansea, 1960. Barrister; called to Bar, Inner Temple, 1969. Member of HM Foreign Service, 1960-64: Foreign Office, 1960-63; 3rd Sec., British Embassy, Budapest, 1963-64; lectured in Dept of

Political Theory and Govt, University Coll., Swansea, 1964-66. MP (Lab) Monmouth, 1966-70; Mem. Estimates Cttee, 1966-69; Vice-Chm., Welsh Labour Group, 1969-70; PPS to Min. of Defence (Administration), 1969-70; PPS to Attorney General, 1974-; Chm., Parly Lab. Party Environment Gp, 1974-; Pres., Gower Soc., 1976-78. Councillor, Kensington and Chelsea, 1971-75. Dir, Campaign for European Political Community, 1967. Methodist local preacher. *Recreations:* church work, walking and talking. *Address:* Lamb Building, Temple, EC4; House of Commons, SW1.

ANDERSON, Prof. Donald Thomas, PhD, DSc, FRS 1977; Professor of Biology, University of Sydney, since 1972; *b* 29 Dec. 1931; *s* of Thomas and Flora Anderson; *m* 1960, Joanne Trevathan (*née* Claridge). *Educ:* King's Coll., London Univ. Lectr in Zoology, Sydney Univ., 1958-61; Sen. Lectr, 1962-66; Reader in Biology, 1967-71. *Publication:* Embryology and Phylogeny, of Annelids and Arthropods, 1973; papers in zool. jls. *Recreations:* gardening, photography. *Address:* 52 Spruson Street, Neutral Bay, NSW 2089, Australia. *T:* (home) 929.7583; (office) 692.2438.

ANDERSON, Sir Duncan (Law), KBE 1960 (CBE 1944); TD; CEng, FICE; consulting civil engineer; *b* 10 June 1901; *s* of J. D. Anderson, MA, Aberdeen, and L. Anderson; *m* 1947, Edens Alcyone, *er d* of Wallace McMullen; no *c. Educ:* Robert Gordon's Coll., Aberdeen. Practised as Civil Engineer on railway, road, bridge and tunnel construction, 1922-39. TA Officer, 1923-61; served with Royal Engineers, War of 1939-45 (despatches, CBE); Deputy Dir of Works, Gen. Eisenhower's staff, N African Campaign, and Dir of Works (Brig.), FM Alexander's Staff, Italian Campaign. Concerned latterly with rehabilitation of Italian Industry as Dep. Vice-Pres. Allied Commn, Rome. Chm. Jt Anglo-American/Jugo-Slav Econ. Commn, Trieste. CCG, 1946-50; Vice-Pres. Econ. Sub-Commn, Berlin, and Dep. Chm. US/UK Control Office, Frankfurt; Mem. two Foreign Office Missions led by Lord Strang to Washington, 1947 (first on rehabilitation of Ruhr coal industry, second, on finance and control of German foreign trade). Gen. Manager, Overseas Food Corp., Southern Prov., Tanganyika, 1950-51; responsible for re-organising and cutting down "Ground-nuts scheme" in that area after its failure. Controller, Caribbean Region, Colonial Development Corp., 1951-53, in charge of the Corporation's interest in Islands of West Indies, Br. Honduras and Br. Guiana; Controller in charge of Corporation's interests in Nyasaland, Rhodesias, Bechuanaland and Swaziland, 1953-55; Chm. Federal Power Bd of Rhodesia and Nyasaland (responsible for construction of Kariba Hydroelectric project on the Zambezi), 1955-61. First Chm., Commn for the New Towns, 1961-64. Director: South Durham Steel and Iron Co., 1961-67; BOAC, 1964-70; British Oxygen Co., 1962-72; Thomas Tilling Ltd, 1965-72. *Address:* Flat 7, 14 Melbury Road, Holland Park, W14. *T:* 01-602 3434. *Club:* Athenæum.

ANDERSON, Sir Edward (Arthur), Kt 1952; JP; Director of A. Anderson & Son (Electrical Engineers) Ltd, Middlesbrough; *b* 4 Jan. 1908; *s* of Arthur and Florence Anderson; *m* 1937, Elsa Mary French; no *c. Educ:* Middlesbrough High Sch.; South Shields Marine Engineering Coll. Entire working life spent in family business, A. Anderson & Son. AIEE 1937. Councillor for County Borough of Middlesbrough, 1945-56; Chairman Middlesbrough Conservative Assoc., 1947-60; JP Middlesbrough, 1950-. *Recreations:* swimming, walking, reading, music and travel. *Address:* Spring Lodge, Guisborough, North Yorkshire. *T:* Guisborough 2581. *Club:* Cleveland (Middlesbrough).

ANDERSON, Prof. Edward William, MD, FRCP; Hon. MSc; Lord Chancellor's Visitor, 1965-73; retired as Professor of Psychiatry, Victoria University of Manchester and Director of Department of Psychiatry, Manchester Royal Infirmary (1949-65), now Professor Emeritus; *b* 8 July 1901; *s* of Edward Ross Anderson and Elizabeth Leith (*née* Dow); *m* 1934, Margaret Mottram Hutton; two *s* one *d. Educ:* Daniel Stewart's Coll., Edinburgh; Univs of Edinburgh, London and Frankfurt-on-Main. MD Edinburgh 1927, MB, ChB 1923, FRCP 1946; DPM London 1925; Founder FRCPsych 1972. Junior hosp. appts in medicine and surgery, 1923-24; various mental hosp. appts, 1924-29; Asst MO, The Maudsley Hosp., 1929-35; Med. Dir Cassel Hosp. for Functional Nervous Disorders, 1935-37; Cons. Psychiatrist, Devon CC, 1938-47; Neuropsychiatric Specialist, Royal Navy (Temp. Actg Surg. Comdr, RNVR), 1940-45. Physician, The Maudsley Hospital and Lecturer in Psychiatry, The Institute of Psychiatry, 1947-49. Govt delegate, WHO Conference on health of Seamen, Marseilles, 1959. Rockefeller Fellow in Psychiatry, 1937-38. Visiting Professor, Univs of Witwatersrand and Cape Town, 1964. Examiner in Psychological Medicine, Univ. of London, 1950-58, and in

Psychological Medicine (Pt I), Conjoint Examining Bd, England, 1956-60; also (in the Membership) to RCP, 1964-70. Pres. Sect. Psychiatry RSM, 1961-62; Pres. (1964) Sect. Med., Manchester Med. Society. Hon. MSc (Vict.) 1953; Hon. Fellow (Psychiatry), Coll. of Medicine of S Africa, 1964. *Publications:* (jointly with W. H. Trethowan) Psychiatry, 1964, 3rd edn 1973; various articles on psychiatric topics in professional journals. *Address:* Fir Trees, The Green, Frant, near Tunbridge Wells TN3 9DN. *Club:* Reform.

ANDERSON, Prof. Ephraim Saul, CBE 1976; FRCP, FRS 1968; Director, Enteric Reference Laboratory, Public Health Laboratory Service, since 1954; *b* 1911; *e s* of Benjamin and Ada Anderson, Newcastle upon Tyne; *m* 1959, Carol Jean (née Thompson); three *s. Educ:* Rutherford Coll., and King's Coll. Med. Sch. (Univ. of Durham), Newcastle upon Tyne. MB, BS 1934; MD Durham, 1953; Dip.Bact. London, 1948; Founder Fellow, Royal Coll. of Pathologists, 1963. GP, 1935-39; RAMC, 1940-46; Pathologist, 1943-46; Registrar in Bacteriology, Postgrad. Med. Sch., 1946-47; Staff, Enteric Reference Lab., 1947-52, Dep. Dir, 1952-54. WHO Fellow, 1953; FIBiol 1973; FRCP 1975. Chm., Internat. Cttee for Enteric Phage Typing of Internat. Assoc. of Microbiol. Socs, 1966- (Jt Chm., 1958-66); Dir, Internat. Ref. Lab. for Enteric Phage Typing of Internat. Fedn for Enteric Phage Typing, 1954-; Dir, Collab. Centre for Phage Typing and Resistance of Enterobacteria of WHO, 1960-; Mem., WHO Expert Adv. Panel for Enteric Diseases. Vis. Prof., Sch. of Biol Sciences, Brunel Univ., 1973-. Hon. DSc Newcastle 1975. *Publications:* contrib. to: The Bacteriophages (Mark Adams), 1959; The World Problem of Salmonellosis (Van Oye), 1964; numerous articles on bacteriophage typing and its genetic basis, microbial ecology, transferable drug resistance, and epidemiology. *Recreations:* music, photography. *Address:* Enteric Reference Laboratory, Public Health Laboratory Service, Colindale Avenue, NW9. *T:* 01-205 7041.

ANDERSON, Eric; *see* Anderson, W. E. K.

ANDERSON, Sir Ferguson; *see* Anderson, Sir W. F.

ANDERSON, Dame Frances Margaret; *see* Anderson, Dame Judith.

ANDERSON, George David, CMG 1967; HM Diplomatic Service, retired; *b* 11 Sept. 1913; *m* 1950, Audrey Rowena Money; one *d. Educ:* King Edward VII Gram. Sch., King's Lynn; Emmanuel Coll., Cambridge. National Association of Boys' Clubs, 1935-37; Macgregor and Co., Rangoon, Burma, 1937-41. Army Service, Burma Rifles, 1941-44; Combined Services Detailed Interrogation Centre (India), 1944-46. Min. of Food, 1946; CRO, 1947. Office of British High Commission in New Delhi and Calcutta, 1947-51; British Embassy, Dublin, 1957-60; Dep. High Comr, Ceylon, 1961-66; Diplomatic Service, 1964; Head of Chancery, British High Commn, Lagos, Nigeria, 1967-69; British High Comr in Botswana, 1969-73. *Recreations:* gardening and the enjoyment of retirement. *Address:* c/o Grindlay's Bank Ltd, 13 St James's Square, SW1. *Club:* Royal Commonwealth Society.

ANDERSON, Rev. Prof. George Wishart, FRSE 1977; FBA 1972; Professor of Hebrew and Old Testament Studies, University of Edinburgh, since 1968 (Professor of Old Testament Literature and Theology, 1962-68); *b* 25 Jan. 1913; *s* of George Anderson and Margaret Gordon Wishart; *m* 1st, 1941, Edith Joyce Marjorie Walter (decd); one *s* one *d*; 2nd, 1959, Anne Phyllis Walter. *Educ:* Arbroath High Sch.; Univs of St Andrews, Cambridge, Lund. United Coll., St Andrews: Harkness Scholar; MA 1st Cl. Hons Classics, 1935. Fitzwilliam House and Wesley House, Cambridge: 1st Cl. Theol Tripos Part I, 1937; 2nd Cl. Theol Tripos Part II, 1938; BA 1937; MA 1946. Asst Tutor, Richmond Coll., 1939-41. Chaplain, RAF, 1941-46; Tutor in OT Lang. and Lit., Handsworth Coll., 1946-56; Lecturer in OT Lit. and Theol., Univ. of St Andrews, 1956-58; Prof. of OT Studies, Univ. of Durham, 1958-62. Hon. Sec., Internat. Organization of Old Testament Scholars, 1953-71 (Pres., 1971-74); Mem. Editorial Bd of Vetus Testamentum, 1950-75; Editor, Book List of Soc. for OT Study, 1957-66; President, Soc. for OT Study, 1963; Hon. Sec. (Foreign Correspondence), Soc. for OT Study, 1964-74; Charles Ryder Smith Meml Lectr, 1964; Fernley-Hartley Lectr, 1969; Speaker's Lectr in Biblical Studies, Univ. of Oxford, 1976-; Henton Davies Lectr, 1977. Hon. DD St Andrews, 1959; Hon. TeolD Lund, 1971. *Publications:* He That Cometh (trans. from Norwegian of S. Mowinckel), 1956; A Critical Introduction to the Old Testament, 1959; The Ras Shamra Discoveries and the Old Testament (trans. from Norwegian of A. S. Kapelrud, US 1963, UK 1965); The History and Religion of Israel, 1966; (ed) A Decade of Bible Bibliography, 1967; articles in: The Old

Testament and Modern Study (ed H. H. Rowley), 1951; The New Peake Commentary (ed M. Black and H. H. Rowley), 1962; The Cambridge History of the Bible, Vol. I (ed P. R. Ackroyd and C. F. Evans), 1970, and in various learned jls. *Recreations:* reading, music, walking. *Address:* 51 Fountainhall Road, Edinburgh EH9 2LH.

ANDERSON, Sir Gilmour M.; *see* Menzies Anderson.

ANDERSON, Rev. Hector David, MVO 1951; MA, BD; Chaplain to the Queen, 1955-77; *b* 16 Aug. 1906; *s* of Rev. David Anderson, LLD, Dublin; *m* 1931, Muriel Louise Peters; one *s. Educ:* The Abbey, Tipperary; Trinity Coll., Dublin. Schol. 1928, BA Mods 1929, MA 1932, BD 1949. Curate, Shirley, Croydon, 1930-33; St Michael's, Chester Square, SW1, 1933-39; CF, Sept. 1939-42; Domestic Chaplain to King George VI, 1942-52, to the Queen, 1952-55; Rector: Sandringham, 1942-55; Lutterworth, 1955-61; Swanage, 1961-69. *Address:* Adare, The Hyde, Langton Matravers, Swanage, Dorset. *T:* Swanage 3206.

ANDERSON, H(ector) John, FRCP; Physician, St Thomas' Hospital, since 1948, Governor since 1968; Physician, Lambeth Hospital, South Western Hospital and French Hospital; *b* Central Provinces, India, 5 Jan. 1915; *s* of H. J. Anderson; *m* 1st, 1940, Frances Pearce (marr. diss.), *er d* of Rev. W. P. Putt; one *s* one *d*; 2nd, 1956, Pauline Mary, *d* of A. Hammond; one *d. Educ:* Exeter Sch.; St Catharine's Coll., Cambridge; St Thomas' Hospital. MA, MB (Cantab), FRCP. Medical Registrar and Res. Asst Physician, St Thomas' Hospital, 1941 and 1942. Hon. Lt-Col RAMC; served MEF, 1944-47. Kitchener Scholar; Mead Prizeman, St Thomas' Hospital; Murchison Scholar, RCP, 1942; Goulstonian Lectr, RCP, 1951; Examiner: MB London; Medicine, Conjoint Bd, London and England; RCP. Mem. AHA, Lambeth, Southwark, Lewisham Area (T). Member: Assoc. of Physicians of Gt Britain; Thoracic Soc.; FRSoc.Med. *Publications:* Brim of Day, 1944; contrib. to medical literature. *Address:* 5 Coombe Rise, Kingston Hill, Surrey; 3 Upper Wimpole Street, W1. *T:* 01-935 5873; 102 Lambeth Road, SE1. *T:* 01-928 1533.

ANDERSON, Hugh Fraser, MA, FRCS; Urological Surgeon, St George's Hospital, London, 1948, now Emeritus; late Surgeon, West Park Hospital, Epsom; *b* 19 April 1910; *s* of late William Thomson Anderson and late Madeline Bertha (née Grubb); *m* 1942, Nancy Singleton; one *s* one *d. Educ:* King William's Coll., I of M; Gonville and Caius Coll., Cambridge (Open Exhibition, 1929); St George's Hospital (Anne Selina Fernee Exhibition, 1932). MA (Cantab) 1939; MB, BCh (Cantab) 1935; LRCP 1935; FRCS 1940. Allingham Prize in Surgery, St George's Hospital, 1938. Served War of 1939-45 (Major, RAMC) (despatches). Examiner in Surgery: Univ. of London, 1958; Univ. of Basrah, 1973; Univ. of Lagos, 1975, 1976, 1977; Mem., Court of Examiners, Royal Coll. of Surgeons, 1966. Member: Assoc. of Surgeons; British Association of Urological Surgeons; International Soc. of Urology. *Publications:* articles on urological subjects and the infected hand in learned journals and textbooks. *Recreations:* golf, railways, gardening. *Address:* 13 Durrington Park Road, Wimbledon, SW20. *T:* 01-946 2114; St George's Hospital, Consulting Suite, 11-13 Knightsbridge, SW1. *T:* 01-235 8157. *Clubs:* MCC, Ski Club of Great Britain; Walton Heath Golf, St Enodoc Golf (Rock, Cornwall).

ANDERSON, Prof. Sir (James) Norman (Dalrymple), Kt 1975; OBE 1945 (MBE 1943); BA 1930, LLB 1931, MA 1934, LLD 1955 (Cantab); Hon. DD St Andrews 1974; FBA 1970; QC 1974; Professor of Oriental Laws in the University of London, 1954-75; Barrister-at-Law; Director of the Institute of Advanced Legal Studies in the University of London, Oct. 1959-Sept. 1976; *b* 29 Sept. 1908; *s* of late William Dalrymple Anderson; *m* 1933, Patricia Hope, *d* of A. Stock Givan; one *s* and two *d* decd. *Educ:* St Lawrence Coll., Ramsgate; Trinity Coll., Cambridge (Senior Scholar). 1st Class, Law Tripos Parts I and II (distinction in Part I); 1st Class LLB. Called to the Bar, Gray's Inn, 1965. Missionary, Egypt General Mission, 1932; served War of 1939-45 in Army as Arab Liaison Officer, Libyan Arab Force, 1940 (Capt.); Sec. for Sanusi Affairs, Civil Affairs Branch, GHQ, MEF, 1941 (Major); Sec. for Arab Affairs, 1943 (Lieut-Col); Political Sec., 1943; Chief Sec. (Col), 1944; Lectr in Islamic Law, Sch. of Oriental and African Studies, 1947; Reader in Oriental Laws in Univ. of London, 1951-53; Hd of Dept of Law, SOAS, 1953-71; Dean of Faculty of Laws, Univ. of London, 1965-69. President, Soc. of Public Teachers of Law, 1968-69. Chm. UK Nat. Cttee of Comparative Law, 1957-59; Vice-Chm. Internat. African Law Assoc.; Visiting Prof., Princeton Univ. and New York Univ. Law Sch., 1958; Harvard Law Sch., 1966; Mem., Denning Cttee on Legal Education for Students from Africa, 1960. Conducted survey of application of Islamic Law in British African possessions for Colonial Office, 1950-51. President:

BCMS; CPAS; Scripture Union; Victoria Inst. Chm. Middle East Christian Outreach; First Chairman, House of Laity in Gen. Synod of Church of England, 1970- (Mem. former Church Assembly, 1965-70); Anglican delegate to the World Council of Churches; Examining Chaplain to the Bishop of London. Libyan Order of Istiqlal, Class II, 1959. *Publications:* Islamic Law in Africa, 1954; Islamic Law in the Modern World, 1959; Into the World: The Need and Limits of Christian Involvement, 1968; Christianity: the witness of history, 1969; Christianity and Comparative Religion, 1970; Morality, Law and Grace, 1972; A Lawyer among the Theologians, 1973; Law Reform in the Muslim World, 1976; Issues of Life and Death, 1976; Editor: The World's Religions, 1950, 4th edn 1975; Changing Law in Developing Countries, 1963; Family Law in Asia and Africa, 1968; numerous articles in periodicals. *Address:* 9 Larchfield, Gough Way, Cambridge. *T:* Cambridge 58778. *Club:* Athenæum.

ANDERSON, John, CB 1956; CBE 1950; CEng, FIEE; retired as Chief Scientist, Admiralty Surface Weapons Establishment, Portsmouth, 1961; *b* 29 Aug. 1896; *s* of John Anderson, Beith, Ayrshire; *m* 1928, Isabella Mary Morton Crerar; no *c.* *Educ:* Spiers Sch., Beith, Ayrshire; Royal Technical Coll., Glasgow (Diploma). Joined RN Scientific Service, 1918; Chief Scientist: HM Underwater Detection Establishment, Portland, 1943-51; Admiralty Signal and Radar Establishment, Portsmouth, 1951. American Medal of Freedom, 1946. *Address:* Blue Hills, Denbigh Road, Haslemere, Surrey. *T:* Haslemere 3575.

ANDERSON, Prof. John, MD, FRCP; Professor of Medicine, King's College Hospital Medical School, since 1964; *b* 11 Sept. 1921; *s* of James and Margaret Anderson; *m* 1952, Beatrice May Venner; three *s.* *Educ:* Durham Univ. BA Hons, Dunelm (Mod. Hist.) 1942; MB, BS Hons, 1950; BSc Hons, 1952 (Physiology); MA (Mod. Hist.), MD. Served War, Lt, RA (Field) (Ayrshire Yeomanry), 1940-45. MRC Fellow in Clin. Med., Univ. Coll. Hosp., London, 1952-55; Rockefeller Travelling Fellowship, 1956-57; Reader in Medicine, King's Coll. Hosp. Med. Sch., Med. Unit, 1962-65. Mem., Med. Research Soc. FRCP 1962; FBCS 1969; FIBiol 1977. *Publications:* A New Look at Medical Education, 1965; Information Processing of Medical Records, 1970; articles in Lancet and BMJ, on: nutron activation, medical computing, cancer, endocrinology, med. educn. *Recreations:* shooting, sailing, fishing. *Address:* 14 Styles Way, Park Langley, Beckenham, Kent. *T:* (office) 01-274 6222. *Club:* University (Durham).

ANDERSON, General Sir John (D'Arcy), GBE 1967 (CBE 1945); KCB 1961 (CB 1957); DSO 1940; DL; Pro-Chancellor, Queen's University, Belfast, since 1969; *b* 23 Sept. 1908; *s* of late Major Reginald D'Arcy Anderson, RGA, and Norah Anderson (*née* Gracey), Ballyhossett, Downpatrick, Co. Down; *m* 1937, Elizabeth, *d* of late Augustus M. Walker. *Educ:* Winchester; New Coll., Oxford (MA). 2nd Lieut 5th Royal Inniskilling Dragoon Guards, 1929; served War of 1939-45, France, Middle East and Italy (wounded, despatches twice); GOC 11th Armoured Div., BAOR, 1955-56. Chief of Staff, Headquarters Northern Army Group and BAOR, 1956-58; Director, RAC, WO, 1958-59; Dir-Gen. of Military Training, 1959-61; DCIGS, 1961-63; Military Sec. to: Sec. of State for War, 1963-64; Min. of Defence, 1964-65. Commandant IDC, 1966-68; Col 5th Royal Inniskilling Dragoon Guards, 1962-67; Col Comdt, RAEC, 1964-70; Col Comdt, UDR, 1969- (Rep., 1969-77); Hon. Col: Oxford Univ. OTC, 1961-67; Queen's Univ., Belfast, OTC, 1964-75. ADC General to the Queen, 1966-68. Mem., Commonwealth War Graves Commn, 1963-71. Chm., Army Museums Ogilby Trust; Vice-Pres. Sandes Soldiers' and Airmen's Homes; Deputy Pres., ACF Assoc. (NI). DL Co. Down 1969, High Sheriff Co. Down 1974. Grand Officer, Order of the Crown (Belgium), 1963. Grand Officer, Order of Leopold (Belgium), 1966. *Recreation:* painting. *Address:* Ballyhossett, Downpatrick, Co. Down, Northern Ireland BT30 7EF. *T:* Ardglass 227. *Clubs:* Cavalry and Guards; Ulster (Belfast).

ANDERSON, Maj.-Gen. Sir John (Evelyn), KBE 1971 (CBE 1963); CEng, FIEE; FBIM; Director General NATO Integrated Communications System Management Agency, since 1977; *b* 28 June 1916; *s* of Lt-Col John Gibson Anderson, Christchurch, NZ, and Margaret (*née* Scott), Edinburgh; *m* 1944, Jean Isobel, *d* of Charles Tait, farmer, Aberdeenshire; one *s* one *d.* *Educ:* King's Sch., Rochester; RMA, Woolwich. Commissioned in Royal Signals, 1936; Lt-Col 1956; Col 1960; Brig. 1964; Maj.-Gen. 1967; Signal Officer in Chief (Army), MoD, 1967-69; ACDS (signals), 1969-72. Col Comdt, Royal Corps of Signals, 1969-74. Hon. Col 71st (Yeomanry) Signal Regt TAVR, 1969-76; Hon. Col Women's Transport Corps (FANY), 1970-76. *Recreation:* fishing. *Address:* 18 Avenue du Capricorne, 1410 Waterloo, Belgium. *T:* 354-1180. *Clubs:* Army and Navy, Flyfishers'.

ANDERSON, Prof. John Kinloch, FSA; Professor of Classical Archaeology, University of California, Berkeley, since 1958; *b* 3 Jan. 1924; *s* of late Sir James Anderson, KCIE, and of Lady Anderson; *m* 1954, Esperance, *d* of Guy Batham, Dunedin, NZ; one *s* two *d.* *Educ:* Trinity Coll., Glenalmond; Christ Church, Oxford (MA). Served War, in Black Watch (RHR) and Intelligence Corps, 1942-46 (final rank, Lieut). Student, British Sch. at Athens, 1949-52; Lecturer in Classics, Univ. of Otago, NZ, 1953-58. FSA 1976. *Publications:* Greek Vases in the Otago Museum, 1955; Ancient Greek Horsemanship, 1961; Military Theory and Practice in the Age of Xenophon, 1970; Xenophon, 1974; articles and reviews in Annual of British Sch. at Athens; Jl of Hellenic Studies, etc. *Recreations:* gardening, riding. *Address:* 1020 Middlefield Road, Berkeley, California 94708, USA. *T:* Berkeley 841-5335.

ANDERSON, Sir John (Muir), Kt 1969; CMG 1957; Commissioner of State Savings Bank of Victoria, since 1962, Chairman of Commissioners, 1967; *b* 14 Sept. 1914; *s* of John Weir Anderson; *m* 1949, Audrey Drayton Jamieson; one *s* one *d.* *Educ:* Brighton Grammar Sch.; Melbourne Univ. 2/6th Commando Co., 1941; Lieut, 1st Australian Parachute Bn, 1944; served SE Asia, 1941-45. Established John M. Anderson & Co. Pty Ltd, Manufacturers, Agents and Importers, 1951; Dir, Bly's (Australia) Pty Ltd; Managing Director, King Oscar Fine Foods Pty Ltd. Pres. of Liberal and Country Party of Victoria, 1952-56 (Treasurer, 1957-61). Comr, Melbourne Harbour Trust, 1972-. Trustee, Melbourne Exhibn, 1960, Chm. of Trustees, 1968. *Recreations:* swimming, fishing. *Address:* 25 Cosham Street, Brighton, Vic 3186, Australia. *T:* 92-4790.

ANDERSON, Professor John Neil; (first) Professor of Dental Prosthetics, since 1964, Dean of Dentistry, 1975-76, University of Dundee; *b* 11 Feb. 1922; *s* of late J. Anderson and Mrs A. Anderson, Sheffield; *m* 1945, Mary G. Croll; one *s* one *d.* *Educ:* High Storrs Gram. Sch., Sheffield; Sheffield Univ. Asst Lectr, Sheffield Univ., 1945-46; Lectr, Durham Univ., 1946-48; Lectr, Birmingham Univ., 1948-52; Sen. Lectr, St Andrews Univ., 1952-64. External Examiner, Univs of Malaya, Baghdad, Newcastle upon Tyne, Bristol, Birmingham, Liverpool, RCSI. *Publications:* Applied Dental Materials, 5th edn, 1976; (with R. Storer) Immediate and Replacement Dentures, 1966, 2nd edn, 1973; contribs to leading dental jls. *Recreations:* music, gardening, carpentry. *Address:* The Bensil, Carnoustie, Angus, Scotland. *T:* Carnoustie 52133.

ANDERSON, Prof. John Russell; Professor of Pathology at the Western Infirmary, Glasgow University, since 1967; *b* 31 May 1918; *s* of William Gregg Anderson and Mary Gordon Adam; *m* 1956, Audrey Margaret Shaw Wilson; two *s* two *d.* *Educ:* Worksop Coll.; St Andrews Univ. BSc (St Andrews) 1939, MB, ChB (St Andrews) 1942, MD (St Andrews) 1955; MRCP 1961; FRCPGlas 1965; FRCPath 1966; FRSE 1968. RAMC, 1944-47 (Emergency Commn). Lecturer and Senior Lecturer in Pathology, Glasgow Univ., 1947-65; George Holt Prof. of Pathology, Liverpool Univ., 1965-67. Rockefeller travelling fellowship in Medicine, at Rochester, NY, 1953-54. Vice-Pres., RCPath, 1975. *Publications:* Autoimmunity, Clinical and Experimental (jtly), 1967; Muir's Textbook of Pathology (jtly), 9th edn 1972, 10th edn 1976; various papers on immunopathology in scientific jls. *Recreations:* squash, ski-ing, gardening. *Address:* Pathology Department, Western Infirmary, Glasgow G11 6NT. *T:* 041-339 8822.

ANDERSON, Prof. John Stuart, FRS 1953; MA, PhD, MSc; Professor of Inorganic Chemistry, Oxford University, 1963-75, now Emeritus; *b* 9 Jan. 1908; *m* 1935, Joan Taylor; one *s* three *d.* Formerly Dep. Chief Scientific Officer, Chemistry Div., Atomic Energy Research Establishment, Harwell, Berks; Prof. of Inorganic and Physical Chemistry and Head of the Dept of Chemistry, Univ. of Melbourne, Australia, 1954-59; Director of the National Chemical Laboratory (Department of Scientific and Industrial Research), Teddington, 1959-63. Pres., Dalton Div. of Chemical Soc., 1974-76. Davy Medal, Royal Soc., 1973. *Address:* Edward Davies Chemical Laboratory, University College of Wales, Aberystwyth, Dyfed; The Cottage, Abermagwr, near Aberystwyth, Dyfed SY23 4AR.

ANDERSON, Dame Judith, DBE 1960; (Dame Frances Margaret Anderson); Actress; *b* Adelaide, South Australia, 10 Feb. 1898; *d* of James Anderson Anderson and Jessie Saltmarsh; *m* 1937, Prof. B. H. Lehman (marr. diss. 1939); *m* 1946, Luther Greene (marr. diss. 1950). *Educ:* Norwood High Sch., South Australia. Started Theatre with Julius Knight; toured Australia and America, 1918; has played in: The Dove, 1925; Behold the Bridegroom, 1927; Strange Interlude, 1930; Mourning becomes Electra, 1931; Come of Age, 1934; The Old Maid, 1935; Hamlet, 1936; Macbeth (London), 1937; Family Portrait, 1939; Three

Sisters, 1942; Medea (New York, 1947-48; toured America, 1948-49; Paris Internat. Drama Festival, 1955); The Seagull, Edin. Fest., 1960, Sept. at Old Vic; The Oresteia, 1966; Hamlet, 1970. *Films:* Rebecca, Edge of Darkness, Laura, King's Row, Spectre of the Rose, The Red House, Pursued, Tycoon, Cat on a Hot Tin Roof, Macbeth, Don't Bother to Knock, A Man Called Horse; TV: The Chinese Prime Minister, 1974. *Recreation:* gardening. *Address:* 808 San Ysidro Lane, Santa Barbara, Calif 93103, USA.

ANDERSON, Sir Kenneth, KBE 1962 (CBE 1946); CB 1955; *b* 5 June 1906; *s* of Walter Anderson, Exmouth; *m* 1932, Helen Veronica Grose; one *s* one *d*. *Educ:* Swindon Secondary Sch.; Wadham Coll., Oxford (MA). Entered India Office, 1928; Asst Sec., 1942; Dep. Financial Adviser to British Military Governor, Germany, 1947-48; Imperial Defence Coll., 1949; Under-Sec., HM Treasury, 1950-51; Dep. Director-General, 1954-66 and Comptroller and Accountant-General, 1952-66, GPO. Officer, Order of Orange-Nassau, 1947. *Address:* 7 Milton Close, N2. *T:* 01-455 8701. *Club:* United Oxford & Cambridge University.

ANDERSON, Hon. Sir Kenneth (McColl), KBE 1972; Kt 1970; Senator for New South Wales, Australia, 1953-75; Government Leader in the Senate, 1968-72; Commonwealth Minister for Health, 1971-72; *b* 11 Oct. 1909; *m*; one *d*. MLA, NSW, for Ryde, 1950-53; Minister for Customs and Excise, 1964-68 (Actg Minister for Civil Aviation, 1966; Actg PMG, 1967); Minister for Supply, 1968-71. Alderman, Ryde Municipal Council, and Mayor of Ryde, 1949-50; Mem., Cumberland CC, 1949-50. Member: Cttee of Disputed Returns and Qualifications, 1953-62; Standing Cttee on Public Works, 1956-64; Jt Cttee on New and Permanent Parliament House, 1967; Standing Cttee on Standing Orders, 1968-72; Chm., Senate Select Cttee to consider problems of Road Safety, 1960. Served with AIF, Lieut, 8 Div. Signals, Malaya (PoW). *Recreation:* bowls. *Address:* 80 East Parade, Eastwood, NSW, Australia. *Clubs:* National, Union, Ryde RSL.

ANDERSON, Dame Kitty, DBE 1961; BA London; PhD London; Vice-President, Girls' Public Day School Trust, since 1976 (Chairman, 1965-75); President, Schoolmistresses and Governesses Benevolent Institution, since 1972; *b* 4 July 1903; *d* of J. H. Anderson, FCA, and L. Anderson. *Educ:* High Sch. for Girls, Saltburn-by-the-Sea; Royal Holloway Coll., Univ. of London. Head Mistress King's Norton Girls' Grammar Sch., Birmingham, 1939-44; Head Mistress, North London Collegiate Sch., 1944-65. FCP, 1966. Hon. LLD, Hull, 1967; DUniv York, 1971. *Address:* 33 Hutchinson Drive, Northallerton, North Yorks. *Club:* University Women's.

ANDERSON, Lindsay (Gordon); film and theatre director; *b* 17 April 1923; 2nd *s* of late Maj.-Gen. A. V. Anderson and Estelle Bell Sleigh. *Educ:* Cheltenham Coll.; Wadham Coll., Oxford. Associate Artistic Director, Royal Court Theatre, 1969-75. Governor, British Film Institute, 1969-70. *Films include:* Wakefield Express, 1953; Thursday's Children (with Guy Brenton), 1954; O Dreamland, 1954; Every Day Except Christmas, 1957; This Sporting Life, 1963; The White Bus, 1966; Raz, Dwa, Trzy (The Singing Lesson), for Warsaw Documentary Studio, 1967; If...., 1968 (Grand Prix, Cannes Fest., 1969); O Lucky Man!, 1973 (Film Critics' Guild award for best film of 1973); In Celebration, 1974. *Productions in theatre:* The Waiting of Lester Abbs, 1957; The Long and the Short and the Tall; Progress to the Park; Jazzetry; Serjeant Musgrave's Dance, 1959; The Lily White Boys; Billy Liar; Trials by Logue, 1960; The Fire-Raisers, 1961; The Diary of a Madman, 1963; Andorra, 1964; Julius Caesar, 1964; The Cherry Orchard, 1966; first Polish production of Inadmissible Evidence (Nie Do Obrony), Warsaw, 1966; In Celebration, 1969; The Contractor, 1969; Home (also NY), 1970; The Changing Room, 1973; The Farm, 1974; Life Class, 1974; What the Butler Saw, 1975; The Sea Gull, 1975; The Bed Before Yesterday, 1975; The Kingfisher, 1977. Editor, film quarterly, Sequence, 1947-51. *Publications:* Making a Film, 1952; contrib. to Declaration, 1957. *Address:* 9 Stirling Mansions, Canfield Gardens, NW6.

ANDERSON, Marian, (Mrs Orpheus H. Fisher); American contralto; *b* Philadelphia, Pa, 17 Feb. 1902; *m* 1943, Orpheus H. Fisher. *Educ:* Philadelphia; New York; Chicago; and in Europe. MusD Howard Univ., 1938. Singing career began in 1924; 1st prize at Lewisohn Stadium competition, New York, 1925. Has made numerous tours in the United States, Europe, Japan, Israel, India, Pakistan, Korea, etc. Ulrica in Verdi's The Masked Ball, Metropolitan Opera House, New York, 1955. US Delegate to UN, 1958. Has made many recordings. Holds numerous American and other hon. doctorates; Bok Award, 1940. Finnish decoration, 1940; Litteris et Artibus Medal, Sweden, 1952; Yukusho Medal, Japan, 1953; Gimbel Award, 1958; Gold

Medal, US Inst. of Arts and Sciences, 1958; US Presidential Medal of Freedom, 1963. *Publication:* My Lord, What a Morning, 1957. *Address:* c/o Speakers Group, 75 East 55th Street, New York City, NY 10022, USA; Danbury, Conn 06810, USA.

ANDERSON, Brig. Hon. Dame Mary Mackenzie; *see* Pihl, Brig. Hon. Dame M. M.

ANDERSON, Sir Norman; *see* Anderson, Sir J. N. D.

ANDERSON, Prof. Philip Warren; Professor of Physics, Princeton University, New Jersey, since 1975; Consulting Director, Physical Research Laboratory, Bell Telephone Laboratories, NJ, since 1976 (Member of Staff, 1949-76); *b* 13 Dec. 1923; *s* of Prof. H. W. Anderson and Mrs Elsie O. Anderson; *m* 1947, Joyce Gothwaite; one *d*. *Educ:* Harvard Univ. BS 1943; MA 1947; PhD 1949, Harvard. Naval Res. Lab., Washington, DC, 1943-45 (Chief Petty Officer, USN). Fulbright Lectr, Tokyo Univ., 1952-53; Overseas Fellow, Churchill Coll., Cambridge, 1961-62; Vis. Prof. of Theoretical Physics, Univ. of Cambridge, 1967-75, and Fellow of Jesus College, Cambridge, 1969-75. Member: Amer. Acad. of Arts and Sciences, 1966; Nat. Acad. of Sciences, US, 1967. O. E. Buckley Prize, Amer. Phys. Soc., 1964; Dannie Heinemann Prize, Akad. Wiss. Göttingen, 1975; (jtly) Nobel Prize for Physics, 1977. *Publications:* Concepts in Solids, 1963; numerous articles in scholarly jls. *Recreations:* go (Japanese game), rank sho-dan, walking. *Address:* Millbrook Road, New Vernon, NJ 07976, USA.

ANDERSON, Reginald, CMG 1974; Deputy Under-Secretary of State, Ministry of Defence, since 1976; *b* 3 Nov. 1921; *s* of late Herbert Anderson and late Anne Mary (*née* Hicks); *m* 1945, Audrey Gabrielle Williams; two *d*. *Educ:* Palmers, Grays, Essex. Cabinet Office, 1938-40. Served War, RAF, Flt Lt, 1941-46. Ministry of: Supply, 1947-57; Supply Staff, Australia, 1957-59; Aviation, 1960-67; Counsellor, British Embassy, Washington, 1967-70; Asst Under-Sec. of State, MoD, 1970-76. *Recreations:* tennis, badminton, golf. *Address:* Reynosa, Heronway, Shenfield, Essex. *T:* Brentwood 213077. *Club:* Royal Air Force.

ANDERSON, Lt-Gen. Sir Richard (Neville), KCB 1961 (CB 1957); CBE 1949; DSO and Bar, 1944; Colonel, The King's Own Royal Border Regiment, 1961-71; Colonel, 10th Princess Mary's Own Gurkha Rifles, 1960-66; *b* 28 April 1907; *s* of Col Sir Neville Anderson, CBE; *m* 1942, Dorrie Norah Wybergh; two *d*. *Educ:* Tonbridge; Royal Mil. Coll., Sandhurst; idc. Served Palestine, 1938-39; War of 1939-45; Italy campaign, 1944-45; Palestine, 1946-48; GOC 17 Gurkha Div., 1955-57; GOC Overseas Forces, Malaya, 1957-58; Vice-Adj.-Gen., War Office, 1958-60; GOC-in-C, MELF, 1960-63; GOC-in-C, NI Command, 1963-65, retd 1965. Director, Civil Defence for Wales, 1965-68. Hon. Fellow Inst. of Civil Defence, 1966. *Recreation:* golf. *Address:* Tarrant Keynston House, Blandford, Dorset.

ANDERSON, Robert Bernerd; lawyer and statesman, United States; Chairman, Robert B. Anderson & Co. Ltd; *b* Burleson, Texas, 4 June 1910; *s* of Robert Lee and Elizabeth (*née* Haskew); *m* 1935, Ollie Mae Anderson; two *s*. *Educ:* Weatherford Coll., Texas; Univ. of Texas (LLB). Admitted to Texas Bar, and began law practice, Fort Worth, Texas, 1932; elected to Texas legislature, 1932; Asst Attorney-Gen., Texas, 1932; Prof. of Law, Univ. of Texas, 1933; State Tax Commr, Texas, 1934; Racing Commr, Texas, 1934; Member State Tax Board, 1934; Chm. and Executive Director, Texas Unemployment Commn, 1936; Gen. Counsel for the Waggoner Estate (oil and ranching), 1937-40 (Gen. Man., 1941-53). Secretary of US Navy, 1953-54; Dep. Secretary of Defense, 1954-55; Secretary of the Treasury, 1957-61. Chairman: American Gas & Chemical Co. Ltd; ITC Commercial Credit Inc.; Tacnavcom Inc.; Director: Pan American World Airways; Goodyear Tire & Rubber Co.; CIT Financial Corp.; Intercontinental Trailsea Corp.; National Bank of N America; Prudential Technology Internat. Mem. Texas Bar Assoc.; Associate of Bar of City of New York. *Address:* 630 Fifth Avenue, Suite 950, New York, NY 10020, USA.

ANDERSON, Robert (Woodruff); playwright; *b* NYC, 28 April 1917; *s* of James Hewston Anderson and Myra Esther (*née* Grigg); *m* 1st, 1940, Phyllis Stohl (*d* 1956); 2nd, 1959, Teresa Wright. *Educ:* Phillips Exeter Acad.; Harvard Univ. AB 1939, MA 1940. Served USNR, 1942-46 (Lt); won prize (sponsored by War Dept) for best play written by a serviceman, Come Marching Home, 1945, subseq. prod, Univ. of Iowa and Blackfriars Guild, NY. Rockefeller Fellowship, 1946; taught playwrighting, American Theatre Wing Professional Trng Prog., 1946-50; organized and taught Playwright's Unit, Actors Studio, 1955; Writer in Residence, Univ. of N Carolina, 1969;

Faculty, Univ. of Iowa Writers' Workshop, 1976. Member: Playwrights Co., 1953-60; Bd of Governors, American Playwrights Theatre, 1963-; Council, Dramatists Guild, 1954- (Pres., 1971-73); New Dramatists Cttee, 1950-60 (Pres., 1955-57); Fac., Salzburg Seminar in American Studies, 1968; Council, Authors' League of America; Chm., Harvard Bd of Overseers' Cttee to visit the Performing Arts, 1970-76. Wrote and adapted plays for TV and Radio. *Plays:* Eden Rose, 1948; Love Revisited, 1952; Tea and Sympathy, 1953; All Summer Long, 1954; Silent Night, Lonely Night, 1959; The Days Between, 1965; You Know I Can't Hear You When the Water's Running (four short plays), 1967; I Never Sang For My Father, 1968; Solitaire/Double Solitaire, 1971; *screenplays:* Tea and Sympathy, 1956; Until They Sail, 1957; The Nun's Story, 1959; The Sand Pebbles, 1965; I Never Sang For My Father, 1970; *novels:* After, 1973; Getting Up and Going Home, 1978. *Recreations:* photography, guitar, gardening. *Address:* Roxbury, Conn 06783 USA. *Clubs:* Harvard, Century Association, Coffee House (New York City).

ANDERSON, Dr Theodore Farnworth, CMG 1956; OBE 1943; HM Overseas Medical Service, retired; *b* 22 Oct. 1901; *s* of Rev. J. F. Anderson; *m* 1928, Isabel Cecile Downey; two *d. Educ:* Rugby Sch.; Trinity Hall, Cambridge; University Coll. Hospital. MA (Cantab), MD, BCh, MRCS, LRCP, DTM & H. General Practice, Kenya, 1925; appointed Medical Officer, Colonial Medical Service, Kenya, 1928. North Persian Forces Memorial Medal, 1930. Commn RAMC, 1939 (despatches); demobilised, 1945, rank of Col. Director of Medical Services, Somaliland Protectorate, 1945-49; Director of Medical Services, HM Overseas Medical Services, Kenya, 1949-57; MLC Kenya, 1950-57, retired. Liveryman Worshipful Soc. of Apothecaries; Freeman, City of London. *Publications:* numerous articles in medical press. *Recreations:* gardening, reading, history, archaeology. *Address:* The Clearing, Hawkhurst, Kent. *T:* Hawkhurst 2217. *Clubs:* Athenæum, Royal Commonwealth Society; Rye Golf; Nairobi; Limuru Country; Muthaiga Country.

ANDERSON, Thomas, CBE 1972; MD, FRCPE, FRCPGlas, FFCM; Henry Mechan Professor of Public Health, University of Glasgow, 1964-71, retired (Professor of Infectious Diseases, 1959-64); *b* 7 Dec. 1904; *e s* of Thomas Anderson and Mary (*née* Johnstone); *m* 1935, Helen Turner Massey (*d* 1974), one *s* three *d. Educ:* The High Sch. of Glasgow; Glasgow Univ. (MB, ChB 1928; MD, Hons and Bellahouston Gold Medal, 1945); MRCPE 1934; FRCPE 1940; FRCPGlas 1947. Dep. Phys., Ruchill Hosp., 1933-41; Phys. Supt, Knightswood Hosp., 1941-47; Sen. Lectr, subseq. Reader, Infectious Diseases, Glasgow Univ., 1947-59. Mem., Industrial Injuries Adv. Council, 1971-77. Formerly Consultant in Infectious Diseases to Western Region of Scotland. Hon. Member: Soc. for Study of Infectious Disease; Royal Medico-Chirurgical Soc., Glasgow; Swedish Med. Assoc.; Soc. for Social Med.; Section of Epidemiology and Preventive Med., RSM. *Publications:* various, on Infectious Diseases, in med. scientific jls. *Recreation:* bowls. *Address:* Braeside, Brodick, Isle of Arran KA27 8AF.

ANDERSON, Walter Charles, CBE 1968; Solicitor; General Secretary, National and Local Government Officers Association, 1957-73; Member, IBA, since 1973; *b* 3 Dec. 1910; *s* of William Walter John Anderson and Mary Theresa McLoughlin; *m* 1941, Doris Jessie Deacon; two *s. Educ:* Bootle Grammar Sch. and Wigan Grammar Sch.; Liverpool Univ. (LLB). Articled Clerk, J. W. Wall & Co., Solicitors, Bootle, Liverpool, 1930-33; Asst Solicitor, Bootle, 1933-34; Dep. Town Clerk, Heywood, 1934-37; Asst Solicitor, Nalgo, 1937-41; Royal Air Force, 1941-45; Legal Officer, Nalgo, 1945-50; Dep. Gen. Sec., Nalgo, 1950-57; Mem., Gen. Council of TUC, 1965-73. Member: Fulton Cttee on Civil Service Recruitment, Structure, Management and Training, 1966-68; Nat. Insurance Adv. Cttee, 1970-74; Industrial Injuries Adv. Council, 1970-74; Nat. Inst. of Econ. and Social Res., 1970; Industrial Arbitration Bd, Workpeople's Rep., 1972; Royal Commn on Civil Liability and Compensation for Personal Injury, 1973-. *Publication:* Simonds' Local Government Superannuation Act, 1937 (rev. and ed), 1947. *Recreations:* sport, gardening. *Address:* 1 The Comyns, Bushey, Watford WD2 1HN. *T:* 01-950 3708.

ANDERSON, (William) Eric (Kinloch), MA, BLitt; Headmaster of Shrewsbury School since 1975; *b* 27 May 1936; *er s* of W. J. Kinloch Anderson, Edinburgh; *m* 1960, Poppy, *d* of W. M. Mason, Skipton; one *s* one *d. Educ:* George Watson's Coll.; Univ. of St Andrews; Balliol Coll., Oxford. Asst Master: Fettes Coll., 1960-64, 1966-67; Gordonstoun, 1964-66; Housemaster, Arniston House, Fettes Coll., 1967-70; Headmaster, Abingdon Sch., 1970-75. Governor, Dragon Sch., 1973. *Publications:* The Written Word, 1964; (ed) The Journal of Sir Walter Scott, 1972;

(contrib.) Scott Bicentenary Essays, 1973; (contrib.) The English Novel, 1974. *Recreation:* golf. *Address:* Shrewsbury School, Salop SY3 7BA. *T:* Shrewsbury 4537. *Club:* Athenæum.

ANDERSON, Professor Sir (William) Ferguson, Kt 1974; OBE 1961; David Cargill Professor of Geriatric Medicine, University of Glasgow, since 1965; *b* 8 April 1914; *s* of James Kirkwood Anderson, Capt. 7th Scottish Rifles (killed on active service Gaza 1917) and late Sarah Barr Anderson; *m* 1940, Margaret Battison Gebbie; one *s* two *d. Educ:* Merchiston Castle Sch.; Glasgow Academy; Glasgow Univ. (MB Hons 1936; MD Hons 1942, with Bellahouston Gold Medal). FRFPSG 1939 (now FRCPG); FRCPE 1961; FRCP 1964; FRCPI 1975; FRCP (C) 1976. Med. Registrar, Univ. Med. Clinic, 1939-41; Army Service, 1941-46, Major (Med. Specialist). Sen. Lectr, Dept of Materia Medica and Therapeutics, Univ. of Glasgow, and Asst Phys., Univ. Med. Clinic, Stobhill Hosp., Glasgow, 1946-49; Sen. Univ. Lectr, Medical Unit, also Hon. Cons. Phys., Cardiff Royal Infirmary, 1949-52; Physician in Geriatric Medicine, Stobhill Gen. Hosp., Adviser in Diseases of Old Age and Chronic Sickness, Western Reg. Hosp. Bd, Scotland, 1952-74. Consultant in organisation of patient care, WHO, 1973-. President: RCPGlas, 1974-76; British Geriatric Soc. Chairman, Glasgow Retirement Council; Hon. Chairman: St Mungo's Old Folks' Club, Glasgow; European Clin. Sect., Internat. Assoc. Gerontology. Fellow, Australasian Coll. of Technologists, 1971. St Mungo Prize, Glasgow, 1968. KStJ 1974. *Publications:* Practical Management of the Elderly, 1967, 3rd edn 1976; Current Achievements in Geriatrics (ed with Dr B. Isaacs), 1964; articles on Geriatric Medicine and Preventive aspects of Geriatrics in current med. jls. *Recreation:* walking. *Address:* Broadgate House, Strathblane, Glasgow. *T:* Blanefield 70525. *Clubs:* Caledonian; University Staff (Glasgow).

ANDERSON, William Galloway Macdonald, CBE 1957; CEng, FICE; Director-General of Works, Air Ministry, 1959-63, retired; *b* 27 Feb. 1905; *s* of late Andrew Syme Anderson, Dundee and of late Mary Anderson (*née* McDonald), Dundee; *m* 1934, Ivy Walker, York; one *s* one *d. Educ:* Dundee High Sch., Dundee; St Andrews Univ. Chief Engineer (Air Ministry) W African Command, 1942-44; Chief Supt Designs, Air Ministry (Works), 1944-46; Chief Engineer (Group Capt.) Far East Command, 1947-48; Deputy Dir of Works, Ministry of Civil Aviation, 1948-52; Dir of Works, Air Ministry, 1952-59. *Recreations:* golfing, motoring and gardening. *Address:* 39 The Barnhams, Bexhill-on-Sea, Sussex. *T:* Cooden 4212. *Clubs:* Devonshire (Eastbourne); Rye Golf.

ANDERTON, (Cyril) James, QPM 1977; Chief Constable, Greater Manchester Police Force, since 1976 (Deputy Chief Constable, 1975); *b* 24 May 1932; *o s* of late James Anderton and late Lucy Anderton (*née* Occleshaw); *m* 1955, Joan Baron; one *d. Educ:* St Matthew's Church Sch., Highfield; Wigan Grammar Sch. Certif. Criminology, Manchester Univ., 1960; Sen. Comd Course, Police Coll., 1967. Corps of Royal Mil. Police, 1950-53; Constable to Chief Inspector, Manchester City Police, 1953-67; Chief Supt (Traffic and Communications), Cheshire Constab., 1967-68; Asst Chief Constable (Admin and Trng), Leicester and Rutland Constab., 1968-72; Asst to HM Chief Inspector of Constab. for England and Wales, Home Office, London, 1972-75; Dep. Chief Constable, Leics Constabulary, 1975. Leader, NW Police District O&M Team, 1964-66; Crown Courts Adv. Cttee, Northampton Gp, Midland and Oxford Circuit, 1972; Manchester Circuit, 1976-; TRRL Traffic and Safety Adv. Cttee, 1972-75; Member: Cttee on Police in the Community, BCC Bd for Soc. Responsibility, 1972-; Adv. Cttee, Law Dept, Manchester Polytechnic, 1976-. Lecture Tour of Far East and SE Asia for FCO, 1973; UK Govt Deleg., European Regional Meeting of 5th UN Congress on Prevention of Crime and Treatment of Offenders, Budapest, 1974; Vis. Lectr, Police Coll., Keele and Manchester Univs; Chm. Governing Council, British Coll. of Accordionists, 1972-77, Vice-Pres., 1977-. Pres., Leics Bn, Boys' Bde, 1972-76; County Dir, St John Amb. Assoc., Greater Manchester, 1976-; Vice-Pres., Manchester YMCA, 1976-. FBIM 1977; Hon. FBCA 1976. Member: RIPA; RSCM; HA; RAC; Corps of Royal Mil. Police Assoc. *Publications:* contrib. Police Review and Police Jl. *Recreations:* public-speaking, theatre, music, books. *Address:* Greater Manchester Police Force, Police Headquarters, Southmill Street, Manchester M60 2NH. *Clubs:* Royal Commonwealth Society, Special Forces; Manchester Luncheon.

ANDERTON, Col Geoffrey, OBE 1944; *b* 23 Jan. 1902; *s* of late Frederic Anderton, Embsay, Yorks, and Jersey, CI; *m* 1930, Edyth Cecile Hastings; two *s* one *d. Educ:* Ermysted's Sch., Skipton-in-Craven, Yorks; St Mary's Hospital, Paddington, W2. MRCS, LRCP 1924; MB, BS London 1925; DRCOG 1947. Entered RAMC Jan. 1927; War of 1939-45 (despatches twice:

Tunisia, 1943; Italy, 1944); Korean War (despatches, Cross of Honour of Norwegian Red Cross, 1952); retd Dec. 1952. Comdt Star and Garter Home for Disabled Sailors, Soldiers and Airmen, Richmond, Surrey, 1953-67. Officer, Legion of Merit (USA), 1954; OStJ 1960. *Recreation:* sailing. *Address:* Lenton, 14 George Road, Milford-on-Sea, Lymington, Hants SO4 0RT. *T:* Milford-on-Sea 3040.

ANDERTON, James, CBE 1966 (OBE 1956); CEng, MIMinE; *b* 3 Nov. 1904; *s* of Richard and Rebecca Anderton; *m* 1st, 1931, Margaret Asbridge (*d* 1945); no *c*; 2nd, 1949, Lucy Mackie; no *c*. *Educ:* Wigan and District Mining and Technical Coll. Manager of various collieries. On nationalisation of mining industry in 1947 became Asst Agent for a group of collieries in St Helens, Lancs; later made Prod. Man., St Helens Area, N Western Div.; Area Gen. Man., St Helens Area, 1949; Dep. Chm., Scottish Div., NCB, 1958. Chm., North Western Div., NCB, 1961-67. Dir, Gullick Ltd, Wigan, 1967-. Hon. MIMinE, 1968. Medal, Instn of Mining Engineers, 1965. *Recreation:* golf. *Address:* The Knoll, Mere Road, Newton-le-Willows, Merseyside. *T:* Newton-le-Willows 5901.

ANDERTON, James; *see* Anderton, C. J.

ANDOVER, Viscount; Alexander Charles Michael Winston Robsahm Howard; *b* 17 Sept. 1974; *s* and *heir* of 21st Earl of Suffolk and Berkshire, *qv*.

ANDRÉ, Brigadier James Richard Glencoe, CBE 1950; DSO 1945; retired; *b* 24 Oct. 1899; *s* of Dr J. E. F. André and Mrs D. K. André (*née* Fowler); *m* 1929, Grace Douglas Darbyshire; two *s* one *d* (and one *s* decd). *Educ:* Killcott; RMC, Sandhurst. Commissioned, 1918, Royal Lincolns. Served European War, with Royal Lincolns, France, 1918-19; Ireland, 1919 and 1920; India, 1920-27; UK, 1927-34; seconded for service with Colonial Office, 1934; served with Malay Regt, 1935-42. Commanded 1st Bn The Malay Regt during Malaya Campaign, 1941-42; in battle for Singapore (DSO); despatches, 1946; Commandant (Col), Malay Regt, 1947; despatches, 1949; Brig. (temp.) 1948, (subs.) 1952; retired 1953. *Recreations:* gardening, handicraft. *Address:* Peaked Croft, Sidlesham Common, Chichester, W Sussex. *T:* Sidlesham 260.

ANDRESKI, Prof. Stanislav Leonard; Professor of Sociology and Head of Department of Sociology, University of Reading, since 1964; *b* 18 May 1919; two *s* two *d*. *Educ:* Secondary sch. in Poznan, 1928-37; Univ. of Poznan (Faculty of Economics and Jurisprudence), 1938-39; London Sch. of Economics, 1942-43. Military service in Polish Army (with exception of academic year 1942-43), 1937-38 and 1939-47 (commissioned, 1944). Lectr in Sociology, Rhodes Univ., SA, 1947-53; Sen. Research Fellow in Anthropology, Manchester Univ., 1954-56; Lectr in Economics, Acton Technical Coll., London, 1956-57; Lectr in Management Studies, Brunel Coll. of Technology, London, 1957-60; Prof. of Sociology, Sch. of Social Sciences, Santiago, Chile, 1960-61; Sen. Res. Fellow, Nigerian Inst. of Social and Economic Research, Ibadan, Nigeria, 1962-64. Vis. Prof. of Sociology and Anthropology, City Coll., City Univ. of New York, 1968-69. *Publications:* Military Organization and Society (Internat. Library of Sociology and Social Reconstruction), 1954 (2nd aug. edn, 1968, USA, 1968, paperback, 1969); Class Structure and Social Development (with Jan Ostaszewski and others), (London), 1964 (in Polish); Elements of Comparative Sociology (The Nature of Human Society Series), 1964, Spanish edn 1972; The Uses of Comparative Sociology (American edn of the foregoing), 1965, paperback 1969; Parasitism and Subversion: the case of Latin America, 1966 (NY, 1967, rev. edn 1968, etc; Buenos Aires (in Spanish with a postscript), 1968; paperback edn, London, 1970); The African Predicament: a study in pathology of modernisation, 1968 (USA, 1969); Social Sciences as Sorcery, 1972, Spanish edn 1973, German edn 1974, French edn 1975; Prospects of a Revolution in the USA, 1973; The Essential Comte, 1974; Reflections on Inequality, 1975; Editor: Herbert Spencer, Principles of Sociology, 1968; Herbert Spencer, Structure, Function and Evolution, 1970; contribs to: A Dictionary of the Social Sciences (UNESCO); A Dictionary of Sociology (ed D. Mitchell); Brit. Jl of Sociology; Japanese Jl of Sociology; The Nature of Fascism (ed S. Woolf); Science Jl, Man, European Jl of Sociology, etc. *Recreation:* sailing. *Address:* University of Reading, Reading, Berks. *T:* Reading 85123.

ANDREW, Prof. Edward Raymond, MA, PhD, ScD (Cambridge); FInstP; FRSE; Lancashire-Spencer Professor of Physics, University of Nottingham, since 1964; Dean of Faculty of Pure Science, since 1975; *b* Boston, Lincs, 27 June 1921; *o s* of late Edward Richard Andrew and Anne Andrew; *m* 1948, Mary Ralph Farnham (*d* 1965); two *d*; *m* 1972, Eunice Tinning. *Educ:*

Wellingborough Sch.; Christ's (Open Scholarship) and Pembroke Colls, Univ. of Cambridge. Scientific Officer, Royal Radar Establishment, Malvern, 1942-45; Cavendish Laboratory, Cambridge, 1945-48; Stokes Student, Pembroke Coll., Cambridge, 1947-49; Commonwealth Fund Fellow, Harvard Univ., 1948-49; Lectr in Natural Philosophy, Univ. of St Andrews, 1949-54; Prof. of Physics, University of Wales, Bangor, 1954-63; Prof. of Experimental Physics, Univ. of Nottingham, 1963-64. Vis. Prof. of Physics, Univ. of Florida, 1969-70. Pres., Groupement Ampère, 1974-78; Chm., Standing Conf. of Profs of Physics, 1976-; Mem. Council, European Physical Soc., 1976-. *Publications:* Nuclear Magnetic Resonance, 1955; scientific papers in learned jls. *Address:* Department of Physics, University of Nottingham, University Park, Nottingham. *T:* Nottingham 56101.

ANDREW, Rev. Sir (George) Herbert, KCMG 1963; CB 1956; Assistant Curate of Edenbridge, Kent; *b* 19 March 1910; *s* of James Andrew and Harriet Rose, Woodley, Cheshire; *m* 1936, Irene Jones; two *s* two *d*. *Educ:* Godley Sch.; Manchester Grammar Sch.; Corpus Christi Coll., Oxford (MA). Patent Office (Asst Examiner), 1931; Transf. to Board of Trade headquarters, 1938; Asst Sec., 1945; Second Secretary: (General) 1955-60, (Overseas) 1960-63, Bd of Trade; Mem., UK delegn to Common Market Conf., 1961-63; Deputy Secretary, Ministry of Education, during 1963, Permanent Secretary, 1963-64; Permanent Under-Sec. of State for Education and Science, 1964-70. Hon. Fellow, Corpus Christi Coll., Oxford, 1965. *Recreations:* walking, talking. *Address:* 18 Stangrove Road, Edenbridge, Kent. *T:* Edenbridge 2569.

ANDREW, Robert John; Deputy Under Secretary of State, Home Office, since 1976; *b* 25 Oct. 1928; *s* of Robert Young Andrew; *m* 1963, Elizabeth, *d* of late Walter de Courcy Bayley; two *s*. *Educ:* King's College Sch., Wimbledon; Merton Coll., Oxford (MA). Intelligence Corps, 1947-49. Joined Civil Service, 1952: Asst Principal, War Office, Principal, 1957; Min. of Defence, 1963; Asst Sec., 1965; Defence Counsellor, UK Delegn to NATO, 1967-70. Private Sec. to Sec. of State for Defence, 1971-73; Under-Sec., CSD, 1973-75; Asst Under-Sec. of State, MoD, 1975-76. Conservator of Wimbledon and Putney Commons. Governor, King's College Sch. *Recreations:* walking, carpentry. *Address:* 3 Camp View, Wimbledon Common, SW19 4UL. *T:* 01-947 2732.

ANDREW, Sydney Percy Smith, FRS 1976; CEng, FIChemE, MIMechE; ICI Senior Research Associate, Group Manager, Catalysts and Chemicals Research, 1963-76; *b* 16 May 1926; *s* of Harold C. Andrew and Kathleen M. (*née* Smith). *Educ:* Barnard Castle Sch.; King's Coll., Durham Univ. (Open Schol.; BSc); Trinity Hall, Cambridge (Schol. and Prizeman; MA). Joined ICI Billingham Div., 1950; Chemical Engrg Res., 1951; Plant Engr, 1953; Section Manager: Reactor Res., 1955; Process Design, 1959. Member: Res. Cttee, IChemE; Nat. Cttee for Theoretical and Applied Mechanics. Fellow, Fellowship of Engineering, 1977. *Publications:* Catalyst Handbook, 1970; various papers in chemical engrg and applied chemistry. *Recreations:* archaeology, ancient and medieval history. *Address:* 83 Hutton Avenue, Hartlepool TS26 9PR. *T:* Hartlepool 5321.

ANDREWES, Antony, MBE 1945; FBA 1957; Wykeham Professor of Ancient History, Oxford, 1953-77; Fellow of New College, Oxford, 1946-77; *b* 12 June 1910; *s* of late P. L. Andrewes; *m* 1938, Alison Blakeway (*née* Hope); two *d*. *Educ:* Winchester; New College, Oxford. Fellow of Pembroke Coll., Oxford, 1933-46. Intelligence Corps, 1941-45. *Publications:* (with R. Meiggs) revised edition of Sir George Hill's Sources for Greek History, 1951; The Greek Tyrants, 1955; The Greeks, 1967; (with K. J. Dover) Vol. IV of A. W. Gomme's Historical Commentary on Thucydides, 1970; articles in Classical Quarterly, etc. *Address:* 13 Manor Place, Oxford. *T:* Oxford 48807.

ANDREWES, Sir Christopher (Howard), Kt 1961; FRS 1939; Deputy Director, National Institute for Medical Research, 1952-June 1961 (Member of Scientific Staff from 1927) and in charge of World Influenza Centre (WHO) until June 1961; *b* 7 June 1896; *s* of late Sir Frederick William Andrewes, MD, FRS and Phyllis Mary Hamer; *m* 1927, Kathleen Helen Lamb; three *s*. *Educ:* Highgate Sch.; St Bartholomew's Hospital. Surgeon Sub-Lt (RNVR), 1918-19; MRCS, LRCP, 1921, MB BS London (Univ. Gold Medal), 1921, MD London (Univ. Gold Medal), 1922, MRCP, 1923; FRCP, 1935; House Physician and Asst to Medical Unit St Bartholomew's Hospital, 1921-23 and 1925-26; Assistant Resident Physician, Hospital of the Rockefeller Institute, New York City, 1923-25; William Julius Mickle Fellowship, Univ. of London, 1931; Oliver-Sharpey Lectureship, Royal Coll. of Physicians, 1934; Bisset-Hawkins Medal, RCP,

1947; Stewart Prize, BMA, 1952. Hon LLD Aberdeen 1963; Hon. MD Lund, 1968. *Publications:* Viruses of Vertebrates, 1964, 3rd edn (with H. G. Pereira), 1972; The Common Cold, 1965; Viruses and Evolution (Huxley lecture), 1966; Natural History of Viruses, 1967; The Lives of Wasps and Bees, 1969; Viruses and Cancer, 1970. *Recreation:* natural history, especially entomology. *Address:* Overchalke, Coombe Bissett, Salisbury, Wilts. *T:* Coombe Bissett 201.

ANDREWES, Edward David Eden; Deputy Chairman and Managing Director, Tube Investments Ltd, 1972-75; a Trustee, Cheshire Foundation; *b* Portmadoc, 4 Oct. 1909; *s* of Edward and Norah Andrewes; *m* 1935, Katherine Sheila, *d* of Brig. W. B. G. Barne, CBE, DSO; one *s* two *d*. *Educ:* Repton Sch.; Oriel Coll., Oxford (BA). Admitted Solicitor, 1935. Joined Tube Investments Ltd, 1935. Dir, Maen Offeren Slate Quarry Co. Ltd. Legion of Merit (USA). *Recreations:* gardening, hunting, shooting, fishing. *Address:* Stockton House, Worcester WR6 6UT. *T:* Eardiston 272. *Club:* Boodle's.

ANDREWS; *see* Burt-Andrews.

ANDREWS, (Arthur) John (Francis), CBE 1970; Chairman, Clark Equipment Ltd, UK, 1962-73; Deputy Chairman, Clark Equipment Co. AG Zürich, 1963-73; Chairman, All Wheel Drive Ltd, 1954-73; *b* 15 May 1906; *s* of Arthur Andrews and Gertrude Ellen Andrews (*née* Francis); *m* 1936, Elsy Maud (*née* Johns); one *d*. *Educ:* Malvern; Paris. Development Engineer, AC Cars Ltd, 1926; Chief Purchasing Manager, Gardner Diesel Engines, 1935. *Recreations:* sailing, golf. *Address:* Blackpool Mill, Dartmouth, Devon. *T:* Stoke Fleming 328. *Clubs:* Royal Automobile, Royal Thames Yacht; Royal Motor Yacht (Poole); Berkshire Golf (Ascot); Ferndown Golf (Ferndown); Isle of Purbeck Golf; Parkstone Golf.

ANDREWS, Dame Cicily; *see* West, Dame Rebecca.

ANDREWS, Cyril Frank Wilton, *b* 22 Dec. 1892; *s* of late Robert Parsons and Mariannellen Wilton Gleadhill Andrews; *m* 1929, Dorothy Constance Lascelles (*d* 1976), *d* of late Major George Thomas and Mrs Pickering; no *c*. *Educ:* abroad. Served European War, RE; Foreign Service, 1920; Vice-Consul at Antwerp, 1920-21; Tunis, 1921-23; Paris, 1923-24; Genoa, 1924-28; Montevideo (with rank of 2nd Sec.), 1929; Naples, 1929-30; Katowice, 1930-32; Philadelphia, 1933-35; Consul and 1st Sec. at Panama, 1935-38; Chargé d'Affaires, 1936 and 1938; Consul at Madeira, 1939-42; Minister to Dominican Republic, 1943-45; Special Ambassador for celebration of Centenary of Independence of Dominican Republic, Feb. 1944; Consul-General at Lourenço Marques, 1946-49; Consul-General at Algiers, 1949-53; retired from HM Foreign Service, 1953; Coronation Medal, 1953. Grand Cross of Dominican Order of Merit Juan Pablo Duarte. *Recreation:* reading. *Address:* c/o Lloyds Bank, Ltd, Lansdowne, Bournemouth, Dorset.

ANDREWS, Derek Henry, CBE 1970; Under-Secretary, Ministry of Agriculture, Fisheries and Food, since 1973; Director of Establishments, since 1976; *b* 17 Feb. 1933; *s* of late Henry Andrews and Emma Jane Andrews; *m* 1956, Catharine May (*née* Childe); two *s* one *d*. *Educ:* LSE. BA (Hons) 1955. Ministry of Agriculture, Fisheries and Food: Asst Principal, 1957; Asst Private Sec. to Minister of Agriculture, Fisheries and Food, 1960-61; Principal, 1961; Asst Sec., 1968; Private Sec. to Prime Minister, 1966-70; Harvard Univ., USA, 1970-71. *Address:* 5a St German's Place, Blackheath, SE3 0NH. *T:* 01-858 4076.

ANDREWS, Éamonn, CBE (Hon.) 1970; Television Compère; Broadcaster; Writer; *b* 19 Dec. 1922; *s* of William and Margaret Andrews; *m* 1951, Gráinne Bourke; one *s* two *d*. *Educ:* Irish Christian Brothers, Synge Street, Dublin. Radio Eireann broadcaster (boxing commentaries, general sports commentating, interview programmes, etc.), 1941-50; first broadcast for the BBC, 1950; first appeared on BBC Television, 1951; BBC programmes included: What's My Line?, This Is Your Life, Sports Report, Crackerjack, Playbox; also boxing commentaries, variety, interview and general sports programmes. Chm. Radio Eireann Statutory Authority, charged with establishment of television in Ireland, 1960-66; joined ABC Television, 1964, Thames Television, 1968; ITV programmes include: This Is Your Life, Today, Time for Business. Former All-Ireland Amateur Junior Boxing Champion (Middle Weight). Knight of St Gregory, 1964. *Publications:* The Moon is Black (play), 1941; This Is My Life (autobiog.), 1963; articles for magazines and newspapers. *Recreations:* walking and talking. *Address:* Windsor House, Heathfield Gardens, Chiswick, W4 4ND. *Clubs:* Irish, Royal Automobile.

ANDREWS, Sir Edwin Arthur C.; *see* Chapman-Andrews.

ANDREWS, Brig. George Lewis Williams, CBE 1960; DSO 1944; *b* 1 July 1910; *o s* of Captain C. G. W. Andrews, The Border Regt (killed in action, 1914) and of late Mrs Diana Gambier-Parry (*née* Norrington); *m* 1938, Marianne, *d* of late Carl Strindberg, Stockholm and Fru Greta Winbergh (*née* Skjöldebrand); one *s*. *Educ:* Haileybury; Sandhurst. Commissioned 2nd Lieut, The Seaforth Highlanders, 1930; active service, Palestine, 1936. Served War of 1939-45; BEF, 1939, MEF, 1941-43, BLA, 1944-45; Comd 2nd Bn The Seaforth Highlanders, 1943-45. Comd 1st Bn Seaforth Highlanders, 1953-54; Comd 152nd Highland Infantry Brigade (TA), 1954-57; Assistant Commandant, RMA Sandhurst, 1957-60. Hon. Col, 2nd Bn 51st Highland Volunteers, 1975-. Lieut-Col, 1953; Colonel, 1955; Hon. Brig., 1960; psc 1940; jssc 1948. Chevalier, Order of Leopold, Belgium, 1945; Croix de Guerre with palm, Belgium, 1945. *Address:* West Kingsteps, Nairn, Scotland. *T:* Nairn 53231.

ANDREWS, Lt-Col Harold Marcus E.; *see* Ervine-Andrews.

ANDREWS, Harry (Fleetwood), CBE 1966; Actor since 1933; *b* 10 Nov. 1911. *Educ:* Tonbridge; Wrekin Coll. With Liverpool Repertory, 1933-35. Played Horatio in Hamlet, New York 1936; John Gielgud's Season, 1937; with Old Vic, 1945-49; Bolingbroke, Mirabel, Warwick in St Joan; Shakespeare Memorial Theatre; Wolsey, Macduff Brutus, Bolingbroke in Henry IV Pts I and II, 1949-51; Enobarbus, Buckingham, Kent, 1953; Othello, Claudius, 1956; Menenius in Coriolanus, 1959; Casanova in Camino Real, Phoenix, 1957; Henry VIII, Old Vic, 1958; Allenby in Ross, Haymarket, 1960; Rockhart in The Lizard on the Rock, Phoenix, 1962; Ekhart in Baal, Phoenix, 1963; Crampton in You Never Can Tell, Haymarket, 1966; Lear, Royal Court, 1971. *Films:* Red Beret, Helen of Troy, Alexander the Great, Hill in Korea, Moby Dick, St Joan, Dreyfus, Ice Cold in Alex, Solomon and Sheba, Question of Larceny, Circle of Deception, The Best of Enemies, The Inspector, Barabbas, Reach for Glory, Nine Hours to Rama, 55 Days at Peking, The Snout, The Best of Everything, The Hill, The Agony and the Ecstasy, The Sands of Kalahari, Modesty Blaise, The Deadly Affair, The Jokers, The Long Duel, A Dandy in Aspic, The Charge of The Light Brigade, The Night They Raided Minsky's, The Southern Star, The Seagull, A Nice Girl Like Me; Too Late The Hero; The Gaunt Woman; Entertaining Mr Sloan; I want what I want; Burke and Hare; Country Dance; Wuthering Heights; Nicholas and Alexandra; The Nightcomers; The Ruling Class; Man of La Mancha; Theatre of Blood; The Mackintosh Man; Man at the Top; Jacob and Esau; The Bluebird; Sky Riders; The Passover Plot; The Prince and the Pauper; Equus; *Television:* Leo Tolstoy; An Affair of Honour; Edward VII; Clayhanger series; The Garth People; Valley Forge; Two Gentle People, adapted from Graham Greene. Served War of 1939-45 (despatches). *Recreations:* cricket, tennis, sailing, gardening. *Address:* Church Farm Oast, Salehurst, Robertsbridge, E Sussex; Flat 7, 1 Bryanston Square, W1.

ANDREWS, Harry Thomson; Director: Consolidated Diamond Mines of South West Africa (De Beers Group); Welkom GM Co. (Anglo-American Corp. of South Africa); *b* Capetown, South Africa, 11 Dec. 1897; *s* of late H. Andrews, Capetown; *m* 1926, R. D. Williams, Pretoria; one *d*. *Educ:* Observatory High Sch., Capetown; Marist Brothers' Coll., Capetown; Univ. of Pretoria. Served European War, 1917-19, in France, South African Signals, RE. Advocate, Supreme Court (Transvaal), 1927; Political Secretary South Africa House, London, 1930-35; Accredited Representative of Union of South Africa to League of Nations, Geneva, 1936-40; Asst Sec. for Defence, Pretoria; Under-Sec. for External Affairs, Pretoria; Head of South Africa Govt Supply Mission to USA, 1942-45; Ambassador of South Africa to USA, 1945-49; Permanent Representative of SA to United Nations, 1945-49; South African Ambassador to France, 1949-57; Minister to Switzerland, 1954-56. Member French-Commonwealth War Graves Commission, 1954-57. Vice-Pres., S Africa Foundn, 1960. *Recreation:* golf. *Address:* 214 Bretton Woods, Killarney, Johannesburg, S Africa. *Clubs:* Kimberley (Kimberley); Rand, Bryanston Country (Johannesburg); West Province Sports (Cape Town).

ANDREWS, James Roland Blake F.; *see* Fox-Andrews.

ANDREWS, John; *see* Andrews, Arthur John Francis.

ANDREWS, Rt. Hon. Sir John (Lawson Ormrod), PC (Northern Ireland) 1957; KBE 1974; DL; Senator, 1964-72; Minister and Leader in the Senate, Northern Ireland, 1964-72; *b* 15 July 1903; *o s* of late Right Hon. John Miller Andrews, CH, DL, LLD, MP,

Maxwell Court, Comber, Co. Down, and Jessie, *er d* of Joseph Ormrod, Morelands, Heaton, Bolton; *m* 1928, Marjorie Elaine Maynard James, *d* of Alfred Morgan James, The Fields, Newport, Mon; three *s* one *d. Educ:* Mourne Grange Preparatory Sch., Kilkeel, Co. Down; Shrewsbury. Served apprenticeship to flax spinning trade and joined family firm, John Andrews & Co. Ltd, Comber, 1922; now Chm. and Man. Dir. Northern Ireland Government: MP (U) Mid-Down, 1953-64; Minister of Health and Local Govt, 1957-61; Minister of Commerce, 1961-63; Minister of Finance, 1963-64; Dep. Prime Minister, 1970-72. President, Ulster Unionist Council, 1969-73. DL Co. Down, N Ireland, 1961. *Recreation:* yachting (Commodore Strangford Lough Yacht Club). *Address:* Maxwell Court, Comber, Co. Down. *T:* Comber 263. *Clubs:* Ulster Reform (Belfast); Royal Ulster Yacht.

ANDREWS, Air Vice-Marshal John Oliver, CB 1942; DSO 1917; MC; idc; *b* 20 July 1896; *s* of John Andrews, Waterloo, Lancs; *m* 1923, Bertha, *d* of Wilfred Bisdée, Hambrook, Glos; two *s*. Lieut Royal Scots; seconded RFC, 1914; served France, 1914-18; S Russia, 1919; India, 1920 (MC and bar, Montenegrin Silver Medal for bravery, DSO, despatches thrice); transferred to RAF, 1919; retired, 1945.

ANDREWS, Julie (Elizabeth); Actress; *b* 1 Oct. 1935; *m* 1st, Anthony J. Walton (marr. diss. 1968); one *d*; 2nd, 1969, Blake Edwards; one step *s* one step *d*, and two adopted *d. Educ:* Woodbrook Girls' Sch., Beckenham and private governess. Appeared in The Boy Friend, Broadway, New York, 1954; My Fair Lady: New York, 1956, London, 1958; Camelot, New York, 1960. *Films:* (Walt Disney) Mary Poppins, 1963 (Academy Award, 1964); Americanisation of Emily, 1964; Sound of Music, 1964; Hawaii, 1965; Torn Curtain, 1966; Thoroughly Modern Millie, 1966; Star, 1967; Darling Lili, 1970; The Tamarind Seed, 1973. *TV:* The Julie Andrews Hour, 1972-73. *Publication:* (as Julie Andrews Edwards) Mandy, 1972; Last of the Really Great Whangdoodles, 1973. *Recreations:* boating, ski-ing, riding. *Address:* Chasin-Park-Citron Agency, 9255 Sunset Boulevard, Los Angeles, Calif 90069, USA.

ANDREWS, Rev. Canon Leonard Martin, CVO 1946; MBE; MC 1917; Rector of Stoke Climsland, Cornwall, 1922-68; Chaplain to the Queen, 1952-69 (to King Edward VIII, 1936, and to King George VI, 1936-52); Hon. Canon of Truro since 1932; *b* 24 Sept. 1886. *Educ:* Queens' Coll., Cambridge. BA 1909; MA 1921; Deacon, 1909; Priest, 1910; Rector of Brewarrina, NSW, 1913-14; Vice-Principal Brotherhood of the Good Shepherd, NSW, 1914-15; Temp. CF, 1914-19; Chaplain at Khartoum, 1920-22; Rural Dean of Trigg Major, 1929-32. *Publication:* Canon's Folly, 1974. *Address:* Climsland, Downderry, Torpoint, Cornwall PL11 3LW.

ANDREWS, Raymond Denzil Anthony, MBE 1953; VRD 1960; Senior Partner, Andrews, Downie & Kelly, Architects, since 1960; *b* 5 June 1925; *s* of Michael Joseph Andrews, BA, and Phylis Marie Andrews (*née* Crowley); *m* 1958, Gillian Whitlaw Small; one *s* one *d. Educ:* Highgate Sch.; Christ's Coll., Cambridge; University Coll. London (DipArch, DipTP); Univ. of Michigan (MArch). RIBA. Lieut, Royal Marines 1943-46; Royal Marines Reserve, 1948-68 (Major). King George VI Meml Fellow of English-Speaking Union of US, 1954-55; Chm., London Region, RIBA, 1968-72; Vice-Pres., RIBA, 1972-74; Good Housing Award Cttee, DoE, 1970-73, Chm. SE Region, 1973; Pres., Architectural Assoc., 1975-77. Editor, Architect, 1968-70. Architectural Design Award, 1968; Civic Trust Award, 1971; 1st Prize, Royal Mint Square Housing Competition, GLC, 1974. Order of AL Rafadain (Iraq), 1956. *Recreation:* sailing. *Address:* 1 Sloane Street, SW1 X9L. *T:* 01-235 8877. *Club:* Bosham Sailing.

ANDREWS, Stuart Morrison; Head Master of Clifton College, since 1975; *b* 23 June 1932; *s* of William Hannaford Andrews and Eileen Elizabeth Andrews; *m* 1962, Marie Elizabeth van Wyk; two *s. Educ:* Newton Abbot Grammar Sch.; St Dunstan's Coll.; Sidney Sussex Coll., Cambridge (MA). Nat. service with Parachute Bde, 1952-53. Sen. History Master and Librarian, St Dunstan's Coll., 1956-60; Chief History Master and Librarian, Repton Sch., 1961-67; Head Master, Norwich Sch., 1967-75. Chm., Direct-grant Sub-cttee of Headmasters' Conf., 1974-75. Editor, Conference. *Publications:* Eighteenth-century Europe, 1965; Enlightened Despotism, 1967; Methodism and Society, 1970; articles in various historical jls. *Recreations:* walking, writing. *Address:* Headmaster's House, Clifton College, Bristol BS8 3HT. *T:* Bristol 35613. *Club:* East India, Devonshire, Sports and Public Schools.

ANDRUS, Francis Sedley; Lancaster Herald of Arms, since 1972; *b* 26 Feb. 1915; *o s* of late Brig.-Gen. Thomas Alchin Andrus,

CMG, JP, and Alice Loveday Parr; unmarried. *Educ:* Wellington Coll.; St Peter's Hall (now Coll.), Oxford (MA). Entered College of Arms as Member of Staff, 1938; Bluemantle Pursuivant of Arms, 1970-72. *Address:* College of Arms, Queen Victoria Street, EC4V 4BT. *T:* 01-248 2659; 8 Oakwood Rise, Longfield, near Dartford, Kent DA3 7PA. *T:* Longfield 5424.

ANFINSEN, Dr Christian Boehmer; Head of Laboratory of Chemical Biology, National Institute for Arthritis and Metabolic Diseases, Bethesda, since 1963; *b* Monessen, Pa, 26 March 1916; *s* of Christian Boehmer Anfinsen and Sophie (*née* Rasmussen); *m* 1941, Florence Bernice Kenenger; one *s* two *d. Educ:* Swarthmore Coll. (BA); Univ. of Pennsylvania (MS); Harvard (PhD). Amer.-Scand. Foundn Fellow, Carlsberg Lab., Copenhagen, 1939; Sen. Cancer Res. Fellow, Nobel Inst. Medicine, Stockholm, 1947; Asst Prof. of Biological Chemistry, Harvard Medical Sch., 1948-50; Head of Lab. of Cellular Physiology and Metabolism, Nat. Heart Inst., Bethesda, Md, 1950-62; Prof. of Biochemistry, Harvard Med. Sch., 1962-63. Rockefeller Fellow, 1954-55; Guggenheim Fellow, Weizmann Inst., Rehovot, Israel, 1958. Mem., Bd of Governors, Weizmann Inst., Rehovot, 1960-. Member: Amer. Soc. of Biol Chemists (Pres., 1971-72); Amer. Acad. of Arts and Scis; Nat. Acad. of Scis; Royal Danish Acad.; Washington Acad. of Scis; Fedn Amer. Scientists (Vice-Chm., 1958-59, and 1974-75). Hon. DSc: Swarthmore, 1965; Georgetown, 1967; NY Med. Coll., Gustavus Adolphus Coll., 1975. (Jtly) Nobel Prize for Chemistry, 1972. *Publication:* The Molecular Basis of Evolution, 1959. *Address:* 6 West Drive, Bethesda, Md 20014, USA; National Institute for Arthritis and Metabolic Diseases, Bethesda, Md 20014.

ANFOM, Emmanuel E.; *see* Evans-Anfom.

ANGELES, Victoria de los; *see* de los Angeles.

ANGELL-JAMES, John, CBE 1967; MD, FRCP, FRCS; Hon. Consulting Surgeon in Otolaryngology, United Bristol Hospitals, since 1966; *b* 23 Aug. 1901; *s* of Dr John Angell James, MRCS, LRCP and Emily Cormell (*née* Ashwin), Bristol; *m* 1930, Evelyn Miriam Everard, *d* of Francis Over and Ada Miriam Everard, Birmingham; one *s* two *d. Educ:* Bristol Grammar Sch.; Univ. of Bristol; London Hosp.; Guy's Hosp. MB ChB 1st Cl. Hons 1924, Bristol; MBBS London (Hons) 1924; MD 1927; FRCS 1928; FRCP 1965. Res. appts, 1924-28, Bristol and London; Hon. ENT Registrar, Bristol Royal Infirmary, 1928-29; Hon. ENT Surg., Bristol Children's Hosp., 1928-48; Cons. ENT Surg., 1948-66; Hon. Asst ENT Surg., later Hon. ENT Surg., Bristol Royal Infirmary, 1929-48; Clin. Tutor, Univ. of Bristol, 1928-55, Lectr and Head of Dept of Otolaryngology, 1955-66; Cons. ENT Surg., United Bristol Hosps, 1948-66. Lt-Col RAMC, 1942-46; Adviser in Otorhinolaryngol., MEF, 1945. Hunterian Prof., RCS, 1962; Semon Lectr in Laryngol., Univ. of London, 1965; James Yearsley Lectr, 1966; Sir William Wilde Meml Lectr, Irish Otolaryngol. Soc., 1966; Vis. Lectr, Univs of Toronto, Vermont, Cornell, Baylor and Chicago. Royal Soc. of Medicine: Former Fellow, Hon. FRSM 1976; Hon. Mem., Sections of Laryngol. (Pres., 1955) and otology. Member: SW Laryngolog. Assoc. (Chm. 1956); Brit. Medical Assoc. (Pres. Sect. of Otolaryngol., 1959; Chm. Bristol Div., 1966-67; Pres., Bath, Bristol and Som Br., 1968-69); Bristol Med.-Chirurg. Soc. (Pres. 1961) and Visiting Assoc. of ENT Surgs of GB, 1948 (Pres. 1965-66); Brit. Assoc. of Otolaryngologists, 1942 (Pres. 1966-69); Collegium Oto-Rhino-Laryngologicum Amicitae Sacrum, 1948 (Councillor, 1966-74; Pres., 1974); Barany Soc. Extern. Examr, Univ. of Manchester, 1964. Hon. Member: Irish Otolaryngol. Soc.; S Africa Soc. of Otolaryngol.; Hon. FRCSE 1971; Jobson Horne Prize, BMA, 1962; Colles Medal, RCSI, 1963; Dalby Prize, RSM, 1963; W. J. Harrison Prize in Laryngology, RSM, 1968. Pres., Gloucester Soc., 1977. Chm. Editorial Cttee, Clinical Otolaryngology. *Publications:* Chapters in: British Surgical Practice, 1951; Diseases of the Ear, Nose and Throat, 1952 (2nd edn 1966); Ultrasound as a diagnostic and surgical tool, 1964; Clinical Surgery, 1966; Ménière's Disease, 1969; articles in learned jls in Eng., USA, Canada, Germany and Sweden. *Recreations:* farming; shooting. *Address:* Sundayshill House, Falfield, near Wotton-under-Edge, Glos; (consulting rooms) Litfield House, Clifton Down, Bristol BS8 3LS. *T:* Bristol 33483.

ANGLESEY, 7th Marquess of, *cr* 1815; **George Charles Henry Victor Paget;** Baron Paget, of Beau Desert, 1549; Earl of Uxbridge, 1784; Bt 1730; Vice-Lieutenant of Anglesey, since 1960; *b* 8 Oct. 1922; *o s* of 6th Marquess of Anglesey, GCVO, and Lady Victoria Marjorie Harriet Manners (*d* 1946), *d* of 8th Duke of Rutland; *S* father, 1947; *m* 1948, Elizabeth Shirley Vaughan Morgan (*see* Marchioness of Anglesey); two *s* three *d. Educ:* Wixenford, Wokingham; Eton Coll. Major, RHG, 1946.

Div. Dir, Wales, Nationwide Building Soc., 1973-. President: Anglesey Conservative Assoc.; Nat. Museum of Wales, 1962-68; Friends of Friendless Churches. Treasurer, Danilo Dolci Trust (Britain). Vice-Chairman: Welsh Cttee, Nat. Trust; Member: Historic Buildings Council for Wales, 1953- (Chm., 1977-); Royal Fine Art Commn, 1965-71; Redundant Churches Fund, 1969-; Council, Nat. Army Museum; Council, Soc. of Army Historical Research. FSA 1952; FRSL 1969; Hon. FRIBA, 1971; FRHistS, 1975. Cdre, Royal Welsh Yacht Club, 1948. Anglesey: CC, 1951-67; JP, 1959-68; DL, 1960. Hon. Fellow, Royal Cambrian Acad. Lord of the Manor of Burton-upon-Trent; Freeman of the City of London. *Publications:* (ed) The Capel Letters, 1814-1817, 1955; One-Leg: the Life and Letters of 1st Marquess of Anglesey, 1961; (ed) Sergeant Pearman's Memoirs, 1968; (ed) Little Hodge, 1971; A History of the British Cavalry, 1816-1919, vol I, 1973, vol. II, 1975. *Recreations:* gardening, music. *Heir: s* Earl of Uxbridge, *qv. Address:* Plâs-Newydd, Llanfairpwll, Gwynedd. *T:* Llanfairpwll 330.
See also Sir C. M. R. V. Duff, Bt.

ANGLESEY, Marchioness of; (Elizabeth) Shirley Vaughan Paget, CBE 1977; Member, Arts Council, since 1972; Chairman, Welsh Arts Council, since 1975; *b* 4 Dec. 1924; *d* of late Charles Morgan, novelist, and of Hilda Vaughan, *qv*; *m* 1948, Marquess of Anglesey, *qv*; two *s* three *d. Educ:* Francis Holland Sch., London; St James', West Malvern; Kent Place Sch., USA. Personal Secretary to Gladwyn Jebb, FO, until marriage. Dep. Chm., Prince of Wales Cttee, 1970-. Member: Civic Trust for Wales, 1967-76; IBA, 1976-; Royal Commn on Environmental Pollution, 1973-; Chm., Nat. Federation of Women's Institutes, 1966-69; Vice-Chm., Govt Working Party on Methods of Sewage Disposal, 1969-70. *Address:* Plâs-Newydd, Llanfairpwll, Gwynedd. *T:* Llanfairpwll 330.
See also R . H . V . C . Morgan .

ANGLIN, Prof. Douglas (George); Professor of Political Science, Carleton University, Ottawa, Canada, since 1958; *b* Toronto, Canada, 16 Dec. 1923; *s* of George Chambers Anglin, MD, and Ruth Cecilia Cale, MD; *m* 1948, Mary Elizabeth Watson; two *d. Educ:* Toronto Univ.; Corpus Christi and Nuffield Colls, Oxford Univ. BA Toronto; MA, DPhil Oxon. Lieut, RCNVR, 1943-45. Asst (later Associate) Prof. of Polit. Sci. and Internat. Relations, Univ. of Manitoba, Winnipeg, 1951-58; Associate Prof. (later Prof.), Carleton Univ., 1958. Vice-Chancellor, Univ. of Zambia, Lusaka, Zambia, 1965-69; Associate Research Fellow, Nigerian Inst. of Social and Economic Research, Univ. of Ibadan, Ibadan, Nigeria, 1962-63; Research Associate, Center of Internat. Studies, Princeton Univ., 1969-70; Pres., Canadian Assoc. of African Studies, 1973-74. *Publications:* The St. Pierre and Miquelon Affair of 1941: a study in diplomacy in the North Atlantic quadrangle, 1966; (ed jtly) Africa: Problems and Prospects 1961; articles on Internat. and African affairs in a variety of learned jls. *Address:* Carleton University, Colonel By Drive, Ottawa, Ontario K1S 5B6, Canada.

ANGLIN, Eric Jack; HM Diplomatic Service; Counsellor (Commercial) and Consul General, Buenos Aires, since 1976; *b* 9 Aug. 1923; *m* 1945, Patricia Farr; three *s* . Joined Foreign Service (subseq. Diplomatic Service), 1948; FO, 1948-52; HM Missions in: Damascus, 1952-56; Rangoon, 1956-59; Madrid, 1960-64; FO, 1964-67; La Paz, 1967-70; Khartoum, 1970-72; Inspector, Diplomatic Service, FCO, 1973-76. *Recreations:* sailing and auctions. *Address:* c/o Foreign and Commonwealth Office, SW1. *Club:* Inglés (Buenos Aires).

ANGLISS, Dame Jacobena Victoria Alice, DBE 1975 (CBE 1949); Chairman, William Angliss Charitable Trust; *b* 23 May 1897; *d* of Francis Grutzner, Thomastown, Vic, Australia; *m* 1919, Hon. Sir William Charles Angliss (*d* 1957). Chairman: Bluff Downs Pastoral Co., Miranda Downs Pty Ltd; Dir, Investors Pty Ltd; Trustee, William Angliss Estate. Pres., Astra Chamber Music Soc.; Dir, Aust. Nat. Memorial Theatre. *Recreations:* gardening, music. *Address:* Harcourt Street, Hawthorne, Melbourne, Vic 3122, Australia. *Clubs:* Lyceum, Alexandra (Melbourne).

ANGUS, Col Edmund Graham, CBE 1944; MC; TD; DL, JP; Chairman: George Angus & Co. Ltd, Newcastle upon Tyne 1933-64, later President; Newcastle upon Tyne Permanent Building Society, since 1969; *b* 9 June 1889; *s* of Col W. M. Angus, CB; *m* 1922, Bridget E. I. Spencer (*d* 1973); one *s* one *d* (and two *s* decd, of whom *e s* was presumed killed in action, Anzio, Italy, 1944). *Educ:* Felsted Sch. Joined George Angus & Co. Ltd, 1906. Commissioned in Volunteer Forces (RA). Served in firm's Boston office, 1910-11, mobilised Aug. 1914; served in France and Flanders with 50th Div. Artillery till Feb. 1919; demobilised with rank of Major; rejoined G. Angus & Co. Ltd, Dir. 1920. Rejoined TA 1920; commanded 74th Northumbrian

Field Regt, 1925-32; subst. Col with effect, 1929. FRSA 1974. DL Co. Durham, 1945; JP Northumberland, 1948. KStJ 1966. *Recreation:* horticulture. *Address:* Ravenstone, Corbridge, Northumberland. *T:* Corbridge 2122. *Clubs:* Carlton; Northern Counties (Newcastle upon Tyne).

ANGUS, Brig. (hon.) Tom Hardy, DSO 1938; psc†; fs; late Indian Army; *b* 22 May 1899; *s* of late J. B. Angus and M. S. D. Hardy; *m* 1954, Lilian Maud, *er d* of late John Emil and Ada Hyort. *Educ:* privately; RMC, Sandhurst. First Commission, 1918; Joined 45th Rattray's Sikhs, now 3rd Bn 11th Sikh Regt (Rattray's Sikhs), 1918; Regimental duty until 1932; Staff Coll., Quetta, 1932-33; RAF Staff Coll., Andover, 1935; Brigade Major, 1st Infantry Brigade, Abbottabad, NWFP, 1936-40; served Waziristan (DSO); Instructor (GSO2) Staff Coll., Quetta, 1940; Brig. Gen. Staff, Ceylon, 1942; Commander 51 Indian Infantry Brigade, 1943-44; DDMT, GHQ, India, 1945; Director of Air, India, 1946-47; retired 1948. *Recreation:* golf. *Address:* c/o Lloyds Bank Ltd, St Mary Street, Weymouth, Dorset. *Club:* Royal Dorset Yacht (Weymouth).

ANNALY, 5th Baron *cr* 1863; **Luke Robert White;** Partner, W. Greenwell & Co., Members of London Stock Exchange; *b* 15 March 1927; *o s* of 4th Baron Annaly and Lady Annaly (formerly Lady Lavinia Spencer); *S* father, 1970; *m* 1st, 1953, Lady Marye Pepys (marr. diss. 1957; she *d* 1958); one *s* ; 2nd, 1960, Jennifer Carey (marr. diss. 1967); two *d. Educ:* Eton. RAF, 1944-48; RAuxAF, 1948-51; Flying Officer (601 Sqdn). Livery, Haberdashers' Company; Freeman of City of London, 1953; Governor, Star and Garter Home. *Recreations:* cricket, golf, theatre. *Heir: s* Hon. Luke Richard White [*b* 29 June 1954. *Educ:* Eton; RMA Sandhurst. Commnd Royal Hussars, 1974]. *Address:* Welches, Bentley, Farnham, Surrey. *T:* Bentley (Hants) 2107. *Clubs:* Turf, Royal Air Force, Beefsteak, Pratt's, MCC.

ANNAMUNTHODO, Sir Harry, Kt 1967; FRCS, FACS; Professor and Head of Department of Clinical Surgery, University of the West Indies, since 1961; *b* 26 April 1920; *s* of George Annamunthodo and Rosaline (*née* Viapree); *m* 1953, Margaret Pullman; one *s* three *d. Educ:* Queen's Coll., Guyana; London Hospital Medical Coll. MB, BS London, 1946; DTM&H, 1947; FRCS, 1951; FACS, 1961. Lectr in Surg., Univ. of the W Indies, 1955-57; Sen. Lectr in Surg., UWI, 1957-61. Rockefeller Research Fellow, 1959-60; Hunterian Prof., Royal Coll. of Surgeons, 1960. *Publications:* (Co-author) Lymphogranuloma Venereum, 1962; papers on: various cancers and diseases of stomach, rectum, etc in British and American Med. Jls. *Recreation:* horticulture. *Address:* 44 Hope Boulevard, Kingston 6, Jamaica, WI. *T:* 70716.

ANNAN, family name of **Baron Annan.**

ANNAN, Baron, *cr* 1965 (Life Peer); **Noël Gilroy Annan,** OBE 1946; Provost of University College, London, since 1966; *b* 25 Dec. 1916; *s* of late James Gilroy Annan; *m* 1950, Gabriele, *d* of Louis Ferdinand Ullstein, Berlin; two *d. Educ:* Stowe Sch.; King's Coll., Cambridge (Exhibitioner and Scholar). Served War of 1939-45: WO, War Cabinet Offices, and Military Intelligence, 1940-44; France and Germany, 1944-46; GSO1, Political Div. of British Control Commn, 1945-46. University of Cambridge: Fellow of King's Coll., 1944-56, 1966; Asst Tutor, 1947; Lectr in Politics, 1948-66; Provost of King's Coll., 1956-66. Romanes Lectr, Oxford, 1965. Chairman: Departmental Cttee on Teaching of Russian in Schools, 1960; Academic Planning Bd, Univ. of Essex, 1965-70; Cttee on Future of Broadcasting, 1974-77, report published 1977. Member: Academic Adv. Cttee, Brunel Coll., 1966-73; Academic Planning Bd, Univ. of East Anglia, 1964-71; Public Schools Commn, 1966-70. Chm., Enquiry on the disturbances in Essex Univ. (report published 1974). Sen. Fellow Eton Coll., 1956-66. Governor: Stowe Sch., 1945-66; Queen Mary Coll., London, 1956-60. Trustee: Churchill Coll., 1958-76; British Museum, 1963-. Dir, Royal Opera House, Covent Garden; Gulbenkian Foundation: Mem., Arts Cttee, 1957-64; Chm., Educn Cttee, 1971-76. FRHistS; Fellow, Berkeley Coll., Yale, 1963; Hon. Fellow, UCL, 1968. For. Hon. Mem., Amer. Acad. of Arts and Sciences, 1973. Hon. DLitt: York; Ontario; DUniv Essex. Le Bas Prize, 1948; Diamond Jubilee Medal, Inst. of Linguists, 1971. Comdr, Royal Order of King George I of the Hellenes (Greece), 1962. *Publications:* Leslie Stephen: his thought and character in relation to his time, 1951 (awarded James Tait Black Memorial Prize, 1951); The Intellectual Aristocracy (in Studies in Social History, a tribute to G. M. Trevelyan, 1956); Kipling's Place in the History of Ideas (in Kipling's Mind and Art, 1964); The Curious Strength of Positivism in English Political Thought, 1959; Roxburgh of Stowe, 1965; articles in Victorian Studies and other periodicals. *Recreation:* Mediterranean travel. *Address:*

University College London, Gower Street, WC1E 6BT. *T:* 01-387 7050. *Club:* Brooks's.

ANNAN, Robert; President, Consolidated Gold Fields Ltd, 1960-73 (Chairman, 1944-60); director of mining companies; *b* 16 May 1885; *er s* of John and Marion Annan; *m* 1st, 1911, Dely (*d* 1967), *yr d* of Everett Loraine Weston, New York; two *s*; 2nd, 1971, Betty, *yr d* of Richard Abenheim. *Educ:* Uppingham Sch.; Columbia Univ., New York City. Served European War, 1915-18, in France, with Royal Engineers (TF). Institution of Mining and Metallurgy: Mem. 1920; Pres. 1936-37; Hon. Treas., 1946-68; Gold Medallist, 1949; Hon. Fellow, Imperial Coll. of Science and Technology, 1951; Egleston Medal, Columbia Univ., 1957. Mem.: South African Institute of Mining and Metallurgy, 1936; Newcomen Soc. *Recreations:* history and early literature of mining and metallurgy; book collecting. *Address:* 132 Bickenhall Mansions, W1. *T:* 01-935 2065.

ANNAND, John Angus; Under Secretary, Welsh Office, since 1975; *b* 13 May 1926; *s* of James Annand and Lilias Annand (*née* Smith); *m* 1971, Julia Dawn Hardman. *Educ:* Hillhead High Sch., Glasgow; Glasgow Univ. (MA, 1st Cl. Hons); Brasenose Coll., Oxford (BLitt). Lecturer: Univ. of Ceylon; Univ. of South Australia, 1951-53; Asst Dir, Civil Service Commn, 1953-57; Principal, 1957, Asst Sec., 1967, HM Treasury; Civil Service Dept, 1968; Welsh Office, 1971; Under Sec., Health and Social Work Dept, Welsh Office, 1975. *Address:* c/o Welsh Office, Cathays Park, Cardiff CF1 3NQ; 21 Fairwater Road, Llandaff, Cardiff. *Club:* Cardiff and County (Cardiff).

ANNAND, Richard Wallace, VC 1940; DL; Personnel Officer at Finchale Abbey Training Centre for the Disabled, near Durham, since 1948; late Captain Durham Light Infantry (RARO); *b* 5 Nov. 1914; *s* of Lt-Comdr Wallace Moir Annand, Royal Naval Division (killed Gallipoli 1915), and late Dora Elizabeth Chapman, South Shields; *m* 1940, Shirley Osborne, JP 1957. *Educ:* Pocklington, East Yorks. Staff of National Provincial Bank, 1933-37; commissioned in RNVR 1933 (Tyne and London Divisions); transferred to Durham Light Infantry, Jan. 1938; served in France and Belgium, 1939-40 (wounded, VC). Invalided, Dec. 1948. Hon. Freeman Co. Borough of South Shields, 1940; Hon. Representative of The Officers' Assoc.; DL Co. of Durham, 1956. *Recreations:* Rugby football, golf; interest: general welfare of the deafened. *Address:* Springwell House, Whitesmocks, Durham City. *Club:* County (Durham).

ANNENBERG, Walter H., KBE (Hon.) 1976; US Ambassador to the Court of St James's, 1969-74; *b* 13 March 1908; *s* of M. L. Annenberg; *m* 1951, Leonore Cohn; one *d. Educ:* Peddie Sch.; Univ. of Pennsylvania. President, Triangle Publications Inc., Philadelphia, Pa; Publisher: Seventeen Magazine; TV Guide; Daily Racing Form. Holds foreign decorations. *Address:* Llanfair Road, Wynnewood, Pa 19096, USA; 250 King of Prussia Road, Radnor, Pa 19088, USA. *Clubs:* White's, Turf; Racquet, Rittenhouse (Philadelphia); Lyford Cay (Bahamas); National Press (Washington, DC); Swinley Forest Golf.

ANNESLEY, family name of **Earl Annesley** and **Viscount Valentia.**

ANNESLEY, 9th Earl, *cr* 1789; **Robert Annesley;** Baron Annesley, 1758; Viscount Glerawly, 1766; Civil Servant, retired; *b* 20 Feb. 1900; *s* of Arthur Albert O'Donel Valentia Annesley (*d* 1947) and Elizabeth Mary (*d* 1909), *d* of late Embertus van Ooms, Consul for the Netherlands; *S* kinsman, 8th Earl of Annesley, 1957; *m* 1922, Nora, *y d* of late Walter Harrison, Sapperton, near Cirencester, Glos; three *s.* Served European War, 1914-18, with Royal Navy; War of 1939-45 with Royal Corps of Signals, France and West Africa. *Heir: s* Viscount Glerawly, *qv. Address:* 67 Vegal Crescent, Englefield Green, Surrey. *T:* Egham 2162.

ANNETT, David Maurice, MA; Headmaster of King's School, Worcester, since 1959; *b* 27 April 1917; *s* of late M. W. Annett and Marguerite, *d* of Rev. W. M. Hobson; *m* 1953, Evelyn Rosemary, *d* of late W. M. Gordon, Headmaster of Wrekin Coll., and *widow* of R. E. Upcott; one *d* (one step-*s* two step-*d*). *Educ:* Haileybury Coll.; Queens' Coll., Cambridge. Head of Classical Dept at Oundle Sch., 1939-53, and Housemaster, 1948-53; Headmaster of Marling Sch., Stroud, 1953-59. Served with 27th Field Regt, RA, in India and Burma (Capt.), 1941-45. *Address:* 14 College Green, Worcester. *T:* Worcester 24989.

ANNETT, Engineer-Captain George Lewis, CIE 1941; RIN, retired; *b* 1887; *s* of late George Samuel Annett, MC; *m* 1918, Hessie Mary (*d* 1963), *d* of late Robert Felpts, Ulverston. Arms Traffic Operations, Persian Gulf, 1909-14; served European War, 1914-19 (despatches twice); Head of Engineering Branch,

Royal Indian Navy; retired, 1941. CA Lancs. *Address:* Rakehead, Ulverston, Cumbria.

ANNIGONI, Pietro, RP; Italian painter; artist in oil, tempera, etching and fresco; *b* Milan, 7 June 1910; *s* of Ricciardo Annigoni, engineer; *m* 1st, Anna Maggini (*d* 1969); one *s* one *d*; 2nd, 1976, Rosa Segreto. *Educ:* Accademia delle Belle Arti, Florence. Member of: Accademia di S Luca, Rome; Accademia delle Arti del Disegno, Florence; Academy of Design, New York. Portraits exhibited: (at Nat. Portrait Gallery) The Queen, 1970; (at Royal Academy, London) The Queen (for the Fishmongers' Company), 1955, Dame Margot Fonteyn, 1956, The Duke of Edinburgh (for the Fishmongers' Company), 1957, Maharanee of Jaipur, 1958. Other works: Portrait of Princess Margaret, 1958; The Immaculate Heart of Mary, 1962; The Last Supper, fresco in San Michele Arcangelo, Ponte Buggianese, 1974-75. Permanent collections showing his works include: Uffizi (Print Room), Florence; Galleria Arte Moderna, Milan; Frescoes: S Martino, Florence; Madonna del Consiglio, Pistoia; Basilica of S Lorenzo, Florence. Exhibitions include: Wildenstein Gall., London, 1954; Royal Academy, 1956; Wildenstein, NY, 1957; Galleries of Fedn of British Artists, 1961; retrospective exhbn, New York and San Francisco, 1969; Arts Unlimited Gall., London, 1971. Has also exhibited in Rome, Turin, Paris, Florence, Milan, etc. *Publication:* (autobiog.) An Artist's Life, 1977. *Address:* Borgo degli Albizi 8, Florence, Italy.

ANOUILH, Jean; French dramatic author; *b* Bordeaux, 23 June 1910. *Educ:* Collège Chaptal; Univ. of Paris. *Plays include:* L'Ermine, 1934 (prod Nottingham, 1955, as The Ermine); Y'avait un prisonnier, 1935; Le Voyageur sans bagages, 1937; Le Bal des Voleurs, 1938 (prod London, 1952, as Thieves' Carnival); La Sauvage, 1938 (prod London, 1957, as Restless Heart); Cavalcade d'Amour, 1941; Le Rendez-vous de Senlis, 1942: Léocadia, 1942 (prod London, 1954, as Time Remembered); Eurydice, 1942 (prod London as Point of Departure, 1950); Humulus le Muet (in collaboration with Jean Aurenche), 1945; Oreste, 1945; Antigone, 1946 (prod London, 1949); Jézébel, 1946; Roméo et Jeannette, 1946 (prod London, 1949, as Fading Mansion); Médée, 1946; L'Invitation au château, 1948 (prod London, 1950, 1968, as Ring Round the Moon); Ardèle ou la Marguerite, 1949; La Répétition, ou l'amour puni, 1950 (prod Edinburgh Festival 1957, and London, 1961); Colombe, 1950 (prod London, 1951); La Valse des toréadors, 1952 (prod London, 1956); L'Alouette, 1953 (prod London, 1955, as The Lark); Ornifle, 1955; L'Hurluberlu, 1958 (prod Chichester and London, 1966, as The Fighting Cock); La Foire d'Empoigne, 1960; Becket (prod London, 1961); La Grotte, 1961 (prod London, 1965, as The Cavern); Poor Bitos (prod London, 1963-64); Le Boulanger, la Boulangère et le Petit Mitson, 1968; Cher Antoine, 1969; Les Poissons Rouges, 1969; Ne Réveillez Pas, Madame, 1970; The Arrest, 1974. *Films include:* Monsieur Vincent (awarded Grand Prix du Cinéma Français); Pattes blanches; Caprice de Caroline, etc. *Address:* c/o Les Éditions de la Table Ronde, 40 rue du Bac, Paris VIIe, France.

ANSCOMBE, Gertrude Elizabeth Margaret, FBA 1967; Professor of Philosophy, University of Cambridge, since 1970; Fellow, New Hall, Cambridge, since 1970; *b* 1919; *d* of Allen Wells Anscombe and Gertrude Elizabeth Anscombe (*née* Thomas); *m* 1941, Prof. Peter Thomas Geach, *qv*; three *s* four *d. Educ:* Sydenham High Sch.; St Hugh's Coll., Oxford (Schol.); Newnham Coll., Cambridge. 2nd cl. Hon. Mods 1939, 1st cl. Greats 1941, Oxford. Research studentships, Oxford and Cambridge, 1941-44; research fellowships, Somerville Coll., Oxford, 1946-64; Fellow, Somerville Coll., 1964-70, Hon. Fellow, 1970-; Hon. Fellow, St Hugh's Coll., Oxford, 1972. *Publications:* Intention, 1957; An Introduction to Wittgenstein's Tractatus, 1959; (with Peter Geach) Three Philosophers, 1961; translator and co-editor of posthumous works of Ludwig Wittgenstein. *Address:* New Hall, Cambridge.

ANSELL, James Lawrence Bunting, MRCS, LRCP; lately Surgeon Apothecary to HM Household at Sandringham. *Educ:* Cambridge Univ.; St Thomas' Hospital. BA Cambridge; MRCS, LRCP, 1940. Formerly: Casualty Officer, Ear, Nose and Throat House Surgeon at St Thomas' Hospital; House Physician and Opthalmic House Surgeon, Royal Hants County Hospital, Winchester; House Physician and Resident Medical Officer, London Chest Hospital. *Address:* The Surgery, Sandringham, Norfolk. *T:* Dersingham 40542.

ANSELL, Sir Michael Picton, Kt 1968; CBE 1951; DSO 1944; DL; First President/Chairman, British Equestrian Federation, 1972-76; Show Director, Royal International Horse Show, and Horse of the Year Show, 1951-75; *b* 26 March 1905; *s* of Lieut-

Col G. K. Ansell and K. Cross; *m* 1st, 1936, Victoria Jacintha Fleetwood Fuller (*d* 1969); two *s* one *d*; 2nd, 1970, Eileen (*née* Stanton) (*d* 1971), *widow* of Maj.-Gen. Roger Evans, CB, MC. *Educ:* Wellington; RMC Sandhurst. Gazetted 5th Royal Inniskilling Dragoon Guards, 1924, Col, 1957-62. War of 1939-45: Lieut-Col to command 1st Lothian & Border Yeo., 1940 (severely wounded and prisoner, 1940); discharged disabled, 1944. Chairman: British Show Jumping Assoc., 1945-64, 1970-71 (Pres., 1964-66); (first) British Horse Soc. Council, 1963-72 (Hon. Dir, British Horse Soc., 1952-73). Yeoman, Worshipful Co. of Saddlers, 1963; Freeman: Worshipful Co. of Farriers, 1962, Worshipful Co. of Loriners, 1962. A Vice-Pres., St Dunstan's, 1970, Vice-Chm., 1975- (Mem. Council, 1958-). DL 1966, High Sheriff 1967, Devon. Chevalier, Order of Leopold, Belgium, 1932; Commander's Cross, Order of Merit, German Federal Republic, 1975. *Publications:* Soldier On (autobiog.), 1973; Riding High, 1974. *Recreations:* show jumping (International, 1931-39), polo International, fishing. *Address:* Pillhead House, Bideford, N Devon. *T:* Bideford 2574. *Club:* Cavalry and Guards.

ANSETT, Sir Reginald (Myles), KBE 1969; Chairman and Managing Director, Ansett Transport Industries Ltd and subsidiary cos; *b* 13 Feb. 1909; *s* of late Charles John and Mary Ann Ansett; *m* 1944, Joan McAuliffe Adams; three *d*. *Educ:* State Sch. and Swinburne Techn. Coll., Victoria. Founded Ansett Roadways, 1931, and Ansett Airways Ltd, 1936; Managing Dir, Ansett Airways Ltd, 1936, later Ansett Transport Industries Ltd, 1946. Subsidiary cos include: Ansett Transport Industries (Ops) Pty Ltd (operating as Ansett Airlines of Australia, Ansett Airlines of NSW, Ansett Airlines of S Australia, MacRobertson Miller Airline Services, Ansett Freight Express, Aviation Engineering Supplies, N.I.C. Instrument Co.; Ansett-Pioneer, Mildura Bus Lines, Barrier Reef Islands; Ansair; Ansett Motors; Provincial Motors; Ansett General Aviation; Ansett Television Films; Wridgways; Albury Border Transport; P. E. Power (Wagga) Transport; Austarama Television Pty Ltd; Universal Telecasters (Qld) Ltd; Ansett Hotels Pty Ltd; Ansett Hotels (P&NG) Pty Ltd; Ansett Niugini Enterprises Ltd; Ansett Brewarrana Holdings Pty Ltd; Transport Industries Insurance Co. Ltd; Sist Constructions Pty Ltd. Director: Diners Club Ltd; Associated Securities Ltd. Chm., Peninsula Church of England Sch. Council, 1965-74; Mem. Council, 1974-. *Recreations:* horse racing (Chm., Port Phillip Dist Racing Assoc.); game shooting. *Address:* (private) Gunyong Valley, Mount Eliza, Vic 3930, Australia; (business) 489 Swanston Street, Melbourne, Vic. 3000, Australia. *T:* 3453144. *Clubs:* Victoria Racing, Victoria Amateur Turf, Moonee Valley Racing, Mornington Racing (Chm.) (all in Victoria).

ANSON, family name of **Earl of Lichfield.**

ANSON, John; Deputy Secretary, HM Treasury, since 1977; *b* 3 Aug. 1930; *yr s* of Sir Edward Anson, 6th Bt, and of Dowager Lady Anson; *m* 1957, Myrica Fergie-Woods; two *s* two *d*. *Educ:* Winchester, Magdalene Coll., Cambridge. Served in HM Treasury, 1954-68; Financial Counsellor, British Embassy, Paris, 1968-71; Asst Sec., 1971-72, Under-Sec., 1972-74, Cabinet Office; Under-Sec., HM Treasury, 1974-77. *Address:* 18 Church Road, Barnes, SW13 9HN. *T:* 01-748 5079.
See also Sir Peter Anson, Bt.

ANSON, Rear-Adm. Sir Peter, 7th Bt, *cr* 1831; CB 1974; CEng, FIERE; Assistant Marketing Director, Marconi Space and Defence Systems Ltd, since 1975; *b* 31 July 1924; *er s* of Sir Edward R. Anson, 6th Bt, and of Alison, *o d* of late Hugh Pollock; *S* father 1951; *m* 1955, Elizabeth Audrey, *o d* of late Rear-Adm. Sir Philip Clarke, KBE, CB, DSO; two *s* two *d*. *Educ:* RNC, Dartmouth. Joined RN 1938; Lieut 1944. Served War of 1939-45, HMS Prince of Wales, HMS Exeter. Lieut-Comdr, 1952; Comdr 1956. Commanding Officer, HMS Alert, 1957-58; Staff of RN Tactical Sch., Woolwich, 1959-61; Commanding Officer, HMS Broadsword, 1961-62; Captain, 1963; Director Weapons, Radio (Naval), 1965-66 (Dep. Director, 1963-65); CO HMS Naiad and Captain (D) Londonderry Squadron, 1966-68; Captain, HM Signal School, 1968-70; Commodore, Commander Naval Forces Gulf, 1970-72; ACDS (Signals), 1972-74, retired 1975. FIERE 1972. *Heir: s* Philip Roland Anson, *b* 4 Oct. 1957. *Address:* Rosefield, Rowledge, Farnham, Surrey. *T:* Frensham 2724.
See also John Anson.

ANSTEY, Edgar, MA, PhD; Deputy Chief Scientific Officer, Civil Service Department, and Head of Behavioural Sciences Research Division, 1969-77; *b* 5 March 1917; British; *s* of late Percy Lewis Anstey and Dr Vera Anstey; *m* 1939, Zoë Lilian Robertson; one *s*. *Educ:* Winchester Coll.; King's Coll,

Cambridge. Assistant Principal, Dominions Office, 1938; Private Sec. to Duke of Devonshire, 1939. 2nd Lieut Dorset Regt, 1940; Major, War Office (DSP), 1941. Founder-Head of Civil Service Commission Research Unit, 1945; Principal, Home Office, 1951; Senior Principal Psychologist, Min. of Defence, 1958; Chief Psychologist, Civil Service Commn, 1964-69. *Publications:* Interviewing for the Selection of Staff (with Dr E. O. Mercer), 1956; Staff Reporting and Staff Development, 1961; Committees-How they work and how to work them, 1962; Psychological Tests, 1966; The Techniques of Interviewing, 1968; (with Dr C. A. Fletcher and Dr. J. Walker) Staff Appraisal and Development, 1976; articles in Brit. Jl of Psychology, Occupational Psychology, etc. *Recreations:* fell-walking, surfing, bridge. *Address:* Sandrock, Higher Tristram, Polzeath, Wadebridge, Cornwall PL27 6TF. *T:* Trebertherick 3324. *Club:* Royal Commonwealth Society.

ANSTEY, Edgar (Harold Macfarlane), OBE 1969; Documentary Film Producer and Critic; *b* 16 Feb. 1907; *s* of Percy Edgar Macfarlane Anstey and Kate Anstey (*née* Clowes); *m* 1949, Daphne Lilly, Canadian film-maker; one *s* one *d*. *Educ:* Watford Grammar Sch. Empire Marketing Board Film Unit, 1931; associated with Grierson group in devel't of sociological and scientific documentaries, 1931-; organised Shell Film Unit, 1934; March of Time: London Dir of Productions, later Foreign Editor, NY, 1936-38. Produced wartime films for Ministries and Services, 1940-46. Film planning and prod. for BOAC, for oil industry in Venezuela and for CO in WI, 1946-49; rep. short films on Cinematograph Films Council, 1947-49; org. and acted as producer-in-charge, British Transport Films, 1949-74. Formerly film critic of The Spectator; regular mem., BBC Radio programme The Critics. Chairman: Brit. Film Acad., 1956; and again (with Soc. of Film and Television Arts), 1967; Pres., Internat. Scientific Film Assoc., 1961-63; Mem. Council RCA, 1963-74 (Sen. Fellow, 1970); led British cultural delegns to USSR, 1964, 1966; Pres., British Industrial and Scientific Film Assoc., 1974- (Chm., 1969-70); Governor, British Film Inst., 1965-75. Hon. Fellow, British Kinematograph Soc., 1974. *Notable films include:* Housing Problems, 1935; Enough to Eat?, 1936; Journey into Spring, 1957 (British Film Acad. and Venice Award); Terminus, 1961 (British Film Acad. and Venice Award); Between the Tides, 1958 (Venice Award); Wild Wings, 1965 (Hollywood Oscar). *Publication:* The Development of Film Technique in Britain (Experiment in the Film), 1948. *Recreations:* formerly football, tennis and walking, now international relations and giving public advice to professional footballers and referees (at Watford and Highbury). *Address:* 6 Hurst Close, Hampstead Garden Suburb, NW11. *T:* 01-455 2385. *Club:* Savile.

ANSTEY, Brig. Sir John, Kt 1975; CBE 1946; TD; DL; President Chairman, National Savings Committee, since 1975 (a Vice-Chairman, 1968-75); retired as Chairman and Managing Director, John Player & Sons; Director, Imperial Tobacco Co., Ltd, 1949-67; *b* 3 Jan. 1907; *s* of late Major Alfred Anstey, Matford House, Exeter, Devon; *m* 1935, Elizabeth Mary, *d* of late William Garnett, Backwell, Somerset; one *s* one *d*. *Educ:* Clifton; Trinity Coll., Oxford. Served War of 1939-45: N Africa, France, SEAC (despatches); Lt-Col 1944; Brig. 1944. Mem. Council, Nottingham Univ.; Mem. (part-time) East Midlands Gas Board, 1968-72. Governor, Clifton Coll. Mem. Council, The Queen's Silver Jubilee Appeal, 1976. High Sheriff of Nottinghamshire, 1967; DL Notts 1970. Hon. LLD Nottingham, 1975. Legion of Honour; Croix de Guerre (France); Legion of Merit (USA). *Address:* The Old House, Epperstone, Notts NG14 6AU.

ANSTEY, Sidney Herbert; HM Diplomatic Service, retired; Consul-General, Atlanta, 1968-70; *b* 4 June 1910; *m* 1937, Winifred Mary Gray; three *s* one *d*. Foreign Office, 1940-49; Vice-Consul, Nantes, 1950; First Sec. and Consul, Port-au-Prince, 1951; Belgrade, 1952; Vienna, 1953; Dep. Finance Officer, Foreign Office, 1957; First Sec., Paris, 1960, Counsellor, 1963; Consul, Bilbao, 1965; Consul-Gen., Bilbao, 1966. *Address:* 17 Hambledon Hill, Epsom, Surrey. *T:* Epsom 25989.

ANSTICE, Vice-Adm. Sir Edmund (Walter), KCB 1953 (CB 1950); retired; *b* 5 May 1899; 2nd *s* of late Major J. C. A. Anstice; *m* 1928, Lesley, *d* of late L. Ritchie, Sydney, NSW; two *s*. *Educ:* RNC, Osborne and Dartmouth. Lieut, 1920; Comdr, 1932; Capt., 1939; Rear-Adm., 1948; Vice-Adm., 1951. Served European War, 1914-18; specialised Naval Aviation, 1924; War of 1939-45, Admty; comd HMS Fencer; Chief of Staff Flag Officer, Carrier Training; 4th Naval Mem. Australian Naval Board, 1946-48; Flag Officer Training Squadron, 1948-49; Flag Officer Flying Training, 1949-51; a Lord Commissioner of the Admiralty, Fifth Sea Lord and Dep. Chief of Naval Staff (Air), 1951-54; retd 1954. *Recreations:* fishing, shooting. *Address:*

Inverdunning House, Dunning, Perthshire. *T:* 207. *Club:* Royal Perth (Perth).

ANSTRUTHER, Sir Ralph (Hugo), 7th Bt, *cr* 1694; KCVO 1976 (CVO 1967); MC 1943; DL; Equerry to the Queen Mother since 1959, also Treasurer, since 1961; *b* 13 June 1921; *o s* of late Capt. Robert Edward Anstruther, MC, The Black Watch, *o s* of 6th Bt; *S* grandfather, 1934. *Educ:* Eton; Magdalene Coll., Cambridge (BA). Major, RARO Coldstream Gds. Served Malaya, 1950 (despatches). Mem. Queen's Body Guard for Scotland (Royal Co. of Archers). DL Fife, 1960, Caithness-shire, 1965. *Heir: cousin,* Ian Fife Campbell Anstruther, Capt. late Royal Corps of Signals [*b* 11 May 1922; *m* 1st, 1951, Honor (marr. diss., 1963), *er d* of late Capt. Gerald Blake, MC; one *d*; 2nd, 1963, Susan Margaret Walker, *e d* of H. St J. B. Paten; two *s* three *d*]. *Address:* Balcaskie, Pittenweem, Fife; Watten, Caithness.
See also Sir T. D. Erskine.

ANSTRUTHER, Sir Windham Eric Francis Carmichael-, 12th Bt, *cr* 1694 and 1798; Hereditary Carver to Royal Household in Scotland; one of the Hereditary Masters of the Household for Scotland; *b* 1900; *s* of late Gerald Yorke Anstruther and Ellen Caroline, *d* of J. Milne, Cradock, Cape Colony; *S* cousin, 1928; *m* 1st, 1932, Fay Sibyl Marie (marr. diss.), *o c* of Ernest Rechnitzer, Berkeley Square (she *m* 1948, Capt. Jerzy Bondorowski); 2nd, 1948, Joan Coates (marr. diss.). *Educ:* Marlborough; RMC, Sandhurst. *Heir:* none. *Address:* Carmichael, Thankerton, Biggar, Lanarks.

ANSTRUTHER-GOUGH-CALTHORPE, Brig. Sir Richard (Hamilton), 2nd Bt *cr* 1929; CBE 1946 (OBE 1940); DL, JP, CA; Croix de Guerre, 1947; Hon. LLD Birmingham 1950; MA (Cantab); *b* 28 March 1908; *o s* of Sir FitzRoy Anstruther-Gough-Calthorpe, 1st Bt; *S* father 1957; *m* 1939, Nancy Moireach (*d* 1976), *o d* of late Vernon Austen Malcolmson, MA, JP, Aston Bury, Stevenage, Herts; two *s* (and one *s* decd). *Educ:* Harrow; Magdalene Coll., Cambridge (MA). 2nd Lieut Royal Scots Greys, 1930, Captain, 1938. Served War of 1939-45, Norway and Middle East; Dep. Director Military Operations, War Office, 1944-47; retd 1947. Director: Rowton Hotels Ltd; Lloyds Bank Ltd. CC 1949, JP 1950, DL 1955, CA 1956, Chm. CC 1967-74, Hants; Chm., Hants Local Govt Reorganisation Jt Cttee, 1972-73. *Heir: g s* Euan Hamilton Anstruther-Gough-Calthorpe, *b* 22 June 1966. *Address:* Elvetham Farm House, Hartley Wintney, Hants. *T:* Hartley Wintney 2117. *Clubs:* Royal Yacht Squadron; Warwickshire County Cricket (Pres.).
See also Baron Luke.

ANSTRUTHER-GRAY, family name of **Baron Kilmany.**

ANTCLIFFE, Kenneth Arthur; Director of Education, City of Liverpool, since 1975. *Address:* Education Offices, 14 Sir Thomas Street, Liverpool. *T:* 051-236 5480.

ANTHONY, Archbishop, (*né* **André Borisovich Bloom);** Metropolitan of Sourozh, since 1965; Head of the Russian Orthodox Patriarchal Church in Britain; Exarch of the Patriarch of Moscow and all Russia in Western Europe, 1965-74; *b* Lausanne, Switzerland, 19 June 1914; *o c* of Boris Edwardovich Bloom (Russian Imperial Diplomatic Service) and Xenia Nikolaevna Scriabina (sister of the composer Alexander Scriabin). *Educ:* Lycée Condorcet and Sorbonne, Paris. Dr of Med., Sorbonne, 1943. Army service, med. corps French Army and Resistance, 1939-45. Gen. Practitioner, 1945-49. Took monastic vows, 1943; Priest, Russian Orthodox Church in Paris, 1948; Chaplain to Fellowship of St Alban and St Sergius, London, 1949-50; Vicar, Russian Orthodox Church of St Philip, London, 1950; apptd Hegumen, 1953, Archimandrite, 1956; consecrated Bishop of Sergievo, Suffragan Bishop, Exarchate of Western Europe, 1957; Archbishop of Sourozh, 1960, acting Exarch, 1962-65. Member: Ecumenical Commn of Russian Orthodox Church; Central Cttee and Christian Medical Commn of World Council of Churches, 1968. Hulsean Preacher, Cambridge, 1972-73. Médaille de Bronze de la Société d'encouragement au bien (France), 1945; Orders of: St Vladimir 1st Cl. (Russia), 1962; St Andrew (Ecumenical Patriarchate), 1963; Lambeth Cross, 1975. *Publications:* Asceticism, 1948; Living Prayer, 1965; School for Prayer, 1970; God and Man, 1971; Meditations on a Theme, 1972; Courage to Pray, 1973. *Address:* Russian Orthodox Cathedral, Ennismore Gardens, SW7. *T:* 01-584 0096.

ANTHONY, C. L.; *see* Smith, Dodie.

ANTHONY, Rt. Hon. Douglas; *see* Anthony, Rt. Hon. J. D.

ANTHONY, Evelyn; author; *b* 3 July 1928; *d* of Christian Stephens and Elizabeth (*née* Sharkey); *m* 1955, Michael Ward Thomas; four *s* two *d*. *Educ:* Convent of Sacred Heart, Roehampton. *Publications:* Imperial Highness, 1953; Curse Not the King, 1954; Far Fly the Eagles, 1955; Anne Boleyn, 1956 (US Literary Guild Award); Victoria, 1957 (US Literary Guild Award); Elizabeth, 1959; Charles the King, 1961; Clandara, 1963; The Heiress, 1964; Valentina, 1965; The Rendezvous, 1967; Anne of Austria, 1968; The Legend, 1969; The Assassin, 1970; The Tamarind Seed, 1971; The Poellenberg Inheritance, 1972; The Occupying Power, 1973 (Yorkshire Post Best Novel); The Malaspiga Exit, 1974; The Persian Ransom, 1975; The Silver Falcon, 1977. *Recreations:* racing (National Hunt), music, going to sale rooms. *Address:* Castlesize, Sallins, Co. Kildare, Ireland.

ANTHONY, Rt. Hon. (John) Douglas, PC 1971; MEC 1963; MP, Parliament of Australia, since 1957; Leader, National Country Party of Australia (formerly Australian Country Party), since 1971; Deputy Prime Minister, and Minister for Overseas Trade and National Resources, since 1975; *b* 31 Dec. 1929; *s* of late H. L. Anthony; *m* 1957, Margot Macdonald Budd; two *s* one *d*. *Educ:* Murwillumbah Primary and High Schs, The King's Sch., Parramatta; Queensland Agricultural Coll. (QDA). Minister for Interior, 1964; Dep. Leader, Australian Country Party, 1966-71; Minister for Primary Industry, 1967-71; Dep. Prime Minister and Minister for Trade and Industry, 1971-72; Minister for Overseas Trade, Minerals and Energy, Nov.-Dec. 1975. *Recreations:* golf, squash, swimming. *Address:* Parliament House, Canberra, ACT 2600, Australia. *T:* 721211. *Club:* Royal Sydney Golf.

ANTHONY, Sir Mobolaji B.; *see* Bank-Anthony.

ANTICO, Sir Tristan, Kt 1973; Managing Director, Pioneer Concrete Services Ltd; Company Director; *b* 25 March 1923; *s* of Terribile Giovani Antico and Erminia Bertin; *m* 1950, Dorothy Brigid Shields; three *s* four *d*. *Educ:* Sydney High Sch. Began career as Accountant; subseq. became Company Secretary, Melocco Bros; Founder of Pioneer Concrete Services Ltd. Knighthood awarded for services to industry and the community in New South Wales. Comdr, Order of Star of Solidarity (Italy), 1967. *Recreations:* horse racing, yachting, water-skiing, boating. *Address:* 161 Raglan Street, Mosman, NSW 2088, Australia. *T:* 969 4070. *Clubs:* Tattersall's, Australian Jockey, Sydney Turf, American National, Royal Sydney Yacht Squadron, Royal Prince Alfred Yacht, Royal Motor Yacht Squadron (all in Sydney).

ANTON, Alexander Elder, CBE 1973; FBA 1972; Full-time Member, Scottish Law Commission, since 1973 (part-time Member, 1966-73); *b* 1922; *m* 1949, Doris May Lawrence; one *s*. *Educ:* Aberdeen Univ. (MA, LLB with dist.). Solicitor, 1949; Lectr, Aberdeen, 1953-59; Prof. of Jurisprudence, Univ. of Glasgow, 1959-73. Literary Dir, Stair Soc., 1960-66. *Publications:* Private International Law, 1967; (co-ed) Amos and Walton's Introduction to French Law, 3rd edn, 1966; contribs to legal and historical jls. *Recreation:* hill walking. *Address:* 41 Braid Farm Road, Edinburgh EH10 6LE.

ANTONIO; *see* Ruiz Soler, Antonio.

ANTONIONI, Michelangelo; Film Director; *b* Ferrara, Italy, 29 Sept. 1912; *s* of Ismaele and Elisabetta Roncagli; *m* (marr. diss.). *Educ:* degree in Economics and Commerce, Univ. of Bologna. Formerly an Asst Dir, Film Critic to newspapers, and Script Writer. Films directed include: 8 documentaries, etc, 1943-50; subseq. long films: Cronaca di un Amore, 1950; one episode in Amore in Città, 1951; I Vinti, 1952; La Signora Senza Camelie, 1953; Le Amiche, 1955; Il Grido, 1957; L'Avventura, 1959-60; La Notte, 1961; L'Eclisse, 1962; Il Deserto Rosso, 1964; one episode in I Tre Volti, 1965; Blow-Up, 1967; Zabriskie Point, 1969; Chung Kuo-China, 1972; The Passenger, 1974. *Recreations:* collecting blown glass, tennis, ping-pong. *Address:* Via Vincenzo Tiberio 18, Rome, Italy.

ANTONY, Jonquil; author; *b* 5 Oct. 1916; *m* 1941, John Wyse. *Educ:* Worthing High Sch. Began writing for BBC in 1937 and has since written over 4,000 scripts: daily serials, plays, adaptations, features for radio and television; wrote The Robinson Family (jointly) for four years, also initiated Mrs Dale's Diary, 1948 and wrote it (jointly) until 1963. *Publications:* The Robinson Family, 1948; The Malindens, 1951; Mrs Dale's Bedside Book, 1951; Paradise Square, 1952; Mrs Dale At Home, 1952; Mrs Dale, 1958; The Dales of Parkwood Hill, 1959; Hark! Hark! The Ark!, 1960; Mrs Dale's Friendship Book, 1961; Eaglemania, 1966; Dear Dr Dale, 1970. *Recreations:* reading, theatres, the country. *Address:* 142

Foundling Court, Brunswick Centre, WC1N 1AN. *T:* 01-278 4506.

ANTRIM, 14th Earl of, *cr* 1620; **Alexander Randal Mark McDonnell;** Viscount Dunluce; Keeper of Conservation, Tate Gallery, since 1975 (Restorer, 1965-75); *b* 3 Feb. 1935; *er s* of 13th Earl of Antrim, KBE, and of Angela Christina, *d* of Sir Mark Sykes, 6th Bt; *S* father, 1977 (but continues to be known as Viscount Dunluce); *m* 1963, Sarah Elizabeth Anne (marr. diss. 1974), 2nd *d* of St John Harmsworth; one *s* two *d*; *m* 1977, Elizabeth Sacher. *Educ:* Downside; Christ Church, Oxford; Ruskin Sch. of Art. Restorer, the Ulster Museum, 1969-71. *Recreations:* painting, vintage cars. *Heir: s* Hon. Randal Alexander St John McDonnell, *b* 2 July 1967. *Address:* Glenarm Castle, Glenarm, Co. Antrim, N Ireland. *T:* Glenarm 229; 35 Durand Gardens, Stockwell, SW9.

ANTROBUS, Maurice Edward, CMG 1943; OBE 1938; *b* 20 July 1895; *er s* of late Sir Reginald Antrobus and late Dame Edith Antrobus, DBE; *m* 1929, Betty, *er d* of late Sir Llewelyn Dalton; two *s. Educ:* Winchester; Trinity Coll., Cambridge (Exhibitioner). BA 1920; served European War, 1914-19, KRRC (wounded twice); Asst Principal, Colonial Office, 1920; Private Sec. to Governor of Ceylon, 1927-30; Principal Dominions Office, 1930; Political Sec., Office of UK High Comr in Union of S Africa, 1935-39; Asst Sec., Colonial Office, 1939; Principal Sec., Office of UK Representative to Eire, 1939-41; Official Sec., Office of UK High Comr in Commonwealth of Australia, 1941-44; Official Sec., Office of UK High Commissioner in New Zealand, 1944-45; Asst Sec., Commonwealth Relations Office, 1945; retd 1955. *Recreations:* golf, gardening. *Address:* Quorndon, Forest Row, East Sussex RH18 5BE. *T:* Forest Row 2159. *Club:* Royal Ashdown Forest Golf (Forest Row).

ANTROBUS, Sir Philip Coutts, 7th Bt, *cr* 1815; *b* 10 April 1908; *s* of late Geoffrey Edward Antrobus and Mary Atherstone, *d* of Hilton Barber, JP, Halesowen, Cradock, Cape Province; *S* cousin, 1968; *m* 1st, 1937, Dorothy Margaret Mary (*d* 1973), *d* of late Rev. W. G. Davis; two *s* one *d*; 2nd, 1975, Doris Primrose, *widow* of Ralph Dawkins. Served War, 1939-45 (POW). *Heir: s* Edward Philip Antrobus [*b* 28 Sept. 1938; *m* 1966, Janet, *d* of Philip Sceales; one *s* two *d*]. *Address:* Amesbury Abbey, Amesbury, Wilts SP4 7EX.

ANTROBUS, Lieutenant-Colonel Ronald Henry, MC 1916; DL; *b* 8 Nov. 1891; *s* of John Coutts Antrobus and Mary, *d* of Lieut-Gen. Hon. Sir James Lindsay, KCMG; *m* 1921, Muriel, *d* of R. H. Gosling, Hawthorn Hill, Berks, and *widow* of Capt. Miles Chetwynd Stapylton (killed in action); one *s. Educ:* Charterhouse. Royal Artillery Special Reserve, 1910-13; Royal Artillery, 1913-44. DL Cheshire, 1952; High Sheriff of Cheshire, 1960. *Address:* Eaton Hall, Congleton, Cheshire. *T:* Congleton 3123.

ANWAR, Mohamed Samih; Order of the Republic, 2nd Class (Egypt), 1958; Order of Merit, 1st Class (Egypt), 1968; Ambassador of the Arab Republic of Egypt to the Court of St James's, since 1975; *b* 10 Dec. 1924; *s* of Ahmed Fouad Anwar and Aziza Tewfik; *m* 1953, Omayma Soliman Hazza; one *s* one *d*. *Educ:* Cairo Univ. (Bachelor of Law, 1945). Min. of Justice, 1946-54; First Sec., Min. of Foreign Affairs, 1954; apptd to Egyptian Embassies in Moscow, 1957, and London, 1963; Ambassador to Kuwait, 1966; Under Sec., Min. of Foreign Affairs, 1968; Ambassador to Iran, 1970; Minister of State for Foreign Affairs, 1974. Order of Hamayon, 1st Cl. (Iran), 1974; Order of the Flag (Yugoslavia), 1970. *Recreations:* rowing, tennis. *Address:* Egyptian Embassy, 26 South Street, W1. *T:* 01-499 2401; Ministry of Foreign Affairs, Cairo, Egypt. *Clubs:* Travellers', Hurlingham, Les Ambassadeurs; Al Ahly (Cairo).

ANWYL-DAVIES, Marcus John, MA, QC 1967; **His Honour Judge Anwyl-Davies;** a Circuit Judge, since 1972; *b* 11 July 1923; *s* of late Thomas Anwyl-Davies and of Kathleen Beryl Anwyl-Davies (*née* Oakshott); *m* 1954, Eva Hilda Elisabeth Paulson; one *s* one *d*. *Educ:* Harrow Sch.; Christ Church, Oxford. Royal Artillery, including service with Hong Kong and Singapore RA, 1942-47 (despatches 1945). Called to Bar, Inner Temple, 1949. Legal Assessor, GMC and GDC, 1969-72; Liaison Judge to Herts Magistrates, 1972. Vice-Pres., Herts Magistrates' Assoc., 1975. *Recreations:* farming, photography.

ANYAOKU, Eleazar Chukwuemeka, (Emeka); Assistant Secretary-General of the Commonwealth, since 1975; *b* 18 Jan. 1933; *e s* of late Emmanuel Chukwuemeka Anyaoku, Ononukpo of Okpuno Ire, Obosi, Nigeria, and Cecilia Adiba (*née* Ogbogu); *m* 1962, Ebunola Olubunmi, *yr d* of late barrister Olusola Akanbi Solanke, of Abeokuta, Nigeria; two *s* one *d. Educ:* Merchants of Light Sch., Oba; Univ. of Ibadan (Schol.), Nigeria;

courses at Cambridge and Inst. of Public Admin (London); also at Cavillam Inst. (France). Management Trainee, and later Regional Asst, Commonwealth Develt Corp., in London and Lagos, 1959-62. Joined Nigerian Diplomatic Service, 1962; served as Mem. Nigerian Permanent Mission to the UN, New York, 1963-66; seconded to Commonwealth Secretariat as Asst Dir, 1966-71, and Dir, 1971-75, Internat. Affairs Div. Served as Secretary: Review Cttee on Commonwealth inter-governmental organisations, June-Aug., 1966; Commonwealth Observer Team for Gibraltar Referendum, Aug.-Sept., 1967; Anguilla Commn, WI, Jan.-Sept. 1970; (Dep. Conf. Sec.) Meeting of Commonwealth Heads of Govt, in London, 1969, and Singapore, 1971; (Conf. Sec.) Meeting of Commonwealth Heads of Govt, Ottawa, 1973, Jamaica, 1975. Dep. Chm., Royal Commonwealth Society, London, 1972-; Mem., Cttee of Management, London University's Inst. of Commonwealth Studies, 1972-; Chm., Africa Centre, London (Director, 1971). *Recreations:* tennis, athletics, swimming, reading. *Address:* Commonwealth Secretariat, Marlborough House, Pall Mall, SW1. *T:* 01-839 3411. *Clubs:* Royal Commonwealth Society, Africa Centre, Travellers'.

AOTEAROA, Bishop of, since 1968; **Rt. Rev. Manu Augustus Bennett,** DD; *b* 10 Feb. 1916; *s* of Rt Rev. F. A. Bennett, Bishop of Aotearoa, 1928-50, and Alice Rangioue Bennett; *m* 1944, Kathleen Clark; one *d. Educ:* Victoria Univ. Coll., Univ. of Hawaii. BSc 1954. Deacon, 1939; Priest, 1940; Vicar of Tauranga, Te Puke Maori District, Dio. Waiapu, 1940-44; Chaplain to 2 NZEF, 1944-46; Pastor of Rangitikei South-Manawatu Pastorate, Dio. Wellington, 1946-52; Asst Vicar of Church of Holy Nativity, Honolulu, 1953-54; Pastor of Wellington Pastorate, 1952-57; Vicar of Ohinemutu Pastorate, 1957-64; Associate Chaplain, Waikeria Youth Centre, Dio. Waikato, 1964-68; Nat. Council of Churches Chaplain, Dept of Justice. Hon. DD Jackson Coll., 1964. *Address:* PO Box 227, Napier, New Zealand.

See also Sir C. M. Bennett.

APEL, Dr Hans Eberhard; Federal Minister of Finance, West Germany, since 1974; Social-democratic Member of Bundestag, since 1965 (Deputy-Chairman of Group, 1969-72); *b* Hamburg, 25 Feb. 1932; *m* 1956, Ingrid Schwingel; two *d. Educ:* Hamburg Univ. Diplom-Volkswirt, 1957, Dr.rer.pol, 1960. Apprentice in Hamburg export and import business, 1951-54; Sec., Socialist Group in European Parlt, 1958-61; Head of Economics, Finance and Transportation Dept of European Parlt, 1962-65. Mem. Bd, Howaldt-Deutsche Werft as elected rep. of workers and employees, 1970-74. Chm., Bundestag Cttee on Transportation, 1969-72. Mem. Nat. Bd, Social-democratic Party (SPD), 1970-; Parly Sec. of State, Min. for Foreign Affairs, 1972-73. *Publications:* Edwin Cannan und seine Schüler (Doct. Thesis), 1961; Raumordnung der Bundesrepublik, in: Deutschland 1975, 1964; Europas neue Grenzen, 1964; Der deutsche Parlamentarismus, 1968; Bonn, den..., Tagebuch eines Abgeordneten, 1972. *Recreation:* soccer. *Address:* Ministry of Finance, 53 Bonn, Rheindorfer Strasse 108, West Germany. *T:* 79-1.

APPEL, Karel Christian; Netherlands Artist (Painter); *b* 25 April 1921; *s* of Jan Appel and Johanna Chevallier. *Educ:* Royal Academy of Art, Amsterdam. Began career as artist in 1938. Has had one-man exhibitions in Europe and America including the following in London: Inst. of Contemporary Art, 1957; Gimpel Fils, 1959, 1960, 1964. UNESCO Prize, Venice Biennale, 1953; Lissone Prize, Italy, 1958; Acquisition Prize, Sao Paulo Biennale, Brazil, 1959; Graphique Internat. Prize, Ljubljana, Jugoslavia, 1959; Guggenheim National Prize, Holland, 1961; Guggenheim International Prize, 1961. *Publications:* Illustrations: De Blijde en Onvoorziene Week, by Hugo Claus, 1950; Atonaal, by Simon Vinkenoog, 1951; De Ronde Kant van de Aarde, by Hans Andreus, 1952; Het Bloed Stroomt Door, by Bert Schierbeek, 1954; Haine, by E. Looten, 1954; Cogne Ciel, by E. Looten, 1954; Rhapsodie de ma Nuit, by E. Looten, 1958; Unteilbare Teil, by André Frénaud, 1960; Een Dier Heeft een Mens Getekend, by B. Schierbeek, 1961. *Address:* c/o Galérie Statler, 51 rue de Seine, Paris, France.

APPLEBY, Brian John, QC 1971; a Recorder of the Crown Court, since 1972; *b* 25 Feb. 1930; *s* of Ernest Joel and Gertrude Appleby; *m* 1958, Rosa Helena (*née* Flitterman); one *s* one *d. Educ:* Uppingham; St John's Coll., Cambridge (BA). Called to Bar, Middle Temple, 1953. Dep. Chm., Notts QS, 1970-71. Mem., Nottingham City Council, 1955-58 and 1960-63. *Recreations:* watching good football (preferably Nottingham Forest: Mem. Club Cttee, 1965-, Vice-Chm., 1972-75, Chm., 1975-); swimming, reading and enjoying, when possible, company of wife and children. *Address:* The Poplars, Edwalton Village, Notts. *T:* Nottingham 232814.

APPLEBY, Maj-Gen. David Stanley, MC 1943; TD 1950; Director of Army Legal Services, since 1976; *b* 4 Dec. 1918; *s* of Stanley Appleby and Mabel Dorothy Mary (*née* Dickson); *m* 1942, Prudence Marianne Chisholm; one *s* one *d* (and one *s* decd). *Educ:* St Peter's School. Barrister, Middle Temple, 1951. Rifleman, London Rifle Bde (TA), 1938; 2nd Lieut, Royal Fusiliers (TA), 1939; Army Legal Services, 1950-; Captain, 1950; Maj.-Gen. 1976. *Recreations:* sailing, military and other history. *Address:* Finches, Lilley Drive, Kingswood, Surrey. *T:* Mogador 3142. *Clubs:* Naval & Military; Island Sailing (Cowes).

APPLEBY, Douglas Edward Marrison; Group Managing Director, The Boots Co. Ltd, since 1977 (Managing Director, 1973-77); *b* 17 May 1929; *s* of late Robert Appleby and Muriel (*née* Surtees); *m* 1952, June; one *s* one *d*. *Educ:* Durham Johnston Sch.; Univ. of Nottingham. BSc London, BSc Nottingham. Chartered Accountant. RAF, 1950-53; Moore, Stephens & Co., Chartered Accountants, London, 1954-57; Distillers Co. Ltd, 1957-58; Corn Products Co., USA, 1959-63; Wilkinson Sword Ltd, 1964-68; The Boots Co. Ltd, 1968-. Mem. Council, Inst. Chartered Accountants, 1971-75; Mem. Council, Loughborough Univ., 1973-75. *Address:* Scarsdale House, Old Woodhouse, Leics.

APPLEBY, Dom Raphael; Head Master of Downside, since 1975; *b* 18 July 1931; *s* of Harold Thompson Appleby and Margaret Morgan. *Educ:* Downside; Christ's Coll., Cambridge (MA). Downside novitiate, 1951. Housemaster at Downside, 1962-75; National Chaplain to Catholic Students' Council, 1974. *Recreations:* books, music, golf. *Address:* Downside School, Bath BA3 4RJ.

APPLEBY, Robert, CBE 1969; Chairman, Black & Decker Ltd, 1956-75 (Managing Director, 1956-72); *b* 1913; *s* of Robert James Appleby; *m* 1957, Elisabeth Friederike (*d* 1975), *d* of Prof. Eidmann. *Educ:* Graham Sea Training and Engineering Sch., Scarborough. Dep. Chm., Black & Decker Manufacturing Co., Maryland, 1968-72. Mem., Post Office Bd, 1972-73. ČEng, FIProdE; FBIM. *Address:* Ridgewood House, Ridgemead, Englefield Green, Surrey. *Club:* Reform.

APPLETON, Rt. Rev. George, CMG 1972; MBE 1946; *b* 20 Feb. 1902; *s* of Thomas George and Lily Appleton; *m* 1929, Marjorie Alice, *d* of Charles Samuel Barrett; one *s* two *d*. *Educ:* County Boys' School, Maidenhead; Selwyn Coll., Cambridge; St Augustine's Coll., Canterbury. BA Cantab 1924 (2nd Cl. Math. Trip. pt 1, 1st Cl. Theological Trip. pt I); MA 1929. Deacon, 1925; Priest, 1926. Curate, Stepney Parish Church, 1925-27; Missionary in charge SPG Mission, Irrawaddy Delta, 1927-33; Warden, Coll. of Holy Cross, Rangoon, 1933-41; Archdeacon of Rangoon, 1943-46; Director of Public Relations, Government of Burma, 1943-46; Vicar of Headstone, 1947-50; Sec., Conf. of Brit. Missionary Societies, 1950-57; Rector of St Botolph, Aldgate, 1957-62; Archdeacon of London and Canon of St Paul's Cathedral, 1962-63; Archbishop of Perth and Metropolitan of W Australia, 1963-69; Archbishop in Jerusalem and Metropolitan, 1969-74. Buber-Rosenzweig Medal, Council of Christians and Jews, 1975. *Publications:* John's Witness to Jesus, 1955; In His Name, 1956; Glad Encounter, 1959; On the Eightfold Path, 1961; Daily Prayer and Praise, 1962; Acts of Devotion, 1963; One Man's Prayers, 1967; Journey for a Soul, 1974; Jerusalem Prayers, 1974; The Word is the Seed, 1976. *Address:* 7-8 Ginge, Wantage, Oxon OX12 8QR.

APPLEYARD, Raymond Kenelm, PhD; Director-General for Scientific and Technical Information and Information Management, Commission of the European Communities, since 1973; *b* 5 Oct. 1922; *s* of late Maj.-Gen. K. C. Appleyard, CBE, TD, DL, and Monica Mary Louis; *m* 1947, Joan Greenwood; one *s* two *d*. *Educ:* Rugby; Cambridge. BA 1943, MA 1948, PhD 1950. Instructor, Yale Univ., 1949-51; Fellow, Rockefeller Foundn, California Inst. of Technology, 1951-53; Research Officer, Atomic Energy of Canada Ltd, 1953-56; Sec., UN Scientific Cttee on effects of atomic radiation, 1956-61; Dir, Biology Div., Commn of European Atomic Energy Community, 1961-73; Exec. Sec., European Molecular Biology Organisation, 1965-73; Sec., European Molecular Biology Conf., 1969-73. Hon. Dr.med Ulm, 1977. *Publications:* contribs to: Nature, Jl Gen. Microbiol., Genetics. *Recreations:* bridge, tennis, squash. *Address:* 5a avenue Grand Air, 1640 St Genesius-Rode, Belgium; 72 boulevard Napoléon, Luxemburg. *Clubs:* Athenæum; Château Ste Anne (Brussels).

ap ROBERT, Hywel Wyn Jones; His Honour Judge ap Robert; a Circuit Judge, since 1975; *b* 19 Nov. 1923; *s* of Rev. Robert John Jones, BA, BD and Mrs Jones (*née* Evans); *m* 1956, Elizabeth Davies; two *d*. *Educ:* Cardiff High Sch.; Corpus Christi Coll., Oxford (MA). War Service, FO and Intell. Corps. 1942-46, in Britain and India. Called to Bar, Middle Temple, 1950. A Recorder of the Crown Court, 1972-75; Stipendiary Magistrate, Cardiff, later S Glamorgan, 1972-75. Contested (Plaid Cymru) Cardiganshire, 1970. Hon. Mem., Gorsedd of the Bards, 1973. *Recreations:* Welsh literature, classical and modern languages. *Address:* Law Courts, Cardiff. *Clubs:* Cardiff and County (Cardiff); Bristol Channel Yacht (Swansea).

APSLEY, Lord; Allen Christopher Bertram Bathurst; *b* 11 March 1961; *s* and *heir* of 8th Earl Bathurst, *qv*.

AQUILECCHIA, Prof. Giovanni; Professor of Italian, University of London, since 1970; *b* Nettuno, Rome, 28 Nov. 1923; *s* of late Gen. Vincenzo Aquilecchia and Maria L. Filibeck; *m* 1951, Costantina M. Bacchetta (marr. diss. 1973); two *s* one *d*. *Educ:* Liceo T. Tasso, Rome; Univ. of Rome. Dott. Lett., 1946, Diploma of Perfezionamento in Filologia Moderna, 1948, Univ. of Rome. Asst in Italian, Univ. of Rome, 1946-49; Boursier du Gouvernement Français at Collège de France, Univ. of Paris, 1949-50; British Council Scholar, Warburg Inst., Univ. of London, 1950-51; Asst, Dept of Italian Studies, Univ. of Manchester, 1951-53; Asst Lectr in Italian, University Coll., London, 1953-55, Lectr, 1955-59; Libero Docente di Letteratura Italiana, Univ. of Rome, 1958-; Reader in Italian, Univ. of London, at University Coll., 1959-61; Prof. of Italian Lang. and Lit., Univ. of Manchester, 1961-70. Corr. Fellow, Arcadia, 1961. MA (Manchester) 1965. *Publications:* Giordano Bruno, 1971; Schede di italianistica, 1976; critical editions of: Giordano Bruno: La Cena de le Ceneri, 1955; Due Dialoghi sconosciuti, 1957; Dialoghi Italiani, 1958; Praelectiones geometricæ e Ars deformationum, 1964; De la causa, principio et uno, 1973; Pietro Aretino: Sei Giornate, 1969, 2nd edn with Introduction, 1975; (co-editor) Collected essays on Italian Language and Literature, 1971; contrib.: Atti dell'Accad. dei Lincei, Atti e Memorie dell'Arcadia, Bull. dell'Accad. della Crusca, Bull. John Rylands Library, Cultura Neolatina, Dizionario Biografico degli Italiani, Enciclopedia Dantesca, Encyclopædia Britannica, English Miscellany, Giornale storico della letteratura italiana, Studi Secenteschi, Studi Tassiani, etc. *Address:* Department of Italian, Bedford College, Regent's Park, NW1.

ARAGON, Louis; poet; novelist; essayist; *b* 3 Oct. 1897; *m* 1939, Elsa Triolet (*née* Kagan). *Educ:* Faculty of Medicine, Paris Univ. Served European War, 1914-18, Infantry; War of 1939-45, Tank Div., 1939-40 (prisoner, escaped to unoccupied France); one of leaders of intellectual Resistance. Co-founder, 1919, and leader since 1924 of former Surrealist Movement, now Socialistic Realism Movement; founder, 1935, and Sec. of Internat. Assoc. of Writers for Defence of Culture; founder, 1944, and co-director, Editeurs français réunis; Vice-Pres., Assoc. des Ecrivains Combattants, 1945-60. Editor: Les Lettres Françaises, 1944-; Ce Soir, Paris, 1950; Member: Cttee of Dirs, Europe review; Nat. Cttee of Authors, 1958-; Goncourt Academy, 1967-68. Mem., French Communist Party Central Cttee. *Publications:* poems: Feu de joie, 1920; Le mouvement perpétuel, 1925; La grande gaîté; Persécuté persécuteur; Hourra l'Oural, 1934; Le crève-coeur, 1941; Les yeux d'Elsa, 1942; Brocéliande; Le Musée Grévin; La Diane Française, 1945; Les yeux et la mémoire, 1954; Elsa, 1959; Le fou d'Elsa, 1963; *novels:* Anicet ou le panorama, 1921; Le libertinage; Le paysan de Paris, 1926 (trans. as Paris Peasant, 1971); Les cloches de Bâle, 1933; Les beaux quartiers, 1936 (awarded Prix Renardot); Les voyageurs de l'Impériale, 1942; Aurélien, 1945; La Semaine Sainte, 1958 (trans. as Holy Week, 1961); La mise à mort, 1965; Blanche ou l'oubli, 1967; Henri Matisse, 1972; *history:* Histoire de l'URSS de 1917-60; (with A. Maurois) Histoire parallèle des USA et de l'URSS, 1962; *essays:* La lumière de Stendhal, 1954; Litterature sovietique, 1955; Traité du style; Les aventures de Télémaque; Pour un réalisme socialiste; La culture et les hommes; Chroniques du Bel-Canto; Matisse ou comme il vous plaira; *translations:* La chasse au Snark by Lewis Carroll, 1928; Cinq sonnets de Pétrarque, 1947. *Address:* 56 rue de Varenne, 75007 Paris, France; 78730 Saint-Arnoult-en-Yvelines, France.

ARAM, Abbas; Senator, Iranian Senate, since 1977; *b* Yazd, Iran, August 1905. *Educ:* Calcutta Univ. (BA). Entered Foreign Service 1935; Sec., Consulate-Gen., New Delhi; 3rd Sec., London, 1938-43; Min. of Foreign Affairs, 1943; 1st Sec., Berne, 1945; 1st Sec. Counsellor, and Chargé d'Affaires, Washington, 1946, 1949, 1950; Min. of Foreign Affairs, 1951; Counsellor, Baghdad, 1953; Chargé d'Affaires and Minister, Washington, 1953 and 1954-56; Dir-Gen. of Political Affairs, Min. of Foreign Affairs, 1958; Ambassador: to Japan 1958 (concurrently to Rep. of China); to Iraq, 1960-62; Minister of Foreign Affairs, 1959-60, 1962-67; Ambassador to the Court of St James's, 1967-69; returned to Teheran, 1969; Ambassador to People's Republic of China, 1972-75; returned to Teheran, 1975. Leader of Iranian Delegn to Gen. Assembly of UN, 1959, 1960, 1963, 1964, 1966. *Address:* The Senate, Teheran, Iran.

ARBUTHNOT, Sir Hugh Fitz-Gerald, 7th Bt, *cr* 1823; Master, Duke of Buccleuch's Hounds, since 1964; late Temporary Captain Welsh Guards; *b* 2 Jan. 1922; *s* of Brig.-Gen. Sir Dalrymple Arbuthnot, 5th Bt, CMG, DSO, and Alice Maude (*d* 1969), *d* of Hugh Arbuthnot; *S* brother 1944; *m* 1949, Elizabeth K. (*d* 1972), *e d* of Sqdn Ldr G. G. A. Williams, Curral Hall, Tenbury Wells; two *s* one *d*. *Educ:* Eton. MFH: Ludlow Hounds, 1948-52; Cotswold Hounds, 1952-64. *Heir:* s Keith Robert Charles Arbuthnot, *b* 23 Sept. 1951. *Address:* Brundeanlaws, Jedburgh, Roxburghshire.

ARBUTHNOT, Sir John (Sinclair-Wemyss), 1st Bt *cr* 1964; MBE 1944; TD 1951; Chairman, Folkestone and District Water Co.; Director, The Ecclesiastical Insurance Co. Ltd; Underwriting Member of Lloyd's; *b* 11 Feb. 1912; *s* of late Major K. W. Arbuthnot, the Seaforth Highlanders; *m* 1943, Margaret Jean, *y d* of Alexander G. Duff; two *s* three *d*. *Educ:* Eton; Trinity Coll., Cambridge. MA Hons in Nat. Sciences. Served throughout War of 1939-45, in RA, Major (wounded); Dep. Inspector of Shell, 1942-45; hon. pac 1944; TARO, 1948-62. Prospective Conservative candidate, Don Valley Div. of Yorks, 1934-35, Dunbartonshire, 1936-45, Dover Div. of Kent, 1945-50, contesting elections in 1935 and 1945. MP (C) Dover Div. of Kent, 1950-64; PPS to Parly Sec., Min. of Pensions, 1952-53, to Minister of Pensions, 1953-56, and Minister of Health, 1956-57; a Chm. of Committees and a Temporary Chm. of the House, 1958-64; Second Church Estates Comr, 1962-64; Church Comr for England and Mem., Bd of Governors, 1962-77 (Dep Chm., Assets Cttee, 1966-77); Mem., Church Assembly and Gen. Synod of Church of England, 1955-75, Panel of Chairmen, 1970-72; Trustee, Lambeth Palace Library, 1964-77; Chm., Archbp of Canterbury's Commn to inquire into the organisation of the Church by dioceses in London and the SE of England, 1965-67. Member: Crathorne Cttee on Sunday Observance, 1961-64; Hodson Commn on Synodical Government for the Church of England, 1964-66; Parliamentary Chm., Dock & Harbour Authorities Assoc., 1962-64; Member: Public Accounts Cttee, 1955-64; Standing Cttee, Ross Inst., 1951-62; Council, Ceylon Assoc., 1951-62; Cttee, South Indian Assoc., 1951-62. Member Parliamentary Delegations: to the Iron and Steel Community, 1955; to West Africa, 1956; to USA, 1957; to The West Indies, 1958; to Zanzibar, Mauritius and Madagascar, 1961; Leader of Parliamentary Delegation to Bulgaria, 1963. Pres., Trustee Savings Bank Assoc., 1962-76; in business in tea industry concerned with India and Ceylon, 1934-74; Chm., Estates & Agency Holdings Ltd, 1955-70; Joint Hon. Sec. Assoc. of British Chambers of Commerce, 1953-59. *Recreation:* gardening. *Heir:* s William Reierson Arbuthnot, *b* 2 Sept. 1950. *Address:* Poulton Manor, Ash, Canterbury, Kent CT3 2HW. *T:* Ash 812516; 7 Fairholt Street, SW7 1EG. *T:* 01-589 1727. *Clubs:* Carlton, Royal Commonwealth Society.

ARBUTHNOTT, family name of **Viscount of Arbuthnott.**

ARBUTHNOTT, 16th Viscount of, *cr* 1641; **John Campbell Arbuthnott,** DSC 1945; Lord-Lieutenant Grampian Region (Kincardineshire), since 1977; President, The Scottish Landowners' Federation, since 1974 (Convener, 1971-74); Director: Northern Area, Clydesdale Bank, since 1975; Aberdeen and Northern Marts, since 1973; President, Wildfowlers' Association of Great Britain and Ireland, since 1973; *b* 26 Oct. 1924; *e s* of 15th Viscount of Arbuthnott, CB, CBE, DSO, MC, and Ursula Collingwood; *S* father, 1966; *m* 1949, Mary Elizabeth Darley (*née* Oxley); one *s* one *d*. *Educ:* Fettes Coll.; Gonville and Caius Coll., Cambridge. Served RNVR (Fleet Air Arm), 1942-46; Near and Far East, British Pacific Fleet, 1945. Cambridge University, 1946-49 (Estate Management), MA 1967. Chartered Surveyor and Land Agent; Agricultural Land Service, 1949-55; Land Agent, The Nature Conservancy, Scotland, 1955-67; Mem., Countryside Commn for Scotland, 1967-71; Chm., Red Deer Commn, 1969-75. *Recreations:* countryside activities, historical research. *Heir:* s Master of Arbuthnott, *qv. Address:* Arbuthnott House, by Laurencekirk, Kincardineshire, Scotland. *T:* Inverbervie 226. *Club:* Army and Navy.

ARBUTHNOTT, Master of; Hon. John Keith Oxley Arbuthnott; *b* 18 July 1950; *s* and *heir* of 16th Viscount of Arbuthnott, *qv*; *m* 1974, Jill Mary, *er d* of Captain Colin Farquharson; one *s* one *d*. *Educ:* Fettes College; Aberdeen Univ. *Address:* Kilternan, Arbuthnott, Laurencekirk, Kincardineshire AB3 1NA. *T:* Inverbervie 226.

ARBUTHNOTT, Hugh James; HM Diplomatic Service; Head of European Integration Department (External), Foreign and Commonwealth Office, 1976-77; *b* 27 Dec. 1936; *m*; three *s*. Joined Foreign (subseq. Diplomatic) Service, 1960; 3rd Sec., Tehran, 1962-64; 2nd, later 1st Sec., FO, 1964-66; Private Sec.,

Minister of State for Foreign Affairs, 1966-68; Lagos, 1968-71; 1st Sec. (Head of Chancery), Tehran, 1971-76. *Address:* c/o Foreign and Commonwealth Office, SW1.

ARBUTHNOTT, Robert, MBE 1945; TD 1941; HM Lord-Lieutenant of the County of Dunbarton, 1968-75; *b* 22 Sept. 1900; *s* of Hugh Corsar Arbuthnott and Marianne Arbuthnott (*née* Gibson); unmarried. *Educ:* Cheltenham Coll. Served War of 1939-45: The Manchester Regt; RAC; REME. Mem., Iron and Steel Consumers' Council, 1951; Dep. Leader, UK Heavy Engineering Mission to India, 1956; Pres., Inst. of Locomotive Engrs, 1958-59. Mem. Queen's Body Guard for Scotland, Royal Company of Archers. CEng, FICE, FIMechE. DL Dunbartonshire, 1961. *Address:* Ardmoy, Rhu, Dunbartonshire G84 8NH. *T:* Rhu 230. *Clubs:* New (Edinburgh); Royal Northern Yacht.

ARCHDALE, Sir Edward (Folmer), 3rd Bt, *cr* 1928; DSC 1943; Captain, RN, retired; serving in Ministry of Defence; *b* 8 Sept. 1921; *s* of Vice-Adm. Sir Nicholas Edward Archdale, 2nd Bt, CBE, and Gerda (*d* 1969), 2nd *d* of late F. C. Sievers, Copenhagen; *S* father 1955; *m* 1954, Elizabeth Ann Stewart, *d* of late Maj-Gen. Wilfrid Boyd Fellowes Lukis, CBE; one *s* two *d*. *Educ:* Royal Naval Coll., Dartmouth. Joined Royal Navy, 1935; served War of 1939-45 (despatches, DSC). *Recreation:* civilization. *Heir:* s Nicholas Edward Archdale, *b* 2 Dec. 1965. *Address:* Hamilton House, Grafton Road, Winchester, Hants. *Club:* Naval.

ARCHER, Archibald, CMG 1961; grazier; company director; *b* 10 Jan. 1902; *s* of late Robert Stubbs Archer and Alice Manon Archer, Gracemere Station, Queensland; *m* 1930, Sarah Beatrice Cameron Crombie, *er d* of late Donald Charles Cameron Crombie and Mildred Ida Lloyd Crombie, Greenhills Station, Longreach, Qld; one *s* two *d*. *Educ:* Church of England Grammar Sch., Sydney, NSW, Australia. Land Consultant to Qld Govt, 1961-63. Dep. Chm., Picture Theatre and Films Commn, 1972-76 (Mem., 1957-76); Vice-Pres., Royal National Assoc., 1961- (Councillor, 1948-); President: Qld Chamber of Agricultural Societies, 1965-; Australian Agricl Socs, 1975-76 (Mem., 1970-); Qld Electoral Commn, 1971-72, 1977-; City of Brisbane, Electoral Wards Commn, 1972. Pres., Royal Geog. Soc. Qld, 1971-72, Fellow, 1972. *Address:* 23 Sefton Avenue, Clayfield, Queensland 4011, Australia. *Clubs:* Queensland (Brisbane); Australasian Pioneers (Sydney).

ARCHER, Lt-Gen. Sir (Arthur) John, KCB 1976; OBE 1964; Commander British Forces Hong Kong, 1976-78; Major-General, Brigade of Gurkhas, 1977-78; *b* 12 Feb. 1924; *s* of Alfred and Mildred Archer, Fakenham; *m* 1950, Cynthia Marie, *d* of Col Alexander and Eileen Allan, Swallowcliffe, Wilts; two *s*. *Educ:* King's Sch., Peterborough; St Catharine's Coll., Cambridge. Entered Army, 1943; commnd 1944; regular commn Dorset Regt, 1946; psc 1956; jssc 1959; GSO1 3rd Div., 1963-65; CO 1 Devon and Dorset Regt, 1965-67; Comdr Land Forces Gulf, 1968-69; idc 1970; Dir of Public Relations (Army), 1970-72; Comdr 2nd Div., 1972-74; Dir of Army Staff Duties, 1974-76. Lt-Col 1963; Brig. 1968; Maj.-Gen. 1972; Lt-Gen. 1976. Col, Devonshire and Dorset Regt, 1977-. *Recreations:* light aviation and gliding. *Address:* Grey Timbers, Silverdale Avenue, Walton-on-Thames, Surrey. *T:* Walton-on-Thames 24979. *Club:* Army and Navy.

ARCHER, Bruce; see Archer, L. B.

ARCHER, Sir Clyde Vernon Harcourt, Kt 1962; Judge of the Court of Appeal, Bahamas, 1971-75; *b* 12 Nov. 1904. *Educ:* Harrison Coll., Barbados; Cambridge Univ. Barrister-at-Law, Gray's Inn; clerk to the Attorney-General Barbados, 1930; police magistrate Barbados, 1935; Judge, Bridgetown Petty Debt Court, 1938; Legal Draftsman, Trinidad and Tobago, 1944; Solicitor-General, Trinidad and Tobago, 1953; Puisne Judge, Trinidad and Tobago, 1954; Chief Justice of the Windward Islands and Leeward Islands, 1958; a Federal Justice, WI, 1958-62. *Publication:* (jointly) Revised Edition of the Laws of Barbados, 1944. *Address:* Belleville, St Michael, Barbados.

ARCHER, Frank Joseph, RE 1960 (ARE 1940); RWS 1976 (ARWS 1972); ARCA 1937; Head of School of Fine Art, Kingston Polytechnic, Kingston upon Thames (formerly Kingston College of Art), 1962-73, retired; *b* 30 June 1912; *s* of Joseph and Alberta Archer; *m* 1939, Celia Cole; one *s* one *d*. *Educ:* Eastbourne Grammar Sch.; Eastbourne Sch. of Art; Royal Coll. of Art. ARCA 1937; Rome Scholar, Engraving, 1938; British Sch. at Rome, 1938. Paintings bought by numerous local authorities and private collectors. *Address:* Plaisance, Luxborough, Watchet, Som. *T:* Washford 708.

ARCHER, Maj.-Gen. Gilbert Thomas Lancelot, CB 1960; FRCPI; retired; *b* 6 April 1903; *s* of Gilbert Archer, Dublin, Ireland, and Kate Archer (*née* Lamb); *m* 1928, Catherine, *d* of Edward O'Malley, Louisburgh, Westport, Co. Mayo, Ireland; two *s* one *d*. *Educ:* St Andrews Coll., Dublin; Dublin Univ. (TCD). MB 1926; Lieut RAMC, 1928; Major, 1937; Deputy Asst Dir of Pathology, China Command, 1937-40; Asst Dir of Pathology, West Africa, 1943-45; Reader in Pathology, Royal Army Medical Coll., 1946-48; Asst Dir of Pathology, Middle East Land Forces, 1949-52; MRCPI, 1953; Officer Commanding David Bruce Laboratories, 1952-53; QHS 1953-61; Dir of Pathology and Consulting Pathologist to the Army, 1953-61; Brig., 1956; Major-General, 1958; FRCPI 1958. *Publications:* Articles on bacteriology, immunity, etc., in Jl of the RAMC, Brit. Med. Jl, etc. *Address:* 7 Nutley Avenue, Ballsbridge, Dublin, Eire.
See also *J . M . Archer*.

ARCHER, Mrs Jean Mary; Under-Secretary, Ministry of Agriculture, Fisheries and Food, since 1973; *b* 24 Aug. 1932; *e d* of late Reginald R. and D. Jane Harvey, Braiseworth Hall, Tannington, Suffolk; *m* 1954, G. Micheal D. Archer, MB, BChir, FFARCS, *er s* of Gen. G. T. L. Archer, *qv*; two *d*. *Educ:* Fleet House, Felixstowe; St Felix Sch., Southwold; Newnham Coll., Cambridge. MA Econs 1954. Asst Principal, Min. of Agriculture, 1954; Private Sec. to successive Perm. Secs, MAFF, 1956-59; Principal 1960; Sec., Reorganisation Commn for Eggs, 1967; Asst Sec. 1968; Under-Sec. i/c Food Policy Gp, MAFF, 1973; Under-Sec., Dept of Prices and Consumer Protection, 1974-76; returned to MAFF, as Under-Sec., Milk and Marketing Group, 1976. *Recreations:* travel, music, tennis, watching sport, swimming administration (Team Man., Chelsea/Kensington Swimming Club; Hon. Sec., Swimmers' Parents' and Supporters' Assoc.). *Address:* 51 Sussex Street, SW1. *T:* 01-828 6296; Friary Cottage, Mendlesham Suffolk. *T:* Mendlesham 395. *Club:* Hurlingham.
See also *A . J . D . McCowan*.

ARCHER, Jeffrey Howard; author and has-been politician; *b* 15 April 1940; *s* of William Archer and Lola Archer (*née* Cook); *m* 1966, Mary Weeden; two *s*. *Educ:* by his wife since leaving Wellington Sch., Somerset; Brasenose Coll., Oxford. Athletics Blues, 1963-65, Gymnastics Blue, 1965, Pres. OUAC 1965; ran for Great Britain (very slowly). Mem. GLC for Havering, 1966-70; MP (C) Louth, Dec. 1969-Sept. 1974. Mem. Exec., British Theatre Museum. Pres., Somerset AAA. FRSA 1973. *Publications:* Not a Penny More, 1975; Shall We Tell the President?, 1977. *Recreation:* theatre. *Address:* 93 Albert Embankment, SE1. *Clubs:* MCC; Louth Working Men's.

ARCHER, Sir John; *see* Archer, Sir A. J.

ARCHER, John Francis Ashweek, QC 1975; a Recorder of the Crown Court since 1974; *b* 9 July 1925; *s* of George Eric Archer, FRCSE, and Frances Archer (*née* Ashweek); *m* 1960, Doris Mary Hennessey. *Educ:* Winchester Coll., 1938-43; New Coll., Oxford, 1947-49 (BA 1949). Served War of 1939-45, 1944-47; Lieut RA, 1948. Called to Bar, Inner Temple, 1950. *Recreations:* motoring, bridge. *Address:* 22a Connaught Square, W2. *T:* 01-262 9406.

ARCHER, John Norman; Under-Secretary, Marine Division, Department of Trade, since 1974; *b* 27 Feb. 1921; *s* of Clifford Banks Archer and Grace Archer; *m* 1952, Gladys Joy (*née* Barnes); one step *d*. *Educ:* Wandsworth School. Served with RA, 1939-46 (Major). Entered Civil Service, Board of Educn, 1937; Asst Principal 1947, Principal 1949, Min. of Educn; attended Admin. Staff Coll., Henley, 1960; Asst Sec. (Joint Head, Architects and Buildings Br.), 1962; technical assistance assignments etc educn, Nigeria, Yugoslavia, Tunisia, 1961-63; Asst Sec., Treasury, O&M Div., 1964; Civil Service Department: Asst Sec., Management Services Development Div., 1968; Under-Sec., Management Services, 1970; Under-Sec., Marine Div., DTI, later Dept of Trade, 1972-. *Recreations:* lawn tennis, watching cricket. *Address:* 1 Dacre Court, Tite Street, SW3. *T:* 01-352 2898. *Clubs:* All England Lawn Tennis, Hurlingham, MCC.

ARCHER, Prof. (Leonard) Bruce, CBE 1976; DrRCA; CEng, MIMechE; Head of Department of Design Research, Royal College of Art, since 1968; Member of Design Council, since 1972; *b* 22 Nov. 1922; *s* of Leonard Castella Archer and Ivy Hilda Archer; *m* 1950, Joan Henrietta Allen; one *d*. *Educ:* Henry Thornton Sch., London; City Univ., London. MIED, ASIA(Ed). Served, Scots Guards, 1942-44. City Univ., 1945-50. Various posts in manufacturing industry, 1950-57; Lectr, Central Sch. of Art and Design, London, 1957-60; Guest Prof., Hochschule für Gestaltung, Ulm, 1960-61; Research Fellow,

later Prof., Royal Coll. of Art, 1961-. Various public appointments in design, educn and industrial and scientific policy, 1968-. *Publications:* varied, on the theory and practice of research, design, develt and educn. *Recreations:* music, the theatre. *Address:* 43 Avenue Road, N6 5DF. *T:* 01-340 2918.

ARCHER, Rt. Hon. Peter (Kingsley), PC 1977; QC 1971; MP (Lab) Warley West, since 1974 (Rowley Regis and Tipton, 1966-74); Solicitor General, since 1974; *b* 20 Nov. 1926; *s* of Cyril Kingsley Archer and May (*née* Baker); *m* 1954, Margaret Irene (*née* Smith); one *s*. *Educ:* Wednesbury Boys' High Sch.; LSE; University Coll., London. Called to Bar, Gray's Inn, 1952; Bencher, 1974; commenced practice, 1953. PPS to Attorney-Gen., 1967-70. UK Deleg. to UN Gen. Assembly (Third Cttee), 1969. Chm., Amnesty International (British Section), 1971-74; Chm., Parly Gp for World Govt, 1970-74; Chm., Soc. of Labour Lawyers, 1971-74; Vice-Chm., Anti-Slavery Soc., 1970-74; Mem., Exec. Cttee, Fabian Soc., 1974-. *Publications:* The Queen's Courts, 1956; ed Social Welfare and the Citizen, 1957; Communism and the Law, 1963; contrib. Trends in Social Welfare, 1965; contrib. Atkins, Court Forms, 1965; (with Lord Reay) Freedom at Stake, 1966; contrib. The International Protection of Human Rights, 1967; Human Rights, 1969; (jtly) Purpose in Socialism, 1973. *Recreations:* music, writing, talking. *Address:* Arvika, 44 Clements Road, Chorleywood, Herts. *T:* Chorleywood 3103.

ARCHER, William George, OBE 1947; MA; DLitt; Keeper Emeritus, Indian Section, Victoria and Albert Museum, since 1959; *b* 11 Feb. 1907; *s* of William Archer; *m* 1934, Mildred Bell; one *s* one *d*. *Educ:* Strand Sch.; Emmanuel Coll., Cambridge. Entered ICS, 1930; posted Bihar, 1931; District Magistrate, Purnea, 1938-39; Superintendent of Census Operations, Bihar, 1939-41; Dist Magistrate Patna, 1941-42; Dep. Comr, Santal Parganas, 1942-45; Special Officer, Santal Law, 1945-46; Addtl Dep. Comr, Naga Hills, 1946-48; retired ICS, 1948; Keeper, Indian Section, Victoria and Albert Museum, 1949-59; re-visited India, 1954, as lecturer (Indian Painting), Govt of India, British Council; research tours India, Ceylon, 1960, 1966, 1968, 1973, 1976; Vis. Lectr, USA, 1958, 1963, 1970. Editor, Man in India, 1942-49; Contrib. Editor, Marg, 1956-; Mem. Editorial Bd, Roopa Lekha, 1959-. Hon. DLitt Punjab Univ., Chandigarh, 1968; Hon. DLit Guru Narak Dev Univ., Amritsar, 1976. *Publications:* The Blue Grove, 1940; The Vertical Man, 1947; The Plains of the Sun, 1948; The Dove and the Leopard, 1948; Forty Thousand Years of Modern Art (with Robert Melville), 1948; Indian Painting in the Punjab Hills, 1952; Kangra Painting, 1952; Bazaar Paintings of Calcutta, 1953; Garhwal Painting, 1954; Indian Painting for the British (with Mildred Archer), 1955; Indian Painting, 1957; The Loves of Krishna, 1957; Indian Paintings from Rajasthan, 1957; Ceylon: Paintings from Temple, Shrine and Rock, 1958; Central Indian Painting, 1958; India and Modern Art, 1959; Indian Painting in Bundi and Kotah, 1960; Indian Miniatures, 1960; Kalighat Drawings, 1962; The Kama Sutra (ed), 1963; Love Songs of Vidyapati (jt), 1963; Kangra Paintings of the Gita Govinda (jt), 1964; The Rose Garden of Sa'di (ed), 1964; The Koka Shastra (preface), 1964; Paintings of the Sikhs, 1966; Rajput Miniatures, 1968; Kalighat Paintings, 1971; Indian Paintings from the Punjab Hills (2 vols), 1973; The Hill of Flutes, 1974; Pahari Miniatures: a concise history, 1975; Visions of Courtly India, 1976. *Recreations:* films, foreign travel. *Address:* 18 Provost Road, NW3 4ST. *T:* 01-722 2713.

ARCHER HOUBLON, Mrs Doreen, CVO 1969 (MVO 1954); *b* 1899; *d* of Lt-Col Walter Charles Lindsay, MVO, and Lady Kathleen Lindsay, OBE, *d* of 6th Earl of Carrick; *m* 1929, Major Richard Archer Houblon, DSO (*d* 1957); no *c*. Spent many years training and remaking horses with her father, and studying in depth the art of horsemanship and adapting it to the side saddle. Has lectured with films, and officiated as a judge at Internat. Horse Shows at Olympia, etc. Farms 300 acres organically and biodynamically. Member: Soil Assoc.; Bio-Dynamic Agric. Assoc. *Publication:* Side Saddle, 1938. *Address:* Kilmurry, Thomastown, Co. Kilkenny, Ireland. *T:* Kilkenny 24130. *Club:* English-Speaking Union.

ARCHIBALD, Barony of, *cr* 1949, of Woodside, Glasgow; title disclaimed by 2nd Baron; *see under* Archibald, George Christopher.

ARCHIBALD, George Christopher; Professor of Economics, University of British Columbia, since 1970; *b* 30 Dec. 1926; *s* of 1st Baron Archibald, CBE, and Dorothy Holroyd Edwards (*d* 1960); *S* father, 1975, as 2nd Baron Archibald, but disclaimed his peerage for life; *m* 1st, 1951, Liliana Barou (marr. diss. 1965); 2nd, 1971, Daphne May Vincent. *Educ:* Phillips Exeter Academy, USA; King's Coll., Cambridge (MA); London Sch. of

Economics (BSc Econ.). Served in Army, 1945-48, Captain RAEC. Formerly: Prof. of Economics, Univ. of Essex; Lectr in Economics, Otago Univ. and LSE; Leon Fellow, London Univ. *Publications:* (ed) Theory of the Firm, 1971; (with R. G. Lipsey) Introduction to a Mathematical Treatment of Economics, 1973. *Address:* c/o Department of Economics, University of British Columbia, Vancouver 8, BC, Canada

ARCHIBALD, Dr Harry Munro, CB 1976; MBE 1945; Deputy Chief Medical Officer (Deputy Secretary), Department of Health and Social Security, 1973-77; *b* 17 June 1915; *s* of James and Isabella Archibald; unmarried. *Educ:* Hillhead High Sch.; Univ. of Glasgow. MB, ChB 1938; DPH 1956. War Service: RAMC, 1940-43; IMS/IAMC, 1943-46; Lt-Col; Italian Campaign (despatches). Colonial Medical Service, Nigeria, 1946-62: Senior Specialist (Malariologist), 1958; Principal Med. Officer, Prevent. Services, N Nigeria, 1960; Med. Officer, Min. of Health, 1962; Sen. Med. Off., 1964; Principal Med. Off., DHSS, 1970; Sen. Principal Med. Off., 1972. Mem. Bd, Public Health Laboratory Service, 1975-. Fellow, Faculty of Community Medicine, 1973. *Recreation:* travel. *Address:* 1 Camborne House, Camborne Road, Sutton, Surrey. *T:* 01-643 1076. *Club:* Caledonian.

ARCHIBALD, James Montgomery, MBE 1945; JP; Chairman and Managing Director, James Archibald & Associates Ltd, since 1963; film producer, writer and director; *b* 3 April 1920; *s* of Brig. Gordon King Archibald, DSO, and Helen Archibald; *m* 1956, Sheila Elizabeth Maud Stafford; two *s*. *Educ:* Westminster Sch.; Merton Coll., Oxford (MA). Rep. Oxford Univ., Foil and Epée, 1939. Served War, 1939-45: Private 1939, Lt-Col 1944 (mentioned in despatches, 1943). Rank Org., 1950-56; Dir, J. Walter Thompson Ltd, 1956-63. Gen. Comr of Income Tax, St Martin's in the Fields, 1961; Chm. Comrs of Income Tax, St Martin's in the Fields and Charing Cross, 1974. Chairman: Nat. Music Council of GB; Arts Panel, Inst. of Dirs; Member: Exec. Cttee, Assoc. for Business Sponsorship of the Arts; BAFTA; Royal Television Soc.; Film Prodn Assoc. of GB; Council, Assoc. of Specialised Film Producers. Governor: BFI; Loughborough Coll. of Art and Design. Member: Ct, Worshipful Co. of Bowyers; Worshipful Co. of Musicians. JP Inner London, 1967. FRAI, FRSA, Hon. FTCL. 60 Internat. Awards for films. *Address:* 35 Morpeth Mansions, Morpeth Terrace, SW1P 1EU. *T:* 01-828 9691; 1 The Coastguards, Thorpeness, Leiston, Suffolk. *T:* Aldeburgh 2922. *Clubs:* Brooks's, Royal Thames Yacht; Myrmidon (Oxford).

ARCHIBALD, Liliana, Head of Division (Credit Insurance and Export Credit), Commission of the European Communities, since 1973; *b* 25 May 1928; *d* of late Noah and Sophie Barou; *m* 1951, George Christopher Archibald (marr. diss. 1965). *Educ:* Kingsley Sch.; Geneva University. Univ. Lectr, Otago Univ., 1952-55; Director: Const & Co. Ltd, 1955-73; Credit Consultants Ltd, 1957-73; Adam Brothers Contingency Ltd, 1970-. Member of Lloyd's, 1973-. *Publications:* (trans. and ed) Peter the Great, 1958; (trans. and ed) Rise of the Romanovs, 1970; contrib. Bankers Magazine. *Recreations:* driving fast cars, ski-ing, gardening. *Address:* 21 Langland Gardens, NW3 6QE.

ARCTIC, Bishop of The, since 1974; **Rt. Rev. John Reginald Sperry;** *b* 2 May 1924; *s* of William Reginald Sperry and Elsie Agnes (*née* Priest); *m* 1952, Elizabeth Maclaren; one *s* one *d* (and one *d* decd). *Educ:* St Augustine's Coll., Canterbury; King's Coll., Halifax (STh). Deacon, 1950; priest, 1951; St Andrew's Mission, Coppermine, NWT, 1950-69; Canon of All Saints' Cathedral, Aklavik, 1957-59; Archdeacon of Coppermine, 1959-69; Rector of St John's, Fort Smith, NWT, 1969-73; Rector of Holy Trinity, Yellowknife, NWT, 1974. Hon. DD Coll. of Emmanuel, St Chad, 1974. *Publications:* translations into Copper Eskimo: Canadian Book of Common Prayer (1962), 1969; Four Gospels and Acts of the Apostles, 1972. *Address:* PO Box 2009, Yellowknife, Northwest Territories, Canada. *T:* 403-873-4517.

ARCULUS, Ronald, CMG 1968; HM Diplomatic Service; Ambassador and Permanent Leader, UK Delegation to United Nations Conference on Law of the Sea, since 1977; *b* 11 Feb. 1923; *s* of late Cecil and of Ethel L. Arculus; *m* 1953, Sheila Mary Faux; one *s* one *d*. *Educ:* Solihull; Exeter Coll., Oxford (BA). 4th Queen's Own Hussars (now Queen's Royal Irish Hussars), 1942-45 (Capt.). Joined HM Diplomatic Service, 1947; FO, 1947; San Francisco, 1948; La Paz, 1950; FO, 1951; Ankara, 1953; FO, 1957; Washington, 1961; Counsellor, 1965; New York, 1965-68; IDC, 1969; Head of Science and Technology Dept, FCO, 1970-72; Minister (Economic), Paris, 1973-77. *Recreations:* travel, music and fine arts. *Address:* c/o Lloyds Bank Ltd, Guards and Cavalry Section, 6 Pall Mall, SW1. *Club:* Cavalry and Guards.

ARDAGH and CLONMACNOIS, Bishop of, (RC), since 1967; **Most Rev. Cahal Brendan Daly;** *b* 1917. *Educ:* St Malachy's, Belfast; Queen's Univ., Belfast (BA Hons, Classics, MA); St Patrick's, Maynooth (DD); Institut Catholique, Paris (LPh). Ordained, 1941. Lecturer in Scholastic Philosophy, Queen's Univ., Belfast, 1946-62; Reader, 1962-67; consecrated Bishop, 1967. *Publications:* Morals, Law and Life, 1962; Natural Law Morality Today, 1965; Violence in Ireland and Christian Conscience, 1973; chapters in: Prospect for Metaphysics, 1961; Intellect and Hope, 1968; New Essays in Religious Language, 1969; Understanding the Eucharist, 1969. *Address:* St Michael's, Longford, Ireland. *T:* Longford 6432.

ARDEE, Lord; John Anthony Brabazon; *b* 11 May 1941; *e s* of 14th Earl of Meath, *qv*; *m* 1973, Xenia Goudime; one *s* one *d*. *Educ:* Harrow. Page of Honour to the Queen, 1956-57. Served Grenadier Guards, 1959-62. *Heir:* s Hon. Anthony Jaques Brabazon, *b* 30 Jan. 1977. *Address:* Furnace House, Rathdrum, Co. Wicklow, Ireland.

ARDEN, Most Rev. Donald Seymour; *see* Central Africa, Archbishop of.

ARDEN, John; playwright; *b* 26 Oct. 1930; *s* of C. A. Arden and A. E. Layland; *m* 1957, Margaretta Ruth D'Arcy; four *s* (and one *s* decd). *Educ:* Sedbergh Sch.; King's Coll., Cambridge; Edinburgh Coll. of Art. Plays produced include: All Fall Down, 1955; The Life of Man, 1956; The Waters of Babylon, 1957; Live Like Pigs, 1958; Serjeant Musgrave's Dance, 1959; Soldier, Soldier, 1960; The Happy Haven, 1960; Wet Fish, 1962; The Workhouse Donkey, 1963; Ironhand, 1963; Armstrong's Last Goodnight, 1964; Left-Handed Liberty, 1965; The True History of Squire Jonathan and his Unfortunate Treasure, 1968; The Bagman, 1970; with Margaretta D'Arcy: The Business of Good Government, 1960; Ars Longa Vita Brevis, 1964; Friday's Hiding, 1966; The Royal Pardon, 1966; The Hero Rises Up, 1968; Island of the Mighty, 1972; The Ballygombeen Bequest, 1972; The Non-Stop Connolly Cycle, 1976. *Publication:* To Present the Pretence (essays), 1977. *Recreations:* antiquarianism, mythology. *Address:* c/o Margaret Ramsay Ltd, 14 Goodwin's Court, WC2.

ARDIZZONE, Edward Jeffrey Irving, CBE 1971; RA 1970 (ARA 1962); RDI 1974; Hon. ARCA; Artist; *b* 16 Oct. 1900; *s* of Auguste Ardizzone and Margaret Irving; *m* 1929, Catherine Berkley Anderson; two *s* one *d*. *Educ:* Claysmore Sch. Worked for 6 years for Eastern Telegraph Co.; studied art at Westminster and Central Schools of Art; Official War Artist, 1940-46; pictures purchased by Tate Gallery, Sheffield, Leeds and Liverpool Art Galleries and Contemporary Art Society. First retrospective exhibn, V&A Museum, 1973. *Publications:* Little Tim and the Brave Sea Captain, 1936; Lucy Brown and Mr Grimes, 1937; Tim and Lucy go to Sea, 1938; Baggage to the Enemy, 1941; Nicholas and the Fast Moving Diesel, 1947; Paul the Hero of the Fire, 1947; Tim to the Rescue, 1949; Tim and Charlotte, 1951; Tim in Danger, 1953; Tim All Alone, 1956 (Kate Greenaway medal of Library Association, for best illustrated children's book in 1956); Johnny the Clockmaker, 1960; Tim's Friend Towser, 1962; Peter the Wanderer, 1963; Diana and Her Rhinoceros, 1964; Tim and Ginger, 1965; Sarah and Simon and No Red Paint, 1965; Tim to the Lighthouse, 1968; Tim's Last Voyage, 1972; Ship's Cook Ginger, 1977; *illustrated:* more than 170 books which include: In a Glass Darkly, 1929; My Uncle Silas, 1939; The Local, 1939; Peacock Pie, 1947; The Poems of François Villon, 1947; The Pilgrim's Progress, 1947; The Blackbird in the Lilac, 1952; The Warden, 1952; The Little Bookroom, 1955; Henry Esmond, 1956; Ding Dong Bell, 1957; Titus in Trouble, 1959; More Prefabulous Animiles, 1975; contrib. Oxford Illustrated Old Testament, 1968; The Young Ardizzone: an autobiographical fragment, 1970; Diary of a War Artist, 1974. *Address:* 5 Vine Cottages, Rodmersham Green, Sittingbourne, Kent. *T:* Sittingbourne 71264.

ARDWICK, Baron *cr* 1970 (Life Peer), of Barnes; **John Cowburn Beavan;** Member of European Parliament, since 1975; *b* 1910; *s* of late Silas Beavan and Alderman Emily Beavan, JP; *m* 1934, Gladys (*née* Jones); one *d*. *Educ:* Manchester Grammar Sch. Blackpool Times, 1927; Evening Chronicle, Manchester, 1928; Manchester Evening News, 1930; London staff, Manchester Evening News, 1933; News Editor, Manchester Evening News, Manchester, 1936; Asst Editor, Londoner's Diary, Evening Standard, and leader writer, 1940; News Editor and Chief Sub, Observer, 1942; Editor, Manchester Evening News; Dir, Manchester Guardian and Evening News Ltd, 1943; London Editor, Manchester Guardian, 1946; Asst Dir, Nuffield Foundation, 1955; Editor, Daily Herald, 1960-62; Political Adviser to the Daily Mirror Group, 1962-76. Chm., Industrial

Sponsors, 1975-. Sec., British Cttee, Internat. Press Inst., 1972-76. *Address:* 10 Chester Close, SW13. *T:* 01-789 3490. *Clubs:* Garrick, Roehampton.

ARGENTINA AND EASTERN SOUTH AMERICA, Bishop in, since 1975; **Rt. Rev. Richard Stanley Cutts;** *b* 17 Sept. 1919; *s* of Edward Stanley and Gabrielle Cutts; *m* 1960, Irene Adela Sack; one *s* three *d*. *Educ:* Felsted School, Essex. Asst Curate, SS Peter and Paul, Godalming, 1951-56; Director of St Cyprian's Mission, Etalaneni and Priest-in-Charge Nkandhla Chapelry, Zululand, 1957-63; Director, Kambula Mission District, 1963-65; Rector, St Mary's, Kuruman and Director, Kuruman Mission District, 1965-71; Archdeacon of Kuruman, 1969-71; Dean of Salisbury, Rhodesia, 1971-75. *Address:* 25 de Mayo 282, Buenos Aires, Argentina.

ARGYLE, Major Michael Victor, MC 1945; QC 1961; **His Honour Judge Argyle;** a Circuit Judge (formerly an Additional Judge of the Central Criminal Court), since 1970; *b* 31 Aug. 1915; *e s* of late Harold Victor Argyle and Elsie Marion, Repton, Derbyshire; *m* 1951, Ann Norah, *d* of late Charles Newton, and of Mrs V. Jobson, Duffield, Nr Derby; three *d*. *Educ:* Shardlow Hall, Derbyshire; Westminster Sch.; Trinity Coll., Cambridge (MA). Served War of 1939-45: with 7th QO Hussars in India, ME and Italy (immediate MC), 1939-47. Called to Bar, Lincoln's Inn, 1938, Bencher, 1967; resumed practice at Bar, 1947 (Midland Circuit); Recorder of Northampton, 1962-65, of Birmingham, 1965-70; Dep. Chm., Holland QS, 1965-71; Lay Judge, Arches Court, Province of Canterbury, 1968-. General Elections, contested (C) Belper, 1950, and Loughborough, 1955. Mem. ABA Council. *Publications:* (ed) Phipson on Evidence, 10th edn. *Recreations:* chess, boxing. *Address:* The Red House, Fiskerton, near Southwell, Notts. *Clubs:* Carlton, Cavalry and Guards, Kennel, RAC; County (Derby); Abbey (Burton-upon-Trent); St Paul's (Birmingham).

ARGYLL, 12th Duke of, *cr* 1701 (Scotland), 1892 (UK); **Ian Campbell;** Marquess of Lorne and Kintyre; Earl of Campbell and Cowal; Viscount Lochow and Glenyla; Baron Inveraray, Mull, Morvern, and Tiry, 1701; Baron Campbell, 1445; Earl of Argyll, 1457; Baron Lorne, 1470; Baron Kintyre, 1633 (Scotland); Baron Sundridge, 1766; Baron Hamilton of Hameldon, 1776; Bt 1627; 36th Baron and 46th Knight of Lochow; Celtic title, Mac Cailein Mhor, Chief of Clan Campbell (from Sir Colin Campbell, knighted 1280); Hereditary Master of the Royal Household, Scotland; Hereditary High Sheriff of the County of Argyll; Admiral of the Western Coast and Isles; Keeper of the Great Seal of Scotland and of the Castles of Dunstaffnage, Dunoon, and Carrick and Tarbert; *b* 28 Aug. 1937; *e s* of 11th Duke of Argyll, TD, and Louise (*d* 1970), *o d* of Henry Clews; *S* father, 1973; *m* 1964, Iona Mary, *d* of Captain Sir Ivar Colquhoun, *qv*; one *s* one *d*. *Educ:* Le Rosey, Switzerland; Glenalmond; McGill Univ., Montreal. Captain (retd) Argyll and Sutherland Highlanders. Member, Queen's Body Guard for Scotland, the Royal Company of Archers. KStJ 1975. Heir: *s* Marquess of Lorne, *qv*. *Address:* Inveraray Castle, Inveraray, Argyll. *T:* Inveraray 2275; 81 Park Walk, SW10. *T:* 01-352 9581. *Clubs:* White's; New (Edinburgh).

ARGYLL AND THE ISLES, Bishop of, since 1977; **Rt. Rev. George Kennedy Buchanan Henderson,** MBE 1974; *b* 5 Dec. 1921; *s* of George Buchanan Henderson and Anna Kennedy Butters; *m* 1950, Isobel Fergusson Bowman. *Educ:* Oban High School; University of Durham (BA, LTh). Assistant Curate, Christ Church, Glasgow, 1943-48; Priest in Charge, St Bride's, Nether Lochaber, 1948-50; Chaplain to Bishop of Argyll and The Isles, 1948-50; Rector, St Andrew's, Fort William, 1950-77; Canon, St John's Cathedral, Oban, 1960; Synod Clerk, 1964-73; Dean of Argyll and The Isles, 1973-77. JP of Inverness-shire, 1963-; Hon. Sheriff, 1971-; Provost of Fort William, 1962-75; Hon. Burgess of Fort William, 1973. *Recreations:* reading, talking. *Address:* The Rectory, Fort William, Inverness-shire PH33 6BA.

ARGYLL AND THE ISLES, Bishop of, (RC), since 1968; **Rt. Rev. Colin MacPherson;** *b* Lochboisdale, South Uist, 5 Aug. 1917; *e s* of Malcolm MacPherson and Mary MacPherson (*née* MacMillan). *Educ:* Lochboisdale School; Daliburgh H. G. School; Blairs Coll., Aberdeen; Pontificium Athenæum Urbanum, Rome. Bachelor of Philosophy 1936; Bachelor of Theology 1938; Licentiate of Theology 1940 (Rome). Assistant Priest, St Columba's Cathedral, Oban, 1940-42. Parish Priest: Knoydart, 1942-51; Eriskay, 1951-56; Benbecula, 1956-66; Fort William, 1966-68. Hon. LLD, Univ. of St Francis Xavier, Canada, 1974. *Address:* Bishop's House, Esplanade, Oban, Argyll. *T:* Oban 2010.

ARGYRIS, Prof. John, DScEng, DE Munich; Professor of Aeronautical Structures in the University of London, at Imperial College of Science and Technology, 1955-75, Visiting Professor since 1975; Director of Institute for Statics and Dynamics, Stuttgart, since 1959; *b* 19 Aug. 1913; *s* of Nicolas and Lucie Argyris; *m* 1953, Inga-Lisa (*née* Johansson). *Educ:* 3rd Gymnasium, Athens; Technical Universities, Athens, Munich and Zurich. With J. Gollnow u. Son, Stettin, Research in Structures, 1937-39; Royal Aeronautical Soc., Research and Technical Officer, 1943-49; Univ. of London, Imperial Coll. of Science and Technology, Dept of Aeronautics: Senior Lecturer, 1949; Reader in Theory of Aeronautical Structures, 1950. Hon. FCGI; Hon. Dott Ing Genoa; Hon. dr.tech Trondheim. Von Kármán Medal, Amer. Soc. of Civil Engrs, 1975. Editor, Jl of Computer Methods in Applied Mechanics and Engineering, 1972-. *Publications:* Handbook of Aeronautics, Vol. I, 1952: Energy Theorems and Structural Analysis, 1960; Modern Fuselage Analysis and the Elastic Aircraft, 1963; Recent Advances in Matrix Methods of Structural Analysis, 1964; articles and publications in Ingenieur Archiv, Reports and Memoranda of Aeronautical Research Council, Journal of Royal Aeronautical Society and Aircraft Engineering, etc. *Recreations:* reading, music, hiking, archæology. *Address:* Imperial College, Prince Consort Road, SW7. *T:* 01-589 5111. *Club:* English-Speaking Union.

ARIAS, Dame Margot Fonteyn de, (Margot Fonteyn), DBE 1956 (CBE 1951); Prima Ballerina; President of the Royal Academy of Dancing, since 1954; *b* 18 May 1919; *m* 1955, Roberto E. Arias, *qv*. Hon. degrees: LittD Leeds; DMus London and Oxon; LLD Cantab; DLitt Manchester; LLD Edinburgh. Benjamin Franklin Medal, RSA, 1974; Internat. Artist Award, Philippines, 1976; Hamburg Internat. Shakespeare Prize, 1977. Order of Finnish Lion, 1960; Order of Estacio de Sa, Brazil, 1973; Chevalier, Order of Merit of Duarte, Sanchez and Mella, Dominican Republic, 1975. *Publication:* Margot Fonteyn, 1975. *Address:* c/o Royal Opera House, Covent Garden, WC2.

ARIAS, Roberto Emilio; *b* 1918; *s* of Harmodio Arias and Rosario Guardia de Arias; *m* 1955, Margot Fonteyn (*see* Dame Margot Fonteyn de Arias). *Educ:* Peddie Sch., New Jersey, USA; St John's Coll., Cambridge. Called to the Bar, Panama, 1939; Fifth Circuit, Court of Appeals, US, 1941; Editor, El Panama-America, 1942-46; Counsellor to Panama Embassy, Chile, 1947; Publisher, La Hora, since 1948; Delegate to UN Assembly, New York, 1953; Panamanian Ambassador to the Court of St James's, 1955-58, 1960-62; Elected Dep. to the Nat. Assembly of Panama, Oct. 1964-Sept. 1968. *Address:* Apartado 6399, Panama 5, Republic of Panama.

ARKELL, Rev. Anthony John, MBE 1928; MC 1918; DLitt; FSA; Vicar of Cuddington with Dinton, in the Diocese of Oxford, 1963-71; Reader in Egyptian Archæology, University of London, 1953-63; Curator of the Flinders Petrie Collection of Egyptian Antiquities at Univ. Coll., London, 1948-63; Hon. Asst Curate, Great Missenden, 1960-63; *b* Hinxhill, Kent, 29 July 1898; *s* of late Rev. John Norris Arkell and late Eleanor Jessy (*née* Bunting); *m* 1st, 1928, Dorothy (*d* 1945), *d* of late John Davidson; one *s* one *d*; 2nd, 1950, Joan Margaret Burnell, *d* of late Col Louis James Andrews, Indian Army. *Educ:* Bradfield Coll. (Schol.); Queen's Coll., Oxford (Jodrell Schol. in Classics). DLitt. (Oxon) 1955; Cuddesdon Coll.; deacon, 1960, priest, 1961. Served European War: RFC 1916-18; RAF 1918-19. Joined Sudan Political Service, 1920; Asst Dist Commr, Darfur Province, 1921-24; Actg Res., Dar Masalit, 1925-26; Dist Comr, Kosti (White Nile Province), 1926-29; Sennar (Blue Nile Province), 1929-32; Actg Dep.-Governor, Darfur Province, 1932-37; Comr for Archæology and Anthropology, Sudan Govt, 1938-48; Chief Transport Officer, Sudan Govt, 1940-44; Ed., Sudan Notes and Records, 1945-48; Archæological Adviser to Sudan Govt, 1948-53; Lecturer in Egyptology, Univ. Coll., London, 1948-53. British Ennedi Expedition, 1957. First Pres., Philosophical Soc. of Sudan, 1947 (Hon. Life Mem., 1949); Hon. Mem., German Archæological Inst., 1953; Mem. Council, Soc. of Antiquaries, 1956-57; Mem. Cttee Egypt Exploration Soc. Order of the Nile, 4th Class (Egypt), 1931. *Publications:* Early Khartoum, 1949; The Old Stone Age in the Anglo-Egyptian Sudan, 1949; Shaheinab, 1953; The History of the Sudan from the earliest times to 1821, 1955, 2nd rev. edn, 1961; Wanyanga, 1964; The Prehistory of the Nile Valley, 1975; articles in Enc. Britannica; numerous articles in Sudan Notes and Records and other learned jls. *Recreations:* travel, photography, natural history and gardening. *Address:* Cuddington, Colam Lane, Little Baddow, Chelmsford, Essex. *T:* Danbury 4221.

ARKELL, John Heward, CBE 1961; Director, The Boots Co. Ltd, since 1970; Chairman, Air Transport and Travel Industry Training Board, since 1970; Director, UK Provident Institution, since 1971; *b* 20 May 1909; *s* of Rev. H. H. Arkell, MA, and Gertrude Mary Arkell; *m* 1st, 1940, Helen Birgit Huitfeldt; two *s* one *d*; 2nd, 1956, Meta Bachke Grundtvig; one *s. Educ:* Dragon Sch.; Radley Coll.; Christ Church, Oxford (MA). Sir Max Michaelis (Investment) Trust, 1931-37. Asst Sec., CPRE, 1937-39, Mem. of Exec. Cttee, 1945-, Vice-Chm., 1967-74, Vice-Pres., 1975-. Commissioned Territorial Officer, KRRC 1939; served War of 1939-45; demobilised 1945, Major. Personnel Manager, J. Lyons, 1945-49; BBC: Controller, Staff Admin, 1949-58; Dir, Staff Admin, 1958-60; Dir of Admin, 1960-70; Lay Mem., Nat. Industrial Relations Ct, 1972-74. Lectr on indust. subjects; occasional indep. management consultancies include P&O and Coates Group of Cos (Dir, 1970-76). Exec. Pres., Christ Church (Oxford) United Clubs (Community Centre, SE London), 1932- (former Gen. Hon. Sec., and Chm.). Chm. Council, British Institute of Management, 1972-74 (Fellow, 1964-; Vice-Chm., 1966-72; Chm. Exec. Cttee, 1966-69); Chm. BIM/CBI Educl Panel, 1971-72; Member Council: CBI, 1973-75; Industry for Management Educn, 1971-; Foundn for Management Educn, 1971-75; National Trust, 1971-; Adv. Council, Business Graduates Assoc., 1973-; Action Resources Centre, 1975-; Chm., Cttee of British Council of Churches responsible for report on further educn of young people, 1960-61; Member: Finance Cttee, C of E Bd of Finance, 1960-68; CS Deptl Cttee to consider application of Fulton Report to Civil Service, 1968-70. Trustee, Visnews, 1960-69; Vis. Fellow, Administrative Staff Coll., 1971-; Governor, Radley Coll., 1965-70. FIPM; FRSA. *Publications:* contrib. to jls on management and indust. subjects. *Recreations:* walking, swimming, music. *Address:* Pinnocks, Fawley, near Henley-on-Thames, Oxon. *T:* Henley 3017; Glen Cottage, Ringstead Bay, Dorchester, Dorset. *T:* Warmwell 852686. *Clubs:* Savile; Leander.

ARKELL, Captain Sir (Thomas) Noël, Kt 1937; DL; Joint Managing Director of J. Arkell and Sons, Ltd, Swindon, Wiltshire; Local Director, Royal Insurance Group; *b* 25 Dec. 1893; 2nd *s* of James Arkell, Redlands Court, Highworth, Wilts, and Laura Jane Rixon; *m* 1919, Olive Arscott Quick, Tiverton, Devon; two *s* three *d* (and one *s* killed in action). *Educ:* Bradfield Coll. Joined 4th Wiltshire Regt (Territorials) in 1912 as 2nd Lieut; served European War in India, Mesopotamia and Palestine (thrice wounded); invalided with rank of Captain, 1919; Chm., Swindon Conservative Assoc., 1927-47, Pres. 1947-52; Chm. Wessex Provincial Area of Conservative Party, 1933-35; Mem. of National Executive Cttee of Conservative Party, 1933-38. DL 1945, High Sheriff 1953-54, Wilts. *Recreation:* fishing. *Address:* Hillcrest, Highworth, near Swindon, Wilts. *T:* Highworth 762 216.

ARKFELD, Most Rev. Leo; *see* Madang, Archbishop of, (RC).

ARLOTT, (Leslie Thomas) John, OBE 1970; cricket correspondent, wine correspondent and general writer, The Guardian; leader-writer, Hampshire Magazine; broadcaster; topographer; *b* Basingstoke, 25 Feb. 1914; *s* of late William John and Nellie Jenvey Arlott; *m* 1st, Dawn Rees; one *s* (and one *s* decd); 2nd, Valerie France (*d* 1976); one *s*; 3rd, 1977, Patricia Hoare. *Educ:* Queen Mary's Sch., Basingstoke. Clerk in Mental Hospital, 1930-34; Police (Detective), 1934-45; Producer, BBC, 1945-50; General Instructor, BBC Staff Training School, 1951-53. Contested (L) Epping Division, Gen. Election, 1955 and 1959. President: Cricketers' Assoc., 1968-; Hampshire Schools Cricket Assoc., 1966-. Hon. MA Southampton, 1973. *Publications:* (with G. R. Hamilton) Landmarks, 1943; Of Period and Place (poems), 1944; Clausentum (poems), 1945; First Time In America (anthology), 1949; Concerning Cricket, 1949; How to Watch Cricket, 1949; Maurice Tate, 1951; Concerning Soccer, 1952; (ed) Cricket (Pleasures of Life series), 1953; The Picture of Cricket, 1955; English Cheeses of the South and West, 1956; Jubilee History of Cricket, 1965; Vintage Summer, 1967; (with Sir Neville Cardus) The Noblest Game, 1969; Fred: portrait of a fast bowler, 1971; The Ashes, 1972; Island Camera: the Isles of Scilly in the photography of the Gibson family, 1973; The Snuff Shop, 1974; (ed) The Oxford Companion to Sports and Games, 1975; (with Christopher Fielden) Burgundy, Vines and Wines, 1976; Krug: House of Champagne, 1977; Jack Hobbs, 1977. *Recreations:* watching cricket, drinking wine, talking, sleeping, golf, collecting aquatints, engraved glass, and books about Gladstone. *Address:* c/o The Guardian, 119 Farringdon Road, EC1R 3ER. *Clubs:* National Liberal, MCC; Master's; Scillonian (Isles of Scilly); Forty, Hampshire CC.

ARMAGH, Archbishop of, and Primate of All Ireland, since 1969; **Most Rev. George Otto Simms,** DD; MRIA 1957; *b* 4 July 1910; 3rd *s* of John F. A. Simms, Crown Solicitor, County Tyrone, and Mrs Simms, Combermore, Lifford, County Donegal; *m* 1941, Mercy Felicia, *o d* of Brian James Gwynn, Temple Hill, Terenure, Dublin; three *s* two *d. Educ:* St Edmund's School, Hindhead; Cheltenham College; Trinity

College, Dublin; Scholar, 1930; Moderator in Classics, and History and Political Science, 1932; Berkeley Medallist; Vice-Chancellor's Latin Medallist; Theological Exhibnr. MA 1935; BD 1936; PhD 1950; DD (*jure dignitatis*, Dublin), 1952; DD (*hc* Huron), 1963; Deacon, 1935; Priest, 1936; Curate-asst, St Bartholomew's Church, Dublin, 1935-38; Chaplain Lincoln Theol. Coll., 1938-39; Dean of Residence, Trinity Coll., Dublin, 1939-52; Asst Lectr to Archbishop King's Prof. of Divinity, Dublin Univ., 1939-52; Chaplain-Secretary, Church of Ireland Training Coll., 1943-52; Hon. Clerical Vicar, Christ Church Cathedral, Dublin, 1937-52; Dean of Cork, 1952; Bishop of Cork, Cloyne, and Ross, 1952-56; Archbishop of Dublin and Primate of Ireland, 1956-69; also Bishop of Glendalough and Bishop of Kildare. Member Governing Body, University College, Cork, 1953-57; President, The Leprosy Mission, 1964-. *Publications:* joint-editor (with E. H. Alton and P. Meyer), The Book of Kells (fac. edn), Berne, 1951; For Better, for Worse, 1945; The Book of Kells: a short description, 1950; The Bible in Perspective, 1953; contributor, The Book of Durrow (fac. edn), 1960; Memoir of Michael Lloyd Ferrar, 1962; Christ within Me, 1975; articles in Hermathena, Theology, and Dublin Magazine, JTS; contrib. to New Divinity, Booklore. *Address:* The See House, Cathedral Close, Armagh BT60 7ES. *T:* Armagh 522851.

ARMAGH, Archbishop of, (RC), and Primate of All Ireland, since 1977; **Most Rev. Tomás Séamus O'Fiaich;** *b* Crossmaglen, 3 Nov. 1923; *s* of Patrick Fee and Annie Fee (*née* Caraher). *Educ:* Cregganduff Public Elem. School; St Patrick's Coll., Armagh; St Patrick's Coll., Maynooth; St Peter's Coll., Wexford; University Coll., Dublin; Catholic Univ. of Louvain. BA (Celtic Studies) 1943, MA (Early Irish History) 1950 (NUI); LicScHist 1952 (Louvain). Ordained, Wexford, 1948; Curate, Moy, Co. Tyrone, 1952-53; St Patrick's College, Maynooth: Lectr in Modern History, 1953-59; Prof. of Modern History, 1959-74; Pres., 1974-77. Chairman: Govt Commn on Restoration of the Irish Language, 1959-63; Irish Language Advisory Council, 1965-68; Pres., Soc. of Irish-speaking Priests, 1955-67; Treas., Catholic Record Soc. of Ireland, 1954-74; Editor, Jl of Armagh Historical Soc. and other jls. *Publications:* Gaelscrinte i gCéin, 1960; Irish Cultural Influence in Europe, 1967; Imeacht na nIarlai, 1972; Má Nuad, 1972; Art MacCumhaigh, 1973; St Columbanus in his own words, 1974; Oliver Plunkett: Ireland's New Saint, 1975. *Address:* Ara Coeli, Armagh, Ireland.

ARMAGH, Auxiliary Bishop of, (RC); *see* Lenny, Most Rev. Francis.

ARMAGH, Dean of; *see* Lillie, Very Rev. H. A.

ARMER, Sir (Isaac) Frederick, KBE 1954; CB 1945; MC 1918; *b* 1891; 2nd *s* of William and Gwenllian Armer; *m* 1925, Elsie Maude Neale; one *s* two *d. Educ:* University Coll., South Wales and Monmouth. BSc (Hons). Served European War, 1914-19. Entered Civil Service Sept. 1919 as Assistant Principal; Sec. Royal Commission on London Squares, 1928; Assistant Sec., 1938; Chm. Welsh Board of Health, 1940-44; Under Sec., Min. of Health, 1946, Dep. Sec., 1951-56; Chm., Board of Control, 1952-60. *Address:* Picketston Cottage, Flemingston, Barry, South Glam.

ARMIDALE, Bishop of, since 1976; **Rt. Rev. Peter Chiswell;** *b* 18 Feb. 1934; *s* of Ernest and Florence Ruth Chiswell; *m* 1960, Betty Marie Craik; two *s* one *d. Educ:* Univ. of New South Wales (BE); Moore Theological College (BD London, Th. Schol.). Vicar of Bingara, 1961-68; Vicar of Gunnedah, 1968-76; Archdeacon of Tamworth, 1971-76. *Address:* Bishopscourt, Armidale, NSW, Australia. *T:* 067-724555.

ARMITAGE, Sir Arthur (Llewellyn), Kt 1975; MA, LLB, LLD; Vice-Chancellor, and Professor of Common Law, Victoria University of Manchester, since 1970; *b* 1 Aug. 1916; *m* 1940, Joan Kenyon Marcroft; two *d. Educ:* Oldham Hulme Grammar Sch.; Queens' Coll., Cambridge. Law Tripos 1936; LLB 1937; Commonwealth Fund Fellow, Yale Univ., USA, 1937-39; called to the Bar, 1940, Inner Temple. Served Army, 1940-45, KRRC and 2nd Army, temp. Major. Fellow Queens' Coll., Cambridge, 1945-58; Asst Tutor, 1945; Tutor, 1946; Senior Tutor, 1957; President, 1958-70; Hon. Fellow, 1970. University Lectr in Law, 1947-70; Vice-Chancellor, Univ. of Cambridge, 1965-67, Dep. Vice-Chancellor, 1967-70. Dep. Chm. QS, Co. Huntingdon, 1963-65, Co. Huntingdon and Peterborough, 1965-71. Mem. and Chm., Wages Councils, 1955-70; Chairman: Trustee Savings Bank Arbitration Tribunal, 1964-; Cttee on Pay of Postmen, 1964; Adv. Cttee on Trng and Supply of Teachers, 1973-; British Cttee of Award of Commonwealth Fund, 1969-74; Cttee of Vice-Chancellors and Principals of Univs of UK, 1974-76; Cttee on

Political Activities of Civil Servants, 1976-; Member: Departmental Cttee on Summary Trial of Minor Offences, 1954-55; Chm.'s Panel Industrial Ct, 1962-; Agric. Wages Bd for England and Wales, 1967-72 (Chm., 1968-72); Nat. Adv. Council on Training of Magistrates, 1964-70; UGC, 1967-70; Lord Chancellor's Cttee on Legal Educn, 1967-71; UNESCO Adv. Mission for Develt of Univ. of W Indies, 1964-70; Standing Adv. Cttee on Grants to Students, 1961-65; Adv. Council on the Penal System, 1976-. Pres., Soc. of Public Teachers of Law, 1967-68; Trustee, Henry Fund, 1961-70; Chm. Governors, Leys Sch., Cambridge, 1971-. Hon. Bencher, Inner Temple. JP City of Cambridge, 1950-70. Hon. LLD Manchester, 1970. Order of Andrés Bello 1st Class (Venezuela), 1968. *Publications:* Case Book on Criminal Law (with J. W. C. Turner), 1952, 1958, 1964; Jt Editor Clerk and Lindsell on Torts, 1954, 1961, 1969, 1975. *Address:* The Firs, Manchester M14 6HE. *Club:* Athenæum.

ARMITAGE, Edward, CB 1974; Comptroller-General, Patent Office and Industrial Property and Copyright Department, Department of Trade (formerly Trade and Industry), 1969-77; *b* 16 July 1917; *s* of Harry and Florence Armitage; *m* 1940, Marjorie Pope; one *s* two *d*. *Educ:* Huddersfield Coll.; St Catharine's Coll., Cambridge. Patent Office, BoT: Asst Examr 1939; Examr 1944; Sen. Examr 1949; Principal Examr 1960; Suptg Examr 1962; Asst Comptroller 1966. Governor, Centre d'Études Internationales de la Propriété Industrielle, Strasbourg, 1975-. *Recreations:* tennis, bridge, gardening. *Address:* 218 Crofton Lane, Orpington, Kent. *T:* Orpington 28188.
See also Peter Armitage.

ARMITAGE, Maj.-Gen. Geoffrey Thomas Alexander, CBE 1968 (MBE 1945); Secretary, Country Landowners' Association Game Fair, since 1974; *b* 5 July 1917; *s* of late Lt-Col H. G. P. Armitage and late Mary Madeline (*née* Drought); *m* 1949, Monica Wall Kent (*widow, née* Poat); one *s* one step *d*. *Educ:* Haileybury Coll.; RMA, Woolwich (Sword of Honour). Commissioned Royal Artillery, 1937. Served War of 1939-45 (despatches, MBE), BEF, Middle East, Italy, NW Europe. Transferred to Royal Dragoons (1st Dragoons), 1951, comd 1956-59; Instructor (GSO1), IDC, 1959-60; Col GS, War Office, 1960-62; Comdt RAC Centre, 1962-65; Chief of Staff, HQ1 (BR) Corps, 1966-68; Dir, Royal Armoured Corps, 1968-70; GOC Northumbrian Dist, 1970-72; retd 1973. *Recreation:* field sports. *Address:* Clyffe, Tincleton, near Dorchester, Dorset. *Clubs:* Cavalry and Guards, Kennel.

ARMITAGE, Henry St John Basil, OBE 1968; HM Diplomatic Service; Consul General and Counsellor, Dubai, since 1974; *b* 5 May 1924; *s* of Henry John Armitage and late Amelia Eleanor Armitage; *m* 1956, Jennifer Gerda Bruford, *d* of Prof. W. H. Bruford, *qv*; one *s* one *d*. *Educ:* St Bede's and Bradford Grammar Schs; Lincoln Christ's Hosp.; Trinity Coll., Cambridge. Served Army, 1943-49; Arab Legion, 1946; British Mil. Mission to Saudi Arabia, 1946-49. Mil. Adviser to Saudi Arabian Minister of Defence, 1949-51; Desert Locust Control, Kenya and Aden Protectorates, 1952; in mil. service of Sultan of Muscat and Oman in Oman and Dhofar, 1952-59; Resident Manager, Gen. Geophysical Co. (Houston), Libya, 1959-60; Oil Conslt, Astor Associates, Libya, 1960-61; Business conslt, Beirut, 1962; joined HM Diplomatic Service, 1962; First Secretary (Commercial): Baghdad, 1963-67; Beirut, 1967-68; First Sec., Jedda, 1968 and 1969-74. *Recreations:* reading, travel. *Address:* c/o Foreign and Commonwealth Office, SW1. *Club:* Travellers'.

ARMITAGE, John; editor and bookseller; *b* 25 Sept. 1910; *s* of C. V. and C. C. Armitage, Lincoln; *m* 1934, Margaret Rosa, *y d* of W. G. Watkins; three *s*. *Educ:* Bedford Sch; Emmanuel Coll., Cambridge. Editor Rackets Publications Ltd, 1932-39; Asst Editor, The Fortnightly, 1937-39, Editor, 1939-54; RAF 1942, Educational Service, Squadron Leader, 1943-46; Times Educational Supplement, 1946-49; Editor, Encyclopædia Britannica Ltd, 1949-67. Councillor, Surbiton Borough Council, 1942-46; Chairman: Education Advisory Cttee, Liberal Party, 1948-56; The Norton Sch., 1964-76; Letchworth Adult Settlement. Pres. Rugby Fives Assoc., 1956-60; Dir, David's Bookshops (Letchworth) Ltd. *Publications:* A History of Ball Games and Rugby Fives (Lonsdale Library), 1934; To Christian England, 1942; Europe in Bondage, 1943; Our Children's Education, 1960; Man at Play, 1977; contributor to: Partnership in Education, 1948; The Unservile State, 1957; The Oxford Companion to Sports and Games, 1975; Man at Play, 1977; Times Lit. Supp., 1947-74; Encyc. Britannica, 14th and 15th edns. *Address:* 100 Wilbury Road, Letchworth, Herts.

ARMITAGE, Prof. John Vernon, PhD; Principal, College of St Hild and St Bede, Durham, since 1975; Special Professor, University of Nottingham, since 1976; *b* 21 May 1932; *s* of Horace Armitage and Evelyn (*née* Hauton); *m* 1963, Sarah Catherine Clay; two *s*. *Educ:* Rothwell Grammar Sch., Yorks; UCL (BSc, PhD); Cuddesdon Coll., Oxford. Asst Master: Pontefract High Sch., 1956-58; Shrewsbury Sch., 1958-59; Lectr in Maths, Univ. of Durham, 1959-67; Sen. Lectr in Maths, King's Coll., London, 1967-70; Prof. of Mathematical Educn, Univ. of Nottingham, 1970-75. Chm., Math. Instruction Sub-Cttee, Brit. Nat. Cttee for Maths, Royal Soc., 1975-. *Publications:* A Companion to Advanced Mathematics (with H. B. Griffiths), 1969; papers on theory of numbers in various jls. *Recreations:* railways, cricket and most games inexpertly. *Address:* The Principal's House, Leazes Lane, Durham DH1 1TA. *T:* Durham 3502.

ARMITAGE, Kenneth, CBE 1969; sculptor; *b* 18 July 1916; *m* 1940. Studied at Slade Sch., London, 1937-39. Served War of 1939-45 in the Army. Teacher of Sculpture, Bath Academy of Art, 1946-56. Regular one-man exhibitions, Gimpel Fils, London, since 1952, and New York since 1954, the last at Paul Rosenberg & Co., 1958; joined Marlborough Fine Art Ltd, London, 1959. Gregory Fellowship in sculpture, Leeds Univ., 1953-55; Guest Artist: Caracas, Venezuela, 1963; City of Berlin, 1967-69. Representations of work shown in: Exhibn of Recent Sculpture in British Pavilion at 26th Venice Biennale, 1952; Internat. Open-Air Exhibns of sculpture in Antwerp, London, Sonsbeek, Varese, and Sydney; British Council Exhibns of sculpture since 1952, which have toured Denmark, Germany, Holland, Norway, Sweden, Switzerland, Canada, USA, and S America; New Decade Exhibn, Museum of Modern Art, New York, 1955; British Section of 4th Internat. São Paulo Biennial, Brazil, 1957; 5th Internat. Exhibn of Drawings and Engravings, Lugano, 1958 (prize-winner); British Pavilion at 29th Venice Biennale, 1958; Art since 1945, Kassel Exhibition, 1959; work in British Sculpture in the 'Sixties' exhibition, Tate Gallery, 1965. Work represented in: Victoria and Albert Museum, Tate Gallery; Museum of Modern Art, Brooklyn Museum, New York; Musée D'Art Moderne, Paris; Galleria Nazionale d' Arti Moderne, Rome, etc. *Address:* 22a Avonmore Road, W14. *T:* 01-603 5800.

ARMITAGE, Prof. Peter; Professor of Biomathematics, and Fellow, St Peter's College, University of Oxford, since 1976; *b* 15 June 1924; *s* of Harry and Florence Armitage, Huddersfield; *m* 1947, Phyllis Enid Perry, London: one *s* two *d*. *Educ:* Huddersfield Coll.; Trinity Coll., Cambridge. Wrangler, 1947; MA Cambridge, 1952; PhD London, 1951; Ministry of Supply, 1943-45; National Physical Laboratory, 1945-46; Mem. Statistical Research Unit of Med. Research Council, London Sch. of Hygiene and Trop. Med., 1947-61; Prof. of Medical Statistics, Univ. of London, 1961-76. Hon. Sec., Royal Statistical Society, 1958-64; Pres., Biometric Soc., 1972-73; Mem., International Statistical Institute, 1961. *Publications:* Sequential Medical Trials, 1960, 2nd edn 1975; Statistical Methods in Medical Research, 1971; papers in statistical and medical journals. *Recreation:* music. *Address:* 71 High Street, Drayton, Abingdon, Oxon OX14 4JW. *T:* Drayton 763.
See also Edward Armitage.

ARMITAGE, Sir Robert (Perceval), KCMG 1954 (CMG 1951); MBE 1944; MA; *b* 21 Dec. 1906; *s* of late F. Armitage, CIE; *m* 1930, Gwladys Lyona, *d* of late Lt-Col H. M. Meyler, CBE, DSO, MC, Croix de Guerre; two *s*. *Educ:* Winchester; New Coll. District Officer, Kenya Colony, 1929; Sec. to Mem. for Agriculture and Natural Resources, 1945; Administrative Sec., 1947; Under Sec., Gold Coast, 1948; Financial Sec., 1948; Min. for Finance, Gold Coast, 1951-53; Governor and C-in-C, Cyprus, 1954-55; Governor of Nyasaland, 1956-61, retired. Trustee of the Beit Trust, 1963-. Mem., St John Council for Dorset, 1962-. KStJ 1954. *Recreations:* golf and gardening. *Address:* South Well, Marnhull, Sturminster Newton, Dorset. *T:* Marnhull 294. *Club:* Royal Commonwealth Society.

ARMITAGE, (William) Kenneth; see Armitage, Kenneth.

ARMOUR, Mary Nicol Neill, RSA 1958 (ARSA 1940); RSW 1956; Teacher of Still Life, Glasgow School of Art, 1952-62, retd; *b* 27 March 1902; *d* of William Steel; *m* 1927, William Armour, *qv. Educ:* Glasgow Sch. of Art. Has exhibited at Royal Academy, Royal Scottish Academy, Soc. of Scottish Artists, and Royal Glasgow Institute. Work in permanent collections: Glasgow Municipal Gallery; Edinburgh Corporation; Art Galleries of Aberdeen, Perth, Dundee, Newport, Paisley, Greenock and Victoria (Australia). *Recreations:* weaving, gardening. *Address:* 2 Gateside, Kilbarchan, Renfrewshire. *T:* Kilbarchan 2873.

ARMOUR, William, RSA 1966 (ARSA 1958); RSW; painter; formerly Head of Drawing and Painting, School of Art, Glasgow, retired; *b* 1903; *s* of Hugh T. Armour; *m* 1927, Mary Nicol Neill (*see* M. N. N. Armour), *d* of William Steel. *Educ:* Camphill Sch., Paisley. Has exhibited: RSA, RSW, etc. *Address:* Kilbarchan, Renfrewshire. *Club:* Glasgow Art.

ARMSTRONG, family name of **Baron Armstrong of Sanderstead.**

ARMSTRONG, 3rd Baron *cr* 1903, of Bamburgh and Cragside; **William Henry Cecil John Robin Watson-Armstrong;** *b* 6 March 1919; *s* of 2nd Baron Armstrong and Zaida Cecile, *e d* of Cecil Drummond-Wolff; *S* father, 1972; *m* 1947, Baroness Maria-Teresa du Four Chiodelli Manzoni, *o c* of late Mme Ruegger (*see* Paul J. Ruegger); one adopted *s* one adopted *d*. *Educ:* Eton; Trinity College, Cambridge. An Underwriting Member of Lloyd's. Served War of 1939-45, Captain Scots Guards. *Heir:* none. *Address:* 237 Knightsbridge, SW7; Bamburgh Castle, Northumberland.

ARMSTRONG OF SANDERSTEAD, Baron *cr* 1975 (Life Peer), of the City of Westminster; **William Armstrong**, PC 1973; GCB 1968 (KCB 1963; CB 1957); MVO 1945; Chairman: The Midland Bank, since 1975; Midland and International Banks Ltd, since 1976; *b* 3 March 1915; *s* of William Armstrong, Stirling, Scotland; *m* 1942, Gwendoline Enid Bennett; one *s* one *d*. *Educ:* Bec Sch., London; Exeter Coll., Oxford. Asst Principal, Board of Educn, 1938; Asst Private Sec. to Pres. of Board of Educn, 1940; Private Sec. to Sec. of War Cabinet, 1943-46; Prin. Private Sec. to successive Chancellors of the Exchequer, 1949-53; Under-Sec., Overseas Finance Div., HM Treasury, 1953-57, and Home Finance Div., 1957-58; Third Sec. and Treasury Officer of Accounts, 1958-62; Jt Permanent Sec., 1962-68; Permanent Sec., Civil Service Dept, and Official Head of Home CS, 1968-74. Dep. Chm., Cttee of London Clearing Bankers, 1976-77. Hon. Fellow, Exeter Coll., Oxford, 1963; Visiting Fellow, Nuffield Coll., Oxford, 1964-72; Fellow, Imperial Coll. of Science and Technology, 1977. Pres., Manpower Soc., 1970-73. Member: Governing Body, London Business Sch., 1970-74; Council, Manchester Business Sch., 1970-74; Council, Oxford Centre for Management Studies, 1970-. Trustee: Wellcome Trust, 1974; Civic Trust, 1975. Hon. Liveryman, Salters' Co., 1974. Hon. DCL Oxford, 1971; Hon. DLitt: City Univ., 1974; Heriot-Watt, 1975; DUniv Open Univ., 1974; Hon. degrees also from: Cranfield Inst of Technol., 1975; Sheffield Univ., 1975. *Recreations:* reading, walking, talking. *Address:* 143 Whitehall Court, SW1A 2EP. *Club:* Athenæum.

ARMSTRONG, Andrew Clarence Francis, CMG 1959; Permanent Secretary, Ministry of Mines and Power, Federation of Nigeria, retired; *b* 1 May 1907; *s* of E. R. C. Armstrong, FSA, MRIA, Keeper of Irish Antiquities and later Bluemantle Pursuivant, Herald's Coll., and Mary Frances, *d* of Sir Francis Cruise; *cousin and heir-pres.* to Sir Andrew St Clare Armstrong, 5th Bt, *qv; m* 1st, 1930, Phyllis Marguerite (*d* 1930), *e d* of Lt-Col H. Waithman, DSO; 2nd, 1932, Laurel May, *d* of late A. W. Stuart; one *s* (and one *s* decd). *Educ:* St Edmund's Coll., Old Hall, Ware; Christ's Coll., Cambridge; BA. Colonial Administrative Service: Western Pacific, 1929; Nigeria, 1940. *Recreation:* golf. *Address:* Fernacre, Little Marlow, Bucks. *T:* Bourne End 22784.

ARMSTRONG, Sir Andrew St Clare, 5th Bt *cr* 1841; *b* 20 Dec. 1912; *s* of Sir Nesbitt William Armstrong, 4th Bt, and Clarice Amy, *d* of John Carter Hodkinson, Maryborough, Victoria, Australia; *S* father 1953. *Educ:* Waitaki; Wellesley Coll. Served War of 1939-45 with RAE, 2nd AIF. *Heir: cousin* Andrew Clarence Francis Armstrong, *qv.*

ARMSTRONG, Anne Legendre; Member, Board of Directors, General Motors, since 1977; *b* New Orleans, Louisiana, 27 Dec. 1927; *d* of Armant Legendre and Olive Martindale; *m* 1950, Tobin Armstrong; three *s* two *d*. *Educ:* Foxcroft Sch., Middleburg, Va; Vassar Coll., NY (BA). Dep. Vice-Chm., Texas Repub. Party, 1958-61 and State Vice-Chm., 1965-66; Deleg. Nat. Conventions, 1964, 1968 and 1972; Mem. Republican Cttee, 1968-73 (Co-Chm., 1971-72); Counselor to the President, with Cabinet rank, 1972-74; while Presidential Counselor, served as Head of Bicentennial Coordinators at White House; Ambassador to the Court of St James's, 1976-77; Member: Domestic Council; Council on Wage and Price Stability; Feceral Property Council (Chm.); US Delegn, World Food Conference, Rome; US Delegn, Internat. Women's Year Conf., Mexico City; Commn on Org. of Govt for the Conduct of Foreign Policy. Trustee, Kennedy County Sch. Bd, 1968-74. Founder, Office for Women's Programs at White House. Phi Beta Kappa. *Address:* Armstrong Ranch, Armstrong, Texas 78338, USA.

ARMSTRONG, Prof. Arthur Hilary, MA Cantab; FBA 1970; Emeritus Professor, University of Liverpool, since 1972; Visiting Professor of Classics and Philosophy, Dalhousie University, Halifax, Nova Scotia, since 1972; *b* 13 Aug. 1909; *s* of the Rev. W. A. Armstrong and Mrs E. M. Armstrong (*née* Cripps); *m* 1933, Deborah, *d* of Alfred Wilson and Agnes Claudia Fox Pease; two *s* two *d* (and one *d* decd). *Educ:* Lancing Coll.; Jesus Coll., Cambridge. Asst Lectr in Classics, University Coll., Swansea, 1936-39; Professor of Classics, Royal University of Malta, Valletta, 1939-43; Classical VIth Form Master, Beaumont Coll., Old Windsor, Berks, 1943-46; Lectr in Latin, University Coll., Cardiff, 1946-50; Gladstone Professor of Greek, Univ. of Liverpool, 1950-72. Killam Sen. Fellow, Dalhousie Univ., 1970-71. *Publications:* The Architecture of the Intelligible Universe in the Philosophy of Plotinus, 1940, repr. 1967; An Introduction to Ancient Philosophy, 1947 (American edn, 1949, 4th edn, 1965); Plotinus, 1953 (American edn, 1963); Christian Faith and Greek Philosophy (with R. A. Markus), 1960 (American edn, 1964); Plotinus I-III (Loeb Classical Library), 1966-67; Cambridge History of Later Greek and Early Mediæval Philosophy (Editor and part author), 1967, repr. 1970; St Augustine and Christian Platonism, 1968. Has contributed to Classical Qly, Mind, Jl Hellenic Studies, Jl Theological Studies, Downside Review, etc. *Recreations:* travel, gardening. *Address:* The Hollins, Whitton, near Ludlow, Salop SY8 3AE. *T:* Cleehillstone 241.

ARMSTRONG, Brig. Charles Douglas, CBE 1945; DSO 1940; MC 1919; late East Surrey Regiment; *b* 11 June 1897; *s* of late C. F. Armstrong, Kitale, Kenya Colony; *m* 1935, Sylvia Holden Earl Bailey; one *s* three *d*. *Educ:* Cheltenham Coll.; RMC, Sandhurst. Served European War (wounded twice, MC); France, 1916-18; North Russia, Mesopotamia, 1920-21; NWF India, 1930-31; War of 1939-45 (wounded twice, DSO, Africa Star, CBE): France, 1939-40; N Africa, 1943; Jugoslavia, 1943-44. Retired 1948. *Address:* Rushetts, Old Green Lane, Camberley, Surrey GU15 4LG. *T:* Camberley 21028. *Club:* Special Forces.

ARMSTRONG, Christopher Wyborne, OBE 1943; farming in Kenya since 1959; *b* 9 May 1899; *s* of Rt Hon. H. B. Armstrong, Dean's Hill, Armagh; *m* 1956, Hilde Ingeburg Kolz, Lübeck; one *s* one *d*. *Educ:* Winchester; Trinity Coll., Cambridge (MA). Lieutenant RFA, BEF, France, 1918; Burmah Oil Co., Burma, 1922-39; Royal Engineers, BEF, France, 1939-40; Burmah Oil Co., Burma, 1940-42; Member, House of Representatives, Burma, 1942; Controller of Petroleum Industry, Burma, 1942; AQMG, MEF, Egypt, 1942-43; GHQ, India, 1944-45; Commissioner, Magwe Division, Burma, 1945-46; farming in Kenya, 1947-54 and 1959-. MP (UU) Co. Armagh, 1954-59. *Address:* Kwetu Farm, Gilgil, Kenya. *Clubs:* Carlton, United Oxford & Cambridge University.

ARMSTRONG, Rev. Canon Claude Blakeley, MA, BD; Canon residentiary of Worcester, 1947-70, Canon Emeritus 1970; Vice-Dean and Treasurer, 1965-70; *b* 31 Oct. 1889; *e s* of late Rev. J. B. Armstrong, MA; *m* 1914, Hester (*d* 1968), *d* of late Sir Samuel Dill, LittD; one *d*. *Educ:* St Stephen's Green School and Trinity Coll., Dublin (First Classical Scholar). Senior Moderator in Classics and Philosophy; Fellowship prizeman; Vice-Chancellor's prizeman and Medallist. Lieut, OTC, 1914-18; Observer Officer, ROC, 1940-45. Deputy for the Professor of Greek, Queen's Univ. Belfast, 1913-14; Headmaster of Cork Grammar Sch., 1914-19; Warden of St Columba's Coll., Rathfarnham, 1920-33; Headmaster of St Andrew's Coll., Grahamstown, SA, 1934-38; Rector of Clannaborough, near Exeter, 1940-43; Rector of Clyst St George, 1943-47; Lectr in Classics, University Coll. of the South-West, Exeter, 1940-47. Pres. Irish Schoolmasters Assoc., 1929; Pres. Exeter Clerical Soc., 1942; Vice-Pres. Classical Assoc. (Chm. Council). Examining Chaplain to the Bishop of Worcester, and Director of Training, 1948; Warden, Worcester Ordination Coll., 1952-64; Founder, Worcester Ordination Coll., 1965. Editor, Veritas (for Anglican Assoc.). *Publications:* The Persians of Aeschylus translated into English verse; Outline of Western Philosophy, 1964; Foundations Unshaken, 1966; Creeds and Credibility, 1969; contributor to Reviews and Punch; Editor Sir S. Dill's Roman Society in Gaul in the Merovingian Age. *Address:* 12a College Green, Worcester. *T:* Worcester 25837. *Club:* Kildare Street and University (Dublin).

ARMSTRONG, Ernest; MP (Lab) North West Durham since 1964; Parliamentary Under-Secretary of State, Department of the Environment, since 1975; *b* 12 Jan. 1915; *s* of John and Elizabeth Armstrong; *m* 1941, Hannah P. Lamb; one *s* one *d*. *Educ:* Wolsingham Grammar Sch. Schoolmaster, 1937-52; Headmaster, 1952-64. Chm., Sunderland Educn Cttee, 1960-65. Asst Govt Whip, 1967-69; Lord Comr, HM Treasury, 1969-70;

an Opposition Whip, 1970-73; Parly Under-Sec. of State, DES, 1974-75. Vice-Pres., Methodist Conf., 1974-75. *Recreation:* walking. *Address:* Penny Well, Witton-le-Wear, Bishop Auckland, Co. Durham. *T:* Witton-le-Wear 397.

ARMSTRONG, Francis William, CB 1977; MVO 1953; *b* 11 July 1919; *s* of late W. T. Armstrong, Gravesend, Kent; *m* 1st, 1945, Brenda Gladys de Wardt (*d* 1967); one *d*; 2nd, 1969, Muriel Ernestine Hockaday, MBE. *Educ:* King's Sch., Rochester; Brasenose Coll., Oxford (Open Scholarship in Classics) (MA). Served War of 1939-45: RA (commissioned, 1940); Western Desert, India, Burma. Asst Principal, War Office, 1947; Private Sec. to Permanent Under-Sec., War Office, 1948-50; Principal Private Sec. to Sec. of State for War, 1957-60; Director of Finance, Metropolitan Police, 1968-69; Asst Under-Sec. of State, MoD, 1969-72; Under Sec., Cabinet Office, 1972-74; Dep. Sec., N Ireland Office, 1974-75; Dep. Sec., MoD, 1975-77, retired 1977. *Recreations:* walking, cricket, reading. *Address:* 50 Nork Way, Banstead, Surrey. *T:* Burgh Heath 54602. *Clubs:* Royal Commonwealth Society, Kent CCC.

ARMSTRONG, Rt. Rev. John, CB 1962; OBE 1942; Assistant Bishop in the Diocese of Exeter; *b* 4 Oct. 1905; *y s* of late John George and Emily Armstrong; *m* 1942, Diana Gwladys Prowse, *widow* of Lieut Geoffrey Vernon Prowse, and 2nd *d* of late Admiral Sir Geoffrey Layton, GBE, KCB, KCMG, DSO; one step *s. Educ:* Durham School and St Francis Coll., Nundah, Brisbane, Qld. LTh, 2nd Class Hons, Australian College of Theology, 1932. Ordained 1933; Mem. Community of Ascension, Goulburn, 1932-33; Curate, St Martin, Scarborough, 1933-35; Chaplain RN, HMS Victory, 1935; Courageous, 1936-39; 6th Destroyer Flotilla, 1939-41 (despatches 1940); RM Div., 1941-43; Commando Group, 1943-45; HMS Nelson, 1945; Sen. Naval Chaplain, Germany, 1946-48; Excellent, 1948-50; RM Barracks, Portsmouth, 1950-53; Indomitable, 1953; RN Rhine Sqdn, 1953-54; HMS Vanguard, 1954; Tyne, 1954; HM Dockyard, Malta, and Asst to Chaplain of the Fleet, Mediterranean, 1955-57; HMS Bermuda, 1957-59; RM Barracks, Portsmouth, 1959-60; Chaplain of the Fleet and Archdeacon of the Royal Navy, 1960-63; Bishop of Bermuda, 1963-68; Vicar of Yarcombe, Honiton, 1969-73. QHC, 1958-63. Life Mem., Guild of Freemen of City of London. *Address:* Foundry Farm, Yarcombe, Honiton EX14 9AZ. *T:* Chard 3332. *Club:* Naval and Military.

ARMSTRONG, John Anderson, OBE 1945, TD 1945; Master of the Court of Protection since 1970; *b* 5 May 1910; *s* of W. A. Armstrong; *m* 1938, Barbara, *d* of Rev. W. L. Gantz; two *d* (and one *s* decd). *Educ:* Wellington Coll.; Trinity Coll., Cambridge. BA 1931, MA 1943. Called to Bar, Lincoln's Inn, 1936. City of London Yeomanry, RHA(T), 1931-40. Served War: Lt-Col Comdg 73 Light AA Regt, 1940-45 (Normandy, 1944). Practice at Chancery Bar, 1946-70; Bencher, Lincoln's Inn, 1969. *Recreations:* gardening, walking, fishing, golf. *Address:* 62 Chelsea Park Gardens, SW3 6AE. *T:* 01-352 0369. *Club:* Brooks's.

ARMSTRONG, Rt. Rev. John Ward; *see* Cashel, Waterford and Lismore, Ossory, Ferns and Leighlin, Bishop of.

ARMSTRONG, Rt. Rev. Mervyn, OBE 1946; Adviser on Industry to the Archbishop of York, and Assistant Bishop of York, 1964-70, retired; *b* 10 Mar. 1906; *o s* of Rev. Evan Armstrong and Sarah Armstrong; *m* 1st, 1933, Charlotte Stewart (*d* 1961), *y d* of Rev. A. Irvine-Robertson, DD, Clackmannan; 2nd, 1963, Mrs Barbara Newborn, *widow* of G. R. Newborn, Epworth. *Educ:* Balliol Coll., Oxford. In business in China, 1928-37; ordained 1938; served War of 1939-45 as Chaplain, RNVR, 1940-43; Adviser on Seamen's Welfare, Min. of War Transport and Dir of Seamen's Welfare, Govt of India, 1944-45; Vicar of Margate, 1946-49; Chaplain to Archbishop of Canterbury, 1949-51; Archdeacon of Stow and Rector of Epworth and of Wroot, 1951-54; Provost of Leicester, 1954-58; Bishop Suffragan of Jarrow, 1958-64. *Address:* Glen Brathay, Skelwith Fold, Ambleside, Cumbria LA22 0HT. *T:* Ambleside 3249.

ARMSTRONG, Prof. Neil A.; NASA Astronaut; Commander, Apollo 11 rocket flight to the Moon; first man to step onto the Moon, 20 July 1969 (Edwin Aldrin being the second); University Professor of Aerospace Engineering, University of Cincinnati, since 1972; *b* Wapakoneta, Ohio, USA, 5 Aug. 1930; *s* of Stephen and Viola Armstrong, Wapakoneta; *m* 1956, Janet Shearon, Evanston, Ill, *d* of Mrs Louise Shearon, Pasadena, Calif; two *s. Educ:* High Sch., Wapakoneta, Ohio; Univ. of Southern California (MS); Purdue Univ. (BSc). Pilot's licence obtained at age of 16. Served in Korea (78 combat missions) being a naval aviator, 1949-52. He joined NASA's Lewis Research Center, 1955 (then NACA Lewis Flight Propulsion Lab.) and later transf. to NASA High Speed Flight Station (now Flight Research Center) at Edwards Air Force Base, Calif, as an aeronautical research pilot for NACA and NASA; in this capacity, he performed as an X-15 project pilot, flying that aircraft to over 200,000 feet and approximately 4,000 miles per hour; other flight test work included piloting the X-1 rocket airplane, the F-100, F-101, F-102, F-104, F5D, B-47, the paraglider, and others; as pilot of the B-29 "drop" aircraft, he participated in the launches of over 100 rocket airplane flights. Selected as an astronaut by NASA, Sept. 1962; served as backup Command Pilot for Gemini 5 flight; as Command Pilot for Gemini 8 mission, launched 16 March 1966; he performed the first successful docking of 2 vehicles in space; served as backup Command Pilot for Gemini 11 mission; assigned as backup Comdr for Apollo VIII Flight, 1969; Dep. Associate Administrator of Aeronautics, Space HQ, Washington, 1970-71. Fellow, Soc. of Experimental Test Pilots; FRAeS. Honours include NASA Exceptional Service Medal, and AIAA Astronautics Award for 1966; RGS Gold Medal, 1970. Presidential Medal for Freedom, 1969. *Recreation:* soaring (FAI gold badge). *Address:* College of Engineering, University of Cincinnati, Cincinnati, Ohio 45221, USA.

ARMSTRONG, Robert George, CBE 1972; MC 1946; TD 1958; Deputy Director and Controller, Savings Bank, Department for National Savings, 1969-74, retired (Deputy Director and Controller, Post Office Savings Bank, 1964); *b* 26 Oct. 1913; *s* of late George William Armstrong; *m* 1947, Clara Christine Hyde; one *s* one *d. Educ:* Marylebone Grammar Sch.; University Coll., London. Post Office Engineering Dept, 1936-50. Served War of 1939-45, Royal Signals. Principal, PO Headquarters, 1950; Asst Sec., 1962; Dep. Dir of Savings, 1963; Under-Sec., 1972. *Address:* Barryleigh, Wheelers Lane, Brockham, Betchworth, Surrey. *T:* Betchworth 3217.

ARMSTRONG, Robert Temple, CB 1974; CVO 1975; Permanent Under Secretary of State, Home Office, since 1977; *b* 30 March 1927; *o s* of Sir Thomas (Henry Wait) Armstrong, *qv*; *m* 1953, Serena Mary Benedicta, *er d* of Sir Roger Chance, 3rd Bt, *qv*; two *d. Educ:* Dragon Sch., Oxford; Eton; Christ Church, Oxford. Asst Principal, Treasury, 1950-55; Private Secretary to: Rt Hon. Reginald Maudling, MP (when Economic Sec. to Treasury), 1953-54; Rt Hon. R. A. Butler, CH, MP (when Chancellor of the Exchequer), 1954-55; Principal, Treasury, 1955-57; Sec., Radcliffe Cttee on Working of Monetary System, 1957-59; returned to Treasury as Principal, 1959-64; Sec., Armitage Cttee on Pay of Postmen, 1964; Asst Sec., Cabinet Office, 1964-66; Sec. of Kindersley Review Body on Doctors' and Dentists' Remuneration and of Franks Cttee on Pay of Higher Civil Service, 1964-66; Asst Sec., Treasury, 1967-68; Jt Princ. Private Sec. to Rt Hon. Roy Jenkins, MP (Chancellor of the Exchequer), 1968; Under Secretary (Home Finance), Treasury, 1968-70; Principal Private Sec. to Prime Minister, 1970-75; Dep. Sec., 1973; Dep. Under-Sec. of State, Home Office, 1975-77. Sec., Bd of Dirs, Royal Opera House, Covent Garden, 1968-; Member: Governing Body, RAM, 1975-; Cttee of Management, Royal Philharmonic Soc., 1975-; Rhodes Trust, 1975-. *Recreation:* music. *Address:* Home Office, SW1. *Clubs:* Athenæum, Brooks's.

ARMSTRONG, Sheila Ann; soprano; *b* 13 Aug. 1942. *Educ:* Hirst Park Girls' Sch., Ashington, Northumberland; Royal Academy of Music, London. Debut Sadler's Wells, 1965 Glyndebourne, 1966, Covent Garden, 1973. Sings all over Europe, Far East, N and S America; has made many recordings. K. Ferrier and Mozart Prize, 1965; Hon. RAM 1970, FRAM 1973. *Recreations:* interior decoration, collecting antique keys, swimming, driving.

ARMSTRONG, Thomas; Author; *b* 3 Sept. 1899; *s* of late Charles Plaxton and late Alice Lily Armstrong, Airedale, Yorks; *m* 1930, Una Dulcie, *er d* of late Edgar and late Amy Jane Bray, Huddersfield. *Educ:* Queen Elizabeth's Sch., Wakefield; Royal Naval Coll., Keyham. Served in Royal Navy during European War, 1914-19. *Publications:* The Crowthers of Bankdam, 1940 (filmed as Master of Bankdam); Dover Harbour, 1942; King Cotton, 1947; Adam Brunskill, 1952; Pilling Always Pays, 1954; A Ring Has No End, 1958; Sue Crowther's Marriage, 1961; The Face of a Madonna, 1964; Our London Office, 1966. *Recreations:* reading, mediæval architecture, outdoor constructional work, country pursuits, any ball game, racing. *Address:* Lawn House, Low Row, Swaledale, North Yorks. *T:* Gunnerside 247.

ARMSTRONG, Sir Thomas Henry Wait, Kt 1958; MA, DMus; FRCM; Hon. FRCO, Hon. RAM; Principal, Royal Academy of Music, 1955-68; Organist of Christ Church, Oxford, 1933-55;

Student of Christ Church, 1939-55; Student Emeritus, 1955; Choragus of the University and University lecturer in music, 1937-54; Conductor of the Oxford Bach Choir and the Oxford Orchestral Society; Musical Director of the Balliol Concerts; Trustee, The Countess of Munster Musical Trust; *b* 15 June 1898; *o s* of A. E. Armstrong, Peterborough, Northants; *m* 1926, Hester, 2nd *d* of late Rev. W. H. Draper; one *s* one *d*. *Educ:* Choir Sch., Chapel Royal, St James's; King's Sch., Peterborough; Keble Coll., Oxford; Royal Coll. of Music. Organist, Thorney Abbey, 1914; sub-organist, Peterborough Cathedral, 1915; Organ Scholar, Keble Coll., Oxford 1916, Hon. Fellow, 1955; served in RA, BEF, France, 1917-19; sub-organist, Manchester Cathedral, 1922; organist, St Peter's, Eaton Square, 1923; organist of Exeter Cathedral, 1928. Cramb Lectr in music, Univ. of Glasgow, 1949. Vice-President, Bruckner-Mahler Chorale, 1970. *Compositions:* various, the larger ones remain unpublished. *Publications:* include choral music, songs and church music, together with many occasional writings on music. *Address:* The Old Rectory, Newton Blossomville, near Turvey, Beds MK43 8AL. *Club:* Athenæum. *See also R. T. Armstrong*.

ARMSTRONG, Prof. Wallace Edwin, MA Cantab; Professor Emeritus since 1961; *b* 24 Feb. 1896; *s* of William Wallace Armstrong and Alice Imeson; *m* 1928, Mary Agnes Canavan; one *s* one *d*. *Educ:* Dulwich Coll.; (Exhibitioner) Sidney Sussex College, Cambridge. Volunteered as Private in RAMC, 1914 (wounded, 1915, with loss of leg). BA Cantab Moral Sciences Tripos, 1918; Anthony Wilkin Studentship for ethnological research in New Guinea, 1919-22; Asst Anthropologist to Papuan Govt, 1921-22; Lecturer in Social Anthropology, Cambridge, 1922-26; Supervisor and occasional lecturer in Economics, Cambridge, 1926-39; Lecturer in Economics, University Coll., Southampton, 1939, Senior Lecturer, 1949; Reader, Univ. of Southampton, 1953; Professor of Economic Theory, Univ. of Southampton, 1958-61. *Publications:* Rossel Island, 1928; Saving and Investment, 1936. Numerous articles in: Man, Anthropos, Economic Journal, Oxford Economic Papers, Review of Economic Studies. *Recreations:* gardening, building. *Address:* Ballards Wood, Straight Mile, Ampfield, near Romsey, Hants. *T:* Romsey 513234.

ARMSTRONG COWAN, Sir Christopher; *see* Cowan, Sir C. G. A.

ARMSTRONG-JONES, family name of **Earl of Snowdon.**

ARMYTAGE, Captain Sir John Lionel, 8th Bt *cr* 1738; *b* 23 Nov. 1901; *s* of Brig.-Gen. Sir George (Ayscough) Armytage, 7th Bt, CMG, DSO, and Aimée (*d* 1955), 3rd *d* of Sir Lionel Milborne Swinnerton-Pilkington, 11th Bt; *S* father 1953; *m* 1st, 1927, Evelyne Mary Jessamine (marr. diss., 1946); *d* of Edward Herbert Fox, Adbury Park, Newbury; one *s* one *d*; 2nd, 1949, Maria Margarete, *o d* of Paul Hugo Tenhaeff, Bruenen, Niederrhein; one *d*. *Educ:* Eton; Royal Military Coll., Sandhurst. Joined King's Royal Rifle Corps, 1921; retired owing to ill-health, 1940. *Heir:* s John Martin Armytage, *b* 26 Feb. 1933. *Address:* (seat) Kirklees Park, Brighouse, West Yorks. *T:* Brighouse 3016. *Clubs:* Naval and Military, Oriental.

ARMYTAGE, Rear-Adm. Sir Reginald William, GC (AM 1928); CBE 1959; retired; *b* 18 May 1903; *s* of Sir George Ayscough Armytage, 7th Bart, CMG, DSO, Kirklees Park, Brighouse; *m* 1928, Sylvia Beatrice Staveley; three *s*. *Educ:* Osborne and Dartmouth. Entered Royal Navy, 1917. Served in HMS: Royal Oak, 1921; Capetown, 1922-24; Emergency Destroyers, 1925; Warspite, 1926-28 (Albert Medal 1928). Qualified in Gunnery, 1929. Served HMS: Devonshire, 1930-32; Mackay, 1932-34; Frobisher, 1935. Took up Naval Ordnance Design, Experiment and Inspection Duties, 1935; Head of Gun Design and Senior Naval Representative at Armament Design Estab., 1946; Deputy Chief Inspector of Naval Ordnance, 1949; Chief Inspector of Naval Ordnance, 1956; Vice-Pres. (Naval), Ordnance Board, 1959; President of The Ordnance Board, 1961-62. *Address:* The Malt House, Downton, Wilts.

ARMYTAGE, Prof. Walter Harry Green; Professor of Education, University of Sheffield, since 1954; *b* 22 Nov. 1915; *e s* of Walter Green Armytage and Harriet Jane May Armytage; *m* 1948, Lucy Frances Horsfall; one *s*. *Educ:* Redruth County School; Downing Coll., Cambridge. 1st Cl. Hist. Trip. 1937, Cert. in Educ., 1938. History Master, Dronfield Grammar Sch., 1938-39; served War of 1939-45 (despatches); Captain, London Irish Rifles. Univ. of Sheffield: Lectr, 1946; Sen. Lectr, 1952; Pro-Vice-Chancellor, 1964-68. Visiting Lectr, Univ. of Michigan, USA, 1955, 1959, 1961, 1963, 1975; Lectures: Ballard-Matthews, University Coll. of North Wales, 1973; Cantor, RSA, 1969; Hawkesley, IMechE, 1969; S. P. Thompson,

IEE, 1972; Galton, Eugenics Soc., 1974. Hon. DLitt NUU, 1977. *Publications:* A. J. Mundella 1825-1897; The Liberal Background of the Labour Movement, 1951; Thomas Hughes: The Life of the Author of Tom Brown's Schooldays, 1953 (with E. C. Mack); Civic Universities: Aspects of a British Tradition, 1955; Sir Richard Gregory: his Life and Work, 1957; A Social History of Engineering, 1961; Heavens Below: Utopian Experiments in England, 1560-1960, 1962; Four Hundred Years of English Education, 1964; The Rise of the Technocracy, 1965; The American Influence on English Education, 1967; Yesterday's Tomorrows: A Historical Survey of Future Societies, 1968; The French Influence on English Education, 1968; The German Influence on English Education, 1969; The Russian Influence on English Education, 1969. *Recreations:* walking and gardening. *Address:* 3 The Green, Totley, Sheffield, South Yorks. *T:* Sheffield 362515. *Clubs:* National Liberal; University Staff (Sheffield).

ARNELL, Richard Anthony Sayer; FTCL; composer; conductor; film maker; Teacher of Composition, Trinity College, London, since 1949; *b* 15 Sept. 1917; *s* of late Richard Sayer Arnell and of Helène Marie Sherf; *m* 1974, Charlotte Jennings. *Educ:* The Hall, Hampstead; University Coll. Sch., NW3; Royal Coll. of Music. Music Consultant, BBC North American Service, 1943-46; Lectr, Royal Ballet Sch., 1958-59. Editor, The Composer, 1961-64; Chairman: Composers' Guild of GB, 1965, 1974-75; Young Musicians' Symph. Orch. Soc., 1973-75. Vis. Lectr (Fulbright Exchange), Bowdoin Coll., Maine, 1967-68; Vis. Prof. Hofstra Univ., New York, 1968-70. Music consultant, London Internat. Film Sch., 1975-. Composer of the Year 1966 (Music Teachers Assoc. Award). Compositions include: 5 symphonies; 2 concertos for violin; concerto for harpsichord; concerto for piano; 5 string quartets; 2 quintets; piano trio; piano works; songs; cantatas; organ works; music for string orchestra, wind ensembles, brass ensembles, song cycles. *Opera:* Love in Transit; Moonflowers; Rain Folly. *Ballet scores:* Punch and the Child, for Ballet Soc., NY, 1947; Harlequin in April, for Arts Council, 1951; The Great Detective, for Sadler's Wells Theatre Ballet, 1953; The Angels, for Royal Ballet, 1957; Giselle (Adam) re-orchestrated, for Ballet Rambert, 1965. *Film Scores:* The Land, 1941; The Third Secret, 1963; The Visit, 1964; The Man Outside, 1966; Topsail Schooner, 1966; Bequest for a Village, 1969; Second Best, 1972; Stained Glass, 1973; Wires Over the Border, 1974. *Other works:* Symphonic Portrait, Lord Byron, for Sir Thomas Beecham, 1953; Landscapes and Figures, for Sir Thomas Beecham, 1956; Petrified Princess, puppet operetta, for BBC, 1959; Robert Flaherty, Impression for Radio Eireann, 1960; Musica Pacifica for Edward Benjamin, 1963; Festival Flourish, for Salvation Army, 1965; 2nd piano concerto, for RPO, 1967; Overture, Food of Love, for Portland Symph. Orch., 1968; My Ladye Greene Sleeves, for Hofstra Univ., 1968; Nocturne: Prague, 1968; I Think of all Soft Limbs, for Canadian Broadcasting Corp., 1971; Astronaut One, 1973; Life Boat Voluntary, for RNLI, 1974. *Address:* c/o National Westminster Bank Ltd, 115 Old Brompton Road, SW7.

ARNEY, Frank Douglas, CBE 1959; *b* 4 Feb. 1899; *s* of Frank Charles Arney; *m* 1925, Mildred, *d* of W. J. Dallin; three *s*. *Educ:* Grammar Sch., Bristol. Formerly: General Manager, Port of Bristol Authority, for 16 years until retd Oct. 1961; Part-time Chm. British Waterways Board, Dec. 1962-June 1963; Mem., National Ports Council, 1963-71. *Recreations:* fly fishing, golf. *Address:* Glenleven, Northumbria Drive, Henleaze, Bristol. *T:* Bristol 628810.

ARNOLD, Prof. Denis Midgley, FBA 1976; Heather Professor of Music, University of Oxford, since 1975; *b* 15 Dec. 1926; *m* 1951, Elsie Millicent Dawrant; two *s*. *Educ:* Sheffield Univ. (MA, BMus). ARCM. Queen's Univ., Belfast: Lectr in Music, Extra-Mural Studies, 1951-60; Reader in Music, 1960-64; Sen. Lectr in Music, Hull Univ., 1964-69; Prof. of Music, Nottingham Univ., 1969-75. Hon. RAM. Foreign Mem., Accademia dei Lincei, 1976. Jt Editor, Music and Letters, 1976-. *Publications:* Monteverdi, 1963; Marenzio, 1965; Monteverdi's Madrigals, 1967; (ed with N. Fortune) Monteverdi Companion, 1968; Beethoven Companion, 1971; Giovanni Gabrieli, 1974; articles in Music and Letters, Musical Qly, Monthly Musical Record, Brass Qly, Musical Times, Galpin Soc. Jl, Rivista Musicale Italiana. *Address:* Faculty of Music, Oxford University, 32 Holywell, Oxford OX1 3SL. *T:* Oxford 47069.

ARNOLD, Mrs Elliott; *see* Johns, Glynis.

ARNOLD, Rt. Rev. George Feversham; *see* Nova Scotia, Bishop of.

ARNOLD, Hon. Sir John Lewis, Kt 1972; Hon. Mr Justice Arnold; a Judge of the High Court, Family Division, since 1972;

b 6 May 1915; *s* of late A. L. Arnold and E. K. Arnold; *m* 1940, Alice Margaret Dorothea (*née* Cookson) (marr. diss., 1963); one *s* one *d*; *m* 1963, Florence Elizabeth, *d* of H. M. Hague, Montreal; one *s* two *d. Educ:* Wellington Coll.; abroad. Called to Bar, Middle Temple, 1937; served War of 1939-45 in Army (despatches, 1945); resumed practice at Bar, 1946; QC 1958; Chm. Bar Council, 1970-72, Chm., Plant Variety Rights Tribunal for proceedings in England and Wales, 1969-72. *Recreations:* cricket, travel. *Address:* Royal Courts of Justice, WC2; Little Horse Leas, Bradfield, Berks. *T:* Bradfield 442; 7 Clareville Grove, SW7. *T:* 01-373 7707. *Club:* Bath.

ARNOLD, Malcolm, CBE 1970; composer; *b* 21 Oct. 1921; *s* of William and Annie Arnold, Northampton; *m*; two *s* one *d. Educ:* Royal Coll. of Music, London (Schol., 1938). Principal Trumpet, London Philharmonic Orchestra, 1941-44; served in the Army, 1944-45; Principal Trumpet, London Philharmonic Orchestra, 1945-48; Mendelssohn Schol. (study in Italy), 1948; Coronation Ballet, Homage to the Queen, performed Royal Opera House, 1953. Awarded Oscar for music for film Bridge on the River Kwai, 1957. Bard of the Cornish Gorsedd, 1969. Hon. DMus Exeter, 1970; Hon. RAM. *Publications: symphonies:* No 1, 1949; No 2, 1953; No 3, 1957; No 4, 1960; No 5, 1961; No 6, 1967; No 7, 1973; *other works:* Beckus the Dandipratt, overture, 1943; Tam O'Shanter, overture, 1955; Peterloo, overture, 1967; twenty three concertos; five ballets; two one-act operas; one string quartet; brass quintet; vocal music; chamber music. *Recreations:* reading and foreign travel. *Address:* 4 De Vesci Terrace, Dun Laoghaire, Co. Dublin, Ireland.

ARNOLD, Thomas Richard; MP (C) Hazel Grove, since Oct. 1974; *b* 25 Jan. 1947; *s* of Thomas Charles Arnold and Helen Breen. *Educ:* Bedales Sch.; Le Rosey, Geneva; Pembroke Coll., Oxford (MA). Theatre producer; Mem., Soc. of West End Theatre; Mem., Assoc. of Touring and Producing Managers. Contested (C): Manchester Cheetham, 1970; Hazel Grove, Feb. 1974. *Address:* House of Commons, SW1A 0AA. *T:* 01-219 4096. *Clubs:* Carlton; St James's (Manchester).

ARNOLD, Vere Arbuthnot, CBE 1970; MC 1945; TD 1953; JP; DL; Chairman, Ross T. Smyth & Co. Ltd, since 1957; Director, D. T. Russell & Baird (Ireland) Ltd; *b* 23 May 1902; *s* of Rev. H. A. Arnold, Wolsingham Rectory, Co. Durham; *m* 1928, Joan Kathleen, *d* of C. J. Tully, Wairarapa, NZ; one *s* one *d. Educ:* Haileybury Coll.; Jesus Coll., Cambridge (BA). Ross T. Smyth & Co. Ltd, 1924, Director, 1931; President Liverpool Corn Trade Association, 1947-48 and 1951-52; Chairman: Liverpool Grain Storage and Transit Co. Ltd; Alexandra Silos Ltd. Chm., Runcorn Develt Corp., 1964-74. Served War of 1939-45 as Major (MC, TD). JP County of Chester, 1949; High Sheriff, Cheshire, 1958; DL Cheshire, 1969. *Recreations:* shooting, fishing. *Address:* Ardmore, Great Barrow, near Chester. *T:* Tarvin 40257.

ARNOLD-BAKER, Charles, OBE 1966; Secretary, National Association of Local Councils, since 1953; *b* 25 June 1918; *s* of Baron Albrecht v. Blumenthal and Alice Wilhelmine (*née* Hainsworth); *m* 1943, Edith (*née* Woods); one *s* one *d. Educ:* Winchester Coll.; Magdalen Coll., Oxford. BA 1940. Called to Bar, Inner Temple, 1948. Army (Private to Captain), 1940-46. Admty Bar, 1948-52; Mem., Royal Commn on Common Lands, 1955-58; Mem. European Cttee, Internat. Union of Local Authorities, 1960-; a Deleg. to European Local Govt Assembly, Strasbourg, 1960-. Gwylim Gibbons Award, Nuffield Coll., Oxford, 1959. King Haakon's Medal of Freedom (Norway), 1945. *Publications:* Norway (pamphlet), 1946; Everyman's Dictionary of Dates, 1954; Parish Administration, 1958; New Law and Practice of Parish Administration, 1966; The 5000 and the Power Tangle, 1967; The Local Government Act 1972, 1973; Local Council Administration, 1975; many contribs to British and European local govt jls. *Recreations:* travel, history, writing, music, cooking, journalism, wine and doing nothing. *Address:* Top Floor, 2 Paper Buildings, Inner Temple, EC4. *T:* 01-353 3490. *Club:* Union (Oxford).

ARNOTT, Most Rev. Felix Raymond; *see* Brisbane, Archbishop of.

ARNOTT, Sir John (Robert Alexander), 5th Bt *cr* 1896, of Woodlands, Shandon, Co. Cork; *b* 9 April 1927; *er s* of Sir Robert John Arnott, 4th Bt, and Emita Amelia (*d* 1948), *d* of Francis James, formerly of Royston, Herts; *S* father, 1966; *m* 1974, Ann Margaret, *d* of late T. A. Farrelly, Kilcar, Co. Cavan; one *s. Educ:* Harrow. Formerly Lt, Royal Irish Fusiliers. Chm., Phoenix Park Racecourse, Dublin; Member, Irish Racing Board. *Heir: s* Alexander John Maxwell Arnott, *b* 18 Sept. 1975. *Address:* Ashtown House, Castlenock, Co. Dublin, Ireland. *Club:* Irish Turf (Dublin).

ARNOTT, Sir Melville; *see* Arnott, Sir W. M.

ARNOTT, Sir (William) Melville, Kt 1971; TD (and clasps) 1944; MD; FRCP; FRCPE, FRSE, FRCPath; British Heart Foundation Professor of Cardiology, University of Birmingham, 1971-74, now Emeritus; Physician, United Birmingham Hospitals, since 1946; Consultant Adviser in Research to West Midlands Regional Health Authority; *b* 14 Jan. 1909; *s* of Rev. Henry and Jeanette Main Arnott; *m* 1938, Dorothy Eleanor, *er d* of G. F. S. Hill, Edinburgh; one *s. Educ:* George Watson's Coll., Edinburgh; Univ. of Edinburgh. MB, ChB (Hons), 1931, BSc (1st Cl. Hons Path.), 1934, MD (Gold Medal and Gunning Prize in Path.), 1937, Edinburgh; McCunn Res. Schol. in Path., 1933-35, Crichton Res. Schol. in Path., 1935, Shaw Macfie Lang Res. Fellow, 1936-38, Edinburgh. MD Birmingham, 1947. 2nd Lieut RA, 1929; TA 1929-39; War of 1939-45, served as specialist physician; five years foreign service (Siege of Tobruk; despatches, NW Europe); Lt-Col 1942. Asst Physician, Edinburgh Municipal Hosps, 1934-36; Hon. Asst Physician: Church of Scotland Deaconess Hosp., Edinburgh, 1938-46; Edinburgh Royal Infirmary, 1946. Dir, Post-grad. studies in Medicine, Edinburgh Univ., 1945-46; William Withering Prof. of Medicine, Univ. of Birmingham, 1946-71. Associate Examr in Medicine, London Univ., 1948-49; Examr in Medicine, to Univs of Cambridge, 1950-56, London, 1951-54, Wales, 1954-57, Queen's, Belfast, 1956-59, Edinburgh, 1959-62, Leeds, 1959-62, St Andrews, 1961-63, Oxford, 1961-68, Newcastle, 1964-67, Manchester, 1964-70, Singapore, 1965, East Africa, 1965, Malaysia, 1973, NUI, 1975-. Member: UGC, 1954-63; MRC, 1965-69; Council, University Coll. of Rhodesia, 1964-70; UGC Hong Kong, 1966-75; Home Office Cttee (Brodrick) on Death Registration and Coroners, 1965-71; Tropical Medicine Res. Bd, 1967-71. Dep. Pres., First Internat. Conf. on Med. Educn, 1953. Editor, Clinical Science, 1953-58, and Mem., Ed. Bd of Brit. Jl of Social Medicine. RCPE: Mem., 1933; Fellow, 1937; John Matheson Shaw Lectr, 1958; Cullen Prize, 1958. RCP: Mem., 1947; Fellow, 1951; Mem. Council, 1954-56; Oliver-Sharpey Lectr, 1955; Examr for Membership, 1957-66; Croonian Lectr, 1963; Censor, 1969-71; Sen. Vice-Pres., and Sen. Censor, 1973. Foundation Fellow, Royal Coll. of Pathologists. FRMedSoc 1929 (late Senior Pres.); Hon. FRCP(C), 1957; Hon. FACP, 1968 (Lilly Lectr, 1968). Member: Assoc. of Physicians; Physiological Soc.; Pathological Soc.; Med. Res. Soc.; Cardiac Soc.; Thoracic Soc.; Internat. Soc. of Internal Medicine. Sir Arthur Sims Commonwealth Trav. Prof. of Medicine, 1957. Lectures: Frederick Price, Trinity Coll., Dublin, 1959; Hall, Cardiac Soc. of Aust. and NZ, 1962; Henry Cohen, Hebrew Univ. of Jerusalem, 1964; Alexander Brown Meml, Univ. of Ibadan, 1972. Pres., Edinburgh Harveian Soc., 1955. Research: Originally into experimental path. of renal hypertension and peripheral vascular disease; at present, into physiology and path. of cardio-respiratory function. Hon. DSc Edinburgh, 1975; Hon. LLD: Rhodesia, 1976; Dundee, 1976. *Publications:* some 50 scientific papers, principally in Lancet, Jl of Physiol., Jl of Path., Brit. Jl of Social Medicine, Edinburgh Med. Jl, etc. *Recreation:* travel. *Address:* 40 Carpenter Road, Edgbaston, Birmingham B15 2JJ. *T:* 021-440 2195. *Clubs:* Athenæum, Naval and Military.

ARON, Prof. Raymond Claude Ferdinand; Officier de la Légion d'Honneur; author; Professor at Collège de France, since 1970; Professor at Ecole Pratique des Hautes Etudes, Paris, since 1960; Columnist, Figaro, 1947-77; *b* Paris, 14 March 1905; *m* 1933, Suzanne Gauchon; two *d* (and one *d* decd). *Educ:* Ecole Normale Supérieur and Sorbonne, Paris. Lectr, Univ. of Cologne, 1931; French Academic House, Berlin, 1931-33; Lycée du Havre, 1933-34; Centre Documentation sociale ENS, 1934-39; Maître de Conférences, Univ. of Toulouse, 1939; Editor, La France Libre, in London, 1940-44; Columnist, Combat, 1946-47; Professor of Sociology at the Sorbonne, 1955-68. Several hon. doctorates from foreign univs, 1958-; For. Hon. Mem., Amer. Acad. of Arts and Sciences, Boston, 1962; Mem., Académie des Sciences Morales et Politiques, Paris, 1963; Mem., Philosophical Soc., Philadelphia, 1967; Corres. Fellow, British Acad., 1970. Hon. Fellow, LSE, 1974. *Publications:* Introduction à la philosophie de l'histoire, 1938 (Introduction to the Philosophy of History, 1961); Le grand schisme, 1948; Les guerres en chaîne, 1951 (Century of Total War, 1954); L'Opium des intellectuels, 1955 (Opium of the Intellectuals, 1957); Espoir et peur du siècle, 1957 (Part III trans. as On War: atomic weapons and global diplomacy, 1958); Diversity of Worlds, 1957; La tragédie algérienne, 1957; Immuable et changeante, 1959 (France: steadfast and changing, 1960); La société industrielle et la guerre, 1959; Dimensions de la conscience historique, 1960 (parts trans. in Evidence and Inference, 1959, and The Dawn of Universal History, 1960); France: the new republic, 1960; Imperialism and Colonialism, 1960; Paix et guerre entre les nations, 1962 (Peace and War, 1967); Dix-huit leçons sur la société industrielle, 1963 (Eighteen Lectures on Industrial Society, 1968); Le grand débat, 1963 (The Great Debate: theories of nuclear strategy, 1965); (ed) World Technology and Human Destiny, 1963; La lutte de classes, 1964; Démocratie et totalitarisme, 1965 (Democracy and Totalitarianism, 1968); Trois essais sur la société industrielle, 1966 (The Industrial Society, 1967); Les étapes de la pensée sociologique, 1967 (Main Currents in Sociological Thought: I, Montesquieu, Comte, Marx, Tocqueville, the sociologist and the revolution of 1848, 1965; II, Durkheim, Pareto, Weber, 1968); De Gaulle, Israël et les juifs, 1968 (De Gaulle, Israel and the Jews, 1969); La révolution introuvable, 1968 (The Elusive Revolution: anatomy of a student revolt, 1970); Les désillusions du progrès, 1969 (Progress and Disillusion, 1968); Etudes politiques, 1972; République impériale, 1973 (The Imperial Republic, 1975); Histoire et Dialectique de la Violence, 1973 (History and the Dialectic of Violence, 1975); Penser la Guerre, Clausewitz, vol. I, L'Age européen, vol. II, L'Age planétaire, 1976. *Address:* 87 Boulevard Saint-Michel, Paris 5, France.

ARONSON, Geoffrey Fraser, CB 1977; Legal Adviser and Solicitor to Ministry of Agriculture. Fisheries and Food, to Forestry Commission, and to (EEC) Intervention Board for Agricultural Produce, since 1974; *b* 17 April 1914; *er s* of late Victor Rees Aronson, CBE, KC, and Annie Elizabeth Aronson (*née* Fraser); *m* 1940, Marie Louise, *e d* of late George Stewart Rose-Innes; one *s* two *d. Educ:* Haileybury. Solicitor (Honours) 1936. Legal Dept, Min. of Agriculture and Fisheries, 1938; served War of 1939-45, Flying Control Officer, RAFVR; Sen. Legal Asst 1949; Asst Solicitor, MAFF, 1960; seconded to Min. of Land and Natural Resources, 1965 and to Min. of Housing and Local Govt, 1966; EEC duties, MAFF, 1967; Principal Asst Solicitor (Under-Sec.), 1971; Dep. Legal Advr and Solicitor, MAFF and Forestry Commn, 1971-74. *Publications:* contribs to legal pubns. *Recreations:* travel, gardening, fishing. *Address:* Cedars Cottage, Church Street, Epsom, Surrey KT17 4QB. *T:* Epsom 22431; Little Thatch, Child Oxeford, Blandford Forum, Dorset. *T:* Hintock 8289. *Clubs:* Royal Commonwealth Society, Royal Automobile.

ARRAN, 8th Earl of, *cr* 1762; **Arthur Kattendyke Strange David Archibald Gore;** Bt 1662; Viscount Sudley, Baron Saunders, 1758; Earl of Arran of the Arran Islands, Co. Galway, 1762; Baron Sudley (UK) 1884; journalist; broadcaster on radio and television; *b* 5 July 1910; *s* of 6th Earl of Arran, KP, PC(Ire.), and Maud, *o d* of Baron Huyssen van Kattendijke; *S* brother, 1958; *m* 1937, Fiona Bryde, *d* of Sir Iain Colquhoun, 7th Bt, of Luss, KT, DSO; one *s* (and one *s* decd). *Educ:* Eton; Balliol Coll., Oxford. Assistant Press Attaché, British Legation, Berne, 1939-40; Attaché, British Embassy, Lisbon, 1941-42; Deputy Dir, Overseas General Div., MOI, 1943-45; Dir of Secretariat, Central Office of Information, 1945-49. Introduced in House of Lords: Sexual Offences Bill (now Act) (3 times); Badger Protection Bill (now Act). Director, Daily Mail and General Trust Ltd; Chm., Children's Country Holidays Fund; Hon. Treasurer of Moorfields Eye Hospital. *Publications:* Lord Arran Writes, 1964; columnist, Evening News; contributions to Encounter, Punch, The Observer, Manchester Guardian, Daily Mail and Evening Standard. *Recreations:* shooting and tennis. *Heir: s* Viscount Sudley, *qv. Address:* Pimlico House, Hemel Hempstead, Herts. *Club:* Beefsteak.

ARRAU, Claudio; Concert Pianist; *b* Chillan, Chile, 6 Feb. 1903; *m* ; two *s* one *d.* Gave first recital at Santiago at age of 5; musical education in Europe financed by Chilean Govt; studied at Stern Konservatorie Berlin, under Martin Krause; won Liszt Prize 1919, 1920 (not awarded in 45 years), Schulhoff prize, Ibach prize (1917), and, in 1927, first place in Geneva International Congress of Pianists. Has appeared in US, Canada, England, France, Holland, Italy, Germany, Scandinavia, Russia, South America, Mexico, Cuba, Hawaii, South Africa, Australia, Israel, Japan, NZ, Iceland, Hong Kong, Singapore, Ceylon and Bombay. Chile has named two streets in his honour. Cycle performances include: all keyboard works of Bach in 12 recitals, Berlin, 1935; all Beethoven Sonatas, 8 recitals, Berlin, Buenos Aires, Santiago; all Beethoven Sonatas, Diabelli Variations, (first BBC broadcast from London, 1952), all Beethoven, NY Season, 1953-54, 1962; renowned also for Chopin, Schumann, Brahms, Liszt. Decorations from France, Germany, Mexico, Chile. *Address:* c/o Hurok Concerts Inc., 540 Madison Avenue, New York City, NY 10022, USA.

ARROW, Kenneth Joseph; University Professor, Harvard University, since 1975 (Professor of Economics, 1968-75); *b* 23 Aug. 1921; *s* of Harry I. and Lillian Arrow; *m* 1947, Selma Schweitzer; two *s. Educ:* City College (BS in Social Science 1940); Columbia Univ. (MA 1941, PhD 1951). Captain, US AAF, 1942-46. Research Associate, Cowles Commn for Research in Economics, Univ. of Chicago, 1947-49; Actg Asst Prof., Associate Prof. and Prof. of Economics, Statistics and Operations Research, Stanford Univ., 1949-68; Staff Mem., US Council of Economic Advisers, 1962. Consultant, The Rand Corp., 1948-. Fellow, Churchill Coll., Cambridge, 1963-64, 1970, 1973. Member: Inst. of Management Sciences (Pres., 1963); Nat. Acad. of Sciences; Amer. Philosoph. Soc.; Econometric Soc. (Pres., 1956); Fellow, Amer. Acad. of Arts and Sciences; Dist. Fellow, Amer. Econ. Assoc. (Pres., 1972); Corresp. Fellow, British Acad., 1976; Foreign Hon. Mem., Finnish Acad. of Sciences. John Bates Clark Medal, American Economic Assoc., 1957; Nobel Meml Prize in Economic Science, 1972. Hon. LLD: Chicago, 1967; City Univ. of NY, 1972; Hon. Dr Soc. and Econ. Sciences, Vienna, 1971; Hon. ScD Columbia, 1973; Hon. DSocSci, Yale, 1974; Hon. Dr: Paris, 1974; Hebrew Univ. of Jerusalem, 1975; Helsinki, 1976. *Publications:* Social Choice and Individual Values, 1951, 2nd edn 1963; (with S. Karlin and H. Scarf) Studies in the Mathematical Theory of Inventory and Production, 1958; (with M. Hoffenberg) A Time Series Analysis of Interindustry Demands, 1959; (with L. Hurwicz and H. Uzawa) Studies in Linear and Nonlinear Programming, 1959; Aspects of the Theory of Risk Bearing, 1965; (with M. Kurz) Public Investment and the Rate of Return, and Optimal Fiscal Policy, 1971; Essays in the Theory of Risk-Bearing, 1971; (with F. Hahn) General Competitive Analysis, 1972; The Limits of Organization, 1974; (with L. Hurwicz) Studies in Resource Allocation Processes, 1977. *Address:* 1737 Cambridge Street, Harvard University, Cambridge, Mass 02138, USA.

ARROWSMITH, Sir Edwin (Porter), KCMG 1959 (CMG 1950); Director of Overseas Services Resettlement Bureau, since 1965; *b* 23 May 1909; *s* of late Edwin Arrowsmith; *m* 1936, Clondagh, *e d* of late Dr W. G. Connor; two *d. Educ:* Cheltenham Coll.; Trinity Coll., Oxford (MA). Assistant District Commissioner, Bechuanaland Protectorate, 1932; in various District posts, Bechuanaland Protectorate, 1933-38; Commissioner, Turks and Caicos Islands, BWI, 1940-46; Administrator, Dominica, BWI, 1946-52; Resident Commissioner, Basutoland, 1952-56; Governor and Commander-in-Chief, Falkland Islands, 1957-64, and High Commissioner, British Antarctic Territory, 1962-64. Chm., Royal Commonwealth Soc. for the Blind, 1970-. Pres., Freshwater Biol Assoc., 1977-. *Recreation:* flyfishing. *Address:* 25 Rivermead Court, SW6 3RU. *T:* 01-736 4757. *Clubs:* Flyfishers', Hurlingham, Royal Commonwealth Society.

ARROWSMITH, Pat; pacifist and socialist; Assistant at Amnesty International, since 1971; *b* 2 March 1930; *d* of George Ernest Arrowsmith and Margaret Vera (*née* Kingham). *Educ:* Farringtons; Stover Sch.; Cheltenham Ladies' Coll.; Newnham Coll., Cambridge (BA history); Univ. of Ohio; Liverpool Univ. (Cert. in Social Science). Homosexual partnership with Wendy Butlin, 1962-76. Has held many jobs, incl.: Community Organizer in Chicago, 1952-53; Cinema Usherette, 1953-54; Social Caseworker, Liverpool Family Service Unit, 1954; Child Care Officer, 1955 and 1964; Nursing Asst, Deva Psychiatric Hosp., 1956-57; Reporter for Peace News, 1965; Gardener for Camden BC, 1966-68; Researcher for Soc. of Friends Race Relations Cttee, 1969-71; Case Worker for NCCL, 1971; and on farms, as waitress in cafes, in factories, as a toy demonstrator, as a 'temp' in numerous offices, as asst in children's home, as newspaper deliverer and sales agent, as charperson, as bartender, and in a holiday camp. Organizer for Direct Action Cttee against Nuclear War, Cttee of 100 and Campaign for Nuclear Disarmament, 1958-68; gaoled 9 times as political prisoner, 1958-74 (adopted twice as Prisoner of Conscience by Amnesty International); awarded Holloway Prison Green Band, 1964; awarded Girl Crusaders knighthood, 1940. Contested Fulham, 1966 (Radical Alliance) and 1970 (Hammersmith Stop the SE Asia War Cttee), on peace issues. Member: War Resisters' Internat.; Troops Out Movement; British Withdrawal from N Ireland Campaign; Campaign for Nuclear Disarmament; TU Campaign against Prevention of Terrorism Act. Mem. TGWU. *Publications:* Jericho (novel), 1965; Somewhere Like This (novel), 1970; To Asia in Peace, 1972; The Colour of Six Schools, 1972; Breakout (poems and drawings from prison), 1975. *Recreations:* water colour painting (has held and contrib. exhibns), swimming, drinking, writing poetry. *Address:* 37 Middle Lane, N8. *T:* 01-340 2661. *Club:* Gateways.

ARTHINGTON-DAVY, Humphrey Augustine, MVO 1977; OBE 1965; High Commissioner to Tonga, since 1973, and Western Samoa, 1973-77; *b* 1920. *Educ:* Eastbourne Coll.; Trinity Coll., Cambridge. Indian Army, 1941; Indian Political Service, 1946; Civil Service of Pakistan, 1947; CRO, 1958; British Representative in the Maldives, 1960; Deputy High Commissioner: Botswana, 1966; Mauritius, 1968; Tonga, 1970.

Recreation: travel. *Address:* c/o Foreign and Commonwealth Office, SW1. *Club:* Naval and Military.

ARTHUR, family name of **Baron Glenarthur.**

ARTHUR, Hon. Sir Basil (Malcolm), 5th Bt, *cr* 1841; MP (Lab) for Timaru, New Zealand, since 1962; Minister of Transport, and Minister in charge of State Insurance Office, New Zealand, 1972-75; *b* 18 Sept. 1928; *o s* of Sir George Malcolm Arthur, 4th Bt, and Doris Fay, *y d* of Joseph Wooding, JP, Woodland Grange, Woodbury, Geraldine, New Zealand; *S* father 1949; *m* 1950, Elizabeth Rita, *d* of late Alan Wells, Wakefield, Nelson, New Zealand; one *s* two *d. Heir: s* Stephen John Arthur, *b* 1 July 1953. *Address:* Seadown, No 3 RD, Timaru, New Zealand.

ARTHUR, Prof. Donald Ramsay, MSc, PhD, DSc; Professor and Head of Department of Zoology, King's College, London University, since 1963, and Director of Studies, School of Human Environmental Studies, since 1975; FKC 1972; *b* 1 May 1917; *s* of Henry and Rachel Arthur; *m* 1945, Iris Doreen (*née* Gingell); one *d. Educ:* Amman Valley Gram. Sch.; UCW, Aberystwyth. School Master, Brockley Co. Sch., London, 1938-39; Scientist, Royal Ordnance Factory, 1939-42; Sen. Entomologist, University Coll. South Wales (working under grant from ARC), 1943-47; Sen. Biology Master, City of Cardiff High Sch., 1947-48; King's Coll., London: Lectr in Zoology, 1948-59; Leverhulme Research Award, 1954-55; Reader in Zoology, 1959-63; Dean, Faculty of Science, 1968-70; Consultant: US Naval Med. Res. Unit, Cairo, 1955-62; Environmental Resources Ltd, 1972; TEST (Transport and Environment Studies), 1970-. Vis. Prof., Univ. of Rhodesia, 1962; Vis. Res. Fellow, Tick Res. Unit, Rhodes Univ., 1972; Mem. Council, Brit. Soc. Parasitol., 1962-64; Chm., Bd of Studies in Zoology, Univ. of London, 1965-67; Pres., London Branch of Assoc. for Science Educn, 1965-66; Member: Exec. Cttee and Finance and Admin. Cttee, Field Studies Council, 1963-72; Council of Environmental Educn, 1968-; Editorial Bd, Parasitology, 1964-; Editorial Bd, Internat. Jl of Environmental Sciences, 1970-; Council, John Cass Coll., 1965-69; Delegacy, King's Coll., 1970-76; Finance Cttee, King's Coll., 1970; Cleaner Thames Consultative Cttee, 1968-; Adv. Cttee of Pollution by oil of the sea, 1970-; Council, Instn of Environmental Sciences, 1970-. Editor, Biological Science Texts, 1966-. President: London Old Aberystwythians, 1967-68; London Carms Soc., 1970-71. FIBiol, 1965. *Publications:* Ticks: a Monograph of the Ixodoidea, Pt V, 1960; Ticks and Disease, 1962; (ed) Aspects of Disease Transmission by Ticks, 1962; British Ticks, 1963; Ticks of the Genus Ixodes in Africa, 1965; (ed) Looking at Animals Again, 1966; Survival: Man and his Environment, 1969; (ed with J. D. Carthy) Oil Pollution and Littoral Organisms, 1968; Joint Editor, Symposium vol., 2nd Internat. Acarological Congress, 1969; Adv. Editor, Encyclopaedia of Zoology, 1970; papers in Parasitology, Jl Parasitology, Proc. Zool. Soc., Bulletin Entomological Research, etc. *Recreation:* Rugby football. *Address:* 57 Rushgrove Avenue, NW9. *T:* 01-205 6375.

ARTHUR, Sir Geoffrey (George), KCMG 1971 (CMG 1963); HM Diplomatic Service, retired; Master of Pembroke College, Oxford, since 1975; *b* 19 March 1920; *s* of G. J. Arthur; *m* 1946, Margaret, *d* of late T. A. Woodcock, OBE; no *c. Educ:* Ashby de la Zouch Grammar Sch.; Christ Church, Oxford. Served in Army, 1940-45. Joined HM Foreign Service, 1947. Served in: Baghdad, 1948-50; Ankara, 1950-53; Foreign Office, 1953-55; Bonn, 1956-58; Cairo, 1959-63; Counsellor in Foreign Office, 1963-67; Ambassador to Kuwait, 1967-68; Asst Under-Sec. of State, FCO, 1968-70; Political Resident in the Persian Gulf, 1970-72; Visiting FCO Fellow, St Antony's Coll., Oxford, 1972-73; Dep. Under-Sec. of State, FCO, 1973-75. Dir, British Bank of the Middle East, 1975-. *Address:* Master's Lodgings, Pembroke College, Oxford. *T:* Oxford 43482. *Clubs:* United Oxford & Cambridge University, Beefsteak.

ARTHUR, Prof. Geoffrey Herbert; Professor of Veterinary Surgery and Head of Department, University of Bristol, since Jan. 1974; *b* 6 March 1916; *s* of William Gwyn Arthur and Ethel Jessie Arthur; *m* 1948, Lorna Isabel Simpson; four *s* one *d. Educ:* Abersychan Secondary Sch.; Liverpool Univ. BVSc 1939; MRCVS 1939; MVSc 1945; DVSc 1957; FRCVS 1957. Lectr in Veterinary Medicine, Liverpool Univ., 1941-48; Reader in Veterinary Surgery, Royal Veterinary Coll., 1949-51; Reader in Veterinary Surgery and Obstetrics, Univ. of London, 1952-65; Prof. of Veterinary Obstetrics and Diseases of Reproduction, Univ. of London, 1965-73. Examiner to Univs of Cambridge, Dublin, Edinburgh, Glasgow, Liverpool, London, Reading, Bristol and Ceylon. Visiting Professor: Univ. of Khartoum, 1974; Pahlavi Univ., 1976. *Publications:* Wright's Veterinary Obstetrics, including Diseases of Reproduction, 3rd edn, 1964;

Veterinary Reproduction and Obstetrics, 4th edn, 1975; papers on medicine and reproduction in Veterinary Record, Veterinary Jl, Jl of Comparative Pathology, Jl Reprod. Fert. and Vet. Jl. *Recreation:* observing natural phenomena. *Address:* Department of Veterinary Surgery, University of Bristol, Langford House, Langford, Bristol.

ARTHUR, James Stanley, CMG 1977; HM Diplomatic Service; British High Commissioner, Suva, since 1974; first British High Commissioner (non-resident), Republic of Nauru, since 1977; *b* 3 Feb. 1923; *s* of Laurence and Catherine Arthur, Lerwick, Shetland; *m* 1950, Marion North; two *s* two *d. Educ:* Trinity Academy, Edinburgh; Liverpool Univ. (BSc). Scientific Civil Service, 1944-46; Asst Principal, Scottish Educn Dept, 1946; Min. of Educn/Dept of Educn and Science, 1947-66: Private Sec. to Parly Sec., 1948-50; Principal Private Sec. to Minister, 1960-62; Counsellor, FO, 1966; Nairobi, 1967-70; Dep. High Comr, Malta, 1970-73. *Recreations:* golf, music. *Address:* c/o Foreign and Commonwealth Office, SW1. *T:* 01-930 8440. *Club:* Travellers'.

ARTHUR, John Rhys, DFC 1944; **His Honour Judge Arthur;** a Circuit Judge, since 1975; *b* 29 April 1923; *s* of late John Morgan Arthur and Eleanor Arthur; *m* 1951, Joan Tremearne Pickering; two *s* one *d. Educ:* Mill Hill; Christ's Coll., Cambridge (MA). Commnd RAF, 1943, demobilised 1946. Cambridge, 1946-48; called to Bar, Inner Temple, 1949. Dep. Chm., Lancs County QS, 1970-71; a Recorder, 1972-75. *Address:* Orovales, Caldy, Wirral L48 1LP. *T:* 051-625 8624. *Clubs:* MCC, Old Millhillians; Racquets, Athenæum (Liverpool).

ARTHUR, Peter Bernard; Deputy Chairman and Chairman of the Sub-Committees of Classification, Lloyd's Register of Shipping, since 1976; *b* 29 Aug. 1923; *s* of Charles Frederick Bernard Arthur and Joan (*née* Dyer); *m* 1954, Irêne Suxy (*née* Schüpbach); one *s* two *d. Educ:* Oundle Sch. Commnd 1943; Mahratta LI, 1943-47 (mentioned in despatches, Italy, 1945); RA, 1947-53. Underwriting Mem. of Lloyd's, 1954-; Mem. Cttee, Lloyd's Register of Shipping, and Vice-Chm., Sub-Cttees of Classification, 1967. Dir, Bolton Steam Shipping Co. Ltd, 1958-; Chairman: London Deep Sea Tramp Shipowners' Assoc., 1970-71; Deep Sea Tramp Sect., Chamber of Shipping of UK, 1972-73; Mem., London Gen. Shipowners Soc., 1965-. *Recreations:* golf, music, gardening. *Address:* Oak Lodge, Peter Avenue, Oxted, Surrey RH8 9LG. *T:* Oxted 2962. *Club:* Tandridge Golf.

ARTHUR, Rt. Rev. Robert Gordon; Priest-in-charge of Bratton, Wilts, since 1975; Rural Dean of Heytesbury, since 1976; *b* 17 Aug. 1909; *s* of George Thomas Arthur and Mary Arthur; *m* Marie Olive Cavell Wheen; two *s* two *d. Educ:* Launceston and Devonport High Schs, Tasmania; Queen's Coll., Univ. of Melbourne. MA (Hons) 1932. Rector of: Berridale, NSW, 1950-53; St John's, Canberra, ACT, 1953-60; Wagga Wagga, NSW, 1960-61; Archdeacon of Canberra, 1953-60; Asst Bp of Canberra and Goulburn, 1956-61; Bishop of Grafton, NSW, 1961-73; Rector of St Philip's, Canberra, 1973-74. *Address:* Bratton Vicarage, Westbury, Wilts. *T:* Bratton 374.

ARTHURE, Humphrey George Edgar, CBE 1969; MD, FRCS, FRCOG; Consulting Obstetric and Gynæcological Surgeon: Charing Cross Hospital; Queen Charlotte's Hospital; Mount Vernon Hospital. MRCS, LRCP 1931; MB, BS 1933; FRCS 1935; MD London 1938; FRCOG 1950 (Hon. Sec. 1949-56; Vice-Pres. 1964-67); FRSM (Pres., Section of Obstetrics and Gynaecology, 1969); co-opted Mem. Council, RCS 1960; Pres., West London Medico-Chirurgical Soc., 1964; Formerly: Chm., Central Midwives Board, and Adviser, Obstetrics and Gynæcology, DHSS; Mem., Standing Maternity and Midwifery Advisory Cttee; Resident Obstetric Officer and Obstetrical Registrar, Charing Cross Hospital; Resident Medical Officer, Chelsea Hospital for Women. Served War of 1939-45, temp. Lt-Col, RAMC. *Publications:* Simpson Oration, 1972; contribs med. jls. *Address:* 12 Eyot Green, Chiswick Mall, W4 2PT. *T:* 01-994 7698.

ARTON, Major A. T. B.-; *see* Bourne-Arton.

ARTRO MORRIS, John Evan; a Registrar of the Supreme Court, Family Division, since 1977; *b* 17 Feb. 1925; *s* of Tudor and Mabel Artro Morris; *m* 1961, Karin Ilse Alide Russell; two *s . Educ:* Liverpool Coll.; The Queen's Coll., Oxford. BA Oxon. Served RN, 1943-47. Called to the Bar, Middle Temple, 1952. *Recreations:* D-I-Y, Rugby (spectator), rough shooting, fishing. *Address:* 6 Billing Street, SW10 9UR. *T:* 01-352 5249. *Club:* London Welsh RFC.

ARUNDEL AND SURREY, Earl of; Edward William Fitzalan-Howard; student; *b* 2 Dec. 1956; *s* and *heir* of 17th Duke of Norfolk, *qv. Educ:* Ampleforth Coll., Yorks; Lincoln Coll., Oxford. *Recreations:* ski-ing, shooting, farming. *Address:* Arundel Castle, Sussex. *T:* Arundel 882173; Carlton Towers, Yorks. *T:* Goole 860 243; Bacres House, Hambleden, Henley-on-Thames. *T:* Hambleden 350.

ARUNDELL; *see* Monckton-Arundell, family name of Viscount Galway.

ARUNDELL, Dennis Drew, (formerly D. D. Arundel); actor, composer, producer, writer for theatre, radio, films and television, since 1926; *b* 22 July 1898; *s* of Arundel Drew Arundel and Rose Lucy Campbell. *Educ:* Tonbridge Sch.; St John's Coll., Cambridge. Lieut, RGA, 1917-19 (gassed, 1918). St John's Coll., 1919-29 (Sizarship, 1917; Strathcona Studentship, 1922); BA (Classics) 1922, MusB 1923, MA 1924. Fellow of St John's Coll., Cambridge, 1923-29; Lecturer in Music and English Drama, Deputy Organist St John's, 1924. First appeared on professional stage at Lyric, Hammersmith, 1926; subseq. joined Old Vic Company, and has since taken many parts, directed and composed music for plays in West End theatres, films, radio and television. Chief Producer, RCM Opera Sch., 1959-73 (Crees Lectr, RCM, 1970; FRCM 1969); Resident Opera Producer and Coach, Royal Northern Coll. of Music, Manchester, 1974. Chm., Internat. Jury of Singing, Jeunesses Musicales, Belgrade, 1972. As an opera director his work has been especially with Sadler's Wells and the BBC; producer of over 50 operas; translator of some 15 operas; arr. Purcell's Indian Queen for Opera da Camera, 1973; directed both operas and plays in Australia, 1956, 1975 and Finland, 1947, 1952, 1957 (scene from 1952 production of Hamlet inc. in centenary prog. of Helsinki Nat. Theatre, 1973). Lecture to Soc. of Theatre Research, 1971. *Publications:* Henry Purcell, 1927 (in German, 1929); (ed) King Arthur, Purcell Soc. edn, 1928; Dryden and Howard, 1929; The Critic at the Opera, 1957; The Story of Sadler's Wells, 1965; Introduction to Le Nozze di Figaro and Cosi fan Tutte (Cassell Opera Guides), 1971; (ed) Congreve's Semele, 1925; (trans.) Morax and Honegger's King David, 1929; (trans.) Weinberger's Schwanda the Bagpiper, 1946; (trans.) Claudel's and Honegger's Jeanne d'Arc au Bûcher, 1939; (trans.) Monteverdi's Il Combattimento di Tancredi e Clorinda, 1974; Sibelius's Kullervo, 1974; various musical compositions and musical articles. *Recreation:* operatic research. *Address:* 21 Lloyd Square, WC1. *T:* 01-837 2942.

ARUNDELL, Brig. Sir Robert (Duncan Harris), KCMG 1950 (CMG 1947); OBE 1943; retired as Governor and Commander-in-Chief, Barbados (1953-59) (Acting Governor-General and C-in-C, The West Indies, 1959); Zanzibar Delimitation Commissioner, 1962; *b* Lifton, Devon, 22 July 1904; *s* of late C. H. Arundell; *m* 1929, Joan, *d* of late Capt. J. A. Ingles, RN; one *s. Educ:* Blundell's Sch.; Brasenose Coll., Oxford. Colonial Administrative Service, Tanganyika Territory, 1927; seconded Colonial Office, 1935-37; Sec. Nyasaland Financial Commission, 1937-38; Tanganyika Territory, 1938-39; Assistant Chief Sec. Uganda, 1939; Army, Civil Affairs, 1941-45; served War of 1939-45 in Middle East and East Africa (despatches, OBE); Chief Civil Affairs Officer MEF (Brig.), 1944-45; British Resident Mem. in Washington of Caribbean Commission, 1946-47; Governor and C-in-C, Windward Islands, 1948-53. KStJ 1952. *Address:* Wakehill, Ilminster, Somerset. *Club:* East India, Devonshire, Sports and Public Schools.

ARUP, Sir Ove (Nyquist), Kt 1971; CBE 1953; FICE, FIStructE, MICEI, MSAICE; Senior Partner of Ove Arup & Partners, Consulting Engineers, since 1949, and Arup Associates, since 1963; *b* Newcastle upon Tyne, 16 April 1895; *s* of Jens Simon Johannes Arup and Mathilde B. Nyquist; *m* 1925, Ruth Sœrensen; one *s* two *d. Educ:* Preparatory Sch., Hamburg, Germany; Public Sch., Sorø; Univ. of Copenhagen, Denmark. MIngF (Medlem Ingeniør Forening), Copenhagen. Designer Christiani & Nielsen, GmbH, Hamburg, 1922-23, transf. to London 1923; Designer, 1923-25, Chief Designer, 1925-34, Christiani & Nielsen, Ltd, London; Director and Chief Designer, J. L. Kier & Co., Ltd, London, 1934-38; Consulting Engineer for: schools, flats, air raid shelters, industrial projects, marine work (Air Min.); Director: Arup Designs, Ltd; Arup & Arup, Ltd; Pipes, Ltd, 1938-45; Chm. Soc. of Danish Civil Engineers in Gt Britain and Ireland, 1955-59; Visiting Lectr, Harvard Univ., 1955; Alfred Bossom Lectr, RSA, 1970; Maitland Lecture, IStructE, 1968. RIBA Royal Gold Medal for Architecture for 1966; Gold Medal, IStructE, 1973. Hon. DSc Durham, 1967; Hon. ScD East Anglia, 1968; Hon. Dr Tekniske Hojskole, Lyngby, Denmark, 1974; Hon. DSc Heriot-Watt, 1976. Fellow Amer. Concrete Inst., 1975. Commander (First Class), Order of the Dannebrog, 1975 (Chevalier, 1965).

Publications: Design, Cost, Construction and Relative Safety of Trench, Surface, Bomb-proof and other Air Raid Shelters, 1939; Safe Housing in War-Time, 1941; various contribs to technical jls. *Recreations:* music and reading. *Address:* 6 Fitzroy Park, Highgate, N6. *T:* 01-340 3388. *Clubs:* Athenæum; Danish.

ARVILL, Robert; *see* Boote, R. E.

ARWYN, Baron, *cr* 1964 (Life Peer); **Arwyn Randall Arwyn;** Chairman, Atkinson Electrical Engineering, Penryn, Cornwall, since 1976; Director of various companies; Chartered Mining Engineer and Industrial Consultant; *b* 17 April 1897; *s* of Rev. William Davies, Congregational Minister, Glamorgan; changed name by deedpoll from Davies to Arwyn, 1964; *m* 1st, 1929, Norah Gwynne (marr. diss. 1945), *d* of Ernest Watkins, Swansea; two *d*; 2nd, 1946, Beatrix Emily Bassett, *d* of Capt. F. H. Organ, St Austell; one *s. Educ:* Ystalyfera Grammar Sch.; Swansea Technical Coll. Served Wars of 1914-18 and 1939-45: Army, Air Force, and specialist duties. Member: Mineral Develt Cttee, 1946-49; China Clay Council, 1948-71; Mil., Sci. and Tech. Cttees, North Atlantic Assembly, 1967-73. Dep. Chm., Bath and Portland Group, 1926-75, now Gp Consultant. Past Pres., Inst. of Cornish Mining Engrs. CEng, FIMinE. *Address:* Ormonde, Lostwithiel, Cornwall. *Clubs:* Reform; Royal Automobile; Royal Cornwall Yacht, House of Lords Yacht, Flushing Sailing.

ASAAD, Prof. Fikry Naguib M.; *see* Morcos-Asaad.

ASFA WOSSEN HAILE SELLASSIE, HIH Merd Azmatch; GCMG (Hon.) 1965; GCVO (Hon.) 1930; GBE (Hon.) 1932; Crown Prince of Ethiopia, since 1930; *b* 27 July 1916; *e s* and *heir* of late Emperor Haile Sellassie, KG, and Empress Menen; *m* 1st, Princess Wallatta Israel; one *d* decd; 2nd, Princess Madfariash Wark Abebe; one *s* three *d. Educ:* privately; Liverpool Univ. Governor of Wollo province; Mem., Crown Council. Fought in Italo-Ethiopian War, 1935-36. Grand Cross: Légion d'Honneur; Belgian Order of Leopold; Order of the Netherlands; Order of Rising Sun, Japan; Order of White Elephant, Siam. *Recreation:* walking. *Heir:* s Prince Zara Yacob, *b* 18 Aug. 1953. *Address:* 82 Portland Place, W1.

ASH, Prof. Eric Albert, FRS 1977; Professor of Electrical Engineering, University of London, at University College London, since 1967; *b* 31 Jan. 1928; *s* of Walter and Dorothea Ash; *m* 1954, Clare (*née* Babb); five *d. Educ:* University College Sch.; Imperial Coll. of Science and Technology. BSc(Eng), PhD, DSc; ACGI, DIC. FIEE; FIEEE; FInstP. Research Fellow: Stanford Univ., Calif, 1952-54; QMC, 1954-55; Res. Engr, Standard Telecommunication Laboratories Ltd, 1955-63; Sen. Lectr, 1963-65, Reader, 1965-67, Dept of Electronic and Electrical Engrg, UCL. Chm., IEE Publications Bd, 1975-; Member: MoD Cttees; IEE Council. *Publications:* patents; papers on topics in physical electronics in various engrg and physics jls. *Recreations:* music, skiing, swimming. *Address:* 11 Ripplevale Grove, N1 1AE. *T:* 01-607 4989.

ASH, Graham Baron; *b* 18 Aug. 1889; *s* of Alfred James Ash, OBE. *Educ:* Radley. Served European War with RFC and RAF, and with RAF, 1939-40; High Sheriff of Warwickshire, 1938-39. *Recreation:* shooting. *Address:* Wingfield Castle, Diss, Norfolk.

ASH, Maurice Anthony, BSc (Econ); Chairman, Dartington Hall Trust, since 1972; Chairman of Executive, Town and Country Planning Association, since 1969; *b* 31 Oct. 1917; *s* of Wilfred Cracroft and Beatrice Ash; *m* 1947, Ruth Whitney Elmhirst, *o d* of late Leonard Knight Elmhirst; three *d* (one *s* decd). *Educ:* Gresham's Sch., Holt; LSE; Yale. Served War of 1939-45, armoured forces in Western Desert, Italy, Greece (despatches 1944). Mem. Executive, TCPA, 1956-; Trustee, Dartington Hall and Dir associated companies, 1964-; Mem., SW Regional Economic Planning Council, 1965-68. Founder, Harlow Arts Trust. *Publications:* The Human Cloud, 1962; Who are the Progressives Now?, 1969; Regions of Tomorrow, 1969; A Guide to the Structure of London, 1972; articles on land use, education, international relations. *Recreation:* applying Wittgenstein. *Address:* Sharpham House, Ashprington, Totnes, Devon TQ9 7UT. *T:* Harbertonford 216. *Club:* Reform.

ASH, Rear-Admiral Walter William Hector, CB 1962; WhSch; CEng; FIEE; *b* Portsmouth, Hants; 2 May 1906; *s* of Hector Sidney and Mabel Jessy Ash; *m* 1932, Louisa Adelaide Salt, Jarrow-on-Tyne; three *d. Educ:* City & Guilds Coll., Kensington; Royal Naval Coll., Greenwich. Whitworth Scholar, 1926; John Samuel Scholar, 1927. Asst Elect. Engr, Admiralty (submarine design), 1932-37; Elect. Engr, Admiralty (battleship design), 1937-39; Fleet Elect. Engr, Staff C-in-C Med., 1939-40; Supt Elect. Engr, Admiralty (supply and prod.), 1940-45; Supt

Elect. Engr, HM Dockyard, Hong Kong, 1945-48; Supt Elect. Engr, Admiralty Engineering Lab., 1948-49; Comdr RN, HMS Montclare, 1950-51; Capt. RN, Admiralty (weapon control design), 1951-54; Capt. RN, Elect. Engr Manager, HM Dockyard, Devonport, 1954-58; Capt. RN, Ship Design Dept, Admiralty, 1959-60; Rear-Adm. 1960; subseq. Ship Dept Directorate, Admty, retd Aug. 1963. Vis. Lectr in electrical machinery design, RN Coll., Greenwich, 1934-37. Chairman IEE, SW Sub Centre, 1957-58. ADC to the Queen, 1958-60. *Recreations:* golf, music (piano and organ). *Address:* Saltash, 14 Beacon Drive, Highcliffe-on-Sea, Christchurch, Dorset BH23 5DH. *T:* Highcliffe 5261.

ASH, Rear-Adm. William Noel, CB 1977; MVO 1959; Director of Service Intelligence, 1974-77; *b* 6 March 1921; *s* of late H. Arnold Ash, MRCS, LRCP; *m* 1951, Pamela, *d* of late Harry C. Davies, Hawkes Bay, NZ; one *s* one *d*. *Educ:* Merchant Taylors' School. Joined RN, 1938; HM Yacht Britannia, 1955-58; Captain 1965; Canadian NDC, 1965-66; Staff of SACLANT (NATO), 1966-69; Cabinet Office, 1969-71; comd HMS Ganges, 1971-73; Rear-Adm. 1974. *Address:* Lynchets, Buriton, Petersfield, Hants. *T:* Petersfield 3470. *Club:* Royal Commonwealth Society.

ASHBEE, Paul; Archaeologist, University of East Anglia, since 1969; *b* 23 June 1918; *s* of Lewis Ashbee and Hannah Mary Elizabeth Ashbee (*née* Brett); *m* 1952, Richmal Crompton Lamburn Disher; one *s* one *d*. *Educ:* sch. in Maidstone, Kent; Univ. of London; Univ. of Leicester (MA). Post-grad. Dip. Prehistoric Archaeology, London. Royal W Kent Regt and REME, 1939-46; Control Commn for Germany, 1946-49; Univ. of London, Univ. of Bristol (Redland Coll.), 1949-54; Asst Master and Head of History, Forest Hill Sch., 1954-68. Excavation of prehistoric sites, mostly barrows both long and round for then Min. of Works, 1949-; Co-dir with R. L. S. Bruce-Mitford of BM excavations at Sutton-Hoo, 1964-69. Mem. Council and Meetings Sec., Prehistoric Soc., 1960-74; Sec. (Wareham Earthwork), British Assoc. Sub-Cttee for Archaeological Field Experiment, 1961-; one-time Sec., Neolithic and Bronze Age Cttee, Council for British Archaeology; Mem. Royal Commn on Historical Monuments (England), 1975-; Mem., Area Archaeological Adv. Cttee (DoE) for Norfolk and Suffolk, 1975-. Pres., Cornwall Archæol Soc., 1976-. FSA 1958. *Publications:* The Bronze Age Round Barrow in Britain, 1960; The Earthen Long Barrow in Britain, 1970; Ancient Scilly, 1974; chapter in Sutton Hoo, Vol. I, 1976; numerous papers, articles and reviews in Archaeologia, Antiquaries Jl, Archaeological Jl, Proc. Prehistoric Soc., Antiquity, Cornish Archaeology, Arch. Cantiana, Proc. Dorset Arch. and Nat. Hist. Soc., Proc. Hants FC, etc. *Recreations:* skiing, historical architecture, bibliophilia, dog ownership. *Address:* The Old Rectory, Chedgrave, Norfolk NR14 6ND; University of East Anglia, Norwich NR4 7TJ. *T:* Loddon 20595.

ASHBOURNE, 3rd Baron, *cr* 1885; **Edward Russell Gibson;** CB 1950; DSO 1943; Vice-Admiral, retired; *b* 1 June 1901; *s* of Hon. Edward Graves Mayne Gibson (3rd *s* of 1st Baron Ashbourne) and Mary Philips Greg; *S* uncle, 1942; *m* 1929, Reta Frances Manning, *e d* of E. M. Hazeland of Hong Kong; one *s* one *d*. *Educ:* Osborne; Dartmouth; Caius Coll., Cambridge. Entered Osborne, 1915; Midshipman, 1917; served in HMS Superb, Dreadnought, Monarch, in War of 1914-18; Lieut, 1922; specialised in submarines, 1925; Commander 1934; served on staff of Admiral of the Fleet Sir Dudley Pound in Mediterranean, 1938-39; Capt., 1939; served War of 1939-45 (DSO, Legion of Merit, US); served on staff of Adm. Sir Max Horton, 1940-42; Sicily Assault (DSO), 1943; commanded HMS Ariadne (Legion of Merit, US), 1943-45; commanded 3rd Submarine Flotilla, 1945; served on Naval Staff at Admiralty, 1946-47; commanded HMS Mauritius, 1947-48; Rear-Adm., 1948; Naval Representative on Military Staff Cttee, UN, 1949-50; Flag Officer, Gibraltar, and Admiral Supt, HM Dockyard, Gibraltar, 1950-52; Vice-Adm. 1952; retired list, 1952. JP Co. of Devon, 1955. County Pres., St John Ambulance Brigade for Devon, 1963. OStJ 1964. *Heir: s* Lieut-Comdr Hon. Edward Barry Greynville Gibson, RN, retired [*b* 28 Jan. 1933; *m* 1967, Yvonne Georgina, *d* of late Major G. W. Ham; two *s*]. *Address:* 56 Chiltley Way, Liphook, Hampshire. *Club:* Army and Navy.

ASHBROOK, 10th Viscount, *cr* 1751; **Desmond Llowarch Edward Flower**, KCVO 1977; MBE 1945; DL; Baron of Castle Durrow, 1733; Member of Council of Duchy of Lancaster, 1957-77; *b* 9 July 1905; *o s* of 9th Viscount and late Gladys, *d* of late Gen. Sir George Wentworth A. Higginson, GCB, GCVO; *S* father, 1936; *m* 1934, Elizabeth, *er d* of late Capt. John Egerton-Warburton, and of late Hon. Mrs Waters; two *s* one *d*. *Educ:* Eton; Balliol Coll., Oxford (BA 1927). Served War of 1939-45, RA. Formerly a Chartered Accountant. JP, 1946-67, DL 1949-,

Vice-Lieutenant, 1961-67, Cheshire. *Heir: s* Hon. Michael Llowarch Warburton Flower [*b* 9 Dec. 1935; *m* 1971, Zoë Engleheart, *y d* of late F. H. A. Engleheart; two *s*. *Address:* Arley Hall, Northwich, Cheshire. *T:* Arley 204. *Club:* Brooks's.

ASHBURNHAM, Captain Sir Denny Reginald, 12th Bt *cr* 1661; Captain South Staffordshire Regiment; *b* 24 March 1916; *o* surv. *s* of Sir Fleetwood Ashburnham, 11th Bt, and Elfrida, *d* of late James Kirkley, JP, Cleadon Park, Co. Durham; *S* father 1953; *m* 1946, Mary Frances, *d* of Major Robert Pascoe Mair, Wick, Udimore, Sussex; one *s* two *d*. *Heir: s* John Anchitel Fleetwood Ashburnham [*b* 25 June 1951; *m* 1975, Corinne, *d* of D. W. J. O'Brien, Nutley, Sussex]. *Address:* Little Broomham, Guestling, Hastings, East Sussex; (seat) Broomham, Hastings.

ASHBURTON, 6th Baron, *cr* 1835; **Alexander Francis St Vincent Baring**, KG 1969; KCVO 1961; JP; DL; Lord Lieutenant and Custos Rotulorum, Hampshire and Isle of Wight, 1960-73 (Vice-Lieutenant, 1951-60); High Steward of Winchester, since 1967; Receiver-General to the Duchy of Cornwall, 1961-74; *b* 7 April 1898; *o s* of 5th Baron and Hon. Mabel Edith Hood (*d* 1904), *d* of 4th Viscount Hood; *S* father, 1938; *m* 1924, Hon. Doris Mary Thérèse Harcourt, *e d* of 1st Viscount Harcourt; two *s*. *Educ:* Eton; Royal Military Coll. Lieut The Greys, 1917-23; Flt-Lt AAF, 1939, retd as Group Captain, 1944. Director: Baring Brothers & Co. Ltd, 1962-68 (Managing Director, 1928-62); Alliance Assurance, 1932-68; Pressed Steel Co. Ltd, 1944-66; Mem. London Cttee, Hongkong & Shanghai Banking Corp., 1935-39. Treasurer, King Edward VII Hospital Fund for London, 1955-64, Governor, 1971-; Trustee: King George's Jubilee Trust, 1949-68; Chantrey Bequest, 1963-; St Cross Hospital of Noble Poverty, Winchester, 1961-. Chm., Hampshire and IoW Police Authy, 1961-71. President: Hampshire and IoW Territorial Assoc., 1960-67 (Mem., 1951-60); Eastern Wessex Territorial Assoc., 1968-70. CC 1945, CA 1955, JP 1951, DL 1973, Hants. KStJ 1960. *Heir: s* Hon. John Francis Harcourt Baring, *qv*. *Address:* Itchen Stoke House, Alresford, Hants. *T:* Alresford 2479. *Clubs:* Lansdowne; Hampshire County (Winchester).

ASHBY, family name of **Baron Ashby**.

ASHBY, Baron *cr* 1973 (Life Peer), of Brandon, Suffolk; **Eric Ashby**, Kt 1956; FRS 1963; DSc London, MA Cantab; DIC; Chancellor, Queen's University, Belfast, since 1970; Fellow of Clare College, Cambridge, 1958, Life Fellow since 1975; *b* 1904; *s* of Herbert Charles Ashby, Bromley, Kent, and Helena Chater; *m* 1931, Elizabeth Helen Farries, Castle-Douglas, Scotland; two *s*. *Educ:* City of London Sch.; Imperial Coll. of Science, Univ. of London; Univ. of Chicago. Demonstrator at Imperial Coll., 1926-29; Commonwealth Fund Fellow in Univ. of Chicago and Desert Laboratory of Carnegie Institution, 1929-31; Lectr, Imperial Coll. of Science, 1931-35; Reader in Botany, Bristol Univ., 1935-37; Prof. of Botany, Univ. of Sydney, Australia, 1938-46; Harrison Prof. of Botany and Dir of Botanical Labs, Univ. of Manchester, 1946-50; Pres. and Vice-Chancellor, Queen's Univ., Belfast, 1950-59; Master of Clare College, Cambridge, 1959-75; Vice-Chancellor, Univ. of Cambridge, 1967-69. Chm., Aust. National Research Council, 1940-42; Chm., Professorial Board, Univ. of Sydney, 1942-44; Mem., Power Alcohol Committee of Enquiry, 1940-41; conducted enquiry for Prime Minister into enlistment of scientific resources in war, 1942; Trustee, Aust. Museum, 1942-46; Dir, Scientific Liaison Bureau, 1942-43; Counsellor and Chargé d'Affaires at Australian Legation, Moscow, USSR, 1945-46; Member of: Advisory Council on Scientific Policy, 1950-53; Nuffield Provincial Hospitals Trust, 1951-59; Advisory Council on Scientific and Industrial Research, 1954-60; Chairman: Scientific Grants Cttee, DSIR, 1955-56; Postgraduate Grants Cttee, DSIR, 1956-60; Northern Ireland Adv. Council for Education, 1953-58; Adult Education Cttee, 1953-54; Cttee of Award of Commonwealth Fund, 1963- (Member, 1956-61); Royal Commn on Environmental Pollution, 1970-73; Member: Univ. Grants Cttee, 1959-67; Commonwealth Scholarship Commn, 1960-; Council of Royal Soc., 1964-65; Governing Body, Sch. of Oriental and African Studies, Univ. of London, 1965-70; Chm., Commn for post-secondary and higher education in Nigeria, 1959-61; Chm., working party on pollution control in connection with UN conf. on the Environment, Stockholm, June 1972. Vice-Chm. Assoc. of Univs of Brit. Commonwealth, 1959-61; Pres., Brit. Assoc. for the Advancement of Science, 1963. Walgreen Prof., Michigan, 1975-77; Lectures: Godkin, Harvard Univ., 1964; Whidden, McMaster Univ., 1970; Bernal, Royal Soc., 1971; Prof-at-large, Cornell Univ., 1967-72; Trustee: Ciba Foundation, 1966-; British Museum, 1969-; Fellow: Imperial Coll. of Science; Davenport Coll., Yale Univ.; Hon. Fellow, Clare Hall; Hon. FRSE; Hon. FRIC. Hon. Foreign Mem., Amer. Acad. of Arts

and Sciences. Hon. LLD: St Andrews; Aberdeen; Belfast; Rand; London; Wales; Columbia; Chicago; Michigan; Windsor; Western Australia; Manchester; Johns Hopkins; Hon. ScD Dublin; Hon. DSc: NUI; Univ. of Nigeria; Southampton; Hon. DLitt: W Ont; Sydney; Hon. DPhil Tech. Univ. Berlin; Hon. DCL East Anglia; Hon. DHL Yale. Jephcott Medal, RSM, 1976. Order of Andrés Bello, first class, Venezuela, 1974. *Publications:* papers on aspects of experimental botany and on education; Environment and Plant Development, translated from German, 1931; German-English Botanical Terminology (with Elizabeth Helen Ashby), 1938; Food Shipment from Australia in Wartime; Challenge to Education, 1946; Scientist in Russia, 1947 (German trans., 1950); Technology and the Academics, 1958 (Japanese trans., 1963; Spanish trans, 1970); Community of Universities, 1963; African Universities and Western Tradition, 1964 (French trans. 1954); Universities: British, Indian, African (with Mary Anderson), 1966 (Spanish trans. 1972); Masters and Scholars, 1970; (with Mary Anderson) The Rise of the Student Estate, 1970; Any Person, Any Study, 1971; (with Mary Anderson) Portrait of Haldane, 1974. *Recreations:* chamber music, mountain walking. *Address:* Norman Cottage, Manor Road, Brandon, Suffolk IP27 0LG. *T:* Thetford 810695.
See also M. F. Ashby.

ASHBY, Francis Dalton, OBE 1975; Comptroller-General, National Debt Office, since 1976; *b* 20 Jan. 1920; *s* of late John Frederick Ashby and late Jessie Ashby; *m* 1948, Mollie Isabel Mitchell; one *s* two *d*. *Educ:* Watford Grammar Sch. Diploma in Govt Admin. War Service, Royal Signals, 1940-46: POW, Far East, 1942-45. National Debt Office: Exec. Officer, 1938; Asst Comptroller and Estabt Officer, 1966-76. *Recreations:* dinghy sailing, walking. *Address:* Moorfield, Carpenters Wood Drive, Chorleywood, Herts.

ASHBY, Dame Margery I. C.; *see* Corbett Ashby.

ASHBY, Prof. Michael Farries; Professor of Engineering Materials, University of Cambridge, since 1973; *b* 20 Nov. 1935; *s* of Lord Ashby, *qv*; *m* 1962, Maureen Ashby; two *s* one *d*. *Educ:* Campbell Coll., Belfast; Queens' Coll., Cambridge (BA, MA, PhD). Post-doctoral work, Cambridge, 1960-62; Asst, Univ. of Göttingen, 1962-65; Asst Prof., Harvard Univ., 1965-69; Prof. of Metallurgy, Harvard Univ., 1969-73. Hon. MA Harvard, 1969. Editor, Acta Metallurgica, 1974-. *Recreations:* music, design. *Address:* 51 Maids Causeway, Cambridge CB5 8DE. *T:* Cambridge 64741.

ASHCOMBE, 4th Baron, *cr* 1892; **Henry Edward Cubitt;** late RAF; Chairman, Cubitt Estates Ltd; *b* 31 March 1924; *er s* of 3rd Baron Ashcombe; *S* father, 1962; *m* 1955, Ghislaine (marr. diss. 1968), *o d* of Cornelius Willem Dresselhuys, Long Island, New York; *m* 1973, Hon. Virginia Carington, *yr d* of Baron Carrington, *qv*. *Educ:* Eton. Served War of 1939-45, RAF. Consul-General in London for the Principality of Monaco, 1961-68. *Heir: cousin* Alick John Archibald Cubitt [*b* 10 Aug. 1927; *m* 1st, 1956, Rosemary Priscilla (*d* 1957), *er d* of T. C. Gouldsmith; 2nd, 1961, Jennifer Faith, *yr d* of late Lt-Col William Henry Ewart Gott, CB, CBE, DSO, MC; two *d*]. *Address:* Denbies, Dorking, Surrey. *Club:* White's.
See also Earl of Harrington.

ASHCROFT, David, TD 1957; MA Cantab; Headmaster, Cheltenham College, 1959-Aug. 1978; *b* 20 May 1920; *s* of late A. H. Ashcroft, DSO; *m* 1949, Joan Elizabeth Young; two *s* three *d*. *Educ:* Rugby Sch.; Gonville and Caius Coll., Cambridge. War Service, 1940-46 (despatches). Asst Master, Rossall Sch., 1946-50; Asst Master, Rugby Sch., 1950-59. *Address:* College House, Cheltenham, Glos. *T:* Cheltenham 24841.

ASHCROFT, James Geoffrey; Assistant Under Secretary of State, Central Finance, Ministry of Defence, since 1976; *b* 19 May 1928; *s* of James Ashcroft and Elizabeth (*née* Fillingham); *m* 1953, Margery (*née* Barratt); one *s*. *Educ:* Cowley Sch., St Helens; Peterhouse, Cambridge. BA (Hons Hist.). Min. of Supply, 1950-59; Min. of Aviation, 1959-61, 1964-65; Min. of Defence, 1961-64, 1965-68, 1970-73; Inst. of Strategic Studies, 1968-70; Under-Sec., Pay Board, 1973-74; Asst Under Sec. of State, Management Services, PE, 1974-76. *Publications:* papers on international collaboration in military logistics. *Recreation:* golf. *Address:* 39 Hill Rise, Hinchley Wood, Esher, Surrey KT10 0AL. *T:* 01-398 5637.

ASHCROFT, Ven. Lawrence; retired as Archdeacon of Stow and Vicar of Burton-on-Stather (1954-62); *b* 1901; *s* of Lawrence Ashcroft; *m* 1927, Barbara Louise Casson; two *s* three *d*. *Educ:* University Coll., Durham; Lichfield Theological Coll. Deacon,

1926; Priest, 1927; Curate of Ulverston, 1926-29, of Egremont, 1929-30; District Sec., Brit. and Foreign Bible Society, 1930-33; Vicar of St Saviour's, Retford, 1934-40; Chaplain to the Forces (Emergency Commission), 1940-43; Rector of St Michael Stoke, Coventry, 1943; Rural Dean of Coventry, 1949; Hon. Canon of Coventry, 1952; Hon. Canon of Lincoln, 1954; Chaplain to British Embassy, Oslo, 1967, Luxembourg, 1968; Rector, St Philip's, Antigua, 1969, Manvers St Crispin, Toronto, 1970-. *Address:* c/o Lloyds Bank Ltd, St Helier, Jersey, Channel Islands.

ASHCROFT, Dame Peggy, (Edith Margaret Emily), DBE 1956 (CBE 1951); actress; Director, Royal Shakespeare Co., since 1968; *b* 22 Dec. 1907; *d* of William Worsley Ashcroft and Violet Maud Bernheim; *m* 1st, 1929, Rupert Hart-Davis (marr. diss.; he was knighted, 1967); 2nd, 1934, Theodore Komisarjevsky (marr. diss.); 3rd, 1940, Jeremy Hutchinson, QC (marr. diss., 1966); one *s* one *d*. *Educ:* Woodford Sch., Croydon; Central Sch. of Dramatic Art. Member of the Arts Council, 1962-64. Ashcroft Theatre, Croydon, named in her honour, 1962. First appeared as Margaret in Dear Brutus, Birmingham Repertory Theatre, 1926; parts include: Bessie in One Day More, Everyman, Eve in When Adam Delved, Wyndham's, 1927, Mary Bruin in The Land of Heart's Desire, Hester in The Silver Cord, 1928; Constance Neville in She Stoops to Conquer, Naomi in Jew Süss, 1929; Desdemona in Othello with Paul Robeson, 1930; Fanny in Sea Fever, 1931; Cleopatra, Imogen, Rosalind, etc, at Old Vic and Sadler's Wells, 1932; Juliet at New, 1935; Nina in Seagull, New, 1936; Portia, Lady Teazle, and, Irina in Three Sisters, Queen's, 1937-38; Yeliena in White Guard and Viola, Phoenix, 1938-39; Cecily Cardew in The Importance of Being Earnest, 1939-40, and Dinah in Cousin Muriel, 1940, both at Globe; revival of Importance of Being Earnest, Phoenix, 1942; Catherine in The Dark River, Whitehall, 1943; Ophelia, Titania, Duchess of Malfi, Haymarket Repertory Season, 1944-45; Evelyn Holt in Edward my Son, His Majesty's, 1947; Catherine Sloper in The Heiress, Haymarket, 1949; Beatrice and Cordelia, Memorial Theatre, Stratford-on-Avon, 1950; Viola, Electra and Mistress Page, Old Vic 1950-51; Hester Collyer in the Deep Blue Sea, Duchess, 1952; Cleopatra, Stratford-on-Avon and Princes, 1953; title-rôle, Hedda Gabler, Lyric, Hammersmith and Westminster, 1954; Beatrice in Much Ado About Nothing, Stratford Festival Company, 1955 (London, provinces and continental tour); Miss Madrigal in The Chalk Garden, Haymarket, 1956; Shen Te in The Good Woman of Setzuan, Royal Court, 1956; Rosalind, Imogen, Cymbeline, Stratford-on-Avon, 1957; Julia Rajk in Shadow of Heroes, Piccadilly, 1958; Stratford-on-Avon Season, 1960: Katharina in The Taming of the Shrew; Paulina in The Winter's Tale; The Hollow Crown, Aldwych, 1961; title rôle in The Duchess of Malfi, Aldwych, 1961; Emilia in Othello, Stratford-on-Avon, 1961, also Madame Ranevskaya in the Cherry Orchard, subseq. Aldwych; Margaret of Anjou in Henry VI and Margaret in Edward IV, also Margaret in Richard III, Stratford-on-Avon, 1963, Aldwych, 1964; Mme Arkadina in The Seagull, Queen's, 1964; Mother in Days in the Trees, Aldwych, 1966; Mrs Alving in Ghosts, 1967; A Delicate Balance, Aldwych, 1969; Beth in Landscape, Aldwych, 1969; Katharine of Aragon in Henry VIII, Stratford-on-Avon, 1969; The Plebeians Rehearse the Uprising, Aldwych, 1970; The Lovers of Viorne, Royal Court, 1971 (Evening Standard Best Actress award, 1972); All Over, Aldwych, 1972; Lloyd George Knew My Father, Savoy, 1972. Beth in Landscape, Flora in A Slight Ache, Ashcroft Theatre, foreign tour and Aldwych, 1973; The Hollow Crown, tour in US, 1973; John Gabriel Borkman, National, 1975; Happy Days, National, 1975, 1977; Old World, Aldwych, 1976. Entered films 1933; subsequent films include: The Wandering Jew, The Thirty-nine Steps, The Nun's Story (played Mother Mathilde), etc. Queen Victoria for BBC Radio, 1973. King's Gold Medal, Norway, 1955; Hon. DLitt: Oxford, 1961; Leicester, 1964; Warwick, 1974; Hon. DLit London, 1965; Hon LittD Cantab, 1972. Hon. Fellow, St Hugh's College, Oxford, 1964. Comdr, Order of St Olav, Norway, 1976. *Address:* Manor Lodge, Frognal Lane, NW3.

ASHCROFT, Philip Giles; Legal Adviser, Department of Energy, since 1974; *b* 15 Nov. 1926; *s* of Edmund Samuel Ashcroft and Constance Ruth Ashcroft (*née* Giles); *m* 1968, Kathleen Margaret Senior; one *s*. *Educ:* Royal Grammar Sch., Newcastle upon Tyne; Durham Univ. Admitted solicitor, 1951. Joined Treasury Solicitor's Dept, 1955; Asst Legal Adviser, Land Commn, 1967; Asst Treasury Solicitor, 1971; Under-Sec. (Legal), DTI, 1973. *Recreations:* reading, listening to music, walking. *Address:* 3 Julian Close, Woking, Surrey GU21 3HD. *T:* Woking 71383.

ASHDOWN, Rt. Rev. Hugh Edward, MA, DD; *b* 5 July 1904; *s* of William Edward and Sarah Annie Constance Ashdown; *m*

1937, Georgina Sylvia (*née* Battye); one *s* two *d. Educ:* St John's, Leatherhead; Keble College, Oxford; Lincoln Theological College. Deacon, 1929; priest, 1930; Curate of St Mary, Portsea, 1929-34; Chaplain and Lecturer, Lincoln Theol Coll., 1934-37; Exam. Chaplain to Bishop of Ripon, 1935-46; Perpetual Curate of St Aidan's, West Hartlepool, 1937-43; Rector of Houghton-le-Spring, 1943-48; Rector of St Saviour with St Peter, Southwark, and Provost of Southwark, 1948-57; Bishop of Newcastle, 1957-72. *Address:* Manor Cottage, Misterton, near Crewkerne, Somerset.

ASHE, Derick Rosslyn, CMG 1966; HM Diplomatic Service; Ambassador and Permanent UK Representative to Disarmament Conference, Geneva, since 1977; *b* 20 Jan. 1919; *s* of late Frederick Allen Ashe and late Rosalind Ashe (*née* Mitchell); *m* 1957, Rissa Guinness, *d* of late Capt. Hon. Trevor Tempest Parker, DSC, Royal Navy (retd) and Mrs Parker; one *s* one *d. Educ:* Bradfield Coll.; Trinity Coll., Oxford. HM Forces, 1940-46 (despatches 1945). Second Sec., Berlin and Frankfurt-am-Main, 1947-49; Private Sec. to Permanent Under-Sec. of State for German Section of FO, 1950-53; First Sec., La Paz, 1953-55; FO, 1955-57; First Sec. (Information), Madrid, 1957-61; FO, 1961-62; Counsellor and Head of Chancery: Addis Ababa, 1962-64; Havana, 1964-66; Head of Security Dept, FCO (formerly FO), 1966-69; Minister, Tokyo, 1969-71; Ambassador to: Romania, 1972-75; Argentina, 1975-77. Knight of the Order of Orange-Nassau (with swords), 1945. *Recreation:* riding. *Address:* c/o Foreign and Commonwealth Office, SW1; 30 Gloucester Square, W2. *T:* 01-262 4647. *Clubs:* Travellers', Beefsteak.

ASHE LINCOLN, Fredman; *see* Lincoln, F. A.

ASHENHEIM, Sir Neville (Noel), Kt 1963; CBE 1958; Leader of Government Business in the Senate and Minister without Portfolio, Jamaica, 1967-72; *b* 18 Dec. 1900; *s* of Lewis Ashenheim and Estelle Lillian de Cordova; *m* 1926, Leonie Vivienne Delevante; three *s. Educ:* Jamaica Coll.; Munro Coll.; Wadham Coll., Oxford. BA 1922, MA 1943. Admitted Solicitor of Supreme Court, 1926, and joined father's firm of Milholland, Ashenheim & Stone. HM's Jamaican Ambassador to the USA, 1962-67. Chairman: "The Gleaner" Company, 1946-67 (newspaper in Caribbean founded by his forbears in 1834); Jamaica Industrial Development Corporation, 1952-57; Caribbean Cement Co., 1965-73; Caribbean Steel Co., 1965-73; Wray & Nephew Gp Ltd (formerly Consolidated Internat. Corporation), 1958-73; Internat. Corp.; Standard Life Assurance Co. (Jamaica Branch), 1958-61, 1967-71; Jamaica Housing Develt Co., 1957-62. Director: Lascelles de Merado & Co. Ltd; Henriques Brothers Ltd, 1950-73; West Indies Glass Co. Ltd, 1961-73. Hon. DHL Hebrew Union Coll., 1964. *Address:* Apartment B5, Roxdene, Pitts Bay Road, Pembroke, Bermuda. *Clubs:* Jamaica, Liguanea, St Andrew, Kingston Cricket, Jamaica Jockey (all in Jamaica); Royal Bermuda Yacht.

ASHERSON, Nehemiah, MA Cape; MB, BS London; FRCS, LRCP; FZS, etc; Fellow International College of Surgeons; Hon. Fellow Surgical Academy, Madrid; Associate, Royal Institute of Chemistry, 1919; Hon. Cons. Surgeon, The Royal National (Central London) Throat, Nose, and Ear Hospital (late Member of Board of Governors, 1948-49-50-58); late Hon. Secretary to the Medical Council; Lecturer to the Institute of Otology and Laryngology (Member Academic Board); Teacher in Oto-laryngology in the University of London; Consulting Surgeon for Diseases of the Ear, Nose, and Throat to the NE, NW and SE regional hospital boards, including the Queen Elizabeth Hospital for Children; FRSocMed (Hon. Mem., late Pres., Section of Laryngology; Member Council, Section History of Medicine; late Member Council Section Otology, and Library Committee); Trustee (Hon. Fellow, late Pres., Hunterian Society); Hon. Treasurer, BMA, St Marylebone Division, and Mem. Ethical Cttee; Fellow and Hon. Librarian, late Councillor, Medical Society of London; *b* 1897; *s* of Isaac Asherson; *m*; one *s* one *d. Educ:* South African Coll.; Univ. of Cape Town (Entrance Scholar); University Coll. and Hospital, London; postgraduate study in speciality in London and Vienna. Medallist in Chemistry; exhibitioner at the BA examination; Jamieson Scholar at MA; Alexander Bruce Gold Medallist in Surgery and Liston Gold Medal in Surgical Pathology, University Coll. Hosp.; Geoffrey Duveen Travelling Scholar of the Univ. of London in Oto-rhino Laryngology; late Harker Smith Cancer (radium) Registrar and Casualty Surgical Officer at University Coll. Hosp.; Chief Asst to the Royal Ear Hosp., University Coll. Hosp.; Chief Asst to the Ear, Nose, and Throat Dept of the Bolingbroke Hosp., etc; Late: Ear Consultant to Army Medical Boards; Surgeon Emergency Medical Service, 1939-45; Consulting Surgeon to LCC and to the Charterhouse Rheumatism Clinic. Hunterian Prof., RCS, 1942. Mem. Royal

Instn (Visitor, 1969-71). Mem., Apothecaries Soc. *Publications:* Diagnosis and Treatment of Foreign Bodies in the Upper Food and Respiratory Passages, 1932; Acute Otitis and Mastoiditis in General Practice, 1934; Chronic Ear Discharge (Otorrhœa) and its complications, 1936; Otogenic Cerebellar Abscess, Hunterian Lecture, 1942; Identification by Frontal Sinus Prints, 1965; The Deafness of Beethoven, 1965; Bibliography of G. J. Du Verney's Traité de l'Organe de l'Ouï, 1683 (first scientific treatise on the ear), 1977; communications in Jl of Laryngology, of the Royal Society of Medicine, in The Lancet and in medical journals on subjects relating to the speciality. *Recreations:* numismatics, book collecting. *Address:* 21 Harley Street, W1. *T:* 01-580 3197; Green Shutters, East Preston, West Kingston, West Sussex. *Clubs:* Reform, Savage.

ASHFORD, (Albert) Reginald, CMG 1962; Assistant Secretary, Board of Customs and Excise, 1952-73; *b* 30 June 1914; *s* of late Ernest Ashford; *m* 1946, Mary Anne Ross Davidson, *d* of late Thomas Davidson; one *s. Educ:* Ealing Grammar Sch.; London Sch. of Economics. UK Delegate to numerous internat. conferences on reduction of trade barriers and simplification of customs formalities, 1946-60. *Recreations:* local amenity societies, walking, gardening. *Address:* Piper's Lawn, 21 Frogmore Close, Hughenden Valley, High Wycombe, Bucks. *T:* Naphill 2440.

ASHFORD, George Francis, OBE 1945; Director: Albright and Wilson Ltd, since 1973; Inveresk Research International, since 1973; Member, Monopolies and Mergers Commission, since 1973; *b* 5 July 1911; *s* of G. W. Ashford and L. M. Redfern; *m* 1950, Eleanor Vera Alexander; two *s. Educ:* Malvern Coll.; Trinity Hall, Cambridge; Birmingham Univ. Served War of 1939-45, Army, N Africa and Italy (despatches 1944). Distillers Co. Ltd, 1937-67: Solicitor, 1937; Legal Adviser, 1945; Dir, 1956; Management Cttee, 1963-67; Dir, BP Co. Ltd, 1967-73; Man. Dir, 1969-73. Pres., British Plastics Fedn, 1966-67; Vice-President: Soc. of Chemical Industry, 1966-69; Chem. Ind. Assoc., 1967-70. Mem. Economic Policy Cttee for Chemical Industry, 1967-74; Chm., Working Party on Industrial Review, 1973. *Recreation:* gardening. *Address:* The Old House, Sonning, Berks. *T:* Reading 692122; 13 Cheyne Gardens, SW3. T: 01-352 1754. *Club:* Royal Automobile.

ASHFORD, Reginald; *see* Ashford, A. R.

ASHIOTIS, Costas; High Commissioner of Cyprus in London since 1966; Cyprus Ambassador to Denmark, Sweden, Norway and Malta; *b* 1908; *m* . 3*Educ:* Pancyprian Gymnasium, Nicosia; London Sch. of Economics. Journalist and editor; joined Govt Service, 1942; Asst Comr of Labour, 1948; Dir-Gen., Min. of Foreign Affairs, 1960. Mem. Cyprus delegns to UN and to internat. confs. MBE 1952. *Publications:* Labour Conditions in Cyprus during the War Years, 1939-45; literary articles. *Address:* Cyprus High Commission, 93 Park Street, W1. *T:* 01-499 8272.

ASHKENAZY, Vladimir; concert pianist; *b* Gorky, Russia, 6 July 1937; *m* 1961, Thorunn Tryggvason, Iceland; two *s* two *d. Educ:* Central Musical Sch., Moscow; Conservatoire, Moscow. Studied under Sumbatyan; Lev Oborin class, 1955: grad 1960. Internat. Chopin Comp., Warsaw, at age of 17 (gained 2nd prize); won Queen Elizabeth Internat. Piano Comp., Brussels, at age of 18 (gold medal). Joint winner (with John Ogdon) of Tchaikovsky Piano Comp., Moscow, 1962. London debut with London Symph. Orch. under George Hurst, and subseq, solo recital, Festival Hall, 1963. Has played in many countries. Makes recordings. Hon. RAM 1972. Icelandic Order of the Falcon, 1971. *Address:* Brekkugerdi 8, Reykjavik, Iceland.

ASHLEY, Lord; Anthony Nils Christian Ashley-Cooper; *b* 24 June 1977; *s* and *heir* of Earl of Shaftesbury, *qv* .

ASHLEY, Jack, CH 1975; MP (Lab) Stoke-on-Trent, South, since 1966; *b* 6 Dec. 1922; *s* of John Ashley and Isabella Bridge; *m* 1951, Pauline Kay Crispin; three *d. Educ:* St Patrick's Elem. Sch., Widnes, Lancs; Ruskin Coll., Oxford; Gonville and Caius Coll., Cambridge. Labourer and cranedriver, 1936-46; Shop Steward, Convener and Nat. Exec. Mem., Chemical Workers' Union, 1946; Scholarship, Ruskin Coll., 1946-48 and Caius Coll., 1948-51 (Chm. Cambridge Labour Club, 1950; Pres. Cambridge Union, 1951); BBC Radio Producer, 1951-57; Commonwealth Fund Fellow, 1955; BBC Senior Television Producer, 1957-66; Mem., General Advisory Council, BBC, 1967-69, 1970-74. PPS to Sec. of State, DHSS, 1974-. Mem., Lab. Party Nat. Exec. Cttee, 1976-. Councillor, Borough of Widnes, 1945. *Publication:* Journey into Silence, 1973. *Recreations:* walking, golf, reading. *Address:* House of Commons, SW1A 0AA.

ASHLEY, Maurice Percy; *b* 4 Sept. 1907; *s* of Sir Percy Ashley, KBE, and Lady Ashley (*née* Hayman); *m* 1935, Phyllis Mary Griffiths; one *s* one *d. Educ:* St Paul's Sch., London; New Coll., Oxford (History Scholar). 1st Class Hons Modern History; DPhil Oxon. Historical Research Asst to Sir Winston Churchill, 1929-33; Editorial Staff, The Manchester Guardian, 1933-37; Editorial Staff, The Times, 1937-39; Editor, Britain Today, 1939-40. Served in Army, 1940-45 (Major, Intelligence Corps). Deputy Editor, The Listener, 1946-58, Editor, 1958-67; Research Fellow, Loughborough Univ. of Technology, 1968-70. Pres. Cromwell Association, 1961-77. *Publications include:* Financial and Commercial Policy under the Cromwellian Protectorate, 1934 (revised, 1962); Oliver Cromwell, 1937; Marlborough, 1939; Louis XIV and the Greatness of France, 1946; John Wildman: Plotter and Postmaster, 1947; Mr President, 1948; England in the Seventeenth Century, 1952, rev. edn, 1973; Cromwell's Generals, 1954; The Greatness of Oliver Cromwell, 1957 (revised 1967); Oliver Cromwell and the Puritan Revolution, 1958; Great Britain to 1688, 1961; The Stuarts in Love, 1963; Life in Stuart England, 1964; The Glorious Revolution of 1688, 1966 (revised, 1968); Churchill as Historian, 1968; A Golden Century, 1598-1715, 1969; (ed) Cromwell: great lives observed, 1969; Charles II: the man and the statesman, 1971; Oliver Cromwell and his World, 1972; The Life and Times of King John, 1972; The Life and Times of King William I, 1973; A History of Europe 1648-1815, 1973; The Age of Absolutism 1648-1775, 1974; A Concise History of the English Civil War, 1975; Rupert of the Rhine, 1976; General Monck, 1977 James II, 1977. *Recreations:* bridge, gardening, painting. *Address:* 34 Wood Lane, Ruislip, Mddx HA4 6EX. *T:* Ruislip 35993. *Club:* Reform.

ASHLEY-COOPER, family name of **Earl of Shaftesbury.**

ASHMOLE, Professor Bernard, CBE 1957; MC; MA, BLitt; Hon. FRIBA, FBA; Fellow of Lincoln College, Oxford; Hon. Fellow, Hertford College, Oxford, 1961; *b* Ilford, 22 June 1894; 2nd *s* of late William Ashmole and Caroline Wharton Tiver; *m* 1920, Dorothy Irene, 2nd *d* of late Everard de Peyer, Newent Court, Glos; one *s* two *d. Educ:* Forest; privately; Hertford Coll., Oxford (Classical Scholar). 11th Royal Fusiliers, 1914-18; Craven Fellow, and Student of the British schools at Athens and Rome, 1920-22; Asst Curator of Coins, Ashmolean Museum, 1923-25; Director of the British Sch. at Rome, 1925-28; Florence Bursar, RIBA, 1937; Hon. Member of the Archæological Institute of America, 1940; RAF 1940-45, Adjutant of 84 Sqdn in Greece, Iraq, Western Desert, Sumatra and India (despatches twice, Hellenic Flying Cross). Yates Professor of Archæology, University of London, 1929-48, Hon. Fellow, UCL, 1974; Keeper of Greek and Roman Antiquities, British Museum, 1939-56; Lincoln Professor of Classical Archæology, Univ. of Oxford, 1956-61; Geddes-Harrower Professor of Greek Art and Archæology, Univ. of Aberdeen, 1961-63; Visiting Professor in Archæology, Univ. of Yale, 1964. Rhind Lectr, 1952; Myres Memorial Lectr, Oxford, 1961; Norton Lectr, Archæological Inst. of America, 1963; Wrightsman Lectr, New York, 1967. Hon. LLD Aberdeen, 1968. *Publications:* Catalogue of Ancient Marbles at Ince Blundell, 1929; Greek Sculpture and Painting (with Beazley), 1932, repr. 1966; The Ancient World (with Groenewegen-Frankfort), 1967; Olympia: sculptures of the temple of Zeus (with Yalouris and Frantz), 1967; Architect and Sculptor in Classical Greece, 1972; articles on Greek sculpture in the Journal of Hellenic Studies and other periodicals. *Address:* 5 Tweed Green, Peebles. *T:* Peebles 21154. *Club:* Athenæum.

ASHMORE, Prof. Alick; Director Daresbury Laboratory, Science Research Council, since 1970; *b* 7 Nov. 1920; *s* of Frank Owen Ashmore and Beatrice Maud Swindells; *m* 1947, Eileen Elsie Fuller; two *s* three *d. Educ:* King Edward VII Sch., Lytham; King's Coll., London. Experimental Officer, RRDE, Malvern, 1941-47; Lecturer in physics, University of Liverpool, 1947-59; Queen Mary Coll., London: Reader in experimental physics, 1960-64; Prof. of Nuclear Physics, 1964-70, also Head of Physics Dept, 1968-70. *Publications:* research publications on nuclear and elementary-particle physics in Proc. Phys. Soc., Nuclear Physics, Physical Review. *Recreations:* walking, camping. *Address:* 3 Dane Bank Road, Lymm, Cheshire WA13 9DQ. *T:* Lymm 3735.

ASHMORE, Adm. of the Fleet Sir Edward (Beckwith), GCB 1974 (KCB 1971; CB 1966); DSC 1942; Chief of the Defence Staff, Feb.-Aug. 1977; *b* 11 Dec. 1919; *er s* of Vice-Admiral L. H. Ashmore, CB, DSO and late Tamara Vasilevna Shutt, Petrograd; *m* 1942, Elizabeth Mary Doveton Sturdee, *d* of late Rear-Admiral Sir Lionel Sturdee, 2nd Bt, CBE; one *s* one *d* (and one *d* decd). *Educ:* RNC, Dartmouth. Served HMS Birmingham, Jupiter, Middleton, 1938-42; qualified in Signals, 1943; Staff of C-in-C Home Fleet, Flag Lieut, 4th Cruiser Sqdn, 1944-45; qualified Interpreter in Russian, 1946; Asst Naval Attaché, Moscow, 1946-47; Squadron Communications Officer, 3rd Aircraft Carrier Squadron, 1950; Commander 1950; comd HMS Alert, 1952-53; Captain 1955; Captain (F) 6th Frigate Sqdn, and CO HMS Blackpool, 1958; Director of Plans, Admiralty and Min. of Defence, 1960-62; Commander British Forces Caribbean Area, 1963-64; Rear-Adm., 1965; Asst Chief of the Defence Staff, Signals, 1965-67; Flag Officer, Second-in-Command, Far East Fleet, 1967-68; Vice-Adm. 1968; Vice-Chief, Naval Staff, Adm. 1970; C-in-C Western Fleet, Sept.-Oct. 1971; C-in-C, Fleet, 1971-74; Chief of Naval Staff and First Sea Lord, 1974-77; First and Principal Naval Aide-de-Camp to the Queen, 1974-77. *Recreations:* usual. *Address:* South Cottage, Headley Down, near Bordon, Hants.
See also Vice-Adm. Sir P. W. B. Ashmore, Sir Francis Sykes, Bt.

ASHMORE, Vice-Adm. Sir Peter (William Beckwith), KCB 1972 (CB 1968); MVO (4th Class) 1948; DSC 1942; Master of HM's Household, since 1973; Extra Equerry to the Queen, since 1952; *b* 4 Feb. 1921; *yr s* of late Vice-Adm. L. H. Ashmore, CB, DSO and late Tamara Vasilevna Shutt, Petrograd; *m* 1952, Patricia Moray Buller, *o d* of late Admiral Sir Henry Buller, GCVO, CB and of Lady Hermione Stuart; one *s* three *d. Educ:* Yardley Court; RN Coll., Dartmouth. Midshipman, 1939. Served War of 1939-45, principally in destroyers (despatches); Lieut, 1941; Equerry (temp.) to King George VI, 1946-48; Extra Equerry, 1948; Comdr, 1951; Captain, 1957; Deputy Director, RN Staff Coll., Greenwich, 1957; Captain (F) Dartmouth Training Squadron, 1960-61; Imperial Defence Coll., 1962; Admiralty, Plans Division, 1963; Rear-Adm. 1966; Flag Officer, Admiralty Interview Board, 1966-67; Chief of Staff to C-in-C Western Fleet and to NATO C-in-C Eastern Atlantic, 1967-69; Chief of Allied Staff, NATO Naval HQ, S Europe, 1970-72, retired 1972. *Recreations:* fishing, golf.
See also Adm . of the Fleet Sir E. B. Ashmore.

ASHMORE, Prof. Philip George; Professor of Physical Chemistry, The University of Manchester Institute of Science and Technology, since 1963; *b* 5 May 1916; *m* 1943, Ann Elizabeth Scott; three *s* one *d. Educ:* Emmanuel Coll., Cambridge. Fellow, Asst Tutor and Dir of Studies of Natural Sciences, Emmanuel Coll., Cambridge, 1949-59; Lecturer in Physical Chem., Univ. of Cambridge, 1953-63; Fellow and Tutor to Advanced Students, Churchill Coll., Cambridge, 1959-63. Vice-Principal Acad. Affairs, UMIST, 1973, 1974. *Publications:* The Catalysis and Inhibition of Chemical Reactions, 1963; (ed) Reaction Kinetics, 1975; RIC Monographs for Teachers: No 5 and No 9; many papers in: TFS, International Symposium on Combustion, Jl of Catalysis. *Address:* Department of Chemistry, University of Manchester Institute of Science and Technology, Manchester M60 1QD. *T:* 061-236 3311.

ASHTON, family name of **Baron Ashton of Hyde.**

ASHTON OF HYDE, 2nd Baron *cr* 1911; **Thomas Henry Raymond Ashton,** DL, JP; Major, late 1st Royal Gloucestershire Hussars, RAC, TA; Joint Master, Heythrop, 1934-36, sole Master, 1936-48, Joint Master, 1948-52; *b* 2 Oct. 1901; *s* of 1st Baron and Eva Margaret (*d* 1938) *d* of J. H. James Kingswood, Watford, Herts; *S* father, 1933; *m* 1925, Marjorie Nell, *d* of late Hon. Marshall Brooks; one *s* (two *d* decd). *Educ:* Eton; New Coll., Oxford (MA). DL 1957, JP 1944, Gloucestershire. *Recreations:* hunting, shooting, deerstalking. *Heir:* *s* Hon. Thomas John Ashton [*b* 19 Nov. 1926; *m* 1957, Pauline Trewlove, *er d* of Lieut-Col R. H. L. Brackenbury, Yerdley House, Long Compton, Shipston-on-Stour; two *s* two *d*]. *Address:* Broadwell Hill, Moreton-in-Marsh, Glos. *T:* Stow-on-the-Wold 30626. *Club:* Boodle's.

ASHTON, Anthony Southcliffe; Director: Provincial Insurance Co., since 1974; Tyzack and Partners Ltd, since 1974; *b* 5 July 1916; *s* of late Prof. Thomas Southcliffe Ashton, FBA, and of Mrs Marion Hague Ashton; *m* 1939, Katharine Marion Louise Vivian; two *d. Educ:* Manchester Grammar Sch.; Hertford Coll., Oxford (MA). Economist, Export Credits Guarantee Dept, 1937. Served War of 1939-45, as driver and Lt-Col, RASC. Asst Financial Editor, Manchester Guardian, 1945; Dep. Asst Dir of Marketing, NCB, 1947; Manager, various depts of Vacuum Oil Co. (later Mobil Oil Co.), 1949; attended Advanced Management Programme, Harvard Business Sch., 1961; Treasurer, and later Finance Director, Esso Petroleum Co., 1961; Mem. Bd (Finance and Corporate Planning), Post Office Corp., 1970-73. Member: Shipbuilding Industry Bd, 1967-71; Council of Manchester Business Sch., 1968-; Dir, Oxford Univ. Business Summer Sch., 1974. Trustee, PO Pension Fund, 1975-. *Address:* Quarry Field, Stonewall Hill, Presteigne, Powys LD8 2HB. *T:* Presteigne 447.

ASHTON, Sir (Arthur) Leigh (Bolland), Kt 1948; Director and Secretary, Victoria and Albert Museum, 1945-55, retired; *b* London, 20 Oct. 1897; *o s* of late A. J. Ashton, KC, Recorder of Manchester; *m* 1952, Mrs Madge Garland. *Educ:* Horris Hill; Winchester; Balliol Coll., Oxford, BA (war degree). Served European War, Lieut RGA, 1916-19. Victoria and Albert Museum: Asst Keeper (2nd class), Dept of Architecture and Sculpture, 1922-25; Dept of Textiles, 1925-31; Dept of Ceramics, 1931-37; Keeper of Special Collections, 1937, Secretary of the Advisory Council, 1935, and Asst to Dir, 1937; Asst Keeper, 1st class, 1932; Keeper (1st class) 1938. Mem. Committee, City Companies Exhibition, 1927; Asst Dir International Exhibition of Persian Art, RA, 1931; Executive Committee and arranger of the Exhibition of Chinese Art, RA, 1935-36; Executive Committee, Exhibition of 17th Century Art, RA, 1937; Dir, Exhibition of the Arts of India and Pakistan, RA, 1947-48; loaned to Ministry of Information, April 1939; Officer i/c Finance, 1939; Dep.-Dir of Foreign Division, 1940; Director of Neutral Countries Division, 1941; Dir of British Information Office, Istanbul, 1942, and head of Press Office, HM Embassy, Ankara, with rank of Counsellor. Comdr of the Dannebrog. *Publications:* Introduction to the History of Chinese Sculpture, 1922; Samplers, 1927; Memoirs of the Prince de Ligne, 1928; Chinese Art (with Basil Gray), 1935; Chinese Art (with others), 1935; (ed) Commemoration Catalogue of Chinese Exhibition, 1936; (ed) Commemorative Catalogue of the Exhibition of the Arts of India and Pakistan, 1950; numerous articles and lectures on the decorative arts. *Recreations:* music, the theatre, travel, bridge.

ASHTON, Lt-Col Edward Malcolm, CIE 1947; OBE 1945; Indian Army (retired); *b* 21 May 1895; 3rd *s* of late H. Bankes Ashton, Bury St Edmunds; *m* 1927, Gwyneth Ena Darcy Smith; one *s* two *d. Educ:* Falconbury Sch., Purley; King Edward VI Sch., Bury St Edmunds. Indian Army; Mil. Officer in Civil Employ; Dir Military Lands and Cantonments; Defence Dept, Govt of India. Served European War, 1914-18 (despatches). *Recreations:* fishing, shooting, tennis. *Address:* 34 Well Street, Bury St Edmunds. *T:* Bury St Edmunds 63937. *Club:* National Liberal.

ASHTON, Sir Frederick (William Mallandaine), CH 1970; Kt 1962; CBE 1950; Founder-choreographer to the Royal Ballet (Principal Choreographer, 1933-70, and Director, 1963-70); *b* Guayaquil, Ecuador, 17 Sept. 1904; *s* of George Ashton and Georgiana Fulcher. *Educ:* The Dominican Fathers, Lima, Peru; Dover Coll., Dover. Best known ballets: Les Patineurs, Apparitions, Horoscope, Symphonic Variations, Façade, Wedding Bouquet, Scènes de Ballet, Cinderella (first English choreographer to do a 3-act ballet), Illuminations, Sylvia, Romeo and Juliet, Ondine, La Fille Mal Gardée, Les Deux Pigeons, Marguerite and Armand, The Dream, Sinfonietta, Jazz Calendar, Enigma Variations, Walk to the Paradise Garden, Birthday Offering, A Month in the Country, etc. Film: The Tales of Beatrix Potter (choreography, and appeared as Mrs Tiggywinkle), 1971. Served in Royal Air Force during War as Flight Lieut. Queen Elizabeth II Coronation Award, Royal Academy of Dancing, 1959. Hon. DLitt: Durham, 1962; East Anglia, 1967; Hon. DMus: London, 1970; Hull, 1971; Oxon, 1976. Legion of Honour (France), 1960; Order of Dannebrog (Denmark), 1964. *Relevant Publication:* Frederick Ashton: a Choreographer and his Ballets, by Z. Dominic and J. S. Gilbert, 1971. *Recreation:* dancing. *Address:* 8 Marlborough Street, SW3.

ASHTON, Gilbert, MC 1916; MA Cantab; DL; Headmaster, Abberley Hall (Preparatory School), near Worcester, 1921-61; *b* 27 Sept. 1896; *s* of Hubert Shorrock Ashton and Victoria Alexandrina, *d* of Maj.-Gen. Sir John Inglis, KCB; *m* 1921, Joan Mary, *d* of Rev. H. R. Huband; four *d. Educ:* Winchester Coll.; Trinity Coll., Cambridge. Served European War (wounded, MC): 2nd Lieut RFA, 1915; Instructor Army Signal Sch., 1918. Underwriter, Lloyd's, 1936. Chm. Incorporated Association of Preparatory Schs, 1937 and 1946. Major, Home Guard, 1940-45; Governor, Abberley Hall Sch., 1961-. Pres., Worcs CC 1967-69. JP 1934, DL 1968, Worcs. *Recreations:* formerly cricket (CU Cricket XI, 1919-21, Capt.; CU Assoc. XI, 1919-20, Capt.). *Address:* Abberley Lodge, near Worcester. *T:* Great Witley 305. *Clubs:* United Oxford & Cambridge University, MCC; Worcester Church House (Worcester).

ASHTON, Sir Hubert, KBE 1959; MC; MA Cantab; DL; Third Church Estates Commissioner, 1962-72; *b* 13 Feb. 1898; *s* of late H. S. Ashton, Trueloves, Ingatestone, Essex, and Mrs V. A. Ashton; *m* 1927, Dorothy Margaret Gaitskell; one *s* two *d* (and one *s* decd). *Educ:* Winchester Coll.; Trinity Coll., Cambridge (Blues for cricket (captain), football and hockey). Royal Field Artillery, 1916-19. Burmah Oil Co., 1922-45; Underwriter at Lloyd's, 1936. MP (C) Chelmsford Division of Essex, 1950-64; Parliamentary Private Secretary to the Chancellor of the Exchequer, 1951-55, to the Lord Privy Seal, Oct. 1955 and to Lord Privy Seal and Home Sec., 1957; Second Church Estates Comr, 1957-62; Third Church Estates Comr, 1962-72. Governor: Brentwood Sch., 1948- (Chm., 1962-76); London Hosp., 1948-70 (Dep. Chm., 1967-70; Vice-Patron, 1970-); Mem. GBA, 1963-, Vice-Chm. 1966-76. Cttee Mem., MCC, 1947-50, 1952-55 and 1957-64, Pres. 1961; Pres., Essex CCC, 1948-70. Church Warden, St Peter's Church, S Weald, 1940-70. DL Essex, 1942; High Sheriff of Essex, 1943; Essex County Councillor, 1946, Vice-Chm., 1949-52; Alderman Essex CC, 1950-61. Dir of public companies. *Recreations:* walking, grandchildren. *Address:* Wealdside, South Weald, Brentwood, Essex. *T:* Coxtie Green 324. *Clubs:* City of London, Oriental.

ASHTON, Joseph William; MP (Lab) Bassetlaw Division of Notts since Nov. 1968; an Assistant Government Whip, since 1976; journalist; *b* 9 Oct. 1933; *s* of Arthur and Nellie Ashton, Sheffield; *m* 1957, Margaret Patricia Lee; one *d. Educ:* High Storrs Grammar Sch.; Rotherham Technical Coll. Engineering Apprentice, 1949-54; RAF National Service, 1954-56; Cost Control Design Engineer, 1956-68; Sheffield City Councillor, 1962-69. PPS to Sec. of State for Energy, formerly Sec. of State for Industry, 1975-76. *Publication:* Grass Roots, 1977. *Recreations:* watching Sheffield Wednesday, reading, do-it-yourself, motoring. *Address:* 16 Ranmoor Park Road, Sheffield. *T:* Sheffield 301763. *Clubs:* Foundry Working Men's (Sheffield); Doncaster Road Working Men's (Langold); various Miners' Institutes, etc.

ASHTON, Kenneth Bruce; General Secretary, National Union of Journalists, since 1977; *b* 9 Nov. 1925; *s* of late Harry Anstice Ashton and of Olive May Ashton; *m* 1955, Amy Anne, *d* of late John Baines Sidebotham and of Amy Sidebotham; four *s. Educ:* Latymer Upper School. Served Army, 1942-46. Reporter: Hampstead and Highgate Express, 1947-50; Devon and Somerset News, Mansfield Reporter, Sheffield Star, 1950-58; Sub-Editor, Sheffield Telegraph, Daily Express, London and Daily Mail, Manchester, 1958-75. Nat. Exec. Cttee Mem., NUJ, 1968-75, Pres., 1975, Regional Organiser, 1975-77. Member: TUC Printing Industries' Cttee, 1975-; Printing and Publishers' Industry Training Bd, 1977; consultative Mem., Press Council, 1977. *Recreation:* gliding. *Address:* Acorn House, 314 Gray's Inn Road, WC1X 8DP. *T:* 01-278 7916. *Clubs:* Manchester Press (Pres. 1971); Derbyshire and Lancashire Gliding.

ASHTON, Sir Leigh; see Ashton, Sir A. L. B.

ASHTON, Rt. Rev. Leonard (James), CB 1970; Bishop in Cyprus and The Gulf, since 1976, Episcopal Church in Jerusalem and the Middle East; Hon. Canon and Prebendary of St Botolph, Lincoln Cathedral, 1969-73, Canon Emeritus since 1973; *b* 27 June 1911; *s* of late Henry Ashton and Sarah Ashton (née Ing). *Educ:* Tyndale Hall, Bristol. Ordained, Chester, 1942; Curate, Cheadle, 1942-45; Chap. RAF, 1945-; N Wales, 1945; AHQ Malaya and Singapore, 1946; BC Air Forces, Japan, 1947-48; Halton, 1948-49; Feltwell, 1949-50; Chap. and Lectr, RAF Chap. Sch., Cheltenham, 1950-53; Sen. Chap., AHQ Iraq, 1954-55; RAF Coll., Cranwell, 1956-60; Br. Forces Arabian Peninsular and Mid. East Command, 1960-61; Asst Chap. Chief, Trng Commands, 1962-65; Res. Chap., St Clement Danes, Strand, 1965-69; Chaplain-in-Chief, (with relative rank of Air Vice-Marshal) RAF, and Archdeacon of RAF, 1969-73; QHC, 1967-73; Asst Bishop in Jerusalem, 1974-76. ChStJ 1976. *Recreations:* gardening, photography. *Address:* 60 Lowndes Avenue, Chesham, Bucks. *T:* Chesham 2952. *Club:* Royal Air Force.

ASHTON, Prof. Norman (Henry), CBE 1976; DSc (London); FRS 1971; FRCP, FRCS; FRCPath; Professor of Pathology, University of London since 1957; Director, Department of Pathology, Institute of Ophthalmology, University of London, since 1948; Consultant Pathologist, Moorfields Eye Hospital, since 1948; *b* 11 Sept. 1913; 2nd *s* of Henry James and Margaret Ann Ashton. *Educ:* King's Coll. and Westminster Hosp. Med. Sch., Univ. of London. Westminster Hospital: Prize in Bacteriology, 1938; Editor Hosp. Gazette, 1939-40; House Surg., House Phys., Sen. Casualty Officer and RMO, 1939-41. Asst Pathologist, Princess Beatrice Hosp., 1939; Dir of Pathology, Kent and Canterbury Hosp., and Blood Transfusion Officer of East Kent, 1941. Lieut-Col RAMC, Asst Dir of Pathology and Officer i/c Central Pathological Lab., Middle East, 1946. Pathologist to the Gordon Hosp., 1947; Reader in Pathology, Univ. of London, 1953; Fellow in Residence, Johns Hopkins Hosp., Baltimore, 1953, and Visiting Prof. there, 1959. Examr in Ophthalmic Pathology, RCSI, 1963-; Chm., Postgrad. Fedn Medical TV Policy Cttee, 1972-. Lectures: Walter Wright,

1959; Banting, 1960; Proctor (USA), 1965; Bradshaw (RCP), 1971; Montgomery, 1973; Edward Nettleship Prize for Research in Ophthalmology, 1953; BMA Middlemore Prize, 1955; Proctor Medal for Research in Ophthalmology (USA), 1957; Doyne Medal (Oxford), 1960; William Julius Mickle Fellow, Univ. London, 1961; Bowman Medal, 1965; Donder's Medal, 1967; Wm Mackenzie Memorial Medal, 1967; Gonin Medal, 1978. Trustee, Fight for Sight; Pres. elect, Assoc. of Clinical Pathologists (Sec. for Internat. Relations; Mem. Council, 1958-61); Member, Board of Governors: Moorfields Eye Hosp.; Hosp. for Sick Children, Gt Ormond St; Royal Nat. Coll. for the Blind; Member: Council, RCPath, 1975-; Med. Adv. Bd, British Retinitis Pigmentosa Soc.; Pathological Soc. of Great Britain and Ireland; British Microcirculation Soc.; European Assoc. for Study of Diabetes; Cttee of Management, Cardio-Thoracic Inst.; Cttee of Management, Inst. of Child Health, 1960-65; Inst. of Opthalmology; Inst. of Rheumatology; Council, RSM; Med. Art Soc.; Soc. Française d'Ophth.; Brit. Nat. Cttee for Prevention of Blindness; Pres. elect, Ophth. Soc. of UK; Past Pres., Ophth. Sect., RSM; Oxford Ophth. Congress; Council, RCPath, 1963-66 (Founder Fellow); Governing Body, British Postgrad. Med. Fedn; Ophth. Hosp. Cttee of Order of St John. Hon. Life Mem., British Diabetic Association; Life Pres. European Ophth. Pathology Soc.; Past Pres. Brit. Div. Internat. Acad. of Pathology, 1962. Hon. Member: Assoc. for Eye Research; Amer. Acad. Ophthal. and Otolaryng.; Hellenic Ophth. Soc. Hon. Fellow, Coll. of Physicians, Philadelphia. Mem. Ed. Bd, Brit. Jl Ophthalmology. FRSocMed; Liveryman and Mem. Court of Assistants, Soc. of Apothecaries of London. Freeman, City of London. Hon. DSc Chicago. KStJ. *Publications:* contrib. to books and numerous scientific articles in Jl of Pathology and Bacteriology, Brit. Jl of Ophthalmology, and Amer. Jl of Ophthalmology. *Recreations:* painting, gardening. *Address:* 2 The Cloisters, Westminster Abbey, SW1. *T:* 01-222 4982. *Clubs:* Athenæum, Garrick.

ASHTON, Rev. Canon Patrick Thomas, MVO; Chaplain to the Queen 1968-77, retired; *b* 27 July 1916; *s* of Lieut-Col S. E. Ashton, OBE; *m* 1942, Mavis St Clair Brown, New Zealand; three *d* (one *s* decd). *Educ:* Stowe; Christ Church, Oxford (MA); Westcott House, Cambridge. Served War of 1939-45 as Captain, Oxfordshire Yeomanry; Curate, St Martin's-in-the-Fields, 1947-51; Rector of All Saints, Clifton, Beds, 1951-55; Rector of Sandringham with West Newton and Appleton, and Domestic Chaplain to the Queen, 1955-70; Rector: Sandringham Gp of Eight Parishes, 1963-70; Swanborough Team of Parishes, 1970-73; Priest-in-charge of Avebury with Winterbourne Monkton and Berwick Bassett, 1974-77; Rector, Upper Kennet team of Parishes, 1975-77; a Canon of Salisbury Cathedral, 1975; Rural Dean of Marlborough, 1976-77. *Address:* Field Cottage, Bottlesford, Pewsey, Wilts. *T:* Woodborough 340.

ASHTON, Prof. Robert, PhD; Professor of English History, University of East Anglia, since 1963; *b* 21 July 1924; *s* of late of Joseph and late Edith F. Ashton; *m* 1946, Margaret Alice Sedgwick; two *d. Educ:* Magdalen Coll. Sch., Oxford; University Coll., Southampton (1942-43, 1946-49); London Sch. of Economics (1949-52). BA 1st Cl. hons (London) 1949; PhD (London) 1953; Asst Lecturer in Economic History, Univ. of Nottingham, 1952; Lecturer, 1954; Senior Lecturer, 1961; Vis. Associate Prof. in History, Univ. of California, Berkeley, 1962-63; Prof. of English History, 1963, and Dean of Sch. of English Studies, 1964-67, Univ. of East Anglia. Vis. Fellow, All Souls Coll., Oxford, 1973-74. FRHistS 1960. *Publications:* The Crown and the Money Market, 1603-1640, 1960; Charles I and the City, in Essays in the Economic and Social History of Tudor and Stuart England in honour of R. H. Tawney (ed F. J. Fisher), 1961; James I by his Contemporaries, 1969; The Civil War and the Class Struggle, in The English Civil War and After 1642-1658 (ed R. H. Parry), 1970; articles in learned periodicals. *Recreations:* music, looking at old buildings, walking. *Address:* The Manor House, Brundall, Norwich NR13 5JY. *T:* Norwich 713368.

ASHTOWN, 5th Baron *cr* 1800; **Dudley Oliver Trench,** OBE 1961; retired as Assistant Chief Constable, War Department Constabulary, 1964; late KRRC; *b* 11 July 1901; *yr s* of 3rd Baron Ashtown (*d* 1946), and Violet Grace (*d* 1945), *d* of Col R. G. Cosby; *S* brother, 1966; *m* 1st, 1932, Ellen Nancy (*d* 1949), *y d* of late William Garton, Brixedone, Bursledon, Hants; two *d*; 2nd, 1955, Sheelah A. S. (*d* 1963), *yr d* of late Brig.-Gen. L. F. Green-Wilkinson, CMG, DSO; 3rd, 1966, Natalie *widow* of Major James de Sales La Terrière. *Educ:* Wellington Coll.; RMC Sandhurst. Adjutant 11th London Regt, 1934-35, and Queen's Westminsters, 1936-38; retd pay, 1939. Served War of 1939-45 (despatches). *Heir:* kinsman Christopher Oliver Trench, *b* 23 March 1931. *Address:* Woodlawn, King's Somborne, Near Stockbridge, Hants. *T:* King's Somborne 333.

ASHWELL, Major Arthur Lindley, DSO 1916; OBE 1946; TD 1926; DL; late 8th Battalion Sherwood Foresters; *b* 19 Jan. 1886; *o s* of Arthur Thomas Ashwell, solicitor, Nottingham; *m* 1932, Sylvia Violet, *widow* of Harold Gallatly, MC, and *d* of Philip Scratchley. *Educ:* Lambrook, Bracknell; Winchester Coll. Served European War, 1915 (wounded thrice, despatches, DSO). DL Notts, 1941. *Address:* Flat 3, 19 The Vale, SW3. *Clubs:* Naval and Military, Royal Automobile.

ASHWORTH, Prof. Graham William; Professor of Urban Environmental Studies, University of Salford, since 1973; *b* 14 July 1935; *s* of Frederick William Ashworth and Ivy Alice Ashworth; *m* 1960, Gwyneth Mai Morgan-Jones; three *d. Educ:* Devonport High Sch., Plymouth; Univ. of Liverpool (Master of Civic Design, BArch). RIBA, PPRTPI, FRSA. LCC (Hook New Town Project), 1959-61; consultancy with Graeme Shankland, 1961-64; architect to Civic Trust, 1964-65; Dir, Civic Trust for North-West, 1965-73. Member: Skeffington Cttee on Public Participation in Planning, 1969; North-West Adv. Council of BBC, 1970-75 (Chm.); NW Economic Planning Council (and Sub-gp Chm.), 1968-; Countryside Commn, 1974-. Governor, Northern Baptist Coll., 1966-; Pres., Royal Town Planning Inst., 1973-74; Chm. Exec. Cttee, Civic Trust for North-West, 1973-. *Publication:* An Encyclopædia of Planning, 1973. *Recreations:* gardening, painting, church and social work. *Address:* Manor Court, Manor Farm, Samlesbury Hall, Preston New Road, Preston PR5 0UP. *Clubs:* National Liberal; Manchester.

ASHWORTH, Harold Kenneth, TD and Clasp 1951; Hon. Consultant Anaesthetist, Charing Cross and Moorfields Hospitals, since 1968; *b* 16 May 1903; *s* of Dr J. H. Ashworth, Manchester. *Educ:* Sedbergh; Manchester Univ. MB, ChB (Vic) 1925; MRCS, LRCP 1925; DA 1934; FFARCS 1948. Formerly: Visiting Anaesthetist, Royal Infirmary, Manchester; Clinical Lecturer in Anaesthesia, Univ. of Manchester; Senior Anaesthetist, Charing Cross and Moorfields Hosps; Director, Dept of Anaesthesia, Charing Cross Hosp. Med. Sch., 1956-68; Consulting Anaesthetist to the Kingdom of Libya, 1968-69. RAMC (TA) 1939-45, BEF France, 1940; Brig., Cons. Anaesthetist, India Command, 1944-45. Councillor: St Marylebone Borough Council, 1949-65; Westminster City Council, 1964-68. Examiner for DA (RCP & S), 1962-68. Sen. Mem., Assoc. of Anæsthetists of Great Britain and Ireland, 1968; Pres., Southern Soc. of Anaesthetists. *Publications:* Practical Points in Anaesthesia, 1936. Contributions to Medical Journals. *Recreations:* watching cricket; formerly Rugby football (Manchester Univ. XV, 1922-26). *Address:* 1 Quelland, Beverley Close, East Ewell, Surrey KT17 3HB. *T:* 01-393 9032. *Clubs:* MCC; XXI (Manchester University).

ASHWORTH, Sir Herbert, Kt 1972; Chairman, Nationwide Building Society (formerly Co-operative Permanent Building Society), since 1970 (Deputy-Chairman, 1968-70); Chairman, Orbit General Housing Association, since 1977 (Deputy Chairman, 1974-77); *b* 30 Jan. 1910; *s* of Joseph Hartley Ashworth; *m* 1936, Barbara Helen Mary, *d* of late Douglas D. Henderson; two *s* one *d. Educ:* Burnley Grammar Sch.; London Univ. (grad. econ. and law). General Manager, Portman Building Soc., 1938-50; General Manager, Co-operative Permanent Building Soc., 1950-61; Director and General Manager, Hallmark Securities Ltd, 1961-66. Dep. Chm., 1964-68, Chm., 1968-73, Housing Corp. Dir, The Builder Ltd, 1975. Chm., Surrey, E and W Sussex Agricl Wages Cttee, 1974-. Vice-President: Building Socs Assoc.; Building Socs Inst. *Publications:* Housing in Great Britain, 1951; Building Society Work Explained, (current edn), 1977. *Address:* 8 Tracery, Park Road, Banstead, Surrey SM7 3DD. *T:* Burgh Heath 52608.

ASHWORTH, Ian Edward; Circuit Administrator, Western Circuit, Lord Chancellor's Office, since 1970; *b* 3 March 1930; *s* of William Holt and Cicely Ashworth, Rochdale; *m* Pauline, *er d* of Maurice James and Gladys Heddle, Westliff-on-Sea; two *s* one *d. Educ:* Manchester Grammar Sch.; The Queen's Coll., Oxford (BCL, MA). Admitted Solicitor, 1956; Asst Solicitor, Rochdale, 1956-58; Dep. Town Clerk, Dep. Clerk of Peace, Canterbury, 1958-63; Town Clerk, Clerk of Peace, Deal, 1963-66; Town Clerk, Rugby, 1966-70. *Recreations:* music, painting, gardening. *Address:* 5 St Hilary Close, Stoke Bishop, Bristol BS9 1DA. *T:* Bristol 685236. *Club:* United Oxford & Cambridge University.

ASHWORTH, James Louis, FIMechE, FIEE, ARTC (Salford); Full-Time Member for Operations, Central Electricity Generating Board, 1966-70, retired; *b* 7 March 1906; *s* of late James and late Janet Ashworth; *m* 1931 Clara Evelyn Arnold; one *s* two *d. Educ:* Stockport Grammar Sch.; Salford Royal Coll. of Technology. Apprenticeship with Mirrlees, Bickerton & Day

Ltd, Stockport (Diesel Oil Engine Manufrs), 1924-29; Metro-Vickers Electrical Co. Ltd, 1929; Manchester Corp. Elec. Dept, Stuart Street Gen. Stn, 1930-32; Hull Corp. Elec. Dept, 1932-35; Halifax Corp. Elec. Dept, 1935-40; Mersey Power Co. Ltd, Runcorn, 1940-48; British Elec. Authority, N West: Chief Generation Engr (O), 1948-57; Dep. Divisional Controller, 1957-58; Central Elec. Gen. Bd, N West, Merseyside and N Wales Region: Dep. Regional Dir, 1958-62; Regional Dir, 1962-66. *Recreations:* gardening, photography, travel, reading. *Address:* Chase Cottage, 23 The Chase, Reigate, Surrey. *T:* Redhill 61279.

ASHWORTH, Brig. John Blackwood, CBE 1962; DSO 1944; DL; retired 1965; *b* 7 Dec. 1910; *s* of Lieut-Col H. S. Ashworth, Royal Sussex Regt (killed in action, 1917) and late Mrs E. M. Ashworth; *m* 1946, Eileen Patricia, *d* of late Major H. L. Gifford (Royal Ulster Rifles) and of Lady Gooch; one *d. Educ:* Wellington Coll.; RMC, Sandhurst. Commissioned Royal Sussex Regt, 1930; Instructor RMC, 1938; War of 1939-45 (despatches twice); OC Training Centre, 1942; OC 1/5 Queen's Royal Regt (wounded, DSO), 1944; GSO1, War Office, 1944; OC 4/5 Royal Sussex, 1945; OC 1st Royal Sussex, 1946; GSO1, Brit. Middle East Office, 1947; AMS War Office, 1948; OC 1st Royal Sussex, 1951; Comdt Joint Sch. of Chemical Warfare, 1954; Commander 133rd Inf. Bde (TA), 1957; Director of Military Training, War Office, 1959-62; Inspector of Boys' Training, War Office, 1962-65. ADC to the Queen, 1961-65. Col The Royal Sussex Regt, 1963-66; Dep. Col, The Queen's Regt (Royal Sussex), 1967-68. DL Sussex 1972. OStJ 1950. Grand Officer, Order of House of Orange, 1967. *Address:* West Common Drive, Hayward's Heath, West Sussex RH16 2AN. *T:* Hayward's Heath 52371.

ASHWORTH, Prof. John Michael, PhD; FIBiol; Professor of Biology, University of Essex, since 1974 (on secondment) Chief Scientist, Central Policy Review Staff, 1976-78; *b* 27 Nov. 1938; *s* of Jack Ashworth and late Constance Mary Ousman; *m* 1963, Ann Knight; one *s* three *d. Educ:* West Buckland Sch., N Devon; Exeter Coll., Oxford (BA, BSc, MA); Leicester Univ. (PhD). FIBiol 1974. Dept of Biochemistry, Univ. of Leicester: Res. Demonstr, 1961-63; Lectr, 1963-71; Reader, 1971-73. Harkness Fellow of Commonwealth Fund, NY, at Brandeis Univ. and Univ. of Calif, 1965-67. Colworth Medal, Biochem. Soc., 1972. *Publications:* Cell Differentiation, 1972; (with J. Dee) The Slime Moulds, 1976; over 50 pubns in prof. jls on biochem., genet., cell biolog. and educnl topics. *Recreation:* sailing. *Address:* 5 Beech Avenue, Wivenhoe, Essex. *T:* Wivenhoe 3576. *Club:* Wivenhoe Sailing (Wivenhoe).

ASHWORTH, Piers, QC 1973; a Recorder of the Crown Court, since 1974; *b* 27 May 1931; *s* of Tom and Mollie Ashworth; *m* 1959, Iolene Jennifer, *yr d* of W. G. Foxley; three *s* one *d. Educ:* Christ's Hospital; Pembroke Coll., Cambridge. BA (Cantab) 1955. Called to Bar, Middle Temple, 1956. *Recreations:* sailing, squash, tennis. *Address:* 14 Heaton Drive, Edgbaston, Birmingham B15 3LW. *T:* 021-454 3069; 2 Harcourt Buildings, Temple, EC4Y 9DB. *T:* 01-353 4746.

ASHWORTH, Prof. William; Professor of Economic and Social History, University of Bristol, since 1958; Pro-Vice-Chancellor, since 1975; *b* 11 March 1920; *s* of Harold and Alice Ashworth; unmarried. *Educ:* Todmorden Grammar Sch.; London Sch. of Economics and Political Science. Served 1941-45, RAPC and REME. BSc (Econ.) 1946; PhD 1950. Research Assistant, London Sch. of Economics and Political Science, 1946-47; on staff of Cabinet Office (Historical Section), 1947-48; Assistant Lecturer and Lecturer in Economic History, London Sch. of Economics and Political Science, 1948-55; Reader in Economic History in the Univ. of London, 1955-58. Dean, Faculty of Social Sciences, Univ. of Bristol, 1968-70. *Publications:* A Short History of the International Economy, 1952 (revised 1962, 1975); contributor to: London, Aspects of Change, ed by Centre for Urban Studies, 1964; Victoria County History of Essex, 1966; The Study of Economic History, ed N. B. Harte, 1971. Articles and reviews in Economic History Review and other jls. *Address:* 91 High Kingsdown, Bristol BS2 8ER. *T:* Bristol 423771.

ASKE, Rev. Sir Conan, 2nd Bt *cr* 1922; Assistant Curate of St John-in-Bedwardine, Worcester, since 1972; *b* 22 April 1912; *s* of Sir Robert William Aske, 1st Bt, TD, QC, LLD, and Edith (*d* 1918), *d* of Sir Walter Herbert Cockerline; *S* father 1954; *m* 1st, 1948, Vera Faulkner (*d* 1960); 2nd, 1965, Rebecca, *d* of Hugh Grant, Wick, Caithness. *Educ:* Rugby; Balliol Coll., Oxford. TA, London Irish Rifles, 1939; served, 1939-49, with East York

Regt, Sudan Defence Force, Somalia Gendarmerie. Major, Civil Affairs Officer, Reserved Area of Ethiopia and The Ogaden, 1949-51; Schoolmaster, Hillstone, Malvern, 1952-69; Asst Curate, Hagley, Stourbridge, 1970-72. *Heir: b* Robert Edward Aske [*b* 21 March 1915; *m* 1940, Joan Bingham, *o d* of Captain Bingham Ackerley, Cobham; one *s*]. *Address:* 167 Malvern Road, Worcester WR2 4NN. *T:* Worcester 422817.

ASKEW, Herbert Royston, QC 1955; BSc; MICE; *e s* of late Leonard Askew; *m* 1st, 1919, Christiana Rachel (decd), *o d* of late C. Wolryche Dixon, Great Roke, Witley, Surrey; one *d* (one *s* killed on active service, 1942; and one *d* decd); 2nd, 1948, Dorothy Beatrice, *o d* of late J. Gale Wilson, Aberdour, Fife. *Educ:* Alleyn's Sch., Dulwich; London Univ. Served European War 1914-18, Capt. Middlesex Regt and Royal Tank Corps. Called to the Bar, Middle Temple, 1926; Master of the Bench, 1963. Mem. Kensington Borough Council, 1931-39. Served War of 1939-45, Lieut-Col, Gen. List (GSO1). *Address:* 24 Palace Court, W2. *T:* 01-727 6033. *Club:* Reform.

ASKEW, John Marjoribanks Eskdale, CBE 1974; *b* 22 Sept. 1908; *o s* of late William Haggerston Askew, JP, Ladykirk, Berwicks, and Castle Hills, Berwick-on-Tweed; *m* 1st, 1933, Lady Susan Egerton (marr. diss., 1966), 4th *d* of 4th Earl of Ellesmere, MVO; one *s* one *d*; *m* 1976, Priscilla Anne, *e d* of late Algernon Ross-Farrow. *Educ:* Eton; Magdalene Coll., Cambridge (BA). Lieut 2 Bn Grenadier Guards, 1932; Capt. 1940; Major 1943. Royal Company of Archers, Queen's Body Guard for Scotland. Convener: Berwicks CC, 1961; Border Regional Council, 1974. *Address:* Ladykirk, Berwicks. *T:* Norham 229; Castle Hills, Berwick-on-Tweed. *Clubs:* Boodle's; New (Edinburgh).
See also Baron Faringdon, Duke of Sutherland.

ASKEW, Rev. Canon Reginald James Albert; Principal of Salisbury and Wells Theological College since 1974; *b* 16 May 1928; *s* of late Paul Askew and Amy Wainwright; *m* 1953, Kate, *yr d* of late Rev. Henry Townsend Wigley; one *s* two *d. Educ:* Harrow; Corpus Christi Coll., Cambridge (MA); Lincoln Theological College. Curate of Highgate, 1957-61; Tutor and Chaplain of Wells Theol Coll., 1961-65, Vice-Principal 1966-69; Priest Vicar of Wells Cath., 1961-69; Vicar of Christ Church, Lancaster Gate, London, 1969-73; Canon of Salisbury Cathedral and Prebendary of Grantham Borealis, 1975-. *Publication:* The Tree of Noah, 1971. *Recreations:* music, gardening, cricket. *Address:* 19 The Close, Salisbury, Wilts. *T:* Salisbury 4223.

ASKEY, Arthur Bowden, OBE 1969; theatrical artiste; *b* 6 June 1900; *s* of Samuel Askey, Liverpool, and Betty Askey (*née* Bowden), Knutsford, Cheshire; *m* 1925, Elizabeth May Swash (*d* 1974); one *d. Educ:* Liverpool Institute. Liverpool Education Offices, 1916-24; concert parties, pantomimes, broadcasts, London and Provincial Concerts, 1924-38. *Films:* Band Waggon, Charlie's Big-Hearted Aunt, The Ghost Train, I Thank You, Back-Room Boy, King Arthur was a Gentleman, Miss London Ltd, Bees in Paradise, 1939-44; The Love Match; Ramsbottom Rides Again; Make Mine a Million; Friends and Neighbours. *Broadcast Series:* Band Waggon, 1938-39, and 1971; Big's Broadcast, 1940; Big Time, 1942; Forever Arthur, 1945; How Do You Do, 1949; Arthur's Inn, 1952; Hello, Playmates, 1954; Askey Galore, 1957; The Arthur Askey Show, 1958. *Television Series:* Before Your Very Eyes, 1953, 1955, 1956, 1957; Living it up, 1958; Arthur's Treasured Volumes, 1960; The Arthur Askey Show, 1961; Raise Your Glasses, 1962. *London Theatres:* The Boy Who Lost His Temper, Garrick, 1937, Cambridge, 1938; Band Waggon, London Palladium, 1939; Jack and Jill, Palace, 1941, His Majesty's, 1942; The Love Racket, Victoria Palace, Prince's and Adelphi, 1944-45; Follow the Girls, His Majesty's, 1945-47; Cinderella, London Casino, 1948; The Kid from Stratford, Prince's, Winter Garden, 1948-49; Goody Two Shoes, London Casino, 1950; Bet Your Life, London Hippodrome, 1951-52; The Love Match, Palace, 1953-54; Babes in the Wood, Golders Green, 1954; Babes in the Wood, Streatham Hill, 1955; Humpty Dumpty, Golders Green Hippodrome, 1956; Robinson Crusoe, Palladium, 1957; Dick Whittington, Golders Green Hippodrome, 1958; Dick Whittington, Streatham Hill Theatre, 1959-60; Cinderella, Golders Green Hippodrome, 1961-62; *Pantomime:* Robin Hood, Coventry Theatre, 1963-64; Babes in the Wood, Wimbledon, 1966-67; Sleeping Beauty, Wimbledon, 1969-70; Cinderella, Manchester, 1970-71; Cinderella, Nottingham, 1971-72; Cinderella, Birmingham, 1972-73; Babes in the Wood, Richmond, 1973-74; Cinderella, Bournemouth, 1974-75; Babes in the Wood, Bristol, 1975-76, Manchester, 1976-77. London Palladium: Aladdin, 1964-65; Babes in the Wood, 1965-66; Robinson Crusoe, 1967-68; Jack and the Beanstalk, 1968-69. Royal Command Performance (Palladium), 1946, 1948, 1952, 1954, 1955, 1957, 1968, 1972; Command Performance

(Manchester), 1959. Australian tour, 1949-50; various radio and television broadcasts and provincial variety tours. Summer seasons: Blackpool, Bournemouth, Southsea, Margate, Shanklin, Hastings, Rhyl, Torquay, Eastbourne, etc. Pres., Stage Golfing Soc. *Publication:* Before Your Very Eyes (autobiog.), 1975. *Recreations:* golfing, motoring. *Club:* Savage.

ASKIN, Hon. Sir Robert William, GCMG 1975 (KCMG 1972); Premier of New South Wales, 1965-75; *b* 4 April 1909; *s* of William James Askin and Ellen Laura Askin (*née* Halliday); *m* 1937, Mollie Isabelle Underhill; no *c. Educ:* Sydney Techn. High Sch.; Central Coaching College. War Service, 1941-45. Mem. NSW Parlt, 1950; Dep. Opposition Leader, 1954; Leader of Opposition, 1959. Hon. DLitt New South Wales, 1966. Order of St Peter and St Paul, Lebanon, 1972; Grand Officer, Order of Cedar of Lebanon, 1972. *Recreations:* gardening, racing, cricket. *Address:* 86 Bower Street, Manly, NSW 2095, Australia. *T:* 977-1844. *Club:* University.

ASKONAS, Brigitte Alice, PhD; FRS 1973; Head of Division of Immunology, MRC, National Institute for Medical Research, London, since 1976; *b* 1 April 1923; *d* of late Charles F. Askonas and Rose Askonas. *Educ:* McGill Univ., Montreal (BSc, MSc); Cambridge Univ. (PhD). Research student, Sch. of Biochemistry, Univ. of Cambridge, 1949-52; Immunology Div., NIMR, 1953-; Dept of Bacteriology and Immunology, Harvard Med. Sch., Boston, 1961-62; Basel Inst. for Immunology, Basel, Switzerland, 1971-72. *Publications:* contrib. scientific papers to various biochemical and immunological jls and books. *Recreations:* art, travel. *Address:* 23 Hillside Gardens, N6 5SU. *T:* 01-348 6792.

ASKWITH, Hon. Betty Ellen, FRSL; *b* 26 June 1909; *o d* of late Baron Askwith, KCB, KC, LLD, and Lady Askwith, CBE; *m* 1950, Keith Miller Jones, *qv. Educ:* Lycée Français, London; North Foreland Lodge, Broadstairs. *Publications:* First Poems, 1928; If This Be Error, 1932; Poems, 1933; Green Corn, 1933; Erinna, 1937; Keats, 1940; The Admiral's Daughters, 1947; A Broken Engagement, 1950; The Blossoming Tree, 1954; The Tangled Web, 1960; A Step Out of Time, 1966; Lady Dilke, 1969; Two Victorian Families, 1971; The Lytteltons, 1975. With Theodora Benson: Lobster Quadrille, 1930; Seven Basketfuls, 1932; Foreigners, 1935; Muddling Through, 1936; How to Be Famous, 1937. *Translations:* The Tailor's Cake, 1947; A Hard Winter, 1947; Meeting, 1950. *Recreation:* reading Victorian novels. *Address:* 9/105 Onslow Square, SW7. *T:* 01-589 7126.

ASLIN, Elizabeth Mary; Keeper, Bethnal Green Museum, since 1974; *b* 23 March 1923; *d* of Charles Herbert Aslin and Ethel Fawcett Aslin. *Educ:* various schools; Slade Sch. of Fine Art, Univ. of London. Res. Asst, Circulation Dept, V & A Museum, 1947; Asst Keeper i/c, Bethnal Green Museum, 1964; Asst Dir, V & A Museum, 1968. Member: Victorian Soc.; Decorative Arts Soc. *Publictions:* Nineteenth Century English Furniture, 1962; The Aesthetic Movement: Prelude to Art Nouveau, 1969. *Recreations:* drawing, etching, travel. *Address:* 9 Pembridge Crescent, W11 3DT. *T:* 01-229 1945.

ASPIN, Norman, CMG 1968; British High Commissioner in Malta, since 1976; *b* 9 Nov. 1922; *s* of Thomas and Eleanor Aspin; *m* 1948, Elizabeth Irving; three *s. Educ:* Darwen Grammar Sch.; Durham Univ. (MA). War Service, 1942-45, Lieut RNVR. Demonstrator in Geography, Durham Univ., 1947-48; Asst Principal, Commonwealth Relations Office, 1948; served in India, 1948-51; Principal, Commonwealth Relations Office, 1952; served in Federation of Rhodesia and Nyasaland, 1954-57; British Deputy High Commissioner in Sierra Leone, 1961-63; Commonwealth Relations Office, 1963-65; British Embassy, Tel Aviv, 1966-69; IDC 1970; Head of Personnel Policy Dept, FCO, 1971-73; Under-Sec., FCO, 1973-76; Comr, British Indian Ocean Territory, 1976. *Recreations:* sailing, tennis. *Address:* c/o Foreign and Commonwealth Office, SW1. *Club:* Naval.

ASPINALL, William Briant Philip, OBE 1945; Headmaster, Queen's School, HQ Northern Army Group, Rheindahlen, 1960-72, retired; *b* 1912; *s* of William Pryce Aspinall and Ethel Eleanor (*née* Ravenscroft); *m* 1st, Aileen, *d* of Major R. FitzGerald; one *s*; 2nd, Phyllis, *d* of Leopold Hill. *Educ:* Royal Masonic Sch.; St John's Coll., Cambridge; Headmaster, Sutton Valence Sch., 1950-53; Windsor Sch., Hamm, BAOR, 1953-58; King Richard Sch., Cyprus, 1959. *Recreations:* cricket, hockey, golf, etc. *Address:* Baker's Farm House, Goudhurst, Kent. *Clubs:* MCC; Rye Golf.

ASPRAY, Rodney George, JP; FCA; Member, Monopolies and Mergers Commission, since 1975; Chief Executive Officer, Norwest Cooperative Society, since 1969; *b* 1934. Formerly Secretary, Manchester and Salford Cooperative Society. FCA 1960. *Address:* Kambara, 4 Green Lane, Higher Poynton, Cheshire; c/o Monopolies and Mergers Commission, New Court, 48 Carey Street, WC2. *T:* 01-831 6111.

ASQUITH, family name of **Earl of Oxford and Asquith.**

ASQUITH, Viscount; Raymond Benedict Bartholomew Michael Asquith; *b* 24 Aug. 1952; *er s* and *heir* of 2nd Earl of Oxford and Asquith, *qv. Educ:* Ampleforth; Balliol College, Oxford. *Address:* Manor House, Mells, Frome, Somerset.

ASSHETON, family name of **Baron Clitheroe.**

ASTAIRE, Fred; actor, motion pictures; *b* 10 May 1899; *s* of F. E. Astaire and Ann Geilus; *m* 1933, Phyllis Livingston Potter (*d* 1954); two *s* one *d. Educ:* private. Stage musical comedy-vaudeville until 1933, then motion pictures. First appearance in London, 1923, in Stop Flirting; American and English successes: Lady Be Good, Funny Face, The Band Waggon, Gay Divorce. *Films:* Flying Down to Rio, Top Hat, Roberta, Gay Divorce, Follow the Fleet, Swingtime, Shall We Dance?, Story of Vernon and Irene Castle, Holiday Inn, Ziegfeld Follies, Blue Skies, Easter Parade, The Barkleys of Broadway, Three Little Words, Let's Dance, Daddy Longlegs, Funny Face, Silk Stockings, On the Beach, The Pleasure of His Company, Finian's Rainbow, The Midas Run, A Run on Gold, The Towering Inferno, Un Taxi Mauve. *Television Shows:* An Evening with Fred Astaire, 1958; Another Evening with Fred Astaire, 1959; Astaire Time, 1960; The Fred Astaire Show, 1968. *Publication:* Autobiography, Steps in Time, 1959. *Recreations:* golf, thoroughbred racing. *Address:* Beverly Hills, California 90210, USA. *Clubs:* Racquet and Tennis, The Brook, Lamb's (New York).

ASTBURY, Sir George, Kt 1966; JP; *b* 10 May 1902; 2nd *s* of Thomas Astbury, Longton, Stoke-on-Trent; *m* 1930, Nellie, 2nd *d* of Albert Bagnall, Sandford Hill, Longton; two *s. Educ:* St James's, Longton. Retired as Co-operative Soc. Insurance Agent. Former Mem. Nat. Wages Bd of Co-op. Union. CC 1937, JP 1938, CA 1951, Hon. Alderman 1974, Cheshire. *Address:* West Winds, Strawberry Roundabout, Backford, near Chester.

ASTBURY, Norman Frederick, CBE 1968; MA, ScD Cantab, CEng, FIEE, FInstP, FRSA; Director, British Ceramic Research Association, 1960-73; *b* 1 Dec. 1908; *y c* of William and Clara Astbury, Normacot, Staffs; *m* 1933, Nora Enid, *yr d* of William and Mary Wilkinson; three *s* one *d. Educ:* Longton High Sch.; St John's Coll., Cambridge (Scholar and Prizeman). National Physical Laboratory, 1929-39; HM Anti-Submarine Experimental Establishment, 1939-45; Dir of Research, J. Sankey & Sons Ltd and Guest, Keen & Nettlefold Ltd, 1945-49; Prof. of Applied Physics, NSW Univ. of Technology, 1949-51; Prof. of Physics, Univ. of Khartoum, 1951-56; Royal Aircraft Establishment, 1956-57; Dep. Dir of Research, Brit. Ceram. Research Assoc., 1957-60. Pres., Brit. Ceram. Soc., 1969; Member: Coun. Inst. of Physics and Phys. Soc., 1963-66; Nat. Coun. for Technological Awards, 1958-64; Coun. for Nat. Academic Awards, 1964-66; Inter-services Metallurgical Research Board, 1964-69; Chm. Cttee of Directors of Research Assocs, 1964-66; Vice-Pres., Parly and Sci. Cttee, 1965-68; Mem., Construction Res. Adv. Council, DoE (formerly MPBW), 1968-71. *Publications:* Industrial Magnetic Testing, 1952; Electrical Applied Physics, 1956; numerous papers in scientific jls. *Recreations:* music, model railways. *Address:* 85 Atlantic Way, Westward Ho!, Devon. *T:* Bideford 5482. *Clubs:* Athenæum; Federation (Stoke-on-Trent).

ASTERLEY JONES, Philip; see Jones, P. A.

ASTLEY, family name of **Baron Hastings.**

ASTLEY, Sir Francis Jacob Dugdale, 6th Bt, *cr* 1821; Head of Classics Department, The Atlantic College, St Donat's Castle, Glamorgan, 1962-69; *b* 26 Oct. 1908; *s* of Rev. Anthony Aylmer Astley (6th *s* of 2nd Bt); *S* kinsman 1943; *m* 1934, Brita Margareta Josefina Nyström, Stockholm; one *d. Educ:* Marlborough; Trinity Coll., Oxford. Sen. Lectr, University Coll. of Ghana, 1948-61. *Heir:* none. *Address:* 21a Lindfield Gardens, NW3 6PX. *T:* 01-435 9945.

ASTON, Bishop Suffragan of, since 1972; **Rt. Rev. Mark Green,** MC 1945; *b* 28 March 1917; *s* of late Rev. Ernest William Green, OBE, and Miranda Mary Green; unmarried. *Educ:* Rossall Sch.; Lincoln Coll., Oxford (MA). Curate, St Catherine's Gloucester, 1940; Royal Army Chaplains' Dept, 1943-46 (despatches, 1945); Dir of Service Ordination Candidates, 1947-48; Vicar of St John,

Newland, Hull, 1948-53; Short Service Commn, Royal Army Chaplains' Dept, 1953-56; Vicar of South Bank, Teesside, 1956-58; Rector of Cottingham, Yorks, 1958-64; Vicar of Bishopthorpe and Acaster Malbis, York, 1964-72; Hon. Chaplain to Archbp of York, 1964-72; Rural Dean of Ainsty, 1964-68; Canon and Prebendary of York Minster, 1963-72. *Recreation:* walking. *Address:* 5 Greenhill Road, Sutton Coldfield, West Midlands B72 1DS. *T:* 021-373 1031.

ASTON, Archdeacon of; see Tytler, Ven. D. A.

ASTON, Arthur Vincent, CMG 1950; MC 1917; b 5 Nov. 1896; m 1922, Rita Bethia Walker Simpson (d 1972); two s. *Educ:* King's Sch., Chester; Queen's Coll., Oxford. Malayan Civil Service, 1919; ADC to Officer Administering the Govt, 1929; Resident Commissioner, Pahang, 1946, Perak, 1947, Penang, 1948-51; retired, 1951. Served European War, 1914-18 (MC); War of 1939-45 (despatches). *Address:* Croylands, Hindon, Salisbury, Wilts. *T:* Hindon 285.

ASTON, Prof. Peter George, DPhil; Professor of Music, University of East Anglia, since 1974; b 5 Oct 1938; s of George William Aston and Elizabeth Oliver Smith; m 1960, Elaine Veronica Neale; one s. *Educ:* Tettenhall Coll.; Birmingham Sch. of Music (GBSM); Univ of York (DPhil); FTCL, ARCM. Lectr in Music, 1964-72, Sen. Lectr, 1972-74, Univ. of York. Dir, Tudor Consort, 1958-65; Conductor: English Baroque Ensemble, 1968-70; Aldeburgh Festival Singers, 1975-. *Compositions:* two song cycles, chamber music, choral and orchestral works, church music, opera. *Publications:* George Jeffreys and the English Baroque, 1970; The Music of York Minster, 1972; Sound and Silence (jtly), 1970, German edn 1972; (ed) The Collected Works of George Jeffreys, 3 vols, 1977; contrib. to internat. music jls. *Recreations:* Association football, cricket, chess. *Address:* University of East Anglia, Music Centre, School of Fine Arts and Music, University Plain, Norwich NR4 7TJ. *T:* Norwich 56161.

ASTON, Thomas William, CMG 1969; HM Diplomatic Service; British Consul-General, Los Angeles, since 1974; b 14 May 1922; s of late Henry Herbert Aston, Birmingham, and of Lilian Perks; m 1947, Eve Dunning; one d. *Educ:* Saltley Grammar Sch., Birmingham. Entered Civil Service as Employment Clerk, Ministry of Labour, 1939. Served with RAF, 1941-46: Middle East, Palestine, Persian Gulf, Egypt, South Africa; Navigator, 1942; Flight-Lieut, 1944. Executive Officer (Inspector), Ministry of National Insurance, 1947; Assistant Principal, Commonwealth Relations Office, 1951; Delhi, 1953-54; Principal, 1954; seconded to Joint Intelligence Cttee, 1954-56; First Secretary, South Africa, 1957-60; CO, 1961-63; First Sec., Kenya, 1963-64; Deputy British High Commissioner, Kampala, 1964-65; Dir, Internat. Affairs Div., Commonwealth Secretariat, 1966-69; Inspector, FCO, 1969-72; Sen. British Trade Comr, Hong Kong, 1972-74. *Recreations:* tennis, cricket, gardening, bird watching. *Address:* c/o Foreign and Commonwealth Office, SW1. *Club:* Royal Commonwealth Society.

ASTON, Hon. Sir William (John), KCMG 1970; JP; Speaker, House of Representatives, Australia, 1967-73; MP for Phillip, 1955-61, 1963-72; Chairman, Kolotex Holdings Ltd; Director; Neilson McCarthy & Partners; b 19 Sept. 1916; s of Harold John Aston and Dorothea (née McKeown); m 1941, Beatrice Delaney Burrett; one s two d. *Educ:* Randwick Boys' High School. Mayor of Waverley, 1952-53. Dep. Govt Whip, 1959-61 and 1963-64; Chief Govt Whip, 1964-67; Trustee, Parlt Retiring Allowances, 1964-67; Mem. and Dep. Chm., Joint Select Cttee on New and Perm. Parlt House, 1965-72; Chairman: House of Reps Standing Orders Cttee, 1967-72; Joint House Cttee, 1967-72; Library Cttee, 1967-72; Joint Cttee on Broadcasting of Parly Proceedings, 1967-72; Jt Chm., Inter-Parliamentary Union (Commonwealth of Aust. Br.) and Commonwealth Parly Assoc. (Aust. Br.), 1967-72; Leader, Aust. Delegn to IPU Conf., Ottawa, 1964; Convenor and Chm., First Conf. of Aust. Presiding Officers, 1968; rep. Australia at: opening of Zambian Parlt Bldg; Funeral of Israeli Prime Minister Eshkol and IPU Symposium, Geneva, 1968; Conf. of Commonwealth Presiding Officers, Ottawa, 1969, New Delhi, 1971; opened Aust. House, Mt Scopus, Univ. of Israel, 1971; led Parly delegn to Turkey, Yugoslavia, UK and to Council of Europe, 1971. JP NSW 1954. Korean Order of Distinguished Service Merit (1st Class), 1969. *Recreations:* cricket, golf, football, fishing, bowls. *Address:* 55 Olola Avenue, Vaucluse, NSW 2030, Australia. *T:* 337-5992. *Clubs:* Royal Automobile of Australia (Sydney); Waverley Bowling.

ASTOR, family name of Viscount Astor and Baron Astor of Hever.

ASTOR, 4th Viscount, cr 1917, of Hever Castle; Baron cr 1916; **William Waldorf Astor;** b 27 Dec. 1951; s of 3rd Viscount Astor; S father 1966; m 1976, Annabel Sheffield, d of T. Jones; one d. *Educ:* Eton Coll. *Recreation:* shooting. *Heir:* uncle Hon. (Francis) David (Langhorne) Astor, qv. *Address:* Ginge Manor, Wantage, Oxon. *Clubs:* White's, Turf.

ASTOR OF HEVER, 2nd Baron cr 1956, of Hever Castle; **Gavin Astor;** Lord-Lieutenant and Custos Rotulorum of Kent, since 1972; Director, Alliance Assurance Co. Ltd, 1954; President, Commonwealth Press Union, since 1972 (Chairman of Council, 1959-72); b 1 June 1918; e s of 1st Baron Astor of Hever, and Lady Violet Mary Elliot (d 1965), y d of 4th Earl of Minto, KG, PC, GCSI, GCMG, GCIE, and widow of Lord Charles Mercer Nairne, 2nd s of 5th Marquess of Lansdowne; S father, 1971; m 1945, Lady Irene Haig, d of late Field Marshal Earl Haig, KT, GCB, OM, GCVO, KCIE; two s three d. *Educ:* Eton; New Coll., Oxford. Served with The Life Guards, 1940-46. Director: C. Townsend Hook Ltd, 1954-65; Reuters Ltd, 1955-61; Electrolux Ltd, 1959-70; Monotype Corp. Ltd, 1952-73; Chm., The Times Publishing Co. Ltd, 1959-66 (Dir, 1952-66); Co-Chief Proprietor of The Times, 1964-66; Pres., Times Newspapers Ltd, 1967-. Chairman: 9th Commonwealth Press Conf., India and Pakistan, 1961; 10th Conf., West Indies, 1965; 11th Conf., UK, 1970; 12th Conf., SE Asia, 1974; Exec. Cttee, Pilgrims Soc. of Gt Britain, 1967-77 (Pres., 1977-); Central Council, Royal Commonwealth Soc., 1972-75. Master of Guild of St Bride's Ch., Fleet St, 1970-. Seneschal of Canterbury Cathedral, 1973-. Mem. Ct of Assts, Goldsmiths' Company, 1973-. High Sheriff 1955-56, DL 1956, Sussex; DL 1966, JP 1973, Kent. FRSA 1965. KStJ 1974. *Heir:* s Hon. John Jacob Astor [b 16 June 1946; m 1970, Fiona Diana, d of Captain R. E. L. Harvey; one d]. *Address:* Hever Castle, Edenbridge, Kent. *T:* Edenbridge 2204. *Clubs:* Bath, White's. *See also Hon. H. W. and Hon. John Astor, Marquess of Lansdowne.*

ASTOR, Hon. (Francis) David (Langhorne); Editor of the Observer, 1948-75; Director, The Observer, since 1976; b 5 March 1912; s of 2nd Viscount Astor and heir-pres. to 4th Viscount Astor, qv; m 1st, 1945, Melanie Hauser; one d; 2nd, 1952, Bridget Aphra Wreford; two s three d. *Educ:* Eton; Balliol, Oxford. Yorkshire Post, 1936. Served War of 1939-45, with Royal Marines, 1940-45. Foreign Editor of the Observer, 1946-48. Croix de Guerre, 1944. *Address:* 9 Cavendish Avenue, St John's Wood, NW8 9JD. *T:* 01-286 0223/4; Manor House, Sutton Courtenay, Oxon. *T:* Sutton Courtenay 221. *Clubs:* Athenæum, Boodle's, Royal Automobile.

ASTOR, Hon. Hugh Waldorf, JP; Director: Hambro's Bank; Phœnix Assurance; Hutchinson Ltd; Winterbottom Trust Ltd; b 20 Nov. 1920; 2nd s of 1st Baron Astor of Hever; m 1950, Emily Lucy, d of Sir Alexander Kinloch, 12th Bt, qv; two s three d. *Educ:* Eton; New Coll., Oxford. Served War of 1939-45; Intelligence Corps, Europe and SE Asia (Lieut-Col). Joined The Times as Asst Middle East Correspondent, 1947; elected to Board of The Times, 1956; Dep. Chm., 1959, resigned 1967 on merger with Sunday Times; Chm., The Times Book Co. Ltd, 1960, resigned 1967 on merger with Sunday Times. Chairman: Times Trust, 1967; Trust Houses Forte Council, 1971 (Mem. Council, 1962); Dep. Chm., Olympia Ltd, 1971-73. Dep. Chm., Middlesex Hosp., 1965-74; Governor: Bradfield Coll.; Gresham's Sch.; Peabody Trust; Hon. Treasurer: Franco-British Soc., 1969-76; Marine Biol Assoc. UK; has served on Council or governing body of: RNLI; RYA; RORC; Air League. Mem. Ct of Assts, Fishmongers' Co. (Prime Warden, 1976-77). In partnership with Sir William Dugdale participated in air races, London-Sydney 1969, London-Victoria 1971. JP Berks, 1953; High Sheriff of Berks, 1963. *Recreations:* sailing, flying, shooting, diving. *Address:* Folly Farm, Sulhamstead, Berks. *T:* Reading 302326; 14 Culross Street, W1. *T:* 01-629 4601. *Clubs:* Brooks's, Buck's, Pratt's; Royal Yacht Squadron, Royal Ocean Racing. *See also Baron Astor of Hever, Hon. John Astor.*

ASTOR, Hon. John; a Director, TPC (Investments) Ltd; b 26 Sept. 1923; 3rd s of 1st Baron Astor of Hever; m 1950, Diana Kathleen Drummond; two s one d. *Educ:* Summerfields, Hastings; Eton Coll. RAFVR, 1942-45. Berkshire County Council, 1953-74; Alderman, 1960; Chairman, Education Cttee, 1961-66. Vice-Chm., South Berkshire Conservative Assoc., 1958 until 1963, when adopted as candidate. MP (C) Newbury, 1964-Feb. 1974. *Recreations:* fishing, shooting. *Address:* Kirby House, Inkpen, Berks. *T:* Inkpen 284. *Clubs:* Buck's; Royal Yacht Squadron. *See also Baron Astor of Hever, Hon. H. W. Astor.*

ASTOR, Major Hon. John Jacob, MBE 1945; DL; Major, Life Guards; b 29 Aug. 1918; 4th s of 2nd Viscount Astor; m 1st,

1944, Ana Inez (marr. diss. 1972), *yr d* of Señor Dr Don Miguel Carcano, *qv*; one *s* one *d*; 2nd, 1976, Susan Sheppard, *d* of Major M. Eveleigh. *Educ:* Eton; New Coll., Oxford. Served War of 1939-45: Italy, France, Germany, Norway; North-West Europe, 1944-45 (MBE, Legion of Honour, French Croix de Guerre). Contested (C) Sutton Div. of Plymouth, 1950; MP (C) Sutton Div. of Plymouth, 1951-Sept. 1959. PPS to Financial Sec. of Treasury, 1951-52. Chairman: Governing Body of Nat. Inst. of Agricultural Engineering, 1963-68; Agric. Res. Council, 1968-. Member: Horserace Totalisator Bd, 1962-68; Horserace Betting Levy Bd, 1976-. Steward of Jockey Club, 1968-71. DL 1962, former JP, Cambs. *Address:* Hatley Park, Hatley St George, Sandy, Beds. *T:* Gamlingay 50266. *Clubs:* White's, Royal Automobile.

ASTOR, Hon. Michael Langhorne; *b* 10 April 1916; *s* of 2nd Viscount Astor; *m* 1st, 1942, Barbara Mary Colonsay (marr. diss., 1961; she *m* 1962, 1st Viscount Ward of Witley, *qv*), *o d* of late Capt. Ronald Fitzroy Rous McNeill; two *s* two *d*; 2nd, 1961, Mrs Pandora Jones (marr. diss. 1968), *d* of late Sir Bede Clifford, GCMG, CB, MVO; 3rd, 1970, Judy, *d* of Paul Innes; one *s* one *d*. *Educ:* Eton; New College, Oxford. Served in Berkshire Yeomanry TA and GHQ Liaison Regt Sept. 1939-June 1945. MP (C) Eastern Division of Surrey, 1945-51. Chm., The London Library; Mem., Arts Council, 1968-71. *Publications:* Tribal Feeling (biog.), 1963; Brand (novel), 1967. *Clubs:* White's, Brooks's.

ASTWOOD, Lt-Col Sir Jeffrey (Carlton), Kt 1972; CBE 1966; OBE (mil.) 1946; ED 1942; Speaker of House of Assembly, Bermuda, 1968-72, retired; *b* 5 Oct. 1907; *s* of late Jeffrey Burgess Astwood, Neston, Bermuda, and Lilian Maude (*née* Searles); *m* 1928, Hilda Elizabeth Kay (*née* Onions); one *s* one *d*. *Educ:* Saltus Grammar School, Bermuda. Served local TA, 1922-60; retired as Lt-Col, having commanded since 1943. House of Assembly, Bermuda, 1948-72; Minister of Agriculture, of Immigration and Labour, of Health; Member of Exec. Council; Dep. Speaker, 1957-68. Pres., Exec. Cttee, Sandys Grammar Sch., 1950-57 (Chm. Trustees, 1950-); Chm., St James' Church Vestry. President: Atlantic Investment and Development Co. Ltd; J. B. Astwood & Son Ltd; Belfield-in-Somerset Ltd; Brewer Distributors Ltd; Aberfeldy Nurseries Ltd. *Recreations:* theatre, horticulture. *Address:* Greenfield, Somerset, Bermuda. *T:* (business) Hamilton 1.1283; (home) Somerset 4.1729. 4.8180. *Clubs:* No 10; Royal Bermuda Yacht, Sandys Boat.

ATCHERLEY, Sir Harold Winter, Kt 1977; Personnel Co-ordinator, Royal Dutch Shell Group, 1964-70, retd; Chairman, Armed Forces Pay Review Body, since 1971; Member, Top Salaries Review Body, since 1971; *b* 30 Aug. 1918; *s* of L. W. Atcherley and Maude Lester (*née* Nash); *m* 1946, Anita Helen (*née* Leslie), *widow* of Sub Lt W. D. H. Eves, RN; one *s* two *d*. *Educ:* Gresham's Sch.; Heidelberg and Geneva Univs. Joined Royal Dutch Shell Gp, 1937. Served War: Queen's Westminster Rifles, 1939; commissioned Intelligence Corps, 1940; served 18th Infty Div., Singapore; PoW, 1942-45. Rejoined Royal Dutch Shell Gp, 1946: served Egypt, Lebanon, Syria, Argentina, Brazil, 1946-59. Recruitment Advisor to Ministry of Defence, 1970-71. Dir, British Home Stores Ltd, 1973-. Member: Nat. Staff Cttee for Nurses and Midwives, 1973-77; Cttee of Inquiry into Remuneration of Members of Local Authorities, 1977. Empress Leopoldina Medal (Brazil), 1958. *Recreations:* music, skiing, good food. *Address:* Flat 14, 30 Bramham Gardens, Kensington, SW5. *T:* 01-370 5882.

ATHA, Bernard Peter; Vice Chairman, Sports Council, since 1976; Chairman, Yorkshire and Humberside Regional Sports Council, since 1966; Principal Lecturer in Business Studies, Huddersfield Technical College, since 1973; *b* 27 Aug. 1928; *s* of Horace Michael Atha and Mary Quinlan; unmarried. *Educ:* Leeds Modern Sch.; Leeds Univ. (LLB Hons). Barrister-at-law, Gray's Inn. Commn, RAF, 1950-52. Variety artist on stage; Mem. Equity; films incl. Kes, and Family Life; TV plays. Elected Leeds City Council, 1957; Chm., Watch Cttee and Leisure Services Cttee. Parly Candidate (Lab), Penrith and the Border, 1959, Pudsey, 1964. Director: Leeds Coop. Soc.; Leeds Grand Theatre and Leeds Playhouse. Mem., Ministerial Working Party on Sport and Recreation, 1974. *Recreations:* dilettante involvement in variety of sports; music, ballet, travel. *Address:* 25 Moseley Wood Croft, Leeds 16, West Yorks. *T:* Leeds 672485.

ATHABASCA, Bishop of, since 1975; **Rt. Rev. Frederick Hugh Wright Crabb,** DD; *b* Luppitt, Devon, 24 April 1915; *s* of William Samuel and Florence Mary Crabb; *m* 1946, Alice Margery Coombs; two *s* two *d*. *Educ:* Luppitt Parochial Sch.; Univ. of London (St John's Hall, Highbury, London). BD Lond.

(1st Cl. Hons); ALCD (1st Cl. Hons). Asst Curate, St James', West Teignmouth, Devon, 1939-41; Asst Priest, St Andrew's, Plymouth, 1941-42; Missionary at Akot, S Sudan, 1942-44; Principal, Bishop Gwynne Divinity Sch., S Sudan, 1944-51; Vice Principal, London Coll. of Divinity, 1951-57; Principal, Coll. of Emmanuel and St Chad, Saskatoon, Sask., 1957-67; Assoc. Priest, Christ Church, Calgary, Alberta, 1967-69; Rector, St Stephen's Church, Calgary, 1969-75. Hon. DD: Wycliffe Coll., Toronto; St Stephen's Coll., Saskatoon. *Recreations:* gardening, mountain hiking. *Address:* Bishop's Lodge, Box 279, Peace River, Alberta T0H 2X0, Canada. *T:* 1-403-624-2419.
[See supplementary pages.

ATHAIDE, Most Rev. D. R.; *see* Agra, Archbishop of, (RC).

ATHENAGORAS, Theodoritos, (né Theodoros G. Kokkinakis), STM, MA, STD; Archbishop Athenagoras, Metropolitan of Thyateira and Great Britain, since 1964; Exarch of Sweden, Norway, Ireland, Iceland, and Malta; *b* Patmos, Dodecanese, 1912. *Educ:* schs in Patmos and Cyprus; Patriarchal Theological Seminary; Gen. Theolog. Seminary, NY; Northwestern Univ., Chicago. Went to USA 1936. Priest, Greek Orthodox Church, 1940. Formerly: served Patriarchal Church of St Sava, Alexandria, St Andrew's Church, Chicago and St Demetrios Church, Astoria, NY; taught theology at Acad. of Pomfret, Conn. and at Acad. of St Basil; Dean and then Pres., Holy Cross Theolog. Sch., Brookline, Mass; rep. The Ecumenical Patriarchate of Constantinople at World Council of Churches Conferences: Amsterdam, Evanston, New Delhi, Uppsala; Bishop, Western States Dio., 1950; Metropolitan Bishop of Canada, 1960-63. Pres. 4th Panorthodox Conference, Belgrade, 1967. Editor, Orthodox Herald; past Editor, Orthodox Observer and Greek Orthodox Theolog. Review. Hon. DD Edinburgh, 1970. *Publications:* several books in English and in Greek. *Address:* Greek Archdiocese, 5 Craven Hill, W2. *T:* 01-723 4787.

ATHERTON, Alan Royle; Under-Secretary, Department of Environment, since 1975; *b* 25 April 1931; *s* of Harold Atherton and Hilda (*née* Royle); *m* 1959, Valerie Kemp; three *s* one *d*. *Educ:* Cowley Sch., St Helens; Sheffield Univ. (BSc (Hons Chem.)). ICI Ltd, 1955-58; DSIR: Sen. Scientific Officer, 1959-64, Private Sec. to Permanent Sec., 1960-64; Principal Sci. Officer, Road Res. Lab., 1964-65; Principal, Min. of Housing and Local Govt, 1965-70; Asst Sec., Ordnance Survey, 1970-74. *Address:* Windhover, Bowers Hill, Redlynch, Salisbury, Wilts SP5 2HD. *T:* Downton (Wilts) 21096.

ATHERTON, David; Resident Conductor, Royal Opera House, Covent Garden, since 1968; *b* 3 Jan. 1944; *s* of Robert and Lavinia Atherton; *m* 1970, Ann Gianetta Drake; two *d*. *Educ:* Cambridge Univ. (MA). LRAM, LTCL. Repetiteur, Royal Opera House, Covent Garden, 1967-68; Founder and Musical Dir, London Sinfonietta, 1967-73. Became youngest conductor in history of Henry Wood Promenade Concerts at Royal Albert Hall, and also at Royal Opera House, 1968; Royal Festival Hall debut, 1969; from 1970 performances in Europe, Middle East, Far East, Australasia, N America. Adapted and arranged Pandora by Roberto Gerhard for Royal Ballet, 1975. Conductor of the year award, 1971, Edison award, 1973, Composers' Guild of GB; Grand Prix du Disque award, 1977. *Publications:* (ed) The Complete Instrumental and Chamber Music of Arnold Schoenberg and Roberto Gerhard, 1973; (ed) Pandora and Don Quixote Suites by Roberto Gerhard, 1973; contrib., The Revised Musical Companion, 1978. *Recreations:* travel, squash, theatre. *Address:* c/o Royal Opera House, Covent Garden, WC2E 7RA. *T:* 01-240 1200.

ATHLONE, Countess of; (HRH Princess Alice Mary Victoria Augusta Pauline; Princess Alice, Countess of Athlone), VA 1898; GCVO 1948; GBE 1937; *b* 25 Feb. 1883; *d* of HRH Prince Leopold George Duncan Albert, 1st Duke of Albany, KG, PC, KT, GCSI, GCMG (4th *s* of Queen Victoria) and HSH Princess Helene Friederike Auguste, VA, CI, RRC (*d* 1922); *m* 1904, Maj.-Gen. the 1st Earl of Athlone, KG, PC, GCB, GCMG, GCVO, DSO, FRS (*d* 1957), 3rd *s* of HH the 1st Duke of Teck, GCB, and brother of HM Queen Mary; one *d* (two *s* decd). Commandant-in-Chief, Women's Transport Service (FANY). Chairman of Governors, Royal Holloway Coll., 1936-Dec. 1958, resigned; Chancellor, Univ. of West Indies, 1950-71. Hon. DLitt: London Univ., 1933; Queen's Univ., Kingston, Ont., 1943; McGill Univ., 1944; Birmingham Univ., 1960; Hon. LLD St Andrews Univ., 1951. Hon. Freeman: Weavers' Co., 1947; Vintners' Co., 1956; Royal Borough of Kensington, 1961. DGStJ. Grand Cross, Legion of Honour, France. *Address:* Clock House, Kensington Palace, W8.
See also Col Sir Henry Abel Smith.

ATHOLL, 10th Duke of, *cr* 1703; **George Iain Murray;** Lord Murray of Tullibardine, 1604; Earl of Tullibardine, Lord Gask and Balquhidder, 1606; Earl of Atholl, 1629; Marquess of Atholl, Viscount Balquhidder, Lord Balvenie, 1676; Marquess of Tullibardine, Earl of Strathtay, Earl of Strathardle, Viscount Glenalmond, Viscount Glenlyon, 1703-all in the peerage of Scotland; Representative Peer for Scotland in the House of Lords, 1958-63; *b* 19 June 1931; *s* of Lieut-Col George Anthony Murray, OBE, Scottish Horse (killed in action, Italy, 1945), and of Hon. Mrs Angela Campbell-Preston, *qv*; *S* kinsman 1957. *Educ:* Eton; Christ Church, Oxford. Director: Westminster Press (Chm., 1974-); Birmingham Post and Mail Gp; Pearson Longman Ltd, 1975-; Bands of Inverness Ltd. Convener, Scottish Landowners Fedn, 1976- (Vice-Convener, 1971-76); Dep. Chm., RNLI, 1972-; Member: Cttee on the Preparation of Legislation, 1973-75; Exec. Cttee, Nat. Trust for Scotland (Vice-Pres., 1977-); Red Deer Commn. *Heir: cousin* Arthur Stewart Pakington Murray, *b* 9 Sept. 1899. *Address:* Blair Castle, Blair Atholl, Perthshire. *T:* Blair Atholl 212; 31 Marlborough Hill, NW8. *Clubs:* Turf, White's; New (Edinburgh).

ATIYAH, Michael Francis, MA, PhD Cantab; FRS 1962; Royal Society Research Professor, Mathematical Institute, Oxford, and Professorial Fellow of St Catherine's College, Oxford, since 1973; *b* 22 April 1929; *e s* of late Edward Atiyah and Jean Levens; *m* 1955, Lily Brown; three *s. Educ:* Victoria Coll., Egypt; Manchester Grammar Sch.; Trinity Coll., Cambridge. Research Fellow, Trinity Coll., Camb., 1954-58, Hon. Fellow, 1976; First Smith's Prize, 1954; Commonwealth Fund Fellow, 1955-56; Professorial Fellow, 1976-; Mem. Inst. for Advanced Study, Princeton, 1955-56, 1959-60, 1967-68; Asst Lectr in Mathematics, 1957-58, Lectr 1958-61, Univ. of Cambridge; Fellow Pembroke Coll., Cambridge, 1958-61; Reader in Mathematics, Univ. of Oxford, and Professorial Fellow of St Catherine's Coll., Oxford, 1961-63; Savilian Prof. of Geometry, and Fellow of New College, Oxford, 1963-69; Prof. of Mathematics, Inst. for Advanced Study, Princeton, NJ, 1969-72. Visiting Lecturer, Harvard, 1962-63 and 1964-65. Mem. Exec. Cttee, Internat. Mathematical Union, 1966-74; Pres., London Mathematical Soc., 1975-77. Foreign Member: Amer. Acad. of Arts and Scis; Swedish Royal Acad. Hon. DSc: Bonn; Warwick, Durham. Fields Medal, Internat. Congress of Mathematicians, Moscow, 1966; Royal Medal, Royal Soc., 1968. *Publications:* papers in mathematical journals. *Recreation:* gardening. *Address:* Mathematical Institute, 24-29 St Giles, Oxford OX1 3LB. *T:* Oxford 54295; Shotover Mound, Headington, Oxford. *T:* Oxford 62359.
See also P. S. Atiyah.

ATIYAH, Prof. Patrick Selim, DCL; Professor of English Law, Oxford University, since 1977; *b* 5 March 1931; *s* of Edward Atiyah and D. J. C. Levens; *m* 1951, Christine Best; four *s. Educ:* Woking County Grammar Sch. for Boys; Magdalen Coll., Oxford (MA 1957, DCL 1974). Called to the Bar, Inner Temple, 1956. Asst Lectr, LSE, 1954-55; Lectr, Univ. of Khartoum, 1955-59; Legal Asst, BoT, 1961-64; Fellow, New Coll., Oxford, 1964-69; Professor of Law: ANU, 1970-73; Warwick Univ., 1973-77. *Publications:* The Sale of Goods, 1957 (5th edn 1976); Introduction to the Law of Contract, 1961 (2nd edn 1971); Vicarious Liability, 1967; Accidents, Compensation and the Law, 1970 (2nd edn 1976); articles in legal jls. *Recreations:* gardening, cooking. *Address:* St John's College, Oxford; The Old Rectory, Middleton Stoney, Oxon.
See also M. F. Atiyah.

ATKINS, Prof. Sir Hedley (John Barnard), KBE 1967; DM, MCh, FRCS, FRCP; Emeritus Professor of Surgery, University of London; formerly Director of the Department of Surgery, Guy's Hospital; *b* 30 Dec. 1905; *s* of Col Sir John Atkins, KCMG, KCVO, FRCS; *m* 1933, Gladwys Gwendolen, *e d* of Frank Harding Jones; two *s. Educ:* Rugby; Trinity Coll., Oxford; Guy's Hospital. War of 1939-45 (despatches): Temp. Lieut-Col RAMC, 1941. Surgeon to Guy's Hosp., 1936; Hunterian Professor, RCS, 1936; Examiner in Surgery at: Cambridge Univ., 1947; London Univ., 1948; Durham Univ., 1950; Univ. of The W Indies 1960; Member: Court of Examiners, RCS, 1950, Council, 1952; Gen. Dental Council, 1954; Gen. Medical Council, 1955; Central Health Services Council, 1956; Dean of the Institute of Basic Med. Sciences, 1957-62; Clinical Research Bd, Med. Research Council, 1959; Pres. Surgical Research Soc., 1960. Visiting Professor: Johns Hopkins Hosp., 1947; UCLA, 1954; Univ. of California, 1956; Univ. of Miami, 1972; Sims Commonwealth Travelling Prof., 1961. Lectures: Syme Oration, Brisbane, 1961; Bradshaw, RCS, 1965; Astor, Middlesex Hosp., 1970; Cavendish, W London Med. Chir. Soc., 1970; Gideon de Laune, Soc. of Apothecaries, 1970; Hunterian Orator, RCS, 1971; Macewen, Glasgow, 1972; First Leah Lederman, RSM, 1973; Purvis Oration, 1975. Mem.

Med. Advisory Cttee of British Council, 1962; Chm., MRC working party, on Tristan da Cunha, 1962; Mem. Med. Consultative Cttee of Nuffield Provincial Hosps Trust, 1962; Chm., Med. Res. Council Cttee on Uses of High Oxygen Tension, 1963, and on Gastric Hypothermia, 1963; Mem., Med. Research Council, 1963; Thomas Vicary Lecturer, Royal Coll. of Surgeons, 1964; Examr in Surgery, at Birmingham Univ., 1964; Vice-Chm., Standing Med. Adv. Cttee (of Central Health Services Council), 1964; Chairman: (MRC) Cttee on Endolymphatic Therapy, 1965; Jt Bd, Clinical Nursing Studies, 1969-; Med. Bd, St John, 1969. Chm. Council, Queen Elizabeth Coll., Univ. of London, 1969-. President: Med. Soc. of London, 1972; RSM, 1971-72 (Hon. Fellow, 1974; Pres., Section of Measurement in Medicine, 1965); RCS, 1966-69 (Vice-Pres. 1964-66). Governor, Strangeways Research Laboratory, Cambridge, 1968. Hon. FACS, 1956; Hon. FRACS, 1961; Hon. FCS (So. Af.), 1968; Hon. FRCS Glas., 1971; Hon. FRCP&S (Can.) 1969; Hon. FDSRCS 1972; Hon. Fellow: Trinity Coll., Oxford, 1968; Queen Elizabeth Coll., Univ. of London, 1968; Assoc. of Surgeons of GB and Ireland, 1973; American Surgical Assoc., 1966; New England Surgical Soc. Thomas and Edith Dixon Medal, 1965. Hon. DSc: East Anglia, 1968; Kent, 1971. KStJ 1968. *Publications:* After-Treatment, 1942; (author of Biographical introduction) Hilton's Rest and Pain, 1950; (ed) Tools of Biological Research, 1959; The Surgeon's Craft, 1965; Down, the Home of the Darwins, 1974; Memoirs of a Surgeon, 1977; numerous articles in med. jls. *Recreation:* gardening. *Address:* Down House, Downe, Kent BR6 7JT. *Clubs:* Athenæum; Vincent's (Oxford), Harlequins.

ATKINS, Henry St J., DSc; President, University College, Cork, 1954-63, retired; *b* 19 March 1896; *s* of Patrick Atkins and Agnes Egan, Cork; *m* 1929, Agnes E. O'Regan (*d* 1960), MB, BCh; one *s* one *d. Educ:* Christian Brothers, North Monastery, Cork; University Coll., Cork. BSc (Math. Science) 1915; post-grad. scholar, MSc 1923. Prof. of Pure Maths, University Coll., Cork, 1936-54; Registrar, 1943-54. Hon. DSc 1955. MRIA, 1957. *Recreations:* golf, fishing. *Address:* Knockrea Park, Cork. *T:* Cork 32448. *Clubs:* National University of Ireland; Cork City and County (Cork).

ATKINS, Rt. Hon. Humphrey Edward, PC 1973; MP (C) Spelthorne since 1970 (Merton and Morden, Surrey, 1955-70); Opposition Chief Whip, since 1974; *b* 12 Aug. 1922; *s* of late Capt. E. D. Atkins, Nyeri, Kenya Colony; *m* 1944, Margaret, *d* of Sir Robert Spencer-Nairn, 1st Bt; one *s* three *d. Educ:* Wellington Coll. Special entry cadetship, RN, 1940; Lieut RN, 1943; resigned, 1948. PPS to Civil Lord of the Admiralty, 1959-62; Hon.. Sec. Conservative Parly Defence Cttee, 1965-67; Opposition Whip, 1967-70; Treasurer of HM Household and Dep. Chief Whip, 1970-73; Parly Sec. to the Treasury and Govt Chief Whip, 1973-74. Vice-Chm., Management Cttee, Outward Bound Trust, 1966-70. *Address:* 3 North Court, Great Peter Street, SW1; Tuckenhams, Waltham St Lawrence, Berks. *Club:* Brooks's.

ATKINS, Ian Robert, OBE 1963; Controller, Programme Services, Television, BBC, 1963-72; *b* 22 Jan. 1912; *s* of late Robert Atkins, CBE, and Mary (*née* Sumner); *m* 1939, Freda Bamford; one *s* one *d. Educ:* St Paul's Sch. Film cameraman, 1930-33; theatre stage manager, 1934-36; asst film dir, 1936-37; theatre stage manager, 1937-39. Royal Artillery, 1939-46; seconded to Min. of Supply, 1942-46. Television, BBC: Television Studio Manager, BBC, 1939 and 1946; Producer, Drama Dept, 1946-58; Asst to Controller, Programme Services, 1958-62; Asst Controller, Programme Services, 1962-63. *Recreations:* gardening, fishing. *Address:* Ash Cottage, Blacksmith Lane, London Street, Chertsey, Surrey. *T:* Chertsey 63161.

ATKINS, John Spencer, DSO 1945; TD; DL; President, Atkins Brothers (Hosiery) Ltd; *b* 28 Oct. 1905; 3rd *s* of late Col E. C. Atkins, CB, DL; *m* 1936, Monica Lucy Standish; one *s* two *d. Educ:* Uppingham Sch. DL Leics 1946. *Recreations:* shooting, fishing. *Address:* White House, Ullesthorpe, Lutterworth, Leics. *T:* Leire 209274. *Club:* Naval and Military.

ATKINS, Leonard B. W.; *see* Walsh Atkins.

ATKINS, Ronald Henry; MP (Lab) Preston North, 1966-70 and since Feb. 1974; *b* Barry, Glam, 13 June 1916; *s* of Frank and Elizabeth Atkins; *m*; three *s* two *d. Educ:* Barry County Sch.; London Univ. (BA Hons). Teacher, 1949-66 (latterly Head, Eng. Dept, Halstead Sec. Sch.); Lectr, Accrington Coll. of Further Educn, 1970-74. Member: Braintree RDC, 1952-61; Preston Dist. Council, 1974-. Contested (Lab) Lowestoft, 1964. *Recreations:* jazz, dancing, walking. *Address:* 22 Linden Grove, Preston, Lancs. *T:* Preston 791692.

ATKINS, Sir William Sydney Albert, Kt 1976; CBE 1966; Chairman: W. S. Atkins & Partners, since 1951; W. S. Atkins & Partners (Ethiopia) Ltd, since 1963; W. S. Atkins Group Ltd, since 1971; W. S. Atkins & Associates Pty Ltd, since 1971; W. S. Atkins (Overseas Projects) Ltd, since 1973; W. S. Atkins International, since 1973; W. S. Atkins Group Consultants, since 1975; Sir William Atkins & Partners, since 1977; *b* 6 Feb. 1902; 2nd *s* of Robert Edward and Martha Atkins; *m* 1928, Elsie Jessie, *d* of Edward and Hilda Barrow, Hockley, Essex; two *d*. *Educ:* Coopers' Sch.; London Univ. Chief Engr, Smith Walker Ltd, 1928; Man. Dir, London Ferro-Concrete Co. Ltd, 1935, Chm. 1937; Founder and Sen. Partner, W. S. Atkins & Partners, 1938. Mem. Council, London Chamber of Commerce. Fellow, UCL. *Publications:* many technical papers. *Recreations:* gardening and horticultural research. *Address:* Chobham Place, Chobham, near Woking, Surrey GU24 8TN. *T:* Chobham 8867. *Club:* Royal Automobile.

ATKINSON, Prof. Anthony Barnes; Professor and Head of Department of Political Economy, University College London, since 1976; *b* 4 Sept. 1944; *s* of Norman Joseph Atkinson and Esther Muriel Atkinson; *m* 1965, Judith Mary (*née* Mandeville); two *s* one *d*. *Educ:* Cranbrook Sch.; Churchill Coll., Cambridge (MA). Fellow, St John's Coll., Cambridge, 1967-71; Prof. of Econs, Univ. of Essex, 1971-76. Vis. Prof. MIT, 1973. Fellow, Econometric Soc., 1975. Editor, Jl of Public Economics, 1972-. *Publications:* Poverty in Britain and the Reform of Social Security, 1969; Unequal Shares, 1972; The Tax Credit Scheme, 1973; Economics of Inequality, 1975; articles in Rev. of Econ. Studies, Econ. Jl, Jl of Public Econs, Jl of Econ. Theory. *Address:* 33 Hurst Green, Brightlingsea, Colchester, Essex. *T:* Colchester 302253.

ATKINSON, Arthur Kingsley Hall; Under Secretary, Cabinet Office, since 1976; *b* 24 Dec. 1926; *er s* of Arthur Hall Atkinson and Florence (*née* Gerrans). *Educ:* Priory Sch., Shrewsbury; Emmanuel Coll., Cambridge (MA). RAF, 1948; MAFF: Asst Principal 1950; Private Sec. 1953; Principal 1956; Asst Sec. 1965; Under Sec., 1973. *Recreations:* travel, music, gardening. *Address:* 24 Pond Place, SW3 6QV. *T:* 01-589 6262.

ATKINSON, Brooks; see Atkinson, J. B.

ATKINSON, Colin Ronald Michael; Headmaster, Millfield School, Somerset, since Jan. 1971 (Acting Headmaster, 1969-70); *b* 23 July 1931; *s* of R. and E. Atkinson; *m* 1957, Shirley Angus; two *s* one *d*. *Educ:* Hummersknott, Darlington, Co. Durham; Durham Univ. (BA); Queen's Univ., Belfast (BA); Nottingham Univ. (Teaching Certif.); Loughborough Coll. of Educn (Physical Educn Dip.); MEd, Univ. of Bath, 1977. Served 5th Fusiliers (Northumberland) in Kenya, 1954-56. The Friends' School, Great Ayton, 1956-58; Haughton School, Darlington, 1958-60; Millfield, 1960-. West of England Hockey and Chief Divl coach; Founder Mem.: Nat. Hockey Coaching Cttee; Nat. Cricket Coaching Cttee, 1967-71; Chm., Phys. Educn Cttee of Schools Council; Minister for Sport and Recreation's Nominee for SW Council Working Party on Centres of excellence. *Publications:* An Experiment in Closed Circuit TV at Millfield School, 1970; various articles. *Recreations:* County Representation in five sports; Pres. and former Captain Somerset CCC XI and County Hockey XI; idealism, theories and planning. *Address:* Millfield School, Street, Somerset. *T:* Street 2291. *Clubs:* MCC, Free Foresters, I Zingari.

ATKINSON, Air Vice-Marshal David William, FFCM; QHP 1977; Director of Health and Research (RAF), since 1974; *b* 29 Sept. 1924; *s* of late David William Atkinson and of Margaret Atkinson; *m* 1948, Mary (*née* Sowerby); one *s*. *Educ:* Edinburgh Univ. (MB, ChB 1948). DPH and DIH, London; FFCM 1976. Joined RAF, 1949; med. officer appts, UK, Jordan and Egypt, 1949-63; Student, RAF Staff Coll., 1963-64; SMO, RAF Brüggen, Germany, 1964-67; Dep. PMO, HQ Air Support Comd, 1967-70; PMO, HQ Brit. Forces Gulf, Bahrain, 1970-71; OC RAF Hosp., Wegberg, Germany, 1971-73. *Publication:* (jtly) Double Crew Continuous Flying Operations: a study of aircrew sleep patterns, 1970. *Recreations:* walking, shooting, reading, looking at pictures. *Address:* 39 Brim Hill, N2. *Club:* Royal Air Force.

ATKINSON, Rt. Hon. Sir Fenton, PC 1968; Kt 1960; a Lord Justice of Appeal, 1968-71; *b* 6 Jan. 1906; *s* of late Hon. Sir Cyril Atkinson; *m* 1929, Margaret Mary, *d* of James Edward and Mary Roy, Scotscraig, Radlett; one *s* two *d*. *Educ:* Winchester; New Coll., Oxford (MA). Called to Bar, 1928; Bencher of Lincoln's Inn, 1958. Joined Northern Circuit and practised in Manchester, 1928-39. Served War of 1939-45: 2/Lieut Royal Norfolk Regt, 1939; Staff Captain and DAAG Madras District,

1940-42; AAG Southern Army, India, 1943; AAG, GHQ, India, 1944; Pres. Military Govt Court, Germany, 1945; released with rank of Colonel, 1945. QC 1953; Judge of the Salford Hundred Court of Record, 1953-60; Deputy Chm., Hertfordshire Quarter Sessions, 1958-60; Judge of High Court, Queen's Bench Div., 1960-68. Member, Royal Commn on Assizes and Quarter Sessions, 1966-67. *Recreations:* gardening, golf and reading. *Address:* Dalbeathie House, Dunkeld, Perthshire. *T:* 230.

ATKINSON, Frederick John, CB 1971; Chief Economic Adviser, HM Treasury, and Head of Government Economic Service, since 1977; *b* 7 Dec. 1919; *s* of George Edward Atkinson and of late Elizabeth Sabina Cooper; *m* 1947, Margaret Grace Gibson; two *d*. *Educ:* Dulwich Coll.; Jesus Coll., Oxford. Lectr, Jesus and Trinity Colls, Oxford, 1947-49; Economic Section, Cabinet Office, 1949-51; British Embassy, Washington, 1952-54; HM Treasury, 1955-62; Economic Adviser, Foreign Office, 1962-63; HM Treasury, 1963-69 (Dep. Dir, Economic Section, Treasury, 1965-69); Controller, Economics and Statistics, Min. of Technology, 1970; Chief Econ. Adviser, DTI, 1970-73; an Asst Sec.-Gen., OECD, Paris, 1973-75; Dep. Sec. and Chief Econ. Advr, Dept of Energy, 1975-77. *Recreation:* reading. *Address:* 26 Lee Terrace, Blackheath, SE3. *T:* 01-852 1040; Tickner Cottage, Aldington, Kent. *T:* Aldington 514. *Club:* Athenæum.

ATKINSON, Prof. James; Professor of Biblical Studies, University of Sheffield, since 1967; *b* 27 April 1914; *s* of Nicholas Ridley Atkinson and Margaret (*née* Hindhaugh); *m* 1939, Laura Jean Nutley (decd); one *s* one *d*. *Educ:* Tynemouth High Sch.; Univ. of Durham. MA 1939, MLitt 1950 Durham; DrTheol, Münster, Germany, 1955. Curate, Newcastle upon Tyne, 1937; Precentor, Sheffield Cath., 1941; Vicar, Sheffield, 1944; Fellow, Univ. of Sheffield, 1951; Canon Theologian: Leicester, 1954-70; Sheffield, 1971-; Reader in Theology, Univ. of Hull, 1956; Vis. Prof., Chicago, 1966. Member: Anglican-Roman Catholic Preparatory Commission, 1967-; Gen. Synod of Church of England. *Publications:* Library of Christian Classics, Vol. XVI, 1962; Rome and Reformation, 1965; Luther's Works, Vol. 44, 1966; Luther and the Birth of Protestantism, 1968; The Reformation, Paternoster Church History, Vol. 4, 1968; The Trial of Luther, 1971; contribs to learned jls, also essays and parts of books. *Recreations:* gardening, music. *Address:* Leach House, Hathersage, Derbyshire. *T:* Hope Valley 50570.

ATKINSON, John Alexander, CB 1976; DFC 1943; Second Permanent Secretary, Department of Health and Social Security, since 1977; *b* 9 June 1919; *yr s* of late Rev. R. F. Atkinson and late Harriet Harrold Atkinson, BSc (*née* Lowdon); *m* 1945, Marguerite Louise Pearson; one *d*. *Educ:* Kingswood Sch.; Queen's Coll., Oxford. Served in RAF, 1939-45. Asst Prin., 1946, Prin., 1949, Min. of Nat. Insce; Cabinet Office, 1950-52; Prin. Private Sec. to Minister of Pensions and Nat. Insce, 1957-58; Asst Sec., 1958; Under-Sec., Min. of Social Security, later DHSS, 1966-73; Dep. Sec., DHSS, 1973-76. *Address:* Bleak House, The Drive, Belmont, Sutton, Surrey. *T:* 01-642 6479. *Club:* United Oxford & Cambridge University.

ATKINSON, Sir (John) Kenneth, Kt 1953; retired as Chief Valuer, Valuation Office, Board of Inland Revenue (1951-66); *b* 21 May 1905; 2nd *s* of late James Oswald and Jane Atkinson, Liverpool; *m* 1930, Ellen Elsie Godwin Dod (*d* 1975); one *d*. *Educ:* The Leys, Cambridge. Joined Valuation Office, 1928; Deputy Chief Valuer, 1950. Fellow of the Royal Institution of Chartered Surveyors. *Recreation:* Rugby football. *Address:* Clouds, High Park Avenue, East Horsley, Leatherhead, Surrey. *T:* East Horsley 3103.

ATKINSON, (Justin) Brooks; US journalist and writer; retired as Staff Writer, New York Times; *b* Melrose, Massachusetts, USA, 28 Nov. 1894; *s* of Jonathan H. Atkinson and Garafelia Taylor; *m* 1926, Oriana Torrey MacIlveen; one step *s*. *Educ:* Harvard Univ. (AB). Reporter, Springfield Daily News, 1917; Teacher of English, Dartmouth Coll., 1917-18; Boston Evening Transcript, Reporter and Asst Drama Critic, 1919-22; New York Times, 1922-65: Editor Book Review, 1922-25; Drama Critic, 1925-42; War Correspondent, China, 1942-44; Correspondent in Russia, 1945-46; Drama Critic, 1946-60; retd, 1965. Pulitzer Prize for Journalism, 1947. Hon. LHD Williams College, Mass, 1941; Hon. LLD: Adelphi Coll., NY; Pace Coll., NY, 1961; Franklin and Marshall Coll., 1962; Brandeis Univ. 1965; Clark Univ., 1966; Washington Coll., 1966; Dartmouth Coll., 1975. *Publications:* Skyline Promenades, 1925; Henry Thoreau, the Cosmic Yankee, 1927; East of the Hudson, 1931; Cingalese Prince, 1935; Once Around the Sun, 1951; Tuesdays and Fridays, 1963; Brief Chronicles, 1966; Broadway, 1970; This Bright Land, 1972; (with Al Hirschfeld) The Lively Years, 1973; (ed) Walden and other writings of Henry David Thoreau, 1937; (ed) Complete Essays and other writings of Ralph Waldo

Emerson, 1940; (ed) Sean O'Casey Reader, 1968. *Address:* Durham, NY 12422, USA.

ATKINSON, Sir Kenneth; *see* Atkinson, Sir J. K.

ATKINSON, Leonard Allan, CMG 1963; *b* 6 Dec. 1906; *s* of L. Atkinson; *m* 1933, Annie R., *d* of A. E. Wells; one *s* two *d*. *Educ:* Wellington Coll. and Victoria Univ. of Wellington, New Zealand. Joined Customs Dept, 1924; Inspector, Public Service Commission, 1941-44; Sec., 1944-47; Asst Comr, 1947-54; Commission Member, 1954-58; Chm., 1958-62; Chm., State Services Commission, NZ, 1963-66. *Recreation:* bowls. *Address:* 181 The Parade, Island Bay, Wellington, NZ. *Club:* Wellington (NZ).

ATKINSON, Maj.-Gen. Sir Leonard Henry, KBE 1966 (OBE 1945); *b* 4 Dec. 1910; *s* of A. H. Atkinson; *m* 1939, Jean Eileen, *d* of C. A. Atchley, OBE; one *s* three *d*. *Educ:* Wellington Coll., Berks; University Coll., London (Fellow, 1977). BSc (Eng) 1932; commnd in RAOC, 1933; transf. to REME, 1942; Comdr REME (Lieut-Col) Guards Armd Div. (NW Europe), 1943-45; DDEME (Col) Brit. Airborne Corps, India, 1945; Staff Coll., Quetta, 1945-46; served in Far East, UK and WO, 1946-50; JSSC, 1950-51; GSO1, REME Trg Centre, 1951-53; DDEME (Col) HQ 1st Corps (Germany), 1953-55; DDEME (Brig.). WO, 1956-58; Comdt (Brig.) REME Training Centre and Commander Berkshire Dist, 1958-63; Dir, Electrical and Mechanical Engineering, Army, 1963-66; Col Comdt, REME, 1967-72. Man. Dir, Harland Simon, 1970-72; Director: Harland Engineering, 1966-69; Simon Equipment, 1966-69; Weir Engineering Industries, 1970-74; United Gas Industries, 1972-76; C. & W. Walker Ltd, 1974-77; Bespoke Securities, 1974-. Chairman: Christopher Gold Associates, 1976-; DTI Cttee on Terotechnology, 1970-75; Council of Engineering Instns, 1974-75 (Vice-Chm., 1973). Member: Court of Bradford Univ., 1968-76; Court of Cranfield Inst. of Technology, 1975-77; Governor, Reading Coll. of Technology, 1968-. FIMechE; FIEE; FIGasE; FIERE (past Pres.); Hon. MIPlantE. Liveryman, Turners' Company, 1966-. *Address:* Pound Cottage, Silchester, Reading, Berks. *T:* Bramley Green 220. *Club:* Naval and Military.

ATKINSON, Leslie, CMG 1965; OBE 1961; Managing Director, Leslie Atkinson Pty Ltd, since 1960; Member of Export Development Council, Sydney, since 1959; *b* 11 Jan. 1913; *s* of J. Atkinson; *m* 1935, Ellen, *d* of J. Kinsey; one *s* one *d*. *Educ:* Wollongong Technical Sch. Controller, Nock and Kirby Ltd, 1943-49, Associate Dir, 1949-53; Dir and General Manager, Carr and Elliott, 1953-59. Pres., Sydney Junior Chamber of Commerce, 1946-47; Vice-Pres. and Hon. Treasurer, Sydney Chamber of Commerce, 1949-53, Pres., 1953-54, 1957-58; Vice-Pres., Associated Chambers of Commerce of the Commonwealth of Australia, 1956-57 (Pres., 1964-65). Mem. of Standing Cttee, NSW Methodist Conference, 1957-62. *Address:* 28 Castlereagh Crescent, Sylvania Waters, NSW 2224, Australia.

ATKINSON, Michael William, MBE 1970; HM Diplomatic Service; Counsellor, Budapest, since 1977; *b* 11 April 1932; *m* 1963, Veronica Bobrovsky; two *s* one *d*. *Educ:* Purley County Grammar School; Queen's College, Oxford (BA Hons). Served FO, Vientiane and Buenos Aires, 1956-69; Permanent Sec., External Affairs, British Honduras, 1969-71; Madrid, 1971-74; FCO 1975; NATO Defence Coll., 1976. *Recreations:* travelling, reading, gardening. *Address:* c/o Foreign and Commonwealth Office, King Charles Street, SW1.

ATKINSON, Norman; MP (Lab) Haringey, Tottenham, since 1974 (Tottenham, 1964-74); Treasurer, Labour Party, since 1976; *b* 25 March 1923; *s* of George Atkinson, Manchester; *m* 1948, Irene Parry. *Educ:* elementary and technical schs. Member of Manchester City Council, 1945-49. Chief Design Engineer, Manchester University, 1957-64. Contested (Lab) Wythenshawe, 1955, Altrincham and Sale, 1959. *Recreations:* walking, cricket, football. *Address:* House of Commons, SW1.

ATKINSON, Prof. Richard John Copland, MA; FSA 1946; Professor of Archaeology, University College, Cardiff, since 1958; *b* 22 Jan. 1920; *e s* of Roland Cecil Atkinson and Alice Noel Herbert Atkinson (*née* Wright); *m* 1942, Hester Renée Marguerite Cobb; three *s*. *Educ:* Sherborne School; Magdalen College, Oxford. Asst Keeper, Department of Antiquities, Ashmolean Museum, Oxford, 1944-49; Lectr in Prehistoric Archaeology, Univ. of Edinburgh, 1949-58; Dep. Principal, UC Cardiff, 1970-74. Member: Ancient Monuments Board for Wales, 1959-; Cttee of Enquiry into Arrangements for Protection of Field Monuments, 1966-68; Royal Commission: on Ancient Monuments (Wales) 1963-; on Historical Monuments (England), 1968-; UGC, 1973-. Vice-President:

Prehistoric Society, 1963-67; Council for British Archaeology, 1970-73 (Hon. Sec., 1964-70); Dir, BBC Silbury Hill project, 1967-69. *Publications:* Field Archaeology, 1946; Stonehenge, 1956; Stonehenge and Avebury, 1959; Archaeology, History and Science, 1960. Articles in archaeological journals. *Recreations:* archaeology, wood-work and wine. *Address:* The Old Rectory, Wenvoe, S Glamorgan CF5 6AN. *Clubs:* Athenæum, United Oxford & Cambridge University.

ATKINSON, William Christopher; Stevenson Professor of Hispanic Studies in University of Glasgow, 1932-72; Director, Institute of Latin-American Studies, 1966-72; *b* Belfast, 9 Aug. 1902; *s* of Robert Joseph Atkinson; *m* 1928, Evelyn Lucy, *d* of C. F. Wakefield, Hampstead; one *s* three *d*. *Educ:* Univs of Belfast and Madrid. Lectr in Spanish at Armstrong Coll., Newcastle upon Tyne, 1926-32; Hon. Sec., Modern Humanities Research Assoc., 1929-36; Head of Spanish and Portuguese sections, Foreign Research and Press Service of Royal Institute of International Affairs, 1939-43; Visiting British Council Lecturer to Latin America, 1946, 1960, 1971; Hon. Prof. National Univ. of Colombia, 1946; Chm. 1st Scottish cultural delegation to USSR, 1954; Carnegie Research Fellow visiting US Univs, 1955; Member, Hispanic Society of America, 1955 (Corres. Mem., 1937); Rockefeller Fellow visiting Latin-American Univs, 1957; Visiting Prof. of Portuguese Studies, University Coll. of Rhodesia and Nyasaland, 1963. Commander, Order of Prince Henry the Navigator, Portugal, 1972. *Publications:* Spain, A Brief History, 1934; The Lusiads of Camoens, 1952; The Remarkable Life of Don Diego, 1958; A History of Spain and Portugal, 1960; The Conquest of New Granada, 1961; The Happy Captive, 1977; contributions to Encyclopædia Britannica, learned periodicals and reviews, and to composite works on Spanish and Portuguese studies. *Recreations:* travel and tramping. *Address:* 39 Manse Road, Bearsden, Glasgow. *T:* 041-942 0368.

ATKINSON, William Reay; Director, Central Computer Agency, Civil Service Department, since 1973; *b* 15 March 1926; *s* of William Edwin Atkinson and Lena Marion (*née* Haselhurst); *m* 1959, Leigh Foster (*née* Burgess); one *s* two *d*. *Educ:* Gosforth Grammar Sch., Newcastle upon Tyne; King's Coll., Durham Univ.; Worcester Coll., Oxford. Served RNVR, 1943-46. Entered Civil Service as Inspector of Taxes, 1950; Secretaries Office, Inland Revenue, 1958-61 and 1962-69; Asst Sec., Royal Commn on the Press, 1961-62; Civil Service Dept, 1969. Principal 1958; Asst Sec. 1965; Under-Sec. 1973. *Recreations:* fell walking, music, tennis. *Address:* 16 Temple Sheen, East Sheen, SW14 7RP. *T:* 01-876 1850.

ATTENBOROUGH, David Frederick, CBE 1974; broadcaster and traveller; *b* 8 May 1926; *s* of late Frederick Levi Attenborough; *m* 1950, Jane Elizabeth Ebsworth Oriel; one *s* one *d*. *Educ:* Wyggeston Grammar Sch. for Boys, Leicester; Clare Coll., Cambridge. Served in Royal Navy, 1947-49. Editorial Asst in an educational publishing house, 1949-52; joined BBC Television Service as trainee producer, 1952; undertook zoological and ethnographic filming expeditions to: Sierra Leone, 1954; British Guiana, 1955; Indonesia, 1956; New Guinea, 1957; Paraguay and Argentina, 1958; South West Pacific, 1959; Madagascar, 1960; Northern Territory of Australia, 1962; the Zambesi, 1964; Bali, 1969; Central New Guinea, 1971; Celebes, Borneo, Peru and Colombia, 1973; Mali, British Columbia, Iran, Solomon Islands, 1974; Nigeria, 1975; Controller, BBC-2, BBC Television Service, 1965-68; Dir of Programmes, Television, and Mem., Bd of Management, BBC, 1969-72. Mem., Nature Conservancy Council, 1973-. Special Award, Soc. of Film and TV Arts, 1961; Silver Medal, Zool Soc. of London, 1966; Silver Medal, Royal Television Soc., 1966; Desmond Davis Award, Soc. of Film and Television Arts, 1970; Cherry Kearton Medal and Award, RGS, 1972. Hon. DLitt: Leicester, 1970; City, 1972; Hon. DSc Liverpool, 1974. *Publications:* Zoo Quest to Guiana, 1956; Zoo Quest for a Dragon, 1957; Zoo Quest in Paraguay, 1959; Quest in Paradise, 1960; Zoo Quest to Madagascar, 1961; Quest under Capricorn, 1963; The Tribal Eye, 1976. *Recreations:* music, books, and natural history. *Address:* 5 Park Road, Richmond, Surrey. *T:* 01-940 5055.
See also Sir R . S . Attenborough .

ATTENBOROUGH, James, CMG 1915; TD; Colonel (retired) TF; solicitor; *b* 7 Aug. 1884; *e s* of Stanley J. Attenborough, 30 Clarges Street, Piccadilly; *m* 1915, Phyllis, *d* of late Edwin J. Layton. *Educ:* Rugby. Served European War, 1914-18 (CMG) and War of 1939-45; commanded 9th Batt. Royal Fusiliers (TF) and Halton Camp RAF. *Recreations:* shooting and golf. *Address:* The Old Rectory, Great Mongeham, near Deal, Kent. *Clubs:* East India, Devonshire, Sports and Public Schools; Royal St George's (Sandwich).

ATTENBOROUGH, John Philip, CMG 1958; CBE 1953 (OBE 1946); retired; *b* 6 Nov. 1901; *s* of late Frederick Samuel and Edith Attenborough; *m* 1947, Lucie Blanche Woods, *y d* of late Rev. J. R. and Mrs Prenter and *widow* of late Dr P. P. Murphy; one step *s*. *Educ:* Manchester Grammar Sch.; Corpus Christi Coll., Oxford (MA). Superintendent of Education, Northern Nigeria, 1924-30; Lecturer and Senior Inspector, Education Dept, Palestine, 1930-37; Dir of Education, Aden, 1937-46; Deputy Dir of Education, Palestine, 1946-48; Asst Educational Adviser, Colonial Office, 1948; Dir of Education, Tanganyika, 1948-55; Mem. for Social Services, Tanganyika, 1955-57; Min. for Social Services, Tanganyika, 1957-58; Consultant: UNICEF, 1963-65; UNESCO, 1967; Devon, CC, 1961-68; Mem. SW Regional Hosp. Bd, 1965-71. Pres. Torbay Conservative Assoc. *Address:* 21 Thorncliff Close, Torquay, Devon. *T:* Torquay 27291.

ATTENBOROUGH, Peter John; Headmaster of Sedbergh School, since 1975; *b* 4 April 1938; *m* 1967, Alexandra Deirdre Campbell Page; one *s* one *d*. *Educ:* Christ's Hospital; Peterhouse, Cambridge. BA Classics 1960, MA 1964. Asst Master, Uppingham Sch., 1960-75 (Housemaster, Senior Classics Master); Asst Master, Starehe Boys' Centre, Nairobi, 1966-67. *Address:* Birksholme, Sedbergh, Cumbria LA10 5HQ. *T:* Sedbergh 20491.

ATTENBOROUGH, Sir Richard (Samuel), Kt 1976; CBE 1967; actor, producer and director; *b* 29 Aug. 1923; *s* of late Frederick L. Attenborough; *m* 1945, Sheila Beryl Grant Sim; one *s* two *d*. *Educ:* Wyggeston Grammar Sch., Leicester. Leverhulme Schol. to Royal Acad. of Dramatic Art, 1941 (Bancroft Medal). First stage appearance as Richard Miller in Ah Wilderness, Intimate Theatre, Palmers Green, 1941. West End début as Ralph Berger in Awake and Sing, Arts Theatre, 1942. First film appearance in In Which We Serve, 1942. In The Little Foxes, Piccadilly Theatre, 1942; Brighton Rock, Garrick, 1943. Joined RAF 1943; seconded to RAF Film Unit, 1944, and appeared in Journey Together; demobilised, 1946. Returned to Stage, Jan. 1949, in The Way Back (Home of the Brave), Westminster; To Dorothy, a Son, Savoy, 1950 (transf. to Garrick, 1951); Sweet Madness, Vaudeville, 1952; The Mousetrap, Ambassadors, 1952-54; Double Image, Savoy, 1956-57, St James's, 1957; The Rape of the Belt, Piccadilly, 1957-58. Films include: School for Secrets, The Man Within, Dancing With Crime, Brighton Rock, London Belongs to Me, The Guinea Pig, The Lost People, Boys in Brown, Morning Departure, Hell is Sold Out, The Magic Box, Gift Horse, Father's Doing Fine, Eight O'Clock Walk, The Ship That Died of Shame, Private's Progress, The Baby and the Battleship, Brothers in Law, The Scamp, Dunkirk, The Man Upstairs, Sea of Sand, Danger Within, I'm All Right Jack, Jet Storm, SOS Pacific. Formed Beaver Films with Bryan Forbes and appeared in, and co-prod, The Angry Silence, 1959; formed Allied Film Makers and appeared in their first film The League of Gentlemen, 1960; prod Whistle Down the Wind, also appeared in Only Two Can Play and All Night Long, 1961; appeared in The Dock Brief, prod The L-Shaped Room and appeared in The Great Escape, 1962; appeared in and prod Séance On a Wet Afternoon (Best actor, San Sebastian Film Fest. and British Film Acad.), and appeared in The Third Secret, 1963; appeared in: Guns at Batasi, 1964 (Best actor, British Film Acad.); The Flight of the Phœnix, 1965; The Sand Pebbles, Dr Dolittle, 1966 (both Hollywood Golden Globe); The Bliss of Mrs Blossom, 1967; Only When I Larf, 1968; directed: Oh! What a Lovely War, 1968 (16 Internat. Awards inc. Hollywood Golden Globe and Soc. of Film & Television Arts UN Award); appeared in: The Last Grenade, A Severed Head, David Copperfield, Loot, 1969; 10 Rillington Place, 1970; dir. Young Winston, 1972 (Hollywood Golden Globe); appeared in Ten Little Indians, Rosebud, Brannigan, 1974, Conduct Unbecoming, 1975; dir. A Bridge Too Far, 1976. Member: British Actors' Equity Council, 1949-73; Cinematograph Films Council, 1967-73; Arts Council of GB, 1970-73; Young Vic Bd, 1974-; Governor, Nat. Film Sch., 1970-; a Trustee, Tate Gall., 1976-; Chairman: RADA, 1970- (Mem. Council, 1963-); Capital Radio, 1973-; Actor's Charitable Trust, 1956-; Combined Theatrical Charities, 1964-; Pro-Chancellor, Sussex Univ., 1970-; Vice-Pres., British Academy of Film and Television Arts (formerly SFTA), 1971- (Chm., 1969-70); Pres., Muscular Dystrophy Gp of GB, 1971- (Vice Pres., 1962-71). Dir, Chelsea Football Club, 1969-. Hon. DLitt Leicester, 1970; Hon. DCL Newcastle, 1974. *Recreations:* listening to music, collecting paintings, watching football. *Address:* Old Friars, Richmond Green, Surrey. *Clubs:* Garrick, Beefsteak, Green Room.
See also D. F. Attenborough.

ATTLEE, family name of **Earl Attlee.**

ATTLEE, 2nd Earl, *cr* 1955; **Martin Richard Attlee;** Viscount Prestwood, 1955; Marketing Director, SOS Talisman Co., since 1977; Owner of Prestwood Publicity, since 1967; *b* 10 Aug. 1927; *o s* of 1st Earl Attlee, KG, PC, OM, CH, FRS, and Violet Helen (*d* 1964), *d* of H. E. Millar; *S* father, 1967; *m* 1955, Anne Barbara, *er d* of late James Henderson, CBE, Bath, Somerset; one *s* one *d*. *Educ:* Millfield Coll.; Southampton University Coll. (now Southampton Univ.). Served in Merchant Navy, 1945-50. Active Mem. Hon. Artillery Company, 1951-55. Asst PRO, Southern Region, British Rail, 1970-76. MIPR 1964. *Publication:* Bluff Your Way in PR, 1971. *Recreations:* cars, carpentry. *Heir: s* Viscount Prestwood, *qv*. *Address:* 125 Hendon Lane, N3 3PR. *Clubs:* Press, Pathfinders'.

ATTLEE, Air Vice-Marshal Donald Laurence, MVO 1964; fruit farmer, since 1977; *b* 2 Sept. 1922; *s* of Major Laurence Attlee; *m* 1952, Jane Hamilton Young; one *s* two *d*. *Educ:* Haileybury. Pilot trng in Canada, 1942-44; Flying Instructor, 1944-48; Staff, Trng Comd, 1949-52; 12 Sqdn, 1952-54; Air Ministry, Air Staff, 1954-55; RAF Staff Coll., 1955; 59 Sqdn, 1957-59; CO, The Queen's Flight (W/Cdr), 1960-63; HQ, RAF Germany, 1964-67; CO, RAF Brize Norton, 1968-69; IDC, 1970; MoD Policy Staff, 1971-72; Dir of RAF Recruiting, 1973-74; Air Cdre, Intell., 1974-75; AOA Trng Comd, 1975-77, retired. *Recreations:* genealogy, Do-it-Yourself, gardening. *Address:* Jerwoods, Culmstock, Cullompton, Devon. *T:* Hemycock 317. *Club:* Royal Air Force.

ATTWELL, Ven. Arthur Henry; Archdeacon of Westmorland and Furness, since 1978; *b* 5 Aug. 1920; *s* of Henry John and Kate Attwell. *Educ:* Wilson School, Reading; Leeds Univ. (BA 1941); College of the Resurrection, Mirfield. MTh 1958, MA 1972 (London). Deacon 1943, priest 1944; Curate of St George, Wolverton, 1943-45; Curate of Wigan, 1945-51; Sub-warden of St Paul's Coll., Grahamstown, S Africa, 1951-52; Dean of Kimberley, S Africa, 1952-60; Rector of Workington, Cumberland, 1960-72; Hon. Canon of Carlisle, 1964-72; Rural Dean of Cockermouth and Workington, 1966-70; Proctor in Convocation, 1965-; Canon Residentiary of Carlisle Cathedral, 1972-77; Exam. Chaplain to Bishop of Carlisle, 1972-. *Recreation:* travel. *Address:* c/o Diocesan Registry, 19 Castle Street, Carlisle, Cumbria CA3 8SY. *T:* 25195.

ATWELL, Sir John (William), Kt 1976; CBE 1970; CEng; FIMechE, FRSE; Member: British Railways (Scottish) Board, since 1975; Board of Royal Ordnance Factories, since 1974; *b* 24 Nov. 1911; *s* of William Atwell and Sarah Workman; *m* 1945, Dorothy Hendry Baxter, *d* of J. H. Baxter and Janet Muir; no *c*. *Educ:* Hyndland Secondary Sch., Glasgow; Royal Technical Coll., Glasgow (ARTC); Cambridge Univ. (MSc). General Management, Stewarts and Lloyds Ltd, 1939-54; Dir 1955-61, Man. Dir 1961-68, G. & J. Weir Ltd; Dir, The Weir Group Ltd, 1961-74, and Chm., Engineering Div., 1968-74. Chm., Scottish Offshore Partnership, 1975-; Director: Anderson Strathclyde Ltd, 1975-; Govan Shipbuilders Ltd, 1975-. Chm., Requirements Bd for Mechanical Engineering and Machine Tools, DTI, 1972-76. Member: University Grants Commn, 1965-69; NEDC Mech. Eng Cttee, 1969-74; Court, Strathclyde Univ., 1967- (Chm., 1975-); Council, RSE, 1974-; Exec. Cttee, Scottish Council of Develt and Industry, 1972; Adv. Council for Applied R&D, 1976-; Council, Scottish Business Sch.; Vice-Pres., IMechE, 1966-73, Pres., 1973-74; Vice-Chm., 1977-78, Chm., 1978-79, CEI. Hon. LLD Strathclyde, 1973. *Recreation:* golf. *Address:* Elmfield, Buchanan Drive, Rutherglen, Glasgow. *T:* 041-647 1824. *Club:* Caledonian.

AUBREY, Henry M. W.; *see* Windsor-Aubrey.

AUBREY-FLETCHER, Sir John (Henry Lancelot), 7th Bt *cr* 1782; a Recorder of the Crown Court, 1972-74; Metropolitan Magistrate, 1959-71; *b* 22 Aug. 1912; *s* of Major Sir Henry Aubrey-Fletcher, 6th Bt, CVO, DSO, and Mary Augusta (*d* 1963), *e d* of Rev. R. W. Chilton; *S* father, 1969; *m* 1939, Diana Fynvola, *d* of late Lieut-Col Arthur Egerton, Coldstream Guards, and late Mrs Robert Bruce; one *s* (one *d* decd). *Educ:* Eton; New Coll., Oxford. Called to Bar, 1937. Served War of 1939-45, Grenadier Guards, reaching rank of temp. Lieut-Col and leaving Army with rank of Hon. Major. Dep. Chm., Bucks Quarter Sessions, 1959-71. High Sheriff, Bucks, 1961. *Heir: s* Henry Egerton Aubrey-Fletcher [*b* 27 Nov. 1945; *m* 1976, Roberta Sara, *d* of Major Robert Buchanan, Blackpark Cottage, Evanton, Ross-shire, and Mrs Ogden White; one *s*]. *Address:* The Gate House, Chilton, Aylesbury, Bucks. *T:* Long Crendon 347.
See also Hon. R. O. Stanley.

AUCHINCLOSS, Louis Stanton; author; Partner, Hawkins Delafield and Wood, NYC, since 1957 (Associate, 1954-57); *b*

NY, 27 Sept. 1917; s of J. H. Auchincloss and P. Stanton; m 1957, Adèle Lawrence; three s. Educ: Groton Sch.; Yale Univ.; Univ. of Virginia (LLB). Lieut USNR; served, 1941-45. Admitted to NY Bar, 1941; Associate Sullivan and Cromwell, 1941-51. Mem. Exec. Cttee, Assoc. of Bar of NY City. Pres., Museum of City of NY, 1967; Trustee, Josiah Macy Jr Foundn. Mem., Nat. Inst. of Arts and Letters. Publications: The Indifferent Children, 1947; The Injustice Collectors, 1950; Sybil, 1952; A Law for the Lion, 1953; The Romantic Egoists, 1954; The Great World and Timothy Colt, 1956; Venus in Sparta, 1958; Pursuit of the Prodigal, 1959; The House of Five Talents, 1960; Reflections of a Jacobite, 1961; Portrait in Brownstone, 1962; Powers of Attorney, 1963; The Rector of Justin, 1964; Pioneers and Caretakers, 1966; The Embezzler, 1966; Tales of Manhattan, 1967; A World of Profit, 1969; Second Chance: tales to two generations, 1970; Edith Wharton, 1972; I come as a thief, 1972; Richelieu, 1972; The Partners, 1974; A Writer's Capital, 1974; Reading Henry James, 1975; The Winthrop Covenant, 1976; The Dark Lady, 1977; pamphlets on American writers. Address: 1111 Park Avenue, New York, NY 10028, USA; (office) 67 Wall Street, New York, NY 10005. Club: Century Association (NY).

AUCHINLECK, Field-Marshal Sir Claude John Eyre, GCB 1945 (CB 1934); GCIE 1940; CSI 1936; DSO 1917; OBE 1919; Hon. LLD Aberdeen, 1948; Hon. LLD St Andrews, 1948; Hon. LLD Manchester, 1970; b 21 June 1884; s of late Col John Claude Auchinleck, RA; m 1921, Jessie (from whom he obtained a divorce, 1946), d of late Alexander Stewart, of Innerhadden, Kinloch-Rannoch, Perthshire. Educ: Wellington Coll.; RMC Sandhurst. 2nd Lieut, Indian Army Unattached List, 1903; joined 62nd Punjabis 1904; served Egypt, 1914-15; Aden, 1915; Mesopotamia, 1916-19; Kurdistan, 1919 (despatches, DSO, Croix de Guerre, OBE, Brevet Lieut-Col); operations against Upper Mohmands, 1933 (despatches, CB); Mohmand Operations, 1935 (despatches, CSI); Imperial Defence Coll., 1927; commanded 1st Batt. 1st Punjab Regt, 1929-30; Instructor Staff Coll., Quetta, 1930-33; Comdr Peshawar Brigade, India, 1933-36; Dep. Chief of General Staff Army Headquarters, India, 1936-38; Comdr Meerut District, India, 1938; Mem., Expert Cttee on the Defence of India, 1938; GOC-in-C, Northern Norway, 1940; GOC-in-C, Southern Command, 1940; C-in-C in India, 1941 and 1943-47; C-in-C Middle East, 1941-42; ADC Gen. to the King, 1941-46; War Mem. of the Viceroy's Executive Council, 1943-46; Field-Marshal, 1946; Supreme Comdr in India and Pakistan, 1947, under Joint Defence Council; Col of 1st Punjab Regt; Col of the Indian Grenadiers, 1939-47, of the Royal Inniskilling Fusiliers, 1941-47; a Governor of Wellington Coll., 1946-59; Pres., London Federation of Boys' Clubs, 1949-55; Pres. National Small-bore Rifle Association, 1956; a Vice-Pres. Forces Help Soc. and Lord Roberts Workshops; Chm., Armed Forces Art Soc., 1950-67. Virtuti Militari (Poland), 1942; War Cross (Czecho-Slovakia), 1944; Order of Chief Comdr, Legion of Merit (USA), 1945; Order of the Star of Nepal, 1st Class, 1945; Grand Cross of Order of St Olaf (Norway), 1947; 1st Class Order of Cloud and Banner (China), 1947; Grand Officer Legion of Honour; Croix-de-Guerre (France), 1918, 1949. Recreations: walking, fishing, sketching. Address: Villa Rikichou, rue Hafid Ibrahim, Marrakech, Morocco; c/o Grindlays Bank, 13 St James's Square, SW1. Clubs: East India, Devonshire, Sports and Public Schools, Naval and Military, Cavalry, Army and Navy, Norwegian; Karachi Yacht.

AUCHMUTY, Prof. James Johnston, CBE 1971; PhD; Vice-Chancellor and Principal, University of Newcastle, New South Wales, 1965-74; Professor of History, 1955-74, now Emeritus Professor; b Portadown, N Ireland, 29 Nov. 1909; s of Canon J. W. Auchmuty, MA; m 1934, Margaret (BA (Vassar), Phi Beta Kappa (Mem., Churchill Fellowship Trust Cttee, NSW, 1965-; Pres., Aust. Fedn of Univ. Women, 1974-77), d of R. F. Walters, Detroit, USA; one s one d (and one s decd). Educ: Armagh Royal Sch.; Trinity Coll., Dublin (Scholar). First Cl. Moderator and Gold Medallist in Hist. and Polit. Science, 1931 (Gold Medallist in Hist., 1930, and Auditor, 1931-32, of College Hist. Soc.); MA 1934, PhD 1935. Lectr in Sch. of Educn, Dublin Univ., 1936-46; Head of Dept of Mod. Hist., Farouk Univ., Alexandria, 1946-52; joined Univ. of NSW, 1952; Dean of Faculty of Humanities and Social Sciences, 1956-59 and Mem. Council, 1959-61; Head of Dept of Arts at Newcastle Univ. Coll., 1954; Warden of the College, 1960-64. Vis. Prof. of Modern Commonwealth Hist., Leeds Univ., 1976-77; Hon. Vis. Fellow, Humanities Res. Centre, ANU, 1975-76. First Chm. of Irish Cttee of Historical Sciences, 1938-44; Mem., Internat. Commn on the Teaching of History, 1938. Chm., Aust. Nat. Humanities Research Council, 1962-65; Chm., Aust. Nat. Commn for UNESCO, 1973-76 (Mem., 1962-76); Member: Aust. Delegn to 4th Commonwealth Educn Conf., Lagos, 1968;

5th Conf., Canberra, 1971; Aust. Educl Mission to S Pacific, 1970; Chm., Aust. Commonwealth Adv. Cttee on the Teaching of Asian Languages and Cultures, 1969; Chm., Aust. Vice-Chancellors' Cttee, 1969-71; Mem. Council, Assoc. of Commonwealth Univs, 1967-74. FRHistS 1938; MRIA 1941; Foundn Fellow, Aust. Acad. of the Humanities, 1970. Hon. DLitt: Sydney, 1974; Newcastle, NSW, 1974; Hon. LLD Dublin, 1974. Silver Jubilee Medal, 1977. Publications: US Government and Latin American Independence 1810-1830, 1937; Irish Education: a historical survey, 1937; Sir Thomas Wyse, 1791-1862, 1939; The Teaching of History, 1940; Lecky, 1946; (ed) The Voyage of Governor Phillip to Botany Bay, 1970; contrib. to: The Australian Dictionary of Biography; The New History of Australia; many papers in historical and other jls. Recreations: golf, swimming. Address: 9 Glynn Street, Hughes, ACT 2605, Australia. T: 815410. Clubs: Athenæum; Pioneers (Sydney); Newcastle (NSW); Commonwealth (Canberra).

AUCKLAND, 9th Baron (cr Irish Barony, 1789; British 1793); **Ian George Eden;** Director, Cargill, Attwood & Thomas Ltd, Management Consultants; b 23 June 1926; s of 8th Baron Auckland; S father 1957; m 1954, Dorothy Margaret, d of H. J. Manser, Eastbourne; one s two d. Educ: Blundell's Sch. Royal Signals, 1945-48; 3/4 County of London Yeomanry (Sharpshooters) (TA), 1948-53. Underwriting Mem. of Lloyd's, 1956-64. Vice-Pres., Royal Society for Prevention of Accidents; Mem., New Zealand Soc. Recreations: music, tennis and walking. Heir: s Hon. Robert Ian Burnard Eden, b 25 July 1962. Address: Tudor Rose House, 30 Links Road, Ashtead, Surrey. T: Ashtead 74393. Clubs: City Livery, Constitutional; Epsom.

AUCKLAND (Dio. Durham), **Archdeacon of;** see Marchant, Ven. G. J. C.

AUCKLAND, (NZ), Bishop of, since 1960; **Rt. Rev. Eric Austin Gowing;** b 11 March 1913; s of late Frederic Lanchester and Beryl Moselle Gowing; m 1940, Muriel, d of late Rt Rev. Thomas Sherwood Jones, DD; two s. Educ: North Sydney High Sch.; Sydney Univ.; Oxford Univ. BA Sydney, 1934; BA Oxon, 1938; MA Oxon, 1943; Curate: St Mary, Deane, 1938-42; St Andrew, Plymouth, 1942-45; Vicar of St Peter, Norbiton, 1945-50; Dean of Nelson, NZ, 1950-56; Archdeacon of Christchurch and Vicar of St Mary's, Merivale, NZ, 1956-60. Address: Bishop's House, 2 Arney Crescent, Remuera, Auckland, NZ. T: 543-473.

AUCKLAND (NZ), Bishop of, (RC), since 1974; **Most Rev. John Mackey.** Educ: Auckland Univ. (MA, DipEd); Notre Dame Univ., USA (PhD). Formerly Professor in Theological Faculty, National Seminary of Mosgiel, Dunedin. Publications: The Making of a State Education System, 1967; Reflections on Church History, 1975. Address: Bishop's House, 36 New Street, Ponsonby, PO Box 47255, Auckland 1, New Zealand. T: 764-244.

AUDLAND, Christopher John, CMG 1973; Deputy Secretary General, Commission of the European Communities, since 1973; b 7 July 1926; s of late Brig. Edward Gordon Audland, CB, CBE, MC, and of Violet Mary, d of late Herbert Shepherd-Cross, MP; m 1955, Maura Daphne Sullivan; two s one d. Educ: Winchester Coll. RA, 1944-48 (Temp. Capt.). Entered Foreign (subseq. Diplomatic) Service, 1948; has served in: Bonn; British Representation to Council of Europe; Washington; UK Delegn to Common Market negotiations, Brussels, 1961-63; Buenos Aires; FCO, 1968-70; Counsellor (Head of Chancery), Bonn, 1970-73. Mem., UK Delegn to Four-Power negotiations on Berlin, 1970-72. Address: Secrétariat-Général, Commission des Communautés Européennes, 200 rue de la Loi, Bruxelles 1049, Belgium. T: Brussels 7350040 ext. 1959. Club: United Oxford & Cambridge University.

AUDLEY, 25th Baron cr 1312-13; **Richard Michael Thomas Souter;** Director, Graham Miller (Maidstone) Ltd, since 1974; b 31 May 1914; s of Sir Charles Alexander Souter, KCIE, CSI (d 1958) and Lady Charlotte Dorothy Souter (née Jesson) (d 1958); S kinswoman, Baroness Audley (24th in line), 1973; m 1941, Pauline, d of D. L. Eskell; three d. Educ: Uppingham. Fellow, CILA. Military Service, 1939-46; Control Commission, Germany, 1946-50. Insurance Broker until 1955; Loss Adjuster, 1955-. Recreations: shooting, gardening. Heir: three co-heiresses. Address: Friendly Green, Cowden, near Edenbridge, Kent TN8 7DU. T: Cowden 682.

AUDU, Dr Ishaya Shu'aibu, FRCPE; Professor of Medicine, Ahmadu Bello University since 1975; b 1 March 1927; s of Malam Bulus Audu and Malama Rakiya Audu; m 1958, Victoria Abosede Ohiorhenuan; one s five d. Educ: Ibadan and London Univs. House Officer, Sen. House Officer, Registrar in

Surgery, Medicine, Obstetrics and Gynæcology and Pædiatrics, King's Coll. Hosp., London and Univ. Coll. Hosp., Ibadan, 1954-58; postgrad. studies, UK, 1959-60; Specialist Physician, Pædiatrician to Govt of Northern Nigeria and Personal Physician to Premier of North Region Govt, 1960-62; Lectr to Associate Professorship in Pæds, Univ. of Lagos Med. Sch., 1962-66; Vis. Res. Associate Prof., Univ. of Rochester Med. Sch., NY, 1964-65; Dep. Chm., Lagos Univ. Teaching Hosp. Man. Bd and Mem. Council, Univ. Lagos Med. Coll., 1962-66; Mem. Senate, Lagos Univ., 1963-66; Vice-Chancellor, Ahmadu Bello Univ., 1966-1975. Hon. LHD Ohio, 1968; Hon DSc Nigeria, 1971; Hon. LLD Ibadan, 1973; FMC (Pæd) Nigerian Med. Council; FRSocMed. *Publications:* contribs to learned jls. *Recreations:* walking, table tennis. *Address:* School of Medicine, Ahmadu Bello University, Zaria, Nigeria. *T:* Zaria 2581-1148.

AUDUS, Prof. Leslie John, MA, PhD, ScD Cantab; FLS, FInstBiol; Hildred Carlile Professor of Botany, Bedford College, University of London, since 1948; *b* 9 Dec. 1911; English; *m* 1938, Rowena Mabel Ferguson; two *d. Educ:* Downing Coll., Cambridge Univ. Downing Coll. Exhibitioner, 1929-31; Frank Smart Research Student (Cambridge Univ.), 1934-35; Lecturer in Botany, University Coll., Cardiff, 1935-40. Served War of 1939-45: RAFVR (Technical, Radar, Officer), 1940-46; PoW South Pacific, 1942-45. Scientific Officer, Agricultural Research Council, Unit of Soil Metabolism, Cardiff, 1946-47; Monsanto Lecturer in Plant Physiology, University Coll., Cardiff, 1948. Recorder, 1961-65, Pres., 1967-68, Section K, British Assoc. for the Advancement of Science. Vis. Prof. of Botany: Univ. of California, Berkeley, 1958; Univ. of Minnesota, Minneapolis, 1965; Vice-Pres. Linnean Soc. of London, 1959-60; Life Mem. New York Academy of Sciences, 1961. Editor, Journal Exp. Botany, 1965-74. *Publications:* Plant Growth Substances, 1953, 3rd edn 1972; (ed) The Physiology and Biochemistry of Herbicides, 1964; (ed) Herbicides: physiology, biochemistry and ecology, 1976; original research on plant respiration, hormones, responses to gravity, soil micro-biology in relation to pesticides, etc in Annals of Botany, New Phytologist, Nature, Journal of Experimental Botany, Weed Research, etc. *Recreations:* music, photography. *Address:* Botany Department, Bedford College, Regent's Park, NW1. *T:* 01-486 4400.

AUERBACH, Charlotte, FRS 1957; PhD, DSc; FRSE; Professor of Animal Genetics in the University of Edinburgh (Institute of Animal Genetics), 1967, Emeritus 1969 (Lecturer, 1947-57; Reader, 1957-67). Has done pioneering work on the chemical induction of mutations. Hon. Mem., Genetics Soc., Japan, 1966; Foreign Mem., Kongelige Danske Videnskabernes Selskab, 1968; Foreign Associate, Nat. Acad. of Sciences, USA, 1970. Hon. Dr Leiden, 1975; Hon. ScD Dublin, 1977; Hon. ScD Cambridge, 1977. Darwin Medal, Royal Soc., 1976. *Publications:* Genetics in the Atomic Age, 1956; The Science of Genetics, 1961; Mutation Pt 1-Methods, 1962; Heredity, 1965; Mutation Research, 1976; papers in various genetical journals. *Address:* Institute of Animal Genetics, The University, West Mains Road, Edinburgh EH9 1SN.

AUERBACH, Frank Helmuth; painter, draughtsman; *b* 29 April 1931; *s* of Max Auerbach, lawyer, and Charlotte Norah Auerbach; *m* 1958, Julia Wolstenholme; one *s. Educ:* privately; St Martin's Sch. of Art; Royal Coll. of Art. *One-man exhibitions:* Beaux Arts Gallery, 1956, 1959, 1961, 1962, 1963; Marlborough Fine Art, 1965, 1967, 1971, 1974; Marlborough-Gerson, New York, 1969; Villiers, Sydney, Australia, 1972; Bergamini, Milan, 1973; Univ. of Essex, 1973; Mun. Gall. of Modern Art, Dublin, 1974; Marlborough, Zurich, 1976. *Mixed exhibitions:* Carnegie International, Pittsburgh, 1958, 1962; Dunn International, Fredericton, 1963; Gulbenkian International, Tate Gallery, 1964; European Painting in the Seventies, USA, 1976; Annual Eshbn, part I, Hayward Gall., 1977, etc. *Public collections:* Brit. Council; Brit. Museum; Tate Gallery, London; National Gallery of Victoria, Melbourne; Nat. Gall. of W Australia; Chrysler Museum, Provincetown, Mass; County Museum of LA, Calif; Univ. of Cincinnati; Bedford, Edinburgh, Hartlepool, Hull, Leeds, Leicester, Manchester, Nottingham, Oldham, Sheffield Galls; Arts Council, Contemporary Art Soc., etc. *Address:* c/o Marlborough Fine Art, 39 Old Bond Street, W1.

AUGER, Pierre Victor, Grand Officer, Legion of Honour; retired as Director-General European Space Research Organisation (ESRO); Professor, Faculty of Sciences, University of Paris, since 1937; *b* 14 May 1899; *s* of Victor E. Auger, Prof., Univ. of Paris, and Eugénie Blanchet; *m* 1921, Suzanne Motteau; two *d. Educ:* Ecole Normale Supérieure, Paris; Univ. of Paris. Université de Paris (Faculté des Sciences): Asst 1927; Chef de Travaux, 1932; Maître de Conférences, 1937. Research Associate, Univ. of Chicago, 1941-43; Head of Physics Div.,

joint Anglo-Canadian research project on atomic energy, 1942-44; Dir of Higher Education, Min. of Education, France, 1945-48; Mem. exec. Board of UNESCO, 1946-48; Membre du comité de l'Energie Atomique, France, 1946-48; Dir, Natural Sciences Dept, UNESCO, 1948-59; Special Consultant, UNO and UNESCO, 1959-60; Chm., French Cttee on Space Research, 1960-62. Mem., French Academy of Sciences, 1977. Feltrinelli International Prize, 1961; Kalinga Internat. Prize, 1972. *Publications:* Rayons cosmiques, 1941; L'Homme microscopique, 1952; Current Trends in Scientific Research, 1961; scientific papers on physics (X-rays, neutrons, cosmic rays), 1923-; papers on philosophy of science, 1949-. *Address:* 12 rue Emile Faguet, Paris XIV. *T:* 540 96 34.

AULD, Margaret Gibson, MPhil, SRN, SCM; Chief Nursing Officer, Scottish Home and Health Department, since 1977; *b* 11 July 1932; *d* of Alexander John Sutton Auld and Eleanor Margaret Ingram. *Educ:* Glasgow; Cardiff High Sch. for Girls; Radcliffe Infirm., Oxford (SRN 1953); St David's Hosp., Cardiff; Queen's Park Hosp., Blackburn (SCM 1954). Midwife Teacher's Dipl., 1962; Certif. of Nursing Admin, 1966, MPhil 1974, Edinburgh. Queen's Park Hosp., Blackburn, 1953-54; Staff Midwife, Cardiff Maternity Hosp., 1955, Sister, 1957; Sister, Queen Mary Hosp., Dunedin, NZ, 1959-60; Deptl Sister, Cardiff Maternity Hosp., 1960-66; Asst Matron, Simpson Meml Maternity Pavilion, Edinburgh, 1966-68, Matron, 1968-73; Actg Chief Reg. Nursing Officer, S-Eastern Reg. Hosp. Bd, Edinburgh, 1973; Chief Area Nursing Off., Borders Health Bd, 1973-76. Member: Cttee on Nursing (Briggs), 1970-72; Maternity Services Cttee, Integration of Maternity Work (Tennent Report), 1972-73; Gen. Nursing Council (Scotland), 1973-76; Central Midwives Bd (Scotland), 1972-76. *Recreations:* reading, music, entertaining. *Address:* Staddlestones, Belwood Road, Milton Bridge, Penicuik, Midlothian. *T:* Penicuik 72858. *Club:* University of Edinburgh Staff (Edinburgh).

AULD, Robin Ernest, QC 1975; a Recorder of the Crown Court, since 1977; *b* 19 July 1937; *s* of Ernest Auld and Adelaide Mary Hellings (formerly Auld, *née* Mackie); *m* 1963, Catherine Eleanor Mary, *er d* of late David Henry Pritchard, MA, BCL; one *s* one *d. Educ:* Brooklands Coll.; King's Coll., Univ. of London (LLB 1st cl. Hons, PhD). Called to Bar, Gray's Inn, 1959 (Macaskie Schol., Lord Justice Holker Sen. Schol.); SE Circuit; Mem., Commn of Inquiry into Casino Gambling in the Bahamas, 1967; Prosecuting Counsel to Dept of Trade at Central Criminal Court, 1969-75; called to N Ireland Bar, 1973; Jt Chm., Disciplinary Tribunal of Inquiry of Inner London Educn Authority, 1974-; Chm., William Tyndale Sch. Inquiry, 1975-76; Dept of Trade Ashbourne Investments Ltd, 1975-77. Liveryman, Woolmen's Co. *Address:* Lamb Building, Temple, EC4Y 7AS. *T:* 01-353 6701; 3ème Etage, 23 Boulevard des Capucines, 75002 Paris, France. *T:* 073-38-44. *Clubs:* City Livery; Moor Park Golf.

AURIC, Georges, Commander, Legion of Honour; Commander, Order of Academic Palms; French composer; General Administrator, Paris Opéra and Opéra Comique, 1962-68; *b* Lodève, 15 Feb. 1899; *m* 1938, Nora Smith. *Educ:* Paris Conservatoire; Schola Cantorum, Paris. Co-founder Les Six movement, 1916. Mem. Acad. des Beaux-Arts, 1962-. Pres., CISAC, 1968-70. *Publications include:* Trois Interludes; Chandelles Romaines; Trio pour Hautbois; *ballet music:* Le Peintre et son Modèle, 1949; Phèdre, 1950; Chemin de Lumière, 1952; Coup de Feu, 1952; *opera:* Sous le Masque; *music for films:* Le Sang d'un Poète; A Nous la Liberté; Entrée des Artistes; L'Eternel Retour; La Belle et la Bête; La Symphonie Pastorale; Torrents; Ruy Blas; L'Aigle à Deux Têtes; Les Parents Terribles; Maya; Orphée: Caroline Chérie; La P... Respectueuse; La Fête à Henriette, etc. *Address:* 36 avenue Matignon, 75008 Paris, France.

AUSTEN-SMITH, Air Vice-Marshal Roy David, CB 1975; DFC 1953; Senior Air Staff Officer, Near East Air Force, since 1975; Commander, British Forces, Cyprus, AOC Air Headquarters, Cyprus, and Administrator, Sovereign Base Areas, Cyprus, since 1976; *b* 28 June 1924; *m* 1951, Ann (*née* Alderson); two *s. Educ:* Hurstpierpoint College. Pilot trng, Canada, 1943-44; 41 Sqn (2 TAF), 1945; 33 Sqdn, Malaya, 1950-53; Cranwell, 1953-56; 73 Sqdn, Cyprus, 1956-59; Air Min., 1960-63; 57 Sqdn, 1964-66; HQ 2 ATAF, 1966-68; CO, RAF Wattisham; MoD, 1970-72; AOC and Comdt, RAF Coll., Cranwell, 1972-75. *Recreation:* golf. *Address:* c/o National Westminster Bank, Swanley, Kent. *Club:* Royal Air Force.

AUSTERBERRY, Ven. Sidney Denham; Archdeacon of Salop and Vicar of Great Ness, since 1959; *b* 28 Oct. 1908; *s* of late Mr and Mrs H. Austerberry; *m* 1934, Eleanor Jane Naylor; two *s* two *d. Educ:* Hanley High Sch.; Egerton Hall, Manchester.

Curate, Newcastle-under-Lyme Parish Church, 1931-38; Vicar of S Alkmund, Shrewsbury, 1938-52; Vicar of Brewood, 1952-59; Hon. Clerical Sec., Lichfield Diocesan Conf., 1954-70; Rural Dean of Penkridge, 1958-59. Hon. Canon, Lichfield Cathedral, 1968. *Address:* Great Ness Vicarage, Shrewsbury, Salop. *T:* Nesscliffe 240.

AUSTICK, David; retail bookseller; *b* 8 March 1920; *m* 1945, Florence Elizabeth Lomath. Member: Leeds City Council (for W Hunslet), 1969-74; Leeds Metropolitan District Council (for Hunslet), 1974-75; W Yorkshire County Council (for Otley and Lower Wharfedale), 1974-. MP (L) Ripon, July 1973-Feb. 1974. Chm., Liberal Candidates' Assoc. Member: Electoral Reform Soc.; European Movement; Fellowship of Reconciliation. *Address:* Austick's Bookshops, 29 Cookridge Street, Leeds LS1 3AN; Cross Green, Otley, Yorks. *Club:* National Liberal.

AUSTIN, Prof. Colin Russell; Charles Darwin Professor of Animal Embryology, University of Cambridge, since 1967; *b* 12 Sept. 1914; *s* of Ernest Russell Austin and Linda Mabel King; *m* 1941, Patricia Constance Jack; two *s. Educ:* Univ. of Sydney, Australia (BVSc 1936; DSc 1954). Mem. Research Staff, CSIRO, Australia, 1938-54; Mem. Scientific Staff of MRC, UK, 1954-64; Editor, Jl of Reproduction and Fertility, 1959-64; Head of Genetic and Developmental Disorders Research Program, Delta Regional Primate Research Center, and Prof. of Embryology, Tulane Univ., New Orleans, 1964-67. *Publications:* The Mammalian Egg, 1961; Fertilization, 1965; Ultrastructure of Fertilization, 1968; numerous research papers. *Recreations:* tennis, swimming, squash. *Address:* Manor Farm House, Toft, Cambridge. *T:* Comberton 2101.

AUSTIN, Hon. Jacob, (Jack), QC (Canada) 1970; Member of the Senate, Canadian Parliament, since 1975; *b* 2 March 1932; *s* of Morris Austin and Clara Edith (*née* Chetner); *m* (marr. diss.); three *d. Educ:* Univ. of British Columbia (BA, LLB); Harvard Univ. (LLM). Barrister and Solicitor, BC and Yukon Territory. Asst Prof. of Law, Univ. of Brit. Columbia, 1955-58; practising lawyer, Vancouver, BC, 1958-63; Exec. Asst to Minister of Northern Affairs and Nat. Resources, 1963-65; contested (Liberal) Vancouver-Kingsway, Can. Federal Election, 1965; practising lawyer, Vancouver, BC, 1966-70; Dep. Minister, Dept of Energy, Mines and Resources, Ottawa, 1970-74; Principal Sec. to Prime Minister, Ottawa, May 1974-Aug. 1975. *Publications:* articles on law and public affairs in Canadian Bar Rev., Amer. Soc. of Internat. Law and other publns. *Recreations:* sailing, squash, reading, theatre. *Address:* Room 668-5, The Senate, Ottawa, Ontario K1A 0A4, Canada. *T:* (613) 992-1437. *Clubs:* Rideau (Ottawa); Cercle Universitaire d'Ottawa; University Club of Vancouver (Vancouver, BC); Metropolitan (NY).

AUSTIN, Sir John (Byron Fraser), 3rd Bt, *cr* 1894; *b* 14 July 1897; *s* of Sir William Austin, 2nd Bt, and Violet Irene (*d* 1962), *d* of Alex. Fraser, Westerfield House, near Ipswich; *S* father, 1940; *m* 1st, 1953, Sheila McNaught (marr. diss., 1958); 2nd, 1960, Rhoda Noreen Rose, *widow* of Col C. V. D. Rose. *Educ:* Downside; Royal Military Coll., Sandhurst. Late Lieut 7th Hussars; Major Indian Army; retired, 1935; served with Somaliland Camel Corps and King's African Rifles, Tanganyika; European War, 1915-18, as Flight-Comdr RFC and RAF; served War of 1939-45, Lieut-Col Comdg Bn (despatches). Director: Baronetcy Properties; St Anthonys Properties Ltd; Austin Properties Ltd; Wrights Motors Ltd. *Heir: b* William Ronald Austin [*b* 20 July 1900; *m* 1st, 1926, Dorothy Mary (*d* 1957), *d* of late L. A. Bidwell, FRCS; two *s*; 2nd, 1958, Mary Helen Farrell]. *Address:* Pax, St George's Lane, Hurstpierpoint, Sussex. *Club:* Royal Air Force.

AUSTIN, Sir John Worroker, Kt 1971; CA; Chairman: Blue Metal Industries Ltd, since 1952; Clutha Development Pty Ltd, 1952-76; TRW (Aust.) Ltd, since 1968; Greater Pacific General Insurance Ltd Group, 1970-76; *b* Sydney, New South Wales; *s* of late J. W. Austin; *m* 1948, Doris, *d* of R. Jenkins; one *s. Educ:* Sydney High School; Sydney Univ. Director: Rank Industries Aust. Pty Ltd, 1974-; Greater Union Organisation Pty Ltd, 1974-; George Kent (ANZ) Pty Ltd; Allied Polymer Group (Holdings) Pty Ltd; Ready Mixed Concrete Ltd. Mem. Cttee. Aust. Jockey Club. *Recreations:* farming, breeding racehorses (stud property, Princes Farm); golf, fishing, surfing. *Address:* Toft Monks, 95 Elizabeth Bay Road, NSW 2011, Australia. *Clubs:* Tattersall's, Union, Royal Sydney Yacht Squadron, Elanora Golf (NSW).

AUSTIN, Professor Lloyd James; FBA 1968; Fellow of Jesus College, Cambridge, since 1961; Drapers Professor of French since 1967; *b* 4 Nov. 1915; *s* of late J. W. A. Austin and late Mrs J. E. Austin (*née* Tymms), Melbourne, Australia; *m* 1939,

Jeanne Françoise Guerin, Rouen, France; three *s* one *d. Educ:* Melbourne Church of England Grammar Sch.; Univ. of Melbourne; Univ. of Paris. French Government Scholar, Paris, 1937-40; Lecturer in French, Univ. of Melbourne, 1940-42. Active Service as Lieut (Special Branch) RANVR, SW Pacific area, 1942-45. Lecturer in French, Univ. of Melbourne, 1945-47; Lecturer in French, Univ. of St Andrews, 1947-51; Research work in Paris, 1951-55; Fellow of Jesus Coll., Cambridge, 1955-56, 1961-; Professor of Modern French Literature, Univ. of Manchester, 1956-61; Lecturer in French, Univ. of Cambridge, 1961-66, Reader, 1966-67; Librarian, Jesus Coll., Cambridge, 1965-68, 1972-73. Herbert F. Johnson Visiting Prof., Inst. for Research in the Humanities, Univ. of Wisconsin, 1962-63; Mem., Editorial Bd, French Studies, 1964-, Gen. Editor, 1967-; Pres., Assoc. Internat. des Etudes Françaises, 1969-72 (Vice-Pres., 1966-69). Docteur *hc* Paris-Sorbonne, 1973. Chevalier de l'Ordre des Arts et des Lettres, 1971; Officier de l'Ordre National du Mérite, 1976. *Publications:* Paul Bourget, 1940; Paul Valéry: Le Cimetière marin, 1954; L'Univers poétique de Baudelaire, 1956; ed (with E. Vinaver and G. Rees) Studies in Modern French Literature, presented to P. Mansell-Jones, 1961; (with H. Mondor) Les Gossips de Mallarmé, 1962; ed (with H. Mondor) Stéphane Mallarmé: Correspondance (1871-1885), 1965, (1886-1889), 1969, (1890-1891), 1973, (1892-1898), 1978; (ed) Baudelaire: L'Art romantique, 1968; contrib. to French Studies, Modern Languages, Modern Language Review, Forum for Modern Language Studies, Bulletin of the John Rylands Library, Mercure de France, Revue des Sciences Humaines, Revue d'Histoire littéraire de la France, Revue de littérature comparée, Romanic Review, Studi francesi, Synthèses, Revue de l'Université de Bruxelles, L'Esprit créateur, Comparative Literature Studies, Wingspread Lectures in the Humanities, Encyclopædia Britannica, Yale French Studies, Meanjin Quarterly, Australian Jl for French Studies, AUMLA, etc. *Recreations:* cricket, tennis, travel. *Address:* 14 Park Terrace, Cambridge CB1 1JH. *T:* 59630; Jesus College, Cambridge.

AUSTIN, Vice-Adm. Sir Peter (Murray), KCB 1976; Operations Director, Mersey Docks and Harbour Co., since 1976; *b* 16 April 1921; *er s* of late Vice-Adm. Sir Francis Austin, KBE, CB, and late Lady Marjorie Austin (*née* Barker); *m* 1959, Josephine Rhoda Ann Shutte-Smith; three *s* one *d. Educ:* RNC, Dartmouth. Cadet, Dartmouth, 1935. Served War of 1939-45: at sea in HMS Cornwall, 1939-40; destroyers, 1941-45. Qualif. as pilot in FAA, 1946; served in 807 Sqdn, 1947-49; CO 736 Sqdn, 1950-52; grad. from RAF Flying Coll., Manby, 1953; comd 850 Sqdn in HMAS Sydney, incl. Korea, 1953-54; Lt-Cmdr (Flying) HMS Bulwark, 1954-56; Comdr (Air), RNAS Brawdy, 1956-58; Comdr (Air), HMS Eagle, 1958-59; Captain, 1961; Captain F7 in HMS Lynx, 1963-65; CO, RNAS Brawdy, 1965-67; Staff of SACLANT, 1967-69; comd aircraft carrier, HMS Hermes, 1969-70; Rear-Adm., 1971; Asst Chief of Naval Staff (Ops and Air), 1971-73; Flag Officer, Naval Air Comd, 1973-76, retired; Vice-Adm., 1974. FBIM. *Recreations:* golf, tennis, squash, sailing, shooting, skiing, caravanning. *Address:* Churchdown, Birkenhead Road, Meols, Wirral L47 0LE. *T:* 051-632 2440. *Clubs:* Army and Navy; Royal Yacht Squadron; Royal Naval, Royal Albert Yacht (Portsmouth).

AUSTIN, Richard, FRCM; Professor, 1946-76, Director of Opera, 1955-76, Royal College of Music; *b* 26 Dec. 1903; *s* of Frederic and Amy Austin; *m* 1935, Lelly, *y d* of Col Wilfred Howell, CBE, DSO. *Educ:* Gresham's Sch., Holt; RCM; Munich. Conductor, Carl Rosa Opera Co., 1929; Musical Dir of the Bournemouth Corporation, 1934-40; Music Advisor Northern Command, 1941-45; Music Dir, New Era Concert Soc., 1947-57. Guest Conductor: Sadler's Wells, London and provincial orchestras, Holland, Belgium, Germany, Spain, Sweden, Switzerland, Finland, Yugoslavia, Czechoslovakia, Cuba, Mexico, South Africa, South America and USA. *Recreations:* squash, tennis. *Address:* Stubbles, Ashampstead, Berks. *T:* Compton 565. *Club:* Savage.

AUSTIN, Sumner Francis, MA Oxon; Hon. FGSM; late Technical Director, Sadler's Wells Opera, London; late Captain Intelligence Corps; *b* Anerley, Kent, *s* of late Ware Plumtre Austin, ICS, and Frances Laura Greenaway; *m* Dorothy Stirling (*née* Blackwell). *Educ:* Bexhill; Magdalen Coll. Sch.; St John's Coll., Oxford. Studied for Indian Forest Service; studied singing and music, Dresden, Germany, 1910-14; first engagement, Royal Theatre, Potsdam; interned Prisoner of War, Ruhleben, 1914-18; Carl Rosa Opera Co., 1919; Surrey Theatre, 1920; Old Vic and later Sadler's Wells, 1919-; recitals in Holland, Berlin, London, and provinces, BBC, and various Choral Societies; Scarborough Open Air Production, 1935; Covent Garden, 1952, 1955, etc; numerous productions. *Publications:* translations from the Italian, French and German. *Address:* Clarendon Cottage, 43 Park Town, Oxford OX2 6SL.

AUSTIN, Thomas Aitken, CMG 1949; LRCP, LRCS, LM (Ireland); DTM&H (Liverpool); DPH (Dublin); late Public Health Officer for East and Central Africa, UN World Health Organisation; *b* 1895. *Educ:* Derry Church Sch.; Royal Coll. of Surgeons, Dublin. Storey Memorial Gold Medal (Anatomy), De Renzy Centenary Prize, 1st place 1st class honours DPH, Royal Coll. of Surgeons, Dublin. Served War of 1939-45, 1939-40; Major. Appointed Zanzibar Protectorate, 1924; Nyasa, 1930; SMO, Tanganyika Territory, 1939; DMS: Nyasa, 1943; Uganda, 1946; PMO, Colonial Office, 1949. *Address:* 38 Sycamore Road, Mount Merrion, Blackrock, Co. Dublin.

AUSTRALIA, North-West, Bishop of, since 1965; **Rt. Rev. Howell Arthur John Witt;** *b* 12 July 1920; *s* of Thomas Leyshon Witt and Harriet Jane Witt; *m* 1949, Gertrude Doreen Edwards; three *s* two *d*. *Educ:* Newport Sec. Sch.; Leeds Univ.; Coll. of the Resurrection, Mirfield. Deacon 1944; Priest 1945. Asst Curate of: Usk, Mon, 1944-47; St George's, Camberwell, 1948-49; Chaplain, Woomera, S Australia, 1949-54; Rector, St Mary Magdalene's, Adelaide, 1954-57; Priest in charge of Elizabeth, 1957-65; Missioner of St Peter's Coll. Mission, 1954-65. *Recreations:* Rugby football coaching; script writing. *Address:* Bishop's House, 11 Mark Way, Tarcoola, Geraldton, WA 6530, Australia. *T:* Geraldton 21.4653. *Club:* Public Schools (Adelaide).

AUSTWICK, Prof. Kenneth, JP; Professor of Education, Bath University, since 1966; *b* 26 May 1927; *s* of Harry and Beatrice Austwick; *m* 1956, Gillian Griffin; one *s* one *d*. *Educ:* Morecambe Grammar Sch.; Sheffield Univ. BSc Maths, DipEd, MSc, PhD Sheffield. Fellow, Royal Statistical Soc.; FRSA. Schoolmaster, Bromsgrove, Frome and Nottingham, 1950-59; Lectr/Sen. Lectr, Sheffield Univ., 1959-65; Dep. Dir, Inst. of Educn, Reading Univ., 1965-66; Pro-Vice-Chancellor, Bath Univ., 1972-75. Vis. Lecturer: Univ. of BC, 1963; Univ. of Michigan, 1963; Univ. of Wits., 1967. Consultant, OECD, 1965; Adviser, Home Office, 1967-; Chm., Nat. Savings SW Regional Educn, 1975-. JP Bath 1970. *Publications:* Logarithms, 1962; Equations and Graphs, 1963; (ed) Teaching Machines and Programming, 1964; (ed) Aspects of Educational Technology, 1972; articles and contribs on maths teaching and educnl technology. *Recreations:* gardening, wine making. *Address:* Brook House, Combe Hay, near Bath. *T:* Combe Down 832541. *Club:* Royal Commonwealth Society.

AUSWILD, Sir James (Frederick John), Kt 1974; CBE 1970; FCA, FAIM; Chartered Accountant and Company Director, Australia; Commissioner of Rural Bank of New South Wales, since 1961; Member, Advanced Education Board, NSW, since 1969; *b* Canbelego, 12 April 1908; *s* of late James Auswild, Temora, and Janet Caroline Auswild (*née* Starr); *m* 1933, Kathleen, *d* of late M. Conway, Lake Cargelligo; two *d*. *Educ:* Temora High Sch. Principal of James F. J. Auswild & Co., Business Consultants and Chartered Accountants, 1930-. Supervisor, Rural Reconstr. Bd, 1932-39. Past Dir: Skandia Aust. Insurance Ltd, 1966-74; Glass Tougheners Pty Ltd, 1967-70. Governing Dir, Auswild Org., embracing 130 associated cos; Chairman, Austwide Corp. Pty Ltd and many private cos; Jt Chm. and Managing Dir, Preston Motors Holdings Ltd and Subsidiary Cos. Director: Boyded Pty Ltd; C. V. Holland Pty Ltd; Finance & Guarantee Co. Ltd; Rossfield House Pty Ltd; Auswild Securities Pty Ltd; Embassy Motel, Statesman Hotel Pty Ltd, Canberra; ACT Motors Pty Ltd; Holden Dealers, Canberra; Ambassador Hotel, Canberra; Mentone Motors Gp; Cooma-Monaro Express Pty Ltd; Canberra Publishing & Printing Co. Pty Ltd; J. F. J. Auswild (Holdings) Pty Ltd; Auswild Properties Pty Ltd; Mindaribba Vineyards Pty Ltd; Roxburgh Vineyards Pty Ltd. Fellow of Local Govt Auditors' Assoc. (FLGA), Aust. *Recreation:* yachting. *Address:* 609 New South Head Road, Rose Bay, Sydney, NSW 2029, Australia. *T:* 36.1711. *Clubs:* American National, Tattersall's, RMYC, CYC, AJC, STC (Sydney); Athenaeum (Melbourne).

AUTY, Richard Mossop, OBE 1968; British Council Representative, France, and Cultural Counsellor, British Embassy, Paris, since 1976; *b* 29 Jan. 1920; *s* of Rev. Thomas Richard Auty and Mrs Edith Blanche Auty (*née* Mossop); *m* 1st, 1944, Noreen Collins (marr. diss. 1949); one *d*; 2nd, 1956, (Anne) Marguerite Marie Poncet; one *s* one *d*. *Educ:* Hanley High Sch.; LSE, Univ. of London (BScEcon). Research Officer: Planning Br., Min. of Agriculture and Fisheries, 1942-46; Bureau of Current Affairs, 1946-49; Lectr, Goldsmiths' Coll. and Morley Coll., 1947-49; British Council, 1949-: Lectr, Milan, 1949-57; Head, Overseas Students Centre, London, 1957-61; Reg. Rep., S India, 1961-65; Cultural Attaché, Brit. Embassy, Budapest, 1965-68; Director: S Asia Dept, 1968-70; Personnel Dept, 1970-72; Controller, European Div., 1972-76. *Recreations:* literature, theatre, ballet, cinema. *Address:* (home)

4 Thurlow Road, NW3. *T:* 01-435 8982; 5 Avenue Franklin Roosevelt, 75008 Paris, France. *T:* 720 9036.

AUTY, Prof. Robert, MA (Cantab and Oxon); DrPhil (Münster); DLitt (Oxon); FBA 1976; Professor of Comparative Slavonic Philology, University of Oxford, and Fellow of Brasenose College, since 1965; *b* Rotherham, 10 Oct. 1914; 2nd *s* of George Auty, schoolmaster, and Martha Louise Richards; *m* 1944, Kathleen Marjorie Milnes-Smith (marr. diss.); one *s* one *d*. *Educ:* Rotherham Grammar School; (Scholar) Gonville and Caius Coll., Cambridge; Münster Univ. Tiarks German Schol., Cambridge Univ., 1935; Faculty Asst Lectr in German, 1937; Univ. Lectr (in German), 1945, (in German and Czech), 1948, (in Slavonic Studies), 1957-62; Head of Dept of Other Languages, 1948-56; Sen. Proctor, 1949-50; Fellow and Coll. Lectr in Modern Langs, Selwyn Coll., 1950-62; Dean of Selwyn Coll., 1953-56; Professor of Comparative Philology of the Slavonic Languages, Univ. of London, and Head of Dept of Languages and Literature, Sch. of Slavonic and East European Studies, 1962-65. War work with Czechoslovak authorities in London, 1939-43, attached to the Foreign Office, 1944-45. Visiting Prof. Slavic Languages, Univ. of California, Los Angeles, 1968; de Carle Lectr, Univ. of Otago, 1975. Sec. Assoc. Internationale des Langues et Littératures Slaves, 1957-60, Pres. 1966-72, Vice-Pres., 1972; Sec., British Univs Assoc. of Slavists, 1957-63, Pres., 1964-67, Vice-Pres., 1967-72; Treas., Philological Society, 1962-65; Vice-Pres., Fédération Internationale des Langues et Littératures Modernes, 1966-72, Hon. Vice-Pres., 1976. Pres., Assoc. of Teachers of Russian, 1967-69; Chm., Modern Humanities Research Assoc., 1968-73; Member: International Cttee of Slavists, 1965 (Vice-Pres., 1966); Exec., Internat. Cttee for Soviet and E European Studies, 1974; Governing Body, GB-E Europe Centre, 1970 (Vice-Chm., 1976); Chm. Council, SSEES, 1977; Editorial Board of Slavonic and East European Review (Chm., 1963-65); Ed. Board, International Journal of Slavic Linguistics and Poetics, 1965; Slavonic Editor, Modern Language Review, 1966; Editor, Oxford Slavonic Papers, 1968; Hon. Member: Slovak Linguistic Soc., 1971; Aust. and NZ Slavists Assoc., 1975; Vice-President: British-Yugoslav Soc.; Anglo-Byelorussian Soc.; Corresp. Mem., Austrian Acad. of Sciences, 1975. Josef Dobrovský Gold Medal, Czechoslovak Acad. of Sciences, 1968. *Publications:* Old Church Slavonic Texts and Glossary, 1960; (ed and contrib.) Cambridge Companion to Russian Studies, 1976-77. Articles in Brit. and foreign learned jls and encyclopædias. *Recreation:* travel, especially in Central and South-Eastern Europe. *Address:* Brasenose College, Oxford. *T:* Oxford 48641. *Clubs:* Athenæum, United Oxford & Cambridge University.

AVEBURY, 4th Baron *cr* 1900; **Eric Reginald Lubbock;** Bt 1806; *b* 29 Sept. 1928; *s* of Hon. Maurice Fox Pitt Lubbock (6th *s* of 1st Baron) (*d* 1957), and Hon. Mary Katherine Adelaide Stanley, *d* of 5th Baron Stanley of Alderley; *S* cousin, 1971; *m* 1953, Kina Maria, *d* of Count Joseph O'Kelly de Gallagh and Mrs I. D. Bruce; two *s* one *d*. *Educ:* Upper Canada Coll.; Harrow Sch.; Balliol Coll., Oxford (BA Engineering; boxing blue). Welsh Guards (Gdsman, 2nd Lieut), 1949-51; Rolls Royce Ltd, 1951-56; Grad. Apprentice; Export Sales Dept; Tech. Assistant to Foundry Manager. Management Consultant: Production Engineering Ltd, 1953-60; Charterhouse Group Ltd, 1960. MP (L) Orpington, 1962-70; Liberal Whip in House of Commons, 1963-70. Consultant, Morgan-Grampian Ltd, 1970-; Chm., Digico Ltd; Director: C. L. Projects Ltd; Industrial Leasing & Finance Ltd. President: Data Processing Management Assoc., 1972-75; Fluoridation Soc., 1972-; Conservation Soc., 1973-. Member: Council, Inst. of Race Relations, 1972-74; Royal Commn on Standards of Conduct in Public Life, 1974-76. MIMechE. *Recreations:* listening to music, reading. *Heir:* s Hon. Lyulph Ambrose Jonathan Lubbock, *b* 15 June 1954. *Address:* Combe House, Sundridge, Sevenoaks, Kent. *Club:* National Liberal.

AVELING, Alan John; Director of Estate Management Overseas, Property Services Agency, Department of the Environment, since 1976; *b* 4 Jan. 1928; *s* of late Herbert Ashley Aveling and Ethel Aveling; *m* 1960, Stella May Reed; one *s* one *d*. *Educ:* Fletton Grammar Sch.; Rugby Technical Coll. CEng; MIEE, MIMechE, MCIBS. Air Min. Works Dir, Newmarket, 1951-52; RAF Airfield Construction, 2nd Allied Tactical Air Force, 1952-55; Air Min. HQ, 1955-61; Sen. Engr, War Office Works Dept, Sen. Engr, 1961-63; BAOR Services, Germany, MPBW, 1963-66; Directorate Personnel, MPBW, 1966-67; Superintending Engr, Overseas Defence and FCO Services, 1967-72; Reg. Works Officer, later Regional Dir, British Forces, Germany, PSA/DoE, 1972-76. *Recreations:* aviculture, reading, skiing, country pursuits. *Address:* Running Hook, Peaslake, Guildford, Surrey. *T:* Shere 2499. *Club:* Royal Air Force.

AVERILL, Leslie Cecil Lloyd, CMG 1961; MC 1918; MD; FRCSE; FRCOG; Specialist in Obstetrics and Gynaecology, Christchurch, NZ, 1934-68; Chairman, North Canterbury Hospital Board, NZ, 1956-74; *b* 25 March 1897; 2nd *s* of late Most Rev. A. W. Averill, CMG, DD (Oxon) (Archbp of NZ, 1925-40); *m* 1925, Isabel Mary Wilkie Roberton, *o d* of Ernest Roberton, MD, Auckland; two *s* two *d. Educ:* Christ's Coll., Christchurch, NZ; Univ. of Edinburgh (medical). War Service with NZ Rifle Brigade: Lieut, France (MC), 1917-19. General medical practice, Christchurch, NZ, 1925-34. Pres. BMA (NZ), 1951-52; Chm. NZ Regional Council, Royal Coll. of Obstetricians and Gynaecologists, 1951-55. Chm., Christchurch Clinical Sch. Council, 1972-74. Pres., NZ Rifle Brigade Assoc., 1972-. Citoyen d'Honneur, Le Quesnoy, France, 1968 (Bronze medal), 1975 (Silver medal); Chevalier de la Légion d'Honneur, 1973. *Publications:* articles in medical journals. *Recreations:* golf, horticulture. *Address:* 41 Wairarapa Terrace, Christchurch 1, New Zealand. *T:* 557751. *Club:* Christchurch (NZ).

AVERY, Gillian Elise, (Mrs A. O. J. Cockshut); writer; *b* 1926; *d* of Norman and Grace Avery; *m* 1952, A. O. J. Cockshut; one *d. Educ:* Dunottar Sch., Reigate. *Publications: fiction:* The Warden's Niece, 1957; Trespassers at Charlcote, 1958; James without Thomas, 1959; The Elephant War, 1960; To Tame a Sister, 1961; The Greatest Gresham, 1962; The Peacock House, 1963; The Italian Spring, 1964; The Call of the Valley, 1966; A Likely Lad (Guardian Award, 1972), 1971; Huck and her Time Machine, 1977; *non -fiction:* 19th Century Children: heroes and heroines in English children's stories (with Angela Bull), 1965; Victorian People in Life and Literature, 1970; The Echoing Green: memories of Regency and Victorian youth, 1974; Childhood's Pattern, 1975. Ed, Gollancz revivals of early children's books, 1967-70, and anthologies of stories and extracts from early children's books. *Recreations:* walking, growing vegetables, cooking. *Address:* 32 Charlbury Road, Oxford.

AVERY, James Royle, (Roy Avery); Headmaster, Bristol Grammar School, since 1975; *b* 7 Dec. 1925; *s* of Charles James Avery and Dorothy May Avery; *m* 1954, Marjorie Louise (*née* Smith); one *s* one *d. Educ:* Queen Elizabeth's Hosp., Bristol; Magdalen Coll., Oxford; Bristol Univ. MA Oxon, CertifEd Bristol; FRSA. Asst History Master, Bristol Grammar Sch., 1951-59; Sen. History Master, Haberdashers' Aske's Sch. at Hampstead, then Elstree, 1960-65; Head Master, Harrow County Boys' Sch., 1965-75. *Publications:* The Story of Aldenham House, 1961; The Elstree Murder, 1962; contrib. Dictionary of World History, 1973; articles, reviews in educnl jls. *Recreations:* ecumenical movement, American studies and international affairs, rugby, cricket, theatre, music, walking. *Address:* Headmaster's House, Bristol Grammar School, 7 Elton Road, Bristol BS8 1SJ. *T:* Bristol 37832.

AVERY JONES, Sir Francis; *see* Jones, Sir F. A.

AVES, Dame Geraldine (Maitland), DBE 1977 (CBE 1963; OBE 1946); *b* 22 Aug. 1898; *er d* of Ernest Aves, MA, FSS, and Eva Mary (*née* Maitland). *Educ:* Frognal Sch., Hampstead; Newnham Coll., Cambridge (MA). Education Dept, LCC: Sch. Care Organiser, 1924-38; assisting planning and develt of war-time evacuation services, 1938-41; Ministry of Health, Chief Welfare Officer and Head of Welfare Divn, 1941-62. Seconded: to UNRRA as Chief Child Care Consultant (Europe), 1945-46; to Home Office, to initiate child care training, 1947-48; various assignments to UN Headqrs, in field of family and child welfare and to direct UN Seminars for European Region, 1949-69. Governor, Nat. Inst. for Social Work Training, 1961-71; Mem. Council for Training in Social Work, 1962-72; Associate Fellow, Newnham Coll., 1962-65 and 1966-69; Chm., Adv. Council of Nat. Corp. for the Care of Old People, 1965-72; Chm., Cttee of Enquiry into Voluntary Workers in the Social Services, 1966-69 (Report: The Voluntary Worker in the Social Services, 1969). Pres., Newnham College Roll, 1969-72; Mem., London Diocesan Synod and Bishop's Council, 1971-; Founder Mem., Governing Body, The Volunteer Centre, 1973-; Chm., Working Party that produced PIVOT (People Involved in Volunteer Organisation and Tasks), published 1976; serves on several local environmental and parochial organisations. *Recreation:* birdwatching. *Address:* 24 North Grove, Highgate Village, N6 4SL. *T:* 01-340 1685. *Club:* University Women's.

AVON, 2nd Earl of, *cr* 1961; **Nicholas Eden,** OBE 1970; TD 1965; DL; *b* 3 Oct. 1930; *o surv. s* of 1st Earl of Avon, KG, PC, MC, and Beatrice Helen (*d* 1957), *d* of Hon. Sir Gervase Beckett, 1st Bt; *S* father, 1977. *Educ:* Eton. Served with KRRC, 1949-51; ADC to the Governor-Gen. of Canada, 1952-53; served in Queen Victoria's Rifles (TA), 1953-61; on amalgamation, served in Queen's Royal Rifles (TA), 1961-67; 4th (Volunteer) Bn,

Royal Green Jackets, 1967-70; Major, 1959; Lt-Col, 1965; Col, TAVR, 1972-75; Hon. Col. ACF, NE Sector Greater London, 1970; Vice-Chm., Greater London TA&VRA, 1976. DL Greater London, 1973. *Recreations:* lawn tennis, Eton fives. *Address:* 6 Boynes Terrace Mews, W11 3LR. *Club:* All England Lawn Tennis.

AVONSIDE, Rt. Hon. Lord; Ian Hamilton Shearer, PC 1962; a Senator of the College of Justice in Scotland since 1964; *b* 6 Nov. 1914; *s* of Andrew Shearer, OBE, and Jessie Macdonald; *m* 1st, 1942; one *s* one *d*; 2nd, 1954, Janet Sutherland Murray (*see* Lady Avonside). *Educ:* Dunfermline High Sch.; Glasgow Univ.; Edinburgh Univ. MA Glasgow, 1934; LLB Edinburgh, 1937. Admitted to Faculty of Advocates, 1938; QC (Scotland) 1952. Served War of 1939-45: RA (Fd), 1939; Capt. 1941; Major 1943; released 1946, Emerg. R of O. Standing Counsel: to Customs and Excise, Bd of Trade and Min. of Labour, 1947-49; to Inland Revenue, 1949-51; to City of Edinburgh Assessor, 1949-51; Junior Legal Assessor to City of Edinburgh, 1951; Sheriff of Renfrew and Argyll, 1960-62; Lord Advocate, 1962-64. Chm., Lands Valuation Appeal Court, 1975-. Chm. Nat. Health Service Tribunal, Scotland, 1954-62; Mem. Scottish Cttee of Coun. on Tribunals, 1958-62; Chm. Scottish Valuation Advisory Coun., 1965-68; Mem., Scottish Univs Cttee of the Privy Council, 1971-. Pres., Stair Soc., 1975-. *Publications:* Purves on Licensing Laws, 1947; Acta Dominorum Concilii et Sessionis, 1951. *Recreation:* golf. *Address:* The Mill House, Samuelston, East Lothian. *T:* Haddington 2396. *Clubs:* Garrick; New (Edinburgh).

AVONSIDE, Lady; Janet Sutherland Shearer, OBE 1958; Scottish Governor, BBC, 1971-76; *b* 31 May 1917; *d* of William Murray, MB, ChB, and Janet Harley Watson; *m* 1953, Ian Hamilton Shearer, Rt Hon. Lord Avonside, *qv. Educ:* St Columba's Sch., Kilmacolm; Erlenhaus, Baden Baden; Univ. of Edinburgh. LLB, Dip. of Social Science. Asst Labour Officer (Scot.), Min. of Supply, 1941-45; Sec. (Scot.), King George's Fund for Sailors, 1945-53; Hon. Sec. (Scot.), Federal Union and United Europe, 1945-64; Scottish Delegate: Congress of Europe, 1947; Council of Europe, Strasburg, 1949. Contested (C), elections: Maryhill, Glasgow, 1950; Dundee East, 1951; Leith, 1955. Lectr in Social Studies, Dept of Educational Studies, Univ. of Edinburgh, 1962-70. *Recreation:* gardening. *Address:* The Mill House, Samuelston, East Lothian, Scotland. *T:* Haddington 2396. *Clubs:* Caledonian (Associate Mem.); New (Edinburgh).

AWAD, Muhammad Hadi; Ambassador of the People's Democratic Republic of Yemen to the Court of St James's since 1973, to Sweden and Spain, since 1974, to Denmark, since 1975; *b* 5 May 1934; Yemeni; *m* 1956, Adla; one *s* three *d. Educ:* Murray House Coll. of Educn. DipEd, Certif. Social Anthrop. Edinburgh. Teacher, 1953-59; Educn Officer, 1960-62; Chief Inspector of Schs, 1963-65; Vice-Principal, As-Shaab Coll., 1965-67; Perm. Rep. to Arab League, Ambassador to UAR and non-resident Ambassador to Sudan, Lebanon, Libya and Iraq, 1968-70; Perm. Sec., Min. of For. Affairs, 1970-73. *Recreation:* photography. *Address:* 57 Cromwell Road, SW7 2ED. *T:* 01-584 6607.

AWDRY, Daniel (Edmund), TD; MP (C) Chippenham Division of Wiltshire, since November 1962; *b* 10 Sept. 1924; *s* of Col Edmund Portman Awdry, MC, TD, DL, Coters, Chippenham, Wilts. and late Mrs Evelyn Daphne Alexandra Awdry, JP (formerly French); *m* 1950, Elizabeth Cattley; three *d. Educ:* Winchester Coll. RAC, OCTU, Sandhurst, 1943-44 (Belt of Honour). Served with 10th Hussars as Lieut, Italy, 1944-45; ADC to GOC 56th London Div., Italy, 1945; Royal Wilts Yeo., 1947-62; Major and Sqdn Comdr, 1955-62. Qualified Solicitor, 1950. Mayor of Chippenham, 1958-59; Pres., Southern Boroughs Assoc., 1959-60. PPS to Minister of State, Board of Trade, Jan.-Oct. 1964; PPS to Solicitor-Gen., 1973-74. Director: BET Omnibus Services, 1966-; Sheepbridge Engineering, 1968-; Rediffusion Ltd, 1973-. *Recreations:* cricket (Mem. Free Foresters and Butterflies), chess. *Address:* Old Manor, Beanacre, near Melksham, Wilts. *T:* Melksham 2315.

AXELROD, Julius, PhD; Chief, Section on Pharmacology, Laboratory of Clinical Science, National Institute of Mental Health, USA, since 1955 (Acting Chief, Jan.-Oct. 1955); *b* NYC, 30 May 1912; *s* of Isadore Axelrod, Michaliev, Poland, and Molly Liechtling, Striej, Poland (formerly Austria); *m* 1938, Sally (*née* Taub); two *s. Educ:* George Washington Univ., Wash., DC (PhD); New York Univ. (MA); New York City Coll. (BS). Lab. Asst. Dept Bacteriology, NY Univ. Med. Sch., 1933-35; Chemist, Lab. Industrial Hygiene, 1935-46; Res. Associate, Third NY Univ.; Research Div., Goldwater Memorial Hosp., 1946-49; Nat. Heart Inst., NIH: Associate Chemist, Section on Chem. Pharmacology, 1949-50; Chemist, 1950-53; Sen.

Chemist, 1953-55. Jt Nobel Prize for Physiology-Medicine, 1970; Mem., Nat. Academy of Sciences, 1971; Fellow, Amer. Acad. of Arts and Sciences. Hon. LLD: George Washington, 1971; College City, NY, 1972; Hon. DSc: Chicago, 1966; Med. Coll., Wisconsin, 1971; New York, 1971; Philadelphia Coll. of Med., 1973; Doctor *hc* Panama, 1972. Winner of 15 awards; holds 23 hon. lectureships; Member: 13 editorial boards; 5 Sci. Adv. Cttees. *Publications:* (with Richard J. Wurtman and Douglas E. Kelly) The Pineal, 1968; numerous original papers and contribs to jls in Biochem., Pharmacol. and Physiology. *Recreations:* reading and listening to music. *Address:* 10401 Grosvenor Place, Rockville, Maryland 20852, USA. *T:* (301) 493-6376.

AXISA, John Francis, MBE 1950; *b* 20 Nov. 1906; *s* of late Emmanuel Axisa and Vincenzina (*née* Micallef); *m* 1939, Ariadne Cachia; three *s* one *d. Educ:* St Paul's Sch., Malta and privately. Joined Malta Civil Service, 1927; Dir of Emigration, 1947-56; Dir of Technical Education, 1956-59; Dir of Emigration, Labour and Social Welfare, 1959-60; Under-Sec., 1960-61; Commissioner-Gen. for Malta in London, 1961-64; Malta's first High Commissioner on Malta's Independence, 1964-69; Ambassador of Malta to: France, 1966-69; Fed. Republic of Germany, 1967-69; Libya, 1966-68; Belgium, 1967-68; Netherlands, 1968-69. *Recreations:* carpentry, fishing, reading. *Address:* Godolphin, San Anton, Attard, Malta, GC. *Clubs:* Royal Commonwealth Society, Royal Over-Seas League; Union (Malta).

AXWORTHY, Geoffrey (John); Artistic Director of Sherman Theatre, University College, Cardiff, since 1970; *b* Plymouth, England, 10 Aug. 1923; *s* of William Henry Axworthy and Gladys Elizabeth Kingcombe; *m* 1951, Irene Dickinson (*d* 1976); two *s* one *d. Educ:* Exeter Coll., Oxford (MA). On staff of: Univ. of Baghdad 1951-56; Univ. of Ibadan, Nigeria, 1956-67. First Director, Univ. of Ibadan Sch. of Drama, 1962-67. Principal, Central School of Speech and Drama, London, 1967-70. Founded Univ. of Ibadan Travelling Theatre, 1961. *Address:* Monkton House, Marine Parade, Penarth, South Glamorgan, S Wales. *T:* Cardiff 703360.

AYALA, Jaime Z. de; *see* Zobel de Ayala.

AYCKBOURN, Alan; playwright; Director of Productions, Theatre-in-the-Round Co., Westwood, Scarborough; *b* 12 April 1939; *s* of Horace Ayckbourn and Irene Maude (*née* Worley); *m* 1959, Christine Helen (*née* Roland); two *s. Educ:* Haileybury. Worked in repertory as Stage Manager/Actor at Edinburgh, Worthing, Leatherhead, Oxford, and with late Stephen Joseph's Theatre-in-the-Round Co., at Scarborough. Founder Mem., Victoria Theatre, Stoke-on-Trent, 1962. BBC Radio Drama Producer, Leeds, 1964-70. Has written numerous full-length plays, mainly for Theatre-in-the-Round Co., 1959-. London productions: Mr Whatnot, Arts, 1964; Relatively Speaking, Duke of York's, 1967; How the Other Half Loves, Lyric, 1970; Time and Time Again, Comedy, 1972; Absurd Person Singular, Criterion, 1973 (Evening Standard Drama Award, Best Comedy, 1973); The Norman Conquests (Trilogy), Globe, 1974 (Evening Standard Drama Award, Best Play; Variety Club of GB Award; Plays and Players Award); Jeeves (musical, with Andrew Lloyd Webber), Her Majesty's, 1975; Absent Friends, Garrick, 1975; Confusions, Apollo, 1976; Bedroom Farce, Nat. Theatre, 1976; Just Between Ourselves, Queen's, 1977. Scarborough: Ten Times Table, 1977. *Publications:* Relatively Speaking, 1968; How the Other Half Loves, 1972; Time and Time Again, 1973; Absurd Person Singular, 1974; The Norman Conquests, 1975 (acting edn, 1975); Three Plays (Absurd Person Singular, Absent Friends, Bedroom Farce), 1977. *Recreations:* music, reading, cricket, films. *Address:* c/o Margaret Ramsay Ltd, 14a Goodwin's Court, St Martin's Lane, WC2N 4LL. *T:* 01-240 0691. *Club:* Garrick.

AYER, Sir Alfred (Jules), Kt 1970; FBA 1952; Wykeham Professor of Logic in the University of Oxford, since 1959; Fellow of New College, Oxford; *b* 29 Oct. 1910; *s* of late Jules Louis Cyprien Ayer; *m* 1932, Grace Isabel Renée Lees; one *s* one *d*; *m* 1960, Alberta Constance Chapman (Dee Wells); one *s. Educ:* Eton Coll. (scholar); Christ Church, Oxford (scholar). 1st class Lit. Hum. 1932; MA 1936; Lecturer in Philosophy at Christ Church, 1932-35; Research Student, 1935-44; Fellow of Wadham Coll., Oxford, 1944-46, Hon. Fellow, 1957; Dean, 1945-46; Grote Professor of the Philosophy of Mind and Logic in the Univ. of London, 1946-59; Visiting Prof. at: NY Univ., 1948-49; City Coll., New York. 1961-62; Lectures: William James, Harvard, 1970; John Dewey, Columbia, 1970; Gifford, St Andrews, 1972-73. Mem., Central Advisory Council for Education, 1963-66; President: Humanist Assoc., 1965-70; Modern Languages Assoc., 1966-67. Hon. Mem. Amer. Acad.

of Arts and Sciences 1963; For. Mem., Royal Danish Acad. of Scis and Letters, 1976. Dr hc Univ. of Brussels, 1962; Hon. DLitt East Anglia, 1972. Chevalier de la Légion d'Honneur, 1977. Enlisted in Welsh Guards, 1940; commissioned, 1940; Capt. 1943. Attaché at HM Embassy, Paris, 1945. *Publications:* Language, Truth and Logic, 1936 (revised edn 1946); The Foundations of Empirical Knowledge, 1940; Thinking and Meaning (Inaugural Lecture), 1947; (ed with Raymond Winch) British Empirical Philosophers, 1952; Philosophical Essays, 1954; The Problem of Knowledge, 1956; (ed) Logical Positivism, 1959; Privacy (British Academy lecture), 1960; Philosophy and Language (Inaugural lecture), 1960; The Concept of a Person and Other Essays, 1963; Man as a Subject for Science (Auguste Comte Lecture), 1964; The Origins of Pragmatism, 1968; (ed) The Humanist Outlook, 1968; Metaphysics and Common Sense, 1969; Russell and Moore: the analytical heritage, 1971; Probability and Evidence, 1972; Russell, 1972; Bertrand Russell as a Philosopher (British Acad. Lecture), 1973; The Central Questions of Philosophy, 1974; Part of my Life, 1977; articles in philos. and lit. jls. *Address:* New College, Oxford; 10 Regent's Park Terrace, NW1. *T:* 01-485 4855. *Clubs:* Garrick, Beefsteak.

AYERS, Herbert Wilfred, CB 1951; CBE 1948; retired; Under Secretary for Finance and Accountant-General, Ministry of National Insurance, 1948-53; *b* 22 May 1889; *s* of Joseph Drake Ayers; *m* Ethel M. Pitcher (decd); two *s*. Entered Civil Service, 1905; Ministry of Labour, 1913-44; joined Ministry of National Insurance, Dec. 1944 (Deputy Accountant-General). *Recreation:* philately. *Address:* 77 Davisville Avenue, Apartment 904, Toronto, Ontario M4S 1G4, Canada. *See also J. G. Ayers.*

AYERS, John Gilbert; Keeper, Far Eastern Section, Victoria and Albert Museum, since 1970; *b* 27 July 1922; *s* of H. W. Ayers, *qv*; *m* 1957, Bridget Elspeth Jacqualine Fanshawe; one *s* two *d. Educ:* St Paul's Sch.; St Edmund Hall, Oxford. Served in RAF, 1941-46 (Sgt). Asst Keeper, Dept of Ceramics, Victoria and Albert Museum, 1950, Dep. Keeper 1963. *Publications:* The Seligman Collection of Oriental Art, II, 1964; The Baur Collection; Chinese Ceramics, I-IV, 1968-74; (with R. J. Charleston) The James A. de Rothschild Collection: Meissen and Oriental Porcelain, 1971; Oriental Ceramics, The World's Great Collections: Victoria and Albert Museum (Tokyo), 1975; (with J. Rawson) Chinese Jade throughout the Ages, exhbn catalogue, 1975. *Address:* 3 Bedford Gardens, W8 7ED. *T:* 01-229-5168.

AYKROYD, Sir Cecil William, 2nd Bt, *cr* 1929; *b* 23 April 1905; *e s* of Sir Frederic Alfred Aykroyd, 1st Bt and late Lily May, *e d* of Sir James Roberts, 1st Bt, LLD, of Strathallan Castle, Perthshire, and Fairlight Hall, near Hastings; *S* father 1949; unmarried. *Educ:* Charterhouse; Jesus Coll., Cambridge. BA 1926. Dir, Nat. Provincial Bank Ltd, 1958-69 (Dir Bradford and District Bd, 1946-69). *Recreations:* fishing and shooting. *Heir: b* Frederic Howard Aykroyd [*b* 10 Oct. 1907; *m* 1932, Ruth Joan, *d* of Carlton Oldfield, Moor Hill, Harewood, Yorks; three *d. Educ:* Rugby; Jesus Coll., Cambridge, BA 1928]. *Address:* Birstwith Hall, near Harrogate, North Yorks. *T:* Harrogate 770250.

AYKROYD, Wallace Ruddell, CBE 1943; MD, ScD; *b* 30 July 1899; *e s* of Alfred Constantine Aykroyd, Bradford and Dublin; *m* 1931, Freda Kathleen Buttery; one *s* two *d. Educ:* The Leys Sch., Cambridge; Trinity Coll., Dublin (Vice-Chancellor's Prizeman in English Prose). MB, BCh 1924; MD 1928; ScD 1938; after various hospital appts Beit Memorial Research Fellow, 1928; Mem. of Health Section, League of Nations, 1931-35; Dir, Nutrition Research Laboratories, Coonoor, S India, 1935-45; Delegate of Govt of India to League of Nations Inter-governmental Conference on Rural Hygiene, Bandoeng, 1937; Far Eastern Representative, 1938, of League of Nations Technical Commission on Nutrition; Delegate to United Nations Conference on Food and Agriculture, Hot Springs, Virginia 1943; Dir, Nutrition Div., FAO, 1946-60; Senior Lectr, Dept of Human Nutrition, London Sch. of Hygiene and Tropical Medicine, 1960-66. Hon. Fellow, Amer. Public Health Assoc., 1954; Hon. Mem. American Nutrition Soc., 1960. *Publications:* Vitamins and other Dietary Essentials, 1933; Three Philosophers, 1935; Nutrition and Public Health, 1935 (with Et. Burnet); Sweet Malefactor: Sugar, Slavery and Human Society, 1967; The Conquest of Famine, 1974; numerous scientific papers on various aspects of nutrition. *Recreations:* reading, walking, gardening. *Address:* Queen Anne House, Charlbury, Oxon.

AYKROYD, Sir William Miles, 3rd Bt *cr* 1920; MC 1944; *b* 24 Aug. 1923; *s* of Sir Alfred Hammond Aykroyd, 2nd Bt, and Sylvia Ambler Aykroyd (*née* Walker), *widow* of Lieut-Col

Foster Newton Thorne; S father, 1965. *Educ:* Charterhouse. Served in 5th Royal Inniskilling Dragoon Guards, Lieut, 1943-47. Dir, Hardy Amies Ltd, 1950-69. *Heir: cousin* Michael David Aykroyd [*b* 14 June 1928; *m* 1952, Oenone Gillian Diana, *o d* of Donald George Cowling, MBE; one *s* three *d*]. *Address:* Buckland Newton Place, Dorchester, Dorset. *T:* Buckland Newton 259. *Club:* Boodle's.

AYLEN, Rear-Adm. Ian Gerald, CB 1962; OBE 1946; DSC 1942; CEng; FIMechE; *b* 12 Oct. 1910; *s* of late Commander A. E. Aylen, RN and Mrs S. C. M. Aylen; *m* 1937, Alice Brough Maltby; one *s* two *d*. *Educ:* Blundell's, Tiverton. RNE Coll., Keyham, 1929-33; served in HMS Rodney; Curacoa; Galatea, 1939-40; Kelvin, 1940-42; Cossack; 30 Assault Unit, 1945; Fleet Engineer Officer, Home Fleet, 1957-58; CO HMS Thunderer, RNE Coll., 1958-60; Rear-Admiral, 1960; Admiral Superintendent, HM Dockyard, Rosyth, 1960-63; Dep. Sec., Instn Mechanical Engineers, 1963-65; Asst Sec., Council of Engineering Instns, 1966-71, retired 1971. *Recreations:* fishing, golf, gardening. *Address:* Tracey Mill, Honiton, Devon. *Club:* St Stephen's.

AYLESFORD, 11th Earl of; Charles Ian Finch-Knightley, JP; Baron Guernsey, 1703; Lord-Lieutenant of West Midlands, since 1974; *b* 2 Nov. 1918; *er s* of 10th Earl of Aylesford; *S* father, 1958; *m* 1946, Margaret Rosemary Tyer; one *s* two *d*. *Educ:* Oundle. Lieut RSF, 1939; Captain Black Watch, 1947. Mem., Water Space Amenity Commn, 1973-. County Comr for Scouts, 1949-74, Patron 1974-. JP 1948, DL 1954, Vice-Lieutenant 1964-74, Warwicks. KStJ 1974. *Recreations:* wild life and nature conservation. *Heir: s* Lord Guernsey, *qv*. *Address:* Packington Hall, Coventry, West Midlands CV7 7HF. *T:* Meriden 22274.

AYLESTONE, Baron *cr* 1967 (Life Peer), of Aylestone; **Herbert William Bowden;** PC 1962; CH 1975; CBE 1953; Chairman, Independent Broadcasting Authority (formerly Independent Television Authority), 1967-75; *b* 20 Jan. 1905; *m* 1928, Louisa Grace, *d* of William Brown, Cardiff; one *d*. RAF, 1941-45. MP (Lab) S Leicester, 1945-50, S-W Div. of Leicester, 1950-67. PPS to Postmaster-Gen., 1947-49; Asst Govt Whip, 1949-50; a Lord Comr of the Treasury, 1950-51; Dep. Chief Oppn Whip, 1951-55; Chief Oppn Whip, 1955-64; Lord Pres. of the Council and Leader of the House of Commons, 1964-66; Secretary of State for Commonwealth Affairs, 1966-67. *Address:* c/o House of Lords, SW1.

AYLING, Air Vice-Marshal Richard Cecil, CB 1965; CBE 1961 (OBE 1948); Adjudicator, Immigration Appeals, since 1970; *b* 7 June 1916; *s* of A. C. Ayling, LDS, Norwood, London; *m* 1st, 1941, Patricia Doreen Wright (*d* 1966); one *s* one *d*; 2nd, 1971, Virginia, *d* of Col Frank Davis, Northwood; two *d*. *Educ:* Dulwich Coll. No 3(F) Sqdn, 1936-39. Served RNZAF, 1940-43; Comd No 51 Sqdn (Bomber Comd), 1944; Station Comdr, Bomber Comd, 1944-45; Staff Coll., 1945. Staff of Central Bomber Estabt, 1946-48; Air Staff (Plans) Far East, 1948-50; Air Min. (OR1 and Dep. Dir Policy Air Staff), 1951-54; Station Comdr, Bomber Comd, 1954-58; Asst Chief of Defence Staff, Min. of Defence, 1958-59; Dir of Organisation (Estabts), Air Min., 1960-61; SASO, Flying Training Command, 1962-65; Min. of Defence, 1965-66; AOA, RAF Air Support (formerly Transport) Comd, 1966-69; retd, 1969. *Recreations:* ski-ing, sailing, gardening. *Address:* Buckler's Spring, Buckler's Hard, Beaulieu, Hants. *T:* Buckler's Hard 204. *Clubs:* various yacht clubs and sailing associations.

AYLMER, family name of Baron Aylmer.

AYLMER, 12th Baron *cr* 1718; **Hugh Yates Aylmer;** Bt 1662; retired; *b* 5 Feb. 1907; *s* of Arthur Lovell Aylmer (*d* 1961) and Georgina Henrietta Emmeline (*d* 1936), *d* of Lt-Col J. F. Sweeny; *S* kinsman, 1977; *m* 1939, Althea, *e d* of late Lt-Col John Talbot; one *d*. *Educ:* Minneapolis, Minnesota, USA. General business career; sales, purchasing and management; retired, 1971. *Recreations:* badminton, fishing, hunting and varied outdoor sports. *Heir: cousin* Michael Anthony Aylmer [*b* 27 March 1923; *m* 1950, Countess Maddalena Sofia Maria Gabriella Cecilia Stefania Francesca, *d* of late Count Arbeno Attems di Santa Croce; one *s* one *d*]. *Address:* 601-1159 Beach Drive, Victoria, BC V8S 2N2, Canada.

AYLMER, Sir Felix, (Sir Felix E. Aylmer-Jones), Kt 1965; OBE 1950; Actor; *b* 21 Feb. 1889; *s* of Lieut-Col T. E. Aylmer-Jones, RE, and Lilian Cookworthy; *m* Cecily Byrne (*d* 1975); one *d* (and two *s* decd). *Educ:* Magdalen Coll. Sch.; Exeter Coll., Oxford. First stage appearance, Coliseum, with Seymour Hicks, 1911; Birmingham Rep. Theatre, 1913. Served European War, 1914-18, RNVR. Pres., British Actors' Equity Assoc., 1949-69.

Principal London appearances: R. E. Lee, 1923; The Terror, 1927; Bird in Hand, 1928; The Nelson Touch, 1931; The Voysey Inheritance, St Joan, 1934; Heroes Don't Care, Waste, 1936; Yes and No, 1937; The Flashing Stream, 1938; Scandal at Barchester, 1944; Daphne Laureola, 1949; Spider's Web, 1955; The Chalk Garden, 1956. New York: 1922, 1925, 1939; The Prescott Proposals, 1953-54. Numerous films and broadcasts. *Principal films:* Tudor Rose, Victoria the Great, The Demi-Paradise, Henry V, Mr Emmanuel, The Ghosts of Berkeley Square, Hamlet, Prince of Foxes, Quo Vadis, The Lady With a Lamp, Ivanhoe, The Knights of the Round Table, The Angel Who Pawned Her Harp, St Joan, Separate Tables, The Doctor's Dilemma, The Mummy, Never Take Sweets from a Stranger, From the Terrace, Exodus, The Chalk Garden. *Publications:* Dickens Incognito, 1959; The Drood Case, 1964. *Address:* 6 Painshill House, Cobham, Surrey. *Clubs:* Garrick, Green Room, Beefsteak.

AYLMER, Sir Fenton Gerald, 15th Bt, *cr* 1622; *b* 12 March 1901; *s* of Sir Gerald Evans-Freke Aylmer, 14th Bt, and Mabel Howard, *d* of late Hon. J. K. Ward, MLC, Province of Quebec; *S* father, 1939; *m* 1928, Rosalind Boultbee, *d* of J. Percival Bell, Hamilton, Ont; one *s* one *d*. *Educ:* Lower Canada Coll., Montreal; Bishop's Coll. Sch., Lennoxville. *Heir: s* Richard John Aylmer [*b* 23 April 1937; *m* 1962, Lise Demers; one *s* one *d*]. *Address:* 29 Church Hill, Westmount, Quebec, Canada.

AYLMER, Prof. Gerald Edward, DPhil; FBA 1976; Professor of History and Head of Department of History, University of York, since 1963; *b* 30 April 1926; *s* of late Captain E. A. Aylmer, RN, and Mrs G. P. Aylmer (*née* Evans); *m* 1955, Ursula Nixon; one *s* one *d*. *Educ:* Winchester; Balliol Coll., Oxford (MA, DPhil). Jane Eliza Proctor Vis. Fellow, Princeton Univ., NJ, USA, 1950-51; Jun. Res. Fellow, Balliol Coll., Oxford, 1951-54; Asst Lectr in History, Univ. of Manchester, 1954-57, Lectr, 1957-62; Vis. Mem., Inst. for Advanced Study, Princeton, 1975. *Publications:* The King's Servants, 1961 (2nd edn 1974); (ed) The Diary of William Lawrence, 1962; The Struggle for the Constitution, 1963 (5th edn 1975); (ed) The Interregnum, 1972 (2nd edn 1974); The State's Servants, 1973; (ed) The Levellers in the English Revolution, 1975; articles and revs in learned jls. *Address:* 48 Marygate, York YO3 7BH. *T:* York 24944; History Department, University of York, Heslington, York YO1 5DD. *T:* York 59861.

AYLMER-JONES, Sir Felix E.; *see* Aylmer, Sir Felix.

AYLWARD, Prof. Francis; Professor and Head of Department of Food Science, University of Reading, 1968-76, now Emeritus; *b* Liverpool, 21 July 1911; *e s* of J. F. and Margaret Aylward, Liverpool; *m* 1947, Nora Gunter, Warwickshire; two *d*. *Educ:* Univ. of Liverpool. BSc 1st cl. Hons Chem.; PhD Biochem.; DSc; Johns Hopkins University, 1935-37; Commonwealth Fund Fellow and Univ. Fellow in Paediatrics. ICI Ltd, 1941-44. Teaching and research posts, 1937-41, 1944-60: at Univ. of Liverpool; Manchester; Borough Polytechnic, London. Field staff, FAO, 1960-65: in Ghana, Scientific Adviser, food and nutrition, Min. of Agric., also Prof. and Head of Dept of Nutrition and Food Science at Univ. of Ghana; in Poland, Dir FAO/UNDP project; Consultant, 1968-, for internat. bodies (inc. FAO, UNESCO, Protein Adv. Gp UN, OECD, EEC) and UK bodies (ODM, IUC), mainly Africa and ME; Hon. Consultant, Nestle Foundn. Dir, Campden Food Preserv. Res. Assoc., 1965-68; Member Council: Nutrition Soc., 1975-; Soc. Chem. Ind., 1975-; former Vice-Pres. Council and Chm., Food Gp; Chm., Overseas Cttee, Univ. of Reading, 1968-76; Mem., IUC Acad. Policy Cttee, 1974-. FRIC; CChem.; FRSM; FRSA; FIFST. Hon. Mem., Agric. Univ., Warsaw, 1965; Internat. Award (US), Inst. of Food Tech., 1973. KSG. *Publications:* (jtly) Protein and Nutrition Policy in Low Income Countries, 1975; research papers and reviews in scientific and other jls. *Recreation:* travel. *Address:* Four Corners, Upper Warren Avenue, Mapledurham, near Reading. *T:* Reading 472 308. *Club:* Athenæum.

AYNSLEY, George Ayton, CMG 1956; CBE 1949; *b* 2 May 1896; *e s* of George Morrison Thomas Aynsley and Annie Sarah Jones Aynsley (*née* Ayton); *m* 1920, Margaret Studdy Oliver; one *d*. *Educ:* Rutherford Coll., Newcastle upon Tyne. Colonial Office, 1912-13; Crown Agents for Colonies, 1913-15; joined London Scottish, 1915; served France, Balkans, Egypt and Palestine, 1916-19; Min. of Pensions, 1919-20; Mercantile Marine Dept,. Bd of Trade, 1920-23; Customs and Excise, 1923-39; Establishment Officer, Min. of Information, 1939-44; recruited personnel for Allied Commission in Austria, and Control Commission for Germany, 1944-45; administration of Commissions under War Office, 1945, Control Office for Germany and Austria, 1946-47, and Foreign Office, 1947. Head of Personnel Dept, Foreign Office (German Section), 1947-56; Establishment Officer, British Council for Aid to Refugees (Hungarian Dept), 1956-57 (reception and administration of refugees from Hungary). Coronation Medal, 1953. *Recreations:* golf, bowls. *Address:* 9 The Grove, St Margarets, Twickenham, Middlesex. *T:* 01-892 8556.

AYOUB, John Edward Moussa, FRCS; Consulting Surgeon, Moorfields Eye Hospital, since 1973 (Surgeon, 1950-73); Consulting Ophthalmic Surgeon, London Hospital, since 1973 (Surgeon, 1947-73); Consulting Ophthalmic Surgeon, Royal Masonic Hospital, since 1973 (Consultant, 1967-73); Consulting Ophthalmic Surgeon, Royal Navy; *b* 7 Sept. 1908; British; *m* 1939, Madeleine Marion Coniston Martin; one *s* one *d*. *Educ:* St Paul's Sch.; Lincoln Coll., Oxford; St Thomas' Hospital. BM, BCh Oxon 1933; FRCS 1935. Fellow, and past Vice-Pres. Section of Ophthalmology, RSM; Past Mem. Council, Faculty of Ophthalmologists (Vice-Pres., 1959-). Served War of 1939-45, Surg. Lieut-Comdr RNVR, specialist in ophthalmology. *Publications:* contributions to medical journals. *Recreations:* rowing, sailing. *Address:* 1 Royal Connaught Square, Alderney, Channel Islands. *Clubs:* Leander; Royal Solent Yacht; Royal Cruising.

AYRE, Captain Leslie Charles Edward, CBE 1941 (OBE 1919); RN, retired; *b* 30 May 1886; *er s* of late Rev. H. E. Ayre, Rector of Brendon, North Devon; *m* 1911, Dorothy Beatrice Agnes, *e d* of late Rev. J. F. Vallings, Vicar of Sopley, Hants; (one *s* killed on active service, Dec. 1941) one *d*. *Educ:* St John's Sch., Leatherhead. Entered Royal Navy, 1904; Paymaster of Royal Yacht Alexandra, 1913-14; HMS Agincourt (Grand Fleet), 1914-15; Secretary to: Admiral Commanding Coastguard, 1917-21; to Rear-Admiral Commanding Destroyer Flotillas, 1922-23; to Asst Chief of Naval Staff, 1923-24; to Rear-Admiral Commanding First Cruiser Squadron, 1924-26; to Commander-in-Chief, China Station, 1928-31; to Commander-in-Chief, Portsmouth, 1931-34; Deputy Paymaster Dir-Gen., 1935-37; Command Accountant Officer, Plymouth Command, 1939-43. Polonia Restituta, 1942. *Recreations:* gardening; played football (Association) for navy. *Address:* 38 Chapel Street, Ely, Cambs. *T:* Ely 2704.

AYRTON, Norman Walter; international theatre and opera director; *b* London, 25 Sept. 1924. Served War of 1939-45, RNVR. Trained as an actor at Old Vic Theatre School under Michael Saint Denis, 1947-48; joined Old Vic Company, 1948; repertory experience at Farnham and Oxford, 1949-50; on staff of Old Vic Sch., 1949-52; rejoined Old Vic Company for 1951 Festival Season; opened own teaching studio, 1952; began dramatic coaching for Royal Opera House, Covent Garden, 1953; apptd Asst Principal of London Academy of Music and Dramatic Art, 1954; taught at Shakespeare Festival, Stratford, Ont, and Royal Shakespeare Theatre, Stratford-upon-Avon, 1959-62; apptd GHQ Drama Adviser to Girl Guide Movement, 1960-74; Principal, LAMDA, 1966-72; Dean World Shakespeare Study Centre, Barkside, 1972. *Director:* Artaxerxes, for Hancel Opera Soc., Camden Festival, 1963; La Traviata, Covent Garden, 1963; Manon, Covent Garden, 1964; Sutherland-Williamson Grand Opera Season, in Australia, 1965; Twelfth Night at Dallas Theatre Center, Texas, 1967; The Way of the World, NY, 1976; Lakmé, Sydney Opera, 1976; *Guest Director:* Australian Council for Arts, Sydney and Brisbane, 1973; Loeb Drama Center, Harvard (and teacher), 1974; Faculty, Juillard Sch., NY, 1974-; Melbourne Theatre Co., 1974-; Nat. Inst. of Dramatic Art, Sydney, 1974; Vancouver Opera Assoc., 1975-; Sydney Opera House, 1976; has directed many student and professional productions of classic and modern plays, as well as operas at Covent Garden, Sadler's Wells, and elsewhere. *Recreations:* reading, music, travel. *Address:* 55A Holland Park Mews, W11 5SS. *T:* 01-727 0375.

AZIKIWE, Rt. Hon. Nnamdi, PC 1960; LLD, DLitt, MA, MSc; Ndichie Chief Owelle of Onitsha, 1973; (First) President of the Federal Republic of Nigeria, 1963-66; Governor-General and Commander-in-Chief of Nigeria, 1960-63; *b* Zungeru, Northern Nigeria, 16 Nov. 1904; *s* of Obededom Chukwuemeka and Rachel Chinwe Azikiwe; *m* 1936, Flora Ogbenyeanu Ogoegbunam, *d* of Chief Ogoegbunam, the Adazia of Onitsha (Ndichie Chief); three *s* one *d*. *Educ:* CMS Central Sch., Onitsha; Methodist Boys' High Sch., Lagos; Storer Coll., Harpers Ferry, W Va, USA; Howard Univ., Washington, DC; Lincoln Univ., Pa; Univ. of Pennsylvania. Overseas Fellow, Inst. Journalists, London, 1962 (Mem., 1933-). Editor-in-Chief, African Morning Post, Accra, 1934-37; Editor-in-Chief, West African Pilot, 1937-45; Correspondent for Associated Negro Press, 1944-47; Gen. Sec., Nat. Council of Nigeria and the Cameroons, 1944-46 (Pres., 1946-60); Correspondent for Reuter's, 1944-46; Chm. African Continental Bank Ltd, 1944-

53. MLC Nigeria, 1947-51; Mem. Foot Commission for Nigerianisation of Civil Service, 1948. Leader of Opposition in the Western House of Assembly, 1952-53; Mem. Eastern House of Assembly, 1954-59; MHR 1954; Minister, Eastern Nigeria, 1954-57; Leader, Educational Missions to UK and USA, for establishment of Univ. of Nigeria, 1955 and 1959; Premier of Eastern Nigeria, 1954-59; Pres., Exec. Council of Govt of E Nigeria, 1957-59; President of Senate of Federation, Jan-Nov. 1960. Ndichie Chief Ozizani Obi of Onitsha, 1963-72. Chm., Provisional Council of Univ. of Nigeria, 1960-61; Chancellor of Univ. of Nigeria, 1961-66, of Univ. of Lagos, 1970-76. Jt Pres., Anti-Slavery Soc. for Human Rights, London, 1970- (Vice-Pres., 1966-69). (Life) FREconS; (Life) FRAI; (Life) Mem. British Association for Advancement of Science; Member: American Soc. of International Law; American Anthropological Assoc. Pres. numerous sporting assocs and boards, 1940-60; Mem., Nigerian Olympic Cttee, 1950-60. Hon. DCL Liberia, 1969; Hon. DSc Lagos, 1972. KStJ 1960-66. *Publications:* Renascent Africa; Political Blueprint of Nigeria; Economic Reconstruction of Nigeria; Meditations: A Collection of Poems; Treasury of West African Poetry; My Odyssey, 1971, etc. *Recreations:* athletics, boxing, cricket, soccer, swimming, tennis, reading. *Address:* Onuiyi Haven, PO Box 7, Nsukka, Nigeria.

AZIZ, Suhail Ibne; Personnel/Industrial Relations Executive, International Mars Group, Melton Mowbray, Leics, since 1974; *b* Bangladesh (then India), 3 Oct. 1937; *s* of Azizur Rahman and Lutfunnessa Khatoon; *m* 1960, Elizabeth Ann Pyne, Dartmouth, Devon; two *d*. *Educ:* Govt High Sec. Sch., Sylhet; Murarichand Coll., Dacca Univ., Sylhet (Intermed. in Science, 1954); Jt Services Pre-Cadet Trng Sch., Quetta; Cadet Trng Sch., PNS Himalaya, Karachi; BRNC, Dartmouth (Actg Sub-Lieut 1958); (mature student) Kingston upon Thames Polytechnic and Trent Polytech., Nottingham (Dipl. in Man. Studies, 1970); (ext. student) London Univ. (BScEcon Hons 1972); (internal student) Birkbeck Coll., London Univ., (MScEcon 1976). AMBIM 1970. Sub-Lieut and Lieut, Pakistan Navy Destroyers/Mine Sweeper (Exec. Br.), 1954-61. Personnel and indust. relations: Unilever (Pakistan); Royal Air Force; Commn on Indust. Relations, London; Ford Motor Co. (GB); Mars Ltd, 1963-. Permanently living in England, 1966-. Leading Mem., Bangladesh Movement in UK, 1971. Member: Exec., Standing Conf. of Asian Orgs in UK, 1972-; N Metropol. Conciliation Cttee, Race Relations Bd, 1971-74; Exec., Post Conf. Constituent Cttee, Black People in Britain—the Way Forward, 1975-76; Adv. Cttee to Gulbenkian Foundn on Area Resource Centre and Nat. Forum on Community Work, 1976-; Exec., Nottingham and Dist Community Relations Council, 1975-; Exec., Fedn of Bangladesh Assocs, UK and Europe, 1972-; Jt Trustee, United Action-Bangladesh Relief Fund, 1971-; Founder Mem., Bangladesh Econ. Soc., UK, 1975-; Exec., National Org. of African, Asian and Caribbean Peoples, 1976-77; Home Sec.'s Standing Adv. Council on Race Relations, 1976-; Labour Econ. Finance Taxation Assoc., 1973-; Cambridge Econ. Soc., 1973-. Deeply interested in community and race relations and believes profoundly that future health of Brit. society depends on achieving good race relations. *Recreations:* travelling, seeing places of historical interest, meeting people, reading (*eg* political economy). *Address:* 29 Trevor Road, West Bridgford, Nottingham NG2 6FS. *T:* Nottingham 234866. *Club:* Royal Air Force.

B

BABCOCK, Horace Welcome; Director, Hale Observatories, since 1964; *b* 13 Sept. 1912; *s* of Harold D. Babcock and Mary G. (*née* Henderson); *m* 1st, 1940; one *s* one *d*; 2nd, 1958, Elizabeth M. Aubrey; one *s* (one step *s* one step *d*). *Educ:* California Institute of Technology (BS); Univ. of California (PhD). Instructor, Yerkes and McDonald Observatories, 1939-41; Radiation Laboratory, Mass Inst. of Tech., 1941-42; Calif Inst. of Tech., 1942-45; Staff Mem., Mount Wilson Observatory, 1946-51; Astronomer, Mount Wilson and Palomar Observatories, 1951-57, Asst Dir, 1957-63, Associate Dir, 1963-64, Dir, 1964. Founded Las Campanas Observatory, Chile, of Carnegie Instn, Washington, 1968. Elected to: National Acad. of Sciences, 1954 (Councillor, 1973-76); American Acad. of Arts and Sciences, 1959; American Philosophical Soc., 1966; Corres. Mem., Société Royale des Sciences de Liège, 1968; Associate, Royal Astronomical Soc., 1969; Member: American Astronomical Soc.; Astronomical Soc. of the Pacific; Internat. Astronomical Union. Hon. DSc Univ. of Newcastle upon Tyne,

1965. US Navy Bureau of Ordnance Develt Award, 1945; Eddington Gold Medal, RAS, 1958; Henry Draper Medal of the National Acad. of Sciences, 1957; Bruce Medal, Astronomical Soc. of the Pacific, 1969; Gold Medal, RAS, 1970. *Publications:* scientific papers in Astrophysical Jl, Publications of the Astronomical Soc. of the Pacific, Jl of Optical Soc. of America, etc, primarily on magnetic fields of the stars and sun, astrophysics, and astronomical instruments. *Address:* Hale Observatories, 813 Santa Barbara Street, Pasadena, California 91101, USA. *T:* (213) 577-1122.

BABER, Hon. Ernest George; Hon. Mr. Justice Baber; Judge of the Supreme Court of Hong Kong, since 1973; *b* 18 July 1924; *s* of Walter Averette Baber and late Kate Marion (*née* Pratt); *m* 1960, Dr Flora Marion, *y d* of Dr Raymond Bisset Smith and late Mrs Jean Gemmell Bisset Smith (*née* Howie); one *s* two *d*. *Educ:* Brentwood; Emmanuel Coll., Cambridge (MA, LLB). Served RN, 1942-47 (Lieut (S)). Called to Bar, Lincoln's Inn, 1951. Resident Magistrate, Uganda, 1954-62; Magistrate and President of Tenancy Tribunal, Hong Kong, 1962; Senior Magistrate, 1963-67; District Judge, 1967-73. *Recreations:* children, music, walking. *Address:* Supreme Court, Hong Kong. *Clubs:* Naval; Hong Kong, United Services Recreation (Hong Kong).

BABINGTON, Anthony Patrick; His Honour Judge Babington; a Circuit Judge, since 1972; *b* 4 April 1920; 2nd *s* of late Oscar John Gilmore Babington, MAI, AMICE, Monkstown, Co. Cork. *Educ:* Reading Sch. Served with Royal Ulster Rifles and Dorset Regt, 1939-45 (wounded twice); Croix de Guerre with Gold Star (France), 1944. Called to the Bar, Middle Temple, 1948; South Eastern Circuit; Prosecuting Counsel to Post Office, SE Circuit (South), 1959-64; Metropolitan Stipendiary Magistrate, 1964-72. Mem., Home Office Working Party on Bail, 1971-73. *Publications:* No Memorial, 1954; The Power to Silence, 1968; A House in Bow Street, 1969; The English Bastille, 1971; The Only Liberty, 1975. *Recreations:* music, theatre, reading. *Address:* 3 Gledhow Gardens, South Kensington, SW5 0BL. *T:* 01-373 4014; Thydon Cottage, Chilham, near Canterbury, Kent. *T:* Chilham 300. *Club:* Garrick.

BABINGTON, Air Marshal Sir John T.; *see* Tremayne, Air Marshal Sir J. T.

BABINGTON, Ven. Richard Hamilton; Archdeacon of Exeter and Canon Residentiary of Exeter Cathedral, 1958-70, Archdeacon Emeritus, 1970; Treasurer of Exeter Cathedral, 1962-70; retired; *b* 30 Nov. 1901; *s* of Very Rev. R. Babington; *m* 1926, Evelyn Ruth Montgomery; two *s* two *d*. *Educ:* Malvern; Keble Coll., Oxford. Curate of Banstead, 1925; Vicar of West End, Southampton, 1929; Vicar of St Mary-le-Tower, Ipswich, 1942; Hon. Canon of St Edmundsbury, 1947. *Recreations:* gardening, trout fishing. *Address:* Thatch End, Whimple, Exeter. *T:* Whimple 479.

BABINGTON, William, CBE 1972; QFSM 1969; Chief Officer, Kent County Fire Brigade, 1966-76, retired; *b* 23 Dec. 1916; *s* of William and Annie Babington; *m* 1940, Marjorie Perdue Le Seelleur; one *d*. *Educ:* King Edward's Grammar Sch., Birmingham. Member of Institution of Fire Engineers. Addtl Supt of Police, Assam, India, 1942-44; Instructor, Fire Service Coll., 1951-53; Divl Officer, Hampshire Fire Service, 1954-59; Asst Chief Officer, Suffolk and Ipswich Fire Service, 1959-62; Dep. Chief Officer, Lancashire Fire Brigade, 1962-66. *Recreations:* sailing, travel. *Address:* Dean Farm, East Farleigh, near Maidstone, Kent. *T:* Maidstone 26301.

BABINGTON SMITH, Michael James, CBE 1945; Consultant, Williams & Glyn's Bank Ltd (late Deputy Chairman); Chairman, London Committee of Ottoman Bank, since 1975; Director of other companies; Brigadier R of O (TA); *b* 20 March 1901; *e s* of Sir Henry Babington Smith, GBE, KCB, CH, and Lady Elisabeth Mary Bruce; *m* 1943, Jean Mary Meade, *yr d* of late Admiral Hon. Sir Herbert Meade-Fetherstonhaugh, GCVO, CB, DSO; one *s* two *d*. *Educ:* Eton; Trinity Coll., Cambridge. Director: Bank of England, 1949-69; Bank for International Settlements, 1965-74; Compagnie Financière de Suez, 1957-74. Sheriff of London, 1953 and 1962. *Recreations:* fishing, shooting, etc. *Address:* Flat 6, 20 Embankment Gardens, SW3 4LW. *T:* 01-352 2854. *Club:* Brooks's.

BACK, Mrs J. H.; *see* Harrison, Kathleen.

BACK, Kenneth John Campbell, MSc, PhD; Vice-Chancellor, James Cook University of North Queensland, since 1970; *b* 13 Aug. 1925; *s* of J. L. Back; *m* 1950, Patricia, *d* of R. O. Cummings; two *d*. *Educ:* Sydney High Sch.; Sydney Univ. (MSc, PhD). Res. Bacteriologist, Davis Gelatine (Aust.) Pty Ltd, 1947-49; Queensland University: Lectr in Bacteriology, 1950-56; Sen. Lectr in Microbiology, 1957-61; Actg Prof. of Microbiology, 1962; Warden, University Coll of Townsville, Queensland, 1963-70. *Publications:* papers on microbiological metabolism. *Recreations:* golf, bridge, sailing. *Address:* James Cook University of North Queensland, Post Office, James Cook University, Qld 4811, Australia; 15 Yarrawonga Drive, Townsville, Qld 4810. *Club:* North Queensland.

BACK, Patrick, QC 1970; a Recorder of the Crown Court, since 1972; *b* 23 Aug. 1917; *s* of late Ivor Back, FRCS, and Barbara Back (*née* Nash). *Educ:* Marlborough; Trinity Hall, Cambridge. Captain, 14th Punjab Regt, 1941-46. Called to Bar, 1940; commenced practice, Western Circuit, 1948; Dep. Chm., Devon QS, 1968. *Recreation:* dinghy racing. *Address:* Paddock Edge, Broadwindoor, Dorset. *T:* Broadwindsor 644; 3 Paper Buildings, Temple, EC4; Flat 3, Marquess House, 74 Marquess Road, N1. *T:* 01-226 0991.

BACKETT, Prof. Edward Maurice; Foundation Professor of Community Health, University of Nottingham, since 1969; *b* 12 Jan. 1916; *o s* of late Frederick and Louisa Backett; *m* 1940, Shirley Paul-Thompson; one *s* two *d*. *Educ:* University Coll., London; Westminster Hospital. Operational Research with RAF; Nuffield Fellow in Social Medicine; Research Worker, Medical Research Council; Lecturer, Queen's Univ., Belfast; Senior Lecturer, Guy's Hospital and London Sch. of Hygiene and Tropical Medicine; Prof. and Head of Dept of Public Health and Social Medicine, Univ. of Aberdeen, 1958-69. *Publications:* papers in scientific journals. *Recreations:* swimming, walking, sailing. *Address:* Department of Community Health, The Medical School, University of Nottingham, Nottingham. *T:* 56101.

BACKHOUSE, Jonathan; director of companies; *b* 16 March 1907; 2nd *s* of late Lieut-Col M. R. C. Backhouse, DSO, TD, and of Olive Backhouse; *m* 1934, Alice Joan Woodroffe; two *s* one *d*. *Educ:* RNC Dartmouth. Served War of 1939-45, Royal Artillery. Merchant Bank, 1924-28; Stock Exchange, 1928-50; Merchant Bank, 1950. *Recreations:* shooting, etc. *Address:* Breewood Hall, Great Horkesley, Colchester, Essex. *T:* Great Horkesley 260. *Club:* Royal Thames Yacht.

BACKHOUSE, Sir Jonathan Roger, 4th Bt, *cr* 1901; Director, W. H. Freeman & Co. Ltd, Publishers; *b* 30 Dec. 1939; *s* of Major Sir John Edmund Backhouse, 3rd Bt, MC, and Jean Marie Frances, *d* of Lieut-Col G. R. V. Hume-Gore, MC, The Gordon Highlanders; *S* father, 1944. *Educ:* Oxford. *Heir: b* Oliver Richard Backhouse, [*b* 18 July 1941; *m* 1970, Gillian Irene, *o d* of L. W. Lincoln, Northwood, Middx]. *Address:* c/o Lloyds Bank, 39 Piccadilly, W1.

BACON, family name of **Baroness Bacon.**

BACON, Baroness *cr* 1970 (Life Peer), of Leeds and Normanton; **Alice Martha Bacon,** PC 1966; CBE 1953; DL; *d* of late County Councillor B. Bacon, miner. *Educ:* Elementary Schs, Normanton, Yorks; Normanton Girls' High Sch.; Stockwell Training Coll.; external student of London Univ. Subsequently schoolmistress. MP (Lab) NE Leeds, 1945-55, SE Leeds, 1955-70; Minister of State: Home Office, 1964-67; Dept of Educn and Science, 1967-70. Mem. National Executive Cttee of Labour Party, 1941-70; Chm., Labour Party, 1950-51. DL W Yorkshire 1974. *Address:* 53 Snydale Road, Normanton, West Yorks. *T:* Wakefield 893229.

BACON, Sir Edmund (Castell), 13th Bt of Redgrave, *cr* 1611, and 14th Bt of Mildenhall, *cr* 1627; KG 1970; KBE 1965 (OBE 1945); TD; JP; Premier Baronet of England; Lord-Lieutenant of Norfolk, since 1949; Church Commissioner, 1955-63; *b* 18 March 1903; *s* of Sir Nicholas Henry Bacon, 12th and 13th Bt, and Constance Alice, CBE (*d* 1962), *y d* of late A. S. Leslie Melville; *S* father 1947; *m* 1936, Priscilla Dora, *d* of Col Sir Charles Ponsonby, 1st Bt, TD, and of Hon. Winifred Gibbs, *d* of 1st Baron Hunsdon; one *s* four *d*. *Educ:* Eton Coll.; Trinity Coll., Cambridge. Served War of 1939-45, Lieut-Col commanding 55 (Suffolk Yeomanry) Anti-tank Regt RA, 1940-44, Normandy and Belgium 1944 (despatches, OBE). Hon. Col, RA (TA), 1947-67. Chairman: British Sugar Corp., Ltd, 1957-68; Agricultural EDC, 1966-71; Dir, Lloyds Bank, 1949-73. Pro-Chancellor, Univ. of East Anglia, 1964-73. High Steward: of Norwich Cathedral, 1956; of Great Yarmouth, 1968-. JP Norfolk. Hon. DCL East Anglia, 1969. *Heir: s* Nicholas Hickman Ponsonby Bacon, *b* 17 May 1953. *Address:* Raveningham Hall, Norwich. *T:* Raveningham 206; Ash Villa, Morton Terrace, Gainsborough, Lincs. *T:* Gainsborough 2898. *Clubs:* Carlton, Pratt's.
See also Sir C. B. Barrington.

BACON, Francis; artist; *b* Dublin 1909. One-man exhibitions: Hanover Gall., London, 1949, 1950, 1951, 1952 (after travelling in S Africa and Kenya), 1954, 1957; Durlacher Gall., New York, 1953; Galerie Rive Droite, Paris, 1957; Galerie D'Arte Galatea, Turin; Galleria Dell' Ariete, Milan; Galleria Obelisco, Rome, 1958; Marlborough Fine Art Gall., London, 1960; Tate Gall., 1962. Exhibitions etc: Beaux Arts Gall., London, 1953; (rep. Great Britain, with Ben Nicholson and Lucien Freud) 27th Venice Biennale, 1954; Hanover Gall., and in New York, 1954; Inst. of Contemporary Arts, London, 1955 (retrospective); New Decade Show, Museum of Modern Art, New York, 1955; New London Gall., 1963, 1965; Solomon Guggenheim Museum, New York, 1963; Gallerie Maeght, Paris, 1966; Marlborough Fine Art, 1967; Marlborough-Gerson Gall., New York, 1968; Grand Palais, Paris, 1971; Kunsthalle, Düsseldorf, 1972; Metropolitan Museum, NY, 1975. Travelling exhibitions: Mannheim, Turin, Zürich, Amsterdam, 1962; Hamburg, Stockholm, Dublin, 1965. Important works include: triptychs: Three Studies for Figures at the Base of a Crucifixion, 1944; Crucifixion, 1962; Sweeney Agonistes, 1967; single oils: Painting, 1946; Man with Dog, 1953; Study after Velazquez's portrait of Pope Innocent X, 1953; Two Figures, 1953; Study for portrait of Van Gogh II, 1957; Portrait of Isabel Rawsthorne standing in a street in Soho, 1967. Paintings acquired by: Tate Gall.; Arts Council; Aberdeen, Belfast and Leeds Museums; Nat. Galls of Adelaide and Canberra; Museums in Berlin, Bochum, Düsseldorf, Hamburg, Hanover, Mannheim, Munich and Stuttgart; CNAC, Paris; MOMA, NY; Amsterdam, Rotterdam, Stockholm etc. Rubens Prize, 1966; Prize, Carnegie Inst., Pittsburgh, 1967. *Address:* c/o Marlborough Fine Art, 6 Albemarle Street, W1X 3HF.

BACON, Francis Thomas, OBE 1967; FRS 1973; consultant on fuel cells, retired; *b* 21 Dec. 1904; 2nd *s* of T. W. Bacon, Ramsden Hall, Billericay; *m* 1934, Barbara Winifred, *y d* of G. K. Papillon, Manor House, Barrasford; one *s* one *d* (and one *s* decd). *Educ:* Eton Coll.; Trinity Coll., Cambridge. With C. A. Parsons & Co. Ltd, Newcastle-on-Tyne, 1925-40 (i/c production of silvered glass reflectors, 1935-39); experimental work on hydrogen/oxygen fuel cell at King's Coll., London, for Merz & McLellan, 1940-41; Temp. Exper. Off. at HM Anti-Submarine Experimental Estbt, Fairlie, 1941-46; exper. work on hydrogen/oxygen fuel cell at Cambridge Univ., 1946-56 (for ERA); Consultant to: NRDC on fuel cells at Marshall of Cambridge Ltd, 1956-62; Energy Conversion Ltd, Basingstoke, 1962-71; Fuel Cells Ltd, AERE, 1971-72. British Assoc. Lecture, 1971; Bruno Breyer Meml Lecture and Medal, Royal Aust. Chem. Inst., 1976. S. G. Brown Award and Medal (Royal Soc.), 1965; British Silver Medal (RAeS), 1969; Churchill Gold Medal, Soc. of Engineers, 1972; Melchett Medal, Inst. of Fuel, 1972. *Publications:* chapter 5 in Fuel Cells (ed G. J. Young), 1960; chapter 4 in Fuel Cells (ed W. Mitchell), 1963; papers on fuel cells for World Power Conf., Royal Instn, Nature, two UN Confs, Amer. Inst. of Chem. Eng., Inst. of Fuel, Electrochimica Acta, Royal Soc. *Recreations:* hill walking, music, photography, fishing. *Address:* Westfield, Little Shelford, Cambridge CB2 5ES. *T:* Shelford 2244. *Club:* Athenæum.

BACON, Prof. George Edward, MA, DSc Cantab, PhD London; Professor of Physics, University of Sheffield, since 1963; *b* 5 Dec. 1917; *s* of late George H. Bacon and Lilian A. Bacon, Derby; *m* 1945, Enid Trigg; one *s* one *d*. *Educ:* Derby Sch.; Emmanuel Coll., Cambridge (Open and Sen. Schol.). Air Ministry, Telecommunications Research Estabt, 1939-46. Dep. Chief Scientific Officer, AERE, Harwell, 1946-63. FInstP. *Publications:* Neutron Diffraction, 1955; Applications of Neutron Diffraction in Chemistry, 1963; X-ray and Neutron Diffraction, 1966; Neutron Physics, 1969; Neutron Scattering in Chemistry, 1977; many scientific pubns on X-ray and neutron crystallographic studies in Proc. Royal Society, Acta Cryst., etc. *Recreations:* gardening, photography, travel. *Address:* Carr House, Hope Road, Edale, Sheffield S30 2ZE. *T:* Hop Valley 70279.

BACON, Sir Ranulph Robert Maunsell, Kt 1966; KPM 1953; Director: Securicor Ltd, since 1966; International Intelligence Inc., USA, since 1970; *b* 6 Aug. 1906; *s* of late Arthur Ranulph and Hester Mary (*née* Ayles), Westgate-on-Sea; *m* 1932, Alfreda Violet (*née* Annett); one *d* decd. *Educ:* Tonbridge Sch; Queens' Coll., Cambridge (BA). Joined Metropolitan Police, 1928; Metropolitan Police Coll., 1935 (Baton of Honour); seconded to Provost Service, 1940; Capt. 1940, Major 1941, Lieut-Col 1941; all service was in Middle East; Dep. Provost Marshal, Ninth Army, 1942; seconded to Colonial Police Service, 1943; Dep. Inspector-Gen., 1943, Inspector-Gen., 1944-47, Ceylon Police; Chief Constable of Devon, 1947-61; Asst Comr, Met. Police, 1961-66; Dep. Comr New Scotland Yard, 1966. Mem., Gaming Board, 1968-75. President: Gun Trade Assoc., 1972-77; Shooting Sports Trust, 1972-77. CStJ 1964. *Address:* 3 Royal Court, 8 King's Gardens, Hove, Sussex BN3 2PF. *T:* Brighton 732396. *Club:* United Oxford & Cambridge University.

BACON, Sir Sidney (Charles), Kt 1977; CB 1971; BSc(Eng); CEng, FIMechE, FIProdE, FTP; Managing Director, Royal Ordnance Factories, since 1972; Deputy Chairman, Royal Ordnance Factories Board, since 1972; *b* 11 Feb. 1919; *s* of Charles and Alice Bacon. *Educ:* Woolwich Polytechnic; London Univ. Military Service, 1943-48, Capt. REME. Min. of Supply, 1948-60; Asst Dir, ROF, Nottingham, 1960-61; Supt, ROF: Leeds, 1961-62; Woolwich, 1962-63; Birtley, 1965; idc, 1964; Dir of Ordnance Factories, Weapons and Fighting Vehicles, 1965-66; Dep. Controller, ROFs, 1966-69; Controller, ROFs, 1969-72. *Recreations:* golf, listening to music. *Address:* 228 Erith Road, Bexleyheath, Kent. *Club:* Shooters Hill Golf.

BADCOCK, Maj.-Gen. John Michael Watson, CB 1976; MBE 1969; Defence Adviser and Head of British Defence Liaison Staff, Canberra, 1974-77; *b* 10 Nov. 1922; *s* of late R. D. Badcock, MC, JP and Mrs J. D. Badcock; *m* 1948, Gillian Pauline (*née* Attfield); one *s* two *d*. *Educ:* Sherborne Sch.; Worcester Coll., Oxford. Enlisted in ranks (Army), 1941; commnd Royal Corps of Signals, 1942; war service UK and BAOR; Ceylon, 1945-47; served in UK, Persian Gulf, BAOR and Cyprus; Comdr 2 Inf. Bde and Dep. Constable of Dover Castle, 1968-71; Dep. Mil. Sec., 1971-72; Dir of Manning (Army), 1972-74. Major 1954; Lt-Col 1964; Brig. 1968; Maj.-Gen. 1972; psc, jssc, idc. Col Comdt, Royal Signals, 1974-. *Recreations:* Rugby football, cricket, hockey, most field sports less horsemanship. *Address:* Palmer's Lodge, Petham, Canterbury, Kent. *T:* Petham 458. *Clubs:* Royal Commonwealth Society, Lansdowne.

BADDELEY, Hermione; actress; *b* Broseley, Shropshire, 13 Nov. 1908; *d* of late W. H. Clinton-Baddeley and Louise Bourdin; *m* 1st, 1928, Hon. David Tennant (marr. diss., 1939); one *s* one *d*; 2nd, Captain J. H. Willis, MC. *Educ:* privately. Appeared on London stage in La Boîte à Joujoux, Court Theatre, 1918; 1919-23; Makebelieve, Lyric, Hammersmith, 1920; West End parts; early success as Florrie Small in The Likes of Her, St Martin's, 1923; Punchbowl revue, Palace, 1924; joined the Co-Optimists, London Pavilion, 1925; continuous appearances in West End theatres in varied plays, including The Greeks had a Word for It; Nine Sharp; Rise Above It; Sky High; Brighton Rock; one and a half years entertaining the troops; A La Carte; Grand National Night; Fallen Angels; Far East and Middle East tour in Cabaret, 1955-56; A Taste of Honey, US tour, 1961-62; The Milk Train Doesn't Stop Here Any More, (New York) 1963; The Killing of Sister George, St Martin's, 1966; The Threepenny Opera, Prince of Wales, 1972. Debut in Commercial Television, 1956; constant appearances in films and TV, 1957-61. *US TV:* Julia (Golden Globe Award, 1976); Mrs Naugutuck in Maude (comedy series) (Emmy nomination, 1976). *Films include:* Caste; Kipps; It Always Rains on Sunday; Brighton Rock; No Room at the Inn; Quartet; Passport to Pimlico; Scrooge; The Belles of St Trinian's; Midnight Lace; Room at the Top (Oscar nomination); Mary Poppins; The Unsinkable Molly Brown; Marriage on the Rocks; Harlow; Do Not Disturb; The Black Windmill. *Recreations:* swimming, reading, entertaining. *Address:* c/o Peter Campbell Personnel Management, 34 Berkeley House, Hay Hill, W1X 7LG.
See also Sir H . A . C . Rumbold , Bt .

BADDELEY, Sir John Beresford, 3rd Bt, *cr* 1922; Managing Director of Baddeley Bros (London) Ltd since 1929; *b* 23 Nov. 1899; *er s* of Sir William Baddeley, 2nd Bt, and Kate (*d* 1956), *d* of Matthew Shaw, Clapton; *S* father, 1951; *m* 1929, Nancy Winifred, *d* of Thomas Wolsey; one *s* two *d*. *Educ:* Lancing Coll. *Heir:* *s* John Wolsey Beresford Baddeley [*b* 27 Jan. 1938; *m* 1962, Sara Rosalind, *o d* of Colin Crofts, Scarborough, and Mrs John Holman, Ferring, Sussex; three *d*]. *Address:* Street Cottage, Bury, Sussex. *T:* Bury 442. *Club:* Royal Automobile.

BADDELEY, Rev. William Pye, BA; Rector of St James's, Piccadilly, since 1967; Rural Dean of Westminster (St Margaret's), since 1974; Member: London Diocesan Synod, since 1970; Bishop's Council, since 1975; *b* 20 March 1914; *s* of W. H. Clinton-Baddeley and Louise Bourdin, Shropshire; *m* 1947, Mary Frances Shirley, *d* of Col E. R. C. Wyatt, CBE, DSO; one *d*. *Educ:* Durham Univ.; St Chad's Coll., Durham; Cuddesdon Coll., Oxford. Deacon, 1941; Priest, 1942; Curate of St Luke, Camberwell, 1941-44; St Anne, Wandsworth, 1944-46; St Stephen, Bournemouth, 1946-49; Vicar of St Pancras (with St James and Christ Church from 1954), 1949-58; Dean of Brisbane, 1958-67; Commissary to: Archbishop of Brisbane, 1967-; Bishop of Wangaratta, 1970-; Bishop, later Archbishop of Papua New Guinea, 1972-; Bishop of Newcastle, NSW, 1976-. Chaplain: Elizabeth Garrett Anderson Hospital, London, 1949-

59; St Luke's Hostel, 1952-54; Qld Univ. Anglican Soc., 1960-64; St Martin's Hosp., Brisbane, 1960; London Companions of St Francis, 1968-; Lord Mayor of Westminster, 1974-75; Actors' Church Union, 1968-70; Royal Acad. of Arts, 1968-. Hon. Chaplain to: Archbishop of Brisbane (Diocesan Chaplain, 1963-67); Union Soc. of Westminster, 1972-. President: Brisbane Repertory Theatre, 1961-64; Qld Ballet Co., 1962-67; Qld Rep. Elizabethan Theatre Trust, 1963-67; Dir, Australian Elizabethan Theatre Trust, 1965-67; Chairman: Diocesan Radio and Television Council, 1961-67; weekly television Panel "Round Table", 1962-66; monthly television Panel "What Do YOU Think", 1960-67. Governor: Burlington Sch., 1967-; Archbishop Tenison's Sch., 1967-; Chairman: Assoc. for Promoting Retreats, 1967-; Trustees, Malcolm Sargent Cancer Fund for Children, 1968-; Cttee for Commonwealth Citizens in China, 1970-73; Mem. Council, Metropolitan Hosp. Sunday Fund, 1968-; Vice-Pres., Cancer Relief Appeal, 1977-. Life Governor of Thomas Coram Foundation, 1955-. ChStJ 1971 (SBStJ 1959). *Recreations:* theatre, music, photography. *Address:* St James's Rectory, 197 Piccadilly, W1V 9LF. *T:* 01-734 0956. *Clubs:* East India, Devonshire, Sports and Public Schools, Junior Carlton, Royal Over-Seas League, Arts.

BADDILEY, Prof. Sir James, Kt 1977; FRS 1961; FRSE 1962; PhD, DSc; Professor of Chemical Microbiology since 1977, Director, Microbiological Chemistry Research Laboratory, and Head of School of Chemistry, since 1968, University of Newcastle upon Tyne; *b* 15 May 1918; *s* of late James Baddiley; *m* 1944, Hazel Mary (*née* Townsend); one *s. Educ:* Manchester Grammar Sch.; Manchester University (BSc 1941, PhD 1944, DSc 1953). Imperial Chemical Industries Fellow, University of Cambridge, 1945-49; Swedish Medical Research Council Fellow, Wenner-Grens Institute for Cell Biology, Stockholm, 1947-49; Mem. of Staff, Dept of Biochemistry, Lister Institute of Preventive Medicine, London, 1949-55; Rockefeller Fellowship, Harvard Med. Sch., 1954; Prof. of Organic Chem., King's Coll., Univ. of Durham, 1955-77 (later Univ. of Newcastle upon Tyne). Member: Council, Chemical Soc., 1962-65; Cttee, Biochemical Soc., 1964-67; Enzyme Chem. and Technol Cttee, SRC 1971; Editorial Boards, Biochemical Preparations, 1960-70, Biochimica et Biophysica Acta, 1970-. Tilden Lectr, Chem. Soc., 1959; Karl Folkers Lectr in Biochemistry, Illinois Univ., 1962; Special Vis. Lectr, Dept of Microbiology, Temple Univ., Pa, 1966; Leeuwenhoek Lectr, Royal Society, 1967. Hon. Mem., Amer. Soc. Biol Chem. Meldola Medal, RIC, 1947; Corday-Morgan Medal, Chem. Soc., 1952; Davy Medal, Royal Soc., 1974. *Publications:* numerous in Journal of the Chemical Society, Nature, Biochemical Journal, etc; articles in various microbiological and biochemical reviews. *Recreations:* photography, music. *Address:* The Microbiological Chemistry Research Laboratory, The University, Newcastle upon Tyne NE1 7RU; 26 Woolsington Park South, Woolsington, Newcastle upon Tyne NE13 8BJ. *T:* Newcastle 860229.

BADEL, Alan; actor; *b* 11 Sept. 1923; *s* of Auguste Firman Joseph Badel and Elizabeth Olive Durose; *m* Yvonne Owen. *Educ:* Burnage High Sch., Manchester; Royal Acad. of Dramatic Art (Bancroft Gold Medallist). First London appearance as Pierrot in L'Enfant Prodigue, Mercury, 1941; Lennox and 1st Murderer in Macbeth, Piccadilly, 1941. Served with 6th Airborne Div., 1942-47 (appearing with Army Play Unit in Egypt, ME, and Germany). Stevie in Peace in Our Time, Lyric, 1947; Sandman in Frenzy, St Martins (and tour), 1948; Stratford-on-Avon, 1950: Claudio in Measure for Measure, Octavius in Julius Caesar, the Fool in King Lear, and others; Stratford Fest. Season, 1951: parts incl.: The Dauphin in Henry V, Ariel in The Tempest, Justice Shallow and Poins in Henry IV Parts I and II; Old Vic Seasons, 1951-53: Quince in A Midsummer Night's Dream, Romeo, François Villon in The Other Heart; Stratford, 1956: Hamlet, Berowne in Love's Labour's Lost, Lucio in Measure for Measure; Tinville in The Public Prosecutor (which he also directed), Arts, 1957; Kreton in Visit to a Small Planet, Alex in The Life of the Party, 1960; Hero in The Rehearsal, Globe, 1961 (first NY appearance in same part, 1963); John Tanner in Man and Superman, New Arts, 1965; Kean, Globe, 1971. Entered management (with Lord Furness), 1957, as Furndel Productions Ltd, and presented: Ulysses Nighttown (played Stephen Dedalus), Arts 1959 (again, in Paris and Holland); The Ark, 1959; Visit to a Small Planet, and others, 1960. Numerous film and television appearances. *Address:* ICM, 22 Grafton Street, W1.

BADEN-POWELL, family name of Baron Baden-Powell.

BADEN-POWELL, 3rd Baron, *cr* 1929, of Gilwell; **Robert Crause Baden-Powell;** Bt, *cr* 1922; *b* 15 Oct. 1936; *s* of 2nd Baron and Carine Crause Baden-Powell (*née* Boardman); *S* father, 1962; *m* 1963, Patience Hélène Mary, *d* of Major D. M.

Batty, S Rhodesia. *Educ:* Bryanston (Blandford). *Recreations:* fishing, camping, scouting. *Heir: b* Hon. David Michael Baden-Powell [*b* 11 Dec. 1940; *m* 1966, Joan Phillips, *d* of H. W. Berryman, Melbourne, Australia; two *s. Address:* Chapel Farm, Ripley, Surrey. *T:* Ripley 2262.

BADENOCH, Alec William, MA, MD, ChM, FRCS; *b* 23 June 1903; *s* of late John Alexander Badenoch, chartered accountant, Banff; *m* 1942, Jean McKinnell, MB, ChB (Edinburgh), *d* of late Alexander Brunton; three *s. Educ:* Banff Academy; Aberdeen Univ. Pres. Student Representation Council of Scotland, 1926. Served RAFVR, 1937-45, as Temp. Wing Comdr, i/c Surgical Divs, RAF Hosps Rauceby, Wroughton and St Athan; Surgeon: Royal Hosp. of St Bartholomew, 1947-68; St Peter's Hosp. for Stone and other Urological Diseases, 1946-68; Visiting Urologist: Royal Masonic Hosp., 1950-70; King Edward VII's Hosp. for Officers; Visiting Professor: Cairo, 1962; Dallas, Texas, 1967; Guest Lectr, Amer. Urological Assoc., 1968; Hon. Civilian Consultant in Urology to RAF. Hunterian Prof., RCS, 1948; Hon. Fellow, British Assoc. of Urological Surgeons (Pres., 1968-69; St Peter's Medal, 1974); Hon. FRSocMed (Hon. Treasurer 1971-76, Hon. Mem. and Past Pres. Section of Urology); Hon. Fellow, Hunterian Soc. (Pres. 1949, Vice-Pres. and Orator, 1957); Chm., Editorial Bd, British Jl of Urology, 1969-72 (Treasurer, 1961-67); Member: BMA (Vice-Pres. Section of Urology, 1955); Internat. Soc. of Urology (Treas. London Congress, 1964, British Delegate, 1966-74); (Founder Mem.) Cttee of Management, European Soc. of Urology, 1972; Council, RCS, 1963-71 (Patron, 1975); GMC, 1966-71; GDC, 1969-71. Hon. Mem. Peruvian and American Urological Assocs; Corresp. Mem. French and Mexican Urological Assocs and Amer. Assoc. of Genito Urinary Surgeons. Jt Editor, European Jl of Urology, 1974. *Publications:* Manual of Urology, 1953, 2nd edn 1974; contrib. to British Surgery, Modern Operative Surgery, and Modern Trends in Urology. Articles in scientific jls. *Recreations:* gardening, music, swimming. *Address:* 123 Harley Street, W1N 1HE. *T:* 01-935 3881. *Club:* Royal Air Force.

BADENOCH, John, DM; FRCP; Consultant Physician, Oxford Area Health Authority (Teaching); University Lecturer in Medicine, Oxford University, and Fellow of Merton College, Oxford; *b* 8 March 1920; *s* of William Minty Badenoch, MB, and Ann Dyer Badenoch (*née* Coutts); *m* 1944, Anne Newnham, *d* of Prof. Lancelot Forster; two *s* two *d. Educ:* Rugby Sch.; Oriel College, Oxford. MA; DM 1952; FRCP 1959. Rockefeller Med. Studentship, Cornell Univ. Med. Coll., 1941. Res. Asst, Nuffield Dept of Clin. Medicine, Oxford, 1949-56; Dir, Clin. Studies, Univ. of Oxford, 1954-65. Former Mem., Board of Governors of United Oxford Hosps; Mem. Board, Oxford AHA(T), 1974-. Royal College of Physicians: Pro-Censor and Censor, 1972-73; Sen. Censor and Sen. Vice-Pres., 1975-76; Goulstonian Lectr, 1960; Lumleian Lectr, 1977. Examiner in Medicine at various times for the Universities of: Oxford, Cambridge, Manchester, QUB and NUI. Member: Assoc. of Physicians of GB and Ireland; Med. Res. Soc.; British Soc. of Haematology; British Soc. of Gastroenterology. Liveryman, Soc. of Apothecaries. *Publications:* (ed jtly) Recent Advances in Gastroenterology, 1965, 2nd edn 1972; various papers in the field of gastroenterology and medicine. *Recreations:* reading, walking, natural history. *Address:* 123 Woodstock Road, Oxford OX2 6HN. *T:* Oxford 55413. *Clubs:* United Oxford & Cambridge University; Hibernian United Services (Dublin).

BADER, Group Captain Sir Douglas (Robert Steuart), Kt 1976; CBE 1956; DSO 1940; DFC 1940; FRAeS; DL; Member, Civil Aviation Authority, since 1972; Director: Trafalgar Offshore Ltd; *b* 21 Feb. 1910; *s* of Frederick Roberts Bader and Jessie Scott-Mackenzie; *m* 1st, 1933, Olive Thelma Exley Edwards (*d* 1971); no *c;* 2nd, 1973, Mrs Joan Eileen Murray. *Educ:* St Edward's Sch., Oxford; RAF Coll., Cranwell. Commissioned 1930. Lost both legs in flying accident, Dec 1931; invalided out of RAF, May 1933; joined Asiatic Petroleum Co. Ltd; re-joined RAF as Flying Officer, Nov. 1939; Flight Lieut April 1940; fought first action during evacuation of BEF from Dunkirk May-June 1940: Squadron Leader, June 1940, commanding first RAF Canadian Fighter Squadron (242); Wing Comdr, March 1941; captured 9 Aug. 1941, after collision with enemy aircraft over Bethune; released 15 April 1945 by American 1st Army from Colditz, near Leipzig (despatches thrice, DSO and Bar, DFC and Bar, Légion d'Honneur, Croix de Guerre); Group Capt. June 1945; retired 1946; rejoined Shell Petroleum Co. (late Asiatic Petroleum Co.); Man. Dir, Shell Aircraft Ltd, 1958-69, retd. Led first post-war Battle of Britain fly-past, 15 Sept. 1945. Chm., Flight Time Limitations Bd, 1974-. FRAeS 1976. DL Greater London, 1977. *Publication:* Fight for the Sky: the story of the Spitfire and the Hurricane, 1973; *relevant publication:* biography, Reach for the Sky, by Paul Brickhill. *Recreation:*

golf. *Address:* 5 Petersham Mews, Gloucester Road, SW7 5NR. *T:* 01-584 0902. *Clubs:* Buck's, Royal Air Force.

BADGE, Peter Gilmour Noto; a Metropolitan Stipendiary Magistrate, since 1975; *b* 20 Nov. 1931; *s* of late Ernest Desmond Badge, LDS and Marie Benson Badge (*née* Clough); *m* 1956, Mary Rose Noble; four *d*. *Educ:* Ruthin Sch., N Wales; Univ. of Liverpool (LLB). National Service, 1956-58: RNVR, lower deck and commnd; UK, ME and FE; RNR, 1958-62. Articled to Lt-Col E. C. Arden, Liverpool, 1950-55; solicitor, 1956; Mem., Solicitor's Dept, New Scotland Yard, 1958-61; Asst Solicitor and later Partner, 1961-75, Notary Public 1964-75, Kidd, Rapinet, Badge & Co.; Clerk to Justices, Petty Sessional Div. of Marlow, 1967-74; Lectr in Magisterial Law, Bucks Magistrates Courts Cttee, 1968-72; Sen. Solicitor to Comr and Detention Appeals Tribunal, NI, 1973-75. Mem., Cttee on Criminal Law, Law Soc., 1971-. *Recreations:* sailing, skiing, fencing, music. *Address:* West London Magistrates' Court, Southcombe Street, Kensington, W14. *Club:* Army and Navy.

BADGER, Geoffrey Malcolm, AO 1975; PhD, DSc, FRIC, FRACI, FACE, FAIM, FAA; Emeritus Professor; Vice-Chancellor, University of Adelaide, 1967-March 1977 (Deputy Vice-Chancellor, 1966-67); President, Australian Academy of Science, 1974-78; Chairman, Australian Science and Technology Council, since 1977; *b* 10 Oct. 1916; *s* of J. McD. Badger; *m* 1941, Edith Maud, *d* of Henry Chevis. *Educ:* Geelong Coll.; Gordon Inst. of Technology; Univs of Melbourne, London, Glasgow. Instructor Lieut, RN, 1943-46. Finney-Howell Research Fellow, London, 1940-41; Research Chemist, ICI, 1941-43; Research Fellow, Glasgow, 1946-49. Univ. of Adelaide: Sen. Lectr, 1949-51; Reader, 1951-54; Prof. of Organic Chemistry, 1955-64. Mem. Executive, CSIRO, 1964-65. *Publications:* Structures and Reactions of Aromatic Compounds, 1954; Chemistry of Heterocyclic Compounds, 1961; The Chemical Basis of Carcinogenic Activity, 1962; Aromatic Character and Aromaticity, 1969; (ed) Captain Cook, 1970; numerous papers in Jl Chem. Soc., etc. *Address:* 240 Childers Street, North Adelaide, SA 5006, Australia. *T:* 267-3029. *Club:* Adelaide (Adelaide).

BADHAM, Douglas George, CBE 1975; JP; DL; company director; Chairman, Development Corporation for Wales, since 1971; *b* 1 Dec. 1914; *s* of late David Badham, JP; *m* 1939, Doreen Spencer Phillips; two *d*. *Educ:* Leys Sch., Cambridge. CA. Exec. Dir, Powell Duffryn Gp, 1938-69; Chm., Nat. Health Service Staff Commn, 1972-75; Member: Wales and the Marches Telecommunications Bd, 1973-; British Gas Corp., 1974-; Forestry Commn, S Wales Reg. Adv. Cttee, 1946-76 (Chm., 1973-76); Western Region Adv. Bd, BR, 1977; Welsh Council (Chm., Industry and Planning Panel), 1971-; Nature Conservancy Council Adv. Cttee for Wales, 1974-; Council, UWIST, 1975-. JP Glamorgan, 1962; DL Mid Glamorgan, 1975; High Sheriff Mid Glamorgan, 1976. *Recreations:* forestry, trout breeding. *Address:* Plas Watford, Caerphilly, Mid Glamorgan, Wales. *T:* Caerphilly 882094. *Clubs:* Royal Automobile; Cardiff and County (Cardiff).

BADHAM, Leonard; Managing Director, J. Lyons Group of Companies, since 1977; *b* 10 June 1923; *s* of John Randall Badham and Emily Louise Badham; *m* 1944, Joyce Rose Lowrie; two *d*. *Educ:* Wandsworth Grammar Sch. Commnd E Surrey Regt, 1943; Royal W Kent Regt, 5th Indian Div., 1944-46; SO II Stats, Burma Comd, 1946-47. J. Lyons & Co. Ltd: Management Trainee, 1939; Main Bd, 1965; Chief Comptroller, 1965; Tech. and Commercial Co-ordinator, 1967; Exec. Dir, Finance and Admin, 1970; Asst Gp Man. Dir, 1971; Dep. Gp Man. Dir, 1975. Fellow, Inst. of Admin. Management; FHCIMA. *Recreations:* bridge, gardening. *Address:* 26 Vicarage Drive, East Sheen, SW14 8RX. *T:* 01-876 4373.

BADIAN, Ernst, FBA 1965; Professor of History, Harvard University, since 1971; *b* 8 Aug. 1925; *s* of Joseph Badian and Sally (*née* Horinger), Vienna (later Christchurch, NZ); *m* 1950, Nathlie Anne (*née* Wimsett); one *s* one *d*. *Educ:* Christchurch Boys' High Sch.; Canterbury Univ. Coll., Christchurch, NZ; University Coll., Oxford (Chancellor's Prize for Latin Prose, 1950; Craven Fellow, 1950; Conington Prize, 1959). MA (1st cl. hons), NZ, 1946; LitD, Victoria, NZ, 1962. BA (1st cl. hons Lit. Hum.) Oxon, 1950; MA 1954; DPhil 1956. Asst Lectr in Classics, Victoria University Coll., Wellington, 1947-48; Rome Scholar in Classics, British Sch. at Rome, 1950-52; Asst Lectr in Classics and Ancient History, Univ. of Sheffield, 1952-54; Lectr in Classics, Univ. of Durham, 1954-65; Prof. of Ancient History, Univ. of Leeds, 1965-69; Prof. of Classics and History, State Univ. of NY at Buffalo, 1969-71. Vis. Professor: Univs of Oregon, Washington and California (Los Angeles), 1961; Univ. of S Africa, 1965, 1973; Harvard, 1967; State Univ. of NY

(Buffalo), 1967-68; Heidelberg, 1973; Univ. of California (Sather Prof.), 1976. Lecturing visits to Australia, Canada, France, Germany, Holland, Israel, Italy, NZ, Rhodesia, and S Africa. Fellow, Amer. Acad. of Arts and Sciences, 1974; Corresp. Mem., Austrian Acad. of Scis, 1975. Editor, Amer. Jl of Ancient History. *Publications:* Foreign Clientelae (264-70 BC), 1958; Studies in Greek and Roman History, 1964; Polybius (The Great Histories Series), 1966; Roman Imperialism in the Late Republic, 1967 (2nd edn 1968); Publicans and Sinners, 1972; contribs to Artemis-Lexikon, Encyc. Britannica, Oxf. Class. Dictionary and to classical and historical journals. *Recreations:* travelling, reading. *Address:* Department of History, Harvard University, Cambridge, Mass 02138, USA.

BADMIN, Stanley Roy, RE 1935 (ARE 1931); (Hon. retired 1965); RWS 1939 (ARWS 1932); ARCA 1927; FSIA 1959; *b* Sydenham, 18 April 1906; 2nd *s* of Charles James and Margaret Badmin, Somersetshire; *m* 1st, 1929; one *s* one *d*; 2nd, 1950, Mrs Rosaline Flew, *widow* of Dr R. Flew; one *d* one step-*d*. *Educ:* private tutor; Royal College of Art. One man exhibns London, New York, Worthing; works bought by Liverpool, Huddersfield, Bradford, Birmingham, V & A Museum, Chicago Inst. of Art, South London Galleries, Newport, Ashmolean, Worthing, Boston Museum, London Museum, etc. *Publications:* Etched Plates; Autolithoed Educational books; Village and Town, Trees in Britain and Farm Crops in Britain; colour prints; illustrations to: British Countryside in Colour; Trees for Town & Country and Famous Trees; Shell Guide to Trees and Shrubs; The Seasons (by Ralph Wightman); Trees of Britain (Sunday Times); Ladybird Book of Trees; Readers' Digest Publications; Royles Publications. *Recreations:* painting and gardening. *Address:* Streamfield, Bignor, Pulborough, West Sussex. *T:* Sutton (Sussex) 229.

BAELZ, Rev. Canon Peter Richard; Canon of Christ Church and Regius Professor of Moral and Pastoral Theology in the University of Oxford, since 1972; *b* 27 July 1923; 3rd *s* of Eberhard and Dora Baelz; *m* 1950, Anne Thelma Cleall-Harding; three *s*. *Educ:* Dulwich Coll.; Cambridge Univ. BA 1944, MA 1948, BD 1971. Asst Curate: Bournville, 1947-50; Sherborne, 1950-52; Asst Chap. Ripon Hall, Oxford, 1952-53; Rector of Wishaw, Birmingham, 1953-56; Vicar of Bournville, 1956-60; Fellow and Dean, Jesus Coll., Cambridge, 1960-72; University Lectr in Divinity, Cambridge, 1966-72. Hulsean Lectr, 1965-66; Bampton Lectr, 1974. *Publications:* Prayer and Providence, 1968; Christian Theology and Metaphysics, 1968; The Forgotten Dream, 1975; Ethics and Belief, 1977; contributor to: Traditional Virtues Reassessed, 1964; Faith, Fact and Fantasy, 1964; The Phenomenon of Christian Belief, 1970; Christianity and Change, 1971; Christ, Faith and History, 1972. *Recreations:* walking, motoring. *Address:* Christ Church, Oxford OX1 1DP. *T:* Oxford 44317.

BAGENAL, (Philip) Hope (Edward), OBE 1956; DCM; FRIBA; architect and writer on architectural subjects; consultant in the acoustics of buildings; *b* 11 Feb. 1888; *s* of Philip Henry Bagenal; *m* 1914, Alison Mary, *d* of Stuart Hogg; two *s* one *d*. *Educ:* Uppingham Sch.; Leeds Univ.; Architectural Assoc. Sch. Articled to Niven & Wigglesworth, FFRIBA. War Service, France, RAMC 27th F. Ambulance. RIBA Prize Essay and Silver Medal; holder of Athens Bursary, etc. Acoustic Consultant for: Free Trade Hall, Manchester; Guild Hall, Portsmouth; Coventry Hippodrome; Fairfield Halls, Croydon; Royal Festival Hall, etc. *Publications:* Fields and Battlefields, 1918; Sonnets in War and Peace, 1940; Practical Acoustics and Planning against Noise; (With Robert Atkinson) Theory and Elements of Architecture, 1926; (with late Dr Alex. Wood) Planning for Good Acoustics, 1931. *Address:* Leaside, Hertingfordbury, Hertford.

BAGGALEY, Ernest James; Bursar of Chichester Theological College, 1968-77, retired; *b* 2 June 1900; *er s* of A. H. Baggaley, Wokefield, Mortimer, Berks; *m* 1929, Sylvia Austen Bell, LRAM; one *s* one *d*. *Educ:* University Coll., Reading (BSc London). Asst Master (later Second Master), Bembridge Sch., IOW, 1923-41; Asst Master (later Second Master) Queen Elizabeth Grammar Sch., Wakefield, 1941-56, Headmaster, 1956-64. Former Mem. of Selection Board, Voluntary Service Overseas. *Publication:* A Geography of New Zealand, 1967. *Recreations:* walking, gardening, writing autobiography of early years, 1910-20. *Address:* 57 Cedar Drive, Chichester, West Sussex. *T:* Chichester 82624.

BAGGE, Sir John (Alfred Picton), 6th Bt *cr* 1867; ED; *b* 27 Oct. 1914; *e s* of Sir Picton Bagge, 5th Bt, CMG, and Olive Muriel Mary (*d* 1965), *d* of late Samuel Mendel; *S* father, 1967; *m* 1939, Elizabeth Helena (Lena), *d* of late Daniel James Davies, CBE, Comr for Newfoundland in London; three *s* three *d*. *Educ:* Eton and abroad. Served Inns of Court Regt, 1936-39; commnd into Cheshire Yeo., 1939; served War of 1939-45, Palestine, Sudan, Liberation Campaign of Ethiopia; Major 1941; GSO 2, Brit. Mil. Mission to Ethiopia, 1941-44; GSO 2, HQ, E Africa Comd Liaison with French, 1944; Mil. Asst to Brit. Comdr Allied Control Commn for Bulgaria, 1944-45; GSO 2, War Office, 1945. KStJ 1975; Chm. Council of St John in Norfolk, 1969. Vice-Chm., W Norfolk DC, 1973-76, Chm., 1976-77; High Sheriff of Norfolk, 1977. *Recreations:* flying, shooting, ski-ing and water ski-ing. *Heir: s* (John) Jeremy (Picton) Bagge [*b* 21 June 1945; Chartered Accountant, 1968]. *Address:* Stradsett Hall, Kings Lynn, Norfolk. *T:* Fincham 215. *Club:* Allsorts (Norfolk).

BAGGLEY, Charles David Aubrey, MA; Headmaster of Bolton School since 1966; *b* 1 Feb. 1923; *s* of A. C. and M. Baggley, Bradford, Yorks; *m* 1949, Marjorie Asquith Wood, *d* of M. H. Wood, Harrogate; one *s* one *d. Educ:* Bradford Grammar Sch.; King's Coll., Cambridge (1942 and 1945-47) (Exhibitioner in Classics, Scholar in History; Class I, Part II of Historical Tripos, 1947; BA 1947, MA 1952). Temp. Sub. Lieut, RNVR, 1942-45. History Master, Clifton Coll., 1947-50; Head of History Side, Dulwich Coll., 1950-57; Headmaster, King Edward VII Sch., Lytham, 1957-66. Chm., HMC, 1978. Member: Bolton Civic Trust; Bolton Branch, Historical Assoc. *Recreations:* walking, gardening, reading. *Address:* Leverhouse, Greenmount Lane, Bolton, Lancs. *T:* Bolton 40202 (School), Bolton 40607 (Home).

BAGIER, Gordon Alexander Thomas; MP (Lab) Sunderland South since 1964; *b* July 1924; *m* 1949, Violet Sinclair; two *s* two *d. Educ:* Pendower Secondary Technical Sch., Newcastle upon Tyne. Signals Inspector, British Railways; Pres., Yorks District Council, NUR, 1962-64. Mem. of Keighley Borough Council, 1956-60; Mem. of Sowerby Bridge Urban Council, 1962-65. PPS to Home Secretary, 1968-69. *Address:* House of Commons, SW1; Rahana, Whickham Highway, Dunston, Gateshead, Durham.

BAGLEY, Desmond; professional novelist since 1962; *b* Kendal, 29 Oct. 1923; *s* of John Bagley and Hannah Marie Bagley (*née* Whittle); *m* 1960, Joan Margaret (*née* Brown). *Educ:* spottily, mainly by reading and travel. British Aircraft Industry, 1940-46. Travelled overland to Africa, 1947; worked in: Uganda, 1947; Kenya, 1948; Rhodesia, 1949; S Africa, 1950-64; variety of jobs incl. nightclub photographer, film scenario writer; freelance journalist from 1956, contrib. S African press; travels extensively. Member: Soc. Authors; Crime Writers' Assoc.; Mystery Writers of America; Writers' Guild (US). *Publications:* The Golden Keel, 1963; High Citadel, 1965; Wyatt's Hurricane, 1966; Landslide, 1967; The Vivero Letter, 1968; The Spoilers, 1969; Running Blind, 1970; The Freedom Trap, 1971; The Tightrope Men, 1973; The Snow Tiger, 1975; The Enemy, 1977; work trans. into many languages. *Recreations:* sailing, travel, military history, reading, recreational mathematics, computer programming. *Address:* Câtel House, Les Rohais de haut, St Andrew, Guernsey, CI. *T:* Guernsey 54345. *Clubs:* Authors'; Aero (Johannesburg); Antarctic Press (McMurdo Sound).

BAGNALL, Frank Colin, CBE 1950; Commercial Director, Imperial Chemical Industries Ltd, 1965-70, also Finance Director, 1967-68; Director, African Explosives and Chemical Industries Ltd, 1965-70; *b* 6 Nov. 1909; *s* of late Francis Edward Bagnall, OBE and Edith Bagnall; *m* 1st, 1933, Ethel Hope (*née* Robertson) (killed by enemy action, 1941), Blechingley; 2nd, 1941, Rona (*née* Rooker Roberts) (marr. diss. 1975), Belmont, Mill Hill; one *s* one *d;* 3rd, 1975, Christine (*née* Gerrard), Westhill, Ledbury. *Educ:* Repton; Brasenose Coll., Oxford (MA); Dept of Business Administration, London Sch. of Economics. ICI Ltd, 1932-38; Urwick, Orr and Partners, 1938-40. War Office, 1940-42; British Nylon Spinners: Dir and Gen.-Man., 1944-45, Man. Dir, 1945-64; Non-Exec. Dir, ICI, 1964. Mem., Oxford Univ. Appts Cttee, 1948-69; Governor, Ashridge Coll., 1958-70; Chm. Regular Forces Resettlement Cttee for Wales, 1958-68. Life Governor, University Coll. of S Wales and Monmouthshire (Pres., 1963-68); Chm. Wales Business Training Cttee, 1946-49; Founder Mem., BIM (Mem. Council, 1949-52); Dir Oxford Univ. Business Summer Sch., 1954; Mem. Govt Cttee of Enquiry into Electricity Supply Industry, 1954-55; Chm. SW Reg. Council, FBI, 1956-57; Mem. Air Transport Licensing Bd, 1960-64; Chm. Man-Made Fibres Producers Cttee, 1961-65; Vice-Pres. British Man-Made Fibres Fedn, 1965-70 (Chm. 1963-65); Pres. Textile Inst., 1964-65. Hon. LLD, Wales, 1969. OStJ. *Address:* Vermont, Budleigh Salterton, Devon. *T:* Budleigh Salterton 3068. *Club:* Boodle's.

BAGNALL, Kenneth Reginald, QC 1973; a Deputy Judge of the Crown Court, since 1975; *b* 26 Nov. 1927; *s* of Reginald and Elizabeth Bagnall; *m* 1st, 1955, Margaret Edith Wall; one *s* one

d; 2nd, 1963, Rosemary Hearn; one *s* one *d. Educ:* King Edward VI Sch., Birmingham; Univ. of Birmingham. LLB (Hons). Served Royal Air Force; Pilot Officer, 1947, Flt Lt, 1948. Called to the Bar, Gray's Inn, 1950. Chm., Hurstwood Timber Co. Ltd, 1972-. Freeman and Liveryman, Barber-Surgeons' Co., 1972. *Publications:* Guide to Business Tenancies, 1956; Atkins Court Forms and Precedents (Town Planning), 1973. *Recreations:* yachting, motoring, travel. *Address:* 11 King's Bench Walk, Temple, EC4Y 7EQ. *T:* 01-353 2484. *Clubs:* Royal Thames Yacht; Island Sailing (Cowes).

BAGNALL, Maj.-Gen. Nigel Thomas, MC 1950 and Bar 1953; Assistant Chief of Defence Staff (Policy), Ministry of Defence, since 1978; *b* 10 Feb. 1927; *s* of Lt-Col Harry Stephen Bagnall and Marjory May Bagnall; *m* 1959, Anna Caroline Church; two *d. Educ:* Wellington Coll. Joined Army, 1945; commnd Green Howards, 1946; Palestine, 1946-48, 6th Airborne Div.; Malaya, 1949-53, Green Howards; GSO1 (Intell.), Dir of Borneo Ops, 1966-67; comd 4/7 Royal Dragoon Guards, NI and BAOR, 1967-69; Sen. Directing Staff (Army), Jt Services Staff Coll., 1970; comd Royal Armoured Corps HQ1 (Br.) Corps, 1970-72; Defence Fellow, Balliol Coll., Oxford, 1972-73; Sec., Chief of Staff Cttee, 1973-75; GOC 4th Div., 1975-77. *Recreations:* country pursuits. *Address:* Blackwell Lodge, Chesham, Bucks HP5 1TN. *T:* Little Chalfont 2221. *Club:* Cavalry and Guards.

BAGNALL, Richard Maurice, MBE 1945; Director since 1969, a Managing Director since 1974 and Deputy Chairman since 1976, Tube Investments Ltd; *b* 20 Nov. 1917; *s* of late Francis Edward Bagnall, OBE and Edith Bagnall; *m* 1946, Irene Pickford; one *s* one *d. Educ:* Repton. Served War, 1939-45: RA, Shropshire Yeomanry, 1939-43 (despatches); Bde Major, 6 AGRA Italy, 1943-45. Joined Tube Investments Ltd, 1937. Chm., Round Oak Steel Works Ltd, 1977- (Dir, 1974-). Bronze Star, USA, 1945. *Recreations:* golf, gardening, photography. *Address:* Oak House Farm, Himbleton, Droitwich, Worcs. *Club:* MCC.
See also F. C. Bagnall.

BAGNALL, Rt. Rev. Walter Edward, DD; *b* 1903. *Educ:* Masonic School, Dublin, Ireland; University of Western Ontario; Huron College, London, Ont. BA, Univ. of Western Ontario, 1927; Licentiate in Theology, Huron Coll., 1927. Deacon, 1927; Priest, 1928; Curate of All Saints, Windsor, Ont, 1927-28; Incumbent of St Mark's, London, Ont, 1928-30; Rector of St John's, Preston, Ont, Canada, 1930-36; Rural Dean of Waterloo, Ont, 1932-36; Rector of All Saints, Hamilton, Ont, 1936-40; Rector of St George's, St Catharine's, Ont, 1940-47; Canon of Niagara, 1944-47; Dean of Niagara and Rector of Ch. Ch. Cathedral, Hamilton, 1947-49; Bishop of Niagara, 1949-73. Hon. degrees: DD Univ. of Western Ontario, 1949; DD Trinity Coll., Toronto, 1953; DCL Bishops Univ., Lennoxville, 1956; LLD McMaster Univ., 1959. *Address:* 252 James Street North, Hamilton, Ont, Canada.

BAGNOLD, Enid, (Lady Jones), CBE 1976; writer; *b* 1889; *d* of late Colonel A. H. Bagnold, CB, CMG; *m* 1920, Sir Roderick Jones, KBE (*d* 1962), for 25 years Chairman of Reuters; three *s* one *d. Educ:* Prior's Field, Godalming; Paris; Marburg. *Publications: general:* A Diary Without Dates, 1916; Sailing Ships (poems), 1917; *novels:* The Happy Foreigner, 1920; Serena Blandish (or the Difficulty of Getting Married), 1924; Alice and Thomas and Jane, 1930; National Velvet, 1935 (filmed and TV); The Squire (in US, The Door of Life), 1938; The Loved and Envied, 1951; The Girl's Journey, 1956; *plays:* Lottie Dundass, (perf. Vaudeville, 1943); National Velvet, (perf. Embassy, 1945); Poor Judas, (perf. Arts, 1951; Arts Theatre Prize, with John Whiting, 1951); Gertie, (perf. New York, 1952; perf. London as Little Idiot); The Chalk Garden, 1956 (perf. New York and London, 1956; Award of Merit Medal, Amer. Acad. of Arts and Letters); The Last Joke, (perf. Phoenix, 1960); The Chinese Prime Minister, (perf. New York, 1964, London, 1965); Call me Jacky, (perf. Oxford, 1967); Four Plays, 1970; A Matter of Gravity, NY, 1975 (tour, with Katharine Hepburn, 1976-77); *translation:* Alexander of Asia (from Princess Marthe Bibesco, Alexandre Asiatique), 1955; *autobiography:* Enid Bagnold's Autobiography, 1969. *Recreations:* "as above." *Address:* North End House, Rottingdean, Sussex, BN2 7HA. *T:* Brighton 32337.

BAGNOLD, Brig. Ralph Alger, OBE 1941; FRS 1944; Consultant on movement of sediments by wind and water, since 1956; Fellow of Imperial College, University of London, since 1971; *b* 3 April 1896; *s* of late Col A. H. Bagnold, CB, CMG; *m* 1946, Dorothy Alice, *d* of late A. E. Plank; one *s* one *d. Educ:* Malvern College; Royal Military Academy, Woolwich; Gonville and Caius Coll., Cambridge. Commission RE, 1915; Capt, 1918; transferred Royal Corps of Signals, 1920; Major, 1927; retired, 1939. Served European War, Western Front, 1915-18 (despatches); North-West Frontier of India, 1930 (despatches). Organised and led numerous explorations on Libyan Desert and elsewhere, 1925-32; Founder's Medal of Royal Geographical Soc., 1935. Called up, 1939. Raised and commanded Long Range Desert Group in Middle East, 1940-41 (despatches); Deputy Signal-Officer-in-Chief, Middle East, 1943-44; released from Army Service, 1944. G. K. Warren Prize, US Acad. of Sciences, 1969; Penrose Medal, Geolog. Soc. of America, 1970; Wollaston Medal, Geolog. Soc. of London, 1971. *Publications*: Libyan Sands, 1935; Physics of Blown Sand and Desert Dunes, 1941; papers, etc, on deserts, hydraulics, and beach formation. *Recreations*: exploration, research. *Address*: Rickwoods, Mark Beech, near Edenbridge, Kent. *T*: Cowden 516. *Club*: Athenæum.

BAGOT, family name of **Baron Bagot.**

BAGOT, 8th Baron *cr* 1780; **Reginald Walter Bagot;** Bt 1627; *b* 24 Aug. 1897; *s* of Charles Frederick Heneage Bagot (*d* 1939) (4th *s* of *g s* of 1st Baron) and Florence Eleanor (*née* Bagot) (*d* 1940); *S* brother, 1973; *m* 1st, 1922, Winifred Gwyneth Bowen (marr. diss. 1934); 2nd, 1934, Millicent Brenda, *o d* of late Henry White Bowden. *Educ*: Wellington. Major, Royal Marines, retired. *Heir: half-b* Heneage Charles Bagot [*b* 11 June 1914; *m* 1939, Muriel Patricia Moore, *y d* of late Maxwell James Moore Boyle; one *s* one *d*]. *Address*: Tower House, Clarendon Gardens, Southsea, Hants.

BAGRIT, Sir Leon, Kt 1962; Chairman, Elliot-Automation Ltd, 1963-73 (Deputy Chairman from its formation, 1957, until 1962); Director, Technology Investments Ltd, since 1963; *b* 13 March 1902; *s* of Manuel and Rachel Bagrit; *m* 1926, Stella Feldman; two *d*. *Educ*: St Olave's; London Univ. Organised the first company in Europe devoted to automation. Mem., Council for Scientific and Industrial Research, 1963-65; Mem., Advisory Council on Technology, 1964-. Dir, Royal Opera House, Covent Garden, 1962-70; Founder, Friends of Covent Garden, Chm., 1962-69. Reith Lecturer, 1964. RSA Albert Medal, 1965. DUniv. Surrey, 1966; DSc Univ. Reading, 1968. *Publication*: The Age of Automation, 1966. *Recreations*: music and visual arts. *Address*: 80F Eaton Square, SW1W 9AP. *Club*: East India, Devonshire, Sports and Public Schools.

BAILEY, family name of **Baron Glanusk.**

BAILEY, Alan Marshall; Under-Secretary, HM Treasury, since 1973; *b* 26 June 1931; *s* of John Marshall Bailey and Muriel May Bailey; *m* 1959, Stella Mary Scott; three *s*. *Educ*: Bedford Sch.; St John's and Merton Colls, Oxford (MA, BPhil). Harmsworth Senior Scholarship, 1954; Harkness Commonwealth Fellowship, USA, 1963-64. Principal Private Sec. to Chancellor of the Exchequer, 1971-73. *Recreations*: sailing, carpentry, children's homework. *Address*: 117 Dacre Park, SE13 5BZ. *T*: 01-852 8680.

BAILEY, Arthur, OBE 1945; FRIBA 1946; Architect; *s* of Charles Hill and Winnifred Bailey; *m* 1930, Phyllis, *d* of William and Harriet Martin; one *s*. Consulting Architect to: King George's Fields Foundn; London Dio.; Rochester Dio.; Min. of Transport (Bridges); GLC (Housing); Worshipful Co. of Vintners; London Electricity Bd; Nat. Council of Social Service; Church Pastoral-Aid Soc; Lloyds Bank Ltd; Hambros Bank Ltd; Nat. Deposit Friendly Soc.; ICAA; Commissions include: remodelling and extensions, Sheffield Cath. (Civic Trust Award, 1969); rebuilding St Nicholas Cole Abbey (Wren) London (Civic Trust Award, 1967); re-building and remodelling St George-in-the-East (Hawksmoor), Stepney (Civic Trust Award, 1967); Churches: New Dutch, Austin Friars, EC2; St James-the-Less, Bethnal Green; St Mary's, Shortlands, Kent; Holy Trinity, Gillingham (Civic Trust Award, 1969); Baptist, Norwood and Paddington; London Electricity Bd: Divl Offices, Ilford and Bexleyheath; Meter Test Stn and Labs, Bexleyheath, also Stores; Offices: Austin Friars; Holborn Circus; St Peter's Square, Manchester; Church Pastoral-Aid Soc., Fleet Street; Divl Offices for Nat. Deposit Friendly Soc. in various cities; new HQ, CMS, SE1; Bridges: Stratford-upon-Avon; Ross-on-Wye; Maidstone By-Pass; M4, Maidenhead; M6, Cheshire and Westmorland; Housing for: LCC, Mortimer Crescent, Tower Hamlets, Hawgood Street; West Ham Corp.; Sevenoaks RDC; Brit. Drug Houses Ltd; Tower Court Flats, Bournemouth; Convalescent Home, Portal House, Bournemouth; Arts Block, Highgate Sch.; Pilgrims Sch., Seaford, and Edith Edwards House Sch., Banstead, ICAA; Highgate Sch. Swimming Bath; many private commissions. Min. of Lab. and Nat. Service, 1940-45; Chief Inspector, Building Labour Supply, and Advisor on War Building Programme. Prize Winner of Open Architectural Competitions: Swansea City Hall, Coun. Offices and Law Cts; Wimbledon Town Hall; Wiggeston Gram. Sch., Leicester;

Bradford Civic Centre Improvement Scheme; Wolverhampton Town Hall; Overhead Motorway; Liverpool RC Cathedral. Member: Architects' Registration Coun. (RIBA Rep.); and Finance Cttee (Vice-Chm.); RIBA Practice Cttee (Vice-Chm. and Past Chm.); Councillor, Artists General Benevolent Instn; Hon. Architect to: ICAA; Nat. Council of Social Service; Queen Alexandra's House; Exhibitor, Royal Academy (Water Colours and Architecture). President's Certificate, 1970, for work with Nat. Playing Fields Assoc. Officer, Order of Orange Nassau, 1954. *Publications*: papers in learned jls. *Recreations*: water colours, fly-fishing. *Address*: 48 Tower Court, West Cliff Road, Bournemouth, Dorset BH2 5HA. *T*: Bournemouth 23991. *Club*: Athenæum.

BAILEY, Brian Harry, OBE 1976; JP; South West District Organisation Officer, National and Local Government Officers' Association (NALGO), since 1951; Chairman, South Western Regional Health Authority, since 1975; *b* 25 March 1923; *s* of Harry Bailey and Lilian (*née* Pulfer); *m* 1948, Nina Olive Sylvia (*née* Saunders); two *d*. *Educ*: Lowestoft Grammar Sch. RAF, 1941-45. S Western Reg. Sec., TUC, 1968-. Member: Somerset CC, 1966-; SW Econ. Planning Council, 1969-. Vice-Chm., BBC Radio Bristol Adv. Council, 1971-; Mem., BBC West Reg. Adv Council, 1973-. JP Somerset, 1964. *Recreations*: football and cricket (watching), tennis (playing), music. *Address*: Runnerstones, 32 Stonegallows, Taunton, Somerset. *T*: Taunton 46265. *Club*: Wyvern (Taunton).

BAILEY, D(avid) R(oy) Shackleton, LittD; FBA 1958; Professor of Greek and Latin, Harvard University, since 1975; *b* 10 Dec. 1917; *y s* of late Rev. J. H. Shackleton Bailey, DD, and Rosamund Maud (*née* Giles); *m* 1967, Hilary Ann (marr. diss. 1974), *d* of Leonard Sidney and Margery Bardwell. *Educ*: Lancaster Royal Grammar Sch.; Gonville and Caius Coll., Cambridge. Fellow of Gonville and Caius Coll., 1944-55, Praelector, 1954-55; Fellow and Dir of Studies in Classics, Jesus Coll., Cambridge, 1955-64; Visiting Lecturer in Classics, Harvard Coll., 1963; Fellow and Dep. Bursar, Gonville and Caius Coll., 1964; Senior Bursar 1965-68; Univ. Lectr in Tibetan, 1948-68; Prof. of Latin, Univ. of Michigan, 1968-74. Andrew V. V. Raymond Vis. Prof., State Univ. of NY at Buffalo, 1973-74. *Publications*: The Satapañcāśatka of Mātrceta, 1951; Propertiana, 1956; Towards a Text of Cicero, *ad Atticum*, 1960; Ciceronis Epistulae ad Atticum IX-XVI, 1961; Cicero's Letters to Atticus, Vols I and II, 1965; Vol. V, 1966, Vol. VI, 1967, Vols III and IV, 1968, Vol. VII, 1970; Cicero, 1971; Two Studies in Roman Nomenclature, 1976; Cicero: *Epistulae ad Familiares*, 2 vols, 1977; articles in Classical and Orientalist periodicals. *Recreation*: cats. *Address*: Department of Classics, Harvard University, Cambridge, Mass 02138, USA.

BAILEY, Rev. Dr (Derrick) Sherwin; Non-residentiary Canon of Wells Cathedral and Prebendary of Ashill, since 1975; *b* 30 June 1910; *s* of William Thomas and Ellen Mary Bailey, Alcester, Warwicks; *m* 1st, 1939, Philippa Eleanor (*d* 1964), *d* of Capt. Philip James and Eleanor Frances Vandeleur Green; one *s* two *d*; 2nd, 1966, Morag Stuart Macdonald, MD, DPM. *Educ*: The Grammar Sch., Alcester, Warwks; Lincoln Theological Coll.; Edinburgh Univ. In business, 1928-40; ACII 1934; Linc. Theol Coll., 1940-42; Univ. of Edin., PhD 1947; DLitt, 1962; Fellow of Eugenics Soc., 1957-74. Deacon, 1942; Priest, 1943; Curate, Mablethorpe St Mary and Theddlethorpe St Helen with Theddlethorpe All Saints, 1942-44; Chaplain to Anglican students at Univ. and Colls of Edinburgh, and Curate of St John Evang., Edin., 1944-51; Anglican Lectr in Divinity, Moray House Trg Coll., Edin., 1948-51; Central Lectr, C of E Moral Welfare Counc., 1951-55; Actg Educ. Sec., 1954-55; Study Sec., 1955-59; Permission to officiate in Dio. B'ham, 1951-59; Rector of Lyndon with Manton, Martinsthorpe and Gunthorpe, 1959-62; Chancellor of Wells, and Prebendary of Litton, 1962-69; Canon Residentiary of Wells Cathedral, 1962-74; Precentor of Wells and Prebendary of Whitchurch, 1968-74. Select Preacher, Univ. of Camb., 1963. Examining Chaplain to Bishop of Bath and Wells, 1963-76. *Publications*: Sponsors at Baptism and Confirmation, 1952; Thomas Becon and the Reformation of the Church in England, 1952; The Mystery of Love and Marriage, 1952; Homosexuality and the Western Christian Tradition, 1955; Sexual Offenders and Social Punishment, 1956; The Man-Woman Relation in Christian Thought, 1959; Common Sense about Sexual Ethics, 1962; (Joint-Author) Celibacy and Marriage, 1944; (ed) Wells Cathedral Chapter Act Book 1666-1683, 1973; contributor: They Stand Apart, 1955; The Human Sum, 1957; Die Religion in Geschichte und Gegenwart, 1959; Westminster Dict. of Christian Educ., 1961; Dictionary of Christian Ethics, 1967; Sexual Ethics and Christian Responsibility, 1970; Oxford Dictionary of the Christian Church, 1974; also contrib. to: Theology; Journal of Ecclesiastical History; Church Quarterly Review; Scottish Jl of

Theol.; London Quarterly and Holborn Review; The Churchman, etc. *Recreations:* stamp collecting, railways. *Address:* 23 Kippax Avenue, Wells, Somerset BA5 2TT. *T:* Wells 75061.

BAILEY, Sir Derrick Thomas Louis, 3rd Bt, *cr* 1919; DFC; *b* 15 Aug. 1918; 2nd *s* of Sir Abe Bailey, 1st Bt, KCMG; *S* half-brother, 1946; *m* 1946, Katharine Nancy Stormonth Darling; four *s* one *d. Educ:* Winchester. Engaged in farming. *Recreations:* all sports, all games. *Heir: s* John Richard Bailey [*b* 11 June 1947; *m* 1977, Jane, *o d* of John Pearson Gregory]. *Address:* de Poort, Colesberg, Cape, South Africa. *Club:* Rand (Johannesburg).

BAILEY, Desmond Patrick; His Honour Judge Bailey; a Circuit Judge (formerly Judge of County Courts), since 1965; *b* 6 May 1907; 3rd *s* of Alfred John Bailey, Bowdon, Cheshire, and of Ethel Ellis Johnson; unmarried. *Educ:* Brighton Coll.; Queens' Coll., Cambridge (BA, LLB). Called to Bar, Inner Temple, 1931. Northern Circuit. Served War of 1939-45: Rifle Brigade, Lancashire Fusiliers, Special Operations Executive, North Africa, Italy (Major). Recorder of Carlisle, 1963-65. *Recreations:* cricket, fishing, gardening. *Address:* Chaseley, Bowdon, Cheshire. *T:* 061-928 0059. *Club:* St James's (Manchester).

BAILEY, Sir Donald Coleman, Kt 1946; OBE 1944; JP; *b* 15 Sept. 1901; *s* of J. H. Bailey, Rotherham, Yorkshire; *m* Phyllis (*d* 1971), *d* of Charles Frederick Andrew, Wick, Bournemouth; one *s. Educ:* The Leys, Cambridge; Univ. of Sheffield (BEng). Posts: Rowntree & Co. Ltd, York, Efficiency Dept; London Midland & Scottish Rly, Civil Engineers Dept; City Engineer's Dept, Sheffield; Dir, Military Engineering Experimental Estabt; Dean, RMCS, 1962-66. Hon. FIW; FIStructE; MICE; Hon. Member: Instn of Royal Engrs; Inst. of Engrg Designers. Hon. DEng Sheffield, 1946. JP Bournemouth, 1946. Commander of the Order of Orange-Nassau, 1947. *Recreation:* golf. *Address:* 14 Viking Close, Southbourne, Bournemouth. *T:* Bournemouth 49181.

BAILEY, Air Vice-Marshal Dudley Graham, CBE 1970; Director General of Personal Services (RAF), Ministry of Defence, since 1976; *b* 12 Sept. 1924; *s* of P. J. Bailey and D. M. Bailey (*née* Taylor); *m* 1948, Dorothy Barbara Lovelace-Hunt; two *d. Educ:* Christ's Coll., Finchley; Teignmouth Grammar Sch. Pilot trng, Canada, 1943-45; Intell. Officer, Air HQ Italy, 1946-47 and HQ 23 Gp, 1948-49; Berlin Airlift, 1949; Flt Comdr No 50 and 61 Sqdns, Lincolns, 1950-52; exchange duties, USAF, B-36 aircraft, 1952-54; Canberra Sqdn: Flt Comdr, 1955; Sqdn Comdr, 1956; Air Min., 1956-58; psc (m) 1959; OC No 57 (Victor) Sqdn, 1960-62; Air Warfare course, Manby, 1962; Wing Comdr Ops, HQ Air Forces Middle East, 1963-65; MoD Central Staffs, 1965-66; MoD (Air) Directorate of Air Staff Plans, 1966-68; OC RAF Wildenrath, 1968-70; Sen. Personnel Staff Officer, HQ Strike Comd, 1970-71; Royal Coll. of Defence Studies, 1972; Dir of Personnel (Air), RAF, 1972-74; SASO, RAF Germany, 1974-75; Dep. Comdr, RAF Germany, 1975-76. *Recreations:* music, photography. *Address:* Brook Cottage, West End, Brampton, Hunts. *T:* Huntingdon 54017. *Club:* Royal Air Force.

BAILEY, Eric; Director, Plymouth Polytechnic, 1970-74, retired; *b* 2 Nov. 1913; *s* of Enoch Whittaker Bailey, Overton Hall, Sandbach, Cheshire; *m* 1942, Dorothy Margaret Laing, Stockport; one *s* one *d. Educ:* King's Sch., Macclesfield; Manchester Univ. BSc Hons; CEng, FRIC, MICHemE; DipEd. Lectr, Stockport Coll. of Technology, 1936-41; Industrial Chemist, 1941-45; Lectr, Enfield Coll. of Technology, 1945-46; Vice-Principal, Technical Coll., Worksop, 1946-51; Principal: Walker Technical Coll., Oakengates, Salop, 1951-59; Plymouth Coll. of Technology, 1959-69. *Recreations:* putting colour into gardens, photography, pursuing leisure and voluntary activities. *Address:* 3 St Bridget Avenue, Crownhill, Plymouth, Devon. *T:* Plymouth 771426. *Club:* Rotary (Plymouth).

BAILEY, George Leo, CBE 1952; MSc, FIM; Director, British Non-Ferrous Metals Research Association, 1944-66; *b* 1 July 1901; *s* of late Charles and Annie Bailey; *m* 1925, Blanche Joy, *d* of late J. A. Pearce; one *s* one *d. Educ:* King Edward VI Grammar Sch., Birmingham; Birmingham Univ. Metallurgist, Research Dept, Woolwich, 1922; Chief Development Officer, BNFMRA, 1930-44. Past-Pres. Inst. of Metals and of Instn of Metallurgists. Hon. DMet (Sheffield). *Publications:* The Casting of Brass Ingots (with R. Genders). Papers on metallurgical and related subjects in Jl of Inst. of Metals and other scientific instns. *Recreations:* walking and bridge. *Address:* Broomfield, Box Lane, Hemel Hempstead, Herts. *T:* Hemel Hempstead 52488.

BAILEY, Harold, CMG 1960; Under-Secretary, Department of Trade and Industry, 1970-74, retired; *b* 26 Feb. 1914; *yr s* of late John Bailey and Elizabeth Watson, Preston, Lancashire; *m* 1946, Rosemary Margaret, *d* of Harold and Irene Brown, Shotesham St Mary, Norfolk; two *s* one *d. Educ:* Preston Grammar Sch.; Christ Church, Oxford. Asst Principal Air Ministry, 1937; Principal, Min. of Aircraft Production, 1942; Served, Royal Air Force, 1942-45; Private Sec. to Minister of Supply and Aircraft Production, 1945-47; Asst Sec., 1947; Min. of Supply Rep. and Adviser (Defence Supplies) to UK High Comr, Ottawa, 1953-55; Under-Secretary: Ministry of Supply, 1957; BoT, 1958; British Senior Trade Comr in India, and Economic Adviser to the British High Comr, 1958-63. *Address:* 83 Redington Road, NW3. *T:* 01-435 8916.

BAILEY, Sir Harold (Walter), Kt 1960; FBA 1944; MA, W Aust.; MA, DPhil Oxon; Professor of Sanskrit, Cambridge Univ., 1936-67, Professor Emeritus, 1967; *b* Devizes, Wilts, 16 Dec. 1899. Was Lecturer in Iranian Studies at Sch. of Oriental Studies. Member of: Danish Academy, 1946; Norwegian Academy, 1947; Kungl. Vitterhets Historie och Antikvitets Akademien, Stockholm, 1948; Governing Body, SOAS, Univ. of London, 1946-70; L'Institut de France; Associé étranger, Académie des Inscriptions et Belles-Lettres, 1968. President: Philological Soc., 1948-52; Royal Asiatic Society, 1964-67 (Gold Medal, RAS, 1972); Soc. for Afghan Studies, 1972. FAHA 1971; Hon. Fellow: SOAS, London Univ., 1963-; Queens' Coll., Cambridge, 1967; St Catherine's Coll., Oxford, 1976. Hon. DLitt: W Aust., 1963; ANU, 1970; Oxon, 1976. *Publications:* in Bulletin of Sch. of Oriental Studies, Journal of Royal Asiatic Soc., Zeitschrift der Deutschen Morgenländischen Gesellschaft, etc. Codices Khotanenses, 1938; Zoroastrian Problems in the Ninth Century Books, 1943; Khotanese Texts I, 1945; Khotanese Buddhist Texts, 1951; Indoscythian Studies, Khotanese Texts II, 1953; III, 1956; IV, 1961; V, 1963; VI, 1967; Corpus inscriptionum iranicarum, Saka Documents, Portfolios I-IV, 1960-67; Saka Documents, text volume, 1968. *Address:* Queens' College, Cambridge.

BAILEY, Jack Arthur; Secretary, MCC, since 1974; Secretary, International Cricket Conference, since 1974; *b* 22 June 1930; *s* of Horace Arthur and Elsie Winifred Bailey; *m* 1957, Julianne Mary Squier; one *s* two *d. Educ:* Christ's Hospital; University Coll., Oxford (BA). Asst Master, Bedford Sch., 1958-60; Reed Paper Group, 1960-67; Rugby Football Correspondent, Sunday Telegraph, 1962-74; Asst Sec., MCC, 1967-74. *Recreations:* cricket (played for Essex and for Oxford Univ.), golf. *Address:* 20 Elm Tree Road, NW8. *T:* 01-286 6246. *Clubs:* MCC; Vincent's (Oxford).

BAILEY, James Vincent; Executive Director, Bank of England, 1964-69; *b* 26 July 1908; *s* of R. H. Bailey; *m* 1946, Ida Hope Weigall; no *c. Educ:* Malvern; Pembroke Coll., Oxford. Entered Bank of England, 1928; Deputy Chief Cashier, 1959-62; Chief Accountant, 1962-64. *Address:* Common Barn, Remenham, Henley-on-Thames, Oxon. *T:* Henley 2480.

BAILEY, John Bilsland; Under-Secretary (Legal), Department of HM Procurator General and Treasury Solicitor, 1973-77; *b* 5 Nov. 1928; *o s* of late Walter Bailey and of Ethel Edith Bailey, FRAM (who *m* 2nd, Sir Thomas George Spencer); *m* 1952, Marion Rosemary (*née* Carroll); two *s* one *d. Educ:* Eltham Coll.; University Coll., London (LLB). Solicitor of Supreme Court. Legal Asst, Office of HM Treasury Solicitor, 1957; Sen. Legal Asst, 1962; Asst Treasury Solicitor, 1971; Principal Asst Treasury Solicitor, 1973. *Recreations:* walking, reading, listening to music. *Address:* Mavins, Greenhill Road, Farnham, Surrey. *T:* Farnham (Surrey) 6725.

BAILEY, John Everett Creighton, CBE 1947; Executive Chairman, Difco Laboratories (UK) Ltd, 1970-75; Chairman and Managing Director, Baird & Tatlock Group of Cos, 1947-69; *b* 2 Nov. 1905; *s* of late John Edred Bailey and late Violet Constance Masters; *m* 1928, Hilda Anne Jones; one *s* four *d. Educ:* Brentwood Sch. Peat Marwick Mitchell & Co., 1925-31; Director: Derbyshire Stone Ltd, 1959-69; Tarmac Derby Ltd, 1969-70; G. D. Searle & Co., 1969-70, and other companies. Mem., Admlty Chemical Adv. Panel, 1940-50; Pres. Scientific Instrument Manufacturers Assoc., 1945-50; Chm. Brit. Laboratory Ware Assoc., 1950-52, Pres., 1974-75; Chm. Brit. Sci. Instr. Research Assoc., 1952-64 (Pres. 1964-71), first Companion, SIRA Inst.; Mem., Grand Council FBI, 1945-58; Mem. BoT Exhibns Adv. Cttee, 1957-65, and Census of Production Adv. Cttee, 1960-68. Formerly Special Member, Prices and Incomes Board. Master, 1957-58 and 1974-75, Co. of Scientific Instrument Makers; Assistant, Worshipful Co. of Needlemakers; Freeman of City of London. Fellow, Inst. of Export; MRI; FBIM. *Recreation:* golf. *Address:* The Haven,

Paternoster Row, Ottery St Mary, South Devon EX11 1DP. *Club:* Athenæum.

BAILEY, Norman Stanley, CBE 1977; operatic and concert baritone; *b* 23 March 1933; *s* of Stanley and Agnes Bailey; *m* 1957, Doreen Simpson; two *s* one *d*. *Educ:* Rhodes Univ., S Africa; Vienna State Academy. BMus; Performer's and Teacher's Licentiate in Singing; Diplomas, opera, lieder, oratorio. Principal baritone, Sadler's Wells Opera, 1967-71; presently leading English-born Wagnerian baritone; regular engagements at world's major opera houses and festivals, including: La Scala, Milan; Royal Opera House, Covent Garden; Bayreuth Wagner Festival (first British Hans Sachs in Meistersinger, 1969); Vienna State Opera (first British Wanderer in Siegfried, 1976); Metropolitan Opera, NY; Paris Opera; Edinburgh Festival; Hamburg State Opera; Munich State Opera. BBC Television performances in Falstaff, La Traviata, The Flying Dutchman. Recordings include The Ring (Goodall); Meistersinger and Der Fliegende Holländer (Solti); Walküre (Klemperer), among others. *Recreations:* Mem., Baha'i world community; chess, notaphily, tropical fish, squash. *Address:* Anston, 63 Kimbolton Road, Bedford MK40 2PQ. *T:* Bedford 66392.

BAILEY, Reginald Bertram, CBE 1976; Director, South-Eastern Postal Region, 1970-76; *b* 15 July 1916; *s* of George Bertram Bailey and Elizabeth Bailey, Ilford; *m* 1942, Phyllis Joan Firman; one *s* one *d*. *Educ:* Owen's School. Served War of 1939-45: RAPC, 1940-42; RE, 1942-46. Entered Post Office as Exec. Officer, 1935; Higher Exec. Officer, 1947; Sen. Exec. Officer, 1948; Principal, 1950; Instructor, Management Trng Centre, 1957; Staff Controller, SW Region, 1958; Comdt, Management Trng Centre, 1962; Asst Sec., 1965; Dir, Wales and the Marches Postal Region, 1967. *Recreations:* walking, gardening, philately, old railway timetables. *Address:* 6 Wanderdown Road, Ovingdean, Brighton BN2 7BT. *T:* Brighton 35670.

BAILEY, Ronald William, CMG 1961; HM Diplomatic Service, retired; *b* 14 June 1917; *o s* of William Staveley and May Eveline Bailey, Southampton; *m* 1946, Joan Hassall, *d* of late A. E. Gray, JP, Stoke-on-Trent; one *s* one *d*. *Educ:* King Edward VI Sch., Southampton; Trinity Hall, Cambridge (Wootton Isaacson Scholar in Spanish). Probationer Vice-Consul, Beirut, 1939-41; HM Vice-Consul, Alexandria, 1941-45; Asst Oriental Sec., British Embassy, Cairo, 1945-48; Foreign Office, 1948-49; 1st Sec., British Legation, Beirut, 1949-52 (acted as Chargé d'Affaires, 1949, 1950 and 1951); 1st Sec., British Embassy, Washington, 1952-55; Counsellor, Washington, 1955-57; Khartoum, 1957-60 (acted as Chargé d'Affaires in each of these years); Chargé d'Affaires, Taiz, 1960-62; Consul-Gen., Gothenburg, 1963-65; Minister, British Embassy, Baghdad, 1965-67; Ambassador to Bolivia, 1967-71; Ambassador to Morocco, 1971-75. Vice-Pres., Soc. for Protection of Animals in N Africa; Chm., British-Moroccan Soc. *Recreations:* walking, photography, gardening. *Address:* Redwood, Tennyson's Lane, Haslemere, Surrey. *T:* Haslemere 2800. *Clubs:* Athenæum, Oriental.

BAILEY, Rev. Dr Sherwin; *see* Bailey, Rev. Dr D. S.

BAILEY, Stanley Ernest, QPM 1975; Chief Constable of Northumbria, since 1975; *b* 30 Sept. 1926; *m* 1954, Marguerita Dorothea Whitbread. Joined Metropolitan Police, 1947; Asst Chief Constable, Staffs, 1966; Dir, Police Res., Home Office, 1970-72; Dep. Chief Constable, Staffs, 1973-75. Chm., Cttee on Burglar Alarms, BSI, 1975-. SBStJ 1969. *Recreations:* gardening, travel. *Address:* Police HQ, Morpeth Road, Ashington, Northumberland. *T:* Ashington 814511.

BAILEY, Prof. Stanley John, LLD; Rouse Ball Professor of English Law in the University of Cambridge, 1950-68; Fellow of St John's College, Cambridge, since 1931; Barrister-at-Law, Inner Temple, 1924; *b* 19 June 1901; *o s* of John Bailey and Evelyn Mary Bailey (*née* Campkin); *m* 1st, 1926, Kathleen Aimée (*d* 1949), *d* of late Rev. F. J. Hamilton, DD; 2nd, 1952, Wilhelmina, *d* of late Dr H. W. Leeksma, The Hague, Holland; one *s*. *Educ:* Queen's Coll., Taunton; St John's Coll., Cambridge. Lecturer in Univ. Coll. of Wales, Aberystwyth, 1926; Reader in English Law in Univ. of Birmingham, 1930; Coll. Lecturer at St John's Coll., Cambridge, 1931-50; Lecturer in Univ. of Cambridge, 1934, Senior Proctor, 1936-37; Tutor of St John's Coll., 1939-46; Reader in Law, Cambridge, 1946-50. Editor, Cambridge Law Jl, 1948-54. *Publications:* Law of Wills, 1935 (6th edn, 1967); contrib. to Law Quarterly Review, Cambridge Law Journal, The Conveyancer. *Address:* St John's College, Cambridge. *T:* Cambridge 61621.

BAILEY, Thomas Aubrey, MBE 1959; Director, Peter Cox Ltd, Building Restoration Specialists (Member of SGB Group of Cos), 1970-76; *b* 20 Jan. 1912; *o s* of late Thomas Edward Bailey and Emma Bailey; *m* 1944, Joan Woodman, *d* of late John Woodman Hooper; one *s*. *Educ:* Adams' Grammar Sch., Newport, Shropshire; Regent Street Polytechnic Sch. of Architecture. Entered HM Office of Works, Ancient Monuments Br., 1935; Asst Architect, 1945-49; Architect, London and E Anglia, 1949-54; Sen. Architect in charge Ancient Monuments Br., Eng., Wales and Overseas, Min. of Public Building and Works, 1954-69; Architectural Adv. to Oxford Historic Bldgs Fund, 1963-69. Served on various cttees on stone decay and preservation; seconded to Sir Giles G. Scott, OM, RA, for Rebuilding of House of Commons, 1944-49. *Principal works:* Direction of MPBW Survey for Oxford Historic Bldg Appeal, 1957-62 and Cambridge Appeal, 1963; re-erection of fallen Trilithons at Stonehenge, 1958-64; Conservation of Claudian Aqueduct and Aurelian Wall, Brit. Embassy at Rome, 1957-69; etc. Resigned professional membership of RIBA and ARCUK, to enter specialised Bldg Industry, 1969. Mem. Conservation Cttee, for Council for Places of Worship, 1968; Mem. Council, Ancient Monuments Soc., 1970-. FSA 1957; FRSA 1969; Fellow of Faculty of Bldg, 1970. Freeman of City of London, 1967; Freeman and Liveryman, Worshipful Company of Masons, 1973. Hon. MA Oxon, 1963. *Publications:* (jointly) The Claudian Aqueduct in the Grounds of the British Embassy, Rome, 1966; many technical reports on conservation of Historic Monuments. *Recreations:* music, photography, travel, motoring. *Address:* 32 Anne Boleyn's Walk, Cheam, Sutton, Surrey SM3 8DF. *T:* 01-642 3185. *Club:* City Livery.

BAILEY, Wilfrid; Chairman, Southern Gas Region (formerly Southern Gas Board), 1969-75; Chartered Accountant; *b* 9 March 1910; *s* of late Harry Bailey and Martha Bailey (*née* Pighills); *m* 1934, Vera (*née* Manchester); two *s* one *d*. *Educ:* Keighley Grammar Sch. Borough Treasurer, Bexley BC, 1945-47; Chief Financial Officer, Crawley Development Corp., 1947-49; Gas Council: Chief Accountant, 1949-58; Secretary, 1958-61; Dep. Chm., Southern Gas Bd, 1961-69. FCA 1935; FBIM 1959. *Recreations:* cricket, motoring, music, photography, gardening. *Address:* (home) Bramble Way, Clease Way, Compton Down, near Winchester. *T:* Twyford 713382.

BAILEY, William John Joseph; journalist; *b* 11 June 1940; *s* of Ernest Robert Bailey and Josephine Smith; *m* 1963, Maureen Anne, *d* of James Gibbs Neenan and Marjorie Dorema Wrigglesworth; four *s* three *d*. *Educ:* St Joseph's, Stanford-le-Hope, Essex; Campion Hall, Jamaica; St George's Coll., Kingston, Jamaica; St Chad's Coll., Wolverhampton. Reporter: Southend Standard, Essex, and Essex and Thurrock Gazette, 1960-63; Northern Daily Mail, 1963-64; Chief Reporter, Billingham and Stockton Express, 1964-72; Sub-Editor, Mail, Hartlepool, 1972-75; Features Editor, Echo, Sunderland, 1975-. Member: Press Council, 1974-; Complaints Cttee, 1974-77; Cttee for Evidence to Royal Commission on Press, 1975-76; Gen. Purposes Cttee, 1976-; Secretariat Cttee, 1976-. Nat. Union of Journalists: Mem., Nat. Exec. Council, 1966-; Vice-Pres., 1972-73; Pres., 1973-74; Gen. Treasurer, 1975-. *Address:* 225 Park Road, Hartlepool, Cleveland TS26 9NG. *T:* Hartlepool 64577. *Club:* Press (Glasgow).

BAILIE, Rt. Hon. Robin John, PC (N Ire) 1971; MP (N Ire) for Newtonabbey, 1969-72; Minister of Commerce, Government of Northern Ireland, 1971-72; *b* 6 March 1937; *m* 1961, Margaret F. (*née* Boggs); one *s* three *d*. *Educ:* Rainey Endowed Sch. Magherafelt, Co. Londonderry; The Queen's Univ. of Belfast (LLB). Solicitor of the Supreme Court of Judicature, Northern Ireland, 1961-. *Recreations:* golf, squash. *Address:* 39a Malone Park, Belfast. *T:* Belfast 668085. *Club:* Ulster (Belfast).

BAILLIE, family name of Baron Burton.

BAILLIE, Sir Gawaine George Hope, 7th Bt, of Polkemmet, *cr* 1823; *b* 8 March 1934; *s* of Sir Adrian Baillie, 6th Bt, and Hon. Olive Cecilia (*d* 1974), *d* of 1st Baron Queenborough, GBE; *S* father, 1947; *m* 1966, Margot, *d* of Senator Louis Beaubien, Montreal; one *s* one *d*. *Heir:* *s* Adrian Louis Baillie, *b* 26 March 1973. *Address:* Freechase, Warninglid, Sussex.

BAILLIE, Ian Fowler, CMG 1966; OBE 1962; Director, The Thistle Foundation, Edinburgh, since 1970; *b* 16 Feb. 1921; *s* of late Very Rev. Principal John Baillie, CH, DLitt, DD, LLD and Florence Jewel (*née* Fowler); *m* 1951, Sheila Barbour (*née* Mathewson); two *s* one *d*. *Educ:* Edinburgh Acad,; Corpus Christi Coll., Oxford (MA). War service, British and Indian Armies, 1941-46. HM Overseas Civil Service (formerly Colonial Service), 1946-66: Admin. Officer (District Comr), Gold Coast,

1946-54; Registrar of Co-operative Socs and Chief Marketing Officer, Aden, 1955; Protectorate Financial Sec., Aden, 1959; Dep. British Agent, Aden, 1962; Brit. Agent and Asst High Comr, Aden, 1963; Dir, Aden Airways 1959-66; Sen. Research Associate and Administrative Officer, Agricultural Adjustment Unit, Dept of Agricultural Economics, Univ. of Newcastle upon Tyne, 1966-69. *Publication:* (ed with S. J. Sheehy) Irish Agriculture in a Changing World, 1971. *Recreation:* angling. *Address:* 4 Grange Loan Gardens, Edinburgh EH9 2EB. *T:* 031-667 2647.

BAILLIE, Isobel, CBE 1951; Hon. MA (Manchester Univ.), 1950; RCM, RAM; Singer; *b* Hawick, Scotland; *m* 1918, H. L. Wrigley; one *d. Educ:* Dover Street High Sch. for Girls, Manchester. Appeared at all leading Festivals, including Three Choirs, Edinburgh, London, etc.; only British singer to appear with Toscanini on three occasions. Concerts with Sir Malcolm Sargent, Sir Adrian Boult, Sir Hamilton Harty, Sir Henry Wood, Bruno Walter, De Sabata, etc. Sang at Covent Garden in Orphée, and in Hollywood Bowl. Toured New Zealand twice; concerts in Malaya, 1948, South Africa, 1952, etc. Professor of Singing: Cornell Univ., USA, 1960-61; Royal Coll. of Music, London. *Address:* 524 Stretford Road, Manchester M16 9AF. *T:* 061-872 1731.

BAILLIE, John Strachan, CBE 1965; *b* 1896; *s* of William T. Baillie, Belfast; *m* 1926, Eileen Mary, *d* of Saxon J. Payne. *Educ:* Queen's Univ., Belfast (BComSc). Joined Harland and Wolff, Belfast, 1913, and (apart from service in RN, 1914-18) was with Co. throughout his career; transf. to Co.'s London Office, 1924; Asst Sec., Harland & Wolff, Belfast, 1937; London Manager, 1945; Dir 1947; Dep. Chm. 1958; Chm. 1962-65; Dir, Short Brothers & Harland Ltd, 1948-67; Dep. Chm. Brown Bros & Co. Ltd, 1962-67. Liveryman, Worshipful Co. of Shipwrights. Commander: Order of St Olav (Norway), 1960; Dannebrog (Denmark) 1964. *Address:* Merrydown, 12 Aldersey Road, Guildford, Surrey.

BAILLIE-GROHMAN, Vice-Admiral Harold Tom, CB 1941; DSO 1917; OBE 1922; RN retired; *b* Victoria, British Columbia, 16 Jan. 1888; *o s* of late W. A. Baillie-Grohman, Kootenay pioneer, author and sportsman; *m* 1915, Evelyn, *e d* of Arthur S. Taylor, MD, FRCS; two *s.* Joined HMS Britannia, 1903; Lieut 1909; Lt-Com. 1917; Captain 1930; Rear-Adm. 1941; Vice-Admiral, 1943 (retd). Served European War, 1914-18, with Grand Fleet, in Dover Patrol in destroyers and minesweepers (DSO, OBE, Chevalier of Order of Leopold, Star of Ethiopia, Order of the Brilliant Jade); in Persian Gulf and Red Sea, 1922-23; as SO 1st Minesweeping Flotilla, 1923-24; and as ACNS and DNI in Navy Office, Melbourne, 1925-27; Military Staff Coll., Camberley, 1928; Head of British Naval Mission to China, 1931-33; in command First Destroyer Flotilla, Mediterranean, 1934-36; in command HMS St Vincent and in charge Boys' Training Establishment, 1936-38; commanded HMS Ramillies, 1st Battle Squadron, Mediterranean, 1939-40; attached to Staff of GOC Mid. East, 1941 (chiefly responsible for shore to ship arrangements, evacuation of British Forces from Greece, 1941); Rear-Admiral Combined Operations, 1942; FOIC, Harwich, 1944, Kiel and Schleswig-Holstein, 1945-46, to eliminate the remains of the German naval forces; hoisted White Ensign over German Naval HQ, Kiel, 8 May 1945. *Publication:* (with A. Heckstall-Smith) Greek Tragedy, 1941. *Address:* 6 St Martin's Square, Chichester, West Sussex. *T:* Chichester 82753. *Clubs:* Naval and Military, Alpine Ski; (Naval Member) Royal Yacht Squadron; RN Sailing Assoc.

BAILLIE-HAMILTON, family name of **Earl of Haddington.**

BAILLIEU, family name of **Baron Baillieu.**

BAILLIEU, 3rd Baron *cr* 1953, of Sefton, Australia and Parkwood, Surrey; **James William Latham Baillieu;** *b* 16 Nov. 1950; *s* of 2nd Baron Baillieu and Anne Bayliss, *d* of Leslie William Page, Southport, Queensland; *S* father, 1973; *m* 1974, Cornelia Masters Ladd, *d* of W. Ladd. *Educ:* Radley College. Joined Army, 1969; commission, Coldstream Guards, 1970-73; served W Germany, N Ireland, London; GSM N Ireland, 1970. *Heir: b* Hon. David Clive Latham Baillieu, *b* 2 Nov. 1952. *Address:* c/o Mutual Trust Pty Ltd, 459 Collins Street, Melbourne, Victoria 3000, Australia. *Clubs:* Boodle's, Bath.

BAIN, Prof. Andrew David; Professor of Economics, University of Strathclyde, since 1977; *b* 21 March 1936; *s* of Hugh Bain and Kathleen Eadie; *m* 1960, Anneliese Minna Frieda Kroggel; three *s. Educ:* Glasgow Academy; Christ's Coll., Cambridge. PhD Cantab 1963. Junior Res. Officer, Dept of Applied Econs, Cambridge Univ., 1958-60; Res. Fellow, Christ's Coll., Cambridge, 1960; Instructor, Cowles Foundn, Yale Univ., 1960-

61; Lectr, Cambridge, 1961-66; Fellow, Corpus Christi Coll., Cambridge, 1962; on secondment to Bank of England, 1965-67; Prof. of Econs, 1967-70, Hd of Econs Dept, 1967-71, Esmee Fairbairn Prof. of Econs of Finance and Investment, 1970-77, Univ. of Stirling. *Publications:* The Growth of Television Ownership in the United Kingdom (monograph), 1964; The Control of the Money Supply, 1970; Company Financing in the UK, 1975; articles on demand analysis, monetary policy and other subjects. *Address:* 7 Pathfoot Avenue, Bridge of Allan, Stirlingshire. *T:* Bridge of Allan 832433. *Club:* Royal Commonwealth Society.

BAIN, Cyril William Curtis, MC; DM Oxford; FRCP; Hon. Consulting Physician, Harrogate General Hospital; Past President BMA; *b* Thornfield, Heaton Mersey, near Manchester, 5 June 1895; *e s* of late William Bain, MD, FRCP, and Ellen, *d* of late John Curtis, Rose Leigh, Heaton Chapel, near Manchester; *m* 1930, Diana Alice, *y d* of late Lt-Col H. R. Pease, and *ggd* of late Joseph Robinson Pease, Hesslewood, near Hull; three *s* one *d. Educ:* Bilton Grange, near Rugby; Wellington Coll.; Christ Church, Oxford; St Thomas's Hospital, London. Served European War, 1914-18; gazetted to the Duke of Wellington's Regt 29 August 1914; Captain, 1916; Major, 1918; served in Machine Gun Corps (despatches, MC); active service in France and Flanders, 1915-17; retired, 1918; Extraordinary member of the Cardiac Society. *Publications:* Recent Advances in Cardiology (with C. F. T. East), 5th edn, 1959; Incomplete Bundle Branch Block; Bilateral Bundle Branch Block; The Oesophageal Lead; Clinical Value of Unipolar Chest and Limb Leads, etc. *Recreation:* gardening. *Address:* Red Willows, The Belyars, St Ives, Cornwall. *T:* St Ives 6298. *Club:* Royal Cornwall Yacht.

BAIN, John Taylor, CBE 1975; JP; Director of Education, Glasgow, 1968-75; *b* 9 May 1912; *m* 1941, Anne Nicoll Dewar; one *s* two *d. Educ:* St Andrews Univ. (BSc, MA); Edinburgh Univ. (BEd). War Service, RAF (Technical Br.), 1939-45. Asst Dir of Educn, Stirlingshire, 1947-49; Depute Dir of Educn, Glasgow, 1949-68. JP Glasgow, 1971. *Recreation:* golf. *Address:* 20 Essex Drive, Glasgow G14 9NA. *T:* 041-959 2390. *Club:* Royal Scottish Automobile (Glasgow).

BAIN, Kenneth Bruce Findlater; *see* Findlater, Richard.

BAIN, Mrs Margaret Anne; MP (SNP) East Dunbartonshire, since Oct. 1974; *b* 1 Sept. 1945; *d* of John and Peggie McAdam; *m* 1968, Donald Straiton Bain. *Educ:* Univs of Glasgow and Strathclyde. MA Glasgow 1967, BA Hons Strathclyde 1973. Asst Teacher, Our Lady's High, Cumbernauld, 1968-70; St Modan's High, Stirling: Special Asst Teacher, 1970-73; Principal Teacher, Remedial Educn, 1973-74. *Recreations:* the arts in general, folk music in particular. *Address:* 60 Galloway Terrace, West High Street, Kirkintilloch, Dunbartonshire.

BAINBRIDGE, Beryl; actress, writer; *b* 21 Nov. 1934; *d* of Richard Bainbridge and Winifred Baines; *m* 1954, Austin Davies (marr. diss.); one *s* two *d. Educ:* Merchant Taylors' Sch., Liverpool; Arts Educational Schools, Ltd, Tring. *Plays:* Tiptoe Through the Tulips, 1976; The Warrior's Return, 1977; Its a Lovely Day Tomorrow, 1977. *Publications:* A Weekend with Claude, 1967; Another Part of the Wood, 1968; Harriet Said...., 1972; The Dressmaker, 1973; The Bottle Factory Outing, 1974 (Guardian Fiction Award); Sweet William, 1975; A Quiet Life, 1976; Injury Time, 1977. *Recreations:* painting, sleeping. *Address:* 42 Albert Street, NW1 7NU. *T:* 01-387 3113.

BAINBRIDGE, Maj.-Gen. Henry, CB 1948; CBE 1944; psc; retired; late Corps of Royal Engineers; *b* 1903. 2nd Lieut Royal Engineers, 1923. Served War of 1939-45, 1939-44 (despatches twice, CBE). Dir of Man-power Planning, War Office, 1949-52; Dep. QMG, War Office, 1952-55, retired 1955. *Address:* Brizlee, Hoe Lane, Peaslake, Surrey.

BAINES, Prof. John Robert, MA, DPhil; Professor of Egyptology, Oxford University and Fellow of Queen's College, Oxford, since 1976; *b* 17 March 1946; *o s* of late Edward Russell Baines and of Dora Margaret Jean (*née* O'Brien); *m* 1971, Jennifer Christine Ann, *e d* of S. T. Smith; one *d. Educ:* Winchester Coll.; New Coll., Linacre Coll., Worcester Coll., Oxford (BA 1967, MA, DPhil 1976). Lectr in Egyptology, Univ. of Durham, 1970-75; Laycock Student, Worcester Coll., Oxford, 1973-75. *Publications:* (trans. and ed) H. Schäfer, Principles of Egyptian art, 1974; articles in Acta Orientalia, Jl Egypt. Archaeol., Orientalia, Studien altägypt. Kultur, etc. *Address:* The Queen's College, Oxford.

BAINS, Lawrence Arthur, FCII; Chairman, Greater London Council, 1977-May 1978; Director: Bains Brothers

Managements Ltd; Crowland Leasings Ltd; Tower Plywood & Boards Ltd; D. R. S. Beers Ltd, and associated companies; *b* 11 May 1920; *s* of late Arthur Bains and Mabel Payn; *m* 1954, Margaret, *d* of Sir William and Lady Grimshaw; two *s* one *d*. *Educ:* Stationers' Company's School. Served War, 1939-45: Middlesex Yeomanry, 1939; N Africa, 1940; POW, 1942, escaped, 1943. Member of Lloyd's. Hornsey Borough Council: Mem., 1949-65; Dep. Leader, 1958-64; Mayor, 1964-65; Council, London Borough of Haringey: Mem., 1964-74; Finance Chm., 1968-71; Greater London Council: Mem. for Hornsey/Haringey, 1967-; Chm., South Area Planning Bd, 1970-73; Mem., Lee Valley Regional Park Authority, 1968-. *Recreation:* riding. *Address:* Crowland Lodge, 100 Galley Lane, Arkley, Barnet EN5 4AL. *T:* 01-440 3499. *Club:* United Wards.

BAINS, Malcolm Arnold; DL; Clerk of the Kent County Council and Clerk to the Lieutenancy of Kent, 1970-74; *b* 12 Sept. 1921; *s* of Herbert Bains, Newcastle-upon-Tyne; *m* 1st, 1942, Winifred Agnes Davies (marr. diss. 1961); three *s*; 2nd, 1968, Margaret Hunter. *Educ:* Hymers Coll.; Durham Univ. (LLB (Hons)); Solicitor. Commnd as Pilot in RAF, 1942-46. Apptd a solicitor, Taunton and Sunderland and with Notts and Hants County Councils, 1946-55; Dep. Clerk of Hants County Council and Dep. Clerk of the Peace, 1955-60; Dep. Clerk of Kent County Council, 1960-70; Chm., Working Group on Local Authority Management Structures which advised Secretary of State for Environment on future management of Local Authorities, 1971-73. Mem. Court, University of Kent at Canterbury. FRSA 1976. DL Kent 1976. *Publications:* The Bains Report, 1972; Principles and Processes of Management for New Local Authorities, 1974. *Recreations:* swimming, walking, travel. *Address:* Flat 2B, 55 Ravensbourne Road, Bromley, Kent.

BAIRAMIAN, Sir Vahé (Robert), Kt 1959; *b* 30 Nov. 1900; 2nd *s* of Dr Bairamian, Cyprus; *m* 1934, Eileen Elsie Connelly; one *s*. *Educ:* English Sch., Nicosia, Cyprus; University Coll., London. Barrister-at-Law, Middle Temple, 1923. Served in the Courts and Land Registry, Cyprus, 1926-44; Legal Asst, Lands and Survey, Nigeria, 1944; Chief Registrar, Supreme Court, Nigeria, 1944; Magistrate, 1946; Puisne Judge, 1949; Senior Puisne Judge, High Court, Northern Region of Nigeria, 1955; Chief Justice, Sierra Leone, 1957-60; Justice, Supreme Court of Nigeria, 1960-68. Fellow UCL, 1963. Jubilee Medal, 1935; Coronation Medal, 1953. *Publications:* Editor, All Nigeria Law Reports of 1963, 1964, 1965 and 1966 (Supreme Court Judgments) (wrote a Synopsis of Criminal Procedure and Evidence in Nigeria based on them). *Address:* 36 The Crescent, Sandgate, Folkestone, Kent CT20 3EE. *T:* Folkestone 38240. *Club:* Royal Commonwealth Society.

BAIRD, Sir David Charles, 5th Bt of Newbyth, *cr* 1809; *b* 6 July 1912; *s* of late William Arthur Baird, of Lennoxlove, and Lady Hersey Baird; *S* uncle, 1941. *Educ:* Eton; Cambridge. *Heir: b* Robert Walter Stuart Baird [*b* 5 March 1914; *m* 1st, 1938, Maxine Christine (marr. diss. 1960), *o c* of Rupert Darrell, New York; one *s*; 2nd, 1960, Maria Florine Viscart; one *d*]. *Address:* Summerhill, Hardgate, Castle Douglas, Kirkcudbright.

BAIRD, Sir Dugald, Kt 1959; MD, FRCOG, Hon. FRCPGlas, BSc, DPH; Belding Scholar, Association for Aid to Crippled Children, New York, 1966-71; Regius Professor of Midwifery in the University of Aberdeen, 1937-65, retired; formerly Obstetrician-in-Chief, Aberdeen Maternity Hospital and Visiting Gynæcologist, Aberdeen Royal Infirmary and Hon. Director, Obstetric Medicine Research Unit, Medical Research Council; *b* 16 Nov. 1899; *er s* of David Baird, MA, Gourock, Renfrewshire; *m* 1928, May Tennant (*see* Lady Baird); two *s* two *d*. *Educ:* Greenock Acad.; University of Glasgow; University of Strasbourg. Formerly with Glasgow Royal Maternity and Women's Hosp., Glasgow Royal Infirmary, and Glasgow Royal Cancer Hosp. Freedom of City of Aberdeen, 1966. Hon. LLD: Glasgow, 1959; Aberdeen, 1966; Hon. DSc: Manchester, 1962; Wales, 1966; Hon. DCL, Newcastle; DUniv Stirling, 1974. *Publications:* various papers on obstetrical and gynæcological subjects. *Recreation:* golf. *Address:* 21 Russell Place, Edinburgh.

BAIRD, Lt-Gen. Sir James (Parlane), KBE 1973; MD, FRCP, FRCPEd; Director General, Army Medical Services, 1973-77; *b* 12 May 1915; *s* of Rev. David Baird and Sara Kathleen Black; *m* 1948, Anne Patricia Anderson; one *s* one *d*. *Educ:* Bathgate Academy; Univ. of Edinburgh. FRCPEd 1952, MD 1958, FRCP 1959. Commissioned, RAMC, 1939; Lt-Col 1956; Prof. of Military Medicine, Royal Army Medical Coll., 1965; Cons. Physician, BAOR, 1967; Dir of Medicine and Consulting Physician to the Army, 1969-71; Comdt and Dir of Studies, Royal Army Med. Coll., 1971-73. QHP 1969. *Publication:* Tropical Diseases Supplement to Principles and Practice of

Medicine, 1968. *Recreation:* golf. *Address:* 30 Stonehills Court, College Road, Dulwich, SE21 7LZ. *T:* 01-693 2735. *Club:* Army and Navy.

BAIRD, Sir James Richard Gardiner, 10th Bt *cr* 1695; MC 1945; Director, Bond Worth Holdings, since 1971; *b* 12 July 1913; *er s* of Captain William Frank Gardiner Baird (killed in action 1914) (2nd *s* of 8th Bt) and Violet Mary (*d* 1947), *d* of late Richard Benyon Croft; *S* uncle, Sir James Hozier Gardiner Baird, 9th Bt, 1966; *m* 1941, Mabel Ann (Gay), *d* of A. Algernon Gill, Toronto, Canada; two *s* one *d*. *Educ:* Eton. Served War of 1939-45. Lieut, Royal Artillery, 1940; Captain, Kent Yeomanry, 1944. *Recreation:* shooting. *Heir: s* James Andrew Gardiner Baird [*b* 2 May 1946. *Educ:* Eton]. *Address:* Wareside, Ware, Herts. *T:* Ware 3695. *Club:* Bath.

BAIRD, Lady, (May Deans), CBE 1962; National Governor of the BBC in Scotland, 1965-70; *b* 14 May 1901; *er d* of Matthew Tennent, Newton, Lanarks; *m* 1928, Sir Dugald Baird, *qv*; two *s* two *d*. *Educ:* Glasgow High Sch. for Girls; Glasgow Univ. BSc 1922; MB, ChB 1924. Hospital appts until marriage; social and local govt work, 1938-54; Chm. of Public Health Cttee, Aberdeen Town Council; Chm. NE Regional Hosp. Bd (Scotland), 1947-66. Freedom of City of Aberdeen, 1966. Hon. LLD Aberdeen Univ., 1958. *Address:* 21 Russell Place, Edinburgh.

BAIRD, Rear-Adm. Thomas Henry Eustace; Director General of Naval Personal Services, since 1978; *b* Canterbury, Kent, 17 May 1924; *s* of Geoffrey Henry and Helen Jane Baird; *m* 1953, Angela Florence Ann Paul, Symington, Ayrshire; one *s* one *d*. *Educ:* RNC, Dartmouth. Served HM Ships: Trinidad, in support of convoys to Russia, 1941, Midshipman; Bermuda, Russian convoys and landings in N Africa, and Orwell, Russian convoys and Atlantic escort force, 1942; Howe, E Indies, 1943, Sub-Lt; Rapid, E Indies, 1944 until VJ Day, Lieut; St James, Home Fleet, 1946; Ganges, Ratings' New Entry Trng, 1948; Plucky, Exec. Officer, mine clearance in Mediterranean, 1950; Lt Comdr 1952; Veryan Bay, Exec. Officer, W Indies and Falkland Is., 1953; O-in-C, Petty Officers' Leadership Sch., Malta, 1954; Exec. Officer, HMS Whirlwind, Home Fleet and Med., for Suez Op., 1956; Comd, HMS Acute, Dartmouth Trng Sqdn, 1958; Comdr 1959; Comd, HMS Ulysses, Home Fleet, 1960; Staff, C-in-C, Home Fleet, Northwood, 1961; Exec. Officer, Jt Anti-Sub. Sch., Londonderry, 1963; EO, HMS Bulwark, Far East, 1965; Ch. Staff Officer to Cdre, Naval Drafting, 1966; Captain 1967; Dep. Dir, Naval Equipment, Adm., Bath, 1967; Captain: Mine Countermeasures; Fishery Protection and HMS Lochinvar (comd); 1969; Comd, HMS Glamorgan, Far East, W Indies, S Amer., Med., and UK Waters, 1971; Captain of the Fleet, 1973; Rear Adm. 1976; Chief of Staff to C-in-C Naval Home Comd, 1976-77. *Recreations:* cricket, golf, shooting, fishing. *Address:* Craigrethill, Symington, Ayrshire KA1 5QN. *T:* Symington 830339. *Clubs:* Army and Navy; Prestwick Golf (Prestwick).

BAIRD, Dr Thomas Terence, CB 1977; Chief Medical Officer, Department of Health and Social Services, Northern Ireland, since 1972; *b* 31 May 1916; *s* of Thomas Baird, Archdeacon of Derry, and Hildegarde Nolan; *m* 1940, Joan Crosbie; two *d*. *Educ:* Haileybury Coll.; Queen's Univ. of Belfast. MB, BCh, BAO, 1939; DPH, 1947; FFCM (RCP), 1972; MRCPI 1973, FRCPI 1975; MRCPEd 1975; FFCM Ireland (Founder Fellow), 1977. Ho. Surg./Ho. Phys., North Lonsdale Hosp., Barrow-in-Furness, 1939-40. Served War, RNVR, 1940-46. Queen's Univ. of Belfast, DPH course, 1946-47. Berks CC: Asst MO, 1947-49; Dep. County MO and Dep. Principal Sch. MO, 1949-54. Welsh Bd of Health: MO, 1954-57; Sen. MO, 1957-62; Min. of Health and Local Govt, Northern Ireland: PMO, 1962-64; Dep. Chief MO, 1964-68; Min. of Health and Social Services, NI, Sen. Dep. Chief MO, 1968-72. Chm., NI Med. Manpower Adv. Cttee; Member: GMC; Faculty of Medicine, QUB; NI Council for Postgrad. Med. Educn. Chief Surgeon for Wales, St John Ambulance Bde, 1959-62. QHP 1974-. CStJ 1959. *Publications:* (jtly) Infection in Hospital-a code of practice, 1971; papers in various learned jls. *Recreations:* fishing, forestry. *Address:* 2 Kensington Road, Belfast BT5 6NF. *T:* Belfast 651420. *Club:* Junior Carlton.

BAIRD, William; Registrar General for Scotland since 1973; *b* 13 Oct. 1927; *s* of Peter and Christina Baird, Airdrie; *m* 1954, Anne Templeton Macfarlane; two *d*. *Educ:* Airdrie Academy; Glasgow Univ. Entered Scottish Home Dept, 1952; Private Sec. to Perm. Under-Sec. of State, Scottish Office, 1957; Principal, Scottish Educn Dept, 1958-63; Private Sec. to Minister of State and successive Secs of State for Scotland, 1963-65; Asst Sec., Scottish Educn Dept, 1965-66; Dept of Agriculture and Fisheries for Scotland, 1966-71; Scottish Office Finance Div.,

1971-73. *Recreations:* reading, music, gardening. *Address:* 18 Lygon Road, Edinburgh EH16 5QB. *T:* 031-667 3054.

BAIRSTO, Air Vice-Marshal Peter Edward, CBE 1973; AFC 1957; Air Officer Commanding Training Units, Royal Air Force Support Command, since 1977; *b* 3 Aug. 1926; *s* of late Arthur Bairsto and of Beatrice (*née* Lewis); *m* 1947, Kathleen (*née* Clarbour); two *s* one *d*. *Educ:* Rhyl Grammar Sch. Pilot, FAA, 1944-46; 1946-62: FO RAF Regt, Palestine, Aden Protectorate; Flying Instr; Fighter Pilot, Fighter Comd and Near East; Flight Comdr, 43 Sqdn, and Leader, RAF Aerobatic Team; Sqdn Comdr, 66 Sqdn; RAF Staff Coll.; Wing Comdr, Flying, Nicosia, 1963-64; Op. Requirements, MoD, 1965-67; JSSC Latimer, 1967; Instr, RAF Staff Coll., 1968-70; Stn Comdr, RAF Honington, 1971-73; Dir, Op. Requirements, MoD, 1974-77. Queen's Commendation for Valuable Services in the Air, 1955 and 1960. *Recreations:* golf, fishing, shooting, argument. *Address:* Ursa Cottage, Fakenham Magna, Bury St Edmunds, Suffolk. *T:* Honington 660. *Clubs:* Royal Air Force; Flempton (Suffolk).

BAKER; see **Noel-Baker.**

BAKER, family name of **Baron Baker.**

BAKER, Baron *cr* 1977 (Life Peer), of Windrush, Gloucestershire; **John Fleetwood Baker,** Kt 1961; OBE 1941; FRS 1956; MA, ScD Cantab; DSc Wales; Hon. LLD Glasgow; Hon. DSc Leeds, Manchester, Edinburgh, Aston, Leicester, Salford, Cranfield, Lancaster; Hon. DEng Liverpool; Hon. DS Ghent; Hon. FIMechE; Hon. ARIBA; Hon. FWeldI; Hon. Mem., Inst. of Royal Engineers; FICE; FIStructE; Associate MASCE; Fellow of Clare College, Cambridge, 1943; Director of Research and Development, IDC Group Ltd; Deputy Chairman, IDC Consultants Ltd; Director, IDC Project Management Consultants Ltd; *b* 19 March 1901; *s* of J. W. Baker, Wallasey, and Emily C. Fleetwood; *m* 1928, Fiona Mary MacAlister, *d* of late John Walker; two *d*. *Educ:* Rossall; Clare Coll., Cambridge (Scholar). Technical Asst, Design Dept, Royal Airship Works, 1925; Asst Lecturer, University Coll., Cardiff, 1926; Scientific Asst, Building Research Station, 1928; Technical Officer to Steel Structures Res. Cttee, 1931-36; Prof. of Civil Engineering, Bristol Univ., 1933-43; Prof. of Mechanical Sciences and Head of Dept of Engineering, Cambridge Univ., 1943-68, Prof. Emeritus, 1977. Chm. Council, Sch. of Physical Sciences, Cambridge Univ., 1945-72. Telford Gold Medal, 1932, Telford Premium, 1936 and 1953; Howard Quinquennial Medal and Prize, 1937; Ewing Medal, 1952; Inst. Lecture to Students, 1936-37. Unwin Memorial Lecture, 1961. Mem. of Council 1947-56, 1958-63, 1964-66, Vice-Pres., 1968-70, Inst. of Civil Engrs; Research Medal 1951, Instn Silver Medal 1951, Gold Medal 1953; Mem. of Council, 1936-39, Chm., Western Counties Br., 1935-39, Midland Lecture, 1971, Instn of Structural Engineers; Royal Medal, Royal Soc., 1970. Member: Civil Defence Research Cttee, 1939-1948; Scientific Adv. Com., Min. of Works, 1945-46; Adv. Council to Military Coll. of Science, 1947-52; UGC, 1953-63; Council, British Welding Res. Assoc.; Pres., Welding Inst., 1971-73 (Brooker Medal, 1977); Pres., British Assoc. for the Advancement of Science, 1975-76; Hon. Fellow, 1977-, Vice-Pres., 1977-, Inst. of Materials Handling; Chm., Naval Educn Adv. Cttee, 1958-64; Consultant, Naval Constructional Research Establishment, Rosyth, 1948-63; Director: Technical Development Capital Ltd, 1962-74; John Brown & Co. Ltd, 1963-71; Cambridge Fender & Engineering Co. Ltd, 1964-74. Scientific Adviser, and in charge of Design and Development Section, Ministry of Home Security, ARP Dept, 1939-43; designer of Morrison indoor shelter, 1940. Founder Fellow, Fellowship of Engineering, 1976. Officier du Mérite pour la Recherche et l'Invention, Paris, 1964. *Publications:* Differential Equations of Engineering Science, 1929; Analysis of Engineering Structures, 1936, 4th edn, 1968; The Steel Skeleton, Vol 1, 1954, Vol. 2, 1956; Plastic designs of frames, Vol. 1, 1969; numerous scientific and technical papers on Theory of Structures and Strength of Materials, etc. *Address:* 100 Long Road, Cambridge, *T:* Trumpington 2152. *Club:* Athenæum.

BAKER, Prof. Alan, FRS 1973; Professor of Pure Mathematics, University of Cambridge, since 1974; Fellow of Trinity College, Cambridge, since 1964; *b* 19 Aug. 1939; *o c* of Barnet and Bessie Baker. *Educ:* Stratford Grammar Sch.; University Coll. London; Trinity Coll., Cambridge. BSc (London); MA, PhD (Cantab). Mem., Dept of Mathematics, UCL, 1964-65; Research Fellow, 1964-68, and Dir of Studies in Mathematics, 1968-74, Trinity Coll., Cambridge; Mem., Dept of Pure Maths and Math. Statistics, Univ. of Cambridge, 1966-; Reader in Theory of Numbers, 1972-74. Visiting Professor: Univs of Michigan and Colorado, USA, Fall term, 1969; Stanford Univ., Calif, USA,

Winter quarter, 1974; Mem., Inst. for Advanced Study, Princeton, USA, Fall term, 1970. Fields Medal (at Internat. Congress of Mathematicians, Nice), 1970; Adams Prize of Univ. of Cambridge, 1971-72. *Publications:* Transcendental Number Theory, 1975; papers in various mathematical jls. *Recreations:* hiking, travel, art. *Address:* Trinity College, Cambridge. *T:* Cambridge 58201.

BAKER, Alex Anthony, CBE 1973; MD, MRCP, DPM; FRCPsych; Consultant Psychiatrist with special interest in the elderly to Gloucestershire Clinical Area, 1973-77, retired; *b* 22 March 1922; *m* 1944; two *s* two *d*. *Educ:* St Mary's Hosp. Med. Sch. Consultant Psychiatrist: Banstead Hosp., 1955; Mother and Baby Unit, Downview Hosp., 1958; St Mary Abbotts Hosp., 1967; Medical Administrator, Banstead Hosp., 1964; sometime Consultant to WHO; Sen. Principal Medical Officer, Dept of Health, 1968; Dir, NHS Hospital Adv. Service, 1969-73. *Publications:* (jtly) Psychiatric Services and Architecture, 1958; (jtly) Social Psychiatry; Psychiatric Disorders in Obstetrics, 1967; Comprehensive Psychiatric Care, 1976; chapters in sundry books; papers in numerous jls on research, psychiatric treatment, organisation of psychiatric services, etc. *Address:* Alpina, Theescombe Lane, Amberley, Stroud, Glos. *T:* Amberley 2329.

BAKER, Alexander Shelley, CB 1977; OBE 1958; DFC 1944; Assistant Under Secretary of State, Home Office, since 1973; *b* 5 June 1915; *s* of late Rev. William Shelley Baker and Mrs Winifred Baker, Staines and Stratford E15; *m* 1944, Cynthia, 2nd *d* of late Charles Mould, Great Easton, Leics; two *d*. *Educ:* West Ham Secondary School. Served RAF, 1939-65 (despatches, 1944; 2 citations French Croix de Guerre); comd Nos 4, 16, 37 and 224 Sqdns and RAF North Front Gibraltar; retd as Group Captain. Principal, Home Office, 1965; Asst Sec., 1969-73. Reader, Church of England. *Recreations:* gardening, bridge. *Address:* 4 Sandford House, Kingsclere, Newbury, Berks. *T:* Kingsclere 298489. *Club:* Royal Air Force.

BAKER, Alfreda Helen, MD; FRCS; Consulting Surgeon: to Elizabeth Garrett Anderson Hospital, 1937-68; to Hounslow Hospital, 1930-68; to Marie Curie Hospital, 1937-68; *b* 2 Oct. 1897; *d* of late Alfred Rawlings and Hannah Mary Baker. *Educ:* Queen's Univ., Belfast. MB, BCh, QU Belfast, 1921 (hons); MD 1926 (Commendation); FRCS, Eng. 1927. Demonstrator of Anatomy, QU Belfast, 1922-24; House Surgeon, Royal Cancer Hosp., 1926; Riddel Research Fellow, Royal Free Hosp., 1924-26; Surgical Registrar, Elizabeth Garrett Anderson Hosp., 1930-33; Surgeon, EMS, 1939-45. Fellow Assoc. of Surgeons of Gt Brit. and Ire., 1950. *Publications:* original work published in: British Journal of Surgery; Lancet; British Journal of Obstetrics and Gynæcology, etc. *Recreations:* water colour painting, oil painting, photography, foreign travel. *Address:* Arkesden, Saffron Walden, Essex. *T:* Clavering 370.

BAKER, Allan; see Baker, J. F. A.

BAKER, Sir (Allan) Ivor, Kt 1972; CBE 1944; JP; DL; Chairman, Baker Perkins Holdings Ltd, 1944-75; *b* 2 June 1908; *s* of late Allan Richard Baker; *m* 1935, Josephine, *d* of late A. M. Harley, KC; three *s* one *d*. *Educ:* Bootham, York; King's Coll., Cambridge; Harvard, USA. Baker Perkins: Student apprentice, 1931; Director, 1935-; Jt Man. Dir., 1942-67; Chm., 1944-. British Engineers' Assoc.: Mem. Council, 1943-68; Pres., 1960-61; Director: Lloyds Bank Ltd, 1973-; Lloyds Bank Eastern Region, 1953-73 (Chm., 1973-); Mitchell Construction Holdings Ltd, 1963-. Member: Economic Planning Council for East Anglia, 1965-69; Peterborough Development Corp., 1968-. JP 1954; High Sheriff, 1968-69, DL 1973, Cambridgeshire. *Recreations:* golf, gardening. *Address:* 29 Westwood Park Road, Peterborough. *T:* Peterborough 3301.

BAKER, Anthony Baxter, JP; Regional Administrator, Northern Regional Health Authority, since 1973; *b* 12 June 1923; *s* of late Anthony Thurlbeck Baker and Robina Frances Jane (*née* Baxter); *m* 1946, Mary Margherita Patterson; one *s* three *d*. *Educ:* Tynemouth High Sch.; Durham Univ. DPA; FHA. RAFVR, UK, Canada and Iceland, 1942-46. Admin. Asst, later Dep. Sec., SE Northumberland HMC, 1949-60; Asst Sec., later Principal Asst Sec., Newcastle Regional Hosp. Bd, 1960-73. JP Tynemouth 1965; Dep. Chm., North Tyneside PSD. *Recreations:* Rugby football, golf. *Address:* 16 Manor Road, Tynemouth, North Shields NE30 4RH. *T:* North Shields 74660.

BAKER, Prof. Arthur Lemprière Lancey, DSc (Eng), FICE, FIStructE, FACI; Professor of Concrete Structures and Technology, University of London (Imperial College), 1945-73, now Emeritus; *b* 16 Dec. 1905; *s* of late W. L. Baker, Exeter; *m* 1930, Lillian Hollings; two *d*. *Educ:* Queen Elizabeth's Sch.,

Crediton; University of Manchester. Asst Engineer, Mersey Tunnel, Edmund Nuttall, Sons & Co. Ltd, 1926-28; Dist Engineer, PWD, Nigeria, 1928-30; Asst Engineer, Christiani & Nielsen Ltd, 1930-33; Senior Design Engineer, Reinforcing Steel Co., Johannesburg, 1933-36; Senior Civil Engineer, Trinidad Leaseholds Ltd, 1936-45. Mem., BSI Cttee for the Structural Use of Concrete, 1970-; Mem., Nuclear Safety Advisory Cttee, 1972-. Hon. ACGI; Hon. DTech Bradford, 1971. *Publications:* Raft Foundations, 1937; Reinforced Concrete, 1949; The Ultimate Load Theory Applied to the Design of Reinforced and Pre-stressed Concrete Frames, 1956; The Inelastic Space Frame, 1967; Limit State Design of Reinforced Concrete, 1970. *Address:* Department of Civil Engineering, Imperial College of Science and Technology, SW7 2BU. *T:* 01-589 5111.

BAKER, Air Marshal Sir Brian Edmund, KBE 1944; CB 1943; DSO 1918; MC; AFC; *b* 31 Aug. 1896; *m* 1926, Jaimsie Derby Robinson; two *d. Educ:* Haileybury. Served European War, 1914-18 (despatches, MC, DSO, AFC); Chief Flying Instructor, RAF Training Base, Leuchars, 1932-34; HMS Eagle, 1934; HMS Courageous, 1936; commanded RAF Station, Gosport, 1937-38; RAF Station, Leuchars, 1938; No 51 Group, 1940-41; RAF Iceland, 1941; No 16 Group, 1941-42; No 19 Group, 1943-44; AOC East Africa, 1945; Senior Air Staff Officer, HQ, Middle East, 1945; AOC-in-C, Transport Command, 1947-50; retd 1950. Hon. Life Governor, RNLI, 1971. *Address:* 3 Howard Place, St Andrews, Fife.

BAKER, Charles A.; see Arnold-Baker.

BAKER, Colin Lewis Gilbert, CBE 1974; FCA; Chairman, Northern Economic Planning Council, 1973-77; Director of companies; *b* 24 Aug. 1913; *m* 1942, Pauleen Denice Hartley; two *s* two *d. Educ:* Queen's Coll., Taunton. Professional accountancy, 1931-39. Served War, Somerset LI, Major, 1939-45. George Angus & Co. Ltd, 1945-73: Director, 1958-63; Dep. Chm., 1963-64; Chm., 1964-73; Exec. Dir, The Dunlop Co. Ltd (later Dunlop Holdings Ltd), 1968-73. Mem., Companies Consultative Gp, (DTI), 1972-. Other interests include: Mem., Northern Regional Bd, Lloyds Bank; Mem., Northern Regional Council, CBI (Chm., 1972-73); Local Dir, Baring Bros & Co. Ltd; Chm., Jobling Purser Ltd; Commissaris, Bos Kalis Westminster Dredging Gp NV. Gen. Comr of Income Tax, 1965-. Mem., Newcastle AHA(T); Chm., Northumberland and Tyne and Wear Red Cross Soc. Finance Cttee. *Recreations:* fishing, gardening, going to cottage in Cornwall. *Address:* Lynton, Apperley Road, Stocksfield, Northumberland. *T:* Stocksfield 3454. *Clubs:* Army and Navy; Northern Counties (Newcastle upon Tyne).

BAKER, Brig. Euston Edward Francis, CB 1957; CBE 1936; DSO 1919; MC 1917 and Bar 1918; TD; JP; Chairman, Amersham Bench, 1954-69; Hon. Colonel 5th Battalion Middlesex Regiment, 1961-63; Chairman: Middlesex T & AFA, 1951-59; Middlesex County Cadet Committee, 1944-51; National Association of Bolt and Nut Stockholders, 1948-59; *b* 5 April 1895; *s* of H. R. Baker; *m* 1920, Mary Helena, *d* of T. Sampson; two *s* one *d* (and *y s* decd). *Educ:* Sherborne (captain of football and shooting, 1913-14). Winner of Spencer Cup, Bisley, 1914. Gazetted to 5th Middlesex Regt, 15 Aug. 1914; served in France, 1914-19, continuously; commanded 2nd Bn Middlesex Regt 1918-19 (DSO, MC and bar, despatches thrice); commanded 8th Bn Middlesex Regt 1923-30 and 1936-37; Brevet Col, 1927; commanded 7th City of London Regt, 1931-36; Col, 1927; Comdr Infantry Bde, TA, 1939-42; ADC to the King, 1941-51; retd (ill-health), 1945; Hon. Col, 2/8th Batt. Middlesex Regt, 1939-47; Hon. Col 11th Bn Parachute Regt, 1948-56; Hon Col 8th Bn Middlesex Regt, 1956-61. DL Mddx (later Greater London) 1938-76; JP Bucks 1945. Citoyen d'Honneur of Douai, France, 1947-. *Address:* Stanbridge House, Amersham, Bucks. *T:* 6230.

BAKER, Geoffrey, QC 1970; a Recorder of the Crown Court, since 1972 (Recorder of Sunderland, 1971); *b* 5 April 1925; *er s* of late Sidney and Cecilia Baker, Bradford; *m* 1948, Sheila (*née* Hill); two *s* one *d. Educ:* Bradford Grammar Sch.; Leeds Univ.; LLB (Hons). Called to Bar, Inner Temple, 1947. Recorder of Pontefract, 1967-71. *Recreations:* gardening, painting, photography. *Address:* 64 The Fairway, off Alwoodley Lane, Leeds LS17 7PD. *T:* Leeds 685181. *Club:* Sheffield (Sheffield).

BAKER, Field-Marshal Sir Geoffrey Harding, GCB 1968 (KCB 1964; CB 1955); CMG 1957; CBE 1946 (OBE 1943); MC 1941; Constable of the Tower of London, since 1975; *b* 20 June 1912; *s* of late Col Cecil Norris Baker, CIE, IA, and Ella Mary Baker; *m* 1946, Valerie, *d* of late Major J. L. Lockhart and Mrs Lockhart; two *s* one *d. Educ:* Wellington Coll.; RMA Woolwich (Sword of Honour). Commnd RA, 1932; India, with 11th Field Bde, RA,

1935; "F" (Sphinx) Battery, RHA, 1937 (Egypt, 1939); Middle East Staff Coll., 1940; Bde Major RA, 4th Indian Div., Western Desert and Eritrea, 1940, 1941; Instructor ME Staff Coll., 1942; GSO1, HQ Eighth Army, 1942-43; CO 127th Field Regt, 51st Highland Div., Sicily, 1943. BGS, HQ 21st Army Gp, North West Europe, 1944; Dep. Dir, War Office, 1947; Commanding Officer 3rd Regt RHA, 1950-52; Dir War Office, 1952-54; Dir of Operations and Chief of Staff to Governor of Cyprus, Nov. 1955-Feb. 1957; CRA, 7th Armd and 5 Divs, BAOR, 1957-59; Asst C of S, HQ, Northern Army Gp, Germany, 1959; Chief of Staff, HQ Southern Command, 1960-61; Chief of Staff, Contingencies Planning, Supreme HQ, Allied Powers Europe, 1961-63; Vice-Chief of the General Staff, 1963-66; GOC-in-C, Southern Command, 1966-68; CGS, 1968-71; Field-Marshal, 1971. Director: Grindlays Bank, 1972-; Central London Reg. Bd, Lloyds Bank. Colonel Commandant: RA, 1964-; RMP, 1968-71; RHA, 1970-. Master Gunner, St James's Park, 1970-76. President: Officers' Assoc.; Army Benevolent Fund, 1971-. Vice-Pres., Wellington Coll., 1976; Mem. Council, Radley Coll., 1973-. Freeman: Haberdashers' Co.; City of London. US Legion of Merit (Comdr), 1946. *Address:* Broomden Oast, Ticehurst, Sussex. *Club:* Army and Navy.

BAKER, Geoffrey Hunter, CMG 1962; HM Diplomatic Service, retired; *b* 4 Aug. 1916; *s* of late Thomas Evelyn Baker and Gladys Beatrice Baker (*née* Marsh); *m* 1963, Anita Wägeler; one *d. Educ:* Haberdashers' Aske's Hampstead Sch.; Royal Masonic Sch., Bushey, Herts; Gonville and Caius Coll., Cambridge (Scholar). Joined Consular Service, 1938; Vice-Consul at Hamburg, 1938, Danzig, 1939, Bergen, 1939; captured by German forces there, April 1940; Vice-Consul, Basra, 1942, Jedda, 1942; Foreign Office, 1945-47; First Sec., Rangoon, 1947-51, Tehran, 1951-52; FO, 1953-54; NATO Def. Coll., Paris, 1954; Consul-Gen., Hanoi, 1954-56; UK Delegation, UN, Nov. 1956-March 1957; Cabinet Office, 1957-60; UK Delegation to the European Free Trade Association, Geneva, 1960-66; Consul-General, Munich, 1966-71, Zagreb, 1971-74. Order of Merit (Bavaria), 1971. *Recreations:* tennis, sailing, reading, and listening to music. *Address:* 10 Leigh Road, Highfield, Southampton SO2 1EF. *Clubs:* United Oxford & Cambridge University; Cambridge University Cruising (Cambridge).

BAKER, Rt. Hon. Sir George (Gillespie), PC 1971; Kt 1961; OBE 1945; President of the Family Division (formerly the Probate, Divorce and Admiralty Division) of the High Court of Justice, since 1971, a Judge in the Division, since 1961; *b* 25 April 1910; *s* of late Captain John Kilgour Baker, Stirling; *m* 1935, Jessie McCall Findlay; three *s. Educ:* Glasgow Academy; Strathallan Sch., Perthshire; Brasenose Coll., Oxford (Hon. Schol.; Sen. Hulme Schol.). Called to the Bar, Middle Temple, 1932 (Harmsworth Schol.); Bencher, 1961; Lent Reader, 1975; Treasurer, 1976. Army, 1939-45; Queen's Own RWK 1939-40; commissioned The Cameronians (Scottish Rifles), 1940; DAAG War Office, 1941-42; AAG Allied Force HQ, 1942-44; Col. 'A' 15 Army Gp, 1945: AAG British War Crimes Executive, Nuremberg, 1945. Contested (C) Southall (Middlesex), 1945. Recorder: of Bridgnorth, 1946-51; of Smethwick, 1951-52; of Wolverhampton, 1952-61. Dep. Chm. QS, Shropshire, 1954-71. QC 1952, Leader of Oxford Circuit, 1954-61; Presiding Judge, Wales and Chester Circuit, 1970-71. Governor, Strathallan Sch., 1947-57, Hon. Governor, 1968-; Governor: Epsom Coll., 1958-72; Wycombe Abbey, 1972-. Commissioner holding Government enquiry, Feb.-April 1956 into objections to proposed British Egg Marketing Scheme and for Kenya Government into pyrethrum industry, 1960; First Chm. of the General Optical Council, 1959-61. Chm., Departmental Cttee on Mechanical Recording of Court Proceedings, 1964-70. Hon. Mem., Canadian Bar Assoc. Hon. Fellow, Brasenose Coll., Oxford, 1966. *Recreations:* golf, fishing. *Address:* Camrie, Overstream, Loudwater, Rickmansworth, Herts. *T:* Rickmansworth 77296; 2 Plowden Buildings, Temple, EC4. *T:* 01-353 4720. *Clubs:* Caledonian; Denham Golf (Captain 1967-68).

See also *T . S . G . Baker.*

BAKER, George William, CBE 1977 (OBE 1971); VRD 1952; HM Diplomatic Service, retired; British High Commissioner to Papua New Guinea, 1975-77; *b* 7 July 1917; *e s* of late George William Baker and of Lilian Turnbull Baker; *m* 1942, Audrey Martha Elizabeth, *e d* of Harry and Martha Day; two *d . Educ:* Chigwell Sch.; Hertford Coll., Oxford (Colonial Service Second Devonshire Course). London Div., RNVR, 1937-62; served War, RN, 1939-45. Colonial Admin. Service, Tanganyika, 1946-62: Asst Colonial Attaché, Washington (incl. service in UK Delegn to Trusteeship Council at UN), 1957; Defence Sec., Tanganyika, 1959; Head of Tanganyika Govt Information Dept, 1959-62; retd after Tanganyika Independence, 1962. Joined CRO, 1962; First Sec. (Information) and Dir of British Inf.

Services, British High Commn, Freetown, 1962-65; served in FCO (Consular and Defence Depts), 1965-69; First Sec. and Head of Chancery, Kinshasa, 1969-72; Dep. British Govt Rep., St Vincent and Grenada, Windward Is, 1972-74; British Commissioner, Port Moresby, Papua New Guinea, 1974-75. A Vice-Pres., Royal African Soc., 1973-. *Publications:* official booklets and contribs to learned jls. *Recreations:* photography, fishing, sailing, climbing, tennis, Rugby Union, cricket, flying. *Address:* Siggswood, Waldron, Sussex. *T:* Heathfield 2847. *Clubs:* East India, Devonshire, Sports and Public Schools, MCC, Royal Commonwealth Society, Royal Photographic Society; Scientific Exploration Society (Hon. Mem.); Papua and Papua Yacht (both Port Moresby).

BAKER, Sir Humphrey D. B. S.; *see* Sherston-Baker.

BAKER, Sir Ivor; *see* Baker, Sir A. I.

BAKER, Dame Janet (Abbott), DBE 1976 (CBE 1970); professional singer; *b* 21 Aug. 1933; *d* of Robert Abbott Baker and May (*née* Pollard); *m* 1957, James Keith Shelley. *Educ:* The College for Girls, York; Wintringham, Grimsby. Daily Mail Kathleen Ferrier Award, 1956; Queen's Prize, Royal College of Music, 1959; Shakespeare Prize, Hamburg, 1971. Hon. DMus: Birmingham, 1968; Leicester, 1974; London, 1974; Hull, 1975; Oxon, 1975. Hon. Fellow St Anne's Coll., Oxford, 1975. *Recreations:* reading, tennis, walking. *Address:* c/o Ibbs & Tillett Ltd, 124 Wigmore Street, W1H 0AX.

BAKER, John Arnold; His Honour Judge Baker; a Circuit Judge, since 1973; *b* Calcutta, 5 Nov. 1925; *s* of late William Sydney Baker, MC and Hilda Dora Baker (*née* Swiss); *m* 1954, Edith Muriel Joy Heward; two *d*. *Educ:* Plymouth Coll.; Wellington Sch., Somerset; Wadham Coll., Oxford (MA, BCL). Treas., Oxford Union, 1948. Admitted Solicitor, 1951; called to Bar, Gray's Inn, 1960. A Recorder, 1972-73. Chm., Nat. League of Young Liberals, 1952-53; contested (L): Richmond, 1959 and 1964; Dorking, 1970; Vice-Pres., Liberal Party, 1968-69; Chm., Liberal Party Exec., 1969-70. *Recreations:* music, boating. *Address:* 1 Rosemont Road, Richmond, Surrey. *T:* 01-940 6983.

BAKER, Rev. Canon John Austin; Canon of Westminster, since 1973; Treasurer, since 1974; *b* 11 Jan. 1928; *s* of George Austin Baker and Grace Edna Baker; *m* 1974, Gillian Mary Leach. *Educ:* Marlborough; Oriel Coll., Oxford (B Litt, MA). Asst Curate, All Saints', Cuddesdon, and Lectr in Old Testament, Cuddesdon Theol Coll., 1954-57; Priest 1955; Asst Curate, St Anselm's, Hatch End, and Asst Lectr in NT Greek, King's Coll., London, 1957-59; Official Fellow, Chaplain and Lectr in Divinity, Corpus Christi Coll., Oxford, 1959-73, Emeritus Fellow, 1977; Lectr in Theology, Brasenose and Lincoln Colls, Oxford, 1959-73; Hebrew Lectr, Exeter Coll., Oxford, 1969-73; Governor of Pusey House, Oxford, 1970-; Exam. Chaplain to Bp of Oxford, 1960-, to Bp of Southwark, 1973-; Governor: Westminster Sch., 1974-; Ripon Coll., Cuddesdon, 1974-; Trustee, Harold Buxton Trust, 1973-; Dorrance Visiting Prof., Trinity Coll., Hartford, Conn, USA, 1967; Visiting Prof., King's Coll., London, 1974-77; Mem.: CofE Doctrine Commn, 1967-76; Faith and Order Advisory Gp, CofE Bd for Mission and Unity, 1976-. *Publications:* The Foolishness of God, 1970; Travels in Oudamovia, 1976; The Living Splendour of Westminster Abbey, 1977; contrib. to: Man: Fallen and Free (ed Kemp), 1969; Thinking about the Eucharist (ed Ramsey), 1972; Church Membership and Intercommunion (ed Kent and Murray), 1973; What about the New Testament? (ed Hooker and Hickling), 1975; Man and Nature (ed Montefiore), 1975; *translations:* W. Eichrodt, Theology of the Old Testament, vol. 1 1961, vol. 2 1967; T. Bovet, That They May Have Life, 1964; J. Daniélou, Theology of Jewish Christianity, 1964; H. von Campenhausen, Ecclesiastical Authority and Spiritual Power, 1969; H. von Campenhausen, The Formation of the Christian Bible, 1972; J. Daniélou, Gospel Message and Hellenistic Culture, 1973; (with David Smith) J. Daniélou, The Origins of Latin Christianity, 1977. *Recreations:* music, walking. *Address:* 3 Little Cloister, SW1P 3PL. *T:* 01-222 4174.

BAKER, John B.; *see* Brayne-Baker.

BAKER, John Burkett, QC 1975; a Recorder of the Crown Court, since 1972; *b* 17 Sept. 1931; *s* of Philip and Grace Baker; *m* 1955, Margaret Mary Smeaton; three *s* seven *d*. *Educ:* Finchley Catholic Grammar Sch.; White Fathers, Bishops Waltham; UC Exeter. LLB London. RAF, 1955-58. Called to Bar, Gray's Inn, 1957; practised from 1958. Prosecuting Counsel to Dept of Health and Social Security, 1969-75; Dep. Chm., Shropshire QS, 1970-71. Marriage Counsellor, Catholic Marriage Adv. Council. *Address:* 1 Essex Court, Temple, EC4Y 9AR. *T:* 01-353 6717.

BAKER, (John Frederic) Allan, CB 1957; CEng, FICE; Ministry of Transport, retired; *b* 5 Oct. 1903; *s* of late H. J. Baker; *m* 1927, Nancy Elizabeth Wells; one *d* (and one *s* decd). *Educ:* St Paul's Sch. After Local Authority experience in Middlesex, 1922-, joined Ministry of Transport, 1929, serving in Exeter, Bedford, Nottingham and London; apptd Divisional Road Engineer for Wales and Mon, at Cardiff, 1947, and Dep. Chief Engineer at Headquarters, 1953; Chief Engineer and Dir of Highway Engineering, 1954-65. Member: Road Research Board, 1954-65; London Roads Cttee, 1959; Traffic Signs Cttee, 1963; Cons. Adviser to Automobile Assoc., 1965-69. Mem. (Past Chm.), Road Engrg Industry Cttee of BSI; Vice-Pres., Internat. Exec. Cttee of Permanent Internat. Assoc. of Road Congresses, 1960-72 and Pres. d'Honneur, Brit. Nat. Cttee; Founder Fellow, Fellowship of Engineering, 1976; Hon. FIMunE; Hon. FInstHE. Viva Shield and Gold Medal, Worshipful Co. of Carmen, 1968. *Recreations:* most outdoor and indoor games. *Address:* 36 Imber Close, Ember Lane, Esher, Surrey. *T:* 01-398 3331.

BAKER, Rt. Rev. John Gilbert Hindley; *see* Hong Kong and Macao, Bishop of.

BAKER, John Randal, MA, DPhil, DSc Oxon; FRS 1958; Emeritus Reader in Cytology, Oxford University (Reader, 1955-67); *b* 23 Oct. 1900; *y s* of Rear-Adm. Julian A. Baker, RN; *m* 1st, 1923, Inezita Davis; one *s* one *d*; 2nd, 1939, Mrs Helen Savage. *Educ:* New Coll., Oxford (1st Class in Honour Sch. of Natural Science). Scientific expeditions to New Hebrides, 1922-23, 1927, 1933-34; Joint editor Quarterly Journal of Microscopical Science, 1946-64; Professorial Fellow, New Coll., Oxford, 1964-67; Pres. Royal Microscopical Society, 1964-65, Hon. Fellow, 1968. Oliver Bird Medal for researches on chemical contraception, 1958. *Publications:* Sex in Man and Animals, 1926; Man and Animals in the New Hebrides, 1929; Cytological Technique, 1933 (5th edn, 1966); The Chemical Control of Conception, 1935; The Scientific Life, 1942; Science and the Planned State, 1945; Abraham Trembley of Geneva, 1952; Principles of Biological Microtechnique, 1958; Race, 1974. *Address:* The Mill, 26 Mill End, Kidlington, Oxford OX5 2EG.

BAKER, Air Chief Marshal Sir John (Wakeling), GBE 1954; KCB 1949 (CB 1942); MC 1918; DFC 1925; RAF retired; *b* Winnipeg, Canada, 23 Oct. 1897; *er s* of late Rev. F. V. Baker, DD, BA; *m* 1927, Hilary, *o d* of late Lieut-Col H. Bonham-Carter; three *s* one *d*. *Educ:* Eastbourne Coll.; RMA Woolwich. Commissioned RA, 1916; transferred RFC 1917; RAF 1918 (MC); 60 Sqdn, India, NWF, 1923-28 (DFC); RAF Staff Coll., 1931; 33 Sqdn, Middle East, 1935-36; Imperial Defence Coll., 1938; Director of Bomber Operations, Air Ministry, 1942 (CB); SASO Air Command, SE Asia, 1943-44 (despatches); AOC 12 (Fighter) Group, 1945-46; Dir-Gen. of Personnel, Air Ministry, 1946-48; AOC-in-C, Coastal Command, 1948-49 (KCB); C-in-C MEAF, 1950-52; DCAS then VCAS, Air Ministry, 1952-53; Controller of Aircraft, Min. of Supply, 1953-56 (GBE). Air ADC to the Queen, 1952-56. *Address:* 10 The Glebe, Chislehurst, Kent BR7 5PX.

BAKER, Sir Joseph; *see* Baker, Sir S. J.

BAKER, Kenneth Wilfred; MP (C) St Marylebone since Oct. 1970; Industrial Consultant; *b* 3 Nov. 1934; *s* of late W. M. Baker, OBE and of Mrs Baker (*née* Harries); *m* 1963, Mary Elizabeth Gray-Muir; one *s* two *d*. *Educ:* St Paul's Sch.; Magdalen Coll., Oxford. Nat. Service, 1953-55: Lieut in Gunners, N Africa; Artillery Instructor to Libyan Army. Oxford, 1955-58 (Sec. of Union). Served Twickenham Borough Council, 1960-62. Contested (C): Poplar, 1964; Acton, 1966; MP (C) Acton, March 1968-70; Public Accounts Cttee, 1969-70; PPS to Minister of State, Dept of Employment, 1970-72; Parly Sec., CSD, 1972-74; PPS to Leader of Opposition, 1974-75; Mem. Exec., 1922 Cttee. Chm., Computer Agency Council, 1973-74. *Recreation:* collecting books. *Address:* House of Commons, SW1. *Club:* Carlton.

BAKER, Maurice S.; Managing Director, F. W. Woolworth & Co. Ltd, 1967-71, retired; *b* 27 Jan. 1911; *s* of Sidney B. Baker and Ellen Elizabeth (*née* Airey); *m* 1935, Helen Johnstone (*née* Tweedie); one *s*. *Educ:* Lowestoft Grammar School. Trainee Manager, F. W. Woolworth & Co. Ltd, 1928; RAOC, 1940-46 (Major); rejoined company; Dir 1962. Officer, Legion of Merit (US), 1945. *Recreation:* bowls (Mem. Exec., English Bowling Assoc.). *Address:* Ness Point, 7a Woodcote Park Avenue, Purley, CR2 3ND. *T:* 01-660 3718.

BAKER, Mrs Noel John Horne; *see* Scott-Moncrieff, J. C.

BAKER, Paul Vivian, QC 1972; *b* 27 March 1923; *er s* of Vivian Cyril Baker and Maud Lydia Baker; *m* 1957, Stella Paterson Eadie, *d* of William Eadie, MD; one *s* one *d*. *Educ:* City of London Sch.; University Coll., Oxford (BCL, MA). Called to Bar, Lincoln's Inn, 1950. Editor, Law Quarterly Review, 1971-. *Recreations:* music, gardening. *Address:* 9 Old Square, Lincoln's Inn, WC2A 3SR. *T:* 01-405 0846. *Clubs:* Athenæum, Authors'.

BAKER, Prof. Peter Frederick, PhD; FRS 1976; Halliburton Professor and Head of Department of Physiology, King's College, London, since 1975; *b* 11 March 1939; *s* of F. T. Baker and D. E. Skelton; *m* 1966, Phyllis Light; one *s* three *d*. *Educ:* Lincoln Sch.; Emmanuel Coll., Cambridge (Scholar; BA Natural Sciences Tripos, Cl. 1, 1960; PhD 1964).Univ. of Cambridge: Demonstrator in Physiol., 1963-66; Lectr in Physiol., 1966-74; Fellow, Emmanuel Coll., Cambridge, 1962-74. Guest Investigator, Rockefeller Univ., NY, 1964. Scientific Medal, RZS, 1975. *Publications:* Calcium Movement in Excitable Cells (with H. Reuter), 1975; papers on cell physiol. in Jl of Physiol. and other sci. jls. *Recreation:* natural history, the Loch Ness Monster. *Address:* Meadow Cottage, Bourn, Cambridge. *T:* Caxton 212.

BAKER, Peter Maxwell, QC 1974; a Recorder of the Crown Court, since 1972; *b* 26 March 1930; *s* of late Harold Baker and of Rose Baker; *m* 1954, Jacqueline Mary Marshall; three *d*. *Educ:* King Edward VII Sch., Sheffield; Exeter Coll., Oxford. MA Oxon. Called to Bar, Gray's Inn, 1956 (Holker Senior Exhibitioner); Junior, NE Circuit, 1960. Chm., Appeal Tribunal, Min. (now Dept) of Social Security, 1966. *Recreations:* yachting, music, watching others garden. *Address:* Five Acres, Curbar, Sheffield S30 1YA. *T:* Hope Valley 30282. *Club:* Sheffield (Sheffield).

BAKER, Richard Douglas James, OBE 1976; broadcaster and author; BBC Television Newsreader since 1954; *b* Willesden, London, 15 June 1925; *s* of Albert and Jane Isobel Baker; two *s*. *Educ:* Kilburn Grammar Sch.; Peterhouse, Cambridge (MA). Served War, Royal Navy, 1943-46. Actor, 1948; Teacher, 1949; Third Programme Announcer, 1950-53. Commentator for State Occasion Outside Broadcasts, 1967-70. TV Introductions to Promenade Concerts, 1960-; Panellist on BBC2's Face the Music, 1966-; on Radio 4: Presenter of Start the Week with Richard Baker, 1970-; These You Have Loved, 1972-. Mem. Exec. Cttee: Youth and Music; National Youth Orchestra; Friends of Covent Garden; Mem. Council, London Philharmonic Orchestra; Vice-Pres., Internat. Voluntary Service 'Master Key' (Multiple Sclerosis Soc.). TV Newscaster of the Year (Radio Industries Club), 1972, 1974. Hon. FLCM 1974. *Publications:* Here is the News (broadcasts), 1966; The Terror of Tobermory, 1972; The Magic of Music, 1975; Dry Ginger, 1977. *Recreations:* RNR (Lt-Cmdr), gardening, the gramophone. *Address:* Hadley Lodge, 12 Watford Road, Radlett, Herts. *T:* 01-242 4388 (Agent). *Clubs:* Garrick, Savage.

BAKER, Richard St Barbe, FIAL; Forestry Adviser and Silviculturist; Founder of The Men of the Trees, 1922; *b* 9 Oct. 1889; *s* of John R. St Barbe Baker and Charlotte Purrott; *m* 1st, 1946, Doreen Whitworth (from whom he obtained a divorce, 1953), *d* of G. H. W. Long, Strensham, Worcs; one *s* one *d*; 2nd, 1959, Catriona Burnett. *Educ:* Dean Close Sch., Cheltenham; Saskatchewan Univ.; Gonville and Caius Coll., Cambridge. Forestry Diploma, Cantab., 1920; Canada, 1909-13; Expeditionary Force, France, King Edward's Horse, Royal Field Artillery and Remounts, 1914-18; Army Sch. of Education, 1919; Asst Conservator of Forests, Kenya, 1920-23, Nigeria, 1924-29; initiated silvicultural experiments in the mahogany forests; delegate to World Forestry Congress, Rome; forest research Oxford and Continent, 1926; lecture tours 1930, 1931; founded Junior Men of the Trees, 1956; travelled 17,000 miles visiting forests of USA and Canada to prepare forestry plan; conf. with Franklin D. Roosevelt developed into Civilian Conservation Corps Camps; Ottawa Conf. on Empire Forestry, 1932-33; forest survey, S. America, 1936; organised Forestry Summer Sch., Oxford, 1938, and others; lectured to Army and RAF Cadets; supervised forestry training and prepared plan for rehabilitation of returning service men; General Meeting of The Men of the Trees, Chelsea, assumed world leadership in earthwide regeneration, 1947; took New Earth Charter to USA, 1950; convened World Forestry Charter Gatherings, 1945-56; led Sahara Univ. Expedn, surveying 9000 miles of desert and equatorial Africa; revisited NZ for Forest and Soil Conservation, 1954; settled in NZ, 1959; Deleg., 5th World Forestry Congress, Seattle; convened 1st Redwood Reunion, Mill Creek, 1960; for UNA covered 1200 miles on horseback in NZ, giving talks to schools on Trees, 1962-63; convened 1st Sahara Reclamation Conf., Rabat; reported 1964; broadcasts, lectures, NZ Schs,Conservation and Sahara Reclamation, 1965; vis. Australia

to check felling and burning high forest, Kenya, Nat. Tree-Planting Week and Reunion of Men of the Trees; deleg., 6th World Forestry Congress, Spain, 1966; fact finding mission for Forestry, NZ and Q'land; rep. NZ, S Island at S Pacific Conf. Sydney, 1967; promoted afforestation, India and Pakistan, and inspected progress, Kuwait, Iran, Lebanon, UAR, Tunisia, and Spain; prepared forestry plans, Jamaica and British Honduras, 1968; conferred FAO, Rome, then visited Tunisian Pre-Sahara with group of scientists; inspected Austrian techniques of dune-stabilisation, Libya; addressed students, Univ. of Vienna, to recruit personnel for Sahara Reclamation Programme, 1969; revisited Silvicultural Experimental Area, Mahogany Forests, Nigeria, expl. S Sahara, Nigerian and Niger frontiers, 1970; conducted seminars on place of trees in farming, Univ. Saskatchewan, 1971; visited UN, NY, re Sahara Reclamation Prog., 1971; completed survey, N Nigeria, route for spiral shelter belt; led delegn, Nairobi, Golden Jubilee Kenya where 500,000 trees planted in 3 days; 7th World Forestry Congress, Argentine, to help launch World Year of the Tree, 1972; Men of the Trees, seminar on Trees and the Environment, 1973; convened 13th World Forestry Charter Gathering, London, 1974. Hon. LLD Saskatchewan, 1971. *Publications:* Tree Lovers Calendar, 1929 and following years; Book of the Seasons, 1940; Africa Drums, 1942; The Redwoods, 1943; I Planted Trees, 1944; Green Glory: Forests of the World, 1947; New Earth Charter, 1949; Famous Trees, 1953; Sahara Challenge, 1954; Land of Tané, 1956; Dance of the Trees, 1957; Kamiti: A Forester's Dream, 1958; The Redwoods (Famous Trees of the World, 1), 1959; Horse Sense: Story of My Horses in War and Peace, 1961; Trees of the World, 1962; Trees of the Bible Lands, Famous Trees of New Zealand, True Book of Trees, 1963; Sahara Conquest, 1966; Caravan Story and Country Notes 1969; My Life, My Trees, 1970; Famous Trees of Bible Lands, 1974. Founder Trees and Life, Journal of The Men of the Trees; many articles and pamphlets on forestry. *Recreations:* riding, gardening, music and tree photography. *Address:* The Priory, Pembury, Kent. *T:* Pembury 3018. *Club:* Naval and Military.

BAKER, Sir Rowland, Kt 1968; OBE 1946; RCNC; Director, Balrena Engrng; *b* 3 June 1908; *s* of Isaac and Lizzie Baker; *m* 1931, Frances Cornish; one *s* three *d*; *m* 1972, Barbara Mary Comley. *Educ:* RNC Greenwich. Assistant Constructor, HM Dockyards, 1933-39; Constructor, Admty, 1939-42; Supt of Landing Craft, 1942-46; Naval Constructor-in-Chief, Royal Canadian Navy, 1948-56; Technical Chief Exec., Dreadnought Project, 1958-63; Tech. Dir, Polaris Exec., MoD (Navy), 1963-68, retired. Medal of Freedom with Silver Palm (US), 1946. *Publications:* contribs to jls. *Recreations:* golf, bridge. *Address:* Newfield, Entry Hill, Bath. *T:* Bath 22452.

BAKER, Sir (Stanislaus) Joseph, Kt 1958; CB 1947; retired as Receiver for the Metropolitan Police District and Courts (1952-60); *b* 7 March 1898; *s* of Henry G. Baker, Liverpool; *m* 1920, Eleonora White; one *d* (and one *d* decd). *Educ:* St Francis Xavier Sch.; Liverpool Univ. BSc 1919, Hons 1920. Served European War, 1914-18, RE 1915-17; Royal Artillery, 1917-18. Local Government Board for Ireland, 1920; Chief Sec.'s Office, Dublin Castle, 1922; Irish Office, 1922; Home Office, 1924; Sec. to Privy Council Cttee on question of contributions to Imperial Funds from the Islands of Jersey, Guernsey and Man, 1925. Asst Under-Sec. of State, Home Office, 1941-52. Chairman: National Police Fund Advisory Council, 1946-52; Police Regional Services Cttee, 1945-48; Police Common Services Cttee, 1948-52; Mem. Board of Governors of Police Coll., 1947-52. Chm., Kenya Police Commission, 1953. *Address:* Grenfields, Grenofen, Tavistock, Devon PL19 9ES. *T:* Tavistock 2702.

BAKER, Stephen; Co-ordinator of Industrial Advisers, Departments of Trade and Industry, since 1974; *b* 27 March 1926; *s* of late Arthur and Nancy Baker; *m* 1950, Margaret Julia Wright; one *s* two *d*. *Educ:* Epsom Coll.; Clare Coll., Cambridge (MA). FIMechE. Engr Officer, RN, 1944-47; Apprentice, Davy United Engineering Co. Ltd, 1947-49; Works Engr, John Baker & Bessemer Ltd, 1949-51; Davy United Engrg Co. Ltd, 1951: Dir of Prodn, 1960; Gen. Man., 1961; Dir, Davy Ashmore Ltd, 1963; Dir of Ops, Davy-Ashmore Engrg Ltd, 1964; Chm. and Chief Exec. of Davy United Engrg Co. Ltd, Ashmore Benson Pease Ltd and Loewy Robertson Engrg Co. Ltd, 1968; Man. Dir, Kearney & Trecker Ltd, 1970; Member: BOTB, 1975-; Construction Exports Adv. Bd, 1975-; Process Plant EDC, 1977-. *Recreations:* shooting, gardening. *Address:* 43A Heathfield Road, SW18. *T:* 01-870 1115. *Club:* United Oxford & Cambridge University.

BAKER, Prof. Stephen Leonard; Professor Emeritus, Manchester University; *b* 24 Oct. 1888; *s* of Arthur de Chair Baker and Sophia Baker (*née* Sandes); *m* 1921, Georgina Mary (*née* Barnes); five *s*. *Educ:* Whitgift Grammar Sch.; London Hospital

Medical Sch. Temp. Surgeon Lieut RN, 1915-18; Pathologist to King Edward VII Sanatorium, Midhurst, 1919-21; Chief Asst, Bland-Sutton Institute, Middlesex Hospital, 1922-31; Proctor Prof. of Pathology, Manchester Univ., 1931-50; Professor of Osteo-pathology, Manchester Univ., 1950-55. John Hunter Medal and Triennial Prize, Royal Coll. of Surgeons, 1955. *Publications:* numerous publications in medical journals. *Recreations:* gardening, photography, geology. *Address:* Sea Winds, Orford, Woodbridge, Suffolk.

BAKER, Very Rev. Thomas George Adames, MA; Dean of Worcester, since 1975; *b* 22 Dec. 1920; *s* of late Walter and Marion Baker, Southampton; unmarried. *Educ:* King Edward VI Sch., Southampton; Exeter Coll., Oxford; Lincoln Theological Coll. Curate of All Saints, King's Heath, Birmingham, 1944-47; Vicar of St James, Edgbaston, 1947-54; Sub-Warden of Lincoln Theological Coll., 1954-60; Principal of Wells Theological College and Prebendary of Combe II in Wells Cathedral, 1960-71; Archdeacon of Bath, 1971-75. Canon Theologian of Leicester Cathedral, 1959-66. Select Preacher, Univ. of Cambridge, 1963, Univ. of Oxford, 1973. Recognised Teacher, Bristol Univ., 1969-74. *Publications:* What is the New Testament?, 1969; Questioning Worship, 1977. *Recreation:* music. *Address:* The Deanery, College Green, Worcester. *T:* Worcester 23501.

BAKER, Thomas Scott Gillespie; a Recorder of the Crown Court, since 1976; *b* 10 Dec. 1937; *s* of Rt Hon. Sir George Baker, *qv*; *m* 1973, Margaret Joy Strange; one *s* one *d*. *Educ:* Haileybury; Brasenose Coll., Oxford. Called to the Bar, Middle Temple, 1961 (Astbury Schol.); Midland and Oxford Circuit. Mem., Chorleywood UDC, 1965-68. *Recreations:* golf, fishing. *Address:* Fern House, Jordans Lane, Jordans, Bucks HP9 3SW. *T:* Chalfont St Giles 4566; 1 Crown Office Row, Temple, EC4Y 7HH. *T:* 01-353 1801. *Clubs:* Caledonian, MCC; Denham Golf.

BAKER, Willfred Harold Kerton, TD; company director; *b* 6 Jan. 1920; *o s* of late W. H. Baker; *m* 1945, Kathleen Helen Sloan (*née* Murray Bisset); one *s* two *d* (and one *step d*). *Educ:* Hardye's Sch.; Edinburgh Univ.; Cornell Univ., USA. Joined TA, and served War of 1939-45 (Major). Edinburgh Univ. (BSc Agriculture), 1946-49. MP (C) Banffshire, 1964-Feb. 1974. *Recreations:* fishing, philately. *Address:* Plancöet, Alderney, Channel Islands. *T:* Alderney 2232.

BAKER, Rt. Rev. William Scott, MA; Assistant Bishop, Diocese of Liverpool, since 1968; *b* 22 June 1902; *s* of late Rev. Canon William Wing Carew Baker, Vicar of Southill, Beds; unmarried. *Educ:* King's Coll. Choir Sch., Cambridge; Aldenham; King's Coll., Cambridge; Cuddesdon. Deacon, 1925; Priest, 1927; Chaplain of King's Coll., Cambridge, and Asst Curate of St Giles with St Peter's Church, Cambridge, 1925-32; Vicar of St John The Baptist's, Newcastle on Tyne, 1932-43; Examining Chaplain to Bishop of Wakefield, 1928-32; to Bishop of Newcastle, 1941-43; Proctor in Convocation for Diocese of Newcastle, 1943; Bishop of Zanzibar and Dar-es-Salaam, 1943-65, of Zanzibar and Tanga, 1965-68; Lectr, St Katherine's Coll., Liverpool, 1968-75. *Publication:* (contributor) The Parish Communion, 1937. *Address:* 11 Woolacombe Road, Liverpool L16 9JG. *T:* 051-722 5035.

BAKER, Wilson, FRS 1946; FRIC; BSc, MSc, PhD, DSc (Manchester); MA (Oxon.); retired; Alfred Capper Pass Professor of Organic Chemistry, University of Bristol, 1945-65 (Dean of the Faculty of Science, 1948-51; Emeritus Professor, University of Bristol, 1965); *b* 24 Jan. 1900; *yr s* of Harry and Mary Baker, Runcorn, Cheshire; *m* 1927, Juliet Elizabeth, *d* of Henry and Julia R. Glaisyer, Birmingham; one *s* two *d*. *Educ:* Liverpool Coll. Upper Sch.; Victoria Univ. of Manchester (Mercer Schol., Baeyer Fellow and Dalton Scholar). Asst Lecturer in Chemistry, Univ. of Manchester, 1924-27; Tutor in Chemistry, Dalton Hall, Manchester, 1926-27; Univ. Lecturer and Demonstrator in Chemistry, Univ. of Oxford, 1927-44; Fellow and Praelector in Chemistry, The Queen's Coll., Oxford, 1937-44. Vice-Pres. of the Chemical Society, 1957-60. *Publications:* numerous original papers on organic chemistry, dealing chiefly with the synthesis of natural products, the development of synthetical processes, compounds of abnormal aromatic type, organic inclusion compounds, and the preparation of large-ring compounds, and the chemistry of penicillin, published mainly in Journal of the Chemical Society; (with T. W. J. Taylor) 2nd Edition of Professor N. V. Sidgwick's The Organic Chemistry of Nitrogen, 1937. *Recreations:* walking, gardening, music, mineralogy. *Address:* Lane's End, Church Road, Winscombe, Avon. *T:* Winscombe 3112.

BAKER-CARR, Air Marshal Sir John (Darcy), KBE 1962 (CBE 1951); CB 1957; AFC 1944; Controller of Engineering and Equipment, Air Ministry, 1962-64, retired; *b* 13 January 1906; *s* of late Brigadier-General C. D. Baker-Carr, CMG, DSO and Sarah Quinan; *m* 1934, Margery Dallas; no *c*. *Educ:* England and USA. Entered RAF as Pilot Officer, 1929; No. 32 Fighter Sqdn 1930, Flying Officer; Flying Boats at home and overseas, 1931; Armament Specialist Course, 1934; Flight-Lieut; Armament and Air Staff appts, 1935-38; Sqdn Ldr, 1938; Armament Research and Development, 1939-45 (AFC); Wing Comdr, 1940; Gp Captain, 1942; Central Fighter Estab., 1946-47; Dep. Dir Postings, Air Min., 1947-48; Air Cdre, 1948; Dir of Armament Research and Development, Min. of Supply, 1948-51 (CBE); idc 1952; Comdt RAF, St Athan, 1953-56; Senior Technical Staff Officer, HQ Fighter Command, RAF, 1956-59; Air Vice-Marshal, 1957; Air Officer Commanding, No. 41 Group, Maintenance Command, 1959-61; Air Marshal, 1962. *Recreations:* sailing and carpentry. *Address:* Thatchwell Cottage, King's Somborne, Hants. *Club:* Royal Air Force Yacht (Hamble, Hants).

BAKER WILBRAHAM, Sir R. J.; *see* Wilbraham.

BAKEWELL, Robert Donald, CMG 1952; Chm. Australian Woolgrowers' Council, 1949-54 (Member, 1940-); Member Australian Wool Realization Commission, 1945-59; *b* 9 Sept. 1899; *s* of late E. H. Bakewell, Adelaide; *m* 1929, Ydonea, *d* of Hylton Dale, Toorak; one *d*. *Educ:* Kyre Coll. (now Scotch Coll.), Adelaide. Man. Dir Farnley Grazing Pty. Ltd, 1935-73; Pres., Graziers' Federal Council of Aust., 1948-49 (Mem. 1940-50); Pres., Graziers' Assoc. of Vic., 1943-46 (Mem. Council and Exec., 1937-, Trustee, 1945-); Mem. Exec. Chamber of Agric. of Vic., 1940-50 (Vice-Pres. 1946-48); Graziers Rep., Primary Producers' Council of Aust., 1947-49; Mem. Wool Industry Conference, 1963-70. *Recreation:* bowls. *Address:* 22 Parkview Parade, Benalla, Vic 3672, Australia. *T:* Benalla 62-3368. *Clubs:* Australian (Melbourne); Adelaide (S Australia); Benalla (Victoria).

BALANCHINE, George Melitonovitch; Choreographer; Artistic director, New York City Ballet Company, since 1948; *b* St Petersburg (now Leningrad), Russia, 22 Jan. 1904; *s* of Meliton Balanchivadze, composer, and Maria Vassiliev; became a citizen of the US. *Educ:* Imperial Academy of Dance, Imperial Academy of Music, St Petersburg. Left Russia on a European tour with the Soviet State Dancers, 1924, playing in Germany, England and France. Ballet-Master: for Serge Diaghilev, 1925-29; staged dances for Cole Porter production of Wake up and Dream, London, 1929; Maître de Ballet at Royal Theatre, Copenhagen, 1930; with Boris Kochno organized Ballets de Théâtre de Monte Carlo, under patronage of Princess of Monaco, 1932; presented Les Ballets, 1933; went to US, 1933, and founded School of American Ballet, 1934 (Chm. of Faculty); Artistic director, Ballet Society, New York, 1946; with Lincoln Kirstein as General director and himself as artistic director the New York City Ballet Company was started, 1948; it has subsequently made many tours in US and abroad. Has composed over 100 ballets and his choreography includes ballets in operas, musical comedies and films. Was guest of Grand Opera, Paris, 1947, and Sadler's Wells, London, 1950. *Publication:* Balanchine's Complete Stories of the Great Ballets, 1954. *Address:* c/o School of American Ballet, Inc., NY State Theatre, NY 10023, USA.

BALCHIN, John Alfred; housing and new towns consultant; *b* 8 Aug. 1914; *er s* of Alfred and Florence Balchin; *m* 1940, Elsie Dormer; one *s* two *d*. *Educ:* Sir Walter St John's Sch., Battersea; Sir John Cass Coll., City of London. DPA (London), DMA, FCIS, FIH. Entered clerical staff of LCC (Clerk's Dept), 1932; admin. grade 1936; civil defence co-ordination work, 1938-45; transf. to Housing Dept: Progress Officer, 1946; Principal Clerk, 1952; Asst Dir (Finance), 1960; Asst Dir (Management), 1963; Sen. Asst Dir of Housing, GLC, 1965-69; Assoc. Sen. Lectr, for Housing Management and Administration, Brunel Univ., 1969-71; Gen. Manager, Stevenage Develt Corp., 1969-76. Mem., Housing Services Adv. Gp, DoE, 1976-. *Publications:* papers to professional bodies and jls on housing and new town topics. *Address:* Westwards, Perran Downs, Goldsithney, Cornwall. *T:* Penzance 710449.

BALCOMBE, Hon. Sir (Alfred) John, Kt 1977; **Hon. Mr Justice Balcombe;** a Judge of the High Court of Justice, Family Division, since 1977; *b* 29 Sept. 1925; *er s* of Edwin Kesteven Balcombe; *m* 1950, Jacqueline Rosemary, *yr d* of late Julian Cowan; two *s* one *d*. *Educ:* Winchester (schol.); New Coll., Oxford (exhibnr). Served, 1943-47: Royal Signals; India and Egypt; 2/Lt 1945, Lt 1946. BA 1949 (1st class Hons Jurisprudence), MA 1950. Called to Bar, Lincoln's Inn, 1950, Bencher 1977; QC 1969; practised at Chancery Bar, 1951-77; Mem., Gen. Council of the Bar, 1967-71. Master, Worshipful

Company of Tin Plate Workers, 1971-72. *Publications:* The Law and Practice relating to Exempt Private Companies, 1953; (ed) Estoppel, in Halsbury's Laws of England, 4th edn. *Address:* 6 Highbury Road, Wimbledon, SW19 7PR. *T:* 01-947 0980. *Club:* Garrick.

BALCOMBE, Frederick James, JP; Lord Mayor of Manchester, 1974-75, Deputy Lord Mayor, 1975-76; *b* 17 Dec. 1911; *s* of late Sidney and late Agnes Balcombe; *m* 1st, 1936, Clarice (*née* Cassel) *d* 1949); two *s* (and two *c* decd); 2nd, 1956, Rhoda (*née* Jaffe); one *d*. *Educ:* St Anthony's RC Sch., Forest Gate; West Ham Secondary Central Sch., Stratford, London. Served War of 1939-45, RAF (commnd). Dir and Sec., commercial building co. and commercial property develt co.; Dir, family co. of insurance loss assessors; Mem. TGWU; active in Labour Party. President: Manchester and District Fedn of Community Assocs; Manchester and District Allotments Council; Higher Blackley Community Assoc.; Vice-President: Blackley Prize Band; Blackley Football League; formerly Mem. Cttee and Hon. Treas., Crumpsall Hosp. League of Friends; connected with 199th Manchester Scout Gp. Mem. Manchester City Council, Crumpsall Ward, 1958, subseq. St Peter's Ward, now Collegiate Church Ward; served as Chm. Central Purchasing Cttee, Gen. and Parly (now Policy), Markets, Airports (Dep. Chm.), Parks and Finance Cttees (Dep. Chm.). Chm., Manchester Internat. Airport, 1975-. Mem., Airport Owners' Assoc. Founder, Hillel House, Manchester Univ. (Hon. Sec., 1958-68, now Sen. Life Vice-Pres.); Former Chm. of Governors, Coll. of Building, Manchester; Past Mem. Council, BBC Radio Manchester; Mem. Council, Manchester and Salford Police Authority, 1968-74; Mem., AMC Rating Cttee, 1973-74. Mem., Bd of Deputies of British Jews, 1956-64; Mem., Council, Manchester and Salford Jews, 1958- (Exec. Mem., 1963-68); Founder Mem., Manchester Jewish Blind Soc. (Hon. Sec. 13 years, now Vice-Pres.); Adjutant, Jewish Lads' Brigade and Club, Manchester, 1946-49, Chm. 1972-; Governor, King David Schs, Manchester, 1954-; Vice-Pres., Fedn of Boys' Clubs; Pres., Manchester Cttee, Central British Fund. Founder Mem., Variety Club of Israel; Barker of Variety Club (Chm. Manchester Cttee, 1976). JP Manchester, 1967. Mem. Jewish Faith. Life long blood donor. *Recreations:* family, communal endeavour, swimming, walking. *Address:* 16 Spath Road, Didsbury, Manchester M20 8GA. *T:* 061-434 2555; (office) 061-436 2663.

BALCOMBE, Hon. Sir John; *see* Balcombe, Hon. Sir A. J.

BALDOCK, John Markham, VRD 1949; Lieutenant Commander RNVR 1948; Chairman Lenscrete Ltd, 1949; Director CIBA-GEIGY (UK) Ltd; *b* 19 Nov. 1915; *s* of late Captain W. P. Baldock, and Mrs H. Chalcraft; *m* 1949, Pauline Ruth Gauntlett; two *s*. *Educ:* Rugby Sch.; Balliol Coll., Oxford. Agric. degree, 1937. Served War of 1939-45, with Royal Navy, Atlantic, Mediterranean, Indian Ocean; Russian convoys, 1942-43. Lloyds, EC3, 1945. Joined Board of Lenscrete, 1946. MP (C) Harborough Div. of Leics, 1950-Sept. 1959, retd, also as Parl. Private Sec. to Rt Hon. D. Ormsby Gore (Minister of State, Foreign Office). *Recreations:* country life, sailing, steam engines, industrial archæology, theatre. *Address:* Hollycombe House, Liphook, Hants. *T:* Liphook 723233; 17 Aylesford Street, SW1; *T:* 01-821 8759. *Club:* Farmers'.

BALDRY, Prof. Harold Caparne; Member, Arts Council of Great Britain, since 1973, and Chairman, Regional Committee, since 1975; *b* 4 March 1907; *s* of William and Gertrude Mary Baldry, Nottingham; *m* 1934, Carina Hetley (*née* Pearson); one *s* two *d*. *Educ:* Nottingham High Sch.; Trinity Hall, Cambridge (Warr Schol., MA). Editor Cambridge Review, 1931. Educational Staff, Trinity Hall, Cambridge, 1931-34; Asst Lecturer in Classics, University Coll. of Swansea, 1934-35; Univ. of Cape Town: Lecturer in Classics, 1936-48, Prof. of Classics, 1948-54; Univ. of Southampton: Prof. of Classics, 1954-72; Dean of Faculty of Arts, 1959-62; Dep. Vice-Chancellor, 1963-66; Public Orator, 1959-67. Chm., Council of University Classical Depts, 1969-72; Pres., Orbilian Soc., 1970; Vice-Pres., Classical Assoc., 1972-; Chm., Southern Arts Assoc., 1972-74. Hon. DLitt Southampton, 1975. *Publications:* The Classics in the Modern World (an Inaugural Lecture), 1949; Greek Literature for the Modern Reader, 1951; Ancient Utopias (an Inaugural Lecture), 1956; The Unity of Mankind in Greek Thought, 1965; Ancient Greek Literature in its Living Context, 1968; The Greek Tragic Theatre, 1971; articles and reviews in classical journals. *Address:* 19 Uplands Way, Highfield, Southampton. *T:* Southampton 555290.

BALDRY, Jack Thomas; Director, Purchasing and Supplies, Post Office, 1969-72; *b* 5 Oct. 1911; *s* of late John and Ellen Baldry; *m* 1936, Ruby Berenice (*née* Frost); three *d*. *Educ:* Framlingham Coll. Post Office: Asst Traffic Supt, 1930; Asst Surveyor, 1935;

Asst Princ., 1940; Princ., 1947 (Private Sec. to PMG, 1950-53); Asst Sec., 1953; Dep. Dir, External Telecommunications, 1960; Dir of Personnel, 1967. Part-time Mem., VAT Appeals Tribunals. *Recreations:* tennis, farming, foreign travel. *Address:* Bruisyard Road, Badingham, Woodbridge IP13 8NA. *T:* Badingham 331.

BALDWIN, family name of **Earl Baldwin of Bewdley.**

BALDWIN OF BEWDLEY, 4th Earl *cr* 1937; **Edward Alfred Alexander Baldwin;** Viscount Corvedale, 1937; *b* 3 Jan. 1938; *o s* of 3rd Earl Baldwin of Bewdley and of Joan Elspeth, *y d* of late C. Alexander Tomes, New York, USA; *S* father, 1976; *m* 1970, Sarah MacMurray, *er d* of Evan James, *qv*; two *s*. *Educ:* Eton; Trinity Coll., Cambridge (MA). *Heir: s* Viscount Corvedale, *qv*. *Address:* Jacaranda Cottage, Water End, Hemel Hempstead, Herts.

BALDWIN, Captain George Clifton, CBE 1966; DSC 1941 and Bar 1944; RN (retd); Chairman, Fleet Air Arm Officers Association, since 1973; Member, Press Council, since 1973; *b* 17 Jan. 1921; *s* of late George and late Louisa Baldwin; *m* 1947, Hasle Mary Macmahon; three *s*. *Educ:* Sleaford Grammar Sch., Lincs; Hitchin Grammar Sch., Herts. Served War: joined RN, 1939, and trained as Pilot in Fleet Air Arm; 801 Sqdn, 1940-41; 807 Sqdn, 1942; in comd: 807 Sqdn, 1943; No 4 Naval Fighter Wing, 1944-45. Qual. at Empire Test Pilots' Sch., 1946; RN, Staff Course, 1951; in comd, 800 Sqdn, 1952; Comdr, RN, 1953; British Naval Staff, Washington, DC, 1955-58; Captain, RN, 1958; in comd, RN Air Station, Lossiemouth, 1961-62; IDC course, 1963; Dir, Naval Air Warfare, MoD, 1964-66; in comd, RN Air Station, Yeovilton, 1966-68; ADC, 1967; retd, 1968. Mem., Royal United Services Inst., 1968. *Publications:* articles in: Air Pictorial, Navy International, Embassy, etc. *Recreations:* gardening, tennis, swimming. *Address:* Three Greens, Level Mare Lane, Eastergate, Chichester, West Sussex. *T:* (home) Eastergate 3040; (office) Chichester 89131. *Club:* Naval and Military.

BALDWIN, Prof. Jack Edward, PhD; Professor of Chemistry, Massachusetts Institute of Technology, 1972-78; Waynflete Professor of Chemistry, University of Oxford, from Oct. 1978; *b* 8 Aug. 1938; *s* of Frederick Charles Baldwin and Olive Frances Headland. *Educ:* Lewes County Grammar Sch.; Imperial Coll., London Univ. (BSc, DIC, PhD). ARCS. Asst Lectr in Chem., Imperial Coll., 1963, Lectr, 1966; Asst Prof. of Chem., Pa State Univ., 1967, Associate Prof., 1969; Associate Prof. of Chem., MIT, 1970, Prof.,' 1972; Daniell Prof. of Chem., King's Coll., London, 1972. Corday Morgan Medal and Prize, Chem. Soc., 1975. *Publications:* res. pubns in Jl of Amer. Chem. Soc. and Jl of Chem. Soc. *Recreation:* hunting. *Address:* (until July 1978) Massachusetts Institute of Technology, Cambridge, Mass 02139, USA; Dyson Perrins Laboratory, South Parks Road, Oxford.

BALDWIN, James (Arthur); Author; *b* Harlem, New York City, 2 Aug. 1924; *s* of David and Berdis Emma Baldwin. *Educ:* DeWitt Clinton High Sch., New York. Various non-literary jobs, 1942-45. Moved to Paris, 1948; lived in Europe until 1956. Active in civil rights movement in USA. Saxton Fellow, 1945; Rosenwald Fellow, 1948; Guggenheim Fellow, 1954; Nat. Inst. of Arts and Letters Award, and Partisan Review Fellow, 1956. Mem. Nat. Inst. of Arts and Letters, 1964. DLitt, Univ. of British Columbia, 1963. *Publications: novels:* Go Tell It on the Mountain, 1953; Giovanni's Room, 1956; Another Country, 1962; Going to Meet the Man, 1965; Tell Me How Long the Train's Been Gone, 1968; If Beale Street Could Talk, 1974; Little Man, Little Man, 1975; *essays:* Notes of a Native Son, 1955; Nobody Knows My Name, 1961; The Fire Next Time, 1963; Nothing Personal (with Richard Avedon), 1964; No Name in the Street, 1971; *plays:* The Amen Corner, 1955 (prod Saville, London, 1965); Blues for Mr Charlie, 1964; One Day when I was Lost, 1972; The Woman at the Well, 1972; essays and short stories in many jls and anthologies, 1946-. *Recreation:* American Negro music. *Address:* 137 West 71st Street, New York, NY, USA. *T:* Trafalgar 7-7773.

BALDWIN, John; General Secretary, Amalgamated Union of Engineering Workers/Construction Section, since 1976; *b* 16 Aug. 1923; *s* of Stephen John Baldwin and Elizabeth (*née* Hutchinson); *m* 1945, Grace May Florence (*née* Wilson); two *d*. *Educ:* Laindon High Road Sen. Sch., Essex. Boy service, RN, HMS Ganges, 1938; returned to civilian life, 1948; Steel Erector, CEU, 1950; played active part as Shop Steward and Site Convenor; elected full-time official, 1957; Asst Gen. Sec., AUEW/Construction Sect., 1969-76. Prominent Mem., Labour Party, 1962-. *Recreations:* most sports. *Address:* 7 Ridge Langley, Sanderstead, South Croydon, Surrey. *T:* 01-651 1643.

BALDWIN, Nelson Mills, OBE 1977; Director General (formerly Secretary-General), Royal Automobile Club, since 1971; *b* 17 March 1923; *s* of Nelson Baldwin and Alice (*née* Mills); *m* 1950, Cynthia Agnes Kienel; three *d*. *Educ:* Tonbridge Sch.; St John's Coll., Cambridge. Admitted as a Solicitor of the Supreme Court, 1948. Chairman, Speedway Control Board, 1964. Member of Court of Assistants, Guild of Loriners. *Recreation:* golf. *Address:* 29 Hurlingham Gardens, SW6. *T:* 01-736 1538; Sarne, Greenway, Frinton-on-Sea, Essex. *T:* Frinton 2729. *Clubs:* Royal Automobile; Hawks, Frinton-on-Sea Golf.

BALDWIN, Maj.-Gen. Peter Alan Charles; Chief Signal Officer, Headquarters British Army of the Rhine, since 1977; *b* 19 Feb. 1927; *s* of Alec Baldwin and Anne Dance; *m* 1953, Judith Elizabeth Mace. *Educ:* King Edward VI Grammar Sch., Chelmsford. Enlisted 1942; commnd R Signals 1947; early service included Berlin, 1948-49 (during airlift), and Korean War, 1950; Staff Coll., 1960; JSSC, 1964; Borneo operations (despatches, 1967); Directing Staff, Staff Coll., 1967-69; Comdr, 13 Signal Regt, BAOR, 1969-71; Sec. for Studies, NATO Defence Coll., 1971-74; Comdr, 2 Signal Group, 1974-76; ACOS Jt Exercises Div., Allied Forces Central Europe, 1976-77; Maj.-Gen. 1977. *Recreations:* tennis, cricket, music, theatre. *Address:* c/o Lloyds Bank Ltd, 6 Pall Mall, SW1. *Club:* Army and Navy.

BALDWIN, Sir Peter Robert, KCB 1977 (CB 1973); Permanent Secretary, Department of Transport, since 1976; *b* 10 Nov. 1922; *s* of Charles Baldwin and Katie Baldwin (*née* Field); *m* 1951, Margaret Helen Moar; two *s*. *Educ:* City of London Sch.; Corpus Christi Coll., Oxford. Foreign Office, 1942-45; Gen. Register Office, 1948-54; HM Treasury, 1954-62; Cabinet Office, 1962-64; HM Treasury, 1964-76; Principal Private Sec. to Chancellor of Exchequer, July 1966-Jan. 1968; Under-Sec., HM Treasury, 1968-72; Dep. Sec., HM Treasury, 1972-76; Second Permanent Sec., DoE, 1976. Chm., Civil Service Sports Council, 1977 (Vice-Chm., 1974-77); Chm., St Catherine's Home and Sch., Ventnor. *Recreations:* painting, watching cricket. *Address:* Sanders, 21 Crescent Road, Beckenham, Kent. *T:* 01-658 6956. *Club:* Royal Over-Seas League.

BALERNO, Baron *cr* 1963, of Currie (Life Peer); **Alick Drummond Buchanan-Smith;** Kt 1956; CBE 1945 (OBE 1939); TD 1938; DL; MA, DSc; MSA Iowa; FRSE; Lecturer in Animal Genetics, University of Edinburgh, 1925-60, retired; *b* 9 Oct. 1898; *s* of late Very Rev. Sir George Adam Smith, DD, LLD, FBA, Principal of Aberdeen Univ., 1909-35 and of late Lilian, *d* of Sir George Buchanan, LLD, FRS; *m* 1926, Mary Kathleen (*d* 1947), *d* of late Captain George Smith of Pittodrie; four *s* one *d*. *Educ:* Glasgow Acad., Glenalmond; University of Aberdeen; Iowa State Univ. Lt-Col Comdg 5/7th, 5th and 9th Bns The Gordon Highlanders, TA, 1936-42; Brigadier and Dir Selection of Personnel, War Office, 1942-45; Col Comdg Edinburgh Univ. Contingent, OTC, 1945-53; Chm. Edinburgh, Lothians and Peebles TA & AFA, 1953-57. Pres. Scottish Unionist Assoc., 1955-56; Dep. Chm., Unionist Party in Scotland, 1960-63. Vice-Chm., Pigs Industry Develt Authority, 1957-69; Vice-Pres. Brit. Council of Churches, 1967-71; Pres., Royal Scottish Geographical Soc., 1968-74. Hon. Mem., BVA, 1976. Mem., Edinburgh Univ. Court, 1961-68; Mem., Heriot-Watt Univ. Court, 1974-77 (Chm., 1966-72). Pres. Edinburgh Bn The Boys' Brigade, 1955-68. Hon. Col 5/6th Bn The Gordon Highlanders, 1958-61, of 3rd Bn, 1961. Hon. DSc Heriot-Watt, 1970. Hon. ARCVS, 1971. Iowa State Univ. Distinguished Achievement Citation, 1967. DL, Midlothian, 1975. *Publications:* papers on breeding of farm livestock, in various sci. jls. *Address:* House of Cockburn, Balerno, Midlothian EH14 7JD. *T:* 031-449 3737. *Clubs:* Caledonian, Royal Automobile; New (Edinburgh).
See also Janet Adam Smith (Mrs John Carleton), A. L. Buchanan-Smith.

BALES, Kenneth Frederick; Regional Administrator, West Midlands Regional Health Authority, since 1973; *b* 2 March 1931; *s* of Frederick Charles Bales and Deborah Alice Bales; *m* 1958, Margaret Hazel Austin; two *s* one *d*. *Educ:* Buckhurst Hill Grammar Sch.; LSE; Univ. of Manchester. BScSoc; DipSocAdmin. Hosp. Sec., Newhall & Hesketh Park Hosps, 1958-62; Regional Trng Officer, Birmingham Regional Hosp. Bd, 1962-65; Regional Staff Officer, Birmingham Regional Staff Cttee, 1965-68; Group Sec., W Birmingham HMC, 1968-73. Associate, Inst. Health Service Administrators. *Recreations:* painting, sport. *Address:* 25 South Road, West Hagley, West Midlands DY9 0JT. *T:* Hagley 2550.

BALFOUR, family name of **Earl of Balfour** and **Barons Balfour of Inchrye, Kinross** and **Riverdale.**

BALFOUR, 4th Earl of, *cr* 1922; **Gerald Arthur James Balfour;** Viscount Traprain 1922; JP; *b* 23 Dec. 1925; *er s* of 3rd Earl of Balfour and Jean, 4th *d* of late Rev. Canon J. J. Cooke-Yarborough; *S* father, 1968; *m* 1956, Natasha Georgina, *d* of late Captain George Anton. *Educ:* Eton; HMS Conway. Holds Master Mariner's certificate. Mem., E Lothian CC, 1960-75. JP East Lothian, 1970. Mem., Internat. Assoc. of Cape Horners, 1960. *Heir: cousin* Eustace Arthur Goschen Balfour [*b* 26 May 1921; *m* 1st, 1946, Anne, *d* of late Major Victor Yule; two *s*; 2nd, 1971, Mrs Paula Cuene-Grandidier]. *Address:* The Tower, Whittingehame, Haddington, Scotland. *Clubs:* English-Speaking Union, Naval and Military; RNVR (Glasgow).

BALFOUR OF BURLEIGH, Baron *cr* 1607 (*de facto* 8th Baron, 12th but for the Attainder); **Robert Bruce,** CEng, FIEE; Director: Bank of Scotland, since 1968; Scottish Investment Trust, since 1971; Chairman, Scottish Arts Council, since 1971; Chairman, Viking Oil Ltd, since 1971; President, Friends of Vellore, since 1973; Treasurer, Royal Scottish Corporation, since 1967; *b* 6 Jan. 1927; *e s* of 11th Baron Balfour of Burleigh and Dorothy (*d* 1976), *d* of late R. H. Done; *S* father, 1967; *m* 1971, Mrs Jennifer Brittain-Catlin, *d* of late E. S. Manasseh; two *d*. Served RN, 1945-48, as Ldg Radio Electrician's Mate. Joined English Electric Co. Ltd, 1951; graduate apprentice, 1951-52; Asst Foreman, Heavy Electrical Plant Dept, Stafford Works, 1952-54; Asst Superintendent, Heavy Electrical Plant Dept, Netherton Works, Liverpool, 1954-57; Manager, English Electric Co. of India (Private) Ltd, Madras, 1957-60; Dir and Gen. Manager, English Electric Co. India Ltd, 1960-64; Dep. Gen. Manager, English Electric Co. Ltd, Netherton, Liverpool, 1964-65, Gen. Manager 1965-66; Dir and Gen. Manager, D. Napier & Son Ltd, 1966-68. Chairman: Fedn of Scottish Bank Employers, 1977-; Jt Negotiating Council of the Scottish Banking Industry, 1977-. Forestry Comr, 1971-74. *Recreations:* music, climbing, woodwork. *Heir: d* Hon. Victoria Bruce, *b* 7 May 1973. *Address:* Brucefield, Clackmannan, Scotland.
See also Hon. G. J. D. Bruce.

BALFOUR OF INCHRYE, 1st Baron *cr* 1945, of Shefford; **Harold Harington Balfour,** PC 1941; MC and Bar; *b* 1 Nov. 1897; *s* of Col N. H. Balfour, Belton, Camberley, Surrey; *m* 1st, 1921, Diana Blanche (marr. diss. 1946), *d* of Sir Robert G. Harvey, 2nd Bt; one *s*; 2nd, 1947, Mary Ainslie Profumo, *d* of late Baron Profumo, KC, and of Baroness Profumo; one *d*. *Educ:* Chilverton Elms, Dover; RN Coll., Osborne. Joined 60th Rifles, 1914; attached RFC 1915; RAF 1918; served European War, 1914-18 (MC and bar); RAF 1918-23; journalism and business since 1923; contested (C) Stratford, West Ham, 1924; MP (C) Isle of Thanet, 1929-45; Parliamentary Under-Sec. of State for Air, 1938-44; Minister Resident in West Africa, 1944-45. President, Federation Chambers of Commerce of the British Empire, 1946-49; President, Commonwealth and Empire Industries Association, 1956-60; Part-time Member, Board of BEA, 1955-66; Chairman, BEA Helicopters Ltd, 1964-66. *Publications:* An Airman Marches, 1935; Wings over Westminster, 1973. *Recreations:* fishing, shooting. *Heir: s* Hon. Ian Balfour [*b* 21 Dec. 1924; *m* 1953, Josephine Maria Jane, *d* of late Mr and of the Hon. Mrs Morogh Bernard, Shankill, Co. Dublin; one *d*]. *Address:* End House, St Mary Abbot's Place, W8. *T:* 01-603 6231; Tressady, Rogart, Sutherland. *T:* Rogart 227. *Clubs:* Carlton, Pratt's.
See also J. D. Profumo.

BALFOUR, David, CBE 1960; FIL; retired diplomat; free-lance conference interpreter; *b* London, 20 Jan. 1903; *s* of Reginald Balfour and Charlotte Warre Cornish; *m* 1948, Louise Fitzherbert; one *d*. *Educ:* Oratory Sch., Edgbaston; and at Angers, Prague, Salzburg, Rome, Athens. Graduate of Oriental Institute, Rome, and of Athens Univ. (1940). On staff of the Institute of English Studies, Athens, 1939-41. Served War of 1939-45 in Army, 1941-43, GSO II, GHQ, Middle East Forces (despatches). Entered HM Foreign Service, 1943, established 1946; served Cairo, Athens, Foreign Office, Tel Aviv (Oriental Sec., 1949-50), Smyrna (Consul-Gen., 1951-55), Genoa (Consul-Gen., 1955-60), and Geneva (Consul-Gen., 1960-63); Interpreter and Translator, FO, 1963-68; retd 1968. Mem., Internat. Assoc. of Conf. Interpreters, 1969. *Recreations:* theology, byzantinology (especially 14th and 15th century). *Address:* The Old Mill, Kingsclere, Hants. *T:* Kingsclere 298610; 9 Rives du Rhône, Pougny, 01630 St Genis (Ain), France. *T:* (50) 59.65.80.

BALFOUR, David Mathers, CBE 1970; MA; CEng, MICE; Director, R. M. Douglas Construction Ltd, since 1975; Chairman, Balfour, Beatty & Co. Ltd, 1971-74 (Managing Director, 1950-72); *b* 11 Jan. 1910; *s* of late George Balfour, MP and Margaret (*née* Mathers); *m* 1938, Elisabeth, *d* of John Murdoch Beddall; two *s* one *d*. *Educ:* Shrewsbury Sch.; Pembroke Coll., Cambridge (MA). Served War of 1939-45, Lt-Col RE. Joined Balfour, Beatty & Co. Ltd, as Civil Engineer, 1930 (Dir, 1942); Chairman: Power Securities Corporation Ltd,

1971-74; Balfour Kilpatrick Ltd, 1971-72 (Dir, 1971-75); Exec. Dir, British Insulated Callender's Cables Ltd, 1970-72. Chm., Export Gp for the Constructional Industries, 1963-65; Vice-Pres., Fedn of Civil Engineering Contractors (Chm. 1966-67). *Recreations:* golf, shooting. *Address:* Little Garnstone Manor, Seal, Sevenoaks, Kent. *T:* Sevenoaks 61221. *Clubs:* East India, Devonshire, Sports and Public Schools; Rye Golf (Rye); Wildernesse Golf (Sevenoaks).

BALFOUR, (Elizabeth) Jean, JP; Chairman, Countryside Commission for Scotland, since 1972; *b* 4 Nov. 1927; 2nd *d* of late Maj.-Gen. Sir James Syme Drew, KBE, CB, DSO, MC, and of Victoria Maxwell, Munches; *m* 1950, John Charles Balfour, MC, JP, Balbirnie; three *s*. *Educ:* Edinburgh Univ. (BSc). Partner, Balbirnie Home Farms; Dir, A. & J. Bowen & Co. Ltd. Pres., Royal Scottish Forestry Soc., 1969-71; Mem., Fife CC, 1958-70; Chm., Fife County and City and Royal Burgh of Dunfermline Joint Probation Cttee, 1967-69; Governor, East of Scotland Coll. of Agriculture, 1958-; Member: Scottish Agric. Develt Council, 1972-77; Verney Working Party on Management of National Resources, 1971-72; Nature Conservancy Council, 1973-; Oil Develt Council, 1973-; Council, Scottish Agricultural Coll., 1974-; Vice-Chm., Scottish Wildlife Trust, 1968-72; Chm., Regional Adv. Cttee, East (Scotland) Conservancy, Forestry Commn, 1976-. JP Fife, 1963. Hon. DSc St Andrews, 1977. *Recreations:* hill walking, fishing, music. *Address:* Kirkforthar House, Markinch, Fife KY7 6LS. *T:* Glenrothes 752233; Scourie, by Lairg, Sutherland. *Clubs:* Royal Commonwealth Society; (Assoc. Mem.) New (Edinburgh).

BALFOUR, Rear-Adm. George Ian Mackintosh, CB 1962; DSC 1943; *b* 14 Jan. 1912; *yr s* of late Dr T. Stevenson Balfour, Chard, Som, and Mrs Balfour; *m* 1939, Pamela Carlyle Forrester, *y d* of late Major Hugh C. C. Forrester, DL, JP, Tullibody House, Cambus, and late Mrs Forrester; two *s* one *d*. *Educ:* Royal Naval Coll., Dartmouth. Served in China, 1930-32; South Africa, 1935-37. Commanded Destroyers for most of War of 1939-45, on various stations. Mediterranean, 1948, Far East, 1949-50, USA 1951-53, Captain (D) 2nd Destroyer Flotilla, 1956-58; Dir of Officer Appointments, 1958-59; Senior Naval Mem., Imperial Defence Coll., 1960-63; retired list, 1963. Chief Appeals Officer, Cancer Res. Campaign, 1963-77. *Address:* Westover, Farnham Lane, Haslemere, Surrey. *T:* 3876.

BALFOUR, Jean; *see* Balfour, E. J.

BALFOUR, Sir John, GCMG 1954 (KCMG 1947; CMG 1941); GBE 1959; *b* 26 May 1894; *s* of Charles Barrington Balfour, CB, Newton Don and Balgonie, and of Lady Nina Balfour; *m* 1933, Frances (CVO 1969; Lady-in-Waiting to HRH Princess Marina, Duchess of Kent, 1961-68), *d* of Prof. Alexander van Millingen, DD. *Educ:* Eton; New Coll., Oxford. Interned in Germany, 1914-18; 3rd Sec. in the Diplomatic Service or Foreign Office, 1919; served in Foreign Office, at HM Legations at Budapest, Sofia and Belgrade, and at HM Embassies at Madrid and Washington; Minister in Lisbon, 1941-43; in Moscow, 1943-45; in Washington, 1945-48; Ambassador to Argentine Republic, 1948-51; Ambassador to Spain, 1951-54; retired from Foreign Service, 1954. UK Commissioner-Gen. to Brussels International Exhibition of 1958. Chairman: British and French Bank, 1959-69; United Bank for Africa, 1961-69. Officier de la Légion d'Honneur, 1972. *Address:* 38 Onslow Square, SW7. *T:* 01-584 1970. *Club:* Brooks's.

BALFOUR, Peter Edward Gerald; Chairman, Scottish & Newcastle Breweries Ltd; *b* 9 July 1921; *y s* of late Brig. Edward William Sturgis Balfour, CVO, DSO, OBE, MC and Lady Ruth Balfour, CBE, MB; *m* 1st, 1948, Grizelda Davina Roberta Ogilvy (marr. diss. 1967); two *s* one *d*; 2nd, 1968, Diana Rosemary Wainman; one *s* one *d*. *Educ:* Eton College. Scots Guards, 1940-54. Joined Wm McEwan & Co. Ltd, 1954. Director: Royal Bank of Scotland, 1971-; Scottish & Newcastle Breweries Ltd, 1961; British Assets Trust Ltd; Edinburgh American Assets Trust. Mem., Hansard Soc. Commn on Electoral Reform, 1975-76. *Address:* Scadlaw House, Humbie, East Lothian. *T:* Humbie 252. *Club:* Cavalry and Guards.

BALFOUR, Raymond Lewis, MVO 1965; HM Diplomatic Service; Counsellor, British Embassy, Tripoli, Libya, since 1976; *b* 23 April 1923; *s* of Henry James Balfour and Vera Alice (née Dunford); *m* 1975, Vanda Gaye Crompton. RMA Sandhurst, 1942; commnd RAC; served with IV Queen's Own Hussars, 1942-47. Diplomatic Service, 1947-; served at Munich, Beirut, Gdansk (Poland), Baghdad, Khartoum, Geneva, Damascus. Order of the Blue Nile, Sudan, 1965. *Recreations:* travel, gardening. *Address:* c/o Foreign and Commonwealth Office, SW1A 2AH.

BALFOUR, Richard Creighton, MBE 1945; Director, Datasaab Ltd, since 1975; *b* 3 Feb. 1916; *s* of Donald Creighton Balfour and Muriel Fonçeca; *m* 1943, Adela Rosemary Welch; two *s*. *Educ:* St Edward's Sch., Oxford. FIB. Joined Bank of England, 1935; Agent, Leeds, 1961-65; Deputy Chief Cashier, 1965-70; Chief Accountant, 1970-75. Naval Service, Lt-Comdr RNVR, 1939-46. Pres., Royal National Rose Soc., 1973 and 1974; Chairman: 1976—The Year of the Rose; Internat. Rose Conf., Oxford, 1976; Classification Cttee, World Fedn of Rose Socs. Liveryman, Worshipful Co. of Gardeners; Freeman, City of London. DHM 1974. *Publications:* articles in Rose Annual and many horticultural magazines. *Recreations:* roses, gardening, photography, dancing, sea floating, collecting rocks and hat pins, travel, watching sport. *Address:* Albion House, Little Waltham, Chelmsford, Essex CM3 3LA. *T:* Chelmsford 360410.

BALFOUR, Sir Robert George Victor FitzGeorge; *see* FitzGeorge-Balfour.

BALFOUR-LYNN, Dr Stanley; Director, American Medical International, Inc., since 1977; Chief Executive, American Medical (Europe) Ltd, since 1969; *b* 21 June 1922; *s* of John Balfour-Lynn and Yetta Balfour-Lynn; *m* 1952, Valerie Eker; three *s* one *d*. *Educ:* City of London Sch.; Guy's Hosp., London (MB, BS). MRCS, LRCP, MRCGP. Prosector and Demonstr of Anatomy, RCS, 1949-51; RMO, Queen Charlotte's Maternity Hosp., 1951-52; Chm. and Man. Dir, Harley Street Clinic, 1960-. Dep. Chm., Indep. Hosp. Gp, 1975-. Underwriting Mem. of Lloyd's, 1977-. *Publications:* contrib. Lancet. *Recreations:* sub-aqua diving, inventing, good food. *Address:* Flat 12, 55 Portland Place, W1N 3DG. *T:* 01-580 8075. *Clubs:* Variety Club of GB, British Sub-Aqua, MCC, Queen's; Coombe Hill Golf (Surrey); Tenterden Golf (Kent).

BALFOUR PAUL, Hugh Glencairn, CMG 1968; HM Diplomatic Service, retired; Director General, Middle East Association, since 1978; *b* 23 Sept. 1917; *s* of late Lt-Col J. W. Balfour Paul, DSO; *m* 1st, 1950, Margaret Clare Ogilvy (*d* 1971); one *s* three *d*; 2nd, 1974, Janet Alison Scott. *Educ:* Sedbergh; Magdalen Coll., Oxford. Served War of 1939-45, Sudan Defence Force. Sudan Political Service, Blue Nile and Darfur, 1946-54; joined Foreign Office, 1955; Santiago, 1957; Beirut, 1960; Counsellor, Dubai, 1964; Dep. Political Resident, Persian Gulf, 1966; Counsellor, FO, attached St Antony's Coll., Oxford, 1968; Ambassador to Iraq, 1969-71; Ambassador to Jordan, 1972-75; Ambassador to Tunisia, 1975-77. *Recreations:* archaeology, modern poetry, tennis. *Address:* 20 Essex Villas, W8 7BN. *Club:* Travellers'.

BALGONIE, Lord; David Alexander Leslie Melville; *b* 26 Jan. 1954; *s* and *heir* of Earl of Leven and Melville, *qv*. *Educ:* Eton. Lieut, Queen's Own Highlanders, 1973 (GSM for N Ireland). *Address:* Glenferness House, Nairn.

BALKWILL, Bryan Havell; conductor; *b* 2 July 1922; *s* of Arthur William Balkwill and Dorothy Silver Balkwill (née Wright); *m* 1949, Susan Elizabeth Roberts; one *s* one *d*. *Educ:* Merchant Taylors' Sch.; Royal Academy of Music. Asst Conductor, New London Opera Co., 1947-48; Associate Conductor, Internat. Ballet, 1948-49; Musical Director and Principal Conductor, London Festival Ballet, 1950-52; Music staff and subseq. Associate Conductor, Glyndebourne Opera, 1950-58; Musical Dir, Arts Council 'Opera For All', 1953-63; Resident Conductor, Royal Opera House, Covent Garden, 1959-65; Musical Director: Welsh Nat. Opera Company, 1963-67; Sadler's Wells Opera, 1966-69; free-lance opera and concert conducting in N America, Europe and GB, 1970-76. Vis. Prof. of Conducting, Indiana Univ., 1976. Guest Conductor: Royal Opera House, Covent Garden, Glyndebourne, Wexford Festival, Aldeburgh, RPO, LPO, Royal Liverpool Ph. Orchestra, Bournemouth Symphony Orch., City of Birmingham Symphony Orch., BBC Promenade Concerts, Festival Ballet. Mem. Royal Philharmonic Society; FRAM. *Recreation:* open air. *Address:* 8 The Green, Wimbledon Common, SW19 5AZ. *T:* 01-947 4250.

BALL, Alan Hugh; Executive Deputy Chairman, Lonrho Ltd, and associated companies, since 1972 (Chairman and Joint Managing Director, 1961-72); *b* 8 June 1924; *s* of late Sir George Joseph Ball, KBE and Mary Caroline Ball; *m* 1948, Eleanor Katharine Turner; two *s* one *d*. *Educ:* Eton. KRRC, 1943-47. Lonrho Ltd and associated cos, 1947-. *Recreations:* fishing, shooting. *Address:* The Old Mill, Ramsbury, Wilts. *T:* Ramsbury 266. *Clubs:* Carlton, City of London, East India, Devonshire, Sports and Public Schools, Royal Automobile.

BALL, Air Marshal Sir Alfred (Henry Wynne), KCB 1976 (CB 1967); DSO 1943; DFC 1942; idc, jssc, psc, pfc; UK

Representative, Permanent Military Deputies Group, Central Treaty Organisation, 1975-77; *b* 18 Jan. 1921; *s* of Captain J. A. E. Ball, MC, BA, BE; *m* 1942, Nan McDonald; three *s* one *d*. *Educ:* Campbell Coll., Belfast; RAF Coll., Cranwell. Served War of 1939-45 (Despatches twice; US Air Medal 1943); Pilot Officer, 1939; Flying Officer, 1940; Flight Lt 1941; Sqdn Ldr 1942; Wing Comdr 1944; air operations, Lysanders, Spitfires, Mosquitoes; commanded: 4 Photo. Reconn. Unit; 682, 542, 540 and 13 Photo. Reconn. Sqdns in N Africa, UK, France and Middle East; E Africa, 1947; Bomber Comd, 1952; Gp Captain, Operations, BJSM, Washington, 1959; Comdr, Honington V Bomber Base, 1963-64; Air Cdre, Air Officer, Administration, Aden, 1965; IDC, 1967; Dir of Operations, (RAF), MoD, 1967-68; Air Vice-Marshal, 1968; ACOS, Automatic Data Processing Div., SHAPE, 1968-71; Dir-Gen. Organisation (RAF), 1971-75; Air Marshal, 1975. Hon. Mem. British Computer Soc., 1974. *Recreation:* golf. *Address:* Tarshyne, Lambridge Wood Road, Henley-on-Thames, Oxon. *Club:* Royal Air Force.

BALL, Charles Irwin; Director, Barclays Bank, 1976-77; Chairman, Barclays Merchant Bank Ltd, 1976-77; *b* 12 Jan. 1924; *s* and *heir* of Sir Nigel Gresley Ball, Bt, *qv*; *m* 1950, Alison Mary, *d* of Lt-Col Percy Holman Bentley, MBE, MC, Farnham, Surrey; one *s* one *d*. *Educ:* Sherborne Sch. Served RA, 1942-47. Chartered Accountant, 1950; Peat, Marwick, Mitchell & Co., 1950-54; joined Robert, Benson, Lonsdale & Co. Ltd (now Kleinwort, Benson Ltd), 1954; Director: Kleinwort, Benson Ltd, 1964-76 (Vice-Chm., 1974-76); Kleinwort, Benson, Lonsdale Ltd, 1974-76; Kleinwort Benson Investment Trust (Chm., 1974-76); Cadbury Schweppes Ltd, 1971-76; Chubb & Son Ltd, 1971-76; Sun Alliance and London Insurance Ltd, 1971-; Telephone Rentals Ltd, 1971-; Tunnel Holdings Ltd, 1976-. Mem., British Transport Docks Board, 1971-. FCA 1960. *Address:* Downlands, Seale, near Farnham, Surrey GU10 1HB. *T:* Runfold 2415.

BALL, Denis William, MBE 1971; Headmaster of Kelly College since 1972; *b* 20 Oct. 1928; *er s* of William Charles Thomas and Dora Adelaide Ball, Eastbourne; *m* 1972, Marja Tellervo Lumijärvi, *er d* of Osmo Kullervo and Leila Tellervo Lumijärvi, Toijala, Finland; two *s*. *Educ:* Brunswick Sch.; Tonbridge Sch. (Scholar); Brasenose Coll., Oxford (MA). Asst Master, The King's Sch., Canterbury, 1953-72 (Housemaster, 1954-72). Sub-Lt, RNR, 1953; Lieut 1954; Lt-Comdr 1958. Governor, St Michael's Sch., Tawstock Court, 1974-. *Recreations:* Elizabethan history, cryptography, literary and mathematical puzzles, cricket, real tennis, squash (played for Oxford Univ. and Kent), golf. *Address:* Kelly College, Tavistock, Devon PL19 0HZ. *T:* Tavistock 3005. *Clubs:* East India, Devonshire, Sports and Public Schools, MCC.

BALL, George T.; *see* Thalben-Ball.

BALL, Dr Harold William; Keeper of Palæontology, British Museum (Natural History), since 1966; *b* 11 July 1926; *s* of Harold Ball and Florence (*née* Harris); *m* 1955, Patricia Mary (*née* Silvester); two *s* two *d*. *Educ:* Yardley Gram. Sch.; Birmingham Univ. BSc 1947, PhD 1949, Birmingham. Geologist, Nyasaland Geological Survey, 1949-51; Asst Lectr in Geology, King's Coll., London, 1951-54; Dept of Palæontology, British Museum (Nat. Hist.), 1954-: Dep. Keeper, 1965; Keeper, 1966. Adrian Vis. Fellow, Univ. of Leicester, 1972-77. Sec., 1968-72, Vice-Pres., 1972-73, Geological Soc. of London; Wollaston Fund, Geological Soc. of London, 1965. *Publications:* papers on the stratigraphy of the Old Red Sandstone and on the palæontology of the Antarctic in several scientific jls. *Recreations:* music, rhododendron species, collecting early books on natural history and voyages. *Address:* Wilderbrook, Dormans Park, East Grinstead, West Sussex. *T:* Dormans Park 426.

BALL, Prof. John Geoffrey; Professor of Physical Metallurgy, Imperial College, University of London, since 1956 and Head of Metallurgy Department, since 1957; *b* 27 Sept. 1916; *s* of late I. H. Ball and late Mrs E. M. Ball; *m* 1941, Joan C. M., *d* of late Arthur Wiltshire, JP, Bournemouth. *Educ:* Wellington (Salop) High Sch.; Univ. of Birmingham. British Welding Res. Assoc., 1941-49; Sen. Metallurgist, 1945-49; AERE, Harwell, 1949-56; Head of Reactor Metallurgy, 1953-56. Min. of Tech. Visitor to British Non-Ferrous Metals Res. Assoc., 1962-72. Dean, Royal Sch. of Mines, Imperial Coll., 1962-65 and 1971-74; Dean, Faculty of Engineering, Univ. of London, 1970-74. Chairman: Res. Bd, 1964-74, and Mem. of Council Br. Welding Res. Assoc., 1964-; Engrg Physics Sub-Cttee, Aeronautical Res. Council, 1964-68; Metallurgy Bd, CNAA, 1965-71; Metallurgy and Materials Cttee and Univ. Science and Technology Bd, SRC, 1967-70; Engrg Bd, SRC, 1969-71; Manpower Utilisation Working Party, 1967-; Mem., Light Water Reactor Pressure

Vessel Study Gp, Dept of Energy, 1974-. Pres., Inst. of Welding, 1965-66. Member: Council, Instn of Metallurgists, 1951-56, 1958-(Pres., 1966-67); Council, Br. Nuclear Forum, 1964-71; Manpower Resources Cttee, 1965-; Council, Inst. of Metals, 1965; Council, Iron and Steel Inst., 1965; Council, City Univ., 1966-; Brain Drain Cttee, 1966-67; Public Enquiry into loss of "Sea Gem", 1967; Materials and Structures Cttee, 1967-70; Technology Sub-Cttee of UGC, 1968-73. Governor, Sir John Cass Coll., 1958-67. Hon. ARSM 1961. *Recreations:* gardening, furniture design and making, travel. *Address:* 3 Sylvan Close, Limpsfield, Surrey. *T:* Oxted 3511.

BALL, Rev. Kenneth Vernon James, MA; *b* 10 July 1906; *s* of Vernon Arthur and Eveline Ball, Brighton; *m* 1939, Isabella Jane Armstrong, MB, ChB, *d* of Archibald Armstrong, JP, and Eleanor Elsie Armstrong, Strachur, Argyll; one *s* one *d*. *Educ:* The College, Swindon; Jesus Coll., Oxford; Wycliffe Hall, Oxford. Acting Headmaster, Busoga High Sch., Uganda, 1930-32; Curate, St Paul, Bedminster, 1932-35; Curate, Temple or Holy Cross Church, Bristol, 1935-38; Vicar, St Barnabas, Bristol, 1938-42; Vicar, St Leonard, Redfield, Bristol, 1942-47; Bishop of Liverpool's Special Service Staff, 1947-50; Vicar, St Nicholas, and Chap. St Bartholomew's Hosp., Rochester, 1950-59; Oriel Canon of Rochester Cath., 1955-59; Vicar of Leatherhead, Surrey, 1959-70; Rector of Piddlehinton, Dorset, 1970-72; retd. *Publication:* Spiritual Approach to Marriage Preparation, 1948. *Recreations:* rowing, walking, camping, singing. *Address:* 1 Gretton Court, Girton, Cambridge.

BALL, Sir Nigel Gresley, 3rd Bt, *cr* 1911; MA, ScD, FLS; *b* 27 Aug. 1892; *s* of late Sir Charles Bent Ball, Bt, MD; *S* brother, 1945; *m* 1922, Florine Isabel, *d* of late Col Herbert Edwardes Irwin; two *s* one *d*. *Educ:* St Columba's Coll., Rathfarnham, Co. Dublin; Trinity Coll., Dublin. Received commission in 8th (S) Bn Royal Dublin Fusiliers, Nov. 1914; demobilised March 1919; Asst to the University Prof. of Botany, Trinity Coll., Dublin, 1920-24; Prof. of Botany, University Coll., Colombo, 1924-43; Lecturer in Botany, University of London, King's Coll., 1944-55, Reader, 1955-57, Special lecturer, 1957-59. *Publications:* chapters on physiology of plant movements in: Vistas in Botany, vol. 3 (ed Turrill), 1963; Plant Physiology, vol. 5A (ed Steward), 1969; Physiology of Plant Growth and Development (ed Wilkins), 1969; various papers on plant physiology in scientific jls. *Heir: s* Charles Irwin Ball, *qv*. *Address:* 19 Bernard Road, West Worthing, West Sussex. *T:* Worthing 47155.

BALL, Rt. Rev. Peter John; *see* Lewes, Bishop Suffragan of.

BALL, Robert Edward, CB 1977; MBE 1946; Chief Master of the Supreme Court of Judicature (Chancery Division) since 1969 (Master, 1954-68); *b* 8 March 1911; *s* of James Ball, LLB, Purley, Surrey, and Mabel Louise (*née* Laver); *m* 1935, Edith Margaret Barbara, *d* of late Dr Patrick Edward Campbell; one *s* two *d* (and one *s* decd). *Educ:* Westminster Sch.; Lycée de Vendôme, France; Germany; London Univ. (LLB). Law Soc.'s Studentship, 1929. Admitted Solicitor, 1933; junior partner, James Ball & Son, 1933-46; served War, 1939-46; commissioned in Queen's Royal Regt, 1940; served KORR and in various staff appts, England, France and India; AA & QMG, Madras; released with rank of Lt-Col, 1946; formed practice of Potts and Ball, Chester and London, with Henry Potts, 1946. Formerly: Hon. Sec., Chester and North Wales Incorp. Law Soc.; Chm. Chester Insurance Tribunal, etc. *Publication:* The Law and the Cloud of Unknowing, 1976. *Recreations:* history, gardening. *Address:* 62 Stanstead Road, Caterham, Surrey. *T:* Caterham 43675. *Club:* Athenæum.

BALL, Prof. Robert James, MA, PhD; Principal, London Graduate School of Business Studies, since 1972; Director: Barclays Bank Trust Company; Tube Investments Ltd; Part-time Member, National Freight Corporation, since 1973; *b* 15 July 1933; *s* of Arnold James Hector Ball; *m* 1st, 1954, Patricia Mary Hart Davies (marr. diss. 1970); one *s* three *d* (and one *d* decd); 2nd, 1970, Lindsay Jackson (*née* Wonnacott); one step *s*. *Educ:* St Marylebone Grammar Sch.; The Queen's College, Oxford; Styring Schol.; George Webb Medley Junior Schol. (Univ. Prizeman), 1956.BA 1957 (First cl. Hons PPE), MA 1960; PhD Univ. of Pennsylvania, 1973. RAF 1952-54 (Pilot-Officer, Navigator). Research Officer, Oxford University Inst. of Statistics, 1957-58; IBM Fellow, Univ. of Pennsylvania, 1958-60; Lectr, Manchester Univ., 1960, Sen. Lectr, 1963-65; Prof. of Economics, London Business School, 1965-, Governor, 1969-, Dep. Principal, 1971-72. Director: Ogilvy and Mather Ltd, 1969-71; Economic Models Ltd, 1971-72. Member: Cttee to Review National Savings (Page Cttee), 1971-73; Economics Cttee of SSRC, 1971-74; Cttee on Social Forecasting, SSRC, 1971-72; Cttee of Enquiry into Electricity Supply Industry (Plowden Cttee), 1974-75; Chm., Treasury Cttee on Policy

Optimisation, 1976-. Governor, NIESR, 1973-. Member Council: REconS, 1973-; BIM, 1974-. Fellow, Econometric Soc., 1973; FBIM, 1974. *Publications:* An Econometric Model of the United Kingdom, 1961; Inflation and the Theory of Money, 1964; (ed) Inflation, 1969; (ed) The International Linkage of National Economic Models, 1972; articles in professional jls. *Recreations:* fishing, chess. *Address:* 1 Sussex Place, Regent's Park, NW1 4SA. *T:* 01-723 8777; 7 Spittis Park, Kingswear, Devon. *Club:* Royal Dart Yacht.

BALLANCE, Rear-Adm. Frank Arthur, CB 1953; DSO 1944; Royal Navy, retired; *b* 16 Nov. 1902; *s* of Sydney Ballance, Sandon, Herts; *m* 1st, 1930, Marie Arundell (*d* 1972), *d* of Reavely Maitland, Loughton, Essex; one *s*; 2nd, 1972, Sybil, *d* of E. C. Lee, Petersfield, and widow of Comdr G. P. U. Morris, DSC, RN. *Educ:* Royal Naval Colls Osborne and Dartmouth. Commander, 1939; HMS Phoebe; HMS Gosling; Capt., 1943; took part in Invasion of Normandy; Admiralty, 1944-46; Ordnance Board, 1946-48; HMS Jamaica, 1949-50; Chief of Naval Staff, New Zealand, 1950-53; Flag Officer Flotilla, Indian Fleet, 1953-55; Rear-Admiral, 1953; Admiralty, 1955; retired, 1957. *Recreation:* shooting. *Address:* Malthouse Cottage, Rogate, Petersfield, Hants. *T:* Rogate 338.

BALLANTRAE, Baron *cr* 1972 (Life Peer), of Auchairne and The Bay of Islands; **Bernard Edward Fergusson,** KT 1974; GCMG 1962; GCVO 1963; DSO 1943; OBE 1950; Chairman, London Board, Bank of New Zealand, since 1968; Chancellor, University of St Andrews, since 1973; *b* 6 May 1911; *y s* of Gen. Sir Charles Fergusson of Kilkerran, 7th Bt, GCB, GCMG, DSO, MVO, and of Lady Alice Boyle (*d* 1958), *d* of 7th Earl of Glasgow; *m* 1950, Laura Margaret, *y d* of Lieut-Col A. M. Grenfell, DSO; one *s*. *Educ:* Eton; RMC Sandhurst. Joined The Black Watch, 1931; Lieut 1934, Capt. 1939; ADC to Maj.-Gen. (later F.-M.) Wavell, 2nd Div. Aldershot, 1935-37; served Palestine, 1937 (medal and clasp); Instructor RMC, 1938-39; served War of 1939-45 (wounded, despatches twice, DSO); Staff Coll., 1940; Bde Major 46th Inf. Bde, 1940; Middle East, 1941; GSO1 Joint Plans India, 1942; Wingate Expeditions into Burma, 1943-44; comd 16th Inf. Bde in 1944 Expedition; Dir of Combined Ops (Military), 1945-46. Asst Inspector-Gen., Palestine Police, 1946-47; commanded 1st Bn The Black Watch, 1948-51; Col Intelligence, Supreme HQ, Allied Powers, Europe, 1951-53; idc 1954; Comdr, 153rd Highland Bde, TA, 1955-56; Allied Force HQ Port Said Operations, 1956; Comdr, 29th Infantry Bde, 1957-58, retd. Governor-General and C-in-C of New Zealand, 1962-67. Internat. Observer Team, Nigeria, Oct. 1968-March 1969. Mem., Cttee to review Defamation Act, 1952, 1971-74; Chm., Scottish Trust for the Physically Disabled, 1971-. Chm., British Council, 1972-76. Lord High Comr to Gen. Assembly of Church of Scotland, 1973, 1974. Col The Black Watch (Royal Highland Regt), 1969-76. Hon. DCL Canterbury, 1965; DUniv Waikato, 1967; Hon. LLD: Strathclyde, 1971; Dundee, 1973; Hon. DLitt St Andrews, 1974. *Publications:* Eton Portrait, 1937; Beyond the Chindwin, 1945; Lowland Soldier (verse), 1945; The Wild Green Earth, 1946; The Black Watch and the King's Enemies, 1950; Rupert of the Rhine, 1952; The Rare Adventure, 1954; The Watery Maze: The Story of Combined Operations, 1961; Wavell: Portrait of a Soldier, 1961; Return to Burma, 1962; The Trumpet in the Hall, 1970; Captain John Niven, 1972. *Address:* Auchairne, Ballantrae, Ayrshire. *T:* 344. *Clubs:* White's; New (Edinburgh).

BALLANTYNE, Alexander Hanson, CVO 1957; CBE 1963; HM Diplomatic Service, retired; Consultant, Organisation for Economic Co-operation and Development, since 1971; *b* 27 Feb. 1911; *s* of late Dr Harold Sherman Ballantyne and of Mrs Gladys Pauline Ballantyne; *m* 1944, Hélène Georgette Contoroussi; one *s* one *d*. *Educ:* Rugby; Christ's Coll., Cambridge. BA (Hons) Cantab. HM Consular Service, 1934. Vice-Consul: Bangkok, 1934-38; Valencia, 1938 and 1939; Tokyo, 1940-42; Antananarivo, 1942-45; Actg Consul-Gen. Antananarivo, 1945 and 1946; Foreign Office, 1946 and 1947; First Sec. (Commercial), Istanbul, 1947-50; Actg Consul-Gen, Istanbul, 1950 and 1951; Foreign Office, 1951 and 1952; First Sec. (Commercial), Bangkok, 1952-55; Counsellor (Commercial) and Consul-General, Copenhagen, 1956-60; Chargé d'Affaires, Ankara, 1962; Counsellor (Commercial), Ankara, 1960-64; Consul-General, Frankfurt-am-Main, 1964-69. Commander of the Dannebrog, 1957. *Recreation:* music. *Address:* 2 Avenue Marie-Christine, 06 Nice, France.

BALLANTYNE, Archibald Morton, OBE 1966; TD 1951; Secretary, Royal Aeronautical Society, 1951-73; *b* 1908; *o s* of late Archibald Morton Ballantyne and of Janet Ballantyne, Pollokshields, Glasgow; *m* 1941, Catherine Mary, 2nd *d* of J. Warner Crofts, Kilsby Grange, Rugby; one *s* one *d*. *Educ:* Hutchesons' Grammar Sch.; Glasgow Univ. BSc (Eng) 1930;

PhD 1936; Diploma in Town Planning; FAIAA. Senior Lecturer in Civil and Municipal Engineering Department, University College, London, 1936-51. Served War of 1939-45, in Royal Artillery, attached to Inspector-Gen. of Armaments; Captain Royal Artillery, TA. Hon. FCASI; Hon. FRAeS, 1973. *Recreations:* golf, writing. *Address:* 27 Clifton Lawns, Chesham Bois, Bucks. *T:* Amersham 3711.

BALLANTYNE, Colin Sandergrove, CMG 1971; President, Arts Council of Australia, since 1974 (Federal Director, 1966-74); *b* 12 July 1908; *s* of James Fergusson Ballantyne, Adelaide; *m* 1934, Gwenneth Martha Osborne Richmond; one *s* two *d*. *Educ:* Adelaide High School. Theatre director, photographer; produced cycle Shakespeare plays, 1948-52; five major productions Adelaide Festival of Arts, 1960-68; directed 100 contemporary plays, 1948-70. Chm. Bd of Governors, SA Theatre Co., 1972-. Dir, 1964-72, Pres., 1972-74, Arts Council of Australia (SA). Hon. FIAP 1971. *Address:* 77 Kingston Terrace, North Adelaide, SA 5006, Australia. *T:* Adelaide 267 1138.

BALLANTYNE, Air Vice-Marshal Gordon Arthur, CBE 1945; DFC 1918; FDSRCS; FDSRCSE; Director of Dental Services, RAF, 1943-54; *b* 12 Feb. 1900; *e s* of late John Alexander and Ida Ballantyne; *m* 1st, 1925, Brenda Muriel, *d* of Rev. Bernard Cuzner; one *d*; 2nd, 1945 Rachel Mary, *er d* of late Francis Reid Brown. *Educ:* King's Coll. Sch.; London Hosp. Probationary Flight Officer, Royal Naval Air Service, 1917; Flying Officer RAF 1918. Served in France with No 8 Squadron, RFC (wounded); LDS, RCS 1923; Lieut Army Dental Corps, 1924; Captain, 1927. Transferred to RAF Dental Branch, 1930; Squadron Leader, 1934; Wing Commander, 1937; Acting Group Captain, 1941; Temp. Group Captain, 1942; Group Captain and Acting Air Commodore, 1943; Temp. Air Commodore, 1944; Air Commodore, 1947; Air Vice-Marshal, 1952; Senior Dental Officer, Iraq, 1935; Inspecting Dental Officer, Home Commands, 1938; Training Officer (Dental), 1941; retd 1954; Hon. Dental Surgeon to King George VI, 1945-52. Member Board of Faculty of Dental Surgery of Royal Coll. of Surgeons of England, 1947-53; Hon. member British Dental Association; Hon. Pres. Armed Forces Commn, Federation Dentaire Internationale, 1953; Hon. Dental Surgeon to the Queen, 1952-54. *Publications:* various professional papers. *Recreations:* painting and motoring. *Address:* 3 St Martin's Hill, Canterbury, Kent. *T:* Canterbury 61103.

BALLANTYNE, Henry, CBE 1968; DL, JP; Chairman and Managing Director, Scottish Worsteds & Woollens Ltd, since 1968; *b* 27 Nov. 1912; *er s* of Lieut-Col David Ballantyne, OBE, Barns Kirkton Manor, Peeblesshire; *m* 1938, Barbara Mary, *d* of late C. S. Gavin, Worthing; one *s* three *d*. *Educ:* Cheltenham Coll.; Pembroke Coll., Cambridge. Entered family business, D. Ballantyne Bros & Co. Ltd, 1937; Dir, 1937; Chm., 1940, also of subsid. cos; merged twelve Border woollen firms to form Scottish Worsteds & Woollens Ltd, 1968, new holding co. Henry Ballantyne & Sons Ltd formed 1977; Dir, Chagford Investment Hldgs Ltd and other cos. Pres., S of Scotland Chamber of Commerce, 1942-44; Pres., Nat. Assoc. of Scottish Woollen Manufrs, 1951-55; Member: BoT Adv. Cttee, 1961-67; Scottish Econ. Planning Cttee, 1965-68; Royal Commn on Local Govt in Scotland, 1967-69; Scottish Constitutional Cttee of Conservative Party, 1969-70. Member of the Royal Company of Archers (Queen's Body Guard for Scotland). DL 1953, JP 1943, Peeblesshire. *Recreations:* shooting, yachting, gardening. *Address:* Caerlee House, Innerleithen, Peeblesshire. *T:* Innerleithen 392. *Clubs:* Caledonian, Lansdowne, Royal Ocean Racing; Leander (Henley-on-Thames).

BALLARAT, Bishop of, since 1975; **Rt. Rev. John Hazlewood;** *b* 19 May 1924; *s* of George Harold Egerton Hazlewood and Anne Winnifred Edeson; *m* 1961, Dr Shirley Shevill; two *s*. *Educ:* Nelson Coll., New Zealand; King's Coll., Cambridge (BA 1948, MA 1952); Cuddesdon Coll., Oxford. Deacon 1949, priest 1950, Southwark; Asst Curate: SS Michael and All Angels, Camberwell, 1949-50, 1953-55; St Jude, Randwick, Sydney, 1950-51; Holy Trinity, Dubbo, NSW, 1951-53; Vice-Principal, St Francis Coll., Brisbane, 1955-60; Asst Lectr in Ecclesiastical History, Univ. of Queensland, 1959-60; Dean of Rockhampton, Qld, 1960-68; Dean of Perth, WA, 1968-75. *Recreations:* travelling, music, gardening, reading, theatre, art. *Address:* Bishopscourt, 454 Wendouree Parade, Ballarat, Victoria 3355, Australia. *T:* 053-392370.

BALLARAT, Bishop of, (RC), since 1971; **Most Rev. Ronald Austin Mulkearns,** DD, DCL; *b* 11 Nov. 1930. *Educ:* De La Salle Coll., Malvern; Corpus Christi Coll., Werribee; Pontifical Lateran Univ., Rome. Ordained, 1956; Coadjutor Bishop, 1968-71. *Address:* 340 Wendouree Parade, Ballarat, Victoria 3350, Australia.

BALLARD, Ven. Arthur Henry; Archdeacon of Manchester and Canon Residentiary of Manchester Cathedral, since 1972; *b* 9 March 1912; 3rd *s* of Alfred and Lillian Ballard; *m* 1943, Phyllis Marion, *d* of Walter East, Theydon Bois, Essex; two *s*. *Educ:* privately; St John's Coll., Univ. of Durham (Van Mildert Scholar). BA 1938; DipTh. 1939; MA 1941. Deacon 1939; Curate of Walthamstow, 1939-43; Rector of Broughton, Manchester, 1943-46; Rector of All Saints, Stand, Manchester, 1946-72. Rural Dean of Radcliffe and Prestwich, 1952-67; Hon. Canon of Manchester, 1958-66; Archdeacon of Rochdale, 1966-72. *Address:* 30 Rathen Road, Withington, Manchester M20 9GH. *T:* 061-445 4703.

BALLARD, Lieut-Col Basil W.; *see* Woods-Ballard.

BALLARD, Prof. Clifford Frederick; Professor Emeritus in Orthodontics, University of London; Hon. Consultant, Eastman Dental Hospital, London; *b* 26 June 1910; *s* of Frederick John Ballard and Eliza Susannah (*née* Wilkinson); *m* 1937, Muriel Mabel Burling; one *s* one *d*. *Educ:* Kilburn Grammar Sch.; Charing Cross Hosp. and Royal Dental Hospital. LDS 1934; MRCS, LRCP 1940. Hd of Dept of Orthodontics, Inst. of Dental Surgery, British Post-Grad. Med. Fedn, Univ. of London, 1947-72; Prof. of Orthodontics, London Univ., 1956-72. Pres. of Brit. Soc. for the Study of Orthodontics, 1957, Senior Vice-Pres., 1963, 1964; Mem. Council of Odontological Section of Royal Society Med., 1954-56, 1959-62 (Sec., 1957, Vice-Pres., 1969-72); Mem. Board, Faculty of Dental Surgery. RCS, 1966-74. FDS 1949; Diploma in Orthodontics, 1954 (RCS); FFDRCS Ire., 1964. Charles Tomes Lectr, RCS, 1966; Northcroft Memorial Lectr, Brit. Soc. for Study of Orthodontics, 1967. Hon. Member: British Soc. for Study of Orthodontics; Israel Orthodontic Soc.; NZ Orthodontic Soc.; European Orthodontic Soc.; Membre d'Honneur, Société Française d'Orthopédie Dento-faciale. Colyer Gold Medal, RCS, 1975. *Publications:* numerous contributions to learned journals, 1948-. *Recreations:* golf, gardening, sailing, motor cruising. *Address:* Winnards Perch, Ridge, Wareham, Dorset BH20 5BQ. *T:* Wareham 3346.

BALLARD, Brig. (Retd) James Archibald William, CBE 1957 (MBE 1940); DSO 1943; *b* 31 July 1905; *s* of late Admiral G. A. Ballard, CB and Mrs M. F. H. Ballard (*née* Paterson); *m* 1st, 1939, Helen Mary (*d* 1941), *d* of late F. Longdon; 2nd, 1945, Ursula Mary (*d* 1962), *d* of late Rev. F. Icely, Naval Chaplain. *Educ:* Rugby. Joined Northamptonshire Regiment, 1925; psc 1939; HQ 2 Corps, BEF, 1940; Military mission to S Africa, 1941-42; in command 2nd Bn Northamptonshire Regt, 1942-43 and 1944; USA, 1943-44; SHAEF Mission to Denmark, 1945; BGS British Troops, Egypt, 1946-48; in comd 2nd Bn Northamptonshire Regt, 1948-50; Chief of Staff British Forces, Trieste, 1950-52; in comd 133 Inf. Bde (TA), 1952-54. War Office, 1954-57. *Address:* Laundry Cottage, Hanmer, Whitchurch, Salop. *Club:* Naval and Military.

BALLENTYNE, Donald Francis; HM Diplomatic Service; Counsellor (Commercial), The Hague, since 1974; *b* 5 May 1929; *s* of late Henry Q. Ballentyne and Frances R. MacLaren; *m* 1950, Elizabeth Heywood, *d* of Leslie A. Heywood; one *s* one *d*. *Educ:* Haberdashers' Aske's Hatcham Sch. FO, 1950-53; Berne and Ankara, 1953-56; Consul: Munich, 1957; Stanleyville, 1961; Cape Town, 1962; First Secretary: Luxembourg, 1965-69; Havana, 1969-72; FCO, 1972-74. *Recreation:* sailing. *Address:* c/o Foreign and Commonwealth Office, SW1; British Embassy, The Hague, Netherlands. *T:* 070-645-800.

BALMAIN, Pierre Alexandre; Chevalier de la Légion d'Honneur, 1962; Couturier, established in 1945; *b* St-Jean-de-Maurienne (Savoie), 18 May 1914; *s* of Maurice Balmain and Françoise Balmain (*née* Ballinari). *Educ:* Lycée of Chambéry; Ecole des Beaux-Arts, Paris. Dress designer with Molyneux, 1934-39; dress designer with Lelong, 1939-45. Mem., Rotary Club of Paris. Kt Order of Dannebrog (Denmark) 1963. Cavaliere Ufficiale del Merito Italiano, 1966. *Publication:* My Years and Seasons, 1964. *Recreations:* horse-riding, yachting. *Address:* 44 rue François 1er, Paris 8e, France. *T:* Balzac 6804.

BALME, Prof. David Mowbray, CMG 1955; DSO 1943; DFC 1943; MA; Professor of Classics, Queen Mary College, London University, since 1964; *b* 8 Sept. 1912; *s* of late Harold Balme, OBE, MD, FRCS; *m* 1936, Beatrice Margaret Rice; four *s* one *d*. *Educ:* Marlborough; Clare Coll., Cambridge. Res. Student, Clare Coll. and Univ. of Halle, Germany, 1934-36; Lecturer, Reading Univ., 1936-37; Research Fellow, Clare Coll., Cambridge, 1937-40; Fellow of Jesus Coll., 1940. Served with No 207 (Bomber) Squadron, 1943; Comd No 49 Squadron, 1945. Tutor of Jesus Coll., 1945-47; Senior Tutor, 1947-48; University Lecturer in Classics, 1947-48; Principal, University College of Ghana, 1948-57; Reader in Classics, Queen Mary

Coll., London, 1957-64. Vis. Prof., Princeton Univ., 1973. Hon. LLD Lincoln, Pa, 1955; Hon. LittD Ghana, 1970. *Publications:* Aristotle's De Partibus Animalium, I, 1972; articles in classical journals on Greek Philosophy. *Recreations:* music, foxhunting. *Address:* Gumley, near Market Harborough, Leics. *T:* Kibworth 2762.

BALMER, Sir Joseph (Reginald), Kt 1965; JP; Retired Insurance Official; *b* 22 Sept. 1899; *s* of Joseph Balmer; *m* 1927, Dora, *d* of A. Johnson; no *c*. *Educ:* King Edward's Grammar Sch., Birmingham. North British and Mercantile Insurance Co. Ltd, 1916-60; National Chairman Guild of Insurance Officials, 1943-47. Pres. Birmingham Borough Labour Party, 1946-54; elected to Birmingham City Council, 1945, 1949, 1952; Alderman 1952-74; Chairman Finance Cttee, 1955-64; Lord Mayor of Birmingham, 1954-55; Hon. Alderman, 1974; City Magistrate, 1956. Hon. Life Mem. Court, Birmingham Univ.; formerly Governor, King Edward VI Schs, Birmingham; Member or ex-member various cttees. Served European War, 1914-18, overseas with RASC and Somerset Light Infantry. *Recreations:* gardening, woodwork and reading. *Address:* 26 Stechford Lane, Ward End, Birmingham B8 2AN. *T:* 021-783 3198.

BALNIEL, Lord; Anthony Robert Lindsay; *b* 24 Nov. 1958; *s* and heir of 29th Earl of Crawford and 12th of Balcarres, *qv*. *Address:* 107 Frognal, NW3.

BALOGH, family name of **Baron Balogh.**

BALOGH, Baron *cr* 1968 (Life Peer), of Hampstead; **Thomas Balogh,** MA, Dr rer. pol. (Budapest); Fellow Emeritus of Balliol College, Oxford, 1973; Deputy Chairman, British National Oil Corporation, since 1976; *b* Budapest, 2 Nov. 1905; *e s* of Emil Balogh; *m* 1945, Penelope (marr. diss. 1970), widow of Oliver Gatty, sometime Fellow of Balliol; two *s* one *d* one step-*d*; *m* 1970, Catherine Storr; three step-*d*. *Educ:* The Gymnasium of Budapest Univ.; Univs of Budapest, Berlin, Harvard. Fellow of Hungarian Coll., Berlin, 1927; Rockefeller Fellow, 1928-30; League of Nations, 1931; economist in the City, 1931-39; National Institute of Economic Research, 1938-42; Oxford Univ. Institute of Statistics, 1940-55; Special Lecturer, 1955-60; Fellow of Balliol Coll., Oxford, 1945-73; Reader in Econs, Oxford Univ., 1960-73. Minister of State, Dept of Energy, 1974-75. Leverhulme Fellow, Oxford, 1973-76. Visiting Prof., Minnesota and Wisconsin, 1951; Delhi and Calcutta, 1955; Member and acting Chairman Minerals Cttee, Min. of Fuel and Power, 1964-68; Consultant: Reserve Bank of Australia, 1942-64; UNRRA Mission to Hungary, 1946; Govt of Malta, 1955-57, of Jamaica, 1956, 1961-62; Food and Agricultural Organisation of UN, 1957-59, 1961-62; UN Economic Commn for Latin America, 1960; Government of India Statistical Inst., 1960, 1971; Greece, 1962; Mauritius, 1962-63; UN Special Fund, 1964, 1970, 1971; OECD, 1964; Turkey, Peru, 1964. Member, Economic and Financial Cttee of the Labour Party, 1943-64, 1971-; Economic Advr to Cabinet, 1964-67; Consultant to Prime Minister, 1968. Chm., Fabian Soc., 1970. Fellow, New York Univ., 1969; Fellow, W. Wilson Center, Washington, 1976. *Publications:* Hungarian Reconstruction and the Reparation Question, 1946; Studies in Financial Organisation, 1946; Dollar Crisis, 1949; Planning through the Price Mechanism, 1950; (with D. Seers) The Economic Future of Malta (Valetta), 1955; Planning and Monetary Organisation in Jamaica, 1956; The Economic Problem of Iraq, 1957; The Economic Development of the Mediterranean (as Head of a Research team), 1957; Economic Policy and Price Mechanism, 1961; Development Plans in Africa, 1961; (with M. Bennett) Sugar Industry in Mauritius; Unequal Partners, 2 vols, 1963; Planning for Progress, 1963; Economics of Poverty, 1966; Labour and Inflation, 1970; Fact and Fancy: an essay in monetary reform, 1973; (co-author): Economics of Full Employment, 1945; War Economics, 1947; Foreign Economic Policy for the US; Fabian International and Colonial Essays; The Establishment, 1960; Crisis in the Civil Service, 1968; Keynes College Essays, 1976; papers in Economic Journal, Bulletin of Oxford Institute of Statistics, etc. *Address:* Old Bank House, 14 Hampstead High Street, NW3. *T:* 01-435 9275; The Cottage, Christmas Common, Watlington, Oxon. *Clubs:* Little French, Reform.

BALTIMORE, Prof. David, PhD; Professor of Biology, Massachusetts Institute of Technology, since 1972; American Cancer Society Professor of Microbiology, since 1973; *b* New York, 7 March 1938; *s* of Richard and Gertrude Baltimore; *m* 1968, Alice Huang; one *d*. *Educ:* Swarthmore Coll.; Rockefeller Univ. Postdoctoral Fellow, MIT, 1963-64; Albert Einstein Coll. of Med., NY, 1964-65; Research Associate, Salk Inst., La Jolla, Calif, 1965-68; Associate Prof., MIT, 1968-72. Eli Lilly Award in Microbiology and Immunology, 1971; US Steel Foundn

Award in Molecular Biology, 1974; (jtly) Nobel Prize for Physiology or Medicine, 1975. *Address:* Center for Cancer Research, Massachusetts Institute of Technology, Cambridge, Mass 02139, USA.

BAMBERG, Harold Rolf, CBE 1968; Chairman, Bamberg Group Ltd and other companies, including Eagle Aircraft Services Ltd; *b* 17 Nov. 1923; *m* 1957, June Winifred Clarke; one *s* two *d* (and one *s* one *d* of a former marriage). *Educ:* Fleet Sch.; William Ellis Sch., Hampstead. FRSA. *Recreations:* polo, shooting, bloodstock breeding. *Address:* Harewood Park, Sunninghill, Berks.

BAMBOROUGH, John Bernard; Principal of Linacre College, Oxford, since 1962; Pro-Vice-Chancellor, Oxford University, since 1966; *b* 3 Jan. 1921; *s* of John George Bamborough; *m* 1947, Anne, *d* of Olav Indrehus, Indrehus, Norway; one *s* one *d*. *Educ:* Haberdashers' Aske's Hampstead Sch. (Scholar); New College, Oxford (Scholar). 1st Class, English Language and Literature, 1941; MA 1946. Service in RN, 1941-46 (in Coastal Forces as Lieut RNVR; afterwards as Educ. Officer with rank of Instructor Lieut, RN). Junior Lectr, New Coll., Oxford, 1946; Fellow and Tutor, Wadham Coll., Oxford, 1947-62 (Dean, 1947-54; Domestic Bursar, 1954-56; Sen. Tutor, 1957-61); Univ. Lectr in English, 1951-62; Mem. Hebdomadal Council, Oxford Univ. Hon. Fellow, New Coll., Oxford, 1967. Editor, Review of English Studies, 1964-. *Publications:* The Little World of Man, 1952; Ben Jonson, 1959; (ed) Pope's Life of Ward, 1961; Jonson's Volpone, 1963; The Alchemist, 1967; Ben Jonson, 1970. *Address:* 40 St Giles', Oxford. *T:* 59886.

BAMFORD, Prof. Clement Henry, FRS 1964; MA, PhD, ScD Cantab; FRIC; Campbell Brown Professor of Industrial Chemistry, University of Liverpool, since 1962; *b* 10 Oct. 1912; *s* of Frederic Jesse Bamford and Catherine Mary Bamford (*née* Shelley), Stafford; *m* 1938, Daphne Ailsa Stephan, BSc Sydney, PhD Cantab, of Sydney, Australia; one *s* one *d*. *Educ:* St Patrick's and King Edward VI Schs, Stafford; Trinity Coll., Cambridge (Senior Scholar). Fellow, Trinity Coll., Cambridge, 1937; Dir of Studies in Chemistry, Emmanuel Coll., Cambridge, 1937. Awarded Meldola Medal of Royal Inst. of Chemistry, 1941. Joined Inter-Services Research Bureau, 1941; joined Fundamental Research Laboratory of Messrs Courtaulds Ltd, at Maidenhead, 1945; head of laboratory, 1947-62; Liverpool University: Dean, Faculty of Science, 1965-68; Pro-Vice-Chancellor, 1972-75. Member: Council, Chem. Soc., 1972-75; Council, Soc. Chem. Ind., 1974-75. Pres., British Assoc. Section B (Chemistry), 1975-76. Mem. Edit. Bd, Polymer, 1958-. *Publications:* Synthetic Polypeptides (with A. Elliott and W. E. Hanby), 1956; The Kinetics of Vinyl Polymerization by Radical Mechanisms (with W. G. Barb, A. D. Jenkins and P. F. Onyon), 1958; (ed with C. F. H. Tipper) Comprehensive Chemical Kinetics (series), 1969-; papers on physical chemistry and polymer science in learned journals. *Recreations:* music, especially playing violin in string quartets, hill walking, gardening. *Address:* Broom Bank, Tower Road, Prenton, Birkenhead, Merseyside L42 8LH. *T:* 051-608 3979.

BAMFORD, Joseph Cyril, CBE 1969; Chairman and Managing Director: J. C. Bamford Excavators Ltd, 1945-76; JCB Farms Ltd; Chairman: JCB Research Ltd; JCB Sales Ltd; JCB Service; JCB Earthmovers Ltd; *b* 21 June 1916; *m* 1941, Marjorie Griffin; two *s*. *Educ:* St John's, Alton, Staffs; Stonyhurst Coll. Founded J. C. Bamford Excavators Ltd, 1945; more than fifty per cent of total production now goes to export market. *Recreations:* yacht designing, landscaping, landscape gardening. *Address:* 16 Rue de Bourg, CH 1003 Lausanne, Switzerland. *Club:* Lighthouse.

BAMPFYLDE, family name of **Baron Poltimore.**

BANBURY, family name of **Baron Banbury of Southam.**

BANBURY OF SOUTHAM, 2nd Baron, *cr* 1924, of Southam; **Charles William Banbury;** 2nd Bt, *cr* 1902; DL; late 12th Lancers; *b* 18 May 1915; *s* of Captain Charles William Banbury, *e s* of 1st Baron (killed in action, Sept. 1914), and Josephine, *d* of José Reixach; *S* grandfather, 1936; *m* 1945, Hilda Ruth (marr. diss. 1958), 2nd *d* of late A. H. R. Carr; one *s* two *d*. *Educ:* Stowe. DL 1965, CC 1967, CA 1967-74, Glos. *Heir:* *s* Hon. Charles William Banbury, *b* 29 July 1953. *Address:* Daglingworth Place, near Cirencester, Glos GL7 7HU. *T:* Cirencester 3521.

BANBURY, (Frederick Harold) Frith; Theatrical director, producer and actor; *b* 4 May 1912; *s* of Rear-Adm. Frederick Arthur Frith Banbury and Winifred (*née* Fink); unmarried. *Educ:* Stowe Sch.; Hertford Coll., Oxford; Royal Academy of

Dramatic Art. First stage appearance in "If I Were You", Shaftesbury Theatre, 1933; for next 14 years appeared both in London and Provinces in every branch of theatre from Shakespeare to revue. Appearances included: Hamlet, New Theatre, 1934; Goodness How Sad, Vaudeville, 1938; (revue) New Faces, Comedy, 1939; Uncle Vanya, Westminster, 1943; Jacobowsky and the Colonel, Piccadilly, 1945; Caste, Duke of York's, 1947. During this time he also appeared in numerous films including The Life and Death of Colonel Blimp and The History of Mr Polly, and also on the television screen. Since 1947 he has devoted his time to production and direction, starting with Dark Summer at Lyric, Hammersmith (later transferred St Martin's), 1947; subseq. many, in both London and New York, including The Holly and the Ivy, Duchess, 1950; Waters of the Moon, Haymarket, 1951; The Deep Blue Sea, Duchess, 1951, and Morosco, New York, 1952; A Question of Fact, Piccadilly, 1953; Marching Song, St Martin's, 1954; Love's Labour's Lost, Old Vic, 1954; The Diary of Anne Frank, Phoenix, 1956; A Dead Secret, Piccadilly, 1957; Flowering Cherry, Haymarket, 1957, and Lyceum, New York, 1959; A Touch of the Sun, Saville, 1958; The Ring of Truth, Savoy, 1959; The Tiger and the Horse, Queen's, 1960; The Wings of the Dove, Lyric, 1963; The Right Honourable Gentleman, Billy Rose, New York, 1965; Howards End, New, 1967; Dear Octopus, Haymarket, 1967; Enter A Free Man, St Martin's, 1968; A Day In the Death of Joe Egg, Cameri Theatre, Tel Aviv, 1968; Le Valet, Théâtre de la Renaissance, Paris, 1968; On the Rocks, Dublin Theatre Festival, 1969; My Darling Daisy, Lyric, 1970; The Winslow Boy, New, 1970; Captain Brassbound's Conversion, Cambridge, 1971; Reunion in Vienna, Chichester Festival, 1971, Piccadilly, 1972; The Day After the Fair, Lyric, 1972, Shubert, Los Angeles, 1973; Glasstown, Westminster, 1973; Ardèle, Queen's, 1975; Family Matters, Watford, 1976; On Approval, Canada and SA, 1977. *Recreation:* playing the piano. *Address:* 4 St James's Terrace, Prince Albert Road, NW8. *T:* 01-722 8481.

BANBURY, Frith; *see* Banbury, Frederick Harold F.

BANCROFT, Sir Ian (Powell), KCB 1975 (CB 1971); Permanent Secretary, Department of the Environment, since 1975; *b* 23 Dec. 1922; *s* of A. E. and L. Bancroft; *m* 1950, Jean Swaine; two *s* one *d*. *Educ:* Coatham Sch.; Balliol Coll., Oxford. Served Rifle Brigade, 1942-45. Entered Treasury, 1947; Private Secretary: to Sir Henry Wilson Smith, 1948-50; to Chancellor of the Exchequer, 1953-55; to Lord Privy Seal, 1955-57; Cabinet Office, 1957-59; Principal Private Sec. to successive Chancellors of the Exchequer, 1964-66; Under-Sec., HM Treasury, 1966-68, Civil Service Dept, 1968-70; Dep. Sec., Dir Gen. of Organization and Establishments, DoE, 1970-72; a Comr of Customs and Excise, and Dep. Chm. of Bd, 1972-73; Second Permanent Sec., CSD, 1973-75. Vis. Fellow, Nuffield Coll., Oxford, 1973-. *Address:* 4 Melrose Road, West Hill, SW18. *T:* 01-874 8020. *Club:* United Oxford & Cambridge University.

BAND, Robert Murray Niven, MC 1944; QC 1974; Barrister-at-Law since 1947; a Recorder of the Crown Court, since 1977; *b* 23 Nov. 1919; *s* of Robert Niven Band and Agnes Jane Band; *m* 1948, Nancy Margery Redhead; two *d*. *Educ:* Trinity Coll., Glenalmond; Hertford Coll., Oxford (MA). Served in Royal Artillery, 1940-46. Junior Treasury Counsel in Probate Matters, 1972-74; Chm. Family Law Bar Assoc., 1972-74. Chm., St Teresa's Hosp., Wimbledon. *Recreations:* the countryside, gardens, old buildings, treen. *Address:* Well Farm, Banstead, Surrey. *T:* Burgh Heath 52288; 3 Dr Johnson's Buildings, Temple, EC4Y 7BA. *T:* 01-353 1866.

BANDA, Hastings Kamuzu, MD; President of Malawi since 1966, Life President, 1971; Chancellor, University of Malawi, since 1965; Member, Malawi Congress Party; *b* Nyasaland, 1905. *Educ:* Meharry Medical Coll., Nashville, USA (MD); Universities of Glasgow and Edinburgh. Further degrees: BSc, MB, ChB, LRCSE. Practised medicine in Liverpool and on Tyneside during War of 1939-45 and in London, 1945-53. Returned to Africa, 1953, and practised in Gold Coast. Took over leadership of Nyasaland African Congress in Blantyre, 1958, and became Pres.-Gen.; was imprisoned for political reasons, 1959; unconditionally released, 1960; Minister of Natural Resources and Local Government, Nyasaland, 1961-63; Prime Minister of Malawi (formerly Nyasaland), 1963-66. *Address:* Office of the President, Zomba, Malawi.

BANDARANAIKE, Mrs Sirimavo; Member of Parliament of Sri Lanka; Prime Minister of Sri Lanka (Ceylon until 1972), 1960-65, and 1970-77, also Minister of Defence and Foreign Affairs, of Planning and Economic Affairs, and of Plan Implementation; President, Sri Lanka Freedom Party, since 1960; *b* 17 April 1916; *d* of Barnes Ratwatte, Ratemahatmaya of Ratnapura Dist,

Mem. of Ceylon Senate; *m* 1940, Solomon West Ridgeway Dias Bandaranaike (*d* 1959), Prime Minister of Ceylon, 1956-59; one *s* two *d. Educ:* Ratnapura Ferguson Sch.; St Bridget's Convent, Colombo. Assisted S. W. R. D. Bandaranaike in political career. Campaigned for Sri Lanka Freedom Party in election campaigns, March and July 1960. Formerly Pres. and Treasurer, Lanka Mahila Samiti. Prime Minister of Ceylon, also Minister of Defence and External Affairs, 1960-65; Minister of Information and Broadcasting, 1964-65; Leader of the Opposition, 1965-70. Ceres Medal, FAO, 1977. *Address:* Horagolla, Nittambuwa, Sri Lanka.

BANDON, 5th Earl of, *cr* 1880; **Percy Ronald Gardner Bernard,** GBE 1961 (KBE 1957); CB 1945; CVO 1953; DSO 1940; Baron Bandon, 1793; Viscount Bandon, 1795; Viscount Bernard, 1800; Air Chief Marshal, Royal Air Force, retired; *b* 30 Aug. 1904; *s* of late Lt-Col Ronald P. H. Bernard and Lettice Mina, *yr d* of late Captain Gerald C. S. Paget (she *m* 2nd, late Hon. Charles C. J. Littleton, DSO); *S* cousin, 1924; *m* 1st, 1933, Elizabeth (marr. diss., 1946; she *m* 1965, Sir Reginald Holcroft, 2nd Bt, *qv*), 2nd *d* of R. W. Playfair; two *d*; 2nd, 1946, Lois White, *d* of Francis Russell, Victoria, Australia. *Educ:* Wellington; RAF Coll., Cranwell. RAF Staff Coll., 1938; served War of 1939-45; commanded No 82 Squadron, 1939-40; commanded RAF Station, West Raynham, 1941-42; AOC No 224 Group, South-East Asia, 1945 (despatches thrice, American DFC and Bronze Star); Commandant, ROC, 1945-48; idc 1949; AOC No 2 Group, BAFO, Germany, 1950-51, No 11 Group, 1951-53; ACAS (Trg), Air Ministry, 1953-Dec. 1955; C-in-C, 2nd Tactical Air Force, and Comdr, 2nd Allied Tactical Air Force, 1955-57; C-in-C, Far East Air Force, 1957-60; Comdr, Allied Air Forces, Central Europe, 1961-63. *Heir:* none. *Address:* Castle Bernard, Bandon, Co. Cork. *Club:* Royal Air Force.

BANERJEA, A. C., CIE 1943; DrPH; *b* 5 Feb. 1894; *s* of late A. T. Banerjea; *m* 1917, Prabhabati; one *s* four *d. Educ:* India, England and USA. MB, BS 1920; DPH 1922; DrPH 1928; Malariologist, UP Govt for ten years. Dir of Public Health, UP, India, 1939; Dir of Medical and Health Services, 1948; retired, 1950. *Publications:* in official files and records. *Address:* 31 Station Road, Lucknow, UP, India. *T:* 2686.

BANERJEE, Rabindra Nath, CSI 1946; CIE 1938; Chairman, Union Public Service Commission, India, 1949-55, retired; *b* 1 Feb 1895; *s* of late Haradhan Banerjee; *m* Manisha (*d* 1953) *d* of late Lieut-Col Upendra Nath Mukerjee, IMS; one *s* one *d. Educ:* Calcutta Univ. (MA 1915); Emmanuel Coll., Cambridge (BA 1918). Entered Indian Civil Service, 1920; Registrar Co-operative Societies and Dir Of Industries, Central Provinces and Berar, 1929-33; Vice-Chm. Provincial Banking Enquiry Cttee, 1929; Sec. to Govt, Central Provinces and Berar, Revenue Dept, 1933; Sec. to Govt, CP and Berar, Local Self-Government Dept, 1936; Mem. CP and Berar Legislative Council, 1929-36; Sec. to the Governor, CP and Berar, 1937; Commissioner, 1941; Commissioner of Food Supply, 1943; Sec. to Govt of India, Commonwealth Relations Dept and Min. of Home Affairs, 1944-48. Mem. Council of State (India), 1944, 1945, 1947; MLA (India), 1946. Mem. of Cttee of Experts of International Labour Organisation, 1956-58. *Address:* 17 Friends' Colony, Mathura Road, New Delhi, India. *T:* New Delhi 630220.

BANGHAM, Alec Douglas, FRS 1977; MD; Research Worker, Agricultural Research Council, Institute of Animal Physiology, Babraham, since 1952 and Head, Biophysics Unit, since 1971; *b* 10 Nov. 1921; *s* of Dr Donald Hugh and Edith Bangham; *m* 1943, Rosalind Barbara Reiss; three *s* one *d. Educ:* Bryanston Sch.; UCL and UCH Med. Sch. (MD). Captain, RAMC, 1946-48. Lectr, Dept of Exper. Pathology, UCH, 1949-52; Principal Scientific Officer, 1952-63, Senior Principal Scientific Officer (Merit Award), 1963-, ARC, Babraham. *Publications:* contrib. Nature, Biochim. Biophys. Acta, and Methods in Membrane Biol. *Recreations:* horticulture, photographic arts, sailing. *Address:* 17 High Green, Great Shelford, Cambridge. *T:* Shelford 3192.

BANGOR, 7th Viscount *cr* 1781; **Edward Henry Harold Ward;** Baron, 1770; free-lance journalist (as Edward Ward); *b* 5 Nov. 1905; *s* of 6th Viscount Bangor, PC (Northern Ireland), OBE and Agnes Elizabeth (*d* 1972), 3rd *d* of late Dacre Hamilton of Cornacassa, Monaghan; *S* father, 1950; *m* 1st, 1933, Elizabeth (who obtained a divorce, 1937), *e d* of T. Balfour, Wrockwardine Hall, Wellington, Salop; 2nd, 1937, Mary Kathleen (marr. diss. 1947), *d* of W. Middleton, Shanghai; 3rd, 1947, Leila Mary (marr. diss. 1951; she died, 1959), *d* of David R. Heaton, Brookfield, Crownhill, S Devon; one *s*; 4th, 1951, Mrs Marjorie Alice Simpson, *d* of late Peter Banks, St Leonards-on-Sea; one *s* one *d. Educ:* Harrow; RMA, Woolwich. Formerly Reuter's correspondent in China and the Far East; BBC War

Correspondent in Finland, 1939-40, ME, 1940-41, and Foreign Correspondent all over world, 1946-60. *Publications:* 1940 Despatches from Finland, 1946; Give Me Air, 1946; Chinese Crackers, 1957; The New Eldorado, 1957; Oil is Where They Find It, 1959; Sahara Story, 1962; Number One Boy, 1969; I've Lived like a Lord, 1970. With his wife, Marjorie Ward: Europe on Record, 1950; The US and Us 1951; Danger is Our Business, 1955. *Heir:* s Hon. William Maxwell David Ward [*b* 9 Aug. 1948; *m* 1976, Mrs Sarah Bradford]. *Address:* 59 Cadogan Square, SW1. *T:* 01-235 3202. *Clubs:* Savile, Garrick.

BANGOR, Bishop of; *see* Wales, Archbishop of.

BANGOR, Dean of; *see* Rees, Very Rev. J. I.

BANHAM, Prof. (Peter) Reyner; Professor of History of Architecture, University College, London, since 1969; *b* 2 March 1922; *m* 1946, Mary Mullett; one *s* one *d. Educ:* King Edward VI Sch., Norwich; Courtauld Institute of Art, London. BA 1952, PhD 1958. Bristol Aeroplane Co., 1939-45. Editorial Staff, Architectural Review, 1952-64; University Coll., London, 1960-. Research Fellow, Graham Foundation (Chicago), 1964-66. Prix Jean Tschumi, 1975. *Publications:* Theory and Design in the First Machine Age, 1960; Guide to Modern Architecture, 1962; The New Brutalism, 1966; Architecture of the Well-tempered Environment, 1969; Los Angeles, 1971; (ed) The Aspen Papers, 1974; The Age of the Masters: a Personal View of Architecture, 1975. *Recreations:* indistinguishable from daily interests in architecture and design. *Address:* School of Environmental Studies, University College London, Wates House, 22 Gordon Street, WC1H 0QB. *T:* 01-387 7050.

BANISTER, Stephen Michael Alvin; Under Secretary, Department of Transport, since 1976; *b* 7 Oct. 1918; *s* of late Harry Banister and Idwen Banister (*née* Thomas); *m* 1944, Rachel Joan Rawlence; four *s. Educ:* Eton; King's Coll., Cambridge (MA). With Foreign Office, 1939-45; Home Guard (Major, 1944). Asst Principal, Min. of Civil Aviation, 1946; Principal, 1947; Private Sec. to six successive Ministers of Transport and Civil Aviation, 1950-56; Asst Sec., Min. of Transport and BoT, 1956-70; Under Sec., DoE, 1970-76. UK Shipping Delegate, UNCTAD, 1964. *Compositions:* (amateur) for singers, including Bluebeard. *Recreations:* countryside, walking, singing (particularly in opera); formerly cricket (Cambridge Crusader); played for CU *v* Australians, 1938. *Address:* Bramshaw, Lower Farm Road, Effingham, Surrey. *T:* Bookham 52778.

BANK-ANTHONY, Sir Mobolaji, KBE 1963 (OBE 1956); Company Director, Lagos, Nigeria; *b* 11 June 1907; *e s* of Alfred Bank-Anthony and Rabiatu Aleshinloye Williams, Lagos; *m* 1935, Olamide Adeshigbin. *Educ:* Methodist Boys' High Sch., Lagos; CMS Gram. Sch., Lagos; Ijebu-Ode Gram. Sch. Postal Clerk in Nigerian P & T Dept, 1924; course in Palm Oil cultivation methods, in England, 1931-33, when returned Nigeria, and gradually built up extensive business, opening stores in many parts of Lagos; Dir of some leading local companies. Fellow of Royal Commonwealth Society; FRSA, FInstD. Stella della Solidarieta (Italy), 1957. *Recreations:* working, reading, newspapers, dancing. *Address:* Executive House, 2a Oil Mill Street, Lagos, Nigeria. *T:* Lagos 24660, 24669; Fountainpen House, 29 Okotie-Eboh Street, Ikoyi, Lagos, Nigeria. *T:* Lagos 21900 and 21363. *Clubs:* Royal Automobile (London); Rotary, Metropolitan, Island, Lagos Race, Lagos Motor, Lagos Amateur Cricket, Yoruba Tennis, Skal, Lodge Academic (Lagos).

BANKES, Henry John Ralph; JP; Barrister, Inner Temple, 1925; *b* 14 July 1902; *s* of Walter Ralph Bankes of Corfe Castle and Kingston Lacy, Dorset; *m* 1935, Hilary (*d* 1966), *d* of late Lieut-Col F. Strickland-Constable, Wassand Hall, Yorks; one *s* one *d. Educ:* Eton; Magdalen Coll., Oxford. JP Dorset, 1936; High Sheriff of Dorset, 1939. RNVR, 1939-45. *Address:* Kingston Lacy, Wimborne, Dorset. *Clubs:* Carlton; Royal Dorset Yacht (Weymouth); Royal Motor Yacht (Sandbanks).

BANKOLE-JONES, Sir Samuel; *see* Jones, Sir S. B.

BANKS, family name of **Baron Banks.**

BANKS, Baron *cr* 1974 (Life Peer), of Kenton in Greater London; **Desmond Anderson Harvie Banks,** CBE 1972; President, Liberal European Action Group, since 1971; Vice-Chairman, Liberal Party Standing Committee, since 1973; Deputy Liberal Whip, House of Lords, since 1977; *b* 23 Oct. 1918; *s* of James Harvie Banks, OBE and Sheena Muriel Watt; *m* 1948, Barbara Wells; two *s. Educ:* Alpha Prep. Sch.; University College Sch. Served with KRRC and RA, 1939-46, Middle East and Italy (Major); Chief Public Relations Officer to Allied Mil. Govt, Trieste, 1946. Joined Canada Life Assce Co., subseq. Life Assoc. of Scotland; life assce broker from 1959; Dir, Tweddle French & Co. (Life & Pensions) Ltd, 1973-. Liberal Party: Pres., 1968-69; Chm. Exec., 1961-63 and 1969-70; Dir of Policy Promotion, 1972-74; Chm. Res. Cttee, 1966; Hon. Sec., Home Counties Liberal Fedn, 1960-61; Chm., Working Party on Machinery of Govt, 1971-74; Mem., For. Affairs and Social Security Panels, 1961-; Hon. Sec., Liberal Candidates Assoc., 1947-52; contested (L): Harrow East, 1950; St Ives, 1955; SW Herts, 1959. Liberal spokesman on social services, 1977-. Elder, United Reformed Church. *Publications:* Clyde Steamers, 1947, 2nd edn 1951; numerous political pamphlets. *Recreations:* pursuing interest in Gilbert and Sullivan opera and in Clyde river steamers; reading. *Address:* 58 The Ridgeway, Kenton, Harrow, Mddx. *T:* 01-907 7369. *Club:* National Liberal.

BANKS, Alan George; HM Diplomatic Service, retired; *b* 7 April 1911; *s* of George Arthur Banks and Sarah Napthen; *m* 1946, Joyce Frances Telford Yates; two *s. Educ:* Preston Gram. Sch. Served in HM Forces, 1939-43; at Consulate-Gen., Dakar, 1943-45; Actg Consul, Warsaw, 1945-48; HM Vice-Consul: Bordeaux, 1948-50; Istanbul, 1950-52; Zagreb, 1952-55; FO, 1955-58; HM Consul, Split, 1958-60; 1st Sec. and Consul, Madrid, 1960-62; 1st Sec., FO, 1962-67; Consul-General, Alexandria, 1967-71. *Recreations:* swimming, classical music, bridge. *Address:* Ferney Field, Parkgate Road, Newdigate, Dorking, Surrey. *T:* Newdigate 434. *Club:* MCC.

BANKS, A(rthur) Leslie, MA Cantab; MD London; FRCP; DPH; Barrister-at-Law (Lincoln's Inn); Professor of Human Ecology, Cambridge, 1949-71, now Emeritus; Fellow, Gonville and Caius College; *b* 12 Jan. 1904; *o s* of late A. C. and E. M. F. Banks; *m* 1933, Eileen Mary (*d* 1967), *d* of Sidney Barrett, Arkley, Herts; two *s. Educ:* Friern Barnet Gram. Sch.; Middlesex Hospital and Medical Sch. Resident hospital appointments, including house-surgeon, resident officer to special depts and acting Registrar, Middlesex Hosp., 1926-28; Locum tenens and asst in general practice, Asst Medical Officer, Gen. Post Office, EC1, 1928-34; Divisional Medical Officer, Public Health Dept, LCC (duties included special public health enquiries and slum clearance), 1934-37; Min. of Health, 1937-49; seconded as Medical Officer of Health to City of Newcastle, 1946. Formerly Principal Medical Officer, Min. of Health. First Viscount Bennett prize, Lincoln's Inn, for essay on the Jurisdiction of the Judicial Cttee of the Privy Council. Member: WHO Expert Advisory Panel on Organisation of Med. Care, 1972-76; Hon. Society of Lincoln's Inn; Middlesex Hosp. Club. FRSocMed. *Publications:* Social Aspects of Disease, 1953; (ed) Development of Tropical and Sub-tropical Countries, 1954; (with J. A. Hislop) Health and Hygiene, 1957; (with J. A. Hislop) Art of Administration, 1961; private and official papers on medical and social subjects. *Address:* 4 Heycroft, Eynsham, Oxford. *T:* Oxford 880791.

BANKS, Air Cdre Francis Rodwell, CB 1946; OBE 1919; RAF (retired); *b* 22 March 1898; *s* of late Bernard Rodwell and Frances Emily Banks; *m* 1925, Christine Constance Grant Langlands; two *d. Educ:* Christ's Coll., London, N. Served in two wars, 1914-19 in Navy and 1939-46 in RAF. Between the two wars specialised in the development of aviation engines and their fuels with The Associated Ethyl Co.; responsible in the recent war successively for the production, the research and development of aero engines, including gas turbines, at MAP. Principal Dir of Engine Research and Development, Min. of Supply, 1952-53; Dir, The Bristol Aeroplane Co., 1954-59; Dir, Hawker Siddeley Aviation Ltd, 1954-59, now Engrg Consultant. Pres. RAeS, 1969. CEng; Hon. CGIA; Hon. FRAeS; Hon. FAIAA; FIMechE; FInstPet. *Publications:* technical papers on aviation engines and their fuels. *Recreation:* golf. *Address:* 5a Albert Court, SW7. *T:* 01-584 2740. *Club:* Royal Air Force.

BANKS, Frank David, FCA; Director, Constructors John Brown Ltd, since 1974; *b* 11 April 1933; *s* of Samuel and Elizabeth Banks; *m* 1st, 1955, Catherine Jacob; one *s* two *d*; 2nd, 1967, Sonia Gay Coleman; one *d. Educ:* Liverpool Collegiate Sch.; Carnegie Mellon Univ. (PFE). British Oxygen Co. Ltd, 1957-58; Imperial Chemical Industries Ltd, 1959-62; English Electric Co. Ltd, 1963-68; Finance Dir, Platt International Ltd, 1969-71. Industrial Advr, DTI, 1972-73. *Recreations:* music, history. *Address:* 27 Pembroke Road, Old Portsmouth, Hants PO1 2NS.

BANKS, James Dallaway, MA, FHA; seconded to Regional and Planning Division, Department of Health and Social Security, 1973-75, retired 1975; *b* 3 Jan. 1917; *s* of late Dr Cyril Banks; *m* 1942, Winifred Holt; one *s* one *d* (and one *s* decd). *Educ:* Nottingham High Sch.; St John's Coll., Cambridge. BA 1938, MA 1943. Indian Civil Service, 1939-47. Dep. House Governor,

King's Coll. Hosp., 1947-53; House Governor: Royal Marsden Hospital 1953-59; The Hospital for Sick Children, Great Ormond Street, 1959-60; Sec. to Bd of Governors, KCH, Denmark Hill, 1960-73. *Address:* 8 Newenham Road, Lymington, Hants. *T:* Lymington 74999. *Club:* Lymington Town Sailing.

BANKS, Sir Maurice (Alfred Lister), Kt 1971; Chairman, Laird Group Ltd, 1970-75; *b* 11 Aug. 1901; *s* of Alfred Banks, FRCS and Elizabeth Maud (*née* Davey); *m* 1933, Ruth Hall, Philadelphia, USA; one *s* two *d. Educ:* Westminster Sch.; Manchester Univ., Coll. of Technology. BSc Tech., FRIC, MIChemE. Coal Research Fellowship under DSIR, 1923; joined Anglo Persian Oil Co., 1924. British Petroleum: a Man. Dir, 1960; a Dep. Chm., 1965; retd from BP, 1967. Chairman: Adv. Council on Calibration for Min. of Technology, 1965-66; Adv. Cttee on Hovercraft for Min. of Technology, 1967-68; Chairman BoT Departmental Cttee to enquire into Patent Law and Procedure, 1967-70. *Recreations:* golf, gardening. *Address:* Beech Coppice, Kingswood, Surrey. *T:* Mogador 2270. *Clubs:* Athenæum; Walton Heath Golf.

BANKS, Richard Alford, CBE 1965; Member of the Water Resources Board, 1964-74; *b* 11 July 1902; *s* of William Hartland Banks, Hergest Croft, Kington, Hereford; *m* 1st, 1937, Lilian Jean (*d* 1974), *d* of Dr R. R. Walker, Presteigne, Radnorshire; two *s* one *d*; 2nd, 1976, Rosamund Gould. *Educ:* Rugby; Trinity Coll., Cambridge (BA). Dir of Imperial Chemical Industries Ltd, 1952-64; Chm. of the Industrial Training Council, 1962-64. JP Hereford, 1963-73. *Recreations:* arboriculture, gardening and travel. *Address:* Ridgebourne, Kington, Hereford.

BANKS, Robert George; MP (C) Harrogate, since Feb. 1974; *b* 18 Jan. 1937; *s* of George Walmsley Banks, MBE, and Olive Beryl Banks (*née* Tyler); *m* 1967, Diana Margaret Payne Crawfurd; four *s* one *d* (of whom one *s* one *d* are twins). *Educ:* Haileybury. Lt-Comdr RNR. Jt Founder Dir, Antocks Lairn Ltd, 1963-67; Partner, Breckland Securities, investment co. Mem., Council of Europe, 1977-. Jt Sec., Cons. Parly Defence Cttee; Vice Chm., Cons. Parly Horticulture Cttee; Sec., All-Party Tourism Gp. *Recreations:* farming, architecture. *Address:* Bretteston Hall, Stanstead, Sudbury, Suffolk; Cow Myers, Galphay, Ripon, Yorks.

BANKS, Captain William Eric, CBE 1943; DSC; RN retired; *b* 17 July 1900; *er s* of late Walter Banks; *m* 1937, Audrey Steel; two *s. Educ:* University Coll. Sch. Joined Navy in 1918; retired list, 1952. *Address:* Villa Fort, Lija, Malta, GC. *Club:* Naval and Military.

BANNER, Mrs Delmar; *see* Vasconcellos, J. de.

BANNER, Sir George Knowles H.; *see* Harmood-Banner.

BANNERMAN, David Armitage, OBE 1961 (MBE 1918); MA, ScD, Hon. LLD; FRSE; *b* 27 Nov. 1886; *o s* of late David Alexander Bannerman; *m* 1911, Muriel (*d* 1945), 2nd *d* of T. R. Morgan of Las Palmas, Grand Canary; twin *d* (one *s* decd); *m* 1952, Winifred Mary (Jane), OBE, *e d* of David Holland, Cardiff. *Educ:* Wellington College; Pembroke College, Cambridge. Graduated 1909; joined temp. Staff Natural History Museum, 1910; travelled extensively West Indies, N, S, and W Africa, S America, Atlantic Isles and Europe; carried out Zoological Survey of Canary Islands, 1908-13. Served with BEF (Europe), first as Ambulance driver, then, as Staff Officer, on HQ Staff BRCS (France), 1915-18 (MBE; OStJ 1919); British and French War Medals, Mons Star; after Armistice rejoined staff of Natural History Museum; Leader, British Museum Expedition to Tunisia, 1925. Assistant Editor, Ibis, 1931-41. On outbreak of Second World War, 1939, appointed Deputy Assistant Censor (Liaison Branch) on Staff of Controller of Postal and Telegraph Censorship, War Office; Assistant Censor, IRB Censorship Hqrs, 1940-42; Sgt in Home Guard. Retd from Natural History Museum, 1952, to take up book-writing and stock-breeding in Kirkcudbrightshire. Carried out ornithological surveys of Morocco, 1950-52, Cyprus, 1954, Madeira and Azores, 1960-64, Cape Verde Islands, 1966. Chairman, British Ornithologists' Club, 1932-35; Brit. representative Internat. Council Bird Preservation, Vienna, 1937, Rouen, 1938; MBOU (Vice-Pres., 1943-45); Member Council: RGS, 1935-38; Zoological Soc., 1943-50; RSPB, 1938-52 (Vice-Pres., 1961); Hon. Associate, British Museum (Natural History), 1950; Hon. Curator, Royal Scottish Museum (Edinburgh), 1971; Hon. Pres., Scottish Ornithologists' Club; Hon. Member: Société Ornithologique de France; Soc. Española de Ornitologia (Madrid); Les Naturalistes de Mons et du Borinage (Belgium); Hon. Fellow, Amer. Ornith. Union. Hon.

LLD Glasgow, 1964. Gold Medal of British Ornithologists' Union, 1959. *Publications:* The Canary Islands, their History, Natural History and Scenery, 1922; Reports on numerous British Museum Expeditions for the advancement of ornithological knowledge; The Birds of Tropical West Africa, by order of the Secretary of State for the Colonies, vols i-viii, 1930-51; The Birds of West and Equatorial Africa (2 vols), 1953; The Birds of the British Isles Vols 1-12 1953-63; The Larger Birds of West Africa, 1958, in Penguin series; (by request of Government) The Birds of Cyprus (in conjunction with W. Mary Bannerman), 1958; Birds of the Atlantic Islands (with W. Mary Bannerman): Vol. 1, Canary Islands, 1963; Vol. 2, Madeira, 1965; Vol. 3, Azores, 1966; Vol. 4, Cape Verde Islands, 1968; Handbook of the Birds of Cyprus and Migrants of the Middle East, 1971; (with Joseph A. Vella) Birds of the Maltese Archipelago. *Recreations:* natural history and travel. *Address:* Bailiff's House, Slindon, by Arundel, West Sussex. *T:* Slindon 212. *Club:* Athenæum.
See also Gen. Sir J. H. Gibbon.

BANNERMAN, Lt-Col Sir Donald Arthur Gordon, 13th Bt, *cr* 1682; *b* 2 July 1899; *s* of Lieut-Col Sir Arthur D'Arcy Gordon Bannerman, KCVO, CIE, 12th Bt and of late Virginia Emilie Bannerman; *S* father 1955; *m* 1932, Barbara Charlotte, *d* of late Lieut-Col A. Cameron, OBE, IMS; two *s* twin *d. Educ:* Harrow; Royal Military Coll., Sandhurst; commissioned into Queen's Own Cameron Highlanders, 1918; served in N Russian Campaign, 1919; 1st Class Interpreter (Russian), 1925; served with 1st and 2nd Bns of his Regt in Egypt and India, 1931-34 and 1936-39; served War of 1939-45: with 4th Indian Div. and in MEF, 1940-43; in NW Europe, 1945, attached to US 9th Army, in closing stages of fighting, and then for 3 yrs with Control Commission as Senior Control Officer; retired from Army as Lieut-Col, 1947. On staff of Gordonstoun Sch., 1948-52, of Fettes Coll., 1952-60. *Publication:* Bannerman of Elsick: a short family history, 1975. *Recreations:* gardening, walking, reading. *Heir:* s Alexander Patrick Bannerman, *b* 5 May 1933. *Address:* 11 Learmonth Place, Edinburgh EH4 1AX. *T:* 031-332 1076.

BANNISTER, Sir Roger (Gilbert), Kt 1975; CBE 1955; DM (Oxon); FRCP; Consultant Physician: National Hospital for Nervous Diseases, Queen Square, WC1; Department of Nervous Diseases, St Mary's Hospital, W2; Consultant Neurologist, Western Ophthalmic Hospital, NW1; Hon. Consultant, King Edward VII Convalescent Home for Officers, Osborne; *b* 23 March 1929; *s* of late Ralph and of Alice Bannister, Harrow; *m* 1955, Moyra Elver, *d* of late Per Jacobsson, Chairman IMF; two *s* two *d. Educ:* City of Bath Boys' Sch.; University Coll. Sch., London; Exeter and Merton Colls, Oxford; St Mary's Hospital Medical Sch., London. Amelia Jackson Studentship, Exeter Coll., Oxford, 1947; BA (hons) Physiology, Junior Demonstrator in Physiology, Harmsworth Senior Scholar, Merton Coll., Oxford, 1950; Open and State Schol., St Mary's Hosp., 1951; BSc Thesis in Physiology, 1952; MRCS, LRCP, 1954; BM, BCh Oxford, 1954; DM Oxford, 1963. William Hyde Award for research relating physical education to medicine; MRCP 1957. Junior Medical Specialist, RAMC, 1958; Radcliffe Travelling Fellowship, at Harvard, USA, 1962-63. Pres. of National Fitness Panel, NABC, 1956-59. Mem. Council, King George's Jubilee Trust, 1961-67; Pres., Sussex Assoc. of Youth Clubs, 1972-; Chm., Res. Cttee, Adv. Sports Council, 1965-71; Mem., Min. of Health Adv. Cttee on Drug Dependence, 1967-70; Chairman: Sports Council, 1971-74; Internat. Council for Sport and Physical Recreation, 1976-. Chadwick Trust Lectr, 1972. Winner Oxford *v* Cambridge Mile, 1947-50; Pres. OUAC, 1948; Capt. Oxford & Cambridge Combined American Team, 1949; Finalist, Olympic Games, Helsinki, 1952; British Mile Champion, 1951, 1953, 1954; World Record for One Mile, 1954; British Empire Mile title and record, 1954; European 1500 metres title and record, 1954. Hon. LLD Liverpool, 1972; Hon. FUMIST, 1974. Hans-Heinrich Siegbert Prize, 1977. *Publications:* First Four Minutes, 1955; (ed) Brain's Clinical Neurology, 4th edn, 1973; papers on physiology of exercise, heat illness and neurological subjects. *Recreations:* sailing, golf, orienteering. *Address:* 16 Edwardes Square, W8. *T:* 01-603 9903; Churchfield, Lyminster, Sussex. *Clubs:* Athenæum; Vincent's (Oxford).

BANNON, John Kernan, ISO 1969; Director of Services, Meteorological Office, 1973-76; *b* 26 April 1916; *s* of Frederick J. Bannon, Clerk in Holy Orders and Eveline Bannon, Muckamore, NI; *m* 1947, Pauline Mary Roch Thomas, Pembroke; one *s* one *d. Educ:* Royal Sch., Armagh; Emmanuel Coll., Cambridge (Braithwaite Batty Scholar). BA (Wrangler) 1938. Technical Officer, Meteorological Office, 1938; commnd RAFVR, 1943-46 (Temp. Sqdn Ldr); Met. Office, 1946-76; idc 1963. *Publications:* some official scientific works; articles in meteorological jls. *Recreations:* walking, gardening. *Address:* 18 Courtenay Drive, Emmer Green, Reading RG4 8XH. *T:* Reading 473696.

BANTOCK, Prof. Geoffrey Herman; Emeritus Professor of Education, University of Leicester, 1975; Leverhulme Emeritus Fellow, 1976; *b* 12 Oct. 1914; *s* of Herman S. and Annie Bantock; *m* 1950, Dorothy Jean Pick; no *c. Educ:* Wallasey Grammar Sch.; Emmanuel Coll., Cambridge. BA 1936, MA 1942, Cantab. Taught in grammar schs, training coll.; Lectr in Educn, University Coll. of Leicester, 1950-54; Reader in Educn, University Coll., Leicester, later Univ. of Leicester, 1954-64; Prof. of Educn, 1964-75. Vis. Prof., Monash Univ., Melbourne, 1971. *Publications:* Freedom and Authority in Education, 1952 (2nd edn 1965); L. H. Myers: a critical study, 1956; Education in an Industrial Society, 1963 (2nd edn 1973); Education and Values, 1965; Education, Culture and the Emotions, 1967; Education, Culture and Industrialization, 1968; T. S. Eliot and Education, 1969 (paperback 1970). *Recreations:* music, art, foreign travel. *Address:* c/o The University, Leicester.

BANTOCK, John Leonard; Assistant Under Secretary of State, Home Office, since 1976; *b* 21 Oct. 1927; *s* of Edward Bantock and Agnes Bantock; *m* 1947, Maureen McKinney; two *s. Educ:* Colfe's Grammar Sch., SE13; King George V Sch., Southport, Lancs; LSE, London Univ. (LLB 1951). Unilever Ltd, 1943-45; Army, 1945-48 (Staff Captain); Colonial Office, 1951-52; Inland Revenue, 1952-69; Secretariat, Royal Commn on Constitution, 1969-73; Cabinet Office, 1973-76; Sec., Cttee of Privy Counsellors on Recruitment of Mercenaries, 1976. *Address:* 1 Heathcote Road, St Margarets, Twickenham, Mddx TW1 1RX. *T:* 01-892 2972.

BANTON, Prof. Michael Parker, PhD, DSc; JP; Professor of Sociology, University of Bristol, since 1965; Director, Social Science Research Council Research Unit on Ethnic Relations, since 1970; *b* 8 Sept. 1926; *s* of Francis Clive Banton and Kathleen Blanche (*née* Parkes); *m* 1952, Rut Marianne (*née* Jacobson), Luleå; two *s* two *d. Educ:* King Edward's Sch., Birmingham; London Sch. of Economics. BSc Econ. 1950; PhD 1954; DSc 1964. Midn, then Sub-Lieut RNVR, 1945-47. Asst, then Lecturer, then Reader, in Social Anthropology, University of Edinburgh, 1950-65; Visiting Professor: MIT, 1962-63; Wayne State Univ., Detroit, 1971; Univ. of Delaware, 1976. Editor, Sociology, 1966-69. Pres., Section N, British Assoc. for the Advancement of Science, 1970-71; Mem., Vetenskaps-societeten, Lund, Sweden, 1972; Mem., SW Regl Hosp. Board, 1966-70. JP Bristol, 1966. *Publications:* The Coloured Quarter, 1955; West African City, 1957; White and Coloured, 1959; The Policeman in the Community, 1964; Roles, 1965; Race Relations, 1967; Racial Minorities, 1972; Police-Community Relations, 1973; (with J. Harwood) The Race Concept, 1975; The Idea of Race, 1977. *Address:* 9 Canynge Road, Bristol BS8 3JZ. *T:* Bristol 36459.

BANWELL, Derick Frank; General Manager, Runcorn Development Corporation, since 1964; *b* 19 July 1919; *s* of Frank Edward Banwell; *m* 1945, Rose Kathleen Worby; two *s* one *d. Educ:* Kent Coll., Canterbury. Admitted as Solicitor, 1947; Asst Solicitor, Southend-on-Sea Co. Borough Coun., 1947-48; Sen. Asst Solicitor, Rochdale Co. Borough Coun., 1948-51; Chief Common Law Solicitor, City of Sheffield, 1951-56; Sen. Asst Solicitor, 1956-59, Asst Town Clerk, 1959-60, Southend-on-Sea Co. Borough Coun.; Dep. Town Clerk and Dep. Clerk of the Peace, Swansea Co. Borough Council, 1960-64. *Recreations:* history, music, model railways. *Address:* 57 Main Street, Halton, Runcorn, Cheshire.

BANWELL, Sir (George) Harold, Kt 1955; Managing Trustee, Municipal Mutual Insurance Co. Ltd; Director, Municipal Journal Ltd; *b* 11 Dec. 1900; *yr s* of late Edward and Marion Banwell, Whitstable, Kent; *m* 1924, Kate Mary, *d* of late Rev. A. B. Bull, Durham; two *s* three *d. Educ:* Tankerton Coll., Kent. Admitted Solicitor, 1922; articled to Town Clerk, Canterbury; Asst Solicitor: West Hartlepool; Cumberland County Council; Sheffield City Council; Dep. Town Clerk, Norwich, 1929-32; Town Clerk, Lincoln, 1932-41; Clerk of the County Council of Lincoln, (Parts of Kesteven), 1941-44; Sec., Association of Municipal Corporations, 1944-Oct. 1962; Chm., Nat. Citizens Advice Bureaux Council, 1961-71; Dep. Chm., Commn for the New Towns, 1964-71. Alderman, Lincoln City Council, 1967-74. Chairman: Cttee on Placing and Management of Contracts for Building and Civil Engineering Work, 1962-64; Congregational Church in England and Wales, 1966-69; Member: Gen. Adv. Council of BBC, 1961-64; Nat. Incomes Commn, 1962-65; Deptl Cttee on the Fire Services, 1967-70; Adv. Council on Commonwealth Immigration, 1962-64; Parly Boundary Commn for England, 1963-74. Hon. LLD Nottingham, 1972. *Address:* 2 Vicars' Court, Lincoln. *T:* Lincoln 28869. *Club:* Royal Commonwealth Society.

BANWELL, Godwin Edward, CBE 1955; MC 1917 and Bar 1918; KPM; Chief Constable of Cheshire 1946-63; *b* 1897; *s* of Edward and Rose Banwell, Polegate, Sussex; *m* 1st, 1924, Kathleen Frances Cole (*d* 1939); 2nd, 1940, Gladys Lilian Banwell; three *s* one *d*. *Educ:* Merchant Taylors' Sch., London. Leics Regiment, TA, 1916-19; Indian Police, Burma, 1920-38; Regional Officer, Min. of Home Security, 1939-41; Actg Inspector of Constabulary, 1941-42; Chief Constable of East Riding of Yorks, 1942-46. KPM 1931. *Address:* Sunnycroft, Manley, via Warrington, Cheshire. *Club:* National Liberal.

BANWELL, Sir Harold; see Banwell, Sir G. H.

BARBACK, Ronald Henry; Head, Economic Research Department, Confederation of British Industry, since 1977; *b* 31 Oct. 1919; *s* of late Harry Barback and Winifred Florence (*née* Norris); *m* 1950, Sylvia Chambers; one *s* one *d*. *Educ:* Woodside Sch., Glasgow; Univ. Coll., Nottingham (BScEcon); Queen's and Nuffield Colls, Oxford (BLitt). Asst Lectr in Econs, Univ. of Nottingham, 1946-48; Lectr in Econs, subseq. Sen. Lectr, Canberra University Coll., Australia, 1949-56; Univ. of Ibadan (formerly University Coll., Ibadan): Prof. of Econs and Social Studies, 1956-63; Dean, Faculty of Arts, 1958-59; Dean, Faculty of Econs and Social Studies, 1959-63; Dir, Nigerian (formerly W African) Inst. of Social and Econ. Res., 1956-63; Sen. Res. Fellow, Econ. Res. Inst., Dublin, 1963-64; Prof. of Econs, TCD, 1964-65; Univ. of Hull: Prof. of Econs, 1965-76; Dean, Faculty of Social Sciences and Law, 1966-69; Head, Dept of Econs and Commerce, 1971-74. Nigeria: Mem., Ibadan Univ. Hosp. Bd of Management, 1958-63; Mem., Jt Econ. Planning Cttee, Fedn of Nigeria, 1959-61; Sole Arbitrator, Trade Disputes in Ports and Railways, 1958; Chm., Fed. Govt Cttee to advise on fostering a share market, 1959. UK Official Delegate, FAO meeting on investment in fisheries, 1970; Mem., FAO mission to Sri Lanka, 1975. Consultant, Div. of Fisheries, Europ. Commn Directorate-Gen. of Agriculture, 1974. Commonwealth Scholarships Commn Adviser on Econs, 1971-76; Mem., Schools Council Social Sciences Cttee, 1971-; Chm., Schs Council Econs and Business Studies Syllabus Steering Gp, 1975-77. Member: Hull and Dist Local Employment Cttee, 1966-73; N Humberside Dist Manpower Cttee, 1973-76; Editorial Bd, Bull. of Economic Research (formerly Yorks Bull. of Social and Economic Research), 1965-76 (Jt Editor, 1966-67); Editorial Adv. Bd, Applied Economics, 1969-. Editor, Humberside Statistical Bull., nos 1-3, 1974, 1975, 1977. *Publications:* (contrib.) The Commonwealth in the World Today, ed J. Eppstein, 1956; (ed with Prof. Sir Douglas Copland) The Conflict of Expansion and Stability, 1957; (contrib.) The Commonwealth and Europe (EIU), 1960; The Pricing of Manufactures, 1964; (contrib.) Insurance Markets of the World, ed M. Grossmann 1964; (contrib.) Webster's New World Companion to English and American Literature, 1973; Forms of Co-operation in the British Fishing Industry, 1976; (with M. Breimer and A. F. Haug) Development of the East Coast Fisheries of Sri Lanka, 1976; contrib. New Internat. Encyc., FAO Fisheries Reports, and jls. *Recreations:* weeding (the cultivation of weeds), walking in wild places, music. *Address:* 21 Tothill Street, SW1H 9LP. *T:* 01-930 6711; Oakhurst, Beaconfields, Sevenoaks, Kent. *T:* Sevenoaks 57917. *Club:* Royal Commonwealth Society.

BARBER, family name of Baron Barber.

BARBER, Baron *cr* 1974 (Life Peer), of Wentbridge; Anthony Perrinott Lysberg Barber, PC 1963; TD; Chairman, Standard Chartered Bank Ltd, since 1974; *b* 4 July 1920; *s* of John Barber, CBE, Doncaster; *m* 1950, Jean Patricia, *d* of Milton Asquith, Wentbridge, Yorks; two *d*. *Educ:* Retford Grammar Sch.; Oriel Coll., Oxford Univ. (PPE, MA) (Hon. Fellow 1971). Served War of 1939-45: commnd in Army (Dunkirk); seconded to RAF as pilot, 1940-45 (despatches; prisoner of war, 1942-45, took Law Degree with 1st Class Hons while POW, escaped from Poland, prisoner of the Russians). Barrister-at-law, Inner Temple, 1948 (Inner Temple Scholarship). MP (C): Doncaster, 1951-64; Altrincham and Sale, Feb. 1965-Sept. 1974; PPS to the Under-Sec. of State for Air, 1952-55; Asst Whip, 1955-57; a Lord Comr of the Treasury, 1957-58; PPS to the Prime Minister, 1958-59; Economic Sec. to the Treasury, 1959-62; Financial Sec. to the Treasury, 1962-63; Minister of Health and Mem. of the Cabinet, 1963-64; Chancellor of the Duchy of Lancaster, June-July 1970; Chancellor of the Exchequer, 1970-74. Chm., Conservative Party Organisation, 1967-70. *Address:* Standard Chartered Bank Ltd, 10 Clement's Lane, EC4. *T:* 01-623 7500. *Club:* Carlton.

BARBER, Alan Theodore, MA (Oxon); Headmaster of Ludgrove Preparatory School, Wokingham, Berks, 1937-73; *b* 17 June 1905; *s* of Harold Priestman Barber, Todwick House, Todwick, Yorks; *m* 1937, Dorothy Shaw; one *s* two *d*. *Educ:* Shrewsbury Sch.; Queen's Coll., Oxford. BA 1929; Triple Blue, captained cricket and football XIs, Oxford; captained Yorks County Cricket XI, 1929 and 1930; played football regularly for Corinthians. Asst master, Ludgrove, 1930. *Recreations:* golf, cricket, Eton Fives. *Address:* The Garden Cottage, Ludgrove, Wokingham, Berks. *T:* Wokingham 782639. *Clubs:* Sports, MCC; Berkshire Golf (Bagshot).

BARBER, Hon. Sir (Edward Hamilton) Esler, Kt 1976; Puisne Judge, Supreme Court of Victoria, Australia, 1965-77; *b* Hamilton, Vic., 26 July 1905; *s* of late Rev. John Andrew Barber and Maggie Rorke; *m* 1954, Constance, *d* of Captain C. W. Palmer; one *s* one *d*. *Educ:* Hamilton Coll., Victoria; Scots Coll., Sydney; Scotch Coll., Melbourne; Melbourne Univ. Barrister-at-law, 1929; QC (Vic.) 1955, Tas. 1956; Judge, County Court, Vic., 1957-65; Actg Judge, 1964-65. Chm., Royal Commn into Failure of King's Bridge, 1962-63; Dep. Chm. Parole Bd, Vic., Nov. 1969-77; Mem. Council of Legal Educn, 1968-77; Chm., Royal Commn into West Gate Bridge Disaster, 1970-71; Mem., Bd of Inquiry into causes and origins of bush and grass fires in Vic. during Jan.-Feb. 1977, 1977-. *Publications:* articles on Matrimonial Law, incl. Divorce—the Changing Law, 1968. *Address:* 1 St George's Court, Toorak, Vic. 3142, Australia. *T:* 24-5104. *Club:* Australian (Melbourne).

BARBER, Elizabeth; see Barber, M. E.

BARBER, Hon. Sir Esler; see Barber, Hon. Sir E. H. E.

BARBER, Sir Herbert (William), Kt 1952; *b* 8 Nov. 1887; *m* 1912, Annie Nora Heys (*d* 1953); one *s*. *Educ:* Salford Technical Coll. Mem. of Southport County Borough Council, 1931-62; Mayor, 1937-39 and 1943-44; Freeman of Southport, 1962. *Recreations:* Rugby Union football and cricket. *Address:* 40 Hesketh Road, Southport, Merseyside. *T:* Southport 31837.

BARBER, Rear-Adm. John L.; see Lee-Barber.

BARBER, John Norman Romney; company director; *b* 22 April 1919; *s* of George Ernest and Gladys Eleanor Barber; *m* 1941, Babette Chalu; one *s*. *Educ:* Westcliff. Served with Army, 1939-46 (Capt.). Min. of Supply, 1946-55 (Princ.). Joined Ford Motor Co. Ltd, 1955, Finance Dir, 1962; Chm., Ford Motor Credit Co. Ltd, 1963; Dir, Henry Ford & Son Ltd, Cork, 1963; Dir Autolite Motor Products Ltd, 1963; Finance Dir, AEI Ltd, 1965; Chm., Telephone Cables Ltd, 1967; Dir of Finance and Planning, 1968-71, Dep. Man. Dir, 1971-73, Dep. Chm. and Man. Dir, 1973-75, British Leyland Motor Corp. Ltd; Chairman, 1973-75: British Leyland International Ltd; Leyland Innocenti, SpA; Leyland Motor Corp. of Australia Ltd; Director: Leyland España SA; Automóviles de Turismo Hispano Ingleses SA; NZ Motor Corp. Ltd; British Leyland Motors Inc.; Metalurgica de Santa Ana SA; Chairman: Pullmaflex International Ltd, 1976-; Aberhurst Ltd, 1976-; A. C. Edwards Engineering Ltd, 1976-; Dir, Acrow Ltd, 1977-. Mem., Royal Commn on Medical Educn, 1965-68; Chm., Adv. Cttee to BoT on Investment Grants, 1967-68; Mem., Adv. Council for Energy Conservation, 1974-75. Vice Pres., SMMT, 1974-76. FBIM; Mem. Council BIM, 1967-71. *Publications:* papers on management subjects in various jls. *Recreations:* motor sport, forestry, photography. *Address:* Copthall Green House, Upshire, Waltham Abbey, Essex EN9 3SZ. *T:* Lea Valley 711273. *Clubs:* British Automobile Racing, British Racing and Sports Car.

BARBER, (Mary) Elizabeth, OBE 1968; MA; General Secretary, Society of Authors, 1963-71; *b* 14 March 1911; *yr d* of Frederic Viccars and Margaret Filmer Barber; unmarried. *Educ:* St Swithun's Sch., Winchester; Somerville Coll., Oxford. Called to the Bar, Gray's Inn, 1935. Asst-Sec., then Sec., Society of Authors, 1936-63. *Publications:* Contrib. on copyright and allied subjects to British and foreign books and periodicals. *Address:* 82 Drayton Gardens, SW10.

BARBER, Samuel; Composer; *b* West Chester, Pennsylvania, 9 March 1910; *s* of Samuel Leroy Barber and Marguerite McCleod Beatty; unmarried. *Educ:* Curtis Institute of Music, Philadelphia. Compositions performed by all leading American orchestras and by many European orchestras; Conductors include Toscanini, Koussevitzky, Walter, etc. Has conducted own works in Prague, Vienna, London, Three Choirs Festival (Hereford, 1946), etc. Member: AAAL; American Society of Composers, Authors and Publishers (Dir, 1969-). Prix de Rome, 1935; Guggenheim Award, 1945; NY Music Critics Award, 1946; Pulitzer prize for music (opera, Vanessa), 1958, (piano concerto), 1963. Hon. Dr Harvard, 1959. Served AUS, 1943. *Compositions:* First Symphony, 1936; Violin Concerto, 1941; Second Essay, 1942; Capricorn Concerto (flute, oboe, trumpet and strings), 1944; Cello Concerto, 1946; Piano Sonata, 1949;

Souvenirs (for piano), 1953; Prayers of Kierkegaard (for chorus, soprano and orch.), 1954; Overture to The School for Scandal, 1932; Music for a Scene from Shelley, 1933; Adagio for Strings, 1936; First Essay for Orchestra, 1942; Medea's Dance of Vengeance (for orch.), 1946; Knoxville: Summer of 1915 (for soprano and orchestra), 1947; Vanessa (opera), 1958; Toccata Festiva (for organ and orch.), 1960; Die Natali (for orch.), 1960; Piano Concerto, 1962; Andromache's Farewell (soprano and orch.), 1963; Antony and Cleopatra (opera), 1966; The Lovers (for baritone, chorus and orch.), 1971; also songs, piano pieces, chamber music, choruses. *Address:* c/o G. Schirmer Inc., 866 Third Avenue, New York, NY 10022, USA.

BARBER, Sir William (Francis), 2nd Bt *cr* 1960; TD; JP; *b* 20 Nov. 1905; *yr* and *o surv. s* of Sir Philip Barber, 1st Bt, DSO, TD, JP, DL, and of Beatrice Mary (*d* 1962), *d* of Lieut-Col W. Ingersoll Merritt; *S* father, 1961; *m* 1936, Diana Constance, *d* of late Lieut-Col Thomas Owen Lloyd, CMG, Minard Castle, Argyll; one *s* one *d*. *Educ:* Eton Coll. South Nottinghamshire Hussars Yeomanry (Commnd, 1924). Royal Horse Artillery; served in Palestine, Egypt, North Africa, NW Europe; Lieut-Col 1947. Hon. Col, South Nottinghamshire Hussars Yeomanry, 1961-66. JP Notts, 1952; High Sheriff, Notts., 1964. *Heir: s* (Thomas) David (Barber) [*b* 18 Nov. 1937; *m* 1972, Amanda Mary (*née* Rabone), *widow* of Maj. Michael Healing; one *s*]. *Address:* Lamb Close, Eastwood, Notts; Dunmaglass, Aberarder, Invernessshire.

BARBER, Prof. William Joseph; Professor of Economics, Wesleyan University, Middletown, Conn, USA, since 1965; American Secretary, Rhodes Scholarship Trust, since 1970; *b* 13 Jan. 1925; *s* of Ward Barber; *m* 1955, Sheila Mary Marr; three *s*. *Educ:* Harvard Univ. (AB); Balliol Coll., Oxford. BA, 1st Cl. Hons, 1951, MA 1955; DPhil (Nuffield Coll.) 1958. Served War, US Army, 1943-46. Dept of Economics, Wesleyan Univ., USA, 1957- (Asst Prof., 1957-61; Associate Prof., 1961-65; Prof., 1965-; Andrews Prof., 1972-). Research Associate: Oxford Univ. Inst. of Economics and Statistics, 1962-63; Twentieth Century Fund, South Asian Study, 1961-62. Lectr in Economics, Balliol Coll., Oxford, 1956. *Publications:* The Economy of British Central Africa, 1961; A History of Economic Thought, 1967; contributor to Asian Drama: an inquiry into the poverty of nations (with Gunnar Myrdal and others), 1968-; British Economic Thought and India 1600-1858, 1975; contribs to professional jls. *Address:* 306 Pine Street, Middletown, Conn, USA. *T:* 203-346-2612.

BARBIERI, Margaret Elizabeth; Senior Principal, Sadler's Wells Royal Ballet, since 1974; *b* 2 March 1947; *d* of Ettore Barbieri and Lea Barbieri. *Educ:* Convent High Sch., Durban, S Africa. Trained with Iris Manning and Brownie Sutton, S Africa; Royal Ballet Sen. Sch., 1963; joined Royal Ballet, 1965; Principal, 1970. Gypsy Girl, Two Pigeons, 1966; 1st Giselle, Covent Garden, 1968; 1st Sleeping Beauty, Leeds, 1969; 1st Swan Lake, Frankfurt, 1977. Other roles with Royal Ballet: La Fille mal Gardée, Two Pigeons, The Dream, Façade, Wedding Bouquet, Rendezvous (Ashton); Lady and the Fool, Card Game, Pineapple Poll (Cranko); The Invitation, Solitaire, (Summer) The Four Seasons (MacMillan); Checkmate, The Rake's Progress (de Valois); Grosse Fugue, Tilt (van Manen); Lilac Garden (Tudor); Fête Etrange (Howard); Grand Tour (Layton); Summer Garden (Hynd); Coppélia, Les Sylphides, Raymonda Act III, Spectre de la Rose. Roles created: Knight Errant (Tudor), 1968; From Waking Sleep (Drew), 1970; Ante-Room (Cauley), 1971; Oscar Wilde (Layton), 1972; Sacred Circles and The Sword (Drew), 1973; The Entertainers (Killar), 1974; Charlotte Brontë (Hynd), 1974; Summertide (Wright), 1977. Travelled with Royal Ballet to France, Germany, Italy, Spain, Portugal, Holland, Switzerland, Egypt, Greece, Israel; guest appearances, Germany, S Africa, France, Norway, Czechoslovakia. TV Appearances in: Spectre de la Rose; Grosse Fugue; Giselle; Coppelia. *Recreations:* music (classical), theatre, gardening, home crafts. *Address:* 19 Merton Avenue, Chiswick, W4 1TA. *T:* 01-995 6554.

BARBOUR, George Brown; MA, PhD, FRSE, FRGS, FGS, FGSAm; Professor Emeritus of Geology, University of Cincinnati; *b* 22 Aug. 1890; *s* of A. H. F. Barbour, MD, and Margaret Nelson Brown; *m* 1920, Dorothy, *d* of Dr R. L. Dickinson of New York; three *s*. *Educ:* Merchiston; Marburg Univ.; Edinburgh Univ.; St John's Coll., Cambridge; Columbia Univ., NY. Active Service, FAU and RFA, Sep. 1914-Jan. 1919. Prof. of Applied Geology, Peking Univ., 1920-22; Head of Dept of Geology, Peiyang Univ., Tientsin, 1922-23; Prof. of Geology, Yenching Univ., Peiping, 1923-32; Lecturer, Columbia Univ., 1928-29; Univ. of Cincinnati, 1932-33; Visiting Physiographer, Cenozoic Laboratory, Peiping, 1934; Visiting Prof., Stanford Univ., 1935; Hon. Lecturer, London Univ., 1934-37; Dean of

McMicken Coll. of Arts and Science, 1938-58. Academic Coordinator US Army Air-Force College Training Programme, 1943-45. Member Royal Society of South Africa; Hon. Member Société Belge de Géologie, de Paléontologie et d'Hydrologie, 1937; Corresp. Fellow R. Belgian Geog. Soc., 1946; Corresp. Member, Geological Survey of China; Foreign Member, Geolog. Soc. of Finland; Member Soc. géol. de France; Geologist, Univ. of California African Expedition, 1947; Pres. Ohio Academy of Science, 1948-49; Corresp. Mem. Ital. Inst. of Hum. Paleontology, 1955. RGS Gill Memorial Award, 1937; Viking Fund Award, Wenner-Gren Foundation, 1951, 1954. Visiting Professor, Duke Univ., 1961-62, Univ. of Louisville, Ky, 1964-65. George Barbour Collection of letters, photographs, articles etc, in Univ. of Cincinnati Library. *Publications:* Geology of the Kalgan Area, 1928; Physiographic History of the Yangtze, 1935; Ape or Man, 1949; In the Field with Teilhard de Chardin, 1965, paperback, 1975; In China When— (letters 1911-34), 1974; Geological Reports and papers in scientific jls. *Recreations:* mountaineering, music. *Address:* University of Cincinnati, Cincinnati, Ohio 45221, USA; 440 Lafayette Avenue, Cincinnati, Ohio 45220. *Club:* Athenæum.

BARBOUR, Rev. Prof. Robert Alexander Stewart, MC 1945; Professor of New Testament Exegesis, University of Aberdeen, since 1971; Chaplain-in-Ordinary to the Queen, since 1976; Prelate of the Priory of Scotland of the Order of St John, 1977; *b* 11 May 1921; *s* of George Freeland Barbour and Helen Victoria (*née* Hepburne-Scott); *m* 1950, Margaret Isobel Pigot; three *s* one *d*. *Educ:* Rugby Sch.; Balliol Coll., Oxford (MA 1946); Univ. of St Andrews (BD 1952); Yale Univ. (STM 1953). Sec., Edinburgh Christian Council for Overseas Students, 1953-55; Lectr and Sen. Lectr in NT Lang., Lit and Theol., Univ of Edinburgh, 1955-71. Hon. Sec., Studiorum Novi Testamenti Societas, 1970-77. *Publications:* The Scottish Horse 1939-45, 1950; Traditio-Historical Criticism of the Gospels, 1972; What is the Church for?, 1973; articles in various jls. *Recreations:* music, walking, forestry. *Address:* 74 Don Street, Old Aberdeen AB2 1UU. *T:* Aberdeen 43645. *Club:* New (Edinburgh).

BARBOUR, Walworth; US Ambassador to Israel, 1961-73; *b* 4 June 1908; *s* of Samuel Lewis Barbour and Clara Hammond; unmarried. *Educ:* Harvard Coll. USA. Vice Consul, Naples, 1932; Athens, 1933; Baghdad, 1936; Sofia, 1939; Dip. Sec., Cairo, 1941; Athens, 1944; Dept of State, Washington, 1945-49; Minister, Moscow, 1949-51; Dept of State, Washington, 1951-55; Deputy Asst Sec. of State for European Affairs, 1954-55; American Minister, London, 1955-61. Hon. Fellow, Weizmann Inst. of Sci., 1970. Hon. PhD: Tel Aviv, 1971; Hebrew Univ. of Jerusalem, 1972; Hon. LLD Dropsie, Pa, 1973. *Recreation:* golf. *Address:* 14 Grapevine Road, Gloucester, Mass 01930, USA. *Clubs:* American; Swinley Forest (Surrey); Chevy Chase (Md, USA).

BARCLAY, Alexander, CBE 1957; ARCS, FRIC; Keeper, Department of Chemistry and Photography, Science Museum, S Kensington, 1938-59; retired; *b* 25 July 1896; *o s* of late Alexander Barclay; *m* 1921, Irene Margaret (*d* 1973), *y d* of late Frank Carrington Falkner, Wisbech. *Educ:* Berkhamsted Sch.; Royal College of Science. Served European War with Special Gas Brigade, RE, 1916-17; invalided, 1917; Postal Censorship Research Dept, 1918; entered Science Museum, 1921; Asst Keeper, 1930; Board of Education, 1940 and 1943; Postal Censorship, 1944-45. Hon. Member Royal Photographic Soc.; Mem. of Nat. Film Library Cttee, British Film Institute, 1938-55. *Publications:* Official Handbooks to the Chemistry Collections, Science Museum, 1927-37; various papers in scientific journals. *Address:* Towers End, Walberswick, Southwold, Suffolk. *T:* Southwold 2146.

BARCLAY, Christopher Francis Robert, CMG 1967; Secretary, Government Hospitality Fund, since 1976; *b* 8 June 1919; *s* of late Captain Robert Barclay, RA (retired) and late Annie Douglas Dowdeswell Barclay (*née* Davidson); *m* 1st, 1950, Clare Justice Troutbeck (marr. diss., 1962); two *s* one *d*; 2nd, 1962, Diana Elizabeth Goodman; one *s* one *d*. *Educ:* Eton Coll.; Magdalen Coll., Oxford (MA). 2nd Lieut The Rifle Bde, 1940; Capt. 1942; Major 1943; served in Egypt; Middle East Centre of Arab Studies, Jerusalem, 1944-45; Political Officer, Northern Iraq, 1945; Asst Information Officer, Brit. Embassy, Baghdad, 1946. Joined Foreign Office, 1946; Second Sec., British Embassy, Cairo, 1947; First Sec., Foreign Office, 1950; Brit. Embassy, Bonn, 1953; FO, 1956; Regional Information Officer, Beirut, 1960; FO, 1961; Counsellor and Head of Information Research Dept, 1962-66; Head of Personnel Dept (Training and General), FCO (formerly DSAO), 1967-69; Asst Sec., CSD, 1969-73, DoE, 1973-76. Mem. Council, City Univ., 1976. Mem. Court of Assistants, Saddlers' Co., 1974. *Recreations:* fishing, travel. *Address:* 88 Redcliffe Gardens, SW10. *T:* 01-373 1677. *Clubs:* Army and Navy, City Livery.

BARCLAY, Sir Colville Herbert Sanford, 14th Bt, *cr* 1668; Painter; *b* 7 May 1913; *s* of late Rt Hon. Sir Colville Adrian de Rune Barclay, 3rd *s* of 11th Bt, and Sarita Enriqueta, *d* of late Herbert Ward; *S* uncle, 1930; *m* 1949, Rosamond Grant Renton Elliott; three *s*. *Educ:* Eton, Trinity Coll., Oxford. Third Sec., Diplomatic Service, 1937-41; enlisted in Navy, Nov. 1941; Sub-Lieut RNVR 1942; Lieut 1943; Lieut Commander 1945; demobilised, 1946. Exhibitor: Royal Academy, RBA, London Group, Bradford City and Brighton Art Galleries. Chm. Royal London Homoeopathic Hospital, 1970-74 (Vice-Chm., 1961-65). *Publications:* articles in botanical jls. *Recreations:* gardening, plant-hunting. *Heir: s* Robert Colraine Barclay, *b* 12 Feb. 1950. *Address:* Pitshill, Petworth, West Sussex. *T:* Lodsworth 341. *Club:* Brooks's.

BARCLAY, Brig. Cyril Nelson, CBE 1945; DSO 1940; Cameronians (Scottish Rifles); free-lance writer; Military Adviser and Contributor to the Encyclopædia Britannica; *b* 20 Jan. 1896; *o s* of late E. J. Barclay; *m* 1934, Margaret (*d* 1976), *d* of G. Roberts; one *d*. *Educ:* Thanet Coll., St Peter's, Kent; Elstow Sch., Beds. Commissioned in Cameronians (Scottish Rifles), 1915; served European War, 1914-18, France and Mesopotamia; 3rd Afghan War, 1919; War of 1939-45: Dunkirk, Holland, Germany and South-East Asia; retired, 1946. Editor, Army Quarterly, 1950-66; Jt Editor, Brassey's Annual, 1950-69. *Publications:* History of The Cameronians (Scottish Rifles), 1933-46; Part-Time Farmer; History of the London Scottish, 1939-45; History of the Royal Northumberland Fusiliers in the Second World War; History of the 3rd QAO Gurkha Rifles, 1927-47; The New Warfare; History of the Duke of Wellington's Regiment, 1919-52; The First Commonwealth Division, Korea, 1950-53; Against Great Odds; History of the 53rd (Welsh) Division in the Second World War; History of the Sherwood Foresters, 1919-57; History of the 16th/5th The Queen's Royal Lancers, 1963; On Their Shoulders, 1964; Battle 1066, 1966; Armistice 1918, 1968. *Recreation:* bridge. *Address:* York House, 35 South Side, Clapham Common, SW4 9BS. *T:* 01-720 5922. *Club:* Army and Navy.

BARCLAY, Sir Roderick (Edward), GCVO 1966 (KCVO 1957; CVO 1953); KCMG 1955 (CMG 1948); Director: Barclays Bank SA, since 1969 (Chairman, 1970-74); Slough Estates, since 1969; Barclays Bank International, 1971-77; Banque de Bruxelles, since 1971; *b* 22 Feb. 1909; *s* of late J. Gurney Barclay and Gillian (*née* Birkbeck); *m* 1934, Jean Cecil, *d* of late Sir Hugh Gladstone; one *s* three *d*. *Educ:* Harrow; Trinity Coll., Cambridge. Entered Diplomatic Service, 1932. Served at HM Embassies at Brussels, Paris, Washington and in FO; Counsellor in FO 1946; Principal Private Sec. to Sec. of State for Foreign Affairs, 1949-51; Asst Under-Sec. of State, 1951; Dep. Under-Sec. of State, 1953-56; HM Ambassador to Denmark, 1956-60; Adviser on European Trade Questions, Foreign Office, and Dep. Under-Sec. of State for Foreign Affairs, 1960-63; Ambassador to Belgium, 1963-69. Knight Grand Cross of the Dannebrog (Denmark) and of the Couronne (Belgium). *Publication:* Ernest Bevin and the Foreign Office 1932-69, 1975. *Recreations:* shooting, fishing. *Address:* Great White End, Latimer, Bucks. *T:* Little Chalfont 2050. *Club:* Brooks's.

BARCLAY, Theodore David; banker; *b* 6 Sept. 1906; *e s* of Rev. Canon David Barclay and Loetitia Caroline Rowley, *d* of late Rt Rev. Rowley Hill, Bishop of Sodor and Man; *m* 1934, Anne Millard, *d* of late T. W. M. Bennett, Hatfield; two *s* one *d*. *Educ:* Harrow; Trinity Coll., Cambridge. Entered Barclays Bank Ltd, 1927; Local Director at 54 Lombard Street, 1934, Director of the Bank, 1948; former Dir and Chm., Sun Alliance and London Insurance Ltd; Dir, The Bank of Scotland. High Sheriff of Suffolk, 1959. *Recreations:* shooting and fishing. *Address:* Desnage Lodge, Higham, Bury St Edmunds. *T:* Newmarket 750254. *Clubs:* Boodle's, Pratt's; New (Edinburgh).

BARCLAY, Prof. William, CBE 1969; Professor of Divinity and Biblical Criticism, University of Glasgow, 1963-74; *b* Wick, 1907; *m* Katherine Barbara Gillespie; one *s* two *d*. *Educ:* Dalziel High Sch., Motherwell; Univs of Glasgow and Marburg; Trinity Coll., Glasgow. Minister, Trinity Church, Renfrew, 1933-46; Lectr in New Testament Language and Literature, Univ. of Glasgow, 1946-63. Vis. Prof., Univ. of Strathclyde, 1975. External Examiner: Edinburgh, St Andrews, Aberdeen, Leeds. Lectures: Bruce, 1935; Croall, 1955; Kerr, 1956; Baird, 1969-70; Sir David Owen Evans, Aberystwyth, 1969; James Reid Memorial, 1969, 1970. Member: Joint Cttee, New English Bible; Soc. of New Testament Studies; Soc. of Old Testament Studies. Hon. Pres., Glasgow YMCA; Hon. Vice-Pres., Boys Bde. *Publications:* Ambassador for Christ, 1950; And Jesus Said, 1953; The Daily Study Bible, 1953-59; And He had Compassion on Them, 1955; A New Testament Word Book, 1955; The Mind of Paul, 1957; Letters to the Seven Churches, 1957; More New

Testament Words, 1958; Educational Ideas in the Ancient World, 1959; The Plain Man's Book of Prayers, 1959; The Master's Men, 1959; The Mind of Jesus, 1960; The Promise of the Spirit, 1960; Crucified and Crowned, 1961; Flesh and Spirit, 1962; Jesus as they saw Him, 1962; More Prayers for the Plain Man, 1962; Prayers for the Young People, 1962; Many Witnesses, One Lord, 1963; Turning to God, 1963; The All-Sufficient Christ, 1964; New Testament Words, 1964; The Plain Man Looks at the Lord's Prayer, 1964; Prayers for the Christian Year, 1964; Prayers for Help and Healing, 1968; The New Testament: a new translation, 1969; Ethics in a Permissive Society, 1972; The Plain Man's Guide to Ethics, 1973; Jesus of Nazareth, 1977; contribs to learned journals. *Address:* 32 Holmhead Road, Cathcart, Glasgow G44 3AR. *T:* 041-637 4917. *Club:* Royal Scottish Automobile (Glasgow).

BARCLAY, Mrs William; see Minton, Y. F.

BARCLAY-SMITH, (Ida) Phyllis, CBE 1971 (MBE 1958); Ornithologist; 2nd *d* of late Prof. Edward Barclay-Smith, MD. *Educ:* Church House Sch., Worthing; Blackheath High Sch.; King's Coll., London. Asst Sec. Royal Society for the Protection of Birds, 1924-35; Asst Sec. Internat. Cttee for Bird Preservation, 1935-46; Foreign Office, 1939-42; Sec. to Business Manager, Bristol Aeroplane Shadow Factory, Corsham, 1942-43; Specialist Local Welfare Officer (Transport Workers), SW Region, Min. of Labour, 1943-45; Hon. Sec. British Ornithologists' Union, 1945-51; Member: Home Office Advisory Cttee on Wild Birds, 1948-53; Exec. Bd of Internat. Union for Protection of Nature, 1950-56; Council, Royal Geographical Soc., 1970-73. Sec. Internat. Council for Bird Preservation, 1946-; Editor Avicultural Magazine, 1939-73; Jt Hon. Sec. Internat. Wildfowl Research Bureau, 1948-69, Sec. of Honour, 1969-; Hon. Sec. Advisory Cttee on Oil Pollution of the Sea, 1952-71; Organising Sec., Internat. Conferences on Prevention of Oil Pollution of the Sea: London, 1953; Copenhagen, 1959; Rome, 1968; Mem. Home Office Advisory Cttee on Protection of Birds for England and Wales, 1954-; Vice-Pres. Commn on Migratory Game-birds of Conseil Internat. de la Chasse, 1950-61; Hon. Vice-Pres. 1965-; Vice-President: British Ornithologists Union 1957-60; Avicultural Soc., 1970-; Pheasant Trust, 1972-; Hon. Vice-Pres., Soc. for the Promotion of Nature Reserves, 1971-. Hon. Member: Avicultural Soc.; British Falconers' Club; Fauna Preservation Soc.; Corresp. Mem. Bavarian, German, Netherlands, S African Ornithological Unions and Hungarian Inst. of Ornithology. Gold Medal, Sveriges Djurskyddsforenigars Riksforbund, 1954; Isidore Geoffroy St Hilaire Gold Medal of Société Nationale de Protection de la Nature et d'Acclimatation de France, 1963; Delacour Gold Medal of the Internat. Council for Bird Preservation, 1970; Gold Medal, Svenska Kvinnors Djurskyddsforening, 1970; Gold Medal, World Wildlife Fund, 1971; Gold Medal, RSPB, 1973; Silver Medals: Soc. d'Acclimatation de France, 1951; RSPB, 1951; V. v. Heidenstams Fond (Sweden), 1958; President's Medal, Avicultural Soc., 1960. Coronation Medal, 1953; Ridder, Most Excellent Order of Golden Ark, Netherlands, 1973. *Publications:* British Birds on Lake, River and Stream, 1939; (with Hugh Pollard) British and American Game Birds, 1939; Garden Birds, 1945; A Book of Ducks, 1951; Woodland Birds, 1955; (trans. from German) The Bird (by Gertrude Hess), 1951; (trans. from French) Birds of the World (by P. Barruel), 1954, 2nd edn, 1973; (trans. from French) Water Birds with Webbed Feet (by P. Géroudet), 1965. *Recreations:* bird-watching, travelling. *Address:* 5 Eton Avenue, NW3.

BARCROFT, Prof. Henry, FRS 1953; MA; MD; FRCP; Professor of Physiology, St Thomas's Hospital Medical School, London, 1948-71, Emeritus since 1971; a Wellcome Trustee, 1966-75; *b* 18 Oct. 1904; *s* of late Sir Joseph Barcroft, CBE, FRS; *m* 1933, Bridget Mary, *d* of late A. S. Ramsey; three *s* one *d*. *Educ:* Marlborough Coll.; King's Coll. Cambridge; Exhibitioner, 1923. Natural Science Tripos Class I, Parts I and II; Harold Fry and George Henry Lewis studentships at Cambridge, 1927-29; Gedge Prize, 1930; Harmsworth Scholar, St Mary's Hospital, London, 1929-32; Lectr in Physiology, University Coll., London, 1932-35; Dunville Prof. of Physiology, Queen's Univ., Belfast, 1935-48. Arris and Gale Lectr, RCS, 1945; Bertram Louis Abrahams Lectr, RCP, 1960; Robert Campbell Meml Orator, Ulster Med. Soc., 1975; Bayliss-Starling Meml Lectr, Physiological Soc., 1976; Vis. Prof., Univ. of Adelaide, 1963. Chairman: Editorial Bd, Monographs of Physiological Soc., 1957-65; Research Defence Soc., 1968-71, Sec. 1972-. Hon. Member: Academic Adv. Cttee, Loughborough Coll. of Technology, 1964-66; Société Française d'Angiologie; Japanese Coll. of Angiology; Czechoslovak Med. Soc. J. E. Purkinje. Hon. DSc Univ. Western Australia, 1963; Hon. MD Leopold-Franzens Univ., Innsbruck, 1969; Hon. DSc QUB,

1975. Pro meritis médaille in silver, Karl Franzens Univ., Graz. *Publications:* (with H. J. C. Swan) Sympathetic Control of Human Blood Vessels, 1953; papers in the Journal of Physiology. *Recreations:* sailing and golf. *Address:* 44 Wood Lane, N6 5UB. *T:* 01-340 2338. *Club:* Athenæum.

BARD, Dr Basil Joseph Asher, CBE 1968; Managing Director, Arlington Technology Services Ltd, since 1976; Chairman, Birmingham Mint Ltd, since 1977; *b* London, 20 Aug. 1914; *s* of Abram Isaac Bard and Anita Bard; *m* 1942, Ena Dora Birk; three *s. Educ:* Owen's Sch.; RCS (Imperial Coll.). BSc(Chem.) 1934, DIC (Chem. Engrg and Fuel Technology) 1935, PhD (Chem. Constitution of Coal) 1936, London; Bar Finals (1st cl. hons) and Studentship, Coun. of Legal Educn, 1937; called to Bar, Gray's Inn (Birkenhead and William Shaw Schol.), 1938. Practised at Bar, 1938-39; Legal Dept, Coal Commn, 1939-41; Explosives Prodn Dept, Min. of Supply, 1941-43; Materials Dept, Min. of Aircraft Production, 1943-45; Depts of Industrial Res., Educn, Design, etc, FBI, 1945-49; NRDC, 1950-73; in turn, Commercial Man., Techn. Dir, Exec. Dir, and Chief Exec., Dept of Applied Science; Mem., NRDC, 1956-73, Man. Dir, 1971-73; Exec. Dir, First National Finance Corp., 1974-76. Founder and Chm., 1968, subsequently Vice-Pres., UK Licensing Execs Soc. (awarded Gold Medal 1973). Consultant to UNIDO, 1972-74; Mem., Management Cttee, Science Policy Foundn; has served on various Govt Cttees; ARCS; FInstD. *Publications:* (ed) Industry and Research, 1947; (ed) The Patent System, 1975; various articles on science, technology, patents, industry, commerce and their inter-relationships. *Recreations:* music, bridge, chess, social life. *Address:* 23 Mourne House, Maresfield Gardens, Hampstead, NW3 5SL. *T:* 01-435 5340. *Club:* Athenæum.

BARDEEN, Prof. John; Professor of Physics and Electrical Engineering, University of Illinois, 1951-75, now Emeritus; *b* Madison, Wisconsin, 23 May 1908; *s* of Dr Charles R. Bardeen and Althea Bardeen (née Harmer); *m* 1938, Jane Maxwell; two *s* one *d. Educ:* Univ. of Wisconsin; Princeton Univ. BS 1928, MS 1929, Univ. of Wisconsin; PhD 1936, Princeton Univ. Geophysicist, Gulf Research and Development Corp., Pittsburgh, Pa, 1930-33; Junior Fellow, Soc. of Fellows, Harvard Univ., 1935-38; Asst Prof. of Physics, Univ. of Minnesota, 1938-41; Physicist, Naval Ordnance Laboratory, Washington, DC, 1941-45; Research Physicist, Bell Telephone Laboratories, Murray Hill, NJ, 1945-51. For. Mem., Royal Soc., 1973. Holds hon. doctorates. Nobel Prize for Physics: (with W. H. Brattain and W. Shockley), 1956; (with L. N. Cooper and J. R. Schrieffer), 1972; National Medal of Science, 1965; Presidential Medal of Freedom, 1977. *Publications:* articles on solid state physics, including semi-conductors, metals, superconductivity in Physical Review and other periodicals and books. *Address:* 55 Greencroft, Champaign, Illinois, USA. *T:* Champaign 352-6497.

BARDER, Brian Leon; HM Diplomatic Service; attending National Defence College, Kingston, Ontario, Canada, since 1977; *b* 20 June 1934; *s* of Harry and Vivien Barder; *m* 1958, Jane Maureen Cornwell; one *s* two *d. Educ:* Sherborne; St Catharine's Coll., Cambridge (BA). 2nd Lieut, 7 Royal Tank Regt, 1952-54. Colonial Office, 1957; Private Sec. to Permanent Under-Sec., 1960-61; HM Diplomatic Service, 1965; First Secretary, UK Mission to UN, 1964-68; FCO, 1968-70; First Sec. and Press Attaché, Moscow, 1971-73; Counsellor and Head of Chancery, British High Commn, Canberra, 1973-77. *Recreations:* music, squash. *Address:* c/o Foreign and Commonwealth Office, SW1; National Defence College, Kingston, Ontario, Canada; 33 Lakeside, Wickham Road, Beckenham, Kent. *T:* 01-650 7458. *Club:* Royal Commonwealth Society.

BARDSLEY, Andrew Tromlow; JP; General Manager and Chief Executive, Harlow Development Corporation, since 1973; *b* 7 Dec. 1927; *o s* of Andrew and Gladys Ada Bardsley; *m* 1954, June Patricia (née Ford); one *s* one *d. Educ:* Ashton-under-Lyne Grammar Sch.; Manchester Coll. of Art. CEng, FIMunE, FInstHE, MBIM. Royal Navy, 1947-49. Entered Local Govt (Municipal Engrg), 1950; various appts leading to Borough Engr and Surveyor, Worksop MB, 1962-69; Director of Technical Services: Corby New Town, 1969-71; Luton CBC, 1971-73. JP Essex, 1975. *Publications:* papers on engrg and associated matters incl. housing and town centre re-development. *Recreations:* golf, music, gardening, most spectator sports. *Address:* Grenville Lodge, Barton Road, Luton, Beds. *T:* Luton 56831.

BARDSLEY, Rt. Rev. Cuthbert Killick Norman, CBE 1952; DD 1957; *b* 28 March 1907; *yr s* of late Canon J. U. N. Bardsley and Mabel Killick; *m* 1972, Ellen Mitchell. *Educ:* Eton; New Coll.,

Oxford. Curate of All Hallows, Barking by the Tower, 1932-34; Rector of Woolwich, 1940-44; Provost of Southwark Cathedral, 1944-47. Suffragan Bishop of Croydon, 1947-56; Bishop of Coventry, 1956-76. Hon. Canon in Canterbury Cathedral, 1948-56; Archbishop of Canterbury's Episcopal Representative with the three Armed Forces, 1948-56; Hon. Chaplain Siemens Bros, 1943-46; Proctor in Convocation, 1945-46. Select Preacher, University of Cambridge, 1958. ChStJ 1976. *Publications:* Bishop's Move, 1952; Sundry Times, Sundry Places, 1962; Him We Declare, 1967; I Believe in Mission, 1970. *Recreations:* golf, sketching. *Address:* Grey Walls, Berkeley Road, Cirencester, Gloucestershire GL7 1TY.

BARENBOIM, Daniel; pianist and conductor; Musical Director, Orchestre de Paris, since 1975; *b* Buenos Aires, 15 Nov. 1942; *s* of Enrique Barenboim and Aida Barenboim (née Schuster); *m* 1967, Jacqueline du Pré, *qv. Educ:* Santa Cecilia Acad., Rome; studied with his father; coached by Edwin Fischer, Nadia Boulanger, and Igor Markevitch. Debut as pianist with: Israel Philharmonic Orchestra, 1953; Royal Philharmonic Orchestra, 1956; Berlin Philharmonic Orchestra, 1963; NY Philharmonic Orchestra, 1964; tours include: Australia, 1958, 1962; South America, 1960; Far East, 1962; regular appearances at Edinburgh, Lucerne, Prague and Salzburg Festivals. Beethoven Medal, 1958; Paderewski Medal, 1963; subsequently other awards. *Address:* c/o Harold Holt Ltd, 134 Wigmore Street, W1.

BARFETT, Ven. Thomas; Archdeacon of Hereford and Canon Residentiary of Hereford Cathedral, since 1977; Chaplain to the Queen, since 1975; *b* 2 Oct. 1916; *s* of Rev. Thomas Clarence Fairchild Barfett and Dr Mary Deborah Barfett, LRCP, LRCS, MA; *m* 1945, Edna, *d* of Robert Toy; one *s* one *d. Educ:* St John's Sch., Leatherhead; Keble Coll., Oxford (BA 1938; MA 1942); Wells Theol Coll. Ordained deacon, Portsmouth, 1939; priest, 1940; Curate: Christ Church, Gosport, 1939-44; St Francis of Assisi, Gladstone Park, London, 1944-47; St Andrew Undershaft with St Mary Axe, City of London, 1947-49; Asst Sec., London Diocesan Council for Youth, 1944-49; Vicar, St Paul, Penzance, dio. of Truro, 1949-55; Rector of Falmouth, 1955-77; Sec., Truro Diocesan Conf., 1952-67; Proctor in Convocation, dio. of Truro, 1958-76; Hon. Canon, Truro, 1964-77. Chm., House of Clergy, and Vice-Pres., Truro Diocesan Synod, 1970-76. Chaplain to lay Sheriff, City of London, 1976-77. Freeman, City of London, 1973; Freeman and Liveryman, Scriveners Co., 1976. Sub ChStJ, 1971 (Asst ChStJ, 1963). *Recreations:* heraldry, genealogy. *Address:* The Archdeacon's House, The Close, Hereford HR1 2NG. *T:* Hereford 2873. *Club:* United Oxford & Cambridge University.

BARFOOT, Most Rev. Walter Foster, DD (Hon.) 1937; DD (Lambeth), 1958; Primate of All Canada, 1951-Dec. 1958; *b* 17 Oct. 1893; *m* 1942. *Educ:* Wycliffe Coll., Toronto, BA 1923; Univ. of Toronto, MA 1930. Deacon, 1922; priest 1923; Tutor at Em. Coll., Saskatoon, 1926-33, Prof., 1933-34; Prof. of St John's Coll., Winnipeg, 1934-35. Warden, 1935-41; Canon of St John's Cathedral, Winnipeg, 1934-41; Bishop of Edmonton 1941-51, Archbishop, 1951-53; Archbishop and Metropolitan of Rupert's Land. 1953-60; retired Dec. 1960. Served European War, 1915-19. Capt. 2nd Royal Sussex Regt (Croix de Guerre). *Address:* 2803 West 41st Avenue, Suite 235, Vancouver, BC V6N 4B4, Canada.

BARFORD, Edward, MC 1918; Landowner; *b* 1898; *m* 1st, 1928, Hon. Grace Lowrey Stanley (from whom he obtained a divorce, 1940), *yr d* of 1st and last Baron Ashfield; one *s* two *d;* 2nd, 1944, Mrs June Johnstone (marr. diss. 1963); one *s;* 3rd, 1964, Hon. Mrs Marian Hubbard (marr. diss. 1970), *er d* of 1st and last Baron Ashfield. *Educ:* Rugby. Enlisted, European War, 1915 (wounded twice, despatches twice), Acting Major 1918. Founded Aveling-Barford Ltd, 1933; Chm., 1933-68. Underwriting Member of Lloyd's. *Address:* 29 Kingston House North, SW7. *T:* 01-584 4425. *Clubs:* Buck's, Boodle's.

BARFORD, Sir Leonard, Kt 1967; Deputy Chairman, Horserace Totalisator Board, 1974-77; (Member since 1973); Chief Inspector of Taxes, Board of Inland Revenue, 1964-73; Commissioner of Inland Revenue, 1970-73; *b* 1 Aug. 1908; *s* of William and Ada Barford, Finsbury Park; *m* 1939, Betty Edna Crichton, Plymouth; two *s. Educ:* Dame Alice Owen's Sch.; St Catharine's Coll., Cambridge Univ. (Exhibitioner in History). Asst Inspector of Taxes, 1930; Administrative Staff Coll., Henley, 1948; President, Assoc. of HM Inspectors of Taxes, 1951-53; Principal Inspector of Taxes, 1953; Senior Principal Inspector of Taxes, 1957; Deputy Chief Inspector, 1960. *Publication:* (jointly) Essay on Management in Tax Offices, 1950. *Recreations:* badminton, tennis, chess, bridge. *Address:* Harley House, 79 Sutton Road, Seaford, East Sussex. *T:* Seaford 893364. *Club:* Civil Service.

BARING, family name of **Baron Ashburton,** of **Earl of Cromer,** of **Baron Howick of Glendale,** of **Baron Northbrook,** and of **Baron Revelstoke.**

BARING, Sir Charles Christian, 2nd Bt, *cr* 1911; JP; DL; *b* 16 Dec. 1898; *s* of Sir Godfrey Baring, 1st Bt, KBE, DL, and Eva Hermione Mackintosh of Mackintosh (*d* 1934); *S* father 1957; *m* 1948 Jeanette (Jan), *d* of Henry Charles Daykin. *Educ:* Eton. Served European War: Lieut Coldstream Guards. 1917-18 (severely wounded); War of 1939-45: Major Coldstream Guards, 1940-45; Political Warfare Executive, 1943-44; Staff, AFHQ, Italy, War Office, 1944-45. Attaché, HM Legation, Warsaw, 1922-23; Cunard White Star Ltd, 1933-36; HM Prison Service, 1936-38; Probation Officer: West London Magistrates' Court, 1938-40; Central Criminal Court, 1945-46; Inspector, Probation Branch Home Office, 1946-49; Colonial Service: Warden of Prisons, Bermuda, 1949-53. Member, Cttee of Management, RNLI (Vice-Pres., 1972). JP Isle of Wight County, 1956; DL Co. Southampton subseq. IoW, 1962; Chm. of Justices, IoW Petty Sessional Div., 1962-70. *Recreations:* golf, swimming, walking. *Heir: nephew* (Charles) Peter Baring [*b* 24 May 1939; *m* 1964, Sarah (marr. diss. 1974), *d* of late Col William Gill Withycombe; two *d*]. *Address:* 4 Sandlands, Seaview, Isle of Wight. *Club:* Army and Navy.

BARING, Hon. John Francis Harcourt; Chairman, Baring Brothers & Co. Ltd, since 1974 (a Managing Director, 1955-74); Receiver-General of Duchy of Cornwall, since 1974; Chairman, Accepting Houses Committee, since 1977; *b* 2 Nov. 1928; *er s* and *heir* of 6th Baron Ashburton, *qv*; *m* 1955, Susan Mary Renwick, *e d* of 1st Baron Renwick, KBE, and Mrs John Ormiston; two *s* two *d*. *Educ:* Eton; Trinity Coll., Oxford (MA). Director: Trafford Park Estates Ltd, 1964-77; Pye Holdings Ltd, 1966-; Outwich Ltd, Johannesburg, 1967-; Dep. Chm., Royal Insurance Co. Ltd, 1975- (Dir, 1964-); Chm., Outwich Investment Trust Ltd, 1968-. Vice-Pres., British Bankers' Assoc., 1977-. Mem., British Transport Docks Bd, 1966-71. Rhodes Trustee, 1970. Hon. Fellow, Hertford Coll., Oxford, 1976. *Address:* Stratton Park, Micheldever, near Winchester, Hants. *T:* Micheldever 283; Flat 7, 34 Bryanston Square, W1. *Club:* Pratt's.

BARING, Mark, CVO 1970; JP; Chairman, Mediplan Ltd, since 1976; General Commissioner for Income Tax, since 1966; Executive Chairman, King Edward VII's Hospital for Officers, since 1969; *b* 9th June 1916; *yr s* of late Hon. Windham Baring and Lady Gweneth Cavendish, 3rd *d* of 8th Earl of Bessborough; *m* 1949, Victoria Winifred Russell, *d* of late Col R. E. M. Russell, CVO, CBE, DSO; two *d*. *Educ:* Eton Coll.; Trinity Coll., Cambridge. Served War of 1939-45, Grenadier Guards; in Italy and UK; Mil. Liaison Officer HM Embassy, Rome, 1945-46 (Major 1945); retd 1946. Man. Dir, Seccombe Marshall and Campion Ltd, Discount Brokers, 1950-76. JP, Inner Area of London, 1963. Treasurer, Inst. of Urology, 1969-74; Mem. Bd of Governors, St Peter's Hosp., 1970-74; Governor, The Peabody Trust, 1971; Mem. Council, Baring Foundn, 1975-; Chm., Assoc. of Independent Hosps; Pres., St Marylebone Housing Assoc. High Sheriff, Greater London, 1975. *Recreations:* tennis, bridge. *Address:* 18 Thurloe Square, SW7. *T:* 01-589 8455. *Clubs:* Brooks's, White's.

BARING, Lady Rose (Gwendolen Louisa), DCVO 1972 (CVO 1964); Extra Woman of the Bedchamber to the Queen, since 1973; *b* 23 May 1909; *er d* of 12th Earl of Antrim and of Margaret, *y d* of late Rt Hon. J. G. Talbot; *m* 1933, Francis Anthony Baring (killed in action, 1940); two *s* one *d*. Woman of the Bedchamber to the Queen, 1953-73. *Address:* 43 Pembroke Square, W8.

BARK, Evelyn (Elizabeth Patricia), CMG 1967; OBE 1952; retired as Director International Affairs Department of British Red Cross (1950-66); *b* 26 Dec. 1900; *e d* of late Frederick William Bark. *Educ:* privately. On staff of Swedish Match Co. (at home and abroad) until 1939, when joined British Red Cross. Served War, 1939-44, VAD (Stars: of 1939-45, of France, and of Germany; Defence Medal, and War Medal, 1939-45). Foreign Relations Officer, 1944-48. Commissioner, NW Europe, 1948-49; Foreign Relations and Relief Adviser, 1950 (title later changed to Dir International Affairs). Serving Sister of St John's, 1953; British Red Cross Certificate First Class, 1966. *Publication:* No Time to Kill, 1960. *Recreations:* reading, music, nordic languages. *Address:* 4 Milton Mansions, Queen's Club Gardens, W14. *T:* 01-385 2181. *Club:* VAD Ladies'.

BARKE, James Allen; Director, Falcon Engineering Co., since 1972; *b* 16 April 1903; *s* of James E. Barke and Emma Livsey; *m* 1st, 1937, Doris Marian Bayne (*d* 1952); two *s* one *d*; 2nd, 1953, Marguerite Amy Sutcliffe (*née* Williams) (*d* 1968); one *step d*.

Educ: Birley Street Central Sch.; Manchester Coll. of Technology. Mather & Platt and general engineering experience, 1922-32; joined Ford Motor Co., 1932; Buyer, Purchase Dept, 1939; Chief Buyer (Tractors), 1947; Manager, Leamington Foundry, 1948; Executive Dir and General Manager, Briggs Motor Bodies Ltd, 1953; Ford Motor Co.: Dir, Product Divs, 1959; Asst Man. Dir, 1961; Man. Dir, 1962; Chief Exec. Officer and Man. Dir, 1963; Vice-Chm., 1965-68; Dir, De La Rue Company Ltd, 1970-73. *Recreations:* golf, rock climbing, walking, reading. *Address:* Thurlestone, Mill Green, Ingatestone, Essex. *Club:* Oriental.

BARKER, Alan; *see* Barker, William A.

BARKER, Sir Alwyn (Bowman), Kt 1969; CMG 1962; BSc, BE; FIEAust; Chairman: Kelvinator Australia Ltd, since 1967 (Managing Director, 1952-67); Tecalemit (Australia) Pty Ltd; *b* 5 Aug. 1900; *s* of late A. J. Barker, Mt Barker, South Australia; *m* 1926, Isabel Barron Lucas, *d* of late Sir Edward Lucas; one *d* (one *s* decd). *Educ:* St Peter's Coll., Adelaide; Geelong C of E Grammar Sch.; Univ. of Adelaide. British Thomson Houston Co. Ltd, England, 1923-24; Hudson Motor Car Co., Detroit, 1924-25; Production Manager, Holden's Motor Body Builders Ltd, Adelaide, 1925-30; Works Manager, Kelvinator Aust. Ltd, Adelaide, 1931-40; Gen. Man., Chrysler Aust. Ltd, Adelaide, 1940-52; Chm., Municipal Tramways Trust SA, 1953-68; Dir, six public companies. Mem. Faculty of Engineering, Univ. of Adelaide, 1937-66 (Lectr in Industrial Engineering, 1929-53). Chm., Industrial Develt Adv. Council, 1968-70; Fellow, Internat. Acad. of Management; Member: Manufacturing Industries Adv. Council, 1958-72; Res. and Develt Adv. Cttee, 1967-72. Hon. Fellow Australian Inst. of Management (Federal Pres., 1952-53, 1959-61; Pres. Adelaide Div., 1952-54); Pres., Australian Council, Inst. of Prodn Engrs, 1970-72. John Storey Meml Medal, 1965; Jack Finlay Nat. Award, 1964. *Publications:* Three Presidential Addresses, 1954; William Queale Memorial Lecture, 1965. *Recreations:* golf; pastoral. *Address:* 51 Hackney Road, Hackney, SA 5069, Australia. *T:* 42.2838; (office) PO Box 1347, Adelaide, SA 5001, Australia. *Clubs:* Adelaide, Royal Adelaide Golf (Adelaide).

BARKER, Lt-Col Arthur James; writer; retired from Army; *b* 20 Sept. 1918; *o s* of late John Robert Barker and Caroline Barker, Hull; *m* 1969, Alexandra Franziska, *o d* of late Eugen Franz Roderbourg, Berlin; one *s* of previous marriage. *Educ:* Hymers Coll., Hull; Royal Mil. Coll. of Science. Commissioned E Yorks Regt, 1936; E African campaign with 1st/4th KAR, 1940-41; Ceylon, India, Burma, 1941-46; Staff Coll., Quetta, 1944. Subseq. service as a Staff Officer in Middle East, 1947-48; WO (Techn. intell.), 1950-52; Far East, 1956-58; a Regtl Officer in Malaya, 1952-53; Mem. Directing Staff, RMCS, 1954-56; retd, 1958, and employed until 1968 by UKAEA; NATO Research Fellowship, 1968; Illinois Inst. of Technology, 1971-72. *Publications:* Principles of Small Arms, 1953; The March on Delhi, 1963; Suez: The Seven Day War, 1964; Eritrea 1941, 1966; The Neglected War, 1967; Townshend of Kut, 1967; The Civilising Mission, 1968; German Infantry Weapons of World War 2, 1969; British and US Infantry Weapons of World War 2, 1969; Pearl Harbour, 1969; The War Against Russia, 1970; The Vainglorious War, 1854-56, 1970; Midway, 1971; The Suicide Weapon, 1971; The Rape of Ethiopia, 1971; Fortune Favours the Brave, 1974; Behind Barbed Wire, 1974; The Red Army Handbook, 1975; Redcoats, 1976; Mortars of the World, 1976; The Japanese Soldier's Weapons in World War II, 1977; Dunkirk, 1977; Panzer at War, 1977; contrib. Warsaw Pact and NATO Infantry and Weapons. *Recreation:* travel. *Address:* c/o National Westminster Bank, 60 Market Place, Beverley, North Humberside HU17 8AH; 37A Friedrichsruherstrasse, 1 Berlin 33. *Club:* Army and Navy.

BARKER, Arthur Vincent, CBE 1974 (OBE 1955); FCIT; Scottish Chartered Accountant; financial planning consultant; Director CFP Ltd; *b* 10 Nov. 1911; *e s* of late Arthur and Susannah Mary Barker; *m* 1936, Dorothy Drew; one *d*. *Educ:* Whitley and Monkseaton High Sch.; London Sch. of Economics. Qual. as CA, 1934; with Price Waterhouse & Co., 1934-35; with NAAFI in Middle East and UK, 1935-62 (Jt Gen. Man., 1955); Asst Gen. Man., Southern Region, British Railways, and Mem., Southern Railway Bd, 1962; Asst Gen. Man., London Midland Region, British Railways, and Mem., LMR Bd, 1965; Chairman: Shipping and Internat. Services Div., British Railways, 1968-69; British Rail Hovercraft, 1970-71; British Transport Hotels Ltd, 1968-74; Mem., British Railways Bd, 1968-74. *Recreation:* fly-fishing. *Address:* 25 West Mount, The Mount, Guildford, Surrey GU2 5HL. *T:* Guildford 39524.

BARKER, Audrey Lilian; writer; *b* 13 April 1918; *d* of Harry and Elsie Barker. *Educ:* County secondary schools in Beckenham,

Kent and Wallington, Surrey. Editorial office, Amalgamated Press, 1936; Publisher's reader, Cresset Press, 1947; BBC, 1949-. Atlantic Award in Literature, 1946; Somerset Maugham Award, 1947; Cheltenham Festival of Literature Award, 1962. FRSL 1970. *Publications:* Innocents, 1947; Apology for a Hero, 1950; Novelette, 1951; The Joy-Ride, 1963; Lost Upon the Roundabouts, 1964; A Case Examined, 1965; The Middling, 1967; John Brown's Body, 1969; Femina Real, 1971; A Source of Embarrassment, 1974. *Address:* 103 Harrow Road, Carshalton, Surrey.

BARKER, Barry, MBE 1960; FCIS; Secretary and Chief Executive, Institute of Chartered Secretaries and Administrators (formerly Chartered Institute of Secretaries), since 1976; *b* 1929; *s* of late Francis Walter Barker and of Amy Barker; *m* 1954, Dr Vira Dubash; two *s. Educ:* Ipswich Sch.; Trinity Coll., Oxford (MA Class. Greats). Associate MBIM. Secretary: Bombay Chamber of Commerce and Industry, 1956-62; The Metal Box Co. of India Ltd, 1962-67. Dir, Shipbuilding Industry Bd, 1967-71; Consultant at Dept of Industry, 1972; Sec., Pye Holdings Ltd, 1972-76. *Recreations:* the theatre and the arts. *Address:* 9/11 Westbourne Terrace, W2 3UL. *T:* 01-402 7056; Worsted Barrows, Babraham, Cambridge CB2 4AX. *T:* Cambridge 83 3298. *Club:* Oriental.

BARKER, Sir (Charles Frederic) James, Kt 1970; MBE 1944; Chairman, Unigate Ltd, 1970-77 (Chief Executive, 1970-72; Joint Chief Executive, 1972-73); *b* 17 Feb. 1914; *s* of Charles F. J. Barker and Ethel (*née* Brooke), Walton-on-the-Naze; *m* 1940, Thora Daphne, *d* of Amos Perry and Nancy (*née* Aspland); two *s. Educ:* Royal Grammar Sch., Colchester. Served War of 1939-45, Wilts Regt (Major): Staff Coll., 1943; GSO2, 43rd Wessex Division. L. Rose & Co. Ltd, 1934-39 and 1948; Man. Dir, 1957; Schweppes Ltd, 1958-69: Dir, 1962; Man. Dir, 1969; Dir, Cadbury Schweppes Ltd, 1962-71. Mem., Central London Regional Board, Lloyds Bank, 1976-. Chairman: CCAHC, 1975-; CBI Employment Policy Cttee, 1976-77. FBIM, 1965; Fellow, Inst. Grocery Distribution, 1973. President: Food Manufacturers Fedn, 1967-70; Dairy Trade Fedn, 1973-75; British Food Manufacturing Industries Res. Assoc., 1974-. Croix de Guerre, 1944. *Recreations:* sailing, reading, family. *Address:* New Hall, Thorpe-le-Soken, Essex. *T:* Thorpe-le-Soken 507. *Clubs:* Carlton; Walton and Frinton Yacht.

BARKER, Rt. Rev. Clifford Conder; see Whitby, Bishop Suffragan of.

BARKER, David, QC 1976; a Recorder of the Crown Court, since 1974; *b* 13 April 1932; *s* of Frederick Barker and Amy Evelyn Barker; *m* 1957, Diana Mary Vinson Barker (*née* Duckworth); one *s* three *d. Educ:* Sir John Deane's Grammar Sch., Northwich; University Coll., London; Univ. of Michigan. 1st cl. hons LLB London; LLM Michigan. RAF, 1956-59. Called to Bar, Inner Temple, 1954; practised Midland and Oxford Circuit. Contested (Lab) Runcorn, 1955. *Recreations:* gardening, walking, sailing. *Address:* Nanhill, Woodhouse Eaves, Leics. *T:* Woodhouse Eaves 890224. *Club:* Northampton and County (Northampton).

BARKER, Prof. David (Faubert), MA, DPhil, DSc; Professor of Zoology, University of Durham, since 1962; *b* 18 Feb. 1922; *s* of Faubert and Doreen Barker; *m* 1945, Kathleen Mary Frances Pocock; three *s* two *d. Educ:* Bryanston Sch.; Magdalen Coll., Oxford. DSc 1972. Senior Demy of Magdalen Coll., 1946; Leverhulme Research Scholar, Royal Coll. of Surgeons, 1946; Demonstrator in Zoology and Comparative Anatomy, Oxford, 1947; DPhil 1948; Rolleston Prizeman, 1948; Prof. of Zoology, Univ. of Hong Kong, 1950-62; led scientific expeditions to Tunisia, 1950, North Borneo, 1952; Dean of Faculty of Science, Hong Kong, 1959-60; Public Orator, Hong Kong, 1961. *Publications:* (Founder) Editor, Hong Kong Univ. Fisheries Journal, 1954-60; Editor, Symposium on Muscle Receptors, 1962; scientific papers, mostly on muscle innervation. *Address:* Department of Zoology, Science Laboratories, South Road, Durham. *T:* Durham 64971.

BARKER, Denis William Knighton; a Managing Director, The British Petroleum Co. Ltd, 1967-72; *b* 21 Aug. 1908; *m* 1938, Esmee Doris Marsh; two *d. Educ:* Holgate Grammar School, Barnsley; Sheffield Univ. (MSc). With the British Petroleum Co. Ltd, 1929-72; President, BP (North America) Ltd, 1959; Asst Gen. Manager, Refineries Dept, 1960; Gen. Manager, Refineries Dept, 1966. Formerly Director: BP Trading Ltd, BP Refineries Ltd, Britannic Estates Ltd, The British Petroleum Co. of Canada Ltd, and others. *Recreations:* golf, gardening. *Address:* Stable Cottage, Upper House Lane, Shamley Green, near Guildford, Surrey. *T:* Cranleigh 2726.

BARKER, Dennis Albert, QC 1968; a Recorder of the Crown Court, since 1972; *b* 9 June 1926; *s* of J. W. and R. E. Barker; *m* 1949, Daphne (*née* Ruffle); one *s* one *d* (and one *d* decd). *Educ:* Nottingham High Sch.; The Queen's Coll. Oxford (Jodrell Schol.). Flying Officer, RAFVR, 1944-47. 1st cl. hons (Jurisprudence), Oxon, 1949; 1st cl. Certif. of Honour and Studentship, Bar Finals, 1950; Harmsworth Law Schol., 1950; Eldon Law Schol., 1950; called to the Bar, Middle Temple, 1950, Bencher, 1975. Mem. Midland Circuit; Dep. Chm., Bucks QS, 1963-71. Mem., Criminal Injuries Compensation Bd. *Recreations:* golf, flying. *Address:* 1 Harcourt Buildings, Temple, EC4. *T:* 01-353 0375; Heathlands, Great Brickhill, Milton Keynes MK17 9AC. *T:* Great Brickhill 251. *Clubs:* Royal Air Force; The Western (Glasgow).

BARKER, Douglas William Ashley, CMG 1966; Secretary to the Treasury, New Zealand, 1965-66; *b* 19 Sept. 1905; *s* of John Joseph and Annie Barker; *m* 1934, Elsie May Owen; one *s* one *d. Educ:* Palmerston North Boys' High Sch.; Victoria Univ. Coll., Wellington; LSE. Joined NZ Treasury, 1922; seconded NZ High Comr's Office, London, 1934; Treasury, NZ, 1937. Dir, Cable Price Downer Ltd, 1967. *Recreations:* bowls, golf, gardening. *Address:* 7 Amritsar Street, Wellington, NZ. *T:* 797151. *Club:* Civil Service (Wellington, NZ).

BARKER, Edward, OBE 1966; QPM 1961; Chief Constable of Sheffield and Rotherham Constabulary, 1967-72; *b* 1 Nov. 1909; *s* of George and Gertrude Barker; *m* 1935, Clare Garth; one *d. Educ:* The Grammar School, Malton. Joined Preston Borough Police, 1931; transf. Lancs Constabulary, 1938; Inspector/Chief Inspector, Comdt of Constabulary Trng Sch., 1946-51; Supt 1954; Vis. Lectr to Bermuda Police, 1955; Chief Supt 1956; Asst Comdt, Police Coll., Bramshill, 1956-57; Chief Constable: Bolton Borough Police, 1957; Sheffield City Police, 1964. Police Long Service and Good Conduct Medal, 1953. SBStJ. *Recreations:* golf, gardening, watching field sports. *Address:* 21 Woodstock Road, Aberdeen. *Club:* Deeside Golf.

BARKER, Eric Leslie; Author and Entertainer; *b* 20 Feb. 1912; *s* of Charles and Maude Barker; *m* 1936, Pearl Hackney; one *d. Educ:* Whitgift Sch. Character actor Birmingham, Oxford and Croydon Repertory Theatres, 1932-33; Comedian, also sketch and lyric writer, Charlot revues, Windmill, and Prince of Wales Theatre, 1933-38. Author and star of radio series: Howdyfolks, 1939-40; Navy Mixture, 1944-45; Merry-Go-Round, 1945-49; Just Fancy, 1950-62; Passing Parade, 1957; Barker's Folly, 1958; Law and Disorder, 1960. Lieut RNVR, 1940-45. Author and star of television series: Eric Barker Half Hour, 1952-55; Absolutely Barkers, 1963. *Films:* Brothers-in-Law; Clean Sweep; Blue Murder at St Trinians; Happy Is The Bride; Carry on, Sergeant; Eye Spy; Bachelor of Hearts; Right, Left and Centre; Carry on, Constable; Dentist in the Chair; Raising the Wind; The Fast Lady; Those Magnificent Men in their Flying Machines; Doctor in Clover; Maroc 7. *Publications:* short stories, 3 novels, 1931-33; The Watch Hunt, 1931; Day Gone By, 1932; Steady Barker (Autobiog.), 1956; Golden Gimmick, 1958. *Recreations:* antiques, photography, gardening, history, cricket, swimming, weight watching. *Address:* c/o Lloyds Bank, Faversham, Kent.

BARKER, Gen. Sir Evelyn Hugh, KCB 1950 (CB 1944); KBE 1945 (CBE 1940); DSO 1918; MC; *b* 22 May 1894; *y s* of late Maj.-Gen. Sir George Barker, KCB, and late Hon. Lady Barker; *m* 1923, Violet Eleanor, *y d* of T. W. Thornton of Brockhall, near Weedon, Northants; one *s. Educ:* Wellington Coll.; RM Coll., Sandhurst. Joined Army, 1913; Capt. 1916; Bt-Maj. 1929; Major 1930; Bt-Col 1934; Lt-Col 1936; Bt-Col 1937; Col 1938; Maj.-Gen., 1941; Lt-Gen., 1944; General, 1948. Served European War, 1914-18, France, Salonica, and South Russia; GSO3, 1917; Bde-Major, 1917; despatches, DSO, MC; GSO3 (War Office), 1919; Brigade-Major 8th Infantry Brigade, 1931-33; commanded 2nd Bn KRRC, 1936-38; commanded 10th Infantry Brigade, 1938-40; commanded 54th Div. 1941-42, and 49th (West Riding) Div. 1943-44; commanded 8 Corps, 1944-April 1946; commanded British Troops in Palestine and Transjordan, 1946; ADC General to the King, 1949-50; GOC-in-C Eastern Command, 1947-50; retd 1950. Col Comdt 2nd Bn KRRC, 1946-56; Hon. Col Loyal Suffolk Hussars (Yeomanry), 1946-50; Hon. Col, Beds Yeo., 1951-60; Hon. Col Herts and Beds Yeo., 1961-62. DL, Beds, 1952-67. Cmdr, Legion of Honour; Croix de Guerre (with palm) France; Silver Medal, Italy; O St Stanislas, Russia; Grand Cross of Dannebrog, Denmark. *Address:* Park House, Bromham, Bedford. *Club:* Royal Automobile.

BARKER, George Granville; writer; *b* 26 Feb. 1913; *s* of George Barker and Marion Frances Barker (*née* Taaffe); *m* 1964, Elspeth Langlands. *Educ:* Marlborough Road London County

Council Sch., Chelsea. Prof. of English Literature at Imperial Tohoku Univ., Japan, 1939; visited America, 1940; returned to England, 1943; lived in Rome, 1960-65. Arts Fellow York Univ., 1966-67; Vis. Prof., Florida Internat. Univ., 1974. *Publications:* Thirty Preliminary Poems, 1933; Alanna Autumnal, 1933; Poems, 1935; Janus, 1935; Calamiterror, 1937; Lament and Triumph, 1940; Eros in Dogma, 1944; News of the World, 1950; The Dead Seagull, 1950; The True Confession of George Barker, 1950; A Vision of Beasts and Gods, 1954; Collected Poems, 1930-55, 1957; The True Confession of George Barker, Book II, 1957; Two Plays, 1958; The View from a Blind I, 1962; Dreams of a Summer Night, 1966; The Golden Chains, 1968; Essays, 1970; Runes & Rhymes & Tunes & Chimes, 1970; To Aylsham Fair, 1970; At Thurgarton Church, 1970; Poems of Places and People, 1971; The Alphabetical Zoo, 1972; In Memory of David Archer, 1973; Dialogues etc, 1976. *Address:* Bintry House, Itteringham, Aylsham, Norfolk. *T:* Saxthorpe 240.

BARKER, Harold; Keeper, Department of Conservation and Technical Services, British Museum, since 1975; *b* 15 Feb. 1919; *s* of William Frampton Barker and Lily (*née* Pack); *m* 1942, Everilda Alice Whittle; one *s* one *d*. *Educ:* City Secondary Sch., Sheffield; Sheffield Univ. (BSc). Experimental Asst, 1940, Experimental Officer, 1942, Chemical Inspectorate, Min. of Supply; British Museum: Experimental Officer, Research Lab., 1947; Sen. Experimental Officer, 1953; Chief Experimental Officer, 1960; Principal Scientific Officer, 1966; Acting Keeper, 1975. *Publications:* papers on radiocarbon dating and scientific examination of antiquities in various jls. *Recreations:* music, walking, cinematography. *Address:* 138 Halfway Street, Sidcup, Kent DA15 8DB. *T:* 01-300 7569.

BARKER, Hugh Purslove; Chairman, 1956-71 and Managing Director, 1945-71, Parkinson Cowan Group; Chairman, Boosey & Hawkes Ltd, since 1974; Vice-President, British Institute of Management, since 1962 (Chairman, 1960-62); *b* 11 March 1909; *s* of Arthur Henry Barker and Florence Barker (*née* Saich); *m* 1935, Joye Frances Higgs; two *s* one *d*. *Educ:* Oundle Sch. Mech. Engr Apprenticeship (concurrently studied Engineering, Accountancy and Law), Waygood-Otis Ltd, 1927-31; private mfg business, 1931-35; Cons. Engr, A. H. Barker & Partners, 1935-39. Dir Mfg Cos. Min. of Aircraft Prodn (Dep. Dir Instrument Prodn), 1940-44. Part-time Mem., British Railways Bd, 1962-67 (British Transport Commn, 1951-62); Chm., EDC for the Rubber Industry, 1968-71. Mem., Royal Commn on Assizes, 1967-70. CEng; FIEE; FIMechE; FInstGasE; FIHVE; FCIT; FBIM. *Publications:* papers and articles to Technical Institutes and press, on engineering subjects, and to financial and econ. press on management. *Recreations:* fishing, music. *Address:* Flat 18, 22 St James's Square, SW1Y 4JH. *T:* 01-930 2618; Rose Cottage, Elkstone, near Buxton, Derbyshire. *T:* Blackshaw 287. *Club:* Junior Carlton.

BARKER, Sir James; see Barker, Sir C. F. J.

BARKER, Air Vice-Marshal John Lindsay, CB 1963; CBE 1946; DFC 1945; RAF (Retired); *b* 12 Nov. 1910; *s* of Abraham Cockroft Barker and Lilian Alice (*née* Woods); *m* 1948, Eleanor Margaret Hannah; one *s*. *Educ:* Trent Coll., Derbys; Brasenose Coll., Oxford. Called to the Bar, Middle Temple, 1947. RAFO, 1930, RAF, 1933. Served War of 1939-45: France, 1939-40; N Africa, 1942-44; Bomber Command, 1944-45; Far East, 1945-48; Egypt, 1950-53; Air Attaché, Rome, 1955-58; Cmdr Royal Ceylon Air Force, 1958-63. Air Vice-Marshal, 1959. Retd, 1963. Order of Merit, Italy, 1958. *Recreations:* golf, photography, sailing. *Address:* Newcomen Cottage, Ridge Hill, Dartmouth, Devon. *Club:* Royal Air Force.

BARKER, John Michael Adrian; a Recorder of the Crown Court, since 1974; barrister-at-law; *b* 4 Nov. 1932; *s* of Robert Henry Barker and Annie Robson Barker (*née* Charlton); *m* 1971, Gillian Marsha (*née* Greenstone). *Educ:* Marist Coll., Hull; Univs of Sheffield and Hull. BSc, LLB. Called to Bar, Middle Temple, 1959. Schoolmaster, Stonyhurst Coll., 1957-59; Lectr in Law, Univ. of Hull, 1960-63. Mem., Hull CC, 1965-71. *Publications:* articles in Conveyancer and Property Lawyer, Solicitors' Jl and Solicitor. *Recreations:* music, cricket. *Address:* 86 Davenport Avenue, Hessle, North Humberside. *T:* Hull 648909.

BARKER, Brig. Lewis Ernest Stephen, CBE 1943; DSO 1941; MC 1918; *b* 5 May 1895; *s* of late Richard Barker, Mulgrave, Vic, Australia; *m* 1921, Alice Hope McEachern; two *s*. *Educ:* Brighton Grammar Sch., Vic.; Royal Military Coll., Duntroon. Permanent Army Officer. European War, 1917-18 (MC). Various staff appointments AMF 1919-39. Comd 2/1 Australian Fd Regt in first Libyan campaign, 1940-41 (DSO);

Dir of Artillery, LHQ Melbourne, 1941-42; CCRA 1 Australian Corps in New Guinea for the operations to the capture of Buna (CBE); subsequently BRA New Guinea up to the capture of Madang, 1944. BRA LHQ Melbourne, July 1945; Commandant, 4th Military District (S Australia), 1946-Dec. 1948; retired. *Address:* 53 Donaldson Street, Corryong, Vic 3707, Australia.

BARKER, Nicolas John; Head of Conservation, British Library Reference Division, since 1976; Editor, Book Collector, since 1965; *b* 6 Dec. 1932; *s* of Sir Ernest Barker, FBA, and Olivia Stuart Horner; *m* 1962, Joanna Mary Sophia Nyda Cotton; two *s* three *d*. *Educ:* Westminster Sch.; New Coll., Oxford (MA). With Bailliere, Tindall & Cox, 1959 and Rupert Hart-Davis, 1959; Asst Keeper, National Portrait Gallery, 1964; with Macmillan & Co. Ltd, 1965; with OUP, 1972-76. *Publications:* The Publications of the Roxburghe Club, 1964; The Printer and the Poet, 1970; Stanley Morison, 1972; (ed) The Early Life of James McBey: an autobiography, 1883-1911, 1977. *Address:* 22 Clarendon Road, W11. *T:* 01-727 4340. *Club:* Garrick.

BARKER, Paul; Editor of New Society since 1968; *b* 24 Aug. 1935; *s* of Donald and Marion Barker; *m* 1960, Sally, *e d* of James and Marion Huddleston; three *s* one *d*. *Educ:* Hebden Bridge Grammar Sch.; Calder High Sch.; Brasenose Coll., Oxford (Hulme Exhibr), BA 1958, MA 1970. Intell. Corps (commn), 1953-55. Lecteur, Ecole Normale Supérieure, Paris, 1958-59; The Times, 1959-64; New Society, staff writer, 1964; The Economist, 1964; New Society, Assistant Editor, 1965-68. Editor of book series, Towards a New Society, 1971-; Gen. Editor, Society Today, 1976-. *Publications:* (ed) A Sociological Portrait, 1972; (ed) One for Sorrow, Two for Joy, 1972; (ed) The Social Sciences Today, 1975; (ed) Arts in Society, 1977; contrib. to various books; numerous articles and broadcasts. *Address:* 26 Patshull Road, NW5. *T:* 01-485 8861.

BARKER, Ronald Hugh, PhD, BSc; CEng, FIEE, FIMechE; Deputy Director, Royal Armament Research and Development Establishment, 1965-75, retired; *b* 28 Oct. 1915; *s* of E. W. Barker and L. A. Taylor; *m* 1943, W. E. Hunt; two *s*. *Educ:* University of Hull. Physicist, Standard Telephones and Cables, 1938-41; Ministry of Supply, 1941-59; Dep. Dir, Central Electricity Research Laboratories, 1959-62; Technical Dir, The Pullin Group Ltd, 1962-65. *Publications:* various, on servomechanisms and control systems. *Address:* Cró Madra, St Monica's Road, Kingswood, Surrey KT20 6HA. *T:* Burgh Heath 55489.

BARKER, Ronnie, (Ronald William Barker); actor; *b* 25 Sept. 1929; *s* of Leonard and Edith Barker; *m* 1957, Joy Tubb; two *s* one *d*. *Educ:* Oxford High Sch. Started acting career, Aylesbury Rep. Co., 1948. *Plays (West End):* Mourning Becomes Electra, 1955; Summertime, 1955; Listen to the Wind, 1955; Double Image, 1956; Camino Real, 1957; Lysistrata, 1958; Irma la Douce, 1958; Platonov, 1960; On the Brighter Side, 1961; Midsummer Night's Dream, 1962; Real Inspector Hound, 1968. *Films include:* Robin and Marion, 1976. *Television: series:* Seven Faces of Jim, 1965; Frost Report, 1966-67; Hark at Barker, 1968-69; Six Dates with Barker, 1970; The Two Ronnies, 1971-; Porridge, 1974, 1975, 1976; Open All Hours, 1976. Awards: Variety Club, 1969, 1974; SFTA, 1971; Radio Industries Club, 1973, 1974; Water Rats, 1975; British Acad. Award, 1975; Royal Television Society's award for outstanding creative achievement, 1975. *Publications:* Book of Bathing Beauties, 1974; Book of Boudoir Beauties, 1975; It's Goodnight From Him, 1976. *Recreations:* writing song lyrics, collecting postcards. *Address:* c/o Peter Eade, 9 Cork Street, W1; Pinner, Middlesex.

BARKER, Thomas Christopher; HM Diplomatic Service; *b* 28 June 1928; *s* of late Rowland Francis Barker and Kathleen Maude Barker (*née* Welch); *m* 1960, Griselda Helen Cormack; two *s* one *d*. *Educ:* Uppingham; New Coll., Oxford (Schol.). MA, Lit Hum, 1952. 2nd Lt, 1st Bn, The Worcestershire Regt, 1947-48. HM Foreign (now Diplomatic) Service, 1952; Third Sec., Paris, 1953-55; Second Sec., Baghdad, 1955-58; FO, 1958-62; First Sec., Head of Chancery and Consul, Mexico City, 1962-67; FO, 1967-69; Counsellor and Head of Chancery, Caracas, 1969-71; FCO, 1971-75; seconded as Under Sec., NI Office, 1976.

BARKER, Sir William, KCMG 1967 (CMG 1958); OBE 1949; Bowes Professor of Russian, University of Liverpool, 1969-76, now retired; *b* 19 July 1909; *s* of Alfred Barker; *m* 1939, Margaret Beirne; one *s* one *d*. *Educ:* Universities of Liverpool and Prague. Employed in Foreign Office, 1943; First Sec., Prague, 1945; Foreign Service Officer, Grade 7, Senior Branch of Foreign Service, 1946; Chargé d'Affaires, Prague, 1947;

transferred Moscow, Aug. 1947; granted rank of Counsellor, Dec. 1948; Grade 6, 1950; Counsellor, Oslo, 1951, also Chargé d'Affaires; Consul-Gen., Boston, Mass, Sept. 1954; Counsellor, Washington, 1955; Minister, Moscow, 1960-63; Fellow, Center for Internat. Affairs, Harvard Univ., 1963-64. Asst Under-Sec. of State, FO, 1965-66; British Ambassador to Czechoslovakia, 1966-68. *Address:* 53 Eshe Road North, Liverpool L23 8UE.

BARKER, (William) Alan; Head Master, University College School, Hampstead, since 1975; *b* 1 Oct. 1923; 2nd *s* of late T. L. Barker, Edinburgh and Beaconsfield; *m* 1954, Jean Alys, JP (Mayor of Cambridge 1971-72), *d* of late Capt. A. E. Campbell-Harris, MC; one *s. Educ:* Rossall Sch.; Jesus Coll., Cambridge (scholar). Lieut Royal Artillery, 69 (WR) Field Regt, NW Europe; wounded, 1944. 1st cl. Hons Hist. Tripos Pt I, 1946, Pt II, 1947; BA 1946, MA 1948. Asst Master, Eton Coll., 1947-53; Commonwealth Fund Fellow, Yale Univ., 1951-52, MA (Yale) 1952. Fellow Queens' Coll., Cambridge, and Dir Studies in History, 1953-55; Asst Master, Eton Coll., 1955-58; Headmaster, The Leys School, 1958-75. Governor: Rossall Sch.; St Felix Sch.; Queenswood Sch.; Malsis Sch. Mem. Eton UDC, 1956-59; Councillor, Cambs and I of Ely, 1959-70, Alderman 1970-74. Select Preacher, Oxford Univ., 1966. Dir, Hobson's Press, 1973-. *Publications:* (jt) A General History of England 1688-1950, 2 vols, 1952, 1953; Religion and Politics (1558-1642), 1957; The Civil War in America, 1961, repr. US 1974; (contrib.) The Rebirth of Britain, 1964. *Recreations:* bridge, American history, golf. *Address:* University College School, Hampstead, NW3 6XH. *T:* 01-435 2215; 5 Redington Road, Hampstead, NW3 7QX; Luckboat House, Sandwich, Kent. *T:* 3007. *Clubs:* Brooks's, East India, Devonshire, Sports and Public Schools; MCC; Pitt (Cambridge); Elizabethan (Yale).

BARKING, Bishop Suffragan of, since 1975; **Rt. Rev. Albert James Adams;** *b* 9 Nov. 1915; *s* of James and Evelyn Adams, Rayleigh, Essex; *m* 1943, Malvena Jones; three *s. Educ:* Brentwood Sch.; King's Coll., London; Community of St Andrew, Whittlesford, Cambridge. Ordained Deacon, 1942; Priest, 1943; Curate of Walkley, Sheffield, 1942-44; Succentor, 1944, Precentor, 1945-47, Sheffield Cathedral. Rector of Bermondsey, 1947-55; Rural Dean of Bermondsey, 1954-55; Rector of: Stoke Damerel, Devonport, 1955-63; Wanstead, 1963-71. Sub-Dean, Wanstead and Woodford, 1968-69; Asst Rural Dean, Redbridge, 1970-71; Archdeacon of West Ham, 1970-75. *Address:* 670 High Road, Buckhurst Hill, Essex. *T:* 01-505 1372.

BARKLEY, Mrs Harry; *see* Ryman, B. E.

BARKLEY, Rev. Prof. John Monteith, Professor of Ecclesiastical History in the Presbyterian College, Belfast, since 1954; Vice-Principal and Secretary of Faculty, 1964, Principal, 1976; *b* 16 Oct. 1910; *s* of Rev. Robert James Barkley, BD, and Mary Monteith; *m* 1936, Irene Graham Anderson; one *d. Educ:* Magee Univ. Coll. Derry; Trinity Coll., Dublin; The Presbyterian Coll., Belfast. BA 1934, MA 1941, BD 1944, PhD 1946, DD 1949, Trinity Coll., Dublin; BA 1952, MA 1953, Queen's Univ., Belfast. Thompson Memorial Prizeman in Philosophy, 1934; Larmour Memorial Exhibitioner in Theology, 1944; Paul Memorial Prizeman in History, 1953; Carey Lecturer, 1954-56; Lecturer in Ecclesiastical History, Queen's Univ., Belfast, 1951-54. FRHistS. Ordained, Drumreagh Presbyterian Church, 1935; installed in II Ballybay and Rockcorry, 1939; installed in Cooke Centenary, Belfast, 1949. *Publications:* Handbook on Evangelical Christianity and Romanism, 1949; Presbyterianism, 1951; Westminster Formularies in Irish Presbyterianism, 1956; History of the Presbyterian Church in Ireland, 1959; Weltkirchenlexikon (arts), 1960; History of the Sabbath School Society for Ireland, 1961; The Eldership in Irish Presbyterianism; The Baptism of Infants, 1963; The Presbyterian Orphan Society, 1966; Worship of the Reformed Church, 1966; St Enoch's 1872-1972, 1972; articles in Scottish Journal of Theology, Verbum Caro, Biblical Theology, Dictionary of Worship. *Recreations:* bowls, golf. *Address:* 55 Cranmore Park, Belfast BT9 5EF.

BARKSHIRE, Robert Hugh, CBE 1968; General Commissioner of Income Tax for City of London, since 1969; Governor, National Institute of Economic and Social Research, since 1970; *b* 24 Oct. 1909; *yr s* of late Lt-Col Charles Robert Barkshire, OBE; *m* 1934, Emily Blunt, *er d* of A. S. Blunt, Bedford; one *s. Educ:* King's Sch., Bruton. Bank of England, 1927-55; Private Sec. to the Governor (C. F. Cobbold, later Lord Cobbold), 1949-53; Sec. to Cttee of London Clearing Bankers, British Bankers' Assoc., Bankers' Clearing House, and Mem., various inter-Bank Cttees, 1955-70; Hon. Sec., Meetings of Officers of European Bankers' Assocs, 1959-72. FIB 1960. Freeman, City of London. *Address:* 22 Clareville Court, SW7. *Clubs:* Gresham; Hurlingham; Royal Wimbledon Golf.

BARLAS, Sir Richard Douglas, KCB 1977 (CB 1968); OBE 1943; Clerk of the House of Commons, since 1976; *b* 19 May 1916; *s* of E. D. M. Barlas and Elena Barlas (*née* Kenyon); *m* 1940, Ann, *d* of Canon R. W. Porter; three *s. Educ:* Westminster; Christ Church, Oxford. War Service, 1939-45, Wing Cmdr, RAF; RAF Staff Coll., 1942. Asst Clerk, House of Commons, 1946; Senior Clerk, 1947. Called to the Bar, Middle Temple, 1949. Fourth Clerk at the Table, House of Commons, 1959; Second Clerk Asst, 1962; Clerk Asst, 1974. *Recreations:* travel, gardening. *Address:* House of Commons, SW1. *Club:* Athenæum.

BARLEY, Lieut-Col Leslie John, DSO 1917; late Royal Engineers and Cameronians; *b* Gosport, 7 July 1890; *s* of Rev. A. G. Barley; *m* 1915, Muriel More, *d* of James Kerr Love, LLD, MD, Glasgow; two *d. Educ:* Taunton Sch.; University Coll., Southampton; Kiel Univ.; Queen's Coll., Oxford. MA (Hons Chemistry) Oxon; BSc (London); Commissioned The Cameronians, June 1913; 1st Batt. France, Dec. 1914; when first gas attack occurred made one of first efficient respirators, instituted the gas-proof dugout and other methods of protection and training of troops in anti-gas measures; Army Chemical Adviser, June 1915; Asst Dir and Head, Gas Services, Italy, Nov. 1917; Superintendent Anti-Gas Dept (Ministry of Munitions), 1919 (despatches thrice, DSO; Croix de Guerre, 1918; Cavalier of the Order of St Maurice and St Lazarus of Jerusalem, 1918; brevet majority, 1918; Officer of the Order of the Crown of Italy, 1919); Head of Development Dept of Nobel Industries Ltd, 1919, and of ICI Ltd, 1926 (ICI Ltd was founded on his Memoranda to Sir Harry McGowan which he now has permission to publish); re-employed with RE, 1939-43, served in most Overseas Commands and USA with Chemical Warfare Liaison Mission, 1942. Pacific Relations Conf., 1947. Overseas Development Controller of ICI Ltd until retirement, 1952. *Publications:* Set of Lectures on Chemical Defence, 1915; Use of Smoke in Mountain Warfare, 1918; The Riddle of Rationalisation, 1932; (part) A Food Plan for India, 1945; working on autobiography (section relating to Chemical Defence in First World War is on tape at Imperial War Museum) and forthcoming publication on world food and population problem. *Address:* West Lodge, West Kingston, Angmering-on-Sea, West Sussex BN16 1SW. *Clubs:* Royal Automobile; Ham Manor Golf.

BARLEY, Prof. Maurice Willmore, MA; Professor of Archaeology, University of Nottingham, 1971-74, now Emeritus; *b* 19 Aug. 1909; *s* of late Levi Baldwin and Alice Barley, Lincoln; *m* 1934, Diana, *e d* of late Dr A. E. Morgan, MA, Hon. LLD; two *s* one *d. Educ:* Lincoln Sch.; Reading Univ. (BA). Asst Lectr, UC Hull, 1935-40; Mins of Information and Labour, 1940-45; Tutor, Adult Educn Dept, Nottingham, 1946-62; Sen. Lectr and Reader, Classics Dept, Nottingham, 1962-71. Sec. 1954-64, Pres. 1964-67, Council for British Archaeology; Vice-Pres., Soc. of Antiquaries, 1965-68; Mem. Royal Commn Hist. Monuments, 1966-76. FSA. *Publications:* Parochial Documents of the East Riding, 1939; Lincolnshire and the Fens, 1952 (repr. 1972); Documents relating to Newark on Trent, 1955; The English Farmhouse and Cottage, 1961; The House and Home, 1963 (repr. 1971); Guide to British Topographical Collections, 1974; The Plans and Topography of Medieval Towns in England and Wales, 1975; European Towns, their Archaeology and early History, 1977; contrib. Agrarian History of England vol. V, Antiquaries Jl and other learned jls. *Address:* 60 Park Road, Chilwell, Nottingham. *T:* Nottingham 257501. *Club:* Athenæum.

BARLOW, Sir Christopher Hilaro, 7th Bt, *cr* 1803; architect; *b* 1 Dec. 1929; *s* of Sir Richard Barlow, 6th Bt, AFC, and Rosamund Sylvia, *d* of late F. S. Anderton (she *m* 2nd, 1950, Rev. Leonard Haslet Morrison, MA); *S* father, 1946; *m* 1952, J. C. de M. Audley, *e d* of J. E. Audley, Bahamas; one *s* two *d* (and one *s* decd). *Educ:* Eton; McGill Univ., Montreal. BArch. MRAIC. Past Pres., Newfoundland Architects' Assoc. Lt Governor's Silver Medal, 1953. *Heir: s* Crispian John Edmund Audley Barlow, *b* 20 April 1958. *Address:* 18 Winter Avenue, St John's, Newfoundland.

BARLOW, Donald Spiers Monteagle, MS London; FRCS; Consulting Surgeon: Hospitals for Diseases of the Chest, since 1971 (Consultant Surgeon 1947-71); Southend Group of Hospitals, since 1970 (Consultant Surgeon 1936-70); Luton Group of Hospitals, since 1970 (Consultant Surgeon 1940-70); Italian Hospital, since 1970 (Hon. Consultant Thoracic Surgeon 1955-70); Penrose-May Surgical Tutor to the Royal College of Surgeons of England, since 1969 (Surgical Tutor, 1962-69); *b* 4 July 1905; *s* of late Leonard Barlow, MIEE, and Katharine Barlow; *m* 1934, Violet Elizabeth (*née* Maciver); one *s* three *d* (and one *d* decd). *Educ:* Whitgift Sch.; University Coll. Hospital

and Medical Sch. MRCS, LRCP 1927; MB, BS London 1928; MS London 1930; FRCS 1930. Formerly: RMO, Wimbledon Hosp., 1927; House Phys., UCH, 1928; House Surg., UCH, 1929; Ho. Surg., Norfolk and Norwich Hosp., 1930-31; Resident Asst Surg., West London Hosp., 1931-35; Surg. Registrar London Lock Hosp., 1936; Research work at UCL, 1936-37; Hon. Surg., St John's Hosp., Lewisham, 1937-47; Cons. Thoracic Surg., LCC, 1945-48. Teacher, 1964-67, Lectr, 1967-71, Inst. of Diseases of the Chest, Univ. of London. Chm., S Beds Div., BMA, 1971-72. Coronation Medal, 1953. *Publications:* contribs to: Progress of Clinical Surgery, 1960 (ed Rodney Smith); Operative Surgery, 2nd edn 1969 (ed Rob and Smith). Many publications in learned jls mostly concerning diseases of oesophagus, chest and abdomen. Also 3 reports (Ceylon Govt White Papers), 1952, 1954, 1967. *Recreations:* golf (Captain, Harpenden Golf Club, 1971-72, Pres., 1976), painting. *Address:* Deacons Field, High Elms, Harpenden, Herts. *T:* Harpenden 3400. *Club:* Carlton.
See also *Prof. H. E. M. Barlow, Michael Miller.*

BARLOW, Prof. Frank, MA, DPhil; FBA 1970; FRSL 1971; Professor of History and Head of Department, University of Exeter, 1953-76, now Emeritus Professor; *b* 19 April 1911; *e s* of Percy Hawthorn and Margaret Julia Barlow; *m* 1936, Moira Stella Brigid Garvey; two *s. Educ:* Newcastle High Sch.; St John's Coll., Oxford. Open Schol., St John's Coll., Oxford, 1929; 1st Cl. Hons Sch. of Modern History, 1933; Bryce Student, 1933; Oxford Senior Student, 1934.; BLitt, 1934; Fereday Fellow, St John's Coll., Oxford, 1935-38; DPhil 1937. Asst Lecturer, University Coll., London, 1936-40; War service in the Army, 1941-46, commissioned into Intelligence Corps, demobilised as Major; Lecturer 1946, Reader 1949, Dep. Vice-Chancellor, 1961-63, Public Orator, 1974-76, University of Exeter. *Publications:* The Letters of Arnulf of Lisieux, 1939; Durham Annals and Documents of the Thirteenth Century, 1945; Durham Jurisdictional Peculiars, 1950; The Feudal Kingdom of England, 1955; (ed and trans.) The Life of King Edward the Confessor, 1962; The English Church, 1000-1066, 1963; William I and the Norman Conquest, 1965; Edward the Confessor, 1970; (with Martin Biddle, Olof von Feilitzen and D. J. Keene) Winchester in the Early Middle Ages, 1976. *Recreation:* gardening. *Address:* Middle Court Hall, Kenton, Exeter. *T:* Starcross 438.

BARLOW, Sir (George) William, Kt 1977; BSc Tech, CEng, FIMechE, FIEE; Chairman of the Post Office, since 1977; Director: Ransome Hoffman Pollard Ltd, since 1977 (Group Chief Executive, 1969-77, Chairman 1971-77); Glynwed Ltd, since 1975; Royal Worcester, since 1976; *b* 8 June 1924; *s* of Albert Edward and Annice Barlow; *m* 1948, Elaine Mary Atherton (*née* Adamson); one *s* one *d. Educ:* Manchester Grammar Sch.; Manchester Univ. (Kitchener Schol., Louis Atkinson Schol.; BSc Tech. 1st cl. Hons Elec. Engrg, 1944). Served as Elec. Lt, RNVR, 1944-47. Various appts, The English Electric Co. Ltd (in Spain, 1952-55, Canada, 1958-62); Gen. Manager, Liverpool and Netherton, 1964-67; Managing Director: English Electric Domestic Appliance Co. Ltd, 1965-67; English Electric Computers Ltd, 1967-68. Member: Industrial Develt adv. Bd, 1972-; Council: IEE, 1969-72; IMechE 1971-74; Engineering Industries Council, 1975-77; Pres., IWM, 1976-77; Chm., Ferrous Foundries Adv. Cttee, 1975-; Chm., Ball & Roller Bearings Manufacturers' Assoc., 1975-76; Independent Mem., Electrical Engrg EDC, 1975-76; Pres., Fedn of European Bearing Manufacturers, 1977. FBIM 1971. *Recreation:* golf. *Address:* 2 Neville Drive, N2. *Clubs:* Army and Navy, Brooks's; Hampstead Golf, Royal Birkdale Golf.

BARLOW, Prof. Harold Everard Monteagle, BSc (Eng.) London, PhD (Sci.), London; FRS 1961; FIEEE; FIEE; MIMechE; Emeritus Professor of Electrical Engineering, University College, London (Jennber Professor, 1950-67); *b* Highbury, 15 Nov. 1899; *s* of late Leonard Barlow, MIEE, and Katharine Monteagle, Glasgow; *m* 1931, Janet Hastings, *d* of the late Rev. J. Hastings Eastwood, BA; three *s* one *d. Educ:* Wallington Grammar School; City & Guilds Engineering College; University College, London. Sub-Lieut. RNVR 1917-19; Student at University College, London, 1919-23; Practical engineering training with East Surrey Ironworks and Barlow & Young Ltd, 1923-25; Member of Academic Staff, Faculty of Engineering, UCL, 1925-67 (absent from University on War Service, Sept. 1939-Oct. 1945). Joined staff of Telecommunications Research Establishment, Air Ministry, to deal with Radar development, Sept. 1939; Superintendent, Radio Dept, RAE, 1943-45. Fellow of University College, 1946, Prof. of Elec. Engineering, 1945-50; Dean of Engineering Faculty, and Mem. UCL Cttee, 1949, 1961. Mem. of: Radar and Signals Advisory Bd, Min. of Supply, 1947; Scientific Advisory

Council, Min. of Supply, 1949; Radio Research Bd, DSIR, 1948 and 1960; London Regional Advisory Council and of Academic Bd for Higher Technological Educn, 1952-67; Academic Council, Univ. of London, 1953-55; BBC Scientific Advisory Committee, 1953-76; Governor, Woolwich Polytechnic, 1948; Dir, Marconi Instruments, 1963. Member of Council of IEE, 1955-58 and 1960-; awarded Kelvin Premium, J. J. Thomson Premium, Oliver Lodge and Fleming Premium of IEE; Faraday Medal, 1967; Mem. Council, IERE, 1973-76. FCGI 1969. For. Mem., Polish Acad. of Science, 1966; Hon. Mem., Japanese Inst. of Electronics and Communications Engineers, 1973. Chm., British Nat. Cttee for Radio Science, 1968; Mem., Nat. Electronics Council, 1969-. Dellinger Gold Medal, Internat. Radio Union, 1969; Harold Hartley Medal, Inst. of Measurement and Control, 1973; Mervin J. Kelly Award, IEEE, 1975. Hon. DSc Heriot-Watt, 1971; Hon. DEng Sheffield, 1973. *Publications:* Micro-waves and Wave-guides, 1947; (with A. L. Cullen) Micro-Wave Measurements, 1950; (with J. Brown) Radio Surface Waves, 1962; many scientific papers. *Recreations:* sailing, walking, reading. *Address:* 13 Hookfield, Epsom, Surrey. *T:* Epsom 21586; University College, Gower Street, WC1. *T:* 01-387 7050. *Club:* Athenæum.
See also *D. S. M. Barlow.*

BARLOW, Prof. Horace Basil, FRS 1969; Royal Society Research Professor, Physiological Laboratory, Cambridge University, since 1973; *b* 8 Dec. 1921; *s* of Sir (James) Alan (Noel) Barlow, 2nd Bt, GCB, KBE (*d* 1968), and of Nora Barlow (*née* Darwin); *m* 1954, Ruthala (marr. diss., 1970), *d* of Dr M. H. Salaman, *qv*; four *d. Educ:* Winchester; Trinity Coll., Cambridge. Research Fellow, Trinity Coll., 1950-54, Lectr, King's Coll., Cambridge, 1954-64. Demonstrator and Asst Dir of Research, Physiological Lab., Cambridge, 1954-64; Prof. of Physiological Optics and Physiology, Univ. of Calif, Berkeley, 1964-73. *Publications:* several, on neurophysiology of vision in Jl of Physiology, and elsewhere. *Address:* Physiological Laboratory, Cambridge CB2 3EG.
See also *Sir T. E. Barlow, Bt.*

BARLOW, Sir John (Denman), 2nd Bt, *cr* 1907; JP for Cheshire; Consultant, Thomas Barlow and Bro., Manchester and London; Emeritus Director, Manchester Chamber of Commerce; Chairman: various Rubber Plantation Companies; United Kingdom Falkland Islands Committee; *b* 15 June 1898; *er s* of Sir John Barlow, 1st Bt, and Hon. Anna Maria Heywood Denman (*d* 1965), *sister* of 3rd Baron Denman, PC, GCMG, KCVO; *S* father, 1932; *m* 1928, Hon. Diana Helen Kemp, *d* of 1st Baron Rochdale, CB, and *sister* of 1st Viscount Rochdale, *qv*; three *s* one *d*. Contested (L) Northwich Division of Cheshire, 1929; MP (Nat Lib) Eddisbury Division of Cheshire, 1945-50; contested (U and Nat Lib) Walsall Div. of Staffordshire, 1950; MP (C) Middleton and Prestwich Division of Lancashire, 1951-66. Led CPA Mission to Malaya, 1959; led Parly Mission to new Malaysian Parlt, taking gift of Speaker's chair, 1963; Chm., Cons. Trade and Industries Cttee, 1955-60. Vice-Chm., Cotton Bd, 1940; Director: Barclays Bank Ltd (Manchester Local Bd), 1940-73; Calico Printers Assoc., 1952-68; The Falklands Islands Co. Mem. Council, RASE, 1942-53. *Heir: s* John Kemp Barlow [*b* 22 April 1934; *m* 1962, Susan, *er d* of Col. Sir Andrew Horsbrugh-Porter, *qv*; four *s*]. *Address:* Bradwall Manor, Sandbach, Cheshire. *T:* Sandbach 2036. *Club:* Brooks's.

BARLOW, Roy Oxspring; solicitor; a Recorder of the Crown Court, since 1975; *b* 13 Feb. 1927; *s* of George and Clarice Barlow; *m* 1957, Kathleen Mary Roberts; two *s* one *d. Educ:* King Edward VII Sch., Sheffield; Queen's Coll., Oxford; Sheffield Univ. (LLB). Local Government, 1952-62; solicitor in private practice, 1962-. *Recreations:* farming, walking, reading. *Address:* The Cottage, Oxton Rakes, Barlow, Sheffield S18 5TH. *T:* Sheffield 890652.

BARLOW, Thomas Bradwall; merchant banker; director of rubber, insurance and other public companies; Joint Senior Consultant in Thomas Barlow & Bro. Ltd, London and Manchester; 2nd *s* of Sir John Emmott Barlow, 1st Bt; *m* 1943, Elizabeth Margaret, *d* of Hon. B. G. Sackville-West; one *s* one *d. Educ:* Leighton Park, Reading; Haverford, Pa, USA. Chairman: Br. Assoc. of Straits Merchants, 1937; Rubber Trade Assoc., 1942-43; Rubber Growers' Assoc., 1945-46; British Assoc. of Malaysia, 1965; Highlands & Lowlands Para Rubber Co. Ltd; Chersonese (F.M.S.) Estates Ltd. *Recreations:* hunting, steeplechasing, and travelling. *Address:* Thornby House, Northampton. *T:* Guilsborough 214. *Clubs:* Brooks's, City of London, Hurlingham.

BARLOW, Sir Thomas (Erasmus), 3rd Bt *cr* 1902; DSC 1945; DL; *b* 23 Jan. 1914; *s* of Sir Alan Barlow, 2nd Bt, GCB, KBE,

and of Nora, *d* of late Sir Horace Darwin, KBE; *S* father, 1968; *m* 1955, Isabel, *d* of late Dr T. M. Body, Middlesbrough, Yorks; two *s* two *d*. *Educ:* Winchester College. Entered RN as cadet, 1932; qualified Submarines, 1937; served in Submarines in Atlantic, Mediterranean, Indian Ocean and Far East during War of 1939-45; Naval Staff Course, 1946; Joint Services Staff Course, 1947, Commander, 1950. British Joint Services Mission, Washington, 1950-53; Captain 1954; Imperial Defence Coll., 1957; Chief Staff Officer to Flag Officer Submarines, 1960-62; Commodore, HMS Drake, Devonport, 1962-64; retired, 1964. Now farms at Wendover, Bucks. Pres. Chiltern Hills Agricultural Assoc., 1968; actively concerned in Wildlife and Countryside Conservation movements: Soc. for Promotion of Nature Reserves; Berks, Bucks and Oxfordshire Naturalists' Trust; RSPB; Charles Darwin Foundn for Galapogos Is. DL Bucks, 1977. *Recreations:* bird watching, the countryside. *Heir:* s James Alan Barlow, *b* 10 July 1956. *Address:* Boswells, Wendover, Bucks. *T:* Wendover 622119. *Clubs:* Athenæum, Savile.
See also Prof. H. B. Barlow.

BARLOW, Sir William; *see* Barlow, Sir G. W.

BARLTROP, Roger Arnold Rowlandson; HM Diplomatic Service; Counsellor and Head of Chancery, Addis Ababa, since 1973; *b* 19 Jan. 1930; *s* of late Ernest William Barltrop, CMG, CBE, DSO, and Ethel Alice Lucy Barltrop (*née* Baker); *m* 1962, Penelope Pierrepont Dalton; two *s* two *d*. *Educ:* Solihull Sch.; Leeds Grammar Sch.; Exeter Coll., Oxford. BA (Hons). Served RN, 1949-50, RNVR/RNR, 1950-64 (Lt-Comdr 1962). Asst Principal, CRO, 1954-56; Second Sec., New Delhi, 1956-57; Private Sec. to Parly Under-Sec. of State and Minister of State, CRO, 1957-60; First Sec., E Nigeria, 1960-62; Actg Dep. High Comr, W Nigeria, 1962; First Sec., Salisbury, Rhodesia, 1962-65; CO and FO, later FCO, 1965-69; First Sec. and Head of Chancery, Ankara, 1969-70; Dep. British Govt Rep., WI Associated States, 1971-73. *Recreations:* cricket, sailing, chess, genealogy. *Address:* c/o Foreign and Commonwealth Office, SW1A 2AH; Cards House, Woodhurst Park, Oxted, Surrey RH8 9HA. *Club:* Royal Commonwealth Society.

BARMAN, Christian, OBE 1963; RDI; Past President, Society of Industrial Artists; *b* 1898. *Educ:* University of Liverpool School of Architecture. Editor, the Architect's Journal and the Architectural Review; Publicity Officer, London Passenger Transport Bd, 1935-41; was generally responsible for the visual presentation of the undertaking to the public; Asst Dir of Post-War Building, Min. of Works, 1941-45; Public Relations Adviser, GWR, 1945-47; Chief Publicity Officer, British Transport Commn, 1947-62; Exec. Mem., BTC Design Panel, 1956-62. *Publications:* Sir John Vanbrugh, 1924; edition of James Gibbs, Rules for Drawing the various Parts of Architecture, 1925; Balbus, or the Future of Architecture, 1926; Architecture: An Introduction for the General Reader, 1927; Next Station, 1947 (repr. as The Great Western Railway's Last Look Forward, 1972); Public Transport (The Things We See Series), 1949; Early British Railways, 1950; Introduction to Railway Architecture, 1950; under pseudonym Christian Mawson: Ramping Cat (a novel), 1941; Portrait of England (an anthology), 1941. *Address:* 12a Hillbrow, Reading, Berks.

BARNA, Prof. Tibor, CBE 1974; Professor of Economics, University of Sussex, since 1962; Member, Monopolies and Mergers Commission, since 1963; *b* 1919. *Educ:* London School of Economics. Lecturer, London School of Economics, 1944; Official Fellow, Nuffield College, Oxford, 1947; senior posts in UN Economic Commission for Europe, 1949; Assistant Director, National Institute of Economic and Social Research, London, 1955. *Publications:* Redistribution of Income through Public Finance in 1937, 1945; Investment and Growth Policies in British Industrial Firms, 1962. Papers in Jl Royal Statistical Soc., Economic Jl. *Address:* Beanacre, Westmeston, Hassocks, West Sussex. *T:* Hassocks 2384.

BARNARD, 11th Baron, *cr* 1698; **Harry John Neville Vane,** TD 1960; Landowner; Lord-Lieutenant and Custos Rotulorum of County Durham, since 1970; *b* 21 Sept. 1923; *er s* of 10th Baron and Sylvia Mary, *d* of Herbert Straker; *S* father, 1964; *m* 1952, Lady Davina Mary Cecil, OStJ, *e d* of 6th Marquess of Exeter, *qv*; one *s* four *d*. *Educ:* Eton. Served War of 1939-45, RAFVR, 1942-46 (Flying Officer, 1945). Lieut Northumberland Hussars, 1948; Captain, 1951; Major, 1957; Lt-Col Commanding, 1964-66. Vice-Pres., N of England TA&VRA, 1970, Pres., 1974-77. County Councillor, Durham, 1952-61. Member: Durham Co. AEC, 1953-72 (Chm., 1970-72); N Regional Panel, MAFF, 1972-76; Dir, NE Housing Assoc.; President: Farmway Ltd; Durham Co. Br. BRCS, 1969-; Durham Co. Br., CLA; Durham Co. St John Council, 1971-; Durham Co. Scout Assoc., 1972-;

Durham Co. Br. RBL, 1973-. DL Durham, 1956, Vice-Lieutenant, 1969-70; JP Durham, 1961. Joint Master of Zetland Hounds, 1963-65. KStJ 1971. *Heir:* s Hon. Henry Francis Cecil Vane, *b* 11 March 1959. *Address:* (Residence) Selaby, Gainford, Darlington, Co. Durham DL2 3HF. *T:* Gainford 206; (Seat) Raby Castle, Staindrop, Darlington, Co. Durham. *Clubs:* Brooks's; Durham County (Durham); Northern Counties (Newcastle upon Tyne).

BARNARD, Sir (Arthur) Thomas, Kt 1958; CB 1954; OBE 1946; Director-General of Inspection, Ministry of Supply, 1956-58, retired; *b* 28 Sept. 1893; *s* of late Arthur Barnard; *m* 1921, Grace, *d* of William Magerkorth, Belvedere, Kent. *Educ:* Erith Technical Coll. Is a Chartered Civil Engineer. Chief Superintendent, Royal Ordnance Factories, Woolwich, 1951-55; Dep. Dir-Gen., Royal Ordnance Factories, Adelphi, London, 1955-56. *Address:* Kentmead, 26 Heathfield, Chislehurst, Kent BR7 6AE.

BARNARD, Prof. Christiaan Neethling, MD, MMed, PhD; Professor of Surgical Science, Cape Town University, since 1968; *b* 8 Nov. 1922; *s* of Adam Hendrik Barnard and Maria Elizabeth Barnard (*née* De Swart); *m* 1st, 1948, Aletta Gertruida Louw (marr. diss. 1970); one *s* one *d*; 2nd, 1970, Barbara Maria Zoellner; two *s*. *Educ:* Beaufort West High Sch.; Univs of Cape Town and Minnesota. MB, ChB 1946, MD 1953, Cape Town; MS, PhD 1958, Minnesota. Private practice, Ceres, CP, 1948-51; Sen. Resident MO, City Hosp., Cape Town, 1951-53; subseq. Registrar, Groote Schuur Hosp.; Registrar, Surgery Dept, Cape Town Univ.; Charles Adams Meml Schol. and Dazian Foundn Bursary for study in USA; US Public Health Grant for further res. in cardiac surgery; Specialist Cardio-Thoracic Surgeon, Lectr and Dir of Surg. Res., Cape Town Univ. and Groote Schuur Hosp., 1958; Head of Cardio-Thoracic Surgery, Cape Town Univ. Teaching Hosps, 1961; Assoc. Prof., Cape Town Univ., 1962. Oppenheimer Meml Trust Bursary for overseas study, 1960. Holds numerous hon. doctorates, foreign orders and awards, hon. citizenships and freedoms, medallions, etc; Dag Hammarskjöld Internat. Prize and Peace Prize, Kennedy Foundn Award, Milan Internat. Prize for Science, etc; hon. fellow or member various colleges, societies, etc. FACS 1963; Fellow NY Cardiological Soc. 1965; FACC 1967. *Publications:* (with V. Schrire) Surgery of Common Congenital Cardiac Malformations, 1968; One Life, 1969; Heart Attack: You Don't Have to Die, 1971; The Unwanted, 1974; South Africa: Sharp Dissection, 1977; The Night Season, 1977; numerous contribs to med. jls. *Recreations:* tennis, music. *Address:* Department of Cardiac Surgery, Medical School, Observatory, Cape Town, South Africa. *T:* 551358.

BARNARD, Eric, CB 1951; CBE 1943; DSO 1917; MA (Oxon); Deputy Secretary, Department of Scientific and Industrial Research, 1945-55; *b* 19 Sept. 1891; *m* 1923; one *s* one *d*. Gloucestershire Regt, 1914-19 (DSO, despatches twice). *Address:* Milland Place Hotel, Liphook, Hants.

BARNARD, Prof. George Alfred, MA, DSc; Professor of Mathematics, University of Essex, 1966-75; part-time at University of Waterloo, Canada, since 1975; Statistical consultant to various organisations; *b* 23 Sept. 1915; *s* of Frederick C. and Ethel C. Barnard; *m* 1st, 1942, Helen J. B. Davies; three *s*; 2nd, 1949, Mary M. L. Jones; one *s*. *Educ:* Sir George Monoux Grammar Sch., Walthamstow; St John's Coll., Cambridge. Math. Trip., Pt III, 1936, Res. Studentship, St John's Coll., spent at Grad. Sch. Princeton, NJ, USA, 1937-39. Plessey Co., Ilford, as Math. Consultant, 1940-42; Ministry of Supply Adv. Unit, 1942-45; Maths Dept, Imperial Coll., London: Lectr, 1945-47; Reader in Math. Statistics, 1948-54, Professor, 1954-66. Vis. Prof., Univ. of Waterloo, 1972-73. Member: UGC, 1967-72; Computer Bd, 1970-72; SSRC, 1971-74. Royal Statistical Society: Council Mem. and Vice-Pres., 1952, 1962, Pres. 1971-72 (Chm. Res. Sect., 1958); Mem. Internat. Statistical Inst., 1952; Statistical Adviser, Brit. Standards Instn (with Prof. E. S. Pearson), 1954; Chm. Inst. of Statisticians, 1960-62; President: Operational Res. Soc., 1962-64; Inst. of Mathematics and its Applications, 1970-71; Fellow: Amer. Statistical Assoc., Inst. of Mathematical Statistics, 1961. *Publications:* (ed) The Foundations of Statistical Inference, 1962; papers in Jl Royal Statistical Society; Technometrics; Biometrika. *Recreations:* viola playing, boating. *Address:* Mill House, Hurst Green, Brightlingsea, Essex. *T:* Brightlingsea 2388.

BARNARD, Captain Sir George (Edward), Kt 1968; Deputy Master of Trinity House, 1961-72; *b* 11 Aug. 1907; 2nd *s* of Michael and Alice Louise Barnard; *m* 1940, Barbara Emma Hughes (*d* 1976); one *s*. Apprenticed at sea, 1922; 1st Command, Blue Star Line, 1945. Elder Brother of Trinity House, 1958-.

Trustee, Nat. Maritime Museum, 1967-74; Treasurer, Internat. Assoc. of Lighthouse Authorities, 1961-72; Hon. Sec., King George's Fund for Sailors, 1967-75; first Chm., Nautical Inst., 1972-73, Pres., 1973-75, Fellow, 1975; Mem. Cttee of Management, RNLI, 1972-. FRSA 1969. *Recreation:* gardening. *Address:* The Lodge, Rayleigh Road, Hutton, Essex CM13 1AJ. *T:* Brentwood 2320.

BARNARD, Sir Henry William, Kt 1944; Judge of High Court of Justice (Probate, Divorce and Admiralty Division), 1944-59; *b* 18 April 1891; *s* of late William Tyndal Barnard, KC. *Educ:* Wellington Coll.; Merton Coll., Oxford. Called to Bar, Gray's Inn, 1913; KC 1939. Bencher Gray's Inn, 1939, Treasurer, 1953. Admiralty Judge of the Cinque Ports. Served European War as a Captain in Royal West Kent Regt (5th Bn). *Address:* Boscobel, Hawkshill, Walmer, Kent. *Club:* Royal Cornwall Yacht.

BARNARD, Howard Clive, MA, BLitt Oxon; MA (Educ), DLitt London, FCP, FTCL; Professor of Education, Reading University, 1937-51; Emeritus since 1951; *b* City of London, 7 June 1884; Freeman of the City and Mem. of the Goldsmiths' Co. by patrimony; *s* of late Howard Barnard, journalist; *m* Edith Gwendolen (*d* 1956), *d* of late John Wish, Civil Servant; one *s* one *d*. *Educ:* University Coll. Sch., London; Brasenose Coll., Oxford (Sen. Hulme Scholar); London Sch. of Economics; King's Coll., London (Advanced Student); also studied in France and Germany. Asst Master at Manchester, Ramsgate, and Bradford; Headmaster, Grammar Sch., Gillingham, Kent; Examiner at various times to Univs of Oxford, Cambridge, London, Durham, Birmingham, Liverpool, Manchester, Leeds, Sheffield, Wales, Nottingham and Hull, the Civil Service Commission, the LCC, the Coll. of Preceptors, etc. Hon. DLitt Reading, 1974. *Publications:* The Little Schools of Port-Royal; The Port-Royalists on Education (source-book); The French Tradition in Education; Madame de Maintenon and Saint-Cyr; Fénelon on Education; Girls at School under the Ancien Régime; Education and the French Revolution (also Italian edn); A History of English Education from 1760 (also Hindi edn); Were those the Days?; An Introduction to Teaching; Principles and Practice of Geography Teaching; Observational Geography and Regional Survey; The Expansion of the Anglo-Saxon Nations (ed); A Handbook of British Educational Terms (with Prof. J. A. Lauwerys); and numerous school books. *Recreations:* walking, organ-playing. *Address:* 54 Grosvenor Road, Caversham, Reading, Berks. *T:* Reading 473001.

BARNARD, Hon. Lance Herbert; Australian Ambassador to Sweden, Norway and Finland, since 1975; *b* 1 May 1919; *s* of Hon. H. C. Barnard and M. M. Barnard (*née* McKenzie); *m* 2nd, 1962, Jill Denise Carstairs, *d* of Senator H. G. J. Cant; one *s* two *d* (and one *d* decd); also one *d* by a former marriage. *Educ:* Launceston Technical Coll. Served War, overseas, AIF 9th Div., 1940. Formerly teacher, Tasmanian Educn Dept. Elected to House of Representatives as Member for Bass, 1954, 1955, 1958, 1961, 1963, 1966, 1969, 1972, 1974. From Dec. 1972: Minister of Defence, Navy, Army, Air, Supply, Postmaster-Gen., Labour and National Service, Immigration, Social Services, Repatriation, Health, Primary Industry, National Development, and of the Interior. Dep. Leader, Federal Parliamentary Labor Party, 1967-72; Deputy Prime Minister, 1973-74; Minister for Defence (Navy, Army, Air and Supply), 1973-75. Captain, Aust. Cadet Corps, post War of 1939-45. State Pres., Tasmanian Br., Aust. Labor Party; Tasmanian deleg., Federal Exec., Aust. Labor Party. *Publication:* Labor's Defence Policy, 1969. *Recreations:* bowls, golf, swimming. *Address:* Australian Embassy, Sergels Torg 12, Stockholm, Sweden. *T:* 244660. *Clubs:* South Launceston Rotary, East Launceston Bowling, Launceston Workingmen's (Launceston).

BARNARD, Sir Thomas; see Barnard, Sir A. T.

BARNARD, Thomas Theodore, MC; MA Oxon; PhD Cantab; *b* 31 Aug. 1898; *e s* of late T. H. Barnard, banker, Bedford; *m* 1924, Gillian Sarah (*d* 1961), *d* of late Lieut-Col Hon. A. S. Byng, DSO; one *s* two *d*. *Educ:* Eton, Christ Church, Oxford; King's Coll., Cambridge. Lieut, Coldstream Guards, 1917-19; Prof. of Social Anthropology, and Dir of the Sch. of African Life and Languages, University of Cape Town, 1926-34. Rejoined Coldstream Guards, 1940-45, Capt., Guards Depôt. VMH 1965. *Address:* Furzebrook, Wareham, Dorset. *Club:* Cavalry and Guards.

BARNBY, 2nd Baron, *cr* 1922; **Francis Vernon Willey;** CMG 1918; CBE 1919; MVO 1918; *b* Bradford, Yorks., 1884; *e s* of 1st Baron and Florence (*d* 1933), *d* of Frederick Chinnock, Dinorbin Court, Hants; *S* father, 1929; *m* 1940, Banning Grange, Bryn Mawr, Pennsylvania. *Educ:* Eton; Magdalen Coll., Oxford. Late Brevet Col Comdg Sherwood Rangers, Notts

Yeomanry (TF). Hon. Col 1948; mobilised, 1914; served Egypt and Gallipoli, 1915; recalled as Asst Dir of Ordnance Stores (Clothing); Controller of Wool Supplies under War Dept, June 1916, and organised the purchase and distribution of the British and Colonial Wool Clips on Government and civilian account; MP (Co. U) South Bradford, Dec. 1918-22; MFH Blankney Hunt, Lincolnshire, 1919-33. Past Pres. CBI; Member: Surplus Govt Property Disposals Board, 1918-21; Central Electricity Board, 1927-46; Overseas Settlement Board, 1937-; a former Director: Lloyds Bank Ltd; Commercial Union Assurance Co. Ltd; President: Textile Institute, 1961-62; Aire Wool Co. Ltd; Past Master, Worshipful Company of Woolmen. Hon. DTech Bradford, 1968. *Heir:* none. *Address:* Hillthorpe, Ashtead, Surrey; 2 Caxton Street, SW1. *T:* 01-222 3003; 35-37 Grosvenor Square, W1. *T:* 01-499 2112. *Clubs:* Carlton, Cavalry and Guards, Bath, Hurlingham.

BARNEBY, Lt-Col Henry Habington, TD 1946; retired from HM Forces 1955; Vice Lord-Lieutenant of Hereford and Worcester, 1974-77; *b* 19 June 1909; *er s* of Richard Hicks Barneby, Longworth Hall, Hereford; *m* 1st, 1935, Evelyn Georgina Heywood; 2nd, 1944, Angela Margaret Campbell; four *s* one *d* (and one *s* decd). *Educ:* Radley Coll.; RMC Sandhurst. QALAS 1939. 2nd Lieut KSLI 1929, retd 1935; Lieut Hereford Regt TA 1936; commanded: Hereford Regt (TA), 1945-46; Hereford LI (TA), 1947-51; Jamaica Bn, 1951-53; regranted commn in KSLI as Major, 1947; retd 1955. Mem., Herefordshire T&AFA, 1955-68; Mem., W Midlands T&AVR, 1968-77. Member: Hereford RDC, 1955-67 (Chm., 1964-67); Dore and Bredwardine RDC, 1966-73; S Herefordshire RDC, 1973-76. DL 1958, Vice Lieut, 1973-74, JP 1960, High Sheriff 1972, Herefordshire. *Address:* Llanerch-y-Coed, Dorstone, Herefordshire. *T:* Clifford 215.

BARNES, family name of **Baron Gorell.**

BARNES, Alan Robert, CBE 1976; JP; Headmaster, Ruffwood School, Kirkby, Liverpool, since 1959; *b* 9 Aug. 1927; *s* of Arthur Barnes and Ida Barnes; *m* 1951, Pearl Muriel Boughton; one *s* (and one *s* decd). *Educ:* Enfield Grammar Sch.; Queens' Coll., Cambridge (MA). National Service, RAEC. Wallington County Grammar Sch., 1951-55; Churchfields Sch., West Bromwich, 1955-59. Treas., Headmasters' Assoc., 1975- (Pres., 1974); Vice-Chm., Jt Four Secondary Assocs, 1976-. JP Knowsley, Merseyside, 1967. *Publications:* (contrib.) Going Comprehensive (ed Halsall), 1970; contrib. to: HMA Rev., Education, BEAS Jl. *Recreations:* bridge, cricket. *Address:* 16 Oaktree Road, St Helens, Merseyside. *T:* St Helens 28073.

BARNES, Dame (Alice) Josephine (Mary Taylor), (Dame Josephine Warren), DBE 1974; FRCP, FRCS, FRCOG; Consulting Obstetrician and Gynaecologist, Charing Cross Hospital and Elizabeth Garrett Anderson Hospital; President, Women's National Cancer Control Campaign, since 1974 (Chairman 1969-72; Vice-President, 1972-74); *b* 18 Aug. 1912; *er d* of late Rev. Walter W. Barnes, MA(Oxon), and Alice Mary Ibbetson, FRCO, ARCM; *m* 1942, Sir Brian Warren, *qv* (marr. diss. 1964); one *s* two *d*. *Educ:* Oxford High Sch.; Lady Margaret Hall, Oxford; University College Hosp. Med. Sch. 1st class Hons Physiology, Oxford, BA 1934, MA, BM, BCh 1937, DM 1941. University College Hospital: Goldschmid Scholar; Aitchison Scholar; Tuke Silver Medal; Fellowes Silver Medal; F. T. Roberts Prize; Suckling Prize. Various appointments at UCH, Samaritan Hosp., Queen Charlotte's Hosp., and Radcliffe Infirmary, Oxford; Dep. Academic Head, Obstetric Unit, UCH, 1947-52; Surgeon, Marie Curie Hosp., 1947-67. Medical Women's Federation: Hon. Sec., 1951-57; Pres., London Assoc., 1958-60; Pres., 1966-67. Royal Society of Medicine: Mem. Council, 1949-50; Pres., Sect. of Obstetrics and Gynaecology, 1972-73; Hon. Editor, Sect. of Obstetrics, 1951-71. President: W London Medico-Chirurgical Soc., 1969-70; Nat. Assoc. of Family Planning Doctors, 1976-; Obstetric Physiotherapists Assoc., 1976-; Union Professionelle Internationale de Gynécologie et d'Obstétrique, 1977-. Examiner in Obstetrics and Gynaecology: Univ. of London; RCOG; Examining Bd in England, Queen's Univ., Belfast; Univ. of Oxford; Univ. of Kampala. Member: Council, Med. Defence Union; Royal Commn on Med. Educn, 1965-68; Council, RCOG, 1965-71 (Jun. Vice-Pres., 1972-74, Sen. Vice-Pres., 1974-75); MRC Cttee on Analgesia in Midwifery; Min. of Health Med. Manpower Cttee; Medico-Legal Soc.; Population Investigation Cttee, Eugenics Soc.; Cttee on the Working of the Abortion Act, 1971-73; Standing Med. Adv. Cttee, DHSS, 1976. Mem. of Honour, French Gynaecological Soc., 1945; Corresp. Mem., Royal Belgian Soc. of Obstetricians and Gynaecologists, 1949. Hon. FRCPI 1977. Governor: Charing Cross Hosp.; Chelsea Coll. of Science and Technology; Member Council: Benenden Sch.; Bedford Coll. Lectures: Fawcett, Bedford Coll., 1969; Rhys-

Williams, Nat. Birthday Trust, 1970; Bartholomew Mosse, Rotunda Hosp., Dublin, 1975. Commandeur du Bontemps de Médoc et des Graves, 1966. *Publications:* Gynaecological Histology, 1948; The Care of the Expectant Mother, 1954; Lecture Notes on Gynaecology, 1966; (ed, jtly) Scientific Foundations of Obstetrics and Gynaecology, 1970; Essentials of Family Planning, 1976; numerous contribs to med. jls, etc. *Recreations:* music, gastronomy, motoring, foreign travel; formerly hockey (Oxford Univ. Women's Hockey XI, 1932, 1933, 1934). *Address:* 8 Aubrey Walk, W8 7JG. *T:* 01-727 9832.
See also F. W. I. Barnes, M. G. J. Neary.

BARNES, Arthur Chapman, CMG 1936; FRIC; BSc (Hons); Sugar Consultant; *b* 1891. *Educ:* Deacon's School, Peterborough; Municipal College of Technology and Victoria Univ., Manchester. Entered Survey Dept, East Africa Protectorate, 1914; agricultural chemist, Nigeria, 1923; Asst Director of Agriculture, Zanzibar, 1927; Director of Agriculture, Fiji, 1929; Director of Agriculture and Island Chemist, Jamaica, 1933; General Manager West Indies Sugar Co. Ltd, 1938; seconded for duty as Director of Research for The Sugar Manufacturers' Association (of Jamaica), Ltd, 1947; retired 1951. *Publications:* Agriculture of the Sugar-cane, 1953; The Sugar Cane, 1964, 2nd edn, 1974. *Address:* 8 Newlands, Musgrave Road, Durban, Natal, South Africa.

BARNES, Clive Alexander, CBE 1975; Dance Critic, The New York Times, since 1965; New York Correspondent of The Times, since 1970; *b* London, 13 May 1927; *s* of Arthur Lionel Barnes and Freda Marguerite Garratt; *m* 1958, Patricia Winckley; one *s* one *d*. *Educ:* King's Coll., London; St Catherine's Coll., Oxford. Served RAF, 1946-48. Admin. Officer, Town Planning Dept, LCC, 1952-61; concurrently freelance journalist; Chief Dance Critic, The Times, 1961-65; Exec. Editor, Dance and Dancers, Music and Musicians, and Plays and Players, 1961-65; a London Correspondent, New York Times, 1963-65, Drama Critic (weekdays only), 1967-77. Knight of the Order of Dannebrog (Denmark), 1972. *Publications:* Ballet in Britain since the War, 1953; (ed, with others) Ballet Here and Now, 1961; Frederick Ashton and his Ballets, 1961; Dance Scene, USA (commentary), 1967; (ed with J. Gassner) Best American Plays, 6th series, 1963-67, 1971, and 7th series, 1974; (ed) New York Times Directory of the Theatre, 1973; contribs to jls, inc. Punch, The New Statesman, The Spectator, The New Republic. *Recreations:* eating, drinking, walking, theatregoing. *Address:* 450 West End Avenue, New York, NY 10024, USA. *Club:* Century (NY).

BARNES, Sir Denis (Charles), KCB 1967 (CB 1964); Director: Glynwed Ltd; General Accident, Fire & Life Assurance Corporation, since 1976; President, Manpower Society, since 1976; *b* 15 Dec. 1914; *s* of Frederick Charles Barnes; *m* 1938, Patricia Abercrombie. *Educ:* Hulme Gram. Sch., Manchester; Merton Coll., Oxford. Postmaster, Merton Coll., Oxford, 1933-37. BA, 1st Cl. Mod. History, 1936; PPE 1937. Entered Min. of Labour, 1937; Private Sec. to Minister of Labour, 1945-47; Dep. Sec., Min. of Labour, 1963, Permanent Sec. 1966; Permanent Sec., Dept of Employment, 1968-73; Chm., Manpower Services Commn, 1974-76. FIPM. Commonwealth Fellowship, 1953. *Address:* The Old Inn, 30 The Street, Wittersham, Kent. *T:* Wittersham 528. *Club:* Savile.

BARNES, Eric Cecil, CMG 1954; Colonial Administrative Service; Provincial Commissioner, Nyasaland, 1949-55, retired; *b* 1899; *m* 1950, Isabel Margaret Lesley, MBE, *d* of late Mrs Isabel Wauchope; one *s* one *d*. *Educ:* Bishop Cotton's Sch., Simla; Bedford Sch. and Cadet Coll., Quetta, India. Indian Army, 1917-23; Administrative Service, Nyasaland, 1925. Deputy Provincial Commissioner, 1946. *Address:* Polmear, Frogham, near Fordingbridge, Hants. *T:* Fordingbridge 53357.

BARNES, Sir (Ernest) John (Ward), KCMG 1974; MBE (mil.) 1946; *b* 22 June 1917; *er s* of Rt Rev. Ernest William Barnes, 3rd Bishop of Birmingham, and Adelaide, *d* of Sir Adolphus Ward, Master of Peterhouse, Cambridge; *m* 1948, Cynthia Margaret Ray, *d* of Sir Herbert Stewart, CIE; two *s* three *d*. *Educ:* Winchester; Trinity Coll., Cambridge. Classical Tripos, Pts I and II, Class I; Porson Scholar, 1939. Royal Artillery, 1939-46 (Lt-Col, MBE, US Bronze Star). HM Foreign Service, 1946; served Washington, Beirut, Bonn and Harvard Univ. (Center for International Affairs); Ambassador to Israel, 1969-72; Ambassador to the Netherlands, 1972-77. *Address:* Hampton Lodge, Hurstpierpoint, Sussex. *Clubs:* Athenæum, Beefsteak, Brooks's; MCC.

BARNES, Francis Walter Ibbetson; a full-time Chairman, Industrial Tribunals, since 1976; *b* 10 May 1914; *s* of late Rev. Walter W. Barnes, MA (Oxon) and Alice Mary Ibbetson,

FRCO, ARCM; *m* 1st, 1941, Heather Katherine (marr. diss. 1953), *d* of Frank Tamplin; two *s*; 2nd, 1955, Sonia Nina (Nina Walker, pianist), *d* of late Harold Higginbottom; two *s* one *d*. *Educ:* Dragon Sch., Oxford; Mill Hill Sch.; Balliol Coll., Oxford. BA Jurisprudence (Hons), Oxford, 1937; MA 1967. Called to Bar, Inner Temple, 1938. Profumo Prize, Inner Temple, 1939. Served War, 1939-46 in Army (Middlesex Regt) and Home Office and Military Fire Services; Sen. Company Officer NFS and Capt. comdg military Fire Fighting Co. on BLA; later Staff Capt., JAG (War Crimes Section). Functioned as Judge Advocate and Prosecutor in various trials of war criminals in Germany. Recorder of Smethwick, 1964-66; Dep. Chm., Oxfordshire QS, 1965-71; Recorder of Warley, 1966-71, Hon. Recorder, 1972; a Recorder of the Crown Court, 1972-76. Life Governor, Mill Hill Sch., 1939-; Mem., Dame Henrietta Barnett Bd (Educl Trust), 1951-. Elected to Bar Council, 1961. Bar Council's rep. (observer) on Cons. cttee of Lawyers of the Common Market countries, 1962-71; contrib. to Common Market Law Review. Union Internat. des Avocats: Mem. Council, 1964-; Rapporteur Général at Vienna Congress, 1967; Rapporteur National at Paris Congress, 1971. *Recreations:* music, outdoor games, motoring. *Address:* 93 Ebury Bridge Road, SW1; 11 Park Hill, Ealing, W5. *T:* 01-997 5501; Southernhay, Diptford, S Devon.
See also Dame A. J. M. T. Barnes.

BARNES, Harold William; Director, Telecommunications Finance, Telecommunications Headquarters, GPO, 1968-72; *b* 7 Nov. 1912; *s* of Edgar and Florence Barnes; *m* 1941, Mary M. Butchart; one *s* one *d*. *Educ:* Chesterfield Grammar Sch. Entered Civil Service as Exec. Officer, 1931. Served HM Forces, RE Postal Services, 1940-46 (final rank, Major). Asst Accountant Gen., GPO, 1952-55; Dep. Dir, Finance and Accounts, GPO, 1955-64; Controller, Post Office Supplies Dept, 1964-68. *Recreations:* golf, choral music, (City of London Choir). *Address:* 3 Little Court, West Wickham, Kent. *T:* 01-777 6785. *Club:* Langley Park Golf (Beckenham).

BARNES, (Harry) Jefferson, CBE 1971; MA; Director (Principal), Glasgow School of Art, since 1964; *b* 3 April 1915; *yr s* of Prof. Alfred Edward Barnes, FRCP; *m* 1941, Joan Alice Katherine, *d* of Prof. Randolph Schwabe, RWS; two *d* (one *s* decd). *Educ:* Repton Sch.; The Slade Sch., Univ. of London. Diploma of Fine Art (Lond) 1936. Tour of Europe, studying the teaching of Art in Schools, 1937-38; Secondary Sch. teaching (refused for mil. service), 1938-44; joined Staff of Glasgow Sch. of Art, 1944; Dep. Dir and Registrar, 1947-64. Dir, Edinburgh Tapestry Co., Dovecot Studios, 1953-; Founder Mem., Scottish Craft Centre (Chm., 1972-). Member: Senate, Glasgow Univ., 1973-; CNAA, 1974-. Mem., Scottish Arts Council, 1972-. Hon. MA Glasgow, 1966. *Recreation:* gardening. *Address:* Castleton House, Lochgilphead, Argyll PA31 8RU. *T:* Lochgilphead 2535. *Club:* Glasgow Art.

BARNES, James Edwin; Under-Secretary, Small Firms and Regional Development Grants, Department of Industry, 1974-75; retired; *b* 23 Nov. 1917; *s* of James Barnes and Kate (née Davies); *m* 1943, Gloria Parkinson; two *s* one *d*. *Educ:* King Edward VI Sch., Nuneaton. Joined Civil Service as Executive Officer, War Office, 1936; Higher Executive Officer, Min. of Supply, 1942; Sen. Exec. Officer 1945, Principal, 1946, Asst Sec. 1952; Under-Secretary: Min. of Aviation, 1964-66; DTI, 1966-70; DTI, 1970-74. Coronation Medal, 1953. *Address:* 12 Encombe, Sandgate, Folkestone, Kent CT20 3DE. *T:* Folkestone 38142.

BARNES, James Frederick; Director General Research (C), Ministry of Defence (Procurement Executive), since 1974; *b* 8 March 1932; *s* of Wilfred and Doris M. Barnes; *m* 1957, Dorothy Jean Drew; one *s* two *d*. *Educ:* Taunton's Sch. Southampton; Queen's Coll., Oxford. BA 1953, MA 1957; CEng, MIMechE, FRAeS. Bristol Aeroplane Co. (Engine Div.), 1953; Min. of Supply, Nat. Gas Turbine Estabt: Sci. Officer 1955; Sen. Sci. Off. 1957; Principal Sci. Off. 1962; Sen. Principal Sci. Off. (Individual Merit) 1965; Min. of Aviation Supply, Asst Dir, Engine R&D, 1970; seconded to HM Diplomatic Service, Counsellor (Science and Technology), British Embassy, Washington, 1972; Under-Sec., MoD, 1974. James Clayton Fund Prize, IMechE, 1964. *Publications:* contrib. books and learned jls on mech. engrg, esp. gas turbine technology, heat transfer and stress analysis. *Recreation:* making things. *Address:* 32 Empress Avenue, Farnborough, Hants. *T:* Farnborough (Hants) 44744.

BARNES, Sir James George, Kt 1976; MBE (mil.); JP; Mayor of Dunedin, New Zealand, since 1968; sharebroker, N. & E. S. Paterson Ltd, Dunedin; *b* Dunedin, NZ; *s* of Richard R. Barnes; *m* 1938, Elsie, *d* of James D. Clark; one *d*. *Educ:* King Edward

Technical High Sch. Served War, RNZAF 75 Sqdn, 1940-46 (POW, 1942-45). Mem., Dunedin City Council, 1947-53 and 1959- (Dep. Mayor 1951-53 and 1959-68); MP, 1951-57. Exec. Mem.: Otago Peninsula Trust; NZ Fedn for the Blind; Chm., Bd of Ocean Beach Domain. Past Pres., Otago Savings Bank. Chm. or Dir, Sch. Bds and Youth orgs. NZ mile champion, 1932; NZ Cross Country Champion, 1933; Manager NZ Empire Games Team, 1950; Asst Man., NZ Olympic Team, 1956; Past Pres., NZ AAA; Mem. Otago AAA; Mem. NZ Trotting Conf.; Past Pres., Forbury Park Trotting Club. *Recreations:* golf, trotting. *Address:* Mayor's Office, Dunedin, New Zealand; (home) 11 Cavell Street, Dunedin; 172 Rattray Street, Dunedin.

BARNES, Jefferson; *see* Barnes, Harry J.

BARNES, Sir John; *see* Barnes, Sir E. J. W.

BARNES, Prof. John Arundel, DSC 1944; Professor of Sociology, University of Cambridge, and Fellow of Churchill College, since 1969; *b* Reading, 9 Sept. 1918; *s* of T. D. and M. G. Barnes, Bath; *m* 1942, Helen Frances, *d* of Charles Bastable; three *s* one *d. Educ:* Christ's Hosp.; St John's Coll., Cambridge; Balliol Coll., Oxford. Fellow, St John's Coll., Cambridge, 1950-53; Simon Research Fellow, Manchester Univ., 1951-53; Reader in Anthropology, London Univ., 1954-56; Prof. of Anthropology, Sydney Univ., 1956-58; Prof. of Anthropology, Inst. of Advanced Studies, ANU, Canberra, 1958-69; Overseas Fellow, Churchill Coll., Cambridge, 1965-66. *Publications:* Marriage in a Changing Society, 1951; Politics in a Changing Society, 1954; Inquest on the Murngin, 1967; Sociology in Cambridge, 1970; Three Styles in the Study of Kinship, 1971; Social Networks, 1972; The Ethics of Inquiry in Social Science, 1977. *Address:* Churchill College, Cambridge CB3 0DS. *T:* Cambridge 61200.

BARNES, Dame Josephine; *see* Barnes, Dame A. J. M. T.

BARNES, Sir Kenneth, KCB 1977 (CB 1970); Permanent Secretary, Department of Employment, since 1976; *b* 26 Aug. 1922; *s* of Arthur and Doris Barnes, Accrington, Lancs; *m* 1948, Barbara Ainsworth; one *s* two *d. Educ:* Accrington Grammar Sch.; Balliol Coll., Oxford. Entered Ministry of Labour, 1948; Asst Sec., 1963; Under-Sec., Cabinet Office, 1966-68; Dep. Sec., Dept of Employment, 1968-75. *Address:* Hill House, 35 Pilgrim's Way, Reigate, Surrey. *T:* Reigate 45237. *Club:* United Oxford & Cambridge University.

BARNES, Kenneth James, CBE 1969 (MBE 1964); Head of Division, Industrial Co-operation, Trade Promotion and Regional Co-operation, Commission of the European Communities, since 1976; *b* 8 May 1930; *s* of Thomas Arthur Barnes and Ethel Maude Barnes; *m* 1953, Lesley Dawn Grummett Wright (*d* 1976); two *s* one *d . Educ:* Dover Coll.; St Catharine's Coll., Cambridge (Crabtree exhibnr; MA); London Univ. MBIM. Pilot Officer, RAF, 1949-50; Administrative Officer, HMOCS Eastern Nigeria, 1954-60; Asst Sec., Min. of Finance, Malawi, 1960-64, Sen. Asst Sec., 1965, Dep. Sec., 1966, Permanent Sec., 1967-71; Asst Sec., British Steel Corp., 1971-73; Principal Administrator, Directorate-Gen. for Development, EEC, 1973-75. *Recreations:* reading, esp. history, listening to music, mediaeval fortifications. *Address:* Commission of the European Communities, 200 rue de la Loi, B1049 Brussels, Belgium. *T:* (office) 735.00.40, ext. 5970; (home) 771.53.27. *Club:* Travellers'.

BARNES, Michael Cecil John; marketing consultant; *b* 22 Sept. 1932; *s* of late Major C. H. R. Barnes, OBE and of Katherine Louise (*née* Kennedy); *m* 1962, Anne Mason; one *s* one *d. Educ:* Malvern; Corpus Christi Coll., Oxford. MP (Lab) Brentford and Chiswick, 1966-Feb. 1974; an Opposition Spokesman on food and food prices, 1970-71; Chairman: Parly Labour Party Social Security Group, 1969-70; ASTMS Parly Cttee, 1970-71; Jt Hon. Sec., Labour Cttee for Europe, 1969-71; Mem., Public Accounts Cttee, 1967-74. Contested (Lab): Wycombe, 1964; Brentford and Isleworth, Feb. 1974. Member: Council of Management, War on Want, 1972-; Nat. Consumer Council, 1975-; Arts Council Trng Cttee, 1977-; Chairman: UK Adv. Cttee on EEC Action Against Poverty Programme, 1975-76; Notting Hill Social Council, 1976-; Organising Secretary: Gulbenkian Foundn Drama Trng Inquiry, 1974-75; Music Trng Inquiry, 1975-76; Sec., Nat. Council for Drama Trng, 1976-; Chm., Hounslow Arts Trust, 1974-; Trustee, Project Hand Trust, 1974-. *Recreations:* lawn tennis, walking, reading. *Address:* 45 Ladbroke Grove, W11. *T:* 01-727 2533.

BARNES, Peter Robert; Assistant Director of Public Prosecutions, since 1974; *b* 1 Feb. 1921; *s* of Robert Stanley Barnes and Marguerite (*née* Dunkels); *m* 1955, Pauline Belinda

Hannen; two *s* one *d. Educ:* Eton Coll.; Trinity Coll., Cambridge (BA). Called to Bar, Inner Temple, 1947. Dir. of Public Prosecutions: Legal Asst, 1951; Sen. Legal Asst, 1958; Asst Solicitor, 1970. *Recreations:* golf, tennis, ski-ing, conjuring. *Address:* Woodhurst, Hydestile, Godalming, Surrey GU8 4AY. *T:* Godalming 5743. *Club:* Boodle's.

BARNES, Dr Robert Sandford; Principal, Queen Elizabeth College, London University, since April 1978; *b* 8 July 1924; *s* of William Edward Barnes and Ada Elsie Barnes (*née* Sutherst); *m* 1952, Julia Frances Marriott Grant; one *s* three *d. Educ:* Univ. of Manchester. BSc 1948, MSc 1959, DSc 1962. Radar Research, Admiralty Signals Estab., Witley, Surrey, 1944-47; AERE, Harwell: Metallurgical Research, 1948-62; Head of Irradiation Branch, 1962-65; Vis. Scientist, The Science Center, N Amer. Aviation Co., Calif, 1965; Head of Metallurgy Div., AERE, Harwell, 1966-68; Dep. Dir, BISRA, 1968-69; Dir, BISRA, 1969-70; Dir R&D, BSC, 1970-75; Chief Scientist, BSC, 1975-78. Chm., Ruthner Continuous Crop Systems Ltd, 1976. Member: CBI Res. and Technol. Cttee, 1968-75; Adv. Council on R&D for Iron and Steel, 1970-75; European Industrial Res. Management Assoc., 1970 (Vice-Pres., 1974); Parly and Scientific Cttee, 1970; Council, Welding Inst., 1970-75; Council, Metals Soc., 1974 (Chm., Coordinating Cttee, 1976); Materials Science and Technology Cttee, SRC, 1975; Chm., European Nuclear Steel-making Club, 1973; UK Representative: Commn de la Recherche Technique Sidérurgique, 1972; Conseil d'Association Européenne pour la Promotion de la Recherche Technique en Sidérurgie, 1972. Lectures: Hatfield Meml, Iron and Steel Inst., 1973; John Player, IMechE, 1976. Hon. Mem. Council, Iron and Steel Inst., 1969-73. Governor, Sheffield Polytechnic, 1968-72; Mem., Court of Univ. of Surrey, 1968. Rosenhain Medallist, Inst. of Metals, 1964. FInstP 1961, FIM 1965 (Mem. Council, 1970). *Publications:* chapters in several specialist books of science; scientific papers in various learned jls. *Recreations:* family yachting, gardening. *Address:* Pigeon Forge, Daneshill, The Hockering, Woking, Surrey. *T:* Woking 61529. *Club:* Athenæum.

BARNES, Roland, CBE 1970; BSc, MB, ChB, FRCS, FRCSE, FRCSGlas; Professor of Orthopaedic Surgery, University of Glasgow, 1959-72, now Professor Emeritus; *b* 21 May 1907; *y s* of Benjamin Barnes and Mary Ann Bridge, Accrington, Lancs.; *m* 1938, Mary Mills Buckley; one *s* two *d. Educ:* University of Manchester. BSc 1927; MB, ChB 1930; Medical and Surgical Clinical prizes. Usual resident appointments; Resident Surgical Officer, Manchester Royal Infirmary, 1934-35; Dickinson Travelling Scholar, Univ. of Manchester, 1935-36; visited orthopaedic clinics in USA; Fellow, Hospital for Ruptured and Crippled, New York. Chief Asst to Sir Harry Platt, Bt, Orthopaedic Department, Royal Infirmary, Manchester, 1937-39; Surgeon in Charge of Orthopædic and Peripheral Nerve Injury Centre, EMS Hospital, Winwick, Lancs, 1940-43. Past Pres., British Orthopædic Assoc.; Hon. Mem. French, Finnish, German and S African Orthopædic Assocs; Corresp. Mem. Amer. Orthopædic Assoc. *Publications:* papers on injuries of the peripheral nerves and spine, fractures of neck of femur, and on tumours of bone. *Recreation:* gardening. *Address:* 35 Boclair Road, Bearsden, Glasgow. *T:* 041-942 2699.

BARNES, Sir William Lethbridge G.; *see* Gorell Barnes.

BARNES, Prof. Winston Herbert Frederick, MA (Oxon); Professor Emeritus, Universities of Manchester and Liverpool; *b* 30 May 1909; *er s* of Frederick Charles and Martha Lilley Barnes; *m* 1938, Sarah, *d* of late Thomas David Davies; two *d. Educ:* Manchester Grammar Sch.; Corpus Christi Coll., Oxford (Hugh Oldham Scholar, Haigh Scholar). 1st Cl., Classical Hon. Mods. 1930; 1st Cl., Lit. Hum. 1932; John Locke Scholar in Mental Philosophy, Oxford, 1932; Sen. Demy, Magdalen Coll., Oxford, 1933-34. Asst Lecturer in Philosophy, 1936-39; Lecturer 1939-41, Univ. of Liverpool; served in RAFVR, 1941-42; Temporary Principal, Ministry of Supply, 1942-45; Prof. of Philosophy, Univ. of Durham (Durham Colls) 1945-59; Prof. of Moral Philosophy, Univ. of Edinburgh, 1959-63, Gifford Lectr in Natural Theology, 1968-69, 1969-70; Vice-Chancellor, Univ. of Liverpool, 1963-69; Vis. Prof. of Philosophy, Univ. of Auckland, NZ, 1970; Sir Samuel Hall Prof. of Philosophy, Manchester Univ., 1970-73. Pres., Mind Assoc., 1948. Mem. Planning Bd, Independent Univ., 1970-73; Mem. Council, University Coll. at Buckingham, 1973-. Hon. DCL Durham, 1964. *Publications:* The Philosophical Predicament, 1950; contributions to Mind, Philosophy, Aristotelian Society Proceedings. *Recreations:* walking, swimming. *Address:* 7 Great Stuart Street, Edinburgh EH3 7TP. *T:* 031-226 3158.

BARNETSON, family name of **Baron Barnetson.**

BARNETSON, Baron *cr* 1975 (Life Peer), of Crowborough, E Sussex; **William Denholm Barnetson,** Kt 1972; Chairman and Managing Director, United Newspapers Ltd, since 1966; Chairman: Reuters Ltd, since 1968; The Observer, since 1976; Bradbury Agnew and Co., since 1969; *b* 21 March 1917; *e s of* late William Barnetson and Ella Moir, Edinburgh; *m* 1940, Joan Fairley, *d of* late W. F. Davidson; one *s* three *d*. *Educ:* Royal High Sch., Edinburgh; Edinburgh Univ. (MA). Served War of 1939-45 in AA Comd (Battery Comdr); detached for special duty on reorganisation of newspaper and book publishing in British Zone of Germany, and in launching Die Welt, 1944-47; successively Leader Writer, Editor and Gen. Man., Edinburgh Evening News, 1948-61; Director: Provincial Newspapers Ltd, 1958- and of parent co., 1962-; Drayton Consolidated Trust; Hill Samuel; Argus Press; Yorkshire Post Newspapers; British Electric Traction Co. (Dep. Chm., 1976-); Earls Court and Olympia; Dep. Chm., Monotype Corp., 1971-73. Extra-mural Lectr, Edinburgh Univ., 1949-57; regular contrib. to BBC radio and TV in Scotland, 1950-61. Pres., Edinburgh Press Club, 1957-59; Dir, Edinburgh Chamber of Commerce, 1957-60; Mem., Press Council, 1958-61, 1968-73; Chm., Nat. Council for Trng of Journalists, 1959-60; Vice-Pres., Scottish Daily Newspaper Soc., 1960-61; Dir, Press Assoc., 1963-70 (Chm., Centenary Year, 1967-68); Chm., Council, Commonwealth Press Union, 1972-77 (UK delegate Quinquennial Conf., 1965, 1970, 1974; Chm., Public Relations Cttee, 1968-69); Vice-Pres., Royal Commonwealth Soc.; Chm., Scottish Internat. Information Cttee, 1971-77; Mem., UK Cttee of Internat. Press Inst., 1964-; Mem. Council, Newspaper Soc., 1967-74; Pres., Press Club, 1973-76; Mem., Punch Table, 1969-; Pres., Periodical Publishers Assoc., 1974-76; Appeals Chm., Newspaper Press Fund, 1974; Pres., Advertising Assoc., 1976-. Chm., 1971-72, Pres., 1975-, Newsvendors' Benevolent Instn; Vice-Pres., Cartoonists Club of GB, 1973-; Mem. Council, Open Univ., 1973-76 (Chm., Marketing Adv. Cttee, 1973-76); Dir, English Nat. Opera, 1975- (Chm., Appeals Cttee, 1975-); Member: Presidential Council, Canada-UK Chamber of Commerce, 1975-; Presidential Council, Italian Chamber of Commerce for GB, 1976-; Council, Queen's Silver Jubilee Appeal, 1976-; Trustee: The Times Trust, 1973-; Visnews, 1968-; Catherine Pakenham Meml Award, 1972-. OStJ. Kt Grand Cross, Order of Merit, Italy, 1973. *Recreations:* books, gardening. *Address:* (business) 23-27 Tudor Street, EC4. *T:* 01-583 9199; (home) Broom, Chillies Lane, Crowborough, East Sussex. *T:* Crowborough 5748. *Clubs:* Beefsteak, Press.

BARNETSON, Maj.-Gen. James Craw, CB 1965; OBE 1945; Director of Medical Services, BAOR, December 1964-66, retired; *b* 26 July 1907; *s of* Dr R. B. Barnetson; *m* 1935, Sylvia Joan Milner Moore; three *s*. *Educ:* Edinburgh Academy; Edinburgh Univ. (MB, ChB). Staff Coll., Camberley, 1942; ADMS, AFHQ, 1942-43; ADMS, 6th Armd Div., 1943-46, ADMS, Scot. Comd, 1946-47; Asst DGAMS, War Office, 1947-50; Joint Staff Coll., Latimer, 1950; ADMS, 11th Armd Div., 1951; ADMS, Plans, SHAPE, 1951-53; OC Commonwealth Mil. Hosp., Japan, 1953-54; ADMS, GHQ, E Africa, 1954-57; ADMS, 6 Armd Div., 1958-59; Comdt Field Trg Centre, HQ, AER, RAMC, 1959-60; DDMS, Northern Comd, 1960-61; Dep. DGAMS, 1961-64. QHP 1961-66. Col Comdt, RAMC, 1968-72. OStJ 1965. *Recreations:* golf and fishing. *Address:* The Old Cottage, Wardley Green, Milland, West Sussex. *T:* Milland 371.

BARNETT, Sir Ben L(ewis), KBE 1952; CB 1948; MC 1918; MA Cantab; *b* London 20 July 1894; *s of* Isaac and Eva Barnett. *Educ:* Christ's Hospital; Trinity Coll., Cambridge. Entered GPO, 1920; Principal, 1930; Telecoms Controller, Scotland, 1935; Asst Sec. (HQ), 1939; Reg. Dir, Home Counties Region, 1945; Dir Inland Telecommunications, 1946; Dep. Dir-Gen., GPO, 1949-56. Chm., Commonwealth Telecommunications Board, 1956-62. Director: Pye Ltd; Telephone Manufacturing Co. Ltd; Unidare Ltd (Dublin); Adviser to: ATV Ltd; Western Union International, 1958-69. Served European War, 1914-18. Lieut RE (TA) (despatches twice, MC). OStJ 1959. Hon. FIEE, 1973. *Address:* c/o Barclays Bank Ltd, 110 Bishopsgate, EC2.

BARNETT, Correlli (Douglas); author; Keeper of the Archives, and a Fellow, Churchill College, Cambridge, since 1977; *b* 28 June 1927; *s of* D. A. Barnett; *m* 1950, Ruth Murby; two *d*. *Educ:* Trinity Sch., Croydon; Exeter Coll., Oxford. Second class hons, Mod. Hist. with Mil. Hist. and the Theory of War as a special subject; MA 1954. Intell. Corps, 1945-48. North Thames Gas Bd, 1952-57; Public Relations, 1957-63. Chm. Literature Panel, and Mem. Exec. Cttee, E Arts Assoc.; Pres., East Anglian Writers; Mem. Organising Cttee, Inter-Univ. Seminar on Armed Forces and Society; Mem. Council, RUSI, 1973. Leverhulme Res. Fellowship, 1976. FRSL. *Publications:* The Hump Organisation, 1957; The Channel Tunnel (with Humphrey Slater), 1958; The Desert Generals, 1960; The Swordbearers,

1963; Britain and Her Army, 1970 (RSL award, 1971); The Collapse of British Power, 1972; Marlborough, 1974; Bonaparte, 1978; (historical consultant and writer to) BBC Television series: The Great War, 1963-64; The Lost Peace, 1965-66; The Commanders, 1972-73; reviews Mil. Hist. for The Sunday Telegraph; contrib. to: Jl of Contemp. Hist.; Horizon Magazine (USA); The Promise of Greatness (a symposium on the Great War), 1968; Governing Elites (a symposium), 1969; Decisive Battles of the Twentieth Century, 1976; The War Lords, 1976. *Recreations:* gardening, interior decorating, idling, eating, mole-hunting. *Address:* Catbridge House, East Carleton, Norwich. *T:* Mulbarton 410. *Club:* Savage.

BARNETT, Air Chief Marshal Sir Denis Hensley Fulton, GCB 1964 (KCB 1957; CB 1956); CBE 1945; DFC 1940; RAF, retired; Member for Weapons Research and Development, Atomic Energy Authority, 1965-72; *b* 11 Feb. 1906; *y s of* late Sir Louis Edward Barnett; *m* 1939, Pamela, *y d of* late Sir Allan John Grant; one *s* two *d*. *Educ:* Christ's Coll., NZ; Clare Coll., Cambridge (BA 1929, MA 1935). Perm. Commn, RAF, 1929; Flt Lieut, 1934; Sqdn Ldr 1938; comd 84 Sqdn, Shaibah, 1938. Served War of 1939-45; Sqdn Comdr, Stn Comdr and G/C Ops, Bomber Comd, 1939-44; Dep. Dir Bomber Ops, Air Min., 1944; Dep. SASO at HQ Bomber Comd, 1945; Actg Wing Cdr, 1940; Gp Capt., 1941; Air Cdre, 1945; Dir of Ops at Air Min., 1945-46; Air Staff, India, 1946-47; Jt Services Staff Coll., 1948; Comdt Central Bomber Estabt, 1949; Dir of Ops Air Min., 1950-52; idc, 1952; Representative of UK Chiefs of Staff at HQ, UN Command, Tokyo, 1952-54; AOC, No. 205 Group, Middle East Air Force, 1954-56; Commandant, RAF Staff Coll., Bracknell, 1956; Commander Allied Air Task Force, Near East, 1956; Air Secretary, Air Ministry, 1957-59; AOC-in-C, RAF Transport Command, 1959-62; Air Officer Commanding-in-Chief, RAF Near East; Commander, British Forces Cyprus, and Administrator of the Sovereign Base Areas, 1962-64; Subst. Air Commodore, 1950; Air Vice-Marshal, 1953; Air Marshal, 1959; Air Chief Marshal, 1962. Comdr, US Legion of Merit, 1954; French Légion d'Honneur (Commandeur) and Croix de Guerre, 1958. *Recreations:* fishing, shooting. *Address:* River House, Rushall, Pewsey, Wilts SN9 6EN.

BARNETT, Guy; see Barnett, N. G.

BARNETT, Dame Henrietta; see Barnett, Dame M. H.

BARNETT, Rt. Hon. Joel, PC 1975; JP; MP (Lab) Heywood and Royton Division of Lancashire, since 1964; Chief Secretary to the Treasury, since 1974 (as a Member of the Cabinet, from 1977); *b* 14 Oct. 1923; *s of* Louis and Ettie Barnett, both of Manchester; *m* 1949, Lillian Goldstone; one *d*. *Educ:* Derby Street Jewish Sch.; Manchester Central High Sch. Certified accountant, retd 1974; formerly in private practice in Manchester. Served RASC and British Military Govt in Germany. Mem. of Prestwich, Lancs, Borough Council, 1956-59; JP Lancs 1960; Hon. Treas. Manchester Fabian Society, 1953-65. Contested (Lab) Runcorn Div. of Cheshire, Oct. 1959. Member: Public Accounts Cttee, 1965-71; Public Expenditure Cttee, 1971-74; Select Cttee on Tax Credits, 1973-74; Chm. Parly Labour Party Economic and Finance Group, 1967-70 and 1972-74 (Vice-Chm., 1966-67); Opposition Spokesman on Treasury matters, 1970-74. *Recreations:* walking, conversation and reading; good food. *Address:* Flat 92, 24 John Islip Street, SW1; 10 Park Lane, Whitefield, Lancs.

BARNETT, Joseph Anthony, OBE 1975; Controller, English Teaching Division, British Council, since 1975; *b* 19 Dec. 1931; *s* of Joseph Edward Barnett and Helen Johnson; *m* 1960, Carolina Johnson Rice; one *s* one *d*. *Educ:* St Albans Sch.; Pembroke Coll., Cambridge (BA (Hons) English and Psychology); Edinburgh Univ. (Diploma in Applied Linguistics). Served Army, 1950-51 (2nd Lieut). Teaching, Aylesford House, St Albans, 1954-55; Unilever Ltd, 1955-58; apptd British Council, 1958; Asst Educn Officer, Dacca, Pakistan, 1958; trng at Sch. of Applied Linguistics, Edinburgh Univ., 1960; Educn Officer, Dacca, 1961; seconded to Inst. of Educn, London Univ., 1963; Head, English Language Teaching Inst., London, 1964; Dir of Studies, Regional Inst. of English, Bangalore, India, 1968; Representative, Ethiopia, 1971. *Publications:* (jtly) Getting on in English, 1960; Success with English (language laboratory materials), Books 1-3, 1966-69. *Recreation:* sport (tennis, cricket, riding). *Address:* The Thatch, Stebbing Green, Dunmow, Essex. *T:* Stebbing 352.

BARNETT, Kenneth Thomas; a Deputy Secretary, Department of the Environment, since 1976; *b* 12 Jan. 1921; *yr s of* late Frederick Charles Barnett and Ethel Barnett (*née* Powell); *m* 1943, Emily May Lovering; one *d*. *Educ:* Howard Gardens High Sch., Cardiff. Entered Civil Service (Min. of Transport), 1937;

Sea Transport Office, Port Said, 1951-54; Asst Sec., 1965; Under-Sec., Cabinet Office (on secondment), 1971-73; Under-Sec., DoE, 1970-76. *Recreations:* gardening, watching Rugby football. *Address:* The Stone House, Frith End, Bordon, Hants. *T:* Bordon 2856.

BARNETT, Dame (Mary) Henrietta, DBE 1958 (CBE 1956; OBE 1950); Director of the Women's Royal Air Force, 1956-60; *d* of Col George Henry Barnett, 60th Rifles, Glympton Park, Woodstock, Oxon. *Educ:* Heathfield, Ascot. Joined Women's Auxiliary Air Force in 1939. *Address:* Hoggrove House, Park Street, Woodstock, Oxon. *T:* Woodstock 811502.

BARNETT, Rev. Dr Maurice; Minister, Westminster Central Hall, London, since 1964; *b* Coppenhall, Crewe, 21 March 1917; *s* of Edward Percy and Beatrice Barnett; *m* 1943, Margaret Brown, Chester; one *s. Educ:* Crewe Grammar Sch.; Hartley Victoria Coll., The University, Manchester. BA Manchester, 1939, BD 1941, MA 1946; PhD Sheffield, 1960. Minister, East Ham Central Hall, 1941-43; Eden Grove Methodist Church, Bristol, 1943-46; Tutor, Cliff Coll., Derbyshire, 1946-47; Minister, Eastbrook Hall, Bradford, 1947-64. Hon. FLCM 1973. *Publications:* The Living Flame, 1953; This Concerns You, 1954; What Next?, 1954; New Life Now, 1976; The Divine Invasion, 1976; articles, etc. *Recreations:* organ and piano. *Address:* Westminster Central Hall, SW1. *T:* 01-930 1801.

BARNETT, (Nicolas) Guy; MP (Lab) Greenwich, since July 1971; Parliamentary Under-Secretary of State, Department of the Environment, since 1976; *b* 23 Aug. 1928; *s* of late B. G. Barnett; *m* 1967, Daphne Anne, *d* of Geoffrey William Hortin, JP; one *s* one *d. Educ:* Highgate; St Edmund Hall, Oxford. Teacher: Queen Elizabeth Gram. Sch., 1953-59; Friends Sch., Kamusinga, Kenya, 1960-61. Famine Relief Sec., Christian Council of Kenya, 1962; on staff VSO, 1966-69; Chief Educn Officer, Commonwealth Inst., 1969-71. Contested (Lab) NR Yorks (Scarborough and Whitby Div.), 1959; MP (Lab) S Dorset Div., Nov. 1962-Sept. 1964. PPS to Minister for Local Govt and Planning, 1974-75; Member: Parly Select Cttee on Race Relations and Immigration, 1972-74; Public Accts Cttee, 1975. Mem., European Parlt, 1975-76. Parly Adviser, Soc. of Civil Servants, 1973-76. Mem., Gen. Adv. Council of BBC, 1973-76; Trustee, Nat. Maritime Museum, 1974-76. *Publication:* By the Lake, 1964. *Recreations:* music, walking. *Address:* 32 Westcombe Park Road, SE3. *Club:* Royal Commonwealth Society.

BARNETT, Sir Oliver (Charles), Kt 1968; CBE 1954 (OBE 1946); QC 1956; *b* 7 Feb. 1907; *er s* of Charles Frederick Robert Barnett, 2nd Lieut Gloucestershire Regt (TA) (killed in action, 1915), and late Cicely Frances Barnett (*née* Cornish); *m* 1945, Joan, *o surv c* of Capt. W. H. Eve, 13th Hussars (killed in action, 1917), *o s* of late Rt Hon. Sir Harry Trelawney Eve, a Judge of the High Court. *Educ:* Eton. Called to Bar, Middle Temple, 1928; Bencher, Middle Temple, 1964, Oxford Circuit; Central Criminal Court Sessions; Dep. Chm., Somerset QS, 1967-71. Dir of Public Prosecutions Office, 1931; Legal Asst, Judge Advocate General's Office, 1934; Second Deputy Judge Advocate, 1937; First Deputy Judge Advocate, 1938; RAF, 1939-47 (OBE); Wing Comdr (RAFVR); Asst Judge Advocate Gen. (RAF), 1942-47; Asst Judge Advocate Gen. (Army and RAF), 1947-54; Deputy Judge Advocate Gen. (Army and RAF) BAOR, BTA and 2nd TAF, 1953-54; Vice Judge Advocate Gen., 1955-62; Judge Advocate Gen., 1963-68. *Address:* Zinch Cottage, Stogumber, near Taunton, Somerset. *T:* Stogumber 264. *Clubs:* Brooks's, Pratt's.

BARNETT, Richard David, CBE 1974; MA, DLitt; FBA 1962; FSA; *b* Acton, 23 Jan. 1909; *o s* of late Lionel David Barnett, CB; *m* 1948, Barbara Joan, *d* of Ralph Pinto; two *s* one *d. Educ:* St Paul's Sch., London; Corpus Christi Coll., Cambridge. Student of British Sch. of Archaeology at Athens, 1930-32; Asst Keeper, Dept of Egyptian and Assyrian Antiquities, British Museum, 1932; Dep. Keeper, 1953; Keeper, Dept of Western Asiatic Antiquities, 1955-74. Vis. Prof., Hebrew Univ., Jerusalem, 1974-75. Sec., British Sch. of Archaeology at Athens, 1933-35; Pres. Jewish Historical Society of England, 1959-61. Corr. Mem., Greek Archaeological Soc.; Ordinary Fellow, German Archaeological Inst., 1961. Served War of 1939-45; Admiralty 1939-40; Foreign Office, 1940-42; Intelligence Officer, RAF, 1942-46, Egypt, Syria, Libya, Turkey. *Publications:* (ed) Treasures of a London Temple, 1951; (with Sir A. Woolley) British Museum Excavations at Carchemish, Vol. III, 1952; Catalogue of Nimrud Ivories in the British Museum, 1957, 2nd edn 1975; (trans.) The Jewish sect of Qumran and the Essenes (by J. Dupont-Sommer), 1954; Assyrian Palace Reliefs, 1960; (with M. Falkner) The Sculptures of Tiglath-pileser III, 1962; Illustrations of Old Testament

History, 1966, 2nd edn 1977; (ed) The Sephardi Heritage, 1971; (ed) Catalogue of the Jewish Museum, London, 1974; (with Amleto Lorenzini) Assyrian Sculpture, 1976; The Sculptures of Ashurbanipal, 1976; articles on archæology and Anglo-Jewish history in various learned jls. *Address:* 14 Eldon Grove, NW3 5PT. *T:* 01-794 2066.

BARNEWALL, family name of **Baron Trimlestown.**

BARNEWALL, Sir Reginald Robert, 13th Bt, *cr* 1622; cattle breeder and orchardist at Mount Tamborine; *b* 1 Oct 1924; *o s* of Sir Reginald J. Barnewall, 12th Bt and of Jessie Ellen, *d* of John Fry; *S* father 1961; *m* 1st, 1946, Elsie Muriel (*d* 1962), *d* of Thomas Matthews-Frederick, Brisbane; three *d* (one *s* decd); 2nd, 1962, Maureen Ellen, *d* of William Joseph Daly, South Caulfield, Vic; one *s. Educ:* Xavier Coll., Melbourne. Served War of 1939-45, overseas with Australian Imperial Forces. Served with Citizen Military Forces Unit, Royal Australian Armoured Corps, 1948-56. Managing Dir, Southern Airlines Ltd of Melbourne, 1953-58; Operation Manager, Polynesian Airlines, Apia, Western Samoa, 1958-62; Managing Dir, Orchid Beach (Fraser Island) Pty Ltd, 1962-71; Dir, Island Airways Pty Ltd, Pialba, Qld, 1964-68; owner and operator, Coastal-Air Co. (Qld), 1971-76; Dir and Vice-Chm., J. Roy Stevens Pty Ltd, to 1975. *Heir: s* Peter Joseph Barnewall, *b* 26 Oct. 1963. *Address:* Mount Tamborine, Queensland 4272, Australia. *Clubs:* United Service (Brisbane); RSL (Surfers Paradise).

BARNSLEY, Alan Gabriel; see Fielding, Gabriel.

BARNSLEY, Thomas Edward, OBE 1975; FCA; a Managing Director, Tube Investments Ltd, since 1974; *b* 10 Sept. 1919; *s* of Alfred E. Barnsley and Ada F. Nightingale; *m* 1947, Margaret Gwyneth Llewellin; one *s* one *d. Educ:* Wednesbury Boys' High Sch. ACMA. Friends' Ambulance Unit, 1940-45. Price Waterhouse Peat & Co., South America, 1948-49; Asst Sec., 1958-62, Group Financial Controller, 1962-65, Tube Investments Ltd; Chm. and Man. Dir, Raleigh Industries Ltd, 1968-74. Chm., Nat. Industrial Cttee, Nat. Savings Movement, 1975-. *Recreations:* gardening, cycling. *Address:* Old Rectory, Cossington, near Leicester LE7 8UU. *T:* Sileby 2623.

BARNSLEY, (William) Edward, CBE 1945; Designer and maker of furniture and building woodwork; Adviser in woodwork design, Loughborough Training College, 1938-65; Consultant in Furniture Design to Rural Industries Bureau, 1945-60; *b* 1900; *s* of Sidney Howard Barnsley, Sapperton, Cirencester; *m* 1925, Tatiana, *d* of late Dr Harry Kellgren; one *s* one *d. Educ:* Bedales. *Address:* Froxfield, Petersfield, Hants. *T:* Hawkley 233.

BARNSTAPLE, Archdeacon of; see Herniman, Ven. R. G.

BARNWELL, Col Ralph Ernest, CBE 1943; retired; *b* 20 Jan. 1895; *s* of late E. F. Barnwell, Rugby; *m* 1927, Lilian Katharine Oliphant, *d* of late C. R. Bradburne, Official Solicitor to the Supreme Court of Judicature; one *d* (one *s* decd). *Educ:* Rugby Sch. HAC 1914; 2nd Lieut Royal Warwicks Regt 1914; served in France in European War, 1914-18 (despatches); Capt. 1923; Adjutant, 7th Bn Royal Warwicks Regt, 1924-27; Staff Coll., Camberley, 1928-29; Staff Capt., War Office, 1930-32; GSO Weapon Training, Eastern Command, 1932-34; Bt Major 1935; Major, 1938; DAAG Lahore District, 1937-39; Lieut-Col 1939; DAA and QMG (France), 1939; AQMG 2nd Corps (France), 1940; Asst Adjutant-Gen., War Office, 1940-45; Col (temp.) 1941; retd pay 1945; Commandant, Duke of York's Royal Military Sch., 1945-53. *Recreation:* painting. *Address:* Woodrow House, Fifehead Neville, Sturminster Newton, Dorset. *T:* Hazelbury Bryan 297. *Club:* Army and Navy.

BARODA, Maharaja of; see Gaekwad, Lt-Col F. P.

BARON, Alexander; Writer; *b* 4 Dec. 1917; *s* of Barnet Baron and Fanny Levinson; *m* 1960, Delores Salzedo; one *s. Educ:* Hackney Downs Sch., London. Asst Editor, The Tribune, 1938-39. Served War of 1939-45, Army. Editor, New Theatre, 1946-49. *Publications: novels:* From the City, From the Plough, 1948; There's No Home, 1950; Rosie Hogarth, 1951; With Hope, Farewell, 1952; The Human Kind, 1953; The Golden Princess, 1954; Queen of the East, 1956; Seeing Life, 1958; The Lowlife, 1963; Strip Jack Naked, 1966; King Dido, 1969; The In-Between Time, 1971; Gentle Folk, 1976; also film scripts and television plays. *Address:* 30 Cranbourne Gardens, NW11. *T:* 01-455 8352. *Club:* PEN.

BARON, Colin; Director General, Weapons Research, Ministry of Defence, since 1976; *b* 20 May 1921; *s* of John Henry Baron and Dorothy May (*née* Crumpler); *m* 1961, Anita Veronica Hale; one *s* one *d* by former marriage. *Educ:* Carlton Grammar

Sch., Bradford; Univ. of Leeds (BSc Hons 1941, MSc 1947). Scientific Civil Service, 1941-; Royal Radar Estabt, Malvern: radar trials and res., 1941-57; weapon systems assessment, 1957-66; RAE, Farnborough: Head, Weapons Res. Gp, 1966-70; Head, Avionics Dept, 1970-74; Head, Flt Systems Dept, 1974-76. *Publications:* contribs to Jl IEE and Jl Applied Physics. *Recreations:* gardening, badminton, economics. *Address:* Tanglewood, Vicarage Lane, The Bourne, Farnham, Surrey. *T:* Farnham 21433. *Club:* Civil Service.

BARON, Cyril Faudel Joseph, MRCS, LRCP; Barrister-at-law; HM Coroner for County of Greater London (Western District), 1965-68 (Surrey, 1939-64); *b* 22 Jan. 1903; *s* of John and Lily Baron; *m* 1933, Kathleen Julia, *d* of Henry and Hilda Jacob; one *d. Educ:* Owen's Sch.; University Coll., London; St Bartholomew's Hospital (Wix Prize, 1923), MRCS, LRCP, 1924; Bar Final (1st Class Criminal Law), 1926. Practised medicine, 1924-36; called to Bar Middle Temple, 1936; practised at Bar (Common Law) from 1936. Pres., Coroners' Soc. of England and Wales; Vice-Pres., Medico-legal Soc.; Hon. Sec., Association of Whole-time Coroners. *Publications:* various articles on medico-legal subjects in learned journals. *Recreations:* tennis, swimming, foreign travel. *Address:* The Spinney, More Lane, Esher, Surrey. *T:* Esher 64240.

BARR, Alfred Hamilton, jun.; Counsellor to the Trustees, Museum of Modern Art, New York; *b* Detroit, Mich, 28 Jan. 1902; *s* of Alfred Hamilton Barr and Annie Elizabeth Wilson; *m* 1930, Margaret Scolari-Fitzmaurice, Rome, Italy; one *d. Educ:* Princeton Univ. AB 1922, AM 1923 (University Fellow, 1922-23); Thayer Fellow, 1924-25. PhD 1946, Harvard; Doctor of Letters (hc), Princeton Univ., 1949; PhD (hc), Univ. of Bonn, 1958; DFA (hc): Univ. of Buffalo, 1962; Adelphi Coll., 1963; Yale, 1967; Columbia Univ., 1969. Instructor, Vassar Coll., Dept of Art, 1923-24; Asst, Dept of Fine Arts, Harvard, 1924-25; Instr, Dept Art and Archaeology, Princeton, 1925-26; Assoc. Prof., Art Dept, Wellesley, 1926-29; Museum of Modern Art, NY: Dir, 1929-43; Vice-Pres. of Bd, 1939-43; Trustee, 1939-; Dir, Research in Painting and Sculpture, 1944-46; Dir of Museum Collections, 1947-67. Mary Flexner Lectureship, Bryn Mawr Coll., 1946; Overseer, Harvard Coll., 1964-70. Member: Adv. Council, Dept of Art and Archaeology, Princeton, 1946-, Columbia Univ., 1964-; Vis. Cttee on Fine Arts, Fogg Museum, Harvard, 1958-70; Pres., Foundation for Arts, Religion and Culture, 1962-65, Mem. Bd of Dirs, 1965-. Special Merit Award for Notable Creative Achievement, Brandeis Univ., 1964; Award of Merit, AIA, 1964; NY State Award, 1968; Nat. Inst. of Arts and Letters Award for Distinguished Service to the Arts, 1968; Art Dealers' Assoc. of Amer. Award, 1972; Skowhegan Gertrude Vanderbilt Whitney Award, 1974; European Art Dealers' Assoc. Award, 1974. Cross of Chevalier, Légion d'Honneur, 1959; Grand Cross, Order of Merit, German Federal Republic, 1959. *Publications:* Author or Editor of: Cézanne, Gauguin, Seurat, van Gogh, 1929; Modern German Painting and Sculpture, 1931; Henri-Matisse, 1931; Edward Hopper, 1933; The Lillie P. Bliss Collection, 1934; Modern Works of Art, 1934; Vincent van Gogh, 1935; Cubism and Abstract Art, 1936; Fantastic Art, Dada and Surrealism, 1936; Trois siècles d'art aux Etats-Unis, Paris, 1938; Art in our Time, 1939; Picasso: Forty Years of his Art, 1939; Italian Masters, 1940; What is Modern Painting?, 1943; Picasso: Fifty Years of his Art, 1946; (with Holger Cahill) Art in America: A Complete Survey, 1936; Painting and Sculpture in the Museum of Modern Art, 1948; Matisse: His Art and His Public, 1951; Masters of Modern Art, 1954; Editor: American Painter series, Penguin Books, London, 1944-45; Picasso 75th Anniversary Exhibition, Museum of Modern Art, NY, 1957; Painting and Sculpture in the Museum of Modern Art, New York, 1975; articles on art, films, architecture in British, Russian, French, German and American periodicals, notably Cézanne d'après les lettres de Marion à Morstatt (Gazette des Beaux-Arts), Jan. 1937. *Recreations:* music, ornithology. *Address:* Museum of Modern Art, 11 West 53 Street, New York, USA; (home) 49 East 96 Street, New York, USA. *TA:* Modernart, New York. *T:* Atwater 9-3936.

BARR, A. W. Cleeve, CBE 1972; FRIBA; FIOB; Managing Director, National Building Agency, 1967-77; *b* 1910; *s* of Albert John Barr and Ellen (*née* Cleeve); *m* 1st, 1935, Edith M. Edwards, BA (*d* 1965); one *s* one *d* (and one *s* decd); 2nd, 1966, Mrs Mary W. Harley (*widow*). *Educ:* Borlase, Marlow; Liverpool Univ. Private offices (Charles Holden and Paul Mauger); Herts CC (schools) and LCC (housing). Dep. Housing Architect, LCC, 1956-57; Development Architect, Ministry of Education, 1957-58; Chief Architect, Min. of Housing and Local Govt, 1959-64. Dir, Nat. Building Agency, 1964-. Hon. Sec. RIBA, 1963-65. *Address:* 72 Eastwick Road, Walton-on-Thames, Surrey KT12 5AR.

BARR, David; a Metropolitan Stipendiary Magistrate, since 1976; *b* 15 Oct. 1925; *s* of Walter and Betty Barr; *m* 1960, Ruth Weitzman; one *s* one *d. Educ:* Haberdashers' Aske's Hampstead Sch.; Brookline High Sch., Boston, USA; Edinburgh Univ.; University Coll., London (LLB). Royal Navy, 1943-47. Solicitor, 1953; private practice, 1953-76 (Partner, Pritchard Englefield & Tobin). JP Inner London Area, 1963-76; Chm., Inner London Juvenile Panel, 1968-76; Dep. Chm., N Westminster PSD, 1968-76. Manager, Finnart House Sch., Weybridge, 1955-, Trustee 1973-. *Recreations:* gardening, bridge, reading. *Address:* 47 Abbey Road, NW8; Hartmoor House, Buckhorn Weston, Dorset. *Clubs:* Garrick, MCC.

BARR, Rev. Prof. James, MA, BD, DD; FBA 1969; Oriel Professor of the Interpretation of Holy Scripture and Fellow, Oriel College, Oxford University, since 1976; *b* 20 March 1924; *s* of Rev. Prof. Allan Barr, DD; *m* 1950, Jane J. S. Hepburn, MA; two *s* one *d. Educ:* Daniel Stewart's Coll., Edinburgh; Edinburgh Univ. (MA 1948, BD 1951); MA Oxon 1976. Served War of 1939-45 as pilot in RNVR (Fleet Air Arm), 1942-45. Minister of Church of Scotland, Tiberias, Israel, 1951-53; Prof. of New Testament Literature and Exegesis, Presbyterian Coll., Montreal, 1953-55; Prof. of Old Testament Literature and Theology, Edinburgh Univ., 1955-61; Prof. of Old Testament Literature and Theology, Princeton Theological Seminary, 1961-65; Prof. of Semitic Languages and Literatures, Manchester Univ., 1965-76. Visiting Professor: Hebrew Univ., Jerusalem, 1973; Chicago Univ., 1975; Strasbourg Univ., 1975-76; lectured in Princeton Univ., 1962-63; in Union Theol. Seminary, New York, 1963; Currie Lectr, Austin Theol. Seminary, Texas, 1964; Guggenheim Memorial Fellowship for study in biblical semantics, 1965; Cadbury Lectr, Birmingham Univ., 1969; Croall Lectr, Edinburgh Univ., 1970; Grinfield Lectr on the Septuagint, Oxford Univ., 1974-. Editor: Jl of Semitic Studies, 1965-76; Oxford Hebrew Dictionary, 1974-. Pres., Soc. for OT Studies, 1973. FRAS 1969. Hon. Fellow, SOAS, 1975. Hon. DD: Knox Coll., Toronto, 1964; Dubuque, 1974; St Andrews, 1974; MA Manchester, 1969. Corresp. Mem., Göttingen Acad. of Sciences, 1976; Mem., Norwegian Acad. of Science and Letters, 1977. *Publications:* The Semantics of Biblical Language, 1961; Biblical Words for Time, 1962; Old and New in Interpretation, 1966; Comparative Philology and the Text of the Old Testament, 1968; The Bible in the Modern World, 1973; Fundamentalism, 1977; articles in Semitic and biblical journals. *Recreation:* bird watching. *Address:* 6 Fitzherbert Close, Iffley, Oxford OX4 4EN. *T:* Oxford 772741.

BARR, Kenneth Glen; Sheriff of South Strathclyde, Dumfries and Galloway at Dumfries, since 1976; *b* 20 Jan. 1941; *s* of Rev. Gavin Barr and Mrs Catherine McLellan Barr (*née* McGhie); *m* 1970, Susanne Crichton Keir. *Educ:* Ardrossan Acad.; Royal High Sch.; Edinburgh Univ. (MA, LLB). Admitted to Faculty of Advocates, 1964. *Address:* Sheriff Court House, Dumfries DG1 2AN.

BARR, Prof. Murray Llewellyn, OC (Canada) 1968; FRS 1972; Professor of Anatomy, University of Western Ontario, since 1949; *b* 20 June 1908; Canadian; *m* 1934, Ruth Vivian King; three *s* one *d. Educ:* Univ. of Western Ontario (BA, MD, MSc). FRSC 1958; FRCP(C) 1964; FACP 1965; FRCOG 1972. Served War of 1939-45 as MO, RCAF (Wing Comdr). Univ. of Western Ontario: Instructor in Anatomy, 1936-45; Associate Prof. of Anatomy, 1945-49 (Chm., Dept of Anatomy, 1951-67). Hon. Degrees: LLD Queen's, 1963; LLD Toronto, 1964; Drmed Basel, 1966; LLD Alberta, 1967; LLD Dalhousie, 1968; LLD Saskatchewan, 1973; DSc Western Ontario, 1974. *Publications:* The Human Nervous System: an anatomical viewpoint, 1972; numerous scientific papers. *Address:* Department of Anatomy, Health Sciences Centre, University of Western Ontario, London, Canada. *T:* 679-3745. *Club:* Harvey (London, Ont.).

BARR, His Honour Judge Reginald Alfred; a Circuit Judge (formerly Judge of County Courts), since 1970; *b* 21 Nov. 1920; *s* of Alfred Charles Barr; *m* 1946, Elaine, 2nd *d* of James William Charles O'Bala Morris, Llanstephan, Carmarthenshire. *Educ:* Christ's Hospital; Trinity Coll., Oxford (MA). Served War, 1941-46, Middle East and Burma. Called to Bar, Middle Temple, 1954; Standing Counsel to Registrar of Restrictive Trading Agreements, 1962-70. Mem. Review Bd for Govt Contracts, 1969-70. *Address:* 42 Bathurst Mews, Hyde Park, W2. *T:* 01-262 5731.

BARR, William Greig, DL; Rector, Exeter College, Oxford, since 1972; *b* 10 June 1917; *s* of late William S. Barr, Glasgow; *m* 1954, Helen Georgopoulos; two *s. Educ:* Sedbergh Sch.; Magdalen Coll., Oxford. Stanhope Prize, 1938; 1st cl., Hon. Sch. of Modern History, 1939. Served War, 1939-45: Lt-Col., Royal Devon Yeomanry. Fellow of Exeter Coll., Oxford, 1945-72; Sub-

Rector, 1947-54; Sen. Tutor, 1960-66. Lectr in Modern History, Univ. of Oxford, 1949-72. Hon. Treas., Oxford Univ. Rugby Football Club, 1948-73; Jun. Proctor, 1951-52. A Rhodes Trustee, 1975-. Visiting Prof. of Hist., Univ. of South Carolina, 1968. Governor: Brighton Coll.; Plymouth Coll.; Sedbergh Sch.; Trustee, Uppingham Sch. DL Oxon 1974. *Address:* Exeter College, Oxford. *T:* Oxford 44681.

BARRACLOUGH, Geoffrey; *b* 10 May 1908; *e s* of late Walter and Edith M. Barraclough. *Educ:* Bootham Sch., York; Oriel Coll., Oxford; Univ. of Munich. Bryce Research Student, 1931; Rome Scholar, British Sch. at Rome, 1931; Fellow of Merton Coll., Oxford, 1934; Fellow and Lectr, St John's Coll., Cambridge, 1936; Univ. Lectr, Cambridge, 1937; Foreign Office, 1940; RAFVR, 1942-45; Prof. of Mediæval History, University of Liverpool, 1945-56. Research Prof. of Internat. History, University of London, 1956-62; Prof. of History, Univ. of California, 1965-68; Springer Prof. of History, Brandeis Univ., 1968-70; Chichele Prof. of Modern History, and Fellow of All Souls Coll., Oxford Univ., 1970-73. President: Historical Assoc., 1964-67; Internat. Soc. Sci. Council, Gp of Twenty, 1975-. Hon. Mem., Austrian Inst. Historical Research. *Publications:* Public Notaries and the Papal Curia, 1934; Papal Provisions, 1935; Mediæval Germany, 1938; The Origins of Modern Germany, 1946; Factors in German History, 1946; The Mediæval Empire, 1950; The Earldom and County Palatine of Chester, 1953; History in a Changing World, 1955; Early Cheshire Charters, 1957; (ed) Social Life in Early England, 1960; European Unity in Thought and Action, 1963; An Introduction to Contemporary History, 1964; The Mediæval Papacy, 1968; (ed) Eastern and Western Europe in the Middle Ages, 1970; The Crucible of Europe, 1976; Management in a Changing Economy, 1976; (with R. F. Wall) Survey of International Affairs, 1955-56; Survey of International Affairs, 1956-58; Survey of International Affairs, 1958-60.

BARRACLOUGH, Henry, CVO 1976 (MVO 1958); *b* 10 Aug. 1894; *s* of late Thomas Barraclough, Shipowner, West Hartlepool; *m* 1922, Ethel Mary, *d* of Wilkinson Dix Sunderland; two *s. Educ:* Giggleswick Sch. On leaving school joined staff of Lambert Bros Ltd, Newcastle on Tyne office, 1911. Served European War, 1914-18, Durham LI, retiring as Capt.; served in Mesopotamia and NW Persia, 1916-19. Silver Line Ltd: Treasury Dir, 1940-48; Chm. and Man. Dir, 1948-60. Chairman, Prince of Wales Dry Dock Co., Swansea, Ltd, 1943-65 (Dir of the company, 1931-66); Dir, Dene Shipping Co. Ltd from formation until 1970 (Chm., 1941-66), and of other cos; Mem. of Lloyd's. Chm. London General Shipowners' Soc., 1946-47; Dep. Chm. and Chm. of Sub-Cttees of Classification of Lloyd's Register of Shipping, 1949-50. Mem. Council, Maritime Trust; Chm. Governors, The "Cutty Sark" Soc. Liveryman of Worshipful Company of Shipwrights. *Address:* Bix Manor, Henley-on-Thames, Oxon. *T:* Henley-on-Thames 5454; Cotehow, Martindale, Penrith.

BARRACLOUGH, Air Chief Marshal Sir John, KCB 1970 (CB 1969); CBE 1961; DFC 1942; AFC 1941; FIPM, MBIM, MIPR; Commandant, Royal College of Defence Studies, 1974-76, retired; *b* 2 May 1918; *s* of late Horatio and Marguerite Maude Barraclough; *m* 1946, Maureen (*née* McCormack), niece of George, Noble Count Plunkett; one *d. Educ:* Cranbrook Sch. Service Artists' Rifles, 1935-38. Commissioned RAF, 1938. Air Vice-Marshal, 1964; Air Marshal, 1970; Air Chief Marshal, 1973. Served Near, Middle and Far East; first single-engined jet flight to S Africa, 1957. On staffs of Central Flying Sch. and IDC, 1949-54; Station Commander, Biggin Hill, 1954-56; Dir of Public Relations, Air Ministry, 1961-64; AOC No 19 and COMMAIRCENTLANT, 1964-67; Harvard Business Sch., 1967; AOA, Bomber Command, 1967-68; AOA, Strike Comd, 1968-70; Vice-Chief of Defence Staff, 1970-72; Air Secretary, 1972-74. Member: Commonwealth War Graves Commn, 1974-; RAF Training and Educn Adv. Bd, 1976-; Air League Council, 1977; Chm., RUSI Council, 1977. Past Pres., RAF Modern Pentathlon Assoc. *Publications:* contribs to professional jls. *Recreations:* sailing, country pursuits. *Address:* Crapstone House, Buckland Monachorum, Yelverton, Devon. *T:* Yelverton 3639. *Clubs:* Boodle's, Royal Air Force, East India, Devonshire, Sports and Public Schools; Royal Western Yacht.

BARRACLOUGH, Brig. Sir John (Ashworth), Kt 1962; CMG 1950; DSO 1941; OBE 1941; MC 1918; DL; Chairman, Engineering Employers' Association, 1950-67. Served European War, 1914-19, with KORR, RFC, and Machine Gun Corps; served in Iraq (severely wounded), 1920, Ireland, 1922, Palestine, 1929, Egypt, 1932, and India, 1934; military commander, Hebron District, Palestine, 1939; War of 1939-45, comd 1st Bn King's Own Royal Regt, Syria, Lebanon and at Siege of Tobruk, 1941 (despatches five times, wounded); reg.

comdr North Rhine Province, 1945-46; dep. reg. cmdr Land North Rhine-Westphalia, 1946-50. Member: Nat. Adv. Council for the Employment of the Disabled; Piercy Cttee on the Rehabilitation of the Disabled, 1953-56. KStJ, 1964. DL Warwicks, 1962. Comdr Order of Orange Nassau with Swords (Netherlands). *Address:* 6 Devonshire Mews South, W1. *T:* 01-935 3680.

BARRACLOUGH, Kenneth James Priestley, CBE 1967 (OBE 1945); TD; JP; Chief Metropolitan Magistrate since 1975; *b* 1907; *s* of Herbert Barraclough, Leeds; *m* 1931, Gladys Evelyn, *d* of Charles Henderson, Liverpool and Rio de Janeiro; two *s* one *d. Educ:* Oundle Sch.; Clare Coll., Cambridge. Barrister, Middle Temple, 1929 (Master of the Bench, 1975), North Eastern Circuit; Inns of Court Regt, TA, 1938; Col 1945. HQ, 21st Army Group (despatches). Metropolitan Magistrate, 1954; Dep. Chm. Appeals Cttee, Hampshire QS, 1957-62; Chm., HO Poisons Board, 1958-76. Member: Adv. Cttee on Drug Dependence, 1966-70; Adv. Council on the Misuse of Drugs, 1972-73; Medicines Commn, 1969-75. JP Hampshire, 1957. *Address:* 18 Fitzroy Road, Fleet, Hants.

BARRAN, Sir David (Haven), Kt 1971; Managing Director, Shell Transport and Trading Co. Ltd, since 1964 (Deputy Chairman, 1964-67; Chairman, 1967-72); *b* 23 May 1912; *s* of Sir John Barran, 2nd Bt and Alice Margarita (*née* Parks); *m* 1944, Jane Lechmere Macaskie; four *s* three *d. Educ:* Winchester; Trinity Coll., Cambridge. BA 1934. Joined Asiatic Petroleum Co., 1934; served in Egypt, Palestine, Sudan, India, 1935-46. Pres., Asiatic Petroleum Corp., New York, 1958; Managing Dir, Royal Dutch/Shell Group, 1961-72; Chm., Shell Oil Co., 1970-72; Director: Midland Bank (Dep. Chm., 1975-); General Accident Insurance; BICC; Glaxo Hldgs; Standard Chartered Bank, 1977-. Chairman: CBI Cttee on Inflation Accounting, 1973-74; Adv. Cttee on Appt of Advertising Agents, 1975- (Mem., 1973-); Ct of Governors, Administrative Staff Coll., 1971-76; Governor, Centre for Environmental Studies, 1972-75. Comdr, Order of Oranje Nassau, 1971. *Recreations:* gardening, shooting, embroidery. *Address:* 36 Kensington Square, W8. *T:* 01-937 5664; Brent Eleigh Hall, Suffolk. *T:* Lavenham 202. *Club:* River (New York).

BARRAN, Sir John (Napoleon Ruthven), 4th Bt *cr* 1895; Head of Television Commercials and Fillers Unit, Central Office of Information, since 1975; *b* 14 Feb. 1934; *s* of Sir John Leighton Barran, 3rd Bt, and Hon. Alison Mary (*d* 1973), 3rd *d* of 9th Baron Ruthven, CB, CMG, DSO; *S* father, 1974; *m* 1965, Jane Margaret, *d* of Sir Stanley Hooker, *qv*; one *s. Educ:* Heatherdown Sch., Ascot; Winchester Coll. National Service, 1952-54, Lieut, 5th Roy. Inniskilling Dragoon Guards; served Canal Zone. Asst Account Executive: Dorland Advertising Ltd, 1956-58; Masius & Fergusson Advertising Ltd, 1958-61; Account Executive, Ogilvy, Benson & Mather (New York) Inc., 1961-63; Overseas TV News Service, COI, 1964; First Sec. (Information), British High Commission, Ottawa, 1965-67; Home Documentary Film Section, COI, 1967-72; Overseas TV and Film News Services, COI, 1972-75. *Recreations:* entertaining, talking, reading, drawing, gardening, shooting, fishing, sailing. *Heir: s* John Ruthven Barran, *b* 10 Nov. 1971. *Address:* 17 St Leonard's Terrace, SW3. *T:* 01-730 2801; The Hermitage, East Bergholt, Suffolk.

BARRATT, Francis Russell, CB 1975; Deputy Secretary, HM Treasury, since 1973; *b* 16 Nov. 1924; *s* of Frederick Russell Barratt; *m* 1949, Janet Mary Sherborne; three *s. Educ:* Durban High Sch., SA; Clifton; University Coll., Oxford. Asst Principal, HM Treasury, 1949; Principal, 1953; First Sec., UK High Commission, Karachi, 1956-58; Asst Sec., 1962, Under Sec., 1968, HM Treasury. *Recreations:* reading, golf, music. *Address:* 25 Highgate Close, N6. *T:* 01-348 1319.

BARRATT, Herbert George Harold, OBE 1966; General Secretary, Confederation of Shipbuilding and Engineering Unions, 1957-70; *b* 12 Jan. 1905; *m* 1926; one *s* three *d. Educ:* Vicarage Street Church of England Sch., Nuneaton. Nuneaton Borough Councillor, 1945-47; Mem. Nat. Cttee AEU, 1943-48; Delegate to USSR, 1946. Chm. Nuneaton Labour Party, 1944-46; Coventry Dist. Cttee AEU, 1943-49; Shop Steward Convener, Daimler Motors, 1940-49; Appeals Board Assessor during war years; Nat. Insurance Tribunal Assessor; elected Nat. Organiser AEU, 1949-57. Formerly Member: Gas Adv. Council; Shipbuilding and Ship repairing Council; Nat. Adv. Council for the Motor Manufacturing Industry; Motor Industry Joint Labour Council; British Railways Productivity Council; Econ. Devel Cttee for Mech. Engrg Industry; Econ. Devel Cttee for Electrical Engrg Industry; Econ. Devel Cttee for Motor Manufacturing Industry; Industrial Training Board, Engrg; Industrial Training Board, Shipbuilding; British

Productivity team to Swedish Shipyards, 1959; visited German Federal Railways, 1960; Exchange Leader Scheme visitor to USA, 1961; Vice-Chm., Sub-Cttee on Programme and Planning, Metal Trades Cttee, ILO, Geneva, 1965. *Recreation:* gardening. *Address:* (home) 58 The Crescent, West Wickham, Kent. *T:* 01-777 7638.

BARRATT, Michael Fieldhouse; broadcaster on radio and television; *b* 3 Jan. 1928; *s* of Wallace Milner Barratt and late Doris Barratt; *m* 1952, Joan Francesca Warner (marr. diss.); three *s* three *d. Educ:* Rossall and Paisley Grammar Sch. Entered journalism, Kemsley Newspapers, 1945; Editor, Nigerian Citizen, 1956; *television:* Reporter, Panorama, 1963; Presenter: 24 Hours, 1965-69; Nationwide, 1969-77; Songs of Praise, 1977-; *radio:* Question-Master, Gardeners' Question Time, 1973-. Mem. Cttee, Yorks and Humberside Develt Assoc., 1975. Rector, Aberdeen Univ., 1973. Hon. LLD Aberdeen, 1975. FRHS. *Publications:* Michael Barratt, 1973; Michael Barratt's Down-to-Earth Gardening Book, 1974; Michael Barratt's Complete Gardening Book, 1977. *Recreations:* golf, cricket, listening. *Address:* 2 Park Steps, St George's Fields, W2. *T:* 01-723 8448. *Club:* Lord's Taverners.

BARRATT, Prof. Michael George; Professor of Mathematics, Northwestern University, Illinois, since 1974; *b* 26 Jan. 1927; *e s* of George Bernard Barratt and Marjorie Holloway Barratt (*née* Oldham); *m* 1952, Jenepher Hudson; one *s* four *d. Educ:* Stationers' Company's Sch.; Magdalen Coll., Oxford. Junior Lecturer, Oxford Univ., 1950-52; Fellow, Magdalen Coll., Oxford, 1952-56; Lectr, Brasenose Coll., Oxford, 1955-59; Sen. Lectr and Reader, 1959-63, Prof. of Pure Maths, 1964-74, Manchester Univ. Vis. Prof., Chicago Univ., 1963-64. *Publications:* Papers in Mathematical Jls. *Address:* Department of Mathematics, Northwestern University, Evanston, Ill 60201, USA.

BARRATT, Richard Stanley, QPM 1974; Chief Constable, South Yorkshire Police, since 1975; *b* 11 Aug. 1928; *s* of Richard Barratt and Mona Barratt; *m* 1952, Sarah Elizabeth Hale; one *s* two *d. Educ:* Saltley Grammar Sch., Birmingham. MBIM. Birmingham City Police (Constable to Chief Inspector), 1949-65; Dir, Home Office Crime Prevention Centre, Stafford, 1963; seconded to Home Office (Res. and Develt), 1964; Sen. Comd Course, Police Coll., 1964; Supt, Cheshire Constab., 1965, Chief Supt, 1966; Asst Chief Constable, Manchester City Police, 1967; Asst Chief Constable, Manchester and Salford Police, 1968, Dep. Chief Constable, 1972; Dep. Chief Constable, Greater Manchester Police, 1974. *Recreations:* reading, caravanning, gardening. *Address:* Police Headquarters, Snig Hill, Sheffield S3 8LY. *T:* Sheffield 78522. *Club:* The Club (Sheffield).

BARRATT-BOYES, Sir Brian (Gerald), KBE 1971 (CBE 1966); Surgeon-in-Charge, Cardio-Thoracic Surgical Unit, Greenlane Hospital, Auckland, since 1964; Hon. Senior Cardio-Thoracic Surgeon, Mater Misericordiae Hospital, Auckland, since 1966; *b* 13 Jan. 1924; *s* of Gerald Cave Boyes and Edna Myrtle Boyes (*née* Barratt); *m* 1949, Norma Margaret Thompson; five *s. Educ:* Wellington Coll.; Univ. of Otago. MB, ChB 1946; FRACS 1952; FACS 1960; ChM 1962. Lectr in Anatomy, Otago Univ. Med. Sch., 1947; House Surg. and Registrar, Wellington Hosp., 1948-50; Surgical Registrar and Pathology Registrar, Palmerston North Hosp., 1950-52; Fellow in Cardio-Thoracic Surgery, Mayo Clinic, USA, 1953-55; Nuffield Trav. Fellowship UK (Bristol Univ.), 1956; Sen. Cardio-Thoracic Surg., Greenlane Hosp., 1957. Hon. Prof. of Surgery, Auckland Univ., 1971. K T. Hall Prize for Distinguished Cardiac Surgery in Austr. and NZ, 1966. FRSNZ 1970. *Publications:* Heart Disease in Infancy: diagnosis and surgical treatment, 1973; numerous in med. jls throughout the world. *Recreations:* farming, trout fishing. *Address:* 27 Rahiri Road, Auckland 4, New Zealand. *T:* 689-414; (consulting rooms) 102 Remuera Road, Auckland 5. *T:* 500176. *Club:* Northern (Auckland).

BARRAULT, Jean-Louis; Officer of the Legion of Honour; actor, director, producer; Director: Odéon-Théâtre de France, 1959-68; Théâtre des Nations, Paris, 1965-67, and since 1971; *b* Vésinet, France, 8 Sept. 1910; *m* Madeleine Renaud, *qv. Educ:* public sch., Paris; Collège Chaptal. Taught at Collège Chaptal, 1931; Atelier Dramatic Sch. and Theatre (schol.), 1931-35; formed experimental theatrical company. Served War of 1939-40. With Comédie-Française as producer-director, 1940-46. At instigation of French Govt formed company with Madeleine Renaud, Marigny Theatre. Has appeared at Venice; Edinburgh Festival, 1948 and 1957: St James's Theatre, London, 1951; Palace Theatre, London, 1956, etc.; produced Duel of Angels, Apollo, 1958; World Theatre Season, Aldwych, 1965, 1968; toured Western Europe, S America, Canada, and US. Films include: Les Beaux Jours, Hélène, Les Perles de la couronne, La

Symphonie fantastique, Les Enfants du Paradis, D'Hommes à hommes, Versailles, Chappaqua, Le Puritain. *Publications:* Une Troupe et ses auteurs, 1950; Reflections on the Theatre (autobiography), 1951; Rabelais, 1971 (prod, Paris 1968-69, tours in Japan and USA, 1969, London 1971); Memories for Tomorrow: the memoirs of Jean-Louis Barrault, 1974; articles in theatrical publications. *Address:* 18 avenue du Président Wilson, Paris XVIe, France.

BARRE, Raymond; Chevalier de la Légion d'Honneur, Chevalier de l'Ordre National du Mérite agricole, Officier des Palmes Académiques; Grand Croix de l'Ordre National du Mérite, 1977; Prime Minister of France, since Aug. 1976; *b* Saint-Denis, Réunion, 12 April 1924; *s* of René Barre and Charlotte Déramond; *m* 1954, Eve Hegedüs; two *s. Educ:* Lycée Leconte-de-Lisle, Saint-Denis-de-la-Réunion; Faculté de Droit, Paris; Institut d'Etudes Politiques, Paris. Professor at Faculté de Droit et des Sciences Economiques: Caen, 1950; Paris (Chair of Political Economy), 1963-; Professor at Institut d'Etudes Politiques, Paris, 1961-. Director of Cabinet of Mr J.-M. Jeanneney (Minister of Industry), 1959-62; Member: Cttee of Experts (Comité Lorain) studying financing of investments in France, 1963-64; Gen. Cttee on Economy and Financing of Fifth Plan, 1966; Vice-Chm., Commn of European Communities (responsible for Economic and Financial Affairs), 1967-72; Mem. Gen. Council, Banque de France, 1973; Chm. Cttee for studying Housing Financing Reform, 1975-76; Minister of Foreign Trade, Jan. 1976. *Publication:* Economie Politique, 1955, and 1974. *Address:* Hôtel Matignon, 57 rue de Varenne, 75007 Paris, France; (home) 6 rue de Bagatelle, 92200 Neuilly sur Seine.

BARRER, Prof. Richard Maling, FRS 1956; PhD Cantab; DSc (NZ); ScD Cantab; FRIC 1939; Hon. ARCS, 1959; Professor of Physical Chemistry, Imperial College of Science and Technology, University of London, 1954-77, now Emeritus; Head of Department of Chemistry, 1955-76; Dean of the Royal College of Science, 1964-66; *b* 16 June 1910; *s* of T. R. Barrer, 103 Renall Street, Masterton, New Zealand; *m* 1939, Helen Frances Yule, Invercargill, NZ; one *s* three *d. Educ:* Canterbury University Coll., NZ (MSc); Clare Coll., Cambridge (1851 Exhibition Scholar). PhD Cantab, 1935; DSc NZ, 1937; ScD Cantab, 1948. Major Research Student, 1935-37, Research Fellow, 1937-39, Clare Coll.; Head of Chemistry Dept, Technical Coll., Bradford, 1939-46; Reader in Chemistry, London Univ., 1946-49; Prof. of Chemistry, Aberdeen Univ., 1949-54. Member Council: Faraday Soc., 1952-55; Chemical Soc., 1956-59, 1974-; Royal Institute of Chemistry, 1961-64; Soc. of Chemical Industry, 1965-68. Governor, Chelsea Coll. of Sci. and Technol., 1960-. Hon. FRSNZ 1965; Hon. DSc Bradford, 1967. *Publications:* Diffusion in and through Solids, 1941. Various research papers in British and foreign scientific journals. *Recreations:* tennis and interest in athletics. Full Blue for cross-country running, 1934. *Address:* Flossmoor, Orpington Road, Chislehurst, Kent. *Clubs:* Hawks (Cambridge); Achilles.

BARRÈRE, Prof. Jean-Bertrand Marie; Croix de Guerre (France), 1940; Légion d'Honneur, 1969; Professor of French Literature, University of Cambridge, since 1954; Fellow of St John's College, Cambridge, 1957; *b* Paris, 15 Dec. 1914; *s* of Alexandre Barrère and Marie-Claire Lavigne; *m* 1941, Micheline, *d* of Henri Cousin and Inès Dumontier; three *s* three *d. Educ:* Lycées Buffon and Louis-le-Grand; Ecole Normale Supérieure and Sorbonne, Paris. MA; Agrégé des Lettres; Docteur ès Lettres. Served War: Sous-Lieut, 32e Régiment d'Infanterie, 1939-40; 1re Armée Française, 1945; Lieut 1945; Capitaine de réserve, 1954; Capitaine Honoraire, 1967. Teacher of French and Classics, Lycée d'Amiens, 1940-42; Asst Lectr on French Literature, Sorbonne, 1942-46; Lectr on French Literature, Institut Français, London, 1946-49; Lectr on French Literature, Univ. of Lyons, 1949-50; appointed Prof. of French Literature, Univ. of Lyons, 1950; seconded as Prof. of French Literature, Ibrahim Univ., Cairo, 1950-52; Prof. at Lyons, 1952-54. *Publications:* Explications françaises, 1946; La Fantaisie de Victor Hugo, 3 vols, 1949, 1960, 1950, rev. edn 1973; Hugo, l'homme et l'œuvre, 1952; Romain Rolland par lui-même, 1955; Le Regard d'Orphée, 1956; La Cure d'amaigrissement du roman, 1964; Critique de chambre, 1964; Un Carnet des Misérables, 1965; Victor Hugo devant Dieu, 1965; Victor Hugo à l'œuvre, 1966; Romain Rolland, l'âme et l'art, 1966; L'Idée de Goût, 1972; Ma Mère qui boite, 1975; L'Echange poétique, 1977. *Recreations:* painting, violin. *Address:* Coleby, 31 Storey's Way, Cambridge.

BARRETT, Sir Arthur George, Kt 1942; *b* Geelong, 7 May 1895; *s* of A. O. and F. M. Barrett, Melbourne; *m* 1922, Jean Beatrice, *d* of late E. S. Mair, Melbourne; two *d. Educ:* Melbourne Church of England Grammar Sch. Served European War, AIF, 1916-19;

Lord Mayor of Adelaide, 1937-41; Alderman, Adelaide City Council, 1941-53; business: maltster. Formerly Wing Comdr Air Training Corps RAAF. *Recreations:* golf, tennis. *Address:* 210 Stanley Street, North Adelaide, South Australia 5006, Australia. *T:* 267.1171. *Club:* Adelaide (Adelaide).

BARRETT, Rev. Prof. Charles Kingsley, DD; FBA 1961; Professor of Divinity, Durham University, since 1958; *b* 4 May 1917; *s* of Rev. F. Barrett and Clara (*née* Seed); *m* 1944, Margaret E. Heap, Calverley, Yorks; one *s* one *d*. *Educ:* Shebbear Coll.; Pembroke Coll., Cambridge; Wesley House, Cambridge. DD Cantab, 1956. Asst Tutor, Wesley Coll., Headingley, 1942; Methodist Minister, Darlington, 1943; Lecturer in Theology, Durham Univ., 1945. Hewett Lecturer (USA), 1961; Shaffer Lecturer (Yale), 1965; Delitzsch Lectr, Münster, 1967; Cato Lecturer (Australia), 1969; Tate-Willson Lectr, Dallas, 1975; McMartin Lectr, Ottawa, 1976. Vice-Pres., British and Foreign Bible Soc.; Pres., Studiorum Novi Testamenti Societas, 1973. Hon. DD: Hull, 1970; Aberdeen, 1972. Burkitt Medal for Biblical Studies, 1966. *Publications:* The Holy Spirit and the Gospel Tradition, 1947; The Gospel according to St John, 1955; The New Testament Background: Selected Documents, 1956; Biblical Preaching and Biblical Scholarship, 1957; The Epistle to the Romans, 1957; Westcott as Commentator, 1959; Yesterday, Today and Forever: The New Testament Problem, 1959; Luke the Historian in Recent Study, 1961; From First Adam to Last, 1962; The Pastoral Epistles, 1963; Reading Through Romans, 1963; History and Faith: the Story of the Passion, 1967; Jesus and the Gospel Tradition, 1967; The First Epistle to the Corinthians, 1968; The Signs of an Apostle, 1970; Das Johannesevangelium und das Judentum, 1970; The Prologue of St John's Gospel, 1971; New Testament Essays, 1972; The Second Epistle to the Corinthians, 1973; The Fourth Gospel and Judaism, 1975; contributions to learned journals and symposia in Britain, the Continent, and USA. *Address:* 8 Princes Street, Durham DH1 4RP. *T:* Durham 61340.

BARRETT, David, MLA since 1960; Leader of the Official Opposition, British Columbia, since 1976; Premier and Minister of Finance, Province of British Columbia, Canada, 1972-75; *b* Vancouver, 2 Oct. 1930; father a business man in East Vancouver, after war service; *m* 1953, Shirley Hackman, West Vancouver; two *s* one *d*. *Educ:* Britannia High Sch., Vancouver; Seattle Univ.; St Louis Univ. BA(Phil) Seattle, 1953; Master of Social Work, St Louis, 1956. Personnel and Staff Trng Officer, Haney Correctional Inst., 1957-59; also gained experience in a variety of jobs. Elected: MLA for Dewdney, Sept. 1960 and 1963; to re-distributed riding of Coquitlam 1966, 1969 and 1972; Vancouver East, by-election 1976; New Democratic Party Leader, June 1970 (first Social Democratic Govt in history of Province). Dr of Laws, *h c*, St Louis Univ., 1974. *Address:* Legislative Buildings, Victoria, British Columbia, Canada. *T:* 387-5571.

BARRETT, Lt-Gen. Sir David William S.; *see* Scott-Barrett.

BARRETT, Denis Everett; a Special Commissioner of Income Tax, 1967-71; *b* 7 Jan. 1911; *o s* of late Walter Everett Barrett, London, and Julia Barrett (*née* MacCarthy), Cork; *m* 1st, 1947, Eilish (*d* 1974), *y d* of late William and Margaret Phelan, Co. Laois; one *s* two *d*; 2nd, 1977, Patricia Madeline (*née* Ruddin), widow of H. A. Cowan, FRCS. *Educ:* Wimbledon Coll.; London Univ. Entered Inland Revenue Dept, 1930; Asst Sec., 1948. *Address:* 30 Little Forest Road, Bournemouth BH4 9NW. *T:* Bournemouth 763066.

BARRETT, Edwin Cyril Geddes, CMG 1958; MA; *b* 15 Feb. 1909; *s* of late Lieut-Col C. C. J. Barrett, CSI, CIE, IA, and late Mrs Mabel Ada Barrett (*née* Geddes); *m* 1936, Eleanor Nelson Raymond (*d* 1970); one *s*. *Educ:* Marlborough Coll.; Jesus Coll., Cambridge. Cadet, Malayan Civil Service, 1931; many appts in Malaya and Borneo, 1931-42. Military Service, 1942-45. Resumed duty in the Malayan CS, 1946; Chief Registration Officer, Fedn of Malaya, 1949; Pres. Municipal Council, Kuala Lumpur, 1951; Comr for Resettlement of Special Constables in Civil Life, Fedn of Malaya, 1952; Acting British Adviser, Perak, 1953; British Adviser, Kedah, 1953; left Malaya on abolition of appt, 1957; Lectr in Malay, SOAS, Univ. of London, 1957-71. *Recreation:* gardening. *Address:* Hillfield, Amlets Lane, Cranleigh, Surrey. *T:* Cranleigh 3533.

BARRETT, Ernest; Joint Managing Director, Henry Barrett & Sons Ltd, since 1968; Chairman: Steel Stockholding Division, Henry Barrett & Sons Ltd, since 1967; John France & Co. (Iron & Steel) Ltd, since 1969; Henry Lindsay Ltd, since 1974; *b* 8 April 1917; *s* of Ernest Barrett and Marian Conyers; *m* 1940, Eileen Maria Peel; one *d*. *Educ:* Charterhouse. Joined Henry

Barrett & Sons Ltd, Bradford, 1934. Served War, RA, and commissioned, 1940; served in Mediterranean Theatre, with 1st Army, 1943-46 (despatches, 1944); Major 1945. Apptd Dir, Henry Barrett & Sons Ltd, 1946. Pres., Nat. Assoc. of Steel Stockholders, 1977- (Chm., Yorks Assoc., 1964-66; Vice-Pres., 1975-77); Pres., Engineering Industries Assoc., 1971 (Chm. Yorks Region, 1960-65; Vice-Pres. of Assoc., 1965-71). *Recreations:* badminton, gardening. *Address:* West Ghyll, Victoria Avenue, Ilkley, W Yorks. *T:* Ilkley 3911.

BARRETT, Hugh Tufnell-; *see* Tufnell-Barrett.

BARRETT, Jack Wheeler, CBE 1971; Director, Monsanto Ltd, since 1955; Chairman, Info-line Ltd, since 1976; Special Professor of Industrial Chemistry, University of Nottingham, since 1968; *b* 13 June 1912; *s* of John Samuel Barrett, Cheltenham; *m* 1935, Muriel Audley Read; two *s* two *d*. *Educ:* Cheltenham Grammar Sch.; Imperial Coll., Univ. of London. BSc, PhD, CEng, ARCS, FRIC, DIC, FIChemE. Chief Chemist, London Essence Co. Ltd, 1936-41; joined Monsanto Chemicals Ltd, 1941: Dir of Research, 1955-71. President: IChemE, 1971-72; Chem. Soc., 1974-75; ICSU Abstracting Bd, 1974-; Chm., Chemical Divl Council, BSI, 1973-; Mem., British Library Bd, 1973-. Fellow, Imperial Coll., London, 1977. *Publications:* articles in Jl Chem. Soc., Chemistry and Industry, Jl ASLIB, Chemistry in Britain. *Recreation:* gardening. *Address:* 195 Latymer Court, Hammersmith Road, W6 7JQ. *T:* 01-748 7080; West Manor House, Bourton-on-the-Water, Cheltenham, Glos GL54 2AP. *T:* Bourton-on-the-Water 20296. *Club:* Athenæum.

BARRETT, Norman Rupert, CBE 1969; FRCS 1930; retired 1970; Surgeon to King Edward VII Sanatorium, Midhurst, 1938-70; Consulting Thoracic Surgeon to Royal Navy and to Ministry of Social Security, 1944-70; Lecturer in Surgery, University of London, 1935-70; Formerly: Senior Surgeon, St Thomas' Hospital; Surgeon, Brompton Hospital; *b* Adelaide, Australia, 16 May 1903; *o s* of late Alfred Barrett, Sussex; *m* 1931, Elizabeth, *d* of late H. Warington Smyth, CMG; two *d*. *Educ:* Eton Coll., Trinity Coll., Cambridge (1st class Hons Natural Science Tripos, 1925, MA 1930); St Thomas' Hosp. (MB 1928, MChir 1931). Rockefeller Travelling Fellowship, 1935; Visiting Professor of Surgery: Royal North Shore Hosp., Sydney, 1963; Cleveland Metropolitan Gen. Hosp., USA. Formerly Examiner in Surgery: Univs of Cambridge, Oxford, Birmingham, London, Khartoum; RCS. Hunterian Prof., RCS, 1955, and Arris and Gale Lectr, RCS, 1957, 1959; Thomas Vicary Lectr, 1970; Tudor Edwards Lectr, 1970. President: Thoracic Surgeons of Great Britain and Ireland, 1962; The Thoracic Soc., 1963. Fellow, Assoc. of Surgeons of Great Britain and Ireland. Member: Council, RCS, 1962-74, Vice-Pres., 1972; Tuberculosis Assoc. Hon. Mem., Amer. Assoc. for Thoracic Surgery. Editor of Thorax, 1946-71. *Publications:* many papers on surgical and historical subjects; contribs to many textbooks of surgery. *Recreation:* yacht cruising. *Address:* Old Palace Place, Richmond Green, Surrey. *T:* 01-940 3834. *Club:* Royal Corinthian Yacht.

BARRETT, Stephen Jeremy; HM Diplomatic Service; Fellow of the Center for International Affairs, Harvard, 1977-78; *b* 4 Dec. 1931; *s* of W. P. Barrett; *m* 1958, Alison Mary Irvine; three *s*. *Educ:* Westminster Sch.; Christ Church, Oxford (MA). FO, 1955-57; 3rd, later 2nd Sec., Political Office with Middle East Forces, Cyprus, 1957-59; Berlin, 1959-62; 1st Sec., FO, 1962-65; Head of Chancery, Helsinki, 1965-68; 1st Sec., FCO, 1968-72; Counsellor and Head of Chancery, Prague, 1972-74; Head of SW European Dept, FCO, later Principal Private Sec. to Foreign and Commonwealth Sec., 1975; Head of Science and Technology Dept, FCO, 1976-77. *Recreations:* climbing small mountains, reading. *Address:* c/o Foreign and Commonwealth Office, SW1. *Clubs:* Travellers', Hurlingham.

BARRETT, William Spencer, FBA 1965; Fellow of Keble College, Oxford, since 1952 and Tutor in Classics since 1939; Reader in Greek Literature, University of Oxford, since 1966; *b* 29 May 1914; *o s* of William Barrett and Sarah Jessie Barrett (*née* Robbins); *m* 1939, Georgina Margaret Elizabeth, *e d* of William and Alma Georgina Annie Hill; one *s* one *d*. *Educ:* Derby Sch; Christ Church, Oxford (Scholar). Ireland and Craven Schol. 1933; 1st Class Classical Hon. Mods, 1934; Gaisford Prize for Greek Verse, 1934; de Paravicini Schol., 1934; 1st Class Lit. Hum., 1937; Derby Schol., 1937; Charles Oldham Prize, 1938. Lectr, Christ Church, Oxford, 1938-39; Lectr, Keble Coll. 1939-52; Librarian, 1946-66; Univ. Lectr in Greek Literature, 1947-66; Sub Warden, Keble Coll., 1968-76. Temp. Civilian Officer, Admty (Naval Intelligence Div.), 1942-45. *Publications:* (ed) Euripides, Hippolytos, 1964; Sophocles, Niobe (in Papyrus Fragments of Sophocles, ed R. Carden), 1974;

articles in learned jls. *Address:* Keble College, Oxford. *T:* Oxford 59201; Sumner House, Mill Street, Kidlington, Oxford. *T:* Kidlington 3170.

BARRETT-LENNARD, Sir (Thomas) Richard F.; *see* Lennard.

BARRIE, Derek Stiven Maxwelton, OBE 1969 (MBE 1945); FCIT; Director, Derwent Valley Railway Company; *b* 8 Aug. 1907; *s* of John Stiven Carruthers Barrie and Dorothea Barrie; *m* 1936, Kathleen Myrra Collins; one *s* one *d. Educ:* Apsley House, Clifton; Tonbridge Sch. London and provincial journalism (Daily Graphic, Allied Newspapers, etc), reporter and sub-editor, 1924-32; joined LMS Railway, 1932; on return from war service, rejoined LMS, 1946; PRO Railway Exec., 1948; Chief PRO British Transport Commn, 1956; Asst Sec.-Gen., BTC, 1958; Asst Gen. Man., York, 1961; Chm., British Railways (Eastern) Bd, and Gen. Man., British Railways Eastern Region, 1968-70. Mem. Council, Inst. of Transport, 1968. Served with Royal Engineers, 1941-46; Hon. Col 74 Movement Control Regt, RE and RCT, 1961-67; Major, Engr. and Rly Staff Corps (T & AVR), 1967, Lt-Col 1968-73. Bronze Star Medal (US), 1945. OStJ 1968. *Publications:* numerous railway historical books and monographs; contribs various transport jls, 1928-. *Recreations:* railways, authorship, country life. *Address:* 1 Norman Close, Castlegate, Pickering, N Yorks YO18 7AZ. *T:* Pickering 73580.

BARRIE, Sir Walter, Kt 1958; Chairman of Lloyd's, 1953, 1954, 1957, 1958; Director: Jos. W. Hobbs Ltd; Westminster Bank Ltd, 1958-68; Ulster Bank, 1964-72; *b* 31 May 1901; *y s* of late Right Hon. H. T. Barrie, MP, DL, JP, and late Katie Barrie; *m* 1927, Noele Margaret (*d* 1968), *d* of G. J. Furness, JP; two *s. Educ:* Coleraine; Merchiston Castle, Edinburgh; Gonville and Caius Coll., Cambridge. Entered Lloyd's, 1926; first served on Cttee of Lloyd's, 1946; Deputy-Chm. of Lloyd's, 1951, 1952. Lloyd's Gold Medal, 1958. Pres., Insurance Inst. of London, 1955-56; Vice-Pres., Chartered Insurance Inst., 1957, 1958, 1959, Dep. Pres. 1961. Pres. 1962-63. *Recreation:* golf. *Address:* Compton Elms, Pinkneys Green, Maidenhead, Berks SL6 6NR. *T:* Maidenhead 27151. *Club:* City of London.

BARRINGTON, family name of Viscount Barrington.

BARRINGTON, 11th Viscount *cr* 1720; **Patrick William Daines Barrington;** Baron Barrington, 1720; Baron Shute (UK) 1880 (sits as Baron Shute); *b* 29 Oct. 1908; *s* of Hon. Walter Bernard Louis Barrington (*d* 1959); *S* uncle, 1960. *Educ:* Eton; Magdalen Coll., Oxford (BA). Called to the Bar, Inner Temple, 1940. Late 2nd Lieut, RA. Formerly Hon. Attaché, HBM's Embassy, Berlin, and sometime in Foreign Office. *Heir: cousin* Eric Rupert Walter Barrington [*b* 13 Dec. 1904; *m* 1st, 1929, Hester Maud Vere, CBE 1963 (marr. diss. 1938), *er d* of Rev. Guy Ronald Campbell; 2nd, 1941, Mabel Susannah, *d* of late Charles Wardrope Taylor].

BARRINGTON, Sir Charles Bacon, 6th Bt, *cr* 1831; Nurseryman (Orchid grower and Carnation specialist); *b* 6 June 1902; *s* of Sir Charles Burton Barrington, 5th Bt, and Mary Rose (*d* 1943), *d* of Sir Henry Hickman Bacon, 10th and 11th Bt; *S* father 1943; *m* 1930, Constance Doris, *d* of E. J. Elkington; two *d. Educ:* Eton. *Recreation:* horticulture. *Heir: b* Capt. Alexander Fitzwilliam Croker Barrington, *b* 19 Nov. 1909. *Address:* Barrihurst, Cranleigh, Surrey GU6 8LQ.

BARRINGTON, Prof. Ernest James William, FRS 1967; Professor of Zoology, Nottingham University, 1949-74, now Emeritus; *b* 17 Feb. 1909; *o s* of late William Benedict and Harriet Barrington; *m* 1943, Muriel Catherine Anne Clinton; one *s* one *d. Educ:* Christ's Hosp.; Oriel Coll., Oxford (Organ Scholar). ARCO 1926; LRAM 1927; BA (Oxford), 1931; BSc 1934; MA 1936; DSc 1947. Lectr in Zoology, Univ. Coll., Nottingham, 1932, Head of Zoology Dept, 1934, Reader, 1945; Dep. Vice-Chancellor, 1956-59; Public Orator, 1964-70. Rockefeller Foundation Fellow in Comparative Physiology at McGill Univ., 1939, and Harvard Univ., 1940; Buell Gallagher Vis. Prof., City Coll., New York, 1966; Royal Soc. Leverhulme Vis. Prof., Univ. of Buenos Aires, 1970; Vis. Prof., Univ. of São Paulo, 1972. European Editor, General and Comparative Endocrinology, 1960-74. Mem. Council, Royal Society, 1970-72, a Vice-Pres., 1971-72. Hon DSc Nottingham, 1975. Frink Medal, Zoological Soc. of London, 1976. Membre d'honneur, European Soc. for Comparative Endocrinology, 1974. *Publications:* Introduction to General and Comparative Endocrinology, 1963, 2nd edn, 1975; Hormones and Evolution, 1964; The Biology of Hemichordata and Protochordata, 1965; Zoological Editor, Contemporary Biology Series, 1966; Invertebrate Structure and Function, 1967; The Chemical Basis of Physiological Regulation, 1968; Perspectives in Endocrinology (Jt Editor with C. B. Jørgensen), 1968; (Jt Editor with M. Hamburgh) Hormones in Development, 1972; (ed) Trends in Comparative Endocrinology, 1975; papers on chordate morphology and physiology in various jls. *Recreation:* music. *Address:* Cornerways, 2 St Margaret's Drive, Alderton, Tewkesbury, Glos GL20 8NY. *T:* Alderton 375. *Club:* United Oxford & Cambridge University.

BARRINGTON, Sir Kenneth (Charles Peto), Kt 1973; *b* 27 Aug. 1911; *er s* of C. W. Barrington; *m* 1938, Eileen Doris Stone; one *d. Educ:* St Paul's School. FCA. Joined Morgan Grenfell & Co. Ltd, Merchant Bankers, 1929; Naval Service, 1939-46; Chartered Accountant, 1952; Director: Morgan Grenfell & Co. Ltd, 1961-76; Morgan Grenfell Holdings Ltd, 1961-76; Vice-Chm., United Biscuits Ltd; Deputy Chairman: BICC Ltd, 1973 (Dir 1966); Baker Perkins Holdings Ltd; Director of other public companies. *Address:* Hall Land, Slinfold, Horsham, West Sussex. *T:* Slinfold 790250.

BARRINGTON, Nicholas John, CVO 1975; HM Diplomatic Service; Head of Information Policy (formerly Guidance and Information Policy) Department, Foreign and Commonwealth Office, since 1976; *b* 23 July 1934; *s* of late Eric Alan Barrington and Mildred (*née* Bill). *Educ:* Repton; Clare Coll., Cambridge (MA 1957). HM Forces, RA, 1952-54. Joined Diplomatic Service, 1957; Tehran (language student), 1958; Oriental Sec., Kabul, 1959; FO, 1961; 2nd Sec., UK Delegn to European Communities, Brussels, 1963; 1st Sec., Rawalpindi, 1965; FO, 1967; Private Sec. to Permanent Under Sec., Commonwealth Office, April 1968; Asst Private Sec. to Foreign and Commonwealth Sec., Oct. 1968; Head of Chancery, Tokyo, 1972-75 (promoted Counsellor and for a period apptd Chargé d'Affaires, Hanoi, 1973). 3rd Cl., Order of the Sacred Treasure, Japan, 1975. *Recreations:* theatre, drawing, prosopography. *Address:* 21 Alwyne Villas, N1. *T:* 01-226 7321; 23 Wingate Way, Trumpington, Cambridge. *Clubs:* Athenæum, Royal Commonwealth Society.

BARRINGTON-WARD, Rev. Canon Simon; General Secretary, Church Missionary Society, since 1975; Hon. Canon of Derby Cathedral, since 1975; *b* 27 May 1930; *s* of Robert McGowan Barrington-Ward and Margaret Adele Barrington-Ward; *m* 1963, Jean Caverhill Taylor; two *d. Educ:* Eton; Magdalene Coll., Cambridge (MA). Lektor, Free Univ., Berlin, 1953-54; Westcott House, Cambridge, 1954-56; Chaplain, Magdalene Coll., Cambridge, 1956-60; Asst Lectr in Religious Studies, Univ. of Ibadan, 1960-63; Fellow and Dean of Chapel, Magdalene Coll., Cambridge, 1963-69; Principal, Crowther Hall, Selly Oak Colls, Birmingham, 1969-74. FRAI. *Address:* 62 Park House Gardens, Twickenham, Mddx TW1 2DE. *T:* 01-892 4852.

BARRITT, Sir David (Thurlow), Kt 1969; BSc, FIChemE; Chairman, Cammell Laird, since 1971; *b* 17 Oct. 1903; *er s* of late David Webster Barritt and Rachel Barritt; *m* 1931, Hilda Marshall Creyke; one *s. Educ:* High Sch., Newcastle-under-Lyme, Staffs; N Staffs Polytechnic. Chairman: Simon Engineering Ltd, 1963-70; Twyfords Holdings Ltd, 1969-71; Davy International, 1970-73. Chm. Govs, The Newcastle-under-Lyme Endowed Schs, Newcastle, Staffs, 1962-72. FInstF; Vice-Pres., IChemE 1974. *Publications:* papers in technical jls. *Recreations:* golf, music, gardening, photography. *Address:* Stone Cottage, Prestbury, Cheshire, SK10 4AH. *T:* Prestbury 49716. *Club:* Carlton.

BARRITT, Rev. Gordon Emerson; Principal, National Children's Home, since 1969; *b* 30 Sept. 1920; *s* of Norman and Doris Barritt; *m* 1947, Joan Mary Alway; two *s* one *d. Educ:* William Hulme's Grammar Sch., Manchester; Manchester Univ.; Cambridge Univ. (Wesley House and Fitzwilliam Coll.). Served War, RAF, 1942-45 (despatches). Methodist Minister: Kempston Methodist Church, Bedford, 1947-52; Westlands Methodist Church, Newcastle-under-Lyme, 1952-57; Chaplain, Univ. of Keele, 1953-57. Treasurer, Nat. Council of Voluntary Child Care Organisations (Chm., 1970-72); Member: Home Office Adv. Council on Child Care, 1968-71; Exec. of Nat. Children's Bureau; Brit. Assoc. of Social Workers. *Publications:* The Edgworth Story, 1972; (ed) Many Pieces—One Aim, 1975; contributor to: Caring for Children, 1969. *Recreations:* music, do-it-yourself. *Address:* (office) National Children's Home, 85 Highbury Park, N5 1UD. *T:* 01-226 2033; (residence) 107 Old Park Ridings, Grange Park, N21 2EJ. *T:* 01-366 1687.

BARRON, Sir Donald (James), Kt 1972; DL; Chairman, Rowntree Mackintosh Ltd, since 1966; *b* 17 March 1921; *o s* of Albert Gibson Barron and Elizabeth Macdonald, Edinburgh; *m* 1956, Gillian Mary, *o d* of John Saville, York; three *s* two *d. Educ:* George Heriot's Sch., Edinburgh; Edinburgh Univ.

(BCom). Member, Inst. Chartered Accountants of Scotland. Joined Rowntree Mackintosh Ltd, 1952; Dir, 1961; Vice-Chm., 1965; Dir, Midland Bank Ltd. Trustee, Joseph Rowntree Memorial Trust, 1966-73, 1975-; Treasurer, York Univ., 1966-72; Member: Council of CBI, 1966-; SSRC, 1971-72; UGC, 1972-. DL N Yorks (formerly WR Yorks and City of York), 1971. *Recreations:* golf, tennis, boating, gardening. *Address:* Greenfield, Sim Balk Lane, Bishopthorpe, York. *T:* York 705675. *Clubs:* Athenæum; Yorkshire (York).

BARRON, Donovan Allaway, CBE 1962; MIEE; Engineer-in-Chief of the Post Office, 1965-67; *b* 1907; *s* of late George Barron; *m* 1941, Margaret Kathleen, *d* of Percival Aylwin Selfe; one *d. Educ:* Bristol Grammar Sch.; Bristol Univ. BSc 1927, MSc 1936. General Post Office: Asst Engineer, 1927-35; Area Engineer, 1936-40; Asst Staff Engineer, 1941-48; Staff Engineer, 1949-53; Asst Engineer-in-Chief, 1954-59; Deputy Engineer-in-Chief, 1960-65. Formerly Member of the Council of the Institution of Electrical Engineers. *Publications:* various contributions to learned journals. *Recreations:* music, gardening, philately. *Address:* 18 Reddons Road, Beckenham, Kent BR3 1LZ. *T:* 01-778 4162.

BARRON, Douglas Shield, CIE 1945; Chairman, Godfrey Phillips, India, Ltd, retired 1973; *b* 18 March 1904; *s* of Thomas Barron; *m* 1934, Doris Katherine (*d* 1970), *o d* of late Henry Deakin; no *c. Educ:* Holgate Grammar Sch.; Corpus Christi Coll., Cambridge. Joined Indian Civil Service, 1926; retired, 1948. *Recreations:* shooting, fishing, golf. *Address:* Eyeworth Lodge, Fritham, Lyndhurst, Hants SO4 7HJ. *T:* Cadnam 2256. *Clubs:* Oriental; Bombay Yacht.

BARRON, Prof. John Penrose, MA, DPhil, FSA; Professor of Greek Language and Literature, University of London, since 1971, and Head of Department of Classics, King's College London, since 1972; *b* 27 Apr. 1934; *s* of George Barron and Minnie Leslie Marks; *m* 1962, Caroline Mary, *d* of late W. D. Hogarth, OBE; two *d. Educ:* Clifton Coll.; Balliol Coll., Oxford (Hon. Exhibnr). 1st Cl., Class. Hon. Mods, 1955; Lit. Hum., 1957; MA 1960, DPhil 1961; Thomas Whitcombe Greene Prizeman, 1955, and Scholar, 1957; Barclay Head Prizeman, 1959; Cromer Prize, British Academy, 1963. Asst Lectr in Latin, Bedford Coll., 1959-61, and Lectr, 1961-64; Lectr in Archaeology, University Coll. London, 1964-67; Reader in Archaeology and Numismatics, Univ. of London, 1967-71; Dean, Faculty of Arts, Univ. of London, 1976-. *Publications:* Greek Sculpture, 1965; Silver Coins of Samos, 1966; articles in Classical Quarterly, Jl of Hellenic Studies, Bulletin of Inst. of Classical Studies, etc. *Recreations:* travel, homes and gardens. *Address:* King's College, Strand, WC2R 2LS. *T:* 01-836 5454.

BARRON, Rt. Rev. Patrick Harold Falkiner; *see* George, Bishop of.

BARRON, Wilfrid P. S.; *see* Shepherd-Barron.

BARROW, Rt. Hon. Errol Walton, PC 1969; MP (Democratic Labour Party), Barbados; *b* 21 Jan. 1920; *s* of Reginald Grant Barrow, LTh, DD (retired), and Ruth Barrow (*née* O'Neal); *m* 1945, Carolyn Plaskett; one *s* one *d. Educ:* Harrison Coll., Barbados; LSE (BSc); Hon. Fellow 1975. Royal Air Force, 1940-47. Barrister, Lincoln's Inn, 1949. Elected House of Assembly, Barbados, 1951; Minister of Finance, 1959-76; Premier, 1961; Prime Minister, 1966-76. Hon. LLD, McGill, 1966. *Recreations:* sailing, flying, diving, tennis. *Address:* PO Box 125, Bridgetown, Barbados.

BARROW, Prof. Geoffrey Wallis Steuart, FRSE; FBA 1976; Professor of Scottish History, University of St Andrews, since 1974; *b* Headingley, Leeds, 28 Nov. 1924; *s* of late Charles Embleton Barrow and Marjorie, *d* of Donald Stuart; *m* 1951, Heather Elizabeth, *d* of James McLeish Lownie; one *s* one *d. Educ:* St Edward's Sch., Oxford; Inverness Royal Acad.; St Andrews Univ.; Pembroke Coll., Oxford. FRSE 1977. Lecturer in History, University Coll., London, 1950-61; Prof. of Mediaeval Hist., King's Coll., Univ. of Durham, later Univ. of Newcastle upon Tyne, 1961-74. Ford's Lectr, Univ. of Oxford, 1977. *Publications:* Feudal Britain, 1956; Acts of Malcolm IV, King of Scots, 1960; Robert Bruce and the Community of the Realm of Scotland, 1965; Acts of William I, King of Scots, 1971; Kingdom of the Scots, 1973; (ed) The Scottish Tradition, 1974; contrib. Scottish Historical Review, etc. *Recreation:* hill walking. *Address:* University of St Andrews, St Andrews, Fife KY16 9AL.

BARROW, John Frederick; HM Diplomatic Service, retired; *b* 28 Dec. 1918; *s* of Frederick William and Caroline Barrow; *m* 1947, Mary Roberta Young; two *d. Educ:* King Edward VII Sch.,

King's Lynn. Home Civil Service, 1936-39; war service in British and Indian Armies, 1939-46 (Major); rejoined Home Civil Service, 1946; Treasury, 1952-62; FCO, 1962; service overseas at Delhi, Kuala Lumpur, Jesselton, Prague, Washington, Hong Kong; retired as Counsellor, 1977. *Address:* 29 Raleigh Court, Lymer Avenue, SE19 1LS; 2 Tomkyns, Hillside Street, Hythe, Kent CT21 5EQ.

BARROW, Rev. Canon John Harrison, MA; Vicar of Stansted Mountfitchet, Essex, 1932-54; Honorary Canon of Chelmsford Cathedral, 1935-75, now Emeritus; *b* 11 Oct. 1881; *s* of James and Elizabeth Agnes Barrow; *m* 1917, Mary Irene Debnam (*d* 1976); one *s. Educ:* Durham Sch.; Pembroke Coll., Oxford. Curate of St Luke, Victoria Docks, E, 1904-10; St Mary's, Chelmsford, 1911-14; Precentor of St Mary's Cathedral, Chelmsford, 1914-17; Rector of St Andrew, Romford, 1917; Curate of Dalton-in-Furness, 1917-19; Sec. of Bishop of Chelmsford's Crusade Fund, 1919-22; Metropolitan Organising Sec. of SPCK, Dioceses Chelmsford, London, St Albans, and Southwark, 1922-32; Surrogate, 1915-75; Proctor in Convocation, Diocese of Chelmsford, 1926-50; Vice-Chm. Council, RSCM, 1945-76. Hon. Chaplain to Bishop of Chelmsford, 1951-61, 1962-70, 1971-75; Chaplain to High Sheriff 1955-56, 1962-63; Chapter Clerk, 1957-75; Priest-in-charge, Margaret Roding, 1955-56, Roxwell, 1957-59. *Recreation:* motoring. *Address:* 189 Kingsdown Avenue, South Croydon, Surrey CR2 6QS. *T:* 01-660 4461. *Club:* Church House.

BARROW, Captain Sir Richard John Uniacke, 6th Bt *cr* 1835; *b* 2 Aug. 1933; *s* of Sir Wilfrid John Wilson Croker Barrow, 5th Bt and (Gwladys) Patricia (*née* Uniacke); *S* father 1960; *m* 1961, Alison Kate, *yr d* of late Capt. Russell Grenfell, RN, and of Mrs Lindsay-Young; one *s* two *d. Educ:* Abbey Sch., Ramsgate; Beaumont Coll., Old Windsor. Commnd. 2nd Lieut Irish Guards, 1952; served: Germany, 1952-53; Egypt, 1953-56; Cyprus, 1958; Germany, 1959-60; retired, 1960; joined International Computers and Tabulators Ltd; resigned 1973. *Heir: s* Anthony John Grenfell Barrow, *b* 24 May 1962. *Address:* 36 South Vale, SE19. *T:* 01-771 0905.

BARROWCLOUGH, Anthony Richard, QC 1974; a Recorder of the Crown Court, since 1972; *b* 24 June 1924; *m* 1949, Mary Agnes Pery-Knox-Gore; one *s* one *d. Educ:* Stowe; New Coll., Oxford. Served RNVR, 1943-46 (Sub-Lieut and later Lieut). Called to the Bar, Inner Temple, 1949. Part-time Member, Monopolies Commn, 1966-69. *Recreation:* country pursuits. *Address:* 13 Hillgate Place, W8; The Old Vicarage, Winsford, near Minehead, Somerset.

BARRY, Geraldine Mary; retired; late Senior Surgeon, Royal Free Hospital, and Senior Surgeon, London Homœopathic Hospital; Examiner in Surgery, University of London; *b* 4 Oct. 1897; *d* of Rev. Walter George and Anna Barry. *Educ:* Queen Anne's Sch., Caversham; London (Royal Free Hosp.); Sch. of Medicine for Women, MRCS, LRCP 1921; MB, BS London Univ. Gold Medal, Distinction Medicine and Surgery, 1922; FRCS, 1926; MS London, 1929; Asst Surgeon, London Homœopathic Hospital, 1929; Asst Surgeon, Royal Free Hospital, 1930; EMS, Surgeon to Three Counties Emergency Hospital, Arlesey, Beds, 1940. *Address:* Three Hedges, Dungells Lane, Yateley, near Camberley, Surrey. *T:* Yateley 873187.

BARRY, Sir (Lawrence) Edward (Anthony Tress), 5th Bt *cr* 1899; *b* 1 Nov. 1939; *s* of Sir Rupert Rodney Francis Tress Barry, 4th Bt, MBE, and Diana Madeline (*d* 1948), *o d* of R. O'Brien Thompson; *S* father, 1977; *m* 1968, Fenella Hoult; one *s* one *d. Educ:* Haileybury. Formerly Captain, Grenadier Guards. *Heir: s* William Rupert Philip Tress Barry, *b* 13 Dec. 1973. *Address:* 3 Sunnyside Cottages, Warehorne Road, Ham Street, Kent. *T:* Ham Street 2464.

BARRY, Michael, (James Barry Jackson); OBE 1956; Principal, London Academy of Music and Dramatic Art, since 1973; *b* 15 May 1910; *s* of A. G. and Helen Jackson; *m* 1st, 1934, Judith Gick (marr. diss. 1947); one *d*; 2nd, 1948, Rosemary Corbett (*d* 1968); one *d*; 3rd, 1973, Pamela Corbett. Studied farming and horticulture in Glos and Herts. Studied for theatre at RADA (Baliol Holloway Award, Best Diploma Performance, 1930) and subsequently as actor, stage-manager, designer and producer at the Northampton, Birmingham, Hull and Croydon Repertory Theatres before working in London. Appointed BBC television producer, 1938. Served Royal Marine Brigade Landing-Craft and as AMS, RM Office, 1939-45 (Major); Producer and writer, BBC television drama and documentary, 1946-51 (Programmes included: The Silence of the Sea, I Want to Be a Doctor, Promise of Tomorrow, The Passionate Pilgrim, Shout Aloud Salvation); Head of Drama, BBC Television, 1952-61; Programme Controller, Irish Television, 1961-63; prod The Wars of the

Roses (TV), 1966; Prof. of Drama and Dept Head, Stanford Univ., Calif, 1968-72. Literary Adviser, Council of Repertory Theatres, 1964-67; Member: Drama Panel, Arts Council, 1955-68; Council, RADA, 1966-69; Nat. Council Drama Training, 1976; Governing Body, Wimbledon Sch. of Art, 1976. Desmond Davis Award, SFTA, 1961. *Publication:* (selected) The Television Playwright, 1960. *Address:* 5 Clarence Gardens, Brighton, East Sussex. *Club:* Savile.

BARRY, Rev. Noel Patrick, OSB; Headmaster of Ampleforth College, since 1964; *b* 6 Dec. 1917; 2nd *s* of Dr T. St J. Barry, Wallasey, Cheshire. *Educ:* Ampleforth Coll.; St Benet's Hall, Oxford. Housemaster, Ampleforth Coll., 1954-64. Governor, Westminster Cathedral Choir Sch., 1977-. Chm., HMC, 1975-76. *Address:* Ampleforth College, York. *T:* Ampleforth 224.

BARRY, Norman, SRN, RMN, RMPA; Divisional Nursing Officer (Mental Illness), South District, Kensington, Chelsea and Westminster Area Health Authority, since 1975; based at Banstead Hospital; Chairman, General Nursing Council, since 1974; *b* 30 July 1916; *s* of Edward and Annie Barry; *m* 1940, Winifred McGowan; two *d. Educ:* Houghton-le-Spring Intermed. Sch. Graylingwell Hosp.: completed Mental Nurse trng, 1939; Staff Nurse, 1939; served RAMC, 1940-47; Staff Nurse, Graylingwell Hosp., 1947-50; qual. SRN, Lambeth Hosp., 1951; Graylingwell Hosp.: Charge Nurse, 1951, Night Supt, 1953; Sen. Asst Chief Male Nurse, Park Prewett Hosp., 1954; Banstead Hosp.: Dep. Chief Male Nurse, 1955, Chief Male Nurse, 1960, Chief Nursing Officer, 1972. Gen. Nursing Council: Mem., 1970- (Mem. Mental Nurses Cttee, Dec. 1960-); Vice-Chm., 1972-74; Mem. DHSS and Nat. Assoc. for Mental Health gps examining care of patients in mental hosps; Chm., Nat. Assoc. Chief and Prin. Nursing Officers. *Recreation:* reading (lay reader, All Saints Church, Banstead). *Address:* 130 Winkworth Road, Banstead, Surrey SM7 2QT. *T:* Burgh Heath 57376.

BARRY, Sir Philip Stuart M.; *see* Milner-Barry.

BARRY, Maj.-Gen. Richard Hugh, CB 1962; CBE 1953 (OBE 1943); retired; *b* 9 Nov. 1908; *s* of Lieut-Col Alfred Percival Barry and Helen Charlotte (*née* Stephens); *m* 1st, 1940, Rosalind Joyce Evans (*d* 1973); one *s* two *d*; 2nd, 1975, Elizabeth Lucia Middleton. *Educ:* Winchester; Sandhurst. 2nd Lieut Somerset LI, 1929; Staff Coll., Camberley, Capt., 1938; served War of 1939-45; BEF, SOE, AFHQ, Algiers. Military Attaché, Stockholm, 1947; Deputy Chief of Staff Europe Land Forces, 1948; Dir, Standing Group, NATO, 1952; Chief of Staff, HQ British Troops in Egypt, 1954-56; Imperial Defence Coll., 1957; Standing Group Representative, North Atlantic Council, 1959-62; retired, 1962. Maj.-Gen. 1959. Africa Star, 1943; 1939-45 Star; Defence, Victory Medals, 1945. *Recreation:* hunting. *Address:* Little Place, Farringdon, Alton, Hants GU34 3DH. *T:* Tisted 216. *Club:* Army and Navy.

BARSON, Derek Emmanuel; Director General, British Red Cross Society, since 1976; *b* 31 Jan. 1922; *s* of Horace Barson and Phyllis Edna (*née* Hathaway); *m* 1948, Maya Renwick; two *s* one *d. Educ:* Westminster Abbey Choir Sch.; The King's Sch., Ely; Downing Coll., Cambridge. FCIS. Served War, UK, ME, E Africa, Burma, Ethiopia: Major, King's Shropshire LI (despatches, Burma, 1944), 1942-47. Cambridge, 1947-49; HM Colonial Admin. Service, Nyasaland, 1949-64. Asst Sec., Royal Nat. Life-Boat Instn, 1964-69; Sec., British Red Cross Soc., 1970-75. *Recreations:* music (esp. choral), conducting, country walking. *Address:* Willow Cottage, Slines Oak Road, Woldingham, Surrey. *T:* Woldingham 2381. *Clubs:* Royal Over-Seas League, Anglo-Belgian.

BARSTOW, Josephine, (Mrs Ande Anderson); opera singer, free-lance since 1971; *b* Sheffield, 27 Sept. 1940; *m* 1969, Ande Anderson; no *c. Educ:* Birmingham Univ. (BA). Debut with Opera for All, 1964; studied at London Opera Centre, 1965-66; Opera for All, 1966; Glyndebourne Chorus, 1967; Sadler's Wells Contract Principal, 1967-68, sang Cherubino, Euridice, Violetta; Welsh Nat. Opera Contract Principal, 1968-70, sang Violetta, Countess, Fiordiligi, Mimi, Amelia, Simon Boccanegra; Covent Garden: Helena, world première, Tippett's The Knot Garden, 1970 (recorded 1974); has sung all parts in Hoffman, Emilia Marty (Makropulos Case), Natasha (War and Peace) and Traviata, Sadler's Wells; Alice in Falstaff, Aix-en-Provence Festival, 1971; Nitocris in Belshazzar, Geneva, 1972; Lady Macbeth in TV recording for Glyndebourne, 1972; Elizabeth (Don Carlos), WNO, 1973; Jeanne, British première, Penderecki's The Devils, 1973; Marguerite, world première, Crosse's The Story of Vasco, 1974; Electra in Idomeneo, Glyndebourne, 1974; Octavian in Der Rosenkavalier, Coliseum, 1975; Alice in Falstaff, Covent Garden, 1975; title rôles, Salome,

Coliseum, 1975, Jenufa, Welsh Nat. Opera, 1975; Elizabeth, Don Carlos, Coliseum, 1976; Tosca, Coliseum, 1976; Fidelio, Jenufa, Scottish Opera, 1977; US debut as Lady Macbeth, Miami, 1977; Musetta in La Bohème, NY Met., 1977; Gayle, world première, Tippett's The Ice Break, 1977. *Recreations:* country cottage where grows all own vegetables and endless flowers. *Address:* c/o John Coast, 1 Park Close, Knightsbridge, SW1X 7PQ.

BARSTOW, Stan; writer; *b* 28 June 1928; *s* of Wilfred Barstow and Elsie Gosney; *m* 1951, Constance Mary Kershaw; one *s* one *d. Educ:* Ossett Grammar Sch. Employed in Engineering Industry, 1944-62, mainly as Draughtsman. Best Drama Series Award, British Broadcasting Press Guild, 1974; Best British Drama Series, SFTA, 1974; Best British Dramatisation, Writers' Guild of GB, 1974; Royal TV Soc. Writers' Award, 1975. *Television:* dramatisations: A Raging Calm, 1974; South Riding, 1974; Joby, 1975; The Cost of Loving, 1977. *Publications:* A Kind of Loving, 1960; The Desperadoes, 1961; Ask Me Tomorrow, 1962; Joby, 1964; The Watchers on the Shore, 1966; A Raging Calm, 1968; A Season with Eros, 1971; The Right True End, 1976; Joby, 1977; *plays:* (with Alfred Bradley): Ask Me Tomorrow, 1966; A Kind of Loving, 1970; Stringer's Last Stand, 1972. *Address:* Goring House, Goring Park Avenue, Ossett, West Yorks. *T:* Ossett 273362.

BART, A. S.; *see* Schwarz-Bart.

BART, Lionel; composer, lyricist and playwright; *b* 1 Aug. 1930. Wrote lyrics for Lock Up Your Daughters, 1959; music and lyrics for Fings Ain't Wot They Used T'be, 1959; music, lyrics and book for Oliver!, 1960; music, lyrics and direction of Blitz!, 1962; music and lyrics of Maggie May, 1964; music of Lionel, 1977. Has also written several film scores and many individual hit songs. *Films:* Serious Charge; In the Nick; Heart of a Man; Let's Get Married; Light up the Sky; The Tommy Steele Story; The Duke Wore Jeans; Tommy the Toreador; Sparrers Can't Sing; From Russia with Love; Man in the Middle; Oliver; The Optimists. Ivor Novello Awards as a song writer: three in 1957; four in 1959; two in 1960. Variety Club Silver Heart as Show Business Personality of the Year, 1960. Broadway, USA; Tony (Antoinette Perry) Award, etc (for Oliver!), best composer and lyricist, 1962. *Address:* c/o Patricia McNaughton, MLR, 194 Old Brompton Road, SW5. *T:* 01-373 1161.

BARTER, John (Wilfred); JP; Chartered Secretary; Management and Financial Consultant; *b* 6 Oct. 1917; *s* of late W. F. Barter; *m* 1st, 1941, Joan Mackay (*d* 1973); two *s* one *d*; 2nd, 1974, Jessica Crabtree. *Educ:* Royal Pinner Sch. Contested (C) East Ham South, 1951; MP (C) Ealing North, 1955-64; PPS to Minister of Health, 1957; PPS to Parly Sec., Min. of Power, 1958-60. Middlesex County Council: Mem., 1949; Alderman, 1961-65; Leader of Majority Party, 1962-63; Vice-Chm., 1963-64; last Chm., 1964-65. Chm. subseq. Pres., Middlesex County Assoc., 1964-76. JP Greater London, Middlesex, 1974.

BARTHOLOMEW, John Eric, OBE 1976, (**Eric Morecambe**); actor comedian; *b* 14 May 1926; *m* 1952, Joan Dorothy Bartlett; one *s* one *d* (and one adopted *s*). *Educ:* Euston Road Elementary Sch., Morecambe. First double act (with E. Wise), at Empire Theatre, Liverpool, 1941; first broadcast, 1943; BBC television series, 1955; BBC TV and ATV series, 1961-. Best Light Entertainment Award, SFTA, 1963, 1971, 1972, 1973, 1974. *Films:* The Intelligence Men, 1964; That Riviera Touch, 1965; The Magnificent Two, 1966. A Vice-Pres., Luton Town Football Club (Dir, 1969-75). Pres., Lord's Taverners', 1977. Freeman, City of London, 1976. *Publications:* (with E. Wise) Eric and Ernie: an autobiography of Morecambe and Wise, 1973; The Best of Morecambe and Wise, ed E. Braben, 1975. *Recreation:* fishing. *Address:* 235/241 Regent Street, W1A 2JT. *T:* 01-734 8851.

BARTINGTON, Dennis Walter, CB 1950; *b* 12 May 1901; *s* of late Walter Bartington; *m* 1934, Margaret Christina Skinner. *Educ:* Dulwich Coll.; Trinity Coll., Cambridge (Sen. Schol., MA). Inland Revenue, 1923; Department of Scientific and Industrial Research, 1925; War Office, 1926-39; Asst Sec., Ministry of Supply, 1939, Principal Asst Sec., 1942; Under-Sec., 1947-59. Min. of Aviation, 1959-61; retired, 1961. *Address:* Kingsfield, Orchard Way, Esher, Surrey KT10 9DY. *T:* Esher 63918. *Club:* United Oxford & Cambridge University.

BARTLE, Ronald David; a Metropolitan Stipendiary Magistrate since 1972; a Deputy Circuit Judge, since 1975; *b* 14 April 1929; *s* of Rev. George Clement Bartle and Winifred Marie Bartle; *m* 1963, Barbara Gloria Teleri Dawn Bartle (*née* Williams); one *s* one *d. Educ:* St John's Sch., Leatherhead; Jesus Coll., Cambridge (MA). Called to Bar, Lincoln's Inn, 1954. Contested

(C) Islington North, 1958 and 1959. A Chm., Inner London Juvenile Courts, 1975-. Freeman, Basketmaker's Co., 1976. Freeman, City of London, 1976. *Publication:* Introduction to Shipping Law, 1958. *Recreations:* music, gardening. *Address:* Thames Magistrates' Court, Aylward Street, Stepney, E1.

BARTLETT, Lt-Col Sir Basil Hardington, 2nd Bt, *cr* 1913; BA; dramatic author; *b* 15 Sept. 1905; *s* of late Hardington Arthur Bartlett, *e s* of 1st Bt and Irene (*d* 1974), *d* of Prof. Henry Robinson; *S* grandfather, 1921; *m* 1937, Mary (marr. diss. 1960), *o d* of late Sir Ian Malcolm, KCMG; three *d. Educ:* Repton; Corpus Christi Coll., Cambridge. Served War of 1939-45 (wounded, despatches); Lt-Col, Intelligence Corps. Drama script supervisor, BBC, Television, 1952-55. *Publications:* My First War, 1940; Next of Kin, 1944. *Plays:* This Seat of Mars, 1938; The Intruder, 1939; The Jersey Lily, produced Gate Theatre, 1940; Less than Kind, 1947; A Fish in the Family, 1947. *Heir: b* Henry David Hardington Bartlett, MBE [*b* 18 March 1912; *m* 1936, Katherine Rosemond (marr. diss.), *d* of Lt-Col W. H. Stanbury; three *s*]. *Clubs:* Garrick, Beefsteak.

BARTLETT, Charles; *see* Bartlett, Harold Charles.

BARTLETT, Charles Vernon Oldfeld; *see* Bartlett, Vernon.

BARTLETT, (Harold) Charles, ARCA 1949; RE 1961 (ARE 1950); RWS 1970 (ARWS 1959); painter and printmaker; *b* Grimsby, 23 Sept. 1921; *s* of Charles Henry and Frances Kate Bartlett; *m* ; one *s. Educ:* Eastbourne Grammar Sch.; Eastbourne Sch. of Art; Royal College of Art. First one man exhibition in London, 1960. *Recreations:* music, sailing. *Address:* St Andrews, Fingringhoe, near Colchester, Essex. *T:* Rowhedge 406.

BARTLETT, Henry Francis, CMG 1975; OBE 1964; Executive Officer, Utah Foundation, Brisbane, since 1976; HM Diplomatic Service, retired; *b* 8 March 1916; *s* of F. V. S. and A. G. Bartlett, London; *m* 1940, A. D. Roy. *Educ:* St Paul's Sch.; Queen's Coll., Oxford; Univ. of California (Commonwealth Fellow). Min. of Inf., 1940-45; Paris, 1944-47; Vice-Consul Lyons, 1948-49; FO, 1949-50; Vice-Consul, Szczecin, 1950; Second, later First, Sec., Warsaw, 1951-53; FO, 1953-55; First Sec. (Commercial), Caracas, 1955-60; First Sec. (Inf.), Mexico City, 1960-63; Consul, Khorramshahr, 1964-67; Dep. High Comr, Brisbane, 1967-69; Counsellor, Manila, 1969-72 (Chargé d'Affaires, 1971); Ambassador to Paraguay, 1972-75. Hon. Prof., Nat. Univ. of Asunción, 1975. Trustee, Queensland Art Gallery, 1977-. *Recreation:* painting (one-man shows Paris, London, Caracas, Mexico City, Brisbane). *Address:* c/o Utah Foundation, PO Box 1297, Brisbane, Qld 4001, Australia; 14 Bowen Place, 341 Bowen Terrace, New Farm, Qld 4005, Australia.

BARTLETT, John Vernon, CBE 1976; MA; CEng, FICE, FASCE, FIE Aust.; Consulting Engineer; Senior Partner and Chairman, Mott, Hay & Anderson; *b* 18 June 1927; *s* of late Vernon F. Bartlett and Olga Bartlett (*née* Testrup); *m* 1951, Gillian, *d* of late Philip Hoffmann, Sturmer Hall, Essex; four *s. Educ:* Stowe; Trinity Coll., Cambridge. Served 9th Airborne Squadron, RE, 1946-48. Engineer with John Mowlem & Co. Ltd, 1951-57; joined staff of Mott, Hay & Anderson, 1957; Partner, 1966-. Mem. Council, ICE, 1974-. Telford Gold Medal, (jointly) 1971, 1973; S. G. Brown Medal, Royal Soc., 1973. FRSA 1975. *Publications:* contrib. various papers to ICE, ASCE, etc. *Recreation:* sailing. *Address:* c/o Mott, Hay & Anderson, 20/26 Wellesley Road, Croydon, Surrey CR9 2UL. *T:* 01-686 5041. *Clubs:* St Stephens; Hawks (Cambridge).

BARTLETT, Prof. Maurice Stevenson, FRS 1961; MA Cambridge, DSc London; Professor of Bio-mathematics in the University of Oxford, 1967-75, now Emeritus; *b* 18 June 1910; *s* of W. S. Bartlett, Scrooby; *m* 1957, Sheila, *d* of C. E. Chapman; one *d. Educ:* Latymer Upper Sch.; Queens' Coll., Cambridge. Wrangler, 1932; Rayleigh Prize, 1934. Asst Lectr in Statistics, University Coll., London, 1933-34; Statistician, Imperial Chemical Industries, Ltd, 1934-38; Lectr in Mathematics, Univ. of Cambridge, 1938-47. National Service, Min. of Supply, 1940-45. Visiting Prof. of Mathematical Statistics, Univ. of North Carolina, 1946; Prof. of Mathematical Statistics, Univ. of Manchester, 1947-60; Prof. of Statistics, Univ. of London (University Coll.), 1960-67. Mem. Internat. Statistical Institute, 1949; President: Manchester Statistical Soc., 1959-60; Biometric Soc. (Brit. Reg.), 1964-66; Internat. Assoc. Statistics Phys. Sci., 1965-67; Royal Statistical Society, 1966-67. Hon. DSc: Chicago, 1966; Hull, 1976. Gold Medal, Royal Statistical Soc., 1969; Weldon Prize and Medal, Oxford, 1971. *Publications:* An Introduction to Stochastic Processes, 1955; Stochastic Population Models in Ecology and Epidemiology, 1960; Essays in Probability and Statistics, 1962; Probability, Statistics and

Time, 1975; Statistical Analysis of Spatial Pattern 1976; papers on statistical and biometrical theory and methodology. *Address:* 117 Littlehampton Road, Worthing, West Sussex BN13 1QU.

BARTLETT, Prof. Neil, FRS 1973; FRIC; Professor of Chemistry, University of California, Berkeley, since 1969, and Principal Investigator, Materials and Molecular Research Division, Lawrence Berkeley Laboratory, since 1977; *b* Newcastle upon Tyne, 15 Sept. 1932; *s* of Norman Bartlett and Ann Willins Bartlett (*née* Voak), both of Newcastle upon Tyne; *m* 1957, Christina I., *d* of J. W. F. Cross, Guisborough, Yorks; three *s* one *d. Educ:* Heaton Grammar Sch., Newcastle upon Tyne; King's Coll., Univ. of Durham, Newcastle upon Tyne. BSc 1954, PhD 1958. Senior Chemistry Master, The Duke's Sch., Alnwick, Northumberland, 1957-58; Mem. Faculty (Dept of Chemistry), Univ. of British Columbia, 1958-66; Prof. of Chemistry, Princeton Univ., and Scientist, Bell Telephone Laboratories, Murray Hill, NJ, USA, 1966-69. Member: Deutsche Akademie der Naturforscher Leopoldina; Amer. Chem. Soc., Amer. Soc. for Advancement of Science, etc. Sigma Xi. Visiting Miller Prof., Univ. of Calif, Berkeley, 1967-68, etc. Hon. DSc: Univ. of Waterloo, Canada, 1970; Colby Coll., Maine, USA, 1972; Dr *hc* Univ. of Bordeaux, 1976. Fellow: Chem. Inst. of Canada; Chem. Soc. (London). Corday-Morgan Medal and Prize of Chem. Soc., 1962; Robert A. Welch Award, 1976; various overseas awards and prizes, 1965-. *Publications:* The Chemistry of the Monatomic Gases, 1975; scientific papers to: Jl of Chem. Soc., Inorganic Chem., etc; Mem. various editorial advisory bds in Gt Britain and USA. *Recreations:* water colour painting; walking in high country; gardening. *Address:* 6 Oak Drive, Orinda, Calif 94563, USA. *T:* (415) 254 5322; Chemistry Dept, University of California, Berkeley, Calif 94720, USA. *T:* (business) (415) 642-7259.

BARTLETT, Peter Geoffrey, FRIBA; Partner, Bartlett & Gray, Chartered Architects/Surveyors, Nottingham, since 1951; *b* Bristol, 15 May 1922; *s* of Percy Bartlett, FRIBA, and Daisy Bartlett (*née* Eungblut); *m* 1944, Joan Trevor Lees; one *s. Educ:* Nottingham High Sch.; Nottingham Sch. of Architecture, 1939-40 and 1946-49 (Governor's Prize 1949). DipArch, MInstRA. LDV, 1939-40. Served War, Pilot, RAF, 1940-46 (Bomber, Middle East and Transport Commands). Lectr, Sch. of Architecture, Nottingham, and Asst Architect, Dudding and Thornely, 1949-51. RIBA Bronze Medal (for Notts, Derbys, Lincs), 1958-61; Civic Trust Awards and Commendations in 1960, 1965, 1968, 1969; Craftmanship Awards in E Midlands, 1967, 1968; Competitions: (Jt winners) Brit. Columbia Lumber Manufrs Assoc. of Canada for Housing of Timber Construction, 1958; Special Collective Insts for the Physically Handicapped, Kuwait, Arabia, 1961; original research into: timber constr. in Canada, 1958; pre-cast concrete constr. in Denmark, 1958; Bldgs in hot climates in Kuwait, 1962. RIBA Part III Examr, Univ. of Nottingham, 1975-; Mem., Court of Governors, Univ. of Nottingham, 1975-; Mem. Council, RIBA, 1973-76; Mem. Press Council, 1973-76; Past Pres., Nottingham and Derby Soc. of Architects. FRSA. Liveryman, Guild of Air Pilots and Air Navigators; Freeman, City of London. Qual. Flying Instr, Gps A and B; Mem. Flying Trng Cttee of Brit. Light Aviation Centre, 1966-68; Bd of Trade Examr for Private Pilot's Licence, 1967-69. *Recreations:* inland waterways, gardening. *Address:* (home) The Pantiles, Mill Road, Elston, near Newark, Notts. *T:* East Stoke 241; (office) Bartlett & Gray, DipArch, F/FRIBA, 14-16 Bridgford Road, West Bridgford, Nottingham NG2 6AF. *T:* Nottingham 866434/8. *Club:* Sherwood Flying (Nottingham) (Hon. Life Mem.).

BARTLETT, Vernon, CBE 1956; author; *b* Westbury, Wilts, 30 April 1894; *s* of late T. O. Bartlett, Swanage; *m* 1st, Marguerite van den Bemden (*d* 1966); two *s* ; 2nd, 1969, Eleanor Needham Ritchie. *Educ:* Blundell's, Tiverton. Travelled abroad, 1911-14; European War, 1914-16; joined staff of Daily Mail, 1916; Reuter's Agency, 1917; Paris Peace Conference for Reuter's, and later, for Daily Herald; joined staff of The Times, 1919; special correspondent of that paper in Switzerland, Germany, Poland, 1919-20; Correspondent in Rome, 1921-22; London Director of the League of Nations, 1922-32; broadcast regularly on foreign affairs, 1928-34 and during the war; Staff of News Chronicle, 1934-54; Political Commentator for the Straits Times, Singapore, 1954-61; SE Asia Correspondent for Manchester Guardian (now The Guardian), 1954-61. MP (Ind Prog) Bridgwater Div. of Som, 1938-50; Mem. of UN Advisory Cttee of Information Experts, 1948. *Publications:* some twenty-eight books including: Calf Love, 1929; (with R. C. Sherriff) Journey's End, 1930; Nazi Germany Explained, 1933; This is My Life, 1937; Tomorrow Always Comes, 1943; East of the Iron Curtain, 1950; Struggle for Africa, 1953; And Now, Tomorrow, 1960; Tuscan Retreat, 1964; A Book about Elba, 1965; Introduction to Italy, 1967; The Past of Pastimes, 1969; The

Colour of their Skin, 1969; Tuscan Harvest, 1971; Central Italy, 1972; Northern Italy, 1973; I Know What I Liked, 1974. *Recreation:* growing grapes and making wine. *Address:* 603 Colle di Compito, I 55062 Lucca, Italy. *T:* 0583.99241. *Clubs:* Garrick, Beefsteak.

BARTON, Arthur Edward Victor, CBE 1936 (OBE 1933); *b* 26 Aug. 1892; *s* of Arthur Moore Barton and Margaret (*née* Bourke); *m* 1st, 1919, Megan Lewis (*d* 1960), *d* of Anthony Matthews, Liverpool; one *s* one *d*; 2nd, 1962, Aileen, widow of Ronald S. Lonergan, Mexico City and London. *Educ:* Manchester Grammar Sch. Imperial Customs and Excise Service, 1912; Asst to Chief of Customs, Kenya and Uganda, 1919; Comptroller Customs and MLC, Br. Guiana, 1924; Collector General and MLC, Jamaica, 1927; Collector of Customs and Excise and MLC, Trinidad and Tobago, 1929; MEC, 1936; Mem. West Indies Cricket Board of Control, 1938-39; Comptroller of Customs and Mem. of Legislative Council, Nigeria, 1939-44; retired from Colonial Service, 1944; Sec. to the West India Cttee, 1949-61. Mem. Council, Football Assoc., 1952-70. *Address:* 64 Seabright, West Parade, Worthing, W Sussex BN11 3QU. *T:* Worthing 33935. *Clubs:* Royal Commonwealth Society (West Indian); Queen's Park Cricket (Port of Spain); West Indian Students' Centre; British Caribbean Association.

BARTON, Cecil James Juxon Talbot, CMG 1937; OBE 1932; MA 1921; *b* 13 April 1891; *e s* of late Rev. R. C. E. Barton, MA, and Emma Isabella Talbot; *m* 1926, Cicely (*d* 1940), *y d* of Lt-Col F. E. Bradshaw, DSO; one *s* one *d*; *m* 1945, Sheila Jean, *d* of A. Macgregor, Dannevirke, NZ. *Educ:* Denstone; Downing Coll., Cambridge, BA 1913. Asst District Comr, E African Protectorate (Kenya), 1914; served in various administrative posts; Asst for Native Affairs, 1923; acted in various Secretariat posts; Senior Asst Colonial Sec. Kenya, 1933; MLC 1934 and 1935; Colonial Sec. Fiji, 1936-41; MLC; Chm. Public Service Reorganisation Cttee, 1936; Administered Government of Fiji and acted as High Commissioner for the Western Pacific and as Consul General for the Western Pacific in 1936, 1938, 1939; Chief Sec. Nyasaland, 1941; MLC; Mem. Central African Council; Chm. Development Cttee; Administered Government of Nyasaland in 1942, 1944; retired 1945. Employed in Colonial Office, 1945-58. *Publications:* various papers on East African tribes and local history. *Recreations:* formerly Rugby, cricket, polo, shooting; now grandchildren, repairing education, stamps, walking. *Address:* The Old Coach House, Rye, East Sussex.

BARTON, Sir Charles Newton, Kt 1974; OBE; ED; BE; FIEAust; FAIM; Chairman: Port of Brisbane Authority, since 1977; Queensland Local Government Grants Commission, since 1977; *b* 5 July 1907; *s* of J. Barton, Maryborough, Qld; *m* 1935, Enid, *d* of W. Wetherell. *Educ:* Maryborough Boys' Grammar Sch.; Queensland Univ. (BE Civil). Consulting Engr, Mackay, 1935-59; Comr of Main Roads, Qld, 1960-68; Co-ordinator-Gen., Qld, 1969-76. Served War, AIF, 1940-41; 2/15th Bn (PW), Europe, 1941-45. CO, 31 Bn, CMF, 1948-52, 42 Bn, 1952-57; Hon. Col, Kennedy Regt, 1958-60; Aust. Cadet Corps, N Comd, 1962-66; Qld Univ. Regt, 1966-73. *Recreations:* gardening, fishing. *Address:* 78 Jilba Street, Indooroopilly, Queensland 4068, Australia. *Clubs:* Queensland, Johnsonian, United Service, Mackay (all in Qld).

BARTON, Sir Derek Harold Richard, Kt 1972; FRS 1954; FRSE 1956; Hofmann Professor of Organic Chemistry, Imperial College of Science and Technology, University of London, 1970- (Professor of Organic Chemistry, 1957-70); Directeur, Institut de Chimie des Substances Naturelles, Gif-sur-Yvette, from Oct. 1978; *b* 8 Sept. 1918; *s* of William Thomas and Maude Henrietta Barton; *m* 1st, 1944, Jeanne Kate Wilkins; one *s*; 2nd, 1969, Christiane Cognet. *Educ:* Tonbridge Sch.; Imperial Coll., Univ. of London. BSc Hons (1st Class) 1940; Hofmann Prizeman; PhD (Organic Chemistry) 1942; DSc London 1949. Research Chemist: on Govt project, 1942-44. Albright and Wilson, Birmingham, 1944-45; Asst Lectr, Dept of Chemistry, Imperial Coll., 1945-46, ICI Research Fellow, 1946-49; Visiting Lectr in Chemistry of Natural Products, Harvard Univ., USA, 1949-50; Reader in Organic Chemistry, Birkbeck Coll., 1950, Prof. of Organic Chemistry, 1953-55; Regius Prof. of Chemistry, Glasgow Univ., 1955-57; Arthur D. Little Vis. Prof., MIT, 1958; Karl Folkers Vis. Prof., Univs of Illinois and Wisconsin, 1959; Lectures: Tilden, Chem. Soc., 1952; Max Tischler, Harvard Univ., 1956; First Simonsen Memorial, Chem. Soc., 1958; Falk-Plaut, Columbia Univ., 1961; Aub, Harvard Med. Sch., 1962; Renaud, Michigan State Univ., 1962; Inaugural 3 M's, Univ. of Western Ontario, 1962; 3 M's, Univ. of Minnesota, 1963; Hugo Müller, Chem. Soc., 1963; Pedler, Chem. Soc., 1967; Sandin, Univ. of Alberta, 1969; Robert Robinson, Chem. Soc., London, 1970; Bakerian, Royal Society, 1970; Bose Endowment, Bose

Inst., Calcutta, 1972; Stieglitz, Chicago Univ., 1974; Bachmann, Michigan, 1975; Woodward, Yale, 1975; First Smissman, Kansas, 1976; Priestley, Pennsylvania State Univ., 1977. President: Section B, British Assoc. for the Advancement of Science, 1969; Organic Chemistry Div., Internat. Union of Pure and Applied Chemistry, 1969; Perkin Div., Chem. Soc., 1971; Pres., Chem. Soc., 1973-74. Mem., Council for Scientific Policy, 1965-. Hon. Member: Sociedad Quimica de Mexico, 1969; Belgian Chem. Soc., 1970; Chilean Chem. Soc., 1970; Polish Chem. Soc., 1970; Pharmaceutical Soc. of Japan, 1970; Royal Acad. Exact Scis, Madrid, 1971; Acad. of Pharmaceutical Scis, USA, 1971; Danish Acad. Scis, 1972; Argentinian Acad. Scis, 1973; Societa Italiana per il Progresso delle Scienze, 1976; Corresp. Mem., Argentinian Chem. Soc., 1970; Foreign Member: Acad. das Ciencias de Lisboa, 1971; Academia Nazionale dei Lincei, Rome, 1975; Foreign Hon. Mem. American Academy of Arts and Sciences, 1960; Foreign Associate, Nat. Acad. of Sciences, USA, 1970. Hon. Fellow: Deutsche Akad. der Naturforscher Leopoldina, 1967; Birkbeck Coll., 1970; ACS Centennial Foreign Fellow, 1976. Hon. DSc: Montpellier Univ., 1962; Dublin, 1964; St Andrews, Columbia NYC, 1970; Coimbra, 1971; Oxon, Manchester, 1972; South Africa, 1973; City, 1975; Hon. Dr: La Laguna, 1975; Univ. of Western Virginia, 1975. Harrison Memorial Prize, Chem. Soc., 1948; First Corday-Morgan Medallist, Chemical Soc., 1951; Fritzsche Medal, Amer. Chem. Soc., 1956; First Roger Adams Medal, Amer. Chem. Soc., 1959; Davy Medal, Royal Society, 1961; Nobel Prize for Chemistry (jointly), 1969; First award in Natural Product Chemistry, Chem. Soc. of London, 1971; Longstaff Medal, Chem. Soc., 1972; B. C. Law Gold Medal, Indian Assoc. for Cultivation of Science, 1972; Medal, Soc. of Cosmetic Chem. of GB, 1972; Royal Medal, Royal Soc., 1972; Second Centennial of Priestly Chemistry Award, Amer. Chem. Soc., 1974. Order of the Rising Sun (2nd class), Japan, 1972; Chevalier, Légion d'Honneur, 1974. *Publications:* numerous, in Journal of Chemical Society. *Address:* (from Oct. 1978) Institut de Chimie des Substances Naturelles, 91190 Gif-sur-Yvette, France; (until Oct. 1978) Department of Chemistry, Imperial College of Science and Technology, Prince Consort Road, SW7 2AY.

BARTON, Maj.-Gen. Francis Christopher, CB 1966; CBE 1964; Voluntary Help Organiser, Royal Victoria Hospitals, Bournemouth, since 1967; *b* 17 Jan. 1916; *s* of Rev. John Bernard Barton, Elphinstone House, Hastings; *m* 1939, Olivia Mary Darroll-Smith; two *d*. *Educ:* Haileybury Coll. 2nd Lieut, Royal Marines, 1934; Lieut-Col, 1956; Brig., 1961; Maj.-Gen., 1964. Comd 45 Commando, RM, 1958-60; Comd 3 Commando Brigade, RM, 1962-63; Comdt, Joint Warfare Establishment, Old Sarum, 1964-66; retired, 1966. Chm., Standing Conf., Voluntary Help Organisers, 1971-72. *Address:* c/o National Westminster Bank, 661 Christchurch Road, Boscombe, Bournemouth, Dorset.

BARTON, John Bernard Adie; Associate Director, Royal Shakespeare Company, since 1964; *b* 26 Nov. 1928; *s* of late Sir Harold Montague Barton and Joyce Wale; *m* 1968, Anne Righter. *Educ:* Eton Coll.; King's Coll., Cambridge (BA, MA). Fellow, King's Coll., Cambridge, 1954-60 (Lay Dean, 1956-59). Joined Royal Shakespeare Company, 1960; Associate Dir, 1964. Has adapted texts and directed or co-directed many plays for Royal Shakespeare Company, including: The Taming of the Shrew, 1960; The Hollow Crown, 1961; The Art of Seduction, 1962; The Wars of the Roses, 1963-64; Henry IV, Parts I and II, and Henry V, 1964-66; Love's Labour's Lost, 1965; Coriolanus and All's Well That Ends Well, 1967; Julius Caesar and Troilus and Cressida, 1968; Twelfth Night and When Thou Art King, 1969; Measure for Measure and The Tempest, 1970; Richard II, Henry V, and Othello, 1971; Richard II, 1973; King John, Cymbeline, and Dr Faustus, 1974; Perkin Warbeck, 1975; Much Ado About Nothing, The Winter's Tale, and Troilus and Cressida, 1976; A Midsummer Night's Dream, Pillars of the Community, 1977. *Publications:* The Hollow Crown, 1962 (and 1971); The Wars of the Roses, 1970. *Recreations:* travel, chess, work. *Address:* Hillborough Manor, near Bidford-on-Avon, Alcester, Warwickshire. *T:* Bidford-on-Avon 2275.

BARTON, Margaret, LRAM; writer; *b* 1897; *y d* of Thomas Lloyd Barton and Fanny Roberta Isaacs. *Educ:* St Paul's Girls' Sch.; Royal Academy of Music. *Publications:* Tunbridge Wells, 1937; Garrick, 1948; (with Sir Osbert Sitwell) Sober Truth, 1930; Victoriana, 1931; Brighton, 1935. *Address:* 18 Kensington Court Place, W8.

BARTON, Sidney James; Part-time Member, London Transport Executive, 1969-76; Additional Chairman, National Health Service Appeal Tribunals, South West Thames/Wessex Regions, since 1974; *b* 5 March 1909; *s* of James George Barton and

Emily Hannah Jury; *m* 1933, Lorna Beatrice Mary Williams; one *s* one *d. Educ:* Elliott Sch., Wandsworth. Laboratory Technician, Metropolitan Asylums Board and LCC, 1927-34; appointed a full-time Officer, National Union of Public Employees, 1934, National Officer, 1962-73. Mem. Exec. Cttee, London Labour Party; Vice-Chm., Greater London Regional Council, Labour Party, 1969-74. Former Member: General Council, Nurses and Midwives Council; Ancillary Staffs Council; Professional and Technical Staffs Council for the Health Services; TUC Local Govt and Nurses Advisory Cttees; Chm., London Trades Council, 1970-74 (Vice-Chm., 1952-70); Former Member: Surrey County Council (1945-49); Sutton and Cheam Borough Council (1945-48); Surrey Exec. Council for Health Services (1947-54); Epsom Group Hosp. Management Cttee and Long Grove Hosp. Management Cttee; South West Metropolitan Regional Hosp. Bd Farming Adv. Cttee. JP 1955; Alderman LCC 1953-65 (Chm. Public Control Cttee, 1954-59); Chm., LCC, 1959-60 (Chm., Primary and Secondary Schools Sub-Cttee, 1960-61); Vice-Chm. General Purposes Cttee, 1961-65. Alderman London Borough of Sutton, 1964-68. Chm., Governors, Garratt Green Comprehensive Sch. 1958-67, 1970- (Vice-Chm., 1967-70); Governor, Hosp. for Sick Children, Great Ormond Street, 1969-75. Member: Met. Regional Exams Bd for Cert. of Secondary Educn, 1964-72; London and Home Counties Regional Advisory Council for Technological Educn, 1965-73; Heathrow Airport London Consultative Cttee. Order of Homayoun Class III (Iraq), 1959; Grand Cross of Order Al Merito (Peru), 1960; Comdr Legion of Honour (France), 1960. *Address:* 14 Chatsworth Road, Cheam, Surrey. *T:* 01-644 9222. *Club:* Ewhurst Bowls (Vice-Pres.).

BARTON-CHAPPLE, Mrs Derek; *see* Tutin, Dorothy.

BARTOSIK, Rear-Adm. Josef C., CB 1968; DSC 1943; Director, Australia New Zealand Europe Container Service, since 1977; *b* Poland, 20 July 1917; *m* 1st, 1943, Cynthia Pamela, *d* of late Humphrey Bowman, CMG, CBE; three *s* one *d*; 2nd, 1969, Mrs Jeannine Scott, *d* of late Paul Bridgeman. *Educ:* in Poland. Joined Polish Navy, 1935; served in Polish destroyers under British operational control, 1939-46; transf. to RN, 1948; commanded: HMS Comus, 1955-56; HMS Scarborough and as Capt. (F) 5th FS, 1960-61; HMS Seahawk (RN Air Station Culdrose), 1962-63, HMS London, 1964-65; Rear-Adm. 1966; Asst Chief of Naval Staff (Ops), 1966-68; retired 1968. Dir, Australia Europe Container Service, 1969-77. Freeman, City of London, 1968. *Recreations:* all outdoor. *Address:* 78 Leadenhall Street, EC3.

BARTTELOT, Major Sir Brian Walter de Stopham, 5th Bt, *cr* 1875; psc; Second in Command, 2nd Battalion, Colstream Guards, since 1977; *b* 17 July 1941; *s* of Lt-Col Sir Walter de Stopham Barttelot, 4th Bt, and Sara Patricia (who *m* 2nd, 1965, Comdr James Barttelot, RN retd), *d* of late Lieut-Col H. V. Ravenscroft; *S* father, 1944; *m* 1969, Hon. Mary Angela Fiona Weld Forester, *y d* of 7th Baron Forester, and of Marie Louise Priscilla, CStJ, *d* of Sir Herbert Perrott, 6th Bt, CH, CB; two *d. Educ:* Eton; RMA, Sandhurst. Temp. Equerry to HM Queen, 1970-71; Camberley Staff Coll., 1974; GSO2, Army Staff Duties Directorate, MoD, 1975-76. *Heir: b* Robin Ravenscroft Barttelot, *b* 15 Dec. 1943. *Address:* Keepers, Stopham, Pulborough, W Sussex RH20 1EB. *T:* Fittleworth 347. *Clubs:* Cavalry and Guards, Pratt's, Buck's.

BARWICK, Rt. Hon. Sir Garfield (Edward John), PC 1964; GCMG 1965; Kt 1953; QC (Australia); Chief Justice of Australia since 1964; *b* 22 June 1903; *s* of late Jabez Edward Barwick and Lilian Grace Ellicott; *m* 1929, Norma Mountier Symons; one *s* one *d. Educ:* Fort Street Boys' High Sch., Sydney; University of Sydney, BA 1923; LLB (Hons) 1925; Hon. LLD Sydney, 1972. New South Wales Bar, 1927; KC 1941; Victorian Bar, 1945; KC (Vic) 1945; Queensland Bar, 1958; QC Queensland, 1958. Practised extensively in all jurisdictions: Supreme Court, High Court of Australia and Privy Council. Pres. NSW Bar Assoc., 1950-52 and 1955-56; Attorney-Gen. Commonwealth of Australia, Dec. 1958-Feb. 1964; Minister for External Affairs, Dec. 1961-April 1964. Judge ad hoc, Internat. Court of Justice, 1973-74. President: Law Council of Australia, 1952-54; Australian Inst. of Internat. Affairs, 1972-. Hon. Bencher, Lincoln's Inn, 1964. Leader: Australian Delegation, SEATO Council, Bangkok, 1961, Paris, 1963; UN Delegation, 1960, 1962-64; Australian Delegation to ECAFE, Manila, 1963; Australian Delegation, ANZUS, Canberra, 1962, Wellington, 1963. Chancellor, Macquarie Univ., 1967-. *Recreations:* fishing, yachting. *Address:* Mundroola, 133 George Street, Careel Bay, Sydney, NSW, Australia; High Court of Australia, Darlinghurst, NSW. *Clubs:* Australian (Sydney); Melbourne (Melbourne); Royal Sydney Yacht Squadron.

BARWICK, Sir Richard (Llewellyn), 3rd Bt, *cr* 1912; *b* 4 Nov. 1916; *o surv. s* of Sir John Storey Barwick, 2nd Bt, and Gwladys Jessie (*d* 1949), 3rd *d* of George William Griffith Thomas, Ystrad Mynach, Co. Glamorgan; *S* father 1953; *m* 1st, 1948, Valerie Maud (Ward) (marr. diss.), *d* of Robert J. Skelton, Nairobi, Kenya Colony; three *d*; 2nd, 1968, Mrs Denise Radcliffe, *widow* of Hugh Christian Radcliffe. *Educ:* Harrow; Christ's Coll., Cambridge. Served Royal Air Force, 1940-46. *Heir:* none. *Address:* Thimbleby Hall, Northallerton, North Yorks. *T:* Osmotherly 212. *Club:* Northern Counties (Newcastle upon Tyne).

See also R. A. Cookson.

BARZEL, Dr Rainer C.; Chairman of the Christian Democratic Union of Germany, 1971-73, and Chairman of the CDU/CSU Group in the German Federal Parliament, 1964-73 (Acting Chairman, Dec. 1963); *b* 20 June 1924; *s* of Dr Candidus Barzel, Senior Asst Master, and Maria Barzel; *m* 1948, Kriemhild Barzel (*née* Schumacher); one *d. Educ:* studied Jurisprudence and Political Economy, Univ. of Cologne (Referendar, Dr jur.). With Govt of North Rhine-Westphalia, 1949-; Member of the German Federal Diet for the Constituency of Paderborn-Wiedenbrück, 1957; Federal Minister in the Adenauer Govt, for all-German affairs, Dec. 1962-Oct. 1963. *Publications:* (all publ. in Germany): Die geistigen Grundlagen der politischen Parteien, 1947; Die deutschen Parteien, 1952; Gesichtspunkte eines Deutschen, 1968. *Recreation:* skating. *Address:* Ferdinandstrasse 4, Paderborn, Germany.

BARZUN, Prof. Jacques; University Professor Emeritus, Columbia University; *b* 30 Nov. 1907; *s* of Henri Barzun and Anna-Rose Martin; *m* 1936, Mariana Lowell; two *s* one *d. Educ:* Lycée Janson de Sailly; Columbia Univ. Instructor in History, Columbia Univ., 1929; Research Fellow, American Council of Learned Socs, 1933-34; Columbia University: Asst Prof., 1938; Associate Prof., 1942; Prof. of History, 1945-75; University Prof., 1967; Dean of Grad. Faculties, 1955-58; Dean of Faculties and Provost, 1958-67. Director: American Friends of Cambridge Univ.; Council for Basic Educn; Peabody Inst.; NY Soc. Library; Mem. Adv. Council, Univ. Coll. at Buckingham. Membre Associé de l'Académie Delphinale, Grenoble, 1952; Member: Nat. Inst. of Arts and Letters, USA (President, 1972-75); Amer. Acad. of Arts and Sciences; American Historical Assoc.; FRSA, USA (Benjamin Franklin Fellow). Seth Low Prof. of History, Columbia Univ., 1960; Extraordinary Fellow, Churchill Coll., Cambridge, 1961-. Literary Advisor, Charles Scribner's Sons Ltd, 1975-. Chevalier de la Légion d'Honneur. *Publications:* The French Race: Theories of its Origin, 1932; Race: A Study in Superstition, 1937 (revd, 1965); Of Human Freedom, 1939 (revd, 1964); Darwin, Marx, Wagner, 1941 (revd, 1958); Teacher in America, 1945 (revd, 1964); Berlioz and the Romantic Century, 1950 (3rd edn 1969); Pleasures of Music, 1951; Selected Letters of Byron, 1953; Nouvelles Lettres de Berlioz, 1954, 2nd edn 1974; God's Country and Mine, 1954; Music in American Life, 1956; The Energies of Art, 1956; The Modern Researcher (with Henry F. Graff), 1957, 3rd edn 1977; The House of Intellect, 1959; Classic, Romantic and Modern, 1961; Science: The Glorious Entertainment, 1964; (ed) Follett's Modern American Usage, 1967; The American University, 1968; (with W. H. Taylor) A Catalogue of Crime, 1971; On Writing, Editing and Publishing, 1971; Berlioz's Evenings with the Orchestra, 1956, 2nd edn 1973; The Use and Abuse of Art, 1974; Clio and the Doctors, 1974; Simple and Direct, 1975; contrib. to leading US journals. *Address:* Charles Scribner's Sons, 597 Fifth Avenue, New York, NY 10017, USA. *T:* 486-4041. *Clubs:* Athenæum, Authors'; Century (New York).

BASHFORD, Humphrey John Charles, MA; Headmaster, Hessle High School, since 1964; *b* 5 Oct. 1920; *s* of late Sir Henry Bashford, MD, FRCP, and late Margaret Eveline Sutton; *m* 1942, Alyson Margaret Liddle; two *s* three *d. Educ:* Sherborne Sch.; Clare Coll., Cambridge. MA Cambridge 1950. Served War of 1939-45: commissioned 2nd Bn Oxford Bucks LI, 1941; GSO3 HQ Airborne Corps 1944-46. Senior History Master, Leys Sch., Cambridge, 1947; Part-time Tutor, WEA, 1950; Headmaster, Wellingborough Sch., 1956-64. *Recreations:* gardening, fly-fishing. *Address:* 16 Main Street, Hotham, York.

BASING, 4th Baron *cr* 1887; **George Lutley Sclater-Booth;** *b* 7 Dec. 1903; *s* of Hon. Charles Lutley Sclater-Booth (*d* 1931) (2nd *s* of 1st Baron) and Ellen Geraldine (*d* 1957), *y d* of George Jones, Mitton Manor, Staffs; *S* cousin, 1969; *m* 1st, 1938, Jeannette (marr. diss. 1944; she *d* 1957), *d* of late N. B. MacKelvie, New York; one *s*; 2nd, 1951, Cynthia, *widow* of Carl H. Beal, Los Angeles, and *d* of late Charles W. Hardy, Salt Lake City, Utah. *Educ:* Winchester. *Heir: s* Hon. Neil Lutley Sclater-Booth [*b* 16 Jan. 1939; *m* 1967, Patricia Ann, *d* of G. B. Whitfield; two *s*]. *Address:* PO Box 301, Pebble Beach,

California, USA. *Clubs:* Bel Air Country (Los Angeles); Eldorado Country (Palm Desert, Calif).

BASINGSTOKE, Bishop Suffragan of, since 1977; **Rt. Rev. Michael Richard John Manktelow;** Residentiary Canon of Winchester Cathedral, since 1977; *b* 23 Sept. 1927; *s* of late Sir Richard Manktelow, KBE, CB, and late Helen Manktelow; *m* 1966, Rosamund Mann; three *d*. *Educ:* Whitgift School, Croydon; Christ's Coll., Cambridge (MA 1952); Chichester Theological Coll. Deacon 1953, priest 1954, Lincoln; Asst Curate of Boston, Lincs, 1953-57; Chaplain of Christ's Coll., Cambridge, 1957-61; Chaplain of Lincoln Theological Coll., 1961-64, Sub-Warden, 1964-66; Vicar of Knaresborough, 1966-73; Rural Dean of Harrogate, 1972-77; Vicar of St Wilfrid's, Harrogate, 1973-77; Hon. Canon of Ripon Cathedral, 1975-77. *Publication:* Forbes Robinson: Disciple of Love, 1961. *Recreations:* music, walking. *Address:* 1 The Close, Winchester, Hants. *T:* Winchester 69374.

BASINGSTOKE, Archdeacon of; *see* Finch, Ven. G. G.

BASNETT, David; General Secretary, General and Municipal Workers Union, since 1973 (National Industrial Officer, General and Municipal Workers', 1960-72); *b* 9 Feb. 1924; British; *m* 1956, Kathleen Joan Molyneaux; two *s*. *Educ:* Quarry Bank High School, Liverpool. Served War of 1939-45, RAF. Trade Union Official, 1948; TUC General Council, 1966. Numerous committees of enquiry including: Royal Commission on Penal Reform; Commission on the Constitution, 1969-71; Royal Commn on the Press, 1974-77. Mem., NEDC, 1973-; Mem., National Enterprise Bd, 1975- (and of Organising Cttee, 1975). *Address:* Thorne House, Ruxley Ridge, Claygate, Esher, Surrey. *T:* Esher 62081.

BASNYAT, Shri Upendra Bahadur, Prasiddha Prabal Gorkha Dakshin Bahu; Long Service, War Service, Defence and Coronation Medals (Nepal); Ambassador of Nepal to the Court of St James's, 1969-73; *b* 1919; *m*; two *s*. *Educ:* Calcutta University. Commnd Lieut, Royal Nepalese Army, 1940; served War of 1939-45 with Nepalese contingent as Adjt. Mil. Attaché (Lt-Col), Royal Nepalese Embassy, New Delhi and Nepalese Liaison Officer to Gorkha Rifles of Indian Army, 1951-56; transf. to Foreign Service of Nepal, 1957; Consul-General in Lhasa, 1958-61; Deputy, Peking, 1961-65; Ambassador to Pakistan, Iran and Turkey, 1965-69. *Address:* c/o Ministry of Foreign Affairs, Rastria Sharsha Griha, Kathmandu, Nepal.

BASOV, Prof. Nikolai Gennadievich; Orders of Lenin, 1967, 1969, 1972, 1975; Hero of Socialist Labour, 1969; Physicist, USSR; Member of the Praesidium of the Academy of Sciences of USSR, since 1967; Deputy of USSR Supreme Soviet, since 1974; Director of the P. N. Lebedev Physical Institute, Moscow, since 1973 (Vice-Director, 1958-72), also Head of the Laboratory of Quantum Radiophysics; Professor, Moscow Institute of Physical Engineers; *b* 1922; *s* of Prof. Gennadiy Fedorovitsch Basov and Zinaida Andreevna Basova; *m* 1950, Kseniya Tikhonovna Basova; two *s*. *Educ:* secondary; Institute of Physical Engineers, Moscow. Joined the P. N. Lebedev Physical Institute, 1948. Editor: Priroda (Nature), Popular Sciences Magazine; Soviet Jl of Quantum Electronics. Corresponding Mem. USSR Acad. of Sciences, 1962; Academician, 1966. Fellow, Optical Soc. of America, 1974 (Mem. 1972); Member: German Acad. of Sciences, 1967; German Acad. of Natural Scis, Leopoldina, 1971; Polish Mil.-Tech. Acad., 1972; Bulgarian Acad. of Scis, 1974; Jena Univ., 1974; Swedish Royal Acad. of Engineering Sciences, 1975. Hon. Dr, Prague Polytechnic Inst., 1975. Awarded Lenin Prize, 1959; Nobel Prize for Physics (jointly with Prof. A. M. Prokhorov of the P. N. Lebedev Physical Institute, Moscow, and Prof. C. H. Townes of MIT Cambridge, Mass, USA), 1964. *Address:* P. N. Lebedev Physical Institute, Academy of Sciences of the USSR, Lenin Prospekt 53, Moscow, USSR.

BASS, Harry Godfrey Mitchell, CMG 1972; HM Diplomatic Service, retired; Chapter Clerk, St George's Chapel, Windsor, since 1974; *b* 26 Aug. 1914; *s* of late Rev. Arthur Edward Bass and Mildred Bass; *m* 1948, Monica Mary, *d* of late Rev. H. F. Burroughs (and eponym of the orchid *Onchidium flexuosum* x *Rodriguezia fragrans*); two *s* one *d*. *Educ:* Marlborough Coll.; Gonville and Caius Coll., Cambridge; St John's Coll., Oxford. British Museum, Dept of Egyptian and Assyrian Antiquities, 1939; Admiralty, 1940; Dominions Office, 1946; Asst Sec., Office of UK High Commissioner, Australia, 1948-51; Mem. of Secretariat, Commonwealth Economic Conference, 1952 and Meeting of Commonwealth Prime Ministers, 1953; Counsellor, Office of UK High Commissioner, Calcutta, 1954-57; Dep. UK High Commissioner, Federation of Rhodesia and Nyasaland, 1959-61; British Minister (Pretoria and Cape Town) in the

Republic of S Africa, 1961-62; seconded to Central African Office, 1963-64; British Dep. High Commissioner, Ibadan, 1965-67; Head of Consular Dept, FCO, 1967-70; High Comr in Lesotho, 1970-73. *Publications:* contrib. to Oxford Review, Journal of Egyptian Archæology. *Recreations:* birdwatching, walking. *Address:* 7 The Cloisters, Windsor Castle, SL4 1NJ; Tyler's Mead, Reepham, Norfolk.

BASSETT, Douglas Anthony; Director, National Museum of Wales, since 1977; *b* 11 Aug. 1927; *s* of Hugh Bassett and Annie Jane Bassett; *m* 1955, Elizabeth Menna Roberts; three *d*. *Educ:* Llanelli Boys' Grammar Sch.; University Coll. of Wales, Aberystwyth. Asst Lectr and Lectr, Dept of Geology, Glasgow Univ., 1952-59; Keeper, Dept of Geology, Nat. Museum of Wales, 1959-77. Member: Water Resources Bd, 1965-73; Nature Conservancy Council (and Chm., Adv. Cttee for Wales), 1973-; Secretary of State for Wales, Celtic Sea Adv. Cttee, 1974-; Founder Mem. and first Chm., Assoc. of Teachers of Geology, 1967-68; Chm., Royal Soc. Cttee on History of Geology, 1972-. *Publications:* Bibliography and Index of Geology and Allied Sciences for Wales and the Welsh Borders, 1897-1958, 1961; A Source-book of Geological, Geomorphological and Soil Maps for Wales and the Welsh Borders (1800-1966), 1967; contribs to various geological and earth science jls. *Recreations:* bibliography, chronology. *Address:* 58 Ely Road, Llandaff, Cardiff CF5 2JG.

BASSETT, Sir Walter (Eric), KBE 1959; MC; FIEAust; Consultant to W. E. Bassett & Partners Pty Ltd, Consulting Engineers; *b* Melbourne, 19 Dec. 1892; *m* 1923, Marnie, *d* of late Sir David Orme Masson; one *s* one *d*. *Educ:* Wesley Coll., Melbourne; Melbourne Univ. (MMechE, BEE). Served European War, 1914-18, with AIF; Lieut 5th Field Co. Engineers and Australian Flying Corps. Senior Lecturer, Mechanical Engineering and Aerodynamics, Melbourne Univ., 1919-28; Mt Lyell M. & R. Co., Australia: Dir, 1948-74; Chm., 1951-68; Pres., 1969-74; Director: Gas and Fuel Corp., Victoria, 1951-75; Renison Ltd, 1958-74 (Chm., 1958-68). Pres. Instn Engrs Australia, 1942. Kernot Memorial Medal, 1948; Peter Nicol Russell Memorial Medal, 1958; James Harrison Medal, 1976. Hon. DrEng Monash, 1970; Hon. LLD Melbourne, 1974. *Recreations:* fishing, sailing, woodwork. *Address:* 133 Kooyong Road, Armadale, Victoria 3143, Australia. *Clubs:* Melbourne, Royal Melbourne Golf (both Melbourne).

BASSETT SMITH, (Newlands) Guy, CVO 1977; Executive Chairman, Blundell-Permoglaze Holdings Ltd, since 1975; *b* 14 July 1910; *s* of Guy Burroughs Smith and Elizabeth Hawkins; *m* 1939, Barbara, *d* of Clement Lionel Tyrer. Joined Dunlop Rubber Co. Ltd, 1927. Served War, Army, 1940-46; passed Staff Coll., Camberley, 1943; Staff appt, 8th Army in Italy, 1944; demobilised 1946, with rank of Lt-Col. Rejoined Dunlop Ltd; General Manager: Dunlop Chem. Products Ltd, 1946-60; Dunlop Footwear Ltd, 1960-69, Dir, 1960-69; Man. Dir, Blundell-Permoglaze Holdings Ltd, 1970; Chm., Blundell Eomite Paints Ltd, Bombay, 1971-76. Chm., British Rubber Adhesive Mfrs Assoc., 1958-60; Council Member: Fedn of British Rubber Mfrs, 1951-60; Inst. of British Carriage and Automobile Mfrs, 1958-77 (Fellow, 1958). Mem. Council, Liverpool Sch. of Tropical Med., 1962. Trustee, Duke of Edinburgh Award Scheme, 1971- (Liaison Officer, 1956-71); Sec., English Tennis and Racquets Assoc., 1972-76. *Recreations:* real tennis, youth work, local municipal affairs. *Address:* The Old Vicarage, Lower Quinton, Warwicks CV37 8SH. *T:* Pebworth 473; 53 Burton Court, SW3 4SY. *T:* 01-730 8769. *Clubs:* Boodle's, Queen's.

BASTEN, Sir Henry (Bolton), Kt 1966; CMG 1947; MA Oxon and Adelaide; University of Adelaide, 1953-67, Vice-Chancellor, 1958-67. Formerly Chairman and General Manager, Singapore & Penang Harbour Boards. Investigated conditions in Australian ports for Commonwealth Government, 1951-52, report published, 1952. Chm., Aust. Univs Commn, 1968-71. Hon. DLitt Flinders Univ. (S Australia), 1967. *Address:* 13 Holmes Crescent, Campbell, ACT 2601, Australia.

BASTIN, Prof. John Andrew, MA, PhD; FRAS; Professor, since 1971, and Head of Department of Physics, since 1975, Queen Mary College, London University; *b* 3 Jan. 1929; *s* of Lucy and Arthur Bastin; *m* 1959, Wendy Susan Jacobsen; one *s* one *d*. *Educ:* George Monoux Grammar Sch., London; Corpus Christi Coll., Oxford. MA, PhD. Univ. of Ibadan, Nigeria, 1952-56; Univ. of Reading, 1956-59; Queen Mary Coll., Univ. of London, 1959-. Initiated a group in far infrared astronomy at Queen Mary College, 1960-70. *Publications:* papers on far infrared astronomy and lunar evolution. *Recreations:* English water colours, Renaissance and Baroque music, tennis, skiing. *Address:* 62 Tycehurst Hill, Loughton, Essex. *T:* 01-508 1255.

BASTYAN, Lt.-Gen. Sir Edric (Montague), KCMG 1962; KCVO 1963; KBE 1957 (CBE 1943; OBE 1942); CB 1944; *b* 5 April 1903; *s* of late Lt.-Col S. J. Bastyan, Ferndown, Dorset; *m* 1944, Victoria Eugénie Helen (*née* Bett), DStJ 1969; one *s*. *Educ:* West Buckland; RMC, Sandhurst. 2nd Lieut Sherwood Foresters, 1923; Capt. West Yorks Regt, 1935; Staff Coll., 1936-37; Royal Irish Fusiliers, 1937; Major, 1940; Temp. Lt.-Col 1941; Temp. Brigadier, 1942; Acting Maj.-Gen, 1944; Col, 1945; Maj.-Gen. (with seniority, 1946), 1948. Served Palestine, 1938-39 (despatches); War of 1939-45, Africa, Italy, SEAC (despatches, OBE, CBE, CB). Chief Admin. Officer, Eighth Army, 1943; Maj.-Gen. i/c Administration Allied Land Forces, SE Asia, 1944-45. Imperial Defence Coll., 1946. Maj.-Gen. i/c Administration, British Army of the Rhine, 1946-48; employed in special duties, War Office, 1949; Chief of Staff Eastern Command, 1949-50; Dir of Staff Duties, WO 1950-52; Comdr 53rd (Welsh) Infantry Div. (TA) and Mid-West District, 1952-55; Vice Adjutant Gen., War Office, 1955-57; Lieut.-Gen., 1957; Comdr, British Forces, Hongkong, 1957-60; retired, 1960. Governor of: South Australia, 1961-68; Tasmania, 1968-74. Exhibn of drawings and paintings, Hahndorf Gall., 1974. Assoc. Mem., Royal S Aust. Soc. of Arts. KStJ, 1961. *Recreations:* golf; tennis; painting. *Address:* Flat 42, 52 Brougham Place, North Adelaide, SA 5006, Australia. *Club:* Adelaide (Adelaide).

BATCHELOR, Alfred Alexander Meston, MA; Headmaster, Temple Grove School, Heron's Ghyll, near Uckfield, 1935-57; *b* 8 March 1901; *s* of late Rev. Canon A. W. Batchelor, and late Agnes Lowe; *m* 1949, Thelma Williams (*d* 1973). *Educ:* Temple Grove; Charterhouse (Scholar); Christ Church, Oxford (Holford Exhibitioner). Hon. Mods. 1922; Lit. Hum. 1924; Senior Asst Master, The Old Ride, Bournemouth, 1926-30; Joint Headmaster, St Christopher's, near Bath, 1930-35; Private Holiday Tutor to the late Duke of Connaught, 1929-34. *Publications:* Contributor to Country Life, Blackwood's, The Times, etc. *Recreations:* natural history, music. *Address:* Hundred End, Fairwarp, near Uckfield, East Sussex. *T:* Nutley 2151.

BATCHELOR, G(eorge) F(rederick) Grant, MB, ChB, LRCP, FRCS; retired as consulting surgeon; *b* 6 April 1902; *s* of Robert and Margaret Grant Batchelor; *m* 1944, Helen Elspeth Mackintosh (*d* 1976), *d* of late Lieut-Col C. H. Simpson, Harrogate. *Educ:* Dundee High Sch.; St Andrews Univ. MB, ChB (St Andrews), 1923; MRCS, LRCP, 1925; FRCS, 1926; Asst Surgeon, West London Hospital, 1929; Hounslow Hospital, 1930; Surgeon: Wembley Hospital, 1930; West London Hospital, 1935; EMS, London, 1939-42; Lieut-Col, RAMC, 1942. Consulting Surgeon, Charing Cross Hosp., 1972. *Recreations:* golf; shooting. *Address:* 14 Lexham House, 45 Lexham Gardens, W8. *T:* 01-373 9008. *Club:* Constitutional.

BATCHELOR, George Keith, FRS 1957; Professor of Applied Mathematics, University of Cambridge, since 1964, and Head of Department of Applied Mathematics and Theoretical Physics, since 1959; *b* Melbourne, 8 March 1920; *s* of George Conybere Batchelor and Ivy Constance Batchelor (*née* Berneye); *m* 1944, Wilma Maud Rätz; three *d*. *Educ:* Essendon and Melbourne High Schs; University of Melbourne. BSc 1940, MSc 1941, University of Melbourne; PhD 1948, Adams Prize, 1951, University of Cambridge; Research Officer, Aeronautical Research Laboratory, Melbourne, 1940-44; Fellow of Trinity Coll., Cambridge, 1947-; Lecturer, University of Cambridge, 1948-59; Reader in Fluid Dynamics, Univ. of Cambridge, 1959-64. Chairman: European Mechanics Cttee, 1965-; Nat Cttee for Theoretical and Applied Mechanics, 1967-72. Editor, Cambridge Monographs on Mechanics and Applied Mathematics, 1953-; Editor, Journal of Fluid Mechanics, 1956-. Mem., Royal Soc. of Sciences, Uppsala, 1972. Foreign Hon. Member: Amer. Acad. of Arts and Scis, 1959; Polish Acad of Scis, 1974. Dr *hc* : Univ. of Grenoble, 1959; Tech. Univ. of Denmark, 1974. *Publications:* The Theory of Homogeneous Turbulence, 1953; An Introduction to Fluid Dynamics, 1967; various papers on fluid mechanics in journals devoted to physical science. *Address:* Cobbers, Conduit Head Road, Cambridge. *T:* Cambridge 56387.

BATCHELOR, Prof. Ivor Ralph Campbell, CBE 1976; FRCPE, FRCPsych, DPM, FRSE; Professor of Psychiatry, University of Dundee, since 1967; *b* 29 Nov. 1916; *s* of Ralph C. L. Batchelor, FRCSE, FRCPE, and Muriel (*née* Shaw); *m* 1941, Honor Wallace Williamson; one *s* three *d*. *Educ:* Edinburgh Academy; Edinburgh Univ. MB ChB. Sqdn Ldr, RAFVR, 1941-46. Asst Phys. and Dep. Phys. Supt, Royal Edinburgh Hosp., and Sen. Lectr in Psyciatry, Univ. of Edinburgh, 1947-56; Phys. Supt, Dundee Royal Mental Hosp., 1956-62; Prof. of Psychiatry, Univ. of St Andrews, 1962-67. Member: Gen. Nursing Council for Scotland (Chm. Educn Cttee), 1964-71; Standing Med. Adv.

Cttee, Scot., 1967-74; Adv. Cttee on Med. Research, Scotland, 1969-73; Scottish Council for Postgraduate Med. Educn, 1970-; Chief Scientist Cttee, Scotland, 1973-. Mem., Med. Services Review (Porritt) Cttee, 1958-62; Chm., Cttee on Staffing Mental Deficiency Hosps, 1967-70; Member: Cttee on Nursing (Briggs Cttee), 1970-72; Cttee on the Working of the Abortion Act (Lane Cttee), 1971-74; MRC (Chm. Clinical Research Bd, 1973-74, Chm. Neuro-Sciences Bd, 1974-75), 1972-76; Royal Commn on the Nat. Health Service, 1976-. *Publications:* Aviation Neuro-Psychiatry, 1945; Henderson and Gillespie's Textbook of Psychiatry, 8th edn 1956 and subseq. edns to 10th edn 1969; contribs to med. jls. *Address:* Department of Psychiatry, Ninewells Hospital, Dundee DD1 9SY. *T:* Dundee 60111. *Club:* Athenæum.

BATCHELOR, John Richard; Director, McIndoe Research Unit, Queen Victoria Hospital, East Grinstead, since 1967; *b* 4 Oct. 1931; *s* of B. W. Batchelor, CBE and Mrs C. E. Batchelor; *m* 1955, Moira Ann (*née* McLellan); two *s* two *d*. *Educ:* Marlborough Coll.; Emmanuel Coll., Cambridge; Guy's Hospital, London. MB, BChir Cantab, 1955; MD Cantab 1965. Nat. Service, RAMC, 1957-59; Dept of Pathology, Guy's Hospital: Res. Fellow, 1959-61; Lectr and Sen. Lectr, 1961-67. Prof. of Transplantation Research, RCS, 1967. *Publications:* scientific articles upon tissue transplantation research in various special jls. *Recreations:* sailing; tennis; walking. *Address:* Little Ambrook, Nursery Road, Walton-on-the-Hill, Tadworth, Surrey. *T:* Tadworth 2028.

BATCHELOR, John Stanley, FRCS; Orthopaedic Surgeon, Guy's Hospital, since 1946; *b* 4 Dec. 1905; *s* of Dr Ferdinand Stanley Batchelor and Florence Batchelor; *m* 1934, Marjorie Blanche Elvina Rudkin; two *s* one *d*. *Educ:* Christ's Coll., Christchurch, NZ; Otago Univ.; Guy's Hospital. MRCS, LRCP 1931; FRCS 1934. Pres., Section of Orthopaedics, RSocMed, 1958-59; British Orthopaedic Assoc.: Hon. Treas. 1960-65; Hon. Sec. 1964; Vice-Pres. 1967-68; Pres. 1970-72. *Publications:* contribs to med. jls. *Recreations:* golf, walking, antiques. *Address:* 37 Albemarle, Parkside, Wimbledon, SW19 5NP.

BATE, Ven. Alban F., MA; DCnL; Archdeacon of St John, 1949-63, retired; Rector of St Paul's Church, St John, New Brunswick, 1936-63, retired; *b* 12 May 1893; *s* of Rev. William John Bate and Alice C. McMullen; *m* 1919, Norah F. Warburton, Charlottetown, PEI; two *s* five *d*. *Educ:* Rothesay Collegiate Sch.; Dalhousie, Superior Sch.; University of King's Coll., Nova Scotia, (made Hon. Fellow 1939), BA, 1914; Divinity Testamur, 1916; MA, 1918; Deacon, 1916; Priest, 1917; Curate of Cathedral, Fredericton, 1916-19; Asst at Parish Church, Fredericton, 1919-20; Rector of Fredericton 1920-36 and Archdeacon of Fredericton, 1932-36; Canon of Christ Church Cathedral, Fredericton, 1946; Chaplain of the Legislature of Province of New Brunswick, 1925-35; Chaplain 7th Machine Gun Bn, 1927; 1936; Chaplain, St George's Soc., 1939-42; Pres. Rotary Club of Fredericton, 1928-29; Saint John, 1941-42. DCnL (King's Univ. Halifax) 1955. *Recreation:* gardening. *Address:* 351 Charlotte Street West, Saint John, NB, Canada. *Clubs:* Rotary, Canadian (St John, NB).

BATE, Maj.-Gen. (Alfred) Christopher, OBE 1968 (MBE 1960); Commandant, National Defence College, since 1977; *b* 18 Aug. 1927; *y s* of late S. C. C. Bate; *m* 1954, Patricia Mary Stuart Bell; twin *s* two *d*. *Educ:* Alleyn's Sch. Commnd Royal Signals, 1949; served Middle East, BAOR, 1949-56; Staff Coll., 1957; HQ Northern Army Gp, 1958-61; 19 Airportable Bde, Cyprus, Kenya, Kuwait, 1961-63; 99 Gurkha Bde, Borneo, 1963-65 (despatches); JSSC, 1965; 7 Armoured Bde, BAOR, 1965-67; Comd 9th Signal Regt, Cyprus, 1967-69; DS, IDC and RCDS, 1969-71; Comdt, Sch. of Signals, 1971-74; Dir, Defence Operational Requirements Staff, 1974-75; MoD (Army), 1975-77. *Recreations:* philately, industrial archaeology. *Address:* Parkfield House, Latimer, Chesham, Bucks.

BATE, David Lindsay, CBE 1968; Hon. Mr Justice Bate; Chief Justice, Benue and Plateau States of Nigeria, 1975-77; Senior Puisne Judge, High Court of Justice, Northern States of Nigeria, 1968-77 (Puisne Judge 1957-68); *b* 3 March 1916; *m* 1948, Thadeen June, *d* of R. F. O'Donnell Peet; two *s*. *Educ:* Marlborough; Trinity Coll., Cambridge. Called to Bar, Inner Temple, 1938. Commissioned, Royal Artillery, 1939 and served, Royal Artillery, 1939-46. Entered Colonial Legal Service, 1947; Crown Counsel, Nigeria, 1947-52; Senior Crown Counsel, Nigeria, 1952-54; Senior Crown Counsel, Northern Nigeria 1954-56; Solicitor-Gen., Northern Nigeria, 1956. *Recreations:* shooting; fishing; riding. *Address:* c/o National Westminster Bank, Ross-on-Wye, Herefordshire. *Club:* Flyfishers'.

BATE, Henry, OBE 1971; Vice-Chairman of Press Council, 1960-75; founder member, 1953-75; b 14 Oct. 1899; m 1st, 1926, Annie Stonehewer (marr. diss.); one s; 2nd, 1949, May Abbott. Journalist, provincial newspapers in Brecon, Cardiff, Aberystwyth, 1918-22; Evening Chronicle, Manchester, 1922-45 (Industrial Corresp. 1933-45); Daily Telegraph, Fleet Street, 1945-70 (Architectural Reporter 1959-70). Mem., Nat. Union of Journalists Appeals Tribunal, 1976- (Mem. Exec. Council, 1946-76; Nat. Pres., 1952-53; Trustee 1956-76); Mem. Exec. Cttee, Internat. Fedn of Journalists, 1957-60; Mem. Newspaper Mergers Panel, Monopolies Commn, 1965-73. Address: 48 Berwyn Road, Richmond, Surrey. T: 01-876 6162. Club: Press.

BATE, Sir (Walter) Edwin, Kt 1969; OBE 1955; Barrister, Solicitor and Notary Public, Hastings, New Zealand, since 1927; b 12 March 1901; s of Peter and Florence Eleanor Bate; m 1925, Louise Jordan; two s one d. Educ: Victoria Univ., Wellington. LLM (first class hons), 1922. Admitted Barrister and Solicitor, 1922; practised: Taumarunui, NZ, 1923; Hastings, NZ, 1927. Mayor, City of Hastings, NZ, 1953-59; Chm., Hawke Bay Hosp. Bd, 1941-74; Pres., Hosp. Bds Assoc. of NZ, 1953-74; Pres., Associated Trustee Savings Banks of NZ, 1968 and 1969. OStJ 1961. Recreations: fishing, gardening. Address: PO Box 749, Hastings, New Zealand. T: 777448.

BATE, Prof. Walter Jackson; Abbott Lawrence Lowell Professor of the Humanities, Harvard University, since 1962; b 23 May 1918; s of William George Bate. Educ: Harvard Univ. AB 1939, PhD 1942. Harvard University: Associate Prof. of English, 1949-55; Prof. of English, 1955-62; Chm., Dept of English, 1955-62. Member: Amer. Acad. of Arts and Sciences; Amer. Philosophical Soc.; Cambridge Scientific Soc. Christian Gauss Award, 1956, 1964, 1970; Pulitzer Prize for Biography, 1964. Publications: Stylistic Development of Keats, 1945; From Classic to Romantic, 1946; Criticism: The Major Texts, 1952; The Achievement of Samuel Johnson, 1955; Prefaces to Criticism, 1959; Yale Edition of Samuel Johnson, Vol. II, 1963, Vols III-V, 1969; John Keats, 1963; Coleridge, 1968; The Burden of the Past and The English Poet, 1971. Recreation: farming. Address: 3 Warren House, Cambridge, Mass, USA. Club: Saturday (Boston, Mass).

BATE, Maj.-Gen. William, CB 1974; OBE 1963; Secretary to the Council of TAVR Associations, since 1975 (Deputy Secretary, 1973-75); b 6 June 1920; s of S. Bate, Warrington; m 1946, Veronica Mary Josephine (née Quinn); two s two d. Commnd, 1941; war service in Burma, 1941-46 (despatches); Senior Instructor, RASC Officers Sch., 1947-50; Co. Comd 7th and 11th Armoured Divs, 1951-53; psc 1954; DAA&QMG Q (Ops), WO, 1955-57; jssc 1957; Admin. Staff Coll., Henley, 1958; Directing Staff, Staff Coll., Camberley, 1958-60; AA&QMG, Ops and Plans, HQ BAOR, 1961-63; CO, 2 Div. Column, BAOR, 1963-65; Col GS, Staff Coll., Camberley, 1965-67; Brig. Q (Maint.), MoD, 1967-68; ADC to the Queen, 1969; idc 1969; Dir of Admin. Planning (Army), 1970; Dir of Movements (Army), MoD, 1971-73. Col Comdt, RCT, 1974-; Hon. Col, 163 Movement Control Regt, RCT(V), TAVR, 1974-. FCIT 1967. Recreations: cricket, tennis, hockey. Address: Netherbury, Belton Road, Camberley, Surrey. T: Camberley 63529. Clubs: East India, Devonshire, Sports and Public Schools, Royal Overseas League.

BATE, Dame Zara (Kate), DBE 1968; b 10 March; d of Sidney Herbert Dickens; m 1st, 1935, Captain James Fell; three s; 2nd, 1946, Rt Hon. Harold Edward Holt, PC, CH (d 1967), Prime Minister of Australia; 3rd, 1969, Hon. Henry Jefferson Percival Bate, MHR. Educ: Ruyton and Toorak Coll. Director: Trading and Agency; Berger & Fell; Magg; John Stafford & Co.; Colebrook Estates. Hon. Dr Lit and Hum, Ewha Women's Univ., Seoul, Korea, 1967. Coronation Medal, 1953. Recreations: tennis, reading, spear fishing. Address: 18 Millicent Avenue, Toorak, Victoria 3142, Australia. T: 24.1128.

BATE-SMITH, Dr Edgar Charles, CBE 1963; FLS 1959; Hon. FIFST; ScD; Director, Low Temperature Research Station, Cambridge, 1947-65, retired; b 24 Aug. 1900; s of Albert Edward Smith and Avis Ellen Jenkinson; m 1934, Margaret Elizabeth Bate Hardy; one s. Educ: Wellingborough Sch.; Manchester Univ.; Gonville and Caius Coll., Cambridge. Mem., Soc. of Chemical Industry Food Group Cttee, 1939-41, 1956-60 (Jubilee Memorial Lectr, 1962-63); formerly Mem. Council, Inst. of Food Science and Technology; Pres., Cambridge Philosophical Soc., 1953-55; Chm., Phytochemical Soc. (formerly Plant Phenolics Group), 1958-60. Publications: Food Science (with T. N. Morris), 1952. Papers in scientific jls on post-mortem physiology of muscle, chemistry and taxonomy of plants. Recreations: plants and animals; sketching. Address: 39 Grange Road, Cambridge. T: Cambridge 52591.

BATELY, Prof. Janet Margaret, (Mrs L. J. Summers); Professor of English Language and Medieval Literature, King's College, University of London, since 1977; b 3 April 1932; d of Alfred William Bately and Dorothy Maud Bately (née Willis); m 1964, Leslie John Summers, sculptor; one s. Educ: Greenhead High Sch., Huddersfield; Westcliff High Sch. for Girls; Somerville Coll., Oxford (Shaw Lefevre Scholar). BA 1954, Dip. in Comparative Philology 1956, MA 1958. Asst Lectr in English, Birkbeck Coll., Univ. of London, 1955-58, Lectr, 1958-69, Reader, 1970-76. Publications: contribs to Medium Aevum, Rev. of English Studies, Anglia, English Studies, Classica et Mediaevalia, Scriptorium, Studies in Philology, Mediev. Arch., Notes and Queries, Archaeologia, England before the Conquest, Anglo-Saxon England, The Dickensian, Jl Soc. of Archivists. Recreations: music, gardening. Address: 86 Cawdor Crescent, W7 2DD. T: 01-567 0486.

BATEMAN, Sir Cecil (Joseph), KBE 1967 (MBE 1944); Chairman, G. Heyn & Sons Ltd, since 1971; Director: Nationwide Building Society, since 1970; Allied Irish Banks, since 1970; Allied Irish Investment Bank Ltd, since 1971; b 6 Jan. 1910; s of Samuel and Annie Bateman; m 1938, Doris M. Simpson; one s one d. Educ: Queen's Univ., Belfast. Served War of 1939-45, Royal Artillery (Major). Entered NI Civil Service, Nov. 1927. Dir of Establishments, Min. of Finance, 1958-63; Sec. to Cabinet and Clerk of Privy Council of N Ireland, 1963-65; Permanent Sec., Min. of Finance, and Head of Northern Ireland Civil Service, 1965-70. Chm., NI Educn and Library Bds Staff Commn, 1973-. Mem. Cttee, London Steam Ship Owners' Mutual Insurance Assoc. Ltd. Recreations: golf, reading. Address: 60 Knocklofty Park, Belfast 4, N Ireland. T: Belfast 650818. Clubs: Royal Commonwealth Society; Shandon Park Golf, Royal Belfast Golf (Craigavad).

BATEMAN, Sir Charles Harold, KCMG 1950 (CMG 1937); MC; b Portsmouth, 4 Jan. 1892; s of late Charles Bateman; m 1940, Bridget Mary, d of late Michael Kavanagh, Co. Wicklow. Educ: London Univ. (BA); Sorbonne, Paris. Served European War, 1914-18, with 2nd London Regt (Royal Fusiliers), Gallipoli and France; Royal Artillery, France and Belgium (MC, twice wounded); entered Diplomatic Service, 1920; Third Sec., Santiago, Chile; Foreign Office, 1924; First Sec., 1929; transferred Bagdad, 1932; Acting Counsellor, 1935; Counsellor, Lisbon, 1937; Minister at Cairo, 1938; transferred Foreign Office, 1940; Minister to Mexico, 1941-44, Ambassador, 1944-47; Asst Under Sec., Foreign Office, 1948-50; British Ambassador to Poland, 1950-52; retired, 1952. Address: 30 Longcroft Avenue, Banstead, Surrey.

BATEMAN, Sir Geoffrey (Hirst), Kt 1972; FRCS; Surgeon, Ear, Nose and Throat Department, St Thomas' Hospital, London, 1939-71; b 24 Oct. 1906; s of Dr William Hirst Bateman, JP, Rochdale, Lancs; m 1931, Margaret, d of Sir Samuel Turner, Rochdale; three s one d. Educ: Epsom Coll.; University Coll., Oxford. Theodore Williams Schol. in Anat., Oxford Univ., 1926; BA Oxon, Hons sch. Physiol., 1927; Epsom schol. to King's Coll. Hosp., 1927; BM, BCh Oxon, 1930; FRCS, 1933; George Herbert Hunt Trav. Schol., Oxford Univ., 1933. RAFVR, Wing Comdr, 1939-45. Mem., Bd Governors, St Thomas' Hosp., 1948; Mem. Collegium Otolaryngologica Amicitiæ Sacrum, 1949; Hon. Corr. Mem. Amer. Laryngological Assoc., 1960; Past Mem. Council, RCS; Editor, Jl of Laryngology and Otology; Formerly Hon. Cons. on Oto-rhino-laryngology to the Army; Cons. Adviser in Otolaryngology, Dept of Health and Social Security. Pres., British Assoc. of Otolaryngologists, 1970-71 (Vice-Pres., 1967-70). Publications: Diseases of the Nose and Throat (Asst Editor to V. E. Negus, 6th edn), 1955; contributor various jls, etc. Recreations: golf, fishing. Address: Thorney, Graffham, Petworth, West Sussex GU28 0QA. T: Graffham 314.

See also Sir R. M. Bateman.

BATEMAN, Leslie Clifford, CMG 1965; FRS 1968; Secretary-General, International Rubber Study Group, since 1976; b 21 March 1915; s of Charles Samuel Bateman; m 1st, 1945, Marie Louise Pakes (d 1967); two s; 2nd, 1973, Mrs Eileen Joyce Jones (née Henwood). Educ: Bishopshalt Sch., Uxbridge; University Coll., London. BSc, 1st cl. Hons Chem., 1935; PhD and Ramsey Memorial Medal, 1938; DSc 1955; Fellow, 1974. Oriel Coll., 1940-41; Chemist, Natural Rubber Producers Research Assoc., 1941-53; Dir of Research, 1953-62; Controller of Rubber Res., Malaysia, 1962-74; Chm., Internat. Rubber R&D Board, 1962-74. Hon. DSc: Malaya, 1968; Aston, 1972. Colwyn Medal, 1963, and Jubilee Foundn Lectr, 1971, Inst. of Rubber Industry. Hon. PSM, Malaysia, 1974. Publications: (ed and contrib.) The Chemistry and Physics of Rubber-like Substances, 1963; numerous scientific papers in Jl Chem. Soc., etc, and articles on technical-economic status of natural rubber and its developments. *Recreations:* golf and other outdoor pursuits. *Address:* 3 Palmerston Close, Welwyn Garden City, Herts. *T:* Welwyn Garden 22391.

BATEMAN, Sir Ralph (Melton), KBE 1975; MA Oxon; Chairman, Turner & Newall Ltd, 1967-76; President, Confederation of British Industry, 1974-May 1976 (Deputy President, 1973-74); *b* 15 May 1910; 3rd *s* of William Hirst Bateman, MB, BCh, and of Ethel Jane Bateman, Rochdale, Lancs.; *m* 1935, Barbara Yvonne, 2nd *d* of Herbert Percy Litton and Grace Vera Litton, Heywood Lancs.; two *s* two *d. Educ:* Epsom Coll.; University Coll., Oxford. Turner & Newall Ltd: joined as management trainee, 1931; held various directorships in Group, 1942-; Dir, 1957; Dep. Chm., 1959. Mem., NEDC, 1973-76. Mem. Council, Manchester Business Sch., 1972-; Governor, NIESR; Chm. of Governors, Ashridge Management Coll.; Chm. of Council, University Coll. at Buckingham; Member Court: Manchester Univ.; Salford Univ. FCIS, FBIM; FRSA 1970. Hon. DSc Salford, 1969. *Recreations:* family and social affairs; tennis. *Address:* Highfield, Withinlee Road, Prestbury, Cheshire. *T:* Prestbury 49071.
See also Sir G. H. Bateman.

BATES, Alan (Arthur); actor; *b* 17 Feb. 1934; *m* 1970, Victoria Ward; twin *s. Educ:* Herbert Strutt Grammar Sch., Belper, Derbyshire; RADA. *Theatre:* English Stage Co. (Royal Court Theatre, London): The Mulberry Bush; Cards of Identity; Look Back in Anger; The Country Wife; In Celebration; London (West End): Long Day's Journey into Night; The Caretaker; The Four Seasons; Hamlet; Butley, London and NY (Evening Standard Best Actor award, 1972; Antoinette Perry Best Actor award, 1973); Poor Richard, NY; Richard III and The Merry Wives of Windsor, Stratford, Ont.; Venice Preserved, Bristol Old Vic; Taming of the Shrew, Stratford-on-Avon, 1973; Life Class, 1974; Otherwise Engaged, Queen's, 1975; The Seagull, Duke of York's, 1976. *Films:* The Entertainer, Whistle Down the Wind, A Kind of Loving, The Running Man, The Caretaker, Zorba the Greek, Nothing but the Best, Georgie Girl, King of Hearts, Far from the Madding Crowd, The Fixer (Oscar nomination), Women in Love, The Three Sisters (National Theatre Co.), A Day in the Death of Joe Egg, The Go-Between, Second Best (also prod.), Impossible Object, Butley, In Celebration, Royal Flash. *Television:* various plays. *Recreations:* swimming, squash, driving, riding, water skiing, reading. *Address:* c/o Michael Linnit, Chatto & Linnit Ltd, Globe Theatre, Shaftesbury Avenue, W1.

BATES, Sir Alfred, Kt 1952; MC 1918; DL; Solicitor; *b* 3 July 1897; *s* of Alfred Bates (Solicitor) and Agnes Bates; *m* 1925, Margaret, *d* of the Rev. J. H. Clarke, MSc, Heywood; three *s* one *d. Educ:* Royal Grammar Sch., Lancaster (Scholar). Member Lancs CC 1931-74; Chm., 1949-52, 1955-58 and 1961-64; CA 1949-74; Chairman: Planning Cttee of County Councils Assoc., 1948-68; Lancs Police Cttee, 1952-74; North West Police Training Centre, 1952-74; Governor, Police Coll., 1957-74. Served on W Lancs T&AFA 1949-61. Deputy Pro-Chancellor, Lancaster Univ., 1964-75. DL 1951. Hon. FRTPI(MTPI 1959); Hon. LLD (Lancaster), 1964. *Address:* 191 Coleherne Court, SW5. *T:* 01-373 4799. *Club:* Royal Automobile.

BATES, Alfred; MP (Lab) Bebington and Ellesmere Port since Feb. 1974; *b* 8 June 1944; *s* of Norman and Alice Bates; single. *Educ:* Stretford Grammar Sch. for Boys; Manchester Univ. (BSc); Corpus Christi Coll., Cambridge. Lectr in Maths, De La Salle Coll. of Educn, Middleton, 1967-74. PPS to Minister of State for Social Security, 1974-76; Asst Govt Whip, 1976-. *Recreation:* cricket umpiring. *Address:* 5 Dunbar Court, Little Sutton, Wirral, Cheshire.

BATES, Allan Frederick, CMG 1958; *b* 15 July 1911; *s* of John Frederick Lawes and Ethel Hannah Bates; *m* 1937, Ena Edith, *d* of John Richard Boxall; three *s. Educ:* Woolwich Central Sch.; London Univ. Qualified as Certified Accountant, 1938; practised in London, 1938-44. Joined Colonial Service (now Overseas Civil Service), 1944; Deputy Comptroller Inland Revenue, Cyprus, 1944-48; Comptroller Inland Revenue, Cyprus, 1948-52; Financial Secretary: Cyprus, 1952-60; Mauritius, 1960-64; Man. Dir, Develt Bank of Mauritius, 1964-70; Financial Advr (IMF) to Govt of Bahamas, 1971-75; Budget Advr (IMF) to Govt of Lesotho, 1975-76. Fellow Inst. of Taxation 1950. *Recreations:* swimming, painting, carving. *Address:* 5 Redford Avenue, Coulsdon, Surrey. *T:* 01-660 7421. *Club:* Royal Commonwealth Society.

BATES, Sir Darrell; *see* Bates, Sir J. D.

BATES, Prof. David Robert, MSc; DSc; FRS 1955; MRIA; Professor of Theoretical Physics, Queen's University, Belfast, since 1968; *b* Omagh, Co. Tyrone, N Ireland, 18 Nov. 1916; *s* of late Walter Vivian Bates and of Mary Olive Bates; *m* 1956, Barbara Bailey Morris; one *s* one *d. Educ:* Royal Belfast Academical Institution; Queen's Univ., Belfast; University Coll., London. Engaged at Admiralty Research Laboratory, 1939-41, and at Mine Design Department, 1941-45; Lecturer in Mathematics, University Coll., London, 1945-50; Consultant at US Naval Ordnance Test Station, Inyokern, Calif., 1950; Reader in Physics, University Coll., London, 1951; Prof. of Applied Mathematics, Queen's Univ., Belfast, 1951-68. Vice-Pres., RIA, 1976-77. Chapman Meml Lectr, Univ. of Colorado, 1973. Vice-Pres., Alliance Party of NI, 1971. Hon. Foreign Mem., Amer. Acad. of Arts and Scis, 1974. Hon. DSc: Ulster, 1972; NUI, 1975. Hughes Medal, Royal Soc., 1970; Chree Medal, Inst. Physics, 1973; Gold Medal, Royal Astron. Soc., 1977. *Publications:* papers in geophysical and physical journals. Editor-in-Chief, Planetary and Space Science. *Recreations:* reading and listening to radio. *Address:* 6 Deramore Park, Belfast BT9 5JT. *T:* Belfast 665640.

BATES, Sir Dawson; *see* Bates, Sir J. D.

BATES, Maj.-Gen. Sir (Edward) John (Hunter), KBE 1969 (OBE 1952); CB 1965; MC 1944; Director, Thomson Regional Newspapers, 1969-77; *b* 5 Dec. 1911; *s* of late Ernest Bates, FRIBA; *m* 1947, Sheila Ann Norman; two *s* two *d. Educ:* Wellington Coll.; Corpus Christi Coll., Cambridge. BA 1933; MA 1963. Commissioned, 1932; Pre-war service in UK and Malaya; War Service in Africa, Middle East, Sicily, Italy and Greece; Senior Army Instructor, JSSC, 1954-57; Student, IDC, 1958; CRA, 2 Div., 1959; CCRA 1 (British) Corps, 1960-61; Dir, RA, War Office, 1961-64; Comdt of RMCS, 1964-67; Dir, Royal Defence Acad., 1967-68. Special Comr, Duke of York's Royal Military Sch., 1972-. Col Comdt, RA 1966-76. Mem. Ct of Assts, 1972-, Warden, 1977, Worshipful Co. of Haberdashers. Chm., RUSI. *Recreations:* fishing, shooting. *Address:* Seymours Oast, Leeds, near Maidstone, Kent. *T:* Maidstone 861275. *Clubs:* Army and Navy; Rye Golf.
See also J . D . Waite.

BATES, Eric; Chairman, Midlands Electricity Board, 1969-72; *b* 1 Nov. 1908; *s* of late John Boon Bates and late Edith Anne Bates; *m* 1933, Beatrice, *d* of late William Henry Herapath and late Beatrice Herapath; one *s* two *d.* Trained Ilford Elec. Dept.; Asst, County of London Elec. Supply Co., 1929-32; Consumers' Engr: West Kent Electric Co., 1933-36; Isle of Thanet Elec. Supply Co., 1937-42; Elec. Engr, Kennedy & Donkin, 1942-44; Consumers' Engr, Luton Elec. Dept, 1944-48; Sect. Head, Eastern Elec. Bd, 1948-49; Dep. Chief Commercial Officer, Eastern Elec. Bd, 1949-57; North Eastern Electricity Board: Chief Commercial Officer, 1957-62; Dep. Chm., 1962-67; Chm., 1967-69. *Publications:* contribs to Proc. IEE. *Recreation:* golf. *Address:* 24 Grange Road, Broadstairs, Kent.

BATES, Sir Geoffrey Voltelin, 5th Bt, *cr* 1880; MC 1942; *b* 2 Oct. 1921; *s* of Major Cecil Robert Bates, DSO, MC (3rd *s* of 2nd Bt) and Hylda, *d* of Sir James Heath, 1st Bt; *S* uncle, 1946; *m* 1st, 1945, Kitty Kendall Lane (*d* 1956); two *s*; 2nd, 1957, Olivia Gwyneth Zoë (*d* 1969) *d* of Capt. Hon. R. O. FitzRoy (now 2nd Viscount Daventry, *qv*); one *d* (and one *d* decd); 3rd, 1971, Mrs Juliet Eleanor Hugolyn Whitelocke-Winter, *widow* of Edward Colin Winter and *d* of late Comdr G. C. A. Whitelocke, RN retd, and of Mrs S. H. Whitelocke, Cerrigllwydion Hall, Denbigh. *Educ:* Radley. High Sheriff, Flintshire, 1969. *Recreations:* hunting, shooting, fishing. *Heir: s* Edward Robert Bates, *b* 4 July 1946. *Address:* Gyrn Castle, Llanasa, near Holywell, Clwyd. *T:* Prestatyn 3500. *Clubs:* Cavalry and Guards; Palatine (Liverpool).

BATES, Harry Stuart, CSI 1947; *b* 16 March 1893; *s* of late Albert Bates, Congleton, Cheshire; *m* 1920, *d* of late William Hammond Walker, Congleton, Cheshire; two *s* one *d. Educ:* Denstone; St Catharine's Coll., Cambridge (BA). Served in British and Indian Armies 1914-19. Joined Indian Civil Service, 1920: Collector, Settlement Offr and Manager, Balrampur Estate, 1926-42; Comr, 1942-45; Mem., Bd of Revenue, UP, 1945-47; retired, 1949. Employed Colonial Office, 1948-57. *Address:* Rowhurst Cottage, Milford-on-Sea, Hants. *T:* Milford 2906.

BATES, James P. M.; *see* Martin-Bates.

BATES, Maj.-Gen. Sir John; *see* Bates, Maj.-Gen. Sir E. J. H.

BATES, Sir John (David), Kt 1969; CBE 1962; VRD; Australian Consul-General in New York, 1970-73; *b* 1 March 1904; *s* of H. W. Bates, Plymouth, Devon; *m* 1930, Phyllis Helen Muller; one *s. Educ:* Plymouth. Joined sea staff of Orient Line, 1925; transf.

to shore staff, in Australia, 1929; RANVR, 1932-57, Comdr; Gen. Manager in Australia of Orient Line, 1954-60; Dep. Chm., P & O Lines of Australia, 1960-67; Chm., Hon. Bd of Australian Nat. Travel Assoc., 1956-67; Chm. Australian Tourist Commn, 1967-69. Federal Pres., Navy League of Australia, 1950-56; Trustee, Art Gallery of NSW, 1962-70; Lay Member, Trade Practices Tribunal, 1968-70. *Recreation:* farming. *Address:* 18 Southern Cross Gardens, 2 Spruson Street, Neutral Bay, NSW 2089, Australia. *Clubs:* Union, Royal Sydney Golf (Sydney).

BATES, Sir (John) Dawson, 2nd Bt, *cr* 1937; MC 1943; Area Land Agent for the National Trust; *b* 21 Sept. 1921; *o s* of Sir (Richard) Dawson Bates, 1st Bt, PC, and Muriel (*d* 1972), *d* of late Sir Chas. Cleland, KBE, MVO, LLD; *S* father, 1949; *m* 1953, Mary Murray, *o d* of late Lieut-Col Joseph M. Hoult, Norton Place, Lincoln; two *s* one *d. Educ:* Winchester; Balliol. BA 1949. FRICS. Served War of 1939-45, Major, Rifle Brigade (MC). *Heir: s* Richard Dawson Hoult Bates, *b* 12 May 1956. *Address:* Eaton Hastings Grange, Faringdon, Oxon.

BATES, Sir (Julian) Darrell, Kt 1966; CMG 1956; CVO 1954; *b* 10 Nov. 1913; *y s* of late E. Stuart Bates; *m* 1944, Susan Evelyn June Sinclair; two *s* one *d. Educ:* Sevenoaks Sch.; Keble Coll., Oxford. Entered Colonial Service, Tanganyika Territory, 1936; served King's African Rifles (despatches), 1940-43; seconded Colonial Office, 1944-46; Officer Administering the Government, Seychelles, 1950-51; Deputy Chief Secretary, Somaliland Protectorate, 1951-53; Colonial Sec., Gibraltar, 1953-64, Permanent Sec., 1964-68. *Publications:* A Fly Switch from the Sultan, 1961; The Shell at My Ear, 1961; The Mango and the Palm, 1962; A Longing for Quails, 1964; Susie, 1964; A Gust of Plumes, 1972; The Companion Guide to Devon and Cornwall, 1976. *Address:* Mellinpons, St Buryan, Cornwall. *Club:* Travellers'.

BATES, Leslie Fleetwood, CBE 1966; FRS 1950; BSc Bristol, PhD Cambridge, DSc London; FInstP; Emeritus Professor of Physics, Nottingham University (formerly University College, Nottingham), since 1964 (Lancashire-Spencer Professor, 1936-64); Deputy Vice-Chancellor, University of Nottingham, 1953-56; *b* 7 March 1897; *e s* of late W. F. Bates, Kingswood, Bristol; *m* 1925, Winifred Frances Furze Ridler, MSc, (*d* 1965), *o d* of late F. Ridler, Bristol; one *s* one *d. Educ:* Merchant Venturers' Sch., Bristol; University of Bristol; Trinity Coll., Cambridge. Served as radiographer, Capt. Unattached List, i/c X-Ray Laboratory IX Division, Secunderabad, Deccan, India, 1916-20; Research at University of Bristol, 1920-22, and Cavendish Laboratory, 1922-24; Lecturer in Physics, University Coll., London, 1924-30, Reader in Physics, 1930-36; Pres. of Physical Soc., 1950-52; Holweck Prizeman (French and English Physical Socs), 1949; Mem. of Board of Institute of Physics, 1947-49; Pres. Association of University Teachers, 1938-39. Consultant to Inter-Services Research Bureau, 1941-45; Vice-Principal, University Coll. Nottingham, 1944-46; Vice-Pres., Lace Research Association, 1955-63; Senior Scientific Adviser for Civil Defence, North Midland Region (No 3), 1951-72. May Lecture, Inst. of Metals, 1954; Rippon Lectures University of Calcutta, 1960; Guthrie Lecture, 1963. Hon. DSc: Nottingham, 1972; Durham, 1975. *Publications:* Modern Magnetism, 1939, 1948, 1951, 1961, 1963; Sir Alfred Ewing, 1946; Recent Advances in Physics, Science Progress, 1928-36; Research publications mainly on electricity and magnetism in various journals. *Address:* Flat 2, Castlethorpe, Newcastle Circus, The Park, Nottingham NG7 1BJ. *T:* Nottingham 42135. *Club:* Athenæum.

BATES, Ven. Mansel Harry, MA; Archdeacon of Lindisfarne and Vicar of Eglingham, Diocese of Newcastle, since 1970; *b* 4 Aug. 1912; *s* of Rev. John Handel Greenhalgh and Alice Bates; *m* 1939, Queenie Mary Fraser Campbell; one *s* three *d. Educ:* Liverpool Institute; Brasenose Coll., Oxford; Wycliffe Hall. BA 1934; Dip. in Theol., 1935; MA 1938. Deacon, 1935, Priest, 1936, Dio. Liverpool. Curate, SS John and James, Litherland, 1935-38; Curate in Charge of Netherton, 1938-41; Vicar: St Saviour, Everton, 1941-47; Jesmond, Newcastle upon Tyne, 1947-59 (Proctor in Convocation, 1950-59); Great Crosby, Liverpool, 1959-70. Hon. Canon of Liverpool Cath., 1964-70. *Address:* Eglingham Vicarage, Alnwick, Northumberland. *T:* Powburn 250.

BATES, Ralph; *b* Swindon, Wilts, 3 Nov. 1899; *s* of Henry Roy and Mabel Stevens Bates; *m* 1940, Eve Salzman; one *s, Educ:* Swindon and North Wilts. Secondary Sch. After service in 16th Queen's Royal West Surreys, 1917-19, worked in Great Western Railway Factory at Swindon; in Spain, 1930-37; took active part in Republican politics in Spain; began literary career in 1933 as consequence of unemployment; Capt. in the Spanish Loyalist Army and in the International Brigade, Madrid sector, 1936-37;

lecture tour in USA 1937-38; one year resident in Mexico, 1938-39; Adjunct Prof. of Literature, New York Univ. 1948-68, now Professor Emeritus of Literature. *Publications:* Sierra, 1933; Lean Men, 1934, Schubert, 1934, The Olive Field, 1936; Rainbow Fish, 1937; The Miraculous Horde, 1939; The Fields of Paradise, 1941; The Undiscoverables, 1942; The Journey to the Sandalwood Forest, 1947; The Dolphin in the Wood, 1949. *Recreations:* small boating, music. *Address:* 37 Washington Square West, New York, NY 10011, USA. *T:* (212) 254-4149.

BATES, Stewart Taverner, QC 1970; *b* 17 Dec. 1926; *s* of John Bates, Greenock; *m* 1950, Anne Patricia, *d* of David West, Pinner; two *s* four *d. Educ:* Univs of Glasgow and St Andrews; Corpus Christi Coll., Oxford. Called to Bar, Middle Temple, 1954, Bencher, 1975; Mem. Bar Council, 1962-66. *Recreations:* theatre, sailing, ski-ing. *Address:* 2 Maids of Honour Row, The Green, Richmond, Surrey. *T:* 01-940 0438. *Club:* Garrick.

BATES, William Stanley, CMG 1971; HM Diplomatic Service; Ambassador to Korea, since 1975; *b* 7 Sept. 1920; *m* 1949, Suzanne Elston. *Educ:* Christ's Hospital; Corpus Christi Coll., Cambridge. Asst Principal, Colonial Office, 1948; Principal, 1951; Commonwealth Relations Office, 1956; Canberra, 1956-59; Asst Sec., 1962. British Deputy High Commissioner, Northern Nigeria, 1963-65; Imperial Defence Coll., 1966; Head of Communications Dept, FCO, 1967-70; High Comr in Guyana, 1970-75. *Address:* c/o Foreign and Commonwealth Office, SW1. *Club:* Travellers'.

BATESON; *see* de Yarburgh-Bateson, family name of Baron Deramore.

BATESON, Andrew James, QC 1971; *b* 29 June 1925; *m* 1954, Janette Mary Poupart (*d* 1970); one *s* three *d. Educ:* Eton. Called to the Bar, Middle Temple, 1951; Bencher, 1977. *Recreations:* shooting, fishing, gardening. *Address:* 10 South Square, Grays Inn, Holborn, WC1; Bracken House, Beechwood Avenue, Weybridge, Surrey. *Clubs:* Bath, Garrick.

BATESON, Frederick Wilse; Fellow and Tutor in English Literature, Corpus Christi College, Oxford, 1946-69, now Emeritus; *b* 25 Dec. 1901; *s* of Alfred Bateson, Styal, Cheshire; *m* 1931, Jan Cancellor, JP; one *s* one *d. Educ:* Charterhouse; Trinity Coll., Oxford. Commonwealth Fellow, Harvard Univ., 1927-29. Editor of Cambridge Bibliography of English Literature, 1930-40; Lecturer WEA, 1935-40; Statistical Officer, Bucks War Agric. Exec. Cttee, 1940-46; Agricultural correspondent, The Observer and The New Statesman, 1944-48; Founder and Editor of Essays in Criticism (Quarterly), 1951-74. Visiting Professor: Cornell Univ., USA, 1955, California Univ. (Berkeley), 1958; Pennsylvania State Univ., 1960, 1962 and 1964. *Publications:* English Comic Drama, 1700-1750, 1929; English Poetry and the English Language, 1934, rev. edn 1973; Towards a Socialist Agriculture, 1946; Mixed Farming and Muddled Thinking, 1946; English Poetry: a Critical Introduction, 1950 (rev. 1966); Pope's Epistles to Several Persons, 1951 (rev. 1961); Wordsworth: a Re-interpretation, 1954; Selected Poems of William Blake, 1957; A Guide to English Literature, 1965, rev. edn 1976; Brill: a Short History, 1966; Essays in Critical Dissent, 1972; The Scholar Critic, 1972. *Recreation:* local history. *Address:* Temple House, Brill, Bucks HP18 9SX. *T:* Brill 255.

BATESON, Mrs Gregory; *see* Mead, Dr M.

BATESON, Air Vice-Marshal Robert Norman, CB 1964; DSO 1943 and Bar, 1944; DFC 1940; idc; jssc; psa; *b* 10 June 1912; *s* of late George Rowland Bateson; *m* 1st, 1942, Elizabeth Lindsay Davidson (*d* 1975); 2nd, 1976, Margaret Graham Craig. *Educ:* Watford Grammar Sch. Joined RAF 1936. Served War of 1939-45. Asst Chief of Air Staff, Operational Requirements, Air Min., 1959-61; Air Officer Comdg No. 12 Group, Fighter Comd, 1961-62; SASO, Fighter Comd, 1963-67. ADC to the Queen, 1958-60. Air Cdre, 1958; actg Air Vice-Marshal, 1959; Air Vice-Marshal, 1960. Dutch Flight Cross, 1943; Order of Dannebrog, 1944. *Recreations:* squash, tennis, sailing, motor sport. *Address:* Greenways, Parsonage Road, Newton Ferrers, Devon. *T:* Newton Ferrers 476. *Clubs:* Royal Air Force; Yealm Yacht (Newton Ferrers).

BATESON, Rear-Adm. Stuart Latham, CB 1950; CBE 1948; MIEE; retired; *b* 7 July 1898; *twin s* of late Sir Alexander Dingwall Bateson, Judge of the High Court, and Isabel Mary (*née* Latham); *m* 1923, Marie Elphinstone Fleming Cullen; one *s* one *d. Educ:* Lockers Park; Rugby; RNC Keyham. Joined Navy, 1916; specialised in Torpedo, 1923; Comdr, 1934; Capt., 1939; Rear-Admiral (L), 1949, the first holder of the rank. Served War of 1939-45; Commanded HMS Latona, 1941; HMS Ajax, 1941-

42; HMS London, 1944-46; Dir of Naval Electrical Department, Admiralty, 1946-51; retd, 1951. County Comr for Boy Scouts of Rutland, 1953-66. Chm. and Sec. Rutland Historic Churches Preservation Trust, 1954-. Sheriff of Rutland, 1958; DL 1957, Vice-Lieut Co. Rutland, 1963-72. *Recreation:* shooting. *Address:* Ridlington, Leics.

BATEY, Charles Edward, OBE 1943; Hon. MA Oxon, 1941 (by Decree, 1946, Lincoln College); JP; *b* 22 Feb. 1893; *e s* of Edward Batey and Christian Allan Morison; *m* 1922, Ethel May, *d* of George Reed; one *d. Educ:* Edinburgh Board Schs.; Heriot Watt College (Hon. Fellow 1954). Apprenticed Leith Observer, 1908-15; served European War, 1915-20, RAMC. Hazell, Watson & Viney, Aylesbury, 1920; Works Manager, Univ. Tutorial Press, 1922-28; Asst Printer, University of Oxford, 1929-46; Printer to the University of Oxford, 1946-58. Mem. Council British Federation of Master Printers, 1944-50, and Mem. of Labour Cttee, 1944-49; Chairman: Jt Industrial Council of Printing and Allied Trades, 1948-49; Apprenticeship Authority, 1946-48; City of Oxford Youth Employment Cttee, 1944-54. Pres. Assoc of Teachers of Printing and Allied Subjects, 1953-58. Mem. various industrial education cttees. Hon. Mem. City and Guilds of London Institute, 1959; Hon. Fellow Inst of Printing, 1961; Hon. City and Guilds Insignia Award, 1965. *Publication:* (with T. W. Chaundy and P. R. Barrett) The Printing of Mathematics, 1954. *Recreations:* calligraphy, gardening. *Address:* Carfax, Up Nately, Basingstoke, Hants. *T:* Hook 2170.

BATEY, Rowland William John S.; see Scott-Batey.

BATH, 6th Marquess of, *cr* 1789; **Henry Frederick Thynne,** Bt 1641; Viscount Weymouth and Baron Thynne, 1682; Major Royal Wiltshire Yeomanry; JP; *b* 26 Jan. 1905; *o surv. s* of 5th Marquess, KG, PC, CB and Violet Caroline (*d* 1928), *d* of Sir Charles Mordaunt, 10th Bt; *S* father, 1946; *m* 1st, 1927, Hon. Daphne (marr. diss., 1953; she *m* 2nd, 1953, Major A. W. Fielding, DSO), *er d* of 4th Baron Vivian, DSO; three *s* one *d*; 2nd, 1953, Mrs Virginia Penelope Tennant, *d* of late Alan L. R. Parsons; one *d. Educ:* Harrow; Christ Church, Oxford. MP (U) Frome Division, Som., 1931-35. Served War of 1939-45 (wounded). Life-long interest in forestry; Longleat has some of the best private woodland in the country. *Heir: s* Viscount Weymouth, *qv. Address:* Job's Mill, Warminster, Wilts BA12 8BB. *T:* Warminster 2279; Longleat, Warminster, Wilts. *Club:* White's.
See also Duke of Beaufort.

BATH and WELLS, Bishop of, since 1975; **Rt. Rev. John Monier Bickersteth;** *b* 6 Sept. 1921; *yr s* of late Rev. Canon Edward Monier Bickersteth, OBE; *m* 1955, Rosemary, *yr d* of late Edward and Muriel Cleveland-Stevens, Gaines, Oxted; three *s* one *d. Educ:* Rugby; Christ Church, Oxford; Wells Theol College. MA Oxon 1953. Captain, Buffs and Royal Artillery, 1941-46, Normandy and India. Priest, 1951; Curate, St Matthew, Moorfields, Bristol, 1950-54; Vicar, St John's, Hurst Green, Oxted, 1954-62; St Stephen's, Chatham, 1962-70; Bishop Suffragan of Warrington, 1970-75. ChStJ 1977. *Recreations:* walking, gardening. *Address:* The Palace, Wells, Somerset. *T:* Wells 72341.

BATH, Archdeacon of; see Burgess, Ven. J. E.

BATH, Alan Alfred; Director, Education and Training, Commission of the European Communities, since 1973; *b* 3 May 1924; *s* of Alfred Edward Bath and Doris Ellen Lawson; *m* 1946, Joy Roselle Thornton, *d* of George Jeune, St Saviour, Jersey; one *s* two *d. Educ:* Frays Coll., Uxbridge; Queen's Univ., Belfast (BSc Econ). RAF, 1942-46. Asst Lectr in Econs, QUB, 1950-53; Admin. Officer, Assoc. of Univs of British Commonwealth, 1953-58; Imperial Coll., Univ. of London, 1958-62 (Develt Sec., 1960-62); Sec., Cttee of Vice-Chancellors and Principals of Univs of UK, 1964-73; Sec., UK Nat. Delegn to Council of Europe Cttee for Higher Educn and Research, 1969-73. *Recreations:* music, sailing, gardening. *Address:* 12 Voltaire, Ennerdale Road, Kew Gardens, Surrey TW9 3PQ. *T:* 01-940 6577; Avenue des Eperviers 47, 1150 Brussels. *T:* 771-12-26. *Club:* Athenæum.

BATHER, Elizabeth Constance, OBE 1946; retired as Chief Superintendent Metropolitan (Women) Police, (1946-60); *b* 11 Oct. 1904; *d* of late Rev. Arthur George Bather, MA, and Lilian Dundas Firth, Winchester. *Educ:* St Swithuns Sch., Winchester. Mem. Hampshire County Council, 1937-46. Served in WAAF, 1939-45; Group Officer, 1944-45. JP Winchester, 1937-46; Councillor, Hartley Witney and Hart DCs, 1967-76. *Address:* Laburnham Cottage, Odiham, Hants.

BATHO, Edith Clara, MA, DLit (London); Principal, Royal Holloway College, University of London, 1945-62, retired; *b* 21 Sept. 1895; 3rd *d* of late William John Batho and Ellen Clara Hooton. *Educ:* Highbury Hill High Sch.; University Coll., London. BA (Hons English), 1915, MA 1920, DLit 1935; war work, 1916-18; on staff of Roedean Sch., 1918-19; Downe House Sch., 1919-21; Quain Student and Asst in English at University Coll., London, 1921; Fellow of University Coll., London, 1934; Reader in English Literature, University Coll., London, 1935-45. Visiting Prof., Univ. of Wisconsin, 1963. An active mem. British Fedn of Univ. Women. Hon. D de l'U Poitiers, 1962. *Publications:* The Ettrick Shepherd, 1927 (reprinted 1969); The Later Wordsworth, 1934 (reprinted, 1964); The Poet and the Past (Warton Lecture of the British Acad.), 1937; The Victorians and After (with Bonamy Dobrée), 1938; Chronicles of Scotland by Hector Boece, tr. Bellenden (ed for STS), Vol. I with R. W. Chambers, 1936, Vol. II with H. W. Husbands, 1941; A Wordsworth Selection, 1962; other articles and reviews. *Recreations:* travelling, languages, needlework. *Address:* 130 Wood Street, Barnet, Herts. *Club:* New Arts Theatre, English-Speaking Union.

BATHO, Sir Maurice Benjamin, 2nd Bt, *cr* 1928; Chairman and Managing Director, Ridgley (Huntingdon) Ltd and associated companies; *b* 14 Jan. 1910; *o surv. s* of Sir Charles Albert Batho, 1st Bt, and Bessie (*d* 1961), 4th *d* of Benjamin Parker, Oulton Broad, Suffolk; *S* father, 1938; *m* 1934, Antoinette, *o d* of Baron d'Udekem d'Acoz, Ghent; two *s* two *d. Educ:* Uppingham; Belgium. Served War of 1939-45: Lt-Col, KRRC. Jt Sub-Dir, Syrian Wheat Collection Scheme of Spears Mission, 1943; Adviser on Cereals Collection, Min. of Finance of Imp. Iranian Govt, 1944; Dep. Dir, Rice Procurement, Bengal, 1945; Managing Dir, Reed Paper & Board Sales Ltd, 1959, resigned 1965; formerly Director: Reed Paper & Board (UK) Ltd; London Paper Mills Co. Ltd; Empire Paper Mills Ltd; Reed Board Mills (Colthorp) Ltd; Reed Brookgate Ltd. *Recreations:* golf. *Heir: s* Peter Ghislain Batho [*b* 9 Dec. 1939; *m* 1966, Lucille Mary, *d* of Wilfrid F. Williamson; three *s*]. *Address:* Carlton Hall, Saxmundham, Suffolk. *T:* 2505. *Clubs:* Naval and Military, Constitutional.

BATHURST, family name of **Earl Bathurst** and **Viscount Bledisloe.**

BATHURST, 8th Earl, *cr* 1772; **Henry Allen John Bathurst,** DL; Baron Bathurst of Battlesden, Bedfordshire, 1712; Baron Apsley of Apsley, Sussex, 1771; Earl Bathurst of Bathurst, Sussex, 1772; Capt. Royal Gloucestershire Hussars (TA); TARO, 1959; *b* 1 May 1927; *s* of late Lord Apsley, DSO, MC, MP (killed on active service, 1942), and late Lady Apsley, CBE; *g s* of 7th Earl; *S* grandfather, 1943; *m* 1959, Judith Mary (marr. diss. 1977), *d* of Mr and Mrs A. C. Nelson, Springfield House, Foulridge, Lancs; two *s* one *d. Educ:* Ridley Coll., Canada; Eton; Christ Church, Oxford, 1948-49. Late Lieut 10th Royal Hussars (PWO). Capt., Royal Glos. Hussars, TA, 1949-57. Hon. Sec. Agricultural Cttee (Conservative), House of Lords, 1957; a Lord-in-Waiting, 1957-61; Joint Parliamentary Under-Sec. of State, Home Office, 1961-July 1962. Governor, Royal Agricultural Coll.; Pres. Glos Branch CPRE. DL County of Gloucester, 1960. Chancellor, Primrose League, 1959-61. Member: CLA Council, 1965 (Chm., Glos Branch of CLA, 1968-71); Timber Growers' Organisation (TGO) Council, 1966; Pres., Royal Forestry Scc., 1976-. *Heir: s* Lord Apsley, *qv. Address:* Cirencester Park, Cirencester, Glos GL7 2BT. *T:* Cirencester 3412. *Club:* White's.

BATHURST, (NSW), Bishop of, since 1959; **Rt. Rev. Ernest Kenneth Leslie,** OBE 1972; *b* 14 May 1911; *s* of Rev. Ernest Thomas Leslie and Margaret Jane Leslie; *m* 1941, Isabel Daisy Wilson; two *s* one *d* (and one *s* decd). *Educ:* Trinity Gram. Sch., Kew, Vict.; Trinity Coll., University of Melbourne (BA). Aust. Coll. of Theology. ThL, 2nd Cl. 1933, Th Schol. 1951, 2nd Cl. 1952; Deacon, 1934; Priest, 1935; Asst Curate, Holy Trinity, Coburg, 1934-37; Priest-in-Charge, Tennant Creek, Dio. Carpentaria, 1937-38; Alice Springs with Tennant Creek, 1938-40; Rector of Christ Church, Darwin, 1940-44; Chaplain, AIF, 1942-45; Rector of Alice Springs with Tennant Creek, 1945-46; Vice-Warden, St John's Coll., Morpeth, NSW, 1947-52; Chap. Geelong Church of Eng. Gram. Sch., Timbertop Branch, 1953-58. *Recreations:* walking, woodwork, cycling. *Address:* Bishopscourt, Bathurst, NSW, Australia. *T:* Bathurst 31.1175.

BATHURST, (NSW), Bishop of, (RC), since 1963; **Rt. Rev. Albert Reuben Edward Thomas;** *b* Farnborough, Hants, 26 Oct. 1908; *s* of Albert Charles Thomas and Esperie Loreto Clarke. *Educ:* St Joseph's College, Hunter's Hill; St Columbia's Coll., St Patrick's Coll., Manly. Diploma of Social Studies, Sydney Univ., 1944. Ordained, 1931. Asst Suburban Parishes, 1931-38; Diocesan Dir, Pontifical Missions, 1938-63, National Dir, 1944-

70. Founder of Catholic Welfare Bureau, 1941. Initiated Australian National Pilgrimage, 1950-63; Hon. Chaplain of House of Lourdes, 1960; Foundation Chm. of St Vincent's Hospital Advisory Board, 1955; Chm. of Unity Movement for Christian Christmas, 1956-63. *Publication:* contrib. to Australian Encyclopaedia, on Catholic Missions and Welfare, 1958. *Address:* Bishop's House, Bathurst, NSW 2795, Australia.

BATHURST, Sir Frederick Peter Methuen Hervey-, 6th Bt, *cr* 1818; *b* 26 Jan. 1903; *s* of Sir Frederick Edward William Hervey-Bathurst, 5th Bt, DSO and Hon. Moira O'Brien, 2nd *d* of 14th Baron Inchiquin; *S* father 1956; *m* 1st, 1933, Maureen (marr. diss. 1956), *d* of Charles Gordon, Boveridge Park, Salisbury; one *s* one *d*; 2nd, 1958, Mrs Cornelia Shepard Riker, *widow* of Dr John Lawrence Riker, Rumson, NJ, USA. *Educ:* Eton. Served War of 1939-45, Capt. Grenadier Guards. *Recreations:* sailing, riding, ski-ing, flying. *Heir: s* Frederick John Charles Gordon Hervey-Bathurst [*b* 23 April 1934; *m* 1957, Caroline Myrtle, *d* of Lieut-Col Sir William Starkey, 2nd Bt, and late Irene Myrtle Francklin; one *s* two *d*]. *Address:* Bellevue Avenue, Rumson, New Jersey 07760, USA. *T:* 842-0791. *Clubs:* Cavalry and Guards, Royal Ocean Racing.

BATHURST, Joan Caroline; *see* Petrie, J. C.

BATHURST, Maurice Edward, CMG 1953; CBE 1947; QC 1964; *b* 2 Dec. 1913; *o s* of Edward James Bathurst and late Annie Mary Bathurst; *m* 1941, Dorothy (marr. diss. 1963), *d* of late W. S. Stevens, LDS, RCS; one *s*; *m* 1968, Joan Caroline Petrie, *qv*. *Educ:* Haberdashers' Aske's, Hatcham; King's Coll., London; Gonville and Caius Coll., Cambridge; Columbia Univ. LLB, First Class Hons. (London), 1937; University Law Schol. (London), 1937; Post-Grad. Research Studentship (London), 1938; Bartle Frere Exhibitioner (Camb.), 1939; Tutorial Fellow (Chicago), 1939; Special Fellow (Columbia), 1940; LLM (Columbia), 1941; Hon. DCL (Sacred Heart, NB), 1946; PhD (Camb.), 1949; LLD (London), 1966. Solicitor of Supreme Court, 1938-56. Called to Bar, Gray's Inn, 1957; Master of the Bench, 1970. Legal Adviser, British Information Services, USA, 1941-43; Legal Adviser, British Embassy, Washington, 1943-46 (First Sec.), 1944; Counsellor, 1946); Legal Member, UK Delegation to United Nations, 1946-48; UK Representative, Legal Advisory Cttee, Atomic Energy Commission, 1946-48; Legal Adviser to British Chm., Bipartite Control Office, Frankfurt, 1949; Dep. Legal Adviser, CCG, 1949-51; Legal Adviser, UK High Commn, Germany, 1951-55; Judge, Supreme Court, British Zone, Germany, 1953-55; Legal Adviser, British Embassy, Bonn, 1955-57; British Judge, Arbitral Commn, Germany, 1968-69. Mem. UK Delegations to UNRRA; United Nations San Francisco Conference; Bermuda Civil Aviation Conference; PICAO; Washington Financial Talks; UN Gen. Assembly; FAO; WHO; Internat. Tin Study Group; UK-US Double Taxation Treaty Negotiations; London Nine-Power Conf.; Paris Conf. on W Eur. Union; NATO Status of Forces Conf., Bonn. Internat. Vice-Pres. UN League of Lawyers; Vice-Chm. Council, Brit. Inst. of International and Comparative Law; a Pres. of Arbitral Tribunals, Internat. Telecommunications Satellite Orgn. Member: Panel of Arbitrators, Internat. Centre for Settlement of Investment Disputes; UK Cttee, UNICEF; Ct of Assistants, Haberdashers' Co. (Fourth Warden, 1973-74); Editorial Cttee, British Yearbook of International Law; *ad eundem,* Inner Temple; Gen. Council of the Bar, 1970-71; Senate of Inns of Court, 1971-73; Council of Legal Educn, 1971-; Senate of the Inns of Court and the Bar, 1974-77. Hon. Vis. Prof. in Internat. Law, King's Coll., London, 1967-; Hon. Fellow, King's Coll., London. Chm. Governors, Haberdashers' Aske's Hatcham Schools. Pres., British Insurance Law Assoc., 1971-75. Freeman of the City of London and of the City of Bathurst, NB. *Publications:* Germany and the North Atlantic Community: A Legal Survey (with J. L. Simpson), 1956; (ed, jtly) Legal Problems of an Enlarged European Community, 1972; notes and articles in legal jls, etc., British and American. *Recreation:* theatre. *Address:* Airlie, The Highlands, East Horsley, Surrey. *T:* East Horsley 3269. *Club:* Garrick.

BATSFORD, Sir Brian (Caldwell Cook), Kt 1974; *b* 18 Dec. 1910; *s* of late Arthur Caldwell Cook, Gerrards Cross, Bucks.; assumed mother's maiden name of Batsford by Deed Poll 1946; *m* 1945, Joan (Wendy), *d* of late Norman Cunliffe, DSc, of Oxford; two *d*. *Educ:* Repton Sch. Joined B. T. Batsford Ltd, Booksellers and Publishers, 1928; Chairman, 1952-74; President, 1974-77. Lectured in Canada under auspices Canadian National Council of Education, 1935, 1937; lectured in Scandinavia and Baltic States under auspices British Council, 1940. Hon. Sec. Empire Youth Sunday Cttee, 1938; Chm. Youth City Cttee of Enquiry, 1939. RAF, 1941-46. Contested Chelmsford Div. of Essex for Nat. Govt, 1945; MP (C) Ealing

South, 1958-Feb. 1974; PPS to Minister of Works, 1959-60; Asst Govt Whip, 1962-64; Opposition Deputy Chief Whip, 1964-67. Chairman: Adv. Cttee on Works of Art in House of Commons, 1970; House of Commons Library Cttee, 1970-74. Alderman, GLC, and Parly Rep. of GLC Majority Party, 1967-70; co-opted Mem., GLC Arts and Recreation Cttee, 1970-72. Pres., London Appreciation Soc., 1955. FRSA 1955, Mem. Council, 1967, Treasurer, 1971-73; Chm., RSA, 1973-75, Vice-Pres., 1975; FSIAD 1971. Mem., Post Office Stamp Adv. Cttee, 1967. Pres., Old Reptonian Soc., 1973; Mem., Governing Body, Repton Sch., 1973. Trustee, Bishop's Palace, Wells; Visitor, Sexey's Hosp., Bruton. *Recreations:* painting, gardening. *Address:* The Manor, Wyke Champflower, Bruton, Somerset. *T:* Bruton 3203; D5, Albany, Piccadilly, W1. *T:* 01-734 4282. Pendower, Polzeath, Cornwall. *T:* Trebetherick 3462. *Clubs:* Carlton, Pratt's, MCC.

BATTEN, Edith Mary, OBE 1948; Principal, William Temple College, 1950-66; *b* 1905, British. *Educ:* High Sch. for Girls, Southport; Liverpool Univ.; London School of Economics; St Anne's Coll., Oxford. BSc Liverpool; BSc (Econ) London; MA Oxon. Asst Industrial Personnel Officer; Sec. North West Ham Branch, Invalid Children's Aid Association; Sub-Warden, St Helen's Settlement, E15; Warden, Birmingham Settlement, 1933-38; JP City of Birmingham, 1937-38; Organising Sec. British Assoc. of Residential Settlements, 1938-42; Mem. Factory and Welfare Advisory Board to Min. of Labour, 1940-42; Min. of Labour and National Service, 1942-47. Res. Officer, Bd for Social Responsibility of Church Assembly, 1967-70. Mem. Panel, Industrial Tribunals. *Recreations:* reading, listening to music. *Address:* Guillard's Oak House, Midhurst, West Sussex. *Club:* Royal Commonwealth Society.

BATTEN, Jean Gardner, CBE 1936; *b* 1909; *d* of Capt. F. H. Batten, Dental Surg., Auckland, New Zealand. *Educ:* Cleveland House Coll., Auckland, NZ. Gained Private pilot's licence at London Aeroplane Club, 1930; commercial pilot's licence London, 1932; solo flight England-Australia (women's record) May 1934; solo flight Australia-England (first woman to complete return flight), April 1935; solo flight England-Argentina (first woman to make solo flight across South Atlantic Ocean to South America), Nov. 1935; world records established: England-Brazil 61 hrs 15 mins; fastest crossing of South Atlantic Ocean by air 13 hrs 15 mins; solo flight England-New Zealand 11 days 45 mins, Oct. 1936; first direct flight from England to Auckland, NZ; solo record England-Australia 5 days 21 hrs; record flight across Tasman Sea, Australia-New Zealand, 9hrs 29 mins; record solo flight Australia-England, 5 days 18 hrs 15 mins, Oct. 1937. Jean Batten Archive estbd RAF Museum, Hendon, 1972; Museum issued 13,000 Jean Batten Commemorative Covers which were flown over route to New Zealand by British Airways to mark 40th anniversary of first direct flight, 1976. Invited to visit Auckland, NZ by Min. of Transport and Technology to open new Pavilion, 1977. Officer of the Order of the Southern Cross, Brazil; Chevalier of the Legion of Honour, France; awarded Britannia Trophy, Royal Aero Club, 1935 and 1936; Harmon Trophy awarded by international vote, 1935, 1936 and 1937; Johnston Memorial Air Navigation Trophy, 1935; Challenge Trophy (USA), Women's International Association of Aeronautics, 1934, 1935 and 1936; Segrave Trophy, 1936; Coupe de Sibour, 1937; gold medals: Fédération Aéronautique Internationale; Royal Aero Club, Aero Club de France, Belgian Royal Aero Club, Académie des Sports, Royal Swedish Aero Club, Ligue International des Aviateurs, Aero Club of Argentine, Royal Danish Aeronautical Society, Royal Norwegian Aero Club, Aero Club of Finland. City of Paris Medal, 1971. *Publication:* My Life, 1938. *Recreations:* walking, swimming, music. *Address:* c/o Barclays Bank Ltd, 25 Charing Cross Road, WC2H 0HZ.

BATTEN, John Charles, MD, FRCP; Physician to HM Royal Household since 1970; Physician to the Queen, since 1974; Physician: St George's Hospital, since 1958; Brompton Hospital, since 1959; King Edward VII Hospital for Officers, since 1968; King Edward VII Hospital, Midhurst, since 1969; Hon. Physician to St Dunstan's and New Victoria Hospital, Kingston; Consultant, King Edward VII Convalescent Home, IoW, since 1975; Chief Medical Referee, Confederation Life Assoc. of Canada, since 1974 (Deputy Chief Medical Referee, 1958-74); *b* 11 March 1924; *s* of Raymond Wallis Batten, JP and Gladys (*née* Charles); *m* 1950, Anne Mary Margaret, *d* of late John Oriel, CBE, MC; one *s* two *d* (and one *d* decd). *Educ:* Mill Hill School; St Bartholomew's Medical School. MB, BS 1946 London Univ.; MRCP 1950; MD London 1951; FRCP 1964. Junior appts, St George's Hosp. and Brompton Hosp., 1946-58. Surgeon Captain, Royal Horse Guards, 1947-49. Dorothy Temple Cross Research Fellow, Cornell Univ. Medical Coll., New York, 1954-55. Examiner in Medicine, London Univ., 1968; Marc Daniels Lectr, RCP, 1969. Member: Board of

Governors, Brompton Hosp., 1966-69; St George's Hosp. Medical School Council, 1969; Council of Royal Society of Medicine, 1970. *Publications:* contributions to medical books and journals. *Recreations:* music and sailing. *Address:* 7 Lion Gate Gardens, Richmond, Surrey. *T:* 01-940 3282.

BATTEN, Mark Wilfrid, RBA 1962; FRBS 1952 (ARBS 1950); Sculptor, direct carver in stone; *s* of Edward Batten; *m* 1933, Elsie May Owston Thorneloe (*d* 1961); one *d. Educ:* Beckenham Co. Sch.; Beckenham Sch. of Art; Chelsea Sch. of Art. Commenced to experiment individually with stone carving, 1927; exhibited only drawings and paintings until 1934; combined experiment in sculpture with learning craft of stone carving mainly in granite mason's yards in Cornwall; first exhibited sculpture, 1936; FRSA 1936. Collaborated with Eric Gill, 1939; first exhibited sculpture at Royal Academy, 1939. War service in Life Guards, 1940-45. Exhibited Paris Salon, 1949, and thereafter frequently at RA and many sculpture exhibitions in Paris, London and provincial cities. Many commissions for stone sculptures on public buildings. President, RBS 1956-61; Council, 1953-; Council, RBA 1964-. Société des Artistes Français: Gold Medal for Sculpture, 1977 (Silver Medal, 1952); Associate, 1970. Hon. Mem. National Sculpture Soc. of the USA, 1956; Syracuse Univ., USA, estab. Mark Batten Manuscripts Collection, 1965, also Wichita State Univ., 1971. *Publications:* Stone Sculpture by Direct Carving, 1957; Direct Carving in Stone, 1966; articles in art magazines. *Recreations:* country life, travel, contemplation of other men's sculptures. *Address:* Christian's River, Dallington, Heathfield, East Sussex TN21 9NX. *Club:* Chelsea Arts.

BATTERSBY, Prof. Alan Rushton, MSc, PhD, DSc, ScD; FRS 1966; Professor of Organic Chemistry, University of Cambridge, since 1969; Fellow of St Catharine's College, Cambridge; Director, Fison's Agrochemicals Division; *b* Leigh, 4 March 1925; *s* of William and Hilda Battersby; *m* 1949, Margaret Ruth, *d* of Thomas and Annie Hart, Whaley Bridge, Cheshire; two *s. Educ:* Grammar Sch., Leigh; Univ. of Manchester (Mercer and Woodiwis Schol.); Univ. of St Andrews. MSc Manchester; PhD St Andrews; DSc Bristol; ScD Cantab. Asst Lectr in Chemistry, Univ. of St Andrews, 1948-53; Commonwealth Fund Fellow at Rockefeller Inst., NY, 1950-51 and at Univ. of Illinois, 1951-52; Lectr in Chemistry, Univ. of Bristol, 1954-62; Prof. of Organic Chemistry, Univ. of Liverpool, 1962-69. Mem. Council, Royal Soc., 1973-75. Mem. Deutsche Akademie der Naturforscher Leopoldina, 1967. Pres., Bürgenstock Conf., 1976. Lectures: Treat Johnson, Yale, 1969; Pacific Coast, USA, 1971; Karl Folkers, Wisconsin, 1972; N-E Coast, USA, 1974; Andrews, NSW, 1975; Middle Rhine, 1976; Visiting Professor: Cornell Univ., 1969; Virginia Univ., 1971; Tohoku Univ., Japan, 1974; ANU, 1975; Technion, Israel, 1977. Tilden Medal and Lectr, Chem. Soc., 1963; Hügo Müller Medal and Lectr, Chem. Soc., 1972; Paul Karrer Medal and Lectr, Univ. Zürich, 1977; Corday-Morgan Medal, Chem. Soc., 1959; Flintoff Medal, Chem. Soc., 1975. Hon. LLD St Andrews, 1977. *Publications:* papers in chemical jls, particularly Jl Chem. Soc. *Recreations:* music, camping, sailing and gardening. *Address:* University Chemical Laboratory, Lensfield Road, Cambridge CB2 1EW. *T:* Cambridge 66499.

BATTERSBY, Edmund James, FRICS; formerly Senior Partner, Edmund Kirby & Sons, Architects and Surveyors, Liverpool; *b* Knowsley, Lancs, 1911; *m* 1942, Mary, *y d* of J. F. W. Ravenhill; one *s* one *d.* Served War of 1939-45: Corps of Royal Engineers; during part of that time commanded Battle Wing of Sapper OCTU; demobilised in rank of Major. Was trained, and has spent whole career, with Edmund Kirby & Sons. Royal Institution of Chartered Surveyors: Council (Branch Rep.), 1960-; Vice-Pres., 1966; Sen. Vice-Pres., 1969; Pres., 8 June 1970-28 June 1971. Past service to the Institution includes many cttees, post-war rehabilitation of Chartered Surveyors, etc. Chm., Unification Cttee of the three Chartered Land Societies (united June 1970). Formerly Member: Bd, Runcorn New Town Development Corp.; Property Cttee, Nat. Freight Corp.; Court, Lancaster Univ. Formerly Governor and Dep. Treas., Liverpool Blue Coat School. Interested in youth and social welfare. Past Mem., Liverpool Regional Hosp. Bd; Past Chm., House Cttee of Liverpool Ear, Nose and Throat Hosp. *Recreations:* gardening, shooting. *Address:* Hornby Castle, near Lancaster. *T:* Hornby 21670.

BATTISCOMBE, Mrs (Esther) Georgina, BA; FRSL 1964; author; *b* 21 Nov. 1905; *d* of late George Harwood, MP, Master Cotton Spinner, Bolton, Lancs, and Ellen Hopkinson, *d* of Sir Alfred Hopkinson, KC, MP, First Vice-Chancellor of Manchester Univ.; *m* 1932, Lt-Col Christopher Francis Battiscombe, OBE, FSA (*d* 1964), Grenadier Guards; one *d. Educ:* St Michael's Sch., Oxford; Lady Margaret Hall, Oxford.

Publications: Charlotte Mary Yonge, 1943; Two on Safari, 1946; English Picnics, 1949; Mrs Gladstone, 1956; John Keble (James Tait Black Memorial Prize for best biography of year), 1963; Christina Rossetti (Writers and their Work), 1965; ed, with M. Laski, A Chaplet for Charlotte Yonge, 1965; Queen Alexandra, 1969; Shaftesbury, 1974. *Recreations:* walking, looking at churches. *Address:* 3 Queen's Acre, King's Road, Windsor, Berks. *T:* Windsor 60460.

BATTLE, Richard John Vulliamy, MBE 1945; FRCS; Plastic Surgeon, retired 1972; Hon. Consultant in Plastic Surgery: St Thomas' Hospital; Westminster Hospital; Queen Elizabeth Hospital for Children; King Edward VII Hospital for Officers; Consultant in Plastic Surgery to the Army, 1955-71; *b* 21 Jan. 1907; *s* of late William Henry Battle and Anna Marguerite (*née* Vulliamy); *m* 1941, Jessie Margaret King; three *s. Educ:* Gresham's Sch.; Trinity Coll., Cambridge. BA 1928, MA 1935, Cantab; MRCS, LRCP, 1931; FRCS, 1933; MChir (Cantab) 1935. Joined Territorial Army; served War of 1939-45 in RAMC, France, 1939-40, Italy, 1943-46; Comd No 1 Maxillo Facial Unit and 98 General Hospital; Major 1940; Lt-Col 1945. Pres., British Assoc. of Plastic Surgs, 1952, 1967, Gillies Gold Medal, 1970. *Publications:* Plastic Surgery, 1964; contrib. on plastic surgery to scientific periodicals. *Recreations:* golf, music. *Address:* Benhall Green, Saxmundham, Suffolk. *T:* Saxmundham 2334. *Clubs:* East India, Devonshire, Sports and Public Schools; Woodbridge Golf.

BATTY, Mrs Ronald; *see* Foyle, C. A. L.

BATTY, Sir William (Bradshaw), Kt 1973; TD 1946; Chairman, Ford Motor Co. Ltd, 1972-75, retired (Managing Director, 1968-73); *b* 15 May 1913; *s* of Rowland and Nellie Batty; *m* 1946, Jean Ella Brice; one *s* one *d* (and one *s* decd). *Educ:* Hulme Grammar Sch., Manchester. Served War of 1939-45, RASC (Lt-Col). Apprentice toolmaker, Ford Motor Co. Ltd, Trafford Park, Manchester, 1930; Co. trainee, 1933; Press liaison, Advertising Dept, 1936; Service Dept, 1937; Tractor Sales Dept, 1945; Asst Man., Tractor Dept, 1948; Man., Tractor and Implement Product Planning, 1953; Man., Tractor Div., 1955; Gen. Man., Tractor Gp, 1961; Dir, Tractor Gp, 1963; Dir, Car and Truck Gp, 1964; Exec. Dir, 1963-75. Chairman: Ford Motor Credit Co. Ltd, 1968 (Dir, 1963-); Automotive Finance Ltd, 1970-75; Director: Henry Ford & Son Ltd, Cork, 1965-75; Ford Lusitana SARL, Portugal, 1973-75. Mem., Engineering Industries Council, 1975-76. Pres., SMMT, 1975-76. Hon. LLD Manchester, 1976. FBIM. *Recreations:* golf, sailing, gardening. *Address:* Glenhaven Cottage, Riverside Road West, Newton Ferrers, South Devon. *Clubs:* Royal Automobile; Royal Western Yacht.

BATTYE, Maj.-Gen. (Retd) Stuart Hedley Molesworth, CB 1960; *b* 21 June 1907; *s* of late Lieut-Col W. R. Battye, DSO, MS, LRCP, Chev. de la Légion d'Honneur, CStJ, and late M. St G. Molesworth; *m* 1940, Evelyn Désirée, *d* of late Capt. G. B. Hartford, DSO and bar, RN; one *s* two *d. Educ:* Marlborough Coll.; RMA, Woolwich; Cambridge Univ. (MA). Commissioned 2nd Lieut, RE, 1927; served with Bengal Sappers and Miners, India, 1930-44 (NW Frontier Campaign, 1930-31); Iraq, 1941-42; India, 1942-44; 21 Army Group, BLA, 1945-47; MELF, 1952-55; War Office, 1955; Dir of Movements, the War Office, 1958-61; Dir, Council for Small Industries in Rural Areas (formerly Rural Industries Bureau), 1963-73. FRSA 1963. *Publications:* contrib. to Blackwood's and RE Journal. *Recreations:* fishing, painting. *Address:* Sunninghill, Ascot, Berks. *Club:* Army and Navy.

See also Baron Hankey.

BATY, Charles Witcomb; *e s* of late Wm Baty and late Margarette Ballinger; *m* 1923, Edith Halina, *d* of late Robert Bevan; one *s* two *d. Educ:* Westminster Sch. (King's Scholar); Christ Church, Oxford (Scholar). Asst Master, later sixth form Master, Bedford Sch. 1923-29; Head Master of the King's Sch., Chester, 1930-46; Dir, Education Div., Allied Commn for Austria, 1946-48; one of Her Majesty's Inspectors of Schools, 1949-62 (Staff Inspector, 1954), retd, 1962. A Vice-Pres., The Classical Assoc., 1966. *Address:* Greenbank, West Street, Mayfield, East Sussex TN20 6DS. *T:* Mayfield 2273.

BAUD, Rt. Rev. Joseph A., BA; Former Bishop of Visakhapatnam (RC); *b* Bellevaux (Haute-Savoie, France), 23 July 1890. *Educ:* Evian-les-Bains; Yeovil; Univ. studies at Fribourg (Switzerland). Came to Vizag in 1914; Teacher in St Aloysius' European High-School, Vizagapatam, 1914-30; Principal there, 1930-40; Vicar-General of Diocese of Vizagapatam in 1940; Coadjutor-Bishop of Vizagapatam (British India), 1942-47; Bishop of Visakhapatnam, 1947-66, retired. *Address:* Salesianum, Visakhapatnam 3, India.

BAUDOUX, Most Rev. Maurice, STD, PhD, DèsL; *b* Belgium, 1902. *Educ:* Prud'homme convent, Saskatchewan; St Boniface College, Manitoba; St Joseph's Seminary, Alberta; Grand Seminary, Quebec. Priest, 1929; Curate then Pastor, Prud'homme, Sask; Domestic Prelate, 1944; First Bishop of Saint Paul in Alberta, 1948; Coadjutor-Archbishop of Saint Boniface, 1952; Archbishop of St Boniface, 1955-74. *Address:* c/o Archbishop's Residence, 151 Cathedral Avenue, St Boniface, Manitoba R2H 0H6, Canada.

BAUER, Prof. Peter Thomas, MA; FBA; Professor of Economics (with special reference to economic development and under-developed countries) in the University of London, at the London School of Economics, since 1960; Fellow of Gonville and Caius College, Cambridge, 1946-60, and since 1968; *b* 6 Nov. 1915; unmarried. *Educ:* Scholae Piae, Budapest; Gonville and Caius Coll., Cambridge. Reader in Agricultural Economics, University of London, 1947-48; University Lecturer in Economics, Cambridge Univ., 1948-56; Smuts Reader in Commonwealth Studies, Cambridge Univ., 1956-60; Woodward Lectr, Yale Univ., 1965; Roush Distinguished Vis. Scholar, Hoover Instn, Stanford, Calif., 1967; Sir William Meyer Lectr, Madras Univ., 1969-70. *Publications:* The Rubber Industry, 1948; West African Trade, 1954; The Economics of Under-developed Countries (with B. S. Yamey), 1957; Economic Analysis and Policy in Under-developed Countries, 1958; Indian Economic Policy and Development, 1961; (with B. S. Yamey) Markets, Market Control and Marketing Reform, 1968; Dissent on Development, 1972; Aspects of Nigerian Development, 1974; articles on economic subjects. *Address:* London School of Economics and Political Science, Houghton Street, Aldwych, WC2.

BAUGHEN, Rev. Michael Alfred; Rector of All Souls, Langham Place, W1, since 1975 (Vicar of All Souls, 1970-75); *b* 7 June 1930; *s* of Alfred Henry and Clarice Adelaide Baughen; *m* 1956, Myrtle Newcomb Phillips: two *s* one *d*. *Educ:* Bromley County Grammar Sch.; Univ. of London; Oak Hill Theol Coll. BD (London). With Martins Bank, 1946-48, 1950-51. Army, Royal Signals, 1948-50. Degree Course and Ordination Trng, 1951-56; Curate: St Paul's, Hyson Green, Nottingham, 1956-59; Reigate Parish Ch., 1959-61; Candidates Sec., Church Pastoral Aid Soc., 1961-64; Rector of Holy Trinity (Platt), Rusholme, Manchester, 1964-70. Editor: Youth Praise, 1966; Youth Praise II, 1969; Psalm Praise, 1973. *Recreations:* music, railways, touring. *Address:* 12 Weymouth Street, W1N 3FB. *T:* 01-580 6029.

BAVERSTOCK, Donald Leighton; Executive Producer, Television, BBC Manchester, since 1975; *b* 18 Jan. 1924; *s* of Thomas Philip Baverstock and Sarah Ann; *m* 1957, Gillian Mary, *d* of late Mrs Kenneth Darrell Waters (Enid Blyton); two *s* two *d*. *Educ:* Canton High Sch., Cardiff; Christ Church, Oxford (MA). Served with RAF, 1943-46; completed tour of operations Bomber Command, 1944; Instructor, Navigation, 1944-46. History Master, Wellington Coll., 1949. Producer, BBC General Overseas Service, 1950-54; Producer, BBC Television Service, 1954-57; Editor, Tonight Programme, 1957-61; Asst Controller, Television Programmes, BBC, 1961-63; Chief of Programmes BBC TV (1), 1963-65; Partner, Jay, Baverstock, Milne & Co., 1965-67; Dir of Programmes, Yorkshire TV, 1967-73; Man. Dir, Granada Video Ltd, 1974-75. *Address:* Low Hall, Middleton, Ilkley, Yorks. *T:* Ilkley 2693. *Club:* Savile.

BAVIN, Alfred Robert Walter, CB 1966; Deputy Secretary, Department of Health and Social Security, 1968-73 (Ministry of Health, 1966-68); *b* 4 April 1917; *s* of late Alfred and Annie Bavin; *m* 1947, Helen Mansfield; one *s* three *d*. *Educ:* Christ's Hosp.; Balliol Coll., Oxford. 1st cl. Hon. Mods 1937; 1st cl. Lit. Hum. 1939. Min. of Health, Asst Principal, 1939, Principal, 1946; Cabinet Office, 1948-50; Min. of Health, Principal Private Sec. to Minister, 1951; Asst Sec. 1952; Under-Sec. 1960. Nuffield Home Civil Service Travelling Fellowship, 1956. *Address:* 7 First Avenue, Felpham, Bognor Regis, W Sussex. *T:* Middleton-on-Sea 3073. *Clubs:* Athenæum, MCC.

BAVIN, Rt. Rev. Timothy John; *see* Johannesburg, Bishop of.

BAWDEN, Edward, CBE 1946; RA 1956 (ARA 1947); RDI 1949; Painter and Designer; Draughtsman; formerly a Tutor in the School of Graphic Design, Royal College of Art; *b* Braintree, Essex, 1903; *m* 1932, Charlotte (*d* 1970), *d* of Robert Epton, Lincoln; one *s* one *d*. *Educ:* Cambridge Sch. of Art; Royal Coll. of Art. As an Official War Artist he travelled in Middle East, 1940-45; visited Canada during 1949 and 1950 as a guest instructor at Banff Sch. of Fine Arts, Alberta. His work is represented in the Tate Gallery, London, and by water-colour drawings in several London, Dominion and provincial galleries;

exhibitions: at Leicester Galleries, 1938, 1949, 1951; at Zwemmer Gallery, 1963; at Fine Art Soc., 1968. Illustrated books include: The Arabs, Life in an English Village, London is London. He has designed and cut blocks for a series of wallpapers printed by Messrs Cole & Son, and has painted mural decorations for the SS Orcades and SS Oronsay, also for Lion and Unicorn Pavilion on South Bank site of Festival of Brtain. Trustee of Tate Gallery, 1951-58. *Relevant publications:* "Edward Bawden" by J. M. Richards (Penguin Modern Painters); "Edward Bawden" by Robert Harling (English Masters of Black and White). *Address:* 2 Park Lane, Saffron Walden, Essex CB10 1DA.

BAWDEN, Nina Mary, (Mrs A. S. Kark), MA; FRSL; JP; novelist; *b* 19 Jan. 1925; *d* of Charles and Ellalaine Ursula May Mabey; *m* 1st, 1946, Henry Walton Bawden: two *s*; 2nd, 1954, Austen Steven Kark; one *d*. *Educ:* Ilford County High Sch.; Somerville Coll., Oxford (BA). Asst, Town and Country Planning Assoc., 1946-47. JP Surrey, 1968. *Publications: novels:* Who Calls the Tune, 1953; The Odd Flamingo, 1954; Change Here for Babylon, 1955; Devil by the Sea, 1958, 2nd edn 1972 (abridged for children, 1976); The Solitary Child, 1956; Just Like a Lady, 1960; In Honour Bound, 1961; Tortoise by Candlelight, 1963; Under the Skin, 1964; A Little Love, a Little Learning, 1965; A Woman of My Age, 1967; The Grain of Truth, 1969; The Birds on the Trees, 1970; Anna Apparent, 1972; George beneath a Paper Moon, 1974; Afternoon of a Good Woman, 1976 (Yorkshire Post Novel of the Year, 1976); *for children:* The Secret Passage; On the Run; The White Horse Gang; The Witch's Daughter; A Handful of Thieves; The Runaway Summer; Squib; Carrie's War; The Peppermint Pig (Guardian award, 1976); Rebel on a Rock, 1978. *Recreations:* travelling, reading, garden croquet. *Address:* 22 Noel Road, N1. *T:* 01-226 2839. *Clubs:* Ski Club of Great Britain, PEN, Society of Authors.

BAWN, Cecil Edwin Henry, CBE 1956; FRS 1952; BSc, PhD; Brunner Professor of Physical Chemistry in the University of Liverpool, 1969-Dec. 1973, now Emeritus (Grant-Brunner Professor of Inorganic and Physical Chemistry, 1948-69); *b* 6 Nov. 1908; British; *m* 1934, Winifred Mabel Jackson; two *s* one *d*. *Educ:* Cotham Grammar Sch., Bristol. Graduated, Univ. of Bristol, 1929; PhD in Chemistry (Bristol), 1932; Asst Lectr in Chemistry, Univ. of Manchester, 1931-34; Lectr in Chemistry, 1934-38; Lectr in Physical Chemistry, Univ. of Bristol, 1938-45; Reader in Physical Chemistry, 1945-49. During War of 1939-45 was in charge of a Physico-Chemical Section in Armament Research Dept, Min. of Supply. Mem., Univ. Grants Cttee, 1965-74. Swinburne Gold Medal, 1966. Hon. DSc: Bradford, 1966; Birmingham, 1968; Bristol, 1974. *Publications:* The Chemistry of High Polymers, 1948; papers in chemical journals. *Address:* Springfields, Stoodleigh, near Tiverton, Devon EX16 9PT. *T:* Oakford 220.

BAX, Rodney Ian Shirley, QC 1966; **His Honour Judge Bax**; a Circuit Judge, since 1973; *b* 16 Sept. 1920; *s* of late Rudolph Edward Victor Bax, Barrister, and of Shirley Winifred, *d* of Canon G. A. Thompson; *m* 1953, Patricia Anne, *d* of late Martin Stuart Turner, MC; one *s* one *d*. *Educ:* Bryanston Sch. (Scholar); Royal Coll. of Music (Exhibitioner). Served with Royal Fusiliers and Intelligence Corps, 1940-46 (Major GS). Called to Bar, Gray's Inn, 1947, Bencher, 1972; S Eastern Circuit. A Recorder, 1972-73. Mem., General Council of the Bar, 1961-65. Asst Comr, Boundary Commn for England, 1965-69. Comr, Central Criminal Court, 1971. *Recreations:* music, books. *Address:* 4 Jocelyn Road, Richmond, Surrey. *T:* 01-940 3395; Alderney, Channel Islands.

BAXANDALL, David Kighley, CBE 1959; Director of National Galleries of Scotland, 1952-70; *b* 11 Oct. 1905; *m* 1931, Isobel, *d* of Canon D. J. Thomas; one *s* twin *d*. *Educ:* King's Coll. Sch., Wimbledon; King's Coll., University of London. Asst Keeper, 1929-39, and Keeper of the Department of Art, 1939-41, National Museum of Wales. Served in RAF, 1941-45. Dir of Manchester City Art Galleries, 1945-52. *Publications:* Ben Nicholson, 1962; numerous articles, gallery handbooks, catalogues and broadcast talks. *Address:* 12 Darnaway Street, Edinburgh EH3 6BG. *T:* 031-225 1417.
See also M. D. K. Baxandall.

BAXANDALL, Michael David Kighley; Reader in the History of the Classical Tradition, Warburg Institute, University of London, since 1973; *b* 18 Aug. 1933; *s* of David Baxandall, *qv*; *m* 1963, Katharina Simon; one *s* one *d*. *Educ:* Manchester Grammar Sch.; Downing Coll., Cambridge (MA); Univs of Pavia and Munich. Jun. Res. Fellow, Warburg Inst., 1959-61; Asst Keeper, Dept of Architecture and Sculpture, Victoria and Albert Museum, 1961-65; Lectr in Renaissance Studies,

Warburg Inst., 1965-73; Slade Prof. of Fine Art, Univ. of Oxford, 1974-75. *Publications:* Giotto and the Orators, 1971; Painting and Experience in Fifteenth-Century Italy, 1972; South German Sculpture 1480-1530 in the Victoria and Albert Museum, 1974. *Address:* The Warburg Institute, Woburn Square, WC1H 0AB.

BAXENDELL, Peter Brian, CBE 1972; Managing Director of Royal Dutch/Shell Group of Companies, since 1973; *b* 28 Feb. 1925; *s* of Lesley Wilfred Edward Baxendell and Evelyn Mary Baxendell (*née* Gaskin); *m* 1949, Rosemary (*née* Lacey); two *s* two *d. Educ:* St Francis Xavier's, Liverpool; Royal School of Mines, London (ARSM, BSc). Joined Royal Dutch/Shell Group, 1946; Petroleum Engr in Egypt, 1947, and Venezuela, 1950; Techn. Dir, Shell-BP Nigeria, 1963; Head of SE Asia Div., London, 1966; Man. Dir, Shell-BP Nigeria, 1969; Chm., Shell UK, 1973. *Publications:* articles on petroleum engrg subjects in scientific jls. *Recreations:* squash, tennis. *Address:* Shell Centre, SE1 7NA. *T:* 01-934 2772.

BAXTER, Prof. Alexander Duncan, CEng; Research Consultant, since 1970; Director, de Havilland Engine Co. Ltd, 1958-63; Chief Executive Rocket Division and Nuclear Power Group, de Havilland Engine Co. Ltd, 1957-63; *b* 17 June 1908; *e s* of Robert Alexander and Mary Violet Baxter; *m* 1933, Florence Kathleen McClean; one *s* two *d. Educ:* Liverpool Institute High Sch.; Liverpool Univ. BEng (1st Cl. Hons MechEng) 1930; MEng 1933. Post-graduate pupil with Daimler Company, 1930-34; commissioned in RAFO, 1930-35; Research Engineer with Instn. of Automobile Engrs, 1934-35; Scientific Officer at RAE, Farnborough, 1935; engaged on aircraft propulsion and gas turbine research until 1947; Supt, Rocket Propulsion, RAE, 1947-50; Prof. of Aircraft Propulsion, Coll. of Aeronautics, Cranfield, 1950-57; Dep. Principal, Cranfield, 1954-57; Sen. Exec., Bristol Siddeley Engines Ltd, 1963-68, Bristol Engine Div. of Rolls Royce Ltd, 1968-70. Mem. Council: InstMechE, 1955-57; RAeS, 1953-70 (Vice-Pres, 1962-66, Pres., 1966-67). Served as member of many educnl bodies, incl.: jt Cttee on Higher Nat. Certificate in Engrg; RAF Educn Adv. Cttee; Aeronautical Board, CNAA; Board of CEI, 1962-69; various Govt advisory cttees. Member of Court: Univ. of Bristol; Cranfield Inst. of Technology. FIMechE, FRAeS, FInstPet, Fellow, British Interplanetary Soc. *Publications:* various reports in government R & M series; papers in Proc. Instn Mech. Engineers and RAeS. *Recreations:* do-it-yourself, grandchildren, cine photography. *Address:* Glebe Cottage, Pucklechurch, Glos. *T:* Abson 2204.

BAXTER, Frederick William; Professor of English Language and Literature in The Queen's University of Belfast, 1949-58, retired (Professor of English Literature, 1930-49); *b* Auckland New Zealand, 29 April 1897; *m* 1925, Marjorie Newsam Coles, Newbury, Berks. *Educ:* Auckland Grammar Sch.; Auckland Univ. Coll.; Worcester Coll., Oxford. Divisional Signal Company, New Zealand Engineers, 1917-19; King's Coll., London, 1921-24; McGill Univ., Montreal, Canada, 1924-26; The University of Leeds, 1926-30. *Address:* 18 Gloucester Road, Painswick, Glos GL6 6RA. *T:* Painswick 812102.

BAXTER, Prof. James Thomson; William Dick Professor of Veterinary Medicine, Edinburgh University, since 1970; *b* Feb. 1925; *e s* of James T. Baxter and Victoria A. D. Montgomery; *m* 1951, Muriel Elizabeth Knox; two *s* one *d. Educ:* Trinity Academy, Edinburgh; Royal (Dick) Veterinary Coll., Edinburgh. MA(Dub), PhD(Dub); MRCVS. Served War, Royal Navy, 1944-46. Gen. veterinary practice, 1950-52; Veterinary Officer, then Veterinary Research Officer, Min. of Agr., N Ireland, 1952-60; Lectr, Loughry Agr. Coll., 1955-60; Asst Lectr in Vet. Sci., Queen's Univ., Belfast, 1958-60; Prof. in Clinical Vet. Practices, Dublin Univ., 1960-70; Dir, Sch. of Veterinary Medicine, Dublin Univ., 1963-70. Mem. Council: Irish Grassland and Animal Production Assoc., 1961-70 (Pres. 1963-64); Royal Coll. of Veterinary Surgeons, 1962-70; Agricl Inst. (An Foras Taluntais), 1964-70. Mem., Irish Veterinary Council, 1962-70. Fellow, Trinity Coll., Dublin, 1965-70. FIBiol; FRSH. *Publications:* articles in vety and other jls. *Address:* 1 Wilton Road, Edinburgh EH16 5NX. *T:* 031-667 3055. *Club:* University (Edinburgh).

BAXTER, Jeremy Richard; Director of Personnel, Commission of the European Communities, since 1973; *b* 20 Jan. 1929; *s* of late Andrew Paterson Baxter and late Ann Winifred Baxter; *m* 1965, Faith Elizabeth Graham; two *s* one *d. Educ:* Sedbergh Sch.; St John's Coll., Cambridge (BA Class. Tripos). Asst Principal, Post Office, 1952; Asst Private Sec. to Postmaster-Gen., 1956; Private Sec. to Asst Postmaster-Gen., 1957; Principal, Post Office, 1958; Principal, Treasury, 1964; Asst Sec., Post Office, 1967; Dir, Postal Personnel, 1971. *Recreations:*

sailing and squash. *Address:* 20 avenue des Aubépines, Uccle, 1180 Brussels, Belgium. *T:* 358 49 05.

BAXTER, John Lawson; *b* 25 Nov. 1939; *s* of John Lawson Baxter and Enid Maud Taggart; *m* 1967; three *s. Educ:* Trinity Coll., Dublin; Queen's Univ., Belfast; BA, BComm, LLM; LLM Tulane Univ., New Orleans. Solicitor. Mem. (U) N Ireland Assembly, for N Antrim, 1973-75; Minister of Information, N Ireland Executive, 1974. *Recreations:* golf, fishing. *Address:* Beardiville, Cloyfin, Coleraine, N Ireland. *T:* Bushmills 31552.

BAXTER, Prof. Sir (John) Philip, KBE 1965 (OBE 1945); CMG 1959; PhD; Chairman, Sydney Opera House Trust, 1968-75; *b* 7 May 1905; *s* of John and Mary Netta Baxter; *m* 1931, Lilian May Baxter (*née* Thatcher); three *s* one *d. Educ:* University of Birmingham. BSc 1925, PhD 1928. University of Birmingham. Research Dir, ICI General Chemicals Ltd and Dir, Thorium Ltd, until 1949; Prof. Chem. Eng, NSW University of Technology, 1950; Vice-Chancellor, Univ. of NSW, 1953-69. Chm, Australian Atomic Energy Commn, 1957-72. Fellow Aust. Acad. of Science. FRACI; MIE(Aust). Hon. LLD Montreal, 1958; Hon. DSc: Newcastle, Queensland; NSW; Hon. DTech Loughborough, 1969. *Address:* 1 Kelso Street, Enfield, NSW 2136, Australia. *T:* 7474261.

BAXTER, John Walter, CBE 1974; Managing Partner, G. Maunsell & Partners, since 1959 (Partner since 1955); *b* 4 June 1917; *s* of late J. G. Baxter and late D. L. Baxter (*née* Phelps); *m* 1941, Jessie, *d* of late T. Pimblott; one *d. Educ:* Westminster City Sch.; City and Guilds Engrg College. BSc(Eng), FCGI, CEng, FICE, FIEAust, FRSA. Civil Engineer: Trussed Concrete Steel Co. Ltd, 1936-41; Shell Refining Co. Ltd, 1941-52; Maunsell Posford & Pavry, 1952-55. Pres., ICE, 1976-77 (Vice-Pres., 1973-76, Mem. Council, 1963-68 and 1970-). *Publications:* contrib. Proc. ICE. *Address:* 17 Chislehurst Road, Bickley, Kent. *T:* 01-467 1985. *Club:* Athenæum.

BAXTER, Prof. Sir Philip; *see* Baxter, Prof. Sir J. P.

BAXTER, Raymond Frederic, FRSA; broadcaster and writer; *b* 25 Jan. 1922; *s* of Frederick Garfield Baxter and Rosina Baxter (*née* Rivers); *m* 1945, Sylvia Kathryn (*née* Johnson), Boston, Mass; one *s* one *d. Educ:* Ilford County High Sch. Joined RAF, 1940; flew Spitfires with 65, 93 and 602 Sqdns, in UK, Med. and Europe. Entered Forces Broadcasting in Cairo still as serving officer, 1945; civilian deputy Dir BFN BBC, 1947-49; subseq. short attachment West Region and finally joined Outside Broadcast Dept, London; with BBC until 1966 Dir, Motoring Publicity, BMC, 1967-68. *Publications:* (with James Burke and Michael Latham) Tomorrow's World, Vol. 1, 1970, Vol. 2, 1971; film commentaries, articles and reports on motoring and aviation subjects, etc. *Recreations:* motoring, riding, boating. *Address:* The Old Rectory, Denham, Bucks. *Clubs:* British Racing Drivers, etc.

BAXTER, Walter; author; *b* 1915. *Educ:* St Lawrence, Ramsgate, Trinity Hall, Cambridge. Worked in the City, 1936-39; served War of 1939-45, with KOYLI in Burma; afterwards, in India, ADC to General Slim, and on Staff of a Corps HQ during reconquest of Burma. After completion of first novel, returned to India to work temporarily on a mission. *Publications:* Look Down in Mercy, 1951; The Image and The Search, 1953. *Address:* 119 Old Brompton Road, SW7.

BAXTER, William; JP; *b* 4 Dec. 1911; *s* of William Baxter, Kilsyth; *m* 1938, Margaret, *d* of Anthony Bassy, Kilsyth; one *s. Educ:* Banton Public Sch. County Councillor, Stirlingshire, 1932; Vice-Convener Stirling CC, 1957-; MP (Lab) West Stirlingshire, 1959-Oct. 1974. JP 1952; Stirling Representative, County Councils Association. *Address:* Gateside Farm, Kilsyth, by Glasgow. *T:* Kilsyth 2167.

BAXTER, William T., BCom Edinburgh; Professor of Accounting, London School of Economics, 1947-73; *b* 27 July 1906; *s* of W. M. Baxter and Margaret Threipland; *m* 1st, 1940, Marjorie Allanson (*d* 1971); one *s* one *d*; 2nd, 1973, Leena-Kaisa Laitakari-Kaila. *Educ:* George Watson's Coll.; Univ. of Edinburgh. Chartered Accountant (Edinburgh), 1930; Commonwealth Fund Fellow, 1931, at Harvard Univ.; Lectr in Accounting, Univ. of Edinburgh, 1934; Prof. of Accounting, Univ. of Cape Town, 1937. *Publications:* Income Tax for Professional Students, 1936; The House of Hancock, 1945; Depreciation, 1971; Accounting Values and Inflation, 1975. *Address:* 1 The Ridgeway, NW11. *T:* 01-455 6810. *Club:* Athenæum.

BAYHAM, Viscount; James William John Pratt; *b* 11 Dec. 1965; *s* and *heir* of Earl of Brecknock, *qv*.

BAYLEY, Gordon Vernon, CBE 1976; FIA, FIMA, FSS; Director, General Manager and Actuary, National Provident Institution, since 1964; *b* 25 July 1920; *s* of late Capt. Vernon Bayley, King's Regt, and Mrs Gladys Maud Bayley; *m* 1945, Miriam Allenby, *d* of late Frederick Walter Ellis and Miriam Ellis, Eastbourne; one *s* two *d. Educ:* Abingdon. Joined HM Forces, 1940; commissioned Royal Artillery, Major 1945. Asst Actuary, Equitable Life Assurance Soc., 1949; Partner, Duncan C. Fraser and Co. (Actuaries), 1954-57; National Provident Institution: Assistant Sec., 1957, Joint Sec. 1959. Mem., Occupational Pensions Bd, 1973-74. Mem., Cttee to Review the Functioning of Financial Institutions, 1977-. Institute of Actuaries: Fellow, 1946; Hon. Sec., 1960-62; Vice-Pres., 1964-67; Pres., 1974-76; Chm., Life Offices Assoc., 1969-70 (Dep. Chm., 1967-68). *Publications:* contribs to Jl Inst. Actuaries, Jl Royal Statistical Soc. *Recreations:* tennis, ski-ing, sailing, water ski-ing. *Address:* The Old Manor, Witley, Surrey. *T:* Wormley 2301. *Clubs:* English Speaking Union; Island Sailing; Sea View Yacht.

BAYLEY, Prof. John Oliver; Warton Professor of English Literature, and Fellow of St Catherine's College, University of Oxford, since 1974; *b* 27 March 1925; *s* of F. J. Bayley; *m* 1956, Jean Iris Murdoch, *qv. Educ:* Eton; New Coll., Oxford. 1st cl. hons English Oxon 1950. Served in Army, Grenadier Guards and Special Intell., 1943-47. Mem., St Antony's and Magdalen Colls, Oxford, 1951-55; Fellow and Tutor in English, New Coll., Oxford, 1955-74. *Publications:* In Another Country (novel), 1954; The Romantic Survival: A Study in Poetic Evolution, 1956; The Characters of Love, 1961; Tolstoy and the Novel, 1966; Pushkin: A Comparative Commentary, 1971; The Uses of Division: unity and disharmony in literature, 1976. *Address:* Cedar Lodge, Steeple Aston, Oxford. *T:* Steeple Aston 40229.

BAYLEY, Mrs John Oliver; *see* Murdoch, J. I.

BAYLEY, Lt-Comdr Oscar Stewart Morris, RN Retd; Director and Chief Secretary, The Royal Life Saving Society, since 1977; *b* 15 April 1926; *er* surv. *s* of late Rev. J. H. S. Bayley. *Educ:* St John's Sch., Leatherhead; King James's Grammar Sch., Knaresborough. Called to Bar, Lincoln's Inn, 1959. Entered RN, 1944: Ceylon, 1956-58; Supply Off., HMS Narvik and Sqdn Supply Off., 5th Submarine Div., 1960-62; Sec. to Comdr British Forces Caribbean Area, 1962-65; retd from RN at own request, 1966. Legal Asst (Unfair Competition), The Distillers Co. Ltd, 1966-68; Clerk, Fishmongers' Co., 1969-74. Director: Anglers Co-operative Assoc. Trustee Co. Ltd; Seed Oysters (UK) Ltd. Clerk to Governors of Gresham's Sch., Holt; Hon. Sec., Salmon and Trout Assoc. and of Shellfish Assoc. of Great Britain; Vice-Chm., National Anglers' Council; Secretary: Atlantic Salmon Research Trust; City and Guilds of London Art Sch. Ltd; Nat. Assoc. of Pension Funds Investment Protection Cttee, 1975-76. *Recreations:* fishing, bridge, assistant gardener. *Address:* 14 Devonshire Street, W1N 2AT.

BAYLEY, Peter Charles; Master of Collingwood College, University of Durham, since 1971; *b* 25 Jan. 1921; *y s* of late William Charles Abell Bayley and Irene (*née* Heath); *m* 1951, Patience, *d* of Sir George (Norman) Clark, *qv*; one *s* two *d. Educ:* Crypt Sch., Gloucester; University Coll., Oxford (Sidgwick Exhibnr; MA 1st Cl. Hons English, 1947). Served RA and Intell. Corps, India, 1941-45. Jun. Fellow, University Coll., Oxon, 1947; Fellow and Praelector in English, 1949-72; Univ. Lectr in English, 1952-72; Domestic Bursar, Tutor for Admissions, Librarian, Editor of University Coll. Record, 1949-71; Proctor, 1957-58; Oxford Univ. Corresp., The Times, 1960-63. Vis. Lectr, Yale Univ., and Robert Bates Vis. Fellow, Jonathan Edwards Coll., 1970. Prepared Macbeth, Brit. Council Recorded Seminars, 1976. *Publications:* (ed) Spenser, The Faerie Queene: Book II, 1965 (2nd edn 1974); Book I, 1966 (2nd edn 1970); (contrib.) Patterns of Love and Courtesy, ed Lawlor, 1966; Edmund Spenser, Prince of Poets, 1971; (contrib.) English Poetry: select bibliographical guides, 1971; Loves and Deaths: short stories by 19th century novelists, 1972 (2nd edn 1974); 'Casebook' on Spenser's The Faerie Queene, 1977. *Recreations:* nature and art. *Address:* The Master's House, Collingwood College, Durham.

BAYLIS, Clifford Henry, CB 1971; Director, Shipbuilders' and Repairers' National Association, 1974-77; *b* 20 March 1915; *s* of late Arthur Charles and Caroline Jane Baylis, Alcester, Warwicks; *m* 1939, Phyllis Mary Clark; two *s. Educ:* Alcester Grammar Sch.; Keble Coll., Oxford. Harrods Ltd, 1937-39. Served with HM Forces, 1940-46: Major RASC. Principal, Board of Trade, 1947; Asst Sec., UK Trade Commissioner, Bombay, 1955; Export Credits Guarantee Dept, 1963-66; Under-Sec., Board of Trade, 1966-67; Under-Sec., Min. of Technology, 1967-69; Controller, HM Stationery Office, and

Queen's Printer of Acts of Parlt, 1969-74. *Address:* 38 Cleaver Street, SE11 4DP. *T:* 01-735 0817. *Club:* Royal Automobile.

BAYLISS, Colonel George Sheldon, CB 1966; OBE 1945; TD 1941; DL; *b* 26 Dec. 1900; *s* of Francis and E. M. Bayliss, Walsall; *m* 1935, Margaret Muriel Williamson (*d* 1962), *widow* of Dr K. B. Williamson, MC, and *d* of J. S. Harker, Penrith; one *s* and one *step s. Educ:* Shrewsbury Sch. Joined TA, 2nd Lieut, 1921; Major 1926-40; Lieut-Col 1940-45 (despatches 4 times, 1941-45). Hon. Col 473 HAA Regt, 1947-53. DL Co. Stafford, 1953; Chm., Staffs T&AFA, 1959-65. Managing Dir, S B & N Ltd, Walsall, 1930-76, retired. Bronze Star (USA). *Address:* Littlefield House, Wall, Lichfield, Staffs WS14 0AU. *T:* Shenstone 480024.

BAYLISS, Richard Ian Samuel, MD, FRCP; Physician to the Queen since 1970, and Head of HM Medical Household, since 1973; Consultant Physician: Westminster Hospital since 1954; King Edward VII Hospital, Midhurst, since 1973; Physician to King Edward VII's Hospital for Officers since 1964; Hon. Consultant Physician, Newspaper Press Fund; Medical Director, Swiss Reinsurance Co.; Civilian Consultant in Medicine, Royal Navy; *b* 2 Jan. 1917; *o s* of late Frederick William Bayliss, Tettenhall, and late Muryel Anne Bayliss; *m* 1st, 1941, Margaret Joan Hardman (marr. diss. 1956); one *s* one *d*; 2nd, 1957, Constance Ellen, *d* of Wilbur J. Frey, Connecticut; two *d. Educ:* Rugby; Clare Coll., Cambridge; St Thomas' Hosp., London. MB, BChir Cambridge 1941; MRCS, LRCP 1941; MRCP 1942; MD Cambridge 1946; FRCP 1956. Casualty Officer, Ho.-Phys., Registrar, Resident Asst Phys., St Thomas' Hosp.; Off. i/c Med. Div., RAMC, India; Sen. Med. Registrar and Tutor, Hammersmith Hosp.; Rockefeller Fellow in Medicine, Columbia Univ., New York, 1950-51; Lectr in Medicine and Physician, Postgrad. Med. Sch. of London; Dean, Westminster Med. Sch., 1960-64; Physician to HM Household, 1964-70. Hon. Sec., Assoc. of Physicians, 1958-63, Cttee 1965-68; Pres., Section of Endocrinology, RSM, 1966-68; Examr in Medicine, Cambridge and Oxford Univs; Examr, MRCP. Member: Bd of Governors, Westminster Hosp., 1960-64, 1967-74; Council, Westminster Med. Sch., 1960-75; Soc. for Endocrinology (Council, 1956-60); Brit. Cardiac Soc., 1952; Council, RCP, 1968-71; Bd of Advrs, Merck Inst. of Therapeutic Res., 1972-76. *Publications:* Practical Procedures in Clinical Medicine, 3rd edn. Various, in med. jls and textbooks, on endocrine, metabolic and cardiac diseases. *Recreations:* ski-ing, music, gardening. *Address:* 9 Park Square West, NW1. *T:* 01-935 2071; Cell Farm Cottage, Loughton, Milton Keynes, Bucks MK8 0AW. *T:* Shenley Church End 272. *Clubs:* Athenæum, Garrick.

BAYLY, Vice-Adm. Sir Patrick (Uniacke), KBE 1968; CB 1965; DSC 1944, and 2 bars, 1944, 1951; Director, The Maritime Trust, since 1971; *b* 4 Aug. 1914; *s* of late Lancelot F. S. Bayly, Nenagh, Eire; *m* 1945, Moy Gourlay Jardine, *d* of Robert Gourlay Jardine, Newtonmearns, Scotland; two *d. Educ:* Aravon, Bray, Co. Wicklow; RN Coll., Dartmouth, Midshipman, 1932; Sub-Lieut, 1934; Lieut, 1935; South Africa, 1936; China station, 1938; Combined operations, 1941-44, including Sicily and Salerno; Lieut-Comdr 1944; HMS Mauritius, 1946; Comdr 1948, Naval Staff, 1948; Korean War, 1952-53, in HMS Alacrity and Constance; Captain 1954, Naval Staff; Imperial Defence Coll., 1957; Capt. (D) 6th Destroyer Sqdn, 1958; Staff of SACLANT, Norfolk, Va, 1960; Chief of Staff, Mediterranean, 1962; Rear-Admiral, 1963; Flag Officer, Sea Training, 1963; Adm. Pres., RN Coll., Greenwich, 1965-67; Chief of Staff, COMNAVSOUTH, Malta, 1967-70; retd, 1970. Vice-Adm. 1967. US Legion of Merit, 1951. *Recreation:* golf. *Address:* Dunning House, Liphook, Hants.

BAYNE, John; Advocate; Sheriff of Glasgow and Strathkelvin, since 1975; Sheriff (formerly Sheriff-Substitute) of Lanarkshire at Glasgow, 1959-74. *Address:* Sheriff Court, Glasgow; Winsford, 7 Milrig Road, Rutherglen G73 2NQ.

BAYNE, Nicholas Peter; HM Diplomatic Service; Financial Counsellor, HM Embassy, Paris, since 1975; *b* 15 Feb. 1937; *s* of Captain Ronald Bayne, RN and Elisabeth Ashcroft; *m* 1961, Diana Wilde; three *s. Educ:* Eton Coll.; Christ Church, Oxford (MA, DPhil). Entered Diplomatic Service, 1961; served at British Embassies in Manila, 1963-66, and Bonn, 1969-72; seconded to HM Treasury, 1974-75. *Recreations:* archaeology, model-making. *Address:* c/o Foreign and Commonwealth Office, King Charles Street, SW1.

BAYNE-POWELL, Robert Lane; Senior Registrar of the Family Division, High Court of Justice, since 1976 (Registrar, 1964-76); *b* 10 Oct. 1910; 2nd *s* of William Maurice and Rosamond Alicia Bayne-Powell; *m* 1938, Nancy Geraldine, *d* of late Lt-Col J. L.

Philips, DSO; one *s* two *d*. *Educ:* Charterhouse; Trinity Coll., Cambridge (BA). Called to Bar, Middle Temple, 1935. Served War of 1939-45, Intell. Corps; Major 1944; Allied Commn for Austria, 1945. Mem., Reviewing Cttee on Export of Works of Art, 1975-. *Publication:* (special editor) Williams and Mortimer on Executors and Probate, 1970. *Recreations:* gardening, miniature collecting, wine-tasting. *Address:* The Mount, Borough Green, Sevenoaks, Kent. *T:* Borough Green 882045. *Club:* Athenæum.

BAYNES, Pauline Diana, (Mrs F. O. Gasch); designer and book illustrator; *b* 9 Sept 1922; *d* of Frederick William Wilberforce Baynes, CIE and Jessie Harriet Maud Cunningham; *m* 1961, Fritz Otto Gasch. *Educ:* Beaufront Sch., Camberley; Farnham Sch. of Art; Slade Sch. of Art. MSIA 1951. Mem., Women's Internat. Art Club, 1938. Voluntary worker, Camouflage Develt and Trng Centre, RE, 1940-42; Hydrogaphic Dept, Admty, 1942-45. Designed world's largest crewel embroidery, Plymouth Congregational Church, Minneapolis, 1970. Kate Greenaway Medal, Library Assoc., 1968. *Publications: illustrated:* Farmer Giles of Ham, and subseq. books and posters by J. R. R. Tolkien, 1949; The Lion, the Witch and the Wardrobe, and subseq. Narnia books by C. S. Lewis, 1950; The Arabian Nights, 1957; The Puffin Book of Nursery Rhymes, 1963; Recipes from an Old Farmhouse, 1966; Dictionary of Chivalry, 1968; Snail and Caterpillar, 1972; numerous other children's books, etc. *Recreation:* going for walks with dogs. *Address:* Rock Barn Cottage, Dockenfield, Farnham, Surrey. *T:* Headley Down 3306.

BAYNES, Sir Rory (Malcolm Stuart), 6th Bt *cr* 1801; retired; *b* 16 May 1886; *s* of Rev. Malcolm Charles Baynes, MA (4th *s* of 3rd Bt) (*d* 1941), and Margaretha (*d* 1936), *d* of Rev. Arthur Cazenove; *S* cousin, 1971; *m* 1925, Ethel Audrey (*d* 1947), *d* of Edward Giles, CIE; one *s*. *Educ:* Harrow School. 3rd Bedford Militia, 1905-08; commissioned in The Cameronians (Scottish Rifles), 1908; served European War, 1914-18; commanded 2nd Bn The Cameronians (Scottish Rifles), 1933-37; served war of 1939-45. County Councillor, Somerset, 1946-58, County Alderman, 1958-68. *Recreations:* fishing, golf (until sight lost). *Heir: s* Lt-Col John Christopher Malcolm Baynes [*b* 24 April 1928; *m* 1955, Shirley Maxwell, *o d* of late Robert Allan Dodds; four *s*]. *Address:* Lake Vyrnwy Hotel, via Oswestry, Salop SY10 0LY. *T:* Llanwddyn 244.

BAYNHAM, Tom, CBE 1975 (OBE 1964); County Councillor, South Yorkshire CC, since 1973 (Chairman, 1973, 1974, 1975); *b* 12 Aug. 1904; *s* of James Baynham and Elizabeth Baynham (*née* Heathcote); *m* 1926, Florence May (*née* Jones); one *s* two *d* . *Educ:* state school. Miner, 1918-69. Adwick Le Street UDC, 1939-74; W Riding CC, 1946-74; W Riding Health Exec. Council, 1948-74. Served on Mental Health Tribunal for approx. nine years to 1974; past Trade Union local official, also Safety Inspector. *Recreations:* reading, gardening. *Address:* 15 Buttercross, Skellow, Doncaster, South Yorkshire. *T:* Adwick Le Street 2226. *Clubs:* Carcroft Village; Skellow Grange Working Men's; Doncaster Trade Union and Labour; Hooton Pagnell.

BAYÜLKEN, Ümit Halûk; Secretary-General, Central Treaty Organisation, since 1975; *b* 7 July 1921; *s* of Staff Officer H. Hüsnü Bayülken and Mrs Melek Bayülken; *m* 1952, Mrs Valihe Salci; one *s* one *d*. *Educ:* Lycée of Haydarpasa, Istanbul; Faculty of Political Science (Diplomatic Sect.), Univ. of Ankara. Joined Min. of For. Affairs, 1944; 3rd Sec., 2nd Political Dept; served in Private Cabinet of Sec.-Gen.; mil. service as reserve Officer, 1945-47; Vice-Consul, Frankfurt-on-Main, 1947-49; 1st Sec., Bonn, 1950-51; Dir of Middle East Sect., Ankara, 1951-53; Mem. Turkish Delegn to UN 7th Gen. Assembly, 1952; Political Adviser, 1953-56, Counsellor, 1956-59, Turkish Perm. Mission to UN; rep. Turkey at London Jt Cttee on Cyprus, 1959-60; Dir-Gen., Policy Planning Gp, Min. of Foreign Affairs, 1960-63; Minister Plenipotentiary, 1963; Dep. Sec.-Gen. for Polit. Affairs, 1963-64; Sec.-Gen. with rank of Ambassador, 1964-66; Ambassador to London, 1966-69, to United Nations, 1969-71; Minister of Foreign Affairs, 1971-74. Mem., Turkish Delegns to 8th-13th, 16th-20th Gen. Assemblies of UN; rep. Turkey at internat. confrs, 1953-66; Leader of Turkish Delegn: at meeting of For. Ministers, 2nd Afro-Asian Conf., Algiers, 1965. Univ. of Ankara: Mem., Inst. of Internat. Relations; Lectr, Faculty of Polit. Scis, 1963-66. Hon. Gov., Sch. of Oriental and African Studies, London. Isabel la Catolica (Spain), 1964; Grand Cross of Merit (Germany), 1965; Hon. GCVO, 1967; Sitara-i-Pakistan (Pakistan), 1970; Star, Order One (Jordan), 1972; Sirdar-i-Ali (Afghanistan), 1972. *Publications:* lectures, articles, studies and essays on subject of minorities, Cyprus, principles of foreign policy, internat. relations and disputes. *Recreations:* music, painting, reading. *Address:* Central Treaty Organisation,

Ankara, Turkey. *Clubs:* Hurlingham, Travellers', Royal Automobile.

BAZALGETTE, Rear-Adm. Derek Willoughby, CB 1976; Principal, Netley Waterside House; *b* 22 July 1924; *yr s* of late H. L. Bazalgette; *m* 1947, Angela Hilda Vera, *d* of Sir Henry Hinchliffe, *qv*; four *d*. *Educ:* RNC Dartmouth. Served War of 1939-45; specialised in Gunnery, 1949; HMS Centaur, 1952-54; HMS Birmingham, 1956-58; SO 108th Minesweeping Sqdn and in comd HMS Houghton, 1958-59; HMS Centaur, 1963-65; Dep. Dir Naval Ops, 1965-67; comd HMS Aurora, 1967-68; idc 1969; Chief Staff Officer to Comdr British Forces Hong Kong, 1970-72; comd HMS Bulwark, 1972-74; Admiral President, RNC Greenwich, 1974-76; Comdr 1958; Captain 1965; Rear-Adm. 1974. ADC 1974. HQ Comr for Water Activities, Scout Assoc., 1976. Freeman, City of London, 1976. *Address:* The Glebe House, Newtown, Fareham, Hants. *Club:* Lansdowne.

BAZELL, Prof. Charles Ernest; Professor of General Linguistics, School of Oriental and African Studies, University of London, 1957-77; *b* 7 Dec. 1909; *s* of Charles Thomas Bazell. *Educ:* Berkhamstead Sch.; Wadham Coll., Oxford; Fellow of Magdalen Coll., Oxford 1934-42; Prof. of English Language and General Linguistics, Univ. of Istanbul, 1942-57. *Publications:* Linguistic Form, 1953; articles and reviews for Archivum Linguisticum, Word, Acta Linguistica, etc. *Address:* c/o Lloyds Bank, 23 Old Woking Road, West Byfleet, Surrey.

BAZIN, Germain René Michel; Officier, Légion d'Honneur; Commandeur des Arts et des Lettres; Conservateur en chef honoraire du Musée du Louvre, since 1971; Professeur honoraire à L'Ecole du Louvre, since 1971; Research Professor Emeritus, York University, Toronto; Membre de l'Institut, 1975; *b* Paris, 1907; *s* of Charles Bazin, Industrialist and engineer of Ecole Centrale de Paris, and J. Laurence Mounier-Pouthot; *m* 1947, Countess Heller de Bielotzerkowka. *Educ:* Ste Croix de Neuilly; Ste Croix d'Orléans; Collège de Pontlevoy; Sorbonne. D ès L; Lic. en Droit; Dipl. Ecole du Louvre. Served French Infantry (Capt.), 1939-45. Prof., Univ. Libre de Bruxelles, since 1934; joined staff of Louvre, 1937; Conservateur en chef du Musée du Louvre, 1951-71; Professeur de muséologie, Ecole du Louvre, 1942-71; lecturer and writer; responsible for more than 30 exhibitions of paintings in France and elsewhere; his books are translated into English, German, Spanish, Italian, Japanese, Portuguese, Yugoslav, Hebrew, Swedish, Dutch, Rumanian, Czech, Danish. Corresponding Mem. of many Academies. Grand Officier, Ordre Léopold, Belgium; Grand Officier, Couronne, Belgium; Commandeur, Mérite, République d'Italie; Officier: Ordre de Santiago, Portugal; Star of the North, Sweden; Cruzeiro do Sul, Brazil, etc. Dr *hc:* Univ. of Rio de Janiero; Villanova, Pa, Univ. *Publications:* Mont St Michel, 1933; Le Louvre, 1935; Les primitifs français, 1937; La peinture italienne aux XIVe et XVe siècles, 1938; Memling, 1939; De David à Cézanne, 1941; Fra Angelico, 1941; Corot, 1942; Le crépuscule des images, 1946; L'Epoque impressioniste, 1947; Les grands maîtres de la peinture hollandaise, 1950; Histoire générale de l'art, 1951; L'Architecture religieuse baroque au Brésil, 1956-58; Trésors de la peinture au Louvre, 1957; Musée de l'Ermitage: écoles étrangères, 1957; Trésors de l'impressionnisme au Louvre, 1958; A gallery of Flowers, 1960; Baroque and Rococo, 1964; Message de l'absolu, 1964; Aleijadinho, 1963; Francesco Messina, 1966; Le Temps des Musées, 1967; La Scultura francese, 1968; Destins du baroque, 1968; La peinture d'avant garde, 1969; Le Monde de la sculpture, 1972 (trans. as Sculpture in the World, 1968); Manet, 1972; numerous articles in principal reviews and French periodicals and foreign art journals of Europe and America. *Recreation:* swimming. *Address:* 4 avenue Raymond Poincaré, 75116 Paris, France. *Clubs:* Army and Navy, Carlton, East India, Devonshire, Sports and Public Schools; Cercle de l'Union, Union Interallié, Fondateur de la Maison de l'Amérique Latine (Paris).

BAZIRE, Rev. Canon Reginald Victor; Archdeacon and Borough Dean of Wandsworth, 1973-75; an Honorary Canon of Southwark, 1959-67 and since 1975; *b* 30 Jan. 1900; *s* of Alfred Arsène Bazire and Edith Mary (*née* Reynolds); *m* 1927, Eileen Crewsdon Brown; two *s*. *Educ:* Christ's Hospital. Missionary, China Inland Mission, 1922-36; Vicar, St Barnabas, Clapham Common, 1949-67; Rural Dean of Battersea, 1953-66; Archdeacon of Southwark, 1967-73. Proctor in convocation: 1959-64, 1970-. *Address:* 7 Grosvenor Park, Bath BA1 6BL. *T:* Bath 317100.

BAZLEY, Rt. Rev. Colin Frederick; *see* Chile, Bolivia and Peru, Bishop of.

BAZLEY, Sir Thomas Stafford, 3rd Bt, *cr* 1869; *b* 5 Oct. 1907; *s* of Capt Gardner Sebastian Bazley, *o s* of 2nd Bt (*d* 1911) and Ruth Evelyn (*d* 1962), *d* of late Sir E. S. Howard (she *m* 2nd, Comdr F. C. Cadogan, RN, retd; he *d* 1970); *S* grandfather, 1919; *m* 1945, Carmen, *o d* of late J. Tulla, 11 Stanley Gardens, W11; three *s* two *d*. *Educ:* Harrow; Magdalen Coll., Oxford. *Heir: s* Thomas John Sebastian Bazley, *b* 31 Aug. 1948. *Address:* Eastleach Folly, near Hatherop, Cirencester, Glos. *T:* Southrop 252.
    See also H . A . Abel Smith .

BB; *see* Watkins-Pitchford, D. J.

BEACH; *see* Hicks-Beach, family name of Earl St Aldwyn.

BEACH, Gen. Sir (William Gerald) Hugh, KCB 1976; OBE 1966; MC 1944; Master-General of the Ordnance, since 1977; *b* 20 May 1923; *s* of late Maj.-Gen. W. H. Beach, CB, CMG, DSO; *m* 1951, Estelle Mary (*née* Henry); three *s* one *d*. *Educ:* Winchester; Peterhouse, Cambridge (MA). Active service in France, 1944 and Java, 1946; comd: 4 Field Sqn, 1956-57; Cambridge Univ. OTC, 1961-63; 2 Div. RE, 1965-67; 12 Inf. Bde, 1969-70; Defence Fellow, Edinburgh Univ. (MSc), 1971; Dir, Army Staff Duties, MoD, 1971-74; Comdt, Staff Coll., Camberley, 1974-75; Dep. C-in-C, UKLF, 1976-77. Colonel Commandant: REME, 1976-; RPC, 1976-; Hon. Colonel, Cambridge Univ. OTC, TAVR, 1977-. *Recreations:* sailing, ski-ing. *Address:* The Ropeway, Beaulieu, Hants. *T:* Beaulieu 612269. *Clubs:* Farmers'; Royal Lymington Yacht.

BEACH, Surgeon Rear-Adm. William Vincent, CB 1962; OBE 1949; MRCS; LRCP; FRCSE; Retd; *b* 22 Nov. 1903; *yr s* of late William Henry Beach; *m* 1931, Daphne Muriel, *yr d* of late Eustace Ackworth Joseph, ICS; two *d*. *Educ:* Seaford Coll.; Guy's Hospital, London. Joined RN Medical Service, 1928. Served War of 1939-45 as Surgical specialist in Hospital ships, Atlantic and Pacific Fleets. Surgical Registrar, Royal Victoria Infirmary, Newcastle upon Tyne; Senior Specialist in Surgery, RN Hospitals, Chatham, Haslar, Malta, Portland; Senior Medical Officer, RN Hospital, Malta; Medical Officer i/c RN Hospital, Portland; Sen. Medical Officer, Surgical Division, RN Hospital, Haslar; Medical Officer in charge of Royal Naval Hospital, Chatham, and Command MO on staff of C-in-C the Nore Command, 1960-61; MO i/c RN Hospital, Malta, and on staff of C-in-C, Mediterranean and as Medical Adviser to C-in-C, Allied Forces, Mediterranean, 1961-63. Surg. Rear-Admiral, 1960. QHS 1960. Senior Surgeon i/c Shaw Savill Passenger Liners, 1966-75. Fellow, Assoc. of Surgeons of Great Britain and Ireland, 1947, Senior Fellow, 1963. *Publications:* Urgent Surgery of the Hand, 1940; Inguinal Hernia-a new operation, 1946; The Treatment of Burns, 1950. *Recreations:* ski-ing, shooting, fishing. *Address:* Cherrytree Cottage, Easton, Winchester. *T:* Itchen Abbas 222. *Club:* Naval and Military.

BEACHAM, Prof. Arthur, OBE 1961; MA, PhD; Deputy Vice-Chancellor, Murdoch University, Western Australia, since 1975; *b* 27 July 1913; *s* of William Walter and Maud Elizabeth Beacham; *m* 1938, Margaret Doreen Moseley; one *s* one *d*. *Educ:* Pontywaun Grammar Sch.; University Coll. of Wales and Univ. of Liverpool. BA Wales 1935, MA Liverpool, 1937, PhD Belfast 1941. Jevons Res. Student, University of Liverpool, 1935-36; Leon Res. Fellow, University of London, 1942-43; Lectr in Economics, Queen's Univ. of Belfast, 1938-45; Sen. Lectr, University Coll. of Wales, 1945-47; Prof. of Indust. Relations, University Coll., Cardiff, 1947-51; Prof. of Economics, University Coll. of Wales, Aberystwyth, 1951-63; Vice-Chancellor, Univ. of Otago, Dunedin, New Zealand, 1964-66; Gonner Prof. of Applied Econs, Liverpool Univ., 1966-75. Chairman: Mid-Wales Industrial Develt Assoc., 1957-63; Post Office Arbitration Tribunal, 1972-73; Member: Advisory Council for Education (Wales), 1949-52; Transp. Consultative Cttee for Wales, 1948-63 (Chm. 1961-63); Central Transp. Consultative Cttee, 1961-63; Economics Cttee of DSIR, 1961-63; North West Economic Planning Council, 1966-74; Merseyside Passenger Transport Authority, 1969-71; Council, Royal Economic Soc., 1970-74. Hon. LLD Otago, 1969. *Publications:* Economics of Industrial Organisation, 1948 (5th edn 1970); Industries in Welsh Country Towns, 1950. Articles in Econ. Jl, Quarterly Jl of Economics, Oxford Econ. Papers, etc. *Recreations:* golf, gardening. *Address:* 35 Hogarth Way, Bateman, WA 6153, Australia.

BEACHCOMBER; *see* Morton, J. C. A. B. M.

BEACHCROFT, Thomas Owen; Author; Chief Overseas Publicity Officer, BBC, 1941-61; *b* 3 Sept. 1902; *s* of Dr R. O. Beachcroft, Dir of Music at Clifton Coll., and Nina Cooke, Beckley Grove, Oxfordshire; *m* 1926, Marjorie Evelyn Taylor;

one *d*. *Educ:* Clifton Coll.; Balliol Coll., Oxford. Scholarship, Balliol. Joined BBC 1924; subsequently in Messrs. Unilevers Advertising Service; rejoined BBC 1941. *Publications: fiction:* A Young Man in a Hurry, 1934; You Must Break Out Sometimes, 1936; The Man Who Started Clean, 1937; The Parents Left Alone, 1940; Collected Stories, 1946; Asking for Trouble, 1948; Malice Bites Back, 1948; A Thorn in The Heart, 1952; Goodbye Aunt Hesther, 1955; (with Lowes Luard) Just Cats, 1936; Calling All Nations, 1942; British Broadcasting, 1946 (booklets about BBC); The English Short Story, 1964; The Modest Art, 1968; contributor of short stories and literary criticism to numerous publications throughout world, and to BBC. Gen. Editor British Council series Writers and their Work, 1949-54. *Recreations:* the arts in general; formerly track and cross-country running (represented Oxford against Cambridge at mile and half-mile). *Address:* The White Cottage, Datchworth Green, Herts SG3 6TL. *Club:* United Oxford & Cambridge University.

BEADLE, Prof. George Wells; President Emeritus and Professor of Biology Emeritus, University of Chicago; *b* Wahoo, Nebraska, 22 Oct. 1903; *s* of Chauncey E. Beadle and Hattie Albro; *m* 1st, 1928, Marion Cecile Hill (marr. diss., 1953); one *s*; 2nd, 1953, Muriel McClure Barnett; one *step s*. *Educ:* Univ. of Nebraska; Cornell Univ. BS 1926, MS 1927, Nebraska; MA Oxford, 1958; PhD Cornell, 1931. Teaching Asst, Cornell, 1926-27; Experimentalist, 1927-31; National Research Fellow, Calif. Institute of Technology, 1931-33; Research Fellow and Instructor, Calif. Institute of Technology, 1933-35; Guest Investigator, Institut de Biologie Physico-Chimique, Paris, 1935; Asst Prof. of Genetics, Harvard Univ., 1936-37; Prof. of Biology, Stanford Univ., 1937-46; Prof. of Biology and Chm. of the Division of Biology, California Institute of Technology, 1946-60, Acting Dean of Faculty, 1960-61; Univ. of Chicago: Pres., 1961-68, Emeritus, 1969. Trustee and Prof. of Biology, 1961-68; William E. Wrather Distinguished Service Prof., 1969-75. Hon. Trustee, Univ. of Chicago, 1971-. Hon. DSc: Yale, 1947; Nebraska, 1949; Northwestern, 1952; Rutgers, 1954; Kenyon Coll., 1955; Wesleyan Univ., 1956; Oxford Univ., 1959; Birmingham Univ., 1959; Pomona Coll., 1961; Lake Forest Coll., 1962; Univ. of Rochester, Univ. of Illinois, 1963; Brown Univ., Kansas State Univ., Univ. of Pennsylvania, 1964; Wabash Coll., 1966; Syracuse, 1967; Loyola, 1970; Eureka Coll., 1972; Butler Univ., 1973; Hon. PhD: Gustavus Adolphus Coll.; Indiana State Univ., 1976; Hon. LLD: UCLA, 1962; Univ. of Miami, Brandeis Univ., 1963; Johns Hopkins Univ., Beloit Coll., 1966; Michigan, 1969; Hon. DHL: Jewish Theological Seminary of America, 1966; DePaul Univ., 1969; Univ. of Chicago, 1969; Canisius Coll., 1969; Knox Coll., 1969; Roosevelt Univ., 1971; Carroll Coll., 1971; DPubSer, Ohio Northern Univ., 1970. Pres., Chicago Horticultural Soc., 1968-71; Trustee: Museum of Sci. and Industry, Chicago, 1967-68; Nutrition Foundn, 1969-73. Member: Twelfth Internat. Congress of Genetics (Hon. Pres.), 1968; National Academy of Sciences (Mem. Council, 1969-72); American Philosophical Soc.; Amer. Assoc. of Adv. Sci. (Pres., 1946); Amer. Acad. of Arts and Sciences; Genetics Soc. of America (Pres., 1955); President's Sci. Adv. Cttee, 1960; Genetics Soc. (Gt Britain); Indian Soc. of Genetics and Plant Breeding; Inst. Lombardo di Scienze E Lettre; Sigma Xi. Hon. Member: Japan Acad.; Phi Beta Kappa. Royal Danish Academy of Sciences; Foreign Member: Royal Society 1960; Indian Nat. Science Acad. Lasker Award, American Public Health Association, 1950; Emil Christian Hansen Prize (Denmark), 1953; Albert Einstein Commemorative Award in Science, 1958; Nobel Prize for Medicine (jointly), 1958; National Award, American Cancer Soc., 1959; Kimber Genetics Award, National Academy of Sciences, 1959; Priestley Memorial Award, 1967; Donald Forsha Jones Award, 1972; (with Muriel B. Beadle) Edison Award for Best science book for youth, 1967. George Eastman Visiting Professor, University of Oxford, 1958-59. Trustee Pomona Coll., 1958-61. *Publications:* An Introduction to Genetics (with A. H. Sturtevant), 1939; Genetics and Modern Biology, 1963; The Language of Life (with Muriel Beadle), 1966. Technical articles in Cytology and Genetics. *Address:* 5533 Dorchester Avenue, Chicago, Illinois 60637, USA. *T:* 493-2119. *Clubs:* Chicago, Tavern (Chicago).

BEADLE, Rt. Hon. Sir (Thomas) Hugh (William), PC 1964; Kt 1961; CMG 1957; OBE 1946; QC 1946; Chief Justice, Rhodesia, 1961-77, retired; *b* 6 Feb. 1905; *s* of late A. W. Beadle, OBE, Sec. to Southern Rhodesia Treasury; *m* 1st, 1934, Leonie Barry (*d* 1953); two *d*; 2nd, 1954, Olive Staley Jackson (*d* 1974); 3rd, 1976, Pleasance Johnson. *Educ:* Salisbury Boys' High Sch.; Diocesan Coll., Rondebosch; University of Cape Town (BA, LLB); Queen's Coll., Oxford (BCL, Hon. Fellow). Advocate, Bulawayo, 1930-39; Seconded Royal WAfFF, Gold Coast, 1939-40; Deputy Judge Advocate-Gen., S Rhodesia Forces, and Parliamentary Sec. to Prime Minister, 1940-46; MP Bulawayo

North (United Party), 1939-50; Southern Rhodesia, 1946-50: Minister of Justice; of Internal Affairs; of Health; of Education; Judge of the High Court, Rhodesia, 1950-61. Cross of the Grand Commander of Royal Hellenic Order of the Phœnix (Greece), 1950. Hon. Fellow Queen's Coll., Oxford, 1966. *Recreations:* shooting, fishing, Boy Scouts, care of physically handicapped. *Address:* 63 Leander Avenue, Hillside, Bulawayo, Rhodesia. *Clubs:* Bulawayo, Salisbury (Rhodesia).

BEAGLEY, Thomas Lorne, CB 1973; Deputy Secretary, Department of the Environment, since 1972; *b* 2 Jan. 1919; *s* of late Captain T. G. Beagley, Royal Montreal Regt; *m* 1942, Heather Blanche Osmond; two *s* one *d. Educ:* Bristol Grammar Sch.; Worcester Coll., Oxford (MA). Served War: 2nd Lieut, Northamptonshire Regt, 1940; Lt-Col, AQMG (Movements), AFHQ, Italy, 1945. Joined Min. of Transport, 1946; Cabinet Office, 1951-52; Min. of Defence, 1952-54; UK Delegn to NATO, 1954-57; UK Shipping Rep., Far East, 1960-63; Asst Under-Sec. of State, Dept of Economic Affairs, 1966-68; Under-Sec., Min. of Transport, 1968-71. FCIT (Pres., 1977). *Recreations:* golf, galleries, gardening. *Address:* 3 Sheen Common Drive, Richmond, Surrey. *T:* 01-876 1216. *Clubs:* Travellers'; Richmond Golf, St Enodoc Golf.

BEALE, Prof. Geoffrey Herbert, MBE 1947; FRS 1959; PhD; Royal Society Research Professor, Edinburgh University, since 1963; *b* 11 June 1913; *s* of Herbert Walter and Elsie Beale; *m* 1949, Betty Brydon McCallum (marr. diss. 1969); three *s. Educ:* Sutton County Sch.; Imperial Coll. of Science, London. Scientific Research Worker, John Innes Horticultural Institution, London, 1935-40. Served in HM Forces (1941-46). Research worker, department of Genetics, Carnegie Institute, Cold Spring Harbor, New York, 1947; Rockefeller Fellow, Indiana Univ., 1947-48; Lecturer, Dept of Animal Genetics, 1948-59, Reader in Animal Genetics, 1959-63, Edinburgh Univ. *Publications:* The Genetics of Paramecium aurelia, 1954; (with Jonathan Knowles) Extranuclear Genetics, 1977. *Address:* 23 Royal Terrace, Edinburgh EH7 5AH. *T:* 557 1329.

BEALE, Hon. Sir Howard; *see* Beale, Hon. Sir O. H.

BEALE, Josiah Edward Michael; Assistant Secretary, Department of Industry (formerly Board of Trade), since 1968; *b* 29 Sept. 1928; *s* of late J. E. Beale and of Mrs P. A. Beale, Upminster, Essex; *m* 1958, Jean Margaret McDonald; two *d* (and one *d* decd). *Educ:* Brentwood Sch.; Jesus Coll., Cambridge. Entered Civil Service, 1950; Principal, Min. of Transport, 1956; Asst Sec., BoT, 1968; British Govt Shipping Representative for Far East, Singapore, 1968-71. *Address:* 43 Shenfield Road, Brentwood, Essex.

BEALE, Hon. Sir (Oliver) Howard, KBE 1961; QC; Australian Ambassador to United States, 1957-64; formerly Barrister-at-Law, Member of Commonwealth Parliament and Cabinet Minister; *b* 1898; *s* of late Rev. Joseph Beale; *m* 1927, Margery Ellen Wood; one *s. Educ:* Sydney High Sch.; University of Sydney. BA 1921; LLB 1925. Called to NSW Bar and High Court of Australia, 1925; served War of 1939-45, RANVR, 1942-45. Elected MHR (L) Parramatta, 1946, re-elected, 1949, 1951, 1954, 1955; Mem. Commonwealth Parly. Public Works Cttee, 1947-49; Austr. Deleg., Internat. Bar Congress at The Hague, 1948; apptd KC 1950. Minister for Information and Minister for Transport (Menzies Govt), 1949-50; Chm., Austr. Transp. Adv. Council, 1949-50; Minister for Supply, 1950-58, including control of guided missiles research and Woomera Rocket Range, and atomic weapons research and Maralinga atomic testing ground; Minister i/c Austr. Aluminium Prod. Commn, 1950-58; Minister i/c Austr Atomic Energy Commn and Rum Jungle uranium project, 1950-56; Minister for Defence Prod., 1956-58, responsible for govt ordnance ammunition, explosives, chemicals, aircraft and engine factories; Actg Minister: for Immigration, 1951-52, 1953 and 1954; for Nat. Development, 1952-53; for Air, 1952; for Defence, 1957; Mem. Austr. Defence Council, 1950-58; Mem. Cabinet Defence Preparations Cttee and Cabinet Cttee on Uranium and Atomic Energy, 1950-58. Austr. rep., Anzus Council, Washington, 1958, 1959, Canberra, 1962; Leader, Austr. Delegn, Colombo Plan Conf., Seattle, 1958; Dep. Leader, Austr. Delegn to UN, New York, 1959; Dep. Leader, later Leader Austr. Delegn to Antarctic Conf., Washington, 1959; Austr. Deleg. SEATO Conf., Washington, 1959, 1960; Alt. Gov., Internat. Monetary Fund, 1960, 1962, 1963; Leader, Austr. Delegn, World Food Congress, Washington, 1963; State Visitor to Mexico and Chile, 1963; Woodward Lectr, Yale Univ., 1960; Dean of British Commonwealth Diplomatic Corps, Washington, 1961-64; Pres., Arts Council of Australia, 1964-68. Dir of various corporations. Regents' Visiting Prof., Univ. of Calif., 1966; Marquette Univ., Wisconsin, 1967, 1969. Holds Hon. degrees. *Address:* 4

Marathon Road, Darling Point, Sydney, NSW 2027, Australia. *Clubs:* Union, Australasian Pioneers' (Sydney).

BEALE, Percival Spencer; *b* 14 Sept. 1906; *m* 1938, Rachel M. H. (née Wilson); two *s. Educ:* St Paul's Sch. Entered Bank of England Oct. 1924; Chief Cashier, Bank of England, 1949-Jan. 1955; General Manager, Industrial Credit and Investment Corporation of India, 1955-58. Director: Samuel Montagu & Co. Ltd, 1960-65; The British Oxygen Co. Ltd, 1958-69; Carpet Manufacturing Co. Ltd, 1958-69. An Underwriting Mem. of Lloyd's, 1971-75. *Address:* Villa Aurore, Route de Genève, 1299 Commugny, Vaud, Switzerland.

BEALE, Thomas Edward, CBE 1966; JP; Chairman, Beale's Ltd; *b* 5 March 1904; *s* of late Thomas Henderson Beale, London; *m* Beatrice May, *d* of William Steele McLaughlin, JP, Enniskillen; one *s. Educ:* City of London Sch. Mem. Bd, British Travel Assoc., 1950-70, Dep. Chm. 1965-70. Vice-Pres. and Fellow, Hotel and Catering Inst., 1949-71; Chm., Caterers' Assoc. of Gt Britain, 1949-52; Pres., Internat. Ho-Re-Ca (Union of Nat. Hotel, Restaurant & Caterers Assocs), 1954-64. Chm., Treasury Cttee of Enquiry, House of Commons Refreshment Dept, 1951. Master, Worshipful Co. of Bakers, 1955. Mem., Islington Borough Council, 1931-34; JP Inner London, 1950 (Chm. EC Div., Inner London Magistrates, 1970-73). FRSH 1957; FRSA 1968. Médaille d'Argent de Paris, 1960. *Recreation:* arboriculture. *Address:* West Lodge Park, Hadley Wood, Herts; Shoreacres, Banks Road, Sandbanks, Poole, Dorset. *Club:* Carlton.

BEALE, Sir William (Francis), Kt 1956; OBE 1945; Director: National Cash Register Co. Ltd; Randalls Group Ltd; Commercial Union Group (local director); *b* 27 Jan. 1908; *y s* of late George and Elizabeth Beale, Potterspury Lodge, Northants; *m* 1934, Dèva Zaloudek; one *s* one *d. Educ:* Downside Sch., Pembroke Coll., Cambridge. Joined Green's Stores (Ilford) Ltd, Dir, 1929-63 (Chm., 1950-63). Navy, Army and Air Force Institutes, UK, 1940-41, Dir, 1949-61 (Chm. 1953-61). EFI, GHQ West Africa, 1942-43; EFI, 21st Army Gp, 1944-46. Jt Master, Tedworth Foxhounds. *Recreations:* hunting, shooting; formerly Rugby football (Eastern Counties Cap, 1932). *Address:* All Cannings Grange, Devizes, Wilts SN10 3NR. *Club:* Bath.

BEALES, Hugh Lancelot; Reader in Economic History in University of London, 1931-56; *b* 18 Feb. 1889; 3rd *s* of Rev. W. Beales; *m*; two *s* one *d. Educ:* Kingswood Sch., Bath; University of Manchester. Lecturer in Economic History, University of Sheffield, 1919-26; Lecturer in Economic History, University of London (London Sch. of Economics), 1926-31. Visiting Prof., Columbia Univ., 1954-55, Harvard Univ., 1956, University of Washington, 1959, USA. Editorial Adviser, Penguin and Pelican Books, to 1945; Ed. of Agenda, a journal of reconstruction issued by London Sch. of Economics to 1945; mem. of Editorial Bd of Political Quarterly; Editor, Kingswood Books on Social History. Mem. of CS Arbitration Tribunal, 1955-65. Hon. Fellow, LSE, 1971. Hon. DLitt: Exeter, 1969; Sheffield, 1971; Hon. DrRCA, 1974. *Publications:* Industrial Revolution, 1929; Early English Socialists, 1932; Making of Social Policy (Hobhouse Lecture), 1945, etc. Contributor to Economic History Review and various periodicals. *Address:* 16 Denman Drive, London, NW11. *T:* 01-455 4091.

BEALES, Reginald Edwin, CBE 1961; Deputy Director, Central Statistical Office, Cabinet Office, 1957-72; *b* 16 Sept. 1909; *s* of Charles Neslen Beales, Norwich; *m* 1938, Margaret Alice Poulton (*d* 1964); one *s* one *d. Educ:* City of Norwich Sch. Norwich Union Life Ins. Soc., 1926; Northern Assce Co., 1931; Central Statistical Office, 1943; Chief Statistician, Inland Revenue, 1949; Dir of Statistics and Intell., Inland Revenue, 1952-57. FIA 1934, FSS 1947 (Mem. Coun., 1965-69; Vice-Pres., 1967-68). *Publications:* articles in: Jl of Royal Statistical Soc.; Review of Income and Wealth. *Recreations:* tennis, gardening. *Address:* Barnet Wood, Barnet Wood Road, Bromley, Kent BR2 8HJ. *T:* 01-462 2813.

BEALEY, Prof. Frank William; Professor of Politics, University of Aberdeen, since 1964; *b* Bilston, Staffs, 31 Aug. 1922; *er s* of Ernest Bealey and Norah (née Hampton), both of Netherton, Dudley; *m* 1960, Sheila Hurst; one *s* two *d. Educ:* Hill Street Elem. Sch.; King Edward VI Grammar Sch., Stourbridge; London Sch. of Economics. Seaman in RN, 1941-46; Student, LSE, 1946-48; Finnish Govt Scholar, 1948-49; Research Asst for Passfield Trust, 1950-51; Extra-Mural Lectr, University of Manchester (Burnley Area), 1951-52; Lectr, University of Keele, 1952-64. *Publications:* (with Henry Pelling) Labour and Politics, 1958; (with J. Blondel and W. P. McCann) Constituency Politics, 1965; The Social and Political Thought of the British Labour Party, 1970; The Post Office Engineering

Union, 1976; articles in academic jls. *Recreations:* reading poetry, eating and drinking, watching football and cricket, darts, playing with the children. *Address:* 355 Clifton Road, Aberdeen. *T:* Aberdeen 44689. *Club:* Economicals Association Football and Cricket.

BEALS, Carlyle Smith, OC (Canada) 1970; FRS 1951; FRSC 1933; Private Scientific Consultant in Celestial and Earth Sciences, since 1964; *b* 29 June 1899; *s* of Rev. F. H. Beals, Inglisville, NS, and Annie F. N. Smith, Albert, NB; *m* 1931, Miriam White Bancroft; one *d. Educ:* Acadia Univ., NS (BA 1919); Toronto Univ. (MA (Physics), 1923); Imperial Coll. of Science and Technology (DIC 1925); London Univ. (PhD 1926, DSc 1934); DSc hon.: Acadia Univ, 1951; Univ. of New Brunswick, 1956; Queen's Univ., 1960; Pittsburgh Univ., 1963. Tory Medal, RSC 1957; Gold Medal of Professional Inst. of the Public Service of Canada, 1958; F. C. Leonard Medal of Meteoritical Soc., 1966. Asst Prof. of Physics, Acadia Univ., 1926-27; Astronomer, Dominion Astrophysical Observatory, Victoria, BC, 1927-40; Asst Dir, 1940-46; Dominion Astronomer, Ottawa, 1946-64. *Publications:* about 87 papers in astronomical and physical journals on analysis of line spectra, emission line stars, interstellar matter, terrestial and lunar impact craters, and the development of scientific instruments. *Recreations:* wild life study, the study of rural photographs, geology. *Address:* Manotick, Ont, Canada. *T:* Manotick 692-3247.

BEAM, Jacob D.; US Ambassador to USSR, 1969-73; *b* Princeton, NJ, 24 March 1908; *s* of Jacob Newton Beam and Mary Prince; *m* 1952, Margaret Glassford; one *s. Educ:* Kent Sch., USA; Princeton Univ. (BA); Cambridge Univ., England (1929-30). Vice-Consul, Geneva, 1931-34; Third Sec., Berlin, 1934-40; Second Sec., London, 1941-45; Asst Political Adviser, HQ, US Forces, Germany, 1945-47; Chief of Central European Div., Dept of State, 1947-49; Counsellor and Consul-Gen., US Embassy, Djakarta, 1949-51; Actg US Rep., UN Commn for Indonesia, 1951; Counsellor, Belgrade, 1951-52; Minister-Counsellor, US Embassy, Moscow, 1952-53 (actg head); Dep. Asst Sec. of State, 1953-57; US Ambassador to Poland, 1957-61; Asst Dir, Internat. Relations Bureau, Arms Control and Disarmament Agency, USA, 1962-66; US Ambassador to Czechoslovakia, 1966-68. Chm., US Delegn to Internat. Telecomm. Union Plenipotentiary Conf., Malaga, 1973. *Address:* 3129 'O' Street NW, Washington, DC 20007, USA. *Club:* Metropolitan (Washington, DC).

BEAMENT, James William Longman, ScD; FRS 1964; Drapers' Professor of Agriculture and Head of the Department of Applied Biology, University of Cambridge, since 1969; Chairman, Natural Environment Research Council, since 1977 (Member, since 1970); *b* 17 Nov. 1921; *o c* of late T. Beament, Crewkerne, Somerset; *m* 1962, Juliet, *o d* of late Prof. Sir Ernest Barker, Cambridge; two *s. Educ:* Crewkerne Grammar Sch.; Queens' Coll., Cambridge; London Sch. of Tropical Medicine. Exhibitioner, Queens' Coll., 1941; BA 1943; MA 1946; PhD London 1945; ScD Cantab 1960. Research Officer with Agricultural Research Council, Cambridge, 1946; Univ. Lectr, and Fellow and Tutor of Queens' Coll., Cambridge, 1961; Reader in Insect Physiology, 1966. Mem., Composers' Guild of Great Britain, 1967. Scientific Medal of Zoological Soc., 1963. *Publications:* many papers on insect physiology in scientific journals; Editor of several review volumes. *Recreations:* acoustics, playing the double-bass. *Address:* 19 Sedley Taylor Road, Cambridge CB2 2PW. *T:* 46045; Queens' College, Cambridge CB3 9ET. *T:* 65511.

BEAMISH, family name of **Baron Chelwood.**

BEAMISH, Air Vice-Marshal Cecil Howard, CB 1970; FDSRCS; Director of Dental Services, Royal Air Force, 1969-73; *b* 31 March 1915; *s* of Frank George Beamish, Coleraine; *m* 1955, Frances Elizabeth Sarah Goucher; two *s. Educ:* Coleraine Acad.; Queen's Univ., Belfast. Joined Royal Air Force, 1936; Group Capt., 1958; Air Cdre, 1968; Air Vice-Marshal, 1969. QHDS 1969-73. *Recreations:* Rugby football, golf, squash. *Address:* East Keal Manor, Spilsby, Lincs.

BEAMONT, Wing Comdr Roland Prosper, CBE 1969 (OBE 1953); DSO 1943, Bar 1944; DFC 1941, Bar 1943; DFC (US) 1946; FRAeS; Director and Manager, Flight Operations, British Aircraft Corporation, Preston, since 1965; Director of Flight Operations, Panavia, since 1971; *b* 10 Aug. 1920; *s* of Lieut-Col E. C. Beamont and Dorothy Mary (*née* Haynes); *m* 1946, Patricia Raworth; three *d. Educ:* Eastbourne Coll. Commissioned in RAF, 1939; served War of 1939-45, Fighter Command, RAF, BEF, Battle of Britain (despatches), Battle of France and Germany. Attached as Test Pilot to Hawker

Aircraft Ltd during rest periods, in 1941-42 and 1943-44; Experimental Test Pilot, Gloster Aircraft Co. Ltd, 1946; Chief Test Pilot, English Electric Co., 1947-61; Special Dir and Dep. Chief Test Pilot, BAC, 1961-64. Events while Chief Test Pilot, English Electric Co. Ltd: 1st British pilot to fly at speed of sound (in USA), May 1948; 1st Flight of Britain's 1st jet bomber (the Canberra), May 1949; holder of Atlantic Record, Belfast-Gander, 4 hours 18 mins. Aug. 1951 and 1st two-way Atlantic Record, Belfast-Gander-Belfast, 10 hrs 4 mins Aug. 1952 (in a Canberra); first flight of P1, 1954 (Britain's first fully supersonic fighter); first British pilot in British aircraft to fly faster than sound in level flight, 1954, and first to fly at twice the speed of sound, Nov. 1958; first flight of Lightning supersonic all-weather fighter, 1957; first flight of TSR2, Sept. 1964 (Britain's first supersonic bomber). Britannia Trophy for 1953; Derry and Richards Memorial Medal, 1955; R. P. Alston Memorial Medal, RAeS, 1960; British Silver Medal for Aeronautics, 1965. Master Pilot and Liveryman, Guild of Air Pilots. *Publications:* Phoenix into Ashes, 1968; Typhoon and Tempest at War, 1975. *Recreations:* sailing, fishing. *Address:* Samlesbury Hall Cottage, Samlesbury, Preston, Lancs. *Club:* Royal Air Force.

BEAN, Ven. Arthur Selwyn, MBE 1939; Chaplain to the Queen, 1952-69, Extra Chaplain, since 1969; *b* 23 April 1886; *s* of Charles and Ellen Annie Bean; *m* 1912, Nellie Lingard Hackwood; two *d* (one *s* decd). *Educ:* Christ's Coll., Christchurch, NZ; Keble Coll., Oxford (MA); University of Manchester (BD). Curate of Rugby, 1910-17; Vicar of Ribby with Wrea, 1917-22; Vicar of Weaste, 1922-27; Vicar of Astley, 1927-34; Archdeacon of Manchester and Canon Residentiary of Manchester Cathedral, 1934-66. Church Comr, 1948-68. Dir, Ecclesiastical Insurance Office Ltd, 1949-66; Chm., C. of E. Pensions Board, 1959-65. Prolocutor, Lower House, York Convocation, 1955-66. Archdeacon Emeritus, 1966. *Address:* 2 The Brae, Longdown Road, Lower Bourne, Farnham, Surrey. *T:* Farnham 5348.

BEAN, Basil; General Manager, Northampton Development Corporation, since 1977; *b* 2 July 1931; *s* of Walter Bean and Alice Louise Bean; *m* 1956, Janet Mary Brown; one *d. Educ:* Archbishop Holgate Sch., York. Mem. CIPFA. York City, 1948-53; West Bromwich Borough, 1953-56; Sutton London Bor., 1957-62; Skelmersdale Develt Corp., 1962-66; Havering London Bor., 1967-69; Northampton Develt Corp., 1969-. *Recreations:* reading, walking, travel. *Address:* 7 Great Close, Chapel Brampton, Northampton. *T:* Northampton 843599. *Club:* Northampton and County (Northampton).

BEAN, Hugh (Cecil), CBE 1970; violinist (freelance); Professor of Violin, Royal College of Music, since 1954; *b* 22 Sept. 1929; *s* of Cecil Walter Claude Bean and Gertrude Alice Chapman; *m* 1963, Mary Dorothy Harrow; one *d. Educ:* Beckenham Grammar Sch. Studied privately, and at RCM, London (principal prize for violin) with Albert Sammons, 1938-57; Boise Trav. Schol., 1952; at Brussels Conservatoire with André Gertler (double premier prix for solo and chamber music playing), 1952-53. National Service, Gren. Gds, 1949-51. Formerly Leader of Harvey Phillips String Orch. and Dennis Brain Chamber Orch.; Leader of Philharmonia and New Philharmonia Orch., 1957-67; Associate Leader, BBC Symph. Orch., 1967-69. Member: Bean-Parkhouse Duo; Music Gp of London. Has made solo commercial records, and has performed as soloist with many major orchestras. Hon. ARCM 1961, FRCM 1968. *Recreations:* design and construction of flying model aircraft; steam-driven passenger hauling model railways; gramophone record collection. *Address:* Rosemary Cottage, 30 Stone Park Avenue, Beckenham, Kent. *T:* 01-650 8774.

BEAN, Leonard, CMG 1964; MBE 1945; MA; Secretary, Southern Gas Region, since 1966; *b* 19 Sept. 1914; *s* of late Harry Bean, Bradford, Yorks, and late Agnes Sherwood Beattie, Worcester; *m* 1938, Nancy Winifred, *d* of Robert John Neilson, Dunedin, NZ; one *d. Educ:* Canterbury Coll., NZ; Queens' Coll., Cambridge. Served War of 1939-45: Major, 2nd NZ Div. (despatches, MBE). Entered Colonial Service, N Rhodesia, 1945; Provincial Comr, 1959; Perm. Sec. (Native Affairs), 1961; acted as Minister for Native Affairs and Natural Resources in periods, 1961-64; Permanent Secretary: to Prime Minister, 1964; also to President, 1964. Adviser to President, Zambia, 1964-66. *Recreations:* golf, gardening. *Address:* Amcotts, Bassett Green Road, Southampton, Hampshire. *T:* Southampton 68293. *Clubs:* MCC; Stoneham Golf.

BEAN, Robert E.; MP (Lab) Rochester and Chatham, since Oct. 1974; *b* 5 Sept. 1935. *Educ:* Rochester Mathematical Sch.; Medway Coll. of Technol. MIOB; AMBIM. Polytechnic Lectr. Joined Labour Party, 1950. Mem., Chatham Borough Council, 1958-74; formerly Member: Fabian Soc.; Co-operative party.

Contested (Lab): Gillingham, 1970; Thanet East, Feb. 1974. Mem., Medway Borough Council, 1974-76. *Address:* House of Commons, SW1A 0AA; 86 Maidstone Road, Chatham, Kent.

BEAN, Thomas Ernest, CBE 1957; *b* 11 Feb. 1900; *s* of Arthur Charles Bean; *m* 1929, Eleanor Child; one *d.* Asst Circulation Manager, Manchester Guardian, 1928-44; General Manager: Hallé Concerts Soc., Manchester, 1944-51; Royal Festival Hall, London, 1951-65; Sec., London Orchestral Concert Bd, 1965-71. Austrian Order of Merit (Officer's Class), 1959. *Recreation:* gardening. *Address:* 5 Pixholme Court, Dorking, Surrey. *T:* Dorking 2900.

BEANEY, Alan; *b* 3 March 1905; *s* of John Beaney, New Silksworth, Co. Durham; *m* 1926, Mary Elizabeth, *d* of William Wass, New Silksworth, Co. Durham; one *s* two *d. Educ:* Elementary Sch.; NCLC. Mem. Dearne Urban District Council, 1938; County Councillor, WR Yorks, 1949; MP (Lab) Hemsworth Div. WR Yorks, 1959-Feb. 1974. Mem., Yorks Executive Cttee, National Union of Mineworkers. *Recreations:* hiking, fishing, reading. *Address:* 190 Houghton Road, Thurnscoe, Rotherham, W Yorks. *T:* Goldthorpe 3304. *Club:* Royal Automobile.

BEAR, Leslie William, CBE 1972; Editor of Official Report (Hansard), House of Commons, 1954-72; *b* 16 June 1911; *s* of William Herbert Bear, Falkenham, Suffolk; *m* 1st, 1932, Betsy Sobels (*d* 1934), Lisse, Holland; 2nd, 1936, Annelise Gross, Trier, Germany; two *s. Educ:* Gregg Sch., Ipswich. Served War, 1943-44, Royal Air Force. Mem. of Official Reporting Staff, League of Nations, Geneva, 1930-36; joined Official Report (Hansard), House of Commons, 1936; Asst Ed., 1951. *Recreations:* ski-ing, gardening, chess. *Address:* Medleys, Ufford, Woodbridge, Suffolk. *T:* Eyke 358.

BEARD, Allan Geoffrey; Under Secretary, Department of Health and Social Security, since 1968 (Ministry of Social Security 1966-68); *b* 18 Oct. 1919; *s* of late Major Henry Thomas Beard and Florence Mercy Beard; *m* 1945, Helen McDonagh; one *d. Educ:* Ormskirk Grammar Sch. Clerical Officer, Air Min., 1936; Exec. Off., Higher Exec. Off., Asst Principal, Assistance Board, 1938-47; Army Service, 1940-46 (Capt., RE); Principal, Nat. Assistance Board, 1950; Asst Sec., 1962. *Recreations:* music, gardening, do-it-yourself. *Address:* 51 Rectory Park, Sanderstead, Surrey CR2 9JR. *T:* 01-657 4197. *Club:* Royal Automobile.

BEARD, Christopher Nigel; Director, London Docklands Development Team, since 1974; *b* 10 Oct. 1936; *o s* of Albert Leonard Beard, Castleford, Yorks, and Irene (*née* Bowes); *m* 1969, Jennifer Anne, *d* of T. B. Cotton, Guildford, Surrey; one *s* one *d. Educ:* Castleford Grammar Sch., Yorks; University Coll. London. BSc Hons, Special Physics. Asst Mathematics Master, Tadcaster Grammar Sch., Yorks, 1958-59; Physicist with English Electric Atomic Power Div., working on design of Hinckley Point Nuclear Power Station, 1959-61; Market Researcher, Esso Petroleum Co., assessing future UK Energy demands and market for oil, 1961. MoD: Scientific Officer, later Principal Scientific Officer, in Defence Operational Analysis Estabt (engaged in analysis of central defence policy and investment issues), 1961-68, and Supt of Studies pertaining to Land Ops; responsible for policy and investment studies related to Defence of Europe and strategic movement of the Army, Dec. 1968-72; Chief Planner, Strategy, GLC, 1973-74. *Publication:* The Practical Use of Linear Programming in Planning and Analysis, 1974 (HMSO). *Recreations:* reading 19th Century history, walking, tennis, the theatre. *Address:* Lanquhart, The Ridgway, Pyrford, Woking, Surrey. *T:* Byfleet 48630.

BEARD, Derek; British Council Representative in Germany, since 1977; *b* 16 May 1930; *s* of Walter Beard and Lily Beard (*née* Mellors); *m* 1st, 1953, Ruth Davies (marr. diss. 1966); two *s;* 2nd, 1966, Renate Else, *d* of late W. E. Kautz, Berlin and Mecklenburg; two *s. Educ:* Hulme Grammar Sch., Oldham; Brasenose Coll., Oxford (MA, DipEd). Stand Grammar Sch., Whitefield, 1954-56; HMOCS, Nyasaland, 1956-59; Asst Educn Officer, WR Yorks, 1959-61; Sen. Asst, Oxfordshire, 1961-63; British Council, Pakistan, 1963-65; Producer, BBC Overseas Educnl Recordings Unit, 1965-66; Dir, Appts, Services Dept, British Council, 1966-70; Dep. Rep., India, 1970-73; Controller, Educn and Science Div., British Council, 1973-77. *Publications:* articles on educn and cultural relns. *Recreations:* sculpture, music, travel. *Address:* Hahnenstrasse 6, 5 Cologne-1, Germany. *T:* Cologne 23-66-77. *Club:* Travellers'.

BEARD, Paul, OBE 1952; FRAM; FGSM; Professor of Violin, Guildhall School of Music, retired 1968; *b* 4 Aug. 1901; *m* 1925, Joyce Cass-Smith; one *s* one *d. Educ:* Birmingham Oratory and

St Philip's. Began violin playing at 4, being taught by father; first public appearance at 6; studied as Scholarship holder at RAM; appointed ARAM, 1921, and FRAM 1939; Principal 1st Violin of following Orchestras: City of Birmingham and Spa, Scarborough, 1920-32; National of Wales, 1929; London Philharmonic, 1932-36; BBC Symphony Orchestra, 1936-62. *Recreations:* golf, gardening. *Address:* 84 Downs Wood, Epsom Downs, Surrey. *T:* Burgh Heath 50759.

BEARD, Paul Michael; a Recorder of Crown Courts since 1972; Barrister-at-Law; *b* 21 May 1930; *s* of late Harold Beard, Sheffield; *m* 1959, Rhoda Margaret, *er d* of late James Henry Asquith, Morley, Yorks; one *s* one *d. Educ:* The City Grammar Sch., Sheffield; King's Coll., London. LLB (Hons). Commissioned RASC, 1949; served BAOR (Berlin), 1949-50. Called to Bar, Gray's Inn, 1955; North-Eastern Circuit. Contested (C): Huddersfield East, 1959; Oldham East, 1966; Wigan, Feb. and Oct. 1974; Prospective Parly Cand. (C), Doncaster; Chm., Brightside Conservative Assoc., 1961-68. *Recreations:* reading, walking. *Address:* Flowerdale, Church Street, East Markham, near Newark, Notts. *T:* Tuxford 870074; 42 Bank Street, Sheffield S1 1EE. *T:* 20606/26826. *Clubs:* St Stephen's; Sheffield (Sheffield).

BEARDS, Paul Francis Richmond; *b* 1 Dec. 1916; *s* of late Dr Clifford Beards and Dorothy (*née* Richmond); *m* 1950, Margaret Elizabeth, *y d* of late V. R. Aronson, CBE, KC; one *s* one *d. Educ:* Marlborough; Queen's Coll., Oxford (Open Scholar; 1st cl. hons Mod. Hist.). Entered Admin. Class of Home Civil Service, 1938; Asst Princ., War Office; served in Army, 1940-44; Principal War Office, 1945; Asst Private Sec. to successive Prime Ministers, 1945-48; Princ. Private Sec. to successive Secs of State for War, 1951-54; Asst Sec., 1954; Imp. Def. Coll., 1961; Asst Under-Sec. of State, MoD, 1964-69; Comr for Administration and Finance, Forestry Commn, 1969; retd, 1970. Coronation Medal, 1953. *Recreations:* fishing, gardening, archæology. *Address:* Thrale Cottage, Budleigh Salterton, Devon EX9 6EA. *T:* Budleigh Salterton 2084. *Club:* Royal Commonwealth Society.

BEARE, Robin Lyell Blin, MB, BS; FRCS; Consultant Plastic Surgeon: Queen Victoria Hospital, East Grinstead, since 1960; Brighton General Hospital and Brighton and Lewes Group of Hospitals, since 1960; Hon. Consulting Plastic Surgeon, St Mary's Hospital, London, since 1976 (Consultant Plastic Surgeon, 1959-76); *b* 31 July 1922; *s* of Stanley Samuel Beare, OBE, FRCS, and late Cecil Mary Guise Beare (*née* Lyell); *m* 1947, Iris Bick; two *s* two *d. Educ:* Radley (scholar). Middlesex Hosp. Medical Sch. MB, BS (Hons) 1952 (dist. Surg.); FRCS (Eng) 1955. Served with RAF Bomber Command (Aircrew) 1940-46. Formerly Ho. Surg., Casualty Officer, Asst Pathologist and Surgical Registrar, The Middlesex Hosp., 1952-56. Surg. Registrar, Plastic Surgery and Jaw Injuries Centre. Queen Victoria Hosp., East Grinstead, 1957-60. Examr in gen. surgery for FRCS, 1972-. Fellow Assoc. of Surgeons of Gt Britain and Ireland; Fellow Royal Society Med.; Mem. Brit. Assoc. of Plastic Surgeons; Mem. of Bd of Trustees, McIndoe Memorial Research Unit, E Grinstead; Hon. Mem. Societé Française de Chirurgie Plastique et Reconstructive. *Publications:* various on surgical problems in BMJ, Amer. Jl of Surgery, etc. *Recreations:* fishing, shooting. *Address:* 149 Harley Street, W1N 2DE. *T:* 01-935 4444; Scraggs Farm, Cowden, Kent. *T:* Cowden 386. *Club:* MCC.

BEARN, Prof. Alexander Gordon, MD; FRCP, FRCPEd, FACP; Stanton Griffis Distinguished Medical Professor, since 1976, Professor of Medicine, Cornell University Medical College, since 1966; Attending Physician, The New York Hospital, since 1966; *b* 29 March 1923; *s* of E. G. Bearn, CB, CBE; *m* 1952, Margaret, *d* of Clarence Slocum, Fanwood, NJ, USA; one *s* one *d. Educ:* Epsom Coll.; Guy's Hosp., London. Postgraduate Medical Sch. of London, 1949-51. Rockefeller Univ., 1951-66; Hon. Research Asst, University Coll. (Galton Laboratory), 1959-60; Prof. and Sen. Physician, Rockefeller Univ., 1964-66, Vis. and Adjunct Prof. 1966-; Chm., Dept of Medicine, Cornell Univ. Med. Coll., 1966-77; Physician-in-Chief, NY Hosp., 1966-77. Trustee, Rockefeller Univ. Mem. Editorial Bd, several scientific and med. jls. Lectures: Lowell, Harvard, 1958; Medical Research Soc., 1969; Lilly, RCP, 1973; Harvey, 1975; Lettsomian, Med. Soc., 1976. Macy Faculty Scholar Award, 1974-75. Member: Nat. Acad. Science; Amer. Philosophical Soc.; Foreign Mem., Norwegian Acad. Science and Letters. *Publications:* articles on Human Genetics and Liver Disease, 1950-; (Co-Editor) Progress in Medical Genetics, Vol. 2, 1962-; (Associate Editor) Cecil and Loeb: Textbook of Medicine. *Recreations:* biography, travel. *Address:* 1225 Park Avenue, New York, NY 10028, USA. *T:* 831-0133. *Clubs:* Bath; Grolier, Century (NY).

BEARN, Col Frederic Arnot, CBE 1945; DSO 1917; MC; MB, ChB Manchester; MD Manchester 1920; Dauntesey, Turner, and Bradley Scholar, Platt Scholar, University of Manchester; Hon. Consultant Physician, District Hospital, Buxton, and Devonshire Royal Hospital, Buxton; retired; *b* 1890; *m* Alice (*d* 1968), *d* of James Bell, JP, Colinton, Edinburgh. Late House Physician and Senior House Surg., Manchester Royal Infirmary; served European War, 1914-19 (despatches, DSO, MC); also in Mesopotamia, 1918; and in India, 1919; war of 1939-45, Col AMS (four Bars to DSO, CBE, King Haakon VII Liberty Cross; gazetted Hon. Col, 1945). County Commissioner, SJAB, Derbys; KStJ. *Recreation:* shooting. *Address:* c/o Bank of Scotland, 16 Piccadilly, W1. *Club:* Caledonian.

BEARNE, Air Vice-Marshal Guy, CB 1956; *b* 5 Nov. 1908; *y s* of late Lieut-Col L. C. Bearne, DSO, AM; *m* 1933, Aileen Cartwright, *e d* of late H. J. Randall, Hove; one *s* two *d*. Commissioned RAF, 1929; served in various Bomber Sqdns, 1930-33; specialist armament course, 1933; armament duties, 1934-44; Bomber Command, 1944-45 (despatches twice); Staff Officer i/c Administration, RAF Malaya, 1946; Joint Services Staff Coll., 1947; Dep. Dir Organisation (Projects), 1947-49; Command of Central Gunnery Sch., 1949-51; SASO, Rhodesian Air Training Gp, 1951-52; AOC Rhodesian Air Training Gp, 1953; Dir of Organisation (Establishments), Air Ministry, 1954-56; Air Officer in Charge of Administration, Technical Training Command, 1956-61; retd, 1961. *Recreation:* golf. *Address:* 2 Mill Close, Hill Deverill, Warminster, Wilts BA12 7EE. *T:* Sutton Veny 533.

BEARSTED, 3rd Viscount, *cr* 1925, of Maidstone; **Marcus Richard Samuel**, TD 1945; DL; Baron, *cr* 1921; Bt *cr* 1903; Chairman: 1928 Investment Trust Ltd, since 1948; Samuel Properties Ltd and subsidiary companies, since 1961; Hill Samuel & Co. (Jersey) Ltd, since 1962; Negit SA, Luxembourg, since 1966; Director: Hill Samuel Group Ltd, since 1933 (formerly Chairman); Sun Alliance & London Insurance Group, since 1949; Lloyds Bank Ltd and subsidiary companies, since 1963; *b* 1 June 1909; *e s* of 2nd Viscount and Dorothea (*d* 1949), *e d* of late E. Montefiore Micholls; *S* father 1948; *m* 1st, 1947, Elizabeth Heather (marr. diss. 1966), *er d* of G. Firmston-Williams; one *d* (and one *d* decd); 2nd, 1968, Mrs Jean Agnew Somerville, *d* of R. A. Wallace. *Educ:* Eton; New Coll., Oxford. Served War of 1939-45, Warwicks Yeomanry (Major), Middle East, Italy (wounded). Chm., Warwicks Hunt, 1960-69. Trustee and Chm. of Whitechapel Art Gallery, 1949-73. Chm., Bearsted Meml Hosp., 1948-; President: Jewish Home and Hosp. at Tottenham, 1948-; St Mary's Hosp. Med. Sch., 1964-; Dep. Chm., St Mary's Hosp., Paddington, 1958-74; Vice-Chm., Tottenham Gp HMC, 1949-74; Board Member: Eastman Dental Hosp., 1970-75; Kensington, Chelsea and Westminster AHA, 1973-; St John's Hosp. for Diseases of the Skin, 1975-. Pres., Nat. Soc. for Epileptics, Chalfont Colony, 1960-; Jt Pres., Barkingside Jewish Youth Centre, 1969-. DL Warwicks, 1950. *Recreations:* hunting, shooting, tapestry. *Heir: b* Hon. Peter Montefiore Samuel, *qv. Address:* 1 Eaton Close, SW1W 8JX. *T:* 01-730 4040; Upton House, Banbury, Oxon OX15 6HT. *T:* Edgehill 242. *Clubs:* White's, Cavalry and Guards.

BEASLEY, Prof. William Gerald, BA, PhD; FRHistS; FBA 1967; Professor of the History of the Far East, University of London, since 1954; *b* 1919; *m* 1955, Hazel Polwin; one *s. Educ:* Magdalen Coll. Sch., Brackley; University Coll., London. Served War, 1940-46, RNVR. Lecturer, Sch. of Oriental and African Studies, University of London, 1947. Mem., 1961-68, British Chm., 1964-68, Anglo-Japanese Mixed Cultural Commn. Vice-Pres., British Acad., 1974-75, Treasurer, 1975-. *Publications:* Great Britain and the opening of Japan, 1951; Select Documents on Japanese foreign policy, 1853-1868, 1955; The Modern History of Japan, 1963; The Meiji Restoration, 1972. *Address:* School of Oriental and African Studies, University of London, WC1E 7HP. *T:* 01-637 2388.

BEASLEY-MURRAY, George Raymond, DD, PhD; Lecturer, Southern Baptist Seminary, Louisville, Ky, since 1973; *b* 10 Oct. 1916; *s* of George Alfred Beasley; *m* 1942, Ruth Weston; three *s* one *d. Educ:* City of Leicester Boys' Sch.; Spurgeon's Coll. and King's Coll., London; Jesus Coll., Cambridge (MA). BD 1941, MTh 1945, PhD 1952, DD 1964, London; DD McMaster, Canada, 1973. Baptist Minister, Ilford, Essex, 1941-48; Cambridge, 1948-50; New Testament Lectr, Spurgeon's Coll., 1950-56; New Testament Prof., Baptist Theological Coll., Rüschlikon, Zürich, 1956-58; Principal, Spurgeon's Coll., 1958-73. Pres., Baptist Union of Great Britain and Ireland, 1968-69. *Publications:* Christ is Alive, 1947; Jesus and the Future, 1956; Preaching the Gospel from the Gospels, 1956; A Commentary on Mark Thirteen, 1957; Baptism in the New Testament, 1962; The Resurrection of Jesus Christ, 1964; Baptism Today and Tomorrow, 1966; Commentary on 2 Corinthians (Broadman Commentary), 1971; The Book of Revelation (New Century Bible), 1974. *Recreation:* music. *Address:* 2825 Lexington Road, Louisville, Kentucky 40206, USA.

BEATON, Arthur Charles, CMG 1954; Assistant Area General Manager, North Staffs Area, West Midlands Division, National Coal Board, 1955-61; National Coal Board Civil Defence Organiser, 1961, retired 1967; *b* 22 Aug. 1904; *s* of Samuel and Alice Ellen Beaton; *m* 1935, Jessie, *d* of Albert and Sarah Burrow; one *s* one *d. Educ:* Leeds Grammar Sch.; Keble Coll., Oxford. BA Litt. Hum. (Oxon), 1927; MA (Oxon), 1935. Sudan Political Service, 1927; District Comr, 1937; Dep. Gov., Equatoria, 1947; Dir, Local Govt Branch, 1950; Dep. Civil Sec., 1952; Actg Civil Sec., 1953; Permanent Under Sec. Ministry of the Interior, Sudan Government, 1954-55. 4th Class, Order of the Nile, 1941. *Publications:* Handbook, Equatoria Province, 1952. Articles in Sudan Notes and Records on anthropological subjects. *Recreations:* gardening, reading. *Address:* 50 Chiltern Road, Sutton, Surrey. *T:* 01-643 7493.

BEATON, Sir Cecil (Walter Hardy), Kt 1972; CBE 1957; photographer and designer; *b* London, 14 Jan. 1904; *s* of late Ernest Walter Hardy Beaton and Etty Sisson. *Educ:* Harrow; Cambridge. Exhibitions of photographs: Cooling Gallery, 1930; Nat. Portrait Gallery, 1968. Exhibitions of painting and stage designs: Redfern Gallery, 1936, 1958, 1965; Lefevre Gallery, 1966; Wright Hepburn Gallery, 1968. Writer; Photographer for Min. of Information; Designer of scenery and costumes for ballet and opera, and for many theatrical productions (London and New York stage); including sets and costumes for Lady Windermere's Fan, Quadrille, The Grass Harp; The School for Scandal (Comédie Française); costumes for: My Fair Lady (New York, London); *films:* Gigi, The Doctor's Dilemma, My Fair Lady. Légion d'Honneur, 1960. *Publications:* The Book of Beauty, 1930; Cecil Beaton's Scrapbook, 1937; Cecil Beaton's New York, 1939; My Royal Past, 1939 (rev. 1960); (with P. Quennell) Time Exposure, 1941; Air of Glory, 1941; Winged Squadrons, 1942; Near East, 1943; British Photographers, 1944; Far East, 1945; Time Exposure, 1946; Portrait of New York, 1949; Ashcombe, 1949; Ballet, 1951; Photobiography, 1951; (with Kenneth Tynan) Persona Grata, 1953; The Glass of Fashion, 1954; It Gives me Great Pleasure, 1955; The Face of the World, 1957; Japanese, 1959; The Wandering Years, 1961; Quail in Aspic, 1962; Royal Portraits, 1963; Images, 1963; Cecil Beaton's Fair Lady 1964; The Years Between, 1965; The Best of Beaton, 1968; My Bolivian Aunt, 1971; The Happy Years, 1972; The Strenuous Years, 1973; The Magic Image, 1975; The Restless Years, 1976. Photograph illustrations and drawings for many books including: History Under Fire (James Pope Hennessy), Bomber Command, The Importance of Being Earnest (Folio Society) 1960; author of play The Gainsborough Girls. *Recreations:* diaries, scrap-books, decoration, travel. *Address:* Reddish House, Broadchalke, near Salisbury. *T:* Broadchalke 211.

BEATON, Surg. Rear-Adm. Douglas Murdo, CB 1960; OBE 1940; retired as Medical Officer in Charge, RN Hospital, Plymouth, and Command Medical Officer, Plymouth Command (1957-60); *b* 27 May 1901; *s* of late Murdo Duncan Beaton, Kishorn, Ross-shire; *m* 1929, Violet, 2nd *d* of late David R. Oswald, MD, Kinross, Scotland; one *s* one *d. Educ:* Bristol Grammar Sch.; Edinburgh, Royal Colleges LDS 1923; LRCPE, LRCSE, LRFPS (Glas), 1924; Surg. Lieut Royal Navy, 1924; Surg. Comdr, 1936; Surg. Capt., 1948; Surg. Rear-Adm., 1957. Asst to Medical Dir-Gen., 1944-46; Medical Officer in Charge, HMHS Maine, 1947-48; MO i/c RN Sick Quarters, Shotley, 1949-51; Senior Medical Officer, Medical Section, RN Hospital, Plymouth, 1951-54; Asst to Medical Dir-Gen., Admiralty, 1954-57. QHP 1956-60; CStJ 1958. *Recreations:* golf, gardening, sailing. *Address:* Ardarroch, Auchterarder, Perthshire. *T:* Auchterarder 2329.

BEATON, Inspector James Wallace, GC 1974; Police Officer to The Princess Anne, since 1973; *b* St Fergus, Aberdeenshire, 16 Feb. 1943; *s* of J. A. Beaton and B. McDonald; *m* 1965, Anne C. Ballantyne; two *d. Educ:* Peterhead Acad., Aberdeenshire. Joined Metropolitan Police, 1962: Notting Hill, 1962-66; Sergeant, Harrow Road, 1966-71; Station Sergeant, Wembley, 1971-73; Royalty Protection Officer, 'A' Division, 1973-; Police Inspector, 1974. Director's Honor Award, US Secret Service, 1974. *Recreations:* reading, keeping fit. *Address:* 12 Embry Way, Stanmore, Mddx HA7 3AZ. *T:* 01-954 5054.

BEATON, John Angus, CB 1975; solicitor; lately Director, Scottish Courts Administration (Deputy Director, 1972-74); *b* 24 July 1909; *s* of Murdoch Beaton, TD, ISO, Inverness, and Barbara Mackenzie Beaton (*née* Rose); *m* 1942, Margaret

Florence McWilliam; two *s* one *d*. *Educ:* Inverness Royal Acad.; Edinburgh Univ. (BL). Scottish Office: Sen. Legal Asst, 1947; Asst Solicitor, 1960; Deputy Solicitor, 1966-72. Vice-Pres., 1960-63 and Hon. Mem., 1963-, Instn of Professional Civil Servants. *Publications:* articles in Encycl. of Scots Law and in legal jls. *Recreations:* curling, golf, fishing. *Address:* 2 Dryden Place, Edinburgh EH9 1RP. *T:* 031-667 3198. *Clubs:* Scottish Arts (Edinburgh); Gullane Golf; New Golf (St Andrews).

BEATTIE, Hon. Sir Alexander (Craig), Kt 1973; **Hon. Mr Justice Beattie;** President, Industrial Commission of New South Wales, Australia, since 1966 (Member, 1955); *b* 24 Jan. 1912; *e s* of Edmund Douglas and Amie Louisa Beattie; *m* 1944, Joyce Pearl Alder; two *s*. *Educ:* Fort Street High Sch., Sydney; Univ. of Sydney (BA, LLB). Admitted to NSW Bar, 1936. Served War of 1939-45: Captain, 2nd AIF, Royal Australian Armoured Corps, New Guinea and Borneo. Trustee, Royal Botanic Gardens and Govt Domain, Sydney, 1976-. *Recreations:* gardening, tennis. *Address:* Queen's Square, Sydney, NSW 2000, Australia. *Club:* Australian (Sydney).

BEATTIE, Prof. Arthur James, FRSE 1957; Professor of Greek at Edinburgh University, since 1951; Dean of the Faculty of Arts, 1963-65; *b* 28 June 1914, *e s* of Arthur John Rait Beattie. *Educ:* Montrose Academy; Aberdeen Univ.; Sidney Sussex Coll., Cambridge. 1st Cl. Hons Classics, Aberdeen, 1935; 1st Cl Classical Tripos, Cambridge, Part I, 1936, Part II, 1938; Wilson Travelling Fellowship, Aberdeen, 1938-40. Served War, 1940-45; RA, 1940-41; Intelligence Corps, 1941-45; Major GSO2; despatches, 1945; Staff Officer, Military Government, Germany, 1945; Fellow and Coll. Lectr, Sidney Sussex Coll., 1946-51; Faculty Asst Lectr and Univ. Lectr in Classics, Cambridge, 1946-51. Chm. Governors, Morrison's Acad., Crieff, 1962-75; Governor, Sedbergh Sch., 1967-. Comdr, Royal Order of the Phœnix (Greece), 1966. *Publications:* articles contributed to classical jls. *Recreations:* walking, bird-watching. *Club:* New (Edinburgh).

BEATTIE, Charles Noel, QC 1962; *b* 4 Nov. 1912; *s* of Michael William Beattie and Edith Beattie (*née* Lickfold); *m* ; one *s* three *d*. *Educ:* Lewes Grammar Sch. LLB (London). Admitted as a solicitor, 1938. Served War of 1939-45 (despatches), Capt. RASC. Called to the Bar, 1946; Bencher 1971. *Address:* 24 Old Buildings, Lincoln's Inn, WC2A 3UJ. *T:* 01-242 2744.

BEATTIE, Colin Panton, MA, MB, ChB, DPH; FRCPath; Professor of Bacteriology, University of Sheffield, 1946-67; now Emeritus Professor; *b* 11 Sept. 1902; *s* of James Beattie, MA, and Eleanor Anne Beattie; *m* 1937, May Hamilton Christison, BA, PhD; no *c*. *Educ:* Fettes Coll., Edinburgh; University of Edinburgh. House appointments in Royal Infirmary, Edinburgh, and Royal Northern Infirmary, Inverness, 1928-30; Asst in Bacteriology Dept., University of Edinburgh, 1930-32; Rockefeller Travelling Fellow, 1932-33; Lecturer in Bacteriology Dept, University of Edinburgh, 1933-37; Prof. of Bacteriology in The Royal Faculty of Medicine of Iraq and Dir of Govt Bacteriology Laboratory, Baghdad, 1937-46. *Publications:* various papers on bacteriological and parasitological subjects. *Recreation:* gardening. *Address:* 39 Stumperlowe Crescent Road, Sheffield S10 3PR. *T:* 302158.

BEATTIE, Brigadier Joseph Hamilton, CBE 1945; DSO 1944; *b* 29 Sept. 1903; *s* of late Malcolm Hamilton Beattie and Maria Isabel Beattie; *m* 1938, Margaret Antonia, *er d* of J. R. Makeig-Jones, CBE, Budleigh Salterton, Devon; three *s* (and one *s* decd), three *d*. *Educ:* Rugby; RMA Woolwich, 2nd Lieut RA, 1924; ADC to Viceroy of India, 1933-34; served Mohmand Campaign, NWF, India, 1935; served War of 1939-45; France, Belgium, Holland, Germany and Burma (despatches twice); Lieut-Col 1942, Brig. 1945; retd, 1956. *Recreations:* shooting, fishing. *Address:* San Anard, Zabbar, Malta.

BEATTIE, Thomas Brunton, OBE 1968; HM Diplomatic Service; Counsellor, British Embassy, Rome, since 1977; *b* 17 March 1924; *s* of Joseph William Beattie and Jessie Dewar (*née* Brunton), Rutherglen; *m* 1956, Paula Rahkola; one *d*. *Educ:* Rutherglen Acad.; Pembroke Coll., Cambridge. MA (Hons). Served RAF, 1943-47. Jt Press Reading Service, British Embassy, Moscow, 1947; Finnish Secretariat, Helsinki, 1951; FO, 1954; Second Sec., Madrid, 1956; FO, 1960; First Sec., Athens, 1964; First Sec., later Counsellor, FCO, 1969. *Recreations:* hill walking, local Scottish history, music. *Address:* Cairnside, Kirkland of Glencairn, Moniaive, Dumfriesshire DG3 4HD. *Clubs:* Carlton, Travellers'; Royal Scottish Automobile (Glasgow).

BEATTIE, Prof. William, CBE 1963; Librarian, National Library of Scotland, 1953-70; Director, Institute for Advanced Studies in the Humanities, Edinburgh University, 1972-77; *b* 27 Aug. 1903; *s* of William Beattie and Elizabeth Vallance; *m* 1932, Agnes Howie, *d* of Henry Wood; two *d* (and one *d* decd). *Educ:* Jedburgh Grammar Sch.; George Watson's Coll.; University of Edinburgh. Asst Librarian, University of Edinburgh, 1926-30; Keeper of Printed Books, National Library of Scotland, 1931-53. Visiting Fellow, Folger Library, 1957. Lyell Reader in Bibliography, University of Oxford, 1964-65. David Murray Lectr, Glasgow Univ., 1976. Chm., Standing Conference of National and University Libraries, 1964-67. Vice-Pres., 1963-75, Pres., 1975-77, Bibliographical Soc.; Pres., Scottish Soc. for Northern Studies, 1976-. Hon. LLD St Andrews, 1957; Hon. LittD, Trinity Coll., Dublin, 1967; Hon. Prof., Univ. of Edinburgh, 1967. St Olav's Medal (Norway), 1977. *Publications:* The Chepman and Myllar Prints, The Taill of Rauf Coilyear (facsimiles, with introductions), 1950, 1966; (with H. W. Meikle) selection of Robert Burns, 1946, rev. edn, 1972; selection of Border Ballads, 1952; articles in Edinburgh Bibliographical Soc. Transactions. *Address:* 7 South Gillsland Road, Edinburgh EH10 5DE. *T:* 031-447 4835.

BEATTIE, William John Hunt Montgomery, MA Cantab; MD, FRCS, FRCOG, FRCGP; Consultant Gynæcologist and Obstetric Surgeon, St Bartholomew's Hospital; Gynæcologist: Leatherhead Hospital; Florence Nightingale Hospital; retired. *Educ:* Cambridge Univ.; London Univ. MRCS; LRCP 1927; BCh (Cantab) 1928; FRCS 1929; MB 1930; MD 1933; FRCOG 1942; Examiner: Central Midwives' Board; Univs. of Oxford, Cambridge and London (Obst. and Gynæcol.); Conjoint Board (Midwifery and Gynæcol.). *Publications:* (jt) Diseases of Women by Ten Teachers, 1941; articles in medical journals. *Address:* Ivy Cottage, Reigate Heath, Surrey.

BEATTY, 3rd Earl *cr* 1919; **David Beatty;** Viscount Borodale of Wexford, Baron Beatty of the North Sea and of Brooksby, 1919; *b* 21 Nov. 1946; *s* of 2nd Earl Beatty, DSC, and Dorothy Rita, *d* of late M. J. Furey, New Orleans, USA; *S* father, 1972; *m* 1971, Ann, *d* of A. Please, Wokingham; one *s*. *Educ:* Eton. *Heir: s* Viscount Borodale, *qv*. *Address:* c/o House of Lords, SW1.

BEATTY, (Alfred) Chester; Chairman: Selection Trust Ltd; Australian Selection (Pty) Ltd; Consolidated African Selection Trust Ltd; Seltrust Investments Ltd; Seltrust Iron Ore Ltd; Selcast Exploration Ltd; Selco Mining Corp. Ltd; Western Selcast (Pty) Ltd; and other companies; Director: Tsumeb Corp. Ltd; Unisel Gold Mines Ltd; and other companies; *b* 1907; *o s* of late Sir (Alfred) Chester Beatty and late Grace Madeline, *d* of Alfred Rickard, Denver, USA; *m* 1st, 1933, Pamela (marr. diss. 1936; she *d* 1957), *o d* of Captain George Belas; one *d*; 2nd, 1937, Enid (marr. diss. 1950), *d* of S. H. Groome, Golfe Juan, France; 3rd, 1953, Helen Gertrude, *widow* of Roger Casalis de Pury. *Educ:* Eton; Trinity Coll., Cambridge. Past-Pres., Overseas Mining Assoc.; Jt Master, Ashford Valley Foxhounds, 1927-31, Master, 1931-53. FID. *Address:* Owley, Wittersham, Kent; 76 Park Street, W1. *Club:* Royal Yacht Squadron.

BEAUCHAMP, 8th Earl, *cr* 1815; **William Lygon,** DL, JP; Baron Beauchamp, 1806; Viscount Elmley, 1815; *b* 3 July 1903; *e s* of 7th Earl and Lady Lettice Grosvenor (*d* 1936), *d* of late Earl Grosvenor and *sister* of 2nd Duke of Westminster, GCVO, DSO; *S* father, 1938; *m* 1936, Else Doronville de la Cour, MBE 1944, Order of the Dannebrog (RDI) 1964, Grand Commander of the Dannebrog, 1970, DStJ 1957, *widow* of Director C. de la Cour. *Educ:* Eton; Magdalen Coll., Oxford. MP (L) Norfolk E, 1929-31 (LNat), 1931-38. Parliamentary Private Sec. to late Lord Hore-Belisha, in four Government Departments, 1931-38; DL 1948, JP 1941, CC 1940-52, Worcs. Pres., Three Counties Show, 1964. Served in RAOC Aug. 1941-45 at home and in Italy. *Heir:* none. *Address:* Madresfield Court, Great Malvern, Worcs. *T:* Malvern 3024; 8 Halkin Place, SW1. *T:* 01-235 5665. *See also Sir Richard Cotterell.*

BEAUCHAMP, Charles Edward; Acting Board Member for Finance and Corporate Planning, Post Office Corporation, since 1977; *b* 1 Feb. 1922; *s* of late John Sampson Beauchamp and Alice Kathleen Beauchamp (*née* Kirby); *m* 1943, Elsie Edith Cull; two *s* one *d*. *Educ:* Owen School, EC1. Various finance posts, Accountant General's Dept, GPO, 1929-67; Financial Advr, PO Nat. Data Processing Service, 1967; Director: PO Central Finance Dept, 1970; Postal Finance and Management Services Dept, 1975; Sen. Dir, PO Central Finance Dept, 1977. *Address:* 39 The Avenue, Potters Bar, Herts EN6 1ED. *T:* Potters Bar 56879.

BEAUCHAMP, Sir Christopher Radstock Proctor-, 9th Bt *cr* 1744; solicitor with Gilbert H. Stephens & Sons, Exeter; *b* 30 Jan. 1935; *s* of Rev. Sir Ivor Cuthbert Proctor-Beauchamp, 8th Bt, and Caroline Muriel, *d* of late Frank Densham; *S* father,

1971; *m* 1965, Rosalind Emily Margot, 3rd *d* of G. P. Wainwright, St Leonards-on-Sea; two *s* one *d. Educ:* Rugby; Trinity College, Cambridge (MA). *Heir: s* Charles Barclay Proctor-Beauchamp, *b* 7 July 1969. *Address:* The White House, Harpford, near Sidmouth, East Devon.

BEAUCHAMP, Sir Douglas Clifford (commonly known as **Sir Peter**), 2nd Bt, *cr* 1918; *b* 11 March 1903; *s* of Sir Frank Beauchamp, 1st Bt, and Mabel Constance (*d* 1957), *e d* of James Norman Bannon, Kent; *S* father 1950; *m* 1st, 1926, Nancy (who obtained a divorce, 1933), *o d* of Laurence E. Moss, Sydney, NSW; 2nd, 1933, Pamela Dorothy May Chandor (*d* 1971); 3rd, 1972, M. Elizabeth, *widow* of J. H. Tilbury. *Educ:* Eton. *Heir:* none. *Address:* The Pebbles, Budleigh Salterton, Devon. *T:* Budleigh Salterton 3197.

BEAUCHAMP, Dr Guy; Manipulative Surgeon since 1935; Consultant: London Transport Friendly Society; Lloyd Memorial Society; Printers Medical Aid Fund; *b* 30 July 1902; *s* of Thomas and Elizabeth Beauchamp, Dudley, Worcs; *m* 1943, Hon. Susan Silence North; *yr d* of late Hon. Dudley North and *sister* of 13th Baron North; three *d. Educ:* Dudley Grammar Sch.; Birmingham Univ. MB, ChB, MRCS, LRCP, FICS, FRSocMed, Mem. Brit. Assoc. of Manip. Med. Hon. Manipulative Surgeon, Charterhouse Clinic, 1938-48; Hon. Physician: Weir Hosp., 1942-48; British Home and Hosp. for Incurables, 1942-70. Kt of Grace, SMO Malta, 1964; Gold Medal of Honour, Soc. d'Encouragement au Progrés, Paris, 1974. *Publications:* (jtly, play) Death on the Table, 1938; (jtly) Honourable Jeux des Gentilhommes, 1944; numerous contrib. med. jls and text books. *Recreations:* fishing, swimming, theatre. *Address:* 38 Harley House, Marylebone Road, NW1 5HF. *T:* 01-935 3088; (home) 19 Beaumont Street, W1 1FF. *T:* 01-935 5958. *Club:* Buck's.

BEAUCHAMP, Sir Peter; *see* Beauchamp, Sir D. C.

BEAUCLERK, family name of **Duke of St Albans.**

BEAUFORT, 10th Duke of, *cr* 1682; **Henry Hugh Arthur FitzRoy Somerset,** KG 1937; PC 1936; GCVO 1930; JP; Royal Victorian Chain, 1953; Baron Botetourt, 1305, confirmed, 1803; Baron Herbert of Raglan, Chepstow, and Gower, 1506; Earl of Worcester, 1514; Marquess of Worcester, 1642; late Royal Horse Guards; Master of the Horse since 1936; Lord-Lieutenant of Gloucestershire, since 1974 (Lord Lieutenant of County of Gloucester and Bristol, 1931-74); Hon. Colonel: Royal Gloucestershire Hussars, TA, 1925-69, T&AVR, 1969-71; A and C Squadrons, The Wessex Yeomanry, T&AVR, since 1972; *b* 4 April 1900; *o s* of 9th Duke and Louise Emily (*d* 1945), *d* of William H. Harford of Oldown, Almondsbury, Glos, and *widow* of Baron Carlo de Tuyll; *S* father, 1924; *m* 1923, Lady Mary Cambridge, *er d* of 1st Marquess of Cambridge. *Educ:* Eton; Sandhurst. Chancellor, Univ. of Bristol, 1966-70. High Steward: Bristol, 1925-; Gloucester, 1925-; Tewkesbury, 1948-. Received Freedom of City of Gloucester 1945. KStJ 1935. *Heir: cousin* David Robert Somerset [*b* 23 Feb. 1928; *m* 1950, Lady Caroline Jane Thynne, *o d* of 6th Marquess of Bath, *qv*; three *s* one *d*]. *Address:* Badminton, Glos GL9 1DB. *TA:* Badminton. *Club:* Turf.

BEAUMAN, Wing Commander Eric Bentley; Librarian, Royal United Service Institution, 1952-57; *b* 7 Feb. 1891; *yr s* of late Bentley Martin Beauman; *m* 1940, Katharine Burgoyne, MA, *yr d* of late F. W. Jones; one *s. Educ:* Malvern Coll.; Geneva Univ.; Royal Aero Flying Certificate, 1913; served European war, 1914-18: commnd RNAS Aug. 1914; Anti-Submarine patrols, Home and Aegean; Home Defence and flying instruction: comd seaplane stations at Dundee and Newhaven (despatches). Major, RAF 1918; psa 1922-23 (first course of RAF Staff College); psc 1929-30; instructor at RAF Staff Coll., 1932-33; retd, 1938; Air Ministry, 1938-51. War of 1939-45; RAF liaison officer with BBC. Expeditions: Mount Kamet, Himalaya, 1931; Coast Range of British Columbia, 1934 (paper to RGS on Coast Range Crossing); climbed the Matterhorn 5 times. Pres. Alpine Ski Club, 1933-35; Hon. Librarian, Alpine Club, 1947-58. Vice-Pres. RAF Mountaineering Assoc. 1951-; Chm., Touring and Mountaineering Cttee of Ski Club of Gt Britain, 1952-54. Broadcasts on many occasions. *Publications:* compiled: Winged Words, 1941 (Book Soc. Choice); The Airmen Speak, 1941; (with Cecil Day Lewis) compiled: We Speak from the Air, 1942; Over to You, 1943; chapters in: Living Dangerously, 1936; Travellers' Tales, 1945; The Boys' Country Book, 1955. Contributor to The Times, The Field, The Listener, National Review, The Geographical Magazine, Alpine Jl, RUSI Jl, British Ski Year Book, Dictionary of National Biography, Encyclopædia Britannica. *Recreations:* mountaineering, exploring, ski-ing, fishing. *Address:* 59 Chester Row, SW1W

8JL. *T:* 01-730 9038. *Clubs:* Alpine, Royal Air Force, Army and Navy, Society of Authors.

BEAUMARCHAIS, Jacques Delarüe Caron de; Hon. GCVO; Commandeur de la Légion d'Honneur 1976; Commandeur de l'Ordre National du Mérite 1968; Ambassadeur de France; French Ambassador to the Court of St James's, 1972-77; *b* Bayonne (Pyrénées Atlantiques), 16 April 1913; *s* of Maurice Delarüe Caron de Beaumarchais, diplomat, and Louise Lagelouze; *m* 1944, Marie-Alice Le Couteulx de Caumont; one *s. Educ:* Ecole des Roches; Faculty of Law, Paris Univ. Licencié en droit, Diplômé de l'Ecole Libre des Sciences Politiques. Attaché d'Ambassade, 1942; Mem. French Delegn to Germany Armistice Commn for Economic Affairs, 1942; escaped from France, 1942; Head of section, Foreign Affairs Commissariat, Algiers, 1943; Second Sec., Rome (Quirinal), 1945; seconded to Commissariat-Général for German and Austrian Affairs, 1946; First Secretary, 1951; Counsellor, 1952; Counsellor, French Embassy, London, 1953; Private Sec. to Minister of Foreign Affairs, 1958; Minister Plenipotentiary, 1959; Minister-Counsellor, Moscow, 1962; Head of European Dept, Min. of Foreign Affairs, 1962; Principal Private Sec. to Minister of Foreign Affairs, 1964; Head of Political Affairs Dept, Min. of Foreign Affairs, 1965. Hon. Fellow, St Antony's Coll., Oxford, 1972. Officier de la Légion d'Honneur 1965. *Address:* 5 Avenue Franklin-Roosevelt, 75008 Paris, France. *Clubs:* Travellers', Beefsteak, Garrick.

BEAUMONT, family name of **Viscount Allendale** and **Baron Beaumont of Whitley.**

BEAUMONT OF WHITLEY, Baron *cr* 1967 (Life Peer), of Child's Hill; **Timothy Wentworth Beaumont,** MA (Oxon); Managing Director, Holystone Productions Ltd, since 1974; *b* 22 Nov. 1928; *o s* of Major and Hon. Mrs M. W. Beaumont; *m* 1955, Mary Rose Wauchope; two *s* two *d. Educ:* Gordonstoun; Christ Church, Oxford; Westcott House, Cambridge. Asst Chaplain, St John's Cathedral, Hong Kong, 1955-57; Vicar, Christ Church Kowloon Tong, Hong Kong, 1957-59; Hon. Curate, St Stephen's Rochester Row, London, 1960-63; resigned orders, 1973. Editor: Prism, 1960-63 and 1964; New Outlook, 1964, 1972-74; Chm., Studio Vista Books Ltd, 1963-68; Proprietor of New Christian, 1965-70. Food Correspondent, Illustrated London News, 1976-. Liberal Party Organisation: Jt Hon. Treas., 1962-63; Chm., Liberal Publications Dept, 1963-64; Head of Org., 1965-66; Chm., Liberal Party's Org. Cttee, 1966; Chm., Liberal Party, 1967-68; Pres., Liberal Party, 1969-70; Alternate Mem., Assemblies of Council of Europe and WEU, 1973-77, Leader of Liberal Delegn, 1977-. Pres., British Fedn of Film Socs, 1973-. Chairman: Albany Trust, 1969-71; Inst. of Res. into Mental and Multiple Handicap, 1971-73. Mem., Exec. Cttee, British Council, 1974-. *Publications:* (ed) Modern Religious Verse, 1965; ed and contrib., The Liberal Cookbook, 1972; (ed) New Christian Reader, 1974; (ed) The Selective Ego: the diaries of James Agate, 1976. *Address:* 1 Hampstead Square, NW3. *Clubs:* Beefsteak, National Liberal.

BEAUMONT, Sir George Howland Francis, 12th Bt, *cr* 1661; late Lieutenant 60th Rifles; *b* 24 Sept. 1924; *s* of 11th Bt and Renée Muriel, 2nd *d* of late Maj.-Gen. Sir Edward Northey, GCMG, CB; *S* father 1933; *m* 1949, Barbara Singleton (marr. annulled, 1951); *m* 1963, Henrietta Anne, *d* of late Dr A. Waymouth and of Mrs J. Rodwell, Riverside Cottage, Donnington, Berks; twin *d. Educ:* Stowe Sch. *Address:* Duntrune Nurseries, Deddington Mill, Deddington, Oxfordshire. *T:* Deddington 277. *Club:* Lansdowne.

BEAUMONT, Herbert Christopher, MBE 1948; **His Honour Judge Beaumont;** a Circuit Judge, since 1972; *b* 3 June 1912; *s* of late Gerald Beaumont, MC, and Gwendolene Beaumont (*née* Haworth); *m* 1940, Helen Margaret Gordon Smail, *d* of William Mitchell Smail; one *s* two *d. Educ:* Uppingham Sch.; Worcester Coll., Oxford. Indian Civil and Political Services, 1936-48; Foreign Office, 1948-52. Called to the Bar, Inner Temple, 1951; Metropolitan Magistrate, 1962-72. Chm. of the London Juvenile Courts, 1964; Dep. Chm., North Riding QS, 1966-71. Mem., Parole Bd, 1974-76. *Recreations:* travel in Europe, bridge. *Address:* Minskip Lodge, Boroughbridge, Yorks. *T:* Boroughbridge 2365. *Clubs:* Brooks's; Yorkshire (York).

BEAUMONT, (John) Michael; Seigneur of Sark since 1974; *b* 20 Dec. 1927; *s* of late Lionel (Buster) Beaumont and Enid Beaumont (*née* Ripley); *m* 1956, Diana (*née* La Trobe-Bateman); two *s. Educ:* Loughborough Coll. (DLC). Aircraft Design Engr, 1952-70; Chief Techn. Engr, Beagle Aircraft, 1969-70; Design Engr, BAC GW Div., 1970-75. *Recreations:* theatre, music, sailing. *Heir: s* Christopher Beaumont, *b* 4 Feb. 1957. *Address:* La Seigneurie, Sark. *T:* Sark 17.

BEAUMONT, Sir Richard Ashton, KCMG 1965 (CMG 1955); OBE 1949; HM Diplomatic Service, retired; Director in Morocco, Michael Rice & Co.; *b* 29 Dec. 1912; *s* of A. R. Beaumont, FRCS, Uppingham, and Evelyn Frances (*née* Rendle); *m* 1942, Alou, *d* of M. Camran, Istanbul; one *d. Educ:* Repton; Oriel Coll., Oxford. Joined HM Consular Service, 1936; posted Beirut, 1936; Damascus, 1938. Served War, 1941-44. Foreign Office, 1945; Mosul, 1946; Jerusalem, 1948; Foreign Office, 1949; Caracas, Venezuela, 1950; Baghdad, 1953; Imperial Defence Coll., 1958; Head of Arabian Department, Foreign Office, 1959; Ambassador: to Morocco, 1961-65; to Iraq, 1965-67; Dep. Under-Sec. of State, FO, 1967-69; Ambassador to the Arab Republic of Egypt, 1969-72. Dir-Gen., Middle East Assoc., 1973-77; Chm., Arab British Centre, 1976-77. Governor, SOAS, 1973-. *Recreations:* riding, shooting, golf. *Address:* 18 rue Zalagh, Agdal, Rabat, Morocco. *T:* Rabat 71243 71248. *Telex:* Morocco 31824 M Agdal. *Club:* United Oxford & Cambridge University.

BEAUREPAIRE, Ian Francis, CMG 1967; Chairman and Chief Executive, Olympic Consolidated Industries Ltd, since 1959; *b* 14 Sept. 1922; *s* of late Sir Frank and Lady Beaurepaire; *m* 1946, Beryl Edith Bedggood; two *s. Educ:* Carey Grammar Sch., Scotch Coll., Melbourne; Royal Melbourne Inst. of Technology. Served RAAF (Flying Officer), 1942-45. Man. Dir, Beaurepaire Tyre Service Pty Ltd, 1953-55; Gen. Man., The Olympic Tyre & Rubber Co. Pty Ltd, 1955-61. Mem., Melbourne Underground Rail Loop Authority, 1971-. Member: Melbourne City Council, 1956-75 (Lord Mayor of Melbourne, 1965-67); Management Cttee of Royal Victorian Eye and Ear Hosp., 1966-. *Recreations:* golf, fishing, sailing. *Address:* PO Box 1, West Footscray, Victoria 3012, Australia. *Clubs:* Athenæum, Naval and Military, Melbourne (Melbourne); Peninsula Country Golf (Frankston).

BEAUVOIR, Simone de; French author; *b* Paris, 9 Jan. 1908; *d* of Georges Bertrand and Françoise (*née* Brasseur). *Educ:* Institut Catholique; Institut Sainte-Marie; Univ. of Paris. Taught, 1931-43. Prix Goncourt, France, 1954. *Publications:* L'Invitée, 1943 (trans. She Came to Stay, 1949); Pyrrhus et Cinéas (essay), 1944; Le Sang des autres, 1944 (trans. The Blood of Others, 1948); Les Bouches Inutiles (play), 1945; Tous les hommes sont mortels, 1947 (trans. All Men are Mortal, 1955); Pour une morale de l'ambiguité (essay), 1947; L'Amérique au jour le jour, 1948 (trans. America Day by Day, 1952); L'Existentialisme et la sagesse des nations (essay), 1948; Le Deuxième Sexe, 1949: vol. I, Les Faits et les myths; vol. II, L'Expérience vécue; Faut-il Brûler Sade?, 1951 (trans. Must We Burn Sade?, 1963); Les Mandarins, 1954 (Prix Goncourt; trans. The Mandarins, 1957); Privilèges (essay), 1955; La Longue marche (essay on China), 1957 (trans. The Long March, 1958); Mémoires d'une jeune fille rangée, 1958 (trans. The Memoirs of a Dutiful Daughter, 1959); La Force de L'âge, 1960 (trans. The Prime of Life, 1963); Brigitte Bardot, 1960; (with G. Halimi) Djamila Boupacha, 1963; La Force des choses, 1963 (trans. Force of Circumstance, 1965); Une mort très douce, 1964 (trans. A Very Easy Death, 1966); Les Belles Images, 1966; La Femme Rompue, 1968 (trans. The Woman Destroyed, 1969); La Vieillesse, 1970 (trans. Old Age, 1972); Tout Compte fait, 1972 (trans. All Said and Done, 1974). *Address:* 11 bis rue Schoelcher, Paris 14e, France.

BEAVAN, family name of **Baron Ardwick.**

BEAVEN, John Lewis, MVO 1974; HM Diplomatic Service; Counsellor (Economic and Commercial), British High Commission, Lagos, since 1975; *b* 30 July 1930; *s* of Charles and Margaret Beaven; *m* 1960, Jane Beeson (marr. diss.); one *s* one *d* ; *m* 1975, Jean McComb Campbell. *Educ:* Newport (Gwent) High Sch. BoT, 1946; RAF, 1948-50; Asst Trade Comr, British High Commn, Karachi, 1956-60; Second Secretary (Commercial), British High Commn, Freetown, 1961-64; First Secretary (Commercial): British High Commn, Nicosia, 1964-66; Nairobi, 1966-68; FCO, 1969-72; Head of Chancery, British Embassy, Jakarta, 1972-74. *Recreations:* music, bridge, riding. *Address:* 30 Boulters Gardens, Maidenhead, Berks. *T:* 32947; Scannell Road, Ghent, NY 12075, USA. *T:* 518-392-2152. *Club:* Reform.

BEAVERBROOK, Barony of (*cr* 1917, of Beaverbrook, New Brunswick and Cherkley, Surrey); title disclaimed by 2nd Baron; *see under* Aitken, Sir (John William) Max, 2nd Bt.

BEAVIS, David, CBE 1976; retired; Chairman, West Midlands Gas Region (formerly West Midlands Gas Board), 1968-77; Part-time Member, British Gas Corporation, 1973-77; *b* 12 Dec. 1913; *s* of David Beavis; *m* 1946, Vera, *d* of F. C. Todd; one *s* one *d. Educ:* Whitehill Secondary Sch.; Royal Technical Coll., Glasgow (now Strathclyde Univ.). Dep. Engineer and Manager, Helensburgh Town Council Gas Dept, 1935-41; Asst Engineer, Camb. Univ. and Town Gas Light Co., 1942-47; Dep. Engineer and Manager, Edin. Corp. Gas Dept, 1947-49; Divisional Gen. Man. Edin. and SE Div., and subseq. Area Manager, Scottish Gas Bd, 1949-64; Mem. Scottish Gas Bd, 1962-64; Dep. Chm., Eastern Gas Bd, 1964-68. Member: W Midlands Economic Planning Council; Council, Univ. of Aston in Birmingham. *Publications:* technical papers presented to Engineering Instns. *Recreations:* technological education, golf. *Address:* 1 Sandal Rise, Solihull, West Midlands. *T:* 021-705 0455. *Club:* Anglo-Belgian.

BEAVIS, Maj.-Gen. Leslie Ellis, CB 1952; CBE 1942; DSO 1918; Australian Staff Corps; *b* 1895; *s* of late H. C. Beavis, Bathurst, New South Wales; *m* Ethel (decd), *d* of L. Blumer, Hunter's Hill, NSW; one *s* one *d*. Served European War, 1915-18 (despatches twice, DSO); psc, pac; War of 1939-45, DOS, AIF, Middle East, 1940-42 (CBE); Master General of the Ordnance HQ, AMF, 1942-46; Defence Dept, 1946-52; High Commissioner for Australia in Pakistan, 1952-54. *Club:* Naval and Military (Melbourne).

BEBBINGTON, Bernard Nicolas, CBE 1969 (OBE 1955); QPM 1962; Adviser to Home Office Community Development Project, 1970-72; *b* 23 Nov. 1910; *yr s* of Canon John Henry and Mabel Edith Bebbington; *m* 1936, Daphne Frizelle Drury; two *s. Educ:* Sutton Valence Sch.; Jesus Coll., Cambridge. Joined Metropolitan Police, 1932; attended Hendon Police Coll., 1935-36; apptd Chief Constable of Cambridge, 1944; Sec. of Assoc. of Chief Police Officers, 1961-63; HM Inspector of Constabulary, 1963-70; Dir, Home Office Police Research and Develt Branch, 1965-69; Home Office Adviser on Police Management Services, 1969-70; retd, 1970. Hon. MA Cantab 1963. OStJ 1959. *Publications:* articles and broadcasts on Police. Several children's books including The Policeman, 1952. *Recreations:* painting, writing. *Address:* 21 Riverside, Shoreham-by-Sea, East Sussex BN4 5RU; 24600 Vanxains, Dordogne, France. *Club:* Pitt (Cambridge).

BECHER, Rear-Adm. Otto Humphrey, CBE 1961; DSO 1950; DSC 1940, and Bar, 1944; retd; *b* 13 Sept. 1908; *m* 1935, Valerie Chisholm Baird; three *s. Educ:* Harvey State Sch.; RAN Coll. Served War of 1939-45 (DSC and Bar): in Norwegian waters, Atlantic, Mediterranean, Indian and Pacific Oceans. Capt. of HMAS: Quickmatch, 1944-45; Warramunga, 1950-51; Vengeance, 1954-55; idc 1956; Capt. of HMAS Melbourne, 1957-58; Deputy Chief of Naval Staff, Australia, 1959-61; Head of Australian Joint Services Staff, London, 1962-63; Flag Officer Comdg Australian Fleet, 1964; Flag Officer in Charge, East Australian Area, 1965-66; Dir-Gen. of Recruiting, 1966-69. Officer, Legion of Merit (USA), 1950. *Address:* 3 Moore Street, Vaucluse, NSW 2030, Australia. *Recreations:* gardening, golf, tennis. *Club:* Royal Sydney Golf.

BECHER, Major Sir William Fane Wrixon-, 5th Bt, *cr* 1831; MC 1943; Temp. Major, Rifle Brigade (SRO); *b* 7 Sept. 1915; *o s* of Sir Eustace W. W. W. Becher, 4th Bt, and Hon. Constance Gough-Calthorpe, *d* of 6th Baron Calthorpe; *S* father, 1934; *m* 1st, 1946, Vanda (marr. diss. 1960; she *m* 1962, Rear-Adm. Viscount Kelburn, now 9th Earl of Glasgow, *qv*), *d* of 4th Baron Vivian; one *s* one *d* ; 2nd, 1960, Hon. Mrs Yvonne Mostyn. *Educ:* Harrow; Magdalene Coll., Cambridge. Served War of 1939-45. Western Desert and Tunisian Campaigns, 1940-43 (MC, wounded twice); Italian Campaign, 1944. *Recreations:* golf and cricket. *Heir: s* John William Michael Wrixon-Becher, *b* 29 Sept. 1950. *Address:* 16 Wilton Place, SW1. *Clubs:* MCC, White's.

BECK, Prof. Arnold Hugh William, BSc (Eng), MA; Professor of Engineering, since 1966, Head of Electrical Division, since 1971, University of Cambridge; Fellow of Corpus Christi College, Cambridge, since 1962; *y s* of Major Hugh Beck and Diana L. Beck; *m* 1947, Katharine Monica, *y* of S. K. Ratcliffe; no *c. Educ:* Gresham's Sch., Holt; University Coll., London. Research Engr, Henry Hughes & Sons, 1937-41; seconded to Admty Signal Estab., 1941-45; Standard Telephones & Cables, 1947-58; Lectr, Cambridge Univ., 1958-64; Reader in Electrical Engrg, 1964-66. FIEEE 1959. *Publications:* Velocity Modulated Thermionic Tubes, 1948; Thermionic Valves, 1953; Space-charge Waves, 1958; Words and Waves, 1967; (with H. Ahmed) Introduction to Physical Electronics, 1968; Handbook of Vacuum Physics, Vol. 2, Parts 5 and 6, 1968; Statistical Mechanics, Fluctuations and Noise, 1976; papers in Jl IEE, Inst. Radio Engrs, etc. *Address:* 12 Rutherford Road, Cambridge. *T:* Trumpington 3324.

BECK, Sir Edgar (Charles), Kt 1975; CBE 1967; Chairman: John Mowlem & Company Ltd; SGB Group Ltd; *b* 11 May 1911; *s* of

Edgar Bee Beck and Nellie Stollard Beck (*née* Osborne); *m* 1933, Mary Agnes Sorapure (marr. diss. 1972); three *s* two *d*; *m* 1972, Anne Teresa Corbould. *Educ:* Lancing Coll.; Jesus Coll., Cambridge (MA). Joined John Mowlem & Co. Ltd as Engineer, 1933: Dir 1940; Man. Dir 1958; Chm. 1961. Director: Scaffolding Great Britain Ltd, 1942 (Chm., 1958-); Builders' Accident Insce Ltd, 1959, Dep. Chm., 1969; Mem., ECGD Adv. Council, 1964-69; President, Fedn of Civil Engrg Contractors, 1971-75 (Chm., 1958-59); Chairman: Export Gp for the Constructional Industries, 1959-63; Brit. Hosps Export Council, 1964-75. Under-writing Mem. of Lloyd's, 1955-. FICE. *Recreations:* golf, salmon fishing. *Address:* 13 Eaton Place, SW1. *T:* 01-235 7455; Logierait House, Ballinluig, Perthshire. *T:* Ballinluig 228. *Clubs:* Buck's; Royal and Ancient Golf (St Andrews); Swinley Forest Golf.

BECK, Most Rev. George Andrew, AA; *b* 28 May 1904; 2nd *s* of late P. T. Beck, journalist. *Educ:* Clapham Coll. and St Michael's Coll., Hitchin. Priest, 1927; BA Hons (History), London, 1934. Staff St Michael's Coll., Hitchin, until 1941, Headmaster, 1941-44; Headmaster, The Becket Sch., Nottingham, 1944-48. Consecrated Titular Bishop of Tigia and Coadjutor Bishop of Brentwood by Cardinal Griffin, 1948; Bishop of Brentwood, 1951-55; Bishop of Salford, 1955-64; Archbishop of Liverpool and Metropolitan of Northern Province, 1964-76. Chm. Catholic Education Council, 1949-70. Hon. LLD Manchester, 1967. *Publications:* Assumptionist Spirituality, 1936; The Family and the Future, 1948; (ed. with A. C. F. Beales) Eng. translation of Gonella's The Papacy and World Peace, 1944; (ed) The English Catholics 1850-1950, 1950; occasional contributions to the Tablet and Clergy Review. *Address:* Upholland Northern Institute, Upholland College, Skelmersdale, Lancs WN8 0PZ. *T:* Upholland 622286. *Clubs:* Athenæum, Royal Automobile.

BECK, James Henry John; Director of Industries and Supply, Prison Department, Home Office, since 1976; *b* 5 April 1920; *s* of James Henry and Elizabeth Kate Beck; *m* 1942, Doris Peacock; two *d*. *Educ:* Polytechnic Secondary Sch., Regent Street, W1. Entered Home Office as Clerical Officer, 1937; HM Forces, 1939; returned to Home Office as Executive Officer, 1946; Higher Exec. Officer, 1950; Sen. Exec. Officer, 1958; Principal, 1963; Asst Sec., 1968. *Address:* Scarlet Oaks, Ridgway, Pyrford, Woking, Surrey GU22 8PN. *T:* Byfleet 46064.

BECK, John Melliar Adams; *see* Adams-Beck.

BECK, Prof. (John) Swanson; Professor of Pathology, University of Dundee, since 1971; *b* 22 Aug. 1928; *s* of late Dr John Beck and Mary (*née* Barbour); *m* 1960, Marion Tudhope Paterson; one *s* one *d*. *Educ:* Glasgow Acad.; Univ. of Glasgow. BSc, MB, ChB, MD, FRCPG, FRCPE, FRCPath. Lectr in Pathology, Univ. of Glasgow, 1958-63; Sen. Lectr in Pathology, Univ. of Aberdeen, 1963-71. *Publications:* various papers in Jl of Pathology and other medical and scientific jls. *Recreations:* walking, gardening, sailing. *Address:* Morar, Hazel Avenue, Dundee DD2 1QD. *T:* Dundee 68606.

BECK, (Richard) Theodore, FRIBA, FSA, FRSA, MRTPI; architect; *b* 11 March 1905; *s* of Alfred Charles Beck and Grace Sophia Beck (*née* Reading); *m* 1950, Margaret Beryl Page; one *s* one *d*. *Educ:* Haileybury; Architectural Association Sch. Past Mem. Council, Royal Archaeological Inst.; Past Master: Broderers Company; Barber-Surgeons Company; Master, Parish Clerks Co., 1976-77; Mem. Court of Common Council, Corporation of London; Sheriff, City of London, 1969-70; former Dep. Governor, the Hon. the Irish Soc.; Chm., Governors, City of London Sch., 1971-75, Dep. Chm., 1976-; Chm., Schools Cttee, Corporation of London, 1977. Governor: Bridewell Royal Hosp.; King Edward's Sch., Witley; Christ's Hospital. Vicary Lectr, 1969; Prestonian Lectr, 1975. *Publication:* The Cutting Edge: early history of the surgeons of London, 1975. *Recreations:* golf, archaeology. *Address:* Great House, Hambledon, Godalming, Surrey. *T:* Wormley 2662. *Clubs:* East India, Devonshire, Sports and Public Schools, City Livery.

BECK, (Rudolph) Rolf, (Baron Rolf Beck); Chairman and Managing Director of Slip and Molyslip Group of Companies since 1939; *b* 25 March 1914; *s* of Baron Dr Otto Beck (famous industrialist and politician in Austrian and Hungarian Empire; also special Envoy and Representative in Switzerland of Emperor Franz Josef of Austria during 1914-19 War) and Baroness Margaret Beck; *m* 1944, Elizabeth Lesley Brenchley, *d* of Captain Fletcher, RN; one *s*. *Educ:* Theresanium Mil. Acad.; Univs of Geneva, Lausanne, Vienna. Degrees in Engrg and Chem. Whilst still at univ. took up racing and rally driving

seriously in a Skoda car; became well known amateur driver, 1935; came to London as rep. of Skoda works to make Skoda cars in UK with 51 per cent British parts and labour and 49 per cent Czechoslovakian parts; outbreak of war ended this develt, 1937; founded Slip Products Ltd, 1939; discovered Milex (petrol economiser), and Dieslip (fuel additive of interest to the Admty and Min. of War Transport); apptd Adviser on gas producer research, 1940; acted as export adviser to Rolls Royce and toured USA twice. Formed cos: Slip Products and Engrg, Slip Trading and Shipping also Slip Auto Sales and Engrg, 1948-49. Invented for automobiles or oil drilling: Molyslip (lubricant); Copaslip (compound), 1959. Founded: Slip Internat. Ltd; Molyslip Trading, 1961; Molyslip Holdings, 1964; Molyslip Chemicals Ltd, 1967; Molytex Internat., 1970. Introduced additives: Multiglide and Molyglide, 1972. Fellow of Scientific Exploration Soc.; FZS. *Recreations:* skiing, water skiing, shooting, sailing. *Heir:* *s* Stephen Rolf Beck, *b* 2 Dec. 1948. *Address:* Layham Hall, near Hadleigh, Suffolk IP7 5LE. *T:* Hadleigh 2137; Cap Davia, Marine de Davia, Ile Rousse, Corsica. *T:* Ile Rousse 600.625; 19 Empire House, Thurloe Place, SW7. *T:* 01-589 7570. *Clubs:* Royal Automobile; Royal Scottish Automobile; Royal Harwich Yacht; West Mersey Yacht; Hurlingham; Union Interalliée (Paris).

BECK, Swanson; *see* Beck, J. S.

BECKE, Mrs Shirley Cameron, OBE 1974; QPM 1972; Vice-Chairman, since 1976, and Regional Administrator, London Region, since 1974, Women's Royal Voluntary Service; *b* 29 April 1917; *er d* of late George L. Jennings, AMIGasE and Marion Jennings; *m* 1954, Rev. Justice Becke, MBE, TD, FCA; no *c*. *Educ:* privately; Ealing Co. Gram. Sch. Trained in Gas Engineering, 1935-40. Joined Metropolitan Police as Constable, 1941; served in various ranks; Woman Commander, 1969-74. *Recreations:* philately, reading, keeping cats. *Address:* 12 Frewin Road, SW18. *T:* 01-874 9053.

BECKE, Lt-Col William Hugh Adamson, CMG 1964; DSO 1945; Personnel Officer, Gas and Fuel Corporation of Victoria, since 1974; *b* 24 Sept. 1916; *er s* of late Brig.-Gen. J. H. W. Becke, CMG, DSO, AFC, and late Mrs A. P. Becke (*née* Adamson); *m* 1945, Mary Catherine, 3rd *d* of late Major G. M. Richmond, Kincairney, Murthly, Perthshire. *Educ:* Charterhouse; RMC Sandhurst. Commissioned in The Sherwood Foresters, 1937. British Military Mission to Greece, 1949-52; Asst Military Adviser to the High Commissioner for the UK in Pakistan, 1957-59; Military Attaché, Djakarta, 1962-64; retd 1966. Private Sec. and Comptroller to Governor of Victoria, 1969-74. *Address:* 3 Chambers Street, South Yarra, Vic 3141, Australia; Priestoun, Edzell, Angus, Scotland. *Clubs:* Army and Navy; Naval and Military, Victoria Racing (Melbourne).

BECKER, Sir Ellerton; *see* Becker, Sir J. E.

BECKER, Harry (Thomas Alfred); Publishers' Representative, Journal of Environmental Health; occupied in encouraging UK imports into USA; *b* Wandsworth, 16 June 1892; *e s* of late Sir Frederick Becker; *m* 1st, 1912; one *d*; 2nd, 1926; one *s* one *d*; 3rd, 1939 (marr. diss., Reno, Nevada, USA, 1952), *d* of John Henry and Elizabeth Newman; one *d*; 4th, 1952, in USA, Mary Beth, *d* of Clyde and Mae Browder, Tenn, USA. *Educ:* Colet Court; Uppingham; Bristol Univ. Served European War, 1914-18; was invalided from the Service through wounds; retd with rank of 2nd Lieut Suffolk Regt, 1918 (medals, 1914-15 Star, etc.); many years spent in newspaper production in Fleet Street; MP Richmond (Ind) 1922-23, (Ind C) 1923-24; contested W Bermondsey, 1918, as ex-Servicemen's candidate. USA Naturalization Certificate, 8 July 1955. *Recreations:* swimming, cricket. *Address:* 300 West Franklin Street, Richmond, Va 23220, USA.

BECKER, Sir (Jack) Ellerton, Kt 1962; FAA; retired; formerly Chairman of Directors of private pastoral companies from 1929; *b* 4 Oct. 1904; *s* of Percy Harold and Mabel Martha Becker, Adelaide, S Australia; *m* 1928, Gladys Sarah, *d* of Percival John and Mary Elizabeth Duggan, Adelaide, S Australia. *Educ:* Unley High Sch.; Adelaide Sch. of Technology and Univ. Manufacturing jeweller, 1920; commenced teaching music, 1926. Founded Adelaide Coll. of Music and, as Principal, built it up to 5000 students and 30 teachers; three world tours; organised Music League of S Australia and directed for charity, theatrical productions. Retired from music 1943, to farm scientifically in S Australia. FAA, 1961 (only the seventh Australian non-scientist ever elected) between Sir R. Menzies, 1958 and Lord Casey, 1966; Academy Building Auditorium named Becker Hall in 1962. Mem. Council of Australian Academy of Science, 1965-68. Acquired important stud cattle and sheep properties, Hereford, England, and NSW, Australia,

1962 and 1964. Fellow: Intercontinental Biographical Assoc., 1975; Internat. Inst. Community Service, 1976. Mem., Imperial Soc. of Knights Bachelor. *Recreations:* overseas travel, antique collecting. *Address:* Blue Highway, Point Shares, Pembroke, Bermuda. *T:* 2 5970.

BECKERMAN, Wilfred, PhD, DPhil; Fellow of Balliol College, Oxford, since 1975; *b* 19 May 1925; *s* of Morris and Mathilda Beckerman; *m* 1952, Nicole Geneviève Ritter; one *s* two *d*. *Educ:* Ealing County Sch.; Trinity Coll., Cambridge (MA, PhD); MA, DPhil Oxon. RNVR, 1943-46. Trinity Coll., Cambridge, 1946-50; Lecturer in Economics, Univ. of Nottingham, 1950-52; OEEC and OECD, Paris, 1952-61; National Inst. of Economic and Social Research, 1962-63. Fellow of Balliol Coll., Oxford, 1964-69; Prof. of Political Economy, Univ. of London, and Head of Dept of Political Economy, UCL, 1969-75; The Economic Adviser to the Board of Trade (leave of absence from Balliol), 1967-69. Mem., Royal Commn on Environmental Pollution, 1970-73. Mem. Exec. Cttee, NIESR, 1973-; Pres., Section F (Economics), BAAS. *Publications:* The British Economy in 1975 (with associates), 1965; International Comparisons of Real Incomes, 1966; An Introduction to National Income Analysis, 1968; (ed and contrib) The Labour Government's Economic Record, 1972; In Defence of Economic Growth, 1974; articles in Economic Jl, Economica, Econometrica, Review of Economic Studies, Review of Economics and Statistics, etc. *Recreations:* various. *Address:* 12 Chadlington Road, Oxford. *T:* Oxford 54384.

BECKETT, family name of **Baron Grimthorpe.**

BECKETT, Prof. Arnold Heyworth; Professor of Pharmaceutical Chemistry and Head, Department of Pharmacy, Chelsea College (University of London); *b* 12 Feb. 1920; *m* 1942, Miriam Eunice Webster; one *s* one *d*. *Educ:* Baines Grammar Sch., Poulton-le-Fylde; Sch. of Pharmacy and Birkbeck Coll., University of London, FPS 1942; BSc 1947; PhD 1950; DSc London, 1959. Prof. of Pharmaceutical Chemistry and Head, Dept of Pharmacy, Chelsea Coll. of Sci. and Technology, 1959-. Member: Council, Pharmaceutical Soc. of Gt Brit., 1965-; Bd of Pharmaceutical Sciences, Fédération Internat. Pharmaceutique, 1960- (Chm.); Olympic Games Medical Commn, 1968. Vis. Prof. to Univs, USA and Canada. Examr in Pharmaceut. Chem., Univs in UK, Nigeria, Ghana, Singapore. Pereira Medal, 1942; STAS Medal, Belg. Chem. Soc., 1962; Hanbury Meml Medal, 1974. Hon. Dr, Univ. of Uppsala, 1977. *Publications:* (co-author) Practical Pharmaceutical Chemistry, 1962; Part 1, 3rd edn, 1975, Part 2, 3rd edn, 1976; founder Co-editor, Jl of Medicinal Chemistry; research contribs to jls. *Recreations:* travel, sport, photography. *Address:* Lynwood, Southill Road, Chislehurst, Kent. *T:* 01-467 5792.

BECKETT, Bruce Probart, FRIBA; Chief Architect, Scottish Development Department, since 1967; *b* 7 June 1924; *s* of J. D. L. Beckett and Florence Theresa (*née* Probart); *m* 1957, Jean McDonald; two *s* three *d* (incl. twin *s* and *d*). *Educ:* Rondebosch Boys' High Sch., Cape Town; Univ. of Cape Town (BArch with distinction, 1950); University Coll. London (Diploma in Town Planning, 1963). Active Service SA Navy, 1943; Midshipman, 1943; Sub-Lieut, 1944; seconded RN, 1944; Lieut, 1946. ARIBA 1950, FRIBA 1968; FRIAS 1968. Mem. Inst. S African Architects, 1950; FRTPI (AMTPI 1966). Private practice in S Africa, 1952-59, London, 1960. Sen. Architect, War Office, 1961; Superintending Grade Arch., Directorate-Gen. of Res. and Development, 1963-67. Dep. Leader, Timber Trade Mission to Canada, 1964. A Vice-Pres., RIBA, 1972-73, 1975-76, 1976-77; Hon. Librarian, 1976-78. Sec. of State for Scotland's nominee on ARCUK; Member Council: EAA, 1970; RIAS, 1971-; RIBA, 1972-; Member: Sec. of State for Environment's Construction and Housing Adv. Cttee, 1968-; Building Res. Estabt Adv. Cttees in England and Scotland, 1970-. Assessor to Scottish Cttee of Design Council, 1974-. *Publications:* papers on industrialised building, contract procedure, etc, in various jls; HMSO publications on Scottish housing, educational and health buildings. *Recreations:* sailing, walking. *Address:* 71 Ravelston Dykes Road, Edinburgh EH4 3NU. *T:* 031-337 7301. *Clubs:* New (Edinburgh); Western Province Sports (Kelvin Grove, Cape Town).

BECKETT, Maj.-Gen. Denis Arthur, CB 1971; DSO 1944; OBE 1960; *b* 19 May 1917; *o s* of late Archibald Beckett, Woodford Green, Essex; *m* 1946, Elizabeth (marr. diss. 1974), *er d* of late Col Guy Edwards, Upper Slaughter, Glos; one *s*. *Educ:* Forest Sch.; Chard Sch. Joined Hon. Artillery Co., 1939; commnd into Essex Regt, 1940; served in W. Africa, Middle East, Italy and Greece, 1940-45; DAA & QMG and Bde Major, Parachute Bdes, 1948-50; Instructor, RMA Sandhurst, 1951-53; Staff Coll., Camberley, 1953-56; Second in Comd 3rd Bn Para. Regt, 1956-

58; comd 2nd Bn Para. Regt, 1958-60; jssc 1960-61; comd 19 Bde, 1961-63; idc 1964; DAG, BAOR, 1965-66; Chief of Staff, Far East Land Forces, 1966-68; Dir of Personal Services (Army), 1968-71, retired 1971. *Address:* 12 Wellington House, Eton Road, NW3. *Clubs:* Army and Navy, Lansdowne; MCC.

BECKETT, Prof. James Camlin, MA; Professor of Irish History, Queen's University of Belfast, 1958-75; *b* 8 Feb. 1912; 3rd *s* of Alfred Beckett and Frances Lucy Bushell. *Educ:* Royal Belfast Academical Instn; Queen's Univ., Belfast. History Master, Belfast Royal Academy, 1934; Lectr in Modern History, Queen's Univ., Belfast, 1945, Reader in Modern History, 1952. Fellow Commoner, Peterhouse, Cambridge, 1955-56; Cummings Lectr, McGill Univ., Montreal, 1976; Mellor Prof., Tulane Univ., New Orleans, 1977; Member: Irish Manuscripts Commn, 1959; Royal Commission on Historical Manuscripts, 1960; FRHistS; MRIA. *Publications:* Protestant Dissent in Ireland, 1687-1780, 1948; Short History of Ireland, 1952; (ed with T. W. Moody) Ulster since 1800: a Political and Economic Survey, 1954; (ed with T. W. Moody) Ulster since 1800: a Social Survey, 1957; (with T. W. Moody) Queen's Belfast, 1845-1949, 1959; The Making of Modern Ireland 1603-1923, 1966; (ed with R. E. Glasscock) Belfast: the Origin and Growth of an Industrial City, 1966; (ed) Historical Studies VII, 1969; The Anglo-Irish Tradition, 1976; contrib. The Ulster Debate, 1972; Confrontations, 1973; articles, reviews, etc., in English Hist. Rev., History, Irish Hist. Studies and other jls. *Recreations:* chess, walking. *Address:* 19 Wellington Park Terrace, Belfast BT9 6DR, N Ireland. *Club:* Ulster (Belfast).

BECKETT, John Angus, CB 1965; CMG 1956; MA; Chairman: William Press Production Systems Ltd, since 1972; Gannet Offshore Production Services, since 1974; Director, William Press (International) Ltd, since 1972; *b* 6 July 1909; *s* of late John Beckett, BA; *m* 1935, Una Joan, *yr d* of late George Henry Wright; one *s* two *d*. *Educ:* privately; Sidney Sussex Coll., Cambridge. BA 2nd Cl. Hons (Geog. Tripos); Mem., Cambridge Iceland Expedition, 1932. Schoolmaster, 1933-40; entered Civil Service, 1940; Principal Private Sec. to Minister of Fuel and Power, 1946-47; Asst Sec., Min. of Fuel and Power, 1947-59; Under-Sec., 1959 (Gas Div., 1959-64, Petroleum Div., 1964-72) Min. of Power, Min. of Technology, DTI; retired 1972. Chm. Petroleum Cttee of OEEC, 1948-50, 1955-59, 1965-72; Petroleum Attaché, British Embassy, Washington, 1950-53. *Publication:* Iceland Adventure, 1934. *Recreations:* rowing, Rugby football, administration. *Address:* The Timber House, Aldercombe Lane, Caterham, Surrey. *T:* Caterham 44054. *Clubs:* American, St Stephen's.

BECKETT, John Michael; Chief Executive, British Sugar Corporation Ltd, since 1975; *b* 22 June 1929; *yr s* of H. N. Beckett, MBE, and C. L. Beckett (*née* Allsop); *m* 1955, Joan Mary, *d* of Percy Rogerson and F. M. Rogerson (*née* Martin); five *d*. *Educ:* Wolverhampton Grammar Sch.; Magdalen Coll., Oxford (BA 1953, MA 1957). Called to Bar, Gray's Inn, 1954 (Lord Justice Holker Sen. Exhibn). Nat. Service Commn, RA, in UK, 1947-49; Reg. Commn, 1949-50; Adjt 23 Fd Regt, RA, Hong Kong, 1950; TA, 1950-60. Bar, 1954-55; Tootal Ltd, 1955-58; Tarmac Ltd, 1958-75; Sec., 1958-62; Asst Man. Dir, Tarmac Roadstone, 1962-63; Man. Dir, Tarmac Roadstone Holdings, 1963-71; Dir, Tarmac Ltd, 1963; Gp Exec. Dir, 1971-75, Non-exec. dir, 1975-. Chairman: British Slag Fedn, 1967-69; Asphalt & Coated Macadam Assoc., 1971-73; Member: Construction and Housing Research Adv. Council, 1971-75; Transport and Road Research Laboratory Adv. Cttee, 1972-. Hon. MIQ. *Recreations:* travel, shooting, squash. *Address:* Belton House, near Uppingham, Leics LE15 9LE. *T:* Belton 682. *Club:* Naval and Military.
See also T . N . Beckett .

BECKETT, Sir Martyn Gervase, 2nd Bt, *cr* 1921; MC 1945; RIBA; Architect; Lieutenant (temp. Captain) Welsh Guards; *b* 6 Nov. 1918; *s* of Hon. Sir Gervase Beckett, 1st Bt, and Lady Marjorie Beckett (*d* 1964); *S* father, 1937; *m* 1941, Hon. Priscilla Brett, *y d* of 3rd Viscount Esher, GBE; two *s* one *d*. *Educ:* Eton; Trinity Coll., Cambridge. Served War of 1939-45 (MC). Renovations and alterations to E end of King's College, Cambridge; private houses and council estates. Trustee, The Wallace Collection, 1972-. *Recreations:* photography, painting, piano. *Heir:* *s* Richard Gervase Beckett [*b* 27 March 1944; *m* 1976, Elizabeth, *d* of Major Hugo and Lady Caroline Waterhouse; one *d*]. *Address:* 3 St Albans Grove, W8. *T:* 01-937 7834; Kirkdale Farm, Nawton, Yorks. *Club:* Brooks's.

BECKETT, Noel George Stanley; HM Diplomatic Service, retired; Consul-General, Casablanca, 1973-76; *b* 3 Dec. 1916; *s* of Captain J. R. Beckett, MC, and Ethel Barker; *m* 1948, Huguette Laure Charlotte Voos; one *s* two *d*. *Educ:* Peterhouse,

Cambridge. MA Hons Cantab 1938, BScEcon Hons London 1961. British Embassy, Paris, 1946; UK Commercial Rep., Frankfurt and Cologne, 1949; Lima, 1956; Bonn, 1959; British Embassy, Addis Ababa, 1963 and liaison officer with Econ. Commn for Africa; Sec., European Conf. on Satellite Communications, FO, 1965; British Embassy, Beirut, 1968. *Recreations:* tennis, photography, reading, travel. *Address:* The Second House, South Drive, Dorking, Surrey. *Club:* Royal Commonwealth Society.

BECKETT, Richard Henry, CSI 1934; CIE 1928; *b* 18*Q2; s* of Richard Beckett; *m* 1928, Doris May (*d* 1974), *d* of W. T. Sutcliffe and *widow* of Capt. Cedric F. Horsfall. *Educ:* Imperial Coll. of Science. Entered Indian Educational Service, 1906; Principal, Coll. of Science, Nagpur, 1908; Officiating Dir of Public Instruction and Sec. for Education to the Govt of the Central Provinces India, 1924; Dir of Public Instruction, Bombay Presidency, 1930-34. *Recreations:* tennis, golf. *Address:* c/o Lloyds Bank (Cox's and King's Branch), 6 Pall Mall, SW1. *Club:* East India, Devonshire, Sports and Public Schools.

BECKETT, Samuel; author and playwright; *b* Dublin, 1906. *Educ:* Portora Royal School; Trinity Coll., Dublin (MA). Lectr in English, Ecole Normale Supérieure, Paris, 1928-30; Lectr in French, Trinity Coll., Dublin, 1930-32; from 1932 has lived mostly in France, in Paris since 1937. Nobel Prize for Literature, 1969. *Publications: verse:* Whoroscope, 1930; Echo's Bones, 1935; Collected Poems in English and French, 1977; *novels:* Murphy, 1938; Watt, 1944; Molloy, 1951 (Eng. trans. 1956); Malone meurt, 1952 (Eng. trans. Malone Dies, 1956); L'Innommable, 1953 (Eng. trans. 1960); Comment C'est, 1961 (Eng. trans. 1964); Imagination Dead Imagine, 1966 (trans. from French by author); First Love, 1973; Mercier and Camier, 1974; *short stories:* More Pricks than Kicks, 1934; Nouvelles et textes pour rien, 1955; Le Depeupleur, 1971 (Eng. trans., The Lost Ones, 1972); Four Novellas, 1977; *plays:* En attendant Godot, 1952 (Eng. trans. Waiting for Godot, 1954); Fin de Partie, 1957 (Eng. trans. End Game); Krapp's Last Tape, 1959; La Dernière Bande, 1961; Happy Days, 1961; Play, 1963; Film, 1972; Breath and Other Short Plays, 1972; Not I, 1973; *radio plays:* All that Fall, 1957; Embers, 1959; Cascando, 1964; *TV plays:* Ghost Trio and... But the Clouds..., 1977. *Address:* c/o Faber & Faber Ltd, 24 Russell Square, WC1.

BECKETT, Terence Norman, CBE 1974; Chairman, since 1976, Managing Director and Chief Executive, since 1974, Ford Motor Co. Ltd; Chairman, Ford Motor Credit Co. Ltd, since 1974; *b* 13 Dec. 1923; *s* of Horace Norman Beckett, MBE and Clarice Lillian (*née* Allsop); *m* 1950, Sylvia Gladys Asprey; one *d. Educ:* London Sch. of Econs. BScEcon, CEng, FIMechE, FBIM, FIMI. Captain REME, British Army (UK, India, Malaya), 1945-48; RARO, 1949-62. Company Trainee, Ford Motor Co. Ltd, 1950; Asst in office of Dep. Chm. and Man. Dir, 1951; Man., Styling, Briggs Motor Bodies Ltd (Ford subsid.), 1954; Admin Man., Engrg, Briggs, 1955; Manager: Product Staff, 1955; Product Planning Staff, 1961; Marketing Staff, 1963; Dir, Car Div., 1964; Exec. Dir, Ford Motor Co. Ltd, 1966 and Dir of Sales, 1968; Vice-Pres., European and Overseas Sales Ops, Ford of Europe Inc., 1969; Director: ICI; various Ford Companies in Europe; Ford Motor Credit Co. Ltd, 1974; Automotive Finance Ltd, 1974. Member: Engineering Industries Council, 1975-; BIM Council, 1976-; CBI Council and President's Cttee, 1976-; Grand Council, Motor and Cycle Trades Benevolent Fund (BEN), 1976-; SMMT Council and Exec. Cttee; Vice Pres. and Hon. Fellow, Inst. of the Motor Industry, 1974-. Pres., Essex County Voluntary Assoc. for the Blind, 1976-. Mem., Governing Body, London Business Sch., 1976-. Hon. DSc Cranfield, 1977. *Recreations:* ornithology, music. *Address:* Ford Motor Company Ltd, Eagle Way, Brentwood, Essex. *T:* Brentwood 253000. *Club:* Royal Automobile.
See also *J . M . Beckett* .

BECKETT, William Cartwright, LLM; Legal Secretary, Law Officers' Department, since 1975; *b* 21 Sept. 1929; *s* of late William Beckett and Emily (*née* Cartwright); *m* 1st, 1956, Marjorie Jean Hoskin; two *s* ; 2nd, 1972, Lesley Margaret Furlonger. *Educ:* Salford Grammar Sch.; Manchester Univ. (LLB 1950, LLM 1952). Called to Bar, Middle Temple, 1952. Joined Treasury Solicitor's Dept, 1956; Board of Trade, 1965; Asst Solicitor, DEP, 1969; Under-Sec., DTI, 1972. *Recreations:* music, golf. *Address:* 12 Wigmore Street, W1H 9DE. *T:* 01-637 0265. *Club:* Reform.

BECKINGHAM, Charles Fraser; Professor of Islamic Studies, University of London, since 1965; *b* 18 Feb. 1914; *o c* of Arthur Beckingham, ARBA and Alice Beckingham, Houghton, Hunts; *m* 1st, 1946, Margery (*d* 1966), *o d* of John Ansell; one *d* ; 2nd,

1970, Elizabeth, *y d* of R. J. Brine (marr. diss. 1977). *Educ:* Grammar Sch., Huntingdon; Queens' Coll., Cambridge (scholar, Members' English prizeman, 1934). Dept of Printed Books, British Museum, 1936-46. Seconded for service with military and naval Intelligence, 1942-46. Foreign Office, 1946-51; Lectr in Islamic History, Manchester Univ., 1951-55; Sen. Lectr, 1955-58. Prof. of Islamic Studies, 1958-65. Mem. Council, Hakluyt Soc., 1958-62, 1964-69, Pres. 1969-72; Treas., Royal Asiatic Society, 1964-67, Pres., 1967-70, 1976-. Jt Editor, 1961-64, Editor, 1965, Jl of Semitic Studies. *Publications:* contribs to Admiralty Handbook of Western Arabia, 1946; (with G. W. B. Huntingford) Some Records of Ethiopia, 1954; Introduction to Atlas of the Arab World and Middle East, 1960; (with G. W. B. Huntingford) A True Relation of the Prester John of the Indies, 1961; Bruce's Travels (ed and selected), 1964; The Achievements of Prester John, 1966; (ed) Islam, in, Religion in the Middle East (ed A. J. Arberry), 1969; articles in learned jls. *Address:* School of Oriental and African Studies, Malet Street, WC1E 7HP. *Club:* Travellers'.

BECKMAN, Michael David, QC 1976; *b* 6 April 1932; *s* of Nathan and Esther Beckman; *m* 1966, Sheryl Robin (*née* Kyle); two *d . Educ:* King's Coll., London (LLB (Hons)). Called to the Bar, Lincoln's Inn, 1954. *Recreations:* various. *Address:* Bullards, Widford, Herts. *T:* Much Hadham 2669.

BECKWITH, John Gordon, FBA 1974; FSA 1968; Keeper, Department of Architecture and Sculpture, Victoria and Albert Museum, since 1974; *b* 2 Dec. 1918; *s* of late John Frederick Beckwith. *Educ:* Ampleforth Coll., York; Exeter Coll., Oxford (Loscombe Richards Exhibnr; Amelia Jackson Student). MA. Served with The Duke of Wellington's Regt, 1939-45. Victoria and Albert Museum: Asst Keeper, Dept of Textiles, 1948; Asst Keeper, Dept of Architecture and Sculpture, 1955, Dep. Keeper, 1958. Vis. Fellow of Harvard Univ. at Dumbarton Oaks Res. Library and Collection, Washington, DC, 1950-51; Visiting Professor: at Harvard Univ. (Fogg Museum of Art), 1964; at Univ. of Missouri, Columbia, Mo, 1968-69; Slade Prof.-elect of Fine Art, Oxford Univ., 1978-79. Reynolds-Stephens Meml Lecture, RBS, 1965. Mem., Centre International des Etudes des Textils Anciens at Lyon, 1953-. *Publications:* The Andrews Diptych, 1958; Coptic Textiles, 1959; Caskets from Cordoba, 1960; The Art of Constantinople, 1961; The Veroli Casket, 1962; Coptic Sculpture, 1963; The Basilewsky Situla, 1963; Early Medieval Art, 1964; The Adoration of the Magi in Whalebone, 1966; Early Christian and Byzantine Art, Pelican History of Art, 1970; Ivory Carvings in Early Medieval England, 1972; Catalogue of Exhibition, Ivory Carvings in Early Medieval England 700-1200, 1974; contrib. Art Bulletin, Burlington Magazine, etc. *Recreation:* music. *Address:* Flat 12, 77 Ladbroke Grove, W11 2PF. *T:* 01-727 7277.

BECTIVE, Earl of; Thomas Michael Ronald Christopher Taylour; *b* 10 Feb. 1959; *s* and *heir* of 6th Marquis of Headfort, *qv . Educ:* Harrow.

BEDDALL, Hugh Richard Muir; Chairman: Muir Beddall & Co. Ltd, since 1964; C. T. Bowring (Continental) Ltd; Member of Lloyd's; *b* 20 May 1922; *s* of Herbert Muir Beddall and Jennie Beddall (*née* Fowler); *m* 1946, Monique Henriette (*née* Haefliger); three *s* one *d. Educ:* Stowe; Ecole de Commerce, Neuchatel, Switzerland. Employee of Muir Beddall & Co., 1939-41. Served War of 1939-45; Royal Marines, 2nd Lieut, 1941; subseq. Captain A Troop 45 RM Commando and No 1 Commando Bde HQ; demob., 1946. Employee, Muir Beddall, Mise & Cie, Paris, 1946-47; returned as employee of Muir Beddall & Co. Ltd, 1947; Dir, 1949; Dep. Chm., 1960; Chm., 1964. Partner in Iver Stud. FCII. Director: C. T. Bowring & Muir Beddall International Ltd; Muir Beddall Boda & Co.; H. M. Beddall & Partners. *Recreations:* shooting, fishing, racing. *Address:* Iver Lodge, Iver, Bucks. *T:* Iver 653007. *Clubs:* Buck's, East India, Devonshire, Sports and Public Schools; Denham Golf; Stoke Poges Golf.

BEDDARD, Dr Frederick Denys, CB 1974; Deputy Chief Medical Officer, Department of Health and Social Security, 1972-77, retired; *b* 28 Feb. 1917; *s* of late Rev. F. G. Beddard and late Mrs Emily Beddard; *m* 1942, Anne (*née* Porter); two *d. Educ:* Haileybury Coll.; St Mary's Hosp. Med. Sch., London Univ. MRCS, LRCP 1939; MB, BS 1940; FRCPE 1972; FFCM 1972. House Phys. and Surg., St Mary's, 1939-41; RAMC, 1941-45 (Lt-Col). St Mary's Hosp. and Brompton Hosp., 1946-49; SE Metrop. Reg. Hosp. Bd, 1950-55; SE Reg. Hosp. Bd (Scotland), 1955-57; NE Reg. Hosp. Bd (Scotland), 1957-68 (seconded to Dept of Health, New Zealand, 1967); Chief Medical Officer, Min. of Health and Social Services, NI, 1968-72. *Publications:* various contribs to Lancet, etc. *Recreations:* gardening, travel. *Address:* Birk Field, Staveley, Kendal, Cumbria. *T:* Staveley 454.

BEDDINGTON, Charles Richard; Metropolitan Magistrate since 1963; *b* 22 Aug. 1911; *s* of late Charles Beddington, Inner Temple, and Stella (*née* de Goldschmidt); *m* 1939, Debbie, *d* of Frederick Appleby Holt; two *s* one *d. Educ:* Eton (scholar); Balliol Coll., Oxford. Barrister, Inner Temple, 1934. Joined TA, 1939; served RA, 1939-45, Major. Practised at the Bar in London and on SE Circuit. Mem. Mental Health Review Tribunal (SE Metropolitan Area), 1960-63. *Recreations:* golf, lawn tennis. *Address:* Rosehill, Cuckfield, Sussex RH17 5EU. *T:* Haywards Heath 54063; 1 Temple Gardens, Temple, EC4. *Clubs:* Royal Ashdown Forest Golf; Lambton Squash.

BEDDINGTON, Nadine Dagmar; architect in own practice, since 1967; *d* of Frank Maurice Beddington and Mathilde Beddington. *Educ:* New Hall; Regent Polytechnic Sch. of Architecture. FRIBA (ARIBA 1940); FSIA; FRSA. Asst in central and local govt, 1940-45; asst in private practice, 1945-55; Chief Architect to Freeman Hardy Willis/Trueform, 1957-67. Vice-Chm., Architects in Industry Group, 1965-67; Mem., RIBA Council, 1969-72, 1975-76, Vice-Pres., RIBA, 1971-72; Mem., ARCUK, 1969-77; Chm., Camberwell Soc., 1970-77; Fellow, Ancient Monuments Soc. Vice Chm., Brixton and District Dog Training Club, 1974-77. *Publications:* articles on shops, shopping centres, building maintenance, building legislation. *Recreations:* reading, riding, people, music, travel, dogs. *Address:* 17 Champion Grove, SE5 8BN; (office) 142 Charing Cross Road, WC2H 0LB. *T:* 01-836 4147.

BEDDOE, Jack Eglinton, CB 1971; Chief Executive, Severn Trent Water Authority, 1974-77; *b* 6 June 1914; *s* of Percy Beddoe and Mabel Ellen Hook; *m* 1st, 1940, Audrey Alison Emelie (*d* 1954); two *s* one *d*; 2nd, 1957, Edith Rosina Gillanders. *Educ:* Hitchin Grammar Sch.; Magdalen Coll., Cambridge. Entered Ministry of Health, 1936; Principal Private Sec. to Minister of Health, 1948-51; to Minister of Housing and Local Government, 1951-53; Asst Sec., 1953; Under-Sec., Ministry of Housing and Local Government, 1961-65; Asst Under-Sec. of State, Dept of Economic Affairs, 1965-66; Chm., SE Planning Board, during 1966; Under-Sec., Min. of Housing and Local Govt, later DoE, 1966-74. *Address:* 29 Regency House, Newbold Terrace, Leamington, Warwickshire.

BEDDY, James Patrick, DEconSc; MRIA; Consultant, The Industrial Credit Company Ltd, since 1972; *b* Cobh, County Cork, 1900. *Educ:* O'Connell Schs, Dublin; National Univ. of Ireland, University Coll., Dublin. Inspector of Taxes, 1927-33; Sec., Industrial Credit Co. Ltd, 1933-49; Dir, The Industrial Credit Co. Ltd, 1949-52, Man. Dir 1952-69, Chm., 1952-72; Chm., Mergers Ltd, 1969-72. Lectr in Commerce, University Coll., Dublin, 1936-51. Pres., Statistical and Social Inquiry Soc. of Ireland, 1954-56; Council Mem., Economic and Social Res. Inst., 1960-75. Chairman: Commn on Emigration and Other Population Problems, 1948-54; Cttee of Inquiry into Internal Transport, 1956-57; An Foras Tionscail, 1952-65; The Industrial Development Authority, 1949-65. Member: Tribunal of Inquiry into Public Transport, 1939; Industrial Res. Cttee of Inst. for Industrial Res. and Standards, 1946-60. LLD (*hc* Dublin). *Publications:* Profits, Theoretical and Practical Aspects, 1940. Various articles on matters of economic interest. *Address:* 15 Spencer Villas, Glenageary, County Dublin. *T:* Dublin 801542. *Club:* Royal Irish Yacht (Dun Laoghaire).

BEDFORD, 13th Duke of, *cr* 1694; **John Robert Russell;** Marquess of Tavistock, 1694; Earl of Bedford, 1550; Baron Russell of Chenies, 1540; Baron Russell of Thornhaugh, 1603; Baron Howland of Streatham, 1695; *b* 24 May 1917; *er s* of 12th Duke and Louisa Crommelin Roberta (*d* 1960), *y d* of Robert Jowitt Whitwell; *S* father 1953; *m* 1st, 1939, Clare Gwendolen Hollway, *née* Bridgman (*d* 1945); two *s*; 2nd, Lydia (marr. diss., 1960), widow of Capt. Ian de Hoghton Lyle, 3rd *d* of 3rd Baron Churston and late Duchess of Leinster; one *s*; 3rd, 1960, Mme Nicole Milinaire, *d* of Paul Schneider. Coldstream Guards, 1939; invalided out, 1940. *Publications:* A Silver-Plated Spoon, 1959; (with G. Mikes) Book of Snobs, 1965; The Flying Duchess, 1968; (with G. Mikes) How to Run a Stately Home, 1971. *Heir: s* Marquess of Tavistock, *qv. Address:* (seat) Woburn Abbey, Beds; San Carlo, 22 Boulevard des Moulins, Monte Carlo. *Clubs:* Brooks's, Pratt's.

BEDFORD, Bishop Suffragan of, since 1977; **Rt. Rev. Andrew Alexander Kenny Graham;** *b* 7 Aug. 1929; *o s* of late Andrew Harrison and Magdalene Graham; unmarried. *Educ:* Tonbridge Sch.; St John's Coll., Oxford; Ely Theological College. Curate of Hove Parish Church, 1955-58; Chaplain and Lectr in Theology, Worcester Coll., Oxford, 1958-70; Fellow and Tutor, 1960-70; Warden of Lincoln Theological Coll., 1970-77; Canon and Prebendary of Lincoln Cathedral, 1970-77. 0Examining Chaplain to: Bishop of Carlisle, 1967-77; Bishop of Bradford,

1972-77; Bishop of Lincoln, 1973-77. *Recreation:* hill walking. *Address:* 168 Kimbolton Road, Bedford MK41 8DN. *T:* Bedford 57551. *Club:* United Oxford & Cambridge University.

BEDFORD, Archdeacon of; *see* Brown, Ven. R. S.

BEDFORD, Alfred William, (Bill), OBE 1961; AFC 1945; FRAeS; Sales Manager, Hawker Siddeley Aviation, since 1968; *b* 18 Nov. 1920; *m* 1941, Mary Averill; one *s* one *d. Educ:* Loughborough College School, Leics. Electrical engineering apprenticeship, Blackburn Starling & Co. Ltd. RAF 1940-51: served Fighter Sqdns, 605 (County of Warwick) Sqdn, 1941; 135 Sqdn, 1941-44; 65 Sqdn, 1945. Qualified Flying Instructor, Upavon, 1945, and Instructor, Instrument Rating Examiner, until 1949; Graduate Empire Flying School all-weather course. Awarded King's Commendation, 1949; Graduate and Tutor, Empire Test Pilots' School, 1949-50; Test Pilot, RAE Farnborough, 1950-51; Experimental Test Pilot, Hawker Aircraft Ltd, 1951-56; Chief Test Pilot, Hawker Aircraft Ltd, 1956-63; Chief Test Pilot (Dunsfold); Hawker Siddeley Aviation Ltd, 1963-67. London-Rome and return world speed records, 1956. Made initial flight, Oct. 1960, on the Hawker P1127 (the World's first VTOL strike fighter), followed by first jet V/STOL operations of such an aircraft from an Aircraft Carrier (HMS Ark Royal) on 8 Feb. 1963; Harrier first flight, Aug. 1966. Holder Gliding Internat. Gold 'C' with two diamonds; held British and UK national gliding records of 257 miles and altitude of 21,340 ft (19,120 ft gain of height); awarded BGA trophies: de Havilland (twice), Manio, and Wakefield, 1950-51. Approved Air Registration Bd glider test pilot. Chm. and founder Mem., Test Pilots' Group, RAeS, 1964-66. Member SBAC Test Pilots' Soc., 1956-67. Member Society of Experimental Test Pilots. RAeS Alston Memorial Medal, 1959; Guild of Air Pilots and Air Navigators Derry Richards Memorial Medal, 1959-60; Segrave Trophy, 1963; Britannia Trophy, 1964; Air League Founders Medal, 1967. *Recreations:* squash, sail-plane flying. *Address:* The Chequers, West End Lane, Esher, Surrey. *T:* Esher 62285. *Clubs:* Royal Air Force; Esher Squash.

BEDFORD, D(avis) Evan, CBE 1963; MD, FRCP, London; FACP (Hon.); MD (Hon.) Cairo; retired; Hon. Consultant Physician, Middlesex, National Heart and Connaught Hospitals; Consultant Emeritus in Cardiology to the Army, 1976; Hon. Civil Consultant in Cardiology, RAF; formerly Chairman Council, British Heart Foundation; *b* 1898; *s* of William Bedford, JP, Boston, Lincs; *m* 1935, Audrey Selina North, *e d* of Milton Ely, CBE; two *s. Educ:* Epsom Coll.; Middlesex Hospital. Medical Registrar, Middlesex Hospital, 1923-25; Paterson Research Scholar, London Hospital Cardiographic Dept, 1926-27; Medical Officer in Charge Cardiac Wards, Ministry of Pensions Hospital, Orpington, 1922; studied in Paris and Lyons, 1926; Surg.-Sub-Lieut RNVR, 1918, 20th Destroyer Flotilla. Served in RAMC, 1939-45, Brig. Cons. Physician, MEF (despatches). Late Pres. British Cardiac Soc.; Corresp. mem., Soc. Française de Cardiologie, Soc. Belge de Cardiologie, Soc. Suisse de Cardiologie; Hon. Member: Cardiac Soc. of Australia and NZ, Brazilian Soc. of Cardiology and Egyptian Cardiological Soc.; Hon. Pres., European Soc. of Cardiology; late Vice-Pres. International Soc. of Cardiology; Corresp. Acad. of Med., Rome. Carey Coombs Lectr, 1963. *Publications:* articles on Diseases of Coronary Arteries, Angina Pectoris and Congenital Heart Disease, in Lancet, Heart, etc, and other papers and addresses on Diseases of the Heart; Strickland Goodall Memorial Lecture, 1939; Bradshaw Lecture, RCP, 1946; St Cyres' Lecture, 1947; Lumleian Lectures, RCP 1960; Harveian Oration, RCP 1968. *Recreation:* gardening. *Address:* 118 St Pancras, Chichester, W Sussex. *T:* Chichester 83993.

BEDFORD, Eric, CB 1959; CVO 1953; Chief Architect, Ministry of Works, 1952-70 (Chief Architect, Directorate General of Works, Ministry of Public Building and Works, 1963-70). ARIBA 1933; Grissell Gold Medal of Royal Institute of British Architects, 1934. Was responsible for Ministry of Works decorations for the Coronation, 1953.

BEDFORD, John, OBE 1948 (MBE 1944); Director: Commercial Union Assurance Co. Ltd, 1959-73; National Building Agency, 1964-77 (Deputy Chairman of Board and Chairman, Finance Committee, 1967-77); Governor, The Leys School, Cambridge; Trustee, The Cottage Homes for Old People; *b* 16 Jan. 1903; *o s* of John and Rosalind Bedford; *m* 1930, Florence Mary Oddy; one *d*. Chm., Debenhams Ltd, 1956-71 (also Man. Dir, 1956-70); Mem., Banwell Cttee to look at Contractual matters in the Construction Industries for MPBW, 1962; Part-time Mem., London Transport Bd, 1962-68. FRSA 1976. *Recreations:* golf, reading, walking. *Address:* 7A North Gate, Regent's Park, NW8. *Club:* MCC.

BEDFORD, Leslie Herbert, CBE 1956 (OBE 1942); retired as Director of Engineering, Guided Weapons Division, British Aircraft Corporation Ltd, 1968; *b* 23 June 1900; *s* of Herbert Bedford; *m* 1928, Lesley Florence Keitley Duff; three *s*. *Educ:* City and Guilds Engineering Coll., London (BSc); King's Coll., Cambridge (MA). Standard Telephones & Cables Ltd, 1924-31; Dir Research, A. C. Cossor Ltd, 1931-47; Chief TV Engr, Marconi's Wireless Telegraph Co. Ltd, 1947-48. Chief Engineer, GW Div., The English Electric Aviation Ltd, 1948-59; Dir, 1959-60. Mem., Council for Scientific and Industrial Research, 1961-. CEng, FCGI, FIEEE, MBritIRE, FIEE, FRAeS. Silver Medal (RAeS), 1963; Gold Medal, Société d'Encouragement pour la Recherche et l'Invention, 1967; Faraday Medal, 1968. *Publications:* Articles in: Proc. Phys. Soc., Jl BritIRE, Jl RSA, Jl RAeS, Jl IEE, Wireless Engineer, Electronic and Radio Engineer, Electronic Technology. *Recreations:* music, sailing. *Address:* 82a Hendon Lane, N3. *T:* 01-346 1558.

BEDFORD, Steuart John Rudolf; Co-Artistic Director, English Music Theatre Co. since 1976; *b* 31 July 1939; *m* 1969, Norma Burrowes, *qv*. *Educ:* Lancing Coll., Sussex; Royal Acad. of Music. Fellow, RCO; FRAM; BA. Artistic Dir, Aldeburgh Festival, 1974; Royal Acad. of Music, 1965; English Opera Gp, now English Music Theatre, 1967-. Has conducted regularly with English Opera Gp and Welsh National Opera; also at Royal Opera House, Covent Garden (operas incl. Owen Wingrave and Death in Venice, by Benjamin Britten, and Cosi Fan Tutte). Debut at Metropolitan, NY, 1974 (Death in Venice); new prodn of The Marriage of Figaro, 1975. *Recreations:* golf, gardening. *Address:* 56 Rochester Road, NW1 9JG. *T:* 01-485 7322.

BEDFORD, Mrs Steuart; see Burrowes, N. E.

BEDFORD, Sybille; author; *b* 16 March 1911; *d* of Maximilian von Schoenebeck and Elizabeth Bernard; *m* 1935, Walter Bedford. *Educ:* privately, in Italy, England and France. Career in writing and literary journalism. FRSL. *Publications:* The Sudden View, A Journey to Don Otavio, 1953, new edn 1962; A Legacy, 1956, 5th edn 1975, televised 1975; The Best We Can Do (The Trial of Dr Adams), 1958; The Faces of Justice, 1961; A Favourite of the Gods, 1962, new edn 1975; A Compass Error, 1968, new edn 1975; Aldous Huxley, a Biography, Vol I, 1973, Vol II, 1974. *Recreations:* wine, reading, travel. *Address:* c/o Messrs Coutts, 440 Strand, WC2N 5LJ. *Club:* PEN.

BEDINGFELD, Sir Edmund; see Paston-Bedingfeld.

BEDINGFIELD, Christopher Ohl Macredie, TD 1968; QC 1976; a Recorder of the Crown Court, since 1972; *b* 2 June 1935; *s* of late Norman Macredie Bedingfield, Nantygroes, Radnorshire and of Mrs Macredie Bedingfield. *Educ:* Rugby; University Coll., Oxford (MA). Called to Bar, Gray's Inn, 1957; Wales and Chester Circuit. Commnd 2 Mon R; NS 24th Regt; Staff Captain TA, 1960-64; Coy Comdr 4 RWF, 1964-69; Lt-Col TAVR, 1973-76, Co. Comdt Denbigh and Flint ACF 1973, Clwyd ACF 1974-76 (resigned on appt as QC). *Recreations:* riding, squash. *Address:* 5 Essex Court, Temple, EC4. *T:* 01-353 2440; (residence) Nantygroes, near Knighton, Powys. *T:* Whitton 220. *Clubs:* Reform, Army and Navy.

BEDNALL, Maj.-Gen. Sir (Cecil Norbury) Peter, KBE 1953 (OBE 1941); CB 1949; MC 1917; director of companies; *b* 1895; *s* of late Peter Bednall, Endon, Staffs; *m* 1937, Eileen Margaret, *d* of late Col C. M. Lewin, Cowfold, Sussex; one *s* one *d*. *Educ:* Hanley; privately. Army Officer since 1915; Chartered Accountant since 1920. Commissioned 1915, RFA; served European War, 1916-19, France and Belgium. Palestine, 1936-37; War of 1939-45 in France, Abyssinia, and East Africa. Maj.-Gen., 1948. Paymaster-in-Chief, the War Office, 1948-55. Col Comdt RAPC, 1955-60. *Recreation:* golf. *Address:* PO Box 454, Blantyre, Malaŵi; Effingham Golf Club, Effingham, Surrey; Sandapple House, Ruwa. *Clubs:* Army and Navy; New, Ruwa Country (Salisbury).

BEDSER, Alec Victor, OBE 1964; company director; *b* 4 July 1918; twin *s* of Arthur and Florence Beatrice Bedser. *Educ:* Monument Hill Secondary Sch., Woking. Served with RAF in UK, France (BEF), N Africa, Sicily, Italy, Austria, 1939-46. Joined Surrey County Cricket Club, as Professional, 1938; awarded Surrey CCC and England caps, 1946, 1st Test Match v India, created record by taking 22 wickets in first two Tests; toured Australia as Member of MCC team, 1946-47, 1950-51, 1954-55; toured S Africa with MCC, 1948-49; held record of most number of Test wickets (236), since beaten, 1953; took 100th wicket against Australia (only English bowler since 1914 to do this), 1953; Asst Man. to Duke of Norfolk on MCC tour to Australia, 1962-63; Manager of MCC team to Australia, 1974-

75; Chm., England Cricket Selection Cttee, 1968- (Mem. 1962-). Founded own company (office equipment and supplies) with Eric Bedser, 1955. *Publications:* (with E. A. Bedser) Our Cricket Story, 1951; Bowling, 1952; (with E. A. Bedser) Following On, 1954. *Recreations:* cricket, golf. *Address:* The Coppice, Carlton Road, Woking, Surrey GU21 4HQ. *T:* Woking 73018. *Clubs:* MCC (Hon. Life), East India, Devonshire, Sports and Public Schools; Surrey County Cricket (Vice-Pres.); West Hill Golf.

BEEBY, Clarence Edward, CMG 1956; PhD; *b* 16 June 1902; *s* of Anthony and Alice Beeby; *m* 1926, Beatrice Eleanor, *d* of Charles Newnham; one *s* one *d*. *Educ:* Christchurch Boys' High Sch.; Canterbury Coll., University of NZ (MA); University Coll., London; University of Manchester (PhD). Lectr in Philosophy and Education, Canterbury Univ. Coll., University of NZ, 1923-34; Dir, NZ Council for Educational Research, 1934-38; Asst Dir of Education, Education Dept, NZ, 1938-40; Dir of Education, NZ, 1940-60 (leave of absence to act as Asst Dir-Gen. of UNESCO, Paris, (1948-49); NZ Ambassador to France, 1960-63; Research Fellow, Harvard Univ., 1963-67; Commonwealth Visiting Prof., Univ. of London, 1967-68; Consultant on Educn in Developing Countries, 1969-; Consultant: to Australian Govt in Papua and New Guinea, 1969; to Ford Foundn in Indonesia, 1970-75; to UNDP in Malaysia, 1976. Leader of NZ Delegs, to Gen. Confs of UNESCO, 1946, 1947, 1950, 1953, 1954, 1956, 1958, 1960, 1962. Hon. Counsellor of UNESCO, 1950; Mem., Exec. Bd, UNESCO, 1960-63 (Chm., Exec. Bd, 1963-64); Mem., Council of Consultant Fellows, Internat. Inst. for Educnl Planning, Paris, 1971-. Mackie Medal, ANZAAS, 1971. Hon. LLD Otago, 1969; Hon. LittD Wellington, 1970. Order of St Gregory (1st cl.), 1964. *Publications:* The Intermediate Schools of New Zealand, 1938; (with W. Thomas and M. H. Oram) Entrance to the University, 1939; The Quality of Education in Developing Countries, 1966; (ed) Qualitative Aspects of Educational Planning, 1969; articles in educational periodicals. *Recreations:* gardening, fishing, cabinet-making. *Address:* 73 Barnard Street, Wellington N2, New Zealand.

BEEBY, George Harry, CBE 1974; PhD, BSc, CEng, FRIC; Chairman, Inveresk Research International, since 1973; *b* 9 Sept. 1902; *s* of George Beeby and Lucy Beeby (née Monk); *m* 1929, Helen Elizabeth Edwards; one *d*. *Educ:* Loughborough Grammar Sch.; Loughborough Coll. BSc Hons 1922; PhD 1924, London Univ. Various appts in rubber and chemical industries, 1924-; Divisional Chm., ICI, 1954-57; Chm., British Titan Ltd, 1957-69. Chairman: EDC for Chemical Industry, 1964-67; Nat. Sulphuric Acid Assoc., 1963-65; British Standards Instn, 1967-70 (Dep. Pres. 1970-73). Pres., Soc. of Chemical Industry, 1970-72 (Vice-Pres., 1966-69); Vice-Pres., RoSPA, 1969-; Hon. Mem., Chemical Industries Assoc. Member: Robens Cttee on Safety and Health at Work, 1970; Parly and Sci. Cttee, 1971; Windeyer Cttee on lead poisoning, 1972. FIChemE; FRSA 1969. Hon. DTech Loughborough Univ. of Technology, 1969. Soc. of Chemical Industry Medal, 1973. *Publications:* contribs to various jls on industrial safety, industrial economics and business administration. *Recreations:* golf, racing. *Address:* The Laurels, Sandy Drive, Cobham, Surrey. *T:* Oxshott 2346. *Club:* Royal Automobile.

BEECH, Patrick Mervyn, CBE 1970; Controller, English Regions, BBC, 1969-72, retired; *b* 31 Oct. 1912; *s* of Howard Worcester Mervyn Beech and Stella Patrick Campbell; *m* 1st, 1935, Sigrid Gunnel Christenson (*d* 1959); two *d*; 2nd, 1960, Merle-Mary Barnes; one *d*. *Educ:* Stowe; Exeter Coll., Oxford. Joined BBC as Producer, West Region, 1935; News Editor, West Region, 1945; Asst Head of programmes, West Region, 1954; Controller, Midland Region, 1964-69. *Recreations:* riding, photography, music, theatre. *Address:* Mill Bank, Cradley, near Malvern, Worcs. *T:* Ridgway Cross 234.

BEECHAM, Sir Adrian (Welles), 3rd Bt cr 1914; *b* 4 Sept. 1904; *er s* of Sir Thomas Beecham, 2nd Bt, CH (*Kt* 1916) and of Utica, *d* of Dr Charles S. Welles, New York; *S* father, 1961; *m* 1939, Barbara Joyce Cairn; two *s* one *d*. *Educ:* privately. MusBac Durham, 1926. *Publications:* Four Songs, 1950; Little Ballet Suite, 1951; Traditional Irish Tunes, 1953; Three part-songs, 1955; Ruth (sacred cantata), 1957; Sonnet cxlvi (Shakespeare), 1962. *Recreation:* country life. *Heir: er s* John Stratford Roland Beecham, *b* 21 April 1940. *Address:* Compton Scorpion Manor, Shipston-on-Stour, Warwicks. *T:* Shipston 61482. *Club:* Savage.

BEECHER, Most Rev. Leonard James, CMG 1961; ARCS, MA, DD; *b* 21 May 1906; *er s* of Robert Paul and Charlotte Beecher; *m* 1930. Gladys Sybil Bazett, *yr d* of late Canon Harry and Mrs Mary Leakey; two *s* one *d*. *Educ:* St Olave's Grammar Sch., Southwark; Imperial Coll. and London Day Trg Coll., University of London. ARCS 1926; BSc 1927; MA (London)

1937. DD Lambeth, 1962. Asst Master, Alliance High Sch., Kikuyu, Kenya, 1927-30; Missionary, Church Missionary Soc., Diocese of Mombasa, 1930-57; Unofficial Mem. of Legislative Council, Colony of Kenya, representing African interests, 1943-47; MEC of the Colony of Kenya, 1947-52; Asst Bishop of Mombasa, Kenya Colony, 1950-53; Archdeacon and Canon of the Diocese, 1945-53; Bishop of Mombasa, 1953-64; Archbishop of East Africa, 1960-70; Bishop of Nairobi, 1964-70; Archbishop Emeritus, 1970. *Publications:* (with G. S. Beecher) A Kikuyu-English Dictionary, 1933; translator of parts of the Kikuyu Old Testament, 1939-49; Ed. of Kenya Church Review, 1941-50. *Recreations:* recorded music, bird-watching, photography. *Address:* PO Box 21066, Nairobi, Kenya. *T:* Nairobi 67485.

BEECHING, family name of **Baron Beeching.**

BEECHING, Baron, *cr* 1965 (Life Peer); **Richard Beeching,** PhD; Director, Lloyds Bank Ltd, since 1965; *b* 21 April 1913; *s* of Hubert J. Beeching; *m* 1938, Ella Margaret Tiley. *Educ:* Maidstone Grammar Sch.; Imperial Coll. of Science and Technology, London. ARCS, BSc, 1st Cl. Hons; DIC; PhD London. Fuel Research Station, 1936; Mond Nickel Co. Ltd 1937; Armaments Design Dept, Min. of Supply, 1943; Dep. Chief Engineer of Armaments Design, 1946. Joined Imperial Chemical Industries, 1948, Dir, 1957-61 and 1965, Dep. Chm. 1966-68. Vice-Pres. ICI of Canada Ltd, 1953; Chm., Metals Div., ICI, 1955. Furness Withy & Co. Ltd: Dir, 1972-75; Chm., 1973-75; Chm., Redland Ltd, 1970-77. Member: Special Adv. Gp on BTC, 1960; NEDC, 1962-64; Top Salaries Review Body, 1971-75; Chairman: British Railways Bd, 1963-65; BTC, 1961-63. Chm., Royal Commn on Assizes and QS, 1966. First Pres., Inst. of Work Study Practitioners, 1967-72; Pres., RoSPA, 1968-73. Fellow, Imperial Coll.; CIMechE, FBIM, FInstP, FCIT; Hon. LLD London; Hon. DSc NUI. *Publication:* Electron Diffraction, 1936. *Address:* Little Manor, East Grinstead, West Sussex.

BEELEY, Sir Harold, KCMG 1961 (CMG 1953); CBE 1946; *b* 15 Feb. 1909; *s* of Frank Arthur Beeley; *m* 1st, 1933, Millicent Mary Chinn (marr. diss., 1953); two *d*; 2nd, 1958, Mrs Patricia Karen Brett-Smith; one *d*. *Educ:* Highgate; Queen's Coll., Oxford. 1st Cl. in Modern History, 1930. Asst Lectr in Modern History, Sheffield Univ., 1930-31; University Coll., London, 1931-35; Junior Research Fellow and Lecturer, Queen's Coll., Oxford, 1935-38; Lecturer in Charge of History Dept, University Coll., Leicester, 1938-39. Mem. of wartime organisation of Royal Institute of International Affairs, and subsequently of Foreign Office Research Dept, 1939-45. Mem. of Secretariat of San Francisco Conf. and of Preparatory Commission of UN, 1945; Sec. of Anglo-American Cttee of Enquiry on Palestine, 1946. Entered Foreign Service, 1946; Counsellor of Embassy, Copenhagen, 1949-50; Baghdad, 1950-53; Washington, 1953-55; Ambassador to Saudi Arabia, during 1955; Asst Under-Sec., Foreign Office, 1956-58; Dep. UK Representative to UN, New York, 1958-61; UK Representative, Disarmament Conf., Geneva, 1964-67; Ambassador to the United Arab Republic, 1961-64, 1967-69. Lectr in History, Queen Mary Coll., Univ. of London, 1969-75. Chm., Unigulf Investments Ltd. Pres., Egypt Exploration Soc., 1969-; Chm., World of Islam Festival Trust, 1973-. *Publications:* Disraeli, 1936; contrib. to Survey of International Affairs, 1936-38. *Address:* 2 Ormond Road, Richmond, Surrey. *Club:* Reform.

BEER, Prof. (Anthony) Stafford; International Consultant and Visiting Professor of Cybernetics at Manchester University (Business School) since 1969, also Adjunct Professor of Statistics and Operations Research at Pennsylvania University (Wharton School) since 1972; *b* London, 25 Sept. 1926; *er s* of late William John and of Doris Ethel Beer; *m* 1st, 1947, Cynthia Margaret Hannaway; four *s* one *d*; 2nd, 1968, Sallie Steadman (*née* Child); one *s* two *d*. *Educ:* Whitgift Sch.; University Coll., London. MBA Manchester. Lieut, 9th Gurkha Rifles 1945; Captain, Royal Fusiliers 1947. Man. of Operational Res. and Prodn Controller, S. Fox & Co., 1949-56; Head of Op. Res. and Cybernetics, United Steel, 1956-61; Man. Dir, SIGMA Science in General Management Ltd and Dir, Metra International, 1961-66; Develt Dir, International Publishing Corp.; Dir, International Data Highways Ltd; Chm., Computaprint Ltd, 1966-69. Vis. Prof. of Gen. Systems, Open Univ., 1970-71. Ex-Pres., Operational Res. Soc.; Ex-Pres., Soc. for Gen. Systems Res. (USA); Mem. UK Automation Council, 1957-69; Mem. Gen. Adv. Council of BBC, 1961-69. Silver Medal, Royal Swedish Acad. for Engrg Scis, 1958; Lanchester Prize (USA) for Ops Res., 1966; McCulloch Award (USA) for Cybernetics, 1970. *Publications:* Cybernetics and Management, 1959; Decision and Control, 1966; Management Science, 1967; Brain of the Firm, 1972; Designing Freedom, 1974; Platform for Change, 1975; Transit (poems), 1977; Heart of the Firm, 1978;

chapters in numerous other books. *Recreations:* spinning, painting, poetry, classics, staying put. *Address:* Cwarel Isaf, Pont Creuddyn, Lampeter, Dyfed, Wales. *Club:* Athenæum. *See also* I. D. S. Beer.

BEER, Ian David Stafford, MA; JP; Head Master, Lancing College, Sussex, since 1969; *b* 28 April 1931; *s* of William Beer, Lloyd's Register of Shipping; *m* 1960, Angela Felce, *d* of Col E. S. G. Howard, MC, RA; two *s* one *d*. *Educ:* Whitgift Sch.; (Exhibitioner) St Catharine's Coll., Cambridge. Second Lieut in 1st Bn Royal Fusiliers, 1950. House Master, Marlborough Coll., Wilts, 1957-61; Head Master, Ellesmere Coll., Salop, 1961-69. Chm., HMC Academic Cttee. *Recreations:* Rugby Football Union Cttee (formerly: played Rugby for England; CURFC (Capt.), Harlequins, Old Whitgiftians), swimming, golf, reading, zoology, meeting people. *Address:* Lancing College, W Sussex. *T:* Shoreham-by-Sea 2213. *Clubs:* East India, Devonshire, Sports and Public Schools; Hawks (Cambridge). *See also* A. S. Beer.

BEER, James Edmund; Director of Finance, Leeds City Council, since 1973; *b* 17 March 1931; *s* of Edmund Huxtable Beer and Gwendoline Kate Beer; *m* 1953, Barbara Mollie (*née* Tunley); two *s* one *d*. *Educ:* Torquay Grammar School. IPFA, FRVA, MBCS, MBIM. Torquay Borough Council, 1951-54; Chatham, 1954-56; Wolverhampton, 1956-58; Doncaster, 1958-60; Chief Accountant, Bedford, 1960-62; Asst Borough Treas., Croydon, 1963-65; Dep. Treas., Leeds, 1965; Chief Financial Officer, Leeds, 1968. Mem. Local Govt Financial Exec., CIPFA; Financial Adviser to AMA; Treas., Soc. of Metrop. Treasurers; Mem. Nat. Savings Exec., Yorks; Vice-Chm., LAMSAC Computer Panel; Treas., Yorks and Humberside Develt Assoc.; Past Examr, CIPFA; an Adviser on Rate Support Grant, AMA; Treas., Leeds Grand Theatre & Opera House Ltd; Mem. Exec. Cttee, Leeds Musical Festival. *Publications:* contrib. professional jls. *Recreations:* golf, theatre, swimming, Rugby (past playing mem., Torquay Athletic RUFC). *Address:* 48 High Ash Avenue, Alwoodley, Leeds LS17 8RG. *T:* Leeds 683907. *Club:* Leeds (Leeds).

BEÉR, Prof. János Miklós, DSc, PhD, Dipl-Ing; Professor of Chemical and Fuel Engineering, Massachusetts Institute of Technology (MIT), since 1976; Programme Director for Combustion, MIT Energy Laboratory, since 1976; *b* Budapest, 27 Feb. 1923; *s* of Sándor Beér and Gizella Trismai; *m* 1944, Marta Gabriella Csató. *Educ:* Berzsenyi Dániel Gymnasium, Budapest; Univ. of Budapest. PhD (Sheffield), 1960, DSc(Tech) Sheffield, 1967. Heat Research Inst., Budapest: Research Officer, 1949-52; Head, Combustion Dept, 1952-56; Princ. Lectr (part-time), University of Budapest, 1953-56; Research Engr, Babcock & Wilcox Ltd, Renfrew, 1957; Research Bursar, University of Sheffield, 1957-60; Head, Research Stn, Internat. Flame Research Foundn, Ijmuiden, Holland, 1960-63; Prof., Dept of Fuel Science, Pa State Univ., 1963-65; Newton Drew Prof. of Chemical Engrg and Fuel Technology and Head of Dept, Univ. of Sheffield, 1965-76; Dean, Faculty of Engineering, Univ. of Sheffield, 1973-75. Member: Adv. Council on R&D for Fuel and Power, DTI, later Dept of Energy, 1973-76; Adv. Bd, Safety in Mines Research, Dept of Energy, 1974-76; Clean Air Council, DoE, 1974-76; Bd of Directors, The Combustion Inst., Pittsburgh, USA, 1974-; Mem., Adv. Cttee, Italian Nat. Res. Council, 1974-. Gen. Superintendent of Research, Internat. Flame Research Foundn, 1971-. Editor, Fuel and Energy Science Monograph Series, 1966-. Moody Award, Amer. Soc. Mech. Eng., 1964. *Publications:* (with N. Chigier) Combustion Aerodynamics, 1972; (ed with M. W. Thring) Industrial Flames, 1972; (ed with H. B. Palmer) Developments in Combustion Science and Technology, 1974; (ed with N. Afgan) Heat Transfer in Flames, 1975; contribs to Nature, Combustion and Flame, Basic Engrg Jl, Amer. Soc. Mech. Engrg, Jl Inst. F, ZVDI, Internat. Gas Wärme, Proc. Internat. Symposia on Combustion, etc. *Recreations:* swimming, rowing, reading, music. *Address:* Department of Chemical Engineering, Massachusetts Institute of Technology, Cambridge, Mass 02139, USA. *T:* 617-253-6661.

BEER, Nellie, (Mrs Robert Beer), OBE 1957; JP; DL; Member of Manchester City Council, 1937-72 (Alderman 1964-72; Lord Mayor of Manchester, 1966); *b* 22 April 1900; *d* of Arthur Robinson and Nelly Laurie Robinson (*née* Hewitt); *m* 1927, Robert Beer; one *d*. *Educ:* Ardwick Higher Grade Sch. JP Manchester, 1942; DL Lancs, 1970. *Address:* 6 Princes Avenue, Didsbury, Manchester. *T:* 061-445 6237.

BEER, Patricia, (Mrs J. D. Parsons); freelance writer; *b* 4 Nov. 1924; *yr d* of Andrew William and Harriet Beer, Exmouth, Devon; *m* 1964, John Damien Parsons. *Educ:* Exmouth Grammar Sch.; Exeter Univ. (BA, 1st cl. Hons English); St

Hugh's Coll., Oxford (BLitt). Lecturer: in English, Univ. of Padua, 1947-49; British Inst., Rome, 1949-51; Goldsmiths' Coll., Univ. of London, 1962-68. *Publications: poetry:* Loss of the Magyar, 1959; The Survivors, 1963; Just Like The Resurrection, 1967; The Estuary, 1971; (ed) New Poems 1975, 1975; Driving West, 1975; (ed jtly) New Poetry 2, 1976; *autobiog.:* Mrs Beer's House, 1968; *criticism:* Reader, I Married Him, 1974; contrib. The Listener, TLS. *Recreations:* travelling, cooking. *Address:* 1 Oak Hill Park, NW3. *T:* 01-435 2470.

BEER, Prof. Stafford; see Beer, Prof. A. S.

BEESLEY, Mrs Alec M.; see Smith, Dodie.

BEESLY, Lewis Rowland, CB 1966; CEng, FIMechE, FIProdE; industrial consultant; Head of Engineering Staff, 1962-73, and Director-General of Aircraft Production, 1960-73, Ministry of Defence; *b* 1 May 1912; *s* of Edward Rowland Beesly, Derby; *m* 1936, Kathleen Lilian, *d* of late Rev. S. Ivan Bell, Glasgow; four *d. Educ:* Bemrose Sch., Derby. Various managerial positions in Royal Ordnance Factories, 1935-49; Asst Dir, Longterm Production Planning (Air), Ministry of Supply, 1950; Dir, Engine Production, Ministry of Supply, 1951-59; Superintendent-Dir, Royal Small Arms Factory, Enfield, 1959-60; Min. of Aviation, 1960. Treasurer, London Derbyshire Soc. *Address:* 58 Wood Ride, Petts Wood, Kent. *T:* Orpington 21185.

BEESON, Prof. Paul Bruce, Hon. KBE 1973; FRCP; Distinguished Physician, United States Veterans Administration, since 1974; Professor of Medicine, University of Washington, since 1974; *b* 18 Oct. 1908; *s* of John Bradley Beeson, Livingston, Mont; *m* 1942, Barbara Neal, *d* of Ray C. Neal, Buffalo, NY; two *s* one *d. Educ:* Univ. of Washington, McGill Univ. Med. Sch. MD, CM, 1933. Intern, Hosp. of Univ. of Pa, 1933-35; Gen. practice of medicine, Wooster, Ohio, 1935-37; Asst Rockefeller Inst., 1937-39; Chief Med. Resident, Peter Bent Brigham Hosp., 1939-40; Instructor in Med., Havard Med. Sch., and Chief Phys., American Red Cross-Harvard Field Hosp. Unit, Salisbury, 1940-42; Asst and Assoc. Prof. of Med., Emory Med. Sch., 1942-46; Prof. of Med. Emory Med. Sch., 1946-52; Prof. of Med. and Chm. Dept of Med., Yale Univ., 1952-65; Nuffield Prof. of Clinical Med., Oxford Univ., and Fellow of Magdalen Coll., 1965-74, Hon. Fellow, 1975; Hon. Fellow RSM, 1976. Vis. Investigator, Wright-Fleming Inst., St Mary's Hosp., 1958-59. Pres., Assoc. Amer. Physicians, 1967; Master, Amer. Coll. of Physicians, 1970. *Alumnus Summa Laude Dignatus,* Univ. of Washington, 1968; Hon. DSc: Emory Univ., 1968; McGill Univ., 1971; Yale Univ., 1975; Albany Med. Coll., 1975. *Publications:* Edited: Cecil-Loeb Textbook of Medicine; Yale Journal Biology and Medicine, 1959-65; numerous scientific publications relating to infectious disease, pathogenesis of fever, pyelonephritis and mechanism of eosinophilia. *Address:* US Veterans Administration Hospital, Seattle, Washington, USA.

BEESON, Rev. Canon Trevor Randall; Canon of Westminster, since 1976; *b* 2 March 1926; *s* of Arthur William and Matilda Beeson; *m* 1950, Josephine Grace Cope; two *d. Educ:* King's Coll., London (AKC 1950); St Boniface Coll., Warminster. RAF Met Office, 1944-47. Deacon, 1951; Priest, 1952; Curate, Leadgate, Co. Durham, 1951-54; Priest-in-charge and subseq. Vicar of St Chad, Stockton-on-Tees, 1954-65; Curate of St Martin-in-the-Fields, London, 1965-71; Vicar of Ware, Herts, 1971-76. Chaplain of St Bride's, Fleet Street, 1967-. Gen. Sec., Parish and People, 1962-64; Editor, New Christian, and Man. Dir, Prism Publications Ltd, 1965-70; European Corresp. of The Christian Century (Chicago), 1970-. Hon. MA (Lambeth) 1976. *Publications:* New Area Mission, 1963; (jtly) Worship in a United Church, 1964; An Eye for an Ear, 1972; The Church of England in Crisis, 1973; Discretion and Valour: religious conditions in Russia and Eastern Europe, 1974. *Recreations:* cricket, travel. *Address:* 2 Little Cloister, Westminster Abbey, SW1.

BEESTON, Prof. Alfred Felix Landon, MA, DPhil; FBA 1965; Laudian Professor of Arabic, Oxford, 1956-Sept. 1978; *b* 1911; *o s* of Herbert Arthur Beeston and Edith Mary Landon. *Educ:* Westminster Sch.; Christ Church, Oxford. James Mew Arabic Scholarship, Oxford, 1934; MA (Oxford), 1936; DPhil (Oxford), 1937. Asst in Dept of Oriental Books, Bodleian Library, Oxford, 1935-40; Sub-Librarian and Keeper of Oriental Books, Bodleian Library, 1946-55. *Publications:* Descriptive Grammar of Epigraphic South Arabian, 1962; Written Arabic, 1968; The Arabic Language Today, 1970. *Address:* St John's College, Oxford OX1 3JP.

BEETHAM, Sir Edward (Betham), KCMG 1955 (CMG 1950); CVO 1947; OBE 1946; retired as Governor and Commander-in-Chief, Trinidad and Tobago (1955-60); *b* 19 Feb. 1905; *s* of late Dr Beetham, Red House, Knaresborough; *m* 1933, Eileen Joy Parkinson, CStJ; one *d. Educ:* Charterhouse; Lincoln Coll., Oxford. District Officer, Kenya, 1928-38; seconded to Colonial Office, 1938; District Commissioner, Sierra Leone, 1938-40; Chief Asst Colonial Sec., Sierra Leone, 1940-46; acted as Colonial Sec. and Governor's Deputy, Sierra Leone, on many occasions; Resident Commissioner of Swaziland, 1946-50; of the Bechuanaland Protectorate, 1950-53; Governor and C-in-C, Windward Is, 1953-55. Chm. Texaco Ltd, and Chief Exec. Officer, Texaco Gp of Cos in UK, 1963-70; Chm., Oaklife Assurance Ltd. KStJ 1953. *Address:* Millstream, Mill End, Hambleden, Henley-on-Thames, Oxon. *Clubs:* Army and Navy; Phyllis Court (Henley-on-Thames).

BEETHAM, Air Chief Marshal Sir Michael (James), KCB 1976; CBE 1967; DFC 1944; AFC 1960; Chief of the Air Staff, since 1977; Air ADC to the Queen, since 1977; *b* 17 May 1923; *s* of Major G. C. Beetham, MC; *m* 1956, Patricia Elizabeth Lane; one *s* one *d. Educ:* St Marylebone Grammar School. Joined RAF, 1941; pilot trng, 1941-42; commnd 1942; Bomber Comd: 50, 57 Sqdns, 1943-46; HQ Staff, 1947-49; 82 (RECCE) Sqdn, E Africa, 1949-51; psa 1952; Air Min. (Directorate Operational Requirements), 1953-56; CO 214 (Valiant) Sqdn Marham, 1958-60; Gp Captain Ops, HQ Bomber Comd, 1962-64; CO RAF Khormaksar, Aden, 1964-66; idc 1967; Dir Ops (RAF), MoD, 1968-70; Comdt, RAF Staff Coll., 1970-72; ACOS (Plans and Policy), SHAPE, 1972-75; Dep. C-in-C, Strike Command, 1975-76; C-in-C RAF Germany, and Comdr, 2nd Tactical Allied Air Force, 1976-77. *Recreations:* golf, tennis. *Address:* Ministry of Defence (Air), Whitehall, SW1. *Clubs:* Royal Air Force; Royal Mid-Surrey Golf.

BEEVOR, John Grosvenor, OBE 1945; Chairman, National and Commercial Development Capital Ltd; Director: The Lafarge Organisation Ltd, since 1965 (Chairman, 1966-76); Lafarge SA, since 1969; *b* 1 March 1905; *s* of Henry Beevor, Newark-on-Trent, Notts; *m* 1st, 1933, Carinthia Jane (marr. diss., 1956), *d* of Aubrey and Caroline Waterfield, Aulla, Italy; three *s* ; 2nd, 1957, Mary Christine Grepe. *Educ:* Winchester; New Coll., Oxford. Solicitor, 1931-53, Slaughter and May, London, EC2. Served HM Army, 1939-45, RA and Gen. Staff. Adviser to British Delegation to Marshall Plan Conf., Paris, 1947; Mem. Lord Chancellor's Cttee on Private Internat. Law, 1952-53; Man. Dir, Commonwealth Development Finance Co. Ltd, 1954-56; Vice-Pres., Internat. Finance Corp., Washington, DC, 1956-64. Chairman: Doulton & Co., 1966-75; Tilbury Contracting Group, 1966-76; Director: Williams & Glyn's Bank Ltd, 1970-75; Glaxo Holdings Ltd, 1965-75. Member Councils: The Officers' Assoc.; Overseas Develt Inst. *Publication:* The Effective Board, a Chairman's View, 1975. *Recreations:* golf, travel. *Address:* 51 Eaton Square, SW1W 9BE. *T:* 01-235 7987. *Clubs:* Royal Automobile; Royal St George's (Sandwich).

BEEVOR, Miles; retired as Solicitor and Director of Companies; *b* 8 March 1900; 2nd *s* of Rowland Beevor; *m* 1st, 1924, Margaret Florence Platt (*d* 1934); one *s* (and one *d* decd); 2nd, 1935, Sybil Gilliat; two *s* one *d. Educ:* Winchester (Scholar); New Coll., Oxford (Scholar), BA 1921. Admitted a Solicitor, 1925. Served European War, 1914-18, in Army (RE Officer Cadet Battalion), 1918; War of 1939-45, RAFVR (Flt-Lieut Admin. and Special Duties Br.), 1941-43. Chief Legal Adviser, LNER, 1943-47; Actg Chief General Manager, LNER, 1947; Chief Sec. and Legal Adviser, British Transport Commission, 1947-51; Managing Dir, Brush Electrical Engineering Co. Ltd (which became The Brush Group Ltd), 1952-56; Deputy Chm. and Joint Managing Dir, 1956-57. *Recreations:* fishing, shooting. *Address:* Parkside, Welwyn, Herts. *T:* Welwyn 4087.

BEEVOR, Sir Thomas Agnew, 7th Bt, *cr* 1784; *b* 6 Jan. 1929; *s* of Comdr Sir Thomas Beevor, 6th Bt, and of Edith Margaret Agnew (who *m* 2nd, 1944, Rear-Adm. R. A. Currie, *qv*); S father 1943; *m* 1st, 1957, Barbara Clare (marr. diss., 1965), *y d* of Capt. R. L. B. Cunliffe, RN (retd); one *s* two *d* ; 2nd, 1966, Carola, *d* of His Honour J. B. Herbert, MC; 3rd, 1976, Mrs Sally Bouwens, White Hall, Saham Toney, Norfolk. *Heir:* s Thomas Hugh Cunliffe Beevor, *b* 1 Oct. 1962. *Address:* Hargham Hall, Norwich.

See also Sir E. C. H. Warner, Bt.

BEEZLEY, Frederick Ernest; His Honour Judge Beezley; a Circuit Judge, since 1976; *b* 30 Jan. 1921; *s* of Frederick William Beezley and Lilian Isabel (*née* Markham); *m* 1969, Sylvia Ruth (*née* Locke). *Educ:* Acton County Sch. Served War, Royal Signals, Combined Operations, 1940-46. Called to Bar, Gray's Inn, 1947. *Recreations:* organ playing, conducting, racing. *Address:* c/o Crown Court, Norwich. *T:* Norwich 29859.

BEGG, Rt. Rev. Ian Forbes, MA, DD; *b* 12 Feb. 1910; *e s* of Rev. John Smith Begg and Elizabeth Macintyre; *m* 1949, Lillie Taylor Paterson. *Educ:* Aberdeen Grammar Sch.; Aberdeen Univ.; Westcott House, Cambridge. Deacon 1933; Priest 1934. Curate, St Paul's, Prince's Park, Liverpool, 1933-35; Priest-in-Charge of St Ninian's Episcopal Church, Seaton, Aberdeen, 1935-73; Dean, United Diocese of Aberdeen and Orkney, 1969-73; Bishop of Aberdeen and Orkney, 1973-77; Canon of St Andrew's Cathedral, Aberdeen, 1965. Chm., Church Guest Houses' Assoc., 1969-. Hon. DD Aberdeen, 1971. *Recreations:* fishing, gardening. *Address:* 430 King Street, Aberdeen. *T:* Aberdeen 572169.

BEGG, Admiral of the Fleet Sir Varyl (Cargill), GCB 1965 (KCB 1962; CB 1959); DSO 1952; DSC 1941; Governor and Commander-in-Chief of Gibraltar, 1969-73; *b* 1 Oct. 1908; *s* of Francis Cargill Begg and Muriel Clare Robinson; *m* 1943, Rosemary Cowan, CStJ; two *s*. *Educ:* St Andrews Sch., Eastbourne; Malvern Coll. Entered RN, special entry, 1926; Qualified Gunnery Officer, 1933; HMS Glasgow, 1939-40; HMS Warspite, 1940-43; Comdr Dec. 1942; Capt. 1947; commanded HM Gunnery Sch., Chatham, 1948-50; 8th Destroyer Flotilla, 1950-52; HMS Excellent, 1952-54; HMS Triumph, 1955-56; idc 1954; Rear-Adm. 1957; Chief of Staff to C-in-C Portsmouth 1957-58; Flag Officer Commanding Fifth Cruiser Squadron and Flag Officer Second-in-Command, Far East Station, 1958-60; Vice-Adm. 1960; a Lord Commissioner of the Admiralty and Vice-Chief of Naval Staff, 1961-63; Admiral, 1963; C-in-C, British Forces in the Far East, and UK Military Adviser to SEATO, 1963-65; C-in-C, Portsmouth, and Allied C-in-C, Channel, 1965-66; Chief of Naval Staff and First Sea Lord, 1966-68. KStJ 1969. PMN 1966. *Recreations:* fishing, gardening. *Address:* Copyhold Cottage, Chilbolton, Stockbridge, Hants. *Club:* Army and Navy.

BEHAN, Sir Harold Garfield, Kt 1977; CMG 1967; MBE 1958; JP; Grazier; *b* 22 Feb. 1901; *s* of Thomas and Mary Behan, Jericho; *m* 1942, Kathleen. *d* of John Costello; two *s* four *d*. *Educ:* Nudgee Coll.; Brisbane Gram. Sch. Member: Jericho Shire Council, 1922-25; Isisford Shire Council, 1926-67 (Chm. 1945-67); Executive Member: Queensland Local Govt Assoc., 1945-67 (Pres. 1952-67); Australian Council of Local Govt Assocs, 1945-67 (Pres. 1967); Graziers' Assoc. of Central and N Queensland, 1942-67 (Pres. 1962-67); Mem. Council and Exec. Council, United Graziers' Assoc. of Queensland, 1939-67. *Address:* Bilbah Downs, Isisford, Qld 4731, Australia. *Clubs:* Longreach, Blackall (Qld).

BEHNE, Edmond Rowlands, CMG 1974; Managing Director, Pioneer Sugar Mills Ltd, Queensland, since 1952; *b* 20 Nov. 1906; *s* of late Edmund Behne; *m* 1932, Grace Elizabeth Ricketts; two *s* one *d*. *Educ:* Bendigo Sch. of Mines; Brisbane Boys' Coll.; Univ. of Queensland. BSc and MSc (App.); ARACI. Bureau of Sugar Experiment Stations, 1930-48 (Director, 1947); Pioneer Sugar Mills Ltd, 1948. *Recreations:* bowls, golf. *Address:* c/o Pioneer Sugar Mills Ltd, GPO Box 266, Brisbane, Queensland 4001, Australia. *T:* (business) 229-1088; Craigston, 217 Wickham Terrace, Brisbane, Qld 4000. *T:* (private) 221-5657. *Clubs:* Brisbane, Queensland, Johnsonian (all in Brisbane).

BEHRENS, Sir Leonard (Frederick), Kt 1970; CBE 1956; MCom; Vice-President, Liberal Party Organisation; Hon. Member, Royal Manchester College of Music; Member of Court, Manchester University; Vice-President, UN Association; Hon. President, World Federation of UN Associations and acting President, Stockholm, 1951; New York, 1963; *b* 15 Oct. 1890; *y s* of late Gustav Behrens; *m* 1920, Beatrice Mary, *y d* of late Dr W. Sandham Symes, Maryborough, Queen's Co. and Chesterfield; two *d*. *Educ:* Ladybarn House Sch.; Manchester Grammar Sch.; Rugby Sch.; Manchester Univ. Partner Sir Jacob Behrens and Sons, 1920-48; Dir Sir Jacob Behrens and Sons Ltd. 1948-54, Dep.-Chm. Cotton and Rayon Merchants' Assoc., 1939-42 and 1954. JP City of Manchester, 1940. Chm. Manchester Information Cttee, and Lecturer to HM Forces, 1940-45; Royal Observer Corps. 1941-52 (now Hon. Mem.). Pres., Manchester Statistical Soc., 1942-44; Dir, Manchester Chamber of Commerce, 1923-67, now Emeritus. Liberal Candidate, Withington, 1945 and 1950; Pres. Liberal Party Org., 1955-57; Chm. of Exec., 1959-61. Pres. Manchester Reform Club, 1956-57; Pres. Manchester Liberal Fedn, 1947-49; Chm. Hallé Concerts Soc., 1952-59 (Cttee Mem., 1932, Hon. Life Cttee Mem., 1974). Order of St Sava (Jugoslavia), 1919; Brilliant Star with Ribbon (China), 1949. *Publications:* pamphlets, articles and letters to the Press. *Recreations:* music and crossword puzzles. *Address:* Netherby, 119 Barlow Moor Road, Didsbury, Manchester M20 8TS. *T:* 061-445 3600. *Clubs:* National Liberal, English-Speaking Union; Manchester (Manchester).

See also Sir B. H. Flowers.

BEHRMAN, Simon, FRCP; Consultant Emeritus in Neurology, Guy's Hospital; Consulting Physician, Moorfields, Eye Hospital; formerly Consulting Neurologist: Regional Neurosurgical Centre, Brook Hospital; Lewisham, Dulwich, St Giles', St Francis', St Leonard's, Bromley and Farnborough Hospitals; *s* of late Leopold Behrman; *m* 1940, Dorothy, *d* of late Charles Engelbert; two *s* two *d*. *Educ:* University Coll. and St Bartholomew's Hosp., London. BSc (Hons) London. 1925; MRCS Eng. 1928; MRCP London 1932. Member: Assoc. of British Neurologists; Ophthalmological Soc. of UK; Academic Bd of Inst of Ophthalmology, University of London; FRSocMed. House Physician and Registrar, Hosp. for Nervous Diseases, Maida Vale, 1930-33; Registrar: Nat. Hosp., Queen Square, 1934-38; Dept of Nervous Diseases, Guy's Hosp., 1935-45. *Publications:* articles on neurology and neuro-ophthalmology. *Address:* 33 Harley Street, W1. *T:* 01-580 3388; The Dower House, Oxney, St Margaret's-at-Cliffe, Kent. *T:* St Margaret's Bay 2161.

BEINART, Prof. Ben Zion; Barber Professor of Jurisprudence, University of Birmingham, since 1975; Dean, Faculty of Law, since 1976; *b* 21 Oct. 1914; *s* of Woolf Beinart and Gitel Apter; *m* 1945, Gladys Beryl Levy; one *s* two *d*. *Educ:* Boys' High Sch., Malmesbury, Cape Province; Univ. of Cape Town (BA, LLB); Univ. of London (LLM). Barrister-at-Law, Gray's Inn, 1940; Advocate, Supreme Ct of SA. War Service, S Af. Def. Force, 1941-45; Lieut. Advocate, Grahamstown, 1945-49; Prof. of Law, Rhodes University Coll., Grahamstown, 1945-49; Dean, Faculty of Law, Univ. of SA, 1948-49; Univ. of Cape Town: W. P. Schreiner Prof. of Roman and Comparative Law, 1950-74; Dean, Faculty of Law, 1953-56 and 1963-66; Asst-Principal, 1969-74; Fellow, 1960-74; Prof. Emeritus, 1975-. Gen. Editor, Acta Juridica, 1958- (Cape Town). *Publications:* (ed and trans. with P. van Warmelo) D. G. van der Keessel, Praelectiones ad Jus Criminale, 4 vols, 1969-76; Dictata ad Institutiones, 2 vols; (ed) S. Groenewegen van der Made, De Legibus abrogatis, 2 vols, 1974-75; (with Riccobono and Wylie) Stipulation and the Theory of Contract, 1957; articles and revs in Mod. Law Rev., SA Law Jl, Tydskrif vir HRHReg and Acta Juridica. *Address:* 54 Hamilton Avenue, Harborne, Birmingham B17 8AR. *T:* 021-427 4314, (univ.) 021-472 1301. *Clubs:* Royal Commonwealth Society; Owl (Cape Town); Albany (Grahamstown).

BEIT, Sir Alfred Lane, 2nd Bt, *cr* 1924; Trustee of the Beit Trust; Trustee of Beit Fellowships for scientific research; *b* London, 19 Jan. 1903; *o surv. s* of 1st Bt and Lilian (*d* 1946), *d* of late T. L. Carter, New Orleans, USA; *S* father, 1930; *m* 1939. Clementine, 2nd *d* of late Major the Hon. Clement Mitford, DSO and Lady Helen Nutting. *Educ:* Eton; Christ Church, Oxford. Contested West Islington in LCC election 1928; South-East St Pancras (C) in general election, 1929; MP (U) St Pancras South-East, 1931-45. Trustee, Beit Memorial Fellowships for Medical Research, 1930-49. *Heir:* none. *Address:* Russborough, Blessington, Co Wicklow, Eire; Gordon's Bay, CP, S Africa. *Clubs:* Buck's, Carlton; Kildare Street and University (Dublin); Civil Service (Cape Town); Muthaiga (Nairobi).

BEITH, Alan James; MP (L) Berwick-upon-Tweed since Nov. 1973; Liberal Chief Whip, since 1976; *b* 20 April 1943; *o s* of James and Joan Beith, Poynton, Ches; *m* 1965, Barbara Jean Ward; one *s*. *Educ:* King's Sch., Macclesfield; Balliol and Nuffield Colls, Oxford. BLitt, MA Oxon. Lectr, Dept of Politics, Univ. of Newcastle upon Tyne, 1966-. Vice-Chm., Northumberland Assoc. of Parish Councils, 1970-71 and 1972-73; Jt Chm., Assoc. of Councillors, 1974-; Member: Gen. Adv. Council of BBC, 1974-; Hexham RDC, 1969-74; Corbridge Parish Council, 1970-74; Tynedale District Council, 1973-74; BBC NE Regional Adv. Council, 1971-74; NE Transport Users' Consultative Cttee, 1970-74. Methodist Local Preacher. *Publications:* chapter in The British General Election of 1964, ed Butler and King, 1965; articles in Public Administration Bull., Policy and Politics, New Society, Local Government Chronicle, District Councils Review, Parish Councils Review, etc. *Recreations:* walking, music, looking at old buildings. *Address:* Overdale, Corchester Terrace, Corbridge, Northumberland. *T:* Corbridge 2494. *Clubs:* National Liberal; Union Society (Oxford); Shilbottle Working Men's (Alnwick).

BEITH, Sir John, KCMG 1969 (CMG 1959); HM Diplomatic Service, retired; *b* 4 April 1914; *s* of late William Beith and Margaret Stanley, Toowoomba, Qld; *m* 1949, Diana Gregory-Hood, *d* of Sir John Little Gilmour, 2nd Bt; one *s* one *d* (and one *d* decd), (one step *s* one step *d*). *Educ:* Eton; King's Coll., Cambridge. Entered Diplomatic Service, 1937, and served in FO until 1940; 3rd Sec., Athens, 1940-41; 2nd Sec., Buenos Aires, 1941-45; served Foreign Office, 1945-49; Head of UK Permanent Delegation to the UN at Geneva, 1950-53; Head of Chancery at Prague, 1953-54; Counsellor, 1954; Counsellor and

Head of Chancery, British Embassy, Paris, 1954-59; Head of Levant Dept, FO, 1959-61; Head of North and East African Dept, Foreign Office, 1961-63; Ambassador to Israel, 1963-65; an Asst Sec.-Gen., NATO, 1966-67; Asst Under-Sec. of State, FO, 1967-69; Ambassador to Belgium, 1969-74. *Recreations:* music, racing, tennis. *Address:* Dean Farm House, Winchester. *T:* Sparsholt 326. *Clubs:* White's, Anglo-Belgian.

BEITH, John William, CBE 1972; Director Special Duties, Massey Ferguson Holdings Ltd, 1971-74, retired; *b* 13 Jan. 1909; *s* of John William Beith and Ana Theresia (*née* Denk); *m* 1931, Dorothy (*née* Causbrook); two *s. Educ:* Spain, Chile, Germany; Llandovery Coll., S Wales. Joined Massey Harris (now Massey Ferguson), 1927, London; occupied senior exec. positions in Argentina, Canada, France and UK; Vice-Pres., Canadian parent co., 1963; Chm., Massey Ferguson (UK) Ltd, 1970. Pres., Agricl Engrs Assoc. Ltd, 1970. *Recreations:* ancient and contemporary history; follower of Rugby; swimming. *Address:* Torre Blanca, Cala Serena, Cala d'Or, Mallorca. *T:* Baleares 657830. *Clubs:* Oriental; Nautico (Palma de Mallorca).

BELAM, Noël Stephen; Regional Director, North-West, Department of Industry, since 1975; *b* 19 Jan. 1920; *s* of Dr Francis Arthur Belam and Hilda Mary Belam; *m* 1948, Anne Coaker; one *s* one *d. Educ:* Cranleigh Sch.; St Edmund Hall, Oxford (MA). Royal Artillery (T/Captain), 1940-46. Board of Trade, 1947; Trade Comr, Karachi, 1955-58; Private Sec. to successive Ministers of State, BoT, 1961-63; Asst Sec., 1963; Principal Trade Comr, Vancouver, 1963-67; Board of Trade: Regional Controller NW Region, 1967-70; Asst Sec., London, 1970-75; Under Sec., 1975. *Recreations:* fishing, Dartmoor ponies. *Address:* Knarrs Nook, Monks Road, Glossop, Derbyshire. *T:* Glossop 64916. *Club:* United Oxford & Cambridge University.

BELCH, Alexander Ross, CBE 1972; Managing Director, Scott Lithgow Ltd, since 1969; *b* 13 Dec. 1920; *s* of Alexander Belch, CBE, and Agnes Wright Ross; *m* 1947, Janette Finnie Murdoch; four *d. Educ:* Morrison's Acad., Crieff, Perthshire; Glasgow Univ. (BSc Naval Arch. 1st Cl. Hons). Lithgows Ltd: Dir and Gen. Man., 1954-59; Asst Man. Dir, 1959-64; Man. Dir, 1964-69. *Address:* Altnacraig, Lyle Road, Greenock, Renfrewshire. *T:* Greenock 21124.

BELCHEM, Maj.-Gen. Ronald Frederick King, CB 1946; CBE 1944; DSO 1943; President, Le Vexin SA France, since 1973; Director: Fitch Lovell Ltd, since 1973; Crown Lion (Singapore), since 1974; *s* of O. K. Belchem and Louise Morris; *m* 1947 (marr. diss. 1954); *m* 1958, Ellen, *d* of late William Cameron, Ross-shire. *Educ:* Guildford; Sandhurst. 2nd Lieut Royal Tank Regt, 1931, Interpreter, Russian, Italian and French. Served Egypt and Palestine, 1936-39 (despatches); War of 1939-45 (despatches seven times); Greece; with Eighth Army; Western Desert (commanded 1st Royal Tank Regiment, 1943); Sicily and Italy, BGS (Ops) North-West Europe (BGS (Ops) 21 Army Group). Comd. 6 Highland Bde BAOR, 1948; Chief of Staff to Field Marshal Viscount Montgomery, 1948-50; retd 1953. Chairman's Staff, Tube Investments Ltd, 1954-59; Chairman's Staff, BSA Group, 1959-61; Managing Dir Metal Components Div. of the BSA Group 1961; Chm. and Man. Dir, GUS Export Corp. Ltd, 1964-70; Dir of Exports, GUS Industrial Div., 1964-70; Chairman: BNEC Hotel and Public Buildings Equipment Group, 1968-69; Scotia Investments, 1972-74; Dir, National Bank Ltd Brunei, 1971-73. Freeman, City of London, 1956. Mem., Worshipful Co. of Barbers, 1956. Legion of Merit (US), Order of White Lion and MC (Czech), 1946; Order of Orange-Nassau (Dutch), 1947. *Publication:* A Guide to Nuclear Energy. *Recreation:* language study. *Address:* c/o Williams & Glyn's Bank, Holt's Branch, Whitehall, SW1. *Club:* Army and Navy.

BELCHER, John Rashleigh, MS 1946; FRCS 1942; Consultant Thoracic Surgeon, NW Metropolitan Regional Hospital Board, since 1950; Surgeon, London Chest Hospital, since 1951; Thoracic Surgeon, Middlesex Hospital, since 1955; *b* 11 Jan. 1917; *s* of late Dr Ormonde Rashleigh Belcher, Liverpool; *m* 1940, Jacqueline Mary, *d* of late C. P. Phillips; two *s* one *d. Educ:* Epsom Coll.; St Thomas' Hosp. MB 1939; FRCS 1942; MS 1946; Resident appointments at St Thomas' Hospital, 1939-40. RAF, 1940-46: Medical Service; general duties and surgical specialist; Squadron Leader. Resident and Asst posts at St Thomas', Brompton, London Chest, and Middlesex Hosps; followed by consultant appointments; co-editor, Brit. Jl of Diseases of the Chest. Member: Assoc. of Thoracic Surgeons; Thoracic Soc.; Cardiac Soc.; Amer. Coll. of Chest Physicians. Toured: for British Council, Far East 1969; Cyprus and Greece 1973; for FCO, Indonesia 1971, Bolivia 1975; Yugoslavia 1977. *Publications:* Thoracic Surgical Management, 1953; chapters in standard text-books; papers in British and foreign medical

journals. *Recreations:* golf, ski-ing, photography. *Address:* 23 Hornton Court, Hornton Street, W8. *T:* 01-937 7006.

BELCHER, Ronald Harry, CMG 1958; Under-Secretary, Ministry of Overseas Development, 1965-75; *b* 5 Jan 1916; *s* of Harry Albert Belcher; *m* 1948, Hildegarde (*née* Hellyer-Jones); one *s. Educ:* Christ's Hosp., Horsham; Jesus Coll., Cambridge; Brasenose Coll., Oxford. BA (Hons Classics) Cantab 1937; Dipl. Class. Arch. Cantab 1938; BA Oxon 1938. Indian Civil Service, Punjab, 1939-48; Commonwealth Relations Office, 1948-65; seconded to Foreign Office for service in British Embassy, Washington, 1951-53; Private Sec., 1953-54; Asst Sec., 1954; Deputy High Commissioner for the UK in S Africa, 1956-59; Asst Under Sec. of State, CRO, 1960-61; British Dep. High Comr, Delhi, 1961-65. *Address:* Fieldview, Lower Road, Fetcham, Surrey. *Club:* Royal Commonwealth Society.

BELDAM, Alexander Roy Asplan, QC 1969; a Recorder of the Crown Court, since 1972; *b* 29 March 1925; *s* of George William Beldam and Margaret Frew Shettle (formerly Beldam, *née* Underwood); *m* 1953, Elisabeth Bryant Farr; two *s* one *d. Educ:* Oundle Sch.; Brasenose Coll., Oxford. Sub-Lt, RNVR Air Branch, 1943-46. Called to Bar, Inner Temple, 1950. *Recreations:* sailing, cricket, naval history. *Address:* Wherries, Riverbank, Thames Ditton, Surrey KT7 0QU. *T:* 01-398 7148. *Club:* Naval.

BELFAST, Earl of; Arthur Patrick Chichester; Serving Officer, Coldstream Guards; *b* 9 May 1952; *s* and *heir* of 7th Marquess of Donegall, *qv*. *Educ:* Harrow. *Recreations:* hunting, shooting, fishing, knitting. *Address:* Dunbrody Park, Arthurstown, Co. Wexford, Eire.

BELFAST, Dean of; *see* Crooks, Very Rev. S. B.

BELFRAGE, Leif Axel Lorentz, GBE (Hon.), 1956; former Swedish Ambassador; *b* 1 Feb. 1910; *s* of J. K. E. Belfrage and G. U. E. Löfgren; *m* 1937, Greta Jering; one *s* three *d. Educ:* Stockholm University. Law degree, 1933. Practised law at Stockholm Magistrates Court; joined Min. of Commerce, 1937; Dir, Swedish Clearing Office, 1940; Dir, war-time Swedish Trade Commn, 1943-45; entered Swedish Diplomatic Service, as Head of Section in Commercial Dept, 1945; Commercial Counsellor, Swedish Embassy, Washington, 1946; Head of Commercial Dept, FO, Stockholm, 1949-53; Dep. Under-Sec. of State, FO, 1953; Perm. Under-Sec. of State FO, 1956; Ambassador to Court of St James's, 1967-72; Ambassador and Head of Swedish Delegn to OECD and UNESCO, 1972-76. Grand Cross, Order of North Star (Sweden). *Address:* Sturegatan 14, 11436 Stockholm, Sweden.

BELHAM, David Ernest, CB 1975; Principal Assistant Solicitor (Under Secretary), Department of Employment, since 1970; *b* 9 Aug. 1914; *s* of Ernest George Belham and Grace Belham (*née* Firth); *m* 1938, Eunice Monica (*née* Vine); two *s* two *d. Educ:* Whitgift Sch.; Law Society's Sch. of Law. Solicitor (Hons), 1937. Private practice, 1937-39. Served War, RAFVR, 1940-46. Entered Solicitor's Department, Min. of Labour, 1946; Asst Solicitor, 1962. *Address:* 18 Ridge Park, Purley, Surrey CR2 3PN. *T:* 01-647 8603.

BELHAVEN and STENTON, 13th Baron, *cr* 1647; **Robert Anthony Carmichael Hamilton;** farming; *b* 27 Feb. 1927; *o s* of 12th Baron; *S* father, 1961; *m* 1st, 1952, Elizabeth Ann, *d* of late Col A. H. Moseley, Warrawee, NSW; one *s* one *d*; 2nd, 1973, Rosemary Lady Mactaggart, only *d* of Sir Herbert Williams, 1st Bt, MP; one *d* (adopted). *Educ:* Eton. Commissioned, The Cameronians, 1947. *Heir:* *s* Master of Belhaven, *qv*. *Address:* Tighcargaman, Port Ellen, Isle of Islay, Argyll.

BELHAVEN, Master of; Hon. Frederick Carmichael Arthur Hamilton; *b* 27 Sept. 1953; *s* of 13th Baron Belhaven and Stenton, *qv*. *Educ:* Eton. *Address:* 11 Edna Street, SW11. *T:* 01-228 3360.

BELL, Adrian Hanbury; author; Compiler of the Times Crosswords, since 1930; *b* 4 Oct. 1901; *e s* of Robert Bell and Frances Hanbury; *m* 1931, Marjorie Gibson; one *s* two *d. Educ:* Uppingham. After leaving school went as pupil on a Suffolk farm, and has farmed in West and East Suffolk. *Publications:* Corduroy, 1930; Silver Ley, 1931; The Cherry Tree, 1932; Folly Field, 1933; The Balcony, 1934; Poems, 1935; By-Road, 1937; Shepherd's Farm, 1939; Men and the Fields, 1939; Apple Acre, 1942, repr. 1964; Sunrise to Sunset, 1944; The Budding Morrow, 1947; The Black Donkey, 1949; The Flower and the Wheel, 1949; The Path by the Window, 1952; Music in the Morning, 1954; A Young Man's Fancy, 1955; A Suffolk Harvest, 1956; The Mill House, 1958; My Own Master, 1961; A Street in

Suffolk, 1964; A Countryman's Notebook, 1975; The Green Bond, 1976; (ed) The Open Air, 1936.

BELL, Alistair Watson; a Recorder of the Crown Court since 1972; *b* Edinburgh, 31 March 1930; *s* of Albert William Bell and Alice Elizabeth Watson; *m* 1957, Patricia Margaret Seed; one *s* two *d. Educ:* Lanark Grammar Sch.; George Watson's Coll.; Univs of Edinburgh (MA) and Oxford (BA, BCL). 2nd Lieut RASC, 1955. Called to Bar, Middle Temple, 1955; Harmsworth Scholar, 1956; entered practice, Northern Circuit, 1957. Contested (L) Chorley, 1964 and Westmorland, 1966. *Recreation:* hill walking, with or without golf clubs. *Address:* Oaklands, Whittingham Lane, Broughton, Preston, Lancs. *T:* Preston (Lancs) 863065. *Club:* (Pres. 1975) Reform (Manchester).

BELL, Archibald Angus, QC (Scot.) 1961; Sheriff of Glasgow and Strathkelvin (formerly Lanark) at Glasgow, since 1973; *b* 13 April 1923; *o s* of James Dunlop Bell, Solicitor, Ayrshire, and Katherine Rachel Gordon Miller; *m* 1949, Dorothy, *d* of Dr Pollok Donald, Edinburgh, and Mrs Dorothy Donald; two *s. Educ:* The Leys Sch., Cambridge; Univ. of St Andrews; Univ. of Glasgow. Served War, Royal Navy, 1941-45; Sub-Lieut RNVR. MA, St Andrews, 1947; LLB, Glasgow, 1949; admitted to Faculty of Advocates, 1949; Reporter, Court of Session Cases, 1952-55. Contested (C and U) Maryhill Div. of Glasgow, Gen. Elec., 1955. Standing Junior Counsel in Scotland: to Board of Trade, 1955-57; to War Dept, 1957-61. Pres., Scottish Cricket Union, 1975. *Recreations:* watching the sun rise, getting fun out of games. Formerly: hockey and cricket blue, St Andrews, and Pres. UAU and Dramatic Soc. *Clubs:* Royal Scots (Edinburgh); MCC; Royal and Ancient (St Andrews); RNVR (Scotland).

BELL, Arthur; *see* Bell, E. A.

BELL, Sir Arthur (Capel Herbert), Kt 1963; FRCS, FRCOG; Past President of the Royal College of Obstetricians and Gynæcologists; Consultant Gynæcological Surgeon: Westminster Hospital; Chelsea Hospital for Women; Consultant Surgeon, Queen Charlotte's Maternity Hospital; Consulting Gynæcological Surgeon, Thames Ditton Cottage Hospital and Edenbridge Memorial Hospital; *b* 18 Sept. 1904; *o s* of late J. H. Bell; *m* 1933, Hilda, *d* of late H. M. F. Faure; three *s* two *d. Educ:* Marlborough Coll.; St Bartholomew's Hosp. MRCS Eng, LRCP London 1927; MB, BS London 1930; FRCS Eng 1930; FRCOG 1946; Hon. MMSA; Hon. FRCPSG. Formerly: House Surgeon to Surg. Prof. Unit, and Obstetric House Surg., St Bartholomew's Hosp.; Obstetric House Surg., Liverpool Royal Infirmary; Obstetric and Gynæcological Registrar and Tutor, Charing Cross Hosp. and Westminster Hosp.; Obstetric Surgeon, Westminster Hosp.; Gynæcological Surgeon, Chelsea Hosp. for Women. Hon. Adviser on Obstetrics and Gynæcology to the Army, 1963-70. Sometime Examr to the Univs of London, Glasgow, Belfast, Durham, Birmingham, Oxford, Conjoint Board of RCP and RCS, RCOG, Soc. of Apothecaries, Central Midwives Board. *Publications:* A Pocket Obstetrics; (jointly) Queen Charlotte's Practice of Obstetrics; Hysterectomy; Total and Subtotal (Jl of Obst. and Gynec. of Br. Empire). *Recreations:* gardening, shooting, fishing, tennis and golf. *Address:* Garden End, Orchard Way, Esher, Surrey. *T:* Esher 62455.

BELL, Charles William, CBE 1968; Chairman of Coats Patons Ltd, 1967-75; *b* 4 June 1907; *s* of Herbert James Bell and Bertha Alice Bell (*née* Jones), Pen-y-Ffordd, Flintshire; *m* 1931, Eileen, *d* of Edwin James Hannaford, Eastham, Cheshire; three *s. Educ:* Chester City Grammar Sch.; Selwyn Coll., Cambridge (Open Exhibr). Joined Coats Patons Ltd, 1930; Dir, Central Agency Ltd (subsid. co.), 1934; Dir, J. & P. Coats Ltd, (Subsid. Co.), 1947; Man. Dir, J. & P. Coats Ltd, 1961; Dir, Coats Patons Ltd, 1961. Dep. Chm., and Nat. Treasurer, Scottish Conservative and Unionist Party, 1971-. *Recreations:* shooting, fishing, golf. *Address:* The White Cottage, 19 Lennox Drive East, Helensburgh, Dunbartonshire. *T:* Helensburgh 4973. *Clubs:* Royal and Ancient (St Andrews); Royal Northern Yacht; Helensburgh Golf.

BELL, Donald L.; *see* Lynden-Bell.

BELL, Donald Munro; international concert and opera artist; freelance; *b* 19 June 1934; one *s. Educ:* South Burnaby High Sch., BC, Canada. Made Wigmore Hall Debut, 1958, since when has sung at Bayreuth Wagner Festival, 1958, 1959, 1960; Lucerne and Berlin Festivals, 1959; Philadelphia and New York debuts with Eugene Ormandy, 1959; Israel, 1962; Russia Recital Tour, 1963; Glyndebourne Festival, 1963, 1973, 1974; with Deutsche Oper am Rhein, Düsseldorf, 1964-66; Scottish National Opera, 1974. Has made recordings. Arnold Bax Medal,

1955. *Address:* c/o Basil Horsfield, 5 Regent's Park Road, NW1 7TC.

BELL, Douglas Maurice, CBE 1972; Chairman and Chief Executive, Tioxide Group Ltd (formerly British Titan Ltd), since 1973; *b* Shanghai, China, 15 April 1914; *s* of Alexander Dunlop Bell; *m* 1947, Elizabeth Mary Edelsten; one *s* two *d. Educ:* The Edinburgh Academy; St Andrews Univ. War Dept, Chemist, Woolwich Arsenal, 1936. Imperial Chemical Industries: Dyestuffs Div., 1937-42; Regional Sales Manager, 1946-53; Billingham Dir, 1953; Billingham Man. Dir, 1955-57; Heavy Organic Chemicals Managing Dir, 1958-61; Chm. of European Council, Imperial Chemical Industries Ltd, 1960-65; Chief Executive, ICI (Europa) Ltd, 1965-72. Director: British Titan Products Ltd; Tioxide Australia Pty Ltd; Tioxide of Canada Ltd; Tioxide SA; Titanio SA. FBIM 1974; FRSA 1976; Soc. of Chemical Industry: Vice-Pres., 1975-76; Pres., 1976-; Mem. Council, Chemical Industry Assoc. Hon. LLD St Andrews, 1977. Comendador de Numero de la Orden de Merito Civil (Spain), 1967; Commandeur, Ordre de Léopold II (Belgium), 1973. *Recreations:* sports and gardens. *Address:* Stocks Cottage, Church Street, West Chiltington, Sussex. *T:* West Chiltington 2284. *Clubs:* Anglo-Belgian; Cercle Royal Gaulois (Brussels); Royal Waterloo Golf, West Sussex Golf.

BELL, Edward Percy, OBE 1974; Member for Newham South, Greater London Council, since 1973 (for Newham, 1964-73); *b* 3 April 1902; *m* 1932, Ethel Mary Bell. *Educ:* Rutherford Coll., Newcastle upon Tyne; King's Coll., London. Teacher in the service of West Ham County Borough, 1922-64; Headmaster, Shipman County Secondary School, West Ham, 1951-64. Chairman: Planning Cttee of GLC, 1973-74; Town Development Cttee, 1974-75; Docklands Jt Cttee, 1974-77. *Recreations:* foreign travel; local and national social history. *Address:* 151c Ham Park Road, E7 9LE. *T:* (private) 01-472 8897; (business) 01-633 7622.

BELL, Prof. (Ernest) Arthur, PhD; CChem, FRIC; Professor of Biology, University of London, and Head of Department of Plant Sciences, King's College, since 1972; *b* 20 June 1926; *s* of Albert Bell and Rachel Enid (*née* Williams), Gosforth, Northumberland; *m* 1952, Jean Swinton Ogilvie; two *s* one *d. Educ:* Dame Allan's Sch., Newcastle upon Tyne; Univ. of Durham (King's Coll., Newcastle upon Tyne) BSc; Trinity Coll., Univ. of Dublin (MA, PhD). CChem, FRIC 1961. Res. Chemist, ICI, Billingham, 1946; Demonstr and holder of Sarah Purser Med. Res. Award, TCD, 1947; Asst to Prof. of Biochem., TCD, 1949; Lectr in Biochem., KCL, 1953; Reader in Biochem., Univ. of London, 1964; Sen. Foreign Scientist Fellow, National Science Foundn, USA, and Vis. Prof. of Biol., Univ. of Kansas, 1966; Prof. of Botany, Univ. of Texas, 1968; Vis. Prof., Univ. of Sierra Leone, 1977. *Publications:* contribs on plant biochem., chemotaxonomy, and chem. ecology to Phytochemistry, and Biochem. Jl. *Recreations:* walking, travel. *Address:* Department of Plant Sciences, King's College, University of London, 68 Half Moon Lane, SE24 9JF. *T:* 01-733 5666.

BELL, Ewart; *see* Bell, W. E.

BELL, Prof. Frank, DSc, PhD; FRIC; FRSE; FSAScot; Professor of Chemistry, Heriot-Watt University (formerly College), Edinburgh, 1950-66 (now Emeritus); *b* 24 Dec. 1904; *o s* of Thomas Bell, Derby; *m* 1930, May Perryman; one *s* one *d. Educ:* Crypt Grammar Sch., Glos; Queen Mary Coll., University of London. Head of Science Dept, Blackburn Tech. Coll. 1935-41; Principal Lancaster Tech. Coll., 1941-46; Prof. of Chemistry, Belfast Coll. of Tech., 1947-50. *Publications:* original papers mainly in Journal of Chemical Soc. *Recreations:* numismatics, walking and field-club activities (Past Pres., Cotteswold Naturalists' Field Club; Past Pres., Edinburgh Natural History Soc.). *Address:* Hilcot, Finchcroft Lane, Prestbury, Cheltenham, Glos.

BELL, Sir Gawain (Westray), KCMG 1957; CBE 1955 (MBE mil. 1942); Secretary-General, South Pacific Commission, 1966-70; *b* 21 Jan. 1909; *s* of late William Westray Bell; *m* 1945, Silvia, *d* of Major Adrian Cornwell-Clyne; three *d. Educ:* Winchester; Hertford Coll., Oxford. Sudan Political Service, 1931; seconded to the Government of Palestine, 1938. 2nd Lt TA, 1929-32; Military Service in Middle East, 1941-45; Kaimakam (Col): Arab Legion, 1942-45; RARO, 1949-59. District Comr, Sudan Political Service, 1945-49; Dep. Sudan Agent, Cairo, 1949-51; Dep. Civil Sec., Sudan Government, 1953-54; Permanent Under-Sec., Ministry of the Interior, 1954-55; HM Political Agent, Kuwait, 1955-57; Governor, Northern Nigeria, 1957-62; Sec Gen., Council for Middle East Trade, 1963-64; engaged, with Sir Ralph Hone, as Constitutional Adviser to Govt of Fedn of S Arabia, 1965-66. Various missions to Arab world, 1970-.

Chm., Exec. Cttee, LEPRA; Member: Governing Body, SOAS, London Univ., 1971-; part-time Chm., CS Selection Bds, 1972-; Chapter Gen., Order of St John, 1964-66, 1970- (KStJ 1958). Order of Independence 3rd Class (Trans Jordan), 1944. *Recreations:* walking, riding, skiing, shooting, rifle shooting (Capt. Oxford Univ., 1931; shot for Sudan). *Address:* Hidcote Bartrim Manor, Chipping Campden, Glos. *T:* Mickleton 305. *Club:* Bath.

BELL, Geoffrey Foxall, MC; MA; *b* 16 April 1896; *s* of late F. R. Bell, Burton-on-Trent; *m* 1926, Margaret, *d* of late R. Austin-Carewe, Montreal, Canada; three *s. Educ:* Repton; Balliol Coll., Oxford. Served in RFA, 1915-19; Asst Master, Upper Canada Coll. and Christ's Hospital; Headmaster, Trent Coll., Derbs, 1927-36; Headmaster, Highgate Sch., 1936-54; Oxford Univ. Cricket XI, 1919. *Publications:* Establishing a Fruit Garden, 1963; Seven Old Testament Figures (Bishop of London's Lent Book), 1968. *Address:* Widford, Haslemere, Surrey.

BELL, George Douglas Hutton, CBE 1965; FRS 1965; PhD; Director, Plant Breeding Institute, Cambridge, 1947-71, retired; a Vice President, Royal Society, since 1976; *b* 18 Oct. 1905; *er s* of George Henry and Lilian Mary Matilda Bell; *m* 1934, Eileen Gertrude Wright; two *d. Educ:* Bishop Gore's Grammar Sch., Swansea; Univ. Coll. of North Wales, Bangor; University of Cambridge. BSc 1928; PhD 1931. Research Officer. Plant Breeding Inst., 1931; University Demonstrator, Cambridge, 1933, Lectr, 1944; Fellow of Selwyn Coll., Cambridge, 1944-54, Hon. Fellow, 1965. Research Medal, Royal Agricultural Soc. of England, 1956; Royal Society Mullard Medal, 1967. Hon. DSc: Reading Univ., 1968; Univ. Wales, 1968; Liverpool Univ., 1970. Massey-Ferguson National Award, 1973. *Publications:* Cultivated Plants of the Farm, 1948; The Breeding of Barley Varieties in Barley and Malt, 1962; Cereal Breeding in Vistas in Botany, Vol. II, 1963; Phylogeny of Temperate Cereals in Crop Plant Evolution, 1965; papers on barley and breeding in Jl of Agricultural Science, etc. *Recreations:* natural history; theatre, music. *Address:* 6 Worts Causeway, Cambridge. *T:* Cambridge 47449.

BELL, Prof. George Howard, MD; FRCPGlas 1946; FRSE 1947; Symers Professor of Physiology in the University of Dundee (formerly Queen's College, Dundee), 1947-75, now Emeritus; Dean of The Faculty of Medicine, 1954-56 and 1963; *b* 24 Jan. 1905; *m* 1934, Isabella Margaret Thomson, MB, ChB; two *s. Educ:* Ayr Academy; Glasgow Univ. BSc 1929; MB (Hons) 1930; MD (Hons) 1943. House Physician, Royal Hosp. for Sick Children, 1930; Asst Lecturer in Physiology Dept, University of Glasgow, 1931-34; Lecturer in Physiology: Univ. of Bristol, 1934-35; Univ. of Glasgow, 1935-47. Mem. Physiological Soc., 1934-, and Sec., 1949-54; Mem. Inter-University Council for Higher Education Overseas, 1957-75; Mem. Eastern Regional Hospital Board, 1957-67 (Vice-Chm., 1966-67); Gen. Dental Council Visitor, 1960-62; Comr, Royal University of Malta, 1962-70. Hon. Fellow, Accademia Anatomico-Chirurgica, Perugia, 1959. *Publications:* (with D. Emslie Smith and C. R. Paterson) Textbook of Physiology and Biochemistry, 9th edn, 1976; papers in Journal of Physiology, Journal of Endocrinology, Lancet, etc. *Address:* Duntulm, 80 Grove Road, Broughty Ferry, Dundee DD5 1LB. *T:* Dundee 78724.

BELL, Sir (George) Raymond, KCMG 1973; CB 1967; Vice-President, European Investment Bank, since 1973; *b* 13 March 1916; *e s* of late William Bell and Christabel Bell (*née* Appleton); *m* 1944, Joan Elizabeth, *o d* of late W. G. Coltham and Christina Coltham; two *s* two *d. Educ:* Bradford Grammar Sch.; St John's Coll., Cambridge (Scholar). Entered Civil Service, Assistant Principal, 1938; Min. of Health, 1938; transf. Treasury, 1939; served War 1941-44, Royal Navy (Lieut RNVR). Principal, Civil Service, 1945; Asst Sec., 1951; Under-Sec., 1960; Dep. Sec., 1966; Dep. Sec. HM Treasury, 1966-72. Sec. (Finance), Office of HM High Commissioner for the UK in Canada, 1945-48; Counsellor, UK Permanent Delegn to OEEC/NATO, Paris, 1953-56; Principal Private Sec. to Chancellor of Exchequer, 1958-60. Mem. UK Delegation to Brussels Conference, 1961-62 and 1970-72. *Recreations:* music, reading, travel. *Address:* European Investment Bank, 2 Place de Metz, Luxembourg. *T:* 43-50-11; 24 rue de Bragance, Luxembourg. *T:* 23-515. *Club:* Athenæum.

BELL, George Trafford, CMG 1961; OBE 1952; retired; *b* 9 March 1912; 2nd *s* of late George H. Bell and of Veronica Jessie Bell, Alderley Edge, Ches; *m* 1944, Eileen Patricia, *d* of late A. Geoffrey Southern, Wilmslow, Ches; two *s* one *d. Educ:* Sedbergh; St John's Coll., Cambridge. Apptd Admin. Offr, Tanganyika, 1936; Sen. Admin. Offr, 1954; Provincial Comr, 1958-62. *Recreations:* golf, fishing. *Address:* Dukenfield Grange, Mobberley, Knutsford, Cheshire.

BELL, Griffin B.; Attorney-General, USA, since 1977; *b* Americus, Georgia, 31 Oct. 1918; *s* of A. C. Bell and Thelma Pilcher; *m* 1943, Mary Foy Powell; one *s . Educ:* Southwestern Coll., Ga; Mercer Univ. (LLB *cum laude* 1948, LLD 1967). Served AUS, 1941-46, reaching rank of Major. Admitted to Georgia Bar, 1947; practice in Savannah and Rome, 1947-53. Partner in King and Spalding, Atlanta, 1953-59, 1976-77, Managing Partner, 1959-61; United States Judge, 5th Circuit, 1961-76. Chief of Staff to Governor of Georgia (Vandiver), 1959-61; Chm., Atlanta Commn on Crime and Delinquency, 1965-66; Mem., Vis. Cttee, Law Sch., Vanderbilt Univ.; Trustee, Mercer Univ.; Mem. Amer. Law Inst. *Address:* Department of Justice, Washington, DC 20530, USA; (home) 3100 Habersham Road, NW Atlanta, Georgia 30305, USA.

BELL, Harold Arthur; Chairman, Gateway Building Society, since 1974; *b* 13 Sept. 1918; *s* of Anthony Bell and Emily Bell (*née* Johnson); *m* 1946, Barbara Joyce Copp; four *s* one *d . Educ:* Westminster City School. Solicitor in private practice, 1940-; Dir, Temperance Permanent Building Soc., 1958, Vice-Chm., 1961; Chm., Jan.-July 1974; merged with Bedfordshire Building Soc., July 1974, to become Gateway Building Soc. Vice-Pres., Metropolitan Assoc. of Building Societies, 1976-; Hon. Solicitor: Baptist Missionary Soc., 1950-67; Home Counties Baptist Assoc., 1958-. *Recreations:* charitable works, golf, reading. *Address:* The Coach House, Chiddingfold, Surrey. *T:* Wormley 2068; Devon House, 172-174 Kingston Road, Ewell, Surrey. *T:* 01-393 0231. *Club:* Royal Automobile.

BELL, Harry, OBE 1945; MA; MEd; Research Fellow, University of St Andrews, since 1972 (Research Scholar, 1967); *b* 11 April 1899; *s* of late John Nicol Bell, Aberdeen, and late Isabella Georgina Reith; *m* 1933, Sophia McDonald, *d* of late Alexander B. Fulton, Kilkerran, Newlands, Glasgow; two *s* one *d. Educ:* Robert Gordon's Coll.; Aberdeen Univ. (Kay Prize and Dey Scholarship); Clare Coll., Cambridge (Foundation Scholar); Glasgow Univ. (MEd). Asst Master, Glasgow Academy, 1927-33; Rector of Elgin Academy, 1933-36; Rector of Dollar Academy, 1936-60. Scottish Educational Adviser Air Training Corps, 1941-45; Mem. of Scottish Youth Advisory Cttee, 1942-45; Pres. of Scottish Association of Headmasters, 1948. Adviser with UNESCO Delegation, Florence, 1950; Mem. of Advisory Council on Scottish Education, 1957-61. Fellow Internat. Inst. of Arts and Letters, 1960. *Publications:* English for Air Cadets; Stevenson's Travels and Essays; Thirteen Short Stories; Selected English Prose; Approach to English Literature; General Editor of Oxford Comprehension Course; articles on literary, historical and educational subjects. *Recreations:* reading, writing, walking. *Address:* Viewpark, 31 Lawhead Road East, St Andrews, Fife. *T:* St Andrews 2867. *Clubs:* Royal Over-Seas League; Scottish Mountaineering.

BELL, Ian Wright, CBE 1964; HM Diplomatic Service, retired; *b* Radlett, Herts, 21 Aug. 1913; *s* of late T. H. D. Bell, Hohenort, Constantia, S Africa; *m* 1940, Winifred Mary Ruth Waterfield, *y d* of late E. H. Waterfield, ICS; three *s. Educ:* Canford Sch.; St Peter's Hall, Oxford. Entered Consular Service, 1938; Vice-Consul: Valparaiso, 1938; Montevideo, 1940; Foreign Office, 1946; First Sec., 1947; First Sec., Addis Ababa, 1949, Chargé d'Affaires, 1949, 1950, 1952 and 1953; Consul, Innsbruck, 1953; First Sec., Prague, 1954, Chargé d'Affaires, 1954 and 1956; Counsellor and Consul-Gen., Jedda, 1956; Counsellor and Official Sec., Office of UK High Commissioner, Canberra, 1957; HM Consul-Gen., Lyons, France, 1960-65; Ambassador, Santo Domingo, Dominican Republic, 1965-69; Consul-Gen., Stuttgart, 1969-73. FRSA. *Publication:* The Scarlet Flower (Poems), 1947. *Recreations:* painting, drama, music, riding, walking. *Address:* Liveras House, Broadford, Skye. *Clubs:* Athenæum, Royal Geographical Society, PEN.

BELL, Very Rev. John, MM 1917; Dean Emeritus of Perth, WA; Dean, 1953-59, retired; *b* 11 Nov. 1898; *s* of Thomas and Isabella McCracken Bell; unmarried. *Educ:* Gair Sch., Dumfriesshire; privately; St John's Coll., Perth, WA. Deacon, 1926, Priest, 1928; Curate of Christ Church, Claremont, 1926-29; Rector of S Perth, 1929-32; Priest-in-Charge of Claremont, 1933, Rector, 1933-43; Canon of St George's Cathedral, Perth, 1938-44; Org. Sec. (for NSW) Austr. Bd of Missions, 1943-46; Dean of Armidale, 1946-48; Exam. Chap. to Bp of Armidale, 1946-48; Rector of Oddington with Adlestrop, Dio. Gloucester, 1948-52. *Publications:* This Way Peace, 1939; Many Coloured Glass, 1943; Facing the Week, 1947; For Comfort and Courage, 1958. *Recreation:* travel. *Address:* 22/8 Darley Street, South Perth, Western Australia 6151. *T:* 67-4434. *Club:* Weld (Perth, WA).

BELL, Rear-Adm. John Anthony, CB 1977; Director, Naval Education Service, since 1975; *b* 25 Nov. 1924; *s* of Mathew Bell, Dundee, and Mary Ann Ellen Bell (*née* Goss), London; *m* 1946,

Eileen Joan Woodman; three d. *Educ:* St Ignatius Coll., Stamford Hill; London Univ. BA, BSc, LLB. Barrister, Gray's Inn, 1970. RM 1943-45; Schoolmaster, RN, Instr Lt, Courses, Reserve Fleet, service with RAN, 1945-52; HMS Implacable, Theseus, Admiralty, HMS Excellent, 1952-59; HMS Centaur, RN Staff Course, Staff of SACLANT, USA, Directing Staff, RN Staff Course, Western Fleet, 1959-69; Naval Educn Service, Dir, Dept of Naval Oceanography and Meteorology, 1969-75; Instr Captain 1969, Rear-Adm. 1975. Member: BEC Educn Cttee, 1975-; TEC, 1976-; C&G Policy Cttee; Governor, SOAS; Pres., United Services Catholic Assoc. *Recreations:* swimming, wines, travelling, France. *Address:* The Beild, Conifer Avenue, Hartley, Dartford, Kent DA3 8BX. *T:* Longfield 2485. *Clubs:* National Liberal; Hartley Country.

BELL, John Elliot; *b* 6 Nov. 1886; *e s* of late David Bell and Elizabeth Elliot; *m* 1924, Olga, *er d* of late Henry Banks and Elizabeth Ritchie, Edinburgh; one *s* one d. *Educ:* George Watson's Coll.; Edinburgh Univ. Vice-Consul at Paris, 1911; Boston, USA 1912; Leopoldville, Belgian Congo, 1913-14; Magallanes, Chile, 1915-19; Santo Domingo, 1920; Consul at Galveston, USA 1920-23; Portland, Ore., 1923-29; Bahia, Brazil, 1930-32; Basle, 1932-34; Consul Gen. at Cologne, 1934-39; at Zurich, 1939-42; at Strasbourg, 1945-46; retired, 1947. *Recreations:* golf, riding. *Address:* 3175 Point Grey Road, Vancouver 8, BC, Canada. *T:* 731-3490.

BELL, John Geoffrey Y.; *see* Yates-Bell.

BELL, Sir John Lowthian, 5th Bt *cr* 1885; *b* 14 June 1960; *s* of Sir Hugh Francis Bell, 4th Bt and of Lady Bell (Mary Howson, MB, ChB, *d* of late George Howson, The Hyde, Hambledon); *S* father, 1970. *Heir: b* David Hugh Bell, *b* 8 Oct. 1961. *Address:* Arncliffe Hall, Ingleby Cross, Northallerton, N Yorks.

BELL, Dr John Stewart, FRS 1972; Physicist, CERN, Geneva, since 1960; *b* 28 July 1928; *s* of John Bell and Annie (*née* Brownlee); *m* 1954, Mary Ross. *Educ:* Technical High Sch., Belfast; Queen's Univ., Belfast (BSc); Univ of Birmingham (PhD). AERE Harwell, 1949-60. *Publications:* various papers on electromagnetic, nuclear, elementary particle, and quantum theory. *Address:* CERN, 1211 Geneva 23, Switzerland.

BELL, Joseph, CBE 1953; Chief Constable, City of Manchester, 1943-58, retired; *b* 15 July 1899; *s* of late Joseph Bell; *m* 1926, Edith, *d* of late Matthew Adamson; one *s* (one *d* decd). *Educ:* Alderman Wood Sch., Stanley, Co. Durham. Royal Naval Volunteer Reserve, 1917-19. Newcastle on Tyne City Police, 1919-33; Chief Constable, Hastings, 1933-41; Asst Chief Constable, Manchester, 1941-43. *Address:* Norwood, 246 Windlehurst Road, Marple, Cheshire.

BELL, Joseph Denis Milburn; Chairman, North Western Electricity Board, since 1976; *b* 2 Sept. 1920; *s* of John Bell, BEM, and Ann Bell; *m* 1949, Wilhelmina Maxwell Miller; one *s* one d. *Educ:* Bishop Auckland Grammar Sch.; St Edmund Hall, Oxford (MA). Lectr in Modern Econ. History, Univ. of Glasgow, 1946; National Coal Board: Indust. Relations Dept, 1954; Dep. Indust. Relations Dir, Durham Div., 1963; Electricity Council: Statistical Officer, Indust. Relations Dept, 1966; Dep. Indust. Relations Adviser (Negotiating), 1967; Indust. Relations Adviser, 1972. *Publications:* Industrial Unionism: a critical analysis, 1949 (repr. in Trade Unions: selected readings, ed W. E. J. McCarthy, 1972); (contrib.) The Scottish Economy (ed A. K. Cairncross), 1953; (contrib.) The System of Industrial Relations in Great Britain (ed A. Flanders and H. A. Clegg), 1954; (contrib.) The Lessons of Public Enterprise (ed M. Shanks), 1963. *Address:* North Western Electricity Board, Cheetwood Road, Manchester M8 8BA. *T:* 061-834 8161.

BELL, Julia, MA; FRCP; retired; *b* 28 Jan. 1879; unmarried. *Educ:* Nottingham Girls' High Sch.; Girton Coll., Cambridge; London Sch. of Medicine for Women; St Mary's Hospital. Mathematical Tripos, Cambridge. Hon. aegrotat degree, 1901; MA granted by Trinity Coll. Dublin (Cambridge degree not then given to women). Research into Solar Parallax, Cambridge Observatory, 1902-08; Statistical Asst, UC London, 1908-14; medical student and research (with Karl Pearson, FRS), 1914-20; MRCS, LRCP; research asst under Med. Res. Council (during much of time on permanent Acad. Staff), working in Galton Lab., University Coll., 1920-65; Hon. Research Associate at University Coll., London, 1944-65; MRCP (on basis of research work), Galton Research Fellow, 1926; FRCP 1938. Weldon Medal and Prize, Oxford Univ., 1941. *Publications:* in Treasury of Human Inheritance, Vol. II, 6 Monographs on Hered. Diseases of the Eye, 1922-33; Vol. IV, 6 monographs on Nerv. Disease and Muscular Dystrophies, 1934-

48; Vol. V, Pts 1 and 2, monographs on Digital Anomalies, 1951-53; Pt 3, on the Lawrence-Moon Syndrome, 1958. A number of papers in Biometrika and Annals of Eugenics, etc. *Recreations:* reading, delights of friendship; chief interests Applied Statistics and Historical side of Medicine and Science.

BELL, Leslie Gladstone, CEng, FRINA; RCNC; Director of Naval Ship Production, Ministry of Defence, since 1977; *b* 20 Oct. 1919; *s* of late John Gladstone Bell and Jessie Gray Bell (*née* Quigley); *m* 1963, Adriana Agatha Jacoba van den Berg; one *s* one d. *Educ:* Portsmouth Dockyard Tech. Coll.; Royal Naval Engineering Coll., Keyham; Royal Naval Coll., Greenwich. Staff Constructor Cdr, Home Fleet, 1953-56; Aircraft Carrier Design, 1956-59; Chief Constructor, Weapon Development, 1959-67; IDC, 1968; Asst Dir, Submarine Design, 1969-72; Director, Submarine Project Team, 1972-77. *Recreations:* gardening, golf, music. *Address:* Haytor, Old Midford Road, Bath, Avon. *T:* Bath 833357. *Club:* Bath Golf.

BELL, His Honour P(hilip) Ingress, TD 1950; QC 1952; a Circuit Judge (formerly Judge of County Courts), 1960-75; *b* 10 Jan. 1900; *s* of Geoffrey Vincent and Mary Ellen Bell; *m* 1933, Agnes Mary Eastwood; two *s* one d. *Educ:* Stonyhurst, Blackburn; Royal Naval College, Keyham; Queen's Coll., Oxford (BA Jurisprudence, BCL). Called to the Bar, Inner Temple, 1925. Cadet RN, 1918; Midshipman RN, 1918-20. Lieut TA, 1939; JAG Dept, 1941, Temp. Major, 1944. MP (C) Bolton East, 1951-60. *Publication:* Idols and Idylls, 1918. *Recreations:* golf; Capt., Oxford University Boxing Club, 1923. *Address:* Blackmoss House, Longridge, Lancs. *Club:* Carlton.

BELL, Prof. Quentin (Claudian Stephen), FRSA; FRSL; Emeritus Professor of the History and Theory of Art, Sussex University; painter, sculptor, potter, author, art critic; *b* 19 Aug. 1910; 2nd *s* of late Clive Bell and Vanessa Stephen; *m* 1952, Anne Olivier Popham; one *s* two d. *Educ:* Leighton Park. Exhibitions, 1935, 1947, 1949, 1972, 1977. Political warfare executive, 1941-43. Lectr in Art Education, King's Coll., Newcastle, 1952; Senior Lecturer, 1956; Prof. of Fine Art, University of Leeds, 1962-67 (Head of Dept of Fine Art, 1959); Slade Professor of Fine Art, Oxford Univ., 1964-65; Ferens Prof. of Fine Art, University of Hull, 1965-66; Prof. of History and Theory of Art, Sussex Univ., 1967-75. MA Dunelm, 1957. Regular contributor to Listener, 1951-. FRSA 1972. *Publications:* On Human Finery, 1947, rev. edn 1976; Those impossible English (with Helmut Gernsheim), 1951; Roger Montané, 1961; The Schools of Design, 1963; Ruskin, 1963; Victorian Artists, 1967; Bloomsbury, 1968; Virginia Woolf, a Biography, 2 vols, 1972 (James Tait Black Meml Prize; Duff Cooper Meml Prize); articles in Burlington Magazine, Jl of Warburg and Courtauld Insts, History Today, Durham Research Review, Critical Inquiry. *Recreations:* none worth speaking of. *Address:* Cobbe Place, Beddingham, Sussex. *T:* Glynde 201. *Club:* Reform.

BELL, Sir Raymond; *see* Bell, Sir G. R.

BELL, Robert Donald Murray, CB 1966; Under-Secretary, Scottish Development Department, 1970-76; *b* 8 Oct. 1916; *s* of Robert William and Mary Caroline Bell; *m* 1941, Karin Anna Smith; one *s* one d. *Educ:* Christ's Hosp.; Clare Coll., Cambridge. First Class Honours, Natural Sciences Tripos (Physics), 1938. Joined Scottish Office, 1938. War of 1939-45: Royal Artillery, 1940-45 (Mil. Coll. of Science, Bury, 1943). Principal, Scottish Home Dept, 1946; Private Sec. to Sec. of State for Scotland, 1947-50; Asst Sec., Scottish Home Dept, 1950; Under-Secretary: Scottish Development Dept, 1959-69; Scottish Educn Dept, 1969-70. *Address:* Smeaton House, Inveresk, Musselburgh, Midlothian. *T:* 031-665 2940.

BELL, Prof. Robert Edward, CC (Canada) 1971; FRS 1965; FRSC 1955; Rutherford Professor of Physics, McGill University, Montreal, since 1960; Principal and Vice-Chancellor, McGill University, since 1970; *b* 29 Nov. 1918; *s* of Edward Richardson Bell and Edith E. Rich, British Columbia; *m* 1947, Jeanne Atkinson; one d. *Educ:* Univ. of British Columbia (BA 1939, MA 1941); McGill Univ. (PhD 1948). Wartime Radar development, Nat. Research Council, Ottawa, 1941-45; Sen. Research Officer, Chalk River Nuclear Laboratories, 1946-56; seconded to Foster Radiation Lab., McGill Univ., 1952-56; Assoc. Prof. of Physics, 1956-60; Dir, Foster Radiation Lab., 1960-69; Vice-Dean for Physical Scis, 1964-67; Dean, Fac. of Grad. Studies and Research, 1969-70, McGill Univ. Visiting scientist, Copenhagen Univ. Inst. for Theoretical Physics, under Niels Bohr, 1958-59. Sec., Sect. III (Science), Royal Society of Canada, 1962-64; Pres. Cdn Assoc. of Physicists, 1965-66. Fellow, American Physical Soc. Hon. DSc: Univ. of New Brunswick; Université Laval; Université de

Montréal; Hon. LLD Univ. of Toronto; Hon. DCL Bishop's Univ. *Publications:* contribs to books: Annual Reviews of Nuclear Science, 1954; Beta and Gamma Ray Spectroscopy, 1955; Alpha, Beta and Gamma Ray Spectroscopy, 1964; papers on nuclear physics and allied topics in scientific jls. *Address:* 363 Olivier Avenue, Westmount, Montreal, Quebec H3Z 2C8, Canada. *T:* (514) 935-3769; Administration Building, McGill University, 845 Sherbrooke Street W, Montreal, H3A 2T5, Canada. *T:* (514) 392-5347.

BELL, Ronald McMillan, QC 1966; MP (C) Beaconsfield, since 1974 (South Buckinghamshire, 1950-74); *b* 14 April 1914; *yr s* of late John Bell, Cardiff; *m* 1954, Elizabeth Audrey, *e d* of late Kenneth Gossell, MC, Burwash, Sussex; two *s* two *d*. *Educ:* Cardiff High Sch.; Magdalen Coll., Oxford (Demy). BA 1936; MA 1941; Sec. and Treas., Oxford Union Soc., 1935; Pres., Oxford Univ. Conservative Assoc., 1935. MP (C) for Newport (Monmouth), May-July 1945. Contested Caerphilly Div. of Glamorgan at by-election 1939, Newport, Monmouth, July 1945. Served RNVR, 1939-46. Called to Bar, Gray's Inn, 1938; practises in London and on South-Eastern circuit. Mem. Paddington Borough Council, 1947-49. *Publication:* Crown Proceedings, 1948. *Recreation:* athletics. *Address:* 2 Mitre Court Buildings, Temple, EC4. *T:* 01-353 6981; First House, West Witheridge, Knotty Green, Beaconsfield, Bucks. *T:* Beaconsfield 4606.

BELL, Ronald Percy, MA; FRS 1944; FRSE 1968; FRIC; Professor of Chemistry, University of Stirling, 1967-75, now Emeritus; Hon. Research Professor of Chemistry, University of Leeds, since 1976; *b* 1907; *e s* of E. A. Bell, Maidenhead; *m* 1931, Margery Mary West; one *s*. *Educ:* County Boys' Sch., Maidenhead; Balliol Coll., Oxford. Bedford Lecturer in Physical Chemistry, Balliol Coll., 1932; Fellow of Balliol Coll., 1933 (Vice-Master, 1966); Hon. Fellow, 1967; Univ. Lecturer and Demonstrator, Oxford Univ., 1938; Univ. Reader, Oxford Univ., 1955. George Fisher Baker Lectr, Cornell Univ., 1958; Nat. Science Foundn Fellow, Brown Univ., 1964; Spiers Meml Lectr, 1975; Vis. Prof., Tech. Univ. of Denmark, Lyngby, 1976. President: Faraday Soc., 1956; Chemistry Section, British Assoc. Meeting, Durham, 1970; Vice-Pres. Chemical Soc., 1958 (Liversidge Lectureship, 1973-74). Foreign Mem. Royal Danish Acad. of Arts and Sciences, 1962; Foreign Associate, Nat. Acad. of Sciences, USA. Hon. LLD Illinois Inst. of Techn., 1965; Hon. DTech, Tech. Univ. of Denmark, 1969; Hon. DSc Kent, 1974; Hon. DUniv. Stirling, 1977. Leverhulme Emeritus Fellow, 1976. Meldola Medal, Inst. of Chemistry, 1936; Chem. Soc. Award in Kinetics and Mechanism, 1974. *Publications:* Acid-Base Catalysis, 1941; Acids and Bases, 1952, 2nd edn 1969; The Proton in Chemistry, 1959, 2nd edn 1974; papers in scientific journals. *Address:* 28 Ayresome Terrace, Roundhay, Leeds LS8 1BH; Bowderbeck, Buttermere, Cumbria.

BELL, Stewart Edward, Advocate; Sheriff of Glasgow and Strathkelvin (formerly Sheriff of Lanarkshire at Glasgow), since 1961; *b* 4 Aug. 1919; *yr s* of late Charles Edward Bell, Shipowner, and Rosalind Stewart; *m* 1948, Isla, 2nd *d* of James Spencer and late Adeline Kelly; three *d*. *Educ:* Kelvinside Academy, Glasgow; Trinity Hall, Cambridge; Glasgow Univ. Trinity Hall, 1937-39 and 1946 (MA Cantab), Glasgow Univ., 1946-48 (LLB). Commissioned, Loyal Regt, 1939; served with 2nd Bn in Singapore and Malaya, 1940-42 (wounded, POW in Singapore and Korea, 1942-45). Admitted Advocate, 1948; practised: in Malacca, Malaya as Advocate and Solicitor, 1949-51; at Scottish Bar, 1951-61. *Recreation:* Highland bagpipe (Hon. Pipe-major, The Royal Scottish Pipers' Soc., 1975-77). *Address:* 23 Cleveden Drive, Glasgow G12 0SD. *T:* 041-339 3481. *Clubs:* Western (Glasgow); Caledonian (Edinburgh).

BELL, Rev. Vicars, MBE 1964; author; Vicar of Clawton; Rector of Tetcott; lecturer; *b* 24 Jan. 1904; *s* of W. A. Bell, Edinburgh; *m* 1926, Dorothy Carley. *Educ:* Radnor Sch., Redhill; Reigate Grammar Sch.; Goldsmiths' Coll., King's Coll., Univ. of London. Asst master at Horley Boys' Council Sch., 1925; Headmaster: Spaldwick Council Sch., 1926; Little Gaddesden C of E Sch., 1929-63. *Publications:* Little Gaddesden: the story of an English Parish, 1949; Death Under the Stars, 1949; The Dodo, 1950; Two by Day and One by Night, 1950; Death has Two Doors, 1950; This Way Home, 1951; Death Darkens Council, 1952; On Learning the English Tongue, 1953; Death and the Night Watches, 1954; To Meet Mr Ellis, 1956; Death Walks by the River, 1959; That Night, a play for the Nativity, 1959; Orlando and Rosalind, three tales, 1960; Steep Ways and Narrow, 1963; The Flying Cat, 1964; (ed) Prayers for Every Day, 1965. *Recreations:* walking, village activities past and present. *Address:* 20 Watts Road, Tavistock, Devon.

BELL, Walter (Fancourt), CMG 1967; *b* 7 Nov. 1909; *s* of Canon George Fancourt Bell; *m* 1948, Katharine Spaatz, Washington, DC, USA; no *c*. *Educ:* Tonbridge Sch. Barrister, Inner Temple. Vice-Consul (Acting): New York, 1935-40; Mexico City, 1940-41; New York, 1941-42; Foreign Office, London, 1942-45; 1st Sec., Brit. Embassy, Washington, DC, 1946-48; attached E Africa High Commn, Nairobi, Kenya, 1949-52; 1st Sec., Brit. High Commn, New Delhi, 1952-55; attached War Office, London, 1956-57; Adviser, Federal Govt, W Indies, 1957-60; attached Govt of Kenya, 1961-63; Counsellor, British High Commn, Nairobi, Kenya, 1963-67. US Medal of Freedom with Bronze Palm, 1946. *Recreations:* tennis, walking. *Address:* 6 Onslow Square, SW7. *Clubs:* Travellers'; Nairobi (Nairobi).

BELL, (William) Ewart; Permanent Secretary, Department of Finance for Northern Ireland, since 1976; *b* 13 Nov. 1924; *s* of late Rev. Dr Frederick G. Bell and of Margaret Jane Ewart; *m* 1957, Kathleen Ross Boucher; two *d*. *Educ:* Methodist Coll., Belfast; Wadham Coll., Oxford (MA). Asst Master, Cheltenham Coll., 1946-48; Northern Ireland Civil Service, 1948-; Min. of Health and Local Govt, 1948-52; Min. (later Dept) of Commerce, 1952-76; Asst Sec., 1963-70; Dep. Sec., 1970-73; Sec., 1973-76. *Recreations:* gardening, golf, Rugby football. *Address:* 39 Tweskard Park, Belfast, N Ireland. *T:* Belfast 63649.

BELL, Sir William H. D. M.; *see* Morrison-Bell.

BELL, William Lewis, CMG 1970; MBE 1945; Information Officer, University of Oxford, since 1977; *b* 31 Dec. 1919; *s* of Frederick Robinson Bell and Kate Harper Bell (*née* Lewis); *m* 1943, Margaret Giles; one *s* one *d*. *Educ:* Hymers Coll., Hull; Oriel Coll., Oxford. Served The Gloucestershire Regt (Major), 1940-46. Colonial Administrative Service, Uganda, 1946-63: Dep. Sec. to the Treasury, 1956-58; Perm. Sec., Min. of Social Services, 1958-63; Fellow, Economic Develt Inst., World Bank, 1958. Chm., Uganda National Parks, 1962; Pres., Uganda Sports Union, 1961-62. Director, Cox & Danks Ltd (Metal Industries Group), 1963-64. Sec. to the Governors, Westfield Coll., Univ. of London, 1964-65; seconded to FCO (ODA) as Head of British Develt Div. in the Caribbean, 1965-72; Dir-Gen., Technical Educn and Training Org. for Overseas Countries, 1972-77. UK Dir, Caribbean Develt Bank, 1970-72. *Recreations:* cricket, writing, Caribbeana. *Address:* Delly End, Hailey, Oxon. *Club:* MCC.

BELL, William Rupert Graham; Under Secretary, Department of Industry, since 1975; *b* 29 May 1920; *m* 1950, Molly Bolton; two *d*. *Educ:* Bradford Grammar Sch.; St John's Coll., Cambridge (Scholar). Served Royal Artillery, 1940-45 (despatches). Asst Principal, Min. of Fuel and Power, 1948; Principal, 1949; Asst Sec., 1959; Under-Sec., Min. of Power, 1966-70, DTI, 1970-72; Deputy Principal, Civil Service Coll., 1972-75. Imperial Defence Coll., 1965. *Address:* 47 Chiswick Staithe, Hartington Road, W4 3TP. *T:* 01-994 2545.

BELL DAVIES, Vice-Adm. Sir Lancelot (Richard), KBE 1977; Supreme Allied Commander Atlantic's Representative in Europe, 1975-78; *b* 18 Feb. 1926; *s* of late Vice-Adm. R. Bell Davies, VC, CB, DSO, AFC, and Mrs M. P. Bell Davies, Holt, Wiltshire; *m* 1949, Emmeline Joan (*née* Molengraaff), Wassenaar, Holland; one *s* two *d*. *Educ:* Boxgrove Preparatory Sch., Guildford; RN Coll., Dartmouth. War of 1939-45: Midshipman, HMS Norfolk, 1943 (Scharnhorst sunk); joined Submarines, 1944. First Command, HMS Subtle, 1953; subseq. commands: HMS Explorer, 1955; Comdr, HMS Leander, 1962; Captain: HMS Forth, also SM7, 1967, and HMS Bulwark, 1972; Rear-Adm., 1973. Ministry of Defence Posts: (Comdr) Naval Staff, 1960; (Captain) Naval Asst to Controller, 1964; Director of Naval Warfare, 1969; Comdr, British Naval Staff, Washington, and UK Rep. to Saclant, 1973-75. *Recreations:* sailing, skiing, gardening. *Address:* Holly Hill Lodge, Barnes Lane, Sarisbury Green, Southampton. *T:* Locks Heath 3131. *Clubs:* Naval and Military; Royal Naval Sailing Association.

BELLAIRS, Prof. Angus d'Albini; Professor of Vertebrate Morphology in the University of London, at St Mary's Hospital Medical School, since 1970; *b* 11 Jan. 1918; *s* of Nigel Bellairs and late Kathleen Bellairs (*née* Niblett); *m* 1949 (Madeline) Ruth (PhD, Reader in Embryology at UCL), *d* of Trevor Morgan; one *d*. *Educ:* Stowe Sch.; Queens' Coll., Cambridge (MA); University Coll. Hosp., London. DSc London, MRCS, LRCP. Served War, RAMC, 1942-46; Major, Operational Research, SE Asia, 1944-46. Lectr in Anat. and Dental Anat., London Hosp. Med. Coll., 1946-51; Lectr in Anat., Univ. of Cambridge, 1951-53; St Mary's Hosp. Med. Sch.: Reader in Anatomy, 1953-66, in Embryology, 1966-70. Vis. Prof. of Zoology, Kuwait Univ., 1970. Scientific Fellow and Hon. Cons.

Herpetologist, Zoological Soc. of London; FLS 1941; FIBiol 1974. *Publications:* Reptiles, 1957 (4th edition with J. Attridge, 1975); The World of Reptiles (with Richard Carrington), 1966; The Life of Reptiles, 1969; contribs to zoological literature, mainly on reptiles. *Recreations:* natural history (especially reptiles and cats), modern fiction, antiques. *Address:* 7 Champion Grove, SE5. *T:* 01-274 1834; Vicarage Cottage, Ramsbury, Wilts.

BELLAMY, Albert Alexander, RIBA, DipTP 1938; Under-Secretary, Department of the Environment, Housing Directorate C, 1972-74 retired; *b* 19 April 1914; *m* 1941, Renée Florence Burge; three *d. Educ:* Clapham Xaverian Coll.; RIBA. Asst Architect in private practice in City of London, 1932-39; LCC: Mem. Abercrombie/Forshaw Team on 'County of London Plan 1943' and until 1946. Architect specialising on housing with MoH and successors, 1946-74. (Dep. Chief Architect, Min. of Housing and Local Govt, 1964-72). Awarded Commonwealth Fund Fellowship (now Harkness), 1956-57, studying design of housing in USA for 12 months. *Recreation:* watercolour painting. *Address:* 1 Buckingham Place, The Steyne, Bognor Regis PO21 1TU.

BELLAMY, Rear-Adm. Albert John, CB 1968; OBE 1956; Deputy Director, Polytechnic of the South Bank, since 1970; *b* Upton-on-Severn, 26 Feb. 1915; *s* of late A. E. Bellamy and late Mrs A. E. Bellamy; *m* 1942, Dorothy Joan Lawson; one *s* one *d. Educ:* Hanley Castle Grammar Sch.; Downing Coll., Cambridge (Buchanan Exhibitioner). 1st cl. hons Pts I and II, Math. tripos. Asst master, Berkhamsted Sch., 1936-39. Joined RN, 1939, as Instructor Lieut; Fleet Instr and Meteorological Officer, America and WI, 1948-50 (HMS Glasgow); Instr Comdr, 1950; Headmaster, RN Schs, Malta, 1951-54; HMS Ark Royal, 1955-56; Dean of the College, RN Engineering Coll., Manadon, Plymouth, 1956-60; Instr Capt., 1958; Staff of Dir, Naval Educn Service, 1960-63; Dir of Studies, RN Electrical, Weapons and Radio Engineering Sch., HMS Collingwood, 1963-65; Instr Rear-Adm., 1965; Dir, Naval Educn Service, MoD, 1965-70. *Recreations:* golf, amateur drama, gardening, show jumping. *Address:* The Cottage, Kington Magna, Gillingham, Dorset. *T:* East Stour 668.

BELLAMY, Alexander (William); retired; Senior Legal Assistant, Council on Tribunals, 1967-76 (temporary Legal Assistant, 1963-67); *b* Aug. 1909; *m* 1931, Lena Marie Lauga Massy. *Educ:* Mill Hill Sch.; Clare Coll., Cambridge. Called to Bar, Gray's Inn, 1934; practised at Bar, London, 1934-38; Magistrate, Straits Settlements and FMS, 1938; seconded as District Magistrate, Gold Coast, 1942; legal staff, Malaya Planning Unit, WO, 1944; Crown Counsel, Singapore, 1946; District Judge (Civil), Singapore, 1948; District Judge and 1st Magistrate, Singapore, 1952; actg Puisne Judge, Fed. of Malaya, 1953-54; Puisne Judge, Supreme Court, Nigeria, 1955; Actg Chief Justice, High Court of Lagos and Southern Cameroons, 1959, 1960; Actg Chief Justice, High Court of Lagos, 1961; a Judge of High Court of Lagos and Southern Cameroons, 1955-62. *Address:* 212 Collingwood House, Dolphin Square, SW1.

BELLAMY, Basil Edmund, CB 1971; Under-Secretary, Department of Trade and Industry (formerly Board of Trade), 1965-74; *b* 9 Feb. 1914; *s* of William Henry and Mary Bellamy; *m* 1943, Sheila Mary Dolan; one *d. Educ:* Whitgift Sch. Joined Board of Trade, 1932; Asst Dir, Min. of War Transport, 1943; Asst Sec., Min. of Transport, 1951; Under-Sec., 1963-65. Joint Services Staff Coll., 1950; Imperial Defence Coll., 1957. *Address:* 52 Denmark Road, Wimbledon, SW19 4PQ.

BELLAMY, Prof. Edmund Henry, MA, PhD; Professor of Physics in the University of London, Westfield College, since 1960; *b* 8 April 1923; *s* of Herbert Bellamy and Nellie (*née* Ablett); *m* 1946, Joan Roberts; three *s. Educ:* Quarry Bank Sch., Liverpool; King's Coll., Cambridge. Lectr in Natural Philosophy, Univ. of Glasgow, 1951-59, Sen. Lectr, 1959-60. Mem., Nuclear Physics Board of Science Research Council, 1965-66. Visiting Prof., Univ. of Stanford, 1966-67. *Publications:* numerous scientific papers in Proc. Phys. Soc. and other journals. *Recreations:* skiing, squash, travel, football. *Address:* 7 Homefield Road, Radlett, Herts. *T:* Radlett 4677.

BELLAMY, Dr Lionel John, CBE 1970; Visiting Professor, University of East Anglia, since 1976; Director: Explosives Research and Development Establishment, Ministry of Defence, 1964-76; Rocket Propulsion Establishment, 1972-76; *b* 23 Sept. 1916; *m* Jill Stanley; one *s* one *d* (and one *s* decd). *Educ:* Clapham Coll.; London Univ. BSc Lond 1st cl. 1937; PhD Lond 1939. Scientific Civil Service: Chemical Inspectorate, Min. of Supply, 1939-59; Explosives Research and Development Establishment, Min. of Aviation, later Min. of Technology,

1954-, Dir, 1964-. Adrian Visiting Fellow, Dept of Chemistry, Univ. of Leicester, 1967-76; Hon. Prof., Univ. of East Anglia, 1968-. *Publications:* The Infra-Red Spectra of Complex Molecules, 1954 (2nd edn 1958); Advances in IR Group Frequencies, 1968; contribs to Jl Chem. Soc., Spectrochimica Acta, Transactions Faraday Soc., etc. *Recreation:* spectroscopy. *Address:* The Lodge, Powdermill Lane, Waltham Abbey, Essex. *T:* Lea Valley 716597.

BELLERBY, Rev. Alfred Courthope Benson, MA Cantab; Headmaster, King Edward School, Witley, Surrey, 1926-51; retired, 1951; *b* 26 Jan. 1888; *s* of late E. J. Bellerby, MusDoc Oxon., LRAM, and Charlotte Bellerby; *m* 1922, Enid Florence Apperly. *Educ:* St Lawrence Coll., Ramsgate; Emmanuel Coll., Cambridge; Ridley Hall, Cambridge. Cambridge Univ. Athletic Blue, 1907, 1908, 1909, 1910; Pres. Cambridge Univ. Athletic Club, 1910; Holder of Univ. Gold Medal for 3 wins in succession against Oxford; Cambridge Univ. Hockey Blue, 1909-10; International Hockey Trials, 1909-10; represented United Kingdom in Olympic Games, 1908 (High Jump). Deacon, 1911; Priest, 1913; Chaplain, Games Master and Senior House Master, St Lawrence Coll., 1911-26. *Publication:* The Lonely Dog. *Recreations:* gardening, lecturing. *Address:* Redcot, Three Gates Lane, Haslemere, Surrey.

BELLEW, family name of **Baron Bellew**.

BELLEW; *see* Grattan-Bellew.

BELLEW, 6th Baron *cr* 1848; **Bryan Bertram Bellew**, MC 1916; Bt 1688; *b* 11 June 1890; 2nd *s* of Hon. Richard Eustace Bellew (*d* 1933) (4th *s* of 2nd Baron), and Ada Kate (*d* 1893), *d* of Henry Parry Gilbey; *S* brother, 1975; *m* 1918, Jeanie Ellen Agnes (*d* 1973), *d* of late James Ormsby Jameson; one *s. Educ:* Stubbington; Trinity Hall, Cambridge. Served European War, 1914-19 (MC); Lieut S Irish Horse. *Heir: s* Hon. James Bryan Bellew [*b* 5 Jan. 1920; *m* 1942, Mary Elizabeth, *d* of Rev. Edward Eustace Hill; two *s* one *d*]. *Address:* Barmeath Castle, Dunleer, Co. Louth, Eire.

BELLEW, Hon. Sir George (Rothe), KCB 1961; KCVO 1953 (CVO 1950; MVO 1935); Kt 1950; FSA 1948; Secretary of the Order of the Garter, 1961-74, Garter Principal King of Arms, 1950-61; Genealogist of the Order of the Bath, 1950-61; Genealogist Order of St John, 1951-61; Knight Principal of Imperial Society of Knights Bachelor, 1957-62 (Deputy Knight Principal, 1962-71); Inspector of Regimental Colours, 1957-61; *b* 13 Dec. 1899; *s* of late Hon. Richard Bellew and Gwendoline, *d* of William R. J. Fitzherbert Herbert-Huddleston of Cliffoney; *m* 1935, Ursula Kennard, *e d* of late Anders Eric Knös Cull, Warfield House, Bracknell; one *s. Educ:* Wellington Coll.; Christ Church, Oxford. Served War of 1939-45: Squadron Leader RAFVR, 1940-45 (despatches). Formerly Portcullis Pursuivant of Arms; Somerset Herald, 1926-50, and Registrar of the Coll. of Arms, 1935-46. KStJ 1951 (Mem. Chapter Gen., 1951-). *Address:* The Grange, Farnham, Surrey.

BELLINGER, Sir Robert (Ian), GBE 1967; Kt 1964; President, Kinloch (Provision Merchants) Ltd; Chairman, National Savings Committee, 1970-75, and President, 1972-75; Director, Rank Organisation, since 1971; *b* Tetbury Glos, 10 March 1910; *s* of David Morgan Bellinger, Cardiganshire, and Jane Ballantine Deans, Edinburgh; *m* 1962, Christiane Marie Louise Janssens, Brussels; one *s* one *d. Educ:* Church of England sch. Elected Court of Common Council, 1953; Chm. City of London Freemen's Sch., 1957; Alderman for Ward of Cheap, 1958; Sheriff, City of London, 1962-63; Lord Mayor of London, 1966-67; one of HM Lieutenants, City of London, 1976-. Chairman: Panel for Civil Service Manpower Review, 1968-71; Adv. Cttee on Magistracy, City of London, 1968-76; Licensing Cttee, City of London; Finance Cttee, BBC; Governor, BBC, 1968-71; Dir, Arsenal Football Club. Past Master, Broderers' Company; Liveryman, Fletchers' Company. Hon. DSc City Univ., 1966. Gentleman Usher of the Purple Rod, Order of the British Empire, 1969-. Chm., Anglo-Danish Soc., 1976. KStJ 1966; Commandeur, Ordre de Léopold, cl. III (Belgium), 1963; Comdr, Royal Order of the Phoenix (Greece), 1963; Officier, Ordre de la Valeur Camerounaise (Cameroons), 1963. *Recreations:* tennis, football, music, motoring. *Address:* Penn Wood, Fulmer, Bucks. *T:* Fulmer 2029. *Club:* City Livery.

BELLINGHAM, Sir Noel (Peter Roger), 7th Bt (2nd creation) *cr* 1796; accountant; *b* 4 Sept. 1943; *s* of Sir Roger Carroll Patrick Stephen Bellingham, 6th Bt, and of Mary, *d* of late William Norman; *S* father, 1973. *Heir: b* Anthony Edward Norman Bellingham, *b* 24 March 1947. *Address:* 20 Davenport Park Road, Davenport, Stockport, Cheshire. *T:* 061-483 7168. *Club:* 64 Society (Cheshire).

BELLIS, Bertram Thomas; Headmaster, The Leys School, Cambridge, since 1975; *b* 4 May 1927; *s* of Rev. Thomas J. Bellis and Mary A. Bellis; *m* 1952, Joan Healey; two *s. Educ:* Kingswood Sch., Bath; St John's Coll., Cambridge (Exhibr in Maths, MA). Rossall Sch., 1951-55; Highgate Sch., 1955-65; Headmaster, Daniel Stewart's Coll., 1965-72; Principal, Daniel Stewart's and Melville Coll., 1972-75. Chm., Scottish Educn Dept Cttee on Computers and the Schools (reports, 1969 and 1972). Pres., Mathematical Assoc., 1971-72. Schoolmaster Fellow, Balliol Coll., Oxford, 1963; FIMA 1964; FRSE 1972. *Recreation:* fell walking. *Address:* The Leys School, Cambridge CB2 2AD.

BELLOW, Saul; American writer; *b* 10 June 1915; *s* of Abraham and Liza Gordon Bellow; three *s. Educ:* Univ. of Chicago: Northwestern Univ. Three one-act plays: Out From Under, Orange Soufflé, and The Wen, prod. London, 1966. Nobel Prize for Literature, 1976. Hon. DLitt, Northwestern Univ., 1962. *Publications:* Dangling Man, 1944 (reissued 1972); The Victim, 1947; The Adventures of Augie March, 1953; Seize the Day, 1956; Henderson the Rain King, 1959; Herzog, 1964; Mosby's Memoirs and Other Stories, 1969; Mr Sammler's Planet, 1970; Humboldt's Gift, 1975 (Pulitzer Prize 1976); To Jerusalem and Back, 1976. Play: The Last Analysis, 1967. *Address:* University of Chicago, Chicago, Ill 60637, USA.

BELLOWS, James Gilbert; Editor, The Washington Star, since Jan. 1975; *b* 12 Nov. 1922; *s* of Lyman Hubbard Bellows and Dorothy Gilbert Bellows; *m* 1950, Marian Raines (marr. diss.); three *d*; *m* 1964, Maggie Savoy (decd); *m* 1970, Keven Ryan; one *d. Educ:* Kenyon Coll. (BA, LLB). Columbus (Ga) Ledger, 1947; News Editor Atlanta (Ga) Jl, 1950-57; Asst Editor, Detroit (Mich.) Free Press, 1957-58; Managing Editor Miami (Fla) News, 1958-61; Exec. Editor (News Ops), NY Herald Tribune, 1961-62; Editor, 1962-66; associate Editor, Los Angeles Times, 1966-75. *Address:* 5044 Millwood Lane, Washington, DC 20016, USA.

BELMORE, 8th Earl of, *cr* 1797; **John Armar Lowry-Corry;** Baron Belmore, 1781; Viscount Belmore, 1789; *b* 4 Sept. 1951; *s* of 7th Earl of Belmore and Gloria Anthea, *d* of late Herbert Bryant Harker, Melbourne, Australia; *S* father 1960. *Educ:* Lancing; Royal Agricultural Coll., Cirencester. *Heir: kinsman* Frederick Henry Lowry-Corry[*b* 23 Dec. 1926; *m* 1949, Hon. Rosemary Diana Lavinia, *y d* of 2nd Viscount Plumer; two *s*]. *Recreations:* fishing, shooting. *Address:* Castlecoole, Enniskillen, Co. Fermanagh, N Ireland. *T:* Enniskillen 2368. *Clubs:* Army and Navy (Associate Mem.), Travellers'.

BELOE, Robert, CBE 1960; Liaison Officer between Anglican Communion and World Council of Churches, 1969-71; *b* 12 May 1905; *s* of late Rev. R. D. Beloe, Headmaster of Bradfield Coll., and of Clarissa, *d* of Rev. Prebendary J. T. Bramston, Winchester Coll.; *m* 1933, Amy (JP), *d* of Capt. Sir Frank Rose, 2nd Bt (killed in action, 1914) and of late Daphne, Lady Rose; one *s* two *d. Educ:* Winchester; Hertford Coll., Oxford. Asst Master: Bradfield, 1927-28; Eton, 1928-30; Reading elementary sch., 1930-31. Kent Education Office, 1931-34; Asst Education Officer, Surrey, 1934-39; Dep. Education Officer, 1939-40; Chief Education Officer, 1940-59; Sec. to Archbishop of Canterbury, 1959-69. Mem. of various commissions and departmental cttees, including Royal Commission on Marriage and Divorce, 1951-55; Mauritius Electoral Boundary Commission, 1957; Higher Agricultural Education Cttee, 1944-46; Secondary Sch. Examinations Council, 1944-64 (Chm. Cttee on Exams other than GCE, 1958-60, leading to establishment of Cert. of Secondary Educn); Hon. Consultant, CSE Sub-Cttee of Schools Council, 1964-; Mem., Home Office Central Training Council for Child Care, 1947-53. Hon. Sec. County Education Officers Soc., 1958-59; Governor of Commonwealth Inst., 1949-67. Trustee of Duke of Edinburgh's Award Scheme, 1960-66. Secretary: Monckton Cttee on Admin of Church Comrs, 1963; Archbishop's Advisers on Needs and Resources, 1963-69; General Synod C of E: Mem., 1970-75; Mem., Standing Cttee, 1971-75. *Recreations:* gardening, travel. *Address:* The Hill House, Queen's Road, Richmond, Surrey. *Club:* United Oxford & Cambridge University.
See also Sir Julian Rose, Bt.

BELOFF, Prof. Max, MA, DLitt (Oxon); FBA 1973; FRHistS; FRSA; Principal, University College at Buckingham, since April 1974; Fellow, St Antony's College, Oxford, since 1975; *b* 2 July 1913; *er s* of late Simon and Mary Beloff; *m* 1938, Helen Dobrin; two *s. Educ:* St Paul's Sch.; Corpus Christi Coll., Oxford (Scholar). Gibbs Schol. in Mod. Hist., 1934; 1st Cl. Hons, School of Modern History, 1935; Senior Demy, Magdalen Coll., Oxford, 1935. Junior Research Fellow, Corpus Christi Coll., 1937; Asst Lecturer in History, Manchester Univ., 1939-

46; Nuffield Reader in Comparative Study of Institutions, Oxford Univ., 1946-56; Fellow of Nuffield Coll., 1947-57; Gladstone Prof. of Govt and Public Admin, Oxford Univ., and Fellow, All Souls Coll., 1957-74, now Professor Emeritus. War of 1939-45, Royal Corps of Signals, 1940-41. Governor, Haifa Univ.; Ex-Trustee and Ex-Librarian, Oxford Union Soc. Hon. LLD Pittsburgh, USA, 1962; Hon. DCL, Bishop's Univ. Canada, 1976; Hon. DLitt Bowdoin Coll., USA, 1976. *Publications:* Public Order and Popular Disturbances, 1660-1714, 1938; The Foreign Policy of Soviet Russia, Vol. 1, 1947, Vol. 2, 1949; Thomas Jefferson and American Democracy, 1948; Soviet Policy in the Far East, 1944-51, 1953; The Age of Absolutism, 1660-1815, 1954; Foreign Policy and the Democratic Process, 1955; Europe and the Europeans, 1957; The Great Powers, 1959; The American Federal Government, 1959; New Dimensions in Foreign Policy, 1961; The United States and the Unity of Europe, 1963; The Balance of Power, 1967; The Future of British Foreign Policy, 1969; Imperial Sunset, vol. 1, 1969; The Intellectual in Politics, 1970; edited: The Federalist, 1948; Mankind and his Story, 1948; The Debate on the American Revolution, 1949; On the Track of Tyranny, 1959; L'Europe du XIXe et XXe siècle, 1960-67; (with V. Vale) American Political Institutions in the 1970's, 1975; articles in English, French, Italian and American journals. *Recreation:* watching cricket. *Address:* University College at Buckingham, Hunter Street, Buckingham MK18 1EG. *T:* Buckingham 4161. *Club:* Reform.

BELOFF, Nora; author and journalist; *b* 24 Jan. 1919. *Educ:* King Alfred Sch.; Lady Margaret Hall, Oxford. BA Hons History 1940. Polit. Intell. Dept, FO, 1941-44; British Embassy, Paris, 1944-45; reporter, Reuters News Agency, 1945-46; Paris corresp., The Economist, 1946-48; Observer corresp., Paris, Washington, Moscow, Brussels etc from 1948; political correspondent, 1964-76, roving correspondent, 1976-. *Publications:* The General Says No, 1963; The Transit of Britain, 1973; Freedom under Foot, 1976. *Address:* 59 Blair Court, Boundary Road, NW8 6NT. *T:* 01-586 0378. *Club:* Le Petit Club français.

BELPER, 4th Baron *cr* 1856; **Alexander Ronald George Strutt;** formerly Major, Coldstream Guards; *b* 23 April 1912; *s* of 3rd Baron and Hon. Eva Isabel Mary Bruce, 2nd *d* of 2nd Baron Aberdare (she *m* 2nd, 6th Earl of Rosebery); *S* father 1956; *m* 1940, Zara Sophie Kathleen Mary (marr. diss. 1949), *y d* of Sir Harry Mainwaring, 5th Bt; one *s. Educ:* Harrow. Served War with Coldstream Guards, 1939-44 (wounded). *Heir: s* Hon. Richard Henry Strutt [*b* 24 Oct. 1941; *m* 1966, Jennifer Vivian, *d* of late Capt. Peter Winser and of Mrs James Whitaker; one *s* one *d*]. *Address:* Kingston Hall, Nottingham.

BELSKY, Franta; sculptor; *b* Brno, 6 April 1921; *s* of Joseph Belsky, economist; *m* 1944, Margaret Constance Owen (cartoonist Belsky). *Educ:* Acad. of Fine Arts, Prague; Royal Coll. of Art, London. ARCA, Hons Dip. 1950. Joined Armed Forces in France, 1940, as gunner; in Britain until Normandy, 1944; service in Europe, 1944-45 (various decorations). Taught in art schs, 1950-55. FRBS (Mem. Council); Pres., Soc. of Portrait Sculptors, 1963-68; Governor, St Martin's Sch. of Art, 1967-. Exhibited in London from 1943; work in collections in Europe and USA. Various public commns, work for numerous co. councils, industrial and private cos and educn authorities: Paratroop Memorial, Prague, 1947; statue of Cecil Rhodes, 8', Bulawayo, 1953; Lt-Col Peniakoff (Popski), Ravenna, 1952; groups: Constellation, Colchester, 1953; Lesson, LCC housing develt, 1957-58; Triga, 16'×16'×16', Knightsbridge, 1958; Joy-ride, Stevenage New Town Centre, 1958; fountains: European Shell Centre, 30', South Bank, 1959-61; Four Seasons, 17', Yate, 1965; portrait bust of the Queen Mother, Birmingham Univ., 1962; reliefs: Epicentre, 11', Doncaster City Centre, 1965; Key West, 27', Slough, 1966; Radiation, St Luke's Hosp., Guildford, 1967; sculpture of Adm. Cunningham, Trafalgar Sq., 1967; Astronomer Herschel Memorial, 18', Slough, 1969; statue of Sir Winston Churchill, 8', for Churchill Meml and Library in US, Fulton, Missouri, 1969-70, and bust in Churchill Archives, Cambridge; sculptured bulkheads in BR ships Hengist, Horsa, Senlac, 1971-72; group, Oracle, 18', Temple Way House, Bristol, 1975; Harry S. Truman bust, Presidential Library, Independence, Mo, 1975; Totem, 32', Manchester Arndale Centre, 1975; Lord Cottesloe, Nat. Theatre, 1976. *Publications:* contrib. various books and jls. *Recreations:* ski-ing, gardening, amateur archaeology. *Address:* 12 Pembroke Studios, W8 6HX. *Club:* Ski Club of Great Britain.

BELSTEAD, 2nd Baron, *cr* 1938; **John Julian Ganzoni;** Bt 1929; JP; Chairman, Association of Governing Bodies of Public Schools, since 1974; *b* 30 Sept. 1932; *o s* of 1st Baron Belstead and Gwendolen Gertrude Turner (*d* 1962); *S* father, 1958. *Educ:*

Eton; Christ Church, Oxford. MA 1961. Parliamentary Under-Secretary of State: DES, 1970-73; NI Office, 1973-74. JP Borough of Ipswich, 1962. *Heir:* none. *Address:* The Old Rectory, Great Bealings, near Woodbridge, Suffolk. *T:* Grundisburgh 278. *Clubs:* Bath; All England Lawn Tennis (Wimbledon); MCC.

BELTRAM, Geoffrey; Under-Secretary, Department of Health and Social Security, since 1973; *b* 7 April 1921; *s* of George and Beatrice Dorothy Beltram; *m* 1945, Audrey Mary (*née* Harkett); one *s* one *d. Educ:* Dame Alice Owen's School. Tax Officer, Inland Revenue, 1938; served in RAF, 1941-46; Exec. Officer and Higher Exec. Officer, Min. of Town and Country Planning, 1947-51; Asst Principal, Nat. Assistance Bd, 1951-55; Principal 1955-63; Asst Sec. 1963-73 (NAB 1963-66, Min. of Social Security 1966-68, DHSS 1968-73). *Recreations:* Literature, listening to music, opera, ballet, walking, tennis. *Address:* 115 Abbots Gardens, East Finchley, N2 0JJ. *T:* 01-883 5776.

BEMROSE, Sir Max, (John Maxwell), Kt 1960; DL; Chairman, Bemrose Corporation Ltd; *b* 1 July 1904; *y s* of late Dr Henry Howe Bemrose and late Mrs Bemrose; *m* 1933, Margaret Le Mare; one adopted *s* and one adopted *d. Educ:* Derby Sch.; Brighton Coll.; Clare Coll., Cambridge. MA (Economics). Joined family firm, 1926. Prospective Conservative Candidate for Derby, 1938; fought Gen. Election, 1945; contested Watford Div., 1950; Chm. East Midlands Provincial Area, Conservative & Unionist Assoc., 1957-61; Mem. Exec. and Gen. Purposes Cttee of Conservative Assoc.; Chm. Nat. Union of Conservative & Unionist Associations, 1964-65; Chm., Printing and Publishing Industry Training Bd, 1972-; Pres., British Fedn of Master Printers, 1967-68, 1971-72. DL Derbyshire, 1967, High Sheriff of Derbyshire, 1969-70. *Recreations:* swimming, music, gardening. *Address:* Hazelbrow, Duffield, Derbyshire. *T:* Derby 840388. *Clubs:* Carlton, Lansdowne.

BENARROCH, Mrs E. J.; *see* Harper, Heather.

BENAUD, Richard, OBE 1961; public relations and media representation; BBC Television Commentator, since 1960; *b* 6 Oct. 1930; *s* of Louis Richard Benaud and Irene Benaud; *m* 1967, Daphne Elizabeth Surfleet; two *s* by previous marr. *Educ:* Parramatta High Sch. Captain, Australian Cricket Team, Tours to England, 1953, 1956, 1961; represented Australia, 63 Tests, 28 as Captain. *Publications:* Way of Cricket, 1960; Tale of Two Tests, 1962; Spin Me a Spinner, 1963; The New Champions, 1965; Willow Patterns, 1972. *Recreation:* golf. *Address:* 19 Tara, 178 Beach Street, Coogee, NSW 2034, Australia. *T:* Sydney 665-6464.

BENCE, Cyril Raymond; *b* 26 Nov. 1902; *s* of Harris Bryant Bence; *m* 1926, Florence Maud Bowler (*d* 1974); one *s* one *d*; *m* 1975, Mrs I. N. Hall (*née* Lewis). *Educ:* Pontywaen Sch.; Newport High Sch., Mon. Apprenticed to Ashworth Son & Co. Ltd of Dock Street, Newport, Mon, Weighing Machine Manufacturers; moved to Birmingham, 1937. Member of National Union of Scalemakers; Mem. of AEU; Mem. of Birmingham Trades Council, 1942-45; Pres. Witton Branch AEU. Contested (Lab) Handsworth Div. of Birmingham, at Gen. Elections of 1945 and 1950, and Bye-election Nov. 1950; MP (Lab) Dunbartonshire East, 1951-70. *Address:* Leda, Sweethay Close, Staplehay, Taunton, Som.

BENDALL, David Vere, CMG 1967; MBE 1945; HM Diplomatic Service, retired; Director, Morgan Grenfell (Holdings) Ltd, since 1971; Director, Banque de Suez (UK) Ltd, since 1975; Comité Consultatif, Banque de l'Indochine et de Suez, since 1974; *b* 27 Feb. 1920; *s* of John Manley Bendall; *m* 1941, Eve Stephanie Merrilees Galpin; one *d. Educ:* Winchester; King's Coll., Cambridge. Served Grenadier Guards, 1940-46. Third Sec., Allied Force HQ, Caserta, 1946; Rome, 1947; FO, 1949; First Sec., Santiago, 1952; FO, 1955; seconded to NATO Secretariat, Paris 1957; FO, 1960; NATO Secretariat, Paris as Dep. Head, Economic and Finance Div. and Special Advisor on Defence Policy, 1962; Counsellor, 1962; Counsellor, Washington, 1965-69; Asst Under-Sec. of State for Western Europe, 1969-71. *Recreations:* golf, tennis, languages. *Address:* 3 Eaton Terrace Mews, SW1. *T:* 01-730 4229; Ashbocking Hall, near Ipswich, Suffolk. *T:* Helmingham 262. *Club:* Boodle's.

BENDALL, Dr Eve Rosemarie Duffield; Registrar, General Nursing Council for England and Wales, 1973-77; *b* 7 Aug. 1927; *d* of Col F. W. D. Bendall, CMG, MA, and Mrs M. L. Bendall, LRAM, ARCM. *Educ:* Malvern Girls' Coll.; London Univ. (MA, PhD); Royal Free Hosp. (SRN). Ward Sister, Dorset County Hosp., 1953-55; Night Supt, Manchester Babies' Hosp., 1955-56; Nurse Tutor: United Sheffield Hosps Sch. of Nursing, 1958-61; St George's Hosp., London, 1961-63;

Principal, Sch. of Nursing, Hosp. for Sick Children, Gt Ormond Street, 1963-69. *Publications:* (jtly) Basic Nursing, 1963, 3rd edn 1970; (jtly) A Guide to Medical and Surgical Nursing, 1965, 2nd edn 1970; (jtly) A History of the General Nursing Council, 1969; So you passed, nurse (research), 1975. *Recreations:* gardening, theatre.

BENDER, Prof. Arnold Eric; Professor of Nutrition, Queen Elizabeth College, University of London, since 1971; *b* 24 July 1918; *s* of Isadore and Rose Bender; *m* 1941, Deborah Swift; two *s. Educ:* Liverpool Inst. High Sch.; Univ. of Liverpool (BSc Hons); Univ. of Sheffield (PhD). Research, Pharmaceutical Industry, 1940-45 and 1950-54; Lectr, Univ. of Sheffield, 1947-49; Research, Food Industry, 1954-64; Teaching and Research, Univ. of London, 1965-. *Publications:* Dictionary of Nutrition and Food Technology, 1960, 4th edn 1975; Nutrition and Dietetic Foods, 1967, 2nd edn 1973; Value of Food, 1970, 2nd edn 1975; Facts of Food, 1975; Nutritional Changes in Food Processing, 1977; research papers and review articles in Brit. Jl of Nutrition, Biochem. Jl, BMJ, and other professional jls, and reports. *Recreations:* writing, gardening. *Address:* 59 Perryn Road, W3 7LS. *T:* 01-743 6419.

BENDIGO, Bishop of, since 1975; **Rt. Rev. Oliver Spencer Heyward;** *b* Launceston, Tasmania, 16 March 1926; *s* of Harold and Vera Heyward; *m* 1952, Peggy Butcher; four *s. Educ:* Church Gram. Sch., Launceston; Univ. of Tasmania (BA Hons 1949); Oriel Coll., Univ. of Oxford (BA 1953, MA 1956); Cuddesdon Coll., Oxford. RAAF, 1944-46. Rhodes Scholar, 1949. Deacon 1953, priest 1954, dio. Chichester; Asst Curate, St Peter's, Brighton, 1953-56; Rector of Sorell, Tasmania, 1956-60; Rector of Richmond, Tasmania, 1960-62; Precentor, St David's Cathedral, Hobart, 1962-63; Warden, Christ Coll., Univ. of Tasmania, 1963-74. *Recreations:* gardening, Royal tennis. *Address:* Bishopscourt, 40 Forest Street, Bendigo, Victoria 3550, Australia. *T:* 436093.

BENEY, Frederick William, CBE 1962; QC 1943; *s* of late William Augustus Beney, JP, Beckenham, Kent; *m* Irene Constance, *e d* of Henry Ward-Meyer, Weybridge; two *s. Educ:* Mill Hill Sch.; New Coll., Oxford (MA). Called to Bar, Inner Temple, 1909, Bencher 1948. Legal Asst, War Office, 1914-20; Recorder of Norwich, 1944-59; Mem., Deptl Ctte on Alternative Remedies, 1944-46; Chm. Deptl Cttee on Nat. Insurance against Industrial Diseases, 1953-54; Commissioner, Central Criminal Court, 1959-64; Commissioner of Assize, SE Circuit, 1959; Western Circuit, 1961; retd from practice, 1961. BBC Broadcasting, 1961-. Mem. Appeal Tribunal, Assoc. of British Travel Agents. *Publications:* contributions to legal journals. *Address:* Longmynd, Burwood Park, Walton-on-Thames, Surrey. *T:* Walton-on-Thames 21295.

BENIN, Oba of; Akenzua II; Godfrey Okoro, CMG 1946; *b* 1899; *e s* of Oba Eweka II and *o s* of Queen Ariowa (titled Queen Ezon); *S* father 1933; first marriage, 1922; over 50 *s* and *d. Educ:* Government Sch., Benin City; King's Coll., Lagos. Transport Clerk, 1922; Private Sec. and Clerk to Oba Eweka II and to Benin Judicial Council, 1924-25; Administrative Training, Abeokuta, 1926-27; District Head, Ekiadolor District in Benin Div., 1928-33. Minister Without Portfolio, Western Nigeria, 1955-60. Chancellor, Ahmadu Bello University, 1966-70. JP 1960. Jubilee medal, 1935; Coronation medal, 1937; Medal for African Chiefs. *Recreations:* snooker, etc. *Heir: s* Solomon Igbinoghodua Aisiokuoba Akenzua, *b* 22 June 1923. *Address:* PO Box 12, Benin City, Western Nigeria. *T:* 1 Benin City.

BENJAMIN, Prof. Bernard; Professor of Actuarial Science, The City University, London, 1973-75; now Visiting Professor; *b* 8 March 1910; *s* of Joseph and Lucy Benjamin, London; *m* 1937, May Pate, Horham, Suffolk; two *d. Educ:* Colfe Grammar Sch.; Sir John Cass Coll. (London University). BSc (Hons); PhD London. LCC, 1928; statistician Public Health Dept, 1940; served War, 1943-46, RAF; statistician, General Register Office, 1952; Chief Statistician, 1954; Dir of Statistics, Ministry of Health, 1963-65; Dir of Research and Intelligence, GLC, 1965-70; Dir of Statistical Studies, CS College, 1970-73; Hon. Cons. in Med. Stats to Army, 1966. Chm., Standing Cttee of Statistics Users, 1971-. Fellow: Inst. of Actuaries (a Vice-Pres. 1963; Pres., 1966-68; Gold Medal, 1975); Royal Statistical Soc. (Pres. 1970-71). *Publications:* Social and Economic Factors in Mortality, 1965; Health and Vital Statistics, 1968; Demographic Analysis, 1969; The Population Census, 1970; (with H. W. Haycocks) The Analysis of Mortality and Other Actuarial Statistics, 1971; Statistics in Urban Administration, 1976; (ed) Medical Records, 1977; General Insurance, 1977; numerous medical and population statistical papers and contribs to Jl of Royal Statistical Society and Jl of Inst. of Actuaries. *Recreations:* gardening, painting (both kinds). *Address:* 39 Dale Wood Road, Orpington, Kent. *T:* Orpington 24092. *Club:* Athenæum.

BENJAMIN, Brooke; see Benjamin, T. B.

BENJAMIN, Mrs Joseph; see Crabbe, Pauline.

BENJAMIN, Dr Ralph, DSc, PhD, BSc, ACGI, CEng, FIEE, FIERE; Chief Scientist, Government Communications Headquarters, since 1971; b 17 Nov. 1922; s of Charles Benjamin and Claire Benjamin (née Stern); m 1951, Kathleen Ruth Bull, BA; two s. Educ: in Germany and Switzerland; St Oswald's Coll., Ellesmere; Imperial Coll. of Science and Technology, London. DSc(Eng) London, 1970. Joined Royal Naval Scientific Service, 1944; Senior Scientific Officer, 1949; Principal Scientific Officer, 1952; Senior Principal Scientific Officer (Special Merit), 1955; Deputy Chief Scientific Officer (Special Merit), 1960; Head of Research and Deputy Chief Scientist, Admiralty Surface Weapons Establishment, 1961; Dir and Chief Scientist, Admiralty Underwater Weapons Estab., 1964-71, and Dir, Underwater Weapons R&D (Navy), 1965-71. Hon. consultant: Univ. of Illinois; US Office of Naval Research, 1956; IEE Marconi Premium, 1964; Council Mem., Brit. Acoustical Soc., 1971; Vis. Prof., Dept of Electrical and Electronic Engineering, Univ. of Surrey, 1973-. Publications: Modulation, Resolution and Signal Processing for Radar Sonar and Related Systems, 1966; contribs to various advisory cttees, working parties, symposia, etc; articles in Jls of Instn of Electrical Engineers and Inst. of Electronic and Radio Engineers, etc. Recreations: work, mountaineering, ski-ing, swimming, sailing, sub-aqua (qualified naval diving officer), canoeing, judo (black belt). Address: c/o Government Communication Headquarters, Cheltenham, Glos. Club: Athenæum.

BENJAMIN, Prof. (Thomas) Brooke, MEng, PhD; FRS 1966; Professor of Mathematics, and Director, Fluid Mechanics Research Institute, University of Essex, since 1970; b 15 April 1929; s of Thomas Joseph Benjamin and Ethel Mary Benjamin (née Brooke); m 1956, Helen Gilda-Marie Rakower Ginsburg (marr. diss. 1974); one s two d. Educ: Wallasey Grammar Sch.; University of Liverpool; Yale Univ. (USA); University of Cambridge. BEng (Liverpool) 1950; MEng. (Yale) 1952; PhD (Cantab) 1955. Fellow of King's Coll., Cambridge, 1955-64; Asst Dir of Research, University of Cambridge, 1958-67; Reader in Hydrodynamics, Univ. of Cambridge, 1967-70. Chm., Mathematics Cttee, SRC, 1975-. Editor, Journal of Fluid Mechanics, 1960-65; Consultant to English Electric Co., 1956-67. William Hopkins Prize, Cambridge Philosophical Soc., 1969. Publications: various papers on theoretical and experimental fluid mechanics. Recreations: music, poetry. Address: Clifton House, Chapel Road, Wivenhoe, Colchester, Essex. T: Wivenhoe 4780.

BENN, Anthony, OBE 1945; b 7 Oct. 1912; s of late Francis Hamilton Benn and Arta Clara Benn (née Boal); m 1943, Maureen Lillian Kathleen Benn (née Denbigh); two s four d. Educ: Harrow; Christ Church, Oxford. Scholar; 1st cl. Hon. Mods; 2nd cl. Greats. Oxford Univ. Cricket XI, 1935. Price & Pierce Ltd, 1935 (Director, 1947, Chm., 1956-72). Joined Surrey and Sussex Yeomanry, 1936. Served War of 1939-45 (OBE): Staff Coll., 1942; Instructor, Middle East Staff Coll., 1943. Comdr, Order of the Lion of Finland, 1958. Recreations: golf, shooting, travel. Address: Rock House, Runfold, Farnham, Surrey GU10 1NR. T: Farnham 5750.

BENN, Edward; Deputy Chief Scientist (RAF), Ministry of Defence, since 1975; b 8 May 1922; s of John Henry Benn and Alice (née Taylor); m 1947, Joan Taylor; one d. Educ: High Storrs Grammar Sch., Sheffield; Sheffield Univ. (BEng; 1st Cl. Hons Civil Engrg; Mappin Medal, 1943). Operational Research with Army, 1943-48; India and Burma, 1944-46 (Major); entered War Office, 1948; tank research, Supt Special Studies, and later Dep. Dir, Army Op. Res. Estabt, 1961; Asst Sci. Adviser to SACEUR, Paris, 1962-65; Dep. Chief Sci. Adviser, Home Offfice, 1966-68; Dir, Defence Policy, MoD, 1968-75; Under Sec., 1975. Recreation: golf. Address: 37 Woodham Waye, Woodham, Woking, Surrey GU21 5SJ. T: Woking 60443. Clubs: MCC; XIXth; West Byfleet Golf.

BENN, Edward Glanvill; Life President, Benn Brothers, Ltd, Publishers, since 1976, Chairman, 1945-75; b 1905; 2nd s of late Sir Ernest Benn, 2nd Bt, CBE; m 1931, Beatrice Catherine, MBE, d of Claude Newbald; one s one d. Educ: Harrow; Clare Coll., Cambridge. Served War of 1939-45, East Surrey Regt, 1940-45; Brigade Major, 138 Infantry Brigade, Italy, 1944 (despatches). Council Member: Nat. Advertising Benevolent Soc., 1937-61 (Trustee, 1951-, and Pres. 1961-62); Advertising Assoc., 1951-67 (Hon. Treasurer 1960-65); Commonwealth Press Union, 1956- (Hon. Treasurer 1967-77, Hon. Life Mem. 1975); Vice Pres., Readers' Pension Cttee, 1950-; Life Vice Pres., Newspaper Press Fund, 1965- (Appeals Pres. 1971); Chm.,

Advertising Advisory Cttee, Independent Television Authority, 1959-64; Dir., Exchange Telegraph Co. Ltd, 1960-72 (Chm. 1969-72); Pres., Periodical Publishers Assoc. 1976-. Mackintosh Medal, 1967. Address: 35 Marsham Court, SW1P 4JY.
See also Sir J. A. Benn.

BENN, Sir John Andrews, 3rd Bt, cr 1914; Consultant, Benn Brothers Ltd and Ernest Benn Ltd; b 28 Jan. 1904; e s of Sir Ernest Benn, 2nd Bt, CBE and Gwendolen, d of F. M. Andrews, Edgbaston; S father, 1954; m 1929, Hon. Ursula Helen Alers Hankey, o d of 1st Baron Hankey, PC, GCB, GCMG, GCVO, FRS; two s three d. Educ: Harrow; Princeton Univ., USA (Class of 1926 Achievement Award 1970); Gonville and Caius Coll., Cambridge. Toured Latin America, founding Industria Britanica to promote British export trade, 1931. Helped to get new industries to Crook, South-West Durham, depressed area, 1936-38. Served War of 1939-45, KOYLI. Contested Bradford N (Nat. C), General Election, 1945. Chm. and Man. Dir, UK Provident Instn, 1949-68; Chairman: Crosby Trust Management Ltd, 1958-61; Cincinnati Milacron Ltd, 1969-76; Founder, 1962, and former Chm., Technical Development Capital Ltd. Chairman: English-Speaking Union of the Commonwealth, 1969-72; Benn Charitable Foundn, 1972; Vice-Pres., Book Trade Benevolent Soc., 1974. Associate, Princeton Univ. Press, 1965; Pres., Princeton Club of London, 1969-70. Publications: Columbus-Undergraduate, 1928; A Merchant Adventurer in South America, 1931; Tradesman's Entrance, 1935; I Say Rejoice, 1942; Something in the City, 1959. Recreations: painting, swimming, reading. Heir: s James Jonathan Benn [b 27 July 1933; m 1960, Jennifer, e d of Dr Wilfred Howells; one s one d. Educ: Harrow]. Address: High Field, Limpsfield, Surrey. Clubs: English-Speaking Union; Nassau, Princeton, NJ.
See also E. G. Benn.

BENN, John Meriton, CB 1969; Senator, Queen's University, Belfast, since 1973; Chairman, Northern Ireland Schools Examinations Council, since 1974; b 16 July 1908; s of late Ernest and Emily Louise Benn, Burnley; m 1933, Valentine Rosemary, d of late William Seward, Hanwell; two d. Educ: Burnley Gram. Sch.; Christ's Coll., Cambridge (Scholar; Modern Languages Tripos, 1st Cl. Hons French, 2nd Cl. Hons German). Asst Master, Exeter Sch., 1931-34; Lektor, Halle Univ., Germany, 1934; Asst Master, Regent Street Polytechnic Secondary Sch., 1935; Inspector of Schs., Ministry of Education for Northern Ireland, 1935-44; Principal, 1944-51; Asst Sec., 1951-59; Senior Asst Sec., 1959-64; Permanent Sec., 1964-69; NI Comr for Complaints, 1969-73; Parly Comr for Administration, NI, 1972-73. Hon. LLD QUB, 1972. Publication: Practical French Prose, 1935. Recreations: gardening, bell-ringing. Address: 3 Croft Gardens, Holywood, Co. Down. T: Holywood 2817.

BENN, Captain Sir Patrick (Ion Hamilton), 2nd Bt cr 1920; Captain, Reserve of Officers, late Duke of Cornwall's Light Infantry; Major, Norfolk Army Cadet Force, 1960; b 26 Feb. 1922; o s of late Col Ion Bridges Hamilton Benn, JP (o s of 1st Bt), Broad Farm, Rollesby, Gt Yarmouth, and late Theresa Dorothy, d of late Major F. H. Blacker, Johnstown, Co. Kildare; S grandfather, 1961; m 1959, Edel Jørgine, d of late Col W. S. Løbach, formerly of The Royal Norwegian Army, Andenes, Vesteraalen; one s one d (both adopted). Educ: Rugby. Served War of 1939-45 (despatches); North Africa, Italy, Greece, 1941-45; Capt. 1943; served Korea, 1951-52; retd, 1955. Recreations: shooting, fishing. Address: Rollesby Hall, Great Yarmouth, Norfolk NR29 5DT. T: Great Yarmouth 740313.

BENNER, Patrick, CB 1975; Deputy Secretary, Department of Health and Social Security, since 1976; b 26 May 1923; s of Henry Grey and Gwendolen Benner; m 1952, Joan Christabel Draper; two d. Educ: Ipswich Sch.; University Coll., Oxford. Entered Min. of Health as Asst Princ., 1949; Princ., 1951; Princ. Private Sec. to Minister, 1955; Asst Sec., 1958; Under-Sec., Min. of Health, 1967-68, DHSS 1968-72; Dep. Sec., Cabinet Office, 1972-76. Address: 44 Ormond Crescent, Hampton, Mddx TW12 2TH. T: 01-979 1099.

BENNET, family name of Earl of Tankerville.

BENNETT, Alan; dramatist and actor; b 9 May 1934; s of Walter Bennett and Lilian Mary Peel; unmarried. Educ: Leeds Modern Sch.; Exeter Coll., Oxford. BA Modern History, 1957. Jun. Lectr, Modern History, Magdalen Coll., Oxford, 1960-62. Co-author and actor, Beyond the Fringe, Royal Lyceum, Edinburgh, 1960, Fortune, London, 1961 and Golden, NY, 1962; author and actor: On the Margin (TV series), 1966; Forty Years On, Apollo, 1968; author: Getting On, Queen's, 1971; A Day Out (BBC TV film), 1972; Habeas Corpus, Lyric, 1973; Sunset Across the Bay (BBC TV film), 1975; A Little Outing, A

Visit from Miss Prothero (BBC TV Plays), 1977; The Old Country, Queen's, 1977. *Publications:* (with Cook, Miller and Moore) Beyond the Fringe, 1962; Forty Years On, 1969; Getting On, 1972; Habeas Corpus, 1973. *Address:* c/o Chatto & Linnit Ltd, Globe Theatre, Shaftesbury Avenue, W1. *T:* 01-439 4371.

BENNETT, Albert Joseph, CBE 1966; Secretary, National Health Service Staff Commission, 1972-75; b 9 April 1913; *er s* of late Albert James Bennett and late Alice Bennett, Stourbridge, Worcs; unmarried. *Educ:* King Edward VI Sch., Stourbridge; St John's Coll., Cambridge (MA) Mathematical Tripos (Wrangler). Admin. Officer, LCC, 1936-39; Central Midwives Board: Asst Sec., 1939-45; Sec., 1945-47; Instructor Lieut, later Lt-Comdr, RN, 1940-45; Sec., NW Met. Regional Hosp. Bd, 1947-65; Principal Officer, NHS Nat. Staff Cttee, 1965-72; Under-Sec., DHSS, 1972-75, seconded as Sec., NHS Staff Commn. Member: Nat. Selection Cttee for Recruitment of Trainee Hospital Admin. Staff, 1955-64; Cttee of Inquiry into the Recruitment, Training and Promotion of Admin. and Clerical Staff in Hospital Service, 1962-63; Adv. Cttee on Hospital Engineers Training, 1967-72; Admin. Training Cttee, Cttee of Vice-Chancellors and Principals, 1970-72. *Recreations:* walking, gardening. *Address:* 19 Garson House, Gloucester Terrace, W2 3DG. *T:* 01-262 8311. *Club:* Athenæum.

BENNETT, Alexander; see Bennett, F. O. A. G.

BENNETT, Andrew Francis; MP (Lab) Stockport North since Feb. 1974; Teacher; *b* Manchester, 9 March 1939; *m* ; two *s* one *d* . *Educ:* Birmingham Univ. (BSocSc). Joined Labour Party, 1957; Member, Oldham Borough Council, 1964-74. Member, National Union of Teachers. Contested (Lab) Knutsford, 1970. Interested especially in social services and education. *Recreations:* photography, walking, climbing. *Address:* 48 College Avenue, Oldham, Lancs; House of Commons, SW1A 0AA.

BENNETT, Sir Arnold (Lucas), Kt 1975; QC (Aust.); Barrister-at-Law of Supreme Courts of Queensland, New South Wales and Victoria and of High Court of Australia, in private practice, since 1932; *b* 12 Nov. 1908; *s* of George Thomas Bennett and Celia Juliana Bennett (*née* Lucas); *m* 1st, 1934, Marjorie Ella May Williams (*d* 1942); two *s* two *d* ; 2nd, 1944, Nancy Margaret Mellor; one *s* three *d* . *Educ:* Brisbane Grammar Sch.; University of Queensland. Called to Bar, 1932, and except for a period of war service, has practised ever since in Australian Courts and in the Privy Council. Served War, AIF (2 service medals), 1939-45: Captain in Artillery; Captain and Major, Sqdn Ldr 2/5 Aust. Armoured Regt, and as 2 i/c of 2/1 Ind. Light Tank Sqdn, and as 2 i/c and Actg CO, 2/7 Aust. Armoured Regt. KC (Qld), 1947 (automatically became KC in High Court of Aust.), Victoria, 1952, NSW, 1953. Served 2/14 Qld Mounted Inf., 1950-54. Has conducted cases in all jurisdictions and increasingly in sphere of constitutional law. At present (1975-) in practice, but serves in Qld Adv. Cttee on constitutional law and as Mem. Qld Treaties Commn. For nearly 30 yrs, Member: Barristers' Bd of Qld (Chm. 1957-); Supreme Court Library Cttee, Qld; Incorp. Council of Law Reporting (Chm. 1957-71); Rotary International (Governor D260 1972-73, in Qld's Fiftieth Rotary Year); (Chm.) Constitution and By-Laws Cttee, RI. Coronation Medal, 1953. *Publications:* articles in Australian Law Jl. *Recreations:* tennis, farming. *Address:* Fairthorpe, 52 Dunmore Terrace, Auchenflower, Qld 4066, Australia. *T:* Brisbane 371 3313 and 370 8485, and Tamborine Mountain 451 215. *Club:* Rotary (Pres., 1959-60) (Brisbane).

BENNETT, Charles John Michael, CBE 1974; FCA; Partner in Barton, Mayhew & Co., Chartered Accountants, 1937-71; *b* 29 June 1906; *e s* of late Hon. Sir Charles Alan Bennett and Constance Radeglance, *d* of Major John Nathaniel Still; *m* 1931, Audrey Thompson; two *d*. *Educ:* Clifton Coll.; Trinity Coll., Cambridge. Served with HM Forces, 1939-45. Member: Electricity Supply Companies Commn, 1959, in Hong Kong; Fiji Sugar Inquiry Commn, 1961; Commn of Inquiry (Sugar Industry) 1962, in Mauritius; Commn of Inquiry into Banana Industry of St Lucia, 1963; Commn of Inquiry (Chm.) into Sugar Industry and Agriculture of Antigua, 1965; Commn of Enquiry into Sugar Industry of Guyana, 1967; Cttee of Enquiry into the pricing of certain contracts for the overhaul of aero-engines by Bristol Siddeley Engines Ltd. Mem. of Council, Institute of Chartered Accountants, 1963-69. Part-time Mem., Commonwealth Development Corp., 1965-73, Dep. Chm. 1970-71, 1972-73; Independent Mem., NEDC for Chemical Industry, and Chm., Pharmaceuticals Working Party, 1969. Mem., E Anglian Regional Cttee of Nat. Trust. *Recreations:* golf, fishing and shooting. *Address:* 15 St Olave's Court, St Petersburgh Place, W2. *T:* 01-229 9554; 2 Orchard Close, Brancaster Staithe, Norfolk.

BENNETT, Sir Charles (Moihi), Kt 1975; DSO 1943; Director, Bank of New Zealand, since 1974; President, New Zealand Labour Party, 1972-76; *b* 27 July 1913; *s* of Rt Rev. Frederick August Bennett, Bishop of Aotearoa, 1928-50, and Rangioue Bennett; *m* 1947, Elizabeth May Stewart. *Educ:* Univ. of New Zealand; Exeter Coll., Oxford. MA, DipSocSci, DipEd. Director of Maori Welfare, 1954-57; High Comr for New Zealand to Fedn of Malaya, 1959-63; Asst Sec., Dept of Maori Affairs, 1963-69. Mem., NZ Prisons Parole Bd, 1974-. Hon. LLD Canterbury Univ. of NZ, 1973. Hon. Kt PMN (Malaysia), 1963. *Address:* Maketu, Bay of Plenty, New Zealand. *T:* Te Puke (NZ) 1377. *Club:* Officers' (Wellington).
See also Bishop of Aotearoa .

BENNETT, Councillor Daniel, JP; Chairman, Greater Manchester Council, 1976-77; *b* 18 Jan. 1900; *s* of Daniel Bennett and Margaret Bennett; *m* 1923, Helen Holt Atherton; two *d* . *Educ:* elementary sch. Elected to Orrell UDC, 1946; served continuously until 1974 (Chm. 3 times); elected to Lancs CC, 1966; elected to Divnl Educn Exec., 1950, Chm., 1969-74; elected to Greater Manchester CC, 1973. JP Lancs 1952. *Recreation:* bowling. *Address:* 56 Lodge Road, Orrell, Wigan, Lancs. *T:* Up Holland 622894.

BENNETT, Air Vice-Marshal Donald Clifford Tyndall, CB 1944; CBE 1943; DSO 1942; late Royal Air Force; Chairman and Managing Director: Fairthorpe Ltd; Dart Aircraft Ltd; Fairtravel Ltd; consultant, director, etc.; *b* 14 Sept. 1910; *s* of G. T. Bennett, Brisbane, Queensland; *m* 1935, Elsa Gubler, Zürich; one *s* one d. Royal Australian Air Force; Royal Air Force; AOC the Pathfinder Force of RAF Bomber Command, war of 1939-45; resigned commission, 1945; Imperial Airways; Empire and Atlantic Air Route Development; holder of the world's long-distance seaplane record (Dundee, Scotland, to Alexandra Bay, South Africa); a founder as Flying Superintendent of the Atlantic Ferry organisation (later Ferry Command); MP (L) Middlesbrough West, 1945; Managing Director and Chief Exec., British South American Airways, 1945-48. Chairman: Exec. Cttee United Nations Assoc. of Gt Britain and N Ireland, 1946-49; Political Freedom Movement; Nat. Council of Anti Common Mkt Organisations; Pres. Radar Assoc., 1952-55; Patron: Pathfinder Assoc.; British League of Rights. FRAeS. Oswald Watt Medallist, 1938, 1946; Johnston Memorial Trophy, 1937-38. Order of Alexander Nevsky, 1944. *Publications:* Complete Air Navigator, 1935, 7th edn. 1967; Air Mariner, 1937, 2nd edn 1943; Freedom from War, 1945; Pathfinder, 1958; Let us try Democracy, 1970. *Recreations:* tennis, ski-ing, car racing, sailing. *Address:* Fairthorpe, Denham, Uxbridge; Monte Carlo; Brisbane. *Club:* Royal Air Force.

BENNETT, Sir Frederic (Mackarness), Kt 1964; MP (C) Torbay, since 1974 (Reading N, 1951-55; Torquay, Dec. 1955-1974); *b* 2 Dec. 1918; 2nd *s* of late Sir Ernest Bennett and of Lady (Marguerite) Bennett; *m* 1945, Marion Patricia, *e d* of Cecil Burnham, OBE, FRCSE. *Educ:* Westminster. Served War of 1939-45, enlisted Middx Yeo., 1939; commissioned RA, 1940; Military Experimental Officer in Petroleum Warfare Dept, 1943-46, when released to reserve with rank of Major. Called to English Bar, Lincoln's Inn, 1946, Southern Rhodesian Bar, 1947. Visited Greece as guest of Greek Govt, 1947 and 1949, to observe Communist war there and children's refugee camps. Retained as diplomatic correspondent, Birmingham Post, Jan. 1950 until election to Parliament. Contested (C) Burslem, 1945, Ladywood Div. of Birmingham, 1950. PPS: to Under-Sec. of State, Home Office, 1953-55, to Minister of Supply, 1956-57, to Paymaster-Gen, 1957-59, and to Pres. of Bd of Trade, 1959-61. Member: Council of Europe, 1977-; WEU Assembly, 1977-; Chm., Bank Credit Commerce International (Hong Kong); Director: Kleinwort Benson Europe SA; Sir Lindsay Parkinson Ltd; Arawak Trust Co. Ltd (Bahamas); Squibb A/S; Commercial Union Assurance Co. Ltd, West End and Exeter Bds; Arawak Trust (Caymans) Ltd; Deltan Ltd (Toronto); Delzotto Enterprises (Toronto); Gibraltar Building Soc. Lord of the Manor of Mawddwy. Comdr, Order of Phœnix, Greece, 1963; (Sithari) Star of Pakistan, 1st cl., 1964. *Recreations:* shooting, fishing, ski-ing. *Address:* Cwmllecoediog, Aberangell, Powys. *T:* Cemmaes Road 430; Kingswear Castle, South Devon; 2 Stone Buildings, Lincoln's Inn, WC2. *Club:* Carlton.

BENNETT, (Frederick Onslow) Alexander (Godwyn), TD; Chairman, Whitbread & Co. Ltd, 1972-77; *b* 21 Dec. 1913; *s* of Alfred Bennett, banker and Marjorie Muir Bremner; *m* 1942, Rosemary, *d* of Sir Malcolm Perks, Bt, *qv*; one *s* four *d*. *Educ:* Winchester Coll.; Trinity Coll., Cambridge (BA). Commnd 2nd Bn London Rifle Bde TA, 1938; Lt-Col 1944, GS01 SHAEF and 21 Army Gp (despatches). Joined Whitbread & Co. Ltd, 1935: Man. Dir, 1949; Dep. Chm., 1958; Chief Exec., 1967-75. Master,

Brewers' Company, 1963-64; Chm., Brewers' Soc., 1972-74. US Bronze Star, 1944. *Recreations:* shooting, gardening, the countryside, music. *Address:* Grove House, Selling, Faversham, Kent ME13 9RW. *T:* Selling 250. *Clubs:* Brooks's, MCC.

BENNETT, Captain Geoffrey Martin, DSC 1944; RN retired; *b* 7 June 1909; *s* of late Rear-Adm. Martin Gilbert Bennett, and of Esme Geraldine Bennett (*née* Hicks); *m* 1932, Rosemary Alys (*née* Béchervaise); two *s. Educ:* Royal Naval Coll., Dartmouth, 1923-26; Flag Lieut, Second Cruiser Squadron, Home Fleet, 1938-40; Fleet Signal Officer, S Atlantic, 1940-42; Signal Officer to Adm. Comdg Force H, 1943; Sig. Off. to Flag Officer Levant and E Med., 1943-44; Admlty, 1945-56; HMS Ajax, 1947; HMS St Bride's Bay, 1948; Naval Attaché, Moscow, Warsaw and Helsinki, 1953-55; City Marshal. Common Cryer and Serjeant-at-Arms (London), 1958-60. Secretary to Lord Mayor of Westminster, 1960-74; Vis. Lectr on War Studies, Univ. of Frederickton, NB, 1973. Gold Medal and Trench-Gascoigne Prize of RUSI, 1934, 1942 and 1943. FRHistS, 1963. Order of Orange Nassau, 1972. *Publications:* Coronel and Falklands, 1962; Cowans' War, 1964; Battle of Jutland, 1964; Charlie B: biography of Admiral Lord Beresford, 1968; Naval Battles of First World War, 1968; Nelson the Commander, 1972; Naval Battles of World War Two, 1975; Battle of Trafalgar, 1977; *novels:* (under Pseudonym "Sea-Lion"): Phantom Fleet, 1946; Sink Me the Ship, 1947; Sea of Troubles, 1947; Cargo for Crooks, 1948; When Danger Threatens, 1949; Invisible Ships, 1950; This Creeping Evil, 1950; Quest of John Clare, 1951; Diamond Rock, 1952; Meet Desmond Drake, 1952; Damn Desmond Drake!, 1953; Desmond Drake Goes West, 1956; Death in Russian Habit, 1958; Operation Fireball, 1959; Down Among the Dead Men, 1961; Death in the Dog Watches, 1962; also books for children; radio scripts, etc. *Address:* Stage Coach Cottage, 57 Broad Street, Ludlow, Salop SY8 1NH. *T:* Ludlow 3863.

BENNETT, Harry Graham, QC 1968; **His Honour Judge Bennett;** a Circuit Judge, since 1972; *b* 19 Sept. 1921; *s* of Ernest and Alice Mary Bennett, Cleckheaton, Yorks. *Educ:* Whitcliffe Mount Grammar Sch., Cleckheaton; King's Coll., London. Royal Artillery, 1943-47. Called to Bar, Gray's Inn, 1948. Recorder: Doncaster, 1966-68; York, 1968-71; Crown Court, 1972; Dep. Chm., ER of Yorks QS, 1964-71. Chm., Agricl Land Tribunal (N Area), 1967-72. *Address:* c/o Leeds Crown Court, Yorks. *Club:* Leeds (Leeds).

BENNETT, Sir Hubert, Kt 1970; FSIA; Executive Director, English Property Corporation Ltd; former Architect to the Greater London Council (formerly London County Council) and Superintending Architect of Metropolitan Buildings, 1956-71; *b* 4 Sept. 1909; *s* of late Arthur Bennett and Eleanor Bennett; *m* 1939, Louise F. C. Aldred; three *d. Educ:* Victoria University, Manchester, School of Architecture. Asst Lecturer, Leeds School of Architecture, 1933-35; Asst Lecturer, Regent Street Polytechnic Sch. of Architecture, 1935-40; Superintending Architect (Lands), War Dept, 1940-43; Borough Architect, Southampton, 1943-45; County Architect, W Riding of Yorks, 1945-56. Mem. of Council, RIBA, 1952-55, 1957-62, 1965-66, 1967-69; Hon. Treas. RIBA, 1959-62; Pres., W Yorks Soc. of Architects, 1954-66; Chm., Technical Panel, Standing Conf. on London Regional Planning, 1962-64; Member: Building Res. Bd, 1959-66; Timber Res. and Develt Assoc. Adv. Panel, 1965-68; Housing Study Mission from Britain to Canada, 1968. Dir, Help the Aged Housing Assoc. (UK) Ltd. Prof., Univ of NSW, 1973. Architect for the Hyde Park Corner-Marble Arch Improvement Scheme, Crystal Palace Recreational Centre and South Bank Arts Centre. RIBA: Silver Medallist for Measured Drawings (Hon. Mention), 1932; Arthur Cates Prize, 1933; Sir John Soane Medallist, 1934; Neale Bursar, 1936; Godwin and Wimperis Bursar, 1948; RIBA London Architecture Bronze Medal, 1959; RIBA Bronze Medal, 1968. Royal Society of Arts Medal, 1934; Rome Scholarship Special Award, 1936; Min. of Housing and Local Govt Housing Medal, 1954, 1963, 1964, 1966, 1968; Civic Trust Awards; Sir Patrick Abercrombie Award (for planning project Thamesmead), Internat. Union of Architects, 1969; Fritz Schumacher Prize, 1970. Hon. Member: Architects in Industry Group; Inst. of Architects of Czechoslovakia; Soc. of Architects of Venezuela. *Address:* Linton House, Bramley, Surrey. *T:* Bramley 3460.

BENNETT, Prof. Jack Arthur Walter, MA, DPhil; FBA 1971; Professor of Medieval and Renaissance English, Cambridge University, 1964-Sept. 1978; Fellow of Magdalene College, Cambridge, since 1964; Keeper of the Old Library, Magdalene College, since 1968; *b* Auckland, New Zealand, 28 Feb. 1911; *s* of Ernest and Alexandra Bennett; *m* 1951, Gwyneth Mary Nicholas; two *s. Educ:* Mt Albert Grammar Sch.; Auckland Univ. Coll.; Merton Coll., Oxford. MA (NZ) 1933; BA Oxon 1st

Cl. Eng. Lang. and Lit., 1935; Harmsworth Scholar, Merton Coll., 1935-38; MA, DPhil, 1938, Res. Fellow, The Queen's Coll., Oxford, 1938-47; Head of Research Dept, later Dir, British Information Services, New York, 1940-45; Fellow and Tutor, Magdalen Coll., Oxford, 1947-64; Alexander Lectr, Univ. of Toronto, 1970-71; Vis. Fellow, Australian National Univ., 1976; Corresp. Fellow, Medieval Acad. of America, 1976; Hon. Foreign Mem., American Acad. of Arts and Scis, 1976. Editor of Medium Ævum; Mem. of Council, Early English Text Soc.; Editor, Clarendon Medieval and Tudor Series. *Publications:* The Knight's Tale, 1954; (with H. R. Trevor-Roper) The Poems of Richard Corbett, 1955; Devotional Pieces in Verse and Prose, 1957; The Parlement of Foules, 1957; (ed.) Essays on Malory, 1963; The Humane Medievalist, 1965; (jointly) Early Middle English Verse and Prose, 1966; Chaucer's Book of Fame, 1968; Selections from John Gower, 1968; (ed) Piers Plowman, 1972; Chaucer at Oxford and at Cambridge, 1974; (trans.) Ordo Missæ, 1975; articles and reviews in Listener, TLS, Review of English Studies, Landfall (NZ), DNB, Dictionnaire de Spiritualité, etc. *Recreations:* collecting books on Oxford and Cambridge, the study of watermills. *Address:* 10 Adams Road, Cambridge. *T:* Cambridge 55322.

BENNETT, James; *b* 18 Dec. 1912; *s* of Samuel and Elizabeth Bennett; *m* 1936, Dorothy Maclaren; one *s* one *d. Educ:* Grove Street Primary and North Kelvinside Secondary Schs., Glasgow. Councillor, Glasgow, 1947-62. JP, Glasgow, 1950-52. MP (Lab) Bridgeton Div. of Glasgow, Nov. 1961-Feb. 1974; PPS to Sec. of State for Scotland, 1964-67. *Recreations:* reading, bowls, gardening. *Address:* 105 Boreland Drive, Glasgow W3. *T:* 041-959 2393.

BENNETT, Jill; actress; *b* Penang, SS, 24 Dec. 1931; *d* of Randle and Nora Bennett; *m* 1st, 1962, Willis Hall, *qv* (marr. diss., 1965); 2nd, 1968, John Osborne, *qv* (marr. diss. 1977). *Educ:* Tortington Park; Priors Field. Stratford-upon-Avon, 1949-50. First London appearance in Captain Carvallo, St James's Theatre, 1950; Iras in Anthony and Cleopatra, and Caesar and Cleopatra (Olivier Season), St James's, 1951; Helen Elliot in Night of the Ball, New, 1955; Masha in The Seagull, Saville, 1956; Sarah Stanham in The Touch of Fear, Aldwych, 1956; Isabelle in Dinner with the Family, New, 1957; Penelope in Last Day in Dream Land, Lyric, Hammersmith, 1959; Feemy Evans and Lavinia in Shaw double bill, Mermaid, 1961; Estelle in In Camera, Oxford Playhouse, 1962; Ophelia in Castle in Sweden, Piccadilly, 1962; Hilary and Elizabeth in double bill of Squat Betty and The Sponge Room, Royal Court, 1962; The Countess in A Patriot for Me, Royal Court, 1965; Anna Bowers in A Lily of Little India, St Martin's, 1965; Katrina in The Storm, and Imogen Parrott in Trelawney of the Wells, National, 1966; Pamela in Time Present, Royal Court (and later) Duke of York's, 1968 (won Evening Standard Award and Variety Club's Best Actress Award); Anna in Three Months Gone, Royal Court and Duchess, 1970; West of Suez, Royal Court and Cambridge, 1971; Hedda Gabler, Royal Court, 1972; Leslie in The Letter, Palace, Watford, 1973; Amanda in Private Lives, Globe, 1973; The End of Me Old Cigar, Greenwich, 1975; Loot, Royal Court, 1975; Watch It Come Down, National, 1976; Separate Tables, Apollo, 1977. *Films include:* Lust for Life; The Nanny; The Criminal; The Charge of the Light Brigade; Inadmissible Evidence; Julius Caesar (Calpurnia); I Want What I Want; Quilp. Numerous TV appearances in classical works, etc. *Recreations:* riding, water ski-ing, ski-ing, having holidays, collecting paintings. *Address:* 147-149 Wardour Street, W1.

BENNETT, Joan, MA; Life Fellow of Girton College, Cambridge; Lecturer in English, Cambridge University, 1936-64; *b* 26 June 1896; *d* of Arthur Frankau and of Julia Frankau (Frank Danby); *m* 1920, Henry Stanley Bennett (*d* 1972), FBA; one *s* three *d. Educ:* Wycombe Abbey; Girton Coll., Cambridge. Visiting Lectr in the University of Chicago, 1952, 1955, and 1958. Warton Lecturer (Brit. Acad.), 1958; Rose Mary Crawshay Prize (Brit. Acad.), 1963. Fellow, Folger Library, 1961. *Publications:* Five Metaphysical Poets, 1965 (formerly Four Metaphysical Poets, 1934); Virginia Woolf; Her Art as a Novelist, 1945, 2nd edn enl. 1964; George Eliot: Her Mind and her Art, 1948; Sir Thomas Browne, 1962; The Love Poetry of John Donne (chapter in Seventeenth Century Studies), 1938. *Address:* Church Rate Corner, Cambridge. *T:* Cambridge 53511.

See also C. F. Eccleshare.

BENNETT, Joan; Actress (films and plays); *b* 27 Feb. 1910; *d* of Richard Bennett and Adrienne Morrison; *m* 1st, 1926, John Fox (marr. diss., 1928); one *d*; 2nd, 1932, Gene Markey (marr. diss., 1936); one *d*; 3rd, 1940, Walter Wanger (marr. diss., at Juarez, Mexico, 1965; he *d* 1968); two *d. Educ:* St Margaret's Sch., Waterbury, Conn.; Mlle Lataple's, Versailles, France. *Films* *include:* (first film) Bulldog Drummond, 1929; Three Live Ghosts; Disraeli; Little Women; Pursuit of Happiness; Private Worlds; The Man in the Iron Mask; Margin for Error; Woman on the Beach; Father of the Bride; Love that Brute; Desire in the Dust. *Plays include:* (first play) Jarnegan, 1928; Bell, Book and Candle; We're no Angels; Love Me Little; Never too Late, Prince of Wales Theatre, London, 1963. Has appeared on Television: (series) Too Young to go Steady; Dark Shadows. *Publication:* The Bennett Playbill (with Lois Kibbee), 1970. *Recreations:* interior decorating, swimming, tennis; particularly likes Shakespeare's works and classical literature. *Address:* 67 Chase Road, North Scarsdale, NY 10583, USA.

BENNETT, John, MBE 1945; HM Senior Chief Inspector of Schools for Scotland, 1969-73; *b* 14 Nov. 1912; *m* 1940, Johanne R. McAlpine, MA; two *s* one *d. Educ:* Edinburgh Univ. MA (first class hons) 1934. Schoolmaster until 1951. Served War of 1939-45: Capt. REME, 79 Armd Div., 1940-46. HM Inspector of Schools, 1951. *Recreations:* mathematics, golf, bridge. *Address:* 35 Cadzow Drive, Cambuslang, Glasgow G72 8NF. *T:* 041-641 1058.

BENNETT, John Sloman, CMG 1955; *b* 22 Nov. 1914; *y s* of late Ralph Bennett, FRCVS, and Constance Elkington; *m* 1955, Mary Fisher (*see* Mrs. M. L. S. Bennett). *Educ:* Royal Liberty Sch., Romford; Magdalene Coll., Cambridge (Schol.). 1st cl. historical tripos, parts 1 and 2, 1935. Entered Colonial Office, 1936; seconded to Office of Minister of State in Middle East, 1941-45; Asst Sec., Colonial Office, 1946; Imperial Defence College, 1953; served Commonwealth Office, subsequently FCO, after merger of Colonial Office in 1966; retired 1976. *Address:* Rock Cottage, Thursley, Surrey. *Club:* United Oxford & Cambridge University.

BENNETT, Rt. Rev. Manu Augustus; *see* Aotearoa, Bishop of.

BENNETT, Mrs Mary Letitia Somerville, MA; Principal, St Hilda's College, Oxford, since 1965; *b* 14 Jan. 1913; *o c* of Rt Hon. H. A. L. Fisher, OM, and Lettice Ilbert; *m* 1955, John Sloman Bennett, *qv. Educ:* Oxford High Sch.; Somerville Coll. (Schol.); 2nd Cl. Mods, 1st Cl. Lit. Hum.; Hon. Fellow, 1977. Mary Ewart Travelling Schol., 1936-37; Jt Broadcasting Cttee, 1940-41; Transcription Service of BBC, 1941-45; Colonial Office, 1945-56. Hon. Sec., Society for the Promotion of Roman Studies, 1960-. *Address:* St Hilda's College, Oxford. *T:* Oxford 41821. *Club:* University Women's.

BENNETT, Patrick, QC 1969; a Recorder of the Crown Court, since 1972; *b* 12 Jan. 1924; *s* of Michael Bennett; *m* 1951, Lyle Reta Pope; two *d. Educ:* Bablake Sch., Coventry; Magdalen Coll., Oxford. State Scholar, 1941, MA, BCL 1949. Served RNVR, 1943-46, Sub Lt. Called to Bar, Gray's Inn, 1949, Bencher 1976; Asst Recorder, Coventry, 1969-71; Dep. Chm., Lindsey QS, 1970-71. *Recreations:* food, flying. *Address:* (home) 22 Wynnstay Gardens, W8. *T:* 01-937 2110; (professional) 2 Crown Office Row, Temple, EC4. *T:* 01-236 9337. *Clubs:* Hurlingham; Spartan Flying (Denham).

BENNETT, Philip Hugh Penberthy, CBE 1972; FRIBA; Senior Partner, T. P. Bennett & Son, architects, since 1967 (Partner since 1948); *b* 14 April 1919; *o s* of Sir Thomas Penberthy Bennett, *qv*; *m* 1943, Jeanne Heal; one *s* one *d. Educ:* Highgate Sch.; Emmanuel Coll., Cambridge (MA). Lieut (G) RNVR, 1940-46. Principal works: town centres at Bootle and Stratford (London); head offices for Norwich Union Insce Socs, Ford Motor Co. and other commercial cos; dept stores for United Africa Co. in Ghana and Nigeria, Bentalls (Kingston) and Fenwicks (Newcastle); extensions to Middlesex Hosp.; hostel for Internat. Students Trust; Cunard Internat. Hotel; flats for local authorities and private developers; buildings for airfield and dock develt. Chm., Building Regulations Adv. Cttee (DoE), 1965-77; RIBA rep. on Jt Contracts Tribunal (Chm. 1973) and Nat. Jt Consultative Cttee (Chm. 1970); Mem. other cttees of RIBA and NEDO; Governor: Sch. of Building, 1952-72; Vauxhall Coll. of Further Educn, 1972-77; Member: Home Office Deptl Cttee enquiring into Fire Service, 1967-70; Adv. Council for Energy Conservation, 1974-76. Mem. Anglo-French Union of Architects. *Publications:* chapter on building, in Britain 1984, 1963; articles in Building, Financial Times, etc. *Recreations:* travel, drawing, theatre. *Address:* 32 York Terrace West, NW1 4QA. *T:* 01-935 8757. *Club:* Garrick.

BENNETT, Ralph Featherstone; Deputy Chairman, since 1971, and Chief Executive, since 1975, London Transport Executive (formerly London Transport Board), (Member, 1968-71); Chairman, London Transport International Services; *b* 3 Dec. 1923; *o s* of late Ralph J. P. Bennett and of Mrs E. M. Bennett, Plymouth, Devon; *m* 1948, Delia Marie, *o d* of late Mr and Mrs

J. E. Baxter, Franklyns, Plymouth; two *s* two *d. Educ:* Plympton Grammar Sch.; Plymouth Technical Coll. Articled pupil to City of Plymouth Transport Manager, 1940-43; Techn. Asst, Plymouth City Transp., 1943-54; Michelin Tyre Co., 1954-55; Dep. Gen. Man., City of Plymouth Transp. Dept, 1955-58; Gen. Manager: Gt Yarmouth Transp. Dept, 1958-60; Bolton Transp. Dept, 1960-65; Manchester City Transp., 1965-68. Mem., SE Economic Planning Council, 1972-76. CEng; FIMechE; FCIT. *Address:* 19 Palace Street, SW1.

BENNETT, Dr Reginald Frederick Brittain, VRD 1944; MA Oxon; BM, BCh, 1942; LMSSA 1937; DPM 1948; MP (C) Fareham, since 1974 (Gosport and Fareham, 1950-74); company director; consultant; formerly psychiatrist; *b* 22 July 1911; *e s* of late Samuel Robert Bennett and Gertrude (*née* Brittain); *m* 1947, Henrietta, *d* of Capt. H. B. Crane, CBE, RN (retd); one *s* three *d. Educ:* Winchester Coll.; New College, Oxford; St George's Hosp. Maudsley Hospital, 1946-49; Institute for Study and Treatment of Delinquency, 1950-54. RNVR, 1934-46; Fleet Air Arm, Medical Officer and Pilot; torpedoed twice. PPS to Rt Hon. Iain Macleod, MP, 1956-63; Chairman: House of Commons Catering Sub-Cttee, 1970-74, 1976- (Dep. Chm., 1974-76); Anglo-Italian Parly Gp, 1971- (Hon. Sec. 1961-71); Parly and Scientific Cttee, 1959-62. Vice-Pres., Franco-British Parly Relations Cttee, 1973, Mem. Executive, 1959-73; Mem. Executive, Inter-Parly Union (Brit. Gp), 1962-; Rapporteur on the Ocean Floor and Seabed, Inter-Parly Conf., The Hague, 1970; Leader, Parly Delegn to: Iceland 1965; European Parliament, Strasbourg, 1971; Conf. on Mediterranean Pollution, Rome 1974, Monaco, 1975; Canadian Govtl Conf., 1974; European Conf. on Security and Co-operation, Belgrade, 1975. Mem. Council, Internat. Inst. of Human Nutrition, 1975. President: Brit. Launderers' Research Association, 1960-77; Southern Boroughs Assoc., 1950-73. Pres., Club Oenologique, 1976-77 (Vice-Pres., 1973-76), Gold Insignia, 1972. Helmsman: International yacht races in Germany, 1934, USA, 1935; Shamrock V, 1934-35; Evaine, 1936-38; Olympic Games (reserve), 1936; in British-American Cup Team, 1949 and 1953 in USA; various trophies since. Chm., Amateur Yacht Research Soc., 1972-. Hon. Lieut-Col, Georgia Militia, 1960; Hon. Citizen of Atlanta, Ga, 1960. Commandeur du Bontemps-Médoc, 1959; Chevalier du Tastevin, 1970; Galant de la Verte Marennes; Chevalier de St Etienne, Alsace, 1971; Chevalier Bretvin (Muscadet), 1973. *Publications:* Assaults on Parliamentary Democracy, Inter-Parly Bulletin, 1972; articles on wine, medicine, psychiatry, politics and yacht racing. *Recreations:* sailing, shooting, painting, foreign travel, basking in the sun, avoiding exercise. *Address:* House of Commons, SW1. *Clubs:* White's; Imperial Poona Yacht (Cdre); Wykehamist Sailing (Cdre); House of Commons Yacht (Vice-Cdre); House of Commons Motor (Vice-Chm.); Royal Colombo Yacht; Bembridge Sailing, etc.

BENNETT, Richard Rodney, CBE 1977; composer; Member of General Council, Performing Right Society, since 1975; *b* 29 March 1936; *s* of H. Rodney and Joan Esther Bennett. *Educ:* Leighton Park Sch., Reading; Royal Academy of Music. Works performed, 1953-, at many Festivals in Europe, S Africa, USA, Canada, Australia, etc. Has written music for numerous films including: Indiscreet; The Devil's Disciple; Only Two Can Play; The Wrong Arm of the Law; Heavens Above; Billy Liar; One Way Pendulum; The Nanny; Far from the Madding Crowd; Billion Dollar Brain; Secret Ceremony; The Buttercup Chain; Figures in a Landscape; Nicholas and Alexandra; Lady Caroline Lamb; Voices; Murder on the Orient Express (Ivor Novello award, PRS, 1976); Permission to Kill; Equus; Sherlock Holmes in New York; also the music for Television series, Hereward the Wake; The Christians. Commissioned to write 2 full-length operas for Sadler's Wells: The Mines of Sulphur, 1965, A Penny for a Song, 1968; commnd to write opera for Covent Garden: Victory, 1970; (children's opera) All the King's Men, 1969; Guitar Concerto, 1970; choral work: Spells, 1975. *Publications include:* chamber music, orchestral music, educational music, song cycles, etc; articles for periodicals, about music. *Recreations:* cinema, modern jazz. *Address:* c/o Mrs Keys, London Management, Regent House, 235 Regent Street, W1.

BENNETT, Ronald Alistair, QC (Scotland) 1959; Sheriff-Principal of Roxburgh, Berwick and Selkirk, 1971-74; *b* 11 Dec. 1922; *s* of Arthur George Bennett, MC and Edythe Sutherland; *m* 1950, Margret Magnusson, *d* of Sigursteinn Magnusson, Icelandic Consul-Gen. for Scotland; three *s* three *d. Educ:* Edinburgh Academy; Edinburgh Univ.; Balliol Coll., Oxford. MA, LLB Univ. of Edinburgh, 1942; Muirhead and Dalgety Prizes for Civil Law, 1942. Lieut, 79th (Scottish Horse) Medium Regt RA, 1943-45; Capt. attached RAOC, India and Japan, 1945-46. Called to Scottish Bar, 1947; Vans Dunlop Schol. in Scots Law and Conveyancing, 1948; Standing Counsel to Min.

of Labour and National Service, 1957-59. Lectr in Mercantile Law: Edinburgh Univ., 1956-68; Heriot-Watt Univ., 1968-75. Chairman: Med. Appeal Tribunals (Scotland), 1971; Agricultural Wages Bd for Scotland, 1973; Local Govt Boundaries Commn for Scotland, 1974; Northern Lighthouse Bd, April-Sept., 1974; Industrial Tribunals, (Scotland), 1977. Arbiter: Motor Insurers' Bureau appeals, 1975; Scottish Medical Practices Cttee, 1976. *Publications:* Bennett's Company Law, 2nd edn, 1950; Fraser's Rent Acts in Scotland, 2nd edn 1952; Editor: Scottish Current Law and Scots Law Times Sheriff Court Reports, 1948-74; Court of Session Reports, 1976. *Recreations:* shooting, swimming, reading, music, gardening. *Address:* Laxamyri, 46 Cammo Road, Barnton, Edinburgh 4. *T:* 031-336 1337.

BENNETT, Sir Ronald (Wilfred Murdoch), 3rd Bt, *cr* 1929; *b* 25 March 1930; *o s* of Sir Wilfred Bennett, 2nd Bt, and Marion Agnes (OBE 1953), *d* of late James Somervell, Sorn Castle, Ayrshire, and step *d* of late Edwin Sandys Dawes; *S* father 1952; *m* 1st, 1953, Rose-Marie Audrey Patricia, *o d* of Major A. L. J. H. Aubépin, France and Co. Mayo, Ireland; two *d*; 2nd, 1968, Anne, *d* of late Leslie George Tooker. *Educ:* Wellington Coll.; Trinity Coll., Oxford. *Heir: cousin* Michael Bennett *b* 15 Feb. 1924; *m* 1952, Jane Hazel Margaret, *d* of Brig. E. J. Todhunter, TD; one *s* two *d*]. *Clubs:* Kampala, Uganda (Kampala).

BENNETT, Roy Grissell, CMG 1971; Chairman, Maclaine Watson & Co. Ltd, London and Singapore, 1970-72 (Director, 1958-72), retired; Chairman: Pilkington (South East Asia) Private Ltd; Beder International and Beder Malaysia; *b* 21 Nov. 1917. *Educ:* RMC Sandhurst. Served War of 1939-45, 17th/21st Lancers (Major). Joined J. H. Vavasseur & Co. Ltd, Penang, 1946; Director, 1949; joined Maclaine, Watson & Co. Ltd, Singapore 1952, Dir London Board 1958, Man. Dir, Eastern interests, 1960; Director Fibreglass Pilkington Ltd (Chm.), and other cos. Mem. Union Insurance Soc. of Canton Ltd; retired from Singapore Internat. Chamber of Commerce (Chm. 1967-68, 1969-70); Singapore Chamber of Commerce Rubber Assoc. (Chm. 1960-63); Rubber Assoc. of Singapore (past Chm., Dep. Chm. 1966-72); Member: Council, Singapore Anti-Tuberculosis Assoc.; Council, United World Colleges; United World Coll. Internat. Council; Chm. Governors, United World Coll., SE Asia. Patron: Nat. Kidney Foundn; Nat. Theatre Trust. *Recreations:* economics, commercial, polo, racing, shooting, swimming, photography, motoring, safaris, camping, gardening, zoology, boating, reading, travelling, people especially of the East, social welfare. *Address:* Beder International, PO Box 49, Bukit Panjang, Singapore; 22 Jalan Perdana, Johore Baru, Malaysia. *T:* Johore Baru 24505. *Clubs:* Cavalry and Guards; Tanglin, Town, Turf (Dep. Chm.), Polo (Patron; Past Chm.), Foreign Correspondents' (Singapore); Turf, Polo (Penang).

BENNETT, Sir Thomas (Penberthy), KBE 1954 (CBE 1942); Kt 1946; FRSA; FRIBA; Hon. FIOB; Hon. FIBD; Chairman: New Town of Crawley, 1947-60; Stevenage Development Corporation, 1951-53; *b* 14 Aug. 1887; *s* of Thomas William Bennett and Anne Frances Penberthy; *m* 1916, Mary Langdon Edis (*d* 1976); one *s*. *Educ:* Royal Academy Schs; Heatherleys, etc. Architectural Staff of LNWR; Staff of HM Office of Works; Head of Northern Polytechnic Sch. of Architecture, Surveying and Building, 1920-28; Dir of Bricks, 1940, Dir of Works, 1941-44, and Controller of Temporary Housing, Min. of Works, 1944-45; Chm., Bd of Trade Boot and Shoe Working Party, 1945; Lecturer Board of Education; Private Practice as Architect: *theatres:* including Saville; *cinemas:* including several Odeons; *offices:* incl. Diamond Corp.; Rank Organisation; Anglo-American: Metal Box; Marks & Spencer; Pearl Assurance; Portman Building Soc.; Esso House, Iraq Petroleum Company; Ford Motor Co.; Rugby Portland Cement; Norwich Union Insurance Co.; South Bank Estates; Hill, Samuel & Co. Ltd; *flats:* incl. Eyre Court; Westminster Gardens; Marsham Court; Caroline House; Campbell Court; Queensmead, St John's Wood; *factories:* for Smiths (Eng.); Kodak; *department stores:* Hammonds, Hull; Harrods (Rackhams); Bentalls; Fenwicks; Grants; stores in Africa for United Africa Co.; *hospital work at:* King Edward VII Hosp. for Officers; London Hosp.; Middlesex Hosp.; Westminster Hosp.; *air terminal and offices* for BOAC; Mormon Temple, chapels (Church of Christ Scientist); *synagogues:* St John's Wood; Great Cumberland Pl.; *banks:* for Westminster; Barclay's; Bank of Ireland; *hotel:* The Royal Lancaster. Liveryman and Mem. Court of Assts, Painter-Stainers Co. *Publications:* The Relation of Sculpture and Architecture; Architectural Design in Concrete; articles in Architectural Press, etc. *Recreations:* architecture, golf. *Address:* The Sycamores, 19 North Road, Highgate Village, N6 4BD. *T:* 01-340 6081. *Clubs:* Reform; Highgate Golf.
See also P. H. P. Bennett.

BENNETT, Sir William Gordon, Kt 1955; Member of Glasgow Royal Exchange; Member of the Glasgow Trades House. Formerly a Magistrate and Member of Glasgow Corporation. Past President of the Scottish Unionist Association. Contested (C) Shettleston Division of Glasgow, July 1945. MP (C) Woodside Division of Glasgow, 1950-55. Served European War, 1914-18 (wounded); Officer in the Tank Corps. *Address:* 3 Hillside Road, Glasgow G43 1DE.

BENNETT, William John, OBE 1946; LLD; President and Director: Iron Ore Company of Canada, Montreal (Vice-President, 1960-65); Quebec North Shore and Labrador Railway Co.; President and Director, Gulf Power Co.; Director: Canadian Reyndds Metals Co. Ltd; The Investors Group; Eldorado Nuclear Ltd; Twin Falls Power Corporation Ltd; Labrador Mining and Exploration Co. Ltd; Hollinger North Shore Exploration Co. Ltd; Canron Ltd; Cominco Ltd; Canadian Pacific Railway; Phillips Cable Ltd; *b* 3 Nov. 1911; *s* of Carl Edward Bennett and Mary Agnes Downey; *m* 1936, Elizabeth Josephine Palleck; three *s* four *d. Educ:* University of Toronto (BA Hons). Private Sec., Minister of Transport, 1935-39; Chief Exec. Asst to Minister of Munitions and Supply, 1939-46; President: Atomic Energy of Canada Ltd, 1953-58; Canadian British Aluminium Co. Ltd, 1958-60. Eldorado Mining & Refining Ltd, 1946-58. Hon. LLD, Toronto Univ., 1955; Hon. Dr of Science, St Francis Xavier Univ., Antigonish, NS, 1956; Hon Dr of Laws, University of Ottawa, 1957. *Recreations:* skiing, music. *Address:* 4304 Montrose Avenue, Montreal, Quebec, Canada. *Clubs:* Mount Royal, Canadian (Montreal); Rideau (Ottawa, Ontario); Union (Cleveland, Ohio).

BENNETT, Hon. William Richards, PC (Can.); Premier of British Columbia, since Dec. 1975; *b* 1932; *y s* of Hon. William Andrew Cecil Bennett, PC (Can.) and Annie Elizabeth May, *d* of J. A. Richards, Edmonton, Alta; *m* Audrey; four *s*. Began a business career. Elected MP for Okanagan South (succeeding to a constituency which had been held by his father), 1973; Leader of Social Credit Group in Provincial House, 1973; formed Social Credit Govt after election of Dec. 1975. *Address:* Provincial House of Legislature, Victoria, BC, Canada.

BENNEY, Prof. (Adrian) Gerald (Sallis), RDI 1971; FSIA; goldsmith and silversmith; Professor of Silversmithing and Jewellery, Royal College of Art, since 1974; *b* 21 April 1930; *s* of late Ernest Alfred Benney and Aileen Mary Benney; *m* 1957, Janet Edwards; three *s* one *d*. *Educ:* Brighton Grammar Sch.; Brighton Coll. of Art (Nat. Dip. in Art); RCA (DesRCA). FSIAD 1975. Estabd 1st workshop, Whitfield Place, London, 1955; Consultant Designer, Viners Ltd, 1957-69; began designing and making Reading civic plate, 1963; discovered technique of texturing on silver, 1964; moved workshop to Bankside, London, 1969; began prodn of Beenham Enamels, 1970. Holds Royal Warrants of Appt to the Queen, the Duke of Edinburgh, and Queen Elizabeth the Queen Mother. Mem., Govt's Craft Adv. Cttee, 1972-77; Metalwork Design Advisor to Indian Govt (UP State), 1977-. Liveryman, Worshipful Co. of Goldsmiths, 1964; Major Exhibn, Worshipful Co. of Goldsmiths, 1973. Hon. MA Leicester, 1963. *Recreations:* walking, barging, landscape gardening. *Address:* Beenham House, Beenham, Berks RG7 5LJ. *T:* Bradfield 370. *Club:* Arts.

BENNION, Francis Alan Roscoe; writer; *b* 2 Jan. 1923; *o s* of Thomas Roscoe Bennion, Liverpool; *m* 1951, Barbara Elisabeth Braendle (separated 1971, marr. diss. 1975); three *d*. *Educ:* John Lyon's, Harrow; Balliol Coll., Oxford. Pilot, RAF, 1941-46. Gibbs Law Scholar, Oxford, 1948. Called to Bar, Middle Temple, 1951 (Harmsworth Scholar). Lectr and Tutor in Law, St Edmund Hall, Oxford, 1951-53; Office of Parly Counsel to HM Treasury, 1953-65, and 1973-75; Dep. Parly Counsel, 1964; Parly Counsel, 1973-75; seconded to Govt of Pakistan to advise on drafting of new Constitution, 1956; seconded to Govt of Ghana to advise on legislation and drafting Constitution converting the country into a Republic, 1959-61. Sec., RICS, 1965-68; Governor, College of Estate Management, 1965-68. Co-founder and first Chm., Professional Assoc. of Teachers, 1968-72; Founder: Statute Law Soc., 1968; Freedom Under Law, 1971; founder and first Chm., World of Property Housing Trust (later WPHT Housing Assoc.), 1968-72. *Publications:* Constitutional Law of Ghana, 1962; Professional Ethics: The Consultant Professions and their Code, 1969; Tangling with the Law, 1970; Anti-Discrimination Law, 1976; Consumer Credit Control, 1976. *Recreation:* creation. *Address:* Flat 4, 24 St Aubyns, Hove, East Sussex BN3 2TD. *T:* Brighton 779992. *Club:* MCC.

BENNITT, Mortimer Wilmot; *b* 28 Aug. 1910; *s* of Rev. F. W. and Honoria Bennitt. *Educ:* Charterhouse; Trinity Coll., Oxford. Entered Office of Works, 1934; Private Sec. to Sir Philip

Sassoon, 1937-38. Served War of 1939-45: RAF, 1943-45. Under Sec., 1951; Dep. Dir, Land Commn, 1967-71; retired 1971. Chairman: Little Theatre Guild of Gt Britain, 1959-60; Tavistock Repertory Company, London, 1975-77. *Publication:* Guide to Canonbury Tower, 1977. *Address:* 3/5 Highbury Grove, N5. *T:* 01-226 5937. *Clubs:* United Oxford & Cambridge University, Tower Theatre.

BENOY, Maj.-Gen. John Meredith, CBE 1943 (OBE 1931); Major-General Retired; *b* 13 July 1896; *s* of late Rev. J. Benoy; *m* 1920, Ursula Hulme Cox; one *s* one *d. Educ:* Denstone Coll., Staffs; Felsted Sch., Essex; RMC, Sandhurst. 2nd Lieut, South Staffs Regt, 1914; served European War, 1914-18, in France and Belgium with South Staffs and Royal Warwicks Regts (wounded twice); GSO3 Supreme War Council, Versailles and Peace Conference, Paris, 1918-20; Internal Security, S Ireland, 1920-21. Palestine Riots, 1929-30 (OBE); Staff Coll., Camberley, 1932-33; GSO3 War Office, 1934-36; Brigade Major, Aldershot, Palestine, and Transjordan, 1936-39; Bt Lieut-Col, 1940; AA&QMG, BEF, France and Belgium, 1940; Dep. Dir, War Office, 1941-42; Col, 1942; Brig., DA&QMG. First Army, BNAF, 1942-43; DA&QMG Second Army, 1943-44; Maj.-Gen. i/c Administration, Anti-Aircraft Command, 1944-45; Chief Administrator, Eritrea, 1945-46. Mem. Council of Industrial Design, 1949-66; Controller, Association of Socs of Art and Design, 1966-70. Consultant, UN Develt Prog., Thailand, 1971. *Address:* c/o National Westminster Bank, 208 Piccadilly, W1.

BENSKIN, Gladys, (Mrs Joseph Benskin), CBE 1918; *d* of Michael Paul Grace, 40 Belgrave Square, SW; *m* 1st, 1912, Major Raymond Sheffield Hamilton-Grace (*d* 1915); 2nd, 1919, Col Joseph Benskin, DSO, OBE (*d* 1953). Was Sec. to Mesopotamian Relief Fund. *Address:* Knowle, Frant, near Tunbridge Wells, Kent.

BENSON, Sir Arthur (Edward Trevor), GCMG 1959 (KCMG 1954; CMG 1952); *b* 21 Dec. 1907; *s* of late Rev. Arthur H. Trevor Benson, Vicar of Ilam, Staffs, formerly of Castle Connell, Co. Limerick and of St Saviour's, Johannesburg, and Emily Maud Malcolmson, Woodlock, Portlaw, Co. Waterford, late of Hanson Mount, Ashbourne, Derbyshire; *m* 1933, Daphne Mary Joyce, *d* of late E. H. M. Fynn, Serui, near Hartley, S Rhodesia; two *d. Educ:* Wolverhampton Sch.; Exeter Coll., Oxford. Colonial Administrative Service; Cadet, N Rhodesia, 1932; seconded to Colonial Office, 1939; to War Cabinet Office, 1940-43; to Colonial Office, 1943-44; Northern Rhodesia, 1944-46; Administrative Sec., Uganda, 1946-49; Chief Sec., Central African Council, 1949-51; Chief Sec. to Govt of Nigeria, 1951-54; Governor of Northern Rhodesia, 1954-59. Hon. Fellow, Exeter Coll., Oxford, 1963. JP Devon, 1962-66. KStJ 1954. *Recreation:* fishing. *Address:* Combe Hill, Combe Raleigh, near Honiton, Devon.

BENSON, Rev. Sir (Clarence) Irving, Kt 1963; CBE 1960 (OBE 1951); DD; Superintendent of the Wesley Church Central Mission, Melbourne, 1926-67; *b* 1 Dec. 1897; *s* of Walter Benson; *m* 1st, 1919, Agnes Lyell (*d* 1947); three *d*; 2nd, 1967, Marjorie Featonby. *Educ:* Hull Technical Coll.; Hymers Coll. and Private Tutors for Ministry. DD 1939. Minister, Hamilton (Victoria) Circuit, 1916-17; Toorak, 1918-23; Brunswick, 1923-26. Bevan Lectr, 1933; Drew (USA) Lectr, 1944. Pres., Methodist Conf., 1943. Pres., Australian Reading Union; Vice-Pres., Library Association of Victoria; Pres. of Trustees, State Library of Victoria; Chm., Free Library Service Board. *Publications:* The Man with the Donkey; A Century of Victorian Methodism; The Craft of Prayer; The Craft of Finding God; contribs to the Melbourne Herald, 1924-. *Recreations:* swimming, book collecting. *Address:* 25 Hoddle Street, Elsternwick, Victoria 3185, Australia. *Club:* Melbourne.

BENSON, Maj.-Gen. Edward Riou, CB 1952; CMG 1950; CBE 1945; *b* 4 April 1903; *yr s* of late Brig.-Gen. Riou Philip Benson, CB, CMG, Guildford, Surrey; *m* 1931, Isolda Mary Stuart, *d* of late Gen. Sir John Stuart Mackenzie Shea, GCB, KCMG, DSO; one *s* (one *d* decd). *Educ:* Cheltenham Coll.; RMA Woolwich, 2nd Lieut, Royal Field Artillery, 1923; Lieut, RA, 1925; Capt. 1936; Major 1940; Temp. Lieut-Col 1941; Temp. Brig. 1942; Col 1946; Maj.-Gen. 1951. Served War of 1939-45, North-West Europe, 1944-46. Dep. Dir Mil. Govt (BE), Berlin, 1948-50; Comdr 4 Anti-Aircraft Group, 1951-53; Chief of Staff, GHQ, Middle East Land Forces, 1954-57, retired. Col. Commandant, Royal Artillery, 1960-65. *Address:* Well House, Aldermaston, Berks. *T:* Woolhampton 3347.

BENSON, Prof. Frank Atkinson, BEng, MEng (Liverpool); PhD, DEng (Sheffield); FIEE, FIEEE, FIllumES; Professor and Head of Department of Electronic and Electrical Engineering, University of Sheffield, since 1967; Pro-Vice Chancellor, 1972-

76; *b* 21 Nov. 1921; *s* of late John and Selina Benson; *m* 1950, Kathleen May Paskell; two *s. Educ:* Ulverston Grammar Sch.; Univ. of Liverpool. Mem. research staff, Admty Signal Estab., Witley, 1943-46; Asst Lectr in Electrical Engrg, University of Liverpool, 1946-49; Lectr 1949-59, Sen. Lectr 1959-61, in Electrical Engrg, University of Sheffield; Reader in Electronics, University of Sheffield, 1961-67. *Publications:* Voltage Stabilizers, 1950; Electrical Engineering Problems with Solutions, 1954; Voltage Stabilized Supplies, 1957; Problems in Electronics with Solutions, 1958; Electric Circuit Theory, 1959; Voltage Stabilization, 1965; Electric Circuit Problems with Solutions, 1967; Millimetre and Submillimetre Waves, 1969; many papers on microwaves, gas discharges and voltage stabilization in learned jls. *Address:* 64 Grove Road, Sheffield S7 2GZ. *T:* Sheffield 363493.

BENSON, Sir Henry (Alexander), GBE 1971 (CBE 1946); Kt 1964; FCA; Partner, Coopers and Lybrand (formerly Cooper Brothers & Co.), Chartered Accountants, 1934-75; Adviser to the Governor of the Bank of England, since 1975; Chairman, Royal Commission on Legal Services, since 1976; *b* 2 Aug. 1909; *s* of Alexander Stanley Benson and Florence Mary (*née* Cooper); *m* 1939, Anne Virginia Macleod; two *s* one *d. Educ:* Johannesburg, South Africa. ACA (Hons) 1932; FCA 1939. Commissioned Grenadier Guards, 1940-45; seconded from Army to Min. of Supply to advise on reorganisation of accounts of Royal Ordnance Factories, 1943-44, and in Dec. 1943 apptd Dir Ordnance Factories, to carry out reorganisation; apptd Controller of Building Materials, Min. of Works, 1945; Special appt to advise Minister of Health on housing production, 1945, and subseq. other appts; also Mem. Cttee (Wilson Cttee) to review work done on, and to make recommendations for further research into, processes for transformation of coal into oil, chemicals and gas, 1959-60. Mem. Crawley Development Corp., 1947-50; Mem. Royal Ordnance Factories Board, 1952-56; Dep. Chm. Advisory Cttee (Fleck Cttee) to consider organisation of National Coal Board, 1953-55. Dir Hudson's Bay Co., 1953-62 (Dep. Governor 1955-62); Director: Finance Corporation for Industry Ltd, 1953-; Industrial and Commercial Finance Corp., 1974-; Hawker Siddeley Gp, 1975-; Council, Institute of Chartered Accountants, 1956-75 (Pres., 1966); Mem. Advisory Cttee on Legal Aid, 1956-60: Mem. Tribunal under Prevention of Fraud (Investments) Act 1939, 1957-75; Mem. Special Advisory Cttee to examine structure, finance and working of organisations controlled by British Transport Commission, 1960; apptd by Minister of Commerce, N Ireland, to investigate position of railways; to make recommendations about their future, and to report on effect which recommendations will have on transport system of Ulster Transport Authority, 1961; apptd Chm. of a Cttee to examine possible economies in the shipping and ancillary services engaged in meat, dairy products and fruit trades of New Zealand, 1962; Mem. Cttee apptd by Chancellor of the Exchequer to investigate practical effects of introduction of a turnover tax, 1963. Joint Comr to advise on integration of Nat. Assoc. of Brit. Manufrs, FBI, Brit. Employers' Confed., and on formation of a Nat. Industrial Organisation (CBI), 1963; Joint Inspector, Bd of Trade, to investigate affairs of Rolls Razor Ltd, 1964; Indep. Chm. of British Iron & Steel Fedn Development Co-ordinating Cttee, 1966; Indep. Chm., Internat. Accounting Standards Cttee (IASC), 1973-76; Member: Permanent Jt Hops Cttee, 1967-74; Dockyard Policy Bd, 1970-75; NCB team of inquiry into Bd's purchasing procedures, 1973; CBI Company Affairs Cttee, 1972; Dir, Finance for Industry Ltd, 1974-; City Liaison Cttee, 1974-75; Vice-Pres., Union Européene des Experts Comptables économiques et financiers (UEC), 1969; Mem. Cttee to enquire into admin and organisation of MoD. Apptd by Nat. Trust as Chm. of adv. cttee to review management, organisation and responsibilities of Nat. Trust, 1967; apptd by Jt Turf Authorities as Chm. of The Racing Industry Cttee of Inquiry to make detailed study of financial structure and requirements of racing industry, 1967. Treasurer, Open Univ., 1975-. Trustee, The Times Trust, 1967-. *Recreations:* shooting, golf, sailing. *Address:* 9 Durward House, 31 Kensington Court, W8 5BH. *T:* 01-937 4850. *Clubs:* Brooks's, Jockey; Royal Yacht Squadron.

BENSON, Horace Burford; *b* 3 April 1904; *s* of Augustus W. Benson and Lucy M. (*née* Jarrett); *m* 1930, Marthe Lanier; one *s* one *d.* Called to Bar, Gray's Inn, 1936; practised as Barrister, Seychelles Islands, 1936-46; District Magistrate, Ghana, 1946; Puisne Judge, Ghana, 1952-57; retired, 1957. Temp. Magistrate, Basutoland, 1958-60; Puisne Judge, Basutoland, Bechuanaland Protectorate and Swaziland, 1960-61; Chief Justice, Basutoland (now Lesotho), 1965; Puisne Judge, Malawi, 1967-69. *Recreations:* bowls, bridge. *Address:* c/o Barclays Bank Ltd, Tulse Hill, SE27.

BENSON, Rev. Sir Irving; see Benson, Rev. Sir C. I.

BENSON, Jeremy Henry; architect, since 1954; *b* 25 June 1925; *s* of late Guy Holford Benson and Lady Violet Benson; *m* 1951, Patricia Stewart; two *s* three *d*. *Educ:* Eton; Architectural Assoc. (AADipl.); FRIBA. Royal Engineers, 1944-47. Vice-Chm., Soc. for Protection of Ancient Buildings, 1971- (Mem. Exec. Cttee, 1959-); Dep. Chm., Georgian Group, 1969- (Mem., Exec. Cttee, 1967-); Vice-Chm., Joint Cttee of SPAB, GG, Victorian Soc., Civic Trust and Ancient Monuments Soc., 1972- (Mem., 1968-); Member: Forestry Commn's Westonbirt Adv. Cttee, 1969-; Historic Buildings Council for England, 1974-; Adv. Cttee on Forestry in the Royal Parks, 1977-. *Recreation:* gardening. *Address:* Walpole House, Chiswick Mall, W4 2PS. *T:* 01-994 1611; Field Barn, Taddington, Temple Guiting, Cheltenham, Glos. *T:* Stanton 228. *Club:* Brooks's.

BENSON, Rev. Niale Shane Trevor, AFC 1942; MA; Vicar of Broadchalke with Bowerchalke, since 1970; Rural Dean of Chalke, since 1974; *b* Johannesburg, SA, 14 Dec. 1911; *s* of late Rev. A. H. T. Benson, Vicar of Ilam, Staffs, formerly of Castle Connell, Co. Limerick and of St Saviour's, Johannesburg, and late Emily Maud Malcolmson, Woodlock, Portlaw, Co. Waterford; *m* 1939, Helen Marjorie, *d* of late Air Chief Marshal Sir John Miles Steel, GCB, KBE, CMG; two *s* one *d*. *Educ:* Wolverhampton Grammar Sch.; St John's Coll., Oxford (Open Classical Scholar). BA 1934; MA 1945. Asst Master, Shrewsbury Sch., 1934; Giggleswick Sch., 1935-39. Served War of 1939-45, RAF (AFC); Sqdn-Ldr, 1941; Dep. Chief-Instructor, Empire Central Flying Sch., 1942-43. Giggleswick Sch., 1945-47; Headmaster: Queen Elizabeth's Grammar Sch., Blackburn, 1948-56; Giggleswick Sch., 1956-60; The Cathedral Sch., Salisbury, 1963-70. Deacon, 1968; priest, 1969. *Address:* Broadchalke Vicarage, near Salisbury, Wilts.

BENSON, Maj.-Gen. Peter Herbert, CBE 1974 (MBE 1954); Director General of Transportation (formerly Transport Officer in Chief, Army), since 1976; *b* 27 Oct. 1923; *s* of Herbert Kamerer Benson and Edith Doris Benson; *m* 1949, Diana Betty Ashmore; one *s* one *d*. *Educ:* Craig-y-Nos Sch., Swansea; Swansea Techn. Coll. FCIT. Joined Army, 1944; commnd into S Wales Borderers, 1945; transf. to RASC, 1948, and Royal Corps of Transport, 1965; served, Palestine, Cyprus, Malaya and Singapore (three times), Borneo, Africa and Australia; Comdr, 15 Air Despatch Regt, 1966-68; GSO1 (DS) Staff Coll., Camberley, and Australian Staff Coll., 1968-70; Col Q (Movements), MoD (Army), 1971-72; Comdr, 2 Transport Gp RCT (Logistic Support Force), 1972-73. Comdr, ANZUK Support Gp Singapore, Sen. British Officer Singapore, and Leader, UK Jt Services Planning Team, 1973-74; Chief Transport and Movements Officer, BAOR, 1974-76. Hon. Col, 161 Regt RCT(V), 1975. *Recreations:* golf, fly-fishing, shooting.

BENSTEAD, Sir John, Kt 1953; CBE 1946; DL; Member British Transport Commission, 1947-61 (Deputy Chairman); *b* 10 Jan. 1897; *m* 1922, Gladys Mary Palmer (*d* 1965); one *d*; *m* 1967, Catherine Ferguson McCabe. *Educ:* King's Sch., Peterborough. RN, 1915-19. Gen. Sec., National Union of Railwaymen, 1943-47; Pres., International Transport Workers' Federation, 1946; Member: Advisory Council for Scientific and Industrial Research, 1943-48; Colonial and Economic Development Council, 1947-48; Royal Commission on Press, 1946; FCIT. DL Cambridgeshire (formerly Huntingdon and Peterborough), 1967. *Address:* 98a Lincoln Road, Peterborough. *T:* Peterborough 62072.

BENTALL, Hugh Henry, MB; FRCS; Professor of Cardiac Surgery, Royal Postgraduate Medical School of London, since 1965; Consultant Thoracic Surgeon, Hammersmith Hospital, since 1955; *b* 28 April 1920; *s* of Henry Bentall and of late Lilian Alice Greeno; *m* 1944, Jean, *d* of late Hugh Cameron Wilson, MD, FRCS; three *s* one *d*. *Educ:* Seaford Coll., Sussex; Medical Sch. of St Bartholomew's Hospital, London. RNVR, Surg Lieut, 1945-47. Lecturer in Thoracic Surgery, Postgraduate Medical Sch., London, 1959; Reader, 1962-65. *Publications:* books and papers on surgical subjects. *Recreation:* sailing. *Address:* Royal Postgraduate Medical School of London, Ducane Road, W12. *T:* 01-743 2030. *Clubs:* Naval; Cruising Association; Royal Naval Sailing Association (Portsmouth).

BENTALL, (Leonard Edward) Rowan, DL; Chairman, Bentalls Ltd, since 1968; Managing Director, since 1963; *b* 27 Nov. 1911; *yr s* of late Leonard H. Bentall and Mrs Bentall; *m* 1937, Adelia E., *yr d* of late David Hawes and Mrs Hawes; three *s* two *d*. *Educ:* Aldro Sch.; Eastbourne Coll. Joined family business, 1930. Served War of 1939-45: joined East Surrey Regt, 1940; commissioned, Royal Welch Fusiliers, 1941; served Middle East, N Africa, Sicily, Italy, France, Belgium, Holland, 231

(Malta) Inf. Bde; now Hon. Captain, Royal Welch Fusiliers. Bentalls: Dep. Chm., 1950; Merchandise Dir, 1946-63. Mem. Council, Inst. of Directors, 1972. DL Greater London, 1977; Freeman of City of London, 1972. President: Kingston Arts Trust; Kingston RFC; Steadfast Sea Cadet Corps. Cavaliere, Order Al Merito della Repubblica Italiana, 1971. *Publication:* My Store of Memories, 1974. *Recreations:* farming, shooting, gardening, ornithology. *Address:* Ridgemount, Ashcombe Avenue, Surbiton, Surrey; Willetts Farm, West Chiltington, Sussex. *Clubs:* Farmers', Royal Automobile.

BENTHALL, Sir (Arthur) Paul, KBE 1950; FLS; Chairman: Amalgamated Metal Corporation Ltd, 1959-72; Bird & Co. (London) Ltd, 1953-73; Director, Chartered Bank, 1953-72; *b* 25 Jan. 1902; *s* of Rev. Charles Francis Benthall and Annie Theodosia Benthall; *m* 1932, Mary Lucy, *d* of John A. Pringle, Horam, Sussex; four *s*. *Educ:* Eton; Christ Church, Oxford. Joined Bird & Co. and F. W. Heilgers & Co., Calcutta, 1924; partner in both firms, 1934; Vice-Pres. Bengal Chamber of Commerce, 1947; Pres. 1948 and 1950; Pres. of Assoc. Chambers of Commerce of India, 1948 and 1950; Member: Calcutta Local Board, Imperial Bank of India, 1946-48 and 1950-53; Central Board, 1948 and 1950-53; Chm. All India Board of Technical Studies in Commerce and Business Administration, 1950-53; Pres. Royal Agri-Horticultural Society of India, 1945-47; Vice-Pres. UK Citizens' Assoc., 1951; Pres. 1952. *Publication:* The Trees of Calcutta and its Neighbourhood, 1946. *Address:* Benthal Hall, Broseley, Salop. *T:* Telford 882254. *Clubs:* Oriental, Landsowne.
See also J. C. M. Benthall.

BENTHALL, Jonathan Charles Mackenzie; Director, Royal Anthropological Institute, since 1974; *b* Calcutta, 12 Sept. 1941; *s* of Sir Arthur Paul Benthall, *qv*; *m* 1975, Zamira, *d* of Yehudi Menuhin, *qv*; one *s* one step *s*. *Educ:* Eton (KS); King's Coll., Cambridge (MA). Sec., Inst. of Contemporary Arts, 1971-73. Chevalier de l'Ordre des Arts et des Lettres (France), 1973. *Publications:* Science and Technology in Art Today, 1972; The Body Electric: patterns of western industrial culture, 1976; (ed) Ecology: the Shaping Enquiry, 1972; (ed) The Limits of Human Nature, 1973; (ed jtly) The Body as a Medium of Expression, 1975. *Address:* 41 Pangbourne Avenue, W10 6DJ.

BENTHALL, Sir Paul; see Benthall, Sir A. P.

BENTINCK; see Cavendish-Bentinck.

BENTLEY, Frederic Herbert, OBE 1944; Professor of Surgery, University of Jordan; *b* 1905; *e s* of Fred Bentley, JP, and Laura Evelyn Bentley; *m* 1946, Radmila Novakovic, of Belgrade. *Educ:* Church Institute Sch., Bolton; University of Manchester. BScManch. 1926; MB, ChB, 1929; FRCS 1932; MD Manchester, 1946; FACS 1955. Bradley Memorial Schol. Clinical Surgery, Manchester Royal Infirmary, 1928. Formerly House Surgeon, Asst RSO; First Asst and Tutor, Manchester Royal Infirmary; formerly House Surg. and Res. Surg. Off., St Mark's Hospital, London; formerly Hon. Surgeon various hospitals in Manchester area. Hunterian Prof., Royal College of Surgeons, England, 1936 and 1937; Prof. of Surgery, the University of Durham, 1945-52; formerly: Mackenzie Mackinnon Research Fellow, RCP London and RCS England; Bernhard Baron Scholar RCS Eng; Dickinson Scholar and Demonst. Anatomy, University of Manchester; Sommer Meml Fellow, Instructor in Surgery, Portland, Oregon, 1953-75; Chm., Oregon State Health Commn; Medical Dir, North Lincoln Hosp. On Active Service with RAMC 1942-45, rank Lieut-Col. First as Officer in charge a Surgical Division and later OC Penicillin Control Team in Mediterranean area; separate mission to Russian Army in Rumania, and Partisan Army in Yugoslavia. *Publications:* various contributions to Medical and Physiological Journals since 1936. *Recreations:* tennis, angling, music. *Address:* Faculty of Medicine, The University, Amman, Jordan. *Clubs:* Waverley, Arlington (Portland); Reform (London, England).

BENTLEY, Rev. Canon Geoffrey Bryan; Canon of Windsor since 1957; *b* 16 July 1909; *s* of late Henry Bentley; *m* 1938, Nina Mary, *d* of late George Coombe Williams, Clerk; two *s* two *d*. *Educ:* Uppingham Sch.; King's Coll., Cambridge (Scholar); Cuddesdon Coll., Oxford. BA and Carus Greek Testament Prize, 1932; MA 1935. Ordained, 1933; Asst Curate, St Cuthbert's, Copnor, 1933-35; Tutor of Scholae Cancellarii, Lincoln, 1935-38; Lecturer, 1938-52; Priest Vicar of Lincoln Cathedral and Chaplain of Lincoln County Hosp., 1938-52; Proctor in Convocation, 1945-55; Rector of Milton Abbot with Dunterton, Dio. Exeter, 1952-57; Examg Chap. to Bp of Exeter, 1952-74; Commissary to Bp of SW Tanganyika, 1952-61; Canon of Windsor, 1957, Precentor, 1958-69, 1970-73, President, May-

Dec. 1962 and Feb.-July 1971, Steward 1969, 1975; Mem., Archbp's Group on Reform of Divorce Law, 1964; William Jones Golden Lectr., 1965; Scott Holland Lectr., 1966. *Publications:* The Resurrection of the Bible, 1940; Catholic Design for Living, 1940; Reform of the Ecclesiastical Law, 1944; God and Venus, 1964; Dominance or Dialogue?, 1965. *Address:* 8 The Cloisters, Windsor Castle, Berks SL4 1NJ. *T:* Windsor 63001. *Club:* National Liberal.

BENTLEY, John Ransome; Chairman, Bentley Securities Ltd; *b* 19 Feb. 1940; *m* 1960 (marr. diss. 1969); one *s* one *d. Educ:* Harrow Sch. Chm. and Man. Dir, Barclay Securities Ltd, 1969-73; Chairman: Weston Holdings, 1973; Lion International, 1973. *Recreation:* living.

BENTLEY, Nicolas Clerihew, FRSA, FSIA; Publisher, Artist, and Author; *b* Highgate, London, 14 June 1907; *yr s* of late Edmund Clerihew Bentley; *m* 1934, Barbara, *e d* of late Sir Patrick Hastings, QC; one *d. Educ:* University Coll. Sch., London; Heatherley Sch. of Art. Dir, André Deutsch Ltd. *Publications:* Die, I Thought I'd Laugh: a book of pictures, 1936; Ballet-Hoo, 1937; The Time of my Life, 1937; Gammon and Espionage, 1938; Le Sport, 1939; Second Thoughts, and other poems, 1939; Animal, Vegetable and South Kensington, 1940; The Tongue-Tied Canary, 1948; The Floating Dutchman, 1950; Third Party Risk, 1953; How can you bear to be Human?, 1957; A Version of the Truth, 1960; The Victorian Scene, 1968; Golden Sovereigns, 1970; Tales from Shakespeare, 1972; The Events of That Week, 1972; An Edwardian Album, 1974; Inside Information, 1974; *edited:* (with L. Russell) The English Comic Album, 1948; Diary by F. Bason, 1950; Treasury of Humorous Comic Quotations by E. Esar, 1951; The Pick of Punch, 1955-56, 1956-57, 1957-58, 1959-60; A Choice of Ornaments, 1959; Comfortable Words by B. Evans, 1963; Dispatches from the Crimea 1854-56 by Sir W. H. Russell, 1966; The Reminiscences of Captain Gronow, 1977; *illustrated:* New Cautionary Tales by H. Belloc, 1930; More Than Somewhat by Damon Runyon, 1937; Old Possum's Book of Practical Cats by T. S. Eliot, 1939; Cautionary Verses by H. Belloc, 1940; Baseless Biography by E. C. Bentley, 1940; The Wind on the Moon by E. Linklater, 1944; How to be an Alien by G. Mikes, 1946; This England, 1940-46, 1946; How to scrape Skies by G. Mikes, 1947; Milk and Honey, Israel Explored by G. Mikes, 1950; Wisdom for Others, by G. Mikes, 1950; Stiff Upper Lip by L. Durrell, 1958; Sauve qui peut by L. Durrell, 1966; On Drink by Kingsley Amis, 1973, etc. *Address:* The Old School, Downhead, Shepton Mallet, Somerset. *Club:* Garrick.

BENTLEY, William, CMG 1977; HM Diplomatic Service; Ambassador to the Philippines, since 1976; *b* 15 Feb. 1927; *s* of Lawrence and Elsie Jane Bentley; *m* 1950, Karen Ellen Christensen; two *s* three *d. Educ:* Bury High Sch.; Manchester Univ.; Wadham Coll., Oxford (1st cl. Mod. Hist.); Coll. of Europe, Bruges. HM Foreign (later Diplomatic) Service, 1952; 3rd (later 2nd) Sec., Tokyo, 1952-57; United Nations Dept, Foreign Office, 1957-60; 1st Sec., UK Mission to United Nations, 1960-63; Far Eastern Dept, FO, 1963-65; Head of Chancery, Kuala Lumpur, 1965-69; Dep. Comr-Gen., British Pavilion, Expo 70, Osaka, 1969-70; Counsellor, Belgrade, 1970-73; Head of Permanent Under-Sec.'s Dept, FCO, 1973-74; Head of Far Eastern Dept, FCO, 1974-76. *Recreations:* golf, skiing, fishing, shooting. *Address:* c/o Foreign and Commonwealth Office, SW1; 6 Landsdowne Close, SW20. *T:* 01-946 1985; Oak Cottage, Oak Lane, Crickhowell, Breconshire. *Clubs:* Brooks's; Roehampton.

BENTON, Gordon William, CIE 1946; *b* 25 March 1893; *s* of William Benton, Cannock, Staffs; *m* 1st, 1922, Ethel Beatrice (*d* 1971), *d* of George Mark Robinson; no *c*; 2nd, 1973, Vera Alicia, *d* of P. W. J. J. Harman-Harris and *widow* of H. W. Trussler. *Educ:* Merchant Taylors' Sch. Joined Indian Police, 1912; Indian Army Reserve of Officers, 1917-19; 45th Rattray's Sikhs, Mesopotamia, 1926-33, 1938; lent to Govt of HEH the Nizam of Hyderabad for CID, and Dir-Gen., Police and Jails, 1935-38; Deputy Dir, Intelligence Bureau, Home Dept, Govt of India; Deputy Inspector-General, Central Provinces and Berar, retd 1947. Mem., two Cttees on aspects of Railway Police admin under the Govt of India Bill then under consideration in parlt.Indian Police Medal, 1940; King's Police Medal, 1945. *Address:* 39 Marine Parade West, Lee-on-the-Solent, Hants PO13 9LW. *Club:* East India, Devonshire, Sports and Public Schools.

BENTON, Kenneth Carter, CMG 1966; *b* 4 March 1909; *s* of William Alfred Benton and Amy Adeline Benton (*née* Kirton); *m* 1938, Peggie, *d* of Maj.-Gen. C. E. Pollock, CB, CBE, DSO; one *s* (and two step *s*). *Educ:* Wolverhampton Sch.; London Univ. Teaching and studying languages in Florence and Vienna,

1930-37; employed British Legation, Vienna, 1937-38; Vice-Consul, Riga, 1938-40; 2nd 1974-76. British Embassy, Madrid, 1941-43; 2nd, later 1st Sec., Rome, 1944-48; FO, 1948-50; 1st Sec., Rome, 1950-53; 1st Sec., Madrid, 1953-56; FO, 1956-62; 1st Sec. and Consul, Lima, 1963-64; FO, 1964-66; Counsellor, Rio de Janeiro, 1966-68; retd from Diplomatic Service, 1968. *Publications:* Twenty-fourth Level, 1969; Sole Agent, 1970; Spy in Chancery, 1972; Craig and the Jaguar, 1973; Craig and the Tunisian Tangle, 1974; Death on the Appian Way, 1974; Craig and the Midas Touch, 1975; A Single Monstrous Act, 1976; The Red Hen Conspiracy, 1977. *Recreations:* writing, enamelling. *Address:* Vine House, Appledore, Ashford, Kent. *T:* Appledore 260. *Clubs:* Authors', Detection.

BENTON JONES, Sir Simon W. F.; *see* Jones.

BENYON, William Richard, JP; DL; MP (C) Buckingham since 1970; *b* 17 Jan. 1930; *e s* of late Vice-Adm. R. Benyon, CB, CBE, and of Mrs. Benyon, The Lambdens, Beenham, Berkshire; *m* Elizabeth Ann Hallifax; two *s* three *d. Educ:* Royal Naval Coll., Dartmouth. Royal Navy, 1947-56; Courtaulds Ltd, 1956-64; Farmer, 1964-. PPS to Minister of Housing and Construction, 1972-74; Conservative Whip, 1974-76. Mem., Berks CC, 1964-74; JP 1962, DL 1970, Berks. *Address:* Englefield House, Englefield, near Reading, Berkshire. *T:* Reading 302221.

BEOVICH, Most Rev. Matthew, DD, PhD; Former Archbishop of Adelaide, (RC) (Archbishop, 1940-71); *b* 1896; *s* of Matthew and Elizabeth Beovich, Melbourne. *Educ:* Melbourne; Propaganda College, Rome. *Address:* 28 Robe Terrace, Medindie, SA 5081, Australia.

BERE, Rennie Montague, CMG 1957; Retired; *b* 28 Nov. 1907; *s* of late Rev. M. A. Bere; *m* 1936, Anne Maree Barber; no *c. Educ:* Marlborough Coll.; Selwyn Coll., Cambridge (MA). Colonial Administrative Service, Uganda, 1930-55; Asst District Officer, 1930; District Officer, 1942; Provincial Commissioner, 1951-55. Commandant, Polish Refugee Settlements, 1943-44; Dir and Chief Warden, Uganda National Parks, 1955-60; Pres., Cornwall Naturalists-Trust, 1967-70. *Publications:* The Wild Mammals of Uganda, 1961; The African Elephant, 1966; Wild Animals in an African National Park, 1966; The Way to the Mountains of the Moon, 1966; Birds in an African National Park, 1969; Antelopes, 1970; Wildlife in Cornwall, 1971; Crocodile's Eggs for Supper, 1973; The Mammals of East and Central Africa, 1975; articles (chiefly of mountaineering and wild life and anthropological interest) in Alpine Jl, Uganda Jl, Oryx, Animals, etc. *Recreations:* mountaineering; game and bird watching; cricket. *Address:* West Cottage, Bude, N Cornwall. *T:* Bude 2082. *Clubs:* Alpine, Royal Commonwealth Society; Uganda Kobs (past Pres.).

BERENS, Herbert Cecil Benyon, MC 1942; Chairman: Evans of Leeds Ltd, since 1972; Siebens Oil and Gas (UK) Ltd, since 1971; Director: Allied Irish Investment Bank Ltd, since 1966; *b* 16 Oct. 1908; *s* of Cecil Berens, JP, St Mary Cray, Kent; *m* 1931, Moyra Nancy Mellard; three *s* one *d. Educ:* Wellington Coll.; Christ Church, Oxford. Hambro's Bank, 1931-39. Served War of 1939-45; Major, 4th County of London Yeomanry (MC); POW, 1941-43. *Recreations:* racing, shooting. *Address:* Bentworth Hall, Alton, Hants. *T:* Alton 62140. *Clubs:* MCC, I Zingari.

BERESFORD, family name of **Baron Decies** and **Marquess of Waterford.**

BERESFORD, His Honour Eric George Harold; a Circuit Judge (formerly Judge of County Courts), 1959-76; *b* 19 Nov. 1901; *s* of Henry Beresford, Sutton Coldfield; *m* 1930, Barbara Muriel, *d* of Wallace Edwin Marley, Sutton Coldfield; one *s* one *d. Educ:* King Edward's Sch., Birmingham; Emanuel Coll., Cambridge (MA, LLB). Called to Bar, Lincoln's Inn, 1926; practised on Midland Circuit. Chm., Licensed Premises Cttee, New Town of Redditch, 1965. *Recreations:* history and literature. *Address:* Saxbys, Rolvenden, Kent. *T:* Rolvenden 403.

BERESFORD, Jack, CBE 1960; Member, British Olympic Council, since 1936; Member, Council for England, British Empire and Commonwealth Games (BE & CG) 1931-74; *b* 1 Jan. 1899; *s* of Julius and Ethel Mary Beresford; *m* 1st, 1940, Mary Leaning (marr. diss.); one *s* one *d*; 2nd, 1958, Stroma Jean Margaret Morrison; two *d. Educ:* Bedford Sch. Served, European War of 1914-18: enlisted Artists' Rifles, 1917; commissioned. Liverpool Scottish Regiment; served 1917-19, Northern France; wounded, 1918. Champion Sculler of Great Britain, 1920-26; winner of Diamond Sculls, 1920, 1924, 1925, 1926; only winner of all five principal events, Henley Royal Regatta; Grand (twice), Stewards, Silver Goblets (twice), Diamonds (four times), Double Sculls; Olympic Games:

(Brussels) 1920 silver medal Olympic Sculls, (Paris) 1924 gold medal Olympic Sculls, (Amsterdam) 1928 silver medal Olympic Eights, (Los Angeles) 1932 gold medal Olympic Fours, (Berlin) 1936 gold medal Olympic Double Sculls; 1930 British Empire Games (Canada) silver medal Empire Sculls. Philadelphia Gold Cup, World Amateur Sculling Championship, 1924-25; Helms Athletic Foundn (USA) Helms World Trophy, Europe, 1926. Leader of British Olympic team, Berlin, 1936; coach and manager, English oarsmen in Argentina and Uruguay, 1947; awarded gold medal of honour of the Fédération Internationale des Sociétés d'Aviron (FISA), Lucerne, 1947; Organising Cttee, Olympic Games, London, 1948; Olympic diploma of merit, Amsterdam, 1949; coach and manager, English crews to New Zealand and Australia, British Empire and Commonwealth Games, 1950; coach and manager, British rowing team, Olympic Games, Finland, 1952; Pres., Bucks, Berks and Oxon branch, British Olympic Assoc., 1971-76; Founder Mem. of the Furniture Makers' Guild; Liveryman of Painter Stainers' Company; Member: Council, National Playing Fields Assoc., British Field Sports Assoc.; Greater London and South East Sports Council, 1966-73; Council, Amateur Rowing Assoc., 1932-67; Selection Cttee for British crews, 1938-64; Steward and Mem. Cttee of Management, Henley Royal Regatta, 1946-73. Mem., Court of Worshipful Co. of Furniture Makers, Master 1971-72. Rowing correspondent of The Field, 1966-71. Played Umpire in film "Half a Sixpence". Freeman of City of London, 1952. *Recreations:* family life, beagling, rowing, and swimming. *Address:* Highlands House, Shiplake-on-Thames, Oxon. *T:* Wargrave 2346. *Clubs:* Thames Rowing (Pres. 1971), Kingston Rowing, Leander; British Sportsman's; Christchurch and Farley Hill Beagles; Remenham; Old Bedfordians.

BERESFORD, Prof. Maurice Warwick; Professor of Economic History, University of Leeds, since 1959; *b* 6 Feb. 1920; *s* of late H. B. Beresford and Mrs N. E. Beresford. *Educ:* Boldmere and Green Lane Elementary Schs; Bishop Vesey's Grammar Sch., Sutton Coldfield; Jesus Coll., Cambridge. Historical Tripos, Pt I class I, 1940, Pt II class I, 1941; MA 1945. On Staff of Birmingham Univ. Settlement, 1941-42; Sub-warden, Percival Guildhouse, Rugby, 1942-43; Warden, 1943-48; University of Leeds: Lecturer, 1948-55; Reader, 1955-59; Dean, 1958-60; Chm., Sch. of Economic Studies, 1965-68, 1971-72; Chm. of Faculty Bd, 1968-70. Harrison Vis. Prof. of History, Coll. of William and Mary, Virginia, 1975-76. Chairman: Yorks Citizens' Advice Bureaux Cttee, 1963-69; Parole Review Cttee, Leeds Prison, 1970-; Northern Area Inst. for Study and Treatment of Delinquency, 1973-; Co-opted Mem., City of Leeds Probation Cttee, 1972-; SSRC, Economic and Social History Cttee, 1972-75. Minister's nominee, Yorkshire Dales National Park Cttee, 1964-71; Member: Consumer Council, 1966-71; Hearing Aids Council, 1969-71. *Publications:* The Leeds Chambers of Commerce, 1951; The Lost Villages of England, 1954; History on the Ground, 1957; (with J. K. S. St Joseph) Medieval England: an Aerial Survey, 1958; Time and Place, 1962; New Towns of the Middle Ages, 1967; (Ed, with G. R. J. Jones) Leeds and Its Region, 1967; (with J. G. Hurst) Deserted Medieval Villages, 1971; (with H. P. R. Finberg) English Medieval Boroughs, 1973. Contributions to Economic History Review, Agricultural History Review, Medieval Archaeology, etc. *Recreations:* music, theatre, maps, delinquency. *Address:* 6 Claremont Avenue, Leeds 3. *T:* Leeds 454563.

BERESFORD-PEIRSE, Sir Henry Grant de la Poer, 6th Bt *cr* 1814; *b* 7 Feb. 1933; *s* of Sir Henry Campbell de la Poer Beresford-Peirse, 5th Bt, CB, and of Margaret, *d* of Frank Morison Seafield Grant, Knockie, Inverness-shire; *S* father, 1972; *m* 1966, Jadranka, *d* of Ivan Njerš, Zagreb, Yugoslavia; two *s. Heir: s* Henry Njerš de la Poer Beresford-Peirse, *b* 25 March 1969.

BERESFORD-STOOKE, Sir George; *see* Stooke.

BERESFORD WEST, Michael Charles, QC 1975; a Recorder of the Crown Court, since 1975; *b* 3 June 1928; *s* of Arthur Charles and Ida Dagmar West; *m* 1956, Patricia Eileen Beresford; two *s* one *d. Educ:* St Peter's, Southbourne; Portsmouth Grammar Sch.; Brasenose Coll., Oxford (MA). Nat. Service, Intell. Corps, Middle East. Called to Bar, Lincoln's Inn, 1952; Western Circuit, 1953-65; SE Circuit, 1965; a Chm., Independent Schools Tribunal and Tribunal (Children's Act 1948), 1974. *Recreations:* swimming, lawn tennis, music. *Address:* 3 King's Bench Walk, Temple, EC4Y 7DQ. *T:* 01-353 0431; Chilterns, 4 Four Hill, Purley, Surrey. *T:* 01-660 3293.

BERGANZA, Teresa; singer (mezzo-soprano); *b* Madrid, Spain; *d* of Guillermo and Maria Ascension Berganza; *m* 1957, Felix Lavilla; one *s* two *d*. Début in Madrid, 1955; début in England,

Glyndebourne, 1958; appeared at Glyndebourne, 1959; Royal Opera House, Covent Garden, 1959, 1960, 1963, 1964, 1976, 1977; Royal Festival Hall, 1960, 1961, 1962, 1967, 1971; appears regularly in Vienna, Milan, Aix-en-Provence, Holland, Edinburgh, Paris, Israel, America. Prizes: Lucretia Arana; Nacional Lírica, Spain; Lily Pons, 1976; Acad. Nat du Disque Lyrique; USA record award; Harriet Cohen Internat. Music Award, 1974. Charles Cross (4 times); Grand Cross, Isabel la Católica, Spain. *Recreations:* music, books, the arts. *Address:* c/o Miss Lies Askonas, 19a Air Street, Regent Street, W1. *T:* 01-734 5459.

BERGEL, Prof. Franz, FRS 1959; DPhil. Nat. (Freiburg), PhD (London), DSc (London), FRIC, FIBiol; Professor Emeritus of Chemistry, University of London; Member, Institute of Cancer Research: Royal Cancer Hospital; *b* Vienna, 13 Feb. 1900; *s* of Moritz Martin Bergel and Barbara Betty Spitz; *m* 1939, Phyllis Thomas. *Educ:* Universities of Vienna and Freiburg im Breisgau. Head of Dept of Medical Chemistry, Inst. Chem., 1927-33, and Privatdoz., Univ. of Freiburg, 1929-33; research worker: Med. Chem. Dept, Univ. of Edinburgh, 1933-36; Lister Inst. of Preventive Med., Dept of Biochemistry, 1936-38; Dir of Research, Roche Products Ltd, Welwyn Garden City, 1938-52; Head, Chemistry Dept, Chester Beatty Res. Inst., 1952-66; Dean, Inst. Cancer Research, 1963-66. Hon. Lectr, Pharmacology Dept, Faculty of Medical Sciences. University Coll., London 1946-73; Consultant, Harvard Med. Sch. and Children's Cancer Research Foundn (now Sidney Farber Cancer Inst.), Boston, Mass, 1959-60, 1967-73; FChemSoc; FRSM; FRSH; FRSA 1957 (Life Mem., 1967-); Member: Soc. Chem. Ind.; Biochem. Soc.; Amer. Assoc. Adv. Sci.; Brit. Pharm. Soc.; NY Acad. Sci. *Publications:* Chemistry of Enzymes in Cancer, 1961; All about Drugs, 1970; Today's Carcinochemotherapy, 1970; papers and reviews in chemical, biochemical and pharmacological journals. *Recreation:* sketching. *Address:* Magnolia Cottage, Bel Royal, Jersey, CI. *T:* Central 33688. *Club:* Athenæum.

BERGER, John; author and art critic; *b* London, 5 Nov. 1926; *s* of late S. J. D. Berger, OBE, MC, and of Mrs Miriam Berger (*née* Branson). *Educ:* Central Sch. of Art; Chelsea Sch. of Art. Began career as a painter and teacher of drawing; exhibited at Wildenstein, Redfern and Leicester Galls, London. Art Critic: Tribune; New Statesman. Numerous TV appearances, incl.: Monitor; two series for Granada TV. Scenario: (with Alain Tanner) La Salamandre; Le Milieu du Monde; Jonas (New York Critics Prize for Best Scenario of Year, 1976). George Orwell Meml Prize, 1977. *Publications:* Marcel Frishman, 1958; A Painter of Our Time (novel), 1958; Permanent Red, 1960; trans. (with A. Bostock) Poems on the Theatre, by B. Brecht, 1960; The Foot of Clive (novel), 1962; Corker's Freedom (novel), 1964; The Success and Failure of Picasso, 1965; (with J. Mohr) A Fortunate Man: the story of a country doctor, 1967; Art and Revolution, 1969; Moments of Cubism and Other Essays, 1969; trans. (with A. Bostock) Return to My Native Land, by Aimé Césaire, 1969; Selected Essays and Articles: The Look of Things, 1972; G (novel), 1972 (Booker Prize 1972; James Tait Black Meml Prize, 1972); Ways of Seeing, 1972; The Seventh Man, 1975 (Prize for Best Reportage, Union of Journalists and Writers, Paris 1977); Poems in Voix, Maspero, Paris 1977. *Address:* c/o Penguin Books, Harmondsworth, Mddx.

BERGER, Vice-Adm. Peter Egerton Capel, MVO 1960; DSC 1949; Chief of Staff to Commander-in-Chief Fleet, since 1976; *b* 11 Feb. 1925; *s* of late Capel Colquhoun Berger and Winifred Violet Berger (*née* Levett-Scrivener); *m* 1956, June Kathleen Pigou; three *d. Educ:* Harrow Sch. Served War of 1939-45: entered RN as a Cadet, 1943; Normandy and South of France landings in HMS Ajax, 1944; Sub-Lt, 1945; Lieut, 1946; Yangtse Incident, HMS Amethyst, 1949; Lt-Comdr, 1953; Comdr, 1956; Fleet Navigating Officer, Home Fleet, 1956-58; Navigating Officer, HM Yacht Britannia, 1958-60; Commanded HMS Torquay, 1962-64; Captain, 1964; Defence, Naval and Military Attaché, The Hague, 1964-66; commanded HMS Phoebe, 1966-68; Commodore, Clyde, 1971-73; Rear-Adm., 1973; Asst Chief of Naval Staff (Policy), 1973-75. *Recreations:* shooting, fishing, history. *Address:* Pincotts, Meadow Way, West Horsley, Surrey KT24 6LL. *T:* East Horsley 3112.

BERGIN, John Alexander; Deputy Secretary, Lord Chancellor's Department, since 1977; *b* 25 May 1920; *s* of late B. A. G. and Mrs L. Bergin; *m* 1953, Pierrette Wack, MA. *Educ:* Varndean Sch., Brighton; St Catharine's Coll., Cambridge. BA Hons (Natural Science) 1947. REME, 1940-46 (T/Major, despatches). Asst Principal, Bd of Trade, 1948; HM Customs and Excise, 1954-56; Office of Chancellor, Duchy of Lancaster, 1960; Dept of Economic Affairs, 1964; IDC, 1966; Under-Sec., BoT, 1968-71; Principal Estabt and Finance Officer, Lord Chancellor's

Dept, 1971-77. *Recreations:* claret; hybridising *Liliaceae*, *Amaryllidaceae*. *Address:* 15 Granard Avenue, SW15 6HH.

BERGIN, Kenneth Glenny, MA, MD Cantab; DPH London; FRAeS; physician; Director, Cavendish Medical Centre, since 1973; President, International Academy of Aviation and Space Medicine, since 1977; *b* 10 June 1911; *er s* of Dr F. Gower Bergin, Clifton, Bristol; *m* 1938, Joan Mary, *o d* of G. H. Sinnott, Clifton, Bristol and *gd* of Maj.-Gen. N. F. J. Sampson-Way, CB, Henbury, Glos; two *s* one *d. Educ:* Clifton Coll.; Queens' Coll., Cambridge; St Bartholomew's Hospital, London. Served with RAF Med. Br., 1939-46 (despatches twice); Flying Trng Bomber (Pathfinder) and Fighter Comds (Wing Comdr, qual. service pilot). BOAC, 1946-64: Dir Personnel and Medical Services, 1959-63; Dir Medical Services, 1963-64. Pres. Airline Med. Directors' Assoc., 1965; Pres., Air League, 1978-(Chm., 1974-77, Vice-Chm., 1960-64); Mem. Council: Brit. Soc. for Internat. Understanding; Aerospace Med. Assoc.; Member: Airline Personnel Directors' Assoc., 1959-64; Nat. Jt Council for Civil Air Transport, 1959-64; Nat. Jt Adv. Council to Minister of Labour, 1959-64; Bd of Govs, Clifton Coll.; Assoc. of Industrial Med. Officers; WHO Cttee on Internat. Quarantine; Nat. Aviation Council; Econ. Research Council; Adv. Council, Coll. of Aeronautical and Automobile Engineering; Vice-Chm., Bd of Govs, Coll. of Air Trng., 1962-64; Chm., Air Centre Trust, 1967-70; Master, Guild of Air Pilots and Air Navigators, 1959-61; Custodian, Guild of Air Pilots Benevolent Fund; Freeman and Liveryman, City of London. Hon. Steward, Westminster Abbey. Invitation Lectr., Oxford, Cambridge and Bristol Univs., Brit. Assoc., Royal Soc. of Health, BMA, etc. Dir, Gp Personnel, Cunard Steamship Co. Ltd, 1969-71. FRSocMed. Internat. Aerospace Med. Assoc. Boothby Award (res. into health of pilots), 1971. JP Inner London, 1970-73. OStJ 1959. *Publications:* Aviation Medicine, 1948; numerous others on Aviation Medicine and allied subjects. *Recreations:* fishing, shooting, riding, sailing, flying. *Address:* The Mill House, Kintbury, Berks RG15 0UR. *T:* Kintbury 292; 99 Harley Street, W1N 1DF. *T:* 01-935 7501. *Clubs:* Athenæum, United Oxford & Cambridge University, Boodle's, Royal Air Force; Pitt (Cambridge).

BERGMAN, (Ernst) Ingmar; Swedish film producer, and Head of Royal Dramatic Theatre, Stockholm, 1963-66 (also Director from 1959); director of productions on television; *b* Uppsala, 14 July 1918; *s* of a Chaplain to the Royal Court at Stockholm; *m* 1971, Mrs Ingrid von Rosen; (eight *c* by previous marriages). *Educ:* Stockholm Univ. Producer, Royal Theatre, Stockholm, 1940-42; Producer and script-writer, Swedish Film Co., 1940-44; Theatre Director: Helsingborg, 1944-46; Gothenburg, 1946-49; Malmo, 1952-1959. Produced: Hedda Gabler, Cambridge, 1970; Show, 1971. Films (British titles) produced include: Torment, 1943; Crisis, 1945; Port of Call, 1948; Summer Interlude, 1950; Waiting Women, 1952; Summer with Monika, 1952; Sawdust and Tinsel, 1953; A Lesson in Love, 1953; Journey into Autumn, 1954; Smiles of a Summer Night, 1955; The Seventh Seal, 1956-57; Wild Strawberries, 1957; So Close to Life, 1957; The Face, 1958; The Virgin Spring, 1960 (shown Edinburgh Fest., 1960); The Devil's Eye, 1961 (shown Edinburgh Fest., 1961); Through a Glass Darkly, 1961; Winter Light, 1962; The Silence, 1963; Now About all these Women, 1964 (first film in colour); Persona, 1967; Hour of the Wolf, 1968; Shame, 1968; The Rite, 1969; The Passion, 1970; The Fâro Document, 1970; The Touch, 1971; Cries and Whispers, 1972 (NY Film Critics Best Film Award, 1972); Scenes from a Marriage, 1974 (BBC TV Series, 1975; published, 1975); Face to Face, 1976. Has gained several international awards and prizes for films; Goethe Prize, 1976. *Publication:* Four Stories, 1977.

BERGMAN, Ingmar; *see* Bergman, E. I.

BERGMAN, Ingrid; actress; *d* of Justus and Friedel Bergman; *m* 1937, Petter Lindstrom (marriage dissolved, 1950, Los Angeles; dissolution ruled not valid by a Rome court, 1960); one *d*; *m* 1950 (by proxy, Mexico), Roberto Rossellini (marriage ruled not valid by a Rome court, 1960); one *s* twin *d*; *m* 1958, (in London), Lars Schmidt. *Educ:* Lyceum for Flickor and Sch. of Royal Dramatic Theatre, Stockholm. Has played in following stage plays: Liliom, 1940; Anna Christie, 1941; Joan of Lorraine, 1947; Tea and Sympathy (Paris), 1956; Hedda Gabler (Paris), 1962; A Month in the Country, Guildford (Yvonne Arnaud), 1965, and Cambridge Theatre, London; More Stately Mansions, New York, 1967-68; Captain Brassbound's Conversion, Cambridge Theatre, 1971; The Constant Wife, Albery, 1973, and in US, 1974-75; Waters of the Moon, Chichester, 1977. *Films:* Intermezzo, 1939; Adam Had Four Sons, 1940; Rage in Heaven, 1941; Dr Jekyll and Mr Hyde, 1941; Casablanca, 1942; For Whom the Bell Tolls, 1943; Gaslight, 1944; Saratoga Trunk, 1945; Spellbound, 1945; The Bells of St Mary's, 1946; Notorious,

1946; Arch of Triumph, 1947; Joan of Arc, 1948; Under Capricorn, 1948; Stomboli, 1950; Anastasia, 1957; Elena et les Hommes; The Inn of the Sixth Happiness; Indiscreet, 1958; Goodbye Again, 1961; The Visit, 1963; The Yellow Rolls-Royce, 1964; Cactus Flower, 1970; A Walk in the Spring Rain, 1970; Murder on the Orient Express, 1974. *Opera:* Joan of Arc at the Stake, 1954. Awarded three Oscars. Has appeared on Television.

BERGNER, Elisabeth; actress; *b* Vienna, 22 Aug. 1900; naturalised British subject, 1938; *m* Dr Paul Czinner. Early stage appearances in Austria, Switzerland and Germany included performances with Wedekind in Spring Awakening, Lulu and Schloss Wetterstein; Ophelia in Hamlet, Zürich; Rosalind in As You Like It, Vienna; Katherine in The Taming of the Shrew, Munich; Julie in Miss Julie; Viola in Twelfth Night; Juliet in Romeo and Juliet; Joan in Saint Joan, 1924; Mrs Cheyney in The Last of Mrs Cheyney, Berlin, 1926; Tessa in The Constant Nymph, Berlin, 1927. First London appearance as Gemma Jones in Escape Me Never, Apollo, 1933, NY, 1935; The Boy David, His Majesty's, 1936; The Two Mrs Carrolls, NY, 1943; Duchess of Malfi, NY, 1946; The Gay Invalid, Garrick, 1951; toured Germany and Austria in Long Day's Journey Into Night, 1957; First Love, United States, 1964; The Madwoman of Chaillot, Oxford, Germany, 1957. Films include: Der Evangelimann, Ariane, Fräulein Else, Escape Me Never, Dreaming Lips, Catherine the Great, Stolen Life, As You Like It. Schiller Prize, 1963; Goldene Band, International Film Festival, Berlin, 1963 and 1965. *Recreations:* walking, music. *Address:* 42 Eaton Square, SW1.

BERIO, Luciano; composer; *b* 24 Oct. 1925; *s* of Ernesto Berio and Ada dal Fiume; *m* 1st, 1950, Cathy Berberian (marr. diss. 1964); one *d*; 2nd, 1964, Susan Oyama (marr. diss. 1971); one *s* one *d. Educ:* Liceo Classico, Oneglia; Conservatorio G. Verdi, Milan. Works include: Differences, 1958; Epifanie, 1959-63; Circles, 1960; Passaggio, 1962; Laborintus II, 1965; Sinfonia, 1968; Concerto for 2 pianos, 1972; Opera, 1969-74; Sequenzas for solo instruments; A-Ronne for eight voices, 1974-75; Coro for chorus and orchestra, 1975-76; La Ritirata Notturna di Madrid, 1975; Ritorno degli Snovidenia, 1977. *Address:* 131 Via della Mendola, Rome, Italy.

BERIOZOVA, Svetlana; Ballerina, The Royal Ballet; *b* 24 Sept. 1932; *d* of Nicolas and Maria Beriozoff (Russian); *m* 1959, Mohammed Masud Khan (marr. diss. 1974). *Educ:* New York, USA. Joined Grand Ballet de Monte Carlo, 1947; Metropolitan Ballet, 1948-49; Sadler's Wells Theatre Ballet, 1950-52; Sadler's Wells Ballet (now The Royal Ballet), 1952-. Has created leading rôles in Designs for Strings (Taras), Fanciulla delle Rose (Staff), Trumpet Concerto (Balanchine), Pastorale (Cranko), The Shadow (Cranko), Rinaldo and Armida (Ashton), The Prince of the Pagodas (Cranko), Antigone (Cranko), Baiser de la Fée (MacMillan), Diversions (MacMillan), Persephone (Ashton), Images of Love (MacMillan). Classical Rôles: Le Lac des Cygnes, The Sleeping Beauty, Giselle, Coppélia, Sylvia, Cinderella. Other rôles currently danced: Les Sylphides, The Firebird, The Lady and Fool, Checkmate, Fête Etrange, Ondine, Nutcracker. Has danced with The Royal Ballet in USA, France, Italy, Australia, S Africa, Russia, and as guest ballerina in Belgrade, Granada, Milan (La Scala), Stuttgart, Bombay, Nervi, Helsinki, Paris, Vienna, New Zealand, Zurich. Played the Princess in The Soldier's Tale (film), 1966. Has frequently appeared on television. *Relevant publications:* Svetlana Beriosova (by C. Swinson), 1956, Svetlana Beriosova (by A. H. Franks), 1958. *Recreation:* the arts. *Address:* Royal Opera House, Covent Garden, WC2. *T:* 01-240 1200.

BERISAVLJEVIĆ, Živan; Yugoslav Ambassador to the Court of St James's, since 1977; *b* 19 Sept. 1935; *s* of Rajko and Ljubica Prodanović; *m* 1963, Slobodanka Koledin; one *d. Educ:* Belgrade Univ. Held leading political functions in Youth League of Socialist Republic of Serbia, 1955-62; Editor-in-Chief, Gledista magazine, 1962-65; held scientific, cultural, educational and press positions, Central Cttee of League of Communists of Serbia, 1962-67; Sec. for Educn, Science and Culture, Serbia, 1967-71; Official of Assembly, Serbia, 1971-72; Advr to Fed. Sec., 1972-74, Asst Fed. Sec., i/c press, information and cultural affairs, 1974-77, Yugoslav Fed. Secretariat for Foreign Affairs. Mem., Comm for Information and Propaganda, Exec. Cttee of Presidency of League of Communists of Yugoslavia, 1972-77. Formerly: Mem. Council, Museum of Contemporary Art, Belgrade; Mem. Federal Cttees for Information, and for Science and Culture. *Publications:* Democratisation of Society and the League of Communists, 1967; Cultural Action, 1972; Education between the Past and Future, 1973; many articles and papers in journals and newspapers. *Recreations:* tennis, football, walking. *Address:*

Yugoslav Embassy, 5 Lexham Gardens, W8 5JJ. *T:* 01-370 6105. *Club:* Travellers'.

BERKELEY, Baroness (17th in line); *(cr* 1421; called out of abeyance, 1967); **Mary Lalle Foley-Berkeley;** *b* 9 Oct. 1905; *e d* of Col Frank Wigram Foley, CBE, DSO (*d* 1949), Royal Berks Regt, and Eva Mary Fitzhardinge, Baroness Berkeley; *S* mother, Baroness Berkeley (16th in line) (*d* 1964). *Heiress presumptive: sister* Hon. Cynthia Ella [*b* 31 Jan. 1909; *m* 1937, Brig. Ernest Adolphus Leopold Gueterbock; one *s*]. *Address:* Pickade Cottage, Great Kimble, Aylesbury, Bucks. *T:* Princes Risborough 3051.

BERKELEY, (Augustus Fitzhardinge) Maurice, CB 1975; MA; Chief Registrar of The High Court in Bankruptcy, 1966-75; Registrar of The Companies Court, 1957-75 and Clerk of the Restrictive Practices Court, 1965-75; *b* 26 Feb. 1903; *s* of late Dr Augustus Frederic Millard Berkeley and Anna Louisa Berkeley; *m* 1931, Elaine Emily, *d* of Adin Simmonds; no *c. Educ:* Aldenham Sch.; Pembroke Coll., Cambridge. Called to the Bar, Inner Temple, 1927. Served War of 1939-45, in The Welch Regiment, 1940-45; Temp. Lieut-Col; AAG, AG3d, War Office. Junior Counsel in Chancery Matters to Ministry of Agriculture, Fisheries and Food, The Commissioners of Crown Lands and the Forestry Commissioners, 1956-57. Bar Council, 1955-57. *Recreations:* watching cricket, travel, theatre, reading. *Address:* 3 Dr Johnson's Buildings, Inner Temple, EC4. *T:* 01-353 2448; Freshwell Cottage, Little Sampford, near Saffron Walden, Essex. *T:* Great Sampford 244. *Club:* Garrick.
See also F. G. Berkeley.

BERKELEY, Frederic George; Master of the Supreme Court (Taxing Office), since 1971; *b* 21 Dec. 1919; *s* of late Dr Augustus Frederic Millard Berkeley and Anna Louisa Berkeley; *m* 1964, Gillian Eugenie Louise Depreux; one *s* two *d* and one step *s. Educ:* Aldenham Sch.; Pembroke Coll., Cambridge (BA). Admitted Solicitor, 1948. Served War of 1939-45, Leics Regt, Normandy (wounded); Major; DADAWS Allied Land Forces SE Asia, 1945-46. Partner in Lewis & Lewis (from 1964 Penningtons and Lewis & Lewis), 1951-70. Mem. No 1 (London) Legal Aid Area Cttee (later No 14), 1954-70, Vice-Chm. 1964-70, Chm. 1970. *Recreations:* reading, travel, gardening. *Address:* Tyrells End Farm, Eversholt, Milton Keynes MK17 9DS. *T:* Ridgmont 308.
See also A. F. M. Berkeley.

BERKELEY, Humphry John; writer and broadcaster; *b* 21 Feb. 1926; *s* of late Reginald Berkeley, author and playwright, former MP (L), and of Mrs Hildegarde Tinne. *Educ:* Dragon Sch., Oxford; Malvern; Pembroke Coll., Cambridge (Exhibitioner); BA 1947, MA 1963; Pres., Cambridge Union, 1948; Chm., Cambridge Univ. Conservative Assoc., 1948. Held various appointments at Conservative Political Centre, 1949-56; Dir Gen., UK Council of European Movement, 1956-57; Chairman of Coningsby Club, 1952-55; Hon. Sec., Carlton Club Political Cttee, 1954-59. MP (C) Lancaster, 1959-66; Member, British Parly Delegn to Council of Europe and Council of WEU, 1963-66; personal representative of Colonial Secretary in constitutional talks in Seychelles, 1965; Hon. Sec., Cons. Parly West Africa Cttee, 1959-64; Hon. Sec., UN Parly Gp, 1962-64; joined Labour Party July 1970; contested (Lab) N Fylde, Oct. 1974. Director: Landmark International Hotels Ltd; Caspair Ltd; City and Beach Hotels (Mauritius) Ltd; Island Developments Ltd. Mem., Pierre Philip's Cttee on Overseas Volunteers, 1966-70; Chm., UNA of GB and NI, 1966-70; Vice-Chm, Nat. Coordinating Cttee for 25th Anniversary of UN, 1970; Mem., UK Nat. Commn for Unesco, 1966-71. Hon. Treasurer, Howard League for Penal Reform, 1965-71; Mem. Governing Body, Inst. for Study of Internat. Relations, Sussex Univ., 1969-. *Publications:* The Power of the Prime Minister, 1968; Crossing the Floor, 1972; The Life and Death of Rochester Sneath, 1974; The Odyssey of Enoch: a political memoir, 1977. *Address:* 3 Pages Yard, Church Street, Chiswick, W4 2PA. *Club:* Savile.

BERKELEY, Sir Lennox (Randal), Kt 1974; CBE 1957; composer; President, Performing Right Society, since 1975; *b* 12 May 1903; *o s* of Capt. Hastings George Fitzhardinge Berkeley, RN, and Aline Carla (*née* Harris); *m* 1946, Elizabeth Freda Bernstein; three *s. Educ:* Gresham's Sch., Holt; Merton Coll., Oxford. BA Oxford, 1926; Hon. DMus Oxford, 1970. Studied music in Paris under Nadia Boulanger, 1927-32. Returned to London, 1935; on staff of BBC Music Dept, 1942-45. Composition Professor, Royal Acad. of Music, 1946-68. Hon. Prof. of Music, Keele Univ., 1976-. Pres., Composers' Guild of Great Britain, 1975-. Hon. Fellow, Merton Coll., Oxford, 1974. Awarded Collard Fellowship in Music, 1946; Cobbett Medal 1962; Ordre de Mérite Culturel, Monaco, 1967; KSG 1973.

Composer of the Year, Composer's Guild of GB, 1973. *Compositions include: orchestra:* Divertimento; Serenade; three symphonies; Concertos for Piano and Orch.; 2 Pianos and Orch.; Flute and Orch.; Violin and Chamber Orch.; Five Pieces for Violin and Orchestra; Winter's Tale Suite; Partita for Chamber Orchestra; Guitar Concerto, 1974. *chamber music:* String Trio; Trio for Horn, Violin and String Quartet; Sextet for Clarinet, Horn and String Quartet; Oboe Quartet; Duo for 'cello and piano; Dialogue for 'cello and chamber orchestra; Quintet for Wind and Piano; *voice and orchestra:* Three Poems of St Teresa for Contralto and Strings; Stabat Mater for Soloists and Chamber Orchestra; Four Ronsard Sonnets for Tenor and Orchestra; Batter My Heart Three-person'd God (Cantata); Signs in the dark (poems by Laurie Lee) for choir and strings; Magnificat for choir and orchestra; Hymn for chorus and organ; The Hill of the Graces for unaccompanied choir; *piano:* Sonata; Six Preludes; Three Mazurkas; *opera:* Nelson (3 Acts); A Dinner Engagement (1 Act); Ruth (1 Act); Castaway (1 Act). *Recreation:* reading. *Address:* 8 Warwick Avenue, W2. *T:* 01-262 3922.

BERKELEY, Maurice; *see* Berkeley, A. F. M.

BERKELEY MILNE, Alexander; *see* Milne.

BERKHOUWER, Cornelis; Chevalier, Order of the Netherlands Lion 1966; Vice-President of the European Parliament, since 1975; *b* Alkmaar, Holland, 19 March 1919; *m* 1966, Michelle Martel; one *s. Educ:* Amsterdam Univ. Dr of Law 1946. Barrister, High Court of Amsterdam, 1942. Pres., European Parliament, 1973-75. Grand Cross of Merit (Italy), 1974. *Publications:* Conversion of Void Legal Acts (thesis), 1946; Medical Responsibilities, 1951; Civil Responsibility for Illegal Publicity, 1954. *Recreations:* tennis, ancient literature, swimming, bibliothèque, vinothèque, chess. *Address:* 56 Stationsweg, Heiloo, Netherlands. *Clubs:* National Liberal; de Witte (The Hague); Cercle Gaulois (Brussels).

BERKIN, John Phillip, CBE 1952; Director: "Shell" Transport & Trading Co. 1957-76; Shell Petroleum Co., 1953-76; Grindlays Bank, 1966-76; Grindlays Holdings Ltd, 1969-76; retired 1976; *b* 23 Oct. 1905; *s* of John Berkin and Leila Louise (*née* Doolittle); *m* 1st, 1934, Elizabeth Mary Joseph Arnold (*d* 1967); one *s*; 2nd, 1968, Mrs Lilian Ivy Beatrice Chisholm, *widow* of Lieut W. B. Chisholm, RNVR. Educ: Taunton Sch.; Sidney Sussex Coll., Cambridge. BA 1927, MA 1956. Joined Royal Dutch/Shell Group of Cos, 1927 and served in Far East, US and London; a Man. Dir, Royal Dutch/Shell Group, 1957-66; Dir, Shell Petroleum NV (formerly Bataafse Petroleum Maatschappij), 1957-68. Part-time Mem., IRC, 1966-68. *Address:* Oriel, Fairfield Road, Southdown, Shawford, Winchester, Hants. *T:* Twyford (Hants) 712331. *Club:* Junior Carlton.

BERKSHIRE, Archdeacon of; *see* Brown, Ven. J. E.

BERLIN, Irving; author and composer; *b* Russia, 11 May 1888; *s* of Moses Baline and Leah Lipkin; brought to USA, 1893; *m* 1st, 1913, Dorothy Goetz (*d* 1913); 2nd, 1926, Ellin, *d* of Clarence H. Mackay, NY; three *d. Educ:* public schools, NY City, for two years only. First song published, Marie from Sunny Italy, 1907; first complete Broadway score, Watch Your Step, 1914; Music Box Revue, 1921-24; Ziegfeld Follies, 1919, 1920, 1927. Pres. Irving Berlin Music Corp. Served as Sergt Infantry at Camp Upton, LI. Hon. Degrees, Bucknell, Temple, and Fordham Univs; Medal of Merit for This Is The Army; awarded a special Gold Medal by Congress for God Bless America; Legion of Honour, France. Has composed about 800 songs, including: Alexander's Ragtime Band; Oh, How I Hate To Get Up In the Morning; When I Lost You; A Pretty Girl Is Like A Melody; Say It With Music; Always; Remember; Blue Skies; Easter Parade; Heat Wave; Isn't This A Lovely Day; Top Hat, White Tie and Tails; I've Got My Love To Keep Me Warm; White Christmas; This Is The Army, Mr Jones; Anything You Can Do; Doin' What Comes Natur'lly; The Girl That I Marry; There's No Business Like Show Business. Musicals (several of which have been filmed) include: As Thousands Cheer; Face The Music; Louisiana Purchase; Annie Get Your Gun; Call Me Madam. US Medal of Freedom, 1977. *Address:* Irving Berlin Music Corp., 1290 Avenue of the Americas, New York City, USA. *Clubs:* Lambs, Friars.

BERLIN, Sir Isaiah, OM 1971; Kt 1957; CBE 1946; FBA 1957; MA; President of the British Academy, since 1974; Fellow of All Souls College, Oxford; *b* 6 June 1909; *s* of Mendel and Marie Berlin; *m* 1956, Aline, *d* of Pierre de Gunzbourg. *Educ:* St Paul's Sch.; Corpus Christi Coll., Oxford. Lectr in Philosophy, New Coll., Oxford, 1932; Fellow: All Souls, 1932-38; New Coll., 1938-50; war service with Min. of Information, in New York,

1941-42, at HM Embassy in Washington, 1942-46, HM Embassy, Moscow, Sept. 1945-Jan. 1946; Fellow, All Souls Coll., Oxford, 1950-66, 1975-; Chichele Prof. of Social and Pol Theory, Oxford Univ., 1957-67; Pres., Wolfson Coll., Oxford 1966-Mar. 1975, Hon. Fellow, 1975. Mem. Cttee of Awards: Commonwealth (Harkness) Fellowships, 1960-64; Kennedy Scholarships, 1967-. Vice-Pres., British Academy, 1959-61; Pres. Aristotelian Soc., 1963-64. Mem., Academic Adv. Cttee., Univ. of Sussex, 1963-66. Visiting Professor: Harvard Univ., 1949, 1951, 1953, 1962; Bryn Mawr Coll., 1952; Chicago Univ., 1955; Princeton Univ., 1965; ANU, Canberra, 1975; Prof. of Humanities, City Univ. of NY, 1966-71. Lectures: Northcliffe, UCL, 1953; Mellon, Nat. Gall. of Art, Washington, DC, 1965; Danz, Washington Univ., 1971. Foreign Member: American Academy of Arts and Sciences; American Academy-Institute of Arts and Letters; American Philosophical Soc. Member, Board of Directors, Royal Opera House, Covent Garden, 1954-65, 1974-; a Trustee, Nat. Gall., 1975-. Governor, Univ. of Jerusalem; Pres., British Friends of the Univ. of Jerusalem. Hon. doctorates of the following universities: Hull, 1965; Glasgow, 1967; E Anglia, 1967; Brandeis (USA), 1967; Columbia, 1968; Cambridge, 1970; London, 1971; Jerusalem, 1971; Liverpool, 1972; Tel Aviv, 1973. Hon. Fellow, Corpus Christi Coll., Oxford. *Publications:* Karl Marx, 1939, 1963; Translation of First Love by I. S. Turgenev, 1950; The Hedgehog and the Fox, 1953; Historical Inevitability, 1954; The Age of Enlightenment, 1956; Moses Hess, 1958; Two Concepts of Liberty, 1959; Mr Churchill in 1940, 1964; Four Essays on Liberty, 1969; Fathers and Children, 1972; Vico and Herder, 1976. *Address:* All Souls College, Oxford. *Clubs:* Athenæum, Brooks's; Century (New York).

BERMAN, Franklin Delow; Legal Counsellor, HM Diplomatic Service, since 1974; *b* 23 Dec. 1939; *s* of Joshua Zelic Berman and Gertrude (*née* Levin); *m* 1964, Christine Mary Lawler; two *s* three *d*. *Educ:* Rondebosch Boys' High Sch., Cape Town; Univ. of Cape Town; Wadham and Nuffield Colls, Oxford. BA, BSc Cape Town; MA Oxford. Rhodes Scholar, 1961; called to Bar (Middle Temple), 1966. Asst Legal Adviser, FO, 1965; Legal Adviser: British Military Govt, Berlin, 1971; British Embassy, Bonn, 1972. *Recreations:* walking, reading, music. *Address:* 12 Ulundi Road, SE3. *T:* 01-858 4397.

BERMAN, Lawrence Sam, CB 1975; Director of Statistics, Departments of Industry, Trade, and Prices and Consumer Protection, since 1974; *b* 15 May 1928; *yr s* of Jack and Violet Berman; *m* 1954, Kathleen D. Lewis; one *s* one *d*. *Educ:* St Clement Danes Grammar Sch.; London Sch. of Economics. BSc (Econ) 1st cl. hons 1947; MSc (Econ) 1950. Res. Asst, LSE, 1947; Nuffield Coll., Oxford, 1948; Econ. Commn for Europe, 1949; Central Statistical Office: Asst Statistician 1952; Statistician 1955; Chief Statistician 1964; Asst Dir 1968; Dir of Stats, DTI later Dept of Industry, 1972-. Editor, National Income Blue Book, 1954-60; Mem. Council, Royal Statistical Soc., 1970-74 (Vice-Pres., 1973-74). *Publications:* articles and papers in Jl of Royal Statistical Soc., Economica, Economic Trends, Statistical News, etc. *Recreations:* travel, theatre, gardening and other do-it-yourself activities. *Address:* 10 Carlton Close, Edgware, Mddx. *T:* 01-958 6938.

BERMUDA, Bishop of, since 1977; **Rt. Rev. Roger Alban Marson Genders, (Father Anselm, CR);** *b* 15 Aug. 1919; *yr s* of John Boulton Genders and Florence Alice (*née* Thomas). *Educ:* King Edward VI School, Birmingham; Brasenose College, Oxford (Sen. Scholar 1938, BA Lit. Hum. 1946, MA 1946). Served War, Lieut RNVR, 1940-46. Joined Community of the Resurrection, Mirfield, 1948; professed, 1952; ordained, 1952; Tutor, College of the Resurrection, 1952-55; Vice-Principal 1955, and Principal 1957-65, Codrington Coll., Barbados; Exam. Chaplain to Bishop of Barbados, 1957-65; Treasurer of St Augustine's Mission, Rhodesia, 1966-75; Archdeacon of Manicaland, 1970-75; Asst Bursar, Community of the Resurrection, Mirfield, 1975-77. *Publications:* contribs to Theology. *Recreation:* sailing. *Address:* Bishop's Lodge, Box 769, Hamilton, Bermuda. *Club:* Royal Bermuda Yacht.

BERNACCHI, Michael Louis, CMG 1955; OBE 1952; *b* 5 May 1911; *s* of late Louis Charles Bernacchi, Physicist and Antarctic explorer, and late Winifred Edith Harris; *m* 1943, Elaine Chapman; one *s* one *d*. *Educ:* RN Colls Dartmouth and Greenwich; Magdalene Coll., Cambridge. Royal Navy, 1925-34; entered Colonial Service as Cadet, Fiji, 1936; District Commissioner, 1937; acting ADC to Governor of Fiji, 1939; served Royal Navy, 1940-44; Lieut Comdr RN (retd); transferred Malayan Civil Service, 1944; special duty, N Borneo, 1944; Military Administration N Borneo (Col), 1945-46; acting Chief Sec., N Borneo, 1946, Malaya, 1947-52; Class Ic Malayan Civil Service, 1951; (Perak Meritorious Service Medal, 1951);

Resident Commissioner, Gilbert and Ellice Islands Colony, 1952-61, retd 1962. *Recreation:* swimming. *Address:* 61 Leinster Road, Merivale, Christchurch 1, New Zealand. *Clubs:* Athenæum; Christchurch (NZ).

BERNARD, family name of **Earl of Bandon.**

BERNARD, Sir Dallas (Edmund), 2nd Bt *cr* 1954; Director, Morgan Grenfell Holdings Ltd, since 1972; *b* 14 Dec. 1926; *o s* of Sir Dallas Gerald Mercer Bernard, 1st Bt, and of Betty, *e d* of late Sir Charles Addis, KCMG; *S* father, 1975; *m* 1959, Sheila Mary, *d* of Arthur Gordon Robey, Hadley Highstone, Herts; three *d*. *Educ:* Eton Coll.; Corpus Christi Coll., Oxford (MA). FCIS. Director: Morgan Grenfell (Holdings) Ltd; Morgan Grenfell & Co. Ltd; Dominion Securities Ltd, Toronto; Dreyfus Intercontinental Investment Fund NV. Mem. Monopolies and Mergers Commn, 1973-. *Heir:* none. *Address:* 36 Marryat Road, Wimbledon, SW19 5BD. *T:* 01-946 5887. *Clubs:* Brooks's; Victoria (Jersey).

BERNARD, Francis Georgius; Chartered Accountant, since 1931; Publishing Consultant, since 1974; *b* 20 Jan. 1908; *m* 1st, 1934, Muriel Florence Bealer; two *s* one *d*; 2nd, 1954, Eileen Theresa Richley; one *s* one *d*. *Educ:* St Edmund's Coll., Ware. Served War, RAPC (Lt-Col), 1939-46. Kelly-Iliffe Holdings: Dir, 1954; Asst Man. Dir, 1961. Associated Iliffe Press Ltd, Jt Man. Dir, Kelly Iliffe Holdings, 1963, and dir of many other cos in UK and abroad; Financial Dir, IPC Business Press Ltd, 1966; Dir, two publishing cos abroad, 1971; Dep. Chm., Price Commission, 1973. *Recreations:* gardening, bee-keeping, photography. *Address:* 52 Manor Road South, Esher, Surrey. *T:* 01-398 1929.

BERNARD, Joan Constance, MA, BD; FKC; Principal of Trevelyan College, University of Durham, and Honorary Lecturer in Theology, since 1966; *b* 6 April 1918; *d* of late Adm. Vivian Henry Gerald Bernard, CB, and Eileen Mary Bernard. *Educ:* Ascham Sch., Sydney, NSW; St Anne's Coll., Oxford Univ. (BA Lit. Hum. 1940, MA 1943); King's Coll., London (BD 1961). War Service, ATS, 1940-46; Regtl duties, AA Comd, 1940-42; SO HQ AA Comd, 1942-44; SO Air Def. Div., SHAEF, 1944-45 (mentioned in despatches 1945); Special Projectile Ops Gp, July-Nov. 1945; SO HQ Northern Comd, 1945-46. Dep. Admin. Officer, NCB, 1946-50; Asst Sec., Educn, Music and Drama, NFWI, 1950-57; full-time student, 1957-61; Warden, Canterbury Hall, Univ. of London, and part-time Lectr, Dept of Theol., KCL, 1962-65; FKC 1976. Mem., Candidates' Cttee, ACCM, 1972-. *Recreations:* music (assisted John Tobin in Handel research for many years); mountaineering, photography. *Address:* Trevelyan College, Elvet Hill Road, Durham DH1 3LN. *T:* Durham 61133.

BERNARD, Madame R. K.; *see* Delysia, A.

BERNERS, Baroness (15th in line) *cr* 1455; **Vera Ruby Williams;** *b* 25 Dec. 1901; *d* of late Hon. Rupert Tyrwhitt, Major RA (5th *s* of Emma Harriet, Baroness Berners) and of Louise I. F. (*née* Wells); *S* cousin, 1950; *m* 1927, Harold Williams, Colonial Civil Service; two *d*. *Educ:* Ladies' Coll., Eastbourne; St Agnes' Sch., East Grinstead. Co-heiresses of [Hon. Mrs Michael Kirkham, *b* (Pamela Vivian Williams) 30 Sept. 1929; *m* 1952; two *s* one *d*]; and *d* [Hon. Mrs Kelvin Pollock, *b* (Rosemary Tyrwhitt Williams) 20 July 1931; *m* 1959; two *s*]. *Address:* Ashwellthorpe, Charlton Lane, Cheltenham, Glos. *T:* Cheltenham 59595.

BERNEY, Sir Julian (Reedham Stuart), 11th Bt *cr* 1620; *b* 26 Sept. 1952; *s* of Lieut John Reedham Erskine Berney (killed on active service in Korea, 1952), Royal Norfolk Regt, and of Hon. Jean Davina (who *m* 2nd, P. W. Jesson), *d* of 1st Viscount Stuart of Findhorn, PC, CH, MVO, MC; *S* grandfather, 1975; *m* 1976, Sheena Mary, *yr d* of Ralph Day and Ann Gordon Day. *Educ:* Wellington Coll.; North-East London Polytechnic. *Recreation:* sailing. *Heir: cousin* Hugh Barton Berney, MB, ChB, New Zealand, *b* 11 Jan. 1902. *Address:* 17 Shrublands Close, Chelmsford, Essex. *T:* Chelmsford 84359. *Club:* Royal Ocean Racing.

BERNSTEIN, family name of **Baron Bernstein.**

BERNSTEIN, Baron *cr* 1969 (Life Peer), of Leigh; **Sidney Lewis Bernstein,** LLD; Chairman, Granada Group Ltd (Granada Television, Granada Publishing, Granada Theatres, Granada TV Rental, Granada Motorway Services, Novello & Co.); *b* 30 Jan. 1899; *s* of Alexander and Jane Bernstein; *m* Sandra, *d* of Charles and Charlotte Malone, Toronto; one *s* two *d*. A founder, Film Society, 1924. Mem., Mddx CC, 1925-31. Films Adviser, Min. of Inf., 1940-45; Liaison, British Embassy, Washington,

1942; Chief Film Section, AFHQ N Africa, 1942-43; Chief, Film Section, SHAEF, 1943-45. Lectr on Film and Internat. Affairs, New York Univ. and Yale. Mem., Resources for Learning Cons. Cttee, Nuffield Foundn, 1965-72. Governor, Sevenoaks Sch., 1964-74. *Address:* 36 Golden Square, W1R 4AH; Coppings Farm, Leigh, Tonbridge, Kent TN11 8PN. *Club:* Garrick.

BERNSTEIN, Alexander; Joint Deputy Chairman, Granada Group Ltd, since 1974; *b* 15 March 1936; *s* of Cecil Bernstein, *qv*; *m* 1962, Vanessa Anne, *d* of Alwyn and Winifred Mills; one *s* one *d. Educ:* Stowe Sch.; St John's Coll., Cambridge. Chm., Granada TV Rental Ltd, 1977- (Man. Dir, 1964-68); Director: Granada TV Ltd, 1970- (Jt Man. Dir, 1971-75; Dep. Chm., 1975-); Barranquilla Investments, 1975-; Waddington Galleries, 1966-; Trustee: Civic Trust for the North-West; Granada Foundn. Mem. Ct, Univ. of Salford. *Recreations:* modern art, ski-ing. *Address:* 22 Kingston House, Princes Gate, SW7 1LM.

BERNSTEIN, Prof. Basil; Professor in Sociology of Education, since 1967, Head of Sociological Research Unit, since 1963, University of London; *b* 1 Nov. 1924; *s* of Percival and Julia Bernstein; *m* 1955, Marion Black; two *s. Educ:* LSE (BScEcon); UCL (PhD). Teacher, City Day Coll., Shoreditch, 1954-60; Hon. Research Asst, UCL, 1960-62; Sen. Lectr, Sociology of Educn, Univ. of London Inst. of Educn, 1963; Reader in Sociology of Educn, 1965. Hon. DLitt Leicester, 1974. *Publications:* Class Codes and Control, Vol. I 1971 (2nd edn 1974), Vol. II 1973, Vol. III 1975; (with W. Brandis) Selection and Control, 1974. *Recreations:* theatre, painting, conversation, etc. *Address:* 90 Farquhar Road, Dulwich, SE19 1LT. *T:* 01-670 6411.

BERNSTEIN, Cecil (George); Executive Director, Granada Group Ltd; Chairman: Granada International Productions Ltd; Granada Television, 1971-74; *b* 28 July 1904; *s* of Alexander and Jane Bernstein; *m* 1929, Myra Ella, *d* of Rachel and Lesser Lesser; one *s* one *d. Educ:* Haberdashers' Aske's. Member, Cinematograph Films Council, 1948-; Pres., Cinema and Television Benevolent Fund. *Address:* 7 Grosvenor Square, W1; Five Trees, Craigweil-on-Sea, Sussex.
See also A. Bernstein.

BERNSTEIN, Leonard; conductor, composer, pianist, lecturer; *b* Lawrence, Mass, 25 Aug. 1918; *s* of Samuel J. and Jennie (Resnick) Bernstein; *m* 1951, Felicia Montealegre Cohn; one *s* two *d. Educ:* Boston Latin Sch.; Harvard Univ.; Curtis Inst. of Music. Asst to Koussevitzky, Berkshire Music Center, 1942, Head of Conducting Dept, 1951-56; Asst Conductor, NY Philharmonic Orch., 1943-44; Conductor, NYC Symphony, 1945-48; Musical Adviser, Israel Philharmonic Orch., 1948-49; Prof. of Music, Brandeis Univ., 1951-56; Charles Eliot Norton Prof. of Poetry, Harvard Univ., 1973-74; co-conductor (with Dimitri Mitropoulos), NY Philharmonic Orch., 1957-58; Music Dir, NY Philharmonic Orch., 1958-69, now Laureate Conductor; Pres., English Bach Festival, 1977-. Has conducted all major orchestras of US and Europe in annual tours, 1944-; has toured N and S America, Europe, Near East, USSR and Japan with NY Philharmonic Orch. Holds decorations from: France, Italy, Finland, Chile and Austria. *Works include:* Clarinet Sonata, 1942; Symphony, No 1, Jeremiah, 1942; Song cycle (I Hate Music), 1943; Seven Anniversaries for Piano, 1943; Fancy Free, 1944; Hashkivenu, 1945; Facsimile, 1946; Five Pieces for Brass Instruments, 1947; Four Anniversaries for Piano, 1948; Symphony, No 2, The Age of Anxiety, 1949; Song Cycle (La Bonne Cuisine), 1949; songs, Afterthought and Silhouette, 1951; Trouble in Tahiti (one-act opera), 1952; Serenade (after Plato's Symposium) for violin solo, with string orch. and percussion, 1954; Symphony, No 3, Kaddish, 1963; Five Anniversaries for Piano, 1964; Chichester Psalms (a choral work with orchestra), 1965; Mass, a theatre piece for singers, players and dancers, 1971; Score for ballet, Dybbuk, 1974; Suite No 1 from Dybbuk, 1975; Seven Dances from Dybbuk, 1975; Scores for Broadway musicals including: On the Town, 1944, Wonderful Town, 1953, Candide, 1956, West Side Story, 1957; Score for Film, On the Waterfront, 1954. Has received Hon. Degrees from universities and colleges. *Publications:* The Joy of Music, 1959; Leonard Bernstein's Young People's Concerts for Reading and Listening, 1962; The Infinite Variety of Music, 1966; The Unanswered Question, 1973. *Address:* 205 West 57th Street, New York, NY 10019, USA.

BERNSTEIN, Ronald Harold, DFC 1944; QC 1969; a Recorder of the Crown Court, since 1974; *b* 18 Aug. 1918; *s* of late Mark and Fanny Bernstein; *m* 1955, Judy, *d* of David Levi, MS, and Vera Levi; three *s* one *d. Educ:* Swansea Grammar Sch.; Balliol Coll., Oxford. BA (Jurisprudence) 1939. Served in RA, 1939-46, and in 654 Air OP Sqdn, RAF, 1942-46. Commanded 661 Air OP Sqdn, RAuxAF, 1954-56. Called to the Bar, Middle Temple,

1948, Bencher, 1975. Mem., Gen. Council of the Bar, 1965-69; Mem., Law Commn Working Party on the Law of Landlord and Tenant, 1966-. Mem., Highgate Soc. (which he founded, 1966). *Publications:* (jointly) The Restrictive Trade Practices Act, 1956; (Ed. jointly) Foa, Landlord and Tenant, 8th edn, 1957. *Address:* (professional) 11 King's Bench Walk, Temple, EC4. *T:* 01-353 2484; *T:* (home) 01-340 9933. *Club:* Athenæum.

BERRIDGE, (Donald) Roy; Chairman, South of Scotland Electricity Board, since 1977 (Deputy Chairman, 1974-77); *b* 24 March 1922; *s* of Alfred Leonard Berridge and Pattie Annie Elizabeth (*née* Holloway); *m* 1945, Marie (*née* Kinder); one *d. Educ:* King's Sch., Peterborough; Leicester Coll. of Art and Technology. CEng, FIMechE. Works and Develt Dept, Taylor, Taylor & Hobson Ltd, Leicester, 1940; Project Engr, James Gordon & Co., 1946; Engrg Asst, British Electricity Authority, 1948; seconded to AERE, Harwell, 1952; Reactor Design Engr, CEGB, 1962; Chief Generation Design Engr, 1964-70; Dir-Gen., Gen. Develt Constr. Div., CEGB, 1970-72; Dir of Engrg, SSEB, 1972-74. Mem., N of Scotland Hydro-Electric Bd, 1977-. *Recreations:* golf, music. *Address:* Whinfell, Broom Road, Newton Mearns, Glasgow G77 5DN. *T:* 041-639 1091. *Club:* Royal Automobile.

BERRILL, Sir Kenneth, KCB 1971; Head of the Central Policy Review Staff, since 1974; *b* 28 Aug. 1920; *m* 1950, June Phillips (marr. diss.); one *s* one *d*; *m* 1977, Jane Marris. *Educ:* London Sch. of Economics; Trinity Coll., Cambridge. BSc London; MA Cantab, 1949. Served War, 1939-45, REME. Economic Adviser to Turkey, Guyana, Cameroons, OECD, and World Bank. Univ. Lectr in Economics, Cambridge, 1949-69; Rockefeller Fellowship Stanford and Harvard Univs, 1951-52; Fellow and Bursar, St Catharine's Coll., Cambridge, 1949-62, Hon. Fellow, 1974; Prof., MIT, 1962; Fellow and First Bursar, King's Coll., Cambridge, 1962-69, Hon. Fellow, 1973; HM Treasury Special Adviser, 1967-69; Chm., UGC, 1969-73; Council for Scientific Policy, 1969-72; Adv. Bd for Research Councils, 1972-77; Head of Govt Econ. Service and Chief Economic Advr, HM Treasury, 1973-74. Member: Brit. Nat. Commn for UNESCO, 1967-70; Inter-Univ. Council, 1969-73; UGC, Univ. of S Pacific, 1972-; Council, Royal Economic Soc., 1972-; Adv. Bd, Royal Coll. of Defence Studies, 1974-. Governor: Administrative Staff Coll., Henley, 1969-. Overseas Develt Inst., 1969-73. Cambridge City Cllr, 1963-67. Chm., General Funds Investment Trust, 1972. Director: Investing in Success Investment Trust, 1965-67; Ionian Bank, 1969-73; Universities' Superannuation Scheme, 1974-. Hon. Fellow: LSE, 1970; Chelsea Coll., London, 1973. Hon. LLD: Cambridge, 1974; Bath 1974; East Anglia 1975; Leicester 1975; DUniv Open, 1974; Hon. DTech Loughborough, 1974; Hon DSc Aston, 1974. *Recreation:* ski-ing. *Address:* Cabinet Office, 70 Whitehall, SW1A 2AS. *T:* 01-233 7765. *Clubs:* Climbers (Hon. Mem.); Himalayan.

BERRILL, Prof. Norman John, FRS 1952; FRSC; PhD, DSc; lately Strathcona Professor of Zoology, McGill University, Montreal; *b* 28 April 1903. *Educ:* Bristol Gram. Sch., Somerset, England; Bristol Univ.; London Univ. BSc Bristol; PhD, DSc London. *Publications:* The Tunicata 1951; The Living Tide, 1951; Journey into Wonder, 1953; Sex and the Nature of Things, 1954; The Origin of Vertebrates, 1955; Man's Emerging Mind, 1955; You and the Universe, 1958; Growth, Development and Pattern, 1962; Biology in Action, 1966; Worlds Apart, 1966; Life of the Oceans, 1967; The Person in the Womb, 1968; Developmental Biology, 1971; Development, 1976. *Address:* 410 Swarthmore Avenue, Swarthmore, Pa 19081, USA.

BERRIMAN, David; Director, Guinness Peat Group Ltd and subsidiaries, since 1973; Managing Director: Guinness Mahon & Co. Ltd, since 1973; Guinness Peat (Overseas) Ltd, since 1975; Director (non-executive), Cable and Wireless Ltd, since 1975; *b* 20 May 1928; *s* of Algernon Edward Berriman, OBE and Enid Kathleen Berriman (*née* Sutcliffe); *m* 1st, 1955, Margaret Lloyd (*née* Owen) (marr. diss. 1970); two *s*; 2nd, 1971, Shirley Elizabeth (*née* Wright). *Educ:* Winchester; New Coll., Oxford (MA, Dip. Econ. and Pol. Sc.); Harvard Business Sch. PMD course, 1961. First National City Bank of New York, 1952-56; AEI Hotpoint, 1960-63; Gen. Manager, United Leasing Corporation Ltd, 1963-64; Morgan Grenfell & Co. Ltd: Manager, 1964; Dir, 1968-73. Mem. Council, MacIntyre Schools Ltd (for mentally handicapped), 1972-. *Recreations:* golf, lawn tennis, squash. *Address:* Roughwood, Bayley's Hill, Sevenoaks, Kent TN14 6HT. *T:* Sevenoaks 51122. *Clubs:* Royal Automobile, International Lawn Tennis.

BERRY, family name of **Viscount Camrose, Baron Hartwell** and **Viscount Kemsley.**

BERRY, Alan Percival; Barrister-at-Law; Director, Coventry & District Engineering Employers' Association, since 1963; *b* 1 Oct. 1926; *s* of Percy Berry and Winifred Berry; *m* 1952, Audrey Gwendolen, *d* of Douglas E. Spalton, Bramley; one *s* one *d*. *Educ:* Jesus Coll., Oxford (MA). Called to the Bar, Middle Temple, 1957. HM Factory Inspectorate, 1951-57; Sec., W of England Engrg Employers' Assoc., 1957-63. Dir, Midland Gp Trng Services Ltd, 1970-; Comr, Manpower Services Commn, 1976-. Member: Coventry Educn Cttee, 1963-; CBI Council, 1972-; Council, Warwick Univ., 1974-; W Midlands Econ. Planning Council, 1975-. Governor, Lanchester Polytechnic, 1970-. OStJ 1968. *Publication:* Worker Participation: the European experience, 1974. *Recreation:* sailing. *Address:* 50 Beverley Road, Leamington Spa, Warwicks. *T:* Leamington Spa 23262.

BERRY, Hon. Anthony George; MP (C) Enfield, Southgate, since 1974 (Southgate, 1964-74); *b* 12 Feb. 1925; *y s* of 1st Viscount Kemsley, GBE; *m* 1st, 1954, Hon. Mary Cynthia Burke Roche (from whom he obtained a divorce, 1966), *er d* of 4th Baron Fermoy; one *s* three *d*; 2nd, 1966, Sarah Anne, *d* of Raymond Clifford-Turner, *qv*; one *s* one *d*. *Educ:* Eton; Christ Church, Oxford (MA). Served as Lieut, Welsh Guards, 1943-47. Asst Editor, Sunday Times, 1952-54; Editor, Sunday Chronicle, 1954; Dir, Kemsley Newspapers, 1954-59; Managing Dir, Western Mail and Echo Ltd, 1955-59. Dep. Chm., Leopold Joseph & Sons Ltd; Dir of other companies. PPS to Rt Hon. Peter Walker, Sec. of State, for the Environment, 1970-72, for Trade and Industry, 1972-74; Vice-Chm., Cons. Transport Cttee, 1969-70, 1974-75; Opposition Whip, 1975-. Pres., Welsh Games Council, 1959-. JP Cardiff, 1961; High Sheriff, Glamorgan, 1962. CStJ. *Publication:* (jt editor) Conservative Oxford, 1949. *Address:* 98 Ebury Mews, SW1. *T:* 01-235 3801; Warbrook House, Eversley, Hants. *T:* Eversley 732174. *Clubs:* Portland, White's; Cardiff and County (Cardiff).

BERRY, Prof. Francis; Professor of English Language and Literature, Royal Holloway College, University of London, since 1970; *b* 23 March 1915; *s* of James Berry and Mary Augusta Jane Berry (*née* Ivens); *m* 1st, 1947, Nancy Melloney (*d* 1967), *d* of Cecil Newton Graham; one *s* one *d*; 2nd, 1970, Patricia, *d* of John Gordon Thomson (marr. diss. 1975). *Educ:* Hereford Cathedral Sch.; Dean Close Sch.; University Coll., Exeter. BA London (1st cl. hons); MA Exeter. Solicitor's articled clerk, 1931; University Coll., Exeter, 1937. War Service, 1939-46. University Coll., Exeter, 1946; successively Asst Lectr, Lectr, Sen. Lectr, Reader in English Literature, and Prof. of English Literature, Univ. of Sheffield, 1947-70. Visiting Lectr: Carleton Coll., Minn, USA, 1951-52; University Coll. of the West Indies, Jamaica, 1957; Lectr for British Council, in India, 1966-67. FRSL 1968. *Publications:* Gospel of Fire, 1933; Snake in the Moon, 1936; The Iron Christ, 1938; Fall of a Tower, 1942; Murdock and Other Poems, 1947; The Galloping Centaur, 1952, 2nd edn 1970; Herbert Read, 1953, 2nd edn 1961; An Anthology of Medieval Poems (ed), 1954; Poets' Grammar: time, tense and mood in poetry, 1958, 2nd edn, 1974; Morant Bay and other poems, 1961; Poetry and the Physical Voice, 1962; The Shakespeare Inset, 1965, 2nd edn 1971; Ghosts of Greenland, 1967; John Masefield: the Narrative Poet, 1968; (ed) Essays and Studies for the English Association, 1969; Thoughts on Poetic Time, 1972; I Tell of Greenland (novel), 1977; Contributor: Essays in Criticism; BBC Radio Three, etc. *Recreations:* devising outdoor games, walking, watching cricket. *Address:* Department of English, Royal Holloway College, Englefield Green, Surrey TW20 0EX. *T:* 01-389 4455.

BERRY, Prof. Harry, BSc London; FPS; FRIC; Dip. Bact. London; ACT Birmingham; retired; Dean, School of Pharmacy, University of London, 1937-56; Professor of Pharmaceutics, 1944-56; Professor Emeritus, 1956; *b* 6 Oct. 1890; *s* of late William Berry and Lois Robinson Blood; *m* 1918, Agnes May, *d* of late Robert Boardman; two *s* one *d*. *Educ:* Nantwich and Acton Grammar Sch. Served European War, 1914-19, Royal Fusiliers, RE, RGA (Lieut). Lecturer in Pharmacy, Robert Gordon Colls, Aberdeen, 1919; Head, Dept of Pharmacy, Tech. Coll., Birmingham, 1919-33; Vice-Dean, 1933, Dean, 1937, College of the Pharmaceutical Soc.; Reader in Pharmaceutics, University of London, 1933. Hon. Fellow, School of Pharmacy, Univ. of London, 1956; Mem. Royal Free Hosp. Sch. of Medicine; Hon. Assoc., Coll. of Technology, Birmingham, 1956; Hon. Mem. Guild of Public Pharmacists 1965. Mem. of the British Pharmacopoeia Commission. Examiner for the Universities of London, Glasgow, Manchester, Wales, and the Pharmaceutical Soc.; Member: British Pharmaceutical Codex Revision Cttee; Central Health Services Council Standing Pharmaceutical Advisory Cttee, and Jt Sub-Cttee of Ministry of Health on Definition of Drugs; Cttee of Management of University of London Inst. of Educ.; Chm. Brit. Pharm. Conf.,

1951. *Publications:* (jt) Whitla's Pharmacy, Materia Medica and Therapeutics, 12th edn, 1933; (jt) Penicillin, Fleming, 1st and 2nd edn, 1949; original contributions to Journal of Pharmacy and Pharmacol., Lancet. *Address:* 3 The Lawns, Hoo Gardens, Willingdon, Eastbourne. *T:* Eastbourne 52537.

BERRY, Sir (Henry) Vaughan, Kt 1949; *b* 28 March 1891; *s* of late John Henry Berry; *m* 1st, 1921, Dorothy Loveday (*d* 1959), *d* of late Charles Baldwin, Bath, Somerset; (two *s* decd); 2nd, 1960, Mrs Joan Ogilvie Kirke, *d* of Percy Lachlan, Wadhurst, Sussex. *Educ:* City of London Sch.; Caius Coll., Cambridge. Somerset Light Infantry and Intelligence Corps, 1914-18; on staff of Inter-Allied Rhineland High Commission, 1919-25; Mem. Union Discount Company of London Ltd, 1925-45; Chm. Southern Region Manpower Board, 1941-44; Mem. Capital Issues Cttee, 1946; Regional Commissioner Hamburg, CCG, 1946-49; British delegate to the Internat. Authority for the Ruhr, 1949-50; Full-time Mem., Iron and Steel Corporation of Great Britain, 1950-53. Hon. Senator, University of Hamburg. *Address:* Dutch House, College Road, Bath, Avon. *T:* Bath 314879.

BERRY, Prof. Jack; Professor, Department of Linguistics, since 1964, and Director, Program of Oriental and African Languages, since 1973, Northwestern University, Evanston, Ill, USA; *b* 13 Dec. 1918; *s* of H. and N. Berry; *m* 1942, Winifred Mary; one *s*. *Educ:* Univ. of Leeds (BA); Univ. of London (PhD). Formerly Reader in West African Languages and subsequently Professor of West African Languages, Oct. 1960-Sept. 1963, at the Sch. of Oriental and African Studies; Prof. of West African Languages at Michigan State Univ., USA, 1963-64. Editor, Journal of African Languages, 1962-64. *Address:* Northwestern University, Evanston, Ill 60201, USA.

BERRY, John, (Cantab), CBE 1968; MA (Cantab) PhD (St Andrews); FRSE 1936; DL; Consultant on Water Impoundment Biology; Conservation and Fisheries Adviser to: North of Scotland Hydro-Electric Board, since 1968; South of Scotland Electricity Board, since 1973; Chairman, Interdepartmental Salmon Research Group (UK and Ireland), since 1971; *b* Edinburgh, 5 Aug. 1907; *o s* of late William Berry, OBE, DL, Tayfield, Newport, Fife; *m* 1936, Hon. Bride Fremantle, MA (Cantab), 3rd *d* of 3rd Baron Cottesloe, CB; two *s* one *d*. *Educ:* Eton; Trinity Coll., Cambridge. BA 1929 (Zoo. Chem. Phys. Pt I and Law Pt II); MA 1933; PhD 1935; Salmon research, Fishery Bd for Scotland, 1930-31; Biological Research Station, University Coll., Southampton, Research Officer, 1932-36 and Dir, 1937-39. Press Censor for Scotland, 1940-44; Biologist and Information Officer, North of Scotland Hydro-Electric Bd, 1944-49; Dir of Nature Conservation in Scotland, 1949-67. Pres. 1954-56, Vice-Pres. 1956-60, and Mem., 1966-72, Commn on Ecology, Internat. Union for Conservation of Natural Resources; UK rep., Exec. Bd, Internat. Wildfowl Research Bureau, 1963-72. Mem. Court, Univ. of Dundee, 1970-; Vice-President: RZS Scotland, 1959-; Wildfowlers' Assoc. of GB and Ireland; Wildfowl Trust. Hon. LLD Dundee, 1970. DL Fife, 1969. *Publications:* The Status and Distribution of Wild Geese and Wild Duck in Scotland, 1939; various papers and articles on fresh-water fisheries, hydro-electric development and ornithology. *Recreations:* wild geese, photography, music. *Address:* Tayfield, Newport-on-Tay, Fife DD6 8HA. *T:* Newport-on-Tay 3118. *Club:* New (Edinburgh).

BERRY, John Hatton, CMG 1946; OBE 1943; retired; *b* 24 Sept. 1898, English; *m* 1925, Joyce Henderson; one *d*. *Educ:* Wallasey, Cheshire. Engineer; European War, Royal Naval Air Service; General Motors Export Corporation in London and Japan; Vauxhall Motors, Ltd, Luton. War of 1939-45; Canadian Government Service; Mem., Joint War Production Cttee (Canada-United States); Vice-Chm., Production Board (Canada); Motor Vehicle Controller; Dir-Gen., Automotive and Tank Production Branch of Dept of Munitions and Supply. Pres., War Assets Corporation, Canada; Chm., Crown Assets Allocation Cttee; Dir-Gen. Import Control Branch, Dept of Trade and Commerce. Dir of Manufacturing, A. V. Roe Canada Ltd, 1950-52; Gen. Manager, Canadian Arsenals Ltd, 1953-63. *Recreations:* cricket, tennis, gardening. *Address:* c/o 317 Lyndeview Drive, Whitby, Ont, Canada.

BERRY, Michael Francis; Director of Robert Fleming & Co. Ltd, Merchant Bankers, since 1937; *b* 17 Oct. 1906; *e s* of C. Seager Berry and Constance, *d* of Rev. D. C. Cochrane; *m* 1939, Prudence *d* of C. G. Atha, Haverbrack House, Milnthorpe; one *d*. *Educ:* Eton; Hertford Coll., Oxford. Entered City, 1929; served War of 1939-45, Royal Artillery. A Crown Estate Commissioner, 1956-65. High Sheriff Northants 1973. *Publications:* A History of the Puckeridge Hunt, 1950; (with C. M. Floyd) A History of the Eton College Hunt 1857-1968, 1969.

Recreations: hunting, farming. *Address:* Benefield House, near Peterborough. *T:* Benefield 219. *Club:* Boodle's.

BERRY, Lady Pamela; see Hartwell, Lady.

BERRY, Rt. Rev. Robert Edward Fraser; see Kootenay, Bishop of.

BERRY, Dr Robert Langley Page; Deputy Chairman, Alcoa of Great Britain Ltd, 1978 (Chairman, 1968-77); Director, National Anti-Waste Programme, since 1976; *b* 22 Nov. 1918; *s*. of Wilfred Arthur and Mabel Grace Berry; *m* 1946, Eleanor Joyce (*née* Cramp); one *s* one *d*. *Educ:* Sir Thomas Rich's Sch., Gloucester; Birmingham Univ. (BSc (Hons), PhD). Served war, Royal Engrs, 1939-45. ICI Metals Div., 1951-66, Director, 1960-66; Man. Dir, Impalco, 1966-68. President: Inst. of Metals, 1973; Aluminium Fedn, 1974. *Publications:* several, in scientific jls. *Recreations:* fly-fishing, gardening. *Address:* Waterloo Cottage, Waterloo Lane, Fairford, Glos GL7 4BP. *T:* Fairford 712038. *Clubs:* Army and Navy, Naval and Military.

BERRY, Air Cdre Ronald, CBE 1965 (OBE 1946); DSO 1943; DFC 1940 and Bar, 1943; RAF retired; Director of Control Operations, Board of Trade, 1965-68; *b* 3 May 1917; *s* of W. Berry, Hull; *m* 1940, Nancy Watson, Hessle, near Hull; one *d*. *Educ:* Hull Technical Coll. VR Pilot, Brough Flying Sch., 1937-39; 603 F Sqdn, Turnhouse/Hornchurch, 1939-41 (Battle of Britain); Sqdn Ldr, and CO 81 F Sqdn, North Africa, 1942; Wing Comdr, and CO 322 F Wing, North Africa, 1942-43; Camberley Army Staff Coll., 1944; CO, RAF Acklington, 1945-46; jssc 1955; various operational appts in Fighter and Bomber Comd; V Sqdn, 1957-59; Group Capt., Air Min. and HQ Bomber Comd, 1959. *Recreations:* motoring, gardening, flying. *Address:* Aldrian, Mereview Avenue, Hornsea, N Humberside HU18 IRR.

BERRY, Sir Vaughan; see Berry, Sir H. V.

BERRYMAN, Lieut-Gen. Sir Frank Horton, KCVO 1954; CB 1944; CBE 1941; DSO 1919; Company Director since 1961; Director and Chief Executive Officer, Royal Agricultural Society, Sydney, 1954-61; *b* 11 April 1894; *s* of William Berryman; *m* 1925, Muriel Whipp, CBE; one *s* one *d*. *Educ:* Melbourne High Sch.; Sydney Univ.; RMC, Duntroon; Staff Coll., Camberley (psc); Artillery Coll., Woolwich (pac). Served European War, 1915-19 (DSO, despatches twice, wounded); served as regimental officer, battery commander in field artillery, and infantry brigade-major. Army Representative High Commissioner's Office, London, 1931; Brigade-Major 14 Infantry Brigade, Sydney, 1932-34; GSO Operations and Asst Dir Military Operations, Army HQ, Melbourne, 1934-37; GSO1 3 Aust. Div., 1938-39; War of 1939-45; GSO1, 6 Australian Div. at capture of Bardia and Tobruk in 1941 (CBE); CRA 7 Aust. Div. and Comdr Berryforce in Syrian Campaign, 1941 (despatches); Brig. Gen. Staff, 1 Aust. Corps, Aug. 1941, and served in Middle East and Java; Maj.-Gen. General Staff, 1st Australian Army, 1942; Dep. Chief of Gen. Staff, Sept. 1942; DCGS and MCGS on New Guinea Force, Dec. 1942-Oct. 1943; Admin Comd, 2 Aust. Corps, Nov. 1943; Lieut-Gen. GOC 2 Aust. Corps, Finchhaven, Huon Peninsula, New Guinea, Jan. 1944 (CB); GOC 1 Aust. Corps, April 1944; Chief of Staff, Advanced Land Force HQ, South-West Pacific Area, July 1944; served with GHQ SWPA in Hollandia, Leyte, and Manila; present on USS Missouri, Tokyo Bay, at official Japanese surrender ceremony as representative of Australian Army, 2 Sept. 1945; Chief of Staff Adv. HQ, AMF, Oct.-Dec. 1945; Chief of Staff HQ Morotai Force, Dec. 1945-March 1946; GOC Eastern Command, Australia, 1946-50, and 1952-53. Awarded Medal of Freedom with Silver Palm by US Govt 1946; Commonwealth Dir Royal Tour (1949), 1948; seconded to Prime Minister's Dept as Dir-Gen. Commonwealth Jubilee Celebrations (1951), and Dir-Gen. Royal Visit (1952), 1951-52; seconded to Prime Minister's Dept as Dir-Gen. Royal Visit (1954), 1953-54; retd list, 1954. Pres., Dr Barnados, Australia, 1966-. Col Comdt, Royal Australian Artillery, 1956-61. *Recreation:* golf. *Address:* 17 Wentworth Street, Point Piper, Sydney, NSW 2027, Australia. *Clubs:* Australian, Royal Sydney Golf (Sydney); Naval and Military (Melbourne).

BERTHOIN, Georges Paul; Médaille militaire, Croix de Guerre, Médaille de la Résistance avec Rosette, France, 1945; Executive Member of the Trilateral Commission (Japan, N America, W Europe), since 1973, Chairman, since 1975; *b* Nérac, France, 17 May 1925; *s* of Jean Berthoin and Germaine Mourgnot; *m* 1st, 1950, Ann White Whittlesey; four *d*; 2nd, 1965, Pamela Jenkins; two *s*. *Educ:* Grenoble Univ.; Ecole Sciences Politiques, Paris; Harvard Univ. Licencié ès Lettres (Philosophie), Licencié en Droit, Laureate for Economics (Grenoble). Lectr, McGill Univ.,

Montreal, 1948; Private Sec. to French Minister of Finance, 1948-50; Head of Staff of Superprefect of Alsace-Lorraine-Champagne, 1950-52. Joined High Authority of European Coal and Steel Community, and then Principal Private Sec. to its Pres. (Jean Monnet), 1952-53-55. Dep. Chief Rep. of ECSC in UK, 1956-67; Chargé d'Affaires for Commission of the European Communities (ECSC Euratom-Common Market), 1968; Principal Adviser to the Commission, and its Dep. Chief Rep. in London, 1969-70, Chief Representative, 1971-73. *Recreations:* art, theatre, walking, collecting objects. *Address:* 95 bis rue de Longchamp, 92200 Neuilly, France.

BERTHON, Vice-Adm. Stephen Ferrier; Assistant Chief of Naval Staff (Operational Requirements), since 1976; *b* 24 Aug. 1922; *s* of late Rear-Adm. C. P. Berthon, CBE and Mrs C. P. Berthon (*née* Ferrier); *m* 1948, Elizabeth Leigh-Bennett; two *s* two *d*. *Educ:* Old Malthouse, Swanage; RNC Dartmouth. Served War of 1939-45 at sea, Mediterranean, Atlantic, Russia; spec. communications, 1945-46; Flag Lieut Singapore, 1946-48; submarines, 1949-51; East Indies Flagship, 1951-52; HMS Mercury, 1952-54; Staff of Flag Officer Aircraft Carriers, 1954-56; Fleet Communications Officer Mediterranean, 1957-59; jssc 1959; Comdr HMS Mercury, 1959-61; Jt Planning Staff, 1961-64; Naval Attaché, Australia, 1964-66; Dir of Defence Policy, MoD, 1968-71; Cdre HMS Drake, 1971-73; Flag Officer Medway and Port Adm. Chatham, 1974-76. *Recreations:* hunting, riding, gardening, walking, painting. *Address:* Stert House, Devizes, Wilts. *T:* Devizes 3713. *Club:* Army and Navy.

BERTHOUD, Sir Eric Alfred, KCMG 1954 (CMG 1945); MA; retired from HM Foreign Service, 1960; *b* 10 Dec. 1900; 2nd *s* of late Alfred E. Berthoud; *m* 1927, Ruth Tilston, *d* of Sir Charles Bright, FRSE; two *s* two *d*. *Educ:* Gresham's Sch., Holt; Magdalen Coll., Oxford; MA. Demy; Hons in Natural Science. Anglo-Austrian Bank Ltd, London, 1922-26; Anglo-Iranian Oil Co. (BP) Ltd, 1926-39; served as board mem. in France, Holland and Germany. Commercial Sec. to HM Legation, Bucharest, 1939-41; Asst Sec., Min. of Fuel and Power (Petroleum Div.), 1942-44; Dir Economic Div., Allied Commission for Austria (British Element), 1944-46; Under-Sec., Petroleum Div., Min. of Fuel and Power, 1946-48; Asst Under-Sec., FO, 1948-52; HM Ambassador to Denmark, 1952-56, to Poland, 1956-60. Jt Chm., International Cttee setting up OEEC in Paris, 1948. Pres., Colchester Constituency Liberal Assoc., 1974-76. Member: Court, Essex Univ.; Council, SSEES, London Univ., 1964-76. Governor, Atlantic College. Mem., Bd of Visitors, Chelmsford Prison, 1960-75; Pres. (formerly Chm.), Katherine Low Settlement, Battersea. DL Essex, 1969-75. Knight Comdr's Cross with star, Order of Polonia Restituta, 1965. *Recreations:* country recreations. *Address:* Becketts, Nayland, Colchester, Essex. *T:* Nayland 262402. *Clubs:* Brooks's, MCC.
See also M. S. Berthoud, R. G. Pentney.

BERTHOUD, Martin Seymour; Inspector, HM Diplomatic Service, since 1977; *b* 20 Aug. 1931; *s* of Sir Eric Berthoud, *qv*; *m* 1960, Marguerite Joan Richarda Phayre; three *s* one *d*. *Educ:* Rugby Sch.; Magdalen Coll., Oxford (BA). Served with British Embassies in: Tehran, 1956-58; Manila, 1961-64; Pretoria/Cape Town, 1967-71; Tehran, 1971-73; Counsellor, Helsinki, 1974-77. *Recreations:* squash, tennis, photography. *Address:* Higham Lodge, Higham, Colchester, Essex. *T:* Higham 217. *Club:* United Oxford & Cambridge University.

BERTIE, family name of **Earl of Lindsey and Abingdon.**

BERTRAM, Anthony, MA; author and lecturer; Editor, History of Art, for Visual Publications; *b* London, 19 Nov. 1897; *s* of Ernest Bertram; *m* 1929, Barbara Randolph; two *s*. *Educ:* Douai Abbey; Pembroke Coll., Oxford. Served in Army, 1915-19 (wounded) and 1940-45 (Legion of Honour and Croix de Guerre); Art Critic to Spectator, 1922-24; to Saturday Review, 1924-27; Lectr to National Portrait Gallery, 1922-24; Stipendiary Lectr to Extramural Delegacy, Oxford, 1927-68; Ed., Design for To-day, 1934; Lectr in Fine Arts, Queen's Univ. Belfast, 1938-39; Dep.-Dir of British Council in France, 1945-46. Vis. Prof., Elmira Coll., NY, USA, 1958. *Publications:* English Portraiture in National Portrait Gallery, 1924; The Pool, 1926; Here We Ride, 1927; Life of Rubens, 1928; The Sword Falls, 1929; To the Mountains, 1929; The Man who made Gottlieb, 1930; They Came to the Castle, 1931; Three Meet, 1932; Pavements and Peaks, 1933; Men Adrift, 1935; The House, 1935; The King Sees Red, 1936; Design in Daily Life, 1937; Design, 1938; Contemporary Painting, 1939; Bright Defiler, 1940; Pleasures of Poverty, 1950; A Century of British Painting, 1951; Paul Nash, 1955; Michelangelo, 1964; 1000 Years of Drawing, 1966; Florentine Sculpture, 1969; various small monographs on artists. *Recreations:* gardening, reading. *Address:* Coates Castle, Fittleworth, Sussex. *T:* Fittleworth 213.

BERTRAM, Dr Christoph; Director, International Institute for Strategic Studies, since Oct. 1974; *b* 3 Sept. 1937; German national; *m* 1967, Renate Edith Bergemann. *Educ:* Free Univ. Berlin and Bonn Univ. (law); Institut d'Etudes Politiques, Paris (political science). Dr of Law 1967. Joined Internat. Inst. for Strategic Studies as Research Associate, 1967, Asst Dir 1969-74; Mem. Planning Staff, West German Min. of Defence, 1969-70. *Publications:* (with Alastair Buchan *et al.*) Europe's Futures—Europe's Choices, 1969; Mutual Force Reductions in Europe: the political aspects, 1972; (ed, with Johan J. Holst) New Strategic Factors in the North Atlantic, 1977. *Recreations:* clocks, sailing. *Address:* International Institute for Strategic Studies, 18 Adam Street, WC2. *T:* 01-930 3757, 01-930 1102. *Club:* Europe House.

BERTRAM, (Cicely) Kate, MA; PhD; JP; President, Lucy Cavendish College, Cambridge, since 1970 (Tutor, 1965-70); *b* 8 July 1912; *d* of late Sir Harry Ralph Ricardo, FRS; *m* 1939, Dr George Colin Lawder Bertram (Fellow and formerly Senior Tutor of St John's Coll., Cambridge); four *s*. *Educ:* Hayes Court, Kent; Newnham Coll., Cambridge. MA, PhD (Cantab), 1940. Jarrow Research Studentship, Girton Coll., Cambridge, 1937-40. Mem. Colonial Office Nutrition Survey, in Nyasaland, 1939; Adviser on Freshwater Fisheries to Govt of Palestine, 1940-43. Mem. Council, New Hall, Cambridge, 1954-66; Associate of Newnham Coll. FLS. JP Co. Cambridge, and Isle of Ely, 1959. *Publications:* 2 Crown Agents' Reports on African Fisheries, 1939 and 1942; papers on African Fish, in zoological jls; papers and articles on Sirenia (with G.C.L. Bertram). *Recreations:* foreign travel, gardening. *Address:* Linton House, Linton, Cambridgeshire. *T:* Cambridge 891368. *Club:* English-Speaking Union.

BERTRAM, Prof. Douglas Somerville; Professor of Medical Entomology and Director of Department of Entomology, London School of Hygiene and Tropical Medicine, 1956-76, now Emeritus; *b* 21 Dec. 1913; *s* of William R. J. Bertram and Katherine Arathoon Macaskill, Glasgow, Scotland; *m* 1st, 1947, Louisa Menzies MacKellar (*d* 1956); two *d*; 2nd, 1973, Mrs Muriel Elizabeth Drury. *Educ:* Hillhead High Sch., Glasgow; Univ. of Glasgow. 1st cl. hons BSc (Zoology), 1935, PhD 1940, DSc 1964, Glasgow Univ.; Strang-Steel Scholar, Glasgow Univ., 1935-36. Demonstrator, Dept of Zoology, Glasgow Univ., 1936-38; Lectr, Liverpool Sch. of Tropical Medicine, 1938-40, and 1946-48; Reader in Entomology, London Sch. of Hygiene and Tropical Medicine, 1948-56. Overseas work in East and West Africa, India and Ceylon, Central America periodically. Served War of 1939-45: Lieut to Major, Royal Army Medical Corps, Middle East, POW Germany, Army Sch. of Health Staff, 1945-46. *Publications:* scientific papers in Annals of Trop. Medicine and Parasitology, Transactions Royal Society Tropical Medicine and Hygiene, Adv. Parasitology, Bulletin WHO, etc. *Recreations:* gardening, painting, travel. *Address:* 33 Parkside Drive, Watford, Herts WD1 3AS.

BERTRAM, Kate; *see* Bertram, C. K.

BERTRAND, Cavalier Léon; Professor at the London Fencing Club; British; father of French extraction; *b* 10 July 1897; unmarried. *Educ:* St George's Coll., Wimbledon; Grenoble Univ. Diplomé L'Accademia Nazionale di Scherma, Naples; studied fencing under Profs Georges and Adolphe Rouleau, Paris, and Maestro Commendatore Guiseppe Nadi, Leghorn; served European War, Artists' Rifles; active service, commnd in RFC and RAF; War of 1939-45: commnd in RAFVR, 1939, and served until Nov. 1945 in France, Middle East, Italy, home stations (African Star with clasp, etc). Past Pres., British Academy of Fencing. Awarded (twice) Gold Medal of the Amateur Fencing Assoc. Order of the Crown of Italy, 1938. *Publications:* Cut and Thrust: The Subtlety of the Sabre; The Fencer's Companion, 1935. *Recreations:* billiards and snooker. *Address:* London Fencing Club, 83 Perham Road, West Kensington, W14. *T:* 01-385 7454; 3 Cutcombe Villas, Cutcombe Road, SE5. *T:* 01-274 8168. *Club:* London Sketch.

BESCH, Anthony John Elwyn; opera and theatre director, since 1950; *b* 5 Feb. 1924; *s* of Roy Cressy Frederick Besch and Ann Gwendolen Besch. *Educ:* Rossall Sch., Lancs; Worcester Coll., Oxford (MA). Dir, opera and theatre, 1950-: Royal Opera House, Covent Garden; English Nat. Opera, London Coliseum; Scottish Opera; Welsh Nat. Opera; New Opera Co., London; Handel Opera Soc.; Edinburgh Festival; Wexford Festival; Deutsche Oper, Berlin; Royal Netherlands Opera; Théâtre de la Monnaie, Brussels; Teatro Colon, Buenos Aires; New York City Opera; San Francisco Opera; Canadian Opera Co.; Nat. Arts Centre, Canada; New Opera, S Australia. *Recreation:* gardening. *Address:* 19 Church Lane, Aston Rowant, Oxfordshire. *Club:* Garrick.

BESLEY, Christopher; a Metropolitan Magistrate since 1964; *b* 18 April 1916; *s* of late C. A. Besley, Tiverton; *m* 1947, Pamela, *d* of Dr W. E. David, Sydney, Australia; four *s* two *d*. *Educ:* King's Coll., Wimbledon; King's Coll., London. Barrister, Gray's Inn, 1938. Served War of 1939-45, Devon Regt. *Address:* Queen Elizabeth Building, Temple, EC4; 15 Belvedere Avenue, SW19. *T:* 01-946 2184.

BESSBOROUGH, 10th Earl of, *cr* 1739, Earl (UK), *cr* 1937; **Frederick Edward Neuflize** Ponsonby; DL; Baron of Bessborough; Viscount Duncannon, 1723; Baron Ponsonby, 1749; Baron Duncannon (UK), 1834; Member, European Parliament, since 1972 (Vice-President, 1973-76); Deputy Leader, European Conservative Group, 1972-77); *b* 29 March 1913; *s* of 9th Earl of Bessborough, PC, GCMG, and Roberte de Neuflize, GCStJ, *d* of late Baron Jean de Neuflize; *S* father, 1956; *m* 1948, Mary, *d* of Charles A. Munn, USA; one *d*. *Educ:* Eton; Trinity Coll., Cambridge (MA). Contested W Div. Islington (Nat. Govt), 1935. Joined Sussex Yeomanry (TA), 1936; Sec., League of Nations High Commission for Refugees, 1936-39. Served War of 1939-45, France, Flanders and Dunkirk; ADC to Comdr, Canadian Corps; Experimental Officer (Capt.) Tank Gunnery; GSO2 (liaison) in West and North Africa; Second and subsequently First Sec., British Embassy, Paris, 1944-49. With Robert Benson, Lonsdale and Co. Ltd and Dir High Definition Films, Associated Broadcasting Development Co. Ltd, ATV, Glyndebourne Arts Trust; English Stage Co. Ltd, etc, 1950-63. Chairman of Governors: Dulwich College, 1972-73; British Soc. for Internat. Understanding, 1939-71; Chairman: International Atlantic Cttee, 1952-55; European Atlantic Group, 1954-61. Mem. of UK Parly Delegn to USSR, 1960. Parly Sec. for Science, Oct. 1963; Jt Parly Under-Sec. of State for Educn and Science, 1964; Cons. front bench spokesman on Science, Technology, Power, Foreign and Commonwealth Affairs, 1964-70; Minister of State, Min. of Technology, June-Oct. 1970. Dep. Chm., Metrication Board, 1969-70; Chm., Cttee of Inquiry into the Res. Assocs, 1972-73. Lectures throughout world on British sci. and ind.; Member: Parly and Scientific Cttee (Vice-Pres.); European Parliament's Cttees on Budgets, Energy, Research and Technology; Adv. Cttee, Science Policy Foundn, 1977-; Rapporteur on European Technological Cooperation; President: SE Assoc. of Building Socs; Men of the Trees; Chichester Cons. Assoc.; Chichester Festival Theatre Trust; Mem. Council, Zoological Soc. DL West Sussex, 1977. OStJ; Chevalier Legion of Honour; MRI; FRGS. *Plays and publications:* Nebuchadnezzar (with Muriel Jenkins), 1939; The Four Men (after H. Belloc), 1951; Like Stars Appearing, 1953; The Noon is Night, 1954; Darker the Sky, 1955; Triptych, 1957; A Place in the Forest, 1958; Return to the Forest, 1962; articles, reviews. *Heir pres.:* *c* Arthur Mountifort Longfield Ponsonby [*b* 11 Dec. 1912; *m* 1939, Patricia (*d* 1952), *d* of Col Fitzhugh Lee Minnigerode, Va, USA; one *s* one *d*; *m* 1956, Princess Anne Marie Galitzine (marr. diss., 1963), *d* of late Baron Sir Rudolph Slatin Pasha; *m* 1963, Madeleine, *d* of Maj.-Gen. Laurence Grand, CB, CIE, CBE; two *s*]. *Address:* 4 Westminster Gardens, SW1. *T:* 01-828 5959; Stansted Park, Rowland's Castle, Hants. *T:* Rowlands Castle 2223. *Clubs:* Turf, Garrick, Beefsteak; Grolier (New York).
See also Lady M. B. M. Browne.

BESSELL, Peter Joseph; *b* Bath, 24 Aug. 1921; *m* 1948; one *s* one *d*. MP (L) Bodmin, 1964-70, retired. *Address:* PO Box 2145, Oceanside, California 92054, USA.

BESSEY, Gordon Scott, CBE 1968; *b* 20 Oct. 1910; *s* of late Edward Emerson and Mabel Bessey, Great Yarmouth; *m* 1937, Cynthia (JP 1966), *d* of late William and Mary Bird, Oxford; one *s* three *d*. *Educ:* Heath Sch., Halifax; St Edmund Hall, Oxford. BA 1932, Dip Ed 1933, MA 1937. Teaching: Keighley and Cheltenham, 1933-37; Admin. Asst, Surrey, 1937-39; Asst, later Dep. Educn Officer, Norfolk, 1939-45; Dep. Educn Officer, Somerset, 1945-49. Mem., Youth Service Development Council, 1960-67; Chm., Working Party on part-time training of Youth Leaders, 1961-62; Pres., Assoc. of Chief Educn Officers, 1963; Treas., Soc. of Educn Officers, 1971-74; Chairman: Educnl Adv. Council of IBA (formerly ITA), 1970-74; County Educn Officers' Soc., 1969-70; Dir of Educn, Cumberland, 1949-74, Cumbria, 1974-75. Chairman: East Cumbria Community Health Council, 1974-; Voluntary Action, Cumbria, 1975-. Hon. DCL Newcastle upon Tyne, 1970. *Recreations:* fishing, golf, fell-walking, ornithology. *Address:* 8 St George's Crescent, Carlisle. *T:* Carlisle 22253. *Clubs:* United Oxford & Cambridge University; Border (Carlisle).

BEST, family name of **Baron Wynford.**

BEST, Alfred Charles, CBE 1962 (OBE 1953); DSc (Wales); Director of Services, Meteorological Office, 1960-66; *b* 7 March

1904; s of late Charles William Best, Barry, Glam; m 1932, Renée Margaret, d of late John Laughton Parry, Blaina, Mon; two s. Educ: Barry Grammar Sch.; University Coll., Cardiff. Professional Asst, Meteorological Office, 1926; appointments: Shoeburyness, 1926; Porton, 1928; Air Min., 1933; Malta, 1936; Larkhill, 1939; Air Min., 1940; Wing Comdr RAFVR, ACSEA, 1945; Air Min., 1945; Research, 1945-54; Meteorological Office Services, 1955-66. Publications: Physics in Meteorology, 1957; meteorological papers in jls. Recreation: photography. Address: Blaina, 10 Flintgrove, Bracknell, Berks. T: Bracknell 21772.

BEST, Charles Herbert, CC (Canada) 1967; CH 1971; CBE 1944; FRS 1938; MA, MD, DSc; FRSC, FRCP(C); Professor of Physiology and Director of Department, University of Toronto, 1929-65, Director Emeritus, 1966; Director of Banting-Best Department of Medical Research, University of Toronto, 1941-67, Director Emeritus, 1967; b West Pembroke, Maine, USA, 27 Feb. 1899 (parents both Canadian); s of Herbert Huestis Best, MD, and Luella May Best; m 1924, Margaret Hooper Mahon; two s. Educ: Univ. of Toronto; Univ. of London. BA 1921, MA 1922, MD 1925, Toronto; DSc 1928, London. FRCP 1961. Went overseas with 70th Battery (2nd Canadian Tanks Corps section), serving as Driver and Sergeant, 1918-19; Surg. Lt-Comdr, RCNVR, 1941; Surg.-Comdr 1942; Surg.-Capt. 1943. Co-discoverer of insulin with late Sir Frederick Banting in 1921; in charge of production of insulin, Connaught Laboratories, Univ. of Toronto, 1922-41. Hon. Mem., American Diabetes Assoc., 1940 (Past Pres., 1948-49; Hon. Pres., 1960); Vice-Pres., British Diabetic Assoc., 1934; Hon. Pres., Internat. Diabetes Fedn, 1949; Hon. Dir, Muscular Dystrophy Assoc. of Canada, 1964; Hon. Mem., European Assoc. for the Study of Diabetes, 1965. Initiated Canadian Serum Project for securing dried human serum for military use, 1939; Dir, RCN Med. Res. Unit 1941-; Scientific Dir, Internat. Health Div., Rockefeller Foundn, 1941-43, re-appointed 1946; Consultant to Nat. Inst. of Health, US Public Health Service, 1946; Member: Research Defence Board, Dept Nat. Defence, Canada, 1946-65; Nat. Research Council of Canada, 1947; Interim Cttee, Nat. Cancer Inst. of Canada, 1947. Mem., Paris Acad. of Medicine, 1945; Hon. Mem., Royal Acad. of Sciences, Amsterdam, 1946; For. Corresp., Académie Royale de Médecine de Belgique, 1946; Corresp. Fellow, NY Acad. of Medicine, 1947; Hon. Life Mem., NY Acad. of Sciences, 1950; For. Assoc., Nat. Acad. of Sciences, 1950; Mem., Amer. Philosophical Soc., 1950; Hon. FRSocMed, 1951; Hon. FRCPE, 1953; Hon. FRSE, 1972; First Pres., Internat. Union of Physiological Sciences, 1953; Mem., Pontifical Acad. of Sciences, 1955; Mem., Royal Danish Acad. of Sciences and Letters, 1956. Hon. Mem., Ont. Med. Assoc., 1959; For. Mem., Royal Swedish Acad. of Science, 1961; Adv. Vice-Pres., Pan American Med. Assoc., 1961; Adv. Cttee on Medical Research, WHO, 1963. Croonian Lectr, Royal Soc., 1955; Hon. DSc: Chicago, 1941; Oxford, 1947; Laval, 1952; Maine, 1955; Northwestern, 1959; Laurentian, 1971; Hon. ScD Cambridge, 1946; Hon. Doctor of Medicine: Amsterdam, 1947; Louvain, 1947; Liège, 1947; Freie Univ. of Berlin, 1966; Zagreb, 1976; Hon. LLD: Dalhousie, 1949; Queen's, 1950; Melbourne, 1952; Edinburgh, 1959; Toronto, 1970; Ottawa, 1972; Hon. Degrees, Univs of Chile, Uruguay, San Marcos (Peru), 1951; Hon. PhD Jerusalem, 1971; Hon. Doctorate: Paris, 1945; Central Univ. of Venezuela, 1958; Aristotelian Univ. of Thessaloniki, 1963. Holds many medals from Canadian, American and European instns; first Brazil Science biennial award, Sao Paulo Biennial Foundn, 1971. Legion of Merit, US, 1947; King Haakon VI Liberty Cross, Norway, 1947; Comdr of Order of the Crown, Belgium, 1948. Publications: (with F. G. Banting) original publication on insulin, 1922; Co-author books: The Human Body, 1932; Physiological Basis of Medical Practice, 1937 (9th edn, 1973); Selected Papers of Charles H. Best, 1963; numerous articles on insulin, carbohydrate and fat metabolism, muscular exercise, heparin, histamine, etc. Recreations: riding, golf. Address: The Charles H. Best Institute, University of Toronto, Toronto, Ontario M5G 1L6, Canada. T: 978-2586. Clubs: Athenæum; (Hon. Life) Canadian (Toronto); York Downs Golf (Toronto); Faculty (Univ. of Toronto).

BEST, Edward Wallace, CMG 1971; JP; Advertising Consultant; Governing Director, Best & Co. (Advertising) Pty Ltd; Chairman, Australian Insurance Brokers Ltd; Director: The Craftsman Press Pty Ltd; Edwin K. Williams & Co. Pty Ltd; Wormald Brothers (Vic) Pty Ltd; b 11 Sept. 1917; s of Edward Lewis Best and Mary Best (née Wallace); m 1940, Joan Winifred Ramsay; three d. Educ: Trinity Grammar Sch. and Wesley Coll., Melbourne. Served War 6 years with AIF; 3½ years PoW (Lieut). Elected to Melbourne City Council, 1960; Lord Mayor of Melbourne, 1969-71; has served on numerous cttees; currently Member: Electric Supply, Finance, Civic Square Bldg, Victoria Market Redevelopment Cttees; Melbourne and Metropolitan Bd

of Works Finance and Publicity Cttee; Sidney Myer Music Bowl, 1967- (Chm. 1969); Victorian Olympic Park Cttee of Management, 1967- (Chm. 1969-); Chm., Sports and Recreation Council to Victoria State Govt; Trustee for Olympic Park (Exec. Mem. on Vic. Olympic Cttee which applied for 1956 Melbourne Olympic Games; Mem. Publicity and Pentathlon Cttees at Melbourne Games); Chm., Exhibn Buildings, 1973-; Melbourne Moomba Festival, 1969- (Pres. 1969-71); Lord Mayor's Holiday Camp, 1969- (Chm. 1969-71); associated 25 years with Lord Mayor's Fund, in an adv. capacity, for appeals; Mem. Cttee: Royal Agricultural Soc. Council, 1970-; Equestrian Fedn of Australia, 1965-; Moonee Valley Racing Club, 1975-. Visited Edinburgh, Commonwealth Games, 1970 to present Melbourne's application for 1974 Commonwealth Games; Victorian Chm., 1972 Aust. Olympic Appeal, 1971-72, 1974 Commonwealth Games Appeal; Pres., XXth World Congress of Sports Medicine; Chm., Victorian Olympic Council, 1970-. Mem., Advertising Inst. Australia. Recreations: racing, hunting, farming; athletics (rep. Australia at 1938 Empire Games; former Victorian champion sprinter). Address: Eildon Park, Kerrie, via Romsey, Vic. Australia. T: 054 270230. Clubs: Australian, Bendigo Jockey, Melbourne Cricket, Moonee Valley Racing, Victorian Amateur Turf, Naval and Military, Richmond Football, Victoria Racing, Royal Automobile Club of Victoria.

BEST, Prof. Ernest; Professor of Divinity and Biblical Criticism, University of Glasgow, since 1974; b 23 May 1917; s of John and Louisa Elizabeth Best; m 1949, Sarah Elizabeth Kingston; two d. Educ: Methodist Coll., Belfast; Queen's Univ., Belfast (BA, MA, BD, PhD); Presbyterian Coll., Belfast. Asst Minister, First Bangor Presbyterian Church, 1943-49; Minister, Caledon and Minterburn Presby. Churches, 1949-63; Lectr (temp.), Presbyt. Coll., Belfast, 1953-54; Guest Prof., Austin Presbyt. Theol Seminary, Texas, 1955-57; Lectr in Biblical Lit. and Theol., St Andrews Univ., 1963-74 (Sen. Lectr 1971-74). Jt Editor, Biblical Theology, 1962-72. Publications: One Body in Christ, 1955; The Temptation and the Passion, 1965; The Letter of Paul to the Romans, 1967; 1 Peter, 1971; 1 and 2 Thessalonians, 1972; From Text to Sermon, 1977; contrib. Biblica, Ecumenical Review, Expository Times, Interpretation, Jl Theol Studies, New Testament Studies, Novum Testamentum, Scottish Jl Theology. Recreations: vegetable growing, golf. Address: Department of Divinity and Biblical Criticism, University of Glasgow, Glasgow G12 8QQ; 8 Park Crescent, Bearsden, Glasgow.

BEST, Prof. Geoffrey Francis Andrew; Professor of History in the School of European Studies, University of Sussex, since 1974; b 20 Nov. 1928; s of Frederick Ebenezer Best and Catherine Sarah Vanderbrook (née Bultz); m 1955, Gwenllyan Marigold Davies; two s one d. Educ: St Paul's Sch.; Trinity Coll., Cambridge (MA, PhD). Army (RAEC), 1946-47; Trinity Coll., Cambridge, 1948-54; Choate Fellow, Harvard Univ., 1954-55; Fellow of Trinity Hall and Asst Lectr, Cambridge Univ., 1955-61; Lectr, Edinburgh Univ., 1961-66; Sir Richard Lodge Prof. of History, Edinburgh Univ., 1966-74. Vis. Prof., Chicago Univ., 1964; Vis. Fellow, All Souls Coll., Oxford, 1969-70; Lees Knowles Lectr, Cambridge, 1970. Jt Editor, Victorian Studies, 1958-68. Jt Editor, War and Society Newsletter, 1973-. FRHistS 1977. Publications: Temporal Pillars, 1964; Shaftesbury, 1964; Bishop Westcott and the Miners, 1968; Mid-Victorian Britain, 1971; (ed) Church's Oxford Movement, 1971; (jt ed) War, Economy and the Military Mind, 1976; contrib. various jls. Recreations: music, Victorian arts and architecture. Address: 7 St Anne's Crescent, Lewes, E Sussex BN7 1SB.

BEST, Giles Bernard; His Honour Judge Best; a Circuit Judge, since 1975; b 19 Oct. 1925; yr s of late Hon. James William Best, OBE. Educ: Wellington Coll.; Jesus Coll., Oxford. Called to Bar, Inner Temple, 1951; Dep. Chm., Dorset QS, 1967-71; a Recorder, 1972-75. Recreations: walking, fishing, shooting. Address: The Cottage, Little Bredy, Dorset.
See also T. W. Best.

BEST, Rear-Adm. Thomas William, CB 1966; DL; b Hoshangabad, India, 1 Sept. 1915; s of late Hon. James William Best, OBE, and Florence Mary Bernarda (née Lees); m 1942, Brenda Joan, d of late F. A. Hellaby, MC, Auckland, New Zealand; two s one d. Educ: Farnborough Sch.; Royal Naval Coll., Dartmouth. Served in NZ Div. of RN (HMS Leander, 1937-41); War of 1939-45 (despatches); Qualified Gunnery Specialist, 1942. Korean War, 1951-52 (despatches); i/c HMS Barrosa, 1952-54; Dep. Dir Naval Ordnance, 1955-58; i/c HMS Ausonia, 1958-60; Capt. Supt, Admiralty Surface Weapons Establishment, 1961-64. ADC to the Queen, 1964; Flag Officer Gibraltar, 1964-66; retd 1967. Governor, Bryanston Sch., 1969-. Chm., Dorset County Branch NFU, 1976. Member: Bath & West & Southern Counties Soc.; Dorset Naturalists' Trust. DL Dorset, 1977. Recreations: beekeeping, fruit farming. Address:

Hincknowle, Melplash, Bridport, Dorset. *T:* Netherbury 221. *Club:* Naval and Military.
See also G. B. Best.

BEST-SHAW, Sir John (James Kenward), 9th Bt *cr* 1665; Commander (E) RN, retired; *b* 11 June 1895; *s* of Rev. Sir Charles J. M. Shaw, 8th Bt, and Louisa (*d* 1961), *d* of J. W. Bosanquet; *S* father, 1922; assumed the name and arms of Best by Royal Licence, 1956; *m* 1921, Elizabeth Mary Theodora, *e d* of Sir Robert Hughes, 12th Bt; three *s* four *d. Educ:* Cheam Sch., Sutton, Surrey; Royal Naval Colls, Osborne and Dartmouth. A lay guardian of the Sanctuary of Our Lady of Walsingham, 1931. Served with Royal Navy, Wars of 1914-18 and 1939-45. High Sheriff, Kent, 1961. Pres., Church Union, 1969. OStJ. *Heir: s* John Michael Robert Best-Shaw [*b* 28 Sept. 1924; *m* 1960, Jane Gordon, *d* of A. G. Guthrie, Hampton Court House, Farningham, Kent; two *s* one *d* (and *e s* decd)]. *Address:* Boxley Abbey, Maidstone, Kent. *T:* Maidstone 52910. *Club:* Naval and Military.
See also J. M. Adams-Beck.

BESTERMAN, Edwin Melville Mack, MD, MA, Cantab; FRCP; Consultant Cardiologist: St Mary's Hospital, London, since 1962; Paddington Green Children's Hospital, since 1972; *b* 4 May 1924; *s* of late Theodore Deodatus Nathaniel Besterman and Evelyn, *y d* of Arthur Mack, NY; *m* 1955, Eleanor Mary Rymer Till, *d* of T. Till, Caerleon; four *s. Educ:* Stowe Sch.; Trinity Coll., Cambridge; Guy's Hospital. BA (Cantab) 1943 (1st cl. hons Physiology); MB, BChir 1947; MRCP 1949; MD 1955 (Raymond Horton Smith Prize); FRCP 1967. Out-patient Officer, Guy's Hosp., 1947; House Physician, Post-graduate Medical Sch., Hammersmith, 1948; Registrar, Special Unit for Juvenile Rheumatism, Canadian Red Cross Memorial Hosp., Taplow, Berks, 1949-52; First Asst (Lectr), Inst of Cardiology and Nat. Heart Hosp., 1953-56; Sen. Registrar, Middlesex Hosp., 1956-62; Cons. Cardiologist, Princess Louise Kensington Hosp. for Children, 1962-72. Member: Brit. Cardiac Soc.; Med. Research Soc.; Harveian Soc.; Faculty of History of Medicine and Pharmacy; Osler Club; Scientific Fellow, Zoological Soc. *Publications:* contribs to Paul Wood, Diseases of the Heart and Circulation, 3rd edn, 1968; articles on phonocardiography, pulmonary hypertension, atherosclerosis, blood platelet function and lipid fractions in Brit. Heart Jl, Brit. Med. Jl, Lancet, Circulation, Atherosclerosis Research, etc. *Recreations:* photography, gardening, fishing, tennis, dogs. *Address:* 29 Harley Street, W1N 1DA. *T:* 01-580 9347; 32 Langbourne Avenue, N6. *T:* 01-348 9572. *Club:* Savile.

BESTOR, Arthur (Eugene); Professor of History, University of Washington, 1962-76, now Emeritus; *b* 20 Sept. 1908; *s* of Arthur Eugene and Jeanette Louise Lemon Bestor; *m* 1st, 1931, Dorothea Nolte (marr. diss.); 2nd, 1939, Anne Carr (*d* 1948); two *s*; 3rd, 1949, Dorothy Alden Koch; one *s. Educ:* Yale Univ. PhB 1930; PhD 1938. Yale University: Instructor in English, 1930-31; Instructor in History, 1934-36; Teachers Coll., Columbia University: Associate in History, 1936-37; Asst Prof. of History, 1937-42; Stanford University: Asst Prof. of Humanities, 1942-45; Associate Prof. of History, 1945-46; Lectr in American History, Univ. of Wisconsin, 1947; University of Illinois: Associate Prof. of History, 1947-51; Prof. of History, 1951-62. Harold Vyvyan Harmsworth Prof. of American History, Oxford, 1956-57; Fulbright Vis. Prof., University of Tokyo, 1967. Editor-in-chief, Chautauquan Daily, Chautauqua, NY, 1931-33. Fellow, Newberry Library, Chicago, Ill., 1946; John Simon Guggenheim Memorial Fellow, 1953-54, 1961-62. President: Ill. State Historical Soc., 1954-55; Council for Basic Education, 1956-57; Pacific Coast Branch, Amer. Historical Assoc., 1976. MA (Oxon) by decree, 1956; LLD Lincoln Univ. (Pa), 1959. John Addison Porter Prize, Yale Univ., 1938; Albert J. Beveridge Award, Amer. Historical Assoc., 1946. *Publications:* Chautauqua Publications, 1934; David Jacks of Monterey, 1945; Education and Reform at New Harmony, 1948; Backwoods Utopias, 1950; Educational Wastelands, 1953; The Restoration of Learning, 1955; State Sovereignty and Slavery (in Jl Ill State Historical Soc.), 1961; The American Civil War as a Constitutional Crisis (in Amer. Historical Review), 1964; Separation of Powers in the Realm of Foreign Affairs (in Seton Hall Law Review), 1974; jointly: Problems in American History, 1952, 3rd edn 1966; Three Presidents and Their Books, 1955; The Heritage of the Middle West, 1958; Education in the Age of Science, 1959; Interpreting and Teaching American History, 1961; The American Territorial System, 1973; contribs to Amer. Hist. Review, Jl of Hist. of Ideas, William and Mary Quarterly, Encounter, Procs Amer. Philosophical Soc., American Scholar, Daedalus, Washington Law Review, New England Quarterly, Jl of Southern History, Harvard Educational Review, New Republic, Scientific Monthly, School and Society. *Recreations:* photography, walking. *Address:* Department of History, DP-20,

Smith Hall, University of Washington, Seattle, Washington 98195, USA; (home) 4553 55th Avenue NE, Seattle, Washington, 98105, USA. *Club:* Elizabethan (New Haven).

BESWICK, Baron, *cr* 1964 (Life Peer); **Frank Beswick,** PC 1968; JP; Chairman, British Aerospace, since 1977 (Chairman, Organising Committee, 1976); *b* 1912; *m* Dora, *d* of Edward Plumb; one *s* one *d.* Joined RAF, 1940; Transport Command (despatches). MP (Lab Co-op.) Uxbridge Div. of Middlesex, 1945-Oct. 1959. PPS to Under-Sec. of State for Air, 1946-49; Parly Sec., Min. of Civil Aviation, 1950-Oct. 1951. UK Govt Observer, Bikini Tests, 1946; Delegate UN General Assembly, 1946. Formerly: Chm., Parly Labour Party Civil Aviation Sub-Cttee; Chm., Co-operative Party Parly Group; a Lord-in-Waiting, 1965; Parly Under-Sec. of State in CO, 1965-67; Captain, Hon. Corps of Gentlemen at Arms, and Govt Chief Whip, House of Lords, 1967-70, Chief Opposition Whip, 1970-74; Minister of State for Industry, and Deputy Leader, House of Lords, 1974-75. Special Adviser to Chm., British Aircraft Corp., 1970-74. Vice-Pres., British Air Line Pilots Assoc., 1965-74. JP Co. of London, 1963. *Address:* 27 Margin Drive, SW19.

BESWICK, John Reginald, CBE 1973; Director, Society of Motor Manufacturers & Traders Ltd, since 1963; *b* 16 Aug. 1919; *s* of Malcolm Holland Beswick and Edythe Beswick (*née* Bednall); *m* 1943, Nadine Caruth Moore Pryde; one *s* two *d. Educ:* Manchester Grammar Sch.; Rossall Sch.; Trinity College, Cambridge (MA). Sub-Lt RNVR, 1940-42: anti submarine trawlers, N and S Atlantic; Lt RNVR, 1942-45: submarines, home waters and Far East. Called to Bar, Lincoln's Inn, 1947. Practised at Chancery Bar, 1947-51. Sec., Mullard Ltd, 1951-62; Jt Sec., Philips Electrical Industries Ltd, 1953-62; Dir, Mullard Equipment Ltd, 1955-62. Member: CBI Council, 1965-; Council, Inst. of Advanced Motorists, 1966-76. UK delegate, Bureau Permanent International des Constructeurs d'Automobiles, 1966-. Asst, Worshipful Co. of Coachmakers, 1973-. *Recreations:* golf, fly-fishing, reading. *Address:* Amberley, 11 Ferncroft Avenue, Hampstead, NW3. *T:* 01-435 5706. *Clubs:* Bath, Royal Automobile, Anglo-Belgian; Royal Scottish Automobile (Glasgow).

BETHE, Prof. Hans Albrecht, PhD; John Wendell Anderson Professor of Physics, Cornell University, USA; Professor of Theoretical Physics since 1937; *b* Strasbourg, Germany, 2 July 1906; *m* 1939, Rose Ewald; one *s* one *d. Educ:* Goethe Gymnasium, Frankfurt on Main; Univs of Frankfurt and Munich. PhD Munich, 1928. Instructor in Theoretical Physics, Univs of Frankfurt, Stuttgart, Munich and Tübingen, 1928-33; Lectr, Univs of Manchester and Bristol, England, 1933-35; Asst Prof., Cornell Univ. Ithaca, 1935-37. Dir, Theoretical Physics Div. of Los Alamos Atomic Scientific Laboratory, 1943-46. Sabbatic leave to Cambridge Univ., academic year, 1955-56. Mem., President's Science Adv. Cttee, 1956-59. Member: Nat. Acad. Science; Amer. Physical Soc.; Amer. Astron. Soc.; For. Mem., Royal Society. Holds hon. doctorates in Science. US Medal of Merit, 1946; Planck Medal, German Physical Soc., 1955; Eddington Medal, Royal Astronomical Soc., 1961; Enrico Fermi Award, US Atomic Energy Commn, 1961; Nobel Prize for Physics, 1967. *Publications:* (jt author) Elementary Nuclear Theory, 1947; Mesons and Fields, 1955; contributions to: Handbuch der Physik, 1933, 1954; Reviews of Mod. Physics, 1936-37; Physical Review. *Address:* Laboratory of Nuclear Studies, Cornell University, Ithaca, NY 14850, USA.

BETHEL, David Percival; Director, Leicester Polytechnic, since 1973; Chairman, CNAA Committee for Art and Design and Research Degrees Sub-Committee (Art and Design), since 1975; *b* Bath, 7 Dec. 1923; *m* 1943, Margaret Elizabeth, *d* of late Alexander Wrigglesworth; one *s* one *d. Educ:* King Edward VII Sch., Bath; Crypt Grammar Sch., Glos; West of England Coll. of Art; Bristol Univ., 1946-51; NDD, ATD, FRSA, FSAE, ASIA, ARWA. Served with RN, Far East, 1939-45. Lectr, Stafford Coll. of Art, 1951-56; Deputy Principal, Coventry Coll. of Art, 1956-65; Principal, Coventry Coll. of Art, 1965-69; Dep. Dir, Leicester Polytechnic, 1969-73. Sometime Design Consultant to Massey Ferguson, Van Heusen, Monotype Corp., etc. British Council Adviser to Hong Kong Govt, 1974; Member: World Council, INSEA; Council of Europe; Trustee, Cyril Wood Meml Trust. Paintings and prints in Glos. Libraries, Stafford Art Gallery, Coventry, RWA, private collections. Mem., Worshipful Co. of Frame-Work Knitters. *Recreations:* travel; study of art, design, architecture; archæology and music.

BETHELL, family name of **Barons Bethell** and **Westbury.**

BETHELL, 4th Baron *cr* 1922, of Romford; **Nicholas William Bethell;** Bt 1911; freelance writer; Member of European Parliament, since 1975; *b* 19 July 1938; *s* of Hon. William

Gladstone Bethell (*d* 1964) (3rd *s* of 1st Baron), and of Ann Margaret Bethell (*née* Barlow, now Thornycroft); *S* kinsman, 1967; *m* 1964, Cecilia Mary (marr. diss. 1971, she *d* 1977), *er d* of Prof. A. M. Honeyman, *qv*; two *s*. *Educ:* Harrow; Pembroke Coll., Cambridge. On editorial staff of Times Literary Supplement, 1962-64; a Script Editor in BBC Radio Drama, 1964-67. A Lord in Waiting (Govt Whip, House of Lords), June 1970-Jan. 1971. *Publications:* Gomulka: his Poland and his Communism, 1969; The War Hitler Won, 1972; The Last Secret, 1974; Russia Besieged, 1977; *translations:* Six Plays, by Slawomir Mrozek, 1967; Elegy to John Donne, by Joseph Brodsky, 1967; Cancer Ward, by A. Solzhenitsyn, 1968; The Love Girl and the Innocent, by A. Solzhenitsyn, 1969; The Ascent of Mount Fuji, by Chingiz Aitmatov, 1975; dramatic works for radio and TV; occasional journalism. *Recreations:* poker, cricket. *Heir:* *s* Hon. James Nicholas Bethell, *b* 1 Oct. 1967. *Address:* 73 Sussex Square, W2. *T:* 01-402 6877; Villa Domino, Tangier, Morocco. *Clubs:* Garrick, Pratt's.

BETHELL, Maj.-Gen. Donald Andrew Douglas Jardine; retired 1975; *b* 6 Feb. 1921; *e s* of D. L. Bethell, Stourbridge, near Birmingham, and L. K. Bethell; *m* 1946, Pamela Mary Woosnam; two *s*. *Educ:* Sherborne Sch., Dorset. Commnd RA, 1940; Regimental Service, 1940-47; Staff and Regimental appts, 1947-66; CRA, 3rd Div., 1966-68; Dep. Commandant, Staff Coll., 1969-72; Pres., Regular Commissions Bd, 1972-75. *Recreations:* sailing, fishing, golf, shooting. *Address:* Rose Cottage, Nutfield, Surrey. *T:* Nutfield Ridge 2206; Yacht Acquest. *Clubs:* Royal Cruising, Flyfishers'.

BETHUNE, Sir Alexander Maitland Sharp, 10th Bt (NS), *cr* 1683; *b* 28 March 1909; *o s* of late Alexander Bethune, JP, DL, of Blebo, Cupar, 9th Bt of Scotscraig, and Elisabeth Constance Carnegie (*d* 1935), 3rd *d* of Frederick Lewis Maitland Heriot, of Ramonie, Fife; *S* father, 1917; *m* 1955, Ruth Mary, *d* of J. H. Hayes; one *d*. *Educ:* Eton; Magdalene Coll., Cambridge. *Address:* 21 Victoria Grove, W8.

BETJEMAN, Sir John, Kt 1969; CBE 1960; CLit 1968; poet and author; Poet Laureate, since 1972; *b* 1906; *s* of late E. E. Betjeman; *m* 1933, Penelope Valentine Hester (author, as Penelope Chetwode, of Two Middle-aged Ladies in Andalusia, 1963, and Kulu, 1972), *d* of Field-Marshal Lord Chetwode, GCB, OM, GCSI; one *s* one *d*. *Educ:* Marlborough; Oxford. UK Press Attaché, Dublin, 1941-42; Admiralty, 1943. Mem., Royal Commn on Historical Monuments (England), 1970-76. A Governor of Pusey House, Church of England. Hon. Fellow: Keble Coll., Oxford, 1972; Magdalen Coll., Oxford, 1975. Hon. LLD Aberdeen; Hon. DLitt: Oxon, Reading, Birmingham, Exeter, City, Liverpool, Hull; Hon. ARIBA. *Publications:* Mount Zion; Ghastly Good Taste, 1933, new edn 1971; Continual Dew; An Oxford University Chest; Shell Guides to Cornwall and Devon, and (with John Piper) Shropshire; Antiquarian Prejudice; Old Lights for New Chancels; Selected Poems, 1948 (Heinemann Award); First and Last Loves, 1952; A Few Late Chrysanthemums, 1954 (Foyle Poetry Prize); Collected Poems, 1958 (Duff Cooper Prize; Foyle Poetry Prize; Queen's Gold Medal for Poetry, 1960); Summoned By Bells (verse autobiography), 1960; High and Low (poems), 1966; A Nip in the Air (poems), 1974; (ed with John Piper): Buckinghamshire Guide, 1948; Berkshire Guide, 1949; (ed with late Geoffrey Taylor): An Anthology of Landscape Verse; English Love Poems; English Churches (with Basil Clarke), 1964; (ed) Pocket Guide to English Parish Churches, 1968; Victorian and Edwardian London, 1969; (with David Vaisey) Victorian and Edwardian Oxford from Old Photographs, 1971; A Pictorial History of English Architecture, 1972; London's Historic Railway Stations, 1972; (contrib.) Westminster Abbey, 1972; (with J. S. Gray) Victorian and Edwardian Brighton from Old Photographs, 1972; West Country Churches, 1973; (with A. L. Rowse) Victorian and Edwardian Cornwall, 1974; A Nip in the Air, 1974. *Address:* c/o John Murray Ltd, 50 Albemarle Street, W1X 4BD. *Clubs:* Royal Automobile, Beefsteak.

BETTLEY, F(rancis) Ray, TD 1945; MD; FRCP; Physician for Diseases of the Skin, Middlesex Hospital, London, 1946-74, retired; Physician, St John's Hospital for Diseases of the Skin, London, 1947-74; formerly Dean, Institute of Dermatology, British Postgraduate Medical Federation; Lieutenant-Colonel RAMC, TARO; *b* 18 Aug. 1909; *yr s* of late Francis James Bettley; *m* 1951, Jean Rogers, 2nd *d* of late Archibald Barnet McIntyre; one *s* (one *d* decd), and one adopted *d*. *Educ:* Whitgift Sch., Croydon; University Coll., London; University Coll. Hosp. Medically qualified, 1932; MD 1935; FRCP 1948. Gazetted RAMC TA, 1932; Resident House-appointments, 1932-33; Radcliffe-Crocker Student (Vienna, Strasbourg), 1936; Hon. Dermatologist to Cardiff Royal Infirmary, 1937; various military hosps in UK and Middle East, 1939-44; Dermatologist

and Venereologist, E Africa Comd, 1944-45. Malcolm Morris Lectr, 1959 and 1970; Watson Smith Lectr (RCP), 1960; Emeritus Mem., Brit. Assoc. of Dermatologists; Hon. or Corresp. Mem. of dermatological assocs of: Belgium, Denmark, France, Holland, India, Israel, Poland, USA, Venezuela. *Publications:* Skin Diseases in General Practice, 1949; Editor, British Jl of Dermatology, 1949-59; medical papers in various medical jls. *Recreation:* painting. *Address:* Friary House, St Michael's Road, Winchester, Hants; Manor Cottage, Newton Valence, Alton, Hants. *Clubs:* Athenæum. MCC; Hampshire.

BETTS, Alan Osborn, PhD, MA, BSc, MRCVS; Principal and Dean, The Royal Veterinary College, University of London, since Oct. 1970; *b* 11 March 1927; *s* of A. O. and D. S. A. Betts; *m* 1952, Joan M. Battersby; one *s* one *d*. *Educ:* Royal Veterinary Coll.; Magdalene Coll., Cambridge. Asst in Gen. Practice, 1949; Animal Health Trust Research Scholar, 1950-52; Demonstrator, Univ. of Cambridge, 1952-56; Commonwealth Fund Fellow, Cornell Univ., USA, 1955-56; University Lectr, Cambridge, 1956-64; Prof. of Veterinary Microbiology and Parasitology, Univ. of London, 1964-70. *Publications:* Viral and Rickettsial Infections of Animals, 1967; papers in microbiological and veterinary jls. *Recreations:* travel, gliding. *Address:* The Royal Veterinary College, College Street, NW1 0TU. *T:* 01-387 2898; Lower Boycott, Stowe, Buckingham. *T:* Buckingham 3287. *Club:* Athenæum.

BETTS, Air Vice-Marshal (Charles) Stephen, CBE 1963; MA; Head of Control and Inspection Division, Agency for the Control of Armaments, WEU, Paris, since 1974; *b* 8 April 1919; *s* of H. C. Betts, Nuneaton; *m* 1st, 1943, Pauline Mary (deceased), *d* of Lt-Col P. Heath; two *d*; 2nd, 1964, Margaret Doreen, *d* of Col W. H. Young, DSO. *Educ:* King Edward's Sch., Nuneaton; Sidney Sussex Coll., Cambridge. Joined RAF 1941; Air Cdre 1966; Asst Comdt (Eng.), RAF Coll., Cranwell, 1971-72; Air Vice-Marshal 1972; AOC No 24 Group, RAF, 1972-73, retired 1974. *Recreations:* travel, music. *Address:* Agence pour le Contrôle des Armaments, UEO, 43 avenue du Président-Wilson, 75116 Paris, France. *T:* 723 5432. *Club:* Royal Air Force.

BETTS, Edward William; journalist and critic; *b* London, 27 March 1881; *e s* of late Edward Betts, London and Tunbridge Wells; *m* 1904, Elizabeth Annie (*d* 1945), 2nd *d* of late William West, Tunbridge Wells. *Educ:* privately. Began journalistic career on Kent and Sussex Courier; afterwards on editorial staff of Sussex Daily News; Actg Ed., Malton Gazette, 1904-12; Asst Ed. and Dramatic Critic, Birmingham Gazette, 1912-19; Asst London Editor and Dramatic Critic, Birmingham Gazette and associated papers, 1919-21; Dramatic and Film Critic, Westminster Gazette, 1921-28; Editor, The Era, to 1939; Associate Editor, Daily Film Renter, retd 1951. Founder, 1955, Pres., 1973, Pinner Gramophone Soc. Mem. of Council, Critics' Circle; contributor to Daily Telegraph, Stage, Weekly Westminster, Theatre and Stage, and other periodicals on theatrical and kinema subjects. *Recreations:* music, seeing and reading plays. *Address:* 24 Chiltern House, Hillcrest Road, Ealing W5 1HL. *T:* 01-997 1071. *Club:* National Liberal.

BETTS, Prof. James Anthony; Professor of Fine Art, University of Reading, 1934-63; Emeritus since 1963; *b* 28 Dec. 1897; *s* of James and Ellen Betts; *m* 1925, Nellie Serena Flexen; one *s*. *Educ:* St Stephens, Skipton; Bradford Coll. of Art; Royal Coll. of Art. Head, Sch. of Painting, Sheffield Coll. of Art, 1926-30; Principal, Kingston-on-Thames Sch. of Art, 1930-34. *Address:* Norfolk House, 28 Kidmore Road, Caversham, Reading, Berks. *T:* Reading 471600. *Club:* Athenæum.

BETTS, Rt. Rev. Stanley Woodley, CBE 1967; *b* 23 March 1912; *yr s* of Hubert Woodley and Lillian Esther Betts. *Educ:* Perse Sch.; Jesus Coll., Cambridge. MA 1937. Curate of St Paul's Cheltenham, 1935-38; Chaplain, RAF, 1938-47 (despatches); Sen. Chaplain of BAFO, Germany, 1946-47; Comdt, RAF Chaplains' Sch., Dowdeswell Court, 1947; Chaplain, Clare Coll., Cambridge, 1947-49; Chaplain, Cambridge Pastorate, 1947-56; Proctor in Convocation, 1952-59; Vicar of Holy Trinity Cambridge, 1949-56; Exam. Chaplain to Bishop of Southwell, 1947-56; Select Preacher to University of Cambridge, 1955; Suffragan Bishop of Maidstone, 1956-66; Archbishop of Canterbury's Episcopal Representative with the three Armed Forces, 1956-66; Dean of Rochester, 1966-77. Chairman: Bd of the Church Army; Council, Wadhurst Coll.; Vice-Pres., Lee Abbey; Member Council, Christ Church Coll., Canterbury. *Address:* 2 Kings' Houses, Old Pevensey, Sussex. *T:* Eastbourne 762421. *Club:* National.

BETTS, Stephen; see Betts, C. S.

BETUEL, Herbert William Norman; Assistant Legal Officer, Foreign Compensation Commission, 1965-75; *b* Johannesburg, 9 July 1908; *s* of Leon Louis Betuel, solicitor and advocate of self-governing Colony of the Transvaal (as it was then known), and Christina Ferran, *d* of a planter, both of Port Louis, Mauritius; *m* 1938, Kathleen Harriette Meredith Welsh, MBE, Dublin. *Educ:* Ecole Publique St Julien, Marseilles; Wandsworth Technical Coll., University Tutorial Coll., University Coll., London; Gray's Inn, London. Lee Prizeman, Gray's Inn, 1932; Barrister, 1933; LLB, London, 1934. Magistrate, 1939, Chief Magistrate, 1953, Nigeria; Judge of the High Court of Eastern Nigeria, 1958-65, retd. Chm. Arbitral Tribunal (arrears of overtime among Maritime Workers), 1941. Fellow, Royal Commonwealth Soc. (formerly Royal Empire Soc.), 1939; FRSA 1969. *Recreations:* walking, travelling, literature, history and Contract Bridge. *Address:* 28 Ashfield Road, W3. *T:* 01-743 7439. *Clubs:* Gray's Inn, Royal Commonwealth Society.

BEVAN, family name of **Baroness Lee of Asheridge.**

BEVAN, Cecil Wilfrid Luscombe, CBE 1965; Principal, University College, Cardiff, since 1966; *b* 2 April 1920; *s* of Benjamin Cecil Bevan and Maud Luscombe; *m* 1944, Elizabeth Bondfield, *d* of Henry Dale Bondfield; four *s. Educ:* University Coll. of Wales, Aberystwyth; University Coll., London. BSc Wales 1940; PhD London 1949; FRIC 1957; DSc London 1971. Served Royal Welch Fusiliers and Nigeria Regt, 1940-46 (despatches). Univ. of Exeter, 1949-53; Prof. and Head of Dept of Chemistry, Univ. of Ibadan, 1953-66, Vice Principal and Dep. Vice-Chancellor, 1960-64; Vice-Chancellor, Univ. of Wales, 1973-75. Member: Tropical Products Inst. Adv. Cttee; Council, University of Cape Coast, Ghana, 1967-74; Welsh Council, 1968-71; Chm., Conciliation Cttee of Wales and SW Race Rel. Bd, 1968-72; Governor Welbeck Coll.; Prof. Associé Univ. de Strasbourg, 1965. Fellow UCL, 1969. Hon. DSc, Univ. of Ibadan, 1973. *Publications:* papers, mainly in Jl of Chemical Soc., 1951-. *Recreation:* labouring. *Address:* University College, Cathays Park, Cardiff. *Clubs:* Athenæum; Cardiff and County.

BEVAN, Rear-Adm. Christopher Martin; Flag Officer Medway and Port Admiral Chatham, since July 1976; *b* London, 22 Jan. 1923; *s* of Humphrey C. Bevan and Mary F. Bevan (*née* Mackenzie); *m* 1948, Patricia C. Bedford; one *s* three *d. Educ:* Stowe Sch., Bucks; Victoria Univ., Wellington, NZ. Trooper in Canterbury Yeoman Cavalry (NZ Mounted Rifles), 1941; joined RN as Ord. Seaman (HO), 1942; served remainder of 1939-45 war, Mediterranean and N Atlantic; Sub-Lt RNVR (Exec.) 1943; Gp Radar Officer with Escort Gps 21 and 10, 1944-45; Radar Officer, HMS Mauritius, 1945-46; transf. to permanent commn as Lieut (L), 1946; Radar Section Officer, Directorate of Radio Equipt (DRE), Adm., London, 1946; Radar Instr, HMS Collingwood, 1947, then as student, 1948; radar section, HM Dockyard Malta, 1949-51; Adm. Surface Weapons Estabt (ASWE), measurements section, 1952-53; Lt Comdr 1952; Electrical Officer, HMS Delight, 1954-55; student, Guided Weapons course, RMC Shrivenham, 1955; GW Trials Officer, RAE, Aberporth, 1956-57; DRE, Adm., Bath, 1957-58; Comdr 1958; Section Officer, Ship Dept (Directorate of Naval Equipment), 1958-61; Exec. Officer, HMS St Vincent, 1961-63; Sen. Weapons Engr and i/c electronic workshops, HM Dockyard Portsmouth, 1963-65; i/c electronics section and leader of 'Lightweight' Gun-fire Control project, Weapons Dept, MoD (N) Bath, 1965-67; Captain 1967; Supt Weapons and Radio, Dockyard Dept, MOD (Navy) Bath, 1967-71; Asst Dir, Weapons Equipt (Surface), later, Captain Surface Weapons Acceptance, Weapons Dept (ASWE), 1971-73; Dir, Naval Officer Appts (Engrs), 1973-76. *Recreations:* photography, theatre, opera and chamber music, gardening. *Address:* 18 Upper Cheyne Row, SW3 5JW. *Club:* Army and Navy.

BEVAN, John Henry, CB 1945; MC 1917; *b* 5 April 1894; *y s* of late David Augustus Bevan and late Hon. Dame Maud Bevan, DBE; *m* 1927, Lady Barbara Bingham (*d* 1963), *d* of 5th Earl of Lucan, PC, GCVO, KBE, CB; one *s* two *d. Educ:* Eton Coll.; Christ Church, Oxford. Served European War, 1914-19, with the Herts Regt; Capt., 1916; Major, 1918; TARO General List, recalled, 1939. *Address:* 232 Cranmer Court, Sloane Avenue, SW3 3HD. *T:* 01-589 9302. *Club:* Brooks's.

BEVAN, John Sage; Managing Director, The Union-Castle Mail Steamship Co. Ltd, 1956-65; *b* 29 Nov. 1900; *er s* of E. H. Bevan, Southampton; *m* 1953, Lilian Ellen, *d* of C. Channing, Exeter; no *c. Educ:* King Edward VI Sch., Southampton. Joined Union-Castle Co., 1917; Chairman's Private Sec., 1932; Asst Head, Freight Dept, 1934; Asst Manager, 1946; Asst Man. Dir, 1953; Dep. Man. Dir, 1955. Ministry of Shipping and War Transport, 1939-46. Chairman: South and East African Confs, 1954-66; Delagoa Bay Agency Co., 1955-66; King Line, 1956-58; London

General Shipowners Soc. Cttee, 1958-60; Dir, British and Commonwealth Shipping Co., 1956-66; Member: Chamber of Shipping Council, 1953-66; Shipping Fedn Council, 1953-66; Lloyds Register Gen. Cttee, 1958-66; Port of London Authority 1958-67 (Chm., Docks and Warehouse Cttee, 1964-67); Old Edwardians Assoc., Southampton (Pres., 1959-60, and Chm., London Br.); Governor, King Edward VI Sch., Southampton. Retired Mem., Baltic Mercantile and Shipping Exchange. FCIS. *Recreations:* gardening, writing, reading. *Address:* Redlands, Rewe, Exeter, Devon. *T:* Stoke Canon 329. *Clubs:* Royal Commonwealth Society, Royal Over-Seas League.

BEVAN, Rt. Rev. Kenneth Graham; Assistant Bishop, Diocese of Wakefield, 1968-77; *b* 27 Sept. 1898; *s* of late Rev. James Alfred Bevan, MA; *m* 1927, Jocelyn Duncan Barber; three *d. Educ:* The Grammar Sch., Great Yarmouth; London Coll. of Divinity. Deacon, 1923; Priest, 1924; Curate of Holy Trinity, Tunbridge Wells, 1923-25; Missionary, Diocese of Western China, 1925-36, Diocese of Eastern Szechwan, 1936-40; Bishop of Eastern Szechwan, 1940-50; Vicar of Woolhope, 1951-66; Rural Dean, Hereford (South) 1955-66; Prebendary de Moreton et Whaddon, Hereford Cathedral, 1956-66; Master of Archbishop Holgate's Hosp., Wakefield, 1966-77. *Address:* 12 Howard Link, Shipton Road, York YO3 6UU. *T:* York 51895.

BEVAN, Leonard; Counsellor (Economic), Brasilia, since 1976; *b* 16 Nov. 1926; *s* of Richard (Dick) and Sarah Bevan; *m* 1953, Muriel Anne Bridger. *Educ:* Swansea and Gowerton Grammar Schs; UCW, Aberystwyth (BA Hons). RAF, 1948-50. BoT, 1950 (Private Sec. to Parly Sec., 1952-54); UK Trade Comr: Karachi, 1954; Kuala Lumpur, 1957; Principal British Trade Comr and Econ. Adviser to High Comr, Accra, 1959; Nairobi, 1964; Commonwealth Office (later FCO), 1968; Counsellor (Econ. and Commercial), Canberra, 1970; Head, SW Pacific Dept, FCO, 1974. *Recreations:* bird spotting, clock repairing and restoring, flower gardening. *Address:* c/o Foreign and Commonwealth Office, SW1; Waun Wen, Abercastle Road, Trefin, Dyfed.

BEVAN, Sir Martyn Evan E.; see Evans-Bevan.

BEVAN, Percy Archibald Thomas, CBE 1958; BSc, DEng, FIEE, FIEEE; retired; Director, Engineering, 1954-67, Consultant Engineer, 1967-69, Independent Television Authority (now Independent Broadcasting Authority); *b* 8 Jan. 1909; *s* of late Albert James Bevan, BA, Abertillery, Mon, and Florence Violet Perkins, Worcester. *Educ:* Newport Grammar Sch.; University Coll. and Welsh Coll. of Advanced Technology, Cardiff (now UWIST); Double Diploma Eng. Graduate Apprentice, British Thomson-Houston Company, Rugby, 1930-34; Design Engineer, Studios and Transmitting Stations, BBC, 1934-46; Cambridge Univ., Consultant, Cavendish Laboratory Atomic Energy Cyclotron, 1940-43; involved in RAF airborne radar (night ops), 1941-45; BBC: Senior Television Engineer, Planning and Construction Dept, 1946-50; Chief Planning Engineer, 1950-54. Member: UK Television Adv. Techn. Cttee; Frequency Adv. Cttee, 1955-69; Radio Intereference Cttee; UK Rep., Internat. Telecommns Union and Radio Consultative Cttee, 1953-68; Member: UK Space and Radio Research Adv. Cttee, 1960-68; European Broadcasting Union Techn. Cttee; Eurovision and Colour Television Cttees, 1955-68; Mem. of Council IEE and Chm. Electronics Bd, 1967-68; Chm., Prof. Group Sound and Television Broadcasting, 1962-66. Awarded IEE Radio Section Premium, 1947, 1949, Duddell Premium, 1951; Electronics Bd Premium, 1963. Fellow, Royal Television Soc., 1957; Hon. Fellow, British Kinematograph and Television Soc., 1967. *Publications:* many technical and scientific papers in the radio and television broadcasting field. *Recreations:* photography, country life, music, exploring France. *Address:* Hulls Farm House, West Chiltington Road, Pulborough, West Sussex. *T:* West Chiltington 2518.

BEVAN, Richard Thomas, MD; FRCP; Chief Medical Officer, Welsh Office, 1965-77, retired; *b* 13 Jan. 1914; *s* of T. Bevan, Bridgend; *m* 1940, Dr Beryl Bevan (*née* Badham); two *s* one *d. Educ:* Welsh Nat. Sch. of Medicine. MB, BCh 1939; DPH 1941; MD 1955; FRCP; FFCM. Resident Medical Officer, St David's Hosp., Cardiff; RAF, 1941-46; Lecturer, Welsh Nat. Sch. of Medicine, 1946-68; Deputy County MO, Glamorgan CC, 1948-62. QHP 1974-. *Address:* West Winds, Rhiwbina Hill, Cardiff. *T:* Cardiff 63423. *Clubs:* Civil Service; Glamorgan County (Cardiff).

BEVAN, Timothy Hugh; Deputy Chairman, Barclays Bank Ltd, since 1973 (Vice-Chairman, 1968-73); Chairman, Barclays Bank UK Management, since 1972; Director: Barclays Bank International Ltd, since 1971; Commercial Union Assurance, since 1974; The Union Discount Company of London Ltd, since

1975; *b* 24 May 1927; *y s* of late Hugh Bevan and Pleasance (*née* Scrutton); *m* 1952, Pamela, *e d* of Norman Smith and late Margaret Smith; two *s* two *d. Educ:* Eton. Lieut Welsh Guards. Called to Bar, 1950. Joined Barclays Bank Ltd, 1950. Dir, London Adv. Board, Bank of New South Wales; Mem., Institut International d'Etudes Bancaires. *Recreations:* sailing, gardening. *Address:* Tyes Place, Staplefield, Haywards Heath, Sussex RH17 6EW. *Clubs:* Cavalry and Guards, Royal Ocean Racing; Royal Yacht Squadron.

BEVERIDGE, John Caldwell; Recorder, Western Circuit, since 1976; *b* 26 Sept. 1937; *s* of William Ian Beardmore Beveridge, *qv*; *m* 1972, Frances Ann Clunes Grant Martineau. *Educ:* privately; Jesus Coll., Cambridge (MA, LLB). Called to the Bar, Inner Temple, 1963; Western Circuit; called to the Bar, NSW, 1975. Partner, Beveridge & O'Malley, The Hague, 1975. Conservative Mem., Westminster City Council, 1968-72. Freeman, City of London. Jt Master, Westmeath Foxhounds, 1976. *Recreations:* hunting, shooting, travelling. *Address:* 28 Arlington House, St James's, SW1. *T:* 01-493 3945; The Astor, Macquarie Street, Sydney, NSW, Australia. *Club:* Turf.

BEVERIDGE, William Ian Beardmore, MA, ScD Cantab; DVSc Sydney; Professor of Animal Pathology, Cambridge, 1947-75; Fellow of Jesus College; *b* 1908; *s* of J. W. C. and Ada Beveridge; *m* 1935, Patricia, *d* of Rev. E. C. Thomson; one *s. Educ:* Cranbrook Sch., Sydney; St Paul's Coll., University of Sydney. ScD Cantab 1974. Research bacteriologist, McMaster Animal Health Laboratory, Sydney, 1930-37; Commonwealth Fund Service Fellow at Rockefeller Inst. and at Washington, 1938-39; Walter and Eliza Hall Inst. for Medical Research, Melbourne, 1941-46; Visiting Worker, Pasteur Inst., Paris, 1946-47; Vis. Prof., Ohio State Univ., 1953; Guest Lectr, Norwegian Veterinary Sch., 1955; first Wesley W. Spink Lectr on Comparative Medicine, Minnesota, 1971. Consultant, WHO, Geneva, 1964-74. Chm. Permanent Cttee of the World Veterinary Assoc., 1957-75. DVM (*hc*) Hanover, 1963; Hon. Associate RCVS, 1963; Hon. Mem., British Veterinary Assoc., 1970; Hon. Foreign Mem., Académie Royale de Médicine de Belgique, 1970; Foundation Fellow, Aust. Coll. Vet. Scientists, 1971; Hon. Mem., Amer. Vet. Med. Assoc., 1973; Mem., German Acad. for Scientific Research, Leopoldina, 1974. *Publications:* The Art of Scientific Investigation, 1950; Frontiers in Comparative Medicine, 1972; Influenza: the last great plague, 1977; articles on infectious diseases of man and domestic animals and comparative medicine, in scientific jls. *Address:* Jesus College, Cambridge; 15 Montpelier Place, SW7. *T:* 01-589 3344. *Club:* Athenæum.
See also J . C . Beveridge .

BEVERLEY, Vice-Adm. Sir (William) York (La Roche), KBE 1952 (CBE 1947); CB 1949; *b* 14 Dec. 1895; *s* of Major W. H. Beverley; *m* 1931, Maria Teresa Matilde (*d* 1957), *d* of Enrico Palazio, Santa-Margherita-Ligure, Italy; one *s* one *d* (and one *s* decd). *Educ:* Royal Naval Colls, Osborne and Dartmouth. Served throughout European War, 1914-18, and War of 1939-45; ADC to the King, 1947-48; Admiral Supt, Portsmouth, 1949-51; Vice-Adm., 1950; Dir of Dockyards, 1951-54, retired Dec. 1954. *Address:* c/o Grindlays Bank Ltd, 13 St James's Square, SW1Y 4LF. *Club:* Bath.

BEVERTON, Raymond John Heaphy, CBE 1968; FRS 1975; Secretary, Natural Environment Research Council, since 1965; *b* 29 Aug. 1922; *s* of Edgar John Beverton and Dorothy Sybil Mary Beverton; *m* 1947, Kathleen Edith Marner; three *d. Educ:* Forest Sch., Snaresbrook; Downing Coll., Cambridge (MA). Cambridge, 1940-42 and 1946-47. Joined Fisheries Research Lab. (MAFF), 1947; Dep. Dir, Fisheries Res., 1959-65. Hon. posts during research career: Chm., Comparative Fishing Cttee of ICES, 1957-62; Chm., Res. and Statistics Cttee of Internat. Commn for Northwest Atlantic Fisheries, 1960-63. *Publications:* (with S. J. Holt) On the Dynamics of Exploited Fish Populations, 1957; papers on mathematical basis of fish population dynamics, theory and practice of fisheries conservation and various fisheries research topics. *Recreations:* fishing, sailing, golf, music. *Address:* 54 Priests Lane, Shenfield, Essex. *T:* Brentwood 3920. *Club:* Athenæum.

BEVINGTON, Eric Raymond, CMG 1961; Senior Housing and Planning Inspector, Department of the Environment, since 1970; *b* 23 Jan. 1914; *s* of late R. Bevington and N. E. Bevington (*née* Sutton); *m* 1939, Enid Mary Selina (*née* Homer); one *s* one *d. Educ:* Monkton Combe Sch.; Loughborough Coll.; Queens' Coll., Cambridge. CEng, MIMechE. Cadet, HM Overseas Service, Gilbert and Ellice Islands, 1937; District Officer, Fiji, 1942; Sec., Commn of Enquiry into Cost of Living Allowances, Nigeria, 1945-46; Admin. Officer Cl I, Fiji, 1950; Asst Col Sec. (Devlt), Fiji, 1951; Devlt Comr, Brunei, 1954; Financial Sec.,

Fiji, 1958-61, Development Commissioner, 1962-63; Mem., Executive Council, Fiji, 1958-63; Senior Project Engineer, Wrigh Rain Ltd, 1964-67; Appeals Inspector, Min. of Housing and Local Govt, 1967-70. *Recreations:* golf, sailing, zymurgy. *Address:* Holmans Cottage, Bisterne Close, Burley, Hants. *T:* Burley 3316. *Club:* National Liberal.

BEVINS, Rt. Hon. John Reginald, PC 1959; *b* 20 Aug. 1908; *e s* of John Milton and Grace Eveline Bevins, Liverpool; *m* 1933, Mary Leonora Jones; three *s. Educ:* Dovedale Road and Liverpool Collegiate Schs. Served War of 1939-45; gunner, 1940; Major, RASC, 1944; MEF and Europe. Mem. Liverpool City Council, 1935-50. Contested West Toxteth Div., 1945, and Edge Hill (bye-election), 1947; MP (C) Toxteth Div. of Liverpool, 1950-64; PPS to the Minister of Housing and Local Government, 1951-53; Parliamentary Sec., Ministry of Works, 1953-57, Ministry of Housing and Local Govt, 1957-59; Postmaster-General, 1959-64. *Publication:* The Greasy Pole, 1965. *Address:* 37 Queen's Drive, Liverpool L18 2DT. *T:* 051-722 8484.
See also K. M. Bevins.

BEVINS, Kenneth Milton, CBE 1973; TD 1951; Chief General Manager and Director, Royal Insurance Co. Ltd, since 1970; Chairman, Trade Indemnity Co. Ltd., since 1975 (Director since 1970); Director: Insurance Technical Bureau; Mutual & Federal Insurance Co. Ltd; Mutual & Federal Investments Ltd; Roins Holding Ltd (Canada); Royal Insurance Australia Ltd; Royal Insurance Fire and General (NZ) Ltd; *b* 2 Nov. 1918; *yr s* of late John Milton Bevins and Grace Eveline Bevins, Liverpool; *m* 1st, 1940, Joan Harding (*d* 1969); two *d* ; 2nd, 1971, Diana B. Sellers, *y d* of Godfrey J. Sellers, Keighley. *Educ:* Liverpool Collegiate Sch. Joined Royal Insurance Co. Ltd, 1937. Served War, 1939-46: 136 Field Regt, RA, incl. with 14th Army in Burma, 1943-46 (Major). Sec., Royal Insurance Co. Ltd, 1957; Gen. Manager, 1963; Dep. Chief Gen. Manager 1966. Dir, Fire Protection Assoc., 1963-77 (Chm., 1966-68). Member: Jt Fire Research Organisation Steering Cttee, 1966-68; Home Secretary's Standing Cttee on Crime Prevention, 1967-73; Chm., British Insurance Assoc., 1971-73 (Dep. Chm., 1966-71). *Address:* Linton, The Drive, Sevenoaks, Kent. *T:* Sevenoaks 56909.
See also Rt Hon . J . R . Bevins .

BEWICK, Herbert; barrister; *b* 4 April 1911; *s* of late James Dicker and Elizabeth Jane Bewick. *Educ:* Whitehill Secondary Sch., Glasgow; Royal Grammar Sch., Newcastle upon Tyne; St Catharine's Coll., Cambridge. Called to Bar, Gray's Inn, 1935. Recorder of Pontefract, 1961-67. Chm. of Industrial Tribunal (Newcastle upon Tyne), 1967-72. *Address:* 51 Westgate Road, Newcastle upon Tyne NE1 1SS. *T:* Newcastle 20541; 27 Mitchell Avenue, Jesmond, Newcastle upon Tyne NE2 3JY. *T:* Newcastle 811138.

BEWICKE-COPLEY; family name of Baron Cromwell.

BEYFUS, Drusilla Norman; writer, editor, broadcaster; *d* of Norman Beyfus and Florence Noel Barker; *m* 1956, Milton Shulman, *qv*; one *s* two *d. Educ:* Royal Naval Sch. Woman's Editor, Sunday Express, 1950; columnist, Daily Express, 1952-55; Associate Editor, Queen magazine, 1956; Home Editor, The Observer, 1963; Associate Editor, Daily Telegraph magazine, 1966; Editor, Brides and Setting Up Home magazine, 1972. TV and radio appearances, incl. Call My Bluff and talks programmes. *Publications:* (with Anne Edwards) Lady Behave, 1956 (rev. edn 1969); The English Marriage, 1968; contrib. to Sunday Times, Picture Post, Punch, New Statesman. *Recreations:* walking, modern art, cooking. *Address:* 51G Eaton Square, SW1. *T:* 01-235 7162.

BEYNON, Albert Gwyn, CB 1972; Chief Veterinary Officer, Ministry of Agriculture, Fisheries and Food, 1970-73; *b* 11 Feb. 1908; *s* of Daniel and Jane Beynon; *m* 1st, 1935, Margaret Markillie, Diss, Norfolk (*d* 1972); one *s* one *d* ; 2nd, 1975, Nicolette Hamilton Rice, Houghton in the Dale, Norfolk. *Educ:* Llanelli Gram. Sch.; Royal Veterinary College, London; Manchester Univ. Joined Animal Health staff of Min. of Agric., Fisheries and Food, 1932; Divisional Veterinary Officer, 1938-52; Regional Vet. Off. for Wales, 1952-60; Dep. Chief Vet. Off., 1960-64; Director of Vet. Field Service, 1965-70. Chairman: European Foot and Mouth Disease Commn, 1971-73; Adv. Cttee, IRAD, 1974-; Pigs Cttee ARC/MAFF; JCO. Mem., ARC, 1970-73. President: Brit. Vet. Assoc., 1961-62; RCVS, 1975-76, Sen. Vice-Pres., 1976-77, Mem. Council, 1976-. Dalrymple-Champneys Award, for services to animal welfare and health both nationally and internationally, 1967. *Publications:* several contribs to veterinary jls on animal disease and control. *Recreations:* travel, golf, gardening. *Address:* Buckland, Houghton in the Dale, Walsingham, Norfolk NR22 6AQ. *T:* Walsingham 312.

BEYNON, Sir Granville; see Beynon, Sir W. J. G.

BEYNON, Ven. James Royston; Archdeacon of Winchester, 1962-73, now Emeritus; *b* 16 Sept. 1907; *s* of James Samuel and Catherine Beynon; *m* 1933, Mildred Maud Fromings; four *d. Educ:* St Augustine's Coll., Canterbury. LTh Durham. Ordained, 1931; Chaplain, Indian Eccl. Estabt, 1933; Senior Chaplain: Peshawar, 1941; Quetta, 1943; Archdeacon of Lahore, 1946-48; Vicar of Twyford, Winchester, 1948-73; Rural Dean of Winchester, 1958-62. Hon. CF, 1945. *Address:* 1511 Geary Avenue, London, Ontario, Canada.

BEYNON, Prof. John Herbert, FRS 1971; DSc; Royal Society Research Professor, University College Swansea, University of Wales, since 1974; *b* 29 Dec. 1923; British; *m* 1947, Yvonne Lilian (*née* Fryer); no *c. Educ:* UC Swansea, Univ. of Wales. BSc (1st cl. hons Physics); DSc; FInstP; CChem; FRIC. Experimental Officer, Min. of Supply, Tank Armament Research, 1943-47; ICI Ltd (Organics Div.), 1947-74; Associate Research Man. i/c Physical Chemistry, 1962-70; Sen. Res. Associate, 1965-74. Hon. Professorial Fellow, and Lectr in Chemistry, UC Swansea, 1967-74; Prof. of Chemistry, Purdue Univ., Indiana, 1969-75; Associate Prof. of Molecular Sciences, Univ. of Warwick, 1972-74; Vis. Prof., Univ. of Essex, 1973-74; Hon. Prof., Univ. of Warwick, 1977-. *Publications:* Mass Spectrometry and its Applications in Organic Chemistry, 1960; Mass and Abundance Tables for use in Mass Spectrometry, 1963; The Mass Spectra of Organic Molecules, 1968; Table of Ion Energies for metastable transitions in mass spectrometry, 1970; Metastable Ions, 1973; papers in Proc. Royal Soc., Nature, Jl Sci. Inst., Jl Applied Physics, Chem. Soc., JACS, Trans Faraday Soc., Int. Jl Mass Spectrom. and Ion Physics, Org. Mass Spectrom., Anal. Chem., etc. *Recreations:* photography, golf. *Address:* Department of Chemistry, University College Swansea, Singleton Park, Swansea SA2 8PP. *T:* Swansea 25678; 17 Coltshill Drive, Mumbles, Swansea SA3 4SN. *T:* Swansea 68718. *Club:* Athenæum.

BEYNON, Prof. Sir (William John) Granville, Kt 1976; CBE 1959; PhD, DSc; FRS 1973; Professor and Head of Department of Physics, University College of Wales, Aberystwyth, since 1958; *b* 24 May 1914; *s* of William and Mary Beynon; *m* 1942, Megan Medi, *d* of Arthur and Margaret James; two *s* one *d. Educ:* Gowerton Grammar Sch.; University Coll., Swansea. Scientific Officer, later Senior Scientific Officer, National Physical Laboratory, 1938-46; Lecturer, later Senior Lecturer in Physics, University Coll. of Swansea, 1946-58. Mem., SRC, 1976-. *Publications:* (ed) Solar Eclipses and the Ionosphere, 1956; (ed) Proceedings Mixed Commission on the Ionosphere, 1948-58; numerous publications in scientific jls. *Recreations:* music, cricket, tennis, Rugby. *Address:* Caebryn, Caergôg, Aberystwyth. *T:* Aberystwyth 3947; Bryn Eithin, 103 Dunvant Road, Swansea. *T:* Swansea 23585.

BHAN, Suraj; Vice-Chancellor, Panjab University, 1965-74; *b* 1 Nov. 1904; *s* of Shri Tota Ram; *m* 1934, Mrs Mohini Suraj Bhan; three *s* one *d. Educ:* DAV High Sch., DAV Coll. and Govt Coll., Lahore; Inst. of Educn, London Univ. 1st cl. hons graduate; MA Panjab; MA (Educn) London. Lectr in English, DAV Coll., Lahore, later Principal and Prof. of English, DAV (Post-grad.) Coll., Sholapur, 1942-47; Asst Educnl Adviser, Govt of India, and Founder-Principal, Central Inst. of Educn, Delhi Univ., 1947; Principal, Lawrence Public Sch., Lovedale-Nilgiris, 1948-49; Principal, DAV (Post-grad.) Coll., Jullundur, 1949-62; Vice-Chancellor, Kurukshetra Univ., 1962-65. MLC, Punjab, 1954-66; Member: Punjab Adv. Bd of Educn, 1956-65; Panjab Univ. Senate, 1949-62; Panjab Univ. Syndicate, 1949-62; Royal Soc. of Teachers, England; Bd of Dirs, US Educnl Foundn in India, 1966-68; Adv. Cttee of Vice-Chancellors to Univ. Grants Commn; Central Adv. Bd of Educn, Govt of India; All India Council of Sports, 1970-. Chairman: Inter-Univ. Bd of India and Ceylon, 1970-71; Panjab Univ. Sports Cttee, 1952-62. Padma Bhushan, India, 1971. *Publications:* Towards a Happier Education; (jtly) Development of Higher Education in India; (jtly) Development of Learning in India; Shikhsha men naye prayoga (New Techniques in Education) (in Hindi). *Recreation:* reading. *Address:* D.A.V. College Managing Committee, Chitra Gupta Road, New Delhi 110055, India.

BHUTTO, Zulfikar Ali, HPK 1964; politician and lawyer, Pakistan; Prime Minister of Pakistan, 1973-77 (President of Pakistan, Dec. 1971-73); Minister for Foreign Affairs and Defence, 1971-77; Founder and Chairman, Pakistan People's Party, since 1967; *b* Larkana, 5 Jan. 1928; *s* of late Sir Shahnawaz Khan Bhutto; *m*; two *s* two *d. Educ:* Univ. of California, Berkeley (grad. Hons Pol. Sci.); Christ Church, Oxford (MA with dist. Jurisprudence). Called to Bar, Lincoln's Inn, 1953. Lectr in Internat. Law, Univ. of Southampton, 1952;

Legal Practice, West Pakistan High Court, Karachi, 1953-58; taught Constitutional Law, Sind Muslim Law Coll., Karachi, 1956-58. Elected Mem., Nat. Assembly of Pakistan for Larkana, 1962; Minister: for Commerce, Pakistan, 1958-60; of Minority Affairs and Nat. Reconstruction and Information, 1960-62, also of Fuel, Power and Nat. Resources and of Kashmir Affairs, April 1960-62; and of Industries and Natural Resources, 1962-63; for Foreign Affairs and Atomic Energy, 1963-66; resigned from Govt, June 1966, returned to legal profession; imprisoned, Sept. 1968; released Feb. 1969; elected Mem., Nat. Assembly, Dec. 1970; Dep. Prime Minister and Foreign Minister of Pakistan, Dec. 1971; Chief Martial Law Administrator, Dec. 1971- April 1972. Sec.-Gen., Pakistan Muslim League, 1964. Mem. Pakistan Delegn to Gen. Assembly, UN, 1957; Leader of various Delegns and Special Missions, including UN Conf. on Law of the Sea, Geneva, 1958, and UN General Assembly, 1959, 1960, 1963, 1965 and 1966. Hon. LLD Sind Univ., 1966. Hilal-i-Pakistan, 1964; holds foreign orders. *Publications:* The Myth of Independence, 1968; The Great Tragedy, 1971. *Recreations:* studies and big game. *Address:* Al-Murtaza, Larkana, Pakistan.

BIBBY, Major Sir (Arthur) Harold, 1st Bt *cr* 1959; Kt 1956; DSO 1917; DL; LLD (Hon.) Liverpool; President, Bibby Line Ltd; *b* 18 Feb. 1889; *s* of late Arthur Wilson Bibby; *m* 1920, Marjorie, *d* of late Charles J. Williamson and late The Lady Royden; one *s* three *d* (and one *s* decd). *Educ:* Rugby. Served in RFA (TF), 1908-19; in France and Flanders, 1915-18 (despatches twice, DSO awarded on field of Cambrai). Senior Partner, Bibby Bros & Co., Shipowners and Bankers, 1935-73; Chm., Bibby Line Ltd, 1935-69, Pres., 1969; Director: Sea Insurance Co. Ltd, 1922-68 (Chm., 1930-56); Liverpool & London Steamship Protection & Indemnity Association, 1921-68; LNER, 1924-47; Martins Bank Ltd, 1929-67 (Chm., 1947-62); Suez Canal Co., 1939-57; Member: Mersey Docks & Harbour Board, 1931-65; Governing Body of Rugby Sch., 1932-67; Chairman: Liverpool Steam Ship Owners' Association, 1927 and 1958 (Centenary Year); Employers' Association of Port of Liverpool, 1938-47; Vice-Chm., National Assoc. of Port Employers, 1941-47; Jt Vice-Chm., General Council of British Shipping, 1958-59; President: Training Ship Indefatigable (Chm., 1931-60); Liverpool Sailors' Home (Chm., 1921-51); Liverpool Conservative Assoc., 1959-66; Northwich Conservative Association, 1960-74. DL, Chester, 1937; High Sheriff of Cheshire, 1934-35. Hon. Freeman, City of Liverpool, 1970. *Heir:* s Derek James Bibby, *qv. Address:* Tilstone Lodge, Tarporley, Cheshire CW6 9HT.

BIBBY, Dr Cyril; Principal of Kingston upon Hull College of Education since 1959; *b* 1914; *s* of William and Elizabeth Jane Bibby, Liverpool; *m* 1936, Frances (Florence Mabel) Hirst, Mddx; two *s* two *d. Educ:* Liverpool Collegiate Sch.; Queens' Coll., Cambridge. Open Major Scholar in natural sciences, 1932; Coll. Prizeman, 1933; Icelandic expedn, 1934; BACantab, 1935. Physics and Chemistry Master, Oulton Sch., Liverpool, 1935-38; Scientific research, Univ. of Liverpool, 1935-40; MACantab, 1939; Sen. Biology Master, Chesterfield Grammar Sch., 1938-40; MSc Liverpool, 1940. Educn Officer to Brit. Social Hygiene Council and then Central Council for Health Educn, 1941-46; Tutor in Biol. (becoming Co-ordinator of Sciences and Sec. to Academic Bd), Coll. of S Mark and S John, London, 1946-59; educational and other research, 1947-59. Visiting Prof., Univ. of Illinois, 1950; PhD London, 1955; Silver Medal of RSA, 1956. Visiting Lecturer at several Univs in USA (also investigatory visits for US Nat. Science Foundn, 1962). Delegate to many internat. congresses, etc., 1947-64. At various periods, Mem. Executive of: Internat. Union of Family Organisations; Fraternité Mondiale; Assoc. of Teachers in Colls and Depts of Educn; Council of Christians and Jews; Eugenics Soc.; Nat. Foundn for Educl Research; Soc. for Research into Higher Educn; School Broadcasting Council of UK, etc. Many political activities. FLS, 1942; FRSA, 1954. *Publications:* Evolution of Man and His Culture, 1938; Heredity, Eugenics and Social Progress, 1939; Experimental Human Biology, 1942; Simple Experiments in Biology, 1943; Sex Education, 1944; How Life is Handed On, 1946; Healthy and Happy, 1948; Healthy Day, 1949; Active Human Biology, 1950; Health Education, 1951; Healthy People, 1954; Human Body, 1955; T. H. Huxley, 1959; Race, Prejudice and Education, 1959; Essence of T. H. Huxley, 1968; Biology of Mankind, 1968; T. H. Huxley on Education, 1971; Scientist Extraordinary, 1972; papers in various scientific, health, educnl, political, sociological and gen. lit. jls. *Recreations:* reading, writing, walking, sun-bathing, film, theatre, travel. *Address:* 246 Cottingham Road, Hull. *T:* Hull 444115; (College) Hull 41451.

BIBBY, Derek James, MC 1945; Chairman, Bibby Line Ltd, since 1969; *b* 29 June 1922; *s* and *heir* of Major Sir (Arthur) Harold Bibby, 1st Bt, *qv; m* 1961, Christine Maud, *d* of late Rt.

Rev. F. J. Okell, MA, DD, Bishop of Stockport; four *s* one *d*. *Educ:* Rugby; Trinity Coll., Oxford (MA). Served War, Army, 1942-46. *Recreations:* shooting, gardening. *Address:* Willaston Grange, Willaston-in-Wirral, Cheshire L64 2UN. *T:* 051-327 4913. *Clubs:* Royal Commonwealth Society; Racquet (Liverpool).

BIBBY, John Benjamin, JP; Chairman, J. Bibby & Sons Ltd, since 1970; *b* 19 April 1929; *s* of J. P. and D. D. Bibby; *m* 1956, Susan Lindsay Paterson; two *s* one *d*. *Educ:* Oundle Sch.; St Catharine's Coll., Cambridge (MA). Has held various positions in J. Bibby & Sons Ltd, 1953-; Director, 1961-. JP Liverpool 1975. *Recreations:* sailing, squash. *Address:* Kirby Mount, Warwick Drive, West Kirby, Wirral, Merseyside. *T:* 051-625 8071. *Clubs:* Liverpool Racquet; West Kirby Sailing; Royal Mersey Yacht; Royal Anglesey Yacht.

BIBBY, Samuel Leslie, CBE 1947 (OBE 1945); DL; *b* 19 Jan. 1897; *s* of Samuel Gawith Bibby, Sutton, Surrey; *m* 1923, Eva Margaret Wood, *d* of Dr G. Benington Wood, Sandown, IoW; one *s* one *d* (and one *s* decd). *Educ:* Malvern. Served European War, 1915-19, Capt. RA(TA) (despatches). Col TA, 1943; Comd 6th (Leatherhead) Bn Surrey Home Guard, 1940-43; Comdt Surrey Army Cadet Force, 1943-49; Chm. Army Cadet Force Sports Council, 1940-49; Military Mem. Surrey T&AFA, 1940-49. DL 1955; High Sheriff of Surrey, 1959. *Address:* Villans Wyk, Headley, Surrey. *T:* Leatherhead 77252. *Clubs:* Bath, Gresham, MCC.

BICESTER, 3rd Baron *cr* 1938, of Tusmore; **Angus Edward Vivian Smith;** *b* 20 Feb. 1932; *s* of Lt-Col Hon. Stephen Edward Vivian Smith (*d* 1952) (2nd *s* of 1st Baron) and Elenor Anderson, *d* of Edward S. Hewitt, New York City; *S* uncle, 1968. *Educ:* Eton. *Heir: b* Hugh Charles Vivian Smith, *b* 8 Nov. 1934.

BICKERSTETH, John Burgon, MC 1918; CM (Canada) 1974; MA; FSA; *b* 1888; 4th *s* of late Rev. Samuel Bickersteth, DD. *Educ:* Charterhouse; Christ Church, Oxford; University of Paris. Gained Blue for Association football, 1908 (Capt., Oxford Univ. AFC 1910-11); in Western Canada as mem. of the Archbishop's Mission, 1911-13; served European War with The Royal Dragoons, 1914-19 (MC and Bar); on staff of University of Alberta, 1919-21; Warden of Hart House, University of Toronto, 1921-47; served War of 1939-45; Personal Asst and Adviser (Educn) to GOC Canadian Corps and then to GOC-in-C First Canadian Army, 1940-42; Dir of Army Education, War Office, 1942-44. Hon. LLD Toronto. *Publications:* The Land of Open Doors (Letters from Western Canada); The History of the 6th Cavalry Brigade. *Address:* 11a The Precincts, Canterbury, Kent.

BICKERSTETH, Rt. Rev. John Monier; *see* Bath and Wells, Bishop of.

BICKERTON, Frank Donald, CBE 1966; Director General, Central Office of Information, 1971-74; *b* 22 June 1917; *s* of F. M. Bickerton and A. A. Hibbert; *m* 1945, Linda Russell; two *s*. *Educ:* Liverpool Collegiate Sch. Min. of Health, in Public Relations Div., 1935-40. Served War, RNVR, 1940-45. Min. of National Insurance (later Min. of Pensions and Nat. Insurance), 1946-61: initially Asst Press Officer and in charge of Information Div., 1952-61; Chief Information Officer, Min. of Transport, 1961-68; Controller (Home), COI, 1968-71. *Recreations:* walking, gardening. *Address:* 6 Diana Close, Granville Rise, Totland, Isle of Wight.

BICKFORD SMITH, John Roger, TD 1950; Master of Supreme Court, Queen's Bench Division, since 1967; *b* 31 Oct. 1915; *er s* of late Leonard W. Bickford Smith, Camborne, Cornwall, For. Man., ICI, and of Anny Grete (*née* Huth); *m* 1st, 1939, Cecilia Judge Heath (marr. diss.), *er d* of W. W. Heath, Leicester; two *s*; 2nd, 1972, Baronin Joaise Miranda et Omnes Sancti von Kirchberg-Hohenheim. *Educ:* Eton (King's Schol.); Hertford Coll., Oxford (Schol.). BA 1937; MA 1952. Commnd in Duke of Cornwall's LI (TA), 1939; served 1939-46: UK, India, Burma and Germany; Dept of JAG, India, 1940-44; AJAG (Major), 1942; Lieut-Col 1944; Legal Div., Control Commn for Germany, 1945-46; SO1 (Lieut-Col). Called to Bar, Inner Temple, 1942. Practised at Common Law Bar in London and on Midland Circuit, 1946-67. *Publications:* The Crown Proceedings Act 1947, 1948; various contribs to legal pubns. *Recreation:* foreign travel. *Address:* Royal Courts of Justice, WC2. *Club:* Garrick.

BICKNELL, Mrs Christine Betty; Chairman, Civil Service Selection Boards, since 1970; Member, Newspaper Panel, Monopolies and Mergers Commission, since 1973; *b* 23 Dec. 1919; *er d* of Walter Edward and Olive Isabelle Reynolds; *m* 1960, Claud Bicknell, *qv* ; one step *s* two step *d* (one step *d* decd). *Educ:* St Martin-in-the-Fields High Sch. for Girls; Somerville Coll., Oxford (Exhibr). BA 1941. Board of Trade, 1941-60: Principal 1945; Sec., UK Trade Mission to Egypt, the Sudan and Ethiopia, 1954; Admin. Staff Coll., Henley, 1954; Asst Sec. 1958; Northern Regional Officer, Min. of Land and Natural Resources, 1965-67. Vice-Chm., Newcastle Family Planning Assoc., 1961-70; Chairman: Prudhoe and Monkton HMC, 1966-70 and Leavesden HMC, 1971-74; Kensington and Chelsea and Westminster AHA (T), 1973-77; Member: Newcastle RHB, 1961-70, and NW Metrop. RHB, 1971-74; Nat. Whitley Council for Nurses and Midwives, 1962-70; Northern Econ. Planning Bd, 1965-67; Nat. Exec., Family Planning Assoc., 1965-67; Bd of Governors, Royal Vic. Infirm., Newcastle upon Tyne, 1965-70 and St Bartholomew's Hosp., 1971-74; Platt Cttee on Med. Staffing (FPA), 1970; Pres., Hosp. Domestic Administrators' Assoc., 1970-74. *Recreations:* gardening, mountaineering and hill walking, sailing, entertaining. *Address:* 20 Miller's Court, Chiswick Mall, W4 2PF. *Clubs:* Alpine, United Oxford & Cambridge University.

BICKNELL, Claud, OBE 1946; a Law Commissioner, 1970-75; a part-time Chairman of Industrial Tribunals, since 1975; *b* Rowlands Gill, near Newcastle upon Tyne, 15 June 1910; 2nd *s* of Raymond Bicknell and Phillis Bicknell (*née* Lovibond); *m* 1st, 1934, Esther Irene (*d* 1958), *e d* of Kenneth Bell; one *s* two *d* (one *d* decd). 2nd, 1960, Christine Betty Reynolds (*see* C. B. Bicknell). *Educ:* Corchester Prep. Sch., Corbridge on Tyne; Oundle Sch.; Queens' Coll., Cambridge (Scholar). MA 1935. Pres., Cambridge Univ. Mountaineering Club, 1930-31. Articled to A. L. Bird, Solicitor, Newcastle upon Tyne, 1931-34; admitted as a solicitor, 1934; Asst Solicitor, 1934-39, and partner, 1939-70, in firm of Stanton, Atkinson & Bird, Newcastle upon Tyne. Dir, Northern Corporation Ltd, 1939-53. Auxiliary Fire Service, Newcastle upon Tyne, 1939-41; Nat. Fire Service, 1941-45; Sen. Fire Staff Officer, Home Office, 1943-45. Mem. Planning Bd, Lake District Nat. Park, 1951-70 (Chm., Development Control Cttee, 1957-70); Mem. Lord Jellicoe's Cttee on water resources in the North-West, 1963; Newcastle upon Tyne Incorporated Law Society: Hon. Sec., 1966-70; Vice-Pres., 1967; Pres., 1969; Chm., Newcastle upon Tyne Housing Improvement Trust Ltd, 1966-70. *Recreation:* mountains. *Address:* 20 Miller's Court, Chiswick Mall, W4 2PF. *Clubs:* Garrick, Alpine; Achilles.
See also Sir J . R . Shelley, Bt .

BIDAULT, Georges; *b* Moulins, 5 Oct. 1899; *s* of Georges Bidault and Augustine Traverse; *m* 1945, Suzanne Borel. *Educ:* Collège des jésuites de Bollengo; Faculté des Lettres, Paris. Before war of 1939-45 was a professor of history and edited L'Aube, the journal of the Christian Democrats; served in the ranks, was taken prisoner but freed after 18 months; became chm. of the resistance council inside France, 1943; Minister for Foreign Affairs in Provisional Govts of 1944 and 1945; Deputy from the Loire, 1945, re-elected 1946, 1951, 1956, 1958; Premier and Foreign Minister, France, 1946; Minister of Foreign Affairs, 1947-48; Pres. of the Council, 1950 and 1951, Vice-Pres., 1951-52 and 1952; Minister of National Defence, 1951-52; Minister of Foreign Affairs, Jan.-July 1954; Premier, April 1958; Pres., Provisional Bureau of Rassemblement pour L'Algérie française, Oct. 1959; charged with plot against security of the State, July 1962; in Brazil, March 1963-July 1967, Belgium 1967-68; returned to France, June 1968. Delegate to Council of Europe, 1949. Grand Croix de la Légion d'honneur; Compagnon de la Libération. *Publications:* D'une Résistance à l'autre, 1965 (Resistance: the political autobiography of Georges Bidault, 1967); Le Point, 1968. *Address:* 21 rue du Colonel Moll, Paris 17e, France.

BIDDULPH, family name of **Baron Biddulph.**

BIDDULPH, 4th Baron *cr* 1903; **Robert Michael Christian Biddulph;** *b* 6 Jan. 1931; *s* of 3rd Baron Biddulph and of Lady Amy Louise Agar, *d* of 4th Earl of Normanton; *S* father, 1972; *m* 1958, Lady Mary Maitland, *d* of Viscount Maitland (killed in action, 1943) and *g d* of 15th Earl of Lauderdale; two *s* one *d*. *Educ:* Canford; RMA, Sandhurst. Lt 16/5 The Queen's Royal Lancers, retd. *Recreations:* shooting, fishing. *Heir: s* Hon. Anthony Nicholas Colin Biddulph, *b* 8 April 1959. *Address:* Makerstoun, Kelso, Roxburghshire, Scotland. *Club:* Cavalry and Guards.

BIDDULPH, Constance; *see* Holt, C.

BIDDULPH, Sir Francis (Henry), 9th Bt *cr* 1664; Grazier, Queensland; *b* Mount Playfair, 8 June 1882; *s* of late Walter John Biddulph and Harriette Sophia Biddulph (*née* Foot); *S* kinsman, Sir Theophilus George Biddulph, 8th Bt, who died 1948 (the title became dormant in that year; succ. proved, 1956); *m* 1907, Janet (*d* 1956), *d* of late Walter Bain Hannah, Brisbane; two *s* (one *d* decd). *Educ:* Mount Playfair. *Heir: er s* Stuart Royden Biddulph [*b* 24 June 1908; *m* 1939, Muriel Margaret, 3rd *d* of Angus Harkness, Hamley Bridge, S Australia; one *s* two *d*]. *Address:* Mount Playfair, Tambo, Qld 4478, Australia. *T:* 4.9U Tambo.

BIDE, Austin Ernest; Chairman and Chief Executive, Glaxo Holdings Ltd, since 1973; *b* 11 Sept. 1915; *o s* of late Ernest Arthur Bide and Eliza Bide (*née* Young); *m* 1941, Irene (*née* Ward); three *d. Educ:* County Sch., Acton; Univ. of London. 1st cl. hons BSc Chemistry; FRIC. Govt Chemist's Dept, 1932-40; Research Chemist, Glaxo, 1940: i/c Chemical Develt and Industrial Property, 1944-54; Dep. Sec., 1954-59; Sec., 1959-65; Dir, 1963-71; Dep. Chm., 1971-73. Member: CBI Council, 1974-; BIM Council, 1976-; Dir, BIM Foundn, 1977-; Chairman: BIM Finance Cttee, 1976-; CBI Res. and Technology Cttee, 1977-. FBIM 1972. *Publications:* papers in learned jls on organic chemical subjects. *Recreations:* fishing, handicrafts. *Address:* Clarges House, 6-12 Clarges Street, W1Y 8DH.

BIDGOOD, John Claude, MIEx; Chairman: Anglo-Dominion Finance Co. Ltd; Anglo-Dominion Construction Co. Ltd; Anglo-Dominion Trading Co. Ltd; Leeds & County Conservative Club House Co. Ltd; *b* 12 May 1914; *s* of late Edward Charles Bidgood, Leeds; *m* 1945, Sheila Nancy Walker-Wood; one *s* two *d. Educ:* London Choir Sch.; Woodhouse Technical Sch. Served early part of War of 1939-45 as Pilot RAF. Mem. Leeds City Council, 1947-55 (late Chm. Works Cttee and City Architects Cttee); contested (C) N E Leeds, 1950, 1951; MP (C) Bury and Radcliffe, 1955-64; PPS to Joint Parly Secs, Min. of Pensions and Nat. Insurance, 1957-58; Mem. Parly Select Cttee on Estimates, 1958-64. Director: Bidgood Holdings Ltd; Edward Bidgood & Co. Ltd; Bidgood Larsson Ltd; Wright & Summerhill Ltd; R. Horsfield & Co. Ltd; Constructional Erection Ltd; Bidgood Larsson (Iraq) Ltd; Chm., Yorks Assoc. for the Disabled, 1950-58; Member: Inst. of Export; Leeds and Bradford Joint Aerodrome Cttee, 1951-55; W Riding Rating Valuation Court, 1955. Gen. Comr of Income Tax. Governor, Bury Grammar Schs, 1955. Freeman, City of London; Liveryman and Mem., Court of Assistants, Worshipful Co. of Horners; Mem., Hon. Soc. of Knights of Round Table. *Recreations:* music, travel. *Address:* Linton, Wetherby, W Yorks. *T:* Wetherby 2791. *Clubs:* City Livery, Naval and Military, Pathfinder; Leeds (Leeds).

BIDSTRUP, (Patricia) Lesley, MD, FRCP, FRACP; Member, Medical Appeals Tribunal, since 1970; Member, Industrial Injuries Advisory Council, since 1970; Clinical Assistant (Hon.), Chest Department, St Thomas' Hospital, since 1958; *b* 24 Oct. 1916; *d* of Clarence Leslie Bidstrup, Chemical Works Manager, South Australia, and Kathleen Helena Bidstrup (*née* O'Brien); *m* 1952, Ronald Frank Guymer, TD, MD, FRCP, FRCS, DPH, DIH; one step *s* one step *d. Educ:* Kadina High Sch. and Walford House, Adelaide, SA. MB, BS (Adel.) 1939; MD (Adel.) 1958; FRACP 1954; FRCP (Lond.) 1964. Resident Ho. Phys. and Registrar, Royal Adelaide Hosp., SA, 1939-41. Hon. Capt., AAMC, 1942-45. MO, UNRRA, Glyn-Hughes Hosp., Belsen, 1945-46. General practice: Acting Hon. Asst Phys., Royal Adelaide Hosp.; Tutor in Med., St Mark's Coll., Adelaide, and in Univ. of Adelaide Med. Sch.; Lectr in Med., Univ. of Adelaide Dental Faculty, 1942-45; Asst, Dept for Research in Industrial Medicine, MRC, 1947-58. Private consulting concerned mainly with industrial medicine, 1958-. Mem., Scientific Sub-Cttee on Poisonous Substances used in Agriculture and Food Storage, 1956-58; Corr. Mem., Amer. Acad. of Occupational Medicine. Visiting Lectr, TUC Centenary Inst. of Occupational Health; Examiner for Diploma in Industrial Health: Conjoint Bd, 1965-71; Society of Apothecaries, 1970-. Mayoress, Royal Borough of Kingston-upon-Thames, 1959, 1960. *Publications:* The Toxicity of Mercury and its Compounds, 1964; chapters in: Cancer Progress, 1960; The Prevention of Cancer, 1967; Clinical Aspects of Inhaled Particles 1972; contribs to Brit. Jl Indust. Med., Lancet, BMJ, Proc. Royal Soc. Med., ILO Encyclopaedia on Industrial Diseases. *Recreations:* people, theatre, music. *Address:* 11 Sloane Terrace Mansions, Sloane Terrace, SW1X 9DG. *T:* 01-730 8720.

BIDWELL, Sydney James; MP (Lab) Ealing- Southall, since 1974 (Southall, 1966-74); *b* Southall, 14 Jan. 1917; *s* of late Herbert Emmett Bidwell; *m* 1941; one *s* one *d. Educ:* Elementary sch., evening classes. Railway worker; Tutor and Organiser, Nat. Council of Labour Colls. Mem., TGWU. TUC Reg. Educn Officer, London, 1963-66. Mem., Southall Bor. Council, 1951-55. Contested (Lab): E Herts, 1959; Herts SW,

1964. Mem., Parly Select Cttee on Race Relations and Immigration. *Publications:* Red White and Black Book on race-relations; articles on TU and Labour history. *Recreations:* watching soccer, painting. *Address:* House of Commons, SW1. *Club:* Southall Social and TU.

BIERER, Joshua, MD, FRCPsych; Medical Director, Institute of Social Psychiatry since 1946; Consultant Psychiatrist, Runwell Hospital, 1948-67; Founder, 1946, and Medical Director, Marlborough Day-Hospital, 1946-67; Founder, International Association of Social Psychiatry; Editor-in-Chief, International Journal of Social Psychiatry; *b* 1 July 1901; *s* of Dr Josef Bierer, X-Ray specialist. *Educ:* Vienna Univ. DEcon and SocSc Vienna; Dipl. IndivPsych. Training in Individual Psychology by Prof. Alfred Adler and Dr A. Neuer (Vienna), 1926-28; Training-Analysis by Dr A. Neuer; private practice as Psychotherapist, 1927-; Lectr, Teaching Inst. of Individual Psychology, Berlin, 1928-29; Research: at Inst. of Physiology, Vienna Univ., 1933; in Psychotherapy and Psychiatry at Mental Hosp., Vienna Univ., 1934-36; at Runwell Hosp., Essex, 1938-40. Psychotherapist, Southend Gen. Hosp. and East Ham Memorial Hosp., 1939-43; Clinical Asst, Guy's Hosp., 1942-44; Visiting Psychotherapist, Runwell Mental Hosp., 1942-44 and 1946-48. Served as Specialist Psychiatrist, Major RAMC, 1944-46. Originated idea of Self-Governed Therapeutic Social Clubs, Day Hosps, Night and Week-end Hosps, Self governed Hostels, Therapeutic Communities, the Total Separation Treatment in Marriage Guidance and a new and revolutionary method in education. Co-Founder, Kibbutz Mishmar Haemek, Israel. *Publications:* (jt) Innovation in Social Psychiatry; The Day-Hospital, 1951; (ed) Therapeutic Social Clubs; pioneer research work in problems of social psychiatry, social psychotherapy, group psychotherapy, psychotherapy of psychotics in mental hosps and in out-patient depts by psychotherapy in Jl of Mental Science, Lancet, Brit. Med. Jl, etc. *Recreations:* golf, swimming, tennis, table tennis, chess, bridge. *Address:* 140 Harley Street, W1. *T:* 01-935 2440; (home) 18 Park Avenue, NW11. *T:* 01-455 2940. *Club:* Garrick.

BIFFEN, (William) John; MP (C) Oswestry Division of Salop since Nov. 1961; *b* 3 Nov. 1930; *s* of Victor W. Biffen; unmarried. *Educ:* Dr Morgan's Grammar Sch., Bridgwater; Jesus Coll., Cambridge (BA). Worked in Tube Investments Ltd, 1953-60; Economist Intelligence Unit, 1960-61. Mem., Scottish Grand Cttee, 1977-. *Address:* Middle Farm, Kinton, Nesscliffe, Salop.

BIGG, Wilfred Joseph, CMG 1948; *b* 20 July 1897; 2nd *s* of late Joseph Henry Bigg; *m* 1925, Ivy Lillian Daniel (*d* 1973); three *d. Educ:* Bournemouth Sch. Entered GPO 1912. Served European War, 1914-19. Entered Colonial Office, 1919; Private Sec. to Permanent Under Sec., Dominions Office, 1930-31; returned to Colonial Office, June 1931; Asst Sec., 1943; retired 1957. Member: Commonwealth Shipping Cttee, 1952-57; Bd of Governors, Coll. of Aeronautics, 1955-58; Commonwealth Telecommunications Board, 1955-62. *Recreations:* gardening, motoring. *Address:* Headley, 35 Manwell Road, Swanage, Dorset. *T:* Swanage 2603.

BIGGAR, (Walter) Andrew, OBE 1967; MC 1945; FRAgS; farming since 1956; *b* 6 March 1915; *s* of Walter Biggar and Margaret Sproat; *m* 1945, Patricia Mary Irving Elliot; one *s* one *d . Educ:* Sedbergh Sch., Cumbria; Edinburgh Univ. (BScAgric). FRAgS 1969. Commnd Royal Signals, 1938; War Service, 51st Highland Div., 1939-46; POW, Germany, 1940-45. Rowett Res. Inst., 1935-54. Member: ARC, 1969-; Scottish Agricultl Develt Council, 1971-. *Recreations:* photography, committees. *Address:* Magdalenehall, St Boswells, Roxburghshire. *T:* St Boswells 3741. *Club:* Farmers'.

BIGGART, Sir John Henry, Kt 1967; CBE 1948; DSc, MD; FRCP, FRCPath; Director of Institute of Pathology, Queen's University, Belfast, 1948-71; Dean of Faculty of Medicine, 1943-71; Professor of Pathology, 1937-71; Pro-Vice-Chancellor, 1967-71; Pro-Chancellor, 1972; *b* 17 Nov. 1905; *s* of John Henry Biggart and Mary Gault; *m* 1934, Mary Isobel Gibson, Knock, Belfast; one *s* one *d. Educ:* Royal Belfast Academical Instn; Queen's Univ., Belfast; Johns Hopkins Medical Sch. MB (Hons) 1928; MD (Gold Medal), 1931; DSc 1937; MRCP 1952; FRCP 1957; FCPath 1964; Hon. FRCPI 1969. Commonwealth Fellowship, Johns Hopkins, 1931-33; Pathologist to Scottish Asylums Board, 1933-37; Lecturer in Neuropathology, Edinburgh Univ., 1933-37; Regional Dir, Blood Transfusion Service, 1939-46. Robert Campbell Orator, 1948; Mem., University Senate, 1948; Chm., Laboratory Services Cttee, Hospitals Authority, 1948-54; Chm., Medical Education and Research Cttee, Hospitals Authority, 1950-64; Gen. Med. Council, 1951; Gen. Dental Council, 1959; Chm., Standing Med.

Adv. Cttee, Min. of Health, NI, 1967-73; Council, Brit. Empire Cancer Campaign, 1968; Council, Coll. of Pathologists, 1968; Chairman: NI Council for Postgraduate Med. Educn, 1971-; Irish br. Council, GMC, 1971-; Belfast Home for the Blind, 1972-; Marie Curie Beaconfield Home, 1969-; Age Action Year (NI), 1976; Vice-President: NI Mental Assoc.; NI Br., British Empire Cancer Campaign; Pres., NI Muscular Dystrophy Assoc., 1972-. Hon. FRCGP, 1971; MD (hc) Dublin, 1957; Hon LLD QUB, 1971; Hon. DSc NUI, 1973. *Publications:* Text Book of Neuropathology, 1936; papers on general and nervous pathology in Brain, Jl Pathology and Bacteriology, Ulster Med. Jl, and Johns Hopkins Bulletin. *Recreations:* reading, writing, gardening, music. *Address:* 64 King's Road, Belfast. *T:* Belfast 653107.

BIGGS, Sir Lionel (William), Kt 1964; *b* 28 May 1906; *s* of William Henry Moore Biggs and Lilian (*née* Bush); *m* 1934, Doris Rose, *d* of late William Davies; one *s*. *Educ:* Manchester Gram. Sch. Served Royal Air Force, 1940-45 (despatches). Lord Mayor of Manchester, 1961-62. JP Manchester 1949. Chm., Aerodrome Owners' Assoc. of GB, 1955. *Recreations:* gardening, swimming. *Address:* 8 Fairlea, 16 West Cliff Road, Bournemouth, Dorset. *T:* Bournemouth 291435.

BIGGS, Brig. Michael Worthington, CBE 1962 (OBE 1944); MA; MICE; Manager, Hatfield and Welwyn Garden City, Commission for New Towns, since 1967; *b* 16 Sept. 1911; *s* of late Lt-Col Charles William Biggs, OBE, Cheltenham and late Winifred Jesse Bell Biggs (*née* Dickinson); *m* 1940, Katharine Mary, *d* of late Sir Walter Harragin, CMG, QC, Colonial Legal Service, and of Lady Harragin; two *d*. *Educ:* Cheltenham Coll.; RMA Woolwich; Pembroke Coll., Cambridge. MA (Cantab) 1966; MICE 1964. 2nd Lieut RE, 1931; served War of 1939-45, E Africa, Abyssinia (Bde Major), and Burma (GSO1 and CRE); Lt-Col 1942; Col 1954; Mil. Adviser to High Comr, Australia, 1954-57; Brig. 1960; Chief of Staff, E Africa Comd, 1960-62; Dir of Quartering (Army), MoD, 1963-66; retd, 1966. Group Building Exec., Forte's (Holdings) Ltd, 1966-67. Pres., KAR and EAF Officers' Dinner Club. *Recreations:* lawn tennis, golf, gardening (FRHS). *Address:* Strawyards, High Street, Kimpton, Herts. *T:* Kimpton 823498. *Club:* Army and Navy.

BIGGS, Sir Norman (Parris), Kt 1977; Chairman: Williams & Glyn's Bank Ltd, 1972-76; United International Bank Ltd, since 1970; Deputy Chairman, National and Commercial Banking Group Ltd, 1974-76; Director: Royal Bank of Scotland, 1974-76; Gillett Bros Discount Co. Ltd, 1963-77; *b* 23 Dec. 1907; *s* of John Gordon Biggs and Mary Sharpe Dickson; *m* 1936, Peggy Helena Stammwitz; two *s* one *d*. *Educ:* John Watson's Sch., Edinburgh. Bank of England, 1927-46; Dir, Kleinwort Sons & Co. Ltd, 1946-52; Esso Petroleum Company, Ltd: Dir, 1952-66, Chm., 1968-72. *Recreations:* sailing, travel. *Address:* Northbrook, Danworth Lane, Hurstpierpoint, Sussex. *T:* Hurstpierpoint 832022.

BIGGS, Peter Martin, PhD, DSc; FRS 1976; Director, Houghton Poultry Research Station, since 1974; *b* 13 Aug. 1926; *s* of Ronald Biggs and Cécile Biggs (*née* Player); *m* 1950, Alison Janet Molteno; two *s* one *d*. *Educ:* Bedales Sch.; Cambridge Sch., USA; Queen's Univ., Belfast; Royal Veterinary Coll., Univ. of London (BSc 1953, DSc 1975); Univ. of Bristol (PhD 1958). MRCVS, MRCPath. Served RAF, 1944-48; Research Asst, Univ. of Bristol, 1953-55, Lectr, 1955-59; Head of Leukosis Experimental Unit, Houghton Poultry Research Station, 1959-74 (Dep. Dir, 1971-74). Hon. DVM Ludwig-Maximilians Univ., 1976; Tom Newman Meml Award, 1964; J. T. Edwards Meml Medal, 1969; Dalrymple-Champneys Cup and Medal, 1973. *Publications:* scientific papers on viruses and infectious disease. *Recreations:* music making, boating. *Address:* Willows, London Road, St Ives, Huntingdon, Cambridgeshire PE17 4ES. *T:* St Ives 63471.

BIGGS-DAVISON, John Alec; MP (C) Epping Forest, since 1974 (Chigwell, 1955-74 (as Ind C 1957-58)); *b* 7 June 1918; *s* of late Major John Norman Biggs-Davison, RGA, retd; *m* 1948, Pamela Mary, 2nd *d* of late Ralph Hodder-Williams, MC; two *s* four *d*. *Educ:* Clifton (scholar); Magdalen Coll., Oxford (exhibitioner, MA). Royal Marines, 1939, Lieut 1940; served in RM Brigade and RM Division. Indian Civil Service: Asst Comr, 1942; Forward Liaison Officer, Cox's Bazar, 1943-44; Sub-Divisional Officer, Pindi Gheb, 1946; Political Asst and Comdt, Border Military Police, subsequently Dep. Comr, Dera Ghazi Khan, during and after transfer of Power to Dominion of Pakistan, 1947; retired from Pakistan Administrative Service, 1948. Conservative Research Dept, 1950-55; Sec., Brit. Conservative Delegn to Council of Europe, 1952, 1953. Contested (C) Coventry South, 1951. Co-founder Pakistan Soc., 1951. Indep. Observer of Malta Referendum, 1956. Mem. Parly

Delegations: West Africa, 1956; Guernsey, 1961; Austria, 1964; France, 1965; Canada (Inter-Parly Union Conf.), 1965; Malawi, 1968; Tunisia, Gibraltar, 1969; Portugal, 1973. Vice-President: Pan-European Union; Franco-British Parly Relations Cttee. An Opposition Front Bench spokesman on NI, 1976. Governor, Clifton Coll., 1972. *Publications:* George Wyndham, 1951; Tory Lives, 1952; The Uncertain Ally, 1957; The Walls of Europe, 1962; Portuguese Guinea: Nailing a Lie, 1970; Africa: Hope Deferred, 1972; The Hand is Red, 1974; contribs to many periodicals. *Recreations:* reading, riding, tennis, walking (Gold Medal London-Brighton Pacesetters' Walk, 1963). *Address:* 35 Hereford Square, SW7; Green Farm Cottage, Stapleford Tawney, Essex.

BIGHAM, family name of **Viscount Mersey** and of **Baroness Nairne.**

BIGLAND, Ernest Frank, MBE (mil.) 1945; TD 1946; Vice-Chairman since 1973, and Managing Director since 1969, Guardian Royal Exchange Assurance Ltd; *b* 7 Dec. 1913; *s* of Robert Taylor Bigland and Helen Inglis Scott Bigland (*née* Hannay); *m* 1936, Mary Dalzell; two *s* one *d*. *Educ:* St Edward's Sch., Oxford. FCII. Joined Guardian Assurance Co. Ltd, 1930. Served Royal Artillery, 1939-45 (MBE, despatches); Lt-Col. Guardian Assurance Co. Ltd: Company Sec., 1950; Asst Gen. Manager, 1952; Dep. Gen. Manager, 1957; Gen. Man., 1960; Gp Gen. Man., 1964; Man. Dir, 1966. *Recreations:* shooting, fishing. *Address:* Lucas Green Manor, Lucas Green Road, West End, Woking, Surrey GU24 9LY. *T:* Brookwood 2234. *Clubs:* Bath, Leander.

BIGNALL, John Reginald, FRCP; Physician, Brompton Hospital, since 1957; Hon. Consultant in Diseases of the Chest, Royal Marsden Hospital, since 1958; *b* 14 Oct. 1913; *s* of Walter and Nellie Bignall; *m* 1939, Ruth Thirtle; one *s* three *d*. *Educ:* Nottingham High Sch.; St John's Coll. Cambridge; London Hospital. MA 1938; MD 1947; FRCP 1961. Served in RAMC, 1941-46, Middle East and Mediterranean (Major). Editor of Tubercle, 1956-. *Publications:* various articles on diseases of the chest. *Address:* Berry Barton, 8 Engliff Lane, Pyrford, Woking, Surrey GU22 8SU. *T:* Byfleet 42603.

BILAINKIN, George; diplomatic correspondent; author; lecturer; *b* 12 Feb. 1903; *m* 1940, Dr Lilian Rivlin (marr. diss., 1949); one *d*. *Educ:* Haberdashers' Aske's Sch., NW; Athenée Royal, Belgium. Joint News Ed., Jamaica Daily Gleaner, 1924-25; Special Writer, Leicester Mail, 1925-27; Sub-Ed., Press Association, 1927-29; Ed., Straits Daily Echo, Penang, 1929-30, and Times Correspondent in N Malaya; Asst Literary Ed., Daily Mail, 1934-36; Editorial Staff, News-Chronicle, 1936-38; Diplomatic Correspondent, Allied Newspapers, 1938-40; Special Correspondent, Russia, 1942, for The Star, London, and American newspapers. Special mission to Paris, Berlin, Prague, and Belgrade for Daily Mail, 1945. Delivered 120 lectures in British Univs, clubs, prisons, schools, on Europe, early in 1946. Since then has visited various personalities and countries every year, from Petsamo to Tierra del Fuego. Contributed since 1920 to Encyclopædia Britannica and leading newspapers and reviews. Hon. Mem., Mark Twain Soc. (USA), 1976. *Publications:* Lim Seng Hooi, 1930; Hail Penang, 1932; Within Two Years, 1934; Front Page News-Once, 1937; Changing Opinions, 1938; Poland's Destiny, 1939; Diary of a Diplomatic Correspondent, 1942; Maisky (a biography), 1944; Second Diary of a Diplomatic Correspondent, 1947; Four Weeks in Yugoslavia, 1948; Tito (a biography), 1949; Cairo to Riyadh Diary, 1950; Destination Tokyo, 1965; Four Guilty Britons, 1972; Joseph Kennedy's Fateful Embassy, 1972. *Recreations:* listening; playing with chow-chow and bull-terrier puppies; major diplomatic receptions; reforming the world. Aversions: cats, chain-smokers, solicitors, interrupters, trains. *Address:* 12 Regency Close, Sheerness, Kent. *Club:* Royal Commonwealth Society.

BILL, Commander Robert, DSO 1940; FRICS; FRGS; RN, retired 1955; Consultant, retired 1975; *b* 1 April 1910; *s* of late R. W. Bill, Penn, Staffs; *m* 1st, 1933, Peggy Shaw (marr. diss. 1952), *d* of late Comdr A. R. S. Warden, AM, RN (retd), Paignton, Devon; 2nd, 1952, Wendy Jean (*d* 1962), *d* of late C. P. Booth, Hampstead, NW2; one *s* one *d*; 3rd, 1965, Mrs Nancy Elizabeth Johnson (*d* 1973), *d* of late Major Arthur Edward Phillips, DSO, MFH, Mompesson House, Salisbury; 4th, 1975, Gillian Ruth, 2nd *d* of late Dr Geoffrey Clarke, and *g d* of late Sir William Clarke of Chatteris. *Educ:* RNC, Dartmouth and Greenwich. Specialised in Hydrographic Survey, 1931, and in Electronic Distance Measurement, 1956; Special Director, Vickers Instruments Ltd, 1956-65; Dir and Man. Dir, Tellurometer (UK) Ltd, 1960-66. *Address:* Sheiling Cottage, North Street, Petworth, West Sussex. *T:* Petworth 42357. *Club:* Royal Automobile.

BILLAM, John Bertram Hardy, DFC 1944; Legal Adviser and Deputy Secretary, Department of Employment, since 1976; *b* 20 Oct. 1920; *s* of late John Wilfred Ambrose Billam and Bertha; *m* 1944, Mary (*née* Armitage); one *s* one *d*. *Educ:* Merchant Taylors'; King's Coll., London (LLB 1947). RAF, 1941-46 (Flt-Lt). Called to Bar, Gray's Inn, 1947; Legal Dept, Min. of Labour, 1948; Asst Solicitor, 1967. *Address:* 32 St James's Square, SW1. *T:* 01-214 8734. *Club:* Athenæum.

BILLING, Melvin George, CMG 1961; retired as Provincial Commissioner, Provincial Administration, Northern Rhodesia (1951-62); *b* 24 June 1906; *s* of Stuart Morrison Billing and Gertrude Roswell Billing; *m* 1934; no *c*. *Educ:* Dulwich Coll.; Worcester Coll., Oxford. Provincial Administration, Northern Rhodesia: Cadet, 1930; District Officer, 1932; Grade II, 1942; Grade I, 1946; Senior, 1950. *Recreations:* bowls, photography. *Address:* c/o Mrs M. A. Emery, Box 67033, Bryanston, Transvaal, S Africa. *Club:* Royal Commonwealth Society.

BILLINGHAM, Prof. Rupert Everett, FRS 1961; MA, DPhil, DSc Oxon; Professor and Chairman, Department of Cell Biology, Southwestern Medical School at Dallas, University of Texas, since 1971; *b* 15 Oct. 1921; *o s* of Albert Everett and Helen Louise Billingham, Oxford; *m* 1951, Jean Mary Morpeth; two *s* one *d*. *Educ:* City of Oxford High Sch.; Oriel Coll., Oxford. Served 1942-46, as Lieut RNVR. Asst Lectr, later Lectr in Zoology, University of Birmingham, 1947; Junior Research Fellow, British Empire Cancer Campaign, 1950; Intermediate Research Fellow, Brit. Emp. Cancer Campaign, 1953; Hon. Res. Asst, later Res. Associate, Dept of Zoology, University Coll., London, 1951; Wistar Prof. of Zoology, Univ. of Pennsylvania, USA, and Mem. of Wistar Institute of Anatomy and Biology, Philadelphia, 1957; Prof. and Chm., Dept of Medical Genetics, Univ. of Pennsylvania Med. Sch., Pa, 1965-71. Member: Allergy and Immunology Study Section, Nat. Insts of Health, US Public Health Service, 1958-62; Transplantation and Immunology Cttee, Nat. Insts of Health, 1968-70, 1971-73; Scientific Adv. Cttee, Massachusetts General Hospital, 1976-79; Pres., Transplantation Soc., 1974. Fellow, New York Acad. of Sciences, 1962; Fellow, Amer. Acad. of Arts and Sciences, 1965; Alvarenga Prize, Coll. Physicians, Philadelphia, 1963; Herman Beerman Lecture, Soc. for Investigative Dermatology, 1963; Hon. Award Medal, American Assoc. of Plastic Surgeons, 1964; AOA Honor Med. Soc., 1974; I. S. Ravdin Lecture, Amer. College of Surgeons, 1964; *Sigma Xi* Lecture, Yale, 1965; National Institutes of Health Lecture, 1965; J. W. Jenkinson Memorial Lecturer, Oxford, 1965-66; Harvey Lectr, New York, 1966. Adair Award, Amer. Gynecological Soc., 1971. Hon. DSc, Trinity Coll., Hartford, Conn, USA. *Publications:* The Immunobiology of Transplantation (with W. K. Silvers), 1971; The Immunobiology of Mammalian Reproduction (with A. E. Beer) 1976; contribs to scien. jls on biology of skin, and immunology of tissue transplantation. *Recreations:* woodwork, gardening. *Address:* Department of Cell Biology, University of Texas, Health Science Center, 5323 Harry Hines Boulevard, Dallas, Texas 75235, USA; (home) 6181 Preston Haven Drive, Dallas, Texas 75230, USA. *T:* (214) 661-9895.

BILLINGS, Rear-Adm. Frederick Stewart, CBE 1953; CEng; FIMechE; *b* 11 Aug. 1900; *s* of F. W. Billings, Cheltenham; *m* 1933, Mary Sheila (*née* Howell); two *s* two *d*. *Educ:* Royal Naval Colls, Osborne and Dartmouth. As Capt. (E): Fleet Engineer Officer on staff of C-in-C, Mediterranean, 1945-47; Asst Engineer-in-Chief (Personnel) at Admiralty, 1947-48; Fleet Engineer Officer (Submarines), 1948-50; Manager, Engineering Dept, HM Dockyard, Portsmouth, 1950-54; retd list, 1954. Local Dir and Chief Engineer, the Consett Iron Co., County Durham, 1956-62. Chilean Order Al Merito, 1932. *Address:* Sideways, Bredon, near Tewkesbury, Glos. *T:* Bredon 72313.

BILLINGTON, Michael; Drama Critic of The Guardian, since 1971; *b* 16 Nov. 1939; *s* of Alfred Billington and Patricia (*née* Bradshaw). *Educ:* Warwick Sch.; St Catherine's Coll., Oxford (BA). Trained as journalist with Liverpool Daily Post and Echo, 1961-62; Public Liaison Officer and Director for Lincoln Theatre Co., 1962-64; reviewed plays, films and television for The Times, 1965-71. Film Critic: Birmingham Post and Illustrated London News, 1968-. Contributor to numerous radio and television Arts programmes, incl. Kaleidoscope, Critics' Forum, The Book Programme, Arena. IPC Critic of the Year, 1974. *Publications:* The Modern Actor, 1974; How Tickled I Am, 1977. *Recreations:* work, travel, cricket. *Address:* 15 Hearne Road, W4. *T:* 01-995 0455. *Club:* Critics' Circle.

BILLINGTON, Prof. Ray Allen; Senior Research Associate, Huntington Library, San Marino, California, since 1963; *b* Bay City, Michigan, USA, 28 Sept. 1903; *s* of Cecil Billington and Nina Allen Billington; *m* 1928, Mabel Ruth Crotty; one *s* one *d*.

Educ: University of Wisconsin (PhB); University of Michigan (MA); Harvard University (PhD). Instructor and Asst Prof. of History, Clark Univ., Worcester, Mass, 1931-37; Asst Prof., Associate Prof., Prof., Smith Coll., Northampton, Mass, 1937-44; William Smith Mason Prof. of History, Northwestern Univ., 1944-63. Visiting Professor: Western Reserve Univ., 1939; Ohio State Univ., 1942; Harvard Univ., 1948. Dir, Massachusetts Federal Writers' Project, 1936-37; Guggenheim Memorial Fellow, 1943-44; History Editor, The Dryden Press, 1949-56; History Editor, Rinehart & Co., 1956-60; Board of Trustees: The Newberry Library, 1952-63; Occidental Coll., 1971-; Dir., Social Science Research Council, 1952. Harold Vyvyan Harmsworth Prof. of American History, Oxford Univ., 1953-54. Hon. Consultant, Library of Congress, 1974-. Hon. MA Oxford, 1953; Hon. LittD: Bowling Green Univ., 1958; Redlands Univ., 1965; Hon. LLD: Park Coll., 1961; Occidental Coll., 1969; Univ. of Toledo, 1970; Hon. LHD: Northwestern Univ., 1971; Clark Univ., 1974. *Publications:* The Protestant Crusade, 1938 (reissued 1953); The United States, American Democracy in World Perspective, 1947; Westward Expansion, 1949 (4th edn 1974); The Making of American Democracy, 1950; American History after 1865, 1950; American History before 1877, 1951; The Journal of Charlotte L. Forten, 1953; The Far Western Frontier, 1830-1860, 1956; The Westward Movement in the United States, 1959; Frontier and Section, 1961; The Historian's Contribution to Anglo-American Misunderstanding, 1966; The Frontier Thesis, 1966; America's Frontier Heritage, 1966; America's Frontier Story, 1969; Dear Lady, 1970; Genesis of the Frontier Thesis, 1971; Frederick Jackson Turner, 1973 (Bancroft Prize); People of the Plains and Mountains, 1973; Allan Nevins on History, 1975; contribs to historical jls. *Address:* 2375 Lombardy Road, San Marino, Calif, USA. *Clubs:* Wayfarers (Chicago); Westerners, Zamorano (Los Angeles); Athenæum, Valley Hunt (Pasadena).

BILLOT, Barbara Kathleen; Deputy Director (Under-Secretary), Department for National Savings, since 1974; *b* 26 May 1920; *d* of Alfred Billot and Agnes Billot (*née* Hiner). *Educ:* Petersfield County High Sch. for Girls. Post Office Savings Bank: Clerical Officer 1938; Exec. Off. 1939; Higher Exec. Off. 1946; Sen. Exec. Off. 1953; Chief Exec. Off. 1957; Principal, Post Office Headquarters, 1960; Sen. Chief Exec. Off., PO Savings Dept, 1961; Principal Exec. Off. (Estabt Off.), 1969; Asst Sec., Dept for Nat. Savings, 1971. *Recreations:* reading, theatre-going. *Address:* 42 Thackeray Court, Hanger Vale Lane, W5 3AT. *T:* 01-998 5705.

BILNEY, Air Vice-Marshal Christopher Neil Hope, CB 1949; CBE 1946 (OBE 1940); RAF, retired; *b* 26 Oct. 1898; *s* of late William A. and late Maud H. Bilney, Fir Grange, Weybridge, Surrey; *m* 1926, Nellie G. Perren; two *d*. *Educ:* Tonbridge Sch. Joined RNAS, 1917; commissioned 1917; served European War, 1914-18, N Sea and Middle East; Flt-Lieut RAF, 1926; India, 1925-30 (despatches); Sqdn Leader, 1935, serving at Air Ministry; Wing Comdr, 1939; served War of 1939-45: Boscombe Down, 1939; MAP, 1940-41; Group Capt, 1941; Air Cdre, Vice-Pres. Ordnance Board, 1942; HQ Bomber Comd as Comd Armament Officer, 1944; AOC No. 25 Group, 1945; Air Ministry, Dir Technical Training, 1947; Air Officer i/c Administration, HQ Maintenance Comd, 1949-51; Dir-Gen. of Technical Services (1), Air Ministry, 1951-52; Pres. Ordnance Board, Ministry of Supply, 1953-54; retd 1954. Took up scouting: District Comr, Andover, 1954; County Comr, Hampshire, 1960-67; awarded Silver Acorn for good service by Chief Scout. *Recreations:* shooting, gardening. *Address:* Middle Acre, Wildhern, Andover, Hants.

BILTON, Percy; Chairman, Percy Bilton Ltd, London, W5, and other companies; *b* 28 Nov. 1896; *s* of Christopher G. Bilton, Ormskirk, Lancs, and Hannah Dunlop, Edinburgh; three *s* two *d*. Founder: Vigzol Oil Co. Ltd, 1919; Percy Bilton Ltd, 1927; and various other property companies. Past Master, Worshipful Co. of Fan Makers, 1959. *Recreations:* yachting, racing, golf, farming (pedigree Jerseys at 5000 acre farm, De Hoek, CP, and Ayrshire pedigree herd at Barnes Farm, King's Langley). *Address:* Barnes House, King's Langley, Herts. *T:* King's Langley 62839. *Clubs:* Royal Thames Yacht; Civil Service (Cape Town), etc.

bin YEOP, Tan Sri Abdul Aziz, Al-Haj; PSM (Malaysia); Hon. GCVO 1972; Member, Malaysian Parliament; Partner in legal firm, Aziz and Mazlan, Advocates and Solicitors, 1966-71, and since 1973; *b* 5 Oct. 1916; *m* 1942, Puan Sri Hamidah Aziz; six *s* three *d*. *Educ:* King Edward VII Sch., Perak, Malaysia. Malay Administrative Service, 1937; called to Bar, Lincoln's Inn, 1950; Malayan Civil Service, 1951; First Asst State Sec., Perak 1954; London Univ. (course in Community Development), 1955. Permanent Sec., Min. of Agriculture, 1958-62; Dep. Sec.,

Malaysian Affairs Div., Prime Minister's Dept, 1962-64; Permanent Sec., Min. of Education, 1964-66. Chm. and Dir of firms in Malaysia, 1966-71. High Comr for Malaysia in London, 1971-73. First Chm., Bd of Governors of BERNAMA (Malaysia's National News Agency); Chairman: Council, Universiti Teknologi, Malaysia; Majlis Amanah Raayat, Malaysia. *Recreations:* walking, reading, fishing. *Address:* c/o Aziz and Mazlan, Jalan Klyne, Kuala Lumpur, Malaysia.

BINCHY, Daniel A.; Senior Professor, Dublin Institute for Advanced Studies, 1950-75; *b* 3 June 1900. *Educ:* Clongowes Wood Coll.; University Coll., Dublin; Munich, Berlin, Paris and The Hague. MA (NUI and Oxford); Dr Phil (Munich). Prof. of Jurisprudence and Legal History, University Coll., Dublin, 1925-45; Senior Research Fellow, Corpus Christi Coll., Oxford, 1945-50, Hon. Fellow, 1971. Envoy Extraordinary and Minister Plenipotentiary for the Irish Free State to Germany, 1929-32. Mem. Council, Royal Irish Academy, 1926, Vice-Pres., 1945. Rhys Lectr, British Academy, 1943; Lowell Lectr, Boston, 1954; Visiting Prof. of Celtic, Harvard Univ., 1962-63; Gregynog Lectr, Univ. of Wales, 1966; O'Donnell Lectr, Oxford, 1967-68. DLitt (*hc*): Dublin, 1956; Wales, 1963; Belfast, 1973; NUI, 1973; DèsL (*hc*) Rennes, 1971. Corresp. Mem., Norwegian Instituttet for Sammenlignende Kulturforsking, 1960; For. Mem., Amer. Acad. of Arts and Sciences, 1962; Corresp. Fellow, British Acad., 1976. *Publications:* Church and State in Fascist Italy, 1941, repr. 1970; Crith gablach, An Early Irish Legal Tract, 1940, repr. 1970; Celtic and Anglo-Saxon Kingship, 1970; papers on Old Irish law; various articles in Irish, English, and German reviews. *Address:* Lisnagree, Castleknock, Co. Dublin. *Club:* United Service (Dublin).

BINDOFF, Prof. Stanley Thomas; Professor of History, Queen Mary College, University of London, 1951-75; *b* 8 April 1908; 2nd *s* of late Thomas Henry and Mary Bindoff, Brighton; *m* 1936, Marjorie, *d* of William George and Helen Blatcher, New Malden; one *s* one *d*. *Educ:* Brighton Grammar Sch.; University Coll., London. BA (History Hons) 1929; MA (with mark of distinction), 1933; Alexander Medallist of the RHistS, 1935. Research Asst, Inst. of Historical Research, 1930-33; Sec., Netherlands Information Bureau, 1933-34; successively Asst Lectr and Lectr in History, University Coll., London, 1935-45; service in Naval Intelligence Div., Admty, 1942-45; Reader in Modern History, University Coll., London, 1945-51. Visiting Prof. in History: Columbia Univ., NY, 1960; Claremont Graduate Sch., Calif., 1966; Wellesley Coll., Mass., Harvard Univ., 1968; Cornell Vis. Prof., Swarthmore Coll., Pa, 1973. FRHistS, 1946; Vice-Pres., 1967. Fellow: University Coll., London, 1958; Queen Mary Coll., London, 1977. Member: Utrecht Historical Soc., 1947; Royal Dutch Soc. of Literature, 1950; Senate, Univ. of London, 1966. *Publications:* (with E. F. Malcolm Smith and C. K. Webster) British Diplomatic Representatives, 1789-1852, 1934; The Scheldt Question to 1839, 1945; Ket's Rebellion (Hist. Assoc. Pamphlet), 1949; Tudor England, 1950; (ed jtly) Elizabethan Government and Society, 1961; articles and reviews in historical journals. *Recreations:* walking and climbing; watching games which he has grown too old to play. *Address:* 2 Sylvan Gardens, Woodlands Road, Surbiton, Surrey. *T:* 01-399 4880. *Club:* Reform.

BING, Sir Rudolf (Franz Joseph), KBE 1971 (CBE 1956); General Manager, Metropolitan Opera, New York, 1950-72; Distinguished Professor, Brooklyn College, City University of New York, 1972-75; Director Columbia Artists Management, since 1973; *b* Vienna, 9 Jan. 1902; *m* 1929, Nina (*née* Schelemskaja). *Educ:* Vienna. Hessian State Theatre, Darmstadt, 1928-30; Civic Opera, Berlin-Charlottenburg, 1930-33. Gen. Manager, Glyndebourne Opera, 1935-49; Artistic Director, Edinburgh Festival, 1947-49. Holds hon. doctorates in music and in letters, from the US. Légion d'Honneur, 1958; Comdr's Cross of Order of Merit, Federal Republic of Germany, 1958; Grand Silver Medal of Honour, Republic of Austria, 1959; Comdr, Order of Merit, Republic of Italy, 1959, Grand Officer, 1970. *Publication:* 5000 Nights at the Opera, 1972. *Address:* Essex House, 160 Central Park South, New York, NY 10019, USA.

BINGHAM, family name of **Baron Clanmorris** and of **Earl of Lucan.**

BINGHAM, Lord; George Charles Bingham; *b* 21 Sept. 1967; *s* and *heir* of 7th Earl of Lucan, *qv.*

BINGHAM, Hon. Charlotte Mary Thérèse; playwright and novelist; *b* 29 June 1942; *d* of Baron Clanmorris, *qv*; *m* 1964, Terence Brady, *qv*; one *s* one *d* (and one *d* decd). *Educ:* The Priory, Haywards Heath. TV series with Terence Brady: Boy Meets Girl; Take Three Girls; Upstairs Downstairs; Away From It All; Play for Today; No—Honestly; Yes—Honestly. *Publications:* Coronet among the Weeds, 1963; Lucinda, 1965; Coronet among the Grass, 1972; with Terence Brady: Victoria, 1972; Rose's Story, 1973; Victoria and Company, 1974; Yes—Honestly, 1977. *Recreations:* horse riding, patchwork, gardening. *Address:* 111 East Sheen Avenue, SW14 8AX; c/o A. D. Peters, Literary Agent, 10 Buckingham Street, WC2N 6BU.

BINGHAM, John; *see* Clanmorris, 7th Baron.

BINGHAM, Lt-Col Ralph Charles, CVO 1953; DSO 1917; *b* 1885; *m* 1913, Dorothy Louisa (*d* 1967), *d* of late Edward Roger Murray Pratt; one *s* one *d*. *Educ:* Eton. Served European War, 1914-18 (DSO, Italian Silver Medal, despatches thrice); commanded 4th Bn City of London Regt (The Royal Fusilliers), 1934-37; Sec. The Order of St John of Jerusalem, 1927-37; Exon in the Yeoman of the Guard, 1938; Clerk of the Cheque and Adjutant of the Yeoman of the Guard, 1950-55. *Recreations:* sailing (passed Board of Trade Yacht Master (Coastal) Exam., 1945); bookbinding and calligraphy. *Address:* 10 Evelyn Gardens, SW7. *T:* 01-373 5543.
See also Baron Alport.

BINGHAM, Richard Martin, TD 1949; QC 1958; **His Honour Judge Bingham;** a Circuit Judge, since 1972; *b* 26 Oct. 1915; *s* of late John and Dorothy Ann Bingham; *m* 1949, Elinor Stephenson; one *d*. *Educ:* Harrow; Clare Coll., Cambridge. Called to Bar, Inner Temple, 1940; Bencher, 1966; joined Northern Circuit, 1946; Recorder of Oldham, 1960-71; Judge of Appeal, IoM, 1965-72. Served with 59th Med. Regt, RA (TA), 1937-46 and 1947-49: Major from 1945; Campaigns, Dunkirk and NW Europe (despatches, 1944). Mem. of Liverpool City Council, 1946-49. MP (C) Garston Division of Liverpool, Dec. 1957-March 1966. Member: HO Departmental Cttee on Coroners, 1965; Royal Commn Assizes and Quarter Sessions, 1966. *Publication:* Cases on Negligence, 1st edn 1961, 2nd edn 1964. *Address:* Lane End, Croft Drive, Caldy, Wirral, Merseyside L48 2JW. *T:* 051-625 6830. *Clubs:* Royal Automobile; Royal Liverpool Golf.

BINGHAM, Robert Porter, CMG 1956; Malayan Civil Service, retired; *b* 3 Jan. 1903; *s* of late Robert William Bingham, Dungannon, Co. Tyrone; *m* 1936, Elizabeth Walker, *d* of late Vincent Andrews Acheson, Castlecaulfield, Co. Tyrone; one *s* one *d*. *Educ:* Royal School, Dungannon; Trinity Coll., Dublin. Entered Malayan Civil Service, 1926; in China, studying Chinese, 1926-28; Protector of Chinese, various parts of Malaya, 1928-41; interned, Singapore, 1942-45; Comr for Labour, Singapore, 1946-50; Sec. for Chinese Affairs, Federation of Malaya, 1950-51; Resident Commissioner, Penang, 1951-57.

BINGHAM, Thomas Henry, QC 1972; Barrister-at-Law; a Recorder of the Crown Court, since 1975; *b* 13 Oct. 1933; *o s* of Dr T. H. Bingham, Reigate; *m* 1963, Elizabeth, *o d* of late Peter Loxley; two *s* one *d*. *Educ:* Sedbergh; Balliol Coll., Oxford (MA). Royal Ulster Rifles, 1952-54 (2nd Lt); London Irish Rifles (TA) 1954-59. Univ. of Oxford: Gibbs Schol. in Mod. Hist., 1956; 1st cl. Hons, Mod. Hist., 1957. Eldon Law Schol., 1957; Arden Schol., Gray's Inn, 1959; Cert. of Honour, Bar Finals, 1959; called to Bar, Gray's Inn, 1959; Standing Jun. Counsel to Dept of Employment, 1968-72. Mem., Lord Chancellor's Law Reform Cttee. *Publication:* Chitty on Contracts, (Asst Editor) 22nd edn, 1961. *Recreations:* walking, theatre. *Address:* 74 Lansdowne Road, W11. *T:* 01-727 8891; Pencommon, Boughrood, Brecon. *Club:* Brooks's.

BINNALL, Rev. Canon Peter Blannin Gibbons, FSA; Canon Residentiary, Sub-Dean and Treasurer of Lincoln Cathedral, 1961-75; *b* 5 Jan. 1907; *s* of late Rev. R. G. Binnall and Geraldine (*née* Pearson); *m* 1936, Stephanie, *d* of late Rev. W. Goss; one *s*. *Educ:* Worksop Coll.; Lichfield Theological Coll. Deacon, Grantham for Lincoln, 1932; priest, Lincoln, 1933. Curate of Caistor with Holton le Moor and Clixby, 1932-36; Vicar of Holland Fen with Amber Hill, 1936-45; Rector of East and West Barkwith with S. Willingham, 1945-61; Hon. Canon of Lincoln, 1956. Hon. Sec., Lincs Old Churches Trust, 1952-68; Pres., Lincs Soc. for History and Archaeology, 1975-; Chairman: Lincoln Dio. Adv. Cttee, 1963-76; Local Cttee, Nat. Trust for Tattershall Castle; Vice-Pres., Tennyson Soc.; Mem., British Soc. of Master Glass-Painters. FSA 1944; MA (Lambeth) 1962. *Publications:* contribs to: Collins' Guide to English Parish Churches; Antiquaries Jl, Jl Brit. Soc. Master Glass Painters, Hibbert Jl, various archæological transactions etc, Folklore. *Recreations:* history, folklore, ornithology. *Address:* Elm Cottage, Hemswell, Gainsborough, Lincs. *T:* Hemswell 264.

BINNEY, H(arry) A(ugustus) Roy, CB 1950; UN Adviser on Standards to Government of Cyprus, since 1974; Adviser, International, British Standards Institution, 1972-73 (Director and Secretary, later Director-General, BSI, 1951-70; Director-General, International, BSI, 1971-72); *b* 18 May 1907; *s* of Harry Augustus Binney, Churston, Devon; *m* 1944, Barbara Poole (*d* 1975); three *s* one *d* (and one *d* decd). *Educ:* Royal Dockyard Sch., Devonport; London Univ. BSc(Eng). Entered Board of Trade, 1929; Under-Sec. of the Board of Trade, 1947-51. Chm., Standardization Cttee, European Productivity Agency, 1953-58; first Chm., Exec. Cttee, ISO, 1967-69 (Mem. Council ISO, and Vice-Pres., 1964-69); Chm., Cttee for European Standardization (CEN), 1963-65; Chm., ISO/CERTICO, 1970-73. Mem. Council, Queen Elizabeth Coll., 1952-68, now Associate; Member: Gen. Bd, and Exec. Cttee, Nat. Physical Laboratory, 1957-63; Glos Small Industries Cttee, 1974-. Hon. Life Fellow, Standards Engineers Soc. of America; Hon. Life Mem., American Soc. for Testing and Materials. *Recreation:* gardening. *Address:* 10 Arlington Corner, Bibury, Cirencester, Gloucestershire GL7 5ND. *T:* Bibury 291; c/o UNDP, PO Box 3521, Nicosia, Cyprus. *Club:* Canning.

BINNIE, Alfred Maurice, FRS 1960; Fellow of Trinity College (1944) and University Reader Emeritus in Engineering, Cambridge; *b* 6 Feb. 1901; *s* of late David Carr Binnie. *Educ:* Weymouth Coll.; Queens' Coll., Cambridge. Jun. Research Engineer, Bridge Stress Cttee, 1923-25; Demonstrator and Lectr, Engrg Lab., Oxford, 1925-44; Rhodes Travelling Fellow, 1932-33; Lectr, New Coll., Oxford, 1933-44; Univ. Lectr, Engrg Lab., Cambridge, 1944-54; Sen. Research Fellow, California Inst. of Technology, 1951-52; Scott Visiting Fellow, Ormond Coll., Univ. of Melbourne, 1966; Vis. Scholar, Univ. of California, Berkeley, 1967-68. FIMechE 1937; FICE 1947; Founder Fellow, Fellowship of Engineering, 1976. *Publications:* articles in scientific and engrg jls. *Recreation:* mountaineering. *Address:* Trinity College, Cambridge. *T:* 58201. *Clubs:* Alpine, United Oxford & Cambridge University.

BINNIE, David Stark; FCIT; FInstM; General Manager, British Rail, London Midland Region, since 1977; *b* 2 June 1922; *s* of Walter Archibald Binnie and Helen (*née* Baxter), Bonkle, Lanarkshire; *m* 1947, Leslie Archibald; one *s* one *d*. *Educ:* Wishaw High School. British Railways: Gen. and Signalling Asst to Gen. Manager Scottish Region, 1955; Asst District Operating Supt 1961, District Operating Supt 1963, Glasgow North; Divisional Movements Manager, Glasgow Div., 1965; Movements Manager, Scottish Region, 1967; Divisional Manager, SE Div., Southern Region, 1969; Asst Gen. Manager, Southern Region, 1970, Gen. Manager, 1972; Exec. Dir, Freight, BR Board, 1974-76. Lt-Col Engineer and Railway Staff Corps, RE (T&AVR). Governor, Sevenoaks Sch. *Recreation:* Highland life. *Address:* Copse Cottage, Oak Hill Road, Sevenoaks, Kent. *T:* Sevenoaks 53425. *Club:* London Press.

BINNIE, Geoffrey Morse, FRS 1975; Consultant to Binnie & Partners since 1973; *b* 13 Nov. 1908; *s* of William Eames Binnie and Ethel Morse; *m* 1st, 1932, Yanka Paryczko (*d* 1964); one *s* one *d*; 2nd, 1964, Elspeth Maud Cicely Thompson. *Educ:* Charterhouse; Trinity Hall, Cambridge (MA); Zurich Univ. FICE, FIWE, FASCE, FGS. Served War of 1939-45, RE (Major). Asst Engr, Gorge Dam, Hong Kong, 1933-37; Chief Asst, Eye Brook Reservoir, Northants, 1937-39; Partner, Binnie & Partners, 1939, resumed practice, 1945; responsible for design and supervision of construction of several water supplies in UK; Sen. Partner 1956-72, resp. for design and supervision of constr. of major projects abroad incl. Dokan dam, Iraq, completed 1960 and Mangla project, W Pakistan, compl. 1970. Chm., Panel advising on design and constr. of 2500 MW Peace River Hydro-electric project, BC, 1962-68. Chief Technical Supervisor, Poechos Dam, Peru, 1972-76; Chm., Advisory Board for Mornos dam, Greece, 1975-76. Chm., ICE Floods Working Party; Chadwick Trustee; Pres., JInstE, 1955; Vice-Pres., ICE, 1970-72; Fellow Imperial Coll. 1972. Telford Gold Medal, 1968; (1st) Smeaton Gold Medal, 1974. Fellow, Fellowship of Engineering, 1976. *Publications:* techn. articles on engrg subjects, papers for World Power Conf., Internat. Commn on Large Dams and ICE. *Recreation:* gardening. *Address:* St Michael's Lodge, Benenden, Cranbrook, Kent TN17 4EZ. *T:* Benenden 498. *Club:* Athenæum.

BINNING, Lord; John George Baillie-Hamilton; *b* 21 Dec. 1941; *o s* of 12th Earl of Haddington, *qv*; *m* 1975, Prudence Elizabeth, *d* of A. Rutherford Hayles. *Educ:* Ampleforth. *Address:* Mellerstain, Gordon, Berwickshire; Tyninghame, Dunbar, East Lothian.

BINNING, Kenneth George Henry, CMG 1976; Under-Secretary, Regional Industrial Finance Division, Department of Industry, since 1976; *b* 5 Jan. 1928; *o s* of late Henry and Hilda Binning; *m* 1953, Pamela Dorothy, *o d* of A. E. and D. G. Pronger; three *s* one *d*. *Educ:* Bristol Grammar Sch.; Balliol Coll., Oxford. Joined Home Civil Service, 1950; Nat. Service, 1950-52; HM Treasury, 1952-58; Private Sec. to Financial Sec., 1956-57; AEA, 1958-65; seconded to Min. of Technology, 1965; rejoined Civil Service, 1968; Dir-Gen. Concorde, 1972-76 and Under-Sec., DTI later Dept of Industry, 1972-. *Recreations:* music, gardening. *Address:* 12 Kemerton Road, Beckenham, Kent. *T:* 01-650 0273.

BINNS, David John; General Manager, Warrington Development Corporation, since 1969; *b* 12 April 1929; *s* of Henry Norman Binns, OBE and Ivy Mary Binns; *m* 1957, Jean Margaret Evans; one *s* (one *d* decd). *Educ:* Fleetwood Grammar Sch.; Rossall Sch.; Sheffield Univ. LLB 1951. Solicitor 1954. Articled Clerk, Sheffield City Council, 1949; Asst Solicitor, Warrington County Borough Council, 1954; Dep. Town Clerk, Warrington County Borough Council, 1958. *Recreations:* walking, gardening, music. *Address:* 4 Cedarways, Appleton, Warrington, Cheshire WA4 5EW. *T:* Warrington 62169. *Club:* Warrington (Warrington).

BINNS, Edward Ussher Elliott E.; *see* Elliott-Binns.

BINNS, Geoffrey John; Partner, Fraser, Woodgate & Beall, Solicitors, Wisbech, Cambs, since 1958; Recorder of the Crown Court, since 1977; *b* 12 Oct. 1930; *s* of Rev. Robert Arthur Geoffrey Binns and Elizabeth Marguerite Binns; *m* 1964, Elizabeth Anne Poole Askew. *Educ:* Perse Sch.; Jesus Coll., Cambridge (MA). Admitted solicitor, 1956. Chm., N Cambs Hosp. Management Cttee, 1970-74; Member: E Anglian Reg. Hosp. Bd, 1972-74; E Anglian RHA, 1974-76; Panel of Chairmen, Cambridge Univ. Ct of Discipline, 1976-. Registrar, Archdeaconry of Wisbech, 1972-. *Recreations:* golf, gardening. *Address:* Fairway, Barton Road, Wisbech, Cambs. *T:* Wisbech 3929.

BINNS, Surgeon Rear-Adm. George Augustus, CB 1975; ophthalmic medical practitioner; *b* 23 Jan. 1918; *s* of Dr Cuthbert C. H. Binns and Julia Binns (*née* Frommel); *m* 1949, Joan Whitaker; one *s* two *d*. *Educ:* Repton Sch.; St Bartholemew's Hosp. MRCS, LRCP, DO. Casualty House Surgeon, Luton and Dunstable Hosp., 1942. Served War of 1939-45: joined RNVR, Dec. 1942. Served as Specialist in Ophthalmology, 1952, and promoted to Sen. Specialist in Ophthalmology, 1962; subseq. Admiralty Medical Bd, HMS Excellent, and RN Hosp., Gibraltar; MO in Charge, RN Hosp., Plymouth, and Command MO, 1972-75. QHS 1972-75. FRSocMed; Member: BMA; Southern and SW Ophthalmological Socs. CStJ 1972. *Recreations:* photography, house and garden maintenance, golf, brewing, wine making. *Address:* Netherseal, Hindhead Road, Haslemere, Surrey GU27 3PJ. *T:* Haslemere 4281. *Club:* Naval and Military.

BINNS, Professor Howard Reed, CMG 1958; OBE 1948; MA (Cantab), BSc (Edin), MRCVS; Visiting Professor and Consultant, University of Guelph, since 1975; Director, Centre for International Programs, and Professor of Veterinary Microbiology, University of Guelph, 1969-75; *b* 3 Aug. 1909; *s* of Cuthbert Evelyn Binns and Edith Mildred Edwards; *m* 1935, Katharine Vroom Lawson; one *s* one *d*. *Educ:* Bootham Sch., York; St John's Coll., Cambridge; Royal (Dick) Veterinary Coll.; Edinburgh Univ. Veterinary Officer, Nyasaland, 1935-39; Veterinary Research Officer, Palestine, 1940-41; Senior Veterinary Research Officer, Palestine, 1941-47; Dep. Dir of Veterinary Services, Palestine, 1947-48; Director, East African Veterinary Research Organization, 1950-67 (Principal Scientific Officer, EAVRO, 1948-50). Scientific missions to: USA and Canada, 1939; Syria and the Lebanon, 1945; India, 1946; USA, 1947; South Africa, 1949; Australia, 1960; USA and Germany, 1966; West Indies and S America, 1970; West Africa, 1971; India, 1973; Kenya, 1975, 1976; Carnegie Corp. Grant, 1956; Rockefeller Foundn Grants, 1966, 1970; Commonwealth Foundn Grant, 1971. Consultant to US Nat. Acad. of Sciences, on animal science in tropical Africa, 1959. Mem. Scientific Council for Africa, 1961-65 (Assoc. Mem., 1955-61). Hon. Prof. of Vet. Science in Univ. of East Africa. *Publications:* contribs to scientific jls. *Recreations:* travel, photography. *Address:* San Diego, Estepona, Malaga, Spain.

BINNS, John; *b* June 1914; *m*; one *s*. *Educ:* Holycroft Sec. Sch., Keighley. Mem., Keighley Borough Council, 1945; Alderman, 1954; Mayor, 1958-59. Joined Labour Party, 1944; MP (Lab) Keighley, 1964-70. Contested (Social Dem.) Keighley, Feb. 1974. Mem. Amalgamated Engineering Union; former Trades Union Officer.

BINNS, Kenneth Johnstone, CMG 1960; Under-Treasurer and Commissioner of State Taxes, Government of Tasmania, 1952-76; now Deputy Chairman: Tasmanian Government Insurance Office; State Library Board of Tasmania; State Grants Commission; Director, Comalco Aluminium (Bell Bay) Ltd; *b* New South Wales, Australia, 3 June 1912; *s* of late Kenneth Binns, CBE; *m* 1940, Nancy H. Mackenzie; no *c. Educ:* Melbourne Church of England Grammar Sch.; Queen's Coll., Univ. of Melbourne (MA, BCom); Harvard Univ., USA. Tasmanian Treasury, 1942-76. First Canberra Scholarship, 1930; Fellow, Commonwealth Fund of New York, 1950; Fiscal Review Comr to Federal Republic of Nigeria, 1964; with IMF as Adviser to Minister of Finance, Indonesia, 1969. *Publications:* Federal-State Financial Relations, Canada and Australia, 1948; Social Credit in Alberta, 1947; various government reports; articles in Economic Record. *Recreation:* fishing. *Address:* 3 Ellington Road, Sandy Bay, Tasmania 7005, Australia. *T:* 25 1863. *Clubs:* Athenæum, Tasmanian, Hobart.

BINNS, Malcolm; concert pianist; *b* 29 Jan. 1936; *s* of Douglas and May Binns. *Educ:* Bradford Grammar Sch.; Royal Coll. of Music (ARCM, Chappell Gold Medal, Medal of Worshipful Co. of Musicians). London début, 1957; Henry Wood Proms début, 1960; Royal Festival Hall début, 1961; Festival Hall appearances in London Philharmonic Orchestra International series, 1969-; concerts at Aldeburgh Festival, Leeds Festival and Three Choirs Festival (1975); regular appearances at Promenade concerts. *Recreation:* collecting etchings and antique gramophone records. *Address:* 233 Court Road, Orpington, Kent. *T:* Orpington 31056.

BINNY, John Anthony Francis; *b* 13 Dec. 1911. *Educ:* Wellington College. Supplementary Reserve of Officers, 15th/19th The King's Royal Hussars, 1936. Served War of 1939-45, France and Burma (despatches). Chairman: Associated Portland Cement Manufacturers; Dir, National Westminster Bank and other cos. A Governor of Wellington Coll., 1968. *Address:* Byways, Pound Lane, Burley, Ringwood, Hampshire. *Clubs:* Cavalry and Guards, White's, MCC.

BIOBAKU, Dr Saburi Oladeni, CMG 1961; MA, PhD; Chairman, Management Consultant Services Ltd, Lagos, since 1972; *b* 16 June 1918; *s* of late Chief S. O. Biobaku, Aré of Iddo, Abeokuta; *m* 1949, Muhabat Folasade, *d* of Alhaji L. B. Agusto, barrister-at-law, Lagos; one *s. Educ:* Govt Coll., Ibadan; Higher Coll., Yaba; University Coll., Exeter; Trinity Coll., Cambridge. BA London, 1945; BA Cantab, 1947, MA 1951; PhD London, 1951. Education Officer, Nigeria, 1947-53; Registrar, University Coll., Ibadan, 1953-57; Dir, Yoruba Historical Research Scheme, 1956-; Sec. to Premier and Executive Council, Western Nigeria, 1957-61; Pro-Vice-Chancellor, Univ. of Ife, Nigeria, 1961-65; Vice-Chancellor, Univ. of Lagos, 1965-72. Created Aré of Iddo, Abeokuta, 1958. *Publications:* The Origin of the Yoruba, 1955; The Egba and Their Neighbours, 1842-1872, 1957; contribs to Africa, jl of Nigerian Historical Soc., Odu (Joint Ed.), etc. *Recreations:* soccer, tennis, badminton, swimming, walking. *Address:* PO Box 7741, Lagos, Nigeria. *T:* (home) 31430. *Clubs:* Metropolitan (Lagos); Dining (Ibadan).

BIRCH, family name of **Baron Rhyl.**

BIRCH, Alexander Hope, CMG 1970; OBE 1961; HM Diplomatic Service, retired; *b* 19 Jan. 1913; *s* of Denys Goldney and Lucy Helen Booth Birch; *m* 1st, 1940, Honor Pengelley (marr. diss., 1948); 2nd, 1953, Joan Hastings-Hungerford; no *c. Educ:* St Catherine's and St Mark's Colls, Alexandria, and privately. Appointed to: HM Embassy, Cairo, 1937; Addis Ababa, 1942; Moscow, 1946; Budapest, 1947; Tel-Aviv, 1949; Second Sec. (Inf.), Baghdad, 1950, First Sec. and Consul, Seoul, 1951, and Djakarta, 1954; First Sec. (Commercial), Khartoum, 1956, and Paris, 1961; Counsellor (Commercial), Paris, 1962, and Baghdad, 1965; Counsellor (Economic and Commercial), Accra, 1967-70; Dep. High Comr, Perth, WA, 1970-73; Administrative Adviser to Premier of Antigua, 1973-75. *Recreations:* reading, walking. *Address:* Woodrow, Edgehill Road, Clevedon, Avon BS21 7BZ. *Club:* Oriental.

BIRCH, Prof. Anthony Harold, PhD; Professor of Political Science, University of Exeter, since 1970; *b* 17 Feb. 1924; *o s* of late Frederick Harold Birch and of Rosalind Dorothy Birch; *m* 1953, Dorothy Madeleine Overton, Bayport, New York; one *s* one *d. Educ:* The William Ellis Sch.; University Coll., Nottingham; London Sch. of Economics. BSc (Econ) London, with 1st cl. hons, 1945; PhD London, 1951. Asst Principal, Board of Trade, 1945-47; University of Manchester: Asst Lectr in Govt, 1947-51; Lectr, 1951-58; Senior Lectr in Government, 1958-61; Prof. of Political Studies, Univ. of Hull, 1961-70. Commonwealth Fund Fellow at Harvard Univ. and University

of Chicago, 1951-52. Consultant to Government of Western Region of Nigeria, 1956-58. Vis. Prof. Tufts Univ., 1968. Vice-President: UK Political Studies Assoc., 1976- (Chm., 1972-75); Internat. Political Science Assoc., 1976-. *Publications:* Federalism, Finance and Social Legislation, 1955; Small-Town Politics, 1959; Representative and Responsible Government, 1964; The British System of Government, 1967; Representation, 1971; Political Integration and Disintegration in the British Isles, 1977; articles in various journals. *Recreation:* sailing. *Address:* University of Exeter, Exeter, Devon. *T:* Exeter 77911.

BIRCH, Prof. Arthur John, DPhil (Oxon), MSc; FRS 1958; FAA, FRIC, FRACI; Professor of Organic Chemistry, Australian National University, Canberra, since 1970; *b* 3 Aug. 1915; *s* of Arthur Spencer and Lily Birch; *m* 1948, Jessie Williams; three *s* two *d. Educ:* Sydney Technical High Sch.; Sydney Univ. Scholar of the Royal Commission for the Exhibition of 1851, Oxford, 1938-41; Research Fellow, Oxford, 1941-45; ICI Research Fellow, Oxford, 1945-48; Smithson Fellow of the Royal Society, Cambridge, 1949-52; Prof. of Organic Chemistry, University of Sydney, 1952-55; Prof. of Organic Chemistry, Manchester Univ., 1955-67; Dean, Research Sch. of Chemistry, ANU, Canberra, 1967-70, 1973-76. Treas., Australian Acad. Science, 1969-73; Chm., Ind. Enquiry into CSIRO, 1976-. Foreign Mem., USSR Acad. of Science, 1976. Davy Medal, Royal Soc., 1972. *Publications:* How Chemistry Works, 1950; about 300 original scientific communications, chiefly in Journal of Chemical Soc. and Australian Journal of Chemistry. *Address:* 3 Arkana Street, Yarralumla, Canberra, ACT 2600, Australia; Research School of Chemistry, Australian National University, Box 4, PO, Canberra, ACT 2600, Australia.

BIRCH, Dr Bryan John, FRS 1972; Reader in Mathematics, University of Oxford, and Fellow of Brasenose College, Oxford, since 1966; *b* 25 Sept. 1931; *s* of Arthur Jack and Mary Edith Birch; *m* 1961, Gina Margaret Christ; two *s* one *d. Educ:* Shrewsbury Sch.; Trinity Coll., Cambridge (MA, PhD). Harkness Fellow, Princeton, 1957-58; Fellow: Trinity Coll., Cambridge, 1956-60; Churchill Coll., Cambridge, 1960-62; Sen. Lectr, later Reader, Univ. of Manchester, 1962-65. *Publications:* articles in learned jls, mainly on number theory; various editorships. *Recreation:* gardening (theoretical). *Address:* Green Cottage, Boars Hill, Oxford. *T:* Oxford 735367; Mathematical Institute, 25-29 St Giles, Oxford. *T:* Oxford 54295.

BIRCH, Dennis Arthur, CBE 1977; Councillor, West Midlands County Council, since 1974; *b* 11 Feb. 1925; *s* of George Howard and Leah Birch; *m* 1948, Mary Therese Lyons; one *d. Educ:* Wolverhampton Municipal Grammar Sch. Wolverhampton County Borough Council: elected, 1952; served, 1952-74; Alderman, 1970-73; Mayor, 1973-74; Leader, 1967-73. Elected (following Local Govt reorganisation) Chm. West Midlands CC, 1974-76. *Address:* 3 Tern Close, Wolverhampton Road East, Wolverhampton WV4 6AU. *T:* Sedgley 3837.

BIRCH, John Anthony, MA; FRCO(CHM), LRAM, ARCM; Organist and Master of the Choristers, Chichester Cathedral, since 1958; University Organist since 1967, and Visiting Lecturer in Music, since 1971, University of Sussex; Organist to the Royal Choral Society, since 1966; Professor, Royal College of Music, since 1959; Examiner to Associated Board, Royal Schools of Music; Musical Adviser, Chichester Festival Theatre; *b* 9 July 1929; *s* of late Charles Aylmer Birch, Leek, Staffs; unmarried. *Educ:* Trent Coll.; Royal Coll. of Music. Organist and Choirmaster, St Thomas's Church, Regent Street, London, 1950-53; Accompanist to St Michael's Singers, 1952-58; Organist and Choirmaster, All Saints Church, Margaret Street, London, 1953-58; Sub-Organist, HM Chapels Royal, 1957-58; Choirmaster, Bishop Otter Coll., Chichester, 1963-69. Rep., 1950-66, and Man. Dir, 1966-73, C. A. Birch Ltd, Staffs. Fellow, Corp. of SS Mary and Nicholas (Woodard Schs). Accompanist, Royal Choral Soc., 1965-70. Special Comr, Royal Sch. of Church Music; Mem. Council, Royal Coll. of Organists. Has made concert appearances in France, Germany and Switzerland; recital tours: Canada and US, 1966 and 1967, Australia and NZ, 1969. Hon. MA Sussex, 1971. *Address:* 2 St Richard's Walk, Cathedral Close, Chichester, W Sussex PO19 1QA. *T:* Chichester 84790. *Clubs:* Athenæum, Garrick, East India, Devonshire, Sports and Public Schools.

BIRCH, Reginald; Chairman, Communist Party of Britain (Marxist Leninist), since 1968; Member, General Council of the TUC, since 1975; Member, Executive Council, AUEW, since 1966; *b* 7 June 1914; *s* of Charles and Anne Birch; *m* 1942, Dorothy; three *s. Educ:* St Augustine's Elementary Sch., Kilburn. Apprentice toolmaker, 1929; at trade (toolmaker), until 1960. Divisional Organiser, AEU, 1960-66. *Recreations:*

swimming, growing herbs. *Address:* 29 Langley Park, NW7. *T:* 01-959 7058.

BIRCH, Robert Edward Thomas; Solicitor to the Metropolitan Police, since 1976; *b* 9 May 1917; *s* of late Robert Birch and Edith Birch; *m* 1946, Laura Pia Busini; two *d*. *Educ:* Dulwich Coll. Served RA, 1940-46; Africa, Italy, NW Europe; Major. Admitted solicitor, 1942; joined Solicitors' Dept, New Scotland Yard, 1946; Dep. Solicitor, 1968. *Recreations:* swimming, travel. *Address:* New Scotland Yard, Broadway, SW1H 0BG. *T:* 01-230 2180.

BIRCH, William, PhD; Director, Bristol Polytechnic, since 1975; *b* 24 Nov. 1925; *s* of Frederick Arthur and Maude Olive Birch; *m* 1950, Mary Vine Stammers; one *s* one *d*. *Educ:* Ranelagh Sch.; Univ. of Reading. BA 1949, PhD 1957. Royal Navy, 1943-46, Sub-Lt RNVR. Lectr, Univ. of Bristol, 1950-60; Prof. of Geography, Grad. Sch. of Geog., Clark Univ., Worcester, Mass, USA, 1960-63; Prof., and Chm. of Dept of Geog., Univ. of Toronto, Canada, 1963-67; Prof., and Head of Dept of Geog., Univ. of Leeds, 1967-75. *Publications:* The Isle of Man: a study in economic geography, 1964; contrib.: geography and planning, Trans Inst. Brit. Geographers, Geog. Jl, Economic Geog., Annals Assoc. Amer. Geographers, Jl Environmental Management, etc. *Address:* 13 Richmond Park Road, Clifton, Bristol BS8 3AS. *T:* 39719.

BIRCHENOUGH, (John) Michael, BSc, PhD; Chief Inspector, Inner London Education Authority, since 1973; *b* 17 Jan. 1923; *s* of John Buckley Birchenough and Elsie Birchenough; *m* 1945, Enid Humphries; two *s*. *Educ:* Ashford Grammar Sch., Kent; Chiswick County Sch.; London Univ. Chemist, May & Baker Ltd, 1943-45; teaching posts, 1946-60; HM Inspector of Schools, 1960; Staff Inspector, 1966; Chief Inspector, 1968-72. Pres., Educn Section, BAAS Annual Meeting, Stirling, 1974. *Publications:* contribs to Jl of Chem. Soc. and other scientific jls. *Address:* 43 Watford Road, Radlett, Herts. *T:* Radlett 5176.

BIRD, Rev. Dr Anthony Peter; Principal of The Queen's College, Edgbaston, Birmingham 15, since 1974; *b* 2 March 1931; *s* of Albert Harry Bird and Noel Whitehouse Bird; *m* 1962, Sabine Boehmig; two *s* one *d*. *Educ:* St John's Coll., Oxford (BA LitHum, BA Theol, MA); Birmingham Univ. (MB, ChB, 1970). Deacon, 1957; Priest, 1958; Curate of St Mary's, Stafford, 1957-60; Chaplain, then Vice-Principal of Cuddesdon Theological Coll., 1960-64. General Medical Practitioner, 1972-73. *Recreations:* water, Wolverhampton Wanderers FC, walking. *Address:* The Queen's College, Somerset Road, Birmingham B15 2QH. *T:* 021-454 1527.

BIRD, Lt-Gen. Sir Clarence August, KCIE 1943; CB 1940; DSO 1917; late RE; *b* 5 Feb. 1885; *m* 1919, Dorothea Marian, MBE 1918, K-i-H 1932, *d* of late Major W. E. Nichols; one *s* (and one *s* died on active service). *Educ:* Cheltenham Coll. Joined Royal Engineers, 1904; served in India, 1907-13, 1917-25, 1930-33, 1939-44; with Indian Expeditionary Force in France, 1914-15; with BEF in France, 1916-17 (Bt Maj.); psc 1921; AHQ India, 1922-25; Army Course, London Sch. of Economics, 1925; Chief Instructor in Fortification, SME, Chatham, 1926-29; Commandant, KGVO Bengal Sappers and Miners, 1930-33; Bt Lieut-Col, 1926; Lieut-Col, 1929; Col, 1933; AQMG Aldershot Command, 1933-35; Chief Engineer, Aldershot Command, 1935-39; Maj.-Gen. 1939; Engineer-in-Chief, Army Headquarters, India, 1939-42; Lieut-Gen. 1941; Master Gen. of Ordnance, India, 1942-44; retd 1944. Col Comdt RE, 1942-52; Col Comdt Indian Electrical and Mechanical Engineers, 1944-48. Dept of Food, Govt of India: Regional Commissioner, NW Region, 1944-45; Special Commissioner, 1945-47; Min. of Food: Divisional Food Officer, North Midland Div., 1947-48; Chm., Rhodesia Railways, 1948-53. FRSA. *Address:* Polesden Lacey, Dorking, Surrey.

BIRD, Sir Cyril (Pangbourne), Kt 1968; Company Director, Perth, Western Australia; *b* 5 April 1906; *s* of late Walter Pangbourne Bird and late Alice Emma Bird; *m* 1st, 1934, Margery Isabel (*d* 1974); two *s* three *d*; 2nd, 1976, Agnes Jarvie. *Educ:* Perth, W Australia. FASA. *Recreations:* fishing, music. *Address:* 4 Riverside Drive, Mosman Park, WA 6012, Australia. *T:* 33884. *Clubs:* Royal Freshwater Bay Yacht; Royal King's Park Tennis.

BIRD, Air Vice-Marshal Frank Ronald, CB 1971; DSO 1945; DFC 1944; AFC 1958; FRAeS 1968; Treasurer, Lady Margaret Hall, Oxford, since 1973; *b* 18 Nov. 1918; *s* of Frank Bird and Minnie (*née* Robinson); *m* 1943, Joan Dodson, WAAF; two *s*. *Educ:* Chesterfield Sch., Halton; RAF Coll., Cranwell. Commnd RAF, 1939; Flying Instruction and Experimental Flying, 1940-

43; 105 Sqdn Bomber Comd (Pathfinder Force), 1943-45; Empire Test Pilots Sch. and A & AEE, 1945-46; RAF Coll., Cranwell (Cadet Wing), 1946-48; Perm. Commng Bds, Air Min., 1948-50; RAF Staff Coll., Andover, 1950-51; Brit. Jt Services Mission, Washington, USA, 1951-54; A & AEE, Boscombe Down, 1954-57; HQ Bomber Comd (Plans), 1957; CO, RAF Gaydon, 1957-60; Bomber Ops Staff, Air Min., 1960-63; Canadian Nat. Def. Coll., Kingston, Ont., 1963-64; Comdt, A & AEE, Boscombe Down, 1964-68; Director Gen. of Organisation (RAF), 1968-71; Asst Chief of Staff, Automatic Data Processing Division, SHAPE, 1971-73. *Recreations:* fell walking, golf, music, photography. *Address:* 36 North Street, Islip, Oxon. *T:* Kidlington 2808. *Club:* Royal Air Force.

BIRD, (George William) Terence; Director: Pilkington Brothers Ltd (Executive Vice-Chairman, 1971-77); Rockware Group Ltd; *b* 27 July 1914; *er s* of George Webber Bird and Jane (*née* Hockin); *m* 1942, Hylda Owen Craven; one d (one *s* decd). *Educ:* Prescot Grammar Sch.; Imperial Coll. of Science and Technology (BSc, ARCS). FBIM 1972. Physicist, Pilkington Bros Ltd, 1935; Laboratory Manager, Triplex Northern Ltd, 1936; Pilkington Bros Ltd: Develt Physicist, 1939; Dir, 1962; Chm., Flat Glass Div., 1966. Mem. Council, Manchester Business Sch., 1971-. *Recreations:* gardening, spectator sports. *Address:* 21 Grange Drive, Eccleston Hill, St Helens, Merseyside WA10 3BG. *Club:* Windermere Motor Boat Racing.

BIRD, James Gurth, MBE 1945; TD 1951; Head Master, William Hulme's Grammar School, Manchester, 1947-74; *b* 30 Jan. 1909; *s* of Charles Harold Bird and Alice Jane Bird (*née* Kirtland); *m* 1940, Phyllis Ellis Pownall; one *s* two *d*. *Educ:* King William's Coll., Isle of Man (Scholar); St Catharine's Coll., Cambridge (exhibnr). Classical Tripos Pts I and II, BA 1931, MA 1933. Asst Master, Rossall Sch., 1931-33; Asst Master and House Master, Denstone Coll., 1933-47 (interrupted by War Service). FRSA 1969. *Recreations:* sailing, caravanning, gardening. *Address:* Ty Deryn, Ravenspoint Road, Trearddur Bay, Holyhead, Gwynedd LL65 2AX.

BIRD, Sir Richard Dawnay Martin-; *see* Martin-Bird.

BIRD, Sir Richard (Geoffrey Chapman), 4th Bt *cr* 1922; *b* 3 Nov. 1935; *er surv. s* of Sir Donald Bird, 3rd Bt, and of Anne Rowena (*d* 1969), *d* of late Charles Chapman; *S* father, 1963; *m* 1st, 1957, Gillian Frances (*d* 1966), *d* of Bernard Haggett, Solihull; two *s* four *d*; 2nd, 1968, Helen Patricia, *d* of Frank Beaumont, Pontefract; two *d*. *Educ:* Beaumont. *Heir:* *s* John Andrew Bird, *b* 19 Jan. 1964. *Address:* 12 Hampton Lane, Solihull, W Midlands.

BIRD, Richard Herries; Under Secretary, Department of Education and Science, since 1975; *b* 8 June 1932; *s* of Edgar Bird and Armorel (*née* Dudley-Scott); *m* 1963, Valerie, *d* of Edward and Mary Sanderson; two *d*. *Educ:* Winchester Coll.; Clare Coll., Cambridge. Min. of Transport and Civil Aviation, 1955; Private Sec. to Permanent Sec., 1958-60; Principal, 1960, Asst Sec., 1966, Min. of Transport; Principal Private Sec. to Minister of Transport, 1966-67; CSD 1969; DoE 1971; DES 1973. *Address:* High Beech, Kippington Road, Sevenoaks, Kent TN13 2LL. *T:* Sevenoaks 56777.

BIRD, Terence; *see* Bird, G. W. T.

BIRD, Terence Frederick, CB 1954; Executive Director, P&O, 1965-71; Chairman, Committee of European Shipowners, 1968-71; *b* 29 Sept. 1906; *s* of F. J. Bird and G. M. Bird (*née* Caulfeild); *m* 1939, Prudence Ann Hutton Moss; one *s* one *d*. *Educ:* Southern Rhodesia; Balliol Coll., Oxford; Harvard Univ. Zoologist and Surveyor to Oxford Univ. Expedition to New Hebrides, 1933-34; Sec., Aerodromes Advisory Board, 1934-35. Entered Civil Service, 1935; Home Civil Service Commonwealth Fellow, 1947-48; Under-Sec., Min. of Transport, 1951-65; Under-Sec., BoT, 1965. Chm., Royal Nat. Inst. for the Deaf, 1972-75. *Address:* 12 Ardleigh Court, Ardleigh, Colchester, Essex CO7 7LA. *Club:* Athenæum.

BIRD, Veronica; Editor, Woman's Realm, 1971-77; *b* 16 Oct. 1932; *o d* of Reginald John Fearn; *m* 1st, 1954, Alec Xavier Snobel (marr. diss. 1974); one *s* one *d*; 2nd, 1974, Michael Bird. *Educ:* Kingsley Sch., Leamington Spa. Editor, Parents magazine, 1963-64; Editor, Mother magazine, 1964-71. *Recreations:* theatre, cinema. *Address:* 5 Glentham Gardens, SW13 9JN. *T:* 01-748 6344.

BIRD-WILSON, Air Vice-Marshal Harold Arthur Cooper, CBE 1962; DSO 1945; DFC 1940 and Bar 1943; AFC 1946 and Bar 1955; *b* 20 Nov. 1919; *m* 1942, Audrey Wallace; one *s* one *d*. *Educ:* Liverpool Coll. Joined RAF, Nov. 1937; No 17 Fighter

Sqdn, Kenley, 1938. Served War of 1939-45 (France, Dunkirk, Battle of Britain): Sqdn Comdr Nos 152 and 66, 1942 (despatches); Wing Leader, No 83 Gp, 1943; Comd and Gen. Staff Sch., Fort Leavenworth, Kansas, USA, 1944; Wing Leader, Harrowbeer, Spitfire Wing and then Bentwater Mustang Wing, 1944-45; CO, Jet Conversion Unit, 1945-46; CO, Air Fighting Development Sqdn, CFE, 1946-47; Op. Staff, HQ, MEAF, 1948; RAF Staff Coll., Bracknell, 1949; Personal Staff Officer to C-in-C, MEAF, 1949-50; RAF Flying Coll., Manby, 1951; OC Tactics, CFE, 1952-54; Staff, BJSM, Washington, USA, 1954-57; Staff, Air Sec. Dept., Air Min., 1957-59; CO, RAF Coltishall, 1959-61; Staff Intell., Air Min., 1961-63; AOC and Comdt, CFS, 1963-65; AOC Hong Kong, 1965-67; Dir of Flying (Research and Develt), Min. of Technology, 1967-70; AOC No 23 Gp, 1970-73; Comdr, S Maritime Air Region, RAF, 1973-74, retired. Czechoslovak Medal of Merit 1st class, 1945; Dutch DFC, 1945. *Address:* Whytecroft, 23 Gong Hill Drive, Farnham, Surrey.

BIRDSALL, Mrs Doris; Lord Mayor of Bradford Metropolitan District, 1975-76; *b* 20 July 1915; *d* of Fred and Violet Ratcliffe; *m* 1940, James Birdsall; one *s* one *d. Educ:* Hanson Girls' Grammar School. Mem. Bradford City Council, 1958, Chm. of Educn Cttee, 1972-74; Mem. Bradford Univ. Council, 1963-. Hon. MA Bradford, 1975; Hon. LHD Lesley Coll., Mass, 1976. *Address:* 26 Markfield Avenue, Low Moor, Bradford, West Yorks. *T:* Bradford 678296.

BIRDWOOD, family name of Baron Birdwood.

BIRDWOOD, 3rd Baron, *cr* 1938, of Anzac and of Totnes; **Mark William Ogilvie Birdwood;** Bt 1919; *b* 23 Nov. 1938; *s* of 2nd Baron Birdwood, MVO, and of Vere Lady Birdwood, CVO; *S* father, 1962; *m* 1963, Judith Helen, *e d* of R. Seymour Roberts, Newton Aycliffe, Darlington, Co. Durham; one *d. Educ:* Radley Coll.; Trinity Coll., Cambridge. *Address:* 7 Bloomfield Terrace, SW1; Stanton, Glos.

BIRGI, Muharrem Nuri; Turkish diplomat, retired; *b* Istanbul, 4 Feb. 1908; *o s* of late Ziya Nuri Birgi Pasha, Prof., Faculty of Med., Univ. of Istanbul, later Mem. Grand Nat. Assembly, Turkey, and of Mme Husniye Birgi, *d* of Hassan Rami Pasha, Minister of Marine; *m* (marr. diss.). *Educ:* Lycée Galata Saray, Istanbul; Sch. of Pol. Sciences, Paris (Grad. 1929); Faculty of Law, Geneva (LLB 1931). Entered Turkish For. Min., 1932; 3rd, 2nd and then 1st Sec., Turkish Embassy, Warsaw, 1935-39; Min. for For. Affairs, 1939-41; 1st Sec., Turkish Embassy, Paris-Vichy, 1941; transferred to Madrid, 1942, later promoted Counsellor there. Min. for For. Affairs, Ankara: Co-Dir-Gen. 1st Political Dept, 1944; Dir-General: Dept of Internat. Affairs, 1945; Dept of Co-ordination, 1946; Dept of Consular Affairs, 1946; 2nd Political Dept, 1950; Dep. Sec.-Gen., 1951; Under-Sec. of State, 1952; Sec.-Gen., 1954-57; Turkish Ambassador to Court of St James's, 1957-60. Turkish Permanent Representative to NATO, 1960-72, retired 1972. *Recreation:* painting. *Address:* Toprakli Sokak 11, Salacak, Üsküdar, Istanbul, Turkey. *T:* Istanbul 331591.

BIRK, family name of Baroness Birk.

BIRK, Baroness *cr* 1967 (Life Peer), of Regent's Park in Greater London; **Alma Birk,** JP; journalist; Parliamentary Under-Secretary of State, Department of the Environment, since 1974; *d* of late Barnett and Alice Wilson; *m* Ellis Birk; one *s* one *d. Educ:* South Hampstead High Sch.; LSE. BSc Econ (Hons) London. Leader of Labour Group, Finchley Borough Council, 1950-53; contested (Lab): Ruislip-Northwood, 1950; Portsmouth West, 1951, 1955. Baroness in Waiting (Govt Whip), March-Oct. 1974. Associate Editor, Nova, 1965-69. Formerly Lectr and Prison Visitor, Holloway Prison. Mem., Youth Service Develt Council, 1967-71; Chm., Health Educn Council, 1969-72; Vice-President: Council for Children's Welfare, 1968-75; H. G. Wells Soc., 1967-; Stamford Hill Associated Clubs, 1967-70; Redbridge Jewish Youth Centre, 1970-; Member: Fabian Soc.; Hea- (Sec., Fabian Soc. Res. Cttee on Marriage and Divorce, 1951-52); Howard League for Penal Reform, 1948-; Hendon Group Hosp. Management Cttee, 1951-59; Panel, London Pregnancy Adv. Service, 1968-; RCOG working party on the unplanned pregnancy, 1969-72; Exec. Council of Christians and Jews, 1971-; Hon. Cttee, Albany Trust; Ct of Governors, LSE, 1971-. JP Highgate, 1952. *Publications:* pamphlets, articles. *Recreations:* travelling, theatre, reading, talking, especially to men. *Address:* 13 Hanover Terrace, NW1.

BIRKENHEAD, 3rd Earl of, *cr* 1922; **Frederick William Robin Smith;** Bt 1918; Baron Birkenhead 1919; Viscount Birkenhead 1921; Viscount Furneaux 1922; *b* 17 April 1936; *o s* of 2nd Earl of Birkenhead, TD, and of Hon. Sheila Berry, 2nd *d* of 1st Viscount Camrose; *S* father, 1975. *Educ:* Eton; Christ Church, Oxford. Mem. Council, RSL, 1975-. *Publications:* (as Robin Furneaux): The Amazon, 1969; William Wilberforce, 1974 (Heinemann Award, 1975). *Address:* 48 Arthur Road, Wimbledon, SW19. *T:* 01-947 3983; The Cottage, Charlton, Banbury, Oxon. *T:* Kings Sutton 224. *Clubs:* Buck's, White's, Portland.

BIRKENHEAD, Bishop Suffragan of, since 1974; **Rt. Rev. Ronald Brown;** *b* 7 Aug. 1926; *s* of Fred and Ellen Brown; *m* 1951, Joyce Hymers; one *s* one *d. Educ:* Kirkham Grammar Sch.; Durham Univ. (BA, DipTh). Vicar of Whittle-le-Woods, 1956; Vicar of St Thomas, Halliwell, Bolton, 1961; Rector and Rural Dean of Ashton-under-Lyne, 1970. *Recreations:* antiques and golf. *Address:* Trafford House, Queen's Park, Chester CH4 7AX. *T:* Chester 25677. *Club:* National Liberal.

BIRKETT, family name of Baron Birkett.

BIRKETT, 2nd Baron *cr* 1958, of Ulverston; **Michael Birkett;** Consultant to National Theatre on Films, Television and Sponsorship, since 1977; film producer since 1961; *b* 22 Oct. 1929; *s* of 1st Baron Birkett, PC and Ruth Birkett (*née* Nilsson, she *d* 1969); *S* father, 1962; *m* 1960, Junia Crawford (*d* 1973). *Educ:* Stowe; Trinity Coll., Cambridge. Asst Dir at Ealing Studios and Ealing Films, 1953-59; Asst Dir, 1959-61, on films including: The Mark; The Innocents; Billy Budd; Associate Producer: Some People, 1961-62; Modesty Blaise, 1965; Producer: The Caretaker, 1962; Marat/Sade, 1966; A Midsummer Night's Dream, 1967; King Lear, 1968-69; Director: The Launching and The Soldier's Tale, 1963; Overture and Beginners, the More Man Understands, 1964; Outward Bound, 1971. Dep. Dir, National Theatre, 1975-77. Master, Curriers' Co., 1975-76. *Recreations:* music, ballet. *Address:* House of Lords, SW1.

BIRKETT, George William Alfred, CBE 1960; CEng, FIEE, FIMechE; Director of Weapons Production, Ministry of Defence (Naval), 1965-70, retired; *b* 16 June 1908; *m* 1939, Doris Lillian Prince; one *s. Educ:* Portsmouth Municipal College. Portsmouth Dockyard, 1929; Techn. Officer, HM Signal Sch., 1938; Prin. Scientific Officer, RNSS, 1946; Sen. Prin. Production Engr, Admty Production Pool, 1953; Supt of Production Pool, Admty, 1956. *Recreation:* sailing. *Address:* 81 Ferndale, Inhurst Wood, Waterlooville, Portsmouth, Hants. *T:* Waterlooville 52695.

BIRKIN, Sir Charles (Lloyd), 5th Bt *cr* 1905; *b* 24 Sept. 1907; *s* of late Col Charles Wilfrid Birkin, CMG (4th *s* of 1st Bt); *S* uncle, 1942; *m* 1940, Janet Johnson; one *s* two *d. Educ:* Eton. Served War of 1939-45, with 112th Regt, 9th Sherwood Foresters. *Publications:* collections of short stories: The Kiss of Death, 1964; The Smell of Evil, 1965; Where Terror Stalks, 1966; My Name is Death, 1966; Dark Menace, 1968; So Cold... So Fair, 1970; Spawn of Satan, 1971. *Heir:* s John Christian William Birkin, *b* 2 July 1953. *Address:* West Kella, Sulby, Isle of Man. *T:* Sulby 544. *Club:* Carlton.

BIRKIN, Air Commodore James Michael, CB 1956; DSO 1944; OBE 1951; DFC 1944; AFC 1942; Director, Birkin & Company Limited, New Basford, Nottingham (Lace Manufacturers); *b* 23 April 1912; *s* of late Major H. L. Birkin, Lincoln House, The Park, Nottingham, and late Olive Isobel, *d* of late Rev. H. C. Russell, Wollaton, Notts; *m* 1956, Antonia Edith (whom he divorced 1977), *d* of late Lt-Col A. F. Stanley Clarke and late Mrs Charles Graves; one *s* one *d. Educ:* Harrow; Trinity Coll., Cambridge (MA). London Stock Exchange until 1939; Birkin & Co. Ltd, 1945-. RAFVR, 1938-47; RAuxAF, 1947-63 (Inspector, 1952-62); Hon. Air Commodore, 1956. ADC to the Queen, 1957-63. High Sheriff, Isle of Wight, 1977. *Address:* c/o Birkin & Co. Ltd, New Basford, Nottingham. *T:* Nottingham 79351. *Clubs:* Royal Automobile, MCC, Pathfinder; Pitt (Cambridge); Royal Yacht Squadron, Royal Victoria Yacht, Cowes Corinthian Yacht.

BIRKINSHAW, Air Commodore George William, CB 1946; *b* 17 June 1896. *Educ:* Downing Coll., Cambridge (BA 1927). RFC and RAF from 1915; served European War, 1914-18, France; India and Iraq, 1920-24; Egypt and Palestine, 1933-38; Dir, Repair and Maintenance, Ministry of Supply, 1943-46; Senior Technical Staff Officer, RAF HQ, India, 1946-47; retired, 1947. Freeman of York, Freeman of London. *Clubs:* Royal Air Force, Pathfinder.

BIRKINSHAW, Prof. John Howard, DSc; FRIC; retired as Professor of Biochemistry and Head of Department of Biochemistry, London School of Hygiene and Tropical

Medicine, University of London (1956-62), now Emeritus; *b* 8 Oct. 1894; *s* of John Thomas and Madeline Birkinshaw, Garforth, near Leeds; *m* 1929, Elizabeth Goodwin Guthrie, Ardrossan, Ayrshire; one *s* one *d*. *Educ:* Leeds Modern Sch.; Leeds Univ. War service, 1915, West Yorks Regt and Machine Gun Corps (POW); demobilised, 1919. BSc Hons 1920, MSc 1921, DSc 1929, Leeds. Research Biochemist to Nobel's Explosives Co. (later ICI), 1920-30; Research Asst to Prof. Raistrick, London Sch. of Hygiene and Tropical Medicine, 1931; Senior Lecturer, 1938; Reader, 1945. *Publications:* about 60 scientific papers in Biochemical Journal, Philos. Trans. Royal Society, etc. *Recreation:* photography. *Address:* 87 Barrow Point Avenue, Pinner, Mddx. *T:* 01-866 4784.

BIRKMYRE, Sir Henry, 2nd Bt *cr* 1921, of Dalmunzie; *b* 24 March 1898; *er s* of Sir Archibald Birkmyre, 1st Bt and Anne, *e d* of Capt. James Black; *S* father, 1935; *m* 1922, Doris Gertrude, *er d* of late Col H. Austen Smith, CIE; one *s* one *d*. *Educ:* Wellington. War Service in France with RFA, 1917. *Heir: s* Archibald Birkmyre [*b* 12 Feb. 1923; *m* 1953, Gillian Mary, *o d* of Eric Downes, OBE; one *s* two *d*]. *Recreation:* golf. *Address:* Springbank, Cooden, Bexhill-on-Sea, E Sussex TN39 4ST. *T:* Cooden 2214.

BIRKS, Maj.-Gen. (retired) Horace Leslie, CB 1945; DSO 1941; *b* 7 May 1897; *m* 1920, Gladys Hester (*d* 1957), MBE, *d* of Lieut-Col Hugh Harry Haworth Aspinall, OBE; one *s*. *Educ:* University College Sch. Enlisted London Rifle Brigade, 1915; 2nd Lieut Machine Gun Corps Heavy Branch, 1917, later Tank Corps; served France, 1915-16 and again 1917 (twice wounded); Instructor RTC Schools, 1919-24; Staff Coll., Quetta, 1927, 1928; General Staff, Western Command and War Office, 1930-37; Instructor Staff Coll., Quetta, 1937-39; India, 1924-29 and 1937-39; GSO1, 7th Armoured Division, Army of the Nile, 1939-40; 2nd in Command 4th Armoured Bde, 1940-41 (DSO, despatches twice); Commander 11th Armoured Brigade, 1941; Commander 10th Armoured Division, 1942; MG, RAC, CMF, 1944 (CB); retired pay, 1946. Secretary, University College Hospital Medical Sch., 1946-63, retired. *Recreations:* travel, golf, squash, swimming in warm water. *Address:* 401 Frobisher House, Dolphin Square, SW1V 3LL. *Clubs:* Army and Navy, Roehampton, Pilgrims (President).

BIRKS, Dr Jack, CBE 1975; Technical Director, BP Trading Ltd, and Deputy Chairman, BP Trading Executive Committee, since 1972; *b* 1 Jan. 1920; *s* of late Herbert Horace Birks and of Ann Birks; *m* 1948, Vere Elizabeth Burrell-Davis; two *s* two *d*. *Educ:* Ecclesfield Grammar Sch.; Univ. of Leeds (BSc, PhD). Served with REME, Europe and India, 1941-46 (despatches, Captain). Exploration Research Div., Anglo Iranian Oil Co., 1948-57; Man., Petroleum Engrg Research, BP Research Centre, Sunbury, 1957-59; Vice-Pres. Exploration, BP North America, NY, 1959-62; various techn. and managerial appts, subseq. Dir and Gen. Man., Iranian Oil Exploration & Producing Co., Teheran and Masjid-i-Sulaiman, 1962-70; Gen. Man., Exploration and Production Dept, British Petroleum Co. Ltd, London, 1970-72. Member: SRC, 1976-; Meteorological Cttee, 1977-. Pres., Soc. for Underwater Technology, 1974. *Publications:* contribs to technical internat. oil jls, sci. papers on oilfields develts and North Sea oil. *Recreations:* tennis, cricket, golf. *Address:* 42 Cromwell Tower, Barbican, EC2Y 8DD. *T:* 01-588 2915; Cliff House, Cromer Road, Trimingham, Norfolk NR11 8DZ. *T:* South Repps 338. *Club:* St George's Hill Golf.

BIRLEY, Anthony Addison; Clerk of Public Bills, House of Commons, since 1973; *b* 28 Nov. 1920; *s* of Charles Fair Birley and Eileen Mia Rouse; *m* 1951, Jane Mary Ruggles-Brise; two *d*. *Educ:* Winchester (exhibnr); Christ Church, Oxford (MA). Served War in RA (Ayrshire Yeomanry), 1940-45, in North Africa and Italian campaigns (wounded). Asst Clerk, House of Commons, 1948; Clerk of Standing Cttees, 1970. *Recreations:* gardening, walking, racing. *Address:* Holtam House, Paxford, Chipping Campden, Glos. *T:* Paxford 318.

BIRLEY, Derek; Director, Ulster College, Northern Ireland Polytechnic, since 1970; *b* 31 May 1926; *s* of late Sydney John and late Margaret Birley; *m* 1948, Margery Duckworth; two *s*. *Educ:* Hemsworth Grammar Sch.; Queens' Coll., Cambridge; Manchester Univ. BA 1950, MA 1954, Cantab. Royal Artillery, 1944-48; Schoolmaster, Queen Elizabeth Grammar Sch., Wakefield, 1952-55; Admin. Asst, Leeds Educn Cttee, 1955-59; Asst Educn Officer: Dorset, 1959-61; Lancs, 1961-64; Dep. Dir of Educn, Liverpool, 1964-70. *Publications:* The Education Officer and his World, 1970; (with Anne Dufton) An Equal Chance, 1971; Planning and Education, 1972. *Recreations:* books, cricket, jazz. *Address:* Gaywood, 127 Circular Road, Newtownabbey, Co. Antrim BT37 0RE. *T:* Whiteabbey 63142.

BIRLEY, Prof. Eric, MBE 1943; FSA 1931; FBA 1969; Professor of Roman-British History and Archæology, University of Durham, 1956-71, now Professor Emeritus; *b* 12 Jan. 1906; *y s* of J. Harold Birley; *m* 1934, Margaret Isabel, *d* of Rev. James Goodlet; two *s*. *Educ:* Clifton Coll.; Brasenose Coll., Oxford. Lecturer, University of Durham, 1931; Reader, 1943. War of 1939-45: Military Intelligence, Lt-Col, GSO1 Military Intelligence Research Section; Chief of German Military Document Section, War Dept. Vice-Master, Hatfield Coll., Durham, 1947-49, Master, 1949-56; first Dean of Faculty of Social Sciences, Univ. of Durham, 1968-70. President: Soc. of Antiquaries of Newcastle upon Tyne, 1957-59; Cumberland and Westmorland Antiquarian and Archaeological Soc., 1957-60; Architectural and Archæological Soc. of Durham and Northumberland, 1959-63; Member: German Archæological Inst.; Ancient Monuments Board for England, 1966-76; Hon. Member, Gesellschaft Pro Vindonissa (Switzerland). Hon. Dr Phil Freiburg i Br, 1970; Hon. DLitt Leicester, 1971. Polonia Restituta, 1944; Legion of Merit, 1947. *Publications:* Roman Britain and the Roman Army, 1953; (ed) The Congress of Roman Frontier Studies 1949, 1952; Research on Hadrian's Wall, 1961; (jt ed) Roman Frontier Studies 1969, 1974; numerous papers on Roman Britain and on the Roman army, excavation reports, etc. *Recreation:* archæology. *Address:* Sele Cottage, Hexham, Northumberland NE46 3LN. *T:* Hexham 3873.

BIRLEY, James Leatham Tennant, FRCP, FRCPsych, DPM; Dean, Institute of Psychiatry, London, SE5, since 1971; *b* 31 May 1928; *s* of late Dr James Leatham Birley and Margaret Edith (*née* Tennant); *m* 1954, Julia Davies; one *s* three *d*. *Educ:* Winchester Coll.; University Coll., Oxford; St Thomas' Hosp., London. Maudsley Hospital: Registrar, 1960; Sen. Registrar, 1963; Mem. Scientific Staff, MRC Social Psychiatry Research Unit, 1965; Consultant Psychiatrist, Bethlem Royal and Maudsley Hosps, 1969. *Publications:* contribs to scientific jls. *Recreations:* music, gardening. *Address:* 133 Sydenham Hill, SE26 6LW.

BIRLEY, Michael Pellew, MA (Oxon); Housemaster at Marlborough College, since 1970; *b* 7 Nov. 1920; *s* of Norman Pellew Birley, *qv*; *m* 1949, Ann Grover (*née* Street); two *s* two *d*. *Educ:* Marlborough Coll.; Wadham Coll., Oxford. 1st class Classical Honour Moderations, 1940; 1st class *Litterae Humaniores,* 1947; MA 1946. Served War of 1939-45 with the Royal Fusiliers; joined up, Sept. 1940; commissioned, April 1941; abroad, 1942-45 (despatches); demobilised, Jan. 1946. Taught Classics: Shrewsbury Sch., 1948-50; Eton Coll., 1950-56; Headmaster, Eastbourne College, 1956-70. *Recreations:* sailing, playing the flute. *Address:* Preshute House, Marlborough, Wilts SN8 4HQ. *T:* Marlborough 2291.

BIRLEY, Norman Pellew, DSO 1918; MC 1916; *b* Pelton Vicarage, Co. Durham, 29 April 1891; *s* of Rev. Hugh Hornby Birley and Florence Lydia Birley; *m* 1919, Eileen Alice Morgan, Underwood, Mumbles, Glamorgan; two *s*. *Educ:* Repton Sch.; New Coll., Oxford. Served European War, 1914-19. History Master, Gresham's Sch., Holt, 1919; Asst Master, Marlborough Coll., 1922-27; Headmaster, King's Sch., Canterbury, 1927-35; Headmaster, Merchant Taylors' Sch., 1935-46; retired, 1946; Mem., Wiltshire Education Cttee, 1948-66. *Recreations:* fishing and gardening. *Address:* Hyde Leaze, Hyde Lane, Marlborough, Wilts.

See also M. P. Birley.

BIRLEY, Sir Robert, KCMG 1967 (CMG 1950); MA; FSA; Chairman, Central Council of the Selly Oak Colleges, since 1969; *b* 14 July 1903; *s* of late Leonard Birley, CSI, CIE; *m* 1930, Elinor Margaret, *d* of Eustace Corrie Frere, FRIBA; two *d*. *Educ:* Rugby Sch.; Balliol Coll., Oxford (Brackenbury Scholar; Hon. Fellow, 1969). Gladstone Memorial Prize, 1924, 1st Class Hons History. Asst Master, Eton Coll., 1926-35; Headmaster, Charterhouse, 1935-47; Educational Adviser to the Military Governor, CCG, 1947-49; Head Master, Eton Coll., 1949-63; Vis. Prof. of Education, Univ. of the Witwatersrand, 1964-67; Prof. and Head of Dept of Social Science and Humanities, City Univ., London, 1967-71. Mem., Fleming Cttee on Public Schools, 1944; Burge Memorial Lecture, 1948; Reith Lectures, 1949; Clark Lectures, 1961; Chancellor's Lecture, University of Witwatersrand, 1965; Chichele Lectures, All Souls Coll., Oxford, Michaelmas Term, 1967. Gresham Professor in Rhetoric, 1967-77. Hon. DCL Oxford, 1972; Hon. DSc Aston, 1972; Hon. Doc. Ing, Technical Univ., Berlin, 1949; Hon. LLD: Edinburgh, 1950; Leeds, 1950; Liverpool, 1953; Witwatersrand, 1965; Hon. DPhil, Frankfurt Univ., 1959. Grosse Verdienstkreuz (Germany), 1955. *Publications:* The English Jacobins, 1925; Speeches and Documents in American History (selected and edited), 1944; Sunk Without Trace (Clark

Lectures), 1962. *Address:* Lomans, West End, Somerton, Somerset. *T:* Somerton 72640. *Club:* Travellers'.
See also B. Rees.

BIRMINGHAM, Archbishop of, (RC), since 1965; **Most Rev. George Patrick Dwyer,** MA, DD, PhD; *b* 25 Sept. 1908; *s* of John William and Ima Dwyer. *Educ:* St Bede's Coll., Manchester; Ven. English Coll., Rome; Christ's Coll., Cambridge. PhD 1929, DD 1934, Gregorian Univ., Rome; ordained Priest, 1932; BA Mod. and Med. Lang. Trip. Cambridge (Lady Margaret Scholar, Christ's Coll.). Teaching, St Bede's, Manchester, 1937-47; Catholic Missionary Society, 1947; Editor of Catholic Gazette, 1947-51; Superior, Catholic Missionary Society, 1951-57; Bishop of Leeds, 1957-65. Pres., RC Bishops' Conference of England and Wales, 1976-. *Publications:* The Catholic Faith, 1954; Mary-Doctrine for Everyman (with Rev. T. Holland, DD), 1956. *Address:* Archbishop's House, St Chad's, Queensway, Birmingham B4 6EX.

BIRMINGHAM, Bishop of, since 1978; **Rt. Rev. Hugh William Montefiore,** MA, BD; *b* 12 May 1920; *s* of late Charles Sebag-Montefiore, OBE, and Muriel Alice Ruth Sebag-Montefiore; *m* 1945, Elisabeth Mary Macdonald Paton, *d* of late Rev. William Paton, DD, and Mrs Grace Paton; three *d*. *Educ:* Rugby Sch.; St John's Coll., Oxford. Served during war, 1940-45; Capt. RA (Royal Bucks Yeo). Deacon 1949, priest 1950. Curate, St George's, Jesmond, Newcastle, 1949-51; Chaplain and Tutor, Westcott House, Cambridge, 1951-53; Vice-Principal, 1953-54; Examining Chaplain: to Bishop of Newcastle, 1953-70; to Bishop of Worcester, 1957-60; to Bishop of Coventry, 1957-70; to Bishop of Blackburn, 1966-70; Fellow and Dean of Gonville and Caius Coll., 1954-63; Lectr in New Testament, Univ. of Cambridge, 1959-63; Vicar of Great Saint Mary's, Cambridge, 1963-70; Canon Theologian of Coventry, 1959-70; Hon. Canon of Ely, 1969-70; Bishop Suffragan of Kingston-upon-Thames, 1970-78. Mem., Archbishops' Commn on Christian Doctrine, 1967-76. Chm., Indep. Commn on Transport, 1973; Pres., Pedestrians Assoc. for Road Safety. Hon. DD Aberdeen, 1976. *Publications:* (contrib.) The Historic Episcopate and the Fullness of the Church, 1954; To Help You To Pray, 1957; (contrib.) Soundings, 1962; Josephus and the New Testament, 1962; (with H. E. W. Turner) Thomas and the Evangelists, 1962; Beyond Reasonable Doubt, 1963; (contrib.) God, Sex and War, 1963; Awkward Questions on Christian Love, 1964; A Commentary on the Epistle to the Hebrews, 1964; Truth to Tell, 1966; (ed) We Must Love One Another Or Die, 1966; (contrib.) The Responsible Church, 1966; Remarriage and Mixed Marriage, 1967; (contrib.) Journeys in Belief, 1968; (ed) Sermons From Great St Mary's, 1968; My Confirmation Notebook, 1968; The Question Mark, 1969; Can Man Survive, 1970; (ed) More Sermons From Great St Mary's, 1971; Doom or Deliverance?, 1972; (ed) Changing Directions, 1974; (ed) Man and Nature, 1976; Apocalypse, 1976; contribs to New Testament and Theological jls. *Address:* Bishop's Croft, Birmingham, W Midlands B17 0BG. *T:* 021-427 0163. *Club:* Royal Commonwealth Society.
See also Rev. Canon D. M. Paton, Prof. W. D. M. Paton.

BIRMINGHAM, Auxiliary Bishops of, (RC); *see* Cleary, Rt Rev. Joseph; McCartie, Rt Rev. P. L.

BIRMINGHAM, Provost of; *see* Moss, Very Rev. B. S.

BIRMINGHAM, Archdeacon of; *see* Hollis, Ven. G.

BIRSAY, Hon. Lord; Harald Robert Leslie, KT 1973; CBE 1963 (MBE 1945); TD 1944; MA 1927, LLB (Glas.) 1930; QC (Scot.), 1949; DL; Chairman, Scottish Land Court, since 1965; *b* 8 May 1905; *s* of Robert Leslie, Master Mariner, Stromness, Orkney, and Margaret Mowat Cochrane, Stromness; *m* 1945, Robina Margaret Marwick, MB, ChB (Edin.), *o d* of ex-Provost J. G. Marwick, FSA (Scot.), Stromness, Orkney; one *s* one *d*. *Educ:* Earlston Public Sch.; Berwickshire High Sch.; Glasgow High Sch.; Glasgow Univ. Served in Glasgow High Sch. (1918-23) and Glasgow Univ. (1923-30) OTCs. Extracted as Solicitor, 1930; called to Scottish Bar, 1937. War of 1939-45 (MBE; despatches); served in the Royal Scots and on HQs 15 (S) Div.; 8 Corps and 21 Army Group; released, 1945, to TARO, as (Hon.) Lieut-Col. Standing Counsel to Dept of Agriculture; Junior Assessor to City of Edinburgh Assessor and Dean of Guild and Burgh Courts, 1949; Senior Assessor, 1960; Advocate-Depute, Scottish Bar, 1947-51; Sheriff of Roxburgh, Berwick and Selkirk, 1956-61; Sheriff of Caithness, Sutherland, Orkney and Zetland, 1961-65. Candidate (Lab) for Orkney and Shetland Constituency, 1950; Chairman: Scottish Advisory Council on the Treatment of Offenders, 1959; Scottish Cttee of British Council, 1963-70; Scottish Joint Council for Teachers' Salaries, 1964; Executive

Edinburgh Council of Social Service, 1956-69; Cttee on Gen. Med. Services in the Highlands and Islands, 1964-67; Nat. Savings Cttee for Scotland, 1965-72, Pres., 1972-; Board of Governors, St Hilary's Sch., Edinburgh, 1959; Salvation Army Adv. Bd, Edinburgh, 1967-77; Scottish Adv. Cttee on the Travelling People, 1971-77; Hon. President: Glasgow, Orkney and Shetland Association also Edinburgh, Orkney and Zetland Association, 1962; Scottish Council for National Parks until 1965; Hon. Vice-President, Boys' Brigade, 1966- (Hon. Pres., Leith Bn, 1963-); Scottish Council of Boys' Clubs and Youth Clubs, 1962; Shipwrecked Fishermen and Mariners' Royal Benevolent Society (Scotland), 1966; Orkney Council of Social Service, 1966; Pres., Scottish Nat. Dictionary Assoc., 1968-. Lord High Commissioner to the General Assembly of the Church of Scotland, 1965 and 1966. Hon. Air Cdre, No 2 (City of Edinburgh) Maritime HQ Unit, RAuxAF, 1967-. DL Orkney, 1965. Hon. LLD: Strathclyde, 1966; Glasgow, 1966. Hon. FEIS, 1966. *Address:* 27 Queensferry Road, Edinburgh EH4 3HB. *T:* 031-332 3315; Queenafjold, Birsay, Orkney KW17 2LZ. *T:* (Orkney) Birsay 286. *Clubs:* Royal Scots, Caledonian, Arts (Edinburgh).

BIRT, Prof. (Lindsay) Michael; Vice-Chancellor, University of Wollongong, Australia, since its foundation, 1975; *b* 18 Jan. 1932; *s* of Robert Birt and Florence Elizabeth Chapman; *m* 1959, Avis Jennypher Tapfield; two *s*. *Educ:* Melbourne Boys' High Sch.; Univ. of Melbourne; Univ. of Oxford. BAgrSc, BSc and PhD (Melb), DPhil (Oxon). Univ. of Melbourne: Lectr in Biochemistry, 1960-63, Sen. Lectr in Biochem., 1964; Sen. Lectr in Biochem., Univ. of Sheffield, 1964-67; Foundn Prof. of Biochemistry, ANU, 1967-73; Vice-Chancellor designate, Wollongong Univ. Coll., Nov. 1973; Emer. Prof., ANU, 1974. *Publication:* Biochemistry of the Tissues (with W. Bartley and P. Banks), 1968 (London), 1970 (Germany, as Biochemie), 1972 (Japan). *Recreations:* music, reading. *Address:* University of Wollongong, PO Box 1144, Wollongong, NSW 2500, Australia. *T:* 042-29-7311. *Clubs:* Union (Sydney); Wollongong; Melbourne Cricket.

BIRT, Ven. William Raymond; Archdeacon of Berkshire, 1973-77; Rector of West Woodhay, since 1971; *b* 25 Aug. 1911; *s* of Rev. Douglas Birt, Rector of Leconfield with Scorborough, and Dorothy Birt; *m* 1936, Marie Louise Jeaffreson; one *s* two *d*. *Educ:* Christ's Hospital; Ely Theological Coll. Journalist until 1940. Major, 22nd Dragoons (RAC), 1941-46 (despatches). Publisher, 1946-55. Deacon 1956; priest, 1957; Curate, Caversham, 1956-59; Vicar, St George, Newbury, 1959-71; Rural Dean of Newbury, 1969-73. *Recreations:* gardens and gardening. *Address:* West Woodhay Rectory, Newbury, Berkshire RG15 0BL. *T:* Inkpen 359.

BIRTWISTLE, Harrison; composer; an Associate Director, National Theatre, since 1975; *b* 1934; *m* Sheila; one *s*. *Educ:* Royal Manchester Coll. of Music; RAM. Dir of Music, Cranborne Chase Sch., 1962-65. Vis. Fellow, Princeton Univ., 1966-68; Cornell Vis. Prof. of Music, Swarthmore Coll., 1973; Vis. Slee Prof., State Univ. of NY at Buffalo, 1974-75. *Publications:* Refrains and Choruses, 1957; Monody for Corpus Christi, 1959; Précis, 1959; The World is Discovered, 1960; Chorales, 1962, 1963; Entre'actes and Sappho Fragments, 1964; Three Movements with Fanfares, 1964; Tragoedia, 1965; Ring a Dumb Carillon, 1965; Carmen Paschale, 1965; The Mark of the Goat, 1965, 1966; The Visions of Francesco Petrarca, 1966; Verses, 1966; Punch and Judy, 1966-67; Three Lessons in a Frame, 1967; Linoii, 1968; Nomos, 1968; Verses for Ensembles, 1969; Down by the Greenwood Side, 1969; Hoquetus David (arr. of Machaut), 1969; Cantata, 1969; Ut Hermita Solvs, 1969; Medusa, 1969-70; Prologue, 1970; Nenia on the Death of Orpheus, 1970; An Imaginary Landscape, 1971; Meridian, 1971; The Fields of Sorrow, 1971; Chronometer, 1971; Epilogue—Full Fathom Five, 1972; Tombeau, 1972; The Triumph of Time, 1972; La Plage: eight arias of remembrance, 1972; Dinah and Nick's Love Song, 1972; Chanson de Geste, 1973; The World is Discovered, 1973; Grimethorpe Aria, 1973; 5 Chorale Preludes from Bach, 1973; Chorales from a Toyshop, 1973; Interludes from a Tragedy, 1973; Orpheus. *Address:* c/o Alfred Kalmus Ltd, Universal Edition (London) Ltd, 2/3 Fareham Street, W1V 4DU.

BISCOE, Rear-Adm. Alec Julian; *see* Tyndale-Biscoe.

BISHOP, Maj.-Gen. Sir Alec, (Alexander); *see* Bishop, Maj.-Gen. Sir W. H. A.

BISHOP, Ann, FRS 1959; ScD; *b* 19 Dec. 1899; *o d* of late James Kimberly and Ellen Bishop. *Educ:* Manchester High Sch. for Girls; Manchester Univ.; Cambridge Univ. BSc 1921, DSc 1932, Manchester; PhD 1926, ScD 1941, Cambridge. Hon. Research

Fellow, Manchester Univ., 1925-26; Research Asst, Medical Research Council, 1926-29; Beit Memorial Research Fellow, 1929-32; Yarrow Fellow of Girton Coll., Cambridge, 1932-37; Research Fellow of Girton Coll., Cambridge, 1937-66, Life Fellow, 1966; Mem., MRC Staff, 1937-42; Director, MRC Chemotherapy Research Unit at the Molteno Inst., Univ. of Cambridge, 1942-64. *Publications:* articles on the biology of Protozoa, and Chemotherapy, published in Scientific Journals. *Address:* 47 Sherlock Close, Cambridge CB3 0HP.

BISHOP, Dr Arthur Clive; Keeper of Mineralogy, British Museum (Natural History), since 1975; *b* 9 July 1930; *s* of late Charles Henry Bishop and Hilda (*née* Clowes); *m* 1962, Helen (*née* Bennison); one *d. Educ:* Wolstanton County Grammar Sch., Newcastle, Staffs; King's Coll., Univ. of London. BSc 1951, PhD 1954. Geologist, HM Geological Survey, 1954; Lectr in Geology, Queen Mary Coll., Univ. of London, 1958; Principal Sci. Officer, British Museum (Natural History), 1969, Deputy Keeper 1972. Geological Society: Daniel Pidgeon Fund, 1958; Murchison Fund, 1970; Mem. Council, 1975-; Mineralogical Society: Gen. Sec., 1965-72; Vice-Pres., 1973-74; Vice-President: Geologists' Assoc., 1973-; Inst. of Science Technology, 1973-. *Publications:* An Outline of Crystal Morphology, 1967; (with W. R. Hamilton and A. R. Woolley) Hamlyn Guide to Minerals, Rocks and Fossils, 1974; papers in various jls, mainly on geology of Channel Is and Brittany, and on dioritic rocks. *Recreations:* drawing and painting. *Address:* 4 Viewfield Road, Bexley, Kent DA5 3EE. *T:* 01-302 9602.

BISHOP, Rt. Rev. Clifford Leofric Purdy; *b* 1908; *s* of Rev. E. J. Bishop; *m* 1949, Ivy Winifred Adams. *Educ:* St John's, Leatherhead; Christ's Coll., Cambridge (MA); Lincoln Theological Coll. Deacon 1932; Priest, 1933; Curacies, 1932-41; Vicar, St Geo., Camberwell, 1941-49; Rural Dean, 1943-49; Curate-in-charge, All Saints, Newington, 1944-47; Rector of: Blakeney, 1949-53 (Rural Dean of Walsingham, 1951-53); Bishop Wearmouth, 1953-62 (Rural Dean of Wearmouth and Surrogate, 1953-62); Hon Canon of Durham, 1958-62; Bishop Suffragan of Malmesbury, 1962-73; Canon of Bristol, 1962-73. *Address:* Rectory Cottage, Cley-next-Sea, Holt, Norfolk. *T:* Cley 250.

BISHOP, Rt. Hon. Edward (Stanley), PC 1977; TEng (CEI), AMRAeS, MIED; JP; MP (Lab) for Newark, Notts, since 1964; Minister of State, Ministry of Agriculture, Fisheries and Food, since Oct. 1974; *b* 3 Oct. 1920; *e s* of Frank Stanley Bishop and Constance Camilla Bishop (*née* Dawbney); *m* 1945, Winifred Mary Bryant, JP, *o c* of Frank and Elizabeth Bryant; four *d. Educ:* S Bristol Central Sch.; Merchant Venturers' Technical Coll.; Bristol Univ. Former Aeronautical Design Engineer, (British Aircraft Corp.). Member Bristol City Council, 1946-59, 1963-66 (Dep. Leader and Chm. Finance and General Purposes Cttee, 1956-59). JP, City and County of Bristol, 1957-73, Notts 1973-; Visiting Magistrate, HM Bristol Prison, 1959-71. Contested (Lab): Bristol West, 1950; Exeter, 1951; S Gloucester, 1955. Chm., SW Reg. Council, Labour Party, 1953-54; Asst Govt Whip, 1966-67; Opposition Spokesman: on Agric., 1970; on Aviation, Trade and Industry, 1970-74; Parly Sec., MAFF, March-Sept. 1974; UK Parly deleg. to N Atlantic Assembly, 1966-74, and Chm., Assembly's Economic Cttee, 1969-72. Promoted Matrimonial Property Bill, 1969-70. Vice-President RDC Assoc., 1965-74; Member: Archbishop of Canterbury's Commn on Organisation of Church by Dioceses in London and SE England, 1965-67; Redundant Churches Fund, 1970-74. A Church Commissioner, 1968-; Second Church Estates Comr, 1974. FAMS. *Recreations:* archæology, genealogy; National Trust visits; being with family. *Address:* House of Commons, SW1A 0AA.

BISHOP, Sir Frederick (Arthur), Kt 1975; CB 1960; CVO 1957; Director-General of the National Trust, 1971-75; *b* 4 Dec. 1915; *o s* of A. J. Bishop, Bristol; *m* 1940, Elizabeth Finlay Stevenson; two *s* one *d. Educ:* Colston's Hospital, Bristol. LLB (London). Inland Revenue, 1934. Served in RAF and Air Transport Auxiliary, 1942-46. Ministry of Food, 1947, where Principal Private Secretary to Ministers, 1949-52; Asst Secretary, Cabinet Office, 1953-55; Principal Private Secretary to the Prime Minister, 1956-59; Deputy Secretary: of the Cabinet, 1959-61; Min. of Agriculture, Fisheries and Food, 1961-64; Perm. Sec., Min. of Lands and Natural Resources, 1964-65, resigned. Chm., Home Grown Timber Advisory Cttee, 1966-73; Member: BBC Gen. Adv. Council, 1971-75; Crafts Adv. Council, 1973-75. Director: Pearson Longman, 1970-; English China Clays Ltd, 1975-; Devon and Cornwall Bd, Lloyds Bank Ltd. Mem., Devon and Cornwall Reg. Cttee, Nat. Trust. *Address:* Lombard Mill, Lanteglos-by-Fowey, Cornwall. *Club:* Reform.

BISHOP, Sir George (Sidney), Kt 1975; CB 1958; OBE 1947; Chairman, Booker McConnell Ltd; Director, since 1961 (Vice-Chairman, 1970-71); Director: Barclays Bank International, since 1972; Barclays Bank Ltd, since 1974; Agricultural Mortgage Co. Ltd, since 1973; Ranks Hovis McDougall, since 1976; *b* 15 Oct. 1913; *o s* of late J. and M. Bishop; *m* 1940, Marjorie Woodruff (marr. diss. 1961); one *d*; *m* 1961, Una Padel. *Educ:* Ashton-in-Makerfield Grammar Sch.; London Sch. of Economics. Social service work in distressed areas, 1935-38; SW Durham Survey, 1939; Ministry of Food, 1940; Private Secretary to Minister of Food, 1945-49; Under-Secretary, Ministry of Agriculture, Fisheries and Food, 1949-59, Dep. Secretary, 1959-61. Chm. Bookers Agricultural Holdings Ltd, 1964-70; Dir, Nigerian Sugar Co. Ltd, 1966-70. Chairman: Internat. Sugar Council, 1957; West India Cttee, 1969-71 (Pres., 1977-); Industry Co-op Programme, FAO, 1976-; Vice-Chm., Internat. Wheat Council, 1959; Member: Panel for Civil Service Manpower Review, 1968-70; Royal Commn on the Press, 1974-77; Tropical Products Inst. Adv. Cttee; Council, CBI, 1973, Chm. Industry Co-operative Programme; Chm. Council, Overseas Develt Inst. Ltd, 1977-; Governor, Nat. Inst. for Economic and Social Research, 1968-. *Recreations:* mountaineering, motoring, photography. *Address:* Brenva, Egham's Wood Road, Beaconsfield, Bucks. *T:* Beaconsfield 3096; 15 West Eaton Place, SW1. *T:* 01-235 9442. *Clubs:* Reform, MCC; Club Alpin Français.

BISHOP, Sir Harold, Kt, *cr* 1955; CBE 1938; FCGI; BSc (Engineering) London; Hon. FIEE, FIMechE; FIEEE; Director, Chemring Ltd, since 1967; *b* 29 Oct. 1900; 3rd *s* of Henry Thomas Bishop; *m* 1925, Madge Adeline, *d* of Frank Harry Vaus; two *d* (one *s* decd). *Educ:* Alleyn's Sch., Dulwich; City and Guilds Coll. Engineer, HM Office of Works, 1920-22; Engineer, Marconi's Wireless Telegraph Co. Ltd, 1922-23; Senior Supt BBC, 1923-29; Asst Chief Engineer, BBC, 1929-43; Chief Engineer, 1943-52; Dir of Engineering, 1952-63; Consultant, BICC Gp, 1963-68. Hon. FIEE (Pres. 1953-54, Vice-Pres. 1948-53); President: Electrical Industries Benevolent Assoc., 1955-56; Association of Supervising Electrical Engineers, 1956-58; Institution of Electrical and Electronic Techn. Engineers, 1965-69; Royal Television Soc., 1960-62; Fellow, Imperial Coll. of Science and Technology. *Address:* Carbis, Harborough Hill, Pulborough, W Sussex. *T:* West Chiltington 3325. *Club:* Athenæum.

BISHOP, Rev. Hugh, (William Fletcher Bishop); Licensed to preach, Diocese of Wakefield; *b* 17 May 1907; *e s* of John and Mary Bishop, Haughton House, Shifnal, Shropshire. *Educ:* Malvern Coll.; Keble Coll., Oxford (MA). Cuddesdon Coll. Oxford, 1932-33; Deacon, 1933; Priest, 1934. Curate of St Michael's, Workington, 1933-35; Curate of Cuddesdon and Lectr, Cuddesdon, 1935-37. Mem., Community of the Resurrection, Mirfield, (taking name of Hugh), 1940-74; Chaplain to the Forces (EC), 1940-45 (POW, 1942-45); Warden, Hostel of the Resurrection, Leeds, 1946-49; Guardian of Novices, Mirfield, 1949-52; Principal of the College, 1956-65, Father Superior of the Community of the Resurrection, 1965-74, released from the Community of the Resurrection, 1974. Mem. (former Chm.), British Council of Churches Race and Community Relations Bd. *Publications:* The Passion Drama, 1955; The Easter Drama, 1958; Life is for Loving, 1961; (contrib. to) Mirfield Essays in Christian Belief, 1962; The Man for Us, 1968. *Address:* 19 St John's Terrace, Leeds LS3 1DY. *T:* Leeds 459180.

BISHOP, Dr John Edward; Senior Lecturer and Tutor, Birmingham School of Music, since 1974; *b* 23 Feb. 1935; *s* of late Reginald John Bishop and of Eva Bishop (*née* Lucas). *Educ:* Cotham Sch., Bristol; St John's Coll., Cambridge (Exhibr); Reading and Edinburgh Univs. MA, MusB Cantab; DMus Edin.; FRCO (CHM); ADCM. John Stewart of Rannoch Schol. (Univ. prize) 1954. Organist and Asst Dir of Music, Worksop Coll., Notts, 1958-69; Dir of Music, Worksop Coll., 1969-73; Dir of Studies, Birmingham Sch. of Music, 1973-74, Head of BSM 1974. President: Sheffield Organists' Assoc., 1972-73; Birmingham Organists' Assoc., 1976-. Hon. Dir of Music, Cotham Parish Church, Bristol, 1976-; Organ recitalist (incl. many broadcasts) and choral conductor, accompanist, examiner and adjudicator, 1960-. *Publications:* various articles on history and practice of church music and 19th century organ design. *Recreations:* walking, ecclesiology, savouring cities and towns, railways, architecture. *Address:* 93 High Kingsdown, Bristol BS2 8ER. *T:* Bristol 423373.

BISHOP, Dame (Margaret) Joyce, DBE 1963 (CBE 1953); MA Oxon; Head Mistress of The Godolphin and Latymer School, Hammersmith, W6, 1935-63, retired; *b* 28 July 1896; 2nd *d* of Charles Benjamin and Amy Bishop. *Educ:* Edgbaston High

Sch., Birmingham; Lady Margaret Hall, Oxford. English Mistress, Hertfordshire and Essex High Sch., 1918-24; Head Mistress, Holly Lodge High Sch., Smethwick, Staffs, 1924-35. Member Working Party set up by Minister of Education to enquire into Recruitment of Women to Teaching Profession, 1947. President, Association of Head Mistresses, 1950-52. Member: Secondary School Examinations Council, 1950-62; University Grants Cttee, 1961-63; Council for Professions Supplementary to Medicine, 1961-70; TV Research Cttee set up by Home Secretary, 1963-69. Chairman, Joint Cttee of the Four Secondary Associations, 1956-58. FKC 1973. *Recreations:* reading, the theatre. *Address:* 22 Malbrook Road, Putney, SW15. *T:* 01-788 5862.

BISHOP, Peter Maxwell Farrow, DM (Oxon); FRCP; FRCOG; Endocrinologist Emeritus, Guy's Hospital; Hon. Consulting Endocrinologist, Chelsea Hospital for Women; late Medical Consultant, Family Planning Association; Past Master, Society of Apothecaries; *b* 14 Aug. 1904; *o s* of late Dr T. H. Bishop; *m* 1937, (Winifred) Phyllis, *o d* of Lt-Col E. O. Thurston, IMS; one *s* two *d*. *Educ:* Berlin; Charterhouse; Trinity Coll., Oxford. Guy's Hosp. Medical Sch.: Senior Demonstrator in Physiology, 1930-33; Lectr in Physiological Chemistry, 1933-38; Lectr in Applied Physiology and Pharmacology, 1938; Warden of the College, 1938-47; Dep. Supt, 1938-45; MO in charge (EMS), Guy's Hosp., 1939-45. First Treas., Member Editorial Board and one of founders of Journal of Endocrinology, 1939; Member Council of Management, Soc. for Endocrinology, 1947, Hon. Mem. 1973; one of first two Hon. Co-Secretaries Section of Endocrinology, Royal Society Medicine, 1946 (Pres. 1955, Hon. Mem. 1973); Hon. Sec. 1959, Chm. 1960-63, Hon. Mem. 1971, Soc. for Study of Fertility. Hon. Dipl. Acad. of Med., Barcelona, 1949; Chm. Council of Management, Jl of Reproduction and Fertility, 1960-63; Ayerst Lectr, 1958, and Hon. Mem., American Soc. for Study of Sterility; Hon. Librarian, Royal Soc. Med., 1963-69. Sir Arthur Sims Commonwealth Travelling Prof., 1964. Hon. Mem., Endocrine Soc., Madrid, 1965; Mem., Torquay Med. Soc., 1973; H. D. Rolleston Lecturer, RCP, 1965; Litchfield Lecturer, Oxford Univ., 1967. *Publications:* Gynæcological Endocrinology, Recent Advances in Endocrinology; Chemistry of the Sex Hormones; various articles on endocrine subjects. *Address:* Moorhaven, Bovey Tracey, Devon TQ13 9HE. *T:* Bovey Tracey 833264.

BISHOP, Prof. Peter Orlebar, DSc; FRS 1977; FAA; Professor and Head of Department of Physiology, John Curtin School of Medical Research, Australian National University, since 1967; *b* 14 June 1917; *s* of Ernest John Hunter Bishop and Mildred Alice Havelock Bishop (*née* Vidal); *m* 1942, Hilare Louise Holmes; one *s* two *d*. *Educ:* Barker Coll., Hornsby; Univ. of Sydney (MB, BS, DSc). Neurol Registrar, Royal Prince Alfred Hosp., Sydney, 1941-42; Surgeon Lieut, RANR, 1942-46; Fellow, Postgrad. Cttee in Medicine (Sydney Univ.) at Nat. Hosp., Queen Square, London, 1946-47 and Dept Anatomy, UCL, 1947-50; Sydney University: Res. Fellow, Dept Surgery, 1950-51; Sen. Lectr, 1951-54, Reader, 1954-55, Prof. and Head, Dept Physiology, 1955-67. Vis. Prof., Japan Soc. for Promotion of Science, 1974. FAA 1967; Fellow, Aust. Postgrad. Fedn in Medicine, 1969. Hon. Member: Neurosurgical Soc. of Aust., 1970; Ophthalmol Soc. of NZ, 1973. *Publications:* contribs on physiological optics and visual neurophysiology. *Recreation:* bushwalking. *Address:* Department of Physiology, John Curtin School of Medical Research, PO Box 334, Canberra City, ACT 2601, Australia. *T:* 062-492593.

BISHOP, Prof. Richard E. D., PhD Stanford, DSc (Eng) London, ScD Cantab; FIMechE, FRINA, MRAeS; Kennedy Professor of Mechanical Engineering in the University of London since 1957; Fellow of University College London, since 1964; *b* London, 1 Jan. 1925; *s* of Rev. Dr N. R. Bishop; *m* 1949, Jean Paterson, London; one *s* one *d*. *Educ:* The Roan Sch., Greenwich. RNVR, 1943-46. University Coll., London, 1946-49; Commonwealth Fund Fellow in Stanford Univ., California, 1949-51; Sen. Scientific Officer, Ministry of Supply, 1951-52; Cambridge Univ.: Demonstrator, 1952; Fellow of Pembroke Coll., 1954; University Lecturer in Engineering, 1955; Visiting Prof.: Massachusetts Institute of Technology, Summer, 1959; Visiting Lecturer, National Science Foundation, USA, Spring, 1961; Member of Council, Instn of Mechanical Engineers, 1961-64, 1969-70; President, British Acoustical Soc., 1966-68; Hon. Member Royal Corps of Naval Constructors, 1968; John Orr Meml Lectr, S Africa, 1971; Originator of Greenwich Forum, 1974; C. Gelderman Foundn Vis. Prof., Technical Univ., Delft, 1976; Fellow, Fellowship of Engineering, 1977. George Stephenson Res. Prize, IMechE, 1959; Thomas Hawksley Gold Medal, IMechE, 1965; Silver Medal of Skoda Works, 1967; Křižík Gold Medal, Acad. Sci. CSSR, 1969; Rayleigh Gold Medal, Brit. Acoustical Soc., 1972; Clayton Prize, IMechE,

1972; RINA Bronze Medal, 1975. *Publications:* (with D. C. Johnson) Vibration Analysis Tables, 1956; (with D. C. Johnson) The Mechanics of Vibration, 1960; (with G. M. L. Gladwell and S. Michaelson) The Matrix Analysis of Vibration, 1965; Vibration, 1965; (with W. G. Price) Probabilistic Theory of Ship Dynamics, 1974; many scientific papers. *Recreation:* dinghy sailing. *Address:* University College London, WC1. *T:* 01-387 7050. *Club:* Royal Naval and Royal Albert Yacht (Portsmouth).

BISHOP, Ronald Eric, CBE 1946; FRAeS; Deputy Managing Director, de Havilland Aircraft Co. Ltd, 1958-64; Design Director, de Havilland Aircraft Co. Ltd, Hatfield, 1946-64; *b* 1903. Joined de Havilland Aircraft Co. Ltd, as an apprentice, 1921; entered Drawing Office; appointed in charge, 1936. Responsible for following designs: Flamingo, Mosquito, Hornet, Vampire, Dove, Venom, Heron, DH 108, DH 110, Comet Jet Airliner. Gold Medal, RAeS, 1964.

BISHOP, Stanley Victor, MC 1944; Director: Massey Ferguson (Europe) Ltd; Goldcrest (Adhesive) Products Ltd; *b* 11 May 1916; *s* of George Stanley Bishop, MA; *m* 1946, Dorothy Primrose Dodds, Berwick-upon-Tweed; two *s* one *d*. *Educ:* Leeds. Articled to Beevers & Adgie, Leeds; CA 1937. Served War of 1939-45: enlisted London Scottish (TA), 1938; commissioned, West Yorkshire Regt, 1940; served overseas, 1940-45, Middle East, India and Burma (MC) (Hon. Major). Joined Albert E. Reed and Co. Ltd, 1946; Brush Group, 1951; Massey Ferguson Ltd, 1959; Perkins Diesel Engine Group, 1963. Man. Dir, British Printing Corp., 1966-70; Chm. and Dir various cos, 1970-73. Has lectured to British Institute of Management, Institute of Chartered Accountants, Oxford Business Summer School, etc. *Publication:* Business Planning and Control, 1966. *Recreations:* golf, swimming, pottering. *Address:* 35 Thickthorn Close, Kenilworth, Warwicks. *Club:* Army and Navy.

BISHOP, Stephen; see Bishop-Kovacevich.

BISHOP, Terence Alan Martyn, FBA 1971; *b* 1907; *s* of Cosby Martyn Bishop. *Educ:* Christ's Hospital; Keble Coll., Oxford. 2nd Mods, 1928; 2nd Hist. 1930; BA 1931, MA 1947. *Publications:* books and articles on palaeography, etc, incl.: Facsimiles of English Royal Writs to AD 1100 (with P. Chaplais), 1957; Scriptores Regis, 1961; (ed) Umbrae Codicum Occidentalium (Vol. 10), 1966 (Holland); English Caroline Minuscule, 1971. *Address:* The Annexe, Manor House, Hemingford Grey, Huntingdon, Cambs.

BISHOP, Instructor Rear-Adm. Sir William (Alfred), KBE 1955 (OBE 1941); CB 1950; MA; Director of Naval Education Service, 1948-56, retired; *b* 29 May 1899; *s* of late Alfred Bishop, Purley, Surrey; *m* 1929, Stella Margaret Macfarlane, MBE; no *c*. *Educ:* Whitgift Sch.; Corpus Christi, Cambridge. 2nd Lieut, RE Signals, 1918; Cambridge 1919. Entered RN as Instructor Lieut, 1922; Instructor Lieut-Comdr, 1928; Instructor Comdr, 1936; Instructor Captain, 1945; Instructor Rear-Adm., 1951. Chief Naval Meteorological Officer, South Atlantic Station, 1939; Asst Director of Naval Meteorological Service, 1944; Dep. Director of Education Dept, 1947. Naval ADC to the King, 1950. Retired Sept. 1956. *Address:* Myrtle Cottage, Burlawn, Wadebridge, Cornwall. *T:* Wadebridge 2773.

BISHOP, Rev. William Fletcher; see Bishop, Rev. Hugh.

BISHOP, Maj.-Gen. Sir (William Henry) Alexander, (Alec), KCMG 1964 (CMG 1961); CB 1946; CVO 1961; OBE 1941; psc; psa; *b* 20 June 1897; *s* of Walter Edward and Elizabeth Bishop; *m* 1926, Mary Patricia (*d* 1977), *d* of Henry Corbett, Physician, Plymouth; one *s*. *Educ:* Plymouth Coll.; RMC Sandhurst. Served European War, 1914-19, Mesopotamia and Palestine; with Dorset Regt; Bt Lt-Col 1938; Col 1941; Brig. 1941; Maj.-Gen. 1944. Served in India, 1919-25, War Office, 1933-35 and Colonial Office, 1937-39; served in East Africa, North Africa, and West Africa during War, 1939-44; Director of Quartering, War Office, 1944-45; Chief of Information Services and Public Relations, CCG, 1945-46; Deputy Chief of Staff, CCG, 1946-48; Regional Commissioner, Land North Rhine/Westphalia, 1948-50; Asst Sec., CRO, 1951; Principal Staff Officer to Secretary of State for Commonwealth Relations, 1953-57; British Dep. High Commissioner in Calcutta, 1957-62; Director of Information Services and Cultural Relations, CRO, 1962-64; British High Commissioner, Cyprus, 1964-65, retired. CStJ 1951. Ehren-Nadel, Johanniter Orden, 1951. *Recreations:* reading, gardening. *Address:* Combe Lodge, Beckley, Sussex. *T:* Beckley 221. *Clubs:* Army and Navy; Dormy House (Rye); Bengal (Calcutta).

BISHOP, Sir William (Poole), Kt 1961; CMG 1947; AASA; Auditor-General, State of South Australia, 1946-59, retired; *b* 8 Aug. 1894; *s* of Henry Bishop, Adelaide, South Australia; *m* 1st, 1922, Leira Viola (*d* 1967); one *s* two *d*; 2nd, 1968, Daphne Rhea, *widow* of Walter Richard Birks. *Educ:* Adelaide High Sch. Official appts: Comr of Taxes for State of South Australia and Federal Dep. Comr of Taxation, 1935-46; Trustee Savings Bank of S Australia, 1946-; Director: Adelaide Cement Co. Ltd (Chm. 1965-70); Johnson & Sons (S Australia) Ltd; Santos Ltd; Chairman City Bricks (Holdings) Ltd., 1963-71. Charitable organisations: Member Exec. and Chairman Finance Cttee, Fighting Forces Comforts Fund (S Australia Div. of Australian Fund), 1939-46; Member Board of Management and Chairman of Finance Cttee, Legacy Club of Adelaide, 1944-56; Member AIF Cemetery Trust, 1928-67 (Chm. 1958-67); Member Exec. War Veterans' Home, Myrtle Bank Inc., 1933-67; Mem. Board of Governors, Burnside War Memorial Hosp., 1959-63; Dir, Nat. Heart Foundn of Australia (and the SA Div.), 1961-70. Served European War, 1914-18, AIF, 1915-19; War of 1939-45, Volunteer Defence Corps, 1942-45. *Clubs:* Naval, Military and Air Force (S Australia); Glenelg Golf.

BISHOP, William Thomas, CBE 1971; retired; Consultant to Drivers Jonas; *b* 27 March 1901; *s* of Thomas Edward and Hannah B. Bishop; *m* 1st, 1929, Freda Bateman Simes (*d* 1935); one *s* one *d*; 2nd, 1936, Marjorie Bateman Leaver; one *d* (one *s* decd). *Educ:* Andover Grammar Sch.; Aldershot County High Sch. Chartered Surveyor, 1924; FRICS 1931; Mem. Council, RICS, 1960-72 (Hon. Sec. 1963-72). Specialised in Urban Estate Management: 25 yrs with Messrs Clutton, then 26 yrs Drivers Jonas as Partner and Sen. Partner, 1952-71. Appts included Surveyor and Receiver for Crown Estate Comrs (London Estate), Corp. of Trinity House, and Ilchester Estates. Mem. Cttee of Management, RNLI; Chm., Oxshott Heath Conservators; Younger Brother of Trinity Hse, 1962. Liveryman, Farmers' Co. *Recreations:* gardening, fishing. *Address:* Bevendean Cottage, Warren Lane, Oxshott, Leatherhead, Surrey. *T:* Oxshott 2007. *Club:* Royal Thames Yacht.

BISHOP-KOVACEVICH, Stephen; pianist; *b* 17 Oct. 1940. *Educ:* studied under Lev Shorr and Myra Hess. Solo and orchestral debut, San Francisco, USA 1951; London debut, Nov. 1961. Concert tours: in England, Europe and USA, with many of the world's leading orchestras, incl. New York Philharmonic, Los Angeles Philharmonic, Israel Philharmonic, Amsterdam Concertgebouw, London Symphony, London Philharmonic, and BBC Symphony. Has appeared at Edinburgh, Bath, Berlin and San Sebastian Festivals. Gave 1st performance of Richard Rodney Bennett's Piano Concerto, 1969 (this work is dedicated to and has been recorded by him, under Alexander Gibson). Performed all Mozart Piano concertos, 1969-71. Edison Award for his recording of Bartok's 2nd Piano Concerto and Stravinsky's Piano Concerto, with BBC Symphony Orchestra, under Colin Davis. *Recreations:* chess, films, tennis. *Address:* c/o Harold Holt Ltd, 122 Wigmore Street, W1. *T:* 01-935 2331.

BISS, Godfrey Charles D'Arcy; Consultant to Ashurst, Morris, Crisp & Co., Solicitors; *b* 2 Sept. 1909; *s* of Gerald Biss and Sarah Ann Coutts Allan; *m* 1946, Margaret Jean Ellis; two *s*. *Educ:* St Paul's Sch. (Scholar); Worcester Coll., Oxford (Exhibitioner). 1st Class Jurisprudence, 1932. Solicitor, 1935; Partner in Ashurst, Morris, Crisp & Co., 1947. Royal Artillery, 1940-46; Staff Capt. RA, 23rd Indian Div. Chairman: The Fairey Company Ltd, 1958-70; UK Optical & Industrial Holdings Ltd; Siebe Gorman & Co. Ltd; Director: Aspro-Nicholas Ltd; International Harvester Co. of Great Britain Ltd; International Harvester Europe; Trafalgar House Investments Ltd; James North & Sons Ltd; International Press Centre Ltd. *Recreations:* gardening, racing. *Address:* Black House Farm, St Lawrence, near Southminster, Essex. *T:* Tillingham 361; 17 Throgmorton Avenue, EC2. *T:* 01-283 1070. *Club:* Oriental.

BISSELL, Claude Thomas, CC 1969; MA, PhD; FRSC 1957; Professor, University of Toronto, since 1971 (President of the University, 1958-71); *b* 10 Feb. 1916; *m* 1945, Christina Flora Gray; one *d*. *Educ:* University of Toronto; Cornell Univ. BA 1936, MA 1937, Toronto; PhD Cornell, 1940. Instructor in English, Cornell, 1938-41; Lecturer in English, Cornell, 1938-41; Lecturer in English, Toronto, 1941-42. Canadian Army, 1942-46; demobilised as Capt. University of Toronto: Asst Prof. of English, 1947-51; Assoc. Prof. of English, 1951-56; Prof. of English, 1962; Asst to Pres., 1948-52; Vice-Pres., 1952-56; Dean in Residence, University Coll., 1946-56; Pres., Carleton Univ., Ottawa, 1956-58; Chm., The Canada Council, 1960-62. President, Nat. Conference of Canadian Universities and Colleges, 1962-; Chairman, Canadian Universities Foundation, 1962-; President, World University Service of Canada, 1962-63.

Visiting Prof. of Canadian Studies, Harvard, 1967-68. Aggrey-Fraser-Guggisberg Meml Lectr, Ghana Univ., 1976. Hon. DLitt: Manitoba, 1958; W Ontario, 1971; Lethbridge, 1972; Leeds, 1976; Toronto, 1977; Hon. LLD: McGill, 1958; Queen's, 1959; New Brunswick, 1959; Carleton, 1960; Montreal, 1960; The St Lawrence, 1962; British Columbia, 1962; Michigan, 1963; Columbia, 1965; Laval, 1966; Prince of Wales Coll., 1967; Windsor, 1968; St Andrews, 1972. *Publications:* The Strength of the University, 1968; Halfway up Parnassus, 1974; (ed) University College, A Portrait, 1853-1953, 1953; (ed) Canada's Crisis in Higher Education, 1957; (ed) Our Living Tradition, 1957; (ed) Great Canadian Writing, 1966; number of articles on literary subjects in Canadian and American jls. *Address:* 229 Erskine Avenue, Toronto, Ontario, Canada. *Clubs:* Arts and Letters, York (Toronto); Cercle Universitaire (Ottawa).

BJARNASON, Sigurdur; Commander with Star, Order of the Icelandic Falcon, 1950; Hon. Emblem, Foundation of the Icelandic Republic, 1944; Ambassador of Iceland to the Court of St James's, the Netherlands and Nigeria, since 1976, and to Ireland since 1970; *b* 18 Dec. 1915; *s* of Bjarni Sigurdsson and Björg Bjornsdóttir; *m* 1956, Olöf Pálsdóttir, sculptress; one *s* one *d*. *Educ:* Univ. of Iceland (Law); Univ. of Cambridge (Internat. and Company Law). Editor of weekly newspaper, 1942-47; Political Editor, Morgunbladid, 1947-56, Editor in Chief, 1956-70. Mem. Icelandic Parlt (Althing), 1942-70; Pres. Lower House, 1949-56 and 1963-70; Chm. Cttee of Foreign Affairs, 1963-70. Mem. govt and municipal cttees, including Pres. Municipal Council of Isfajördur, 1946-50; Mem. Council of State Radio of Iceland, 1947-70, Chm. 1959 and Vice-Chm. 1960-70. Pres. Icelandic Sect. of Soc. for Inter-scandinavian Understanding, 1965-70. Member Nordic Council, 1952-59 and 1963-70; Vice-Pres., 1952-56 and 1959; Pres., 1965 and 1970. Delegate of Iceland to UN Gen. Assembly, 1960, 1961 and 1962; Mem. Cultural Cttee of Nordic Countries, 1954-70. Mem. Icelandic Cttee on territorial rights, 1957-58. Ambassador to Denmark, 1970-76; to Turkey, 1970-76; to China, 1973-76. Commander of the Finnish Lion, 1958; Commander, Order of the Vasa (Sweden), 1958; Grand Cross, Order of Dannebrog (Denmark), 1970. *Publications:* articles for foreign periodicals, especially within the field of culture and Scandinavian co-operation. *Recreations:* fishing, bird watching. *Address:* 101 Park Street, W1. *T:* 01-629 8660.

BJELKE-PETERSEN, Hon. Johannes, MLA; Premier of Queensland, since 1968; *b* Dannevirke, NZ, 13 Jan. 1911; *s* of late C. G. Bjelke-Petersen, Denmark; *m* 1952, Florence Isabel, *d* of J. P. Gilmour; one *s* three *d*. *Educ:* Taabinga Valley Sch.; corresp. courses, and privately. MLA National Party (formerly Country Party): for Nanango, 1947-50; for Barambah, 1950-. Minister for Works and Housing, Qld, 1963-68. *Address:* (office) Premier's Department, George Street, Brisbane, Queensland 4000, Australia; (home) Bethany, Kingaroy, Queensland 4610.

BJÖRNSSON, Henrik Sveinsson, KBE (Hon.) 1963; Icelandic diplomat; Permanent Under Secretary, Ministry for Foreign Affairs, Iceland, since 1976; *b* 2 Sept. 1914; *s* of Sveinn Björnsson (late President of Iceland) and Georgia Hoff-Hansen; *m* 1941, Gróa Torfhildur Jónsdóttir; one *s* two *d*. *Educ:* Reykjavik Grammar Sch.; Univ. of Iceland. Graduated in Law, 1939. Entered Foreign Service, 1939; served in Copenhagen, Washington, DC, Oslo, Paris and Revkjavik; Secretary to President of Iceland, 1952-56; Secretary-General of Min. of Foreign Affairs, Iceland, 1956-61; Ambassador to: the Court of St James's, 1961-65, also to Royal Netherlands Court, and Minister to Spain and Portugal, 1961-65; Belgium and Permanent Representative to NATO, 1965-67, France, Luxembourg, Yugoslavia, 1965-76, UAR and Ethiopia, 1971-76, and concurrently Permanent Rep. to Council of Europe, 1968-70, and OECD and UNESCO, 1965-76. Kt Comdr of the Order of the Icelandic Falcon, 1963. Holds various foreign decorations. *Address:* Ministry for Foreign Affairs, Reykjavik, Iceland.

BLACHE-FRASER, Louis Nathaniel, HBM 1971; CMG 1959; Chairman, Insurance Brokers West Indies Ltd; Director, Furness Withy Ltd; George Wimpey (Caribbean) Ltd; Central Bank of Trinidad and Tobago; Trinidad Building and Loan Association; National Insurance Board; *b* 19 Feb. 1904; *s* of late Winford and Emma Blache-Fraser, Trinidad; *m* 1941, Gwenyth, *d* of George Kent, Grenada; two *s* one *d* (and one *d* decd). *Educ:* Queen's Royal Coll., Trinidad. Joined Trinidad and Tobago Government Service, 1924; Dep. Accountant-General, 1947; Accountant-General, 1948; Dep. Financial Secretary, 1952; Financial Secretary, 1953; Financial Secretary, The West Indies, 1956-60; Chairman, Public Service Commission of The West Indies, 1961-62. Asst Sec., Alstons Ltd, 1962-65, Sec., 1965-70. Past Pres., Trinidad Chamber of Commerce. *Address:* 14

Coblentz Gardens, St Ann's, Trinidad. *Clubs:* Queen's Park Cricket, Harvard Sports (Trinidad).

BLACK, family name of **Baron Black.**

BLACK, Baron *cr* 1968 (Life Peer), of Barrow in Furness; **William Rushton Black;** Kt 1958; Chairman and Managing Director, Associated Commercial Vehicles Ltd; Chairman, Park Royal Vehicles Ltd; Director of other companies; *b* 12 Jan. 1893; *s* of J. W. and F. M. Black; *m* 1916, Patricia Margaret Dallas (*d* 1976); one *d* (one *s* decd). *Educ:* Barrow Secondary Sch.; Barrow Technical Coll. Apprenticed Vickers Ltd (Engineer), 1908; Works Manager, Vickers Crayford, 1924; General Manager, Weymanns Motor Bodies, 1928; Director and General Manager, Park Royal Vehicles Ltd, 1934, Man. Dir 1939, Chairman 1962; Director, Associated Commercial Vehicles Ltd, 1949, Managing Dir 1957. President, Society of Motor Manufacturers and Traders Ltd, 1953; Chairman: National Research Development Corporation, 1957-69; Leyland Motor Corporation, 1963-67. *Recreations:* golf, gardening. *Address:* Birchwood Grange, Ruxley Crescent, Claygate, Surrey. *T:* Esher 62823. *Club:* Royal Automobile.

BLACK, Archibald Niel; Professor of Engineering, University of Southampton, 1968-72, retired; *b* 10 June 1912; *s* of late Steuart Gladstone Black, Glenormiston, Victoria, Australia, and Isabella McCance (*née* Moat); *m* 1940, Cynthia Mary Stradling; one *s* two *d. Educ:* Farnborough Sch.; Eton Coll.; Trinity Coll., Cambridge. 1st cl. hons with distinction in Applied Mechanics in Mech. Sciences Tripos, Cambridge, 1934; MA 1938. Lectr and Demonstrator in Engrg Science, Oxford Univ., 1935; Donald Pollock Reader in Engrg Science, Oxford Univ., 1945-50; Prof. of Mech. Engrg, Southampton Univ., 1950-67. Dep. Chm., Universities Central Council on Admissions, 1964-72. Hon. DSc Southampton, 1975. *Publications:* (with K. Adlard Coles) North Biscay Pilot, 1970; papers in Proc. Royal Soc. and technical jls. *Recreation:* sailing. *Address:* Little Pensbury, Compton Street, Compton, Winchester, Hants SO21 2AS. *T:* Twyford 712360. *Club:* Royal Ocean Racing.

BLACK, Sir Cyril (Wilson), Kt 1959; DL, JP; *b* 1902; *s* of Robert Wilson Black, JP, and Annie Louise Black (*née* North); *m* 1930, Dorothy Joyce, *d* of Thomas Birkett, Wigston Hall, Leicester; one *s* two *d. Educ:* King's College Sch. Chartered Surveyor, FRICS; Consultant to Knight & Co., Arthur Road, SW19. Chairman: Temperance Permanent Building Soc., 1939-73; Beaumont Properties Ltd; London Shop Property Trust Ltd; M. F. North Ltd, and other companies. JP County of London, 1942; Member Wimbledon Borough Council, 1942-65; Mayor, 1945-46, 1946-47; Alderman, 1942-65; Member, London Borough of Merton Council, 1965-; Mayor, 1965-66; Member Surrey County Council, 1943-65; County Alderman, 1952-65, and Chm., 1956-59; MP (C) Wimbledon, 1950-70. DL Surrey, 1957-66; DL Greater London, 1966. Governor of King's College Sch., Wimbledon Coll., Ursuline Convent Sch., Wimbledon, and other Schools. Freedom of City of London, 1943; Freedom of Wimbledon, 1957. Chm., Moral Law Defence Assoc.; Hon. Mem., Houses of Parliament Christian Fellowship; Patron, Wimbledon Youth Cttee; Chairman, Wimbledon Community Assoc.; Member: SW Metrop. Regional Hospital Board, 1959-62; Baptist Union Council (Pres., 1970-71); Free Church Federal Council; Vice-President: Council of Christians and Jews; Girls' Bde, 1969- (Hon. Treasurer, 1939-69); Hon. Vice-Pres., Boys' Bde, 1970- (Hon. Treasurer, 1962-69). Pres., United Nations Association (London Region), 1964-65. *Recreations:* public work, music, reading. *Address:* Rosewall, Calonne Road, Wimbledon, SW19. *T:* 01-946 2588. *Clubs:* Carlton, City Livery, Inner London Justices'.

BLACK, Donald Harrison, CMG 1956; PhD, MSc, FInstP; *b* 18 June 1899; *s* of Robert Black, Nelson, NZ; *m* 1927, Winifred Maida Robertson; two *s* one *d. Educ:* Nelson Coll., New Zealand; Canterbury University Coll., New Zealand; Emmanuel Coll. and Cavendish Laboratory, Cambridge. Standard Telephones and Cables Ltd (and associates), 1925-39; Supt of Research, Radar Research and Development Establishment, Min. Supply, 1939-43 and 1945-47; Admiralty Liaison Officer in USA, 1943-45; Asst Director Telecommunication Research and Development, Ministry of Supply, 1947-49; Director, Electronics Research and Development, Ministry of Supply, 1949-53; Head of UK Ministry of Supply Staff, Australia, 1953-56; Director-General of Electronics Research and Development, Ministry of Supply, 1956-58; Director, Royal Armament Research and Development Establishment, WO, Fort Halstead, Sevenoaks, Kent, 1958-62; Electronics Adviser to Chief Scientist, WO, 1962-66. *Publications:* contributions to Proc. Royal Society, Phil. Mag., Proc. Cambridge Phil. Soc., Jl Sci. Inst. *Recreations:* gardening, woodworking. *Address:* 8 Little Green, Alverstoke, Gosport, Hants PO12 2EV.

BLACK, Sir Douglas (Andrew Kilgour), Kt 1973; MD, PRCP; Professor of Medicine, Manchester University and Physician, Manchester Royal Infirmary, since 1959; Chief Scientist, Department of Health and Social Security, 1973-77 (on secondment); *b* 29 May 1913; *s* of Walter Kilgour Black and Mary Jane Crichton; *m* 1948, Mollie Thorn; one *s* two *d. Educ:* Forfar Academy; St Andrews Univ. BSc 1933; MB, ChB 1936; MD 1940; MRCP 1939; FRCP 1952. MRC Research Fellow, 1938-40; Beit Memorial Research Fellow, 1940-42. Major RAMC, 1942-46. Lecturer, then Reader, in Medicine, Manchester Univ., 1946-58. Horder Travelling Fellow, 1967; Sir Arthur Sims Commonwealth Travelling Prof., 1971. Lectures: Goulstonian, RCP, 1953; Bradshaw, RCP, 1965; Lumleian, RCP, 1970; Harben, RIPH&H, 1973; Crookshank, RCR, 1976. Secretary, Manchester Medical Soc., 1957-59. Member: Medical Research Council, 1966-70 and 1971- (Chm., Clinical Res. Bd, 1971-73); Assoc. of Physicians; Medical Research Soc.; Renal Assoc., etc. Pres., RCP, 1977-; Pres. Section X, British Assoc., 1977. Trustee, 1968-77, Chm., 1977-, Smith Kline & French Foundn. Hon. DSc St Andrews, 1972. *Publications:* Sodium Metabolism in Health and Disease, 1952; Essentials of Fluid Balance (4th edn), 1967; The Logic of Medicine, 1968; (ed) Renal Disease (3rd edn), 1972; contributions to various medical journals. *Recreations:* reading and writing. *Adddress:* c/o Royal College of Physicians, Regent's Park, NW1. *Club:* Athenæum.

BLACK, Eugene R(obert); Banker, United States; Consultant, American Express Co., since 1970; Chairman: Blackwell Land Co. Inc.; Scandinavian Securities Corp.; Director, Warner Communications; *b* Atlanta, Ga, USA, 1 May 1898; *s* of Eugene R. Black and Gussie Grady; *m* 1st, 1918, Elizabeth Blalock (decd); one *s* one *d*; 2nd, 1930, Susette Heath; one *s. Educ:* Univ. of Georgia. Atlanta Office, Harris, Forbes & Co. (NY Investment Bankers), 1919; Manager, Atlanta Office, Chase-Harris, Forbes Corp., in charge of Atlanta, New Orleans, Houston and Dallas offices, 1933; Chase National Bank of the City of NY: 2nd Vice-Pres., 1933; Vice-Pres., 1937; Senior Vice-Pres., 1949, resigned. US Executive Director, Internat. Bank for Reconstruction and Development, 1947-49, President, 1949-53. Consultant and Dir, Chase Manhattan Bank, 1963-70. Special Adviser to President Johnson on SE Asia development, 1965-69; Member Adv. Boards: Colonial Fund; Colonial Growth Shares; Colonial Income Fund. Trustee, Corporate Property Investors, and other financial trusteeships. Medal of Freedom (US), 1969. Holds numerous hon. doctorates and has been decorated by many countries. *Publications:* The Diplomacy of Economic Development, 1963 (trans. other languages); Alternative in Southeast Asia, 1969. *Recreations:* golf, fishing; student of William Shakespeare. *Address:* (office) American Express Company, American Express Plaza, New York, NY 10004, USA. *T:* 212-480-3527; (home) 178 Columbia Heights, Brooklyn, New York 11201. *Clubs:* Athenæum (London, England); Lotos, River (New York); International (Washington, DC); National Golf Links of America (Southampton, NY), etc.

BLACK, George Joseph, DSO 1944; DFC 1942 and Bar 1944; **His Honour Judge Black;** a Circuit Judge, since 1977; *b* 24 Jan. 1918; *s* of Tom Walton Black and Nellie Black; *m* 1955; one *s* one *d. Educ:* Queens Coll., Taunton. LLB. Articled Clerk, C. James Hardwick & Co., Solicitors, Cardiff, 1935-39; joined RAF, Sept. 1939; Sgt Pilot 1940; commnd 1942; Sqdn Ldr 1944; fighter bombers, Middle East, Sicily, Italy, 1941-44; Sen. Personnel Staff Officer, 1944-45; released from service, 1946; admitted Solicitor, 1947; private practice, 1947-49; Legal Dept, New Scotland Yard, 1950-58; Partner, Adams & Black, Cardiff, 1958-77. A Recorder of the Crown Court, 1972-77. *Recreations:* sailing. *Address:* 11 Sealawns, Cold Knap, Barry, S Glamorgan.

BLACK, Prof. Gordon; Professor of Computation, Faculty of Technology, University of Manchester, since 1964; Director, University of Manchester Regional Computing Centre, since 1969; Member, National Electronics Council, since 1967; *b* 30 July 1923; *s* of Martin Black and Gladys (*née* Lee), Whitehaven, Cumberland; *m* 1953, Brenda Janette, *y d* of H. Josiah Balsom, London; two *s* two *d. Educ:* Workington Grammar Sch.; Hatfield Coll., Durham Univ.; Imperial Coll., London Univ. BSc Durham, 1945; MSc Manchester, 1968; PhD, DIC London, 1954; FInstP 1952; FBCS 1968. Physicist, British Scientific Instrument Research Assoc., 1946-56. UKAEA, 1956-66; Principal Sci. Officer, 1956-58; Senior Principal Sci. Officer, 1958-60; Dep. Chief Sci. Officer, 1960-64. Dir, Nat. Computing Centre, 1965-69. Dir, Internat. Computers Ltd, 1976-. *Publications:* scientific papers in learned jls (physics and computers). *Recreations:* piano playing; listening to piano players; old clocks. *Address:* Manchester University Institute of Science and Technology, Sackville Street, Manchester. *T:* 061-236 3311; Highlawn, Alan Drive, Hale, Cheshire. *T:* 061-980 4644.

BLACK, Sir Harold, Kt 1970; Deputy Secretary, Northern Ireland Office, Belfast, 1972-74; *b* 9 April 1914; *s* of Alexander and Adelaide Black, Belfast; *m* 1940, Margaret Saxton; one *s* one *d. Educ:* Royal Belfast Academical Institution. Joined Northern Ireland Civil Service, 1934; Asst Sec., NI Cabinet, 1959-63; Dir of Establishments, Min. of Finance, NI, 1963-65; Sec. to the Cabinet and Clerk of the Privy Council, NI, 1965-72. *Recreations:* photography, sailing. *Address:* 19 Rosepark, Belfast BT5 7RG, Northern Ireland. *T:* Dundonald 2151. *Club:* Strangford Lough Yacht.

BLACK, Sir Hermann David, Kt 1974; Chancellor of the University of Sydney, New South Wales, Australia, since 1970; Fellow, University of Sydney, since 1949; Part-time Lecturer in Economics and Education; also a radio commentator on economics and international affairs, in Australia; *b* 1905. Hon. DLitt Univ. of Newcastle, NSW. *Address:* University of Sydney, Sydney, New South Wales 2006, Australia; 99 Roseville Avenue, Roseville, NSW 2069, Australia.

BLACK, Iain James, QC 1971; barrister-at-law. Called to the Bar, Gray's Inn, 1947; Dep. Chm., Staffs QS, 1965-71. Mem., Criminal Injuries Compensation Bd, 1975-. *Address:* 3 Fountain Court, Steelhouse Lane, Birmingham B4 6DR. *T:* 021-236 5854; 3 Pump Court, Temple, EC4.

BLACK, James Walter; a Recorder of the Crown Court, since 1976; *b* 8 Feb. 1941; *s* of Dr James Black and Mrs Clementine M. Black (*née* Robb); *m* 1964, Jane Marie Keyden; two *s* one *d. Educ:* Harecroft Hall, Gosforth, Cumbria; Trinity Coll., Glenalmond, Perthshire; St Catharine's Coll., Cambridge (MA). Called to the Bar, Middle Temple, 1964. *Recreations:* fishing, sailing, golf. *Address:* August Hill, West Hay, Wrington, Bristol BS18 7NW. *T:* Wrington 862435. *Club:* Constitutional (Bristol).

BLACK, Prof. James Whyte, FRS 1976; FRCP; Director of Therapeutic Research, Wellcome Research Laboratories, since 1978; *b* 14 June 1924. *Educ:* Beath High Sch., Cowdenbeath; Univ. of St Andrews (MB, ChB). Asst Lectr in Physiology, Univ. of St Andrews, 1946; Lectr in Physiology, Univ. of Malaya, 1947-50; Sen. Lectr, Univ. of Glasgow Vet. Sch., 1950-58; ICI Pharmaceuticals Ltd, 1958-64; Head of Biological Res. and Dep. Res. Dir, Smith, Kline & French, Welwyn Garden City, 1964-73; Prof. and Head of Dept of Pharmacology, University College, London, 1973-77. Mem., British Pharmacological Soc., 1961-. *Address:* Wellcome Research Laboratories, Langley Court, South Eden Park Road, Beckenham, Kent BR3 3BS.

BLACK, John Nicholson, MA, DPhil, DSc, FRSE; Principal, Bedford College, London University, since Oct. 1971; *b* 28 June 1922; *e s* of Harold Black, MD, FRCP, and Margaret Frances Black (*née* Nicholson); *m* 1st, 1952, Mary Denise Webb (*d* 1966); one *s* one *d*; 2nd, 1967, Wendy Marjorie Waterston; two *s. Educ:* Rugby Sch.; Exeter Coll., Oxford. MA 1952, DPhil 1952, Oxford; DSc 1965, Adelaide; FRSE 1965. Served War, RAF, 1942-46. Oxford Univ., 1946-49; BA Hons Cl. 1 (Agri.) 1949; Agricl Research Council Studentship, 1949-52; Lectr, Sen. Lectr, Reader, Univ. of Adelaide (Waite Agricl Research Inst.), 1952-63; André Mayer Fellowship (FAO), 1958; Prof. of Forestry and Natural Resources, Univ. of Edinburgh, 1963-71. Mem., Nat. Environment Research Council, 1968-74. *Publications:* The Dominion of Man, 1970; many papers on ecological subjects in scientific jls. *Recreations:* music, philately. *Address:* Westholm, Orchehill Avenue, Gerrards Cross, Bucks.

BLACK, Prof. Joseph, PhD; FIMechE, FRAeS; Professor of Engineering, University of Bath, since 1960, Head of School of Engineering, 1960-70 and since 1973; *b* 25 Jan. 1921; *s* of Alexander Black and Hettie Black; *m* 1946, Margaret Susan Hewitt; three *s* one *d. Educ:* Royal Belfast Academical Instn; QUB (BScEng, MSc). PhD Bristol; FIMechE 1964, FRAeS 1961. Scientific Officer, RAE, 1941-44; Res. Fellow, QUB, 1944-45; Aerodynamicist, de Havilland Aircraft, 1945-46; Lectr/Sen. Lectr in Engrg, Univ. of Bristol, 1946-59. Gillette Fellow, USA, 1963. Pro-Vice-Chancellor, Univ. of Bath, 1970-73. Member: Planning and Bldg Cttees, Univ. of Bath, 1965-73; UGC, 1964-74 (Chm. Educnl Technol. Cttee); (founder) Council for Educnl Technol., 1974-; A/M Cttee, SRC, 1975-; Naval Educn Adv. Cttee, 1972-; Design Council, 1977- (Chm. Engrg Components Awards 1976, Engrg Products Awards 1977). Silver Jubilee Medal, 1977. *Publications:* Introduction to Aerodynamic Compressibility, 1950; contrib. aeronaut., mech. engrg and printing jls (UK and Europe). *Recreations:* photography, antiquarian books, fine art, music. *Address:* 20 Summerhill Road, Bath BA1 2UR. *T:* Bath 23970. *Club:* Shearwater Sailing (Wilts).

BLACK, Kenneth Oscar, MA, MD Cantab, FRCP, BChir, MRCS; Consulting Physician, St Bartholomew's Hospital; *b* 10 Nov. 1910; *s* of late George Barnard Black, Scarborough; *m* 1959, Virginia, *d* of Herbert Lees, Petersham, Surrey; two *d. Educ:* Bootham Sch., York; King's Coll., Cambridge (1st Class Nat. Science Tripos part 1, Senior Exhibitioner); St Bartholomew's Hospital, London. Demonstrator of Physiology and Medical Chief Asst, St Bartholomew's Hospital; Physician, St Bartholomew's Hospital, 1946. MB, BChir 1937; MRCP 1937; MD 1942; FRCP 1946. War service temp. Lt-Col RAMC; served W. Africa and India as Medical Specialist and OC Medical Div. Mem., Assoc. of Physicians; Fellow Royal Society Medicine (Councillor Med. Sect. 1952); Fellow, Med. Soc. of London (Councillor 1953). Examiner in Medicine: University of London, 1953; Soc. of Apothecaries, 1957; for MRCP London, 1967. Dir, Clerical, Medical & General Life Assurance Soc., 1964. *Publications:* contributions to journals and textbooks on diabetes and other medical topics. *Recreation:* natural history. *Address:* 149 Harley Street, W1N 2DE. *T:* 01-935 4444; (home) 28 Palmeira Avenue, Hove, East Sussex BN3 3GB. *Club:* Bath.

BLACK, Margaret McLeod; Head Mistress, Bradford Girls' Grammar School, 1955-75; *b* 1 May 1912; *d* of James Black and Elizabeth Malcolm. *Educ:* Kelso High Sch.; Edinburgh Univ. (MA). Classics Mistress, Lancaster Girls' Grammar Sch., 1936-44, and Manchester High Sch. for Girls, 1944-50; Head Mistress, Great Yarmouth Girls' High Sch., 1950-55. President: Leeds Branch of Classical Assoc., 1963-65; Joint Assoc. of Classical Teachers, 1967-69; Yorkshire Divl Union of Soroptimist Clubs, 1968-69. *Recreation:* music. *Address:* 246 Leaventhorpe Lane, Thornton, Bradford BD13 3BL. *T:* Bradford 881320. *Club:* Royal Over-Seas League.

BLACK, Very Rev. Matthew, DD, DLitt, Theol; FRSE; FBA 1955; Professor of Divinity and Biblical Criticism, and Principal of St Mary's College, University of St Andrews, 1954-Oct. 1978; Dean of the Faculty of Divinity, 1963-67; *b* 3 Sept. 1908; *s* of James and Helen Black, Kilmarnock, Ayrshire; *m* 1938, Ethel M., *d* of late Lt-Comdr A. H. Hall, Royal Indian Navy; one *s* one *d. Educ:* Kilmarnock Academy; Glasgow Univ. Glasgow: 1st cl. hons MA Classics, 1930; 2nd cl. hons Mental Philosophy, 1931; BD with distinction in Old Testament, 1934; DLitt 1944. Dr Phil Bonn, 1937; DTheol Münster. Hon. DD: Glasgow, 1954; Cambridge, 1965; Queen's, Ontario, 1967. Buchanan Prize, Moral Philosophy, 1929; Caird Scholar, Classics, 1930; Crombie Scholar, Biblical Criticism, 1933 (St Andrews award); Brown Downie Fellow, 1934; Maxwell Forsyth Fellow and Kerr Travelling Scholarship, Trinity Coll., Glasgow, 1934. Asst to Prof. of Hebrew, Glasgow, 1935-37; Warden of Church of Scotland Students' Residence, 1936-37; Asst Lecturer in Semitic Languages and Literatures, University of Manchester, 1937-39; Bruce Lectr, Trinity Coll., Glasgow, 1940; Lectr in Hebrew and Biblical Criticism, Univ. of Aberdeen, 1939-42; Minister of Dunbarney, Church of Scotland, 1942-47; Officiating CF, Bridge of Earn, 1943-47; Lecturer in New Testament Language and Literature, Leeds Univ., 1947-52; Prof. of Biblical Criticism and Biblical Antiquities, University of Edinburgh, 1952-54. Chm., Adv. Cttee of Peshitta Project of Univ. of Leiden, 1968-. Morse Lectr, 1956 and de Hoyt Lectr, 1963, Union Theological Seminary, NY; Thomas Burns Lectr, Otago, 1967. President, Soc. for Old Testament Study, 1968. FRSE 1977. Corresponding Member, Göttingen Akademie der Wissenschaften, 1957. Hon. Member: American Soc. of Biblical Exegesis, 1958; American Bible Soc., 1966. British Academy Burkitt Medal for Biblical Studies, 1962. *Publications:* Rituale Melchitarum (Stuttgart), 1938; An Aramaic Approach to the Gospels and Acts, 3rd edn, 1967; A Christian Palestinian Syriac Horologion, Texts and Studies, Contributions to Patristic Literature, New Series, Vol. I, 1954; The Scrolls and Christian Origins, 1961; General and New Testament Editor, Peake's Commentary on the Bible (revised edn, 1962); Bible Societies' edn of the Greek New Testament (Stuttgart), 1966; (Jt Editor) In Memoriam Paul Kahle (Berlin), 1968; (Editor and contributor) The Scrolls and Christianity, 1968; (with A. M. Denis) Apocalypsis Henochi Graece Fragmenta Pseudepigraphorum, 1970; Commentary on Romans, 1973; (organising Editor) The History of the Jewish People in the Age of Jesus Christ, 1973; Editor, New Testament Studies, to 1977; articles in learned journals. *Address:* St Mary's College, St Andrews, Fife; St Michael's, 40 Buchanan Gardens, St Andrews, Fife. *Clubs:* Athenæum; Royal and Ancient.

BLACK, Peter Blair, JP; Chairman, Thames Water Authority, since 1973; Senior Partner, P. Blair Black & Partners, since 1948; *b* 22 April 1917; *s* of Peter Blair Black and Cissie Crawford Samuel; *m* 1952, Mary Madeleine Hilly, Philadelphia; one *s* three *d. Educ:* Sir Walter St John's, Battersea; Bearsden Acad.; Sch. of Building. CC 1949, Alderman 1961, Middlesex; Mem., GLC, 1963-, Chm., 1970-71, Leader, Policy Cttee, 1977-.

Pres., Pure Rivers Soc., 1976-. Former Member: Thames Conservancy Bd; Metrop. Water Bd; Jager Cttee on Sewage Disposal; PLA; Council, Nat. Fedn of Housing Socs; Soc. of Engrs; RSH. Founder and Chm., Omnium Housing Assoc., 1962; Chm., Abbeyfield, London Region. Steward, Henley Royal Regatta. JP Thames Div., 1961. *Recreations:* small boats and fishing. *Address:* Westhorpe Cottage, Tenterden Grove, NW4. *T:* 01-203 5456; 101 Limmer Lane, Felpham, Sussex. *T:* Middleton-on-Sea 2054.

BLACK, Sir Robert Andrew Stransham, 2nd Bt *cr* 1922; ED 1942; JP; *b* 17 Jan. 1902; *s* of 1st Bt and Ellen Cecilia, 2nd *d* of late Gen. W. P. La Touche, IA; *S* father, 1925; *m* 1927, Ivy, *o d* of late Brig.-Gen. Sir Samuel Wilson, GCMG, KCB, KBE; one *s. Educ:* Eton; Cambridge Univ. JP 1934, High Sheriff 1934, Berks. *Heir: s* Robert David Black [*b* 29 March 1929; *m* 1953, Rosemary Diana (marr. diss. 1972), *d* of Sir Rupert Hardy, 4th Bt, *qv*; three *d*]. *Address:* Elvendon Priory, Goring, near Reading, Berks. *T:* Goring 160. *Club:* Bath.

BLACK, Sir Robert (Brown), GCMG 1962 (KCMG 1955; CMG 1953); OBE 1949 (MBE 1948); *b* 3 June 1906; *s* of late Robert and Catherine Black, formerly of Blair Lodge, Polmont, Stirlingshire; *m* 1937, (Elsie) Anne Stevenson, CStJ; two *d. Educ:* George Watson's Coll.; Edinburgh Univ. Colonial Administrative Service, 1930; served in Malaya, Trinidad, N Borneo, Hong Kong. Served War of 1939-45, commissioned in Intelligence Corps, 1942; 43 Special Military Mission; POW Japan, 1942-45. Colonial Secretary, Hong Kong, 1952-55; Governor and C-in-C: Singapore, 1955-57; Hong Kong, 1958-64. Chancellor: Hong Kong Univ., 1958-64; Chinese University of Hong Kong, 1963-64. Mem., Commonwealth War Graves Commn. Chairman: Clerical, Medical and General Life Assurance Soc.; General Reversionary and Investment Co. Ltd. LLD (*hc*): Univ. of Hong Kong; Chinese Univ. of Hong Kong. KStJ. Grand Cross Order of Merit, Peru. *Recreations:* walking, fishing. *Address:* Mapletons House, Ashampstead Common, near Reading, Berks RG8 8QN. *Club:* East India, Devonshire, Sports and Public Schools.

BLACK, Prof. Robert Denis Collison, FBA 1974; Professor of Economics, and Head of Department of Economics, Queen's University Belfast, since 1962; *b* 11 June 1922; *s* of William Robert Black and Rose Anna Mary (*née* Reid), Dublin; *m* 1953, Frances Mary, *o d* of William F. and Mary Weatherup, Belfast; one *s* one *d. Educ:* Sandford Park Sch. and Trinity Coll., Dublin. BA 1941, BComm 1941, PhD 1943, MA 1945. Dep. for Prof. of Polit. Economy, Trinity Coll., Dublin, 1943-45; Asst Lectr in Economics, Queen's Univ., Belfast, 1945-46, Lectr, 1946-58, Sen. Lectr, 1958-61, Reader, 1961-62. Rockefeller Post-doctoral Fellow, Princeton Univ., 1950-51; Visiting Prof. of Economics, Yale Univ., 1964-65; Dean of Faculty of Economics and Social Sciences, QUB, 1967-70; Pro-Vice-Chancellor, 1971-75. Mem. Council, Royal Economic Soc., 1963-; MRIA 1974. *Publications:* Centenary History of the Statistical Society of Ireland, 1947; Economic Thought and the Irish Question 1817-1870, 1960; Catalogue of Economic Pamphlets 1750-1900, 1969; Papers and Correspondence of William Stanley Jevons, Vol. I, 1972, Vol. II, 1973; articles in Economic Jl, Economica, Oxford Econ. Papers, Econ. History Review, etc. *Recreations:* travel, music, golf. *Address:* 14 Malone Court, Belfast, Northern Ireland BT9 6PA. *T:* Belfast 665880.

BLACK, Sheila (Psyche); Special Feature Writer for The Times, since 1973; Chairman, Interflex Data Systems (UK) Ltd, since 1975; Director: Cole Black & Partners Ltd, since 1975; Mills and Allen International, since 1976; *b* 6 May 1920; *d* of Clement Johnston Black, CA, and Mildred Beryl Black; *m* 1st, 1939, Geoffrey Davien, Sculptor (marr. diss. 1951); one *d* (one *s* decd); 2nd, 1951, L. A. Lee Howard (from whom she obtained a divorce, 1973), *qv. Educ:* Dorset; Switzerland; RADA. Actress, until outbreak of War of 1939-45, she became Asst to production manager of an electrical engineering factory. Post-war, in advertising; then in journalism, from the mid-fifties; Woman's Editor, Financial Times, 1959-72; Dir of Marketing and Financial Consultancy, John Addey Associates, 1972-73; Dir, Debenhams Ltd, 1975-76, Consultant, 1976-77. Features writer for The Director and Vogue. Member: Furniture Develt Council, 1967-70; Liquor Licensing Laws Special Cttee, 1971-72; (part-time) Price Commn, 1973-. Mem. Council, Inst of Directors, 1975-. *Publication:* The Black Book, 1976. *Recreations:* mini-horticulture in London mews patio, grandchildren, football. *Address:* 34 Hesper Mews, SW5 0HH. *Club:* Chelsea Arts.

BLACK, Stanley Matthew; HM Diplomatic Service, retired; Commercial Counsellor, British Embassy, Oslo, 1973-77; *b* 10 Jan. 1924; *s* of late David Thomas Black and Jean McKail

Gourlay Black; *m* 1950, Pamela Margaret, *d* of Alfred Herbert Vincent; one *s* two *d. Educ:* Allan Glen's Sch.; Glasgow Univ. Commissioned, RA, 1942; served, 1942-46. Third Sec., HM Foreign Service, 1949. Has served in: Formosa, 1951; West Berlin, 1954; Lebanon, 1959; Kuwait, 1960; Iran, 1964; Lille, 1969. *Recreations:* lawn tennis, golf. *Address:* c/o Foreign and Commonwealth Office, SW1.

BLACK-HAWKINS, Clive David, MA (Cantab); Head Master, University College School, Hampstead, 1956-75; *b* 2 July 1915; *o c* of late Capt. C. C. R. Black-Hawkins, Hants Regt, and Stella Black-Hawkins (*née* Stein); *m* 1941, Ruth Eleanor, 3rd *d* of late H. Crichton-Miller, MA, MD, FRCP; one *s* one *d. Educ:* Wellington Coll.; Corpus Christi Coll., Cambridge. Asst Master, University College Sch., 1938; Vice-Master, 1953. Intelligence Corps, Capt., 1940-46; GHQ Middle East, 1942-44. *Recreations:* travel, reading memoirs. *Address:* 14A Wedderburn Road, Hampstead, NW3 5QG.

BLACKALL, Sir Henry (William Butler), Kt 1945; QC (Cyprus); Hon. LLD (*jd*) (Dublin); Vice-President, Irish Genealogical Research Society; *b* 19 June 1889; *s* of Henry Blackall, Garden Hill, Co. Limerick, and Isabella, *d* of William Butler, JP, Bunnahow, Co. Clare (descended from Hon. Piers Butler, 2nd *s* of 10th Baron Dunboyne); *m* 1934, Maria, *o d* of D. Severis, MLC, Chairman, Bank of Cyprus. *Educ:* Stonyhurst; Trinity Coll., Dublin. BA (Senior Mod., Gold Medallist); LLB (1st place); 1st of 1st Class Hons Mod. Hist.; 1st Prizeman Roman Law; 1st Prizeman International Law and Jurisprudence (TCD); John Brooke Scholar and Victoria Prizeman (King's Inn); called to Irish Bar, 1912; served European War, 1914-18; Crown Counsel, Kenya, 1919; Member Legislative Council, 1920; Sen. Crown Counsel, Nigeria, 1923; Acting Solicitor-General, various periods, 1923-31; Attorney-General, Cyprus, 1932-36; Attorney-General, Gold Coast, 1936-43; MEC, MLC; Governor's Deputy, 1940; Chairman, Cttee of Enquiry into Native Tribunals, 1942; Chief Justice of Trinidad and Tobago, and President of the West Indian Court of Appeal, 1943-46; Chief Justice of Hong Kong, 1946-48; President of the West African Court of Appeal, 1948-51; retired, 1951. *Publications:* The Butlers of Co. Clare; The Galweys of Munster; articles in various historical and genealogical journals. *Recreation:* genealogy. *Address:* Halkedon Street, Lycavitos, PO Box 1139, Nicosia, Cyprus. *T:* Nicosia 76362. *Clubs:* Travellers'; Kildare Street and University (Dublin).➤

BLACKBURN, Bishop of, since 1972; Rt. Rev. Robert Arnold Schürhoff Martineau, MA; *b* 22 Aug. 1913; *s* of late Prof. C. E. Martineau, MA, MCom, FCA, and Mrs Martineau, Birmingham; *m* 1941, Elinor Gertrude Ap-Thomas; one *s* two *d. Educ:* King Edward's Sch., Birmingham; Trinity Hall, Cambridge; Westcott House, Cambridge. Tyson Medal for Astronomy, 1935. Deacon 1938, priest 1939; Curate, Melksham, 1938-41. Chaplain: RAFVR, 1941-46; RAuxAF, 1947-52. Vicar: Ovenden, Halifax, 1946-52; Allerton, Liverpool, 1952-66; St Christopher, San Lorenzo, Calif, 1961-62. Hon. Canon of Liverpool, 1961-66; Rural Dean of Childwall, 1964-66. Proctor in Convocation, 1964-66. Bishop Suffragan of Huntingdon, 1966-72; Residentiary Canon of Ely, 1966-72. First Jt Chm., C of E Bd of Educn and Nat. Soc. for Promoting Religious Educn, 1973-. Chm., Central Readers Bd, C of E, 1971-76. *Publications:* The Church in Germany in Prayer (ed jtly), 1937; Rhodesian Wild Flowers, 1953; The Office and Work of a Reader, 1970; The Office and Work of a Priest, 1972; Moments that Matter, 1976; Preaching through the Christian Year; Truths that Endure, 1977. *Recreations:* gardening, swimming. *Address:* Bishop's House, Clayton-le-Dale, Blackburn, Lancs.
See also C. H. Martineau.

BLACKBURN, Archdeacon of; see Carroll, Ven. C. W. D.

BLACKBURN, Provost of; see Jackson, Very Rev. Lawrence.

BLACKBURN, Lt-Comdr David Anthony James, RN; Equerry-in-Waiting to the Duke of Edinburgh, since 1976; *b* 18 Jan. 1945; *s* of late Lieut J. Blackburn, DSC, RN, and of Mrs M. J. G. Pickering-Pick; *m* 1973, Elizabeth Barstow; two *d. Educ:* Taunton Sch. RNC Dartmouth, 1963; HMS Kirkliston (in comd), 1972-73. *Address:* 143 The Keep, Kings Road, Kingston-upon-Thames, Surrey KT2 5UE. *T:* 01-549 4057. *Club:* Royal Cruising.

BLACKBURN, (Evelyn) Barbara; novelist and playwright; *b* Brampton Brien, Hereford, July 1898; *d* of late E. M. Blackburn, Fairway Cottage, Henley-on-Thames; *m* 1927, Claude Leader; two *s* one *d. Educ:* Eversley, Folkestone. *Publications:* novels: Return to Bondage, 1926; Season Made for Joy, 1927; Sober Feast, 1929; Courage for Martha, 1930; Marriage and Money,

1931; The Club, 1932; The Long Journey, 1933; Lover be Wise, 1934; Good Times, 1935; Abbots Bank, 1947; Georgina Goes Home, 1951; Star Spangled Heavens, 1953; The Briary Bush, 1954; Summer at Sorrelhurst, 1954; The Buds of May, 1955; The Blackbird's Tune, 1957; Spinners Hall (as Barbara Leader), 1957; Green for Lovers, 1958; Story of Alix, 1959; The Little Cousin, 1960; Love Story of Mary Britton, 1961; Doctor and Debutante, 1961; Lovers' Meeting, 1962; Learn Her by Heart, 1962; City of Forever, 1963; Come Back My Love, 1963; (as Frances Castle, with Peggy Mundy Castle) The Sisters' Tale, 1968; as Frances Castle: Tara's Daughter, 1970; The Thread of Gold, 1971; *play:* (with Mundy Whitehouse) Poor Man's Castle; *biography:* Noble Lord, 1949. *Address:* Anchor Cottage, Latchingdon, Chelmsford, Essex. *T:* Maldon 740367.

BLACKBURN, Fred; *b* 29 July 1902; *s* of Richley and Mary Blackburn, Mellor; *m* 1930, Marion, *d* of Walter W. and Hannah Fildes, Manchester; two *s. Educ:* Queen Elizabeth's Grammar Sch., Blackburn; St John's Coll., Battersea; Manchester Univ. Teacher. MP (Lab) Stalybridge and Hyde Div. of Cheshire, 1951-70, retired 1970. *Publications:* The Regional Council; Local Government Reform; George Tomlinson. *Address:* 114 Knutsford Road, Wilmslow, Cheshire. *T:* Wilmslow 23142.

BLACKBURN, Guy, MBE 1944; MChir, FRCS; Consultant Surgeon Emeritus, Guy's Hospital; *b* 20 Nov. 1911; *s* of Dr A. E. Blackburn, Beckenham; *m* 1953, Joan, *d* of Arthur Bowen, Pontycymmer, Wales; one *d. Educ:* Rugby; Clare Coll., Cambridge (MA). MRCS, LRCP 1935; MB, BChir 1935; FRCS 1937; MChir 1941. House appointments, St Bartholomew's Hospital, 1935-37; Brackenbury Scholar in Surgery, 1935; Demonstrator of Anatomy and Chief Asst in Surgery, 1938-39; Military Service, 1942-46; Lt-Col i/c Surgical Div., 1945-46; served in N Africa and Italy. Hunterian Prof., RCS, 1946; late Examiner in Surgery, Univs of Cambridge and London; Member Court of Examiners, RCS, 1962-68. Hon. Visiting Surgeon, Johns Hopkins Hospital, Baltimore, USA, 1957; President, Medical Society of London, 1964-65. Hon. Consulting Surgeon, British Army at Home, 1967-76. Pres., Assoc. of Surgeons of GB and Ireland, 1976-77. *Publications:* various publications in medical journals and books; (co-ed) A Textbook of Surgery, 1958. *Address:* 92 Harley Street, W1. *T:* 01-935 2255. *Club:* Garrick.

BLACKBURN, Ronald Henry Albert; Clerk to the Northern Ireland Assembly, since 1973; *b* 9 Feb. 1924; *s* of late Sidney James and Ellen Margaret Selina Blackburn; *m* 1950, Annabell Hunter; two *s. Educ:* Royal Belfast Academical Institution; Univ. of London (LLB (Hons)). Intelligence Service, 1943; Dept of the Foreign Office, 1944-46. Parly Reporting Staff (N Ire.), 1946-52; Second Clerk Asst, Parlt of N Ire., 1952-62; Clerk Asst, 1962-71; Clerk of the Parliaments, 1971-73; Clerk to NI Constitutional Convention, 1975-76. *Recreations:* golf, gardening. *Address:* Trelawn, Jordanstown Road, Newtownabbey, Co. Antrim, N Ireland. *T:* Whiteabbey 62035.

BLACKBURNE, Rt. Rev. Hugh Charles; *see* Thetford, Bishop Suffragan of.

BLACKBURNE, Sir Kenneth (William), GCMG 1962 (KCMG 1952; CMG 1946); GBE 1962 (OBE 1939); *b* 12 Dec. 1907; *er s* of late Very Rev. H. W. Blackburne; *m* 1935, Bridget Senhouse Constant, *d* of James Mackay Wilson, DL, Currygrane, Co. Longford; one *s* one *d. Educ:* Marlborough; Clare Coll., Cambridge. Asst District Officer, Nigeria, 1930; Asst District Comr, Nazareth, Palestine, 1935; Actg District Comr, Galilee District, Palestine, May-Sept. 1938; Actg Asst Princ. and Princ., CO, 1938; Colonial Sec., The Gambia, 1941; Administrative Sec. to the Comptroller for Development and Welfare in the West Indies, 1943-47 (Actg Comptroller, 1944 and 1946); Dir of Information Services, CO, 1947-50; Governor and C-in-C of the Leeward Islands, 1950-56; Capt.-General and Governor-in-Chief, Jamaica, 1957-62; Governor-General of Jamaica, 1962; retd 1963; Chm., Sussex Church Campaign, 1963-70. KStJ, 1952. *Publication:* Lasting Legacy: a story of British Colonialism, 1976. *Recreations:* sailing, gardening. *Address:* Garvagh, Ballasalla, Isle of Man. *T:* Castletown (IoM) 3640. *Club:* Athenæum.
See also Bishop Suffragan of Thetford.

BLACKER, Gen. Sir Cecil (Hugh), GCB 1975 (KCB 1969; CB 1967); OBE 1960; MC 1944; Adjutant-General, Ministry of Defence (Army), 1973-76, retired; ADC (General) to the Queen, 1974-76; *b* 4 June 1916; *s* of Col Norman Valentine Blacker and Olive Georgina (*née* Hope); *m* 1947, Felicity Mary, *widow of* Major J. Rew and *d* of Major I. Buxton, DSO; two *s. Educ:* Wellington Coll. Joined 5th Royal Inniskilling Dragoon Guards,

1936; Commanded 23rd Hussars, 1945; Instructor, Staff Coll., Camberley, 1951-54; Commanded 5th Royal Inniskilling Dragoon Guards, 1955-57; Military Asst to CIGS, 1958-60; Asst Commandant, RMA, Sandhurst, 1960-62; Commander, 39 Infantry Brigade Group, 1962-64; GOC 3rd Div., 1964-66; Dir, Army Staff Duties, MoD, 1966-69; GOC-in-C Northern Command, 1969-70; Vice-Chief of the General Staff, 1970-73. Colonel Commandant: RMP, 1971-76; APTC, 1971-76; Col, 5th Royal Inniskilling Dragoon Guards, 1972-. FBIM 1973. *Publications:* The Story of Workboy, 1960; Soldier in the Saddle, 1963. *Recreations:* painting and reading. Amateur Steeplechase rider, 1947-54; represented GB in World Modern Pentathlon Championships, 1951; represented GB in Showjumping, 1959-61. *Address:* Whitchurch House, Whitchurch, Aylesbury, Bucks. *Club:* Cavalry and Guards.

BLACKER, Captain Derek Charles, RN; Director of Public Relations (Royal Navy), since 1977; *b* 19 May 1929; *s* of Charles Edward Blacker and Alexandra May Farrant; *m* 1952, Brenda Mary Getgood; one *s* one *d. Educ:* County Sch., Isleworth; King's Coll., Univ. of London (BSc Hons 1950). Entered RN, 1950; specialisations: navigation, meteorology, oceanography; HMS Birmingham, HMS Albion, BRNC Dartmouth, HMS Hermes, 1956-69; Comdr 1965; NATO Commands: SACLANT, 1969; CINCHAN, 1972; SACEUR, 1974; Captain 1975. *Recreations:* music, tennis, fishing, shooting, sailing. *Address:* Barnsfield, Buckfastleigh, Devon. *T:* Buckfastleigh 2504. *Club:* Army and Navy.

BLACKETT, Sir George (William), 10th Bt *cr* 1673; *b* 26 April 1906; *s* of Sir Hugh Douglas Blackett, 8th Bt, and Helen Katherine (*d* 1943), *d* of late George Lowther; *S* brother, 1968; *m* 1st, 1933, Euphemia Cicely (*d* 1960), *d* of late Major Nicholas Robinson; 2nd, 1964, Daphne Laing, *d* of late Major Guy Laing Bradley, TD, Hexham, Northumberland. Served with Shropshire Yeomanry and CMP, 1939-45. *Recreations:* hunting, forestry, farming. *Heir:* *b* Major Francis Hugh Blackett [*b* 16 Oct. 1907; *m* 1950, Elizabeth Eily Barrie, 2nd *d* of late Howard Dennison; two *s* two *d*]. *Address:* Colwyn, Corbridge, Northumberland. *T:* Corbridge 2252. *Club:* English-Speaking Union.

BLACKETT-ORD, Andrew James; His Honour Vice-Chancellor Blackett-Ord; a Circuit Judge since 1972; Vice-Chancellor, County Palatine of Lancaster, since 1973; Member, Council of Duchy of Lancaster, since 1973; *b* 21 Aug. 1921; 2nd *s* of late John Reginald Blackett-Ord, Whitfield, Northumberland; *m* 1945, Rosemary Bovill; three *s* one *d. Educ:* Eton; New Coll., Oxford (MA). Scots Guards, 1943-46; called to Bar, 1947; County Court Judge, 1971. Chancellor, dio. of Newcastle-upon-Tyne, 1971-. *Recreations:* reading, shooting. *Address:* Helbeck Hall, Brough, Kirkby Stephen, Cumbria. *T:* Brough 323. *Clubs:* Garrick, Lansdowne; St James's (Manchester).

BLACKFORD, 4th Baron *cr* 1935; **William Keith Mason;** Bt 1918; at Harrow School; *b* 27 March 1962; *s* of 3rd Baron Blackford, DFC, and of Sarah (now Mrs Eric Hopton), *d* of Sir Shirley Worthington-Evans, 2nd Bt; *S* father, 1977. *Address:* 37 Chesham Place, SW1. *T:* 01-235 3071.

BLACKHAM, Rear-Adm. Joseph Leslie, CB 1965; DL; *b* 29 Feb. 1912; *s* of Dr Walter Charles Blackham, Birmingham, and Margaret Eva Blackham (*née* Bavin); *m* 1938, Coreen Shelford Skinner, *er d* of Paym. Captain W. S. Skinner, CBE, RN; one *s* one *d. Educ:* West House Sch., Edgbaston; RNC Dartmouth. Specialised in Navigation; served war of 1939-45; JSSC 1950; Comdr, RNC Greenwich, 1953-54; Captain 1954; Admty, 1955-57; Sen. Officer, Reserve Fleet at Plymouth, 1957-59; Admty Naval Staff, 1959-61; Cdre. Supt, HM Dockyard, Singapore, 1962-63; Rear-Adm. 1963; Admiral Supt, HM Dockyard, Portsmouth, 1964-66; retired. Mem., IoW Hosp. Management Cttee, 1968-74; Vice-Chm., IoW AHA 1974-; Chm., Family Practitioners Cttee, IoW, 1974-; Mem., Bd of Visitors, HM Prison, Parkhurst, 1967- (Chm. 1974-). CC Isle of Wight, 1967-77 (Chm., 1975-77); DL Hants and IoW, 1970-; High Sheriff, IoW, 1975. Mentioned in despatches for service in Korea, 1951. *Address:* Downedge, The Mall, Brading, Isle of Wight PO36 0BS. *T:* Brading 218.

BLACKIE, John Ernest Haldane, CB 1959; retired as Chief Inspector of the Department of Education (1951-66); *b* 6 June 1904; *e s* of late Rt Rev. E. M. Blackie, sometime Bishop of Grimsby and Dean of Rochester and late Caroline, *d* of Rev. J. Haldane Stewart of Ardsheal; *m* 1st, 1933, Kathleen Mary (*d* 1941), *d* of F. S. Creswell; no *c*; 2nd, 1942, Pamela Althea Vernon, *d* of A. J. Margetson, HMI; two *s* two *d. Educ:* Bradfield; Magdalene Coll., Cambridge (MA). Asst Master: Lawrenceville Sch., NJ, USA, 1926-27; Bradfield, 1928-33; Asst

Director, Public Schools Empire Tour to NZ, 1932-33; HM Inspector of Schools, 1933; District Inspector, Manchester, 1936-47; Divisional Inspector, Eastern Divn, 1947-51; Chief Inspector of: Further Educn, 1951-58; Primary Educn, 1958-66; Secretary of State's Assessor on Central Advisory Council (Plowden), 1963-66. Lectr (part-time), Homerton Coll. of Educn, Cambridge, 1966-70. Mem. Directorate, Anglo-American Primary Project, 1969. Sen. Counsellor, Open Univ., 1970-73. Trustee, Nat. Extension Coll. 47th County of Lancaster Home Guard, 1940-44. FRES. *Publications:* Family Holidays Abroad (with Pamela Blackie), 1961; Good Enough for the Children?, 1963; Inside the Primary School, 1967; English Teaching for Non-Specialists, 1969; Inspecting and the Inspectorate, 1970; Changing the Primary School, 1974; Bradfield 1850-1975, 1976; various books and articles on education, travel and entomology. *Recreations:* travel, gardening, natural history. *Address:* The Bell House, Alconbury, Huntingdon Cambs. *T:* Huntingdon 890270. *Club:* Pitt (Cambridge).

BLACKIE, Dr Margery Grace; Physician to the Queen since 1969; Hon. Consulting Physician to the Royal London Homœopathic Hospital since 1966; Dean of the Faculty of Homœopathy since 1965; *y d* of Robert and Elizabeth Blackie, Trafalgar House, Downham Market, Norfolk. *Educ:* Royal Free Hosp. and Medical School. MRCS, LRCP 1923; MB, BS 1926; MD London 1928. Asst Phys., Children's Dept, Royal London Homœopathic Hosp., 1929-36; Asst Phys., Royal London Homœopathic Hosp., 1937-57; Sen. Consultant Phys., 1957-66. Pres., Internat. Homœopathic Congress, 1965. *Publications:* The Place of Homœopathy in Modern Medicine (Presidential address), 1950; The Richards Hughes Memorial Lecture 1959. *Address:* 18 Thurloe Street, SW7 2SU. *T:* 01-589 2776; Hedingham Castle, Halstead, Essex. *T:* Hedingham 60261.

BLACKLEY, Travers Robert, CMG 1952; CBE 1949 (OBE 1946); farmer; *b* 10 March 1899; *o s* of late Travers R. Blackley, Drumbar, Cavan, and of Ethel, *d* of Col E. W. Cuming, Crover, Mount Nugent, Co. Cavan; *m* 1932, Elizabeth, *o d* of late Major A. Deane, Royal Warwickshire Regt, and *g d* of Lt-Col Charles Deane, Gurrane, Fermoy; three *s* two *d* (and one *s* decd). *Educ:* Charterhouse (Scholar); Worcester Coll., Oxford (Senior Exhibitioner). Served European War, 1914-18, in Royal Artillery; joined Sudan Political Service 1922, and served in Blue Nile, Kordofan and Kassala Provinces; seconded for service in Occupied Territory Administrations, 1940. Lt-Col 1940-41; Col 1942; Brig. 1943. Served in Ethiopia and Tripolitania. Chief Administrator, Tripolitania, 1943-51; British Resident in Tripolitania, 1951. Order of the Nile (4th Class), 1936. *Recreations:* farming, shooting, fishing. *Address:* Gurrane, Fermoy, Co. Cork, Eire. *T:* Fermoy 31036. *Club:* Friendly Brothers (Dublin).

BLACKLOCK, Captain Ronald William, CBE 1944; DSC 1917; RN (retired); *b* 21 June 1889; *s* of late J. H. Blacklock, JP, Overthorpe, Banbury; *m* 1920, Aline Frances Anstell (*d* 1975); one *s. Educ:* Preparatory Sch.; HMS Britannia. Midshipman, 1906. Specialised in Submarines in 1910. Served European War in Submarines (despatches twice, DSC); Captain 1931; retd owing to ill-health, 1938; War of 1939-45, Director of Welfare Services, Admiralty. *Address:* 3 Tipperlinn Road, Edinburgh EH10 5ET. *Clubs:* Naval and Military; Royal Yacht Squadron.

BLACKMAN, Rear-Adm. Charles Maurice, DSO 1919; *b* 7 March 1890; 2nd *surv s* of late Charles W. Blackman; *m* 1917, Brenda Olive (*d* 1969), *y d* of late Lawrence Hargrave; two *d. Educ:* Stubbington House, Fareham; HMS Britannia. Lieut 1910; Lieut-Commander, 1918; Commander, 1924; Captain 1931; retired list, 1941; promoted to Rear-Adm. for war services, 1946; a Younger Brother of Trinity House; served European War, 1914-18 (DSO); Baltic Operations, 1919-20; lent for service League of Nations, 1925-28; Disarmament Conference, 1932-33; War of 1939-45. *Address:* Ripa, Shore Lane, Bishops Waltham, Hants S03 1EA. *T:* Bishops Waltham 2329. *Club:* Army and Navy.

BLACKMAN, Prof. Geoffrey Emett, FRS 1959; Sibthorpian Professor of Rural Economy, University of Oxford, 1945-70, now Emeritus Professor, and Director of Agricultural Research Council Unit of Experimental Agronomy, 1950-70; *b* 17 April 1903; *er s* of late Prof. V. H. Blackman, FRS, and Edith Delta Emett; *m* 1931, Audrey Babette, *o d* of Richard Seligman and Hilda McDowell; no *c. Educ:* King's College Sch.; St John's Coll., Cambridge. Head of Botany Section, Jealott's Hill Agricultural Research Station, Warfield, Berks, 1927-35; Lecturer in Ecology, Imperial Coll. of Science and Technology, London, 1935-45; Dir, APV Holdings, 1937-73. Directed research under the aegis of Agricultural Research Council on

introduction of new crops, principles of selective toxicity and development of selective herbicides, 1941-70. Delegate of the Clarendon Press, 1950-70; Secretary of the Biology War Cttee, 1942-46. Chairman Advisory Cttee enquiring into Production Development and Consumption Research, in Natural Rubber Industry, 1956. Member, Sub-Cttees, UGC: Technology, 1960-68, Biological Sciences, 1960-70; Mem., Nat. Acad. of Sciences Cttee on the effects of herbicides in Vietnam, 1971-74. President, Institute of Biology, 1963-64; Vice-President, Royal Society, 1967-68; Fellow, Imperial Coll. of Science and Technology, 1968-. *Publications:* papers in scientific jls on agricultural, ecological, physiological and statistical investigations. *Recreations:* gardening with the Ericaceae, collecting water-colours. *Address:* Woodcroft, Foxcombe Lane, Boars Hill, Oxford. *Club:* Athenæum.

BLACKMAN, Gilbert Albert Waller, OBE 1973; CEng, FIMechE, FInstF; Member, Central Electricity Generating Board, since 1977; *b* 28 July 1925; *s* of Ernest Albert Cecil Blackman and Amy Blackman; *m* 1948, Lilian Rosay. *Educ:* Wanstead County High Sch.; Wandsworth Tech. Coll. (CEng, FIMechE 1967). FInstF 1964. Trainee Engr, London Div., Brit. Electricity Authority, 1948-50; various appts in power stns, 1950-63; Central Electricity Generating Board: Stn Supt, Belvedere, 1963-64; Asst Reg. Dir, E Midlands Div., 1964-67; Asst Reg. Dir, Midlands Reg., 1967-70; Dir of Generation, Midlands Reg., 1970-75; Dir Gen., N Eastern Reg., 1975-77. *Recreations:* shooting, photography, walking. *Address:* Central Electricity Generating Board, 15 Newgate Street, EC1. *T:* 01-248 1202.
See also *L . C . F . Blackman* .

BLACKMAN, Dr Lionel Cyril Francis; Director: Fibreglass Ltd (subsidiary co. of Pilkington Brothers Ltd), since 1972; Compocem Ltd, since 1975; Cemfil Corporation (US), since 1975; Cementos y Fibras S.A. (Spain), since 1976; *b* 12 Sept. 1930; *s* of Ernest Albert Cecil Blackman and Amy McBain; *m* 1955, Susan Hazel Peachey; one *s* one *d. Educ:* Wanstead High Sch.; Queen Mary Coll., London. BSc 1952; PhD 1955. Scientific Officer, then Senior Research Fellow, RN Scientific Service, 1954-57; ICI Research Fellow, then Lectr in Chemical Physics of Solids, Imperial Coll., London, 1957-60; Asst Dir (London), then Dir, Chemical Research Div., BR, 1961-64; Dir of Basic Research, then Dir Gen., British Coal Utilisation Research Assoc., 1964-70. CEng; FRIC; DIC; SFInstF; AICeram. *Publications:* (ed) Modern Aspects of Graphite Technology, 1970; papers in various scientific and technical jls on dropwise condensation of steam, ferrites, sintering of oxides, graphite and its crystal compounds, glass surface coatings. *Address:* Grange Court, Higher Lane, Dalton, near Wigan, Lancs. *T:* Parbold 2096.

BLACKMAN, Prof. Moses, FRS 1962; Professor of Physics, Imperial College of Science and Technology, London, 1959-76, now Professor Emeritus; Senior Research Fellow, Imperial College, since 1976; *b* 6 Dec. 1908; *e s* of late Rev. Joseph Blackman and Esther Oshry; *m* 1959, Anne Olivia, *d* of late Arthur L. Court, Sydney, Australia. *Educ:* Victoria Boys' High Sch., Grahamstown, SA; Rhodes University Coll., Grahamstown; Universities of Göttingen, London and Cambridge. MSc (SA) 1930; DPhil (Göttingen) 1933; PhD (London) 1936; PhD (Cantab) 1938. Queen Victoria Scholar (University of SA) 1931; Beit Scholar (Imperial Coll.) 1933; DSIR Sen. Res. Scholar, 1935; Member staff Physics Dept, Imperial Coll., 1937-. Mem. British Cttee on Atomic Energy, 1940-41; scientific work for Min. of Home Security, 1942-45. Member Internat. Commn on Electron Diffraction, 1957-66. Member Safety in Mines Research Advisory Board, Min. of Power, 1963-74. *Publications:* scientific papers on the physics of crystals. *Address:* 48 Garden Royal, Kersfield Road, SW15. *T:* 01-789 1706.

BLACKMAN, Raymond Victor Bernard, MBE 1970; CEng, FIMarE, FRINA; Editor of Jane's Fighting Ships, 1949-50 to 1972-73 editions; Author and Journalist; *b* 29 June 1910; *e s* of late Leo Albert Martin Blackman and late Laura Gertrude, *e d* of Albert Thomas; *m* 1935, Alma Theresa Joyce, *y d* of late Francis Richard Hannah; one *s* one *d. Educ:* Southern Grammar Sch., Portsmouth. Contrib. to general and technical press, and associated with Jane's Fighting Ships since 1930; Naval Correspondent, Hampshire Telegraph and Post, 1936-46, Sunday Times, 1946-56. Served Royal Navy, 1926-36 and War of 1939-45, HMS Vernon, Mine Design Dept, Admiralty. Member of The Press Gang. Broadcaster on naval topics. *Publications:* Modern World Book of Ships, 1951; The World's Warships, 1955, 1960, 1963, 1969; Ships of the Royal Navy, 1973; contrib. to The Statesman's Year Book, The Diplomatist, Encyclopædia Britannica Book of the Year, Warships and

Navies 1973, The Motor Ship, The Engineer, Navy, Lloyd's List, etc. *Recreations:* seagoing, foreign travel, philately. *Address:* 72 The Brow, Widley, Portsmouth, Hants. *T:* Cosham 76837. *Clubs:* Anchorites; Press; Royal Naval and Royal Albert Yacht (Portsmouth).

BLACKMUN, Harry A(ndrew); Associate Justice, United States Supreme Court, since 1970; *b* Nashville, Illinois, 12 Nov. 1908; *s* of late Corwin Manning Blackmun and of Theo Huegely (*née* Reuter); *m* 1941, Dorothy E. Clark; three *d. Educ:* Harvard Univ.; Harvard Law Sch. AB, LLB. Admitted to Minnesota Bar, 1932; private legal practice with Dorsey, Colman, Barker, Scott & Barber, Minneapolis, 1934-50: Associate, 1934-38; Jun. Partner, 1939-42; General Partner, 1943-50; Instructor: St Paul Coll. of Law, 1935-41; Univ. of Minnesota Law Sch., 1945-47; Resident Counsel, Mayo Clinic, Rochester, 1950-59; Judge, US Ct of Appeals, 8th Circuit, 1959-70. Member: American Bar Assoc.; Amer. Judicature Soc.; Minnesota State Bar Assoc.; 3rd Judicial Dist (Minn) Bar Assoc.; Olmsted Co. (Minn) Bar Assoc.; Bd of Mems, Mayo Assoc. Rochester, 1953-60; Bd of Dirs and Exec. Cttee, Rochester Methodist Hosp., 1954-70; Trustee: Hamline Univ., St Paul, 1964-70; William Mitchell Coll. of Law, St Paul, 1959-74. Hon. LLD: De Pauw Univ., 1971; Hamline Univ., 1971; Ohio Wesleyan Univ., 1971; Morningside Coll., 1972; Wilson Coll., 1972; Dickinson Sch. of Law 1973; Drake Univ., 1975; Southern Illinois, 1976; Pepperdine Univ., 1976; Emory, 1976; Hon. DPS, Ohio Northern Univ., 1973; Hon. DHL Oklahoma City, 1976. *Publications:* contrib. legal and medical jls. *Recreations:* gardening, reading, music. *Address:* Supreme Court Building, 1 First Street NE, Washington, DC 20543, USA.

BLACKSHAW, Alan, VRD 1970; Director General, Offshire Supplies Office, since 1977 (Deputy Director General, 1974-76); *b* 7 April 1933; *s* of Frederick William and late Elsie Blackshaw; *m* 1956, Jane Elizabeth Turner; one *d. Educ:* elem. schs; Merchant Taylors' Sch., Crosby (Foundn Schol.); Wadham Coll., Oxford (Open Major Schol., MA). Royal Marines, 1954-56: commnd into 42nd Royal Marines Commando, 1955; served as instructor in Cliff Assault Wing; subseq. Royal Marines Reserve until 1974. Asst Principal, Petroleum Div., Min. of Power, 1956; Private Sec. to Parly Sec., 1958-61; Principal 1961, Gen. and Electricity Divs; 1st Sec., UK Delegn to OECD, Paris, 1965-66 (on loan to FO); Principal Private Sec. to Minister of Power, 1967-69; Asst Sec., Min. of Power, 1969, Iron and Steel Div.; with Charterhouse Gp on loan, 1972-73; Asst Sec., DTI Petroleum Div., 1973; Under Sec., Dept of Energy, 1974. Member: Offshore Energy Technol. Bd, 1977-; Ship and Marine Technol. Requirements Bd, 1977-. Pres., Oxford Univ. Mountaineering Club, 1953-54; Editor, Alpine Climbing, 1954-55; Sec., Climbers' Club, 1956-61, Vice-Pres. 1973-76; Editor, Alpine Jl, 1968-70; Leader, British Alpine Ski Traverse, 1972; Ski Club of Great Britain: Mem. Council, 1973-76; Vice-Pres., 1977-; Pery Medal 1977; Mem. Cttee of Management, Mount Everest Foundn Trust, 1968-73; Pres., British Mountaineering Council, 1973-76. FRGS; FInstPet. *Publication:* Mountaineering, 1965, 3rd revision 1975. *Recreations:* mountaineering and ski-ing. *Address:* Friarsbrae House, Friarsbrae, Linlithgow, West Lothian EH49 6BQ. *T:* Linlithgow 2482. *Clubs:* Alpine, Ski Club of Great Britain, Royal Automobile.

BLACKSHAW, James William, CMG 1951; MBE 1920; Assistant Secretary, Ministry of Supply, 1946-55, retired; *b* 8 June 1895; *s* of Arthur Joseph Blackshaw; *m* 1927, Edith Violet, *d* of George Hansford. *Educ:* Doncaster Grammar Sch. Civil Service from 1911. *Address:* 70 Victoria Avenue, Shanklin, Isle of Wight. *T:* Shanklin 2336.

BLACKSHAW, William Simon; Headmaster of Brighton College, since 1971; *b* 28 Oct. 1930; *s* of late C. B. Blackshaw, sometime Housemaster, Cranleigh School and Kathleen Mary (who *m* 1965, Sir Thomas McAlpine, Bt, *qv*); *m* 1956, Elizabeth Anne Evans; two *s* one *d. Educ:* Sherborne Sch.; Hertford Coll., Oxford. 2nd cl. hons Mod. Langs. Repton School: Asst Master, 1955-71; Head of Modern Languages Dept, 1961-66; Housemaster, 1966-71. *Publication:* Regardez! Racontez!, 1971. *Recreations:* philately, painting, cricket, golf. *Address:* Brighton College, Eastern Road, Brighton BN2 2AL. *T:* Brighton 65788.

BLACKWELL, Basil Davenport, MA, BSc(Eng), CEng; Vice-Chairman and Chief Executive, Westland Group of Companies, since 1974; *b* Whitkirk, Yorks, 8 Feb. 1922; *s* of late Alfred Blackwell and of Mrs H. Lloyd; *m* 1948, Betty Meggs, *d* of late Engr Captain Meggs, RN; one *d. Educ:* Leeds Grammar Sch.; St John's Coll., Cambridge (MA; Hughes Prize); London Univ. (BScEng). FIMechE; FRAeS; FBIM. Sci. Officer, Admiralty, 1942; Rolls-Royce Ltd, 1945; Engine Div., Bristol Aeroplane

Co. Ltd, 1949; Bristol Siddeley Engines Ltd: Dep. Chief Engr, 1959; Sales Dir, 1963; Man. Dir, Small Engine Div., 1965 (subseq. Small Engines Div. of Rolls-Royce Ltd). Commercial Dir, Westland Aircraft Ltd, 1970; Man. Dir, Westland Helicopters Ltd, 1972, Dep. Chm. 1974, Chm. 1976-: Chm., Westland Engineers Ltd, 1975- (Dep. Chm., 1974); Dep. Chairman: British Hovercraft Corp., 1974-; Normalair-Garrett Ltd, 1975-. Member Council: CBI; SBAC. *Publications:* contrib. professional jls. *Recreations:* gardens and gardening. *Address:* Charters, The Avenue, Sherborne, Dorset. *T:* Sherborne 3516.

BLACKWELL, Sir Basil Henry, Kt 1956; JP; President of B. H. Blackwell Ltd (Chairman, 1924-69); Chairman, Basil Blackwell and Mott Ltd, 1922-69, and The Shakespeare Head Press, 1921-69; *b* 29 May 1889; *s* of late Benjamin Henry and late Lydia Blackwell; *m* 1914, Marion Christine (*d* 1977), *d* of late John Soans; two *s* three *d. Educ:* Magdalen College Sch.; Merton Coll., Oxford. 2nd Class Lit. Hum; studied publishing at the Oxford Press, Amen Corner; joined father in Oxford, 1913; started publishing independently, 1919; formed the Shakespeare Head Press Ltd to carry on and develop the work of the late A. H. Bullen, 1921; formed Basil Blackwell and Mott Ltd (publishers), 1922; succeeded father (the founder of the firm) as Chairman of B. H. Blackwell Ltd (booksellers), 1924; President: International Association of Antiquarian Booksellers, 1925 and 1926; Associated Booksellers of Great Britain and Ireland, 1934 and 1935; The Classical Assoc., 1964-65; William Morris Soc., 1968-; English Assoc., 1969-70. Hon. Mem., Company of Stationers, 1973. Hon. Freeman of Oxford City. Hon. Fellow, Merton Coll., Oxford; Hon. LLD Manchester Univ., 1965. Officier d'Académie, France. *Recreations:* boating, perennial outdoor swimming, reading. *Address:* Osse Field, Appleton, Abingdon, Oxon. *T:* Cumnor 2436. *Clubs:* Athenæum; Leander.

BLACKWELL, Prof. Donald Eustace, MA, PhD; Savilian Professor of Astronomy, University of Oxford, and Fellow of New College, Oxford, since 1960; *b* 27 May 1921; *s* of John Blackwell and Ethel Bowe; *m* 1951, Nora Louise Carlton; two *s* two *d. Educ:* Merchant Taylors' Sch.; Sandy Lodge; Sidney Sussex Coll., Cambridge. Isaac Newton Student, University of Cambridge, 1947; Stokes Student, Pembroke Coll., Cambridge, 1948; Asst Director, Solar Physics Observatory, Cambridge, 1950-60. Various Astronomical Expeditions: Sudan, 1952; Fiji, 1955; Bolivia, 1958 and 1961; Canada, 1963; Manuae Island, 1965. Pres., RAS, 1973-75. *Publications:* papers in astronomical journals. *Address:* Department of Astrophysics, South Parks Road, Oxford.

BLACKWELL, John Humphrey, CBE 1937; MC; *b* 25 April 1895; *e s* of John Thomas Blackwell, Architect, Kettering, Northants; *m* 1922, Jessie Pauline Luard Pears; one *s* two *d. Educ:* Bedford Sch. Served European War (France), Bedfordshire Regt, 1914-18 (despatches, MC and Bar); Beds and Herts Regt, India, 1919-20; joined staff of Asiatic Petroleum Co. (India) Ltd, 1920; MLA (Central), 1935; Chairman, Karachi Chamber of Commerce, 1939-40 and 1943-44; Trustee, Karachi Port Trust. Director, Burmah-Shell (India) Ltd (Pakistan) Ltd, 1946-50; Resident Manager, Shell Training Centre, Teddington, Middlesex, 1951-54. *Address:* Yew Tree Cottqge, Bridge of Weir, Renfrewshire PA11 3BE. *T:* Bridge of Weir 612020.

BLACKWELL, John Kenneth, CBE 1965; HM Diplomatic Service, retired; *b* 8 May 1914; *s* of late J. W. Blackwell; *m* 1951, Joan Hilary, *d* of late D. W. Field; two *s* one *d. Educ:* Downing Coll., Cambridge (MA). HM Foreign Service, 1938; Vice-consular posts, in China and Mozambique, 1938-45; Second Secretary, British Embassy, Copenhagen, 1946; Consul, Canton, 1947; served in FO, 1950; Consul: Recife, 1952; Basle, 1956; First Secretary and Head of Chancery, British Embassy, Seoul, 1957; served in FO, 1959; First Secretary with UK Delegn to the European Communities in Brussels, 1961; Consul-General: Hanoi, 1962; Lille, 1965; Sen. Trade Comr, Hong Kong, 1969-72; Ambassador to Costa Rica, 1972-74. *Recreations:* linguistics and entomology; walking. *Address:* Oakley Hay, Vincent Road, Selsey, Sussex. *Club:* Royal Commonwealth Society.

BLACKWELL, Thomas Francis, MBE (mil.) 1944; DL; Chairman: Colne Valley Water Company, since 1963; Turf Newspapers Ltd, since 1955; *b* 31 July 1912; *s* of Thomas Geoffrey Blackwell and Shirley Maud Lawson-Johnston; *m* 1948, Lisette Douglas Pilkington (marr. diss. 1959); one *s* one *d. Educ:* Harrow, Magdalene Coll., Cambridge (MA). Mem. London Stock Exchange, 1935-42. Served War, Coldstream Guards, 1940-45: Bde Major, 5th Gds Armd Bde, 1944-45. Member of Lloyds, 1946. Captain Royal and Ancient Golf Club, 1963; Senior Steward of the Jockey Club, 1965 (Dep. Sen. Steward, 1973-); Mem., Horserace Betting Levy Board, 1976-. Chm., St John's Council for Suffolk, 1970-. Governor, Harrow

School, 1975-. DL Suffolk, 1974. *Recreations:* racing, shooting, golf. *Address:* Langham Hall, Bury St Edmunds, Suffolk. *T:* Walsham-le-Willows 271. *Clubs:* White's, Pratt's; Jockey (Newmarket).

BLACKWOOD, HAMILTON-TEMPLE-; family name of **Marquess of Dufferin.**

BLACKWOOD, Sir Francis Elliot Temple, 6th Bt, *cr* 1814; Assistant Vice-President, retired, Crocker-Citizens National Bank, San Francisco; *b* 11 March 1901; *s* of late Henry Robert Temple Blackwood (*e s* of 4th Bt) and Rebecca Paffard (she *m* 2nd, 1930, Walter G. C. Stevenson), *d* of J. Scullard; *S* brother, 1948; *m* 1921, Lily M. *d* of H. F. MacGougan. *Heir: cousin,* Francis George Blackwood [*b* 10 May 1916; *m* 1941, Margaret, *d* of Hector Kirkpatrick, Lindfield, NSW; two *s* one *d*]. *Address:* 114-1050 West Capitol Avenue, West Sacramento, Calif 95691, USA.

BLACKWOOD, Wing Comdr George Douglas; Chairman, William Blackwood & Sons Ltd, publishers and printers, since 1948; Editor of Blackwood's Magazine, and Managing Director of William Blackwood & Sons Ltd, 1948-76; *b* 11 Oct. 1909; *e s* of late James H. Blackwood and *g g g s* of Wm Blackwood, founder of Blackwood's Magazine; *m* 1936, Phyllis Marion, *y d* of late Sir John Caulcutt, KCMG; one *s* one *d. Educ:* Eton; Clare Coll., Cambridge. Short Service Commission in RAF, 1932-38; re-joined 1939. Formed first Czech Fighter Squadron, 1940-41; Battle of Britain (despatches); commanded Czech Wing of Royal Air Force 2nd TAF, 1944 (despatches); retired 1945. Czech War Cross, 1940; Czech Military Medal 1st class, 1944. *Recreations:* countryside activities. *Address:* Airhouse, Oxton, Berwickshire; 32 Thistle Street, Edinburgh. *T:* 031-225 3411.

BLACKWOOD, Sir Robert (Rutherford), Kt 1961; Chairman: Dunlop Australia Ltd, since 1972 (General Manager, 1948-66); Humes Ltd; *b* Melbourne, 3 June 1906; *s* of Robert Leslie Blackwood and Muriel Pearl (*née* Henry); *m* 1932, Hazel Lavinia McLeod; one *s* one *d. Educ:* Melbourne C of E Grammar Sch.; Univ. of Melbourne. BEE 1929, MCE 1932, Melbourne. Senior Demonstrator and Res. Scholar, University of Melbourne, 1928-30; Lecturer in Agric. Engineering, 1931-33; Res. Engineer Dunlop Rubber, Australia, Ltd, 1933-35; Tech. Man., 1936-46; Prof. of Mech. Engineering, University of Melbourne, 1947. Chm. Interim Council, Monash Univ., 1958-61; Chancellor, Monash Univ., 1961-68. Member Cttee on Medical Education, Victoria, 1960. Trustee, National Museum of Victoria, 1964-, Pres. Council, 1971-; Pres., Royal Soc. of Victoria, 1973-74. FIE Aust, 1948; Hon. LLD Monash, 1971. *Publications:* Monash University: the first ten years, 1968; Beautiful Bali, 1970; papers in engrg jls. *Recreations:* marine biology, painting. *Address:* 8 Huntingfield Road, Melbourne, Victoria 3186, Australia. *T:* 92-5925. *Clubs:* Melbourne, Athenæum (Melbourne).

BLACKWOOD, Prof. William; Professor of Neuropathology, University of London, at The Institute of Neurology, The National Hospital, Queen Square, 1958-76, now Professor Emeritus; *b* 13 March 1911; *m* 1940, Cynthia Gledstone; one *s* one *d. Educ:* Cheltenham Coll.; Edinburgh Univ. MB, ChB Edinburgh 1934; FRCSEd 1938; FRCPEd 1961; FRCPath (FCPath 1963). Pathologist, Scottish Mental Hospitals Laboratory; Neuropathologist, Edinburgh Royal Infirmary, and Municipal Hospitals, 1939; Senior Lecturer in Neuropathology, University of Edinburgh, 1945; Asst Pathologist, 1947, Pathologist, 1949, The National Hospital, Queen Square, London. *Publications:* Atlas of Neuropathology, 1949; (ed jtly) Greenfield's Neuropathology, 3rd 3dn, 1976. *Address:* 71 Seal Hollow Road, Sevenoaks, Kent. *T:* Sevenoaks 54345. *Club:* Scottish Mountaineering (Edinburgh).

BLADES, family name of **Baron Ebbisham.**

BLADIN, Air Vice-Marshal Francis Masson, CB 1950; CBE 1943; *b* 26 Aug. 1898; *s* of F. W. Bladin, Melbourne, Victoria; *m* 1927, Patricia Mary (decd), *d* of P. J. Magennis, Jeir Station, Yass, NSW; one *s* two *d. Educ:* Melbourne; RMC, Duntroon. Attached Royal Field Artillery, 1920-22; joined Royal Australian Air Force, 1923; served War of 1939-45, in Pacific and North-West Europe (despatches, CBE, American Silver Star); AOC North Australia, 1942; SASO, 38 Group, Royal Air Force, 1943-44; Chief of Staff, British Commonwealth Occupation Forces, Japan, 1946-47; Air Member for Personnel, RAAF, 1949-53, retired 1953. Hon. National Treasurer, Returned Servicemen's League of Australia, 1951-69. *Address:* 1 Dale Street, Deepdene, Vic. 3103, Australia.

BLAGDEN, Sir John (Ramsay), Kt 1970; OBE 1944; TD 1943; Regional Chairman of Industrial Tribunals for East Anglia, since 1969; *b* Davos, Switzerland, 25 July 1908; *s* of John William Blagden, PhD, MA, and Johanna Alberta (*née* Martin); *m* 1937, Pauline Catherine Robinson; three *d. Educ:* Hawtreys; Marlborough; Emmanuel Coll., Cambridge (MA). Joined 7th Bn The Essex Regt TA, 2nd Lieut, 1928; Capt. 1935; Major 1938; called to Bar, Lincoln's Inn, 1934; Practised at Bar, 1934-39; War Service, 1939-45; Lt-Col, CO 64th HAA Regt, RA, 1943; BNAF, 1943; CMF and Land Forces Adriatic, 1944-45; BLA, 1945 (OBE, despatches twice, TD two clasps). Col 1945, Perm. Pres., Mil. Govt Courts, BAOR, Nov. 1945; Judge of Control Commn Courts, Germany, 1947; Sen. Magistrate, Sarawak, 1950; Actg Puisne Judge and Sen. Magistrate, Sarawak, 1951-56; Co-Ed. Sarawak Gazette, 1955; Puisne Judge, Trinidad, 1956-60; Trinidad Ed., West Indian Reports, 1959-60; Puisne Judge, Northern Rhodesia, 1960-64; Justice of Appeal, Northern Rhodesia and Zambia, 1964-65; Chief Justice, Zambia, 1965-69. Grand Cordon of Order of Star of Honour of Ethiopia, 1965. *Recreations:* photography, ski-ing, riding, walking, tennis, alpinism; watching cricket and motor racing. *Address:* Jackdaws Ford, Chelsworth, Ipswich, Suffolk. *T:* Bildeston 740461. *Club:* Special Forces.

BLAIKLEY, Robert Marcel; HM Diplomatic Service, retired; *b* 1 Oct. 1916; *s* of late Alexander John Blaikley and late Adelaide Blaikley (*née* Miller); *m* 1942, Alice Mary Duncan; one *s* one *d. Educ:* Christ's Coll., Finchley; St John's Coll., Cambridge. Served HM Forces, 1940-46. Inland Revenue, 1946-48; General Register Office, 1948-65, Asst Secretary, 1958; transferred to Diplomatic Service as Counsellor, 1965; on loan to Colonial Office, 1965-66; Head of Aviation and Telecommunications Dept, CO, 1966-68; Counsellor, Jamaica, 1968-71; Ghana, 1971-73. *Recreations:* walking, choral singing. *Address:* 17 Chestnut Grove, Upper Westwood, Bradford-on-Avon, Wilts.

BLAIR, Sir Alastair Campbell, KCVO 1969 (CVO 1953); TD 1950; WS; JP; *b* 16 Jan. 1908; 2nd *s* of late William Blair, WS, and late Emelia Mylne Campbell; *m* 1933, Catriona Hatchard, *o d* of late Dr William Basil Orr; four *s. Educ:* Cargilfield; Charterhouse; Clare Coll., Cambridge (BA); Edinburgh Univ. (LLB). Writer to the Signet, 1932; Partner: Dundas & Wilson, CS; Davidson & Syme, WS, Edinburgh; retired 1977 as Partner, Dundas & Wilson, CS. Director: Bank of Scotland; Scottish Widows Fund & Life Assurance Society; British Assets Trust Ltd (Chm.) and other Companies. RA (TA) 1939; served 1939-45 (despatches); Secretary, Queen's Body Guard for Scotland, Royal Company of Archers, 1946-59; appointed Brig., 1961; Lieut 1974. Purse Bearer to The Lord High Commissioner to the General Assembly of the Church of Scotland, 1961-69. Chm., Edinburgh Area Scout Council, 1965-. JP Edinburgh, 1954. *Recreations:* archery, curling, golf, shooting. *Address:* 14 Ainslie Place, Edinburgh EH3 6AS. *T:* 031-225 3081. *Club:* New (Edinburgh).

BLAIR, Rev. Andrew Hamish; Member of the Community of the Resurrection, Mirfield, Yorks, since 1935; *b* 19 June 1901; *s* of Andrew Buchanan Blair, Edinburgh, and Banwell, Somerset, and Constance Elizabeth Blair; unmarried. *Educ:* Merchiston Castle; Exeter Coll., Oxford. BA 1923, MA 1926. Deacon, 1924; Priest, 1925; Curate of St Mark, Swindon, 1924; CR Missionary in Borneo, 1936; Subwarden, Hostel of the Resurrection, Leeds Univ., 1937, Warden, 1940; Prior of Mirfield, 1943-49 and 1956-61; Principal, College of the Resurrection, Mirfield, 1949-55; Proctor in Convocation, Wakefield, 1958-61; Prior, St Paul's Priory, Holland Park, W11, 1963-66. *Publication:* The Why and Wherefore of the Church, 1946. *Recreations:* various. *Address:* House of the Resurrection, Mirfield, West Yorks. *T:* Mirfield 4318.

BLAIR, Lt-Gen. Sir Chandos, KCVO 1972; OBE 1962; MC 1941 and bar, 1944; GOC Scotland and Governor of Edinburgh Castle, 1972-76; *b* 25 Feb. 1919; *s* of Brig.-Gen. Arthur Blair and Elizabeth Mary (*née* Hoskyns); *m* 1947, Audrey Mary Travers; one *s* one *d. Educ:* Harrow; Sandhurst. Commnd into Seaforth Highlanders, 1939; comd 4 KAR, Uganda, 1959-61; comd 39 Bde, Radfan and N. Ireland. GOC 2nd Division, BAOR, 1968-70; Defence Services Secretary, MoD, 1970-72. Col Comdt, Scottish Div., 1972-76; Col, Queen's Own Highlanders, 1975-. *Recreations:* golf, tennis, fishing, shooting, hunting. *Address:* c/o Royal Bank of Scotland, 44 Brompton Road, SW3. *Club:* Naval and Military.

BLAIR, Charles Neil Molesworth, CMG 1962; OBE (mil.) 1948; Lt-Col; *b* 22 Oct. 1910; *o s* of late Col J. M. Blair, CMG, CBE, DSO, Glenfoot, Tillicoultry, Scotland; *m* 1938, Elizabeth Dorothea, *d* of late Lord Justice Luxmoore, PC; one *d* (one *s* decd). *Educ:* Stowe; RMC Sandhurst. 2nd Lieut The Black

Watch, 1930. Served War of 1939-45 in Europe, North Africa and Sicily; Instructor, Army Staff Coll., 1941 and 1944; commanded 1st Black Watch, 1943. Retired from Army on account of war wounds, 1951. Attached FO, 1951-67. *Recreations:* fishing, model engineering, writing, philately. *Address:* Portbane, Kenmore, Perthshire. *T:* Kenmore 229. *Club:* Army and Navy.

BLAIR, Claude; Keeper, Department of Metalwork, Victoria and Albert Museum, since 1972; *b* 30 Nov. 1922; *s* of William Henry Murray Blair and Lilian Wearing; *m* 1952, Joan Mary Greville Drinkwater; one *s*. *Educ:* William Hulme's Grammar Sch., Manchester; Manchester Univ. (MA). Served War, Army (Captain RA), 1942-46. Manchester Univ., 1946-51; Asst, Tower of London Armouries, 1951-56; Asst Keeper of Metalwork, V&A, 1956-66; Dep. Keeper, 1966-72. Hon. Editor, Jl of the Arms and Armour Soc., 1953-. FSA 1956. Liveryman: Goldsmiths' Co.; Armourers and Brasiers' Co. Medal of Museo Militar, Barcelona, 1969. *Publications:* European Armour, 1958 (2nd edn, 1972); European and American Arms, 1962; The Silvered Armour of Henry VIII, 1965; Pistols of the World, 1968; Three Presentation Swords in the Victoria and Albert Museum, 1972; The James A. de Rothschild Collection: Arms, Armour and Miscellaneous Metalwork, 1974; numerous articles and reviews in Archaeological Jl, Jl of Arms and Armour Soc., Connoisseur, Waffen-und Kostümkunde, etc. *Recreations:* travel, looking at churches, listening to music. *Address:* 90 Links Road, Ashtead, Surrey KT21 2HW. *T:* Ashtead 75532. *Club:* Anglo-Polish.

BLAIR, David Arthur, MBE 1943; MC 1944; Director, The Distillers Co. Ltd; Chairman, United Glass Ltd; Chairman, Export Committee (Scotch Whisky); *b* 25 Aug. 1917; *s* of Brig.-Gen. A. Blair, DSO; *m* 1947, Elizabeth Adela Morton; two *s* one *d* (and one *d* decd). *Educ:* Harrow; Sandhurst. Commnd Seaforth Highlanders, 1937; served War of 1939-45, Middle East and Europe; psc, India 1945; resigned commn and entered Distillers Co. Ltd as export representative. *Recreations:* golf, field sports. *Address:* Wellisford House, Finchampstead, Berks. *T:* Eversley 732321. *Clubs:* White's; New (Edinburgh); Royal and Ancient (St Andrews).

BLAIR, G. W. S.; *see* Scott Blair.

BLAIR, Rev. Canon Harold Arthur, MA, BD; Canon Residentiary and Chancellor of Truro Cathedral, 1960-75, now Emeritus; *b* 22 Sept. 1902; *s* of Rev. A. A. Blair, SPG Mission, India, some time rector of Saxlingham, Holt, Norfolk; *m* 1933, Honor MacAdam, *d* of Col W. MacAdam, CB, RE; two *s* one *d*. *Educ:* Lancing Coll.; St Edmund Hall, Oxford. BA (2nd cl. Hons Theol.) 1925; MA 1937; BD (Oxon) 1945. Classical Tutor, Dorchester Missionary Coll., 1925-27; Gold Coast Administrative Service, 1927; Asst District Comr, 1928; District Comr, 1935, retd 1939. Ordained Deacon, 1939, Priest, 1940; Asst Curate, Sherborne, 1939-41; Vicar of: Horningsham, Wilts, 1941-45; Winterbourne Earls with Winterbourne Dauntsey and Winterbourne Gunner, 1945-54; St James, Southbroom, Devizes, 1954-60. Hon. Canon of Salisbury, 1953 (prebend of Alton Australis); Examining Chaplain: to Bishop of Salisbury, 1952-60; to Bishop of Truro, 1960-. *Publications:* A Creed before the Creeds, 1954; The Ladder of Temptations, 1960; A Stranger in the House, 1963; essay in Agreed Syllabus of Religious Education (Cornwall), 1964; two essays in Teilhard Re-assessed (symposium), 1970; various articles in Church Quarterly Review. *Recreations:* gardening, cycling, story-telling. *Address:* Beech Cottage, Acreman Street, Sherborne, Dorset. *T:* Sherborne 2353.

BLAIR, Rt. Rev. James Douglas, CBE 1975; *b* 22 Jan. 1906; *s* of Rev. A. A. Blair; unmarried. *Educ:* Marlborough; Keble Coll., Oxford; Cuddesdon Coll. 2nd class Lit. Hum., 1928. Deacon, Penistone, Yorks, 1929; Priest, 1930; Oxford Mission Brotherhood of the Epiphany, Calcutta, 1932-; Asst Bishop of Calcutta, with charge of East Bengal, 1951; Bishop of East Bengal, 1956; title of diocese changed to Dacca, 1960; retired as Bishop of Dacca, 1975. *Recreation:* walking. *Address:* Oxford Mission, Barisha, Calcutta 700008, India.

BLAIR, Sir James H.; *see* Hunter Blair.

BLAIR, Thomas Alexander, QC (NI) 1958; Chief National Insurance Commissioner (Northern Ireland), since 1969; *b* 12 Dec. 1916; *s* of late John Blair and of Wilhelmina Whitla Blair (*née* Downey); *m* 1947, Ida Irvine Moore; two *s* one *d*. *Educ:* Royal Belfast Academical Instn; Queen's Univ. Belfast (BA, LLB). Served War, in Royal Navy, 1940-46 (commissioned, 1941). Called to Bar of N Ireland, 1946. Chairman: Wages Councils; War Pensions Appeal Tribunal. Sen. Crown Counsel

for Co. Tyrone; Mem. Departmental Cttee on Legal Aid. Apptd Dep. Nat. Insurance Umpire, 1959; Pres., Industrial Tribunals (NI), 1967-69; Chief Nat. Insurance Commissioner (NI), 1969. *Recreation:* golf. *Address:* 10 Knockdene Park, Belfast BT5 7AD. *T:* 655182.

BLAIR-CUNYNGHAME, Sir James (Ogilvy), Kt 1976; OBE 1945 (MBE 1943); Chairman: National and Commercial Banking Group Ltd, since 1968; Royal Bank of Scotland Ltd, 1971-76; Williams & Glyn's Bank Ltd, since 1976; Director: Provincial Insurance Co. Ltd; Scottish Mortgage and Trust Co. Ltd; *b* 28 Feb. 1913; 2nd *s* of late Edwin Blair Cunynghame and Anne Tod, both of Edinburgh. *Educ:* Sedbergh Sch.; King's Coll., Cambridge (MA). Elected Fellow, St Catharine's Coll., 1939. Served War of 1939-45 (MBE, OBE); RA and Intelligence, Mediterranean and Europe, Lt-Col 1944. FO, 1946-47; Chief Personnel Officer, BOAC, 1947-55; Dir-Gen. of Staff, National Coal Board, 1955-57; Mem. for Staff of Nat. Coal Bd, 1957-59; part-time Mem., Pay Board, 1973-74. Member: Scottish Economic Council, 1965-74; Exec. Cttee Scottish Council Develt and Industry; Council of Industry for Management Educn; Ct of Governors London Sch. of Economics and Political Science; Council Industrial Soc.; Governor, Sedbergh Sch.; Trustee, Internat. Centre for Res. in Accountancy. FBIM; CIPM. Mem., Queen's Body Guard for Scotland. Hon. LLD St Andrews, 1965; Hon. DSc (Soc. Sci.) Edinburgh, 1969. *Publications:* various articles on aspects of personnel management and the economy. *Recreation:* fishing. *Address:* Broomfield, Moniaive, Thornhill, Dumfriesshire. *T:* Moniaive 217. *Clubs:* Savile, Flyfishers'; New, Scottish Arts (Edinburgh).

BLAIR-KERR, Sir William Alexander, (Sir Alastair Blair-Kerr), Kt 1973; Senior Puisne Judge, Supreme Court, Hong Kong, 1971-73; on occasion, Acting Chief Justice of Hong Kong; *b* 1 Dec. 1911; *s* of William Alexander Milne Kerr and Annie Kerr (*née* Blair), Dunblane, Perthshire, Scotland; *m* 1942, Esther Margaret Fowler Wright; one *s* one *d*. *Educ:* McLaren High Sch., Callander; Edinburgh Univ. (MA, LLB). Solicitor in Scotland, 1939; Advocate (Scots Bar), 1951. Advocate and Solicitor, Singapore, 1939-41; Straits Settlements Volunteer Force, 1941-42; escaped from Singapore, 1942; Indian Army: Staff Capt. "A" Bombay Dist. HQ, 1942-43; DAAG 107 Line of Communication area HQ, Poona, 1943-44; British Army: GSO2, War Office, 1944-45; SO1 Judicial, BMA Malaya, 1945-46. Colonial Legal Service (HM Overseas Service): Hong Kong: Magistrate, 1946-48; Crown Counsel, 1949; Pres. Tenancy Tribunal, 1950; Crown Counsel, 1951-53; Sen. Crown Counsel, 1953-59; District Judge, 1959-61; Puisne Judge, Supreme Court, 1961-71. Pres., various Commns of Inquiry. *Recreations:* golf, walking, music. *Address:* Gairn, Kinbuck, Dunblane, Perthshire. *T:* Dunblane 823377. *Clubs:* Royal Over-Seas League; United Services Recreation (Hong Kong).

BLAIR-OLIPHANT, Air Vice-Marshal David Nigel Kington, CB 1966; OBE 1945; *b* 22 Dec. 1911; *y s* of Col P. L. K. Blair-Oliphant, DSO, Ardblair Castle, Blairgowrie, Perthshire, and Laura Geraldine Bodenham; *m* 1942, Helen Nathalie Donald, *yr d* of Sir John Donald, KCIE; one *s* (and one *s* and one *d* decd). *Educ:* Harrow; Trinity Hall, Cambridge (BA). Joined RAF, 1934; Middle East and European Campaigns, 1939-45; RAF Staff Coll., 1945-48; Group Capt. 1949; Air Cdre 1958; Director, Weapons Engineering, Air Ministry, 1958-60; British Defence Staffs, Washington, 1960-63; Acting Air Vice-Marshal, 1963; Pres., Ordnance Board, 1965-66; Air Vice-Marshal, 1966. *Address:* 9 Northfield Road, Sherfield-on-Lodon, Basingstoke, Hants. *Clubs:* Royal Air Force.

BLAKE, family name of **Baron Blake.**

BLAKE, Baron *cr* 1971 (Life Peer), of Braydeston, Norfolk; **Robert Norman William Blake,** FBA 1967; JP; Provost of The Queen's College, Oxford, since 1968; Pro-Vice-Chancellor, Oxford University, since 1971; *b* 23 Dec. 1916; *er s* of William Joseph Blake and Norah Lindley Daynes, Brundall, Norfolk; *m* 1953, Patricia Mary, *e d* of Thomas Richard Waters, Great Plumstead, Norfolk; three *d*. *Educ:* King Edward VI Sch., Norwich; Magdalen Coll., Oxford (MA), 1st Cl. Final Honour Sch. of Modern Greats, 1938; Eldon Law Scholar, 1938. Served War of 1939-45; Royal Artillery; North African campaign, 1942; POW in Italy, 1942-44; escaped, 1944; despatches, 1944. Lectr in Politics, Christ Church, Oxford, 1946-47; Student and Tutor in Politics, Christ Church, 1947-68, Emeritus Student, 1969; Censor, 1950-55; Senior Proctor, 1959-60; Ford's Lectr in English History for 1967-68; Mem., Hebdomadal Council, 1959-. Mem., Royal Commn on Historical Manuscripts, 1975-. Chm., Hansard Soc. Commn on Electoral Reform, 1975-76. Mem. (Conservative) Oxford City Council, 1957-64. Governor of Norwich Sch., and of Trent, Bradfield and Malvern Colls; Rhodes Trustee, 1971. Hon. Student, Christ Church, Oxford, 1977. Hon. DLitt Glasgow, 1972. *Publications:* The Private Papers of Douglas Haig, 1952; The Unknown Prime Minister (Life of Andrew Bonar Law), 1955; Disraeli, 1966; The Conservative Party from Peel to Churchill, 1970; The Office of Prime Minister, 1975; (ed with John Patten) The Conservative Opportunity, 1976. *Address:* The Queen's College, Oxford; Riverview House, Brundall, Norfolk. *Clubs:* Beefsteak, Brooks's, United Oxford & Cambridge University; Vincent's (Oxford); Norfolk County.

BLAKE, Alfred (Lapthorn), CVO 1975; MC 1945; Director, The Duke of Edinburgh's Award Scheme, since 1967; Partner in Blake, Lapthorn, Rea & Williams & Co., Solicitors, Portsmouth and area; *b* 6 Oct. 1915; *s* of late Leonard Nicholson Blake and Nora Woodfall Blake (*née* Lapthorn); *m* 1st, 1940, Beatrice Grace Nellthorp (*d* 1967); two *s*; 2nd, 1969, Mrs Alison Kelsey Dick, Boston, Mass, USA. *Educ:* Dauntsey's Sch. LLB (London), 1938. Qual. Solicitor and Notary Public, 1938. Royal Marines Officer, 1939-45: Bde Major 2 Commando Bde, 1944; Lieut-Col comdg 45 (RM) Commando and Holding Operational Commando, 1945 (despatches). Mem., Portsmouth CC, 1950-67 (Past Chm., Portsmouth Educn Cttee); Lord Mayor of Portsmouth, 1958-59. Mem., Youth Service Development Coun., 1960-66; Pres., Portsmouth Youth Organisations Cttee and Youth Action. Lay Canon, Portsmouth Cathedral, 1962-72. *Recreations:* golf (playing), football (non-playing), youth work. *Address:* Little Orchard, The Drive, Bosham, West Sussex. *T:* Bosham 572228. *Club:* Royal Naval and Royal Albert Yacht (Portsmouth).

BLAKE, Charles Henry, CB 1966; a Commissioner of Customs and Excise, 1968-72; European Adviser, British American Tobacco Co., 1972-76; *b* 29 Nov. 1912; *s* of Henry and Lily Blake, Westbury on Trym, Bristol; *m* 1938, M. Jayne McKinney (*d* 1974), *d* of James and Ellen McKinney, Castle Finn, Co. Donegal; three *d*. *Educ:* Cotham Grammar Sch.; Jesus Coll., Cambridge (Major Scholar). Administrative Class, Home Civil Service, 1936; HM Customs and Excise: Princ., 1941; Asst Sec., 1948; Comr and Sec., 1957-64; Asst Under-Sec. of State, Air Force Dept, MoD, 1964-68. *Recreation:* gardens. *Address:* Belshade, Shepherds Way, Rickmansworth, Herts. *T:* Rickmansworth 2924. *Clubs:* United Oxford & Cambridge University; Moor Park.

BLAKE, Prof. Christopher; Bonar Professor of Applied Economics, University of Dundee, since 1974; *b* 28 April 1926; *s* of George Blake and Eliza Blake; *m* 1951, Elizabeth McIntyre; two *s* two *d*. *Educ:* Dollar Academy; St Andrews Univ. MA St Andrews 1950, PhD St Andrews 1965. Served in Royal Navy, 1944-47. Teaching posts, Bowdoin Coll., Maine, and Princeton Univ., 1951-53; Asst, Edinburgh Univ., 1953-55; Stewarts & Lloyds Ltd, 1955-60; Lectr and Sen. Lectr, Univ. of St Andrews, 1960-67; Sen. Lectr and Prof. of Economics, Univ. of Dundee, 1967-74. *Publications:* articles in economic and other jls. *Recreation:* golf. *Address:* 3 Strathkinness High Road, St Andrews, Fife. *T:* St Andrews 2732. *Clubs:* Royal Commonwealth Society; Royal and Ancient (St Andrews).

BLAKE, Dr Eugene Carson; General Secretary, World Council of Churches, 1966-72; *b* St Louis, Mo, USA, 7 Nov. 1906; *s* of Orville P. Blake and Lulu (*née* Carson); *m* 1st, 1929, Valina Gillespie; 2nd, 1974, Jean Ware Hoyt. *Educ:* Princeton Univ.; New Coll., Edinburgh; Princeton Theological Seminary. Taught at Forman Christian Coll., Lahore, 1928-29; Asst Pastor, St Nicholas, NYC, 1932-35; Pastor: First Presbyterian Church, Albany, 1935-40; Pasadena Presbyterian Church, 1940-51. Stated Clerk, Gen. Assembly: Presbyterian Church of USA, 1951-58; United Presbyterian Church in USA, 1958-66. National Council of Churches of Christ in USA: Pres., 1954-57; subseq. Mem., Gen. Board; Chm., Commn on Religion and Race. Member: Central Cttee, Exec. Cttee, World Council of Churches, 1954-66. Trustee: Princeton Seminary; Occidental Coll.; San Francisco Theol Seminary. Visiting Lectr, Williams Coll., 1938-40. Has many hon. degrees. *Publications:* He is Lord of All, 1956; The Church in the Next Decade, 1966. *Recreation:* golf. *Address:* 204 Davenport Drive, Stamford, Conn 06902, USA.

BLAKE, Sir Francis Michael, 3rd Bt *cr* 1907; *b* 11 July 1943; *o s* of Sir F. Edward C. Blake, 2nd Bt and Olive Mary (*d* 1946) *d* of Charles Liddell Simpson; *S* father, 1950; *m* 1968, Joan Ashbridge, *d* of F. C. A. Miller; two *s*. *Educ:* Rugby. *Heir:* s Francis Julian Blake, *b* 17 Feb. 1971. *Address:* The Dower House, Tillmouth Park, Cornhill-on-Tweed, Northumberland. *T:* Coldstream 2443.

BLAKE, Henry Elliott, TD 1955; MA; FRCS, FRCSE; Hon. Plastic Surgeon, St George's Hospital; Emeritus Consultant Plastic Surgeon, St Helier Hospital, Carshalton; *b* 25 Dec. 1902; *s* of Henry Thomas Blake, JP, of Herefordshire, and Maud Blake; *m* 1945, Mary, Baroness Swaythling, *d* of Hon. Mrs Ionides. *Educ:* Dean Close, Cheltenham; Cambridge Univ.; St Thomas's Hospital, London. MRCS; LRCP 1929; MA, BChir (Cambridge) 1931; FRCS 1941; FRCSE 1941; late Major (surg. specialist), RAMC (TA). Founder Mem. British Assoc. Plastic Surgeons; FRSocMed (late Pres., Section of Plastic Surgery). Sometime Consultant Plastic Surgeon: Victoria Hosp. for Children, Tite Street; Royal Alexandra Hosp. for Sick Children, Brighton, Royal Sussex County Hosp., Brighton, Westminster Hosp. Gp (Queen Mary's Hosp., Roehampton), and Senior Surgeon to the Ministry of Pensions. Founder Mem. Medical Art Soc. Exhibited: Royal Soc. of Portrait Painters; Royal Academy of Arts; ROI; Armed Forces Art Soc. *Publications:* four chapters in: Operative Surgery (ed Prof. Charles Rob and Rodney Smith); Butterworths Operative Surgery-Service Vol. 3(b), The Reconstruction of the Penile Urethra in Hypospadias; articles in medical journals. *Address:* 55 Harley Street, W1. *T:* 01-580 6360; 17 Cadogan Square, SW1. *T:* 01-235 5398. *Clubs:* Boodle's; Hawks (Cambridge); Dunkirk Veterans' Assoc.

BLAKE, (Henry) Vincent; marketing consultant; Secretary, Glassfibre Reinforced Cement Association, since 1977; *b* 7 Dec. 1912; *s* of Arthur Vincent Blake and Alice Mabel (*née* Kerr); *m* 1938, Marie Isobel Todd; one *s*. *Educ:* King Edward's High Sch., Birmingham. Pupil apprentice, Chance Brothers, Lighthouse Engineers, Birmingham, 1931-34; subseq. Asst Sales Manager, 1937 and Sales Manager there, of Austinlite Ltd, 1945; Textile Marketing Manager, Fibreglass Ltd, 1951; Commercial Manager: Glass Yarns and Deeside Fabrics Ltd, 1960; BTR Industries Ltd, Glass and Resin Div., 1962-63, Plastics Group, 1963-66; Gen. Manager, Indulex Engineering Co. Ltd, 1966-71. Mem. Council and Chm., Reinforced Plastics Gp, British Plastics Fedn, 1959. *Publications:* articles in technical jls on reinforced plastics. *Recreations:* sailing, motoring, reading, and talking about reinforced plastics. *Address:* Farthings End, Dukes Ride, Gerrards Cross, Bucks. *T:* Gerrards Cross 82606. *Club:* Datchet Water Sailing (Commodore).

BLAKE, John Clifford, CB 1958; *b* 12 July 1901; *s* of late Alfred Harold and Ada Blake, Prestwich, Lancs; *m* 1928, Mary Lilian Rothwell; one *s* two *d*. *Educ:* Manchester Grammar Sch.; Queen's Coll., Oxford (MA). Admitted solicitor, 1927. Ministry of Health Solicitor's Dept, 1929; Solicitor and Legal Adviser to Ministries of Health and Housing and Local Government, and to Registrar Gen., 1957-65; Mem., Treasurer and Jt Exec. Sec., Anglican-Methodist Unity Commn, 1965-69; Vice-Pres., Methodist Conference, 1968. *Recreations:* music, especially organ and choral. *Address:* 3 Clifton Court, 297 Clifton Drive South, St Anne's on Sea, Lancs FY8 1HN. *T:* St Anne's 728365.

BLAKE, John William, CBE 1972; Professor of History, New University of Ulster, 1972-77, now Emeritus; *b* 7 Dec. 1911; *s* of Robert Gay Blake and Beatrice Mary Blake (*née* Tucket); *m* 1938, Eileen Florence Lord; two *s* one *d*. *Educ:* Kilburn Grammar Sch.; King's Coll., London (MA). Inglis Student and Derby Scholar, 1933-34; QUB: Asst Lectr, 1934; Lectr, 1944; Sen. Lectr, 1945; served War of 1939-45 in Civil Defence and as Offical War Historian to NI Govt; Prof. of History, Univ. of Keele (until 1962 University Coll. of N Staffs), 1950-64; Acting Principal of University Coll. of N Staffs, 1954-56; Vice-Chancellor, Univ. of Botswana, Lesotho and Swaziland (formerly Basutoland, Bechuanaland Protectorate and Swaziland), 1964-71. Mem. Staffs Co. Educn Cttee, 1955-61; Mem. Inter-Univ. Council for Higher Educn Overseas, 1955-64; FRHistS. Hon. DLitt: Keele 1971; Botswana, Lesotho and Swaziland, 1971. *Publications:* European Beginnings in West Africa, 1937; Europeans in West Africa, 2 vols 1942; Offical War History of Northern Ireland, 1956; contribs to historical jls. *Recreations:* hockey, cricket. *Address:* Willow Cottage, Myroe, Limavady, Northern Ireland.

BLAKE, Mary Netterville, MA; Headmistress, Manchester High School for Girls, since 1975; first President, Secondary Heads Association, since 1978 (President, Association of Headmistresses, 1976-77); *b* 12 Sept. 1922; *d* of John Netterville Blake and Agnes Barr Blake. *Educ:* Howell's Sch., Denbigh; St Anne's Coll., Oxford (MA). Asst Mistress, The Mount Sch., York, 1945-48; Head of Geography Dept, King's High Sch., Warwick, 1948-56; Associate Gen. Sec., Student Christian Movement in Schools, 1956-60; Head Mistress, Selby Grammar Sch., 1960-75. *Address:* Manchester High School for Girls, Grangethorpe Road, Manchester M14 6HS. *T:* 061-224 2456.

BLAKE, Peter Thomas, ARA 1974; painter; *b* 25 June 1932; *s* of Kenneth William Blake; *m* Jann Haworth. *Educ:* Gravesend Tech. Coll.; Gravesend Sch. of Art; RCA. Works exhibited: ICA, 1958, 1960; Guggenheim Competition, 1958; Cambridge, 1959; RA, 1960; Musée d'Art Moderne, Paris, 1963; retrospective exhibn, City Art Gall., Bristol, 1969. Works in permanent collections: Trinity Coll., Cambridge; Carlisle City Gall.; Tate Gall. *Publications:* illustrations for Oxford Illustrated Old Testament, 1968; contribs to: Times Educnl Supp.; Ark; Graphis 70; World of Art; Architectural Rev.; House and Garden; Painter and Sculptor. *Address:* The Station, Wellow, near Bath, Avon.

BLAKE, Quentin Saxby; freelance artist and illustrator, since 1957; Senior Tutor, School of Graphic Arts, Royal College of Art, since 1977 (Tutor, 1965); *b* 16 Dec. 1932; *s* of William Blake and Evelyn Blake. *Educ:* Downing Coll., Cambridge (MA). MSIAD. Cartoonist and illustrator for Punch, Spectator and other magazines; illustrator and storyteller for children's television. Exhibns of watercolour drawings, Workship Gallery: Invitation to the Dance, 1972; Runners and Riders, 1973; Creature Comforts, 1974; Water Music, 1976. *Publications:* (author and illustrator) for children: Patrick, 1968; Jack and Nancy, 1969; Angelo, 1970; Snuff, 1973; The Adventures of Lester, 1977; (illustrator) for children: Russell Hoban, How Tom Beat Captain Najork and his Hired Sportsmen, 1974 (Whitbread Lit. Award, 1975; Hans Andersen Honour Book, 1975); Russell Hoban, A Near Thing for Captain Najork, 1976; books by John Yeoman, Joan Aiken, Clement Freud, Sid Fleischman, Michael Rosen, Sylvia plath, Margaret Mahy and Dr Seuss; (illustrator) for adults: Aristophanes, The Birds, 1971; Lewis Caroll, The Hunting of the Snark, 1976; Stella Gibbons, Cold Comfort Farm, 1977. *Address:* 30 Bramham Gardens, SW5 0HF. *T:* 01-373 7464.

BLAKE, Sir Richard; see Blake, Sir T. R. V.

BLAKE, Sir (Thomas) Richard (Valentine), 17th Bt *cr* 1622, of Menlough; *b* 7 Jan. 1942; *s* of Sir Ulick Temple Blake, 16th Bt, and Elizabeth Gordon (she *m* 1965, Vice-Adm. E. Longley-Cook, *qv*); *S* father, 1963; *m* 1976, Mrs Jacqueline Hankey. *Educ:* Bradfield Coll., Berks. *Recreations:* shooting; Royal Naval Reserve. *Heir: kinsman* Anthony Teilo Bruce Blake, *b* 5 May 1951. *Address:* c/o Fletcher's, West Lavant, Chichester, West Sussex.

BLAKE, Vincent; see Blake, H. V.

BLAKE, Mrs William J.; see Stead, Christina E.

BLAKELY, Colin George Edward; actor and director since 1957; *b* 23 Sept. 1930; *s* of Victor Charles and Dorothy Margaret Ashmode Blakely; *m* 1961, Margaret Elsa Whiting; three *s*. *Educ:* Sedbergh School. Manager, Athletic Stores Ltd, Belfast, 1948-57; 1st prof. acting job, Children's Touring Theatre (Gwent), 1957; Group Theatre, Belfast, 1957-59; Cock a Doodle Dandy, Royal Court, 1959; Moon for the Misbegotten, Arts, 1960; The Naming of Murderers Rock, Royal Court, 1960; entered TV and films (Saturday Night and Sunday Morning), 1960-61; Hastings, in Richard III, and Touchstone, in As You Like It, Royal Shakespeare Co., Stratford, 1961; subseq. various films, TV, etc; Nat. Theatre, 1963-68: Pizarro, in Royal Hunt of the Sun; Captain Boyle, in Juno and the Paycock; Proctor, in Crucible; Philoctetes, in Philoctetes; Kite, in Recruiting Officer; Volpone, in Volpone; Hobson, in Hobson's Choice; Captain Shot-over, in Heartbreak House; Astrov, in Uncle Vanya, and Schmidt, in Fire Raisers, Royal Court; Torvald, in A Doll's House, Criterion, 1973; Vukhow, in Judgement, Royal Court, 1976; Dysart, in Equus, Albery, 1976; Dennis, in Just Between Ourselves, Queen's, 1977. Principal films include: This Sporting Life; Decline and Fall; Watson, in The Private Life of Sherlock Holmes; The National Health; It Shouldn't Happen to a Vet; The Pink Panther Strikes Again; Equus; TV appearances incl. Christ, in Son of Man, and Peer Gynt, in Peer Gynt. *Recreations:* piano, painting, sketching, golf. *Address:* c/o Leading Artists, 60 St James's Street, SW1. *T:* 01-491 4400.

BLAKEMORE, Alan, CBE 1976; Town Clerk and Chief Executive (formerly Town Clerk), Croydon, since 1963; *b* 17 May 1919; *s* of John William and Mary Blakemore, Salford; *m* 1956, José Margaret Cavill; two *s*. *Educ:* North Manchester School. Solicitor, 1943. Articled to Town Clerk, Salford, 1936; RASC (TA), 1939; Army service to 1946; released with hon. rank Lt-Col. Asst Solicitor, Salford, 1946-48; Deputy Town Clerk: Wigan, 1948-52; Bolton, 1952-57; Town Clerk, Stockport, 1957-63. Hon. Clerk, General Purposes Cttee, London Boroughs Assoc., 1971-. *Address:* Chaseley, 4 Waterfield Drive, Warlingham, Surrey CR3 9HP. *Club:* Royal Over-Seas League.

BLAKEMORE, Dr Colin Brian; Fellow and Director of Medical Studies, Downing College, Cambridge, since 1971; University Lecturer in Physiology, since 1972; Royal Society Locke Research Fellow, Cambridge, since 1976; *b* 1 June 1944; *s* of Cedric Norman Blakemore and Beryl Ann Smith; *m* 1965, Andrée Elizabeth Washbourne; two *d*. *Educ:* King Henry VIII Sch., Coventry; Corpus Christi Coll., Cambridge (Smyth Scholar; BA 1965, MA 1969); Univ. of Calif, Berkeley (PhD 1968). Harkness Fellow, Neurosensory Lab., Univ. of Calif, Berkeley, 1965-68; Univ. Demonstr in Physiol., Cambridge, 1968-72; Leverhulme Fellow, 1974-75. Vis. Professor: NY Univ., 1970; MIT, 1971; Royal Soc. Study Visit, Keio Univ., Tokyo, 1974. Mem. Central Council, Internat. Brain Res. Org., 1973-. BBC Reith Lectr, 1976. Robert Bing Prize for res. in neurol. and neurophysiol., Swiss Acad. of Med. Sciences, 1975; Richardson Cross Medal, S Western Ophthalmol Soc., 1978. *Publications:* Handbook of Psychobiology (with M. S. Gazzaniga), 1975; Mechanics of the Mind, 1977; res. reports in Jl of Physiol., Brit. Med. Bull., Nature, etc. *Recreations:* theatre and art, sailing and ski-ing. *Address:* Physiological Laboratory, University of Cambridge, Cambridge CB2 3EG.

BLAKEMORE, Michael Howell; Associate Artistic Director, National Theatre, 1971-76, now freelancing; *b* Sydney, NSW, 18 June 1928; *s* of Conrad Blakemore and Una Mary Blakemore (*née* Litchfield); *m* 1960, Shirley (*née* Bush); one *s*. *Educ:* The King's Sch., NSW; Sydney Univ.; Royal Academy of Dramatic Art. Actor with Birmingham Rep. Theatre, Shakespeare Memorial Theatre, etc, 1952-66; Co-dir, Glasgow Citizens Theatre (1st prod., The Investigation), 1966-68. London productions include: A Day in the Death of Joe Egg; Arturo Ui; Forget-me-not Lane; Design for Living; Knuckle; Separate Tables; Privates on Parade; Candida; and at the National Theatre: The National Health (Dir), 1969, and prods incl.: Long Day's Journey Into Night; The Front Page; Macbeth; The Cherry Orchard; Plunder. Voted best Dir, by London Critics, 1972. *Publication:* Next Season, 1969 (novel). *Recreation:* surfing. *Address:* 15 Gardnor Mansions, Church Row, NW3. *T:* 01-435 9951.

BLAKENEY, Hon. Allan Emrys; Premier of Saskatchewan since 1971, Member of Legislative Assembly since 1960; *b* Bridgewater, NS, 7 Sept. 1925; *m* 1st, 1950, Mary Elizabeth (Molly) Schwartz (*d* 1957), Halifax, NS; one *s* one *d*; 2nd, 1959, Anne Gorham, Halifax; one *s* one *d*. *Educ:* Dalhousie Univ. (BA, LLB); Queen's Coll., Oxford (MA). Univ. Medal for Achievement in Coll. of Law, Dalhousie; Rhodes Schol. Sec. and Legal Adviser, Saskatchewan Crown Corps, 1950; Chm., Saskatchewan Securities Commn, 1955-58; private law practice, 1958-60 and 1964-70. Formerly Minister of Educn, Provincial Treas. and Health Minister; Chm., Wascana Centre Authority, 1962-64; Opposition Financial Critic, 1964-70; Dep. Leader, 1967-70; Federal New Democratic Party President, 1969-71; Saskatchewan NDP Leader and Leader of Opposition, 1970. Formerly Dir and Vice-Pres., Sherwood Co-op. and Sherwood Credit Union. *Recreations:* reading, swimming, formerly hockey and badminton. *Address:* Office of the Premier, Regina, Saskatchewan S4S 0B3, Canada. *T:* (306)565-6271.

BLAKENEY, Frederick Joseph, CBE 1968; Australian Ambassador and Permanent Representative to the United Nations, Geneva, since 1977; *b* Sydney, NSW, 2 July 1913; *s* of Frederick Joseph Blakeney, Sydney; *m* 1943, Marjorie, *d* of John Martin, NSW; one *d*. *Educ:* Marist Darlinghurst and Mittagong; Univ. of Sydney. AMF, 1940-41; RAAF Flt Lieut (Navigator), 1942-45. Teaching Fellow, Univ. of Sydney, 1946; Dept of External Affairs, Canberra, 1946; 2nd Sec. and 1st Sec., Austr. Embassy, Paris, 1947; 1st Sec., then Chargé d'Affaires, Austr. Embassy, Moscow, 1949-51; Dept of Ext. Affairs, Canberra, 1952-53; Counsellor, Austr. Embassy, Washington, 1953-56; Minister to Vietnam and Laos, 1957-59, and to Cambodia, 1957; Asst Sec. (S and SE Asia), Dept of Ext. Affairs, Canberra, 1959-62; Australian Ambassador to Federal Republic of Germany, 1962-68; Australian Ambassador to USSR, 1968-71; First Asst Sec. (Defence), Dept of Foreign Affairs, Canberra, 1972-74; Australian Ambassador to the Netherlands, 1974-77. *Address:* c/o Department of Foreign Affairs, Canberra, ACT 2600, Australia.

BLAKENHAM, 1st Viscount *cr* 1963, of Little Blakenham; **John Hugh Hare,** PC 1955; OBE 1945 (MBE 1943); VMH; DL; *b* 22 Jan. 1911; *s* of 4th Earl of Listowel; *m* 1934, Hon. Beryl Nancy Pearson, *d* of 2nd Viscount Cowdray; one *s* two *d*. *Educ:* Eton Coll. Business, London County Council, Territorial Army, Suffolk Yeomanry, then served during War of 1939-45 in England, North Africa and Italy (despatches, MBE, OBE, Legion of Merit, USA). Alderman LCC, 1937-52; Chm. of London Municipal Soc., 1947-52. MP (C) Woodbridge Div. of

Suffolk, 1945-50, Sudbury and Woodbridge Div. of Suffolk, 1950-63. A Vice-Chm. Conservative Party Organisation, (Dec.) 1951-55; Minister of State for Colonial Affairs, Dec. 1955-Oct. 1956; Sec. of State for War, Oct. 1956-Jan. 1958; Minister of Agriculture, Fisheries and Food, Jan. 1958-60; Minister of Labour, 1960-63; Chancellor of the Duchy of Lancaster, also Dep. Leader of the House of Lords, 1963-64; Chairman: Conservative Party Organisation, 1963-65; Council, Toynbee Hall, 1966-; Governing Body, Peabody Trust, 1967-. Treasurer, Royal Horticultural Soc., 1971- (Victoria Medal of Honour, 1974). DL, Suffolk, 1968. *Recreations:* golf, gardening. *Heir:* s Hon. Michael John Hare [*b* 25 Jan. 1938; *m* 1965, Marcia, *o d* of Hon. Alan Hare, *qv*; one *s* two *d*]. *Address:* 10 Holland Park, W11; Cottage Farm, Little Blakenham, near Ipswich, Suffolk. *T:* Ipswich 830344. *Clubs:* White's, Buck's.

BLAKER, George Blaker, CMG 1963; Under-Secretary, HM Treasury, 1955-63, and Department of Education and Science, 1963-71 retired; *b* Simla, India, 30 Sept. 1912; *m* 1938, Richenda Dorothy Buxton; one *d*. *Educ:* Eton; Trinity Coll., Cambridge. Private Sec. to Ministers of State in the Middle East, 1941-43; Cabinet Office, 1943; Private Sec. to Sec. of War Cabinet, 1944; Principal Private Sec. to Minister of Production and Presidents of the Board of Trade, 1945-47; accompanied Cabinet Mission to India, 1946; Sec. of UK Trade Mission to China, 1946; HM Treasury, 1947; UK Treasury Representative in India, Ceylon and Burma, 1957-63. Pres., Surrey Trust for Nature Conservation, 1969-. Jt Hon. Sec., Scientific and Medical Network, 1973-. Gold Medal, Royal Soc. for the Protection of Birds, 1934. *Address:* Lake House, Ockley, Surrey RH5 5NS.

BLAKER, Sir John, 3rd Bt *cr* 1919; *b* 22 March 1935; *s* of Sir Reginald Blaker, 2nd Bt, TD, and of Sheila Kellas, *d* of Dr Alexander Cran; *S* father, 1975; *m* 1st, 1960, Catherine Ann (marr. diss. 1965), *d* of late F. J. Thorold; 2nd, 1968, Elizabeth Katherine, *d* of late Col John Tinsley Russell, DSO. *Address:* Barton Hill Farm, Barton-on-the-Heath, Moreton-in-Marsh, Glos.

BLAKER, Nathaniel Robert, QC 1972; **His Honour Judge Blaker;** a Circuit Judge, since 1976; *b* 31 Jan. 1921; *s* of Major Herbert Harry Blaker and Annie Muriel Blaker (*née* Atkinson); *m* 1951, Celia Margaret Hedley; two *d*. *Educ:* Winchester; University College, Oxford (MA). Royal Signals, 1940-47. Called to the Bar, Inner Temple, 1948; Bencher, 1971. Dep. Chm., Dorset QS, 1970; a Recorder of the Crown Court, 1972-76. Wine Treasurer, Western Circuit, 1964-77. *Address:* 16 Embankment Gardens, SW3 4LW. *T:* 01-352 0792

BLAKER, Peter Allan Renshaw, MA; MP (C) Blackpool South, since 1964; *b* Hong Kong, 4 Oct. 1922; *s* of late Cedric Blaker, CBE, MC; *m* 1953, Jennifer, *d* of late Sir Pierson Dixon, GCMG, CB; one *s* two *d*. *Educ:* Shrewsbury; Trinity Coll., Toronto (BA, 1st class, Classics); New Coll., Oxford (MA). Served 1942-46: Argyll and Sutherland Highlanders of Canada (Capt., wounded). Admitted a Solicitor, 1948. New Coll., Oxford, 1949-52; 1st Class, Jurisprudence, Pass degree in PPE. Pres. Oxford Union. Called to Bar, Lincoln's Inn, 1952. Admitted to HM Foreign Service, 1953; HM Embassy, Phnom Penh, 1955-57; UK High Commn, Ottawa, 1957-60; FO, 1960-62; Private Sec. to Minister of State for Foreign Affairs, 1962-64. Attended Disarmament Conf., Geneva; UN Gen. Assembly, 1962 and 1963; signing of Nuclear Test Ban Treaty, Moscow, 1963. An Opposition Whip, 1966-67; PPS to Chancellor of Exchequer, 1970-72; Parliamentary Under-Secretary of State: (Army), MoD, 1972-74; FCO, 1974; Joint Secretary: Conservative Party Foreign Affairs Cttee, 1965-66; Trade Cttee, 1967-70; Exec. Cttee of 1922 Cttee, 1967-70; Vice-Chairman: Cons. For. and Commonwealth Affairs Cttee, 1974-; All-Party Tourism Cttee, 1974-; Mem., Select Cttee on Conduct of Members, 1976-77; Chm., Hong Kong Parly Gp, 1970-72; Mem. Exec. Cttee, British-American Parly Gp, 1975-. Chm., Bd, Royal Ordnance Factories, 1972-74; Chm. Governors, Welbeck Coll, 1972-74. *Address:* Woodsland Farm, Lindfield, West Sussex. *T:* Lindfield 2381. *Club:* Travellers'.

BLAKEWAY, John Denys; HM Diplomatic Service; Consul-General, Istanbul, since 1975; *b* 27 May 1918; *s* of late Sir Denys Blakeway, CIE; *m* 1946, Jasmine Iremonger; one *s* two *d*. *Educ:* Rugby (Schol.); Magdalen Coll., Oxford (Schol., MA). British and Indian Army, 1939-46. Joined Foreign (subseq. Diplomatic) Service, 1946; served Sofia, Lyons, Athens (twice), Tripoli, FO (twice), Bologna, Rome, Ibadan, The Hague. *Recreation:* Far Eastern ceramics. *Address:* c/o Foreign and Commonwealth Office, SW1A 2AL. *Club:* Brooks's.

BLAKISTON, Sir (Arthur) Norman (Hunter), 8th Bt *cr* 1763; solicitor; *b* 26 April 1899; *s* of Reginald Norman Blakiston (*d*

1946) (*g s* of 3rd Bt) and Annie Constance (*d* 1955), *d* of late William Henry Hunter; *S* kinsman, Sir Arthur Frederick Blakiston, 7th Bt, MC, 1974; *m* 1962, Mary Ferguson, *d* of late Alfred Ernest Gillingham, Cave, S Canterbury, NZ; two *s*. *Educ:* Christ's Coll., Christchurch, NZ; Victoria Univ., Wellington, NZ. Barrister and solicitor, Supreme Court of NZ, 1921-. *Recreations:* general. *Heir: s* Ferguson Arthur James Blakiston, *b* 19 Feb. 1963. *Address:* 28 McKenzie Street (or Box 55), Geraldine, South Canterbury, New Zealand. *T:* 160 Geraldine.

BLAMEY, Norman Charles, RA 1975 (ARA 1970); Senior Lecturer, Chelsea School of Art, London, since 1963; *b* 16 Dec. 1914; *s* of Charles H. Blamey and Ada Blamey (*née* Beacham); *m* 1948, Margaret (*née* Kelly); one *s*. *Educ:* Holloway Sch., London; Sch. of Art, The Polytechnic, Regent Street, London. ROI 1952; Hon. ROI 1974. Exhibited at: RA, RHA, ROI, RBA, NEAC, and provincial galleries; *mural decorations in:* Anglican Church of St Luke, Leagrave, Beds, 1956; Lutheran Church of St Andrew, Ruislip Manor, Middx, 1964; *works in permanent collections:* Municipal Gall., Port Elizabeth, S Africa; Beaverbrook Gall., Fredericton, NB; Beecroft Art Gall., Southend-on-Sea; Towner Art Gall., Eastbourne; Preston Art Gall.; Pennsylvania State Univ. Mus of Art; Chantry Bequest purchase, 1972; works in private collections in UK and USA. *Recreation:* walking. *Address:* 39 Lyncroft Gardens, NW6. *T:* 01-435 9250.

BLAMIRE-BROWN, John, DL; County Clerk and Chief Executive, Staffordshire County Council, since 1973; *b* 16 April 1915; *s* of Rev. F. J. Blamire Brown, MA; *m* 1945, Joyce Olivia Pearson; two *s*. *Educ:* Cheam Sch.; St Edmund's Sch., Canterbury. Solicitor 1937. Served War of 1939-45, Royal Marines (Captain). Asst Solicitor, Wednesbury, 1937; West Bromwich, 1946; Staffs CC, 1948; Deputy Clerk of County Council and of Peace, 1962; Clerk, Staffs CC, 1972; Clerk to Lieutenancy, 1972; Sec., Staffs Probation and After Care Cttee; Hon. Sec., W Mids Planning Authorities Conf., 1972. DL Staffs, 1974. *Recreations:* beagling, gardening. *Address:* The Mount, Codsall Wood, Wolverhampton, West Midlands. *T:* Codsall 2044.

BLANCH, Mrs Lesley, FRSL; author; *b* 1907; *m* 2nd, 1945, Romain Gary Kacew (*see* Romain Gary) (marr. diss. 1962). *Educ:* by reading, and listening to conversation of elders and betters. FRSL 1969. *Publications:* The Wilder Shores of Love (biog.), 1954; Round the World in Eighty Dishes (cookery), 1956; The Game of Hearts (biog.), 1956; The Sabres of Paradise (biog.), 1960; Under a Lilac Bleeding Star (travels), 1963; The Nine Tiger Man (fict.), 1965; Journey into the Mind's Eye (autobiog.), 1968; Pavilions of the Heart (biog.), 1974. *Recreations:* travel, opera, acquiring useless objects, animal welfare, gardening. *Address:* Roquebrune Village, Cap Martin, AM, France. *Club:* Taharir (formerly Mahommed Ali) (Cairo).

BLANCH, Most Rev. Stuart Yarworth; *see* York, Archbishop of.

BLANCHARD, Francis; Director-General, International Labour Office, Geneva, since 1974; *b* Paris, 21 July 1916; *m* 1940, Marie-Claire Boué; two *s*. *Educ:* Univ. of Paris. French Home Office; Internat. Organisation for Refugees, Geneva, 1947-51; Internat. Labour Office, Geneva, 1951-, Asst Dir-Gen., 1956-68, Dep. Dir-Gen., 1968-74. *Recreations:* ski-ing, hunting, riding. *Address* (office) International Labour Office, 4 chemin des Morillons, Geneva, Switzerland. *T:* 985211; (home) Prébailly, 01170 Gex, France. *T:* 41-51-70 Gex.

BLANCO WHITE, Amber, OBE; *b* 1 July 1887; *d* of William Pember Reeves and Magdalen Stuart Robison; *m* George Rivers Blanco White; one *s* two *d*. *Educ:* Kensington High School; Newnham College, Cambridge. Director of Women's Wages, Ministry of Munitions, 1916-19; Member National Whitley Council for Civil Service, 1919-20; University Tutorial Lectr on Moral Science, Morley Coll.; retired 1965. Editor, The Townswoman, 1933; contested Hendon Division, 1931 and 1935. *Publications: as Amber Reeves:* The Reward of Virtue, 1911; A Lady and Her Husband, 1914; Helen in Love, 1916; Give and Take, 1923; *as Amber Blanco White:* The Nationalisation of Banking, 1934; The New Propaganda, 1939; Worry in Women, 1941; Ethics for Unbelievers, 1949; (with H. G. Wells) The Work, Wealth and Happiness of Mankind, 1932; articles on literature and finance. *Address:* 44 Downshire Hill, Hampstead, NW3.
See also T. A. *Blanco White.*

BLANCO WHITE, Thomas Anthony, QC 1969; *b* 19 Jan. 1915; *s* of late G. R. Blanco White, QC, and of Amber Blanco White, *qv*; *m* 1950, Anne Katherine Ironside-Smith; two *s* one *d*. *Educ:*

Gresham's Sch.; Trinity Coll., Cambridge. Called to Bar, Lincoln's Inn, 1937, Bencher 1977. Served RAFVR, 1940-46. *Publications:* Patents for Inventions, 1950, 1955, 1962, 1974, etc. *Recreations:* gardening, photography. *Address:* Francis Taylor Building, EC4.

BLAND, Francis Christopher Buchan; Deputy Chairman, Independent Broadcasting Authority, since 1972; Chairman, Sir Joseph Canston & Sons, since 1977; *b* 29 May 1938; *e s* of James Franklin MacMahon Bland and Jess Buchan Bland (*née* Brodie). *Educ:* Sedbergh; The Queen's Coll., Oxford (Hastings Exhibnr). 2nd Lieut, 5th Royal Inniskilling Dragoon Guards, 1956-58; Lieut, North Irish Horse (TA), 1958-69. Dir, NI Finance Corp., 1972-76. Mem. GLC, for Lewisham, 1967-70; Chm., ILEA Schs Sub-Cttee, 1970; Mem. Burnham Cttee, 1970; Chm., Bow Group, 1969-70; Editor, Crossbow, 1971-72. Governor, Prendergast Girls Grammar Sch. and Woolwich Polytechnic, 1968-70. *Publications:* Bow Group pamphlet on Commonwealth Immigration. *Recreations:* fishing, skiing; formerly: Captain, OU Fencing Team, 1961; Captain, OU Modern Pentathlon Team, 1959-60; Mem. Irish Olympic Fencing Team, 1960. *Address:* 10 Catherine Place, SW1E 6HF. *T:* 01-834 0021. *Club:* Cavalry and Guards.

BLAND, Sir Henry (Armand), Kt 1965; CBE 1957; FRSA; Deputy Chairman, Blue Circle Southern Cement Ltd; Director: Australian Mining and Smelting Ltd; Tubemakers of Australia Ltd; P. Rowe Pty Ltd; Associated National Insurance Co. Ltd; *b* 28 Dec. 1909; *s* of Emeritus Prof. F. A. Bland, CMG, and Elizabeth Bates Jacobs; *m* 1933, Rosamund, *d* of John Nickal; two *d* (and one *d* decd). *Educ:* Sydney High Sch.; Univ. of Sydney. LLB (Hons) 1932. Admitted Solicitor Supreme Court of NSW, 1935. Entered NSW Public Service, 1927; Alderman, Ryde (NSW) Municipal Council, 1937-39; Acting Agent-Gen. for NSW in London, 1940-41; Adviser on Civil Defence to NSW and Commonwealth Govts, 1941; Princ. Asst to Dir-Gen. of Manpower, 1941-45; Asst Sec., First Asst Sec., 1946-51, Sec. 1952-67, Dept of Labour and National Service; Sec., Dept of Defence, Australia, 1967-70. Leader, Austr. Govt Delegns to Confs: 1948, 1953, 1957, 1960, 1962, 1963, 1964, 1966; Austr. Govt Rep. on the Governing Body of ILO, 1963-67; Adviser on industrial relations to Singapore Govt, 1958. Bd of Inquiry into Victorian Land Transport System, 1971; Chairman: Cttee on Administrative Discretions, 1972-73; Bd of Inquiry into Victorian Public Service, 1973-75; Commonwealth Admin. Rev. Cttee, 1976; ABC, 1976. *Address:* 4/1 Monaro Road, Kooyong, Victoria 3144, Australia. *T:* 5095270. *Club:* Athenæum (Melbourne).

BLAND, Lt-Col Simon Claud Michael, CVO 1973 (MVO 1967); Comptroller, Private Secretary and Equerry to Princess Alice Duchess of Gloucester and the Duke and Duchess of Gloucester, since 1972; *b* 4 Dec. 1923; *s* of late Sir Nevile Bland, KCMG, KCVO; *m* 1954, Olivia, *d* of Major William Blackett; one *s* three *d*. *Educ:* Eton College. Served War of 1939-45, Scots Guards, in Italy; BJSM, Washington, 1948-49; 2nd Bn, Scots Guards, Malaya, 1949-51; Asst Mil. Adviser at UK High Commn, Karachi, 1959-60; Comptroller and Asst Private Sec. to late Duke of Gloucester, 1961-74 and Private Sec. to late Prince William, 1968-72. Dir, West End Bd, Commercial Union. OStJ 1973. *Recreation:* shooting. *Address:* Tower Flat, Kensington Palace, W8 4PY. *T:* 01-937 6374; Gabriels Manor, Edenbridge, Kent. *T:* Edenbridge 2340. *Club:* Buck's.

BLANDFORD, Marquess of; Charles James Spencer-Churchill; with Marine Insurance Broker Company (Seascope); *b* 24 Nov. 1955; *e s* and *heir* of 11th Duke of Marlborough, *qv. Educ:* Pinewood; Harrow. *Address:* Lee Place, Charlbury, Oxon. *Club:* Turf.

BLANDFORD, Eric George, CBE 1967; Deputy Assistant Registrar of Criminal Appeals, Royal Courts of Justice, since 1968; *b* 10 March 1916; *s* of George and Eva Blanche Blandford; *m* 1940, Marjorie Georgina Crane; one *s. Educ:* Bristol Grammar Sch. Admitted Solicitor Supreme Court, England, 1939; LLB (London) 1939. War Service, 1939-46 (despatches): India, Burma, Malaya; rank on release Temp. Major RA. Solicitor in London, 1946-51; Asst Comr of Lands, Gold Coast, 1951; Dist Magistrate, Gold Coast, 1952; called to the Bar, Inner Temple, 1955; Chief Registrar, Supreme Court, Gold Coast, 1956; Registrar of High Court of Northern Rhodesia, 1958; Judge, Supreme Court of Aden, 1961-68. Chm. Aden Municipality Inquiry Commn, 1962. *Publication:* Civil Procedure Rules of Court, Aden, 1967. *Recreations:* photography, travel. *Address:* Royal Courts of Justice, Strand, WC2A 2LL. *Club:* Royal Commonwealth Society.

BLANDFORD, Heinz Hermann; Chairman, Ulvir Ltd, since 1936; Chairman, Finance and General Purposes Committee, and Hon. Treasurer: Royal Postgraduate Medical School at Hammersmith Hospital, since 1962; British Postgraduate Medical Federation, since 1969; School of Pharmacy, London University, since 1975; Member Committee of Management, Institute of Ophthalmology (Moorfields Eye Hospital), since 1974; *b* Berlin, Germany, 28 Aug. 1908; *s* of late Judge Richard Blumenfeld and Hedwig Kersten; *m* 1933, Hilde Kleczewer; one *s* one *d. Educ:* Augusta Gymnasium; (classical scholar) Univs of Berlin and Hamburg. Controller of continental cos in ceramic, pharmaceutical, iron and steel industries, 1933-39. Pioneered synthesis, manufacture and use of Liquid Fertilisers in the UK, 1945-60; Horticultural Adviser to Fisons Ltd, 1959-60. Founded (Mem. Bd of Trustees), Blandford Trust for advancement of health and prevention and relief of sickness by med. research and teaching at Royal Postgraduate Med. Sch. of London Univ., 1964, Fellow 1973. Member: Org. Cttee, 6th World Congress of Cardiology, London, 1971; Bd of Governors, Hammersmith and St Mark's Hospitals, 1972-74. *Publications:* various essays and papers in chemical and horticultural jls. *Recreations:* farming, shooting, skiing, gardening. *Address:* Holtsmere End, Redbourn, Herts. *T:* Redbourn 2206. *Club:* Farmers'.

BLANDY, Prof. John Peter, MA, DM, MCh, FRCS; Consultant Surgeon: The London Hospital, since 1964; St Peter's Hospital for the Stone, since 1969; Professor of Urology, University of London, since 1969; *b* 11 Sept. 1927; *s* of late Sir E. Nicolas Blandy, KCIE, CSI, ICS and Dorothy Kathleen (*née* Marshall); *m* 1953, Anne, *d* of Hugh Mathias, FRCS, Tenby; four *d. Educ:* Clifton Coll.; Balliol Coll., Oxford; London Hosp. Med. Coll. BM, BCh 1951; MA 1953; FRCS 1956; DM 1963; MCh 1963. House Phys. and House Surg., London Hosp., 1952; RAMC, 1953-55; Surgical Registrar and Lectr in Surgery, London Hosp., 1956-60; exchange Fellow, Presbyterian St Luke's Hosp., Chicago, 1960-61; Sen. Lectr, London Hosp., 1961; Resident Surgical Officer, St Paul's Hosp., 1963-64. Member: BMA; RSM; Internat. Soc. Pædiatric Urol. Surg.; Internat. Soc. of Urological Surgeons; British Assoc. Urological Surgeons; Fellow, Assoc. of Surgeons. Hon. Fellow: Urological Soc. of Australasia, 1973; Mexican Coll. of Urology, 1974. Hunterian Prof., Royal College of Surgeons, 1964. *Publications:* (with A. D. Dayan and H. F. Hope-Stone) Tumours of the Testicle, 1970; Transurethral Resection, 1971; (ed) Urology, 1976; Lecture Notes on Urology, 1976; papers in surgical and urological jls. *Recreation:* painting. *Address:* The London Hospital, Whitechapel, E1. *T:* 01-247 5454.

BLANKENHORN, Herbert, GCVO (Hon.) 1965; Consultant to Director-General, UNESCO, since 1977 (Member and Vice-President, Executive Board, 1970-76); *b* 15 Dec. 1904; *s* of Erich Blankenhorn; *m* 1944, Gisela Krug; two *s* two *d. Educ:* Gymnasiums in Strasbourg, Berlin, and Karlsruhe; Universities of Munich, London, Heidelberg and Paris. Entered Foreign Service, 1929; served in: Athens, 1932-35; Washington, 1935-39; Helsinki, 1940; Berne, 1940-43; Foreign Office, Berlin (Protocol Section), 1943-45; Dep. Sec.-Gen., Zonal Advisory Council, Hamburg, 1946-48; Sec.-Gen. Christian Democratic Party (British Zone), 1948; Private Sec. to President of Parliamentary Council, Bonn (Dr Adenauer), 1948-49; Political Dir, Foreign Office, 1950-55; German Ambassador: to NATO, 1955-58; to France, 1958-63; to Italy, 1963-65; to London, 1965-70. *Address:* 7847 Badenweiler, Hintere Au 2, Germany.

BLANTYRE, Archbishop of, (RC), since 1968; Most Rev. James Chiona; *b* 1924. *Educ:* Nankhunda Minor Seminary, Malaŵi; Kachebere Major Seminary, Malaŵi. Priest, 1954; Asst Parish Priest, 1954-57; Prof., Nankhunda Minor Seminary, 1957-60; study of Pastoral Sociology, Rome, 1961-62; Asst Parish Priest, 1962-65; Auxiliary Bishop of Blantyre and Titular Bishop of Bacanaria, 1965; Vicar Capitular of Archdiocese of Blantyre, 1967. *Recreation:* music. *Address:* Archbishop's House, PO Box 385, Blantyre, Malaŵi. *T:* 33516.

BLASCHKO, Hermann Karl Felix, MD, FRS 1962; Emeritus Reader in Biochemical Pharmacology, Oxford University, and Emeritus Fellow, Linacre College, Oxford, since 1967; *b* Berlin, 4 Jan. 1900; *o s* of late Prof. Alfred Blaschko, MD and late Johanna Litthauer; *m* 1944, Mary Douglas Black, *d* of late John Robert Black, Yelverton, S Devon; no *c. Educ:* Universities of Berlin, Freiburg im Breisgau and Göttingen. MD Freiburg; PhD Cambridge; MA Oxon. Research Asst to late Prof. O. Meyerhof at Berlin-Dahlem and Heidelberg at various periods, 1925-32; University Asst in Physiology, Univ. of Jena, 1928-29; worked at UCL, 1929-30 and 1933-34; Physiological Lab., Cambridge Univ., 1934-44; came to Oxford, 1944. Visiting Professor: Yale Univ., 1967-68; Upstate Medical Center, Syracuse, NY, 1968; RCS, 1968-73; Univ. of Pennsylvania, 1969; Univ. of Bergen,

Norway, 1969-70. Hon. Prof., Faculty of Medicine, Heidelberg, 1966. Member of Editorial Board of: Pharmacological Reviews, 1957-64; British Journal of Pharmacology and Chemotherapy, 1959-65; Journal of Physiology, 1965-72; Neuropharmacology, 1962-72; Naunyn-Schmiedebergs Arch. Exp. Pharmak., 1966; Molecular Pharmacol., 1966. Mem. Neuropharmacology Panel, International Brain Research Organisation (IBRO); Corresp. Mem., German Pharmacolog. Soc. Schmiedeberg Plakette, 1972. First Thudichum Lectr and Medallist, London, 1974; Aschoff Lectr, Freiburg, 1974. Hon. MD Berlin (Free Univ.), 1966. *Publications:* numerous papers in scientific publications. *Address:* Department of Pharmacology, South Parks Road, Oxford OX1 3QT; 24 Park Town, Oxford OX2 6SH.

BLAXTER, Sir Kenneth (Lyon), Kt 1977; FRS 1967; FRSE 1965; Director, Rowett Research Institute, Bucksburn, Aberdeen, and Consultant Director, Commonwealth Bureau of Nutrition (formerly Animal Nutrition), since 1965; *b* 19 June 1919; *s* of Gaspard Culling Blaxter and Charlotte Ellen Blaxter; *m* 1957, Mildred Lillington Hall; two *s* one *d. Educ:* City of Norwich Sch.; University of Reading; University of Illinois. BSc(Agric.), PhD, DSc, NDA (Hons). Scientific Officer, Nat. Inst. for Research in Dairying, 1939-40 and 1941-44. Served RA, 1940-41. Research Officer, Ministry of Agriculture Veterinary Laboratory, 1944-46; Commonwealth Fellow, University of Ill, 1946-47; Head of Dept of Nutrition, Hannah Inst., Ayr, Scotland, 1948-65. President: British Soc. of Animal Production, 1970-71; Nutrition Soc., 1974. For. Mem., Lenin Acad. of Agric. Sciences, 1970. Hon. DSc QUB; Hon. DAgric Agricl Univ., Norway. Thomas Baxter Prize and Gold Medal, 1960; Gold Medal, RASE, 1964; Wooldridge Gold Medal, British Vet. Assoc., 1973; De Laval medal, Royal Swedish Acad. Engrg Scis, 1976; Messel Medal, Soc. of Chem. Industry, 1976; Keith Medal and Prize, RSE, 1977. *Publications:* Energy Metabolism of Ruminants, 1962; Energy Metabolism, 1965. Scientific papers in Jl Endocrinology, Jl Agricultural Science, British Jl Nutrition, Research in Veterinary Science, etc. *Recreation:* painting. *Address:* Wardenhill, Bucksburn, Aberdeen AB2 9SA. *T:* Bucksburn 2751.

BLEAKLEY, Rt. Hon. David Wylie, PC (NI) 1971; Member (NILP), for E Belfast, Northern Ireland Constitutional Convention, 1975-76; *b* 11 Jan. 1925; *s* of John Wesley Bleakley and Sarah Bleakley (*née* Wylie); *m* 1949, Winifred Wason; three *s. Educ:* Ruskin Coll., Oxford; Queen's Univ., Belfast. MA, DipEconPolSci (Oxon). Belfast Shipyard, 1940-46; Oxford and Queen's Univ., 1946-51; Tutor in Social Studies, 1951-55; Principal, Belfast Further Educn Centre, 1955-58; Lectr in Industrial Relations, Kivukoni Coll., Dar-es-Salaam, 1967-69; Head of Dept of Economics and Political Studies, Methodist Coll., Belfast, 1969-71. MP (Lab) Victoria, Belfast, Parliament of N Ireland, 1958-65; contested: (Lab) East Belfast, General Elections, 1970, Feb. and Oct. 1974. Minister of Community Relations, Govt of NI, March-Sept. 1971; Mem. (NILP), E Belfast, NI Assembly, 1973-75. Irish Deleg. to Anglican Consultative Council, 1976; Deleg. to World Council of Churches; WEA and Open Univ. tutor; Vis. Sen. Lectr in Peace Studies, Univ. of Bradford, 1974-. Hon. MA Open, 1975. *Publications:* Ulster since 1800: regional history symposium, 1958; Young Ulster and Religion in the Sixties, 1964; Peace in Ulster, 1972; Faulkner: a biography, 1974; regular contribs to BBC and to press on community relations and industrial studies. *Address:* 10 Ardgreenan Drive, Belfast BT4 3FQ, Northern Ireland. *T:* 655391.

BLEANEY, Prof. Brebis, CBE 1965; FRS 1950; MA, DPhil; Warren Research Fellow, Royal Society, since 1977; Senior Research Fellow, Wadham College, Oxford, since 1977 (Fellow, 1957-77); Dr Lee's Professor of Experimental Philosophy, University of Oxford, 1957-77; *b* 6 June 1915; *m* 1949, Betty Isabelle Plumpton; one *s* one *d. Educ:* Westminster City Sch.; St John's Coll., Oxford. Lecturer in Physics at Balliol Coll., Oxford, 1947-50. Research Fellow, Harvard Univ. and Mass Institute of Technology, 1949. University Demonstrator and Lectr in Physics, Univ. of Oxford, 1945-57; Fellow and Lectr in Physics, St John's Coll., Oxford, 1947-57; Tutor, 1950-57; Hon. Fellow, 1968. Visiting Prof. in Physics in Columbia Univ., 1956-57; Harkins Lectr, Chicago Univ., 1957; Kelvin Lectr, Instn Electrical Engineers, 1962; Visiting Professor: Univ. of California, Berkeley, 1961; Univ. of Pittsburgh, 1962-63; Manitoba, 1968; La Plata, Argentina, 1971. Mem. Council for Scientific and Industrial Res., 1960-62. FRSA 1971. Corr. Mem. Acad. of Sciences, Inst. of France, 1974. Charles Vernon Boys Prize, Physical Soc., 1952; Hughes Medal, Royal Society, 1962. *Publications:* (with B. I. Bleaney) Electricity and Magnetism, 1957, 3rd edn, 1976; (with A. Abragam) Electron Paramagnetic Resonance, 1970; various papers in Proceedings of the Royal Society and Proceedings of the Physical Society, etc.

Recreations: music and tennis. *Address:* Clarendon Laboratory, Oxford.

BLEASE, William John, JP; Industrial Relations Consultant; Northern Ireland Officer, 1959-75, Executive Consultant, 1975-76, Irish Congress of Trade Unions; *b* 28 May 1914; *e s* of late William and Sarah Blease; *m* 1939, Sarah Evelyn Caldwell; three *s* one *d. Educ:* elementary and technical schs; Nat. Council of Labour Colls; WEA. Retail Provision Trade (apprentice), 1929; Retail Grocery Asst (Branch Manager), 1938-40; Clerk, Belfast Shipyard, 1940-45; Branch Manager, Co-operative Soc., Belfast, 1945-59. Trade Union Side Sec., NI CS Industrial Jt Council, 1975-76. NI Mem., IBA, 1974-; Mem., Reg. Bd, BIM, 1972-. Hon. Res. Fellow, New Univ. of Ulster, 1976-; Jt Hon. Res. Fellow, TCD, 1976-. JP 1976. Hon. DLitt New Univ. of Ulster, 1972. *Recreations:* walking, talking. *Address:* 27 Ferguson Drive, Belfast BT4 2AZ. *T:* Belfast 749481. *Clubs:* Sloane; Northern Ireland Labour (Belfast).

BLECH, Harry, OBE 1962; Hon. RAM, 1963; Musical Director, Haydn-Mozart Society, and Founder, and Conductor, London Mozart Players, since 1949; *b* 2 March 1910; British; *m* 1935, Enid Marion Lessing (*d* 1977); one *s* two *d*; *m* 1957, Marion Manley, pianist; one *s* three *d. Educ:* Central London Foundation; Trinity Coll. of Music (Fellow); Manchester Coll. of Music (Fellow). Violin soloist, 1928-30; joined BBC Symphony Orchestra, 1930-36. Responsible for formation of: Blech Quartet, 1933-50; London Wind Players, 1942 (conductor); London Mozart Players, 1949; Haydn-Mozart Soc., 1949; London Mozart Choir, 1952. Dir of Chamber Orchestra, RAM, 1961-65. FRSA. *Address:* The Owls, 70 Leopold Road, Wimbledon, SW19 7JQ.

BLEDISLOE, 2nd Viscount, *cr* 1935; **Benjamin Ludlow Bathurst,** QC 1952; *b* 2 Oct. 1899; *er s* of 1st Viscount Bledisloe, PC, GCMG, KBE, and Hon. Bertha Susan Lopes (*d* 1926), *y d* of 1st Baron Ludlow, PC; *S* father 1958; *m* 1933, Joan Isobel Krishaber; two *s. Educ:* Eton; Magdalen Coll., Oxford (BA). Served European War, 1914-18, 2nd Lieut RA. Called to Bar, Inner Temple, 1927. War of 1939-45: Squadron Leader, RAF, 1939-40; Senior Comdr, ATA, 1940-45. Bencher, Lincoln's Inn, 1956. Late Chm., Plant Variety Rights Tribunal; Vice-President: West London Flying Club; British Light Aviation Centre. Past-Pres., St Moritz Tobogganing Club; Verderer of Forest of Dean. *Recreations:* mountaineering, ski-ing, tobogganing, shooting, flying, rowing, gardening, photography. *Heir:* s Hon. Christopher Hiley Ludlow Bathurst, 11th Hussars [*b* 24 June 1934; *m* 1962, Elizabeth Mary, 2nd *d* of Sir Edward Thompson, *qv*; two *s* one *d. Educ:* Eton. Barrister-at-Law]. *Address:* 14 Mulberry Walk, SW3. *T:* 01-352 7533; 4 Stone Buildings, Lincoln's Inn, WC2. *T:* 01-242 5524; Lydney Park, Glos. *T:* Lydney 2538. *Clubs:* Garrick, Green Room, Portland, Alpine, Alpine Ski; Vincent's (Oxford); Leander (Henley-on-Thames); West London Aero (White Waltham).

BLEE, David, CBE 1955; FCIT; *b* 7 Aug. 1899; *m* 1926, Catharine Rosetta Vaughan (*d* 1972); one *s.* Served European War, 1917-19, France, Belgium, Germany. Apptd Chief Goods Manager, GWR, 1946; Mem. of Railway Executive, 1947-53; Chief of Commercial Services, British Transport Commission, 1953-55; becoming Traffic Adviser, 1955; Gen. Manager of the London Midland Region of British Railways, 1956-61. Col, Eng. & Rly Staff Corps RE (TA). Former Mem. Council and Vice-Pres., Institute of Transport. Director: Atlantic Steam Navigation Co.; Birmingham & Midland Motor Omnibus Co. Member: Permanent Commn of Internat. Rly Congress Assoc.; Internat. Chamber of Commerce. *Publications:* papers and lectures on transport subjects. *Recreations:* walking, travel. *Address:* 1 Hull Place, Sholden, near Deal, Kent. *T:* Deal 5260.

BLEEHEN, Prof. Norman Montague; Cancer Research Campaign Professor of Clinical Oncology and Hon. Director of MRC Unit of Clinical Oncology and Radiotherapeutics, University of Cambridge, since 1975; Fellow of St John's College, Cambridge, since 1976; *b* 24 Feb. 1930; *s* of Solomon and Lena Bleehen; *m* 1969, Tirza, *d* of Alex and Jenny Loeb. *Educ:* Manchester Grammar Sch.; Haberdashers' Aske's Sch.; Exeter Coll., Oxford; Middlesex Hosp. Med. School. BA 1951, BSc 1953, MA 1954, BM, BCh 1955, Oxon; MRCP 1957, FRCP 1973; FRCR 1964; DMRT 1962. MRC Res. Student, Biochem. Dept, Oxford, 1951; house appts: Middlesex Hosp., 1955-56; Hammersmith Hosp., 1957; Asst Med. Specialist Army, Hanover, 1957; Med. Specialist Army, Berlin, 1959 (Captain); Jun. Lectr in Medicine, Dept of Regius Prof. of Medicine, Oxford, 1959-60; Registrar and Sen. Registrar in Radiotherapy, Middlesex Hosp. Med. Sch., 1961-66; Lilly Res. Fellow, Stanford Univ., 1966-67; Locum Consultant, Middlesex Hosp., 1967-69; Prof. of Radiotherapy, Middlesex Hosp. Med. Sch.,

1969-75. Member: Jt MRC/CRC Cttee for jtly supported insts, 1971-74; Coordinating Cttee for Cancer Res., 1973-; Council, Imperial Cancer Res. Fund, 1973-; Council, Brit. Inst. of Radiology, 1974-; Chm., British Assoc. for Cancer Res. Chm., MRC Cancer Therapy Cttee. *Publications:* (Scientific Editor) British Medical Bulletin 24/1, The Scientific Basis of Radiotherapy; various on medicine, biochemistry cancer and radiotherapy. *Recreations:* gardening, sailing, ski-ing, television. *Address:* New Addenbrooke's Hospital, Cambridge.

BLELLOCH, Ian William, CMG 1955; retired; *b* 2 Aug. 1901; *s* of late John Stobie Blelloch and late Christina Macdonald; *m* 1st, 1929, Leila Mary Henderson (*d* 1936); one *s* (and one *s* decd); 2nd, 1946, Margaret Rachel Stevenson. *Educ:* Dunfermline High Sch.; Edinburgh University. MA 1st Class Hons, 1924. Cadet, Federated Malay States, 1926; Class V, 1929; District Officer, Raub, Class IV, 1933; Legal Adviser and Deputy Public Prosecutor, Perak, 1935-37; Sec. to Resident, Negri Sembilan, Class III, 1938; Legal Adviser, Public Prosecutor, Kedah, 1939-41; interned by Japanese, 1942-45; Class II, 1943; Class IB, 1946; Secretary, Resident Commissioner, Perak, 1946-47; Acting British Adviser, Trengganu, 1948-50; British Adviser, Perak, Federation of Malaya, 1951; retired 1957. Perak Meritorious Service Medal, 1953; created Datoh Kurnia Bakti, Perak, 1956; CStJ 1964 (OStJ 1956). *Recreation:* golf. *Address:* The Garth, Blairgowrie, Perthshire. *T:* Blairgowrie 567. *Club:* East India, Devonshire, Sports and Public Schools.
See also *J . N . H . Blelloch* .

BLELLOCH, John Niall Henderson; Assistant Under Secretary of State (Air), Ministry of Defence (Procurement Executive), since 1976; *b* 24 Oct. 1930; *s* of Ian William Blelloch, *qv* ; *m* 1958, Pamela, *d* of late James B. Blair and E. M. Blair; two *s* . *Educ:* Fettes Coll.; Gonville and Caius Coll., Cambridge (BA). Nat. Service, RA, 1949-51 (commnd 1950). Asst Principal, War Office, 1954; Private Sec. to successive Parly Under Secs of State, 1956-58; Principal, 1958; MoD, 1964-; London Business Sch. (EDP 3), 1967; Asst Sec., 1968; RCDS, 1974. *Recreations:* golf, squash, skiing, learning the piano. *Address:* 19 Ullswater Crescent, Kingston Vale, SW15. *T:* 01-546 8939. *Clubs:* Roehampton; Royal Mid-Surrey Golf.

BLENKINSOP, Arthur; MP (Lab) South Shields since 1964; *b* 30 June 1911; *s* of John Matthewson Blenkinsop and Anne Douglas Rowell; *m* 1939, Mary Norman Harrold; two *s* one *d. Educ:* Newcastle Royal Grammar Sch. MP (Lab) for Newcastle upon Tyne East, 1945-59; Parly Sec., Min. of Health, 1949-51; Mem., Chairmen's Panel, House of Commons. Chm., Shipping Gp, Parly Lab Party. Vice-President, Health Inspectors Assoc.; Delegate to Council of Europe, 1966-70 (Pres. Social Commission, 1968-70). Member, Exec. Cttee, National Trust; Chm., Council, Town and Country Planning Assoc.; Mem., Adv. Council on Misuse of Drugs. *Recreations:* walking and reading. *Address:* 233 Wingrove Road, Newcastle upon Tyne NE4 9DD. *T:* Newcastle 35187.

BLENKINSOP, Dorothy; Regional Nursing Officer, Northern Regional Health Authority, since 1973; *b* 15 Nov. 1931; *d* of late Joseph Henry Blenkinsop, BEM, and Thelma Irene (*née* Bishop). *Educ:* South Shields Grammar Sch. for Girls. SRN 1953; SCM 1954; Health Visitors Cert. 1962. Ward Sister, Royal Victoria Infirm., Newcastle upon Tyne, 1955-61; Health Visitor, South Shields, 1962-64; Dep. Matron, Gen. Hosp., South Shields, 1964-67; Durham Hosp. Management Cttee: Principal Nurse, Durham City Hosps, 1967-69; Principal Nursing Officer (Top), 1969-71; Chief Nursing Officer, 1971-73. Mem. Methodist Church (Circuit Steward, 1968-; Sunday School Teacher). *Publications:* (with E. G. Nelson): Changing the System, 1972; Managing the System, 1976; articles in Nursing Times. *Recreations:* walking, reading, football. *Address:* 98 Stanhope Road, South Shields, Tyne and Wear. *T:* South Shields 561429.

BLENNERHASSETT, Francis Alfred, QC 1965; a Recorder, and Honorary Recorder of New Windsor, since 1972; *b* 7 July 1916; 2nd *s* of John and Annie Elizabeth Blennerhassett; *m* 1948, Betty Muriel Bray; two *d. Educ:* Solihull Sch. Served War of 1939-45 RA and Royal Warwicks Regt, Britain and East Africa (Captain). Called to Bar, Middle Temple, 1946; Bencher, 1971; Oxford Circuit. Dep. Chm., Staffordshire QS, 1963-71; Recorder of New Windsor, 1965-71. Legal Assessor to GMC and Dental Council, 1971-; Chm., Govt Cttee on Drinking and Driving, 1975-76. *Recreation:* golf. *Address:* Broome Cottage, Old Station Road, Hampton in Arden, Warwickshire. *T:* Hampton in Arden 2660; Lamb Building, Temple, EC4. *T:* 01-353 6701. *Clubs:* Garrick; Union (Birmingham); Copt Heath Golf.

BLENNERHASSETT, Sir (Marmaduke) Adrian (Francis William), 7th Bt, *cr* 1809; *b* 25 May 1940; *s* of Lieut Sir Marmaduke Blennerhassett, 6th Bt, RNVR (killed in action, 1940), and Gwenfra (*d* 1956), *d* of Judge Harrington-Morgan, Churchtown, Co. Kerry, and of Mrs Douglas Campbell; *S* father 1940; *m* 1972, Carolyn Margaret, *yr d* of late Gilbert Brown; one *s* one *d. Educ:* Michael Hall, Forest Row; McGill Univ.; Imperial Coll., Univ. of London (MSc); Cranfield Business Sch. (MBA). *Recreations:* flying (private pilot's licence), ocean racing (sailing), ski-ing. *Heir:* *s* Charles Henry Marmaduke Blennerhassett, *b* 18 July 1975. *Address:* 41 Park Road, Chiswick, W4. *Club:* Royal Ocean Racing.

BLESSLEY, Kenneth Harry, CBE 1974 (MBE 1945); ED; Valuer and Estates Surveyor, Greater London Council, 1964-77; *b* 28 Feb. 1914; *s* of Victor Henry le Blond Blessley and Ellen Mary Blessley; *m* 1946, Gwendeline MacRae; two *s. Educ:* Haberdashers' Aske's Hampstead Sch.; St Catharine's Coll., Cambridge (MA); Coll. of Estate Management. FRICS. Private practice, West End and London suburbs. Served War of 1939-45, TA Royal Engrs, Persia, Middle East, Sicily, Italy (despatches 1942 and 1944). Sen. Property Adviser, Public Trustee, 1946-50; Dep. County Valuer, Mddx CC, 1950-53; County Valuer, Mddx CC, 1953-65. Mem. Urban Motorways Cttee, 1970-72; Chm., Covent Garden Officers' Steering Gp, 1970-77; Chm., Thamesmead Officers' Steering Gp, 1971-76; Mem. Management Cttee, Multiple Sclerosis Housing Assoc., 1969-77; Pres., Assoc. of Local Authority Valuers and Estate Surveyors, 1962 and 1972; Mem. Gen. Council, RICS, 1972-77, Pres., Gen. Practice Div., 1976-77. Pres., Old Haberdashers' Assoc., 1963 (Pres. RFC, 1966-68). *Publications:* numerous articles and papers on compensation, property valuation and development. *Recreations:* music, drama, sport, motoring. *Address:* 99 Maplehurst Road, Summersdale, Chichester, West Sussex. *Clubs:* United Oxford & Cambridge University, MCC.

BLIGH, family name of **Earl of Darnley.**

BLIN-STOYLE, Prof. Roger John, FRS 1976; Professor of Theoretical Physics, University of Sussex, since 1962; *b* 24 Dec. 1924; *s* of Cuthbert Basil St John Blin-Stoyle and Ada Mary (*née* Nash); *m* 1949, Audrey Elizabeth Balmford; one *s* one *d . Educ:* Alderman Newton's Boys' Sch., Leicester; Wadham Coll., Oxford (Scholar). MA, DPhil Oxon; FInstP; ARCM. Pressed Steel Co. Res. Fellow, Oxford Univ., 1951-53; Lectr in Math. Physics, Birmingham Univ., 1953-54; Sen. Res. Officer in Theoret. Physics, Oxford Univ., 1952-62; Fellow and Lectr in Physics, Wadham Coll., Oxford, 1956-62; Vis. Associate Prof. of Physics, MIT, 1959-60; Vis. Prof. of Physics, Univ. of Calif, La Jolla, 1960; Sussex University: Dean, Sch. of Math. and Phys. Sciences, 1962-68; Pro-Vice-Chancellor, 1965-67; Dep. Vice-Chancellor, 1970-72; Pro-Vice-Chancellor (Science), 1977-. Member: Royal Greenwich Observatory Cttee, 1966-70; Nuclear Physics Bd, SRC, 1967-70. Rutherford Medal and Prize, IPPS, 1976. *Publications:* Theories of Nuclear Moments, 1957; Fundamental Interactions and the Nucleus, 1973; papers on nuclear and elementary particle physics in scientific jls. *Recreation:* making music. *Address:* 14 Hill Road, Lewes, E Sussex BN7 1DB. *T:* Lewes 3640.

BLISHEN, Edward; author; *b* 29 April 1920; *s* of William George Blishen and Elizabeth Anne (*née* Pye); *m* 1948, Nancy Smith; two *s. Educ:* Queen Elizabeth's Grammar Sch., Barnet. Weekly Newspaper reporter, 1937-40; agricultural worker, 1941-46. Teaching: Prep. Schoolmaster, 1946-49; Secondary Modern School Teacher, 1950-59. *Publications:* Roaring Boys, 1955; This Right Soft Lot, 1969; (with Leon Garfield) The God Beneath the Sea, 1970; (with Leon Garfield) The Golden Shadow, 1972; A Cackhanded War, 1972; Uncommon Entrance, 1974; Sorry, Dad, 1978; edited: Junior Pears Encyclopaedia, 1961-; Oxford Miscellanies, 1964-69; Blond Encyclopaedia of Education, 1969; The School that I'd Like, 1969; The Thorny Paradise, 1975; compiled: Oxford Book of Poetry for Children, 1964; Come Reading, 1967. *Recreations:* walking, photography, listening to music. *Address:* 12 Bartrams Lane, Hadley Wood, Barnet EN4 0EH. *T:* 01-449 3252.

BLISS, John Cordeux, QPM; retired as Deputy Assistant Commissioner, Metropolitan Police, 1971 (seconded as National Co-ordinator of Regional Crime Squads of England and Wales from inception, 1964-71); *b* 16 March 1914; *s* of late Herbert Francis Bliss and Ida Muriel (*née* Hays); *m* 1947, Elizabeth Mary, *d* of Charles Gordon Howard; one *s* two *d. Educ:* Haileybury Coll. Metropolitan Police Coll., Hendon, 1936-37. Served in RAF, 1941-45, Flt Lt, 227 Sqdn, MEF. Various ranks of Criminal Investigation Dept of Metropolitan Police, 1946-62; seconded as Dir of Criminal Law at Police Coll., Bramshill, 1962-63; Dep. Comdr, 1963-64. Barrister, Middle Temple, 1954.

Mem., Parole Bd, 1973-76. Liveryman, Merchant Taylors' Company. Churchill Memorial Trust Fellowship, 1967; Queen's Police Medal, 1969. *Recreations:* squash rackets, hillwalking; but mostly gardening; formerly: Rugby football, tennis. *Address:* Foxhanger Down, Hurtmore, Godalming, Surrey. *T:* Godalming 22487. *Club:* Royal Air Force.

BLISS, Kathleen Mary, (Mrs Rupert Bliss), MA Cantab 1934; Lecturer in Religious Studies, University of Sussex, 1967-72; *b* 5 July 1908; *née* Moore; *m* 1932, Rev. Rupert Bliss; three *d. Educ:* Girton Coll., Cambridge. Educational work in India, 1932-39; Editor, the Christian Newsletter, 1945-49; organized Christian-humanist debate, BBC, 1951-55; Studies of education in industry, 1956-57; General Sec., Church of England Board of Education, 1958-66. Member of Public Schools Commn, 1967-70. Hon. DD (Aberdeen), 1949. Select Preacher before the Univ. of Cambridge, 1967. *Publications:* The Service and Status of Women in the Churches, 1951; We the People, 1963; The Future of Religion, 1969.

BLISS, Mrs Rupert; *see* Bliss, K. M.

BLOCH, Prof. Felix, PhD; Professor of Physics, Stanford University, USA, 1934-71, Professor Emeritus, since 1971; *b* 23 Oct. 1905; *s* of Gustav Bloch and Agnes Mayer; *m* 1940, Lore Misch; three *s* one *d. Educ:* Zurich, Switzerland. PhD Leipzig, 1928. Asst Zurich, 1928-29; Lorentz Fellow, Holland, 1929-30; Asst Leipzig, 1930-31; Oersted Fellow, Copenhagen, 1931-32; Lecturer, Leipzig, 1932-33; Rockefeller Fellow, Rome, 1933-34; Director-General European Council for Nuclear Research, Geneva, 1954-55. Hon. DSc: Grenoble, 1959; Oxon, 1960; Jerusalem, 1962; Hon. DPhil Zurich, 1966. Fellow American Phys. Society (Pres., 1965-66); Member: Nat. Academy of Sciences, 1948; RSE; Royal Dutch Acad. of Sciences; Hon. Mem., French Physical Soc.; Hon. Fellow, Weizmann Inst., 1958. (jointly) Nobel Prize for Physics, 1952. *Publications:* about 80 articles on atomic and nuclear physics in various European and American scientific journals. *Recreations:* ski-ing, mountaineering, piano. *Address:* 1551 Emerson Street, Palo Alto, Calif 94301, USA. *T:* 327-8156.

BLOCH, Prof. Konrad E.; Higgins Professor of Biochemistry, Harvard University, since 1954; *b* 21 Jan. 1912; *s* of Frederick D. Bloch and Hedwig (*née* Striemer); *m* 1941, Lore Teutsch; one *s* one *d. Educ:* Technische Hochschule, Munich; Columbia Univ., New York. Instructor and Research Associate, Columbia Univ., 1939-46; Univ. of Chicago: Asst Prof., 1946-48; Associate Prof., 1948-50; Prof., 1950-54. Nobel Prize for Medicine (jointly), 1964. *Publications:* Lipide Metabolism, 1961; numerous papers in biochemical journals. *Address:* 16 Moon Hill Road, Lexington, Mass 02173, USA. *T:* Volunteer 2-9076; 38 Oxford Street, Cambridge, Mass 02138, USA.

BLOCH, Mrs. Sidney; *see* Park, Merle F.

BLOCK, Maj.-Gen. Adam Johnstone Cheyne, CB 1962; CBE 1959 (OBE 1951); DSO 1945; *b* 13 June 1908; *s* of late Col Arthur Hugh Block, RA; *m* 1945, Pauline Bingham, *d* of late Col Norman Kennedy, CBE, DSO, TD, DL, Doonholm, Ayr; two *d* (and one *d* decd). *Educ:* Blundell's; RMA Woolwich. 2nd Lieut RA 1928; served War of 1939-45 (France, UK, N Africa and Italy); CO 24th Field Regt, RA, 1943-45. GSO1, RA and AMS, GHQ, 1945-47; AQMG and GSO1 Trg AA Comd, 1947-50; Lieut-Col, 1950; Senior Directing Staff (Army). Joint Services Staff College, 1950-53; Col, 1953; CRA 6 Armd Div., 1953; Comdt, School of Artillery, Larkhill, 1956; Maj.-Gen. 1959; GOC Troops, Malta, 1959-62; retd. Chief Information Officer to General Synod (formerly Church Assembly), 1965-72. Col Comdt, Royal Regt of Artillery, 1965-73. *Recreations:* all country pursuits. *Address:* St Cross House, Whitchurch, Hants. *T:* Whitchurch 2344. *Club:* Army and Navy.

BLOCK, Brig. David Arthur Kennedy William, CBE 1961; DSO 1945; MC 1943; retired; *b* 13 June 1908; *s* of late Col Arthur Hugh Block; *m* 1949, Elizabeth Grace (*d* 1975), *e d* of Lieut-Col E. G. Troyte-Bullock, Zeals House, Wiltshire, and *widow* of Major G. E. Sebag-Montefiore, D'Anvers House, Culworth, near Banbury; no *c. Educ:* Blundell's; RMA, Woolwich. Served War of 1939-45 (despatches, MC, DSO); CO 152nd (Ayrshire Yeomanry) Field Regt, RA, 1943-45. CO 2nd Regt RHA, 1950-53; CRA, 7th Armoured Div., 1954-57; Comd 18th Trg Bde, RA, 1958-61; retired, 1961. ADC to the Queen, 1959. *Recreations:* hunting, shooting, golf. *Address:* Benville Manor, Evershot, Dorset. *T:* Corscombe 354. *Club:* Army and Navy.

BLOCK, His Honour Commander Leslie Kenneth Allen, DSC 1945; DL; Commissioner, Central Criminal Court, 1955-69; *b* 9 Aug. 1906; *s* of Harry Allen Block, Esher; *m* 1930, Maud Marion (*née* Hicks); two *s* one *d. Educ:* RN Colleges Osborne and Dartmouth. Joined Royal Navy, 1920; Emergency List, RN, 1933; called to Bar, Inner Temple, 1936; served War of 1939-45; Navigating Officer, HMS Hermes, 1939-42; Rosyth Escort Force, 1942-43; HMS Duke of York, 1943-44; Fleet Navigating Officer, Home Fleet, 1944-45; Commander, 1945. Chairman Agricultural Land Tribunal, SE Area, 1948-54; Asst Judge of Mayor's and City of London Court, 1954-69; Dep. Chm., 1955-67, Chm., 1967-71, W Sussex QS. Freeman, City of London; Liveryman, Tallowchandlers Co. (Master, 1971-72). JP 1947, DL 1960, Sussex. *Address:* Shiprods, Henfield, West Sussex. *T:* Henfield 2004.

BLODGET, Mrs A. S.; *see* Skinner, Cornelia O.

BLOEMFONTEIN, Bishop of, since 1967; **Rt. Rev. Frederick Andrew Amoore;** *b* 6 June 1913; *s* of Harold Frederick Newnham Amoore and Emily Clara Amoore, Worthing; *m* 1948, Mary Dobson; three *s. Educ:* Worthing Boys' High Sch.; University of Leeds. BA (Hons Hist) Leeds, 1934. Curate of: Clapham, London, 1936; St Mary's, Port Elizabeth, S Africa, 1939; Rector of St Saviour's, E London, S Africa, 1945; Dean of St Albans Cathedral, Pretoria, 1950; Exec. Officer for Church of Province of S Africa, 1962. *Recreations:* music, italic script. *Address:* Bishop's House, 16 York Road, Bloemfontein, South Africa. *T:* 7-3861. *Club:* Bloemfontein.

BLOFELD, John Christopher Calthorpe, QC 1975; a Recorder of the Crown Court, since 1975; *b* 11 July 1932; *s* of T. R. C. Blofeld, CBE; *m* 1961, Judith Anne, *er d* of Alan Mohun and Mrs James Mitchell; two *s* one *d. Educ:* Eton; King's Coll., Cambridge. Called to Bar, Lincoln's Inn, 1956. Chancellor, Dio. St Edmundsbury and Ipswich, 1973. *Recreations:* cricket, gardening. *Address:* Harlequin House, Ickleton, Saffron Walden, Essex. *Clubs:* Boodle's, MCC;

BLOFIELD, Edgar Glanville, DSO 1940; Lieutenant (E) RN, retired; *b* 1 June 1899; *s* of Shipwright Lieut-Comdr C. Blofield, RN; *m* 1926, Gladys Enid Learmouth; one *d. Educ:* Esplanade House Sch., Portsmouth. Joined Royal Navy, 1915; served in various ships in Home Fleet, Mediterranean and China Stations; was serving in HM Yacht Victoria and Albert on outbreak of war; retired list, 1949; joined Merchant Navy and served in supertankers and cargo liners until 1963. *Recreations:* those connected with country and sea. *Address:* 91 Festing Grove, Southsea, Hants.

BLOIS, Sir Charles (Nicholas Gervase), 11th Bt, *cr* 1686; farming since 1965; *b* 25 Dec. 1939; *s* of Sir Gervase Ralph Edmund Blois, 10th Bt and Mrs Audrey Winifred Blois (*née* Johnson); *S* father, 1968; *m* 1967, Celia Helen Mary Pritchett; one *s* one *d. Educ:* Harrow; Trinity Coll., Dublin; Royal Agricultural Coll., Cirencester. Australia, 1963-65. *Recreations:* yachting, shooting. *Heir: s* Andrew Charles David Blois, *b* 7 Feb. 1971. *Address:* Red House, Westleton, Saxmundham, Suffolk. *T:* Westleton 200. *Club:* Cruising Association.

BLOM-COOPER, Louis Jacques, QC 1970; JP; Joint Director of Legal Research Unit, Dept of Sociology, Bedford College, University of London, since 1967; *b* 27 March 1926; *s* of Alfred Blom-Cooper and Ella Flesseman, Rotterdam; *m* 1952 (marr. diss. 1970); two *s* one *d*; *m* 1970, Jane Elizabeth, *e d* of Maurice and Helen Smither, Woodbridge, Suffolk; two *d. Educ:* Port Regis Prep. Sch.; Seaford Coll.; King's Coll., London; Municipal Univ. of Amsterdam; Fitzwilliam Coll., Cambridge. LLB London, 1952; Dr Juris Amsterdam, 1954. HM Army, 1944-47: Capt., E Yorks Regt. Called to Bar, Middle Temple, 1952. Mem., Home Secretary's Adv. Council on the Penal System, 1966-. Chm., Howard League for Penal Reform, 1973-. Chm., BBC London Local Radio Adv. Council, 1970-73. Joint Editor, Common Market Law Reports. JP Inner London, 1966 (transf. City of London, 1969). *Publications:* Bankruptcy in Private International Law, 1954; The Law as Literature, 1962; The A6 Murder (A Semblance of Truth), 1963; (with T. P. Morris) A Calendar of Murder, 1964; Language of the Law, 1965; (with O. R. McGregor and Colin Gibson) Separated Spouses, 1970; (with G. Drewry) Final Appeal: a study of the House of Lords in its judicial capacity, 1972; (ed) Progress in Penal Reform, 1975; (ed with G. Drewry) Law and Morality, 1976; contrib. to Modern Law Review, Brit. Jl of Criminology, Brit. Jl of Sociology. *Recreations:* watching and reporting on Association football, reading, music, writing, broadcasting. *Address:* 25 Richmond Crescent, N1 0LY. *T:* 01-607 8045; Goldsmith Building, EC4Y 7BL. *T:* 01-353 6802. *Club:* MCC.

BLOMEFIELD, Peregrine Maitland; His Honour Judge Blomefield; a Circuit Judge (formerly County Court Judge), since 1969; *b* 25 Oct. 1917; 2nd *s* of Lt-Col Wilmot Blomefield,

OBE; *m* 1941, Angela Catherine, *d* of Major Geoffrey Hugh Shenley Crofton, Heytesbury, Wilts; one *s. Educ:* Repton Sch.; Trinity Coll., Oxford (MA). Royal Signals, 1940-46 (Captain). Called to the Bar, Middle Temple, 1947, Bencher, 1967; Oxford Circuit; Recorder of Burton-on-Trent, 1969; Dep. Chm., Berkshire QS, 1967-71. *Address:* The Coach House, Frilsham, Newbury, Berks. *T:* Hermitage 201421.

BLOMEFIELD, Sir Thomas Edward Peregrine, 5th Bt, *cr* 1807; *b* 31 May 1907; *s* of late Commander T. C. A. Blomefield, *e s* of 4th Bt and Margaret, *e d* of E. P. Landon; *S* grandfather, 1928; *m* 1947, Ginette Massart, Paris; one *s. Educ:* Wellington; Trinity Coll., Oxford. Temp. Lieut-Comdt RNVR, 1939-46. *Heir: s* Thomas Charles Peregrine Blomefield [*b* 24 July 1948; *m* 1975, Georgina, *d* of Commander Charles Over]. *Address:* 16 Campden House, Sheffield Terrace, W8. *T:* 01-229 8729.

BLOMFIELD, Douglas John, CIE 1941; ACGI; Regional Technical Adviser, Home Office, 1941-52; *b* 20 Dec. 1885; *s* of Charles Edward Blomfield; *m* 1915, Coralie (*d* 1967), *d* of F. H. Tucker, Indian Police; one *s* one *d. Educ:* St Dunstan's Coll.; City and Guilds Central Technical Coll. Joined Indian Service of Engineers, 1908; retired as Chief Engineer (Communications and Works Branch), Bengal, 1940. *Address:* c/o Grindlay's Bank Ltd, 13 St James's Square, SW1.
See also *J. R. Blomfield.*

BLOMFIELD, Brig. John Reginald, OBE 1957; MC 1944; New Towns Commission Manager for Hemel Hempstead since 1969; *b* 10 Jan. 1916; *s* of Douglas John Blomfield, *qv*; *m* 1939, Patricia Mary McKim; two *d. Educ:* Clifton Coll.; RMA, Woolwich; Peterhouse, Cambridge (MA). Commissioned Royal Engineers, 1936; Lt-Col 1955; Col 1961; Brig. 1965. Retired as Dep. Director, Military Engineering Experimental Establishment, 1969. MBIM 1966. *Recreations:* cruising, ocean racing. *Address:* (office) Swan Court, Waterhouse Street, Hemel Hempstead, Herts HP1 1DU; Moreton's Piece, Meadway, Berkhamsted, Herts. *Club:* Royal Ocean Racing.

BLOMFIELD, Maj.-Gen. Valentine, CB 1947; DSO 1944; *b* 29 March 1898; *e s* of late Frederick Charles Blomfield; *m* 1925, Gladys Edith, *d* of late Col A. M. Lang, CB, RE; three *s. Educ:* Rugby; RMC, Sandhurst. Commissioned Border Regt, 1916; served in France, 1916-18 (despatches); NWF India, 1922-23; graduated Staff Coll., Camberley; served in France, 1939-40 (despatches) and 1944 (DSO). Director of Prisoners of War, Aug. 1945-47; Director of Personal Services, War Office, 1947-50; Commander, North-West District and 42nd (Lancs) Div., TA, 1950-53; retired pay, 1954. Col The Border Regt, 1952-59; Col The King's Own Royal Border Regt, 1959-61. *Address:* c/o Lloyds Bank Ltd, 6 Pall Mall, SW1. *Club:* Naval and Military.

BLONDEL, Prof. Jean Fernand Pierre; Professor of Government, University of Essex, since 1964; Executive Director, European Consortium for Political Research, since 1970; *b* Toulon, France, 26 Oct. 1929; *s* of Fernand Blondel and Marie Blondel (*née* Santelli); *m* 1954, Michèle (*née* Hadet); two *d. Educ:* Collège Saint Louis de Gonzague and Lycée Henri IV, Paris; Institut d'Etudes Politiques and Faculté de Droit, Paris; St Antony's Coll., Oxford. Asst Lectr, then Lectr in Govt, Univ. of Keele, 1958-63; Visiting ACLS Fellow, Yale Univ., 1963-64. Dean, Sch. of Comparative Studies, Univ. of Essex, 1967-69; Visiting Prof., Carleton Univ., Canada, 1969-70. *Publications:* Voters, Parties and Leaders, 1963; (jtly) Constituency Politics, 1964; (jtly) Public Administration in France, 1965; An Introduction to Comparative Government, 1969; (jtly) Workbook for Comparative Government, 1972; Comparing Political Systems, 1972; Comparative Legislatures, 1973; The Government of France, 1974; Thinking Politically, 1976; articles in: Political Studies, Parliamentary Affairs, Public Administration, Revue Française de Science Politique, etc. *Recreation:* holidays in Provence. *Address:* 13 Beverley Road, Colchester, Essex. *T:* Colchester 77615; 9 rue Général de Partouneaux, Mourillon, Toulon, France.

BLOOM, André Borisovich; *see* Anthony, Archbishop.

BLOOM, Claire; *b* London, 15 Feb. 1931; *d* of late Edward Bloom and of Elizabeth Bloom; *m* 1st, 1959, Rod Steiger (marr. diss. 1969); one *d*; 2nd, 1969, Hillard Elkins. *Educ:* Badminton, Bristol; America and privately. First work in England, BBC, 1946. Stratford: Ophelia, Lady Blanche (King John), Perdita, 1948; The Damask Cheek, Lyric, Hammersmith, 1949; The Lady's Not For Burning, Globe, 1949; Ring Round the Moon, Globe, 1949-50. Old Vic: 1952-53: Romeo and Juliet; 1953: Merchant of Venice; 1954: Hamlet, All's Well, Coriolanus, Twelfth Night, Tempest; 1956: Romeo and Juliet (London, and N American tour). Cordelia, in Stratford Festival Company,

1955 (London, provinces and continental tour); Duel of Angels, Apollo, 1958; Rashomon, NY, 1959; Altona, Royal Court, 1961; The Trojan Women, Spoleto Festival, 1963; Ivanov, Phoenix, 1965; A Doll's House, NY, 1971; Hedda Gabler, 1971; Vivat! Vivat Regina!, NY, 1971; A Doll's House, Criterion, 1973 (filmed 1973); A Streetcar Named Desire, Piccadilly, 1974. First film, Blind Goddess, 1947. *Films include:* Limelight; The Man Between; Richard III; Alexander the Great; The Brothers Karamazov; The Buccaneers; Look Back in Anger; Three Moves to Freedom; The Brothers Grimm; The Chapman Report; The Haunting; 80,000 Suspects; Alta Infedelta; Il Maestro di Vigevano; The Outrage; The Spy Who Came in From The Cold; Charly; Three into Two won't go; A Severed Head; Red Sky at Morning; Islands In The Stream. First appearance on television programmes, 1952, since when she has had frequent successes on TV in the US; In Praise of Love, 1975; BBC TV series: A Legacy, 1975. *Recreations:* ballet, skating, reading. *Address:* c/o Larry Dalzell, 3 Goodwin's Court, WC2.

BLOOM, G(eorge) Cromarty, CBE 1974; Deputy Chairman, London Broadcasting Co. Ltd; Director: Beacon Broadcasting Ltd; Cablevision (Wellingborough) Ltd; Radio Forth Ltd; Radio Victory (Portsmouth) Ltd; Selkirk Communications Ltd; *b* 8 June 1910; *s* of late George Highfield Bloom and Jessie Bloom (*née* Cromarty); *m* 1st, 1940, Patricia Suzanne Ramplin (*d* 1957); two *s*; 2nd, 1961, Sheila Louise Curran; one *s. Educ:* Australia and China, privately; Keble Coll., Oxford. With Reuters, 1933-60. Gen. Manager and Chief Exec., The Press Assoc. Ltd, 1961-75. Vice-Chm., Internat. Press Telecommunications Council, 1971-75; Vice-Pres., Alliance Européenne des Agences de Presse, 1971-75; Chm., CPU Telecommunications Cttee, 1973-77. *Address:* 1 Tivoli Court, Tivoli Road, Cheltenham GL50 2TD. *T:* Cheltenham 39413.

BLOOM, Ursula, (Mrs Gower Robinson); authoress; *b* Chelmsford, Essex; *o d* of late Rev. J. Harvey Bloom, MA; *m* 1st, 1916, Capt. Arthur Brownlow Denham-Cookes, 24th London Regt (Queen's) (*d* 1918); one *s*; 2nd, 1925, Paymaster Comdr Charles Gower Robinson, RN (retired). *Educ:* privately. First book, Tiger, published privately when seven years old. Writing under the names of Ursula Bloom, Lozania Prole, Sheila Burnes, Mary Essex and Rachel Harvey has published some 500 books. *Publications include:* The Great Beginning, 1924; Vagabond Harvest, 1925; The Driving of Destiny, 1925; Our Lady of Marble, 1926; The Judge of Jerusalem, 1926; Candleshades, 1927; Spilled Salt, 1927; Base Metal, 1928; An April After, 1928; Tarnish, 1929; To-morrow for Apricots, 1929; The Passionate Heart, 1930; The Secret Lover, 1930; Lamp in the Darkness: a volume of Religious Essays, 1930; Fruit on the Bough, 1931; Packmule, 1931; The Pilgrim Soul, 1932; The Cypresses Grow Dark, 1932; The Log of an NO's Wife, 1932; Wonder Cruise, 1933; Mistress of None, 1933; Rose Sweetman, 1933; Pastoral, 1934; Holiday Mood, 1934; The Questing Trout, 1934; The Gypsy Vans Come Through, 1935; Harvest of a House, 1935; The Laughing Lady, 1936; Laughter on Cheyne Walk, 1936; Three Cedars, 1937; Leaves Before the Storm, 1937; The Golden Venture, 1938; Without Makeup, 1938; The ABC of Authorship, 1938; A Cad's Guide to Cruising, 1938; Lily of the Valley, 1938; Beloved Creditor, 1939; These Roots Go Deep, 1939; The Woman Who Was To-morrow, 1940; Log of No Lady, 1940; The Flying Swans, 1940; Dinah's Husband, 1941; The Virgin Thorn, 1941; Lovely Shadow, 1942; Time, Tide and I, 1942; Age Cannot Wither, 1942; No Lady Buys a Cot, 1943; Robin in a Cage, 1943; The Fourth Cedar, 1943; The Faithless Dove, 1944; No Lady in Bed, 1944; The Painted Lady, 1945; The Changed Village, 1945; Rude Forefathers, 1945; No Lady With a Pen, 1946; Four Sons, 1946; Adam's Daughter, 1947; Three Sisters, 1948; Façade, 1948; No Lady Meets No Gentleman, 1948; Next Tuesday, 1949; Elinor Jowitt, Antiques; No Lady in the Cart; Song of Philomel, 1950; The King's Wife, 1950; Mum's Girl was no Lady, 1950; Pavilion, 1951; Nine Lives, 1951; How Dark, My Lady!, 1951; The Sentimental Family, 1951; As Bends the Bough, 1952; Twilight of a Tudor, 1952; Sea Fret, 1952; The Gracious Lady, 1953; The First Elizabeth, 1953; Hitler's Eva, 1954; Trilogy, 1954; Curtain Call for the Guvnor, 1954; Matthew, Mark, Luke and John, 1954; Daughters of the Rectory, 1955; The Silver Ring, 1955; The Tides of Spring Flow Fast, 1955; Victorian Vinaigrette, 1956; No Lady Has a Dog's Day, 1956; Brief Springtime, 1957; The Elegant Edwardian, 1957; Monkey Tree in a Flower Pot, 1957; He Lit the Lamp, 1958; The Abiding City, 1958; Down to the Sea in Ships, 1958; The Inspired Needle, 1959; Youth at the Gate, 1959; Undarkening Green, 1959; Sixty Years of Home, 1960; The Thieving Magpie, 1960; Prelude to Yesterday, 1961; The Cactus has Courage, 1961; War Isn't Wonderful, 1961; Ship in a Bottle, 1962; Harvest Home Come Sunday, 1962; Parson Extraordinary, 1963; The Gated Road, 1963; Mrs Bunthorpe's Respects, 1963; The House That Died Alone, 1964; The Rose of

Norfolk, 1964; The Ring Tree, 1964; The Ugly Head, 1965; The Quiet Village, 1965; Rosemary for Stratford-on-Avon, 1965; Price Above Rubies, 1965; The Dandelion Clock, 1966; The Mightier Sword, 1966; The Old Adam, 1967; A Roof and Four Walls, 1967; Two Pools in a Field, 1967; The Dragon Fly, 1968; Yesterday is To-morrow, 1968; Flight of the Peregrine, 1969; The House of Kent, 1969; The Hunter's Moon, 1970; Rosemary for Frinton, 1970; The Tune of Time, 1970; The Great Tomorrow, 1971; Perchance to Dream, 1971; Rosemary for Chelsea (autobiog.), 1971; The Caravan of Chance, 1972; The Cheval Glass, 1972; The Duke of Windsor, 1972; The Old Rectory, 1973; Princesses in Love, 1973; Requesting the Pleasure, 1973; The Old Elm Tree, 1974; Miracle on the Horizon, 1974; Royal Baby, 1975; Twisted Road, 1975; Turn of Life's Tide, 1976; Life is no Fairy Tale (autobiog.), 1976; The Great Queen Consort, 1976. *Address:* 191 Cranmer Court, SW3. *T:* 01-589 8966.

BLOOMER, Rt. Rev. Thomas, DD 1946 (TCD); *b* 14 July 1894; *s* of Thomas and Mary Bloomer; *m* 1935, Marjorie Grace (*d* 1969), *d* of late Rev. David Hutchison; one *s* two *d*; *m* 1973, Marjorie, widow of I. M. Orr. *Educ:* Royal Sch., Dungannon, N Ireland; Trinity Coll., Dublin. Ordained to curacy of Carrickfergus, N Ireland, 1918; Curate of Castleton, Lancs, 1922; Cheltenham, Glos, 1923; Vicar of St Mark's, Bath, 1928; Vicar of Barking, 1935-46; Rural Dean of Barking and Canon of Chelmsford Cathedral, 1943-46; Bishop of Carlisle, 1946-66. Chaplain to: the King, 1944-47; House of Lords, 1953-66. Proctor in Convocation of Canterbury, 1945. Freedom of City of Carlisle, 1966. *Publications:* A Fact and a Faith, 1943; A Fact and an Experience, 1944. *Recreations:* golf, gardening. *Address:* 33 Greengate, Levens, Kendal, Cumbria. *T:* Sedgwick 60771.

BLOOMFIELD, Hon. Sir John (Stoughton), Kt 1967; QC (Victoria) 1965; LLB; Member for Malvern, Legislative Assembly, Victoria, 1953-70, retired; *b* 9 Oct. 1901; *s* of Arthur Stoughton Bloomfield, Chartered Accountant, Melbourne, and Ada Victoria Bloomfield; *m* 1931, Beatrice Madge, *d* of W. H. Taylor, Overnewton, Sydenham, Victoria; one *s* one *d*. *Educ:* Geelong Grammar Sch.; Trinity Coll., Melbourne Univ. Served AIF, 1940-45; Lieut-Col retired. Solicitor, 1927-45; called to Victorian Bar, 1945. Government of Victoria: Minister of Labour and Industry and of Electrical Undertakings, 1955-56; Minister of Education, 1956-67. Mem. Council, University of Melbourne, 1956-70. *Publications:* Company Law Amendments, 1939; Screens and Gowns: Some Aspects of University Education Overseas, 1963; articles in professional journals. *Recreation:* painting. *Address:* 25 Mercer Road, Armadale, Victoria 3143, Australia. *T:* 20-2947. *Clubs:* Melbourne, Naval and Military (Melbourne).

BLOOMFIELD, Kenneth Percy; Permanent Secretary, Department of the Environment, Northern Ireland, since 1976; *b* 15 April 1931; *o c* of Harry Percy Bloomfield and Doris Bloomfield (*née* Frankel), Belfast; *m* 1960, Mary Elizabeth Ramsey; one *s* one *d*. *Educ:* Royal Belfast Academical Instn; St Peter's Coll., Oxford (MA). Min. of Finance, N Ireland, 1952-56; Private Sec. to Ministers of Finance, 1956-60; Dep. Dir, British Industrial Develt Office, NY, 1960-63; Asst and later Dep. Sec. to Cabinet, NI, 1963-72; Under-Sec., Northern Ireland Office, 1972-73; Sec. to Northern Ireland Executive, Jan.-May 1974; Permanent Secretary: Office of the Executive, NI, 1974-75; Dept of Housing, Local Govt and Planning, NI, 1975-76. *Recreations:* reading history and biography, swimming. *Address:* Shanoge, Ballymullan Road, Crawfordsburn, Co. Down, N Ireland. *T:* Helen's Bay 2268.

BLOSSE, Sir Richard Hely L.; see Lynch-Blosse.

BLOUGH, Roger M.; former Partner, White & Case; former Chairman of the Board of Directors, United States Steel Corporation; *b* 19 Jan. 1904; *s* of Christian E. Blough and Viola (*née* Hoffman); *m* 1928, Helen Martha Decker; twin *d*. *Educ:* Susquehanna Univ. (AB); Yale Law Sch. (LLB). General practice of law with White & Case, New York City, 1931-42; General Solicitor, US Steel Corp. of Delaware, 1942-51; Exec. Vice-President law and Secretary, US Steel Corp., 1951; Vice-Chairman, Director and Member Finance Cttee, US Steel Corp., 1952; General Counsel, 1953-55; Chairman, Chief Exec. Officer and Member Exec. Cttee, 1955-69; Dir and Mem. Finance and Exec. Cttees, 1969-. Holds numerous hon. degrees. *Publication:* Free Man and the Corporation, 1959. *Address:* (business) 300 Keystone Street, Hawley, Pa 18428, USA; (home) Blooming Grove, Hawley, Pennsylvania 18428, USA. *Clubs:* Blooming Grove Hunting and Fishing (Pa); Board Room, Recess, Links (NYC); Pine Valley Golf; and numerous others.

BLOUNT, Bertie Kennedy, CB 1957; DrPhilNat; *b* 1 April 1907; *s* of late Col G. P. C. Blount, DSO, and late Bridget Constance, *d* of Maj.-Gen. J. F. Bally, CVO; unmarried. *Educ:* Malvern Coll.; Trinity Coll., Oxford (MA 1932, BSc 1929); Univ. of Frankfurt (DrPhilNat 1931). Ramsay Memorial Fellow, 1931; 1851 Senior Student, 1933; Dean of St Peter's Hall, Oxford, 1933-37; Messrs Glaxo Laboratories Ltd: Head of Chemical Research Laboratory, 1937; Principal Technical Executive, 1938-40. Served Army (Intelligence Corps), War of 1939-45; Capt. 1940; Major 1942; Col 1945. Asst Director of Research, The Wellcome Foundation, 1947; Director of Research Branch, Control Commission for Germany, 1948, and subsequently also Chief of Research Div. of Military Security Board; Director of Scientific Intelligence, Min. of Defence, 1950-52; Dep. Secretary, DSIR, 1952; Min. of Technology, 1964; retired 1966. Chairman Steering Cttees: Torry Res. Station and Forest Products Res. Lab., 1958-66; Lab. of the Govt Chemist, 1962-66; Building Res. Station, Joint Fire Res. Organisation, Hydraulics Res. Stat., Water Pollution Res. Lab., Warren Spring Lab., 1965-66. Member Exec. Cttee, British Council, 1957-66. Royal Society of Arts: Armstrong Lecturer, 1955; Cantor Lecturer, 1963. Member Parry Cttee to review Latin American Studies in British Universities, 1962; Pres., Exec. Cttee, Internat. Inst. of Refrigeration, 1963-71, Hon. Pres. 1971; Hon. Mem., (British) Inst. of Refrigeration, 1971. FRIC. *Publications:* papers in scientific and other journals. *Address:* Tarrant Rushton House, Blandford, Dorset. *T:* Blandford 256. *Club:* Athenæum.

BLOUNT, Sir Edward Robert, 11th Bt, *cr* 1642; retired; *b* 2 Dec. 1884; *s* of Sir Walter Blount, 9th Bt; *S* brother (Sir Walter Blount, 10th Bt) 1958; *m* 1914, Violet Ellen (*d* 1969), *d* of Alpin Grant Fowler; one *s* one *d*. *Educ:* Convent, Bath; Wimbledon Coll. (RC). Lieut RFC and RAF, 1914-18. British Sugar Corporation Ltd, 1924-50. *Recreation:* sailing. *Heir:* *s* Walter Edward Alpin Blount, DSC, MA [*b* 31 Oct. 1917; *m* 1954, Eileen Audrey, *o d* of late Hugh B. Carritt; one *d*]. *Clubs:* Seaview Yacht Club, Seaview, Isle of Wight; Island Sailing (Cowes).

BLOW, Prof. David Mervyn, FRS 1972; Professor of Biophysics, Imperial College, University of London, since 1977; *b* 27 June 1931; *s* of Rev. Edward Mervyn and Dorothy Laura Blow; *m* 1955, Mavis Sears; one *s* one *d*. *Educ:* Kingswood Sch.; Corpus Christi Coll., Cambridge (MA, PhD). FInstP. Fulbright Scholar, Nat. Inst. of Health, Bethesda, Md, and MIT, 1957-59; MRC Unit for Study of Molecular Biological Systems, Cambridge, 1959-62; MRC Lab. of Molecular Biology, Cambridge, 1962-77; College Lectr and Fellow, Trinity Coll., Cambridge, 1968-77. Biochem. Soc. CIBA Medal, 1967. *Publications:* papers and reviews in scientific jls. *Recreations:* hill walking, sailing. *Address:* Imperial College, University of London, SW7 2AZ.

BLOW, Sandra, ARA 1971; Tutor, Painting School, Royal College of Art, since 1960; *b* 14 Sept. 1925; *d* of Jack and Lily Blow. *Educ:* St Martin's School of Art; Royal Academy Sch.; Accademia di Belle Arti, Rome. *One-man Exhibitions:* Gimpel Fils, 1952, 1954, 1960, 1962; Saidenburg Gallery, NY, 1957; New Art Centre, London, 1966, 1968, 1971, 1973. Represented in group exhibitions in Britain (including British Painting 74, Hayward Gall.), USA, Italy, Denmark, France. Won British Section of Internat. Guggenheim Award, 1960; 2nd prize, John Moore's Liverpool Exhibition, 1961; Arts Council Purchase Award, 1965-66. *Official Purchases:* Peter Stuyvesant Foundation; Nuffield Foundation; Arts Council of Great Britain; Arts Council of N Ireland; Walker Art Gallery, Liverpool; Allbright Knox Art Gallery, Buffalo, NY; Museum of Modern Art, NY; Tate Gallery; Gulbenkian Foundation; Min. of Public Building and Works; Contemp. Art Society; silk screen prints: Victoria and Albert Museum; Fitzwilliam Museum, Cambridge; City of Leeds Art Gall.; Graves Art Gall., Sheffield; painting purchased for liner Queen Elizabeth II. *Address:* 12 Sydney Close, SW3. *T:* 01-589 8610.

BLOY, Rt. Rev. Francis Eric Irving, DD, STD; *b* Birchington, Isle of Thanet, Kent, England, 17 Dec. 1904; *s* of Rev. Francis Joseph Field Bloy and Alice Mary (*née* Poynter); *m* 1929, Frances Forbes Cox, Alexandria, Va; no *c*. *Educ:* University of Missouri (BA); Georgetown Univ. of Foreign Service; Virginia Theological Seminary (BD). Rector, All Saints Ch., Reisterstown, Maryland, 1929-33; Assoc. Rector, St James-by-the-Sea, La Jolla, Calif, 1933-35, Rector, 1935-37; Dean, St Paul's Cathedral, Los Angeles, Calif, 1937-48; Bishop of Los Angeles, 1948-73. DD: Ch. Divinity Sch. of the Pacific, Berkeley, Calif, 1942; Occidental Coll., Los Angeles, 1953; Va Theol Sem., 1953; STD: Ch. Divinity Sch. of the Pacific, 1948; Univ. of S Calif, 1955. Pres., Church Federation of Los Angeles,

1946-47; Pres., Univ. Religious Conf., 1956; Hon. Chm. Bd of Trustees, Good Samaritan Hosp.; Trustee, Occidental Coll.; Mem. Town Hall. *Address:* 1220 W 4th Street, Los Angeles, Calif 90017, USA. *Clubs:* California; Jonathan (Los Angeles).

BLUCKE, Air Vice-Marshal Robert Stewart, CB 1946; CBE 1945; DSO 1943; AFC 1936, Bar 1941; RAF, retired; *b* 22 June 1897; *s* of late Rev. R. S. K. Blucke, Monxton Rectory, Andover, Hants; *m* 1926, Nancy, *d* of late Frank Wilson, Auckland, NZ; one *d* (one *s* decd). *Educ:* Malvern Coll. Dorset Regt and RFC, 1915-18; Mesopotamia, 1916-18; Royal Air Force, 1922; India, 1927-32; Test Pilot Royal Aircraft Establishment, Farnborough, 1933-37; Air Ministry, 1938-42; served in Bomber Comd, 1942-46; AOC No 1 Group RAF, 1945; SASO, AHQ, India, 1947; AOA, Technical Trg Comd, 1947-49; AOA, Far East Air Force, 1949-50; AOC Malaya, 1951; AOC-in-C Transport Comd, 1952; retired 1952. General Manager, National Assoc. for Employment of Regular Sailors, Soldiers and Airmen, 1952-65. *Recreation:* golf. *Address:* 9 Royal Chase, Tunbridge Wells, Kent. *T:* Tunbridge Wells 20912. *Club:* RAF.

BLUETT, Maj.-Gen. Douglas, CB 1958; OBE 1942; MA, MB; *b* 23 Aug. 1897; *s* of Rev. R. D. Bluett, BD, The Rectory, Delgany, Co. Wicklow, Ireland; *m* 1st, 1940, Johanna Catharine (*d* 1960), *d* of Mr Simpson-Smith, Huddersfield, Yorks; no *c*; 2nd, 1964, Noeline (*d* 1971), *widow* of Col C. Day; 3rd, 1974, Mary (*née* Merrick), *widow* of Francis Power. *Educ:* St Andrews Coll., and Trinity Coll., Dublin. Served European War, 1914-18, in Greek Macedonia, Bulgaria, Serbia, European Turkey and Islands of the Aegean Sea; War of 1939-45, with RAMC, ADMS 10th and 11th Armoured Divs, Western Desert, France and Germany; Lieut-Col, 1943; Col, 1945; Brig., 1953; Maj.-Gen., 1956; QHP 1956-58; retired, 1958. Col Comdt, RAMC, 1958-63. CStJ. Officer, Order of Leopold II avec Palme and Croix de Guerre avec Palme (Belgium), 1945. *Recreation:* golf. *Address:* c/o Williams & Glyn's Bank Ltd, Kirkland House, Whitehall, SW1; Galtymore, 111 Rochester Road, Aylesford, Kent.

BLUMBERG, Prof. Baruch Samuel, MD, PhD; Associate Director for Clinical Research, The Institute for Cancer Research, since 1964; Professor of Medicine and Professor of Anthropology, University of Pennsylvania, since 1970; *b* 28 July 1925; *s* of Meyer Blumberg and Ida Blumberg; *m* 1954, Jean Liebesman Blumberg; two *s* two *d*. *Educ:* Union Coll. (BS Physics, 1946); Columbia University Coll. of Physicians and Surgeons (MD 1951); Balliol Coll., Oxford Univ. (PhD Biol Sciences, 1957). US Navy, 1943-46 (Lieut JG); US Public Health Service (rank of med. dir, col) and Chief, Geographic Medicine and Genetics Sect., Nat. Insts. of Health, Bethesda, Md, 1957-64. Mem. Nat. Acad. of Sciences, Washington, DC. Hon. Fellow, Balliol Coll., Oxford, 1977. Hon. DSc: Univ. of Pittsburgh, 1977; Union Coll., Schenectady, NY, 1977; Med. Coll. of Pa, 1977; Dickinson Coll., Carlisle, Pa, 1977; Hahnemann Med. Coll., Philadelphia, Pa, 1977. (Jt) Nobel Prize in Physiology or Medicine, 1976. *Publications: chapters in:* McGraw-Hill Encyclopedia of Science and Technology Yearbook, 1962; The Genetics of Migrant and Isolate Populations, ed E. Goldschmidt, 1963; Hemoglobin: its precursors and metabolites, ed F. W. Sunderman and F. W. Sunderman, Jr, 1964; McGraw-Hill Yearbook of Science and Technology, 1970; (also co-author chapter) Viral Hepatitis and Blood Transfusion, ed G. N. Vyas and others, 1972; Hematology, ed W. J. Williams and others, 1972; Progress in Liver Disease, Vol. IV, ed H. Popper and F. Schaffner, 1972; Australia Antigen, ed J. E. Prier and H. Friedman, 1973; Drugs and the Liver, ed. W. Gerok and K. Sickinger, 1975 (Germany); (*jtly*) *chapters in:* Progress in Medical Genetics, ed A. G. Steinberg and A. G. Bearn, 1965 (also London); Viruses Affecting Man and Animals, ed M. Sanders and M. Schaeffer, 1971; Perspectives in Virology, 1971; Transmissable Disease and Blood Transfusion, ed T. J. Greenwalt and G. A. Jamieson, 1975; Physiological Anthropology, ed A. Damon, 1975; Hepatite a Virus B et Hemodialyse, 1975 (Paris); Onco-Developmental Gene Expression, 1976; (ed) Genetic Polymorphisms and Geographic Variations in Disease, 1961; (ed jtly) Medical Clinics of North America: new developments in medicine, 1970; contrib. symposia; over 260 articles in scientific jls. *Recreations:* squash, canoeing, middle distance running, cattle raising. *Address:* The Institute for Cancer Research, 7701 Burholme Avenue, Philadelphia, Pa 19111, USA. *T:* 215-728-2203. *Clubs:* Provincetown Yacht (Provincetown, Mass); Chesapeake and Ohio Canal Association.

BLUMENTHAL, W(erner) Michael, PhD; Secretary of the Treasury of the United States, since 1977; *b* Germany, 3 Jan. 1926; *s* of Ewald Blumenthal and Rose Valerie (*née* Markt) (father escaped to Shanghai from Buchenwald Concentration Camp where he was sent by the Nazis in 1938; family interned by Japanese, 1943); *m* 1951, Margaret Eileen Polley; three *d*. *Educ:* Univ. of California at Berkeley; Princeton Univ. Went to USA, 1947; naturalised, 1952; worked as waiter, doorman, etc, to finance univ. studies; Research Associate, Princeton Univ., 1954-57; Labor Arbitrator, State of New Jersey, 1955-57; Vice-Pres., Dir, Crown Cork Internat. Corp., 1957-61. Dep. Asst Sec. of State for Econ. Affairs, Dept of State, 1961-63; also USA Rep. to UN Commn on Internat. Commodity Trade; Mem. US Delegn to Punta del Este Conf. (Alliance for Progress), 1961; Dep. Special Rep. of the President (with rank Ambassador) for Trade Negotiations, 1963-67. Chm., US Delegn to Kennedy Round Tariff talks, Geneva, 1963-67. Pres., Bendix Internat., 1967-70; Dir, Bendix Corp., 1967-77; Vice-Chm., June-Dec. 1970; Pres. and Chief Operating Officer, 1971-72; Chm. and Chief Exec. Officer, 1972-77. Trustee Princeton Univ. *Recreations:* tennis, skiing. *Address:* US Treasury Department, 15th Street NW, Washington, DC 20020, USA.

BLUNDELL, Commandant Daphne Mary, CB 1972; Director, WRNS, 1970-73; *b* 19 Aug. 1916. *Educ:* St Helen's Sch., Northwood; Bedford Coll., London. Worked for LCC as Child Care Organiser. Joined WRNS, Nov. 1942; commnd 1943; served in Orkneys, Ceylon, E Africa; Malta, 1954-56; Staff of Flag Officer Naval Air Comd, 1964-67; Staff of C-in-C Portsmouth, 1967-69; Supt WRNS Training and Drafting, 1969-70. Supt 1967; Comdt 1970, retd 1973; Hon. ADC to the Queen, 1970-73. Governor, St Helen's Sch., Northwood. *Address:* 22 Marsham Court, Marsham Street, SW1P 4JY.

BLUNDELL, Sir (Edward) Denis, GCMG 1972; GCVO 1974; KBE 1967 (OBE (mil.) 1944); Governor-General of New Zealand, 1972-77; *b* 29 May 1907; British; *m* 1945; one *s* one *d*. *Educ:* Waitaki High Sch. (NZ); Trinity Hall, Cambridge Univ. Called to Bar, Gray's Inn, 1929; admitted as Barrister and Solicitor of the Supreme Court of New Zealand at end of 1929. Served War, 1939-44 with 2nd NZ Div. in Greece, Crete, ME and Italy. Formerly Sen. Partner, Bell, Gully & Co., Barristers and Solicitors, Wellington, NZ. President of the New Zealand Law Society, 1962-68. High Comr for NZ in London, 1968-72. Pres., NZ Cricket Council, 1957-60. KStJ 1972. *Recreations:* cricket (cricket Blue Cambridge, 1928, 1929; rep. NZ, 1936-37), golf, swimming, tennis. *Address:* 655 Riddell Road, Glendowie, Auckland, New Zealand. *Clubs:* Wellington; Wellesley (New Zealand).

BLUNDELL, Sir Michael, KBE 1962 (MBE 1943); *b* 7 April 1907; *s* of Alfred Herbert Blundell and Amelia Woodward Blundell (*née* Richardson); *m* 1946, Geraldine Lötte Robarts; one *d*. *Educ:* Wellington Coll. Settled in Kenya as farmer, 1925. 2nd Lieut, RE, 1940; Major, 1940; Lieut-Col, 1941; Col, 1944; served Abyssinian campaign and SEAC. Commissioner, European Settlement, 1946-47; MLC, Rift Valley Constituency, Kenya, 1948-62; Leader European Members, 1952; Minister on Emergency War Council, Kenya, 1954-55; Minister of Agriculture, Kenya, 1955-59 and April 1961-June 1962; Leader of New Kenya Group, 1959-63. Chairman: Pyrethrum Board of Kenya, 1949-54; Egerton Agricultural Coll., 1962-72; EA Breweries Ltd, 1964-; Uganda Breweries Ltd, 1965-76; Dir, Barclays Bank DCO Ltd (Kenya), 1968-. *Publication:* So Rough a Wind, 1964. *Recreations:* gardening, music, 18th century English porcelain. *Address:* Box 30181, Nairobi, Kenya. *T:* Nairobi 63278. *Clubs:* Brooks's; Muthaiga (Nairobi).

BLUNDEN, George; Executive Director, Bank of England, since 1976; *b* 31 Dec. 1922; *s* of late George Blunden and Florence Holder; *m* 1949, Anne, *d* of late G. J. E. Bulford; two *s* one *d*. *Educ:* City of London Sch.; University Coll., Oxford (MA). Royal Sussex Regt, 1942-45; Bank of England, 1947-55; IMF, 1955-58; Bank of England: rejoined 1958; Dep. Chief Cashier, 1968-73; Chief of Management Services, 1973-74; Head of Banking Supervision, 1974-76. On staff of Monopolies Commn, 1968; Chm., Group of Ten Cttee on Banking Regulations and Supervisory Practices at Bank for Internat. Settlements, Basle, 1974-. Hon. Treasurer: Inst. of Urology, 1975-; Dovedale Almshouses Trust, 1973-. Governor: St Peter's Gp of Hosps, 1976-; Chinthurst Sch., 1976-; Trustee, St Peter's Trust for Kidney Res., 1971-. *Address:* Bank of England, Threadneedle Street, EC2R 8AH. *T:* 01-601 4444. *Clubs:* Overseas Bankers, MCC.

BLUNDEN, Sir William, 6th Bt, *cr* 1766; RN, retired; *b* 26 April 1919; *s* of 5th Bt and Phyllis, *d* of P. C. Creaghe; *S* father, 1923; *m* 1945, Pamela Mary Purser, 2nd Officer WRNS, *d* of John Purser, Prof. of Civil Engineering, TCD; six *d. Educ:* Repton. Lieut-Comdr, RN, 1949; retired 1958. *Heir: b* Philip Overington Blunden [*b* 27 Jan. 1922; *m* 1945, Jeanette Francesca (WRNS), *e d* of Captain D. Macdonald, RNR, Portree, Isle of Skye; two *s* one *d*]. *Address:* Castle Blunden, Kilkenny. *T:* Kilkenny 21128.

BLUNT, Sir Anthony Frederick, KCVO 1956 (CVO 1947); FBA 1950; FSA 1960; Professor of History of Art, University of London, and Director, Courtauld Institute of Art, 1947-Sept. 1974; Surveyor of the Queen's Pictures, 1952-72 (of the Pictures of King George VI, 1945-52); Adviser for the Queen's Pictures and Drawings, since 1972; *b* 26 Sept. 1907; *y s* of late Rev. A. S. V. Blunt, Vicar of St John's, Paddington. *Educ:* Marlborough Coll.; Trinity Coll., Cambridge. Served War of 1939-45: France, 1939-40; WO, 1940-45. Fellow, Trinity Coll., Cambridge, 1932-36; on staff of Warburg Inst., London, 1937-39; Reader in History of Art, London Univ., and Dep. Dir, Courtauld Inst. of Art, 1939-47. Slade Prof. of Fine Art: Oxford, 1962-63; Cambridge, 1965-66. Hon. Fellow, Trinity Coll., Cambridge, 1967. Hon. FRIBA, 1973. Hon. DLitt: Bristol, 1961; Durham, 1963; Oxon, 1971; DèsL *hc* Paris, 1966. Commander: Order of Orange Nassau (Holland), 1948; Legion of Honour (France), 1958. *Publications:* (with Walter Friedlaender), The Drawings of Nicolas Poussin, 1939-75; Artistic Theory in Italy, 1940; François Mansart, 1941; French Drawings at Windsor Castle, 1945; (with Margaret Whinney) The Nation's Pictures, 1951; Rouault's Miserere, 1951; Poussin's Golden Calf, 1951; Art and Architecture in France, 1500-1700, 1953, rev. edn 1970; The Drawings of G. B. Castiglione and Stefano della Bella at Windsor Castle, 1954; Venetian Drawings at Windsor Castle, 1957; Philibert de l'Orme, 1958; The Art of William Blake, 1960; (with H. L. Cooke) The Roman Drawings at Windsor Castle, 1960; (with Phoebe Pool) Picasso: The Formative Years, 1962; Nicolas Poussin: Catalogue raisonné, 1966; Nicolas Poussin (2 vols), 1967; Sicilian Baroque, 1968; Picasso's Guernica, 1969; Supplement to Italian and French Drawings at Windsor, 1971; Neapolitan Baroque and Rococo Architecture, 1975; articles in Burlington Magazine, Jl of Warburg and Courtauld Insts, Spectator, etc. *Address:* 45 Portsea Hall, Portsea Place, W2. *Club:* Travellers'.

BLUNT, Christopher Evelyn, OBE 1945; FBA 1965; retired; *b* 16 July 1904; 2nd *s* of Rev. A. S. V. Blunt and Hilda Violet Blunt; *m* 1930, Elisabeth Rachel Bazley; one *s* two *d. Educ:* Marlborough (Foundation Scholar). Entered merchant banking firm of Higginson & Co., 1924; partner, 1947; executive director of successor companies, 1950-64. Served War, 1939-46; 52 AA (TA) Regt; GHQ (Gen. Staff), BEF (despatches), Home Forces, 21 Army Group; SHAEF; retired 1946 (Col). FSA 1936; President: British Numismatic Soc., 1946-50; Royal Numismatic Soc., 1956-61; Wilts Arch. Soc., 1970-74. Medals of Royal British and Amer. Numismatic Socs. Officer Legion of Merit (USA), 1945. *Publications:* The Coinage of Athelstan, 1974; contributions to Numismatic Chronicle, British Numismatic Journal, Archæologia, etc. *Recreations:* travel and archæology. *Address:* Ramsbury Hill, Ramsbury, Marlborough, Wilts. *T:* Ramsbury 358; H4 Albany, Piccadilly, W1. *T:* 01-734 5320. *Clubs:* Travellers', Pratt's.

BLUNT, Sir David Richard Reginald Harvey, 12th Bt *cr* 1720; *b* 8 Nov. 1938; *s* of Sir Richard David Harvey Blunt, 11th Bt and Elisabeth Malvine Ernestine, *d* of Comdr F. M. Fransen Van de Putte, Royal Netherlands Navy (retd); *S* father, 1975; *m* 1969, Sonia Tudor Rosemary (*née* Day); one *d*. Joined Hospital Service, 1964; specialised in administration in Hospital Supplies; on staff of Royal Free Hosp., Hampstead. *Heir: uncle* Charles Harvey David Blunt, *b* 18 Sept. 1919. *Address:* 74 Kirkstall Road, SW2.

BLUNT, Maj.-Gen. Peter, MBE 1955; GM 1959; Assistant Chief of Personnel and Logistics (Army), Ministry of Defence, since 1977; *b* 18 Aug. 1923; *s* of A. G. Blunt and M. Blunt; *m* 1949, Adrienne, *o d* of Gen. T. W. Richardson; three *s*. Joined Army aged 14 yrs, 1937; commnd Royal Fusiliers; served Duke of Cornwall's LI and Royal Scots Fusiliers, until 1946; foreign service, 1946-49; Staff Coll., 1957; Jt Services Staff Coll., 1963; RCDS, 1972; comd 26 Regt, Bridging, 1965; CSO 1 Def. Plans, FARELF, 1968; Comdr RCT 1 Corps, 1970; Dep. Transport Officer-in-Chief (Army), later Transp. Off.-in-Chief, 1973. *Recreation:* fishing. *Address:* Greenbank, Bracknell Lane, Hartley Wintney, Hants. *T:* Hartley Wintney 2313. *Club:* Army and Navy.

BLUNT, Wilfrid Jasper Walter; Curator of the Watts Gallery, Compton, since 1959; *b* 19 July 1901; *s* of late Rev. Arthur Stanley Vaughan Blunt and Hilda Violet Master. *Educ:* Marlborough Coll.; Worcester Coll., Oxford; Royal College of Art. Art Master, Haileybury Coll., 1923-38; Drawing Master, Eton Coll., 1938-59. ARCA (London) 1923. Introduced into the Public Schs the craft of pottery (Haileybury, 1927) and Italic handwriting (Eton, 1940). FLS 1969. *Publications:* The Haileybury Buildings, 1936; Desert Hawk, 1947; The Art of Botanical Illustration, 1950; Tulipomania, 1950; Black Sunrise, 1951; Sweet Roman Hand, 1952; Japanese Colour Prints, 1952; Georg Dionysius Ehret, 1953; Pietro's Pilgrimage, 1953; Sebastiano, 1956; Great Flower Books (with Sacheverell Sitwell and Patrick Synge), 1956; A Persian Spring, 1957; Lady Muriel, 1962; Of Flowers and a Village, 1963; Cockerell, 1964; Omar, 1966; Isfahan, 1966; John Christie of Glyndebourne, 1968; The Dream King, 1970; The Compleat Naturalist, 1971; The Golden Road to Samarkand, 1973; On Wings of Song, 1974; 'England's Michelangelo', 1975; The Ark in the Park, 1976; Splendours of Islam, 1976. *Recreations:* writing, singing and travel. *Address:* The Watts Gallery, Compton, near Guildford, Surrey. *T:* Guildford 810235.

BLYDE, Sir Henry (Ernest), KBE 1969 (CBE 1952); Chairman, Taranaki Harbours Board, since 1953; Chairman Lepperton Dairy Co. since 1942; *b* 25 Oct. 1896; *s* of James Blyde; *m* 1929, Mary, *d* of W. J. McCormick; two *s* two *d. Educ:* St Paul's School, St Leonards-on-Sea, Sussex. Formerly Chairman, Taranaki Hospital Bd. JP. *Recreations:* bowling, billiards. *Address:* 233 Carrington Street, New Plymouth, New Zealand. *T:* 88928 New Plymouth. *Club:* Taranaki (New Plymouth).

BLYTH, family name of **Baron Blyth.**

BLYTH, 3rd Baron, *cr* 1907; **Ian Audley James Blyth;** Bt, *cr* 1895; *s* of late Hon. James Audley Blyth (2nd *s* of 1st Baron); *b* 28 Oct. 1905; *S* uncle, 1943; *m* 1928, Edna Myrtle, *d* of Ernest Lewis, Wellington, NZ; two *s* three *d. Heir: s* Hon. Anthony Audley Rupert Blyth [*b* 3 June 1931; *m* 1st, 1954, Elizabeth Dorothea (marr. diss. 1962), *d* of R. T. Sparrow, Vancouver, BC; one *s* one *d*; 2nd, 1963, Oonagh Elizabeth Ann, *yr d* of late W. H. Conway, Dublin; one *s* one *d*]. *Address:* Rockfield House, Athenry, Co. Galway.

BLYTH, Charles, (Chay Blyth), CBE 1972; BEM; Director, Sailing Ventures (Hampshire) Ltd, since 1969; *b* 14 May 1940; *s* of Robert and Jessie Blyth; *m* 1962, Maureen Margaret Morris; one *d. Educ:* Hawick High School. HM Forces, Para. Regt, 1958-67. Cadbury Schweppes, 1968-69. Rowed North Atlantic with Captain John Ridgway, June-Sept. 1966; circumnavigated the world westwards solo in yacht British Steel, 1970-71; circumnavigated the world eastwards with crew in yacht Great Britain II, 1973-74. *Publications:* A Fighting Chance, 1966; Innocent Aboard, 1968; The Impossible Voyage, 1971; Theirs is the Glory, 1974. *Recreation:* sailing. *Address:* Box 1 Dartmouth, South Devon. *Club:* Royal Southern Yacht.

BLYTHE, James Forbes, TD 1946; a Recorder of the Crown Court, since 1972; HM Coroner for the City of Coventry, since 1964; Solicitor; *b* Coventry, 11 July 1917; *s* of J. F. Blythe; *m* 1949, Margaret, *d* of P. D. Kinsey; two *d. Educ:* Wrekin Coll.; Birmingham Univ. (LLB). 7th Bn, Royal Warwickshire Regt (TA), 1936-53 (Major). Served War of 1939-45 with BEF in France and in Tunisian and Italian campaigns. Admitted solicitor, 1947; private practitioner in partnership in Coventry and Leamington Spa, 1948-. HM Deputy Coroner for City of Coventry and Northern Dist. of Warwickshire, 1954-64. *Recreations:* real tennis, shooting, sailing; past player and Sec. Coventry Football Club (RU). *Address:* Hazlewood, Upper Ladyes' Hill, Kenilworth, Warwickshire. *T:* Kenilworth 54168. *Clubs:* Royal Automobile, Law Society's Yacht; Drapers (Coventry); Tennis Court (Leamington Spa).

BLYTON, family name of **Baron Blyton.**

BLYTON, Baron, *cr* 1964 (Life Peer); **William Reid Blyton;** Secretary, Harton Miners' Lodge, Durham Miners' Association, 1941-45 (Chairman, 1928-41); Councillor South Shields Borough Council, 1936-45; *b* 2 May 1899; *s* of late Charles H. Blyton, retired labourer, and Hannah A. Blyton; *m* 1919, Jane B. Ord; three *d. Educ:* Elementary Education Holy Trinity Sch. and Dean Road Sch., South Shields. Chm. South Shields Labour Party, 1928-29, 1931-32; Mem. Durham Miners' Executive Cttee, 1930-32, 1942-43; Chm. of South Shields Education Cttee, 1943, and of South Shields Electrical Cttee, 1937-40; MP (Lab) Houghton-le-Spring Div. of County Durham, 1945-64; late PPS to Ministry of Civil Aviation; resigned, 1949. Chm. High Sch. Governors and Chm. Secondary and Technical Cttee of South Shields. Served in HM Submarines in European War, 1914-18. *Address:* 139 Brockley Avenue, South Shields, Tyne and Wear; Dylan Hotel, 14 Devonshire Terrace, W2.

BOAG, Prof. John Wilson; Professor of Physics as Applied to Medicine, University of London, Institute of Cancer Research, 1965-76, retired; *b* Elgin, Scotland, 20 June 1911; *s* of John and Margaret A. Boag; *m* 1938, Isabel Petrie; no *c. Educ:* Universities of Glasgow, Cambridge and Braunschweig. Engineer, British Thomson Houston Co., Rugby, 1936-41; Physicist, Medical Research Council, 1941-52; Visiting Scientist, National Bureau of Standards, Washington, DC, 1953-54; Physicist, British Empire Cancer Campaign, Mount Vernon Hospital, 1954-64; Royal Society (Leverhulme) Visiting Prof. to Poland, 1964. President: Hosp. Physicists' Assoc., 1959; Assoc. for Radiation Res. (UK), 1972-74; Internat. Assoc. for Radiation Res., 1970-74; British Inst. of Radiology, 1975-76. L. H. Gray Medal, ICRU, 1973; Barclay Medal, BIR, 1975. *Publications:* papers on radiation dosimetry, statistics, radiation chemistry, radiodiagnosis. *Address:* 40 Overton Road, Sutton, Surrey.

BOARDMAN, Harold; MP (Lab) Leigh, since 1945; Trade Union Official; *b* 12 June 1907; *m* 1936, Winifred May, *d* of Jesse Thorlby, Derbys; one *d. Educ:* Bolton and Derby. Joined Labour party, 1924; formerly Chm., Derby Labour Party; for 3 yrs Mem. Derby Town Council. PPS to Ministry of Labour, 1947-51. ILO Confs in Geneva, 1947, 1949, 1950, and San Francisco, 1948; Delegate to Council of Europe, 1960, 1961. Exec. Mem., NW Industrial Develt Assoc., 1946-. *Address:* House of Commons, SW1; 18 Norris Road, Brooklands, Sale, Manchester.

BOARDMAN, John, FBA 1969; Reader in Classical Archaeology, University of Oxford, since 1959; Fellow of Merton College, Oxford, since 1963; *b* 20 Aug. 1927; *s* of Frederick Archibald Boardman; *m* 1952, Sheila Joan Lyndon Stanford; one *s* one *d. Educ:* Chigwell Sch.; Magdalene Coll., Cambridge. BA 1948, MA 1951, Walston Student, 1948-50; Cromer Greek Prize, 1959. 2nd Lt, Intell. Corps, 1950-52. Asst Dir, British Sch. at Athens, 1952-55; Asst Keeper, Ashmolean Museum, Oxford, 1955-59. Geddes-Harrower Prof., Aberdeen Univ., 1974. Editor, Journal of Hellenic Studies, 1958-65. Conducted excavations on Chios, 1953-55, and at Tocra, in Libya, 1964-65. FSA 1957; FBA 1969. *Publications:* Cretan Collection in Oxford, 1961; Date of the Knossos Tablets, 1963; Island Gems, 1963; Greek Overseas, 1964, rev. edn 1973; Greek Art, 1964, rev. edn 1973; Excavations at Tocra, vol. I 1966, vol. II 1973; Pre-Classical, 1967; Greek Emporio, 1967; Engraved Gems, 1968; Archaic Greek Gems, 1968; Greek Gems and Finger Rings, 1970; (with D. Kurtz) Greek Burial Customs, 1971; Athenian Black Figure Vases, 1974; Athenian Red Figure Vases, 1975; Intaglios and Rings, 1975; Corpus Vasorum, vol. 3, 1975; articles in jls. *Address:* House of Winds, Harcourt Hill, North Hinksey, Oxford. *T:* Oxford 43758.

BOARDMAN, Thomas Gray, MC 1944; TD 1952; DL; President, Association of British Chambers of Commerce, since 1977; *b* 12 Jan. 1919; *s* of John Clayton Boardman, late of Daventry, and Janet Boardman, formerly Houston; *m* 1948, Norah Mary Deirdre, *widow* of John Henry Chaworth-Musters, Annesley Park, Nottingham, and *d* of Hubert Vincent Gough; two *s* one *d. Educ:* Bromsgrove. Served Northants Yeomanry, 1939-45 and subsequently; Commanding Northants Yeomanry, 1956. Qualified as a Solicitor, 1947. MP (C) Leicester SW, Nov. 1967-74, Leicester South Feb.-Sept. 1974; Minister for Industry, DTI, 1972-74; Chief Sec. to Treasury, 1974. Chm. Chamberlain Phipps Ltd, 1958-72; Director: The Steetley Co. Ltd, 1975-; Allied Breweries Ltd, 1968-72 and 1974-77 (Vice-Chm., 1975-76). Pres., Internat. Coil Winding Assoc., 1975-. DL Northants, 1977. *Recreation:* riding. *Address:* 29 Tufton Court, Tufton Street, SW1. *T:* 01-222 6793; The Manor House, Welford, Northampton. *T:* Welford 235. *Club:* Cavalry and Guards.

BOAS, Leslie, OBE 1961; HM Diplomatic Service, retired; *b* Buenos Aires, Argentine, 25 Feb. 1912; *s* of late Gustavus Thomas Boas and late Flora Shield McDonald; *m* 1st, 1944, Margaret Ann Jackson (marr. diss. 1951); one *s*; 2nd, 1951, Patricia Faye Fenning (*d* 1972); 3rd, 1972, Natalie K. Prado (*née* Kitchen). *Educ:* Spain; Gibraltar; Granada University. In business, 1933-39. Joined Coldstream Guards, 1940; commissioned in Royal Ulster Rifles, 1940; invalided out of Army as result of injuries, 1944. Joined Latin American Section of BBC, 1944. Apptd Temp. Press Attaché, Panama, 1946; Temp. First Sec. (Inf.), Bogotá, 1948; Temp. First Sec. (Inf.), Caracas, 1952; estab. as a Permanent First Sec., 1959; Regional Inf. Counsellor, Caracas, 1962-69; Chargé d'Affaires, Panama, April-May 1964; Ambassador to Santo Domingo, 1969-72. Dir, Secretariat of British Bicentennial Liaison Cttee of FCO, 1973-75. *Recreations:* golf, chess, Latin American studies. *Address:* c/o The Royal Bank of Scotland Ltd, 97 New Bond Street, W1Y 0EU. *Clubs:* Bucks; Jockey (Bogotá, Colombia).

BOASE, Alan Martin, MA, PhD; Officier de la Légion d'Honneur; *b* 1902; *s* of late W. Norman Boase, CBE, St Andrews; *m* 1931, Elizabeth Grizelle (*d* 1977), *e d* of late Prof. E. S. Forster; four *s. Educ:* Eton Coll.; New College, Oxford; Trinity Coll., Cambridge; Univ. of Paris. Lectr in French, Univ. of Sheffield, 1929-36; Prof. of French, University Coll., Southampton, 1936-37; Marshall Prof. of French, Univ. of Glasgow, 1937-65. Ex-Chm. of Assoc. of Heads of French Depts. Visiting Professor: Univ. of Calif (Berkeley), 1962; Monash Univ., Australia, 1969; Collège de France, 1974. Chm., Consultative Cttee, Inst. Français d'Ecosse. *Publications:* Montaigne, Selected Essays (with Arthur Tilley), 1934; The Fortunes of Montaigne, 1935, repr. (NY) 1970; Contemporary French Literature (in France: A Companion to French Studies, ed R. L. G. Ritchie), 1937; Les Poèmes de Jean de Sponde, 1950; The Poetry of France, Part III, 1952, Part I, 1964, Part IV, 1969, Part II, 1973; Les Méditations de Jean de Sponde, 1954; articles and reviews in periodicals. *Recreation:* gardening. *Address:* 39 Inverleith Place, Edinburgh. *T:* 031-552 3005.

BOASE, Arthur Joseph, CMG 1968; OBE 1951; Warden, Ophthalmic Hospital of the Order of St John, Jerusalem, 1956, retired; *b* 23 June 1901; 2nd *s* of William George Boase, medical practitioner; *m* 1929, Alice Mary, *d* of Sir Charles Griffin, QC; four *s* five *d* (and one *s* decd). *Educ:* Mount St Mary's Coll., Derbyshire; St Thomas' Hosp., London. MRCS, LRCP 1923; DOMS 1933; FRCS 1952. Uganda Med. Service, 1924; Sen. Med. Off., 1937; Specialist (Ophthalmology), 1945; Sen. Specialist, 1954; retd from Uganda, 1956. Past Pres., E African Assoc. of Surgs. Coronation Medal, 1953. Kt, Order of St Gregory (Papal), 1951; KStJ 1961; Kt, Order of Holy Sepulchre (Greek Orthodox), 1965; Kt, Order of Holy Sepulchre (Armenian), 1969. Istiqlal (Independence) Order, 2nd cl. (Jordan), 1967. *Recreation:* woodworking. *Address:* Kilworth, Maresfield, Uckfield, East Sussex.

See also Sir J. B. Griffin.

BOATENG, Prof. Ernest Amano, GM 1968; Executive Chairman, Environmental Protection Council, Ghana, since 1973; *b* 30 Nov. 1920; 2nd *s* of Rev. Christian Robert Boateng and Adelaide Akonobea, Aburi, Ghana; *m* 1955, Evelyn Kensema Danso, *e d* of Rev. Robert Opong Danso, Aburi; four *d. Educ:* Achimota Coll.; St Peter's Hall, Oxford (Gold Coast Govt Schol.). Henry Oliver Beckit Meml Prize, 1949; BA (Geog.) 1949, MA 1953, BLitt 1954. UC Ghana: Lectr in Geography, 1950-57; Sen. Lectr, 1958-61; Prof. of Geography, 1961-73; Dean, Faculty of Social Studies, 1962-69; Principal, 1969-71, Vice-Chancellor, 1971-73, Univ. of Cape Coast, Ghana. Vis. Asst Prof., Univ. of Pittsburgh and UCLA, 1960-61. Pres., Ghana Geographical Assoc., 1959-69; Foundn Fellow, Ghana Acad. of Arts and Sciences (Sec. 1959-62, Pres., 1973-76); Mem., Unesco Internat. Adv. Cttee on Humid Tropics Research, 1961-63; Mem., Scientific Council for Africa, 1963-; Mem., Nat. Planning Commn of Ghana, 1961-64; Smuts Vis. Fellow, Univ. of Cambridge, 1965-66; Vis. Prof., Univ. of Pittsburgh, 1966; Deleg., UN Conf. on geographical names, Geneva, 1967; Mem., Council for Scientific and Industrial Research, Ghana, 1967-75; Dir, Ghana Nat. Atlas Project; Chm., Geographical Cttee, Ghana 1970 population census; Member: Nat. Economic Planning Council of Ghana, 1974-; Nat. Council for Higher Educn, 1975-; Chm., W African Exams Council, 1977-. Pres., Ghana Wildlife Soc., 1974-. Alternate Leader, Ghana Delegn to UN Conf., Vancouver, 1976. FRSA 1973. *Publications:* A Geography of Ghana, 1959; (contrib.) Developing Countries of the World, 1968; (contrib.) Population Growth and Economic Development in Africa, 1972; Independence and Nation Building in Africa, 1973; various pamphlets, Britannica and other encyclopaedia articles and articles in geographical and other jls and reference works. *Recreations:* photography, gardening. *Address:* Environmental Protection Council, Parliament House, Accra, Ghana. *T:* Accra 64181.

BOCK, Prof. Claus Victor, MA, DrPhil; Professor of German Language and Literature, Westfield College, University of London, since 1969; *b* Hamburg, 7 May 1926; *o s* of Frederick Bock, merchant and manufacturer, and Margot (*née* Meyerhof). *Educ:* Quaker Sch., Eerde, Holland; Univs of Amsterdam, Manchester, Basle. DrPhil (insigni cum laude) Basle 1955. Asst Lectr in German, Univ. of Manchester, 1956-58; Lectr, Queen Mary Coll., London, 1958-69; Reader in German Lang. and Lit., Univ. of London, 1964. Mem. Council, English Goethe Soc., 1965-; Chm., Bd of Studies in Germanic Langs and Lit., Univ. of London, 1970-73; Mem. Council, Stichting Castrum Peregrini, 1971-; Hon. Dir, Inst. of Germanic Studies, Univ. of London, 1973-; Hon. Pres., Assoc. of Teachers of German, 1973-75. *Publications:* Deutsche erfahren Holland 1725-1925, 1956; Q. Kuhlmann als Dichter, 1957; ed (with Margot Ruben) K.

Wolfskehl Ges. Werke, 1960; ed (with G. F. Senior) Goethe the Critic, 1960; Pente Pigadia und die Tagebücher des Clement Harris, 1962; ed (with L. Helbing) Fr. Gundolf Briefwechsel mit H. Steiner und E. R. Curtius, 1963; Wort-Konkordanz zur Dichtung Stefan Georges, 1964; ed (with L. Helbing) Fr. Gundolf Briefe Neue Folge, 1965; A Tower of Ivory?, 1970; (with L. Helbing and K. Kluncker) Stefan George: Dokumente seiner Wirkung, 1974; articles in English and foreign jls and collections. *Recreation:* foreign travel. *Address:* Westfield College, Kidderpore Avenue, NW3 7ST. *T:* 01-435 7141; 4/8 Heath Drive, NW3 7SN. *T:* 01-435 8598.

BOCKETT, Herbert Leslie, CMG 1961; Chairman, Workers' Compensation Board, New Zealand, since 1960; Professional Accountant, and Member New Zealand Society of Accountants; *b* 29 June 1905; *s* of C. F. Bockett and L. M. Bockett (*née* Bridger); *m* 1932, Constance Olive Ramsay; two *d*. *Educ:* Dilworth Sch.; Seddon Memorial Technical Coll. Joined NZ Public Service, 1921; Accountant, Unemployment Board, 1934; Asst Director: Social Security Dept, 1939; National Service Dept, 1940; Controller of Man-power, 1942; Dir of National Service, 1944; Sec. of Labour, New Zealand, 1947-64; retd Dec. 1964. Mem., Shipping Industry Tribunal. *Recreation:* bowls. *Address:* 189 The Parade, Island Bay, Wellington, NZ. *T:* 838-549.

BODDIE, Donald Raikes; Consultant in Public Affairs, since 1975; *b* 27 June 1917; *o* s of William Henry and Violet May Boddie; *m* 1941, Barbara Stuart Strong; one *s*. *Educ:* Colston's Sch., Bristol. Joined: London Star, 1942-47; Natal Mercury, Durban, 1947-52; London Evening News, 1953 (held various exec. posts, to Dep. Editor, 1966 and Editor, 1972-74); Dir, Harmsworth Publications Ltd, 1973-74; Vice-Chm., Evening News Ltd, 1974. *Recreations:* travel, theatre, cinematography. *Address:* 87 Regent Street, W1. *T:* 01-439 6992. *Club:* London Press.

BODDIE, George Frederick, BSc Edinburgh; FRCVS; FRSE; William Dick Chair of Veterinary Medicine, Edinburgh University (in the Royal Dick School of Veterinary Studies), 1953-70; *b* 23 Jan. 1900; *m* 1st, 1926 (she *d* 1968); one *s* two *d*; 2nd, 1971. *Educ:* Merchiston Castle Sch.; Edinburgh Univ.; Royal (Dick) Veterinary College, Edinburgh. Clinical Asst Royal (Dick) Veterinary College, 1924; gen. veterinary practice, 1924-30; veterinary inspector local authority; Prof. of Medicine and Pharmacology Royal (Dick) Veterinary College, Edinburgh, 1930. Pres., RCVS, 1964-65, Vice-Pres., 1959-60, 1963-64 and 1965-66. Director: Hill Farm Research Organisation, 1957-66; Scottish Soc. for Prevention of Cruelty to Animals; former Chm. of Cttee, Edinburgh Dog and Cat Home; formerly Hon. Advisory Officer, Highlands and Islands Veterinary Services Scheme. Member: Medicine Commn, 1969-71; Poisons Bd, 1964-76. *Publications:* Diagnostic Methods in Veterinary Medicine, 1944, sixth edn, 1969; An Introduction to Veterinary Therapeutics, 1952; Editor Hoare's Veterinary Materia Medica and Therapeutics (6th edn), 1942 (jointly); many articles in veterinary and scientific jls. *Address:* 21 Cadogan Road, Edinburgh EH16 6LY.

BODDINGTON, Lewis, CBE 1956; *b* 13 Nov. 1907; *s* of James and Anne Boddington; *m* 1936, Morfydd, *d* of William Murray; no *c*. *Educ:* Lewis' Sch., Pengam; City of Cardiff Technical Coll.; University Coll. of S Wales and Monmouthshire. Pupil Engineer, Fraser & Chalmers Engineering Works, Erith, 1928-31; Asst to Major H. N. Wylie, 1931-36; Royal Aircraft Establishment, 1936; Head of Catapult Section, 1938; Supt of Design Offices, 1942-45; Head of Naval Aircraft Dept, 1945-51; Asst Dir (R&D) Naval, Min. of Supply, 1951-53; Dir Aircraft R&D (RN), 1953-59; Dir-Gen., Aircraft R&D, 1959-60; Dir and Consultant, Westland Aircraft, 1961-72. Medal of Freedom of USA (Bronze Palm), 1958. *Address:* 7 Pine House, Lingwood Close, Southampton.

BODEN, Edward Arthur; Agent-General for Saskatchewan, Canada, since 1973; *b* 13 Nov. 1911; *s* of English and Welsh parents; *m* 1939, Helen Harriet Saunders; one *s* one *d*. *Educ:* Cutknife, Saskatchewan, Canada. Born and raised on a Saskatchewan farm and actively farmed until 1949, retaining interest in farm until 1973. Royal Canadian Mounted Police, 1937-39. Saskatchewan Wheat Pool and Canadian Fedn of Agriculture, 1939-73; held several active positions in these organisations and retired, as 1st Vice-Pres., 1973; in this field acted on various provincial and national govtl bds and cttees; with others, rep. Canada at internat. agricultural confs in different parts of the world. *Recreations:* boxing, hunting. *Address:* (office) Saskatchewan House, 14-16 Cockspur Street, SW1Y 5BL. *T:* 01-930 7491; (private) Flat 3, 2 Avenue Road, NW8. *T:* 01-586 0830. *Clubs:* Farmers', East India, Devonshire, Sports and Public Schools, Belfry.

BODEN, Leonard, FRSA; portrait painter; *b* Greenock, Scotland, 1911; *s* of John Boden; *m* Margaret Tulloch (portrait painter, as Margaret Boden). *Educ:* Sedbergh; Sch. of Art, Glasgow; Heatherley Sch. of Art, London. Has exhibited at: The Royal Scottish Academy, Royal Society of Portrait Painters, etc. *Official portraits* include: HM Queen Elizabeth II, HRH The Prince Philip, Duke of Edinburgh; HH Pope Pius XII; Field Marshal Lord Milne; *work reproduced in:* The Connoisseur, The Artist, Fine Art Prints. *Address:* 27 Warwick Gardens, Kensington, W14. *Clubs:* Savage, Chelsea Arts.

BODILLY, Sir Jocelyn, Kt 1969; VRD; Chairman, Industrial Tribunals for London, since 1976; Chief Justice of the Western Pacific, 1965-75; *b* 1913. *Educ:* Munro Coll., Jamaica; Schloss Schule, Baden; Wadham Coll., Oxford. Called to Bar, Inner Temple, 1937; engaged in private practice until War; Royal Navy until 1946; RNVR, 1937-56 (Lt-Comdr (S)). High Court Judge, Sudan, 1946-55; Crown Counsel, Hong Kong, 1955, Principal Crown Counsel, 1961-65. *Address:* Vine House, Kingston Blount, Oxon. *Club:* Royal Ocean Racing.

BODLEY SCOTT, Sir Ronald, GCVO 1973 (KCVO 1964); DM; FRCP; Physician to: the Queen, 1952-73; Florence Nightingale Hospital, since 1958; King Edward VII Hospital for Officers, since 1963; King Edward VII Hospital, Midhurst, since 1965; Principal Medical Officer, Equity and Law Life Assurance Society, since 1952; Consulting Physician to: St Bartholomew's Hospital, since 1971 (Physician, 1946; Senior Physician, 1965; Member Board of Governors, 1966-71); Woolwich Memorial Hospital, since 1971 (Physician, 1936-71); British Railways (Eastern Region), since 1957; Royal Navy, since 1963; Chairman, Medicines Commission, since 1973; *b* 10 Sept. 1906; *s* of late Maitland Bodley Scott, OBE, FRCSE, and Alice Hilda Durancé George; *m* 1931, Edith Daphne, *d* of late Lt-Col E. McCarthy, RMA; two *d*. *Educ:* Marlborough Coll.; Brasenose Coll., Oxford. BA Oxon, Hons Sch. of Nat. Sci., 1928; MA, BM, BCh, Oxon, 1931; MRCP, 1933; DM Oxon, 1937; FRCP 1943. Chief Asst to Medical Unit, St Bartholomew's Hospital, 1934, Physician 1946-71; Physician, Surbiton Gen. Hosp., 1946-64. Served in Middle East, 1941-45, Lt-Col RAMC; Officer i/c Medical Div. in No 63 and No 43 Gen. Hospitals; Physician to the Household of King George VI, 1949; Hon. Consultant in haematology to the Army at Home, 1957-65; Consulting Physician, 1965-71. Lectures: Langdon Brown, RCP, 1957; Lettsomian, Medical Soc. of London, 1957; Thom Bequest Lectr, RCPE, 1965; Croonian, RCP, 1970; Harveian Orator, RCP, 1976. President: Med. Soc. of London, 1965-66, Trustee, 1972-; British Soc. for Hæmatology, 1966-67; Section of Medicine, Royal Society Med., 1967-68. Chairman: Trustees, Migraine Trust, 1971-73; Medicines Commn, 1973-75; Council, British Heart Foundn, 1975-; Member: Council, Imperial Cancer Res. Fund, 1968-; Research Grants Cttee, British Heart Foundn (Chm. 1970-); Council, RCP, 1963-66 (Censor, 1970-72, Sen. Censor and Sen. Vice-Pres., 1972); Court of Assistants, Soc. of Apothecaries of London, 1964- (Master 1974); Temporary Registration Assessment Bd, GMC, 1973-76; Treas., RSM, 1973-76; Trustee, Nuffield Medical Benefaction. Formerly Examiner in Medicine, Universities of Oxford, London, Edinburgh, Glasgow, Cairo, Singapore, to the RCP, London and Edinburgh, and to the Conjoint Board. Order of Crown of Brunei, 1970; Order of the Family, Brunei, 1973. Editor: The Medical Annual, 1959-; Price's Textbook of the Practice of Medicine. *Publications:* various papers in medical jls. *Address:* 99 New Cavendish Street, W1. *T:* 01-637 8941; Old Barn, Churchill, Oxon. *T:* Kingham 401. *Club:* Athenæum.

BODMER, Prof. Walter Fred, FRS 1974; Professor of Genetics, University of Oxford, since 1970; *b* 10 Jan. 1936; *s* of Dr Ernest Julius and Sylvia Emily Bodmer; *m* 1956, Julia Gwynaeth Pilkington; two *s* one *d*. *Educ:* Manchester Grammar Sch.; Clare Coll., Cambridge. BA 1956, MA, PhD 1959, Cambridge. Research Fellow 1958-61, Official Fellow 1961, Clare Coll., Cambridge; Demonstrator in Genetics, Univ. of Cambridge, 1960-62; Asst Prof. 1962-66, Assoc. Prof. 1966-68, Prof. 1968-70, Dept of Genetics, Stanford Univ. For. Hon. Mem., Amer. Acad. Arts and Scis, 1972. *Publications:* The Genetics of Human Populations (with L. L. Cavalli-Sforza), 1971; (with A. Jones) Our Future Inheritance: choice or chance?, 1974; (with L. L. Cavalli-Sforza) Genetics, Evolution and Man, 1976; research papers in genetical, statistical and mathematical jls, etc. *Recreations:* playing the piano, swimming. *Address:* Manor House, Mill Lane, Old Marston, Oxford.

BODMIN, Archdeacon of; see Meyer, Ven. C. J. E.

BODY, Richard Bernard; Barrister-at-law; MP (C) Holland with Boston, since 1966; *b* 18 May 1927; *s* of Lieut-Col Bernard Richard Body, formerly of Hyde End, Shinfield, Berks; *m* 1959,

Marion, *d* of late Major H. Graham, OBE; one *s* one *d*. Called to the Bar, Middle Temple, 1949. Contested (C) Rotherham, 1950; Abertillery bye-election, 1950; Leek, 1951; MP (C) Billericay Div., Essex, 1955-Sept. 1959. Chm., Open Seas Forum. *Publications:* The Architect and the Law, 1954; (contrib.) Destiny or Delusion, 1971; (ed jtly) Freedom and Stability in the World Economy, 1976. *Address:* Jewell's House, Stanford Dingley, Berks. *T:* Bradfield 295. *Club:* Carlton.

BOEGNER, Jean-Marc; Officier Légion d'Honneur; Commandeur, Ordre National du Mérite; Ambassadeur de France; *b* 3 July 1913; *s* of Marc and Jeanne Boegner; *m* 1945, Odilie de Moustier; three *d*. *Educ:* Lycée Janson-de-Sailly; Ecole Libre des Sciences Politiques; Paris University (LèsL). Joined French diplomatic service, 1939; Attaché: Berlin, 1939; Ankara, 1940; Beirut, 1941; Counsellor: Stockholm, 1945; The Hague, 1947; Ministry of Foreign Affairs, Paris, 1952-55; Minister to Pres. of Council, 1955-58; Counsellor to Charles de Gaulle, 1958-59; Ambassador to Tunisia, 1959-61; Permanent Representative of France to EEC, 1961-72. *Recreations:* music, golf. *Address:* 214 Boulevard Saint-Germain, Paris 7e, France.

BOERMA, Addeke Hendrik; Director-General, Food and Agriculture Organisation of the United Nations, 1968-75; *b* 3 April 1912; *m* 1953, Dinah Johnston; five *d*. *Educ:* Agricultural Univ., Wageningen. Netherlands Farmers' Organisation, 1935-38; Ministry of Agriculture of the Netherlands, 1938-45; Commissioner for Foreign Agricultural Relations, 1946; FAO positions: Regional Representative for Europe, 1948-51; Dir, Economics Div., 1951-58; Head of Programme and Budgetary Service, 1958-62; Asst Dir-Gen., 1960; Exec. Dir, World Food Programme, 1962-67. Holds Hon. Degrees from Univs in USA, Netherlands, Belgium, Hungary, Canada, Italy and Greece. Wateler Peace Prize, Carnegie Foundn, The Hague, 1976. Comdr, Netherlands Order of Lion; Commander, Order of Leopold II, Belgium; Officer, Ordre Mérite Agricole, France; Cavaliere di Gran Crose (Italy). *Address:* Via Erodoto 11, Casalpalocco, Rome, Italy.

BOEVEY, Sir Thomas (Michael Blake) C.; *see* Crawley-Boevey.

BOGARDE, Dirk; *see* Van den Bogaerde, D. N.

BOGDANOVICH, Peter; director, producer, writer, actor; President: Saticoy Productions; Copa de Oro Productions; *b* Kingston, NY, 30 July; *s* of Borislav Bogdanovich and Herma Robinson; *m* Polly Platt (marr. diss.); two *d*. *Educ:* Collegiate Sch., New York; Stella Adler Theatre Studio. *Theatre:* Actor, NY Shakespeare Fest., Amer. Shakespeare Fest., and others; also television, 1955-58; Dir-Prod., The Big Knife, off-Broadway revival, 1959; Artistic Dir, Phoenicia Playhouse, NY, and dir revivals of Camino Real, Ten Little Indians, Rocket to the Moon, etc., 1961; Dir-co-prod., Once in a Lifetime, off-Broadway revival, 1964. *Films, TV, etc:* Second unit director-writer, The Wild Angels, 1966; filmed TV interview, The Great Professional: Howard Hawks Talks with Peter Bogdanovich, BBC-TV, 1967; Dir-prod.-writer-actor, Targets, 1968; Dir-writer, The Last Picture Show, 1971; Dir-writer, Directed by John Ford, documentary with film clips from Ford's movies, interviews with John Wayne, James Stewart, Henry Fonda, John Ford, 1971; Dir-prod., What's Up, Doc?, 1972; Paper Moon, 1973; Daisy Miller, 1974; Dir-prod.-writer, At Long Last Love, 1975; Dir-writer, Nickelodeon, 1976. Moving picture critic and feature writer, 1958-68. *Publications:* John Ford, 1968; Fritz Lang in America, 1969; Allan Dwan: the last pioneer, 1971; Pieces of Time, 1973 (Picture Shows, Eng., 1975); monographs on Cinema of: Orson Welles, 1961; Howard Hawks, 1962; Alfred Hitchcock, 1963; articles in Esquire, NY Times, Variety, Village Voice, Movie, Cahiers du Cinéma, New York, Film Culture, Film Qly, Vogue, Saturday Evening Post, etc. *Address:* 8899 Beverly Boulevard, Los Angeles, Calif 90048, USA.

BOGGIS-ROLFE, Hume, CB 1971; CBE 1962; farmer; *b* 20 Oct. 1911; *s* of Douglass Horace Boggis-Rolfe and Maria Maud (*née* Bailey); *m* 1941, Anne Dorothea, *e d* of Capt. Eric Noble, Henley-on-Thames; two *s* one *d*. *Educ:* Westminster Sch.; Freiburg Univ.; Trinity Coll., Cambridge. Called to Bar, Middle Temple, 1935. Army, Intelligence Corps, 1939-46 (Lieut-Col). Private Sec. to Lord Chancellor, 1949-50; Asst Solicitor in Lord Chancellor's Office, 1951-65; Sec. to Law Commn, 1965-68; Deputy Clerk of the Crown in Chancery, 1968-75, and Deputy Secretary, Lord Chancellor's Office, 1970-75. Master, Merchant Taylors' Co., 1971-72. *Recreations:* gardening, travelling. *Address:* 22 Victoria Square, SW1W 0RB. *T:* 01-834 2676; The Grange, Wormingford, Colchester, Essex. *T:* Bures 227303. *Club:* Athenæum.

BOGGON, Roland Hodgson, MS, MB London; FRCS, LRCP; *b* 11 Aug. 1903; *s* of late Richard Octavius Boggon, OBE, Civil Servant; *m* 1932, Mollie Daphne, *d* of T. H. Newall; one *s* one *d*. *Educ:* St Paul's Sch. Retired as Consulting Surg. to St Thomas' Hospital, London. Mem. Court of Examiners of the Royal College of Surgeons; Examiner in Surgery, Univ. of London. *Publications:* numerous medical. *Recreation:* gardening. *Address:* 1 Beauvale Close, Ottery St Mary, Devon EX11 1ED.

BOGLE, David Blyth, CBE 1967; formerly Senior Partner, Lindsays, WS, Edinburgh; Member of Council on Tribunals, 1958-70, and Chairman of Scottish Committee, 1962-70; *b* 22 Jan. 1903; *s* of late Very Rev. Andrew Nisbet Bogle, DD and Helen Milne Bogle; *m* 1955, Ruth Agnes Thorley. *Educ:* George Watson's Coll., Edinburgh; Edinburgh Univ. (LLB). Writer to the Signet, 1927. Commissioned in the Queen's Own Cameron Highlanders, 1940, and served in UK and Middle East, 1942-45; demobilised, with rank of Major, 1945. *Recreations:* golf, curling, stalking. *Address:* Hartwood House, West Calder, Midlothian. *T:* West Calder 248. *Club:* New (Edinburgh).

BOHEMAN, Erik, Order of the Seraphim; Grand Cross, Order of Vasa; KBE (hon.) 1948; Swedish diplomat; Chairman, Swedish Match Co., since 1973; Director of companies; *b* 19 Jan. 1895; *s* of Carl Boheman and Ellen Abramson; *m* 1932, Margaret Mattsson; two *s* two *d*. *Educ:* Stockholm Univ. Lieut 4th Hussars, 1915; entered Foreign Service, 1918, served at legations in Paris and London, 1918-19: Sec., Councillor and Director. Political Dept, Foreign Office, Stockholm, 1919-31; Minister to Ankara and Athens, 1931-34, to Warsaw, 1934-37; Sec. Gen., Foreign Office, 1938-45; Minister to Paris, 1945-47, to London, 1947; Ambassador to London, 1947-48; Ambassador to Washington, 1948-58. Attended council meetings and assemblies, League of Nations, as Sec. and Deleg., 1920-32. Conducted negotiations for commercial treaties with several countries. Headed Swedish Delegation for War Trade Agreements with Gt Britain during War of 1939-45; Deleg. to Gen. Assembly of UN, 1949-50, 1960-62. Mem of Swedish Parliament (First Chamber) for City of Gothenburg, 1959-70; Speaker of First Chamber, 1965-70. Grand Cross: Order of Danish Dannebrog; Finnish White Rose; Grand Officer, Legion of Honour (France). *Publications:* På Vakt (memoires), 3 vols, 1963-68. *Recreations:* travelling, farming, golf. *Address:* Anneberg, Gränna, Sweden.

BOHM, Prof. David (Joseph), PhD; Professor of Theoretical Physics, Birkbeck College, University of London, since 1961; *b* 20 Dec. 1917; *s* of Samuel and Freda Bohm; *m* 1956, Sarah Woolfson; no *c*. *Educ:* Pa State Coll. (BS); University of Calif (PhD). Research Physicist, University of Calif, Radiation Laboratory, 1943-47; Asst Prof., Princeton Univ., 1947-51; Prof., University de São Paulo, Brazil, 1951-55; Prof., Technion, Haifa, Israel, 1955-57; Research Fellow, Bristol Univ., 1957-61. *Publications:* Quantum Theory, 1951; Causality and Chance in Modern Physics, 1957; one chapter in Observation and Interpretation, 1957; Special Theory of Relativity, 1965; various papers in Physical Review, Nuovo Cimento, Progress of Theoretical Physics, British Jl for Philosophy of Science, etc. *Recreations:* walking, conversation, music (listener), art (viewer). *Address:* Physics Department, Birkbeck College, Malet Street, WC1.

BOHR, Prof. Aage Niels, DSc,DrPhil; physicist, Denmark; Professor of Physics, Univ. of Copenhagen, since 1956; Director, Nordita, since 1975 (Director, Niels Bohr Institute, 1962-70); *b* Copenhagen, 19 June 1922; *s* of Prof. Niels Bohr and Margrethe Nørlund; *m* Marietta Bettina (*née* Soffer); two *s* one *d*. *Educ:* Univ. of Copenhagen. Associate, Dept of Scientific and Industrial Research, London, 1943-45; Research Asst, Inst. of Theoretical Physics, Copenhagen, 1946. Member: Danish Acad. of Science; Nat. Acad. of Sciences, USA; Amer. Acad. of Arts and Sciences; Norwegian and Swedish Acads of Science; Amer. Philosophical Soc. Awards: Dannie Heineman Prize, 1960; Pius XI Medal, 1963; Atoms for Peace Award, 1969; Ørsted Medal, 1970; Rutherford Medal, 1972; John Price Wetherill Medal, 1974; (jointly) Nobel Prize for Physics, 1975; Rømer Medal, 1976. *Publications:* Rotational States of Atomic Nuclei, 1954; (with Ben R. Mottelson) Nuclear Structure, vol. I, 1969, vol. II 1975. *Address:* Granhøjen 10, Hellerup, Copenhagen, Denmark. *T:* 650346.

BOILEAU, Sir Gilbert George Benson, 6th Bt, *cr* 1838; MOH for City of Dandenong; *b* 13 Feb. 1898; *e s* of Sir Francis James Boileau, 5th Bt; *S* father 1945; *m* 1st, 1924, Chica Patricia, *d* of late J. L. Edgeworth-Somers; two *d*; 2nd, 1941, Mary Catherine, *d* of late Lawrence Riordan; three *d*. *Educ:* Xavier Coll., Kew, Vic; Newman Coll., University of Melbourne. MB, BS, Melbourne 1923. Service with rank of Major, 1940-44, AAMC

Australian Military Forces, now on Reserve. *Recreation:* Turf. *Heir: b* Edmond Charles Boileau, Capt. AIF [*b* 28 May 1903; *m* 1933, Marjorie, *d* of late C. M. D'Arcy, Launceston, Tasmania; two *s*]. *Address:* Minto Lodge, 1480 Heatherton Road, Dandenong, Vic 3175, Australia. *T:* 792 2853. *Clubs:* Athenæum, Naval and Military, Savage (Melbourne).

BOK, Derek Curtis; President, Harvard University, since 1971, Professor of Law, since 1961; *b* 22 March 1930, Bryn Mawr, Pa; *s* of late Curtis and of Margaret Plummer Bok (now Mrs William S. Kiskadden); *m* 1955, Sissela Ann Myrdal, *d* of Karl Gunnar and Alva Myrdal, *qqv*; one *s* two *d*. *Educ:* Stanford Univ., BA; Harvard Univ., LLB; Inst. of Political Science, Univ. of Paris (Fulbright Scholar); George Washington Univ., MA in Economics. Served AUS, 1956-58. Asst Prof. of Law, Harvard Univ., 1958-61, Dean of Law Sch., 1968-71. *Publications:* The First Three Years of the Schuman Plan, 1955; (ed with Archibald Cox) Cases and Materials on Labor Law, 5th edn 1962, 6th edn 1965, 7th edn 1969; (with John Dunlop) Labor in the American Community, 1970. *Recreations:* gardening, tennis, skiing. *Address:* Office of the President, Harvard University, Cambridge, Mass 02138, USA.

BOLAND, Bridget; author; *b* 13 March 1913; *d* of late John Boland. *Educ:* Sacred Heart Convent, Roehampton; Oxford Univ. (BA 1935). Screenwriter 1937-; numerous films. Served War, 1941-46, in ATS; Senior Comdr. Stage plays: Abca Play Unit productions, 1946; Cockpit, 1948; The Damascus Blade, 1950; Temple Folly, 1952; The Return, 1953; The Prisoner, 1954 (adapted film version, 1955); Gordon, 1961; The Zodiac in the Establishment, 1963; Time out of Mind, 1970. *Publications: novels:* The Wild Geese, 1938; Portrait of a Lady in Love, 1942; Caterina, 1975; *non -fiction:* (with M. Boland) Old Wives' Lore for Gardeners, 1976; Gardener's Magic and Other Old Wives' Lore, 1977. *Address:* Bolands, Hewshott Lane, Liphook, Hants.

BOLAND, Frederick Henry; former Irish diplomat; Director, Arthur Guinness Son & Co. and other companies; Chancellor, Dublin University; *b* 1904; 2nd *s* of Henry Patrick Boland and Charlotte (*née* Nolan), Dublin; *m* 1935, Frances Kelly, Drogheda; one *s* four *d*. *Educ:* Clongowes Wood Coll.; Trinity Coll., Dublin; King's Inns, Dublin. BA; LLB 1925; LLD (jure dignitatis), 1950. University Studentship in Classics, TCD, 1925; Rockefeller Research Fellowship in Social Sciences (Harvard and University of Chicago), 1926-28; 3rd Sec., Dept of External Affairs, 1929; 1st Sec., Paris, 1932; Principal Officer Dept of Industry and Commerce, 1936; Dept of External Affairs: Asst Sec., 1938; Permanent Sec., 1946; Irish rep., Cttee on European Economic Co-operation, Paris, 1947; Irish Ambassador to the Court of St James's, 1950-56; Permanent Representative of Eire at UN, 1956-63 (Pres., 1960); Irish Representative UN Security Council, 1962-63. Member: Cttee on Seasonal Migration, 1936; Cttee on Design in Industry, 1938; Royal Irish Acad. Pres., Coll. Historical Soc., TCD. Knight Comdr, Order of St Gregory the Great, 1948; Grand Cross, Order of the North Star of Sweden, 1950. *Recreations:* reading, piano, fishing. *Address:* 60 Ailesbury Road, Dublin, Eire. *T:* Dublin 693599. *Clubs:* Stephens Green; Royal Irish Yacht.

BOLES, Sir Jeremy John Fortescue, 3rd Bt, *cr* 1922; *b* 9 Jan. 1932; *s* of Sir Gerald Fortescue Boles, 2nd Bt, and Violet Blanche (*d* 1974), *er d* of late Major Hall Parlby, Manadon, Crown Hill, S Devon; *S* father 1945; *m* 1st, 1955, Dorothy Jane (marr. diss. 1970), *yr d* of James Alexander Worswick; two *s* one *d*; 2nd, 1970, Elisabeth Gildroy, *yr d* of Edward Phillip Shaw; one *d*. *Heir: s* Richard Fortescue Boles, *b* 12 Dec. 1958. *Address:* Lime House, Tilford, Farnham, Surrey.

BOLES, John Dennis, MBE 1960; Director General of the National Trust, since 1975; *b* 25 June 1925; *s* of late Comdr Geoffrey Coleridge Boles and Hilda Frances (*née* Crofton); *m* 1st, Benita (*née* Wormald) (*d* 1969); two *s* three *d*; 2nd, 1971, Lady Anne Hermione, *d* of 12th Earl Waldegrave, *qv*. *Educ:* Winchester Coll. Rifle Brigade, 1943-46. Colonial Administrative Service (later Overseas Civil Service), North Borneo (now Sabah), 1948-64; Asst Sec., National Trust, 1965, Sec., 1968. *Address:* The Old Rectory, Englefield, near Reading, Berks. *T:* Reading 302497. *Club:* Travellers'.

BOLINGBROKE and ST JOHN, 7th Viscount *cr* 1712; **Kenneth Oliver Musgrave St John;** Bt 1611; Baron St John of Lydiard Tregoze, 1712; Viscount St John and Baron St John of Battersea, 1716; *b* 22 March 1927; *s* of Geoffrey Robert St John, MC (*d* 1972) and Katherine Mary (*d* 1958), *d* of late A. S. J. Musgrave; *S* cousin, 1974; *m* 1st, 1953, Patricia Mary McKenna (marr. diss. 1972); one *s*; 2nd, 1972, Jainey Anne McRae; two *s*. *Educ:* Eton; Geneva Univ. Chairman, A&P Gp of Cos, 1958-75; Director: Shaw Savill Holidays Pty Ltd; Bolingbroke and Partners Ltd;

Wata Investment Inc., Panama. Pres., Travel Agents Assoc. of NZ, 1966-68; Dir, World Assoc. of Travel Agencies, 1966-75; Chm., Aust. Council of Tour Wholesalers, 1972-75. Fellow, Aust. Inst. of Travel; Mem., NZ Inst. of Travel. *Recreations:* golf, cricket, tennis, history. *Heir: s* Hon. Henry Fitzroy St John, *b* 18 May 1957. *Address:* PO Box 211, Christchurch, New Zealand; Andover Street, Christchurch, New Zealand. *Clubs:* Bath; Christchurch (Christchurch, NZ).

BOLITHO, Major Simon Edward, MC 1945; JP; Director: Barclays Bank, 1959 (Local Director, Penzance, 1953); English China Clays; Vice-Lord-Lieutenant of Cornwall, since 1970; *b* 13 March 1916; *s* of late Lieut-Col Sir Edward Bolitho, KBE, CB, DSO; *m* 1953, Elizabeth Margaret, *d* of late Rear-Adm. G. H. Creswell, CB, DSO, DSC; two *s* two *d*. *Educ:* Royal Naval Coll., Dartmouth; RMC Sandhurst. Grenadier Guards, 1936-49; Lt-Col, DCLI, 1957-60. DL Cornwall, 1964; High Sheriff of Cornwall, 1956-57; JP 1959; CC 1953-67. *Recreations:* shooting, fishing, hunting, sailing. *Address:* Trengwainton, Penzance, Cornwall. *T:* Penzance 3106. *Clubs:* Pratt's, MCC, Royal Yacht Squadron.

BÖLL, Heinrich Theodor; author; *b* Cologne, 21 Dec. 1917; *s* of Victor Böll and Maria Hermanns; *m* 1942, Annemarie Cech; three *s*. *Educ:* Gymnasium, Cologne; Univ. of Cologne. Member: German Acad. for Language and Poetry; Bavarian Acad. Fine Arts; Hon. Mem., Union of German Translators. Pres., Internat. PEN, 1971-74; a Founder, World Producers Union, 1970; Mem., Gruppe 47, 1950-. Hon. DSc Aston, 1973; Hon. DTech Brunel, 1973; Hon. LittD TCD, 1973. Winner of numerous prizes and awards, incl. Nobel Prize for Literature, 1972. *Publications:* Der Zug war Pünktlich, 1949 (The Train was on Time, UK, 1967); Wanderer, kommst du nach Spa..., 1950; Wo warst du, Adam?, 1951 (And Where Were You, Adam?, UK, 1975); Die schwarzen Schafe, 1951; Nicht nur zur Weihnachtszeit, 1952; Und sagte kein einziges Wort, 1953 (Acquainted with the Night, UK, 1954); Haus ohne Hüter, 1954 (The Unguarded House, UK, 1957); Die Waage der Baleks, 1954; Dr Murkes gesammeltes Schweigen und andere Satiren, 1955; Das Brot der frühen Jahre, 1955 (The Bread of those Early Years, 1977); So ward Abend und Morgen, 1955; Unbenehenbare Gäste; Heitere Erzählungen, 1956; Im Tal der donnernden Hufe, 1957; Irisches Tagebuch, 1957; Der Bahnhof von Zimpren, 1958; Abenteuer eines Brotbeutels, und andere Geschichten, 1958; Brief an einen jungen Katholiken, 1958; Billard um Halbzehn, 1959 (Billiards at Half Past Nine, UK, 1965); Als der Krieg ausbrach, 1961; Als der Krieg zu Ende war, 1962; Anekdote zur Senkung der Arbeitsmoral, 1963; Erzählungen, Hörspiele, Aufsätze, 1961; Ein Schluck Erde (play), 1962; Ansichten eines Clowns, 1963 (The Clown, UK, 1965); Entfernung von der Truppe, 1964 (Absent Without Leave, UK, 1967); Frankfurter Vorlesungen, 1966; Ende einer Dienstfahrt, 1966 (End of a Mission, UK, 1968); Aufsätze, Kritiken, Reden, 1967; Veränderung in Staech, 1969; Hausfriedensbruch, 1970; Aussatz (play), 1970; Gruppenbild mit Dame, 1971 (Group Portrait with a Lady, UK, 1973); Erzählungen 1950-1970, 1972; Neue politische und literarische Schriften, 1973; Gedichte, 1973; Die velorene Ehre der Katharina Blum, 1974 (The Lost Honour of Katharina Blum, UK, 1975); Neue politische und literarische Schriften, 1975; Berichte zur Gesinnungslage der Nation, 1975; Einmischung erwünscht, 1977; radio plays, translations, etc. *Address:* 5 Köln 1, Hülchrather Strasse 7, Federal Republic of Germany.

BOLLAND, Edwin, CMG 1971; HM Diplomatic Service; Head of British Delegation to Negotiations on Mutual Reductions of Forces and Armaments and Associated Measures in Central Europe, since 1976; *b* 20 Oct. 1922; *m* 1948, Winifred Mellor; one *s* three *d* (and one *s* decd). *Educ:* Morley Grammar Sch.; University Coll., Oxford. Served in Armed Forces, 1942-45. Foreign Office, 1947; Head of Far Eastern Dept, FO, 1965-67; Counsellor, Washington, 1967-71; St Antony's Coll., Oxford, 1971-72; Ambassador to Bulgaria, 1973-76. *Recreation:* gardening. *Address: c/o* Foreign and Commonwealth Office, SW1; Lord's Spring Cottage, Godden Green, Sevenoaks, Kent. *T:* Sevenoaks 61105.

BOLLAND, Group Captain Guy Alfred, CBE 1943; Chief Intelligence Officer, BJSM (AFS), Washington, USA, 1956-59, retired; *b* 5 Nov. 1909; 3rd *s* of late Capt. L. W. Bolland; *m* 1935, Sylvia Marguerite, 2nd *d* of late Oswald Duke, Cambridge; one *s* three *d*. *Educ:* Gilbert Hannam Sch., Sussex. Commissioned RAF, 1930. Served in Iraq and Home Squadrons. Served War of 1939-45: commanded 217 Squadron during attacks on French ports, 1940; North African Operations, 1943 (despatches, CBE). *Recreation:* golf. *Address:* The Oaks, Shaftesbury Road, Woking, Surrey. *T:* Woking 60548.

BOLLAND, John; His Honour Judge Bolland; a Circuit Judge since 1974; *b* 30 March 1920; *s* of late Dominic Gerald Bolland and Gladys Bolland; *m* 1947, Audrey Jean Toyne (*née* Pearson); one *s* one step *s* one step *d. Educ:* Malvern Coll.; Trinity Hall, Cambridge (BA). Commnd Royal Warwicks Regt, 1939; 2nd Bn 6th Gurkha Rifles, 1941-46. Called to Bar, Middle Temple, 1948. *Recreations:* cricket, Rugby, golf, theatre. *Address:* 144 Old Fort Road, Shoreham-by-Sea, Sussex. *T:* Shoreham-by-Sea 3877.

BOLLERS, Hon. Sir Harold (Brodie Smith), Kt 1969; Chief Justice of Guyana, since 1966; *b* 5 Feb. 1915; *s* of late John Bollers; *m* 1st, 1951, Irene Mahadeo (*d* 1965); two *s* one *d*; 2nd, 1968, Eileen Hanoman; one *s. Educ:* Queen's Coll., Guyana; King's Coll., London; Middle Temple. Called to the Bar, Feb. 1938; Magistrate, Guyana, 1946, Senior Magistrate, 1959; Puisne Judge, Guyana, 1960. *Recreations:* reading, walking. *Address:* Chief Justice's Residence, 245 Vlissengen Road, Georgetown, Guyana. *T:* 5204. *Club:* Royal Commonwealth Society (West Indian).

BOLS, Hon. Maj.-Gen. Eric Louis, CB 1945; DSO 1944, and bar 1945; *b* 8 June 1904; *s* of Lt-Gen. Sir Louis Bols, KCB, KCMG, DSO; *m* 1st, 1930, Rosa Vaux (marr. diss., 1947); one *s*; 2nd, 1948, Marion du Plessis (marr. diss., 1965); 3rd, 1967, Barbara Brown. *Educ:* Wellington Coll.; Royal Military Coll., Sandhurst. 2nd Lieut Devonshire Regt 1924; Capt The King's Regt 1935; Major, 1940; Temp. Lieut-Col 1941; Temp Col 1944; Temp. Brig. 1944; Temp. Maj.-Gen. and War Subs. Col 1945; Comdr 6th Airborne Div., 1945; retd pay, 1948. War Service in Ceylon, UK, and NW Europe. *Address:* Stone Cottage, Peppering Eye, near Battle, East Sussex.

BOLSOVER, George Henry, CBE 1970 (OBE 1947); Director, School of Slavonic and East European Studies, University of London, 1947-76; *b* 18 Nov. 1910; *yr s* of Ernest and Mary Bolsover; *m* 1939, Stephanie Kállai; one *d. Educ:* Leigh Grammar Sch.; Univ. of Liverpool; Univ. of London. BA 1931, MA (Liverpool), PhD (London), 1933. Univ. of Birmingham, Resident Tutor in Adult Education in Worcs, 1937-38; Asst Lectr in Modern European History, Univ. of Manchester, 1938-43; Attaché and First Sec., HM Embassy, Moscow, 1943-47; Mem. of Editorial Board, Slavonic and East European Review, 1947-63, and Chm., 1958-63; Member: UGC Sub-Cttee on Oriental, African, Slavonic and East European Studies, 1961-71; Treasury Cttee for Studentships in Foreign Languages and Cultures, 1948-58; Inst. of Historical Res. Cttee, 1948-75; Adv. Cttee on Educn of Poles in Gt Britain, 1948-67; Ct of Govs of London Sch. of Economics and Political Science, 1955-77; Council and Exec. Cttee of St Bartholomew's Med. Coll., 1962-76; Council of Royal Dental Hosp. London Sch. of Dental Surgery, 1966-; Min. of Educn Cttee on Teaching of Russian, 1960-62; Senior Treasurer of University of London Union, 1958-77; Chm., Tutorial Classes Cttee of Council for Extra-Mural Studies of Univ. of London, 1965-76; Chm., Council for Extra-Mural Studies, 1968-76; Treas., British Nat. Historical Cttee, 1966-72; Mem. Governing Body, GB/East Europe Centre, 1967-77. *Publications:* essays in: Essays presented to Sir Lewis Namier, 1956, Transactions of Royal Historical Society, 1957; articles in English Historical Review, Journal of Modern History, Slavonic and East European Review, International Affairs, etc. *Recreations:* music, travel. *Address:* 7 Devonshire Road, Hatch End, Mddx. *T:* 01-428 4282.

BOLT, Rear-Adm. Arthur Seymour, CB 1958; DSO 1951; DSC 1940 and bar 1941; *b* 26 Nov. 1907; *s* of Charles W. Bolt, Alverstoke, Hants; *m* 1933, Evelyn Mary June, *d* of Robert Ellis, Wakefield, Yorks; four *d. Educ:* Nautical Coll., Pangbourne; RN Coll., Dartmouth. Joined RN, 1923. Served War of 1939-45; HMS Glorious and Warspite (DSC and Bar), and at Admiralty. Capt. HMS Theseus (Korea), 1949-51; Dir Naval Air Warfare, Admty, 1951-53; Chief of Staff to Flag Officer Air (Home), 1954-56; Dep. Controller of Military Aircraft, Min. of Supply, 1957-60; retd Capt. 1947; Rear-Adm. 1956. *Recreations:* tennis, squash, sailing. *Address:* Dolphins, Derby Road, Haslemere, Surrey. *T:* Haslemere 4410. *Clubs:* Junior Carlton; Royal Naval and Royal Albert Yacht (Portsmouth); Royal Naval Sailing Association; Royal Dart Yacht; Junior Offshore Group; Bosham Sailing.

BOLT, Air Marshal Richard Bruce, CB 1977; CBE 1973; DFC 1945; AFC 1959; Chief of Defence Staff, New Zealand, since 1976; *b* 16 July 1923; *s* of George Bruce Bolt and Mary (*née* Best); *m* 1946, June Catherine South; one *s* one *d. Educ:* Nelson Coll., NZ. Began service with RNZAF in mid 1942; served during 2nd World War in RAF Bomber Command (Pathfinder Force); Chief of Air Staff, NZ, 1974-76. *Recreations:* fly fishing, golf. *Address:* 12 Monaghan Avenue, Karori, Wellington, NZ. *Club:* Wellington (Wellington, NZ).

BOLT, Robert Oxton, CBE 1972; playwright; *b* 15 Aug. 1924; *s* of Ralph Bolt and Leah Binnion; *m* 1st, 1949, Celia Ann Roberts (marr. diss., 1967); one *s* two *d*; 2nd, 1967, Sarah Miles (marr. diss. 1976); one *s. Educ:* Manchester Grammar Sch. Left sch., 1941; Sun Life Assurance Office, Manchester, 1942; Manchester Univ., 1943; RAF and Army, 1943-46; Manchester Univ., 1946-49; Exeter Univ., 1949-50; teaching, 1950-58; English teacher, Millfield Sch., 1952-58. Author of plays: Flowering Cherry, produced Haymarket, 1958; A Man for All Seasons, prod Globe, 1960 (filmed 1967); The Tiger and The Horse, prod Queen's, 1960; Gentle Jack, prod Queen's, 1963; The Thwarting of Baron Bolligrew, 1966; Vivat! Vivat Regina! prod Piccadilly, 1970; State of Revolution, prod Nat. Theatre, 1977. Has also had produced: The Critic and the Heart, Oxford Playhouse, 1957; several radio plays and one play on TV; screenplays: Lawrence of Arabia, 1962; Dr Zhivago, 1965 (Academy Award); Man for all Seasons, 1967 (Academy Award); Ryan's Daughter, 1970; Lady Caroline Lamb, 1972 (also dir.). *Address:* c/o Margaret Ramsay Ltd, 14a Goodwins Court, St Martin's Lane, WC2. *Club:* The Spares (Somerset) (Hon. Life Mem.).

BOLTE, Dame Edith (Lilian), (Lady Bolte), DBE 1973 (CBE 1959); *d* of D. F. M. Elder; *m* 1934, Hon. Sir Henry E. Bolte, *qv.* Mem., State Council, Girl Guide Movement, Victoria. *Recreations:* tennis, golf. *Address:* Kialla, Meredith, Vic 3333, Australia. *Clubs:* Alexandra, Royal Commonwealth Society, Liberal Women's, Victoria League.

BOLTE, Hon. Sir Henry (Edward), GCMG 1972 (KCMG 1966); MLA; Premier and Treasurer of the State of Victoria, Australia, 1955-72; *b* Skipton, Victoria, 20 May 1908; *s* of J. H. Bolte; *m* 1934, Edith Lilian (*see* Dame Edith Bolte). *Educ:* Skipton State Sch.; Ballarat C of E Grammar Sch. Grazier, with sheep property near Meredith in western district of Victoria. Entered Parliament as MLA for Hampden, 1947; Minister of: Water Supply and Mines, 1948-50; Soil Conservation, 1949-50; Water Supply and Soil Conservation, 1950; Leader of Liberal Party (formerly Liberal and Country Party), 1953-72 (Dep. Leader, Nov. 1950-53). Freedom, City of Melbourne, 1975. Hon. LLD: Melbourne Univ., 1965; Monash Univ., 1967. *Recreations:* golf, shooting, turf. *Address:* Kialla, Meredith, Victoria 3333, Australia. *Clubs:* Australian, Athenæum (Melbourne).

BOLTON, 7th Baron, *cr* 1797; **Richard William Algar Orde-Powlett,** JP; *b* 11 July 1929; *s* of 6th Baron Bolton; *S* father, 1963; *m* 1951, Hon. Christine Helena Weld Forester, *e d* of 7th Baron Forester, and of Marie Louise Priscilla, CStJ, *d* of Sir Herbert Perrott, 6th Bt, CH, CB; two *s* one *d. Educ:* Eton; Trinity Coll., Cambridge (BA). Chairman, Richmond Div., Conservative Assoc., 1957-60; Chairman Yorkshire Div., Royal Forestry Soc., 1962-64; Member Council, Timber Growers' Organization. Chm., Waterers Group; Director, Yorkshire General Life Co. JP, North Riding of Yorkshire, 1957. FRICS. *Recreations:* shooting, fishing. *Heir:* *s* Hon. Harry Algar Nigel Orde-Powlett, *b* 14 Feb. 1954. *Address:* Bolton Hall, Leyburn, North Yorkshire. *T:* Leyburn 2303. *Clubs:* White's; Central African Deep Sea Fishing.

BOLTON, Sir Frederic (Bernard), Kt 1976; MC; FIMarE; FCIB; Chairman, The Bolton Group, since 1953; Chairman or Director of other companies (subsidiaries); *b* 9 March 1921; *s* of late Louis Hamilton Bolton and of Beryl Bolton; *m* 1st, 1950, Valerie Margaret Barwick (decd); two *s*; 2nd, 1971, Vanessa Mary Anne Robarts; two *s* two *d. Educ:* Rugby. Served War, with Welsh Guards, 1940-46 (MC 1945, Italy), Major. Northants Yeomanry, 1952-56 (Major). Member: Lloyd's, 1945-; Baltic Exchange, 1946-. Chm., Atlantic Steam Nav. Co. & Subs, 1960-71; Dir, Associated Humber Lines Ltd, 1963 (Chm. 1967-72); Dir, B.P. Tanker Co., 1968-; Mem., Brit. Rail Shipping & Int. Services Bd, 1970-. Pres., Chamber of Shipping of UK, 1966 (Mem. Council, 1954-, and Chm. of various cttees); Mem., Lloyd's Register of Shipping Gen. Cttee, 1961-; Mem. Council, Brit. Ship Research Assoc., 1958, and Chm. Shipowners' Cttee, 1964-66 and 1967-72; Chairman: London Deep Sea Tramp Shipowners' Assoc., 1956-57; Ship & Marine Technol. Requirements Bd, 1977-; Member: Dover Harbour Bd, 1957-62; London General Shipowners' Soc., 1959- (Chm. 1972-74); PLA, 1964-71; Nat. Ports Council, 1967-74 (Chm. Research Cttee, 1970-74); Pres., Inst. of Marine Engineers, 1968-69 and 1969-70; President: British Shipping Fedn, 1972-75; Internat. Shipping Fedn, 1973-; Gen. Council of British Shipping, 1975-76. Grafton Hunt: Jt Master, 1956-67, Chm., 1967-72. *Recreations:* country sports. *Address:* Pudlicote, near Charlbury, Oxon OX7 3HX. *Club:* City of London.

BOLTON, Col Geoffrey George Hargreaves, CBE 1960 (MBE 1946); MC 1916; DL; Chairman, North Western Division, National Coal Board, 1951-60 (Marketing Director, 1946-49,

Deputy Chairman, 1950-51); *b* 5 Aug. 1894; 4th and *o surv. s* of late Henry Hargreaves Bolton, MBE, Newchurch-in-Rossendale, Lancs; *m* 1st, 1919, Ethel (*d* 1942), 2nd *d* of late Rev. James Robinson, Broughton, Preston; one *s* one *d* (and one *s* decd); 2nd, 1943, Margaret, *y d* of late Rev. James Robinson. *Educ:* Clifton Coll., Bristol. Served European War, 1914-18, East Lancs Regt (Gallipoli, Sinai, France); Comd East Lancs Regt TA, 1920-28 (retired 1928). Associated with Coal Industry, 1912-; Dir, Hargreaves Collieries Ltd, 1932-46; Exec. Officer, Lancashire Associated Collieries, 1935-46. DL 1935, JP 1935, Lancaster; High Sheriff, Lancashire, 1962-63. KStJ 1969. *Address:* Fairfield House, Chatburn, Clitheroe, Lancs BB7 4BB. *T:* Clitheroe 41335.

BOLTON, Sir George (Lewis French), KCMG 1950; Hon. Pres., Bank of London and South America since 1970 (Chairman, 1957-70); Chairman: London United Investments Ltd, since 1971; Commonwealth Development Finance Co., since 1968; Premier Consolidated Oilfields, 1974-76; Deputy Chairman, Lonrho, since 1973; *b* 16 Oct. 1900; *s* of William and Beatrice Bolton; *m* 1928, May, *er d* of Charles and Amelia Howcroft; one *s* two *d.* Helbert, Wagg & Co. Ltd, 1920; Bank of England to assist in management of Exchange Equalisation Funds, 1933; Tripartite Monetary Agreement, 1936; Adviser to Bank of England, 1941-48; Exec. Director, 1948-57; Director, Bank for Internat. Settlements, 1949-57; UK Alternate Governor of Internat. Monetary Fund, 1952-57 (UK Exec. Director, 1946-52). Director, Bank of England, 1948-68. Director: Sun Life Assurance Co. of Canada (UK) Ltd; Canadian Pacific Steamships Ltd; Canadian Pacific Oil & Gas of Canada Ltd. Sheriff of the County of London, 1952 and 1961. Gran Oficial de la Orden de Mayo (Argentina), 1960; Orden del Merito (Chile), 1965. *Publication:* A Banker's World, 1970. *Recreations:* reading, gardening. *Address:* Pollards Cross, Hempstead, near Saffron Walden, Essex. *T:* Radwinter 270.

BOLTON, Guy; Playwright; *b* Broxbourne, Herts, 23 Nov. 1884; *o s* of Reginald Pelham Bolton and Katherine Behenna; *m* 1st, Julia Currie; one *s* one *d* ; 2nd, Marguerite Namara; one *s* one *d* ; *m* Virginia De Lanty. *Educ:* Private tutors; Ecole des Beaux Arts. Started life as an architect practising in NY City; engaged by War Dept for special work on the rebuilding of West Point; concurrently wrote magazine stories, the first being published when the writer was 19; in 1913, started career as a playwright and is the author of more than fifty plays and musical comedies; among these are: Polly-with-a-Past, Sally, Kissing-Time, The Dark Angel, Tiptoes, Lady Be Good, Polly Preferred, Oh Boy, Song of the Drum, Anything Goes, Who's Who, Seeing Stars, Swing Along, This'll Make You Whistle, Going Greek, The Fleet's Lit Up, Magyar Melody, Hold On To Your Hats, Follow the Girls, Don't Listen Ladies, Larger than Life (adapted from W. Somerset Maugham's Theatre), The Shelley Story, Music at Midnight, Anastasia, Child of Fortune, Guardian Angel, Fireworks in the Sun. Author of films: Transatlantic, The Love Parade, Words and Music, 'Til the Clouds Roll By, Weekend at the Waldorf, A Man and his Wife, Jennie Kissed Me, Very Good Eddie. *Publications:* (joint autobiography with P. G. Wodehouse) Bring on the Girls, 1954; The Olympians (novel); 1961; The Enchantress (novel); Gracious Living (novel), 1965; Anya (musical play), 1965; A Man and his Wife, 1970; Jeeves, a musical (with P. G. Wodehouse). *Recreation:* travelling. *Address:* Remsenburg, Long Island, USA.

BOLTON, Captain Sir Ian Frederick Cheney, 2nd Bt *cr* 1927; KBE 1957 (OBE 1946); DL; Captain 3rd Bn Argyll and Sutherland Highlanders; chartered accountant and retired partner, Arthur Young, McClelland, Moores and Co., Glasgow and London; *b* 29 Jan. 1889; *s* of Sir Edwin Bolton, 1st Bart, and Elinor, *d* of Sir John H. N. Graham, 1st Bt; *S* father, 1931. *Educ:* Eton. Served European War, 1914-19 (despatches). Past President Institute of Accountants and Actuaries in Glasgow; Past President Institute of Chartered Accountants of Scotland; Member (part-time) British Transport Commission, 1947-59; Chairman Scottish Area Board, British Transport Commission, 1955-59; President, Scottish Boy Scout Assoc., 1945-58; Lord Dean of Guild, Glasgow, 1957-59. DL Stirling, 1965 (re-appointed, with seniority 1939); HM Lieut of Stirlingshire, 1949-64. Hon. LLD Glasgow Univ., 1955. *Recreation:* Boy Scouts. *Heir:* none. *Address:* West Plean, Stirling FK7 8HA. *TA* and *T:* Bannockburn 812208. *Clubs:* Western (Glasgow); County (Stirling).

BOLTON, John; Chief Works Officer (Director General of Works), Department of Health and Social Security, since 1977; *b* 30 Dec. 1925; *s* of John and Elizabeth Ann Bolton, Great Harwood, Lancs; *m* 1950, Nell Hartley Mount, *d* of John and Kathleen Mount; three *d.* *Educ:* Blackburn Coll. of Technology and Art. LLB (Hons) London; CEng, FICE, FIMechE, FInstF,

FIArb; Hon. FIHospE. Mech. Engrg Apprentice, Bristol Aeroplane Co. Ltd; Civil Engrg Pupil, Courtaulds Ltd; subseq. with English Electric Co. Ltd and NW Gas Board. Entered Health Service as Group Engr, W Manchester HMC, 1954; subseq. Chief Engr to Board of Govs of United Liverpool Hosps, Dep. Regional Engr to Leeds Regional Hosp. Board and Regional Engr to E Anglian Regional Hosp. Board; Chief Engr, DHSS, 1969-77. Part-time lectr in building and engrg subjects for many years and Principal, 1955-59, Irlam Evening Inst., Manchester. *Publications:* contribs to: British Hosps Export Council Yearbooks, 1973, 1974, 1975; The Efficient Use of Energy, 1975; papers to internat. confs and to British learned Societies; technical articles in various jls. *Recreations:* theatre, music, reading, gardening, swimming. *Address:* Allsprings House, High Street, Little Shelford, Cambs. *T:* Shelford 2591.

BOLTON, Sir John (Brown), Kt 1977; OBE 1973; Member, Legislative Council of Isle of Man, since 1962; *b* 20 Jan. 1902; *s* of Rev. Richard Bolton and Charlotte Bolton; *m* 1930, Mary Smith; one *s* one *d.* *Educ:* Hull Grammar Sch.; Keighley Trade and Grammar Sch. Chartered Accountant, 1924, in public practice, IoM, 1928-68. Member: Douglas Corp., 1940-46; House of Keys, 1946-62; IoM Exec. Council, 1951-62, 1966-77; Chairman: IoM Highway Bd, 1956-61, 1963-66; IoM Finance Bd, 1966-76. *Recreations:* golf, gardening. *Address:* Amberley, Woodlands Close, Douglas, Isle of Man. *T:* Douglas 3204 and 21267. *Club:* Douglas Golf (Pres.).

BOLTON, John Eveleigh, CBE 1972; DSC 1945; DL; Chairman and Managing Director, Growth Capital Ltd, since 1968; Chairman: Atesmo Ltd; Crosshold Ltd; Small Business Capital Fund Ltd; Riverview Investments Ltd; Crellon Holdings Ltd; Keith Prowse Organisation (Reservations) Ltd; Development Capital Ltd; Director: NCR Co. Ltd; Black & Decker Ltd; Black & Decker Manufacturing Co. Inc.; Plasmec Ltd; ICFC-Numas Ltd; Dawson International Ltd; Johnson Wax Ltd; Keith Prowse Travel Ltd; Redland Ltd; *b* 17 Oct. 1920; *s* of late Ernest and Edith Mary Bolton; *m* 1948, Gabrielle Healey Hall, *d* of late Joseph and Minnie Hall; one *s* one *d.* *Educ:* Ilkley Sch.; Wolverhampton Sch.; Trinity Coll., Cambridge; Harvard, USA. Articled pupil to Chartered Acct, 1937-40; intermed. exam. of Inst. of Chartered Accts, 1940. Served War of 1939-45 (DSC). Destroyers, Lt RNVR, 1940-46. Cambridge, Hons Economics, MA; Cassel Travelling Schol., 1948; Harvard Business Sch., 1948-50; Baker Scholar, 1949; Master in Business Admin. (with Dist.), 1950. Research for Harvard in British Industry, 1950-51; Finance Dir, Solartron Laboratory Instruments Ltd, Kingston-upon-Thames, 1951-53 (Chm., 1953); Chm. and Man. Dir: Solartron Engineering Ltd, 1952; The Solartron Electronic Group Ltd, Thames Ditton and subseq. Farnborough, Hants, 1954-63 (Dep. Chm., 1963-65). Life Vice-Pres. (Chm. Council, 1964-66) Brit. Inst. of Management; Bowie Medal 1969, FBIM; Chm. and Founder Subscriber: Advanced Management Programmes Internat. Trust; Foundn for Management Educn; Dir, Management Publications Ltd, 1966-73 (Chm., 1969); Mem. Exec. Cttee, Automobile Assoc.; Hon. Treasurer, Surrey Univ. (Past Chm.); Member: Sub-Cttee on Business Management Studies, Univ. Grants Cttee; Council of Industry for Management Educn; Harvard Business Sch. Vis. Cttee. Mem. Org. Cttee, World Research Hospital. Member: UK Automation Council, 1964-65; Adv. Cttee for Management Efficiency in Nat. Health Service, 1964-65; Cttee for Exports to New Zealand, 1965-68; Adv. Cttee, Queen's Award to Industry; Chm., Economic Develt Cttee for the Rubber Industry, 1965-68; Vice-Chm., Royal Commn on Local Govt in England, 1966-69; Chm., Committee of Inquiry on Small Firms, 1969-71. DL Surrey, 1974. *Publications:* articles in: Scope; Control; The Listener; Christian Science Monitor; various radio and TV broadcasts on industrial topics. *Recreations:* shooting, swimming, tennis, gardening, opera, antiques. *Address:* Brook Place, Chobham, Woking, Surrey. *T:* Chobham 8157. *Clubs:* Harvard Business School Club of London, Harvard Club of London; Philippics (Surrey).

BOLTON, Percy, MA Cantab; *b* 1889; *s* of James Bolton, Blackburn; *m* Florence Madeleine (*d* 1976), 2nd *d* of late Rev. D. L. Scott, MA, LLD Cantab; one *s* one *d.* *Educ:* Blackburn Grammar Sch.; King's Coll., Cambridge (Scholar). Mathematical Tripos, Wrangler, 1911; Natural Science Tripos, Part II, 1912. Asst Master, Cheltenham Coll.; eleven years Head of Physics and Engineering Dept of Oundle Sch.; Headmaster of Dean Close Sch., Cheltenham, 1924-38; Headmaster of Watford Grammar Sch., 1938-51; retired 1951. *Address:* Brabourne, Kimpton, near Hitchin, Hertfordshire. *T:* Kimpton 832362.

BOMBAY, Cardinal Archbishop of; His Eminence Valerian Cardinal Gracias; Archbishop of Bombay since Dec. 1950; Cardinal since Jan. 1953; *b* 23 Oct. 1900; *s* of José Antonio and

Charlotte. *Educ:* St Patrick's High Sch., Karachi; St Joseph's Seminary, Mangalore; Papal Seminary, Kandy; Gregorian Univ., Rome. Secretary to Archbishop of Bombay, 1929-36; Chancellor of Archdiocese, 1929; Rector of Pro-Cathedral, Dec. 1941; Titular Bishop of Tannis and Auxiliary to Archbishop of Bombay, 1946-50; Consultor to Sacred Congregation for the Oriental Churches, Sacred Congregation of the Sacraments and Sacred Congregation for the Propagation of the Faith; Member: Council for the Implementation of the Constitution on the Sacred Liturgy; Commission for the Revision of the Code of Canon Law; Pontifical Commission for the Study of Family and Population Problems. Awarded Padma Vibhushan (India), 1966. *Publications:* Features of Christian Life; Heaven and Home; The Vatican and International Policy; The Decline of Public Morals; The Chief Duties of Christians as Citizens. *Address:* Archbishop's House, Bombay 400039, India. *T:* 231 093 and 231 193.

BOMFORD, Richard Raymond, CBE 1964; DM Oxon; FRCP; Physician to London Hospital, 1938-70, Consulting Physician since 1970; *b* 15 May 1907; *s* of Raymond Bomford, Evesham, and Evelyn Mary Perkins; unmarried. *Educ:* Bromsgrove Sch.; Wadham Coll., Oxford; London Hospital. Hon. Colonel: late Consultant Physician, 14th Army (despatches); Treasurer, Royal Coll. of Physicians, 1957-70. Mem., Assoc. of Physicians. Hon. FACP. *Publications:* contributions to medical journals and text-books. *Recreation:* gardening. *Address:* 3 Green Lane, Roxwell, Chelmsford CM1 4NA. *T:* Roxwell 321. *Club:* Oriental.

BOMPAS, Donald George, CMG 1966; Secretary, Guy's Hospital Medical and Dental Schools, since 1969 (Deputy Secretary, 1966-69); *b* 20 Nov. 1920; *yr s* of Rev. E. Anstie Bompas; *m* 1946, Freda Vice, *y d* of F. M. Smithyman, Malawi; one *s* one *d. Educ:* Merchant Taylors' Sch., Northwood; Oriel Coll., Oxford. MA Oxon, 1947. Overseas Audit Service, 1942-66, retired; Nyasaland, 1942-47; Singapore, 1947-48; Malaya (now Malaysia), 1948-66; Deputy Auditor-General, 1957-60; Auditor-General, Malaysia (formerly Malaya), 1960-66. Liveryman, Merchant Taylors' Co. JMN (Hon.) Malaya, 1961. *Address:* 8 Birchwood Road, Petts Wood, Kent. *T:* Orpington 21661.

BONALLACK, Michael Francis, OBE 1971; Managing Director, Miller Buckley Golf Services Ltd, since 1974; Director, Buckley Investments Ltd; *b* 31 Dec. 1934; *s* of Sir Richard (Frank) Bonallack, *qv*; *m* 1958, Angela Ward; one *s* three *d. Educ:* Chigwell; Haileybury ISC. National Service, 1953-55 (1st Lieut, RASC). Joined family business, 1955; Director, 1962-74. *Recreation:* golf (British Amateur Champion, 1961, 1965, 1968, 1969, 1970; English Amateur Champion, 1962-63, 1965-67 and 1968; Captain, British Walker Cup Team, 1971; Bobby Jones Award for distinguished sportsmanship in golf, 1972). *Address:* The Old Rectory, North Fambridge, Chelmsford, Essex. *T:* Maldon 740397. *Clubs:* Eccentric, Golfers'; Royal and Ancient (St Andrews).

BONALLACK, Sir Richard (Frank), Kt 1963; CBE 1955 (OBE 1944); MIMechE; President, Freight Bonallack, since 1974 (Chairman, 1971-74, formerly of Bonallack & Sons, Ltd, 1953-71); *b* 2 June 1904; *s* of Francis and Ada Bonallack; *m* 1930, Winifred Evelyn Mary Esplen; two *s* one *d. Educ:* Haileybury. War service in TA; transferred to TA Reserve, 1946, with rank of Colonel. Chm., Freight Container Section, SMMT. Member, Basildon Development Corporation, 1962-77. *Recreation:* golf. *Address:* 4 The Willows, Thorpe Bay, Essex. *T:* Southend 588180.
See also M. F. Bonallack.

BONAR, Sir Herbert (Vernon), Kt 1967; CBE 1946; Chairman, 1949-74, and Managing Director, 1938-73, The Low & Bonar Group Ltd; retired 1974; *b* 26 Feb. 1907; *s* of George Bonar and Julia (*née* Seehusen); *m* 1935, Marjory (*née* East); two *s. Educ:* Fettes Coll.; Brasenose Coll., Oxford (BA). Joined Low & Bonar Ltd, 1929; Director, 1934; Managing Director, 1938; Chairman and Managing Director, 1949. Jute Control, 1939-46; Jute Controller, 1942-46. Hon. LLD: St Andrews, 1955; Birmingham, 1974. Comdr, Order of the Golden Ark, Netherlands, 1974. *Recreations:* golf, fishing, photography, wild life preservation. *Address:* St Kitts, Albany Road, Broughty Ferry, Dundee, Angus. *T:* Dundee 79947. *Clubs:* Eastern (Dundee); Blairgowrie Golf; Panmure Golf.

BOND, Arthur, CBE 1972; Chairman, Yorkshire Electricity Board, 1962-71; *b* 19 July 1907; *s* of Rev. A. and Mrs Anne Bond, Darwen, Lancs; *m* 1935, Nora Wadsworth; one *s* one *d. Educ:* Darwen Grammar Sch. Solicitor to Cleethorpes Corporation, 1930; Dep. Town Clerk, Luton, 1935; Town Clerk:

Macclesfield, 1938; Stockport, 1944; Secretary, Eastern Electricity Board, 1948; Dep. Chairman, Yorkshire Electricity Board, 1952. Solicitor, Legal Member, TPI; Comp. IEE; FBIM. *Address:* 5 Linton Road, Wetherby, West Yorks. *T:* Wetherby 2847.

BOND, Rt. Rev. (Charles) Derek; *see* Bradwell, Bishop Suffragan of.

BOND, Edward; playwright; *b* 18 July 1934; *m* 1971, Elisabeth Pablé. George Divine Award, 1968; John Whiting Award, 1968. Opera libretto: We come to the River (music by Hans Werner Henze), 1976. *Publications:* (plays): Saved, 1965; Narrow Road to the Deep North, 1968; Early Morning, 1968; The Pope's Wedding, 1971; Passion, 1971; Black Mass, 1971; Lear, 1972; The Sea, 1973; Bingo, 1974; The Fool, 1976; A-A-merica! (Grandma Faust, and The Swing), 1976; Stone, 1976; The Woman, 1977; (Libretto): We Come to the River, 1976. *Address:* c/o Margaret Ramsay, 14A Goodwins Court, St Martin's Lane, WC2N 4LL.

BOND, Prof. George, FRS 1972; Hooker Professor of Botany, University of Glasgow, 1973-76, now Emeritus Professor (Titular Professor, 1965-73); *b* 21 Feb. 1906; *m* 1st, 1931, Gwendolyne Kirkbride (*d* 1960); two *s* one *d*; 2nd, 1961, Mary Catherine McCormick; two *s. Educ:* The Brunts Sch., Mansfield; UC Nottingham. BSc, PhD, DSc, FIBiol. Asst Lectr, Dept of Botany, Univ. of Glasgow, 1927; subseq. Lectr, then Reader. Technical Officer, Min. of Food, Dehydration Div., 1942-45. *Publications:* articles in various learned jls on symbiotic fixation of nitrogen. *Recreation:* gardening. *Address:* 23 Westland Drive, Glasgow G14 9NY. *T:* 041-959 4201.

BOND, Maj.-Gen. George Alexander, CB 1956; CBE 1953 (OBE 1942); late RASC; *b* 31 Dec. 1901; *s* of late Alexander Maxwell Bond, Dover; *m* 1929, Dora Margaret, *d* of late H. A. Gray; two *s. Educ:* Dover Grammar Sch.; RMC. Served War of 1939-45 (despatches, OBE); Brig. 1948; Director of Supplies and Transport, BAOR, 1950-53; DDST, Southern Command, 1953-54; Maj.-Gen. 1955; Inspector RASC, War Office, 1954-57; Dir, Supplies and Transport, 1957, retd. Col Comdt, RASC, 1960-65; Col Comdt, Royal Corps of Transport, 1965-66. *Address:* Three Horseshoes, Kirdford, Billingshurst, West Sussex. *T:* Kirdford 340.

BOND, Maj.-Gen. Henry Mark Garneys, JP; DL; *b* 1 June 1922; *s* of W. R. G. Bond, Tyneham, Dorset; unmarried. *Educ:* Eton. Enlisted as Rifleman, 1940; commnd in Rifle Bde, 1941; served Middle East and Italy; seconded to Parachute Regt, 1947-50; ADC to Field Marshal Viscount Montgomery of Alamein, 1950-52; psc 1953; served in Kenya, Malaya, Cyprus and Borneo; Comd Rifle Bde in Cyprus and Borneo, 1964-66; Comd 12th Inf. Bde, 1967-68; idc 1969; Dir of Defence Operational Plans and Asst Chief of Defence Staff (Ops), 1970-72; retd 1972. Pres., Dorset Natural History and Archaeological Soc., 1972-75; Chm., Dorset Br., CPRE, 1975. Mem., Dorset CC, 1973-. JP Dorset, 1972, High Sheriff of Dorset, 1977, DL Dorset, 1977. *Recreations:* shooting, forestry, reading. *Address:* Moigne Combe, Warmwell, Dorchester, Dorset. *T:* Warmwell 852265. *Club:* Boodle's.

BOND, Sir Kenneth (Raymond Boyden), Kt 1977; Deputy Managing Director, General Electric Company Ltd, since 1966 (Financial Director 1962-66); Member: Industrial Development Advisory Board, since 1972; Committee to Review the Functioning of Financial Institutions, since 1977; *b* 1 Feb. 1920; *s* of late James Edwin Bond and of Gertrude Deplidge Bond; *m* 1958, Jennifer Margaret, *d* of late Sir Cecil and Lady Crabbe; three *s* three *d. Educ:* Selhurst Grammar School. Served TA, Europe and Middle East, 1939-46. FCA 1960 (Mem. 1949). Partner, Cooper & Cooper, Chartered Accountants, 1954-57; Dir, Radio & Allied Industries Ltd, 1957-62. *Recreation:* golf. *Address:* White Gables, Austenwood Common, Gerrards Cross, Bucks. *T:* Gerrards Cross 83513. *Club:* Addington Golf.

BOND, Maurice Francis, MVO 1976; OBE 1955; Clerk of the Records, since 1946, and Principal Clerk, Information Services, since 1974, House of Lords; *b* 29 Oct. 1916; *s* of William Francis Bond and Ada Louise Bond (*née* Lightfoot), Windsor; *m* 1954, Shelagh Mary (*d* 1973), *d* of Hulbert Lionel and Katharine Lewis, Northampton. *Educ:* Windsor Grammar Sch.; Selwyn Coll., Cambridge (Exhibnr 1933, BA 1936, Cert. of Educn 1937, MA 1941). Head of dept of History and Geography, Beaumont Coll., 1937-46. Clerk, House of Lords, 1946-. Hon. Custodian of the Muniments, St George's Chapel, Windsor Castle, 1947-75; Mem. Council, British Records Assoc., 1948-66 (Chm. Records Preservation section, 1961-66); Mem. Cttee, Windsor and Eton Soc., 1948-63; Hon. Archivist, Borough of Windsor, 1950-;

Mem. Tech. Cttee, Soc. of Archivists, 1956-74; Governor, Windsor Grammar Sch., 1957-; Hon. Gen. Editor: St George's Chapel Monographs, 1960-; Windsor Records Publications, 1966-; Dir, Simon de Montfort Exhibn, Houses of Parliament, 1965; Mem. Cttee of Management, Inst. of Historical Research, 1968-77; Vice-Pres., Berkshire Archaeological Soc., 1973-; Dir, Chapel of Kings Exhibn, Windsor Castle, 1975. FSA 1947, FRHistS 1971. Hon. Associate, Royal Holloway Coll., London Univ., 1975-. *Publications:* (ed) The Inventories of St George's Chapel, 1947; (jtly) The Romance of St George's Chapel, 1947; (ed jtly) The Dictionary of English Church History, 1948; (ed) The Manuscripts of the House of Lords 1710-1714, 2 vols, 1949, 1953, and Addenda, 1514-1714, 1962; (jtly) The Manuscripts of St George's Chapel, 1957; The Seventh Centenary of Simon de Montfort's Parliament, 1965; Pictorial History of the Houses of Parliament, 1967; Guide to the Records of Parliament, 1971; St George's Chapel, Quincentenary Souvenir Book, 1975; The Diaries and Papers of Sir Edward Dering, 1644-1684, 1976; Royal Windsor, 1977; contributions to: Eng. Hist. Review; Bulletin of Inst. of Hist. Research; Jl of Eccles. Hist.; Theology; Jl of Soc. of Archivists; The Times, etc. *Address:* 19 Bolton Crescent, Windsor, Berks. *T:* Windsor 65132.

BOND, Michael; author; *b* 13 Jan. 1926; *s* of Norman Robert and Frances Mary Bond; *m* 1950, Brenda Mary Johnson; one *d.* *Educ:* Presentation College, Reading. RAF and Army, 1943-47; BBC Cameraman, 1947-66; full-time author from 1966. Paddington TV series, 1976. *Publications:* A Bear Called Paddington, 1958; More About Paddington, 1959; Paddington Helps Out, 1960; Paddington Abroad, 1961; Paddington at Large, 1962; Paddington Marches On, 1964; Paddington at Work, 1966; Here Comes Thursday, 1966; Thursday Rides Again, 1968; Paddington Goes to Town, 1968; Thursday Ahoy, 1969; Parsley's Tail, 1969; Parsley's Good Deed, 1969; Parsley's Problem Present, 1970; Parsley's Last Stand, 1970; Paddington Takes the Air, 1970; Thursday in Paris, 1970; Michael Bond's Book of Bears, 1971; Michael Bond's Book of Mice, 1972; The Day the Animals Went on Strike, 1972; Paddington Bear, 1972; Paddington's Garden, 1972; Parsley the Lion, 1972; Parsley Parade, 1972; The Tales of Olga da Polga, 1972; Olga Meets her Match, 1973; Paddington's Blue Peter Story Book, 1973; Paddington at the Circus, 1973; Paddington Goes Shopping, 1973; Paddington at the Sea-side, 1974; Paddington at the Tower, 1974; Paddington on Top, 1974; Windmill, 1975; How to make Flying Things, 1975; Eight Olga Readers, 1975; Paddington's Loose End Book, 1976; Paddington's Party Book, 1976; Olga Carries On, 1976. *Recreations:* photography, travel, cars, wine. *Address:* Fairacre, Farnham Lane, Haslemere, Surrey GU27 1HA. *T:* Haslemere 4614. *Club:* Wig and Pen.

BOND, Ralph Norman, CMG 1953; OBE 1950; *b* 31 Aug. 1900; *s* of Ralph Bond, Morecambe, Lancs; *m* 1929, Dorothy Ward; three *d. Educ:* Royal Grammar Sch., Lancaster; St John's Coll., Cambridge. BA Classical Tripos, 1922; MA 1929. Eastern Cadetship in Colonial Service, Dec. 1923; arrived in Ceylon, Jan. 1924; Revenue and judicial posts, 1924-36; Customs (Landing Surveyor and Deputy Collector), 1936-39; Import, Export and Exchange Control, 1939-42; Assistant Chief Secretary, 1942-45; Secretary to C-in-C, Ceylon, 1945-46; Permanent Secretary to Ministry of Posts and Broadcasting, Ceylon, 1947-55; retired, 1955. *Recreations:* formerly Rugby, soccer, hockey, cricket, tennis and swimming; now gardening. *Address:* 48 Stuart Avenue, Morecambe, Lancs. *T:* Morecambe 418799.

BOND, Maj.-Gen. Richard Lawrence, CB 1943; CBE 1937; DSO 1915; MC 1918; Hon. FRAM 1954; *s* of late Maj.-Gen. Sir F. G. Bond, KBE; *b* 10 June 1890; *m* Isabelle Helewise (*d* 1943), *y d* of late Col T. J. R. Mallock; one *d* (one *s* killed in action, 1941); *m* 1949, Dorothy Mary, *d* of late Sydney How. Entered Army, 1910; Major, 1926; Bt Lieut-Col, 1931; Lieut-Col, 1934; Col, 1937; Maj.-Gen., 1940; served European War, 1914-19 (despatches, DSO for gallantry in the successful attack on the Railway Embankment at Cuinchy); Waziristan Operations, 1936-37 (CBE); GSO 2nd Grade, War Office, 1930-31; Imperial Defence Coll., 1933; CRE India, 1934-37; AQMG, War Office, 1937-39; Chief Engineer, Aldershot Command, 1939; Chief Engineer, 1 Corps BEF, 1939-40, Maj.-Gen. i/c Administration, 1940; Deputy Quartermaster-General in India, 1941-42; Engineer-in-Chief in India, 1942-43; Commander, 1943 and 1944-46; retired pay, 1946. *Address:* The Dykeries, Compton, Guildford, Surrey.

BOND-WILLIAMS, Noel Ignace; Director: Delta Metal Co. Ltd, 1967-77; Joseph Lucas (Industries) Ltd, since 1972; National Exhibition Centre Ltd, since 1970; Pro-Chancellor, University of Aston in Birmingham, since 1970; *b* 7 Nov. 1914; *s* of late W. H. Williams, Birmingham; *m* 1939, Mary Gwendoline Tomey; one *s* two *d. Educ:* Oundle Sch.; Birmingham Univ.

(BSc). FIM, FBIM. Pres. Guild of Undergrads 1936-37, Pres. Guild of Grads 1947, Birmingham Univ. Various appts in metal industry; Dir, Enfield Rolling Mills Ltd, 1957-65; Industrial Adviser, DEA, 1965-67. Pres., Birmingham Chamber of Commerce, 1969. Member: Commn on Industrial Relations, 1971-74; Price Commn, 1977-. Mem. Council, Industrial Soc., 1947-; Pres., Brit. Non-ferrous Metals Fedn, 1974-75. Feoffee of Lapworth Charity. Hon. DSc Aston, 1975. *Publications:* papers and articles on relationships between people in industry. *Recreation:* sailing. *Address:* Kiftsgate, Weston Subedge, Chipping Campden GL55 6QH. *T:* Evesham 840088. *Clubs:* Metallics; Royal Ocean Racing, Royal Cruising, Royal Lymington Yacht.

BONDI, Prof. Sir Hermann, KCB 1973; FRS 1959; FRAS; Chief Scientist, Department of Energy, since 1977; Professor of Mathematics, King's College, London, since 1954 (on leave of absence 1967-71); *b* Vienna, 1 Nov. 1919; *s* of late Samuel and Helene Bondi, New York; *m* 1947, Christine M. Stockman, *d* of H. W. Stockman, *qv*; two *s* three *d. Educ:* Realgymnasium, Vienna; Trinity Coll., Cambridge (MA). Temporary Experimental Officer, Admiralty, 1942-45; Fellow Trinity Coll., Cambridge, 1943-49, and 1952-54; Asst Lecturer, Mathematics, Cambridge, 1945-48; University Lecturer, Mathematics, Cambridge, 1948-54. Dir-Gen., ESRO, 1967-71; Chief Scientific Advr, MoD, 1971-77. Research Associate, Cornell Univ., 1951; Lecturer, Harvard Coll. Observatory, 1953; Lowell Lecturer, Boston, Mass, 1953; Visiting Prof. Cornell Univ., 1960; Halley Lecturer, Oxford, 1962; Tarner Lectr, Cambridge, 1965; Lees-Knowles Lectr, Cambridge, 1974. Chairman: Space Cttee, MoD, 1964-65; Nat. Cttee for Astronomy, 1963-67; Secretary, Royal Astronomical Soc., 1956-64; Mem., SRC, 1973-. Pres., Inst. of Mathematics and its Applications, 1974-75. Member: Rationalist Press Assoc. Ltd; British Humanist Assoc.; Science Policy Foundn; Hon. Vice-President Advisory Centre for Education (ACE); Mem., Ct, London Univ., 1963-67. Fellow, King's Coll., London, 1968. Hon. DSc: Sussex 1974; Bath 1974; Surrey 1974. *Publications:* Cosmology, 1952 (2nd edn, 1960); The Universe at Large, 1961; Relativity and Commonsense, 1964; Assumption and Myth in Physical Theory, 1968; papers on astrophysics, etc, in Proc. Royal Society, Monthly Notices, Royal Astronomical Society, Proc. Cam. Phil. Society, etc. *Recreation:* travelling. *Address:* East House, Buckland Corner, Reigate Heath, Surrey. *T:* Reigate 45945.

BONE, Captain Howard Francis, CBE 1957; DSO 1940, and Bar 1941; DSC 1940 and Bar, 1942; RN (retired); *b* 20 Oct. 1908; *s* of late Engineer Rear-Adm. H. Bone, CB, and late Mrs A. S. Bone; *m* 1932, Heather Maud Marion Fletcher; one *d. Educ:* Felsted; RNC, Dartmouth. Entered RN, 1922; served in submarines, 1930-50. Comdr 1941; Captain, 1947; Dep. Director of Naval Equipment, 1952-54; Captain-in-Charge, Simonstown, and Captain Superintendent, Simonstown Dockyard, 1954-57. ADC to the Queen, Jan. 1956-May 1957. Retired, 1957. *Address:* Inner Meadow, Combe Hay, near Bath, Avon. *T:* Combe Down 833363. *Clubs:* Western Province Sports, Kelvin Grove (Newlands, Cape Town).

BONE, Mrs Stephen; *see* Adshead, Mary.

BONHAM, Major Sir Antony Lionel Thomas, 4th Bt, *cr* 1852; late Royal Scots Greys; *b* 21 Oct. 1916; *o s* of Maj. Sir Eric H. Bonham, 3rd Bt, and Ethel (*d* 1962), *y d* of Col Leopold Seymour; *S* father 1937; *m* 1944, Felicity, *o d* of late Col. Frank L. Pardoe, DSO, Bartonbury, Cirencester; three *s. Educ:* Eton; RMC. Served Royal Scots Greys, 1937-49; retired with rank of Major, 1949. *Heir: s* George Martin Antony Bonham, *b* 18 Feb. 1945. *Address:* Ash House, Ampney Crucis, Cirencester, Glos. *T:* Poulton 391. *Club:* Cavalry and Guards.

BONHAM-CARTER, Sir (Arthur) Desmond, Kt 1969; TD 1942; Director, Unilever Ltd, 1953-68, retired; *b* 15 Feb. 1908; 2nd *s* of Gen. Sir Charles Bonham-Carter, GCB, CMG, DSO, and Beryl, *née* Codrington; *m* 1st, 1933, Ann Parker Hazelwood (*d* 1972); one *s* ; 2nd, 1973, Diane Anastasia, *d* of Mervyn Madden. *Educ:* Winchester; Magdalene Coll., Cambridge. Served with Royal Tank Regt, 1938-45. Joined J. Crosfield & Sons Ltd, 1929; Director, Crosfield, Watson & Gossage, 1938; Chairman, J. Knight Ltd, 1948; Member: Royal Commission to consider Pay of Doctors and Dentists, 1957-60; Advisory Cttee, Recruitment for the Forces, 1958; Plowden Cttee on Representational Services Overseas, 1962-64; Central Health Services Council, 1965. Trustee, Nightingale Fund, 1961; Chairman: Board of Governors, University College Hospital, 1963-74; S-W Metropolitan Regional Hospital Board, 1968-74; Mem., Camden and Islington Area Health Authy, 1974-. *Address:* 146 Thomas More House, Barbican EC2Y 8BU. *T:* 01-628 4823. *See also* V. *Bonham-Carter.*

BONHAM-CARTER, John Arkwright, CVO 1975; DSO 1942; OBE 1967; ERD 1952; Chairman and General Manager, British Railways London Midland Region, 1971-75; *b* 27 March 1915; *s* of late Capt. Guy Bonham-Carter, 19th Hussars, and Kathleen Rebecca (*née* Arkwright); *m* 1939, Anne Louisa Charteris; two *s. Educ:* Winchester Coll.; King's Coll., Cambridge (Exhibitioner). 1st class hons Mech. Scis, Cantab, 1936; MA 1970. Joined LNER Co. as Traffic Apprentice, 1936; served in Royal Tank Regt, 1939-46 (despatches, 1940 and 1942); subsequently rejoined LNER; held various appointments; Asst General Manager, BR London Midland Region, 1963-65; Chief Operating Officer, BR Board, 1966-68; Chm. and Gen. Manager, BR Western Region, 1968-71. Lieut-Col, Engr and Rly Staff Corps RE (T&AVR IV), 1966-71, Col 1971-. FCIT. OStJ 1970; Comr, St John Ambulance Brigade, Dorset, 1976-. *Recreations:* theatre, foreign travel, cabinet making and carpentry. *Address:* Redbridge House, Crossways, Dorchester, Dorset DT2 8DY. *T:* Warmwell 852669. *Club:* Army and Navy.

BONHAM CARTER, Hon. Mark Raymond; Chairman, Outer Circle Policy Unit, since 1976; a Director, Royal Opera House, Covent Garden, since 1958; Governor, The Royal Ballet; Vice-Chairman and a Governor, BBC, since 1975; *b* 11 Feb. 1922; *e s* of late Sir Maurice Bonham Carter, KCB, KCVO, and Violet, *d* of 1st Earl of Oxford and Asquith, KG, PC (Baroness Asquith of Yarnbury, DBE); *m* 1955, Leslie, *d* of Condé Nast, NY; three *d. Educ:* Winchester; Balliol Coll., Oxford (Scholar); University of Chicago (Commonwealth Fund Fellowship). Served Grenadier Guards, 1941-45; 8th Army (Africa) and 21st Army Group (NW Europe); captured, 1943; escaped; (despatches). Contested (L) Barnstaple, 1945; MP (L), Torrington Div. of Devonshire, March 1958-59; Mem., UK Delegn to the Council of Europe, 1958-59; contested (L) Torrington, 1964. Director, Wm Collins & Co. Ltd, 1955-58. First Chm., Race Relations Bd, 1966-70; Chm., Community Relations Commn, 1971-77; Vice-President: Consumers' Assoc., 1972- (Mem. Council, 1966-71); Educnl Interchange Council, 1972-; Mem. Council, Inst. of Race Relations, 1966-72. Mem. Court of Governors, LSE. *Publications:* (ed) The Autobiography of Margot Asquith, 1962; contributor to: Radical Alternative (essays), 1962. *Address:* 49 Victoria Road, W8. *T:* 01-937 4142; The Manor House, Ripe, Lewes, Sussex. *Clubs:* Brooks's, MCC.
See also Hon . R . H . Bonham Carter .

BONHAM CARTER, Hon. Raymond Henry; on secondment as Director, Industrial Development Unit, Department of Industry, since 1977; Executive Director, S. G. Warburg & Co. Ltd, 1967-77; *b* 19 June 1929; *s* of Sir Maurice Bonham Carter, KCB, KCVO, and Lady Violet Bonham Carter, DBE (later Baroness Asquith of Yarnbury); *m* 1958, Elena Propper de Callejon; two *s* one *d . Educ:* Winchester Coll.; Magdalen Coll., Oxford (BA 1952); Harvard Business Sch. (MBA 1954). Irish Guards, 1947-49. With J. Henry Schröder & Co., 1952-58; acting Advr, Bank of England, 1958-63; Alternate Exec. Dir for UK, IMF, and Mem., UK Treasury and Supply Delegn, Washington, 1961-63; S. G. Warburg & Co. Ltd, 1964-; Director: Transport Development Group Ltd, 1969-77; Banque de Paris et des Pays Bas NV, 1973-77; Mercury Securities Ltd, 1974-77. Mem. Council and Hon. Treasurer, Internat. Inst. for Strategic Studies, 1974-. *Recreation:* skiing. *Address:* 7 West Heath Avenue, NW11 7QS. *T:* 01-455 8434. *Clubs:* Brooks's, MCC.
See also Hon . M . R . Bonham Carter .

BONHAM CARTER, Richard Erskine; Physician to the Hospital for Sick Children, Great Ormond Street, 1947-75, to University College Hospital, 1948-66; *b* 27 Aug. 1910; *s* of late Capt. A. E. Bonham-Carter and late M. E. Bonham-Carter (*née* Malcolm); *m* 1946, Margaret (*née* Stace); three *d. Educ:* Clifton Coll.; Peterhouse, Cambridge; St Thomas' Hospital. Resident Asst Physician, Hospital for Sick Children, Great Ormond Street, 1938. Served War of 1939-45 in RAMC; DADMS 1 Airborne Div., 1942-45; despatches, 1944. *Publications:* contributions to Text-Books of Pædiatrics and to medical journals. *Recreations:* gardening, fishing. *Address:* 18 Doughty Mews, WC1N 2PF. *T:* 01-405 3062; Castle Sweyn Cottage, Achnamara, Argyll.

BONHAM-CARTER, Victor; Joint Secretary, Society of Authors, since 1970; Secretary, Royal Literary Fund, since 1966; *b* 13 Dec. 1913; *s* of Gen. Sir Charles Bonham-Carter, GCB, CMG, DSO, and Gabrielle Madge Jeanette (*née* Fisher); *m* 1938, Audrey Edith Stogdon; two *s. Educ:* Winchester Coll.; Magdalene Coll., Cambridge (MA); Hamburg and Paris. Worked on The Countryman, 1936-37; Dir, School Prints Ltd, 1937-39, 1945-60; Army, R Berks Regt and Intell. Corps, 1939-45; farmed in W Somerset, 1947-59; historian of Dartington Hall Estate, Devon, 1951-66; joined staff of Soc. of Authors, 1963; active in Exmoor National Park affairs, 1955-; Editor, Exmoor Review, 1968-73; Partner, Exmoor Press, 1969-. *Publications:* The English Village, 1952; (with W. B. Curry) Dartington Hall, 1958; Exploring Parish Churches, 1959; Farming the Land, 1959; In a Liberal Tradition, 1960; Soldier True, 1965; Surgeon in the Crimea, 1969; The Survival of the English Countryside, 1971; many contribs to jls, radio, etc on country life and work; also on authorship matters, esp. Public Lending Right. *Recreations:* music, bathing in warm climates, conversation. *Address:* Halsdown Cottage, Waterrow, Wiveliscombe, Somerset. *Club:* Authors'.
See also Sir A . D . Bonham -Carter .

BONINGTON, Christian John Storey, CBE 1976; mountaineer, writer and photographer; *b* 6 Aug. 1934; *s* of Charles Bonington, journalist, and Helen Anne Bonington (*née* Storey); *m* 1962, Muriel Wendy Marchant; two *s* (and one *s* decd). *Educ:* University Coll. Sch., London. RMA Sandhurst, 1955-56; commnd Royal Tank Regt, 1956-61. Unilever Management Trainee, 1961-62; writer and photographer, 1962-. Climbs: Annapurna II, 26,041 ft (1st ascent) 1960; Central Pillar Freney, Mont Blanc (1st ascent), 1961; Nuptse, 25,850 ft (1st ascent), 1961; North Wall of Eiger (1st British ascent), 1962; Central Tower of Paine, Patagonia (1st ascent), 1963; Mem. of team, first descent of Blue Nile, 1968; Leader: successful Annapurna South Face Expedition, 1970; British Everest Expedition, 1972; (1st ascent) Brammah, Himalayas, 1973; (1st ascent) Changabang, Himalayas (co-leader), 1974; British Everest Expedition, 1975. FRGS (Founders' Medal, 1974). Hon. Fellow, UMIST, 1976; Hon. MA Salford, 1973; Hon. DSc Sheffield, 1976. *Publications:* I Chose to Climb (autobiog.), 1966; Annapurna South Face, 1971; The Next Horizon (autobiog.), 1973; Everest, South West Face, 1973; Everest the Hard Way, 1976. *Recreation:* mountaineering. *Address:* Badger Hill, Nether Row, Hesket Newmarket, Wigton, Cumbria. *T:* Caldbeck 286. *Clubs:* Alpine, Alpine Ski, Army and Navy, Climbers.

BONNER, Frederick Ernest, CBE 1974; Deputy Chairman, Central Electricity Generating Board, since 1975; *b* 16 Sept. 1923; *s* of George Frederick Bonner and late Mrs Bonner, Hammersmith; *m* 1957, Phyllis (*d* 1976), *d* of late Mr and Mrs H. Holder. *Educ:* St Clement Danes Holborn Estate Grammar Sch. BSc(Econ) London; DPA, JDipMA. Local Govt (Fulham and Ealing Borough Councils), 1940-49. Central Electricity Authority: Sen. Accountant, 1949-50; Asst Finance Officer, 1950-58; Central Electricity Generating Board: Asst Chief Financial Officer, 1958-61; Dep. Chief Financial Officer, 1961-65; Chief Financial Officer, 1965-69; Member, 1969-75. Mem., UKAEA, 1977-. FCA, IPFA, FBIM. *Recreations:* music, gardening, reading. *Address:* c/o Central Electricity Generating Board, Sudbury House, 15 Newgate Street, EC1A 7AU.

BONNET, C. M.; *see* Melchior-Bonnet.

BONNEY, George Louis William, MS, FRCS; Consultant Orthopædic Surgeon to St Mary's Hospital, London; Consulting Orthopædic Surgeon to the Dispensaire Français; *b* 10 Jan. 1920; *s* of late Dr Ernest Bonney and Gertrude Mary Williams; *m* 1950, Margaret Morgan; two *d. Educ:* Eton (Scholar); St Mary's Hospital Medical Sch. MB, BS, MRCS, LRCP 1943; FRCS 1945; MS (London) 1947. Formerly: Surg.-Lieut RNVR; Research Assistant and Senior Registrar, Royal National Orthopædic Hospital; Consultant Orthopædic Surgeon, Southend Group of Hospitals. Travelling Fellowship of British Postgraduate Med. Fedn, Univ. of London, 1950. Mem. Council, Medical Defence Union. Associate Editor, Journal of Bone and Joint Surgery. *Publications:* Chapters in Operative Surgery, 1957; papers in medical journals on visceral pain, circulatory mechanisms, nerve injuries and on various aspects of orthopædic surgery. *Recreations:* fishing, shooting, photography, music. *Address:* 71 Porchester Terrace, W2 3TT. *T:* 01-262 4236; 107 Harley Street, W1N 1DG; Wyeside Cottages, Much Fawley, Hereford HR1 4SP. *Club:* Leander.

BONSALL, Sir Arthur Wilfred, KCMG 1977; OBE 1957; Director, Government Communications Headquarters, since 1973; *b* 25 June 1917; *s* of late Wilfred Bonsall and Sarah Bonsall; *m* 1941, Joan Isabel Wingfield; four *s* three *d. Educ:* Bishop's Stortford Coll.; St Catharine's Coll., Cambridge. 2nd Cl. Hons Mod. Langs. Joined Air Ministry, 1940; transf. to FO (GCHQ), 1942; idc 1962. *Recreation:* gardening. *Address:* c/o Foreign and Commonwealth Office, SW1A 2AL. *Club:* Athenæum.

BONSALL, Prof. Frank Featherstone, FRS 1970; Professor of Mathematics, University of Edinburgh, since 1965; *b* 1920; *m* 1947, Gillian Patrick. *Educ:* Bishop's Stortford Coll.; Merton Coll., Oxford. *Publications* (all with J. Duncan): Numerical

Ranges of Operators on Normed Spaces and of Elements of Normed Algebras, 1971; Numerical Ranges II, 1973; Complete Normed Algebras, 1973. *Recreations:* walking, climbing. *Address:* Department of Mathematics, James Clerk Maxwell Building, Mayfield Road, Edinburgh EH9 3JZ.

BONSER, Air Vice-Marshal Stanley Haslam, CB 1969; MBE 1942; CEng, FRAeS; Director, Easams Ltd, since 1972; *b* 17 May 1916; *s* of late Sam Bonser and late Phoebe Ellen Bonser; *m* 1941, Margaret Betty Howard; two *s. Educ:* Sheffield University. BSc 1938; DipEd 1939. Armament Officer, Appts, 1939-44; British Air Commn, Washington, DC, 1944-46; Coll. of Aeronautics, 1946-47; RAE, Guided Weapons, 1947-51; Chief Instr (Armament Wing) RAF Techn. Coll., 1951-52; Staff Coll., Bracknell, 1953, psa 1953; Project Officer, Blue Streak, Min. of Technology, 1954-57; Asst Dir, GW Engineering, 1957-60; Senior RAF Officer, Skybolt Development Team, USA, 1960-62; Dir, Aircraft Mechanical Engineering, 1963-64; Dir, RAF Aircraft Development (mainly Nimrod), 1964-69; Dep. Controller: of Equipment, Min. of Technology and MoD, 1969-71; Aircraft C, MoD, 1971-72. *Recreations:* scout movement, gardening. *Address:* Chalfont, Waverley Avenue, Fleet, Aldershot, Hants. *T:* Fleet 5835. *Club:* Royal Air Force.

BONSOR, Sir Nicholas (Cosmo), 4th Bt *cr* 1925; *b* 9 Dec. 1942; *s* of Sir Bryan Cosmo Bonsor, 3rd Bt, MC, TD, and of Elizabeth, *d* of late Captain Angus Valdimar Hambro; *S* father, 1977; *m* 1969, Hon. Nadine Marisa Lampson, *d* of 2nd Baron Killearn, *qv*; one *s* one *d. Educ:* Eton; Keble College, Oxford (MA). Barrister-at-law, Inner Temple. Served Royal Buckinghamshire Yeomanry, 1964-69. Practised at the Bar, 1967-75. FRSA 1970. Prospective Parly Cand. (C), Nantwich, Cheshire. *Publications:* political pamphlets on law and trades unions. *Recreations:* sailing, shooting, military history. *Heir: s* Alexander Cosmo Walrond Bonsor, *b* 8 Sept. 1976. *Address:* Liscombe Park, Leighton Buzzard, Beds; Calveley House, Bunbury, Cheshire. *Clubs:* White's; Royal Yacht Squadron; Potters' (Stoke-on-Trent).

BONY, Prof. Jean V., MA; Professor of the History of Art, University of California at Berkeley, since 1962; *b* Le Mans, France, 1 Nov. 1908; *s* of Henri Bony and Marie Normand; *m* 1st, 1936, Clotilde Roure (*d* 1942); one *d*; 2nd, 1953, Mary England. *Educ:* Lycée Louis-le-Grand, Paris; Sorbonne. Agrégé d'Histoire Paris; MA Cantab; Hon. FSA. Bulteau-Lavisse Research Scholarship, 1935-37; Asst Master, Eton Coll., 1937-39 and 1945-46. Served War of 1939-45; 1st Lieut, French Infantry, 1939-44; POW, Germany, June 1940-Dec. 1943. Research Scholar, Centre Nat. de la Recherche Scientifique, 1944-45; Lecturer in History of Art at the French Inst. in London, 1946-61. Focillon Fellow and Vis. Lectr, Yale Univ., 1949; Slade Prof. of Fine Art, University of Cambridge, and Fellow of St John's Coll., Cambridge, 1958-61; Vis. Prof. and Mathews Lectr, Columbia Univ., 1961; Lecturer in History of Art at the University of Lille, France, 1961-62; Wrightsman Lectr, New York Univ., 1969. Corres. Fellow, British Acad., 1972. *Publications:* Notre-Dame de Mantes, 1946; French Cathedrals (with Dr Martin Hürlimann), 1951 (revised edn, 1967); (ed) H. Focillon: The Art of the West in the Middle Ages, English edn 1963; articles in Bulletin Monumental, Congrès Archéologiques de France, Journal of Warburg and Courtauld Institutes, Journal of British Archæological Assoc., etc. *Address:* Department of Art and History of Art, University of California, Berkeley, California 94720, USA.

BONYNGE, Richard, CBE 1977; Musical Director, Australian Opera Company, since 1975; Artistic Director, Vancouver Opera Association, since 1974; *b* Sydney, 29 Sept. 1930; *s* of C. A. Bonynge, Epping, NSW; *m* 1954, Joan Sutherland, *qv*; one *s. Educ:* Sydney Conservatorium (pianist). Official debut, as Conductor, with Santa Cecilia Orch. in Rome, 1962; conducted Faust (1st opera, stage), in Vancouver, 1963; Covent Garden debut, 1964. Has since made numerous concert and operatic appearances. Artistic Dir, Principal Conductor, Sutherland/Williamson Internat. Grand Opera Co., Aust., 1965. Has conducted in major opera houses in Australia, America, Europe, etc. Florence, 1968: Semiramide, etc; Hamburg and New York, 1969-71: Giulio Cesare, Lucia; New York, 1970: Norma, Orfeo; 1973: Tales of Hoffman; also Sydney Opera House, 1974. Records: opera, orchestral works, ballet. *Recreations:* collector of antiques (espec. Staffordshire china), also autographed letters. *Address:* c/o Ingpen & Williams, 14 Kensington Court, London W8, England.

BONYNGE, Mrs Richard; *see* Sutherland, Joan.

BOOLELL, Sir Satcam, Kt 1977; Minister of Agriculture and Natural Resources, Mauritius, since 1959; *b* New Grove,

Mauritius, 11 Sept. 1920; *m* 1948, Inderjeet Kissoodaye; two *s* one *d. Educ:* primary and secondary schs in New Grove, Mare d'Albert, Rose Belle, and Port-Louis; LSE (LLB Hons 1951). Called to the Bar, Lincoln's Inn, 1952. Civil servant, Mauritius, 1944-48. Mem. Central Exec., Mauritius Labour Party, 1955-. Rep. Mauritius, internat. confs. Founder, French daily newspaper, The Nation. *Recreations:* reading travel books, gardening, walking in the countryside. *Address:* (office) Ministry of Agriculture and Natural Resources, Port-Louis, Mauritius. *T:* 2-1378; (home) 4bis Bancilhon Street, Port-Louis. *T:* 2-0079.

BOON, John Trevor, CBE 1968; Chairman, Mills & Boon Ltd, since 1972; *b* 21 Dec. 1916; 3rd *s* of Charles Boon and Mary Boon (*née* Cowpe); *m* 1943, Felicity Ann, *d* of Stewart and Clemence Logan; four *s. Educ:* Felsted Sch.; Trinity Hall, Cambridge (scholar). 1st Cl. Pts I and II History Tripos. Joined Mills & Boon, 1938. Served War, 1939-45: with Royal Norfolk Regt and S Wales Borderers (despatches). Historical Section of War Cabinet, 1945-46. Deputy Chairman: Wood Bros Glass Works Ltd, 1975- (Chm., 1973-75); Harlequin Enterprises Ltd, Toronto, 1972. Director: Book Tokens Ltd; Book Trade Improvements Ltd; Open University Educational Enterprises Ltd. Chm., Publishers' Panel, British Council; Mem. Council, Publishers' Assoc. (Pres., 1961-63); Pres., The International Publishers' Assoc., 1972-76. Over-seas missions: for British Council, to SE Asia, USSR, Czechoslovakia; for Book Development Council, to Malaysia, Singapore, and New Zealand. *Recreations:* walking, swimming, wine, books, friends. *Address:* 48 Molyneux Street, W1H 5HW. *T:* 01-723 0692; The Old Granary, Cley-next-the-sea, Holt, Norfolk. *Clubs:* Garrick, Royal Automobile; Hawks (Cambridge).

BOON, Dr William Robert, FRS 1974; retired; *b* 20 March 1911; *s* of Walter and Ellen Boon; *m* 1938, Marjorie Betty Oury; one *s* two *d. Educ:* St Dunstan's Coll., Catford; King's Coll., London. BSc, PhD, FRIC, FKC 1976. Research, Chemotherapy and Crop Protection, ICI, 1936-69; Dir, Jealott's Hill Res. Station, 1964-69; Man. Dir, Plant Protection Ltd, 1969-73. Vis. Prof., Reading Univ., 1968. Member: Adv. Bd for the Research Councils, 1972-76; NERC, 1976-. Mullard Medal of Royal Society, 1972. *Publications:* papers in Jl Chem. Soc., Jl Soc. Chem. Ind., etc. *Recreations:* gardening, photography, woodwork. *Address:* The Gables, Sid Road, Sidmouth, Devon EX10 9AQ. *T:* Sidmouth 4069. *Club:* Farmers'.

BOORD, Sir Nicolas (John Charles), 4th Bt *cr* 1896; scientific translator; English training specialist; *b* 10 June 1936; *s* of Sir Richard William Boord, 3rd Bt, and of Yvonne, Lady Boord, *d* of late J. A. Hubert Bird; *S* father, 1975; *m* 1965, Françoise Renée Louise Mouret. *Educ:* Eton (Harmsworth Lit. Prize, 1952); Sorbonne, France; Societa Dante Alighieri, Italy; Univ. of Santander, Spain. *Publications:* (trans. jtly) The History of Physics and the Philosophy of Science—Selected Essays (Armin Teske), 1972; numerous translations of scientific papers for English and American scientific and technical jls. *Recreations:* English and French literature and linguistics. *Heir: b* Antony Andrew Boord [*b* 21 May 1938; *m* 1960, Anna Christina von Krogh; one *s* one *d*]. *Address:* Résidence Les Aloadès, Bâtiment L, 94 Traverse Prat, 13008 Marseille, France. *T:* 73.13.95.

BOORMAN, Edwin Roy Pratt; Managing Director, Kent Messenger Group, since 1965; Chairman: South Eastern Newspapers Ltd; South Eastern Magazines Ltd; Adverkit International; Apricot Investments; Bilabel Ltd; Moadford Ltd; Seacoast Newspapers Ltd; Union Motors Ltd; Managing Director: Messenger Print Ltd; Kentish Express Ltd; Partner, E. A. Powdrill consultancy; *b* 7 Nov. 1935; *m* Merrilyn Ruth Pettit; four *d. Educ:* Rydal, Colwyn Bay, N Wales; Queen's Coll., Cambridge (MA Econ. History). National Service, 1954-56. Cambridge Univ., 1956-59; Kent Messenger, 1959; Editor: South Eastern Gazette, 1960-62; Kent Messenger, 1962-65. Summer sch., S Illinois Univ., Carbondale, St Louis, 1962; Kentucky Colonel 1962. Vice Pres., Kent Co. branch Royal British Legion; Member: Appeals Cttee, St John Ambulance; Kent Co. Show Exec. Cttee; Kent Co. Playing Fields Exec. Cttee; Vice President: Maidstone Rugby Club; Maidstone United Football Club; President: Dickens Area Newsagents' Benevolent Assoc.; Maidstone Surgical Aid; Chm. Publicity Cttee, Medway Regatta; Hon. Sec. Linton Conservative Assoc. *Recreation:* sailing. *Address:* The White Lodge, Linton, Maidstone, Kent. *T:* Maidstone 43129. *Clubs:* Press, Veteran Car, Locomotive of GB; Kent CCC; Royal Yachting Association, Medway Yacht.

BOORSTIN, Dr Daniel J.; (12th) Librarian of Congress, since Nov. 1975; *b* 1 Oct. 1914; *s* of Samuel Boorstin and Dora (*née* Olsan); *m* 1941, Ruth Carolyn Frankel; three *s. Educ:* schs in

Tulsa, Okla; Harvard Univ. (AB, summa cum Laude); Balliol Coll., Oxford (Rhodes Schol., BA Juris. 1st Cl. Hons, BCL 1st Cl. Hons); Yale Univ. Law Sch. (Sterling Fellow, JSD). Called to Bar, Inner Temple, 1937; admitted Mass Bar, 1942. Instr, tutor in history and lit., Harvard Univ. and Radcliffe Coll., 1938-42; Lectr, legal history, Law Sch., Harvard, 1939-42; Sen. Attorney, Office of Lend Lease Admin, Washington, DC, 1942-43; Office of Asst SG, USA, 1942-43; Asst Prof. of History, Swarthmore Coll., 1942-44; Univ. of Chicago, 1944-69: Asst Prof., 1944-49; Associate Prof., Preston and Sterling Morton Distinguished Prof. of Amer. History, 1956-69. During his 25 years tenure at Chicago, Visiting Lectr at Rome and Kyoto Univs, Sorbonne and Cambridge (Fellow, Trinity Coll., and Pitt Prof. of Amer. History and Instns; LittD 1968). Smithsonian Institution: Dir, Nat. Museum History and Techn., 1969-73; Sen. Historian, 1973-75. Many public service membership assignments, trusteeships, and active concern with a number of Amer. Assocs, esp. those relating to Amer. history, educn and cultural affairs. Past Pres., American Studies Assoc. Hon. LittD Michigan, 1976. *Publications: include:* The Mysterious Science of the Law, 1941; The Lost World of Thomas Jefferson, 1948; The Genius of American Politics, 1953; The Americans: The Colonial Experience, 1958 (Bancroft Prize); America and the Image of Europe, 1960; The Image, 1962; The Americans: The National Experience, 1965 (Parkman Prize); The Decline of Radicalism, 1969; The Sociology of the Absurd, 1970; The Americans: The Democratic Experience, 1973 (Pulitzer Prize for History and Dexter Prize, 1974); Democracy and Its Discontents, 1974; The Exploring Spirit (BBC 1975 Reith Lectures), 1976; (for young readers) Landmark History of the American People, vol. I, From Plymouth to Appomattox, 1968; vol. II, From Appomattox to the Moon, 1970; (ed) Delaware Cases 1792-1830, 1943; (ed) An American Primer, 1966; (ed) American Civilization, 1971; (ed) The Chicago History of American Civilization (27 vols). *Address:* (home) 3541 Ordway Street, NW, Washington, DC 20016, USA; (office) Library of Congress, Washington, DC 20540. *T:* Library of Congress 426-5000. *Clubs:* Cosmos, National Press (Washington); Elizabethan (Yale).

BOOSEY, Leslie Arthur; Hon. President: International Confederation of Societies of Authors and Composers; Performing Right Society; President, Boosey & Hawkes Ltd; *b* 26 July 1887; *s* of Arthur and Lucy Ashton Boosey; *m* 1921, Ethel Torfrida, *d* of Frank Marchant; three *s* one *d. Educ:* Malvern Coll.; abroad. Served with 22nd London Regt The Queens, 1908-19; France, 1915-18. Chevalier, Légion d'Honneur. *Address:* Meadowlands, Hambledon Road, Denmead, Hants. *T:* Waterlooville 55995. *Clubs:* Savile, Oriental.

BOOT, Dr Henry Albert Howard; Senior Principal Scientific Officer, Royal Naval Scientific Service, 1954-77 (Principal Scientific Officer, 1948-54); *b* 29 July 1917; *s* of late Henry James and late Ruby May Boot; *m* 1948, Penelope May Herrington; two *s. Educ:* King Edward's High Sch., Birmingham (Scholar); Univ. of Birmingham. BSc 1938; PhD 1941. Invention of the cavity magnetron (with Prof. J. T, Randall, FRS), 1939; research on the cavity magnetron at Univ. of Birmingham, 1939-45; Nuffield Research Fellow in Physics at Univ. of Birmingham, 1945-48. Royal Society of Arts Thomas Gray Memorial Prize (with J. T. Randall), 1943; Award by Royal Commission on Awards to Inventors, 1949; John Price Wetherill Medal of the Franklin Institute, 1958; John Scott Award, 1959 (with Prof. J. Randall). *Publications:* various papers on the production of high power ultra high frequency oscillation and controlled thermonuclear fusion, also optical masers. *Recreation:* sailing. *Address:* The Old Mill Cottage, Rushden, near Buntingford, Herts. *T:* Broadfield 231. *Club:* Athenæum.

BOOTE, Col Charles Geoffrey Michael, MBE 1945; TD 1943; DL; Vice Lord-Lieutenant of Staffordshire, 1969-76; *b* 29 Sept. 1909; *s* of Lt-Col Charles Edmund Boote, TD, The North Staffordshire Regt (killed in action, 1916); *m* 1937, Elizabeth Gertrude, *er d* of Evan Richard Davies, Market Drayton, Salop; three *s. Educ:* Bedford Sch. 2nd Lt 5th Bn North Staffordshire Regt, 1927. Served 1939-45, UK and NW Europe; despatches, 1945; Lt-Col, 1947. Director, H. Clarkson (Midlands) Ltd, 1969-75. Dir, Brit. Pottery Manufacturers' Fedn (Trustee) Ltd, 1955, retd Dec. 1969; Pres., Brit. Pottery Manufacturers' Fedn, 1957-58; Vice-Chm., Glazed and Floor Tile Manufacturers' Assoc., 1953-57. Hon. Col 5/6 Bn North Staffordshire Regt, 1963-67; Mem. Staffs TAVR Cttee, retd 1976. JP, Stoke-on-Trent, 1955-65; DL 1958, JP 1959, High Sheriff, 1967-68, Staffordshire. Chm., Eccleshall PSD, 1971-76; Mem. Court of Governors, Keele Univ., 1957. *Recreations:* salmon fishing; British Racing Drivers' Club (Life Mem.); North Staffordshire

Hunt (Hon. Sec. 1948-59). *Address:* Morile Mhor, Tomatin, Inverness-shire. *T:* Tomatin 319. *Club:* Army and Navy.

BOOTE, Robert Edward, CVO 1971; Director, Nature Conservancy Council, since 1973; *b* 6 Feb. 1920; *s* of Ernest Haydn Boote and Helen Rose Boote; *m* 1948, Vera (*née* Badian); one *s* one *d. Educ:* London Univ. (BSc Econ). DPA, FCIS. War service, 1939-46, Actg Lt-Col, Hon. Major. Admin. Officer, City of Stoke-on-Trent, 1946-48; Chief Admin. Officer, Staffs County Planning and Develt Dept, 1948-54; Principal, 1954-64, Dep. Dir, 1964-73, Nature Conservancy. Sec. 1965-71, formerly Dep. Sec., Countryside in 1970 Confs, 1963, 1965, 1970 and numerous study groups; UK Deleg. to Council of Europe Cttee for Conservation of Nature and Natural Resources, 1963-71, Chm. and Mem. various working parties, etc; Chm. Preparatory Gp for Conservation Year 1970; Chm. Organising Cttee for European Conservation Conf. 1970 (Conf. Vice-Pres.); Chm. European Cttee, 1969-71; Consultant for European Architectural Heritage Year 1975. Mem., Governing Bd and Council, IUCN, 1975-. Greek Distinguished Service Medal, 1946. Hon. AILA 1971. *Publications:* (as Robert Arvill) Man and Environment, 1967 (4th edn 1976); various papers and articles. *Recreations:* walking, music. *Address:* 27 Woodhayes Road, Wimbledon Common, SW19 4RF. *T:* 01-946 1551. *Club:* Athenæum.

BOOTH; see Gore-Booth and Sclater-Booth.

BOOTH, Alan Shore, QC 1975; **His Honour Judge Alan Booth;** a Circuit Judge, since 1976; *b* Aug. 1922; 4th *s* of Parkin Stanley Booth and Ethel Mary Shore; *m* 1954, Mary Gwendoline Hilton; one *s* one *d. Educ:* Shrewsbury Sch.; Liverpool Univ. (LLB). Served War of 1939-45, RNVR, Fleet Air Arm (despatches 1944): Sub-Lt 1942; HMS Illustrious, 1943-45; Lieut 1944. Called to Bar, Gray's Inn, 1949. A Recorder of the Crown Court, 1972-76. Governor, Shrewsbury Sch., 1969. *Recreations:* golf, beagling, sailing, reading. *Address:* Little Paddocks, Croft Drive East, Caldy, Wirral, Merseyside. *T:* 051-625 5796. *Clubs:* Royal Liverpool Golf; Royal and Ancient (St Andrews).

BOOTH, Rt. Hon. Albert Edward, PC 1976; MP (Lab), Barrow-in-Furness since 1966; Secretary of State for Employment, since 1976; *b* 28 May 1928; *e s* of Albert Henry Booth and Janet Mathieson; *m* 1957, Joan Amis; three *s. Educ:* St Thomas's Sch., Winchester; S Shields Marine Sch.; Rutherford Coll. of Technology. Engineering Draughtsman. Election Agent, 1951 and 1955. County Borough Councillor, 1962-65. Contested (Lab) Tynemouth, 1964. Minister of State, Dept of Employment, 1974-76. Chm., Select Cttee on Statutory Instruments, 1970-74. *Address:* 145 Woodwarde Road, SE22.

BOOTH, Catherine B.; see Bramwell-Booth.

BOOTH, Charles Leonard, MVO 1961; HM Diplomatic Service; Counsellor, Belgrade, since 1973; *b* 9 March 1925; *s* of Charles Leonard and Marion Booth; *m* 1958, Mary Gillian Emms, two *s* two *d. Educ:* Pembroke Coll., Oxford Univ., 1942-43 and 1947-50. Served RA (Capt.), 1943-47. Joined HM Foreign Service, 1950; Foreign Office, 1950-51; Third and Second Secretary, Rangoon, 1951-55; FO, 1955-60 (Private Sec. to Parly Under-Sec. of State, 1958-60); First Sec., Rome, 1960-63; Head of Chancery, Rangoon, 1963-64, and Bangkok, 1964-67; FO, 1967-69. Counsellor, 1968; Deputy High Comr, Kampala, 1969-71; Consul-General and Counsellor (Administration), Washington, 1971-73. Officer of Order of Merit of Italian Republic, 1961. *Recreations:* Italian opera, gardening, walking, tennis. *Address:* c/o Foreign and Commonwealth Office, SW1. *Club:* Travellers'.

BOOTH, Prof. Christopher Charles; Director, Clinical Research Centre, Medical Research Council, since 1978; *b* 22 June 1924; *s* of Lionel Barton Booth and Phyllis Petley Duncan; *m* 1st, 1959, Lavinia Loughridge, Belfast; one *s* one *d*; 2nd, 1970, Soad Tabaqchali; one *d. Educ:* Sedbergh Sch., Yorks; University of St Andrews; MB 1951, MD 1958 (Rutherford Gold Medal). Junior appointments at Dundee Royal Infirmary, Hammersmith Hosp. and Addenbrooke's Hosp., Cambridge; successively Medical Tutor, Lecturer in Medicine and Senior Lecturer, Postgraduate Medical School of London; Prof. and Dir of Dept of Medicine, RPMS, London Univ., until 1977. FRCP 1964; FRCPEd 1967; Hon. FACP 1973. Docteur (hc) Paris, 1975. Dicke Gold Medal, Dutch Soc. of Gastroenterology, 1973. *Publications:* (with Betsy C. Corner) Chain of Friendship: Letters of Dr John Fothergill of London, 1735-1780; papers in med. jls on relationship of nutritional disorders to disease of the alimentary tract, and on medical history. *Recreations:* fishing, history. *Address:* 39 Inner Staithe, Hartington Road, W4. *T:* 01-994 4914.

BOOTH, Rev. Canon David Herbert, MBE 1944; Provost, Shoreham Grammar School, Sussex, since 1977 (Headmaster, 1972-77); Chaplain to the Queen, 1957-77; *b* 26 Jan. 1907; *s* of Robert and Clara Booth; *m* 1942, Diana Mary Chard; two *s* one *d. Educ:* Bedford Sch.; Pembroke Coll., Cambridge; Ely Theological Coll. BA (3rd cl. Hist. Trip. part II), 1931; MA 1936; deacon, 1932; priest, 1933; Curate, All Saints', Hampton, 1932-34; Chaplain, Tonbridge Sch., 1935-40; Chaplain, RNVR, 1940-45; Rector of Stepney, 1945-53; Vicar of Brighton, 1953-59; Prebendary of Waltham in Chichester Cathedral, 1953-59; Archdeacon of Lewes, 1959-71; Prebendary of Bury in Chichester Cathedral, 1972-76; Canon Emeritus of Chichester, 1976. Select Preacher, University of Cambridge, 1947. Mem. of Archbishop's Commission on South East, 1965. *Recreations:* horses, gardening and family life. *Address:* Hurst Mill Cottage, Ram Lane, Hothfield, Ashford, Kent. *T:* Pluckley 549.

BOOTH, Sir Douglas Allen, 3rd Bt, *cr* 1916; writer and publisher; *b* 2 Dec. 1949; *s* of Sir Philip Booth, 2nd Bt, and Ethel, *d* of Joseph Greenfield, NY, USA; *S* father 1946. *Educ:* Beverly Hills High Sch.; Harvard Univ. (Harvard Nat. Scholarship, Nat. Merit Scholarship, 1967); BA (magna cum laude) 1975. *Recreations:* music, film, back-packing. *Heir: b* Derek Blake Booth, *b* 7 April 1953. *Address:* 1255 Daniels Drive, Los Angeles, Calif 90035, USA.

BOOTH, Eric Stuart, CBE 1971; FRS 1967; Chairman, Yorkshire Electricity Board, since 1972; Member Central Electricity Generating Board, 1959-71; *b* 14 Oct. 1914; *s* of Henry and Annie Booth; *m* 1945, Mary Elizabeth Melton; two *d. Educ:* Batley Grammar Sch.; Liverpool Univ. Apprentice, Metropolitan Vickers Electrical Co. Ltd, 1936-38; Technical Engineer, Yorks Electric Power Co., 1938-46; Dep., later City Electrical Engineer and Manager, Salford Corporation, 1946-48; various posts associated with construction of Power Stations with British, later Central, Electricity Authority, 1948-57, Dep. Chief Engineer (Generation Design and Construction), 1957; Chief Design and Construction Engineer, Central Electricity Generating Bd, 1958-59. Part-time Mem., UKAEA, 1965-72; Pres., IEE, 1976-77. *Address:* Pinecroft, Upper Dunsforth, York YO5 9RU. *T:* Boroughbridge 2821. *Club:* Royal Automobile.

BOOTH, Gordon, CMG 1969; CVO 1976; HM Diplomatic Service; HBM Consul-General, New York, and Director-General of Trade Development in the USA, since 1975; *b* 22 Nov. 1921; *s* of Walter and Grace Booth, Bolton, Lancs; *m* 1944, Jeanne Mary Kirkham; one *s* one *d. Educ:* Canon Slade Sch.; London Univ. (BCom). Served War of 1939-45: Capt. RAC and 13/18th Royal Hussars, 1941-46. Min. of Labour and Bd of Trade, 1946-55; Trade Comr, Canada and West Indies, 1955-65; Mem. HM Diplomatic Service, 1965-; Counsellor (Commercial), British Embassy in Copenhagen, 1966-69; Dir, Coordination of Export Services, DTI, 1969-71; Consul-General, Sydney, 1971-74. *Recreations:* golf, bridge. *Address:* c/o Foreign and Commonwealth Office, SW1.

BOOTH, James; His Honour Judge Booth; a Circuit Judge (formerly a County Court Judge), since 1969; *b* 3 May 1914; *s* of James and Agnes Booth; *m* 1954, Joyce Doreen Mather; two *s* one *d. Educ:* Bolton Sch.; Manchester Univ. Called to Bar, Gray's Inn, 1936 (Arden Scholar, Gray's Inn). Town Clerk, Ossett, Yorks 1939-41. RAFVR, 1941-46 (Flt-Lieut). Contested (L): West Leeds, 1945; Darwen, 1950. Recorder of Barrow-in-Furness, 1967-69. *Recreation:* fell walking. *Address:* Spinney End, Worsley, Lancs M28 4QN. *T:* 061-790 2003. *Club:* Manchester (Manchester).

BOOTH, John Antony W.; *see* Ward-Booth.

BOOTH, John Wells; Director: Unit Construction Co. Ltd; Alfred Booth & Co. Ltd (formerly Chairman); *b* 19 May 1903; *s* of late Charles and Grace Wells Booth, Liverpool; *m* 1929, Margaret, *d* of late Mr and Mrs S. J. Lawry; two *s* one *d. Educ:* Royal Naval Colls Osborne and Dartmouth. Royal Navy, 1917-25 (Lieut Comdr). Booth Steamship Co. Ltd., 1926-45 (Chm., 1939-45). Civil Aviation, 1945-50. Chm., British South American Airways Corporation, 1946-49; Dep. Chm., BOAC, 1949-50; Bd Mem., BOAC, 1950-65; Dir, Phoenix Assurance Co. Ltd, 1945-73. Former Chairman: Liverpool Seamens' Welfare Cttee (Mem. Seamens' Welfare Bd); Liverpool Steamship Owners' Assoc.; former JP for Co. of Cheshire. *Address:* Park House, Easebourne, Midhurst, West Sussex. *Club:* Flyfishers'.

BOOTH, Margaret Myfanwy Wood, QC 1976; *b* 1933; *d* of Alec Wood Booth and Lilian May Booth. *Educ:* Northwood Coll.; University Coll., London (LLM). Called to the Bar, Middle Temple, 1956. Chm., Family Law Bar Assoc., 1976-78.

Governor, Northwood Coll., 1975-. *Publications:* (co-ed) Rayden on Divorce, 10th, 11th, 12th edns; (co-ed) Clarke Hall and Morrison on Children, 9th edn 1977. *Address:* 1 Mitre Court Buildings, Temple, EC4. *T:* 01-353 0137.

BOOTH, Sir Michael Savile Gore-, 7th Bt, *cr* 1760; *b* 24 July 1908; *s* of 6th Bt and Mary (*d* 1968), *d* of Rev. S. L'Estrage-Malone; *S* father, 1944. *Educ:* Rugby; Trinity Coll., Cambridge. *Heir: b* Angus Josslyn Gore-Booth [*b* 25 June 1920; *m* 1948, Hon. Rosemary Vane (marr. diss., 1954), *o d* of 10th Baron Barnard; one *s* one *d*]. *Address:* Lissadell, Sligo.

BOOTH, Richard George William Pitt; Chairman, Richard Booth (Booksellers) Ltd, since 1961; *b* 12 Sept. 1938; *m* (marr. diss.). *Educ:* Rugby; Univ. of Oxford. Established Richard Booth (Booksellers) Ltd, 1961. *Publications:* Country Life Book of Book Collecting, 1976; Independence for Hay, 1977. *Recreations:* creating a monarchy in Hay (began home rule movement, 1 April 1977); gardening. *Address:* Hay Castle, Hay-on-Wye, via Hereford.

BOOTH, Sir Robert (Camm), Kt 1977; CBE 1967; TD; Chairman, National Exhibition Centre Ltd, since 1975 (also Chief Executive, 1977); Director, Birmingham Chamber of Industry and Commerce, since 1965; *b* 9 May 1916; *s* of late Robert Wainhouse Booth; *m* 1939, Veronica Courtenay, *d* of late F. C. Lamb; one *s* three *d. Educ:* Altrincham Grammar Sch.; Manchester Univ. (LLB). Called to Bar, Gray's Inn. War Service 8th (A) Bn Manchester Regt, France, Malta, Middle East, Italy, 1939-46. Manchester Chamber of Commerce, 1946-58; Sec., Birmingham Chamber of Industry and Commerce, 1958-75. Overseas travel with 15 Trade Missions. Life Mem. Court of Governors 1969-, Mem. Council 1973-, Birmingham Univ.; Governor, Sixth Form Coll., Solihull, 1974-. Mem. W Mids Econ. Planning Council, 1974-; Mem. BOTB Adv. Council, 1975-. Hon. FInstM. Hon. DSc Aston, 1975. Midland Man of the Year Press Radio and TV Award, 1970. *Address:* White House, 7 Sandal Rise, Solihull B9 13ET. *T:* 021-705 5311. *Club:* Naval and Military.

BOOTH, Rev. William James; Chaplain, Westminster School, London, since 1974; *b* 3 Feb. 1939; *s* of William James Booth and Elizabeth Ethel Booth (*née* Leckey). *Educ:* Ballymena Acad., Co. Antrim; TCD (MA). Curate, St Luke's Parish, Belfast, 1962-64; Chaplain, Cranleigh Sch., Surrey, 1965-74. Priest-in-Ordinary to the Queen, 1976-. *Recreations:* music, hi-fi, cooking. *Address:* 14 Barton Street, SW1P 3NE. *T:* 01-222 3707.

BOOTHBY, family name of **Baron Boothby.**

BOOTHBY, Baron *cr* 1958, of Buchan and Rattray Head (Life Peer); **Robert John Graham Boothby,** KBE 1953; President, Anglo-Israel Association, 1962-75; *b* 1900; *o s* of late Sir Robert Tuite Boothby, KBE, Beechwood, Edinburgh, and Mabel, *d* of late H. H. Lancaster; *m* 1st, 1935, Diana (marr. diss. 1937), *d* of late Lord Richard Cavendish, PC, CB, CMG; 2nd, 1967, Wanda, *d* of Giuseppe Sanna, Sardinia. *Educ:* Eton; Magdalen Coll., Oxford. BA 1921, MA 1959. Contested Orkney and Shetland, 1923; MP (U) East Aberdeenshire, 1924-58; Parliamentary Private Sec. to the Chancellor of the Exchequer (Rt Hon. Winston S. Churchill, MP), 1926-29; Parliamentary Sec., Ministry of Food, 1940-41; a British delegate to the Consultative Assembly of the Council of Europe, 1949-57; Vice-Chm. Cttee on Economic Affairs, 1952-56; Hon. Pres., Scottish Chamber of Agriculture, 1934. Rector, University of St Andrews, 1958-61. Chairman, Royal Philharmonic Orchestra, 1961-63, Hon. Life Mem., 1976; Vice-Pres., Delius Soc. Radner Lectr, Columbia Univ., NY, 1960. Hon. LLD St Andrews, 1959. Hon. Burgess of the Burghs of Peterhead, Fraserburgh, Turriff and Rosehearty. Officer of the Legion of Honour, 1950. *Publications:* The New Economy, 1943; I Fight to Live, 1947; My Yesterday, Your Tomorrow, 1962. *Address:* 1 Eaton Square, SW1. *Clubs:* White's; Royal and Ancient (St Andrews).

BOOTHBY, Basil; *see* Boothby, E. B.

BOOTHBY, (Evelyn) Basil, CMG 1958; HM Diplomatic Service, retired; Tutor, London University Extra-Mural Studies, since 1970; *b* 9 Sept. 1910; *s* of Basil T. B. Boothby and Katherine Knox; *m* 1946, Susan Asquith; two *s* one *d* (and one *s* decd). *Educ:* Winchester; CCC, Cambridge. Student Interpreter, China Consular Service, 1933; appointed a Vice-Consul in China, 1936; served at Shanghai and Hankow (periods Acting Consul); Vice-Consul, Boston, 1940; employed at New York, Dec. 1941-June 1942, when reappointed a Vice-Consul in China and transf. to Chungking; seconded to Govt of India for service in Chinese Relations Office, Calcutta, Oct. 1943-July 1944; Actg Consul

Kweilin and Kunming, also Athens, successively, 1944-45; promoted Consul, Sept. 1945; apptd Foreign Service Officer, Grade 7, in Foreign Office, Nov. 1946; promoted Counsellor, Foreign Service Officer, Grade 6, and became Head of UN (Economic and Social) Dept, Sept. 1949; seconded to Commonwealth Relations Office for service in Ontario and attached to Canadian National Defence Coll., Sept. 1950; apptd Counsellor, Rangoon, Nov. 1951 (Chargé d'Affaires, 1952); Counsellor, British Embassy, Brussels, 1954; Head of African Dept, Foreign Office, 1959; British Ambassador to Iceland, 1962-65; Permanent British Rep. to Council of Europe, 1965-69. Lectr, Morley Coll., 1969-70. *Address:* 23 Holland Park Avenue, W11.
See also P. P. Read.

BOOTHBY, Sir Hugo (Robert Brooke), 15th Bt, *cr* 1660; JP; Lieutenant, South Glamorgan, since 1974 (Vice-Lieutenant of Glamorgan, 1957-74); *b* 10 Aug. 1907; *s* of Sir Seymour William Brooke Boothby, 14th Bt, and Clara Margaret (*d* 1969), *d* of late Robert Valpy; *S* father 1951; *m* 1938, Evelyn Ann, *o d* of H. C. R. Homfray; one *s* two *d. Educ:* Lancing; Hertford Coll., Oxford. Served War of 1939-45, Capt. RA 53 (Welsh) Div., 1942-44. Capt. RA (TA). Dir, Wales Tourist Bd, 1965-70; S Wales Regional Dir, Lloyds Bank, 1963; Dir, Divisional Bd for Wales, Nationwide Building Soc., 1971-; Member: Cardiff Rural Dist Council, 1936-58 (Chm. 1948-49 and 1949-50); Representative Body, Church in Wales, 1955-65; National Broadcasting Council for Wales, 1953-56; Glamorgan County Agricultural Executive Cttee, 1953-62; Court and Council, Nat. Museum of Wales, 1955. Chm., Historic Houses Assoc. in Wales. Fellow, Woodard Corporation, 1961-. JP 1950, DL 1953, Glamorgan; High Sheriff, Glamorgan, 1953. *Recreation:* shooting. *Heir: s* Brooke Charles Boothby [*b* 6 April 1949; *m* 1976, Georgiana Alexandra, *d* of Sir John (Wriothesley) Russell, *qv*; one *d*]. *Address:* Fonmon Castle, Barry, South Glamorgan CF6 9ZN. *T:* Rhoose 710206. *Clubs:* Travellers', Brooks's; Cardiff and County (Cardiff).

BOOTHE, Clare; *see* Luce, Mrs Henry R.

BOOTHROYD, Betty; MP (Lab) West Bromwich West, since 1974 (West Bromwich, May 1973-1974); *b* Yorkshire, 8 Oct. 1929; *d* of Archibald and Mary Boothroyd. *Educ:* Dewsbury Coll. of Commerce and Art. Personal/Political Asst to Labour Ministers. Accompanied Parly delegns to: European Confs, 1955-60; Soviet Union, China and Vietnam, 1957; N Atlantic Assembly, 1974; Commonwealth Parly Conference, Sri Lanka, 1974. An Asst Govt Whip, Oct. 1974-Nov. 1975. Mem., European Parlt, 1975-77. Worked with late President Kennedy's election campaign, 1960; Legislative Asst to US Congressman, 1960-62. Councillor, Hammersmith Borough Council, 1965-68. Contested (Lab): SE Leicester (by-elec.), 1957; Peterborough (gen. elec.), 1959; Nelson and Colne (by-elec.), 1968; Rossendale (gen. elec.), 1970. *Recreations:* dominoes, scrabble. *Address:* House of Commons, SW1A 0AA.

BOOTHROYD, Edith Hester, (Mrs Francis Boothroyd); Member, Board of the Crown Agents, since 1975; Associate of Newnham College, Cambridge, since 1975; *b* 11 Jan. 1915; *d* of late Stanley John Benham; *m* 1940, Francis Boothroyd; two *d. Educ:* St Felix Sch., Southwold; Newnham Coll., Cambridge. Min. of Economic Warfare, 1939-44; BoT, 1945-49; Statistician and Prin., Treasury, 1949-64; Asst Sec., DEA, 1965-67, Asst Under-Sec. of State, DEA, 1967-69; Under-Sec., Treasury, 1969-75. Hon. Treasurer, Aldeburgh Fest. Assoc., 1976-. *Recreations:* gardening, music, travel. *Address:* Ranworth House, Nayland, near Colchester, CO6 4CJ. *T:* Nayland 262331. *Club:* Royal Commonwealth Society.

BOOTHROYD, (John) Basil; writer and broadcaster; *b* 4 March 1910; *m* 1939, Phyllis Barbara Youngman; one *s. Educ:* Lincoln Cathedral Choir Sch.; Lincoln Sch. Bank Clerk, 1927. Served with RAF Police, 1941-45; Personal Asst to Provost-Marshal from 1943. Punch contributor continuously from 1938, an Asst Editor, 1952-70, Mem. Punch Table, 1955. Much broadcasting and miscellaneous frivolous journalism; some television, lecturing and public speaking. *Publications:* Home Guard Goings-On, 1941; Adastral Bodies, 1942; Are Sergeants Human? 1945; Are Officers Necessary?, 1946; Lost, A Double-Fronted Shop, 1947; The House About a Man, 1959; Motor If You Must, 1960; To My Embarrassment, 1961; The Whole Thing's Laughable, 1964; You Can't be Serious, 1966; Let's Stay Married, 1967 (and US, 1967); Stay Married Abroad, 1968; Boothroyd at Bay (radio talks), 1970; Philip (an approved biography of HRH the Duke of Edinburgh), 1971 (and US, 1971); Accustomed As I Am, 1975; Let's Move House, 1977. *Recreations:* playing the piano, working. *Address:* 56 Oathall Road, Haywards Heath, Sussex RH16 3EN. *T:* Haywards Heath 54340. *Club:* Savage.

BOOTLE-WILBRAHAM, family name of **Baron Skelmersdale.**

BOR, Walter George, CBE 1975; RIBA DisTP; FRTPI; Consultant, Llewelyn-Davies Weeks Forestier-Walker & Bor, London, since 1966, and Llewelyn-Davies Associates, New York, since 1969; *b* 1916, Czech parentage; father chemical engineer; *m* 1954, Glen (*née* Conolly); two *s* one *d. Educ:* Prague Univ. (degree of Arch.); Bartlett Sch. of Architecture and Sch. of Planning and Regional Research, London (Dip.). Private architectural practice, London, 1946-47; London County Council, 1947-62 (in charge of planning of London's East End, 1958; Dep. Planning Officer with special responsibility for city design, 1960-62); Liverpool City Planning Officer, 1962-66. Mem. Minister's Planning Advisory Gp, 1964-65. In private practice as architect and planning consultant, 1966-. Pres., Town Planning Inst., 1970-71; Vice-Pres., Housing Centre Trust, 1971-. Vis. Prof., Princeton Univ., 1977. *Publications:* Liverpool Interim Planning Policy, 1965; Liverpool City Centre Plan (jt), 1966; The Milton Keynes Plan (jt), 1970; Airport City (Third London Airport urbanisation studies) (jt), 1970; The Making of Cities, 1972; Urban Motorways Studies for DOE (jt), 1972; SE London and the Fleet Line for LTE (jt), 1973; Bogota Urban Development for UNDP (jt), 1974; Concept Plan for Tehran new city centre, 1974; Shetland Draft Structure Plan, 1975; (jtly) Birmingham Inner Area Study, 1977; articles for jls of RTPI, RIBA, TCPA, ICE, RICS, Amer. Inst. of Planners, Princeton Univ.; L'Architecture d'aujourd'hui. *Recreations:* music, theatre, skiing, tennis, swimming, sketching. *Address:* 99 Swains Lane, Highgate, N6 6PJ. *T:* 01-340 6540. *Club:* Reform.

BORDEN, Henry, OC 1969; CMG 1943; QC 1938; Canadian Lawyer; Director: Canadian Investment Fund Ltd; Canadian Fund Inc.; IBM Canada Ltd; Massey-Ferguson Ltd; Hon. Director, Huron and Erie Mortgage Corporation; *b* Halifax, NS, 25 Sept. 1901; *s* of Henry Clifford and Mabel (Ashmere) Barnstead Borden, both of Halifax, NS; *m* 1929, Jean Creelman, *d* of late Dr D. A. MacRae, Toronto, Ont; three *s* two *d. Educ:* King's Coll. Sch., Windsor, NS; McGill Univ.; Dalhousie Law Sch.; Exeter Coll., Oxford (Rhodes Schol.). BA Political Science and Economics, McGill, 1921; BA Oxon, 1926. With Royal Bank of Canada, 1921-22. Called to Bar, Lincoln's Inn, 1927; to Bar of Nova Scotia, 1927; to Bar of Ont, 1927. Senior Mem., Borden, Elliot, Kelley, Palmer, 1936-46; Gen. Counsel, Dept of Munitions and Supply, Ottawa, 1939-42; Chairman: Wartime Industries Control Bd, Ottawa, and Co-ordinator of Controls, Dept of Munitions and Supply, Sept. 1942-43; Royal Commission on Energy, 1957-59. Pres., Brazilian Traction, Light & Power Co., 1946-63, Chm., 1963-65; Chm. and Pres., Brinco Ltd (formerly British Newfoundland Corporation Ltd), 1965-69; Dir Emeritus, Canadian Imperial Bank of Commerce; Hon. Dir, Brascan Ltd. Dir, Mem. Exec. Cttee and Past Pres., Royal Agric. Winter Fair. Formerly Lectr, Corp. Law, Osgoode Hall Law Sch.; Past Pres. Canadian Club of Toronto. Past Chm., Bd of Governors, Univ. of Toronto. Hon. LLD: St Francis Xavier, 1960; Dalhousie, 1968; Toronto, 1972; Hon. DCL Acadia, 1960. Is an Anglican. Grand Officer, Nat. Order of the Southern Cross (Brazil), 1962; Canada Centennial Medal, 1967. *Publications:* (jtly) Fraser & Borden, Hand Book of Canadian Companies, 1931; ed, Robert Laird Borden: His Memoirs, 1938; ed, Letters to Limbo, by Rt Hon. Sir Robert L. Borden, 1971. *Recreations:* farming, fishing. *Address:* Tannery Hill Farm, RR No 2, King, Ont., Canada. *Clubs:* York, Toronto (Toronto).

BORDER, Hugh William; *b* 26 Nov. 1890; *s* of William Border and Mary Abbott; *m* 1917, Mabel Evelyn Watts (*d* 1975); one *d. Educ:* Latymer Upper Sch., Hammersmith. Employed in the Ministry of Labour, 1912-14; Consulate-Gen., Rotterdam 1914-20; Probationer Vice-Consul at Colon, July 1920; Acting Consul, 1921 and 1923; Acting Vice-Consul at Constantsa and Braila, 1924; Vice-Consul at Braila, 1924; Acting Consul-Gen., Galatz, 1925 and 1926; Vice-Consul, 1926; Acting Consul-General, Galatz, 1927, 1928 and 1929; Chargé d'Affaires a.i., Managua, 1930; HM Consul, Managua, July 1930; HM Consul-Gen. (local rank) Havana, 1932; Chargé d'Affaires, Havana, Feb.-June 1933; HM Consul, Havre, 1934-37; HM Consul, Bordeaux, 1937; HM Consul Nantes, 1939-40; HM Consul-Gen. at Seville, 1945-50; retired, 1950. *Address:* 36 Bonfields Avenue, Swanage BH19 1PL. *T:* Swanage 2508.

BOREEL, Sir Francis (David), 13th Bt, *cr* 1645; Consul-General, Netherlands Foreign Service, since 1974 (Attaché, 1956); *b* 14 June 1926; *s* of Sir Alfred Boreel, 12th Bt and Countess Reiniera Adriana (*d* 1957), *d* of Count Francis David Schimmelpenninck; *S* father 1964; *m* 1964, Suzanne Campagne; three *d. Educ:* Utrecht Univ. *Recreations:* tennis, sailing. *Heir:* kinsman Stephen Gerard Boreel, *b* 9 Feb. 1945. *Address:* Netherlands Consulat-General, Avenida Paulista 2073/20, São Paulo, Brazil.

BOREHAM, Arthur John, CB 1974; Deputy Director, Central Statistical Office, since 1972 (Assistant Director, 1971-72); *b* 30 July 1925; 3rd *s* of late Ven. Frederick Boreham, Archdeacon of Cornwall and Chaplain to the Queen, and late Caroline Mildred Boreham; *m* 1948, Heather, *o d* of Harold Edwin Horth, FRIBA, and Muriel Horth; three *s* one *d. Educ:* Marlborough; Trinity Coll., Oxford. Agricultural Economics Research Inst., Oxford, 1950; Min. of Food, 1951; Min. of Agric., 1952; Gen. Register Office, 1955; Central Statistical Office, 1958; Chief Statistician, Gen. Register Office, 1963; Dir of Economics and Statistics, Min. of Technology, 1967-71. *Recreation:* music. *Address:* Piperscroft, Brittain's Lane, Sevenoaks, Kent. *T:* Sevenoaks 54678.

BOREHAM, Hon. Sir Leslie Kenneth Edward, Kt 1972; Hon. Mr Justice Boreham; a Judge of the High Court, Queen's Bench Division, since 1972; Presiding Judge, North Eastern Circuit, since 1974; Deputy Chairman, Agricultural Lands Tribunal; *m* ; one *s* one *d.* Served War of 1939-45, RAF. Called to the Bar at Lincoln's Inn, Nov. 1947; Bencher 1972. QC 1965. Recorder of Margate, 1968-71. Joined South-Eastern Circuit. Dep. Chm. 1962-65, Chm. 1965-71, East Suffolk QS. *Recreations:* gardening, golf. *Address:* 1 Paper Buildings, Temple, EC4.

BORG COSTANZI, Prof. Edwin J.; Rector Magnificus, Royal University of Malta, since 1964; *b* 8 Sept. 1925; 2nd *s* of late Michael Borg Costanzi and M. Stella (*née* Camilleri); *m* 1948, Lucy Valentino; two *s* one *d. Educ:* Lyceum, Malta; Royal University of Malta (BSc); Balliol College, Oxford (BA 1946, MA 1952); Malta Rhodes Scholar, 1945. Professor of Mathematics, Royal University of Malta, 1950-64. Chm., 1976-77, Mem., 1965-66, 1968-69 and 1972-74, Council of ACU. *Recreations:* fishing, photography. *Address:* University of Malta, Msida, Malta; 35 Don Rua Street, Sliema, Malta. *T:* 32958. *Club:* Casino Maltese (Valletta, Malta).

BORG OLIVIER, George, LLD; Prime Minister and Minister of Commonwealth and Foreign Affairs, Malta, 1965-71; Leader of the Nationalist Party, Malta, 1950-76; *b* 5 July 1911; *s* of Oliviero Borg Olivier, Architect and Civil Engineer; *m* 1943, Alexandra (*née* Mattei); two *s* one *d. Educ:* Lyceum and Royal University of Malta. Mem. of Council of Government, Malta, 1939-45; Mem. of Legislative Assembly, 1947; Minister of Works and Reconstruction, 1950-55; Minister of Education, and of Justice, 1950-51; Prime Minister, 1950-55; Leader of the Opposition, 1955-58; Minister of Economic Planning and Finance, 1962-65. Hon. DLitt, Royal University Malta, 1964. Kt Grand Cross: Order of St Sylvester, 1962; Order of Pope Pius IX, 1964. *Adddress:* 55 Victoria Avenue, Sliema, Malta. *T:* 30393; 27 St Paul by the Sea, St Paul's Bay, Malta. *T:* 73471.

BORGES, Jorge Luis; poet; Director, National Library of Argentina, 1955-73; *b* Buenos Aires, 24 Aug. 1899; *s* of late Jorge Borges and of Leonor Acevedo de Borges. *Educ:* Collège de Géneve; Univ. of Cambridge. Prof. of English and N American Literature, Univ. of Buenos Aires, 1955-70. Member: Argentine Nat. Acad., 1955; Uruguayan Acad. of Letters; Goethe Acad. of Sâo Paulo, Brazil; Pres., Argentine Writers' Assoc., 1950-53 (grand prize 1945); Hon. Pres., Argentine branch, Dickens Fellowship of London; Vice-Pres., Amigos de la Literatura Inglesa. Hon. DLitt Oxford 1970; Hon Dr Jerusalem 1971. Premio de Honor, Prix Formentor (with Samuel Beckett), 1961; Fondo de las Artes, 1963. Hon. KBE. *Publications: poems:* Fervor de Buenos Aires, 1923; Luna de Enfrente, 1925; Cuaderno San Martín, 1929; Elogio de la Sombra, 1969 (trans. as In Praise of Darkness, 1975); Selected Poems 1923-1967, 1972; *essays:* Inquisiciones, 1925; El Idioma de los Argentinos, 1928; Evaristo Carriego, 1930; Discusión, 1932; Historia de la Eternidad, 1936; Antología Clásica de la Literatura Argentina, 1942; Nueva Refutación del Tiempo, 1947; Otras Inquisiciones, 1937-52, 1952 (trans. as Other Inquisitions, 1964); *stories:* Historia Universal de la Infamia, 1935; Tlön, Uqbar, Orbis Tertius, 1938; El Jardín de Senderos que se bifurcan, 1941; Ficciones, 1945 (trans. 1962); El Aleph, 1949 (trans. 1973); La Muerte y la Brújula, 1951; El Informe de Brodie, 1971 (trans. as Dr Brodie's Report, 1974); El libro de arena, 1975; Obras completas, 1975; *collections:* El Hacedor, 1960 (trans. as Dreamtigers, 1964); Antología Personal, 1961 (trans. as A Personal Anthology, 1962); Labyrinthe, 1960 (trans. as Labyrinths, 1962); El Libra de los Seres Imaginarios (with Margarita Guerrero), 1967 (trans. as The Book of Imaginary Beings, 1969); Prólogos, 1975. *Recreations:* study of Old English and of Old Norse. *Address:* Maipú 994, Buenos Aires, Argentina.

BORINGDON, Viscount; Mark Lionel Parker; *b* 22 Aug. 1956; *s* and *heir* of 6th Earl of Morley, *qv. Educ:* Eton. Commissioned, Royal Green Jackets, 1976. *Address:* Pound House, Yelverton, Devon.

BORLAND, David Morton; former Chairman, Cadbury Ltd; Director: Cadbury Schweppes Ltd; UBM Group Ltd, since 1976; *b* 17 Jan. 1911; *s* of David and Annie J. Borland; *m* 1947, Nessa Claire Helwig; one *s* one *d. Educ:* Glasgow Academy; Brasenose Coll., Oxford (BA). Management Trainee, etc., Cadbury Bros Ltd, Bournville, Birmingham, 1933. War service, Royal Marines (Lieut-Col), 1940-46. Sales Manager, J. S. Fry & Sons Ltd, Somerdale, Bristol, 1946; Sales Dir and a Man. Dir, J. S. Fry & Sons Ltd, 1948; a Man. Dir, British Cocoa & Chocolate Co. Ltd, 1959, and of Cadbury Bros Ltd, 1963. Mem. Council of Bristol Univ. and of Univ. Appts Bd, 1962; Mem. Govt Cttee of Inquiry into Fatstock and Meat Marketing and Distribution, 1962. *Recreations:* golf, sailing. *Address:* Cotswold Lodge, Hollymead Lane, Stoke Bishop, Bristol BS9 1LN. *T:* Bristol 683978. *Clubs:* Bath; Achilles; Vincent's (Oxford).

BORLAUG, Norman Ernest, PhD; Director of Wheat Improvement Program, International Center for Maize and Wheat Improvement; *b* 25 March 1914; *s* of Henry O. and Clara Vaala Borlaug; *m* 1937, Margaret Gibson; one *s* one *d. Educ:* Univ. of Minnesota; BS 1937; MS 1940; PhD 1942. US Forest Service (USDA), 1935-1937-1938; Biologist, Dupont de Nemours & Co, 1942-44; Plant Pathologist and Genetist, Wheat Improvement, employed by Rockefeller Foundn (Associate Dir of Agricultural Sciences) and Dir of Wheat Program, International Center for Maize and Wheat Improvement (CIMMYT), 1944-. Dir, Population Crisis Cttee, 1971; Asesor Especial, Fundación para Estudios de la Población (Mexico), 1971-; Member: Adv. Council, Renewable Natural Resources Foundn, 1973-; Citizens' Commn on Science, Law and Food Supply, 1973-; Council for Agricl Science and Tech., 1973-; Commn on Critical Choices for Americans 1973-. Outstanding Achievement Award, Univ. of Minnesota, 1959; Mem., Nat. Acad. of Sciences (USA), 1968; Sitara-Imtiaz (Star of Distinction) (Pakistan), 1968; Nobel Peace Prize, 1970. Holds numerous hon. doctorates in Science, both from USA and abroad; and more than 30 Service Awards by govts and organizations. *Publications:* more than 70 scientific and semi-popular articles. *Recreations:* hunting, fishing, baseball, wrestling, football, golf. *Address:* c/o International Center for Maize and Wheat Improvement (CIMMYT), Apartado Postal 6-641, Londres 40, Mexico 6 DF, Mexico. *T:* 585-43-55.

BORLEY, Lester; Chief Executive, English Tourist Board, since 1975; *b* 7 April 1931; *er s* of Edwin Richard Borley and Mary Dorena Davies; *m* Mary Alison, *e d* of Edward John Pearce and Kathleen Florence Barratt; three *d. Educ:* Dover Grammar Sch.; Queen Mary Coll. and Birkbeck Coll., London Univ. Pres. of Union, QMC, 1953; Dep. Pres., Univ. of London Union, 1954; ESU debating team tour of USA, 1955. Joined British Travel Assoc., 1955; Asst to Gen. Man., USA, 1957-61; Manager: Chicago Office, 1961-64; Australia, 1964-67; West Germany, 1967-69; Chief Executive, Scottish Tourist Bd, 1970-75. *Recreations:* listening to music, looking at pictures, walking in the countryside. *Address:* 27 Blandy Road, Henley-on-Thames, Oxon. *T:* Henley-on-Thames 6613. *Clubs:* Caledonian; Royal Automobile.

BORN, Gustav Victor Rudolf, FRS 1972; FRCP 1976; Sheild Professor of Pharmacology, University of Cambridge, since 1973; Fellow, Gonville and Caius College, Cambridge, since 1973; *b* 29 July 1921; *s* of late Prof. Max Born, FRS; *m* 1st, 1950, Wilfrida Ann Plowden-Wardlaw (marr. diss., 1961); two *s* one *d*; 2nd, 1962, Dr Faith Elizabeth Maurice-Williams; one *s* one *d. Educ:* Oberrealschule, Göttingen; Perse Sch., Cambridge; Edinburgh Academy; University of Edinburgh. Vans Dunlop Scholar; MB, ChB, 1943; DPhil (Oxford), 1951, MA 1956. Med. Officer, RAMC, 1943-47; MRC Studentship, 1949-52; Mem. Scientific Staff, MRC, 1952-53; Grad. Asst, later Research Officer, Nuffield Inst. for Med. Research, University of Oxford, 1953-60; Deptl Demonstrator in Dept of Pharmacology, 1956-60, and Lectr in Med. Subjects, St Peter's Hall, University of Oxford, 1959-60; Vandervell Prof. of Pharmacology, RCS and Univ. of London, 1960-73. Vis. Prof. in Chem., NW Univ., Illinois, 1970-; William S. Creasy Vis. Prof. in Clin. Pharmacol., Brown Univ., 1977. Hon. Dir, MRC Thrombosis Res. Gp, 1964-73. Member: Ed. Board, Heffters' Handbook of Experimental Pharmacology; Cttee of Enquiry into Relationship of Pharmaceut. Industry with Nat. Health Service (Sainsbury Cttee), 1965-67. Lectures: Beyer, Wisconsin Univ., 1969; Sharpey-Schäfer, Edinburgh Univ., 1973; Cross, RCS, 1974; Wander, Bern Univ., 1974; Johnson Meml, Paris, 1975. Mem., Akad. Leopoldina; Corresp. Mem., German Pharmacological Soc. Hon. Fellow, St Peter's Coll., Oxford, 1972. *Publications:* articles in scientific jls and books. *Recreations:* music, walking. *Address:* Department of Pharmacology, University Medical School, Hills Road, Cambridge; Gonville and Caius College, Cambridge; 58B Redington Road, NW3. *T:* 01-435 7202.

BORNEMAN, Roy Ernest, QC 1952; *b* 1904; *s* of Ernest Borneman, London; *m* 1st, 1932, Winifred Dixon, *d* of Dr William Hunter, Aberdeen; two *s*; 2nd, 1973, Sarah Anderson, *d* of Thomas Paterson, North Berwick. *Educ:* University Coll., Reading; University Coll., London. BA 1924. Called to the Bar, Gray's Inn, 1929; Bencher, 1956; Treasurer, 1972; Vice-Treasurer, 1973. Chm., Board of Referees and Finance Act 1960 Tribunal, 1960. Served War of 1939-45, Wing Comdr, Royal Air Force. *Recreations:* golf, music, travel. *Address:* 11 New Square, Lincoln's Inn, WC2; Hollands, Langhurst Hill, Petworth, Sussex. *T:* Kirdford 486.

BORODALE, Viscount; Sean David Beatty; *b* 12 June 1973; *s* and *heir* of 3rd Earl Beatty, *qv.*

BORODIN, George; *see* Sava, George.

BORRADAILE, Maj.-Gen. Hugh Alastair, CB 1959; DSO 1946; Vice Adjutant-General, War Office, 1960-63, retired; *b* 22 June 1907; *s* of late Lt-Col B. Borradaile, RE, Walnut Cottage, Wylye, Wilts; *m* 1936, Elizabeth Barbara, *d* of late R. Powell-Williams, Woodcroft, Yelverton, Devon; one *s* one *d. Educ:* Wellington Coll.; RMC Sandhurst. Commissioned Devon Regt, 1926; King's African Rifles, 1931-37; Staff Coll., Camberley, 1939; GSO1, GHQ West Africa, 1942-43; CO 5, E Lancs Regt, 1944; CO 7 Somerset LI, 1944-45; GSO1, 30 Corps, 1945; Asst Chief of Staff (Exec.), CCG, 1945-46; CO 1 Devon, 1946-48; Dep. Chief Intelligence Div., CCG, 1948-50; National Defence Coll., Canada, 1950-51; Brig. A/Q AA Command, 1951-53; Comd 24 Inf. Bde, 1953-55; Dept Military Sec. (A), War Office, 1955-57; Gen. Officer Commanding South-West District and 43rd (Wessex) Infantry Div., TA, 1957-60. Col, Devon and Dorset Regt, 1962-67. Master, Worshipful Co. of Drapers', 1971-72 (Liveryman 1956-). *Recreations:* golf, shooting, fishing. *Address:* Almora, 33 Park Avenue, Camberley, Surrey. *T:* Camberley 21827. *Club:* Army and Navy.

BORRETT, Ven. Charles Walter; Archdeacon of Stoke-upon-Trent and Hon. Canon of Lichfield Cathedral since 1971; Priest-in-charge of Sandon, Diocese of Lichfield, since 1973; *b* 15 Sept. 1916; *s* of Walter George Borrett, farmer, and Alice Frances (*née* Mecrow); *m* 1941, Jean Constable, *d* of Charles Henry and Lilian Constable Pinson, Wolverhampton; one *s* two *d. Educ:* Framlingham Coll., Suffolk; Emmanuel Coll., Cambridge (MA); Ridley Hall, Cambridge. Deacon, 1941; Priest, 1943; Curate: of All Saints, Newmarket, 1941-45; of St Paul, Wolverhampton, 1945-48; of Tettenhall Regis, 1948-49; Vicar of Tettenhall Regis, 1949-71; Rural Dean of Trysull, 1958-71; Prebendary of Flixton in Lichfield Cathedral, 1964-71. Chm., C of E Council for Deaf, 1976-. Fellow, Woodard Schs. *Recreations:* golf, riding. *Address:* Sandon Vicarage, Stafford ST18 0DB. *T:* Sandon 261. *Club:* Hawks (Cambridge).

BORRIE, Gordon Johnson; Director General of Fair Trading, since 1976; *b* 13 March 1931; *s* of Stanley Borrie, Solicitor; *m* 1960, Dorene, *d* of Herbert Toland, Toronto, Canada; no *c. Educ:* John Bright Grammar Sch., Llandudno; Univ. of Manchester (LLB, LLM). Barrister-at-Law and Harmsworth Scholar of the Middle Temple; called to Bar, Middle Temple, 1952. Nat. Service: Army Legal Services, HQ Brit. Commonwealth Forces in Korea, 1952-54. Practice as a barrister, London, 1954-57. Lectr and later Sen. Lectr, Coll. of Law, 1957-64; Sen. Lectr in Law, Univ. of Birmingham, 1965-68; Prof. of English Law and Dir, Inst. of Judicial Admin, Birmingham Univ., 1969-76, and Dean of Faculty of Law, 1974-76. Member: Law Commn Adv. Panel on Contract Law, 1966-; Parole Bd for England and Wales, 1971-74; CNAA Legal Studies Bd, 1971-76; Circuit Adv. Cttee, Birmingham Gp of Courts, 1972-74; Council, Consumers' Assoc., 1972-75; Consumer Protection Adv. Cttee, 1973-76; Equal Opportunities Commn, 1975-76. Sen. Treasurer, Nat. Union of Students, 1955-58. Contested (Lab): Croydon, NE, 1955; Ilford, S, 1959. Gov., Birmingham Coll. of Commerce, 1966-70. *Publications:* Public Law (2nd edn), 1970; The Consumer, Society and the Law (with Prof. A. L. Diamond) (3rd edn), 1973; Law of Contempt (with N. V. Lowe), 1973; Stevens and Borrie's Mercantile Law (16th edn), 1973; Commercial Law (4th edn), 1975; contributor to Modern Law Review, New Law Journal, New Society. *Recreations:* gardening, gastronomy, piano playing, travel. *Address:* Manor Farm, Abbots Morton, Worcestershire. *T:* Inkberrow 792330; 33 Sloane Gardens, SW1. *T:* 01-730 5443. *Club:* Reform.

BORRIE, Peter Forbes, MD, FRCP; Physician in charge of the Skin Department, St Bartholomew's Hospital, since 1968; Consultant Dermatologist to Moorfields, Westminster and Central Eye Hospitals, since 1950, and to Barnet General Hospital since 1954; *b* 26 March 1918; *s* of late Dr David Forbes Borrie and Martha Ruth Downing; *m* 1942, Helen Patricia, *e d* of Major H. G. Chesney; two *s* two *d. Educ:* Rugby Sch.; Clare Coll., Cambridge; St Bartholomew's Hospital. BA (Nat. Sci. Tripos) 1939; MB, BChir Cantab 1942; MRCP 1948; FRCP 1960; MA Cantab 1950; MD Cantab 1951. House Physician, St Bartholomew's Hospital, 1942; Senior Registrar, Skin Dept, St Mary's Hospital, Paddington, 1948; Chief Asst, Skin Dept, St Bartholomew's Hospital, 1950. Fellow Royal Society of Medicine; Mem. British Association of Dermatology; Lecturer at the Institute of Dermatology. *Publications:* Editor, Roxburgh's Common Skin Diseases, 11th-14th edns, 1959-75; Modern Trends in Dermatology, Series iv, 1971; many articles in medical journals. *Address:* 115a Harley Street, W1. *T:* 01-935 6465.

BORTHWICK OF BORTHWICK, Major John Henry Stuart, TD 1943; JP; The Borthwick of Borthwick; 24th Lord Borthwick; Baron of Heriotmuir, Borthwick and Locherwart; Chairman: Heriotmuir Properties Ltd, since 1965; Heriotmuir Exporters Ltd, since 1972; Partner in Crookston Farms, since 1971; Director, Ronald Morrison & Co. Ltd, since 1972; *b* 13 Sept. 1905; *s* of Henry, 23rd Lord Borthwick (*d* 1937); *m* 1938, Margaret Frances (*d* 1976), *d* of Alexander Campbell Cormack, Edinburgh; twin *s. Educ:* Fettes Coll., Edinburgh; King's Coll. Newcastle (DipAgric 1926). Formerly RATA, re-employed 1939; served NW Europe, Allied Mil. Govt Staff (Junior Staff Coll., SO 2), 1944; CCG (CO 1, Lt-Col), 1946. Dept of Agriculture for Scotland, 1948-50; farming own farms, 1950-71; National Farmers Union of Scotland: Midlothian Branch Cttee, 1963; Mid and West Lothian Area Cttee, 1967-73 (Pres. 1970-72); Mem. Council, 1968-72 (served on Legal and Commercial, Labour and Machinery, and Press and Publicity Cttees); Member: Lothians Area Cttee, NFU Mutual Insurance Soc., 1969; Scottish Southern Regional Cttee, Wool Marketing Bd, 1966. Chm., Area Cttee, South of Scotland Electricity Bd Consultative Council, 1972-76. Chm., Monitoring Cttee for Scottish Tartans, 1976. County Councillor, Midlothian, 1937; JP 1938; DL Midlothian (now Lothian Region), 1965; Member: Local Appeal Tribunal (Edinburgh and the Lothians), 1963-75; Midlothian Valuation Appeal Cttee, 1966. Member: Standing Council of Scottish Chiefs; The Committee of the Baronage of Scotland (International Delegate); Mem. Corresp., Istituto Italiano di Genealogia e Araldica, Rome and Madrid, 1964; Hon. Mem., Council of Scottish Clans Assoc., USA, 1975. Hon. Mem., Royal Military Inst. of Canada, 1976. KSLJ, GCKLJ 1975; Comdr, Rose of Lippe, 1971. *Recreations:* shooting, travel, history. *Heir: er twin s* John Hugh, Master of Borthwick [*b* 14 Nov. 1940; *m* 1974, Adelaide, *d* of A. Birkmyre; one *d*]. *Address:* Crookston, Heriot, Midlothian EH38 5YS. *Clubs:* New, Puffins (Edinburgh).

BORTHWICK, Sir John Thomas, 3rd Bt *cr* 1908; MBE 1945; *b* 5 Dec. 1917; *s* of Hon. James Alexander Borthwick (*d* 1961), and Irene, *d* of late George Wise, Sydney, Australia; *S* to Btcy of uncle (1st and last Baron Whitburgh), 1967; *m* 1st, 1939, Irene (marr. diss. 1961), *o c* of Joseph Heller; three *s*; 2nd, 1962, Irene, *d* of Leo Fink; two *s. Educ:* Eton; Trinity Coll., Oxford. Formerly Major, Rifle Brigade, TA. Served War of 1939-45 (MBE). *Heir: s* Antony Thomas Borthwick [*b* 12 Feb. 1941; *m* 1966, Gillian Deirdre Broke, *d* of late Lieut Nigel Vere Broke Thurston, RN; one *s* two *d*]. *Address:* Fox Hills Dower House, Long Cross, Surrey; 23 Lennox Gardens, SW1.

BORTHWICK, Kenneth W.; Rt Hon. Lord Provost of Edinburgh and Lord Lieutenant of the City of Edinburgh, since 1977; *Educ:* Edinburgh. Served War of 1939-45: Air-crew officer, RAF. Started career with Aberdeen Police; went to S Africa, to start own business, 1947; returned to Edinburgh to set up family confectioner's business, 1956. Mem., Edinburgh Council, representing Portobello, 1963-; has served on all cttees. Magistrate and Senior Baillie; Mem., organising cttee, Commonwealth Games, Edinburgh, 1970; Rep. Jock's Lodge/Willowbrae, Lothian Regional Council, 1967-77. *Address:* City Chambers, High Street, Edinburgh EH1 1YJ; 7 Duddingston Crescent, Edinburgh EH15 3AS.

BORTHWICK, William Jason Maxwell, DSC 1942; Director of various companies; *b* 1 Nov. 1910; *er s* of late Hon. William Borthwick and Ruth (*née* Rigby); *m* 1937, Elizabeth Elworthy, Timaru, NZ; one *s* three *d. Educ:* Winchester; Trinity Coll., Cambridge (BA). Called to Bar, Inner Temple, 1933. Commnd RNVR, 1940, Comdr (QO) 1945. Joined Thomas Borthwick & Sons Ltd, 1934, Dir 1946-76; Dir, International Commodities Clearing House Ltd and subsids, 1954; Dir, Commonwealth Develt Corp., 1972; Mem., Central Council of Physical Recreation, 1955-; Chm., Nat. Sailing Centre, 1965. *Recreations:* yachting, shooting. *Address:* Brancaster Staithe, King's Lynn, Norfolk. *T:* Brancaster 475. *Clubs:* United Oxford & Cambridge University, Royal Thames Yacht.

BORWICK, family name of **Baron Borwick**.

BORWICK, 4th Baron, cr 1922; **James Hugh Myles Borwick**; Bt cr 1916; MC 1945; Major HLI retired; b 12 Dec. 1917; s of 3rd Baron and Irene Phyllis, d of late Thomas Main Paterson, Littlebourne, Canterbury; S father 1961; m 1954, Hyllarie Adalia Mary, y d of late Lieut-Col William Hamilton Hall Johnston, DSO, MC, DL, Bryn-y-Groes, Bala, N Wales; four d. Educ: Eton; RMC, Sandhurst. Commissioned as 2nd Lieut HLI, 1937; Capt. 1939; Major 1941; retired, 1947. Recreations: field sports, sailing and ocean racing. Heir: half b Hon. George Sandbach Borwick, b 18 Oct. 1922. Address: Knap Farm, Owermoigne, Dorchester, Dorset. T: Warmwell 352365. Club: Royal Ocean Racing.

BORWICK, Lt-Col Michael George; farmer; Director, Blair Trust Co.; Vice-Lieutenant for Ayr and Arran, since 1974; b 27 March 1916; s of late Col Malcolm Borwick; m 1946, Veronica, d of late Lt-Col J. F. Harrison and Hon. Mrs Harrison; two s decd. Educ: Harrow; in France. Joined Leicestershire Yeomanry, 1935; joined Royal Scots Greys, 1937; joined Middle East Commandos, 1940, fought in Dodecanese Islands and in Crete, 1941 (POW); rejoined Greys, 1945; comd 1954-57. Chm., Royal Scots Greys Assoc., 1963. Joint Master, Eglinton Foxhounds, 1960-63 and 1972-75. Mem., Royal Company of Archers, Queen's Body Guard for Scotland. Mem. Ayrshire CC, 1958-66, resigned; DL Ayrshire, 1960. Recreations: hunting, shooting. Address: Blair, Dalry, Ayrshire KA24 4ER. Club: Cavalry and Guards.

BORWICK, Lt-Col Sir Thomas Faulkner, Kt 1946; CIE 1941; DSO 1917; BMechE; FIMechE; late AIF; b 1890; s of Harry Barton Borwick, Melbourne; m 1918, Elsa, y d of Eduardo and Fanny de Ambrosis, Florence; one s one d. Educ: Scotch Coll. and University, Melbourne. Served European War, 1914-18 (twice wounded, despatches twice, DSO, Croix de Guerre). Worshipful Master, Kitchener Lodge, Simla, 1939. Chm., Indian Advisory Cttee, Institution of Mechanical Engineers, 1950; Dir-Gen. Ordnance Factories, India, 1943-47; Gen. Manager, National Machinery Manufacturers, Ltd, Bombay, 1947-52; joined The Plessey Co., Ilford, 1952; Divisional Manager, 1957; Group Gen. Manager, 1958; Gen. Manager, Swindon Region, 1959-60. Director: The Amar Tool & Gauge Co., 1958-60; Hawley Products Ltd, 1959-60. Chm. of Governors, Farmor's Sch., Fairford, 1967-75. Address: Swallowfield Park, Swallowfield, near Reading, Berks RG7 1TG. T: Reading 882383.

BOSANQUET, Charles Ion Carr, MA; DL; Vice-Chancellor of University of Newcastle upon Tyne, 1963-68 (Rector of King's College, Newcastle upon Tyne, 1952-63); b 19 April 1903; s of Robert Carr Bosanquet and Ellen S. Bosanquet; m 1931, Barbara, d of William Jay Schieffelin, New York; one s three d. Educ: Winchester; Trinity Coll., Cambridge (Scholar). Asst Gen. Manager, Friends Provident and Century Life Office, 1933-39; Principal Asst Sec., Ministry of Agriculture and Fisheries, 1941-45; Treasurer of Christ Church, Oxford, 1945-52. Fellow of Winchester Coll., 1951-73; Chm., Reorganisation Commission for Pigs and Bacon, 1955-56; Development Comr, 1956-70; Chm. Min. of Agric. Cttee of Enquiry into Demand for Agricultural Graduates. Hon DCL Durham; Hon LLD Cincinnati; Hon. DLitt Sierra Leone; Hon. DSc City. High Sheriff, 1948-49, DL 1971, Northumberland. Comdr, Order of St Olav. Address: Rock Moor, Alnwick, Northumberland. T: Charlton Mires 224. Clubs: Brooks's; Northern Counties (Newcastle).

BOSCAWEN, family name of **Viscount Falmouth**.

BOSCAWEN, Hon. Robert Thomas, MC 1944; MP (C) Wells since 1970; b 17 March 1923; 4th s of 8th Viscount Falmouth and of Dowager Viscountess Falmouth, CBE; m 1949, Mary Alice, JP London 1961, e d of Col Sir Geoffrey Ronald Codrington, KCVO, CB, CMG, DSO, OBE, TD; one s two d. Educ: Eton; Trinity College, Cambridge. 2nd Lieut, Coldstream Guards, 1942, Captain 1945; served in NW Europe. Mem., London Exec. Council, Nat. Health Service, 1954-65; Underwriting Mem. of Lloyds, 1952-. Contested Falmouth and Camborne (C), 1964, 1966. Vice-Chm., Conservative Parly Health and Social Security Cttee, 1974. Recreation: sailing. Address: House of Commons, SW1A 0AA. Clubs: Pratt's; Royal Yacht Squadron.

BOSCH, Baron Jean van den, Hon. GCVO 1966; Belgian Ambassador to the Court of St James's and Belgian Permanent Representative to the Council of Western European Union, 1966-72; Director, Lloyds Bank International, since 1972; Chairman, Lloyds Bank International (Belgium) SA, since 1973

(Director, since 1972); b 27 Jan. 1910; s of Baron Firmin van den Bosch and Anne de Volder; m 1944, Hélène Cloquet; two d. Educ: Ecole Abbatiale, Maredsous; Notre-Dame de la Paix, Namur; Université Catholique de Louvain. Docteur en droit; licencié en sciences historiques; licencié en sciences politiques et diplomatiques. Entered Belgian Diplomatic Service, 1934; Attaché, London and Paris, 1934; Sec., Pekin, 1937; 1st Sec., Ottawa, 1940; Chargé d'Affaires to Luxembourg Govt in London, 1943; Counsellor, Prince Regent's Household, 1944; Counsellor and Chargé d'Affaires, Cairo, 1948; Counsellor, 1949, Minister, 1953, Paris; Minister, Consul-Gen., Hong Kong, Singapore and Saigon, 1954; Ambassador, Cairo, 1955; accredited Minister, Libya, 1956; Sec.-Gen. of Min. of For. Aff. and For. Trade, 1959-June 1960, and again, Sept. 1960-1965; Ambassador, Congo, July-Aug. 1960. Grand Officier, Ordres Léopold, Couronne, Léopold II. Médaille Civique (1st cl.). Holds foreign decorations. Address: 1 avenue de l'Hippodrome, 1050 Brussels, Belgium. T: 648.79.03. Clubs: Beefsteak, White's.

BOSE, Vivian; b Ahmedabad, India, 9 June 1891; s of late Lalit Mohun Bose and g s of late Sir Bipin Krishna Bose; m 1930, Irene, d of late Dr John R. Mott (winner of Nobel Prize, 1946); one s one d. Educ: Dulwich Coll.; Pembroke Coll., Cambridge. (BA, LLB). Called to Bar, Middle Temple, 1913; practised at the Nagpur Bar; Principal, University Coll. of Law, Nagpur, 1924-30; Govt Advocate and Standing Counsel to the Govt of the Central Provinces and Berar, 1930-36; Additional Judicial Commissioner, Nagpur, for short periods, 1931-34; Puisne Judge, Nagpur High Court, 1936-49; Chief Justice, High Court of Judicature, Nagpur, 1949-51; Puisne Judge, Supreme Court of India, New Delhi, 1951-56, retd; recalled as ad hoc Judge, Supreme Court, Sept. 1958-Aug. 1959; Chm., two Government Commissions of Inquiry, 1958-62. Member International Commission of Jurists, 1958-; Pres., 1959-66 (Actg Sec.-Gen. March-Oct. 1963); Hon. Pres. 1966 (toured, on Commission's behalf: Europe, Asia Minor, Australia, Indonesia, Malaya, Burma, East and West Africa, UK, Ireland, Eire, USA, Brazil, 1961 and 1962-63). Hon. Provincial Sec., Boy Scouts Assoc. Central Provinces and Berar, 1921-34; Provincial Commissioner, 1934-37; Chief Commissioner for India, 1948; National Commissioner, 1959-62; Silver Wolf, 1942; Capt. the Nagpur Regt, Indian Auxiliary Force. Volunteer Long Service Medal, 1929; King's Silver Jubilee Medal, 1935; Kaisar-i-Hind Silver Medal, 1936. Recreations: photography, wireless, motoring (from and to India, etc), travel; amateur magic, mainly stage illusions. Address: Vishranti Farm, Doddakallasandra Post, Bangalore 560 141, India. Club: Gondwana (Nagpur).

BOSSOM, Hon. Sir Clive, 2nd Bt, cr 1953; b 4 Feb. 1918; s of late Baron Bossom (Life Peer); S to father's Baronetcy, 1965; m 1951, Lady Barbara North, sister of 9th Earl of Guilford, qv; three s one d. Educ: Eton. Regular Army, The Buffs, 1939-48; served Europe and Far East. Kent County Council, 1949-52; Chm. Council Order of St John for Kent, 1951-56; Mem. Jt Cttee, Order of St John and British Red Cross Soc. (Chm., Ex-Services War Disabled Help Cttee). Contested (C) Faversham Div., 1951 and 1955. MP (C) Leominster Div., Herefordshire, 1959-Feb. 1974; Parliamentary Private Secretary: to Jt Parly Secs, Min. of Pensions and Nat. Insce, 1960-62; to Sec. of State for Air, 1962-64; to Minister of Defence for RAF, 1964; to Home Secretary, 1970-72. Chm., Europ Assistance Ltd; Director: Northern Star Insurance Co. Ltd; Vosper Ltd. President: Anglo-Belgian Union, 1970-73 (Chm., 1967-70; Vice-Pres., 1974-); Industrial Fire Protection Assoc. Member Council: RAC (Chm., 1975-); RGS; Vice-Pres., Fédération Internationale de l'Automobile, 1975-; Chairman: RAC Motor Sports Council, 1975; Iran Soc., 1973-76. Liveryman of Worshipful Companies of Grocers, Paviors, Needlemakers. FRSA. KStJ 1961. Comdr, Order of Leopold II; Order of Homayoun III (Iran), 1977. Recreation: travel. Heir: s Bruce Charles Bossom, b 22 Aug. 1952. Address: Parsons Orchard, Eastnor, near Ledbury, Herefordshire. T: Ledbury 2318; 3 Eaton Mansions, Cliveden Place, SW1. T: 01-730 1108. Clubs: Royal Automobile, Carlton, MCC.

BOSSY, Rev. Michael Joseph Frederick, SJ; Headmaster, Stonyhurst College, since 1972; b 22 Nov. 1929; s of F. J. Bossy and K. Bossy (née White). Educ: St Ignatius Coll., Stamford Hill; Heythrop Coll., Oxon (STL); Oxford Univ. (MA). Taught at: St Ignatius Coll., Stamford Hill, 1956-59; St Francis Xavier's Coll., Liverpool, 1963-64; Stonyhurst Coll., 1965-. Recreation: watching games. Address: Stonyhurst College, via Blackburn, Lancashire BB6 9PZ. T: Stonyhurst 345.

BOSTOCK, James Edward, RE 1961 (ARE 1947); ARCA London; Academic Development Officer, Bristol Polytechnic, since 1970; b Hanley, Staffs, 11 June 1917; s of William George Bostock, pottery and glass-worker, and Amy (née Titley); m

1939, Gwladys Irene (*née* Griffiths); three *s. Educ:* Borden Grammar Sch., Sittingbourne; Royal College of Art. War Service as Sgt in Durham LI and Royal Corps of Signals. Full-time Teacher, 1946-; Vice-Principal, West of England Coll. of Art, 1965-70. Elected Mem. of Soc. of Wood Engravers, 1950. Mem. Council. Soc. of Staffs Artists, 1963. Exhibited water-colours, etchings, wood engravings and drawings at RA, NEAC, RBA, and other group exhibitions and in travelling exhibitions to Poland, Czechoslovakia, South Africa, Far East, New Zealand, USA, and the provinces. One-man shows: Mignon Gall., Bath; Univ. of Bristol; Bristol Polytechnic. Works bought by V & A Museum, British Museum, British Council, Hull, Swindon, Stoke-on-Trent and Bristol Education Cttees, Hunt Botanical Library, Pittsburgh and private collectors. Commissioned work for: ICI Ltd, British Museum (Nat. Hist.), Odhams Press, and other firms and public authorities. *Publications:* Roman Lettering for Students, 1959; articles in: Times, Guardian, Staffordshire Sentinel, Studio, Artist. *Address:* 16 Claremont Road, Bishopston, Bristol BS7 8DQ. *T:* Bristol 47376.

BOSTOCK, John, CBE 1972; Business Consultant; Director: British Hartford Fairmont Ltd; British Hartford Fairmont Investments Ltd; Unibin Ltd; *b* 30 Sept. 1916; *s* of William Bostock and Lucy (*née* Booth); *m* 1942, Sybil Field; one *s . Educ:* Sheffield Univ. CEng, MIEE. Exper. Officer, Admty Engrg Labs, W Drayton, 1942-45; Develt Engr, English Electric Co. Ltd, Preston and Bradford, 1945-48; Engrg and Project Man., Sperry Gyroscope Div., Brentford, 1948-62; Gen. Man. 1962-67, Man. Dir 1967-71, Sperry Gyroscope Div., Sperry Rand Ltd. *Recreations:* music, painting, Stock Exchange activities. *Address:* Dial House, 25 Sutton Avenue, Slough, Berks. *T:* Slough 21733.

BOSTOCK, Rev. Canon Peter Geoffrey, MA; Clergy Appointments Adviser, 1973-76; Deputy Secretary, Board for Mission and Unity, General Synod of Church of England, 1971-73; Canon Emeritus, Diocese of Mombasa, 1958; *b* 24 Dec. 1911; *s* of Geoffrey Bostock; *m* 1937, Elizabeth Rose; two *s* two *d. Educ:* Charterhouse; The Queen's Coll., Oxon; Wycliffe Hall, Oxon. Deacon, 1935; Priest, 1937; CMS Kenya, 1935-58; became Canon of Diocese of Mombasa, 1952; Archdeacon, 1953-58; Vicar-Gen., 1955-58. Examining Chaplain to Bishop of Mombasa, 1950-58; Chm., Christian Council of Kenya, 1957-58; Archdeacon of Doncaster and Vicar, High Melton, 1959-67; Asst Sec., Missionary and Ecumenical Council of Church Assembly, 1967-71. *Recreations:* home and gardening. *Address:* 10 Moreton Road, Oxford OX2 7AX. *T:* Oxford 55460. *Club:* Royal Commonwealth Society.

BOSTON, family name of **Baron Boston of Faversham.**

BOSTON, 9th Baron *cr* 1761; **Gerald Howard Boteler Irby,** MBE 1918; Bt 1704; *b* 29 Aug. 1897; *s* of Leonard Paul Irby, OBE (*g g s* of 2nd Baron) (*d* 1936), and Ethel Maud (*d* 1957), *d* of Captain William John Casberd Boteler, RN; *S* cousin, 1972; *m* 1st, 1926, Katherine Gertrude (marr. diss. 1931), *d* of Captain C. M. H. Edwards; one *d*; 2nd, 1936, Erica, *d* of T. H. Hill; one *s.* Served European War, 1914-18 as Lieutenant, KRRC (MBE); War of 1939-45 as Major, RASC. *Heir: s* Hon. Timothy George Frank Boteler Irby [*b* 27 March 1939; *m* 1967, Rhonda Anne, *d* of R. A. Bate, Sydney, Australia; two *s* one *d*]. *Address:* Flat 11, Gunters Mead, Copsem Lane, Esher, Surrey.

BOSTON OF FAVERSHAM, Baron *cr* 1976 (Life Peer), of Faversham, Kent; **Terence George Boston;** *b* 21 March 1930; *yr* surv. *s* of George T. Boston and Kate (*née* Bellati); *m* 1962, Margaret Joyce (Member: SE Metropolitan Regional Hospital Board, 1970-74; Mental Health Review Appeals Tribunal (SE Metropolitan area); market research consultant), *er d* of late R. H. J. Head and of Mrs H. F. Winters, and step *d* of late H. F. Winters, Melbourne, Australia. *Educ:* Woolwich Polytechnic Sch.; King's Coll., University of London. Dep. President (for a time Acting Pres.), University of London Union, 1955-56. Commnd in RAF during Nat. Service, 1950-52; later trained as pilot with University of London Air Sqdn. Called to the Bar: Inner Temple, 1960; Gray's Inn, 1973; BBC News Sub-Editor, External Services, 1957-60; Senior BBC Producer (Current Affairs), 1960-64; also Producer of Law in Action series (Third Programme), 1962-64. Joined Labour Party, 1946; contested (Lab) Wokingham, 1955 and 1959; MP (Lab) Faversham, Kent, June 1964-70; PPS to: Minister of Public Building and Works, 1964-66; Minister of Power, 1966-68; Minister of Transport, 1968-69; Asst Govt Whip, 1969-70. UK Deleg. to UN Gen Assembly (XXXIst Session), 1976. Member: Executive Cttee, International Union of Socialist Youth, 1950; Nat. Cttee, Council for Education in World Citizenship (UNA), 1950-51; Standing Joint Cttee on New Towns, 1954-59; Fabian Soc.; Soc.

of Labour Lawyers; Nat. Union of Journalists; Nat. Union of General and Municipal Workers; Select Cttee on Broadcasting Proceedings of Parliament, 1966; Speaker's Conference on Electoral Law, 1965-68. Trustee, Parly Lab. Party Benevolent Fund, 1967-74. Founder Vice-Chm., Great Britain—East Europe Centre, 1967-69; Chm., The Sheppey Gp, 1967-. *Recreations:* opera (going, not singing), flying. *Address:* 27 Capstan Square, Isle of Dogs, E14; 1 Gray's Inn Square, Gray's Inn, WC1R 5AA.

BOSTON, David Merrick, OBE 1976; MA; Director (formerly Curator), Horniman Museum and Library, London, since 1965; *b* 15 May 1931; *s* of Dr H. M. Boston, Salisbury; *m* 1961, Catharine, *d* of Rev. Prof. E. G. S. Parrinder, *qv*; one *s* two *d. Educ:* Rondebosch, Cape Town; Bishop Wordsworth's, Salisbury; Selwyn Coll., Cambridge; Univ. of Cape Town. BA History Cantab 1954; MA 1958. RAF, 1950-51; Adjt, Marine Craft Trng School. Field survey, S African Inst. of Race Relations, 1955; Keeper of Ethnology, Liverpool Museums, 1956-62; Asst Keeper, British Museum, New World archaeology and ethnography, 1962-65. Chm., British Nat. Cttee of Internat. Council of Museums, 1976; Mem. Council: Museums Assoc., 1969; Royal Anthropological Inst., 1969 (Vice-Pres., 1972-75, 1977). Vis. Scientist, National Museum of Man, Ottawa, 1970. FRAS; FRGS. *Publications:* contribs to learned jls and encyclopaedias and on Pre-European America, in World Ceramics (ed R. J. Charleston). *Address:* 10 Oakleigh Park Avenue, Chislehurst, Kent. *T:* 01-467 1049.

BOSVILLE MACDONALD of Sleat, Sir Ian Godfrey, 17th Bt, *cr* 1625; ARICS; 25th Chief of Sleat; *b* 18 July 1947; *er s* of Sir (Alexander) Somerled Angus Bosville Macdonald of Sleat, 16th Bt, MC, 24th Chief of Sleat and of Mary, Lady Bosville Macdonald of Sleat; *S* father 1958; *m* 1970, Juliet Fleury, *o d* of Maj.-Gen. J. M. D. Ward-Harrison, *qv*; one *d. Educ:* Pinewood Sch.; Eton Coll.; Royal Agricultural Coll. ARICS 1972; MRSH 1972. *Heir: b* James Alexander Bosville Macdonald of Sleat, *b* 11 April 1949. *Recreation:* ornithology. *Address:* Thorpe Hall, Rudston, Driffield, North Humberside. *T:* Kilham 239. *Clubs:* Lansdowne; Puffin's (Edinburgh).

BOSWALL, Sir Thomas; *see* Houstoun-Boswall.

BOSWORTH, George Herbert; retired; *b* 17 May 1896; *s* of John Henry Bosworth. *Educ:* Peter Symonds, Winchester; University of Southampton. Served European War: RNAS and RAF; Air Ministry, 1919; Private Secretary to Marshal of RAF Sir Cyril (later Lord) Newall, 1932; Asst Secretary, 1939; Dir of Housing, Ministry of Aircraft Production, 1940; Asst Secretary Min. of Works, 1944; Under Secretary, 1952-59. *Publications:* How To Be Happy in France, 1930; Prelude (novel), 1932; Where Shall We Go?, 1939. *Recreations:* music, salmon fishing. *Address:* 31 Church Street, Willingdon, Eastbourne, E Sussex. *Club:* National Liberal.

BOSWORTH, George Simms, CBE 1968; CEng, FIMechE, FIEE; Director of Newcastle upon Tyne Polytechnic since 1969; *b* 12 Aug. 1916; *s* of George Bosworth and Mabel Anne Simms; *m* 1940, Helen Cowan Rusack; two *s* two *d. Educ:* Herbert Strutt Grammar Sch.; Gonville and Caius Coll., Cambridge. MA (Mechanical Sci. Tripos). Served RAF, Engineer Officer; Sqdn Ldr, 1940-46. English Electric Co., London, 1946-69: Chief of Technical Personnel Administration; Director of Group Personnel Services; Director of Personnel. Mem. CNAA, 1976-. Hon. DTech Bradford, 1968. *Address:* Craig Holme, 4 Jesmond Park West, Newcastle upon Tyne NE7 7BU. *T:* Newcastle upon Tyne 810771. *Clubs:* Athenæum, Royal Air Force.

BOSWORTH, John Michael Worthington, CBE 1972; FCA; Deputy Chairman, British Railways Board, since 1972 (Vice-Chairman, 1968-72); *b* 22 June 1921; *s* of Humphrey Worthington Bosworth and Vera Hope Bosworth; *m* 1955, Patricia Mary Edith Wheelock; one *s* one *d. Educ:* Bishop's Stortford Coll. Served Royal Artillery, 1939-46. Peat, Marwick, Mitchell & Co., 1949-68, Partner, 1960. Chairman: British Rail Engineering Ltd, 1969-71; British Rail Property Bd, 1971-72; British Rail Shipping and International Services Ltd, 1976-; BR Hovercraft Ltd, 1976-. *Recreations:* ski-ing, vintage cars. *Address:* Southview, Cookhams, Sharpthorne, Sussex. *Club:* Royal Automobile.

BOSWORTH, Neville Bruce Alfred; Senior Partner, Bosworth, Bailey Cox & Co., Solicitors, Birmingham; *b* 18 April 1918; *s* of W. C. N. Bosworth; *m* 1945, Charlotte Marian Davis; one *s* two *d. Educ:* King Edward's Sch., Birmingham; Birmingham Univ. LLB. Admitted Solicitor, 1941. Birmingham City Council, 1950-74; Councillor (Erdington Ward), 1950-61; Alderman, 1961-74; Chm., Gen. Purposes Cttee, 1966-69; Lord Mayor of

Birmingham, 1969-70; Dep. Mayor, 1970-71; Cons. Gp Leader, Birmingham City Council, 1972- (Dep. Gp Leader, 1971-72); County Councillor (Edgbaston Ward), W Midlands CC, 1973-; Dist Councillor (Edgbaston Ward), Birmingham Dist Council, 1973-. Trustee, several charitable trusts; Governor King Edward VI Schools, Birmingham; Chm., Sutton Coldfield Cons. and Unionist Assoc., 1963-66; Vice-Chm., Birmingham Cons. and Unionist Assoc., 1971, Dep. Chm., 1972-; Vice-Pres., Birmingham and Dist Property Owners Assoc.; Dir, Nat. Exhibn Centre Ltd, 1970-72, 1974-. Pres., BP Scout Guild, Birmingham Co., 1970-. *Recreations:* politics, football (Dir, Birmingham City Football Club Ltd). *Address:* Hollington, Luttrell Road, Four Oaks, Sutton Coldfield, Birmingham B74 2SR. *T:* 021-308 0647; 54 Newhall Street, Birmingham B3 3QG. *T:* 021-236 8091. *Club:* St Paul's (Birmingham).

BOTHA, Matthys (Izak); South African Ambassador to the Court of St James's, since 1977; *b* 31 Oct. 1913; *s* of Johan Hendrik Jacobus Botha and Anna Botha (*née* Joubert); *m* 1940, Hester le Roux (*née* Bosman); two *s*. *Educ:* Selborne Coll.; Pretoria Univ. BA, LLB. Called to the Transvaal Bar. Dept of Finance, Pretoria, 1931-44; S African Embassy, Washington, 1944-51; S African Permanent Mission to UN, NY, 1951-54; Head, Political Div., Dept Foreign Affairs, Pretoria, 1955-59; Envoy Extraordinary and Minister Plenipotentiary, Switzerland, 1959-60; Minister, London, 1960-62; Ambassador and Permanent Rep., UN, NY, 1962-70; Ambassador to: Canada, 1970-73; Italy, 1973-77. Knight of Grand Cross, Order of Merit (Italy), 1977. *Recreations:* swimming, skiing, cycling. *Address:* South African Embassy, South Africa House, Trafalgar Square, WC2N 5DP. *T:* 01-930 4488. *Clubs:* Les Ambassadeurs, Hurlingham, Eccentric, Royal Automobile, Travellers'.

BOTHA, Roelof Frederik, (Pik Botha); Minister of Foreign Affairs, South Africa, since 1977; MP (National Party) for Westdene, since 1977; *b* 27 April 1932. *Educ:* Volkskool, Potchefstroom; Univ. of Pretoria. Dept of Foreign Affairs, 1953; diplomatic missions, Europe, 1956-62; Mem. team from S Africa, in SW Africa case, Internat. Court of Justice, The Hague, 1963-66, 1970-71; Agent for S African Govt, Internat. Court of Justice, 1965-66; Legal Adviser, Dept of Foreign Affairs, 1966-68; Under-Sec. and Head of SW Africa and UN Sections, 1968-70. National Party, MP for Wonderboom, 1970-74. Mem., SA Delegn to UN Gen. Assembly, 1967-69, 1971, 1973-74. Served on select Parly Cttees, 1970-74. South African Permanent Representative to the UN, NY, 1974-77; South African Ambassador to the USA, 1975-77. *Address:* House of Assembly, Cape Town, South Africa; c/o Department of Foreign Affairs, Pretoria, South Africa.

BOTT, Ian Bernard; Deputy Director Underwater Weapons Projects (S/M), Ministry of Defence, since 1977; *b* 1 April 1932; *s* of Edwin Bernard and Agnes Bott; *m* 1955, Kathleen Mary (*née* Broadbent); one *s* one *d*. *Educ:* Nottingham High Sch.; Southwell Minster Grammar Sch.; Stafford Technical Coll.; Manchester Univ. BSc Hon. Physics; FIEE, FInstP. Nottingham Lace Industry, 1949-53. Royal Air Force, 1953-55. English Electric, Stafford, 1955-57; Royal Radar Estabt, 1960-75 (Head of Electronics Group, 1973-75); seconded to FCO as Counsellor, Defence Research and Development, at British Embassy, Washington DC, 1975-77. *Publications:* papers on physics and electronics subjects in jls of learned socs. *Recreations:* building, horology, music, travel. *Address:* The Grey House, Colwall, Malvern, Worcs WR13 6ET. *T:* Colwall 40538. *Club:* Cosmos (Washington DC, USA).

BOTT, Prof. Martin Harold Phillips, FRS 1977; Professor of Geophysics, University of Durham, since 1966; *b* 12 July 1926; *s* of Harold Bott and Dorothy (*née* Phillips); *m* 1961, Joyce Cynthia Hughes; two *s* one *d*. *Educ:* Clayesmore Sch. Dorset; Magdalene Coll., Cambridge (Scholar). MA, PhD. Nat. Service, 1945-48 (Lieut, Royal Signals). Durham University: Turner and Newall Fellow, 1954-56; Lectr, 1956-63; Reader, 1963-66. Anglican Lay Reader. Murchison Medallist, Geological Soc. of London, 1977. *Publications:* The Interior of the Earth, 1971; papers in learned jls. *Recreations:* walking, mountains. *Address:* 11 St Mary's Close, Shincliffe, Durham. *T:* Durham 64021.

BOTTINI, Reginald Norman, CBE 1974; General-Secretary, National Union of Agricultural and Allied Workers, 1970-78; Member, General Council of TUC, since 1970; *b* 14 Oct. 1916; *s* of Reginald and Helena Teresa Bottini; *m* 1946, Doris Mary Balcomb; no *c*. *Educ:* Bec Grammar School. Apptd Asst in Legal Dept of Nat. Union of Agricultural Workers, 1945; Head of Negotiating Dept, 1954; elected Gen.-Sec., Dec. 1969. Member: Agricultural Wages Bd, 1963-78; Agricultural Economic Development Cttee, 1970-; (part-time) SE Electricity

Bd, 1974-; Food Hygiene Adv. Council, 1973-; BBC Agric. Adv. Cttee, 1973-78; Econ. and Soc. Cttee, EEC, 1975-; Clean Air Council, 1975-; Adv. Cttee on Toxic Substances, 1977-. Meat and Livestock Commn, 1977- (and Chm. of its Consumers Cttee); Central Transport Consultative Cttee, 1977-; Panel Mem., Central Arbitration Cttee, 1977-. Formerly: Secretary: Trade Union Side, Forestry Commn Ind. and Trades Council; Trade Union Side, British Sugar Beet Nat. Negotiating Cttee; Chm., Trade Union Side, Nat. Jt Ind. Council for River Authorities; formerly Member: Central Council for Agric. and Hort. Co-operation; Nat. Jt Ind. Council for County Roadmen. *Recreations:* gardening, driving. *Address:* 43 Knights End Road, Great Bowden, Market Harborough, Leics LE16 7EY. *T:* Market Harborough 4229. *Club:* Farmers'.

BOTTOMLEY, Rt. Hon. Arthur George, PC 1951; OBE 1941; MP (Lab) Teesside, Middlesbrough, since 1974 (Middlesbrough East, 1962-74); *b* 7 Feb. 1907; *s* of late George Howard Bottomley and Alice Bottomley; *m* 1936, Bessie Ellen Wiles (*see* Dame Bessie Bottomley); no *c*. *Educ:* Gamuel Road Council Sch.; Extension Classes at Toynbee Hall. London Organiser of National Union of Public Employees, 1935-45, 1959-62. Walthamstow Borough Council, 1929-49; Mayor of Walthamstow, 1945-46; Chairman of Emergency Cttee and ARP Controller, 1939-41. Dep. Regional Commissioner for S-E England, 1941-45. MP (Lab) Chatham Division of Rochester, 1945-50, Rochester and Chatham 1950-59. Parliamentary Under-Secretary of State for Dominions, 1946-47; Sec. for Overseas Trade, Board of Trade, 1947-51; Sec. of State for Commonwealth Affairs, 1964-66; Minister of Overseas Develt, 1966-67. Land Tax Comr, Becontree Div. of Essex; Member: Parliamentary Mission to India, 1946; Special Govt Mission to Burma, 1947; Deleg. to UN, New York, 1946, 1947 and 1949; Leader: UK delegation to World Trade and Employment Conference, Havana, 1947; UK Delegn to Commonwealth Conference, Delhi, 1949; Trade Mission to Pakistan, 1950; Special Mission to West Indies, 1951; Member: Consultative Assembly, Council of Europe, 1952, 1953 and 1954; Special Parliamentary Mission to Kenya, 1954; Parliamentary Mission to Ghana, 1959; Leader: Parliamentary Labour Party Mission to Burma, 1962; to Malaysia, 1963; UK Delegation to CPA Conference, Ottawa, 1966; Member: Parliamentary Mission to Cyprus, 1963; Special Mission to Hong Kong, 1964. Chairman: Commonwealth Relations and Colonies Group, Parly Labour Party, 1963; Select Parly Cttee on Race Relations and Immigration, 1969; Select Cttee on Cyprus, 1975; Special Parly Cttee on Admin and Orgn of House of Commons Services, 1976; Treasurer, Commonwealth Parly Assoc., 1974- (Vice-Chm., UK Branch, 1968 and 1974-77). Governor, Commonwealth Inst., 1968. Hon. Freeman of Chatham, 1959; Freeman of Middlesbrough, 1976. *Publications:* Why Britain should Join the Common Market, 1959; Two Roads to Colonialism, 1960; The Use and Abuse of Trade Unions, 1961. *Recreations:* walking and theatre-going. *Address:* 19 Lichfield Road, Woodford Green, Essex.

BOTTOMLEY, Dame Bessie (Ellen), DBE 1970; *b* 28 Nov. 1906; *d* of Edward Charles Wiles and Ellen (*née* Estall); *m* 1936, Rt Hon. Arthur George Bottomley, *qv*; no *c*. *Educ:* Maynard Road Girls' Sch.; North Walthamstow Central Sch. On staff of NUT, 1925-36. Member: Walthamstow Borough Council, 1945-48; Essex CC, 1962-65; Chm., Labour Party Women's Section, E Walthamstow, 1946-71, Chingford, 1973-. Mem., Forest Group Hosp. Man. Cttee, 1949-73; Mem., W Roding Community Health Council, 1973-76. Chm., Walthamstow Nat. Savings Cttee, 1949-65; Vice-Pres., Waltham Forest Nat. Savings Cttee, 1965- (Chm., 1975-). Mayoress of Walthamstow, 1945-46. Mem., WVS Regional Staff (SE England), 1941-45. Past Mem., Home Office Adv. Cttee on Child Care. Chm. of Govs of two Secondary Modern Schools, 1948-68, also group of Primary and Infant Schools; Chm. of Governors of High Schools. JP 1955-76 and on Juvenile Bench, 1955-71; Dep. Chm., Waltham Forest Bench. *Recreations:* theatre, gardening. *Address:* 19 Lichfield Road, Woodford Green, Essex.

BOTTOMLEY, Sir James (Reginald Alfred), KCMG 1973 (CMG 1965); HM Diplomatic Service; Permanent UK Representative to UN and other International Organisations at Geneva, since 1976; *b* 12 Jan. 1920; *s* of Sir (William) Cecil Bottomley, KCMG, and Alice Thistle Bottomley (*née* Robinson), JP; *m* 1941, Barbara Evelyn (Vardon); two *s* two *d* (and one *s* decd). *Educ:* King's College Sch., Wimbledon; Trinity Coll., Cambridge. Served with Inns of Court Regt, RAC, 1940-46. Dominions Office, 1946; Pretoria, 1948-50; Karachi, 1953-55; Washington, 1955-59; UK Mission to United Nations, 1959; Dep. High Commissioner, Kuala Lumpur 1963-67; Asst Under-Sec. of State, Commonwealth Office (later FCO), 1967-70; Dep. Under-Sec. of State, FCO, 1970-72; Ambassador to

South Africa, 1973-76. Mem., British Overseas Trade Bd, 1972. *Recreation:* golf. *Address:* c/o Foreign and Commonwealth Office, SW1A 2AL; Chiltern Rise, Aldbury, Tring, Herts. *T:* Aldbury Common 304.
See also P . J . Bottomley .

BOTTOMLEY, Peter James; MP (C) for Greenwich, Woolwich West, since June 1975; *b* 30 July 1944; *er s* of Sir James Bottomley, *qv*; *m* Virginia Garnett, JP, *er d* of W. John Garnett, *qv*; one *s* one *d*. *Educ:* comprehensive sch.; Westminster Sch.; Trinity Coll., Cambridge (BA Econ, MA). Driving, industrial sales, industrial relations, industrial economics. Contested (C) GLC elect., Vauxhall, 1973; (C) Woolwich West, Gen. Elecs, 1974. Chm., British Union of Family Organisations; Mem., Transport House Br., T&GWU; Vice-Pres., Cons. Trade Unionists' Nat. Adv. Cttee. *Recreation:* children. *Address:* 2 St Barnabas Villas, SW8 2EH. *T:* 01-720 4282.

BOTTRALL, (Francis James) Ronald, OBE 1949; MA; FRSL; *b* Camborne, Cornwall, 2 Sept. 1906; *o s* of Francis John and Clara Jane Bottrall; *m* 1st, 1934, Margaret Florence (marr. diss., 1954), *o d* of Rev. H. Saumarez Smith; one *s*; 2nd, 1954, Margot Pamela Samuel. *Educ:* Redruth County Sch.; Pembroke Coll., Cambridge. Foundress' Scholar; First Class English Tripos, Parts I and II (with distinction); Charles Oldham Shakespeare Scholarship, 1927. Lector in English, Univ. of Helsingfors, Finland, 1929-31; Commonwealth Fund Fellowship, Princeton Univ., USA, 1931-33; Johore Prof. of English Language and Literature, Raffles Coll., Singapore, 1933-37; Asst Dir, British Inst., Florence, 1937-38; Sec., SOAS, London Univ., 1939-45; Air Ministry: Temp. Admin. Officer, 1940; Priority Officer, 1941; British Council Representative: in Sweden, 1941; in Italy, 1945; in Brazil, 1954; in Greece, 1957; in Japan (and Cultural Counsellor, HM Embassy, Tokyo), 1959; Controller of Educ. 1950-54. Chief, Fellowships and Training Br., Food and Agriculture Org. of UN, 1963-65. Syracuse Internat. Poetry Prize, 1954. FRSL 1955. Grande Ufficiale dell'Ordine al Merito della Repubblica Italiana, 1973. KStJ 1972. Coronation Medal, 1953. *Publications:* The Loosening and other Poems, 1931; Festivals of Fire, 1934; The Turning Path, 1939; (with Gunnar Ekelöf) T. S. Eliot: Dikter i Urval, 1942; Farewell and Welcome, 1945; (with Margaret Bottrall) The Zephyr Book of English Verse, 1945; Selected Poems, 1946; The Palisades of Fear, 1949; Adam Unparadised, 1954; Collected Poems, 1961; Rome (Art Centres of the World), 1968; Day and Night, 1974; Poems 1955-73, 1974. *Recreations:* music, travel. *Address:* c/o FAO Regional Office for the Near East, PO Box 2223, Cairo, Egypt. *Club:* Athenæum.

BOTVINNIK, Mikhail Moisseyevich; Order of Lenin, 1957; Order of the Badge of Honour, 1936 and 1945; Order of the Red Banner of Labour, 1961; Senior Scientist, USSR Research Institute for Electro-energetics, since 1955; *b* Petersburg, 17 Aug. 1911; *s* of a dental technician; *m* 1935, Gayane Ananova; one *d*. *Educ:* Leningrad Polytechnical Institute (Grad.). Thesis for degree of: Candidate of Technical Sciences, 1937; Doctor of Technical Sciences, 1952; Professor, 1972. Chess master title, 1927; Chess grandmaster title, 1935. Won Soviet chess championship in 1931, 1933, 1939, 1941, 1944, 1945, 1952; World chess title, 1948-57, 1958 and 1961. Honoured Master of Sport of the USSR, 1945. *Publications:* Flohr-Botvinnik Match, 1934; Alekhin-Euwe Return Match, 1938; Selected Games, 1937, 1945, 1960; Tournament Match for the Absolute Champion Title, 1945; Botvinnik-Smyslov Match, 1955; Eleventh Soviet Chess Championship, 1939; Smyslov-Botvinnik Return Match, 1960; Regulation of Excitation and Static Stability of Synchronous Machines, 1950; Asynchronized Synchronous Machines, 1960; Algorithm Play of Chess, 1968; Controlled AC Machines (with Y. Shakarian), 1969; Computers, Chess and Long-Range Planning, 1971; Botvinnik's Best Games 1947-70, 1972; Three matches of Anatoly Karpov, 1975; On Cybernetic Goal of Game, 1975. *Address:* 3 Frunsenskaja 7 (flat 154), Moscow. *T:* 242.15,86.

BOUCHIER, Air Vice-Marshal Sir Cecil Arthur, KBE 1953 (CBE 1941; OBE 1936); CB 1945; DFC 1918; *b* 14 Oct. 1895, British; *m* 1st, 1927, Gladys Dorothy Sherwood (*d* 1964); one *s*; 2nd, 1968, Isabella Dorothy Guyver, *d* of Frank Guyver Britton, Yokohama. *Educ:* Chichester; RAF Staff Coll. Served in "A" Battery HAC, 1915-17, in Palestine; commissioned RFC 1918; served with RAF in Middle East and N Russia, 1918-19; India and Iraq, 1920-21; RAE Experimental Pilot, Farnborough, 1922-25; No 41 (F) Squadron, 1926-28; Test Pilot, Egypt, 1929; graduated RAF Staff Coll., Andover, 1930; HQ RAF India, 1931-32; formed and commanded Indian Air Force, 1932-35; commanded: No 54 (F) Sqdn, 1936-37; No 11 Group, 1938-39; commanded RAF Sector, Hornchurch (Battle of Britain), 1940 (CBE and despatches); No 11 Group and RAF Station, Kenley,

1941; Air Ministry, 1942; No 11 (F) Group, 1943-45 (in control Fighter "umbrella" at Normandy Beach landings) (CB); AOC No 221 Group in Burma, 1945; AOC, British Commonwealth Air Forces of Occupation, Japan, 1945-48; AOC No 21 Group, Swinderby, Lincs, 1948-49; retired list, 1949; re-instated on active list, 1950; Personal Representative of British Chiefs of Staff to Generals MacArthur, Ridgway and Mark Clark throughout Korean War, 1950-53; retired list 1953. Order of St Anne (Russia), 1919; Legion of Merit (Commander), USA, 1945. *Recreations:* golf, chess. *Address:* 2275 Isshiki, Hayama, Kanagawa-ken, Japan. *T:* 0468-75-1217. *Club:* Royal Air Force.

BOUCHIER, Prof. Ian Arthur Dennis; Professor of Medicine, University of Dundee, since 1973; *b* 7 Sept. 1932; *s* of E. A. and M. Bouchier; *m* 1959, Patricia Norma Henshilwood; two *s*. *Educ:* Rondebosch Boys' High Sch., Cape Town; Univ. of Cape Town. MB, ChB, MD, FRCP, FRCPE. Groote Schuur Hospital: House Officer, 1955-58; Registrar, 1958-61; Asst Lectr, Royal Free Hosp., 1962-63; Instructor in Medicine, Boston Univ. Sch. of Medicine, 1964-65; Sen. Lectr 1965-70, Reader in Medicine 1970-73, Univ. of London. *Publications:* Clinical Investigation of Gastrointestinal Function, 1969; Gastroenterology, 1973; Clinical Skills, 1976. *Recreations:* music, history of whaling, sailing. *Address:* Department of Medicine, Ninewells Hospital, Dundee DD1 9SY. *T:* Dundee 60111.

BOUGHEY, John Fenton C.; *see* Coplestone-Boughey.

BOUGHEY, Sir Richard (James), 10th Bt, *cr* 1798; JP; DL; *b* 30 July 1925; *s* of Sir George Menteth Boughey, 9th Bt; *m* 1st, 1950, Davina Julia (marr. diss. 1975), 2nd *d* of Fitzherbert Wright; two *s* three *d*; 2nd, 1976, Gillian Claire, *d* of late Major Robert Moubray. *Educ:* Eton. Served with Coldstream Guards, 1943-46, in France and Germany, Lieut. Chairman, Apple and Pear Development Council, 1967-72; Liaison Officer to Minister of Agriculture, Fisheries and Food, 1965-71; Chairman, East Sussex Agricultural Exec. Cttee, 1958-67; Pres., Nat. Fedn of Young Farmers Clubs, 1970; Mem., Adv. Council for Agriculture and Horticulture in England and Wales, 1973-. High Sheriff of Sussex, 1964; DL, Sussex, 1970-. OStJ. *Heir: s* John George Fletcher Boughey, *b* 12 Aug. 1959. *Address:* Ringmer Park, Lewes, E Sussex. *T:* Ringmer 310. *Club:* Boodle's.

BOULANGER, Nadia (Juliette), Hon. CBE; Grand Officier de la Légion d'Honneur; teacher of composition; conductor; lecturer; *b* Paris, 16 Sept. 1887; *d* of Ernest and Raïssa (Princess Mychetsky) Boulanger. Studied at Paris Nat. Conservatory. Formerly head of theory dept, Ecole Normale de Musique, Paris. Went to US in 1924, 1935, 1940, 1958, 1962; was faculty member in many American Schools. Now Conservatory of Music, Paris (Hon. Prof.); Prof. and Director, Conservatoire Americain, Fontainebleau; Guest Conductor: Boston Symphony Orchestra; Royal Philharmonic, London; NY Philharmonic; Philadelphia Orchestra; Washington Symphony. Maître de Chapelle to the Prince of Monaco. Has lectured and conducted in many European countries and in US. Has made numerous recordings. FRCM. Dr *hc:* Oxford; Harvard, Newcastle, etc; holds several other hon. doctorates. Gold Medal, Acad. des Beaux Arts. Commander, Arts et Lettres (France); Commander: Order of Polonia Restituta (Poland); Ordre de la Couronne (Belgium); Commander of St Charles (Monaco). *Address:* 3 Place Lili Boulanger (anciennement 36 Rue Ballu), Paris IXe, France.

BOULEZ, Pierre; composer; Director, Institut de Recherche et de Coordination Acoustique/Musique, since 1976; *b* Montbrison, Loire, France, 26 March 1925. *Educ:* Saint-Etienne and Lyon (music and higher mathematics); Paris Conservatoire. Studied with Messiaen and René Leibowitz. Theatre conductor, Jean-Louis Barrault Company, Paris, 1948; visited USA with French Ballet Company, 1952. Has conducted major orchestras in his own and standard classical works in Great Britain, Europe and USA, including Edinburgh Festival, 1965; also conducted Wozzeck in Paris and Frankfurt; Parsifal at Bayreuth, 1966; Chief Conductor, BBC Symphony Orchestra, 1971-75; Chief Conductor and Music Dir, NY Philharmonic, 1971-77; Dir, Bayreuth Festival, 1976. Interested in poetry and aesthetics of Baudelaire, Mallarmé and René Char. *Compositions include:* Trois Psalmodies (Piano solo), 1945; Sonata No 1 (piano), 1946; Sonatine for flute and piano, 1946; Sonata No 2 (piano), 1948; Polyphonie X for 18 solo instruments, 1951; Visage nuptial (2nd version), 1951; Structures for 2 pianos, 1952; Le Marteau sans Maître (voice and 6 instruments), 1954; Sonata No 3 (piano), 1956; Deux Improvisations sur Mallarmé for voice and 9 instruments, 1957; Doubles for orchestra, 1958; Poésie pour Pouvoir for voices and orchestra, 1958; Soleil des Eaux (text by

René Char) for chorus and orchestra, 1958; Pli selon Pli: Hommage à Mallarmé, for voices and orchestra, 1960; Eclat (in progress), 1964; Domaines for solo clarinet, 1968; Cummings ist der Dichter (16 solo voices and instruments), 1970; Explosante Fixe (8 solo instruments), 1972; Rituel, for orchestra, 1975. *Publications:* Penser la musique d'aujourd'hui, 1966 (Boulez on Music Today, 1971); Relevés d'apprenti, 1967; Par volonté et par hasard, 1976. *Address:* IRCAM, 31 rue St Mervi, 75004 Paris, France. *T:* 278.39.42.

BOULIND, Mrs (Olive) Joan, CBE 1975; Tutor, Hughes Hall, Cambridge, since 1974; *b* 24 Sept. 1912; *e d* of Douglas Siddall and Olive Raby; *m* 1936, Henry F. Boulind, MA, PhD; two *s* one *d. Educ:* Wallasey High Sch., Cheshire; Univ. of Liverpool. BA 1st class Hons History, Medieval and Modern; DipEd. Fellow of Hughes Hall, Cambridge, 1973; MA Cantab 1974. Teacher: Wirral Co. Sch. for Girls, 1934-36; Cambridgeshire High Sch. for Girls, 1963. Mem., Domestic Consumers' Cttee, Min. of Power, 1948-52; Founder Chm., Eastern Regional Cttee, Women's Adv. Council on Solid Fuel, 1962-66; Nat. Pres., Nat. Council of Women, 1966-68 (Sen. Vice-Pres., 1964-66); Co-Chm., Women's Consultative Council, 1966-68; Leader, British delegn to conf. of Internat. Council of Women, Bangkok, 1970; Co-Chm., Women's Nat. Commn, 1973-75; Co-Chm., UK Co-ordinating Cttee for Internat. Women's Year, 1975. Founder Chm., primary sch. Parents Assoc., 1947-50; Chm., Parents Assoc., Cambridgeshire High Sch. for Boys, 1953-57. Member: Commn on the Church in the Seventies, Congregational Church in England and Wales, 1970-72 (Vice-Chm., 1971-72); Ministerial Trng Cttee, United Reformed Church, 1972-; East Adv. Council, BBC, 1976-. Deacon, Emmanuel Congregational Ch., Cambridge, 1958-66. Trustee, Homerton Coll. of Educn, 1955-. *Recreations:* reading, travel, music. *Address:* 14 Queen Edith's Way, Cambridge CB1 4PN. *T:* Cambridge 47826. *Club:* University Women's.

BOULT, Sir Adrian, CH 1969; Kt 1937; MA, DMus, Oxon; FRCM; Vice-President, Council of Royal College of Music, since 1963; *b* Chester, 8 April 1889; *o s* of late Cedric R. Boult, JP, formerly of Liverpool, and Katharine Florence Barman; *m* 1933, Ann, *yr d* of late Capt. F. A. Bowles, RN, JP, Dully, Sittingbourne, Kent. *Educ:* Westminster Sch.; Christ Church, Oxford; Leipzig Conservatorium. President, Oxford Univ. Musical Club, 1910. Musical Staff, Royal Opera, 1914; Asst Director of Music, 1926. During European War, served in War Office and Commission Internationale de Ravitaillement. Teaching staff of Royal College of Music, 1919-30 and 1962-66; Conductor of Patron's Fund, 1919-29; Musical Director, Birmingham City Orchestra, 1924-30 and 1959-60; Vice-President, City of Birmingham Symphony Orchestra, 1960-; Director of Music, BBC, 1930-42; Conductor, BBC Symphony Orchestra, 1930-50; Conductor, London Philharmonic Orchestra, 1950-57, President, 1966-. Since 1922, has conducted all over Europe, in Canada, USA and USSR, introducing British music; has conducted all permanent orchestras in England, Scotland and Wales and directed many schools for conductors, recently for Schools' Music Assoc. and Surrey CC. Has also conducted: Bach Choir, 1928-33; Promenade Concerts, 1942-50; Petersfield Festival, 1920-39; Three Choirs Festivals, Worcester, Gloucester and Hereford, and many amateur festivals. Assisted at Coronation Services, 1937, 1953, and took part in concerts and services during Westminster Abbey 900th Anniversary Year, 1966. President: Incorp. Society of Musicians, 1928-29; Nat. Youth Orchestra, 1947-57; Schools' Music Assoc., 1947-; Leith Hill Musical Festival, 1959-; Royal Scottish Academy of Music, 1959-. Hon. LLD (Birmingham, Liverpool); Hon. MusDoc (Edinburgh, Cambridge); Hon. RAM; Hon. Student, Christ Church, Oxon; Hon. Fellow, Manchester Coll., Oxford; Hon. Member Royal Academy of Music, Sweden; Hon. GSM; Hon. TCL; Gold Medal, Royal Philharmonic Soc., 1944; Harvard Medal, with Dr Vaughan Williams, 1956. OStJ. *Publications:* A Handbook on The Technique of Conducting, 1920, rev. edn 1968; (joint) Bach's Matthew Passion, 1949; Thoughts on Conducting, 1963; My Own Trumpet (autobiog.), 1973; contribs on musical subjects to various journals. *Address:* 96 West Street, Farnham, Surrey GU9 7EN. *T:* Farnham 26345. *Clubs:* Athenæum (Life Mem.); Leander.

BOULTER, Eric Thomas; Director-General, Royal National Institute for the Blind, since 1972; *b* 7 July 1917; *s* of Albert and Ethel Boulter; *m* 1946, Martha Mary McClure; one *s* one *d. Educ:* St Marylebone Grammar School. World Council for Welfare of Blind: Sec.-General, 1951-59; Vice-Pres., 1959-64; Pres., 1964-69; Hon. Life Mem., 1969. Chm., Council of World Organisations for Handicapped, 1958-61; Mem. Exec., Internat. Council of Educators of Blind Youth, 1962-70; Assoc. Dir, American Foundn for Overseas Blind, 1956-70; Dep. Dir-Gen., RNIB, 1971-72; Sec., British Nat. Cttee for Prevention of

Blindness, 1976-. Order of the Andes (Bolivia), 1960. *Address:* 40 Snaresbrook Drive, Stanmore, Mddx. *T:* 01-958 8681. *Club:* National Liberal.

BOULTING, John Edward; Producer-Director: Charter Film Productions Ltd (Joint Managing Director), since 1973; BLC Films Ltd; *b* 21 Nov. 1913; *s* of Arthur Boulting and Rose Bennett. *Educ:* Reading Sch. Office boy in Wardour Street, 1933. Spent eighteen months selling bad films to reluctant exhibitors; joined independent producer as general factotum on production, 1935; served hard but educative apprenticeship, in small studios. Went to Spain, served in International Brigade, front line ambulance driver, 1937; returned to England. Nov. 1937 formed independent film production company with twin brother Roy. Served War of 1939-45; joined RAF as AC2, 1940; retired Flt-Lieut, 1946. Continued film production; since War has produced Fame is the Spur, The Guinea Pig, Seagulls over Sorrento, Josephine and Men, Brothers in Law; has directed Brighton Rock, Seven Days to Noon, The Magic Box, Lucky Jim (Edinburgh Festival 1957); directed, and co-author of, screen-play Private's Progress, 1955; produced Carlton-Browne of the FO, 1958; directed and co-author screenplay, I'm All Right Jack, 1959; produced The Risk and The French Mistress, 1960; co-author novel and screen-play and director, Heavens Above!, 1962; produced films: The Family Way, 1966; There's a Girl in my Soup, 1970; Soft Beds, Hard Battles, 1974. Dir, 1958-72, Man. Dir, 1966-72, Consultant, 1972, British Lion Films Ltd. Former Chm., Local Radio Assoc. *Recreations:* cricket, tennis, reading, film making, horse riding and irritating the conservative minded in all stratas. *Address:* Charter Film Productions, 8a Glebe Place, Chelsea, SW3.

BOULTING, Roy; Producer and Joint Managing Director, Charter Film Productions Ltd, since 1973; *b* 21 Nov. 1913; *s* of Arthur Boulting and Rose Bennett. *Educ:* HMS Worcester; Reading Sch. Formed independent film production company with twin brother John, 1937. Served War of 1939-45, RAC, finishing as Capt.; films for Army included Desert Victory and Burma Victory. Producer: Brighton Rock, 1947; Seven Days to Noon, 1950; Private's Progress, 1955; Lucky Jim (Edinburgh Festival), 1957; I'm All Right Jack, 1959; Heavens Above!, 1962. Director: Pastor Hall, 1939; Thunder Rock, 1942; Fame is the Spur, 1947; The Guinea Pig, 1948; High Treason, 1951; Singlehanded, 1952; Seagulls over Sorrento, Crest of the Wave, 1953; Josephine and Men, 1955; Run for the Sun, 1955; Brothers in Law, 1956; Happy is the Bride, 1958; Carlton-Browne of the FO, 1958-59; I'm All Right Jack, 1959; The Risk, 1960; The French Mistress, 1960; Suspect, 1960; The Family Way, 1966; Twisted Nerve, 1968; There's a Girl in my Soup, 1970; Soft Beds, Hard Battles, 1974. Dir, British Lion Films Ltd, 1958-72. *Publication:* (with Leo Marks) Favourites (play), 1977. *Address:* Charter Film Productions Ltd, 8a Glebe Place, Chelsea, SW3. *Club:* Lord's Taverners.

BOULTING, S. A.; *see* Cotes, Peter.

BOULTON, Sir Christian; *see* Boulton, Sir H. H. C.

BOULTON, Edward Henry Brooke, MC; MA; FIWSc; Timber and Forestry Consultant; Forestry and Timber Counsellor to Marquess of Bath; *b* 1897; *s* of Joseph Henry and Florence Helena Boulton; *m*; one *s. Educ:* Portora Royal Inniskillen; St Catharine's Coll., Cambridge. Served with Royal Naval Division, 1915-16, Gallipoli and France; Royal Field Artillery, Capt., 1917-19; School of Forestry, Cambridge, 1920-22; Degree in Forestry and Post-grad. Diploma with Distinction in Timber Technology; University Lecturer in Forestry, 1922-34; Manager Timber Development Assoc. Ltd, 1934; Technical Dir, Timber Development Assoc., Ltd, 1936-48; Past President and Fellow, Inst. of Wood Science; Past Pres., British Wood Preserving Assoc.; Chm., Bristol Channel and S Wales Timber R&D Assoc. *Publications:* A Pocket Book of British Trees, 1937, 2nd edn 1941; Timber Houses, 1937; A Dictionary of Wood, 1938; Timber Buildings for the Country, 1938; British Timbers, 1944, 3rd edn 1947; many papers on Forestry and Identification of Timbers. *Recreations:* riding, golf, fishing. *Address:* The Island, Horningsham, Warminster, Wilts. *Clubs:* British Empire, Farmers'.

BOULTON, Major Sir Edward (John), 2nd Bt, *cr* 1944; *b* 11 April 1907; *s* of Sir William Whytehead Boulton, 1st Bt and Rosalind Mary (*d* 1969), *d* of Sir John D. Milburn, 1st Bt of Guyzance, Northumberland; *S* father, 1949; unmarried. *Educ:* Eton; Trinity Coll., Cambridge (BA). Joined Staffordshire Yeomanry, 1939. Served War of 1939-45, Middle East, Italy, 1940-44 (despatches); North West Europe (HQ 21 Army Group), 1944-45, Major 1944. Contested Southern Division of Ilford (C), 1945. Retired from membership of London Stock

WW—9

Exchange, 1970. *Heir: b* Sir William Whytehead Boulton, *qv.* *Address:* Ouaisné Lodge, Portelet, Jersey, CI. *T:* Jersey 42935. *Club:* Cavalry and Guards.

BOULTON, Sir (Harold Hugh) Christian, 4th Bt *cr* 1905; *b* 29 Oct. 1918; *s* of Sir (Denis Duncan) Harold (Owen) Boulton, 3rd Bt, and Louise McGowan, USA; *S* father, 1968. *Educ:* Ampleforth College, Yorks. Late Captain, Irish Guards (Supplementary Reserve). *Address:* c/o Bank of Montreal, City View Branch, 1481 Merivale Road, Ottawa 5, Ontario, Canada.

BOULTON, Prof. James Thompson; Professor of English Studies and Head of Department of English Language and Literature, University of Birmingham, since 1975; *b* 17 Feb. 1924; *e s* of Harry and Annie M. P. Boulton; *m* 1949, Margaret Helen Leary; one *s* one *d.* *Educ:* University College, Univ. of Durham; Lincoln Coll., Oxford. BA Dunelm 1948; BLitt Oxon 1952; PhD Nottingham 1960. FRSL 1968. Served in RAF, 1943-46 (Flt-Lt). Lectr, subseq. Sen. Lectr and Reader in English, Univ. of Nottingham, 1951-64; John Cranford Adams Prof. of English, Hofstra Univ., NY, 1967; Prof. of English Lit., Univ. of Nottingham, 1964-75; Dean, Faculty of Arts, 1970-73. Editorial Adviser, Studies in Burke and his Time, 1960-; Mem. Exec. Cttee, Anglo-American Associates (NY), 1968-75. Editor, Renaissance and Modern Studies, 1969-75. General Editor: The Letters of D. H. Lawrence, 1973-; The Works of D. H. Lawrence, 1975-. *Publications:* (ed) Edmund Burke: A Philosophical Enquiry into... the Sublime and Beautiful, 1958; (ed) C. F. G. Masterman: The Condition of England, 1960; The Language of Politics in the Age of Wilkes and Burke, 1963, 2nd edn 1975; (ed) Dryden: Of Dramatick Poesy etc, 1964; (ed) Defoe: Prose and Verse, 1965; (with James Kinsley) English Satiric Poetry: Dryden to Byron, 1966; (ed) Lawrence in Love: Letters from D. H. Lawrence to Louie Burrows, 1968; (ed) Samuel Johnson: The Critical Heritage, 1971; (with S. T. Bindoff) Research in Progress in English and Historical Studies in the Universities of the British Isles, vol. 1, 1971, vol. 2, 1976; (ed) Defoe: Memoirs of a Cavalier, 1972; (contrib.) Renaissance and Modern Essays (ed G. R. Hibbard), 1966; (contrib.) The Familiar Letter in the 18th Century (ed H. Anderson), 1966; papers in Durham Univ. Jl, Essays in Criticism, Renaissance and Modern Studies, Modern Drama, etc. *Recreations:* tennis, gardening. *Address:* Department of English Language and Literature, University of Birmingham, PO Box 363, Birmingham B15 2TT.

BOULTON, Prof. Norman Savage, DSc, FICE; Emeritus Professor of Civil Engineering, University of Sheffield, since 1964 (Professor, 1955-64); *b* 8 May 1899; *s* of late Professor William Savage Boulton; *m* 1929, Constance (*d* 1968), *d* of late H. Deakin; one *d.* *Educ:* King Edward's Sch., Birmingham; University of Birmingham. RGA, 1918; BSc (Birmingham), First Class Hons and Bowen Research Schol., 1922; MSc and Dudley Docker Res. Schol., 1923; DSc (Civil Engineering), 1966. Engineering Asst, Public Works Dept, City of Birmingham, 1924-29; University Lecturer in Civil Engineering, King's Coll., Newcastle upon Tyne, 1929-36; Sen. Lecturer in charge of Dept of Civil Engineering, University of Sheffield, 1936-55. Chairman, Yorkshire Assoc. Inst. Civil Engineers, 1947-48 and 1961-62. AMICE, 1927; MICE, 1950. *Publications:* various technical papers in Proc. Instns Civil and Mechanical Engineers, Philosophical Magazine, Jl of Hydrology, Water Resources Research, etc. *Recreations:* music, swimming. *Address:* 68 Endcliffe Vale Road, Sheffield S10 3EW. *T:* Sheffield 661049.

BOULTON, Very Rev. Walter, MA Oxon; *s* of Walter and Clara Elizabeth Boulton, Smallthorne, Staffs.; *m* 1932, Kathleen Lorna York Batley; one *s* four *d.* *Educ:* Balliol Coll., Oxford. Exhibitioner of Balliol, 2nd Class Modern History, 1922, BA 1923, MA 1930. Cuddesdon Coll., 1923. Deacon, 1924; Priest, 1925; Curate of St Mark, Woodhouse, Leeds, 1924-27; Asst Chaplain at the Cathedral Church, Calcutta, 1927-34; Chaplain of Lebong, 1934-35. Furlough, 1937. Chaplain, Shillong, 1935-39; St Paul's Cathedral, Calcutta, 1939-45; Canon of Calcutta, 1940-48. Furlough, 1945. Chaplain, Shillong, 1945-47; Vicar of Fleet, Hampshire, 1948-52; Provost of Guildford and Rector of Holy Trinity with St Mary, Guildford, 1952-61; Rector of Market Overton with Thistleton, 1961-72. *Address:* Milton House, Lindfield, Haywards Heath, W Sussex.

BOULTON, Sir William (Whytehead), Kt 1975; CBE 1958; TD 1949; Secretary, Senate of the Inns of Court and the Bar, 1974-75; *b* 21 June 1912; *s* of Sir William Boulton, 1st Bt, and *b* and *heir* of Sir Edward Boulton, 2nd Bt, *qv; m* 1944, Margaret Elizabeth, *o d* of late Brig. H. N. A. Hunter, DSO; one *s* two *d.* *Educ:* Eton; Trinity Coll., Cambridge. Called to Bar, Inner Temple, 1936; practised at the Bar, 1937-39. Secretary, General Council of the Bar, 1950-74. Served War of 1939-45: with 104th Regt RHA (Essex Yeo.) and 14th Regt RHA, in the Middle East, 1940-44; Staff Coll., Camberley, 1944. Control Commission for Germany (Legal Div.), 1945-50. Gazetted 2nd Lieut TA (Essex Yeo.), 1934; retired with rank of Hon. Lieut-Col. *Publications:* A Guide to Conduct and Etiquette at the Bar of England and Wales, 1st edn 1953, 6th edn, 1975. *Address:* The Quarters House, Alresford, near Colchester, Essex. *T:* Wivenhoe 2450; 53 Montpelier Walk, SW7. *T:* 01-589 1663.

BOURASSA, Robert; Prime Minister of Québec, 1970-76; Member of Québec National Assembly for Mercier, 1966-76; *b* 14 July 1933; *s* of Aubert Bourassa and Adrienne Courville; *m* 1958, Andrée Simard; one *s* one *d.* *Educ:* Jean-de-Brébeuf Coll.; Univs of Montreal, Oxford and Harvard. Gov.-Gen.'s Medal Montreal 1956. MA Oxford 1959. Admitted Quebec Bar 1957. Fiscal Adviser to Dept of Nat. Revenue and Prof. in Econs and Public Finance, Ottawa Univ., 1960-63; Sec. and Dir of Research of Bélanger Commn on Public Finance, 1963-65; Special Adviser to Fed. Dept of Finance on fiscal and econ. matters, 1963-65; financial critic for Quebec Liberal Party, Pres. Polit. Commn and Mem. Liberal Party's Strategy Cttee; Leader, Quebec Liberal Party, 1970-77; Minister of Finance, May-Nov. 1970; Minister of Inter-govtl Affairs, 1971-72.

BOURDILLON, Henry Townsend, CMG 1952; Assistant Under-Secretary of State, Department of Education and Science, 1964-73; *b* 19 Aug. 1913; 2nd *s* of late Sir Bernard Henry Bourdillon, GCMG, KBE, and of Lady (Violet Grace) Bourdillon; *m* 1942, Margareta d'Almaine (*née* Tham); one *s* two *d.* *Educ:* Rugby Sch.; Corpus Christi Coll., Oxford. Asst Principal, Colonial Office, 1937; Acting Principal, Colonial Office, 1940; lent to: Foreign Office, 1942; Cabinet Office, 1943; Ministry of Production, 1944; returned to Colonial Office, 1944; Asst Secretary, 1947-54; Asst Under-Secretary of State, Colonial Office, 1954-59; Deputy UK Commissioner for Singapore, 1959-61; returned to Colonial Office, 1961; Under-Secretary, Ministry of Education, 1962-64. *Recreations:* gardening, music. *Address:* Orchard House, Horsenden Lane, Princes Risborough, Bucks. *T:* Princes Risborough 5416.

BOURDILLON, Mervyn Leigh, JP, DL; a Forestry Commissioner, 1973-76; *b* 9 Aug. 1924; *s* of late Prebendary G. L. Bourdillon; *m* 1961, Penelope, *d* of late P. W. Kemp-Welch, OBE; one *s* three *d.* *Educ:* Haileybury. Served RNVR, 1943-46. Mem. Brecon County Council, 1967-73; DL 1962, JP 1970, High Sheriff 1970, Brecon. *Address:* Llwyn Madoc, Beulah, Llanwrtyd Wells, Powys LD5 4TU.

BOURKE, family name of **Earl of Mayo.**

BOURKE, Christopher John; Metropolitan Stipendiary Magistrate, since 1974; *b* 31 March 1926; *e s* of late John Francis Bourke of the Oxford Circuit and late Eileen Winifred Bourke (*née* Beddoes); *m* 1956, Maureen, *y d* of late G. A. Barron-Boshell; two *s* one *d.* *Educ:* Stonyhurst; Oriel Coll., Oxford. Called to Bar, Gray's Inn, 1953; Oxford Circuit, 1954-55; Dir of Public Prosecutions Dept, 1955-74. *Recreations:* history of art, music. *Address:* 22 Queens Gate Gardens, SW7. *T:* 01-584 0328.

BOURKE, Sir Paget John, Kt 1957; Judge of the Courts of Appeal, Bahamas and Bermuda, since 1965, British Honduras, since 1968 (President of Courts, 1970-75), Gibraltar since 1970; *b* 1906; *s* of H. C. Bourke, Amana, Ballina, Co. Mayo, Ireland; *m* 1936, Susan Dorothy (*née* Killeen); three *s* one *d.* *Educ:* Mount St Mary's Coll., Chesterfield; Trinity Coll., Dublin (Mod. BA, LLB). Barrister-at-law, King's Inn, 1928, Gray's Inn, 1957. Legal Adviser and Crown Prosecutor, Seychelles, 1933; MEC and MLC; Chief Magistrate, Palestine, 1936; Relieving President, District Court, 1941; President, 1945; Judge of Supreme Court of Kenya, 1946; Chief Justice, Sierra Leone, 1955-57; Cyprus, 1957-60. Senior Counsel, Irish Bar, 1961. Acting Chief Justice, Gibraltar, Oct.-Dec., 1965. *Publication:* (ed) Digest of Cases, Seychelles, 1870-1933. *Address:* 9 Barnacoille Park, Dalkey, Co. Dublin.

BOURN, James; HM Diplomatic Service, retired; *b* 30 Aug. 1917; *s* of James and Sarah Gertrude Bourn; *m* 1944, Isobel Mackenzie; one *s.* *Educ:* Queen Elizabeth's Grammar Sch., Darlington. Executive Officer, Ministry of Health, 1936. War of 1939-45; served (Royal Signals), in India, North Africa and Italy; POW; Captain. Higher Exec. Officer, Ministry of National Insurance, 1947; Asst Principal, Colonial Office, 1947; Principal, 1949; Secretary to the Salaries Commission, Bahamas, 1948-49; Private Sec. to Perm. Under-Sec., 1949; seconded to Tanganyika, 1953-55; UK Liaison Officer to Commn for Technical Co-operation in Africa (CCTA), 1955-57; Commonwealth Relations Office, 1961; seconded to Central

African Office, 1962; Dar es Salaam, 1963; Deputy High Commissioner in Zanzibar, Tanzania, 1964-65; Counsellor and Dep. High Comr, Malawi, 1966-70; Ambassador to Somalia, 1970-73; Consul-General, Istanbul, 1973-75. *Address:* c/o Lloyds Bank Ltd, 46 Victoria Street, SW1.

BOURN, John Bryant; Assistant Under-Secretary of State, Ministry of Defence, since 1977; *b* 21 Feb. 1934; *s* of Henry Thomas Bryant Bourn and Beatrice Grace Bourn; *m* 1959, Ardita Ann Fleming; one *s* one *d. Educ:* Southgate County Grammar Sch.; LSE. 1st cl. hons BScEcon 1954, PhD 1958. Air Min. 1956-63; HM Treasury, 1963-64; Private Sec. to Perm. Under-Sec., MoD, 1964-69; Asst Sec. and Dir of Programmes, Civil Service Coll., 1969-72; Asst Sec., MoD, 1972-74; Under-Sec., Northern Ireland Office, 1974-77. *Publications:* articles and reviews in professional jls. *Recreations:* swimming, squash rackets. *Address:* Ministry of Defence, Main Building, Whitehall, SW1A 2HB.

BOURNE, Baron *cr* 1964 (Life Peer), of Atherstone; **Geoffrey Kemp Bourne,** GCB 1960; KBE 1954; CMG 1952; *b* 5 Oct. 1902; *s* of Col. W. K. Bourne, Sway, Hants; *m* 1928, Agnes Evelyn, *d* of late Sir Ernest Thompson, Prestbury, Cheshire; one *s* one *d. Educ:* Rugby; RMA Woolwich. Commissioned into RA, 1923; served in Hong Kong, 1930-32; Gibraltar, 1933-34; Staff Coll., Camberley, 1935-36; Colchester, 1937; War Office, 1938-41. Served War of 1939-45; Comdr 5th Indian Div., May-Sept. 1946 (Java and India); idc 1947; Head of British Services Mission to Burma, 1948; GOC Berlin (British Sector), 1949-51; GOC 16th Airborne Div. (TA), 1951-52; GOC-in-C, Eastern Command, 1953; GOC Malaya Command, and Director of Operations, 1954-56; C-in-C Middle East Land Forces, 1957; Commandant, Imperial Defence Coll., 1958-59; ADC General to the Queen, 1959-60. Col. Commandant RA, 1954-67; Hon. Col 10th Bn The Parachute Regt, TA., 1960-65. Retired April 1960. Director-General, Aluminium Federation, 1960-63; Chm., Nat. Building Agency, 1967-73. US Silver Star and Legion of Merit (degree of officer); Duncan Essay Gold Medal, 1935 (RA Institution). *Recreations:* golf, shooting. *Address:* Drove House, Cranborne, Wimborne, Dorset. *T:* Cranborne 321. *Club:* Army and Navy.

BOURNE, Sir Frederick Chalmers, KCSI 1946 (CSI 1944); CIE 1941; late ICS; *b* 12 Aug. 1891; *s* of late Sir Frederick Bourne, CMG, Mayfield, Sussex; *m* 1918, Heather Frances, *d* of late Lieut-Col F. W. Burbury. *Educ:* Rugby; Christ Church, Oxford; MA. Served in 4th Bn Queen's Own (RW Kent Regt), 1910-20. Entered Indian Civil Service, 1920; Sec. to Government, Punjab, Electricity and Industries Dept, 1934-37; Dep. Commissioner, Lahore, 1937-40; Sec. to Government of Punjab, Home Dept, 1940-41; Chief Sec. to Govt, Punjab, 1941-45; Acting Governor Central Provinces and Berar, May-Oct, 1945; Acting Governor of Assam, 1946; Governor of Central Provinces and Berar, 1946-47; Governor of East Bengal, Aug. 1947-50. Appointed as Adviser, Gold Coast, 1955. *Address:* Eachen Hill, Buxted, Sussex. *T:* Buxted 3108.

BOURNE, Lt-Col Geoffrey (H.), FRSM, FZS; DPhil, DSc; *b* West Perth, Western Australia, 17 Nov. 1909; *s* of Walter Howard Bourne and Mary Ann Mellon; *m* 1935, Gwenllian Myfanwy Jones, BA; two *s*; *m* 1965, Maria Nelly Golarz, PhD. *Educ:* Perth Modern Sch., W Australia; University of Western Australia (BSc 1930, BSc Hons 1931; MSc 1932, DSc 1935); University of Melbourne. DPhil (Oxford), 1943; Hackett Research Student, University of W Australia, 1931-33; Biologist and in charge of Experimental Work, Australian Institute of Anatomy, Canberra, 1933-35; Biochemist Commonwealth of Austr. Advisory Council on Nutrition, 1935-37; Beit Memorial Fellow for Medical Research, Oxford, 1938-41; Mackenzie-Mackinnon Research Fellow of Royal College of Physicians of London and Royal College of Surgeons of England, 1941-44; Demonstrator in Physiology, Oxford, 1941-44, 1946, 1947; in charge of research and development (rations and physiological matters) for Special Forces in South-East Asia, 1944-45; Nutritional Adviser to British Military Administration, Malaya, 1945-46; Reader in Histology, University of London, at the London Hospital Medical Coll., 1947-57; Prof. and Chm. of Anatomy, Emory Univ., Atlanta, Ga, USA, 1957-63; Dir, Yerkes Regional Primate Research Center of Emory Univ., 1962-. Member: Soc. Experimental Biology; Nutrition Soc. (foundation Mem.); Anatomical Soc. of Gt Brit. and N Ireland, Internat. Soc. for Cell Biology; Aerospace Med. Soc., etc. *Publications:* Nutrition and the War, 1940; Wartime Food for Mother and Child, 1942; Cytology and Cell Physiology (ed and part author), 1942, 2nd edn 1951; Starvation in Europe, 1943; How Your Body Works, 1949; The Mammalion Adrenal Gland, 1949; Aids to Histology, 1950; (ed jtly) International Review of Cytology, 1952; (ed jtly) Biochemistry and Physiology of

Nutrition, Vols 1, 2; Introduction to Functional Histology; Biochemistry and Physiology of Bone; (ed jtly) The Biology of Ageing; Structure and function of Muscle; The Division of Labour in Cells; (ed jtly) Muscular Dystrophy in Man and Animals; World Review of Nutrition and Dietetics, 1962; Atherosclerosis and its origins; Structure and Function of Nervous Tissue, 1969; The Ape People, 1971; Primate Odyssey, 1974; The Gentle Giants, 1975; contributor on Famine to Encyclopædia Britannica; contributions to scientific and medical journals. *Recreations:* water ski-ing, tennis, ballet and running (State Mile Championship and Record Holder, Australia). *Address:* Yerkes Primate Research Center, Emory University, Atlanta, Ga 30322, USA.

BOURNE, Gordon Lionel, FRCS, FRCOG; Consultant, since 1961, and Head of Department, since 1975, Department of Obstetrics and Gynæcology, St Bartholomew's Hospital, London; Consultant Gynæcologist to Royal Masonic Hospital since 1973 and Florence Nightingale BUPA Hospital since 1964; *b* 3 June 1921; *s* of Thomas Holland Bourne and Lily Anne (*née* Clewlow); *m* 1948, Barbara Eileen Anderson; three *s* one *d. Educ:* Queen Elizabeth Grammar Sch., Ashbourne; St Bartholomew's Hosp.; Harvard Univ. MRCS, LRCP 1945, FRCS 1954; MRCOG 1956, FRCOG 1962; FRSocMed. Highlands Hosp., 1948; Derbs Royal Infirm., 1949; City of London Mat. Hosp., 1952; Hosp. for Women, Soho, 1954; Gynæcol Registrar, Middlesex Hosp., 1956; Sen. Registrar, Obsts and Gynae., St Bartholomew's Hosp., 1958; Nuffield Trav. Fellow, 1959; Res. Fellow, Harvard, 1959; Cons. Gynæcol., St Luke's Hosp., 1963. Arris and Gale Lectr, RCS, 1964; Mem. Bd of Professions Suppl. to Medicine, 1964; Regional Assessor in Maternal Deaths, 1974; Examr in Obsts and Gynae., Univs of London, Oxford and Riyadh, Jt Conjt Bd and RCOG, Central Midwives Bd; Mem. Ct of Assts, Haberdashers' Co., 1968, Junior Warden, 1975; Mem. Bd of Governors, Haberdashers' Aske's Schs, Hatcham, 1971. *Publications:* The Human Amnion and Chorion, 1962; Shaw's Textbook of Gynæcology, 9th edn, 1970; Recent Advances in Obstetrics and Gynæcology, 11th edn, 1966, 12th edn, 1977; Modern Gynæcology with Obstetrics for Nurses, 4th edn, 1969 and 5th edn, 1973; Pregnancy, 1972, 2nd edn 1975; numerous articles in sci. and professional jls. *Recreations:* ski-ing, water-ski-ing, shooting, swimming, writing. *Address:* 147 Harley Street, W1N 1DL. *T:* 01-935 4444; Oldways, Bishop's Avenue, N2 0BN. *T:* 01-458 4788. *Club:* Junior Carlton.

BOURNE, James Gerald, MA, MD (Cantab); FFARCS; Consulting Anæsthetist: St Thomas' Hospital, London; Salisbury Hospital Group; *b* 6 March 1906; *y s* of late W. W. Bourne, Garston Manor, Herts and of late Clara (*née* Hollingsworth); *m* 1957, Jenny Liddell (*d* 1967); one *s*; *m* 1968, Susan Clarke; two *s. Educ:* Rugby; Corpus Christi Coll., Cambridge; St Thomas' Hospital. 1st class Geographical Tripos Part I, 1925; 1st class Geographical Tripos Part II, 1926; Exhibition and Prizes; MRCS, LRCP 1937; MB, BChir Cantab 1939; DA England 1945; FFARCS 1953; MD (Cantab), 1960. Major RAMC, 1939-45. *Publications:* Nitrous Oxide in Dentistry: Its Danger and Alternatives, 1960; Studies in Anæsthetics, 1967; contributions to medical literature. *Recreations:* ski-ing, riding, fishing. *Address:* Melstock, Nunton, Salisbury, Wilts. *T:* Salisbury 29734.

BOURNE, (John) Wilfrid, CB 1975; Clerk of the Crown in Chancery, and Permanent Secretary, Lord Chancellor's Office, since 1977; Barrister-at-Law; *b* 27 Jan. 1922; *s* of late Capt Rt Hon. R. C. Bourne, MP, and of Lady Hester Bourne; *m* 1958, Elizabeth Juliet, *d* of late G. R. Fox, of Trewardreva, Constantine, Cornwall; two *s. Educ:* Eton; New Coll., Oxford (MA). Served War, Rifle Brigade, 1941-45. Called to Bar, Middle Temple, 1948, Bencher 1977; practised at Bar, 1949-56; Lord Chancellor's Office, 1956-; Principal Assistant Solicitor, 1970-72, Deputy Sec., 1972-77. *Recreations:* gardening, sailing. *Address:* Povey's Farm, Ramsdell, Basingstoke, Hants. *Clubs:* Army and Navy; Leander (Henley-on-Thames).

BOURNE, Stafford, MA Cantab; President for life since Sept. 1972 of Bourne & Hollingsworth Ltd (Chairman, 1938-72); *b* 20 Feb. 1900; *e s* of late Walter William and Clara Louisa Bourne (*née* Hollingsworth), Garston Manor, Herts; *m* 1940, Magdalene Jane, *d* of Frederick and Anne Leeson; one *s* one *d* (and one *s* decd). *Educ:* Rugby; Corpus Christi, Cambridge; and in France. War of 1939-45, Admiralty Ferry Crews. Entire career with Bourne & Hollingsworth Ltd. Co-Founder and First Pres., Oxford Street Assoc., 1958-68. Is actively interested in interchange of young people between UK and W Europe for business and cultural purposes. *Recreations:* yachting, painting, chess. *Address:* Drokes, Beaulieu, Brockenhurst, Hants SO4 7XE. *T:* Bucklers Hard 252; 58 Gower Street, WC1. *T:* 01-636

6962. *Clubs:* United Oxford & Cambridge University, Royal Cruising; Royal Lymington Yacht.

BOURNE, Wilfrid; *see* Bourne, J. W.

BOURNE-ARTON, Major Anthony Temple, MBE 1944; JP; *b* 1 March 1913; 2nd *s* of W. R. Temple Bourne, Walker Hall, Winston, Co. Durham, and Evelyn Rose, 3rd *d* of Sir Frank Wills, Bristol; assumed surname of Bourne-Arton, 1950; *m* 1938, Margaret Elaine, *er d* of W. Denby Arton, Sleningford Park, Ripon, Yorks; two *s* two *d. Educ:* Clifton. Served Royal Artillery, 1935-48; active service, 1936, Palestine; 1939-45: France, N Africa, Sicily and Italy (despatches, MBE); Malaya, 1947-48. Gen. Commissioner Income Tax; has served on Bedale RDC, and N Riding County Agric. Cttee; County Councillor, N Riding of Yorks, 1949-61; CC, W Riding of Yorks, 1967-70; Chm., Yorkshire Regional Land Drainage Cttee, 1973-. MP (C) Darlington, 1959-64; PPS to the Home Sec., 1962-64. JP N Riding of Yorks, 1950-. *Recreations:* fishing and shooting. *Address:* Tanfield Lodge, Ripon, N Yorks. *T:* Well 333.

BOURNS, Prof. Arthur Newcombe; President and Vice-Chancellor since 1972, Professor of Chemistry since 1953, McMaster University; *b* 8 Dec. 1919; *s* of Evans Clement Bourns and Kathleen Jones; *m* 1943, Marion Harriet Blakney; two *s* two *d. Educ:* schs in Petitcodiac, NB; Acadia Univ. (BSc); McGill Univ. (PhD). Research Chemist, Dominion Rubber Co., 1944-45; Lectr, Acadia Univ., 1945-46; Asst Prof. of Chemistry, Saskatchewan Univ., 1946-47; McMaster Univ.: Asst Prof., 1947-49; Associate Prof., 1949-53; Dean, Faculty of Grad. Studies, 1957-61; Chm., Chemistry Dept, 1965-67; Vice-Pres., Science and Engrg Div., 1967-72; Actg Pres., 1970; Mem. Bd of Governors, 1961 and 1967-; Mem. Senate, 1949- (Vice-Chm. 1969-72; Chm. 1972-). Nuffield Trav. Fellow in Science, University Coll., London, 1955-56. Chm., Gordon Res. Conf. on Chem. and Physics of Isotopes (Vice-Chm. 1959-60; Chm., 1961-62); Nat. Res. Council of Canada: Mem. Grant Selection Cttee in Chem., 1966-69 (Chm. 1968-69); Mem. Council, 1969-75; Mem. Exec. Cttee, 1969-75; Mem. or Chm. various other cttees; Mem. Adv. Bd to Div. of Chem., 1969-75; Mem. Adv. Cttee on Special Projects and on Regional Develt Program, 1971-75. Member: Ancaster Public Sch. Bd, 1963-64; Bd, Royal Botanic Gdns, 1972-; Mem., Scientific Adv. Council of Canadian Bd, Weizman Inst. of Sci., 1974-; Cttee on Univ. Affairs, Prov. Ontario (Chm. Sub-cttee on Grad. Studies and Res., 1964-69; Mem. Capital Studies Cttee, 1967-71); Council of Ontario Univs, 1972- (Exec. Cttee, 1974-; Vice-Chm., Exec. Cttee, 1976-78; Chm., Cttee on Nominations, 1976-78); Bd of Dirs and Exec. Cttee, Assoc. of Univs and Colleges of Canada, 1974-; Mohawk Coll. Bd of Dirs, 1975-; Pres. and Chm. Exec. Cttee, Canadian Bureau for Internat. Educn, 1973-76. Dir, Slater Steel Industries Ltd, 1975-. British Council Lectr, 1963. Assoc. Editor, Canadian Jl Chemistry, 1966-69; Mem. Editorial Bd, Science Forum, 1967-73. FCIC 1954 (Chm. Hamilton Section, 1952-53; Mem. Educn Cttee, 1953-59; Mem. Council, 1966-69; Montreal Medal, 1976); FRSC 1964; FCS 1968; Mem. Sigma Xi 1971. Hon. DSc Acadia, 1968. *Address:* President's Office, McMaster University, Hamilton, Ontario, Canada, L8S 4L8. *T:* 525-9140.

BOURTON, Cyril Leonard, CB 1977; Deputy Secretary (Finance), and Accountant General, Department of Health and Social Security, 1974-76; *b* 28 Dec. 1916; *s* of late Leonard Victor Bourton; *m* 1940, Elizabeth Iris Savage; two *s* one *d. Educ:* St Dunstan's Coll., Catford. Nat. Debt Office, 1933-37; Min. of Health, later DHSS: Dep. Accountant-Gen., 1958; Asst Sec., Exec. Councils Div., 1964; Under-Sec. for Finance and Accountant Gen., 1967. *Recreations:* fishing, canal cruising. *Address:* 58 Manor Way, Beckenham, Kent BR3 3LJ. *T:* 01-658 6121.

BOUSSAC, Marcel; French industrialist; President and Director-General, Société des parfums Christian Dior, since 1970; *b* Châteauroux, Indre, 17 April 1889; *s* of Louis-Alexandre Boussac and Primitive Jeanne (*née* Mette); *m* 1939, Margarita Deceuninck (Fanny Heldy), Chevalier de la Légion d'Honneur (*d* 1973). Since 1917 has been Dir, Managing Dir, Chm., and Dir-Gen. of many companies (dealing in textiles, chemicals, dyes, printing, sizing, etc.). Founder and proprietor, Christian Dior; Chm. and Dir-Gen. of the Comptoir de l'Industrie Cotonnière, 1963-70, Pres., 1970-. Is a leading racehorse owner and his horses have won numerous international trophies. *Address:* (business) 21 rue Poissonnière, 75002 Paris, France; (home) 74 boulevard Maurice-Barrès, 92200 Neuilly-sur-Seine, France.

BOUSTEAD, Col Sir (John Edmund) Hugh, KBE 1965 (OBE 1934); CMG 1954; DSO 1941; MC and Bar; Vladimir with cross swords; St George's Military Medal with one Palm (Ethiopia); FRGS; late Gordon Highlanders; British Political Agent, Abu Dhabi, Nov. 1961-May 1965, retired; Development Secretary to Sultanate of Muscat and Oman, Oct. 1958-Oct. 1961; Resident Adviser, Hadhramaut States and British Agent, East Aden Protectorate, Southern Arabia, Oct. 1949-Oct. 1958; *b* 14 April 1895; *s* of Lawrence Twentyman Boustead and Ethel Margaret Alers-Hankey; unmarried. *Educ:* RNC Osborne and Dartmouth; HMS Cornwall; Oxford Univ. Midshipman and acting Sub Lieut, 1913-15; Royal Navy, German East and German South West Africa and Cape Station; S African Bde, Egypt, Western Desert and France, 1915-19; Capt. S African Brigade attached General Denikin's Army in South Russia, 1919; Worcester Coll., Oxford (while still serving in South African Brigade), 1920; appointed Gordon Highlanders, Malta, Constantinople, Chanak and Eastern Thrace, 1921-24; Sudan Camel Corps, 1924-29; Gen. Staff SDF, Khartoum, 1930; commanded Sudan Camel Corps, 1931; retired from Army 1935 to Sudan Political Service; District Commissioner Western District, Darfur, 1935-40; recalled to service with temp. rank of Lieut-Col 1940, raised and trained Sudan Frontier Bn SDF and commanded it, Jan.-July 1941, in operations in Central Abyssinia against the Italians (despatches, DSO); 2nd in command SDF Bde, Eritrea, 1943, with temp. rank of Col; Commanded 2nd SDF Brigade, April 1945; recalled to Political Service, Aug. 1945; late District Commissioner Sudan Political Service; Hon. rank of Col on ceasing to belong to R of O. Captained British Olympic Team Modern Pentathlon, Antwerp, and winner Army Lightweight Championships, 1920; Mem. of Fourth Everest Expedition, 1933. BBC TV programme, The World About Us, 1972. Awarded Lawrence of Arabia Memorial Medal by Royal Central Asian Society, 1966. *Publication:* The Wind of Morning, 1971. *Recreations:* riding, shooting, mountaineering, and ski-ing. *Clubs:* Athenæum, Naval and Military.

BOUTWOOD, Rear-Adm. Laurence Arthur, CB 1955; OBE 1940; DL; *b* 7 Sept. 1898; *yr s* of W. A. Boutwood, Luton; *m* 1925, Audrey Winifred, *d* of H. Dale Morris, Polperro; one *s* two *d. Educ:* Bedford Sch. Royal Navy, 1916; served European War, 1916-18; Cambridge Univ., 1919-21; HM Ships, in E Indies, Home Fleet, etc., 1921-31; Sec. to Rear-Adm., Aircraft Carriers, 1931-33; Sec. to Third Sea Lord and Controller, 1934-39; HMS Glasgow (despatches), 1939-42; Base Supply Officer, Greenock, 1942-43; Sec. to Fourth Sea Lord, 1943-44; Base Supply Officer, Kilindini, 1944; Fleet Supply Officer, Brit. Pacific Fleet, 1945-46; Asst Dir of Plans, Admty, 1946-48; RN Barracks, Lee-on-Solent, 1948-50; Fleet Supply Officer, Mediterranean Stn, 1950-53; Comd Supply Officer, Portsmouth, 1953-56; retired, 1956. County Comr St John Ambulance Brigade, Cornwall, 1958-71. DL Cornwall, 1965. KStJ 1966. *Address:* Golden Cap, Tideford, Saltash, Cornwall. *T:* Landrake 237.

BOUVERIE; *see* Pleydell-Bouverie, family name of Earl of Radnor.

BOVELL, Hon. Sir (William) Stewart, Kt 1976; JP; Agent-General for Western Australia, in London, 1971-74; *b* 19 Dec. 1906; *s* of A. R. Bovell, Busselton, Western Australia. *Educ:* Busselton, WA. Banking, 1923-40. Served War, RAAF, 1941-45, Flt Lt. MLA: for Sussex, WA, 1947-50; for Vasse, WA, 1950-71. Minister: for Labour, WA, 1961-62; for Lands, Forests and Immigration, WA, 1959-71. Govt Whip, WA, 1950-53; Opposition Whip, WA, 1953-57. Rep., Australian States Gen. Council, at British Commonwealth Parly Assoc., in Nairobi, Kenya and Victoria Falls, S Rhodesia, 1954. Mem. Bd of Governors, Bunbury CofE Cathedral Grammar Sch., 1974. Hon. Lay Canon, St Boniface CofE Cathedral, Bunbury, WA, 1975. JP 1949, WA. Patron, Polocrosse Assoc. of WA. *Recreations:* swimming, tennis, walking. *Address:* 24 West Street, Busselton, WA 6280, Australia.

BOVENIZER, Vernon Gordon Fitzell, CMG 1948; Assistant Under-Secretary of State, Ministry of Defence, 1964-68, retired; *b* 22 July 1908; *s* of Rev. Michael Fitzell Bovenizer and Mary Gordon; *m* 1937, Lillian Cherry (*d* 1970), *d* of John Henry Rowe, Cork; two *s* two *d. Educ:* Liverpool Coll.; Sidney Sussex Coll., Cambridge (Scholar). War Office, 1931-45; Control Commission for Germany, 1945, until return to War Office, 1948; Asst Private Sec. to Secretaries of State for War, 1936, and 1940-42; Resident Clerk, 1934-37; Asst Sec., 1942, civilian liaison with US Armies in the UK; Establishment Officer and Dir of Organisation, CCG, 1945-47; Asst Sec. and Dep. Comptroller of Claims, War Office, 1948-58; Counsellor, UK Delegation to NATO, 1958-60; Asst Under-Sec. of State, War Office, 1960-64. US Medal of Freedom, 1945. *Recreations:* tennis and squash. *Address:* 6 Cambanks, Union Lane, Cambridge; 9 The Square, Annalong, Co. Down. *Club:* Reform.

BOVENSCHEN, Sir Frederick Carl, KCB 1943 (CB 1927); KBE 1938; *s* of late C. and Mrs Bovenschen; *m* Mabel Alice (*d* 1975), *o d* of the late Right Hon. Sir A. H. D. Acland, 13th Bart; one *d. Educ:* King's Sch., Canterbury; Corpus Christi Coll., Oxford (Scholar). 1st Class Classical Mods, 1905; 1st Class Lit. Hum., 1907. Asst Private Sec. to Viscount Haldane, Sec. of State for War, 1908-12; Private Sec. to Sir Charles Harris, KCB, 1912-15; Principal, War Office, 1920; Asst Sec., 1921; lent to Government of India to serve on Army Retrenchment Cttee, 1931; Dir of Army Contracts, 1932; Dir of Finance, 1936; Dep. Under-Sec. of State for War, 1936-42; Joint Permanent Under-Sec. of State for War, and Mem. of the Army Council, 1942-45. Chevalier Légion d'Honneur, 1920. A Governor of Westminster Hospital and Chm. of its Finance Cttee, 1948-60; a Governor of King's Sch., Canterbury; Mem. Kent County Council, 1949-55; Councillor, Hythe Town Council; Baron of the Cinque Ports, 1953. *Address:* Dunkery, Church Road, Hythe, Kent. *T:* Hythe 67854. *Club:* Athenæum.

BOVET, Prof. Daniel; Nobel Prize for Physiology and Medicine, 1957; Professor of Psychobiology, Faculty of Science, University of Rome, Italy, since 1971; Director, Laboratorio di Psicobiologia e Psicofarmacologia di Consiglio Nazionale delle Ricerche, Rome, since 1969; *b* Neuchatel, Switzerland, 23 March 1907; *s* of Pierre Bovet and Amy Babut; *m* Filomena Nitti; three *s*. Institut Pasteur, Paris, 1929-47 (first as an asst and afterwards Chief of the Laboratory of Therapeutic Chemistry); Chief of the Laboratory of Therapeutic Chemistry, Instituto Superiore di Sanità, Rome, 1947-64; Prof. of Pharmacology, Fac. of Medicine, Univ. of Sassari, Italy, 1964-71. Mem. of the Accademia Nazionale dei XL, 1949; Mem. of Accademia naz. dei Lincei, 1958; Foreign Mem., Royal Soc., 1962. Chevalier de la Légion d'Honneur, 1946; Grande Ufficiale Dell' Ordine della Repubblica Italiana, 1959. *Publications:* (in collaboration with F. Bovet-Nitti) Structure chimique et activité pharmacodynamique du système nerveux végétatif, 1948 (Bale, Switzerland); (in collaboration with F. Bovet-Nitti and G. B. Marini-Bettolo) Curare and Curare-like Agents, 1957 (Amsterdam, Holland; (in collaboration with R. Blum and others) Controlling Drugs, 1974 (San Francisco). *Recreation:* wandering in Amazonia. *Address:* 33 Piazza S Apollinare, 00186 Rome, Italy. *T:* 565297; Laboratorio di Psicobiologia e Psicofarmacologia CNR, 1 via Reno, 00198 Rome, Italy.

BOVEY, Dr Leonard; Head of Technological Requirements Branch, Department of Industry, since 1977; *b* 9 May 1924; *s* of late Alfred and Gladys Bovey; *m* 1943, Constance Hudson; one *s* one *d. Educ:* Heles Sch., Exeter; Emmanuel Coll., Cambridge (BA, PhD). FInstP. Dunlop Rubber, 1943-46; Post-doctoral Fellow, Nat. Res. Council, Ottawa, 1950-52; AERE Harwell, 1952-65; Head W Mids Regional Office, Birmingham, Min. of Technology, 1966-70; Regional Dir, Yorks and Humberside, DTI, 1970-73; Counsellor (Scientific and Technological Affairs), High Commn, Ottawa, 1974-77. *Publications:* Spectroscopy in the Metallurgical Industry, 1963; papers on spectroscopy in Jl Optical Soc. Amer., Spectrochimica Acta, Jl Phys. Soc. London. *Recreations:* repairing neglected household equipment, work, reading (particularly crime novels), walking, theatre, music. *Address:* 32 Radnor Walk, Chelsea SW3 4BN. *T:* 01-352 4142. *Club:* Civil Service.

BOWATER, Sir Ian (Frank), GBE 1970; Kt 1967; DSO 1945; TD 1953; one of HM's Lieutenants for the City of London since 1938; *b* 1904; *y s* of late Major Sir Frank Henry Bowater, 1st Bt, TD; *m* 1927, Hon. Ursula Margaret, *d* of late Viscount Dawson of Penn, PC, GCVO, KCB, KCMG, MD; one *s* two *d. Educ:* Eton; Magdalen Coll., Oxford. Territorial Commission Berks & Bucks Yeo., 1926-27; rejoined TA, 1938. Served War of 1939-45; Staff Capt. 1st AA Div., London, 1940; E Africa, Madagascar, 1942; CRA Islands area, 1942; CMF Sicily and Italy; Comd 53rd LAA (KOYLI) Regt, 1943-45. Comd 490 (M) HAA Regt (TA), 1947-48; Hon. Col 553 LAA Regt (KOYLI), 1953. Joined family Business, W. V. Bowater & Sons, 1926; later Dir Bowater Sales Co. and subseq. of Bowater Paper Corp. until resignation, 1953; Director, Spicers Ltd, 1953-58; Chm., Bowater Hotels 1937-; Dir, GKN Birfield Industries, 1968, retired 1969. Dep. Chm., Country Gentlemen's Assoc., 1957; First Pres., City and Metropolitan Bldg Soc., 1965-72 (Dir 1963-65). Junior Warden, Haberdashers' Company, 1955 and 1961; Master, 1967; Alderman, Coleman Street Ward, 1960-74; Sheriff, City of London, 1965-66; Lord Mayor of London, 1969-70. Chancellor, The City Univ., 1969-70. Hon. DSc The City Univ., 1970. KStJ 1970. *Recreations:* painting, travel, art. *Address:* Hasker House, Woolley Firs, Maidenhead Thicket, Berks. *T:* Littlewick Green 3282; Bowater Hotels Ltd, c/o The Compleat Angler Hotel, Marlow Bridge, Marlow, Bucks SL7 1RG. *T:* Marlow 4444. *Clubs:* White's, City Livery, Coleman Street Ward, United Wards.

BOWATER, Sir J(ohn) Vansittart, 4th Bt *cr* 1914; *b* 6 April 1918; *s* of Captain Victor Spencer Bowater (*d* 1967) (3rd *s* of 1st Bt) and Hilda Mary (*d* 1918), *d* of W. Henry Potter; *S* uncle, Sir Thomas Dudley Blennerhassett Bowater, 3rd Bt, 1972; *m* 1943, Joan Kathleen, *d* of late Wilfrid Scullard; one *s* one *d. Educ:* Branksome School, Godalming, Surrey. Served Royal Artillery, 1939-46. *Heir: s* Michael Patrick Bowater [*b* 18 July 1949; *m* 1968, Alison, *d* of Edward Wall; three *d*]. *Address:* 214 Runnymede Avenue, Bournemouth, Dorset BH11 9SP. *T:* Northbourne 71782.

BOWATER, Sir Noël Vansittart, 2nd Bt, *cr* 1939; GBE 1954; MC 1917; *b* 25 Dec. 1892; *s* of Sir Frank H. Bowater, 1st Bt and Ethel Anita (*d* 1943), *d* of late Mark Fryar, Burmah; *S* father 1947; *m* 1921, Constance Heiton Bett; one *s* two *d. Educ:* Rugby. Commnd Territorial Force RA, 1913; served in France, 1915-19 (MC). Sheriff of City of London, 1948, Lord Mayor, 1953-54; Master, Company of Vintners, 1954-55. KStJ; Kt Comdr Royal Order of the North Star; Kt Comdr Order of Menelik the Second. *Heir: s* Euan David Vansittart Bowater, BA Cantab [*b* 9 Sept. 1935; *m* 1964, Susan Mary Humphrey, *d* of A. R. O. Slater, FCA, and Mrs N. M. Slater; two *s* two *d*]. *Address:* Conifers, St George's Hill, Weybridge, Surrey. *T:* Weybridge 42744; Riscombe, Exford, Somerset. *T:* Exford 280. *Clubs:* City Livery, United Wards, Guildhall.

BOWDELL, Wilfred, CBE 1973; Management Consultant since 1974; *b* 28 Nov. 1913; *s* of Harry Bowdell and Sarah Alice Bowdell (*née* Roscoe); *m* 1939, Alice Lord. *Educ:* Bury High Sch.; Univ. of London (BScEcon); Inst. of Public Finance and Accountancy (Pres., 1972-73). Finance Asst, Bury County Borough Council, 1930-36; Chief Accountancy Asst, Swinton and Pendlebury Borough Council, 1936-39; Chief Accountant, York City Council, 1939-46; Dep. Treas., Enfield Urban District Council, 1946-48; Dep. Treas. 1948-62, Borough Treas. 1962-65, St Marylebone Borough Council; City Treas., Westminster City Council, 1965-74. Mem., Public Works Loan Bd, 1975-. *Recreations:* music, photography, gardening. *Address:* 72 Highfield Way, Rickmansworth, Herts. *T:* Rickmansworth 73459.

BOWDEN, family name of **Baron Aylestone** and **Baron Bowden.**

BOWDEN, Baron, *cr* 1963, of Chesterfield (Life Peer); **Bertram Vivian Bowden,** MA, PhD, FIEE, FIEEE, MScTech; Principal, The University of Manchester Institute of Science and Technology (called Manchester College of Science and Technology until May 1966), 1964-76; *b* 18 Jan. 1910; *s* of B. C. Bowden, Chesterfield; *m* 1939, Marjorie Browne (marr. diss., 1954; she *d* 1957); one *s* two *d*; *m* 1967, Mary Maltby (*d* 1971); *m* 1974, Mrs Phyllis James (*see* Lady Bowden). *Educ:* Chesterfield Grammar Sch.; Emmanuel Coll., Cambridge. Worked with late Lord Rutherford, 1931-34; PhD 1934; University of Amsterdam, 1934-35. Physics Master, Liverpool Collegiate Sch., 1935-37; Chief Physics Master, Oundle Sch., 1937-40; Radar Research in England, 1940-43; Radar Research in USA, 1943-46; Sir Robert Watson Watt and Partners, 1947-50; Ferranti Ltd, Manchester (Digital Computers), 1950-53; Dean of the Faculty of Technology, Manchester Univ., and Principal, Manchester Coll. of Science and Technology, 1953-64. Chm. Electronics Research Council of Ministry of Aviation, 1960-64; Minister of State, Dept of Education and Science, 1964-65 (on leave of absence as Principal of Manchester Coll. of Science and Technology). Pres. The Science Masters Assoc., 1962. Pres., Nat. Television Rental Assoc., 1975-. Hon. FICE 1975; Hon. DS Rensellaer Polytechnic, USA, 1974; Hon. LLD Manchester, 1976. Pioneer Award, IEEE Aerospace & Electronic Systems Gp, 1973. *Publications:* Faster Than Thought, 1953; The Development of Manchester College of Science and Technology; numerous papers on education. *Recreation:* listening to music. *Address:* Pine Croft, Stanhope Road, Bowdon, Altrincham, Cheshire WA14 3LB. *T:* 061-928 4005. *Club:* Athenæum.

BOWDEN, Lady; Phyllis Bertha Mabel Bowden; Member: Monopolies and Mergers Commission, since 1975; Local Government Boundary Commission for England, since 1977; *b* 10 June 1918; *d* of Stanley Ernest and Bertha Myson; *m* 1st, 1941, John Henry Lewis James (*d* 1962); one *d*; 2nd, 1974, Baron Bowden, *qv. Educ:* Wimbledon High Sch; Newnham Coll, Cambridge (MA). BoT, 1941; Principal 1947; Asst Sec., 1960; DEA, 1964-69; Min. of Technology, 1969-70; Dept of Trade and Industry, 1970-; Asst Under-Sec. of State 1972; Regional Dir, NW Region, DTI, subseq. DoI, 1972-75. Commonwealth (now Harkness) Fellow, 1957-58. Mem. Court, Manchester Univ., 1976-. *Publications:* The Concept of Growth Centres, 1968; Gardens through the Ages, 1971; contrib. Public Administration, Encycl. Britannica. *Recreations:* landscape architecture, collecting art nouveau. *Address:* Pinecroft, Stanhope Road, Bowdon, Altrincham, Cheshire. *Club:* United Oxford & Cambridge University.

BOWDEN, Andrew, MBE 1961; MP (C) Kemp Town Division of Brighton since 1970; *b* 8 April 1930; *s* of William Victor Bowden, Solicitor, and Francesca Wilson; *m* 1970, Benita Napier; one *s* one *d. Educ:* Ardingly College. Paint industry, 1955-68; Man. Dir, Personnel Assessments Ltd, 1969-71; Man. Dir, Haymarket Personnel Selection Ltd, 1970-71; Director: Sales Education & Leadership Ltd, 1970-71; Jenkin and Purser (Holdings) Ltd, 1973-. Jt Chm., All Party Old Age Pensioners Parly Gp, 1972-; Chm., All Party BLESMA Gp; Mem. Select Cttee on Expenditure, 1973-74, on Abortion, 1975. Contested (C): North Hammersmith, 1955; North Kensington, 1964; Kemp Town, Brighton, 1966. Nat. Chm., Young Conservatives, 1960-61; Mem., Wandsworth Borough Council, 1956-62. *Recreations:* fishing, chess, golf. *Address:* House of Commons, SW1. *Club:* Junior Carlton.

BOWDEN, Major Aubrey Henry, DSO 1918; Chairman, Bowden Bros Ltd; *e s* of Henry White Bowden, MICE, Great Missenden; *m* 1st, 1918, Helen (*d* 1939), *o d* of late R. G. Modera, Wilbury Lodge, Hove; one *s* one *d* ; 2nd, 1941, Andrée Marguerite July; one *s* two *d. Educ:* Oundle. Electrical Engineer. Training: Brompton and Kensington Electricity Supply Co.; London Underground Railway; Metropolitan Railway; Oerlikon Co.; from here commissioned: to 11th Service Batt. Royal Warwicks Regt, to Capt. and Brigade Machine Gun Officer, to Machine Gun Corps. *Address:* 28 Berkeley Court, Baker Street, NW1.

BOWDEN, Sir Frank Houston, 3rd Bt *cr* 1915; MA Oxon; industrialist and landowner; *b* 10 Aug. 1909; *o s* of Sir Harold Bowden, 2nd Bt, GBE, and of Vera, *d* of Joseph Whitaker, JP, FZS; *S* father 1960; *m* 1st, 1935; one *s* ; 2nd, 1937, Lydia Eveline, *d* of Jean Manolovici, Bucharest; three *s. Educ:* Rugby; Merton Coll., Oxford. Served with RNVR, 1939-44. President: University Hall, Buckland, 1967-71; British Kendo Association, 1969. Hon. Vice-Pres., 3rd World Kendo Championships, 1976. *Recreation:* collecting weapons and armour, particularly Japanese (Vice-Chm. Japan Soc. of London, 1970-75; Member: Soc. for Preservation of Art Swords of Japan, Tokyo; Japanese Sword Soc. of US; To-Ken Soc. of GB). *Heir: s* Nicholas Richard Bowden, *b* 13 Aug. 1935. *Address:* Thame Park, Oxon. *Clubs:* White's, Bath, Royal Thames Yacht.

BOWDEN, Prof. Kenneth Frank, DSc, FInstP; Professor of Oceanography in the University of Liverpool since 1954; *b* 23 Dec. 1916; *s* of Frank and Margaret N. Bowden; *m* 1946, Lilias T. M. Nicol; one *d. Educ:* Itchen Secondary Sch.; University Coll., Southampton. Scientific Officer, Anti-Submarine Experimental Establishment (Admiralty), 1939-45; Lecturer in Oceanography, University of Liverpool, 1945-52; Principal Scientific Officer, Nat. Inst. of Oceanography, 1952-54; Dean, Faculty of Science, 1959-62, Pro-Vice-Chancellor, 1968-71, Univ. of Liverpool. *Publications:* papers on physical oceanography in various scientific journals. *Address:* 100 Meols Parade, Hoylake, Wirral, Merseyside. *T:* 051-632 4083.

BOWDEN, Logan S.; *see* Scott Bowden.

BOWDEN, Dr Richard Charles, OBE 1941; PhD, MSc, FRIC, FCS; Consultant, Ministry of Aviation (formerly Ministry of Supply), 1952-60; *b* 31 Aug. 1887; *s* of Richard Charles Bowden, Bristol, and Minnie Clara Thatcher; *m* 1913, Nina Adeline, *er d* of Thomas Fisher, Bristol; no *c. Educ:* Merchant Venturers Sch., Bristol; Merchant Venturers Technical Coll., Bristol; Bristol Univ. (Hons, Physical Chemistry). Asst Chemist, Research Dept, Royal Arsenal, Woolwich, 1911; Chemist, Royal Gunpowder Factory, 1912; Chemist 2nd Class, 1915; Chemist in Charge, 1923; Technical Asst (temp.) under Dir of Ordnance Factories, War Office, 1930; Technical Asst, 1932; Chemical Engineer, 1934; Superintendent, Royal Ordnance Factories, 1934-41; Asst Dir of Ordnance Factories (X); Dep Dir of Ordnance Factories (X), 1941; Dir, of Ordnance Factories (X), 1942-52. Patentee or Joint Patentee of various patents relating to chemical processes and chemical plant. Medals: Silver Jubilee, 1935; Coronation, 1937 and 1953. *Publications:* Author or Joint Author of publications in Journal of Chemical Society, 1911, 1912, 1923. *Address:* The Mount, 77 Cheam Road, Sutton, Surrey. *T:* 01-642 7834.

BOWDEN, Prof. Ruth Elizabeth Mary, DSc London, MB, BS, FRCS; Professor of Anatomy, Royal Free Hospital School of Medicine, University of London, since 1951; *b* 21 Feb. 1915; *o c* of late Frank Harold and Louise Ellen Bowden. *Educ:* Westlands Sch.; St Paul's Girls' Sch.; London (Royal Free

Hospital) Sch. of Medicine for Women, University of London. House Surg. and later House Physician, Elizabeth Garrett Anderson Hosp. (Oster House branch), 1940-42; House Surg., Royal Cancer Hosp., 1942; Grad. Asst in Nuffield Dept of Orthopædic Surgery, Peripheral Nerve Injury Unit, Oxford, 1942-45; Asst Lecturer in Anatomy, Royal Free Hospital Sch. of Medicine, 1945; later Lecturer, then University Reader in Human Anatomy, 1949; Rockefeller Travelling Fellowship, 1949-50; Hunterian Prof., RCS, 1950. Pres., Anat. Soc. of Gt Brit. and Ireland, 1970; FRSM; Fellow: Brit. Orthopædic Assoc.; Linnaean Soc. Vice-President: Council of Chartered Soc. of Physiotherapy (Chm., 1960-70); Inst. of Science Technology (Pres., 1960-65); Riding for the Disabled Assoc. CLJ 1962. *Publications:* contribs to Peripheral Nerve Injuries Report of Medical Research Council; Peripheral Nerve Injuries; contribs to medical and scientific jls. *Recreations:* reading, music, painting, walking, gardening, carpentry. *Address:* 6 Hartham Close, Hartham Road, N7. *T:* 01-607 3464.

BOWEN, Edmund John, FRS 1935; MA, DSc Oxon; Hon. Fellow of University College, Oxford; lately Aldrichian Praelector in Chemistry; *b* 29 April 1898; *s* of Edmund Riley Bowen and Lilias Kamester; *m* 1924, Edith Moule; one *s* one *d. Educ:* Royal Grammar Sch., Worcester; Balliol Coll., Oxford (Brackenbury Scholar). BA, 1920; MA, 1922; Fellow of University Coll., Oxford, 1922; Junior Proctor, 1935-36; Lieut 13th Siege Battery, RGA (France), 1917-18. Davy Medal, Royal Society, 1963; Niels Finsen Medal, 1968. *Publications:* The Chemical Aspects of Light, 1942; papers on physical chemical subjects in scientific journals. *Address:* 10 Park Town, Oxford. *T:* Oxford 57631.

BOWEN, Edward George, CBE 1962; FRS 1975; FAA; Counsellor (Scientific) at the Australian Embassy in Washington, DC, USA, 1973-76; *b* 14 Jan. 1911; *s* of G. Bowen, Swansea. *Educ:* Univ. of Wales (MSc); London Univ. (PhD); DSc Sydney. Mem., Radar Develt Team, 1935; Air Ministry Research Station, Bawdsey, 1936-40; British Air Commn Washington, 1940-42; Radiation Lab., MIT, 1943; Chief, Div. of Radiophysics, CSIRO, 1946-71. Chairman: Anglo-Australian Telescope Board, 1967-73. Vice-Pres., Aust. Acad. of Science, 1962-63. *Address:* 5010 Maxwell Avenue, West River, Md 20881, USA. *T:* (301) 261 5715. *Clubs:* Athenæum; Cosmos (Washington).

BOWEN, (Evan) Roderic, QC 1952; MA, LLB; Master Emeritus of the Middle Temple; National Insurance Commissioner, since 1967; *b* 6 Aug. 1913; 2nd *s* of late Evan Bowen, JP, and late Margaret Ellen Twiss, The Elms, Cardigan. *Educ:* Cardigan Schs; University Coll., Aberystwyth; St John's Coll., Cambridge. Practised at the bar with chambers in Cardiff until 1940; served in HM Forces, 1940-45, in the ranks and subsequently as an officer on staff of Judge Advocate-Gen. MP (L), County of Cardigan, 1945-66; Dep. Chm. of Ways and Means, House of Commons, 1965-66. Recorder of: Carmarthen, 1950; Merthyr Tydfil, 1953-60; Swansea, 1960-64; Cardiff, 1964-67; Chm., Montgomeryshire QS, 1959-71. Chm. Welsh Parliamentary Party, 1955. Pres., St David's UC, Lampeter, 1977-. Hon. LLD Wales, 1972. *Address:* Portcullis House, 21 Cowbridge Road East, Cardiff. *T:* Cardiff 388531; Pencartws, Aberporth, Cardigan. *T:* Aberporth 810273. *Clubs:* National Liberal; County (Cardiff).

BOWEN, Sir Geoffrey Fraser, Kt 1977; Managing Director, Commercial Banking Company of Sydney Ltd, Australia, since 1973 (General Manager, 1970-73); *m* Ruth, *d* of H. E. Horsburgh; two *s* one *d* . Director: Australian Resources Develt Bank Ltd; Aust. Bankers Export Re-finance Corp. Ltd; Commercial and General Acceptance Ltd. *Address:* 25 Chilton Parade, Warrawee, NSW 2074, Australia. *Clubs:* Athenæum (Melbourne); Union, Imperial Service (Sydney); Warrawee Bowling.

BOWEN, Gordon, CB 1962; CMG 1956; Director, Metrication Board, 1969-74; *b* 17 June 1910; *e s* of late Arthur Thomas Bowen and late Dora Drinkwater; *m* 1938, Elsa Catriona, *y d* of late Rev. Dr Alexander Grieve, MA, PhD; one *s* (and one *s* decd). *Educ:* Birkenhead Institute Sch.; University of Liverpool. Asst Lecturer in Geography, University of Glasgow, 1933-36; Commonwealth Fund Fellow, University of Calif., 1936-38; Lecturer in Geography, University of Glasgow, 1938-41; Principal, Board of Trade, 1941-44; Asst Sec., Board of Trade, 1944-53; United Kingdom Senior Trade Commissioner in Canada, 1953-58; Under Secretary: Board of Trade, 1958-66; Min. of Technology, 1966-69. *Address:* 17 Somerset Lodge, Briar Walk, SW15. *T:* 01-788 5311.

BOWEN, Ian; see Bowen, Ivor I.

BOWEN, Ivor, CMG 1954; MSc, FRAeS, MIEE; Consultant in Aeronautical Engineering; b 21 Feb. 1902; o s of James and Barbara Bowen, Oxton, Ches; m 1941, Hilda, o d of Arthur and Florence Mary Fakes, Cambridge; one s one d. Educ: Birkenhead Institute; University of Liverpool; Trinity Coll., Cambridge. Oliver Lodge Fellow, University of Liverpool, 1923-24; Research Asst to Sir J. J. Thomson, OM, FRS, 1924-26; Demonstrator in Physics, Cavendish Laboratory, Cambridge, 1925-26; Founder Mem. of Cambridge Univ. Air Squadron, 1925. Lecturer in Air Navigation and Aircraft Instruments, Imperial Coll. of Science, 1938-40; Hon. Sec. Instn of Professional Civil Servants, 1938-40; Dep. Dir of Armament Research, Min. of Aircraft Production, 1940; Dir of Instrument Research and Development, Min. of Supply, 1941-47; Chm. Air Photography Research Cttee, 1945-47; Mem. of Council, British Scientific Instrument Research Assoc., 1945-47; Chief Superintendent, Aeroplane and Armament Experimental Establishment, Boscombe Down, 1947-50; Scientific Adviser to UK High Comr to Australia, and Head of UK Min. of Supply Staff, Australia, 1951-53; Principal Dir of Aircraft Equipment Research and Development, Ministry of Supply, 1953-54; Chm. Air Navigation Cttee of Aeronautical Research Council, 1958-61; Mem. Council, Air League of the British Empire; Mem. Air Traffic Control and Navigation Cttee of Electronics Research Council, 1961-68. Mem., Ct of Common Council, City of London, Ward of Broad Street, 1970-; Liveryman of Worshipful Company of Carpenters, 1959 (Freeman 1954), and of Worshipful Company of Scientific Instrument Makers. Freeman of City of London, 1955. Publications: numerous scientific papers on Physics and Aeronautics. Recreations: archæology, arboriculture, shooting. Address: Stancote, Kippington Road, Sevenoaks, Kent. T: Sevenoaks 52495. Clubs: Athenæum, Savage, City Livery, Royal Air Force.

BOWEN, Prof. (Ivor) Ian, MA Oxon; Editor, Finance and Development (IMF and World Bank Group), 1974-77; b Cardiff, 3 Dec. 1908; s of Ivor Bowen, KC, later County Court Judge, and Edith May (née Dummett); m 1st, 1935, Erica Baillie (marr. diss., 1950); one s one d; 2nd, 1951, Isobel Margaret Lindsay Smith; one s one d. Educ: Westminster Sch.; Christ Church, Oxford. Fellow, All Souls Coll., 1930-37, and 1968; Lecturer, Brasenose Coll., 1931-40; Chief Statistical Officer, Ministry of Works, 1940-45; Lectr, Hertford Coll., 1946-47; Prof. of Economics and Commerce, Hull Univ., 1947-58; Prof. of Economics, Univ. of WA, 1958-73. Publications: Cobden (Great Lives Series), 1934; Britain's Industrial Survival, 1947; Population (Cambridge Economic Handbooks), 1954; Acceptable Inequalities, 1970; Economics and Demography, 1976. Recreation: golf. Address: Xalet Verena, Els Plans, La Massana, Andorra. Club: Reform.

BOWEN, John Griffith; Playwright and Novelist; b 5 Nov. 1924; s of Hugh Griffith Bowen and Ethel May Cook; unmarried. Educ: Queen Elizabeth's Grammar Sch., Crediton; Pembroke Coll., Oxford; St Antony's Coll., Oxford. Frere Exhibition for Indian Studies, Oxford, 1951-52 and 1952-53. Asst Editor, The Sketch, 1954-57; Advertising Copywriter and Copy Chief, 1957-60; Consultant on TV Drama, Associated TV, 1960-67. Publications: The Truth Will Not Help Us, 1956; After the Rain, 1958; The Centre of the Green, 1959; Storyboard, 1960; The Birdcage, 1962; A World Elsewhere, 1965; The Essay Prize, 1965; plays: I Love You, Mrs Patterson, 1964; After the Rain, 1967; Fall and Redemption, 1967; Little Boxes, 1968; The Disorderly Women, 1968; The Corsican Brothers, 1970; The Waiting Room, 1970; Robin Redbreast, 1972; Heil Caesar, 1973; Florence Nightingale, 1975; Which Way Are You Facing?, 1976; Singles, 1977; criticism for London Magazine, Sunday Times and New York Times. Recreations: science fiction, cooking. Address: Old Lodge Farm, Sugarswell Lane, Edgehill, Banbury, Oxon. T: Tysoe 401. Club: PEN.

BOWEN, Very Rev. Lawrence; Dean of St Davids Cathedral since 1972; b 9 Sept. 1914; s of William and Elizabeth Ann Bowen; m 1941, Hilary Myrtle Bowen; two d. Educ: Llanelli Gram. Sch.; Univ. Coll. of Wales, Aberystwyth (BA 1st Cl.); St Michael's Coll., Llandaff (Crossley Exhibnr and Sen. Student). Ordained in St Davids Cathedral, 1938; Curate of Pembrey, 1938-40; Minor Canon, St Davids Cathedral, 1940-46; Vicar of St Clears with Llanginning, 1946-64; Rector of Tenby, 1964-72; Rector of Rectorial Benefice of Tenby with Gumfreston and Penally, 1970-72; Canon of St Davids Cathedral (Mathry), 1972. Surrogate. Recreations: golf, cricket, writing Welsh poetry. Address: The Deanery, St Davids, Dyfed. T: St Davids 202.

BOWEN, Most Rev. Michael George; see Southwark, Archbishop and Metropolitan of, (RC).

BOWEN, Hon. Sir Nigel (Hubert), KBE 1976; Chief Judge, Federal Court of Australia, since 1976; Judge of Court of Appeal of New South Wales, since 1973; b Summerland, BC, Canada, 26 May 1911; s of late O. P. Bowen, Ludlow, England; m 1947, Eileen C., d of F. J. Mullens; three d. Educ: King's Sch., Sydney; St Paul's Coll., Sydney Univ. (BA, LLB). Admitted NSW Bar 1936, Victorian Bar 1954; QC (Austr.) 1953; Vice-Pres., Law Council of Australia, 1957-60; Pres., NSW Bar Council, 1959-61. Lectr in Company Law and Taxation, Sydney Univ., 1957-58; Editor, Australian Law Jl, 1946-58. MHR (L) Australia for Parramatta, NSW, 1964-73; Attorney-General, Australia, 1966-69 and March-Aug. 1971; Minister for Educn and Science, 1969-71; Minister for Foreign Affairs, Aug. 1971-Dec. 1972. Chief Judge in Equity, 1974-76. Head of Austr. Delegn and Vice-Pres. of UN Internat. Conf. on Human Rights, 1968; Leader of Austr. Delegn: to Unesco Inter-Govtl Conf. of Ministers on Cultural Policies, 1970; to UN, 1971 and 1972. Recreations: swimming, music. Address: 43 Grosvenor Road, Wahroonga, NSW 2076, Australia. Club: Union (Sydney).

BOWEN, Roderic; see Bowen, (Evan) Roderic.

BOWEN, Stanley, CBE 1972; Hon. Sheriff, Lothian and Borders, since 1975; b Carnoustie, Angus, 4 Aug. 1910; s of late Edward Bowen and Ellen Esther Bowen, (née Powles), Birmingham; m 1943, Mary Shepherd Greig, d of late Alexander Greig and Mary Shand Greig (née Shepherd), Carnoustie; two s one d. Educ: Barry Sch., Angus; Grove Academy, Dundee; University Coll., Dundee. Enrolled Solicitor, in Scotland, 1932; entered Procurator Fiscal Service, in Scotland, 1933; Procurator Fiscal Depute at Hamilton, Lanarkshire, 1937; Interim Procurator Fiscal at Airdrie, Lanarkshire, 1938; Crown Office, Edinburgh: Legal Asst, 1941; Principal Asst, 1945; Crown Agent for Scotland, 1967-74. Chm., Sec. of State for Scotland's working party on forensic pathology services, 1975; Member: Sec. of State for the Environment's working party on drinking and driving offences, 1975; Sub-Cttee for legislation on transplantation of human tissues, Council of Europe, 1975-76; Police Adv. Bd for Scotland, and sub-cttee on police discipline, 1976; Sec. of State for Scotland's working group on identification evidence in criminal cases, 1977. Recreations: golf, gardening. Address: Achray, 20 Dovecot Road, Corstorphine, Edinburgh EH12 7LE. T: 031-334 4096. Clubs: New, Press (Edinburgh); Carnoustie Golf.

BOWEN, Thomas Edward Ifor L.; see Lewis-Bowen.

BOWEN, Sir Thomas Frederic Charles, 4th Bt cr 1921; b 11 Oct. 1921; s of 2nd Bt and May Isobel (d 1972), d of John Frederick Roberts; S brother, 1939; m 1947, Jill, d of Lloyd Evans, Gold Coast; one s two d. Heir: s Mark Edward Mortimer Bowen, b 17 Oct. 1958. Address: Beechcroft, St George's Avenue, Weybridge, Surrey.

BOWEN, Prof. William G(ordon), PhD; President, Princeton University, since 1972; Professor of Economics, Princeton University, since 1958; b 6 Oct. 1933; s of Albert A. and Bernice C. Bowen; m 1956, Mary Ellen Maxwell; one s one d. Educ: Denison Univ. (AB); Princeton Univ. (PhD). Princeton Univ.: Asst Prof. of Economics, Associate Prof. of Economics; Provost, 1967-72. Hon. LLD: Denison, Rutgers, Pennsylvania and Yale, 1972; Harvard, 1973; Jewish Theol Seminary, 1974; Seton Hall Univ., 1975. Publications: Economic Aspects of Education, 1964; (with W. J. Baumol) Performing Arts: the Economic Dilemma, 1966; (with T. A. Finegan) Economics of Labor Force Participation, 1969, etc; contribs to Amer. Econ. Review, Economica, Quarterly Jl of Economics, etc. Address: 1 Nassau Hall, Princeton University, Princeton, NJ, USA. T: 609-452-6100. Club: Century (NY).

BOWER; see Dykes Bower.

BOWER, Sir Frank, Kt 1960; CBE 1948; b 25 Aug. 1894; s of Herbert Austin Bower; m 1920, Ethel Shaw (d 1970); one s two d. Educ: Lancaster Royal Grammar Sch.; St Catharine's Coll., Cambridge. Served European War of 1914-18; 2/5th King's Own Royal Lancaster Regt, 2/5 Prince Albert Victoria Rajputs, IARO. BA (Classics), 1920; MA 1924. HM Inspector of Taxes, 1920-24; Taxation Officer, Unilever Group, 1924-59. Late Chairman of Tax Cttees of Business Groups; late Director of industrial companies. Past President, Association of British Chambers of Commerce. Publication: United Kingdom Volume, World Tax Series, Harvard Law School; contribs to professional journals on tax subjects. Recreation: gardening. Address: 31 Traps Hill, Loughton, Essex. T: 01-508 3030.

BOWER, Air Marshal Sir Leslie William Clement, KCB 1962 (CB 1954); DSO 1945; DFC 1944; b 11 July 1909; s of William

Clarke Bower, Co. Cork, Eire; *m* 1963, Clare (*d* 1971), widow of Commander Jasper Abbott, RN, Uppaton, Yelverton, S Devon, and *d* of H. W. Etkins, OBE, Curlews, Constantine Bay, N Cornwall. *Educ:* Harvey Grammar Sch., Folkestone; Cranwell. Royal Air Force 1929; served War of 1939-45 (despatches twice, DFC, DSO), in Europe and Canada; OC 217 (TB) Sqdn, 1941-42; Dir Op. Trg, HQ, RCAF, Ottawa, 1942-43; Group Capt., 1942; Air Cdre, 1952; Air Vice-Marshal, 1954; OC 138 Wing 2nd TAF, 1943-45; AOC 81 (Fighter) Group, 1952-54; Senior Air Staff Officer, HQ Fighter Command, 1954-57; Senior Air Staff Officer, MEAF, 1957-58; Dep. Commander-in-Chief, Middle East Air Force, 1958-59; Air Officer Commanding No 19 Group, RAF Coastal Command, 1959-61; UK Representative in Ankara on Permanent Military Deputies Group of Central Treaty Organisation (Cento), 1962-65; retired. Air Marshal, 1962. *Address:* c/o Lloyds Bank Ltd, Cox's & King's Branch, 6 Pall Mall, SW1. *Club:* Royal Air Force.

BOWER, Michael Douglas; Journalist, The Star, Sheffield, since 1968; *b* 25 Aug. 1942; *s* of Stanley Arthur Bower and Rachael Farmer; *m* 1966, Susan Millington; two *d* . *Educ:* Colwyn Bay Grammar Sch.; Royal Coll. of Advanced Technol., Salford. Civil engr, 1961-64; journalist, 1965-. Mem., Press Council, 1976-. *Recreations:* walking, golf. *Address:* 8 St Quentin Drive, Bradway, Sheffield S17 4PP. *T:* Sheffield 362737. *Club:* Carlton Working Men's (Gleadless, Sheffield).

BOWER, Norman; *b* 18 May 1907. *Educ:* Rugby; Wadham Coll., Oxford. Called to Bar, Inner Temple, 1935; contested West Bermondsey, 1931, North Hammersmith, 1935; MP (C) Harrow West, 1941-51; Member Westminster City Council, 1937-45. *Recreations:* golf, cricket, theatre. *Club:* Carlton.

BOWER, Lt.-Gen. Sir Roger (Herbert), KCB 1959 (CB 1950); KBE 1957 (CBE 1944); *b* 13 Feb. 1903; *s* of Herbert Morris Bower and Eileen Francis Fitzgerald Bower, Ripon; *m* 1939, Hon. Catherine Muriel Hotham, *d* of late Capt. H. E. Hotham, and *y sister* of 7th Baron Hotham, CBE; (one adopted *s*) one *d* (and one *s* decd). *Educ:* Repton; RMC, Sandhurst. Served in India with KOYLI, 1923-30; Staff Coll., Camberley, 1935-36; Bde Major, Hong Kong, 1937-38. Served War of 1939-45; NW Europe with HQ Airborne Corps, 1944; Norway, 1945; Comd 1 and 6 Air Landing Bdes; Palestine, 1945-46 (despatches); Comd Hamburg District, 1948-49, with rank of Maj.-Gen.; Director Land/Air Warfare, War Office, 1950-51; Director of Military Training and Director of Land/Air Warfare, 1951-52; Commander East Anglian District, 1952-55; Chief of Staff, Allied Forces, Northern Europe, 1955-56; GOC and Director of Operations, Malaya, 1956-57; Commander-in-Chief, Middle East Land Forces, 1958-60, retired. Col The KOYLI, 1960-66. Treasurer to HRH Princess Margaret, Nov. 1960-Feb. 1962; Lieut HM Tower of London, 1960-63. US Bronze Star, 1944; King Haakon VII Liberty Cross, 1945. *Recreations:* sailing, shooting, fishing. *Address:* Ash House, St Mary Bourne, Andover, Hants. *T:* St Mary Bourne 263. *Clubs:* Army and Navy, Royal Cruising.

BOWERMAN, David Alexander; Director: Jamaica Producers Marketing Co. Ltd; JP Fruit Distributors Ltd; Horticultural Exports (GB) Ltd; Director and Chairman: Linden Hall Hotel, Bournemouth; Kandic Ltd, Bournemouth; *b* 19 April 1903; *s* of Frederick and Millicent Bowerman; *m* 1925, Constance Lilian Hosegood (*d* 1959); four *s* one *d* ; *m* 1962, June Patricia Ruth Day. *Educ:* Queen's Coll., Taunton. Farmer, 1923-36; Wholesale Fruit and Potato Merchant (Director), 1936-60. Chairman, Horticultural Marketing Council, 1960-63. *Recreations:* sailing, golf, gardens. *Address:* The Spinney, Brenchley, Kent. *T:* Brenchley 2149. *Clubs:* Farmers'; Lamberhurst Golf; Isle of Purbeck Golf.

BOWERMAN, Brig. John Francis, CBE 1946; Indian Army (retired); *b* 28 Nov. 1893; *s* of John Bowerman, Cullompton, Devon; *m* 1931, Mary Monica Faed Macmillan; one *d*. *Educ:* Queen Elizabeth's Sch., Crediton. Commissioned West Yorks Regt, 1915; served European War, 1914-18, Mesopotamia, Marri Field Force, 1914-18 (wounded); transferred 129th Duke of Connaught's Own Baluchis, Nov. 1918; active service Afghanistan, 1919, Zhob, 1919-21, Waziristan, 1921-23 and NW Frontier, 1930; Burma Rebellion, 1931-32. Served War of 1939-45, Burma; Chief Liaison Officer, 6th Chinese Army, 1942; Brigadier 1942, as Inspector General Burma Frontier Force; with Chinese-American Forces, Burma, 1943-45; despatches, 1946; retired 1946. King's Police Medal, 1928; American Bronze Star, 1945. FRGS, FRSA. *Publications:* Report on exploration, China, Burma, Tibet Border (MacGregor Memorial Medal of United Services Institution, India, 1928); paper on Frontier Areas of Burma (Silver Medal of RSA, 1947). *Recreations:* golf, fishing. *Address:* Arlington, Woodcock Hill, East Grinstead, W Sussex. *T:* East Grinstead 111.

BOWERS, Prof. Fredson Thayer; Linden Kent Professor of English, University of Virginia, USA, 1969-75, now Emeritus; *b* 25 April 1905; *s* of Fredson Eugene Bowers and Hattie May Quigley; *m* 1st, 1924, Hyacinth Sutphen; three *s* one *d* ; 2nd, 1942, Nancy Hale. *Educ:* Brown Univ. (PhB); Harvard Univ. (PhD). Instructor in English: Harvard Univ., 1926-36; Princeton Univ., 1936-38; Asst Prof., Univ. of Virginia, 1938-46. USNR, Comdr, 1942-46. Associate Prof., Univ. of Virginia, 1946-48, Prof., 1948-75, Alumni Prof., 1959-68 (Dean of the Faculty, 1968-69). Fulbright Fellow for Research in UK, 1953; Guggenheim Fellow, 1959, 1972; Sandars Reader in Bibliography, Cambridge, 1958; Lyell Reader in Bibliography, Oxford, 1959; Vis. Fellow, All Souls Coll., Oxford, 1972, 1974; Fellow Commoner, Churchill Coll., Cambridge, 1975; Exec. Council, Mod. Lang. Assoc. of Amer., 1964-68 (Pres., S Atlantic MLA, 1969); Corresp. FBA, 1968; Fellow Amer. Acad. Arts and Scis, 1972. Gold Medal, Bibliographical Soc., 1969; Thomas Jefferson Award, 1971. Editor, Studies in Bibliography, 1948-. Hon. DLitt: Brown, 1970; Clark, 1970; Hon. MA Oxon, 1972; Hon. LHD Chicago, 1973. *Publications:* Elizabethan Revenge Tragedy, 1940; Randolph's Fairy Knight (ed), 1942; Principles of Bibliographical Description, 1949; George Sandys: A Bibliographical Catalogue, 1950; Dramatic Works of Thomas Dekker (ed, 4 vols), 1953-61; On Editing Shakespeare and the Elizabethan Dramatists, 1955; Whitman's Manuscripts, 1955; Textual and Literary Criticism, 1959; Bibliography and Textual Criticism, 1964; Dramatic Works in the Beaumont and Fletcher Canon (ed), 1966-; Works of Stephen Crane (ed), 1969-75; Works of Christopher Marlowe (ed, 2 vols), 1973; (ed) Tom Jones, 1975; Works of William James (ed), 1975-; Essays in Bibliography, Text and Editing, 1975. *Recreations:* philately, music, dogs. *Address:* Woodburn, Route 8, Charlottesville, Virginia 22901, USA. *T:* 703-973-3629.

BOWES, Sir (Harold) Leslie, KCMG 1968; CBE 1943; Chairman, The Pacific Steam Navigation Company, 1960-65, Managing Director, 1952-65 (Deputy Chairman 1959-60); Chairman, Royal Mail Lines Ltd, 1960-65, Managing Director, 1958-65 (Deputy Chairman 1959-60); *b* 18 Nov. 1893; *m* 1st, 1921; two *s* one *d* ; 2nd 1950; one *d*. Served European War, RFC and RAF. The Pacific Steam Navigation Company: Manager for Chile, 1921-48; Director and General Manager, 1949-51. Director: Rea Bros Ltd; Ocean Wilsons (Holdings) Ltd; Member: General Purposes Cttee of Shipping Federation, 1958-61; Central Transport Consultative Cttee, 1959-61; Chairman Liverpool Steam Ship Owners' Assoc., 1954; Chairman General Council of British Shipping, 1954; Chairman Liverpool Port Welfare Cttee, 1955-58; Chairman Liverpool Marine Engineers' and Naval Architects Guild, 1955-56; Chairman Govt Cttee of Inquiry into Canals and Inland Waterways, 1956-58; Member General Cttee of Lloyd's Register of Shipping, 1956-65; Director, "Indefatigable" and Nat. Sea Training Sch. for Boys, 1954-58; Chairman Liverpool Chamber of Commerce, 1957-58; Governor, City of Liverpool College of Commerce, 1958-60; President: Institute of Shipping and Forwarding Agents, 1957-58; Vice-President: British Ship Adoption Society, 1968- (Chm. 1958-68); Institute of Transport, 1958-59 (Mem. Council, 1959-; Chairman Shipping Advisory Cttee, 1959-65); Member: Mersey Docks and Harbour Board, 1956-58; Shipping Advisory Council of BTC, 1960-62; Shipping and International Services Cttee of British Railways Board, 1963; Chairman, BNEC Cttee for Exports to Latin America, 1966-67 (Dep. Chm. 1964-66). Member Exec. Cttee: Anglo-Chilean Society, 1960-70 (Vice-Pres., 1970); Anglo-Peruvian Society (Vice-Pres. 1970); Hispanic and Luso-Brazilian Councils, 1960-69 (Vice-Pres. 1969-; Chm. 1963-64 and 1965-66); Anglo-Brazilian Soc.; Member: Cttee of Management, Canning Club; Exec. Cttee, Anglo-Portuguese Society; Vice-Pres., British Mexican Soc., 1974. Liveryman Worshipful Company of Shipwrights (Past Prime Warden). Comdr of Chilean Order of Merit, 1942, Grand Officer, 1952; Comdr, Ecuadorian Order of Merit, 1956; Comdr, Peruvian Order of Merit, 1957, Grand Cross, 1959; Order of Vasco Nuñez de Balboa, 1963; Grand Officer, Orden de Mayo, Argentina, 1964; Grand Cross, Order of San Carlos (Colombia), 1966; Comdr, Cruziero do Sul, Brazil, 1975. *Address:* 7 Chester Row, SW1W 9JF. *T:* 01-730 1523. *Clubs:* Canning, City Livery, Naval and Military.

BOWES LYON, family name of **Earl of Strathmore.**

BOWES-LYON, Maj.-Gen. Sir (Francis) James (Cecil), KCVO 1973; CB 1970; OBE 1972; MC and Bar, 1944; a Gentleman Usher to the Queen, 1974-76, an Extra Gentleman Usher, since 1976; *b* 19 Sept. 1917; *o s* of Capt. Geoffrey Bowes-Lyon; *m* 1941, Mary, 2nd *d* of Sir Humphrey de Trafford, 4th Bart, MC; two *s* one *d*. *Educ:* Eton; Royal Military Coll., Sandhurst. Commissioned into Grenadier Guards, 1938; served War of 1939-45, Guards Armoured Division; Commandant, Guards

Depot, 1955-57; comd 2nd Bn Grenadier Guards, 1957-59; Mil. Assistant (GSO1) to CIGS, 1960-62; comd 157 Lowland Bde (Scotland), 1963; GOC 52nd Lowland Division District, 1966-68; GOC Berlin (British Sector), 1968-70; GOC London District, and Maj-Gen. commanding Household Div., 1971-73. Pres., Nat. Small Bore Rifle Assoc., 1974-; Chm. Bd of Governors, The Queen Alexandra Hospital Home for Disabled Sailors, Soldiers and Airmen, 1974-. *Recreations:* shooting, gardening, racing. *Address:* Beltingham House, Bardon Mill, Northumberland. *Clubs:* White's, Pratt's.

BOWETT, Derek William, LLD; President, Queens' College, Cambridge, since 1969; Reader in Law, Cambridge University, since 1976; *b* 20 April 1927; *s* of Arnold William Bowett and Marion Wood; *m* 1953, Betty Northall; two *s* one *d*. *Educ:* William Hulme's Sch., Manchester; Downing Coll., Cambridge. MA, LLB, LLD (Cantab), PhD (Manchester). Called to the Bar, Middle Temple, 1953, Hon. Bencher, 1975. Lectr, Law Faculty, Manchester Univ. 1951-59; Legal Officer, United Nations, New York, 1957-59; Lectr, Law Faculty, Cambridge Univ., 1960-76; Fellow of Queens' Coll., 1960-69; Gen. Counsel, UNRWA, Beirut, 1966-68. Mem., Royal Commn on Environmental Pollution, 1973-. *Publications:* Self-defence in International Law, 1958; Law of International Institutions, 1964; United Nations Forces, 1964; Law of the Sea, 1967; Search for Peace, 1972. *Recreations:* music, cricket, tennis. *Address:* The President's Lodge, Queens' College, Cambridge. *T:* Cambridge 65511.

BOWEY, Olwyn, RA 1975 (ARA 1970); practising artist (painter); *b* 10 Feb. 1936; *o d* of James and Olive Bowey. *Educ:* William Newton Sch., Stockton; West Hartlepool Sch. of Art; Royal Coll. of Art. One-man shows: Zwemmer Gall., 1961; New Grafton Gall., 1969; also exhibited at Leicester Gall., Royal Academy; work purchased through Chantrey Bequest for Tate Gall., Royal Academy, Min. of Works, etc. *Recreations:* natural history, music. *Address:* Folley Cottage, Barlavington, Petworth, West Sussex GU28 0LG. *T:* Petworth 7231.

BOWEY, William, FCIT, FBIM; Managing Director and Member of the Board, Port of London Authority, since 1976; *b* 5 July 1925; *s* of William Bowey and Elizabeth; *m* 1949, Joyce Mary Parvin. *Educ:* Rutherford Grammar Sch., Newcastle upon Tyne; King's Coll., Durham Univ. Solicitor (Hons) 1956. Asst Legal Adviser, Proctor & Gamble Ltd (formerly Thomas Hadley & Co. Ltd), 1947-58; Legal Adviser and Dep. Sec., Smiths Industries Ltd, 1959-62; Exec. Dir, and Sec., Air Products Ltd, 1962-65; Port of London Authority: Dir of Admin, 1967; Dir of Marketing, 1968-69; Asst Dir-Gen., 1969-74. Alternate Dir, Internat. Assoc. of Ports and Harbours, 1976; Dir, Port Publishing Co. Ltd, 1976; rep. UK ports, EEC Commn's Directorates of Transport and Reg. Policy, 1972-74. Mem., Law Soc., 1956. Freeman: City of London, 1976; Worshipful Co. of Watermen and Lightermen, 1977. *Recreations:* music, theatre, philately. *Address:* Haslemere, Surrey.

BOWICK, David Marshall, CBE 1977; Chief Executive (Railways), British Railways Board, since 1971; Member, since 1976, Vice-Chairman and Chief Executive, since 1977, British Railways Board; *b* 30 June 1923; *s* of George Bowick, Corstorphine, Edinburgh; *m* Gladys May (*née* Jeffries); one *d*. *Educ:* Boroughmuir Sch., Edinburgh; Heriot-Watt Coll., Edinburgh. Served with Fleet Air Arm, 1942-46. Movements Supt, Kings Cross, 1962; Planning Officer, British Railways Board Headquarters, 1963; Asst Gen. Man., London Midland Region, BR, 1965; Exec. Dir, Personnel, BRB Headquarters, 1969; Gen. Manager, London Midland Region, BR, 1971. Mem. Council, Manchester Business Sch. FInstM; FREconS; FCIT; MBIM; FRSA. *Recreations:* sailing, swimming, golf, travel, theatre. *Address:* 25 Rossmore Court, Park Road, NW1. *Club:* Caledonian.

BOWIE, Stanley Hay Umphray, DSc; FRS 1975; FRSE, FIMM; Consultant Geologist; Assistant Director, Chief Geochemist, Institute of Geological Sciences, 1968-77; *b* 24 March 1917; *s* of Dr James Cameron and Mary Bowie; *m* 1948, Helen Elizabeth, *d* of Dr Roy Woodhouse and Florence Elizabeth Pocock; two *s*. *Educ:* Grammar Sch. and Univ. of Aberdeen (BSc, DSc). Meteorological Office, 1942; commissioned RAF, 1943; HM Geological Survey of Gt Britain: Geologist, Sen. Geologist and Principal Geologist, 1946-55; Chief Geologist, Atomic Energy Div., 1955-67; Chief Consultant Geologist to UKAEA, 1955-. Visiting Prof. of Applied Geology, Univ. of Strathclyde, 1968-; Chm., Internat. Mineralogical Assoc., Commn on Ore Microscopy, 1970-. Vice-Pres., Geological Soc., 1972-74. FGS 1959; FMSA 1963; FRSE 1970; FIMM 1972 (Pres. 1976-77). Silver Medal, RSA, 1959. *Publications:* contributions to Nuclear

Geology, 1954; Physical Methods in Determinative Mineralogy, 1967, 2nd edn 1977; (ed jtly) Uranium Prospecting Handbook, 1972; Uranium Exploration Methods, 1973; numerous papers in scientific and technical jls on uranium geology and economics, mineralogy, geophysics and geochemistry. *Recreations:* fishing, shooting, sailing, gardening, photography. *Address:* Tanyard Farm, Clapton, Crewkerne, Somerset. *T:* Crewkerne 72093. *Club:* Geological Society's.

BOWKER, Sir (Reginald) James, GBE 1961; KCMG 1952 (CMG 1945); Member, London Committee of Ottoman Bank, since 1961; *b* 2 July 1901; *yr s* of Lieut-Col F. J. Bowker, Hampshire Regt, and Edith Sophie Mary Elliott; *m* 1947, Elsa, *d* of Michel Gued and Mme Gued Vidal. *Educ:* Charterhouse; Oriel Coll., Oxford. 3rd Secretary, Foreign Office and Diplomatic Service, 1925. Served in Paris, Berlin, Ankara, Oslo and Madrid. British Minister in Cairo, 1945-47; High Commissioner in Burma, 1947-48; Ambassador to Burma, 1948-50; an Asst Under-Secretary of State, FO, 1950-53; Ambassador to Turkey, 1954-58; Ambassador to Austria, 1958-61; retired from Foreign Service, 1961. *Address:* 3 West Eaton Place, SW1X 8LU. *T:* 01-235 3852. *Club:* Brooks's.

BOWLBY, Sir Anthony Hugh Mostyn, 2nd Bt, *cr* 1923; President, British Standards Institution, since 1973; *b* 13 Jan. 1906; *e s* of Sir Anthony Bowlby, 1st Bt and Maria Bridget (*d* 1957), *d* of Rev. Canon Hon. Hugh W. Mostyn; *S* father, 1929; *m* 1930, Dora Evelyn, *d* of John Charles Allen; two *d*. *Educ:* Wellington Coll.; New Coll., Oxford. Chm., Working Together campaign. *Heir:* *b* Edward John Mostyn Bowlby, *qv*. *Address:* The Old Rectory, Ozleworth, near Wotton-under-Edge, Glos. *See also* Sir E. H. P. *Brown, J. Dromgoole.*

BOWLBY, (Edward) John (Mostyn), CBE 1972; MD; FRCP, FRCPsych, FBPsS; Hon. Consultant Psychiatrist, Tavistock Clinic, London, since 1972; *b* 26 Feb. 1907; 2nd *s* of late Sir Anthony A. Bowlby, 1st Bt, and late Maria Bridget, *d* of Rev. Canon Hon. Hugh W. Mostyn; *heir -pres.* to *b* Sir Anthony Hugh Mostyn Bowlby, 2nd Bt, *qv*; *m* 1938, Ursula, 3rd *d* of late Dr T. G. Longstaff (Pres. Alpine Club, 1947-49) and Mrs D. H. Longstaff, JP; two *s* two *d*. *Educ:* RNC Dartmouth; Trinity Coll., Cambridge (MA Nat. Scis); UCH (MD). FRCP 1964, FRCPsych (Foundation Fellow) 1971, FBPsS 1945; Mem., Brit. PsychoAnalyt. Soc. Staff Psych., London Child Guidance Clinic, 1937-40; Consultant Psychiatrist: RAMC, 1940-45 (Temp. Lt-Col, 1944-45); Tavistock Clinic, 1946-72 (Chm., Dept for Children and Parents, 1946-68). Consultant: in mental health, WHO, 1950-; Nat. Inst. of Mental Health, Bethesda, Md, 1958-63. Fellow, Center for Advanced Studies in Behavioral Sciences, Stanford, Calif, 1957-58; Vis. Prof. in Psych., Stanford Univ., Calif, 1958; H. B. Williams Trav. Prof., Aust. and NZ Coll. of Psychiatrists, 1973. Pres., Internat. Assoc. for Child Psych. and Allied Professions, 1962-66; part-time Mem., ext. scientific staff, MRC, 1963-72. Hon. DLitt Leicester, 1971; Hon. ScD Cambridge, 1977. Sir James Spence Medal, Brit. Paediatric Assoc., 1974; G. Stanley Hall Medal, Amer. Psychol Assoc., 1974. *Publications:* Personal Aggressiveness and War (with E. F. M. Durbin), 1938; Forty-four Juvenile Thieves, 1946; Maternal Care and Mental Health, 1951 (12 trans); Child Care and the Growth of Love, 1953 (2nd edn 1963); Attachment and Loss (6 trans): Vol. 1, Attachment, 1969; Vol. 2, Separation: anxiety and anger, 1973; papers in Brit. and US jls of psych., psychol. and psychoanalysis. *Recreations:* natural history and outdoor activities. *Address:* Wyldes Close Corner, Hampstead Way, NW11 7JB.

BOWLBY, Hon. Mrs Geoffrey, CVO 1937; Extra Woman of the Bedchamber to Queen Elizabeth, the Queen Mother; 4th *d* of 11th Viscount Valentia, Bletchington Park, Oxford; *m* 1911, Capt. Geoffrey Vaux Salvin Bowlby, Royal Horse Guards (killed in action, 1915); one *s* one *d*. Commandant of Auxiliary Hospital, 1916-19 (despatches twice); a Lady-in-Waiting to Duchess of York, 1932; Woman of the Bedchamber to the Queen, 1937-45. *Address:* Flat 10, Ritchie Court, 380 Banbury Road, Oxford. *T:* Oxford 50414. *See also Earl of Meath.*

BOWLBY, John; *see* Bowlby, E. J. M.

BOWLBY, Rt. Rev. Ronald Oliver; *see* Newcastle, Bishop of.

BOWLE, Horace Edgar; Consul-General in HM's Foreign Service (retired); *b* 13 Aug. 1886; *y s* of late Edward Bowle, Salisbury, Wilts; *m* 1917, Letitia Constance, *y d* of late Charles Penruddocke, Compton Park, Wilts. *Educ:* Pembroke Coll., Cambridge (BA 1908); abroad. Served in USA, Colombia (Chargé d'Affaires, 1914), France, Belgium, Argentina and Portuguese E Africa; retired on pension, Nov. 1944. *Address:* 23 Merrywood Park, Reigate, Surrey RH2 9PA. *T:* Reigate 46103.

BOWLE, John Edward; historian; *b* 19 Dec. 1905; *o s* of Edward Francis Bowle, Salisbury, and Edith Beatrice, *y d* of late Silas Taunton, Fugglestone, Wilton, Wilts. *Educ:* The Old Malthouse, Langton Matravers; Marlborough Coll. (Council and Keith Rae Exhibitioner); Balliol Coll., Oxford (Brackenbury Scholar, 1924; BA 1927; MA 1932). Senior History Master, Westminster Sch., 1932-40; History Master, Eton, 1940-41. Air Ministry and Foreign Office, 1941-45. Lecturer in Modern History, Wadham Coll., Oxford, 1947-49; Leverhulme Research Fellow, 1949-50; Visiting Prof., Columbia Univ., NY, 1949; Dir, Preparatory Session, College of Europe, Bruges, 1949; Prof. of Political Theory, Bruges, 1950-67. Visiting Professor: Grinnell Coll., Iowa, 1961; Occidental Coll., Los Angeles, 1965; Indiana Univ., 1966; Lecturer, Smith Coll., Northampton, Mass, 1967. Editor, The World To-day, for RIIA, 1949-51. *Publications:* Western Political Thought, 1947 (Arts Council Prize, 1966); The Unity of European History, 1948, rev. edn, 1970; Hobbes and his Critics, 1951; Politics and Opinion in the Nineteenth Century, 1954; Viscount Samuel, a biography, 1957; (ed) The Concise Encyclopædia of World History, 1958; A New Outline of World History, 1963; Henry VIII, a biography, 1964, repr. 1973; England, a portrait, 1966; The English Experience, 1971; The Imperial Achievement, 1974; Napoleon, 1974; Charles I, a biography, 1975; Man Through the Ages, 1977; contrib. to various periodicals; writes for radio and broadcasts. *Recreations:* travel, painting. *Address:* 24 Woodstock Close, Oxford. *T:* 58379. *Club:* Travellers'.

BOWLER, Geoffrey, FCIS; Chief General Manager, Sun Alliance & London Insurance Group, since 1977; *b* 11 July 1924; *s* of James Henry Bowler and Hilda May Bowler. *Educ:* Sloane Sch., Chelsea. FCIS 1952. *Address:* 13 Green Lane, Purley, Surrey. *T:* 01-660 0756.

BOWLER, Ian John, CBE 1971 (OBE 1957); President, Iranian Management & Engineering Group Ltd, since 1965; Chairman: International Management & Engineering Group Ltd, since 1973; Kinhill/IMEG, Australia, since 1971; *b* 1920; *s* of Major John Arthur Bowler; *m* 1963, Hamideh, *d* of Prince Yadollah Azodi, GCMG; two *d,* and one step *s* one step *d. Educ:* King's Sch., Worcester; privately; Oxford Univ. Director of Constructors, John Brown, 1961-64; Man. Dir, Internat. Management & Eng. Group Ltd, 1964-68. MInstPet. *Publication:* Predator Birds of Iran, 1973. *Recreations:* ornithology, yachting. *Address:* 4 Kucheh, Bagh Bank, Golhak, Tehran, Iran; 28 Mallord Street, SW3. *T:* 01-351 3322. *Clubs:* Travellers', Royal Thames Yacht, Goat; S.R.R. (La Rochelle, France).

BOWLES, Dame Ann P.; *see* Parker Bowles.

BOWLES, Chester; United States Ambassador to India, 1963-69; *b* Springfield, Mass, 5 April 1901; *s* of Allen Bowles and Nellie Harris; *g s* of Samuel Bowles, Founder of the Springfield Republican; *m* 1934, Dorothy Stebbins Bowles; two *s* three *d. Educ:* Choate Sch., Wallingford, Conn.; Yale Univ., New Haven, Conn. Founded advertising and marketing research agency in NY City with William Benton, 1929; Chm. Board of this agency (Benton & Bowles, Inc.), 1936-41, when sold out interests. Administrator of Office of Price Administration, 1943-46, appointed by President Roosevelt; Mem. of War Production Bd, 1943-46; appointed Dir of Economic Stabilization by President Truman, 1946, and resigned from that post, 1946; Special Asst to UN Sec.-Gen., 1946-48; Governor of Connecticut, 1949-51; American Ambassador to India, and first American Ambassador to Nepal, 1951-53; Mem., 86th Congress, House of Representatives, 1959-60 (2nd Dist. Conn); Under-Sec. of State, USA, Jan.-Nov. 1961; President's Special Representative and Adviser on African, Asian and Latin American Affairs with rank of Ambassador, Nov. 1961-May 1963; Mem. of Congress, US (2nd Dist Conn). Member: Democratic Advisory Council on Foreign Policy; Institute of International Education; American African Soc.; American National Commission for United Nations Economic, Scientific and Cultural Organizations Conference in Paris, 1946; (Internat. Chm.) UN Appeal for Children, 1947; Board of Advisers, Fletcher Sch. of Law and Diplomacy, Medford, Mass; Delivered The Anna Howard Shaw Memorial Lectures at Bryn Mawr Coll., 1953-54; Godkin Lectr, Harvard Univ., 1956; Berkeley Lectr, University of Calif, 1956; Chubb Lectr, Yale Univ., 1957; Rosenfeld Lectr, Grinnell Coll., 1959. Conn Delegate to Democratic Nat. Convention, 1940, 1944, 1948, 1956, 1960; Chm., Platform Cttee, Democratic National Convention, July 1960. Franklin Delano Roosevelt Award for fight against racial discrimination, 1950; Roosevelt Coll. Award for outstanding public service, 1953. Associate Fellow Silliman Coll., Yale Univ.; Hon. DSc The New Sch. for Social Research, New York; Hon. Dr of Laws, Howard Univ., Washington, DC, Hon. Dr of Law: Oberlin Coll., 1957; Bard Coll., 1957; Hon. LLD: American Univ., Washington, DC; Univ. of Rhode Island, 1958; Yale, 1968; Davidson Coll., 1972. *Publications:* Tomorrow Without Fear, 1946; Ambassador's Report, 1954; The New Dimensions of Peace, 1955; American Politics in a Revolutionary World, 1956; Africa's Challenge to America, 1956; Ideas, People and Peace, 1958; The Coming Political Breakthrough, 1959; Conscience of a Liberal, 1962; Makings of a Just Society, 1963; A View from New Delhi, 1969; Promises to Keep: my years in public life, 1941-1969, 1971; and many articles on economic problems and foreign policy. *Recreation:* sailing. *Address:* Hayden's Point, Essex, Conn 06426, USA. *TA:* Essex, Conn. *Clubs:* Essex Yachting (Essex, Conn); Cruising Club of America, Yale (New York).

BOWLES, Rt. Rev. Cyril William Johnston; *see* Derby, Bishop of.

BOWMAN, Sir James, 1st Bt *cr* 1961; KBE 1957 (CBE 1952); JP; DCL; *b* 8 March 1898; *m* 1922, Jean, *d* of Henry Brook, Ashington, Northumberland; one *s* one *d.* Served European War, 1914-18, Royal Marines. Gen. Sec., Northumberland Miners' Association (later National Union of Mineworkers, Northumberland Area), 1935-49; Vice-Pres., National Union of Mineworkers, 1938-49; Mem. of Gen. Council of TUC, 1945-49; Chm., National Coal Board Northern (N & C) Div., 1950-55; Dep. Chm., National Coal Board, 1955-56; Chm., National Coal Board, 1956-61. JP, Northumberland, 1935. Mem., Court of Governors of Administrative Staff Coll., 1957-. Former member: National Miners' Welfare Joint Council; DSIR; Royal Commission on the Press. *Heir: s* George Bowman [*b* 2 July 1923; *m* 1960, Olive (*née* Case); three *d*]. *Address:* Woodlands, Killingworth Drive, Newcastle upon Tyne NE12 0ES. *T:* Newcastle 661252. *Club:* Reform.

BOWMAN, James Thomas; counter-tenor; *b* Oxford, 6 Nov. 1941; *s* of Benjamin and Cecilia Bowman. *Educ:* Ely Cathedral Choir Sch.; King's Sch., Ely; New Coll., Oxford. MA (History) 1967; DipEd 1964. Schoolmaster, 1965-67. Many concert performances with: English Opera Gp, 1967-; Early Music Consort, 1967-76; operatic performances with: Sadler's Wells Opera, 1970-; Glyndebourne Festival Opera, 1970-; in USA at Santa Fe and Wolf Trap Festivals; operatic roles include: Oberon, in A Midsummer Night's Dream; Endymion, in La Calisto; the Priest, in Taverner; Polinesso, in Ariodante; Apollo, in Death in Venice; Astron, in Ice Break; Ruggiero in Alcina; title rôle in Gulio Cesare. Has made recordings of oratorio and Medieval and Renaissance vocal music. Lay Vicar, Westminster Abbey, 1969. *Recreations:* ecclesiastical architecture; collecting records. *Address:* 19a Wetherby Gardens, SW5 0JP.

BOWMAN, Prof. John Christopher, PhD; FIBiol; Professor of Animal Production, since 1966, and Director of University Farms, since 1967, University of Reading; Head of Department of Agriculture, 1967-71; Director, Centre for Agricultural Strategy, University of Reading, since 1975; *b* 13 Aug. 1933; *s* of M. C. Bowman and C. V. Simister; *m* 1961, S. J. Lorimer; three *d. Educ:* Manchester Grammar Sch.; Univ. of Reading (BSc); Univ. of Edinburgh (PhD). Geneticist, later Chief Geneticist, Thornbers, Mytholmroyd, Yorks, 1958-66. Post-doctoral Fellow, North Carolina State Univ., Raleigh, NC, USA, 1964-65. *Publications:* An Introduction to Animal Breeding, 1974; Animals for Man, 1977; papers published in: Heredity; British Poultry Science; Animal Production; Animal Breeding Abstracts; Genetical Research. *Recreations:* tennis, gardening. *Address:* University Farm House, Sonning, Berks. *T:* (office) Reading 85123. *Club:* Farmers'.

BOWMAN, Sir John Paget, 4th Bt, *cr* 1884; *b* 12 Feb. 1904; *s* of Rev. Sir Paget Mervyn Bowman, 3rd Bt, and Rachel Katherine (*d* 1936), *d* of late James Hanning, Kilcrone, Co. Cork; *S* father 1955; *m* 1st, 1931, Countess Cajetana Hoyos (*d* 1948), *d* of Count Edgar Hoyos, Schloss Soss, Lower Austria; one *s* one *d* ; 2nd, 1948, Frances Edith Marian, *d* of Sir Beethom Whitehead, KCMG (*d* 1928), Efford Park, Lymington. *Educ:* Eton. Formerly 2nd Lieut 98th (Surrey and Sussex Yeomanry) Field Brigade RA. *Heir: s* David Anthony Paget Bowman [*b* 16 Oct. 1935; *m* 1968, Valerie Winifred, *o d* of R. C. Tatham, N Ferriby, Yorks.] *Address:* Bishops Green House, Newbury, Berks.

BOWMAN, (Mary) Elaine K.; *see* Kellett-Bowman.

BOWMAN, Thomas Patrick; Chairman: PA Management Consultants Ltd, 1966-75; PA International Management Consultants, 1971-75; Governor, Sundridge Park Management Centre, 1961-75; *b* 25 Sept. 1915; *s* of Thomas Marshall Bowman and Louisa Hetherington Macfarlane; *m* 1950, Norma Elizabeth Deravin; one *s. Educ:* Oundle Sch.; Hertford Coll.,

Oxford. Joined Industrial Engineering Div. of Thomas Hedley & Co. (now Proctor & Gamble Ltd), 1937; P A Management Consultants Ltd, 1945 (Dir, 1955; Managing Dir, 1961). Member: Monopolies Commn, 1969-72; Council, CBI, 1970-74. Chairman, UK Management Consultants Assoc., 1966, 1974; Founder Member and Fellow of Inst. of Management Consultants; Pres., European Fedn of Management Consultants, 1967-69. Chm., Wimbledon and Putney Conservators Bd, 1976-. FBIM 1959. *Address:* 9 Clement Road, Wimbledon, SW19 7RJ. *T:* 01-946 3828. *Club:* Royal Thames Yacht.

BOWMAN-SHAW, (George) Neville; Chairman: Lancer Boss Rentals Ltd, since 1971; Lancer Boss France SA, since 1967; Lancer Boss Fördergeräte Vertriebsgesellschaft, mbH (Austria), since 1966; Lancer Boss Ireland Ltd, since 1966; Lancer Boss Group Ltd, since 1966; Lancer Boss Ltd, since 1967; Boss Trucks & Equipment, since 1959; Lancer Boss International SA Lausanne (formerly BS Exports SA Geneva), since 1962; Boss Engineers Ltd, since 1961; *b* 4 Oct. 1930; *s* of George Bowman-Shaw and Hazel Bowman-Shaw (*née* Smyth); *m* 1962, Georgina Mary Blundell; three *s* one *d. Educ:* Caldicott Preparatory Sch.; then private tutor. Farming Trainee, 1947; Management Trainee in Engineering Co., 1948. Commissioned in 5th Royal Inniskilling Dragoon Guards, 1950. Sales Manager: Matling Ltd, Wolverhampton, 1953; Materials Handling Equipment (GB) Ltd, London, and Matbro Ltd, London, 1955. Mem., Development Commn, 1970-77. Vice-Pres., Bedfordshire Rural Community Council. Governor, Hawtreys School. *Recreations:* shooting, skiing, wildfowl collection. *Address:* Toddington Park, Toddington, Bedfordshire. *T:* Toddington 2576. *Clubs:* Constitutional, Cavalry and Guards, Hurlingham.

BOWNESS, Alan, CBE 1976; Reader in the History of Art, Courtauld Institute, University of London, since 1967; *b* 11 Jan. 1928; *er s* of George Bowness and Kathleen (*née* Benton); *m* 1957, Sarah Hepworth-Nicholson, *d* of Ben Nicholson, *qv*, and late Dame Barbara Hepworth, DBE; one *s* one *d. Educ:* University Coll. Sch.; Downing Coll., Cambridge; Courtauld Inst. of Art, Univ. of London. Worked with Friends' Ambulance Unit and Friends' Service Council, 1946-50; Reg. Art Officer, Arts Council of GB, 1955-57; Courtauld Inst., 1957-. Vis. Prof., Humanities Seminar, Johns Hopkins Univ., Baltimore, 1969. Mem. Internat. Juries: Premio Di Tella, Buenos Aires, 1965; São Paulo Bienal, 1967; Lehmbruck Prize, Duisburg, 1970. Arts Council: Mem., 1973-75; Mem., Art Panel, 1960- (Vice-Chm., 1973-75); Mem., Arts Film Cttee, 1968- (Chm., 1972-75). Member: Fine Arts Cttee, Brit. Council, 1960-69 and 1970-; Exec. Cttee, Contemp. Art Soc., 1961-69 and 1970-; Cultural Adv. Cttee, UK National Commn for UNESCO, 1973-. Governor, Chelsea Sch. of Art, 1965-; Hon. Sec., Assoc. of Art Historians, 1973-76; Dir, Barbara Hepwoth Museum, St Ives, Cornwall, 1976-. Exhibitions arranged and catalogued include: 54:64 Painting and Sculpture of a Decade (with L. Gowing), 1964; Dubuffet, 1966; Sculpture in Battersea Park, 1966; Van Gogh, 1968; Rodin, 1970; William Scott, 1972; French Symbolist Painters (with G. Lacambre), 1972; Ceri Richards, 1975; Courbet (with M. Laclotte), 1977. Chevalier, l'Ordre des Arts et des Lettres, France, 1973. *Publications:* William Scott Paintings, 1964; Impressionists and Post Impressionists, 1965; Henry Moore: complete sculpture 1955-64, 1965; Modern Sculpture, 1965; Barbara Hepworth Drawings, 1966; Alan Davie, 1967; Recent British Painting, 1968; Gauguin, 1971; Barbara Hepworth: complete sculpture 1960-70, 1971; Modern European Art, 1972; Ivon Hitchens, 1973; (contrib.) Picasso 1881-1973, ed R. Penrose, 1973; (contrib.) The Genius of British Painting, ed D. Piper, 1975; Henry Moore: complete sculpture 1964-73, 1977; articles in Burlington Magazine, TLS, Observer, and Annual Register. *Recreations:* listening to music; reading, especially poetry and 19th century fiction. *Address:* 91 Castelnau, SW13 9EL. *T:* 01-748 9696; 16 Piazza, St Ives, Cornwall. *T:* St Ives 5444.

BOWRING, Edgar Rennie; *b* 8 Feb. 1899; *yr s* of Henry A. Bowring, St John's, NF, and Liverpool; *m* 1929, Jean Douglas (*d* 1971), *d* of C. A. C. Bruce. *Educ:* Shrewsbury Sch. Formerly Director: C. T. Bowring & Co. Ltd. and assoc. companies; Martins Bank Ltd (a former Dep. Chm. and Chm. of London Bd); Royal Insurance Company Ltd (a former Dep. Chm.) The Liverpool and London and Globe Insurance Co. Ltd; The London and Lancs Insurance Co. Ltd; Cunard Steam-Ship Co. Ltd. Served European War, 1914-18, Lieut RFA. High Sheriff of Cheshire, 1948-49. *Address:* 116 Grosvenor House, Park Lane, W1.

BOWRING, Edgar Rennie Harvey, MC 1945; Chairman, The Bowring Group of Companies, since 1973; Solicitor; *b* 5 Nov. 1915; *y s* of Arthur Bowring; *m* 1940, Margaret Grace (*née* Brook); two *s* one *d. Educ:* Eastbourne Coll.; Clare Coll.,

Cambridge (MA); Berkeley Coll., Yale, USA. War of 1939-45: commissioned Kent Yeomanry, RA, 1939; served in Iceland, France and Germany (despatches, 1944); demobilised, 1946. Solicitor, 1949; Partner in Cripps Harries Hall & Co., 1950-55. Member of Lloyd's, 1962. Joined C. T. Bowring & Co. (Insurance) Ltd, 1956 (Dir, 1960); Dir, C. T. Bowring & Co. Ltd, 1963; Dep. Chm. and Chief Exec., C. T. Bowring (Insurance) Holdings Ltd, 1970-73. Pres., Insurance Inst. of London, 1971-72 (Dep. Pres., 1970-71); Vice-Pres., Corporation of Insurance Brokers. *Recreations:* gardening, golf. *Address:* Millstream, Horam, Sussex. *T:* Horam Road 2687; 18 Denbigh House, Hans Place, SW1X 0EX. *T:* 01-584 0781.

BOWRING, Maj.-Gen. John Humphrey Stephen, CB 1968; OBE 1958; MC 1941; FICE; Colonel, The Gurkha Engineers, 1966-71; Colonel Commandant, Corps of Royal Engineers, 1968-73; *b* 13 Feb. 1913; *s* of late Major Francis Stephen Bowring and late Mrs Maurice Stonor; *m* 1956, Iona Margaret (*née* Murray); two *s* two *d. Educ:* Downside; RMA Woolwich; Trinity Coll., Cambridge. MA 1936. Commissioned, 1933; Palestine, 1936; India, 1937-40; Middle East, 1940-42; India and Burma, 1942-46; British Military Mission to Greece, 1947-50; UK, 1951-55; CRE, 17 Gurkha Div., Malaya, 1955-58; Col GS, War Office, 1958-61; Brig., Chief Engineer, Far East, 1961-64; Brig. GS, Ministry of Defence, 1964-65; Engineer-in-Chief, 1965-68. Dir, Consolidated Gold Fields. *Recreation:* riding. *Address:* The Upper House, Chedglow, near Malmesbury, Wilts. *T:* Crudwell 238. *Clubs:* Army and Navy, Royal Ocean Racing.

BOWRING, Air Vice-Marshal John Ivan Roy, CB 1977; CBE 1971; CEng, FRAeS; MBIM; Senior Air Staff Officer, RAF Support Command, since 1974; *b* 28 March 1923; *s* of Hugh Passmore Bowring and Ethel Grace Bowring; *m* 1945, Irene Mary Rance; two *d. Educ:* Great Yarmouth Grammar Sch., Norfolk; Aircraft Apprentice, RAF Halton-Cosford, 1938-40; Leicester Tech. Coll.; commissioned, RAF, 1944; NW Europe, 1944-47; RAF, Horsham St Faith's, Engrg duties, 1947-48; RAF South Cerney, Pilot trng, 1949; Engr Officer: RAF Finningly, 1950-51; RAF Kai-Tak, 1951-53; Staff Officer, AHQ Hong Kong, ADC to Governor, Hong Kong, 1953-54; Sen. Engr Officer, RAF Coltishall, 1954-56; exchange duties with US Air Force, Research and Develt, Wright Patterson Air Force Base, Ohio, 1956-60; RAF Staff Coll., Bracknell, 1960; Air Min. Opl Requirements, 1961-64; OC Engrg Wing, RAF St Mawgaw, 1964-67; Head of F111 Procurement Team, USA, 1967-68; OC RAF Aldergrove, NI, 1968-70; RCDS, 1971; Dir of Engrg Policy, MoD, 1972-73; AO Engrg, RAF Germany, 1973-74. *Recreations:* sailing, golf. *Address:* 13 Oxford Road, Breachwood Green, Hitchin, Herts. *T:* Whitwell 536. *Club:* Royal Air Force.

BOWRON, John Lewis; solicitor; Secretary-General, The Law Society, since 1974; *b* 1 Feb. 1924; *e s* of John Henry and Lavinia Bowron; *m* 1950, Patricia, *d* of Arthur Cobby; two *d. Educ:* Grangefield Grammar Sch., Stockton-on-Tees; King's Coll., London (LLB, FKC 1976). Principal in Malcolm Wilson & Cobby, Solicitors, Worthing, 1952-74. Member of the Council of the Law Society, 1969-74. *Recreations:* golf, music. *Address:* Elton Lodge, Palmers Way, High Salvington, Worthing, W Sussex. *T:* Worthing 60444. *Club:* Junior Carlton.

BOWSER, David Stewart, JP; a Forestry Commissioner since 1974; landowner since 1947; *b* 11 March 1926; *s* of David Charles Bowser, CBE and Maysie Murray Bowser (*née* Henderson); *m* 1951, Judith Crabbe; one *s* four *d. Educ:* Harrow; Trinity Coll., Cambridge (BA Agric). Captain, Scots Guards, 1944-47. Mem., Nat. Bd of Scottish Woodland Owners' Assoc., 1960- (Chm. 1972-74); Pres., Highland Cattle Soc., 1970-72; Mem., Regional Adv. Cttee, West Scotland Conservancy, Forestry Commn, 1964-74 (Chm. 1970-74). Mem. Perth CC, 1954-61; JP Co. Perth, 1956. *Recreations:* shooting, fishing, stalking. *Address:* Argaty and the King's Lundies, Doune, Perthshire. *T:* Doune 287. *Clubs:* Army and Navy; Royal Perth Golfing Society.

BOWYER, family name of **Baron Denham.**

BOWYER, William, ARA 1974; RP, RBA, RWS; Head of Fine Art, Maidstone College of Art, since 1971; *b* 25 May 1926; *m* 1951, Vera Mary Small; two *s* one *d. Educ:* Burslem School of Art; Royal College of Art (ARCA). Hon. Sec., New English Art Club. *Recreations:* cricket (Chiswick Cricket Club), snooker. *Address:* 12 Cleveland Avenue, Chiswick, W4 1SN. *T:* 01-994 0346. *Club:* Chelsea Arts.

BOWYER-SMYTH, Sir P. W.; *see* Smyth.

BOX, Betty Evelyn, (Mrs P. E. Rogers), OBE 1958; Film Producer; *b* 25 Sept. 1915; *m* 1949, Peter Edward Rogers; no *c. Educ:* home. Dir, Welbeck Film Distributors Ltd. *Films include:* Dear Murderer; When the Bough Breaks; Miranda; Blind Goddess; Huggett Family series; It's Not Cricket; Marry Me; Don't Ever Leave Me; So Long at the Fair; Appointment with Venus; Venetian Bird; A Day to Remember; The Clouded Yellow; Doctor in the House; Mad About Men; Doctor at Sea; The Iron Petticoat; Checkpoint; Doctor at Large; Campbell's Kingdom; A Tale of Two Cities; The Wind Cannot Read; The 39 Steps; Upstairs and Downstairs; Conspiracy of Hearts; Doctor in Love; No Love for Johnnie; No, My Darling Daughter; A Pair of Briefs; The Wild and the Willing; Doctor in Distress; Hot Enough for June; The High Bright Sun; Doctor in Clover; Deadlier than the Male; Nobody Runs Forever; Some Girls Do; Doctor in Trouble; Percy; The Love Ban; Percy's Progress. *Address:* Pinewood Studios, Iver, Bucks.

BOX, Donald Stewart; Member, The Stock Exchange and Partner, Lyddon & Co., Stockbrokers; *b* 22 Nov. 1917; *s* of late Stanley Carter Box and Elizabeth Mary Stewart Box; *m* 1st, 1940, Margaret Kennington Bates (marr. diss. 1947); 2nd, 1948, Peggy Farr, *née* Gooding (marr. diss. 1973); 3rd, 1973, Margaret Rose Davies; one *d. Educ:* Llandaff Cathedral Sch.; St John's Sch., Pinner; County Sch., Harrow. RAF ranks, 1939, commissioned, 1941; overseas service Egypt, Palestine, Transjordan, 1941-44; demobbed with rank of Flt-Lieut, 1945. MP (C) Cardiff North, 1959-66. *Recreations:* indifferent tennis, studying race form, doodling and doggerel. *Address:* Laburnum Cottage, Sully Road, Penarth, S Glam. *T:* Penarth 707966. *Clubs:* Junior Carlton; Little Ship; Cardiff and County (Cardiff).

BOX, Sydney; author and film producer; *b* 29 April 1907; *m* 1st, 1929, Katherine Knight (marr. diss. 1934); 2nd, 1935, Muriel Baker (marr. diss. 1969); one *d* ; 3rd, 1969, Sylvia Knowles. In 1939 founded Verity Films Ltd, which produced more than 100 documentary and training films for War Office, Ministry of Information, etc; Producer, Two Cities Films, Denham Studios, 1941-42; Producer, Riverside Studios, 1943-45; Man. Dir and Executive Producer, Gainsborough Pictures, 1946-50. Films include: The Seventh Veil (Academy award for best original screen play, 1946); Quartet; Trio; Holiday Camp; Portrait from Life; The Years Between; The Man Within; The Passionate Stranger, and The Truth About Women (both with Muriel Box). Author (often in collaboration with Muriel Box) of more than 50 one-act plays, including Not This Man, winner of British Drama League National Festival at Old Vic, 1937. In charge of production London Independent Producers, 1951. Dir, Tyne Tees Television (ITA), 1958-65; Chairman: London Independent Television Producers Ltd, 1963; National Film Corp. Ltd, 1965; Triton Publishing Co. Ltd. Mem., W Australia Arts Council, 1974-77. *Publications:* Diary of a Drop Out, 1969; The Golden Girls, 1971; Alibi in the Rough, 1977; The Lion That Lost Its Way, 1978. *Address:* 21/71 Mount Street, Perth, WA 6000, Australia.

BOXALL, Bernard, CBE 1963; Chairman, Plastic Research Laboratories Ltd; Director: Export Packing Service Ltd; A. J. Mills (Holdings) Ltd; Lancer Boss Group Ltd; Erma Ltd; *b* 17 Aug. 1906; *s* of late Arthur Boxall and of Mrs Maud Mary Boxall (*née* Mills); *m* 1931, Marjorie Lilian, *d* of late William George Emery and Mrs Emery; one *s* one *d. Educ:* King's Coll. Sch., Wimbledon; Imperial Coll., London Univ. (BSc (Hons), FCGI), Fellow 1971. James Howden & Co. Ltd, 1928-33; J. A. King & Co. Ltd, 1934-42; Production-Engineering Ltd, 1942-59; Management Consultant, 1959-. Chm., British United Trawlers Ltd, 1969-71. Dir, Lindustries Ltd, and Chm. of its engineering cos, 1960-71. Member: Highland Trnspt Bd, 1963-66; IRC, 1966-71; Scottish Economic Planning Council, 1967-71; Monopolies Commn, 1969-74. Mem., Company of Coachmakers and Coach Harness Makers (Master, 1977-78). FIMechE, FIProdE, Assoc. CIT. *Recreations:* golf, sailing. *Address:* Gilridge, Sandy Lane, Kingswood, Surrey. *T:* Mogador 2125. *Clubs:* Royal Automobile, Royal Western Yacht; Walton Heath Golf, Cryptics Cricket.

BOXALL, Mrs Lewis; see Buss, Barbara Ann.

BOXER, Air Vice-Marshal Sir Alan (Hunter Cachemaille), KCVO 1970; CB 1968; DSO 1944; DFC 1943; *b* 1 Dec. 1916; *s* of late Dr E. A. Boxer, CMG, Hastings, Hawkes Bay, NZ; *m* 1941, Pamela Sword; two *s* one *d. Educ:* Nelson Coll., New Zealand. Commissioned in RAF, 1939. Served War of 1939-45; Trng Comd until 1942; flying and staff appts, Bomber Comd, 1942-45. RAF Staff Coll., 1945; Jt Staff, Cabinet Offices, 1946-47; Staff Coll., Camberley, 1948; Strategic Air Comd, USAF and Korea, 1949-51; Central Fighter Estabt, 1952-53; Mem. Directing Staff, RAF Staff Coll., 1954-56; CO No 7 Sqdn, RAF,

1957; Group Capt. and CO, RAF Wittering, 1958-59; Plans, HQ Bomber Comd, 1960-61; Air Cdre, idc, 1962; SASO: HQ No 1 Gp, RAF, 1963-65; HQ Bomber Comd, 1965-67; Defence Services Sec., MoD, 1967-70. Virtuti Militari (Polish), Bronze Star (US), Air Medal (US). *Recreations:* fishing and sailing. *Address:* Lisle Farmhouse, Lymington, Hampshire SO4 8SH. *Club:* Royal Air Force.

BOXER, Charles Ian; Director, Community Affairs and Liaison Division, Commission for Racial Equality, since 1977; *b* 11 Feb. 1926; *s* of Rev. William Neville Gordon Boxer and Margaret Boxer; *m* 1968, Hilary Fabienne Boxer. *Educ:* Glasgow High Sch.; Edinburgh Univ. (BL). Church of England ministry, 1950-54; apprentice to solicitors, 1954-58; Mem., Dominican Order (RC), 1958-67; Sen. Community Relations Officer for Wandsworth, 1967-77. *Recreation:* music. *Address:* 9 Frogmore, SW18 1HW. *T:* 01-870 4400.

BOXER, Prof. Charles Ralph, FBA 1957; Emeritus Professor of Portuguese, University of London, since 1968; Fellow, King's Coll., 1967; *b* 8 March 1904; *s* of Col Hugh Boxer and Jane Boxer (*née* Patterson); *m* 1945, Emily Hahn; two *d. Educ:* Wellington Coll.; Royal Military Coll., Sandhurst. Commissioned Lincs Regt, 1923. Served War of 1939-45 (wounded, POW in Japanese hands, 1941-45). Retired with rank of Major, 1947. Camoens Prof. of Portuguese, London Univ., 1947-51; Prof. of the History of the Far East, London Univ., 1951-53; resigned latter post and re-apptd Camoens Prof., 1953-67; Prof. of History of Expansion of Europe Overseas, Yale, 1969-72. Visiting Research Prof., Indiana Univ., 1967-76; Emeritus Prof. of History, Yale, 1972-. Hon. Fellow, SOAS, 1974. A Trustee of National Maritime Museum, 1961-68. For. Mem., Royal Netherlands Acad. of Scis, 1976. Dr *hc* Universities of Utrecht (1950), Lisbon (1952), Bahia (1959), Liverpool (1966), Hong Kong (1971); Order of Santiago da Espada (Portugal); Grand Cross of the Order of the Infante Dom Henrique (Portugal); Kt Order of St Gregory the Great, 1969. *Publications:* The Commentaries of Ruy Freyre de Andrade, 1929; The Journal of M. H. Tromp, *Anno* 1639, 1930; Jan Compagnie in Japan, 1600-1817, 1936 (2nd edn 1950); Fidalgos in the Far East, 1550-1770, 1948; The Christian Century in Japan, 1549-1640, 1951, 2nd edn 1967; Salvador de Sá and the Struggle for Brazil and Angola, 1952; South China in the 16th Century, 1953; The Dutch in Brazil, 1624-1654, 1957; The Tragic History of the Sea, 1589-1622, 1959; The Great Ship from Amacon, 1959; Fort Jesus and the Portuguese in Mombasa, 1960; The Golden Age of Brazil, 1695-1750, 1962; Race Relations in the Portuguese Colonial Empire, 1415-1825, 1963; The Dutch Seaborne Empire, 1600-1800, 1965; Portuguese Society in the Tropics, 1966; Further Selections from the Tragic History of the Sea, 1969; The Portuguese Seaborne Empire, 1415-1825, 1969; Anglo-Dutch Wars of the 17th Century, 1974; Mary and Misogyny, 1975; numerous articles in learned periodicals. *Address:* Ringshall End, Little Gaddesden, Herts HP4 1NF. *Clubs:* Athenæum; Yale (New York).

BOXER, Air Cdre Henry Everard Crichton, CB 1965; OBE 1948; idc, ndc, psc; *b* 28 July 1914; *s* of late Rear-Adm. Henry P. Boxer; *m* 1938, Enid Anne Louise, *d* of late Dr John Moore Collyns; two *s* two *d. Educ:* Shrewsbury Sch.; RAF Coll., Cranwell. Commissioned RAF, 1935; No 1 Fighter Squadron, 1935-37; No 1 Flying Training Sch. (Chief Instructor), 1937-39; Specialist Navigator, 1939. Served War of 1939-45, in UK, S Africa and Europe. BJSM, Washington, DC, 1945-48; directing Staff, RAF Staff Coll., 1949-50; Coastal Command, 1951-52; Nat. Defence Coll., Canada, 1952-53; Air Ministry, 1953-56; OC, RAF Thorney Island, 1956-58. ADC to the Queen, 1957-59; IDC, 1959; Sen. Air Liaison Officer and Air Adviser to British High Comr in Canada, 1960-62; AO i/c Admin, HQ Coastal Comd, 1962-65; Dir of Personnel (Air), MoD (RAF), 1965-67; retd, 1967. Counsellor (Defence Equipment), British High Commn, Ottawa, 1967-74; retd, 1975. *Address:* Holmans, Bisterne Close, Burley, Hants. *Club:* Royal Air Force.

BOYCE, Air Vice-Marshal Clayton Descou Clement, CB 1946; CBE 1944; Assistant Controller of Aircraft, Ministry of Supply, 1957-59, retired; *b* 19 Sept. 1907; *er s* of Col C. J. Boyce, CBE, late IA; *m* 1928, Winifred, *d* of late J. E. Mead, Castletown, Isle of Man; one *s. Educ:* Bedford Sch.; Cranwell. Sec.-Gen., Allied Air Forces, Central Europe, 1953; AOC, Cyprus, 1954-56. *Address:* c/o Lloyds Bank, Cox's and King's Branch, 6 Pall Mall, SW1.

BOYCE, Guy Gilbert L.; see Leighton-Boyce.

BOYCE, Sir Robert (Charles) Leslie, 3rd Bt *cr* 1952; *b* 2 May 1962; *s* of Sir Richard (Leslie) Boyce, 2nd Bt, and of Jacqueline Anne, *o d* of Roland A. Hill; *S* father, 1968. *Heir:* uncle John

Leslie Boyce [b 16 Nov. 1934; m 1957, Finola Mary, d of late James Patrick Maxwell; one s three d].

BOYCE, Walter Edwin, OBE 1970; Director of Social Services, Essex County Council, since 1970; b 30 July 1918; s of Rev. Joseph Edwin Boyce and Alice Elizabeth Boyce; m 1942, Edna Lane (née Gargett); two d. Educ: High Sch. for Boys, Trowbridge, Wilts. Admin. Officer, Warwickshire CC, 1938-49. Served war, commnd RA; Gunnery sc, 1943; demob. rank Major, 1946. Dep. County Welfare Officer: Shropshire, 1949-52; Cheshire, 1952-57; Co. Welfare Officer, Essex, 1957-70. Adviser to Assoc. of County Councils, 1965-; Mem., Sec. of State's Adv. Personal Social Services Council, 1973-; Mem., nat. working parties on Health Service collaboration, 1972-74. Pres., County Welfare Officers Soc., 1967-68. Recreations: sailing, interest in sports, particularly Rugby and athletics, voluntary services, travel. Address: Highlanders Barn, Newmans Green, Long Melford, Suffolk CO10 0AD.

BOYCOTT, Prof. Brian Blundell, FRS 1971; Medical Research Council Senior Scientific Research Staff, Professor of Biology by title, since 1971; b 10 Dec. 1924; s of Percy Blundell Boycott and Doris Eyton Lewis; m 1950, Marjorie Mabel Burchell; one s (and one s decd). Educ: Royal Masonic Sch. Technician, Nat. Inst. Medical Research, and undergraduate, Birkbeck Coll., London, 1942-46; University Coll., London: Asst Lectr, Zoology, 1946-47; Hon. Res. Asst, Anatomy, 1947-52; Lectr, Zoology, 1952-62; Reader in Zoology, Univ. of London, 1962, Prof. of Zoology, 1968-70. Vis. Lectr, Harvard Univ., 1963. Member: Adv. Council, British Library Board, 1976-; Council, Open Univ., 1975-; Council, Royal Soc., 1976-; Comr, 1851 Exhibition, 1974-. Scientific medal, Zoological Soc. London, 1965. Publications: various articles in learned jls on structure and function of nervous systems. Recreations: nothing of special notability. Address: c/o Department of Biophysics, King's College, 26-29 Drury Lane, WC2. T: 01-836 8851.

BOYCOTT, Rev. D. M.; see Morse-Boycott.

BOYD, family name of **Baron Kilmarnock.**

BOYD OF MERTON, 1st Viscount cr 1960; **Alan Tindal Lennox-Boyd,** PC 1951; CH 1960; DL; Joint Vice-Chairman of Arthur Guinness, Son & Co. Ltd, since 1967 (Managing Director, 1960-67); Director, Imperial Chemical Industries, 1967-75; b 18 Nov. 1904; 2nd s of Alan Walter Lennox-Boyd, and Florence, d of James Warburton Begbie; m 1938, Lady Patricia Guinness, 2nd d of 2nd Earl of Iveagh, KG, CB, CMG, FRS; three s. Educ: Sherborne; Christ Church, Oxford (Scholar; MA; Beit Prizeman; Hon. Student, 1968). Pres. of the Oxford Union, 1926. Lieut RNVR, 1940-43. Contested Gower Div. of Glamorgan, 1929; MP (C) Mid-Beds, 1931-60; Parliamentary Sec., Ministry of Labour, 1938-39; Parliamentary Sec., Ministry of Home Security, 1939; Parliamentary Sec., Ministry of Food, 1939-40; Called to the Bar, Inner Temple, 1941; Parliamentary Sec., Ministry of Aircraft Production, 1943-45; Minister of State for Colonial Affairs, 1951-52; Minister of Transport and Civil Aviation, 1952-54; Sec. of State for the Colonies, 1954-Oct. 1959. Dir, Tate & Lyle, 1966-74. President: British Leprosy Relief Assoc., 1960-; Royal Commonwealth Soc., 1965- (Chm., 1961-64); Chairman: Voluntary Service Overseas, 1962-64; Brewers Soc., 1965; Trustee, BM, 1962-; Trustee, Natural History Museum, 1963-76; Governor, Sherborne Sch., 1962-, Chm. of Governors, 1968; Mem. Council, Institute of Directors, 1962-; Pres. Overseas Employers Federation, 1962-; Prime Warden, Goldsmiths' Co., 1964-65. Hon. Fellow, London Sch. of Hygiene and Tropical Medicine, 1977. Messel Medal, Soc. of Chemical Industry, 1966. DL Beds, 1954-61, Cornwall 1965. Heir: s Hon. Simon Donald Rupert Neville Lennox-Boyd [b 7 Dec. 1939; m 1962, Alice, d of late Major Meysey Clive, Whitfield, Hereford and of Lady Mary Clive; two s two d]. Address: Iveagh House, Ormond Yard, SW1. T: 01-839 4296; Ince Castle, Saltash, Cornwall. T: Saltash 2274. Clubs: Carlton, Pratt's, Buck's, Naval; Royal Yacht Squadron, Royal Western.

BOYD, Sir Alexander Walter, 3rd Bt, cr 1916; b 16 June 1934; s of late Cecil Anderson Boyd, MC, MD, and Marjorie Catharine, e d of late Francis Kinloch, JP, Shipka Lodge, North Berwick; S uncle, 1948; m 1958, Molly Madeline, d of late Ernest Arthur Rendell; two s three d. Heir: s Ian Walter Rendell Boyd, b 14 March 1964. Address: RR 3, Vernon, British Columbia, Canada.

BOYD, Arthur Merric Bloomfield, OBE 1970; painter; b 24 July 1920; s of William Merric Boyd and Doris Lucy Eleanor Gough; m 1945, Yvonne Hartland Lennie; one s two d. Educ: State Sch., Murrumbeena, Vic., Australia. Was taught painting and sculpture by parents and grandfather, Arthur Merric Boyd; first

exhibited painting in Melbourne, 1937; served in Australian Army, 1940-43; painted and exhibited, 1944-59, also sculptured and exhibited ceramics, 1953-56, in Australia; first visited Europe, 1959; first one-man exhibn painting, London, 1960; designed for Ballet at Edinburgh Festival and Sadler's Wells Theatre, 1961, and at Covent Garden Royal Opera House, 1963; retrospective exhibn of painting at Whitechapel Gallery, 1962; retrospective exhbn, Nat. Gallery of S Australia, Adelaide, 1964. Relevant publication: Arthur Boyd, by Franz Philipp, 1967. Address: c/o The Commercial Bank of Australia Ltd, 34 Piccadilly, W1.

BOYD, Christopher; see Boyd, T. C.

BOYD, Sir Francis; see Boyd, Sir J. F.

BOYD, Gavin, CBE 1977; Senior Partner, Boyds, solicitors, since 1974; Chairman: Stenhouse Holdings Ltd, since 1971; Scottish Opera Theatre Royal Ltd, since 1973; b 4 Aug. 1928; s of Gavin and Margaret Boyd; m 1954, Kathleen Elizabeth Skinner; one s. Educ: Glasgow Acad.; Univ. of Glasgow. MA (Hons); LLB. Partner, Boyds, solicitors, Glasgow, 1955-74. Director: Stenhouse Holdings Ltd, 1970-; Scottish Opera, 1970-; North Sea Assets Ltd 1972-; R. Paterson & Sons Ltd, 1972-; Scottish Television Ltd, 1973-; Ferranti Ltd, 1975-. Mem., Law Soc. of Scotland. Recreations: music and the performing arts, particularly opera; yacht racing and cruising. Address: 23 Cleveden Gardens, Glasgow G12 0PU. Clubs: Glasgow Art; Royal Northern Yacht.

BOYD, Maj.-Gen. Ian Herbert Fitzgerald, CB 1962; CBE 1957 (OBE 1950); b 21 Dec. 1907; s of late Sir Donald James Boyd, KCIE, Indian Civil Service, Punjab, and late Laura Caroline (née Hope); m 1931, Dorothy Margaret, d of Lewis French, CIE, CBE, ICS; two s one d. Educ: Fettes; RMA, Woolwich; Christ's Coll., Cambridge (BA). Commissioned RE 1927; served Mohmand, 1933; Waziristan, 1936 (despatches); Instr Staff Coll., Quetta, 1943-44; served Burma and Malaya, 1944-45 (despatches 4 times). Chief Instr SME, 1946-47; AA and QMG, War Office, 1948-50 (OBE); Col, Q (Movements), Far ELF, 1950-53; DQMG, BAOR, 1954-57; Chief Engineer, Far ELF, 1957-59; Chief Engineer, Northern Army Group and BAOR, 1959-62; retd, 1963. Col Comdt, Corps of Royal Engineers, 1966-72. Chm., Lewes Div., Cons. Assoc., 1972-75. Recreations: sailing, shooting, fishing, horology. Address: Primrose Hill, Barcombe, Lewes, E Sussex. T: Barcombe 203.

BOYD, Ian Robertson; HM Stipendiary Magistrate, sitting at Hull, since 1972; b 18 Oct. 1922; s of Arthur Robertson Boyd, Edinburgh, and Florence May Boyd (née Kinghorn), Leeds; m 1952, Joyce Mary Boyd (née Crabtree); one s one d. Educ: Roundhay Sch.; Leeds Univ. (LLB (Hons)). Served Army, 1942-47: Captain Green Howards; Royal Lincolnshire Regt in India, Burma, Malaya, Dutch East Indies. Leeds Univ., 1947; called to Bar, Middle Temple, 1952; practised North Eastern Circuit, 1952-72. Sometime Asst/Dep. Recorder of Doncaster, Newcastle, Hull and York. Recreation: gardener manqué. Address: Brooklands, Carr Lane, Thorner, near Leeds. T: Leeds 892232.

BOYD, James Fleming; Director General (Management), Board of Inland Revenue, since 1978; b 28 April 1920; s of late Walter and late Mary Boyd; m 1949, Daphne Steer, Hendon; one s one d. Educ: Whitehill Sch., Glasgow. Tax Officer, Inland Revenue, 1937; served with HM Forces, RAF, 1940-46; Inspector of Taxes, 1950; Principal Inspector, 1964; Senior Principal Inspector, 1970; Dep. Chief Inspector of Taxes, 1973; Dir of Operations, Inland Revenue, 1975-77. Recreations: history, gardening. Address: 2A The Avenue, Potters Bar, Herts EN6 1EB. T: Potters Bar 55905.

BOYD, Sir (John) Francis, Kt 1976; b 11 July 1910; s of John Crichton Dick Boyd and Kate Boyd, Ilkley, Yorks; m 1946, Margaret, d of George Dobson and Agnes Dobson, Scarborough, Yorks; one s two d. Educ: Ilkley Grammar Sch.; Silcoates Sch., near Wakefield, Yorks. Reporter: Leeds Mercury, 1928-34; Manchester Guardian, 1934-37; Parly Correspondent, Manchester Guardian, 1937-39. Aux. Fire Service, London, 1939; Monitoring Unit, BBC, 1940; Army, 1940-45. Political Correspondent, Manchester Guardian and Guardian, 1945-72; Political Editor, 1972-75. Chm., Lobby Journalists, 1949-50. Hon. LLD Leeds, 1973. Publications: Richard Austen Butler, 1956; (ed) The Glory of Parliament, by Harry Boardman, 1960; British Politics in Transition, 1964. Recreations: reading, walking, choral singing, gardening. Address: 17 Highgate Avenue, N6 5SB. T: 01-340 0812.

BOYD, John McFarlane, CBE 1974; General Secretary, Amalgamated Union of Engineering Workers, since 1975; *b* 8 Oct. 1917; *s* of James and Mary Boyd; *m* 1940, Elizabeth McIntyre; two *d. Educ:* Hamilton St Elem. Sch.; Glencairn Secondary Sch. Engrg apprentice, 1932-37; Engr, 1937-46. AUEW: Asst Div. Organiser, 1946-50; Div. Organiser, 1950-53; Mem. Executive, 1953-75. *Recreations:* brass banding, gardening. *Address:* Dalzell, 113 Woolstone Road, SE23. *T:* 01-699 9542.

BOYD, Brig. Sir John (Smith Knox), Kt 1958; OBE 1942; FRS 1951; MD, FRCP, DPH; *b* 18 Sept. 1891; *s* of J. K. Boyd, Largs, Ayrshire; *m* 1st, 1918, Elizabeth Edgar (*d* 1956); 2nd, 1957, Mary Bennett (*d* 1968), *d* of late Denis Harvey Murphy, Northwood. *Educ:* Largs Sch.; Glasgow Univ. (MB, ChB, 1913, Hons, Brunton Meml Prize; MD 1948, Hons, Bellahouston Gold Medal). Entered RAMC 1914; Lieut-Col 1938; Col 1944; Brig. 1945. Served European War, 1914-18; France and Belgium, 1914-15, Salonika, 1916-18. War of 1939-45, Middle East Force, 1940-43, North-West Europe, 1944-45; Dir of Pathology, War Office, 1945-46. KHP 1944-46; retired, 1946. Dir, Wellcome Laboratories of Tropical Medicine, 1946-55. Wellcome Trustee, 1956-66; Scientific Consultant to Wellcome Trust, 1966-68. Mem. of Colonial Medical Research Cttee, 1945-60; Member: Tropical Medicine Research Board, 1961-63; Army Pathology Advisory Cttee, 1946-74; Managing Cttee, Bureau of Hygiene and Trop. Diseases, 1956-1973. Chairman: Research Defence Soc., 1956-68; Medical Research Council Malaria Cttee and Leprosy Cttee, 1961-63; Royal Society Trop. Diseases Cttee, 1956-64. Hon. Sec., Royal Society of Trop. Medicine and Hygiene, 1946-57, Pres., 1957-59. Hon. FRCPE 1960; Hon. FRCPath, 1968; Hon. LLD Glasgow 1957; Hon. DSc Salford, 1969. Manson Medal, 1968. *Publications:* scientific papers on the pathology of tropical diseases and on bacterial viruses. *Recreation:* golf. *Address:* Mossbank, 6 The Covert, Northwood, Mddx. *T:* Northwood 22437. *Clubs:* Athenæum; Royal and Ancient (St Andrews).

BOYD, Lachlan Macpherson, CMG 1955; *b* 29 Sept. 1904; *s* of late Hugh Boyd, S Uist; *m* 1936, Betty Pinkerton, MBE 1958, *d* of late Dr Robert Scott, Exeter. *Educ:* Portree Secondary Sch.; Edinburgh Univ. Colonial Administrative Service, Uganda, 1930-46; Resident, Buganda, 1947-51; Sec. for African Affairs, 1951-55; Minister of Local Government, Uganda, 1955-60; retired, 1960. *Address:* Devoran, 33 Granary Lane, Budleigh Salterton, Devon. *T:* Budleigh Salterton 2452. *Clubs:* Royal Commonwealth Society, East Africa House.

BOYD, Leslie Balfour, CBE 1977; Courts Administrator, Central Criminal Court, 1972-77; *b* 25 Nov. 1914; *e s* of late Henry Leslie Boyd, Mem. of Lloyds, of Crowborough, Sussex, and Beatrix Boyd, *d* of Henry Chapman, for many years British Consul at Dieppe; *m* 1936, Wendy Marie, *d* of George and Nancy Blake, Oswestry, Salop; one *s* one *d. Educ:* Evelyn's; Royal Naval College, Dartmouth. Invalided out of Royal Navy, 1931. Called to the Bar, Gray's Inn, 1939; joined staff of Central Criminal Court, 1941; Dep. Clerk of Court, 1948; Clerk of the Court, 1955-71; Dep. Clerk of Peace, 1949-55, Clerk of the Peace, 1955-71, City of London and Town and Borough of Southwark. Master, Worshipful Company of Gold and Silver Wyre Drawers, 1969. *Publications:* contributor to Criminal Law and Juries titles, 3rd edn, Juries title, 4th edn, of Halsbury's Laws of England. *Recreations:* gardening and travel. *Address:* 12 Burgh Street, Islington, N1. *Club:* Bar Yacht.

BOYD, Prof. Maurice James; Professor of Latin, Queen's University, Belfast, 1939-76, now Emeritus; Chairman, N Ireland GCE Examinations Board; *b* 7 Jan. 1911; *s* of James Boyd, MA, LLB, Londonderry and Belfast; *m* 1936, Constance Eveline, *d* of Harry Marlow, JP, Croydon; two *s* one *d. Educ:* Royal Academical Instn, Belfast; Queen's Univ., Belfast (BA 1931); Trinity Coll., Oxford (MA). Asst and Junior Lecturer in Latin, Queen's Univ., Belfast, 1933-39; Dean of the Faculty of Arts, 1944-47 and 1956-57; Dean of the Faculty of Theology, 1962-68; Editor of Annual Record of QUB, 1940-49, 1959-71; Pres. QU Assoc., 1954; Chm. of Convocation, QUB, 1956-65. Mem., Belfast Educn and Library Bd, 1976-. MRIA 1968. *Publications:* articles in Classical Periodicals. *Address:* 8 Maryville Park, Belfast BT9 6LN. *T:* Belfast 665610.

BOYD, Prof. Robert Lewis Fullarton, CBE 1972; PhD; FRS 1969; Professor of Physics in the University of London since 1962; Director, Mullard Space Science Laboratory of Department of Physics and Astronomy of University College, London, since 1965; *b* 1922; *s* of late William John Boyd, PhD, BSc; *m* 1949, Mary, *d* of late John Higgins; two *s* one *d. Educ:* Whitgift Sch.; Imperial Coll., London; University Coll., London. BSc 1943, PhD 1949; FIEE 1967; FInstP 1972. Exp.

Officer at Admty Mining Estabt, 1943-46; DSIR Res. Asst, 1946-49; ICI Res. Fellow, 1949-50, Maths Dept, UCL; ICI Res. Fellow, Physics Dept, UCL, 1950-52; Lectr in Physics, UCL, 1952-58, Reader in Physics, UCL, 1959-62. Prof. of Astronomy (part-time), Royal Institution, 1961-67; IEE Appleton Lectr, 1976. Member: BBC Science Cons. Gp, 1970-; SRC, 1977-; Council, Physical Soc., 1958-60; Council, RAS, 1962-66 (Vice-Pres., 1964-66); Pres., Victoria Inst., 1965-76. Governor: Croydon Coll. of Tech. and Design, 1966-; St Lawrence Coll., 1965-. *Publications:* The Upper Atmosphere (with H. S. W. Massey), 1958; Space Research by Rocket and Satellite, 1960; Space Physics, 1975; papers in sci. jls on space sci. and other topics. *Recreation:* vintage Rolls Royce motor cars. *Address:* Ariel House, Holmbury St Mary, Dorking, Surrey.

BOYD, Robert Stanley; Under-Secretary (Principal Assistant Solicitor), Inland Revenue, since 1971; *b* 6 March 1927; *s* of Robert Reginald Boyd (formerly Indian Police) and Agnes Maria Dorothea, *d* of Lt-Col Charles H. Harrison; *m* 1965, Ann, *d* of Daniel Hopkin. *Educ:* Wellington; Trinity Coll., Dublin (BA, LLB). Served RN, 1945-48. Called to Bar, Inner Temple, 1954. Joined Inland Revenue, 1959. *Address:* 28 Canonbury Grove, N1 2HR.

BOYD, (Thomas) Christopher; farmer; *b* 1916; *m* ; one *s* two *d.* Army, 1940-44; civil servant, 1939 and 1944-48; MP (Lab) Bristol NW, 1955-59; Chelsea Borough Councillor, 1953-59. *Address:* Middlegill, Moffat, Dumfriesshire. *T:* Beattock 415.

BOYD, William, CC (Canada) 1968; *b* 21 June 1885; *s* of Dugald Cameron and Eliza M. Boyd; *m* Enid G. Christie. *Educ:* Trent Coll., Derbyshire; Edinburgh Univ. MB, ChB 1908; MD Edinburgh (Gold Medal), 1911; Diploma in Psychiatry, Edinburgh, 1912; MRCPE 1912; FRCP 1932; LLD Saskatchewan, 1937; MD Oslo, 1945; DSc Manitoba, 1948; FRCS Canada, 1949; FRCPE 1955; FRCSEd 1966; LLD Queen's, 1956. MO, Derby Borough Asylum, Derby, England, 1909-12; Pathologist, Winwick Asylum, Warrington, England, 1912-13; Pathologist, Royal Wolverhampton Hosp., Wolverhampton, 1913-14; Prof. of Pathology, University of Manitoba, Winnipeg, 1915-37; Prof. of Pathology and Bacteriology, University of Toronto, 1937-51, Prof. of Pathology, University of British Columbia, 1951-53. Capt. 3rd Field Ambulance, 46th Div. Imperial Forces, France, 1914-15. *Publications:* With a Field Ambulance at Ypres, 1917; The Physiology and Pathology of the Cerebrospinal Fluid, 1920; Pathology for the Surgeon, 8th edn, 1967; Pathology for the Physician, 7th edn, 1965; Text-Book of Pathology, 8th edn, 1970; Introduction to the Study of Disease, 6th edn, 1971; The Spontaneous Regression of Cancer, 1966. *Recreations:* mountaineering, golf, gardening. *Address:* 40 Arjay Crescent, Toronto, Ont, Canada.

BOYD-CARPENTER, family name of **Baron Boyd-Carpenter.**

BOYD-CARPENTER, Baron *cr* 1972 (Life Peer), of Crux Easton in the County of Southampton; **John Archibald Boyd-Carpenter,** PC 1954; DL; Chairman, Rugby Portland Cement, since 1977 (Deputy Chairman, 1976-77, Director, 1970-76); *b* 2 June 1908; *s* of late Sir Archibald Boyd-Carpenter, MP; *m* 1937, Margaret, *e d* of Lieut-Col G. L. Hall, OBE; one *s* two *d. Educ:* Stowe; Balliol Coll., Oxford. Pres. Oxford Union, 1930; BA (History, 1930); Diploma Economics, 1931; toured USA with Oxford Univ. Debating Team, 1931; Harmsworth Law Scholar, Middle Temple, 1933; Council of Legal Education's Prize for Constitutional Law, 1934; called to Bar, Middle Temple, 1934, and practised in London and SE Circuit. Contested (MR) Limehouse for LCC, 1934. Joined Scots Guards, 1940; held various staff appointments and served with AMG in Italy, retired with rank of Major. MP (C) for Kingston-upon-Thames, 1945-72; Financial Sec., to the Treasury, 1951-54; Minister of Transport and Civil Aviation, 1954-Dec. 1955; Minister of Pensions and National Insurance, Dec. 1955-July 1962; Chief Sec. to the Treasury and Paymaster-Gen., 1962-64; Opposition Front Bench Spokesman on Housing, Local Government and Land, 1964-66; Chm., Public Accounts Cttee, 1964-70. Chairman: Greater London Area Local Govt Cttee, Conservative Party, 1968; London Members Cttee, 1966-. Chm., CAA, 1972-77. Chairman: Orion Insurance Co., 1969-72; CLRP Investment Trust, 1970-72; Dir of other cos; Mem. Council, Trust Houses Forte Ltd, 1977-. High Steward, Royal Borough of Kingston-upon-Thames, 1973. DL Greater London, 1973. *Recreations:* tennis and swimming. *Address:* 12 Eaton Terrace, SW1. *T:* 01-730 7765; Crux Easton House, Crux Easton, near Highclere, Hants. *T:* Highclere 253037. *Club:* Carlton.

See also Baron Hailsham of Saint Marylebone.

BOYD-ROCHFORT, Sir Cecil (Charles), KCVO 1968 (CVO 1952); Trainer of Racehorses, Newmarket, retired 1968; *b* 16 April 1887; 3rd *s* of late Major R. H. Boyd-Rochfort, 15th Hussars, Middleton Park, Westmeath; *m* 1944, Hon. Mrs Henry Cecil, *d* of Sir James Burnett, of Leys, 13th Bt, CB, CMG, DSO; one *s. Educ:* Eton. Late Capt. Scots Guards (SR); served European War, 1914-18 (wounded, Croix de Guerre). *Relevant publication:* The Captain, by B. Curling, 1970. *Address:* Kilnahard Castle, Ballyheelan, Co. Cavan, Eire. *T:* Ballyheelan 112. *Clubs:* Turf; Kildare Street and University (Dublin).

BOYDELL, (The Worshipful Chancellor) Peter Thomas Sherrington, QC 1965; Chairman, Planning and Local Government Committee of the Bar, since 1973; Leader, Parliamentary Bar, since 1975; Chancellor of Dioceses of Truro since 1957, Oxford since 1958 and Worcester since 1959; *b* 20 Sept. 1920; *s* of late Frank Richard Boydell, JP, and late Frances Barton Boydell, Blenheim Lodge, Whitegate Drive, Blackpool; unmarried. *Educ:* Arnold Sch., Blackpool; Manchester Univ. LLB Manchester 1940. Served War of 1939-45; Adjt, 17th Field Regt, RA, 1943; Bde Major, 1st Armoured Div., RA, 1944; Bde Major, RA, 10th Indian Div., 1945. Qualified as Solicitor, 1947. Called to Bar, Middle Temple, 1948, Bencher, 1970. Mem., Legal Board of Church Assembly, 1958-71. Contested (C) Carlisle, 1964. *Recreations:* mountaineering, music, travel. *Address:* 45 Wilton Crescent, SW1. *T:* 01-235 5505; 2 Harcourt Buildings, Temple, EC4. *T:* 01-353 8415. *Clubs:* Garrick, Royal Automobile; Climbers.

BOYDEN, (Harold) James; MP (Lab) Bishop Auckland since Oct. 1959; *b* 19 Oct. 1910; *s* of late Claude James and late Frances Mary Boyden; *m* 1935, Emily Pemberton. *Educ:* Elementary Sch., Tiffin Boys, Kingston; King's Coll., London. BA (History), 1932; BSc (Econ), London External, 1943; Barrister-at-law, Lincoln's Inn, 1947. Pres., King's Coll. Union Soc., 1931-32. Master: Henry Mellish Grammar Sch., 1933-35; Tiffin Boys Sch., 1935-40; Lectr, Extra-Mural Depts of London, Nottingham and Southampton Univs, 1934-47. RAF, 1940-45; Sqdn-Ldr, 1944-45; Chief Training Officer, Admiralty, 1945-47; Dir Extra-Mural Studies, Durham Univ., 1947-59. Durham City and County Magistrate since 1951; CC for Durham City, 1952-59; Chm. Durham County Education Cttee, 1959. Vice-Chm. 1957-59; Chm., Exec. Cttee Nat. Inst. for Adult Education, 1958-61; Mem. Newcastle Regional Hospital Board, 1958-64; Fabian Soc. Executive, 1961-65. Jt Parly Under-Sec. of State, Dept of Education and Science, 1964-65; Parliamentary Sec., Ministry of Public Building and Works, 1965-67; Parly Under-Sec. (Army), MoD, 1967-69. Chm., Select Cttee of Expenditure, 1974-; Sec., Anglo-French Parly Cttee, 1974-. Overseas Lecture Tours: for Foreign Office, Germany, 1955 and 1957; for British Council, Ghana, Sierra Leone, 1956; Sierra Leone, 1961; for Admiralty, Malta, 1959. Member: WEA; Fabian Soc.; Nat. Union of General and Municipal Workers; National Trust; Council of Europe, 1970-73, WEU, 1970-73. FKC 1969. *Recreations:* walking, gardening, foreign travel, swimming, local government. *Address:* Appledown, The Avenue, Kingston, near Lewes, E Sussex. *T:* Lewes 3724. *Clubs:* South Church Workman's, Eldon Lane Workman's (Bishop Auckland); Southerne (Newton Aycliffe).

BOYES, Sir Brian Gerald B.; see Barratt-Boyes.

BOYES, James Ashley; Headmaster of City of London School since 1965; *b* 27 Aug. 1924; *s* of late Alfred Simeon Boyes and of Edith May Boyes; *m* 1st, 1949, Diana Fay (*née* Rothera), MA Cantab; two *d*; 2nd, 1973, April Tanner (*née* Rothery). *Educ:* Rugby Sch.; Clare Coll., Cambridge. Lieut RNVR; N Russian convoys and Brit. Pacific Fleet, 1942-46. Cambridge Univ., 1942, 1946-48; 1st class Hons Mod. Hist., 1948; Mellon Fellowship, Yale Univ., 1948-50; MA Yale, 1950. Asst Master, Rugby Sch., 1950-55; Headmaster, Kendal Grammar Sch., Westmorland, 1955-60; Dir of Studies, Royal Air Force Coll., Cranwell, 1960-65. *Recreations:* squash racquets, sailing. *Address:* City of London School, EC4; 12 Linver Road, SW6. *Clubs:* Royal Automobile, Hurlingham; Harlequins RUFC (Hon. Mem.); Hawks (Cambridge); Royal Windermere Yacht.

BOYES, Prof. John, FRCSE, FDS England, FDS Edinburgh; Professor of Dental Surgery, Edinburgh, since 1958; Hon. Dental Surgeon, Royal Victoria Infirmary, Newcastle; *b* 23 June 1912; *o s* of John and Helen Boyes; *m* 1946, Jean Wood; one *s. Educ:* George Watson's Coll., Edinburgh; Dental Sch. and Sch. of Medicine of the Royal Colleges, Edinburgh. House Surg. and Clinical Asst, Edinburgh Dental Hosp.; House Surg., Middx Hosp.; Res. Surgical Officer and Dental Surg., Plastic and Jaw Unit, Bangour EMS Hosp.; Br. Corresp. of Amer. Dental Assoc.; Mem. of Dental Advisory Cttee of RCSE; Nuffield Prof. of Oral Medicine, University of Durham; Sub-Dean of King's Coll., at Dental Sch.; Dir Newcastle upon Tyne Dental Hospital. *Publications:* Dental Analgesia in A Textbook of Anaesthetics, by Minnitt & Gillies. *Recreations:* book and picture collecting; hill walking. *Address:* University of Edinburgh, Edinburgh EH8 9YL. *Clubs:* Oral Surgery; Scottish Arts (Edinburgh); Cairngorm (Aberdeen).

BOYES, Kate Emily Tyrrell, (Mrs C. W. Sanders); Under-Secretary, Department of Trade, since 1972; *b* 22 April 1918; *e d* of S. F. Boyes, Sandiacre, Derbyshire; *m* 1944, Cyril Woods Sanders, *qv*; one *s* three *d. Educ:* Long Eaton Grammar Sch.; (Scholar) Newnham Coll., Cambridge. Economics Tripos, 1939; MA (Cantab). Administrative Class, Home Civil Service, 1939; Private Sec. to Parly Sec., 1942-45; Principal, 1945; Sec. to Council on Prices, Productivity and Incomes, 1958-60; Asst Sec., 1961; Speechwriter to President of Bd of Trade, 1963-64; Under-Sec., Europe, Industry and Technology Div., DTI, later Dept of Trade, 1972-. Mem., Council, National Trust, 1967-. *Recreations:* climbing, sailing, ski-ing, archæology. *Address:* 41 Smith Street, SW3 1NQ. *T:* 01-352 8053; Giles Point, Winchelsea, Sussex; Canower, Cashel, Connemara, Ireland. *Clubs:* Ski Club of Gt Britain; Island Cruising (Salcombe).

BOYLAND, Prof. Eric, PhD London, DSc Manchester; Professor of Biochemistry, University of London, at Chester Beatty Research Institute, Institute of Cancer Research, Royal Marsden Hospital (Free), Fulham Road, SW3, 1948-70, now Emeritus Professor; Visiting Professor in Environmental Toxicology, London School of Hygiene and Tropical Medicine, since 1970; *b* Manchester, 24 Feb. 1905; *s* of Alfred E. and Helen Boyland; *m* 1931, Margaret Esther, *d* of late Maj.-Gen. Sir Frederick Maurice, KCMG, CB; two *s* one *d. Educ:* Manchester Central High Sch.; Manchester Univ. BSc Tech. 1926; MSc 1928; DSc 1936. Research Asst in Physiology, Manchester Univ., 1926-28; Grocers' Company Scholar and Beit Memorial Fellow for Med. Research at Lister Institute for Preventive Medicine, 1928-30, and Kaiser Wilhelm Institut für Medizinische Forschung, Heidelberg, 1930-31; Physiological Chemist to Royal Cancer Hosp., London, 1931; Reader in Biochemistry, University of London, 1935-47. Research Officer in Ministry of Supply, 1941-44; Ministry of Agriculture, 1944-45. Consultant to Internat. Agency for Research on Cancer, Lyon, 1970-72; Member WHO Panel on Food Additives. Judd Award for Cancer Research, New York, 1948. *Publications:* The Biochemistry of Bladder Cancer, 1963; Modern Trends in Toxicology, vol. I, 1962, vol. II, 1974; scientific papers in biochemistry and pharmacology. *Recreations:* walking, looking at paintings. *Address:* 42 Bramerton Street, SW3. *T:* 01-352 2601; Maltmayes, Warnham, Horsham, Sussex. *T:* Oakwood Hill 428. *Clubs:* Athenæum; Chelsea Arts; Rucksack (Manchester).

BOYLE, family name of **Earls of Cork, Glasgow, and Shannon** and of **Baron Boyle of Handsworth.**

BOYLE, Viscount; Richard Henry John Boyle; *b* 19 Jan. 1960; *s* and *heir* of 9th Earl of Shannon, *qv*.

BOYLE OF HANDSWORTH, Baron *cr* 1970 (Life Peer), of Salehurst, Sussex; **Edward Charles Gurney Boyle;** Bt 1904; PC 1962; Vice-Chancellor of Leeds University, since 1970; Director, Penguin Books Ltd, since 1965; Chairman, Top Salaries Review Body, since 1971; *b* 31 Aug. 1923; *s* of 2nd Bt, and Beatrice (*d* 1961), *er d* of Henry Greig, Belvedere House, Kent; *S* father, 1945. *Educ:* Eton; Christ Church Oxford (Schol.) (MA). Temp. Junior Admin. Officer, FO, 1942-45; Mem., Oxford Union Debating Team, USA, Oct. 1947-Feb. 1948; Pres., Oxford Union Soc., Summer 1948; Parliamentary Candidate (U) Birmingham (Perry Bar), 1950; MP (C) Handsworth Div. of Birmingham, (Nov.) 1950-70; Parliamentary Private Sec. to the Under-Sec. for Air, 1951-52 and to the Parliamentary Sec. to the Ministry of Defence, 1952-53; Parliamentary Sec., Ministry of Supply, 1954-April 1955; Economic Sec. to the Treasury, 1955-56; Parliamentary Sec., Ministry of Education, 1957-59; Financial Sec. to the Treasury, Oct. 1959-July 1962; Minister of Education, 1962-64; Minister of State, Dept of Education and Science, April-Oct. 1964. Chm., Youth Service Development Council, 1962-64; President: Soc. of British Gas Industries, 1965-66; Johnson Soc., 1965-66; Incorporated Soc. of Preparatory Schools, 1970-74; Pro-Chancellor, Sussex Univ., 1965-70. Member: Fulton Cttee on Civil Service, 1966-68; IBRD Commn on Internat. Devolt, 1968-69; a UK Rep., High Council, European Univ. Inst., Florence, 1973-; Chm., Cttee of Vice-Chancellors and Principals, 1977-78. Trustee: British Museum; Acton Soc. Trust; Pilgrim Trust; a Governor: Ditchley Foundation; Brit. Inst. of Recorded Sound (Pres.). Lectures: Richard Feetham Memorial, on Academic Freedom, Univ. of Witwatersrand, 1965; Earl Grey, Univ. of Newcastle, 1966;

Sidney Ball Meml, Oxford, 1967; Eleanor Rathbone, Reading, 1969; Gregynog, UCW, 1972. Hon. FRCS 1976. Hon LLD: Leeds and Southampton, 1965; Bath, 1968; Sussex, 1972; Hon. DSc Aston in Birmingham, 1966. Hon. Freeman, Clothworkers' Co., 1975. *Publications:* (with C. A. R. Crosland and Prof. Kogan) The Politics of Education, 1971; (contrib.) The Philosophy of Karl Popper, 1974. *Heir* (to Baronetcy only): *b* Richard Gurney Boyle [*b* 14 May 1930; *m* 1961, Elizabeth Anne, *yr d* of Norman Dennes]. *Address:* The Vice-Chancellor's Lodge, Grosvenor Road, Leeds LS6 2DZ. *Clubs:* Athenæum, Carlton, Pratt's, Beefsteak.

BOYLE, Archibald Cabbourn, MD; FRCP; DPhysMed; Director, Department of Rheumatology, Middlesex Hospital; Senior Consultant Rheumatologist, Charterhouse Rheumatism Clinic; Consultant to BOAC; Hon. Clinical Adviser, Department of Rheumatological Research, Middlesex Hospital Medical School; *b* 14 March 1918; *s* of late Arthur Hislop Boyle and of Flora Ellen Boyle; *m* 1st, Patricia Evelyn Tallack (*d* 1944); one *d*; 2nd, Dorothy Evelyn, *widow* of Lieut G. B. Jones; one *s. Educ:* Dulwich Coll.; St Bartholomew's Hospital. House Physician, St Bartholomew's Hosp., 1941-42. Served War of 1939-45 in Far East, and later as Command Specialist in Physical Medicine. Registrar and Sen. Asst, 1946-49, and Asst Physician, 1949-54, Mddx Hosp.; Consultant in Physical Medicine, Bromley Gp of Hosps, 1950-54; Physician, Arthur Stanley Inst. for Rheumatic Diseases, 1950-65. Member: Bd of Governors, Mddx Hosp.; Bd of Governors, Charterhouse Rheumatism Clinic; Bd of Studies in Medicine, Univ. of London; Council, British Assoc. for Rheumatology and Rehabilitation (Pres., 1973-74); British League against Rheumatism (Vice-Pres., 1972-); Council, Section of Physical Medicine, RSM, 1950- (Pres., 1956-58; Vice-Pres., 1970-); Heberden Soc.; Cttee on Rheumatology and Rehabilitation, RCP. Ernest Fletcher Meml Lectr, RSM, 1971. Formerly: Examnr in Physical Medicine, RCP; Examnr to Chartered Soc. of Physiotherapy; Editor, Annals of Physical Medicine, 1956-63; Sec., Internat. Fedn of Physical Medicine, 1960-64; Chm., Physical Medicine Gp, BMA, 1956-58; Pres., London Br., Chartered Soc. of Physiotherapy. Former Member: Council, British Assoc. of Physical Medicine and Rheumatology, 1949-72 (Vice-Pres., 1965-68; Pres., 1970-72); Cttee on Chronic Rheumatic Diseases, RCP; Regional Scientific, and Educn, Sub-Cttees, Arthritis and Rheumatism Council; Physiotherapists Bd, Council for Professions Supplementary to Medicine; Central Consultants and Specialists Cttee, BMA; Med. Adv. Cttee, British Rheumatism and Arthritis Assoc. *Publications:* A Colour Atlas of Rheumatology, 1974; contribs to medical jls, mainly on rheumatic disease. *Recreation:* gardening. *Address:* 103 Harley Street, W1. *T:* 01-935 6111; Stall House, North Heath, Pulborough, Sussex. *T:* Pulborough 2137.

BOYLE, Marshal of the Royal Air Force Sir Dermot (Alexander), GCB 1957 (CB 1946); KCVO 1953; KBE 1953 (CBE 1945); AFC 1939; Vice-Chairman, British Aircraft Corporation, 1962-71; *b* 2 Oct. 1904; 2nd and *e* surv. *s* of A. F. Boyle, Belmont House, Queen's Co., Ire.; *m* 1931, Una Carey; two *s* one *d* (and one *s* decd). *Educ:* St Columba's Coll., Ireland; RAF (Cadet) Coll., Cranwell. Commissioned RAF 1924; Air ADC to the King, 1943; Air Commodore, 1944; Air Vice-Marshal, 1949; Air Marshal, 1954; Air Chief Marshal, 1956; Marshal of the Royal Air Force, 1958; Dir-Gen. of Personnel, Air Ministry, 1948-49; Dir-Gen. of Manning, Air Ministry, 1949-51; AOC No. 1 Group Bomber Command, 1951-53; AOC-in-C, Fighter Command, 1953-55; Chief of Air Staff, 1956-59. Master, Guild of Air Pilots and Air Navigators, 1965-66. Chairman: Bd of Trustees, RAF Museum, 1965-74; Ct of Governors, Mill Hill Sch., 1969-76; Dep. Chm., RAF Benevolent Fund, 1971-. J. P. Robertson Meml Trophy, Air Public Relations Assoc., 1973. *Address:* Pauls Place, Sway, Lymington, Hants. *Club:* Royal Air Force.

BOYLE, Rev. Desmond; *see* Boyle, Rev. J. D.

BOYLE, Prof. John Andrew; Professor of Persian Studies, University of Manchester, since 1966; *b* Worcester Park, Surrey, 1916; *e s* of William Andrew and Florence May Boyle; *m* 1945, Margaret Elizabeth, *er d* of Charles and Rose Dunbar; three *d. Educ:* Univs of Birmingham, Göttingen, Berlin and London. BA 1st cl. hons Birmingham 1936; PhD London 1947. Service with Royal Engrs, 1941; seconded to a special dept of FO, 1942-50; Manchester Univ.: Sen. Lectr in Persian Studies, 1950-59; Reader, 1959-66. Vis. Prof. of Persian, Univ. of California, Berkeley, 1959-60. Member: Governing Council, British Inst. of Persian Studies, 1964-; Editorial Bd, Cambridge History of Iran, 1966-; Adv. Bd, Iran-Shenasi (Tehran), 1969-; Gibb Memorial Trust, 1970-; Council, British Soc. for Middle Eastern Studies, 1973-; Cttee, Folklore Soc., 1973-. Chm., Anglo-Mongolian

Soc., 1970-. Hon. Fellow, Körösi Csoma Soc., 1973. Hon. MA Manchester, 1970. Order and Decoration of Sepass, Iran, 1958. *Publications:* A Practical Dictionary of the Persian Language, 1949; (trans.) Juvaini: History of the World-Conqueror, 1958; Modern Persian Grammar, 1966; (ed and contrib.) Cambridge History of Iran, Vol. V, 1968; (with Karl Jahn) Rashid al-Din Commemoration Volume (1318-1968), 1970; (trans.) Rashid al-Din: The Successors of Genghis Khan, 1971; The Mongol World Empire 1206-1370, 1977; (trans.) Farid al-Din 'Attar: The Ilahi-nama or Book of God, 1977; contrib. learned jls and encyclopaedias on Persian history and literature and the Mongol world empire. *Recreation:* motoring. *Address:* 266 Rye Bank Road, Manchester M21 1LY. *T:* 061-881 1161.

BOYLE, Rev. (John) Desmond, SJ; Chaplain at St John's, Beaumont, since 1967; *b* 29 Aug. 1897; 2nd *s* of late Patrick J. Boyle, Donamon, County Roscommon, Ireland, and Ellen Mary Ryan. *Educ:* Wimbledon Coll.; St Francis Xavier's Coll., Liverpool; Campion Hall, Oxford. Entered Soc. of Jesus, 1913; ordained Priest, 1929; Prefect of Studies, Beaumont Coll., 1931-50; Rector, Beaumont Coll., 1947-50; Rector, Heythrop Coll., 1950-52; Provincial of Eng. Prov. of Soc. of Jesus, 1952-58; Rector of Stonyhurst Coll., 1958-64; Chaplain, Beaumont Coll., 1964-67. *Address:* St John's, Beaumont, Old Windsor, Berks. *T:* Egham 2428.

BOYLE, Kay, (Baroness Joseph von Franckenstein); writer; Professor in English Department, California State University, San Francisco; *b* St Paul, Minn, USA, 19 Feb. 1903; *d* of Howard Peterson Boyle; *m* 1921, 1931 and 1943; one *s* five *d.* Mem. National Institute of Arts and Letters, 1958. O Henry Memorial Prize for best short story of the year, 1936, 1941; Guggenheim Fellowship, 1934, 1961; Center for Advanced Studies Wesleyan Univ. Fellowship, 1963; Radcliffe Inst. for Independent Study, 1965. Writer-in-residence, Hollins Coll., Virginia, 1971. Hon. DLitt, Columbia Coll., Chicago, 1971; Hon. DHL Skidmore Coll., 1977. *Publications: novels:* Plagued by the Nightingale; Year Before Last; Gentlemen, I Address You Privately; My Next Bride; Death of a Man; Monday Night; Primer for Combat; Avalanche; A Frenchman Must Die; "1939": His Human Majesty; The Seagull on the Step, 1955; Three Short Novels, 1958; Generation Without Farewell, 1959; The Underground Woman, 1975; *volumes of short stories:* Wedding Day; The First Lover; The White Horses of Vienna; The Crazy Hunter; Thirty Short Stories; The Smoking Mountain; Nothing Ever Breaks Except the Heart, 1966; The Autobiography of Emanuel Carnevali, 1967; Being Geniuses Together, 1968; Breaking the Silence (essay), 1962; The Long Walk at San Francisco State and other essays, 1970; *poetry:* A Glad Day; American Citizen; Collected Poems, 1962; Testament for my Students and other poems, 1970. *For Children:* The Youngest Camel; Pinky, the Cat Who Liked to Sleep, 1966; Pinky in Persia, 1968. *Recreations:* ski-ing, mountain climbing. *Address:* c/o Ann Watkins Inc., 77 Park Avenue, New York, NY 10016, USA.

BOYLE, Lawrence, JP; Chief Executive, Strathclyde Regional Council, since 1974; *b* 31 Jan. 1920; *s* of Hugh Boyle and Kate (*née* Callaghan); *m* 1952, Mary McWilliam; one *s* three *d. Educ:* Holy Cross Acad., Leith, Edinburgh; Edinburgh Univ. BCom, PhD; IPFA; FBIM. Depute County Treasurer, Midlothian CC, 1958-62; Depute City Chamberlain, Glasgow, 1962-70; City Chamberlain, Glasgow, 1970-74. JP Glasgow, 1971. *Publications:* Equalisation and the Future of Local Government Finance, 1966; numerous articles and papers in economic jls, etc. *Recreation:* music. *Address:* 24 Broomburn Drive, Newton Mearns, Glasgow. *T:* 041-639 3776.

BOYLE, Leonard Butler, CBE 1977; Director since 1971 and General Manager since 1956, Principality Building Society, Cardiff; *b* 13 Jan. 1913; *s* of Harold and Edith Boyle; *m* 1938, Alice Baldwin Yarborough; two *s. Educ:* Roundhay Sch., Leeds. FBS. Chief of Investment Dept, Leeds Permanent Building Soc., 1937; Asst Man., Isle of Thanet Bldg Soc., 1949; Jt Asst Gen. Man., Hastings and Thanet Bldg Soc., 1951, Sec. 1954. Building Socs Assoc.: Mem. Council, 1956- (Chm. Gen. Purposes Cttee, 1958-60; Chm. Develt Cttee, 1967-71); Chm. of Council, 1973-75 (Dep. Chm. 1971-73). *Recreations:* gardening, walking, golf. *Address:* Greenlawns, Robinswood Crescent, Penarth, South Glamorgan. *T:* Penarth 701204. *Club:* Cardiff and County (Cardiff).

BOYLES, Edgar William; Under Secretary, Inland Revenue, since 1975; *b* 24 March 1921; *s* of William John Boyles and Jessie Louisa Boyles; *m* 1950, Heather Iris Hobart, SRN; three *s* one *d. Educ:* Bedford Modern Sch. RAF, 1940-46. Tax Officer, Inland Revenue, 1939; Principal Inspector of Taxes, 1962; Sen. Principal Inspector, 1967. *Recreations:* chess, gardening, watching cricket. *Address:* The Angles, 2 Limes Avenue, Horley, Surrey RH6 9DH. *T:* Horley 4546.

BOYNE, 10th Viscount *cr* 1717; **Gustavus Michael George Hamilton-Russell,** DL; JP; Baron Hamilton, 1715; Baron Brancepeth, 1866; Deputy Chairman, Telford Development Corporation, since 1975 (Member, since 1963); *b* 10 Dec. 1931; *s* of late Hon. Gustavus Lascelles Hamilton-Russell and *g s* of 9th Viscount; *S* grandfather, 1942; *m* 1956, Rosemary Anne, 2nd *d* of Major Sir Dennis Stucley, Bt, *qv*; one *s* three *d. Educ:* Eton; Sandhurst; Royal Agricl Coll., Cirencester. Commissioned Grenadier Guards, 1952. JP 1961, DL 1965, Salop. Dir, Nat. Westminster Bank, 1976- (Chm., W Midlands and Wales Regional Bd). Governor, Wrekin Coll., Telford. Pres., St John Ambulance Brigade, Salop. CStJ. *Heir: s* Hon. Gustavus Michael Stucley Hamilton-Russell, *b* 27 May 1965. *Address:* Burwarton House, Bridgnorth, Salop. *T:* Burwarton 203. *Club:* Turf.
See also Baron Forbes.

BOYNE, Sir Henry Brian, (Sir Harry Boyne), Kt 1976; CBE 1969; Political Correspondent, The Daily Telegraph, London, 1956-76; *b* 29 July 1910; 2nd *s* of late Lockhart Alexander Boyne, Journalist, Inverness, and late Elizabeth Jane Mactavish; *m* 1935, Margaret Little Templeton, Dundee; one *d. Educ:* High Sch. and Royal Academy, Inverness. Reporter, Inverness Courier, 1927; Dundee Courier and Advertiser, 1929. On active service, 1939-45, retiring with rank of Major, The Black Watch (RHR). Staff Correspondent, Glasgow Herald, at Dundee, 1945, and Edinburgh, 1949; Political Correspondent, Glasgow Herald, 1950. Chairman: Parly Lobby Journalists, 1958-59 (Hon. Sec., 1968-71); Parly Press Gallery, 1961-62. Political Writer of Year, 1972. *Recreations:* reading, playgoing, cycling. *Address:* 11 Marsham Court, Westminster, SW1P 4JY. *T:* 01-834 8863. *Clubs:* Victory; Western (Dundee).

BOYNTON, John Keyworth, MC 1944; LLB; MRTPI; DL; Chief Executive, Cheshire County Council, since 1974; solicitor; *b* 14 Feb. 1918; *s* of late Ernest Boynton, Hull; *m* 1947, Gabrielle Stanglmaier, Munich; two *d. Educ:* Dulwich Coll. Served War, 15th Scottish Reconnaissance Regt, 1940-46 (despatches, MC). Dep. Clerk, Berks CC, 1951-64; Clerk, Cheshire CC, 1964-74. Member: Planning Law Cttee of Law Soc., 1964; Economic Planning Council for NW, 1965; Exec. Council of Royal Inst. of Public Admin., 1970; Council of Industrial Soc., 1974. Pres., RTPI, 1976. DL Cheshire 1975. *Publications:* A Practical Guide to Compulsory Purchase and Compensation, 1964 (4th edn 1977); articles for: The Times; legal and local papers. *Recreation:* golf. *Address:* 3 Hough Green, Chester CH4 8JG. *T:* Chester 22703. *Club:* Army and Navy.

BOYS-SMITH, Captain Humphry Gilbert, DSO 1940; DSC 1943; RD; RNR, retired; *b* 20 Dec. 1904; *s* of late Rev. Edward Percy Boys Smith, MA, Rural Dean of Lyndhurst, Hants, and Charlotte Cecilia, *d* of late Thomas Backhouse Sandwith, CB, HM Consular Service; *m* 1935, Marjorie Helen, *d* of Capt. Matthew John Miles Vicars-Miles, JP; no *c. Educ:* Pangbourne Nautical Coll. Joined Royal Naval Reserve, 1921; Merchant Navy, 1922-35; Extra Master's Certificate, 1930; HM Colonial Service, 1935-40 (Palestine) and 1946-50 (Western Pacific High Commission as Marine Supt); Addnl Mem. RNR Advisory Cttee, 1949-51; War Course, Royal Naval Coll., Greenwich, 1950-51. Courtaulds Ltd, Central Staff Dept, 1951-68. Placed on Retired List of RNR, 1952; Younger Brother of Trinity House, 1944; Mem. of Hon Company of Master Mariners, 1946; Assoc. Instn Naval Architects, 1948; served War of 1939-45 (DSO and Bar, DSC, despatches and American despatches). *Address:* Mark Beacon, Mockbeggar, Ringwood, Hants. *T:* Ringwood 3469.

BOYS SMITH, Rev. John Sandwith, MA; Master of St John's College, Cambridge, 1959-69 (Fellow, 1927-59 and since 1969; Senior Bursar, 1944-59); Vice-Chancellor, University of Cambridge, 1963-65; Canon Emeritus of Ely Cathedral since 1948; *b* 8 Jan. 1901; *s* of late Rev. E. P. Boys Smith, formerly Vicar of Hordle, Hants, and Charlotte Cecilia, *e d* of late T. B. Sandwith, CB; *m* 1942, Gwendolen Sara, *o d* of late W. J. Wynn; two *s. Educ:* Sherborne Sch.; St John's Coll., Cambridge. Economics Tripos Part I, Class II, division 2, 1921; BA, Theological Tripos, Part I, Sec. B, Class I, 1922; Scholar and Naden Student in Divinity, St John's Coll., 1922; Theological Tripos Part II, Sec. V, Class 1, 1924; Burney Student, 1924; Marburg University, 1924-25; Deacon, 1926; Curate of Sutton Coldfield, Birmingham, 1926-27; Priest, 1927; Chaplain of St John's Coll., Cambridge, 1927-34, and Director of Theological Studies, 1927-40, and 1944-52; Assistant Tutor, 1931-34; Tutor, 1934-39; Junior Bursar, 1939-40; University Lecturer in Divinity, Cambridge, 1931-40; Stanton Lecturer in the

Philosophy of Religion, Cambridge Univ., 1934-37; Ely Professor of Divinity in the University of Cambridge and Canon of Ely Cathedral, 1940-43. Hon. Fellow: Trinity Coll., Dublin, 1968; Darwin Coll., Cambridge, 1969. Hon. LLD, Cambridge, 1970. *Publication:* (with late J. M. Creed) Religious Thought in the Eighteenth Century, 1934. *Address:* Trinity House, 2 Castle Street, Saffron Walden, Essex CB10 1BP. *T:* Saffron Walden 23692; St John's College, Cambridge.

BOYSE, Edward Arthur, MD; FRS 1977; Member, Sloan-Kettering Institute for Cancer Research, New York, since 1967; *b* 11 Aug. 1923; *s* of late Arthur Boyse, FRCO, and Dorothy Vera Boyse (*née* Mellersh); *m* 1951, Jeanette (*née* Grimwood); two *s* one *d. Educ:* St Bartholomew's Hosp. Med. Sch., Univ. of London. MB BS 1952; MD 1957. Aircrew, RAF, 1941-46, commnd 1943. Various hospital appts, 1952-57; research at Guy's Hosp., 1957-60; research appts at NY Univ. and Sloan-Kettering Inst., 1960-. Prof. of Biology, Cornell, 1969. Mem., Amer. Acad. of Arts and Scis, 1977. Cancer Research Institute Award in Tumor Immunology, 1975; Isaac Adler Award, Rockefeller and Harvard Univs, 1976. *Publications:* papers relating genetics and immunology to development and cancer. *Address:* 245 East 68th Street, New York, NY 10021, USA. *T:* (212) 861-2373.

BOYSON, Dr Rhodes; MP (C) Brent North, since Feb. 1974; *b* 11 May 1925; *s* of Alderman William Boyson, MBE, JP and Mrs Bertha Boyson, Haslingden, Rossendale, Lancs; *m* 1st, 1946, Violet Burletson (marr. diss.); two *d*; 2nd. 1971, Florette MacFarlane. *Educ:* Haslingden Grammar Sch.; UC Cardiff; Manchester Univ.; LSE; Corpus Christi Coll., Cambridge. BA, MA, PhD. Served with Royal Navy. Headmaster: Lea Bank Secondary Modern Sch., Rossendale, 1955-61; Robert Montefiore Secondary Sch., Stepney, 1961-66; Highbury Grammar Sch., 1966-67; Highbury Grove Sch., 1967-74. Chairman: Nat. Council for Educnl Standards; Churchill Press; Constitutional Book Club; Councillor: Haslingden, 1957-61; Waltham Forest, 1968-74 (Chm. Establishment Cttee, 1968-71); Chm., London Boroughs Management Services Unit, 1968-70. Formerly Youth Warden, Lancs Youth Clubs. Contested (C) Eccles, 1970. Vice-Chm., Cons Parly Educn Cttee, 1975-76; Hon. Sec. Cons. Adv. Cttee on Educn, 1975-; Opposition spokesman on educn, 1976-. Educnl columnist, Spectator, 1969. *Publications:* The North-East Lancashire Poor Law 1838-1871, 1965; The Ashworth Cotton Enterprise, 1970; (ed) Right Turn, 1970; (ed) Down with the Poor, 1971; (ed) Goodbye to Nationalisation, 1972; (ed) Education: Threatened Standards, 1972; (ed) The Accountability of Schools, 1973; Oversubscribed: the story of Highbury Grove, 1974; Crisis in Education, 1975; (jt ed) Black Papers on Education; (ed) 1985: An Escape from Orwell's 1984, 1975. *Recreations:* gardening, reading, writing, talk, hard work, meeting friends, inciting the millenialistic Left in education and politics. *Address:* Laneham, 71 Paines Lane, Pinner, Harrow, Mddx. *T:* 01-866 2071; House of Commons, SW1. *Club:* St Stephen's.

BOZZOLI, Guerino Renzo, DSc(Eng); Vice-Chancellor and Principal, University of the Witwatersrand, Johannesburg, since 1969; *b* Pretoria, 24 April 1911; *s* of late B. Bozzoli; *m* 1936, Cora Collins, *d* of late L. N. B. Collins; one *s* three *d. Educ:* Sunnyside Sch. and Boys' High Sch., Pretoria; Witwatersrand Univ. BSc(Eng) 1933, DSc(Eng) 1948; PrEng. Major, SA Corps of Signals, 1940-45 (commendation 1944). Asst Engr, African Broadcasting Co., 1934-36; Jun. Lectr, Dept of Electrical Engrg, Witwatersrand Univ., Lectr, 1939, Sen. Lectr, 1942; apptd Prof. and Head of Dept of Electrical Engineering, 1948. Dean, Univ. Residence, Cottesloe, 1948-56; Dean, Faculty of Engrg, 1954-57 and 1962-65; Senate Mem., Council of the Univ., 1957-68; Deputy Vice-Chancellor, 1965-68. Member: Straszacker Commn of Enquiry into Univ. Educn of Engineers, 1957-68; de Vries Commn of Enquiry into SA Univs, 1968-75; Nat. Educn Council, 1975-. President: SAIEE, 1955; AS&TS of SA, 1969-70; SA Assoc. for Advancement of Science, 1972. Hon. FSAIEE; Hon LLD, Univ. of Cape Town. *Publications:* numerous articles and papers on engineering education. *Recreations:* swimming, woodwork, electronics. *Address:* 13 Jubilee Road, Parktown, Johannesburg, South Africa. *T:* 642-4969. *Clubs:* Rand, Johannesburg. Scientific and Technical (all in Johannesburg).

BRAADLAND, Erik; diplomat, retired; *b* 21 Nov. 1910; *m* 1940, Aase Rydtun; one *s* two *d. Educ:* Oslo Univ. (Degree in Economics). Served in Hamburg, Marseille, Stockholm, Berlin; various periods Ministry of Foreign Affairs, Oslo; Acting Head of Military Mission in Berlin, 1949; Chargé d'Affaires at Bonn, 1951; Minister in Belgrade, 1952; Ambassador in Moscow, 1954-58, in London, 1959-61, for Norway; Mem. of Storting, 1961-69. Knight Commander, Order of St Olav; Order of the Yugoslav

Flag, 1st Class. *Address:* Oer, 1750 Halden, Norway. *Clubs:* Norwegian, London; Norske Selskab (Oslo).

BRABAZON, family name of **Earl of Meath.**

BRABAZON OF TARA, 3rd Baron *cr* 1942; **Ivon Anthony Moore-Brabazon;** Member of the Stock Exchange, since 1972; *b* 20 Dec. 1946; *s* of 2nd Baron Brabazon of Tara, CBE, and of Henriette Mary, *d* of late Sir Rowland Clegg; *S* father, 1974. *Educ:* Harrow. *Recreations:* sailing, Cresta Run. *Heir:* none. *Address:* 24 Sloane Gardens, SW1. *T:* 01-730 6376; The Watch House, Bembridge, Isle of Wight. *Clubs:* White's; Bembridge Sailing, St Moritz Tobogganing.

BRABHAM, John Arthur, (Jack Brabham), OBE 1966; retired, 1970, as Professional Racing Driver; Managing Director: Jack Brabham (Motors) Ltd; Jack Brabham (Worcester Park) Ltd; Brabham Racing Organisation Ltd; Engine Developments Ltd; *b* Sydney, Australia, 2 April 1926; *m* 1951, Betty Evelyn; three *s*. *Educ:* Hurstville Technical Coll., Sydney. Served in RAAF, 1944-46. Started own engineering business, 1946; Midget Speedway racing, 1946-52; several championships (Australian, NSW, South Australian); numerous wins driving a Cooper-Bristol, Australia, 1953-54; to Europe, 1955; Australian Grand Prix, 1955 and 1963 (debut of Repco Brabham); World Champion Formula II, 1958, also many firsts including Casablanca, Goodwood, Brands Hatch, NZ Grand Prix, Belgian Grand Prix; Formula II Champion of France, 1964. World Champion Driver: (after first full Formula I Season with 2½-litre car), 1959-60, 1960-61, 1966. First in Monaco and British Grandes Epreuves, 1959; won Grand Prix of: Holland, Belgium, France, Britain, Portugal, Denmark, 1960; Belgium, 1961. Elected Driver of the Year by Guild of Motoring Writers, 1959, 1966 and 1970, Sportsman of the Year by Australian Broadcasting Co., 1959; left Cooper to take up building own Grand Prix cars, 1961; debut, 1962; first ever constructor/driver to score world championship points, 1963; cars finished first: French GP; Mexican GP, 1964; Formula II and Formula III cars world-wide success, 1963; awarded Ferodo Trophy, 1964 and again, 1966; won French Grand Prix and British Grand Prix, 1966; won French Grand Prix, 1967. RAC Gold Medal, 1966; BARC Gold Medal, 1959, 1966, 1967; Formula I Manufacturers' Championship, 1966, 1967. *Publications:* Jack Brabham's Book of Motor Racing, 1960; When the Flag Drops, 1971; contribs to British journals. *Recreations:* photography, water ski-ing, under-water swimming, flying. *Address:* c/o 248 Hook Road, Chessington, Surrey. *T:* 01-397 4343. *Clubs:* Royal Automobile, British Racing and Sports Car, British Racing Drivers'; Australian Racing Drivers'.

BRABOURNE, 7th Baron, *cr* 1880; **John Ulick Knatchbull,** 16th Bt, *cr* 1641; film and television producer; *b* 9 Nov. 1924; *s* of 5th Baron and Lady Doreen Geraldine Browne (Order of the Crown of India; DStJ), *y d* of 6th Marquess of Sligo; *S* brother, 1943; *m* 1946, Lady Patricia Edwina Victoria Mountbatten, CD, JP, DL, *er d* of Earl Mountbatten of Burma, *qv*; five *s* (including twin *s*) two *d. Educ:* Eton; Oxford. Films Produced: Harry Black, 1958; Sink the Bismarck!, 1959; HMS Defiant, 1961; Othello, 1965; The Mikado, 1966; Romeo and Juliet; Up the Junction, 1967; Dance of Death, 1968; Tales of Beatrix Potter, 1971; Murder on the Orient Express, 1974. TV Series: National Gallery, 1974; A Much-Maligned Monarch, 1976. Pres., Kent Trust for Nature Conservation; Vice-Pres., RSA; Chairman: Council, Caldecott Community; Governors, Norton Knatchbull Sch.; Governor: Wye Coll.; Gordonstoun Sch.; United World Colleges; Mem. Council, Univ. of Kent. *Heir: s* Hon. Norton Louis Philip Knatchbull, *b* 8 Oct. 1947. *Address:* Newhouse, Mersham, Ashford, Kent. *T:* Ashford 23466; GW Films Ltd, 41 Montpelier Walk, SW7 1JH. *T:* 01-589 8829.

BRABY, Frederick Cyrus, CBE 1962; MC 1918; DL; CEng, FIMechE; Hon. Major; retired, from Frederick Braby and Co. Ltd, etc.; *b* 1 May 1897; *e s* of late Cyrus and Mabel Braby (*née* Weddell), of Sutton, Surrey, and High Hurstwood, Sussex; *m* 1931, Margaret Isabel (*d* 1975), *e d* of late F. H. Marshall, Sutton and Hove; no *c. Educ:* Charterhouse; Manchester Univ. (BSc (Eng.)). Served 1915-19 with Lancashire Fusiliers (wounded twice, despatches, MC), and 1921-23 in TA. Apprenticeship with Metropolitan-Vickers Electrical Co. Ltd, Manchester, 1922-24; joined Frederick Braby & Co. Ltd (estab. 1839), 1925, and held various appointments; Director, 1929; Chairman, 1942-65. President: Engineering and Allied Employers' London & District Assoc., 1941-43; Nat. Council, Building Material Producers, 1960-65; Chairman: Industrial Coal Consumers' Council, 1958-65; British Non-Ferrous Metals Res. Assoc., 1958-64. Member of UK Employer/Trade Union Mission to USA, 1941; Vice-President, Engineering and Allied Employers' National Federation, 1952-56; President, 1956-58.

County Commissioner (Kent), Boy Scouts Assoc., 1952-67; Member, Sevenoaks RDC, 1963-70; a Governor, Star and Garter Home for Disabled Sailors, Soldiers and Airmen, 1963-73, Vice-Pres., 1974-; Master, Carpenters' Company, 1968-69 (Warden, 1965-68). DL (Kent), 1955. *Recreations:* fishing, photography. *Address:* Great Maythan Hall, Rolvenden, Cranbrook, Kent.

BRACEGIRDLE, Dr Brian, FRPS, FIBiol; Keeper, Wellcome Museum of the History of Medicine, Science Museum, London, since 1977; *b* 31 May 1933; *o c* of Alfred Bracegirdle; *m* 1st, 1958, Margaret Lucy Merrett (marr. diss. 1974); one *d* ; 2nd, 1975, Patricia Helen Miles; no *c. Educ:* King's Sch., Macclesfield; Univ. of London (BSc, PhD). DipRMS. FRPS 1969; FIBiol 1976. Technician in industry, 1950-57; Biology Master, Erith Grammar Sch., 1958-61; Sen. Lectr in Biol., S Katharine's Coll., London, 1961-64; Head, Depts of Nat. Science and Learning Resources, Coll. of All Saints, London, 1964-77. Recognised Teacher, Univ. of London, 1969-; Chief Examr in Zool., London, 1970-76; Hon. Res. Fellow, University Coll. London. Sec., then Chm., Inst. of Med. and Biol Illustration, 1971-75; Past Chm., Fellowship and Associateship panel, Royal Photographic Soc. Member: Council, RMS; Council, Brit. Soc. for History of Science. *Publications:* Photography for Books and Reports, 1970; The Archaeology of the Industrial Revolution, 1973; The Evolution of Microtechnique, 1978; (with W. H. Freeman): An Atlas of Embryology, 1963; An Atlas of Histology, 1966; An Atlas of Invertebrate Structure, 1971; An Advanced Atlas of Histology, 1976; (with P. H. Miles): An Atlas of Plant Structure, vol. I, 1971; An Atlas of Plant Structure, Vol. II, 1973; Thomas Telford, 1973; The Darbys and the Ironbridge Gorge, 1974; An Atlas of Chordate Structure, 1977; papers on photography for life sciences, on scientific topics, and on history of science/medicine. *Recreations:* walking, music, travel. *Address:* 67 Limerston Street, Chelsea SW10 0BL. *T:* 01-351 0548.

BRACEWELL, Joyanne Winifred, (Mrs Roy Copeland); a Recorder of the Crown Court, since Nov. 1975; barrister-at-law; *b* 5 July 1934; *d* of Jack and Lilian Bracewell; *m* 1963, Roy Copeland; one *s* one *d. Educ:* Manchester Univ. (LLB, LLM). Called to Bar, Gray's Inn, 1955; pupillage at the Bar, 1955-56; in practice, Northern Circuit, 1956-. *Recreations:* antiques, cooking, reading, walking, bridge. *Address:* (home) Springfield, Macclesfield Road, Alderley Edge, Cheshire SK9 7BW. *T:* Alderley 582000; (chambers) Sunlight House, 12th Floor, Quay Street, Manchester M3 3LA. *T:* 061-236 8418.

BRACEWELL-SMITH, Sir Guy, 3rd Bt *cr* 1947; *b* 12 Dec. 1952; *er s* of Sir George Bracewell Smith, 2nd Bt, MBE, and Helene Marie (*d* 1975), *d* of late John Frederick Hydock, Philadelphia, USA; *S* father, 1976. *Educ:* Harrow. *Heir: b* Charles Bracewell-Smith, *b* 13 Oct. 1955. *Address:* Park Lane Hotel, Piccadilly, W1A 4UA.

BRADBROOK, Prof. Muriel Clara, MA, PhD, 1933; LittD Cantab 1955; *b* 27 April 1909; *d* of Samuel Bradbrook, Supt HM Waterguard at Liverpool and Glasgow. *Educ:* Hutchesons' Sch., Glasgow; Oldershaw Sch., Wallasey; Girton Coll., Cambridge. English Tripos, Class I, 1929, 1930; Harness Prize, 1931, Allen Scholar, 1935-36; in residence, Somerville Coll., Oxford, 1935-36. Cambridge University: Univ. Lecturer, 1945-62; Reader, 1962-65; Professor of English, 1965-76; Mistress of Girton College, 1968-76 (Vice-Mistress, 1962-66; Fellow, 1932-35 and 1936-75). Board of Trade, Industries and Manufactures Depts 2 and 3, 1941-45; in residence at Folger Library, Washington, and Huntington Library, California, 1958-59; Tour of the Far East for Shakespeare's Fourth Centenary, 1964; Trustee, Shakespeare's Birthplace, 1967; Freedom of the City of Hiroshima; Visiting Professor: Santa Cruz, California, 1966; Kuwait, 1969; Tokyo, 1975; Clark Lecturer, Trinity Coll., Cambridge, 1968. FRSL 1947. Hon. LittD: Liverpool, 1964; Sussex, 1972; London, 1973; Hon. LLD Smith Coll., USA, 1965; Hon. PhD, Gothenburg, 1975. Foreign Member Norwegian Acad. of Arts and Sciences, 1966; Hon. Mem., Mod. Lang. Assoc. of America, 1974. *Publications:* Elizabethan Stage Conditions, 1932; Themes and Conventions of Elizabethan Tragedy, 1934; The School of Night, 1936; Andrew Marvell (with M. G. Lloyd Thomas), 1940; Joseph Conrad, 1941; Ibsen the Norwegian, 1947; T. S. Eliot, 1950; Shakespeare and Elizabethan Poetry, 1951; The Queen's Garland, 1953; The Growth and Structure of Elizabethan Comedy, 1955; Sir Thomas Malory, 1957; The Rise of the Common Player, 1962; English Dramatic Form, 1965; That Infidel Place, 1969; Shakespeare the Craftsman, 1969; Literature in Action, 1972; Malcolm Lowry: his art and early life, 1974; The Living Monument, 1976; numerous articles and reviews. *Recreations:* travel, theatre. *Address:* 91 Chesterton Road, Cambridge CB4

3AP. *T:* Cambridge 52765. *Clubs:* University Women's; ADC (Cambridge).

BRADBURY, family name of **Baron Bradbury.**

BRADBURY, 2nd Baron, *cr* 1925, of Winsford; **John Bradbury;** *b* 7 Jan. 1914; *s* of 1st Baron Bradbury, GCB, and Hilda (*d* 1949), 2nd *d* of W. A. Kirby; *S* father 1950; *m* 1st, 1939, Joan, *o d* of W. D. Knight, Darley, Addlestone, Surrey; one *s* one *d*; 2nd, 1946, Gwerfyl, *d* of late E. S. Roberts, Gellifor, Ruthin; one *d. Educ:* Westminster; Brasenose Coll., Oxford. *Heir:* s Hon. John Bradbury [*b* 17 March 1940; *m* 1968, Susan, *d* of late W. Liddiard, East Shefford, Berks; one *s*]. *Address:* Sunridge, Downsway, Merrow, Guildford, Surrey. *T:* Guildford 66204.

BRADBURY, Edgar; Managing Director, Skelmersdale Development Corporation, since 1976; *b* 5 June 1927; *s* of Edgar Furniss Bradbury and Mary Bradbury; *m* 1954, Janet Mary Bouchier Lisle; two *s* one *d. Educ:* Grove Park Sch., Wrexham; The High Sch., Newcastle, Staffs; King's Coll., Durham Univ. LLB (Hons). Solicitor. Asst Solicitor: Scarborough BC, 1952-54; St Helens CBC, 1954-57; Dep. Town Clerk, Loughborough, 1957-59; Town Clerk and Clerk of the Peace, Deal, 1960-63; Legal Dir, Skelmersdale Develt Corp., 1963-76. *Recreations:* tennis, bridge. *Address:* Overdale, Granville Park, Aughton, Ormskirk. *T:* Aughton Green 422308.

BRADBURY, (Elizabeth) Joyce, CBE 1970; Headmistress of Thornhill School (co-educational comprehensive), Sunderland, since 1972; *b* Newcastle upon Tyne, 12 Dec. 1918; *o c* of Thomas Edwin and Anne Bradbury. *Educ:* private sch.; Queen Elizabeth's Grammar Sch., Middleton, near Manchester; Univ. of Leeds. BA (Hons Hist.); Dip. in Educn. Various teaching appts, 1941-57; Dep. Headmistress, Stand Grammar Sch. for Girls, Whitefield, near Manchester, 1957-59; Headmistress: Bede Grammar Sch. for Girls, Sunderland, 1959-67; Pennywell Sch. (co-educnl comprehensive), 1967-72. President, Association of Headmistresses, 1974-76. *Recreations:* travel at home and abroad, walking, pursuing historical interests, music and the theatre, domestic 'arts'. *Address:* 6 Cliffe Court, Roker, Sunderland SR6 9NT. *T:* Sunderland 77135. *Clubs:* Soroptimist, British Federation of University Women.

BRADBURY, Surgeon Vice-Adm. Sir **Eric (Blackburn),** KBE 1971; CB 1968; FRCS 1972; Medical Director-General of the Navy, 1969-72; *b* 2 March 1911; *s* of late A. B. Bradbury, Masse, Co. Antrim; *m* 1939, Elizabeth Constance Austin; three *d. Educ:* Royal Belfast Academical Instn; Queen's Univ., Belfast; MB, BCh 1934; DMRD (London) 1949; Hon. LLD 1973. Joined RN (Medical Service), 1934; served at sea in HMS Barham, HMS Endeavour, HMS Cumberland, 1935-38 and in HMS Charybdis and HMHS Oxfordshire, 1941-45; served in RN Hospitals: Haslar, Chatham, Plymouth and Malta; Med. Officer-in-Charge, RN Hosp., Haslar, and Comd MO, Portsmouth, 1966-69. QHP 1966-72. *Address:* The Gate House, Nevill Park, Tunbridge Wells, Kent. *T:* 27661. *Club:* Army and Navy.

BRADBURY, Joyce; see Bradbury, E. J.

BRADBURY, Prof. Malcolm Stanley; FRSL; Professor of American Studies, University of East Anglia, since 1970; *b* 7 Sept. 1932; *s* of Arthur Bradbury and Doris Ethel (*née* Marshall); *m* 1959, Elizabeth Salt; two *s. Educ:* University Coll. of Leicester (BA); Queen Mary Coll., Univ. of London (MA); Univ. of Manchester (PhD). Staff Tutor in Literature and Drama, Dept of Adult Education, Univ. of Hull, 1959-61; Lectr in English Language and Literature, Dept of English, Univ. of Birmingham, 1961-65; Lectr (later Sen. Lectr and Reader) in English and American Literature, Sch. of English and American Studies, Univ. of East Anglia, 1965-70. Visiting Prof., Univ. of Zürich, 1972. *Publications:* Eating People is Wrong (novel), 1959; Evelyn Waugh, 1962; E. M. Forster: a collection of critical essays (ed), 1965; Stepping Westward (novel), 1965; What is a Novel?, 1969; A Passage to India: a casebook, 1970; (ed) Penguin Companion to Literature, vol. 3: American (with E. Mottram), 1971; The Social Context of Modern English Literature, 1972; Possibilities: essays on the state of the novel, 1973; The History Man (novel), 1975; (with J. W. McFarlane) Modernism, 1976; Who Do You Think You Are? (short stories), 1976; (ed) The Novel Today, 1977. *Recreations:* none. *Address:* School of English and American Studies, University of East Anglia, Norwich NR4 7TJ. *T:* Norwich 56161.

BRADBURY, Ray Douglas; author; *b* Waukegan, Ill, USA, 22 Aug. 1920; *s* of Leonard S. Bradbury and Esther Moberg; *m* 1947, Marguerite Susan McClure; four *d. Educ:* Los Angeles High Sch. First Science-Fiction stories, 1941-44; stories sold to Harpers', Mademoiselle, The New Yorker, etc., 1945-56. Stories selected for: Best American Short Stories, 1946, 1948, 1952, 1958; O. Henry Prize Stories, 1947, 1948; and for inclusion in numerous anthologies. Benjamin Franklin Award for Best Story Published in an American Magazine of General Circulation, 1954; 1000 dollar Grant from Institute of Arts and Letters, 1954. *Publications:* Dark Carnival, 1947; The Martian Chronicles, 1950; The Illustrated Man, 1951; The Golden Apples of the Sun, 1953; Fahrenheit 451, 1953; Switch on the Night, 1955; The October Country, 1955; Dandelion Wine (novel), 1957; A Medicine for Melancholy (English publication as The Day It Rained Forever), 1959; Something Wicked This Way Comes (novel), 1962; R Is For Rocket (short stories), 1962; The Anthem Sprinters (one-act plays), 1963; The Machineries of Joy (short stories), 1964; The World of Ray Bradbury (one-act plays), 1964; The Wonderful Ice Cream Suit and The Day It Rained Forever (one-act plays), 1965; The Vintage Bradbury (stories), 1965; I Sing the Body Electric (short stories), 1969; When Elephants Last in the Dooryard Bloomed (poems), 1973; Pillar of Fire (plays), 1975; Long After Midnight (stories), 1976; Where Robot Mice and Robot Men Run Round in Robot Towns (Poems), 1977; *screenplays for:* Moby Dick; The Dreamers; And The Rock Cried Out. *Recreations:* oil painting, ceramics, collecting native masks. *Address:* 10265 Cheviot Drive, Los Angeles, Calif 90064, USA.

BRADBURY, Rear-Adm. Thomas Henry; Flag Officer, Admiralty Interview Board, since 1977; *b* 4 Dec. 1922; *s* of Thomas Henry Bradbury and Violet Buckingham; *m* 1945, Beryl Doreen Evans; one *s* one *d. Educ:* Christ's Hosp. rcds 1972. CO HMS Jufair, 1960-62; Supply Officer, HMS Hermes, 1965-67; Sec. to Controller of Navy, MoD, 1967-70; CO HMS Terror, 1970-71; RCDS, 1972; Dir, Naval Admin. Planning, MoD, 1974-76. *Recreations:* sailing, gardening. *Address:* Dean House, Court Road, Lee-on-Solent, Hants. *T:* Portsmouth 22351, ext. 842387.

BRADBY, Edward Lawrence; Principal, St Paul's College, Cheltenham, 1949-72; *b* 15 March 1907; *y s* of late H. C. Bradby, Ringshall End, near Berkhamsted, Herts; *m* 1939, Bertha Woodall, *y d* of late Henry Woodall, Yotes Court, Mereworth, Maidstone; three *s* one *d. Educ:* Rugby Sch.; New College, Oxford (MA). Asst Master, Merchant Taylors' Sch., 1930-34; International Student Service, 1934-39; Secretary to Cttee for England and Wales, 1934-36; Asst General Secretary, Geneva, 1936-37; General Secretary, Geneva, 1937-39; Principal, Royal Coll., Colombo, Ceylon, 1939-46; Principal, Eastbourne Emergency Training Coll., 1946-49. Hon. MEd Bristol, 1972. *Publications:* Editor, The University Outside Europe, a collection of essays on university institutions in 14 countries, 1939. *Address:* Beech House, Seend, Melksham, Wilts. *T:* Seend 456. *Club:* Royal Commonwealth Society.

BRADDELL, Dorothy Adelaide; decorative-artist; *b* London; *d* of J. L. Bussé; *m* 1914, Darcy Braddell (*d* 1970); one *s* one *d. Educ:* Miss Manville's Sch.; King's Coll., London. Studied art at Regent Street Polytechnic and at Byam Shaw School of Art; won National Gold Medal for decorative design; is chiefly known as a designer of interior decoration and a domestic planner and has been associated largely with all kinds of exhibition work, being responsible for rooms at the Royal Academy Exhibition of Industrial Art, the British Pavilion, Paris Exhibition, 1938, Dorland Hall Exhibitions of British Industrial Art, Ideal Home Exhibitions, the Empire Exhibition, Glasgow, 1938, and Britain Can Make It Exhibition, 1946. *Address:* 8 Lansdowne Road, Holland Park, W11. *T:* 01-727 5487.
See also Sir John G. N. Brown.

BRADDON, Russell Reading; author; *b* 25 Jan. 1921; *s* of Henry Russell Braddon and Thelma Doris Braddon (*née* Reading). *Educ:* Sydney Church of England Grammar Sch.; Sydney Univ. (BA). Failed Law finals; began writing, by chance, 1949; been writing ever since. *Publications:* The Piddingtons, 1950; The Naked Island, 1951; Those in Peril, 1954; Cheshire, VC, 1954; Out of the Storm, 1956; Nancy Wake, 1956; End of a Hate, 1958; Gabriel Comes to 24, 1958; Proud American Boy, 1960; Joan Sutherland, 1962; The Year of the Angry Rabbit, 1964; Roy Thomson of Fleet Street, 1965; Committal Chamber, 1966; When the Enemy is Tired, 1968; The Inseparables, 1968; Will You Walk a Little Faster, 1969; The Siege, 1969; Prelude and Fugue for Lovers, 1971; The Progress of Private Lilyworth, 1971; End Play, 1972; Suez: splitting of a nation, 1973; The Hundred Days of Darien, 1974; All the Queen's Men, 1977; The Finalists, 1977. *Recreations:* reading, bridge, squash, not writing. *Address:* c/o John Farquharson Ltd, 15 Red Lion Square, WC1.

BRADEN, Bernard; free-lance actor and dabbler; television performer; *b* 16 May 1916; *s* of Rev. Dr Edwin Donald Braden and Mary Evelyn Chastey; *m* 1942, Barbara Kelly; one *s* two *d. Educ:* Maple Grove Public Sch., Point Grey Junior High Sch., Magee High Sch., Vancouver, Canada. Radio engineer, announcer, singer, actor in Vancouver, Canada, 1937-40; wrote and performed in plays for Canadian Broadcasting Corporation, 1940-43; went to Toronto, 1943; wrote and produced plays for Canadian Broadcasting Corporation, 1943-49; came to England, 1949. London plays include: Street-Car Named Desire; Biggest Thief in Town; The Man; No News From Father; Anniversary Waltz; The Gimmick; Period of Adjustment; Spoon River Anthology. Also performs for radio, television and films. Hon. Chancellor, London School of Economics, 1955. *Publication:* These English (Canada), 1948. *Recreations:* family, tennis, swimming.

BRADFORD, 6th Earl of, *cr* 1815; **Gerald Michael Orlando Bridgeman**, TD; JP; Bt 1600; Baron Bradford, 1794; Viscount Newport, 1815; Captain Shropshire Yeomanry, TARO (retired); Vice-Lieutenant of Shropshire, 1970-74; *b* 29 Sept. 1911; *o s* of 5th Earl of Bradford and Hon. Margaret Cecilia Bruce (*d* 1949), *e d* of 2nd Baron Aberdare; *S* father, 1957; *m* 1946, Mary Willoughby, *er d* of Lt-Col T. H. Montgomery, DSO, Cadogan House, Shrewsbury; two *s* two *d. Educ:* Harrow; Trinity Coll., Cambridge (MA). Served War of 1939-45 (despatches). President, Country Landowners' Assoc., 1955-57; Crown Estate Commissioner, 1956-67. President Timber Growers' Organisation, 1962-64; Chairman: NW Midland Region, Nat. Trust; Forestry Cttee of Great Britain, 1964-66; President, Soil Assoc., 1951-70, Patron, 1970. Chairman of Governors, Harper Adams Agricultural Coll., 1956-73. JP 1949, DL 1951, Salop. *Heir: s* Viscount Newport, *qv. Address:* Weston Park, Shifnal, Salop. *T:* Weston-under-Lizard 218; 61d Eaton Square, SW1. *T:* 01-235 4942. *Clubs:* Farmers', Ski, MCC.
See also Sir Valentine Abdy, Bt.

BRADFORD, Bishop of, since 1972; **Rt. Rev. Ross Sydney Hook,** MC 1945; *b* 19 Feb. 1917; *o s* of late Sydney Frank and Laura Harriet Hook; *m* 1948, Ruth Leslie, *d* of late Rev. Herman Masterman Biddell and Violet Marjorie Biddell; one *s* one *d. Educ:* Christ's Hosp.; Peterhouse, Cambridge (MA); Ridley Hall, Cambridge, Asst Curate, Milton, Hants, 1941-43. Chaplain, RNVR (Royal Marine Commandos), 1943-46. Chaplain, Ridley Hall, Cambridge, 1946-48. Select Preacher, University of Cambridge, 1948; Rector, Chorlton-cum-Hardy, Manchester, 1948-52; Rector and Rural Dean, Chelsea, 1952-61; Chaplain: Chelsea Hosp. for Women, 1954-61; St Luke's Hosp., Chelsea, 1957-61; Residentiary Canon of Rochester and Precentor, 1961-65; Treasurer, 1965; Diocesan Dir of Post Ordination Training, 1961-65; Bishop Suffragan of Grantham, 1965-72. Examining Chaplain to Bishop of Rochester, 1961-65, to Bishop of Lincoln, 1966-72; Prebendary of Brampton (Lincoln Cathedral), 1966-72; Dean of Stamford, 1971-72. Chm., Inspections Cttee, Central Advisory Council for the Ministry, 1966-71 (Sec., 1960-66). *Recreation:* cricket. *Address:* Bishopscroft, Ashwell Road, Bradford, W Yorks BD9 4AU. *Club:* Army and Navy.

BRADFORD, Provost of; *see* Jackson, Very Rev. B. D.

BRADFORD, Archdeacon of; *see* Sargeant, Ven. F. P.

BRADFORD, (Sir) Edward Alexander Slade, 5th Bt, *cr* 1902 (but does not use the title); *b* 18 June 1952; *s* of Major Sir Edward Montagu Andrew Bradford, 3rd Bt (*d* 1952) and his 2nd wife, Marjorie Edith (*née* Bere); *S* half-brother, Sir John Ridley Evelyn Bradford, 4th Bt, 1954. *Heir: uncle* Donald Clifton Bradford [*b* 22 May 1914; *m* 1949, Constance Mary Morgan; three *d*]. *Address:* Faith Cottage, Pett, near Hastings, E Sussex.

BRADFORD, Prof. Eric Watts, MDS (Sheffield); DDSc (St Andrews); Professor of Dental Surgery, University of Bristol, since 1959; Dean of the Faculty of Medicine, since 1975; *b* 4 Nov. 1919; *e s* of E. J. G. and C. M. Bradford; *m* 1946, Norah Mary Longmuir; two *s* three *d. Educ:* King Edward VII Sch., Sheffield; High Storrs Grammar Sch., Sheffield; Univ. of Sheffield (Robert Styring Scholar). LDS, Sheffield, 1943; BDS, Sheffield, 1944; MDS, Sheffield, 1950; DDSc St Andrews, 1954. Lieut, Army Dental Corps, Nov. 1944; Capt. Nov. 1945. Lectr, Univ. of Sheffield, 1947-52; Senior Lectr, Univ. of St Andrews, 1952-59. *Publications:* many papers on dental anatomy in British and other journals. *Address:* 11 Grove Road, Coombe Dingle, Bristol BS9 2RQ. *T:* 681849.

BRADFORD, Ernle; independent free-lance writer, principally on historical subjects; *b* 11 Jan. 1922; *s* of Jocelyn Ernle Bradford and Ada Louisa (*née* Dusgate); *m* 1957, Marie Blanche Thompson; one *s. Educ:* Uppingham Sch. RNVR, 1940-46 (despatches 1943). Founder Editor, Antique Dealer and

Collectors' Guide, 1947. *Publications:* Contemporary Jewellery and Silver Design, 1950; Four Centuries of European Jewellery, 1953 (new edn 1968); The Journeying Moon, 1958; The Mighty 'Hood', 1959 (paperback 1974, new edn 1975); English Victorian Jewellery, 1959 (new edn 1968); The Wind off the Island, 1960; Southward the Caravels: the story of Henry the Navigator, 1961; The Great Siege, 1961 (paperback 1964); The Touchstone, 1962; Antique Collecting, 1963; Companion Guide to the Greek Islands, 1963 (3rd edn 1975); Dictionary of Antiques, 1963; Ulysses Found, 1963; Three Centuries of Sailing, 1964; The America's Cup, 1964; Drake, 1965; Wall of England, 1966; The Great Betrayal: Constantinople, 1204, 1967 (new edn 1975); The Sultan's Admiral: the life of Barbarossa, 1969; Antique Furniture, 1970; Cleopatra, 1971 (paperback 1974); Gibraltar: the history of a fortress, 1971; Mediterranean: portrait of a sea, 1971; The Shield and the Sword: the Knights of St John, 1973 (paperback 1974); Christopher Columbus, 1973; The Sword and the Scimitar: the saga of the crusades, 1974; Paul the Traveller, 1975; Nelson, 1977. *Recreations:* swimming, sailing, idling. *Address:* Marina House, Kalkara, Malta. *T:* Malta 20191. *Club:* Casino Maltese (Malta).

BRADFORD, Ven. Richard Bleaden; Archdeacon of Carlisle, 1970-78; Chaplain to The Queen, since 1973; *b* 12 Jan. 1913; *s* of Percival Richard and May Anne Bradford; *m* 1939, Beryl Elizabeth Stanley; two *s* three *d. Educ:* LSE. BA London, 1st cl. hons Med. and Mod. History. Vicar: of St Luke, Barrow-in-Furness, 1942; of St Aidan, Carlisle, 1951; Chaplain to Bp of Carlisle, 1946-66; Proctor in Convocation, 1951-67; Vicar: of Ainstable and Armathwaite, 1957; of Penrith, 1960; Residentiary Canon, Carlisle Cathedral, 1966-78; Church Comr, 1968-73; Mem., General Synod, 1971-78. *Address:* c/o 19 Castle Street, Carlisle, Cumbria.

BRADFORD, Rev. Robert John; MP (UU) Belfast South since 1974; Minister of Suffolk Methodist Church; *b* 1941. *Educ:* Queen's Univ., Belfast. Worker in Lenadoon area of Belfast, 1970-; contested (Vanguard) Assembly election, Northern Ireland. *Recreation:* formerly Association football (Soccer blue, Queen's Univ.). *Address:* House of Commons, SW1A 0AA.

BRADFORD, Rt. Hon. Roy Hamilton, PC (NI) 1969; Member (U) for East Belfast, Northern Ireland Assembly, 1973-75; Minister for the Environment, Northern Ireland Executive, 1973-74; *b* 7 July 1921; *s* of Joseph Hamilton Bradford, Rockcorry, Co. Monaghan, and Isabel Mary (*née* McNamee), Donemana, Co. Tyrone; *m* 1946, Hazel Elizabeth, *d* of Capt. W. Lindsay, Belfast; two *s. Educ:* Royal Belfast Academical Institution; Trinity Coll., Dublin. Foundation Schol. 1940; First Class Hons (BA) German and French (with Gold Medal) 1942 (TCD). Army Intelligence, 1943-47 (France, Belgium, Germany). BBC and ITV Producer and Writer, 1950-. Dir, Geoffrey Sharp Ltd, 1962-. MP (U) for Victoria, Parlt of NI, 1965-73; Asst Whip (Unionist Party), 1966; Parly Sec., Min. of Educn, 1967; Chief Whip, Sept. 1968-April 1969; Minister of Commerce, NI, 1969-71; Minister of Develt, NI, 1971-72. Contested (Off U) North Down, 1974. *Publication:* Excelsior (novel), 1960. *Recreations:* golf, architecture. *Address:* Ardkeen, Carnalea, Bangor, Co. Down, N Ireland. *T:* Bangor 65012. *Club:* Ulster (Belfast).

BRADFORD HILL, Sir Austin; *see* Hill.

BRADING, Keith, CB 1974; MBE 1944; Chief Registrar of Friendly Societies and Industrial Assurance Commissioner, since 1972; *b* 23 Aug. 1917; *s* of late Frederick C. Brading and late Lilian P. Brading (*née* Courtney); *m* 1949, Mary Blanche Robinson. *Educ:* Portsmouth Grammar Sch. Called to Bar, Gray's Inn, 1950. Entered Inland Revenue (Estate Duty Office), 1936. Served War, Royal Navy, 1941-46 (Lieut RNVR); Solicitor's Office, Inland Revenue, 1950; Asst Solicitor, 1962; Asst Registrar of Friendly Societies and Dep. Industrial Assurance Commissioner, 1969. *Address:* 35 Chiswick Staithe, W4. *T:* 01-995 0517. *Clubs:* Savile; Royal Naval and Royal Albert Yacht (Portsmouth).

BRADING, Brig. Norman Baldwin, CMG 1958; CBE 1945; retired; *b* 25 May 1896; *s* of late Rev. F. C. Brading, Ditton, Kent; *m* Helen Margaret, *d* of G. Gatey, Windermere; one *s* one *d. Educ:* Whitgift; Royal Military College, Sandhurst. 2nd Lieut East Surrey Regt, 1915; served European War, 1914-19 (wounded); War of 1939-45; France, Holland, Germany; despatches, 1945; Lieut-Col 1940, Col 1943, Brig. 1944. Lent to UNO as Dep. Dir for Ops in Brit. Zone of Germany; National Health Services, 1949; lent to Nigerian Govt as House Governor, University Coll. Hospital, Ibadan, Nigeria, 1952. FHA. Knight Comdr Order of Orange Nassau, with swords (Netherlands), 1945. *Recreations:* polo, swimming. *Address:*

Newlands, Sion Hill, Bath. *T:* Bath 317805. *Club:* Royal Over-Seas League.

BRADLAW, Prof. Sir Robert (Vivian), Kt 1965; CBE 1950; Hon. Professor of Oral Pathology, Royal College of Surgeons of England, since 1948; Emeritus Professor of Oral Medicine, University of London; Consultant, Royal Navy; Chairman, Advisory Council on the Misuse of Drugs, since 1976; *b* 14 April 1905; *s* of Philip Archibald Bradlaw, Blackrock, Co. Dublin; unmarried. *Educ:* Cranleigh; Guy's Hosp.; University of London. Hilton Prize, etc, Guy's Hosp.; Hon. Degrees, Univs of Belfast, Boston, Durham, Malta, Melbourne, Meshed, Montreal and Newcastle upon Tyne; Fellow, Royal Colleges of Surgeons of England, Edinburgh, Glasgow, Ireland, etc; Hon. Fellow, RSM, 1975. Tomes Prize for Research, RCS 1939-41; Howard Mummery Prize for Research, BDA, 1948-53; Colyer Gold Medal, RCS; Hunterian Prof., RCS 1955; Hon. Gold Medal, RCS, 1972; Chevalier de la Santé Publique (France), 1950; Knight, Order of St Olaf, Norway; Commander, Order of Homayoun, Iran. *Recreations:* fishing, shooting, orchids, oriental ceramics. *Address:* The Manse, Stoke Goldington, Newport Pagnell, Bucks. *Club:* Athenæum.

BRADLEY, Clive; Chief Executive and Secretary, Publishers Association, since 1976; *b* 25 July 1934; *s* of Alfred and Kathleen Bradley. *Educ:* Felsted Sch., Essex; Clare Coll., Cambridge (MA); Yale Univ. (Mellon Fellow). Barrister-at-Law. Broadcasting Officer, Labour Party, 1963-64; Political Editor, Statist, 1965-67; Gp Labour Adviser, Internat. Publishing Corp. Ltd, 1967-69; Newspaper Exec. (IPC and Observer), 1969-75. Broadcaster on current affairs. Governor, Felsted Sch. *Publications:* various articles and pamphlets on politics, economics, the press, television, industrial relations. *Recreations:* walking, travel. *Address:* 2 Upper Wimpole Street, W1. *Clubs:* Reform; Elizabethan (Yale).

BRADLEY, Prof. Daniel Joseph, PhD; FRS 1976; Professor of Optics since 1973 and Head of Physics Department since 1976, Imperial College of Science and Technology, London; *b* 18 Jan. 1928; *s* of John Columba Bradley and Margaret Mary Bradley; *m* 1958, Winefride Marie Therese O'Connor; four *s* one *d*. *Educ:* St Columb's Coll., Londonderry; St Mary's Trng Coll., Belfast; Birkbeck and Royal Holloway Colls, London (BSc Maths, BSc Physics, PhD). Primary Sch. Teacher, Londonderry, 1947-53; Secondary Sch. Teacher, London area, 1953-57; Asst Lectr, Royal Holloway Coll., 1957-60; Lectr, Imperial Coll. of Science and Technol., 1960-64; Reader, Royal Holloway Coll., 1964-66; Prof. and Head of Dept of Pure and Applied Physics, QUB, 1966-73. Vis. Scientist, MIT, 1965; Consultant, Harvard Observatory, 1966. Lectures: Scott, Cambridge, 1977; Tolansky Meml, RSA, 1977. Chm., Laser Facility Cttee, SRC, 1976-; Mem., Rutherford Lab. Estab. Cttee, SRC, 1977-. MRIA 1969; Fellow, Optical Soc. of America, 1975. Thomas Young Medal, Inst. of Physics, 1975. *Publications:* papers on optics, lasers, spectroscopy, chronoscopy and astronomy in Proc. Roy. Soc., Phil. Mag., Phys. Rev., J. Opt. Soc. Amer., Proc. IEEE, Chem. Phys. Letts, Optics Communications. *Recreations:* television, walking, manual labour. *Address:* 73 Lambton Road, SW20. *T:* 01-946 1459. *Club:* Athenæum.

BRADLEY, Edgar Leonard; Metropolitan Stipendiary Magistrate, since 1967; *b* 17 Nov. 1917; 2nd *s* of Ernest Henry and Letitia Bradley, W. Felton, Oswestry; *m* 1942, Elsa, *o d* of Colin and Elizabeth Matheson, Edinburgh; two *s* three *d*. *Educ:* Malvern Coll.; Trinity Hall, Cambridge. BA 1939; MA 1944. Called to Bar, Middle Temple, 1940. Served 1940-46, RA; Capt. and Adjt, 1943-45; Major, GSO2, Mil. Govt of Germany, 1946. Practised at Bar, 1946-51, SE Circuit, Central Criminal Ct, S London and Surrey Sessions. Legal Dept of Home Office, 1951-54. Sec., Departmental Cttee on Magistrates' Courts Bill, 1952; Sec. of Magistrates' Courts Rule Cttee, 1952-54; Clerk to Justices: Wrexham and Bromfield, 1954-57; Poole, 1957-67. Justices' Clerks Society: Mem. Council, 1957-67; Hon. Sec., 1963-67. Mem., Nat. Adv. Council on Trng of Magistrates, 1965-67; Magistrates' Association: Mem. Council, 1968-; Chm. Legal Cttee, 1973-. Adv. tour of Magistrates' Courts in Ghana, 1970. *Publications:* (with J. J. Senior) Bail in Magistrates' Courts, 1977; articles in legal jls. *Recreations:* gardening, golf. *Address:* Camberwell Green Magistrates' Court, SE5. *T:* 01-703 0909.

BRADLEY, Gladys Lilian; Head Mistress, Fairfield High School for Girls, Droylsden, Manchester, 1941-60; *d* of late T. R. Bradley. *Educ:* The Cowley Sch. for Girls, St Helens; Chester City and County High Sch. for Girls (now City High Sch. for Girls, Chester); Manchester Univ. (Scholar). BA (Hons Eng.). Asst Mistress: Withington Girls' Sch., Manchester; Havergal Coll., Toronto; Miss Edgar's and Miss Cramp's Sch., Incorp.,

Montreal; Gunnerside Sch., Plymouth; Head of English Dept, Cowley Sch. for Girls, St Helens; Head Mistress, Farringtons Sch., Chislehurst, Kent (at Trecarn, Babbacombe, S Devon) Sept. 1939-Dec. 1940 (closed for duration of War). *Publications:* Punctuation Hints and Exercises, 1934; sundry articles on youth and Girl Guide work, 1925-30. *Recreations:* walking, boating, swimming, riding, travelling. *Address:* 6 Belvedere Court, Mooragh Promenade, Ramsey, Isle of Man. *T:* Ramsey 814049. *Club:* University Women's.

BRADLEY, Harry, CBE 1951; (First) Director, British Boot, Shoe and Allied Trades Research Association (SATRA), 1922-63, retired; Emeritus President, British Boot and Shoe Institution; *b* 1897; *s* of late George Craven Bradley, Silsden, Yorks; *m* 1921, Bertha Ceridwen, *d* of late Rev. T. Henry Jones, USA and North Wales; one *s* two *d*. *Educ:* Keighley Grammar Sch.; Royal College of Science; Imperial Coll. of Science and Technology. Served European War, 1914-18, RFC and RNVR Anti-submarine Div. On demobilisation completed ARCS (hons), BSc (1st cl. hons); 1 yr research for Admiralty; 1 yr Lectr/Demonstrator, 3rd yr Physics, Royal College of Science. John Arthur Wilson Memorial Lectures, Amer. Leather Chemists' Assoc., 1966. Mem., Royal Institution. *Publications:* many research reports, scientific papers and articles in various jls. *Recreations:* music, gardening, reading; fond of dogs and horses. *Address:* Volta, 38 Piper's Hill Road, Kettering, Northants. *T:* Kettering 3210.

BRADLEY, Air Marshal Sir John Stanley Travers, KCB 1942; CBE 1941 (OBE 1919); RAF retired; *b* 11 April 1888; *m* (she *d* 1948). Director of Equipment, Air Ministry, 1935-38; Air Commodore, 1935; Air Vice-Marshal, 1938; Air Officer Commanding, Maintenance Command, 1938; Temp. Air Marshal, 1942; Deputy Air Member for Supply and Organisation, Air Ministry, 1942-45; Air Marshal, 1944; retired, 1945. *Address:* Beech Lodge, Rowlands Hill, Wimborne, Dorset. *T:* Wimborne 2709. *Club:* Naval and Military.

BRADLEY, General of the Army Omar Nelson, KCB (Hon.) 1944 (CB (Hon.) 1944); DSM (US) 1943 (with 3 oak leaf clusters); DSM (US Navy); Legion of Merit, etc; Chairman Bulova Watch Company Inc., 630 5th Avenue, NY, since 1958; *b* 12 Feb. 1893; *s* of John S. and Sarah Elizabeth Hubbard Bradley; *m* 1st, 1916, Mary Quayle (*d* 1965); one *d* ; 2nd, 1966, Kitty Buhler. *Educ:* United States Military Academy, West Point. 2nd Lieut US Army, 1915; Lieut-Col, 1936; Brig.-Gen. (temp.), 1941, (perm.) 1943; Maj.-Gen. (temp.), 1942, (perm.) 1944; Lieut-Gen. (temp.), 1943; Gen. (temp.), 1945, (Perm.) 1949; General of the Army (perm.), 1950. Commanded II United States Corps in Northern Tunisia and in Sicily, April-Sept. 1943; commanded US troops in invasion of France, June 1944; commanded Twelfth Army Group (American First, Third, Ninth and Fifteenth Armies), 1944; Administrator of Veterans Affairs, 1945-47; Chief of Staff US Army, 1948-49; Chm. of Joint Chiefs of Staff, 1949-53. Freedoms Foundation at Valley Forge George Washington Award, 1971; US Medal of Freedom, 1977; Grand Officer, French Legion of Honour, and many other foreign decorations. *Publication:* A Soldier's Story, 1951. *Recreations:* shooting, golf, fishing. *Address:* 630 Fifth Avenue, New York, NY 10020, USA. *Clubs:* Army Navy Country, Burning Tree Country (Washington, DC).

BRADLEY, Prof. Peter Colley S.; *see* Sylvester-Bradley.

BRADLEY, Maj.-Gen. Peter Edward Moore, CB 1968; CBE 1964 (OBE 1955); DSO 1946; Secretary, Vindolanda Trust, since 1975; *b* 12 Dec. 1914; *s* of late Col Edward de Winton Herbert Bradley, CBE, DSO, MC, DL; *m* Margaret, *d* of Norman Wardhaugh of Haydon Bridge, Northumberland; three *s*. *Educ:* Marlborough; Royal Military Academy, Woolwich. 2nd Lieut, Royal Signals, 1934. Served War of 1939-45; India, Middle East, Italy and North West Europe (DSO 6th Airborne Div.). Lieut-Col 1954; Col 1957; Brig. 1962; Maj.-Gen. 1965; Signal Officer in Chief (Army), Ministry of Defence, 1965-67; Chief of Staff to C-in-C Allied Forces Northern Europe, Oslo, 1968-70, retired. Dunlop Ltd, 1970-75. Col Comdt, Royal Signals, 1967-, Master of Signals, 1970-; Col, Gurkha Signals, 1967-74. CEng, FIEE, 1966; MBIM, 1970. *Address:* Hill House, Haydon Bridge, near Hexham, Northumberland. *T:* Haydon Bridge 234. *Club:* Army and Navy.

BRADLEY, Reginald Livingstone, CBE 1955; MC 1916; Commissioner of Prisons, 1949-57, retired; *b* 9 Aug. 1894; *s* of Frederick L. and Florence Bradley; *m* 1920, Phyllis Mary Richardson; one *s* three *d*. *Educ:* Repton; Oriel Coll., Oxford (MA). Oxford, 1913-14 and 1919-20. Served European War, 1914-18 (despatches, MC); 22nd London Regt, The Queen's; Capt. Sec., Oxford and Bermondsey Club, SE1, 1920-21; Prison

Service: Dep. Governor, 1922-26, HM Borstal, Portland; Dep. Governor, 1926-29, Governor, 1929-36, HM Borstal, Rochester; Governor Cl. II, 1936-38, HM Prison, Wormwood Scrubs; Asst Commissioner, Prison Commission, 1938-52; Dir of Borstal Administration, 1948-57; Commissioner and Dir of Borstal Administration, 1952-57. Coronation Medal, 1953. *Recreations:* walking, reading, chores. *Address:* Avonmore, 4 Malbrook Road, Putney, SW15 6UF. *T:* 01-788 9768. *Clubs:* United Oxford & Cambridge University; Vincent's (Oxford); Surrey County Cricket.
See also R. A. Bradley.

BRADLEY, Richard Alan; Headmaster, Ridley College, Canada, since 1971; *b* 6 Oct. 1925; *s* of Reginald Livingstone Bradley, *qv*; *m* 1971, Mary Ann Vicary; one *s* two *d* by previous marriage. *Educ:* Marlborough Coll.; Trinity Coll., Oxford (Scholar). 2nd cl. hons Mod. History. Royal Marines, 1944-46; Oxford, 1946-48; Club Manager, Oxford and Bermondsey Club, 1949. Asst Master: Dulwich Coll., 1949-50; Tonbridge Sch., 1950-66 (Head of History Dept, 1957-66; Housemaster of Ferox Hall, 1961-66); Warden of St Edward's Sch., Oxford, 1966-71. *Recreations:* games, dramatics, mountains. *Address:* The Headmaster's House, Ridley College, St Catharines, Ontario, Canada. *Club:* Vincent's (Oxford).

BRADLEY, Thomas George; MP (Lab) Leicester East, since 1974 (Leicester NE, July 1962-1974); President, Transport Salaried Staffs' Association since 1964 (Branch Officer, 1946-58; Member Exec. Cttee, 1958-; Treas., 1961-64); Member, Labour Party National Executive, since 1966; *b* 13 April 1926; *s* of George Henry Bradley, Kettering; *m* 1953, Joy, *d* of George Starmer, Kettering; two *s*. *Educ:* Kettering Central Sch., Northants. Elected to Northants County Council, 1952, County Alderman, 1961; Mem., Kettering Borough Council, 1957-61. Contested (Lab) Rutland and Stamford, 1950, 1951 and 1955, Preston South, 1959. PPS: to Minister of Aviation, 1964-65; to Home Secretary, 1966-67; to Chancellor of the Exchequer, 1967-70. Vice-Chm., Labour Party, 1974-75, Chm., 1975-76. Dir, Kettering Town Football Club. *Address:* The Orchard, 111 London Road, Kettering, Northants. *T:* Kettering 3019.

BRADLEY, William Ewart; Special Commissioner of Income Tax 1950-75; *b* 5 Sept. 1910; *s* of W. E. Bradley, Durham City; *m* 1949, Mary Campbell Tyre; two *s*. *Educ:* Johnston Sch., Durham; LSE, London Univ. Inland Revenue, 1929-50. *Address:* 3 Bourne Lane, Tonbridge, Kent. *T:* Tonbridge 352880.

BRADLEY GOODMAN, Michael; *see* Goodman, M. B.

BRADLEY-WILLIAMS, Col William Picton, DSO 1919; *b* 9 Oct. 1890; *s* of late Herbert Edward Bradley, The Grange, Bitton, Glos (took name of Williams from late Capt. William Williams, Pontypridd, Glamorgan); *m* 1918, Frances Mary (*d* 1970), *y d* of late John Selwin Calverley of Oulton, near Leeds; two *s* two *d*; *m* 1947, Sylvia Mary Maxwell Jackson, Ferriby, East Yorks (*d* 1969); one *d*. *Educ:* Haileybury. Served European War, 1914-19 (despatches, DSO); Mesopotamia, 1920-21; North West Frontier, India, 1930; Chief Instructor Army Sch. of PT, Aldershot, 1927-30. Commanded 1st Bn The King's Own Yorks Light Infantry, 1936-39; Garrison Comdr, Hull, 1940-41; Commandant Army Physical Training Corps, 1941-44; Comdr No. 1 War Material Reconnaissance Team BAOR, Dec. 1944-June 1945; Army Welfare Officer, HQ Colchester, 1946-54. *Address:* Burstall House, Burstall, near Ipswich, Suffolk IP8 3DP. *T:* Hintlesham 277. *Club:* Naval and Military.

BRADMAN, Sir Donald (George), Kt 1949; President of South Australian Cricket Association, 1965-73; Chairman, Australian Cricket Board, 1960-63 and 1969-72; *b* Cootamundra, NSW, 27 Aug. 1908; *s* of George and Emily Bradman; *m* 1932, Jessie, *d* of James Menzies, Mittagong, NSW; one *s* one *d*. *Educ:* Bowral Intermediate High Sch. Played for NSW 1927-34; for S Australia, 1935-49; for Australia 1928-48, Capt. 1936-48; records include: highest aggregate and greatest number of centuries in England v Australia test matches; highest score for Australia v England in test matches (334 at Leeds, 1930). Formerly stock and share broker and Mem. Stock Exchange of Adelaide Ltd. *Publications:* Don Bradman's Book, 1930; How to Play Cricket, 1935; My Cricketing Life, 1938; Farewell to Cricket, 1950; The Art of Cricket, 1958. *Recreations:* cricket, golf, tennis, billiards, squash. *Address:* 118 King William Street, Adelaide, South Australia. *Clubs:* MCC (Hon. Life Mem.); Commerce (Adelaide).

BRADSHAW, Kenneth Anthony; Principal Clerk, Table Office, House of Commons, since 1976; *b* 1 Sept. 1922; *s* of late Herbert and Gladys Bradshaw. *Educ:* Ampleforth Coll.; St Catharine's

Coll., Cambridge (1st Cl. Hons History); MA 1947. War Service, 1942-45; served with Royal Ulster Rifles (2nd Bn), NW Europe (despatches). Temp. Asst Principal, Min. of Supply, Oct.-Dec. 1946; Asst Clerk, House of Commons, 1947; Sen. Clerk, 1950; seconded as Clerk of the Saskatchewan Legislature, 1966 session; Clerk of Overseas Office, 1972-76. Jt Sec., Assoc. of Secs Gen. of Parlts, 1955-71. *Publication:* (with David Pring) Parliament and Congress, 1972. *Address:* 8 Cornwall Mansions, Cremorne Road, SW10. *Club:* Garrick.

BRADSHAW, Maurice Bernard; Secretary-General, Federation of British Artists, since 1958; *b* 7 Feb. 1903; 7th *s* of John Bradshaw; *m* 1927, Gladys, 2nd *d* of Henry Harvey Frost; one *d*. *Educ:* Christ's Coll., Finchley. Jun. Clerk, Furness Withy & Co., 1918. Dir, Art Exhibns Bureau, 1926-; Asst Sec., British Artists Exhibns, 1927-35; Organising Sec., Floating Art Gall. aboard Berengaria, 1928; Sec., Empire Art Loan Exhibn Soc., 1932-; Sec., Modern Architectural Res. Gp, 1938. Commissioned RAFVR, 1941-45. Sec. following art socs: Royal Inst. Oil Painters, 1966-74, Royal Inst. Painters in Watercolours, 1969-, Royal Soc. British Artists, 1958-74, Royal Soc. Marine Artists, 1938-72, Royal Soc. Portrait Painters, 1955-, Royal Soc. Miniature Painters, Sculptors and Gravers, 1959-72, Royal British Colonial Soc. of Artists (temp. known as Commonwealth Soc. of Artists), 1930-, Artists of Chelsea, 1949-72, National Soc., 1968-74, New English Art Club, 1955-74, Pastel Soc., 1968-, Soc. Aviation Artists, 1954-, Soc. Graphic Artists, 1968-75, Soc. Mural Painters, 1968-, Soc. Portrait Sculptors, 1969-, Soc. Wildlife Artists, 1963-, Soc. Women Artists, 1968-, Senefelder Gp, 1968-. *Recreation:* woodwork. *Address:* Flat Two, 110 Elm Park Gardens, Chelsea, SW10 9PF. *T:* 01-352 7242. *Clubs:* Army and Navy, Chelsea Arts.

BRADSHAW, Lt-Gen. Sir Richard Phillip, KBE 1977; QHP 1975; Director General, Army Medical Services, since April 1977; *b* 1 Aug. 1920; *s* of late John Henderson Bradshaw and late May Bradshaw (*née* Phillips); *m* 1946, Estelle, *d* of late Emile Meyer; one *d*. *Educ:* Newport High Sch.; London Univ.; Westminster Hosp. MRCS, LRCP 1945; FRCPath 1967; MFCM 1974; DTM&H 1953; FRSocMed, FRSTM&H, Mem. BMA. House appts Westminster and Kent and Canterbury Hosps. Commnd RAMC, 1946; appts as Hosp. Pathologist, Mil. Hosps in UK and Ceylon; Staff appts in Path., WO, 1950-52; Comd Cons. Pathologist, E Africa, 1954-57; Exch. Officer, Armed Forces Inst. of Path., Washington, 1958-59; Demonstr in Path., Royal Army Med. Coll., Millbank, 1961-63; Asst Dir of Path., BAOR, 1966-69; Prof. of Path., Royal Army Med. Coll., Millbank, 1969-71; CO, Cambridge Mil. Hosp., Aldershot, 1971-73; Comdt RAMC Trng Centre, 1973-75; DMS, BAOR, 1975-77. CStJ 1977. *Publications:* various articles and reports in professional jls. *Recreations:* sailing, bird-watching, gardening, joinery. *Address:* Ministry of Defence (Army), Lansdowne House, Berkeley Square, W1X 6AA.

BRADSHAW-ISHERWOOD, C. W.; *see* Isherwood.

BRADWELL, Bishop Suffragan of, since 1976; **Rt Rev. (Charles) Derek Bond;** *b* 4 July 1927; *s* of Charles Norman Bond and Doris Bond; *m* 1951, Joan Valerie Meikle; two *s* two *d*. *Educ:* Bournemouth Sch.; King's Coll., London. AKC (2nd hons). Curate of Friern Barnet, 1952; Midlands Area Sec. of SCM in Schools and Public Preacher, dio. Birmingham, 1956; Vicar: of Harringay, 1958; of Harrow Weald, 1962; Archdeacon of Colchester, 1972-76. *Recreation:* travel. *Address:* 188 New London Road, Chelmsford CM2 0AR. *T:* Chelmsford 84235.

BRADY, Very Rev. Ernest William; Priest-in-Charge, Priory Church of St Mary of Mount Carmel, South Queensferry, since 1974 and Dean of Edinburgh, since 1976; *b* 10 Nov. 1917; *s* of Ernest and Malinda Elizabeth Brady; *m* 1948, Violet Jeanne Louise Aldworth; one *s* one *d*. *Educ:* Harris Academy, Dundee (Dux and Classics Medallist, 1936); Univ. of St Andrews; Edinburgh Theological Coll. (Luscombe Schol. 1942). LTh (Dunelm) 1942. Deacon 1942, priest 1943; Asst Curate, Christ Church, Glasgow, 1942; Asst Curate, St Alphage, Hendon, 1946; Rector, All Saints, Buckie, 1949; Rector, All Saints, Edinburgh, 1957; Chaplain, Royal Infirmary of Edinburgh, 1959-74; Canon of St Mary's Cathedral, Edinburgh, 1967; Synod Clerk, Diocese of Edinburgh, 1969. *Recreations:* Holy Land pilgrimage; choral music; ecclesiastical vestments and embroidery. *Address:* St Mary's House, South Queensferry EH30 9NY. *T:* 031-331 1055.

BRADY, Terence Joseph; playwright, novelist and actor, since 1962; *b* 13 March 1939; *m* Charlotte Mary Thérèse Bingham, *qv*; one *s* one *d*. *Educ:* Merchant Taylors', Northwood; TCD (BA Moderatorship, History and Polit. Science). Actor: Would Anyone who saw the Accident?, The Dumb Waiter, Room at the

Top, 1962; Beyond the Fringe, 1962-64; Present from the Corporation, In the Picture, 1967; Quick One 'Ere, 1968; films include: Baby Love; Foreign Exchange; TV appearances include plays, and comedy series and shows. Writer for TV: Broad and Narrow; TWTWTW; Lines from my Grandfather's Forehead; TV series with Charlotte Bingham: Boy Meets Girl; Take Three Girls; Upstairs Downstairs; Away From It All; Play for Today; Plays of Marriage; No—Honestly; Yes—Honestly. *Publications:* Rehearsal, 1972; The Fight Against Slavery, 1976; with Charlotte Bingham: Victoria, 1972; Rose's Story, 1973; Victoria and Company, 1974; Yes—Honestly, 1977. *Recreations:* painting, music, horse-riding, gardening. *Address:* 111 East Sheen Avenue, SW14 8AX; c/o A.D. Peters, Literary Agent, 10 Buckingham Street, WC2. *Clubs:* Roehampton; Stage Golfing.

BRAGG, Melvyn; writer; Presenter and Editor, new Arts Programme for ITV, since Jan. 1978; *b* 6 Oct. 1939; *s* of Stanley Bragg and Mary Ethel (*née* Parks); *m* 1st, 1961, Marie-Elisabeth Roche (decd); one *d*; 2nd, 1973, Catherine Mary Haste; one *d*. *Educ:* Nelson-Thomlinson Grammar Sch., Wigton; Wadham Coll., Oxford (MA). BBC Radio and TV Producer, 1961-67; writer and broadcaster, 1967-. Novelist, 1964-. FRSL. Mem. ACTT. Presenter, BBC TV series: 2nd House, 1973-77; Read all About It (also editor), 1976-77. Mem. Arts Council, and Chm. Literature Panel of Arts Council, 1977-. *Play:* Mardi Gras, Prince of Wales, 1976 (musical); *Screenplays:* Isadora; Jesus Christ Superstar. *Publications:* For Want of a Nail, 1965; The Second Inheritance, 1966; Without a City Wall, 1968; The Hired Man, 1969; A Place in England, 1970; The Nerve, 1971; Josh Lawton, 1972; The Silken Net, 1974; Speak for England, 1976; A Christmas Child, 1976; articles for various English jls. *Recreations:* walking, books. *Address:* 9 Gayton Road, NW3 1TX. *T:* 01-435 7215. *Clubs:* Garrick, PEN.

BRAGG, Stephen Lawrence, MA, SM; Vice-Chancellor, Brunel University, since Sept. 1971; *b* 17 Nov. 1923; *e s* of late Sir Lawrence Bragg, CH, MC, FRS; *m* 1951, Maureen Ann (*née* Roberts); three *s*. *Educ:* Rugby Sch.; Cambridge Univ.; Massachusetts Inst. of Technology. BA 1945, MA 1949 (Cambridge); SM 1949 (MIT). Rolls-Royce Ltd, 1944-48; Commonwealth Fund Fellow, 1948-49; Wm Jessop Ltd, Steelmakers, 1949-51; Rolls-Royce Ltd, 1951-71: Chief Scientist, 1960-63; Chief Research Engineer, 1964-68; Dir, Aero Div., 1969-71. Member: Univ. Grants Cttee, 1966-71; Aeronautical Research Council, 1970-73; Court of ASC, 1972-; SRC Engineering Bd, 1976-; Chm., Adv. Cttee on Falsework, 1973-75. Governor, Brighton Coll., 1974-. Hon. DEng (Sheffield), 1969. Corres. Mem. Venezuelan Acad. Sci., 1975. *Publications:* Rocket Engines, 1962; articles on Jet Engines, Research Management, University/Industry Collaboration, etc. *Recreation:* railway history. *Address:* Brunel University, Uxbridge, Mddx UB8 3PH. *T:* Uxbridge 37188. *Club:* Athenæum.

BRAHAM, Harold, CBE 1960; HM Diplomatic Service (Retired); *b* Constantinople, 11 Oct. 1907; *er s* of late D. D. Braham, of The Times; *m* 1941, Cicely Edith Norton Webber; one *s* one *d*. *Educ:* St Peter's Coll., Adelaide; New College, Oxford. Entered HM Consular Service, China, 1931. Retired as HM Consul-Gen., Paris, 1966. *Recreations:* gardening, carpentry. *Address:* Torret 19, San Luis, Menorca, Balearic Islands, Spain. *Club:* Athenæum.

BRAHIMI, Lakhdar; Ambassador of Algeria to the Court of St James's since 1971; *b* 1934; *m* 1964; two *s* one *d*. *Educ:* Faculté de Droit and Institut des Sciences Politiques, Algiers; then Paris. Permanent Rep. of FLN and later of Provisional Govt of Algeria, in SE Asia, 1956-61; Gen. Secretariat, Min. of External Affairs, 1961-63; Ambassador to UAR and Sudan, and Permanent Rep. to Arab League, 1963-70. *Address:* Algerian Embassy, 6 Hyde Park Gate, SW7. *T:* 01-584 9502.

BRAHMS, Caryl; critic and novelist; journalist specialising in criticism of the theatre arts; ballet critic; writer of film, broadcast and television scripts; *b* Surrey. *Educ:* privately and at Royal Academy of Music. Wrote stage versions of: Cindy-Ella, 1962; Sing a Rude Song (stage biography of Marie Lloyd), 1970; Television: The Great Inimitable Mr Dickens, 1970; Ooh! La! La!, adapted series of Feydeau farces, 1973. Ivor Novello Award (with Ned Sherrin), 1966. *Publications:* The Moon on my Left, 1930; Footnotes To The Ballet, 1936; Robert Helpmann, Choreographer, 1943; Seat at the Ballet, 1951; Away went Polly, 1952; No Castanets, 1963; The Rest of the Evening's My Own (theatre criticism), 1964; (with S. J. Simon): A Bullet in the Ballet, 1937; Casino for Sale, 1938; The Elephant is White, 1939; Envoy on Excursion, 1940; Don't, Mr Disraeli, 1940 (Evening Standard Book of the Year); No Bed for Bacon, 1941; No Nightingales, 1944 (filmed); Titania Has a Mother, 1944; Six

Curtains for Stroganova, 1945; Trottie True, 1946 (filmed); To Hell with Hedda, 1947; You Were There, 1950; (with Ned Sherrin): Cindy-Ella or I gotta Shoe, 1962; Rappel 1910, 1964; Benbow was his Name, 1966; film script: Girl/stroke/Boy, 1971; Paying the Piper (play; adapted from Feydeau), 1972; After You Mr Feydeau, 1975; Gilbert and Sullivan: Lost Chords and Discords, 1975; Nickleby and Me, 1975; Reflections in a Lake, 1976. *Recreations:* collecting Edwardian postcards and glass walking-sticks. *Address:* 3 Cambridge Gate, Regent's Park, NW1. *T:* 01-935 6439.

BRAILSFORD, Prof. Frederick, PhD; FIEE; Professor of Electrical Engineering, University College, London, 1951-70, now Emeritus Professor; *b* 22 Sept. 1903; *s* of John James and Frances Ann Brailsford; *m* 1934, Sarah Remington Smyth, Knock, County Down; one *d*. *Educ:* University Coll., Swansea. Whitworth Scholar, 1923; BSc(Eng) London (1st Class Hons), 1927; PhD, London, 1939. Apprentice in HM Dockyard, Pembroke, 1919-23; Electrical Engineer with Metropolitan-Vickers Electrical Co., Manchester, 1926-50. *Publications:* Magnetic Materials, 1960; Physical Principles of Magnetism, 1966; Introduction to the Magnetic Properties of Materials, 1968; various papers to Institution of Electrical Engineers and elsewhere. *Address:* Locks Green, 244 Brooklands Road, Weybridge, Surrey. *T:* Weybridge 47548.

BRAILSFORD, John William; Keeper, Department of Prehistoric and Romano-British Antiquities, British Museum, 1969-73; *b* 14 July 1918; *o s* of Alfred and Dorothy H. M. Brailsford; *m* 1945, Mary Freeman Boaden; one *s* one *d*. *Educ:* Bedales; Emmanuel College, Cambridge. Sen. Exhibnr and Scholar, BA, MA 1943. Royal Artillery (Survey), 1939-45; Intell. (Air Photo Interpretation), 1945-46. Asst Keeper, Dept of British and Medieval Antiquities, Brit. Mus., 1946; Dep. Keeper, 1963. FMA; FSA 1949; Fellow, German Archaeolog. Inst., 1967. *Publications:* Museum Handbooks to Mildenhall Treasure, 1947; Antiquities of Roman Britain, 1951; Later Prehistoric Antiquities of the British Isles, 1953; Antiquities from Hod Hill in the Durden Collection, 1962; (ed) Hod Hill: Excavations, 1951-58; 1968; Early Celtic Masterpieces from Britain in the British Museum, 1975; papers in learned jls. *Recreations:* various. *Address:* Sunnyside, Brook End, Chadlington, Oxon. *T:* Chadlington 378.

BRAIN, family name of **Baron Brain.**

BRAIN, 2nd Baron *cr* 1962, of Eynsham; **Christopher Langdon Brain;** Bt 1954; *b* 30 Aug. 1926; *s* of 1st Baron Brain, MA, DM, FRS, FRCP and Stella, *er d* of late Reginald L. Langdon-Down; *S* father 1966; *m* 1953, Susan Mary, *d* of George P. and Ethelbertha Morris; three *d*. *Educ:* Leighton Park Sch., Reading; New College, Oxford. MA 1956. Royal Navy, 1946-48. Liveryman, 1955, Upper Warden, 1974-75, Worshipful Company of Weavers. Chm., Rhone-Alps Regional Council, British Chamber of Commerce, France, 1967. *Recreations:* bird watching, sailing, ski-ing. *Heir:* *b* Hon. Michael Cottrell Brain, MA, DM, FRCP, FRCP Canada, Prof. of Medicine, McMaster Univ. [*b* 6 Aug. 1928; *m* 1960, Dr The Hon. Elizabeth Ann Herbert, *e d* of Baron Tangley, KBE; one *s* two *d*.]. *Clubs:* Savile; Royal Harwich Yacht; Oxford and Cambridge Sailing Society.

BRAIN, Albert Edward Arnold; Regional Director (East Midlands), Department of the Environment, and Chairman of Regional Economic Planning Board, since 1972; *b* 31 Dec. 1917; *s* of Walter Henry and Henrietta Mabel Brain; *m* 1947, Patricia Grace Gallop; two *s* one *d*. *Educ:* Rendcomb Coll., Cirencester; Loughborough College. BSc (Eng) London, external; DLC hons Loughborough; CEng, MICE, MIMunE. Royal Engineers, 1940-46; Bristol City Corp., 1946-48; Min. of Transport: Asst Engr, London, 1948-54; Civil Engr, Wales, 1954-63; Sen. Engr, HQ, 1963-67; Asst Chief Engr, HQ, 1967-69; Divl Road Engr, W Mids, now Regional Controller (Roads and Transportation), 1969-72. *Recreations:* gardening, campanology. *Address:* Patarno, Nicker Hill, Keyworth, Nottingham. *T:* Plumtree 2800. *Club:* Royal Automobile.

BRAIN, Sir (Henry) Norman, KBE 1963 (OBE 1947); CMG 1953; *b* 19 July 1907; *s* of late B. Brain, Rushall, Staffs; *m* 1939, Nuala Mary, *d* of late Capt. A. W. Butterworth; one *s* (and one *s* decd). *Educ:* King Edward's Sch., Birmingham; The Queen's Coll., Oxford (MA). Entered the Consular Service, 1930, and served at Tokyo, Kobe, Osaka, Tamsui, Manila, Mukden, Shanghai and Dairen; interned by Japanese, 1941-42; repatriated and served in Foreign Office, 1943; appointed to Staff of Supreme Allied Comdr, South-East Asia, 1944-46; Political Adviser to Saigon Control Commission, 1945; served with Special Commissioner in South-East Asia, at Singapore, 1946-

48; Counsellor in Foreign Office, 1949; Inspector of HM Foreign Service Estabts, 1950-53; Minister, Tokyo, 1953-55; Ambassador to Cambodia, 1956-58; Asst Under-Sec. of State, FO, 1958-61; Ambassador to Uruguay, 1961-66, retired, 1966. Chairman: Royal Central Asian Soc., 1970-74; Japan Soc. of London, 1970-73; Pres., British Uruguayan Soc., 1974-. *Recreations:* music, golf. *Address:* St Andrews, Abney Court, Bourne End, Bucks. *Clubs:* Canning, Special Forces.

BRAIN, Ronald, CB 1967; Chairman, London and Quadrant Housing Trust, since 1977; *b* 1 March 1914; *s* of T. T. G. Brain, RN, and E. C. Brain (*née* Fruin); *m* 1943, Lilian Rose (*née* Ravenhill); one *s* one *d*. *Educ:* Trowbridge High Sch. Audit Asst, Min. of Health, 1932; Principal, Min. of Health, 1946; Asst Sec., Min. of Housing and Local Govt, 1952; Under-Sec., 1959; Dep. Sec., Dept of Environment (formerly Min. of Housing and Local Govt), 1966-74. *Recreations:* music, chess. *Address:* Flat 4, Badminton, Galsworthy Road, Kingston-upon-Thames, Surrey.

BRAINE, Sir Bernard (Richard), Kt 1972; MP (C) South-East Division of Essex since 1955 (Billericay Division of Essex, 1950-55); *b* Ealing, Middx, 24 June 1914; *s* of Arthur Ernest Braine; *m* 1935, Kathleen Mary Faun; three *s*. *Educ:* Hendon County Grammar Sch. Served North Staffs Regt in War of 1939-45: West Africa, SE Asia, NW Europe; Staff Coll., Camberley, 1944 (sc); Lt-Col. Chm., British Commonwealth Producers' Organisation, 1958-60; Parly Sec., Min. of Pensions and National Insurance, 1960-61; Parly Under-Sec. of State for Commonwealth Relations, 1961-62; Parly Sec., Min. of Health, 1962-64; Conservative front bench spokesman on Commonwealth Affairs and Overseas Aid, 1967-70; Chm., Select Cttees on Overseas Aid, 1970-71, on Overseas Develt, 1973-74; Treasurer, UK Branch of Commonwealth Parly Assoc., 1974-77 (Dep. Chm., 1964 and 1970-74); a Governor, Commonwealth Inst., 1968-; Chairman: Anglo-German Parly Group, 1970-; Anglo-Ethiopian Soc., 1973-77; SOS Children's Villages, UK, 1970-; Nat. Council on Alcoholism, 1973-; UK Chapter, Soc. of Internat. Develt, 1976-. Associate Mem., Inst. of Develt Studies, Univ. of Sussex, 1971-. FRSA 1971. CStJ. Grand Cross, German Order of Merit, 1974. *Address:* King's Wood, Rayleigh, Essex. *Clubs:* Carlton, Beefsteak.

BRAINE, John (Gerard); Author; *b* 13 April 1922; *s* of Fred and Katherine Braine; *m* 1955, Helen Patricia Wood; one *s* three *d*. *Educ:* St Bede's Grammar Sch., Bradford. Furniture-shop asst, bookshop asst, laboratory asst, progress chaser, in rapid succession, 1938-40; Asst, Bingley Public Library, 1940-49; HM Navy, 1942-43; Chief Asst, Bingley Public Library, 1949-51; free-lance writer, London and Yorks, with interval in hospital, 1951-54; Branch Librarian, Northumberland County Library, 1954-56; Branch Librarian, West Riding of Yorks County Library, 1956-57. ALA 1950. *Publications:* Room at the Top, 1957 (filmed 1958); The Vodi, 1959; Life at the Top, 1962 (filmed 1965); The Jealous God, 1964; The Crying Game, 1968; Stay with Me till Morning, 1970; The Queen of a Distant Country, 1972; Writing a Novel, 1974; The Pious Agent, 1975; Waiting for Sheila, 1976 (adapted for TV, 1977); Finger of Fire, 1977. *TV Series:* Man the Top, 1970, 1972. *Recreations:* walking, talking, Victoriana, and dieting. *Address:* Pentons, Onslow Crescent, Woking, Surrey. *Club:* PEN.

BRAINE, Rear-Adm. Richard Allix, CB 1956; Retired; *b* 18 Nov. 1900; *m* 1922; one *s*. *Educ:* Dean Close Memorial Sch., Cheltenham. Joined RN as asst clerk, 1918; Comdr (S), Dec. 1938; Capt. (S), Dec. 1948; Rear-Adm. 1954. Command Supply Officer, Staff of Flag Officer Air (Home), 1954-56, Portsmouth, 1956-57. *Recreation:* fishing. *Address:* The Old Cottage, Littlewick Green, near Maidenhead, Berks. *T:* Littlewick Green 4484.

BRAININ, Norbert, OBE 1960; Leader of Amadeus String Quartet; *b* Vienna, 12 March 1923; *s* of Adolph and Sophie Brainin; *m* 1948, Kathe Kottow; one *d*. *Educ:* High Sch., Vienna. Commenced musical training in Vienna at age of seven and continued studies there until 1938; emigrated to London in 1938 and studied with Carl Flesch and Max Rostal; won Carl Flesch prize for solo violinists at the Guildhall Sch. of Music, London, 1946. Formed Amadeus String Quartet, 1947. DUniv York, 1968. *Address:* 19 Prowse Avenue, Bushey Heath, Herts. *T:* 01-950 7379.

BRAITHWAITE, Bernard Richard; His Honour Judge Braithwaite; a Circuit Judge (formerly County Court Judge), since 1971; *b* 20 Aug. 1917; *s* of Bernard Leigh Braithwaite and Emily Dora Ballard Braithwaite (*née* Thomas); unmarried. *Educ:* Clifton; Peterhouse, Cambridge. BA (Hons), Law. Served War: 7th Bn Somerset LI, 1939-43; Parachute Regt, 1943-46;

Captain, Temp. Major. Called to Bar, Inner Temple, 1946. *Recreations:* hunting, sailing. *Address:* 48 Campden Street, W8. *T:* 01-727 5386. *Clubs:* Boodle's, Little Ship.

BRAITHWAITE, Eustace Edward Adolph Ricardo; writer; Ambassador of Guyana to Venezuela, 1968-69; *b* 27 June 1922. *Educ:* New York Univ.; Cambridge Univ. Served War of 1939-45, RAF. Schoolteacher, London, 1950-57; Welfare Officer, LCC, 1958-60; Human Rights Officer, World Veterans Foundation, Paris, 1960-63; Lecturer and Education Consultant, Unesco, Paris, 1963-66; Permanent Rep. of Guyana to UN, 1967-68. Ainsfield-Wolff Literary Award, 1961; Franklin Prize. *Publications:* To Sir With Love, 1959; Paid Servant, 1962; A Kind of Homecoming, 1962; Choice of Straws, 1965; Reluctant Neighbours, 1972; Honorary White, 1976. *Recreations:* dancing and tennis. *Address:* Billingsley Trail, Golders Bridge, New York 10526, USA.

BRAITHWAITE, Prof. Richard Bevan, FBA 1957; Emeritus Knightbridge Professor of Moral Philosophy in the University of Cambridge; *b* 15 Jan. 1900; *s* of William Charles Braithwaite, Banbury; *m* 1st, 1925, Dorothea Cotter (*d* 1928), *d* of Sir Theodore Morison; 2nd, 1932, Margaret Mary, *d* of Rt Hon. C. F. G. Masterman; one *s* one *d*. *Educ:* Sidcot Sch., Somerset; Bootham Sch., York; King's Coll., Cambridge (Scholar, Prizeman, Research Student). MA Camb. 1926; Fellow of King's Coll., Camb. 1924-; University Lectr in Moral Science, 1928-34; Sidgwick Lectr in Moral Science, 1934-53; Knightbridge Prof. of Moral Philosophy, 1953-67; Tarner Lectr at Trinity Coll., Camb., 1945-46; Pres. Mind Assoc., 1946; Pres. Aristotelian Soc., 1946-47; Annual Philosophical Lectr to British Academy, 1950; Pres. Brit. Soc. for the Philosophy of Science, 1961-63; Deems Lectr, New York Univ., 1962; Forwood Lectr, Liverpool Univ., 1968; Visiting Prof. of Philosophy: Johns Hopkins Univ., 1968; Univ. of Western Ontario, 1969; City Univ. of New York, 1970. Syndic Cambridge Univ. Press, 1943-62; Mem. Gen. Bd of Faculties, 1945-48; Mem. Council Senate, 1959-64. Hon. DLitt Bristol, 1963. *Publications:* Moral Principles and Inductive Policies (British Acad. Lecture, 1950); Scientific Explanation, 1953; Theory of Games as a tool for the Moral Philosopher (Inaugural Lecture), 1955; An Empiricist's view of the nature of Religious Belief (Eddington Lecture), 1955; Introd. to trans. of Gödel, 1962. Articles in Mind, Proc. Aristotelian Soc., etc. *Recreations:* walking, reading novels. *Address:* King's College, Cambridge. *T:* Cambridge 50411; 11 Millington Road, Cambridge. *T:* Cambridge 50822.

BRAITHWAITE, Rodric Quentin; HM Diplomatic Service; Head of Chancery, Office of Permanent Representative to European Economic Community, Brussels, since 1975; *b* 17 May 1932; *s* of Henry Warwick Braithwaite and Lorna Constance Davies; *m* 1961, Gillian Mary Robinson; three *s* one *d* (and one *s* decd). *Educ:* Bedales Sch.; Christ's Coll., Cambridge. 1st cl. Mod. Langs, Pts I and II. Mil. Service, 1950-52. Joined Foreign (subseq. Diplomatic) Service, 1955; 3rd Sec., Djakarta, 1957-58; 2nd Sec., Warsaw, 1959-61; FO, 1961-63; 1st Sec. (Commercial), Moscow, 1963-66; 1st Sec., Rome, 1966-69; FCO, 1969-72; Vis. Fellow, All Souls Coll., Oxford, 1972-73; Head of European Integration Dept (External), FCO, 1973-75. *Recreations:* chamber music (viola); sailing; Russia. *Address:* c/o Foreign and Commonwealth Office, SW1A 2AL.

BRAMALL, Sir Ashley; see Bramall, Sir E. A.

BRAMALL, Gen. Sir Edwin (Noel Westby), KCB 1974; OBE 1965; MC 1945; Commander-in-Chief, United Kingdom Land Forces, since 1976; *b* 18 Dec. 1923; *s* of Major Edmund Haselden Bramall and Mrs Katherine Bridget Bramall (*née* Westby); *m* 1949, Dorothy Avril Wentworth Vernon; one *s* one *d*. *Educ:* Eton College. Commnd into KRRC, 1943; served in NW Europe, 1944-45; occupation of Japan, 1946-47; Instructor, Sch. of Infantry, 1949-51; psc 1952; Middle East, 1953-58; Instructor, Army Staff Coll., 1958-61; on staff of Lord Mountbatten with special responsibility for reorganisation of MoD, 1963-64; CO, 2 Royal Green Jackets, Malaysia during Indonesian confrontation, 1965-66; comd 5th Airportable Bde, 1968-69; idc 1970; GOC 1st Div. BAOR, 1972-73; Lt-Gen., 1973; Comdr, British Forces, Hong Kong, 1973-76; Gen., 1976. Col Comdt, 3rd Bn Royal Green Jackets, 1973-; Col, 2nd Goorkhas, 1976-. *Recreations:* cricket, painting, tennis, travel. *Address:* 8 The Close, Winchester, Hants. *Clubs:* Travellers', Pratt's, MCC, I Zingari, Free Foresters, Butterflies.
See also Sir E. A. Bramall.

BRAMALL, Sir (Ernest) Ashley, Kt 1975; Leader of the Inner London Education Authority, since 1970; *b* 6 Jan. 1916; *er s* of Major E. H. Bramall; *m*; three *s*. *Educ:* Westminster and

Canford Schs; Magdalen Coll., Oxford. Served in Army, 1940-46; Major; psc 1945. Contested Fareham Div. of Hants, 1945; MP (Lab) for Bexley, 1946-50; contested Bexley, 1950, 1951, 1959; Watford, 1955. Barrister, Inner Temple. Member: LCC (Lab) Bethnal Green, 1961; Greater London Council (Lab) Tower Hamlets, 1964, Bethnal Green and Bow, 1973-; Westminster City Council, 1959-68; Chm., Inner London Education Authority, 1965-67; Chm., Council of LEAs, 1975-76, Vice-Chm., 1976-77; Leader, Management Panel, Burnham Cttee (Primary and Secondary), 1973-. *Address:* 21 Hugh Street, SW1. *T:* 01-828 0973.
See also Sir E. N. W. Bramall.

BRAMALL, Margaret Elaine, OBE 1969; MA; JP; Director, National Council for One Parent Families (formerly National Council for the Unmarried Mother and her Child), since 1962; *b* 1 Oct. 1916; *d* of Raymond Taylor, MA and Nettie Kate Taylor, BA; *m* 1939, Sir Ashley Bramall (marr. diss.); two *s. Educ:* St Paul's Girls' Sch., Hammersmith; Somerville Coll., Oxford (BA 1939, MA 1942); LSE (Social Science Hon. Certif. 1950); Inst. of Almoners (Certif. 1951). Medical Social Worker: Ashford Hosp.; Surrey and Mddx CCs; seconded to London Sch. of Econs and Polit. Science. JP Richmond 1965. Member: Juvenile Court Panel; Probation Case Cttee; Co. After-Care Cttee. *Publications:* contrib., One Parent Families, ed Dulan Barber, 1975; contrib. social work jls. *Recreations:* gardening, literature, family. *Address:* 5 Trafalgar Road, Twickenham, TW2 5EJ. *T:* (home) 01-894 3998, (office) 01-267 1361.

BRAMBLE, Courtenay Parker, CIE 1946; *b* 10 June 1900; *s* of Frank Bramble and Violet, *d* of Col M. G. Totterdell, VD; *m* 1st, 1928, Margaret Louise Lawrence, MBE, 1943, *d* of late Sir Henry Lawrence, KCSI; two *s* one *d* : 2nd, 1958, Doreen, *d* of C. E. Cornish, Lytham St Annes, Lancs. *Educ:* St Paul's Cathedral Choir Sch. (Coronation Medal, 1911); Cranleigh Sch.; King's Coll., Cambridge (MA, LLB). Barrister-at-law, Middle Temple; with The Bombay Co. Ltd, India, 1922-33; Senior partner Drennan & Co., Bombay, 1933-52; Silver Jubilee Medal, 1935; Coronation Medal, 1937. Man. Dir, Abercrombie, Bramble & Co. Ltd, 1954-73. Dir, East India Cotton Assoc., Bombay, 1925-33; Mem., Indian Central Cotton Cttee, 1935-50. Mem. of Legislature, Bombay, 1935-50 (Leader, Progress Party); JP and Hon. Magistrate, Bombay; Chm., Children's Aid Soc., Bombay, 1931-39; Pres. Bombay Chamber of Commerce, 1940, 1945-46; Dep. Pres. Associated Chambers of Commerce, India, 1945; Chm. European Assoc., Bombay Branch, 1942-44; Mem., Bombay Presidency War Cttee, 1941-45; Trustee of Port of Bombay, 1949. Music critic, Times of India, 1925-41. Chairman: All India Quadrangular Cricket Cttee, 1935-39; UK Citizens Assoc. (Bombay), 1948-50; National Service Advisory Cttee, 1940-45; Bombay European Hospital Trust, 1943-50; Hon. Lieut, RINVR, 1940-45. Dir (Pres. 1962), Liverpool Cotton Association; Member Council: Cotton Research Corp., 1960-; Liverpool Sch. of Tropical Medicine, 1974-. *Address:* Lyndhurst, Childer Thornton, Cheshire. *T:* 051-339 3545. *Clubs:* United Oxford & Cambridge University; Royal Yacht (Bombay).

BRAMMA, Harry Wakefield, FRCO; Organist, Southwark Cathedral, since 1976; *b* 11 Nov. 1936; *s* of Fred and Christine Bramma. *Educ:* Bradford Grammar Sch.; Pembroke Coll., Oxford (MA). FRCO 1958. Dir of Music, King Edward VI Grammar Sch., Retford, Notts, 1961; Asst Organist, Worcester Cathedral, 1963; Dir of Music, The King's Sch., Worcester, 1965. *Recreations:* travel, walking. *Address:* 52 Bankside, Southwark, SE1. *T:* 01-261 1291.

BRAMMER, Leonard Griffith, RE 1956 (ARE 1932); painter and etcher; Supervisor of Art and Crafts, Stoke-on-Trent Education Authority, 1952-69; *b* 4 July 1906; *s* of Frederick William Brammer and Minnie Griffith; *m* 1934, Florence May, *d* of William and Mary Barnett, Hanley; one *d. Educ:* Burslem Sch. of Art; Royal College of Art (Diploma Associate); awarded Travelling Scholarship, School of Engraving, Royal College of Art, 1930; represented in Tate Gallery, Victoria & Albert Museum, Ashmolean, Oxford, City of Stoke-on-Trent Art Gallery, City of Carlisle Art Gallery, Wedgwood Museum, Barlaston, Keele Univ., Collection of Contemporary Art Soc., The Collections of The British Council, etc.; exhibitor at Royal Academy and all leading English and American exhibitions. *Recreation:* golf. *Address:* Sŵn-y-Wylan, Lon Wydryn, Morfa Bychan, Porthmadog, Gwynedd.

BRAMWELL-BOOTH, Catherine, CBE 1971; a Commissioner of the Salvation Army; *b* London, 1883; *e c* of late General Bramwell Booth. Entered Salvation Army as an Officer, 1903; engaged in training Cadets at International Training Coll., 1907-17; International Sec. for Salvation Army in Europe, 1917;

command of Women's Social Work in Great Britain and Ireland, 1926; International Sec. for Europe, 1946-48; retired 1948. *Publications:* Messages to the Messengers; A Few Lines; Bramwell Booth, 1933; (compiler) Bramwell Booth Speaks, 1947; Verse, 1947; Catherine Booth, the story of her loves, 1970. *Address:* North Court, Finchampstead, Berks.

BRANCH, Sir William Allan Patrick, Kt 1977; Managing Director and Grenada Representative on the Windward Islands Banana Association (Mirabeau, Capitol, Hope Development and Dougalston Estates); *b* 17 Feb. 1915; *m* Thelma (née Rapier); one *s. Educ:* Grenada Boys' Secondary Sch. Dep. Manager, Mt Horne Agricl Estate, 1936; Manager Mt Horne, Boulogne, Colombier, Industry and Grand Bras Agricl Estates, 1941. Chairman, Eastern Dist Agricl Rehabilitation Cttee; Dep. Chm. Bd of Dirs, Grenada Banana Co-op Soc.; Director: Grenada Cocoa Industry; Parochial and Island Anglican Church Council; Managing Cttee: Grenada Boy Scouts Assoc.; St Andrew's Anglican Secondary Sch; Member, Central Agricl Rehabilitation Cttee. Knighthood awarded for services to agriculture, Grenada, Windward Islands. *Address:* The Windward Islands Banana Association, St George's, Grenada, Windward Islands.

BRANCKER, Sir (John Eustace) Theodore, Kt 1969; President of the Senate, Barbados, 1971-76; *b* 9 Feb. 1909; *s* of Jabel Eustace and Myra Enid Vivienne Brancker; *m* 1967, Esme Gwendolyn Walcott. *Educ:* Harrison Coll., Barbados. Called to Bar, Middle Temple, 1933; in private practice; QC (Barbados) 1961. Mem., House of Assembly, Barbados, 1937-71 (Speaker, 1961-71). Hon. LLD, Soochow Univ., 1973; FZS; FRSA. Coronation Medal, 1953. *Recreations:* classical music, chess, drama. *Address:* Valencia, St James's, Barbados. *T:* 04138. *Clubs:* Challoner (London); Empire (Barbados); Rotary International.

BRAND, family name of Viscount Hampden.

BRAND, Hon. Lord; David William Robert Brand; a Senator of the College of Justice in Scotland, since 1972; *b* 21 Oct. 1923; *s* of late James Gordon Brand, Huntingdon, Dumfries, and Frances (née Bull); *m* 1st, 1948, Rose Josephine Devlin (*d* 1968); four *d* ; 2nd, Bridget Veronica Lynch (née Russell), widow of Thomas Patrick Lynch, Beechmount, Mallow, Co. Cork. *Educ:* Stonyhurst Coll.; Edinburgh Univ. Served War of 1939-45; Commissioned Argyll and Sutherland Highlanders, 1942; Capt. 1945. Admitted to Faculty of Advocates, 1948; Standing Junior Counsel to Dept of Education for Scotland, 1951; Advocate-Depute for Sheriff Court, 1953; Extra Advocate-Depute for Glasgow Circuit, 1955; Advocate-Depute, 1957-59; QC Scot. 1959; Senior Advocate-Depute, 1964; Sheriff of Dumfries and Galloway, 1968; Sheriff of Roxburgh, Berwick and Selkirk, 1970; Solicitor-General for Scotland, 1970-72. *Publications:* Joint Editor, Scottish Edn of Current Law, 1948-61; Scottish Editor, Encyclopedia of Road Traffic Law and Practice, 1960-64; contributor to Scots Law Times. *Recreation:* golf. *Address:* Gospatric House, Dalmeny, W Lothian EH30 9TT. *T:* 031-331 1224. *Clubs:* New (Edinburgh); Honourable Company of Edinburgh Golfers.

BRAND, Alexander George, MBE 1945; Deputy Solicitor to the Secretary of State for Scotland, since 1972; *b* 23 March 1918; *s* of David Wilson Brand and Janet Ramsay Brand (née Paton); *m* 1947, Helen Constance Campbell; one *s* one *d. Educ:* Ayr Academy; Univ. of Glasgow. MA 1940, LLB 1948. Admitted Solicitor, 1948. Served in Royal Air Force, 1940-46 (Flt Lt). Legal Asst: Dumbarton CC, 1948; in Office of Solicitor to the Secretary of State for Scotland, 1949; Sen. Legal Asst, 1955; Asst Solicitor, 1964. Sec. of Scottish Law Commn, 1965-72. *Recreations:* golf, theatre, music, reading. *Address:* 16 Queen's Avenue, Edinburgh EH4 2DF. *T:* 031-332 4472. *Clubs:* Civil Service, Royal Commonwealth Society; Bruntsfield Links Golfing Society (Edinburgh).

BRAND, Sir Alfred; see Brand, Sir W. A.

BRAND, Prof. Charles Peter; Professor of Italian, University of Edinburgh, since 1966; *b* 7 Feb. 1923; *er s* of Charles Frank Brand and Dorothy (née Tapping); *m* 1948, Gunvor, *yr d* of Col I. Hellgren, Stockholm; one *s* three *d. Educ:* Cambridge High Sch.; Trinity Hall, Cambridge. War Service, Intelligence Corps, 1943-46. Open Maj. Scholar, Trinity Hall, 1940; 1st Class Hons. Mod. Languages, Cantab., 1948; PhD, Cantab., 1951. Asst Lecturer, Edinburgh Univ., 1952; Asst Lecturer, subsequently Lecturer, Cambridge Univ., 1952-66. Cavaliere Ufficiale, al Merito della Repubblica Italiana, 1975. General Editor, Modern Language Review, 1971-. *Publications:* Italy and the English Romantics, 1957; (Joint Ed.) Italian Studies presented to E. R.

Vincent, 1962; Torquato Tasso, 1965; Ariosto: a preface to the Orlando Furioso, 1974; contributions to learned journals. *Recreations:* sport, travel, gardening. *Address:* 21 Succoth Park, Edinburgh EH12 6BX. *T:* 031-337 1980.

BRAND, Hon. Sir David, KCMG 1969; *b* Dongara, WA, 1 Aug. 1912; *s* of late Albert John Brand and late Hilda (*née* Mitchell), Dongara, WA; *m* 1944, Doris Elspeth, *d* of H. McNeill, Arrino, WA; two *s* one *d. Educ:* Mullewa Sch., WA. Joined AIF, 1939; served in Middle East and Greece (wounded, 1941, and discharged on med. grounds, 1942); joined Volunteer Defence Force, 1942, and apptd Chief Instr, Geraldton Area, WA. Member, WA Legislative Assembly (for Greenough), 1945-75; Junior Minister for Housing, Local Govt and Forests, 1949; Minister for Works and Water Supplies, 1950-53; Leader of Opposition, 1957-59 and 1971-72; Premier, Treasurer and Minister for Tourists, 1959-71. Hon. LLD (Univ. of WA). *Recreations:* golf, tennis. *Address:* 24 Ednah Street, Como, WA, Australia. *T:* 67.2906. *Club:* West Australian (Perth).

BRAND, David William Robert; *see* Brand, Hon. Lord.

BRAND, Geoffrey Arthur; Under-Secretary, Incomes Division, Department of Employment, since 1972; *b* 13 June 1930; *s* of Arthur William Charles Brand and Muriel Ada Brand; *m* 1954, Joy Trotman; two *d. Educ:* Andover Grammar Sch.; University Coll., London. Entered Min. of Labour, 1953; Private Sec. to Parly Sec., 1956-67; Colonial Office, 1957-58; Private Sec. to Minister of Labour, 1965-66; Asst. Sec., Industrial Relations and Research and Planning Divisions 1966-72. *Address:* Cedarwood, Seer Green, Beaconsfield, Bucks. *T:* Beaconsfield 6637.

BRAND, Sir (William) Alfred, Kt 1965; CBE 1958; *b* 22 Aug. 1888; *m* 1913, Myrtle M. Kingston; one *s* two *d* (and one *d* decd). *Educ:* Childers and Appletree Creek State Schools. Canefarmer. Pres., Australian Sugar Producers' Assoc. Ltd, 1943. MLA for Burrum, Qld, 1920-32, for Isis, 1932-50; MP for Wide Bay, Qld, 1954-58. *Recreations:* cricket and bowls. *Address:* 38 North Street, Childers, Qld 4660, Australia. *T:* Childers 33. *Clubs:* Childers, Isis (Queensland).

BRANDES, Lawrence Henry; Under Secretary, HM Treasury, since 1975; *b* 16 Dec. 1924; *m* 1950, Dorothea Stanyon; one *s* one *d. Educ:* Beltane Sch.; London Sch. of Economics. Min. of Health, 1950; Principal Private Sec. to Minister, 1959; Nat. Bd for Prices and Incomes, 1966; Dept of Employment and Productivity, 1969; Under-Sec., DHSS, 1970. *Address:* 29 Temple Fortune Hill, NW11.

BRANDO, Marlon; American actor, stage and screen; *b* Omaha, Nebraska, 3 April 1924; *s* of Marlon Brando; *m* 1957, Anna Kashfi (marr. diss., 1959); one *s. Educ:* Libertyville High Sch., Illinois; Shattuck Military Academy, Minnesota. Entered Dramatic Workshop of New School for Social Research, New York, 1943; has studied with Elia Kazan and Stella Adler. *Plays include:* I Remember Mama, Broadway, 1944; Truckline Café, 1946; Candida, 1946; A Flag is Born, 1946; The Eagle Has Two Heads, 1946; A Streetcar Named Desire, 1947. *Films include:* The Men; A Streetcar Named Desire; Viva Zapata!; Julius Cæsar; The Wild One; Désirée; On the Waterfront; Guys and Dolls; Tea House of the August Moon; Sayonara; The Young Lions; The Fugitive Kind; Mutiny on the Bounty; The Ugly American; The Saboteur, Code Name-Morituri; The Chase; Southwest to Sonora; A Countess from Hong Kong; Reflections in a Golden Eye; The Night of the Following Day; Candy; Queimad!; The Nightcomers; The Godfather; Last Tango in Paris; The Missouri Breaks. Directed, produced and appeared in One-Eyed Jacks, 1959. Academy Award, best actor of year, 1954. *Address:* Box 809, Beverly Hills, Calif, USA.

BRANDON, Henry; *see* Brandon, O. H.

BRANDON, Hon. Sir Henry (Vivian), Kt 1966; MC 1942; **Hon. Mr Justice Brandon;** Judge of the High Court of Justice, Family Division, and Judge of the Admiralty Court, since 1971; *b* 3 June 1920; *y s* of late Captain V. R. Brandon, CBE, RN, and Joan Elizabeth Maud Simpson; *m* 1955, Jeanette Rosemary, *e d* of J. V. B. Janvrin; three *s* one *d. Educ:* Winchester Coll. (Scholar); King's Coll., Cambridge (Scholar 1938, Stewart of Rannoch Scholar 1939). Commnd 2nd Lieut RA 1939; Major 1944; served Madagascar, 1942, India and Burma, 1942-45. BA 1946. Barrister, Inner Temple, 1946 (Entrance and Yarborough Anderson Scholar); Member Bar Council, 1951-53; QC 1961; Judge of the High Court of Justice, Probate, Divorce and Admiralty Division, 1966-71. Member panel of Lloyd's arbitrators in salvage cases, 1961-66; Member panel from which Wreck Commissioners chosen, 1963-66. *Recreation:* cricket. *Address:* 18 Regent's Park Terrace, NW1. *T:* 01-485 3033; Royal Courts of Justice, Strand, WC2. *Club:* MCC.

BRANDON, (Oscar) Henry; Associate Editor and Chief American correspondent of the Sunday Times; *b* 9 March 1916; *m* 1970, Mabel Hobart Wentworth; one *d. Educ:* Univ. of Prague and Lausanne. Joined Sunday Times, 1939; War Correspondent, N Africa and W Europe, 1943-45; Paris Correspondent, 1945-46; Roving Diplomatic Correspondent, 1947-49; Washington Correspondent, 1950-. Foreign corresp. award, Univ. of California, Los Angeles, 1957; award, Lincoln Univ., Jefferson City, Missouri, 1962; Hannen Swaffer award, 1964. *Publications:* As We Are, 1961; In The Red, 1966; Conversations with Henry Brandon, 1966; The Anatomy of Error, 1970; The Retreat of American Power, 1973. *Recreations:* ski-ing, tennis, swimming, photography. *Address:* 814 National Press Building, Washington, DC 20004, USA. *T:* 628-4310. *Clubs:* Federal City, National Press, Overseas Writers (Washington, DC).

BRANDON, Prof. Percy Samuel, (Prof. Peter Brandon); Professor of Electrical Engineering, University of Cambridge, since 1971; *b* 9 Nov. 1916; *s* of P. S. Brandon, OBE; *m* 1942, Joan Edith Marriage, GRSM (London), LRAM; two *s. Educ:* Chigwell Sch.; Jesus Coll., Cambridge (MA). Joined The Marconi Company, 1939; Research Div., 1940-71. Frequency Measurement, 1940-44: Aerial Section, 1944-45. FM Radar, 1945-53; Chief of Guidance Systems, 1953-57; Chief of Mathematics and Systems Analysis Gp, 1957-65; Manager of Theoretical Sciences Laboratory, 1965-68; Asst Dir of Research, 1965-68; Manager of Research Div. of GEC-Marconi Electronics, 1968-71. Part-time lecturing at Mid-Essex Technical Coll., and others, 1945-66. FInstP, FIEE. *Publications:* contribs to Marconi Review, IEE Proc., Agardograph, Electronic Engineering, etc. *Recreation:* colour photography. *Address:* University Engineering Laboratory, Trumpington Street, Cambridge CB2 1PZ. *T:* Cambridge 66466; New Courts, 8 Bridge Lane, Little Shelford, Cambs CB2 5HE. *T:* Shelford 2541.

BRANDT, Peter Augustus; Director, Edward Bates (Holdings) Ltd, since 1972; Chairman, Edward Bates & Sons Ltd, since 1974 (Director since 1972); *b* 2 July 1931; *s* of Walter Augustus Brandt and Dorothy Gray Brandt (*née* Crane); *m* 1962, Elisabeth Margaret (*née* ten Bos); two *s* one *d. Educ:* Eton Coll.; Trinity Coll., Cambridge (BA). Joined Wm Brandt's Sons & Co. Ltd, Merchant Bankers, 1954; Mem. Bd, 1960; Chief Executive, 1966; resigned, 1972. Director: London Life Assoc., 1962; Corp. of Argentine Meat Producers (CAP) Ltd and affiliates, 1970. *Recreations:* sailing, rowing, steam engines, wild fowl. *Address:* 25 Holland Villas Road, W14 8DH. *T:* 01-603 9926. *Clubs:* Carlton; Leander (Henley-on-Thames); Royal Harwich Yacht (Ipswich).

BRANDT, William, (Bill Brandt); photographer; *b* 1904; parents of Russian descent. *Educ:* studied under Man Ray, Paris, in 1930s. Spent much of early youth in Germany and Switzerland; worked in Paris for many years. At age of 25 became a photo-journalist; settled in London, 1931; towards the end of War of 1939-45 he began to photograph nudes and did portraits and landscapes. Exhibition at Museum of Modern Art, New York, Oct.-Nov. 1969; the Arts Council put on this exhibition at the Hayward Gallery, London, Apr.-May 1970 (Prof. Aaron Scharf wrote introd. to catalogue, Herbert Spencer designed catalogue and poster); subseq. the exhibits were shown at 12 centres outside London and then returned to New York. Selected The Land exhibition, V and A, 1975-76, Edinburgh, Belfast and Cardiff, 1976. *Publications:* Shadow of Light, 1966, rev. edn 1977; Perspective of Nudes series, 1961-; contrib. to magazines in Europe, USA, etc.

BRANDT, Willy; Chairman, Social Democratic Party (SPD), Federal Republic of Germany, since 1964; *b* 18 Dec. 1913; *m* 1948, Rut Hansen; three *s* one *d. Educ:* Johanneum, Lübeck; University of Oslo. Fled from Lübeck to Norway, 1933. Chief Editor, Berliner Stadtblatt, 1950-51. Mem., Social Democratic Party (SPD), 1931-; Rep. Federal Board of SPD (German Social Democratic Party) in Berlin, 1948-49, Deputy Chairman of SPD, 1962-63. Member German Federal Parliament, 1949-57 and 1969-; President Berlin House of Representatives, 1955-57; Governing Mayor of W Berlin, 1957-66; President German Conference of Mayors, 1958-63; President German Federal Council, 1957-58; Vice-Chancellor and Foreign Minister, 1966-69, Chancellor 1969-74, Federal Republic of Germany. Pres., Socialist International, 1976. Dr (*hc*): Pennsylvania Univ., 1959; Maryland Univ., 1960; Harvard Univ., 1963; Hon. DCL, Oxford Univ., 1969. Nobel Prize for Peace, 1971. Grosskreuz des Verdienstordens der Bundesrepublik Deutschland, 1959. *Publications:* Krigen i Norge, 1945; Forbrytere og andre tyskere, 1946; (with Richard Löwenthal) Ernst Reuter: Ein Leben für die Freiheit, 1957; Von Bonn nach Berlin, 1957; Mein Weg nach

Berlin (recorded by Leo Lania), 1960; Plädoyer für die Zukunft, 1961; The Ordeal of Co-existence, 1963; Begegnungen mit Kennedy, 1964; (with Günter Struve) Draussen, 1966 (UK, as In Exile, 1971); Friedenspolitik in Europa, 1968; Essays, Reflections and Letters 1933-47, 1971; Der Wille zum Frieden, 1971; Uber den Tag hinaus, 1974; Begegnungen und Einsichten, 1976; many publications on topical questions in Sweden and Norway; articles in home and foreign journals. *Address:* (office) Erich-Öllenhauer-Strasse 1, 5300 Bonn 1, Germany. *T:* 5321.

BRANIGAN, Sir Patrick (Francis), Kt 1954; QC; JP; Chairman: Agricultural Land Tribunal for South West Area of England; Mental Health Review Tribunal for SW Region of England; National Insurance Medical Appeal Tribunal for SW Region; Pensions Appeal Tribunal; *b* 30 Aug. 1906; *e s* of late D. Branigan and Teresa, *d* of Thomas Clinton, Annagassan, Co. Louth; *m* 1935, Prudence, *yr d* of late Dr A. Avent, Seaton, Devon; one *s* one *d*. *Educ:* Newbridge Coll., Co. Kildare; Trinity Coll., Dublin. BA 1st Class Hons in Law and Political Science and gold medallist, 1928; called to Irish Bar, Certificate of Honour, 1928 (1st Victoria Prize, 1927); called to Bar, Gray's Inn, 1935. Practised at Irish Bar, 1928-30; Downing Coll., Cambridge, 1930-31; Colonial Administrative Service, Kenya, 1931; Crown Counsel, Tanganyika, 1934; Solicitor-General, N. Rhodesia, 1938; Chairman NR Man-power Cttee, 1939-41; Chairman Conciliation Board, Copperbelt Strike, 1940; Member NR Nat. Arbitration Tribunal, 1940-46; Member Strauss Arbitration Tribunal, Bulawayo, 1944; Chairman, Road Transport Services Board and Electricity Board of N. Rhodesia, 1939-46; Legal Secretary to Govt of Malta and Chairman Malta War Damage Commission, 1946-48; periodically acting Lieut-Governor of Malta, 1947-48. Minister of Justice and Attorney-General, Gold Coast, 1948-55; QC Gold Coast, 1949; retired, 1955. Chairman of Commission of inquiry into Copperbelt industrial unrest, 1956; Member Industrial Disputes Tribunal, 1955-59. Dep. Chm. Devon QS, 1958-71; a Recorder of the Crown Court, 1972-75. JP Devon 1955. Knight Commander of Order of St Gregory, 1956. *Recreations:* golf, fishing. *Address:* Willhayne, Colyton, Devon. *T:* Colyton 52435.

BRANNAN, Charles Franklin; lawyer; *b* 23 Aug. 1903; *s* of John Brannan and Ella Louise Street; *m* 1932, Eda Seltzer; no *c*. *Educ:* Regis Coll., and University of Denver Law Sch., Denver, Colorado, USA. Private law practice, Denver, Colorado, 1929-35; Asst Regional Attorney: Resettlement Administration, Denver, 1935-37; Regional Attorney, Office of the Solicitor, US Dept of Agriculture, Denver, 1937-41; Regional Director of Farm Security Administration, US Dept of Agriculture, Denver, 1941-44; Asst Administrator, Farm Security Administration, US Dept of Agriculture, Washington, DC, April-June 1944; Asst Secretary of Agriculture, Washington, DC, June 1944-48; Secretary of Agriculture, USA, 1948-Jan. 1953. Pres., Bd of Water Commissioners, Denver, 1976. Hon. Degrees: Doctor of Laws from the University of Denver and Doctor of Science from the Colorado Agricultural and Mechanical Coll. *Address:* (home) 3131 East Alameda, Denver, Colorado 80209, USA; (office) 12025 E 45th Avenue, Denver, Colo 80239. *Club:* Denver Athletic (Denver, Colorado).

BRANSON, Rear Adm. Cecil Robert Peter Charles, CBE 1975; Assistant Chief of Naval Staff (Operations), Ministry of Defence, 1975-77, retired; *b* 30 March 1924; *s* of Cecil Branson and Marcelle Branson; *m* 1946, Sonia Moss; one *d*. *Educ:* RNC, Dartmouth. Served, HMS Dragon, W Africa, S Atlantic, Indian Ocean and Far East (present during time of fall of Singapore and Java), 1941-42; Sub-Lieut's Courses, 1942-43; qual. as submarine specialist, served in HM S/M Sea Rover, Far East, 1944-45; various appts in S/Ms, 1945-53; First Lieut, HMS Defender, 1953-55; jssc; CO, HMS Roebuck, Dartmouth Trng Sqdn, 1957; Staff, Flag Officer Flotillas Mediterranean, 1959-60; Jt Planning Staff, MoD, 1960-62; Exec. Officer, HMS Victorious, Far East, 1962-64; CO, HMS Rooke, Gibraltar, 1965; NATO Def. Coll., 1965; Defence Planning Staff, MoD, 1966-68; CO, HMS Phoebe, and Captain (D) Londonderry Sqdn, 1968-70; Naval Attaché, Paris, 1970-73; CO, HMS Hermes, 1973-74 (Hermes headed RN task force evacuating Brit. and foreign subjects from Cyprus beaches after Turkish invasion, 1973). Comdr 1957, Captain 1965, Rear Adm. 1975. *Club:* Army and Navy.

BRANSON, Col Sir Douglas (Stephenson), KBE 1954; CB 1950; DSO 1918, and 2 bars; MC 1917; TD; MA; *b* 25 July 1893; *s* of Col George Ernest Branson, JP, Broomgrove, Sheffield; *m* 1st, 1930, Edith Eileen (*d* 1959), *d* of Joseph Bradbury, Sheffield; 2nd, 1961, Ailie (*widow* of Brig. John Malcolm Fisher), *d* of late Sir William Bell. *Educ:* Marlborough; New Coll., Oxford. Admitted a Solicitor, 1920 and practised until 1970. Served European War, 1914-18, The Hallamshire Bn York and

Lancaster Regt. Col, 1924; Commander 148 Infantry Brigade (TA), 1925-29; Additional ADC to the King, 1927. DL West Riding of Yorks, 1934. High Sheriff of Hallamshire, 1963. *Address:* 6 Paradise Square, Sheffield, S Yorks. *T:* 737346; 385 Fulwood Road, Sheffield S10 3GA. *T:* Sheffield 302149.

BRANSON, Edward James, MA; a Metropolitan Stipendiary Magistrate, since 1971; barrister-at-law; *b* 10 March 1918; *s* of late Rt Hon. Sir George Branson, PC, sometime Judge of High Court, and late Lady (Mona) Branson; *m* 1949, Evette Huntley, *e d* of late Rupert Huntley Flindt; one *s* two *d*. *Educ:* Bootham Sch., York; Trinity Coll., Cambridge. Served War, 1939-46, Staffordshire Yeomanry: Palestine, Egypt, and Western Desert 1941-42; GSO 3 (Ops) attd 2 NZ Div. for Alamein, 1942; GSO2 (Ops), attd 6 (US) Corps for Salerno and Anzio landings, 1943-44; subseq. GSO2 (Ops) 53 (W) Div. in Germany. Called to the Bar, Inner Temple, 1950; practised London and SE Circuit. *Recreations:* shooting, riding, fishing, archaeology. *Address:* Tanyard Farm, Shamley Green, near Guildford, Surrey. *T:* Bramley 3133, 8136; 150 Ifield Road, SW10. *T:* 01-373 3957; Casa Candi, Binibeca, near San Luis, Menorca.

BRANSON, William Rainforth, CBE 1969; retired; *b* 2 Jan. 1905; *s* of late A. W. Branson, JP; *m* 1932, Dorothy Iris Green; no *c*. *Educ:* Rydal Sch.; University of Leeds. BSc, 1st Class Hons (Fuel and Gas Engrg), 1927; MSc 1930. Asst Engineer, Gas Light & Coke Co., London, 1927-37; Asst Engineer, later Dep. Engineer, Cardiff Gas Light & Coke Co., 1937-45; Dep. Controller, later Controller, Public Utilities Br., Control Commn for Germany, 1945-49; Planning Engineer, Wales Gas Board, 1949-51; Technical Officer, E. Midlands Gas Board, 1952-54; Dep. Chairman, W. Midlands Gas Board, 1954-65; Chm., Scottish Gas Bd, 1965-68; Dir, Woodall-Duckham Group Ltd, 1969-73. President, Instn of Gas Engineers, 1964-65. *Recreation:* music. *Address:* 32 Poolfield Drive, Solihull, West Midlands. *T:* 021-704 9240.

BRANT, Colin Trevor; HM Diplomatic Service; Counsellor (Energy), Washington, since 1973; *b* 2 June 1929; *m* 1954, Jean Faith Walker; one *s* two *d*. *Educ:* Christ's Hospital, Horsham, Sussex; Sidney Sussex Coll., Cambridge (MA). 4th Hussars, RAC, 1948-49. Joined Sen. Br., Foreign Office, 1952; MECAS, Lebanon, 1953-54; Bahrain, 1954; Amman, Jordan, 1954-56; FO, 1956-59; Stockholm, 1959-61; Cairo, 1961-64; Joint Services Staff Coll., Latimer, Bucks, 1964-65 (jssc); FO, 1965-67; First Sec., Head of Chancery and Consul, Tunis, 1967-68; Foreign and Commonwealth Office, 1969-71; Counsellor (Commercial), Caracas, 1971-73. *Recreations:* music, painting, history. *Address:* British Embassy, Washington; East Wing, Wethersfield Manor, Braintree, Essex. *Clubs:* Travellers', Royal Commonwealth Society; International (Washington).

BRASH, Rev. Alan Anderson, OBE 1962; Deputy General Secretary, World Council of Churches, since 1974; *b* 5 June 1913; *s* of Thomas C. Brash, CBE, New Zealand, and Margaret Brash (*née* Allan); *m* 1938, Eljean Ivory Hill; one *s* one *d*. *Educ:* Dunedin Univ., NZ (MA); Edinburgh Univ. (BD). Parish Minister in NZ, 1938-46 and 1952-56; Gen. Sec., NZ Nat. Council of Churches, 1947-52 and 1957-64, East Asia Christian Conf., 1958-68; Dir, Christian Aid, London, 1968-70; Dir, Commn on Inter-Church Aid, Refuge and World Service, WCC, 1970-73. Hon. DD Toronto, 1971. *Address:* c/o World Council of Churches, 150 Route de Ferney, Geneva, Switzerland.

BRASH, Robert; HM Diplomatic Service; Counsellor, Vienna, since 1974; *b* 30 May 1924; *s* of Frank and Ida Brash; *m* 1954, Barbara Enid Clarke; three *s* one *d*. *Educ:* Trinity Coll., Cambridge. War Service, 1943-46. Entered Foreign Service, 1949; Djakarta, 1951-55; FO, 1955-58; First Sec., 1956; Jerusalem, 1958-61; Bonn, 1961-64; Bucharest, 1964-66; FCO, 1966-70; Counsellor, 1968; Canadian Nat. Defence Coll., 1970-71; Counsellor and Consul-Gen., Saigon, 1971-73. *Recreations:* walking, gardening, some golf. *Address:* c/o Foreign and Commonwealth Office, SW1. *Club:* Royal Automobile.

BRASHER, Christopher William; Reporter/Producer, BBC Television, since 1972; Columnist and Olympic Correspondent, The Observer, since 1961; *b* 21 Aug. 1928; *s* of William Kenneth Brasher and Katie Howe Brasher; *m* 1959, Shirley Bloomer; one *s* two *d*. *Educ:* Rugby Sch.; St John's Coll., Cambridge (Hons Degree Nat. Sciences). Pres., Mountaineering Club and Athletic Club, Cambridge Univ. Management Trainee and Jun. Executive, Mobil Oil Co., 1951-57; Sports Editor, The Observer, 1957-61; BBC Television: Reporter, Tonight, 1961-65; Editor, Time Out, and Man Alive, 1964-65; Head of Gen. Features, 1969-72. Rep. GB, Olympic Games, 1952 and 1956; Gold Medal for 3,000 metres Steeplechase, 1956. National Medal of Honour, Finland, 1975. *Publications:* The Red Snows (with Sir John

Hunt), 1960; Sportsmen of our Time, 1962; Tokyo 1964: a diary of the XVIIIth Olympiad, 1964; Mexico 1968: a diary of the XIXth Olympics, 1968; Munich 72, 1972. *Recreations:* mountains, orienteering, social running. *Address:* The Navigator's House, River Lane, Richmond, Surrey. *T:* 01-940 8822. *Clubs:* Alpine, Hurlingham; Hawks (Cambridge).

BRASNETT, Rev. Dr Bertrand Rippington, DD Oxon, 1935; *b* 22 Jan. 1893; *e s* of Stanley Brasnett, The Manor House, Marham, Norfolk, *gs* of Edward Rowing Brasnett, West Bilney House, Norfolk; unmarried. *Educ:* Oxford High Sch.; private tutor; Keble Coll., Oxford; Cuddesdon Theological Coll. Squire Scholar of the University of Oxford, 1911-15, 2nd class Classical Moderations, 2nd class Literæ Humaniores, BA, MA, Diploma in Theology with Distinction, BD; Deacon, 1916; Priest, 1918; Chaplain and Asst Master, Bradfield Coll., Berks, 1916-18; Priest-in-charge, Coleshill, Bucks, 1918-22; Chaplain and Lecturer, Bishops' Coll., Cheshunt, 1922-25; Vice-Principal, 1925-29, Principal and Pantonian Prof., 1930-42, of the Theological Coll. of the Scottish Episcopal Church, Edinburgh; Hon. Chaplain of St Mary's Cathedral, Edinburgh, 1926-29; Canon, 1930-42, and Chancellor, 1940-42, of St Mary's Cathedral, Edinburgh; Examining Chaplain to the Bishop of Edinburgh, 1930-42; Select Preacher, University of Oxford, 1941-43. *Publications:* The Suffering of the Impassible God, 1928; The Infinity of God, 1933; God the Worshipful, 1935. *Address:* Pleasant View, 15 Jack Straw's Lane, Headington, Oxford.

BRASS, John, CBE 1968; BSc, CEng, FIMinE, MICE; FRSA; Member, National Coal Board, 1971-73; Regional Chairman, Yorkshire and North-Western Areas, National Coal Board, 1967-71; *b* 22 Oct. 1908; 2nd *s* of late John Brass, Mining Engineer, and late Mary Brass (*née* Swainston); *m* 1934, Jocelyn Constance Cape, Stroud, Glos; three *s* one *d. Educ:* Oundle Sch.; Birmingham Univ. (BSc Hons). Various appointments, all in mining; Chairman W Midlands Division, NCB, 1961-67. *Address:* The Old Granary, Linton, near Wetherby, W Yorks.

BRASSEY, family name of **Baron Brassey of Apethorpe.**

BRASSEY OF APETHORPE, 3rd Baron, *cr* 1938, of Apethorpe; **David Henry Brassey;** Bt 1922; JP; DL; *b* 16 Sept. 1932; *er s* of 2nd Baron Brassey of Apethorpe, MC, TD, and late Lady Brassey of Apethorpe; *S* father, 1967; *m* 1958, Myrna Elizabeth (*d* 1974), *o d* of Lieut-Col John Baskervyle-Glegg; one *s.* Commissioned, Grenadier Guards, 1951; Major, 1966, retired, 1967. JP 1970, DL 1972, Northants. *Heir: s* Hon. Edward Brassey, *b* 9 March 1964. *Address:* The Manor House, Apethorpe, Peterborough. *T:* Kingscliffe 231. *Club:* White's.

BRASSEY, Brevet-Col Hugh Trefusis, OBE 1959; MC 1944; Vice-Lord-Lieutenant of Wiltshire, since 1968; *b* 5 Oct. 1915; *s* of Lieut-Col Edgar Hugh Brassey, MVO, and Margaret Harriet (*née* Trefusis); *m* 1939, Joyce Patricia, *d* of Captain Maurice Kingscote; two *s* two *d* (and one *d* decd). *Educ:* Eton; Sandhurst. Regular Commission, The Royal Scots Greys, 1935-46; served Palestine, Africa, Italy and NW Europe, Lieut-Col Comdg Royal Wilts Yeomanry, 1955-58. ADC (TA) to the Queen, 1964-69; Exon, Queen's Bodyguard, Yeoman of the Guard, 1964-70, Ensign, 1970-, Adjutant and Clerk of the Cheque, 1971. Col, The Royal Scots Dragoon Guards, 1974-. Chairman, Chippenham Conservative Assoc., 1951-53, 1966-68 (Pres. 1968). Pres., Wilts Assoc. of Boys Clubs, 1968. JP 1951, DL 1955, High Sheriff 1959, Wilts. Regional Dir (Salisbury), Lloyds Bank. Croix de Guerre (France), 1944. *Recreation:* country. *Address:* Manor Farm, Little Somerford, Chippenham, Wilts. *T:* Malmesbury 2255. *Club:* Cavalry and Guards.

BRASSEY, Lt-Col Hon. Peter (Esmé); Lord-Lieutenant of Cambridgeshire, since 1975; *b* 5 Dec. 1907; *o* surv. *s* of 1st Baron Brassey of Apethorpe; *m* 1944, Lady Romayne Cecil, 2nd *d* of 5th Marquess of Exeter, KG, CMG; two *s* one *d. Educ:* Eton; Magdalene Coll., Cambridge. Barrister-at-Law, Inner Temple, Midland Circuit, 1931. Northamptonshire Yeomanry, Lieut-Col, 1945; served NW Europe (wounded). Dir, The Essex Water Co. Ltd. DL 1961, High Sheriff, 1966, and Vice-Lieutenant, 1966-74, County of Huntingdon and Peterborough; DL County of Cambridge, 1974. KStJ 1976. *Recreations:* shooting, fishing. *Address:* The Close House, Barnack, Stamford, Lincs PE9 3DY. *T:* Stamford 740 238. *Clubs:* Carlton, Farmers'.

BRATBY, Jean Esme Oregon; see Cooke, J. E. O.

BRATBY, John Randall, RA 1971 (ARA 1959); ARCA; FIAL; RBA; Painter and Writer; Member of London Group; Editorial Adviser for Art Quarterly; *b* 19 July 1928; *s* of George Alfred Bratby and Lily Beryl Randall; *m* 1953, Jean Esme Oregon

Cooke, ARA (*see* Jean E. Cooke) (marr. diss. 1977); three *s* one *d*; *m* 1977, Patti Prime. *Educ:* Tiffin Boys' Sch.; Kingston School of Art; Royal College of Art. Teacher: Carlisle College of Art, 1956; Royal College of Art, 1957-58. Gained prizes and scholarships, 1954-57. Numerous one-man exhibitions at Beaux Arts Gallery from 1954; Zwemmer Gallery from 1959; Thackeray Gallery; Furneaux Gallery; also in galleries abroad. Exhibited: Royal Academy (yearly) from 1955; has also shown pictures in various international exhibitions and festivals. Guggenheim Award for Great Britain, 1956 and 1958; Paintings for film The Horse's Mouth, 1958. Works in public collections: Tate Gallery; Arts Council of Great Britain; British Council; Contemporary Arts Society. National Galleries: Canada; New Zealand; NSW and Victoria; galleries in many cities and towns of Great Britain; Victoria and Albert Museum; Ashmolean Museum; Museum of Modern Art, New York; also in many other public and private art collections, in Great Britain, the Commonwealth and USA. Has made television appearances and sound broadcasts. FRSA. *Publications:* fiction: Breakdown, 1960; Breakfast and Elevenses, 1961; Break-Pedal Down, 1962 (also TV play); Break 50 Kill, 1963; non-fiction: studio publication of colour reproductions of own work, 1961; contrib., illustrations, Oxford Illustrated Old Testament, 1968; Stanley Spencer, 1969. *Address:* 7A Hardy Road, The Coach House and the Studio, Blackheath, SE3.

BRATT, Guy Maurice, CMG 1977; MBE 1945; HM Diplomatic Service; Counsellor, British Embassy, Washington, since 1975; *b* 4 April 1920; *s* of late Ernst Lars Gustaf Bratt and late Alice Maud Mary Bratt (*née* Raper); *m* 1945, Françoise Nelly Roberte Girardet; two *s* one *d. Educ:* Merchant Taylors' Sch.; London Univ. (BA). Served Army, 1939-46 (MBE): Major, Royal Signals. Solicitor 1947. Asst Sec., Colonial Develt Corp.; joined HM Foreign (subseq. Diplomatic) Service, 1952; served FO, 1952-54; Berlin, 1954-56; Brussels, 1956-58; FO, 1958-62; Vienna, 1962-66; FCO, 1966-70; Geneva, 1970-72; FCO, 1972-74. *Recreations:* music, railways, mountaineering. *Address:* c/o Foreign and Commonwealth Office, SW1A 2AL; 2 Orchehill Rise, Gerrards Cross, Bucks SL9 8PR. *T:* Gerrards Cross 83106. *Clubs:* Travellers'; Cosmos (Washington, DC).

BRATTAIN, Dr Walter H(ouser); Research Physicist, Bell Telephone Laboratories, Inc., 1929-67; Overseer Emeritus, Whitman College; engaged with others in research investigating the properties of lipid membranes in salt solutions; *b* Amoy, China, 10 Feb. 1902; *s* of Ross R. Brattain and Ottilie Brattain (*née* Houser); *m* 1st, 1935, Keren Gilmore (*d* 1957); one *s*; 2nd, 1958, Emma Jane Miller (*née* Kirsch). *Educ:* Whitman Coll., Walla Walla, Washington; University of Oregon, Eugene, Oregon; University of Minnesota, Minneapolis, Minn. BS 1924, Whitman Coll.; MA 1926, University of Oregon; PhD 1929, University of Minnesota. Asst Physicist, Bureau of Standards, 1928-29; Technical Staff, Bell Telephone Labs, Inc., 1929-67. Division of War Research, Columbia Univ., 1942-44. Visiting Lecturer, Harvard Univ., 1952-53; Visiting Prof. of Physics (part-time) Whitman Coll., 1963-72. Hon. Dr of Science: Portland Univ., 1952; Union Coll., 1955; Whitman Coll., 1955; University of Minnesota, 1957; Gustavus Adolphus Coll., 1963; Hon. LHD Hartwick Coll., 1964. Stuart Ballantine Medal, Franklin Institute, 1952; John Scott Medal, City of Philadelphia, 1955; Nobel Prize for Physics (with J. Bardeen and W. Shockley), 1956. Fellow: American Academy of Arts and Sciences, 1956; National Academy of Sciences, 1959. *Publications:* many scientific papers on Thermionics and Semiconductors in various physics journals. *Recreation:* golf. *Address:* Whitman College, Walla Walla, Washington 99362, USA. *T:* (509) 529-5100.

BRAY, Denis Campbell, CMG 1977; CVO 1975; Hong Kong Commissioner in London, since 1977; *b* 24 Jan. 1926; *s* of Rev. Arthur Henry Bray and Edith Muriel Bray; *m* 1952, Marjorie Elizabeth Bottomley; four *d* (one *s* decd). *Educ:* Kingswood Sch.; Jesus Coll., Cambridge (MA). BScEcon London. RN, 1947-49. Devonshire, 1949-50; Admin. Officer, Hong Kong, 1950; Dist Comr, New Territories, 1971; Sec. for Home Affairs, Hong Kong, 1973-77. *Recreations:* ocean racing and cruising. *Address:* Hong Kong Commission, 6 Grafton Street, W1X 3LB. *T:* 01-499 9821. *Cables:* Hongaid, London W1. *Clubs:* London Rowing, Royal Ocean Racing; Leander (Henley-on-Thames); Hong Kong, Royal Hong Kong Jockey, Royal Hong Kong Yacht; Tai Po Boat.
See also J. W. Bray.

BRAY, Frederick, CB 1949; MA Oxon; Consultant to the City and Guilds of London Institute, 1959-70; *b* 1895; *y s* of late Herbert James Bray; *m* 1926, Emily Lloyd, *d* of Richard Poole; two *s. Educ:* Queen Elizabeth's, Tamworth; Pembroke Coll., Oxford. War Service, 1914-18. Master, Clifton Coll., 1922-25;

Asst Director of Education, Leeds, 1925-28; Board of Education: HM Inspector of Schools, 1928-38; Staff Inspector, 1938-40; Divisional Inspector, 1940-45; Ministry of Education; Principal Asst Secretary, 1945-46, Under-Secretary, 1946-56. Technical Adviser to City and Guilds of London Institute; Educational Adviser to the British Assoc. for Commercial and Industrial Education, 1956; Dean of College of Preceptors, 1957; Adviser on Technical Education to the Federal Govt of Rhodesia and Nyasaland and to the Govt of Southern Rhodesia, 1957-63. *Publications:* Light, 1927; General Science, 1928. *Recreation:* golf. *Address:* 24 Pall Mall, 97 Third Street, Salisbury, Rhodesia. *Clubs:* Chelsea Arts; Royal Salisbury Golf.

BRAY, Jeremy William; MP (Lab) Motherwell and Wishaw, since Oct. 1974; *b* 29 June 1930; *s* of Rev. Arthur Henry Bray and Mrs Edith Muriel Bray; *m* 1953, Elizabeth (*née* Trowell); four *d. Educ:* Aberystwyth Grammar Sch.; Kingswood Sch.; Jesus Coll., Cambridge. Researched in pure mathematics at Cambridge, 1953-55; Choate Fellow, Harvard Univ., USA, 1955-56; Technical Officer, Wilton Works of ICI. Contested (Lab) Thirsk and Malton, General Election, 1959; MP (Lab) Middlesbrough West, 1962-70. Member, Select Cttee on Nationalised Industries, 1962-64; Chairman: Labour, Science and Technology Group, 1964-66; Economic Affairs Estimates Sub-Cttee, 1964-66; Parliamentary Secretary, Min. of Power, 1966-67; Jt Parly Sec., Min. of Technology, 1967-69. Dir, Mullard Ltd, 1970-73; Consultant, Battelle Res. Centre, Geneva, 1973; Sen. Res. Fellow, 1974, Vis. Prof., 1975, Univ. of Strathclyde. Dep. Chm., Christian Aid, 1972-; Co-Dir, Programme of Res. into Econometric Methods, Imperial Coll., 1971-74. Chm., Fabian Soc., 1971-72. *Publications:* Decision in Government, 1970; Fabian pamphlets and articles in jls. *Recreation:* sailing. *Address:* 4 Stafford Street, Helensburgh, Dunbartonshire.
See also D . C . Bray .

BRAY, Hon. Dr John Jefferson; Chief Justice of Supreme Court of South Australia since 1967; *b* 16 Sept. 1912; *s* of Harry Midwinter Bray and Gertrude Eleonore Bray (*née* Stow). *Educ:* St Peter's Coll., Adelaide; Univ. of Adelaide. LLB 1932, LLB Hons 1933, LLD 1937. Admitted to South Australian Bar, 1933; QC 1957. Univ. of Adelaide: Actg Lectr in Jurisprudence, 1941, 1943, 1945, 1951; Actg Lectr in Legal History, 1957-58; Lectr in Roman Law, 1959-66. *Publications:* Poems, 1962; Poems 1961-1971, 1972; contrib. Australian Law Jl. *Address:* c/o Supreme Court House, Victoria Square, Adelaide, South Australia 5000. *T:* 87-8700. *Club:* Amateur Sports of South Australia.

BRAY, Gen. Sir Robert (Napier Hubert Campbell), GBE 1966 (CBE 1952); KCB 1962 (CB 1957); DSO 1944, and Bar 1945; retired; late Duke of Wellington's Regiment (Colonel of the Regiment, 1965-75); *b* 1908; *s* of late Brig.-Gen. Robert Napier Bray, CMG, DSO; *m* 1936, Nora, *d* of G. C. G. Gee, Rothley, Leics.; three *s. Educ:* Gresham's Sch., Holt; Royal Military Coll. 2nd Lieut, Duke of Wellington's Regt, 1928. Served War of 1939-45 Norway, Middle East and North Western Europe (despatches, DSO and Bar); Lieut-Col 1941; Brig., 1945; Brig. General Staff British Army of the Rhine, 1950-52; Korea, 1954; Director of Land-Air Warfare, and Director of North Atlantic Treaty Organisation Standardisation, War Office, 1954-57; Maj.-Gen., 1954; General Officer Commanding 56 Infantry Div. (TA), 1957-59; Commander, Land Forces, Arabian Peninsula, 1959; GOC, MELF, 1961; Lieut-Gen. 1961; General Officer Commanding-in-Chief, Southern Command, 1961-63; Commander-in-Chief, Allied Forces, Northern Europe, 1963-67; Dep. Supreme Comdr Allied Powers Europe, 1967-70; General 1965; ADC General to the Queen, 1965-68. *Recreations:* sailing, shooting. *Address:* The Farmhouse, Sherrington, via Warminster, Wilts. *Clubs:* Army and Navy, Royal Cruising.

BRAY, Ronald William Thomas; mechanical engineer; farmer; Underwriting Member of Lloyd's; *b* 5 Jan. 1922; *s* of William Ernest Bray, mech. engr and co. dir, Earls Court, and Ada Bray, Killington, Westmorland; *m* 1944, Margaret Florence, *d* of James B. Parker, St Margarets-on-Thames; no *c. Educ:* Latymer Upper School. Joined family business, 1938; Man. Dir 1946; pioneered develt of British construction equipment incl. heavy earthmoving equipment, four-wheel-drive tractor shovels; travelled extensively, Europe, N and S Africa, America, Canada, Caribbean and Middle East, developing exports; served on numerous professional and British Standards cttees; resigned 1959. Mem., Woking UDC, 1959-62; Chm./Vice-Chm. of various cttees. Commenced farming activities, 1962, specialising in beef production, large breeder of Fell Ponies. Contested (C) Stockton-on-Tees, 1964; MP (C) Rossendale, 1970-Sept. 1974; Mem. Parly delegns to India, Malawi, Sri Lanka, Sweden. Vice-Chm., Assoc. of Cons. Clubs, 1972-75; Vice-Pres., Lancashire Fedn of Cons. Clubs. FFB. *Recreations:* swimming, riding, walking. *Address:* Greenfield, Buckden, Skipton, N Yorks. *T:* Kettlewell 832. *Clubs:* Constitutional, Royal Automobile; Royal Automobile Country (Epsom).

BRAY, Sir Theodor (Charles), Kt 1975; CBE 1964; Chancellor, Griffith University, Brisbane; Director, Queensland Newspapers, since 1956; *b* 11 Feb. 1905; *s* of Horace and Maude Bray; *m* 1931, Rosalie, *d* of Rev. A. M. Trengove; three *s* two *d* (and one *s* one *d* decd). *Educ:* state schs; Adelaide Univ. Apprentice Printer, Reporter, Register, Adelaide; Sub-editor, Chief Sub-editor, Editor (26 yrs), Editor-in-Chief, Jt Man. Dir, Courier Mail & Queensland Newspapers Pty Ltd, 1936-70; Chm., Australian Associated Press, 1968-70; Mem., Austr. Council for the Arts, 1969-73; Austr. Chm., Internat. Press Inst., 1962-70; Chm., Griffith Univ. Council, 1970-75. *Recreations:* gardening, travel. *Address:* 210 Clarence Road, Indooroopilly, Qld 4068, Australia. *T:* 370-7442. *Clubs:* Queensland, Johnsonian, Twelfth Night Theatre (Brisbane).

BRAY, William John, CBE 1975; Director of Research, Post Office, 1966-75 (Dep. Director, 1965); *b* 10 Sept. 1911; British; *m* 1936, Margaret Earp; one *d* (and one *d* decd). *Educ:* Imperial Coll., London Univ. Electrical engineering apprenticeship, Portsmouth Naval Dockyard, 1928-32; Royal and Kitchener Scholarships, Imperial Coll., 1932-34; entered PO Engineering Dept as Asst Engineer, 1934; Commonwealth Fund Fellowship (Harkness Foundation) for study in USA, 1956-57; Staff Engineer, Inland Radio Br., PO Engineering Dept, 1958. Vis. Prof., UCL, 1974-. Participation in work of International Radio Consultative Cttee of International Telecommunication Union and European Postal and Telecommunication Conferences; Consultant to UK Council for Educnl Technology, 1976-. MSc(Eng), FCGI, DIC, CEng, FIEE; DUniv. Essex, 1976. *Publications:* papers in Proc. IEE (IEE Ambrose Fleming Radio Sect. and Electronics Div. Premium Awards). *Recreations:* sailing, travel. *Address:* The Pump House, Bredfield, Woodbridge, Suffolk IP13 6AH. *T:* Woodbridge 5838.

BRAY, Winston, CBE 1970; Deputy Chairman and Deputy Chief Executive, BOAC, 1972-74; Member Board, BOAC, 1971-74; Member Board, BAAC Ltd (formerly BOAC (AC Ltd), 1969-74; *b* 29 April 1910; *s* of late Edward Bray and Alice Walker; *m* 1937, Betty Atterton Miller; one *s* two *d. Educ:* Highgate Sch.; London Univ. (BCom). Missouri Pacific Railroad, USA, 1932; Asst to Traffic Manager, British Airways, 1938; Traffic Dept, BOAC, 1940; Sales Promotion Supt, 1946; Sales Manager, 1950; Sales Planning Manager, 1954; Dir of Planning, 1964; Planning Dir, 1969; Dep. Managing Dir, 1972. FCIT. *Recreations:* sailing, gardening. *Address:* Greenacres, Frith Hill, Great Missenden, Bucks. *Club:* Royal Automobile.

BRAYBROOK, Edward John, CB 1972; *b* 25 Oct. 1911; *s* of late Prior Wormsley Braybrook and Kate Braybrook; *m* 1937, Eva Rosalin Thomas; one *s* two *d. Educ:* Edmonton Latymer Secondary Sch. Asst Naval Store Officer, Admty, Chatham, Malta and Devonport, 1930-37; Deputy Naval Store Officer, Admty, 1938-39; Naval Store Officer, Admty and Haslemere, 1940-43; Suptg Naval Store Officer, Levant, 1943; Comdr/Captain (SP) RNVR Suptg Naval Store Officer, Ceylon and Southern India, 1944-46; Supt, Perth, Scotland, 1946-47; Asst Director of Stores, Admty, 1947-53; Suptg Naval Store Officer, Chatham, 1953-55; Deputy Director of Stores, Admty, 1955-64; Director of Stores (Naval), MoD, 1964-70; Dir-Gen. Supplies and Transport (Naval), MoD, 1970-73. *Recreations:* gardening, photography, painting, handicrafts. *Address:* 22 Church Drive, North Harrow, Middlesex. *T:* 01-427 0838.

BRAYBROOKE, 9th Baron *cr* 1788; **Henry Seymour Neville; JP;** Hon. MA Camb. 1948; Hereditary Visitor of Magdalene College, Cambridge; Patron of four livings; *b* 5 Feb. 1897; *er s* of late Rev. Hon. Grey Neville (2nd *s* of 6th Baron) and late Mary Peele, *e d* of late Canon Francis Slater; *S* cousin, 1943; *m* 1st, 1930, Muriel Evelyn (*d* 1962), *d* of late William C. Manning and *widow* of E. C. Cartwright; one *s* ; 2nd, 1963, Angela Mary, *d* of late William H. Hollis and *widow* of John Ree. *Educ:* Shrewsbury Sch. (Scholar); Magdalene Coll., Cambridge. Served European War, 1914-18, in RNA Service and RAF; later held various appointments with Anglo-Iranian and Shell Groups of oil companies. Chm., Diocesan Bd of Finance, Chelmsford, 1950-68. JP Saffron Walden, 1953; DL, 1950-74. *Heir:* s Hon. Robin Henry Charles Neville [*b* 29 Jan. 1932; *m* 1st, 1955, Robin Helen (marr. diss. 1974), *d* of late T. A. Brockhoff, Sydney, Australia; five *d* ; 2nd, 1974, Linda Norman; one *d*]. *Address:* Bruncketts, Wendens Ambo, Saffron Walden, Essex CB11 4JL. *T:* Saffron Walden 40200.

BRAYBROOKE, Neville Patrick Bellairs; writer; *b* 30 May 1925; *s* of Patrick Philip William Braybrooke and Lettice Marjorie Bellairs; *m* 1953, June Guesdon Jolliffe; one step *d. Educ:* Ampleforth. *Publications:* This is London, 1953; London Green: The Story of Kensington Gardens, Hyde Park, Green Park and St James's Park, 1959; London, 1961; The Idler: novel, 1961; The Delicate Investigation (play for BBC), 1969; *edited:* The Wind and the Rain: quarterly, 1941-1951; T. S. Eliot: a symposium for his 70th birthday, 1958, 3rd edn 1970; A Partridge in a Pear Tree: a celebration for Christmas, 1960; Pilgrim of the Future: a Teilhard de Chardin symposium, 1966, 2nd edn, 1968; The Letters of J. R. Ackerley, 1975; contrib. Guardian, Saturday Review, Times, Times Lit. Suppl., Sunday Telegraph, Tablet. *Recreations:* cats, walking, reading little reviews. *Address:* Grove House, Castle Road, Cowes, IoW PO31 7QZ. *T:* Cowes 3950; 10 Gardnor Road, NW3 1HA. *T:* 01-435 1851. *Club:* Island Sailing.

BRAYE, 7th Baron *cr* 1529; **Thomas Adrian Verney-Cave;** JP; DL; Major, late 13/18th Royal Hussars; *b* 26 July 1902; *er s* of 6th Baron Braye and Ethel Mary (*d* 1955), *d* of Capt. Edward Bouverie Pusey, RN; *S* father, 1952; *m* 1934, Dorothea, *yr d* of late Daniel C. Donoghue, Philadelphia; one *d. Educ:* Eton. Was Flying Officer, RAF; re-employed 13/18th Royal Hussars, 1939; Major, 1942; served on personal staff of The Prince of the Netherlands, 1945-46 (Order of Orange Nassau). Former Dir, George Spencer Ltd. JP Leicestershire, 1953, DL, 1954. *Heir: d* Hon. Penelope Mary Verney-Cave, *b* 28 Sept. 1941. *Address:* Stanford Hall, Lutterworth, Leics LE17 6DH. *T:* Swinford 250. *Club:* Cavalry and Guards.

BRAYNE, Richard Bolding, MBE 1957; Clerk of the Worshipful Company of Ironmongers, since 1973; *b* 28 Oct. 1924; 3rd *s* of late Brig. Frank Lugard Brayne, MC, CSI, CIE, ICS, and late Iris Goodeve Brayne, K-i-H; *m* 1947, Anne Stoddart Forrest; one *s* two *d. Educ:* Sherborne Sch.; Pembroke Coll., Cambridge. Indian Army, 3rd (Peshawar) Indian Mountain Battery, India, Burma and Far East, 1942-46. Entered Colonial Service as DO, Tanganyika, 1948; Staff Officer to HRH The Princess Margaret's tour of Tanganyika, 1956; Dist Comr, 1957; Principal, Admin. Trng Centre and Local Govt Trng Centre, 1960. Prin. Asst Sec., Min. of Educn, 1963; Mem., E African UGC and Makerere Univ. College Council, 1963; retd from Colonial Service, 1964. Sec., Brit. Paper and Board Makers' Assoc., 1964; Trng Adviser and Develt Manager, Construction Industry Trng Bd, 1966. Asst Clerk of Worshipful Co. of Ironmongers, 1971. *Recreations:* shooting, tennis, squash. *Address:* Ironmongers' Hall, Barbican EC2Y 8AA. *T:* 01-606 2725; Thriftwood Cottage, Broomlands Lane, Limpsfield, Surrey RH8 0SP. *T:* Limpsfield Chart 2300.

BRAYNE-BAKER, John, CMG 1957; Colonial Administrative Service, Nigeria (retired); *b* 13 Aug. 1905; *s* of Francis Brayne-Baker and Dorothea Mary Brayne-Baker (*née* Porcher); *m* 1947, Ruth Hancock; no *c. Educ:* Marlborough Coll.; Worcester Coll., Oxford. Nigeria: Asst District Officer, 1928; District Officer, 1938; Senior District Officer, 1948; Resident, 1953. Senior Resident and Deputy Commissioner of the Cameroons, 1954-56; retired 1956. Member, Tiverton RDC, 1959-74, Tiverton DC, 1973-76. *Recreations:* gardening and golf. *Address:* East Grantlands, Uffculme, Cullompton, Devon. *T:* Craddock 236. *Club:* Tiverton Golf (Tiverton).

BRAYNE-NICHOLLS, Rear-Adm. Francis Brian Price, CB 1965; DSC 1942; General Secretary, Officers Pensions Society; *b* 1 Dec. 1914; *s* of late Dr G. E. E. Brayne-Nicholls and *gs* of Sir Francis W. T. Brain; *m* 1939, Wendy (*née* Donnelly); one *d. Educ:* RNC, Dartmouth. Sub-Lieut and Lieut, HMS Bee on Yangtse River, 1936-39; specialised in Navigation, 1939; Navigating Officer of: HM Ships Nelson, Rodney, Cardiff, 1939-41, Manxman (during many mining ops, Malta convoys and Madagascar op.), 1941-42; Combined Ops, taking part in Sicily (despatches), Salerno, and Normandy landings. Navigating Officer: HMS Glory, 1944-46; HMS Vanguard, 1948; Comdr 1948; Comdg Officer: HMS Gravelines, 1952-53; HMS St Kitts, 1953-54; Capt 1954; Naval Asst to First Sea Lord, 1954-55; Comdg Officer, HMS Apollo, 1955-57; NATO Standing Group, Washington, 1957-59; Captain of Navigation Direction Sch., HMS Dryad, 1959-61; Admiralty, 1961-63; Rear-Adm. 1963; Chief of Staff to Commander, Far East Fleet, 1963-65. *Recreation:* golf. *Address:* 3 Tedworth Square, SW3 4DU. *T:* 01-352 1681. *Club:* Naval and Military.

BRAYNEN, Sir Alvin (Rudolph), Kt 1975; JP; High Commissioner for the Commonwealth of the Bahamas in London, 1973-77; *b* 6 Dec. 1904; *s* of William Rudolph Braynen and Lulu Isabelle Braynen (*née* Griffin); *m* 1969, Ena Estelle (*née* Elden); (one *s* one *d* by a previous marriage). *Educ:* Public Sch., The Current, Eleuthera, Bahamas; Boys' Central Sch., Nassau, Bahamas (teacher trng). Public Sch. Headmaster, 1923-25. Entered commercial world, 1925, as clerk; founded his own petroleum commn firm, 1930, disposing of it in 1965. MP for Cat Island, 1935-42 and constituency for what is now known as St John, 1942-72; Dep. Speaker of House of Assembly, 1949-53, and 1963-66; MEC, 1953-58; Speaker of House of Assembly, 1967-72. During years 1952-58 he was Chairman of several Boards, incl. those responsible for Educn, Public Works, Prisons and Traffic; past Member: Bds of Agriculture, Health, Tourism, Out Island Develt and Educn; Mem., both Constitutional Confs from the Bahamas to London in 1963 and 1968; Chm., Exec. Cttee of Conf. of Commonwealth Caribbean Parliamentary Heads and Clerks; also served as either Chm. or Dep. Chm. of important Nat. Festivities for many years, such as Coronation of the Queen, visit of Princess Margaret, First Constitutional Day, 1964, and supervised arrangements for Conf. of Delegates of Commonwealth Parliamentary Conf. held at Nassau, 1968. JP Bahamas 1952. *Recreations:* swimming; collects books on the Bahamas; collects coins and stamps. *Address:* PO Box N42, Nassau, Bahamas.

BRAYSHAW, (Alfred) Joseph, CBE 1975 (OBE 1964); JP; Secretary, The Magistrates' Association, 1965-77; *b* Manchester, 20 Dec. 1912; *er s* of late Shipley Neave Brayshaw and Ruth Cotterell (*née* Holmes), JP; *m* 1st, Joan Pauline Comley Hawkes (*d* 1940); 2nd, 1943, Marion Spencer, *y d* of late John S. C. Johnson, Bury St Edmunds; three *s. Educ:* Sidcot Sch., Somerset; engineering factories; Dalton Hall, Univ. of Manchester. Brayshaw Furnaces & Tools Ltd, 1934-40; Central Board for Conscientious Objectors, 1941-46; Asst Sec., then Gen. Sec., Friends' Relief Service, 1946-48; Gen. Sec., Nat. Marriage Guidance Council, 1949-64 (a Vice-Pres., 1964-); Vice-Pres., Guildford and District Marriage Guidance Council, 1974-. JP Surrey, 1958. *Publications:* articles and broadcasts on magistrates' courts and related subjects. *Recreations:* gardening, walking. *Address:* Apple Trees, Beech Road, Haslemere, Surrey GU27 2BX. *T:* Haslemere 2677.

BRAZENDALE, George William, CMG 1958; FCA; *b* 1909; *s* of late Percy Ridout Brazendale, and late Edith Mary Brazendale (*née* Maystre); *m* 1938, Madeleine, *o d* of Thomas and Betty Wroe; two *d. Educ:* Arnold Sch., Blackpool, Lancs. Chief Accountant, Colclough China Ltd, Stoke-on-Trent, 1936-41; Asst Area Officer, MAP, 1941-42; Chief Progress Officer, ROF Swynnerton, 1942-43; Secretary, Midland Regional Board, 1943-45; Regional Controller Board of Trade; Northern Region, 1945-46; North-Western Region, 1946-50; Asst Secretary, Board of Trade, 1946; Trade Commissioner for the UK in charge Calcutta, 1950-60. Principal British Trade Commissioner: in the Federation of Rhodesia and Nyasaland, 1961-63; also Economic Adviser to British High Commissioner in Rhodesia, 1964-65; Economic Adviser to Special British Representative in East and Central Africa, 1966-67; retired from HM Diplomatic Service, 1967. ACA 1931. *Recreations:* golf, fishing, gardening. *Address:* 61 Ashley Drive South, Ashley Heath, Ringwood, Hants BH28 2JP. *Clubs:* Oriental; Brokenhurst Manor Golf.

BRAZIER, Rt. Rev. Percy James; *b* 3 Aug. 1903; *m* 1933, Joan Cooper, MB, BS; one *s* four *d. Educ:* Weymouth Coll., Dorset; Emmanuel Coll., Cambridge. 2nd class Hist. Trip., Part I, 1924, 2nd class, Part II, and BA, 1925; MA 1939. Ridley Hall, Cambridge, 1925-27, Deacon, 1927; Priest, 1928; Curate of St John the Evangelist, Blackheath, 1927-29; CMS (Ruanda Mission), 1930; Kabale, 1930-34; Kigeme, Diocese of Uganda, 1934-50; Archdeacon of Ruanda-Urundi, 1946-51; Asst Bishop of Uganda for Ruanda-Urundi, 1951-60; Bishop of Rwanda and Burundi, 1960-64 (name of diocese changed when Ruanda-Urundi was granted independence, 1962); retired 1964. Rector of Padworth and Vicar of Mortimer West End, Diocese of Oxford, 1964-70. Chevalier de l'Ordre Royal du Lion (Belgium), 1955. *Recreations:* photography, gardening and golf. *Address:* Lark Rise, Peasemore, Newbury, Berks. *T:* Chieveley 548.

BRAZIER-CREAGH, Maj.-Gen. Sir (Kilner) Rupert, KBE 1962 (CBE 1947); CB 1954; DSO 1944; Secretary of the Horse Race Betting Levy Board, 1961-65; Director of Staff Duties, War Office, 1959-61, retired; *b* 12 Dec. 1909; 2nd *s* of late Lt-Col K. C. Brazier-Creagh; *m* 1st, 1938, Elizabeth Mary (*d* 1967), *d* of late E. M. Magor; one *s* two *d*; 2nd, 1968, Mrs Marie Nelson. *Educ:* Rugby; RMA, Woolwich. 2nd Lieut, 1929; served War of 1939-45 (despatches, DSO); Bde Major, 9th Armoured Div., 1941; GSO1 12th Corps, 1943; Commanded 25th Field Regt, 1944; BGS 21st Army Group and BAOR, 1945-48 (CBE); idc 1949; DDRA, War Office, 1950; CRA 11th Armoured Div., 1951-52; Chief of Staff Malaya Command, 1952-55 (despatches, CB); Asst Comdt, Staff Coll., 1955-57; Chief of Staff, Eastern Command, 1957-59. Officer, American Legion of Merit, 1945.

Recreation: racing. *Address:* Travis Corners Road, Garrison, New York, USA.

BREADALBANE and HOLLAND, 10th Earl of, *cr* 1677; **John Romer Boreland Campbell;** Mac Chailein Mhic Dhonnachaidh (celtic designation); Viscount of Tay and Paintland; Lord Glenorchy, Benederaloch, Ormelie and Weik, 1677; Bt of Glenorchy; Bt of Nova Scotia, 1625; *b* 28 April 1919; *o s* of 9th Earl of Breadalbane and Holland, MC; *S* father, 1959; *m* 1949, Coralie (marr. diss.), *o d* of Charles Archer. *Educ:* Eton; RMC, Sandhurst; Basil Patterson Tutors; Edinburgh Univ. Entered Black Watch (Royal Highlanders), 1939; served France, 1939-41 (despatches); invalided, 1942. *Recreations:* piobaireachd, Scottish highland culture. *Heir:* none. *Address:* House of Lords, SW1; 29 Mackeson Road, Hampstead, NW3.

BREAM, Julian, OBE 1964; guitarist and lutenist; *b* 15 July 1933; *e s* of Henry G. Bream. *Educ:* Royal College of Music (Junior Exhibition Award, 1945 and Scholarship, 1948). Began professional career at Cheltenham, 1946; London début, Wigmore Hall, 1950; subsequently has appeared in leading world festivals in Europe, USA, Australia and Far East. A leader in revival of interest in Elizabethan Lute music, on which he has done much research; has encouraged contemporary English compositions for the guitar. Formed Julian Bream Consort, 1960; inaugurated Semley Festival of Music and Poetry, 1971. DUniv Surrey, 1968. *Recreations:* playing the guitar; cricket; table tennis, gardening, backgammon. *Address:* c/o Harold Holt Ltd, 122 Wigmore Street, W1. *Club:* Garrick.

BREARE, William Robert Ackrill; Chairman and Managing Director: R. Ackrill Ltd since 1955; Lawrence & Hall Ltd since 1963; *b* 5 July 1916; *s* of late Robert Ackrill Breare and late Emily Breare (*née* Waddington); *m* 1942, Sybella Jessie Macduff Roddick, *d* of late John Roddick, Annan; one *s* two *d*. *Educ:* Old College, Windermere; Charterhouse; Wadham Coll., Oxford (MA). BCL Oxon 1938. Sub-Lt RNVSR, 1935-39; Comdr RNVR, 1942-44. Dir, R. Ackrill Ltd, newspaper publishers, 1938. Pres., Yorks Newspaper Soc., 1953 and 1972; Mem. Council, Newspaper Soc., 1967; Mem. Press Council, 1972. Contested (C) Rother Valley, 1950. *Recreations:* cruising under sail, shooting; formerly cricket, swimming, ocean racing. *Address:* Harrison Hill House, Starbeck, Harrogate, N Yorks. *T:* Harrogate 883302. *Clubs:* Cruising Association; Stewards' Enclosure, Henley; Island Sailing, Oxford University Yacht.

BREARLEY, Sir Norman, Kt 1971; CBE 1965; DSO 1916; MC; AFC; FRAeS; Company Director, Western Australia; *b* Geelong, Vic., 22 Dec. 1890; *s* of late Robert Hillard Brearley, Perth, WA; *m* 1917, Violet, *d* of late Hon. Sydney Stubbs, CMG, MLA, Perth; one *s* one *d*. *Educ:* state and private schs, Geelong; Technical Coll., Perth, WA. Enlisted, after engineering training. Served War, RFC and RAF, also Major in Liverpool Regt, France and England, 1914-1919 (wounded, despatches, AFC, MC, DSO); War of 1939-45: Gp Capt., RAAF. Founder (1921) of West Australian Airways; was the first airmail contractor to Australian Govt. Pioneer of Australian Air Services. *Publication:* Australian Aviator, 1971. *Recreations:* tennis, golf. *Address:* 6 Esplanade, Peppermint Grove, Cottesloe, WA 6011, Australia. *T:* 312293. *Club:* Weld (Perth, WA).

BREBNER, Sir Alexander, Kt 1938; CIE 1920; BSc Edinburgh; Indian Service of Engineers, retired; Member of Council and Executive of National Trust for Scotland, retired 1961; Board of Scottish Special Housing Association (appointed by Secretary of State for Scotland), 1954-61; Acting Secretary, Royal Scottish Academy, Edinburgh, 1954-55, retired; *b* 19 Aug. 1883; *s* of R. C. Brebner, Edinburgh; *m* 1911, Margaret Patricia (*d* 1974), *d* of W. Cunningham, Edinburgh; two *d* (one *s* decd). *Educ:* George Watson's Coll., Edinburgh; Edinburgh Univ. Asst Engineer, PWD, 1906; Executive Engineer, 1912; Under-Secretary, Bihar and Orissa, 1919; Under-Secretary to Govt of India, 1919-23; Superintending Engineer, 1923. Consulting Engineer to Govt of India, 1927 and 1929; Chief Engineer, Govt of India, 1931-38, retired, 1938; one-time Member Council of State; employed in Chief Divisional Food Office for Scotland, Ministry of Food, 1940-42; Ministry of Works (Licensing Officer, Scotland), 1942-54. *Recreation:* golf. *Address:* 4 Ainslie Place, Edinburgh. *T:* 031-225 1991. *Clubs:* New (Edinburgh); Hon. Co. Edinburgh Golfers; Royal and Ancient (St Andrews).

BRECHIN, Bishop of, since 1975; **Rt. Rev. Lawrence Edward Luscombe;** *b* 10 Dec. 1924; *s* of Reginald John and Winifred Luscombe; *m* 1946, Doris Carswell Morgan, BSc, MB, ChB; one *d*. *Educ:* Torquay Grammar Sch.; Kelham Theological Coll.; King's Coll., London. CA 1952, ASAA 1957. Served Indian Army, 1942-47. Partner, Galbraith, Dunlop & Co, Chartered Accountants, Glasgow, 1952-63. Ordained deacon, 1963; priest, 1964; Curate, St Margaret's, Glasgow, 1963-66; Rector, St Barnabas', Paisley, 1966-71; Provost of St Paul's Cathedral, Dundee, 1971-75. Hon. DLitt Geneva Theological Coll., 1972. *Recreations:* reading, Indian affairs. *Address:* 7 Shaftesbury Road, Dundee DD2 1HF.

BRECHIN, Sir Herbert Archbold, KBE 1971 (CBE 1961; OBE 1952); Kt 1968; JP; DL; Lord Provost of the City of Edinburgh, 1966-69; Lord Lieutenant, County of the City of Edinburgh, 1966-69; Chartered Quantity Surveyor; *b* 3 Nov. 1903; *s* of late David Brechin and Katharine Mary (*née* O'Brien); *m* 1934, Jane Richmond Cameron; two *s*. *Educ:* Edinburgh. Senior Partner, H. A. Brechin & Co., FRICS, Chartered Quantity Surveyors, Edinburgh, Kelso and Rothesay, Isle of Bute, Chm. 9th British Commonwealth Games, 1955-70. A Dist. Comr, Scout Assoc.; Holder of Scout Wood Badge, 1944; Scout Medal of Merit; and awarded Scout Silver Acorn by Chief Scout (1962); retired from Movement 1962 after 45 years' service; awarded Silver Wolf, 1969, by Chief Scout, in recognition of services of exceptional character in Edinburgh. Chairman: Scottish Br., RICS, 1948; Scottish Cttee for Award of Nat. Certs in Bldg; Scottish Bldg and Engrg Services Cttee, BSI; Scottish Codes of Practice Cttee on Bldg (Min. of Works); Mem., Bldg Industry Working Party set up by Govt in 1948. Member Edinburgh Town Council, 1949-69; City Treasurer, 1962-65. Chm. Bd of Governors, Heriot-Watt Coll., 1966, Chm. Ct, Heriot-Watt Univ., 1972-. Chm., Edinburgh Festival Soc, 1966-69; Hon. President: The Bohemians Lyric Opera Co; The Scottish Paraplegic (Spinal Injuries) Assoc.; Hon. Vice-President: Commonwealth Games Council for Scotland; Scout Assoc. of Scotland; Scout Assoc. of Edinburgh Area Scout Council; Gilbert and Sullivan Assoc.; Scottish Amateur Boxing Assoc.; Scottish Badminton Union; Royal Scottish Country Dance Soc.; Mem., Co. of Merchants of City of Edinburgh (Master's Court, 1969-72). FRSE 1969; FRICS; FH-WC (*hc*) 1962. Hon. DLitt Heriot-Watt, 1967. JP 1966, DL 1970, City of Edinburgh. Grand Officer, Order of Al-Kawkab Al-Urduni, Jordan, 1966; Grand Ufficiale dell' Ordine al Merito della Repubblica Italiana, 1969; Hon. Citizen, Dallas, Texas, 1966; Hon. Cedar Rapidian, 1966. *Address:* The Garth, Colinton, Edinburgh EH13 0DN. *T:* 031-441 2226; 13 Great King Street, Edinburgh EH3 6QP. *T:* 031-556 5441.

BRECKNOCK, Earl of; David George Edward Henry Pratt; late Lieutenant, Scots Guards; *b* 13 Aug. 1930; *o s* of 5th Marquess Camden, *qv*, and Marjorie, Countess of Brecknock, *qv*; *m* 1961, Virginia Ann, *o d* of late F. H. H. Finlaison, Arklow Cottage, Windsor, Berks; one *s* one *d* (and one *s* decd). *Educ:* Eton. Dir, Clive Discount Co. Ltd, 1958-69. *Heir:* *s* Viscount Bayham, *qv*. *Address:* Cowdown Farm House, Andover, Hants. *T:* Andover 2085.

BRECKNOCK, Marjorie Countess of, DBE 1967; Superintendent-in-Chief, St John Ambulance Brigade, 1960-70, Retired, Chief President, 1972; *b* 28 Mar. 1900; *o c* of late Col A. E. Jenkins and of late Mrs Anna Jenkins, Wherwell Priory, Andover, Hants; *m* 1920, Earl of Brecknock (now Marquess Camden; from whom she obtained a divorce, 1941); one *s* one *d*. *Educ:* at home and Heathfield, Ascot. A Lady-in-waiting to Princess Marina, Duchess of Kent, 1937-39. War of 1939-45: Company Asst, ATS, 1940; Junior Commander, 1941; Senior Commander, 1942 (Senior ATS Officer SHAEF, 1944-45); despatches 1945; Bronze Star (USA), 1945. Commanded 310 (Southern Command) Bn WRAC (TA), 1948-54. Joined St John Ambulance Brigade HQ, 1947; appointed Controller Overseas Dept, 1950. GCStJ 1971 (DStJ 1958). Mem. Order of Mercy. *Publication:* Edwina Mountbatten-her life in pictures, 1961. *Recreations:* gardening, shooting, travelling, fishing. *Address:* 23 South Audley St, W1. *T:* 01-499 1305; Wherwell Priory, Andover, Hampshire. *T:* Chilbolton 388.

BRECON, Dean of; *see* Jacob, Very Rev. W. U.

BREDIN, George Richard Frederick, CBE 1947; MA; Sudan Political Service (retired); Hon. Fellow of Pembroke College, Oxford; *b* 8 June 1899; *s* of late Dr Richard Bredin, Valparaiso, Chile; *m* 1932, Dorothy Wall, *d* of late T. R. Ellison, West Kirby, Cheshire; one *s* one *d*. *Educ:* Clifton College; Oriel College, Oxford. MA (Oxon) 1925; served European War, 1914-18, Lieut RE (64th Field Company) (despatches). Oriel College, Oxford, 1919-21; Hons Degree in Lit. Hum. (Distinction), 1921. Asst District Comr, Sudan Political Service, 1921; District Comr, 1930; Dep. Governor, 1935; Dep. Civil Sec., 1939; Governor Blue Nile Province, Sudan, 1941-48; Mem., Governor-General's Council, 1945-48; Chm., Governing Body of Gordon Meml University Coll., Khartoum, 1945-48; retired, 1948. Asst Registrar, Univ. of Liverpool, 1949; Fellow and Bursar, Pembroke Coll., Oxford, 1950-66; a Church Comr, 1951-; Chm., Oxford Diocesan Board of Finance, 1956-58;

Chm., Oxford Diocesan Trusts Corp., 1965-70; a Curator of the Oxford Univ. Chest, 1957-69. Chm. of Governors of Abingdon Sch., 1966-72; Vice-Chm., Dorset House Sch. of Occupational Therapy, Oxford; Treas., Gordon Boys School, Woking; Oxford City Councillor, 1965-67. Order of the Nile (3rd Cl.), 1937. *Recreations:* golf, bridge. *Address:* Rough Lea, Boar's Hill, Oxford. *T:* Oxford 735375.

BREDIN, Maj.-Gen. Humphrey Edgar Nicholson, CB 1969; DSO 1944 (and bars, 1945 and 1957); MC 1938 (and bar, 1939); Appeals Secretary, Cancer Research Campaign, Essex and Suffolk, since 1971; *b* 28 March 1916; *s* of Lieut-Colonel A. Bredin, late Indian Army, and Ethel Bredin (*née* Homan); *m* 1st, 1947, Jacqueline Geare (marr. diss., 1961); one *d*; 2nd, 1965, Anne Hardie; two *d. Educ:* King's School, Canterbury; RMC, Sandhurst. Commissioned Royal Ulster Rifles, 1936; Commanded: 6th Royal Inniskilling Fusiliers, 1944; 2nd London Irish Rifles, 1945; Eastern Arab Corps, Sudan Defence Force, 1949-53; 2nd Parachute Regt, 1956-57; 99th Gurkha Infty Bde Group, 1959-62. Campaigns: Dunkirk, 1940; N Africa, 1943; Italy, 1943-45; Palestine, 1937-39 and 1946-47; Suez, 1956; Cyprus, 1956-57; Singapore-Malaya Internal Security, 1959-62; Chief of British Commander-in-Chief's Mission to Soviet Forces in Germany, 1963-65; Commanded 42nd Div. (TA), 1965-68. Brig. 1964; Maj.-Gen. 1965; Dir, Volunteers, Territorials and Cadets, 1968-71; retired 1971. Col Comdt, The King's Division, 1968-71. *Recreations:* shooting, fishing, gardening. *Address:* Bovills Hall, Ardleigh, Essex. *T:* Colchester 230217. *Club:* Army and Navy.

BREDIN, James John; Managing Director, Border Television Ltd, since 1964; *b* 18 Feb. 1924; *s* of John Francis and late Margaret Bredin; *m* 1958, Virginia Meddowes, *d* of John Meddowes and Mrs K. Thomas; one *s* two *d. Educ:* Finchley Catholic Grammar Sch.; London University. Served Fleet Air Arm, RNVR, S/Lieut, 1943-46. Scriptwriter, This Modern Age Film Unit, 1946-50; Producer, current affairs programmes, BBC TV, 1950-55; Sen. Producer, Independent Television News, 1955-59; Smith-Mundt Fellowship, USA, 1957; Producer of Documentaries, Associated Television, 1959-64. Chm., Guild of Television Producers and Directors, 1961-64. Director: Independent Television News Ltd, 1970-72; Independent Television Publications Ltd; James Archibald & Associates. Mem., Gen. Council, Northern Arts Assoc. *Address:* The Gatehouse, Naworth Castle, Brampton, Cumbria. *T:* Brampton 2460. *Clubs:* Beefsteak, Reform; County (Carlisle).

BREECH, Ernest Robert; industrialist; Honorary Chairman and Director Emeritus, Trans World Airlines Inc. (Chairman, 1961-69); Director: Dart Industries Inc.; The Lehman Corporation; One William Street Fund Inc.; *b* Lebanon, Missouri, 24 Feb. 1897; *s* of Joseph F. E. Breech; *m* 1917, Thelma Rowden; two *s. Educ:* Drury Coll., Springfield, Mo; Walton Sch. of Commerce. Accountant, Fairbanks, Morse & Co., 1917-20; Auditor, Adams & Westlake, 1920-22; Comptroller, Yellow Cab Mfg Co., 1923-29; Dir Yellow Truck & Coach Mfg Co., Chicago, 1927-33; Gen. Asst Treas., Gen. Motors Corp., NYC, 1929-33, Vice-Pres. i/c household appliance div. and aviation subsids, also Mem. administration cttee, 1939-42; Dir N Amer. Aviation Inc., 1933-1946 (Chm., 1933-42); Pres., and Dir Bendix Aviation Corp., 1942-46; with Ford Motor Co. as Exec. Vice-Pres., 1946-55; Chairman, 1955-60; Chm. Finance Cttee, 1960-61; Dir, 1946-67. *Address:* 12723 Telegraph Road, Detroit, Michigan 48239, USA.

BRENAN, (Edward Fitz-) Gerald, MC 1918; Author; *b* 7 April 1894; English; *m* 1931, Elisabeth Gamel Woolsey (*d* 1968); one *d. Educ:* self-educated. Served War: Croix de Guerre, 1918. *Publications:* The Spanish Labyrinth, 1943; The Face of Spain, 1950; The Literature of the Spanish People, 1953; South from Granada, 1957; A Holiday by the Sea, 1961; A Life of One's Own (autobiog.), 1962; The Lighthouse Always Says Yes, 1966; St John of the Cross: his life and poetry, 1971; Personal Record (autobiog.), 1974. *Recreations:* walking and talking. *Address:* c/o Jonathan Cape, 30 Bedford Square, WC1B 3EL.

BRENAN, Gerald; see Brenan, Edward Fitz-Gerald.

BRENAN, John Patrick Micklethwait, MA, BSc Oxon; FLS; FIBiol; Director, Royal Botanic Gardens, Kew, since 1976; *b* 19 June 1917; *s* of Alexander Richard Micklethwait Brenan, MD, and Jill Fraser Brenan (*née* Parker); *m* 1950, Jean Helen Edwardes; one *s* two *d. Educ:* Tonbridge; Brasenose Coll., Oxford. At Imperial Forestry Inst., Oxford, 1940-48; Mem. Cambridge Botanical Expedn to Nigeria and Cameroons, 1948; apptd Sen. Scientific Officer in the Herbarium, Royal Botanic Gardens, Kew, 1948; Principal Sci. Off., 1954; i/c Tropical African Section, 1959-65; Keeper of the Herbarium, and Dep.

Dir, Royal Botanic Gardens 1965-76. Pres., Assoc. for Tropical Biology, 1970-71. Botanical Sec., Linnean Soc. of London, 1965-72. *Publications:* Check List of the Forest Trees and Shrubs of Tanganyika Territory, 1949 (with Dr P. J. Greenway); contrib. various accounts to Flora of Tropical East Africa, etc.; numerous papers on flowering plants of Europe and Africa in scientific jls. *Recreations:* reading, fishing, natural history, walking. *Address:* 49 The Green, Kew, Richmond, Surrey, *T:* 01-940 1173. *Club:* Athenæum.

BRENCHLEY, Thomas Frank, CMG 1964; MA Oxon; HM Diplomatic Service, retired; Deputy Secretary General, Arab-British Chamber of Commerce, since 1976; *b* 9 April 1918; *m* 1946, Edith Helen Helfand; three *d.* Served with Royal Corps of Signals, 1939-46; Major on Staff of Military Attaché, Ankara, 1943-45; Director, Telecommunications Liaison Directorate, Syria and Lebanon, 1945-46. Civil Servant, 1947; transferred to Foreign Office, 1949; First Secretary: Singapore, 1950-53; Cairo, 1953-56; FO, 1956-58; MECAS, 1958-60; Counsellor, Khartoum, 1960-63; Chargé d'Affaires, Jedda, 1963; Head of Arabian Department, Foreign Office, 1963-67; Assistant Under-Secretary of State, Foreign Office, 1967-68; Ambassador to: Norway, 1968-72; Poland, 1972-74; Dep. Sec., Cabinet Office, 1975-76. *Recreations:* tennis, collecting (and sometimes reading) books. *Address:* 15 Cadogan Square, SW1. *Club:* Travellers'.

BRENDEL, Alfred; concert pianist since 1948; *b* 5 Jan. 1931; *s* of Albert Brendel and Ida Brendel (*née* Wieltschnig); *m* 1960, Iris Heymann-Gonzala (marr. diss. 1972); one *d*; *m* 1975, Irene Semler, one *s*. Studied piano with: S. Deželić, 1937-43; L. V. Kaan, 1943-47; also under Edwin Fischer, P. Baumgartner and E. Steuermann; composition with Artur Michl. Vienna State Diploma, 1947; Premio Bolzano Concorso Busoni, 1949. Hon. RAM. Concerts: most European countries, North and Latin America, Australia and New Zealand, also N and S Africa and Near and Far East. Many appearances Vienna and Salzburg Festivals, 1960-. Other Festivals: Athens, Granada, Bregenz, Würzburg, Aldeburgh, York, Cheltenham, Edinburgh, Bath, Puerto Rico, Barcelona, Prague, Lucerne, Dubrovnik, etc. Many long playing records (Haydn to Schoenberg) incl. first complete recording of Beethoven's piano works (Grand Prix du Disque, 1965). Cycle of Beethoven Sonatas: London, 1962, 1977; Copenhagen, 1964; Vienna, 1965; Puerto Rico, 1968; BBC and Rome, 1970; Munich and Stuttgart, 1977. *Publications:* Musical Thoughts and Afterthoughts (Essays), 1976; essays on music, in: HiFi Stereophonie, Music and Musicians, Phono, Fono Forum, Osterreichische Musikzeitschrift, etc. *Recreations:* literature, art galleries, architecture, unintentional humour, "kitsch". *Address:* Ingpen & Williams, 14 Kensington Court, W8.

BRENIKOV, Prof. Paul, FRTPI; Professor and Head of Department of Town and Country Planning, University of Newcastle upon Tyne, since 1964; *b* 13 July 1921; *o s* of Pavel Brenikov and Joyce Mildred Jackson, Liverpool; *m* 1943, Margaret, *e d* of Albert McLevy, Burnley, Lancs; two *s* one *d. Educ:* St Peter's Sch., York; Liverpool Coll.; Univ. of Liverpool (BA (Hons Geog.), MA, DipCD). War service with RNAS, 1941-46. Sen. Planning Officer, Lancs CC, 1950-55; Lectr, Dept of Civic Design, Univ. of Liverpool, 1955-64; Planning Corresp., Architect's Jl, 1957-63; Environmental Planning Consultant: in UK, for Bootle CB, 1957-64; Govt of Ireland, 1963-67; overseas, for UN; Chile, 1960-61; E Africa, 1964; OECD; Turkey, 1968. Royal Town Planning Institute: Mem. Council, 1967-; Chm., Northern Br., 1973-74. Mem., Subject Cttee of UGC, 1975-. *Publications:* contrib. Social Aspects of a Town Development Plan, 1951; contrib. Land Use in an Urban Environment, 1961; (jtly) The Dublin Region: preliminary and final reports, 1965 and 1967; other technical pubns in architectural, geographical, planning and sociological jls. *Recreations:* listening to music, walking, reading. *Address:* Department of Town and Country Planning, The University, Newcastle upon Tyne NE1 7RU. *T:* Newcastle upon Tyne 28511.

BRENNAN, Anthony John Edward; Deputy Under-Secretary of State, Home Office, since 1977; *b* 24 Jan. 1927; 2nd *s* of late Edward Joseph Brennan and Mabel Brennan (*née* West); *m* 1958, Pauline Margery, *d* of late Percy Clegg Lees; two *s* one *d. Educ:* St Joseph's; London Sch. of Economics (Leverhulme Schol.). BSc Econ 1946. Served Army, RA, RAEC, 1946-49; Asst Principal, Home Office, 1949; Private Sec. to Parly Under-Sec. of State, 1953-54; Principal, 1954; Principal Private Sec. to Home Sec., 1963; Asst Sec., 1963; Asst Under Sec. of State, Criminal Dept, 1971-75, Immigration Dept, 1975-77. Sec., Royal Commn on Penal System, 1964-66. *Recreations:* bridge, theatre, athletics. *Address:* 74 The Crescent, Belmont, Surrey.

BRENNAN, Lieut-General Michael; retired as Chief Superintendent of Divisions, Office of Public Works, Dublin.

Chief of Staff, Irish Army, 1931-40. *Address:* South Hill, Killiney, Co. Dublin.

BRENNAN, William Joseph, Jr; Legion of Merit, 1945; Associate Justice, Supreme Court of the US since 1956; *b* 25 April 1906; *s* of William J. Brennan and Agnes McDermott; *m* 1928, Marjorie Leonard; two *s* one *d. Educ:* University of Pennsylvania; Harvard. BS Univ. of Pennsylvania, 1928; LLB Harvard, 1931. Admitted to New Jersey Bar, 1931; practised in Newark, New Jersey, 1931-49, Member Pitney, Hardin, Ward & Brennan; Superior Court Judge, 1949-50; Appellate Division Judge, 1950-52; Supreme Court of New Jersey Justice, 1952-56; served War of 1939-45 as Colonel, General Staff Corps, United States Army. Hon. LLD: Pennsylvania, 1957; Wesleyan, 1957; St John's, 1957; Rutgers, 1958; Notre Dame, 1968; Harvard, 1968; Hon. DCL: New York Univ., 1957; Colgate, 1957; Hon. SJD Suffolk Univ., 1956. *Address:* 3037 Dumbarton Avenue, Washington, DC 20007, USA. *Club:* University (Washington, DC).

BRENNER, Sydney, FRS 1965; DPhil Oxon; Member of Scientific Staff of Medical Research Council at the Medical Research Council Laboratory of Molecular Biology, Cambridge, since 1957; Fellow of King's College, Cambridge, since 1959; *b* Germiston, South Africa, 13 Jan. 1927; *s* of Morris Brenner and Lena (*née* Blacher); *m* 1952, May Woolf Balkind; one *s* two *d* (and one step *s*). *Educ:* Germiston High School; University of the Witwatersrand, S Africa; Oxford University. MSc 1947, MB, BCh 1951, Univ. of the Witwatersrand; DPhil Oxon., 1954. Carter-Wallace Lectr, Princeton, 1966, 1971. Foreign Hon. Member, American Academy of Arts and Sciences, 1965; Foreign Associate, Nat. Acad. of Sciences, USA, 1977; Mem., Deutsche Akademie der Naturforscher, Leopoldina, 1976 (Gregor Mendel Medal, 1970). Hon. DSc: Dublin, 1967; Witwatersrand, 1972; Chicago, 1976. Warren Triennial Prize, 1968; William Bate Hardy Prize, Cambridge Philosophical Soc., 1969; (jtly) Lasker Award for Basic Medical Research, 1971; Royal Medal, Royal Soc., 1974; (jtly) Prix Charles Leopold Mayer, French Acad. of Science, 1975. *Publications:* papers in scientific journals. *Recreation:* conversation. *Address:* MRC Laboratory of Molecular Biology, University Postgraduate Medical School, Hills Road, Cambridge. *T:* Cambridge 48011.

BRENT, Prof. Leslie, FIBiol; Professor of Immunology, St Mary's Hospital Medical School, London, since 1969; *b* 5 July 1925; *s* of Charlotte and Arthur Baruch; *m* 1954, Joanne Elisabeth Manley; one *s* two *d. Educ:* Bunce Court Sch., Kent; Birmingham Central Technical Coll.; Univ. of Birmingham; UCL. BSc Birmingham, PhD London; FIBiol 1964. Laboratory technician, 1941-43; Army service, 1943-47; Lectr, Dept of Zoology, UCL, 1954-62; Rockefeller Res. Fellow, Calif Inst. of Technology, 1956-57; Res. scientist, Nat. Inst. for Med. Res., 1962-65; Prof. of Zoology, Univ. of Southampton, 1965-69. European Editor, Transplantation, 1963-68; Gen. Sec., British Transplantation Soc., 1971-75, Pres., The Transplantation Society, 1976-78. Pres., Guild of Undergrads, Birmingham Univ., 1950-51. Vice-Chancellor's Medal, Birmingham Univ., 1951; Scientific Medal, Zool. Soc., 1963. Played hockey for UAU and Staffs, 1949-51. *Publications:* (ed) Progress in Immunology, 1974; articles in scientific and med. jls on immunology of tissue transplantation and immunological tolerance. *Recreations:* music, walking/climbing, gardening, cycling, chess, squash, social services, community relations, politics. *Address:* 8 Wood Vale, N10.

BRENTFORD, 3rd Viscount, *cr* 1929; Bt, *cr* 1919 and 1956; **Lancelot William Joynson-Hicks;** solicitor; formerly Senior Partner of Joynson-Hicks & Co.; elected Member, Church Assembly, 1934-70; *b* 10 April 1902; 2nd *s* of 1st Viscount Brentford, PC, DL, and Grace Lynn (*d* 1952), *o c* of Richard Hampson Joynson, JP, Bowdon, Cheshire; *S* brother, 1958; *m* 1931, Phyllis, *o d* of late Major Herbert Allfrey, Newnton House, Tetbury, Gloucestershire; one *s. Educ:* Winchester College; Trinity College, Oxford (MA). Admitted a Solicitor, 1926. Served War of 1939-45 as acting Lt-Comdr, RNVR. MP (C) Chichester Division of West Sussex, 1942-58; Parliamentary Secretary, Ministry of Fuel and Power, Nov. 1951-Dec. 1955. Chairman, Automobile Association, 1956-74. Pres., Southern Regional Assoc. for the Blind, 1972-. *Heir:* s Hon. Crispin William Joynson-Hicks [*b* 7 April 1933; *m* 1964, Gillian Evelyn, *er d* of G. E. Schluter, OBE, Valehyrst, Sevenoaks; one *s* two *d. Educ:* Eton; New College, Oxford]. *Address:* Newick Park, Sussex.

BRENTWOOD, Bishop of, (RC), since 1969; **Rt. Rev. Patrick Joseph Casey;** *b* 20 Nov. 1913; *s* of Patrick Casey and Bridget Casey (*née* Norris). *Educ:* St Joseph's Parochial Sch., Kingsland; St Edmund's Coll., Ware. Ordained priest, 1939; Asst, St

James's, Spanish Place, 1939-61; Parish Priest of Hendon, 1961-63; Vicar Gen. of Westminster, 1963; Domestic Prelate, and Canon of Westminster Cathedral, 1964; Provost of Westminster Cathedral Chapter, 1967; Auxiliary Bishop of Westminster and Titular Bishop of Sufar, 1966-69. *Address:* Bishop's House, 38 The Drive, South Woodford, E18. *T:* 01-989 1347.

BRESSON, Robert; film producer since 1934; *b* 25 Sept. 1907; *s* of Léon Bresson and Marie-Elisabeth Clausels; *m* 1926, Leidia Van der Zee. *Educ:* Lycée Lakanal, Sceaux. Started as painter; then producer of short films, Affaires Publiques. Full-length films produced include: Les Anges du Péché, 1943; Les Dames du Bois de Boulogne, 1948; Journal d'un Curé de Campagne, 1951 (Internat. Grand Prix, Venice); Un Condamné à Mort s'est Echappé, 1956; Pickpocket, 1960; Le Procès de Jeanne d'Arc, 1962 (Jury's special prize, Cannes); Au Hasard Balthazar, 1966; Mouchette, 1967; Une Femme Douce, 1969; Quatre nuits d'un rêveur, 1971; Lancelot du Lac, 1974; Le diable, probablement, 1977. *Publication:* Notes sur le cinématographe, 1976. *Address:* 49 quai de Bourbon, 75004 Paris, France.

BRETHERTON, Russell Frederick, CB 1951; Under-Secretary, the Treasury, 1961-68; *b* 3 Feb. 1906; *s* of F. H. Bretherton, Solicitor, Gloucester; *m* 1930, Jocelyn Nina Mathews; three *s* one *d. Educ:* Clifton College; Wadham College, Oxford. Fellow of Wadham College, 1928-45, Lecturer and Tutor in Economics and Modern History; University Research Lecturer, 1936-39. Temporary Civil Servant, Ministry of Supply and Board of Trade, 1939-45; Under-Secretary, Raw Materials Dept, Board of Trade, 1946-48; Cabinet Office (Economic Section), 1949-51; Under-Secretary: Min. of Materials, 1951-54; Board of Trade, 1954-61; Treasury, 1961-68. *Publications:* (with R. L. Lennard and others) Englishmen at Rest and Play (17th Century Studies), 1932; (with Burchardt and Rutherford) Public Investment and the Trade Cycle, 1941; articles in Social Survey of Oxford, Economic Journal, Econometrica, and in various entomological journals, etc. *Recreations:* walking, mountaineering, entomology. *Address:* Folly Hill, Birtley Green, Bramley, Surrey. *T:* Bramley 3377.

BRETT, family name of Viscount Esher.

BRETT, George P., jun.; retired from The Macmillan Company, New York, 1961; *b* Darien, Conn., 9 Dec. 1893; *s* of George Platt and Marie Louise (Tostevan) Brett; *m* 1917, Isabel Yeomans; two *s. Educ:* Collegiate School, New York City; Salisbury School, Salisbury, Conn. Joined staff of The Macmillan Company, Sept. 1913; six months training with competing publishing house, Doubleday, 1915. Served European War, 1914-18, with US Army, private 1916, 2nd Lieut 1917, 1st Lieut Jan. 1918, Capt. July 1918, 16 months service in France, 1918-19; Maj. Reserve Corps until 1940; Lieut-Col, Asst Chief of Staff, NY Guard, 1940-43; Adviser to War Production Board, State Dept, 1943-45. Returned to Macmillan, 1919; Dir and Sales Manager, 1920; Treas., 1920-31; General Manager, 1928-34; Pres., 1931-58; Chairman of the Board, 1959-61. Trustee: Union Square Savings Bank, New York City, 1926-61; Southport (Connecticut) Savings Bank, 1954-58. President: Sasquanaug Assoc. for Southport Improvement, 1954-56; Pequot Library, Southport, Connecticut, 1955-56. *Publications:* occasional contributor to trade journals. *Recreations:* walking, sailing, fishing. *Address:* (home) 648 Harbor Road, Southport, Connecticut 06490, USA. *Clubs:* Century, Players, Cruising of America (New York); Pequot Yacht (Cdre, 1951-53); Fairfield County Hunt (Conn); Lake Placid (NY); Key Largo Anglers' (Fla).

BRETT, Jeremy, (Peter Jeremy William Huggins); actor; *b* 3 Nov. 1935; *s* of Lt-Col H. W. Huggins, DSO, MC, DL, and late Elizabeth Huggins; *m* 1958 (marr. diss.); one *s. Educ:* Eton; Central Sch. of Drama. National Theatre, 1967-70: Orlando, in As You Like It; Berowne, in Love's Labour's Lost; Tesman, in Hedda Gabler; Bassanio, in The Merchant of Venice; Che Guevara, in Macrune's Guevara; The Son, in Voyage round my Father, Haymarket, 1972; Otto, in Design for Living, Phoenix, 1973-74; The Way of the World, Stratford, Ont, 1976. Films include: Nicholas, in War and Peace, 1955; Freddie, in My Fair Lady, 1965; also TV appearances. *Recreation:* archery. *Address:* 19 Hillsleigh Road, Camden Hill, W8 7LE. *T:* 01-727 8946. *Clubs:* Garrick; Woodmen of Arden (Meriden).

BRETT, John Alfred, MA; Headmaster, Durham School, Durham, 1958-67; *b* 26 Oct. 1915; *s* of Alfred Brett, Harrogate, Yorks; *m* 1939, Margaret Coode; one *s* three *d. Educ:* Durham School; St Edmund Hall, Oxford. MA (Hons Modern History). Temp. teacher, Stowe School, 1938; Teacher of History and English, Diocesan College, Rondebosch, South Africa, 1939; restarted Silver Tree Youth Club for non-Europeans, Cape

Town. Served in Army, Gunner to Major, RA, 1940-44; Instructor 123 OCTU Catterick; wounded in invasion of Normandy, 1944, and lost right eye; Military testing officer, War Office Selection Boards, finally Senior Military Testing Officer, War Office Selection Centre. Returned to post at Diocesan College, Rondebosch, 1946; Housemaster, 1948; Temp. teacher, Canford School, Wimborne, Dorset, 1954; Headmaster, Shaftesbury Grammar School, 1954. Diocesan Lay Reader. Member Council: Brathay Hall Centre; McAlpine Educnl Endowments Ltd. Governor, Bernard Gilpin Society. *Recreations:* sport (Captain Oxford University Rugby Football Club, 1937, and Member British Touring XV to Argentina, 1936); travel; reading. *Address:* Dun Cow Cottage, Wass, York.

BRETT, Lionel; *see* Esher, 4th Viscount.

BRETT, Sir Lionel, Kt 1961; *b* 19 Aug. 1911; 3rd *s* of late Very Rev. H. R. Brett, Dean of Belfast, and Constance Brett (*née* White). *Educ:* Marlborough; Magdalen College, Oxford. BA 1934; MA 1946. Called to Bar, Inner Temple, 1937. War service, 1939-46, released as Major. Joined Colonial Legal Service as Crown Counsel, Nigeria, 1946; Justice, Supreme Court of Nigeria, 1958-68. *Recreations:* reading, walking. *Address:* The Cottage, Puckington, near Ilminster, Somerset. *Club:* United Oxford & Cambridge University.

BRETT, Prof. Raymond Laurence; G. F. Grant Professor of English, University of Hull, since 1952; *b* 10 January 1917; *s* of late Leonard and Ellen Brett, Clevedon, Avon; *m* 1947, Kathleen Tegwen, *d* of late Rev. C. D. Cranmer; two *s*. *Educ:* Bristol Cathedral School; University of Bristol; University College, Oxford (Plumptre Exhibitioner). 1st Class Hons BA, English and Philosophy, Bristol, 1937; Taylor Prizeman, Hannam-Clark Prizeman, Haldane of Cloan Post-Grad. Studentship; BLitt, Oxf., 1940. Service in Admiralty, 1940-46; on Staff of First Lord; Lecturer in English, University of Bristol, 1946-52. Visiting Professor, University of Rochester, USA, 1958-59; Dean of Faculty of Arts, University of Hull, 1960-62. *Publications:* The Third Earl of Shaftesbury: A Study in 18th Century Literary Theory, 1951; Coleridge's Theory of Imagination (English Essays), 1949; George Crabbe, 1956; Reason and Imagination, 1961; (with A. R. Jones) a critical edition of Lyrical Ballads by Wordsworth and Coleridge, 1963; Thomas Hobbes (The English Mind), 1964; (ed) Poems of Faith and Doubt, 1965; An Introduction to English Studies, 1965; Fancy and Imagination, 1969; (ed) S. T. Coleridge, 1971; William Hazlitt, 1978; (ed) Barclay Fox's Journal, 1978; articles in: The Times, Time and Tide, Essays and Studies, Review of English Studies, Modern Language Review, Philosophy, English, South Atlantic Quarterly, etc. *Address:* The Gables, Station Walk, Cottingham, North Humberside. *T:* Hull 847115.

BRETT-JAMES, (Eliot) Antony; author (Military History); Head of War Studies and International Affairs Department, Royal Military Academy Sandhurst, since 1970 (Deputy Head, 1968-69); *b* 4 April 1920; *er surv. s* of late Norman George Brett-James, MA, BLitt, FSA, Mill Hill, and Gladys Brett-James. *Educ:* Mill Hill Sch.; Paris; Sidney Sussex Coll., Cambridge. 2nd cl. Mod. Langs Tripos, 1947; MA. Served War of 1939-45: Royal Signals, 2nd Lt, 1941; 2nd Air Formation Signals; Lebanon, Syria; 5th Indian Divl Signals, in Alamein Line, 1942; Iraq, India; Capt., 1943; commanded 9th Indian Inf. Bde Signals, Arakan, Imphal, Burma (despatches), 1944; Burma, 1945. Entered publishing: George G. Harrap (mod. langs editor), 1947-52; Chatto & Windus (reader and publicity manager), 1952-58; Cassell, 1958-61 (educl manager, 1960-61). Lectr, then Sen. Lectr, in Mil. Hist., RMA Sandhurst, 1961-67. Mil. Advr, BBC TV for Tolstoy's War and Peace, 1971-72. Mem., RUSI; FRHistS 1970. *Publications:* Report My Signals, 1948; Ball of Fire: the 5th Indian Division in the Second World War, 1951; The Triple Stream, 1953; General Graham, Lord Lynedoch, 1959; Wellington at War, 1794-1815, 1961; (with Lt-Gen. Sir G. Evans) Imphal, 1962; The Hundred Days, 1964; 1812, 1966; The British Soldier 1793-1815, 1970; Europe against Napoleon, 1970; Daily Life in Wellington's Army, 1972; articles in: Dictionary of National Biography, History Today, Purnell's History of the Second World War; reviews in TLS. *Recreations:* meeting people, cricket, browsing in antiquarian bookshops, gardening, music. *Address:* 18 Station Road, Petersfield, Hants. *T:* Petersfield 4927. *Club:* The Sette of Odd Volumes.

BRETTON; *see* Monk Bretton.

BREW, Richard Maddock; Member of Greater London Council; Deputy Leader of the Council, and Leader of Policy Committee, since 1977; *b* 13 Dec. 1930; *s* of late Leslie Maddock Brew and Phyllis Evelyn Huntsman; *m* 1953, Judith Anne Thompson Hancock; two *s* two *d*. *Educ:* Rugby Sch.; Magdalene Coll.,

Cambridge (BA). Called to the Bar, Inner Temple, 1955. After practising for short time at the Bar, joined family business, Brew Brothers Ltd, SW7, 1955, and remained until takeover, 1972. Dir, Alexander Hughes & Associates (UK) Ltd; Chm., Budget Lifts Ltd. Farms in Essex. Member: Royal Borough of Kensington Council, 1959-65; Royal Borough of Kensington and Chelsea Council, 1964-70; Greater London Council: Alderman, 1968-73; Vice-Chm., Strategic Planning Cttee, 1969-71; Chm., Covent Garden Jt Development Cttee, 1970-71 and Environmental Planning Cttee, 1971-73; Mem. for Chingford, 1973-; Dep. Leader, Cons. Party, GLC. *Recreations:* Pony Club, hunting, tennis. *Address:* The Abbey, Coggeshall, Essex. *T:* Coggeshall 61246. *Clubs:* Carlton, Royal Automobile.

BREWER, Dr Derek Stanley, FSA; Master of Emmanuel College, Cambridge, since 1977, and Reader in Medieval English, University of Cambridge, since 1976; *b* 13 July 1923; *s* of Stanley Leonard Brewer and Winifred Helen Forbes; *m* 1951, Lucie Elisabeth Hoole; three *s* two *d*. *Educ:* elementary school; The Crypt Grammar Sch.; Magdalen Coll., Oxford (Matthew Arnold Essay Prize, 1948; BA, MA 1948); Birmingham Univ. (PhD 1956). Commnd 2nd Lieut, Worcestershire Regt, 1942; Captain and Adjt, 1st Bn Royal Fusiliers, 1944-45. Asst Lectr and Lectr in English, Univ. of Birmingham, 1949-56; Prof. of English, Internat. Christian Univ., Tokyo, 1956-58; Lectr and Sen. Lectr, Univ. of Birmingham, 1958-64; Lectr in English, Univ. of Cambridge, 1965-76; Fellow of Emmanuel Coll., Cambridge, 1965-77 (Seatonian Prize, 1969, 1972). Founder, D. S. Brewer Ltd, for the publication of academic books, 1972. Sir Israel Gollancz Meml Lectr, British Academy, 1974. FSA 1977. *Publications:* Chaucer, 1953, 3rd edn 1973; Proteus, 1958 (Tokyo); (ed) The Parlement of Foulys, 1960; Chaucer in his Time, 1963; (ed and contrib.) Chaucer and Chaucerians, 1966; (ed) Malory's Morte Darthur: Parts Seven and Eight, 1968; (ed and contrib.) Writers and their Backgrounds: Chaucer, 1974; (ed) Chaucer: the Critical Heritage, 1978; Chaucer and his World, 1978; numerous articles in learned jls, reviews, etc. *Recreations:* reading, walking, opera, looking at paintings and antiquities, travelling, publishing other people's books. *Address:* The Master's Lodge, Emmanuel College, Cambridge CB2 3AP. *T:* Cambridge 50484.

BREWER, Frank, CMG 1960; OBE 1953; Foreign and Commonwealth Office (formerly Foreign Office), 1960-76; *b* 1915; *s* of late Lewis Arthur Brewer; *m* 1950, Eileen Marian, *d* of A. J. Shepherd. *Educ:* Swindon Commonweal School; Pembroke College, Oxford (MA). Malayan Civil Service, 1937-39; War Service, 1941-45, Special Forces (POW Sumatra) Chinese Secretariat, Labour Dept; Secretary for Chinese Affairs and Dep. Chief Sec., Fed. of Malaya, 1955-57; Sec. for Defence, 1957-59. *Address:* 18 Forest Way, Tunbridge Wells, Kent. *T:* Tunbridge Wells 24850. *Clubs:* Royal Commonwealth Society, Special Forces.

BREWER, Rt. Rev. John; Titular Bishop of Britonia and Auxiliary Bishop of Shrewsbury, (RC), since 1971; Parish Priest of St Mary's, Middlewich, since 1971; *b* 24 Nov. 1929; *s* of Eric W. Brewer and Laura H. Brewer (*née* Webster). *Educ:* Ushaw College, Durham; Ven. English College, Rome, and Gregorian Univ. PhL, STL, JCL. Ordained priest, 1956; Parish Assistant, 1959-64; Vice-Rector, Ven. English Coll., Rome, 1964-71. Officiating Chaplain, RN, 1966-71; Representative of RC Bishops of England and Wales in Rome, 1964-71. Chaplain to HH Pope Paul VI, 1965. *Recreations:* walking, golf. *Address:* St Mary's, Middlewich, Cheshire. *T:* Middlewich 2359.

BREWIS, Henry John, DL; Chairman, Scottish Conservative Group for Europe; Managing Director, Ardwell Estates, Stranraer; farming; *b* 8 April 1920; *s* of Lt-Col F. B. Brewis, Norton Grove, Malton, Yorks; *m* 1949, Faith A. D. MacTaggart-Stewart, Ardwell, Wigtownshire; three *s* one *d*. *Educ:* Eton; New College, Oxford. Served Royal Artillery, 1940-46 (despatches twice); on active service, North Africa and Italy; demobilized with rank of Major. Barrister-at-law, 1946. Wigtownshire County Council, 1955; Convener, Finance Cttee, 1958. MP (C) Galloway, April 1959-Sept. 1974; PPS to The Lord Advocate, 1960-61; Speaker's Panel of Chairmen, 1965; Chm., Select Cttee on Scottish Affairs, 1970; Member British Delegn: to Council of Europe, 1966-69; to European Parlt, Strasbourg, 1973-75; Vice-Chm., Cons. Agric. Cttee, 1971; Mem., BBC NE Adv. Council, 1976-; Dist Chm., Queen's Jubilee Appeal, 1976-; Reg. Chm., Scottish Landowners' Fedn, 1977-. DL Wigtownshire, 1966. *Recreations:* golf, tennis, shooting. *Address:* Ardwell House, Stranraer. *T:* Ardwell 227; Norton Grove, Malton, N Yorks. *Club:* Caledonian.

BREWIS, John Fenwick, CMG 1962; CVO 1957; HM Diplomatic Service (retired); *b* 26 April 1910; *s* of late Arthur

Brewis and Mary Brewis; *m* 1948, Rachel Mary, *d* of late Hilary G. Gardner; one *s* one *d*. *Educ:* Repton; CCC, Camb. Entered China Consular Service in 1933 and served in China till 1944; First Secretary, Baghdad, 1946-49; Consul, Bordeaux, 1950-52; Foreign Office, 1945-46, 1954-55 and 1959-65; Counsellor, Lisbon, 1955-59; Consul-General, Lyons, 1965-67. Tourist and Publicity Officer for Winchester, 1968-75. *Recreations:* gardening, historical reading. *Address:* 49 St Cross Road, Winchester. *T:* Winchester 4187.

BREWSTER, George, CVO 1969; MD; practitioner of medicine, retired 1977; formerly Surgeon Apothecary to HM Household at Holyrood Palace, Edinburgh, resigned 1970; formerly Medical Officer to French Consulate-General in Scotland; *b* 27 Sept. 1899; *m* 1930; two *s*. *Educ:* High School, Stirling; Edinburgh Univ. MB, ChB, Edin., 1921; DPH Edin., 1924; MD (with distinction) Edin., 1926. House Surgeon, Edin. Royal Infirmary. Chevalier de la Légion d'Honneur (France), 1957. *Address:* 53 Bruntsfield Place, Edinburgh. *T:* 031-229 2301.

BREWSTER, Kingman, United States Ambassador to the Court of St James's, since 1977; *b* Longmeadow, Massachusetts, 17 June 1919; *s* of Kingman Brewster and Florence Besse; *m* 1942, Mary Louise Phillips; three *s* two *d*. *Educ:* Yale University; Harvard University. AB Yale, 1941; LLB Harvard, 1948. Military Service: Lieut (Aviation) USNR, 1942-46. Special Asst Coordinator Inter-American Affairs, 1941; Research Assoc., Dept Economics, Massachusetts Inst. of Technology, 1949-50; Asst. General Counsel, Office US Special Representative in Europe, 1948-49; Cons., Pres. Materials Policy Commission, 1951, Mut. Security Agency, 1952; Asst Prof. of Law, Harvard, 1950-58; Prof. of Law, Harvard, 1953-60; Provost, Yale, 1961-63; Pres., Yale Univ., 1963-77. Chm., Nat. Policy Panel of UN; Mem. Bd of Dirs: Amer. Council of Learned Socs; Amer. Council on Educn; Nat. Educn Television; Carnegie Endowment Fund for Internat. Peace; Kaiser Family Foundn; Mem., Council on Foreign Relations. Holds many Hon. Degrees. *Publications:* Antitrust and American Business Abroad, 1959; (with M. Katz) Law of International Transactions and Relations, 1960. *Recreation:* sailing. *Address:* American Embassy, Grosvenor Square, W1; 43 Hillhouse Avenue, New Haven, Connecticut. *T:* 203:432-4180. *Clubs:* Yale, Century Association (New York); Tavern (Boston, Mass); Vineyard Haven Yacht (Vineyard Haven, Mass); Yale Sailing Associates, Graduates (New Haven, Conn).

BREZHNEV, Leonid Ilyich; Hero of the Soviet Union (two awards); five Orders of Lenin; two Orders of the Red Banner; Order of Bogdan Khmelnitsky (2nd cl.); Order of the Patriotic War (1st cl.); Order of the Red Star; Hero of Socialist Labour; Chairman of the Presidium, Supreme Soviet of USSR, since 1977; General Secretary of Central Cttee, CPSU, since 1966; Member, Presidium of Supreme Soviet (President, 1960-64); *b* Kamenskoye (now Dnieprodzerzhinsk), Ukraine, 19 Dec. 1906. *Educ:* Institute of Metallurgy, Dnieprodzerzhinsk (graduate). Began career as engineer and was active in social work. Joined Communist Party, 1931; 1st Secretary, Central Cttee, Communist Party of Moldavia, 1950. Elected to Supreme Soviet of USSR, 1950, 1954, 1958, 1962. Member, Central Cttee, CPSU, 1952-; Alternate Member Presidium of Central Cttee, CPSU, 1952-57; Secretary, Central Cttee, Communist Party, Kazakhstan, 1954-56; Member Presidium of Central Cttee, CPSU, 1957-; Member Party Secretariat, Central Cttee, 1952-53, 1956-57, 1963-, First Secretary, 1964-66. Maj.-Gen. 1943; Lieut-Gen. 1953. Lenin Peace Prize, 1972. *Address:* Central Committee, CPSU, Kremlin, Moscow, USSR.

BRIAN, Prof. Percy Wragg, CBE 1975; FRS 1958; Professor of Botany, University of Cambridge, 1968-77, now Emeritus Professor; *b* 5 Sept. 1910; *s* of Percy Brian, Macclesfield, and Adelaide Wragg, Shirley, nr Birmingham; *m* 1st, 1935, Iris Neville Hunt (marr. diss. 1947); one *s* two *d*; 2nd, 1948, Margaret Audrey Gilling. *Educ:* King Edward's School, Birmingham; King's College, Cambridge. Univ. of Cambridge. Frank Smart Univ. Student in Botany, 1933-34; PhD 1936; ScD 1951. Assistant Mycologist, Long Ashton Research Station, 1934; Mycologist, Jealott's Hill Research Station, ICI Ltd, 1936; Head of Dept of Microbiology, Akers Research Labs ICI Ltd, Welwyn, 1946; Associate Research Manager, Pharmaceuticals Div., 1961-62; Regius Prof. of Botany, Glasgow Univ., 1962-68; Clive Behrens Lectr in Agric., Leeds Univ., 1964-65. President: British Mycological Society, 1959, 1965; Assoc. of Applied Biologists, 1961; Society for General Microbiology, 1965; Mem., ARC, 1966-; Leeuwenhoek Lectr, Royal Soc., 1966; Mem. Council, Royal Soc., 1968-70. *Publications:* many in learned journals on subjects concerned with plant pathology, microbiology and plant physiology. *Recreation:* gardening. *Address:* Walkers Field, Kingston, Cambridge CB3 7NG. *T:* Comberton 2200.

BRIANCE, John Albert, CMG 1960; HM Diplomatic Service, retired; *b* 19 Oct. 1915; *s* of late Albert Perceval and Louise Florence Briance; *m* 1950, Prunella Mary, *d* of Col. E. Haldane Chapman; one *s* one *d*. *Educ:* King Edward VII School. Colonial Police, Palestine, 1936-48; Foreign Office, 1949; British Embassy, Tehran, 1950-52; British Middle East Office, 1953; Foreign Office, 1954-57; Counsellor, British Embassy, Washington, 1958-60; Counsellor, Office of UK Commissioner for SE Asia Singapore, 1961-63; FCO (formerly FO), 1964-70; retired 1970. *Address:* 14 Pitt Street, W8. *Clubs:* Bath, Hurlingham.

BRIAULT, Dr Eric William Henry, CBE 1976; Education Officer, Inner London Education Authority, 1971-76; *b* 24 Dec. 1911; *s* of H. G. Briault; *m* 1935, Marie Alice (*née* Knight); two *s* one *d*. *Educ:* Brighton, Hove and Sussex Grammar Sch.; Peterhouse, Cambridge (Robert Slade Schol.). 1st cl. hons Geography, 1933; MA Cantab 1937; PhD London 1939. School teaching, 1933-47; Inspector of Schools, LCC, 1948-56; Dep. Educn Officer, ILEA, 1956-71. Vis. Prof. of Educn, Univ. of Sussex, 1977-. Hon. Sec., RGS, 1953-63. Hon. DLitt Sussex, 1975. *Publications:* Sussex, East and West (Land Utilisation Survey report), 1942; (jtly) Introduction to Advanced Geography, 1957; (jtly) Geography In and Out of School, 1960. *Recreations:* travel, gardening, music, theatre and ballet; formerly athletics (Cambridge blue) and cross-country running (Cambridge half-blue). *Address:* Woodedge, Hampers Lane, Storrington, Sussex. *T:* Storrington 3919. *Club:* Athenæum.

BRICE, Air Cdre Eric John, CBE 1971 (OBE 1957); CEng; AFRAeS; MBIM; RAF retd; stockbroker; *b* 12 Feb. 1917; *s* of Courtenay Percy Please Brice and Lilie Alice Louise Brice (*née* Grey); *m* 1942, Janet Parks, Roundhay, Leeds, Yorks; two *s* one *d*. *Educ:* Loughborough Coll. (DLC). Joined RAF, 1939; served War, MEAF, 1943-46 (Sqdn Ldr). Air Ministry, 1946-50; Parachute Trg Sch., 1950-52; Wing Comdr, 1952; RAE, Farnborough, 1952-58; Comd, Parachute Trg Sch., 1958-60; RAF Coll., Cranwell, 1960-61; Gp Capt., 1961; RAF Halton, 1961-64; Comd, RAF Innsworth, Glos, 1964-66; Dir, Physical Educn, RAF, MoD, 1966-68; Air Cdre, 1968; Dep. AOA, RAF Headqrs, Maintenance Comd, 1968-71; April 1971, retd prematurely. *Recreations:* athletics (Combined Services and RAF athletic blues); Rugby football (RAF trialist and Blackheath Rugby Club); captained Loughborough Coll. in three sports. *Address:* Durns, Boldre, Hampshire. *T:* Lymington 72196. *Clubs:* Royal Air Force; Royal Lymington Yacht.

BRICKER, John William, LLB; Lawyer, USA; Republican; *b* 6 Sept. 1893; *s* of Lemuel Spencer Bricker and Laura (*née* King) *m* 1920, Harriet Day; one *s*. *Educ:* State Univ., Ohio. AB 1916; admitted to Bar, Ohio, 1917; LLB 1920. Solicitor, Grandview Heights, 1920-28; Assistant Attorney-General of Ohio, 1923-27; Attorney-General, 1933-37. Governor of Ohio, 1939-41, 1941-43, 1943-45. Candidate (Republican) for US Vice-Presidency, 1944; Senator from Ohio, 1947-58. Member firm of Bricker, Evatt, Barton & Eckler. Member Public Utilities Commission, Ohio, 1929-32. LLD Ohio State University, 1940. Served European War, 1917-18, 1st Lieut. Holds various trusteeships. *Address:* 100 East Broad Street, Columbus, Ohio 43215, USA; 2407 Tremont Road, Columbus, Ohio 43221, USA.

BRICKHILL, Paul Chester Jerome; author; *b* 20 Dec. 1916; 3rd *s* of G. R. Brickhill, Sydney, Aust.; *m* 1950, Margaret Olive Slater, Sydney (marr. diss., 1964); one *s* one *d*. *Educ:* North Sydney High School; Sydney University. Journalist in Sydney, 1935-40; joined RAAF 1940; service in United Kingdom and Middle East as fighter pilot; three times wounded; shot down in Tunisia, 1943; POW Germany; Flight Lieut; Foreign Correspondent in Europe and USA, 1945-47; left journalism to concentrate on books, 1949. *Publications:* Escape to Danger (with Conrad Norton), 1946; The Great Escape, 1951; The Dam Busters, 1951; Escape or Die, 1952; Reach for the Sky, 1954; The Deadline, 1962. *Recreation:* golf. *Address:* c/o John Farquharson Ltd, Bell House, Bell Yard, WC2A 2JR. *T:* 01-242 2445. *Club:* Royal Air Force.

BRICKMAN, Brig. Ivan Pringle, CB 1949; CBE 1942 (OBE 1929); Regular Army retired; *b* 14 May 1891; *s* of Francis Brickman, Edinburgh, and Eliza Macdonald; *m* 1920, Mildred Ducker (*d* 1977); one *d*. *Educ:* Edinburgh Academy; Bowdon College. Served European War, 1914-18, France (despatches); War of 1939-45; ME, 1941 (despatches); BNAF, 1943; CMF, 1944 (despatches), Bronze Star (USA), 1946. *Recreations:* fishing, golf. *Address:* 10 Brynllys East, Meliden, Clwyd. *T:* Prestatyn 3442.

BRICKWOOD, Sir Basil (Greame), 3rd Bt *cr* 1927; *b* 21 May 1923; *s* of Sir John Brickwood, 1st Bt and Isabella Janet Gibson (d 1967), d of James Gordon; S half-brother, 1974; m 1956, Shirley Anne Brown; two d. *Educ:* Clifton College. *Club:* Royal Air Force.

BRIDGE, Very Rev. Antony Cyprian; Dean of Guildford since 1968; b 5 Sept. 1914; s of late Comdr C. D. C. Bridge, RN; m 1937, Brenda Lois Streatfeild; one s two d. *Educ:* Marlborough College. Scholarship to Royal Academy School of Art, 1932. Professional painter thereafter. War of 1939-45: joined Army, Sept. 1939; commissioned Buffs, 1940; demobilised as Major, 1945. Ordained, 1955; Curate, Hythe Parish Church till 1958; Vicar of Christ Church, Lancaster Gate, London, 1958-68. Mem., Adv. Council V&A Museum, 1976-. *Publication:* Images of God, 1960. *Recreations:* bird-watching, reading. *Address:* The Deanery, 1 Cathedral Close, Guildford, Surrey GU2 5TL. *T:* Guildford 60328.
See also Hon. Sir Nigel Bridge.

BRIDGE, John, GC 1944; GM 1940 and Bar 1941; Director of Education for Sunderland Borough Council (formerly Sunderland County Borough Council), 1963-76, retired; b 5 Feb. 1915; s of late Joseph Edward Bridge, Culcheth, Warrington; m 1945, F. J. Patterson; three d. *Educ:* London Univ. BSc Gen. Hons, 1936 and BSc Special Hons (Physics), 1937; Teacher's Dip., 1938. Schoolmaster: Lancs CC, Sept.-Dec. 1938; Leighton Park, Reading, Jan.-Aug. 1939; Firth Park Grammar Sch., Sheffield, Sept. 1939-Aug. 1946 (interrupted by war service). Served War: RNVR June 1940-Feb. 1946, engaged on bomb and mine disposal; demobilised as Lt Comdr RNVR. *Address:* 37 Park Avenue, Roker, Sunderland, Tyne and Wear. *T:* Sunderland 72963.

BRIDGE, Keith James; County Treasurer, Greater Manchester Council, since 1973; b 21 Aug. 1929; s of James Henry Bridge and late Lilian Elizabeth (*née* Nichols); m 1960, Thelma Ruby (*née* Hubble); three d (and one s decd). *Educ:* Sir George Monoux Grammar Sch.; Corpus Christi Coll., Oxford (MA). CIPFA 1959. Local govt service, 1953; Dep. City Treasurer, York, 1965; Borough Treas., Bolton, 1967; City Treas., Manchester, 1971. Financial Adviser to Assoc. of Metrop. Authorities, 1971; Mem. Council, Chartered Inst. of Public Finance and Accountancy, 1972. *Publications:* papers in profess. jls. *Recreations:* gardening, literature, music. *Address:* Kragero, The Clough, Chorley New Road, Bolton BL1 5BB. *T:* Bolton 42372.

BRIDGE, Rt. Hon. Sir Nigel (Cyprian), PC 1975; Kt 1968; **Rt. Hon. Lord Justice Bridge;** a Lord Justice of Appeal, since 1975; b 26 Feb. 1917; s of late Comdr C. D. C. Bridge, RN; m 1944, Margaret Swinbank; one s two d. *Educ:* Marlborough College. Army Service, 1940-46; commnd into KRRC, 1941. Called to the Bar, Inner Temple, 1947; Junior Counsel to Treasury (Common Law), 1964-68; a Judge of High Court, Queen's Bench Div., 1968-75; Presiding Judge, Western Circuit, 1972-74. *Address:* The Old Rectory, Dowdeswell, near Cheltenham, Glos. *T:* Andoversford 249.
See also Very Rev. A. C. Bridge.

BRIDGE, Roy Arthur Odell, CMG 1967; Advisor to the Chairman, Mellon Bank N. A., Pittsburgh, since 1970; Director (since 1970): Julius Baer International Ltd, London; Bär Holding A. G. Zürich; Baer Securities Corporation, New York; Scandinavian Bank Ltd, London; b 27 June 1911; s of late A. S. W. Bridge and late Mary E. Bridge; m 1st, 1938, Mary Ethel (d 1972), d of late E. N. Ruddock; two s two d (and one d decd); 2nd, 1974, Jane Catliffe Glover. *Educ:* Dulwich College. Bank of England, 1929-69: UK Alternate on Managing Bd of European Payments Union, Paris, 1950-52; Dep. Chief Cashier, Bank of England, 1957-63; Adviser to the Governors, 1963-65; Asst to the Governors, 1965-69. Pres., Assoc. Cambiste Internationale, Paris, 1962-67 (Hon. Pres., 1967). FRSA 1969. *Recreations:* people, music, eating and drinking. *Address:* 16 St Leonard's Court, West Hill Road, St Leonards-on-Sea, E Sussex. *T:* Hastings 433098. *Clubs:* Bath, Overseas Bankers; Forex (Paris).

BRIDGEMAN, family name of **Earl of Bradford** and **Viscount Bridgeman.**

BRIDGEMAN, 2nd Viscount, cr 1929, of Leigh; **Robert Clive Bridgeman,** KBE 1954; CB 1944; DSO 1940; MC; psc; JP; HM Lieutenant of County of Salop, 1951-Dec. 1969; b April 1896; e s of 1st Viscount and Caroline Beatrix, DBE (d 1961), er d of Hon. Cecil Parker; S father, 1935; m 1930, Mary Kathleen, 2nd d of Baron Bingley, PC; three d. *Educ:* Eton College. 2nd Lieut, The Rifle Bde, 1914; Lieut, 1916; Captain, 1921; Bt Major, 1932; Bt. Lieut-Col, 1935, acting Maj.-Gen., 1941; Col and Temp. Maj.-Gen., 1942; served European War (France), 1915-18; Private Secretary to his father when Parliamentary Secretary to Minister of Labour, 1918; Brigade Major, 7th Infantry Brigade, 1932-34; GSO2 War Office, 1935-37; retired pay, 1937; served War of 1939-45 (DSO); Deputy Director, Home Guard, 1941; Director-General, Home Guard and Territorial Army, 1941-44; Deputy Adjt-General, 1944-45. Pres., West Midland TA&VRA, 1968-69. Vice-Chm., Trust Houses Forte Council, 1971-. Alderman, Salop CC, 1951-74. JP Salop, 1951. *Heir: nephew* Robin John Orlando Bridgeman [b 5 Dec. 1930; m 1966, Harriet Lucy Turton; three s. *Address:* Leigh Manor, Minsterley, Salop SY5 0EX. *T:* Worthen 210. *Clubs:* Beefsteak, Naval and Military.
See also Hon. Sir Maurice Bridgeman, Rev. N. D. Stacey.

BRIDGEMAN, John Michael; Under Secretary, HM Treasury, since 1975; b 26 April 1931; s of John Wilfred Bridgeman, qv; m 1958, June Bridgeman, qv; one s four d. *Educ:* Marlborough Coll.; Trinity Coll., Cambridge. Asst Principal, BoT, 1954; HM Treasury, 1956-. *Address:* Bridge House, Culverden Park Road, Tunbridge Wells, Kent.

BRIDGEMAN, John Wilfred, CBE 1960; BSc London, AKC; retired as Principal, Loughborough Training College, 1950-63; Principal, Loughborough Summer School, 1931-63; b 25 Jan. 1895; s of late John Edward Bridgeman and Alice Bridgeman, Bournemouth; m 1st, 1928, Mary Jane Wallace (d 1961); one s; 2nd, 1963, Helen Ida Mary Wallace. *Educ:* King's College, University of London; London Day Training College. Industry, 1910-15; taught at technical colleges, Bournemouth, Bath and Weymouth, 1915-20; Asst Master, Lyme Regis Grammar School, 1923; Senior Maths. Master, Wolverhampton Secondary Gram. Sch., 1926; Head of Dept for Training of Teachers, Loughborough Coll., 1930. Chm., Assoc. of Teachers in Colls and Depts of Education, 1952; Leader of Staff Panel, Pelham Cttee, 1955-63. Hon. MA Nottingham, 1961. *Recreations:* chess and walking. *Address:* 33 Old Rectory Gardens, Felpham, Sussex PO22 7ER. *T:* Bognor 21730.
See also J. M. Bridgeman.

BRIDGEMAN, Mrs June; Under-Secretary, Central Policy Review Staff, Cabinet Office, since 1977; b 26 June 1932; d of Gordon and Elsie Forbes; m 1958, John Michael Bridgeman, qv; one s four d. *Educ:* variously, England and Scotland; Westfield Coll., London Univ. (BA). Asst Principal, BoT, 1954; subseq. served in DEA, NBPI, Min. of Housing and Local Govt, DoE; Under-Sec., DoE, 1974-76. *Address:* Bridge House, Culverden Park Road, Tunbridge Wells, Kent TN4 9QX.

BRIDGEMAN, Hon. Sir Maurice (Richard), KBE 1964 (CBE 1946); Chairman of British Petroleum Company, 1960-69; Member, Industrial Reorganisation Corporation, 1969-71; b 26 Jan. 1904; 3rd s of 1st Viscount Bridgeman; m 1933, Diana Mary Erica Wilson; four d. *Educ:* Eton; Trinity Coll., Cambridge. Joined Anglo-Persian Oil Co., 1926; Petroleum Adviser Ministry of Economic Warfare, 1939; Asst Secretary Petroleum Dept and Joint Secretary Oil Control Board, 1940; temporarily loaned as Petroleum Adviser Govt of India, 1942; Principal Assistant Secretary Petroleum Division, Ministry of Fuel and Power, 1944-46; Mem. Advisory Council on Middle East Trade, 1958-63; Pres., Middle East Assoc., 1965-76. Hon. Fellow, Fitzwilliam Coll., Cambridge, 1967. Hon. LLD Leeds Univ., 1969. Cadman Memorial Medal, 1969. KStJ 1961 (CStJ 1957). Knight Grand Cross of the Italian Republic, 1966; Grand Officer, Order of Orange Nassau, 1968; Order of Homayun (Iran), 2nd Class, 1968. *Address:* The Glebe House, Selham, Petworth, West Sussex. *T:* Lodsworth 205; 10 Kylestrome House, Ebury Street, SW1. *T:* 01-730 1700. *Club:* White's.
See also J. L. Harman.

BRIDGER, Pearl, MBE 1947; Director, Central Personnel, Post Office, 1968-72, retired; b 9 Dec. 1912; d of Samuel and Lottie Bridger. *Educ:* Godolphin and Latymer Girls' Sch., London, W6. BA Open Univ., 1976. Entered Post Office as Executive Officer, 1931; Asst Telecommunications Controller, 1938; Principal, 1947; Asst Sec., 1954; Director, 1968. MIPM. *Recreation:* voluntary work with housing associations. *Address:* 95 Deanhill Court, SW14. *T:* 01-876 8877. *Clubs:* Royal Overseas League, Civil Service, Soroptimist.

BRIDGES, family name of **Baron Bridges.**

BRIDGES, 2nd Baron cr 1957; **Thomas Edward Bridges,** CMG 1975; HM Diplomatic Service; Minister (Commercial), Washington, since 1976; b 27 Nov. 1927; s of 1st Baron Bridges, KG, PC, GCB, GCVO, MC, FRS, and Hon. Katharine Dianthe, d of 2nd Baron Farrer; S father, 1969; m 1953, Rachel Mary, y d of late Sir Henry Bunbury, KCB; two s one d. *Educ:* Eton; New Coll., Oxford. Entered Foreign Service, 1951; served in Bonn, Berlin, Rio de Janeiro and at FO (Asst Private Sec. to Foreign Secretary, 1963-66); Head of Chancery, Athens, 1966-

68; Counsellor, Moscow, 1969-71; Private Sec. (Overseas Affairs) to Prime Minister, 1972-74. RCDS 1975. *Heir: s* Hon. Mark Thomas Bridges, *b* 25 July 1954. *Address: c/o* Foreign and Commonwealth Office, SW1.

BRIDGES, John Gourlay, OBE 1954 (MBE 1944); Consultant: Tourism Promotion, Travel and Capital Development; Supervisor, Press, Publicity and Information to Church of Scotland, 1967-72; Director-General, British Travel and Holidays Association, 1945-63, retd; *b* 5 Dec. 1901; *e s* of late David McKay Bridges and late Margaret Gourlay Bridges, Glasgow; *m* 1931, Marion, *d* of late Andrew Bell, MBE, JP, Glasgow; one *s* one *d. Educ:* elementary and secondary schools, Glasgow; Glasgow and West of Scotland Commercial College and School of Accountancy. Secretary, and latterly Director-Secretary, of private Ltd. Co., Glasgow and London, 1922-24; Accountant, Straits Trading Co. Ltd., Singapore and FM States, 1924-30; Sec. at Edinburgh, and later Gen. Sec. for Scotland, of The Overseas League, 1931-35; then Development Sec. of the movement; Development Sec., Overseas League and Gen. Sec., Overseas League in Canada, 1935-38; Gen. Tours Manager, Donaldson Atlantic Line, Great Britain, Canada and USA, 1939. Served in RAF as Embarkation Officer (Personnel) Liverpool, 1940-45; demobilized with rank of Squadron Leader, 1945. Pres. 1960, and Mem., Council of Honour, International Union of Official Travel Organizations (with consultative status UN). Director of Studies and Professor of Tourism, Hawaii Univ., 1964-65. FRGS; Associate Institute of Transport. Member: Association of Scientific Tourism Experts; Exec. Cttee, Scottish Council for Development and Industry; Scottish Tourist Cons. Council. *Publications:* numerous articles on Travel and allied subjects. *Recreations:* motoring, fishing, gardening. *Address:* 35A Cluny Drive, Edinburgh EH10 6DT. *T:* 031-447 4966. *Club:* Royal Over-Seas League.

BRIDGES, Ven. Peter Sydney Godfrey; Archdeacon of Coventry since 1977; Canon-Theologian of Coventry Cathedral, since 1977; *b* 30 Jan. 1925; *s* of Sidney Clifford Bridges and Winifred (*née* Livette); *m* 1952, Joan Penlerick (*née* Madge); two *s. Educ:* Raynes Park Grammar Sch.; Kingston upon Thames Sch. of Architecture; Lincoln Theol College. ARIBA 1950, Dip. Liturgy and Architecture 1967. Gen. and ecclesiastical practice, 1950-54; Lectr, Nottingham Sch. of Architecture, 1954-56. Deacon, 1958; Priest, 1959. Asst Curate, Hemel Hempstead, 1958-64; Res. Fellow, Inst. for Study of Worship and Religious Architecture, Univ. of Birmingham, 1964-67 (Hon. Fellow, 1967-72); Warden, Anglican Chaplaincy and Chaplain to Univ. of Birmingham, 1965-68; Lectr, Birmingham Sch. of Arch., 1967-72; eccles. architect and planning consultant, 1968-75; Chm., New Town Ministers Assoc., 1968-72; Co-Dir, Mids Socio-Religious Res. Gp, 1968-75; Dir, Chelmsford Diocesan R&D Unit, 1972-77; Archdeacon of Southend, 1972-77. *Publications:* Socio-Religious Institutes, Lay Academies, etc, 1967; contrib. Church Building, res. bulletins (Inst. for Study of Worship and Relig. Arch.), Clergy Review, Prism, Christian Ministry in New Towns, Cathedral and Mission, Church Architecture and Social Responsibility. *Recreations:* architecture, singing. *Address:* Baginton Rectory, Coventry, Warwicks. *T:* Coventry 302508. *Club:* Royal Commonwealth Society.

BRIDGES, Hon. Sir Phillip (Rodney), Kt 1973; CMG 1967; **Hon. Mr Justice Bridges;** Chief Justice of The Gambia, since 1968; *b* 9 July 1922; *e s* of late Captain Sir Ernest Bridges, and of Lady Bridges, Bedford; *m* 1st, 1951, Rosemary Ann Streeten (marr. diss. 1961); two *s* one *d* ; 2nd, 1962, Angela Mary (*née* Dearden), widow of James Huyton. *Educ:* Bedford School. Military Service (Capt., RA) with Royal W African Frontier Force in W. Africa, India and Burma, 1941-47. Admitted Solicitor (England), 1951; Colonial Legal Service, 1954; Barrister and Solicitor, Supreme Court of The Gambia, 1954; Solicitor-General of The Gambia, 1963; QC (Gambia) 1964; Attorney-General of The Gambia, 1964-68. *Address:* Weavers, Coney Weston, Bury St Edmunds, Suffolk; Supreme Court, Banjul, The Gambia. *Club:* Travellers'.

BRIDGES-ADAMS, John Nicholas William; a Recorder of the Crown Court, since 1972; *b* 16 Sept. 1930; *s* of late William Bridges-Adams, CBE; *m* 1962, Jenifer Celia Emily, *d* of David Sandell, FRCS. *Educ:* Stowe; Oriel Coll., Oxford (Scholar; MA, DipEd). Commnd Royal Artillery, 1949, transf. to RAFVR 1951 and served with Oxford and London Univ. Air Sqdn. Called to Bar, Lincoln's Inn, 1958. Mem., Young Barristers Cttee, Bar Council, 1960-61; Actg Junior, Mddx Sessions Bar Mess, 1965-67. Mem., Exec. Cttee, Soc. of Cons. Lawyers, 1967-69 (Chm., Rates of Exchange sub-cttee); Chm., panel from which representations Cttees under Dumping at Sea Act 1974 are drawn, 1976-. Contested (C) West Bromwich West, Oct.

1974. Member: RIIA; IISS. *Publication:* contrib. on collisions at sea, 3rd edn of Halsbury's Laws of England, Vol. 35. *Recreations:* sailing, flying, cooking. *Address:* 5 Paper Buildings, Temple, EC4. *T:* 01-583 3724; Fornham Cottage, Fornham St Martin, Bury St Edmunds, Suffolk. *T:* Bury St Edmunds 5307. *Clubs:* Savile, Garrick; Tiger (Redhill Aerodrome).

BRIDGEWATER, Bentley Powell Conyers; Secretary of the British Museum, 1948-73; *b* 6 Sept. 1911; *s* of Conyers Bridgewater, OBE, Clerk to Commissioners of Taxes for City of London, and Violet Irene, *d* of Dr I. W. Powell, Victoria, BC. *Educ:* Westminster School (King's Schol.); Christ Church, Oxford (Schol., BA 1933, MA 1965). Asst Keeper, British Museum, 1937; Asst Sec., 1940. Seconded to Dominions Office, 1941-42, and to Foreign Office, 1942-45; returned to British Museum, 1946; Deputy Keeper, 1950; Keeper, 1961; retired, 1973. *Recreation:* music. *Address:* 4 Doughty Street, WC1N 2PH. *Club:* Athenæum.

BRIDGMAN, Leonard; AMRAeS; *b* 15 Feb. 1895; *o s* of late A. H. Bridgman, ISO; unmarried. *Educ:* Cambridge House; Strand School; King's Coll., London. Hon. Artillery Company, 1915-18 and 1921-; Royal Air Force, 1918-19; Editorial Staff, The Aeroplane, 1919-40; Joint Editor and Compiler, All the World's Aircraft, 1923-40, Editor, 1941-60; International Aviation Associates, 1939-47; Esso Export Ltd, 1947-60; Executive Editor, Esso Air World, 1939-60, Advisory Editor, 1960-66. FAI Paul Tissandier Diploma, 1956, in recognition of 35 years' work on All the World's Aircraft. *Publications:* Aircraft of the British Empire, 1935-1939; (with O. Stewart) The Clouds Remember, 1935, new edn 1972; also illustrated several air historical books. *Address:* 35 Bancroft Avenue, N2 0AR. *T:* 01-340 3962. *Club:* Naval and Military.

BRIDLE, Rear-Adm. Gordon Walter, CB 1977; MBE 1952; *b* 14 May 1923; *s* of Percy Gordon Bridle and Dorothy Agnes Bridle; *m* 1944, Phyllis Audrey Page; three *s. Educ:* King Edward's Grammar Sch., Aston, Birmingham; Northern Grammar Sch., Portsmouth; Royal Dockyard Sch., Portsmouth (Whitworth Scholar); Imperial Coll., London (ACGI). CEng, FIEE 1969. Loan Service Pakistan, 1950-52; Naval Electrical Dept, Bath; jssc; subseq. HMS Newfoundland, Min. of Aviation, HMS Devonshire; Project Man. Sea Dart, Min. of Technology; comd HMS Collingwood, 1969-71; Dir, Surface Weapons/Electronic Projects, Portsmouth, 1972-74; Asst Controller of the Navy, 1974-77, retired. Temp. Instr. Lieut 1944; Lieut 1946; Lt-Comdr 1952; Comdr 1957; Captain 1965; Rear-Adm. 1974. *Publications:* contribs. to Naval Electrical Review and O&M Bulletin. *Recreations:* sailing, walking. *Address:* 25 Heatherwood, Midhurst, Sussex GU29 9LH. *T:* Midhurst 2838. *Clubs:* Naval; Royal Naval Sailing.

BRIDLE, Ronald Jarman; Chief Highway Engineer, Department of Transport, since 1976; *b* 27 Jan. 1930; *s* of Raymond Bridle and Dorothy (*née* Jarman); *m* Beryl Eunice (*née* Doe); two *d. Educ:* West Monmouth Grammar Sch.; Bristol Univ. (BSc). FICE, FIHE. Graduate Asst, Monmouthshire CC, 1953-55; Exec. Engr, Gold Coast Govt, 1955-57; Sen. Engr, Cwmbran Develt Corp., 1957-60; Principal Designer, Cardiff City, 1960-62; Project Engr, Sheffield-Leeds Motorway, West Riding CC, 1962-65; Dep. County Surveyor II, Cheshire CC, 1965-67; Dir, Midland RCU, DoE, 1967-71; Dep. Chief Highway Engr, 1971-73, Under-Sec., Highways 1, 1973-75, Chief Highway Engr, 1975-76, DoE. FRSA. *Publications:* papers in jls of ICE, IHE and internat. confs. *Recreations:* golf, painting. *Address:* L'Escalier, 204 Thames Side, off Blacksmith Lane, Laleham, near Staines, Mddx. *T:* Staines 61017. *Club:* Royal Automobile.

BRIDPORT, 4th Viscount, *cr* 1868; **Alexander Nelson Hood;** Baron Bridport, 1794; 7th Duke of Bronte in Sicily (*cr* 1799); *b* 17 March 1948; *s* of 3rd Viscount Bridport and Sheila Jeanne Agatha, *d* of Johann van Meurs; *S* father, 1969; *m* 1972, Linda Jacqueline Paravicini, *d* of Lt-Col and Mrs V. R. Paravicini, Nutley Manor, Basingstoke, Hants; one *s. Educ:* Eton; Sorbonne. With Merchant Bank. *Heir: s* Hon. Peregrine Alexander Nelson Hood, *b* 30 Aug. 1974. *Address:* Castello di Maniace, 95030 Maniace di Bronte, Catania, Sicily. *T:* Catania 698320; *TA:* Ducea Maletto. *Club:* Brooks's.

BRIEN, Alan; Film Critic, Sunday Times, since 1976; Columnist, Punch, since 1972; *b* 12 March 1925; *s* of late Ernest Brien and Isabella (*née* Patterson); *m* 1st, 1947, Pamela Mary Jones; three *d* ; 2nd, 1961, Nancy Newbold Ryan; one *s* one *d* ; 3rd, 1973, Jill Sheila Tweedie, *qv. Educ:* Bede Grammar Sch., Sunderland; Jesus Coll., Oxford. BA (Eng Lit). Associate Editor: Mini-Cinema, 1950-52; Courier, 1952-53; Film Critic and Columnist, Truth, 1953-54; TV Critic, Observer, 1954-55; Film Critic, 1954-

56, New York Correspondent, 1956-58, Evening Standard; Drama Critic and Features Editor, Spectator, 1958-61; Columnist, Daily Mail, 1958-62; Columnist, Sunday Dispatch, 1962-63; Political Columnist, Sunday Pictorial, 1963-64; Drama Critic, Sunday Telegraph, 1961-67; Columnist, Spectator, 1963-65; Columnist, New Statesman, 1966-72; Diarist, Sunday Times, 1967-75; Contributor various American publications: Saturday Evening Post, Holiday, Vogue, Mademoiselle, Theatre Arts. Regular broadcaster on radio, 1952-, and television, 1955-. Hannen Swaffer Critic of Year, 1966, 1967. *Publications:* contrib. novel by several hands, I Knew Daisy Smuten, 1970; various collections of Spectator and Punch pieces. *Recreations:* eating, drinking, walking, talking, and sleeping in libraries. *Address:* 119 St Mary's Mansions, St Mary's Terrace, W2. *T:* 01-262 1893; Pinkie, Golden Street, Deal, Kent. *Club:* Garrick.

BRIERLEY, Captain Henry, CBE 1960 (OBE 1942); MC 1917; House Governor, The London Hospital, 1939-62, retired; *b* 10 Aug. 1897; *s* of James William and Zoe Brierley, Rochdale; *m* 1931, Bettine Ariana (*d* 1969), *d* of Sir William Curtis, 4th Baronet, Caynham, Ludlow, Salop; one *d. Educ:* Shrewsbury. Commissioned Rifle Bde, 1916; served European War, 1914-18, Iraq, 1919-20; Adjt 1st Bn, 1921-24; Adjt London Rifle Brigade, 1925-29; retired 1929. The London Hospital, 1929; Secretary, 1938. Joint Master Eridge Foxhounds, 1962-68. *Recreation:* foxhunting. *Address:* Stile House, Mark Cross, Crowborough, East Sussex. *T:* Rotherfield 2883.

BRIERLEY, John David; Under-Secretary, Department of Education and Science, since 1969; *b* 16 March 1918; *s* of late Walter George Brierley and late Doris Brierley (*née* Paterson); *m* 1956, Frances Elizabeth Davis; one (adopted) *s* one (adopted) *d. Educ:* elementary schools, London and Croydon; Whitgift Sch., Croydon; Lincoln Coll., Oxford. *Lit. Hum.,* BA Hons, 1940. Served War: Army, RASC, 1940-46. Ministry of Education: Asst Principal, 1946; Principal, 1949; Dept of Education and Science: Asst Sec., 1960; Under-Sec., 1969; Principal Finance Officer, 1969-75. *Recreations:* fell-walking, cycling, photography, music. *Address:* 98 Arundel Avenue, Sanderstead, Surrey. *T:* 01-657 7508.

BRIERS, Richard; actor since 1955; *b* 14 Jan. 1934; *s* of Joseph Briers and Morna Richardson; *m* 1957, Ann Davies; two *d. Educ:* Rokeby Prep. Sch., Wimbledon; private tuition. RADA, 1954-56 (silver medal). First appearance in London in Gilt and Gingerbread, Duke of York's, 1959. *Plays:* (major parts in): Arsenic and Old Lace, 1965; Relatively Speaking, 1966; The Real Inspector Hound, 1968; Cat Among the Pigeons, 1969; The Two of Us, 1970; Butley, 1972; Absurd Person Singular, 1973; Absent Friends, 1975. *Television series:* Brothers-in-Law; Marriage Lines; The Good Life; OneUpManShip; The Other One. *Recreations:* reading, golf. *Address:* c/o ICM Ltd, 22 Grafton Street, W1.

BRIGDEN, Wallace, MA, MD, FRCP; Physician: London Hospital, and Cardiac Department, London Hospital; National Heart Hospital; Consulting Cardiologist to the Royal Navy; *b* 8 June 1916; *s* of Wallis Brigden and Louise Brigden (*née* Clarke). *Educ:* Latymer School; University of Cambridge; King's College Hospital; Yale University. Senior Scholar, King's College, Cambridge; First Class Natural Sciences Tripos, Parts I and II, 1936, 1937; Henry Fund Fellowship, Yale University, USA, 1937-38; Burney Yeo Schol., King's College Hospital, 1938. RAMC, 1943-47, Med. Specialist and O/C Medical Division. Lecturer in Medicine, Post-Grad. Med. School of London; Physician, Hammersmith Hospital, 1948-49; Asst Physician, London Hospital and Asst Physician, Cardiac Dept, 1949; Asst Physician, National Heart Hospital, 1949; Cons. Cardiologist, Special Unit for Juvenile Rheumatism, Taplow, 1955-59; Director Inst. of Cardiology, 1962-66. St Cyres Lectr, 1956; R. T. Hall Lectr, Australia and New Zealand, 1961; Hugh Morgan Vis. Prof., Vanderbilt Univ., 1963. Late Assistant Editor, British Heart Journal. Mem. British Cardiac Society and Assoc. of Physicians. *Publications:* Section on Cardio-vascular disease in Price's Textbook of Medicine; Myocardial Disease, Cecil-Loeb Textbook of Medicine; contributor to the Lancet, British Heart Jl, British Medical Jl. *Recreation:* painting. *Address:* 45 Wimpole Street, W1. *T:* 01-935 1201; Willow House, Totteridge Common, N20 8NE. *T:* 01-959 6616.

BRIGGS, family name of **Baron Briggs.**

BRIGGS, Baron *cr* 1976 (Life Peer), of Lewes, E Sussex; **Asa Briggs,** MA, BSc (Econ); Provost, Worcester College, Oxford, since 1976; *b* 7 May 1921; *o s* of William Walker Briggs and Jane Briggs, Keighley, Yorks; *m* 1955, Susan Anne Banwell, *o d* of Donald I. Banwell, Keevil, Wiltshire; two *s* two *d. Educ:* Keighley Grammar School; Sidney Sussex College, Cambridge

(1st cl. History Tripos, Pts I and II, 1940, 1941; 1st cl. BSc (Econ.), Lond., 1941). Gerstenberg studentship in Economics, London, 1941. Served in Intelligence Corps, 1942-45. Fellow of Worcester College, Oxford, 1945-55; Reader in Recent Social and Economic History, Oxford, 1950-55; Member, Institute for Advanced Study, Princeton, USA, 1953-54; Faculty Fellow of Nuffield College, Oxford, 1953-55; Professor of Modern History, Leeds Univ., 1955-61; University of Sussex: Professor of History, 1961-76; Dean, School of Social Studies, 1961-65; Pro Vice-Chancellor, 1961-67; Vice-Chancellor, 1967-76. Visiting Professor: ANU, 1960; Chicago Univ., 1966, 1972. Dep. Pres., WEA, 1954-58, Pres., 1958-67. Mem., UGC, 1959-67; Chm., Cttee on Nursing, 1970-72 (Cmnd 5115, 1972). Trustee: Glyndebourne Arts Trust, 1966-; Internat. Broadcasting Inst., 1968-; Heritage Educn Gp, 1976-; Chairman: Standing Conf. for Study of Local History, 1969-76; Council, European Inst. of Education, 1975-; Vice-chm. of Council, UN Univ., 1974-; Governor, British Film Institute, 1970-77; Pres., Social History Soc., 1976-. Mem., Ct of Governors, Administrative Staff Coll., 1971-. Mem., Amer. Acad. of Arts and Sciences, 1970. Hon. Fellow: Sidney Sussex Coll., Cambridge, 1968; Worcester Coll., Oxford, 1969. Hon. DLitt: East Anglia, 1966; Strathclyde, 1973; Leeds, 1974; Cincinnati, 1977; Liverpool, 1977; Hon. DSc Florida Presbyterian, 1966; Hon. LLD: York, Canada, 1968; New England, 1972; Sussex, 1976. Marconi Medal for Communications History, 1975. *Publications:* Patterns of Peace-making (with D. Thomson and E. Meyer), 1945; History of Birmingham (1865-1938), 1952; Victorian People, 1954; Friends of the People, 1956; The Age of Improvement, 1959; (ed) Chartist Studies, 1959; (ed with John Saville) Essays in Labour History, Vol. I, 1960, Vol. II, 1971, Vol. III, 1977; (ed) They Saw it Happen, 1897-1940, 1961; A Study of the Work of Seebohm Rowntree, 1871-1954, 1961; History of Broadcasting in the United Kingdom: vol. I. The Birth of Broadcasting, 1961; vol. II, The Golden Age of Wireless, 1965; vol. III, The War of Words, 1970; Vol. IV, Sound and Vision, 1977; Victorian Cities, 1963; William Cobbett, 1967; How They Lived, 1700-1815, 1969; (ed) The Nineteenth Century, 1970; (ed with Susan Briggs) Cap and Bell: Punch's Chronicle of English History in the Making 1841-1861, 1973; (ed) Essays in the History of Publishing, 1974. *Recreation:* travelling. *Address:* The Provost's Lodgings, Worcester College, Oxford; (private) The Caprons, Keere Street, Lewes, Sussex. *Clubs:* Savile, Garrick.

BRIGGS, Hon. Sir Francis Arthur, Kt 1961; a Federal Justice of Supreme Court, Federation of Rhodesia and Nyasaland, 1958-63, retired; *b* 9 July 1902; *yr s* of late William Francis Briggs, Preston, Lancs, and late Jane Greig, *yr d* of late Thomas Macmillan, Glasgow; *m* 1953, Edna Dorothy, *d* of late William Thomas Keylock; no *c. Educ:* Charterhouse (Schol.); Trinity College, Oxford (Open Classical Schol.). Called to Bar, Inner Temple (Cert. of Honour and Jardine Studentship), 1927. Advocate and Solicitor, FMS, SS and Johore, 1928-40. Served in RAFVR, 1940-46 (despatches), Wing Commander. Colonial Legal Service, 1947; Registrar, Supreme Court, Federation of Malaya, 1948; Puisne Judge, Malaya, 1949; Justice of Appeal, E African Court of Appeal, 1953, Vice-President, 1957. *Address:* Shillingford, La Brecque, Alderney, Channel Islands. *T:* 2019.

BRIGGS, Hon. Sir Geoffrey (Gould), Kt 1974; **Hon. Mr Justice Briggs;** Chief Justice: Hong Kong, since 1973; Brunei, since 1973; *b* 6 May 1914; 2nd *s* of late Reverend C. E. and Mrs Briggs, Amersham, Buckinghamshire; unmarried. *Educ:* Sherborne; Christ Church, Oxford (BA, BCL). Called to Bar (Gray's Inn), 1938; served War of 1939-45, County of London Yeomanry (Major). Attorney-General, E Region, Nigeria, 1954-58; QC (Nigeria), 1955; Puisne Judge, Sarawak, N Borneo and Brunei, 1958-62; Chief Justice of the Western Pacific, 1962-65; a Puisne Judge, Hong Kong, 1965-73. DSNB 1974. *Address:* The Courts of Justice, Hong Kong.

BRIGGS, Rt. Rev. George Cardell; *see* Seychelles, Bishop of.

BRIGGS, Prof. George Edward, MA; FRS 1935; Fellow of St John's College, Cambridge (President, 1952-63); Professor Emeritus of Botany, Cambridge University; Professor of Botany, 1948-60; Professor of Plant Physiology, 1946-48, Cambridge University; *b* 25 June 1893; *m* 1920, Nora Burman; one *s* one *d. Educ:* Wintringham Grammar School; St John's College, Cambridge. *Publications:* Electrolytes and Plant Cells (with A. B. Hope and R. N. Robertson), 1961; Movement of Water in Plants, 1967. *Address:* 10 Luard Road, Cambridge CB2 2PJ. *T:* Cambridge 47181.

BRIGGS, George Henry, DSc Sydney; PhD Cantab; FInstP; retired, 1958, as Chief CSIRO Division of Physics, then Hon. Research Fellow, Australian National Standards Laboratory; *b* Sydney, 1893; *o s* of William and Hannah Briggs; *m* 1923, Edna

Dorothy Sayce; two d. *Educ:* Fort Street High School, Sydney; Sydney University. Lecturer in Physics, Sydney University 1916, research at Cavendish Laboratory, Cambridge (Emmanuel College), 1925-26 and 1936. Asst Professor of Physics, University of Sydney, 1928-39. Lyle medal of Australian National Research Council, 1941. Scientific adviser to Australian delegate, Atomic Energy Commission of United Nations, 1946-47. President, Australian Branch, Institute of Physics, 1950-51; Chairman Australian Unesco Committee for Natural Sciences, 1953-55; Member Australian National Advisory Committee for Unesco, 1953-61. Hon. Fellow Australian Institute of Physics, 1964. *Publications:* papers on radioactivity, units of measurement of electrical quantities, properties of high-load resistance standards. *Recreation:* flyfishing. *Address:* Unit 64, St Davids Village, Cook Street, Forestville, NSW, Australia.

BRIGGS, Percy, CBE 1966; Member, Electricity Council, 1962-66; *b* 4 Sept. 1903; *s* of late Alfred and late Caroline Briggs; *m* 1927, Annie M. Folker; one *s*. *Educ:* Deacon's School, Peterborough; Northampton Polytechnic. Supt, Fulham Power Station, 1945; Chief Generation Engr, SE Div., British Elect. Authy, 1948-53; Controller, Merseyside and N Wales Div., 1954-56, Yorks Div., 1957; Regional Dir, NE Region, CEGB, 1958-61. CEng, FIMechE; MInstF. *Recreations:* gardening, fishing. *Address:* 7 Thackers Close, Wansford, Peterborough PE8 6LD. *T:* Stamford 782248.

BRIGGS, Maj.-Gen. Raymond, CB 1943; DSO 1942; psc†; President, Metropolitan Area, Royal British Legion; *b* 19 Jan. 1895; *yr s* of late James Burnett Briggs, Claughton, Cheshire; *m* 1927, Helen Wainwright, *d* of Charles Edward Kenworthy, Liverpool and New Orleans; one *d*. Served European War, 1914-18, France, Belgium, and Mesopotamia, Liverpool Scottish, King's Own Regt, and MGC, 2nd Lieut, 1915 (wounded twice); Royal Tank Corps, 1920; Bt Major, 1933; Bt Lt-Col, 1938; Colonel, 1941; Acting Brig., 1940; Major-General, 1944. Served War of 1939-45, France and Belgium, 1940 (GSO 1), Middle East and North Africa, 1941-43 (Comd 2 Armd Bde, GOC 1 Armd Division); Director, Royal Armoured Corps, War Office, 1943-47. Member Tank Board, 1943-46 (wounded, despatches twice, DSO, CB, Commander Legion of Merit, USA); retired, 1947. *Address:* 1 Linden Gardens, W2 4HA. *T:* 01-229 3711. *Clubs:* Army and Navy, Royal Automobile.

BRIGGS, Rear-Admiral Thomas Vallack, CB 1958; OBE (mil.) 1945; Representative Deputy Lieutenant (Greater London) for Royal Borough of Kingston upon Thames, since 1970; a Vice-Patron, Royal Naval Association; *b* 6 April 1906; *s* of late Admiral Sir Charles John Briggs, and Lady Briggs (*née* Wilson); *m* 1947, Estelle Burland Willing, Boston, USA; one *step s*. *Educ:* The Grange, Stevenage, Herts; Imperial Service College, Windsor. Joined Royal Navy 1924; Rear-Admiral 1956. Advanced Gunnery Specialist. Served War of 1939-45: HMS Ark Royal, 1939-40; HMS Newcastle, 1943-44; staff of Flag Officer 2nd in Command, Eastern Fleet, 1944-45 (despatches twice). US Naval War Coll., Newport, RI, 1947-48; commanded 5th Destroyer Flotilla, HMS Solebay, 1949-50, and HMS Cumberland, 1954-55; IDC, 1951; Chief of Staff: Plymouth, 1952-53, Home Fleet and Eastern Atlantic, 1956-57; Asst Controller of the Navy, 1958, retired. Director: Hugh Stevenson & Sons Ltd, 1958-69; Hugh Stevenson & Sons (North East) Ltd, 1964; Bowater-Stevenson Containers Ltd, 1969-71; Free-Stay Holidays Ltd, 1971; Internat. Consumer Incentives Ltd. Vice-Chm., City of Westminster Soc. for Mentally Handicapped Children, 1969; Member: European Atlantic Group, 1964; Management Cttee, Haileybury and ISC Junior Sch., Windsor; Life Governor and Mem. Council, Haileybury and Imperial Service College, 1959; Pres., Haileybury Soc., 1973-74. Fellow, Inst. of Marketing, 1970. *Address:* King's Legend, Aldeburgh, Suffolk IP15 5QB. *Clubs:* White's; RN Golfing Society, Aldeburgh Yacht and Golf; RN Sailing Association (Pres., 1971-76); RN Ski.

BRIGHTLING, Peter Henry Miller; Assistant Under Secretary of State, Ministry of Defence, since 1973; *b* 12 Sept. 1921; *o s* of late Henry Miller Brightling and Eva Emily Brightling (*née* Fry); *m* 1951, Pamela Cheeseright; two *s* two *d*. *Educ:* City of London Sch.; BSc(Econ), London. War of 1939-45: Air Ministry, 1939-40; MAP, 1940-41; served in RAF, 1941-46. Ministry of: Supply, 1946-59; Aviation, 1959-67; Technology, 1967-70; Aviation Supply, 1970-71; MoD (Procurement Executive), 1971. *Address:* 5 Selwyn Road, New Malden, Surrey KT3 5AU. *T:* 01-942 8014.

BRIGHTMAN, Hon. Sir John (Anson), Kt 1970; **Hon. Mr Justice Brightman;** Judge of the High Court of Justice, Chancery Division, since 1970; *b* 20 June 1911; 2nd *s* of William Henry Brightman, St Albans, Herts; *m* 1945, Roxane Ambatielo; one *s*. *Educ:* Marlborough College; St John's College, Cambridge. Called to the Bar, Lincoln's Inn, 1932; Bencher 1966. QC 1961. RNVR (Lieut-Commander), 1940-46; Assistant Naval Attaché, Ankara, 1944. Attorney-General of the Duchy of Lancaster, and Attorney and Serjeant within the County Palatine of Lancaster, 1969-70; Judge, Nat. Industrial Relns Court, 1971-74. Member, General Council of the Bar, 1956-60, 1966-70. *Recreations:* sailing, ski-ing, topiary. *Address:* Royal Courts of Justice, Strand, WC2.

BRIGINSHAW, family name of **Baron Briginshaw.**

BRIGINSHAW, Baron *cr* 1974 (Life Peer), of Southwark; **Richard William Briginshaw;** General Secretary, National Society of Operative Printers, Graphical and Media Personnel, 1951-75; Member, Council, Advisory, Conciliation and Arbitration Service, since 1974; *b* Lambeth; married. *Educ:* Stuart School, London. Later studied economics, trade union and industrial law. Elected Asst Secretary, London Machine Branch of Union, 1938. Joined Services, 1940; subseq. in Army, saw service overseas in India, Iraq, Persia, Palestine, Egypt, France, etc; left Army, 1946. Returned to printing trade; re-elected to full-time trade union position, 1949. Vice-Pres. 1961-72, Mem. Exec. Council 1951-72, Printing and Kindred Trades Fedn; TUC: Mem. Gen. Council, 1965-75; Member of Finance and General Purposes, Economic, Organisation, and International Cttees; Member: BOTB, 1975-; British Nat. Oil Corp., 1976-. Pres. of two London Confs on World Trade Development, 1963. Member: Joint Committee on Manpower, 1965-70; Bd of Govs, Dulwich Coll., 1967-72; Court, Cranfield Inst. of Technology. Hon. LLD New Brunswick, 1968. *Publications:* (two booklets): Britain's World Rating; Britain and the World Trade Conference. *Recreations:* swimming, painting, music. *Address:* House of Lords, SW1.

BRIGSTOCKE, Mrs Heather Renwick; High Mistress of St Paul's Girls' School since 1974; *b* 2 Sept. 1929; *d* of late Sqdn-Ldr J. R. Brown, DFC and of Mrs M. J. C. Brown, MA; *m* 1952, Geoffrey Brigstocke (*d* 1974); three *s* one *d*. *Educ:* Abbey Sch., Reading; Girton Coll., Cambridge (MA). Univ. Winchester Reading Prize, 1950. Classics Mistress, Francis Holland Sch., London, SW1, 1951-53; part-time Classics Mistress, Godolphin and Latymer Sch., 1954-60; part-time Latin Teacher, National Cathedral Sch., Washington, DC, 1962-64; Headmistress, Francis Holland Sch., London, NW1, 1965-74. A Trustee, Nat. Gall., 1975-; Member: London House for Overseas Graduates, 1965- (Vice-Chm., 1975-); Council, Middlesex Hosp. Med. Sch., 1971-; A. A. Cttee, 1975-; Royal Holloway Coll., 1977-; Governor: Wellington Coll., 1975-; The Royal Ballet Sch., 1977-. *Address:* 48 Rowan Road, W6 7DU.

BRIMACOMBE, Prof. John Stuart, FRSE, FRIC; Roscoe Professor of Chemistry, University of Dundee, since 1969; *b* Falmouth, Cornwall, 18 Aug. 1935; *s* of Stanley Poole Brimacombe and Lillian May Kathleen Brimacombe (*née* Candy); *m* 1959, Eileen (*née* Gibson); four *d*. *Educ:* Falmouth Grammar Sch.; Birmingham Univ. ((DSc). DSc Dundee Univ. Meldola Medallist, 1964. *Publications:* (co-author) Mucopolysaccharides, 1964; numerous papers, reviews, etc, in: Jl Chem. Soc., Carbohydrate Research, etc. *Recreations:* sport, swimming. *Address:* 29 Dalhousie Road, Barnhill, Dundee. *T:* Dundee 79214.

BRIMELOW, family name of **Baron Brimelow.**

BRIMELOW, Baron *cr* 1976 (Life Peer), of Tyldesley, Lancs; **Thomas Brimelow,** GCMG 1975 (KCMG 1968; CMG 1959); OBE 1954; *b* 25 Oct. 1915; *s* of late William Brimelow and Hannah Smith; *m* 1945, Jean E. Cull; two *d*. *Educ:* New Mills Grammar School; Oriel College, Oxford; Hon. Fellow, 1973. Laming Travelling Fellow of the Queen's College, Oxford, 1937, Hon. Fellow, 1974. Probationer Vice-Consul, Danzig, 1938; served in Consulate, Riga, 1939 and Consulate-Gen., New York, 1940; in charge of Consular Section of Embassy, Moscow, 1942-45; Foreign Office, 1945; Foreign Service Officer, Grade 7, 1946; First Sec. (Commercial), and Consul, Havana, 1948; trans. to Moscow, 1951; Counsellor (Commercial), Ankara, 1954; Head of Northern Department of the Foreign Office, 1956; Counsellor, Washington, 1960-63; Minister, British Embassy, Moscow, 1963-66; Ambassador to Poland, 1966-69; Dep. Under-Sec. of State, FCO, 1969-73; Permanent Under-Sec. of State, FCO, and Head of the Diplomatic Service, 1973-75. Mem., European Parlt, 1977-. *Address:* 12 West Hill Court, Millfield Lane, N6 6JJ. *Club:* Athenæum.

BRINCKMAN, Colonel Sir Roderick (Napoleon); 5th Bt, *cr* 1831; DSO 1940; MC 1941; *b* 27 Dec. 1902; 2nd *s* of Colonel Sir

Theodore Brinckman, 3rd Bt, CB; *S* brother 1954; *m* 1st, 1931, Margaret Southam, Ottawa, Canada; two *s*; 2nd, 1942, Rosemary Marguerite Gilbey, *yr d* of late Lt-Col J. C. Hope Vere, Blackwood, Lanarkshire; one *d. Educ:* Osborne; Dartmouth. Served in Royal Navy two years (HMS Temeraire, Barham); joined Grenadier Guards in 1922; ADC to Lord Somers (Governor of Victoria), 1926-27; ADC to Lord Willingdon (Governor-General of Canada), 1930-31; served in Egypt, 1931-32, and France, 1940 (DSO, MC, despatches); commanded 2nd (Armoured) Bn Grenadier Guards, 1943; Chief of Staff Military Mission in Moscow, 1944-45; head of British Military Mission to the Netherlands Government in London, 1945-46. *Heir: s* Theodore George Roderick Brinckman [*b* 20 March 1932; *m* 1958, Helen Mary Anne, *d* of A. E. Cook, Toronto; two *s* one *d*]. *Address:* Mornington House, Parkside, Wimbledon Common, SW19. *T:* 01-946 2124; Crosskeys, Sandwich, Kent; St Helena, Barbados, BWI. *Clubs:* White's, Turf.

BRIND, (Arthur) Henry, CMG 1973; HM Diplomatic Service; Ambassador to Somali Democratic Republic, since 1977; *b* 4 July 1927; *o s* of late T. H. Brind and late N. W. B. Brind; *m* 1954, Barbara Harrison; one *s* one *d. Educ:* St John's Coll., Cambridge. HM Forces, 1947-49. Colonial Administrative Service: Gold Coast/Ghana, 1950-60; Regional Sec., Trans-Volta Togoland, 1959. HM Diplomatic Service, 1960-: Acting High Comr, Uganda, 1972-73, High Comr, Mauritius, 1974-77. *Recreations:* walking, swimming, books. *Address:* c/o Foreign and Commonwealth Office, SW1; 20 Grove Terrace, NW5. *Clubs:* Reform, Royal Commonwealth Society.

BRIND, George Walter Richard; Secretary-General, The Stock Exchange, 1971-75; *b* 13 Oct. 1911; *er s* of late Walter Charles and late Mary Josephine Brind; *m* 1942, Joyce, *er d* of late Matthew and Mary Graham; two *d. Educ:* Chiswick. Joined staff of Council of Stock Exchange, London, 1928, and has had no other employment than that with the Exchange. *Recreation:* bowls. *Address:* 7 Amberley Close, Send, Woking, Surrey. *T:* Guildford 223762.

BRIND, Henry; see Brind, A. H.

BRIND, Maj.-Gen. Peter Holmes Walter; CBE 1962 (OBE 1948); DSO 1945; DL; Director, Surrey Branch, British Red Cross Society, since 1968; *b* 16 Feb. 1912; *yr s* of late General Sir John Brind, KCB, KBE, CMG, DSO; *m* 1942, Patricia Stewart Walker, *er d* of late Comdr S. M. Walker, DSC, RN, Horsalls, Harrietsham, Kent; three *s. Educ:* Wellington College; RMC, Sandhurst. Commissioned Dorset Regt, 1932. ADC to Governor of Bengal, 1936-39; Adjt, NW Europe, 1940; GSO 3 War Office, 1940-41; DAAG, HQ 12 Corps and Canadian Corps, 1941-42; Bde Major 1942; GSO 2 (MO) War Office, 1942; Comdt, Battle School, 1944, Comdg 2 Devons, NW Europe, 1944-45; GSO 1 (MT) War Office, 1946; GSO 1 (Ops), Palestine, 1948; GSO 1 (Plans), Egypt, 1949; GSO 1 (SD), War Office, 1950-54; Bt Lt-Col, 1952; Comdg 5th KAR (Kenya), 1954; Lt-Col, 1954; Col, 1955; Comdg 5 Inf. Bde Gp (BAOR), 1956; IDC 1959; Brig., 1960; Brig., AQ Middle East, 1960; BGS Eastern Comd, 1962; ADC to the Queen, 1964; Maj.-Gen., 1965; COS, Northern Comd, 1965-67. Governor, St Catherine's School, 1968. DL Surrey, 1970. *Recreations:* gardening, music. *Address:* Pine Ridge, Hill Road, Haslemere, Surrey.

BRINDLEY, Prof. Giles Skey, MA, MD; FRS 1965; FRCP; Professor of Physiology in the University of London at the Institute of Psychiatry, since 1968; Hon. Director, Medical Research Council Neurological Prostheses Unit, since 1968; *b* 30 April 1926; *s* of Arthur James Benet Skey and Dr Margaret Beatrice Marion Skey (*née* Dewhurst), later Brindley; *m* 1st, 1959, Lucy Dunk Bennell (marr. diss.); 2nd, 1964, Dr Hilary Richards; one *s* one *d. Educ:* Leyton County High School; Downing College, Cambridge (Hon. Fellow, 1969); London Hospital Medical College. Various jun. clin. and res. posts, 1950-54; Russian lang. abstractor, British Abstracts of Medical Sciences, 1953-56; successively Demonstrator, Lectr and Reader in physiology, Univ. of Cambridge, 1954-68; Fellow: King's Coll., Cambridge, 1959-62; Trinity Coll., Cambridge, 1963-68. Chm. of Editorial Board, Journal of Physiology, 1964-66 (Member 1959-64). Visiting Prof., Univ. of California, Berkeley, 1968. Liebrecht-Franceschetti Prize, German Ophthalmological Soc., 1971; Feldberg Prize, Feldberg Foundn, 1974. *Publications:* Physiology of the Retina and Visual Pathway, 1960, 2nd edn 1970; papers in scientific, musicological and medical journals. *Recreations:* ski-ing, orienteering, designing, making and playing various musical instruments (inventor of the logical bassoon). *Address:* 102 Ferndene Road, SE24. *T:* 01-274 2598.

BRINK, Prof. Charles Oscar, LittD Cambridge; PhD Berlin; FBA; Kennedy Professor of Latin in the University of Cambridge, 1954-74, and Fellow of Gonville and Caius College, since 1955; *b* 13 March 1907; *m* 1942, Daphne Hope Harvey; three *s. Educ:* School and University, Berlin; Travelling Scholarship, Oxford. Member of editorial staff, Thesaurus linguæ Latinæ, 1933-38; Member of editorial staff, Oxford Latin Dictionary, 1938-41; Acting Classical Tutor, Magdalen College, Oxford, 1941-45; Member of Faculty of Literæ Humaniores, Oxford, 1941-48; MA Oxford (decree, 1944); Senior Classics Master, Magdalen College School, Oxford, 1943-48; Senior Lecturer in Humanity, University of St Andrews, 1948-51; Professor of Latin, University of Liverpool, 1951-54; MA Cambridge (BIII 6), 1954. Member Inst. for Advanced Study, Princeton, US, 1960-61, 1966. De Carle Lecturer, University of Otago, NZ, 1965; Vis. Prof., Univ. of Bonn, 1970; Professore Ospite Linceo, Scuola Normale Superiore, Pisa, 1977. Hon. Member, Jt Assoc. of Classical Teachers (Pres. 1969-71). Chm., Classics Committee, Schools Council, 1965-69; Trustee, Robinson Coll., Cambridge, 1973- (Chm., 1975-). Corresp. Mem., Bayerische Akad. der Wissenschaften, Munich. Founding Jt Editor, Cambridge Classical Texts and Commentaries, 1963-. *Publications:* Imagination and Imitation (Inaug. Lect., Liverpool, 1952), 1953; Latin Studies and the Humanities (Inaug. Lect., Cambridge, 1956), 1957; On reading a Horatian Satire, 1965; Horace on Poetry: vol. I, Prolegomena, 1963; vol. II, The Ars Poetica, 1971; papers on Latin and Greek subjects. *Address:* Gonville and Caius College, Cambridge.

BRINKWORTH, George Harold, CBE 1960; Legal Adviser and Solicitor to Pay Board, 1973-74; *b* 16 Nov. 1906; *yr s* of George Alban Brinkworth and Hana Mary Brinkworth; *m* 1935, Dorothy Betty Suffield; one *s* one *d. Educ:* Wimbledon College; University College, London. LLB (Lond.) 1927. Admitted Solicitor, 1931. Entered Solicitor's Dept, Ministry of Labour, 1935; transf. to Ministry of Nat. Insce, 1945; Asst Solicitor, Min. of Pensions and Nat. Insce, 1948; Principal Asst Sol., DHSS (formerly Min. of Social Security), 1965-71. *Address:* Valency Cottage, Forrabury, Boscastle, Cornwall. *T:* Boscastle 385.

BRINTON, Denis Hubert, DM Oxon; FRCP; retired; *b* 9 Dec. 1902; *er s* of Hubert Brinton, Eton College; *m* 1st, 1928, Joan Violet (*d* 1971), *d* of James A. Hood; one *s* (and one *s* decd); 2nd, 1972, Rosemary Cockerill. *Educ:* Eton; New College, Oxford University; St Mary's Hospital, London University. MRCS, LRCP 1927; BM, BCh, 1928; MRCP 1929; DM Oxon 1937; FRCP 1938. Served War of 1939-45 (despatches), Air Commodore, RAF, Consultant in Neuropsychiatry. Member Internat. Neurological Congress, London, 1935; Physician-in-charge, Department of Nervous Diseases, St Mary's Hospital, 1935-63; Dean, St Mary's Hospital Medical School, 1946-51; Physician, National Hospital for Nervous Diseases, 1935-65; Council RCP, 1956-59. Member Assoc. British Neurologists; Member Assoc. Physicians Great Britain; Ed. Quart. Jl Med., 1954-68. *Publications:* Cerebrospinal Fever, 1941; articles in medical jls. *Address:* Bromfields, Vereley Lane, Burley, Hants. *T:* Burley 2319. *Club:* Garrick.

BRINTON, Major Sir (Esme) Tatton (Cecil), Kt 1964; DL; Chairman, Brintons Ltd, Kidderminster, since 1968 (Joint Managing Director, since 1952); *b* 4 Jan. 1916; *o s* of Colonel Cecil Charles Brinton, JP, and Cathleen Cecil Brinton (*née* Maude); *m* 1st, 1938, Mary Elizabeth Fahnestock (*d* 1960); four *s* one *d*; 2nd, 1961, Mrs Irene Sophie Borthwick. *Educ:* Eton; Caius College, Cambridge; and in Vienna and Paris. Served with XIIth R. Lancers, France, Desert, Italy, 1939-45. Technical Intelligence, Germany, 1945-46. Contested (C) Dudley, 1945; MP (C) Kidderminster, 1964-Feb. 74; Mayor of Kidderminster, 1953-54; High Sheriff of Worcestershire, 1961-62; Chm., Kidderminster Conservative Assoc., 1955-56 and 1958-61; Pres., W Midlands Cons. Union, 1972-75 (Treasurer, 1958-61; Chm., 1962-64); Jt Treasurer of Conservative Party, 1966-74. Pres., Fedn of British Carpet Manufrs, 1974-76 (Chm., Home Exec. Cttee, 1960-64); Pres., British Carpet Manufrs Assoc., 1976-; Chm. British Carpets Promotion Council, 1960-66. DL Worcs, 1968. OStJ 1962. *Address:* Kyrewood House, Tenbury Wells, Worcs. *T:* Tenbury Wells 810736; 34 de Vere Gardens, W8. *T:* 01-937 5727. *Clubs:* Carlton, Bath.

BRISBANE, Archbishop of, since 1970 (Metropolitan of Queensland); **Most Rev. Felix Raymond Arnott,** MA (Oxon); ThD; MACE; *b* Ipswich, Suffolk, 8 March 1911; *s* of late Richard Girling Arnott, Ipswich; *m* 1938, Anne Caroline, *d* of W. A. P. Lane, Kingston Gorse, Sussex; two *s* two *d. Educ:* Ipswich Sch.; Keble Coll., Oxford; Cuddesdon Theol Coll. Curate, Elland, Yorks, 1934-38; Exam. Chaplain, Bp of Wakefield, 1936-39; Vice-Prin., Cheshunt, 1938; Warden, St John's Coll., Brisbane, 1939-46; Warden, St Paul's Coll., Univ.

of Sydney, 1946-63; Lectr i/c of Ecclesiastical History, Univ. of Sydney, 1951-63; a Co-Adjutor Bishop of Melbourne, 1963-70. Member: Monash Univ. Council, 1964-70; Anglican-Roman Catholic Internat. Cttee, 1969-; Queensland Univ. Senate, 1971-. Comr, Royal Commn on Human Relations, Australia, 1974-. A Founder of Blake Prize for Religious Art, 1951. *Publications:* The Anglican Via Media in the Seventeenth Century, 1948; contribs to learned jls. *Recreations:* walking, music, golf. *Address:* Bishopsbourne, Hamilton, Qld 4007, Australia. *Clubs:* Melbourne, Royal Automobile (Victoria); Australian (Sydney); Queensland; Royal Sydney Golf.

BRISBANE, Archbishop of, (RC), since 1973; **Most Rev. Francis Roberts Rush,** DD; *b* 11 Sept. 1916; *s* of T. J. Rush. *Educ:* Christian Brothers' Coll., Townsville; Mt Carmel, Charters Towers; St Columba's Coll., Springwood; Coll. de Propaganda Fide, Rome. Assistant Priest, Townsville, Mundingburra and Ingham; Parish Priest, Abergowrie and Ingham; Bishop of Rockhampton, 1960-73. *Address:* Wynberg, 790 Brunswick Street, New Farm, Queensland 4005, Australia.

BRISBANE, Assistant Bishop of; *see* Wicks, Rt Rev. R. E.

BRISCO, Sir Donald Gilfrid, 8th Bt *cr* 1782; JP; *b* 15 Sept. 1920; *s* of Sir Hylton (Musgrave Campbell) Brisco, 7th Bt and Kathleen, *d* of W. Fenwick McAllum, New Zealand; *S* father, 1968; *m* 1945, Irene, *o d* of Henry John Gage, Ermine Park, Brockworth, Gloucestershire; three *d.* Served War of 1939-45 with Royal New Zealand Air Force and Royal Air Force (prisoner of war in Germany and Italy). Retired Farmer. JP Hawke's Bay, 1967. *Heir:* uncle Oriel Arthur Brisco [*b* 6 June 1892; *m* 1921, Lilian Frederica, *d* of E. E. D. Saunderson, Christchurch, NZ; *m* 1960, Sarah Louise, RRC (*d* 1971), *d* of R. O. Clark, Auckland, NZ]. *Address:* Longworth, PO Box 165, Havelock North, Hawke's Bay, New Zealand.

BRISCOE, Capt. Henry Villiers, CIE 1945; OBE 1943; RN (retd); *b* 9 Nov. 1896; *s* of late Maj. A. V. Briscoe, late RA, and G. M. Briscoe; *m* 1925, Lily Miller, *widow* (*decd*); one *s*; *m* 1948, Adaline Mary, *d* of Adam McIntosh, South Bantaskine, Falkirk, Stirling. *Educ:* Yarlet Hall, Staffs; RN Colleges, Osborne and Dartmouth. Royal Navy, 1909-22: Commercial Employment, 1922-31. Colonial Civil Servant, 1931-51; recalled to RN 1941-45; retd from Colonial Service, 1951. *Address:* Flat 3, Balmoral House, Bugibba, St Paul's Bay, Malta, GC.

BRISCOE, Sir John (Leigh Charlton), 4th Bt *cr* 1910; DFC 1945; *b* 3 Dec. 1911; *er s* of Sir Charlton Briscoe, 3rd Bt, MD, FRCP, and Grace Maud (*d* 1973) *d* of late Rev. W. S. Stagg; *S* father 1960; *m* 1948, Teresa Mary Violet, OBE 1972, *d* of late Brig.-Gen. Sir Archibald Home, KCVO, CB, CMG, DSO; two *s* one *d.* *Educ:* Harrow; Magdalen College, Oxford, BA 1933; ACA 1937; MA 1949. Served War of 1939-45 (DFC); RAFVR, 1942-46; Director of Aerodromes, Ministry of Aviation, 1961-66; Dir of Operations, British Airports Authy, 1966-72. *Recreations:* old cars, castles, and carpets. *Heir:* *s* John James Briscoe, *b* 15 July 1951. *Address:* Little Acres, Grays Park Road, Stoke Poges, Bucks. *T:* Farnham Common 2394. *Club:* Royal Air Force.

BRISE; *see* Ruggles-Brise.

BRISTOL, 6th Marquess of, *cr* 1826; **Victor Frederick Cochrane Hervey;** Baron Hervey, 1703; Earl of Bristol, 1714; Earl Jermyn, 1826; *b* 6 Oct. 1915; *s* of 5th Marquess of Bristol; *S* father 1960; *m* 1st, 1949, Pauline Mary (marr. diss., 1959), *d* of late Herbert Coxon Bolton; one *s*; 2nd, 1960, Lady Anne Juliet Wentworth Fitzwilliam (marr. diss. 1972), *o c* of 8th Earl Fitzwilliam, DSC, and of Olive Countess Fitzwilliam, Co. Wicklow; one *s*; 3rd, 1974, Yvonne Marie, *d* of Anthony Sutton; one *d.* *Educ:* Eton; Royal Military College. The Hereditary High Steward of the Liberty of St Edmund; Grand Master, High Stewards' Assoc.; Patron of 30 Livings; has estates in W, N and E Suffolk, Lincs, Essex, Dominica. Owner of Ickworth Stud. Vice Pres., Income Tax Payers' Union; Member: West India Cttee; Monday Club; Nat. Yacht Harbour Assoc.; Council, Bristol Soc. (Pres.); European Atlantic Group; Chancellor and Mem. Grand Council, Monarchist League. Chairman: Ickworth Forestry Contractors Ltd; Estate Associates Ltd; Sleaford Investments Ltd; Eastern Caravan Parks Ltd; The Bristol Publishing Company; Ickworth Automatic Sales Ltd; Radio Marina; British International Airways Ltd; Bristol Powersport Co.; Dominica Paradise Ltd; Marquis of Bristol & Co.; VLC Associated Ltd; Ickworth Bahamas (Australia), Ltd; Atlantis Project, Cyprus; Governing Dir, Cyprus Enterprises Co.; Director of 30 other companies. Formerly: an expert on Central American Affairs and adviser to Govts; Chm. Jersey & Co. (Finland) Ltd; Mil. Advr to Finnish Govt (1960). KLJ. Grand Officer, Royal Bulgarian House Order of St Alexander (1292

AD) with Cordon; Grand Officer, Crown of Afghanistan. *Recreations:* yachting, shooting, antiques. *Heir:* *s* Earl Jermyn, *qv. Address:* 3 Belgrave Place, SW1X 8BU; (seat) Ickworth, Bury St Edmunds, Suffolk. *Clubs:* Hurlingham, Clermont, Eccentric, Marks, House of Lords Motoring; Royal Worlington Golf, House of Lords Yacht; East Hill (Nassau).

BRISTOL, Bishop of, since 1976; **Rt. Rev. Ernest John Tinsley;** Special Lecturer in Theology, University of Bristol, since 1976; *b* 22 March 1919; *s* of Ernest William and Esther Tinsley; *m* 1947, Marjorie Dixon (*d* 1977); two *d.* *Educ:* St John's Coll., Univ. of Durham (BA, MA, BD); Westcott House, Cambridge. Priest, 1942; Curate: S Mary-le-Bow, Durham, 1942-44; South Westoe, 1944-46. Lectr in Theology, University Coll. of Hull, 1946-61; Sen. Lectr and Head of Dept of Theology, Univ. of Hull, 1961-62; Lectr of St Mary, Lowgate, Hull, 1955-62; Prof. of Theology, 1962-75, and Dean of Faculty of Arts, 1965-67, Univ. of Leeds. Examining Chaplain: to Archbp of York, 1957-63; to Bp of Sheffield, 1963-75. Mem., Doctrinal Commn, 1967-69. Hon. Canon of Ripon Cath., 1966-75. *Publications:* The Imitation of God in Christ, 1960; The Gospel according to Luke, 1965; (ed) Modern Theology, 5 vols, 1973; contributor to: The Church and the Arts, 1960; Vindications, 1966; A Dictionary of Christian Ethics, 1967; A Dictionary of Christian Theology, 1969; Art and Religion as Communication, 1974. *Recreations:* France, Romanesque art, gardening. *Address:* Bishop's House, Clifton Hill, Bristol BS8 1BW. *T:* Bristol 30222. *Club:* Athenæum.

BRISTOL, Dean of; *see* Dammers, Very Rev. A. H.

BRISTOL, Archdeacon of; *see* Williams, Ven. Leslie Arthur.

BRISTOW, Alan Edgar, OBE 1966; Chairman, Bristow Helicopter Group Ltd, since 1967; *b* 3 Sept. 1923; *m* 1945; one *s* one *d.* *Educ:* Portsmouth Grammar School. Cadet, British India Steam Navigation Co., 1939-43; Pilot, Fleet Air Arm, 1943-46; Test Pilot, Westland Aircraft Ltd, 1946-49; Helicopair, Paris/Indo-China, 1949-51; Man. Dir, Air Whaling Ltd (Antarctic Whaling Expedns), 1951-54; Man. Dir, Bristow Helicopters Ltd, 1954-68; Dir, British United Airways Ltd, 1960-70, Man. Dir 1967-70. Cierva Memorial Lectr, RAeS, 1967. FRAeS 1967. Croix de Guerre (France), 1950. *Publications:* papers to RAeS. *Recreations:* flying, shooting, sailing, farming, four-in-hand driving. *Address:* Baynards Park Estate, Cranleigh, Surrey. *T:* Cranleigh 4674. *Club:* Lansdowne.

BRISTOW, Hon. Sir Peter (Henry Rowley), Kt 1970; **Hon. Mr Justice Bristow;** a Judge of the High Court, Queen's Bench Division, since 1970; Judge of the Commercial Court and Employment Appeals Tribunal, since 1976; Member, Parole Board, since 1976; *b* 1 June 1913; *s* of Walter Rowley Bristow, FRCS and Florence (*née* White); *m* 1st, 1940, Josephine Noel Leney (*d* 1969); one *s* one *d*; 2nd, 1975, Elsa, *widow* of H. B. Leney. *Educ:* Eton; Trinity College, Cambridge. Served with RAFVR, 1936-45. Called to the Bar, Middle Temple, 1936, Bencher 1961, Treasurer 1977; QC 1964; Mem., Inns of Court Senate, 1966-70 (Hon. Treas., 1967-70); Judge, Court of Appeal, Guernsey, and Court of Appeal, Jersey, 1965-70; Dep. Chm., Hants QS, 1964-71. *Recreations:* sailing, fishing, shooting. *Address:* Royal Courts of Justice, Strand, WC2; 36 Eaton Place, SW1; The Folly, Membury, Axminster, Devon. *Club:* Royal Ocean Racing.

BRISTOWE, William Syer, MA, ScD Cantab; *b* 1 Sept. 1901; *s* of Bertram Arthur Bristowe and Mary Rosa (*née* Johnston), Stoke d'Abernon, Surrey; *m* 1934, Helen Mary Harper (marr. diss., 1962); three *d* (and one *d* decd). *Educ:* Wellington Coll; Cambridge. Cambridge Scientific Expeditions to Jan Mayen, 1921, and Brazil, 1923. Joined Brunner Mond, 1925, subsequently merged in ICI 1926; Head of Far East Department, 1936, and Director of Eastern subsidiary companies; Head of Central Staff Department, 1948-62. Member ECA special productivity mission to USA studying education and the employment of graduates, 1950; Member FBI cttee studying shortage of science teachers, 1954. Pres. Ray Society, 1959-62; Master of Armourers and Braziers, 1965-66; Member, Court of City University. Stamford Raffles Award for Zoology, 1961. *Publications:* The Comity of Spiders, 2 vols, 1939-41; Spiders, 1947; The World of Spiders, 1958; Victorian China Fairings, 1964; Natural History of the Garden of Buckingham Palace (pt author), 1964; Emma, the Resolute Queen, 1966; A Book of Islands, 1969; Louis and the King of Siam, 1976; occasional papers on athletics, explorations, early naturalists, giants, Sherlock Holmes and staff management. *Recreations:* lawn tennis, visiting small islands, studies of Viking and Saxon history, Siamese history, Arctic Exploration, genealogy, folklore and curios, biological research; formerly athletics (Camb. Blue, 1922-24; Pres. CUAC, 1924; Capt. Jt Oxf.

and Camb. Team to USA, 1924), Rugby football (Harlequins and Sale). *Address:* Mill House, Whatlington, Battle, East Sussex.

BRITISH COLUMBIA; see Columbia, British.

BRITTAIN, Rear-Admiral Wilfred Geoffrey, CB 1956; CBE 1945; *b* 19 June 1903; *m* 1st, 1935, May Russell Shorto (*d* 1964); two *d*; 2nd, 1968, Mary Clifton, *d* of late Dennis Hughes. *Educ:* RNC Osborne and Dartmouth. Joined Royal Navy, 1917; Comdr 1939; Captain 1944; Rear-Adm. 1954; Retired 1957. Last appointment Flag Officer, Malta, and Admiral Superintendent, HM Dockyard, Malta, 1954-57. Officer, Legion of Merit, 1946. *Address:* 1 Little Stodham House, Liss, Hants. *T:* 3189.

BRITTAN, Leon; MP (C) Cleveland and Whitby since Feb. 1974; *b* 25 Sept. 1939; *s* of late Dr Joseph Brittan and Mrs Rebecca Brittan. *Educ:* Haberdashers' Aske's Sch.; Trinity Coll., Cambridge (MA); Yale Univ. (Henry Fellow). Chm., Cambridge Univ. Conservative Assoc., 1960; Pres., Cambridge Union, 1960; debating tour of USA for Cambridge Union, 1961. Called to Bar, Inner Temple, 1962. Chm., Bow Group, 1964-65; contested (C) North Kensington, 1966 and 1970. Editor, Crossbow, 1966-68; Mem. Political Cttee, Carlton Club; Vice-Chm. of Governors, Isaac Newton Sch., 1968-71; Mem. European North American Cttee; Vice-Chm., Nat. Assoc. of School Governors and Managers; Dep. Chm. of Research Cttee, Soc. of Conservative Lawyers (Mem. Exec. Cttee); Vice-Chm., Parly Cons. Party Employment Cttee, 1974-76; opposition front bench spokesman on Devolution, 1976-. *Publications:* (contrib.) The Conservative Opportunity; (jtly) Millstones for the Sixties, Rough Justice, Infancy and the Law, How to Save Your Schools (pamphlets). *Recreations:* opera, art, cricket, walking, travel. *Address:* 20 Kensington Park Gardens, W11 3HD. *T:* 01-727 7935; Lease Rigg Farm, Grosmont, Whitby, Yorks. *T:* Grosmont 280. *Clubs:* Carlton, MCC.
See also Samuel Brittan.

BRITTAN, Samuel; Principal Economic Commentator, Financial Times, since 1966; *b* 29 Dec. 1933; *s* of late Joseph Brittan, MD, and of Riva Brittan (*née* Lipetz). *Educ:* Kilburn Grammar Sch.; Jesus Coll., Cambridge. 1st Class in Economics, 1955; MA Cantab. Various posts in Financial Times, 1955-61; Economics Editor, Observer, 1961-64; Adviser, DEA, 1965. Fellow, Nuffield Coll., Oxford, 1973-74, Vis. Fellow, 1974-; Vis. Prof. of Economics, Chicago Business Sch., 1978. Financial Journalist of the Year Award 1971. *Publications:* The Treasury under the Tories, 1964, rev. edn, Steering the Economy, 1969, 1971; Left or Right: The Bogus Dilemma, 1968; The Price of Economic Freedom, 1970; Capitalism and the Permissive Society, 1973; Is There an Economic Consensus?, 1973; Second Thoughts on Full Employment Policy, 1975; (with P. Lilley) The Delusion of Incomes Policy, 1977; articles in various jls. *Address:* Flat 10, The Lodge, Kensington Park Gardens, W11.
See also L. Brittan.

BRITTEN, Brig. Charles Richard, OBE 1966; MC 1916; DL, JP; Extra Gentleman Usher to the Queen, since 1955; *b* 25 June 1894; 2nd *s* of late Rear-Admiral R. F. Britten and Hon. Blanche Cecile Colville, *o d* of 11th Baron Colville of Culross; *m* 1st, 1915, Dorothy (*d* 1970), *d* of late Hon. P. Allsopp; one *s*; 2nd, 1971, Pamela, *yr d* of E. G. Attenborough. *Educ:* Eton; RMC Sandhurst. Served European War, 1914-19, and War of 1939-45; Grenadier Guards, 1914; Capt. 1917; Lieut-Col 1935; Bt. Col 1937; Col 1938; Brig. 1939; Comdg Grenadier Guards, 1937-39, and 1st (London) Infantry Bde, 1937-41; attached RAF Regiment, 1942; retired, 1946. Pres., Worcs and Hereford Branch, Gren. Guards Assoc. Mem., Worcs CC, 1946-74 (CA 1963); Mem., Martley RDC, 1948-74. DL 1947, JP 1946, High Sheriff 1952, Worcs. *Recreations:* shooting, hunting (Chm., Wyre Forest Beagles) and fishing. *Address:* Kenswick Manor, Worcester. *T:* Worcester 640210. *Clubs:* Cavalry and Guards; Union and County (Worcester).

BRITTEN, Brig. George Vallette, CBE 1947 (OBE 1942, MBE 1940); HM Diplomatic Service, retired; *b* 19 March 1909; *s* of John Britten, Bozeat Manor, Northamptonshire, and Elizabeth Franziska Britten (*née* Vallette); *m* 1937, Shirley Jean Stewart Wink; three *s*. *Educ:* Wellingborough; RMC Sandhurst. Regtl duty in UK, 1929-38; Staff Coll., Camberley, 1938-39. Served War: HQ 2 Corps, France and Belgium, 1939-40; Staff appts in UK, 1940-41; with 1st Airborne Div. in UK, N Africa and Sicily, 1942-43; DCS, 5(US) Army, N Africa and Italy, 1943-44; HQ, 21st Army Gp, NW Europe, 1944-45. DCS, Brit. Military Govt, Germany, 1945-47. Regtl Duty, Berlin and Austria, 1947-49; WO, 1949-51; Comdt, Sch. of Infty, Hythe, 1952-54; Instr, US Army Staff Coll., Kansas, 1954-56; Planning Staff, NATO,

Fontainebleau, 1956-58; Mil. Attaché, Brit. Embassy, Bonn, 1958-61; retired from Army, 1961; Ghana Desk, Commonwealth Office, 1961-62; with British High Commissions, Enugu, Kaduna, and Bathurst, 1962-66; Head of Chancery, British Embassy, Berne, 1967-71. American Legion of Merit, 1946; W German Grosses Verdienst Kreuz, 1959. *Recreation:* gardening. *Address:* 67 Bradbourne Park Road, Sevenoaks, Kent.

BRITTEN, Rae Gordon, CMG 1972; HM Diplomatic Service; Head of South-West Pacific Department, Foreign and Commonwealth Office, since 1976; *b* 27 Sept. 1920; *s* of Leonard Arthur Britten and Elizabeth Percival Taylor; *m* 1952, Valentine Alms (marr. diss. 1974); one *s* three *d*. *Educ:* Liverpool Institute High School; Magdalen College, Oxford. Served War 1941-45 (artillery and infantry). Research Assistant with Common Ground Ltd, 1947; apptd Commonwealth Relations Office, 1948; 2nd Sec., Brit. High Commn in India (Calcutta, 1948-49, Delhi, 1949-50): 1st Sec. Brit. High Commn., Bombay, 1955-58, Karachi, 1961-62; Deputy High Commissioner: Peshawar, March 1962; Lahore, June 1962-July 1964; Kingston, Jamaica, 1964-69; Head of Trade Policy Dept, FCO, 1968-71; Dep. High Comr, Dacca, 1971-72; Counsellor and Head of Chancery, Oslo, 1973-76. *Address:* c/o Foreign and Commonwealth Office, SW1. *Club:* Royal Commonwealth Society.

BRITTEN, Maj.-Gen. Robert Wallace Tudor, CB 1977; MC; Defence Marketing Consultant, Lucas Electrical Ltd, since 1977; *b* 28 Feb. 1922; *s* of Lt-Col Wallace Ernest Britten, OBE; *m* 1947, Elizabeth Mary, *d* of Edward H. Davies, Pentre, Rhondda; one *s* one *d*. *Educ:* Wellington Coll.; Trinity Coll., Cambridge. FBIM. 2nd Lieut RE, 1941; served War of 1939-45, Madras Sappers and Miners, 19th Indian Div., India and Burma; Comdr 21 Fd Pk Sqn and 5 Fd Sqn RE, 1947-50; on staff WO, 1951-53; British Liaison Officer to US Corps of Engrs, 1953-56; comd 50 Fd Sqn RE, 1956-58; on staff WO, 1958-61; on staff of 1 (BR) Corps BAOR, 1961-64; Lt-Col in comd 1 Trg Regt RE, 1964-65; GSO1 (DS), Jt Services Staff Coll., 1965-67; Comd 30 Engr Bde (V) and Chief Engr Western Comd, 1967; idc 1969; Dir of Equipment Management, MoD (Army), 1970-71; DQMG, 1971-73; GOC West Midland Dist, 1973-76, retired. Brig. 1967; Maj.-Gen. 1971. *Recreations:* sailing, fishing, dowsing (Mem. Council, Brit. Soc. Dowsers). *Address:* Birch Trees, Fernden Lane, Haslemere, Surrey. *T:* Haslemere 2261. *Clubs:* Army and Navy; Bosham Sailing.

BRITTENDEN, (Charles) Arthur; Deputy Editor, The Sun, since 1972; *b* 23 Oct. 1924; *o s* of late Tom Edwin Brittenden and Caroline (*née* Scrivener); *m* 1st, 1953, Sylvia Penelope Cadman (marr. diss., 1960); 2nd, 1966, Ann Patricia Kenny (marr. diss. 1972); 3rd, 1975, Valerie Arnison. *Educ:* Leeds Grammar School. Served in Reconnaissance Corps, 1943-46. Yorkshire Post, 1940-43, 1946-49; News Chronicle, 1949-55; joined Sunday Express, 1955: Foreign Editor, 1959-62; Northern Editor, Daily Express, 1962-63; Dep. Editor, Sunday Express, 1963-64; Exec. Editor, 1964-66, Editor, 1966-71, Daily Mail. Dir, Harmsworth Publications Ltd, 1967-71. Man. Dir, Wigmore Cassettes, 1971-72. *Address:* 6 Strathearn Place, W2 2NG. *T:* 01-402 6789.

BRITTON, Prof. Denis King; Professor of Agricultural Economics at Wye College, since 1970; *b* 25 March 1920; *s* of Rev. George Charles Britton and Harriet Rosa (*née* Swinstead); *m* 1942, Margaret Alice Smith; one *s* two *d*. *Educ:* Caterham School; London School of Economics, London University (BSc (Econ.)). Asst Statistician, Ministry of Agriculture and Fisheries, 1943-47; Lecturing and Research at University of Oxford, Agricultural Economics Res. Inst., 1947-52; MA Oxon 1948 (by decree); Economist, United Nations Food and Agriculture Organisation, Geneva, 1952-59; Gen. Manager, Marketing and Economic Res., Massey-Ferguson (UK) Ltd, 1959-61; Prof. of Agricultural Economics, Univ. of Nottingham, 1961-70; Dean, Faculty of Agriculture and Horticulture, Univ. of Nottingham, 1967-70. Member: EDC for Agriculture, 1966-; Home Grown Cereals Authy, 1969-; Adv. Council for Agriculture and Horticulture, 1973-; Chairman: Council, Centre for European Agricl Studies, Wye Coll., 1974-; Adv. Cttee, Nuffield Centre for Agric. Strategy, 1975-. Pres., Internat. Assoc. of Agric. Economists, 1976-. Vis. Prof., Uppsala, 1973. Farmers' Club Cup, 1966. FSS 1943; FRAgSS 1970. Hon. DAgric, Univ. of Bonn, 1975. *Publications:* Cereals in the United Kingdom, 1969; (with Berkeley Hill) Size and Efficiency in Farming, 1975; articles in Jl of Royal Statistical Society, Jl of Agricultural Economics, Jl of RSA, Farm Economist, Incorporated Statistician, etc. *Recreations:* music, golf. *Address:* 29 Chequers Park, Wye, Ashford, Kent. *Club:* Farmers'.

BRITTON, Sir Edward (Louis), Kt 1975; CBE 1967; Senior Research Fellow, Education Division, Sheffield University, since 1975; *b* 4 Dec. 1909; *s* of George Edwin and Ellen Alice Britton; *m* 1936, Nora Arnald; no *c. Educ:* Bromley Grammar School, Kent; Trinity College, Cambridge. Teacher in various Surrey schools until 1951; Headmaster, Warlingham County Secondary School, Surrey, 1951-60; General Secretary, Association of Teachers in Technical Institutions, 1960-68. National Union of Teachers: President, 1956-57; General Secretary, 1970-75. Member: TUC General Council, 1970-74; Beloe Cttee on Secondary Schs Exams, 1960; Schools Council, 1964-75; Adv. Cttee for Supply and Trng of Teachers, 1973-75; Burnham Primary and Secondary Cttee, 1956-75 (Jt Sec. and Leader of Teachers' Panel, 1970-75); Burnham Further Educn Cttee, 1959-69 (Jt Sec. and Leader of Teachers' Panel, 1961-69); Officers' Panel, Soulbury Cttee (and Leader), 1970-75; Staff Panel, Jt Negotiating Cttee Youth Leaders (and Leader), 1970-75; Warnock Cttee on Special Educn, 1974-; Council and Exec, CGLI, 1974-77. Fellow College of Preceptors, 1967; Hon. FEIS, 1974. Hon. DEd CNAA, 1969. *Publications:* many articles in educational journals. *Address:* 40 Nightingale Road, Guildford, Surrey.

BRITTON, Prof. Karl William; Professor of Philosophy, University of Newcastle upon Tyne, 1951-75; *b* Scarborough, Yorks, 12 Oct. 1909; *s* of Rev. J. Nimmo Britton and Elsie Clare Britton (*née* Slater); *m* 1936, Sheila Margaret Christie; one *s* two *d* (and one *s* one *d* decd). *Educ:* Southend High School; Clare College, Cambridge. Pres. Cambridge Union Society, 1931. Choate Fellow at Harvard University, USA, 1932-34; Lecturer in Philosophy: University College of Wales, 1934-37; University College of Swansea, 1937-51. War of 1939-45, Regional Commissioner's Office, Reading, 1941-45. Public Orator, Durham University, 1959-62; Dean of the Faculty of Arts, Newcastle upon Tyne, 1961-63 and 1966-69. Examiner, Moral Sciences Tripos: 1949, 1954, 1955, 1964, 1966. Mill Centenary Lectr, Toronto Univ., 1973. Sec., Mind Assoc., 1948-60, Pres. 1963. Hon. DLitt Durham, 1976. *Publications:* Communication: A Philosophical Study of Language, 1939, repr. 1971; John Stuart Mill, 1953, repr. 1969; Philosophy and the Meaning of Life, 1969; contrib. to: The Times, Proc. Aristotelian Society, Mind, Philosophy, Analysis, Jl of Philosophy, Cambridge Review, etc. *Address:* Harthope, Millfield Road, Riding Mill, Northumberland. *T:* Riding Mill 354.

BROACKES, Nigel; Chairman, Trafalgar House Investments Ltd; *b* Wakefield, 21 July 1934; *s* of late Donald Broackes and Nan Alford; *m* 1956, Joyce Edith Horne; two *s* one *d. Educ:* Stowe. Nat. Service, commnd 3rd Hussars, 1953-54. Stewart & Hughman Ltd, Lloyds Underwriting agents, 1952-55; various property developments, etc, 1955-57; Trafalgar House Investments Ltd: Man. Dir 1958; Dep. Chm. and Jt Man. Dir 1968; Chm. 1969. Chm., Ship and Marine Technology Requirements Bd, 1972-77; Dep. Chm., Offshore Energy Technology Bd, 1975-. Hon. Treas., Kensington Housing Trust, 1963-69; Vice-Chairman: Mulberry Housing Trust, 1965-69; London Housing Trust, 1967-70; Mem. Council, Nat. Assoc. of Property Owners, 1967-73. Governor, Stowe Sch., 1974-. Trustee, Royal Opera House Trust. Dir, Horserace Totalisator Bd, 1976-. *Recreation:* silversmith. *Address:* 41 Chelsea Square, SW3; The Deanery, Thames Street, Sonning, Berks.

BROADBENT, Donald Eric, CBE 1974; MA, ScD; FRS 1968; on External Staff, Medical Research Council, since 1974; *b* 6 May 1926; *m* 1st, 1949, Margaret Elizabeth Wright; two *d*; 2nd, 1972, Margaret Hope Pattison Gregory. *Educ:* Winchester College; Pembroke College, Cambridge. RAF Engrg short course, 1st cl., 1944; Moral Science Tripos (Psychology), 1st cl., 1949. Scientific Staff, Applied Psychology Res. Unit, 1949-58 (Dir, 1958-74). Fellow, Pembroke College, Cambridge, 1965-74. Pres., British Psychol. Society, 1965; Pres., Sect. J. Brit. Assoc. for Advancement of Science, 1967; Vis. Fellow, All Souls College, Oxford, 1967-68; Fellow, Wolfson Coll., Oxford, 1974. Member: Biol. Res. Bd, MRC, 1966-70; Psychology Cttee, SSRC, 1969-75; SSRC, 1973-75; Fellow, Acoustical Soc. of Amer.; past or present Council Member: British Acoustical Society; British Psychol Soc.; Ergonomics Res. Soc.; Experimental Psychology Soc.; Fellow, Human Factors Soc.; Lectures: Lister, Brit. Assoc.; Gregynog, Aberystwyth; Pillsbury, Cornell; Fitts, Michigan; William James, Harvard. For. Associate, US Nat. Acad. Sci., 1971. Hon. DSc Southampton, 1973. APA Dist. Scientist Award, 1975. *Publications:* Perception and Communication, 1958; Behaviour, 1961; Decision and Stress, 1971; In Defence of Empirical Psychology, 1973; many papers in jls of above societies and of Amer. Psychol Assoc. *Recreations:* reading, camping, photography. *Address:* Department of Experimental Psychology, 1 South Parks Road, Oxford OX1 3UD.

BROADBENT, Dr Edward Granville, FRS 1977; FRAeS, FIMA; Deputy Chief Scientific Officer (IM), Aerodynamics Department, Royal Aircraft Establishment, since 1969; *b* 27 June 1923; *s* of Joseph Charles Fletcher Broadbent and Lucetta (*née* Riley); *m* 1949, Elizabeth Barbara (*née* Puttick). *Educ:* Huddersfield Coll.; St Catharine's Coll., Cambridge (State Scholarship, 1941; Eng Scholar; MA, ScD). FRAeS 1959; FIMA 1965. Joined RAE (Structures Dept), 1943; worked on aero-elasticity (Wakefield Gold Medal, RAeS, 1960); transf. to Aerodynamics Dept, 1960; worked on magnetohydrodynamics, high speed propulsion, and (currently) aircraft noise reduction. *Publication:* The Elementary Theory of Aero-elasticity, 1954. *Recreations:* duplicate bridge, chess, music, theatre. *Address:* 11 Three Stiles Road, Farnham, Surrey GU9 7DE. *T:* Farnham 714621.

BROADBENT, Ewen, CB 1973; CMG 1965; Deputy Under Secretary of State (Civilian Management), Ministry of Defence, since 1975; *b* 9 Aug. 1924; *s* of late Rev. W. Broadbent and of Mrs Mary Broadbent; *m* 1951, Squadron Officer Barbara David, *d* of F. A. David, Weston-super-Mare; one *s. Educ:* King Edward VI School, Nuneaton; St John's College, Cambridge. Served with Gordon Highlanders, 1943-47 (Captain); Cambridge, 1942-43 and 1947-49; Air Ministry, 1949; Private Sec. to Secretary of State for Air, 1955-59; Asst Secretary, 1959; Dep. Chief Officer, Sovereign Base Areas, Cyprus, 1961, Chief Officer, 1964; MoD 1965-; Private Sec. to Sec. of State for Defence, 1967-68; Asst Under-Sec. of State, 1969-72; Dep. Under-Sec. of State (Air), 1972-75. *Recreation:* golf. *Address:* 18 Park Hill, Ealing, W5. *T:* 01-997 1978. *Club:* Royal Commonwealth Society.

BROADBENT, Sir William Francis, 3rd Bt, *cr* 1898; *b* 29 Nov. 1904; *s* of Sir John Francis Harpin Broadbent, MD, FRCP, Bt and Margaret Elizabeth Field (*d* 1958); *S* father 1946; *m* 1935, Veronica Pearl Eustace (*d* 1951); no *c. Educ:* Winchester College; Trinity College, Oxford (MA). Solicitor, 1933-72, retired. *Heir: cousin* George Walter Broadbent [*b* 23 April 1935; *m* 1962, Valerie Anne, *o d* of C. F. Ward; one *s* one *d*]. *Address:* Flat 43, Ritchie Court, 380 Banbury Road, Oxford. *Club:* United Oxford & Cambridge University.

BROADBRIDGE, family name of **Baron Broadbridge.**

BROADBRIDGE, 3rd Baron *cr* 1945, of Brighton; **Peter Hewett Broadbridge;** Bt 1937; Management Consultant, Peat Marwick Mitchell & Co., EC2, since 1971; *b* 19 Aug. 1938; *s* of 2nd Baron Broadbridge and Mabel Daisy (*d* 1966), *o d* of Arthur Edward Clarke; *S* father, 1972; *m* 1967, Mary, *o d* of W. O. Busch; two *d. Educ:* Hurstpierpoint Coll., Sussex; St Catherine's Coll., Oxford (MA, BSc). Unilever Ltd, 1963-65; Colgate Palmolive Ltd, 1966; Gallaher Ltd, 1967-70. *Recreations:* tennis, squash, antiques. *Heir: uncle* Hon. Ralph George Cameron Broadbridge [*b* 20 Nov. 1901; *m* 1925, Emma Rose Hancock (*d* 1965), *d* of Harry Van der Weyden; three *d*]. *Address:* 31 Ockendon Road, Islington, N1. *T:* 01-226 5231.

BROADBRIDGE, Stanley Robertson; General Secretary, National Association of Teachers in Further and Higher Education (NATFHE), since 1977; *b* 16 March 1928; *s* of Robert Harriss Broadbridge and Lily May Broadbridge; *m* 1951, Eva Bollington; two *d. Educ:* Queen Elizabeth's Sch., Barnet; Univ. of Manchester (MA Econ). National Service, RAF, 1950-52; Sen. Econs Master, Boteler Grammar Sch., Warrington, 1952-57; Lectr, Leigh Tech. Coll., Lancs, 1957-64; Lectr, subseq. Principal Lectr, N Staffs Polytechnic (formerly Staffs Coll. of Technology), 1965-77. *Publications:* Birmingham Canal Navigations 1768-1846, 1974; articles in Transport Hist. and Jl Indust. Archaeol. *Recreations:* collecting antiques, canals, English Baroque music. *Address:* c/o NATFHE, Hamilton House, Mabledon Place, WC1H 9BH. *T:* 01-387 6806.

BROADHURST, Air Chief Marshal (retd) Sir Harry, GCB 1960 (KCB 1955; CB 1944); KBE 1945; DSO and Bar, 1941; DFC 1940, and Bar, 1942; AFC 1937; Director, 1961-76, Deputy Managing Director 1965-76, Hawker Siddeley Aviation Ltd; Director, Hawker Siddeley Group Ltd, 1968-76; *b* 1905; *m* 1st, 1929, Doris Kathleen French; one *d*; 2nd, 1946, Jean Elizabeth Townley; one *d.* SASO to AOC Western Desert, 1942; AOC Allied Air Forces, W. Desert, 1943; 83 Group Commander Allied Expeditionary Air Force, 1944-45; AO i/c Admin. Fighter Command, 1945-46; AOC 61 Group, 1947-48; idc 1949; SASO, BAFO (now 2nd TAF), Germany, 1950-51; ACAS (Ops), 1952-53; C-in-C 2nd Tactical Air Force, Germany, 1954-56; Air Officer Commanding-in-Chief, Bomber Command, Jan. 1956-May 1959; Cmdr Allied Air Forces, Central Europe, 1959-61. Vice-Pres., 1973-74, Pres., 1974-75, SBAC. Kt Grand Cross of Order of Orange Nassau, 1948; Legion of Merit (US).

Address: Lock's End House, Birdham, Chichester, W Sussex. *T:* Birdham 512717. *Clubs:* Royal Air Force; Royal Thames Yacht.

BROADLEY, Sir Herbert, KBE 1947 (CBE 1943); Representative in Britain of United Nations Children's Fund, 1958-68; *b* 23 Nov. 1892; *s* of late Stephenson S. Broadley, Louth, Lincs; *m* 1927, Kathleen May, *d* of late Alfred J. Moore, Camden Square, London; no *c. Educ:* King Edward VI Grammar Sch., Louth; Birkbeck Coll., Univ. of London. Pres. Students' Union; Editor, Coll. Magazine Lodestone, 1922-23. Civil Service, 1912; served in India Office (Military Dept), 1912-1920; served in BoT, 1920-26; Sec., Imperial Customs Conf., 1921, German (Reparations) Act Cttee, 1921, and Imperial Economic Cttee, 1925-26; Asst Sec., Anglo-Soviet Commercial Treaty, 1924; Sec., Anglo-German Commercial Treaty, 1925; Asst Sec., Imperial Econ. Conf., 1926; resigned from Civil Service, 1926, and joined firm of W. S. Crawford Ltd (Advertising Agents), 1927; Dir, W. S. Crawford Ltd and Man. Dir of their Berlin Branch, 1927-32; i/c Distribution and Res. Dept, W. S. Crawford Ltd, London, 1932-39; Fellow and Mem. Council, Inst. of Incorp. Practitioners in Advertising and Chm., Res. Cttee, 1936-39; joined Ministry of Food at outbreak of War, 1939; Asst Sec., Nov. 1939; Principal Asst Sec., 1940; Dep. Sec., 1941; Second Sec., 1945-48; Leader, UK Delegn to Internat. Wheat Confs, 1947 and 1948; UK repr. at UNFAO Confs: Quebec, 1945; Copenhagen, 1946; Dep. Dir-Gen., UNFAO, 1948-58 (Acting Dir-Gen., 1955-56), retd. Trustee, UK Nat. Freedom from Hunger (Mem. Cttee, 1960-). Hon. Freeman of Louth (Lincs) 1961. Hon. Fellow, Birkbeck Coll., Univ. of London, 1963; a Governor, Birkbeck Coll., 1965-. Haldane Meml Lecture on Food and People, Univ. of London, 1964. Commander of the Order of the Crown of Belgium, 1948. *Publication:* The People's Food (with Sir William Crawford), 1938. *Address:* Hollingsworth, Redlands Lane, Ewshot, Farnham, Surrey GU10 5AS. *T:* Aldershot 850437. *Club:* Naval and Military.

BROATCH, James, CBE 1961; Deputy Chairman of the Cotton Board, 1963; Deputy Chairman, Textile Council, 1967-68; *b* 13 May 1900; *s* of Alfred and Mary Broatch; *m* 1927, Mary Booth. *Educ:* Manchester Grammar School; University College, Oxford. Editor, Manchester Guardian Commercial, 1930-39; Assistant Secretary, The Cotton Board, 1939-43; Secretary 1943-53; Director-General, 1953-62. *Address:* 5 Lynton Drive, Hillside, Southport, Merseyside. *T:* Southport 67976.

BROCAS, Viscount; Patrick John Bernard Jellicoe; *b* 29 Aug. 1950; *s* and *heir* of 2nd Earl Jellicoe, *qv*; *m* 1971, Geraldine Ann Jackson; one *s. Educ:* Eton. *Address:* 20 Chapel Street, Belgrave Square, SW1.

BROCK, family name of Baron Brock.

BROCK, Baron, *cr* 1965 (Life Peer), of Wimbledon; **Russell Claude Brock;** Kt 1954; Director, Department of Surgical Sciences, Royal College of Surgeons, since 1968; Surgeon to: Guy's Hospital, 1936-68; Brompton Hospital, 1936-68; *b* 24 Oct. 1903; *s* of Herbert and Elvina Brock; *m* 1927, Germaine Louise Ladevèze; two *d* (and one *d* decd). *Educ:* Christ's Hospital; Guy's Hospital (Schol.). MB, BS London, Hons med. surg. and anat., 1927; MS London 1932. Rockefeller Travelling Fellow, 1929-30; Demonstrator in Pathology and Anatomy, Surgical Registrar and Tutor, Guy's Hospital, 1932; Research Fell., Assoc. Surg. of Great Britain, 1932; Hunterian Prof., RCS, 1938; Cons. Thoracic Surgeon, LCC, 1935-46; Surgeon, Min. of Pensions (Queen Mary's, Roehampton), 1936-45; Thoracic Surgeon and Regional Adviser in Thoracic Surgery, EMS, 1939-46; Exchange Prof. of Surgery, Johns Hopkins Hospital, Baltimore, 1949. MRCS 1926; FRCS 1928; Member Council RCS, 1949-67; a Vice-Pres., RCS, 1956-58; Pres., 1963-66. President, Thoracic Society of Great Britain and Ireland, 1952; Med. Society London, 1968. LRCP 1926; FRCP 1965; FACS 1949; Hon. FRACS 1957; Hon. ScD Cantab., 1968; Hon. LLD Leeds 1965; Hon. MD: Hamburg, 1962; Munich, 1972. Hon. Fellow: Surgical section of RSM, 1951; Brazilian College of Surgeons, 1952; RCSEd 1966; RCSI, 1966; RCSCan. 1966. Hon. Mem., AU-Union Soviet Soc. of Surgeons, 1974. Lectures: Lettsomian, Med. Soc. London, 1952; Bradshaw, RCS, 1957; Tudor Edwards Memorial, 1963; Hunterian Orator, RCS, 1961; Lister Orator, 1967; Astley Cooper Orator, 1968; BMA Prize Essay, 1926; Jacksonian Prize Essay, RCS, 1935; Julius Mickle Prize, London Univ., 1950-51; Cameron Prize, Edinburgh Univ., 1954; Gairdner Award, 1960-61. Treasurer's Gold Medal for Clin. med. and Clin. Surg., 1926; Golding Bird Gold Medal for Pathology, 1926; Fothergillian Gold Medal, Med. Soc. London, 1953; Leriche Medal, Internat. Soc. Surg., 1953; Gold Medal, Soc. Apoth., 1955; Gold Medal, W. London Med.-Chir. Soc., 1955; Lannelongue Medal, Acad. de Chirurgie, 1963;

Bronze Medal of City of NY, 1965; Lister Medal, RCS, 1966. KStJ. *Publications:* Anatomy of the bronchial tree, 1946; Life and Work of Astley Cooper, 1952; Lung Abscess, 1952; Anatomy of Pulmonary Stenosis, 1957; numerous articles in surgical and medical journals. *Recreations:* writing, reading, antiquities and topography of London. *Address:* The Old Rectory House, 84 Church Road, Wimbledon, SW19; 2 Harley Street, W1. *T:* 01-580 1441. *Club:* Athenæum.

BROCK, Arthur Guy C.; *see* Clutton-Brock.

BROCK, Michael George; Professor of Education and Director of the School of Education, Exeter University, 1977-78; Warden of Nuffield College, Oxford, from Aug. 1978; *b* 9 March 1920; *s* of Sir Laurence George Brock and late Ellen Margery Brock (*née* Williams); *m* 1949, Eleanor Hope Morrison; three *s. Educ:* Wellington Coll. (Schol.); Corpus Christi Coll., Oxford (Open Schol.; First Cl. Hons Mod. Hist. 1948; MA 1948). FRHistS 1965. War service (Middlesex Regt), 1940-45. Corpus Christi Coll., Oxford: Jun. Res. Fellow, 1948-50; Fellow and Tutor in Modern History and Politics, 1950-66, Fellow Emeritus, 1977; Oxford University: Jun. Proctor, 1956-57; Univ. Lectr, 1951-70; Mem., Hebdomadal Council, 1965-76; Vice Pres. and Bursar, Wolfson Coll., Oxford, 1966-76. Hon. Fellow, Wolfson Coll., Oxford, 1977. *Publications:* The Great Reform Act, 1973; many articles on historical topics and on higher education. *Address:* 16 St Leonard's Road, Exeter EX2 4LA. *T:* Exeter 33753; (from Aug. 1978) c/o Nuffield College, Oxford. *Clubs:* Athenæum; Oxford Union.

BROCK, Rear-Admiral Patrick Willet, CB 1956; DSO 1951; RN retd; Chairman, The Naval Review, since 1967; *b* 30 Dec. 1902; *e s* of R. W. and M. B. Brock, Kingston, Ontario; *m* 1st, 1931, M. D. Collinson (*d* 1974); 2nd, 1976, Mrs Rosemary Harrison Stanton. *Educ:* Royal Royal Naval College of Canada. Transferred from Royal Canadian Navy to RN, 1921; Commander 1938; Exec. Officer, HMS Mauritius, 1942-44 (despatches); Captain 1944; Senior Naval Officer, Schleswig-Holstein, 1946; commanded HMS Kenya, Far East, 1949-51 (despatches, DSO); Director Operations Div., 1951-53; Rear-Admiral, 1954; Flag Officer, Middle East, 1954-56; Admiralty Material Requirements Committee, 1956-58, retired. Chm., Kipling Soc., 1973-76. Trustee, National Maritime Museum, 1960-74; a Vice-Pres., Soc. for Nautical Research, 1970-. Croix de Guerre (France), 1945; Bronze Star Medal (US), 1951. *Publications:* RUSI Eardley-Wilmot Gold Medal Essay, 1935; (with Basil Greenhill) Steam and Sail in Great Britain and North America, 1973. *Recreations:* gardening, naval history. *Address:* Kiln Cottage, Critchmere, Haslemere, Surrey. *T:* Haslemere 2542.

BROCK, Prof. William Ranulf; Professor of Modern History, University of Glasgow, since 1967; *b* 16 May 1916; *s* of Stewart Ernst Brock and Katherine Helen (*née* Temple Roberts); *m* 1950, Constance Helen (*née* Brown); one *s* one *d. Educ:* Christ's Hosp.; Trinity Coll., Cambridge (MA, PhD). Exhibr, Trinity Coll., 1933, Sen. Schol. 1936, Earl of Derby Res. Student 1937, Prize Fellow 1940 (in absentia). Military service (Army), 1939-45; Asst Master, Eton Coll., 1946-47; Fellow of Selwyn Coll., Cambridge, 1947-67. Commonwealth Fund Fellow, Berkeley, Calif, Yale and Johns Hopkins, 1952-53, 1958; Vis. Professor: Michigan Univ., 1968; Washington Univ., 1970. *Publications:* Lord Liverpool and Liberal Toryism, 1941; The Character of American History, 1960; An American Crisis, 1963; The Evolution of American Democracy, 1970; Conflict and Transformation 1844-1877, 1973; The Sources of History: the United States 1790-1890, 1975; contrib. New Cambridge Mod. History, Vols VII and XI; articles and reviews in Eng. Hist. Review, History, Jl Amer. Hist. etc. *Recreation:* antiques. *Address:* 50 Downside Road, Glasgow G12 9DW. *T:* 041-334 4718.

BROCKBANK, Maj.-Gen. John Myles, CBE 1972; MC 1943; Director, British Field Sports Society, since 1976; *b* 19 Sept. 1921; *s* of Col J. G. Brockbank, CBE, DSO, and Eireine Marguerite Robinson; *m* 1953, Gillian Findlay, three *s* one *d. Educ:* Eton Coll.; Oxford Univ. Commissioned into 12 Royal Lancers, 1941. Served War, North Africa, Italy, 1941-45. Served Germany: 1955-58, 1964-68 and 1970-72; Cyprus, 1959; USA, 1961-64; Staff Coll., 1950; IDC 1969; CO, 9/12 Royal Lancers; Comdr, RAC, HQ 1 Corps; Chief of Staff, 1 Corps; Dir, RAC, 1972-74; Vice-Adjutant General, MoD, 1974-76. *Recreations:* field sports, gardening, bird watching. *Address:* Manor House, Steeple Langford, Salisbury, Wilts. *T:* Stapleford 353. *Club:* Cavalry and Guards.

BROCKBANK, Russell Partridge; free-lance artist; *b* Niagara Falls, Canada, 15 April 1913; *s* of Clarence and Caroline

Brockbank; m 1933, Eileen Hames; one s one d. Educ: Ridley College, Ontario; Chelsea School of Art, London. Came to England, 1929, and studied Art; forsook Art for Industry, 1932; forsook Industry for Art, 1936; Free-lance until 1941. Served War of 1939-45, Lieut RNVR, Northern Convoys, British Pacific Fleet; demobilised, 1946. Free-lanced until 1949; Art Editor of Punch, 1949-60. Publications: Round the Bend, 1948; Up the Straight, 1953; Over the Line, 1955; The Brockbank Omnibus, 1957; Manifold Pressures, 1958; Move Over, 1963; The Penguin Brockbank, 1963; Motoring Through Punch, 1900-1970, 1970; Brockbank's Grand Prix, 1973; The Best of Brockbank, 1975. Recreations: motoring, sport. Address: Zephyrs, 14 Goulds Ground, Frome, Somerset. Club: Savage.

BROCKBANK, William, TD 1946; MA, MD Cambridge; FRCP; Consulting Physician, Royal Infirmary, Manchester, 1965-75, retired; Hon. Medical Archivist Manchester University, 1965-75, Hon. Archivist and Keeper, since 1975; b Manchester, 28 Jan. 1900; s of Edward Mansfield and Mary Ellwood Brockbank; unmarried. Educ: Bootham School, York; Caius College, Cambridge; Manchester University. Medical Officer, Manchester Grammar School, 1929-46; Physician, Manchester Royal Infirmary, 1932-65. Lecturer in Medicine, Manchester University, 1933-65; Dean of Clinical Studies, Manchester University, 1939-65. RAMC, Major, 1939-41; Lieut-Colonel, 1941-46. Director, Asthma Clinic, Manchester Royal Infirmary, 1946-65. Fitzpatrick Lecturer, Royal College of Physicians, 1950-51; Chairman Manchester University Medical Library Cttee, 1951-54; Member Council, Royal College of Physicians, 1955-58; President Manchester Medical Society, 1955-56; Vicary Lecturer, Royal College of Surgeons, 1956; Member Hinchliffe Cttee (Cost of Prescribing), 1957-59; Gideon de Laune Lectr, Soc. of Apothecaries, 1963. Dist Comr (now Hon.) Boy Scouts Assoc.; awarded Silver Acorn, 1950. Vice-President, Lancashire CC Club, 1967-. Hon. MSc Manchester, 1972. Publications: Portrait of a Hospital, 1952; Ancient Therapeutic Arts, 1954; The Honorary Medical Staff of the Manchester Royal Infirmary 1830-1948, 1965; The Diary of Richard Kay, 1716-51, 1968; The History of Nursing at the Manchester Royal Infirmary, 1752-1929, 1970; numerous papers to the Lancet, mostly on asthma, and to Medical History. Recreations: Medical History, archaeology; collecting cricket literature and water colours. Address: 51 Palatine Road, Manchester M20 9LJ. T: 061-445 3259. Club: National Liberal.

BROCKET, 3rd Baron, cr 1933; **Charles Ronald George Nall-Cain,** Bt 1921; b 12 Feb. 1952; s of Hon. Ronald Charles Manus Nall-Cain (d 1961), and of Elizabeth Mary (who m 2nd, 1964, Colin John Richard Trotter), d of R. J. Stallard; S grandfather, 1967. Educ: Eton. 2nd Lieut, 14/20 Hussars, 1971; Lieut, 1974. Heir: b Lieut Hon. Richard Philip Christopher Nall-Cain, Royal Green Jackets, b 5 April 1953. Address: Brocket Hall, Welwyn, Herts.

BROCKHOLES, Michael John F.; see Fitzherbert-Brockholes.

BROCKHOUSE, Dr Bertram Neville, FRS 1965; Professor of Physics, McMaster University, Canada, since 1962; b 15 July 1918; s of Israel Bertram Brockhouse and Mable Emily Brockhouse (née Neville); m 1948, Doris Isobel Mary (née Miller); four s two d. Educ: University of British Columbia (BA); University of Toronto (PhD). Served War of 1939-45 with Royal Canadian Navy. Lectr, University of Toronto, 1949-50; Research Officer, Atomic Energy of Canada Ltd, 1950-59; Branch Head, Neutron Physics Br., 1960-62. Hon. DSc Waterloo, 1969. Publications: some 75 papers in learned journals. Address: Department of Physics, McMaster University, Hamilton, Ontario, Canada L8S 4M1. T: (416) 648-6329.

BROCKHURST, Gerald L., RA 1937 (ARA 1928, now Hon. Retired Senior Member of Royal Academy); m 1947, Kathleen Nancy Woodward; no c. Painter, chiefly of portraits; exhibited at the Royal Academy, 1915-49; portrait of Bishop Fulton J. Sheen exhibited 1949. Has been living in the United States since 1939. Address: 239 Woodside Avenue, Franklin Lakes, NJ 07417, USA.

BROCKINGTON, Prof. Colin Fraser; Professor of Social and Preventive Medicine, Manchester University, 1951-64, Emeritus, 1964; b 8 Jan. 1903; s of late Sir William Brockington; m 1933, Dr Joyce Margaret Furze; three s one d. Educ: Oakham Sch.; Gonville and Caius Coll., Cambridge; Guy's Hosp., London. MD, MA, DPH, BChir Cantab, MSc Manchester, MRCS, MRCP; barrister-at-law, Middle Temple. Medical Superintendent, Brighton Infectious Diseases Hosp. and Sanatorium, 1929; Asst County Medical Officer, Worcs CC, 1930-33; general medical practice, Kingsbridge, Devon, 1933-

36; Medical Officer of Health, Horsham and Petworth, 1936-38; Dep. County Medical Officer of Health, Warwickshire CC, 1938-42; County Medical Officer of Health: Warwickshire CC, 1942-46; West Riding CC, 1946-51. Member: Central Adv. Council for Educn (Eng.), 1945-56; Central Training Council in Child Care (Home Office), 1947-53; Adv. Council for Welfare of Handicapped (Min. of Health), 1949-54; Nursing Cttee of Central Health Services Council (Min. of Health), 1949-51; Council of Soc. of Med. Officers of Health, 1944-66; Public Health Cttee of County Councils Assoc., 1945-49. Chairman: WHO Expert Cttee on School Health, 1950; Symposium on "Mental Health-Public Health Partnership," 5th Internat. Congress on Mental Health, Toronto, 1954; WHO Research Study Group on Juvenile Epilepsy, 1955; UK Cttee of WHO, 1958-61. Took part as Expert in Technical Discussions on Rural Health at World Health Assembly, 1954; Far Eastern Lecture Tour for British Council, 1956-57; visited India, 1959, 1962, S America 1960, Jordan 1966-67, Spain 1967, Arabia 1968, Turkey 1955, 1969, 1970, 1972, Greece 1970, for WHO. Lecture Tour: S Africa and Middle East, 1964. Publications: Principles of Nutrition, 1952; The People's Health, 1955; A Short History of Public Health, 1956 (2nd edn 1966); World Health, 1958 (3rd edn 1975); The Health of the Community, 1955, 1960, 1965; Public Health in the Nineteenth Century, 1965; The Social Needs of the Over-Eighties, 1966; wide range of contribs to learned jls. Recreations: bookbinding, travel. Address: Werneth, Silverburn, Ballasalla, Isle of Man. T: Castletown (Isle of Man) 3465.

BROCKLEBANK, Sir Aubrey (Thomas), 6th Bt cr 1885; Student Chartered Accountant; Director, Augill Castle Antiques Ltd; b 29 Jan. 1952; s of Sir John Montague Brocklebank, 5th Bt, TD, and of Pamela Sue, d of late William Harold Pierce, OBE; S father, 1974. Educ: Eton; University Coll., Durham (BSc Psychology). Heir: kinsman John Daniel Brocklebank [b 29 Sept. 1945; m 1971, Donna J., d of Major Clixby Fitzwilliams; one s]. Address: 27 Richford Street, W6.

BROCKLEBANK-FOWLER, Christopher, MP (C) Norfolk North West, since 1974 (King's Lynn, 1970-74); Director, Creative Consultants Ltd; b 13 Jan. 1934; 2nd s of Sidney Stratton Brocklebank Fowler, MA, LLB; m 1st, 1957, Joan Nowland (marr. diss. 1975); two s ; 2nd, 1975, Mrs Mary Berry. Educ: Perse Sch., Cambridge. Farm pupil on farms in Suffolk, Cambridgeshire and Norfolk, 1950-55. National service (submarines), Sub-Lt, RNVR, 1952-54. Farm Manager, Kenya, 1955-57; Lever Bros Ltd (Unilever Cos Management Trainee), 1957-59; advertising and marketing consultant with various advertising agencies, 1959-66. Mem. Bow Group, 1961- (Research Cttee, 1965-69; Council, 1965-70; Sec., 1966-68; Chm., 1968-69; Dir, Bow Publications, 1968-71). Mem. London Conciliation Cttee, 1966-67; Vice-Chm. Information Panel, Nat. Cttee for Commonwealth Immigrants, 1966-67; Mem. Exec. Cttee, Africa Bureau, 1970-74. Jt Sec., UN Parly Gp, 1971-; Chm., Conservative Parly Sub-Cttee on Horticulture, 1972-74; Vice-Chm., Cons. Parly Cttee on Agriculture, 1974-75; Mem., Select Cttee for Overseas Develt, 1973-; Jt Sec., Cons. Parly Foreign and Commonwealth Affairs Cttee, 1974-75, 1976-. Contested (C) West Ham (North), Gen. Elec., 1964. FRGS; MInstM; M CAM. Publications: pamphlets and articles on immigration, race relations, African affairs. Recreations: painting, shooting, swimming. Address: Long Cottage, Flitcham, near King's Lynn, Norfolk. T: Hillington 255. Club: Junior Carlton (Political Cttee, 1964-68; General Cttee, 1970-72).

BROCKLEHURST, Major-General Arthur Evers, CB 1956; DSO 1945; late RA; b 20 July 1905; m 1940, Joan Beryl Parry-Crooke; twin d. Educ: King's School, Canterbury; RMA Woolwich. 2nd Lieut, RA, 1925; CRA 6th Armoured Div., 1951; IDC 1954; DDPS (B) 1955; Chief of Staff, Malaya Comd, 1956-57; GOC, Rhine Dist., BAOR, 1958-59; Dep. Comdr BAOR, 1959-61; Retired 1961. Recreations: fishing, shooting, gardening. Address: Woodborough Manor, Pewsey, Wilts. Club: Army and Navy.

BROCKLEHURST, Sir John Ogilvy, 3rd Bt cr 1903; b 6 April 1926; s of Lt-Col Henry Courtney Brocklehurst (2nd s of 1st Bt) (killed in action, 1942) and Lady Helen Alice Willington, d of 11th Earl of Airlie; S uncle, 1975.

BROCKLEHURST, Mrs Mary D.; see Dent-Brocklehurst.

BROCKLEHURST, Robert James, DM; Emeritus Professor of Physiology, University of Bristol, since 1965; b Liverpool, 16 Sept. 1899; e s of George and Sarah Huger Brocklehurst, Liverpool; m 1st, 1928, Sybille (d 1968), y d of Captain R. H. L. Risk, CBE, RN; two s one d; 2nd, 1970, Dora Millicent, y d of late Alexander Watts. *Educ:* Harrow Sch.; University College, Oxford (Scholar; 1st Class Honours in Physiology); St Bartholomew's Hospital. BA 1921; MA, BM, BCh, 1924; DM, 1928; MRCS, LRCP, 1925; Demonstrator of Physiology, St Bartholomew's Hosp. Medical Coll., 1925-26; Radcliffe Travelling Fellow, 1926-28; Lecturer, 1928-29, and Senior Lecturer, 1929-30, in Dept of Physiology and Biochemistry, Univ. Coll., London; Prof. of Physiology, 1930-65, and Dean of Med. Fac., 1934-47, Univ. of Bristol, and Univ. Rep. on GMC, 1935-65 (Jt Treas., 1962-65); Long Fox Meml Lectr, 1952; Mem. Inter-departmental Cttee on Dentistry, 1943; Mem. Dental Bd of UK, 1945-56; Additional Mem., GDC, 1956-65; Pres., Bath, Bristol and Somerset Branch, BMA 1959-60; Fellow BMA, 1967; Pres. Bristol Medico-Chirurgical Society, 1960-61; Member Council, 1958-63, and President Sect. I (Physiology), 1950, British Association; Mem., S-W Regional Hosp. Bd, and Bd of Govs of United Bristol Hosps, 1947-66; Chm, Moorhaven Hosp. Management Cttee, 1966-71; a representative of Diocese of Bristol in the Church Assembly, 1945-65; Member, Central Board of Finance, 1957-65; Chm., Bristol Diocesan Bd of Finance, 1951-65. Mem., Council Westonbirt School, 1955-75 (Chm., 1956-68); Member Council, Christ Church College, Canterbury, 1961-73; Churchwarden, Stoke Bishop, 1939-60; a Vice-President Gloucester and Bristol Diocesan Association of Church Bell Ringers. Chm., Glos, Somerset and N Devon Regional Group, YHA, 1934-45. Served in Tank Corps, 1918-19. *Publications:* Papers on physiological, biochemical and educational subjects in medical and scientific jls. *Recreation:* gardening. *Address:* Cleeve, Court Road, Newton Ferrers, Plymouth, Devon PL8 1DE. *T:* Plymouth 872397. *Clubs:* Alpine, Royal Commonwealth Society, Royal Over-Seas League.

BROCKMAN, Vice-Admiral Sir Ronald, KCB 1965; CSI 1947; CIE 1946; CBE 1943; DL; Gentleman Usher to the Queen; Comptroller to the Governor of the Isle of Wight; *b* 8 March 1909; *er s* of late Rear-Adm. H. S. Brockman, CB; *m* 1932, Marjorie Jean Butt; one *s* three *d*. *Educ:* Weymouth Coll., Dorset. Entered Navy, 1927; Assistant Secretary to First Sea Lord, Admiral of the Fleet Sir Roger Backhouse, 1938-39; Lieut-Commander 1939; Admiral's Secretary to First Sea Lord, Admiral of the Fleet Sir Dudley Pound, 1939-43; Commander 1943; Admiral's Secretary to Admiral of the Fleet Lord Mountbatten in all appointments, 1943-59; Private Secretary to Governor-General of India, 1947-48. Principal Staff Officer to the Chief of Defence Staff, Min. of Defence, 1959-65. Captain, 1953; Rear-Admiral, 1959; Vice-Admiral, 1963; retired list, 1965. Mem., Rugby Football Union Cttee. County Pres., St John Ambulance, Devon; Chm., Dartmoor Nat. Park Cttee; Mem., Devon and Exeter Steeplechases Exec. Cttee; Mem. Exec. Council and Senior Steward, Devon County Show. Governor, Royal Western Sch. for Deaf, Exeter. County Councillor, Devon; DL Devon. OStJ. Special Rosette of Cloud and Banner (China), 1946; Chevalier Legion of Honour and Croix de Guerre, 1946; Bronze Star Medal (USA), 1947. *Address:* 3 Court House, Basil Street, SW3. *T:* 01-584 1023; The Chance, Coastguard Road, Budleigh Salterton, Devon. *T:* Budleigh Salterton 2687. *Clubs:* Army and Navy, White's; MCC; Royal Western Yacht Club of England; Liverpool Racquet.

BROCKWAY, family name of **Baron Brockway.**

BROCKWAY, Baron *cr* 1964 (Life Peer); **Archibald Fenner Brockway;** *b* Calcutta, 1888; *s* of Rev. W. G. Brockway and Frances Elizabeth Abbey; *m* 1914, Lilla, *d* of Rev. W. Harvey-Smith; four *d*; *m* 1946, Edith Violet, *d* of Archibald Herbert King; one *s*. *Educ:* Sch. for the Sons of Missionaries (now Eltham Coll.). Joined staff Examiner, 1907; sub-editor Christian Commonwealth, 1909; Labour Leader, 1911; editor, 1912-17; secretary No Conscription Fellowship, 1917; sentenced to one month's imprisonment under DORA Aug. 1916, and to three months, six months, and two years hard labour under Military Service Act, Dec. 1916, Feb. 1917, and July 1917; Joint Secretary British Committee of Indian National Congress and editor India, 1919; Joint Secretary Prison System Enquiry Cttee, 1920; Organising Secretary ILP 1922; General Secretary ILP, 1928 and 1933-39; Editor of New Leader, 1926-29, and 1931-46; Labour candidate Lancaster, 1922; Chairman No More War Movement and War Resister's International, 1923-28; Labour candidate Westminster 1924; Exec. Labour and Socialist International, 1926-31; Fraternal Delegate Indian Trade Union Congress and Indian National Congress, 1927; MP (Lab) East Leyton, 1929-31; Chairman ILP, 1931-33; took part in last public Socialist campaign against Hitler in Germany, 1932; Political Secretary ILP, 1939-46; Chairman British Centre for Colonial Freedom, 1942-47; ILP candidate, Upton Division of West Ham, 1934, Norwich, 1935, Lancaster, 1941, and Cardiff East, 1942; ILP Fraternal Delegate Hamburg Trade Union May

Day Demonstrations and German Social Democratic Party Conference, Hanover, 1946. Resigned from ILP, 1946, and rejoined Labour Party; MP (Lab) Eton and Slough, 1950-64. Member Internat. Cttee of Socialist Movement for United Europe, 1947-52; first Chairman of Congress of Peoples against Imperialism, 1948-; Fraternal Delegate, Tunisian Trade Union Conf., 1951; Mem. unofficial Fact-finding mission, Kenya, 1952; Chairman: Liberation (formerly Movement for Colonial Freedom), 1954-67 (President, 1967-); British Asian and Overseas Socialist Fellowship, 1959-66; Peace in Nigeria Cttee, 1967-70; Peace Mission to Biafra and Nigeria, 1968; Brit. Council for Peace in Vietnam, 1965-69; Pres., British Campaign for Peace in Vietnam, 1970-. *Publications:* Labour and Liberalism, 1913; The Devil's Business, 1915 (proscribed during the war); Socialism and Pacifism, 1917; The Recruit, 1919; Non-Co-operation, 1919; The Government of India, 1920; English Prisons To-day (with Stephen Hobhouse), 1921; A Week in India, 1928; A New Way with Crime, 1928; The Indian Crisis, 1930; Hungry England, 1932; The Bloody Traffic, 1933; Will Roosevelt Succeed?, 1934; Purple Plague (a novel), 1935; Workers' Front, 1938; Inside the Left: a Political Autobiography, 1942; Death pays a Dividend (with Frederic Mullally), 1944; German Diary, 1946; Socialism Over Sixty Years; The Life of Jowett of Bradford, 1946; Bermondsey Story: Life of Alfred Salter, 1949; Why Mau Mau?, 1953; African Journeys, 1955; 1960-Africa's Year of Destiny, 1960; Red Liner (novel in dialogue), 1961; Outside the Right, 1963; African Socialism, 1964; Commonwealth Immigrants: What is the Answer? (with Norman Pannell), 1965; Woman Against the Desert (with Miss Campbell-Purdie) 1967; This Shrinking Explosive World, 1968; The Next Step to Peace, 1970; The Colonial Revolution, 1973; Towards Tomorrow (autobiog.), 1977; numerous ILP and Movement for Colonial Freedom pamphlets. *Address:* 67 Southway, N20 8DE. *T:* 01-445 3054.

BRODIE, Sir Benjamin David Ross, 5th Bt *cr* 1834; *b* 29 May 1925; *s* of Sir Benjamin Collins Brodie, 4th Bt, MC, and Mary Charlotte (*d* 1940), *e d* of R. E. Palmer, Ballyheigue, Co. Kerry; *S* father, 1971. *Educ:* Eton. Formerly Royal Corps of Signals. *Heir: b* Colin Alexander Brodie [*b* 19 April 1929; *m* 1955, Julia Anne Irene, *yr d* of Norman Edward Wates; two *s*].

BRODIE, Rabbi Sir Israel, KBE 1969; BA, BLitt, Hon. DD; Hon. DCL; Chief Rabbi of the United Hebrew Congregations of the British Commonwealth of Nations, 1948-65, now Emeritus Chief Rabbi; *b* 10 May 1895; *s* of Aaron Brodie, Newcastle upon Tyne; *m* 1946, F. Levine. *Educ:* Rutherford Coll., Newcastle upon Tyne; Jews' Coll., London; Univ. Coll., London; Balliol Coll., Oxford. CF, 1917-19; Social Service, East End, London, 1921-23; Rabbi, Melbourne, Australia, 1923-37; Lecturer and Tutor, Jews' Coll., 1939-48; Pres., Jews' Coll.; CF, Army and RAF, 1940-44; Senior Jewish Chaplain, 1944-48; Fellow, University College, London; Hon. officer of several public bodies. *Publications:* A Word in Season, 1958; (ed) The Etz Hayyim by Rabbi Jacob ben Jehuda Hazan of London, Vols 1, 2, 3, 1962, 1964, and 1967. *Address:* Flat R, 82 Portland Place, W1N 3DH.

BRODIE of Brodie, (Montagu) Ninian (Alexander), DL; JP; landowner since 1953; *b* 12 June 1912; *s* of late I. A. M. Brodie of Brodie and late C. V. M. Brodie of Brodie (*née* Hope); *m* 1939, Helena Penelope Mills Budgen; one *s* one *d*. *Educ:* Eton. Stage, films, TV, 1933-40 and 1945-49. Served Royal Artillery, 1940-45. JP Morayshire, 1958; Hon. Sheriff-Substitute, 1958; DL Nairn, 1970. *Recreations:* shooting, collecting pictures. *Heir: s* Alastair Ian Ninian Brodie, Younger of Brodie [*b* 7 Sept. 1943; *m* 1968, Mary Louise Johnson; two *s* one *d*]. *Address:* Brodie Castle, Forres, Moray IV36 0TE, Scotland. *T:* Brodie 202.

BRODIE, Peter Ewen, OBE 1954; QPM 1963; an Assistant Commissioner, Metropolitan Police, 1966-72; *b* 6 May 1914; 2nd *s* of late Captain E. J. Brodie, Lethen, Nairn; *m* 1st, 1940, Betty Eve Middlebrook Horsfall (*d* 1975); one *s*; 2nd, 1976, Millicent Joyce Mellor. *Educ:* Harrow School. Metropolitan Police, 1934-49 (Seconded to Ceylon Police, 1943-47); Chief Constable, Stirling and Clackmannan Police force, 1949-58; Chief Constable, Warwicks Constabulary, 1958-64; HM Inspector of Constabulary for England and Wales, 1964-66. Member: Adv. Cttee on Drug Dependence, 1967-70; Exec. Cttee, Internat. Criminal Police Organisation-Interpol, 1967-70. OStJ 1960. *Address:* The Old Vicarage, Lower Shuckburgh, Daventry, Northants NN11 6DX. *T:* Daventry 71590.

BRODIE, Stanley Eric, QC 1975; a Recorder of the Crown Court, since 1975; *b* 2 July 1930; *s* of Abraham Brodie, MB, BS and Cissie Rachel Brodie; *m* 1956, Gillian Rosemary Joseph; two *d*; *m* 1973, Elizabeth Gloster. *Educ:* Bradford Grammar Sch.; Balliol Coll., Oxford (MA). Pres., Oxford Univ. Law Soc.,

1952. Called to Bar, Inner Temple, 1954; Mem. NE Circuit, 1954; Lectr in Law, Univ. of Southampton, 1954-55. *Recreations:* opera, boating, winter sports. *Address:* 21 Campden Hill Square, W8 7JY. *T:* 01-727 3241. *Club:* United Oxford & Cambridge University.

BRODIE, Maj.-Gen. Thomas, CB 1954; CBE 1949; DSO 1951; late The Cheshire Regt; *b* 20 Oct. 1903; *s* of Thomas Brodie, Bellingham, Northumberland; *m* 1938, Jane Margaret Chapman-Walker; three *s* one *d*. Commanded: 2 Manchester Regt, 1942-43; 14th Infantry Brigade in Wingate Expedition, 1944; 1 Cheshire Regt, 1946-47; Palestine, 1947-48 (CBE and despatches); commanded 29 Inf. Bde, Korea, 1951 (DSO, US Silver Star Medal, US Legion of Merit); GOC 1 Infantry Div., MELF, 1952-55; Colonel The Cheshire Regiment 1955-61; retired 1957. *Address:* Chapmore End House, Chapmore End, Ware, Herts. *Club:* Army and Navy.

BRODNEY, Spencer; Writer; *b* Melbourne, Australia, 29 Aug. 1883; *m* 1918, Edith Siebel, New York; two *s*. *Educ:* Scotch College, Melbourne; Universities of Melbourne and London. Has been on staffs of, or written for, Australian, English, and American Newspapers and magazines; editor, Current History, 1931-36 and 1941-43; editor Events, 1937-41; author of a play produced in London in 1912, and Rebel Smith (a play for the Australian theatre), 1925. *Address:* 298 Emerson Lane, Berkeley Heights, New Jersey 07922, USA.

BRODRICK, family name of Earl of Midleton.

BRODRICK, Norman John Lee, QC 1960; JP; MA; **His Honour Judge Brodrick**; a Circuit Judge (formerly a Judge of the Central Criminal Court), since 1967; *b* 4 Feb. 1912; 4th *s* of late William John Henry Brodrick, OBE; *m* 1940, Ruth Severn, *d* of late Sir Stanley Unwin, KCMG; three *s* one *d*. *Educ:* Charterhouse; Merton College, Oxford. Called to Bar, Lincoln's Inn, 1935, Bencher, 1965; Mem. Senate of Four Inns of Court, 1970-71. Western Circuit, 1935. Temporary civil servant (Ministry of Economic Warfare and Admiralty), 1939-45. Bar Council, 1950-54 and 1962-66. Recorder: of Penzance, 1957-59; of Bridgwater, 1959-62; of Plymouth, 1962-64. Chairman, Mental Health Review Tribunal, Wessex Region, 1960-63; Deputy Chairman, Middlesex Quarter Sessions, 1961-65; Recorder of Portsmouth, 1964-67; Chm., IoW QS, 1964-67, Dep. Chm. 1967-71. Chm., Deptl Cttee on Death Certification and Coroners, 1965-71. JP Hants, 1967. *Recreations:* gardening, model railways. *Address:* 19 Old Buildings, Lincoln's Inn, WC2. *T:* 01-405 2980; Packhurst Farm House, Clanfield, near Portsmouth, Hants PO8 0RR. *T:* Horndean 593150. *Club:* Hampshire (Winchester).

BROGAN, Lt-Gen. Sir Mervyn (Francis), KBE 1972 (CBE 1964; OBE 1944); CB 1970; Chief of the General Staff, Australia, 1971-73, retired; Chairman, Australian Services Council; *b* 10 Jan. 1915; *s* of Bernard Brogan, Dubbo, NSW; *m* 1941, Sheila, *d* of David S. Jones, Canberra; two *s*. *Educ:* RMC Duntroon; Wesley Coll., Univ. of Sydney. Commnd 1935; BEng Sydney, 1938. Served War of 1939-45: New Guinea, 1942-45 (despatches 1943); trng UK and BAOR, 1946-47; Chief Instructor, Sch. of Mil. Engrg, 1947-49; trng UK and USA, 1950-52; jssc 1952; Chief Engr, Southern Comd, 1953-54; Dir of Mil. Trng, 1954-55; BGS: Army HQ, 1956; FARELF, 1956-58; idc 1959; Comdt Australian Staff Coll., 1960-62; GOC Northern Comd, 1962-64; Dir Jt Service Plans, Dept of Defence, 1965-66; QMG 1966-68; GOC Eastern Comd, 1968-71. Col Comdt, Royal Australian Engineers; Hon. Col, Univ. of NSW Regt. Director: Simon Engineering (Aust.) Pty Ltd; Swift & Co. Ltd; Shield Life Assurance Ltd; Consultant, J. B. Meling and Co. (Australasia) Pty Ltd. Hon. FIEAust; FAIM; MACE. JP. *Recreations:* surfing, tennis. *Address:* 71/53 Ocean Avenue, Double Bay, NSW 2028, Australia. *T:* 32-9509. *Clubs:* Imperial Service, Union, Royal Sydney Golf (Sydney).

BROINOWSKI, John Herbert, CMG 1969; Chairman, and Chief Executive since 1976, Sims Consolidated Ltd; Chairman: Aquila Steel Ltd; Hoyts Theatres Ltd; Formfit Australia Ltd; Deputy Chairman, Schroder Darling Holdings Ltd; *b* 19 May 1911; *s* of late Dr G. H. Broinowski and late Mrs Ethel Broinowski (*née* Hungerford); *m* 1939, Jean Gaerloch Broinowski (*née* Kater); one *s* one step *s*. *Educ:* Sydney Church of England Grammar Sch. Served Australian Imperial Forces (Captain), 1940-44, New Guinea. J. H. Broinowski and Storey, Chartered Accountants, 1944-54; Founder and Managing Dir, Consolidated Metal Products Ltd, 1954-62; Chief Exec., Darling & Co., 1963-73. Dir, Peko-Wallsend Ltd. President: Aust. Council for Rehabilitation of the Disabled, 1964-68; NSW Soc. for Crippled Children, 1970-77; Vice-Pres., Internat. Soc. for Rehabilitation of the Disabled, 1966-72. *Recreation:* cattle breeding. *Address:* 1c Wentworth Place, Point Piper, Sydney,

NSW 2027, Australia. *T:* 362057. *Clubs:* Union, Australian, Royal Sydney Golf (all in Sydney).

BROKE; see Willoughby de Broke.

BROKE, Major George Robin Straton, RA; Equerry-in-Waiting to the Queen, since 1974; *b* 31 March 1946; *s* of Maj.-Gen. R. S. Broke, *qv*. *Educ:* Eton. Commissioned into Royal Artillery, 1965. *Recreation:* country sports. *Address:* Holme Hale Hall, Thetford, Norfolk. *T:* Holme Hale 225. *Clubs:* Army and Navy, MCC.

BROKE, Maj.-Gen. Robert Straton, CB 1967; OBE 1946; MC 1940; Director, Wellman Engineering Corporation, since 1968, and Chairman of eight companies within the Corporation; *b* 15 March 1913; *s* of Rev. Horatio George Broke and Mary Campbell Broke (*née* Adlington); *m* 1939, Ernine Susan Margaret Bonsey; two *s*. *Educ:* Eton College; Magdalene College, Cambridge (BA). Commissioned Royal Artillery, 1933. Commander Royal Artillery: 5th Division, 1959; 1st Division, 1960; 1st (British) Corps 1961; Northern Army Group, 1964-66, retired. Col Comdt, RA, 1968-; Representative Col Comdt, 1974-75. Chm., Iron and Steel Plant Contractors Assoc., 1972, 1977. Pres., Metallurgical Plantmakers' Fedn, 1977. *Recreations:* country sports. *Address:* Holme Hale Hall, Thetford, Norfolk. *T:* Holme Hale 225. *Clubs:* Army and Navy, MCC.

See also G . R . S . Broke .

BROME, Vincent; author; *s* of Nathaniel Gregory and Emily Brome. *Educ:* Streatham Grammar School; Elleston School; privately. Formerly: Feature Writer, Daily Chronicle; Editor, Menu Magazines; Min. of Information; Asst Editor, Medical World. Since then author biographies, novels, plays and essays; broadcaster. Mem., British Library Adv. Cttee, 1975-. *Plays:* The Sleepless One (prod. Edin), 1962; BBC plays. *Publications:* Anthology, 1936; Clement Attlee, 1947; H. G. Wells, 1951; Aneurin Bevan, 1953; The Last Surrender, 1954; The Way Back, 1956; Six Studies in Quarrelling, 1958; Sometimes at Night, 1959; Frank Harris, 1959; Acquaintance With Grief, 1961; We Have Come a Long Way, 1962; The Problem of Progress, 1963; Love in Our Time, 1964; Four Realist Novelists, 1964; The International Brigades, 1965; The World of Luke Jympson, 1966; Freud and His Early Circle, 1967; The Surgeon, 1967; Diary of A Revolution, 1968; The Revolution, 1969; The Imaginary Crime, 1969; Confessions of a Writer, 1970; The Brain Operators, 1970; Private Prosecutions, 1971; Reverse Your Verdict, 1971; London Consequences, 1972; The Embassy, 1972; The Day of Destruction, 1975; The Happy Hostage, 1976; contrib. The Times, Sunday Times, Observer, Manchester Guardian, New Statesman, New Society, Encounter, Spectator, TLS etc. *Recreations:* writing plays and talking. *Address:* 45 Great Ormond Street, WC1. *T:* 01-405 0550. *Club:* Savile.

BROMET, Air Vice-Marshal Sir Geoffrey R., KBE 1945 (CBE 1941; OBE 1919); CB 1943; DSO 1917; DL; *b* 28 Aug. 1891; *e s* of late G. A. Bromet, Tadcaster; *m* 1917, Margaret (*d* 1961), *e d* of late Maj. Ratliffe, Hardingstone, Northampton; one *d*; *m* 1965, Jean Conan Doyle (*see* Air Commandant Dame Jean Bromet). *Educ:* Bradfield; Royal Naval Colls, Osborne and Dartmouth. Royal Navy, 1904-14; RNAS, 1914-18; RAF, 1918-38; retired list, 1938; re-employed Sept. 1939; SASO HQ Coastal Command, 1940-41; AOC 19 Group Plymouth, 1941-43; Senior British Officer Azores Force, 1943-45; reverted to retired list, Oct. 1945; Lieutenant-Governor, Isle of Man, 1945-52; a Life Vice-President: Royal Air Force Association; RNLI. DL Kent, 1958. *Address:* Home Green, Littlestone-on-Sea, Kent; 72 Cadogan Square, SW1. *Club:* Royal Air Force.

BROMET, Air Comdt Dame Jean (Lena Annette), (Lady Bromet); see Conan Doyle, Air Comdt Dame J. L. A.

BROMHEAD, Sir Benjamin (Denis Gonville), 5th Bt, *cr* 1806; OBE 1943; Lieut-Col (Retd) Frontier Force Regt (Indian Army); *b* 7 May 1900; *s* of late E. G. Bromhead (*er s* of 4th Bt); *S* grandfather, Colonel Sir Benjamin Parnell Bromhead, 4th Bt, CB, 1935; *m* 1938, Nancy Mary, *o d* of late T. S. Lough, Buenos Aires; one *s* two *d*. *Educ:* Wellington College; RMC Sandhurst. Entered Indian Army, 1919; Iraq, 1920 (medal with clasp); Waziristan, 1922-24 (Wounded, medal with clasp); NW Frontier of India, 1930 (despatches, medal with clasp); Waziristan, 1937 (despatches); Political Agent, N Waziristan, NW Frontier Province, 1945-47; retd, 1949. *Heir:* *s* John Desmond Gonville Bromhead [*b* 21 Dec. 1943. *Educ:* Wellington and privately]. *Address:* Thurlby Hall, Aubourn, Lincoln. *Club:* Naval and Military.

BROMLEY, Archdeacon of; *see* Cragg, Ven. H. W.

BROMLEY, Lance Lee, MA; MChir; FRCS; Consultant Thoracic Surgeon, St Mary's Hospital, W2 and W9; Consulting Surgeon, Teddington Hospital; *b* 16 Feb. 1920; *s* of late Lancelot Bromley, MChir FRCS, of London and Seaford, Sussex, and Dora Ridgway Bromley, Dewsbury, Yorks; *m* 1952, Rosemary Anne Holbrook; three *d. Educ:* St Paul's School; Caius Coll., Cambridge. Late Capt. RAMC. Late Travelling Fell. Amer. Assoc. for Thoracic Surgery. Vis. Thoracic Surgeon, St Bernard's Hosp., Gibraltar. *Publications:* various contributions to medical journals. *Recreations:* sailing, golf. *Address:* 2 Hyde Park Crescent, W2. *T:* 01-262 7175. *Club:* Royal Ocean Racing.

BROMLEY, Leonard John, QC 1971; Barrister-at-Law; *b* 21 Feb. 1929; 2nd *s* of George Ernest and Winifred Dora Bromley; *m* 1962, Anne (*née* Bacon); three *d. Educ:* City of Leicester Boys' Sch.; Selwyn Coll., Cambridge (exhibnr). MA, LLB (Cantab). National Service: 2nd Lt, RA, Hong Kong, 1947-49. Selwyn Coll., Cambridge, 1949-53; called to Bar, Lincoln's Inn, 1954; Greenland Scholar, Lincoln's Inn. In practice, Chancery Bar, 1954-. Gen. Council of the Bar: Mem., 1970-74; Chm., Law Reform Cttee, 1972-74; Mem., Exec. Cttee, 1972-74. Vice Cdre, Bar Yacht Club, 1971-75. *Recreations:* sailing, walking. *Address:* (home) 106 Queen Elizabeth's Drive, Southgate, N14. *T:* 01-886 6113; (professional) 7 Stone Buildings, Lincoln's Inn, WC2. *T:* 01-405 3886. *Club:* United Oxford & Cambridge University.

BROMLEY, Sir Rupert Charles, 10th Bt, *cr* 1757; *b* 2 April 1936; *s* of Major Sir Rupert Howe Bromley, MC, 9th Bt, and Dorothy Vera, *d* of late Sir Walford Selby, KCMG, CB, CVO; *S* father, 1966; *m* 1962, Priscilla Hazel, *d* of late Maj. Howard Bourne, HAC; three *s. Educ:* Michaelhouse, Natal; Rhodes Univ.; Christ Church, Oxford. *Recreations:* equestrian. *Heir: s* Charles Howard Bromley, *b* 31 July 1963. *Address:* Brendon House, Selwyn Road, Kenilworth, CP, South Africa.

BROMLEY, Sir Thomas Eardley, KCMG 1964 (CMG 1955); HM Diplomatic Service, retired; Secretary, Churches Main Committee, Dec. 1970-72; *b* 14 Dec. 1911; *s* of late Thomas Edward Bromley, ICS; *m* 1944, Diana Marion, *d* of Sir John Pratt, KBE, CMG; *m* 1966, Mrs Alison Toulmin. *Educ:* Rugby; Magdalen College, Oxford. Entered Consular Service, 1935; Vice-Consul, Japan, 1938; Asst Private Sec. to the Permanent Under-Secretary of State, 1943, and Private Secretary, 1945; Grade 7, 1945; served in Washington, 1946; Bagdad, 1949; Counsellor, 1953; Head of African Department, Foreign Office, March 1954-Jan. 1956; Imperial Defence College, 1956; Foreign Office Inspectorate, 1957; seconded to Cabinet Office, Oct. 1957; Consul-General at Mogadishu, 1960; Ambassador: to Somali Republic, 1960-61; to Syrian Arab Republic, 1962-64; to Algeria, 1964-65; FO, 1966; Ambassador to Ethiopia, 1966-69. *Address:* Pusey Furze, Buckland, near Faringdon, Oxon.

BROMLEY-DAVENPORT, Lt-Col Sir Walter Henry, Kt 1961; TD; DL; *b* 1903; *s* of late Walter A. Bromley-Davenport, Capesthorne, Macclesfield, Cheshire, and late Lilian Emily Isabel Jane, DBE 1954, JP, *d* of Lt-Col J. H. B. Lane; *m* 1933, Lenette F., *d* of Joseph Y. Jeanes, Philadelphia, USA; one *s* one *d. Educ:* Malvern. Joined Grenadier Guards, 1922; raised and comd 5 Bn Cheshire Regt, Lt-Col 1939. MP (C) Knutsford Div. 1945-70; Conservative Whip, 1948-51. DL Cheshire, 1949. British Boxing Board of Control, 1953. *Address:* 39 Westminster Gardens, Marsham Street, SW1. *T:* 01-834 2929; Capesthorne Hall, Macclesfield, Cheshire. *T:* Chelford 221; Fiva, Aandalsnes, Norway. *Clubs:* White's, Cavalry and Guards, Carlton, Pratt's.

BROMMELLE, Norman Spencer; Keeper, Department of Conservation, Victoria and Albert Museum, since 1960; *b* 9 June 1915; *s* of James Valentine Brommelle and Ada Louisa Brommelle (*née* Bastin); *m* 1959, Rosa Joyce Plesters. *Educ:* High Pavement School, Nottingham; University College, Oxford. Scientific research in industry on Metallography and Spectroscopy, 1937-48; Picture Conservation, National Gallery, 1949-60. Secretary-General, International Institute for Conservation of Historic and Artistic Works, 1957-64, 1966- (Vice-President, 1964-66). Governor, Central Sch. of Art and Design, 1971-. *Publications:* contributions to: Journal of the Institute of Metals; Studies in Conservation; Museums Journal. *Recreation:* gardening. *Address:* 5 Lyndhurst Square, SE15. *T:* 01-701 0607.

BROOK, Caspar; Director, David Owen Centre for Population Growth Studies, University College Cardiff, since 1974; *b* 24 Aug. 1920; *m* 1948, Dinah Fine; one *s* one *d. Educ:* UCW, Cardiff. Royal Tank Regt, Glider Pilot Regt, 1940-46. British Export Trade Research Organisation, 1947; Machine Tool and Electrical Engrs, 1947-53; Publications Ed., Economist Intelligence Unit Ltd, 1953-58; Dir, Consumers' Assoc., 1958-64; Man. Dir, Equipment Comparison Ltd, 1964-67; Dir, Industrial Training and Publishing Div., Pergamon Press, 1966-67; Dir, Family Planning Assoc., 1968-74. Mem., Welsh Consumer Council, 1975-. Hon. Treasurer, Adv. Centre for Educn, Cambridge. *Recreations:* talking, sailing. *Address:* 19 Penylan Road, Cardiff. *T:* Cardiff 373751. *Club:* Reform.

BROOK, Prof. George Leslie, MA, PhD; Professor of English Language 1945-77, and of Medieval English Literature, 1951-77, University of Manchester; Dean of the Faculty of Arts, 1956-57; Pro-Vice-Chancellor, 1962-65; Presenter of Honorary Graduands, 1964-65; *b* 6 March 1910; 3rd *s* of late Willie Brook, Shepley, Huddersfield; *m* 1949, Stella, *d* of Thomas Maguire, Salford. *Educ:* University of Leeds; Ripon English Literature Prize, 1931. Visiting Professor, University of California, Los Angeles, 1951. *Publications:* An English Phonetic Reader, 1935; English Sound-Changes, 1935; Glossary to the Works of Sir Thomas Malory, 1947; An Introduction to Old English, 1955; A History of the English Language, 1958; English Dialects, 1963; The Modern University, 1965; The Language of Dickens, 1970; Varieties of English, 1973; The Language of Shakespeare, 1976; edited: The Harley Lyrics, 1948; The Journal of the Lancashire Dialect Society, 1951-54; (with R. F. Leslie) Layamon's Brut, Vol. I, 1963; (with C. S. Lewis) Selections from Layamon's Brut, 1963. *Address:* 8 Priory Lane, Kents Bank, Grange-Over-Sands, Cumbria LA11 7BH.

BROOK, Gerald Robert; Chief Executive, National Bus Company, since 1977; *b* 19 Dec. 1928; *s* of Charles Pollard Brook and Doris Brook (*née* Senior); *m* 1957, Joan Marjorie Oldfield; two *s* one *d. Educ:* King James Grammar Sch., Knaresborough. FCIS, FCIT. Served Duke of Wellington's Regt, 1947-49. Appointments in bus companies, from 1950; Company Secretary: Cumberland Motor Services Ltd, 1960; Thames Valley Traction Co. Ltd, 1963; General Manager: North Western Road Car Co. Ltd, 1968; Midland Red Omnibus Co. Ltd, 1972; Regional Director, National Bus Company, 1974. *Publications:* papers for professional instns and learned socs. *Recreation:* reading military history. *Address:* Hallow Cottage, Crimple Lane, Crimple, near Harrogate, Yorks. *T:* Harrogate 885548.

BROOK, Helen, (Lady Brook); Founder, 1963, and President, Brook Advisory Centre for Young People (Chairman, 1964-74); *b* 12 Oct. 1907; *d* of John and Helen Knewstub; *m* 1937, Sir Ralph Ellis Brook, *qv*; two *d* (and one *d* of previous marriage). *Educ:* Convent of Holy Child Jesus, Mark Cross, Sussex. Voluntary Worker, Family Planning Association, 1949-. *Recreations:* painting, gardening. *Address:* 31 Acacia Road, NW8 6AS. *T:* 01-722 5844; Claydene Garden Cottage, Cowden, Kent.

BROOK, Leopold, BScEng, FICE, FIMechE; Chairman, Simon Engineering Ltd, 1970-77 (Deputy Chairman and Chief Executive 1967-70); *b* 2 Jan. 1912; *s* of Albert and Kate Brook, Hampstead; *m* 1st, 1940, Susan (*d* 1970), *d* of David Rose, Hampstead; two *s*; 2nd, 1974, Mrs Elly Rhodes; two step *s* one step *d. Educ:* Central Foundation School, London; University College, London. L. G. Mouchel & Partners, Cons. Engineers, 1935-44; Simon Engineering Ltd, 1944-77. Fellow, UCL, 1970-. *Recreations:* music, theatre, golf. *Address:* 55 Kingston House North, Prince's Gate, SW7 1LW. *T:* 01-584 2041. *Clubs:* Royal Automobile, Hurlingham.

BROOK, Peter Stephen Paul, CBE 1965; Producer; Co-Director, The Royal Shakespeare Theatre; *b* 21 March 1925; 2nd *s* of Simon Brook; *m* 1951, Natasha Parry, stage and film star; one *s* one *d. Educ:* Westminster, Greshams and Magdalen College, Oxford. Productions include: The Tragedy of Dr Faustus, 1942; The Infernal Machine, 1945; Birmingham Repertory Theatre: Man and Superman, King John, The Lady from the Sea, 1945-46; Stratford: Romeo and Juliet, Love's Labour's Lost, 1947; London: Vicious Circle, Men Without Shadows, Respectable Prostitute, The Brothers Karamazov, 1946; Director of Productions, Royal Opera House, Covent Garden, 1947-50: Boris Godunov, La Bohème, 1948; Marriage of Figaro, The Olympians, Salome, 1949. Dark of the Moon, 1949; Ring Round the Moon, 1950; Measure for Measure, Stratford, 1950; The Little Hut, 1950; The Winter's Tale, 1951; Venice Preserved, 1953; The Little Hut, New York, Faust, Metropolitan Opera House, 1953; The Dark is Light Enough; Both Ends Meet, 1954; House of Flowers, New York, 1954; The Lark, 1955; Titus Andronicus, Stratford, 1955; Hamlet, 1955; The Power and the Glory, 1956; Family Reunion, 1956; The Tempest, Stratford, 1957; Cat on a Hot Tin Roof, Paris, 1957; View from the Bridge, Paris, 1958; Irma la Douce, London, 1958; The Fighting Cock,

New York, 1959; Le Balcon, Paris, 1960; The Visit, Royalty, 1960; King Lear, Stratford and Aldwych, 1962; The Physicists, Aldwych, 1963; Sergeant Musgrave's Dance, Paris, 1963; The Persecution and Assassination of Marat..., Aldwych, 1964 (New York, 1966); The Investigation, Aldwych, 1965; US, Aldwych, 1966; Oedipus, National Theatre, 1968; A Midsummer Night's Dream, Stratford, 1970, NY, 1971; Timon of Athens, Paris, 1974 (Grand Prix Dominique, 1975; Brigadier Prize, 1975); The Ik, Paris, 1975, London, 1976; work with Internat. Centre of Theatre Research, Paris, Iran, W Africa, and USA, 1971, Sahara, Niger and Nigeria, 1972-73. *Directed films:* The Beggar's Opera, 1952; Moderato Cantabile, 1960; Lord of the Flies, 1962; The Marat/Sade, 1967; Tell Me Lies, 1968; King Lear, 1969. Hon. DLitt Birmingham. Chevalier de l'Ordre des Arts et des Lettres, 1965; Freiherr von Stein Foundn Shakespeare Award, 1973. *Publication:* The Empty Space, 1968. *Recreations:* painting, piano playing and travelling by air. *Address:* c/o CIRT, 9 rue du Cirque, Paris 8, France.

BROOK, Sir Ralph Ellis; *see* Brook, Sir Robin.

BROOK, Sir Robin, Kt 1974; CMG 1954; OBE 1945; Chairman: Ionian Bank; Leda Investment Trust Ltd; Carclo Ltd; Deputy Chairman, United City Merchants; Director, Dimplex Ltd, etc; Chairman, The Sports Council, since 1975 (Member since 1971, Vice-Chairman 1974; Chairman, Sports Development Committee, 1971-74); Vice-Chairman, City and E London Area Health Authority; *b* 19 June 1908; *s* of Francis Brook, FRCS, Harley Street, and Mrs E. I. Brook; *m* 1937, Helen (*see* Helen Brook), *e d* of John Knewstub; two *d. Educ:* Eton; King's College, Cambridge. Served 1941-46; Brig., 1945 (OBE, despatches, Legion of Merit (Commander), Legion of Honour, Croix de Guerre and Bar, Order of Leopold (Officer), Belgian Croix de Guerre). Director, Bank of England, 1946-49. Chm., 1966-68, Pres., 1968-72, London Chamber of Commerce and Industry; Pres., Assoc. of British Chambers of Commerce, 1972-74; Pres., Assoc. of Chambers of Commerce of EEC, 1974-; HM Govt Dir, BP Co., 1970-73; Deputy Chairman: British Tourist and Holidays Board, 1946-50; Colonial Development Corp., 1949-53. Member: Cttee on Invisible Exports, 1969-74; Mem. Council, City Univ.; Hon. Treasurer: CCPR, 1961-; Family Planning Association, 1966-75. High Sheriff of County of London, 1950; Mem. Council, Festival of Britain. Mem. Council and Exec. Cttee, King Edward's Fund; St Bartholomew's Hospital: Governor, 1962-74; Treasurer and Chm., 1969-74; Chm., Special Trustees, 1974-; Pres., St Bartholomew's Med. Coll., 1969-; Governor, Royal Free Hosp., 1962-74. Past Master, Haberdashers' Co. *Recreation:* British Sabre Champion, 1936; Olympic Games, 1936, 1948; Capt. British Team, 1933, etc. *Address:* 31 Acacia Road, NW8 6AS.

BROOKE, family name of **Viscount Alanbrooke,** of **Baron Brooke of Cumnor,** of **Baroness Brooke of Ystradfellte** and of **Viscount Brookeborough.**

BROOKE OF CUMNOR, Baron (Life Peer), *cr* 1966; **Henry Brooke,** PC 1955; CH 1964; *b* 9 April 1903; *y s* of L. Leslie Brooke and Sybil Diana, *d* of Rev. Stopford Brooke; *m* 1933, Barbara (*see* Baroness Brooke of Ystradfellte), *y d* of Canon A. A. Mathews; two *s* two *d. Educ:* Marlborough; Balliol College, Oxford. MP (C) West Lewisham, 1938-45, Hampstead, 1950-66. Deputy Chairman, Southern Railway Company, 1946-48. Member of Central Housing Advisory Committee, 1944-54; Member of London County Council, 1945-55, and of Hampstead Borough Council, 1936-57. Financial Secretary to the Treasury, 1954-57; Minister of Housing and Local Government and Minister for Welsh Affairs, 1957-61; Chief Secretary to the Treasury and Paymaster-General, 1961-62; Home Secretary, 1962-64. Chm., Jt Select Cttee on Delegated Legislation, 1971-73. *Address:* The Glebe House, Mildenhall, Marlborough, Wilts.
See also Hon. *P. L. Brooke*.

BROOKE OF YSTRADFELLTE, Baroness *cr* 1964 (Life Peer); **Barbara Brooke,** DBE 1960; *b* 14 Jan. 1908; *y d* of late Canon A. A. Mathews; *m* 1933, Henry Brooke (*see* Baron Brooke of Cumnor); two *s* two *d. Educ:* Queen Anne's School, Caversham. Joint Vice-Chm., Conservative Party Organisation, 1954-64. Member: Hampstead Borough Council, 1948-65; North-West Metropolitan Regional Hospital Board, 1954-66; Management Cttee, King Edward's Hospital Fund for London, 1966-71; Chairman: Exec. Cttee Queen's Institute of District Nursing, 1961-71; Governing Body of Godolphin and Latymer School, Hammersmith. Hon. Fellow, Westfield College. *Address:* The Glebe House, Mildenhall, Marlborough, Wilts.
See also Hon. *P. L. Brooke*, *Rev. A. K. Mathews*.

BROOKE, Lord; David Robin Francis Guy Greville, *b* 15 May 1934; *s* and *heir* of 7th Earl of Warwick, *qv*; *m* 1956, Sarah Anne (marr. diss. 1967), *d* of Alfred Chester Beatty and Mrs Pamela Neilson; one *s* one *d. Educ:* Eton. Life Guards, 1952; Warwicks Yeo. (TA), 1954. *Address:* Warwick Castle, Warwick. *T:* Warwick 45421. *Clubs:* White's; The Brook (NY); Travellers' (Paris); Eagle Ski (Gstaad).

BROOKE, Arthur Caffin, CB 1972; Permanent Secretary, Department of Education for Northern Ireland, since 1973; *b* 11 March 1919; *s* of Rev. James M. Wilmot Brooke and late Constance Brooke; *m* 1942, Margaret Florence Thompson; two *s. Educ:* Abbotsholme Sch.; Peterhouse, Cambridge (MA). Served War, Royal Corps of Signals, 1939-46 (Lt-Col 1945). Northern Ireland Civil Service, 1946-; Ministry of Commerce, 1946-73: Principal, 1952; Asst Sec., Head of Industrial Development Div., 1955; Sen. Asst Sec., Industrial Development, 1963; Second Sec., 1968; Permanent Sec., 1969. *Recreations:* music, history. *Address:* 53 Osborne Park, Belfast, Northern Ireland. *T:* 669192.

BROOKE, Vice-Admiral (Retd) Basil Charles Barrington, CB 1949; CBE 1947; *b* 6 April 1895; *s* of John C. E. H. Brooke and Hon. Violet M. Barrington; *m* 1925, Nora Evelyn Toppin; two *s* two *d. Educ:* Malvern College. Royal Navy, 1913; Captain, 1938; Rear-Admiral, 1947; retired, 1949. Vice-Admiral (Retd), 1950. *Address:* Robin Hill, Blyth Bridge, West Linton, Peeblesshire. *T:* Drochil Castle 237.

BROOKE, Prof. Bryan Nicholas, MD, MChir, FRCS; Professor of Surgery, University of London, at St George's Hospital 1963-75, now Emeritus Professor; consultant surgeon, St James' Hospital, Balham; *b* 21 Feb. 1915; *s* of George Cyril Brooke, LittD, FSA (numismatist) and Margaret Florence Brooke; *m* 1940, Naomi Winefride Mills; three *d. Educ:* Bradfield College, Berkshire; Corpus Christi College, Cambridge; St Bartholomew's Hospital, London. FRCSEng 1942; MChir (Cantab.) 1944; MD (Birm.) with hons 1954. Lieut-Colonel, RAMC, 1945-46. Lecturer in Surgery, Aberdeen Univ., 1946-47; Reader in Surgery, Birmingham Univ., 1947-63; Hunterian Prof. RCS, 1951. Examiner in Surgery, Universities of: Birmingham, 1951-63; Cambridge, 1958-; Bristol, 1961-; London, 1962-; Glasgow, 1970; Oxford, 1970; Hong Kong, 1972; Nigeria, 1975; RCS, 1973. Member, Medical Appeals Tribunal, 1948-. Copeman Medal for Scientific Research, 1960; Graham Award (Amer. Proctologic Soc.), 1961; Award of NY Soc., Colon and Rectal Surgeons, 1967. Hon. FRACS. *Publications:* Ulcerative Colitis and its Surgical Treatment, 1954; You and Your Operation, 1957; United Birmingham Cancer Reports, 1953, 1954, 1957; (co-editor) Recent Advances in Gastroenterology, 1965; (co-author) Metabolic Derangements in Gastrointestinal Surgery, 1966; Understanding Cancer, 1971; Editor, Jl Clinics in Gastroenterology; contrib. to various surgical works. Numerous articles on large bowel disorder, medical education, steroid therapy. *Recreations:* painting, pottery. *Address:* 112 Balham Park Road, SW12 8EA.

BROOKE, Prof. Christopher Nugent Lawrence, MA; FSA; FRHistS; FBA 1970; Dixie Professor of Ecclesiastical History, University of Cambridge, since 1977; *b* 1927; *y s* of late Professor Zachary Nugent Brooke and Rosa Grace Brooke; *m* 1951, Rosalind Beckford, *d* of Dr and Mrs L. H. S. Clark; three *s. Educ:* Winchester College (Scholar); Gonville and Caius College, Cambridge (Major Scholar). BA 1948; MA 1952; LittD 1973. Army service in RAEC, Temp. Captain 1949. Cambridge University: Fellow of Gonville and Caius College, 1949-56; College Lecturer in History, 1953-56; Praelector Rhetoricus, 1955-56; Asst Lectr in History, 1953-54; Lectr, 1954-56; Prof. of Mediæval History, University of Liverpool, 1956-67; Prof. of History, Westfield Coll., Univ. of London, 1967-77. Mem., Royal Commn on Historical Monuments (England), 1977-. *Publications:* The Dullness of the Past, 1957; From Alfred to Henry III, 1961; The Saxon and Norman Kings, 1963; Europe in the Central Middle Ages, 1964; Time the Archsatirist, 1968; The Twelfth Century Renaissance, 1970; Structure of Medieval Society, 1971; Medieval Church and Society (sel. papers), 1971; (with W. Swaan) The Monastic World, 1974; (with G. Keir) London, 800-1216, 1975; part Editor: The Book of William Morton, 1954; The Letters of John of Salisbury, vol. I, 1955; Carte Nativorum, 1960; (with A. Morey) Gilbert Foliot and his letters, 1965 and (ed jtly) The Letters and Charters of Gilbert Foliot, 1967; (with D. Knowles and V. London) Heads of Religious Houses, England and Wales 940-1216, 1972; contributed to A History of St Paul's Cathedral, 1957; Studies in the Early British Church, 1958; Celt and Saxon, 1963; Studies in Church History, Vol. I, 1964, Vol. VI, 1970; general editor: Oxford (formerly Nelson's) Medieval Texts, Nelson's History of England; articles and reviews in English Historical Review,

Cambridge Historical Journal, Bulletin of Inst. of Historical Research, Downside Review, Traditio, Bulletin of John Rylands Library, Jl of Soc. of Archivists, etc. *Address:* Faculty of History, West Road, Cambridge CB3 9EF.

BROOKE, Maj.-Gen. Frank Hastings, CB 1958; CBE 1954; DSO 1945; Chief Army Instructor, Imperial Defence College, 1960-62, retd; *b* 1909; *s* of Lt-Col G. F. Brooke, DSO; *m* 1st, 1935, Helen Mary (*d* 1973), *d* of late Major R. Berkeley; two *s*; 2nd, 1974, Mrs S. N. Carson. *Educ:* RMC Sandhurst. 2nd Lieut, The Welch Regt, 1929; Captain 1938. Served NWF, India (Medal and clasp), 1935; staff and regtl appts, 1939-45; Instr Staff College, Camberley, 1945-47; Dep. Comd (Brig.) Burma Mission, 1948-49; WO, 1950-52; Comdr 1st Malay Inf. Bde, 1953-54 (despatches); GOC Federation Army, Malaya, 1956-59. Col, The Welch Regt, 1965-69; Comr, Royal Hosp., Chelsea, 1969-72. Bronze Star Medal, USA, 1945. *Publications:* contrib. on military subjects to Chambers's Encyclopædia. *Recreation:* sailing. *Club:* Army and Navy.

BROOKE, Sir George (Cecil Francis), 3rd Bt, *cr* 1903; MBE 1949; Major, 17/21 Lancers, retired; *b* 30 March 1916; *s* of Sir Francis Brooke, 2nd Bt, and Mabel, *d* of Sir John Arnott, 1st Bt; *S* father 1954; *m* 1959, Lady Melissa Wyndham-Quin, *er d* of 6th Earl of Dunraven, CB, CBE, MC; one *s* one *d*. *Educ:* Stowe. Served War of 1939-45 (wounded, despatches twice), in North Africa and Italy. *Heir:* *s* Francis George Windham Brooke, *b* 15 Oct. 1963. *Address:* Glenbevan, Croom, Co. Limerick. *Clubs:* Cavalry and Guards, Pratt's, White's; Kildare Street and University (Dublin).

BROOKE, Humphrey; *see* Brooke, T. H.

BROOKE, John; Chairman, Brooke Bond Liebig Ltd, retired 1971; *b* 7 March 1912; *m* 1936, Bridget (*née* May); two *s* one *d*. *Educ:* Bedales, Petersfield, Hants. Joined Brooke Bond & Co. Ltd, Oct. 1930, as Trainee Salesman. *Address:* 10 Parsonage Lane, Market Lavington, near Devizes, Wilts. *T:* Lavington 2204.

BROOKE, Major Sir John Weston, 3rd Bt, *cr* 1919; TD; DL; JP; Lovat Scouts; *b* 26 Sept. 1911; *s* of Major Sir Robert Weston Brooke, 2nd Bt, DSO, MC, DL, and Margery Jean, MBE (*d* 1975), *d* of Alex. Geddes of Blairmore, Aberdeenshire; *S* father, 1942; *m* 1st, 1945, Rosemary (marr. diss. 1963), *d* of late Percy Nevill, Birling House, West Malling, Kent; two *s*; 2nd, 1966, Lady Macdonald (*née* Phoebe Napier Harvey) (*d* 1977), MB, FFARCS, DA, widow of Sir Peter Macdonald, Newport, IoW. *Educ:* Repton; Trinity College, Cambridge. Apprenticed in engineering trade with Crompton Parkinsons, Electrical Engineers, Chelmsford; employed previous to hostilities as Constructional Engineer with Associated Portland Cement Manufacturers. DL, Ross and Cromarty, 1964; JP Ross-shire, 1960. *Recreations:* shooting, sailing, ski-ing, farming. *Heir:* *s* Alistair Weston Brooke, *b* 12 Sept. 1947. *Address:* Midfearn, Ardgay, Ross-shire. *T:* Ardgay 250. *Club:* Royal Ocean Racing.

BROOKE, Sir (Norman) Richard (Rowley), Kt 1964; CBE 1958; FCA; *b* 23 June 1910; *s* of William Brooke, JP, Scunthorpe, Lincs; *m* 1st, 1948, Julia Dean (marr. diss. 1957); one *s* one *d*; 2nd, 1958, Nina Mari Dolan. *Educ:* Charterhouse School. Joined Guest, Keen & Nettlefolds Ltd, 1935; Dir, Guest, Keen & Nettlefolds Ltd, 1961-67; Dir and/or Chm. of several GKN subsidiary cos until retirement in 1967; Director: Eagle Star Insurance Co. (S Wales Bd); L. Ryan Hldgs Ltd; a Founder Dir, Develt Corp. for Wales, until 1967, now Hon. Vice-Pres. Founder Mem. and Dep. Chm., British Independent Steel Producers Assoc., 1967-. Hon. Life President, Wales Conservative and Unionist Council, 1966; President, Cardiff Chamber of Commerce, 1960-61; Member Exec. Cttee and Council, British Iron and Steel Federation (Joint Vice-Pres., 1966-67); Vice-Pres., University College, Cardiff, 1965. JP Glamorgan, 1952-64, 1970-74. OStJ 1953. *Address:* New Sarum, Pwllmelin Lane, Llandaff, Cardiff. *T:* Cardiff 563692. *Clubs:* Cardiff and County (Cardiff); Royal Porthcawl Golf.

BROOKE, Hon. Peter Leonard; MP (C) City of London and Westminster South, since Feb. 1977; *b* 3 March 1934; *s* of Lord Brooke of Cumnor, *qv*, and Lady Brooke of Ystradfellte, *qv*; *m* 1964, Joan Margaret Smith; three *s* (and one *s* decd). *Educ:* Marlborough (Scholar); Balliol College, Oxford (MA); Harvard Business School (MBA). Vice-Pres., Nat. Union of Students, 1955-56; Pres., Oxford Union, 1957; Harkness Fellow, 1957-59. Research Assistant, IMEDE, Lausanne, 1960-61. Spencer Stuart & Associates, Management Consultants, 1961- (Director of parent company, 1965-), Chairman 1974-). Director, Ecole St Georges, Switzerland, 1964-. Mem., Camden Borough Council, 1968-69. Contested (C) Bedwellty, Oct. 1974. Governor:

Marlborough Coll.; Old Malthouse. *Recreations:* church-crawling, cricket, gardening. *Address:* 110A Ashley Gardens, SW1. *T:* 01-834 1563. *Clubs:* Brooks's, City Livery, MCC, I Zingari, St Stephen's.

BROOKE, Lieut-Colonel Ralph, OBE 1940; PhD, MS, FRCS, MB, LRCP; late RAMC, TA; Hon. Consulting Orthopædic Surgeon, Royal Sussex County Hospital; late: Hon. Surgeon and Hon. Orthopædic Surgeon, Hove Hospital; Hon. Surgeon and Hon. Orthopædic Surgeon, Royal West Sussex Hospital; Hon. Orthopædic Surgeon, Royal Sussex County Hospital; Hon. Surgeon, Worthing Hospital; Consulting Surgeon Bognor War Memorial Hospital; Consulting Surgeon, Midhurst Hospital; also Barrister-at-law, Inner Temple; *b* Bexhill-on-Sea, 2 April 1900; *s* of Herbert Brooke and E. Bones; *m* Marjorie, *d* of H. W. Lee, Managing Director, Messrs Stones, Ltd, Engineers; one *s* three *d*. *Educ:* Christ's College; Guy's Hospital. Late Demonstrator, Anatomy, Physiology, Operative Surgery, Guy's Hospital; late Medical Officer Hackney Hospital. *Publications:* A Shorter Orthopædics; papers in the professional journals. *Address:* Woodend, Linbrook, Ringwood, Hants.

BROOKE, Sir Richard; *see* Brooke, Sir N. R. R.

BROOKE, Sir Richard Christopher, 9th Bt, *cr* 1662; *b* 8 Aug. 1888; *s* of 8th Bt and Alice, *d* of J. S. Crawley, Stockwood Park, Luton; *S* father, 1920; *m* 1st, 1912, Marian Dorothea (*d* 1965) *o d* of late Arthur Charles Innes, MP, of Dromantine, Co. Down; one *s* one *d*; 2nd, 1967, Kathleen Enda, *d* of Francis Gildea, Dun Laoghaire, Dublin. *Educ:* Eton; Christ Church, Oxford. MA. Late Scots Guards. High Sheriff of Worcestershire, 1931; Worcestershire CC, 1928-46; Vice-Chairman Worcestershire War Emergency Cttee for Civil Defence, 1939; Chairman Bewdley Division, Conservative Association, 1945-46. Late JP and DL Worcestershire. *Recreations:* racing, horse breeding, fishing. *Heir:* *s* Richard Neville Brooke, late Scots Guards; Chartered Accountant [*b* 1 May 1915; *m* 1st, 1937, Lady Mabel Kathleen Jocelyn (marr. diss., 1959), *yr d* of 8th Earl of Roden; two *s*; 2nd, 1960, Jean Evison, *d* of Lt-Col A. C. Corfe, DSO]. *Address:* Oaklands, St Saviour, Jersey, Channel Islands. *T:* Jersey 62072. *Clubs:* Cavalry and Guards; Kildare Street and University (Dublin).

BROOKE, (Thomas) Humphrey, CVO 1969 (MVO 1958); Secretary, Royal Academy of Arts, Piccadilly, W1, 1952-68; *b* 31 Jan. 1914; *y s* of late Major Thomas Brooke, Grimston Manor, York, and late B. Gundreda, *d* of Sir Hildred Carlile, 1st and last Bt; *m* 1946, Countess Nathalie Benckendorff, *o d* of Count Benckendorff, DSO; one *d* (one *s* one *d* decd). *Educ:* Wellington Coll; Magdalen Coll., Oxford. 1st Cl. Hons Mod. History Oxon, 1935; BLitt 1937. Asst Keeper, Public Record Office, 1937. Served War of 1939-45; commissioned KRRC, 1943. Controller, Monuments and Fine Arts Branch, Allied Commission for Austria, 1946; Dep. Keeper, Tate Gallery, 1948; Ministry of Town and Country Planning, 1949; Resigned from Civil Service on appointment to Royal Acad., 1951. Member Order of Santiago (Portugal), 1955; Commander Ordine al Merito della Republica Italiana, 1956; Officier de l'Ordre de l'Etoile Noire (France), 1958. *Recreations:* shooting, fishing, gardening. *Address:* 8 Pelham Crescent, SW7. *T:* 01-589 5690; Lime Kiln, Claydon, Suffolk. *T:* Ipswich 830334. *Club:* Chelsea Arts.

BROOKE-LITTLE, John Philip Brooke, MVO 1969; Richmond Herald since 1967; Registrar and Librarian, College of Arms, since 1974; *b* 6 April 1927; *s* of late Raymond Brooke-Little, Unicorns House, Swalcliffe; *m* 1960, Mary Lee, *o c* of late John Raymond Pierce and Mrs E. G. Pierce, Colehill, Wimborne Minster; three *s* one *d*. *Educ:* Clayesmore Sch; New Coll., Oxford (MA). Earl Marshal's staff,1952-53; Gold Staff Officer, Coronation, 1953; Bluemantle Pursuivant of Arms, 1956. Founder of Heraldry Soc. and Chm., 1947; Hon. Editor-in-Chief, The Coat of Arms, 1950; Governor, Clayesmore Sch. (Chm. 1971-); Fellow, Soc. of Genealogists, 1969. Freeman and Liveryman, Scriveners' Co. of London. FSA 1961. KStJ 1975; Knight of Malta, 1955 (Chancellor, 1973-77); Comdr Cross of Merit of Order of Malta, 1964; Cruz Distinguida (1st cl.) de San Raimundo de Peñafort, 1955. *Publications:* Royal London, 1953; Pictorial History of Oxford, 1954; Boutell's Heraldry, 1970 and 1973 (1963 and 1966 edns with C. W. Scott-Giles); Knights of the Middle Ages, 1966; Prince of Wales, 1969; Fox-Davies' Complete Guide to Heraldry, annotated edn, 1969; (with Don Pottinger and Anne Tauté) Kings and Queens of Great Britain, 1970; An Heraldic Alphabet, 1973; (with Marie Angell) Beasts in Heraldry, 1974; The British Monarchy in Colour, 1976; Royal Arms, Beasts and Badges, 1977; genealogical and heraldic articles. *Recreations:* cooking, painting. *Address:* Heyford House, Lower Heyford, near

Oxford. *T:* Steeple Aston 40337; 82A Queen's Gate, SW7. *T:* 01-373 4105; College of Arms, EC4. *T:* 01-248 1310. *Clubs:* Carlton, City Livery, Chelsea Arts (Hon. Member).

BROOKE-ROSE, Prof. Christine; novelist and critic; Professor of English Language and Literature, University of Paris, since 1975 (Lecturer, 1969-75). *Educ:* Oxford and London Univs. MA Oxon 1953, PhD London 1954. Research and criticism, 1957-. Reviewer for: The Times Literary Supplement, The Times, The Observer, The Sunday Times, The Listener, The Spectator, and The London Magazine, 1956-68; took up post at Univ. of Paris VIII, Vincennes, 1969. Has broadcast in book programmes on BBC, and on 'The Critics', and ABC Television. Travelling Prize of Society of Authors, 1964; James Tait Black Memorial Prize, 1966; Arts Council Translation Prize, 1969. *Publications: novels:* The Languages of Love, 1957; The Sycamore Tree, 1958; The Dear Deceit, 1960; The Middlemen, 1961; Out, 1964; Such, 1965; Between, 1968; Thru, 1975; *criticism:* A Grammar of Metaphor, 1958; A ZBC of Ezra Pound, 1971; *short stories:* Go when you see the Green Man Walking, 1970; short stories and essays in various magazines, etc. *Recreations:* people, travel. *Address:* c/o Hamish Hamilton Ltd, 90 Great Russell Street, WC1B 3PT.

BROOKE TURNER, Alan; HM Diplomatic Service; Civil Deputy Commandant and Director of Studies, NATO Defense College, Rome, since 1976; *b* 4 Jan. 1926; *s* of late Arthur Brooke Turner, MC; *m* 1954, Hazel Alexandra Rowan Henderson; two *s* two *d. Educ:* Marlborough; Balliol Coll., Oxford (Sen. Schol.). 1st cl Hon. Mods 1949; 1st cl. Lit. Hum. 1951. Served in RAF, 1944-48. Entered HM Foreign (subseq. Diplomatic) Service, 1951; FO, 1951; Warsaw, 1953; 3rd, later 2nd Sec. (Commercial), Jedda, 1954; Lisbon, 1957; 1st Sec., FO, 1959 (UK Delegn to Nuclear Tests Conf., Geneva, 1962); Cultural Attaché, Moscow, 1962; FO, 1965; Fellow, Center for Internat. Affairs, Harvard Univ., 1968; Counsellor, Rio de Janeiro, 1969-71; Head of Southern European Dept, FCO, 1972-73; Counsellor and Head of Chancery, British Embassy, Rome, 1973-76. *Address:* c/o Foreign and Commonwealth Office, SW1; Poultons, Dormansland, Lingfield, Surrey. *T:* Lingfield 832079. *Club:* Travellers'.

BROOKEBOROUGH, 2nd Viscount *cr* 1952, of Colebrooke; **John Warden Brooke,** PC (NI) 1971; DL; Bt 1822; Member (UPNI) for North Down, Northern Ireland Constitutional Convention, 1975-76; *b* 9 Nov. 1922; *s* of 1st Viscount Brookeborough, KG, PC, CBE, MC, and Cynthia Mary, DBE 1959 (*d* 1970), *d* of late Captain Charles Warden Sergison; *S* father, 1973; *m* 1949, Rosemary Hilda Chichester; two *s* three *d. Educ:* Eton. Joined Army, 1941; Captain 10th Royal Hussars; wounded, Italy, 1942; subseq. ADC to Field Marshal Alexander in Italy and to Gen. Sir Brian Robertson in Germany; ADC to Viceroy of India, Field Marshal Lord Wavell, 1946; invalided, 1947. Fermanagh County Councillor, 1947-, Chairman, 1961-; pioneered streamlining of local govt by voluntary amalgamation of all councils in the county, 1967. MP (U) Lisnaskea Div., Parlt of NI, 1968-73; Mem. (U), N Down, NI Assembly, 1973-75; Parly Sec. to Min. of Commerce with special responsibilities for tourism, Apr. 1969; Parly Sec. to Dept of the Prime Minister (still retaining Commerce office), with responsibility for general oversight of Government's publicity and information services, Jan. 1970; Minister of State, Min. of Finance and Govt Chief Whip, 1971-72. DL Co. Fermanagh, 1967. *Recreations:* shooting, fishing, riding. *Heir: s* Hon. Alan Henry Brooke, *b* 30 June 1952. *Address:* Ashbrooke, Brookeborough, Enniskillen, Co. Fermanagh. *T:* Brookeborough 242.

BROOKES, family name of **Baron Brookes.**

BROOKES, Baron *cr* 1975 (Life Peer), of West Bromwich; **Raymond Percival Brookes,** Kt 1971; Life President, Guest, Keen & Nettlefolds Ltd (Group Chairman and Chief Executive, 1965-74); Director, BHP-GKN Holdings Ltd; *b* 10 April 1909; *s* of William and Ursula Brookes; *m* 1937, Florence Edna Sharman; one *s.* Part-time Mem., BSC, 1967-68. First Pres., British Mechanical Engrg Confedn, 1968-70; a Vice-Pres., Engrg Employers' Fedn, 1967-75. Member: Council, UK S Africa Trade Assoc. Ltd, 1967-74; Council, CBI, 1968-75; BNEC, 1969-71; Wilberforce Ct of Inquiry into electricity supply industry dispute, Jan. 1971; Industrial Develt Adv. Bd, 1972-75. Member: Exec. Cttee, 1970-, Council, 1969-, Pres., 1974-75, Soc. of Motor Manufacturers & Traders Ltd; Court of Governors, Univ. of Birmingham, 1966-75; Council, Univ. of Birmingham, 1968-75. Pres., Motor Ind. Res. Assoc., 1973-75. Chm., Rea Brothers (Isle of Man) Ltd; Director: Plessey Co Ltd; Mannin Industries Ltd; AMF Inc. (USA). *Recreations:* golf, fly-fishing. *Address:* Guest, Keen & Nettlefolds Ltd, Group Head Office, Smethwick, Warley, Worcs; (private) Dolphins, Mount Gawne Road, Port St Mary, Isle of Man.

BROOKES, Hon. and Rev. Edgar Harry, MA, DLitt; Hon. LLD; Author; late Senator representing the natives of Natal and Zululand in the Union of South Africa Parliament; late Professor of Public Administration and Political Science, University of Pretoria, and Principal, Adams College, Natal; *b* Smethwick, England, 4 Feb. 1897; *s* of J. H. Brookes and E. E. Thomas; *m* 1925, Heidi Genevieve, *d* of Rev. C. Bourquin, Mission Suisse, Pretoria; three *s* two *d. Educ:* Pietermaritzburg College; University of South Africa; London School of Economics. Professor of Public Administration and Political Science, Transvaal University College (later University of Pretoria), 1924; SA Delegate to the League of Nations Assembly, 1927; Observer for Union Government at World Population Conference, 1927; President of SA Institute of Race Relations, 1932 and 1946; Member of Union Social and Economic Planning Council, 1942-52; Member, Native Affairs Commission, 1945-50; Professor of History and Political Science, University of Natal, 1959-62. *Publications:* History of Native Policy in South Africa, 1923; Native Education in South Africa, 1929; A Retrospect and a Forecast; History of the Swiss Mission in South Africa, 1875-1925, 1926; The Colour Problems of South Africa, 1934; South Africa in a Changing World, 1954; The Native Reserves of Natal, 1957; The Commonwealth, 1959, 1959; The City of God and the Politics of Crisis, 1959; Power, Law, Right, and Love: A Study in Political Values, 1963; The History of Natal, 1965; Freedom, Faith and the Twenty-First Century, 1966; A History of the University of Natal, 1967; Apartheid: a Documentary Study of Modern South Africa, 1968; White Rule in South Africa 1830-1910, 1974; collaborated in: Coming of Age: Studies in South African Citizenship and Politics, 1930; Western Civilisation and the Bantu of South Africa, 1934; Civil Liberty in South Africa, 1958; White Rule in South Africa 1830-1910, 1976; A South African Pilgrimage, 1977. *Address:* 4 Chapter Close, 6 Taunton Road, Pietermaritzburg, South Africa. *T:* Pietermaritzburg 22714.

BROOKES, Air Vice-Marshal Hugh Hamilton, CB 1954; CBE 1951; DFC 1944; RAF retd; *b* 14 Oct. 1904; *s* of late W. H. Brookes and of Evelyn, *d* of J. Forster Hamilton (she married 2nd Sir John Simpson, KBE, CIE); *m* 1932, Elsie Viola Henry; one *d. Educ:* Bedford School; Cranwell. Bomber Command, 1924; 84 Sqdn Iraq, 1929; Staff College, 1933; Sqdn Bomber Command, 1937; Iraq, 1938; Western Desert, 1939; Aden, 1941; Station Bomber Command, 1943; Iraq, 1946; Director of Flying Training, 1949; AOC Rhodesia, 1951; AOC Iraq, 1954; AOC No 25 Group, Flying Training Command, 1956-58, retd. *Club:* Royal Air Force.

BROOKING, Allan John; Administrator, South Western Regional Health Authority, since 1973; *b* 28 March 1934; *s* of Harold Nicholas Brooking and Margaret Ethel Brooking; *m* 1957, Audrey Irene (*née* Walton); two *s* one *d. Educ:* Okehampton Grammar Sch.; University Coll., Oxford (MA). FHA. Sec., Salisbury General Infirmary, 1959-62; Dep. Sec., Lewisham HMC, 1962-65; Group Sec., Lewisham HMC, 1965-70; Sec., Bd of Governors, United Liverpool Hosps, 1971-73. Mem., NHS Nat. Training Council, 1975-. *Recreations:* singing, walking, surfing. *Address:* Black Wicket, 128 Westbury Road, Westbury-on-Trym, Bristol BS9 3AR. *T:* Bristol 628050.

BROOKNER, Prof. Anita; Lecturer, Courtauld Institute of Art, since 1964; *b* 16 July 1928; *o c* of Newson and Maude Brookner. *Educ:* James Allen's Girls' Sch.; King's Coll., Univ. of London; Courtauld Inst.; Paris. Vis. Lectr, Univ. of Reading, 1959-64; Slade Professor, Univ. of Cambridge, 1967-68. Fellow, New Hall, Cambridge. *Publications:* Watteau, 1968; The Genius of the Future, 1971; Greuze: the rise and fall of an Eighteenth Century Phenomenon, 1972; articles in Burlington Magazine, etc. *Address:* 68 Elm Park Gardens, SW10. *T:* 01-352 6894.

BROOKS, family name of **Baron Crawshaw.**

BROOKS, Prof. Cleanth; Gray Professor of Rhetoric, Yale University, USA, 1947-75, now Emeritus Professor; *b* 16 Oct. 1906; *s* of Rev. Cleanth and Bessie Lee Witherspoon Brooks; *m* 1934, Edith Amy Blanchard; no *c. Educ:* The McTyeire School; Vanderbilt, Tulane and Oxford Universities. Rhodes Scholar, Louisiana and Exeter, 1929; Lecturer, later Prof., Louisiana State Univ., 1932-47; Prof. of English, later Gray Prof. of Rhetoric, Yale Univ., 1947-75. Visiting Professor: Univ. of Texas; Univ. of Michigan; Univ. of Chicago; Univ. of Southern California; Bread Loaf School of English; Univ. of South Carolina, 1975; Tulane Univ., 1976. Cultural Attaché at the American Embassy, London, 1964-66. Managing Editor and Editor (with Robert Penn Warren), The Southern Review, 1935-42. Fellow, Library of Congress, 1953-63; Guggenheim Fellow, 1953 and 1960; Sen. Fellow, Nat. Endowment for the Humanities, 1975. Member: Amer. Acad. of Arts and Scis;

Amer. Acad. Inst. of Arts and Letters; Amer. Philos. Soc.; RSL. Hon. DLitt: Upsala Coll., 1963; Kentucky, 1963; Exeter, 1966; Washington and Lee, 1968; Tulane, 1969; Univ. of the South, 1974; Hon. LHD: St Louis, 1968; Centenary Coll., 1972; Oglethorpe Univ., 1976. *Publications:* Modern Poetry and the Tradition, 1939; The Well Wrought Urn, 1947; (with R. P. Warren) Understanding Poetry, 1938; (with R. P. Warren) Modern Rhetoric, 1950; (with W. K. Wimsatt, Jr) Literary Criticism: A Short History, 1957; The Hidden God, 1963; William Faulkner: The Yoknapatawpha Country, 1963; A Shaping Joy, 1971; (with R. W. B. Lewis and R. P. Warren) American Literature: the Makers and the Making, 1973; (Gen. Ed., with David N. Smith and A. F. Falconer) The Percy Letters; contrib. articles, reviews to literary magazines, journals. *Address:* Forest Road, Northford, Conn 06472, USA. *Club:* Athenæum.

BROOKS, Douglas; Personnel Director, Hoover Ltd, since 1973; *b* 3 Sept. 1928; *s* of Oliver Brooks and Olive Brooks; *m* 1952, June Anne (*née* Branch); one *s* one *d*. *Educ:* Newbridge Grammar Sch.; University Coll., Cardiff (Dip. Soc. Sc.). CIPM. Girling Ltd: factory operative, 1951-53; Employment Officer, 1953-56; Hoover Ltd: Personnel Off., 1956-60; Sen. Personnel Off., 1960-63; Dep. Personnel Man., 1963-66; Indust. Relations Advr, 1966-69; Gp Personnel Man., 1969-73. Mem. Council, SSRC, 1976-. Vice-Pres., IPM, 1972-74. *Recreations:* talking, music, reading, gardening, cooking. *Address:* Bull Farm House, Park Lane, Beaconsfield, Bucks. *T:* Beaconsfield 5253.

BROOKS, Edwin, PhD; Dean of Business and Liberal Studies, Riverina College of Advanced Education, Wagga Wagga, New South Wales, since 1977; *b* Barry, Glamorgan, 1 Dec. 1929; *s* of Edwin Brooks and Agnes Elizabeth (*née* Campbell); *m* 1956, Winifred Hazel Soundie; four *s* one *d*. *Educ:* Barry Grammar Sch.; St John's Coll., Cambridge. PhD (Camb) 1958. National Service, Singapore, 1948-49. MP (Lab) Bebington, 1966-70. Univ. of Liverpool: Lectr, Dept of Geography, 1954-66 and 1970-72; Sen. Lectr, 1972-77; Dean, College Studies, 1975-77. Councillor, Birkenhead, 1958-67. *Publications:* This Crowded Kingdom, 1973; (ed) Tribes of the Amazon Basin in Brazil, 1973. *Recreations:* gardening, do-it-yourself. *Address:* Riverina College of Advanced Education, PO Box 588, Wagga Wagga, NSW 2650, Australia. *T:* 069-21-11-22.

BROOKS, Eric Arthur Swatton, MA; Head of Claims Department, Foreign Office, 1960 until retirement, 1967; *b* 9 Oct. 1907; *yr s* of late A. E. Brooks, MA, Maidenhead; *m* 1947, Daphne Joyce, *yr d* of late George McMullan, MD, FRCSE, Wallingford; one *s* one *d*. *Educ:* Reading Sch.; New Coll., Oxford (MA). 2nd cl. hons Jurisprudence, 1929. Solicitor, 1932; practised in London, 1932-39. Mem. Law Soc., 1934- (Mem. Overseas Relations Cttee, 1949-). Served War of 1939-45 in Admty and Min. of Aircraft Production, and in Operational Research as Hon. Ft-Lieut RAFVR until 1944; Disposal of Govt Factories of Min. of Aircraft Production, 1944-Dec. 1945. Foreign Office, 1946-. Served on Brit. Delegns in negotiations with: Polish and Hungarian Governments, 1953, 1954; Bulgarian Government, 1955; Rumanian Government, 1955, 1956, 1960; USSR, 1964, 1965, 1966, 1967. British Representative on Anglo-Italian Conciliation Commn, until 1967. Councillor: Borough of Maidenhead, 1972-74; Royal Borough of Windsor and Maidenhead, 1973-. *Publications:* articles, on Compensation in International Law, and Distribution of Compensation, in legal jls, and on local history and amenities. *Recreations:* golf (Oxford Univ. team *v* Cambridge Univ., 1929; various later Amateur European Championships); ski-ing; skating; gardening. *Address:* Kitoha, 116b Grenfell Road, Maidenhead, Berks. *T:* Maidenhead 21621.

BROOKS, Most Rev. Francis Gerard; *see* Dromore, Bishop of, (RC).

BROOKS, Leslie James, CEng, FRINA; RCNC; Deputy Director of Engineering (Constructive), Ship Department, Ministry of Defence (Procurement Executive), 1973-76, retired; *b* 3 Aug. 1916; *yr s* of late C. J. D. Brooks and Lucy A. Brooks, Milton Regis, Sittingbourne, Kent; *m* 1941, Ruth Elizabeth Olver, Saltash, Cornwall; two *s*. *Educ:* Borden Grammar Sch.; Sittingbourne, Kent; HM Dockyard Schs, Sheerness and Chatham; Royal Naval Engrg Coll., Keyham; RNC, Greenwich. War of 1939-45: Asst Constructor, Naval Construction Dept, Admty, Bath, 1941-44; Constr Lt-Comdr on Staff of Allied Naval Comdr, Exped. Force, and Flag Officer, Brit. Assault Area, 1944. Constr in charge Welding, Naval Constrn Dept, Admty, Bath, 1945-47; Constr Comdr, Staff of Comdr-in-Chief, Brit. Pacific Fleet, 1947-49; Constr in charge, No 2 Ship Tank, Admty Experiment Works, Haslar, Gosport, 1949-54. Naval Constrn Dept, Admty, Bath: Constr, Merchant

Shipping Liaison, 1954-56; Chief Constr in charge of Conversion of First Commando Ships, and of Operating Aircraft Carriers, 1956-62; Dep. Supt, Admty Exper. Works, Haslar, 1962-65; Ship Dept, Bath: Asst Dir of Naval Constrn, Naval Constrn Div., MoD(N), 1965-68; Asst Dir of Engrg (Ships), MoD(PE), 1968-73; Dep. Dir of Engrg/Constr., MoD(PE), 1973. Mem., Royal Corps of Naval Constructors. *Recreations:* Do-it-Yourself, natural history, walking. *Address:* Merrymeet, Perrymead, Bath BA2 5AY. *T:* Bath 832856.

BROOKS, Mrs Richard; *see* Simmons, Jean.

BROOKS, Ronald Clifton, OBE 1944; MC 1918; Chairman, Commercial Union Assurance Co. Ltd, 1959-72; retired; *b* 3 March 1899; 2nd *s* of Robert Brooks; *m* 1928, Iris Winifred, *er d* of M. W. Payne; two *s* one *d*. *Educ:* Haileybury College; Trinity College, Cambridge. Joined The Queen's (Royal West Surrey) Regt, with rank 2nd Lieut, 1917 (MC). Cambridge (BA), 1919-20. Partner, Robert Brooks & Co., Merchants, 1924-68; Chm., Crosby House Group, retd 1972; Director: Dalgety Ltd, retd 1972; Yeoman Investment Trust Ltd, retd 1973. DAG, SHAEF, 1945. Legion of Merit, USA, 1945; Chevalier, Légion d'Honneur, 1945. *Recreations:* fishing, shooting, golf. *Address:* 14 Whitelands House, Chelsea, SW3. *T:* 01-730 1950. *Clubs:* Bath, City of London.

BROOKS, William Donald Wykeham, CBE 1956; MA, DM (Oxon); FRCP; Consulting Physician: St Mary's Hospital; Brompton Hospital; to the Royal Navy; to the King Edward VII Convalescent Home for Officers, Osborne; Chief Medical Officer, Eagle Star Insurance Co.; *b* 3 Aug. 1905; *er s* of A. E. Brooks MA (Oxon), Maidenhead, Berks; *m* 1934, Phyllis Kathleen, *e d* of late F. A. Juler, CVO; two *s* two *d*. *Educ:* Reading School; St John's College, Oxford (White Scholar); St Mary's Hospital, London (University Scholar); Strong Memorial Hospital, Rochester, New York. First Class Honours, Final Honour School of Physiology, 1928; Cheadle Gold Medallist, 1931; Fereday Fellow St John's College, Oxford, 1931-34; Rockefeller Travelling Fellow, 1932-33; Goulstonian Lecturer, 1940; Marc Daniels Lecturer, RCP, 1957. Asst Registrar, 1946-50, RCP; Censor, RCP, 1961- (Council, 1959-61, Senior Vice-President and Senior Censor, 1965); Member Association of Physicians of Great Britain and Ireland. Served War 1940-45 as Surgeon Captain, RNVR. *Publications:* numerous articles on general medical topics and on chest diseases in various medical journals; Sections on Chest Wounds, Respiratory Diseases and Tuberculosis, Conybeare's Textbook of Medicine; Respiratory Diseases section in the Official Naval Medical History of the War. *Recreations:* golf, shooting, gardening, bridge. *Address:* Two Acres, Fryern Road, Storrington, Sussex. *T:* Storrington 2159.

BROOKS GRUNDY, Rupert Francis; *see* Grundy, R. F. B.

BROOKSBANK, Col Sir (Edward) William, 2nd Bt, *cr* 1919; TD 1953; DL; Yorkshire Hussars; *b* 15 June 1915; *e s* of late Col Edward York Brooksbank and Hazel, *d* of late H. F. Brockholes Thomas; *S* grandfather, 1943; *m* 1943, Ann, 2nd *d* of Col T. Clitheroe; one *s*. *Educ:* Eton. Colonel, Comdg Queen's Own Yorkshire Yeomanry, 1957. Hon. Col, Queen's Own Yorkshire Yeomanry (TA), 1963-69, T&AVR, 1969-71, 1972-75. DL East Riding of Yorks, and City and County of Kingston upon Hull, 1959. *Heir:* s Edward Nicholas Brooksbank, Captain, Blues and Royals [*b* 4 Oct. 1944; *m* 1970, Emma, *o d* of Rt Hon. Richard Frederick Wood, *qv*]. *Address:* Menethorpe Hall, Malton, North Yorks. *Club:* Turf, Yorkshire.

BROOKSBANK, Kenneth, DSC and Bar, 1944; Chief Education Officer, Birmingham, 1968-77; *b* 27 July 1915; *s* of Ambrose and Ethel Brooksbank; *m* 1939, Violet Anne Woodrow; two *d*. *Educ:* High Storrs Gram. Sch., Sheffield; St Edmund Hall, Oxford; Manchester University. Asst Master, Hulme Gram. Sch., Oldham, 1937-41; Royal Navy, 1941-46; Dep. Educn Off., York, 1946-49; Sen. Admin. Asst, Birmingham, 1949-52; Asst Sec. for Educn, NR Yorks CC, 1952-56; Dep. Educn Off., Birmingham, 1956-68. Leader, Unesco Educn Planning Mission to Bechuanaland, Basutoland and Swaziland, 1964. Member: Engineering Ind. Trng Bd, 1970-; Ind. Trng Service Bd, 1974-. President: Educnl Equipment Assoc., 1970-71; Soc. of Educn Officers, 1971-72. *Address:* 29 Wycome Road, Hall Green, Birmingham B28 9EN. *T:* 021-777 4407.

BROOKSBANK, Sir William; *see* Brooksbank, Sir E. W.

BROOKSBY, John Burns, CBE 1973; Director, Animal Virus Research Institute, Pirbright, since 1964; *b* 25 Dec. 1914; *s* of George B. Brooksby, Glasgow; *m* 1940, Muriel Weir; one *s* one *d*. *Educ:* Hyndland Sch., Glasgow; Glasgow Veterinary Coll.;

London University. MRCVS 1935; BSc (VetSc) 1936; PhD 1947; DSc 1957; FRSE 1968. Research Officer, Pirbright, 1939; Dep. Dir, 1957; Dir, 1964. *Publications:* papers on virus diseases of animals in scientific jls. *Address:* Heatherdale House, Compton Way, Farnham, Surrey. *T:* Runfold 2164. *Club:* Farmers'.

BROOM, Air Marshal Sir Ivor (Gordon), KCB 1975 (CB 1972); CBE 1969; DSO 1945; DFC 1942 (Bar to DFC 1944, 2nd Bar 1945); AFC 1956; Controller, National Air Traffic Services, 1974-77 (Deputy Controller, 1972-74); Member, Civil Aviation Authority, since 1974; *b* Cardiff, 2 June 1920; *s* of Alfred Godfrey Broom and Janet Broom; *m* 1942, Jess Irene Broom (*née* Cooper); two *s* one *d*. *Educ:* West Monmouth Grammar Sch.; Pontypridd County Sch., Glam. Joined RAF, 1940; commissioned, 1941; 114 Sqdn, 107 Sqdn, 1941; CFS Course, 1942; Instr on: 1655 Mosquito Trg Unit; 571 Sqdn, 128 Sqdn, and 163 Sqdn, 1943-45; HQ, ACSEA, 1945-46. Commanded 28 (FR) Sqdn, 1946-48; RAF Staff Coll. Course, Bracknell, 1949; Sqdn Comdr, No 1 ITS, 1950-52; No 3 Flying Coll. Course, Manby, 1952-53; commanded 57 Sqdn, 1953-54; Syndicate Leader, Flying Coll., Manby, 1954-56; commanded Bomber Command Development Unit, Wittering, 1956-59; Air Secretary's Dept, 1959-62; commanded RAF Bruggen, 1962-64; IDC, 1965-66; Dir of Organisation (Establishments), 1966-68; Commandant, Central Flying School, 1968-70; AOC No 11 (Fighter) Gp, Strike Comd, 1970-72. *Recreations:* golf, skiing. *Address:* c/o 172 Valley Road, Ipswich, Suffolk. *Club:* Royal Air Force.

BROOME, F. N.; retired, 1961, as Judge-President, Natal Provincial Division, Supreme Court of South Africa; *b* 1891; *s* of late William Broome, formerly Judge of Supreme Court of S. Africa; *m* 1918, Mary Caroline Jervois; one *s* one *d*. *Educ:* Hilton College, Natal; Oriel College, Oxford (Rhodes Scholar). BA(Oxon) 1912; Barrister-at-law, Inner Temple, 1913; Advocate of Supreme Court of S Africa, 1914; Natal Carbineers and Royal Field Artillery, 1914-19, SW Africa and France, Captain (MC); KC 1931; MP for Pietermaritzburg District, 1938; Chairman: Natal Education Commission, 1936-38; Indian Penetration Commission, 1940; Natal Indian Judicial Commission, 1944; Durban Native Enquiry Commission, 1947; Stock Exchange Inquiry Commission, 1962; Courts Commn, Rhodesia, 1970. Hon. LLD Natal, 1968. *Publications:* Not the Whole Truth, 1962; Speeches and Addresses, 1973. *Address:* 94 Roberts Road, Pietermaritzburg, South Africa. *Club:* Victoria (Pietermaritzburg).

BROOMHALL, Maj.-Gen. William Maurice, CB 1950; DSO 1945; OBE 1932; *b* 16 July 1897; *o s* of late Alfred Edward Broomhall, London. *Educ:* St Paul's School; Royal Military Academy, Woolwich. Commissioned Royal Engineers, 1915; France and Belgium, 1914-21 (wounded twice); Waziristan, 1921-24 (medal and clasp); NW Frontier of India, 1929-31 (despatches, clasp, OBE); Staff College, Camberley, 1932-33. Served North-West Europe, 1939-45 (Despatches, DSO); Chief Engineer, Allied Forces, Italy, 1946; Chief Engineer, British Army of the Rhine, 1947-48; Chief Engineer, Middle East Land Forces, 1948-51; retired, 1951. *Address:* The Cottage, Park Lane, Beaconsfield, Bucks HP9 2HR. *Club:* Army and Navy.

BROPHY, Brigid (Antonia), FRSL; author and playwright; *b* 12 June 1929; *o c* of late John Brophy; *m* 1954, Michael Levey, *qv*; one *d*. *Educ:* St Paul's Girls' Sch.; St Hugh's Coll., Oxford. Awarded Jubilee Scholarship at St Hugh's Coll., Oxford, 1947 and read classics. Exec. Councillor, Writers Guild of GB, 1975-; a Vice-Chm., British Copyright Council, 1976-. Awarded Cheltenham Literary Festival First Prize for a first novel, 1954; London Magazine Prize for Prose, 1962. *Publications:* Hackenfeller's Ape, 1953; The King of a Rainy Country, 1956; Black Ship to Hell, 1962; Flesh, 1962; The Finishing Touch, 1963; The Snow Ball, 1964; Mozart the Dramatist, 1964; Don't Never Forget, 1966; (in collaboration with Michael Levey and Charles Osborne) Fifty Works of English Literature We Could Do Without, 1967; Black and White: a portrait of Aubrey Beardsley, 1968; In Transit, 1969; Prancing Novelist, 1973; The Adventures of God in his Search for the Black Girl, and other fables, 1973; Pussy Owl, 1976; Beardsley and his World, 1976. *Plays:* The Burglar, Vaudeville, 1967 (published with preface, 1968); The Waste Disposal Unit, Radio (published 1968). *Visual Art:* (with Maureen Duffy) Prop Art, exhibn, London, 1969. *Address:* Flat 3, 185 Old Brompton Road, SW5. *T:* 01-373 9335.

BROSAN, Dr George Stephen, TD 1960; Director, North East London Polytechnic, since 1970; *b* 8 Aug. 1921; *o s* of Rudolph and Margaret Brosan; *m* 1952, Maureen Dorothy Foscoe; three *d*. *Educ:* Kilburn Grammar Sch.; Faraday House; The Polytechnic; Birkbeck Coll., London. Faraday Scholar, 1939. 1st

cl. hons BSc (Eng) 1944, BSc 1947; PhD 1951; DFH hons 1957; FIProdE 1963; FIEE 1964; FIMA 1966; FIMechE 1971; FBIM 1975. Hon. MIED 1968. KRRC, 1945-46; Dir, British Diamix Ltd, 1945-49; teaching staff: Woolwich Polytechnic, 1949-50; Regent Street Polytechnic, 1950-58; Head of Dept, Willesden Coll. of Technology, 1958-60; Further Educn Officer, Middlesex CC, 1960-62; Principal, Enfield Coll. of Technology, 1962-70. Pres., Tensor Club of GB, 1973-; Pres., IProdE, 1975-77; Member: Cttee for Higher Educn and Res.; Council, BIM, 1975-. *Publications:* (jtly) Advanced Electrical Power and Machines, 1966; (jtly) Patterns and Policies in Higher Education, 1971; numerous articles and papers in academic and professional press. *Address:* North East London Polytechnic, Romford Road, E15 4LZ. *T:* 01-555 0811. *Club:* Reform.

BROSIO, Manlio; *b* 10 July 1897; *s* of late Edoardo Brosio and Fortunata Curadelli; *m* 1936, Clotilde Brosio. *Educ:* Turin University (graduated in Law), Officer in Alpine Troops, European War, 1915-18 (Silver Medal and Cross for Valour). Young political leader, Member of Liberal Party, Central Secretary of "Rivoluzione Liberale" movement, Turin, 1922-25; retired from politics after Fascism took power. Barrister in Turin, in continuous contact with anti-fascist groups, 1926-43; Member of Nat. Liberation Cttee in Rome under German occupation, 1943-44; General Sec. of Liberal Party, 1944-45. Minister without portfolio in Bonomi Cabinet, 1944; Vice-President of Cabinet in De Gasperi Govt, 1945; Minister of War in De Gasperi Govt, 1945-46; Ambassador: in Moscow, Jan. 1947-Dec. 1951; in London, 1952-54; in Washington, 1955-61; in Paris, 1961-64; Sec.-Gen. of NATO, 1964-71; Senator of Italian Republic for Turin, 1972-76, retired. *Publications:* juridical and political articles. *Address:* Corso Re Umberto 29 bis, Torino, Italy. *T:* 532441, 548597.

BROTHERHOOD, Air Cdre William Rowland, CBE 1952; retired as Director, Guided Weapons (Trials), Ministry of Aviation (formerly Supply), 1959-61; *b* 22 Jan. 1912; *s* of late James Brotherhood, Tintern, Mon.; *m* 1939, Margaret, *d* of late Ernest Sutcliffe, Louth, Lincs; one *s* one *d*. *Educ:* Monmouth School; RAF College, Cranwell. Joined RAF, 1930; Group Captain, 1943; Air Commodore, 1955; Director, Operational Requirements, Air Ministry, 1955-58. *Address:* Inglewood, Llandogo, Gwent. *T:* St Briavels 333. *Club:* Royal Air Force.

BROTHERS, Air Cdre Peter Malam, CBE 1964; DSO 1944; DFC 1940, and Bar, 1943; *b* 30 Sept. 1917; *s* of late John Malam Brothers; *m* 1939, Annette, *d* of late James Wilson; three *d*. *Educ:* N. Manchester Sch. (Br. of Manchester Grammar). Joined RAF, 1936; Flt-Lieut 1939; RAF Biggin Hill, Battle of Britain, 1940; Sqdn-Ldr 1941; Wing Comdr 1942; Tangmere Fighter Wing Ldr, 1942-43; Staff HQ No. 10 Gp, 1943; Exeter Wing Ldr, 1944; US Comd and Gen. Staff Sch., 1944-45; Central Fighter Estab., 1945-46; Colonial Service, Kenya, 1947-49; RAF Bomber Sqdn, 1949-52; HQ No. 3 Gp, 1952-54; RAF Staff Coll., 1954; HQ Fighter Comd, 1955-57; Bomber Stn, 1957-59; Gp Capt., and Staff Officer, SHAPE, 1959-62; Dir of Ops (Overseas), 1962-65; Air Cdre, and AOC Mil. Air Traffic Ops, 1965-68; Dir of Public Relations (RAF), MoD (Air), 1968-73; retired 1973. Freeman, Guild Air Pilots and Air Navigators, 1966 (Liveryman, 1968; Warden, 1971; Master, 1974-75); Freeman, City of London, 1967. MBIM; MIPR. *Recreations:* golf, sailing, fishing, swimming, flying. *Address:* c/o National Westminster Bank, Topsham, Devon. *Clubs:* Royal Air Force, Royal Air Force (Reserves); RAF Yacht; Honiton Golf.

BROTHERSTON, Sir John (Howie Flint), Kt 1972; Professor of Community Medicine, University of Edinburgh, since 1977; Hon. Physician to the Queen, 1965-68; *b* Edinburgh, 9 March 1915; *s* of late William Brotherston, WS, Edinburgh, and Dr Margaret M. Brotherston, MBE, Edinburgh; *m* 1939, Elizabeth Irene Low; two *s* two *d*. *Educ:* George Watson's College, Edinburgh; University of Edinburgh. Graduated: MA 1935, MB, ChB 1940, MD 1950, Edinburgh Univ.; FRSE 1950; FRCPE 1958; FRCPGlas 1964; FFCM 1973; DrPH Johns Hopkins University 1952. DPH London University, 1947. Served War of 1939-45 with RAMC, 1941-46. Rockefeller Fellow in Preventive Medicine, 1946-48; Lecturer in Social and Preventive Medicine at Guy's Hospital Medical School and London School of Hygiene and Tropical Medicine, 1948-51; Senior Lecturer, subsequently Reader, Public Health, London School of Hygiene and Tropical Medicine, 1951-55; Prof. of Public Health and Social Medicine, University of Edinburgh, 1955-64; Dean of the Faculty of Medicine, University of Edinburgh, 1958-63; Chief MO, Scottish Home and Health Dept, 1964-77. Mem. MRC, 1974-. Hon. FRSH 1967. Hon. LLD Aberdeen, 1971. Bronfman Prize, 1971. *Publications:* Observations on the early Public Health Movement in Scotland, 1952; various contribs to medical and other jls on social medicine and medical education. *Address:* 26 Mortonhall Road, Edinburgh EH9 2HN. *T:* 031-667 2849.

BROTHERTON, Harry George, CBE 1949; President of the Confederation of Shipbuilding and Engineering Unions, 1948-58; General Secretary of the National Union of Sheet Metal Workers and Braziers, 1941-55; *b* 3 Dec. 1890; *s* of Henry William Brotherton; *m* 1915, Daisy Beatrice (*d* 1953), *d* of Walter Henry King; *m* 1958, May, *d* of John Summers. *Recreation:* reading. *Address:* 18 Cornwallis Gardens, Broadstairs, Kent.

BROTHERTON, Michael Lewis; MP (C) Louth since Oct. 1974; *b* 26 May 1931; *s* of John Basil Brotherton and Maud Brotherton; *m* 1968, Julia, *d* of Austin Gerald Comyn King and Katherine Elizabeth King, Bath; three *s* one *d*. *Educ:* Prior Park; RNC Dartmouth. Served RN, 1949-64; qual. Observer 1955; Cyprus, 1957 (despatches); Lt-Comdr 1964, retd. Times Newspapers, 1967-74. Chm., Beckenham Conservative Political Cttee, 1967-68; contested (C) Deptford, 1970; Pres., Hyde Park Tories, 1975. *Recreations:* cricket, cooking. *Address:* The Old Vicarage, Wrangle, Boston, Lincs. *T:* Old Leake 688. *Clubs:* Army and Navy, MCC; Conservative Working Men's (Louth).

BROTHWOOD, John, MB, DPM; MRCP, FFCM, FRCPsych; Senior Principal Medical Officer, Department of Health and Social Security, since 1975; *b* 23 Feb. 1931; *s* of Wilfred Cyril Vernon Brothwood and Emma Bailey; *m* 1957, Dr Margaret Stirling Meyer; one *s* one *d*. *Educ:* Marlborough Coll.; Peterhouse, Cambridge (Schol.); Middlesex Hosp. MB BChir (Cantab) 1955; MRCP 1960, DPM (London) 1964, FFCM 1972, FRCPsych 1976. Various posts in clinical medicine (incl. Registrar, Maudsley Hosp. and military service as Captain RAMC), 1955-64; joined DHSS (then Min. of Health) as MO, 1964; posts held in mental health, regional liaison, chronic disease policy and medical manpower and educn. *Publications:* various, on NHS matters, especially mental health policy and related topics. *Recreations:* diverse. *Address:* 13 Great Spilmans, SE22. *T:* 01-693 8273.

BROUGH, Edward; Chairman, Adriaan Volker (UK) Ltd, since 1974; *b* 28 May 1918; *s* of late Hugh and Jane Brough; *m* 1941, Peggy Jennings; two *s*. *Educ:* Berwick Grammar School; Edinburgh University (MA). Joined Unilever Ltd, 1938. War service, KOSB, 1939-46 (Captain). Rejoined Unilever, 1946; Commercial Dir, 1951, Man. Dir, 1954, Lever's Cattle Foods Ltd; Chairman, Crosfields (CWG) Ltd, 1957; Lever Bros & Associates Ltd: Development Dir, 1960; Marketing Dir, 1962; Chm., 1965; Hd of Unilever's Marketing Div., 1968-71; Dir of Unilever Ltd and Unilever NV, 1968-74, and Chm. of UK Cttee, 1971-74. Mem., NBPI, 1967-70. FBIM 1967. *Recreations:* flyfishing, golf. *Address:* Far End, The Great Quarry, Guildford, Surrey. *T:* Guildford 4064; St John's, Chagford, Devon. *Club:* Farmers'.

BROUGH, Prof. John, MA, DLitt; FBA 1961; Professor of Sanskrit, University of Cambridge, since 1967; Fellow of St John's College; *b* 1917; *er s* of Charles and Elizabeth Brough, Maryfield, Dundee; *m* 1939, Marjorie Allan, *d* of Dr W. A. Robertson; one *d*. *Educ:* High School, Dundee; University of Edinburgh; St John's College, Cambridge. First Class Hons in Classics, Edinburgh, 1939; First Class in Classical Tripos, Part II, 1940; First Class in Oriental Langs Tripos, Parts I and II, 1941 and 1942; Fellow St John's College, Cambridge, 1945-48. DLitt Edinburgh, 1945. Worked in agriculture, 1940-43, and as asst in agricultural research, 1943-44. Asst Keeper, Dept of Oriental Printed Books and MSS, British Museum, 1944-46; Lecturer in Sanskrit, School of Oriental and African Studies, University of London, 1946-48; Prof. of Sanskrit in the University of London, 1948-67. *Publications:* Selections from Classical Sanskrit Literature, 1951; The Early Brahmanical System of Gotra and Pravara, 1953; The GāndhārīDharmapada, 1962; Poems from the Sanskrit, 1968; articles in Chambers's Encyclopædia and Encyclopædia Britannica; and in specialist journals. *Recreations:* music, gardening. *Address:* 5 Thorn Grove, Bishop's Stortford, Herts CM23 5LB. *T:* Bishop's Stortford 51407.

BROUGHAM, family name of **Baron Brougham and Vaux.**

BROUGHAM AND VAUX, 5th Baron *cr* 1860; **Michael John Brougham;** *b* 2 Aug. 1938; *s* of 4th Baron and Jean, *d* of late Brig.-Gen. G. B. S. Follett, DSO, MVO; *S* father, 1967; *m* 1963, Olivia Susan (marr. diss. 1968), *d* of Rear-Admiral Gordon Thomas Seccombe Gray; one *d*; *m* 1969, Catherine Gulliver, *d* of W. Gulliver; one *s*. *Educ:* Lycée Jaccard, Lausanne; Millfield School. *Heir: s* Hon. Charles William Brougham, *b* 9 Nov. 1971. *Address:* 28 Westmoreland Place, SW1. *Club:* Turf.

BROUGHSHANE, 2nd Baron (UK), *cr* 1945; **Patrick Owen Alexander Davison;** *b* 18 June 1903; *er s* of 1st Baron and Beatrice Mary, *d* of Sir Owen Roberts; *S* father 1953; *m* 1929, Bettine, *d* of Sir Arthur Russell, 6th Bt; one *s*. *Educ:* Winchester; Magdalen College, Oxford. Barrister, Inner Temple, 1926. Served War of 1939-45: with Irish Guards, 1939-41; Assistant Secretary (Military), War Cabinet, 1942-45. Has US Legion of Merit. *Heir: s* Hon. Alexander Davison, *b* 1936. *Address:* 21 Eaton Square, SW1; 28 Fisher Street, Sandwich, Kent. *Clubs:* White's, Garrick.

BROUGHTON, family name of **Baron Fairhaven.**

BROUGHTON, Sir Alfred Davies Devonsher, Kt 1969; DL; MP (Lab) for Batley and Morley, Yorkshire, since Feb. 1949; retired physician; *b* 18 Oct. 1902; *s* of A. G. S. Broughton, MB, JP; *m* 1st, 1930, Dorothy, MA, PhD (marr. diss. 1967), *d* of late Commander W. D. Parry Jones, RD, RNR; one *s* one *d*; 2nd, 1967, Joyce Diana, *d* of H. S. Denton; Leeds. *Educ:* Rossall School; Cambridge Univ.; London Hosp. MRCS (Eng.), LRCP (Lond.), 1929; MA, MB, BChir (Cantab.), 1936; DPM (Leeds), 1936; DPH (Leeds), 1937; Casualty Officer at Poplar Hospital, 1929-30. Receiving Room Officer at London Hospital, 1930; Resident MO at Rossall School, 1930-32; Medical Practitioner in Batley, 1932-40 and 1945-50. Served War of 1939-45, RAFVR (Squadron Leader), 1940-45. Member of Batley Borough Council, 1946-49. Opposition Whip, 1960-64. UK delegate to Council of Europe and to Assembly of WEU, 1956-58. Member of Speaker's Panel of Chairmen, 1964-76. Hon. Treasurer, Commonwealth Parly Assoc., 1969-70. Vice-Pres., Leeds Trustee Savings Bank, 1974-. DL W Yorks, 1971. Hon. Freeman of Morley, 1972, of Batley, 1973. SBStJ 1946, OStJ 1951. *Publication:* Clean Handling of Food, 1953. *Address:* Stockwell Shay Farm, Batley, W Yorkshire. *T:* 474321.

BROUGHTON, Air Marshal Sir Charles, KBE 1965 (CBE 1952); CB 1961; RAF retired; Air Member for Supply and Organization, Ministry of Defence, 1966-68; *b* 27 April 1911; *s* of Charles and Florence Gertrude Broughton; *m* 1939, Sylvia Dorothy Mary Bunbury; one *d* (and one *d* decd). *Educ:* New Zealand; RAF College, Cranwell. Commissioned, 1932; India, 1933-37; Flying Instructor, 1937-40. Served War of 1939-45 in Coastal Command and Middle East (despatches four times). Flying Training Command, 1947-49; Air Ministry, 1949-51; Imperial Defence College, 1952; NATO, Washington DC, 1953-55; Far East, 1955-58; Transport Command, 1958-61; Dir-General of Organization, Air Min. (subseq. Min. of Defence), 1961-64; UK Representative in Ankara on Permanent Military Deputies Group of Central Treaty Organization (Cento), 1965-66. *Address:* c/o 52 Shrewsbury House, Cheyne Walk, SW3. *Club:* Royal Air Force.

BROUGHTON, Major Sir Evelyn Delves, 12th Bt, *cr* 1660; *b* 2 Oct. 1915; *s* of Major Sir Henry Delves Broughton, 11th Bt, and Vera Edyth Boscawen (*d* 1968); *S* father, 1942; *m* 1st, 1947, Hon. Elizabeth Florence Marion Cholmondeley (marr. diss., 1953), *er d* of 4th Baron Delamere, *qv*; 2nd, 1955, Helen Mary (marr. diss. 1974), *d* of J. Shore, Wilmslow, Cheshire; three *d* (one *s* decd); 3rd, 1974, Mrs Rona Crammond. *Educ:* Eton; Trinity Coll., Cambridge. Formerly 2nd Lieut Irish Guards and Major RASC. *Heir presumptive: kinsman* David Delves Broughton, *b* 7 May 1942. *Address:* 3 Dunraven Street, W1. *T:* 01-409 0423; Doddington, Nantwich, Cheshire. *T:* Bridgmere 240.

See also Baron Lovat.

BROUGHTON, Leonard, DL; Chairman, Lancashire County Council, since 1974; *b* 21 March 1924; *s* of Charles Cecil Broughton and Florence (née Sunman); *m* 1949, Kathleen Gibson; one *d*. *Educ:* Kingston-upon-Hull. Served RASC, 1942-47. Estates Manager, Bedford Borough Council, 1957; business man. Member: Blackpool County Borough Council, 1961-74 (Leader, 1968-73); Blackpool Bor. Council, 1974-; Leader, Lancs CC, 1974-; Member: NW Co. Boroughs' Assoc., 1968-74; NW Economic Planning Council, 1970-72; Assoc. of Co. Councils, 1973-; Board, Central Lancs Develt Corp., 1976-. Mem. Courts, Lancaster and Salford Univs, 1974-; Lay Mem., Greater Manch. and Lancs Rent Assessment Panel, 1971-; Vice-President: Lancs Youth Clubs Assoc., 1974-; NW Arts Assoc., 1974-; Blackpool Social Service Council, 1974-; Chm., Blackpool and Fylde Civilian Disabled Soc. 1964-. Freeman, Co. Borough of Blackpool, 1973. DL Lancs, 1975. *Recreations:* gardening, overseas travel. *Address:* Kingsmede, 157 Whitegate Drive, Blackpool, Lancs FY3 9ER. *Club:* Royal Over-Seas League.

BROUMAS, Nikolaos; retired General; Hon. Deputy Chief, Hellenic Armed Forces; Ambassador of Greece to the Court of

St James's, 1972-74; *b* 22 Aug. 1916; *s* of Taxiarches and Kostia Broumas; *m* 1945, Claire Pendelis; two *d. Educ:* Greek Military Academy. US Infantry Coll., 1947-48; Greek Staff Coll., 1952; Greek Nat. Defence Coll., 1954. Co. Comdr, Greece, 1940-41, Western Desert, 1942-43 and Italy, 1944; Co. and Bn Comdr, Greek Guerrilla War, 1946-49; Liaison Officer, Allied Comd Far East, Korean War, 1951; Dep. Nat. Rep. to NATO Mil. Cttee, 1959-61; Dep. Chief of Greek Armed Forces, 1969-72. Kt Comdr, Orders of George I and of the Phoenix. (Greek) Gold Medal for Valour (4 times); Military Cross (twice); Medal for Distinguished Services (twice); Medal of Greek Italian War; Medal of Middle East War; UN Medal of Korean War, 1951; US Bronze Star Medal with oak leaf cluster, 1951. *Recreation:* hunting. *Address:* 5 Argyrokastrou Street, Papagos, Athens, Greece.

BROUN, Sir Lionel John Law, 12th Bt, *cr* 1686; *b* 25 April 1927; *s* of 11th Bt and Georgie, *y d* of late Henry Law, Sydney, NSW; *S* father 1962. *Heir: c* William Windsor Broun [*b* 1917; *m* 1952, D'Hrie King, NSW; two *d*]. *Address:* 89 Penshurst Street, Willoughby, NSW 2068, Australia.

BROWN; *see* Clifton-Brown.

BROWN; *see* George-Brown.

BROWN, Baron *cr* 1964 (Life Peer); **Wilfred Banks Duncan Brown,** PC 1970; MBE 1944; lately Chairman, The Glacier Metal Co. Ltd (1939-65), and Director, Associated Engineering Ltd; *b* 29 Nov. 1908; British; *m* 1939, Marjorie Hershell Skinner; three *s. Educ:* Rossall Sch. Joined The Glacier Metal Co. Ltd, 1931; Sales Manager, 1935; Director, 1936; Joint Managing Director, 1937; Managing Director and Chairman, 1939-65. A Minister of State, Board of Trade, 1965-70. Mem., Industrial Develt Adv. Bd, 1975-; Chm., Machine Tool Adv. Cttee, 1975-. Pro-Chancellor, Brunel University, 1966. Hon. Degrees: DTech Brunel, 1966; Doctor of Laws Illinois, 1967; DSc Cranfield, 1972. *Publications:* (with Mrs W. Raphael) Managers, Men and Morale, 1947; Exploration in Management, 1960; Piecework Abandoned, 1962; (with Elliott Jaques) Product Analysis Pricing, 1964; (with Elliott Jaques) Glacier Project Papers, 1965; Organization, 1971; The Earnings Conflict, 1973. *Recreation:* golf. *Address:* Flat 13, 23 Prince Albert Road, NW1. *T:* 01-722 8040. *Club:* Reform.

BROWN, Alan Brock; Supernumerary Fellow, Worcester College, Oxford, since 1971 (Fellow since 1937); Hon. Bencher, Inner Temple, since 1972; *b* 30 April 1911; *s* of Harold Rinder Brown and Elsie Clara Burnet Brown (*née* Lord), Brisbane; *m* 1940, Elizabeth Muriel McCarthy, Moss Vale, NSW; four *s. Educ:* Geelong Grammar Sch.; New Coll., Oxford (BCL, MA). Vinerian Law Scholar, Oxford, 1935; called to Bar, Inner Temple, 1935; admitted to Bar of NSW, 1936. Commnd into Scots Guards, 1940; served in UK, N Africa, Italy (Captain, wounded, despatches). Worcester College: Domestic Bursar, 1947-58; Estates Bursar, 1957-66; Senior Tutor, 1961-66; Vice-Provost, 1967-71. University Member, Oxford City Council, 1939-65; Mayor of Oxford, 1953-54. Sen. Proctor, Oxford Univ., 1950-51; Mem. Hebdomadal Council, 1951-65. Sen. Mem., Oxford Univ. Law Soc., 1945-65; Hon. Treasurer: Oxford Univ. Athletic Club, 1945-54; Oxford Univ. Boxing Club, 1945-53; Sen. Mem., Oxford Univ. Penguins Lawn Tennis Club, 1945-65 and Oxford Univ. Australian Club, 1945-66; Pres., Oxford Consumers Group; Pres., UK Br. Old Geelong Grammarians. *Recreations:* gardening, music, reading, talking, making speeches. *Address:* Worcester College, Oxford. *T:* Oxford 47251. *Club:* Vincent's (Oxford).

BROWN, Alan James; HM Diplomatic Service, retired; Deputy Commissioner-General, UN Relief and Works Agency for Palestine Refugees, since 1977; *b* 28 Aug. 1921; *s* of W. Y. Brown and Mrs E. I. Brown; *m* 1966, Joy Aileen Key Stone (*née* McIntyre); one *s,* and two step *d. Educ:* Magdalene College, Cambridge (MA). Served with HM Forces, 1941-47; CRO 1948; 2nd Sec., Calcutta, 1948-50; CRO, 1951; Private Sec. to Parly Under-Secretary of State, 1951-52; 1st Secretary, Dacca, Karachi, 1952-55; CRO, 1955-57; Kuala Lumpur, 1957-62; CRO, 1962-63; Head of Information Policy Dept, 1963-64; Dep. High Comr, Nicosia, 1964; Head of Far East and Pacific Dept, CRO, 1964-66; Dep. High Comr, Malta, 1966-70; Dep High Comr, later Consul-Gen., Karachi, 1971-72; Ambassador to Togo and Benin, 1973-75; Head of Nationality and Treaty Dept, FCO, 1975-77. *Recreation:* sailing. *Address:* UNRWA HQ, Museitbeh Quarter, Beirut, Lebanon. *Club:* United Oxford & Cambridge University.

BROWN, Alan Winthrop; Chief Executive, Employment Service Agency, since 1976; *b* 14 March 1934; *s* of James Brown and

Evelyn V. Brown (*née* Winthrop); *m* 1959, Rut Berit (*née* Ohlson); two *s* one *d. Educ:* Bedford Sch.; Pembroke Coll., Cambridge (BA Hons); Cornell Univ., NY (MSc). Joined Min. of Labour, 1959; Private Sec. to Minister, 1961-62; Principal, 1963; Asst Sec., 1969. Dir of Planning, Employment Service Agency, 1973-74; Head of Incomes Div., Dept of Employment, 1975. *Publications:* papers on occupational psychology and industrial training. *Recreations:* cross-country jogging, tennis, squash, gardening. *Address:* Groton, Ballfield Road, Godalming, Surrey GU7 2HE.

BROWN, Albert Peter Graeme; Director of Information, Department of Health and Social Security, and Adviser to the Secretary of State for Social Services, since 1968; *b* 5 April 1913; *s* of William Edward Graeme Brown, accountant, and Amy Powell Brown; unmarried. *Educ:* Queen Elizabeth's Sch., Darlington. Reporter, Sub-Editor, Dep.-Chief Sub-Editor, Westminster Press, 1932-40. Served War of 1939-45: Royal Navy, Officer, Western Approaches; Normandy; Far East; destroyers and assault ships. Information Divs, Ministries of Health, Local Govt and Planning, also Housing and Local Govt, 1946; Chief Press and Inf. Officer, Min. of Housing and Local Govt, 1958. *Recreations:* cricket, opera (Mem. Friends of Covent Garden), classical music. *Address:* 107 Hamilton Terrace, St John's Wood, NW8. *T:* 01-286 9192. *Club:* MCC.

BROWN, Alexander Cosens Lindsay; Chief Veterinary Officer, Ministry of Agriculture, Fisheries and Food, since 1973; *b* Glasgow, 30 Jan. 1920; *s* of William Tait Brown and Margaret Rae; *m* 1945, Mary McDougal Hutchison; two *s* one *d. Educ:* Hutchesons' Grammar Sch., Glasgow; Glasgow Veterinary Coll. Diploma of RCVS; MRCVS 1943. Ministry of Agriculture, Fisheries and Food: appointed Vet. Officer to Dorset, 1943; Divisional Vet. Officer, HQ Tolworth, 1955; Divisional Vet. Officer, Essex, 1958-62; Dep. Regional Vet. Officer, W Midland Region, Wolverhampton, 1962-63; Regional Vet. Officer, Eastern Region, Cambridge, 1963; HQ Tolworth, 1967; Dep. Dir, Veterinary Field Services, 1969-70, Dir, 1970-73. Mem. ARC, 1975-. *Publications:* contribs to Jl of Royal Soc. of Medicine, Veterinary Record, State Veterinary Jl. *Recreations:* gardening, swimming, reading. *Address:* 36 Links Road, Ashtead, Surrey. *T:* Ashtead 72487.

BROWN, Alexander Douglas G.; *see* Gordon-Brown.

BROWN, Sir Allen (Stanley), Kt 1956; CBE 1953; MA; LLM; Australian Commissioner for British Phosphate Commissioners and Christmas Island Phosphate Commission, since 1970; *b* 3 July 1911; *m* 1936, Hilda May Wilke; one *s* two *d. Educ:* Sec. of Post-War Reconstruction, 1948. Sec., PM's Dept and Sec. to Cabinet, Commonwealth Govt, 1949-58; Deputy Australian High Commissioner to UK, 1959-65; Australian Ambassador to Japan, 1965-70. *Address:* Phosphate House, 515 Collins Street, Melbourne, Vic 3000, Australia. *Clubs:* Savage, Melbourne (Melbourne); Commonwealth (Canberra).

BROWN, Anthony Geoffrey Hopwood G.; *see* Gardner-Brown.

BROWN, Gen. Arnold; International Leader, and General, Salvation Army, since 1977; *b* 13 Dec. 1913; *s* of Arnold Rees Brown and Annie Brown; *m* 1939, Jean Catherine Barclay; two *d . Educ:* Belleville Collegiate, Canada. Commnd Salvation Army Officer, 1935; Editor, Canadian War Cry, 1937-47; Nat. Publicity Officer, Canada, 1947-62; Nat. Youth Officer, Canada, 1962-64; Head of Internat. Public Relations, Internat. HQ, London, 1964-69; Chief of Staff, 1969-74; Territorial Comdr, Canada and Bermuda, 1974-77. *Publication:* What Hath God Wrought?, 1952. *Recreations:* reading, writing, music. *Address:* 101 Queen Victoria Street, EC4P 4EP. *T:* 01-236 5222. *Club:* Rotary of London.

BROWN, Prof. Arthur; Professor of English, Monash University, since 1973; *b* 8 March 1921; *s* of Herbert Brown and Edith Mary Honour; *m* 1946, Eudora Margaret Whitehead (marr. diss. 1975); four *s* one *d. Educ:* Urmston Grammar Sch.; University Coll. London. BA 1947, MA 1949, DLit 1965. Undergraduate, Dept of English, UCL, 1939-41, 1946-47. Served RAF, 1941-46. Dept of English, UCL: Quain Student, 1947-50; Lectr, 1950-56; Commonwealth Fund Fellow, 1953-54 (held mainly at Folger Shakespeare Library, Washington, Huntington Library, Calif, libraries of Harvard and Yale and Univs of Texas and Virginia.); Foyle Research Fellow, Shakespeare Inst., Stratford-upon-Avon (Univ. of Birmingham), 1958-59; Reader in English, UCL, 1956-62 (by conferment of title); Prof. of English, UCL, 1962-69 (by conferment of title); Prof. of Library Studies and Dir of Sch. of Library, Archive and Inf. Studies, UCL, 1969-73. Sen. Fellow, South Eastern Inst. of Medieval and Renaissance Studies, Duke Univ., North Carolina, Summer 1966; Commonwealth Vis.

Prof. of English, Sydney Univ., 1972. Gen. Editor, The Malone Society, 1961-71. Pres., Bibliographical Soc. of Aust. and NZ, 1974-76. Fellow of UCL, 1971. *Publications:* Editor (alone and in collab.) of numerous vols for Malone Society; A Whole Theatre of Others (anthology of Elizabethan and Jacobean Drama), 1960; ed (with P. G. Foote) Early English and Norse Studies, 1963; Edmond Malone and English Scholarship, 1963; articles and studies in Mod. Lang. Review, Mod. Lang. Quarterly, Shakespeare Survey, The Library, Studies in Bibliography, Year's Work in English Studies, Philological Quarterly, etc. *Recreations:* taking snuff, walking, talking, reading booksellers' catalogues, amateur printing, maps. *Address:* Department of English, Monash University, Clayton, Victoria 3168, Australia. *Clubs:* Athenæum; United Arts (Dublin).

BROWN, Arthur Godfrey Kilner, MA; Headmaster, Worcester Royal Grammar School, since 1950; *b* 21 Feb. 1915; *s* of Rev. Arthur E. Brown, CIE, MA, BSc, and Mrs Brown, formerly of Bankura, India; *m* 1939, Mary Denholm Armstrong; one *s* three *d. Educ:* Warwick Sch.; Peterhouse, Cambridge. BA Cantab 1938; MA 1950. Assistant Master, Bedford School, 1938-39; King's School, Rochester, 1939-43; Cheltenham College, 1943-50. Elected to Headmasters' Conference, 1950. *Recreations:* athletics (Olympic Games, 1936); music, gardening. *Address:* Whiteladies, The Tything, Worcester. *T:* Worcester 23753. *Clubs:* Achilles; Hawks (Cambridge); Rotary (Worcester).
See also Hon. Sir R. K. Brown.

BROWN, A(rthur) I(vor) Parry, FFARCS; Anæsthetist: London Hospital, 1936-73; London Chest Hospital, 1946-73; Harefield Hospital, 1940-73; Royal Masonic Hospital, 1950-73; retired; *b* 23 July 1908; *s* of A. T. J. Brown; *m* Joyce Marion Bash. *Educ:* Tollington Sch., London; London Hospital. MRCS, LRCP, 1931; MB, BS London, 1933; DA, 1935; FFARCS, 1951. Member of the Board of the Faculty of Anæsthetists, RCS; Pres., Sect. of Anæsthetics, RSM, 1972-73; Fellow, Assoc. of Anæsthetists; Member, Thoracic Soc. *Publications:* chapter in Diseases of the Chest, 1952; contributions to: Thorax, Anæsthesia. *Address:* Long Thatch, Church Lane, Balsham, Cambridge. *T:* West Wratling 270.

BROWN, Sir (Arthur James) Stephen, KBE 1967; CEng, MIMechE; Chairman, Molins Ltd, since 1971; Director, Porvair Ltd, since 1971; Chairman, Stone-Platt Industries Ltd, 1968-73 (Deputy Chairman, 1965-67); Deputy Chairman, Chloride Group, 1965-73; *b* 15 Feb. 1906; *s* of Arthur Mogg Brown, and Ada Kelk (*née* Upton); *m* 1935, Margaret Alexandra McArthur; one *s* one *d. Educ:* Taunton School; Bristol University (BSc(Eng.)). Apprenticed British Thomson-Houston Co. Ltd, 1928-32; joined J. Stone & Co. Ltd, 1932, Dir, 1945; Man. Dir J. Stone & Co. (Deptford) Ltd (on formation), 1951; Divisional Dir, Stone-Platt Industries Ltd (on formation), 1958; Dir, Fairey Co., 1971-76. Pres., Engineering Employers' Fedn, 1964-65; Pres., Confedn of British Industry, 1966-68, Vice-Pres., 1969-; Founder Mem., Export Council for Europe, 1960 (Dep. Chm. 1962-63); Mem., NEDC, 1966-71. Hon. DSc, Aston Univ., 1967. *Recreations:* shooting, fishing, golf. *Address:* Cut Hedges, Bolney, Sussex. *T:* Bolney 225. *Club:* Brooks's.

BROWN, Prof. Arthur Joseph, CBE 1974; FBA 1972; Professor of Economics, University of Leeds, since 1947; Pro-Vice-Chancellor, Leeds University, 1975-77; *b* 8 Aug. 1914; *s* of J. Brown, Alderley Edge, Cheshire; *m* 1938, Joan H. M., *d* of Rev. Canon B. E. Taylor, Holy Trinity, Walton Breck, Liverpool; two *s* (and one *s* decd). *Educ:* Bradford Grammar School; Queen's College, Oxford. First Class Hons in Philosophy, Politics and Economics, 1936. Fellow of All Souls College, Oxford, 1937-46; Lectr in Economics, Hertford College, Oxford, 1937-40; on staff of: Foreign Research and Press Service, 1940-43; Foreign Office Research Dept, 1943-45; Economic Section, Offices of the Cabinet, 1945-47. Head of Dept of Economics and Commerce, University of Leeds, 1947-65. Visiting Professor of Economics, Columbia University, City of New York, Jan.-June 1950. President Section F, British Assoc. for the Advancement of Science, 1958; Member: East African Economic and Fiscal Commn, 1960; UN Consultative Group on Economic and Social Consequences of Disarmament, 1961-62; First Secretary of State's Advisory Group on Central Africa, 1962; Hunt Cttee on Intermediate Areas, 1967-69; Council, Royal Economic Society, 1950-68 and 1974- (Pres., 1976-78); UGC, 1969-. Chairman, Adv. Panel on Student Maintenance Grants, 1967-68. Vis. Prof. ANU, 1963; directing Regional Economics project, National Institute of Economic and Social Research, 1966-72. Hon. DLitt Bradford, 1975. *Publications:* Industrialisation and Trade, 1943; Applied Economics-Aspects of the World Economy in War and Peace, 1948; The Great Inflation, 1939-51, 1955; Introduction to the World Economy, 1959; The Framework of Regional

Economics in the United Kingdom, 1972; (with E. M. Burrows) Regional Economic Problems, 1977; articles in various journals. *Recreations:* gardening and walking. *Address:* 24 Moor Drive, Leeds LS6 4BY. *T:* Leeds 755799. *Club:* Athenæum.

BROWN, Brig. Athol Earle McDonald, CMG 1964; OBE 1956; *b* 2 Jan. 1905; *s* of W. J. C. G. and Alice Catherine Brown, Armidale, NSW; *m* 1929, Millicent Alice Heesh, Sydney; two *s* one *d. Educ:* The Armidale Sch., NSW; Royal Australian Naval Coll.; Sydney Univ. Served War of 1939-45: Royal Australian Artillery, AIF, Middle East and New Guinea; Director, War Graves Services, AIF, 1944-46; Lt-Col, 1944; Brigadier, 1946. Secretary-General: Imperial War Graves Commn, 1946-60; Commonwealth-Japanese Jt Cttee, 1956-69; Dir and Sec.-Gen., Commonwealth War Graves Commn, Pacific Region, 1960-69. *Recreations:* golf, bowls, motoring. *Address:* 351 Belmore Road, North Balwyn, Victoria 3104, Australia. *T:* 357 7544. *Club:* Royal Automobile (Victoria).

BROWN, Dame Beryl P.; *see* Paston Brown.

BROWN, Carter; *see* Brown, John C.

BROWN, Lt-Col Sir Charles Frederick Richmond, 4th Bt, *cr* 1863; TD; DL; *b* 6 Dec. 1902; *er s* of Frederick Richmond Brown (*d* 1933; 2nd *s* of 2nd Bt); *S* uncle, 1944; *m* 1st, 1933, Audrey (marr. diss., 1948), 2nd *d* of late Col Hon. Everard Baring, CVO, CBE, and late Lady Ulrica Baring; one *s* two *d*; 2nd, 1951, Hon. Gwendolen Carlis Meysey-Thomson (marr. diss. 1969), *y d* of 1st (and last) Baron Knaresborough; 3rd, 1969, Pauline, widow of Edward Hildyard, Middleton Hall, Pickering, Yorks. *Educ:* Eton. Joined Welsh Guards, 1921; Captain 1932; retired with a gratuity, 1936; joined 5th Bn Green Howards, Territorial Army, as a Major, March 1939; Lieut-Colonel comdg 7th Bn Green Howards, July 1939, and proceeded to France with 7th Bn, April 1940. DL, North Riding of County of York, 1962. *Heir:* *s* George Francis Richmond Brown, *b* 3 Feb. 1938. *Address:* Stonely Woods, Fadmoor, York. *T:* Kirby Moorside 31293. *Clubs:* Cavalry and Guards, Pratt's; Yorkshire (York).

BROWN, Sir (Charles) James Officer, Kt 1969; Consultant Thoracic Surgeon: Alfred Hosp.; St Vincent's Hosp.; Queen Victoria Memorial Hosp.; Austin Hosp. (all in Melbourne); *b* 24 Sept. 1897; *s* of David Brown; *m* 1932, Esme Mai Frankenberg; two *d. Educ:* Scotch Coll., Melbourne; Melbourne Univ. MB BS 1920, MD 1922, FRCS 1924, FRACS 1928. Surgeon, Alfred Hosp., 1929-57; Surgeon, Austin Hosp., 1926-67. Mem. Council, Royal Australian Coll. of Surgeons, 1956-68; Pres., National Heart Foundation (Victorian Division), 1966-72. *Publications:* papers in surgical journals. *Recreation:* golf. *Address:* 2/1 Monaro Road, Kooyong, Victoria 3144, Australia. *T:* 207313. *Clubs:* Melbourne, Royal Melbourne Golf (Melbourne); Victoria Racing.

BROWN, Admiral Charles Randall, Bronze Star 1943; Legion of Merit 1944; Presidential Unit Citation, 1945; DSM 1960; United States Navy, retired, 1962; *b* Tuscaloosa, Alabama, USA, 13 Dec. 1899; *s* of Robison Brown and Stella Seed Brown; *m* 1921, Eleanor Green, Annapolis, Maryland; two *s. Educ:* US Naval Academy; US Air University; US Naval War College. Graduated from US Naval Academy, 1921. During War served on original US Joint Chiefs of Staff and US-British Combined Chiefs of Staff organisations; later, Captain of USS Kalinin Bay and USS Hornet and Chief of Staff of a Fast Carrier Task Force. Commander, US Sixth Fleet, Mediterranean, 1956; C-in-C, Allied Forces Southern Europe, 1959-61. Vice-President for European Affairs, McDonnell Aircraft Corp. of St Louis, Mo, 1962-65. *Recreation:* gardening. *Address:* 4000 Massachusetts Avenue NW, Apartment 1428, Washington, DC 20016, USA. *Clubs:* Army and Navy, Army and Navy Country (Washington, DC); The Brook, New York Yacht (NY).

BROWN, Rev. Cyril James, OBE 1956; Rector of Warbleton, 1970-77; Chaplain to the Queen, 1956-74; *b* 12 Jan. 1904; *s* of late James Brown, Clifton, Bristol; *m* 1931, Myrtle Aufrère, *d* of late Mark Montague Ford, London; no *c. Educ:* Westminster Abbey Choir School; Clifton College; Keble College, Oxford; St Stephen's House, Oxford. Curate of St Gabriel's, Warwick Square, 1927-31; Chaplain, Missions to Seamen, Singapore, 1931-34, Hong Kong, 1934-41; Chaplain, Hong Kong RNVR, 1941-46; Youth Secretary, Missions to Seamen, 1946-47, Superintendent, 1947-51, General Superintendent, 1951-59, General Secretary, 1959-69; Prebendary of St Paul's, 1958-69. *Publications:* contributions to East and West Review, World Dominion, etc. *Recreation:* choral music. *Address:* c/o National Westminster Bank, 19 High Street, Heathfield, Sussex.

BROWN, Sir (Cyril) Maxwell Palmer, (Sir Max), KCB 1969 (CB 1965); CMG 1957; Director: Schroder International; John Brown & Co.; Ransome Hoffmann Pollard Ltd; Electrical Research Association; Deputy Chairman, Monopolies and Mergers Commission, since 1976 (Member since 1975); *b* 30 June 1914; *s* of late Cyril Palmer Brown; *m* 1940, Margaret May Gillhespy; three *s* one *d*. *Educ:* Wanganui College; Victoria University College, NZ; Clare College, Cambridge. Princ. Private Secretary to Pres. Board of Trade, 1946-49; Monopolies Commn, 1951-55; Counsellor (Commercial) Washington, 1955-57; Board of Trade: Under-Sec. 1961-64; Second Sec., 1964-67; Second Permanent Sec., 1968-70; Sec. (Trade), DTI, 1970-74; Permanent Sec., Dept of Trade, March-June 1974. *Address:* 20 Cottenham Park Road, Wimbledon, SW20. *T:* 01-946 7237.

BROWN, Sir David, Kt 1968; Chairman of The David Brown Corporation Ltd, since 1951; *b* 10 May 1904; *s* of Francis Edwin (Frank) and Caroline Brown; *m* 1st, 1926, Daisie Muriel Firth (marr. diss. 1955); one *s* one *d*; 2nd, 1955, Marjorie Deans. *Educ:* Rossall School; Private Tutor in Engineering; Huddersfield Technical Coll.; CEng, FIMechE; AFRAeS. David Brown and Sons (Hudd.), Ltd, 1921; Dir, 1929; Man. Dir, 1932. Founded David Brown Tractors Ltd (first company to manufacture an all-British tractor in England), 1935; formed, 1951, The David Brown Corp. Ltd embracing gears, machine tools, castings, etc. Chairman: Vosper Ltd; John I. Thornycroft & Co. Ltd; Director, Sonnerdale, Richardson, David Brown Ltd, Australia; President: Aston Martin Lagonda; David Brown Tractors. Underwriting Member of Lloyd's; Past Member: Board of Governors of Huddersfield Royal Infirmary; Council of Huddersfield Chamber of Commerce. First Englishman to open Canadian Farm and Industrial Equipment Trade Show, Toronto, 1959; inaugurated Chief Flying Sun of Iroquois Tribe of Mohawk Nation, Toronto, 1959. Owner of 1550 acres in Bucks, most of which he farms, and 2000 acres in NSW. *Recreations:* hunting, polo, yachting. *Address:* Chequers Manor, Cadmore End, Nr High Wycombe, Bucks. *T:* High Wycombe 881282; 96/97 Piccadilly, W1. *T:* 01-629 7373. *Clubs:* Royal Thames Yacht, Royal Automobile, British Racing Drivers; Guards Polo, Ham Polo.

BROWN, Rt. Rev. David Alan; *see* Guildford, Bishop of.

BROWN, Denise Lebreton, (Mrs Frank Waters), RE 1959 (ARE 1941); Artist; *d* of Jeanne Lebreton and Frederick Peter Brown; *m* 1938, Frank William Eric Waters; one *s*. *Educ:* Lyzeum Nonnenwerth im Rhein; Royal College of Art. British Instn Schol. in Engraving, 1932; ARCA 1935; prox. acc, 1936; Rome scholarship in engraving; Royal College of Art Travelling Schol., 1936. Has exhibited at: Royal Academy regularly, 1937-71; Royal Society of Painter-Etchers and Engravers; also in Canada, USA and S Africa. *Publications:* books illustrated include: several on gardening; children's books, etc. *Recreations:* music, gardening. *Address:* Casula, Sarratt Lane, Loudwater, Rickmansworth, Herts. *T:* Rickmansworth 75505.

BROWN, Denys Downing, CMG 1966; MM 1945; an Executive Director, Peninsular and Oriental Steam Navigation Co., since 1971; *b* 16 Dec. 1918; *s* of A. W. Brown, Belfast, and Marjorie Downing; *m* 1954, Patricia Marjorie, *e d* of late Sir Charles Bartley; one *s* one *d*. *Educ:* Hereford Cathedral School; Brasenose College, Oxford (Scholar). Oxf. and Bucks LI, 1939-45 (prisoner-of-war, 1940; escaped, 1945). Entered Foreign Service, 1946; served in Poland, Germany, Egypt, Yugoslavia, Sweden, and FO; Minister (Economic), Bonn, 1970-71, retired 1971. *Recreations:* reading, winter sports. *Address:* Beechcroft, Priorsfield Road, Godalming, Surrey. *T:* Godalming 6635. *Club:* Travellers'.

BROWN, Derek Ernest D.; *see* Denny-Brown.

BROWN, Derrick H.; *see* Holden-Brown.

BROWN, Douglas Dunlop, QC 1976; a Recorder, since 1972; *b* 22 Dec. 1931; *s* of late Robert Dunlop Brown, MICE, and of Anne Cameron Brown; *m* 1960, June Margaret Elizabeth McNamara; one *s*. *Educ:* Ryleys Sch., Alderley Edge; Manchester Grammar Sch.; Manchester Univ. (LLB). Served in RN, 1953-55; Lieut, RNR. Called to Bar, Gray's Inn, 1953; practised Northern Circuit from 1955; Mem. General Council of Bar, 1967-71; Asst Recorder, Salford City QS, 1971. *Recreations:* cricket, golf, music. *Address:* Byeways, Moss Road, Alderley Edge, Cheshire. *T:* Alderley Edge 582027. *Club:* East India, Devonshire, Sports and Public Schools.

BROWN, Douglas James, MBE 1959; HM Diplomatic Service; Consul-General, St Louis, since 1977; *b* 6 May 1925; *s* of James Stephen Brown and Hilda May (*née* Hinch); unmarried. *Educ:*

Edinburgh Univ. (MA). HMOCS, Nigeria, 1951-62 (Private Sec. to Governor-General, 1955-58); joined Diplomatic Service, 1962; Private Sec. to Comr-Gen. for SE Asia, 1962-63; FO, 1963-66; Asst to Special Representative in Africa, 1966-67; British High Commn, Nairobi, 1967-68; British Embassy, Djakarta, 1968-71; Inspector, FCO, 1971-73; Counsellor and Consul-Gen., Algiers, 1974-77. *Address:* c/o Foreign and Commonwealth Office, SW1; 9 Amherst Avenue, Ealing, W13 8NQ. *T:* 01-997 7125; Via Privata Oliveta 41/18, 16035 Rapallo, Italy. *Club:* Royal Over-Seas League.

BROWN, Sir Edward (Joseph), Kt 1961; MBE 1958; JP; MP (C) Bath since 1964; Laboratory Technician (non-ferrous metals); company director; *b* 15 April 1913; *s* of Edward Brown; *m* 1940, Rosa, *d* of Samuel Feldman; one *s* one *d*. *Educ:* Greencoat Elementary; Morley College (Day Continuation). Leading Aircraftsman, RAF, 1942-46. Formerly Mem. Assoc. Supervisory Staffs Executives and Technicians (Chm., Enfield Branch, 1953-63); Dist Councillor for Union. Member Tottenham Borough Council, 1956-64. Chm., National Union of Conservative and Unionist Associations, 1959, 1960; Chm. Conservative Party Conference, 1960; Vice-Chm., Assoc. of Conservative Clubs. Contested Stalybridge and Hyde (C), 1959. JP (Middlesex) 1963. *Recreation:* campanology. *Address:* 71 Holly Walk, Enfield, Middlesex. *T:* 01-363 3450; The Gate House, Bathwick Hill, Bath. *Clubs:* Tottenham Conservative; Harringay-West Green Constitutional; Bath and County.

BROWN, Edwin Percy; Director of Social Services, North Yorkshire County Council, since 1973; Supplementary Benefits Commissioner, since 1976; *b* 20 May 1917; *s* of late James Percy Brown and of Hetty Brown; *m* 1958, Margaret (*née* Askey); one *s* one *d*. *Educ:* Mundella Grammar Sch., Nottingham; Nottingham Univ. (Certif. in Social Studies). Social worker, Nottinghamshire CC, 1951-54; Sen. social worker, Lancashire CC, 1954-59; Children's Officer: Southampton CC, 1959-65; Wiltshire CC, 1965-71; Dir of Social Services, N Riding CC, 1971-74. Adviser to Assoc. of County Councils, 1974-; Pres., Assoc. of Directors of Social Services, 1977-78. *Recreations:* boating, gardening, cricket. *Address:* 21 The Green, Romanby, Northallerton, N Yorkshire.

BROWN, Captain Eric Melrose, CBE 1970 (OBE 1945; MBE 1944); DSC 1942; AFC 1947; RN; Chief Executive, British Helicopter Advisory Board, since 1970; *b* 21 Jan. 1919; *s* of Robert John Brown and Euphemia (*née* Melrose); *m* 1942, Evelyn Jean Margaret Macrory; one *s*. *Educ:* Royal High Sch., Edinburgh; Edinburgh University. MA 1947. Joined Fleet Air Arm as Pilot, 1939; Chief Naval Test Pilot, 1944-49; Resident British Test Pilot at USN Air Test Center, Patuxent River, 1951-52; CO No 804 Sqdn, 1953-54; Comdr (Air), RN Air Stn, Brawdy, 1954-56; Head of British Naval Air Mission to Germany, 1958-60; Dep. Dir (Air), Gunnery Div., Admty, 1961; Dep. Dir, Naval Air Warfare and Adviser on Aircraft Accidents, Admty, 1962-64; Naval Attaché, Bonn, 1965-67; CO, RN Air Stn, Lossiemouth, 1967-70. FRAeS 1964; Chm., RAeS Rotocraft Sect., 1973. British Silver Medal for Practical Achievement in Aeronautics, 1949. *Publications:* Wings on My Sleeve, 1961; (jtly) Aircraft Carriers, 1969; Wings of the Luftwaffe, 1977; contribs to aviation and naval jls. *Recreations:* tennis, golf, ski-ing, bridge. *Address:* Carousel, New Domewood, Copthorne, Sussex. *T:* Copthorne 712610. *Clubs:* Naval and Military, Steering Wheel.

BROWN, Sir (Ernest) Henry Phelps, Kt 1976; MBE 1945; FBA 1960; Professor of Economics of Labour, University of London, 1947-68, now Emeritus Professor; *b* 10 Feb. 1906; *s* of E. W. Brown, Calne, Wiltshire; *m* 1932, Dorothy Evelyn Mostyn, *d* of Sir Anthony Bowlby, 1st Bt, KCB; two *s* one *d*. *Educ:* Taunton School; Wadham College, Oxford (Scholar). Secretary of Oxford Union, 1928; 1st Class Hons Modern History, 1927; Philosophy, Politics and Economics, 1929. Fellow of New College, Oxford, 1930-47; Hon. Fellow, Wadham College, Oxford, 1969-; Rockefeller Travelling Fellow in USA, 1930-31. Served War of 1939-45, with Royal Artillery; BEF; ADGB; First Army; Eighth Army (MBE). Member: Council on Prices, Productivity and Incomes, 1959; Nat. Economic Development Council, 1962; Royal Commn on Distribn of Income and Wealth, 1974-. Chairman, Tavistock Inst. of Human Relations, 1966-68. Hon. DLitt Heriot-Watt, 1972. *Publications:* The Framework of the Pricing System, 1936; A Course in Applied Economics, 1951; The Balloon (novel), 1953; The Growth of British Industrial Relations, 1959; The Economics of Labor, 1963; A Century of Pay, 1968; The Inequality of Pay, 1977. *Recreations:* walking; represented Oxford *v* Cambridge cross-country running, 1926. *Address:* 16 Bradmore Road, Oxford. *T:* Oxford 56320. *Club:* Athenæum.

BROWN, Sir (Frederick Herbert) Stanley, Kt 1967; CBE 1959; BSc; CEng, FIMechE, FIEE; Chairman, Central Electricity Generating Board, 1965-72 (Deputy-Chairman, 1959-64); *b* 9 Dec. 1910; *s* of Clement and Annie S. Brown; *m* 1937, Marjorie Nancy Brown; two *d. Educ:* King Edward's School, Birmingham; Birmingham University. Corp. of Birmingham Electric Supply Dept, 1932-46; West Midlands Joint Electricity Authority, 1946-47; Liverpool Corporation Electricity Supply Department, 1947-48; Merseyside and N. Wales Division of British Electricity Authority; Generation Engineer (Construction), 1948-49; Chief Generation Engineer (Construction), 1949-51; Deputy Generation Design Engineer of British Electricity Authority, 1951-54; Generation Design Engineer, 1954-57, Chief Engineer, 1957, of Central Electricity Authority; Member for Engineering, Central Elec. Generating Board, 1957-59. President: Instn. of Electrical Engineers, 1967-68; EEIBA, 1969-70. Member: Council, City and Guilds of London Inst., 1969-; Court of Govs, Univ. of Birmingham, 1969-. Hon. DSc: Aston, 1971; Salford, 1972. *Publications:* various papers to technical institutions. *Recreations:* gardening, motoring. *Address:* Cobbler's Hill, Compton Abdale, Glos. *T:* Withington 233. *Club:* Royal Automobile.

BROWN, Hon. Geoffrey E.; *see* Ellman-Brown.

BROWN, Hon. George Arthur, CMG; Governor, Bank of Jamaica, since 1967; *b* 25 July 1922; *s* of Samuel Austin Brown and Gertrude Brown; *m* 1964, Leila Leonie Gill; two *d* (and one *s* one *d* by previous marriage). *Educ:* St Simon's College, Jamaica; London School of Economics. Jamaica Civil Service: Income Tax Dept, 1941; Colonial Secretary's Office. 1951; Asst Secretary, Min. of Finance, 1954; Director, General Planning Unit, 1957; Financial Secretary, 1962. *Publications:* contrib. Social and Economic Studies (University College of the West Indies). *Recreations:* hiking, boating, fishing. *Address:* Beau Monde, 1 Harbour View Road, Constant Spring, Jamaica. *Clubs:* Jamaica; Kingston Cricket (Jamaica).

BROWN, George Frederick William, CMG 1974; Member, Victorian Railway Board, since 1973; Member, Melbourne Underground Railway Loop Authority, since 1971; *b* 12 April 1908; *s* of late G. Brown; *m* 1933, Catherine Mills; one *d* (and one *d* decd). *Educ:* Christian Brothers' Coll., Essendon; Phahran Techn. Coll.; Royal Melbourne Inst. Technology. FIE (Aust.), AMIME (Aust.), FCIT, FAIM. Victorian Railways, 1923; Asst Engr 1929; Country Roads Bd, 1934; Plant Engr Newport Workshops, 1939-43; Supt Loco. Maintenance, 1943-53; Chief Mech. Engr, 1953-58; Comr, 1958-61; Dep. Chm., 1961-67; Chm., 1967-73. Mem. Council, Royal Melb. Inst. Technology, 1958-74, Pres. 1970. *Publications:* articles in techn. jls on rail transport. *Recreation:* golf. *Address:* 66 Baird Street, East Brighton, Victoria 3187, Australia. *Clubs:* Kelvin Victoria, Victoria Golf.

BROWN, George Mackay, OBE 1974; author; *b* 17 Oct. 1921; *s* of John Brown and Mary Jane Mackay. *Educ:* Stromness Acad.; Newbattle Abbey Coll.; Edinburgh Univ. (MA). Hon. MA Open Univ., 1976; Hon. LLD Dundee, 1977. *Publications: fiction:* A Calendar of Love, 1967; A Time to Keep, 1969; Greenvoe, 1972; Magnus, 1973; Hawkfall, 1974; The Two Fiddlers, 1975; The Sun's Net, 1976; Pictures in the Cave, 1977; *play:* A Spell for Green Corn, 1970; *poetry:* Winterfold, 1976; Selected Poems, 1977; *essays, etc:* An Orkney Tapestry, 1969; Letters from Hamnavoe, 1975. *Recreations:* ale drinking, watching television. *Address:* 3 Mayburn Court, Stromness, Orkney KW16 3DH.

BROWN, Prof. George Malcolm, FRS 1975; FRSE 1967; Professor of Geology, Durham University, since 1967; *b* 5 Oct. 1925; *s* of George Arthur Brown and Anne Brown (*née* Fellows); *m* 1963, Valerie Jane Gale. *Educ:* Sir William Turner's Sch., Redcar; Durham Univ. (BSc, DSc); Oxford Univ. (MA, DPhil). FGS. Commonwealth Fund (Harkness) Fellow, Princeton Univ., 1954-55; Lectr in Petrology, Oxford Univ., 1955-66; Fellow, St Cross Coll., Oxford, 1965-67; Carnegie Instn Res. Fellow, Geophysical Lab., Washington DC, 1966-67. Daniel Pidgeon Fund Award, 1952, and Wollaston Fund Award, 1963, Geol Soc. of London. *Publications:* (with L. R. Wager) Layered Igneous Rocks, 1968; (contrib.) Methods in Geochemistry, 1960; (contrib.) Basalts, 1967; papers in several sci. jls. *Recreations:* exploration, music. *Address:* Department of Geological Sciences, South Road, Durham DH1 3LE. *T:* Durham 64971. *Club:* United Oxford & Cambridge University.

BROWN, Gilbert Alexander M.; *see* Murray-Brown.

BROWN, Gillian Gerda, CMG 1971; HM Diplomatic Service; Under-Secretary, Department of Energy, since 1975; *b* 10 Aug. 1923; *er d* of late Walter Brown and late Gerda Brown (*née* Grenside). *Educ:* The Spinney, Gt Bookham; Stoatley Hall, Haslemere; Somerville Coll., Oxford. FO, 1944-52; 2nd Sec., Budapest, 1952-54; FO, 1954-59; 1st Sec., Washington, 1959-62; 1st Sec., UK Delegn to OECD, Paris, 1962-65; FO, 1965-66; Counsellor and Head of Gen. Dept, FO, subseq. Head of Aviation, Marine and Telecommunications Dept, later Marine and Transport Dept, FCO, 1967-70; Counsellor, Berne, 1970-74. *Address:* c/o Foreign and Commonwealth Office, SW1.

BROWN, Prof. Godfrey Norman; Professor of Education and Director, Institute of Education, University of Keele, since 1967; *b* 13 July 1926; *s* of Percy Charles and Margaret Elizabeth Brown; *m* 1960, Dr Freda Bowyer; three *s. Educ:* Whitgift Sch.; School of Oriental and African Studies, London; Merton Coll., Oxford (MA, DPhil). Army service, RAC and Intelligence Corps, 1944—48. Social Affairs Officer, UN Headquarters, NY, 1953-54; Sen. History Master, Barking Abbey Sch., Essex, 1954-57; Lectr in Educn, University Coll. of Ghana, 1958-61; Sen. Lectr, 1961, Prof., 1963, Univ. of Ibadan, Nigeria. Visiting Prof., Univ. of Rhodesia and Nyasaland, 1963; Chm., Assoc. for Recurrent Educn, 1976-77. *Publications:* An Active History of Ghana, 2 vols, 1961 and 1964; Living History, 1967; ed (with J. C. Anene) Africa in the Nineteenth and Twentieth Centuries, 1966; ed, Towards a Learning Community, 1971; ed (with M. Hiskett) Conflict and Harmony in Education in Tropical Africa, 1975; contrib. educnl jls. *Recreations:* family life; art history. *Address:* Betley Court, Betley, near Crewe, Cheshire.

BROWN, Harold, PhD; Secretary of Defense, United States of America, since 1977; *b* 19 Sept. 1927; *s* of Abraham Howard Brown and Gertrude Cohen Brown; *m* 1953, Colene McDowell; two *d. Educ:* Columbia Univ. (AB 1945, AM 1946, PhD in Physics 1949). Res. Scientist, Columbia Univ., 1945-50, Lectr in Physics, 1947-48; Lectr in Physics, Stevens Inst. of Technol., 1949-50; Res. Scientist, Radiation Lab., Univ. of Calif, Berkeley, 1951-52; Gp Leader, Radiation Lab., Livermore, 1952-61; Dir, Def. Res. and Engrg, Dept of Def., 1961-65; Sec. of Air Force, 1965-69; Pres., Calif Inst. of Technol., Pasadena, 1969-77. Sen. Sci. Adviser, Conf. on Discontinuance of Nuclear Tests, 1958-59; Delegate, Strategic Arms Limitations Talks, Helsinki, Vienna and Geneva, 1969-77. Member: Polaris Steering Cttee, 1956-58; Air Force Sci. Adv. Bd, 1956-61; (also Consultant) President's Sci. Adv. Cttee, 1958-61. Hon. DEng Stevens Inst. of Technol., 1964; Hon. LLD: Long Island Univ., 1966; Gettysburg Coll., 1967; Occidental Coll., 1969; Univ. of Calif, 1969; Hon. ScD Univ. of Rochester, 1974. One of Ten Outstanding Young Men of Year, US Jun. Chamber of Commerce, 1961; Columbia Univ. Medal of Excellence, 1963; Air Force Exceptl Civil. Service Award, 1969; Dept of Def. Award for Exceptionally Meritorious Service, 1969; Joseph C. Wilson Award, 1976. *Address:* Department of Defense, Washington, DC 20301, USA. *Clubs:* Athenæum; Bohemian (San Francisco); Cosmos (Washington, DC); University (NYC).

BROWN, Harold Arthur Neville, CMG 1963; CVO 1961; HM Diplomatic Service, retired; *b* 13 Dec. 1914; *s* of Stanley Raymond and Gladys Maud Brown; *m* 1939, Mary McBeath Urquhart; one *s* one *d. Educ:* Cardiff High School; University College, Cardiff. Entered Ministry of Labour as 3rd Class Officer, 1939; Asst Principal, 1943; Private Sec. to Permanent Sec. of Min. of Labour and Nat. Service, 1944-46; Principal, 1946; Labour Attaché, Mexico City (and other countries in Central America and the Caribbean), 1950-54; transferred to Foreign Office, 1955; Head of Chancery, Rangoon, 1958 and 1959; British Ambassador in Liberia, 1960-63; Corps of Inspectors, Foreign Office, 1963-66; Ambassador to Cambodia, 1966-70; Consul-General, Johannesburg, 1970-73; Minister, Pretoria, Cape Town, 1973-74. Knight Great Band of the Humane Order of African Redemption, 1962. *Address:* 14 Embassy Court, King's Road, Brighton BN1 2PX.

BROWN, Harold James, BSc, ME; FIE(Australia); FIREE; Technical Director, Philips Industries Holdings Ltd, Sydney, since 1961; director of several companies; *b* 10 July 1911; *s* of Allison James and Hilda Emmy Brown; *m* 1936, Hazel Merlyn Dahl Helm; two *s* two *d. Educ:* Fort Street Boys' High Sch.; Univ. of Sydney, NSW, Australia. BSc 1933; BE (Univ. Medal) 1935; ME (Univ. Medal) 1945. Research Engineer, Amalgamated Wireless Australasia Ltd, 1935-37; Electrical Engineer, Hydro-electric Commission of Tasmania, 1937-39; Research Officer and Principal Research Officer, Council for Scientific and Industrial Research, 1939-45; Chief Communications Engineer, Australian Nat. Airways Pty Ltd, 1945-47; Prof. of Electrical Engineering, Dean of Faculty of Engineering and Asst Director, NSW Univ. of Technology, 1947-52; Controller, R&D Dept of Supply, Melbourne, 1952-54; Controller, Weapons Research Establishment, Department of Supply, Commonwealth Government of Australia, 1955-58;

Technical Director, Rola Co. Pty Ltd, Melbourne, 1958-61. Chairman: Engineering Course Assessment Cttee of NSW Advanced Educn Bd; Australian Council of Awards in Advanced Educn; Member: Council, Canberra Coll. of Advanced Educn; Australian Telecommunications Develt Assoc.; Engineering Ind. Adv. Cttee; Metric Conversion Bd (Chm. Electrical and Electronic Sector Cttee). *Publications:* numerous technical articles in scientific journals. *Recreations:* gardening, bowling. *Address:* 39c Boronia Avenue, Cheltenham, Sydney, NSW 2119, Australia. *Club:* University (Sydney).

BROWN, Sir Henry Phelps; *see* Brown, Sir E. H. P.

BROWN, Henry Thomas C.; *see* Cadbury-Brown.

BROWN, Herbert Macauley Sandes; a Judge of the High Court of Nigeria, 1945-58, retd; *b* Dublin, Feb. 1897; *o s* of late William Herbert Brown, KC, sometime County Court Judge, of Glenfern, Blackrock, Co. Dublin, and Elizabeth Rose (*née* Sandes); *m* 1928, Catherine Mary (*née* Hutchinson) (*d* 1971); one *d. Educ:* The Abbey Tipperary; Trinity College, Dublin. Served War of 1914-18 in Royal Marines. Called to the Irish Bar, 1921. Entered Administrative Service, Nigeria, 1924; Magistrate, 1934; Assistant Judge, 1943; Puisne Judge, 1945. *Address:* 9 Astra House, King's Road, Brighton BN1 2HJ.

BROWN, Prof. H(oward) Mayer; Ferdinand Schevill Distinguished Service Professor of Music, University of Chicago, since 1976; *b* 13 April 1930; *s* of Alfred R. and Florence Mayer Brown; unmarried. *Educ:* Harvard Univ. AB 1951, AM 1954, PhD 1959. Walter Naumburg Trav. Fellow, Harvard, 1951-53; Instructor in Music, Wellesley Coll., Mass, 1958-60; Univ. of Chicago: Asst Prof., 1960-63; Assoc. Prof., 1963-66; Prof., 1967-72; Chm., 1970-72; Dir of Collegium Musicum, 1960-72; King Edward Prof. of Music, KCL, 1972-74. Guggenheim Fellow, Florence, 1963-64; Villa I Tatti Fellow, Florence, 1969-70; Andrew D. White Prof.-at-large, Cornell Univ., 1972-76; Prof. of Music, Univ. of Chicago, 1974-. *Publications:* Music in the French Secular Theater, 1963; Theatrical Chansons, 1963; Instrumental Music Printed Before 1600, 1965; (with Joan Lascelle) Musical Iconography, 1972; Sixteenth-Century Instrumentation, 1972; Music in the Renaissance, 1976; Embellishing Sixteenth-Century Music, 1976; contrib. Jl Amer. Musicological Soc., Acta musicologica, Musical Quarterly, etc. *Address:* 1415 E 54th Street, Chicago, Ill 60615, USA. *Club:* Reform.

BROWN, Hugh Dunbar; MP (Lab) Provan Division of Glasgow since 1964; Parliamentary Under-Secretary of State, Scottish Office, since 1974; *b* 18 May 1919; *s* of Neil Brown and Grace (*née* Hargrave); *m* 1947, Mary Glen Carmichael; one *d. Educ:* Allan Glen's School and Whitehill Secondary School, Glasgow. Formerly Civil Servant, Ministry of Pensions and National Insurance. Member of Glasgow Corporation, 1954; Magistrate, Glasgow, 1961. *Recreation:* golf. *Address:* 29 Blackwood Road, Milngavie, Glasgow.

BROWN, Prof. James Alan Calvert, MA; Professor of Applied Economics, Oxford University, and Fellow of Merton College, since 1970; *b* Bury, Lancs, 8 July 1922; *s* of Harry and Mary Brown. *Educ:* Bury Grammar Sch.; Emmanuel Coll., Cambridge (BA 1946, MA 1951); MA Oxon 1970. War Service, 1942-46. Min. of Agriculture, Fisheries and Food, 1947-52; Research Officer, Dept of Applied Economics, Cambridge Univ., 1952-65, Fellow of Queens' Coll., 1961-65; Prof. of Econometrics, Bristol Univ., 1965-70. Mem., SW Electricity Bd, 1966-72. *Publications:* monographs: (with J. Aitchison) Lognormal Distribution, 1957; (with R. Stone) Computable Model of Economic Growth, 1962; Exploring, 1970; contribs to econ. and statistical lit. *Recreation:* travel. *Address:* Institute of Economics and Statistics, Manor Road, Oxford OX1 3UL. *T:* Oxford 49631.

BROWN, Sir James Officer; *see* Brown, Sir (Charles) James Officer.

BROWN, Sir James (Raitt), Kt 1948; Third Church Estates Commissioner, 1954-62, retired; a Vice-Patron SPCK, since 1973 (Vice-President and Member, Board of Governors, 1958-72); a Trustee of Toc H since 1954; *b* 9 May 1892; *s* of James Brown and Margaret Laing, 2nd *d* of David Raitt; *m* 1926, Joanna Martin (*d* 1971), *d* of late Lewis Bennett. *Educ:* Merchant Taylors' School, London. Junior Clerk, Ecclesiastical Commission, 1912; Secretary, 1937; Steward of the Manors, 1937; Financial Adviser, 1944; Secretary of Church Comrs for England, 1948-54. Member, Church Assembly (co-opted), 1955-65. Chm., Ecclesiastical Insurance Office Ltd, 1961-71. A Governor, Westfield Coll., Univ. of London, 1954-69; Trustee,

City Parochial Foundn, 1963-69; Trustee, Highgate Literary and Scientific Instn (Pres., 1954-73), and Trustee of other local educnl trusts. Served European War, 1914-19, First Surrey Rifles (TA) and Oxford and Buckinghamshire LI (despatches twice). LLD (Lambeth), 1962. *Publication:* Number One, Millbank, 1944. *Address:* 20 Southwood Lawn Road, Highgate, N6 5SF. *T:* 01-340 6147. *Clubs:* Athenæum; Highgate Golf (Highgate).

BROWN, Joe, MBE 1975; Freelance Guide and Climber; *b* 26 Sept. 1930; *s* of J. Brown, Longsight, Manchester; *m* 1957, Valerie Gray; two *d. Educ:* Stanley Grove, Manchester. Started climbing while working as plumber in Manchester; pioneered new climbs in Wales in early 1950's; gained internat. reputation after climbing West Face of Petit Dru, 1954; climbed Kanchenjunga, 1955; Mustagh Tower, 1956; Mt Communism, USSR, 1962; Climbing Instructor, Whitehall, Derbs, 1961-65; opened climbing equipment shops, Llanberis, 1965, Capel Curig, 1970; Leader of United Newspapers Andean Expedn, 1970; Roraima Expedn, 1973. Hon. Fellow, Manchester Polytechnic, 1970. *Publication:* (autobiog.) The Hard Years, 1967. *Recreations:* mountaineering, ski-ing, fishing, canoeing. *Address:* Menai Hall, Llanberis, Gwynedd. *T:* Llanberis 327. *Club:* Climbers'.

BROWN, Prof. John; FIEE; Professor of Electrical Engineering, and Head of Electrical Engineering Department, Imperial College of Science and Technology, since 1967; *b* 17 July 1923; *s* of George Brown and Margaret Ditchburn Brown; *m* 1947, Maureen Dorothy Moore; one *d. Educ:* Edinburgh University. Radar Research and Development Estab., 1944-51; Lectr, Imperial Coll., 1951-54; University Coll., London: Lectr, 1954-56; Reader, 1956-64; Prof., 1964-67; seconded to Indian Inst. of Technology as Prof. of Electrical Engrg, 1962-65. Mem., SRC, 1977-. Vice-Pres., IEE, 1975-. *Publications:* Microwave Lenses, 1953; (with H. M. Barlow) Radio Surface Waves, 1962; Telecommunications, 1964; papers in Proc. IEE, etc. *Recreations:* photography, gardening. *Address:* 1 Longfield Road, Ealing, W5.

BROWN, John B.; *see* Blamire-Brown.

BROWN, (John) Carter; Director, National Gallery of Art, Washington, DC, since 1969; Chairman, Commission of Fine Arts, since 1971; *b* 8 Oct. 1934; *s* of John Nicholas Brown and Anne Kinsolving Brown; *m* 1976, Pamela Braga Drexel. *Educ:* Harvard (AB *summa cum laude* 1956; MBA 1958); Inst. of Fine Arts, NY Univ. (Museum Trng Prog., Metropol. Museum of Art; MA 1962). Studied: with Bernard Berenson, Florence, 1958; Ecole du Louvre, Paris, 1958-59; Rijksbureau voor Kunsthistoriche Documentatie, The Hague, 1961. National Gallery of Art: Asst to Dir, 1961-63; Asst Dir, 1964-68; Dep. Dir, 1968-69. Hon. Mem., Amer. Inst. of Architects, 1975. Hon. LLD Brown Univ., RI, 1970; Hon. LHD: Mount St Mary's Coll., Md, 1974; Georgetown Univ., Washington, DC, 1975. Gold Medal of Honour, National Arts Soc., 1972. Commandeur, l'Ordre des Arts et des Lettres, France, 1975; Chevalier de la Légion d'Honneur, France, 1976. Phi Beta Kappa, 1956. Author/Dir, (film), The American Vision, 1966. *Publications:* contrib. professional jls and exhibn catalogues. *Recreations:* sailing, riding, photography. *Address:* 700 New Hampshire Avenue NW, Washington, DC 20037, USA. *T:* (office) (202) 737-4215. *Clubs:* Knickerbocker, Century Association, New York Yacht, Cruising Club of America (New York); Metropolitan, Cosmos, 1925 F Street (Washington).

BROWN, Sir John (Douglas Keith), Kt 1960; Chairman: McLeod Russel & Co., Ltd, London, since 1972 (Director since 1963); Robb Caledon Shipbuilders Ltd; Titaghur Jute Factory Co. Ltd; Barnagore Jute Factory Co. Ltd, since 1972; Director of other companies; *b* 8 Sept. 1913; *s* of late Ralph Douglas Brown and Rhoda Miller Keith; *m* 1940, Margaret Eleanor, *d* of late William Alexander Burnet; two *s. Educ:* Glasgow Acad. CA 1937. Joined Messrs. Lovelock & Lewes, Chartered Accountants, Calcutta, October 1937 (Partnership, 1946; retired 1948); joined Jardine Henderson, Ltd, as a Managing Director, 1949; Chairman, 1957-63. Pres. Bengal Chamber of Commerce and Industry and Associated Chambers of Commerce of India, 1958-60; Pres. UK Citizens' Assoc. (India), 1961. Mem. Eastern Area Local Bd, Reserve Bank of India, 1959-63; Mem. Advisory Cttee on Capital Issues, 1958-63; Mem. Technical Advisory Cttee on Company Law, 1958-63; Mem. Companies Act Amendment Cttee, 1957; Mem. Central Excise Reorganisation Cttee, 1960. *Recreations:* gardening, walking. *Address:* Windover, Whitmore Vale Road, Hindhead, Surrey. *T:* Hindhead 4173. *Clubs:* Oriental, City of London; Bengal (Calcutta).

BROWN, Ven. John Edward; Archdeacon of Berkshire, since 1978; *b* 13 July 1930; *s* of Edward and Muriel Brown; *m* 1956, Rosemary (*née* Wood); one *s*. *Educ:* Wintringham Grammar Sch., Grimsby; Kelham Theological Coll., Notts. BD London. Deacon 1955, priest 1956; Master, St George's School, Jerusalem; Curate, St George's Cathedral, Jerusalem; Chaplain of Amman, Jordan, 1954-57; Curate-in-Charge, All Saints, Reading, 1957-60; Missionary and Chaplain, All Saints Cathedral, Khartoum, Sudan, 1960-64; Vicar: Stewkley, Buckingham, 1964-69; St Luke's, Maidenhead, 1969-73; Bracknell, Berkshire, 1973-77; Rural Dean of Sonning, 1974-77. Commissary of Archbishop of the Sudan and of Bishop of Omdurman. *Recreations:* walking; Middle East and African studies. *Address:* Beech Hill Vicarage, Reading, Berks. *T:* Reading 882569.

BROWN, Sir John (Gilbert Newton), Kt 1974; CBE 1966; MA; Publisher, Oxford University Press since 1956; *b* 7 July 1916; *s* of John and Molly Brown, Chilham, Kent; *m* 1946, Virginia, *d* of late Darcy Braddell and of Dorothy Braddell, *qv*; one *s* two *d*. *Educ:* Lancing Coll.; Hertford Coll., Oxford (MA Zoology). Bombay Branch Oxford University Press, 1937-40; commissioned Royal Artillery, 1941; served with 5th Field Regiment, 1941-46; captured by the Japanese at Fall of Singapore, 1942; prisoner of war, Malaya, Formosa and Japan, 1942-45; returned Oxford University Press, 1946; Sales Manager, 1949; Chm., University Bookshops (Oxford) Ltd; Director: Harlequin Enterprises Toronto Ltd; Infoline Ltd; Bookbinders of London Ltd; Book Tokens Ltd; Willshaw Booksellers Ltd, Manchester. President, Publishers' Association, 1963-65. Member: Board of British Council; Nat. Libraries Cttee; EDC for Newspapers, Printing and Publishing Industry, 1967-; Adv. Cttee on Scientific and Technical Information, 1969-73; Communication Adv. Cttee for UK Nat. Cttee for UNESCO; Royal Literary Fund (Asst Treasurer); Bd of British Library. Professorial Fellow, Hertford Coll., Oxford, 1974. FRSA 1964. *Recreation:* gardening. *Address:* Milton Lodge, Great Milton, Oxon. *T:* Great Milton 217; 8 Lansdowne Road, Holland Park, W11. *T:* 01-727 5487. *Club:* Garrick.

BROWN, Prof. John Russell; Professor of English, Sussex University, since 1971; Associate Director, The National Theatre, since 1973; *b* 15 Sept. 1923; *yr s* of Russell Alan and Olive Helen Brown, Coombe Wood, Somerset; *m* 1961, Hilary Sue Baker; one *s* two *d*. *Educ:* Monkton Combe Sch.; Keble Coll., Oxford. Sub-Lieut (AE) RNVR, 1944-46. Fellow, Shakespeare Inst., Stratford-upon-Avon, 1951-55; Lectr and Sen. Lectr, Dept of English, Birmingham Univ., 1955-63; Hd of Dept of Drama and Theatre Arts, Univ. of Birmingham, 1964-71; Reynolds Lectr, Colorado Univ., 1957; Vis. Prof. Graduate Sch., New York Univ., 1959; Mellon Prof. of Drama, Carnegie Inst., Pittsburgh, 1964; Vis. Prof., Zürich Univ., 1969-70; Univ. Lectr in Drama, Univ. of Toronto, 1970. Robb Lectr, Univ. of Auckland, 1976. Dir, Orbit Theatre Co. Member: Adv. Council of British Theatre Museum; Drama Panel, SE Arts Assoc. *Theatre productions include:* Twelfth Night, Playhouse, Pittsburgh, 1964; Macbeth, Everyman, Liverpool, 1965; The White Devil, Everyman, 1969; Crossing Niagara, Nat. Theatre at the ICA, 1975; They Are Dying Out, Young Vic, 1976; Old Times, British Council tour of Poland, 1976. Gen. Editor: Stratford-upon-Avon Studies, 1960-67; Stratford-upon-Avon Library, 1964-. *Publications:* (ed) The Merchant of Venice, 1955; Shakespeare and his Comedies, 1957; (ed) The White Devil, 1960; Shakespeare: The Tragedy of Macbeth, 1963; (ed) The Duchess of Malfi, 1965; (ed) Henry V, 1965; Shakespeare's Plays in Performance, 1966; Effective Theatre, 1969; Shakespeare's The Tempest, 1969; Shakespeare's Dramatic Style, 1970; Theatre Language, 1972; Free Shakespeare, 1974; articles in Shakespeare Survey, Critical Quarterly, Tulane Drama Review, Studies in Bibliography, etc. *Recreations:* gardening, travel. *Address:* c/o The National Theatre, SE1 8AE.

BROWN, Joseph Lawler, TD 1953; FInstM; DL; Chairman and Managing Director, The Birmingham Post & Mail Ltd, since 1973; *b* 22 March 1921; *s* of late Neil Brown; *m* 1950, Mabel Smith, SRN, SCM; one *s* one *d*. *Educ:* Peebles; Heriot-Watt Coll., Edinburgh. FInstM 1976. Served War, The Royal Scots, 1939-46 (Major). The Scotsman Publications Ltd, 1947-60; Coventry Newspapers Ltd: Gen. Man., 1960; Jt Man. Dir, 1961; Man. Dir, 1964-69; The Birmingham Post & Mail Ltd: Dep. Man. Dir, 1970; Man. Dir, 1971. Director: Cambridge Newspapers Ltd, 1965-69; Press Assoc., 1968-75 (Chm. 1972); Reuters Ltd, 1972-75; BPM (Holdings) Ltd, 1973-. Vice-Pres., Birmingham Chamber of Industry and Commerce, 1975-. DL County of W Midlands, 1976. Commendatore, Order Al Merito Della Repubblica Italiana, 1973. *Recreations:* gardening, fishing, Japanese woodcuts. *Address:* Westerly, 37 Mearse Lane, Barnt Green, Birmingham B45 8HH. *T:* 021-445 1234.

BROWN, Sir Kenneth (Alfred Leader), Kt 1963; *b* 26 Jan. 1906; *s* of late Henry Robert Brown; *m* 1931, Emily Agnes (*d* 1967), *d* of W. J. Pugsley; two *s* one *d*. *Educ:* Worcester Cathedral King's School.·Marine Engineer and Surveyor; Company Director. *Recreations:* shooting, fishing. *Address:* The White House, Whitley Batts, Pensford, Avon. *Clubs:* Constitutional, Bristol, University (all Bristol).

BROWN, Kenneth Vincent, CMG 1954; Senior Judge, Supreme Court, Trinidad, 1943-52, retired; *b* 1 Nov. 1890; *m* 1942, Vere Alice Edghill (*d* 1944); one *s*. *Educ:* St George's Coll., Weybridge, Surrey. Barrister, Gray's Inn, 1915; Magistrate, Trinidad, 1925; Puisne Judge, 1936. Coronation Medals, 1937, 1953. *Recreations:* cricket, racing. *Address:* 1 Taylor Street, Woodbrook, Port-of-Spain, Trinidad. *Clubs:* Union, Trinidad Turf, Queen's Park Cricket (Port-of-Spain).

BROWN, Rt. Rev. Laurence Ambrose, MA; *b* 1 Nov. 1907; 2nd *s* of Frederick John Brown; *m* 1935, Florence Blanche, *d* of late William Gordon Marshall; three *d*. *Educ:* Queens' College, Cambridge (MA); Cuddesdon Theological College, Oxford. Asst Curate, St John-the-Divine, Kennington, 1932-35; Curate-in-Charge, St Peter, Luton, Beds, 1935-40; Vicar, Hatfield Hyde, Welwyn Garden City, 1940-46; Sec. Southwark Dio. Reorganisation Cttee, 1946-60; Sec. S London Church Fund and Southwark Dio. Bd of Finance, 1952-60; Canon Residentiary, Southwark, 1950-60; Archdeacon of Lewisham and Vice-Provost of Southwark, 1955-60; Suffragon Bishop of Warrington, 1960-69; Bishop of Birmingham. 1969-77. Mem. Church Assembly, later General Synod, and Proctor in Convocation, 1954-77; Chairman: Advisory Council for Church's Ministry, 1966-71; Industrial Christian Fellowship, 1971-77; Mem., Religious Adv. Bd, Scout Assoc., 1953-. Mem., House of Lords, 1973-77. *Publications:* pamphlets on church building in post-war period. *Address:* 7 St Nicholas Road, Salisbury, Wilts. *Club:* Royal Commonwealth Society.

BROWN, Leslie; Deputy Chairman, Prudential Assurance Co. Ltd, 1970-74 (a Director, 1965-77); *b* 29 Oct. 1902; *s* of late W. H. Brown and late Eliza J. Fiveash; *m* 1930, Frances V., *d* of T. B. Lever; two *s* one *d*. *Educ:* Selhurst Grammar School. Joined Prudential Assurance Co. Ltd, 1919; Secretary and Chief Investment Manager, Prudential Assurance Co. Ltd, 1955-64 (Joint Secretary 1942); Chairman: Prudential Unit Trust Managers Ltd, 1968-75; Prudential Pensions Ltd, 1970-75. Member, Jenkins Committee on Company Law Amendment, 1960. Deputy-Chairman, Insurance Export Finance Co. Ltd, 1962-65. Inst. of Actuaries: FIA 1929; Vice-Pres., 1949-51. *Recreation:* bowls. *Address:* 12 Park View, Christchurch Road, Purley, Surrey CR2 2NL.

BROWN, Leslie F.; *see* Farrer-Brown.

BROWN, Air Vice-Marshal Sir Leslie Oswald, KCB, *cr* 1948 (CB 1945); CBE 1941; DSC 1916; AFC 1918; *b* Durban, 11 June 1893; *m* 1926, P. M. Widowson (whom he divorced); one *s*; *m* 1945, Irene, *widow* of H. F. Seymour, MD, FRCS, FRCOG. *Educ:* Hilton College, Natal, South Africa. South African Defence Force (Artillery) commencement of 1914-18 war; served in German West Africa, 1914-15; commissioned Royal Naval Air Service, Oct. 1915; served in France and East Africa (DSC, despatches, AFC); RAF Staff College, 1929; served in India commanding 20 Squadron and at Karachi, 1930-35; commanded first Reconnaissance Wing at Odiham, 1936-38; Group Captain, 1939; served Middle East, Western Desert, Sept. 1939-April 1941 (despatches); Air Commodore, 1941; AOC Levant, 1941, 1942 (despatches twice, Commander Greek Order of George I with cross swords); Acting Air Vice-Marshal, 1943; AOC No. 84 Group AEAF, 1943-44; Air Vice-Marshal, 1944; Commandant School of Land/Air Warfare, RAF, Old Sarum, 1944-49; retired, 1949. King Haakon VII Liberty Medal. *Address:* 149 North Ridge Road, Durban, S Africa. *T:* 882794. *Clubs:* RAF; Durban (Durban).

BROWN, Rt. Rev. Leslie Wilfrid; *see* St Edmundsbury and Ipswich, Bishop of.

BROWN, Prof. Lionel Neville; Professor of Comparative Law, University of Birmingham, since 1966; *b* 29 July 1923; *s* of Reginald P. N. Brown and Fanny Brown (*née* Carver); *m* 1957, Mary Patricia Vowles; three *s* one *d*. *Educ:* Wolverhampton Grammar Sch.; Pembroke Coll., Cambridge (Scholar; MA, LLB); Lyons Univ. (Dr en Droit). RAF, 1942-45; Cambridge, 1945-48; articled to Wolverhampton solicitor, 1948-50; Rotary Foundn Fellow, Lyons Univ., 1951-52; Lectr in Law, Sheffield Univ., 1953-55; Lectr in Comparative Law, Birmingham Univ., 1956, Sen. Lectr, 1957; Sen. Res. Fellow, Univ. of Michigan, 1960. Vis. Prof., Univ. of Tulane, New Orleans, 1968, Univ. of

Nairobi, 1974, Laval, 1975. Commonwealth Foundn Lectr (Caribbean), 1975-76. *Publications:* (with F. H. Lawson and A. E. Anton) Amos and Walton's Introduction to French Law, 2nd edn 1963 and 3rd edn 1967; (with J. F. Garner) French Administrative Law, 1967, 2nd edn 1973; (with F. G. Jacobs) Court of Justice of the European Communities, 1977; articles in Encycl. Britannica, Chambers's Encycl., Modern Law Review, Amer. Jl of Comparative Law, etc. *Recreations:* landscape gardening, country walking, music. *Address:* Willow Rise, Waterdale, Compton, Wolverhampton, West Midlands. *T:* Wolverhampton 26666.

BROWN, (Marion) Patricia; Under-Secretary (Economics), Treasury, since 1972; *b* 2 Feb. 1927; *d* of late Henry Oswald Brown and Elsie Elizabeth (*née* Thompson). *Educ:* Norwich High Sch. for Girls; Newnham Coll., Cambridge. Central Economic Planning Staff, Cabinet Office, 1947; Treasury, 1948-54; United States Embassy, London, 1956-59; Treasury, 1959-. Godmother of Lucy Harland. *Recreations:* bird watching, gardening, walking. *Address:* 28 The Plantation, SE3 0AB. *T:* 01-852 9011.

BROWN, Sir Max; see Brown, Sir C. M. P.

BROWN, Mervyn, CMG 1975; OBE 1963; High Commissioner in Tanzania, since 1975, and concurrently non-resident Ambassador to Madagascar; *b* 24 Sept. 1923; *m* 1949, Elizabeth Gittings. *Educ:* Ryhope Gram. Sch., Sunderland; St John's Coll., Oxford. Served in RA, 1942-45. Entered HM Foreign Service, 1949; Third Secretary, Buenos Aires, 1950; Second Secretary, UK Mission to UN, New York, 1953; First Secretary, Foreign Office, 1956; Singapore, 1959; Vientiane, 1960; again in Foreign Office, 1963-67; Ambassador to Madagascar, 1967-70; Inspector, FCO, 1970-73; Head of Communications Operations Dept, FCO, 1973-74; Asst Under-Sec. of State (Dir of Communications), 1974. *Recreations:* music, tennis, history. *Address:* c/o Foreign and Commonwealth Office, SW1. *Clubs:* Royal Commonwealth Society, Hurlingham.

BROWN, Ven. Michael René Warneford; Archdeacon of Nottingham, 1960-77; *b* 7 June 1915; *s* of late George and Irene Brown. *Educ:* King's School, Rochester; St Peter's College, Oxford; St Stephen's House, Oxford (MA). Deacon 1941; priest, 1942; Asst Master, Christ's Hospital, 1939-43; Curate of West Grinstead, 1941-43. Chap. RNVR, 1943-46; chaplain and Dean of St Peter's College and Curate of St Mary the Virgin, Oxford, 1946; Lecturer, RN College, Greenwich, 1946-47; Librarian, 1948-50 and Fellow, 1948-52, of St Augustine's Coll., Canterbury; Priest-in-charge of Bekesbourne, 1948-50; Asst Secretary, CACTM, 1950-60. Examining Chaplain: to Bishop of Southwell, 1954-; to Archbishop of Canterbury, 1959-60; Commissary to Bishop of Waikato, 1958-70. Mem., Church of England Pensions Board, 1966-; Church Commissioner, 1968-. *Recreations:* antiquarian and aesthetic, especially marine paintings and Eastern carpets. *Address:* 52 Dover Road, Walmer, Deal, Kent CT14 7JN. *T:* Deal 61326. *Clubs:* Athenæum; Royal Over-Seas League.

BROWN, Ormond John; Principal Clerk of Session and Justiciary, Scotland, since 1975; *b* 30 Jan. 1922; *s* of Herbert John Brown and Janie Lee; *m* 1949, Margaret Eileen Beard; two *d*. *Educ:* Gourock High Sch.; Greenock High Sch. Served War, 1941-45: N Africa, Italy, Greece, Austria. Sheriff Clerk Service, Scotland, 1939; Trng Organiser, Scottish Ct Service, 1957; Sheriff Clerk of Perthshire, 1970; Clerk of Justiciary, 1971. *Recreations:* fine music, coarse golf. *Address:* 29 Atholl Place, Dunblane, Perthshire. *T:* Dunblane 822186. *Clubs:* Dunblane New Golf (Dunblane); Royal Dornoch (Dornoch).

BROWN, Rev. Canon Oscar Henry, CIE 1947; OBE 1938; BA, LLB; Barrister-at-Law; *b* 4 July 1896; *s* of Frank and Winifred Brown; *m* 1918, Daisy Cormac (*d* 1967); two *s* three *d*; *m* 1973, Margaret Roggendorf. *Educ:* Cathedral High School, St Xavier's Coll., and Govt Law Coll., Bombay; Gray's Inn, London. Barrister-at-Law, and Advocate of High Court of Bombay; Presidency Magistrate, 1929; Chief Presidency Magistrate, and Revenue Judge, Bombay, 1941-51. Ordained Priest, 1969. Hon. Canon, St Thomas's Cathedral, Bombay, 1970. *Recreations:* yachting, golf, philosophy. *Address:* 19 Waudby Road, Fort, Bombay 1, India.

BROWN, Patricia; see Brown, M. P.

BROWN, Prof. Peter Robert Lamont, FBA 1971; FRHistS; Professor of History, Royal Holloway College, University of London, since 1975; *b* 26 July 1935; *s* of James Lamont and Sheila Brown, Dublin; *m* 1959, Friedl Esther (*née* Löw-Beer); two *d*. *Educ:* Aravon Sch., Bray, Co. Wicklow, Ireland;

Shrewsbury Sch.; New Coll., Oxford (MA). Harmsworth Senior Scholar, Merton Coll., Oxford and Prize Fellow, All Souls Coll., Oxford, 1956; Junior Research Fellow, 1963, Sen. Res. Fellow, 1970-73, All Souls Coll.; Fellow, All Souls Coll., 1956-75; Lectr in Medieval History, Merton Coll. Oxford, 1970-75; Special Lectr in late Roman and early Byzantine History, 1970-73, Reader, 1973-75, Univ. of Oxford. *Publications:* Augustine of Hippo: a biography, 1967; The World of Late Antiquity, 1971; Religion and Society in the Age of St Augustine, 1971. *Address:* Hillslope, Pullen's Lane, Oxford. *T:* Oxford 61429; Royal Holloway College, Englefield Green, Surrey TW20 0EX.

BROWN, Philip Anthony Russell, CB 1977; Deputy Secretary, Department of Trade, since 1974; *b* 18 May 1924; *e s* of late Sir William Brown, KCB, KCMG, CBE, and of Elizabeth Mabel (*née* Scott); *m* 1954, Eileen (*d* 1976), *d* of late J. Brennan; *m* 1976, Sarah, *d* of Sir Maurice Dean, *qv*. *Educ:* Malvern; King's Coll., Cambridge. Entered Home Civil Service, Board of Trade, 1947; Private Sec. to Perm. Sec., 1949; Principal, 1952; Private Sec. to Minister of State, 1953; Observer, Civil Service Selection Board, 1957; returned to BoT, 1959; Asst Sec., 1963; Head of Overseas Information Co-ordination Office, 1963; BoT, 1964; Under-Sec., 1969; Head of Establishments Div. 1, BoT, later DTI, 1969; Head of Cos Div., DTI, 1971. *Publication:* contrib. to Multinational Approaches: corporate insiders, 1976. *Recreations:* reading, gardening, music. *Address:* 32 Cumberland Street, SW1. *T:* 01-821 9342. *Club:* United Oxford & Cambridge University.

BROWN, Ralph, RA 1972 (ARA 1968); ARCA 1955; sculptor; *b* 24 April 1928; *s* of W. W. Brown and M. Brown; *m* 1st, 1952, M. E. Taylor (marr. diss. 1963); one *s* one *d*; 2nd, 1964, Caroline Ann Clifton-Trigg; one *s*. *Educ:* Leeds Grammar School. Studied Leeds, Hammersmith, Royal College of Art, 1948-56; in Paris with Zadkine, 1954; travel scholarships to Greece 1955, Italy 1957. Tutor, RCA, 1958-64. Sculpture Prof., Salzburg Festival, Summer 1972. Work exhibited: John Moores, Liverpool (prizewinner 1957 and 1959), Tate Gallery, Religious Theme 1958, British Sculpture in the Sixties 1965; Arnhem Internat. Open Air Sculpture, 1958; Middelheim Open Air Sculpture, 1959; Battersea Park Open Air Sculpture, 1960, 1963, 1966, 1977; Tokyo Biennale, 1963; British Sculptors '72, RA, 1972; Holland Park Open Air, 1975. One man Shows: Leicester Galls, 1961, 1963; Bangor Univ. and Forum Gall., 1964; Archer Gall., 1972; Salzburg, 1972; Munich 1973; Montpellier 1974; Marseilles 1975; Oxford 1975; Taranman Gall., 1976. Work in Collections: Tate Gallery, Arts Council, Contemp. Art Society, Kröller-Müller, Gallery of NSW, Stuyvesant Foundation, City of Salzburg, Nat. Gallery of Wales and at Leeds, Bristol, Norwich, Aberdeen, RCA, Huddersfield, Halifax, Southport, etc. Public Sculpture: at Hatfield, Harlow, LCC Tulse Hill, Loughborough Univ., Newnham Coll., Liverpool Univ., Hanover Bank, Kodak House, etc. *Address:* 2 Prospect Place, Beechen Cliff, Bath, Avon.

BROWN, Hon. Sir Ralph Kilner, Kt 1970; OBE 1945; TD 1952; DL; Hon. Mr Justice Kilner Brown; a Judge of the High Court, Queen's Bench Division, since 1970; a Judge of Employment Appeal Tribunal, since 1976; *b* 28 Aug. 1909; *s* of Rev. A. E. Brown, CIE, MA, BSc; *m* 1943, Cynthia Rosemary Breffit; one *s* two *d*. *Educ:* Kingswood School; Trinity Hall, Cambridge (Squire Law Scholar). Barrister, Middle Temple; Midland Circuit, 1934 (Harmsworth Scholar). TA 1938; War Service, 1939-46; DAQMG NW Europe Plans; DAAG HQ53 (Welsh) Div.; AQMG (Planning), COSSAC; Col Q (Ops) and Brig. Q Staff HQ 21 Army Group (despatches, OBE). QC 1958; Recorder of Lincoln, 1960-64; Recorder of Birmingham, 1964-65. Master of the Bench, Middle Temple, 1964; Chairman, Warwicks QS, 1964-67; a Judge of the Central Criminal Court, 1965-67; Recorder of Liverpool, and Judge of the Crown Court at Liverpool, 1967-69; Presiding Judge, N Circuit, 1970-75. Chairman, Mental Health Review Tribunal, Birmingham RHB Area, 1962-65. Contested (L) Oldbury and Halesowen, 1945 and 1950; South Bucks, 1959 and 1964; Pres., Birmingham Liberal Organisation, 1946-56; Pres., and Chm., W Midland Liberal Fedn, 1950-56; Mem., Liberal Party Exec., 1950-56. Pres., Birmingham Bn, Boys Bde, 1946-56; Mem., Exec., Boys Bde, 1950-55. DL Warwickshire, 1956. Guild of Freemen, City of London. *Recreations:* watching athletics (Cambridge University; Great Britain; British AAA Champion 440 yds hurdles, 1934); cricket, Rugby football. *Address:* Victoria Cottage, Best Beech Hill, Wadhurst, Sussex. *Clubs:* Naval and Military; Hawks (Cambridge).
See also A. G. K. Brown.

BROWN, Mrs Ray; see Vaughan, Elizabeth.

BROWN, Rev. Raymond; Principal, Spurgeon's College, London, since 1973; *b* 3 March 1928; *s* of Frank Stevenson Brown and Florence Mansfield; *m* 1966, Christine Mary Smallman; one *s* one *d*. *Educ:* Spurgeon's Coll., London (BD, MTh); Fitzwilliam Coll., Cambridge (MA,PhD). Minister: Zion Baptist Church, Cambridge, 1956-62; Upton Vale Baptist Church, Torquay, 1964-71; Tutor in Church History, Spurgeon's Coll., 1971-73. Pres., Evangelical Alliance, 1975-76. *Publications:* Their Problems and Ours, 1969; Let's Read the Old Testament, 1971; Skilful Hands, 1972. *Recreations:* music, fell walking. *Address:* Spurgeon's College, South Norwood Hill, SE25 6DJ. *T:* 01-653 1235.

BROWN, Sir Raymond (Frederick), Kt 1969; OBE; CompIEE; FIERE; Chairman, since 1972 and Managing Director since 1970, Muirhead Ltd; Chairman, Racecourse Technical Services Ltd; *b* 19 July 1920; *s* of Frederick and Susan Evelyn Brown; *m* 1942, Evelyn Jennings (marr. diss. 1949); one *d*; *m* 1953, Carol Jacquelin Elizabeth, *d* of H. R. Sprinks, Paris; two *s* one *d*. *Educ:* Morden Terrace LCC School; SE London Technical College; Morley College. Joined Redifon as engineering apprentice, 1934; Sales Man., Communications Div., Plessey Ltd, 1949-50; formerly Chm., Man. Dir and Pres., Racal Electronics Ltd (Joint Founder, 1950), and subsidiary companies. Head of Defence Sales, MoD, 1966-69; Consultant Adviser on commercial policy and exports to DHSS, 1969-72. Mem., Brit. Overseas Trade Bd Working Gp on Innovation and Exports, 1972-74; Adviser to NEDO, to promote export of equipment purchased by nationalised industries, 1976-. Pres. Electronic Engrg Assoc., 1975. Liveryman, Scriveners' Co. *Recreations:* golf, farming, shooting, polo. *Address:* Westcroft Park, Windlesham Road, Chobham, Surrey. *Clubs:* City Livery, Travellers', Canada, Australia; Sunningdale Golf; Guards Polo (life mem.); Swinley Forest Golf.

BROWN, Prof. Reginald Francis, PhD; (First) Cowdray Professor of Spanish Language and Literature in the University of Leeds, 1953-75, retired; *b* 23 April 1910; *m* 1939, Rica Eleanor Jones; one *s* one *d*. *Educ:* Lancaster Royal Grammar School; Liverpool University. BA First Class Hons. Spanish, 1932; PhD, 1939; University Fellowship, Liverpool, 1934. On Staff of Spanish Departments in Universities of Liverpool, Columbia, and New York, NYC, and Dartmouth College, NH, USA, 1939-43. War of 1939-45: service in RAF Intelligence (FO). Head of Dept of Spanish, University of Leeds, 1945-53. Vis. Prof. of Spanish, Princeton Univ., 1958-59. Pres., Modern Language Assoc., 1970. Diamond Jubilee Gold Medal, Inst. of Linguists, 1972. *Publications:* Bibliografía de la Novela Española, 1700-1850, (Madrid) 1953; Spanish-English, English-Spanish Pocket Dictionary, (Glasgow) 1954, 2nd edn, 1956; Spain, A Companion to Spanish Studies (ed. E. Allison Peers), 5th edn revised and enlarged, 1956; D. F. Sarmiento, Facundo, ed. Boston, 1960. Articles in Bulletin of Hispanic Studies, Hispania, Hispanic Review, Modern Languages, Year's Work in Modern Language Studies. *Address:* Rivington House, Clarence Road, Horsforth, near Leeds. *T:* Leeds 582443.

BROWN, Maj.-Gen. Reginald Llewellyn, CB 1950; CBE 1941; MA; FRICS (Council 1950-53); late RE; Hon. Colonel 135 Survey Engineer Regt TA, 1954-60; Consultant Surveyor; *b* 23 July 1895; *m* 1928, Nancy Katharine Coleridge, one *s*. *Educ:* Wellington College; Royal Military Acad. European War, pow, 1914-18. Served in Middle East, North Africa, Italy, 1939-45. Director of Military Survey, War Office, 1946; Director-General, Ordnance Survey, 1949-53. MA Oxon by decree, 1954 (Member of New College). Senior Lecturer in Surveying, 1954-55. FRGS (Hon. Vice-President, 1969). Consultant to: the Times Atlas, 1955-59; Spartan Air Services of Ottawa, 1956-71. Chm. Meridian Airmaps Ltd. President Photogrammetric Society, 1957-59; President International Society for Photogrammetry, 1956-60 (Vice-President, 1960-64). Legion of Honour (USA), 1945. FRPSL 1975. *Recreations:* golf, philately. *Address:* Cricket Hill Cottage, Yateley, Hants. *T:* Yateley 872130. *Club:* Naval and Military.

BROWN, Prof. Robert, DSc London; FRS 1956; Regius Professor of Botany, Edinburgh University, 1958-77; *b* 29 July 1908; *s* of Thomas William and Ethel Minnie Brown; *m* 1940, Morna Doris Mactaggart. *Educ:* English School, Cairo; University of London. Assistant Lecturer in Botany, Manchester University, 1940-44; Lecturer in Botany, Bedford College, London, 1944-46; Reader in Plant Physiology, Leeds University, 1946-52; Professor of Botany, Cornell University, 1952-53; Director, Agricultural Research Council Unit of Plant Cell Physiology, 1953-58. *Publications:* various papers on plant physiology in the Annals of Botany, Proceedings of Royal Society and Journal of Experimental Botany. *Recreation:* gardening. *Address:* 5 Treble House Terrace, Blewbury, Didcot, Oxfordshire. *T:* Blewbury 850415.

BROWN, Sir Robert C.; *see* Crichton-Brown.

BROWN, Robert Crofton; MP (Lab) Newcastle upon Tyne West since 1966; Parliamentary Under-Secretary of State for Defence for the Army, since Oct. 1974; *b* 16 May 1921; *m* 1945, Marjorie Hogg, Slaithwaite, Yorks; one *s* one *d*. *Educ:* Denton Road Elementary School; Atkinson Road Technical School; Rutherford Coll. Apprenticed plumber and gasfitter, Newcastle & Gateshead Gas Co., 1937. War Service, 1942-46. Plumber from 1946; Inspector, 1949; in service of Northern Gas Board until 1966. Secretary of Constituency Labour Party and Agent to MP for 16 years. Parly Sec., Ministry of Transport, 1968-70; Parly Under-Sec., Social Security, March-Sept. 1974. Vice-Chm., Parly Lab Party Transport Gp, 1970-. Member Newcastle Co. Borough Council (Chief Whip, Lab. Gp), retd 1968. *Recreations:* walking, reading, gardening. *Address:* 82 Beckside Gardens, Newcastle upon Tyne NE5 1BQ.

BROWN, Prof. Robert Hanbury, FRS 1960; Professor of Physics (Astronomy), in the University of Sydney since 1964; *b* 31 Aug. 1916; *s* of Colonel Basil Hanbury Brown and Joyce Blaker; *m* 1952, Hilda Heather Chesterman; two *s* one *d*. *Educ:* Tonbridge School; Brighton Technical College; City and Guilds College, London. Air Ministry, Bawdsey Research Station, working on radar, 1936-42; British Air Commission, Washington, DC, 1942-45; Principal Scientific Officer, Ministry of Supply, 1945-47; ICI Research Fellow of Manchester University, 1949; Professor of Radio-Astronomy in the University of Manchester, 1960-63. Holweck Prize, 1959; Eddington Medal, 1968; Lyle Medal, 1971; Britannica Australia Award, 1971; Hughes Medal, 1971. FAA 1967; Hon. FNA 1975; Hon. FASc 1975. *Publications:* The Exploration of Space by Radio, 1957; The Intensity Interferometer, 1974; publications in Physical and Astronomical Journals. *Address:* School of Physics, Sydney University, Sydney, NSW 2006, Australia.

BROWN, Robert Ross Buchanan, CBE 1968; Chairman, Southern Electricity Board, 1954-74; *b* 15 July 1909; 2nd *s* of Robert and Rhoda Brown, Sydney, Australia; *m* 1940, Ruth Sarah Aird; one *s* two *d*. *Educ:* The King's School, Sydney; Sydney University; Cambridge University. BA (Cantab.), BSc. Deputy Gen. Manager, Wessex Electricity Co., 1938. Captain 4th County of London Yeomanry, 1940-45. Gen. Manager, Wessex Electricity Co., 1945; Deputy Chairman, Southern Electricity Board, 1948. *Recreations:* gardening, golf. *Address:* Wargrave Court, Wargrave, Reading, Berks.

BROWN, Ven. Robert Saville; Archdeacon of Bedford, since 1974; *b* 12 Sept. 1914; *s* of John Harold Brown and Frances May Brown; *m* 1947, Charlotte (*née* Furber); one *s*. *Educ:* Bedford Modern Sch.; Selwyn Coll., Cambridge (MA). Curate: Gt Berkhamsted, 1940-44; St Mary's, Hitchin, 1944-47; Vicar, Wonersh, 1947-53; Rector, Gt Berkhamsted, 1953-69; Canon of St Albans Cath., 1965; Vicar of St Paul's, Bedford, 1969-74. *Recreations:* reading, travel, chess. *Address:* Old Warden Vicarage, Biggleswade, Beds. *T:* Northill 259. *Club:* Rotary (Bedford).

BROWN, Roland George MacCormack; at the Institute of Development Studies, University of Sussex; *b* 27 Dec. 1924; 2nd *s* of late Oliver and of Mona Brown; *m* 1964, Irene Constance, *d* of Rev. Claude Coltman; two *s* one *d*. *Educ:* Ampleforth College; Trinity College, Cambridge. Called to the Bar, Gray's Inn, Nov. 1949. Practised at the Bar, Nov. 1949-May 1961; Attorney-Gen., Tanganyika, later Tanzania, 1961-65. *Publication:* (with Richard O'Sullivan, QC) The Law of Defamation. *Recreation:* swimming. *Address:* c/o Institute of Development Studies, University of Sussex, Falmer, Brighton BN1 9RH.

BROWN, Rt. Rev. Ronald; *see* Birkenhead, Bishop Suffragan of.

BROWN, Ronald William; JP; MP (Lab) Hackney South and Shoreditch, since 1974 (Shoreditch and Finsbury, 1964-74); *b* 7 Sept. 1921; *s* of George Brown; *m* 1944, Mary Munn; one *s* two *d*. *Educ:* Elementary School, South London; Borough Polytechnic. Sen. Lectr in Electrical Engineering, Principal of Industrial Training Sch. Member: Council of Europe Assembly and WEU, 1965-68; European Parlt, 1977-. Chm., Energy Commn, Rapporteur on Science, Technology and Aerospace questions; Parly Advr to Furniture, Timber and Allied Trades Union. Leader, Camberwell Borough Council, 1956; Alderman and Leader, London Bor. of Southwark, 1964. Asst Govt Whip, 1966-67. MBIM; Assoc. Mem., Inst. of Engineering Designers. JP Co. London, 1961. *Address:* House of Commons, SW1; 76 Beauval Road, Dulwich, SE22.
See also Baron George-Brown.

BROWN, Ronald William; Deputy Legal Adviser and Solicitor to Ministry of Agriculture, Fisheries and Food, to Forestry Commission and to (EEC) Intervention Board for Agricultural Produce since 1974; *b* 21 April 1917; *o s* of late William Nicol Brown and Eleanor Brown (*née* Dobson); *m* 1958, Elsie Joyce, *er d* of late Sir Norman Guttery, KBE, CB; two *s. Educ:* Dover Coll.; Corpus Christi Coll., Cambridge (MA). War service, 1939-45, King's Own Royal Regt (Lancaster), France, W Desert, Burma (Chindits) (Major). Called to Bar, Gray's Inn, 1946. Entered Legal Dept, Min. of Agric. and Fisheries, 1948; Asst Solicitor, MAFF, 1970. *Address:* 5 Gomshall Road, Cheam, Surrey SM2 7JZ. *T:* 01-393 4061.

BROWN, Rear-Adm. Roy S. F.; *see* Foster-Brown.

BROWN, Rt. Rev. Russel Featherstone; *b* Newcastle upon Tyne, 7 Jan. 1900; *s* of Henry John George Brown and Lucy Jane Ferguson; *m* 1940, Priscilla Marian Oldacres (*d* 1948); three *s. Educ:* Bishop's Univ., Lennoxville, PQ, Canada. BA (Theo.) 1933. RAF, 1918-19; business, 1919-29; University, 1929-33; Deacon, 1933; Priest, 1934; Curate, Christ Church Cathedral, Montreal, 1933-36; Priest-in-Charge, Fort St John, BC, 1936-40; Rector of Sherbrooke, PQ, 1940-54; Canon, Holy Trinity Cathedral, Quebec, 1948; Rector, St Matthew's, Quebec, PQ, 1954-60; Archdeacon of Quebec, 1954-60; Bishop of Quebec, 1960-71; subsequently teaching in Papua New Guinea. Hon. DCL Bishop's Univ., Lennoxville, 1961; Hon. DD, Montreal Diocesan Theological College, 1968. *Address:* Montreal Diocesan Theological College, 3473 University Street, Montreal, Que H3A 2A8, Canada.

BROWN, Spencer C.; *see* Curtis Brown.

BROWN, Sir Stanley; *see* Brown, Sir F. H. S.

BROWN, Sir Stephen; *see* Brown, Sir A. J. S.

BROWN, Hon. Sir Stephen, Kt 1975; Hon. Mr Justice Stephen Brown; a Judge of the High Court, Queen's Bench Division, since 1977 (Family Division, 1975-77); Presiding Judge, Midland and Oxford Circuit, since 1977; *b* 3 Oct. 1924; *s* of Wilfrid Brown and Nora Elizabeth Brown, Longdon Green, Staffordshire; *m* 1951, Patricia Ann, *d* of Richard Good, Tenbury Wells, Worcs; two *s* (twins) three *d. Educ:* Malvern College; Queens' College, Cambridge. Served RNVR (Lieut), 1943-46. Barrister, Inner Temple, 1949; Bencher, 1974. Dep. Chairman, Staffs QS, 1963-71; Recorder of West Bromwich, 1965-71; QC 1966; a Recorder, and Honorary Recorder of West Bromwich, 1972-75. Mem., Parole Board, England and Wales, 1967-71; Chairman: Adv. Cttee on Conscientious Objectors, 1971-75; Council of Malvern Coll., 1976-. *Recreation:* sailing. *Address:* 78 Hamilton Avenue, Harborne, Birmingham B17 8AR. *T:* 021-427 1313; Royal Courts of Justice, Strand, WC2. *Clubs:* Garrick, Naval; Birmingham (Birmingham).

BROWN, Sir Thomas, Kt 1974; Chairman, Eastern Health and Social Services Board, Northern Ireland (formerly NI Hospitals Authority), since 1967; *b* 11 Oct. 1915; *s* of Ephraim Hugh and Elizabeth Brown. *Educ:* Royal Belfast Academical Institution. Admitted Solicitor, 1938. Mem., Royal Commn on NHS, 1976-. *Recreations:* boating, chairmanship. *Address:* Westgate, Portaferry, Co. Down, Northern Ireland. *T:* Portaferry 309. *Club:* Ulster (Belfast).

BROWN, Prof. Thomas Julian, MA, FSA; Professor of Palæography, University of London, since 1961; *b* 24 Feb. 1923; *s* of Tom Brown, land agent, Penrith, Cumberland, and Helen Wright Brown, MBE; *m* 1959, Alison Macmillan Dyson; two *d. Educ:* Westminster School (KS); Christ Church, Oxford. 2nd class, Class. Hon. Mods, 1942, and Lit.Hum, 1948. The Border Regt, 1942-45, mostly attached Inf. Heavy Weapons School, Netheravon. Asst Keeper Dept of MSS, British Museum, 1950-60. FSA 1956. Member, Inst. for Advanced Study, Princeton, NJ, 1966-67. Lyell Reader in Bibliography, Univ. of Oxford, 1976-77; Vis. Fellow, All Souls Coll., Oxford, 1976-77. FKC, 1975. *Publications:* contrib. (with R. L. S. Bruce-Mitford, A. S. C. Ross, E. G. Stanley and others) to Codex Lindisfarnensis, vol. ii, 1960; Latin Palæography since Traube (inaugural lecture), Trans. Camb. Bibliographical Society, 1963; The Stonyhurst Gospel (Roxburghe Club), 1969; The Durham Ritual, 1969; Northumbria and the Book of Kells (Jarrow Lect.), 1972. *Address:* King's College, Strand, WC2R 2LS. *T:* 01-836 5454.

BROWN, Thomas Walter Falconer, CBE 1958; Consultant in Marine Engineering; *b* 10 May 1901; *s* of Walter Falconer Brown, MB, ChB, DPH, and Catherine Edith (*née* McGhie); *m* 1947, Lucy Mason (*née* Dickie); one *s* one *d. Educ:* Ayr Academy; Glasgow University; Harvard University. BSc

(special dist. in Nat. Philos.), 1921; DSc (Glas.), 1927; SM (Harvard), 1928; Assoc. of Royal Technical College, Glasgow, 1922. Asst General Manager, Alex Stephen & Sons Ltd, Linthouse, 1928-35; Technical Manager, R. & W. Hawthorn Leslie & Co. Ltd, Newcastle upon Tyne, 1935-44; Director of Parsons and Marine Engineering Turbine Research and Development Assoc., Wallsend, 1944-62; Director of Marine Engineering Research (BSRA), Wallsend Research Station, 1962-66. Liveryman, Worshipful Co. of Shipwrights, Freedom City of London, 1946. Eng Lieut, and Eng Lt-Comdr RNVR, Clyde Div., 1924-36. De Laval Gold Medal, Sweden, 1957. *Publications:* various technical papers in: Trans Instn Mech. Engineers, Inst. Marine Engineers, NE Coast Instn of Engineers & Shipbuilders, etc. *Recreations:* model-making and gardening. *Address:* Dumbreck, Wylam, Northumberland NE41 8JB. *T:* Wylam 2228.

BROWN, Air Cdre Sir Vernon, Kt 1952; CB 1944; OBE 1937; MA; CEng; FRAeS; *b* 10 Jan. 1889; *s* of Ernest J. Brown and H. M. Messent, Blackheath; *m* 1st, 1914, Constance Mary (*d* 1967), *d* of late F. E. Duckham (Port of London Authority) and Maud McDougall, Blackheath; one *d* ; 2nd, 1971, Sheila Rigby, *d* of late T. M. Rigby and Agnes Carter. *Educ:* Eastbourne College; Jesus College, Cambridge (MA). Gas Engineering prior to 1915, then RFC (French Croix de Guerre). Served in UK, France, and after war in Iraq and Egypt. Retired 1937 and became Chief Inspector of Accidents, Air Ministry and later Ministry of Civil Aviation; retired as Permanent Civil Servant, 1952. Hon. FSLAET. *Recreation:* music. *Address:* Eastholme, Station Road, Yarmouth, Isle of Wight PO41 0QT. *T:* Yarmouth (IoW) 760189. *Clubs:* Naval and Military; Royal Solent Yacht.

BROWN, Walter Graham S.; *see* Scott-Brown.

BROWN, William, CBE 1971; Deputy Chairman since 1974, and Managing Director, since 1966, Scottish Television Ltd; Director, Independent Television Publications Ltd, since 1968; *b* 24 June 1929; *s* of Robert C. Brown, Ayr; *m* 1955, Nancy Jennifer, 3rd *d* of Prof. George Hunter, Edmonton, Alta; one *s* three *d. Educ:* Ayr Academy; Edinburgh University. Lieut, RA, 1950-52. Scottish Television Ltd: London Sales Manager, 1958; Sales Dir, 1961; Dep. Man. Dir, 1963. Director: Radio Clyde Ltd, 1973-; Scottish Nat. Orchestra Soc., 1973-; Scottish Television & Grampian Sales Ltd, 1970-; Scottish and Global Television Enterprises Ltd, 1970-; ITN, 1972-77; Laurel Bank School Co. Ltd, 1973-; STV Entertainments Ltd. Mem., Royal Commn on Legal Services in Scotland, 1976-. *Recreations:* gardening, golf, music. *Address:* Ardencraig, 90 Drymen Road, Bearsden, Glasgow. *T:* 041-942 0115. *Club:* Caledonian.

BROWN, Sir William B. P.; *see* Pigott-Brown.

BROWN, Maj.-Gen. William Douglas Elmes, CB 1967; CBE 1962; DSO 1945; Secretary, The Dulverton Trust, since 1969; *b* 8 Dec. 1913; *s* of late Joseph William Brown, Manor House, Knaresborough, Yorks; *m* 1947, Nancy Ursula, *d* of Colonel W. F. Basset, Netherton, nr Andover. *Educ:* Sherborne; RMA, Woolwich. 2nd Lieut, RA, 1934. Served War of 1939-45, RA 50 (Northumbrian) Division, E. Africa and N. Africa (despatches). Seconded to Royal Iraqi Army, 1947-50; Chief of Staff, Northern Ireland, 1961-62; Commandant, School of Artillery, 1962-64; ADC to the Queen, 1963-64; Director of Army Equipment Policy, 1964-66; Dep. Master-Gen. of the Ordnance, 1966-69. Lt-Col 1955; Brigadier, 1961; Major-General, 1964. Col Comdt, RA, 1970-. *Recreations:* shooting, fishing, golf. *Address:* Gunner's Cottage, Littlewick Green, Maidenhead, Berks. *T:* Littlewick Green 2083. *Clubs:* Army and Navy; Hon. Co. of Edinburgh Golfers.

BROWN, William Eden T.; *see* Tatton Brown.

BROWN, W(illiam) Glanville, TD; Barrister-at-Law; Member, Mental Health Review Tribunal for North Eastern Metropolitan Regional Hospital Board Area, since 1960; *b* 19 July 1907; *s* of late Cecil George Brown, formerly Town Clerk of Cardiff, and late Edith Tyndale Brown; *m* 1st, 1935, Theresa Margaret Mary Harrison (decd); one *s* ; 2nd, 1948, Margaret Isabel Dilks, JP, *o d* of late Thomas Bruce Dilks, Bridgwater. *Educ:* Llandaff Cathedral School; Magdalen College School and Magdalen College, Oxford; in France, Germany and Italy. Called to Bar, Middle Temple, 1932. Contested (L) Cardiff Central, 1935, St Albans, 1964. Served War of 1939-45, in Army (TA), Aug. 1939-Dec. 1945; attached to Intelligence Corps; served overseas 3½ years in E Africa Command, Middle East and North-West Europe. Junior Prosecutor for UK Internat. Military Tribunal for the Far East, Tokyo, 1946-48; Member: the National Arbitration Tribunal, 1949-51; Industrial Disputes Tribunal, 1959; Deputy-Chairman of various Wages Councils, 1950-64;

Joint Legal Editor of English Translation of Common Market Documents for Foreign Office, 1962-63; Lectr in Germany on behalf of HM Embassy, Bonn, 1965-73. Life Mem., RIIA. Fellow, Inst. of Linguists. *Publication:* Translation of Brunschweig's French Colonialism, 1871-1914, Myths and Realities. *Recreations:* walking, reading, watching cricket, travel. *Address:* 3 Middle Temple Lane, Temple, EC4. *T:* 01-583 0659. *Club:* National Liberal.

BROWN, William John, MC 1943; Vice President of the Law Society, 1977; Partner, Bristows Cooke & Carpmael; *b* 18 July 1911; *s* of John Brown and Edith Mary Stevens; *m* 1950, Jenifer Chesterman; one *s* two *d*. *Educ:* Magdalen Coll. Sch., Oxford. Solicitor. Employed by Westminster Bank, 1928-30; taught in prep. school while reading for the Bar, 1931-34; called to the Bar, Gray's Inn, 1934; Asst to J. W. Robertson-Scott on the Countryman, 1935; produced Law Journal, 1935-39. War of 1939-45: served in 2nd Bn Scots Guards (Major), N Africa and Italy. Qualified as Solicitor and joined firm of Bristows Cooke & Carpmael, 1946. Mem., Scott-Henderson Cttee on Cruelty to Wild Animals, 1949. Mem. Council, Law Soc., 1962; Dep. Chm., Council of Law Reporting, 1967; Chm. Governors, Coll. of Law, 1972-77. Dir, BPB Industries Ltd. *Publications:* The Gods had Wings, 1936, 1938; Cartel Law of the EEC, 1963; contribs to The Field as legal correspondent. *Recreations:* reading, hill-walking, growing vegetables. *Address:* The Vane, The Avenue, Northwood, Middlesex. *T:* Northwood 26494. *Club:* Bath.

BROWN, Rev. William Martyn; Headmaster, Bedford School, 1955-75; *b* 12 July 1914; *s* of Edward Brown, artist; *m* 1939, Elizabeth Lucy Hill; one adopted *s*. *Educ:* Bedford School; Pembroke College, Cambridge (Scholar). 1st Class Honours in Modern Languages, 1936, MA 1947. Assistant Master, Wellington College, 1936-47; Housemaster 1943-47; Headmaster, The King's School, Ely, 1947-55. Commissioner of the Peace, 1954. Ordained 1976. *Recreation:* watercolour painting. *Address:* Lodge Cottage, Field Dalling, Holt, Norfolk. *T:* Binham 403.

BROWNE, family name of **Baron Craigton, Baron Kilmaine, Baron Oranmore, Marquess of Sligo.**

BROWNE, Major Alexander Simon Cadogan; JP; DL; *b* 22 July 1895; *e s* of late Major Alexander Browne of Callaly Castle, Northumberland; *m* 1918, Dorothy Mary, *d* of late Major F. J. C. Howard, 8th Hussars of Moorefield, Newbridge, Co. Kildare and Baytown, Co. Meath; one *d*. *Educ:* Eton; RMC Sandhurst. Major 12th Royal Lancers; served European War, 1914-18; retired, 1925; re-employed, 1939-45; served with BEF 1940 (despatches) and with BLA 1945. Secretary to the Duke of Beaufort's Fox Hounds, 1928-38; Joint Master, Percy Hounds, 1938-46. Pres., Berwick-upon-Tweed Conservative Assoc., 1970-73. Chairman, Rothbury RDC, 1950-55; CC, 1950-67, CA, 1967-74, Hon. Alderman, 1974, Northumberland; High Sheriff of Northumberland, 1958-59; JP 1946, DL 1961, Northumberland. *Address:* Callaly Castle, Alnwick, Northumberland NE66 4TA. *T:* Whittingham 663. *Clubs:* Cavalry and Guards; Northern Counties (Newcastle upon Tyne).

BROWNE, Anthony Arthur Duncan M.; *see* Montague Browne.

BROWNE, Air Cdre Charles Duncan Alfred, CB 1971; DFC 1944; MBIM; RAF, retired; *b* 8 July 1922; *s* of Alfred Browne and Catherine (*née* MacKinnon); *m* 1946, Una Felicité Leader; one *s*. *Educ:* City of Oxford School. War of 1939-45: served Western Desert, Italy, Corsica and S France in Hurricane and Spitfire Sqdns; post war service in Home, Flying Training, Bomber and Strike Commands; MoD; CO, RAF Brüggen, Germany, 1966-68; Comdt, Aeroplane and Armament Exp. Estab., 1968-71; Air Officer i/c Central Tactics and Trials Orgn, 1971-72. *Address:* c/o Midland Bank, Summertown, Oxford. *Club:* Royal Air Force.

BROWNE, Coral (Edith), (Mrs Vincent Price); actress; *b* Melbourne, Australia, 23 July 1913; *d* of Leslie Clarence Brown and Victoria Elizabeth (*née* Bennett); *m* 1950, Philip Westrope Pearman (*d* 1964); *m* 1974, Vincent Price. *Educ:* Claremont Ladies' Coll., Melb. Studied painting in Melbourne. First stage appearance, in Loyalties, Comedy Theatre, Melb., 1931; acted in 28 plays in Australia, 1931-34. First London appearance in Lover's Leap, Vaudeville, 1934, and then continued for some years playing in the West End. From 1940, successes include: The Man Who Came to Dinner, 1941; My Sister Eileen, 1943; The Last of Mrs Cheyney, 1944; Lady Frederick, 1946; Canaries Sometimes Sing, 1947; Jonathan, 1948; Castle in the Air, 1949; Othello, 1951; King Lear, 1952; Affairs of State, 1952; Simon

and Laura, 1954; Nina, 1955; Macbeth, 1956; Troilus and Cressida, 1956; (Old Vic season) Hamlet, A Midsummer Night's Dream and King Lear, 1957-58; The Pleasure of His Company, 1959; Toys in the Attic, 1960; Bonne Soupe, 1961-62; The Rehearsal, 1963; The Right Honourable Gentleman, 1964-66; Lady Windermere's Fan, 1966; What the Butler Saw, 1969; My Darling Daisy, 1970; Mrs Warren's Profession, 1970; The Sea, 1973; The Waltz of the Toreadors, 1974; Ardèle, 1975; Charley's Aunt, 1976; The Importance of Being Ernest, 1977; Travesties, 1977. Has also appeared in United States and Moscow. *Films:* Auntie Mame; The Roman Spring of Mrs Stone; Dr Crippen; The Night of the Generals; The Legend of Lylah Clare; The Killing of Sister George, 1969; The Ruling Class, 1972; Theatre of Blood, 1973; The Drowning Pool, 1975. *Recreation:* needlepoint. *Address:* 16 Eaton Place, SW1.

BROWNE, Brig. Dominick Andrew Sidney, CBE 1945 (OBE 1943); *b* 29 Feb. 1904; *s* of Major Dominick S. Browne, DL, JP, and Naomi, *d* of Hon. R. Dobell, Quebec; *m* 1930, Iris, *d* of Major G. H. Deane, Littleton House, Winchester; one *s* three *d*. *Educ:* Eton; RMC Sandhurst. 1st Bn Royal Scots Fusiliers, 1924; retired 1929; Jt Master Co. Galway Hounds, 1933-36. Served War of 1939-45 (CBE). *Recreations:* shooting, fishing. *Address:* Corin, Glann, Oughterard, Co. Galway. *Clubs:* Boodle's; Kildare Street and University (Dublin).

BROWNE, Sir (Edward) Humphrey, Kt 1964; CBE 1952; Chairman: British Transport Docks Board, since 1971; Bestobell Ltd, since 1973 (Director, since 1969); Director, Haden Carrier Ltd, since 1973; *b* 7 April 1911; *m* 1934, Barbara Stone (*d* 1970); two *s*. *Educ:* Repton; Magdalene College, Cambridge (BA 1931, MA 1943); Birmingham University (Joint Mining Degree). Manager, Chanters Colliery; Director and Chief Mining Engineer, Manchester Collieries Ltd, 1943-46; Production Director, North-Western Divisional Coal Board, 1947-48; Director-General of Production, National Coal Board, 1947-55; Chm., Midlands Div., NCB, 1955-60; Dep. Chm., NCB, 1960-67; Chairman: John Thompson Group, 1967-70; Woodall Duckham Gp, 1971-73 (Dep. Chm., 1967-71). Mem., Commonwealth Develt Corp., 1969-72. President: The British Coal Utilisation Research Assoc., 1963-68; Inst. of Freight Forwarders, 1976-77. Director, National Industrial Fuel Efficiency Service, 1960-69; Pres., Institution of Mining Engineers, 1957. Pro-Chancellor, Univ. of Keele, 1971-75. *Address:* Beckbury Hall, near Shifnal, Salop. *T:* Ryton 207; 31 Dorset House, Gloucester Place, NW1. *T:* 01-935 8958. *Club:* Brooks's.

BROWNE, (Edward) Michael (Andrew); QC 1970; *b* 29 Nov. 1910; *yr s* of Edward Granville Browne, Fellow of Pembroke Coll., Cambridge, and Alice Caroline Browne (*née* Blackburne Daniell); *m* 1937, Anna Florence Augusta, *d* of James Little Luddington; two *d*. *Educ:* Eton; Pembroke Coll., Cambridge (Scholar); 1st class History Tripos, 1932; MA. Barrister, Inner Temple, 1934, *ad eundem* Lincoln's Inn. Bencher, Inner Temple, 1964. Served War of 1939-45: RA (anti aircraft) and GS, War Office (finally GSO3, Capt.). *Address:* 19 Wallgrave Road, SW5. *T:* 01-373 3055. Wiveton Cottage, Wiveton, near Holt, Norfolk. *T:* Cley 203. *Club:* Athenæum.

BROWNE, E(lliott) Martin, CBE 1952; FRSL 1955; DLitt Lambeth, 1971; *b* 29 Jan. 1900; *s* of Lieut-Col Percy J. Browne, CB, and Bernarda Gracia (*née* Lees); *m* 1st, 1924, Henzie Raeburn (*d* 1973); two *s*; 2nd, 1974, Audrey (*née* Tuck), widow of John Rideout. *Educ:* Eton; Christ Church, Oxford. Warden of Educational Settlement, Doncaster, 1924-26; Assistant Professor of Drama, Carnegie Institute of Technology, Pittsburgh, Pa, 1927-30; first Director of Religious Drama, Diocese of Chichester, 1930-34; Producer (London and New York), including all the plays of T. S. Eliot and many of Christopher Fry, since 1934; Director, the Pilgrim Players, including three seasons of New Plays by Poets at Mercury Theatre, 1939-48; Director, British Drama League, 1948-57; revived York Cycle of Mystery Plays at York, 1951-54-57-66; Visiting Professor in Religious Drama, Union Theological Seminary, New York, 1956-62; Hon. Drama Adviser to Coventry Cathedral, 1962-65. Danforth Visiting Lecturer to American Colleges, 1962-65. Directed Murder in the Cathedral, Canterbury Cathedral, 1970. President, RADIUS (The Religious Drama Society of Great Britain). *Publication:* The Making of T. S. Eliot's Plays, 1969. *Address:* 20 Lancaster Grove, NW3 4PB. *T:* 01-794 4322. *Club:* Garrick.

BROWNE, Hablot Robert Edgar, CMG 1955; OBE 1942; HM Diplomatic Service, retired; employed in Commonwealth Office (formerly CRO), 1959-67; *b* 11 Aug. 1905; *s* of Dr Hablot J. M. Browne, Hoylake, Cheshire; *m* 1933, Petra Elsie, *d* of Peter Tainsh, OBE; one *d*. *Educ:* St George's, Harpenden; Christ's

College, Cambridge. Colonial Administrative Service, Nigeria, 1928; Assistant Colonial Secretary, Barbados, 1939; Asst. Secretary, Jamaica, 1943; Deputy Colonial Secretary, Jamaica, 1945; acted as Colonial Secretary on various occasions, 1945-49; Admin. Officer, Class I, Nigeria, 1950; Civil Secretary, Northern Region, Nigeria, 1951-55; Actg Lieut Governor, Northern Region, Nigeria, Sept. 1954; Actg Governor, Northern Region, Nigeria, Oct. 1954; retired from Colonial Administrative Service, 1955. Assistant Adviser to the Government of Qatar, Persian Gulf, 1956-57. *Recreation:* watching cricket. *Address:* 85 Bishop's Mansions, Bishop's Park Road, SW6. *T:* 01-731 3209. *Clubs:* Travellers', MCC.

BROWNE, Sir Humphrey; *see* Browne, Sir E. H.

BROWNE, Prof. John Campbell McClure, CBE 1975; FRCOG, FRCSE; Professor of Obstetrics and Gynaecology, University of London, since 1952, at Royal Postgraduate Medical School and Institute of Obstetrics and Gynæcology; Consultant Obstetrician and Gynæcologist, Hammersmith Hospital, since 1948; *b* 7 Feb. 1912; *s* of late Prof. F. J. Browne; *m* 1940, Veronica Evelyn Partridge; one *s* one *d. Educ:* Edinburgh Academy; University College, London University (BSc Hons 1934; MB, BS 1938). MRCOG 1948; FRCOG 1954; FRCSEd 1948. Qualified 1937; served War of 1939-45; RAFVR, 1939-46 (despatches twice). Asst Lectr, 1948. Chm., DHSS Cttee on Gynæcological Cytology. Mem. Council, RCOG. Hon. Fellow: American Assoc. of Obstetricians and Gynæcologists (Joseph Price Orator, 1962); Finnish Gynæcological Assoc.; Hon. Mem. Ankara Gynæcological Assoc.; Hon. For. Mem., Royal Belgian Soc. of Obstetricians and Gynæcologists. *Publications:* Co-author Antenatal and Postnatal Care, 11th edn 1977; Postgraduate Obstetrics and Gynæcology, 4th edn 1973; numerous articles in medical jls. *Address:* 6 Devon Court, Links Road, W3. *Clubs:* Royal Air Force, Anglo-Belgian.

BROWNE, Rev. Laurence Edward, DD (Cantab); MA (Manchester); Emeritus Professor, University of Leeds, since 1952; Vicar of Highbrook, Sussex, 1957-64; *b* 17 April 1887; *s* of late E. Montague Browne, Solicitor, Northampton; *m* 1st, 1920, Gladys May Dearden; one *s* two *d*; 2nd, 1938, Margaret Theresa Wingate Carpenter; two *d. Educ:* Magdalen College School, Brackley; Sidney Sussex College, Cambridge. Lecturer and Fellow of St Augustine's College, Canterbury, 1913-20; Lecturer at Bishops' College, Calcutta, 1921-25; studying Islam in Cairo, Constantinople and Cambridge, 1926-29; Lecturer at the Henry Martyn School of Islamic Studies, Lahore, 1930-34; Rector of Gayton, Northants, 1935-46; Prof. of Comparative Religion at the University of Manchester, 1941-46; Professor of Theology, University of Leeds, 1946-52; Vicar of Shadwell, near Leeds, 1952-57. Examining Chaplain to Bp of Peterborough, 1937-50, to Bp of Ripon, 1946-57. Hulsean Lecturer, Cambridge, 1954; Godfrey Day Lectr, Trin. Coll., Dublin, 1956. *Publications:* Parables of the Gospel, 1913; Early Judaism, 1920 and 1929; Acts, in Indian Church Commentaries, 1925; From Babylon to Bethlehem, 1926, 1936 and 1951 (Telugn translation, 1932, Chinese translation 1935); The Eclipse of Christianity in Asia, 1933, New York, 1967; Christianity and the Malays, 1936; Prospects of Islam, 1944; Where Science and Religion Meet, 1951; The Quickening Word (Hulsean Lectures), 1955; Contrib. to New Peake's Commentary, 1962. *Address:* 71 Maisemore Gardens, Emsworth, Hants PO10 7JX. *T:* Emsworth 3248.

BROWNE, Martin; *see* Browne, E. M.

BROWNE, Mervyn Ernest, CBE 1976; ERD 1954; HM Diplomatic Service, retired 1976; private trade and travel consultant; *b* 3 June 1916; *s* of late Ernest Edmond Browne and of Florence Mary Browne; *m* 1942, Constance (*née* Jarvis); three *s. Educ:* Stockpost Sec. Sch.; St Luke's Coll., Exeter; University Coll., Exeter. BScEcon London; BA Exeter. RA, 1940-46; TA, 1947-53; AER, RASC, 1953-60. Distribution of industry res., BoT, 1948-56; HM Trade Comr Service: Trade Comr, Wellington, NZ, 1957-61 and Adelaide, 1961-64; Principal Trade Comr, Kingston, Jamaica, 1964-68; HM Diplomatic Service: Counsellor (Commercial), Canberra, 1968-70; Dir, Brit. Trade in S Africa, Johannesburg, 1970-73; Consul-Gen., 1974-76 and Chargé d'Affaires, 1974 and 1976, Brit. Embassy, Manila. *Recreations:* militaria, lepidoptery, squash rackets. *Address:* 21 Dartmouth Hill, Greenwich, SE10 8AJ. *T:* 01-691 2993.

BROWNE, Most Rev. Michael, DD, DCL, LLD; *s* of Michael Browne, Westport, Co. Mayo. *Educ:* St Jariath's Coll., Tuam; St Patrick's Coll., Maynooth. BA Hons Classics, National Univ. of Ireland, 1916; ordained, 1920; DD Rome, 1921; DCL 1924; Prof. of Theology, Maynooth, 1921-37; Sec. Maynooth Union, 1929-37; Mem. of Senate, Nat. University of Ireland, 1934-76;

Bishop of Galway and Kilmacduagh, 1937-76; Apostolic Administrator of Kilfenora, 1937-76. Hon. LLD Nat. Univ. of Ireland, 1971. Freedom of Galway City, 1973. Retired, 1976. *Publications:* various articles in Irish Ecclesiastical Record on Theological subjects. *Address:* St Anne's, Maunsell's Road, Galway.

BROWNE, Michael; *see* Browne, E. M. A.

BROWNE, Lady Moyra (Blanche Madeleine), DBE 1977 (OBE 1962); Superintendent-in-Chief, St John Ambulance Brigade, since 1970; *b* 2 March 1918; *d* of 9th Earl of Bessborough, PC, GCMG; *m* 1945, Sir Denis John Browne, KCVO, FRCS (*d* 1967); one *s* one *d. Educ:* privately. State Enrolled Nurse, 1946. Dep. Supt-in-Chief, St John Ambulance Bde, 1964; Vice-Chm. Central Council, Victoria League, 1961-65; Vice-Pres., Royal Coll. of Nursing, 1970. DStJ 1970. *Recreations:* music, shooting, fishing, travel. *Address:* 16 Wilton Street, SW1. *T:* 01-235 1419.

BROWNE, Rt. Hon. Sir Patrick (Reginald Evelyn), PC 1974; Kt 1965; OBE (mil.) 1945; TD 1945; **Rt. Hon. Lord Justice Browne;** a Lord Justice of Appeal, since 1974; *b* 28 May 1907; *er s* of Edward Granville Browne, Sir Thomas Adams's Prof. of Arabic, Fellow of Pembroke Coll., Cambridge, and Alice Caroline (*née* Blackburne-Daniell); *m* 1st, 1931, Evelyn Sophie Alexandra (*d* 1966), *o d* of Sir Charles and Lady Walston; two *d*; 2nd, 1977, Lena, *y d* of late Mr and Mrs James Atkinson. *Educ:* Eton; Pembroke Coll., Cambridge (Hon. Fellow, 1975). Barrister-at-law, Inner Temple, 1931; QC 1960; Bencher, 1962. Deputy Chairman of Quarter Sessions, Essex, Co. Cambridge and Isle of Ely, 1963-65; a Judge of the High Court of Justice, Queen's Bench Div., 1965-74. Served Army, 1939-45. *Address:* 7 Hillsleigh Road, W8. *T:* 01-727 4224; Thriplow Bury, Thriplow, Cambs. *T:* Fowlmere 234. *Clubs:* Garrick; Cambridge County.

BROWNE, Percy Basil; Director, Western Counties Building Society, since 1965; *b* 2 May 1923; *s* of late Lt-Col W. P. Browne, MC; *m* 1953, Jenefer Mary, *d* of late Major George Gerald Petherick and the late Lady Jeane Petherick (*née* Pleydell-Bouverie), Hall Barn, Beaconsfield, Bucks. *Educ:* The Downs, Colwall; Eton College. Served War of 1939-45 (commnd in Royal Dragoons): in Sicily, Italy and NW Europe. Farmer. Rode in Grand National, 1953. MP (C) Torrington Division of Devon, 1959-64. Dir, Appledore Shipbuilders Ltd, 1965-72. N Devon District Councillor, 1974-. Mem., SW Reg. Hosp. Bd, 1967-70; Vice-Chm., N Devon HMC, 1967-74. *Address:* Torr House, Westleigh, near Bideford, Devon. *T:* Instow 387.

BROWNE, Prof. Richard Charles, MA, DM, FRCP; Nuffield Professor of Industrial Health, University of Newcastle upon Tyne, 1946-76, retired; Chairman, Division of Social Medicine, University of Newcastle upon Tyne, 1970-75; Consultant Physician, Department of Industrial Health, Royal Victoria Infirmary, Newcastle upon Tyne; *b* 6 July 1911; *s* of Dr Frederick William and Edith Maud Darvel Browne; *m* 1941, Barbara, *o d* of late Ebenezer Cunningham, Fellow of St John's Coll., Cambridge, and Ada Collins; one *s* three *d. Educ:* Clifton; Wadham College, Oxford; Oxford and Bristol Medical Schools. BA honours in human physiology, 1934; Theodore Williams Scholar in Pathology, 1935-36; BM and MA 1937; House Appts, Depts of Medicine, Univs of Oxford and Bristol; MRCP 1940; FRCP 1964; DM Oxon, 1946. Research Asst and Registrar, Dept of Medicine, Oxford; MRC Grant, 1940; Sqdn Ldr (Research Specialist), RAF Medical Br. Nuffield Visitor in Industrial Health to East and Central Africa, 1949 and 1952. Regional Med. Adviser, CEGB, 1948-; Main Bd Med. Industrial Consultant, CEGB, 1970-77. Dir, N of England Industrial Health Service, 1960-76. Council of Europe Fellow in Medicine, 1961; WHO Consultant, 1965. British Editor, Internat. Archives of Occupational Health, 1974-. Lectures: Ernestine Henry, RCP, 1964; John Holmes Meml, Univ. of Newcastle upon Tyne, 1969; Apothecaries', Soc. of Occupational Medicine, 1972; Pres., Sect. of Occupational Medicine, RSM, 1970. Church Warden and Vice-Chm., Parochial Church Council, St Andrews, Corbridge, 1966-68. *Publications:* Health in Industry, 1961; Chemistry and Therapy of Industrial Pulmonary Disease, 1965; articles in British Medical Jl, Lancet and British Journal of Industrial Medicine. *Recreations:* fell walking, swimming, gardening, photography. *Address:* Sele House, Dunkirk Terrace, Corbridge on Tyne NE45 5AQ.

BROWNE, Sheila Jeanne, CB 1977; Senior Chief Inspector, Department of Education and Science, since 1974; *b* 25 Dec. 1924; *d* of Edward Elliott Browne. *Educ:* Lady Margaret Hall, Oxford (MA); Ecole des Chartes, Paris. Asst Lectr, Royal Holloway Coll., Univ. of London, 1947-51; Tutor and Fellow of St Hilda's Coll., Oxford and Univ. Lectr in French, Oxford, 1951-61; HM Inspector of Schools, 1961-70; Staff Inspector,

Secondary Educn, 1970-72; Chief Inspector, Secondary Educn, 1972; Dep. Sen. Chief Inspector, DES, 1972-74. *Recreations:* medieval France, language, mountains. *Address:* 9 Rossmore Court, Park Road, NW1 6XX. *T:* 01-402 9931.

BROWNE, Stanley George, CMG 1976; OBE 1965; MD, FRCP, FRCS, DTM, FKC; Director, Leprosy Study Centre, London, since 1966; Consultant Adviser in Leprosy, Department of Health and Social Security; Hon. Consultant in Leprosy, UCH; Secretary-Treasurer, International Leprosy Association; Medical Secretary, British Leprosy Relief Association, 1968-73; Medical Consultant, Leprosy Mission; Consultant Leprologist to: St Giles' Homes; Order of Charity; Association of European Leprosy Associations; All-Africa Leprosy Training and Rehabilitation Centre, Addis Ababa; *b* 8 Dec. 1907; *s* of Arthur Browne and Edith Lillywhite; *m* 1940, Ethel Marion Williamson, MA (Oxon); three *s*. *Educ:* King's Coll. and KCH, London Univ.; Inst. de Méd. Tropicale Prince Léopold, Antwerp. MRCS, LRCP, MB, BS (London) (Hons, Dist. in Surg., Forensic Med., Hygiene), AKC, 1933, FKC 1976; MRCP 1934 (Murchison Schol. RCP); FRCS 1935; DTM (Antwerp), 1936; MD (London), 1954; FRCP 1961. Leverhulme Res. Grant for investigating trng of African med. auxiliaries, 1954; Consultant, WHO Expert Cttee on Trng of Med. Auxiliaries; WHO Travel Grant to visit Leprosy Res. Instns, 1963. Med. Missionary, Baptist Miss. Soc., Yakusu, Belg. Congo, 1936-59; Médecin Directeur, Ecole agréée d'Infirmiers, Yakusu, 1936-59; Léproserie de Yalisombo, 1950-59; Mem. several Govt Commns concerned with health in Belgian Congo; Sen. Specialist Leprologist and Dir of Leprosy Res. Unit, Uzuakoli, E Nigeria, 1959-66; Associate Lectr in Leprosy, Ibadan Univ., 1960-65, 1968-; Vis. Lectr in leprosy in univs and med. schs in many countries. Sec.-Gen., Internat. Leprosy Congress, London, 1968, Bergen, 1973, Mexico City, 1978. Associate Editor and Dir, Internat. Jl of Leprosy of Internat. Leprosy Assoc., Inc. FRSocMed; Mem. Council, 1967-71, and Fellow, Royal Soc. Trop. Med. Hygiene (Vice-Pres., 1971-73; Pres., 1977-); Fellow, Hunterian Soc., 1974. President: Christian Med. Fellowship, 1969-71; Ludhiana British Fellowship, 1974-; Co-founder and first Chm., Christian Med. Fellowship of Nigeria; Chairman: Internat. Congress of Christian Physicians, 1972-75 (Vice-Pres., 1975-); Editorial Board of Leprosy Review, 1968-73; Founder Member: Internat. Filariasis Assoc.; Internat. Soc. of Tropical Dermatology (and Mem., Bd of Dirs). Member: Leprosy Expert Cttee, WHO (Chm., 1976); Assoc. de Léprologues de langue française (Conseiller technique); Sections Dermatology, Med. Educn, RSM; Medical Policy Cttee, Methodist Missionary Soc.; Medical Adv. Cttee, Baptist Missionary Soc.; British Council, Dr Schweitzer's Hosp. Fund; Comité de Directeurs, Assoc. Internat. du Dr Schweitzer; Medical Commn, European Co-ordinating Cttee of Anti-Leprosy Assocs, 1966- (Chm. 1971-74); Med. Cttee, Hosp. for Tropical Diseases, London; Editorial Bd, Tropical Doctor; Inst. of Religion and Medicine; Soc. for Health Educn; Anglo-Ethiopian Soc.; Acid-Fast Club. Hon. Member: Assoção Brasileira de Leprologia; Sociedad Argentina de Leprologia; Korean Leprosy Assoc.; Sociedad Mexicana de Dermatologia, 1975; Sociedad Mexicana de Leprologia, 1976; Dermatol. Soc. of S Africa; Hon. Life Mem., Nigeria Soc. of Health. Lectures: A. B. Mitchell Meml, QUB, 1967; Godfrey Day Meml, Dublin, 1974. Sir Charlton Briscoe Prize for Research, 1934; Medal, Royal African Soc., 1970 (Life Mem.); Stewart Prize for Epidemiology, BMA, 1975. Holds foreign orders incl.: Chevalier de l'Ordre Royal du Lion, 1948; Officier de l'Ordre de Léopold II, 1958; Comdr, Order of Malta, 1973. *Publications:* As the Doctor sees it-in Congo, 1950; Leprosy: new hope and continuing challenge, 1967; numerous articles on trop. diseases, esp. leprosy and onchocerciasis, and on med. educn in learned jls; booklets on med. missionary work, med. ethics, etc. *Relevant publication:* Bonganga: the story of a missionary doctor, by Sylvia and Peter Duncan, 1958. *Recreations:* photography, reading, writing. *Address:* 57a Wimpole Street, W1. *T:* 01-935 5848; (home) 16 Bridgefield Road, Sutton, Surrey. *T:* 01-642 1656.

BROWNE, Thomas Anthony G.; *see* Gore Browne.

BROWNE, Ven. Thomas Robert; Archdeacon of Ipswich, 1946-63, now Archdeacon Emeritus; *b* 15 June 1889; *s* of Horace Browne, London, and Jessie Drury; *m* 1915, Ellen Gertrude Fowler. *Educ:* King's College, University of London. Captain 3rd Battalion Dorsetshire Regt, 1914-19; Deacon, 1919; Priest, 1920; Curate of Christ Church, West Green, Tottenham, 1919-23; Vicar of Edwardstone, Suffolk, 1923-28; Rector of Earl Soham, Suffolk, 1928-36; Vicar of All Saints, Newmarket, Suffolk, 1936-46; Rector of Elmsett and Aldham, Suffolk, 1946-56. Canon of St Edmundsbury, Ipswich, 1936-46; Rural Dean of Hadleigh, 1946-49; Rector of Shotley, Suffolk, 1956-64. FKC, 1957. *Recreations:* tennis and bowls. *Address:* Ellesborough Manor, Aylesbury, Bucks HP17 0XF. *T:* Wendover 622336.

BROWNE-CAVE, Sir Robert C.; *see* Cave-Browne-Cave.

BROWNE-WILKINSON, Hon. Sir Nicolas Christopher Henry, Kt 1977; Hon. Mr Justice Browne-Wilkinson; a Judge of the High Court, Chancery Division, since 1977; *b* 30 March 1930; *s* of late Canon A. R. Browne-Wilkinson and Molly Browne-Wilkinson; *m* 1955, Ursula de Lacy Bacon; three *s* two *d*. *Educ:* Lancing; Magdalen Coll., Oxford (BA). Called to Bar, 1953, Bencher, Lincoln's Inn, 1977; QC 1972. Junior Counsel: to Registrar of Restrictive Trading Agreements, 1964-66; to Attorney-General in Charity Matters, 1966-72; in bankruptcy, to Dept of Trade and Industry, 1966-72; a Judge of the Courts of Appeal of Jersey and Guernsey, 1976-77. *Publication:* (ed) chapter on Charities in Halsbury's Laws of England, 4th edn. *Recreations:* tennis, squash, gardening. *Address:* 11 Old Square, Lincoln's Inn, WC2A 3TS. *T:* 01-405 3930.

BROWNING, Amy Katherine, RP, ROI, ARCA; 2nd *d* of J. D. Browning; *m* 1916, T. C. Dugdale, RA, RP (*d* 1952). *Educ:* Privately. Studied painting, Royal College of Art and Paris; exhibits regularly in Royal Academy, New English Art Club, and other London Exhibitions; one-man show Fine Art Society, 1925; Smiths Gallery, Manchester, 1935; leading provincial exhibitions; Pittsburgh; Salon des Artistes Français, Silver Medal, Gold Medal, HC, two pictures purchased by Luxembourg Gallery; represented in permanent collections, Glasgow, Southport, Manchester, Wolverhampton, National Gallery, Wellington, NZ, Luton; figure subjects, plein air, portraits, flowers. *Recreations:* gardening and open air. *Address:* 58 Glebe Place, SW3. *T:* 01-352 9969.

BROWNING, (David) Peter (James); Chief Education Officer of Bedfordshire, since 1973; *b* 29 May 1927; *s* of late Frank Browning and of Lucie A. (*née* Hiscock); *m* 1953, Eleanor Berry, *d* of late J. H. Forshaw, CB, FRIBA; three *s*. *Educ:* Christ's Coll., Cambridge (MA (Engl. and Mod. Langs Tripos)); Sorbonne; Univs of Strasbourg and Perugia. Personal Asst to Vice Chancellor, Liverpool Univ., 1952-56; Asst Teacher, Willenhall Comprehensive Sch., 1956-59; Sen. Admin. Asst, Somerset LEA, 1959-62; Asst Dir of Educn, Cumberland LEA, 1962-66; Dep. Chief Educn Officer, Southampton LEA, 1966-69; Chief Educn Officer of Southampton, 1969-73. Member: Schools Council Governing Council and 5-13 Steering Cttee, 1969-75; Council, Univ. of Southampton, 1970-73; CofE Bd of Educn Schools Cttee, 1970-75; Council, Nat. Youth Orch., 1972; Merchant Navy Trng Bd, 1973; British Educnl Administration Soc. (Chm., 1974); UGC, 1974; Taylor Cttee of Enquiry into Management and Govt of Schs, 1975; Governing Body, Centre for Inf. on Language Teaching and Research, 1975; Consultant, Sudan Min. of Educn, 1976. *Publications:* Editor: Julius Caesar for German Students, 1957; Macbeth for German Students, 1959; contrib. London Educn Rev., Educnl Administration Bull., and other educnl jls. *Recreations:* gardening, music, travel. *Address:* 70 Putnoe Lane, Bedford MK41 9AF. *T:* Bedford 62117. *Club:* English-Speaking Union.

BROWNING, Rt. Rev. Edmond Lee; Bishop of Diocese of Hawaii, since 1976; *b* 11 March 1929; *s* of Edmond Lucian Browning and Cora Mae Lee; *m* 1953, Patricia A. Sparks; four *s* one *d*. *Educ:* Univ. of the South (BA 1952); School of Theology, Sewanee, Tenn (BD 1954). Curate, Good Shepherd, Corpus Christi, Texas, 1954-56; Rector, Redeemer, Eagle Pass, Texas, 1956-59; Rector, All Souls, Okinawa, 1959-63; Japanese Lang. School, Kobe, Japan, 1963-65; Rector, St Matthews, Okinawa, 1965-67; Archdeacon of Episcopal Church, Okinawa, 1965-67; first Bishop of Okinawa, 1967-71; Bishop of American Convocation, 1971-73; Executive for National and World Mission, on Presiding Bishop's Staff, United States Episcopal Church, 1974-76. Hon. DD, Univ. of the South, Sewanee, Tenn, 1970. *Address:* Queen Emma Square, Honolulu, Hawaii 96813, USA.

BROWNING, Colonel George William, OBE 1946; Welsh Guards, retired; *b* 1 Sept. 1901; *e s* of Rev. B. A. Browning; *g s* of Col M. C. Browning, Brantham Court, Suffolk; *m* 1937, Rosemary Sybil, *y d* of Hubert Edgar Hughes, Flempton, Bury St Edmunds, Suffolk, *g d* of Sir Alfred Collingwood Hughes, Bt, East Bergholt, Suffolk; one *s* two *d*. *Educ:* Repton; RMC, Sandhurst. Commissioned Suffolk Regt, 1922; transf. Grenadier Guards, 1924; transf. Welsh Guards, 1939. Served War of 1939-45 (wounded); Comd 3rd Bn Welsh Guards, 1941; psc 1942; Comd 1st Bn Welsh Guards, 1944. AQMG, London District, 1945-48; Comd Welsh Guards, 1948-51; retired, 1951. DL Pembrokeshire, 1955. *Address:* Weatherhill Farm, Icklingham, Bury St Edmunds, Suffolk. *T:* Culford 258. *Club:* Army and Navy.

BROWNING, Peter; *see* Browning, D. P. J.

BROWNING, Rex Alan; Under-Secretary, Ministry of Overseas Development, since 1976; *b* 22 July 1930; *s* of Gilbert H. W. Browning and Gladys (*née* Smith); *m* 1961, Paula McKain; three *d*. *Educ:* Bristol Grammar Sch.; Merton Coll., Oxford (Postmaster) (MA). HM Inspector of Taxes, 1952; Asst Principal, Colonial Office, 1957; Private Sec. to Parly Under-Sec. for the Colonies, 1960; Principal, Dept of Techn. Co-operation, 1961; transf. ODM, 1964; seconded to Diplomatic Service as First Sec. (Aid), British High Commn, Singapore, 1969; Asst Sec., 1971; Counsellor, Overseas Develt, Washington, and Alternate UK Exec. Dir, IBRD, 1973-76. *Address:* 10 Fieldway, Petts Wood, Kent. *T:* Orpington 23675.

BROWNLEE, Prof. George; Professor of Pharmacology, King's College, University of London, since 1958; *b* 1911; *s* of late George R. Brownlee and of Mary C. C. Gow, Edinburgh; *m* 1940, Margaret P. M. Cochrane (*d* 1970), 2nd *d* of Thomas W. P. Cochrane and Margaret P. M. S. Milne, Bo'ness, Scotland; three *s*. *Educ:* Tynecastle Sch.; Heriot Watt Coll., Edinburgh, BSc 1936, DSc 1950, Glasgow; PhD 1939, London. Rammell Schol., Biological Standardization Labs of Pharmaceutical Soc., London; subseq. Head of Chemotherapeutic Div., Wellcome Res. Labs, Beckenham; Reader in Pharmacology, King's Coll., Univ. of London, 1949. Editor, Jl of Pharmacy and Pharmacology, 1955-. FKC, 1971. *Publications:* (with Prof. J. P. Quilliam) Experimental Pharmacology, 1952; papers on: chemotherapy of tuberculosis and leprosy; structure and pharmacology of the polymyxins; endocrinology; toxicity of drugs; neurohumoral transmitters in smooth muscle, etc., in: Brit. Jl Pharmacology; Jl Physiology; Biochem. Jl; Nature; Lancet; Annals NY Acad. of Science; Pharmacological Reviews, etc. *Recreations:* collecting books, making things. *Address:* 602 Gilbert House, Barbican, EC2. *T:* 01-638 9543. *Club:* Athenæum.

BROWNLIE, Prof. Ian, DCL; Professor of International Law at the London School of Economics, University of London, since 1976; *b* 19 Sept. 1932; *s* of John Nason Brownlie and Amy Isabella (*née* Atherton); *m* 1957, Jocelyn Gale; one *s* two *d*. *Educ:* Alsop High Sch., Liverpool; Hertford Coll., Oxford (Gibbs Scholar, 1952; BA 1953); King's Coll., Cambridge (Humanitarian Trust Student, 1955). DPhil Oxford, 1961; DCL Oxford, 1976. Called to the Bar, Gray's Inn, 1958. Lectr, Nottingham Univ., 1957-63; Fellow and Tutor in Law, Wadham Coll., Oxford, 1963-76 and Lectr, Oxford Univ., 1964-76. Reader in Public Internat. Law, Inns of Ct Sch. of Law, 1973-76. Vis. Professor: Univ. of E Africa, 1968-69; Ghana, 1971; Florence, 1977. Editor, British Year Book of International Law, 1974-. Assoc. Mem., Inst. of Internat. Law, 1977. *Publications:* International Law and the Use of Force by States, 1963; Principles of Public International Law, 1966 (2nd edn 1973); Russian edn, ed G. I. Tunkin, 1976; Certif. of Merit, Amer. Soc. of Internat. Law, 1976); Basic Documents in International Law, 1967 (2nd edn 1972); The Law Relating to Public Order, 1968; Basic Documents on Human Rights, 1971; Basic Documents on African Affairs, 1971. *Recreations:* travel, philately. *Address:* 43 Fairfax Road, Chiswick, W4 1EN. *T:* 01-995 3647.

BROWNLOW, family name of **Baron Lurgan.**

BROWNLOW, 6th Baron, *cr* 1776; **Peregrine Francis Adelbert Cust; Bt** 1677; *b* 27 April 1899; *o s* of 5th Baron and Maud, *d* of Capt. S. Buckle, RE; *S* father, 1927; *m* 1st, 1927, Katherine Hariot (*d* 1952), *y d* of Brig.-Gen. Sir David Kinloch, 11th Bt; one *s* one *d*; 2nd 1954, Mrs Dorothy Power Beatty (*d* 1966), Broomfield House, Ashford, Co. Wicklow; 3rd, 1969, Leila, widow of 2nd Baron Manton. *Educ:* Eton; Royal Military College, Sandhurst. Served European War, 1918; entered Grenadier Guards 1918; Adjutant of the 3rd Battalion, 1923-26; sometime ADC to the GOC London District; resigned, 1926; joined Royal Air Force VR as Flight Lieut, 1939; Parliamentary Private Secretary to Lord Beaverbrook, Minister of Aircraft Production, 1940; attached Bomber Command, 1941; Staff Officer to Air Vice-Marshal J. Slessor, Assistant Chief of Air Staff, 1942, and to Deputy Chief of Staff 8th US Air Force, 1943; resigned comm. with rank of Sqn Leader, 1944. Personal Lord in Waiting to King Edward VIII, 1936; Lord Lieut and Custos Rotulorum of Lincolnshire, 1936-50; JP and DL for Lincs; Mayor of Grantham, 1934-35. *Heir:* *s* Hon. Edward John Peregrine Cust [*b* 25 March 1936; *m* 1964, Shirlie, *d* of John Yeomans, Upton-on-Severn, Worcs; one *s*]. *Address:* 2 Belgrave Mews West, SW1; Belton House, Grantham, Lincs. *T:* Grantham 3278; The Great House, Roaring River, Jamaica, West Indies; Sagesse Estates, St Davids, Grenada, West Indies. *Clubs:* White's; Travellers' (Paris).

BROWNLOW, Air Cdre Bertrand, OBE 1967; AFC 1962; Commandant, Aeroplane and Armament Experimental Establishment, Boscombe Down, since 1977; *b* 13 Jan. 1929; *s* of Robert John Brownlow and Helen Louise Brownlow; *m* 1958, Kathleen Shannon; two *s* one *d*. *Educ:* Beaufort Lodge Sch. Joined RAF, 1947; 12 and 101 Sqdns, ADC to AOC 1 Gp, 103 Sqdn, 213 Sqdn, Empire Test Pilots' Sch., OC Structures and Mech. Eng Flt RAE Farnborough, RAF Staff Coll., Air Min. Op. Requirements, 1949-64; Wing Comdr Ops, RAF Lyneham, 1964-66; Jt Services Staff Coll., 1966-67; DS RAF Staff Coll., 1967-68; Def. and Air Attaché, Stockholm, 1969-71; CO Experimental Flying, RAE Farnborough, 1971-73; Asst Comdt, Office and Flying Trng, RAF Coll., Cranwell, 1973-74; Dir of Flying (R&D), MoD, 1974-77. *Recreations:* squash, tennis, golf, gliding (Gold C with one diamond). *Address:* (home) The Baulk House, 66 Bromham Road, Biddenham, Beds MK40 4AQ. *T:* Bedford 65595. *Club:* Royal Air Force.

BROWNRIGG, Sir Nicholas (Gawen), 5th Bt, *cr* 1816; *b* 22 Dec. 1932; *s* of late Gawen Egremont Brownrigg and Baroness Lucia von Borosini, *o d* of Baron Victor von Borosini, California; *S* grandfather, 1939; *m* 1959, Linda Louise Lovelace (marr. diss. 1965), Beverly Hills, California; one *s* one *d*; *m* 1971, Valerie Ann, *d* of Julian A. Arden, Livonia, Michigan, USA. *Educ:* Midland Sch.; Stanford Univ. *Heir:* *s* Michael Gawen Brownrigg, *b* Oct. 1961. *Address:* PO Box 548, Ukiah, Calif 95482, USA.

BROWNRIGG, Philip Henry Akerman, CMG 1964; DSO 1945; OBE 1953; TD 1945; Director (appointed by Government of Zambia): Nchanga Consolidated Copper Mines Ltd; Roan Consolidated Mines Ltd; Metal Marketing Corporation of Zambia Ltd; *b* 3 June 1911; *s* of late Charles E. Brownrigg, Headmaster of Magdalen Coll. Sch., Oxford; *m* 1936, Marguerite Doreen Ottley; three *d*. *Educ:* Eton; Magdalen Coll., Oxford (BA). Journalist, 1934-52; Editor, Sunday Graphic, 1952. Joined Anglo American Corp. of S Africa, 1953: London Agent, 1956; Dir in Rhodesia, 1961-63; Dir in Zambia, 1964-65; retd, 1969. Joined TA, 1938; served War of 1939-45 with 6 R Berks, and 61st Reconnaissance Regt (RAC); Lieut-Col 1944; CO 4/6 R Berks (TA) 1949-52. *Recreations:* golf, sport on TV. *Address:* Wheeler's, Checkendon, near Reading, Berks. *T:* Checkendon 680328.

BRUBECK, David Warren; musician, USA; composer; *b* Concord, Calif, 6 Dec. 1920; *s* of Howard Brubeck and Elizabeth Ivey; *m* 1942, Iola Whitlock; five *s* one *d*. *Educ:* Pacific Univ. (BA); Mills Coll. (postgrad.). Hon. PhD: Univ. of Pacific; Fairfield Univ. Pianist with dance bands and jazz trio, 1946-49; own trio, touring USA, 1950; formed Dave Brubeck Quartet, 1951; tours to festivals and colls, incl. tour of Europe and Middle East (for US State Dept); Europe and Australia, 1960; Europe, Australia, Canada, S America, with 3 sons, as Two Generations of Brubeck; Quartet at Festival Hall, London, 1961, etc. Fellow, Internat. Inst. of Arts and Sciences. Exponent of progressive Jazz; many awards from trade magazines; numerous recordings. Has composed: over 250 songs; Points of Jazz (ballet); Elementals (orch.); The Light in the Wilderness (oratorio; perf. Cincinnati Symph. Orch. and mixed chorus of 100 voices, 1968); Gates of Justice (Cantata); Truth (Cantata); They All Sang Yankee Doodle, variations for orch., 1975; Christmas Cantata, 1975. *Address:* c/o Sutton Artists Corporation, 505 Park Avenue, New York, NY 10022, USA.

BRUCE, family name of **Barons Aberdare, Balfour of Burleigh** and **Bruce of Donington,** and of **Earl of Elgin.**

BRUCE; *see* Cumming-Bruce and Hovell-Thurlow-Cumming-Bruce.

BRUCE, Lord; Charles Edward Bruce; *b* 19 Oct. 1961; *s* and *heir* of 11th Earl of Elgin, *qv*, A Page of Honour to HM the Queen Mother, 1975-.

BRUCE OF DONINGTON, Baron *cr* 1974 (Life Peer), of Rickmansworth; **Donald William Trevor Bruce;** economist; Chartered Accountant; writer; Member of European Parliament, since 1975; *b* 3 Oct. 1912; *s* of late W. T. Bruce, Norbury, Surrey; *m* 1939, Joan Letitia Butcher; one *s* two *d* (and one *d* decd). *Educ:* Grammar School, Donington, Lincs; FCA 1947. Re-joined Territorial Army, March 1939; commissioned, Nov. 1939; Major, 1942; served at home and in France until May 1945 (despatches). MP (Lab) for North Portsmouth, 1945-50; Parliamentary Private Sec. to Minister of Health, 1945-50; Member Min. of Health delegn to Sweden and Denmark, 1946, and of House of Commons Select Cttee on Public Accounts, 1948-50. *Publications:* miscellaneous contributions on political science and economics to newspapers and periodicals. *Address:*

Pinecroft, Heronsgate, Rickmansworth, Herts. *T:* Chorleywood 2382. *Club:* Reform.

BRUCE, Alastair Henry, CBE 1951; DL; Chairman and Managing Director, The Inveresk Paper Company Ltd, 1964-68; Member, Monopolies Commission, 1964-68; Chairman, Paper and Paper Products Industry Training Board, 1968-71; *b* 14 April 1900; *s* of Patrick Chalmers Bruce and Lucy Walmsley Hodgson; *m* 1921, Jean Newton Callender; one *s*. *Educ:* Cargilfield, Midlothian; Uppingham. President British Paper and Board Makers Association, 1938-42 and 1948-51; President British Paper and Board Research Association, 1948-51. DL Midlothian, 1943-. *Recreations:* shooting, and fishing. *Address:* Torduff, Juniper Green, Midlothian. *T:* 031-441 2274. *Club:* Bath.

BRUCE, Alexander Robson, CMG 1961; OBE 1948; Assistant Secretary, Board of Trade, 1963-67, retired; *b* 17 April 1907; *m* 1936, Isobel Mary Goldie; four *d*. *Educ:* Rutherford Coll., Newcastle upon Tyne; Durham Univ. Asst Trade Comr, 1933-42, Trade Commissioner, 1942-43, Montreal; Commercial Sec., British Embassy, Madrid, 1943-46; Trade Comr, Ottawa, 1946-50; Asst Sec., Bd of Trade, 1950-54 and 1963-; Principal British Trade Commissioner in NSW, 1955-63. *Recreation:* golf. *Address:* 37 North Road, Highgate, N6. *Club:* Highgate Golf.

BRUCE, Sir Arthur Atkinson, KBE 1943; MC 1917; Director: Wallace Brothers & Co. Ltd, 1947-65; Chartered Bank of India, 1949-70; *b* 26 March 1895; *s* of late John Davidson Bruce, Jarrow-on-Tyne; *m* 1928, Kathleen Frances (*d* 1952), *d* of John Emeris Houldey, ICS (retd), Penn, Bucks; three *d*. *Educ:* Cambridge. Director Reserve Bank of India, 1935-46; Chairman Burma Chamber of Commerce, 1936, 1942, 1946. Member of Council, London Chamber of Commerce, 1960-65. *Address:* Little Tylers, Warwicks Bench, Guildford, Surrey. *Club:* Oriental.

BRUCE, David (Kirkpatrick Este); US Ambassador to NATO, 1974-76; *b* 12 Feb. 1898; *s* of William Cabell Bruce and Louise Este Bruce (*née* Fisher); *m* 1st, 1926, Ailsa Mellon (*d* 1969); one *d* (decd); 2nd, 1945, Evangeline Bell; two *s* (and one *d* decd). *Educ:* Princeton Univ.; Univ. of Virginia; Univ. of Maryland. Served in US Army, 1917-19 and 1942-45. Admitted to Maryland Bar, 1921; Member Maryland House of Delegates, 1924-26; practised law in Baltimore, Md, 1921-25; Amer. Vice-Consul, Rome, 1926-28; engaged in business and farming, 1928-40; Mem. Virginia House of Delegates, 1939-42; Chief Rep. in Gt Brit. for Amer. Red Cross, 1940; with Office of Strategic Services, 1941-45 (Dir European Theater of Ops, 1943-45); Asst Sec. of Commerce, 1947-48; Chief, Econ. Co-op. Admin, to France, 1948-49; US Ambassador to France, 1949-52; Under Secretary of State, 1952-53; apptd Special US Observer at interim cttee of European Defense Community, 1953; Special Amer. Rep. to European High Authority for Coal and Steel, 1953-54; US Ambassador to: Federal Republic of Germany, 1957-59; UK, 1961-69; US Rep., Vietnam Peace Talks, Paris, 1970-71; Chief, US Mission to Peoples' Republic of China, 1973-74. Hon. CBE (mil.) 1945; military decorations from USA, France, Poland, Norway, Czechoslovakia, Denmark. *Publication:* Sixteen American Presidents, 1938. *Address:* 1405 34th Street NW, Washington, DC 20007, USA. *Clubs:* Buck's, White's, Brooks's, Turf; Jockey (Paris), Travellers' (Paris); various (USA).

BRUCE, Sir (Francis) Michael Ian; see Bruce, Sir Michael Ian.

BRUCE, Prof. Frederick Fyvie, MA Aberdeen, Cantab, Manchester, DD Aberdeen; FBA 1973; Rylands Professor of Biblical Criticism and Exegesis, University of Manchester, since 1959; *b* 12 Oct. 1910; *e s* of late P. F. Bruce, Elgin, Morayshire; *m* 1936, Betty, *er d* of late A. B. Davidson, Aberdeen; one *s* one *d*. *Educ:* Elgin Acad.; Univs of Aberdeen, Cambridge, Vienna. Gold Medallist in Greek and Latin; Fullerton Schol. in Classics, 1932; Croom Robertson Fellow, 1933; Aberdeen Univ.; Scholar of Gonville and Caius Coll., Camb., 1932; Sandys Student. Camb., 1934; Ferguson Schol. in Classics, 1933, and Crombie Scholar in Biblical Criticism, 1939, Scottish Univs; Diploma in Hebrew, Leeds Univ., 1943. Asst in Greek, Edinburgh Univ., 1935-38; Lectr in Greek, Leeds Univ., 1938-47: Professor of Biblical History and Literature, University of Sheffield, 1955-59 (Head of Dept, 1947-59). Lectures: John A. McElwain, Gordon Divinity School, Beverly Farms, Massachusetts, 1958; Calvin Foundation, Calvin Coll. and Seminary, Grand Rapids, Michigan, 1958; Payton, Fuller Theolog. Seminary, Pasadena, Calif, 1968; Norton, Southern Baptist Theolog. Seminary, Louisville, Kentucky, 1968; Smyth, Columbia Theological Seminary, Decatur, Ga, 1970; Earle, Nazarene Theological Seminary, Kansas City, Mo, 1970; N. W. Lund, N Park

Theological Seminary, Chicago, 1970; Thomas F. Staley, Ontario Bible Coll., Toronto, 1973. Examr in Biblical Studies: Leeds University, 1943-47, 1957-60, 1967-69; Edinburgh University, 1949-52, 1958-60; Bristol University, 1958-60; Aberdeen University, 1959-61; London University, 1959-60; St Andrews University, 1961-64; Cambridge University, 1961-62; University of Wales, 1965-68; Sheffield University, 1968-70; Newcastle University, 1969-71; Keele Univ., 1971-73; Dublin Univ., 1972-75; Dean of Faculty of Theology, University of Manchester, 1963-64; President: Yorkshire Soc. for Celtic Studies, 1948-50; Sheffield Branch of Classical Association, 1955-58; Victoria Inst., 1958-65; Manchester Egyptian and Oriental Society, 1963-65; Soc. for Old Testament Study, 1965; Soc. for New Testament Studies, 1975. Editor: Yorkshire Celtic Studies, 1945-57; The Evangelical Quarterly, 1949-; Palestine Exploration Quarterly, 1957-71. *Publications:* The NT Documents, 1943; The Hittites and the OT, 1948; The Books and the Parchments, 1950; The Acts of the Apostles, Greek Text with Commentary, 1951; The Book of the Acts, Commentary on English Text, 1954; Second Thoughts on the Dead Sea Scrolls, 1956; The Teacher of Righteousness in the Qumran Texts, 1957; Biblical Exegesis in the Qumran Texts, 1959; The Spreading Flame, 1958; Commentary on the Epistle to the Colossians, 1958; The English Bible, 1961; The Epistle to the Ephesians, 1961; Paul and his Converts, 1962; The Epistle of Paul to the Romans, 1963; Israel and the Nations, 1963; Commentary on the Epistle to the Hebrews, 1964; Expanded Paraphrase of the Epistles of Paul, 1965; New Testament History, 1969; This is That, 1969; Tradition Old and New, 1970; St Matthew, 1970; The Epistles of John, 1970; First and Second Corinthians (Century Bible), 1971; The Message of the New Testament, 1972; Jesus and Christian Origins outside the New Testament, 1974; Paul and Jesus, 1974; First-Century Faith, 1977; contribs to classical and theological journals. *Recreation:* walking. *Address:* The University, Manchester; The Crossways, Temple Road, Buxton, Derbyshire. *T:* Buxton 3250.

BRUCE, Hon. George John Done, RP 1959; painter of portraits, landscapes, still life, ships, flowers; *b* 28 March 1930; *s* of 11th Baron Balfour of Burleigh and Violet Dorothy Done, Delamere Forest, Tarporley, Cheshire; *b* of 12th Baron Balfour of Burleigh, *qv*. *Educ:* Westminster Sch.; Byam Shaw Sch. of Drawing and Painting. Hon. Sec., Royal Soc. of Portrait Painters, 1970-. *Recreations:* sail wing flying, ski-ing on snow and water. *Address:* 6 Pembroke Walk, W8. *T:* 01-937 1493. *Club:* Athenæum.

BRUCE, Sir Hervey (James Hugh), 7th Bt *cr* 1804; Captain, The Grenadier Guards; *b* 3 Sept. 1952; *s* of Sir Hervey John William Bruce, 6th Bt, and of Crista, *y d* of late Lt-Col Chandos De Paravicini, OBE; *S* father, 1971. *Educ:* Eton; Officer Cadet School, Mons. *Heir:* uncle Ronald Cecil Juckes Bruce [*b* 22 Aug. 1921; *m* 1960, Jean, *d* of L. J. W. Murfitt; one *s*]. *Address:* Petersham House, Falmouth Gardens, Newmarket, Suffolk.

BRUCE, Mrs H. J.; *see* Karsavina, Tamara.

BRUCE, Sir Michael (Ian), 12th Bt, *cr* 1629; partner, Gossard-Bruce Co., from 1953; owner, The Eye Witness (legal photo service), from 1956; *b* 3 April 1926; *s* of Sir Michael William Selby Bruce, 11th Bt and Doreen Dalziel, *d* of late W. F. Greenwell; *S* father 1957; is an American citizen; has discontinued first forename, Francis; *m* 1st, 1947, Barbara Stevens (marr. diss., 1957), *d* of Frank J. Lynch; two *s*; 2nd, 1961, Frances Keegan (marr. diss., 1963); 3rd, 1966, Marilyn Ann, *d* of Carter Mallaby. *Educ:* Forman School, Litchfield, Conn; Pomfret, Conn. Served United States Marine Corps, 1943-46 (Letter of Commendation); S Pacific area two years, Bismarck Archipelago, Bougainville, Philippines. *Recreations:* sailing, spear-fishing. *Heir:* *s* Michael Ian Richard Bruce, *b* 10 Dec. 1950. *Clubs:* Rockaway Hunt; Lawrence Beach.

BRUCE, Michael Stewart Rae, QC (Scot.) 1975; *b* 26 July 1938; *s* of late Alexander Eric Bruce, Advocate in Aberdeen, and of Mary Gordon Bruce (*née* Walker); *m* 1963, Alison Mary Monfries Stewart; two *d*. *Educ:* Loretto Sch.; Aberdeen Univ. (MA, LLB). Admitted Faculty of Advocates, 1963; Standing Counsel: to Dept of Agriculture and Fisheries for Scotland, 1973; to Highlands and Islands Develt Bd, 1973. *Recreations:* fishing, golf. *Address:* 17 Heriot Row, Edinburgh EH12 5LR. *T:* 031-337 5883. *Clubs:* New (Edinburgh); Honourable Company of Edinburgh Golfers.

BRUCE of Sumburgh, Robert Hunter Wingate, CBE 1967; Lord-Lieutenant for Shetland (formerly for the County of Zetland), since 1963; *b* 11 Oct. 1907; *s* of John Bruce of Sumburgh and Isobel Abel; *m* 1935, Valmai Muriel, *d* of Charles Frederick Chamberlain and Lillian Muriel Smith; no *c*. *Educ:* Rugby

School; Balliol College, Oxford. LMS Railway, 1930-46; on loan to Min. of Economic Warfare, 1941-43; Manager, Northern Counties Rly, Belfast, 1943-46. Retired from LMS to manage Shetland property, 1946. Rep. Rio Tinto Co. in N and S Rhodesia and S Africa, Africa, 1952-57. Member Zetland CC, 1948-52, 1958-61. Member: Advisory Panel on Highlands and Islands, 1948-52, 1957-65; Crofters Commn, 1960. Chairman, Highland Transport Board, 1963-66. Medal of Freedom with Silver Palm, USA, 1948. *Recreations:* farming, reading history, tennis, golf, convivial argument. *Address:* Sand Lodge, Sandwick, Shetland. *T:* Sandwick 209. *Clubs:* New (Edinburgh); Highland (Inverness).

BRUCE, Robert Nigel (Beresford Dalrymple), CBE 1972 (OBE (mil.) 1946); TD; CEng, Hon. FIGasE; *b* 21 May 1907; *s* of Major R. N. D. Bruce, late of Hampstead; *m* 1945, Elizabeth Brogden, *d* of J. G. Moore; twin *s* two *d*. *Educ:* Harrow School (Entrance and Leaving Scholar); Magdalen College, Oxford (Exhibitioner). BA (Hons Chem.) and BSc. Joined Territorial Army Rangers (KRRC), 1931; Major, 1939; served Greece, Egypt, Western Desert, 1940-42; Lt-Col Comdg Regt, 1942; GHQ, MEF, Middle East Supply Centre, 1943-45; Col, Dir. of Materials, 1944. Joined Gas, Light and Coke Co., as Research Chemist, 1929; Asst to Gen. Manager, 1937, Controller of Industrial Relations, 1946; Staff Controller, 1949, Dep. Chm., 1956, North Thames Gas Bd; Chm., S Eastern Gas Bd, 1960-72. President: British Road Tar Assoc., 1964 and 1965; Coal Tar Research Assoc., 1966; Institution of Gas Engineers, 1968; Mem. Bd and Exec. Cttee, CEI. Chm. Governing Body, Westminster Coll., 1958-76. FBIM; MIPM. Sec., Tennis and Rackets Assoc., 1975-. *Publications:* Chronicles of the 1st Battalion the Rangers (KRRC), 1939-45; contribs to Proc. Royal Society, Jl Soc. Chemical Industry, Jl Chemical Society. *Recreations:* tennis, lawn tennis, golf. *Address:* Fairwater, Orchard Gate, Esher, Surrey. *T:* 01-398 3135. *Clubs:* United Oxford & Cambridge University; Royal Tennis Court.

BRUCE, Hon. Mrs Victor, (Mildred Mary), FRGS; *b* 1895; *d* of Lawrence Joseph Petre, Coptfold Hall, Essex; *m* 1926, Hon. Victor Bruce (marr. diss., 1941), *y s* of 2nd Baron Aberdare. *Educ:* Convent of Sion. Travelled furthest north into Lapland by motor car; holds record for Double Channel Crossing, Dover to Calais, by motor boat; holder of 17 World Records, motoring, and of 24-hour record; single-handed drive, covered longest distance for man or woman, 2164 miles, in 24 hours; Coupe des Dames, Monte Carlo Rally, 1927. Flying records: first solo flight from England to Japan, 1930; longest solo flight, 1930; record solo flight, India to French Indo-China, 1930; British Air refuelling endurance flight, 1933. Holds 24 hour record by motor boat, covering 674 nautical miles, single handed, 1929; first crossing of Yellow Sea. Show Jumping, 1st Royal Windsor Horse Show, 1939. Order of the Million Elephants and White Umbrella (French Indo-China). Fellow, Ancient Monuments Society. *Publications:* The Peregrinations of Penelope; 9000 Miles in Eight Weeks; The Woman Owner Driver; The Bluebird's Flight. *Address:* Priory Steps, Bradford-on-Avon, Wiltshire. *T:* Bradford-on-Avon 2230; 18 Cumberland Terrace, Regent's Park, NW1. *Clubs:* Royal Motor Yacht, British Racing Drivers, Rolls Royce Enthusiasts'.

BRUCE-CHWATT, Prof. Leonard Jan, CMG 1976; OBE 1953; FRCP; FIBiol; Professor of Tropical Hygiene and Director of Ross Institute, London School of Hygiene and Tropical Medicine, University of London, 1969-74, now Emeritus Professor; Editor, Tropical Doctor (Royal Society of Medicine); *b* 9 June 1907; *s* of Dr Michael Chwatt and Anna Marquitant; *m* 1948, Joan Margaret Bruce; two *s*. *Educ:* Univ. of Warsaw (MD); Paris (Dipl. Méd. Col.); Univ. of London (DTM&H); Harvard (MPH). Wartime service Polish Army Med. Corps and RAMC, 1939-45; Colonial Medical Service (Senior Malariologist, Nigeria), 1946-58; Chief Research and Technical Intelligence, Div. of Malaria Eradication, WHO, Geneva, 1958-68. Mem. Expert Cttee on Malaria, WHO, Geneva, 1956-. Vice-Pres., Royal Soc. Tropical Med. and Hygiene; Associate, Wellcome Mus. of Med. Science, 1975. Duncan Medal, 1942; North Persian Forces Memorial Medal, 1952; Darling Medal and Prize, 1971. KStJ 1975. *Publications:* Terminology of Malaria, 1963; chapter on malaria in Cecil and Loeb Textbook of Medicine, 1967 and 1970; Dynamics of Tropical Disease, 1973; The Rise and Fall of Malaria in Europe, 1976; numerous papers in medical jls. *Recreations:* travel, music, walking. *Address:* 21 Marchmont Road, Richmond, Surrey. *T:* 01-940 5540.

BRUCE-GARDNER, Sir Douglas (Bruce), 2nd Bt, *cr* 1945; Deputy Chairman: Guest, Keen & Nettlefolds Ltd; Guest, Keen & Nettlefolds (UK) Ltd; *b* 27 Jan. 1917; *s* of Sir Charles Bruce-Gardner, 1st Bt; *S* father, 1960; *m* 1st, 1940, Monica Flumerfelt

(marr. diss. 1964), *d* of late Sir Geoffrey Jefferson, CBE, FRS; one *s* two *d*; 2nd, 1964, Sheila Jane, *d* of Roger and late Barbara Stilliard, Seer Green, Bucks; one *s* one *d*. *Educ:* Uppingham; Trinity College, Cambridge. Dep. Chairman, GKN Steel Co. Ltd, 1962, Gen. Man. Dir, 1963-65, Chm., 1965-67; Dir, Guest, Keen & Nettlefolds Ltd, 1960; Chairman: GKN Rolled & Bright Steel Ltd, 1968-72; GKN (South Wales) Ltd; Exors of James Mills Ltd; Parson Ltd, 1968-72; Exec. Vice-Chm., UK Ops, Gen. Products, Guest, Keen & Nettlefolds Ltd, 1972-74. Dir, Henry Gardner & Co. Ltd, 1952-68. President: Iron and Steel Inst., 1966-67; British Indep. Steel Producers' Assoc., 1972. *Recreations:* fishing, photography. *Heir:* *s* Robert Henry Bruce-Gardner, *b* 10 June 1943. *Address:* Bishopswood Grange, near Ross-on-Wye, Herefordshire. *T:* Lydbrook 444. *Clubs:* Junior Carlton; Cardiff and County (Cardiff).

BRUCE-GARDYNE, John, (Jock); *b* 12 April 1930; 2nd *s* of late Capt. E. Bruce-Gardyne, DSO, RN, Middleton, by Arbroath, Angus and Joan (*née* McLaren); *m* 1959, Sarah Louisa Mary, *o d* of Comdr Sir John Maitland, *qv*; two *s* one *d*. *Educ:* Winchester; Magdalen College, Oxford. HM Foreign Service, 1953-56; served in London and Sofia; Paris correspondent, Financial Times, 1956-60; Foreign Editor, Statist, 1961-64. MP (C) South Angus, 1964-Oct. 1974; PPS to Secretary of State for Scotland, 1970-72. Vice-Chm., Cons. Parly Finance Cttee, 1972-74. *Publications:* Whatever happened to the Quiet Revolution?, 1974; Scotland in 1980, 1975; (with Nigel Lawson) The Power Game, 1976. *Address:* 13 Kelso Place, W8.

BRUCE LOCKHART, John Macgregor, CB 1966; CMG 1951; OBE 1944; *b* 9 May 1914; *e s* of late John Harold Bruce Lockhart, and Mona Brougham; *m* 1939, Margaret Evelyn, *d* of late Rt Rev. C. R. Hone; two *s* one *d*. *Educ:* Rugby School; St Andrews University (Harkness Scholar). MA 2nd Class Hons Modern Languages, 1937. Asst Master, Rugby School, 1937-39; TA Commission, Seaforth Highlanders, 1938; served War of 1939-45, in UK, Middle East, North Africa, Italy (Lt-Col); Asst Military Attaché, British Embassy, Paris, 1945-47; Control Commission Germany, 1948-51; First Secretary, British Embassy, Washington, 1951-53; served Foreign Office, London, until resignation from the Diplomatic Service, 1965; in charge of planning and development, Univ. of Warwick, 1965-67; Head of Central Staff Dept, Courtaulds Ltd, 1967-71. Advisor on Post Experience Programme, Graduate Business Centre, City Univ.; Chm., Business Educn Council; Member: Nat. Adv. Council on Educn for Industry and Commerce; Naval Educn Adv. Cttee; London and Home Counties Regional Management Council. *Recreations:* music, real tennis, golf, pictures. *Address:* 45 Wynnstay Gardens, Allen Street, W8. *Clubs:* Reform, Boodle's; Rye Dormy; Queen's.

BRUCE LOCKHART, Logie, MA; Headmaster of Gresham's School, Holt, since 1955; *b* 12 Oct. 1921; *s* of late John Harold Bruce Lockhart; *m* 1944, Josephine Agnew; two *s* two *d* (and one *d* decd). *Educ:* Sedbergh School; St John's College, Cambridge (Schol. and Choral Studentship). RMC Sandhurst, 1941; served War of 1939-45; 9th Sherwood Foresters, 1942; 2nd Household Cavalry (Life Guards), 1944-45. Larmor Award, 1947; Asst Master, Tonbridge School, 1947-55. Sponsor, Nat. Council for Educnl Standards. *Recreations:* fishing, writing, natural history, games; Blue for Rugby football, 1945, 1946, Scottish International, 1948, 1950, 1953. *Address:* Church Farm House, Holt, Norfolk. *T:* Holt 2137. *Club:* East India, Devonshire, Sports and Public Schools.

BRUCE LOCKHART, Rab Brougham, MA Cantab; Headmaster, Loretto School, Musselburgh, Edinburgh, 1960-76; *b* 1 Dec. 1916; *s* of late J. H. Bruce Lockhart; *m* 1941, Helen Priscilla Lawrence Crump; two *s* one *d*. *Educ:* Edinburgh Academy; Corpus Christi College, Cambridge. BA (Mod. Lang.) 1939; MA 1946. Assistant Master, Harrow, 1939. Served War of 1939-45: Commissioned RA, 1940; Middle East, 1942-44; Major RA 1944; Intelligence, Italy and Austria, 1945. Assistant Master, Harrow, 1946-50; Housemaster, Appleby College, Oakville, Ont, Canada, 1950-54; Headmaster, Wanganui Collegiate School, Wanganui, New Zealand, 1954-60. *Recreations:* squash, golf and photography; formerly: a Scotland cricket XI, 1935; Scotland XV, 1937, 1939; Rugby "Blue" 1937, 1938. *Address:* Saul Hill, Burneside, near Kendal, Cumbria. *T:* Selside 646.

BRUCE-MITFORD, Rupert Leo Scott, FBA 1976; Research Keeper in the British Museum, 1975-77 (Keeper of British and Mediæval Antiquities, 1954-69, of Mediæval and Later Antiquities, 1969-75); *b* 14 June 1914; 4th *s* of C. E. Bruce-Mitford, Madras, and Beatrice (*née* Allison), British Columbia; *m* 1st, 1941, Kathleen Dent (marr. diss. 1972); one *s* two *d*; 2nd, 1975, Marilyn Roberta, *o d* of Robert J. Luscombe, Walton on the Hill, Staffs. *Educ:* Christ's Hospital; Hertford College, Oxford (Baring Scholar). Temp. Asst Keeper, Ashmolean Museum, 1937; Asst Keeper, Dept of British and Mediæval Antiquities, British Museum, 1938; Royal Signals, 1939-45; Deputy Keeper, British Museum, 1954. FSA 1947 (Sec., Soc. of Antiquaries, 1950-54, Vice-Pres., 1972-76). Slade Professor elect of Fine Art, Univ. of Cambridge, 1978-79. Vis. Fellow, All Souls Coll., Oxford, 1978-79. Member: German Archæological Inst.; Italian Inst. of Prehistory and Protohistory; Corres. Member, Jutland Archæological Society; Hon. Mem., Suffolk Inst. of Archaeology; Member of Ancient Monuments Board, England, 1954-; Member, Permanent Council, Internat. Congress of Prehistoric and Protohistoric Sciences, 1957-; President, Society for Mediæval Archæology, 1957-59. Lectures: Dalrymple, Glasgow, 1961; Thomas Davis Radio, Dublin, 1964; Jarrow, 1967; O'Donnell, Wales, 1971; Garmonsway, York, 1974. Hon. LittD Dublin 1966. *Publications:* The Society of Antiquaries of London; Notes on its History and Possessions (with others), 1952; Editor and contributor, Recent Archæological Excavations in Britain, 1956; (with T. J. Brown, A. S. C. Ross and others), Codex Lindisfarnensis (Swiss facsimile edn), 1957-61; (trans. from Danish) The Bog People, by P. V. Glob, 1969; The Sutton Hoo Ship-burial, a handbook, 1972; Aspects of Anglo-Saxon Archaeology, 1974; The Sutton Hoo Ship-burial, Vol. I, 1975, Vol. II, 1978; Vol. III in press; (ed) Recent Excavations in Europe, 1975; papers and reviews in learned journals. *Address:* 10 Nelson Road, Harrow on the Hill, Mddx. *T:* 01-422 0967. *Clubs:* Athenæum, Garrick, MCC.

BRÜCK, Prof. Hermann Alexander, CBE 1966; DPhil (Munich); PhD (Cantab); Astronomer Royal for Scotland and Regius Professor of Astronomy in the University of Edinburgh, 1957-Sept. 1975; now Professor Emeritus; Dean of the Faculty of Science, 1968-70; *b* 15 Aug. 1905; *s* of late H. H. Brück; *m* 1st, 1936, Irma Waitzfelder (*d* 1950); one *s* one *d*; 2nd, 1951, Dr Mary T. Conway; one *s* two *d*. *Educ:* Augusta Gymnasium, Charlottenburg; Universities of Bonn, Kiel, Munich, and Cambridge. Astronomer, Potsdam Astrophysical Observatory, 1928; Lectr, Berlin University, 1935; Research Associate, Vatican Observatory, Castel Gandolfo, 1936; Asst Observer, Solar Physics Observatory, Cambridge, 1937; John Couch Adams Astronomer, Cambridge University, 1943; Asst Director, Cambridge Observatory, 1946; Director, Dunsink Observatory and Professor of Astronomy, Dublin Institute for Advanced Studies, 1947-57. Mem., Bd of Governors, Armagh Observatory, NI, 1971-. MRIA, 1948; FRSE, 1958; Member Pontif. Academy of Sciences, Rome, 1955, Mem. Council, 1964-; Corr. Member Academy of Sciences, Mainz, 1955; Vice-President Royal Astronomical Society, 1959-61. Hon. DSc: NUI, 1972; St Andrews, 1973. *Publications:* scientific papers in journals and observatory publications. *Recreation:* music. *Address:* Craigower, Penicuik, Midlothian EH26 9LA. *T:* Penicuik 75918. *Club:* New (Edinburgh).

BRUDENELL-BRUCE, family name of **Marquess of Ailesbury.**

BRUFORD, Walter Horace, MA; FBA 1963; *b* Manchester, 1894; *s* of Francis J. and Annie Bruford; *m* 1925, Gerda (*d* 1976), *d* of late Professor James Hendrick; one *s* two *d*. *Educ:* Manchester Grammar School; St John's College, Cambridge; University of Zürich. BA Cambridge, 1915 (1st Class Hons. Med. and Mod. Langs). Bendall Sanskrit Exhibitioner; Master Manchester Grammar School; served Intelligence Division, Admiralty, with rank of Lieut RNVR. On demobilisation, research in University of Zürich; Lecturer in German, University of Aberdeen, 1920, Reader, 1923; Professor of German, University of Edinburgh, 1929-51. Seconded to Foreign Office, 1939-43. Schröder Professor of German, University of Cambridge, 1951-61. Corresponding member Deutsche Akademie für Sprache und Dichtung, 1957; Goethe-Medal in Gold, of Goethe-Institut, Munich, 1958; President: Mod. Lang. Assoc., 1959; Mod. Humanities Research Assoc., 1965; English Goethe Soc., 1965-75; Corresponding Member, Sächsische Akademie der Wissenschaften, Leipzig, 1965. Hon. LLD Aberdeen, 1958; Hon. DLitt: Newcastle, 1969; Edinburgh, 1974. *Publications:* Sound and Symbol (with Professor J. J. Findlay); Germany in the eighteenth century; Die gesellschaftlichen Grundlagen der Goethezeit; Chekhov and His Russia; two chapters in Essays on Goethe (ed. by W. Rose); Theatre, Drama and Audience in Goethe's Germany; Literary Interpretation in Germany; Goethe's Faust (introd., revised and annotated, Everyman's Library); Chekhov (Studies in Modern European Literature and Thought); The Organisation and Rise of Prussia and German Constitutional and Social Development, 1795-1830 (in Cambridge Modern History, New Series, Vols VII and IX); Culture and Society in Classical Weimar; Deutsche Kultur der Goethezeit; Annotated edition and interpretation of Goethe's Faust, Part I; The German Tradition of Self-

Cultivation: *Bildung* from Humboldt to Thomas Mann; articles and reviews in modern language periodicals. *Address:* 15 Strathfillan Road, Edinburgh EH9 2AG.
See also H . St J . B . Armitage .

BRUHN, Erik Belton Evers; Danish Ballet Dancer; Ballet-director, Royal Opera, Stockholm, 1967-71; *b* Copenhagen, Denmark, 3 Oct. 1928; *s* of Ernst Emil Bruhn, CE, and Ellen (*née* Evers); unmarried. *Educ:* Royal Danish Theatre, Copenhagen. Started at Royal Danish Ballet School, 1937. Principal rôles include those in: Giselle, Swan Lake, Carmen, La Sylphide, Les Sylphides, The Sleeping Beauty, Miss Julie, Night Shadow, Spectre de la Rose, A Folk Tale; also classical pas de deux and various abstract ballets. *Publication:* Bournonville and Ballet Tecnic. *Address:* Landsretssagfører Esther, Tonsgaard, Niels Hemmingsensgade 8-10, 1153 Copenhagen, Denmark. *T:* 115704.

BRULLER, Jean; see Vercors.

BRUNE, Sir Humphrey I. P.; see Prideaux-Brune.

BRUNER, Jerome Seymour, MA, PhD; Watts Professor of Psychology, University of Oxford, since 1972; *b* New York, 1 Oct. 1915; *s* of Herman and Rose Bruner; *m* 1st, 1940, Katherine Frost (marr. diss. 1956); one *s* one *d*; 2nd, 1960, Blanche Marshall McLane. *Educ:* Duke Univ. (AB 1937); Harvard Univ. (AM 1939, PhD 1941). US Intelligence, 1941; Assoc. Dir, Office Public Opinion Research, Princeton, 1942-44; govt public opinion surveys on war problems, 1942-43; political intelligence, France, 1943; Harvard University: research, 1945-72; Prof. of Psychology, 1952-72; Dir, Centre for Cognitive Studies, 1961-72. Lectr, Salzburg Seminar, 1952; Bacon Prof., Univ. of Aix-en-Provence, 1965. Editor, Public Opinion Quarterly, 1943-44; Syndic, Harvard Univ. Press, 1962-63. Member: Inst. Advanced Study, 1951; White House Panel on Educnl Research and Develt. Guggenheim Fellow, Cambridge Univ., 1955; Fellow: Amer. Psychol Assoc. (Pres., 1964-65; Distinguished Scientific Contrib. award, 1962); Amer. Acad. Arts and Sciences; Swiss Psychol Soc. (hon.); Soc. Psychol Study Social Issues (past Pres.); Amer. Assoc. Univ. Profs; Puerto Rican Acad. Arts and Sciences (hon.). Hon. DHL Lesley Coll., 1964; Hon. DSc: Northwestern Univ., 1965; Sheffield, 1970; Bristol, 1975; Hon. MA, Oxford, 1972; Hon. DSocSci, Yale, 1975; Hon. LLD: Temple Univ., 1965; Univ. of Cincinnati, 1966; Univ. of New Brunswick, 1969; Hon. DLitt: North Michigan Univ., 1969; Duke Univ., 1969; Dr *hc*: Sorbonne, 1974; Leuven, 1976. *Publications:* Mandate from the People, 1944; (with Krech) Perception and Personality: A Symposium, 1950; (with Goodnow and Austin) A Study of Thinking, 1956; (with Smith and White) Opinions and Personality, 1956; (with Bresson, Morf and Piaget) Logique et Perception, 1958; The Process of Education, 1960; On Knowing: Essays for the Left Hand, 1962; (ed) Learning about Learning: A conference report, 1966; (with Olver, Greenfield, and others) Studies in Cognitive Growth, 1966; Toward a Theory of Instruction, 1966; Processes of Cognitive Growth: Infancy, Vol III, 1968; The Relevance of Education, 1971; (ed Anglin) Beyond the Information Given: selected papers of Jerome S. Bruner, 1973; (with Connolly) The Growth of Competence, 1974; (with Jolly and Sylva) Play: Its role in evolution and development, 1975; contribs technical and professional jls. *Recreation:* sailing. *Address:* Department of Experimental Psychology, South Parks Road, Oxford OX1 3PS. *Clubs:* Harvard (New York); Eastern Point Yacht.

BRUNNER, Sir Felix (John Morgan), 3rd Bt, *cr* 1895; Director of various Companies, retired; *b* 13 Oct. 1897; *o s* of Sir John Brunner, 2nd Bt, and Lucy Marianne Vaughan (*d* 1941), *d* of late Octavius Vaughan Morgan, MP; *S* father 1929; *m* 1926, Dorothea Elizabeth, OBE 1965, JP, *d* of late Henry Brodribb Irving and late Dorothea Baird; three *s* (and two *s* decd). *Educ:* Cheltenham; Trinity College, Oxford (MA). Served European War, 1916-18, as Lieut RFA; contested (L) Hulme Division Manchester, 1924, Chippenham, Wilts, 1929, and Northwich, Cheshire, 1945. Chairman, Henley Rural District Council, 1954-57. Chairman, Commons, Open Spaces and Footpaths Preservation Society, 1958-70. President, Liberal Party Organisation, 1962-63. *Heir: s* John Henry Kilian Brunner [*b* 1 June 1927; *m* 1955, Jasmine Cecily, *d* of late John Wardrop-Moore; two *s* one *d*]. *Address:* Greys Court, Henley-on-Thames, Oxon. *T:* Rotherfield Greys 296. *Clubs:* Bath, Reform.
See also Laurence Irving.

BRUNNER, Dr Guido; Ambassador; Member, Commission of the European Communities, since 1974 (responsible for Energy, Research, Science and Education); *b* Madrid; 27 May 1930; *m* 1958, Christa (*née* Speidel). *Educ:* Bergzabern, Munich; German Sch., Madrid; Univs of Munich, Heidelberg and Madrid (law and econs). LLD Munich; Licentiate of Law Madrid. Diplomatic service, 1955-74; Foreign Minister's office, 1956; Office, Sec. of State for For. Affairs, 1958-60; Office, German Observer at UN, NY, 1960-68; Min. for Foreign Affairs: Dept of scientific and technol relns, Political Div., 1968; Press Spokesman, 1970; Head of Planning Staff, 1972-74; Ambassador and Head of Delegn of Fed. Rep. of Germany, Conf. for Security and Coop. in Europe, Helsinki/Geneva, 1972-74. *Publications:* Bipolarität und Sicherheit, 1965; Friedenssicherungsaktionen der Vereinigten Nationen, 1968; contrib. Vierteljahreshefte für Zeitgeschichte, Aussenpolitik, Europa-Archiv. *Address:* Commission of the European Communities, 200 rue de la Loi, B-1049 Brussels, Belgium. *T:* 735 00 40.

BRUNSKILL, Catherine Lavinia Bennett, CBE 1919; *d* of Robert Bennett, Eastbourne; *m* 1918, Brig. George Stephen Brunskill, *qv* (from whom she obtained a divorce, 1946); one *d*. Private Secretary to Adjutant-General to the Forces, War Office, 1916-18; and to Commissioner of Metropolitan Police, New Scotland Yard, 1918-19. Defence Medal London Ambulance Service, 1945. *Address:* Room C, 126 Sloane Street, SW1.

BRUNSKILL, Brig. George Stephen, CBE 1941; MC 1914; *b* 26 Aug. 1891; *s* of late Major Arthur Stephen Brunskill, The King's Own Regt and West India Regt, of Buckland Tout Saints, S Devon, and Annie Louisa Churchward; *m* Moira Wallace (*née* Wares); one *s* one *d*. *Educ:* Eastbourne College; Royal Military College, Sandhurst; Staff College, Camberley (psc). Commissioned into Indian Army, 1911, and joined 47th Sikhs; served European War, 1914-18, in France, where twice severely wounded, and Italy as DAAG (MC, Corona d'Italia and Order of St Maurice and Lazarus, Brevet Major); transferred to King's Shropshire Light Infantry, 1918; commanded First Battalion, 1934; Colonel 1937, and served on the staff as Temp. Brigadier in Palestine (CBE), in the Greece and Crete campaigns of 1941 (despatches twice, Greek MC, 1939-43 Star, N. African Star, Defence Medal, Czecho Slovak Order of White Lion, 3rd class); and on the Congo-Cairo War Supply Route, 1942-43; retired, 1945. Agent, Slingsby Estate, 1948-66. Councillor, Nidderdale RDC, 1950-66. *Address:* Cob Cottage, Woolstone, Faringdon, Oxon. *T:* Uffington 283.

BRUNSKILL, Muriel; contralto; *b* 18 Dec. 1899; *d* of Edmund Capstick Brunskill; *m* 1925, Robert Ainsworth (*d* 1947), conductor, pianist; two *s*. *Educ:* Kendal High School. Studied in London and Germany, pupil of Blanche Marchesi; debut, Aeolian Hall, 1920; sang with British National Opera Company at Covent Garden, His Majesty's Theatre, and provincial theatres, 1922-27; has sung regularly at Three Choirs, Handel, Norwich, and Leeds Festivals, etc., Royal Choral, Royal Philharmonic, Liverpool Philharmonic, and Hallé Societies, etc.; Toronto Symphony Orchestra and Canadian Tour, 1930; Cincinatti May Festival, 1931; Canadian Recitals, Chicago Symphony Orchestra and New York, 1932; Opera Seasons in Melbourne and Sydney and Concert Tour in Australia and New Zealand, 1934-35; frequent appearances in Holland; sang Tanta in Golden City, Adelphi Theatre, 1950. Gilbert and Sullivan Film, 1952; Gilbert and Sullivan Tour in Australia and New Zealand, 1956-57. *Address:* Downrew House, Bishops Tawton, Devon. *T:* Barnstaple 2497.

BRUNT, Peter Astbury, FBA 1969; Camden Professor of Ancient History, Oxford University, and Fellow of Brasenose College, since 1970; *b* 23 June 1917; *s* of Rev. Samuel Brunt, Methodist Minister, and Gladys Eileen Brunt. *Educ:* Ipswich Sch.; Oriel Coll., Oxford. Open Schol. in History, Oriel Coll., Oxford, 1935; first classes in Class. Mods, 1937, and Lit. Hum., 1939; Craven Fellowship, 1939. Temp. Asst Principal and (later) Temp. Principal, Min. of Shipping (later War Transport), 1940-45. Sen. Demy, Magdalen Coll., Oxford, 1946; Lectr in Ancient History, St Andrews Univ., 1947-51; Fellow and Tutor of Oriel Coll., Oxford, 1951-67, Dean, 1959-64, Hon. Fellow, 1973; Fellow and Sen. Bursar, Gonville and Caius Coll., Cambridge, 1968-70. Editor of Oxford Magazine, 1963-64; Chm., Cttee on Ashmolean Museum, 1967; Deleg., Clarendon Press, 1971-; Mem. Council, British Sch. at Rome, 1972-. *Publications:* Thucydides (selections in trans. with introd.), 1963; Res Gestae Divi Augusti (with Dr J. M. Moore), 1967; Social Conflicts in the Roman Republic, 1971; Italian Manpower 225 BC-AD 14, 1971; ed, Arrian's Anabasis (Loeb Classical Library), vol. I, 1976; articles in classical and historical jls. *Address:* 34 Manor Road, South Hinksey, Oxford. *T:* Oxford 739923.

BRUNT, Robert Nigel Bright, CBE 1947; *b* 13 April 1902; *s* of Henry Robert and Mary Madeline Brunt, Leek, Staffs, afterwards of Belle Isle, Co. Fermanagh; *m* 1943, Joan, *er d* of Sir Richard Pierce Butler, 11th Bt, Ballin Temple, Co. Carlow;

two *s* one *d*. *Educ:* Repton; King's College, Cambridge. Served in India and Pakistan with Burmah-Shell Oil Companies and Associates, 1922-50; a Director in London, 1951-55. Chairman, Punjab Chamber of Commerce, 1940-41; Chairman, National Service Advisory Cttee, Delhi Area, 1939-42; Adviser to Government of India for Petroleum Products, 1941-45; Member, Advisory Cttee for Development of New Delhi, 1940-45; a Trustee of Port of Karachi, 1949-50. A Governor of Queen Charlotte's and Chelsea Hospitals, 1962-65. *Address:* Oak Cottage, Cranleigh, Surrey.
See also Col Sir Thomas Pierce Butler, Bt.

BRUNTISFIELD, 1st Baron, *cr* 1942, of Boroughmuir; **Victor Alexander George Anthony Warrender,** MC 1918; 8th Bt of Lochend, East Lothian, *cr* 1715; late Grenadier Guards; *b* 23 June 1899; *s* of 7th Bt and Lady Maud Warrender (*d* 1945), *y d* of 8th Earl of Shaftesbury; *S* to father's Baronetcy, 1917; *m* 1920, Dorothy (marr. diss., 1945), *y d* of late Colonel R. H. Rawson, MP, and Lady Beatrice Rawson; three *s*; *m* 1948, Tania, *yr d* of Dr Kolin, St Jacob, Dubrovnik, Jugoslavia; one *s* one *d*. *Educ:* Eton. Served European War, 1917-18 (MC, Russian Order of St Stanislas, Star of Roumania, St Ann of Russia with sword); MP (U) Grantham Division of Kesteven and Rutland, 1923-42; an assistant Whip, 1928-31; Junior Lord of the Treasury, 1931-32; Vice-Chamberlain of HM Household, 1932-35; Comptroller of HM Household, 1935; Parliamentary and Financial Secretary to Admiralty, 1935; Financial Secretary, War Office, 1935-40; Parliamentary and Financial Secretary, Admiralty, 1940-42; Parliamentary Secretary, Admiralty, 1942-45. *Heir:* *s* Col Hon. John Robert Warrender, *qv*. *Address:* Chalet les Pommiers, 3780 Gstaad, OB, Switzerland. *T:* 030 42384. *Clubs:* Turf; Royal Yacht Squadron.

BRUNTON, Sir (Edward Francis) Lauder, 3rd Bt, *cr* 1908; Physician; *b* 10 Nov. 1916; *s* of Sir Stopford Brunton, 2nd Bt, and Elizabeth, *o d* of late Professor J. Bonsall Porter; *S* father 1943; *m* 1946, Marjorie, *o d* of David Sclater Lewis, MSc, MD, CM, FRCP (C); one *s* one *d*. *Educ:* Trinity College School, Port Hope; Bryanston School; McGill Univ. BSc 1940; MD, CM 1942; served as Captain, RCAMC. Hon. attending Physician, Royal Victoria Hosp., Montreal. Fellow: American Coll. of Physicians; Internat. Soc. of Hematology; Member American Society of Hematology; Life Mem., Montreal Mus. of Fine Arts. *Heir:* *s* James Lauder Brunton [*b* 24 Sept. 1947; *m* 1967, Susan, *o d* of Charles Hons; one *s* one *d*]. *Address:* PO Box 140, Guysborough, Nova Scotia, Canada. *Club:* Royal Nova Scotia Yacht Squadron.

BRUNTON, Gordon Charles; Managing Director and Chief Executive, The Thomson Organisation Ltd, since 1968; *b* 27 Dec. 1921; *s* of late Charles Arthur Brunton and late Hylda Pritchard; *m* 1st, 1946, Nadine Lucile Paula Sohr (marr. diss. 1965); one *s* two *d* (and one *s* decd); 2nd, 1966, Gillian Agnes Kirk; one *s* one *d*. *Educ:* Cranleigh Sch.; London Sch. of Economics. Commnd into RA, 1942; served Indian Army, Far East; Mil. Govt, Germany, 1946. Joined Tothill Press, 1947; Exec. Dir, Tothill, 1956; Man. Dir, Tower Press Gp of Cos, 1958; Exec. Dir, Odhams Press, 1961; joined Thomson Organisation, 1961; Man. Dir, Thomson Publications, 1961; Dir, Thomson Organisation, 1963; Chm., Thomson Travel, 1965-68; Director: Times Newspapers Ltd, 1967; Bemrose Corp., 1974; Dir of other printing and publishing cos. President: Periodical Publishers Assoc., 1972-74; Nat. Advertising Benevolent Soc., 1973-75; Mem., Printing and Publishing Ind. Trng Bd, 1974. Governor, LSE; Mem. Council, Oxford Centre for Management Studies. *Recreations:* books, breeding horses. *Address:* North Munstead, Godalming, Surrey. *T:* Godalming 6313. *Club:* Garrick.

BRUNTON, John Stirling, CB 1960; *b* 8 May 1903; *s* of John Brunton, Glasgow; *m* 1934, Mary G. Cameron, Bo'ness; one *s* one *d*. *Educ:* Albert Road Academy, Glasgow; Glasgow University. Appointed HM Inspector of Schools, 1932; seconded to Dept of Health for Scotland, for work on Emergency Hospital Scheme, 1939-42; HM Inspector in charge of counties of Stirling, Perth and Kinross, 1942-48; HM Inspector in charge of Glasgow, 1948-50; Assistant Secretary, Scottish Education Department, 1951-55; HM Senior Chief Inspector of Schools, Scottish Education Department, 1955-66, retd. Chm., Scottish Nat. Camps Assoc. *Recreations:* golf, motoring. *Address:* 1/12 Pentland Drive, Edinburgh EH10 6PU. *T:* 031-445 2848.

BRUNTON, Sir Lauder; see Brunton, Sir E. F. L.

BRUSH, Lt-Col Edward James Augustus Howard, CB 1966; DSO 1945; OBE 1946; *b* 5 March 1901; *s* of Major George Howard Brush, Drumnabreeze, Co. Down; *m* 1937, Susan Mary, *d* of Major F. H. E. Torbett, Britford, Salisbury; one *d*.

Educ: Clifton Coll.; RMC. Commnd Rifle Brigade, 1920. Served War of 1939-45 (France; wounded; prisoner of war); retired 1946. Chairman, T&AFA, Co. Down, 1954-65. JP, DL Co. Down, 1953-74; Vice-Lieutenant, 1957-64; High Sheriff, 1953. Member, Irish Nat. Hunt Steeplechase Cttee. *Publication:* The Hunter Chaser, 1947. *Address:* Drumnabreeze, Magheralin, Craigavon, N Ireland. *T:* Moira 611284.

BRYAN, Sir Andrew (Meikle), Kt 1950; DSc; Hon. LLD (Glasgow); CEng, FICE, FIMinE, FRSE; Consulting Mining Engineer; Member of National Coal Board, 1951-57; *b* 1 March 1893; 2nd *s* of John Bryan, Burnbank, Hamilton, Lanarkshire; *m* 1922, Henrietta Paterson (*d* 1977), *y d* of George S. Begg, Allanshaw, Hamilton; one *s*. *Educ:* Greenfield Public School; Hamilton Acad.; Glasgow University, graduated 1919 with Special Distinction. Served in University OTC and HM Forces, 1915-18. Obtained practical mining experience in the Lanarkshire Coalfield; HM Junior Inspector of Mines in the Northern Division, 1920; Senior rank, 1926; Dixon Professor of Mining, University of Glasgow, Professor of Mining, Royal College of Science and Technology, Glasgow, 1932-40; Gen. Manager, 1940, Dir, 1942, Managing Director, 1944, Shotts Iron Co. Ltd; also Director Associated Lothian Coal Owners Ltd; Deputy-Director of Mining Supplies, Mines Department, 1939-40; Chief Inspector of Mines, 1947-51; Hon. Member: IMinE, 1957 (Pres., 1950 and 1951; Inst. Medal, 1954; Chm., Mining Qualifications Bd, 1962-72; former Mem. Council); Inst. Mining and Metallurgy, 1951; Nat. Assoc. of Colliery Managers, 1957 (Futers Gold Medal, 1937; former Mem. Council; Past Pres.); Geol Soc. of Edinburgh; former Mem. Council and Past Pres., Mining Inst. of Scotland; John Buddle Medal, N England Inst. of Mining and Mech. Engrs, 1967. Fellow, Imperial College of Science and Technology. *Publications:* St George's Coalfield, Newfoundland, 1937; The Evolution of Health and Safety in Mines, 1976; contribs to technical journals. *Address:* 3 Hounslow Gardens, Hounslow, Mddx TW3 2DU.

BRYAN, Sir Arthur, Kt 1976; Chairman, Wedgwood Ltd, Barlaston, Staffs, since 1968, and Managing Director since 1963; Lord-Lieutenant of Staffordshire, since 1968; *b* 4 March 1923; *s* of William Woodall Bryan and Isobel Alan (*née* Tweedie); *m* 1947, Betty Ratford; one *s* one *d*. *Educ:* Longton High Sch., Stoke-on-Trent. Trainee, Barclays Bank. Served with RAFVR, 1941-45. Josiah Wedgwood & Sons Ltd, 1947-49; London Man., 1953-57; General Sales Man., 1959-60; Director and President, Josiah Wedgwood & Sons Inc. of America, 1960-62; Director: Josiah Wedgwood & Sons Ltd, Barlaston, 1962; Josiah Wedgwood & Sons (Canada) Ltd; Josiah Wedgwood & Sons (Australia) Pty Ltd; Phoenix Assurance Co., 1976-. Pres., British Ceramic Manufacturers' Fedn, 1970-71; Mem., Design Council, 1977-. FRSA 1964; Fellow, Inst. of Marketing (grad. 1950); FBIM 1968; Comp. Inst. Ceramics. KStJ 1972. *Recreations:* walking, tennis, swimming and reading. *Address:* Parkfields Cottage, Tittensor, Stoke-on-Trent, Staffs. *T:* Barlaston 2686.

BRYAN, Denzil Arnold, CMG 1960; OBE 1947; HM Diplomatic Service, retired; *b* 15 Oct. 1909; *s* of James Edward Bryan; *m* 1965, Hope Ross, (*née* Meyer). *Educ:* in India; Selwyn Coll., Cambridge. Appointed to Indian Civil Service in 1933 and posted to Punjab. Dep. Commissioner, Hissar, 1938; Registrar, Lahore High Court, 1939-41; Dep. Comr, Dera Ghazi Khan, 1941-44; Sec. to Prime Minister, Punjab, 1944-47; and to Governor of Punjab, 1947; retired from ICS, 1947. Appointed to UK Civil Service, Bd of Trade, as Principal, 1947; Asst Sec., 1950; Under Secretary, 1961; served as a Trade Comr in India, 1947-55; UK Senior Trade Comr: in New Zealand, 1955-58; in Pakistan, 1958-61; in South Africa, 1961; Minister (Commercial, later Economic), S Africa, 1962-69. *Recreation:* golf. *Address:* 29 Wildcroft Manor, Wildcroft Road, SW15; c/o Lloyds Bank Ltd, 6 Pall Mall, SW1.

BRYAN, Dora, (Mrs William Lawton); actress; *b* 7 Feb. 1924; *d* of Albert Broadbent and Georgina (*née* Hill); *m* 1954, William Lawton; one *s* (and one *s* one *d* adopted). *Educ:* Hathershaw Council Sch., Lancs. Pantomimes: London Hippodrome, 1936; Manchester Palace, 1937; Alhambra, Glasgow, 1938; Oldham Repertory, 1939-44; followed by Peterborough, Colchester, Westcliff-on-Sea. ENSA, Italy, during War of 1939-45. Came to London, 1945, and appeared in West End Theatres: Peace in our Time; Travellers' Joy; Accolade; Lyric Revue; Globe Revue; Simon and Laura; The Water Gypsies; Gentlemen Prefer Blondes; Six of One; Too True to be Good; Hello, Dolly!; They Don't Grow on Trees. Chichester Festival seasons, 1971-74; London Palladium season, 1971; London Palladium Pantomime season, 1973-74. Has also taken parts in farces televised from Whitehall Theatre. *Films include:* The Fallen Idol, 1949; A Taste of Honey, 1961; Two a Penny, 1968. *TV series:*

appearances on A to Z; Sunday Night at the London Palladium; According to Dora, 1968; Both Ends Meet, 1972. Cabaret in Canada, Hong Kong and Britain. *Recreation:* reading, patchwork quilts. *Address:* 111 Marine Parade, Brighton, East Sussex. *T:* 63235.

BRYAN, Gerald Jackson, CMG 1964; CVO 1966; OBE 1960; MC 1941; General Manager, Bracknell Development Corporation, since 1973; *yr s* of late George Bryan, OBE, LLD, and Ruby Evelyn (*née* Jackson), Belfast; *m* 1947, Georgiana Wendy Cockburn, OStJ, *d* of late William Baraud and Winnifred Hull; one *s* two *d*. *Educ:* Wrekin Coll.; RMA, Woolwich; New Coll., Oxford. Regular Commn, RE, 1940; served Middle East with No. 11 (Scottish) Commando, 1941; retd 1944, Capt. (temp. Maj.). Apptd Colonial Service, 1944; Asst District Comr, Swaziland, 1944; Asst Colonial Sec., Barbados, 1950; Estabt Sec., Mauritius, 1954; Administrator, Brit. Virgin Is, 1959; Administrator of St Lucia, 1962-67; Govt Sec. and Head of Isle of Man Civil Service, 1967-69; Gen. Man., Londonderry Develt Commn, NI, 1969-73. MBIM. CStJ. *Recreation:* riding. *Address:* Whitehouse, Murrell Hill, Binfield, Berks; 30 Queen Street, Castletown, Isle of Man.

BRYAN, Sir Paul (Elmore Oliver), Kt 1972; DSO 1943; MC 1943; MP (C) Howden Division of Yorkshire (East Riding), since 1955; *b* 3 Aug. 1913; *s* of Reverend Dr J. I. Bryan, PhD; *m* 1st, 1939, Betty Mary (*née* Hoyle) (*d* 1968); three *d*; 2nd, 1971, Cynthia Duncan (*née* Ashley Cooper), *d* of late Sir Patrick Ashley Cooper and of Lady Ashley Cooper, Hexton Manor, Herts. *Educ:* St John's School, Leatherhead (Scholar); Caius College, Cambridge (MA). War of 1939-45; 6th Royal West Kent Regt; enlisted, 1939; commissioned, 1940 Lieut-Col, 1943; served in France, N Africa, Sicily, Italy; Comdt 164th Inf. OCTU (Eaton Hall), 1944. Sowerby Bridge UDC, 1947; contested Sowerby, By-Election, 1948, and General Elections, 1950 and 1951. Member Parliamentary Delegation: to Peru, 1955, to Algeria, 1956, to Germany, 1960, to USA and Canada, 1961, to India, 1966, to Uganda and Kenya, 1967, to Hong Kong, 1969, to Japan and Indonesia, 1969, to China, 1972. Assistant Government Whip, 1956-58; Parliamentary Private Secretary to Minister of Defence, 1956; a Lord Commissioner of the Treasury, 1958-61; Vice-Chairman, Conservative Party Organisation, 1961-65; Conservative Front Bench Spokesman on Post Office and broadcasting, 1965; Minister of State, Dept of Employment, 1970-72. Chm., All Party Hong Kong Parly Gp, 1974-. Director: Granada TV Rental Ltd, 1966-70; Granada Television, 1972-; Granada Theatres, 1973-; Greater Manchester Independent Radio Ltd, 1972- *Address:* Park Farm, Sawdon, near Scarborough, North Yorks. *T:* Snainton 370; 5 Westminster Gardens, Marsham Street, SW1. *T:* 01-834 2050. *Club:* Carlton.

BRYAN, Willoughby Guy, TD 1945; Director, Barclays Bank, since 1957 (Vice-Chairman, 1964-70, Deputy Chairman, 1970-74); Director: Barclays Bank Trust Company Ltd (Chairman, 1970-74); Barclays Unicorn Ltd, since 1970; Barclays Unicorn International Ltd, since 1974; Barclays Life Assurance Company Ltd, since 1970; *b* 16 Jan. 1911; *e s* of late C. R. W. Bryan; *m* 1936, Esther Victoria Loveday, *d* of late Major T. L. Ingram, DSO, MC; one *d*. *Educ:* Winchester; Hertford College, Oxford. Barclays Bank Ltd, 1932; various appointments including: Local Director, Oxford, 1946; Local Director, Reading, 1947; Local Director, Birmingham, 1955; Chm. Local Bd, Birmingham, 1957-64. Served War of 1939-45, Queen's Own Oxfordshire Hussars. *Recreation:* golf. *Address:* The Oast House, Sandhurst, Hawkhurst, Kent TN18 5LE. *T:* Sandhurst 376. *Club:* Army and Navy.

BRYANS, Dame Anne (Margaret), DBE 1957 (CBE 1945); DStJ; Chairman, Order of St John of Jerusalem and BRCS Service Hospitals Welfare and VAD Committee, since 1960; Vice-Chairman, Joint Committee, Order of St John and BRCS, since 1976; Member, Camden and Islington Area Health Authority, since 1974; *b* 29 Oct. 1909; *e d* of late Col Rt Hon. Sir John Gilmour, 2nd Bt, GCVO, DSO, MP of Montrave and late Mary Louise Lambert; *m* 1932, Lieut-Comdr J. R. Bryans, RN, retired; one *s*. *Educ:* privately. Joined HQ Staff British Red Cross Society, 1938; Deputy Commissioner British Red Cross and St John War Organisation, Middle East Commission, 1943; Commissioner Jan.-June 1945. Dep. Chm., 1953-64, Vice-Chm., 1964-76, Exec. Cttee, BRCS; Lay Mem., Council for Professions Supplementary to Med.; Member: Ethical practices Sub-Cttee, Royal Free Hosp., 1974-; Royal Free Hosp. Sch. Council, 1968-; Bd of Governors, Eastman Dental Hosp, 1973-; former Member: ITA, later IBA; Govt Anglo-Egyptian Resettlement Bd; BBC/ITA Appeals Cttee; Med. Sch. St George's Hosp.; former Chairman: Royal Free Hosp. and Friends of Royal Free Hosp.; Bd of Governors, Royal Free Hosp.; Council, Florence

Nightingale Hosp.; Vice-Pres., Royal Coll. of Nursing; former Governor, Westminster Hosp. FRSM 1976; Vice-Pres., Open Section, RSM, 1975-. *Address:* 57 Elm Park House, Elm Park Gardens, SW10. *Clubs:* VAD Ladies; Royal Lymington Yacht.

BRYANS, Tom, MBE 1975; Chief General Manager, Trustee Savings Bank Central Board, since 1976; *b* 16 Sept. 1920; *s* of Thomas and Martha Bryans; *m* 1947, Peggy Irene Snelling; two *s* . *Educ:* Royal Belfast Academical Instn. AIB 1950; FSBI 1972. Served War, 1939-46. Joined Belfast Savings Bank, 1938; Asst Gen. Man., 1969; Gen. Man., 1971; Chief Gen. Man., TSB Association Ltd, 1975. *Recreations:* sailing, golfing, gardening and music. *Address:* 26 Ibis Lane, Chiswick, W4 3UP. *T:* 01-995 2831.

BRYANT, Sir Arthur, Kt 1954; CH 1967; CBE 1949; Hon. LLD: Edinburgh; St Andrews; New Brunswick; MA (Oxon); FRHistS; FRSL; Council, Society Society of Authors; Royal Literary Fund; Trustee: Historic Churches Preservation Trust; National Folk Music Fund; *b* 18 Feb. 1899; *e s* of late Sir Francis Bryant, CB, CVO, CBE, ISO, JP, The Pavilion, Hampton Court; *m* 1st, 1924, Sylvia Mary (marr. diss. 1939; she *m* 2nd, F. D. Chew, and *d* 1950), *d* of Sir Walter Shakerley, Bt, Somerford Park, Cheshire; 2nd, 1941, Anne Elaine (marr. diss. 1976), *y d* of Bertram Brooke (HH Tuan Muda of Sarawak). *Educ:* Harrow; BEF France; Queen's Coll., Oxford. Barrister-at-law, Inner Temple. Principal, Cambridge School of Arts, Crafts and Technology, 1923-25; Lectr in History to Oxford Univ. Delegacy for Extra-Mural Studies, 1925-36; Watson Chair in American History, London Univ., 1935; Corres. Member of La Real Academia de la Historia of Madrid; succeeded G. K. Chesterton as writer of Our Note Book, Illustrated London News, 1936-. Chairman: Ashridge Council, 1946-49; Soc. of Authors, 1949; St John and Red Cross Library Dept, 1945-74. President: English Association, 1946; Common Market Safeguards Campaign; Friends of the Vale of Aylesbury. Trustee: English Folk Music Fund; Historic Churches Preservation Trust. Chesney Gold Medal, RUSI; Gold Medal, RICS. Hon. Freedom and Livery, Leathersellers' Company; Hon. Member: Southampton Chamber of Commerce; Rifle Brigade Club; Light Infantry Club. KGStJ. *Publications:* King Charles II, 1931; Macaulay, 1932; Samuel Pepys, the Man in the Making, 1933; The National Character, 1934; The England of Charles II, 1934; The Letters and Speeches of Charles II, 1935; Samuel Pepys, the Years of Peril, 1935; George V, 1936; The American Ideal, 1936; Postman's Horn, 1936; Stanley Baldwin, 1937; Humanity in Politics, 1938; Samuel Pepys, the Saviour of the Navy, 1938; Unfinished Victory, 1940; English Saga, 1940; The Years of Endurance, 1942; Dunkirk, 1943; Years of Victory, 1944; Historian's Holiday, 1947; The Age of Elegance, 1950 (Sunday Times Gold Medal and Award for Literature); The Turn of the Tide, 1957; Triumph in the West, 1959; Jimmy, 1960; The Story of England: Makers of the Realm, 1953; The Age of Chivalry, 1963; The Fire and the Rose, 1965; The Medieval Foundation, 1966; Protestant Island, 1967; The Lion and the Unicorn, 1969; Nelson, 1970; The Great Duke, 1971; Jackets of Green, 1973; Thousand Years of British Monarchy, 1975. *Address:* Myles Place, The Close, Salisbury, Wilts. *Clubs:* Athenæum, Beefsteak, Grillion's, Pratt's, Royal Automobile, Saintsbury, MCC.

BRYANT, Rear-Adm. Benjamin, CB 1956; DSO 1942 (two bars, 1943); DSC 1940; *b* 16 Sept. 1905; *s* of J. F. Bryant, MA, FRGS, ICS (retd); *m* 1929, Marjorie Dagmar Mynors (*née* Symonds) (*d* 1965); one *s* one *d* ; *m* 1966, Heather Elizabeth Williams (*née* Hance). *Educ:* Oundle; RN Colls Osborne and Dartmouth. Entered submarine branch of RN, 1927; Commanded: HMS/M Sea Lion, 1939-41; HMS/M Safari, 1941-43; comd 7th and 3rd Submarine Flotillas, 1943-44; comd 4th s/m Flotilla, British Pacific Fleet, 1945-47; comd HMS Dolphin Submarine School, and 5th Submarine Flotilla, 1947-49; Commodore (submarines), 1948; idc 1950; Commodore, RN Barracks, Devonport, 1951-53; Flag Captain to C-in-C Mediterranean, 1953-54; Rear-Admiral, 1954. Deputy Chief of Naval Personnel (Training and Manning), 1954-57; retired, 1957. Staff Personnel Manager, Rolls Royce Scottish Factories, 1957-68. *Recreations:* fishing, golf, shooting. *Address:* Pines, Symington, Biggar, Lanarkshire.

BRYANT, Rt. Rev. Denis William, DFC 1942; Rector of Dalkeith, W Australia, since 1975; *b* 31 Jan. 1918; *s* of Thomas and Beatrice Maud Bryant; *m* 1940, Dorothy Linda (*née* Lewis); one *d*. *Educ:* Clark's Coll., Ealing; Cardiff Techn. Coll. Joined RAF; Wireless Operator/Air Gunner, 1936; Navigator, 1939; France, 1940 (despatches); Pilot, 1941; commn in Secretarial Br., 1950; Adjt, RAF Hereford, 1950; Sqdn-Ldr i/c Overseas Postings Record Office, Gloucester, 1951; Sqdn-Ldr DP7, Air Min., 1953. Ordinand, Queen's Coll., Birmingham, 1956; Deacon, 1958; Priest, 1959. Bishop of Kalgoorlie, 1967 until

1973 when Kalgoorlie became part of Diocese of Perth; Asst Bishop of Perth, and Archdeacon and Rector of Northam, 1973-75. *Recreations:* squash, tennis, oil painting. *Address:* St Lawrence Church, The Rectory, 42 Alexander Road, Dalkeith, WA 6009, Australia.

BRYANT, Richard Charles, CB 1960; Under-Secretary, Board of Trade, 1955-68; *b* 20 Aug. 1908; *s* of Charles James and Constance Byron Bryant, The Bounds, Faversham, Kent; *m* 1938, Elisabeth Ellington, *d* of Dr. A. E. Stansfeld, FRCP; two *s* two *d. Educ:* Rugby; Oriel College, Oxford. Entered Board of Trade, 1932; Ministry of Supply, 1939-44. *Address:* Marsh Farm House, Brancaster, Norfolk. *T:* Brancaster 206. *Club:* Travellers'.

BRYCE, Gabe Robb, OBE 1959; Sales Manager (Operations) British Aircraft Corporation, 1965-75; now occupied in breeding dogs and boarding cats; *b* 27 April 1921; *m* 1943, Agnes Lindsay; one *s* one *d. Educ:* Glasgow High School. Served in RAF, 1939-46. Vickers-Armstrongs (Aircraft) Ltd, 1946-60 (Chief Test Pilot, 1951-60). Participated as First or Second Pilot, in Maiden Flights of following British Aircraft: Varsity; Nene Viking; Viscount 630, 700 and 800; Tay Viscount; Valiant; Pathfinder; Vanguard; VC-10; BAC 1-11; Chief Test Pilot, British Aircraft Corporation, 1960-64. Fellow Soc. of Experimental Test Pilots (USA), 1967. *Recreations:* squash, tennis. *Address:* Meadows, Elm Corner, Ockham, Ripley, Surrey. *T:* Ripley 3916.

BRYCE, Sir Gordon; *see* Bryce, Sir W. G.

BRYCE, Dame Isabel G.; *see* Graham Bryce.

BRYCE, Sir (William) Gordon, Kt 1971; CBE 1963; Chief Justice of the Bahamas, 1970-73; *b* 2 Feb. 1913; *s* of James Chisholm Bryce and Emily Susan (*née* Lees); *m* 1940, Molly Mary, *d* of Arthur Cranch Drake; two *d. Educ:* Bromsgrove Sch.; Hertford Coll., Oxford (MA). Called to Bar, Middle Temple. War Service, 1940-46 (Major). Colonial Service: Crown Counsel, Fiji, 1949; Solicitor General, Fiji, 1953; Attorney General: Gibraltar, 1956; Aden, 1959; Legal Adviser, S Arabian High Commn, 1963; Attorney General, Bahamas, 1966. Comr, revised edn of Laws: of Gilbert and Ellice Islands, 1952; of Fiji, 1955; Comr, Bahamas Law Reform and Revision Commn, 1976. *Recreations:* riding, gardening. *Address:* Broom Croft, Lydeard St Lawrence, Taunton, Somerset.

BRYDEN, William James, CBE 1970; QC (Scot.) 1973; Sheriff Principal of the Lothians and Borders, since 1975; Sheriff of Chancery in Scotland, since 1973; *b* 2 Oct. 1909; *y s* of late James George Bryden, JP and late Elizabeth Brown Tyrie; *m* 1937, Christina Mary, *e d* of late Thomas Bannatyne Marshall, CBE, JP; two *s* one *d. Educ:* Perth Academy; Brasenose College, Oxford; Edinburgh University. Barrister-at-Law, Inner Temple, 1933; Advocate of the Scottish Bar, 1935; External Examiner in English Law, Edinburgh University, 1937-40; served in RNVR, 1940-45; Hon. Sheriff-Substitute of Dumfries and Galloway, 1946; Sheriff-Substitute of Lanarkshire at Hamilton, 1946-53; Sheriff-Substitute, later Sheriff, of Lanarkshire at Glasgow, 1953-73; Sheriff Principal, Lothians and Peebleshire, 1973-75. Member: Law Reform Cttee for Scotland, 1957-61; Scottish Adv. Council on the Treatment of Offenders, 1959-63; Deptl Cttee on Adoption of Children, 1969-72. Hon. Sec. Assoc. of Sheriffs-Substitute, 1950-53. *Address:* 1A Learmonth Gardens Mews, Edinburgh. *Club:* New (Edinburgh).

BRYHER, (Annie) Winifred; Author; *d* of Sir John Reeves Ellerman, 1st Bt, CH, and late Hannah Ellerman (*née* Glover); *m* 1st, 1921, Robert McAlmon (marr. diss., 1926); 2nd, 1927, Kenneth Macpherson (marr. diss., 1947); no *c. Educ:* Queenwood, Eastbourne. *Publications:* Development, 1920, etc; The Fourteenth of October, 1952; The Player's Boy, 1953; Roman Wall, 1954; Beowulf, 1956; Gate to the Sea, 1958; Ruan, 1960; The Heart to Artemis, 1963; The Coin of Carthage, 1964; Visa for Avalon, 1965; This January Tale, 1966; The Colors of Vaud, 1970; The Days of Mars, 1972. *Recreations:* travel, the sea, archæology. *Address:* Kenwin, Burier, Vaud, Switzerland.

BRYMER, Jack, OBE 1960; Hon. RAM; Principal Clarinettist, London Symphony Orchestra, since 1972; *b* 27 Jan. 1915; *s* of J. and Mrs M. Brymer, South Shields, Co. Durham; *m* 1939, Joan Richardson, Lancaster; one *s. Educ:* Goldsmiths' College, London University. Schoolmaster, Croydon, general subjects, 1935-40. RAF, 1940-45. Principal Clarinettist: Royal Philharmonic Orchestra, 1946-63; BBC Symphony Orchestra, 1963-72; Prof., Royal Acad. of Music, 1950-58; Prof., Royal Military Sch. of Music, Kneller Hall, 1969-; Member of Wigmore, Prometheus and London Baroque ensembles;

Director of London Wind Soloists. Has directed recordings of the complete wind chamber music of Mozart, Beethoven, Haydn and J. C. Bach. Hon. RAM 1955; Hon. MA Newcastle upon Tyne, 1973. *Publication:* The Clarinet (Menuhin Guides), 1976. *Recreations:* golf, tennis, swimming, carpentry, gardening, music. *Address:* Underwood, Ballards Farm Road, South Croydon, Surrey. *T:* 01-657 1698. *Club:* Croham Hurst Golf.

BRYSON, Rear-Adm. Lindsay Sutherland; Director-General Weapons (Naval), since 1977; *b* 22 Jan. 1925; *s* of James McAuslan Bryson and Margaret Bryson (*née* Whyte); *m* 1951, Averil Curtis-Willson; one *s* two *d. Educ:* Allan Glen's Sch., Glasgow; London Univ. (External) (BSc (Eng)); FIEE, FRAeS. Engrg Cadet, 1942; Electrical Mechanic, RN, 1944; Midshipman 1946; Lieut 1948; Comdr 1960; Captain 1967; comd HMS Daedalus, RNAS Lee-on-Solent, 1970-71; RCDS 1972; Dir, Naval Guided Weapons, 1973; Dir, Surface Weapons Project (Navy), 1974-77. *Publications:* contrib. Jl RAeS, Seaford Papers, Control Engineering. *Recreations:* fair weather sailing, gardening, badminton. *Address:* 74 Dyke Road Avenue, Brighton BN1 5LE. *T:* Brighton 553638. *Club:* Naval and Military.

BUCCLEUCH, 9th Duke of, *cr* 1663, **and QUEENSBERRY,** 11th Duke of, *cr* 1684; **Walter Francis John Montagu Douglas Scott;** VRD; JP; Baron Scott of Buccleuch, 1606; Earl of Buccleuch, Baron Scott of Whitchester and Eskdaill, 1619; Earl of Doncaster and Baron Tynedale (Eng.), 1662; Earl of Dalkeith, 1663; Marquis of Dumfriesshire, Earl of Drumlanrig and Sanquhar, Viscount of Nith, Torthorwold, and Ross, Baron Douglas, 1684; Buchan-Hepburn [*b* 27 the Queen's Body Guard for Scotland, Royal Company of Archers; Lord-Lieutenant of Roxburgh, since 1974, of *Clubs:* New, Puffin's (Edinburgh). since 1975; *b* 28 Sept. 1923; *o s* of 8th Duke of Buccleuch, KT, PC, GCVO, and of Vreda Esther Mary, *er d* of late Major W. F. Lascelles and Lady Sybil Lascelles, *d* of 10th Duke of St Albans; *S* father, 1973; *m* 1953, Jane, *d* of John McNeill, QC, Appin, Argyll, and Hongkong; three *s* one *d. Educ:* Eton; Christ Church, Oxford. Served War of 1939-45, RNVR. MP (C) Edinburgh North, 1960-73; PPS to the Lord Advocate, 1961-62 and to the Sec. of State for Scotland, 1962-64; Chm., Cons. Party Forestry Cttee, 1967-73. Chm., British Assoc. for Disability and Rehabilitation; President: Royal Highland & Agricultural Soc. of Scotland, 1969; St. Andrew's Ambulance Assoc.; Royal Scottish Agricultural Benevolent Inst.; Scottish Nat. Inst. for War Blinded; Royal Blind Asylum & School; Galloway Cattle Soc.; East of England Agricultural Soc., 1976; Vice-Pres., RSSPCC; Hon. President: Animal Diseases Research Assoc.; Scottish Agricultural Organisation Soc. DL, Selkirk 1955, Midlothian 1960, Roxburgh 1962, Dumfries 1974; JP Roxburgh 1975. *Heir: s* Earl of Dalkeith, *qv. Address:* Bowhill, Selkirk. *T:* Selkirk 20732; 46 Bedford Gardens, W8. *T:* 01-727 4358.

BUCHAN, family name of **Baron Tweedsmuir** and **Baroness Tweedsmuir of Belhelvie.**

BUCHAN, 16th Earl of, *cr* 1469; **Donald Cardross Flower Erskine;** Lord Auchterhouse, 1469; Lord Cardross, 1606; Baron Erskine, 1806; *b* 3 June 1899; *s* of 6th Baron Erskine and Florence (*d* 1936), *y d* of Edgar Flower; *S* father, 1957 (as Baron Erskine); and kinsman, 1960 (as Earl of Buchan); *m* 1927, Christina, adopted *d* of Lloyd Baxendale, Greenham Lodge, Newbury; one *s* two *d. Educ:* Charterhouse; Royal Military College, Sandhurst. Lieut 9th Lancers, 1918; Captain, 1928; retired, 1930; re-employed, 1939; Lieut-Colonel 1943. *Heir: s* Lord Cardross, *qv. Address:* The Manor, Bourton-on-the-Water, Gloucestershire. *T:* 20383.

BUCHAN of Auchmacoy, Captain David William Sinclair, JP; *b* 18 Sept. 1929; *o s* of late Captain S. L. Trevor, late of Lathbury Park, Bucks, and late Lady Olivia Trevor, *e d* of 18th Earl of Caithness; *m* 1961, Susan Blanche Fionodbhar Scott-Ellis, *d* of 9th Baron Howard de Walden, *qv.*; four *s* one *d. Educ:* Eton; RMA Sandhurst. Commissioned 1949 into Gordon Highlanders; served Berlin, BAOR and Malaya; ADC to GOC, Singapore, 1951-53; retired 1955. Member of London Stock Exchange. Sen. Partner, Messrs Gow and Parsons, 1963-72. Changed name from Trevor through Court of Lord Lyon King of Arms, 1949, succeeding 18th Earl of Caithness as Chief of Buchan Clan. Member: Queen's Body Guard for Scotland; The Pilgrims; Friends of Malta GC; Worshipful Company of Broderers. JP London, 1972-. *Recreations:* cricket, tennis, squash. *Address:* 28 The Little Boltons, SW10. *T:* 01-373 0654; Auchmacoy House, Aberdeenshire. *T:* Ellon 20229. *Clubs:* White's, Royal Automobile, Turf, MCC, City of London; Puffin's (Edinburgh).

BUCHAN, Ven. Eric Ancrum; Archdeacon of Coventry, 1965-77, Archdeacon Emeritus, since 1977; *b* 6 Nov. 1907; *s* of late Frederick Samuel and Florence Buchan. *Educ:* Bristol Grammar School; St Chad's College, University of Durham (BA). Curate of Holy Nativity, Knowle, Bristol, 1933-40. Chaplain RAFVR, 1940-45. Vicar of St Mark's with St Barnabas, Coventry, 1945-59; Hon. Canon of Coventry Cathedral, 1953; Chaplain Coventry and Warwickshire Hospital, 1945-59; Sec. Laymen's Appeal, Dio. of Coventry, 1951-53; Rural Dean of Coventry, 1954-63; Rector of Baginton, 1963-70. Member Central Board of Finance, 1953- (Chm., Develt and Stewardship Cttee, 1976; Mem., Church Commrs and CBF Joint Liaison Cttee, 1976-); Mem. Schools Council, 1958-65; Chm. Dio. Board of Finance, 1958-77; Organiser of Bishop's Appeal, 1958-61; Dio. Director of Christian Stewardship, 1959-65; Domestic Chaplain to Bishop of Coventry, 1961-65; Church Commissioner, 1964-78; Member, Governing Body, St Chad's College, Durham University, 1966-. Awarded Silver Acorn for outstanding services to the Scout Movement, 1974. *Address:* c/o Church House, Palmerston Road, Coventry CV5 6FJ.

BUCHAN, Sir John, (Sir Thomas Johnston Buchan), Kt 1971; CMG 1961; Chairman and Managing Director, Buchan, Laird and Buchan, Architects and Engineers; *b* 3 June 1912; *s* of Thomas Johnston Buchan; *m* 1948, Virginia, *d* of William Ashley Anderson, Penn., USA; one *s* two *d. Educ:* Geelong Grammar School. Served Royal Aust. Engineers (AIF), 1940-44 (Capt.). Member Melbourne City Council, 1954-60. Member Federal Exec., Liberal Party, 1959-62; President, Liberal Party, Victorian Division, Australia, 1959-62, Treasurer, 1963-67; Pres., Australian American Assoc., Victoria, 1964-68, Federal Pres., Australian American Assoc., 1968-70. Member: Council, Latrobe University, 1964-72; Cttee of Management, Royal Melbourne Hosp., 1968-. Co-Founder Apex Association of Australia. *Recreations:* golf, reading. *Address:* 11 Fairlie Court, South Yarra, Vic 3141, Australia. *Clubs:* Melbourne, Athenæum (Melbourne).

BUCHAN, Norman Findlay; MP (Lab) Renfrewshire West since 1964; *b* Helmsdale, Sutherlandshire, 27 Oct. 1922; *s* of John Buchan, Fraserburgh, Aberdeenshire; *m* 1945, Janey, *d* of Joseph Kent, Glasgow; one *s. Educ:* Kirkwall Grammar School; Glasgow University. Royal Tank Regt (N Africa, Sicily and Italy, 1942-45). Teacher (English and History). Parly Under-Sec., Scottish Office, 1967-70. Opposition Spokesman on Agriculture, Fisheries and Food, 1970-74; Minister of State, MAFF, March-Oct. 1974 (resigned). *Publications:* (ed) 101 Scottish Songs; The Scottish Folksinger, 1973; contributions to New Statesman, Tribune and other journals. *Address:* 72 Peel Street, Glasgow G11 5LR. *T:* 041-339 2583.

BUCHAN, Dr Stevenson, CBE 1971; Chief Scientific Officer, Deputy Director, Institute of Geological Sciences, 1968-71; *b* 4 March 1907; *s* of late James Buchan and Christian Ewen Buchan (*née* Stevenson), Peterhead; *m* 1937, Barbara, *yr d* of late Reginald Hadfield, Droylsden, Lancs; one *s* one *d. Educ:* Peterhead Acad.; Aberdeen Univ. BSc 1st cl. hons Geology, James H. Hunter Meml. Prize, Senior Kilgour Scholar, PhD; FRSE, FGS, FIWES, Hon. FIPHE. Geological Survey of Great Britain: Geologist, 1931; Head of Water Dept, 1946; Asst Dir responsible for specialist depts in GB and NI, 1960; Chief Geologist, Inst. of Geological Sciences, 1967. Mem. various hydrological cttees; Chm. Hydrology Subcttee of Royal Soc.'s Brit. Nat. Cttee for Geodesy and Geophysics; Founder Mem., Internat. Assoc. of Hydrogeologists, Pres., 1972-; Pres., Internat. Ground-Water Commn of Internat. Assoc. of Hydrological Sciences, 1963-67; British Deleg. to Internat. Hydrological Decade; Scientific Editor, Hydrogeological Map of Europe; Vis. Internat. Scientist, Amer. Geol Inst.; Pres. Section C (Geology), Brit. Assoc., Dundee, 1968. Awarded Geol Soc.'s Lyell Fund, and J. B. Tyrell Fund for travel in Canada. *Publications:* Water Supply of County of London from Underground Sources; papers on hydrogeology and hydrochemistry. *Recreations:* travel, photography, gardening, philately. *Address:* Far End, 14 Monks Road, Banstead, Surrey SM7 2EP. *T:* Burgh Heath 54227.

BUCHAN, Sir Thomas Johnston; *see* Buchan, Sir John.

BUCHAN-HEPBURN, Sir Ninian (Buchan Archibald John), 6th Bt, *cr* 1815; *b* 8 Oct. 1922; *s* of Sir John Buchan-Hepburn, 5th Bt; *S* father 1961; *m* 1958, Bridget (*d* 1976), *er d* of late Sir Louis Greig, KBE, CVO. *Educ:* St Aubyn's, Rottingdean, Sussex; Canford School, Wimborne, Dorset. Served QO Cameron Hldrs, India and Burma, 1939-45. Member, Queen's Bodyguard for Scotland, Royal Company of Archers. *Heir: kinsman* John Alistair Trant Kidd Buchan-Hepburn [*b* 27 June 1931; *m* 1957,

Georgina Elizabeth Turner; one *s* three *d*]. *Address:* Logan, Stranraer, Wigtownshire. *T:* Ardwell 239. *Clubs:* New, Puffin's (Edinburgh).

BUCHANAN, Most Rev. Alan Alexander; Archbishop of Dublin and Primate of Ireland, 1969-77; *m* 1935, Audrey Kathryn, *d* of W. A. Crone, Knock, Belfast; two *d*. *Educ:* Trinity College, Dublin. Exhibitioner, Moderator, 1928, TCD Deacon, 1930; Priest, 1931. Assistant Missioner, Church of Ireland Mission, Belfast, 1930-33, Head Missioner, 1933-37; Incumbent of Inver, Larne, 1937-45; Incumbent of St Mary, Belfast, 1945-55; Rural Dean of Mid-Belfast, 1951-55; Rector of Bangor, Co. Down, 1955-58; Canon of St Patrick's Cathedral, Dublin, 1957-58; Bishop of Clogher, 1958-69. Chaplain to the Forces, Emergency Commission, 1942-45. *Address:* Kilbride, Castleknock, Co. Dublin.

BUCHANAN, Andrew George; farmer; chartered surveyor in private practice; *b* 21 July 1937; *s* and *heir* of Major Sir Charles Buchanan, Bt, *qv*; *m* 1966, Belinda Jane Virginia (*née* Maclean), widow of Gresham Neilus Vaughan; one *s* and *d*, and one steps and one step *d*. *Educ:* Eton; Trinity Coll., Cambridge; Wye Coll., Univ. of London. Nat. Service, 2nd Lieut, Coldstream Guards, 1956-58. Chartered Surveyor with Smith-Wolley & Co, 1965-70. Commanded A Squadron (SRY), 3rd Bn Worcs and Sherwood Foresters (TA), 1971-74. High Sheriff, Notts, 1976-77. *Recreations:* skiing, stalking, gardening (under protest). *Address:* Hodsock Priory, Blyth, Worksop, Notts S81 0TY. *T:* Blyth (Notts) 204. *Clubs:* Farmers'; Strafford (Cambridge).

BUCHANAN, Sir Charles Alexander James L.; *see* Leith-Buchanan.

BUCHANAN, Major Sir Charles James, 4th Bt, *cr* 1878; HLI; retired; *b* 16 April 1899; *s* of 3rd Bt and Constance (*d* 1914), *d* of late Commander Tennant, RN; *S* father, 1928; *m* 1932, Barbara Helen, *o d* of late Lieut-Colonel Rt Hon. Sir George Stanley, PC, GCSI, GCIE; two *s* two *d*. *Educ:* Harrow; Sandhurst. Served in North Russian Relief Force, 1919; with BEF France, 1939-40 and with AMG in Italy, 1943-44; retired 1945. ADC to Governor of Madras, 1928-32. A member of the Queen's Body Guard for Scotland (Royal Company of Archers); County Commissioner Nottinghamshire, Boy Scouts Association, 1949-62. JP 1952; DL 1954, Notts; High Sheriff of Nottinghamshire, 1962. *Recreations:* fishing and gardening. *Heir:* *s* Andrew George Buchanan, *qv*. *Address:* St Anne's Manor, Sutton Bonington, Loughborough. *Club:* Lansdowne.

BUCHANAN, Prof. Sir Colin (Douglas), Kt 1972; CBE 1964; Lieut-Colonel; Visiting Professor, Imperial College London; consultant with Colin Buchanan & Partners, 47 Princes Gate, London; *b* 22 Aug. 1907; *s* of William Ernest and Laura Kate Buchanan; *m* 1933, Elsie Alice Mitchell; two *s* one *d*. *Educ:* Berkhamsted School; Imperial College, London. Sudan Govt Public Works Dept, 1930-32; Regional planning studies with F. Longstreth Thompson, 1932-35; Ministry of Transport, 1935-39. War Service in Royal Engineers, 1939-46. Ministry of Town and Country Planning (later Ministry of Housing and Local Govt), 1946-61; Urban Planning Adviser, Ministry of Transport, 1961-63; Prof. of Transport, Imperial Coll., London, 1963-72; Prof. of Urban Studies and Dir, Sch. for Advanced Urban Studies, Bristol Univ., 1973-75. Member: Commn on Third London Airport, 1968-70; Royal Fine Art Commn, 1972-74. Hon. DCL Oxon, 1972; Hon. DSc: Leeds, 1972; City, 1972. *Publications:* Mixed Blessing, The Motor in Britain, 1958; Traffic in Towns (Ministry of Transport report), 1963, (paperback edn), 1964; The State of Britain, 1972; numerous papers on town planning and allied subjects. *Recreations:* photography, carpentry, caravan touring. *Address:* Tunnel House, Box, near Minchinhampton, Glos GL6 9HB. *T:* Nailsworth 2951.

BUCHANAN, Brig. Edgar James Bernard, DSO 1918; retired; *b* 1892; *s* of Robert Eccles Buchanan, of Templemore Park, Londonderry; *m* 1st, 1923, Evelyn Constance (*d* 1970), *d* of Richard Charles Holland, of Glanty House, Egham, Surrey; one *s*; 2nd, 1971, Kathleen Hannah Frances, *d* of S. Crosby Halahan, Chiddingford. Served European War, 1914-18; commanded 1st Bn RE, 1918 (wounded, DSO); Bt Lt-Col 1935. Served War of 1939-45; Senior Royal Engineer, Allied Force HQ, 1943; Director of Fortification and Works, War Office, 1945 (despatches); retired 1946. Officer of Legion of Merit, USA. *Address:* Bridge Meadow, Harting, Petersfield, Hants GU31 5LS.

BUCHANAN, George (Henry Perrott); writer; *b* 9 Jan. 1904; 2nd *s* of Rev. C. H. L. Buchanan, Kilwaughter, Co. Antrim, and Florence Moore; *m* 1st, 1938, Winifred Mary Corn (marr. diss.

1945; she *d* 1971); 2nd, 1949, Noel Pulleyne Beasley (*d* 1951), widow of Major J. A. Ritter, RA; 3rd, 1952, Hon. Janet Hampden Margesson (*d* 1968), *e d* of 1st Viscount Margesson, PC, MC; two *d*; 4th, 1974, Sandra Gail McCloy, Vancouver. *Educ:* Campbell College; Queen's University, Belfast. On editorial staff of The Times, 1930-35; literary critic, TLS, 1928-40; columnist, drama critic, News Chronicle, 1935-38; Operations Officer, RAF Coastal Command, 1940-45; Chm. Town and Country Development Cttee, N Ireland, 1949-53; Member, Exec. Council, European Soc. of Culture, 1954-. *Publications:* Passage through the Present, 1932; A London Story, 1935; Words for To-Night, 1936; Entanglement, 1938; The Soldier and the Girl, 1940; Rose Forbes, 1950; A Place to Live, 1952; Bodily Responses (poetry), 1958; Green Seacoast, 1959; Conversation with Strangers (poetry), 1961; Morning Papers, 1965; Annotations, 1970; Naked Reason, 1971; Minute-book of a City (poetry), 1972; Inside Traffic (poetry), 1976; The Politics of Culture, 1977; *plays:* A Trip to the Castle, 1960; Tresper Revolution, 1961; War Song, 1965. *Address:* 27 Ashley Gardens, Westminster, SW1. *T:* 01-834 5722. *Clubs:* Athenæum, Savile.

BUCHANAN, John David, MBE 1944; Headmaster of Oakham School, Rutland, 1958-77; *b* 26 Oct. 1916; *e s* of late John Nevile Buchanan, and Nancy Isabel (*née* Bevan); *m* 1946, Janet Marjorie, *d* of late Brig. J. A. C. Pennycuick, DSO; three *s* four *d* (and one *s* decd). *Educ:* Stowe; Trinity College, Cambridge. Served with Grenadier Guards, 1939-46; Adjutant, 3rd Bn Grenadier Guards, 1941-43; Brigade Major, 1st Guards Bde, 1944-45; Private Secretary to Sir Alexander Cadogan, Security Council for the UN, 1946. Assistant Master, Westminster Under School, 1948; Assistant Master, Sherborne School, 1948-57. *Recreation:* golf. *Address:* Rose Cottage, Owston, Leics.

BUCHANAN, Rear-Adm. Peter William; Naval Secretary, since 1976; *b* 14 May 1925; *s* of Lt-Col Francis Henry Theodore Buchanan and Gwendolen May Isobel (*née* Hunt); *m* 1953, Audrey Rowena Mary (*née* Edmondson); three *s* one *d*. *Educ:* Malvern Coll. HMS King George V, 1944-45; destroyers and frigates, 1946-56; qual. navigation, 1950; staff Britannia RNC, Dartmouth, 1956-58; HMS Birmingham, 1958-60; Comdr 1961; comd HMS Scarborough, 1961-62; Fleet Ops Officer, Far East, 1963-65 (mentioned in despatches); HMS Victorious, 1965-67; jssc 1967; Captain 1967; British Antarctic Survey, 1967-68; comd HMS Endurance, 1968-70; Dir, Naval Officers Appts (X), 1970-72; comd HMS Devonshire, 1972-74; Dir, Naval Manpower Planning, 1974-76; Rear-Adm. 1976. Younger Brother, Trinity House, 1963; MNI 1972 (Mem. Council, 1976). *Recreations:* sailing, walking. *Address:* Whitewalls, 30 The Square, Titchfield, Fareham, Hants. *T:* Titchfield 42146. *Clubs:* Caledonian, Naval; Royal Naval Sailing Association.

BUCHANAN, Major Sir Reginald Narcissus M.; *see* Macdonald-Buchanan.

BUCHANAN, Richard, JP; MP (Lab) Springburn Div. of Glasgow since 1964; *b* 3 May 1912; *s* of late Richard Buchanan and late Helen Henderson; *m* 1st, 1938, Margaret McManus (*d* 1963); six *s* two *d*; 2nd, 1971, Helen Duggan, MA, DipEd. *Educ:* St Mungo's Boys' School; St Mungo's Academy; Royal Technical Coll. Councillor, City of Glasgow, 1949-64 (Past Chm. Libraries, Schools and Standing Orders Cttees); Hon. City Treasurer, 1960-63; PPS to Treasury Ministers, 1967-70; Mem. Select Cttees: Public Accounts; Services. Chm., West Day School Management, 1958-64; Governor, Notre Dame College of Education, 1959-64, etc. Chm., Belvidere Hospital; Member Board of Managers, Glasgow Royal Infirmary; Hon. Pres., Scottish Library Assoc. (Pres., 1963; Chairman: Scottish Central Library; Adv. Cttee, Nat. Library of Scotland; Cttee on Burrell Collection; Director, Glasgow Citizens Theatre. JP Glasgow, 1954. *Recreations:* theatre, golf, snooker, walking, reading. *Address:* 18 Gargrave Avenue, Garrowhill, Glasgow. *T:* 041-771 7234. *Club:* St Mungo's Centenary (Glasgow).

BUCHANAN, Prof. Robert Ogilvie; Emeritus Professor, University of London; *b* 12 Sept. 1894; *s* of Duncan and Janet Buchanan; *m* 1931, Kathleen Mary Parnell; one *s* two *d*. *Educ:* University of Otago, New Zealand; University of London. Served European War, 1914-18, NZEF (Otago Regt), 1915-19, in France. Mount Albert Grammar School, Auckland, NZ, 1922-25; student at London School of Economics, 1925-28. University College, University of London; Asst Lecturer in Geography, 1928. Lecturer, 1930. Reader in Economic Geography, 1938-49; Prof. of Geography, London School of Economics, 1949-61; Hon. Fellow, 1970. War of 1939-45, RAF, maps organisation, Air Ministry and War Office. Member Senate, University of London, 1951-67; President: Section E (Geography) British Assoc. for the Advancement of Science,

1952; Inst. of British Geographers, 1953; Geographical Association, 1958. Member Nature Conservancy, 1965-71. *Publications:* Pastoral Industries of New Zealand, 1935; An Economic Geography of the British Empire, 1936; articles on various topics in economic geography in geographical periodicals in UK, USA, NZ and India. *Address:* 13B Westleigh Avenue, Putney, SW15 6RF. *T:* 01-789 4350.

BUCHANAN-DUNLOP, Commodore David Kennedy, DSC 1945; RN retired; *b* 30 June 1911; *s* of Colonel Archibald Buchanan-Dunlop, OBE and Mary (*née* Kennedy); *m* 1945, Marguerite, *d* of William Macfarlane; no *c. Educ:* Loretto; RNC, Dartmouth. Served as young officer in submarines in Mediterranean and Far East, then Specialist in Fleet Air Arm. Served War of 1939-45 (despatches) in aircraft-carriers world-wide. Asst Naval Attaché, Paris, 1949-52; Dep. Director Nav. Air Org. Naval Staff, 1954-56; Staff of NATO Defence College, Paris, 1957-59; Naval and Military Attaché, Santiago, Lima, Quito, Bogotá and Panama, 1960-62; Captain, Royal Naval College, Greenwich, 1962-64, President, 1964. *Recreation:* fishing. *Address:* Les Nereides, 20110-Propriano, Corsica. *Club:* Flyfishers'.

BUCHANAN-DUNLOP, Richard, QC 1966; *b* 19 April 1919; *s* of late Canon W. R. Buchanan-Dunlop and Mrs R. E. Buchanan-Dunlop (*née* Mead); *m* 1948, Helen Murray Dunlop; three *d. Educ:* Marlborough College; Magdalene College, Cambridge. Served in Royal Corps of Signals, 1939-46 (Hon. Major). BA (Hons.) Law, Cambridge, 1949; Harmsworth Scholar, 1950. Called to the Bar, 1951. *Recreations:* painting, ski-ing, sailing. *Address:* Skiathos, Greece.

BUCHANAN-JARDINE, Sir A. R. J.; *see* Jardine.

BUCHANAN-SMITH, family name of Baron Balerno.

BUCHANAN-SMITH, Alick Laidlaw; MP (U) North Angus and Mearns since 1964; *b* 8 April 1932; 2nd *s* of Baron Balerno, *qv* and late Mrs Buchanan-Smith; *m* 1956, Janet, *d* of late Thomas Lawrie, CBE; one *s* three *d. Educ:* Edinburgh Academy; Trinity College, Glenalmond; Pembroke College, Cambridge; Edinburgh University. Commissioned Gordon Highlanders, National Service, 1951; subseq. Captain, TA (5th/6th Gordon Highlanders). Parly Under-Sec. of State, Scottish Office, 1970-74. *Address:* House of Cockburn, Balerno, Midlothian. *T:* 031-449 4242; Bogindollo, Fettercairn, Laurencekirk, Kincardineshire. *T:* Fettercairn 273. *Clubs:* Caledonian; New (Edinburgh).

BUCHER, Gen. Sir Francis Robert Roy; *see* Bucher, Gen. Sir Roy.

BUCHER, General Sir Roy, KBE 1948 (OBE 1943); CB 1945; MC 1919; DL; psc; *b* 1895; *m* 1922, Edith Margaret Reid (*d* 1944); one *d*; *m* 1946, Maureen, OBE, *e d* of late Captain Thomas George Gibson, DL, Welham Hall, Malton, Yorks. *Educ:* Edinburgh Academy; RMC Sandhurst. Served European War, 1914-19, with 1st Bn The Cameronians (wounded 1915, France); India, 1915, attached 55th Coke's Rifles (FF); transferred 31st Duke of Connaught's Own Lancers, 1916; Mahsud, 1917; Afghanistan, Waziristan, 1919-20; Staff Coll., Camberley, 1926-27; DAAG, Deccan District, 1930-32; Bt. Lieut-Colonel 13 Duke of Connaught's Own Lancers, 1937; Comdt Sam Browne's Cav., Nov. 1939-Feb. 1940; Colonel, 1940; Comdt No. 2 ACTC, Lucknow, 1940; AAG, GHQ, Jan.-June 1941; AQMG, Iraq, 1941; Major-General in charge Administration, Southern Army, India, 1942-45; GOC Bengal and Assam Area, 1946; officiating GOC-in-C Eastern Command, 1946-Jan. 1947; Chief of Staff, AHQ, India, Aug.-Dec. 1947; C-in-C, Army of India, 1948-49; Officer on special duty, Indian Defence Ministry, 1949; retired, 1949. Past National Chairman, The Royal British Legion (Life Member, Nat. Exec. Council); Member of Council of Officers' Association; Vice-President Not-Forgotten Association; Chm., Yorkshire Area Council, Royal Society of St George. Chairman, Anglo Polish Society. DL, NR Yorks, 1962. Order of Star of Nepal Class I; Order of Polonia Restituta 1st Cl. *Address:* Normanby House, Sinnington, York Y06 6RH. *T:* Kirkby Moorside 31483. *Club:* Army and Navy.

BUCHTHAL, Hugo, FBA 1959; PhD; Ailsa Mellon Bruce Professor, 1970-75, Professor of Fine Arts, 1965-70, New York University Institute of Fine Arts; now Emeritus Professor; *b* Berlin, 11 Aug. 1909; *m* 1939, Amalia Serkin; one *d. Educ:* Universities of Berlin, Heidelberg, Paris and Hamburg. PhD, Hamburg, 1933; Resident in London from 1934; Lord Plumer Fellowship, Hebrew University, 1938; Librarian, Warburg Institute, 1941; Lecturer in History of Art, University of

London, 1944; Reader in the History of Art, with special reference to the Near East, 1949; Professor of the History of Byzantine Art in the University of London, 1960. Visiting Scholarship, Dumbarton Oaks, Harvard University, 1950-51, 1965, 1974, 1978; Temp. Member Inst. for Advanced Study, Princeton, NJ, 1959-60, 1968, 1975-76; Visiting Professor Columbia University, New York, 1963. Prix Schlumberger, Académie des Inscriptions et Belles Lettres, 1958; Guggenheim Fellow, 1971-72; membre corres. étranger, Société des Antiquaires de France, 1975; Corres. Mem., Oesterreichische Akad. der Wissenschaften, 1975; Hon. Fellow, Warburg Inst., 1975. *Publications:* The Miniatures of the Paris Psalter, 1938; (with Otto Kurz) A Handlist of illuminated Oriental Christian Manuscripts, 1942; The Western Aspects of Gandhara Sculpture, 1944; Miniature Painting in the Latin Kingdom of Jerusalem, 1957; Historia Trojana, studies in the history of mediaeval secular illustration, 1971; (jtly) The Place of Book Illumination in Byzantine Art, 1976; numerous articles in learned journals. *Address:* 22 Priory Gardens, N6. *T:* 01-348 1664.

BUCHWALD, Art, (Arthur); American journalist, author, lecturer and columnist; *b* Mount Vernon, New York, 20 Oct. 1925; *s* of Joseph Buchwald and Helen (*née* Kleinberger); *m* 1952, Ann McGarry, Warren, Pa; one *s* two *d. Educ:* University of Southern California. Sergeant, US Marine Corps, 1942-45. Columnist, New York Herald Tribune: in Paris, 1949-62; in Washington, 1962-. Syndicated columnist whose articles appear in numerous newspapers throughout the world. *Publications:* (mostly published later in England) Paris After Dark, 1950; Art Buchwald's Paris, 1954; The Brave Coward, 1957; I Chose Caviar, 1957; More Caviar, 1958; A Gift from the Boys, 1958; Don't Forget to Write, 1960; Art Buchwald's Secret List to Paris, 1961; How Much is That in Dollars?, 1961; Is it Safe to Drink the Water?, 1962; I Chose Capitol Punishment, 1963;... and Then I told the President, 1965; Son of the Great Society, 1966; Have I Ever Lied to You?, 1968; The Establishment is Alive and Well in Washington, 1969; Sheep on the Runway (Play), 1970; Oh, to be a Swinger, 1970; Getting High in Government Circles, 1971; I Never Danced at the White House, 1973; I Am not a Crook, 1974; Bollo Caper, 1974; Irving's Delight, 1975; Washington is Leaking, 1976. *Recreations:* tennis, chess, squash. *Address:* 1750 Pennsylvania Avenue NW, Washington, DC 20006, USA. *T:* Washington 298-7990. *Club:* Overseas Press (NY).

BUCK, Albert Charles; consultant industrial adviser; *b* 1 March 1910; *y s* of William and Mary Buck; *m* 1st, 1937, Margaret Court Hartley; one *d*; 2nd, 1951, Joan McIntyre; one *d*; 3rd, 1970, Mrs Aileen Ogilvy. *Educ:* Alderman Newton's Sch., Leicester; Selwyn Coll., Cambridge (MA). Joined J. J. Colman Ltd, as management trainee, 1931; Export Manager, 1939; Director: Reckitt & Sons Ltd, 1941; Joseph Farrow & Co. Ltd, 1947-69; Thomas Green & Son, 1950-60; Reckitt & Colman (Household) Div.; Industrial Adviser to HM Govt, 1969-73. Member: Incorporated Soc. of British Advertisers (Pres., 1961-63); Internat. Union of Advertiser Societies (Pres. 1963-65); Advertising Standards Authority, 1962-71; Internat. Foundation for Research in Advertising (Pres., 1965-71). Mackintosh medal for personal and public services to Advertising, 1965. *Publications:* sundry articles to jls and newspapers. *Recreations:* winter sports, shooting, fishing. *Address:* Mill Farm, Burton Pidsea, East Yorkshire. *T:* Burton Pidsea 328.

BUCK, Antony; *see* Buck, P. A. F.

BUCK, Leslie William; Member, British Aerospace, since 1977 (Member Organising Committee, 1976-77); *b* 30 May 1915; *s* of Walter Buck and Florence Greenland; *m* 1941, Dorothea Jeanne Bieri; two *s. Educ:* Willesden County Grammar Sch. Apprentice panel beater; shop steward; Nat. Union of Sheet Metal Workers and Braziers: District Officer, 1957-60; Dist Sec., 1960-62; Gen. Sec., Nat. Union of Sheet Metal Workers, Coppersmiths, Heating and Domestic Engineers, 1962-77. Member: Confedn of Shipbuilding and Engineering Unions Executive, 1964-75, Pres., 1975-76; Engrg Industry Trng Bd, 1964-75; General Council, TUC, 1971-77. *Recreations:* music, gardening, reading. *Address:* 33 Dover Street, W1; 178 Meadvale Road, Ealing, W5. *T:* 01-998 3943.

BUCK, (Philip) Antony (Fyson), QC 1974; MP (C) Colchester since 1961; Barrister-at-Law; *b* 19 Dec. 1928; *yr s* of late A. F. Buck, Ely, Cambs; *m* 1955, Judy Elaine, *o d* of Dr C. A. Grant, Cottesloe, Perth, W Australia, and late Mrs Grant; one *d. Educ:* King's School, Ely; Trinity Hall, Cambridge. BA History and Law, 1951, MA 1954. Chm. Cambridge Univ. Cons. Assoc. and Chm. Fedn of Univ. Conservative and Unionist Associations,

1951-52. Called to the Bar, Inner Temple, 1954; Legal Adviser, Nat. Association of Parish Councils, 1957-59, Vice-Pres., 1970-74; sponsored and piloted through the Limitation Act, 1963. PPS to Attorney-General, 1963-64; Parly Under-Sec. of State for Defence (Navy), MoD, 1972-74. Sec., Conservative Party Home Affairs Cttee, 1964-70, Vice-Chm., 1970-72, Chm. Oct./Nov. 1972; Mem. Exec., 1922 Cttee, Oct./Nov. 1972; Chm., Select Cttee on Parly Comr for Administration (Ombudsman), 1977-. *Recreations:* most sports, reading. *Address:* Pete Hall, Abberton, near Colchester, Essex. *T:* Peldon 230; 4 Paper Buildings, Temple, EC4. *T:* 01-353 8408/0196. *Club:* United Oxford & Cambridge University.

BUCKEE, Henry Thomas, DSO 1942; **His Honour Judge Buckee;** a Circuit Judge (formerly Judge of County Courts), since 1961; *b* 14 June 1913; *s* of Henry Buckee; *m* 1939, Margaret Frances Chapman; two *d. Educ:* King Edward VI School, Chelmsford. Called to Bar, Middle Temple, 1939. Served RNVR, 1940-46; Lieut-Comdr 1944. *Address:* Rough Hill House, East Hanningfield, Chelmsford, Essex. *T:* Chelmsford 400226.

BUCKHURST, Lord; William Herbrand Sackville; *b* 10 April 1948; *s* and *heir* of 10th Earl De La Warr, *qv. Educ:* Eton.

BUCKINGHAM, Bishop Suffragan of, since 1974; **Rt. Rev. Simon Hedley Burrows;** *b* 8 Nov. 1928; *s* of Very Rev. H. R. Burrows, *qv*; *m* 1960, Janet Woodd; two *s* three *d. Educ:* Eton; King's Coll., Cambridge (MA); Westcott House, Cambridge. Curate of St John's Wood, 1954-57; Chaplain of Jesus Coll., Cambridge, 1957-60; Vicar of Wyken, Coventry, 1960-67; Vicar of Holy Trinity, Fareham, 1967-74, and Rector of Team Ministry, 1971-74. *Address:* Sheridan, Grimms Hill, Great Missenden, Bucks. *T:* Great Missenden 2173.

BUCKINGHAM, Amyand David, FRS 1975; Professor of Chemistry, University of Cambridge, since 1969, Fellow of Pembroke College, since 1970; *b* 28 Jan. 1930; 2nd *s* of late Reginald Joslin Buckingham and of Florence Grace Buckingham (formerly Elliot); *m* 1965, Jillian Bowles; one *s* two *d. Educ:* Barker Coll., Hornsby, NSW; Univ. of Sydney; Corpus Christi Coll., Cambridge (Shell Postgraduate Schol.), Univ. Medal 1952, MSc 1953, Sydney; PhD Cantab 1956. 1851 Exhibn Sen. Studentship, 1955-57; Lectr and subseq. Student, Tutor, and Censor of Christ Church, Oxford, 1955-65; Univ. Lectr in Inorganic Chem. Lab., Oxford, 1958-65; Prof. of Theoretical Chem., Univ. of Bristol, 1965-69. Vis. Lectr, Harvard, 1961; Visiting Professor: Princeton, 1965; Univ. of California (Los Angeles), 1975; Univ. of Illinois, 1976. FRACI 1961 (Masson Meml Schol. 1952; Rennie Meml Medal, 1958); FCS (Harrison Meml Prize, 1959; Tilden Lectr 1964; Theoretical Chemistry and Spectroscopy Prize, 1970; Member Faraday Div. (Council, 1965-67, 1975-)); FRIC (FInstP; Member: Amer. Chem. Soc.; Amer. Physical Soc.; Optical Soc. of America. Associate Editor, Jl of Chem. Physics, 1964-66; Editor, Molecular Physics, 1968-72. Mem., Chemistry Cttee, SRC, 1967-70. Senior Treasurer: Oxford Univ. Cricket Club, 1959-64; Cambridge Univ. Cricket Club, 1976-. *Publications:* The Laws and Applications of Thermodynamics, 1964; papers in various scientific jls. *Recreations:* walking, woodwork, cricket, tennis, travel. *Address:* 37 Millington Road, Cambridge. *T:* Cambridge 50012.

BUCKINGHAM, George Somerset; retired; *b* 11 May 1903; *s* of Horace Clifford Buckingham, Norwich; *m* 1927, Marjorie Lanaway Bateson; one *s* (one *d* decd). *Educ:* Norwich Sch.; Faraday House Electrical Engrg Coll. (Gold Medallist; Dipl.). BSc (Eng); CEng; FIEE; FBIM. Asst Engr, Yorks Electric Power Co., Leeds, 1924-26; District Engr and Br. Man., Birmingham, for Pirelli-General Cable Works Ltd of Southampton, 1928-48; Midlands Electricity Board: Chief Purchasing Officer, 1948-57; Chief Engr, 1957-62; Dep. Chm., 1962-64; Chm., 1964-69. Member: Electricity Council, 1964-69; Electricity Supply Industry Trng Bd, 1965-69; W Midlands Sports Council, 1966-71; Mem. Council, Univ. of Aston in Birmingham; Mem. Council, Electrical Research Assoc., 1967-72; various sci. and profl Instns and Cttees; Pres. Birmingham Branch, Institute of Marketing, 1967-68. Chairman: South Midland Centre, IEE, 1966-67; Midland Centre, Council of Engineering Instns, 1968-70; Past President, Council of Birmingham Electric Club, 1965; Past President, Faraday House Old Students' Assoc., 1962; Vice-President, Outward Bound Schs Assoc. (Birm. and Dist), 1964-72. *Publications:* papers, articles and reviews in scientific and electrical engrg jls and works of professional engrg bodies. *Recreations:* walking, bridge. *Address:* Parklands, Blossomfield Road, Solihull, West Midlands. *T:* 021-705 2066.

BUCKINGHAM, John, CB 1953; Director of Research Programmes and Planning, Admiralty, 1946-Dec. 1959, retired; *b* 23 Dec. 1894; *e s* of late John Mortimer Buckingham, South Molton, N Devon; unmarried. *Educ:* Berkhamsted Sch.; St John's Coll., Cambridge (MA). Joined Admiralty scientific staff for anti-submarine duties under Lord Fisher, 1917, and was, until 1959, engaged continuously upon scientific work for the Admiralty; Deputy Director of Scientific Research, 1932; Apptd Chief Scientific Officer in RN Scientific Service on its formation in 1946. *Publications:* Matter and Radiation, 1930. Various publications in scientific journals. *Address:* 71 Pall Mall, SW1. *T:* 01-930 4152. *Clubs:* Brooks's, Travellers', United Oxford & Cambridge University.

BUCKINGHAM, Prof. Richard Arthur; Professor of Computer Education, Birkbeck College, University of London, since 1974; *b* 17 July 1911; *s* of George Herbert Buckingham and Alice Mary Watson (*née* King); *m* 1939 Christina O'Brien; one *s* two *d. Educ:* Gresham's Sch., Holt; St John's Coll., Cambridge. Asst Lecturer in Mathematical Physics, Queen's University, Belfast, 1935-38; Senior 1851 Exhibitioner, University College, London and MIT, 1938-40. At Admiralty Research Laboratory, Teddington, and Mine Design Dept, Havant, 1940-45. University Coll., London: Lecturer in Mathematics, 1945-50; Lecturer in Physics, 1950-51; Reader in Physics, 1951-57; Dir, Univ. of London Computer Unit, later Inst. of Computer Science, 1957-73, and Prof. of Computing Science, 1963-74. FBCS; FRSA. *Publications:* Numerical Methods, 1957; papers in Proc. Royal Soc., Proc. Phys. Soc., London, Jl Chem. Physics, Trans. Faraday Soc., Computer Journal, etc. *Recreation:* travel. *Address:* Arunlea, Kentwyn's Drive, Horsham, West Sussex.

BUCKINGHAMSHIRE, 9th Earl of, cr 1746; Vere Frederick Cecil Hobart-Hampden; Bt 1611; Baron Hobart, 1728; *b* 17 May 1901; *s* of Arthur Ernest and Henrietta Louisa Hobart-Hampden; *S* kinsman, 1963; *m* 1972, Margot Macrae, *widow* of F. C. Bruce Hittmann, FRACS, Sydney, Australia. *Educ:* St Lawrence College, Ramsgate; Switzerland. Left England for Australia via Canada, 1919; sheep farming and wool business. Served in Royal Australian Air Force, 1942-46; returned to England, 1949. *Heir: kinsman* (George) Miles Hobart-Hampden [*b* 15 Dec. 1944; *m* 1968, Susan Jennifer, *d* of R. W. Adams]. *Address:* c/o Barclay's Bank, 160 Piccadilly, W1.

BUCKLAND, Maj.-Gen. Ronald John Denys Eden, CB 1974; MBE 1956; Chief Executive Adur District Council, since 1975; *b* 27 July 1920; *s* of late Geoffrey Ronald Aubert Buckland, CB and Lelgarde Edith Eleanor (*née* Eden); *m* 1968, Judith Margaret Coxhead; two *d. Educ:* Winchester; New College, Oxford (MA). Commissioned into Coldstream Gds, Dec. 1940. Served War of 1939-45: NW Europe, with 4th Coldstream Gds, 1944-45 (wounded twice). GSO3, Gds Div., BAOR, 1946; Adjt, 1st Bn Coldstream Gds, Palestine and Libya, 1948; DAA&QMG, 2nd Gds Bde, Malaya, 1950; DAAG, 3rd Div., Egypt, 1954; Bde Major, 1st Gds Bde, Cyprus, 1958; commanded 1st Bn, Coldstream Gds, 1961, British Guiana, 1962; GSO1, 4th Div., BAOR, 1963; Comdr, 133 Inf. Bde (TA), 1966; ACOS, Joint Exercises Div., HQ AFCENT, Holland, 1967; idc 1968; DA&QMG, 1st British Corps, BAOR, 1969; Chief of Staff, HQ Strategic Command, 1970; Maj.-Gen. i/c Admin, UKLF, 1972-75. *Recreations:* cricket, travel, philately. *Address:* c/o Lloyds Bank Ltd, 6 Pall Mall, SW1. *Clubs:* Pratt's, Leander.

BUCKLE, (Christopher) Richard (Sandford); writer; critic; exhibition designer; Member, Advisory Council, Theatre Museum; *b* 6 Aug. 1916; *s* of late Lieut-Col C. G. Buckle, DSO, MC, Northamptonshire Regt, and of Mrs R. E. Buckle (*née* Sandford). *Educ:* Marlborough; Balliol. Founded "Ballet", 1939. Served Scots Guards, 1940-46; in action in Italy (despatches, 1944). Started "Ballet" again, 1946; it continued for seven years. Ballet critic of the Observer, 1948-55: ballet critic of the Sunday Times, 1959-75; advised Canada Council on state of ballet in Canada, 1962; advised Sotheby & Co. on their sales of Diaghilev Ballet material, 1967-69. First play, Gossip Column, prod Q Theatre, 1953; Family Tree (comedy), prod Connaught Theatre, Worthing, 1956. *Organised:* Diaghilev Exhibition, Edinburgh Festival, 1954, and Forbes House, London, 1954-55; The Observer Film Exhibition, London, 1956; Telford Bicentenary Exhibition, 1957; Epstein Memorial Exhibition, Edinburgh Festival, 1961; Shakespeare Exhibition, Stratford-upon-Avon, 1964-65; a smaller version of Shakespeare Exhibition, Edinburgh, 1964; Treasures from the Shakespeare Exhibition, National Portrait Gallery, London, 1964-65; The Communities on the March area in the Man in the Community theme pavilion, Universal and Internat. Exhibition of 1967, Montreal; Exhibition of Beaton Portraits, 1928-68, National Portrait Gallery, 1968; Gala of ballet, Coliseum, 1971; exhibn of

Ursula Tyrwhitt, Ashmolean Mus., Oxford, 1974; exhibn Omaggio ai Disegnatori di Diaghilev, Palazzo Grassi, Venice, 1975; exhibn of ballet, opera and theatre costumes, Salisbury Fest., 1975; exhibn Happy and Glorious, 130 years of Royal photographs, Nat. Portrait Gallery, 1977; presented Kama Dev in recital of Indian dancing, St Paul's Church, Covent Garden, 1970; *designed:* (temporary) Haldane Library for Imperial College, South Kensington; new Exhibition Rooms, Harewood House, Yorks, 1959; redesigned interior of Dundee Repertory Theatre, 1963 (burnt down 3 months later). *Publications:* John Innocent at Oxford (novel), 1939; The Adventures of a Ballet Critic, 1953; In Search of Diaghilev, 1955; Modern Ballet Design, 1955; The Prettiest Girl in England, 1958; Harewood (a guide-book), 1959 and (re-written and re-designed), 1966; Dancing for Diaghilev (the memoirs of Lydia Sokolova), 1960; Epstein Drawings (introd. only), 1962; Epstein: An Autobiography (introd. to new edn only), 1963; Jacob Epstein: Sculptor, 1963; Monsters at Midnight: the French Romantic Movement as a background to the ballet Giselle (limited edn), 1966; The Message, a Gothick Tale of the A1 (limited edn), 1969; Nijinsky, 1971; Nijinsky on Stage: commentary on drawings of Valentine Gross, 1971. *Recreations:* caricature, light verse. *Address:* 34 Henrietta Street, Covent Garden, WC2.

BUCKLE, Maj.-Gen. (Retd) Denys Herbert Vintcent, CB 1955; CBE 1948 (OBE 1945); Legion of Merit (USA) 1944; FCIT; Trustee, South Africa Foundation, since 1969; Member Council, South Africa-Britain Trade Association, since 1969; Director, Prince Vintcent & Co. (Pty) Ltd, Mossel Bay; *b* Cape Town, South Africa, 16 July 1902; *s* of Major H. S. Buckle, RMLI and ASC and of Agnes Buckle (*née* Vintcent), Cape Town; *m* 1928, Frances Margaret Butterworth; one *d. Educ:* Boxgrove School, Guildford; Charterhouse, Godalming; RMC Sandhurst. 2nd Lieut, E Surrey Regt, 1923; transf. to RASC, 1926; Shanghai Def. Force, 1927-28; Asst Adjt, RASC Trg Centre, 1929-32; Adjt 44th (Home Counties) Divnl RASC, TA, 1932-36; Student Staff Coll., Camberley, 1936-37; Adjt Ceylon ASC, 1938; Bde Maj., Malaya Inf Bde, 1938-40; GSO 2, Trg Directorate, WO, 1940; AA & QMG, 8th Armd Div., 1940-41; GSO 1, Staff Coll., Camberley, 1941-42; Brig. Admin. Plans, GHQ Home Forces, "Cossac" and SHAEF, 1942-44; Brig. Q Ops, WO, 1944; DDST and Brig. Q, 21 Army Gp and BAOR, 1945-46; DQMG, FARELF, 1946-48; DDST, S Comd, 1948-49; Spec. Appts (Brig.), USA, 1949-50; Dir of Equipment, WO, 1950-51, and special appt, Paris, 1951; Comdt RASC Trg Centre, 1952-53; DST, MELF, 1953-56; Maj.-Gen. i/c Admin, GHQ, MELF, 1956-58; despatches, 1956 (Suez); retd 1958; ADC to King George VI 1951, to the Queen, 1952-54. FCIT 1971. Bursar, Church of England Training Colleges, Cheltenham, 1958-59. Divisional Manager SE Division, British Waterways, 1961-63; Director of Reorganisation, British Waterways, 1963-65. Dir, UK-S Africa Trade Assoc., 1965-68; Administrative Mem., Southern Africa Cttee, BNEC, 1967-68. Col Comdt RASC, 1959-64; Representative Col Comdt, RASC, 1961; Hon. Col 44th (Home Counties), RASC, 1962-65, Regt, RCT, 1965-67. Legion of Merit (USA), 1944. *Publication:* History of 44th Division, RASC, TA, 1932. *Recreations:* reading, book reviewing, walking, swimming, travel. *Address:* 2 Chelsea Cloisters, Durban Road, Wynberg, Cape 7800, South Africa. *Clubs:* Army and Navy; City and Civil Service, Western Province Sports (Cape Town).

BUCKLE, Richard; see Buckle, C. R. S.

BUCKLEY, family name of **Baron Wrenbury.**

BUCKLEY, Anthony James Henthorne; *b* 22 May 1934; *s* of late William Buckley, FRCS; *m* 1964, Celia Rosamund Sanderson, *d* of late C. R. Sanderson; one *s* two *d. Educ:* Haileybury and ISC; St John's Coll., Cambridge. MA, LLB, FCA. Peat Marwick Mitchell & Co, 1959-62; Rank Organisation Ltd, 1962-66; joined Slater Walker Securities Ltd, 1966; Man. Dir, 1972-75; Chm., Floreat Investment, 1975-76. *Address:* 66 Addison Road, W14 8JL. *Clubs:* Eccentric, MCC.

BUCKLEY, Rt. Hon. Sir Denys (Burton), PC 1970; Kt 1960; MBE 1945; **Rt. Hon. Lord Justice Buckley;** Lord Justice of Appeal, since 1970; *b* 6 Feb. 1906; 4th *s* of 1st Baron Wrenbury; *m* 1932, Gwendolen Jane, *yr d* of late Sir Robert Armstrong-Jones, CBE, FRCS, FRCP; three *d. Educ:* Eton; Trinity College, Oxford. Called to the Bar, Lincoln's Inn, 1928, Bencher, 1949, Pro-Treasurer, 1967, Treasurer, 1969, Pres., Senate of the Inns of Court, 1970-72. Served War of 1939-45, in RAOC, 1940-45; Temporary Major; GSO II (Sigs Directorate), War Office. Treasury Junior Counsel (Chancery), 1949-60; Judge of High Court of Justice, Chancery Div., 1960-70. Member, Restrictive Practices Ct, 1962-70, President, 1968-70; Member: Law Reform Cttee, 1963-73; Cttee on Departmental Records, 1952-

54; Advisory Council on Public Records, 1958-. Hon. Fellow, Trinity Coll., Oxford, 1969. Master, Merchant Taylors' Co., 1972. CStJ 1966. Medal of Freedom (USA), 1945. *Address:* 11 Selwood Place, SW7. *T:* 01-373 4752; Stream Farm, Dallington, Sussex. *T:* Rushlake Green 223; Plâs Dinas, near Caernarvon, Gwynedd. *T:* Llanwnda 830274. *Clubs:* United Oxford & Cambridge University, Beefsteak.

BUCKLEY, George Eric; Counsellor, Atomic Energy, British Embassy, Tokyo, since 1976; *b* 4 Feb. 1916; *s* of John and Florence Buckley; *m* 1941, Mary Theresa Terry; one *s* one *d. Educ:* Oldham High Sch.; Manchester Univ. BSc (Hons) Physics; MInstP. Lectr in Physics, Rugby Coll. of Technol., 1938. War service, Sqdn Ldr, RAF, 1940-46. Manager, Health Physics and Safety, Windscale Works, 1949; Works Manager, Capenhurst Works, 1952; Chief Ops Physicist, Risley, 1956; Chief Tech. Manager, Windscale and Calder Works, 1959; Superintendent: Calder Hall and Windscale Advanced Gas Cooled Reactors, 1964; Reactors and Head of Management Services, 1974. *Recreations:* travel, good food, golf. *Address:* 410 Homat President, 3-20 Roppongi 1-chome, Minato-Ku, Tokyo 106, Japan. *T:* 03-583-6076.

BUCKLEY, James Arthur, CBE 1975; Member, British Gas Corporation, 1973-76 (Gas Council, 1968-72); *b* 3 April 1917; *s* of late James Buckley and of Elizabeth Buckley; *m* 1939, Irene May Hicks; two *s. Educ:* Christ's Hosp., Horsham, Sussex; Westminster Technical Coll.; Bradford Technical Coll. RAFVR, 1940-46. Gas Light & Coke Co.; Gas Supply Pupil, 1934; Actg Service Supervisor, 1939; Service Supervisor, 1946; North Thames Gas Board: Divisional Man., 1954; Commercial Man., 1962; Commercial Man. and Bd Mem., 1964; East Midlands Gas Board: Dep. Chm., 1966-67; Chm., 1967-68.

BUCKLEY, Sir John (William), Kt 1977; Chairman: Davy International Ltd, since 1973; Alfred Herbert Ltd, since 1975; *b* 9 Jan. 1913; *s* of John William and Florence Buckley; *m* 1st, 1935, Bertha Bagnall (marr. diss. 1967); two *s* ; 2nd, 1967, Molly Neville-Clarke; one step *s* (and one step *s* decd). *Educ:* techn. coll. (Dipl. Engrg). George Kent Ltd, 1934-50 (Gen. Man. 1945-50); Man. Dir, Emmco Pty Ltd, 1950-55; Man. Dir, British Motor Corp. Pty Ltd, 1956-60; Vice Chm. and Dep. Chm., Winget, Gloucester Ltd, 1961-68; Man. Dir and Dep. Chm., Davy International Ltd, 1968-73; Dir, British Overseas Trade Bd, 1973-76. Chm., EDC for Process Plant Industry, 1977-. Hon. FIChemE 1975. Order of the Southern Cross (Brazil), 1977. *Recreations:* gardening, music, fishing, painting. *Address:* Ashton House, Ashton Keynes, Wilts. *T:* Ashton Keynes 373. *Clubs:* Carlton; Union (Sydney).

BUCKLEY, Rear-Adm. Sir Kenneth (Robertson), KBE 1961; FIEE, MBritIRE; *b* 24 May 1904; 2nd *s* of late L. E. Buckley, CSI, TD; *m* 1937, Bettie Helen Radclyffe Dugmore; one *s* two *d. Educ:* RN Colleges Osborne and Dartmouth. Joined Navy Jan. 1918. Served War of 1939-45 (despatches). Comdr 1942; Capt. 1949; Rear-Adm. 1958. ADC to the Queen, 1956-58. Director of Engineering and Electrical Training of the Navy, and Senior Naval Electrical Officer, 1959-62. *Recreations:* golf, gardening. *Address:* Meadow Cottage, Cherque Lane, Lee-on-Solent, Hants. *T:* Lee 550646.

BUCKLEY, Rear-Adm. Peter Noel, CB 1964; DSO 1945; retd; Head of Naval Historical Branch, Ministry of Defence, 1968-75; *b* 26 Dec. 1909; *s* of late Frank and Constance Buckley, Hooton, Cheshire; *m* 1945, Norah Elizabeth Astley St Clair-Ford, *widow* of Lt-Comdr Drummond St Clair-Ford; one *d* (and two step *s* one step *d*). *Educ:* Holmwood School, Formby, Lancs; RNC, Dartmouth. Midshipman, HMS Tiger, 1927, HMS Cornwall, 1928-30; Lieut: qual. 1931. Submarine Service, 1931-38, in submarines; Lieut-Comdr, CO of HMS Shark, 1938. War of 1939-45 (despatches): POW Germany, 1940-45. Comdr 1945; HMS: Rajah and Formidable, 1946; Siskin, 1947; Glory, 1949; RN Barracks, Portsmouth, 1951; Capt. 1952; Capt. D, Plymouth, 1953; Capt. of Dockyard, Rosyth, 1954; Chief Staff Officer to Flag Officer Comdg Reserve Fleet, 1957; Capt of Fleet, Med. Fleet, 1959; Rear-Adm. 1962; Dir-Gen., Manpower, 1962-64; retd 1965. *Address:* Forest Cottage, Sway, Lymington, Hants. *T:* Sway 2442.

BUCKLEY, Lt-Comdr (Peter) Richard, CVO 1973 (MVO 1968); Private Secretary to the Duke and Duchess of Kent since 1961; *b* 31 Jan. 1928; 2nd *s* of late Alfred Buckley and of Mrs E. G. Buckley, Crowthorne, Berks; *m* 1958, Theresa Mary Neve; two *s* one *d. Educ:* Wellington Coll. Cadet, RN, 1945. Served in HM Ships: Mauritius, Ulster, Contest, Defender, and BRNC, Dartmouth. Specialised in TA/S. Invalided from RN (Lt-Comdr), 1961. *Recreations:* fishing, sailing. *Address:* Coppins Cottages, Iver, Bucks SL0 0AT. *T:* Iver 653004. *Clubs:* Royal Automobile; Royal Dart Yacht.

BUCKLEY, Hon. Dame Ruth (Burton), DBE 1959; JP; *b* 12 July 1898; 4th *d* of 1st Baron Wrenbury, PC. *Educ:* Cheltenham Ladies' College. Called to Bar, Lincoln's Inn, 1926. E Sussex County Council: Member of Council, 1936-74; Alderman, 1946-74; Vice-Chm. 1949-52; Chm. 1952-55. Member of South Eastern Metropolitan Regional Hospital Board, 1948-69; Part-time member of Local Govt Boundary Commn for England, 1958-66. JP Sussex, 1935-. Hon. LLD Sussex, 1977. *Address:* Toll Wood Cottage, Netherfield, Battle, East Sussex. *T:* Brightling 222.

BUCKLEY, Lt-Col William Howell, DL; Landed Proprietor; Chairman, Buckleys Brewery Ltd, Llanelly, 1947-72, President, since 1972; *b* 7 Feb. 1896; *s* of William Joseph Buckley and Muriel Howell; *m* 1st, 1920, Karolie Kathleen Kemmis; one *s* one *d*; 2nd, 1952, Helen Josephine Turner; one *d*. *Educ:* Radley. 2nd Lieut Glamorgan Imperial Yeomanry, 1914; Lieut The Inniskillings (6th Dragoons), 1915; Capt. 5th Inniskilling Dragoon Guards, 1926; Capt. 1930; served War of 1939-45, 6th Cavalry Bde, Palestine, 1939; Deputy Provost Marshal S Area, Palestine, Malta, Western Command. High Sheriff of Carmarthenshire, 1950-51; DL Carmarthen, 1955. Master: Carmarthenshire Fox Hounds, 1931-62; Tivyside Fox Hounds, 1964-66. *Recreation:* hunting. *Address:* Castell Gorfod, St Clears, Dyfed, S Wales. *TA:* St Clears. *T:* St Clears 230210. *Clubs:* Cavalry and Guards, Buck's, Leander.
See also Major W. K. Buckley.

BUCKLEY, Major William Kemmis, MBE 1959; DL; Chairman, Buckley's Brewery Ltd, since 1972 (Director, 1960, Vice-Chairman, 1963-72); *b* 18 Oct. 1921; *o s* of Lt-Col William Howell Buckley, qv. *Educ:* Radley Coll.; New Coll., Oxford (MA). Commnd into Welsh Guards, 1941; served N Africa, Italy (despatches, 1945); ADC, 1946-47, Mil. Sec., 1948, to Governor of Madras; Staff Coll., Camberley, 1950; GSO2, HQ London Dist, 1952-53; OC Guards Indep. Para. Co., 1954-57; Cyprus, 1956; Suez, 1956; War Office, 1957; Mil. Asst to Vice-Chief of Imp. Gen. Staff, 1958-59; US Armed Forces Staff Coll., Norfolk, Va., 1959-60. Director: Rhymney Breweries Ltd, 1962; Whitbread (Wales) Ltd, 1969; Felinfoil Brewery Co., 1975; Guardian Assurance Co. (S Wales), 1966 (Dep. Chm., 1967-). Mem. Council, Brewers' Soc., 1967; Chm., S Wales Brewers' Assoc., 1971-74; Dep. Chm. and Treas., Nat. Trade Develt Assoc., 1966 (Chm., S Wales Panel, 1965); Lay Mem., Press Council, 1967-73. Chm., Council of St John of Jerusalem for Carms, 1966; Pres., Carms Antiquarian Soc., 1971- (Chm., 1968); Mem., Nat. Trust Cttee for Wales, 1962-70; Mem., T&AFA (Carms), 1962 and T&AFA (S Wales and Mon.), 1967; Jt Master and Hon. Sec., Pembrokeshire and Carms Otter Hounds, 1962. High Sheriff of Carms, 1967-68, DL Dyfed (formerly Carms) 1969. CStJ 1966. *Publications:* contributions in local history journals. *Recreations:* gardening, bee-keeping (Pres. Carmarthenshire Bee-Keepers Assoc., 1972-). *Address:* Briar Cottage, Ferryside, Dyfed, S Wales. *T:* Ferryside 359. *Clubs:* Brooks's; Cardiff and County (Cardiff).

BUCKMASTER, family name of Viscount Buckmaster.

BUCKMASTER, 3rd Viscount *cr* 1933, of Cheddington; **Martin Stanley Buckmaster;** Baron 1915; HM Diplomatic Service; Head of Chancery, Yemen Arab Republic, since 1977; *b* 11 April 1921; *s* of 2nd Viscount Buckmaster and Joan, Viscountess Buckmaster (*d* 1976), *d* of Dr Garry Simpson; *S* father, 1974. *Educ:* Stowe. Joined TA, 1939; served Royal Sussex Regt (Captain) in UK and Middle East, 1940-46. Foreign Office, 1946; Middle East Centre for Arab Studies, Lebanon, 1950-51; qualified in Arabic (Higher Standard); served in Trucial States, Sharjah (1951-53) and Abu Dhabi (Political Officer, 1955-58) and subsequently in Libya, Bahrain, FO, Uganda, Lebanon and Saudi Arabia, 1958-73; First Sec., FCO, 1973-77. FRGS 1954. *Recreations:* walking, music, railways; Arab and African studies. *Heir: b* Hon. Colin John Buckmaster [*b* 17 April 1923; *m* 1946, May, *o d* of late Charles Henry Gibbon; three *s* two *d*]. *Address:* 8 Redcliffe Square, SW10 9JZ. *T:* 01-370 2247. *Club:* Travellers'.

BUCKMASTER, Rev. Cuthbert Harold Septimus; *b* 15 July 1903; *s* of Charles John and Evelyn Jean Buckmaster; *m* 1942, Katharine Mary Zoë (*d* 1974), 3rd *d* of Rev. Canon T. N. R. Prentice, Stratford-on-Avon; two *d*. *Educ:* RN Colls, Osborne and Dartmouth. Asst Curate St John's, Middlesbrough, 1927-30; Curate of Wigan, 1930-33; Chaplain of Denstone Coll., 1933-35; Warden of St Michael's Coll., Tenbury, Worcs, 1935-46; Rector of: Ashprington, with Cornworthy, 1957-59; Chagford, 1959-71. Chaplain RNVR, 1940; RN 1947. *Address:* 12A Bridgetown Court, Totnes, Devon.

BUCKNALL, Lt-Gen. Gerard Corfield, CB 1943; MC; psc; ns; lately Colonel, The Middlesex Regiment; Assistant Lieutenant for Greater London, 1965-70; *b* 14 Sept. 1894; *s* of Harry Corfield Bucknall and Alice Oakshott; *m* 1925, Kathleen Josephine Moore-Burt; two *s* one *d*. *Educ:* Repton; Sandhurst. Commissioned 1st Battalion Middlesex Regiment, 1914; served throughout European War, 1914-18, France and Flanders, latterly on General Staff (wounded, MC and Bar, despatches, Bt Major); in Sudan with Egyptian Army, 1920-21; Brevet Lieut-Colonel 1936; General Staff Canadian Forces, 1937-38; commanded 2nd Bn Middx, 1939; Colonel on Staff, War Office, 1939; commanded 5th Div. in Sicily and Italy, and 30th Corps in Army of Invasion, 1944; GOC N Ireland, 1945-47; Lord Lieut of Middlesex, 1963-65. *Address:* 25 Belvedere Avenue, Wimbledon, SW19. *Clubs:* Army and Navy, MCC; Royal Wimbledon Golf.

BUCKNILL, Peter Thomas, QC 1961; *b* 4 Nov. 1910; *o s* of late Rt Hon. Sir Alfred Bucknill, PC, OBE; *m* 1935, Elizabeth Mary Stark; three *s* two *d* (and one *d* decd). *Educ:* Gresham's Sch., Holt; Trinity Coll., Oxford (MA). Called to the Bar, Inner Temple, 1935, Bencher, 1967. Appointed Junior Counsel to the Treasury (Admiralty), 1958; resigned on becoming QC. On rota for Lloyd's Salvage Arbitrators, Wreck Commissioner, 1962-. *Publications:* contributed to Halsbury's Laws of England, shipping vol., 2nd and 3rd edns. *Recreation:* gardening. *Address:* High Corner, The Warren, Ashtead, Surrey KT21 2SL; Queen Elizabeth Building, Temple, EC4Y 9BS. *T:* 01-353 5728, 0132.

BUCKTON, Baron *cr* 1966 (Life Peer), of Settrington; **Samuel Storey;** Bt, *cr* 1960; *b* 1896; *er s* of late Frederick George Storey, JP; *m* 1929, Elisabeth, JP (*d* 1951) *d* of late Brig.-Gen. W. J. Woodcock, DSO; one *s* one *d*. *Educ:* Haileybury Coll.; Trinity Coll., Cambridge, MA. Barrister, Inner Temple, 1919; MP (C) Sunderland, 1931-45 and Stretford, 1950-66; Chairman of Ways and Means, and Dep. Speaker, House of Commons, 1965-66; (Dep. Chm. of Ways and Means, 1964-65); Member Chairman's Panel, House of Commons, 1957-64. E Riding CC, 1946-64. *Heir* (to Baronetcy only): *s* Hon. Richard Storey [*b* 23 Jan. 1937; *m* 1961, Virginia Anne, 3rd *d* of Sir Kenelm Cayley, 10th Bt; one *s* two *d*]. *Address:* Settrington House, Settrington, Malton, North Yorks YO17 8NP. *T:* North Grimston 200. *Club:* Carlton.

BUCKTON, Raymond William; General Secretary, Associated Society of Locomotive Engineers and Firemen, since 1970; *b* 20 Oct. 1922; *s* of W. E. and H. Buckton; *m* 1954, Barbara Langfield; two *s*. *Educ:* Appleton Roebuck School. MCIT. Employed in Motive Power Department, British Railways, 1940-60. Elected Irish Officer of ASLEF, 1960 (Dublin); District Organiser, York, Jan. 1963; Assistant General Secretary, July 1963; General Secretary, 1970. Member: Gen. Council, TUC, 1973-; IBA Gen. Adv. Council, 1976-; Occupational Pensions Bd, 1976-; Health Services Bd, 1977-. Member: CIT Council, 1970-; Industrial Soc., 1973-; Standing Adv. Cttee, TUC Centenary Inst. of Occupational Health, 1974-; Nat. Adv. Council on Employment of Disabled People, 1975-; Industrial Injuries Adv. Council, 1976-; Dangerous Substances Adv. Cttee, 1976-; Adv. Cttee on Alcoholism, 1977-. Councillor, York City Council, 1952-55, Alderman, 1955-57. *Address:* 9 Arkwright Road, Hampstead, NW3. *T:* 01-435 6300.

BUDAY, George, RE 1953 (ARE 1939); wood engraver; author on graphic arts subjects; *b* Kolozsvar, Transylvania, 7 April 1907; *s* of late Prof. Arpad Buday, Roman archaeologist, and Margaret Buday. *Educ:* Presbyterian Coll., Kolozsvar; Royal Hungarian Francis Joseph Univ., Szeged (Dr). Apptd Lectr in Graphic Arts, Royal Hungarian F. J. Univ., 1935-41; Rome Scholar, 1936-37; won travelling schol. to England (and has stayed permanently) 1937. Broadcaster, BBC European Service, 1940-42; in a Dept of Foreign Office, 1942-45. Dir, Hungarian Cultural Inst., London, 1947-49, resigned. Illustrated numerous folk-tale and folk-ballad collections, vols of classics and modern authors, publ. in many countries. Since 1938 exhib. Royal Acad., Royal Soc. of Painter-Etchers and Engravers, Soc. of Wood Engravers, and in many countries abroad. Works represented in: Depts of Prints and Drawings, Brit. Mus.; Victoria and Albert Mus.; Glasgow Univ.; New York Public Library; Florence Univ.; Museums of Fine Arts, Budapest, Prague, Warsaw; Phillips Memorial Gall., Washington, DC; etc. Grand Prix, Paris World Exhibn, 1937 (for engravings); subsequently other art and bibliophile prizes. Officer's Cross, Order of Merit (Hungary), 1947. *Publications:* Book of Ballads, 1934; The Story of the Christmas Card, 1951; The History of the Christmas Card, 1954 (1964); (wrote and illustr.): The Dances of Hungary, 1950; George Buday's Little Books, I-XII, incl. The Language of Flowers, 1951; The Cries of London, Ancient and

Modern, 1954; Proverbial Cats and Kittens, 1956 (1968); The Artist's Recollections, for a volume of his 82 Selected Engravings, 1970; 25 engraved images and an essay, in, Poetical Anthology, 1977; contrib. articles to periodicals. *Relevant publication:* George Buday by Curt Visel, in Illustration 63, 1971. *Recreations:* bibliophile hand-printing on his 1857 Albion hand-press and collecting old Christmas cards (probably most representative collection of Victorian cards extant). *Address:* Downs House, Netherne, PO Box 150, Coulsdon, Surrey CR3 1YE.

BUDD, Bernard Wilfred, MA; QC 1969; *b* 18 Dec. 1912; *s* of late Rev. W. R. A. Budd; *m* 1944, Margaret Alison, *d* of late Rt Hon. E. Leslie Burgin, PC, LLD, MP; two *s. Educ:* Cardiff High Sch.; W Leeds High Sch.; Pembroke Coll., Cambridge (schol. in natural sciences). Joined ICS, 1935; various Dist appts incl. Dep. Comr, Upper Sind Frontier, 1942-43; Collector and Dist Magistrate, Karachi, 1945-46; cont. in Pakistan Admin. Service, 1947; Dep. Sec., Min. of Commerce and Works, Govt of Pakistan, 1947; Anti-corruption Officer and Inspector-Gen. of Prisons, Govt of Sind, 1949. Called to Bar, Gray's Inn, 1952. Contested (L), Dover, 1964 and 1966, Folkestone and Hythe, Feb. and Oct. 1974. *Recreations:* squash, birds, hill walking. *Address:* Highlands, Elham, Canterbury, Kent. *T:* Elham 350; 68 Cliffords Inn, Fetter Lane, EC4. *T:* 01-405 2491; 3 Pump Court, Temple, EC4. *T:* 01-353 4122. *Clubs:* United Oxford & Cambridge University, National Liberal; Sind (Karachi).

BUDD, Hon. Sir Harry Vincent, Kt 1970; President of the Legislative Council of New South Wales since 1966 (MLC since 1946); *b* 18 Feb. 1900; *s* of Arthur Eames Budd and Anne (*née* Knight); *m* 1930, Colina Macdonald White, *d* of Alfred White; one *s* two *d* (and one *s* decd). *Educ:* privately. Editor, Tweed Daily, Murwillumbah, 1921-23; Editorial Staff, Sydney Daily Telegraph, 1923-30; Managing Editor, The Land, 1930-70. *Recreations:* music, gardening. *Address:* 26 Mistral Avenue, Mosman, Sydney, NSW 2088, Australia. *T:* 969-4810. *Clubs:* Australian, American.

BUDD, Stanley Alec; Scottish Representative, Commission of the European Communities, since 1975; *b* 22 May 1931; *s* of Henry Stanley Budd and Ann Mitchell; *m* 1955, Wilma McQueen Cuthbert; three *s* one *d*. *Educ:* George Heriot's Sch., Edinburgh. Newspaper reporter, feature writer and sub-editor, D. C. Thomson & Co, Dundee, 1947-57 (National Service, 1949-51). Research writer, Foreign Office, 1957-60; 2nd Secretary, Beirut, Lebanon, 1960-63; 1st Sec., Kuala Lumpur, Malaysia, 1963-69; FO, 1969-71; Dep. Head of Information, Scottish Office, 1971-72; Press Secretary to Chancellor of Duchy of Lancaster, 1972-74; Chief Information Officer, Cabinet Office, 1974-75. *Recreations:* music, painting, oriental antiques, bridge. *Address:* 2 Bellevue Crescent, Edinburgh EH3 6ND; 7 Alva Street, Edinburgh EH2 4PH. *T:* 031-225 2058. *Clubs:* Press (Edinburgh); Royal Selangor (Malaysia).

BUDDEN, Kenneth George, FRS 1966; MA, PhD; Reader in Physics, University of Cambridge, since 1965; Fellow of St John's College, Cambridge, since 1947; *b* 23 June 1915; *s* of late George Easthope Budden and Gertrude Homer Rea; *m* 1947, Nicolette Ann Lydia de Longesdon Longsdon; no *c. Educ:* Portsmouth Grammar Sch.; St John's College, Cambridge (MA, PhD). Telecommunications Research Establishment, 1939-41; British Air Commn., Washington, DC, 1941-44; Air Command, SE Asia, 1945. Research at Cambridge, 1936-39 and from 1947. *Publications:* Radio Waves in the Ionosphere, 1961; The Wave-Guide Mode Theory of Wave Propagation, 1961; Lectures on Magnetoionic Theory, 1964; numerous papers in scientific jls, on the propagation of radio waves. *Recreation:* gardening. *Address:* 15 Adams Road, Cambridge. *T:* 54752.

BUDGEN, Nicholas William; MP (C) Wolverhampton South-West, since Feb. 1974; *b* 3 Nov. 1937; *s* of Captain G. N. Budgen; *m* 1964, Madeleine E. Kittoe; one *s* one *d*. *Educ:* St Edward's Sch., Oxford; Corpus Christi Coll., Cambridge. Called to Bar, Gray's Inn, 1962; practised Midland and Oxford Circuit. *Recreations:* hunting, racing. *Address:* Malt House Farm, Colton, near Rugeley, Staffs. *T:* Rugeley 77059.

BUFFET, Bernard; Chevalier de la Légion d'Honneur; artist, painter; *b* Paris, 10 July 1928; *m* 1958, Annabel May Schwob de Lure; one *s* two *d*. Début at Salon des Moins de Trente Ans, 1944. From 1948 has had one-man shows, annually, at Drouant-David and Visconti Galleries, from 1956 at Galerie Maurice Garnier. Grand Prix de la Critique, 1948. Solo retrospective exhibition of his works was held at Charpentier Gallery, Paris, 1958. He has exhibited, oils, water colours and drawings and is a lithographer, mural painter and illustrator of books. Work represented in permanent collections: Musée du Petit Palais and

Musée National d'Art Moderne, in Paris; Buffet Museum founded in Japan, 1973; large room of his mystic works in Vatican Museum; work shown at Venice Biennale, 1956; exhibitions: Lefevre Gallery, London, 1961, 1963, 1965. Stage designs: Le Rendez-vous manqué (ballet), 1959; Patron (musical comedy), 1959; ballets at L'Opéra, Paris, 1969. Mem. Salon d'Automne and Salon des Indépendants. Officier des Arts et des Lettres; Membre de l'Institut, 1974. *Address:* Château de Villiers le Mahieu, 78770 Thoiry, France.

BUFFEY, Brig. William, DSO 1940; TD 1940; DL; *b* 24 Sept. 1899; *s* of late William Buffey, Bromley, Kent; *m* 1926, Dorothy Wensley, *d* of late William Rogers, Nelson, New Zealand; two *d*. *Educ:* St Dunstan's College, Catford. Served War of 1939-45, Cmd 91st Fd Regt RA, France, Belgium (DSO), India, Persia, 1939-43; CRA 5 Div. Middle East, Italy, BLA, 1943-45 (despatches thrice); Hon. Col 291st Airborne Fd Regt RA (TA), 1946-55. Governor, St Dunstan's College. DL Co. London, subseq. Greater London, 1954. *Recreation:* golf. *Address:* Jenners, Groombridge, Tunbridge Wells, Kent. *T:* Groombridge 309.

BUFTON, Air Vice-Marshal Sydney Osborne, CB 1945; DFC 1940; *b* 12 Jan. 1908; 2nd *s* of late J. O. Bufton, JP, Llandrindod Wells, Radnor; *m* 1943, Susan Maureen, *d* of Colonel E. M. Browne, DSO, Chelsea; two *d*. *Educ:* Dean Close School, Cheltenham. Commissioned RAF 1927; psa, 1939; idc, 1946. Served War of 1939-45, Bomber Comd, Nos 10 and 76 Sqdns, RAF Station, Pocklington, 1940-41; Dep. Dir Bomber Ops, 1941-43; Dir of Bomber Ops, Air Min., 1943-45; AOC Egypt, 1945-46; Central Bomber Establishment, RAF, Marham, Norfolk, 1947-48; Dep. Chief of Staff (Ops/Plans), Air Forces Western Europe, 1948-51; Dir of Weapons, Air Min., 1951-52; AOA Bomber Command, 1952-53; AOC Brit. Forces, Aden, 1953-55; Senior Air Staff Officer, Bomber Comd, 1955-58; Assistant Chief of Air Staff (Intelligence), 1958-61; retired Oct. 1961. Temp. Gp Capt. 1941; Temp. Air Cdre 1943; Subst. Gp Capt. 1946; Air Cdre 1948; Actg Air Vice-Marshal, 1952; Air Vice-Marshal, 1953. FRAeS 1970. High Sheriff of Radnorshire, 1967. Comdr Legion of Merit (US); Comdr Order of Orange Nassau (with swords), Netherlands. *Recreations:* hockey (Welsh International 1931-37, Combined Services, RAF), golf, squash. *Address:* 1 Castle Keep, London Road, Reigate. *T:* Reigate 43707. *Club:* Royal Air Force.

BUHLER, Robert, RA 1956 (ARA 1947); painter; Hon. Fellow, Royal College of Art; tutor, RCA, 1948-75; *b* London, 23 Nov. 1916; *s* of Robert Buhler, journalist; *m* Evelyn Rowell (marr. diss. 1951); one *s*; *m* 1962, Prudence Brochocka (*née* Beaumont) (marr. diss. 1972); two *s*. *Educ:* Bolt Court; St Martin's School of Art; Royal College of Art. Exhibited at: Royal Academy, New English Art Club, London Group, London galleries. Work in permanent collections: Chantrey Bequest; Stott Fund; provincial art galleries; galleries in USA, Canada, Australia, NZ. *Address:* 33 Alderney Street, SW1V 4ES. *T:* 01-828 2825.

BUIST, Comdr Colin, CVO 1961 (MVO 1927); RN (Retired); Extra Equerry to the Queen since 1952 (to King George VI, 1937-52); President, Coalite and Chemical Products Ltd (Chairman, 1953-70); *b* 10 April 1896; *s* of Col Frederick Braid Buist; *m* 1928, Gladys Mary (*d* 1972), 4th *d* of late Sir William Nelson, Bt. *Educ:* RN Colleges, Osborne and Dartmouth. Served European War, 1914-18; also 1939-44. *Address:* 9 Cumberland Mansions, George Street, W1H 5TE. *T:* 01-723 2890; Highmoor Farm, Henley-on-Thames RG9 5DH. *T:* Nettlebed 275. *Club:* White's.

BUIST, John Latto Farquharson; Under Secretary, International Division, Ministry of Overseas Development, since 1976; *b* 30 May 1930; *s* of Lt-Col Thomas Powrie Buist, RAMC, and Christian Mary (*née* Robertson). *Educ:* Dalhousie Castle Sch.; Winchester Coll.; New Coll., Oxford (MA). Asst Principal, CO, 1952-54; Sec., Kenya Police Commn, 1953; seconded Kenya Govt (Min. of Commerce and Industry, Cabinet Office, and Dist Officer Kitui), 1954-56; Principal, CO, 1956-61; Dept of Tech. Cooperation, 1961-62; Brit. High Commn, Dar-es-Salaam, 1962-64; Consultant on Admin, E African Common Services Org./Community, 1964-69; Sec., Commn on E African Cooperation and related bodies, 1966-69; Asst Sec., Min. of Overseas Develt, 1966-76. Co-founder and several times Pres., Classical Assoc. of Kenya; Member: Campaign for Homosexual Equality; John Bate Choir; United Reformed Church. *Recreations:* singing and other music-making, friends, walking. *Address:* 9 Manor Gate, St John's Avenue, SW15. *T:* 01-789 4490.

BÜLBRING, Edith, MA Oxon; MD Bonn; FRS 1958; Professor of Pharmacology, Oxford University, 1967-71, now Emeritus

(University Reader, 1960-67) and Honorary Fellow, Lady Margaret Hall, 1971; *b* 27 Dec. 1903; *d* of Karl Daniel Bülbring, Professor of English, Bonn University, and Hortense Leonore Bülbring (*née* Kann). *Educ:* Bonn, Munich and Freiburg Universities. Postgraduate work in Pharmacology Department of Berlin University, 1929-31; Pediatrics, University of Jena, 1932; Virchow Krankenhaus University of Berlin, 1933; Pharmacological Laboratory of Pharmaceutical Society of Great Britain, University of London, 1933-38; Pharmacological Dept, University of Oxford, 1938-71. Research work on: autonomic transmitters, suprarenals, smooth muscle, peristalsis. Schmiedeberg-Plakette der Deutschen Pharmakologischen Gesellschaft, 1974. Hon. Mem. Pharmaceutical Soc., Torino, Italy, 1957; Hon. Mem., British Pharmacological Soc., 1975. *Publications:* mainly in Jl of Physiology, Brit. Jl of Pharmacology and Proc. Royal Soc. of London, Series B. *Recreation:* music. *Address:* 15 Northmoor Road, Oxford. *T:* Oxford 57270; Lady Margaret Hall, Oxford.

BULGER, Anthony Clare, BA, BCL; **His Honour Judge Bulger;** a Circuit Judge (formerly County Court Judge), since 1963; *b* 1912; *s* of Daniel Bulger; *m* Una Patricia Banks; one *s* one *d*. *Educ:* Rugby; Oriel Coll., Oxford. Called to the Bar, Inner Temple, 1936. Oxford Circuit; Dep Chm., 1958-70, Chm. 1970-71, Glos QS; Dep. Chm. Worcs QS, 1962-71. Recorder of Abingdon, 1962-63. *Address:* Forthampton, Glos.

BULKELEY, Sir Richard H. D. W.; *see* Williams-Bulkeley.

BULL, Amy Frances, CBE 1964; Head Mistress, Wallington County Grammar School for Girls, 1937-64, retired; *b* 27 April 1902; *d* of Herbert Bull, Head Master of Pinewood Preparatory Sch., Farnborough, until 1919, and Ethel Mary Atkinson. *Educ:* Roedean Sch.; Somerville Coll., Oxford. Asst Mistress, Cheltenham Ladies' Coll., 1925-32; Head of History Dept, Portsmouth Northern Secondary Sch., 1932-37; Pres. Head Mistresses' Assoc., 1960-62; Member: Surrey Educn Cttee, 1946-60; National Youth Employment Council, 1959-68; Secondary School Examination Council, 1960-64; Exec. Cttee Central Council for Physical Recreation, 1963-73; Fountain and Carshalton Gp Management Cttee, 1964-74; Sutton Borough Education Cttee, 1966-74; St Helier Hosp. House Cttee; Women's Nat. Commn, 1969-76. Governor: St Michael's Sch., Limpsfield, 1965-; Queen Mary's and Fountain Hospital Schs, 1972-; St Ebba's, Brooklands and Ellen Terry Hospital Schs, 1972-. *Recreations:* gardening, walking in mountains, watching games. *Address:* Firtree Lodge, 16 Broomfield Park, Westcott, Dorking, Surrey. *Clubs:* University Women's, English-Speaking Union.

BULL, Anthony, CBE 1968 (OBE 1944); Transport Consultant: Kennedy and Donkin, since 1971; Freeman Fox and Partners, and Freeman Fox Associates, since 1971; *b* 18 July 1908; 3rd *s* of Rt Hon. Sir William Bull, 1st Bt, PC, MP, JP, FSA (*d* 1931), and late Lilian, 2nd *d* of G. S. Brandon, Oakbrook, Ravenscourt Park; *m* 1946, Barbara (*d* 1947), *er d* of late Peter Donovan, Yonder, Rye, Sussex; one *d*. *Educ:* Gresham's Sch., Holt; Magdalene Coll., Cambridge (Exhibitioner; MA). Joined Underground Group of Cos, 1929; served in Staff, Publicity and Public Relations Depts and Chairman's Office. Sec. to Vice-Chm. London Passenger Transport Board, 1936-39. Served War, 1939-45; RE; Transportation Br., War Office, 1939-42; GHQ, Middle East, 1943; Staff of Supreme Allied Comdr, SE Asia (end of 1943); Col 1944; Transp. Div., CCG, 1945-46. Returned to London Transport as Chief Staff and Welfare Officer, 1946; Member: LTE, 1955-62; LTB, 1962-65; Vice-Chm., LTE (formerly LTB), 1965-71. Inst. of Transport: served on Council, 1956-59; Vice-Pres., 1964-66; Hon. Librarian, 1966-69; Pres., 1969-70. Mem. Regional Advisory Council for Technological Educ., 1958-62 (Transp. Adv. Cttee, 1950-62; Chm. Cttee, 1953-62); Mem., King's Lynn Area Hosps Management Cttee, 1972-74. CStJ 1969. Bronze Star (USA), 1946. *Publications:* contrib. to transport journals. *Recreation:* travel. *Address:* 27 Pelham Place, SW7 2NQ. *T:* 01-589 1511; Trowland Cottage, Burnham Norton, Norfolk. *T:* Burnham Market 297. *Club:* United Oxford & Cambridge University.
See also Sir George Bull, Bt, Sir Robin Chichester-Clark.

BULL, Sir George, 3rd Bt *cr* 1922, of Hammersmith; Senior Partner of Bull & Bull, Solicitors, 11 Stone Buildings, Lincoln's Inn, and 4 Castle Street, Canterbury; *b* 19 June 1906; 2nd *s* of Rt Hon. Sir William Bull, 1st Bt, and late Lilian, 2nd *d* of G. S. Brandon, Oakbrook, Ravenscourt Park, and Heene, Worthing, Sussex; *S* brother 1942; *m* 1933, Gabrielle, 2nd *d* of late Bramwell Jackson, MC, Bury St Edmunds; one *s* one *d*. *Educ:* RN Colleges, Osborne and Dartmouth; Paris; Vienna. Admitted Solicitor, 1929. Served War of 1939-45 in RNVR; Comdr, 1942. Vice-Chm. Governors, Godolphin and Latymer Sch.; Governor,

Latymer Foundation; Trustee Hammersmith United Charities; Chm., London Rent Assessment Cttees; Member, Hammersmith Borough Council, 1968-71. Liveryman Fishmongers' Company; Freeman of City of London; Hon. Solicitor, Royal Society of St George, Royal Life Saving Society. Pres., London Corinthian Sailing Club. *Recreations:* sailing, travelling. *Heir: s* Simeon George Bull [*b* 1 Aug. 1934; *m* 1961, Annick, *y d* of late Louis Bresson and of Mme Bresson, Chandai, France; one *s* two *d*]. *Address:* 3 Hammersmith Terrace, W6. *T:* 01-748 2400; 11 Stone Buildings, Lincoln's Inn. *T:* 01-405 7474. *Clubs:* 1900, MCC, Arts.
See also A. Bull.

BULL, Sir Graham (MacGregor), Kt 1976; Director, Medical Research Council, Clinical Research Centre, 1966-78; *b* 30 Jan. 1918; *s* of Dr A. B. Bull; *m* 1947, Megan Patricia Jones (*see* M. P. Bull); three *s* one *d*. *Educ:* Diocesan Coll., Cape Town; Univ. of Cape Town (MD). FRCP. Tutor in Medicine and Asst, Dept of Medicine, Univ. of Cape Town, 1940-46; Lecturer in Medicine, Postgraduate Medical Sch. of London, 1947-52; Professor of Medicine, The Queen's Univ., Belfast, 1952-66. Research Fellow, SA Council for Scientific and Industrial Research, 1947; Member, Medical Research Council, 1962-66. *Publications:* contrib. to medical journals. *Address:* 29 Heath Drive, NW3 7SB. *T:* 01-435 1624.

BULL, Prof. Hedley Norman, MA, BPhil (Oxon); BA (Sydney); Montague Burton Professor of International Relations, University of Oxford, and Fellow of Balliol College, Oxford, since 1977; *b* Sydney, 10 June 1932; *s* of J. N. Bull, Sydney; *m* 1954, Frances M., *d* of F. A. E. Lawes; one *s* two *d*. *Educ:* Fort Street High Sch.; Univ. of Sydney; University Coll., Oxford. Asst Lectr, Internat. Relations, London Sch. of Economics, 1955-57, Lectr 1959; also Rockefeller Fellow, Harvard Univ., 1957-58; Research Associate, Princeton Univ., 1963; Reader in Internat. Relations, London Sch. of Economics, 1963; Dir, Arms Control and Disarmament Research Unit, Foreign Office, London, 1965-67; Prof. of Internat. Relns, Aust. Nat. Univ., 1967-77. Mem. Council, Inst. for Strategic Studies, London, 1968-77. Res. Dir, Aust. Inst. of Internat. Affairs, 1968-73. Visiting Professor: Polit. Sci., Columbia Univ., 1970-71; Jawaharlal Nehru Univ., New Delhi, 1974-75; Vis. Fellow, All Souls Coll., Oxford, 1975-76. FASSA 1968. *Recreation:* walking. *Address:* Balliol College, Oxford OX1 3BJ. *Club:* Travellers'.

BULL, James William Douglas, CBE 1976; MA, MD, FRCP, FRCS, FRCR; Honorary Consultant Radiologist (diagnostic): National Hospital for Nervous Diseases, Queen Square; Maida Vale Hospital for Nervous Diseases; St Andrew's Hospital, Northampton; St George's Hospital; University Hospital, West Indies; Teacher, Institute of Neurology (University of London); Consultant Adviser in Diagnostic Radiology, Department of Health and Social Security, until 1975; Consultant Neuroradiologist to Royal Navy, until 1975; *b* 23 March 1911; *o s* of late D. W. A. Bull, MD, JP, Stony Stratford, Bucks; *m* 1941, Edith, *e d* of late Charles Burch, Henley-on-Thames; one *s* one *d*. *Educ:* Repton; Gonville and Caius Coll., Cambridge; St George's Hospital. Entrance schol., 1932. Usual house appts: Asst Curator of Museum, Med. registrar, St George's Hospital, Rockefeller Travelling Schol. (Stockholm), 1938-39. Served War, 1940-46. Temp. Major RAMC (pow Singapore). Dean, Inst. of Neurology, Univ. of London, 1962-68. President: 4th Internat. Symposium Neuroradiologicum, London, 1955; British Inst. of Radiology, 1960; Section of Radiology, 1968-69, Section of Neurology, 1974-75, RSM; Pres., Faculty of Radiologists, 1969-72 (Vice-Pres., 1963). Member: Assoc. of British Neurologists; Brit. Soc. of Neuroradiologists; Pres., European Soc. of Neuroradiology, 1972-75. Examiner in Diagnostic Radiology: Conjoint Board, 1957; Univ. of Liverpool, 1959; for Fellowship, Faculty of Radiologists, London, 1965. Watson Smith Lectr, RCP, 1962; Skinner Lectr, Faculty of Radiologists, 1965; Dyke Meml Lectr, Columbia Univ., New York, 1969; Mackenzie Davidson Meml Lectr, Brit. Inst. Radiol., 1972; Langdon Brown Lectr, RCP, 1974. Member: Council, RCP London, 1964-67; Council, RCS, 1968-73. FRSM; Hon. Fellow: American Coll. of Radiologists; Italian Neuroradiological Soc.; Brazilian Radiological Soc.; Royal Australian Coll. of Radiology; Fac. Radiol. RCSI. Hon. Member: Canadian Neurological Soc.; American Neurological Assoc.; French Radiological Soc.; Amer. Soc. of Neuroradiology. *Publications:* Atlas of Positive Contrast Myelography (jointly), 1962. Contrib. to A. Feiling's Modern Trends in Neurology; various papers in medical journals, mostly connected with neuroradiology. *Recreations:* golf, travel. *Address:* 20 Devonshire Place, W1. *T:* 01-935 4444; Springalls, Park Corner, Nettlebed, Henley-on-Thames, Oxon RG9 6DR. *T:* Nettlebed 365. *Club:* United Oxford & Cambridge University.

BULL, Dr John Prince, CBE 1973; Director of MRC Industrial Injuries and Burns Unit, since 1952; *b* 4 Jan. 1917; *s* of Robert James Bull and Ida Mary Bull; *m* 1939, Irmgard Bross; four *d*. *Educ:* Burton-on-Trent Grammar Sch.; Cambridge Univ.; Guy's Hospital. MA, MD, BCh Cantab; MRCS, FRCP. Casualty Res. Officer, Min. of Home Security, 1941; RAMC, 1942-46; Mem. Research Staff 1947, Asst Dir 1948, MRC Unit, Birmingham Accident Hosp.; Hon. Reader in Traumatology, Univ. of Birmingham. Mem., MRC, 1971-75 (Chm., MRC Environmental (Research Policy) Cttee, 1973-75). Mem., Med. Res. Soc. FRSocMed. *Publications:* contrib. scientific and med. jls. *Recreations:* bricolage, gardening. *Address:* MRC Unit, Accident Hospital, Bath Row, Birmingham B15 1NA. *T:* 021-643 7041.

BULL, Megan Patricia, (Lady Bull); Governor, Holloway Prison, since 1973; *b* Naaupoort, S Africa, 17 March 1922; *d* of Dr Thomas and Letitia Jones; *m* 1947, Sir Graham MacGregor Bull, *qv*; three *s* one *d*. *Educ:* Good Hope Seminary, Cape Town; Univ. of Cape Town. MB, ChB Cape Town 1944, DCH London 1947, MSc QUB 1961, DPM London 1970, MRCP 1974. Lectr in Physiology, Belfast Coll. of Technology, 1954-61; Med. Officer Student Health Dept, QUB, 1961-66; Prison Med. Officer, Holloway Prison, 1967-73. *Publications:* papers in various medical jls. *Address:* HM Prison, Holloway, Parkhurst Road, N7. *T:* 01-607 0231.

BULL, Oliver Richard Silvester; Headmaster, Oakham School, Rutland, since 1977; *b* 30 June 1930; *s* of Walter Haverson Bull and Margaret Bridget Bull; *m* 1956, Anne Hay Fife; one *s* four *d*. *Educ:* Rugby Sch.; Brasenose Coll. Oxford (MA). Mil. Service (21st Beds and Herts), 1949-51. Asst Master, Eton Coll., 1955-77 (Housemaster, 1968-77). *Recreations:* music, walking, reading, ball games. *Address:* Headmaster's House, Oakham School, Rutland. *T:* Oakham 2179.

BULL, Richard; *see* Bull, O. R. S.

BULL, Sir Walter (Edward Avenon), KCVO 1977 (CVO 1957); FRICS; Consultant, Vigers, chartered surveyors, since 1974; *b* 17 March 1902; *s* of Walter Bull, FRICS, and Florence Bull; *m* 1933, Moira Christian Irwin; one *s*. *Educ:* Gresham's Sch.; Aldenham. Sen. Partner, Vigers, 1942-74. Dir, City of London Building Soc., 1957-74. Mem. Council, Duchy of Lancaster, 1957-74. Pres., RICS, 1956. Liveryman, Merchant Taylors' Co. Silver Jubilee Medal, 1977. *Publications:* papers to RICS on Landlord and Tenant Acts. *Recreations:* music, golf, bowls. *Address:* The Garden House, 1 Park Crescent, Brighton BN2 3HA. *T:* Brighton 681196. *Clubs:* Naval and Military, Gresham.

BULLARD, Major-General Colin, CB 1952; CBE 1943; *b* 23 Feb. 1900; *s* of late Canon J. V. Bullard, MA; *m* 1932, Evelyn May Spencer; one *s*. *Educ:* Sedbergh; Ellesmere; Richmond, Yorks; Univ. of Liverpool (BEng). Engineer; apprenticeship, Cammell Laird, Birkenhead. RAOC and REME, 1925-53; retired, 1953. Principal, Royal Technical Coll. of East Africa, 1953-57. ADC to the King during 1950; Maj.-Gen., 1950. CEng; FIMechE; FIEE. *Address:* 4 Meadsway, Staveley Road, Eastbourne, E Sussex. *T:* Eastbourne 26688.

BULLARD, Denys Gradwell; Member, Anglian Water Authority and Chairman, Broads Committee, since 1974; *b* 15 Aug. 1912; *s* of John Henry Bullard; *m* 1970, Diana Patricia Cox; one *s*; one *d*. *Educ:* Wisbech Grammar Sch.; Cambridge Univ. Farmer. Broadcaster on agricultural matters both at home and overseas. MP (C) SW Div. of Norfolk, 1951-55; MP (C) King's Lynn, 1959-64. PPS: to Financial Sec., Treasury, 1955; to Min. of Housing and Local Govt, 1959-64. *Address:* Elm House, Elm, Wisbech, Cambs. *T:* Wisbech 21. *Club:* Farmers'.

BULLARD, Sir Edward (Crisp), Kt 1953; FRS 1941; MA, PhD, ScD; Fellow of Churchill College, Cambridge, since 1960; Professor, University of California at San Diego, since 1963; *b* 21 Sept. 1907; *s* of Edward John Bullard and Eleanor Howes Crisp; *m* 1st, 1931, Margaret Ellen Thomas; four *d*; 2nd, 1974, Mrs Ursula Curnow, *d* of late Dr E. J. Cooke, Christchurch, NZ, and Mrs E. J. Cooke. *Educ:* Repton; Clare Coll., Cambridge. Research in Physics, 1929-31; Geophysics, 1931-; Demonstrator in Geodesy at Cambridge Univ., 1931-35; Smithson Research Fellow of Royal Society, 1936-43; Experimental Officer HMS Vernon and Admiralty, 1939-45; Asst Dir of Naval Operational Research, 1944-45; Fellow of Clare, 1943-48 and 1956-60; Reader in Experimental Geophysics at Cambridge Univ., 1945-48; Prof. of Physics at Univ. of Toronto, 1948-49; Director National Physical Laboratory, 1950-55; Fellow of Caius Coll., Cambridge, 1956; Asst Dir of Research, Cambridge Univ., 1956-60; Reader in Geophysics, 1960-64, Prof., 1964-74. Centennial Prof., Univ. of Toronto, 1967; Hitchcock Prof., Univ. of

California, Berkeley, 1975. Formerly Dir IBM UK. Foreign Corresp. Geol. Soc. Amer., 1952; Foreign Hon. Mem. Amer. Acad. Arts and Sci., 1954; Foreign Assoc. US Nat. Acad. Sci., 1959; Foreign Mem., Amer. Philos. Soc., 1969. Segdwick Prize, 1936; Hughes Medal of Royal Soc., 1953; Chree Medal of Physics Soc., 1956; Day Medal of Geol. Soc. Amer., 1959; Gold Medal, Royal Astronomical Soc., 1965; Agassiz Medal, US Nat. Acad. of Sci., 1965; Wollaston Medal of Geol. Soc. of London, 1967; Bakerian Lecturer of the Royal Society, 1967; Vetlesen Prize, 1968; Bowie Medal, Amer. Geophysical Union, 1975; Royal Medal of Royal Soc., 1975. *Publications:* scientific papers. *Address:* IGPP AO25, University of California, La Jolla, Calif 92093, USA. *Club:* Athenæum.

BULLARD, Giles Lionel; HM Diplomatic Service Inspectorate, since 1974; *b* 24 Aug. 1926; 2nd *s* of late Sir Reader Bullard and late Miriam (*née* Smith); *m* 1952, Hilary Chadwick Brooks; two *s* two *d*. *Educ:* Blundell's Sch.; Balliol Coll., Oxford. Army service, 1944-48; Oxford Univ., 1948-51 (2nd cl. hons Modern History, Capt. OURFC); H. Clarkson & Co. Ltd, Shipping and Insurance Brokers, 1952-55; HM Foreign (later Diplomatic) Service, 1955; 3rd Sec., Bucharest, 1957; 2nd Sec., Brussels, 1958; 1st Sec., Panama City, 1960; FO, 1964; DSAO, 1965; Head of Chancery, Bangkok, 1967; Counsellor and Head of Chancery, Islamabad, 1969; FCO Fellow, Centre of South Asian Studies, Cambridge, 1973. *Address:* The Manor House, West Hendred, Wantage, Oxon. *T:* East Hendred 373.

See also J. L. Bullard.

BULLARD, Julian Leonard, CMG 1975; HM Diplomatic Service; Minister, Bonn, since 1975; *b* 8 March 1928; *s* of late Sir Reader Bullard, KCB, KCMG, CIE, and late Miriam, *d* of late A. L. Smith, Master of Balliol Coll., Oxford; *m* 1954, Margaret Stephens; two *s* two *d*. *Educ:* Rugby; Magdalen Coll., Oxford. Fellow of All Souls Coll., Oxford, 1950-57; Army, 1950-52; HM Diplomatic Service, 1953-: served at: FO, 1953-54; Vienna, 1954-56; Amman, 1956-59; FO, 1960-63; Bonn, 1963-66; Moscow, 1966-68; Dubai, 1968-70; Head of E European and Soviet Dept, FCO, 1971-75. *Address:* Vine Cottage, Filkins, near Lechlade, Glos. *T:* Filkins 304.

See also G. L. Bullard.

BULLEN, Air Vice-Marshal Reginald, CB 1975; GM 1945; MA; Senior Bursar and Fellow, Gonville and Caius College, Cambridge, since 1976; *b* 19 Oct. 1920; *s* of Henry Arthur Bullen and Alice May Bullen; *m* 1952, Christiane (*née* Phillips); one *s* one *d*. *Educ:* Grocers' Company School. 39 Sqdn RAF, 458 Sqdn RAAF, 1942-44; Air Min., 1945-50; RAF Coll. Cranwell, 1952-54; psa 1955; Exchange USAF, Washington, DC, 1956-58; RAF Staff Coll., Bracknell, 1959-61; Admin. Staff Coll., Henley, 1962; PSO to Chief of Air Staff, 1962-64; NATO Defence Coll., 1965; HQ Allied Forces Central Europe, 1965-68; Dir of Personnel, MoD, 1968-69; idc 1970; Dep. AO i/c Admin, HQ Maintenance Comd, 1971; AOA Training Comd, 1972-75. MA Cantab, 1975. MBIM, 1971. *Publications:* various articles. *Recreations:* walking, reading, boating. *Address:* Gonville and Caius College, Cambridge; c/o Lloyds Bank Ltd, Cox's & King's Branch, 6 Pall Mall, SW1Y 5NH. *Clubs:* Athenæum, Royal Air Force.

BULLEN, Dr William Alexander; Chairman since 1975 and Managing Director, 1967-77, Thomas Borthwick & Sons Ltd; Chairman: Whitburgh Investments Ltd, since 1976; Matthews Holdings, since 1977; Director, National Bank of New Zealand, since 1977; *s* of Francis Lisle Bullen and Amelia Morgan; *m* 1st, 1949, Phyllis (marr. diss. 1955), *d* of George Leeson; three *d*; 2nd, 1956, Mary, *d* of Leigh Crutchley; two step *s*. *Educ:* Merchant Taylors' Sch., Crosby; London Hosp. Med. Coll. MRCS, LRCP, MRCGP. Royal Tank Regt, UK and Middle East, 1939-45 (Hon. Major). Med. Dir, Boehringer Pfizer, 1957, Sales Man. 1958; Pres., Pfizer Canada, 1962; Gen. Man., Pfizer Consumer Opns UK, 1964-66; Chm., Coty (England), 1965; Man. Dir, Scribbans Kemp, 1966; Dep. Chm., Borthwicks, 1974; Chm., Freshbake Foods, 1975 (Dep. Chm. 1973). Liveryman, Butchers' Co.; Freeman, City of London. *Publication:* paper on acute heart failure in London Hosp. Gazette. *Recreations:* sailing, reading, music. *Address:* Priory House, St John's Lane, EC1. *T:* 01-253 8661. *Club:* Royal Thames Yacht.

BULLER; *see* Manningham-Buller, family name of Viscount Dilhorne.

BULLER; *see* Yarde-Buller, family name of Baron Churston.

BULLER, Prof. Arthur John, ERD 1969; FRCP; Professor of Physiology since 1965, and Dean, Faculty of Medicine, since 1976, University of Bristol; Honorary Consultant in Clinical

Physiology, Bristol District Hospital (T); *b* 16 Oct. 1923; *s* of Thomas Alfred Buller and Edith May Buller (*née* Wager); *m* 1946, Helena Joan (*née* Pearson); one *s* one *d* (and one *d* decd). *Educ:* Duke of York's Royal Military Sch., Dover; St Thomas's Hosp. Med. Sch. (MB, BS); BSc; FRCP 1976. Kitchener Scholar, 1941-45; Lectr in Physiology, St Thomas' Hosp., 1946-49. Major, RAMC (Specialist in Physiology; Jt Sec., Military Personnel Research Cttee), 1949-53. Lectr in Medicine, St Thomas' Hosp., 1953-57. Royal Society Commonwealth Fellow, Canberra, Aust., 1958-59. Reader in Physiology, King's Coll., London, 1961-65; Gresham Prof. of Physic 1963-65; Visiting Prof., Monash Univ., Aust., 1972. Mem., Avon Health Authority (T), 1974-; Mem., MRC, 1975-; Chm., Neurosciences and Mental Health Bd, MRC, 1975-77. *Publications:* contribs to books and various jls on normal and abnormal physiology. *Recreations:* clarets and conversation. *Address:* Flat 8, Seawalls, Seawalls Road, Bristol BS9 1PG. *T:* Bristol 683225. *Club:* Athenæum.

BULLERWELL, Dr William, FRS 1972; FRSE 1973; Deputy Director, Institute of Geological Sciences, since 1976 (Chief Geophysicist (Assistant Director), 1967-76); *b* Newcastle-on-Tyne, 27 Sept. 1916; *s* of John William Bullerwell and Alice Bullerwell (*née* Wilkinson); *m* 1942, Eileen Nora Field; no *c*. *Educ:* Rutherford Coll., Newcastle-on-Tyne; Armstrong Coll. (later King's Coll.), Newcastle-on-Tyne (Univ. of Durham). BSc (Physics) 1937, BSc (Geology) 1939, PhD (Mining Geophysics) 1951. Served War, 1940-46: with Min. of Supply, RAOC and REME. Geological Survey of Gt Britain: Geologist, 1946; Chief Geophysicist, 1962. *Publications:* scientific papers on geophysical exploration and geological structure of UK land mass and continental shelf. *Recreations:* music, travel. *Address:* Institute of Geological Sciences, Exhibition Road, SW7 2DE. *T:* 01-589 3444.

BULLEY, Rt. Rev. Sydney Cyril; *b* 12 June 1907; 2nd *s* of late Jethro Bulley, Newton Abbot, Devon; unmarried. *Educ:* Newton Abbot Grammar Sch.; Univ. of Durham. BA 1932; MA 1936; DipTh 1933; Van Mildert Scholar, Univ. of Durham, 1932; Hon. DD Dunelm 1972. Deacon, 1933; priest, 1934; Curate of Newark Parish Church, 1933-42; Director of Religious Education, Diocese of Southwell, 1936-42; Vicar of St Anne's, Worksop, 1942-46; Chaplain to High Sheriff of Notts, 1943; Hon. Canon of Southwell Minster, 1945; Vicar and Rural Dean of Mansfield, 1946-51; Proctor in Convocation of York, 1945-51; Vicar of Ambleside with Rydal, 1951-59; Archdeacon of Westmorland and Dir Religious Education, Diocese Carlisle, 1951-58; Archdeacon of Westmorland and Furness, 1959-65; Suffragan Bishop of Penrith, 1959-66; Hon. Canon of Carlisle Cathedral, 1951-66; Examining Chaplain to the Bishop of Carlisle, 1952-66; Bishop of Carlisle, 1966-72; Chaplain and Tutor, All Saints' Coll., Bathurst, NSW, 1973-74. Chaplain to the Queen, 1955-59. Chairman: Southwell Diocese Education Cttee, 1942-51; Worksop Youth Cttee, 1943-45; Mansfield Youth Cttee, 1947-48; Member: Southwell Diocese Board of Finance, 1942-51; Central Council of the Church for Education, 1951-54; Westmorland Education Cttee, 1951-64. Gov. Derby Training Coll., 1938-51, Ripon Training Coll., 1953-58, Lancaster Coll. of Education, 1963-69; Chairman of Governing Body: Casterton Sch., 1962-72; St Chad's Coll., Durham Univ., 1969. *Address:* The Manor, Longcot, Faringdon, Oxon.

BULLOCK, family name of **Baron Bullock**.

BULLOCK, Baron *cr* 1976 (Life Peer), of Leafield, Oxon; **Alan Louis Charles Bullock**, Kt 1972; FBA 1967; Master of St Catherine's College, Oxford, since 1960; Vice-Chancellor, Oxford University, 1969-73; *b* 13 Dec. 1914; *s* of Frank Allen Bullock; *m* 1940, Hilda Yates, *d* of Edwin Handy, Bradford; three *s* one *d* (and one *d* decd). *Educ:* Bradford Grammar Sch.; Wadham Coll., Oxford (Scholar). MA; 1st Class Lit Hum, 1936; 1st Class, Modern Hist., 1938. DLitt Oxon, 1969. Fellow, Dean and Tutor in Modern Hist., New Coll., 1945-52; Censor of St Catherine's Soc., Oxford, 1952-62; Chairman: Research Cttee of RIIA; Nat. Advisory Council on the Training and Supply of Teachers, 1963-65; Schools Council, 1966-69; Cttee on Reading and Other Uses of English Language, 1972-74 (Report, A Language for Life, published 1975); Trustees, Tate Gallery; Friends of Ashmolean Museum; Cttee of Enquiry on Industrial Democracy, 1976 (Report publ. 1977); Member: Arts Council of Great Britain, 1961-64; SSRC, 1966; Adv. Council on Public Records, 1965-77; Organising Cttee for the British Library, 1971-72. Trustee: Aspen Inst.; The Observer, 1957-69. Dir, The Observer, 1977-. Raleigh Lectr, British Acad., 1967; Stevenson Meml Lectr, LSE, 1970; Leslie Stephen Lectr, Cambridge, 1976. Hon. Fellow: Merton Coll.; Wadham Coll.; Linacre Coll.; Wolfson Coll. For. Mem., Amer. Acad. Arts and Sciences, 1972. Hon. Dr Univ. Aix-Marseilles; Hon. DLitt: Bradford; Reading;

Open 1976. Chevalier Légion d'Honneur, 1970. *Publications:* Hitler, A Study in Tyranny, 1952 (rev. edn 1964); The Liberal Tradition, 1956; The Life and Times of Ernest Bevin, Vol. I, 1960, Vol. II, 1967; (ed) The Twentieth Century, 1971; (ed with Oliver Stallybrass) Dictionary of Modern Thought. Gen. Editor (with F. W. Deakin) of The Oxford History of Modern Europe. *Address:* Master's Lodgings, St Catherine's College, Oxford. *T:* Oxford 49541.

BULLOCK, Edward Anthony Watson; HM Diplomatic Service; HM Consul-General, Marseilles, since 1977; *b* 27 Aug. 1926; *yr s* of the late Sir Christopher Bullock, KCB, CBE, and late Lady Bullock (*née* Barbara May Lupton); *m* 1953, Jenifer Myrtle, *e d* of late Sir Richmond Palmer, KCMG, and late Lady Palmer (*née* Margaret Isabel Abel Smith); two *s* one *d*. *Educ:* Rugby Sch. (Scholar); Trinity Coll., Cambridge (Exhibitioner). HM Forces, 1944-47; Joined Foreign Service, 1950; served: FO, 1950-52; Bucharest, 1952-54; Brussels, 1955-58; FO, 1958-61; La Paz, 1961-65; ODM, 1965-67; FCO, 1967-69; Havana, 1969-72; HM Treasury, 1972-74; Head of Pacific Dependent Territories Dept, FCO, 1974-77. *Address:* c/o National Westminster Bank Ltd., 36 St James's Street, SW1. *Clubs:* United Oxford & Cambridge University; Union (Cambridge). *See also R . H . W . Bullock .*

BULLOCK, Sir Ernest, Kt 1951; CVO 1937; MusD (Dunelm); Hon. LLD (Glasgow, 1955); FRCM; FRCO; FRSCM; FRSAMD; Hon. RAM; Director of the Royal College of Music, 1953-60; *b* 15 Sept. 1890; *y s* of late Thos Bullock, Wigan, Lancs; *m* 1919, Margery, *d* of late George H. Newborn, Epworth, Lincolnshire; two *s* one *d*. *Educ:* Wigan Grammar Sch.; privately; musically under Sir E. C. Bairstow, MusD, at Leeds Parish Church; Asst Organist, Leeds Parish Church, and Organist of St Mary, Micklefield and Adel Church, 1906-12; Sub-organist of Manchester Cathedral, 1912-15; served in HM Forces as Captain and Adjutant, 1915-19; Organist of St Michael's Coll., Tenbury, 1919; of Exeter Cathedral, 1919-28; of Westminster Abbey, 1928-41. Joint Musical Director and Conductor of the Coronation Service, 1937. Professor of Music, Glasgow Univ. and Principal Royal Scottish Academy of Music and Drama, Glasgow, 1941-52. Pres. Incorporated Assoc. of Organists, 1946-48; Pres. Incorporated Soc. of Musicians, 1947; Pres. Royal Coll. of Organists, 1951-52; Pres. Union of Graduates in Music, 1947-48. *Publications:* Church and organ music, songs, part-songs, etc. *Address:* Welby Cottage, Long Crendon, Aylesbury, Bucks.

BULLOCK, Hugh, Hon. GBE 1976 (Hon. KBE 1957; Hon. OBE 1946); FRSA 1958; Chairman and Chief Executive Officer, Calvin Bullock Ltd; *b* 2 June 1898; *s* of Calvin Bullock and Alice Katherine (*née* Mallory); *m* 1933, Marie Leontine Graves; two *d*. *Educ:* Hotchkiss Sch.; Williams Coll. (BA). Investment banker since 1921; President and Director: Calvin Bullock, Ltd, 1944-66; Bullock Fund, Ltd; Canadian Fund, Inc.; Canadian Investment Fund, Ltd; Dividend Shares, Inc.; Chairman and Director: Carriers & General Corp.; Nation-Wide Securities Co.; US Electric Light & Power Shares, Inc. Civilian Aide to Sec. of the Army, for First Army Area, United States, 1952-53 (US Army Certificate of Appreciation). Trustee: Roosevelt Hospital; Estate and Property of Diocesan Convention of New York; Williams Coll., 1960-68. President: Pilgrims of US; Calvin Bullock Forum. Member Exec. Cttee, Marshall Scholarship Regional Cttee, 1955-58. Member: Amer. Legion; Academy of Political Science; Amer. Museum of Nat. History; Acad. of Amer. Poets (Dir.); Assoc. Ex-mems Squadron A (Gov. 1945-50); Council on Foreign Relations; Ends of the Earth; English-Speaking Union; Foreign Policy Assoc.; Investment Bankers Assoc. of Amer. (Gov. 1953-55); New England Soc.; Nat. Inst. of Social Sciences (Pres. 1950-53); Newcomen Soc.; St George's Soc. Hon. LLD; Hamilton Coll., 1954; Williams Coll., 1957. 2nd Lieut Infantry, European War, 1914-18; Lieut-Col, War of 1939-45 (US Army Commendation Ribbon). Distinguished Citizens' Award, Denver, 1958; Exceptional Service Award, Dept of Air Force, 1961; US Navy Distinguished Public Service Award, 1972. Assoc. KStJ 1961, and Vice-Pres. Amer. Society. Knight Comdr, Royal Order of George I (Greece), 1964. Is an Episcopalian. *Publication:* The Story of Investment Companies, 1959. *Address:* (office) 33rd Floor, 1 Wall Street, New York, NY 10005. *T:* Bowling Green 9-8800; (home) 1030 Fifth Avenue, New York, NY 10028. *T:* Trafalgar 9-5858. *Clubs:* White's (London); Bond, Century, Racquet and Tennis, Recess, River, Union, Williams, Church, New York Yacht (New York); Denver County (Denver, Colo.); Chevy Chase, Metropolitan (Washington); Edgartown Yacht (Cdre) (Mass); West Side Tennis (Forest Hills, NY); Mount Royal (Montreal).

BULLOCK, Prof. Kenneth, PhD, MSc, FRIC, MChemA, FPS; Professor of Pharmacy, Manchester University, 1955-70,

Emeritus 1970; *b* 27 Dec. 1901; *s* of late James William Bullock, Wigan, Lancashire; *m* 1926, Winifred Mary, *d* of late Rev. F. Ives Cater. *Educ:* Wigan Grammar Sch.; Manchester Univ. Research and Technical Chemist, 1925-32; joined teaching staff of Pharmacy Dept, Manchester Univ., 1932; Lecturer, 1937; Senior Lecturer, 1946; Reader, 1950. Chairman, British Pharmaceutical Conf., 1956. Formerly Examiner for Univs of Dublin, London, Nottingham, and Manchester and for Pharmaceutical Socs of Great Britain and Ireland. *Publications:* original contributions to science, mainly in Journal of Pharmacy and Pharmacology. *Recreations:* gardening and biology. *Address:* 39 Knutsford Road, Wilmslow, Cheshire SK9 6JB. *T:* Wilmslow 22892.

BULLOCK, Richard Henry Watson, CB 1971; Deputy Secretary, Department of Industry, since 1974 (Department of Trade and Industry, 1970-74); *b* 12 Nov. 1920; *er s* of late Sir Christopher Bullock, KCB, CBE; *m* 1946, Beryl Haddan, *o d* of late Haddan J. Markes, formerly Malay Civil Service; one *s* one *d. Educ:* Rugby Sch. (Scholar); Trinity Coll., Cambridge (Scholar). Joined 102 OCTU (Westminster Dragoons), Nov. 1940; Commnd Westminster Dragoons, (2nd County of London Yeo.), 1941; served in England, NW Europe (D-day), Italy, Germany, 1941-45; Instructor, Armoured Corps Officers' Training Sch., India, 1945-46; demobilized 1947, rank of Major. Established in Home Civil Service by Reconstruction Competition; joined Min. of Supply as Asst Principal, 1947; Principal, 1949; Asst Sec., 1956; on loan to War Office, 1960-61; Ministry of Aviation, 1961-64; Under-Sec., 1963; Min. of Technology, 1964-70, Head of Space Div., 1969-70, Dep. Sec., 1970. Mem., BOTB, 1975-. *Recreations:* fly-fishing, hockey (Pres. Dulwich Hockey Club, 1962-), watching cricket. *Address:* 17 Deodar Road, SW15 2NP. *T:* 01-788 5378. *Clubs:* Army and Navy, MCC, Hurlingham; Union (Cambridge).
See also E . A . W . Bullock .

BULLOUGH, Geoffrey, MA; FBA 1966; Emeritus Professor, University of London; *b* 27 Jan. 1901; *s* of James Arthur Bullough and Elizabeth Ford; *m* 1928, Doris Margaret Wall; one *s* one *d. Educ:* Stand Grammar Sch., Whitefield; Manchester Univ. BA 1922, MA 1923 (Vict.), Teachers' Diploma 1923, Gissing Prize 1921, Withers Prize in Education 1923, John Bright Fellowship in English Literature, 1923-24; studied in Italy. Master, Grammar Sch. of Queen Elizabeth in Tamworth, 1924-26; Asst Lecturer in English Literature, Manchester Univ., 1926-29; Lecturer, Edinburgh Univ., 1929-33; Professor of English Literature, Univ. of Sheffield, 1933-46; Professor of English Language and Literature, KCL, 1946-68. Vice-Chm., Sheffield Repertory Co., 1938-46; Governor of Chelsea Coll. of Science and Technology, 1952-68. FKC 1964; Hon. Fellow, Chelsea Coll., 1973. Hon. LittD: Manchester, 1969; Glasgow, 1970; Alfred Univ., NY, 1974. *Publications:* Philosophical Poems of Henry More, 1931; The Oxford Book of Seventeenth-Century Verse (with Sir H. J. C. Grierson), 1934; The Trend of Modern Poetry, 1934, 1949; Poems and Dramas of Fulke Greville, 1939; ed (with C. L. Wrenn) English Studies Today, 1951; ed Essays and Studies, 1953; Narrative and Dramatic Sources of Shakespeare, 1957-75; Milton's Dramatic Poems (with D. M. B.), 1958; Mirror of Minds, 1962; reviews and articles. *Recreations:* music, painting, travel. *Address:* 182 Mayfield Road, Edinburgh EH9 3AX.

BULLOUGH, Prof. William Sydney, PhD, DSc Leeds; Professor of Zoology, Birkbeck College, University of London, since 1952; *b* 6 April 1914; *o s* of Rev. Frederick Sydney Bullough and Letitia Anne Cooper, both of Leeds; *m* 1942, Dr Helena F. Gibbs (*d* 1975), Wellington, NZ; one *s* one *d. Educ:* William Hulme Grammar Sch., Manchester; Grammar Sch., Leeds; Univ. of Leeds. Lecturer in Zoology, Univ. of Leeds, 1937-44; McGill Univ., Montreal, 1944-46; Sorby Fellow of Royal Society of London, 1946-51; Research Fellow of British Empire Cancer Campaign, 1951-52; Hon. Fellow, Soc. for Investigative Dermatology (US). *Publications:* Practical Invertebrate Anatomy, 1950; Vertebrate Sexual Cycles, 1951; (for children) Introducing Animals, 1953; Introducing Animals-with-Backbones, 1954; Introducing Man, 1958; The Evolution of Differentiation, 1967; scientific papers on vertebrate reproductive cycles, hormones, and chalones published in a variety of journals. *Recreation:* gardening. *Address:* Oktober, Uplands Road, Kenley, Surrey. *T:* 01-660 9764.

BULLUS, Wing Comdr Sir Eric (Edward), Kt 1964; journalist; *b* 20 Nov. 1906; 2nd *s* of Thomas Bullus, Leeds; *m* 1949, Joan Evelyn, *er d* of H. M. Denny; two *d. Educ:* Leeds Modern Sch.; Univ. of Leeds. Commnd RAFVR Aug. 1940; served War of 1939-45; Air Min. War Room, 1940-43; joined Lord Louis Mountbatten's staff in SE Asia, 1943; Wing Comdr, 1944; served India, Burma and Ceylon; demobilized, 1945. Journalist

Yorkshire Post, Leeds and London, 1923-46. Mem. Leeds City Council, 1930-40; Sec., London Municipal Soc., 1947-50; Mem., Harrow UDC, 1947-50; Vice-Pres. Assoc. of Municipal Corps, 1953. MP (C) Wembley N, 1950-Feb. 1974; PPS to Secretary for Overseas Trade, and to Minister of State, 1953-56, to Minister of Aviation, 1960-62, to Secretary of State for Defence, 1962-64. FRGS, 1947; Fellow Royal Statistical Society, 1949. Foundation Mem. of Brotherton Collection Cttee of Univ. of Leeds, 1935; Member: Archdeaconry Council of Delhi, 1944; Management Board, Cambridge Mission to Delhi, 1954; House of Laity, Church Assembly, 1960. Ripon Diocesan Reader, 1929; London Diocesan Reader, 1947; St Alban's Diocesan Reader, 1960; Canterbury Diocesan Reader, 1967; Central Readers' Board, 1960; London Readers' Board, 1954; Council Westfield Coll., Univ. of London. Pres., Soc. of Yorkshiremen in London, 1969-70. *Publications:* History of Leeds Modern School, 1931; History of Church in Delhi, 1944; History of Lords and Commons Cricket, 1959. *Recreations:* played Headingley RU Football Club 15 years and Yorkshire Amateurs Assoc. Football Club; cricket and swimming (bronze and silver medallions). *Address:* Westway, Herne Bay, Kent. *Clubs:* Constitutional, MCC.

BULMER, Esmond; *see* Bulmer, J. E.

BULMER, Dr Gerald; Rector of Liverpool Polytechnic, since April 1970; *b* 17 Nov. 1920; *s* of Edward and Alice Bulmer; *m* 1943, Greta Lucy Parkes, MA; two *d. Educ:* Nunthorpe Sch., York; Selwyn Coll., Cambridge. BA 1941; PhD 1944; MA 1945; FRIC 1955. Asst Master, King's Sch., Canterbury, 1945-49; Sen. Lecturer, Woolwich Polytechnic, 1949-53; Head of Dept of Science and Metallurgy, Constantine Technical Coll., Middlesbrough, 1954-57; Vice-Principal, Bolton Technical Coll., 1958-59; Principal, West Ham Coll. of Technology, 1959-64; Dir, Robert Gordon's Inst. of Technology, Aberdeen, 1965-70. Mem. Council CNAA, 1967-. Freeman City of York, 1952. *Publications:* papers on organic sulphur compounds in Jl Chem. Soc. and Nature. *Address:* Liverpool Polytechnic, Liverpool; 11 Capilano Park, Winifred Lane, Aughton, Ormskirk, Lancs.

BULMER, (James) Esmond; MP (C) Kidderminster, since Feb. 1974; *b* 19 May 1935; *e s* of late Edward Bulmer and Margaret Rye; *m* 1959, Morella Kearton; three *s* one *d. Educ:* Rugby; King's Coll., Cambridge (BA); and abroad. Commissioned Scots Guards, 1954; University, 1956-59. Training in Industry, 1959-60; H. P. Bulmer Ltd, 1960-74 (Director, 1962-). Chairman: Hereford Div. Conservative Assoc., 1966-70; Hereford Diocesan Bd of Finance, 1968-72. *Recreations:* gardening, fishing. *Address:* The Old Rectory, Pudleston, Leominster, Herefordshire HR6 0RA. *T:* Steensbridge 234. *Club:* Boodle's.

BULMER-THOMAS, Ivor, FSA 1970; writer; Chairman, Ancient Monuments Society; Chairman, Faith Press; Hon. Director, Friends of Friendless Churches; Vice-President, Church Union; *b* 30 Nov. 1905; *s* of late A. E. Thomas, Cwmbran, Newport, Mon.; *m* 1st, 1932, Dilys (*d* 1938), *d* of late Dr W. Llewelyn Jones, Merthyr Tydfil; one *s*; 2nd, 1940, Margaret Joan, *d* of late E. F. Bulmer, Adam's Hill, Hereford; one *s* two *d.* Assumed additional surname Bulmer by deed poll, 1952. *Educ:* West Monmouth Sch., Pontypool; Scholar of St John's and Senior Demy of Magdalen Coll., Oxford. 1st Class Math. Mods, 1925; 1st Class Lit. Hum., 1928; Liddon Student, 1928; Ellerton Essayist, 1929; Junior Denyer and Johnson Scholar, 1930; MA 1937; represented Oxford against Cambridge at Cross-country Running, 1925-27, and Athletics, 1926-28, winning Three Miles in 1927; Welsh International Cross-country Runner, 1926; Gladstone Research Student at St Deiniol's Library, Hawarden, 1929-30; on editorial staff of Times, 1930-37; chief leader writer to News Chronicle, 1937-39; acting deputy editor, Daily Telegraph, 1953-54. Served War of 1939-45 with Royal Fusiliers (Fusilier), 1939-40, and Royal Norfolk Regt (Captain, 1941), 1940-42, 1945. Contested (Lab) Spen Valley div., 1935; MP Keighley, 1942-50 (Lab 1942-48; C 1949-50); contested Newport, Mon (C), 1950. Parliamentary Secretary, Ministry of Civil Aviation, 1945-46; Parliamentary Under-Sec. of State for the Colonies, 1946-47. Delegate to Gen. Assembly, UN, 1946; first UK Mem., Trusteeship Council, 1947. Mem. of the House of Laity of the Church Assembly, 1950-70, of General Synod, 1970-. Lately Chm., Executive Cttee, Historic Churches Preservation Trust; Chm., Redundant Churches Fund, 1969-76. Stella della Solidarietà Italiana, 1948. *Publications:* Coal in the New Era, 1934; Gladstone of Hawarden, 1936; Top Sawyer, a biography of David Davies of Llandinam, 1938; Greek Mathematics (Loeb Library), 1939-42; Warfare by Words, 1942; The Problem of Italy, 1946; The Socialist Tragedy, 1949;(ed) E. J. Webb, The Names of the Stars, 1952; The Party System in Great Britain, 1953; The Growth of the British Party System, 1965; (ed) St Paul, Teacher and

Traveller, 1975; contrib. to Dictionary of Scientific Biography. *Address:* 12 Edwardes Square, W8 6HG. *T:* 01-602 6267; Old School House, Farnborough, Berks; Ty'n Mynydd, Rhoscolyn, Anglesey. *Clubs:* Athenæum; Vincent's (Oxford).

BULPITT, Cecil Arthur Charles; Chairman: Rest Assured Ltd, since 1971; Pretty Polly Ltd, since 1973; Gascoigne, Gush & Dent Ltd, since 1976; Tilling Construction Services Ltd, since 1976; Director, Thomas Tilling Ltd, since 1973; *b* 6 Feb. 1919; *s* of A. E. Bulpitt; *m* 1943, Joyce Mary Bloomfield; one *s* one *d*. *Educ:* Spring Grove Sch., London; Regent Street Polytechnic. Territorial Army, to rank of Staff Capt., RA, 1937-45. Carreras Ltd: joined firm, 1935; Gen. Manager, 1960; Asst Managing Dir, 1962; Dep. Chm. and Chief Exec., 1968; Chm. 1969-70. MIPM, 1955; FBIM, 1963; Vice-Chm., BIM, 1971-. *Recreations:* fishing, climbing, reading, travelling. *Address:* 3 Potters Cross, Iver Heath, Bucks. *T:* Iver Heath 4571. *Clubs:* Travellers', Lansdowne; Stoke Poges Golf.

BULTEEL, Christopher Harris, MC 1943; Headmaster, Ardingly College, since 1962; *b* 29 July 1921; *er s* of late Major Walter Bulteel and Constance (*née* Gaunt), Charlestown, Cornwall; *m* 1958, Jennifer Anne, *d* of late Col K. E. Previté, OBE and of Frances (*née* Capper), Hindgaston, Marnhull, Dorset; one *s* two *d*. *Educ:* Wellington Coll.; Merton Coll., Oxford. Served War with Coldstream Guards, 1940-46 (MC). Assistant Master at Wellington Coll., 1949-61; Head of history dept, 1959-61. Hon. Sec., Wellington Coll. Mission, 1959-61. *Recreations:* natural history, sailing. *Address:* Ardingly College, Haywards Heath, W Sussex. *T:* Ardingly 892330.

BUMBRY, Grace; opera singer and concert singer; *b* 4 Jan. 1937. *Educ:* Boston Univ.; Northwestern Univ.; Music Academy of the West (under Lotte Lehmann). Debut: Paris Opera, 1960; Vienna State Opera, 1963; Salzburg Festival, 1964; Metropolitan Opera, 1965; La Scala, 1966. Appearances also include: Bayreuth Festival, 1961, 1962, 1963; Royal Opera Covent Garden, London, 1963, 1968, 1970, 1971, 1973, 1974, 1976, 1977. Film, Carmen, 1968. Richard Wagner Medal, 1963. Hon. Dr of Humanities, St Louis Univ., 1968; Hon. doctorates: Rust Coll., Holly Spring, Miss; Rockhurst Coll., Kansas City. Has made numerous recordings. *Recreations:* mountain climbing, tennis, sewing, flying, body building, psychology, entertaining. *Address:* c/o Columbia Artists Management, attention Amy Sperling, 165 West 57th Street, New York, NY 10019, USA; Villa Arasio, CH 6926 Montagnola, Switzerland.

BUMSTEAD, Kenneth, CBE 1952; CVO 1958; *b* 28 April 1908; *s* of Ernest and Nellie Bumstead; *m* 1940, Diana, *e d* of Archibald Smollett Campbell; three *s*. *Educ:* Wallasey Grammar Sch.; Emmanuel Coll., Cambridge. Entered China Consular Service, 1931; served Peking, Tsingtao, Canton, Chungking, Shanghai, 1932-42 (Consul 1939); Madagascar, 1943; London, 1944; Chicago, 1945-48; Shanghai, 1949-52 (Consul-General, 1950); Seattle, 1953-56; Consul-General, Rotterdam, 1957-61; retired, 1961. Commander, Order of Oranje Nassau. *Address:* 4 Perry Way, Hilland, Headley, Hants GU35 8NE.

BUNBURY; *see* McClintock-Bunbury, family name of Baron Rathdonnell.

BUNBURY, Bishop of, since 1977; **Rt. Rev. Arthur Stanley Goldsworthy;** *b* 18 Feb. 1926; *s* of Arthur and Doris Irene Goldsworthy; *m* 1952, Gwen Elizabeth Reeves; one *s* one *d*. *Educ:* Dandenong High School, Vic; St Columb's Theological Coll., Wangaratta. Deacon 1951, priest 1952; Curate of Wodonga, in charge of Bethanga, 1951-52; Priest of Chiltern, 1952; Kensington, Melbourne, 1955; Yarrawonga, Wangaratta, 1959; Shepparton (and Archdeacon), 1972; Parish Priest of Wodonga, and Archdeacon of Diocese of Wangaratta, 1977. Chaplain to Community of the Sisters of the Church, 1956-77. *Recreations:* music, bush walking. *Address:* Bishopscourt, Bunbury, WA 6230, Australia. *T:* 097.21-2163.

BUNBURY, Brig. Francis Ramsay St Pierre, CBE 1958; DSO 1945, Bar 1953; *b* 16 June 1910; *s* of late Lt-Col Gerald Bruce St Pierre Bunbury, Indian Army, and Frances Mary Olivia (*née* Dixon); *m* 1933, Elizabeth Pamela Somers (*née* Liscombe) (*d* 1969); one *s* one *d*. *Educ:* Rugby and Sandhurst. Commissioned into The Duke of Wellington's Regiment, 1930; Staff Coll., 1941; commanded 1st Bn, The King's Own Royal Regt, Italian Campaign, 1944-45 (despatches, DSO); commanded 1st Bn The Duke of Wellington's Regt, 1951-54, Germany, Korea (Bar to DSO), Gibraltar; AAG, War Office, 1954-56; commanded 50 Independent Infantry Brigade, Cyprus, 1956-59 (despatches, CBE). Dep. Adjt-Gen., Rhine Army, 1959-61; retired 1962. *Address:* 16 Lancaster Road, Wimbledon, SW19.

BUNBURY, Sir (John) William Napier, 12th Bt, *cr* 1681; *b* 3 July 1915; *s* of Sir Charles H. N. Bunbury, 11th Bt, and Katherine (*d* 1965), *d* of H. E. Reid; *S* father, 1963; *m* 1940, Pamela, *er d* of late T. Sutton, Westlecott Manor, Swindon; three *s* (and one *s* decd). *Educ:* Eton; Jesus Coll., Cambridge. 2nd Lieut (TA), 1936. Commissioned, KRRC, 1940; Capt. 1942. High Sheriff of Suffolk 1972. *Recreations:* golf, shooting, fishing. *Heir: e* surv. *s* Michael William Bunbury, [*b* 29 Dec. 1946; *m* 1976, Caroline, *d* of Col A. D. S. Mangnall]. *Address:* Hollesley House, Hollesley, Woodbridge, Suffolk. *T:* Shottisham 250. *Clubs:* Army and Navy, MCC.

BUNBURY, Sir Michael; *see* Bunbury, Sir R. D. M. R.

BUNBURY, Lt-Comdr Sir (Richard David) Michael (Richardson-), 5th Bt, *cr* 1787; RN; *b* 27 Oct. 1927; *er s* of Richard Richardson-Bunbury (*d* 1951) and Florence Margaret Gordon, *d* of Col Roger Gordon Thomson, CMG, DSO, late RA; *S* kinsman 1953; *m* 1961, Jane Louise, *d* of late Col Alfred William Pulverman, IA; two *s*. *Educ:* Royal Naval College, Dartmouth. Midshipman (S), 1945; Sub-Lieut (S), 1947; Lieut (S), 1948; Lieut-Comdr, 1956; retd 1967. *Heir: s* Roger Michael Richardson-Bunbury, *b* 2 Nov. 1962. *Address:* Woodlands, Mays Hill, Worplesdon, Guildford, Surrey. *T:* Worplesdon 2034.

BUNBURY, Sir William; *see* Bunbury, Sir J. W. N.

BUNCH, Austin Wyeth, MBE 1974; Deputy Chairman, Electricity Council, since 1976; *b* 1918; *s* of Horace William and Winifred Ada Bunch; *m* 1944, Joan Mary Peryer; four *d*. *Educ:* Christ's Hospital. FCA, CompIEE. Deloitte, Plender, Griffiths, 1935-48; Southern Electricity Board, 1949-76; Area Man., Newbury, 1962; Area Man., Portsmouth, 1966; Dep. Chm., 1967; Chm., 1974. *Recreation:* sports for the disabled. *Address:* Sumner, School Lane, Cookham, Berks. *T:* Bourne End 21551.

BUNDY, McGeorge; President of the Ford Foundation, USA, since 1966; *b* 30 March 1919; *s* of Harvey Hollister Bundy and Katharine Lawrence Bundy (*née* Putnam); *m* 1950, Mary Buckminster Lothrop; four *s*. *Educ:* Yale Univ. AB 1940. Political analyst, Council on Foreign Relations, 1948-49. Harvard University: Vis. Lectr, 1949-51; Associate Prof. of Government, 1951-54; Prof., 1954-61; Dean, Faculty of Arts and Sciences, 1953-61. Special Asst to the Pres. for National Security Affairs, 1961-66. Mem., American Political Science Assoc. *Publications:* (with H. L. Stimson) On Active Service in Peace and War, 1948; The Strength of Government, 1968; (ed) Pattern of Responsibility, 1952. *Address:* The Ford Foundation, 320 East 43rd Street, New York, NY 10017, USA.

BUNFORD, John Farrant, MA, FIA; Hon.FFA; Director, National Provident Institution for Mutual Life Assurance, since 1964 (Manager and Actuary 1946-64); *b* 4 June 1901; *s* of late John Henry Bunford and Ethel Farrant Bunford; *m* 1929, Florence Louise, *d* of late John and Annie Pearson, Mayfield, Cork; two *s* one *d*. *Educ:* Christ's Hosp.; St Catharine's Coll., Cambridge. (MA). Scottish Amicable Life Assurance Soc., 1923-29. Royal Exchange Assurance, 1929-32; National Provident Institution: Dep. Asst Actuary, 1932; Asst Sec., 1933; Asst Manager, 1937. Institute of Actuaries: Fellow, 1930; Hon. Sec., 1944-45; Vice-Pres., 1948-50; Treas., 1952-53; Pres., 1954-56. Hon. Fellow the Faculty of Actuaries, 1956. *Recreation:* gardening. *Address:* 14 Shepherds Way, Liphook, Hants. *T:* Liphook 722594.

BUNKER, Albert Rowland, CB 1966; Deputy Under Secretary of State, Home Office, 1972-75, retired; *b* 5 Nov. 1913; *er* and *o* surv. *s* of late Alfred Francis Bunker and late Ethel Trudgian, Lanjeth, St Austell, Cornwall; *m* 1939, Irene Ruth Ella, 2nd *d* of late Walter and late Ella Lacey, Ealing; two *s*. *Educ:* Ealing Gram. Sch. Served in Royal Air Force, 1943-45. Service in Cabinet Office, HM Treasury, Ministry of Home Security and Home Office. *Recreation:* golf. *Address:* 35 Park Avenue, Ruislip. *T:* Ruislip 35331. *Clubs:* Royal Air Force; Denham Golf.

BUNN, Dr Charles William, FRS 1967; Dewar Research Fellow of the Royal Institution of Great Britain, 1963-72; *b* 15 Jan. 1905; *s* of Charles John Bunn and Mary Grace Bunn (*née* Murray); *m* 1931, Elizabeth Mary Mold; one *s* one *d*. *Educ:* Wilson's Grammar Sch., London, SE; Exeter Coll., Oxford. BA, BSc, (Oxon.), 1927; DSc (Oxon.), 1953; FInstP, 1944. Mem. Research Staff, Imperial Chemical Industries, Winnington, Northwich, Cheshire (now Mond Div.), 1927-46; transf. to ICI Plastics Div., 1946 (Div. Leader of Molecular Structure Div. of Research Dept, and later of Physics Div.); retd 1963. Chm., X-Ray Analysis Group of The Inst. of Physics and The Physical

Soc., 1959-62. Amer. Physical Soc. Award in High Polymer Physics (Ford Prize), 1969. *Publications:* Chemical Crystallography, 1945 (2nd edn 1961); Crystals, Their Role in Nature and in Science, 1964; papers in: Proc. Royal Society; Trans. Faraday Soc.; Acta Crystallographica. *Recreations:* music and horticulture. *Address:* 6 Pentley Park, Welwyn Garden City, Herts. *T:* Welwyn Garden 23581.

BUNN, Douglas Henry David; Chairman: All England Jumping Course, Hickstead; White Horse Caravan Co. Ltd; *b* 1 March 1928; *s* of late G. H. C. Bunn and A. A. Bunn; *m* 1st, 1952, Rosemary Pares Wilson; three *d*; 2nd, 1960, Susan Dennis-Smith; two *s* one *d. Educ:* Chichester High Sch.; Trinity Coll., Cambridge (BA). Called to Bar, Lincoln's Inn; practised at Bar, 1953-59; founded Hickstead, 1960; British Show Jumping Team, 1957-68; Vice-Chm., British Show Jumping Assoc. (Chm. 1969); Mem. British Equestrian Fedn; founded White Horse Caravan Co. Ltd, 1958; Chm., Southern Aero Club, 1968-72. *Recreations:* horses, flying, books. *Address:* Hickstead Place, Sussex. *T:* Bolney 268. *Clubs:* Buck's, Saints and Sinners.

BUNSTER, Don Alvaro; Fellow, Institute of Development Studies, University of Sussex, since 1977; *b* 25 May 1920; *m* 1965, Raquel de Bunster (*née* Parot); three *s. Educ:* National Institute, Santiago; School of Law, Univ. of Chile; Faculty of Law, Central Univ. of Brazil, Rio de Janeiro; Faculty of Jurisprudence, Univ. of Rome, Italy. Judge Advocate of the Army, Chile, 1950-57; Prof. of Penal Law, Univ. of Chile, 1953-73; Gen. Sec., Univ. of Chile, 1957-69. Vis. Prof., Univ. of Calif., Berkeley, 1966-67. Vice-Pres., Inst. of Penal Sciences, 1969-70; Dir, Enciclopedia Chilena, 1970; Chilean Ambassador to Court of St James's, 1971-73; lecturing at Univs of Oxford and Liverpool, 1973-74; Senior Vis. Fellow, Centre of Latin-American Studies, Univ. of Cambridge, 1974-77. *Publications:* La malversación de caudales públicos, 1948; La voluntad del acto delictivo, 1950; articles, descriptive commentaries, etc, in various nat. and foreign magazines. *Recreations:* music, theatre. *Address:* Institute of Development Studies, University of Sussex, Falmer, Brighton BN1 9RE.

BUNT, Rev. F(rederick) Darrell, CB 1958; OBE 1950; retired as Chaplain of the Fleet and Archdeacon of the Royal Navy (1956-60); Hon. Chaplain to the Queen, 1952-60; *b* 3 July 1902; *o s* of F. W. M. Bunt; *m* 1960, Marianne E. Watson; one *d. Educ:* City of London Sch.; St Chad's Coll., Durham (BA 1923, DipTh 1924, MA 1926). Deacon, 1926; Priest, 1927, Diocese of Chelmsford; St Luke's, Victoria Docks, 1926; St Augustine's, Wembley Park, 1928; Chaplain, Royal Navy, 1930. Served in various ships from 1930; HMS President (Asst to Chaplain of the Fleet), 1948-50; HMS Excellent, 1950-51; RN College, Dartmouth, 1951-53; HM Dockyard, Portsmouth, 1953-56. *Recreations:* golf, sailing. *Address:* Ringer's Plat, Lymore, Milford-on-Sea, Hants. *T:* Milford-on-Sea 3213.

BUNTING, Prof. Arthur Hugh, CMG 1971; Professor of Agricultural Development Overseas, Reading University, since 1974; *b* 7 Sept. 1917; *e s* of S. P. and R. Bunting; *m* 1941, Elsie Muriel Reynard; three *s. Educ:* Athlone High Sch., Johannesburg, S Africa; Univ. of the Witwatersrand, Johannesburg; Oriel Coll., University of Oxford. BSc 1937. BSc (Hons Botany), MSc 1938, Witwatersrand; Rhodes Scholar for the Transvaal, 1938; DPhil Oxford, 1941; FIBiol. Asst Chemist, Rothamsted Experimental Station, 1941-45; Member Human Nutrition Research Unit, Medical Research Council, 1945-47; Chief Scientific Officer, Overseas Food Corporation, 1947-51; Senior Research Officer, Sudan Min. of Agriculture, 1951-56; Prof. of Agricultural Botany, 1956-73, Dean, Faculty of Agriculture, 1965-71, Univ. of Reading. Pres., Assoc. of Applied Biologists, 1963-64; Jt Editor, Journal of Applied Ecology, 1964-68. Foundn Mem., 1968-72, and Mem., 1974-, Vice-Chm. 1975-77, and Chm. 1977-, Board of Trustees, Internat. Inst. of Tropical Agriculture, Ibadan, Nigeria; Foundn Mem., Internat. Bd for Plant Genetic Resources, 1974-. LLD *hc* Ahmadu Bello Univ., 1968. *Publications:* (ed) Change in Agriculture, 1970; (ed jtly) Policy and Practice in Rural Development, 1976; numerous papers in scientific and agricultural journals. *Recreation:* music. *Address:* 27 The Mount, Caversham, Reading, Berks. *T:* Reading 472487.

BUNTING, Basil; poet; *b* 1 March 1900; *s* of T. L. Bunting, MD, and Annie Bunting (*née* Cheesman); *m* 1st, 1930, Marian Culver; two *d* (one *s* decd); 2nd, 1948, Sima Alladadian; one *s* one *d. Educ:* Ackworth Sch.; Leighton Park Sch.; Wormwood Scrubbs; London Sch. of Economics. Has had a varied undistinguished career. President: The Poetry Soc., 1972-76; Northern Arts, 1973-76. Hon. DLitt Newcastle upon Tyne, 1971. *Publications:* Redimiculum Matellarum, 1930; Poems, 1950; The Spoils, 1965; Loquitur, 1965; First Book of Odes,

1965; Briggflatts, 1966; Collected Poems, 1968. *Address:* Shadingfield, Wylam, Northumberland. *T:* Wylam 3255.

BUNTING, Sir (Edward) John, KBE 1977 (CBE 1960); Kt 1964; BA; High Commissioner for Australia in the United Kingdom, 1975-77; *b* Ballarat, Vic, 13 Aug. 1918; *s* of late G. B. Bunting; *m* 1942, (Pauline) Peggy, *d* of late D. C. MacGruer; three *s. Educ:* Trinity Grammar School, Melbourne; Trinity Coll., Univ. of Melbourne (BA Hons). Asst Sec., Prime Minister's Dept, Canberra, 1949-53; Official Sec., Office of the High Commissioner for Australia, London, 1953-55; Deputy Sec., Prime Minister's Dept, Canberra, 1955-58; Secretary: Australian Cabinet, 1959-75; Prime Minister's Dept, 1959-68; Dept of the Cabinet Office, 1968-71; Dept of the Prime Minister and Cabinet, 1971-75. *Recreations:* cricket, golf, music. *Address* 8 Arnhem Place, Red Hill, ACT 2603, Australia. *Clubs:* Commonwealth (Canberra); Athenæum (Melbourne); Melbourne Cricket; Royal Canberra Golf.

BUNTING, John Reginald, CBE 1965; author and literary consultant; *b* 12 Nov. 1916; *s* of John Henry and Jane Bunting, Mansfield; *m* 1940, May Hope Sturdy, Malvern, Jamaica; no *c. Educ:* Queen Elizabeth's Grammar Sch., Mansfield; Queen's Coll., Oxford (MA, DipEd). Sen. English Master and Housemaster, Munro Coll., Jamaica, 1939-42; Headmaster, Wolmer's Sch., Jamaica, 1943-49; Principal, King's Coll., Lagos, 1949-54; Actg Dir of Broadcasting, Nigeria, June-Oct. 1952; Actg Inspector of Educn, Western Region, Nigeria, April-Oct. 1954; Dep. Chief Federal Adviser on Educn, Nigeria, 1954-58; Chief Federal Adviser on Educn, Nigeria, 1958-61; Educn Adviser, W Africa, Brit. Council, 1961 and Head, Graduate VSO Unit, 1962; Asst Controller, Educn Div., 1964; Evans Bros Ltd: Editorial Consultant, 1965-68; Dir, Overseas Sales and Publications, 1969; Dir-Gen., Centre for Educnl Develt Overseas, 1970-74; Adviser on Educn to British Council, 1974-76. Hon. Jt Editor, W African Jl of Educn, 1956-61. *Publications:* Civics for Self-Government, 1956; New African English Course (Book 5), 1960; (jtly) Caribbean Civics, 1960; (jtly) Civics for East Africa, 1961; Primary English Course (Book 6): for Ghana, 1962, for Sierra Leone, 1969, for West Cameroon, 1971; Civics: a course in citizenship and character training, 1973; To Light a Candle, 1976. *Recreations:* crickejket, tennis, golf, fishing, painting, bowls. *Address:* Churchmeadow Cottage, 5 High Street, Brill, Bucks. *T:* Brill 7726. *Clubs:* MCC; Chesterton Country Golf.

BUNTON, George Louis, MChir (Cantab), FRCS; Consultant Surgeon to University College Hospital, London, since 1955, to Metropolitan Hospital, 1957-70, and to Northwood Hospital since 1958; *b* 23 April 1920; *s* of late Surg. Capt. C. L. W. Bunton, RN, and Marjorie Denman; *m* 1948, Margaret Betty Edwards; one *d. Educ:* Epsom; Selwyn Coll., Cambridge; UCH. MB, BChir Cantab 1951; MRCS, LRCP 1944; FRCS 1951; MChir Cantab 1955. Served in RNVR 1944-47. Fellow, Assoc. of Surgeons; Fellow, British Assoc. of Pædiatric Surgeons. *Publications:* contribs. to journals and books on surgical subjects. *Recreations:* gardening, music, ski-ing. *Address:* Heathersett, West Heath Road, NW3. *T:* 01-794 3078.

BUÑUEL, Luis; film director; *b* Calanda, Spain, 22 Feb. 1900; *s* of Leonardo and Maria Buñuel; *m* Jeanne Rucar; two *s. Educ:* Univ. of Madrid; Académie du Cinéma, Paris. *Films include:* Un Chien Andalou, 1929; L'Age d'Or, 1930; Las Hurdes (Land Without Bread), 1936; España, 1936; Gran Casino, 1947; El Gran Calavera, 1949; Los Olivados (The Young and the Damned), 1950 (Best Dir Award, Cannes Film Festival, 1951); Subida al Cielo (Mexican Bus Ride), 1952 (best avant-garde film, Cannes, 1952); El (This Strange Passion), 1952; Abismos de Pasión, 1952; The Adventures of Robinson Crusoe, 1953; Ensayo de un Crimen (The Criminal Life of Archibald de la Cruz), 1955; Cela S'Appelle l'Aurore, 1955; La Mort en ce Jardin, 1956; Nazarin, 1958 (Special Internat. Jury Prize, Cannes, 1959); La Jeune Fille, 1959; La Fièvre Monte à El Pau, 1960; The Young One, 1960; The Republic of Sin, 1960; Viridiana, 1961 (jtly, Golden Palm Award, Cannes, 1961); Island of Shame, 1961; El Angel Exterminador, 1962 (Best film, Cannes, 1962); Le Journal d'une Femme de Chambre, 1964; Simon of the Desert, 1965; Belle de Jour, 1966 (Golden Lion of St Mark Award, Venice Film Festival, 1967); La Voie Lactée, 1969; Tristana, 1970; The Discreet Charm of the Bourgeoisie, 1972; Le Fantôme de la liberté, 1974. *Address:* c/o Directores Cinematográficos, Chihuahua 167, Mexico DF.

BURBIDGE, (Eleanor) Margaret, (Mrs Geoffrey Burbidge), FRS 1964; Professor of Astronomy, University of California at San Diego, since 1965; *d* of late Stanley John Peachey, Lectr in Chemistry and Research Chemist, and of Marjorie Peachey; *m* 1948, Geoffrey Burbidge, *qv*; one *d. Educ:* Francis Holland

Sch., London; University Coll., London (BSc); Univ. of London Observatory (PhD). Asst Director, 1948-50, Actg Director, 1950-51, Univ. of London Observatory; fellowship from Internat. Astron. Union, held at Yerkes Observatory, Univ. of Chicago, 1951-53; Research Fellow, California Inst. of Technology, 1955-57; Shirley Farr Fellow, later Associate Prof., Yerkes Observatory, Univ. of Chicago, 1957-62; Research Astronomer, Univ. of California at San Diego, 1962-65; Dir, Royal Greenwich Observatory (on leave of absence), 1972-73. Abby Rockefeller Mauzé Vis. Prof., MIT, 1968. Hon. DSc: Smith Coll., Massachusetts, USA, 1963; Sussex, 1970; Bristol, 1972; Leicester, 1972; City, 1974. Fellow University Coll., London, 1967; Hon. Fellow, Lucy Cavendish Collegiate Soc., 1971. Pres., American Astronomical Soc., 1976-78. *Publications:* Quasi-Stellar Objects (with Geoffrey Burbidge), 1967 (also USA, 1967); contribs to learned jls (mostly USA), Handbuch der Physik, etc. *Recreations:* travel (some done for recreation as well as work!); music (listening-no longer time to play in amateur string orchestra as she used to do). *Address:* Department of Physics, C-011, University of California at San Diego, La Jolla, California 92093, USA. *T:* (714) 452-4479. *Club:* University Women's.

BURBIDGE, Geoffrey (Ronald), FRS 1968; Professor of Physics, University of California, San Diego, since 1963; *b* 24 Sept. 1925; *s* of Leslie and Eveline Burbidge, Chipping Norton, Oxon; *m* 1948, Margaret Peachey (*see* E. M. Burbidge); one *d. Educ:* Chipping Norton Grammar Sch.; Bristol University; Univ. Coll., London. BSc (Special Hons Physics) Bristol, 1946; PhD London, 1951. Asst Lectr, UCL, 1950-51; Agassiz Fellow, Harvard Univ., 1951-52; Research Fellow, Univ. of Chicago, 1952-53; Research Fellow, Cavendish Lab., Cambridge, 1953-55; Carnegie Fellow, Mount Wilson and Palomar Observatories, Caltech, 1955-57; Asst Prof., Dept of Astronomy, Univ. of Chicago, 1957-58; Assoc. Prof., 1958-62; Assoc. Prof., Univ. of California, San Diego, 1962-63. Phillips Vis. Prof., Harvard Univ., 1968. Fellow, UCL, 1970-. Pres., Astronomical Soc. of the Pacific, 1974-76; Trustee, Assoc. Universities Inc., 1973-; Editor, Annual Review Astronomy and Astrophysics, 1973-. *Publications:* (with Margaret Burbidge) Quasi-Stellar Objects, 1967; scientific papers in Astrophysical Jl, Nature, Rev. Mod. Phys, Handbuch der Physik, etc. *Address:* Department of Physics, C-011, University of California at San Diego, La Jolla, California 92093, USA.

BURBIDGE, Mrs Geoffrey; *see* Burbidge, E. M.

BURBIDGE, Sir Herbert (Dudley), 5th Bt *cr* 1916; *b* 13 Nov. 1904; *s* of Herbert Edward Burbidge (*d* 1945) 2nd *s* of 1st Bt, and Harriet Georgina (*d* 1952), *d* of Henry Stuart Hamilton, Londonderry; *S* cousin, 1974; *m* 1933, Ruby Bly, *d* of Charles Ethelbert Taylor; one *s. Educ:* University Sch., Victoria, BC, Canada. Harrods Ltd, Knightsbridge, 1923-28; R. P. Clarke (Stock Brokers), Vancouver, BC, 1929-31; Merchandising Manager, Silverwood Industries of Vancouver, BC, 1931-70; retired 1970. President: Vancouver Executive Club, 1942; Vancouver Sales Executive Club, 1948. Mem. Bd of Referees, Workmen's Compensation Bd, 1943-61. *Recreation:* landscape gardening. Heir: *s* Peter Dudley Burbidge [*b* 20 June 1942; *m* 1967, Peggy Marilyn, *d* of Kenneth Anderson, Ladner, BC; one *d*]. *Address:* 12549/27th Avenue, Surrey, British Columbia V4A 2M6, Canada. *Club:* Vancouver Executive.

BURBIDGE, Mrs Margaret; *see* Burbidge, E. M.

BURBIDGE, Prof. Percy William, CBE 1957; MSc NZ; BARes Cambridge; Professor Emeritus of Physics, University of Auckland; *b* 3 Jan. 1891; *s* of R. W. Burbidge and Agnes Mary Edwards; *m* 1923, Kathleen Black, Wellington; one *s* three *d. Educ:* Wellington Boys' Coll.; Victoria Univ. Coll., Wellington; Trinity Coll., Cambridge. Took 1st class honours in Physics (NZ); gained 1851 Exhibition Research Scholarship, 1913; volunteered NZEF, 1917; took BA Research at Cavendish Laboratory, 1920; Carnegie Corporation Travel Grants, 1933, 1951; Mem. NZ Defence Scientific Advisory Cttee, 1940-47. *Publications:* papers on Fluctuations of Gamma Rays, Absorption of X-Rays, Humidity, Frictional Electricity, Photoconduction in Rock Salt. *Address:* University, Auckland, NZ.

BURBRIDGE, Ven. (John) Paul, MA Oxon and Cantab; Archdeacon of Richmond and Canon Residentiary of Ripon Cathedral, since 1976; *b* 21 May 1932; *e s* of John Henry Gray Burbridge and Dorothy Vera Burbridge; *m* 1956, Olive Denise Grenfell; four *d. Educ:* King's Sch., Canterbury; King's Coll., Cambridge; New Coll., Oxford; Wells Theolog. Coll. Nat. Service Commn in RA, 1957. Jun. Curate, 1959, Sen. Curate, 1961, Eastbourne Parish Church; Vicar Choral of York Minster,

1962-66; Chamberlain, 1962-76; Canon Residentiary, 1966-76; Succentor Canonicorum, 1966; Precentor, 1969-76. *Recreation:* model engineering. *Address:* The Old Vicarage, Sharow, Ripon. *T:* Ripon 5771.

BURBURY, Hon. Sir Stanley Charles, KCVO 1977; KBE 1958; Governor of Tasmania, since 1973; *b* 2 Dec. 1909; *s* of Daniel Charles Burbury and Mary Burbury (*née* Cunningham); *m* 1934, Pearl Christine Barren; no *c. Educ:* Hutchins Sch., Hobart; The Univ. of Tasmania. LLB 1933; Hon. LLD 1970. Admitted to Bar, 1934; QC 1950; Solicitor-Gen. for Tasmania, 1952; Chief Justice, Supreme Court of Tasmania, 1956-73. Pres., Nat. Heart Foundn of Australia, 1967-73; Dir, Winston Churchill Memorial Trust. KStJ 1974. Hon. Col, Royal Tasmanian Regt, 1974. *Recreations:* music and lawn bowls. *Address:* Government House, Hobart, Tasmania 7000, Australia. *Clubs:* Tasmanian, Athenæum, Royal Hobart Bowls (Hobart).

BURCH, Cecil Reginald, CBE 1958; FRS 1944; BA; DSc; Research Associate, 1936-44 and Fellow, since 1944, of H. H. Wills Physics Laboratory, Bristol University; Warren Research Fellow in Physics, 1948-66; *b* 12 May 1901; *s* of late George James Burch, MA, DSc, FRS, and of Constance Emily Jeffries, sometime Principal of Norham Hall, Oxford; *m* 1937, Enid Grace, *o d* of Owen Henry Morice, Ipswich; one *d. Educ:* Oxford Preparatory School; Oundle Sch.; Gonville and Caius Coll., Cambridge. Physicist, Research Dept, Metropolitan Vickers Co., Trafford Park, Manchester, 1923-33; Leverhulme Fellow (in Optics), Imperial Coll. of Science and Technology, 1933-35. Rumford Medal, Royal Society, 1954. *Publications:* A Contribution to the Theory of Eddy Current Heating (with N. Ryland Davis); scientific papers on various subjects in physics and technology in Phil. Mag., Proc. Royal Society, etc. *Recreation:* walking. *Address:* 2 Holmes Grove, Henleaze, Clifton, Bristol BS9 4EE. *T:* Bristol 627322.

BURCH, Maj.-Gen. Frederick Whitmore, CSI 1946; CIE 1944; MC 1916; DL; late Indian Army; *b* 1 Nov. 1893; 2nd *s* of late Major Frederick Burch, Elvington, York; *m* 1929, Marigold (*d* 1977), 2nd *d* of P. U. Allen, late ICS; one *s* one *d. Educ:* Framlingham Coll. Served European War, 1914-19, in Egypt, France, Belgium with E Yorks Regt, and India (wounded, despatches, MC, 1914-15 Star, 2 War Medals, Afghanistan, 1919); Indian Army: 7th Gurka Rifles and Royal Garhwal Rifles; held various staff appointments including AMS (Personal) to C-in-C India, DSD, GHQ, India; War of 1939-45, India and Italy (4 war medals); Bt Major 1930; Bt Lt-Col 1938; Maj.-Gen. 1942; organised India's Victory Celebrations, New Delhi, 1946; Chief of Staff and C-in-C Baroda State Forces, 1946; retired, 1949. Raised and commanded NE Sector Essex Home Guard (5 Bns), 1951; Area Controller, Civil Defence, NE Essex, 1950-64. DL Essex, 1956; Chm., Lexden and Winstree Rural District Council, 1959-63. Hon. Treasurer, Chelmsford Diocesan Bd of Finance, 1968-73. *Recreations:* golf, tennis, fishing, polo. *Address:* The Well House, Dedham, Colchester, Essex CO7 6AB. *T:* Colchester 322223. *Club:* Army and Navy.

BURCH, Maj.-Gen. Geoffrey, CB 1977; Director of Management Careers Development, Courtaulds Group, since 1978; *b* 29 April 1923; *s* of late Henry James Burch, LDS, RCS (Eng); *m* 1948, Jean Lowrie Fyfe; one *s. Educ:* Felsted Sch. Served War: commissioned 2/Lt RA, 1943; served in Italy, 1943-45. India, 1946-47; ptsc 1951; psc 1953; British Defence Liaison Staff, Ottawa, 1962-65; Comd Flintshire and Denbighshire Yeomanry, 1965-66. Programme Director UK/Germany/Italy 155mm project, 1968-71; Dep. Commandant, Royal Military Coll. of Science, 1971-73; Dir-Gen. Weapons (Army), 1973-75; Dep. Master-General of the Ordnance, 1975-77. MBIM. *Recreations:* cricket, golf, squash, tennis, bridge. *Address:* c/o Lloyds Bank Ltd, Cox's & King's Branch, 6 Pall Mall, SW1Y 5NH. *Clubs:* Naval and Military, MCC.

BURCH, Rt. Rev. William Gerald, DD; *m* 1942, Carroll Borrowman; four *d. Educ:* University of Toronto (BA); Wycliffe Coll., Toronto. Deacon, 1936; Priest, 1938. Curate, Christ Church, Toronto, 1936-40; Incumbent, Scarborough Junction with Sandown Park, 1940-42; Rector: St Luke, Winnipeg, 1942-52; All Saints, Windsor, 1952-56; Exam. Chaplain to Bishop of Huron, 1955-56; Canon of Huron, 1956; Dean and Rector, All Saints Cathedral, Edmonton, 1956-60; Suffragan Bishop of Edmonton, 1960-61; Bishop of Edmonton, 1961-76. *Address:* 2358 Estevan Avenue, Victoria, BC V8R 2S5, Canada. *T:* (604) 598 4369.

BURCHAM, Prof. William Ernest, FRS 1957; Oliver Lodge Professor of Physics, University of Birmingham, since 1951; *b* 1 Aug. 1913; *er s* of Ernest Barnard and Edith Ellen Burcham; *m* 1942, Isabella Mary, *d* of George Richard Todd and of Alice

Louisa Todd; two d. *Educ:* City of Norwich Sch.; Trinity Hall, Cambridge. Stokes Student, Pembroke Coll., Cambridge, 1937; Scientific Officer, Ministry of Aircraft Production, 1940, and Directorate of Atomic Energy, 1944; Fellow of Selwyn Coll., Cambridge, 1944; Univ. Demonstrator in Physics, Cambridge, 1945; Univ. Lecturer in Physics, Cambridge, 1946. Mem. SRC, 1974-. *Publications:* Nuclear Physics: an Introduction, 1963; papers in Proc. Royal Society, Proc. Physical Soc. and in *Philosophical Magazine. Address:* 95 Witherford Way, Birmingham B29 4AN. *T:* 021-472 1226.

BURCHFIELD, Robert William, CBE 1975; Editor, A Supplement to the Oxford English Dictionary, since 1957; Chief Editor, The Oxford English Dictionaries, since 1971; Fellow and Tutor in English Language, St Peter's College, Oxford, since 1963; *b* Wanganui, NZ, 27 Jan. 1923; *s* of Frederick Burchfield and Mary Burchfield (*née* Blair); *m* 1949, Ethel May Yates (marr. diss. 1976); on *s* two *d*; *m* 1976, Elizabeth Austen Knight. *Educ:* Wanganui Technical Coll., New Zealand, 1934-39; Victoria University Coll., Wellington, NZ, 1940-41, 1946-48; MA (NZ) 1948; Magdalen Coll., Oxford, 1949-53; BA (Oxon) 1951, MA 1955. Served War, Royal NZ Artillery, NZ and Italy, 1941-46. NZ Rhodes Scholar, 1949. Junior Lectr in English Lang., Magdalen Coll., Oxford, 1952-53; Lectr in English Lang., Christ Church, Oxford, 1953-57; Lectr, St Peter's Coll., Oxford, 1955-63. Hon. Sec., Early English Text Society, 1955-68 (Mem. Council, 1968-); Editor, Notes and Queries, 1959-62. *Publications:* (with E. M. Burchfield) The Land and People of New Zealand, 1953; (with C. T. Onions and G. W. S. Friedrichsen) The Oxford Dictionary of English Etymology, 1966; A Supplement of Australian and New Zealand Words, in the Pocket Oxford Dictionary (5th edn), 1969; A Supplement to the Oxford English Dictionary, vol. I (A-G), 1972, vol. II (H-N), 1976; contribs to: Medium Ævum, Notes and Queries, Times Lit. Supp., Trans Philological Soc., Encounter, etc. *Recreations:* adapting to village life, domestic gardening, travelling. *Address:* The Barn, 14 Green End, Sutton Courtenay, Oxon. *T:* Sutton Courtenay 645.

BURCHMORE, Air Cdre Eric, CBE 1972 (OBE 1963; MBE 1945); *b* 18 June 1920; *s* of Percy William Burchmore and Olive Eva Ingledew; *m* 1941, Margaret Ovendale; one *d. Educ:* Robert Atkinson Sch., Thornaby; RAF Halton; Heriot-Watt Coll., Edinburgh. CEng, MRAeS. Royal Air Force: Aircraft Apprentice, 1936-39; Fitter 2, 1939-41; Engr Officer, 1941: served in Fighter Comd; Air Comd SE Asia, 1943-45; Air Min. and various home postings; Far East, 1952-55; London and Staff Coll.; Near East, 1960-62; comd RAF Sealand, 1963-66; Far East, 1967-68; Dir RAF Project (subseq. Dir Harrier Projects), MoD(PE), 1969-75; retired 1975. Dep. Dir of Housing, London Borough of Camden, 1975-. *Address:* 3 Broad Walk, Caterham, Surrey CR3 5EP. *T:* Caterham 44391. *Club:* Royal Air Force.

BURDEN, family name of **Baron Burden**.

BURDEN, 2nd Baron *cr* 1950, of Hazlebarrow, Derby; **Philip William Burden;** *b* 21 June 1916; *s* of 1st Baron Burden, CBE, and of Augusta, *d* of David Sime, Aberdeen; *S* father, 1970; *m* 1951, Audrey Elsworth, *d* of Major W. E. Sykes; three *s* three *d. Educ:* Raines Foundation School. *Heir: s* Hon. Andrew Philip Burden, *b* 20 July 1959. *Address:* Northdown House Farm, Churchinford, near Taunton, Somerset.

BURDEN, Derrick Frank; HM Diplomatic Service; Counsellor and Head of Claims Department, Foreign and Commonwealth Office, since 1973; *b* 4 June 1918; *s* of late Alfred Burden and Louisa Burden (*née* Dean); *m* 1942, Marjorie Adeline Beckley; two *d. Educ:* Bec Sch., London. Crown Agents, 1936. Served War, King's Royal Rifle Corps, 1939-41. Joined Foreign Office, 1945; Comr-Gen.'s Office, Singapore, 1950-53; 2nd Sec., Moscow, 1954-56; 2nd Sec., Tokyo, 1957-59; HM Consul, Lourenço Marques, 1959-61; FO, 1962-67 (Asst Head of Protocol Dept, 1965); HM Consul, Khorramshahr (Iran), 1967-69; 1st Sec., Nairobi, 1969-71; HM Consul, Luanda (Angola), 1972-73. *Recreations:* golf, gardening. *Address: c/o* Foreign and Commonwealth Office, SW1A 2AL; 12 Strathmore Drive, Charvil, Reading, Berks RG10 9QT. *T:* Twyford (Berks) 340564. *Clubs:* Travellers'; Nairobi (Nairobi); Badgemore Park Golf (Henley-on-Thames).

BURDEN, Sqn Ldr Frederick Frank Arthur; MP (C) Gillingham, Kent, since 1950; *b* 27 Dec. 1905; *s* of A. F. Burden, Bracknell, Berks; *m* Marjorie Greenwood; one *d. Educ:* Sloane Sch., Chelsea. Company Director. Served War of 1939-45, RAF: first with a Polish unit, later with SE Asia Command, and on the staff of Lord Louis Mountbatten. Chm. Parliamentary Animal Welfare Group. Freeman of Gillingham, 1971. *Recreation:* fishing. *Address:* 291 Latymer Court, W6. *T:* 01-748 1916; The Knapp, Portesham, Dorset. *T:* Abbotsbury 366.

BURDEN, Major Geoffrey Noel, CMG 1952; MBE 1938; *b* 9 Dec. 1898; *s* of late A. G. Burden, Exmouth, Devon; *m* 1927, Yolande Nancy, *d* of late G. H. B. Shaddick, Kenilworth, Cape Town; one *s* one *d. Educ:* Exeter Sch.; Royal Military College, Sandhurst. Served European War, 1914-18, Devon Regt, 1915-18; Indian Army, 1918-23. Joined Colonial Administrative Service, Nyasaland, 1925; Director of Publicity, 1936; Nyasaland Labour Officer to S Rhodesia, 1937-38; Nyasaland/N Rhodesian Labour Officer in the Union of South Africa, 1939; Chief Recruiting Officer, Nyasaland, 1940. War of 1939-45: military service in Somaliland, Abyssinia, and N Rhodesia, King's African Rifles, 1941-43. Asst Chief Sec., Nyasaland, 1945-46; Commissioner of Labour, Gold Coast, 1946-50; Chief Commissioner, Northern Territories, Gold Coast, 1950-53. Nyasaland Govt Representative in S Rhodesia, 1954-63. *Address:* The Croft, Hillside Road, Frensham, Surrey. *T:* Frensham 2584.

BURDER, Sir John Henry, Kt 1944; ED; *b* 30 Nov. 1900; *s* of late H. C. Burder; *m* 1928, Constance Aileen Bailey; two *d. Educ:* Eton College. Joined Jardine Skinner & Co., 1920; Chm., Indian Tea Market Expansion Bd, 1939; President: Local Board, Imperial Bank of India, 1943-44; Bengal Chamber of Commerce, 1943-44; Associated Chambers of Commerce of India, 1943-44; Royal Agricultural and Horticultural Soc. of India, 1938-41; Calcutta Soc. for the Prevention of Cruelty to Animals, 1939-41; Lt-Col Commanding Calcutta Light Horse, 1944; Member of Council of State, 1943-44. *Address:* Pytts Piece, Burford, Oxon. *T:* Burford 2287; Achaglachgach, Tarbert, Argyll. *Club:* Oriental.

BURDETT, Sir Savile (Aylmer), 11th Bt, *cr* 1665; Managing Director, Rapaway Ltd; *b* 24 Sept. 1931; *s* of Sir Aylmer Burdett, 10th Bt; *S* father, 1943; *m* 1962, June E. C. Rutherford; one *s* one *d. Educ:* Wellington Coll.; Imperial Coll., London. *Heir: s* Crispin Peter Burdett, *b* 8 Feb. 1967. *Address:* Farthings, 35 Park Avenue, Solihull, West Midlands B91 3EJ. *T:* 021-705 3360.

BURFORD, Earl of; Murray de Vere Beauclerk; *b* 19 Jan. 1939; *s* and *heir* of 13th Duke of St Albans, *qv* and 1st wife (now Mrs Nathalie C. Eldrid); *m* 1st, 1963, Rosemary Frances Scoones (marr. diss. 1974); one *s* one *d*; 2nd, 1974, Cynthia (Lady Hooper), *d* of late Lt-Col W. J. H. Howard, DSO. *Educ:* Tonbridge. Chartered Accountant, 1962. *Heir: s* Lord Vere of Hanworth, *qv. Address:* 3 St George's Court, Gloucester Road, SW7. *T:* 01-589 1771. *Clubs:* Hurlingham, MCC.

BURFORD, Eleanor; *see* Hibbert, Eleanor.

BURGE, James, QC 1965; a Recorder, 1972-75; *b* 8 Oct. 1906; *s* of George Burge, Masterton, New Zealand; *m* 1938, Elizabeth, *d* of Comdr Scott Williams, RN, Dorset; two *s* one *d. Educ:* Cheltenham Coll.; Christ's Coll., Cambridge. Barrister, 1932, Master of the Bench, 1971, Inner Temple; Yarborough Anderson Scholar, Profumo Prizeman, Paul Methuen Prizeman. Pilot Officer RAFVR, 1940; Sqdn Ldr; Dep. Judge Advocate, 1941-44. Formerly Prosecuting Counsel, GPO, at CCC; Deputy Chairman, West Sussex Quarter Sessions, 1963-71. *Address:* Casa Burge, Denia, Spain.

BURGE, Stuart, CBE 1974; Artistic Director, Royal Court Theatre, since 1977; *b* 15 Jan. 1918; *s* of H. O. Burge and K. H. Haig; *m* 1949, Josephine Parker; three *s* two *d. Educ:* Eagle House, Sandhurst; Felsted Sch., Essex. Served War of 1939-45, Intell. Corps. Actor; trained Old Vic, 1936-37; Oxford Rep., 1937-38; Old Vic and West End, 1938-39; Bristol Old Vic, Young Vic, Commercial Theatre, 1946-49; 1st Dir, Hornchurch, 1951-53; productions for theatre and TV, 1953-; Dir., Nottingham Playhouse, 1968-74. *Theatre:* Measure for Measure, The Devil is an Ass, Edinburgh Fest. and Nat. Theatre, 1977. *Television:* Fall of Eagles; Bill Brand, etc. Hon. Prof. of Drama, Nottingham Univ. *Publication:* (ed) King John (Folio Society), 1973. *Address: c/o* Barclay's Bank Ltd, 150b King Street, Hammersmith, W6.

BURGEN, Sir Arnold (Stanley Vincent), Kt 1976; FRS 1964; Director, National Institute for Medical Research, since 1971; *b* 20 March 1922; *s* of late Peter Burgen and Elizabeth Wolfers; *m* 1946, Judith Browne; two *s* one *d. Educ:* Christ's Coll., Finchley. Student, Middlesex Hospital Med. Sch., 1939-45; Ho. Phys., Middlesex Hospital, 1945; Demonstrator, 1945-48, Asst Lectr, 1948-49, in Pharmacology, Middlesex Hospital Med. Sch. Prof. of Physiology, McGill Univ., Montreal, 1949-62; Dep. Dir, Univ. Clinic, Montreal Gen. Hospital, 1957-62; Sheild Prof. of Pharmacology, Univ. of Cambridge, 1962-71; Fellow of Downing Coll., Cambridge, 1962-71, Hon. Fellow 1972; Hon. Dir, MRC Molecular Pharmacology Unit, 1967-72; Mem.

MRC, 1969-71, 1973-; Pres., Internat. Union of Pharmacology, 1972-75; Member: Nat. Biol. Standards Bd, 1975-; Med. Cttee, British Council, 1973-. Hon. DSc: Leeds, 1973; McGill, 1973. *Publications:* Physiology of Salivary Glands, 1961; papers in Journals of Physiology and Pharmacology. *Recreation:* sculpture. *Address:* National Institute for Medical Research, The Ridgeway, Mill Hill, NW7 1AA. *T:* 01-959 3666; Penshurst, Hill Crescent, Totteridge, N20.

BURGER, Warren Earl; Chief Justice of the United States since 1969; *b* St Paul, Minn, 17 Sept. 1907; *s* of Charles Joseph Burger and Katharine Schnittger; *m* 1933, Elvera Stromberg; one *s* one *d. Educ:* Univ. of Minnesota; St Paul Coll. of Law, later Mitchell Coll. of Law (LLB *magna cum laude,* LLD). Admitted to Bar of Minnesota, 1931; Mem. Faculty, Mitchell Coll. of Law, 1931-48. Partner in Faricy, Burger, Moore & Costello until 1953. Asst Attorney-Gen. of US, 1953-56; Judge, US Court of Appeals, Washington, DC, 1956-69. Chm., ABA Proj. Standards for Criminal Justice. Past Lectr, Law Schools in US and Europe. Hon. Master of the Bench of the Middle Temple, 1969. Pres. Bentham Club, UCL, 1972-73. Chancellor and Regent, Smithsonian Instn, Washington, DC; Hon. Chm., Inst. of Judicial Admin; Chm. and Trustee, Nat. Gall. of Art, Washington, DC; Trustee, Nat. Geographic Soc.; Trustee Emeritus: Mitchell Coll. of Law, St Paul, Minn; Macalester Coll., St Paul, Minn; Mayo Foundn, Rochester, Minn. *Publications:* articles in legal and professional jls. *Address:* Supreme Court, Washington, DC 20543, USA.

BURGES, (Norman) Alan, MSc, PhD; FIBiol; FLS; Vice-Chancellor, New University of Ulster, Coleraine, Northern Ireland, 1966-Sept. 1976; *b* 5 Aug. 1911; *s* of late Lieut J. C. Burges, East Maitland, NSW; *m* 1940, Florence Evelyn (*née* Moulton); three *d. Educ:* Sydney Univ., Australia; Emmanuel Coll., Cambridge. Graduated, Sydney, BSc Hons., 1931; MSc, 1932; PhD Cambridge, 1937. Senior 1851 Scholar, 1937. Research Fellow, Emmanuel Coll., 1938; Prof. of Botany, Sydney Univ., 1947-52; Dean of Faculty of Science and Fellow of Senate, 1949-52; Holbrook Gaskell Prof. of Botany, Univ. of Liverpool, 1952-66, Acting Vice-Chancellor, 1964-65; Pro-Vice-Chancellor, 1965-66. Hon. Gen. Sec., ANZAAS, 1947-52; President: British Ecological Soc., 1958, 1959; British Mycological Soc., 1962; Mem. Cttee, Nature Conservancy, England, 1959-66; Mem., Waste Management Adv. Council; Joint Editor, Flora Europæa Project, 1956-. Chm., NI Adv. Council for Education, 1966-; Chairman: Ulster American Folk Park, 1975-; NI American Bicentennial Cttee, 1975-77; Member: Nat. Trust NI Cttee, 1977-; Royal Irish Acad., 1977. Served War of 1939-45 (despatches). Hon. LLD QUB, 1973; Hon. DTech Loughborough, 1975; Hon. DSc Ulster, 1977. *Publications:* Micro-organisms in the Soil, 1958; (with F. Raw) Soil Biology, 1967; various in scientific journals on plant diseases and fungi. *Recreation:* sailing. *Address:* Beechcroft, Glenkeen Road, Aghadowey, Coleraine, Co. Londonderry. *T:* Aghadowey 224.

BURGES, Maj.-Gen. Rodney Lyon Travers, CBE 1963; DSO 1946; *b* 19 March 1914; *s* of Richard Burges and Hilda Christine Burges (*née* Lyon); *m* 1946, Sheila Marion Lyster Goldby, *d* of H. L. Goldby; one *s* one *d. Educ:* Wellington; RMA, Woolwich. 2nd Lieut RA, 1934; war service in Burma, 1942 and 1944-45; CO The Berkshire Yeomanry (145 Fd Regt, RA), 1945; Comdr, E Battery, RHA, 1949-51; Bt Lt-Col 1953; 2nd in comd, 1 RHA, 1954-55; CO 3 RHA, 1955-57; CRA 3 Div., 1958-59; IDC, 1960; Brig. Q (Ops) WO, 1961-63; CCRA, 1 Corps, BAOR, 1963-64; Maj.-Gen. 1964; GOC, Cyprus District, 1964-66; VQMG, MoD, 1966-67. Joined Grieveson, Grant & Co., 1968, Partner 1971. Freeman and Liveryman, Fishmongers' Co., 1974. *Recreations:* racing, drinking wine in the sun. *Address:* Freemantle, Over Wallop, Hants. *Club:* Buck's.

BURGES WATSON, Richard Eagleson Gordon; *see* Watson, R. E. G. B.

BURGESS, Anthony, BA; FRSL; novelist and critic; *b* 25 Feb. 1917; *s* of Joseph Wilson and Elizabeth Burgess; *m* 1942, Llewela Isherwood Jones, BA (*d* 1968); *m* 1968, Liliana Macellari, *d* of Contessa Maria Lucrezia Pasi della Pergola; one *s . Educ:* Xaverian Coll., Manchester; Manchester Univ. Served Army, 1940-46. Lecturer: Birmingham Univ. Extra-Mural Dept., 1946-48; Ministry of Education, 1948-50; English Master, Banbury Grammar Sch., 1950-54; Education Officer, Malaya and Brunei, 1954-59. Vis. Fellow, Princeton Univ., 1970-71; Distinguished Prof., City Coll., NY, 1972-73. *Publications:* Time for a Tiger, 1956; The Enemy in the Blanket, 1958; Beds in the East, 1959 (these three, as The Malayan Trilogy, 1972); The Right to an Answer, 1960; The Doctor is Sick, 1960; The Worm and the Ring, 1961; Devil of a State, 1961; A Clockwork Orange,

1962 (filmed, 1971); The Wanting Seed, 1962; Honey for the Bears, 1963; The Novel Today, 1963; Language Made Plain, 1964; Nothing like the Sun, 1964; The Eve of Saint Venus, 1964; A Vision of Battlements, 1965; Here Comes Everybody-an introduction to James Joyce, 1965; Tremor of Intent, 1966; A Shorter Finnegans Wake, 1966; The Novel Now, 1967; Enderby Outside, 1968; Urgent Copy, 1968; Shakespeare, 1970; MF, 1971; Joysprick, 1973; Napoleon Symphony, 1974; The Clockwork Testament, 1974; Moses, 1976; A Long Trip to Teatime, 1976; Beard's Roman Women, 1976; Abba, Abba, 1977; New York, 1977; scripts of TV Series Moses the Lawgiver and Jesus of Nazareth, 1977; trans. Rostand, Cyrano de Bergerac, 1971; trans. Sophocles: Oedipus the King, 1973; as *Joseph Kell:* One Hand Clapping, 1961; Inside Mr Enderby, 1963; as *John Burgess Wilson:* English Literature: A Survey for Students, 1958; contributor to Observer, Spectator, Listener, Encounter, Queen, Times Literary Supplement, Hudson Review, Holiday, Playboy, American Scholar, etc. *Recreations:* music composition (symphony in C performed, Iowa, 1975), piano-playing, painting, language-learning, travel. *Address:* 44 rue Grimaldi, Monaco; 1 and 2 Piazza Padella, Bracciano, Italy; 168 Triq Il-Kbira, Lija, Malta.

BURGESS, Claude Bramall, CMG 1958; OBE 1954; Minister for Hong Kong Commercial Relations with the European Communities and the Member States, since 1974; *b* 25 Feb. 1910; *s* of late George Herbert Burgess, Weaverham, Cheshire, and Martha Elizabeth Burgess; *m* 1952, Margaret Joan Webb (marr. diss. 1965); one *s*; *m* 1969, Linda Nettleton, *e d* of William Grothier Beilby, New York. *Educ:* Epworth Coll.; Christ Church, Oxford. Eastern Cadetship in HM Colonial Administrative Service, 1932. Commissioned in RA, 1940; POW, 1941-45; demobilized with rank of Lieut-Col, RA, 1946. Colonial Office, 1946-48. Attended Imperial Defence Coll., London, 1951. Various Government posts in Hong Kong; Colonial Secretary (and Actg Governor on various occasions), Hong Kong, 1958-63, retd; Head of Co-ordination and Develt Dept, EFTA, 1964-73. *Recreations:* tennis, golf. *Address:* British Embassy, Hong Kong Government Office, Avenue Louise 228, B 1050 Brussels, Belgium. *T:* 648.38.33; 56 rue Jules Lejeune, 1060 Brussels, Belgium. *T:* 343.32.20. *Club:* Junior Carlton.

BURGESS, Maj.-Gen. Edward Arthur, OBE 1972; Director of Combat Development (Army), since 1977; *b* 30 Sept. 1927; *s* of Edward Burgess and Alice Burgess; *m* 1954, Jean Angelique Leslie Henderson; one *s* one *d . Educ:* All Saints Sch., Bloxham; Lincoln Coll., Oxford; RMA, Sandhurst. Commnd RA 1948; served Germany and ME, 1949-59; psc 1960; GSO 2 WO, 1961-63; served Germany and Far East, 1963-65; jssc 1966; Mil. Asst to C-in-C BAOR, 1966-67; GSO I (DS) Staff Coll., 1968-70; CO 25 Light Regt, RA, 1970-72; CRA 4th Div., 1972-74; Dir of Army Recruiting, 1975-77. *Publications:* articles in military jls. *Recreations:* sailing, fishing, music, reading, gardening. *Address:* Home Close, Grayswood, Haslemere, Surrey. *T:* Haslemere 2750. *Club:* Army and Navy.

BURGESS, Geoffrey Harold Orchard; Director, Torry Research Station, Ministry of Agriculture, Fisheries and Food, since 1969; *b* 28 March 1926; *s* of Harold Frank and Eva M. F. Burgess, Reading; *m* 1952, Barbara Vernon, *y d* of late Rev. Gilbert Vernon Yonge; two *s. Educ:* Reading Grammar Sch.; Univ. of Reading; UC Hull. BSc Reading, 1951 (Colin Morley Prizewinner 1950); PhD London, 1955. FIFST 1966; FRSE 1971. Special research appt, Univ. of Hull, 1951; Sen. Scientific Officer, DSIR, Humber Lab., Hull, 1954; Principal Scientific Officer, Torry Res. Stn, 1960; Officer i/c, Humber Lab., Hull, 1962. Hon. Res. Lectr in Fish Technology, Univ. of Aberdeen, 1969-; Buckland Lectr, 1964; Hon. Lectr in Fish Technology, Univ. of Leeds, 1966-69; Mem. Adv. Cttee on Food Science, Univ. of Leeds, 1970-; Mem., Panel of Fish Technology Experts, FAO, 1962-. Assoc. Editor, Jl of Food Technology, 1966. *Publications:* Developments in the Handling and Processing of Fish, 1965; (with Lovern, Waterman and Cutting) Fish Handling and Processing, 1965; The Curious World of Frank Buckland, 1967; scientific and technical papers, reviews, reports etc concerning handling, processing, transport and preservation for food, of fish, from catching to consumption. *Recreations:* music, book collecting, walking. *Address:* 45 Deeview Road South, Cults, Aberdeen. *T:* Aberdeen 47119.

BURGESS, Ven. John Edward; Archdeacon of Bath, since 1975; *b* 9 Dec. 1930; *s* of Herbert and Dorothy May Burgess; *m* 1958, Jonquil Marion Bailey; one *s* one *d . Educ:* Surbiton County Gram. Sch.; London Univ. (St John's Hall). BD (2nd Cl.), ALCD (1st Cl.). Shell Chemicals Ltd, 1947-53. Asst Curate, St Mary Magdalen, Bermondsey, 1957-60; Asst Curate, St Mary, Southampton, 1960-62; Vicar of Dunston with Coppenhall,

Staffs, 1962-67; Chaplain, Staffordshire Coll. of Technology, 1963-67; Vicar of Keynsham with Queen Charlton and Burnett, Somerset, 1967-75; Rural Dean of Keynsham, 1971-74. *Recreation:* history of railways. *Address:* The Archdeaconry, Corston Rectory, Bath, Avon BA2 9AP. *T:* Saltford 3609.

BURGESS, Sir John (Lawie), Kt 1972; OBE 1944; TD 1945; DL; JP; Chairman, Cumbrian Newspapers Group Ltd, since 1945; Chairman, Border Television Ltd, since 1960; *b* 17 Nov. 1912; *s* of late R. N. Burgess, Carlisle and Jean Hope Lawie, Carlisle; *m* 1948, Alice Elizabeth, *d* of late F. E. Gillieron, Elgin; two *s* one *d. Educ:* Trinity Coll., Glenalmond. Served War of 1939-45, Border Regt, France, Middle East, Tobruk, Syria, India and Burma; comd 4th Bn, Chindit Campaign, Burma, 1944 (despatches, OBE); Hon. Col 4th Bn The Border Regt, 1955-68. Chm., Reuters Ltd, 1959-68; Dir, Press Assoc. Ltd, 1950-57 (Chm. 1955); Mem. Council, Newspaper Soc., 1947-. Mem. Council, Commonwealth Press Union. DL Cumberland, 1955; High Sheriff of Cumberland, 1969; JP City of Carlisle, 1952. *Recreations:* walking; anything to do with Cumbria. *Address:* The Limes, Cavendish Terrace, Carlisle, Cumbria. *T:* Rockcliffe 252. *Clubs:* Garrick, Army and Navy.

BURGESS, Russell Brian, MBE 1975; Director of Music, Wandsworth School, since 1954; Associate Chorus Master, New Philharmonia Chorus, since 1971; *b* 3 July 1931. *Educ:* Royal Academy of Music, London. GRSM(Lond), LRAM, ARAM 1973, ARCM. Founder, Wandsworth School Boys' Choir which has made numerous broadcasts and TV programmes (including BBC's Omnibus, The Wandsworth Sound) and records for every major company. Asst to Wilhelm Pitz, 1964-71, and succeeded him as Associate Chorus Master. He is still closely associated with the music of Lord Britten (*d* 1976), and with performances of Bach and Purcell; he conducted the world première of Britten's Children's Crusade, in St Paul's Cathedral, 1969. Has taken choirs to Holland, Spain, Sweden, France; conducted at: Henry Wood Promenade Concerts; Royal Festival Hall; the Maltings, Snape. *Recreations:* cricket, studying cooking and wine, photography; exploring his beloved Scotland. *Address:* 60 Sandringham Road, Leyton, E10. *T:* 01-539 7119.

BURGH, 7th Baron, *cr* 1529 (title called out of abeyance, 1916; by some reckonings he is 9th Baron (from a *cr* 1487) and his father was 8th and grandfather 7th); **Alexander Peter Willoughby Leith;** *b* 20 March 1935; *s* of 6th (or 8th) Baron Burgh; *S* father 1959; *m* 1957, Anita Lorna Eldridge; two *s* one *d*. *Educ:* Harrow; Magdalene Coll., Cambridge (BA). *Heir: s* Hon. Alexander Gregory Disney Leith, *b* 16 March 1958.

BURGH, John Charles, CB 1975; Deputy Secretary, Department of Prices and Consumer Protection, since 1974; *b* 9 Dec. 1925; *m* 1957, Ann Sturge; two *d*. *Educ:* Friends' Sch., Sibford; London Sch. of Economics (BSc Econ.). Leverhulme post-intermediate Schol.; Pres. of Union, 1949. Asst Principal, BoT, 1950; Private Sec. to successive Ministers of State, BoT, 1954-57; Colonial Office, 1959-62; Mem., UK Delegation to UN Conf. on Trade Develt, 1964; Asst Sec., DEA, 1964; Principal Private Sec. to successive First Secretaries of State and Secretaries of State for Econ. Affairs, 1965-68; Under-Sec., Dept of Employment, 1968-71; Dep.-Chm., Community Relations Commn, 1971-72; Dep. Sec., Cabinet Office (Central Policy Rev. Staff), 1972-74. Mem. Executive, PEP, 1972-; Sec., Nat. Opera Co-ordinating Cttee, 1972-; Asst Sec., Bd of Dirs, Royal Opera House, Covt Gdn, 1972-. *Recreation:* music. *Address:* Department of Prices and Consumer Protection, 1 Victoria Street, SW1H 0ET. *Club:* Little French.

BURGHARD, Rear-Adm. Geoffrey Frederic, CB 1954; DSO 1946; retired; *b* 15 Oct. 1900; *m* 1931, Constance Louise Sheppard; one *s* one *d*. *Educ:* RN Colleges, Osborne and Dartmouth. Naval Cadet, 1913; Captain, 1942; Rear-Admiral, 1952; Deputy Controller Electronics, Min. of Supply, 1952-55; retired list, 1955. MIEE 1956-61. *Address:* Gosfield Hall, Halstead, Essex CO9 1SF. *T:* Halstead 5941.

BURGHERSH, Lord; Anthony David Francis Henry Fane; *b* 1 Aug. 1951; *s* and *heir* of 15th Earl of Westmorland, *qv*. *Educ:* Eton. *Address:* Kingsmead, Didmarton, Badminton, Avon.

BURHOP, Prof. Eric Henry Stoneley, FRS 1963; MSc, PhD; Professor of Physics, University College, London, since 1960; *b* 31 Jan. 1911; *s* of Henry A. and Bertha Burhop, Melbourne, Australia; *m* 1936, Winifred, *d* of Robert Stevens, Melbourne, Australia; two *s* one *d*. *Educ:* Ballarat and Melbourne High Schools, Australia; Melbourne Univ.; Trinity Coll., Cambridge. BA 1932, MSc 1933, Melbourne; PhD 1937, Cambridge. Exhibition of 1851 Schol., 1933-35; Research at Cavendish Laboratory, Cambridge, 1933-35; Research Physicist and

Lecturer, Univ. of Melbourne, 1935-45; Dep. Dir., Radio Research Laboratory, Melbourne, 1942-44; Technical Officer, DSIR Mission to Berkeley, California, 1944-45; University Coll., London: Lectr in Mathematics, 1945-49; Reader in Mathematics, 1949-50; Reader in Physics, 1950-60. Pres., World Fedn of Scientific Workers, 1971. Foreign Mem., Acad. of Science, German Democratic Republic, 1974. Hon. DSc Open Univ., 1975. Joliot-Curie Medal, 1966; Lenin Peace Prize, 1972. *Publications:* The Challenge of Atomic Energy, 1951; The Auger Effect, 1953; Electronic and Ionic Impact Phenomena (with H. S. W. Massey), 1953; High Energy Physics (ed), Vols I, II, 1967, Vols III, IV, 1969. Various publications on atomic and nuclear physics. *Recreation:* furtherance of international scientific co-operation. *Address:* 206 Gilbert House, Barbican, EC2. *T:* 01-638 8816.

BURKE, Adm. Arleigh Albert; Navy Cross; DSM (3 Gold Stars); Legion of Merit (with 2 Gold Stars and Army Oak Leaf Cluster); Silver Star Medal, Purple Heart, Presidential Unit Citation Ribbon (with 3 stars), Navy Unit Commendation Ribbon; retired as Chief of Naval Operations, US Navy and Member of Joint Chiefs of Staff (1955-61); Member of Board of Directors: Financial General Corporation; United Services Life Insurance Corporation; Freedoms Foundation, at Valley Forge; National Capital Area Council, Boy Scouts of America; *b* 19 Oct. 1901; *s* of Oscar A. and Claire Burke; *m* 1923, Roberta Gorsuch; no *c*. *Educ:* United States Naval Academy; Univ. of Michigan (MSE). Commnd ensign, USN, 1923, advancing through grades to Admiral, 1955. USS Arizona, 1923-28; Gunnery Dept, US Base Force, 1928; Post-graduate course (explosives), 1929-31; USS Chester, 1932; Battle Force Camera Party, 1933-35; Bureau of Ordnance, 1935-37; USS Craven, 1937-39; USS Mugford, Captain, 1939-40; Naval Gun Factory, 1940-43; Destroyer Divs 43 and 44, Squadron 12 Comdg, 1943; Destroyer Squadron 23 Comdg, 1943-44; Chief of Staff to Commander Task Force 58 (Carriers), 1944-45; Head of Research and Development Bureau of Ordnance, 1945-46; Chief of Staff, Comdr Eighth Fleet and Atlantic Fleet, 1947-48; USS Huntington, Captain, 1949; Asst Chief of Naval Ops, 1949-50; Cruiser Div. 5, Comdr, 1951; Dep. Chief of Staff, Commander Naval Forces, Far East, 1951; Director Strategic Plans Div., Office of the Chief of Naval Operations, 1952-53; Cruiser Division 6, Commanding, 1954; Commander Destroyer Force, Atlantic, 1955. Member: American Legion; American Soc. of Naval Engineers and numerous other naval assocs, etc.; National Geographic Society; also foreign societies, etc. Holds several hon. degrees. Ul Chi Medal (Korea), 1954; Korean Presidential Unit Citation, 1954. *Recreations:* reading, gardening. *Address:* 8624 Fenway Drive, Bethesda, Maryland 20034, USA. *Clubs:* Army-Navy Town, Metropolitan, Chevy Chase, Alfalfa, Circus Saints and Sinners, Ends of the Earth, etc (Washington, DC); Quindecum (Newport, US); The Brook, Lotos, Salmagundi, Inner Wheel, Seawanhaka Corinthian Yacht (New York); Bohemian (San Francisco).

BURKE, Sir Aubrey (Francis), Kt 1959; OBE 1941; Vice-Chairman retired from Executive Duties, 1969; *b* 21 April 1904; *m* 1936, Rosalind Laura, *d* of Rt Hon. Sir Henry Norman, 1st Bt, PC, OBE, and Hon. Lady Norman, CBE, JP; one *s* three *d* (and one *d* decd). Pres., SBAC, 1958-1959-1960. FCIT; FRSA. High Sheriff of Hertfordshire, 1966-67. *Recreations:* shooting, fishing, sailing. *Address:* Rent Street Barns, Bovingdon, Hertfordshire; Ramster, Chiddingfold, Surrey; Clos de la Garoupe, Antibes, AM, France. *Club:* Royal Automobile.

BURKE, Desmond Peter Meredyth, MA Oxon; Headmaster, Clayesmore School, 1945-66; *b* 10 May 1912; *yr s* of late Maj. Arthur Meredyth Burke. *Educ:* Cheltenham Coll.; Queen's Coll., Oxford. Honours, Modern Greats, 1933. Housemaster and Senior Modern Language Master, Clayesmore School, 1936-40; served in Army Intelligence Corps at home, Belgium and Germany, 1940-45. *Recreations:* the theatre, travel, tennis, bridge. *Address:* The Old Lodge, 92 Alumhurst Road, Bournemouth West. *T:* Westbourne 762329.

BURKE, Rt. Rev. Geoffrey; Titular Bishop of Vagrauta and Auxiliary Bishop of Salford (RC), since 1967; *b* 31 July 1913; *s* of Dr Peter Joseph Burke and Margaret Mary (*née* Coman). *Educ:* St Bede's Coll., Manchester; Stonyhurst Coll.; Oscott Coll., Birmingham; Downing Coll., Cambridge (MA). Taught History, St Bede's Coll., 1940-66; Prefect of Studies, 1950; Rector, 1966. Consecrated Bishop 29 June 1967. *Address:* St John's Cathedral, 250 Chapel Street, Salford, Lancashire M3 5LL. *T:* 061-834 0333.

BURKE, John Barclay; Managing Director: Royal Bank of Scotland Ltd, since 1970; National and Commercial Banking Group Ltd, since 1976; Chairman, Loganair Ltd; Vice-

Chairman, Lloyds and Scottish Ltd; *b* 12 Feb. 1924; *m* 1953; one *s* one *d*. *Educ:* Hutchesons' Boys' Grammar Sch., Glasgow. Joined former National Bank of Scotland Ltd, 1941. Served Royal Navy, 1942-46. Gen. Manager, Nat. Commercial & Schroders Limited, 1965-66; Gen. Manager and Dir: Nat. Commercial Bank of Scotland Ltd, 1968-69; Royal Bank of Scotland Ltd, 1969-70; Director: Williams & Glyn's Bank Ltd, 1974-75 and 1976-; Scottish Agricultural Securities Corp. Ltd. Chm., Cttee of Scottish Clearing Bankers, 1970-73; Pres., The Inst. of Bankers in Scotland, 1973-75; FIB (Scot.). *Recreations:* golf, shooting, flying. *Address:* 3 Cammo Gardens, Edinburgh EH4 8EJ. *T:* 031-336 2872. *Clubs:* Caledonian; New (Edinburgh); Royal and Ancient (St Andrews).

BURKE, Joseph Terence Anthony, CBE 1973 (OBE 1946); MA; Professor of Fine Arts, University of Melbourne, since 1946; Fellow, Trinity College Melbourne, since 1973; *b* 14 July 1913; *s* of late R. M. J. Burke; *m* 1940, Agnes, *d* of late Rev. James Middleton, New Brunswick, Canada; one *s*. *Educ:* Ealing Priory Sch.; King's Coll., Univ. of London; Courtauld Institute of Art; Yale Univ., USA. Entered Victoria and Albert Museum, 1938; lent to Home Office and Min. of Home Security, Sept. 1939; private sec. to successive Lord Presidents of the Council (Rt Hon. Sir John Anderson, Rt Hon. C. R. Attlee, Rt Hon. Lord Woolton), 1942-45; and to the Prime Minister (Rt Hon. C. R. Attlee), 1945-46; Trustee of Felton Bequest; Mem., Australian UNESCO Cttee for Visual Arts. Fellow, Australian Acad. of the Humanities, Pres., 1971-73. *Publications:* Hogarth and Reynolds: A Contrast in English Art Theory, 1943; ed William Hogarth's Analysis of Beauty and Autobiographical Notes, 1955; (with Colin Caldwell) Hogarth: The Complete Engravings, 1968; vol. IX, Oxford History of English Art, 1714-1800, 1976; articles in Burlington Magazine, Warburg Journal and elsewhere. *Recreations:* golf, swimming. *Address:* Trinity College, Melbourne, Victoria, Australia; Dormers, Falls Road, Mount Dandenong, Victoria 3766. *Clubs:* Athenæum; Melbourne (Melbourne).

BURKE, Richard; Member, Commission of the European Communities, since 1977; *b* 29 March 1932; *s* of David Burke and Elisabeth Burke; *m* 1961, Mary Freeley; two *s* three *d*. *Educ:* University Coll., Dublin (MA). Called to the Bar, King's Inns. Mem., Dáil Eireann, South County Dublin, 1969-77; Minister for Education, 1973. *Recreations:* music, golf, walking. *Address:* Commission of the European Communities, 200 rue de la Loi, 1049 Brussels, Belgium. *T:* 02-735-0040.

BURKE, Sir Thomas (Stanley), 8th Bt, *cr* 1797; *b* 20 July 1916; *s* of Sir Gerald Howe Burke, 7th Bt and Elizabeth Mary (*d* 1918), *d* of late Patrick Mathews, Mount Hanover, Drogheda; *S* father 1954; *m* 1955, Susanne Margaretha, *er d* of Otto Salvisberg, Thun, Switzerland; one *s* one *d*. *Educ:* Harrow; Trinity Coll., Cambridge. *Heir:* *s* James Stanley Gilbert Burke, *b* 1 July 1956. *Address:* 18 Elmcroft Avenue, NW11 0RR. *T:* 01-455 9407.

BURKE-GAFFNEY, Maj.-Gen. (Hon.) Edward Sebastian, CBE 1944; RA, retired; *b* 17 Aug. 1900; *s* of Francis Sebastian Burke-Gaffney; *m* 1926, Margot Lawrence; one *s* one *d*. *Educ:* Downside Sch.; RMA, Woolwich. 2nd Lieut RA 1920; Captain, 1933; Major, 1938; Col, 1945; Brig., 1949; Maj.-Gen. 1954; Officer Co. Gentleman Cadets, 1933; Staff Coll., Camberley, 1935-36; AHQ, India, 1937; General Officer Commanding, Aldershot District, 1953-54; retired 1954. *Recreations:* cricket, hockey, golf, shooting. *Address:* 29 Fore Street, Kingsbridge, Devon TQ7 1PG.

BURKE-GAFFNEY, Michael Anthony Bowes, QC 1977; *b* Dar-es-Salaam, Tanzania, 1 Aug. 1928; *s* of Henry Joseph O'Donnell Burke-Gaffney and Constance May (*née* Bishop); *m* 1961, Constance Caroline (*née* Murdoch); two *s* one *d*. *Educ:* Douai Sch.; RMA, Sandhurst. Commissioned Royal Irish Fusiliers, 1948; served with 1st Bn, Suez Canal Zone, Akaba, Gibraltar, BAOR and Berlin; served with Royal Ulster Rifles, Korean War, 1951, and in Hong Kong; qual. as interpreter in Turkish (studied at London Univ. and in Istanbul), 1955; Staff Captain, HQ 44 Div., 1956-58, when resigned commn and read for the Bar; joined Gray's Inn, 1956; called to the Bar, 1959. *Recreations:* family, cricket, wildlife (esp. birds and moths), plant breeding. *Address:* Lamb Building, Temple, EC4. *T:* 01-353 6701.

BURKILL, John Charles, FRS 1953; ScD; Honorary Fellow, Peterhouse, Cambridge; Emeritus Reader in Mathematical Analysis; *b* 1 Feb. 1900; *m* 1928, Margareta, *d* of Dr A. Braun; one *s* one *d* (and one *d* decd). *Educ:* St Paul's; Trinity Coll., Cambridge (Fellow 1922-28). Smith's Prize, 1923; Professor of Pure Mathematics in the University of Liverpool, 1924-29; Fellow of Peterhouse, 1929-67; Master of Peterhouse, 1968-73.

Adams Prize, 1949. *Address:* 2 Archway Court, Barton Road, Cambridge CB3 9LW.

BURKITT, Denis Parsons, CMG 1974; MD, FRCSE; FRS 1972; Medical Research Council External Scientific Staff, 1964-76; Hon. Senior Research Fellow, St Thomas's Hospital Medical School, since 1976; *b* Enniskillen, NI, 28 Feb. 1911; *s* of James Parsons Burkitt and Gwendoline (*née* Hill); *m* 1943, Olive Mary (*née* Rogers); three *d*. *Educ:* Dean Close Sch., Cheltenham; Dublin Univ. BA 1933; MB, BCh, BAO 1935; FRCSE 1938; MD 1946. Surgeon, RAMC, 1941-46. Joined HM Colonial Service: Govt Surgeon, in Uganda, 1946-64, and Lectr in Surgery, Makerere University Coll. Med. Sch.; final appt: Sen. consultant surgeon to Min. of Health, Uganda, 1961. First described a form of cancer common in children in Africa, now named Burkitt's lymphoma. Mem. Editorial Bd, Tropical Doctor. Foundn Fellow, E Africa Assoc. of Surgeons; Hon. Fellow, Sudan Assoc. of Surgeons; Pres., Christian Medical Fellowship; a Vice-Pres., CMS. Hon. FRCSI, 1973; Hon. FRCPI, 1977. Hon. DSc East Africa, 1970. Harrison Prize, ENT Section of RSM, 1966; Stuart Prize, BMA, 1966; Arnott Gold Medal, Irish Hosps and Med. Schs Assoc., 1968; Katharine Berkan Judd Award, Sloan-Kettering Inst., New York, 1969; Robert de Villiers Award, Amer. Leukaemia Soc., 1970; Walker Prize for 1966-70, RCS, 1971; Paul Ehrlich-Ludwig Darmstaedter Prize, Paul Ehrlich Foundn, Frankfurt, 1972; Soc. of Apothecaries' Medal, 1972; Albert Lasker Clinical Chemotherapy Award, 1972; Gairdner Foundn Award, 1973. *Publications:* Co-editor: Treatment of Burkitt's Lymphoma (UICC Monograph 8), 1967; Burkitt's Lymphoma, 1970; Refined Carbohydrate Foods and Disease, 1975; over 150 contribs to scientific jls. *Recreations:* photography, carpentry. *Address:* The Knoll, Shiplake, Oxon. *T:* Wargrave 2186.

BURLEIGH, Very Rev. John H. S., DD, BLitt; Professor of Ecclesiastical History, Edinburgh University, 1931-64, Emeritus, since 1964; Dean of the Faculty of Divinity, 1956-64; Moderator of the General Assembly of the Church of Scotland, May 1960-May 1961; *b* Ednam, Kelso, 19 May 1894; *s* of Rev. J. Burleigh; *m* 1926, Mary, *d* of Rev. C. Giles; one *s* one *d*. *Educ:* Kelso High Sch., George Watson's Coll. and Univ., Edinburgh; Strasbourg; Oxford. Parish Minister of Fyvie, Aberdeenshire, and St Enoch's, Dundee. Principal, New Coll., Edinburgh, 1956-64. *Publications:* Christianity in the New Testament Epistles; City of God; a Study of St Augustine's Philosophy; St Augustine: Earlier Writings; A Church History of Scotland. *Address:* 21 Kingsmuir Drive, Peebles EH45 9AA. *T:* Peebles 20224.

BURLEIGH, Thomas Haydon, CBE 1977; Director, John Brown & Co. Ltd, 1965-77; *b* 23 April 1911; *s* of late J. H. W. Burleigh, Great Chesterford; *m* 1933, Kathleen Mary Lenthall, *d* of late Dr Gurth Eager, Hertford; two *s*. *Educ:* Saffron Walden Sch. RAF, short service commission, No 19 (F) Sqdn, 1930-35; Westland Aircraft Ltd, 1936-45; Thos. Firth & John Brown Ltd, 1945-48; Firth Brown Tools Ltd, 1948-77. Pres., Sheffield Chamber of Commerce, 1963-64; Pres. Nat. Fedn of Engineers' Tool Manufacturers, 1968-70; Master of Company of Cutlers in Hallamshire in the County of York, 1970-71. *Recreations:* golf, gardening. *Address:* Kirkgate, Holme next Sea, Hunstanton, Norfolk. *T:* Holme 387. *Clubs:* Royal Air Force; Royal and Ancient Golf (St Andrews).

BURLINGTON, Earl of; William Cavendish; *b* 6 June 1969; *s* and *heir* of Marquess of Hartington, *qv*.

BURMAN, Sir (John) Charles, Kt 1961; DL; JP; Director and Chairman, South Staffs Waterworks Co.; *b* 30 Aug. 1908; *o s* of Sir John Burman, JP; *m* 1936, Ursula Hesketh-Wright, JP; two *s* two *d*. *Educ:* Rugby Sch. City Council, 1934-66 (Lord Mayor of Birmingham, 1947-49); General Commissioner of Income Tax, 1941-73; Indep. Chm., Licensing Planning Cttee, 1949-60; Chm. Birmingham Conservative and Unionist Assoc., 1963-72; County Pres. St John Ambulance Brigade, 1950-63; Member, Govt Cttee on Administrative Tribunals, 1955; Member Royal Commission on the Police, 1960. Dir, Tarmac Ltd, 1955-71 (Chm., 1961-71). Life Governor, also Trustee, Barber Institute, at University of Birmingham. JP 1942; High Sheriff, Warwickshire, 1958, DL 1967. KStJ, 1961. *Address:* Packwood Hall, Hockley Heath, Warwickshire B94 6PU. *T:* Lapworth 3104. *Club:* Birmingham (Birmingham).

BURMAN, Sir Stephen (France), Kt 1973; CBE 1954 (MBE 1943); MA; Chairman, Serck Ltd, Birmingham, 1962-70; Director: Averys, Ltd, 1951-73; Imperial Chemical Industries Ltd, 1953-75; Imperial Metal Industries Ltd, 1962-75; J. Lucas Industries Ltd, 1952-75, and of other industrial companies; *b* 27 Dec. 1904; *s* of Henry Burman; *m* 1931, Joan Margaret Rogers;

one s (and one s decd). *Educ:* Oundle. Pres. Birmingham Chamber of Commerce, 1950-51 (Vice-Pres. 1949); Chm. United Birmingham Hosps., 1948-53; Dep. Chm. 1953-56. Dir, Midland Bank Ltd, 1959-76. Governor Birmingham Children's Hosp., 1944-48; Dep. Chm. Teaching Hosps. Assoc., 1949-53; Member, Midlands Electricity Board, 1948-65; Chm. Birmingham and District Advisory Cttee for Industry, 1947-49; Member Midland Regional Board for Industry, 1949-65, Vice-Chm. 1951-65; Member of Council and Governor, Univ. of Birmingham, 1949-76, Pro-Chancellor, 1955-66; General Commissioner for Income Tax, 1950-68. Member Royal Commission on Civil Service, 1953-56. Hon. LLD Birmingham, 1972. *Recreation:* shooting. *Address:* 12 Cherry Hill Road, Barnt Green, Birmingham B45 8LJ. *T:* 021-445 1529.

BURN, Andrew Robert, historian; *b* 25 Sept. 1902; *s* of Rev. A. E. Burn and Celia Mary, *d* of Edward Richardson; *m* 1938, Mary, *d* of Wynn Thomas, OBE, Ministry of Agriculture. *Educ:* Uppingham Sch.; Christ Church, Oxford. Sen. Classical Master, Uppingham Sch., 1927-40; British Council Rep. in Greece, 1940-41; Intelligence Corps, Middle East, 1941-44; 2nd Sec., British Embassy, Athens, 1944-46; Sen. Lectr and sole Mem. Dept of Ancient History, Univ. of Glasgow, 1946; Reader, 1965; resigned, 1969; Vis. Prof. at "A College Year in Athens", Athens, Greece, 1969-72. Pres. Glasgow Archæological Soc., 1966-69. *Publications:* Minoans, Philistines and Greeks, 1930; The Romans in Britain, 1932; The World of Hesiod, 1936; This Scepter'd Isle: an Anthology, 1940 (Athens); The Modern Greeks, 1942 (Alexandria); Alexander and the Hellenistic World, 1947; Pericles and Athens, 1948; Agricola and Roman Britain, 1953; The Lyric Age of Greece, 1960; Persia and the Greeks, 1962; The Pelican History of Greece, 1966; The Warring States of Greece (illustrated), 1968; Greece and Rome (Hist. of Civilisation Vol. II), 1970 (Chicago); contributions to encyclopædias and historical journals. *Recreation:* travel. *Address:* 23 Ritchie Court, 380 Banbury Road, Oxford OX2 7PW. *T:* Oxford 50423.

BURN, Duncan (Lyall); economist, historian; *b* 10 Aug. 1902; *s* of Archibald William and Margaret Anne Burn; *m* 1930, Mollie White; two *d. Educ:* Holloway County Sch.; Christ's Coll. (Scholar), Cambridge. Hist. Tripos, Pts I and II, Cl. I, Wrenbury Schol. 1924, Bachelor Research Schol. 1924, Christ's Coll., Cambridge. Lecturer in Economic History: Univ. of Liverpool, 1925; Univ. of Cambridge, 1927. Min. of Supply (Iron and Steel Control), 1939; Member US-UK Metallurgical Mission, New York and Washington, 1943; leader writer and Industrial Correspondent of the Times, 1946-62. Director of the Economic Development Office set up by AEI, English Electric, GEC, and Parsons, 1962-65. Visiting Professor of Economics: Manchester Univ., 1967-69; Bombay Univ., 1971. Member: Advisory Cttee on Census of Production, 1955-65; Exec. Cttee, Nat. Inst. of Econ. and Social Research, 1957-69; Econ. Cttee, DSIR, 1963-65. *Publications:* Economic History of Steelmaking, 1867-1939, 1940; The Steel Industry, 1939-59, 1961; The Political Economy of Nuclear Energy, 1967; Chemicals under Free Trade, two industry studies (with B. Epstein), 1972; Nuclear Power and the Energy Gap: politics and the atomic industry, 1977; ed and contrib. The Structure of British Industry, 2 vols, 1958; also contrib. to Journals, Bank Reviews, etc. *Recreations:* walking, gardening. *Address:* 5 Hampstead Hill Gardens, NW3 2PH. *T:* 01-435 5344. *Club:* United Oxford & Cambridge University.

BURN, Joshua Harold, FRS 1942; MA, MD, Cantab; Emeritus Professor of Pharmacology, Oxford University, Emeritus Fellow of Balliol College; *b* 6 March 1892; *s* of J. G. Burn, Barnard Castle; *m* 1st, 1920, Margaret Parkinson (*d* 1927); 2nd, 1928, Katharine F. Pemberton (*d* 1971); two *s* four *d* ; 3rd, 1971, Mrs Elizabeth Haslam-Jones. *Educ:* Barnard Castle Sch.; Emmanuel Coll., Cambridge (Scholar); 1st Class Pt 2 Natural Science Tripos; Michael Foster Student and Raymond Horton-Smith Prizeman; temp. Lieut RE, 1914-18; Guy's Hospital, 1918-20; member of staff of Medical Research Council, 1920-25; Director of Pharmacological Laboratories of Pharmaceutical Soc., 1926-37; Dean of Coll. of Pharmaceutical Soc. and Prof. of Pharmacology, Univ. of London, 1933-37; Prof. of Pharmacology, Oxford Univ., 1937-59. Member of 1932 Pharmacopœia Commn; Hon. Fellow, Indian Nat. Science Acad.; Hon. Member Soc. of Pharmacology and Therapeutics of Argentine Medical Assoc. Abraham Flexner Lecturer, Vanderbilt Univ., 1956; Nathanson Memorial Lecturer Univ. of Southern California, 1956; Dixon Memorial Lecturer Royal Soc. of Medicine, 1956; Herter Lecturer, Johns Hopkins Univ., 1962; Visiting Prof. to Washington Univ., St Louis, 1959-68. Hon. DSc: Yale, 1957; Bradford, 1971; Hon. MD Johannes Gutenberg Univ., Mainz, 1964; Dr (*hc*), Univ. of Paris, 1965; Hon. Pres., Internat. Union of Pharmacology, 1975; Hon. Member: Deutsche Pharmakologische Gesellschaft (by whom

awarded the Schmiedeberg Plakette); British Pharmacological Society; Deutsche Akademie der Naturforscher (Leopoldina); Czechoslovak Medical Society J. E. Purkyně. Gairdner Foundation Prize, 1959. *Publications:* Methods of Biological Assay, 1928; Recent Advances in Materia Medica, 1931; Biological Standardization, 1937; Background of Therapeutics, 1948; Lecture Notes on Pharmacology, 1948; Practical Pharmacology, 1952; Functions of Autonomic Transmitters, 1956; The Principles of Therapeutics, 1957; Drugs, Medicines and Man, 1962; The Autonomic Nervous System, 1963; Our most interesting Diseases, 1964; A Defence of John Balliol, 1970. *Address:* 3 Squitchey Lane, Oxford. *T:* Oxford 58209.

BURN, Michael Clive, MC 1945; writer; *b* 11 Dec. 1912; *s* of late Sir Clive Burn; *m* 1947, Mary Booker (*née* Walter); no *c. Educ:* Winchester; New Coll., Oxford (open scholar). Journalist, The Times, 1936-39; Lieut 1st Bn Queens Westminsters, KRRC, 1939-40; Officer in Independent Companies, Norwegian Campaign, 1940, subseq. Captain No. 2 Commando; taken prisoner in raid on St Nazaire, 1942; prisoner in Germany, 1942-45. Foreign Correspondent for The Times in Vienna, Jugoslavia and Hungary, 1946-49. Keats Poetry First Prize, 1973. *Plays:* The Modern Everyman (prod. Birmingham Rep., 1947); Beyond the Storm (Midlands Arts Co., and Vienna, 1947); The Night of the Ball (prod. New Theatre, 1956). *Publications:* novels: Yes, Farewell, 1946, repr. 1975; Childhood at Oriol, 1951; The Midnight Diary, 1952; The Trouble with Jake, 1967; *sociological:* Mr Lyward's Answer, 1956; The Debatable Land, 1970; *poems:* Poems to Mary, 1953; The Flying Castle, 1954; Out On A Limb, 1973; *play:* The Modern Everyman, 1948. *Address:* Beudy Gwyn, Minffordd, Gwynedd, North Wales.

BURN, Rodney Joseph, RA 1962 (ARA 1954); Artist; *b* Palmers Green, Middlesex, 11 July 1899; *s* of Sir Joseph Burn, KBE, and Emily Harriet Smith; *m* 1923, Dorothy Margaret, *d* of late Edward Sharwood-Smith; one *s* two *d. Educ:* Harrow Sch. Studied art at Slade Sch.; Asst Teacher at Royal Coll. of Art, South Kensington, 1929-31 and since 1946; Director of School of the Museum of Fine Arts, Boston, Mass., USA, 1931; returned to England, 1934; Asst Master, City & Guilds of London Art Sch.; Tutor, Royal Coll. of Art, 1947-65. Hon. Secretary New English Art Club until 1963; Member Royal West of England Academy, 1963; Pres. St Ives Soc. of Artists, 1963; Hon. Fellow Royal Coll. of Art, 1964; Fellow University Coll. London, 1966; Hon. Mem., Soc. of Marine Artists, 1975. *Address:* 1 The Moorings, Strand on the Green, Chiswick, W4. *T:* 01-994 4190.

BURNABY, Rev. Prof. John; Regius Professor of Divinity (Emeritus), Cambridge University; *b* 28 July 1891; 2nd *s* of Rev. J. C. W. Burnaby and Ina, *d* of Maj.-Gen. J. P. Battersby; *m* 1922, Dorothy Helen (*d* 1971), *d* of Rev. J. B. Lock, and widow of Capt. W. Newton; one *s* one *d* (one step-*d*) (and one *s* decd). *Educ:* Haileybury Coll.; Trinity Coll., Cambridge. Craven Univ. Scholar, 1912; Chancellor's Classical Medalist, 1914. Served European War, 1914-19, 1st Bn The London Regt, Gallipoli and France. Fellow of Trinity Coll., Cambridge, 1915; Junior Dean, 1919; Steward and Prælector, 1921; Junior Bursar, 1921-31; Tutor, 1931-38; Senior Tutor, 1938-45; Dean of Chapel, 1943-58; Hulsean Lecturer, 1938; College Lecturer in Theology, 1939-51; University Lecturer in Divinity, 1945-52; Regius Professor of Divinity, 1952-58. Deacon, 1941; Priest, 1942. *Publications:* Amor Dei: a study in the religion of St Augustine, 1938; Is the Bible Inspired?, 1949; Later Works of St Augustine (trans. and ed) in Library of Christian Classics, 1955; Christian Words and Christian Meanings, 1955; The Belief of Christendom, 1959. *Recreation:* reading aloud. *Address:* 6 Hedgerley Close, Cambridge. *T:* 50395.

BURNE, Sir Lewis (Charles), Kt 1959; CBE 1955; *b* West Leederville, WA, 14 Jan. 1898; *s* of late William Charles and Sarah Ellen Burne; *m* 1922, Florence Mary Stafford; two *s* two *d. Educ:* Xavier Coll., Melbourne. President: Master Builders Assoc. of Victoria, 1941-44; Master Builders' Federation of Australia, 1947; Victorian Employers' Federation, 1948-50 and 1953-61; Australian Council of Employers' Federations, 1957-58. Pres. Royal Melbourne Inst. of Technology, 1961; Chairman: Federation Insurance Ltd, 1956-; VEF Corporate Investments Ltd, 1958. Australian Employers' Deleg. at ILO, 1950-52-55-57-66; Australian Employers' Rep. Asian Advisory Cttee of ILO, 1951-65; Employer Member at Governing Body meetings of ILO, 1950-66, and elected Member Governing Body, 1957-66. Fellow Australian Inst. of Builders (Foundation Member). Australian Flying Corps, 1918. *Recreations:* golf and bowls. *Address:* 20 Rockingham Street, Kew, Vic. 3101, Australia. *T:* 86-8354. *Clubs:* Victoria Racing, RAC of Victoria (all in Melbourne).

BURNELL, (Susan) Jocelyn (Bell), PhD; FRAS; astronomer; part-time research, Mullard Space Science Laboratory, University College London, since 1974; *b* 15 July 1943; *d* of G. Philip and M. Allison Bell; *m* 1968, Martin Burnell; one *s*. *Educ:* The Mount Sch., York; Glasgow Univ. (BSc); New Hall, Cambridge (PhD). FRAS 1969. Res. Fellowships, Univ. of Southampton, 1968-73. An Editor, The Observatory, 1973-76. Michelson Medal, Franklin Inst., Philadelphia (jtly with Prof. A. Hewish), 1973. *Publications:* papers in Nature, Astronomy and Astrophysics, Jl of Geophys. Res. *Recreations:* Quaker interests, walking. *Address:* Mullard Space Science Laboratory, Holmbury St Mary, near Dorking, Surrey. *T:* Forest Green 292.

BURNES, Sheila; *see* Bloom, Ursula.

BURNET, Alastair; *see* Burnet, J. W. A.

BURNET, Sir (Frank) Macfarlane, OM 1958; KBE 1969; Kt 1951; FRS 1942; MD, ScD (Hon.) Cambridge, 1946; DSc (Hon.) Oxford, 1968; FRCP 1953; Past Director, Walter and Eliza Hall Institute for Medical Research, Melbourne, and Professor of Experimental Medicine, Melbourne University, 1944-1965 (Assistant Director, 1928-31 and 1934-44); Emeritus Professor, Melbourne University, 1965; Chairman, Commonwealth Foundation, 1966-69; *b* 3 Sept. 1899; *s* of Frank Burnet, Traralgon, Victoria; *m* 1st, 1928, Edith Linda (*d* 1973), *d* of F. H. Druce; one *s* two *d*; 2nd, 1976, Hazel Jenkin (*née* Foletta). *Educ:* Geelong Coll., Melbourne Univ. (MD). Resident Pathologist, Melbourne Hosp., 1923-24; Beit Fellow for Medical Research at Lister Institute, London, 1926-27; Visiting worker at National Institute for Medical Research, Hampstead, 1932-33; Dunham Lecturer Harvard Medical Sch., Jan. 1944; Croonian Lecturer, 1950 (Royal Society); Herter Lecturer, 1950 (Johns Hopkins Univ.); Abraham Flexner Lecturer (Vanderbilt Univ.), 1958. Pres., Australian Acad. of Science, 1965-69. Hon. FRCS 1969. Royal Medal of Royal Society, 1947; Galen Medal in Therapeutics, Society of Apothecaries, 1958; Copley Medal, Royal Society, 1959; Nobel Prize for Medicine, 1960. *Publications:* Biological Aspects of Infectious Disease, 1940 (4th edn (with D. O. White) Natural History of Infectious Disease, 1972); Virus as Organism, 1945; Viruses and Man (Penguin), 1953; Principles of Animal Virology, 1955; Enzyme Antigen and Virus, 1956; Clonal Selection Theory of Acquired Immunity, 1959; Integrity of the Body, 1962; (with I. R. Mackay) Autoimmune Diseases, 1962; Changing Patterns (autobiography), 1968; Cellular Immunology, 1969; Dominant Mammal, 1970; Immunological Surveillance, 1970; Genes, Dreams and Realities, 1971; Walter and Eliza Hall Institute 1915-65, 1971; Auto-immunity and Auto-immune Disease, 1972; Intrinsic Mutagenesis, 1974; Immunology, 1976; Immunity, Aging and Cancer, 1976; technical papers. *Address:* School of Microbiology, University of Melbourne, Parkville, Victoria 3052; 48 Monomeath Avenue, Canterbury, Victoria 3126, Australia.

BURNET, James William Alexander, (Alastair Burnet); broadcaster with Independent Television News, since 1976; *b* 12 July 1928; *s* of late Alexander and Schonaid Burnet, Edinburgh; *m* 1958, Maureen Campbell Sinclair. *Educ:* The Leys Sch., Cambridge; Worcester Coll., Oxford. Sub-editor and leader writer, Glasgow Herald, 1951-58; Commonwealth Fund Fellow, 1956-57; Leader writer, The Economist, 1958-62; Political editor, Independent Television News, 1963-64; Editor, The Economist, 1965-74; Editor, Daily Express, 1974-76. Member: Cttee of Award, Commonwealth Fund, 1969-76; Cttee on Reading and Other Uses of English Language, 1972-75; Monopolies Commn specialist panel on newspaper mergers, 1973-. Richard Dimbleby Award, British Academy of Film and Television Arts, 1966, 1970; Political Broadcaster of the Year Award, 1970. *Address:* 43 Hornton Court, Campden Hill Road, W8. *T:* 01-937 7563; 33 Westbourne Gardens, Glasgow. *T:* 041-339 8073. *Club:* Reform.

BURNET, Mrs Pauline Ruth, CBE 1970; JP; Chairman, Cambridgeshire Area Health Authority (Teaching), since 1973; *b* 23 Aug. 1920; *d* of Rev. Edmund Willis and Constance Marjorie Willis (*née* Bostock); *m* 1940, John Forbes Burnet, Fellow of Magdalene Coll., Cambridge; one *s* one *d* (and one *s* decd). *Educ:* St Stephen's Coll., Folkestone (now at Broadstairs), Kent. Member: Windsor and Eton Hosp. Management Cttee, 1948-50; Fulbourn and Ida Darwin HMC, 1951-74 (Chm., 1969-74). Member: E Anglian Regional Hosp. Bd, 1968-74; Bd of Governors of United Cambridge Hosps, 1966-74; Mem. Council, Assoc. of Hosp. Management Cttees until 1974 (Chm., 1966-68). Chm., Cambridgeshire Mental Welfare Assoc., 1964-. Mem., Farleigh Hosp. Cttee of Inquiry, 1970. JP City of Cambridge, 1957-. *Recreations:* walking, swimming. *Address:* 28 Selwyn Gardens, Cambridge CB3 9AZ. *T:* Cambridge 50726.

BURNETT, of Leys, Baronetcy of (unclaimed); *see under* Ramsay, Sir Alexander William Burnett, 7th Bt.

BURNETT, Most Rev. Bill Bendyshe; *see* Cape Town, Archbishop of.

BURNETT, Air Chief Marshal Sir Brian (Kenyon), GCB 1970 (KCB 1965; CB 1961); DFC 1942; AFC 1939; RAF, retired; Chairman, All England Lawn Tennis Club, Wimbledon, since 1974; President, Squash Rackets Association, 1972-75; *b* 10 March 1913; *s* of late Kenneth Burnett and Anita Catherine Burnett (*née* Evans); *m* 1944, Valerie Mary (*née* St Ludger); two *s*. *Educ:* Charterhouse; Wadham Coll., Oxford (Hon. Fellow, 1974); Joined RAFO 1932; RAF 1934; Long Distance Record Flight of 7,158 miles from Egypt to Australia, Nov. 1938. Served War of 1939-45, in Bomber and Flying Training Commands; RAF Staff Coll. Course, 1944; Directing Staff, RAF Staff Coll., 1945-47; UN Military Staff Cttee, New York, 1947-48; Joint Planning Staff, 1949-50; SASO HQ No. 3 (Bomber) Group, 1951-53; CORAF Gaydon, 1954-55; ADC to the Queen, 1953-57; Director of Bomber and Reconnaissance Ops, Air Ministry, 1956-57; Imperial Defence Coll., 1958; Air Officer Administration, HQ Bomber Command, 1959-61; AOC No 3 Gp, Bomber Command, 1961-64; Vice-Chief of the Air Staff, 1964-67; Air Secretary, MoD, 1967-70; C-in-C, Far East Command, Singapore, 1970-71; retired 1972. Air ADC to the Queen, 1969-72. *Recreations:* tennis, squash rackets, golf, skiing. *Address:* Heather Hill, Littleworth Cross, Seale, Farnham, Surrey. *Clubs:* Royal Air Force; Vincent's (Oxford); All England Lawn Tennis; Ski Club of Great Britain; Jesters Squash; International Lawn Tennis Club of Great Britain; Hankley Common Golf.

BURNETT, Sir David Humphery, 3rd Bt, *cr* 1913; MBE 1945; TD; Chairman, since 1965, Proprietors of Hay's Wharf Ltd; Director, Guardian Royal Exchange Assurance and other companies; one of HM Lieutenants of the City of London; *b* 27 Jan. 1918; *s* of Sir Leslie Trew Burnett, 2nd Bt, CBE, TD, DL, and Joan, *d* of late Sir John Humphery; *S* father 1955; *m* 1948, Geraldine Elizabeth Mortimer, *d* of Sir Godfrey Arthur Fisher, KCMG; two *s* (and one *s* decd). *Educ:* Harrow; St John's Coll., Cambridge, MA. Served War of 1939-45 (despatches, MBE), in France, N Africa, Sicily and Italy; Temp. Lt-Col GSO1, 1945. Chairman: South London Botanical Institute; London Assoc. of Public Wharfingers, 1964-71. Mem. PLA, 1962-75. Mem. Council, Brighton Coll. Master: Company of Watermen and Lightermen of the River Thames, 1964; Girdlers Company, 1970. FRICS 1970; FBIM 1968. *Heir:* *s* Charles David Burnett, *b* 18 May 1951. *Address:* Tandridge Hall, near Oxted, Surrey; Tillmouth Park, Cornhill-on-Tweed, Northumberland. *Club:* Turf.

BURNETT, Maj.-Gen. Edward John Sidney, CB 1975; DSO 1964; OBE 1965 (MBE 1955); MC 1945; *b* 8 Feb. 1921; *s* of Dr A. H. Burnett; *m* 1967, Christine Adrienne de Jenner; two *d* (and two *s* one *d* by a previous *m*). *Educ:* Kelly Coll., Tavistock. Commissioned into Indian Army, 1941; served with 4th PWO Gurkha Rifles until 1947; transferred to 10th PMO Gurkha Rifles, 1948; served in Hong Kong and Malaya. Military Attaché, Katmandu, 1957-58; College Commander, RMAS, 1967; commanded 48 Gurkha Inf. Bde in Hong Kong, 1968-70; commanded Gurkha L of C, in Nepal, 1970-71; Dep. Comdr Land Forces and Maj.-Gen. Brigade of Gurkhas, in Hong Kong, 1971-75. Col, 10 PMO Gurkha Rifles, 1975-77. Managing Dir, Tehran Racing, PO Box 12/1635 Iran. Star of Nepal, 1954. *Recreations:* golf, shooting. *Address:* c/o Lloyds Bank, 6 Pall Mall, SW1; Whitehouse Farm, near Shaftesbury, Dorset. *Club:* Naval and Military.

BURNETT, Prof. George Murray; Principal and Vice-Chancellor, Heriot-Watt University, since 1974; *b* 12 July 1921; *s* of G. Burnett, Messina, South Africa; *m* 1946, Anne Edith, *d* of S. M. Bow, Aberdeen; one *s* three *d*. *Educ:* Robert Gordon's Coll., Aberdeen; Aberdeen Univ. DSIR Senior Fellow, 1947-48. Lectr, Birmingham Univ., 1949-55; Prof. of Chemistry, Univ. of Aberdeen, 1955-74, Vice-Principal, 1966-69. Member: Science Bd, SRC, 1975-; Council, Open Univ., 1975. FRSE 1957; FRIC 1961. JP Aberdeen 1967-74. *Publications:* Mechanism of Polymer Reactions, 1954; contrib. to Proc. Royal Society, Trans. Faraday Soc., etc. *Address:* Hermiston House, Hermiston, Edinburgh. *T:* 031-449 5595.

BURNETT, Prof. John Harrison; Sibthorpian Professor of Rural Economy, Oxford, since 1970; *b* 21 Jan. 1922; *s* of Rev. T. Harrison Burnett; *m* 1945, E. Margaret, *er d* of Rev. Dr E. W. Bishop; two *s*. *Educ:* Kingswood Sch., Bath; Merton Coll., Oxford. BA, MA 1947; DPhil 1953; Christopher Welch Scholar, 1946. Lecturer, Lincoln Coll., 1948-49; Fellow (by Exam.)

Magdalen Coll., 1949-53; Univ. Lecturer and Demonstrator, Oxford, 1949-53; Lecturer, Liverpool Univ., 1954-55; Prof. of Botany: Univ. of St Andrews, 1955-60; King's Coll., Newcastle, Univ. of Durham, 1961-63, Univ. of Newcastle, 1963-68; Dean of Faculty of Science, St Andrews, 1958-60, Newcastle, 1966-68; Public Orator, Newcastle, 1966-68; Regius Prof. of Botany, Univ. of Glasgow, 1968-70. Chm. Scottish Horticultural Research Inst., 1959-74; Mem., Nature Conservancy (Scottish Cttee), 1961-66; Trustee, The New Phytologist, 1962-; Mem. Academic Adv. Council, Univs of St Andrews and Dundee, 1964-66. Served 1942-46 as Lieut RNVR (despatches). FRSE 1957. *Publications:* The Vegetation of Scotland, ed and contrib., 1964; Fundamentals of Mycology, 1968, 2nd edn 1976; Mycogenetics, 1975; papers in various scientific journals. *Address:* St John's College, Oxford. *T:* Oxford 47671.

BURNETT, Lt-Col Maurice John Brownless, DSO 1944; JP; DL; *b* 24 Sept. 1904; *o* s of late Ernest Joseph Burnett, MBE, JP, The Red House, Saltburn-by-the-Sea, Yorks, and late Emily Maud Margaret, 2nd *d* of John Brownless, Whorlton Grange, Barnard Castle and Dunsa Manor, Dalton; *m* 1930, Crystal, *d* of late Col H. D. Chamier, The Connaught Rangers; one *s. Educ:* Aysgarth Sch.; Rugby Sch.; RMA, Woolwich; Staff Coll., Camberley. 2nd Lieut RA 1924; psc 1937; Lt-Col 1942; served 1939-45; comd 127th (Highland) Field Regt in 51st Highland Division, Normandy to the Rhine; retd 1948. JP, 1957, DL, 1958, N Yorks. Member: N Riding Yorks Education Cttee, 1956-69; NR Yorks Standing Joint Cttee, and York and NE Yorks Police Cttee, 1958-74; Richmond, Yorks, RDC 1958-74 (Chm., 1967-69); N Riding CC, 1962-74 (Chm., Civil Protection Cttee, 1969-74); N Yorks CC, 1974- (Chm., Public Protection Cttee, 1974-); Church Assembly, 1955-70, General Synod, 1970-; Ripon Diocesan Bd of Finance, 1953 (Vice-Chm. 1956); Exec. Cttee, N Riding Yorks Assoc. of Youth Clubs, 1950-71 (Chm. 1952 and 1965, Pres. 1971). Governor, Barnard Castle Sch., 1959-63, 1973-; Chm. of Governors, Richmond Sch., 1970-; District Comr, Scouts Assoc., (formerly Boy Scouts Assoc.), NR Yorks, 1950, County-Comr, 1961-69. Sec., N Riding Yorks Territorial and Auxiliary Forces Assoc., 1950-68. *Recreations:* country sports and pursuits, interest in local government and youth work. *Address:* Dunsa Manor, Dalton, Richmond, N Yorks. *T:* East Layton 251. *Club:* Army and Navy.

BURNETT, Rev. Canon Philip Stephen; Church of England Board of Education, since 1970; *b* 8 Jan. 1914; *s* of late Philip Burnett and Mrs Burnett, Salton, York; *m* 1954, Joan Hardy, *e d* of C. F. Hardy, Sheffield; one *s* one *d. Educ:* Scarborough Coll.; Balliol Coll., Oxford; Westcott House, Cambridge. Admitted Solicitor, 1936; Lay Missionary, Dio. Saskatchewan, Canada, 1939-41. Intelligence Corps, 1942-44; Staff Capt., GHQ, New Delhi, 1944-45, Deacon, 1947, Priest, 1948; Curate of St Andrew's, Chesterton, Cambridge, and Staff Sec., Student Christian Movement, 1947-49; Asst Gen. Sec., SCM, 1949-52; Vicar of St Mary, Bramall Lane, Sheffield, 1952-61; Rural Dean of Ecclesall, 1959-65; Canon Residentiary of Sheffield Cathedral, and Educn Secretary, Diocese of Sheffield, 1961-70, Canon Emeritus 1970.- *Address:* 91 Chelverton Road, Putney, SW15 1RW. *T:* 01-789 9934.

BURNETT, Rear-Adm. Philip Whitworth, CB 1957; DSO 1945; DSC 1943, and Bar, 1944; *b* 10 Sept. 1908; *s* of Henry Ridley Burnett; *m* 1947, Molly, *widow* of Brig. H. C. Partridge, DSO, and *d* of H. M. Trouncer; one *s* two *d. Educ:* Preparatory Sch., Seascale; Royal Naval Coll., Dartmouth. Served War of 1939-45; HMS Kelly, 1939-41; HMS Osprey, 1941-43; Western Approaches Escort Groups, 1943-45. Chief of Staff to Comdr-in-Chief, Portsmouth, 1955-57; retd list 1958. Lieut 1930; Comdr 1940; Capt. 1945; Rear-Adm. 1955. Sec. of the Royal Institution of Chartered Surveyors, 1959-65. *Address:* Priory Farm, Waverley Abbey, Farnham, Surrey GU9 8EW.

BURNETT, William George Esterbrooke, CB 1946; Commissioner of Inland Revenue and Secretary, Board of Inland Revenue, 1942-49, retired; *b* 1886; *s* of late William Burnett, Belturbet, Co. Cavan; *m* 1918, Dorothea, *y d* of late J. E. Kingsbury, Crawley Down, Sussex; two *s. Educ:* Royal School, Cavan; Trinity Coll., Dublin. *Address:* Brookside, 7 Guildford Road, Horsham, West Sussex. *T:* 65284.

BURNEY, Sir Anthony (George Bernard), Kt 1971; OBE 1945; BA, FCA; Chairman, Debenhams Ltd; Director, Commercial Union; *b* 3 June 1909; *o* s of Theodore and Gertrude Burney; *m* 1947, Dorothy Mary Vere, *d* of Col Clements Parr; no *c. Educ:* Rugby; Corpus Christi Coll., Cambridge (Hon. Fellow 1975). BA; FCA. Partner, Binder, Hamlyn & Co., Chartered Accountants, 1938-71. Served War of 1939-45, Army: RE and RASC, Europe (Lt-Col). Dir of Reorganisation, The Cotton Bd, 1959-60; Mem. Shipbuilding Inquiry Cttee, 1965-66; Chm.,

Freight Integration Council, 1968-75; Mem. National Ports Council, 1971; Chm., Charities Aid Foundn. *Publication:* Illustrations of Management Accounting in Practice, 1959. *Recreations:* gardening, photography. *Address:* 6 Greville Place, NW6. *T:* 01-624 4439. *Clubs:* Buck's, Garrick.

BURNEY, Sir Cecil (Denniston), 3rd Bt *cr* 1921; Managing Director since 1951, and Chairman since 1968, Northern Motors Ltd; Chairman: Hampton Trust Ltd; Customagic Manufacturing Co. Ltd; Director, Mooloya Investments Ltd; *b* 8 Jan. 1923; *s* of Sir Charles Dennistoun Burney, 2nd Bt, CMG, and of Gladys, *d* of George Henry High; *S* father, 1968; *m* 1957, Hazel Marguerite de Hamel, *yr d* of late Thurman Coleman; two *s. Educ:* Eton; Trinity Coll., Cambridge. Dir, Security Building Soc., 1959-71. Member of Legislative Council, N Rhodesia, 1959-64; MP Zambia, 1964-68; Chairman, Public Accounts Cttee, Zambia, 1963-67. *Recreations:* tennis, skiing. *Heir: s* Nigel Dennistoun Burney, *b* 6 Sept. 1959. *Address:* PO Box 672, Ndola, Zambia; 5 Lyall Street, SW1. *T:* 01-235 4014. *Clubs:* Carlton, Turf, Buck's; Leander; Salisbury, Bulawayo (Rhodesia); Ndola (Zambia).

BURNHAM, 5th Baron, *cr* 1903; **William Edward Harry Lawson,** Bt 1892; JP; DL; Lieutenant-Colonel; Scots Guards, retired 1968; *b* 22 Oct. 1920; *er s* of 4th Baron Burnham, CB, DSO, MC, TD, and of (Marie) Enid (*see* Lady Burnham); *S* father, 1963; *m* 1942, Anne, *yr d* of late Major Gerald Petherick, The Mill House, St Cross, Winchester; three *d* (one *s* decd). *Educ:* Eton. Royal Bucks Yeomanry, 1939-41; Scots Guards, 1941-68; commanded 1st Bn, 1959-62. Chm., Sail Training Assoc.; Vice-Chm. (Bucks), East Wessex TAVRA. JP Bucks 1970, DL Bucks 1977. *Recreations:* sailing, shooting, ski-ing. *Heir: b* Hon. Hugh John Frederick Lawson [*b* 15 Aug. 1931; *m* 1955, Hilary Mary, *d* of Alan Hunter; one *s* two *d*]. *Address:* Hall Barn, Beaconsfield, Bucks. *T:* Beaconsfield 3315. *Clubs:* Garrick, Turf; Royal Yacht Squadron.

BURNHAM, Enid, CBE 1957; **(Enid Lady Burnham);** Vice-President, Girl Guides Association for England, since 1971 (President, 1961-71); President, Buckinghamshire Red Cross, 1936-64; *d* of Hugh Scott Robson, Buenos Aires; *m* 1920, 4th Baron Burnham, CB, DSO, MC, TD; two *s* one *d. Educ:* Heathfield Sch., Ascot. Pres. Bucks Federation of Women's Institutes, 1947-52; Chief Commissioner for England, Girl Guides, 1951-60. Vice-Pres., Bucks County CPRE, 1969. *Publication:* (with Geoffrey Toye) Military Menus. *Recreations:* riding, country life, dogs. *Address:* Wycombe End House, Beaconsfield, Bucks. *Club:* Guide.

BURNHAM, Forbes; *see* Burnham, L. F. S.

BURNHAM, James; Writer; Editor, National Review, since 1955; *b* 22 Nov. 1905; *s* of Claude George Burnham and Mary May Gillis; *m* 1934, Marcia Lightner; two *s* one *d. Educ:* Princeton Univ.; Balliol Coll., Oxford Univ. Prof. of Philosophy, New York Univ., 1932-54. *Publications:* (jtly) A Critical Introduction to Philosophy, 1932; The Managerial Revolution, 1941, rev. edn 1972; The Machiavellians, 1943; The Struggle for the World, 1947; (jtly) The Case for De Gaulle, 1948; The Coming Defeat of Communism, 1950; Containment or Liberation, 1953; The Web of Subversion, 1954; Congress and the American Tradition, 1959; Suicide of the West, 1964; The War We Are In, 1967. *Address:* Kent, Conn. 06757, USA. *T:* Kent, Conn., 203-927-3117.

BURNHAM, (Linden) Forbes (Sampson), OE (Guyana) 1973; SC (Guyana); MP; Prime Minister of Guyana, since 1964 (of British Guiana, 1964-66); Leader, People's National Congress, since 1957; *b* 20 Feb. 1923; *s* of J. E. Burnham, Headteacher of Kitty Methodist Sch., and Rachel A. Burnham (*née* Sampson); *m* 1st, 1951, Sheila Bernice Lataste; three *d*; 2nd, 1967, Viola Victorine Harper; two *d. Educ:* Kitty Methodist Sch., Central High Sch., Queen's Coll.; London Univ. British Guiana Scholarship, 1942; BA (London) 1944; Best Speaker's Cup at Univ. of London, 1947; Pres. W Indian Students Union (Brit.), 1947-48; Delegate, Internat. Union of Students, Paris and Prague, 1947, 1948; LLB (Hons) 1947. Called to the Bar, 1948; QC (British Guiana), 1960, SC 1966. Entered local politics, 1949; Co-founder and Chm., People's Progressive Party, 1949; Minister of Education, 1953; re-elected to Legislature, 1957 and 1961; Founder and Leader, People's Nat. Congress, 1957; Leader of Opposition, 1957-64. Pres. Kitty Brotherhood, 1947-48, 1949-50; Town Councillor, 1952; Mayor of Georgetown, 1959, 1964; Pres. Bar Association, 1959; Pres. Guyana Labour Union, 1953-56, 1963-65 (Pres. on leave, 1965-). *Publication:* A Destiny to Mould, 1970. *Recreations:* horse-riding, swimming, fishing, hunting, chess (Pres., Guyana Chess Assoc.); special interest, farming. *Address:* Office of the Prime Minister, Public Buildings,

Georgetown, Guyana; The Residence, Vlissengen Road, Georgetown, Guyana. *Clubs:* Demerara Cricket, Malteenoes Sports, Guyana Sports, Cosmos Sports, Georgetown Cricket, Non Pareil, Park Tennis, Guyana Motor Racing (Patron) (all in Guyana).

BURNINGHAM, John Mackintosh; free-lance author-designer; *b* 27 April 1936; *s* of Charles Burningham and Jessie Mackintosh; *m* 1964, Helen Gillian Oxenbury; one *s* one *d*. *Educ:* Summerhill School, Leiston, Suffolk; Central School of Art, Holborn, 1956-59 (Diploma). Now free-lance: illustration, poster design, exhibition, animated film puppets, and writing for children. *Publications:* Borka, 1963 (Kate Greenaway Medal, 1963); Trubloff, 1964; Humbert, 1965; Cannonball Simp, 1966; Harquin, 1967; Seasons, 1969; Mr Gumpy's Outing, 1970 (Kate Greenaway Award, 1971); Around the World in Eighty Days, 1972; Mr Gumpy's Motor Car, 1973; "Little Books" series: The Baby, The Rabbit, The School, The Snow, 1974; The Blanket, The Cupboard, The Dog, The Friend, 1975; The Adventures of Humbert, Simp and Harquin, 1976; Come Away from the Water, Shirley, 1977. *Address:* c/o Jonathan Cape Ltd, 30 Bedford Square, WC1.

BURNISTON, Dr George Garrett, CMG 1972; OBE 1968; Chairman and Director, Division of Rehabilitation Medicine, Department of Medicine, Prince Henry, Prince of Wales and Eastern Suburbs Hospitals, NSW, since 1963; Associate Professor, School of Community Medicine, University of NSW, since 1977; *b* Sydney, NSW, 23 Nov. 1914; *s* of George Benjamin Burniston, Melbourne, Vic.; unmarried. *Educ:* Sydney High Sch.; Sydney Univ. (MB, BS). Served in RAAF Medical Service, 1940-47 (RAF Orthopaedic Service, UK, 1941-43). Dep. Co-ordinator of Rehabilitation, Min. of Post-War Reconstruction (Aust.), 1946-48. SMO, Dept of Social Services, 1948-53; Fulbright Fellow, USA and UK, 1953-54; PMO, Dept of Social Services, 1954-62; Sen. Lectr, Sch. of Medicine, Univ. of NSW, 1963-77. Mem., WHO Expert Advisory Panel on Medical Rehabilitation, 1958-. Gp Captain, RAAF Med. Reserve (retired); Foundation Fellow, Aust. Coll. of Med. Administrators, 1968; Foundn Diplomate, Physical and Rehabilitation Medicine, 1971; FRSH 1973; MRACP 1976. *Recreations:* golf, swimming, painting, reading. *Address:* 701 Tradewinds, Boorima Place, Cronulla, NSW 2230, Australia. *T:* 523-8383. *Club:* University (Sydney).

BURNLEY, Suffragan Bishop of, since 1970; **Rt. Rev. Richard Charles Challinor Watson;** Rector of Burnley since 1970; Hon. Canon of Blackburn Cathedral since 1970; *b* 16 Feb. 1923; *o s* of Col Francis W. Watson, CB, MC, DL, The Glebe House, Dinton, Aylesbury, Bucks; *m* 1955, Anna, *er d* of Rt Rev. C. M. Chavasse, OBE, MC, MA, DD, then Bishop of Rochester; one *s* one *d*. *Educ:* Rugby; New Coll., Oxford; Westcott House, Cambridge. Served Indian Artillery, Lt and Capt. RA, 1942-45. Oxford Hon. Sch. Eng. Lang. and Lit., 1948, Theology 1949; Westcott House, Cambridge, 1950-51. Curate of Stratford, London E, 1952-53; Tutor and Chaplain, Wycliffe Hall, Oxford, 1954-57; Chaplain of Wadham Coll. and Chaplain of Oxford Pastorate, 1957-61; Vicar of Hornchurch, 1962-70; Examining Chaplain to Bishop of Rochester, 1956-61, to Bishop of Chelmsford, 1962-70; Asst. Rural Dean of Havering, 1967-70. *Recreations:* reading, gardening. *Address:* Palace House, Burnley, Lancashire. *T:* Burnley 23564. *Club:* Lansdowne.

BURNLEY, Christopher John; Financial Director, British Airports Authority, since 1975; *b* 1 May 1936; *s* of John Fox Burnley and Helena Burnley; *m* 1960, Carol Joan Quirk; two *d*. *Educ:* King William's College, Isle of Man. Chartered Accountant. Articled Clerk, 1953-59; Military service, 1959-62; Computer Systems Analyst, IBM, 1962-66; Management Consultant, Peat Marwick, 1966-67; Systems Planning Manager, Castrol, 1967-68; Sen. Planner, IBM, 1969-72; Financial Dir, Foseco FS, 1972-74; Group Treasurer, Foseco Minsep, 1974-75. *Recreation:* railway enthusiast. *Address:* Thirlmere, 173 Worcester Road, West Hagley, West Midlands DY9 0PB. *T:* Hagley 3592. *Club:* Royal Automobile.

BURNS, Sir Alan Cuthbert, GCMG 1946 (KCMG 1936; CMG 1927); Knight of Order of St John of Jerusalem, 1942; *b* 9 Nov. 1887; *s* of James Burns, Treas. of St Christopher-Nevis; *m* 1914, Kathleen Hardtman, CStJ (*d* 1970); two *d*. *Educ:* St Edmund's Coll., Ware. Colonial Civil Service, Leeward Islands, 1905-12; Nigeria, 1912-24; Colonial Sec., Bahama Islands, 1924-29; administered Govt of Bahamas, May-Oct. 1924, Sept.-Nov. 1925, Sept. 1926-March 1927, June-Sept. 1928; Member Bahamas House of Assembly, 1925-28; Dep. Chief Sec. to Govt of Nigeria, 1929-34; Governor and C-in-C of British Honduras, 1934-40; Assistant Under-Sec. of State for the Colonies, 1940-41; Governor and C-inC, Gold Coast, 1941-47; Acting Governor of Nigeria, 1942; Permanent UK Representative on Trusteeship Council of United Nations, 1947-56. Represented Bahamas at West Indies Conference in London, 1926; served with Cameroons Expeditionary Force, 1914-15, and during Egba rebellion, 1918. Chm., Commission of Enquiry into Land and Population Problems, Fiji, 1959-60. *Publications:* Index to Laws of Leeward Islands (joint compiler); Nigeria Handbook 1917-23; History of Nigeria, 1929 (rev. and enl. edn, 1972); Colour Prejudice, 1948; Colonial Civil Servant, 1949; History of the British West Indies, 1954; In Defence of Colonies, 1957; Fiji, 1963. *Address:* 16 Pall Mall, SW1. *T:* 01-839 4258. *Club:* Athenæum.

BURNS, Mrs Anne, (Mrs D. O. Burns); British Gliding Champion, 1966; Principal Scientific Officer, Royal Aircraft Establishment, Farnborough, Hants, 1953-77; *b* 23 Nov. 1915; *d* of late Major Fleetwood Hugo Pellew, W Yorks Regt, and of late Violet Pellew (*née* Du Pré); *m* 1947, Denis Owen Burns; no *c*. *Educ:* The Abbey Sch., Reading; St Hugh's Coll., Oxford (BA). Joined Min. of Supply, 1940. Engaged in aircraft research at RAE, Farnborough, Hants, under various ministries, 1940-. Feminine International Records: 4 gliding records in S Africa, 1961; records, S Africa, 1963, 1965; Colorado USA, 1967. Queen's Commendation for Valuable Services in the Air, 1955 and 1963. Lilienthal Medal, Fédération Aéronautique Internationale, 1966. *Publications:* contrib. scientific jls. *Recreations:* gliding, fishing. *Address:* Clumps End, Lower Bourne, Farnham, Surrey. *T:* Frensham 3343.

BURNS, Arthur F.; economist and statistician; Chairman, Board of Governors of the Federal Reserve System in the United States, since 1970; Alternate Governor, International Monetary Fund, since 1973; *b* Stanislau, Austria, 27 April 1904; *s* of Nathan Burns and Sarah Juran; *m* 1930, Helen Bernstein; two *s*. *Educ:* Columbia Univ. AB and AM 1925, PhD 1934. Rutgers Univ.: Instructor in Economics, 1927-30; Asst Prof., 1930-33; Associate Prof., 1933-43; Prof., 1943-44; Columbia Univ.: Vis. Prof., 1941-44; Prof., 1944-59; John Bates Clark Prof., 1959-69. Nat. Bureau of Econ. Research: Res. Associate, 1930-31; Mem. Res. Staff, 1933; Dir of Res., 1945-53; Pres., 1957-67; Chm. of Bureau, 1967-69; Counsellor to the President of the US, 1969-70. Dir and Trustee of various orgs; Member (or Past Mem. or Consultant) of govt and other advisory bds. Chm., President's Coun. of Economic Advisors, 1953-56; Mem., President's Adv. Cttee on Labor-Management Policy, 1961-66, etc. Fellow: Amer. Statistical Assoc.; Econometric Soc.; Philos. Soc.; Amer. Acad. of Arts and Sciences; Amer. Econ. Assoc. (Pres. 1959); Acad. of Polit. Sci. (Pres., 1962-68); Phi Beta Kappa. Many hon. doctorates, 1952-. Alexander Hamilton Medal, Columbia Univ.; Dist. Public Service Award, Tax Foundn. Mugungwha Decoration, S Korea. *Publications:* Production Trends in the United States since 1870, 1934; Economic Research and the Keynesian Thinking of our Times, 1946; Frontiers of Economic Knowledge, 1954; Prosperity Without Inflation, 1957; The Management of Prosperity, 1966; The Business Cycle in a Changing World, 1969; (jointly) Measuring Business Cycles, 1946. *Address:* Federal Reserve Board, Washington, DC 20551, USA; (home) Watergate East, 2510 Virginia Avenue NW, Washington, DC 20037. *Clubs:* Men's Faculty (Columbia), Century Association (New York); Cosmos (Washington).

BURNS, Dr B(enedict) Delisle, FRS 1968; MRC External Staff, Department of Anatomy, since 1976, and Honorary Professor of Neurobiology, since 1977, Bristol University; *b* 22 Feb. 1915; *s* of C. Delisle Burns and Margaret Hannay; *m* 1st, 1938, Angela Ricardo; four *s*; 2nd, 1954, Monika Kasputis; one *d*. *Educ:* University Coll. Sch.; Tübingen Univ.; King's Coll., Cambridge; University Coll. Hospital. MRCS, LRCP 1939. Univ. extension lecturing for WEA, 1936-38; operational research, 1939-45; Research Asst, Nat. Inst. for Med. Research, 1945-49; Assoc. Prof of Physiology, McGill Univ., Canada, 1950-58; Scientific Advisor to Dept of Veterans' Affairs, 1950-67; Prof. of Physiology, 1958-67, Chm., Dept of Physiology, 1965-67, McGill Univ., Canada; Head, Div. of Physiology and Pharmacology, Nat. Inst. of Medical Research, 1967-76. *Publications:* The Mammalian Cerebral Cortex, 1958; The Uncertain Nervous System, 1968; about 60 articles on neurophysiology in scientific jls. *Recreations:* tennis, ski-ing, painting, interior decoration. *Address:* Department of Anatomy, The Medical School, University Walk, Bristol BS8 1TD. *T:* Bristol 24161.

BURNS, Bryan Hartop; Hon. Consulting Orthopædic Surgeon: St George's Hospital; St Peter's Hospital, Chertsey; Heatherwood Hospital, Ascot; *b* 14 Dec. 1896; *s* of Hartop Burns, Grendon, Northampton; *m* 1938, Hon. Dorothy Garthwaite, *d* of late Lord Duveen. *Educ:* Wellingborough Sch.; Clare Coll., Cambridge; St George's Hospital Medical Sch.

Allingham Scholarship in surgery, St George's Hospital, 1924; served 1914-18, Northants Regt. Orthopædic Surgeon, Royal Masonic Hospital, 1945-61. Ex-Pres. Orthopædic Section, Royal Society Med.; Mem. of Court of Examiners, Royal College of Surgeons, 1943-46; Emer. Fellow, British Orthopædic Association; Member Société Internationale de Chirurgie Orthopédique. *Publications:* Recent Advances in Orthopædic Surgery, 1937 (jointly); articles on orthopædic subjects. *Address:* 6 Chesterfield Hill, W1. *T:* 01-493 3435. *Clubs:* Boodle's, Brooks's.

BURNS, Sir Charles (Ritchie), KBE 1958 (OBE 1947); MD, FRCP; FRACP; Consulting Physician and Consulting Cardiologist, Wellington Hospital, since 1958; Director, Clinical Services, National Society on Alcoholism (Inc.), NZ, since 1970; Consultant Physician, National Society on Alcoholism and Drug Dependence, since 1975; *b* Blenheim, Marlborough, NZ, 27 May 1898; *s* of Archibald Douglas Burns, Lands and Survey Dept, NZ; *m* 1st, 1935, Margaret Muriel (decd 1949), *d* of John Laffey, Dunedin, NZ; one *s* one *d*; 2nd, 1963, Doris Ogilvy, *d* of Keith Ramsay (sen.), Dunedin, New Zealand. *Educ:* St Mary's Sch., Blenheim, NZ; Marlborough and Nelson Colls, NZ. MB, ChB (NZ) 1922 (Batchelor Memorial Medal); MRCP 1925; MD (NZ) 1925; Foundation Fellow RACP 1937; FRCP (Lond.) 1943; FMANZ. Med. Registrar Dunedin Hospital, and Medical Tutor Otago Univ., 1925-27; Asst Phys., Dunedin Hospital, 1927-37; Senior Phys. and Cardiologist, Wellington Hospital, NZ, 1940-58; Phys., Home of Compassion, Island Bay, NZ, 1940-68; Mem. Med. Council, NZ, 1943-55; Examr in Medicine, Univ., of NZ, 1947-53, 1959, 1963. Sixth Leonard Ball Oration, Melbourne, 1973. Mem. NZ Bd of Censors for RACP, 1954-61; Corresp. Mem. Brit. Cardiac Soc., 1952-71; Life Mem. Cardiac Soc. of Australia and NZ, 1972 (Mem., 1952-72; Mem. Council, 1956-58; Chm. 1964-65); Member: Council and NZ Vice-Pres., RACP, 1956-58; NZ Lepers' Trust Bd, 1958-; Advisory Cttee, The Nat. Soc. on Alcoholism (NZ); Council, Wellington Med. Research Foundn; Patron: NZ Asthma Soc.; NZ Diabetic Soc. (Wellington Br.); Deaf Children's Parents Soc. (Wellington Br.); Soc. for Promotion of Community Standards. Leonard Ball Oration, Melbourne, 1973. Served War, 1944-47, Military Hospitals, 2nd NZEF, Italy and Japan (OBE). Hon. DSc Otago, 1975. *Publications:* contrib. medical journals and jls of anciliary medical services. *Recreations:* walking and medical writing. *Address:* Flat One, Clifton Towers, 202 Oriental Parade, Wellington, New Zealand. *T:* Wellington 849-249. *Club:* Wellington (Wellington, NZ).

BURNS, Mrs Denis Owen; *see* Burns, Mrs Anne.

BURNS, Lt-Gen. Eedson Louis Millard, CC (Canada) 1967; DSO 1944; OBE 1935; MC; idc; *b* 17 June 1897; *m* 1927, Eleanor Phelan; one *d*. *Educ:* Royal Military Coll., Kingston, Canada; Staff Coll., Quetta. Served European War, 1916-18 (France, Belgium) with Royal Canadian Engineers, Signals, Staff; Can. Perm. Force, 1918-39. War of 1939-45; GOC 2nd Can. Div., 1943 (Maj.-Gen.); 5th Can. Div., 1944; 1st Can. Corps, 1944. Dir-Gen. of Rehabilitation, Dept Veteran Affairs, 1945-46, Asst Dep. Minister, 1946-50, Dep. Minister, 1950-54. Chief of Staff, UN Truce Supervision Organisation, Palestine, 1954-56; Comdr UN Emergency Force, 1956-59; Adviser to Govt of Canada on Disarmament, 1960-69, retd; Leader of Canadian Delegation to 18-Nation Disarmament Conference, Geneva, 1962-68. Res. Fellow, Carleton Univ., 1970-71, Prof. of Strategic Studies, 1971-73. Nat. Pres. UNA, Canada, 1952-53 (Altern. Deleg. to UN, 1949). Officier Légion d'Honneur. *Publications:* Manpower in the Canadian Army, 1939-45, 1955; Between Arab and Israeli, 1962; Megamurder, 1966; General Mud, 1970; A Seat at the Table, 1972; Defence in the Nuclear Age, 1976. *Address:* RR 1, Box 132, Manotick, Ont. KOA 2NO, Canada.

BURNS, Maj.-Gen. Sir George; *see* Burns, Maj.-Gen. Sir W. A. G.

BURNS, James, CBE 1967; GM 1941; Chairman, Southern Gas Board, 1967-69, retired; *b* 27 Feb. 1902; *s* of William Wilson Burns and Isobella MacDonald; *m* 1934, Kathleen Ida Holt (*d* 1976); one *d* (one *s* decd). *Educ:* Inverness Royal Academy; Aberdeen Univ.; Cambridge Univ. BSc 1st cl. Hons 1925, PhD 1928, Aberdeen. Entered Research Dept, Gas Light & Coke Co., 1929; worked as Chem. Engr with Chemical Reactions Ltd, in Germany, 1930-32; Production Engr, Gas Light & Coke Co., 1941, dep. Chief Engr, 1945; Chief Engr, North Thames Gas Board, 1949, Dep-Chm. 1960-62; Chm, Northern Gas Board, 1962-67. President: Instn Gas Engrs, 1957-58; Inst. Fuel, 1961-62, etc. *Publications:* contrib. Jls Instn Gas Engrs, Inst. Fuel, etc. *Recreations:* golf, shooting, country pursuits. *Address:* 4 Corfu, Chaddesley Glen, Canford Cliffs, Dorset. *T:* Canford Cliffs 707370.

BURNS, Prof. James Henderson; Professor of the History of Political Thought, University College London, since 1966; *b* 10 Nov. 1921; *yr s* of late William Burns and of Helen Craig Tait Henderson; *m* 1947, Yvonne Mary Zéla Birnie, *er d* of late Arthur Birnie, MA, and of Yvonne Marie Aline Louis; two *s* (and one *d* decd). *Educ:* George Watson's Boys' Coll., Edinburgh; Univ. of Edinburgh; Balliol Coll., Oxford. MA (Edinburgh and Oxon), PhD (Aberdeen). Sub-Editor, Home News Dept, BBC, 1944-45; Lectr in Polit. Theory, Univ. of Aberdeen, 1947-60; Head of Dept of Politics, 1952-60; Reader in the History of Political Thought, University Coll. London, 1961-66; Head of History Dept, UCL, 1970-75. Gen. Editor, The Collected Works of Jeremy Bentham, 1961-; Hon. Sec., Royal Historical Soc., 1965-70; Sec., Bentham Cttee, 1966-. FRHistS 1962. *Publications:* Scottish University (with D. Sutherland Graeme), 1944; Scottish Churchmen and the Council of Basle, 1962; contributor to: (with S. Rose) The British General Election of 1951, by D. E. Butler, 1952; Essays on the Scottish Reformation, ed D. McRoberts, 1962; Mill: a collection of critical essays, ed J. B. Schneewind, 1968; Bentham on Legal Theory, ed M. H. James, 1973; Jeremy Bentham: ten critical essays, ed B. Parekh, 1974; ed (with H. L. A. Hart) Jeremy Bentham, An Introduction in the Principles of Morals and Legislation, 1970; articles and reviews in: Scottish Historical Review, Innes Review, Political Studies, History, Trans of RHistSoc, etc. *Address:* 39 Amherst Road, Ealing, W13. *T:* 01-997 7538.

BURNS, Sir John (Crawford), Kt 1957; Director, James Finlay & Co. Ltd, 1957-74; *b* 29 Aug. 1903; *s* of William Barr Burns and Elizabeth Crawford; *m* 1941, Eleanor Margaret Haughton James; one *s* three *d*. *Educ:* Glasgow High Sch. Commissioned 2/16th Punjab Regt (Indian Army), 1940-46 (despatches). *Recreations:* golf, fishing. *Address:* Glenorchard, Dunblane, Perthshire. *Clubs:* Oriental; Western (Glasgow).

BURNS, Sir Malcolm (McRae), KBE 1972 (CBE 1959); Principal, Lincoln Agricultural College, New Zealand, 1952-73; *b* 19 March 1910; *s* of J. E. Burns and Emily (*née* Jeffrey); *m* 1936, Ruth, *d* of J. D. Waugh, St Louis, USA; one *s* two *d*. *Educ:* Rangiora High Sch.; Univs of Canterbury (NZ), Aberdeen and Cornell. Plant Physiologist, DSIR, NZ, 1936; Sen. Lectr, Lincoln Agric. Coll., 1937-48; Dir, NZ Fert. Manuf. Res. Assoc., 1948-52. Chm., Physical Environment Commn, 1968-70; Mem., Nat. Develt Council, 1969-74. FNZIC; FNZIAS; FRSNZ; FAAAS. Chm., DSIR Research Council, 1959-62. NZ Representative, Harkness Fellowships. Hon. DSc Canterbury, 1974. *Publications:* articles in scientific jls. *Recreations:* golf, fishing, gardening. *Address:* 7 Royds Street, Christchurch 1, New Zealand.

BURNS, Thomas Ferrier; Editor of The Tablet, since 1967; Chairman of Burns & Oates Ltd, 1948-67; Director, The Tablet Publishing Company, since 1936; *b* 21 April 1906; *s* of late David Burns and late Clara (*née* Swinburne); *m* 1941, Mabel Marañon; three *s* one *d*. *Educ:* Stonyhurst. Press Attaché, British Embassy, Madrid, 1940-45. *Recreations:* painting and gardening. *Address:* 14 Ashley Gardens, SW1. *T:* 01-834 1385. *Clubs:* Garrick, Pratt's.

BURNS, Prof. Tom; Professor of Sociology, University of Edinburgh, since 1965; *b* 16 Jan. 1913; *s* of John and Hannah Burns; *m* 1944, Mary Elizabeth Nora Clark; one *s* four *d*. *Educ:* Hague Street LCC Elementary Sch.; Parmiters Foundation Sch.; Univ. of Bristol (BA). Bookseller's Asst, 1928-30; Univ. of Bristol, 1930-33; teaching in private schools in Tunbridge Wells and Norwich, 1935-39. Friends' Ambulance Unit, 1939-45 (PoW, Germany, 1941-43). Research Asst, W Midland Gp on Post-war Reconstruction and Planning, 1945-49; Lectr, Sen. Lectr and Reader, Univ. of Edinburgh, 1949-65. Vis. Prof., Harvard, 1973-74. Mem., SSRC, 1969-70. *Publications:* Local Government and Central Control, 1954; The Management of Innovation (with G. M. Stalker), 1961; (ed) Industrial Man, 1969; (ed with E. Burns) Sociology of Literature and Drama, 1973; The BBC: Public Institution and Private World, 1977; articles in a number of jls in Britain, USA, France, etc. *Recreations:* music, walking. *Address:* 4 Ann Street, Edinburgh EH4 1PJ.

BURNS, Maj.-Gen. Sir (Walter Arthur) George, KCVO 1962; CB 1961; DSO 1944; OBE 1953; MC 1940; retired; Lord-Lieutenant of Hertfordshire since Dec. 1961; *b* 29 Jan. 1911; *s* of Walter Spencer Morgan and Evelyn Ruth Burns. *Educ:* Eton; Trinity Coll., Cambridge. BA Hons History. Commissioned Coldstream Guards 1932; ADC to Viceroy of India, 1938-40; Adjt 1st Bn, 1940-41 (MC); Brigade Major: 9 Inf. Bde, 1941-42; Sp. Gp Gds Armd Div., 1942; 32 Gds Bde, 1942-43; CO 3rd Bn Coldstream Gds, Italy, 1943-44 (DSO); Staff Coll., Camberley,

1945. Brigade Major, Household Bde, 1945-47; CO 3rd Bn Coldstream Gds, Palestine, 1947-50; AAG, HQ London Dist, 1951, 1952; Regimental Lt-Col Coldstream Gds, 1952-55; Comdg 4th Gds Bde, 1955-59. GOC London District and The Household Brigade, 1959-62; Col, Coldstream Guards, 1966-. Steward, The Jockey Club, 1964-. KStJ 1972. *Recreations:* shooting and racing. *Address:* North Mymms Park, Hatfield, Herts. *T:* Bowmansgreen 22096. *Clubs:* Cavalry and Guards, Jockey, Pratt's.

BURNS, Wilfred, CB 1972; CBE 1967; MEng, PPRTPI, MICE; Chief Planner, since 1968, and Deputy Secretary, since 1971, Department of the Environment (formerly Ministry of Housing and Local Government); *b* 11 April 1923; *m* 1945, Edna Price; one *s* one *d. Educ:* Ulverston Grammar Sch.; Liverpool Univ. Admty, 1944-45; Leeds Corp., 1946-49; Prin. Planning Officer, Coventry Corp., 1949-58; Dep. Planning Officer, Surrey CC, 1958-60; City Planning Officer, Newcastle upon Tyne, 1960-68. Hon. DSc, Univ. of Newcastle upon Tyne, 1966. *Publications:* British Shopping Centres, 1959; New Towns for Old, 1963; Newcastle upon Tyne: A Study in Planning, 1967. *Address:* 29a Sydenham Hill, SE26. *T:* 01-670 3525.

BURNS, Prof. William, CBE 1966; Emeritus Professor of Physiology, University of London; Professor of Physiology, Charing Cross Hospital Medical School, 1947-77; Hon. Consultant Otologist, Charing Cross Group of Hospitals; *b* 15 Oct. 1909; *e s* of late Charles Burns, MB, ChB, JP, and Mary Sillars, lately of Stonehaven, Scotland; *m* 1936, Margaret, *o d* of late W. A. Morgan, Glasgow; one *s* one *d. Educ:* Mackie Acad., Stonehaven; Aberdeen Univ. BSc 1933, MB ChB 1935, DSc 1943 Aberdeen. FRCP 1973. Asst in Physiology, Aberdeen, 1935; Lectr in Physiology, Aberdeen, 1936; War-time duty with Admiralty, 1942; established in RN Scientific Service, 1946; Supt RN Physiological Laboratory, 1947; Consultant in Acoustic Science to RAF; Hon. Civil Consultant to RN in Audiology. Member: Physiological Soc.; Council, British Association for the Advancement of Science, 1956-61; British Medical Association; British Inst. of Acoustics; British Soc. Audiology. *Publications:* Noise and Man, 1968, 2nd edn 1973; (with D. W. Robinson) Hearing and Noise in Industry, 1970; articles on various aspects of hearing, in Journal of the Acoustical Soc. of America, Annals of Occupational Hygiene, Proc. Assoc. of Industrial Med. Officers, etc. *Recreations:* working in wood and metal; interested in engineering in general. *Address:* Cairns Cottage, Blacksmith's Lane, Laleham-on-Thames, Mddx TW18 1UB. *T:* Staines 53066.

BURNSIDE, Dame Edith, DBE 1976 (OBE 1957); *m* W. K. Burnside. Awarded DBE for services to hospitals and the community, Toorak, Victoria. *Address:* Flat 61, 9 Struan Street, Toorak, Victoria 3142, Australia.

BURNSTOCK, Prof. Geoffrey; Professor of Anatomy, University of London, and Head of Department of Anatomy and Embryology, University College London, since 1975; *b* 10 May 1929; *s* of James Hyman Burnstock and Nancy Green; *m* 1957, Nomi Hirschfeld; three *d. Educ:* King's Coll., London; Melbourne Univ. BSc 1953, PhD 1957 London; DSc Melbourne 1971. National Inst. for Medical Res., Mill Hill, 1956-57; Dept of Pharmacology, Oxford Univ., 1957-59; Rockefeller Travelling Fellowship, Univ. of Ill, 1959; Dept of Zoology, Univ. of Melbourne: Sen. Lectr, 1959-62; Reader, 1962-64; Prof. of Zoology and Chm. of Dept, 1964-75; Associate Dean (Biological Sciences), 1969-72. Vis. Prof., Dept of Pharmacology, Univ. of Calif, LA, 1970. Hon. MSc Melbourne 1962; FAA 1970. Silver Medal, Royal Soc. of Victoria, 1970. *Publications:* (with M. Costa) Adrenergic Neurons: their organisation, function and development in the peripheral nervous system, 1975; (with Y. Uehara and G. R. Campbell) An Atlas of the fine structure of Muscle and its innervation, 1976; papers on smooth muscle and autonomic nervous system in sci. jls. *Recreations:* tennis, wood sculpture. *Address:* Department of Anatomy and Embryology, University College London, Gower Street, WC1E 6BT. *T:* 01-387 7050.

BURNTWOOD, Baron *cr* 1970 (Life Peer), of Burntwood, Staffs; **Julian Ward Snow;** *b* 24 Feb. 1910; *s* of late H. M. Snow, CVO, Mottingham, Kent; *m* 1948, Flavia, *d* of late Sir Ralph Blois, 9th Bt, and Lady Blois, Cockfield Hall; one *d. Educ:* Haileybury. Royal Artillery, 1939-45. A member of the Union of Shop Distributive and Allied Workers. MP (Lab) Portsmouth Central, 1945-50, Lichfield and Tamworth Div. of Staffs, 1950-70; Vice-Chamberlain to the Household, 1945-46; a Lord Comr of HM Treasury, 1946-50; Parliamentary Secretary: Min. of Aviation, 1966-67; Min. of Health, 1967-68; Parly Under-Sec. of State, Dept of Health and Social Security, 1968-69. *Address:* 37 Chester Way, SE11.

BURR, Eric Cyril; Under-Secretary, Ministry of Overseas Development, since 1974; *b* 30 Dec. 1920; *s* of Cyril Herbert and Mary Bell Burr; *m* 1949, Myrtle Waters; two *s* one *d. Educ:* Hackney Downs School. Military Service, E Africa, 1942-46. Clerical Officer, Colonial Office, 1937, Exec. Officer 1946; Asst Principal 1948; Private Sec. to Parly Under-Sec. of State, 1952; Principal 1954; Asst Sec., Min. of Overseas Develt, 1964. *Address:* 50 Red Post Hill, SE24 9JQ.

BURRELL, Derek William; Headmaster, Truro School, since 1959; *b* 4 Nov. 1925; *s* of late Thomas Richard Burrell and of Flora Frances Burrell (*née* Nash). *Educ:* Tottenham Grammar Sch.; Queens' Coll., Cambridge. Assistant Master at Solihull Sch. (English, History, Religious Instruction, Music Appreciation), 1948-52. Senior English Master, Dollar Academy, 1952-59. *Recreations:* music of any kind, theatre, wandering about London. *Address:* Truro School, Cornwall. *T:* Truro 2763. *Club:* East India, Devonshire, Sports and Public Schools.

BURRELL, Vice-Adm. Sir Henry Mackay, KBE 1960 (CBE 1955); CB 1959; RAN retired, now a grazier, Illogan Park, Braidwood, NSW; *b* 13 Aug. 1904; British (father *b* Dorset; mother *b* Australia, of Scottish parents); *m* 1944, Ada Theresa Weller; one *s* two *d. Educ:* Royal Australian Naval Coll., Jervis Bay, Australia. Cadet-Midshipman, 1918; specialist in navigation, psc Greenwich, 1938; Commands: HMAS Norman, 1941-42 (despatches); Bataan, 1945; Dep. Chief of Naval Staff, Navy Office, Melbourne, 1947-48; HMAS Australia, 1949; idc 1950; HMAS Vengeance, 1953-54; Second Naval Mem., Australian Commonwealth Naval Board, 1956-57; Flag Officer Commanding HM Australian Fleet, 1955 and 1958; Chief of the Australian Naval Staff, 1959-62. *Recreations:* tennis and lawn tennis. *Address:* 87 Endeavour Street, Red Hill, Canberra, ACT 2603, Australia. *Clubs:* Naval and Military (Melbourne); Commonwealth (Canberra, ACT).

BURRELL, John Glyn, QC 1961; **His Honour Judge Burrell;** a Circuit Judge (formerly County Court Judge), since 1964; *b* 10 Oct. 1912; *o s* of Lewis Morgan Burrell and Amy Isabel Burrell; *m* 1941, Dorothy, 2nd *d* of Prof. T. Stanley Roberts, MA Cantab, Aberystwyth; two *d. Educ:* Friars Sch., Bangor; Univ. Coll. of Wales. Called to Bar, Inner Temple, 1936. Practised Northern Circuit (Liverpool); Recorder of Wigan, 1962-64; Chm., Radnorshire QS, 1964-71. Army service, 1940-45. *Address:* Longhedge, Spittal, Haverfordwest, Dyfed.

BURRELL, Joseph Frederick, CVO 1976; Partner, Farrer & Co., Lincoln's Inn Fields, 1938-76; Solicitor to the Duchy of Cornwall, 1972-76; *b* 17 July 1909; *s* of Arthur J. T. Burrell and Marie Birt; *m* 1940, Diana Margaret Beachcroft, *d* of Cyril Beachcroft and Vivien Hughes. *Educ:* Eton; Trinity College, Cambridge. Sapper, TA, 1938-40; Gunner, 1940-45. Governor and Mem. Bd of Management, Royal Hosp. and Home for Incurables. *Address:* 54 Murray Road, Wimbledon, SW19. *Club:* Travellers'.

BURRELL, Peter, CBE 1957; Director, The National Stud, 1937-71; *b* 9 May 1905; *s* of Sir Merrik R. Burrell, 7th Bt; *m* 1st, 1929, Pamela Pollen (marr. diss., 1940); two *s*; 2nd, 1971, Mrs Constance P. Mellon. *Educ:* Eton; Royal Agricultural Coll., Cirencester. *Recreations:* shooting, stalking, hunting. *Address:* Huntland Downs, Ligonier, Penn 15658, USA. *Clubs:* Boodle's; Kildare Street and University (Dublin).

BURRELL, Robert John, QC 1973; *b* London, 28 Nov. 1923; *s* of late Robert Burrell, QC; *m* 1948, Thelma Louise Mawdesley Harris; no *c. Educ:* Rugby; Trinity Hall, Cambridge (MA). Served War, Royal Navy, 1942-46: Fleet Minesweepers and Motor Torpedo Boats, English Channel and Adriatic; participated in D Day landings, 1944; demobilised, 1946, Lieut RNVR. Called to Bar, Inner Temple, 1948. Mem., Paddington Borough Council, 1949-56 (Chm. Housing Cttee, 1953-56); Chm., Plant Varieties and Seeds Tribunal, 1974-; Hon. Treas., Ligue Internationale contre la Concurrence Deloyale (Paris); Mem., EEC Working Cttee, EEC Trade Mark Law, 1975-. *Recreations:* music (piano), mountain walking. *Address:* 1 Essex Court, Temple, EC4Y 9AR. *T:* 01-353 8507. *Club:* Royal Welsh Yacht.

BURRELL, Sir Walter (Raymond), 8th Bt, *cr* 1774; CBE 1956 (MBE 1945); TD; DL; Trustee Royal Agricultural Society of England, since 1948, President 1964, Chairman of Council, 1967-72; *b* 11 Dec. 1903; *er s* of Sir Merrik Burrell, 7th Bt, CBE; *S* father 1957; *m* 1931, Hon. Anne Judith Denman, OBE, *o d* of 3rd Baron Denman, PC, GCMG, KCVO; two *s* two *d. Educ:* Eton. Major 98th Field Regt (Surrey and Sussex Yeo.), Royal Artillery (TA), 1938; Lt-Col (Chief Instructor) 123 OCTU,

1942; Lt-Col BAS (Washington), 1943; Comd 3 Super Heavy Regt, RA 1945 (MBE). Pres. Country Landowners' Assoc., 1952-53; Pres., South of England Agricultural Soc., 1974-. DL Sussex, 1937, West Sussex 1974; County Alderman, 1950; Vice-Chm. West Sussex County Council, 1953. *Heir:* s John Raymond Burrell [b 20 Feb. 1934; m 1st, 1959, Rowena Pearce (marr. diss. 1971); one s one d; 2nd, 1971, Margot Lucy, d of F. E. Thatcher, Sydney, NSW; one s. *Educ:* Eton]. *Address:* Knepp Castle, West Grinstead, Horsham, West Sussex. *T:* Coolham 247; 43a Reeves Mews, South Audley Street, W1. *T:* 01-499 1318. *Club:* Boodle's.
See also Peter Burrell.

BURRETT, (Frederick) Gordon, CB 1974; Deputy Secretary, Civil Service Department, since 1972; b 31 Oct. 1921; s of Frederick Burrett and Marion Knowles; m 1943, Margaret Joan Giddins; one s two d. *Educ:* Emanuel Sch.; St Catharine's Coll., Cambridge. Served in Royal Engrs, N Africa, Italy, Yugoslavia, Greece, 1942-45 (despatches). HM Foreign Service, 1946; 3rd Sec., Budapest, 1946-49; FO, 1949-51; Vice-Consul, New York, 1951-54; FO, 1954-57; 1st Sec., Rome, 1957-60; transf. to HM Treasury, 1960; Private Sec. to Chief Sec., Treasury, 1963-64; Asst Secretary: HM Treasury, 1964; Cabinet Office, 1967-68; Secretary: Kindersley Review Body on Doctors' and Dentists' Remuneration; Plowden Cttee on Pay of Higher Civil Service, 1967-68; Civil Service Dept, 1968, Under-Sec. 1969. *Recreations:* music, books, walking, cruising on inland waterways. *Address:* Trinity Cottage, Church Road, Claygate, Surrey. *T:* Esher 62783.

BURROUGH, Alan, CBE 1970; Chairman, James Burrough Ltd; b 22 Feb. 1917; s of Ernest James Burrough and Sophie (née Burston); m 1939, Rosemary June Bruce; two s one d. *Educ:* St Paul's Sch., London; Jesus Coll., Cambridge Univ. (MA). Joined James Burrough Ltd, 1935. War of 1939-45: 91st Field Regt, RA, and 5th RHA (Captain). Rejoined James Burrough Ltd, 1945: Director, 1946; Deputy Chairman, 1967; Chairman, 1968. *Address:* Manor Garden, Henley-on-Thames, Oxon. *Clubs:* Bath; Leander (Henley-on-Thames).

BURROUGH, Admiral Sir Harold Martin, GCB 1949 (KCB 1944; CB 1939); KBE 1942; DSO 1942 (and Bar 1943); DSM (USA), 1943; Legion of Merit (USA), 1946; Knight Grand Cross Orange Nassau (Netherlands), 1947; Grand Officer, Legion of Honour (France), 1949; b 4 July 1888; s of Rev. Charles Burrough, MA; m 1914, Nellie Wills Outhit (d 1972), Halifax, Nova Scotia; two s three d. *Educ:* St Edward's Oxford; HMS Britannia. Gunnery Officer of HMS Southampton at the Battle of Jutland; Comdr, 1922; Capt., 1928; commanded HMS London, 1930-32; 5th Destroyer Flotilla, 1935-37; HMS Excellent, 1937-38; served War of 1939-45 (DSO and Bar, KBE); Assistant Chief of Naval Staff, Admiralty, 1939-40; commanding Cruiser Squadron, 1940-42; commanding Naval Forces, Algiers, 1942; Flag Officer Commanding, Gibraltar and Mediterranean Approaches, 1943-45; Allied Naval C-in-C. Expeditionary Force, 1945; British Naval C-in-C, Germany, 1945-46; C-in-C The Nore, 1946-48. Rear-Admiral, 1939; Vice-Admiral, 1942; Admiral, 1945; retired list, 1949. *Address:* Barn House, Aldbourne, Marlborough, Wilts. *Club:* Naval and Military.
See also J. O. H. Burrough and Rear-Adm. A. Davies.

BURROUGH, John Outhit Harold, CB 1975; CBE 1963; Director, Racal Communications Systems Ltd, since 1976; b 31 Jan. 1916; s of Adm. Sir Harold M. Burrough, qv; m 1944, Suzanne Cecile Jourdan; one s one d. *Educ:* Manor House, Horsham; RNC Dartmouth. Midshipman, 1934; Sub-Lt 1936; Lieut 1938; Lt-Comdr 1944; retd 1947. Foreign Office (GCHQ), 1946-65; IDC 1964; British Embassy, Washington, 1965-67; Under-Sec., Cabinet Office, 1967-69; an Under Sec., FCO (Govt Communications HQ), 1969-76. *Address:* The Little Warrens, Stanton, Broadway, Worcs. *T:* Stanton 260. *Club:* Naval and Military (Chm., 1969-72).

BURROUGH, Rt. Rev. John Paul; see Mashonaland, Bishop of.

BURROUGHS, Ronald Arthur, CMG 1966; HM Diplomatic Service, retired; company director; b 4 June 1917; s of Rev. Henry Frederick Burroughs and Ada Burroughs. *Educ:* St John's Sch., Leatherhead; Trinity Coll., Cambridge. Fleet Air Arm, 1940-45. FO, 1946; 2nd Sec., HM Embassy, Rio de Janeiro, 1947-49; HM Consul, Marseilles, 1949-50; 1st Sec., HM Embassy, Cairo, 1950-53; FO, 1953-55; Canadian National Defence Coll., 1955-56; 1st Sec., HM Embassy, Vienna, 1956-59; Counsellor, FO, 1959-62; Counsellor and Head of Chancery, Rio de Janeiro, 1962-64; Counsellor, HM Embassy, Lisbon, 1964-67; British Chargé d'Affaires, South Yemen, 1967-68; Assistant Under-Sec. of State, FCO, 1968-71, seconded to Home

Office as UK Rep. to NI Govt, March 1970-April 1971; Ambassador to Algeria, 1971-73. *Recreations:* reading, fishing. *Address:* The Post House, Graffham, near Petworth, W Sussex. *Club:* Travellers'.

BURROW, Prof. Harold, MRCVS, DVSM; Professor of Veterinary Medicine, Royal Veterinary College, University of London, 1944-63; Professor Emeritus since 1963; b 24 Aug. 1903; s of Henry Wilson and Elizabeth Jane Burrow, Hest Bank Lodge, near Lancaster; m 1933, Frances Olivia, d of Orlando Atkinson Ducksbury, MRCVS, and Mrs Frances Mary Ducksbury, Lancaster; one d. *Educ:* Lancaster Royal Grammar Sch.; Royal (Dick) Veterinary Coll., Edinburgh. Asst Veterinary Officer, City of Birmingham, 1927-30; Chief Veterinary Officer: Birkenhead, 1930-35; Derbyshire CC, 1935-38; Divisional Veterinary Officer, Min. of Agriculture, 1938-42; Private Veterinary Practice, 1942-44. Examiner: to Royal Coll. of Veterinary Surgeons, 1937-44; to Univs. of Liverpool, London, Reading, Edinburgh, Bristol and Ceylon (various dates). Pres. Old Lancastrian Club, 1953; Member of Council, Royal Society Health, 1950-64 (Chairman, 1956-57, Vice-Pres. 1958-65, Life Vice-Pres., 1965). *Publications:* numerous contributions to veterinary scientific press. *Recreation:* gardening. *Address:* Primrose Cottage, Donnington, Moreton-in-Marsh, Glos.

BURROW, Prof. Thomas, MA, PhD; FBA 1970; Boden Professor of Sanskrit in the University of Oxford, and Fellow of Balliol College, 1944-76; Emeritus Fellow of Balliol, 1976; b 29 June 1909; e s of Joshua and Frances Eleanor Burrow; m 1941, Inez Mary (d 1976), d of Herbert John Haley. *Educ:* Queen Elizabeth's Sch., Kirkby Lonsdale; Christ's Coll., Cambridge. Research Fellow of Christ's Coll., Cambridge, 1935-37; Asst Keeper in Dept of Oriental Printed Books and Manuscripts, British Museum, 1937-44. Leverhulme Research Fellow, 1957-68. Hon. Fellow, Sch. of Oriental and African Studies, 1974. *Publications:* The Language of the Kharosthi Documents from Chinese Turkestan, 1937; A Translation of the Kharosthi Documents from Chinese Turkestan, 1940; (with S. Bhattacharya) The Parji Language, 1953; The Sanskrit Language, 1955; (with M. B. Emeneau) A Dravidian Etymological Dictionary, 1961; Supplement, 1968; (with S. Bhattacharya) The Pengo Language, 1970. *Address:* 1 Woodlands, Mill End, Kidlington, Oxford OX5 2ER. *T:* Kidlington 5283.

BURROWES, Edmund Stanley Spencer, CMG 1959; Financial Secretary, Barbados, 1951-66; b 16 Dec. 1906; m 1st, 1934, Mildred B. Jackson (decd); one s three d; 2nd, 1965, Gwen Searson. *Educ:* Queen's Coll., British Guiana. British Guiana Colonial Secretariat, 1924; Inspector of Labour, 1940; Deputy Commissioner, 1945; Labour Commissioner, Barbados, 1947. *Publication:* Occupational Terms on Sugar Estates in British Guiana, 1945. *Recreations:* diving, gardening. *Address:* 66 Meadow Mount, Churchtown, Dublin 14. *T:* 985830.

BURROWES, Norma Elizabeth, (Mrs Steuart Bedford); opera and concert singer; b 24 April 1944; d of Henry and Caroline Burrowes; m 1969, Steuart Bedford, qv. *Educ:* Sullivan Upper Sch., Holywood, Co. Down; Queen's Univ., Belfast (BA); Royal Academy of Music (ARAM). Rôles include: Zerlina in Don Giovanni, Glyndebourne Touring Opera (début); Blöndchen in Die Entführung aus dem Serail, Salzburg Festival, and again Blöndchen, Paris Opera, 1976 (début); Fiakermili, Royal Opera House (début); also Oscar, Despina, Woodbird; recent rôles include: Oscar in Ballo in Maschera and Sophie in Der Rosenkavalier, for ENO; Vixen in Cunning Little Vixen, for Glyndebourne Fest. Opera; Zerbinetta in Ariadne auf Naxos, for Scottish Opera, etc. Television operas include: Nanetta in Falstaff; Susanna in Marriage of Figaro and Lauretta in Gianni Schicchi. Gives concerts and recitals regularly in this country and abroad and records for the BBC and with the major recording companies. *Recreations:* swimming, gardening, needlework. *Address:* 56 Rochester Road, NW1 9JG. *T:* 01-485 7322.

BURROWS, Sir Bernard (Alexander Brocas), GCMG 1970 (KCMG 1955; CMG 1950); Consultant, Federal Trust for Education and Research (Director-General, 1973-76); b 3 July 1910; s of Edward Henry Burrows and Ione, d of Alexander Macdonald; m 1944, Ines, d of late John Walter; one s one d. *Educ:* Eton; Trinity Coll., Oxford. Entered HM Foreign Service (later Diplomatic Service), 1934; served at HM Embassy, Cairo, 1938-45; Foreign Office, 1945-50; Counsellor HM Embassy, Washington, 1950-53; Political Resident in the Persian Gulf, 1953-58; Ambassador to Turkey, 1958-62; Dep. Under-Secretary of State, FO, 1963-66; Permanent British Representative to N Atlantic Council, 1966-70, retired 1970. Chairman: Council, British Inst. of Archaeology, Ankara;

Anglo-Turkish Soc. *Publication:* (with C. Irwin) Security of Western Europe, 1972. *Address:* Steep Farm, Petersfield, Hants. *T:* Petersfield 2287. *Club:* Travellers'.

BURROWS, Fred; Legal Counsellor, HM Diplomatic Service, since 1968; *b* 10 Aug. 1925; *s* of late Charles Burrows; *m* 1955, Jennifer Winsome Munt; two *s. Educ:* Altrincham Grammar Sch.; Trinity Hall, Cambridge (MA). Served in RAF, 1944-47. Called to Bar, Gray's Inn, 1950; Asst Legal Adviser, Foreign Office, 1956-65; Legal Adviser, British Embassy, Bonn, 1965-67; returned to FO, 1967; Legal Counsellor, FCO, 1968. *Recreations:* sailing, carpentry.

BURROWS, Harold Jackson, CBE 1967; MD; FRCS, FRACS; Civil Consultant to Royal Navy in Orthopaedic Surgery, since 1949 (Honorary since 1977); Hon. Consulting Orthopaedic Surgeon: St Bartholomew's Hospital; Royal National Orthopaedic Hospital; Star and Garter Home for Disabled Sailors, Soldiers and Airmen; *b* 9 May 1902; *s* of late Harold Burrows, CBE, and Lucy Mary Elizabeth (*née* Wheeler); unmarried. *Educ:* Cheltenham Coll.; King's Coll., Cambridge (MA); St Bartholomew's Hosp. Served War of 1939-45 as Surgeon Comdr RNVR. Beaverbrook Res. Scholar, RCS, 1930-31; Hunterian Prof., RCS, 1932; Asst Orthopaedic Surgeon, 1937, Orthopaedic Surgeon, 1946 and Surgeon i/c Orthopaedic Dept and Clinical Lectr on Orthopaedic Surgery, St Bartholomew's Hosp., 1958-67; Asst Surgeon, 1946, and Orthopaedic Surgeon, Royal Nat. Orthopaedic Hosp., 1948-67; Orthopaedic Surgeon, Nat. Hosp. for Diseases of the Nervous System, 1937-46; Consultant Adviser in Orthopaedics to Min. of Health 1964-71; Orthopaedic Surgeon, The Heritage, Chailey, 1937-70; Dean, Inst. of Orthopaedics, British Postgraduate Med. Fedn, Univ. of London, 1946-64, 1967-70. Nuffield Vis. Fellow to British WI on behalf of CO, 1955; Samuel Higby Camp Vis. Prof., Univ. of Calif., San Francisco, 1963. Chm., British Editorial Bd, Jl of Bone and Joint Surgery, 1961-73 (Asst Ed., 1948-49; Dep. Ed., 1949-60). Fellow: RSM (Hon. Mem. and Past Pres., Orthopaedic Section); Assoc. of Surgeons of Great Britain and Ireland; British Orthopaedic Assoc. (Past Pres.). Member: Council, RCS, 1964-72; Soc. Internat. de Chirurgie Orthopédique et de Traumatologie; Standing Adv. Cttee on Artificial Limbs, 1957-71 (Chm., 1964-71); Corresp. Member: Australian Orthopaedic Assoc.; Amer. Orthopaedic Assoc.; Hon. Member: NZ Orthopaedic Assoc; Internat. Skeletal Soc. Robert Jones Gold Medal, British Orthopaedic Assoc., 1937. *Publications:* papers on surgical subjects. *Address:* 16 Wood Lane, Highgate, N6.

BURROWS, Very Rev. Hedley Robert; Dean Emeritus of Hereford; Dean of Hereford, 1947-61, resigned in Oct. 1961; *b* 15 Oct. 1887; *s* of late Rt Rev. L. H. Burrows; *m* 1921, Joan Lumsden (*d* 1964), *d* of late Rt Rev. E. N. Lovett, CBE; one *s* (*er s* died on active service, 1945), two *d. Educ:* Charterhouse; New Coll., Oxford; Wells Theological Coll. Deacon, 1911; Priest, 1912; Curate of Petersfield, Hants, 1911-14; Temp. CF European War, 1914-16, invalided; Hon. CF; Priest in charge St Columba's, Poltalloch, Argyll, 1917-18; Domestic Chaplain to Dr Lang, when Archbishop of York, 1918-19; Curate in charge Dock Street Mission, Southampton, 1919-21; Rector of Stoke Abbott, Dorset, 1921-25; Vicar of St Stephen's, Portsea, 1925-28; Hon. Chaplain to 1st Bishop of Portsmouth, 1927-28. Vicar of Grimsby and Rural Dean of Grimsby and Cleethorpes, 1928-36; Vicar of St Peter's, Bournemouth, 1936-43; Rural Dean of Bournemouth, 1940-43; Prebendary and Canon of Sutton-in-Marisco, Lincoln Cathedral, 1933-43; Archdeacon of Winchester, and Residentiary Canon of the Cathedral, 1943-47. Chm., Midland Region Religious Cttee of the BBC, 1952-57 (*ex-officio:* Member Midland Council of BBC and Member Headquarters Council of BBC Central Religious Cttee, London). Elected a Church Commissioner for England, and Member Board of Governors, 1952-63. OStJ, 1947. *Publication:* Hereford Cathedral, 1958. *Address:* Chilland Rise, Itchen Abbas, Winchester. *Club:* Athenæum.
See also Bishop of Buckingham.

BURROWS, Comdr Henry Montagu, CB 1964; CBE 1956; Royal Navy (retired); Clerk-Assistant of the Parliaments, House of Lords, 1961-63, retired (Reading-Clerk and Clerk of the Journals, 1959-61; Principal Clerk of Public Bills, 1950-59); *b* 24 March 1899; *er s* of late Rev. Montagu John Burrows; *m* 1939, Harriet Elizabeth, *o d* of late Ker George Russell Vaizey, Star Stile, Halstead, Essex; one *s* one *d. Educ:* RNC Osborne and Dartmouth. Went to sea at outbreak of European War, 1914-18, as a midshipman in HMS Benbow and served in her at Battle of Jutland. Transferred to RAF, 1923, Flt-Lt in No 1 (Fighter) Sqdn in Irak. Appointed a Clerk in the House of Lords, 1925. Rejoined Royal Navy as Lieut-Comdr at outbreak of War of 1939-45 and commanded a motor boat at Dunkirk evacuation;

later appointed 1st Lieut of HMS Argus (despatches while serving in her in N African landings, 1942); Comdr 1945. Trustee, Attlee Meml Foundn, 1969. Royal Humane Society's bronze medal for life saving, 1920. *Recreation:* golf. *Address:* East House, Long Crendon, near Aylesbury, Bucks. *T:* Long Crendon 208 498. *Club:* Travellers'.

BURROWS, Sir John; see Burrows, Sir R. J. F.

BURROWS, Lionel John, CBE 1974; Chief Inspector of Schools, Department of Education and Science, 1966-73; Educational Adviser, Methodist Residential Schools, since 1974; *b* 9 March 1912; *s* of H. L. Burrows, HM Inspector of Schools, and Mrs C. J. Burrows; *m* 1939, Enid Patricia Carter; one *s* one *d. Educ:* King Edward VI Sch., Southampton; Gonville and Caius Coll., Cambridge. BA Cantab (1st cl. hons Mod. Langs Tripos) 1933. West Buckland Sch., Devon, Tiffin Sch., Kingston-upon-Thames and primary schools in London and Surrey, 1934-41; HM Forces (RASC and Intell. Corps), 1941-46; Commendation from US Army Chief of Staff, 1945; HM Inspector of Schools, 1946; Divisional Inspector, Metropolitan Div., 1960. Vice-Pres., Nat. Assoc. for Gifted Children, 1975-. *Recreations:* natural history, fell-walking. *Address:* 49 Courtfield Avenue, Harrow HA1 2LB. *Club:* English-Speaking Union.

BURROWS, Rev. Millar; Winkley Professor of Biblical Theology, Yale University, 1934-June 1958; Member of the Standard Bible Committee since 1938, Vice-Chairman, 1954-63; *b* 26 Oct. 1889; *s* of Edwin Jones Burrows and Katharine Millar Burrows; *m* 1915, Irene Bell Gladding (*d* 1967); one *s. Educ:* Cornell Univ. (BA 1912), Union Theological Seminary (BD 1915), Yale Univ. (PhD 1925). Rural Pastor in Texas, 1915-19; Rural survey supervisor for Texas, Interchurch World Movement, 1919-20; College pastor and professor of Bible, Tusculum Coll., 1920-23; Asst Professor, Assoc. Professor, and Professor of Biblical Literature and Hist. of Religions, Brown Univ., 1925-34; Visiting Professor of Religion, Amer. Univ. of Beirut, 1930-31; Director, Amer. Sch. of Oriental Research, Jerusalem, 1931-32 and 1947-48; Chm. Dept. of Near Eastern Languages and Literatures, Yale Univ. 1950-58. Pres., Amer. Schools of Oriental Research, 1934-48. Pres., Amer. Middle East Relief, 1954-56. Fellow Amer. Academy of Arts and Sciences, 1949. Hon. DD: Oberlin Coll., 1960; Brown Univ.; Yale Univ., 1961. *Publications:* Founders of Great Religions, 1931; Bible Religion, 1938; Basis of Israelite Marriage, 1938; What Mean These Stones?, 1941; Outline of Biblical Theology, 1946; Palestine is Our Business, 1949; The Dead Sea Scrolls, 1955; More Light on the Dead Sea Scrolls, 1958; Diligently Compared-The Revised Standard Version and the King James Version of the Old Testament, 1964; Jesus in the First Three Gospels, 1977. Editor, The Dead Sea Scrolls of St Mark's Monastery, 1950-51. Articles in many learned journals. *Address:* 1670 Woodland Avenue, Winter Park, Florida 32789, USA. *T:* 1-305-647-0070.

BURROWS, Reginald Arthur, CMG 1964; Assistant Under Secretary of State, HM Diplomatic Service, since 1976; *b* 31 Aug. 1918; *s* of late Arthur Richard Burrows; *m* 1952, Jenny Louisa Henriette Campiche; one *s* one *d. Educ:* Mill Hill Sch.; St Catharine's Coll., Cambridge. Served with Royal Air Force during War; comd No. 13 (bomber) Sqdn, 1945. Entered the Foreign Service (now the Diplomatic Service), 1947; served in: Paris; Karachi; Tehran; Saigon; The Hague; Istanbul; Foreign Office; Minister, Islamabad, 1970-72; Univ. of Leeds, 1972-73; on secondment as Under-Sec., Civil Service Selection Bd, 1974-75. *Recreations:* ski-ing, tennis, squash and small boat sailing. *Address:* c/o Foreign and Commonwealth Office, SW1. *Clubs:* United Oxford & Cambridge University, Ski Club of Great Britain.

BURROWS, Sir (Robert) John (Formby), Kt 1965; MA, LLB; Solicitor; *b* 29 May 1901; *s* of Rev. Canon Francis Henry and Margaret Nelson Burrows; *m* 1926, Mary Hewlett, *y d* of Rev. R. C. Salmon; one *s* one *d. Educ:* Eton Coll. (Scholar); Trinity Coll., Cambridge (Scholar); Harvard Law Sch. Governor of the London Sch. of Economics; Pres. of The Law Soc., 1964-65. *Recreation:* forestry. *Address:* Ridlands Cottage, Limpsfield Chart, Surrey. *T:* Limpsfield Chart 3288. *Clubs:* United Oxford & Cambridge University, Buck's.
See also W. Hamilton.

BURROWS, Rt. Rev. Simon Hedley; see Buckingham, Bishop Suffragan of.

BURSTALL, Prof. Aubrey Frederic; Emeritus Professor (Mechanical Engineering), University of Newcastle upon Tyne (formerly King's College, University of Durham); Dean of Faculty of Applied Science, 1955-57; *b* 15 Jan. 1902; *s* of Prof.

Frederic William Burstall of Univ. of Birmingham and Lilian Maud Burstall (*née* Adley); *m* 1923, Nora Elizabeth (*née* Boycott); two *s* one *d. Educ:* King Edward VI Grammar Sch., Birmingham, Univ. of Birmingham; St John's Coll., Cambridge. BScEng Birmingham, 1922, First Class Hons; MScEng Birmingham, 1923; PhD Cantab 1925; DSc Melbourne; Hon. DSc (NUI), 1959. Research student, St John's Coll., Cambridge, 1923-25. Employed on the staff of Synthetic Ammonia and Nitrates Ltd (later merged into ICI Ltd) as research engineer, asst chief engineer and works engineer at Billingham Factory, 1925-34; Aluminium Plant and Vessel Co., London, as Technical Adviser to the Board responsible for design of chemical plant, 1934-37; Prof. of Engineering and Dean of Faculty of Engineering, Univ. of Melbourne, Australia, 1937-45. Developed mechanical respirators for infantile paralysis epidemic, 1937-38; gas producers for motor vehicles, and built new workshops at the Univ.; part-time Comr of State Electricity Commn of Victoria, 1941-43; leave of absence to work for British Min. of Supply in Armaments Design Dept, Fort Halstead, Kent, 1943-44. Member of Nat. Advisory Cttee on Technical Educ., 1948-; Chm. North Eastern Branch IMechE, 1956; Member Board of Governors, United Newcastle upon Tyne Hospitals, 1964-67;. Member Council of Univ. of Durham, 1964-67; Fellow, NEC Inst. Engineers and Shipbuilders; FIMechE. *Publications:* A History of Mechanical Engineering, 1963; Simple Working Models of Historic Machines, 1968; numerous in engineering journals in Britain and Australia. *Address:* The Firs, Kilmington, Axminster, Devon. *T:* Axminster 32385.

BURSTEIN, Hon. Dame Rose; see Heilbron, Hon. Dame R.

BURSTON, Sir Samuel (Gerald Wood), Kt 1977; OBE 1966; Grazier at Noss Estate, Casterton, Victoria, since 1945; President, Australian Woolgrowers and Graziers Council, since 1976; *b* 24 April 1915; *s* of Maj.-Gen. Sir Samuel Burston, KBE, CB, DSO, VD, late RAAMC, and late Lady Burston; *m* 1940, Verna Helen Peebles; one *s* one *d. Educ:* St Peter's Coll., Adelaide. Major, AIF, 1939-45 (despatches). Chm., Country Fire Authority, Vic, 1964-65; Pres., Graziers Assoc. of Vic, 1973-76; Member: Nat. Employers Policy Cttee, 1970-; Australian Wool Industry Policy Cttee, 1976-; Aust. Sci. and Technol. Council, 1976; Aust. Stats Adv. Council, 1976; Aust. Govt Econ. Consultative Gp, 1976; Nat. Labour Consultative Council, 1977. Mem., Victorian Selection Cttee, Winston Churchill Meml Trust, 1967-. *Recreations:* golf, swimming. *Address:* Noss Estate, Casterton, Vic 3311, Australia. *T:* 055 811147. *Clubs:* Melbourne (Melbourne); Adelaide, Naval, Military and Air Force of South Australia (Adelaide); Royal Adelaide Golf.

BURT, Clive Stuart Saxon, QC 1954; a Metropolitan Magistrate, 1958-73; *b* 11 June 1900; *m* 1st, 1926, Edith Benning, Montreal; 2nd, 1939, Lilian Bethune, Glasgow; one *s* three *d. Educ:* Eton; Oxford Univ. Served War, 1940-45 (despatches). Called to the Bar, Gray's Inn, 1925; Western Circuit. Chairman, The Performing Right Tribunal, 1957-58. Croix de Guerre. *Address:* Townley House, Woodbridge, Suffolk. *Club:* Garrick.

BURT, Hon. Sir Francis (Theodore Page), KCMG 1977; Lieutenant-Governor of Western Australia, since 1977; Chief Justice of the Supreme Court of Western Australia, since 1977 (a Judge of the Supreme Court since 1969); *b* Perth, WA, 14 June 1918; *s* of A. F. G. Burt; *m* 1943, Margaret, *d* of Brig. J. E. Lloyd; two *s* two *d. Educ:* Guildford Grammar Sch.; Univ. of Western Australia (LLB, LLM); Hackett Schol., 1941; admitted to Bar of WA, 1941. Served War, RAN and RAAF, 1940-45. QC 1960; Pres., Law Soc. of WA, 1960-62. Visiting Lectr in Law, Univ. of WA, 1945-65. Chairman: Inst. of Radiotherapy, WA, 1960-62; Bd of Management, Sir Charles Gairdner Hosp., Hollywood, WA, 1962-72; Queen Elizabeth II Medical Centre Trust, 1966-; Mem., Senate of Univ. of WA, 1968-76. *Recreations:* tennis, fishing. *Address:* 64 Leake Street, Cottesloe, WA 6011, Australia. *Club:* Weld (Perth).

BURT, Leonard James, CVO 1954; CBE 1957; Commander of Special Branch, New Scotland Yard, 1946-58, retired; *b* 20 April 1892; *s* of Charles Richard Burt; *m* 1918, Grace Airey; one *s. Educ:* Totton High Sch., Hants. CID, 1919-40; Chief Superintendent, CID, 1940; Intelligence Corps (Lieut-Col) 1940-46. Officer Legion of Honour, 1950; Officer Order of Orange Nassau, 1951; Chevalier Order of Danebrog, 1951. *Publication:* Commander Burt of Scotland Yard, 1959. *Address:* Flat 1, Hedley Court, 67/69 Putney Hill, SW15. *T:* 01-788 4598.

BURT-ANDREWS, Air Commodore Charles Beresford Eaton, CB 1962; CBE 1959; RAF retired; *b* 21 March 1913; *s* of late Major C. Burt-Andrews, RE; *m* 1st, 1941, Elizabeth Alsina Helen, *d* of late Sir Maurice Linford Gwyer, GCIE, KCB, KCSI; one *s* one *d*; 2nd, 1977, Joan Tresor (*née* Cayzer-Evans). *Educ:* Lindisfarne Coll.; Collège des Frères Chrétiens Sophia. Commnd RAF, 1935; served NWF India, 1937-42; S Waziristan ops, 1937; Burma, 1942; comd Army Co-op. Sqdn RAF, 1943; special ops, 1943-44; Air Attaché, British Embassy, Warsaw, 1945-47; Staff Coll., 1948; Sec. Gen. Allied Air Forces Central Europe, Fontainebleau, 1950-52; directing Staff RAF Staff Coll., 1953-55; Head of Far East Defence Secretariat, Singapore, 1955-58; First Comdt, Pakistan Air Force Staff Coll., 1959-61; UK Nat. Mil. Rep., SHAPE, Paris, 1962-65; Asst Comdt, RAF Staff Coll., Bracknell, 1965-68; retd, 1968. *Recreation:* painting. *Address:* Treovis, Upton Cross, Liskeard, Cornwall. See also S. G. Burt-Andrews.

BURT-ANDREWS, Stanley George, CMG 1968; MBE 1948; retired; *b* 1 Feb. 1908; *s* of Major Charles and Menie Celina Burt-Andrews; *m* 1937, Vera Boyadjieva; one *d. Educ:* Lindisfarne Coll., Westcliff-on-Sea; St Andrew's Coll., Bloemfontein, S Africa. Vice-Consul, 1946-47, Consul, 2nd Secretary, Sofia, 1948; Consul, Barranquilla, 1949-52; Commercial Secretary, British Embassy, Buenos Aires, 1952-53; Consul: Baltimore, 1953-59; Bilbao, 1959-62; Venice, 1962-64; Consul-General, St Louis, Mo., 1965-67. *Recreations:* golf, fishing. *Address:* Villa Verial, 1 Aldwick Place, Fish Lane, Aldwick, Bognor Regis, W Sussex. *Club:* Bognor Regis Golf. See also Air Cdre C. B. E. Burt-Andrews.

BURTON, family name of Baroness Burton of Coventry.

BURTON, 3rd Baron, *cr* 1897; **Michael Evan Victor Baillie;** *b* 27 June 1924; *er s* of Brig. Hon. George Evan Michael Baillie, MC, TD (*d* 1941) and *g s* of Baroness Burton (2nd in line); S grandmother, 1962; *m* 1948, Elizabeth Ursula Forster, *er d* of Capt. A. F. Wise; two *s* four *d. Educ:* Eton. Lieut, Scots Guards, 1944. Mem., CC, 1948-75, JP 1961-75, DL 1963-65, Invernessshire. *Heir:* s Hon. Evan Michael Ronald Baillie [*b* 19 March 1949; *m* 1970, Lucinda, *e d* of Robert Law, Newmarket; one *s* one *d*]. *Address:* Dochfour, Inverness. *T:* Dochgarroch 252. *Clubs:* Cavalry and Guards, Brooks's; New (Edinburgh); Highland (Inverness).

BURTON OF COVENTRY, Baroness, *cr* 1962, of Coventry (Life Peer); **Elaine Frances Burton;** Chairman, Mail Order Publishers' Authority, and President, Association of Mail Order Publishers, since 1970; President, Institute of Travel Managers in Industry and Commerce; *b* Scarborough, 2 March 1904; *d* of Leslie and Frances Burton. *Educ:* Leeds Girls' Modern Sch.; City of Leeds Training Coll. Leeds elementary schools and evening institutes, 1924-35; South Wales Council of Social Service and educational settlements, 1935-37; National Fitness Council, 1938-39; John Lewis Partnership. 1940-45. Writer, lecturer, broadcaster, public relations consultant, 1945-50. MP (Lab) Coventry South, 1950-59. Member of parliamentary delegation to Netherlands, 1952 and to Soviet Union, 1954; Siam, 1956; South America, 1958; deleg. to Council of Europe; first woman Chm., Select Cttee on Estimates (sub-Cttee); Mem., Select Cttee on Practice and Procedure (House of Lords). Chairman: Domestic Coal Consumers' Council, 1962-65; Council on Tribunals, 1967-73; Member: Council Industrial Design, 1963-68; ITA, 1964-69; Sports Council, 1965-71. Consultant to: John Waddington Ltd, 1959-61; The Reader's Digest, 1969-70; Courtaulds Ltd, 1960-73; Director: Consultancy Ltd, 1949-73; Imperial Domestic Appliances Ltd, 1963-66. *Publications:* What of the Women, 1941; And Your Verdict?, 1943; articles for press, magazines and political journals. *Recreations:* reading, ballet, opera; World's Sprint Champion, 1920; Yorkshire 1st XI (hockey), 1924-32. *Address:* 47 Molyneux Street, W1. *T:* 01-262 0864.

BURTON, Prof. Alan Chadburn, MBE 1947; FRSC 1952; FRSA (UK) 1954; Professor of Biophysics, University of Western Ontario, Canada, since 1949, now part-time; *b* 18 April 1904; *s* of Frank Burton, Dental Surgeon, and Annie Grey (*née* Tyrrell), N Ireland; *m* 1933, Clara Ballard, Niagara Falls, Ontario; one *s. Educ:* Strand Sch., Streatham Hill; Univ. Coll., London (Fellow, 1971). BSc Physics and Maths, UCL, 1925. Demonstrator in Physics, Univ. Coll., 1925-26; Science Master, Liverpool Collegiate Sch., 1926-27; Demonstrator and lecturer, Univ. of Toronto, Physics Dept., 1927-32; Fellow of Nat. Res. Council, Canada, 1930-32; PhD Physics, Univ. of Toronto, 1932; Research Asst, Dept of Vital Economics, Univ. of Rochester, NY, 1932-34; Rockefeller Gen. Ed. Board Fellow, Univ. of Pennsylvania, 1934-36; Fellow, Johnson Foundation for Medical Physics, 1936-40; Research Assoc., Nat. Research Council of Canada, 1941-46. War Research on Protective Clothing and Equipment for RCAF. Asst Prof., 1946, later Assoc. Prof. of Biophysics, Univ. of W. Ontario. President: American Physiological Soc., 1956-57; Canadian Physical Soc.,

1962-63; Biophysical Soc., 1958. Hon. LLD Alberta, 1963; Hon. DSc Western Ontario, 1974. Gairnder Internat. Award for Cardiovascular Research, 1961. *Publications:* The Science of Field Testing of Clothing and Equipment (Monograph of Defence Research Board of Canada), 1947; (with O. G. Edholm) Man in a Cold Environment, 1955; The Physiology and Biophysics of the Circulation, 1965; about 150 publications in journals of Physiology and Biophysics, 12 in Journals of Physics. *Recreations:* formerly Rugby and tennis, now golf; interested in penal reform and prisoner rehabilitation (John Howard Society). *Address:* 243 Epworth Avenue, London, Ontario, Canada. *T:* 434-9938.

BURTON, Sir George (Vernon Kennedy), Kt 1977; CBE 1972 (MBE (mil.) 1945); Chairman, Fisons Ltd, since 1973 (Chief Executive, 1966-76, Senior Vice-Chairman, 1966-71, Deputy Chairman, 1971-72); Director: Matthews Holdings Ltd; Barclays Bank International Ltd; Thomas Tilling, since 1976; Rolls-Royce Ltd, since 1976; *b* 21 April 1916; *s* of late George Ethelbert Earnshaw and of Francesca Burton; *g s* of Sir Bunnell Burton, Ipswich; *m* 1st, 1945, Sarah Katherine Tcherniavsky (marr. diss.); two *s*; 2nd, 1975, Priscilla Margaret Gore, *d* of Cecil H. King, *qv*. *Educ:* Charterhouse; Germany. Served RA, 1939-45, N Africa, Sicily, Italy, Austria. Member: Council, CBI, 1970- (Chm., CBI Overseas Cttee, 1975-); BOTB, 1972-73 (BOTB European Trade Cttee, 1972-; British Overseas Trade Adv. Council, 1975-); Investment Insce Adv. Cttee, ECGD 1971-76; Council on Internat. Develt of ODM, 1977-; Council, BIM, 1968-70 (FBIM); NEDC, 1975-; Dep. Chm., Export Council for Europe, 1967-71 (Mem., 1965-71). Mem., Whitford Cttee to Consider Law on Copyright and Designs, 1974-77. Member: Ipswich County Borough Council, 1947-51; Ipswich Gp HMC; formerly Chm., Aldeburgh Cottage Hosp. Pres., Ipswich Young Conservatives, 1946-50. Liveryman, Worshipful Co. of Farmers. Commander: Order of Ouissam Alaouite, Morocco, 1968; Order of Léopold II, Belgium, 1974. *Recreation:* music. *Address:* 9 Grosvenor Street, W1. *T:* 01-493 4134.

BURTON, Air Marshal Sir Harry, KCB 1971 (CB 1970); CBE 1963 (MBE 1943); DSO 1941; Air Officer Commanding-in-Chief, Air Support Command, 1970-73, retired; *b* 2 May 1919; *s* of Robert Reid Burton, Rutherglen; *m* 1945, Jean, *d* of Tom Dobie; one *s* one *d*. *Educ:* Glasgow High Sch. Joined RAF 1937; served War of 1939-45, Europe, India, and Pacific (POW, 1940, escaped 1941; despatches); CO, RAF Scampton, 1960-62; SASO 3 (Bomber) Group, RAF, 1963-65; Air Executive to Deputy for Nuclear Affairs, SHAPE, 1965-67; AOC 23 Group, RAF, 1967-70. Group Captain 1958; Air Cdre 1963; Air Vice-Marshal 1965; Air Marshal 1971. *Address:* Mayfield, West Drive, Middleton-on-Sea, Sussex. *Club:* Royal Air Force.

BURTON, Humphrey McGuire; Head of Music and Arts, BBC Television, since 1975; *b* 25 March 1931; *s* of Harry (Philip) and Kathleen Burton; *m* 1st, 1957, Gretel (*née* Davis); one *s* one *d*; 2nd, 1970, Christina (*née* Hellstedt); one *s* one *d*. *Educ:* Long Dene Sch., Chiddingstone; Judd Sch., Tonbridge; Fitzwilliam House, Cambridge (BA). BBC Radio, 1955-58; BBC TV, 1958-67: Editor, Monitor, 1962; Exec. Producer Music Programmes, 1963; Head of Music and Arts Programmes, 1965, programmes inc. Workshop, Master Class, In Rehearsal, Britten at 50, Conversations with Glenn Gould. Since return to BBC in 1975, Exec. Producer opera relays from Covent Garden (Cav and Pag) and Glyndebourne (Capriccio); Producer, Omnibus at Santa Fe Opera; Host of weekly Omnibus series and other arts and music programmes for BBC TV. London Weekend TV: Head of Drama, Arts and Music, 1967; Editor/Introducer, Aquarius, 1970-75, programmes incl. Mahler Festival, Verdi Requiem, Trouble in Tahiti, The Great Gondola Race, Anatomy of a Record, etc; Independent TV: 5 Glyndebourne operas, adapted and produced for Southern TV, 1972-74; The Beach at Falesa, World Premiere for Harlech TV, 1974; UN Day Concert with Pablo Casals, 1971; French TV: Berlioz' Requiem at Les Invalides, 1975; many free-lance prodns in Austria, Germany and USA. Desmond Davis Award, SFTA, 1966; Royal TV Soc. Silver Medal, 1971; Emmy, 1971 for 'Beethoven's Birthday' (CBS TV); Peabody Award, 1972; SFTA Best Specialised Series, 1974 (for Aquarius). *Recreations:* playing piano duets, singing, tennis, swimming, travel. *Address:* 144 Richmond Hill, Richmond, Surrey. *T:* 01-940 5063. *Club:* Garrick.

BURTON, Rev. John Harold Stanley, MA Oxon; General Secretary, Church Lads' Brigade, 1954-64 and 1973-Jan. 1977; Member, Church of England Youth Council, 1954-64; *b* 6 Feb. 1913; *o s* of late John Stanley Burton, Grenadier Guards (killed in action 1916), and Lilian Bostock; *m* 1st, 1943, Susan Lella (*d* 1960), *o d* of Sir John Crisp, 3rd Bt; two *d*; 2nd, 1960, Jacqueline Mary Margaret, *o d* of P. L. Forte, Clifton, Bristol; one *d*. *Educ:* Marlborough; University Coll., Oxford; Westcott House,

Cambridge. BA 2nd Class Hons. in Theology, Oxford, 1935; MA 1937; Deacon, 1936; Priest, 1938; Curate of Christ Church, Woburn Square, WC1, 1936-39; Cranleigh, Surrey, 1939-40; Head of Cambridge Univ. Settlement, Camberwell, 1940-43; Chaplain RAFVR, 1943; Fighter Command, 1943-44; 2nd Tactical Air Force, 1944; Bomber Command, 1945; Ordination Secretary, Air Command, SE Asia, and Chaplain 9 RAF General Hospital, Calcutta, 1945-46; demobilised Aug. 1946. Chaplain of Middlesex Hospital, W1, 1946-50; Chaplain of the Royal Free Hospital, 1950-54; Chairman of Hospital Chaplains Fellowship, 1953-54. *Publications:* (contrib.) A Priest's Work in Hospital, 1955; (contrib.) Trends in Youth Work, 1967. *Recreations:* Beagling, fishing, shooting, most games. *Address:* 45 Westbourne Terrace, W2. *T:* 01-262 8470; Millrace House, Durrus, near Bantry, Co. Cork. *T:* Durrus 18. *Club:* Royal Air Force.

BURTON, Prof. Kenneth, FRS 1974; Professor of Biochemistry, University of Newcastle-upon-Tyne, since 1966; *b* 26 June 1926; *s* of Arthur Burton and Gladys (*née* Buxton); *m* 1955, Hilda Marsden; one *s* one *d*. *Educ:* High Pavement Sch., Nottingham; Wath-upon-Dearne Grammar Sch.; King's Coll., Cambridge (MA, PhD). Asst Lectr in Biochem., Univ. of Sheffield, 1949, Lectr 1952; Res. Associate, Univ. of Chicago, 1952-54; MRC Unit for Research in Cell Metabolism, Oxford, 1954-66. Vis. Lectr in Medicine, Harvard, 1964; Mem. Biological Research Bd, MRC, 1967-71. *Publications:* (ed) Nucleic Acids, 1974; papers in Biochemical Jl, etc. *Recreations:* music, hill-walking. *Address:* University of Newcastle upon Tyne, Newcastle upon Tyne NE1 7RU.

BURTON, Maurice, DSc; retired 1958; now free-lance author and journalist; *b* 28 March 1898; *s* of William Francis and Jane Burton; *m* 1928, Margaret Rosalie Maclean; two *s* one *d*. *Educ:* Holloway County Sch.; London Univ. Biology Master, Latymer Foundation, Hammersmith, 1924-27; Zoology Dept, British Museum (Natural History), SW7, 1927-58. Science Editor, Illustrated London News, 1946-64; Nature Correspondent, Daily Telegraph, 1949-. FRSA, FZS. *Publications:* The Story of Animal Life, 1949; Animal Courtship, 1953; Living Fossils, 1954; Phœnix Re-born, 1959; Systematic Dictionary of Mammals, 1962; (jtly) Purnell's Encyclopedia of Animal Life, 1968-70; Encyclopaedia of Animals, 1972; Introduction to Nature (for children), 1972; Prehistoric Animals, 1974; Deserts, 1974; How Mammals Live, 1975, etc; numerous publications on Sponges in a variety of scientific journals. *Recreation:* gardening. *Address:* Weston House, Albury, Guildford, Surrey GU5 9AE. *T:* Shere 2369.

BURTON, Neil Edward David; Director of Competition Policy, Office of Fair Trading, since 1977; *b* 12 May 1930; *s* of Edward William Burton and Doris Burton; *m* 1954, Jane-Anne Crossley Perry; three *s*. *Educ:* Welwyn Garden City Grammar Sch.; City of London Sch.; Trinity Coll., Oxford (MA). Asst Principal, Min. of Supply, MAFF, 1966, subseq. CSD and Price Commn; Asst Dir, Office of Fair Trading, 1976; Dir, Restrictive Trade Practices, 1976. *Recreations:* reading, walking, travel. *Address:* 29 Brittains Lane, Sevenoaks, Kent. *T:* Sevenoaks 55608.

BURTON, Richard, CBE 1970; stage and film actor; *b* Pontrhydfen, South Wales, 10 Nov. 1925; *m* 1st, 1949, Sybil Williams (marr. diss., 1963; she *m* 1965, Jordan Christopher); two *d*; 2nd, 1964, Elizabeth Taylor (marr. diss. 1974, remarried 1975, marr. diss. 1976), *qv*; 4th, 1976, Susan Hunt. *Educ:* Port Talbot Secondary Sch.; Exeter Coll., Oxford. Hon. Fellow, St Peter's Coll., Oxford, 1972. First appeared on stage as Glan in Druid's Rest, Royal Court Theatre, Liverpool, 1943; played same rôle, St Martin's, London, 1944. Served with Royal Air Force, 1944-47. Returned to stage in Castle Anna, Lyric, Hammersmith, 1948; subsequent stage appearances include: Richard in the Lady's Not For Burning, Globe, 1949, New York, 1950; Cuthman in The Boy With a Cart, Lyric, Hammersmith, 1950. Played Hamlet with Old Vic Company, Edinburgh Festival, 1953, and subsequently; has also appeared with Old Vic Company in King John, The Tempest, Twelfth Night, Coriolanus, etc. Old Vic Season, 1955-56: Othello, Iago, Henry V; Time Remembered, New York, 1957-58; Camelot, New York, 1960; Hamlet, New York, 1964; Equus, NY, 1976. *Films include:* The Last Days of Dolwyn; My Cousin Rachel; The Desert Rats; The Robe; The Prince of Players; Alexander the Great; The Rains of Ranchipur; Sea Wyf and Biscuit; Bitter Victory; Look Back in Anger; Bramblebush; Ice Palace; Cleopatra; The VIP's; Becket; Hamlet (from Broadway prod.); The Night of the Iguana; The Sandpiper; The Spy Who Came in from the Cold; Who's Afraid of Virginia Woolf; The Taming of the Shrew; Dr Faustus; The Comedians; Boom; Where Eagles Dare; Candy; Staircase; Anne of the Thousand Days; Villain; Hammersmith is Out; Raid on Rommel; Under Milk Wood; The

Assassination of Trotsky; Bluebeard; The Kinsman; Massacre in Rome; Exorcist II: The Heretic. *Relevant publication:* Richard Burton, by J. Cottrell and F. Cashin, 1971. *Address:* c/o Major Donald Neville-Willing, 85 Kinnerton Street, SW1. *T:* 01-235 4640.

BURTON, Sydney Harold, FBS; JP; Managing Director, Gateway Building Society, since 1975; *b* 6 April 1916; *s* of Sydney Collard Burton and Maud Burton; *m* 1941, Jean Cowling; one *d*. *Educ:* Belle Vue High Sch., Bradford. Various appts with Bradford Equitable Building Soc. (excl. war years), 1932-63; joined Temperance Permanent Building Soc., 1963; Jt Gen. Manager, 1965; Gen. Man. and Sec., 1972; following merger of Temperance Permanent and Bedfordshire Bldg Socs became Chief Gen. Man. and Sec. of Gateway Bldg Soc., 1974. Pres., Building Societies Inst., 1976-77; Mem. Council, Building Societies Assoc. JP Worthing, 1974. *Recreations:* music and theatre, social and religious work. *Address:* Gull's Croft, 34 Oval Waye, Ferring, Sussex BN12 5RA. *T:* Worthing 46207. *Club:* Junior Carlton.

BURTON-CHADWICK, Sir Robert, 2nd Bt, *cr* 1935; (Sir Peter); *b* 22 June 1911; *s* of Sir Robert Burton-Chadwick, 1st Bt and Catherine Barbara (*d* 1935), *d* of late Thomas Williams; *S* father 1951; *m* 1st, 1937, Rosalind Mary (marr. diss., 1949), *d* of Harry John Stott; two *d*; 2nd, 1950, Beryl Joan, *d* of Stanley Frederick J. Brailsford; one *s* one *d*. *Educ:* St George's Sch., Harpenden, Herts. Served War of 1939-45, with NZMF, N Africa, Italy, 1942-45. *Heir: s* Joshua Kenneth Burton-Chadwick, *b* 1 Feb. 1954. *Address:* 102 Meadowbank Road, Remuera, Auckland 5, New Zealand.

BURTON-TAYLOR, Sir Alvin, Kt 1972; FCA (Aust.); FAIM; Chairman: P&O Australia Ltd; Bishopsgate Insurance Australia Ltd; Country Television Services Ltd; Demag Industrial Equipment Pty Ltd; Pirelli Cables (Aust.) Ltd; Slumberland (Aust.) Pty Ltd; Director: Email Ltd; Formica Plastics Pty Ltd; International Combustion Australia Ltd; NSW Division, National Heart Foundation of Australia; O'Connell Street Associates Pty Ltd; *b* 17 Aug. 1912; *s* of A. A. W. Taylor, Adelaide, and Ruby Ella Burton, Adelaide; *m* 1949, Joan L. Toole; two *s* two *d*. *Educ:* Sydney Church of England Grammar Sch. Cooper Bros Way & Hardie, 1930-37; Asst Gen. Manager, then Gen. Manager, Rheem Aust. Ltd, 1937-57; Man. Dir, Email Ltd (Group), 1957-74; Dir, Commonwealth Banking Corporation, 1959-75. *Recreations:* sailing, golf, fishing. *Address:* Unit 6 Gainsborough, 50-58 Upper Pitt Street, Kirribilli, NSW 2061, Australia. *Clubs:* Union, Royal Sydney Yacht Squadron, Elanora Country (all in NSW).

BURY, Viscount; Rufus Arnold Alexis Keppel; *b* 16 July 1965; *s* of Derek William Charles Keppel, Viscount Bury (*d* 1968), and Marina, *yr d* of late Count Serge Orloff-Davidoff; *g s* and *heir* of 9th Earl of Albemarle, *qv. Address:* Piazza di Bellosguardo 10, 50124 Florence, Italy.

BURY, John; Associate Director (Head of Design), National Theatre, since 1973; free-lance designer for theatre, opera and film; *b* 27 Jan. 1925; *s* of C. R. Bury; *m* 1st, 1947, Margaret Leila Greenwood (marr. diss.); one *s*; 2nd, 1966, Elizabeth Rebecca Blackborrow Duffield; two *s* one *d*. *Educ:* Cathedral Sch., Hereford; University Coll., London. Served with Fleet Air Arm (RN), 1942-46. Theatre Workshop, Stratford, E15, 1946-63; Assoc. Designer, Royal Shakespeare Theatre, 1963-73, Head of Design, 1965-68. FRSA 1970. Co-winner, Gold Medal for Scene Design, Prague Quadrienale, 1976. *Address:* 14 Woodlands Road, Barnes, SW13.

BURY, Hon. Leslie Harry Ernest, MHR (Lib) for Wentworth, NSW, since 1956; *b* London, 25 Feb. 1913; *s* of late Rev. E. Bury, Bournemouth, England; *m* 1940, Anne Helen, *d* of late C. E. Weigall; four *s. Educ:* Queens' Coll., Cambridge (MA). Bank of NSW, 1935-45. Served War of 1939-45, AIF, 12th Aust. Radar Det. Commonwealth Dept of External Affairs, i/c Economic Relations, 1945-47; Treasury, 1948-51; Alternate Dir, IBRD, IMF, 1951-53, Exec. Dir, 1953-56. Minister: for Air, 1961-62; for Housing, 1963-66; for Labour and Nat. Service, 1966-69; Treasurer, 1969-71; Minister for Foreign Affairs, March-Aug. 1971, resigned. Aust. Rep., Commonwealth Finance Ministers' internat. meetings, etc. *Recreations:* carpentry, gardening, home repairs. *Address:* Parliament House, Canberra, ACT 2600; (home) Vaucluse Road, Vaucluse, NSW 2030, Australia. *Clubs:* Union, Royal Sydney Golf (Sydney).

BURY, Michael Oswell, OBE 1968; Director, Education, Training and Technology, Confederation of British Industry, since 1970; Commissioner, Manpower Services Commission, since 1974; *b* 20 Dec. 1922; *o s* of Lt-Col Thomas Oswell Bury,

TD, and Constance Evelyn Bury; *m* 1954, Jean Threlkeld Wood, *d* of late William Threlkeld Wood; two *s* one *d*. *Educ:* Charterhouse; London Sch. of Economics. Served War of 1939-45: The Rifle Brigade (ranks of Rifleman to Captain), 1941-47. Steel Company of Wales, 1947-49; British Iron and Steel Fedn, 1949-64 (Dep. Dir, Labour and Trng, 1962-64); Dir, Iron and Steel Industry Trng Bd, 1964-70. *Recreations:* gardening, fishing, travel. *Address:* Hull Bush, Mountnessing, Brentwood, Essex CM13 1UH. *T:* Ingatestone 3958. *Club:* Reform.

BURY, Air Cdre Thomas Malcolm Grahame, CB 1972; OBE 1962; *b* 11 Sept. 1918; *s* of late Ernest Bury, OBE; *m* 1951, Dillys Elaine Jenkins, MBE, *d* of Dr Aneurin Jenkins, Swansea; two *s* one *d*. *Educ:* Forest Sch., E17. Served War, 1939-45, NW Europe, Arabia. Joined RAF, 1935; STSO, HQ, 1 Gp, 1961-64; DDME, MoD, 1965-66; Senior Engr Officer, Air Forces Gulf, 1967-68; Command Mech. Engr, HQ Strike Command, 1968-73; retired 1973. *Address:* c/o Lloyds Bank, 6 Pall Mall, SW1. *Club:* Royal Air Force.

BURY ST EDMUNDS, Provost of; *see* Maddock, Rt Rev. D. R.

BUSBY, Sir Matthew, Kt 1968; CBE 1958; Director, Manchester United Football Club, since 1971 (General Manager, 1969-71, Manager, 1945-69); Member, Central Lancashire New Town Development Corporation, since 1971; *b* 26 May 1909; *m* 1931, Jean Busby; one *s* one *d* (and four *s* decd). *Educ:* St Brides, Bothwell. Footballer: Manchester City, 1929-36; Liverpool, 1936-39. Served Army, 1939-45. Freeman of Manchester, 1967. KCSG. *Publication:* My Story, 1957. *Recreations:* golf, theatre. *Address:* 210 Kings Road, Manchester M21 1XQ. *T:* 061-881 3326.

BUSH, Alan, MC 1944; Assistant Master, Campbell College, Belfast, since 1970; *b* 18 July 1914; *5th s* of Arthur and Sarah Bush, Endmoor, Westmorland; *m* 1946, Kathleen Olivia Guthrie, *e d* of Dr and Mrs Bryson, Dore, Derbyshire; two *s* one *d*. *Educ:* Heversham Grammar Sch.; The Queen's Coll., Oxford (Hons. History). Asst Master, Scarborough Coll., 1935-37; Asst Master, Mill Hill Sch., 1937. Commissioned into Border Regt, 1940; transferred to Parachute Regt. Housemaster of Ridgeway House, Mill Hill Sch., 1950-58; Headmaster, Merchiston Castle Sch., 1958-69. *Recreations:* most games; gardening. *Address:* Campbell College, Belfast BT4 2ND.

BUSH, Alan, Composer; Conductor; Pianist; Professor of Composition, Royal Academy of Music, since 1925; *b* 22 Dec. 1900; *s* of Alfred Walter Bush and Alice Maud (*née* Brinsley); *m* 1931, Nancy Rachel Head; two *d* (and one *d* decd). *Educ:* Highgate Sch.; Royal Academy of Music; Univ. of Berlin. ARAM 1922; Carnegie Award 1924; FRAM 1938; BMus London, 1940; DMus London, 1968. Arts Council Opera Award, 1951; Händel Prize, City Council of Halle (Saale), 1962; Corresp. Member, Deutsche Akademie der Künste, 1955. FRSA 1966. Hon. DMus Dunelm, 1970. Appeared as piano-recitalist, London, Berlin, etc., 1927-33; played solo part in own Piano Concerto, BBC, 1938, with Sir Adrian Boult conducting. Toured Ceylon, India, Australia as Examiner for Assoc. Board of Royal Schools of Music, London, 1932-33; concert tours as orchestral conductor, introducing British Music and own compositions, to USSR, 1938, 1939, 1963, Czechoslovakia, Yugoslavia, Poland, Bulgaria, 1947, Czechoslovakia and Bulgaria again, 1949, Holland, 1950, Berlin (German Democratic Republic) and Hungary, 1952, and Berlin again, 1958; Première of opera "Wat Tyler" at the Leipzig Opera House, 1953; Première of opera "Men of Blackmoor" at the German National Theatre, Weimar, 1956; Première of opera "The Sugar Reapers" at the Leipzig Opera House, 1966; Première of opera "Joe Hill (The Man Who Never Died)", German State Opera, Berlin, 1970. Musical Adviser, London Labour Choral Union, 1929-40; Chairman Workers' Music Assoc., 1936-41 (President 1941-). Chairman Composers' Guild of Great Britain, 1947-48. *Publications: operas:* Wat Tyler; Men of Blackmoor; The Sugar Reapers; Joe Hill (The Man Who Never Died); and children's operettas; *choral works:* The Winter Journey, Op. 29; Song of Friendship, Op. 34; The Ballad of Freedom's Soldier, Op. 44 (mixed voices); The Dream of Llewelyn ap Gruffydd, Op. 35 (male voices); The Alps and Andes of the Living World, Op. 66 (mixed chorus); Song for Angela Davis; Africa is my Name, Op. 85; Folksong arrangements, etc; *songs:* Voices of the Prophets, Cantata for tenor and piano, Op. 41; Seafarers' Songs for baritone and piano, Op. 57; The Freight of Harvest, Song-Cycle for Tenor and Piano, Op. 69; Four Songs for mezzo-soprano and piano, Op. 77; Two Songs for Baritone and Piano, Op. 80; *orchestral works:* Dance Overture, Op. 12; Piano Concerto, Op. 18; Symphony No 1 in C, Op. 21; Overture "Resolution", Op. 25; English Suite for strings, Op. 28; Piers Plowman's Day Suite, Op. 30; Violin

Concerto, Op. 32; Symphony No 2 "The Nottingham", op. 33; Concert Suite for 'cello and orchestra, Op. 37; Dorian Passacaglia and Fugue, Op. 52; Symphony No 3 "The Byron Symphony", op. 53; Variations, Nocturne and Finale on an English Sea Song for piano and orchestra, Op. 60; Partita Concertante, Op. 63; Time Remembered for Chamber Orchestra, Op. 67; Scherzo for Wind Orchestra with Percussion, Op. 68; Africa: Symphonic Movement for piano and orchestra, Op. 73; Concert Overture for an Occasion, Op. 74; The Liverpool Overture, Op. 76; *chamber music:* String Quartet, Op. 4; Piano Quartet, Op. 5; Five Pieces for Violin, Viola, Cello, Clarinet and Horn, Op. 6; Dialectic for string quartet, Op. 15; Three Concert Studies for piano trio, Op. 31; Suite for Two Pianos, Op. 65; Time Remembered for Chamber Orchestra, Op. 66; Serenade for String Quartet, Op. 70; Suite of six for String Quartet, Op. 81; *instrumental solos:* Prelude and Fugue for piano, Op. 9; Relinquishment for piano, Op. 11; Concert Piece for 'cello and piano, Op. 17; Meditation on a German song of 1848 for violin and String Orchestra or piano, Op. 22; Lyric Interlude for violin and piano, Op. 26; Le Quatorze Juillet for piano, Op. 38; Trent's Broad Reaches for French horn and piano, Op. 36; Three English Song Preludes for organ, Op. 40; Northumbrian Impressions for oboe and piano, Op. 42a; Autumn Poem for French Horn and piano, Op. 45; Two Ballads of the Sea for piano, Op. 50; Two Melodies for viola with piano accompaniment, Op. 47; Suite for harpsichord or piano, Op. 54; Three African Sketches for flute with piano accompaniment, Op. 55; Two Occasional Pieces for organ, Op. 56; Prelude, Air and Dance for violin with accompaniment for string quartet and percussion, Op. 61; Meditation on the Ballad Geordie for double-bass and piano, Op. 62; Two Dances for Cimbalom, Op. 64; Pianoforte Sonata in A flat, Op. 71; Corentyne Kwe-Kwe for piano, Op. 75; sonatina for recorders and piano; Twenty-four Preludes for Piano, Op. 84. *Textbook:* Strict Counterpoint in Palestrina Style. *Recreations:* walking, foreign travel. *Address:* 25 Christchurch Crescent, Radlett, Herts. *T:* Radlett 6422.

BUSH, Hon. Sir Brian Drex, Kt 1976; **Hon. Mr Justice Bush;** a Judge of the High Court, Family Division, since 1976; *b* 5 Sept. 1925; *s* of William Harry Bush; *m* 1954, Beatrice Marian Lukeman; one *s* one *d. Educ:* King Edward's Sch., Birmingham; Birmingham Univ. (LLB). Served, RNVR, 1943-46. Called to the Bar, Gray's Inn, 1947, Bencher, 1976. Dep. Chm., Derbyshire Quarter Sessions, 1966-71; a Circuit Judge, 1969-76. Chm., Industrial Tribunal, 1967-69; Member: Parole Bd, 1971-74; W Midlands Probation and After Care Cttee, 1975-77. *Recreations:* sailing, golf. *Address:* 12 Middlepark Close, Weoley Hill, Birmingham B29 4BT. *Clubs:* Royal Naval Sailing Association, Bar Yacht.

BUSH, Douglas; *see* Bush, J. N. D.

BUSH, Captain Eric Wheler, DSO 1940 (and Bars 1942 and 1944); DSC 1915; RN; psc; *b* 12 Aug. 1899; *s* of late Rev. H. W. Bush, Chaplain to the Forces, and Edith Cornelia (*née* Cardew); *m* 1938, Mollie Noël, *d* of Col B. Watts, DSO; two *s. Educ:* Stoke House, Stoke Poges; Royal Naval Colleges, Osborne and Dartmouth. Midshipman in HMS Bacchante, 1914; present at Battle of Heligoland Bight, 28 Aug. 1914; took part in defence of Suez Canal Jan.-March 1915; present at original landing at Anzac, Gallipoli, 25 April 1915, and subsequent operations, also original landing at Suvla Bay 1915 (despatches twice, DSC); Midshipman HMS Revenge 1916 and present at Battle of Jutland, 31 May 1916; Sub-Lieut 1917; Lieut 1920; Qualified Interpreter in Hindustani, 1924; Lt-Comdr 1927; Qualified RN Staff Coll., 1931; Commander, 1933; Captain, 1939; Chief of Staff and afterwards Captain Auxiliary Patrol, Dover Command, 1939-40 (DSO); HMS Euryalus in Command, Mediterranean, 1941-43 (Bar to DSO); Senior Officer Assault Group S3, invasion of Normandy, 1944 (2nd Bar to DSO); afterwards in Command of HMS Malaya; Chief of Staff, Naval Force 'W', SEAC, 1945 (despatches twice); in Command HMS Ganges, Boys' Training Establishment, Shotley, Suffolk, 1946-48; Sec. Sea Cadet Council, 1948-59. Gen. Manager, Red Ensign Club, Stepney, 1959-64. School Liaison British-India Steam Navigation Co. Ltd, 1965-71. Retired list, 1948. *Publications:* How to Become a Naval Officer (Special Entry); Bless our Ship; The Flowers of the Sea; How to Become a Naval Officer (Cadet Entry); Salute the Soldier; Gallipoli. *Address:* Hunters, Langton Green, Kent. *T:* Tunbridge Wells 21768.

BUSH, George Herbert Walker; Director: Eli Lilly; Texas Gulf Inc.; First International Bancshares, Dallas; Chairman, Executive Committee, First International Bank in Houston; *b* Milton, Mass, 12 June 1924; *s* of Prescott Sheldon Bush and Dorothy (*née* Walker); *m* 1945, Barbara, *d* of Marvin Pierce, NY; four *s* one *d. Educ:* Phillips Acad., Andover, Mass; Yale Univ. (BA Econs 1948). Served War, USNR, Lieut, pilot (DFC,

three Air Medals). Co-founder and Dir, Zapata Petroleum Corp., 1953-59; Founder, Zapata Offshore Co., Houston, 1954, Pres., 1956-64, Chm. Bd, 1964-66. Chm., Republican Party, Harris Co., Texas, 1963-64; Delegate, Republican Nat. Convention, 1964, 1968; Republican cand. US Senator from Texas, 1964, 1970; Mem., 90th Congress, 7th District of Texas, 1967-70; US Perm. Rep. to UN, 1971-73; Chm., Republican Party Nat. Cttee, 1973-74; Chief, US Liaison Office, Peking, 1974-75; Dir, US Central Intelligence Agency, 1976-77. State Chm., Heart Fund. Hon. degrees from Beaver Coll., Adelphi Univ., Austin Coll., N Michigan Univ. *Recreation:* tennis. *Address:* 1079 Houston Club Building, Houston, Texas 77002, USA.

BUSH, Prof. Ian (Elcock), MA; PhD; MB, BChir; Research Professor of Psychiatry and Physiology, Department of Neurology, Dartmouth Medical School, USA, since 1977 (Senior Research Associate, 1974-77); Professor of Physiology, New York University Medical School; *b* 25 May 1928; *s* of late Dr Gilbert B. Bush and of Jean Margaret Bush; *m* 1st, 1951, Alison Mary Pickard (marr. diss., 1966); one *s* two *d*; 2nd, 1967, Joan Morthland (marr. diss. 1972); one *s* one *d. Educ:* Bryanston Sch.; Pembroke Coll., Cambridge BA 1949. Natural Sciences Tripos, 1st class I and II; MA, PhD 1953; MB, BChir. 1957. Medical Research Council Scholar (Physiology Lab. Cambridge; National Institute for Medical Research), 1949-52; Commonwealth Fellow 1952 (University of Utah; Mass. General Hospital); Part-time Research Asst, Med. Unit, St Mary's Hosp. London and med. student, 1953-56; Grad. Asst, Dept Regius Prof. of Med., Oxford, 1956-59; Mem. ext. Scientific Staff, Med. Research Council (Oxford), 1959-61. Hon. Dir Med. Research Council Unit for research in chem. pathology of mental disorders, 1960; Bowman Prof. of Physiology and Dir of Dept of Physiology, Univ. of Birmingham, 1960-64; Senior Scientist, The Worcester Foundation for Experimental Biology, 1964-67; Chm. of Dept and Prof. of Physiology, Medical Coll. of Virginia, 1967-70; Pres. and Dir of Laboratories, Cybertek Inc., New York, 1970-72. Fellow, Amer. Acad. of Arts and Sciences, 1966. *Publications:* Chromatography of Steroids, 1961. Contributions to: Jl Physiol.; Biochem. Jl; Jl Endocrinol.; Nature; The Analyst; Jl Biolog. Chem.; Brit. Med. Bulletin; Acta Endocrinologica; Experientia; Biochem. Soc. Symposia, etc. *Recreations:* music, chess, sailing, fishing, philosophy. *Address:* c/o Dartmouth Medical School, Hanover, NH 03755, USA.

BUSH, Adm. Sir John (Fitzroy Duyland), GCB 1970 (KCB 1965; CB 1963); DSC 1941, and Bars, 1941, 1944; Rear-Admiral of the United Kingdom, since 1976; *b* 1 Nov. 1914; *s* of late Fitzroy Bush, Beach, Glos; *m* 1938, Ruth Kennedy Horsey; three *s* two *d. Educ:* Clifton Coll. Entered Navy, 1933; served in Destroyers throughout War. Commanded HM Ships: Belvoir, 1942-44; Zephyr, 1944; Chevron, 1945-46. Comdr Dec. 1946; Plans Div., Admiralty, 1946-48; graduated Armed Forces Staff Coll., USA, 1949; Comd, HMS Cadiz, 1950-51; Capt. June 1952; Dep. Sec. Chiefs of Staff Cttee, 1953-55; Capt. (F) Sixth Frigate Sqdn, 1955-56; Cdre, RN Barracks, Chatham, 1957-59; Dir. of Plans, Admiralty, 1959-60; Rear-Adm. 1961; Flag Officer Flotillas (Mediterranean), 1961-62; Vice-Adm. 1963; Comdr, British Naval Staff and Naval Attaché, Washington, 1963-65; Vice-Chief of the Naval Staff, Ministry of Defence, 1965-67; C-in-C Western Fleet, C-in-C Eastern Atlantic, and C-in-C Channel (NATO), 1967-70; Admiral 1968; retd, 1970. Dir, Gordon A. Friesen International Inc., Washington, DC, 1970-73. Adm., Texas (USA) Navy. Governor, Clifton Coll., 1973-. Pres., Old Cliftonians Soc., 1967-69. Mem., E Hants District Council, 1974-76. *Recreations:* fishing, gardening. *Address:* Becksteddle House, Colemore, near Alton, Hants. *T:* Tisted 367.

BUSH, (John Nash) Douglas; Professor of English, Harvard University, 1936-66, Gurney Professor, 1957-66; *b* Morrisburg, Ontario, Canada, 21 March 1896; *s* of Dexter C. and Mary E. Bush; *m* 1927, Hazel Cleaver; one *s. Educ:* Univ. of Toronto, Canada; Harvard Univ. USA. Sheldon Fellow in England, 1923-24; Instructor in English, Harvard, 1924-27; Department of English, Univ. of Minnesota, 1927-36; Guggenheim Fellow, in England, 1934-35; Member American Philosophical Society; Pres. Modern Humanities Research Association, 1955; Corr. Fellow, British Academy, 1960. Hon. LittD: Tufts Coll., 1952; Princeton Univ., 1958; Toronto Univ., 1958; Oberlin Coll., 1959; Harvard Univ., 1959; Swarthmore Coll., 1960; Boston Coll., 1965; Michigan State Univ., 1968; Merrimack Coll., 1969; LHD Southern Illinois Univ., 1962; LHD, Marlboro Coll., 1966. *Publications:* Mythology and the Renaissance Tradition in English Poetry, 1932 (revised edition, 1963); Mythology and the Romantic Tradition in English Poetry, 1937; The Renaissance and English Humanism, 1939; Paradise Lost in Our Time, 1945; English Literature in the Earlier Seventeenth Century, 1600-

1660 (Oxford History of English Literature), 1945 (revised edition 1962); Science and English Poetry, 1950; Classical Influences in Renaissance Literature, 1952; English Poetry: The Main Currents, 1952; John Milton, 1964; Prefaces to Renaissance Literature, 1965; John Keats, 1966; Engaged and Disengaged, 1966; Pagan Myth and Christian Tradition in English Poetry, 1968; Matthew Arnold, 1971; Jane Austen, 1975; Editor: The Portable Milton, 1949; Tennyson: Selected Poetry, 1951; John Keats: Selected Poems and Letters, 1959; (with A. Harbage), Shakespeare's Sonnets, 1961; Complete Poetical Works of John Milton, 1965; Variorum Commentary on Milton, vol. 1, Latin and Greek Poems, 1970, vol. 2, (with A. S. P. Woodhouse and E. Weismiller) Minor English Poems, 1972. *Address:* 3 Clement Circle, Cambridge, Mass 02138, USA.

BUSH, Maj.-Gen. Peter John, OBE 1968; Chief of Staff and Head of United Kingdom Delegation to Live Oak, SHAPE, since 1977; *b* 31 May 1924; *s* of Clement Charles Victor Bush and Kathleen Mabel Peirce; *m* 1948, Jean Mary Hamilton; two *s* one *d*. *Educ:* Maidenhead County Sch., Maidenhead. Commnd Somerset LI, 1944; comd LI Volunteers, 1966; GSO 1 HQ 14 Div./Malaya Dist, 1968; Comdr 3 Inf. Bde, 1971 (mentioned in despatches, 1973); Asst Comdt RMA Sandhurst, 1974. Col, The Light Infantry, 1977-. *Recreations:* natural history, golf, tennis, walking, reading. *Address:* c/o Barclays Bank Ltd, High Street, Maidenhead, Berks.

BUSH, Ronald Paul, CMG 1954; OBE 1946; Colonial Administrative Service, retired; *b* 22 Aug. 1902; *s* of late Admiral Sir Paul Bush; *m* 1938, Anthea Mary Fetherstonhaugh; two *s* one *d*. *Educ:* Marlborough Coll. Appointed to Colonial Administrative Service, 1925; service in Northern Rhodesia: confirmed as District Officer, 1927; promoted Provincial Commissioner, 1947, Sec. for Native Affairs, 1949; retired, 1954; on Commission to enquire into Local Government in Basutoland, 1954. *Address:* Sandbrow, Churt, near Farnham, Surrey. *T:* Frensham 2832. *Club:* Royal Commonwealth Society.

BUSHE-FOX, Patrick Loftus, CMG 1963; *b* 4 May 1907; *o s* of late Loftus Henry Kendal Bushe-Fox and of Theodora Bushe-Fox (*née* Willoughby). *Educ:* Charterhouse; St John's Coll., Cambridge (MA, LLM). 1st Class Historical Tripos, Pt II, and Whewell Schol. in Internat. Law, 1928. Called to the Bar, Inner Temple, 1932. Ministry of Economic Warfare, 1941-45; HM Embassy, Washington, 1945; Control Office for Germany and Austria, 1945-47; Foreign Office (German Section), 1947-50; Asst Legal Adviser, Foreign Office, 1950-60; Legal Counsellor, Foreign Office, 1960-67; retired, 1967. *Address:* Flat 3E, Artillery Mansions, 75 Victoria Street, SW1H 0HZ. *T:* 01-222 5002. *Clubs:* Athenæum, United Oxford & Cambridge University.

BUSHELL, John Christopher Wyndowe, CMG 1971; HM Diplomatic Service; Ambassador to Pakistan, since 1976; *b* 27 Sept. 1919; *s* of late Colonel C. W. Bushell, RE, and Mrs Bushell, Netherbury, Dorset; *m* 1964, Mrs Theodora Todd, *d* of late Mr and Mrs Senior; one *s* (and one step *s* one step *d*). *Educ:* Winchester; Clare Coll., Cambridge. Served War of 1939-45, RAF. Entered FO, 1945; served in Moscow, Rome, FO; 1st Sec., 1950; NATO Defence Coll., Paris, 1953-54; Deputy Sec.-Gen., CENTO, 1957-59; Counsellor, 1961; Political Adviser to the Commander-in-Chief, Middle East, 1961-64; UK Delegn to NATO, Brussels, 1964-68; seconded to Cabinet Office, 1968-70; Minister and Deputy Commandant, British Mil. Govt, Berlin, 1970-74; Ambassador to Saigon, 1974-75; FCO 1975-76. *Recreations:* varied. *Address:* c/o Foreign and Commonwealth Office, SW1; 19 Bradbourne Street, SW6. *Club:* Travellers'.

BUSHNELL, Alexander Lynn, CBE 1962; County Clerk and Treasurer, Perth County Council, 1946-75; *b* 13 Aug. 1911; *s* of William and Margaret Bushnell; *m* 1939, Janet Braithwaite Porteous; two *d*. *Educ:* Dalziel High Sch., Motherwell; Glasgow University. Hon. Sheriff at Perth. *Recreation:* golf. *Address:* 18 Fairies Road, Perth, Scotland. *T:* Perth 22675. *Clubs:* County and City (Perth); Royal Perth Golfing Society.

BUSHNELL, Geoffrey Hext Sutherland, MA, PhD, FBA 1970; Fellow of Corpus Christi College, Cambridge, since 1963; author; Curator, University Museum of Archaeology and Ethnology, Cambridge, 1948-70, retd; Reader in New World Archaeology, 1966-70, now Emeritus; *b* 31 May 1903; *s* of Rev. G. D. S. Bushnell and Mildred Mary (*née* Earle); *m* 1936, Patricia Louise Egerton Ruck; four *s*. *Educ:* Wellington; Downing Coll., Cambridge. Geologist, Anglo-Ecuadorian Oilfields Ltd, in Ecuador, 1926-38. Served War: Lincolnshire Regt, 1940, RE 1941-46, Major 1946. Asst Curator, Cambridge Univ. Museum of Archaeology and Ethnology, 1947; Curator, 1948; FSA 1934, Vice-Pres., 1961-65. Mem., Cathedrals

Advisory Cttee, 1955-; Trustee, Historic Churches Preservation Trust, 1964-. Comendador, Al Mérito of Ecuador, 1971. *Publications:* Archaeology of the Santa Elena Peninsula, SW Ecuador, 1951; Ancient American Pottery (with A. Digby), 1955; Peru (Ancient Peoples and Places), 1956, 2nd edn 1963; Ancient Arts of the Americas, 1965; The First Americans, 1968. *Recreations:* gardening, visiting ancient buildings. *Address:* 4 Wordsworth Grove, Cambridge CB3 9HH. *T:* Cambridge 59539.

BUSIA, Dr Kofi Abrefa, GM; Prime Minister of Ghana, 1969-72; *b* 11 July 1913; *m* 1950; two *s* two *d*. *Educ:* Mfantsipim Sch., Gold Coast (Methodist Synod Schol., 1927-30); Achimota Coll.; Oxford Univ. (Achimota Council Schol., 1935-36, 1939-41). Carnegie Res. Student, Oxford, 1941-42, 1945-47; Nuffield Coll. Student Oxford, 1946-47. BA London; MA, DPhil Oxon. Mem. Staff: Wesley Coll., Kumasi, 1932-34; Achimota Coll., Accra, 1936-39; Admin. Officer (District Comr), Govt of Gold Coast, 1942-49; Officer i/c Sociological Surveys, 1947-49; UC Gold Coast: Res. Lectr in African Studies, 1949-51; Sen. Lectr in Sociology, 1952-54; Prof. of Sociology, 1954-59; Prof. of Sociology, Inst. of Social Studies, The Hague, 1959-62; Prof. of Sociology and Culture of Africa, Univ. of Leiden, 1960-62; Dir of Studies for World Council of Churches, Birmingham, 1962-64; Prof. of Sociology, St Antony's Coll., Oxford, 1964-66. Vis. Professor: Northwestern Univ., Ill, 1954; Nuffield Coll., Oxford, 1955; Agricultural Univ. of Wageningen, Holland, 1956; El Colegio de México, 1962; Univ. of York. Member: Exec. Cttee, Internat. Sociological Assoc., 1953-62; Internat. Social Science Council (Unesco), 1955-61. Mem., Nat. Assembly of Ghana, 1951-59 (Leader of Parly Opposition, 1956-59). Chairman: Nat. Adv. Cttee, NLC, 1967; Centre for Civic Educn, 1967. Hon. DLitt Ghana, 1970. *Publications:* The Position of the Chief in the Modern Political System of Ashanti, 1951; The Challenge of Africa, 1962; Purposeful Education for Africa, 1964; Urban Churches in Britain, 1966; Africa in Search of Democracy, 1967, etc. *Recreations:* music, walking. *Address:* 93 Abingdon Road, Standlake, Witney, Oxon OX8 7QN.

BUSK, Sir Douglas Laird, KCMG 1959 (CMG 1948); *b* 15 July 1906; *s* of late John Laird Busk, Westerham, Kent, and late Eleanor Joy; *m* 1937, Bridget Anne Moyra, *d* of late Brig.-Gen. W. G. Hemsley Thompson, CMG, DSO, Warminster, Wilts; two *d*. *Educ:* Eton; New Coll., Oxford; Princeton Univ., USA (Davison Scholar). Joined Diplomatic Service, 1929; served in Foreign Office and Tehran, Budapest, Union of S Africa (seconded to United Kingdom High Commission), Tokyo, Ankara, Baghdad; Ambassador to Ethiopia, 1952-56; to Finland, 1958-60; to Venezuela, 1961-64. *Publications:* The Delectable Mountains, 1946; The Fountain of the Sun, 1957; The Curse of Tongues, 1965; The Craft of Diplomacy, 1967; Portrait d'un guide, 1975. *Recreations:* mountaineering and skiing. *Address:* Broxton House, Chilbolton, near Stockbridge, Hants. *T:* Chilbolton 272. *Clubs:* Alpine, Travellers', United Oxford & Cambridge University, Lansdowne.

BUSS, Barbara Ann, (Mrs Lewis Boxall); freelance journalist, since 1976; Editor-in-Chief, Woman magazine, 1974-75; Consultant, IPC Magazines Ltd, 1975-76; *b* 14 Aug. 1932; *d* of late Cecil Edward Buss and Victoria Lilian (*née* Vickers); *m* 1966, Lewis Albert Boxall; no *c*. *Educ:* Lady Margaret Sch., London. Sec., Conservative Central Office, 1949-52; Sec./journalist, Good Taste magazine, 1952-56; Journalist: Woman and Beauty, 1956-57; Woman, 1957-59; Asst Editor, Woman's Illustrated, 1959-60; Editor, Woman's Illustrated, 1960-61; Journalist, Daily Herald, 1961; Associate Editor, Woman's Realm, 1961-62; Editor: Woman's Realm, 1962-64; Woman, 1964-74. *Recreations:* reading, theatre, cinema. *Address:* 1 Arlington Avenue, N1. *T:* 01-226 3265.

BUSVINE, Prof. James Ronald; Professor of Entomology as applied to Hygiene in the University of London, 1964-76, Emeritus Professor 1977; *b* 15 April 1912; *s* of William Robert and Pleasance Dorothy Busvine; *m* 1960, Joan Arnfield; one *s* one *d*. *Educ:* Eastbourne Coll.; Imperial Coll. of Science and Technology, London Univ. BSc Special (1st Class Hons) 1933; PhD 1938; DSc 1948, London. Imperial Chemical Industries, 1936-39; MRC Grants, 1940-42; Entomological Adviser, Min. of Health, 1943-45; London Sch. of Hygiene and Tropical Medicine: Lecturer 1946; Reader 1954; Professor 1964. Member: ODM Panel of Consultants on Tropical Pesticides, 1963-70; Dept of Educn and Science's Cttee on Pesticides and Other Toxic Chemicals; WHO Expert Cttee on Insecticides, 1956- (Chm. 1959 and 1968). Has travelled professionally in Malaya, Ceylon, Africa, USA, India, etc. *Publications:* Insects and Hygiene, 1951 (2nd edn 1966); A Critical Review of the Techniques for Testing Insecticides, 1957, 2nd edn 1971; Anthropod Vectors of Disease, 1975; Insects, Hygiene and

History, 1976; numerous scientific articles. *Recreations:* painting, golf. *Address:* Musca, 26 Braywick Road, Maidenhead, Berks. *T:* Maidenhead 22888.

BUTCHER, Anthony John, QC 1977; *b* 6 April 1934; *s* of F. W. Butcher and O. M. Butcher (*née* Ansell); *m* 1959, Maureen Workman; one *s* two *d*. *Educ:* Cranleigh Sch.; Sidney Sussex Coll., Cambridge (MA, LLB). Called to the Bar, Gray's Inn, 1957; in practice at English Bar, 1957-. *Recreations:* enjoying the Arts and acquiring useless information. *Address:* Anthony Cottage, Polecat Valley, Hindhead, Surrey. *T:* Hindhead 4155; 22 Old Buildings, Lincoln's Inn, WC2A 3UJ. *T:* 01-405 2072. *Club:* Garrick.

BUTE, 6th Marquess of, *cr* 1796; **John Crichton-Stuart,** JP; Viscount Ayr, 1622; Bt 1627; Earl of Dumfries, Lord Crichton of Sanquhar and Cumnock, 1633; Earl of Bute, Viscount Kingarth, Lord Mountstuart, Cumrae, and Inchmarnock, 1703; Baron Mountstuart, 1761; Baron Cardiff, 1776; Earl of Windsor; Viscount Mountjoy, 1796; Hereditary Sheriff of Bute; Hereditary Keeper of Rothesay Castle; Lieutenant (RARO) Scots Guards, 1953; *b* 27 Feb. 1933; *er s* (twin) of 5th Marquess of Bute and of Eileen, Marchioness of Bute, *yr d* of 8th Earl of Granard; *S* father, 1956; *m* 1955, Nicola, *o d* of late Lt-Comdr W. B. C. Weld-Forester, CBE; two *s* two *d*. *Educ:* Ampleforth Coll.; Trinity Coll., Cambridge. Pres., Scottish Standing Cttee for Voluntary Internat. Aid, 1968-75 (Chm., 1964-68); Chairman: Council and Exec. Cttee, National Trust for Scotland, 1969; Scottish Cttee, National Fund for Res. into Crippling Diseases, 1966-; Member: Countryside Commission for Scotland, 1970-; Development Commission, 1973-; Oil Develt Council for Scotland, 1973. Hon. Sheriff-Substitute, County of Bute. Mem., Design Council, Scottish Cttee, 1972-76. Fellow, Inst. of Marketing, 1967; Hon. FIStructE, 1976. Pres., Scottish Veterans' Garden City Assoc. (Inc.), 1971-. Buteshire CC, 1956-75; Convener, 1967-70; DL Bute, 1961, Lord Lieutenant, 1967-75; JP Bute 1967. Hon. LLD Glasgow, 1970. *Heir: s* Earl of Dumfries, *qv. Address:* Mount Stuart, Rothesay, Isle of Bute. *T:* Rothesay 2730. *Clubs:* Turf, White's; New, Puffin's (Edinburgh); Cardiff and County (Cardiff).

BUTEMENT, William Alan Stewart, CBE 1959 (OBE 1945); DSc (Adel.); Chief Scientist Department of Supply, Australia (in exec. charge Australian Defence Scientific Research and Development which includes the Rocket Range at Woomera), 1949-67; a Director of Plessey Pacific, since 1967; *b* Masterton, NZ, 18 Aug. 1904; *s* of William Butement, Physician and Surgeon, Otago, and Amy Louise Stewart; *m* 1933, Ursula Florence Alberta Parish; two *d*. *Educ:* Scots Coll., Sydney; University Coll. Sch.; Hampstead, London; University Coll., London Univ. (BSc). Scientific Officer at Signals Exptl Estabt, War Office Outstation, Woolwich (now SRDE, Christchurch, Hants), 1928-38; Senior Scientific Officer Bawdsey Research Stn, War Office Outstation; later, under Min. of Supply, Radar Research, 1938-39 (Station moved to Christchurch, Hants, 1939; now RRE, Malvern); Prin. Scientific Officer, Sen. Prin. Scientific Officer, Asst Dir of Scientific Research, Min. of Supply, HQ London, 1940-46; Dep. Chief Scientific Officer of party to Australia under Lt-Gen. Sir John Evetts to set up Rocket Range, 1947; First Chief Supt of Long Range Weapons Estabt (now Weapons Research Establishment), of which Woomera Range is a part, 1947-49. FIEE, CEng, FInstP, FAIP, FIREE (Aust.). *Publications:* Precision Radar, Journal IEE, and other papers in scientific journals. *Address:* 5a Barry Street, Kew, Victoria 3101, Australia. *T:* 86 8375.

BUTENANDT, Prof. Adolf; Dr phil.; Dr med. hc; Dr med. vet. hc; Dr rer. nat. hc; Dr phil. hc; Dr sci. hc; Dr ing. eh; President, Max Planck Society, 1960-72, Hon. President since 1972; Director, Max Planck Institute for Biochemistry, München (formerly Kaiser Wilhelm Institute for Biochemistry, Berlin-Dahlem), 1936-72; Professor Ord. of Physiological Chemistry, München, 1956-71; Nobel Prize for Chemistry, 1939; *b* Bremerhaven-Lehe, 24 March 1903; *m* 1931, Erika von Ziegner; two *s* five *d*. *Educ:* Universities of Marburg and Göttingen. Privatdozent, Univ. of Göttingen, 1931; Prof. Ord. of Organic Chemistry, Technische Hochschule, Danzig, 1933; Honorarprofessor, Univ. Berlin, 1938; Prof. Ord. of Physiological Chemistry, Tübingen, 1945. Foreign Member: Royal Society, 1968; Académie des Sciences, Paris, 1974. *Publications:* numerous contribs to Hoppe-Seyler, Liebigs Annalen, Berichte der deutschen chemischen Gesellschaft, Zeitschrift für Naturforschung, etc. *Address:* München 60, Marsop Str. 5, Germany. *T:* (089) 885490.

BUTLAND, Sir Jack (Richard), KBE 1966; Founder and Chairman: J. R. Butland Pty Ltd, 1922; NZ Cheese Ltd, 1926; Butland Tobacco Co. Ltd, 1936; Butland Industries Ltd, 1949;

Chairman: Greenacres (Morrinsville) Ltd; Blandford Lodge Ltd; Rothmans (NZ) Ltd, 1956; Director, Dairy Industries (Jamaica) Ltd; *s* of late Henry Butland, Westport, NZ; *m* Gretta May Taylor (*d* 1962); two *s* one *d*; *m* Joan Melville Bull. *Educ:* Hokitika High Sch. Chairman: NZ Honey Control Board, 1933-38; NZ Packing Corp., 1953-60. Pres., Food Bank of NZ, 1970; Dir, Rothmans Industries, 1971. Hon. LLD Auckland, 1967. *Address:* (home) 542 Remuera Road, Remuera, Auckland, NZ; (office) J. R. Butland Pty Ltd, Queen Street, Auckland, NZ. *Club:* Northern (Auckland).

BUTLER, family name of **Baron Butler of Saffron Walden,** of **Earl of Carrick,** of **Baron Dunboyne,** of **Earl of Lanesborough,** of **Viscount Mountgarret,** and of **Marquess of Ormonde.**

BUTLER OF SAFFRON WALDEN, Baron *cr* 1965 (Life Peer); **Richard Austen Butler,** KG 1971; PC 1939; CH 1954; MA; Master of Trinity College, Cambridge, since 1965; *b* Attock Serai, India, 9 Dec. 1902; *e s* of late Sir Montagu S. D. Butler, KCSI; *m* 1st, 1926, Sydney (*d* 1954), *o c* of late Samuel Courtauld; three *s* one *d*; 2nd, 1959, Mollie, *d* of late F. D. Montgomerie and *widow* of Augustine Courtauld. *Educ:* Marlborough; Pembroke Coll., Cambridge. President, Union Society, 1924; Fellow, Corpus Christi Coll., Cambridge, 1925-29 (Double First Class; Modern Language Tripos French Section, 1924; Historical Tripos Part II, 1925, First Division First Class). Hon. Fellow: Pembroke Coll., Cambridge, 1941; Corpus Christi Coll., Cambridge, 1952; St Anthony's Coll., Oxford, 1957; Hon. LLD: Cambridge, 1952; Nottingham, 1953; Bristol, 1954; Sheffield, 1955; St Andrews, 1956; Glasgow, 1959; Reading, 1959; Hon. DLitt Leeds, 1971; Hon. DCL: Oxon, 1952; Durham, 1968; Calgary, 1968; Liverpool, 1968; Witwatersrand, 1969. MP (C) Saffron Walden, 1929-65; Under-Secretary of State, India Office, 1932-37; Parliamentary Secretary, Ministry of Labour, 1937-38; Under-Secretary of State for Foreign Affairs, 1938-41; Minister of Education, 1941-45; Minister of Labour, June-July 1945; Chancellor of the Exchequer, 1951-55; Lord Privy Seal, 1955-59; Leader of the House of Commons, 1955-61; Home Secretary, 1957-62; First Secretary of State, July 1962-Oct. 1963; Deputy Prime Minister, July 1962-Oct. 1963; Minister in Charge of Central African Office, 1962-Oct. 1963; Secretary of State for Foreign Affairs, 1963-64. Chairman: Conservative Party Organisation, 1959-61; Conservative Research Dept, 1945-64; Conservative Party's Advisory Cttee on Policy, 1950-64. Mem., Indian Franchise Cttee, 1932; Chm., Scientific Advisory Cttee and Engineering Advisory Cttee, 1942; Chairman of Council of National Union of Conservative Associations, 1945-56, President, 1956-. Chm., Home Office Cttee on Mentally Abnormal Offenders, 1972-75. President: Modern Language Assoc.; National Assoc. of Mental Health, 1946-; Royal Society of Literature, 1951-; Rector of Glasgow Univ., 1956-59; High Steward, Cambridge Univ., 1958-66; High Steward, City of Cambridge, 1963-; Chancellor of Sheffield Univ., 1960-; Chancellor of Univ. of Essex, 1962-. Azad Memorial Lecture, Delhi, 1970. Freedom of Saffron Walden, 1954. *Publication:* The Art of the Possible, 1971. *Recreations:* travel, shooting, agriculture. *Address:* The Master's Lodge, Trinity College, Cambridge. *T:* 58201; Flat 142, Whitehall Court, SW1. *T:* 01-930 0847 and 01-930 3160. *Clubs:* Carlton, Farmers', Beefsteak, Grillions.
See also Hon. A. C. Butler, Hon. R. C. Butler.

BUTLER, Hon. Adam Courtauld, MP (C) Bosworth since 1970; *b* 11 Oct. 1931; *s* of Baron Butler of Saffron Walden, *qv*; *m* 1955, Felicity Molesworth-St Aubyn; two *s* one *d*. *Educ:* Eton; Pembroke College, Cambridge. National Service, 2nd Lieut KRRC, 1949-51. Cambridge (BA History/Economics), 1951-54. ADC to Governor-General of Canada, 1954-55; Courtaulds Ltd, 1955-73; Director: Aristoc Ltd, 1966-73; Kayser Bondor Ltd, 1971-73; Capital and Counties Property Co., 1973-. PPS to: Minister of State for Foreign Affairs, 1971-72; Minister of Agriculture, Fisheries and Food, 1972-74; PPS to Leader of the Opposition, 1975-; an Asst Govt Whip, 1974; an Opposition Whip, 1974-75. Mem. NFU. Liveryman of Goldsmiths' Co. *Recreations:* field sports, music, pictures. *Address:* The Old Rectory, Lighthorne, near Warwick. *T:* Moreton Morrell 214.
See also Hon. R. C. Butler.

BUTLER, Rt. Rev. Arthur Hamilton; *see* Connor, Bishop of.

BUTLER, Rt. Rev. (Basil) Christopher, OSB, MA; Auxiliary Bishop to the Cardinal Archbishop of Westminster since Dec. 1966; President, St Edmund's College, Ware, 1968-77, and Chairman of the Board of Governors, 1969-77; Titular Bishop of Nova Barbara; Hon. Fellow, St John's College, Oxford; *b* 1902; 2nd *s* of late W. E. Butler, Reading. *Educ:* Reading Sch.; St John's Coll., Oxford (White Schol.; Craven Schol.; Gaisford Greek Prose Prize; prox. acc. Hertford Schol.; 1st Class

Classical Mods Greats and Theology). Tutor of Keble Coll., Oxford; Classical Master, Brighton Coll., 1927; Downside Sch., 1928; received into Catholic Church, 1928; entered the noviciate at Downside, 1929; Priest, 1933; Headmaster of Downside Sch., 1940-46; Abbot of Downside, 1946-66. Abbot-President of English Benedictine Congregation, 1961-67. Chm., Editorial Bd, Clergy Review, 1966-; Mem., Editorial Bd, New English Bible, 1972-. Member: Anglican/Roman Catholic Preparatory Commn, 1967-69; Jt Permanent Commn of Roman Catholic Church and Anglican Communion, 1969-70; Anglican-Roman Catholic Internat. Commn, 1970-. President, Social Morality Council, 1968-. Consultor, Congregation for Catholic Education, 1968-73; Member, Congregation for the Doctrine of the Faith, 1968-73. Hon. LLD: Notre Dame Univ.; Catholic Univ. of America. *Publications:* St Luke's Debt to St Matthew (Harvard Theological Review, 1939); The Originality of St Matthew, 1951; The Church and Infallibility, 1954; Why Christ?, 1960; The Church and the Bible, 1960; Prayer: an adventure in living, 1961; The Idea of the Church, 1962; The Theology of Vatican II, 1967; In the Light of the Council, 1969; A Time to Speak, 1972; Searchings, 1974; articles in Dublin Review, Downside Review, Journal of Theological Studies, Clergy Review. *Address:* St Edmund's College, Old Hall Green, Ware, Herts SG11 1DS. *Club:* Athenæum.

BUTLER, Dr Clifford Charles, FRS 1961; BSc, PhD; Vice-Chancellor of Loughborough University of Technology, since 1975; *b* 20 May 1922; *s* of C. H. J. and O. Butler, Earley, Reading; *m* 1947, Kathleen Betty Collins; two *d. Educ:* Reading Sch.; Reading Univ. BSc 1942, PhD 1946, Reading. Demonstrator in Physics, Reading Univ., 1942-45; Asst Lecturer in Physics, 1945-47, Lecturer in Physics, 1947-53, Manchester Univ.; Reader in Physics, 1953-57, Professor of Physics, 1957-63, Asst Dir, Physics Dept, 1955-62; Prof. of Physics and Head of Physics Dept, 1963-70, Imperial College; Dean, Royal Coll. of Science, 1966-69; Dir, Nuffield Foundn, 1970-75. Charles Vernon Boys Prizeman, London Physical Soc., 1956. Member: Academic Planning Board, Univ. of Kent, 1963-71; Schools Council, 1965-; Nuclear Physics Board of SRC, 1965-68; University Grants Cttee, 1966-71; Council, Charing Cross Hosp. Med. Sch., 1970-73; Council, Open Univ., 1971-; Chairman: Standing Education Cttee, Royal Society, 1970-; Council for the Educn and Training of Health Visitors, 1977-. First Vice-Pres., Internat. Union of Pure and Applied Physics, 1972-75, Pres., 1975- (Sec.-Gen., 1963-72). Hon. DSc Reading, 1976. *Publications:* scientific papers on electron diffraction, cosmic rays and elementary particle physics in Proc. Royal Society and Physical Society, Philosophical Magazine, Nature, and Journal of Scientific Instruments, etc. *Address:* University of Technology, Loughborough, Leics LE11 3TU. *T:* Loughborough 63171; Low Woods Farm House, Low Woods Lane, Belton, near Loughborough, Leics. *Club:* Athenæum.

BUTLER, Dr Colin Gasking, OBE 1970; FRS 1970; retired as Head of Entomology Department, Rothamsted Experimental Station, Harpenden, 1972-76 (Head of Bee Department, 1943-72); *b* 26 Oct. 1913; *s* of Rev. Walter Gasking Butler and Phyllis Pearce; *m* 1937, Jean March Innes; one *s* one *d. Educ:* Monkton Combe Sch., Bath; Queens' Coll., Cambridge. MA 1937, PhD 1938, Cantab. Min. of Agric. and Fisheries Research Schol., Cambridge, 1935-37; Supt Cambridge Univ. Entomological Field Stn, 1937-39; Asst Entomologist, Rothamsted Exper. Stn, 1939-43. Hon. Treas., Royal Entomological Soc., 1961-69, Pres., 1971-72; Pres., Internat. Union for Study of Social Insects, 1969-73. FRPS 1957; FIBiol. Silver Medal, RSA, 1945. *Publications:* The Honeybee: an introduction to her sense physiology and behaviour, 1949; The World of the Honeybee, 1954; (with J. B. Free) Bumblebees, 1959; scientific papers. *Recreations:* nature photography, fishing, sailing. *Address:* Silver Birches, Porthpean, St Austell, Cornwall PL26 6AU. *T:* St Austell 2480.

BUTLER, David Edgeworth; Fellow of Nuffield College, Oxford, since 1954; *b* 1924; *yr s* of late Professor Harold Edgeworth Butler and Margaret, *d* of Prof. A. F. Pollard; *m* 1962, Marilyn, *d* of Sir Trevor Evans, *qv*; three *s. Educ:* St Paul's; New Coll., Oxford (MA, DPhil). J. E. Procter Visiting Fellow, Princeton Univ., 1947-48; Student, Nuffield Coll., 1949-51; Research Fellow, 1951-54; Dean and Senior Tutor, 1956-64. Served as Personal Assistant to HM Ambassador in Washington, 1955-56. *Publications:* The British General Election of 1951, 1952; The Electoral System in Britain 1918-51, 1953; The British General Election of 1955, 1955; The Study of Political Behaviour, 1958; (ed) Elections Abroad, 1959; (with R. Rose) The British General Election of 1959, 1960; (with J. Freeman) British Political Facts, 1900-1960, 1963; (with A. King) The British General Election of 1964, 1965; The British General Election of 1966, 1966; (with D. Stokes) Political Change in Britain, 1969; (with M. Pinto-Duschinsky) The British General Election of 1970, 1971; The

Canberra Model, 1973; (with D. Kavanagh) The British General Election of February 1974, 1974; (with A. Sloman) British Political Facts 1900-75, 1975; (with D. Kavanagh) The British General Election of October 1974, 1975; (with U. Kitzinger) The 1975 Referendum, 1976. *Address:* Nuffield College, Oxford. *T:* Oxford 48014. *Club:* United Oxford & Cambridge University.

BUTLER, Edward Clive Barber, FRCS; Surgeon: The London Hospital, E1, 1937-69; Haroldwood Hospital, Essex, 1946-69; retired; *b* 8 April 1904; *s* of Dr Butler, Hereford; *m* 1939, Nancy Hamilton Harrison, Minneapolis, USA; two *s* one *d. Educ:* Shrewsbury Sch.; London Hospital. MRCS, LRCP 1928; MB, BS London, 1929; FRCS 1931. Resident posts London Hosp., 1928-32; Surgical Registrar, London Hosp., 1933-36; Surgeon, RMS Queen Mary, Cunard White Star Line, 1936. Hunterian Prof., RCS, 1939; examinerships at various times to London Univ. and Coll. of Surgeons. Pres. section of Proctology, Royal Soc. of Medicine, 1951-52; Member: Medical Soc. London; Royal Soc. Medicine. *Publications:* chapter on bacteraemia, in British Surgical Practice, 1948; on hand infections, in Penicillin (by Fleming), 1950; (jointly) on combined excision of rectum, in Treatment of Cancer and Allied Diseases (New York), 1952; articles on various surgical subjects in Lancet, BMJ, Proc. Royal Soc. Med., British Journal Surgery. *Recreations:* golf, gardening and yachting. *Address:* Flat 519, Enterprise House, Chingford, E4. *Club:* United Hospitals Sailing.

BUTLER, Air Vice-Marshal Eric Scott, CB 1957; OBE 1941; RAF; AOA HQ Fighter Command, 1957-61; *b* 4 Nov. 1907; *s* of Archibald Butler, Maze Hill, St Leonards-on-Sea, Sussex; *m* 1936, Alice Evelyn Tempest Meates; three *s* one *d. Educ:* Belfast Academy. Commissioned RAF 1933; Bomber Command European War, 1939-45; idc 1952; Director of Organisation, Air Ministry, 1953-56. *Address:* Camden Cottage, High Street, Pevensey, Sussex BN24 5JP. *T:* Westham 353. *Club:* Royal Air Force.

BUTLER, Esmond Unwin, CVO 1972; Secretary to the Governor-General of Canada, since 1959; Secretary-General, Order of Canada, since 1967 and Order of Military Merit, since 1972; *b* 13 July 1922; *s* of Rev. T. B. Butler and Alice Lorna Thompson; *m* 1960, Georgiana Mary North; one *s* one *d. Educ:* Weston Collegiate; Univs of Toronto and Geneva; Inst. Internat. Studies, Geneva. BA, Licence ès Sciences politiques. Journalist, United Press, Geneva, 1950-51; Asst Sec.-Gen., Internat. Union of Official Travel Organizations, Geneva, 1951-52; Information Officer, Dept of Trade and Commerce, Dept of Nat. Health and Welfare, 1953-54; Asst Sec. to Governor-Gen., 1955-58; Asst Press Sec. to Queen, London, 1958-59 and Royal Tour of Canada, 1959. CStJ 1967. *Recreations:* fishing, shooting, collecting Canadiana, ski-ing. *Address:* Rideau Cottage, Government House, Ottawa, Ont K1A OA1. *T:* (office) 749-5933. *Clubs:* Zeta Psi Fraternity (Toronto); White Pine Fishing.

BUTLER, Frank Chatterton, CBE 1961; MA 1934; retd from HM Diplomatic Service, 1967, and re-employed in Foreign Office Library until 1977; *b* 23 June 1907; *s* of late Leonard Butler and late Ada Chatterton Rutter; *m* 1945, Iris, *d* of late Ernest Strater and of Ida Mary Vinall; two *s. Educ:* Central Secondary Sch., Sheffield; Gonville and Caius Coll., Cambridge (Scholar); University of Grenoble. 1st Class Hons, Modern and Medieval Langs Tripos; Exhibitioner of the Worshipful Company of Goldsmiths, 1927, German Prize Essayist, 1928 and 1929. Consular Service, 1930 (head of list); Vice-Consul: Paris, 1931; New York, 1932; Mexico City, 1933-36; Panama, 1936-39; Naples, 1939-40; Barcelona, 1940-43; Consul, Barcelona, 1943-45; First Secretary (Commercial), Bogota, 1945-47; Consul General, Düsseldorf, 1948-52; Consul, Bordeaux, 1952-54; Consul General, Dakar, 1955, and Frankfurt, 1956-60; Counsellor at Shanghai, 1960-62; Consul-General at Cape Town, 1962-67. *Recreations:* golf, riding, motoring. *Address:* Wedgwood, Knowl Hill, Woking, Surrey.

BUTLER, (Frederick Edward) Robin; Under Secretary, General Expenditure Policy Group, HM Treasury, since 1977; *b* 3 Jan. 1938; *s* of Bernard Butler and Nora Butler; *m* 1962, Gillian Lois Galley; one *s* two *d. Educ:* Harrow Sch.; University Coll., Oxford (BA Lit. Hum., 1961). Joined HM Treasury, 1961; Private Sec. to Financial Sec. to Treasury, 1964-65; Sec., Budget Cttee, 1965-69; seconded to Cabinet Office as Mem., Central Policy Rev. Staff, 1971-72; Private Secretary: to Rt Hon. Edward Heath, 1972-74; to Rt Hon. Harold Wilson, 1974-75; returned to HM Treasury as Asst Sec. i/c Gen. Expenditure Intell. Div., 1975. Governor, Harrow Sch., 1977. *Recreation:* competitive games. *Address:* 6 Rockhill, SE26 6SW. *T:* 01-670 6616. *Clubs:* Anglo-Belgian.

BUTLER, Maj.-Gen. Geoffrey Ernest, CB 1957; CBE 1955; *b* Quetta, 1 Jan. 1905; *s* of Major E. G. Butler, W Yorks Regt; *m* 1934, Marjorie Callender (*née* Laine); one *d. Educ:* Appleby Grammar Sch.; Leeds Univ. ICI, 1928-30; Lieut, RAOC, 1930; Asst Inspector of Armaments, 1936; Asst Supt of Design, 1937; British Supply Board, N America, 1939-40; British Army Staff, Washington, 1940-43; Asst Chief Supt, Armaments Design, 1943-44; Comdt 3 Base Workshop, REME, 1944-47; Dep. Dir (Production), War Office, 1947-49; Comdt, REME Training Centre, 1949-53; Dir of Mechanical Engineering, Northern Army Group, 1953-56; Inspector, REME, 1956-57; Commandant Base Workshop Group, REME, 1957-60. *Recreations:* golf, gardening. *Address:* Cornerways, 7 Ashley Road, New Milton, Hants BH25 6BA.

BUTLER, George, RWS 1958; RBA; NEAC; painter, principally in water-colour, in England and Provence; *b* 17 Oct. 1904; *s* of John George Butler; *m* 1933, Kcenia Kotliarevskaya; one *s* one *d. Educ:* King Edward VII School, Sheffield; Central School of Art. Director and Head of Art Dept, J. Walter Thompson Co. Ltd, 1933-60. Hon. Treasurer: RWS; Artists' General Benevolent Institution. Mem., Société des Artistes Indépendants Aixois. *Address:* Riversdale, Castle Street, Bakewell, Derbyshire. *T:* Bakewell 2204. *Club:* Arts.

BUTLER, George William P.; see Payne-Butler.

BUTLER, Gerald Norman, QC 1975; a Recorder of the Crown Court, since 1977; *b* 15 Sept. 1930; *s* of Joshua Butler and Esther Butler (*née* Lampel); *m* 1959, Stella, *d* of Harris Isaacs; one *s* two *d. Educ:* Ilford County High Sch.; London Sch. of Economics; Magdalen Coll., Oxford. LLB London 1952, BCL Oxon 1954. Called to Bar, Middle Temple, 1955. 2nd Lieut, RASC, 1956-57. *Recreations:* athletics, bridge, golf, Victorian paintings. *Address:* 28 St John's Road, Loughton, Essex. *T:* 01-508 7439.

BUTLER, Maj.-Gen. Hew Dacres George, CB 1975; Chief of Staff (Contingencies Planning), SHAPE, 1975-76; retired 1977; *b* 12 March 1922; *s* of late Maj.-Gen. S. S. Butler, CB, CMG, DSO; *m* 1954, Joanna, *d* of late G. M. Puckridge, CMG, ED; two *s* one *d. Educ:* Winchester. Commnd Rifle Bde, 1941; Western Desert, 1942-43; POW, 1943-45; psc 1951; BM 7th Armd Bde, 1951-53; Kenya, 1954-55; Instructor, Staff Coll., 1957-60; CO 1 RB, 1962-64; Cyprus (despatches, 1965); comd 24 Inf. Bde, Aden, 1966-67; idc 1969; ACOS G3 Northag, 1970-72; GOC Near East Land Forces, 1972-74. *Recreations:* shooting, golf, horticulture. *Address:* Bury Lodge, Hambledon, Hants. *Clubs:* Boodle's, MCC.

BUTLER, James Walter, RA 1972 (ARA 1964); Tutor, Sculpture and Drawing, City and Guilds of London Art School, since 1960; *b* 25 July 1931; *m* (marr. diss.); one *d*; *m* 1975, Angela, *d* of Col Roger Berry, Johannesburg, South Africa; two *d . Educ:* Maidstone Grammar Sch.; Maidstone Coll. of Art; St Martin's Art Sch.; Royal Coll. of Art. National Diploma in Sculpture, 1950. Worked as Architectural Carver, 1950-53, 1955-60. Major commissions include: Portrait statue of Pres. Kenyatta, Nairobi, 1973; Monument to Freedom Fighters of Zambia, Lusaka, 1974; Statue, The Burton Cooper, Burton-on-Trent, 1977. *Address:* Old School House, Greenfield, Beds. *T:* Flitwick 2028.

BUTLER, John Manton, MSc; *b* 9 Oct. 1909; *m* 1940, Marjorie Smith, Melbourne; one *s* one *d. Educ:* Southland, NZ; Univ. of Otago (Sen. Schol., NZ, Physics; BSc 1929; Smeaton Schol. Chemistry, 1930, John Edmond Fellow, 1930; MSc 1st class Hons). Pres., Students' Union; Graduate Rep. Univ. Council. Joined Shell, NZ, 1934; served various Shell cos in UK, Australia and S Africa until 1957; Man. Dir, Lewis Berger (GB) Ltd, 1957; Dir, Berger, Jenson & Nicholson Ltd, 1969-74. Chm., BNEC Cttee for Exports to NZ, 1967 (Dep. Chm., 1965). Pres., NZ Soc., 1971. Mem., Cttee, Spastics Soc. Consultant. *Recreations:* golf, photography. *Address:* Wood End, 24 Wool Road, Wimbledon, SW20. *T:* 01-946 0887. *Clubs:* Hurlingham; Royal Mid-Surrey Golf, Royal Wimbledon Golf.

BUTLER, Mrs Joyce Shore; MP (Lab & Co-op) Haringey, Wood Green, since 1974 (Wood Green, 1955-74); *m* ; one *s* one *d. Educ:* King Edward's High Sch., Birmingham. Member: Wood Green Council, 1947-64 (Leader, 1954-55; Deputy Mayor, 1962-63); First Chm., London Borough of Haringey, 1964-65; First Mayoress, 1965-66. Vice-Chm., Labour Parly Housing and Local Govt Gp, 1959-64; Member: Estimates Cttee, 1959-60; Chairman's Panel, House of Commons; Jt Chm., Parly Cttee on Pollution; PPS to Minister for Land and Natural Resources, 1965. A Vice-Chm., Parly Labour Party, 1968-. Exec. Mem., Housing and Town Planning Council; Founder and First Pres., Women's Nat. Cancer Control Campaign; Pres., London Passenger Action Confedn. *Address:* 25 Maidstone Road, N11.

BUTLER, Keith Stephenson, CMG 1977; HM Consul-General, Naples, 1974-77; *b* 3 Sept. 1917; *s* of late Raymond R. Butler and Gertrude Stephenson; *m* 1952, Geraldine Marjorie Clark; no *c. Educ:* King Edward's Sch., Birmingham; Liverpool Coll.; St Peter's Coll., Oxford (MA). HM Forces, 1939-47 (despatches): served, RA, in Egypt, Greece and Crete; POW, Germany, 1941-45. Foreign Correspondent for Sunday Times and Kemsley Newspapers, 1947-50. Joined HM Foreign Service, 1950; served: First Sec., Ankara and Caracas; Canadian Nat. Defence Coll.; Paris; Montreal. HM Consul-General: Seville, 1968; Bordeaux, 1969. *Publications:* contrib. historical and political reviews. *Recreation:* historical research. *Address:* c/o Foreign and Commonwealth Office, SW1. *Clubs:* Bath, English-Speaking Union.

BUTLER, Lionel Harry, FRHistS; MA; DPhil; Principal, Royal Holloway College, University of London, since 1973; *b* 17 Dec. 1923; *yr s* of late W. H. and M. G. Butler, Dudley, Worcs; *m* 1949, Gwendoline Williams (author of detective stories), *o d* of A. E. Williams, Blackheath; one *d. Educ:* Dudley Grammar Sch.; Magdalen Coll., Oxford (exhibitioner). Royal Air Force, 1941-43; First Class, Modern History, Oxford, 1945; Sen. Mackinnon Scholar and Junior Lectr, Magdalen Coll., Oxford, 1946; Fellow of All Souls Coll., 1946 (re-elected, 1953); University of St Andrews: Prof. of Mediaeval History, 1955-73; Dean, Fac. of Arts, 1966-71; Mem., Univ. Ct, 1968-73; Vice-Principal, 1971-73. Chatterton Lectr, British Acad., 1955; Leverhulme Lectr, Royal Univ. of Malta, 1962-63; Visiting Prof. of History, Univ. of Pennsylvania, Pa, 1964; Dir, Historical Assoc. Vacation Sch., 1965 and 1966. Convener, Scottish Univs Council on Entrance, 1968-73. Mem., Scottish Cert. of Educn Exam. Bd, 1969-73; Member, Management Committee: Inst. of Latin American Studies, Univ. of London, 1974-; Warburg Inst., Univ. of London, 1977-; Member: Extra-Mural Council, Univ. of London, 1976-; Standing Conf. on Univ. Entrance, and SCUE Executive, 1976-; Chairman: Centre of Internat. and Area Studies, Univ. of London, 1974-; Library Resources Co-ordinating Cttee, London Univ., 1975-. Governor, Strode's School, Egham, 1973-. Librarian, Venerable Order of St John in the British Realm, 1969-; Historical Dir, 13th Council of Europe Exhibn (on Order of St John in Malta), 1970 (introd. and contribs to Catalogue on Exhibn). KStJ 1969. *Publications:* trans. (with R. J. Adam) R. Fawtier, The Capetian Kings of France, 1960; articles in journals and reviews. *Address:* Royal Holloway College, Egham, Surrey. *Club:* Royal and Ancient (St Andrews).

BUTLER, Sir Michael; see Butler, Sir R. M. T.

BUTLER, Michael Dacres, CMG 1975; HM Diplomatic Service; Deputy Under-Secretary of State, Foreign and Commonwealth Office, since 1976; *b* 27 Feb. 1927; *s* of T. D. Butler, Almer, Blandford, and Beryl May (*née* Lambert); *m* 1951, Ann, *d* of Rt Hon. Lord Clyde; two *s* two *d. Educ:* Winchester; Trinity Coll., Oxford. Joined HM Foreign Service, 1950; served in: UK Mission to UN, New York, 1952-56; Baghdad, 1956-58; FO, 1958-61 and 1965-68; Paris, 1961-65; Counsellor, UK Mission in Geneva, 1968-70; Fellow, Center for Internat. Affairs, Harvard, 1970-71; Counsellor, Washington, 1971-72; Head of European Integration Dept, FCO, 1972-74; Asst Under-Sec. in charge of European Community Affairs, FCO, 1974-76. *Recreations:* collecting Chinese porcelain, ski-ing, tennis. *Address:* 11 Carlyle Square, SW3. *T:* 01-352 9360; c/o Foreign and Commonwealth Office, SW1.

BUTLER, Hon. Sir Milo (Broughton), GCMG 1973; GCVO 1975; Kt 1973; Governor-General, The Commonwealth of the Bahamas, since 1973; *b* 11 Aug. 1906; *s* of George Raleigh and Frances M. Butler; *m* Caroline Lorette (*née* Watson), Morrisville, Long Island, Bahamas; seven *s* three *d. Educ:* George Washington Sch., Florida, USA; a Public Sch., Rum Cay, Bahamas; Central Sch., Nassau Court, Bahamas, Formerly candidate at various elections and a harbinger of the Progressive Liberal Party. Became an Independent Mem., Bahamas Legislative Council. Recent government posts included: Minister of Labour, Welfare, Agriculture and Fisheries, 1968-72; Minister without Portfolio, 1972. Finally Member for Bains Town, New Providence Constituency, after representing other areas. Was Pres., Milo B. Buller and Sons Ltd. Member, Synod of Anglican Church; interested in hospital welfare, etc. Became Governor-General (Independence Day, 10 July), Aug. 1973. *Address:* Government House, Nassau, Bahamas.

BUTLER, Reg, (Reginald Cotterell Butler); sculptor; *b* Buntingford, Herts, 1913. ARIBA 1937. Gregory Fellow in Sculpture, Leeds Univ., 1951-53; Associé, Académie Royale des Sciences, des Lettres et des Beaux-Arts de Belgique, 1965. First one-man show, London, 1949. Winner International

Competition, The Unknown Political Prisoner, 1953. Retrospective Exhibition: J. B. Speed Art Museum, Louisville, USA, 1963. Pierre Matisse Gallery, New York. *Publication:* Creative Development, 1962. *Address:* Ash, Berkhamsted Place, Berkhamsted, Herts. *T:* Berkhamsted 2933.

BUTLER, Sir (Reginald) Michael (Thomas), 3rd Bt *cr* 1922; QC (Canada); Barrister and Solicitor; Partner of Butler, Angus, Victoria, BC; Director: Teck Corporation Ltd; Elco Mining Ltd; *b* 22 April 1928; *s* of Sir Reginald Thomas, 2nd Bt, and Marjorie Brown Butler; *S* father, 1959; *m* Marja McLean (marr. diss.); three *s*; one *s* adopted. *Educ:* Brentwood Coll., Victoria, BC; Univ. of British Columbia (BA). Called to Bar (Hons) from Osgoode Hall Sch. of Law, Toronto, Canada, 1954. Governor, Brentwood Coll. Assoc. *Heir: s* (Reginald) Richard Michael Butler, *b* 3 Oct. 1953. *Address:* Box 381, Brentwood Bay, BC, Canada. *Clubs:* Vancouver (Vancouver); Union (Victoria).

BUTLER, Hon. Richard Clive, DL; Deputy President, National Farmers' Union, since 1971; farmer since 1953; *b* 12 Jan. 1929; *e s* of Rt Hon. Lord Butler of Saffron Walden, *qv*; *m* 1952, Susan Anne Maud Walker; twin *s* one *d*. *Educ:* Eton Coll.; Pembroke Coll., Cambridge (MA). 2nd Lieut, Royal Horse Guards, 1947-49. Mem. Council, NFU, 1962-, Vice-Pres. 1970-71. Member: Agricultural Adv. Council, 1968-72; Central Council for Agricultural and Horticultural Co-operation, 1970-. Man. Dir, Essex Peas Ltd; Dir, British Farmer & Stockbreeder Ltd. DL Essex, 1972. *Recreations:* hunting, shooting, tennis. *Address:* Penny Pot, Halstead, Essex. *T:* Halstead 2828. *Club:* Farmers'. *See also* Hon. A. C. Butler.

BUTLER, Robin; *see* Butler, F. E. R.

BUTLER, Rohan D'Olier, CMG; MA; FRHistS; Historical Adviser to Secretary of State for Foreign and Commonwealth Affairs (to first Secretary of State and successors), since 1968; Fellow of All Souls since 1938 (a Senior Research Fellow since 1956; Sub-Warden, 1961-63; representative at 12th International Historical Congress at Vienna, 1965); Member of Court, University of Essex, since 1971; on management of Institute of Historical Research, University of London, since 1967; *b* St John's Wood, 21 Jan. 1917; surv. *s* of late Sir Harold Butler, KCMG, CB, MA, and Lady Butler, *y c* of late Asst Inspector-General S. A. W. Waters, RIC; *m* 1956, Lucy Rosemary (Lady of the Manor of White Notley, Essex), *y c* of late Eric Byron, Lord of the Manor. *Educ:* Eton; abroad and privately; Balliol Coll., Oxford (Hall Prizeman, 1938). BA (1st Class Hons in History), 1938; on International Propaganda and Broadcasting Enquiry, 1939; on staff of MOI, 1939-41 and 1942-44, of Special Operations Executive, 1941; served with RAPC, 1941-42, with HG, 1942-44 (Defence Medal, War Medal); on staff of FO, 1944-45; Editor of Documents on British Foreign Policy (1919-39), 1945-65 (with late Sir Llewellyn Woodward, FBA, 1945-54; Senior Editor, 1955-65); Leverhulme Research Fellow, 1955-57; Noel Buxton Trustee, 1961-67. Historical Adviser to Sec. of State for Foreign Affairs (from 14th Earl of Home to last Foreign Sec.), 1963-68. Governor, Felsted Sch., 1959-77, representative on GBA 1964-77; Trustee, Felsted Almshouses, 1961-77. *Publications:* The Roots of National Socialism; Documents on British Foreign Policy, 1st series, vols i-ix, 2nd series, vol. ix; The Peace Settlement of Versailles (in New Cambridge Modern History); Paradiplomacy (in Studies of Diplomatic History in honour of Dr G. P. Gooch, OM, CH, FBA); Introduction to Anglo-Soviet historical exhibition of 1967. *Recreation:* idling. *Address:* All Souls College, Oxford; White Notley Hall, near Witham, Essex. *Club:* Beefsteak.

BUTLER, Col Sir Thomas Pierce, 12th Bt *cr* 1628; CVO 1970; DSO 1944; OBE 1954; Resident Governor and Major, HM Tower of London, 1961-71, Keeper of the Jewel House, 1968-71; *b* 18 Sept. 1910; *o s* of Sir Richard Pierce Butler, 11th Bt, OBE, DL, and Alice Dudley (*d* 1965), *d* of Very Rev. Hon. James Wentworth Leigh, DD; *S* father, 1955; *m* 1937, Rosemary Liège Woodgate Davidson-Houston, *d* of late Major J. M. Davidson-Houston, Pembury Hall, Kent; one *s* two *d*. *Educ:* Harrow; Trinity Coll., Cambridge. BA (Hons) Cantab, 1933. Grenadier Guards, 1933; served War of 1939-45 (wounded, POW, escaped); BEF France; 6th Bn, Egypt, Syria, Tripoli, N Africa; Staff Coll., 1944 (psc); Comd Guards Composite Bn, Norway, 1945-46; Comd 2nd Bn Grenadier Guards, BAOR, 1949-52; AQMG, London District, 1952-55; Col, Lt-Col Comdg the Grenadier Guards, 1955-58; Military Adviser to UK High Comr in New Zealand, 1959-61. Pres., London (Prince of Wales's) District, St John Ambulance Brigade. JP Co. of London 1961-71. CStJ. *Recreations:* shooting, fishing, travelling. *Heir: s* Richard Pierce Butler [*b* 22 July 1940; *m* 1965, Diana, *yr d* of Col S. J. Borg, London; three *s* one *d*.]. *Address:* 6 Thurloe Square, SW7. *T:* 01-584 1225; Ballin Temple, Co. Carlow. *Club:*

Cavalry and Guards.
See also R. N. B. Brunt.

BUTLER-SLOSS, (Ann) Elizabeth (Oldfield), (Mrs J. W. A. Butler-Sloss); Registrar, Principal Registry of Family Division (formerly Probate Division), since 1970; *b* 10 Aug. 1933; *d* of Sir Cecil Havers, QC, and late Enid Snelling; *m* 1958, Joseph William Alexander Butler-Sloss, *qv*; two *s* one *d*. *Educ:* Wycombe Abbey Sch. Called to Bar, Inner Temple, Feb. 1955. Practice at Bar, 1955-70. A Vice Pres., Medico-Legal Soc. *Publications:* Joint Editor: Phipson on Evidence (10th edn); Corpe on Road Haulage (2nd edn). *Recreation:* hunting. *Address:* 10 King's Bench Walk, Temple, EC4. *T:* 01-583 4649; Downham's Cottage, Woodbury Salterton, Exeter, Devon EX5 1PQ. *T:* Woodbury 32464.
See also Rt . Hon . Sir R. M. O. Havers.

BUTLER-SLOSS, Joseph William Alexander; a Recorder of the Crown Court, since 1972; *b* 16 Nov. 1926; 2nd and *o* surv. *s* of Francis Alexander Sloss and Alice Mary Frances Violet Sloss (*née* Patchell); *m* 1958, Ann Elizabeth Oldfield Havers (*see* Mrs A. E. O. Butler-Sloss); two *s* one *d*. *Educ:* Bangor Grammar Sch., Co. Down; Hertford Coll., Oxford. Ordinary Seaman, RN, 1944; Midshipman 1945, Sub-Lieut 1946, RNVR. MA (Jurisprudence) Hertford Coll., Oxford, 1951. Called to Bar, Gray's Inn, 1952; joined Western Circuit, 1954; joined Inner Temple. Joint Master, East Devon Foxhounds, 1970-76. *Recreations:* hunting; the violin. *Address:* 10 King's Bench Walk, Temple, EC4Y 7EB. *T:* 01-583 4649; Downham's Cottage, Woodbury Salterton, Exeter, Devon EX5 1PQ. *T:* Woodbury 32464. *Club:* Junior Cairlton.

BUTLIN, Martin Richard Fletcher; Keeper of Historic British Collection, Tate Gallery, since 1967; *b* 7 June 1929; *s* of Kenneth Rupert Butlin and Helen Mary (*née* Fletcher); *m* 1969, Frances Caroline Chodzko. *Educ:* Rendcomb Coll.; Trinity Coll., Cambridge (MA); Courtauld Inst. of Art, London Univ. (BA). Asst Keeper, Tate Gall., 1955-67. *Publications:* A Catalogue of the Works of William Blake in the Tate Gallery, 1957, 2nd edn 1971; Samuel Palmer's Sketchbook of 1824, 1962; Turner Watercolours, 1962; (with Sir John Rothenstein) Turner, 1964; (with Mary Chamot and Dennis Farr) Tate Gallery Catalogues: The Modern British Paintings, Drawings and Sculpture, 1964; The Later Works of J. M. W. Turner, 1965; William Blake, 1966; The Blake-Varley Sketchbook of 1819, 1969; (with Andrew Wilton and John Gage) (exhibn cat.) Turner 1775-1851, 1974; articles and reviews in Burlington Mag., Connoisseur, Master Drawings, Blake Newsletter, Blake Studies. *Recreations:* music, travel. *Address:* Tate Gallery, Millbank, SW1P 4RG. *T:* 01-828 1212.

BUTLIN, Sir William (Edmund), Kt 1964; MBE 1944; Chairman and Joint Managing Director of Butlin's Ltd and Butlin Properties Ltd, 1935-68; retired, 1968; President, since 1972; *b* 29 Sept. 1899; *s* of William Butlin, an engineer, and Bertha; *m* 1959, Norah Faith Butlin (*née* Cheriton) (marr. diss.; she *d* 1976); one *s* three *d*. *Educ:* Canada and Bristol. Founder of Butlin's Ltd, holiday camp proprietors. Three times President of Variety Club of Great Britain. Member, Worshipful Companies of Gardeners and Gold and Silver Wyre Drawers. *Recreations:* President Vaudeville Golfing Society; Companion of the Water Rats; Vice-Pres., Variety Club International. *Address:* c/o 439-441 Oxford Street, W1. *T:* 01-629 6616. *Clubs:* Eccentric, Saints and Sinners, Variety Club of Great Britain; National Sporting; Anglo-American Sporting; World Sporting.

BUTT, Sir (Alfred) Kenneth (Dudley), 2nd Bt *cr* 1929; Underwriting Member of Lloyd's; farmer and bloodstock breeder; *b* 7 July 1908; *o s* of Sir Alfred Butt, 1st Bt and Lady Georgina Mary Butt (*née* Say); *S* father, 1962; *m* 1st, 1938, Kathleen Farmar (marr. diss., 1948); 2nd, 1948, Mrs Ivor Birts (*née* Bain), *widow* of Lt-Col Ivor Birts, RA (killed on active service). *Educ:* Rugby; Brasenose Coll., Oxford. Lloyd's, 1929-39. Royal Artillery, 1939-45, Major RA. Chairman, Parker Wakeling & Co. Ltd, 1946-54. Managing Director, Brook Stud Co., 1962. Pres., Aberdeen-Angus Cattle Soc., 1968-69; Chm., Thoroughbred Breeders Assoc., 1973. *Recreations:* tennis, golf, horse-racing, travelling, paintings. *Address:* Wheat Hill, Sandon, Buntingford, Herts. *T:* Kelshall 203; Flat 29, 1 Hyde Park Square, W2. *T:* 01-262 3988. *Clubs:* Junior Carlton, etc.

BUTT, Sir Kenneth; *see* Butt, Sir A. K. D.

BUTTER, Major David Henry, MC 1941; JP; landowner and farmer; company director; HM Lord-Lieutenant of Perth and Kinross, since 1975; *b* 18 March 1920; *s* cf late Col Charles Butter, OBE, DL, JP, Pitlochry, and Agnes Marguerite (Madge), *d* of late William Clark, Newark, NJ, USA; *m* 1946,

Myra Alice, d of Hon. Maj.-Gen. Sir Harold Wernher, 3rd Bt, GCVO, TD; one s four d. *Educ:* Eton; Oxford. Served War of 1939-45: 2nd Lieut Scots Guards, 1940, Western Desert and North Africa, Sicily (Staff), 1941-43; Italy (ADC to GOC 8th Army, Gen. Sir Oliver Leese, 1944); Temp. Major, 1946; retd Army, 1948. County Councillor, Perth, 1955-74; Member Queen's Body Guard for Scotland (Royal Company of Archers). DL Perthshire, 1956, Vice-Lieutenant of Perth, 1960-71; HM Lieutenant of County of Perth, 1971-75, and County of Kinross, 1974-75. Governor of Gordonstoun School. *Recreations:* shooting, golf, ski-ing, travel. *Address:* Cluniemore, Pitlochry, Scotland. *T:* Pitlochry 2006; 15 Grosvenor Square, W1. *T:* 01-499 1484. *Clubs:* Turf; Royal and Ancient (St Andrews).
See also Lord Ramsay.

BUTTER, John Henry, CMG 1962; MBE 1946; Financial Director to Government of Abu Dhabi, since 1970; *b* 20 April 1916; *s* of late Captain A. E. Butter, CMG, and of Mrs Baird (now of Gordon, Berwickshire); *m* 1950, Joyce Platt; three *s*. *Educ:* Charterhouse; Christ Church, Oxford. Indian Civil Service, 1939-47; Pakistan Admin. Service, 1947-50 (served in Punjab except for period 1942-46 when was Asst to Political Agent, Imphal, Manipur State). HM Overseas Civil Service, Kenya, 1950-65 (Perm. Sec. to the Treasury, 1959-65); Financial Adviser, Kenya Treasury, 1965-69. *Recreations:* golf, bridge. *Address:* Box 246, Abu Dhabi, United Arab Emirates, Arabian Gulf. *Club:* East India, Devonshire, Sports, and Public Schools.
See also Prof. P. H. Butter.

BUTTER, Neil (McLaren), QC 1976; a Recorder of the Crown Court, since 1972; *b* 10 May 1933; *s* of late Andrew Butter, MA, MD and Ena Butter, MB, ChB; *m* 1974, Claire Marianne Miskin. *Educ:* The Leys Sch.; Queens' Coll., Cambridge (MA). Called to Bar, Inner Temple, 1955. An Asst and Dep. Recorder of Bournemouth, 1971. Mem. Senate of the Inns of Court and the Bar, 1976-. *Recreations:* motoring, France, browsing through Who's Who. *Address:* Carpmael Building, Temple, EC4Y 7AT. *T:* 01-353 5537; 54 Linton Street, N1 7AS. *T:* 01-359 8939. *Clubs:* United Oxford & Cambridge University; Hampshire (Winchester).

BUTTER, Prof. Peter Herbert; Regius Professor of English, Glasgow University, since 1965; *b* 7 April 1921; *s* of Archibald Butter, CMG, and Helen Cicely (*née* Kerr); *m* 1958, Bridget Younger; one *s* two *d*. *Educ:* Charterhouse; Balliol Coll., Oxford. Served in RA, 1941-46. Assistant, 1948, Lecturer, 1951, in English, Univ. of Edinburgh; Professor of English, Queen's Univ., Belfast, 1958-65. *Publications:* Shelley's Idols of the Cave, 1954; Francis Thompson, 1961; Edwin Muir, 1962; Edwin Muir: Man and Poet, 1966; (ed) Shelley's Alastor and Other Poems, 1971; (ed) Selected Letters of Edwin Muir, 1974; articles in periodicals. *Address:* Ashfield, Bridge of Weir, Renfrewshire. *T:* Bridge of Weir 613139. *Club:* New (Edinburgh).
See also J. H. Butter.

BUTTERFIELD, Charles Harris, QC (Singapore) 1952; HMOCS, retired; *b* 28 June 1911; 2nd *s* of William Arthur Butterfield, OBE, and Rebecca Butterfield; *m* 1st, 1938, Monica, *d* of Austin Harrison, London; one *d*; 2nd, by special permission of the Holy See, Ellen, *d* of Ernest John Bennett, Singapore and widow of J. E. King, Kuala Lumpur, Singapore and Hooe. *Educ:* Downside; Trinity Coll., Cambridge. Barrister-at-law, Middle Temple, 1934. Entered Colonial Legal Service, 1938; Crown Counsel, Straits Settlements, 1938. Served Singapore RA (Volunteer) and RA, 1941-46; POW, 1942-45. Solicitor-General, Singapore, 1948-55, Attorney-General, 1955-57; Legal Adviser's Dept CRO and FCO, 1959-69; DoE and Sec. of State's Panel of Inspectors (Planning), 1969-74. *Address:* 18 Kewhurst Avenue, Cooden, Bexhill on Sea, E Sussex. *Clubs:* Royal Thames Yacht; Bewl Valley Sailing; Cooden Golf.

BUTTERFIELD, Sir Herbert, Kt 1968; FBA 1965; MA; Hon. LLD, Aberdeen, 1952; Hon. DLitt: UC, Dublin, 1954; Hong Kong, 1961; Sheffield, 1962; Hull, 1963; Warwick, 1967; Bonn, 1968; Hon. DLit: Belfast, 1955; London, 1968; Hon. LittD: Harvard and Columbia, 1956; Manchester, 1966; Bradford, 1973; Cambridge, 1974; Master of Peterhouse, 1955-68; Professor of Modern History, University of Cambridge, 1944-63, Regius Professor, 1963-68 (now Emeritus), and Fellow of Peterhouse, 1923-55 (now an Hon. Fellow); *b* 7 Oct. 1900; *e s* of Albert Butterfield and Ada Mary Buckland; *m* 1929, Edith Joyce (Pamela) Crawshaw; two *s* (and one *s* decd). *Educ:* Trade and Grammar Sch., Keighley; Peterhouse, Cambridge (Scholar). Jane Eliza Procter Visiting-Fellow, Univ. of Princeton, NJ, 1924-25; Lecturer in History, Peterhouse, Cambridge, 1930-44; Editor, Cambridge Historical Journal, 1938-52; President, Historical Assoc., 1955-58; Chm., British Cttee on Theory of Internat. Politics, 1958-68; Member, Administrative Board of

International Association of Universities, 1960-65; Commn on Higher Education in Ireland, 1960-67; Court of Governors, LSE, 1961-68; Adv. Council on Public Records, 1962-72; Inst. of Historical Research Cttee, 1963-68. Vice-Chancellor, Univ. of Cambridge, 1959-61; Fellow, Center for Advanced Studies, Wesleyan Univ., Middletown, Conn., 1965. Gifford Lecturer, Glasgow Univ., 1965-67. Hon. Vice-Pres., RHistS, 1968-. Foreign Hon. Mem., American Acad. of Arts and Sciences, 1967; Hon. MRIA, 1967; Hon. Mem., American Historical Assoc., 1968. Pres., Bd of Dirs, Jl of the History of Ideas, 1974-75. *Publications:* The Historical Novel, 1924; The Peace-tactics of Napoleon, 1806-8, 1929; The Whig Interpretation of History, 1931; (ed.) Select Documents of European History, Vol. III, 1715-1920, 1931; Napoleon (Great Lives), 1939; The Statecraft of Machiavelli, 1940; The Englishman and his History, 1944; Inaugural Lecture on The Study of Modern History, 1944; George III, Lord North and the People, 1949; The Origins of Modern Science, 1949; Christianity and History, 1949; History and Human Relations, 1951; Christianity in European History, 1951; Christianity, Diplomacy and War, 1953; Man on his Past, 1955; George III and the Historians, 1957; International Conflict in the Twentieth Century, 1960; The University and Education Today, 1962; Inaugural Lecture on The Present State of Historical Scholarship, 1965; (jt ed. with Martin Wight) Diplomatic Investigations, 1966; Sincerity and Insincerity in Charles James Fox, 1972; The Discontinuities between the Generations in History (Rede Lecture), 1972. *Address:* 26 High Street, Sawston, Cambridge CB2 4BG.

BUTTERFIELD, Prof. William John Hughes, OBE 1953; DM; FRCP; Regius Professor of Physic, University of Cambridge, since 1976; Professorial Fellow, Downing College, Cambridge, since 1975; Chairman, Medicines Commission, since 1976; *b* 28 March 1920; *s* of late William Hughes Butterfield and of Mrs Doris North; *m* 1st, 1946, Ann Sanders (decd); one *s*; 2nd, 1950, Isabel-Ann Foster Kennedy; two *s* one *d*. *Educ:* Solihull Sch.; Univ. of Oxford; Johns Hopkins Univ. Repr. Oxford Univ.: Rugby football, *v* Cambridge, 1940-41; hockey, 1940-42 (Captain); cricket, 1942 (Captain). Member, Scientific Staff, Medical Research Council, 1946-58: Major RAMC, Army Operational Research Group, 1947-50; Research Fellow, Medical Coll. of Virginia, Richmond, Va, USA, 1950-52; seconded to Min. of Supply, 1952; seconded to AEA, 1956; Prof. of Experimental Medicine, Guy's Hospital, 1958-63; Prof. of Medicine, Guy's Hosp. Med. Sch., and Additional Physician, Guy's Hosp., 1963-71; Vice-Chancellor, Nottingham Univ., 1971-75. Chairman: Bedford Diabetic Survey, 1962; Woolwich/Erith New Town Medical Liaison Cttee, 1965-71; SE Met. Reg. Hospital Board's Clinical Research Cttee, 1960-71; Scientific Advisory Panel, Army Personnel Research Cttee, 1970-; Council for the Education and Training of Health Visitors, 1971-76; East Midlands Economic Planning Council, 1974-75; Member: UGC Medical Sub-Cttee, 1966-71; Council, British Diabetic Assoc., 1963- (Chm. 1967-74, Vice-Pres. 1974-); DHSS Cttee on Medical Aspects of Food Policy, 1964-; DHSS Panel on Medical Research, 1974-; MRC Cttee on General Epidemiology, 1965-74; MRC Clinical Res. Grants Bd, 1969-71; MRC, 1976-; Anglo-Soviet Consultative Cttee; Minister of Health's Long Term Study Group; Health Educn Council, DHSS, 1973-; Trent RHA, 1973-75; IUC Council and Exec. Cttee, 1973-; British Council Med. Adv. Cttee, 1971-; Northwick Park Adv. Cttee, 1971-; Council, European Assoc. for Study of Diabetes, 1968-71 (Vice-Pres.); Hong Kong Univ. and Polytechnic Grants Cttee, 1975-; Consultant, WHO Expert Cttee on Diabetes, 1964-; Visitor, King Edward's Hospital Fund, 1964-71; Examiner in Medicine: Oxford Univ., 1960-66; Univ. of E Africa, 1966; Cambridge Univ., 1967-; Pfizer Vis. Professor, NZ and Australia, 1965; Vis. Professor, Yale, 1966. Oliver-Sharpey Lectr, 1967; Rock Carling Fellow, 1968; Banting Lectr, 1970. Member: Editorial Board, Diabetaloga, 1964-69; Jl Chronic Diseases, 1968-. Hon. Fellow, NY Acad. Science, 1962; Corres. FACP, 1973. Patron, Richmond Soc., 1968-71. FRSA 1971. *Publications:* (jointly) On Burns, 1953; Tolbutamide after 10 years, 1967; Priorities in Medicine, 1968; Health and Sickness: the choice of treatment, 1971; various contribs to medical jls. *Recreations:* tennis (not lawn), cricket (village) and talking (too much). *Address:* 22 Long Road, Cambridge CB2 2PQ. *T:* Cambridge 40747. *Clubs:* Athenæum, MCC, Queen's.

BUTTERWORTH, Sir (George) Neville, Kt 1973; DL; Chairman, Tootal Ltd (formerly English Calico Ltd), 1968-74; Director, Renold Ltd, since 1974; Member, Royal Commission on Distribution of Income and Wealth, since 1974; *b* 27 Dec. 1911; *s* of Richard Butterworth and Hannah (*née* Wright); *m* 1947, Barbara Mary Briggs; two *s*. *Educ:* Malvern; St John's Coll., Cambridge. Served with Royal Artillery, at home and overseas, 1939-45. Joined English Sewing Cotton Co. Ltd, 1933; Commercial Dir, 1948; Dep. Man. Dir, 1961; Jt Man. Dir, 1964;

Man. Dir, 1966; Dep. Chm., 1967; Chm., 1968, on merger with The Calico Printers' Assoc. Ltd. Dir, National Westminster Bank (North Regional Board), 1969. Chm., NW Regional Council of CBI, 1968-70; Former Mem., Grand Council of CBI; Trustee, Civic Trust for the North-West, 1967; Mem., Textile Council, 1970; CompTI 1973. Member: Court of Governors, Manchester Univ., 1973-; Council, UMIST, 1973-. FBIM 1968. High Sheriff 1974, DL 1974, Greater Manchester. *Recreation:* farming. *Address:* Oak Farm, Ollerton, Knutsford, Cheshire. *T:* 061-567 3150. *Club:* St James's (Manchester).

BUTTERWORTH, Prof. Ian; Professor of Physics, Imperial College of Science and Technology, since 1971; *b* 3 Dec. 1930; *s* of Harry and Beatrice Butterworth; *m* 1964, Mary Therese (*née* Gough); one *d*. *Educ:* Bolton County Grammar Sch.; Univ. of Manchester. BSc 1951; PhD 1954. Sen. Scientific Officer, UK Atomic Energy Authority, 1954-58; Lectr, Imperial Coll., 1958-64; Vis. Physicist, Lawrence Radiation Laboratory, Univ. of California, 1964-65; Sen. Lectr, Imperial Coll., 1965-68; Group Leader, Bubble Chamber Research Gp, Rutherford High Energy Laboratory, 1968-71; Mem., Nuclear Physics Bd, SRC, 1972-75; Chairman: Film Analysis Grants Commn, SRC, 1972-75; Super Proton Synchrotron Cttee, European Organisation for Nuclear Research, 1976-. *Publications:* numerous papers in learned jls (on Strong Interaction Physics): Annual Review of Nuclear Science; Physical Review; Nuovo Cimento; Nuclear Physics; Physical Review Letters; Physics Letters, etc. *Recreations:* history of art; archaeology. *Address:* c/o Physics Department, Imperial College, Prince Consort Road, SW7. *T:* 01-589 5111.

BUTTERWORTH, John Blackstock; JP; DL; Vice-Chancellor, University of Warwick, since 1963; *b* 13 March 1918; *o s* of John William and Florence Butterworth; *m* 1948, Doris Crawford Elder; one *s* two *d*. *Educ:* Queen Elizabeth's Grammar Sch., Mansfield; The Queen's Coll., Oxford. Served in Royal Artillery, 1939-46. MA 1946. Called to Bar, Lincoln's Inn, 1947. New Coll., Oxford: Fellow, 1946-63; Dean, 1952-56; Bursar and Fellow, 1956-63; Sub Warden, 1957-58. Junior Proctor, 1950-51; Faculty Fellow of Nuffield Coll., 1953-58; Member of Hebdomadal Council, Oxford Univ., 1953-63. Managing Trustee, Nuffield Foundation, 1964-. Chairman: Inter-Univ. Council for Higher Educn Overseas, 1968-; Universities Cttee for Non-teaching Staffs, 1970-; Inquiry into work of Probation Officers and Social Workers in Local Authorities and Nat. Service, 1971-73; Member: Royal Commn on the Working of the Tribunals of Inquiry (Act), 1921, 1966; Intergovernmental Cttee on Law of Contempt in relation to Tribunals of Inquiry, 1968; Noise Advisory Council, 1974-. Governor, Royal Shakespeare Theatre, 1964-; Trustee, Shakespeare Birthplace Trust, 1966. DL Warwickshire, 1967-74, DL West Midlands 1974-; JP City of Oxford, 1962, Coventry, 1963-. Hon DCL, Univ. of Sierra Leone, 1976. *Address:* The University of Warwick, Coventry CV4 7AL. *T:* Coventry 24011. *Club:* Athenæum.

BUTTERWORTH, Sir Neville; *see* Butterworth, Sir G. N.

BUTTFIELD, Archie Montague Carey, CMG 1959; Chairman, Advisory Board, NSW, National Bank of Australasia Ltd; Director: Mauri Bros & Thomson Ltd; Mount Isa Mines Ltd; Dellingham Corporation of Australia; Member, Principal Board, National Bank of Australasia Ltd; *b* Wagin, WA, 27 Aug. 1898; *s* of late F. Montgomery Buttfield, Wagin; *m* 1930, Ella, *d* of E. Warner; one *s* two *d*. *Educ:* Perth Modern Sch. Joined Australian Mutual Provident Society, 1914; General Manager, 1948-60. Past Chairman, Life Offices' Assoc. for Australasia; Past Member Council, Aust. Administrative Staff Coll. AAII 1926. *Recreations:* trout fishing, golf, tennis, bowls. *Address:* 146 Middle Harbour Road, Lindfield, NSW 2070, Australia. *Clubs:* Union, Royal Sydney Yacht Squadron (Sydney); Elanora Country; Warrawee Bowling.

BUTTFIELD, Dame Nancy (Eileen), DBE 1972; formerly Senator for South Australia; *b* 12 Nov. 1912; *d* of Sir Edward Wheewall Holden and Hilda May Lavis; *m* 1936, Frank Charles Buttfield; two *s*. *Educ:* Woodlands Church of England Girls' Grammar Sch., Adelaide; Composenea; Paris; Univ. of Adelaide, SA. Senator for South Australia, Oct. 1955-June 1965, re-elected July 1968-74. Exec. Mem., Commonwealth Immigration Adv. Council, 1955-; Vice-President: Good Neighbour Council of SA, 1956-62; Phoenix Soc. for the Physically Handicapped, 1959-. Dir, Co-operative Building Soc. of SA, 1959-. Mem. Council, Bedford Industries, 1965-. Mem., Nat. Council of Women of SA. *Recreations:* farming, dress-making, gourmet cooking, music. *Address:* 52 Strangways Terrace, North Adelaide, SA 5006, Australia. *Clubs:* Queen Adelaide, Lyceum, Royal Adelaide Golf (all SA).

BUTTIGIEG, Dr Anton; President of the Republic of Malta, since 1976; *b* Gozo, 19 Feb. 1912; *s* of Saviour Buttigieg and Concetta (*née* Falzon); *m* 1st, 1944, Carmen Bezzina (decd); two *s* one *d*; 2nd, 1953, Connie Scicluna (decd); 3rd, 1975, Margery Patterson. *Educ:* Royal Univ. of Malta (BA, LLD). Notary Public 1939; Advocate 1941. Police Inspector during Second World War; Law Reporter and Leader Writer, Times of Malta, 1944-48; Actg Magistrate 1955; Editor, The Voice of Malta, 1959. MP, 1955-76; Pres., Malta Labour Party, 1959-61, Dep. Leader, 1962-76; Dep. Prime Minister, 1971-76; Minister of Justice and Parly Affairs, 1971-76. Deleg., Malta Constitutional Confs, London, 1958 and 1964; Rep. to Consult. Assembly, Council of Europe, 1966-71, Vice-Pres., 1967-68. Mem., Acad. of Maltese Language. 1st Prize for poetry, Govt of Malta, 1971; Guze Muscat Azzopardi Prize for poetry, 1972; Silver Plaque for poetry, Circolo Culturale Rhegium Julii, Reggio, Calabria, 1975. *Publications:* lyric poetry: Mill-Gallerija ta' Zghoziti (From the Balcony of my Youth), 1945; Fanali bil-Lejl (Lamps in the Night), 1949; Qasba mar-Rih (A Reed in the Wind), 1968; Fl-Arena (In the Arena), 1970; humorous poetry: Ejjew Nidhku Ftit (Let us Laugh a Bit), 1963; Ejjew nidhku ftit iehor (Let us laugh a Bit More), 1966; *Haikus and Tankas:* Il-Muza bil-Kimono (The Muse in Kimono), 1968 (English and Japanese trans); Ballati Maltin (Maltese Ballads), 1973; Il Mare di Malta, 1974; Il Ghanja tas-Sittin (The Song of the Sixty Year Old), 1975. *Recreations:* horse racing, gardening. *Address:* (home) The White Lodge, Kappara, Malta; (official residence) San Anton Palace. *T:* 40354; (office) The Palace, Valletta. *T:* 21221.

BUTTLE, Gladwin Albert Hurst, OBE 1942; MA, MB Cantab; FRCP; retired as Wellcome Professor of Pharmacology, School of Pharmacy, London University (1946-66); *b* 11 April 1899; *s* of William and Mary Buttle; *m* 1936, Eva Korella; one *s*. *Educ:* Whitgift Sch.; St John's Coll., Cambridge. Qualified University Coll. Hospital, 1924; Pharmacologist Wellcome Physiological Research Laboratories for 14 years. RMA Woolwich, 1917; Lieut RE, 1918. Served War of 1939-45. RAMC (Lt-Col); adviser in Blood Transfusion, MEF and BLA, 1940-45. Expert, FAO, Mexico City, 1967-69; Professor of Pharmacology: Addis Ababa, 1972-74; Riyadh Univ., 1974-. Trustee, Buttle Trust for Children. *Publications:* contribs on chemotherapy and pharmacology to medical jls. *Recreations:* gardening, tennis. *Address:* Park View, Woldingham, Surrey. *T:* Woldingham 2191; 30 Witley Court, Coram Street, WC1. *T:* 01-837 8940; 300 Vauxhall Bridge Road, SW1. *Clubs:* Savage, Medical Research.

BUTTON, Air Vice-Marshal Arthur Daniel, CB 1976; OBE 1959; CEng, MRAeS; Editor, RAF Quarterly; Director of RAF Educational Services, 1972-76; *b* 26 May 1916; *o s* of late Leonard Daniel Button and of Agnes Ann (*née* Derbyshire); *m* 1944, Eira Guelph Waterhouse, *o d* of late Reginald Waterhouse Jones; one *s* decd. *Educ:* County High Sch., Ilford; University Coll., Southampton (BSc(Hons), (Lond)). Joined RAF Educnl Service, 1938; Gen. Duties Br., RAF, 1941-46; (Queen's Commendation for Valuable Service in the Air, 1946); returned to RAF Educn Br., 1946. *Recreations:* music, listening and performing; do-it-myself, rowing. *Address:* Dragons, 23 Upper Icknield Way, Aston Clinton, Aylesbury, Bucks HP22 5NF. *Club:* Royal Air Force.

BUTTON, Henry George; author; *b* 1 Aug. 1913; *e s* of late Rev. Frank S. and Bertha B. Button; *m* 1938, Edith Margaret Heslop (*d* 1972); two *d*. *Educ:* Manchester Grammar Sch.; Christ's Coll., Cambridge (Scholar). Mod. and Medieval Langs Tripos, Part II, 1st Class (with dist.) 1934; MLitt 1977; Tiarks German Scholar (research at Univ. of Bonn), 1934-35; Sen. Studentship of Goldsmiths' Company, 1935-36. Entered Civil Service, 1937; Board of Trade, 1937-57 (served in Min. of Production, 1942; Counsellor, UK Delegn to OEEC, Paris, 1952-55; on staff of Monopolies Commn, 1955-56); transf. Min. of Agriculture, Fisheries and Food, 1957; Under-Sec., Min. of Agriculture, Fisheries and Food, 1960-73 (Principal Finance Officer, 1965-73). Res. Student, Christ's Coll., Cambridge, 1974-76 (MLitt). Mem. Agricultural Research Council, 1960-62. Leader of various UK Delegns to FAO in Rome. BBC Brain of Britain for 1962; rep. Great Britain in radio quiz in Johannesburg, 1966; Bob Dyer's TV show, Sydney, 1967. *Publications* (with A. Lampert) The Guinness Book of the Business World, 1976; contribs to various jls both learned and unlearned, and to newspapers. *Recreations:* reading, writing, studying old businesses (hon. review ed., Business Archives Council, 1966-75); Hon. Sec., Tercentenarians' Club. *Address:* 7 Amhurst Court, Grange Road, Cambridge CB3 9BH. *T:* 55698. *Clubs:* Civil Service, Royal Commonwealth Society.

BUTTROSE, Murray; A Deputy Circuit Judge, since 1976; *b* 31 July 1903; *s* of William Robert and Frances Buttrose, both British; *m* 1935, Jean Marie Bowering; one *s*. *Educ:* St Peter's

Coll. and Adelaide Univ., South Australia. Admitted and enrolled as a barrister and solicitor of the Supreme Court of S Australia, 1927; apptd to HM Colonial Legal Service, 1946; Crown Counsel, Singapore, 1946, Senior Crown Counsel, 1949, and Solicitor-General, Singapore, 1955; Puisne Judge, Singapore, 1956-68, retired. Admitted and enrolled as a solicitor of the Supreme Court of Judicature in England, 1955; a Recorder of the Crown Court, 1972-74. Formerly Temp. Dep. Chm. (part time), London QS. Served with Royal Air Force (RAFVR), 1940-45. *Recreations:* reading, tennis, and golf. *Address:* 62 Embassy Court, Kings Road, Brighton, Sussex BN1 2PY. *Clubs:* Singapore (Singapore); Royal Singapore Golf.

BUXTON, family name of **Baron Noel-Buxton.**

BUXTON, Adrian Clarence; HM Diplomatic Service; Ambassador to Bolivia, since 1977; *b* 12 June 1925; *s* of Clarence Buxton and Dorothy (*née* Lintott); *m* 1958, Leonora Mary Cherkas; three *s. Educ:* Christ's Hosp., Horsham; Trinity Coll., Cambridge. RNVR, 1944-46; FO, 1947; 3rd Sec., Bangkok, 1948-52; FO, 1952-53; 2nd Sec., Khartoum, 1953-55; 2nd later 1st Sec., Bonn, 1955-58; 1st Sec. (Commercial) and Consul, Bogota, 1958-62; FO, 1962-64; 1st Sec., Saigon, 1964-67; 1st Sec. (Commercial), Havana, 1967-69; UK Dep. Permanent Rep. to UN and other internat. organisations at Geneva, 1969-73; Univ. of Surrey, 1973-74; Head of Training Dept and Dir Language Centre, FCO, 1974-75; Head of Maritime and Gen. Dept, FCO, 1975-77. *Recreations:* golf, choral singing. *Address:* c/o Foreign and Commonwealth Office, SW1; 7 Grove Road, Guildford, Surrey. *Club:* Travellers'.

BUXTON, Aubrey Leland Oakes, MC 1943; DL; Director: Anglia Television, since 1958; Survival Anglia Ltd; Trident Anglia SA; *b* 15 July 1918; *s* of Leland Wilberforce Buxton and Mary, *d* of Rev. Thomas Henry Oakes; *m* 1946, Pamela Mary, *d* of Sir Henry Birkin, 3rd Bt; two *s* four *d. Educ:* Ampleforth; Trinity Coll., Cambridge. Served 1939-45, RA; combined ops in Arakan, 1942-45 (despatches, 1944). Extra Equerry to Duke of Edinburgh, 1964. A Trustee of the British Museum (Natural History), 1971-73. Member: Countryside Commn, 1968-72; Royal Commission on Environmental Pollution, 1970-74; British Trustee, World Wildlife Fund; Trustee, Wildfowl Trust; Treasurer, London Zoological Soc.; Former Pres., Royal Television Soc.; Chm., Independent Television Cos Assoc., 1972-75. Wildlife Film Producer, Anglia TV; has made more than 200 TV films. Golden Awards, Internat. TV Festival, 1963 and 1968; Silver Medal, Zoological Society of London, 1967; Finalist, Internat. Film Festival, NY, 1968; Silver Medal, Royal TV Society, 1968; major award, Chicago Television Festival, 1972; Emmy award, NY, 1973; Queen's Award to Industry, 1974; Prince Rainier's Special Prize, Monte Carlo Internat. Film Festival, 1974; Golden Gate Award, 1975; Christopher Award, 1976, 1977; Ohio State Award, 1976. High Sheriff of Essex 1972; DL Essex, 1975. *Publications:* (with Sir Philip Christison) The Birds of Arakan, 1946; The King in his Country, 1955; numerous articles and papers on wildlife and exploration. *Recreations:* travel, natural history, painting, sport. *Address:* Stiffkey Old Rectory, Wells-next-sea, Norfolk. *T:* Binham 347. *Club:* White's.

BUXTON, Major Desmond Gurney, DL; 60th Rifles, retired; retired as Local Director (Norwich) Barclays Bank, 1958; Member Norfolk County Council, 1958-74; *b* 4 Jan. 1898; *e s* of late Edward G. Buxton, Catton Hall, Norwich, and of late Mrs Buxton, The Beeches, Old Catton, Norwich; *m* 1930, Rachel Mary, *yr d* of late Colonel A. F. Morse, Coltishall Mead, Norwich; two *s* three *d* (and one *d* decd). *Educ:* Eton; RMC Sandhurst. 60th Rifles, 1917-29; France and Belgium, 1917-18; NW Europe, 1945. Sheriff of Norwich, 1936-37; Lieut-Colonel Royal Norfolk Regt (TA), 1939-40. High Sheriff, Norfolk, 1960; DL Norfolk, 1961. CStJ 1972. *Recreations:* fishing, chess, bridge. *Address:* Hoveton Hall, Wroxham, Norwich.

BUXTON, Paul William Jex; Assistant Secretary, Northern Ireland Office, since 1974; *b* 20 Sept. 1925; *s* of late Denis Buxton and Emily Buxton (*née* Hollins); *m* 1st, 1950, Katharine Hull (marr. diss. 1971); two *s* one *d*; 2nd, 1971, Hon. Margaret Aston (*née* Bridges); two *d. Educ:* Rugby Sch.; Balliol Coll., Oxford. Coldstream Guards, 1944-47. HM Foreign, later Diplomatic, Service, 1950-71; served India, UN, Guatemala and Washington. Investment banking, 1972-74. *Address:* Castle House, Chipping Ongar, Essex. *T:* Ongar 2642. *Club:* Brooks's.

BUXTON, Raymond Naylor, OBE 1975; BEM 1957; QPM 1971; HM Inspector of Constabulary, since 1977; *b* 16 Sept. 1915; *s* of late Tom Bird Buxton and Ethel Buxton, Rushall, Walsall; *m* 1939, Agatha, *d* of late Enoch and Elizabeth Price, Essington, Wolverhampton; three *s. Educ:* King Edward VI Grammar

Sch., Stafford. Constable to Chief Supt in Staffordshire Co. Police. Served War, RAF, Navigator, 1943-45 (FO). Police Coll. Staff, 1958-61; Asst Chief Constable, then Dep. Chief Constable of Herts, 1963-69, Chief Constable, 1969-77. Mem., various Home Office, DoE and Police Cttees. Member: Herts Council for Order of St John; Medico-Legal Soc.; Herts Soc.; Administrative Council, Pendley Arts Centre; Herts AAA. *Address:* 130 Frankwell, Shrewsbury, Salop SY3 8JX.

BUXTON, Dame Rita (Mary), DBE 1969 (CBE 1955; OBE 1944); *b* 1900; *d* of Charles James Neunhoffer and Alice Neunhoffer (*née* O'Connor), Melbourne, Australia; *m* 1922, Leonard R. Buxton; three *d. Educ:* Sacré-Coeur Convent. Interested in philanthropic work. Member of the Victoria League. *Recreations:* golf, tennis, bridge. *Address:* 48 Hampden Road, Armadale, Victoria, Australia. *T:* 50-3333; Glynt, Mount Martha, Victoria, Australia. *T:* Mount Martha 741-216. *Clubs:* English-Speaking Union; Alexandra (Melbourne); Metropolitan Golf, Peninsula County Golf, Frankston Golf.

BUXTON, Ronald Carlile; MA Cantab; *b* 20 Aug. 1923; *s* of Murray Barclay Buxton and Janet Mary Muriel Carlile; *m* 1959, Phyllida Dorothy Roden Buxton; two *s* two *d. Educ:* Eton; Trinity Coll., Cambridge. Chartered Structural Engineer (AMIStructE). Director of H. Young & Co., London and associated companies. MP (C) Leyton, 1965-66. *Recreations:* travel, music, riding. *Address:* Kimberley Hall, Wymondham, Norfolk; 67 Ashley Gardens, SW1. *Club:* Carlton.

BUXTON, St John Dudley, MB, BS (London), FRCS; Hon. Consultant Orthopædic Surgeon to King's College Hospital, and Emeritus Lecturer in Orthopædics to the Medical School; Hon. Consultant Orthopædic Surgeon to the Ministry of Pensions; formerly Consultant Orthopædic Surgeon to the Army, Orthopædic Surgeon to Royal Masonic Hospital, Queen Mary's Hospital, Roehampton and Chairman Standing Advisory Committee on Artificial Limbs; *b* 26 Dec. 1891; 2nd *s* of late Dudley W. Buxton, MD; *m* Winifred, 2nd *d* of Picton Warlow; one *s* one *d. Educ:* St Peter's Coll., Radley; University Coll. Hospital. Served European War 1914-18 in BEF and Salonika Exp. Force (Croix de Guerre); BEF, 1940 and MEF, 1941-42, Brig. Consultant Orthopædic Surgeon. Regional Adviser to EMS; Formerly Lecturer in Orthopædic Surgery and Examiner in Surgery, Univ. of London; Past Pres. Med. Defence Union; Past Pres. Brit. Orthopædic Assoc.; Examiner for Diploma in Phys. Medicine, RCP and RCS; Hunterian Prof. RCS; Past Pres. Section of Orthopædics, Royal Soc. of Medicine; Mem. Soc. International Chirurg. Orth. Traumatol., Hellenic Surg. Soc. and French and Hellenic Soc. Orth. Surg. and Traumatology. Silver Cross of Royal Order of Phœnix (Greece). *Publications:* Arthroplasty; (jointly) Surgical Pathology; Orthopædics, in Post-Graduate Surgery, ed by R. Maingot; Two Visits to Greece; Amputations, In Butterworth's British Encycl. Med. Practice; Memoirs in RCS library; articles in Lancet, Proc. Royal Soc. of Med., etc. *Recreations:* writing, gardening. *Address:* Tollgate, 35 Church Road, Shanklin, IoW PO37 6QY. *T:* 2506.

BUXTON, Sir Thomas Fowell Victor, 6th Bt *cr* 1840; *b* 18 Aug. 1925; *s* of Sir Thomas Fowell Buxton, 5th Bt, and Hon. Dorothy Cochrane (*d* 1927), *yr d* of 1st Baron Cochrane of Cults; *S* father, 1945; *m* 1955, Mrs D. M. Chisenhale-Marsh (*d* 1965). *Educ:* Eton; Trinity Coll., Cambridge. *Heir: cousin* Jocelyn Charles Roden Buxton [*b* 8 Aug. 1924; *m* 1960, Ann Frances, *d* of Frank Smitherman, *qv*; three *d*].

BUZZARD, Sir Anthony (Farquhar), 3rd Bt *cr* 1929; educational consultant and tutor; Teacher of modern languages, The American School in London, since 1974; *b* 28 June 1935; *s* of Rear-Admiral Sir Anthony Wass Buzzard, 2nd Bt, CB, DSO, OBE, and of Margaret Elfreda, *d* of Sir Arthur Knapp, KCIE, CSI, CBE; *S* father, 1972; *m* 1970, Barbara Jean Arnold, Mendon, Michigan, USA; two *d. Educ:* Charterhouse; Christ Church, Oxford (MA); Ambassador Coll., Pasadena, USA (BA). ARCM. Lecturer in French, Ambassador Coll., Pasadena, 1962-65; Peripatetic Music Teacher for Surrey County Council, 1966-68; Lectr in French and Hebrew, Ambassador Coll., Bricket Wood, Herts, 1969-74. *Recreations:* tennis, squash, music. *Heir: b* Timothy Macdonnell Buzzard [*b* 28 Jan. 1939; *m* 1970, Jennifer Mary, *d* of late Peter Patching; one *d*]. *Address:* Robin Hill, Amersham Road, Chalfont St Giles, Bucks. *T:* Chalfont St Giles 2136.

BUZZARD, John Huxley; His Honour Judge Buzzard; a Circuit Judge at the Central Criminal Court, since 1974; *b* 12 Aug. 1912; *s* of late Brig.-Gen. Frank Anstie Buzzard, DSO, and Joan, *d* of late Hon. John Collier; *m* 1946, Hilary Ann Courtney Buzzard (*née* Antrobus); two *s* one *d. Educ:* Wellington Coll.; New Coll.,

Oxford. Open Classical Scholar, New Coll., 1931; commissioned 4th Queen's Own Royal West Kent Regt, TA, 1931; transferred to TA Reserve of Officers, 1935. Called to Bar, 1937 (Master of the Bench, Inner Temple, 1965). Served with RAFVR, in UK, Iceland, and SE Asia, 1940-45 (despatches). Recorder: Great Yarmouth, 1958-68; Dover, 1968-71; Crown Court, 1971-74; Second Sen. Prosecuting Counsel to the Crown, 1964-71, First Sen. Prosecuting Counsel, 1971-74. *Recreations:* mountaineering, ski-ing, sailing. *Address:* Central Criminal Court, Old Bailey, EC4. *Clubs:* Alpine, Lansdowne, Climbers', Cruising Association.

BYAM SHAW, Glencairn Alexander, CBE 1954; a Director, Sadler's Wells, since 1966; *b* 13 Dec. 1904; *s* of Byam Shaw, artist, and Evelyn Pyke-Nott; *m* 1929, Angela Baddeley, CBE (*d* 1976); one *s* one *d. Educ:* Westminster Sch. First stage appearance, Pavilion Theatre, Torquay, 1923; Mem. J. B. Fagan's Company at Oxford Repertory Theatre; played Trophimof, in The Cherry Orchard, New York; Konstantin Treplev, in The Seagull and Baron Tusenbach, in The Three Sisters, London. Was in Max Reinhardt's production of The Miracle. Went to S Africa with Angela Baddeley in repertory of plays. Played Darnley in Queen of Scots and Laertes in John Gielgud's production of Hamlet; was mem. of company for Gielgud's season at Queen's Theatre. Produced plays in London, New York and Stratford-upon-Avon. A Director of Old Vic Theatre Centre; a Governor, Royal Shakespeare Theatre, 1960-; Mem. Directorate, English Nat. Opera, 1974-. Co-Dir, with Anthony Quayle, of Shakespeare Memorial Theatre, Stratford-upon-Avon, 1952-56; Director, 1956-59; directed: Ross, Haymarket, 1960; The Lady From the Sea, Queen's, 1961; The Complaisant Lover and Ross, New York, 1961; The Rake's Progress and Idomeneo, Sadler's Wells, 1962; The Tulip Tree, Haymarket, 1962; Cosi fan Tutte, Der Freischütz, Hansel and Gretel, Sadler's Wells, 1963; Where Angels Fear to Tread, St Martin's, 1963; The Right Honourable Gentleman, Her Majesty's, 1964; Faust, Sadler's Wells, 1964; A Masked Ball, Sadler's Wells, 1964; You Never Can Tell, Haymarket, 1966; Die Fledermaus, Sadler's Wells, 1966; The Rivals, Haymarket, 1966; The Dance of Death, National Theatre, 1967; Orpheus and Eurydice, Sadler's Wells, 1967; The Merchant of Venice, Haymarket, 1967; The Wild Duck, Criterion, 1970; Duke Bluebeard's Castle, 1972; with John Blatchley: The Mastersingers of Nuremberg, 1968; The Valkyrie, 1970; Twilight of the Gods, 1971; The Rhinegold, 1972; Siegfried, 1973; The Ring Cycle, 1973. In the Royal Scots during War of 1939-45. Hon. DLitt Birmingham, 1959. *Address:* 169 Ashley Gardens, SW1. *Club:* Reform.
See also J. J. Byam Shaw.

BYAM SHAW, (John) James, CBE 1972; *b* 12 Jan. 1903; *er* surv. *s* of John Byam Shaw and Evelyn Pyke-Nott; *m* 1st, 1929, Eveline (marr. diss., 1938), *d* of Capt. Arthur Dodgson, RN; 2nd, 1945, Margaret (*d* 1965), *d* of Arthur Saunders, MRCVS; one *s*; 3rd, 1967, Christina, *d* of Francis Ogilvy and widow of W. P. Gibson. *Educ:* Westminster; Christ Church, Oxford. Scholar of Westminster and Christ Church; MA 1925; Hon. DLitt Oxford 1977. Worked independently in principal museums of Europe, 1925-33; Lecturer and Assistant to the Director, Courtauld Institute of Art, Univ. of London, 1933-34; joined P. & D. Colnaghi & Co., 1934; Director, 1937-68. Served in Royal Scots, UK, India and Burma, 1940-46 (wounded); Major, 1944. Associate Curator of pictures, Christ Church, Oxford, 1973-74; Hon. Student of Christ Church, 1976. Member: Council of the Byam Shaw Sch. of Drawing and Painting; Exec. Cttee, Nat. Art Collections Fund; Council, British Museum Soc., 1969-74; Gulbenkian Cttee on conservation of paintings and drawings, 1970-72; Conservation Cttee, Council for Places of Worship, 1970-77; Adv. Cttee, London Diocesan Council for Care of Churches, 1974-76. Trustee, Watts Gall. Lecturer, Christ Church, Oxford, 1964-73. FSA; FRSA. Hon. Fellow: Pierpont Morgan Library, NY; Ateneo Veneto. *Publications:* The Drawings of Francesco Guardi, 1951; The Drawings of Domenico Tiepolo, 1962; Catalogue of Paintings by Old Masters at Christ Church Oxford, 1967; Catalogue of Drawings by Old Masters at Christ Church, Oxford, 1976; publications in Old Master Drawings (1926-39), Print Collectors' Quarterly, Burlington Magazine, Apollo, Master Drawings (New York), Art Quarterly (Detroit), Arte Veneta, etc. *Address:* 4 Abingdon Villas, Kensington, W8. *T:* 01-937 6944. *Club:* Athenæum.
See also G. A. Byam Shaw.

BYATT, Hugh Campbell; HM Diplomatic Service; Deputy High Commissioner, Nairobi, since 1977; *b* 27 Aug. 1927; *e s* of late Sir Horace Byatt, GCMG, and late Olga Margaret Campbell, MBE; *m* 1954, Fiona, *d* of Ian P. Coats; two *s* one *d. Educ:* Gordonstoun; New College, Oxford. Served in Royal Navy, 1945-48; HMOCS Nigeria, 1952-57; Commonwealth Relations Office, 1958; Bombay, 1961-63; CRO, 1964-65; seconded to Cabinet Office, 1965-67; Head of Chancery, Lisbon, 1967-70; Asst, South Asian Dept, FCO, 1970-71; Consul-General, Lourenço Marques, 1971-73; Inspector, HM Diplomatic Service, 1973-75; RCDS, 1976. *Recreations:* sailing, fishing, gardening. *Address:* c/o Foreign and Commonwealth Office, SW1; Leargnahension, Tarbert, Argyll. *Clubs:* Royal Ocean Racing; Leander; Grémio Literário (Lisbon).
See also R . A . C . Byatt .

BYATT, Ian Charles Rayner; Under Secretary, HM Treasury, since 1972; *b* 11 March 1932; *s* of Charles Rayner Byatt and Enid Marjorie Annie Byatt (*née* Howat); *m* 1959 (marr. diss. 1969); one *s* one *d. Educ:* Kirkham Grammar Sch.; Oxford University. Commonwealth Fund Fellow, Harvard, 1957-58; Lectr in Economics, Durham Univ., 1958-62; Economic Consultant, HM Treasury, 1962-64; Lectr in Economics, LSE, 1964-67; Sen. Economic Adviser, Dept of Educn and Science, 1967-69; Dir of Econs and Stats, Min. of Housing and Local Govt, 1969-70; Dir Economics, DoE, 1970-72. *Publications:* articles on economics in learned jls. *Address:* 33 Ridgmount Gardens, WC1. *T:* 01-636 6533.

BYATT, Ronald Archer Campbell; HM Diplomatic Service; Counsellor and Head of Chancery, UK Mission to United Nations, New York, since 1977; *b* 14 Nov. 1930; *s* of late Sir Horace Byatt, GCMG and late Olga Margaret Campbell, MBE; *m* 1954, Ann Brereton Sharpe, *d* of C. B. Sharpe; one *s* one *d. Educ:* Gordonstoun; New Coll., Oxford; King's Coll., Cambridge. Served in RNVR, 1949-50. Colonial Admin. Service, Nyasaland, 1955-58; joined HM Foreign (now Diplomatic) Service, 1959; FO, 1959; Havana, 1961; FO, 1963; UK Mission to UN, NY, 1966; Kampala, 1970; Head of Rhodesia Dept, FCO, 1972-75; Vis. Fellow, Glasgow Univ., 1975-76. *Recreations:* sailing, boating (OUBC 1953), bird-watching, gardening. *Address:* c/o Foreign and Commonwealth Office, SW1; Drim-na-Vullin, Lochgilphead, Argyll. *T:* Lochgilphead 2615. *Clubs:* United Oxford & Cambridge University; Leander (Henley-on-Thames).
See also H. C. Byatt.

BYERS, family name of **Baron Byers.**

BYERS, Baron *cr* 1964 (Life Peer); **Charles Frank Byers,** PC 1972; OBE 1944; DL; Liberal Leader, House of Lords, since 1967; Chairman of the Liberal Party, 1950-52, 1965-67 (Vice-President, 1954-65); Liberal Chief Whip, 1946-50; MP (L) North Dorset, 1945-50; *b* 24 July 1915; *e s* of late C. C. Byers, Lancing, Sussex; *m* 1939, Joan Elizabeth Oliver; one *s* three *d. Educ:* Westminster; Christ Church, Oxford (MA Hons); Exchange Scholar at Milton Acad., Mass, USA. Blue for Athletics, Oxford, 1937, 220 yds Hurdles; Pres. OU Liberal Club, 1937. Enlisted Sept. 1939, RA; commissioned March 1940; served MEF, CMF, 1940-44; GSO1 Eighth Army, Lt-Col, 1943; served NW Europe, 1944-45, GSO1 HQ, 21 Army Group (despatches thrice); Chevalier Legion of Honour, Croix de Guerre (palmes). Chm., Company Pensions Information Centre, 1973-. FBIM 1965. DL Surrey, 1974. *Address:* Hunters Hill, Blindley Heath, Lingfield, Surrey.

BYERS, Dr Paul Duncan; Dean, Institute of Orthopaedics, University of London, since 1971; *b* Montreal, 1922; *s* of A. F. Byers and Marion Taber; *m* 1959, Valery Garden. *Educ:* Bishops College Sch., PQ, Canada; McGill Univ. (BSc, MD, CM); Univ. of London (DCP, PhD). FRCPath. Alan Blair Memorial Fellow, Canadian Cancer Soc., 1955-57. Asst Morbid Anatomist, Inst. of Orthopaedics, 1960; Reader in Morbid Anatomy, Univ. of London, 1974. Hon. Consultant, Royal National Orthopaedic Hosp., 1965; Hon. Senior Lectr, Royal Postgrad. Med. Sch., 1969. *Publications:* articles in medical press on arthritis, metabolic bone disease, bone tumours, medical education. *Recreation:* arts. *Address:* 18 Wimpole Street, W1M 7AD. *T:* 01-580 5206.

BYFORD, Donald, CBE 1963; Founder D. Byford & Co. Ltd, retired 1971; *b* 11 Jan. 1898; 4th *s* of Charles Watson Byford, JP, Clare, Suffolk; *m* 1922, Marjorie Annie, *d* of Ald. W. K. Billings, JP, Leicester (Lord Mayor, 1933-34); two *s* one *d. Educ:* Bishop's Stortford Coll. 2nd Lieut, Royal Tank Corps, 1917-19. Hosiery Manufacturer, 1919-71. Past President: Leicester Hosiery Manufacturers' Assoc.; Nat. Fedn Hosiery Manufacturers. Past Master: Worshipful Co. Framework Knitters; Worshipful Co. Gardeners. Mem. Court and past Treasurer, Corp. of the Sons of the Clergy. *Recreations:* shooting, farming. *Address:* Thurcaston Grange, Leicester LE7 7JQ. *T:* Anstey 2544. *Club:* Farmers'.

BYGRAVES, Max Walter; entertainer; *b* 16 Oct. 1922; *s* of Henry and Lilian Bygraves, Rotherhithe, SE16; *m* 1942, Gladys Blossom Murray; one *s* two *d*. *Educ*: St Joseph's, Rotherhithe. Began in advertising agency, carrying copy to Fleet Street, 1936. Volunteered for RAF, 1940; served 5 years as fitter. Performed many shows for troops; became professional, 1946; has appeared in venues all over English-speaking world, incl. 18 Royal Command Performances; best selling record artist. *Publications*: I Wanna Tell You a Story (autobiog.), 1976; The Milkman's on his Way (novel), 1977. *Recreations*: golf, painting, reading, writing. *Address*: Roebuck House, Victoria, SW1E 5BE. *T*: 01-839 1711. *Club*: 21.

BYNG, family name of **Earl of Strafford,** and of **Viscount Torrington.**

BYNOE, Dame Hilda Louisa, DBE 1969; in General Medical Practice, Port of Spain, Trinidad, since 1975; *b* Grenada, 18 Nov. 1921; *d* of Thomas Joseph Gibbs, CBE, JP, Estate Proprietor, and late Louisa Gibbs (*née* La Touche); *m* 1947, Peter Cecil Alexander Bynoe, ARIBA, Dip. Arch., former RAF Flying Officer; two *s*. *Educ*: St Joseph's Convent, St George's, Grenada; Royal Free Hospital Medical Sch., Univ. of London. MB, BS (London), 1951, MRCS, LRCP, 1951. Teacher, St Joseph's Convents, Trinidad and Grenada, 1939-44; hospital and private practice, London, 1951-53; public service with Govt of Trinidad and Tobago, 1954-55, with Govt of Guyana (then British Guiana), 1955-58, with Govt of Trinidad and Tobago, 1958-65; private practice, Trinidad, 1965-68; Governor of Associated State of Grenada, WI, 1968-74. Patron, Caribbean Women's Assoc., 1970-. *Recreations*: swimming, music, reading, poetry-writing. *Address*: 5A Barcant Avenue, Maraval, Trinidad.

BYRNE, Sir Clarence (Askew), Kt 1969; OBE 1964; DSC 1945; Company Director, Mining, Insurance and Construction, Queensland; *b* 17 Jan. 1903; *s* of George Patrick Byrne, Brisbane, Qld, and Elizabeth Emma Askew, Dalby, Qld; *m* 1928, Nellie Ann Millicent Jones; one *s* one *d*. *Educ*: Brisbane Technical Coll. Mining Develt and Exploration, 1925-30; Oil Exploration, Roma, Qld, 1930-40. Served War, 1940-46 (DSC, Amer. Bronze Star Medal): Lt-Comdr; CO, HMAS Warrego, 1944-45. Pres., Qld Chamber of Mines, 1961-70; Exec. Dir, Conzinc Riotinto of Australia Ltd (Resident, Qld, 1957-68); Director: Mary Kathleen Uranium Ltd; Qld Alumina Ltd; Thiess Holdings Ltd; Mines Administration Pty Ltd; Walkers Ltd; Drilling International Pty Ltd. Mem. Aust. Mining Industries Council, Canberra. *Recreations*: fishing, ocean cruising. *Address*: Culverston, Dingle Avenue, Caloundra, Qld 4551, Australia. *T*: Caloundra 91-1228. *Clubs*: Athenæum (Melbourne); Brisbane, United Service, Queensland (Brisbane); Australasian Pioneers (Sydney).

BYRNE, Douglas Norman; Head of Fair Trading Division, Department of Prices and Consumer Protection, since 1977; *b* 30 Jan. 1924; *s* of Leonard William Byrne and Clarice Evelyn Byrne; *m* 1949, Noreen Thurlby Giles; one *s* one *d*. *Educ*: Portsmouth Grammar Sch.; St John's Coll., Cambridge (MA). RAF, 1942-46. Asst Principal, Min. of Supply, 1949; BoT, 1956; Cabinet Office, 1961-64; Asst Sec., 1964; on staff of Monopolies Commn, 1966-68; Under-Sec., Dept of Industry, 1974-77. *Recreations*: hill walking, natural history. *Address*: 27 Greenlands Road, Staines, Mddx TW18 4LR. *T*: Staines 52936.

BYRNE, Rt. Rev. Herbert Kevin, OSB, MA; Abbot of Ampleforth Abbey, 1939-63; *b* 7 Sept. 1884; 3rd *s* of late Andrew Byrne, Croney Byrne, Co. Wicklow. *Educ*: Ampleforth Coll. Joined Benedictine Order, 1902; at the Ampleforth House of Studies, Oxford, 1905-09; Classical Master, Ampleforth Coll., 1909-35; priest, 1911; parish work at St Peter's, Liverpool, 1935-39. *Address*: Ampleforth Abbey, York.

BYRNE, John Keyes; see Leonard, Hugh.

BYRNE, Muriel St Clare, OBE 1955; writer and lecturer; engaged in research on The Lisle Letters (1533-40) (edition now in the press with University of Chicago Press); *b* 31 May 1895; *o c* of Harry St Clare Byrne, Hoylake, Ches, and Artemisia Desdemona Burtner, Iowa, USA. *Educ*: Belvedere, Liverpool (GPDST); Somerville Coll., Oxford. English Hons, 1916, BA and MA 1920. Teaching: Liverpool Coll., 1916-17; S Hampstead High Sch., 1917-18; English Lectr in Rouen, Army Educn (YMCA), 1918-19; Temp. Asst English Tutor, Somerville, 1919, and English coaching for Final Hons at Oxford, 1920-25; Oxford and London Univ. Extension Lectr, 1920-37; Lectr, Royal Academy of Dramatic Art, London, 1923-55; Eng. Lectr, Bedford Coll., 1941-45; Leverhulme Res. Grant, 1945; Bedford Coll. Research Fellowship, 1955; Brit. Acad. Pilgrim Trust Res.

Grants, 1958 and 1959; Phoenix Trust Res. Grant, 1970; Twenty Seven Foundn Res. Grant, 1971; Brit. Acad. Research in the Humanities Grant, 1964, 1965, 1966; Leverhulme Research Fellowship, 1968. Examr, London Univ. Dipl. in Dramatic Art, 1951-60. Hon. Sec., Malone Soc., 1926-37; Mem. Council, Bibliographical Soc., 1932-39; Mem. Bd, 1952-, Exec., 1959-, Friends of Girls' Public Day Sch. Trust; Mem., Cttee of Soc. for Theatre Research; History Selection Cttee, Nat. Film Archive, 1968; Mem. Council, RADA, 1973. Governor: Royal Shakespeare Theatre, 1960; Bedford Coll., 1968. Mem., Literary Advisory Panel, Shakespeare Exhibn 1564-1964. FSA 1963. *Publications*: History of Somerville College (with C. H. Godfrey), 1921; Elizabethan Life in Town and Country, 1925 (8th revised edn 1961, American edn 1962, Polish edn 1971); The Elizabethan Home, 1925 (3rd rev. edn 1949); The Elizabethan Zoo, 1926; Letters of King Henry VIII, 1936, 2nd edn 1968, US edn 1968; Common or Garden Child, 1942; contributed: Shakespeare's Audience, to Shakespeare in the Theatre, 1927; The Social Background, to A Companion to Shakespeare Studies, 1934; Queen Mary I, to Great Tudors, 1935; History of Stage Lighting and History of Make-Up, to Oxford Companion to the Theatre, 1951; The Foundations of Elizabethan Language, to Shakespeare in his own Age, 1964; Elizabethan Life in the Plays, to The Reader's Encyclopedia of Shakespeare, 1966; Dramatic Intention and Theatrical Realization, to The Triple Bond; essays in honor of Arthur Colby Sprague, 1975; edited: Anthony Munday's John a Kent (Malone Society), 1923; Massinger's New Way to Pay Old Debts, 1949; The French Litleton of Claudius Holyband, 1953; Essays and Studies, Vol. 13 (Eng. Assoc.), 1960; 4-vol. paperback illustr. edn of Granville Barker's Prefaces to Shakespeare, with Introd. and Notes, 1963; plays produced: England's Elizabeth, 1928 and 1953; "Well, Gentlemen..." (with Gwladys Wheeler), 1933; Busman's Honeymoon (with Dorothy L. Sayers), 1936; No Spring Till Now (Bedford Coll. Centenary Play), 1949; Gen. Ed. Pubns for Soc. for Theatre Research, 1949-59; Eng. edit. rep. of and contrib. to Enciclopedia dello Spettacolo, 1955-58; prep. Arts Council's exhibn and Catalogue, A History of Shakespearian Production in England, 1947 (repr. USA 1970); contributor to: The Times Lit. and Educ. Suppts; The Library; Review of Eng. Studies; Mod. Lang. Review; Shakespeare Survey; Shakespeare Quarterly; Drama; Theatre Notebook; Sunday Times; Theatre Research; Essays and Studies Vol. 18 (Eng. Assoc.), etc. *Recreations*: play-going and all theatrical activities. *Address*: 28 St John's Wood Terrace, NW8. *T*: 01-722 0967.

BYRNE, Prof. Patrick Sarsfield, CBE 1975 (OBE 1966); FRCGP; Professor and Director of Department of General Practice, University of Manchester, since 1969; *b* 17 April 1913; *s* of John Stephen Byrne and Marie Anne Byrne; *m* 1937, Dr Kathleen Marianne Pearson; two *s* four *d*. *Educ*: St Edward's Coll., Liverpool; Liverpool Univ. (State Scholarship; MB, ChB 1936). MSc Manchester, 1976; FRCGP 1967. GP, Milnthorpe, Cumbria, 1936-68. Pres., RCGP, 1973-76; Chm., Armed Services Gen. Practice Approval Bd, MoD, 1973-; Cons. Adviser in Gen. Practice to DHSS, 1973-; Mem., Jt Trng Cttee in Gen. Practice (UK), 1976-. Fellow, RSocMed; Hon. Fellow, Coll. of Medicine of SA, 1975; Hon. Mem., Canadian Coll. of Family Physicians, 1976. Sesquicentennial Medal, Med. Univ. of SC, 1974; Hippocratic Medal, SIMG, 1974. *Publications*: Learning to Care—person to person (with B.E.L. Long), 1973 (2nd edn 1975); (with J. Freeman) Assessment of Postgraduate Training for General Practice, 1972 (2nd edn 1973); (with B. E. L. Long) Doctors talking to Patients, 1976; (ed with H. W. Proctor) A Handbook of Medical Treatment, 1976; chapters in books; ubns in med. jls in Britain and overseas. *Recreations*: fishing and wine. *Address*: Grievegate, Leasgill, Milnthorpe, Cumbria. *T*: Milnthorpe 3121.

BYRNE, Rev. Father Paul Laurence, OMI; 1976; Vicar Provincial, Oblates of Mary Immaculate, since 1976; *b* 8 Aug. 1932; *s* of late John Byrne and Lavinia Byrne. *Educ*: Synge Street Christian Brothers' Sch. and Belcamp Coll., Dublin; University Coll., Dublin (BA,Hons Phil.); Oblate Coll., Piltown. Teacher, Belcamp Coll., 1959-65; Dean of Belcamp Coll., 1961-65; Dir, Irish Centre, Birmingham, 1965-68; Dir, Catholic Housing Aid Soc. (Birmingham) and Family Housing Assoc., Birmingham, 1965-69; Nat. Dir, Catholic Housing Aid Soc., and Dir, Family Housing Assoc., London, 1969-70; Dir SHAC (a housing aid centre) 1969-76. Board Member: Hearth and Home, Kensington and Chelsea Geriatric Day Hosp.; Threshold Centre; Deptford Housing Aid Centre; Family Housing Assoc.; Mem. Bd, Housing Corp., 1974. Associate, Inst. of Housing Managers, 1972. *Recreations*: golf, squash, theatre-going. *Address*: 170 Merrion Road, Ballsbridge Road, Dublin 4. *T*: 0001-693658. *Clubs*: West Middlesex Golf; Foxcock Golf.

BYRON, 11th Baron *cr* 1643; **Rupert Frederick George Byron;** farmer and grazier since 1921; *b* 13 Aug. 1903; *er s* of late Col Wilfrid Byron, Perth, WA, and of Sylvia Mary Byron, 12 College Street, Winchester, England, *o d* of late Rev. C. T. Moore; *S* kinsman, 1949; *m* 1931, Pauline Augusta, *d* of T. J. Cornwall, Wagin, W Australia; one *d. Educ:* Gresham's Sch., Holt. Served War of 1939-45, Lieut RANVR, 1941-46. *Heir: kinsman,* Richard Geoffrey Gordon Byron, DSO [*b* 3 Nov. 1899; *m* 1st, 1926, Margaret Mary Steuart (marr. diss. 1946); 2nd, 1946, Dorigen, *o c* of P. Kennedy Esdaile; two *s. Educ:* Eton]. *Address:* 6 Barnsby Road, Swanbourne, WA 6010, Australia. *Club:* Naval and Military (Perth, WA).

BYRT, Henry John, QC 1976; a Recorder of the Crown Court, since 1976; *b* 5 March 1929; *s* of Dorothy Muriel Byrt and Albert Henry Byrt, CBE; *m* 1957, Eve Hermione Bartlett; one *s* two *d. Educ:* Charterhouse; Merton Coll., Oxford (BA, MA). Called to the Bar, Middle Temple, 1953; called within the Bar, 1976. *Recreations:* building, gardening, sailing, walking, music, golf. *Address:* 65 Gloucester Crescent, NW1. *T:* 01-485 0341.

BYWATER, Thomas Lloyd, BSc, MS; Emeritus Professor, University of Leeds; *b* 19 Aug. 1905; *m* 1935, Ishobel McL. Millar; two *s* one *d. Educ:* Lucton Sch.; University Coll. of North Wales; Univ. of Wisconsin, USA. Lecturer in Agriculture, Univ. of Leeds, 1929-46; Prof. of Agriculture: Aberdeen Univ., 1946-53; Leeds Univ., 1953-69. *Address:* 1 Balmoral Terrace, Shaw Lane, Leeds LS6 4EA.

BYWATERS, Eric George Lapthorne, CBE 1975; MB (London); FRCP; Emeritus Professor of Rheumatology, Royal Postgraduate Medical School, University of London; late Director, Medical Research Council Rheumatism Research Unit, Taplow; Hon. Consultant Physician, Hammersmith Hospital and Canadian Red Cross Memorial Hospital, Taplow, Bucks; *b* 1 June 1910; *s* of George Ernest Bywaters and Ethel Penney; *m* 1935, Betty Euan-Thomas; three *d. Educ:* Sutton Valence Sch., Kent; Middx Hosp. (Sen. Broderip Schol., Lyell Gold Medallist). McKenzie McKinnon Fellow, RCP, 1935; Asst Clin. Pathologist, Bland Sutton Inst., 1936; Rockefeller Travelling Fellow and Harvard Univ. Research Fellow in Med., 1937-39; Beit Memorial Fellow, 1939; Actg Dir, MRC Clin. Res. Unit (Shock), 1943; Lectr in Med., Postgrad. Med. Sch., 1945. Hon. FACP, 1973; Hon. FRCP&S (Canada), 1977. Hon. MD Liège, 1973. Gairdner Foundation Medical Award, 1963; Heberden Orator and Medallist, 1966; Bunim Lectr and Medallist, 1973; Ewart Angus Lectr, Toronto, 1974. Hon. Mem. Dutch, French, Amer., German, Czech, Spanish, Portuguese, Aust., Indian, Canadian, Chilean, Peruvian, Jugoslav and Argentine Rheumatism Assocs. *Address:* Long Acre, 53 Burkes Road, Beaconsfield, Bucks.

C

CABALLÉ, Montserrat; Cross of Lazo de Dama of Order of Isabel the Catholic, Spain; opera and concert singer; *b* Barcelona, 12 April 1933; *d* of Carlos and Ana Caballé; *m* 1964, Bernabé Marti, tenor; one *s* one *d. Educ:* Conservatorio del Liceo, Barcelona. Continued to study singing under Mme Eugenia Kemeny. Carnegie Hall début as Lucrezia Borgia, 1965. London début in this role, with the London Opera Society, at the Royal Festival Hall, 1968. Has sung at Covent Garden, Glyndebourne, Metropolitan Opera, La Scala, Mexico City, and other main opera venues. Major roles include Maria Stuarda, Luisa Miller, Queen Elizabeth in Roberto Devereux, Imogene in Il Pirata, Violetta in La Traviata, Marguerite in Faust, Desdemona in Otello, Norma and also those of contemporary opera. Has made many recordings. *Address:* c/o Columbia Artists Management Inc., 165 W 57th Street, New York, NY 10019, USA.

CABLE, Sir James (Eric), KCVO 1976; CMG 1967; HM Diplomatic Service; Ambassador to Finland, since 1975; *b* 15 Nov. 1920; *s* of late Eric Grant Cable, CMG; *m* 1954, Viveca Hollmerus; one *s. Educ:* Stowe; CCC, Cambridge. PhD 1973. Served Royal Signals, 1941-46, Major. Entered Foreign (now Diplomatic) Service, 1947; 2nd Sec., 1948; Vice-Consul, Batavia, 1949; 2nd Sec., Djakarta, 1949; acted as Chargé d'Affaires, 1951 and 1952; Helsinki, 1952; FO, 1953; 1st Sec., 1953; Mem. of British Delegn to Geneva Conf. on Indo-China, 1954; 1st Sec. (Commercial), Budapest, 1956; Head of Chancery and Consul, Quito, 1959; acted as Chargé d'Affaires, 1959 and 1960; FO,

1961 and Head of SE Asia Dept, Dec. 1963; Counsellor, Beirut, 1966; acted as Chargé d'Affaires at Beirut, 1967, 1968 and 1969; Research Associate, Institute for Strategic Studies, 1969-70; Head of Western Organisations Dept, FCO, 1970-71; Counsellor, Contingency Studies, FCO, 1971; Head of Planning Staff, 1971-75, and Asst Under-Sec. of State, 1972-75, FCO. *Publication:* Gunboat Diplomacy, 1971. *Address:* c/o Foreign and Commonwealth Office, SW1. *Clubs:* Athenæum, Royal Automobile.

CABLE-ALEXANDER, Sir Desmond William Lionel, 7th Bt (1809); *b* 1910; *S* 1956; *m* 1st, Mary Jane (who obtained a divorce), *d* of James O'Brien, JP, Enniskillen; one *s*; 2nd, Margaret Wood, *d* of late John Burnett, Dublin; two *d. Educ:* Harrow; Oxford. Assumed addtl name of Cable before that of Alexander, by deed poll, 1931. *Heir: s* Patrick Desmond William Cable-Alexander [*b* 19 April 1936; *m* 1961, Diana Frances Rogers; two *d*]. *Address:* c/o Barclays Bank Ltd, 16 Whitehall, SW1.

CACCIA, family name of **Baron Caccia.**

CACCIA, Baron *cr* 1965 (Life Peer), of Abernant; **Harold Anthony Caccia,** GCMG 1959 (KCMG 1950; CMG 1945); GCVO 1961 (KCVO 1957); Provost of Eton, 1965-77; *b* 21 Dec. 1905; *s* of late Anthony Caccia, CB, MVO; *m* 1932, Anne Catherine, *d* of late Sir George Barstow, KCB; one *s* two *d. Educ:* Eton; Trinity Coll., Oxford. Laming Travelling Fellowship, Queen's Coll., Oxford, 1928, Hon. Fellow, 1974. Entered HM Foreign Service as 3rd Sec., FO, 1929; transferred to HM Legation, Peking, 1932; 2nd Sec., 1934; FO 1935; Asst Private Sec. to Sec. of State, 1936; HM Legation, Athens, 1939; 1st Sec. 1940; FO 1941; seconded for service with Resident Minister, North Africa, 1943, and appointed Vice-Pres., Political Section, Allied Control Commission, Italy; Political Adviser, GOC-in-C Land Forces, Greece, 1944; Minister local rank, HM Embassy, Athens, 1945; Asst Under-Sec. of State, 1946, Dep. Under-Sec. of State, 1949, Foreign Office; British Ambassador in Austria, 1951-54, and also British High Comr in Austria, 1950-54; Dep. Under-Sec. of State, FO, 1954-56; British Ambassador at Washington, 1956-61; Permanent Under-Sec. of State, FO, 1962-65; Head of HM Diplomatic Service, 1964-65, retired. Hon. Fellow, Trinity Coll., Oxford, 1963. Chm., Standard Telephones & Cables, 1968-; Director: Prudential Assurance Co. Ltd; Foreign & Colonial Investment Trust Co. Ltd; Orion Bank (Chm., 1973-74). Chm., Gabbitas-Thring Educational Trust, 1967-73. Mem., Advisory Council on Public Records, 1968-73. Pres., MCC, 1973-74. Lord Prior of the Order of St John of Jerusalem, 1969-; GCStJ. *Address:* 1 Chester Place, Regent's Park, NW1. *T:* 01-935 0302; Abernant, Builth-Wells, Breconshire. *T:* Erwood 233.

CACOYANNIS, Michael; director, stage and screen, since 1954; *b* 11 June 1922; *s* of Sir Panayotis Cacoyannis, *qv. Educ:* Greek Gymnasium; Gray's Inn and Old Vic Sch., London. Radio Producer, BBC, Greek Service, 1941-50. Actor on English stage, 1946-51; parts included: Herod, in Salome, 1946; Caligula, in Caligula, 1949, etc. Directed films: Windfall in Athens, 1953; Stella, 1954; Girl in Black, 1956; A Matter of Dignity, 1958; Our Last Spring, 1960; The Wastrel, 1961; Electra, 1962; Zorba the Greek, 1964; The Day the Fish Came Out, 1967; The Trojan Women, 1971; Attila '74, 1975; Iphigenia, 1977. Directed plays: produced several of these in Athens for Ellie Lambetti's Company, 1955-61; The Trojan Women, in New York, 1963-65, in Paris, 1965; Things That Go Bump in the Night, and The Devils, New York, 1965; Mourning Becomes Electra, Metropolitan Opera, NY, 1967; Iphigenia in Aulis, New York, 1968; La Bohème, Juillard, NY, 1972; King Oedipus, Abbey Theatre, Dublin, 1973; Miss Margarita, Athens, 1975; The Bacchae, Comédie Française, 1977. Order of the Phœnix (Greece), 1965. *Recreations:* walking, swimming. *Address:* 15 Mouson Street, Athens 401, Greece.

CACOYANNIS, Hon. Sir Panayotis (Loizou), Kt 1936; LLB; Advocate; Member of Town School Committee, Limassol (Cyprus), since 1925, Chairman, 1946-61; *b* 20 Sept. 1893; *s* of Loizos Cacoyannis, Limassol, Cyprus; *m* 1915, Angeliki, *d* of George M. Efthyvoulos and Zoe Constantinides, Limassol, Cyprus; two *s* two *d.* MLC, Cyprus, 1925-30; MEC, Cyprus, 1929-46; Mem. of Advisory Council, 1933-46; Mem. of Council of Cyprus Anti-Tuberculosis League until 1946. Attended the Coronation Ceremony of King George VI and Queen Elizabeth as representative of Cyprus, 1937. *Address:* POB 122, Limassol, Cyprus.
See also M. Cacoyannis.

CADBURY, Sir (George) Adrian (Hayhurst), Kt 1977; Chairman, Cadbury Schweppes Ltd, since 1975; a Director of the Bank of England, since 1970; Chairman, Economic Policy Committee, CBI, since 1974; *b* 15 April 1929; *s* of Laurence John Cadbury, *qv*; *m* 1956, Gillian Mary, *d* of late E. D. Skepper, Neuilly-sur-Seine; two *s* one *d. Educ:* Eton Coll.; King's Coll., Cambridge (MA Economics). Coldstream Guards, 1948-49; Cambridge, 1949-52. Cadbury Schweppes Ltd: Jt Man. Dir, 1969-70; Man. Dir, 1970-73; Dep. Chm., 1969-73; Exec. Dep. Chm., 1974; Director: Cadbury Group Ltd, 1962; Cadbury Bros Ltd, 1958; J. S. Fry & Sons, 1964; James Pascall, 1964; R. S. Murray, 1964; IBM UK Ltd, 1975-. Chm., West Midlands Economic Planning Council, 1967-70. Mem., Covent Garden Market Authority, 1974-. Mem. Council: Univ. of Aston in Birmingham; Industry for Management Educn; Industrial Soc.; Governor, Bromsgrove Sch. Hon. DSc Aston, 1973. *Address:* Rising Sun House, Baker's Lane, Knowle, Solihull, West Midlands B93 8PT. *T:* Knowle 2931. *Clubs:* Boodle's; Hawks (Cambridge); Leander (Henley).

CADBURY, George Woodall; Chairman Emeritus, Governing Body of International Planned Parenthood Federation, since 1975 (Chairman, 1969-75, Vice-Chairman, and Chairman of the Executive, 1963-69, and Special Representative, since 1960); Member, Executive Committee, Conservation Council of Ontario (Chairman, 1972-74 and 1976-78); *b* 19 Jan. 1907; *s* of George Cadbury and Edith Caroline Cadbury (*née* Woodall); *m* 1935, Mary Barbara Pearce; two *d. Educ:* Leighton Park Sch., Reading; King's Coll., Cambridge; MA (Economics Tripos); Wharton Sch. of Finance and Commerce, Univ. of Pennsylvania. Man. Dir, British Canners Ltd, 1929-35; Marketing Controller and Man. Dir, Alfred Bird & Sons Ltd, 1935-45; Dep. Dir Material Production, Min. of Aircraft Production and British Air Commn (USA), 1941-45; Chm. Economic Advisory and Planning Bd, and Chief Industrial Executive, Prov. of Saskatchewan, 1945-51; Dir, Technical Assistance Administration, UN, 1951-60 (Dir of Ops, 1951-54; Adviser to Govts of Ceylon, Burma, Indonesia, Jamaica and Barbados, 1954-60). New Democratic Party of Canada: Pres., Ont, 1961-66; Fed. Treasurer, 1965-69; Mem., Fed. Council, 1961-71. Trustee: Bournville Village Trust, 1928-; Youth Hostels Trust, 1931-; Sponsor and Council Mem., Minority Rights Group, 1967-; Member: TGWU (Life Mem., 1973); League for Industrial Democracy, NY, 1928, Bd Mem., 1951-. Dir, Glenford Paper Co., 1966-. Mem. Meetings Cttee, RIIA, 1931-35; Sec., W Midland Group for Post-War Reconstruction and Planning, 1939-41; Resident, Toynbee Hall, 1929-35, 1941-43. *Publications:* (jointly) When We Build Again, 1940; English County, 1942; Conurbation, 1942; Essays on the Left, 1971; A Population Policy for Canada, 1973. *Address:* 35 Brentwood Road, Oakville, Ont L6J 4B7, Canada. *T:* 416-845 3171.

CADBURY, Kenneth Hotham, CBE 1974; MC 1944; Assistant Managing Director, Telecommunications, Post Office, since 1975; *b* 25 Feb. 1919; *s* of J. Hotham Cadbury, manufacturer, Birmingham; *m* 1st, Margaret R. King (marr. diss.); one *s* one *d* ; 2nd, Marjorie I. Lilley; three *d. Educ:* Bootham Sch., York; Univ. of Birmingham. Served in Royal Artillery in Middle East and Italy, 1939-46 (despatches, MC; Major). Joined Foreign Service, 1946. Transferred to GPO, 1947; served in Personnel Dept and Inland Telecommunications Dept; Cabinet Office, 1952-55; PPS to PMG, 1956-57; Dep. Director, 1960, Director, 1962, Wales and Border Counties GPO; Director: Clerical Mechanisation and Buildings, GPO, 1964-65; Inland Telecommunications, GPO, 1965-67; Purchasing and Supply, GPO, 1967-69; Sen. Dir, Planning and Purchasing, PO, 1969-75. Trustee, PO Staff Superannuation Fund, 1969-75. *Recreation:* gardening. *Address:* Pendle, Burdenshott Hill, Worplesdon, Surrey. *T:* Worplesdon 2084.

CADBURY, Laurence John, OBE 1919; *b* 1889; *s* of late George Cadbury; *m* 1925, Joyce, *d* of Lewis O. Matthews, Birmingham; three *s* one *d* (and one *s* one *d* decd). *Educ:* Leighton Park Sch.; Trinity Coll., Cambridge (MA). Economics Tripos. Man. Dir, Cadbury Bros Ltd and associated cos, 1919-59; Chm., Cadbury Bros Ltd, 1944-49 and of J. S. Fry & Sons Ltd, 1952-59; Dir, Bank of England, 1936-61. Director: British Cocoa & Chocolate Co. Ltd, 1920-59; Nation Proprietory Co. Ltd, Tyne Tees Television Ltd, 1958-67; Daily News Ltd; News Chronicle, 1930-60 and Star, 1930-60; Cocoa Investments Ltd, 1937-64; EMB Co. Ltd; Chm., Bournville Village Trust; Treasurer, Population Investigation Cttee, 1936-76. Trustee, Historic Churches Preservation Trust (Exec. Cttee); Head, Economic Section, Mission to Moscow, 1941. High Sheriff of County of London, 1947-48 and 1959-60. Hon. LLD Birmingham, 1970. Mons Medal; 1914 Star; Croix de Guerre. *Publications:* This Question of Population; numerous contribs to the press and periodicals on economics and demographic subjects. *Address:* The Davids, Northfield, Birmingham. *T:* 021-475 1441. *Clubs:* Athenæum, United Oxford & Cambridge University; Leander

(Henley); Hawks (Cambridge).
See also Sir G. A. H. Cadbury.

CADBURY, Paul Strangman, CBE 1948; Chairman, Cadbury Bros Ltd, 1959-65; *b* 3 Nov. 1895; *s* of late Barrow Cadbury; *m* 1919, Rachel E. Wilson; two *s* two *d. Educ:* Leighton Park Sch., Reading. Friends' Ambulance Unit, 1915-19; Chm. Friends Ambulance Unit, 1939-48; Bournville Village Trust. Hon. DSc Aston, 1971. *Publication:* Birmingham-Fifty Years On, 1952. *Address:* Low Wood, 32 St Mary's Road, Harborne, Birmingham B17 0HA. *T:* 021-427 1636. *Clubs:* Reform; Birmingham (Birmingham).

CADBURY, Peter (Egbert); Executive Chairman, Westward Television Ltd, since 1960 (Managing Director, 1960-73); Chairman: Alfred Hays Ltd, 1955-71; Ashton & Mitchell Ltd, 1959-71; TTM Holdings Ltd; *b* Great Yarmouth, Norfolk, 6 Feb. 1918; *s* of late Sir Egbert Cadbury, DSC, DFC; *m* 1st, 1947, Eugenie Benedicta (marr. diss. 1968), *d* of late Major Ewen Bruce, DSO, MC and of Mrs Bruce; one *s* one *d* ; 2nd, 1970, Mrs Jennifer Morgan-Jones (marr. diss. 1976), *d* of Major Michael Hammond-Maude, Ramsden, Oxon; one *s* ; 3rd, 1976, Mrs Jane Mead. *Educ:* Leighton Park Sch.; Trinity Coll., Cambridge (BA, MA). Called to Bar, Inner Temple, 1946; practised at Bar, 1946-54. Served Fleet Air Arm, 1940, until released to Ministry of Aircraft Production, 1942, as Research and Experimental Test Pilot; contested (L) Stroud (Glos), 1945. Member, London Travel Cttee, 1958-60; Chm. and Man. Dir, Keith Prowse & Co. Ltd, 1954-71; Director: Independent Television News Ltd, 1972-; Willett Investments Ltd. Freeman of City of London, 1948. *Recreations:* theatre, racing, flying. *Address:* Westward Television Ltd, Sloane Square House, Sloane Square, SW1W 8NT. *Clubs:* Garrick, Bath, MCC; Royal Western Yacht (Plymouth), Royal Motor Yacht, RAF Yacht.

CADBURY-BROWN, Henry Thomas, OBE 1967; TD; RA 1975 (ARA 1971); FRIBA; Professor of Architecture, Royal Academy, since 1975; Hon. Fellow RCA; architect; *b* 20 May 1913; *s* of Henry William Cadbury-Brown and Marion Ethel Sewell; *m* 1953, Elizabeth Romeyn, *d* of Prof. A. Elwyn, Croton on Hudson, NY. *Educ:* Westminster Sch.; AA Sch. of Architecture (Hons Diploma). Architect in private practice since winning competition for British Railways Branch Offices, 1937. Work includes pavilions for "The Origins of the People", main concourse and fountain display at Festival of Britain; schools, housing, display and interiors. Architect for new civic centre at Gravesend and halls for residence for Birmingham Univ. and, with Sir Hugh Casson and Prof. Robert Goodden, for new premises for Royal College of Art; awarded London Architecture Bronze Medal, 1963; lecture halls for Univ. of Essex; in group partnership with Eric Lyons, Cunningham Partnership for W Chelsea redevelopment for RBK&C. Taught at Architectural Association Sch., 1946-49; Tutor at Royal Coll. of Art, 1952-61. Invited as Visiting Critic to Sch. of Architecture, Harvard Univ., 1956. Member: RIBA Council, 1951-53; British Cttee Internat. Union of Architects, 1951-54; MARS (Modern Architectural Research) group. Pres. Architectural Assoc., 1959-60. TA and military service, 1931-45; Major RA (TD). *Recreations:* numerous, including work. *Address:* 32 Neal Street, WC2. *T:* 01-240 3353; Church Walk, Aldeburgh, Suffolk. *T:* Aldeburgh 2591.

CADELL, Colin Simson, CBE 1944; Air Cdre RAF, retired; Vice Lieutenant for West Lothian since 1972; *b* 7 Aug. 1905; *s* of late Lt-Col J. M. Cadell, DL, Foxhall, Kirkliston, W Lothian; *m* 1939, Rosemary Elizabeth, *d* of Thomas Edward Pooley; two *s* one *d. Educ:* Merchiston; Edinburgh Univ.; Ecole Supérieur d'électricité, Paris. MA; AMIEE; Ingénieur ESE. Commnd RAF, 1926; Dir of Signals, Air Min., 1944; retd 1947. Man. Dir, International Aeradio, 1947-58; Director: Carron Company, 1958-67; Royal Bank of Scotland, 1963-71. Chm., Edinburgh Airport Consultative Cttee, 1972. Mem. Queen's Body Guard for Scotland (Royal Company of Archers). DL: Linlithgowshire, 1963-72. Officer, US Legion of Merit, 1945. *Recreations:* shooting, gardening. *Address:* Whinmill Brae, Coltbridge Gardens, Edinburgh EH12 6AQ. *Club:* New (Edinburgh).

CADIEUX, Hon. Léo, PC 1965; OC 1975; Ambassador of Canada to France, 1970-75; *b* 28 May 1908; *s* of Joseph E. Cadieux and Rosa Paquette, both French Canadian; *m* 1962, Monique, *d* of Placide Plante; one *s. Educ:* Commercial Coll. of St Jerome and Seminary of Ste Thérèse de Blainville, Quebec. Editorial staff of La Presse, Montreal, Quebec, 1930-41; Associate Dir of Public Relations, Can. Army, 1941-44; War Corresp. for La Presse, Montreal, 1944; Mayor of St Antoine des Laurentides, Que., 1948. First elected to House of Commons, gen. elec., 1962; re-elected gen. elec., 1963, 1965, 1968; apptd Associate Minister of Nat. Defence, 1965; Minister of National

Defence, Canada, 1967-70. *Address:* 20 Driveway, Appt 1106, Ottawa, Canada.

CADMAN, family name of **Baron Cadman.**

CADMAN, 3rd Baron *cr* 1937, of Silverdale; **John Anthony Cadman;** farmer since 1964; *b* 3 July 1938; *s* of 2nd Baron Cadman and Marjorie Elizabeth Bunnis; *S* father, 1966; *m* 1975, Janet Hayes. *Educ:* Harrow; Selwyn Coll., Cambridge; Royal Agricultural Coll., Cirencester. *Heir: b* Hon. James Rupert Cadman, *b* 9 June 1944. *Address:* Eakley Manor Farm, Stoke Goldington, Newport Pagnell, Bucks. *T:* Stoke Goldington 249.

CADMAN, Surg. Rear-Adm. (D) Albert Edward; CB 1977; Director of Naval Dental Services, 1974-77; *b* 14 Oct. 1918; *m* 1st, 1946, Margaret Henrietta Tomkins-Russell (*d* 1974); one *s* one *d*; 2nd, 1975, Mary Croil Macdonald, Superintendent, WRNS. *Educ:* Dover Grammar Sch.; Guy's Hosp. Dental Sch. LDS RCS 1941. Surg. Lieut (D) RNVR, 1942; transf. to RN, 1947; Surg. Lt-Comdr (D) 1950; Surg. Comdr (D) 1956; Surg. Captain (D) 1967; served as Asst to Dir, Naval Dental Services, 1967-70; Comd Dental Surgeon on staff of Flag Officer, Naval Air Comd, 1970-74. QHDS 1974. *Recreations:* music, gardening, cricket, tennis, golf. *Address:* Solent House, 2 Solent Way, Alverstoke, Hants. *T:* Gosport 86648.

CADOGAN, family name of **Earl Cadogan.**

CADOGAN, 7th Earl, *cr* 1800; **William Gerald Charles Cadogan,** MC 1943; DL; Baron Cadogan, 1718; Viscount Chelsea, 1800; Baron Oakley, 1831; Lieut-Colonel Royal Wiltshire Yeomanry, RAC; Captain Coldstream Guards R of O until 1964 (retaining hon. rank of Lieut-Colonel); *b* 13 Feb. 1914; *s* of 6th Earl and Lilian Eleanora Marie (who *m* 2nd, 1941, Lt-Col H. E. Hambro, CBE; she *d* 1973), *d* of George Coxon, Craigleith, Cheltenham; *S* father, 1933; *m* 1st, 1936, Hon. Primrose Lillian Yarde-Buller (from whom he obtained a divorce, 1959), *y d* of 3rd Baron Churston; one *s* three *d*; 2nd, 1961, Cecilia, *y d* of Lt-Col H. K. Hamilton-Wedderburn, OBE. *Educ:* Eton; RMC Sandhurst. Served war of 1939-45 (MC); Hereditary Trustee of the British Museum, 1935-63; Mem. Chelsea Borough Council, 1953-59; Mayor of Chelsea, 1964. DL County of London, 1958. *Heir: s* Viscount Chelsea, *qv. Address:* 28 Cadogan Square, SW1. *T:* 01-584 2335; Snaigow, Murthly, Perthshire. *T:* Caputh 223. *Club:* White's.
See also Baron Lurgan, Baron Rockley.

CADOGAN, Prof. John Ivan George, FRS 1976; PhD, DSc London; FRSE, CChem, FRIC; Forbes Professor of Organic Chemistry, since 1969, and Head of Department, since 1974, Edinburgh University; *b* Pembrey, Carmarthenshire, 1930; *er s* of Alfred and Dilys Cadogan; *m* 1955, Margaret Jeanne, *d* of late William Evans, iron founder, Swansea; one *s* one *d*. *Educ:* Grammar Sch., Swansea; King's Coll., London, FKC 1976. Research at KCL, 1951-54. Civil Service Research Fellow, 1954-56; Lectr in Chemistry, King's Coll., London, 1956-63; Purdie Prof. of Chemistry and Head of Dept, St Salvator's Coll., Univ. of St Andrews, 1963-69. Member: Chemistry Cttee, SRC, 1967-71 (Chm. 1972-75); Science Bd, SRC, 1972-75; Council, Chem. Soc., 1966-69, 1973-76. Member: Council of Management, Macaulay Inst. for Soil Res., Aberdeen, 1969-; Council, St George's Sch. for Girls, 1974-; Council, RSE, 1975-. Tilden Lectr, Chem. Soc., 1971. Samuel Smiles Prize, KCL, 1950; Millar Thomson Medallist, KCL, 1951; Meldola Medallist, Soc. of Maccabaeans and Royal Inst. of Chemistry, 1959; Corday-Morgan Medallist, 1965, Chem. Soc. *Publications:* numerous scientific papers, mainly in Jl Chem. Soc. *Address:* Department of Chemistry, The King's Buildings, West Mains Road, Edinburgh EH9 3JJ. *T:* 031-667 1081. *Club:* Athenæum.

CADWALLADER, Air Vice-Marshal Howard George, CB 1974; RAF retd; Controller of Contracts to the Post Office, since 1974; *b* 16 March 1919; British; *m* 1950, Betty Ethel Samuels; no *c*. *Educ:* Hampton Grammar Sch., Mddx. MBIM, FInstPS. Sen. Equipment Staff Officer: HQ Transport Comd, 1963-65; HQ FEAF Singapore, 1965-68; Dep. Dir of Equipment 14 MoD (Air), 1968-69; Comdt of RAF Supply Control Centre, Hendon, 1969-72; Dir of Movts (RAF), MoD (Air), 1972-73; SASO HQ Support Comd, RAF, 1973-74. *Recreations:* golf, bridge. *Address:* 3 Greenway Close, Totteridge, N20 8ES. *Club:* Royal Air Force.

CADWALLADER, Sir John, Kt 1967; Chairman and Managing Director of Allied Mills Ltd since 1949; President, Bank of New South Wales, since 1959; *b* 25 Aug. 1902; *m* 1935, Helen Sheila Moxham; two *s* one *d*. *Educ:* Sydney Church of England Grammar Sch., NSW. *Recreations:* reading, golf. *Address:* 27 Marian Street, Killara, NSW 2071, Australia. *T:* 498 1974.

Clubs: Commonwealth (Canberra, ACT); Australian, Union, Royal Sydney Golf (all Sydney, NSW); Elanora Country (NSW).

CADZOW, Sir Norman (James Kerr), Kt 1959; VRD 1943; *s* of late William Cadzow and Jessie, *d* of James Kerr; *b* 21 Dec. 1912. *Educ:* Sedbergh Sch., Yorkshire. President, Unionist Party in Scotland, 1958; contested (U) Bothwell Div. of Lanarkshire, 1950 and 1951. Rector's Assessor, Glasgow Univ., 1959-63. Joined RNVR 1931, active service, 1939-45 (despatches). *Recreations:* golf and bridge. *Address:* Arden, Bothwell, Glasgow. *T:* Bothwell 853164.

CÆSAR, Irving; author-lyrist; Past President of Songwriters' Protective Association; Member Board of Directors, American Society of Composers, Authors and Publishers; *b* New York, 4 July 1895; *s* of Rumanian Jews. *Educ:* public school; Chappaqua Quaker Inst.; City Coll. of New York. Protégé of Ella Wheeler Wilcox, who, when he was a boy of nine, became interested in bits of verse he wrote and published at the time; at twenty became attached to the Henry Ford Peace Expedition, and spent nine months travelling through neutral Europe (during the War) as one of the secretaries of the Ford Peace Conference; returned to America, and became interested in writing for the musical comedy stage. *Publications:* most important work up to present time, No, No, Nanette; has written hundreds of songs and collaborated in many other musical comedies; writer and publisher of Sing a Song of Safety, a vol. of children's songs in use throughout the public and parochial schools of USA; also Sing a Song of Friendship, a series of songs based on human rights; in England: The Bamboula, Swanee, Tea for Two, I Want to be Happy, I Was So Young; author of "Peace by Wireless" proposal for freedom of international exchange of radio privilege between governments. *Recreations:* reading, theatre, swimming. *Address:* 1619 Broadway, New York, NY 10019, USA. *TA:* Cæsaring. *T:* Columbus 5-7868. *Clubs:* Friars, Green Room, City (New York).

CAFFIN, Albert Edward, CIE 1947; OBE 1946; Indian Police (retired); *b* 16 June 1902; *s* of Claud Carter and Lilian Edith Caffin, Southsea; *m* 1929, Hilda Elizabeth Wheeler, Bournemouth; no *c. Educ:* Portsmouth. Joined Indian Police as Asst Supt, Bombay Province, 1922; Asst Inspector General, Poona, 1939; Dep. Comr, Bombay, 1944, Comr of Police, Bombay, 1947. *Recreations:* yachting, tennis, etc. *Address:* 402 Belvedere, Main Road, Three Anchor Bay, Cape Town, S Africa. *Club:* Royal Bombay Yacht.

CAFFIN, A(rthur) Crawford; a Recorder of the Crown Court since 1972; solicitor since 1932; *b* 10 June 1910; *s* of Charles Crawford Caffin and Annie Rosila Caffin; *m* 1933, Mala Pocock; one *d. Educ:* King's Sch., Rochester. Asst Solicitor: to Norfolk CC, 1933-37; to Bristol Corporation, 1937-46. Partner in firm of R. L. Frank & Caffin, Solicitors, Truro, 1946-72; Consultant with that firm, 1972-. Pres., Cornwall Law Soc., 1960; Mem. Council, the Law Society, 1966-; Dep. Chm., Traffic Commissioners for Western Traffic Area, 1964-. *Recreation:* swimming. *Address:* Cotna House, Gorran, St Austell, Cornwall. *Clubs:* Junior Carlton; The Club (St Austell).

CAFFYN, Brig. Sir Edward (Roy), KBE 1963 (CBE 1945; OBE 1942); CB 1955; TD 1950; DL; Chairman, County of Sussex Territorial and Auxiliary Forces Association, 1947-67; Vice-Chairman, Council of Territorial and Auxiliary Forces Associations, 1961-66; *b* 27 May 1904; *s* of Percy Thomas Caffyn, Eastbourne; *m* 1st, 1929, Elsa Muriel, *d* of William Henry Nurse, Eastbourne; two *s*; 2nd, 1946, Delphine Angelique, *d* of Major William Chilton-Riggs. *Educ:* Eastbourne and Loughborough Colleges. Commissioned RE (TA), 1930. Raised and commanded an Army Field Workshop, 1939; served with 51st Highland Division in France, 1940; Brigadier, 1941; a Deputy Director, War Office, on formation of REME, 1942; served on Field Marshal Montgomery's staff as Director of Mechanical Engineering (despatches twice), 1943-45. JP Eastbourne, 1948, transferred East Sussex, 1960; Chairman, Hailsham Bench, 1962-74; DL Sussex, 1956; Chairman, Sussex Agricultural Wages Board, 1951-74. CC for East Sussex, 1958-69, Alderman, 1964, Vice-Chairman 1967; Chm., Sussex Police Authy, 1971-74. *Recreations:* shooting, fishing. *Address:* Norman Norris, Vines Cross, Heathfield, East Sussex. *T:* Horam Road 2674. *Club:* Royal Automobile.

CAGE, Edward Edwin Henry; General Manager, Craigavon Development Commission, 1966-73; *b* 15 May 1912; *s* of Edward H. Cage and A. M. Windiate; *m* 1938, Hilda W. M. Barber; no *c. Educ:* Cannock House Sch., Eltham; King's Coll., London. Articles, Chartered Accts, 1929-34; Kent CC, 1935-41; Borough Councils: Dagenham, 1941-42; Willesden, 1942-44;

Treas., Eton RDC, and Clerk, Jt Hosp Bd, 1944-47; Local Govt BC, 1947-48; Crawley Development Corp.: Chief Finance Officer, 1948-58, Gen. Manager, 1958-61; Chief Finance and Development Officer, Commn for New Towns, 1961-66. *Publications:* contrib. professional, etc., jls and newspapers. *Recreations:* golf, gardening. *Address:* Charters, Pitnie Lortie, Langport, Somerset. *Club:* English-Speaking Union.

CAHAL, Dr Dennis Abraham; Senior Principal Medical Officer, Department of Health and Social Security (formerly Ministry of Health), since 1963; *b* 1 Oct. 1921; *s* of Henry Cahal and Helen Wright; *m* 1948, Joan, *d* of Allan and Laura Grover; one *s*. *Educ:* Bradford Grammar Sch.; Univ. of Leeds. MB, ChB (Hons) Leeds, 1953; MD (Dist.) Leeds, 1959; MRCP 1968. RA, Indian Artillery and Special Allied Airborne Reconnaissance Force, 1939-46. Hospital appointments and general practice, 1953-55; Lecturer in Pharmacology, Univ. of Leeds, 1955-59; industrial research into drugs, 1959-62. Vis. Prof. of Pharmacology and Therapeutics, St Mary's Hosp. Med. Sch., London, 1967-69. Med. Assessor, Cttee on Safety of Drugs, 1963-70. *Publications:* various articles on drugs in scientific jls. *Recreations:* reading, cricket, the application of statistical methods to equine behaviour. *Address:* 207 Merryhill Road, Bushey, Herts.

CAHILL, Patrick Richard, CBE 1970 (OBE 1944); *b* 21 Feb. 1912; *er s* of late Patrick Francis and Nora Christina Cahill; *m* 1st, 1949, Gladys Lilian May Kemp (*d* 1969); one *s*; 2nd, 1969, Mary Frances Pottinger. *Educ:* Hitchin Grammar Sch. Joined Legal & General Assurance Soc. Ltd, 1929; Pensions Manager, 1948; Agency Manager, 1952; Asst Manager, 1954; Asst General Manager, 1957; Gen. Manager, 1958; Chief Exec., 1969-71; Mem. Board, 1969-77. Served War with RASC, 1940-45 (despatches, OBE); N Africa, Italy, and N Europe, 1st, 7th and 11th Armd Divs; rank of Lt-Col. Managing Dir, Gresham Life Assurance Soc. Ltd and Dir, Gresham Fire and Accident Insurance Soc. Ltd, 1958-72. A Vice-Pres., Chartered Insurance Inst., 1961-63, Pres., 1969; Pres., Insurance Charities, 1965-66; Chm., London Salvage Corps, 1964-65; Chm., British Insurance Assoc., 1967-69. *Address:* Flat G, 47 Beaumont Street, W1. *T:* 01-935 2608; Thorndene, Pluckley, Kent. *T:* Pluckley 306.

CAHILL, Most Rev. Thomas; *see* Canberra, Archbishop of, (RC).

CAHN, Sir Albert Jonas, 2nd Bt, *cr* 1934; Company Director; *b* 27 June 1924; *s* of Sir Julien Cahn, 1st Bt, and Phyllis Muriel, *d* of A. Wolfe, Bournemouth; *S* father, 1944; *m* 1948, Malka, *d* of late R. Bluestone; two *s* two *d*. *Educ:* Headmaster's House, Harrow. *Recreations:* cricket, horse riding, photography. *Heir: s* Julien Michael Cahn, *b* 15 Jan. 1951. *Address:* 10 Edgecoombe Close, Warren Road, Kingston upon Thames, Surrey. *T:* 01-942 6956.

CAHN, Charles Montague, CBE 1956; *b* 27 Dec. 1900; *yr s* of Gottfried Cahn and Lilian Juliet Cahn (*née* Montague); *m* 1939, Kathleen Rose, *d* of Auguste and Kathleen Thoumine; two *d*. *Educ:* Westminster Sch.; Christ Church, Oxford. BA 1923; MA 1968. Called to the Bar, Inner Temple, 1924. Served War of 1939-45 in Army (France and Middle East). Deputy Judge Advocate, 1945; Asst Judge Advocate-General, 1946; Deputy Judge Advocate-General, BAOR and RAF Germany (2 TAF), 1957-60; Vice Judge Advocate-General, 1963-67, retired 1967. Legal Chairman, Pensions Appeal Tribunals, 1967-77. *Recreation:* walking up and down hills. *Address:* Bowhill House, West Stoke, near Chichester, West Sussex.

CAIN; *see* Nall-Cain.

CAIN, Sir Edward (Thomas), Kt 1972; CBE 1966; Commissioner of Taxation, Australia, 1964-76; retired; *b* Maryborough, Qld, Australia, 7 Dec. 1916; *s* of Edward Victor and Kathleen Teresa Cain; *m* 1942, Marcia Yvonne Cain (*née* Parbery); one *s* one *d*. *Educ:* Nudgee Coll., Queensland; Univ. of Queensland (BA, LLB). Commonwealth Taxation Office: in Brisbane, Sydney, Perth and Canberra, 1936-. Served War, 2/9th Bn, AIF, 1939-43. *Recreations:* golf, fishing. *Address:* 99 Buxton Street, Deakin, Canberra, Australia. *T:* 811462. *Clubs:* Commonwealth, Royal Canberra Golf (Canberra); Royal Automobile (Melbourne).

CAIN, Maj.-Gen. George Robert T.; *see* Turner Cain.

CAINE, Michael; actor; *b* Old Kent Road, London, 14 March 1933 (Maurice Joseph Micklewhite); *s* of late Maurice and of Ellen Frances Marie Micklewhite; *m* 1st, 1955, Patricia Haines (marr. diss.); one *d*; 2nd, 1973, Shakira Baksh; one *d*. *Educ:* Wilson's Grammar Sch., Peckham. Began acting in youth club

drama gp. Served in Army, Berlin and Korea, 1951-53. Asst Stage Manager, Westminster Rep., Horsham, Sx, 1953; actor, Lowestoft Rep., 1953-55; Theatre Workshop, London, 1955; numerous TV appearances (over 100 plays), 1957-63; *play:* Next Time I'll Sing for You, Arts, 1963; *films:* A Hill in Korea, 1956; How to Murder a Rich Uncle, 1958; Zulu, 1964; The Ipcress File, 1965; Alfie, 1966; The Wrong Box, 1966; Gambit, 1966; Hurry Sundown, 1967; Woman Times Seven, 1967; Deadfall, 1967; The Magus, 1968; Battle of Britain, 1968; Play Dirty, 1968; The Italian Job, 1969; Too Late the Hero, 1970; The Last Valley, 1971; Get Carter, 1971; Zee & Co., 1972; Kidnapped, 1972; Pulp, 1972; Sleuth, 1973; The Black Windmill, Marseilles Contract, The Wilby Conspiracy, 1974; Fat Chance, The Romantic Englishwoman, The Man who would be King, Harry and Walter Go to New York, 1975; The Eagle has Landed, A Bridge too Far, The Bankers, 1976. *Recreations:* cinema, theatre, travel, gardening. *Address:* Clewer, Berkshire.

CAINE, Michael Harris; Vice-Chairman, since 1973, Chief Executive, since 1975, Director, since 1964, Booker McConnell Ltd; *b* 17 June 1927; *s* of Sir Sydney Caine, *qv*; *m* 1952, Janice Denise (*née* Mercer); one *s* one *d*. *Educ:* Bedales; Lincoln Coll., Oxford; George Washington Univ., USA. Joined Booker McConnell Ltd, 1952; Chm., Bookers Shopkeeping Holdings Ltd, 1963; Director, Acklands Ltd. 1967. Chm., Council for Technical Educn and Training for Overseas Countries, 1973-75. Member: Council, Inst. of Race Relations, 1969-72; Council, Bedford Coll., London, 1966-; Governing Body, Inst. of Develt Studies, Sussex Univ., 1975-. *Address:* Wilton House, 33 High Street, Hungerford, Berks. *T:* Hungerford 2861. *Club:* Reform.

CAINE, Sir Sydney, KCMG 1947 (CMG 1945); Director of the London School of Economics and Political Science, 1957-Sept. 1967; *b* 27 June 1902; *s* of Harry Edward Caine; *m* 1st, 1925, Muriel Anne (*d* 1962), *d* of A. H. Harris, MA; one *s*; 2nd, 1965, Doris Winifred Folkard (*d* 1973); 3rd, 1975, Elizabeth, *d* of late J. Crane Nicholls and *widow* of Sir Eric Bowyer, KCB, KBE. *Educ:* Harrow County Sch.; London Sch. of Economics. BSc (Econ.) 1st Class Hons 1922. Asst Inspector of Taxes, 1923-26; entered Colonial Office, 1926; Sec., West Indian Sugar Commn, 1929; Sec., UK Sugar Industry Inquiry Cttee, 1934; Fin. Sec., Hong Kong, 1937; Asst Sec., Colonial Office, 1940; Member Anglo-American Caribbean Commission, 1942; Financial Adviser to Sec. of State for the Colonies, 1942; Assistant Under-Secretary of State, Colonial Office, 1944; Deputy Under-Secretary of State, Colonial Office, 1947-48; Third Secretary, Treasury, 1948; Head of UK Treasury and Supply Delegn, Washington, 1949-51; Mem., Financial Mission to Ceylon, 1951; Vice-Chancellor, Univ. of Malaya, 1952-56. Chairman: British Caribbean Federation Fiscal Commission, 1955; Internat. Inst. of Educational Planning, 1963-70; Governor (new bd), Reserve Bank of Rhodesia, 1965-67; Planning Bd of Independent Univ., 1969-76. Mem., ITA, 1960-67 (Dep. Chm., 1964-67). Coordinator, Indonesian Sugar Study, 1971-72. Hon. LLD Univ. of Malaya, 1956. *Publications:* The Foundation of the London School of Economics, 1963; British Universities: Purpose and Prospects, 1969. *Recreations:* reading, walking. *Address:* Buckland House, Tarn Road, Hindhead, Surrey. *Club:* Reform.

See also M. H. Caine.

CAINES, John; Secretary, National Enterprise Board, since 1977; *b* 13 Jan. 1933; *s* of John Swinburne Caines and Ethel May Stenlake; *m* 1963, Mary Large; one *s* two *d*. *Educ:* Westminster Sch.; Christ Church, Oxford (MA). Asst Principal, Min. of Supply, 1957; Asst Private Sec., Min. of Aviation, 1960-61; Principal, Min. of Aviation, 1961-64; Civil Air Attaché in Middle East, 1964-66; Manchester Business Sch., 1967; Asst Sec., BoT, 1968; Sec., Commn on Third London Airport, 1968-71; Asst Sec., DTI, 1971-72; Principal Private Sec. to Sec. of State for Trade and Industry, 1972-74; Under-Sec., Dept of Trade, 1974-77. *Recreations:* travel, music, gardening, theatre. *Address:* 19 College Road, Dulwich, SE21 7BG. *T:* 01-693 5537.

CAIRD, Most Rev. Donald Arthur Richard; *see* Meath and Kildare, Bishop of.

CAIRD, Rev. George Bradford, MA(Cantab), DPhil, DD(Oxon); FBA 1973; Dean Ireland's Professor of Exegesis of Holy Scripture, Oxford, since 1977; *b* 9 July 1917; *s* of George Caird and Esther Love Caird (*née* Bradford), both of Dundee; *m* 1945, Viola Mary Newport; three *s* one *d*. *Educ:* King Edward's Sch., Birmingham; Peterhouse, Cambridge; Mansfield Coll., Oxford. Minister of Highgate Congregational Church, London, 1943-46; Prof. of OT Lang. and Lit., St Stephen's Coll., Edmonton, Alberta, 1946-50; Prof. of NT Lang. and Lit., McGill Univ., Montreal, 1950-59; Principal, United Theological Coll., Montreal, 1955-59; Sen. Tutor, 1959-70, Principal, 1970-77,

Mansfield Coll., Oxford; Reader in Biblical Studies, Oxford Univ., 1969-77. Grinfield Lecturer on the Septuagint, Oxford Univ., 1961-65. Moderator of General Assembly of URC, 1975-76. Hon. DD: St Stephen's Coll., Edmonton, 1959; Diocesan Coll., Montreal, 1959; Aberdeen Univ., 1966. *Publications:* The Truth of the Gospel, 1950; The Apostolic Age, 1955; Principalities and Powers, 1956; The Gospel according to St Luke, 1963; The Revelation of St John the Divine, 1966; Our Dialogue with Rome, 1967; Paul's Letters from Prison, 1976; contribs to: Interpreter's Dictionary of the Bible; Hastings Dictionary of the Bible; Jl of Theological Studies; New Testament Studies; Expository Times. *Recreations:* bird-watching, chess, music. *Address:* The Queen's College, Oxford.

CAIRD, William Douglas Sime; Registrar, Family Division of High Court (formerly Probate, Divorce and Admiralty Division), since 1964; *b* 21 Aug. 1917; *er s* of William Sime Caird and Elsie Amy Caird; *m* 1946, Josephine Mary, *d* of Peter and Elizabeth Seeney, Stratford on Avon; no *c. Educ:* Rutlish Sch., Merton. Entered Principal Probate Registry, 1937; Estabt Officer, 1954; Sec., 1959; Mem., Matrimonial Causes Rule Cttee, 1968. *Publications:* Consulting Editor, Rayden on Divorce, 10th edn 1967, 11th edn 1971, 12th edn 1974. *Recreation:* sailing. *Address:* 107 Salisbury Road, Worcester Park, Surrey. *T:* 01-337 0456.

CAIRNCROSS, Sir Alexander Kirkland, (Sir Alec Cairncross), KCMG 1967 (CMG 1950); FBA 1961; Master of St Peter's College, Oxford, since 1969; Chancellor, University of Glasgow, since 1972; *b* 11 Feb. 1911; 3rd *s* of Alexander Kirkland and Elizabeth Andrew Cairncross, Lesmahagow, Scotland; *m* 1943, Mary Frances Glynn; three *s* two *d. Educ:* Hamilton Academy; Glasgow and Cambridge Univs. Univ. Lectr, 1935-39; Civil Servant, 1940-45; Dir of Programmes, Min. of Aircraft Production, 1945; Economic Advisory Panel, Berlin, 1945-46; Mem. of Staff of The Economist, 1946. Mem. of Wool Working Party, 1946; Economic Adviser to Board of Trade, 1946-49; Economic Adviser to Organisation for European Economic Co-operation, 1949-50; Prof. of Applied Economics, Univ. of Glasgow, 1951-61; Dir, Economic Development Inst., Washington DC, 1955-56; Economic Adviser to HM Govt, 1961-64; Head of Govt Economic Service, 1964-69. Chm., independent advrs on reassessment of Channel Tunnel project, 1974-75; Chm., Local Development Cttee, 1951-52; Member: Crofting Commn, 1951-54; Phillips Cttee, 1953-54; Anthrax Cttee, 1957-59; Radcliffe Cttee, 1957-59; Cttee on N Ireland, 1971; Council of Management, Nat. Inst. of Economic and Social Research; Council, Trade Policy Res. Centre; Court of Governors, London Sch. of Economics; Council, Royal Economic Soc. (Pres., 1968-70); Council, Oxford Centre for Management Studies. President: Scottish Economic Soc., 1969-71; Section F, British Assoc. for Advancement of Science, 1969; British Assoc. for Advancement of Science, 1970-71; GPDST, 1972-; Trustee, Urwick Orr and Partners. Editor, Scottish Journal of Political Economy, 1954-61. For. Hon. Mem., Amer. Acad. of Arts and Scis, 1973. Hon. LLD: Mount Allison Univ., 1962; Glasgow Univ., 1966; Exeter Univ., 1969; Hon. DLitt: Reading Univ., 1968; Heriot-Watt Univ., 1969; Hon, DSc(Econ.): Univ. of Wales, 1971; QUB, 1972; DUniv Stirling, 1973. *Publications:* Introduction to Economics, 1944; Home and Foreign Investment, 1870-1913, 1953; Monetary Policy in a Mixed Economy, 1960; Economic Development and the Atlantic Provinces, 1961; Factors in Economic Development, 1962; Essays in Economic Management, 1971; Control over Long-term International Capital Movements, 1973; Inflation, Growth and International Finance, 1975; (ed) Britain's Economic Prospects Reconsidered, 1971; (jtly) Economic Policy for the European Community, 1975; (ed jtly) Employment, Income Distribution and Development Strategy, 1976. *Recreations:* colour photography, travel. *Address:* The Master's Lodgings, St Peter's College, Oxford. *T:* Oxford 40554. *Club:* United Oxford & Cambridge University.

CAIRNCROSS, Neil Francis, CB 1971; Deputy Under-Secretary of State, Home Office, since Nov. 1972; *b* 29 July 1920; *s* of late James and Olive Hunter Cairncross; *m* 1947, Eleanor Elizabeth Leisten; two *s* one *d. Educ:* Charterhouse; Oriel Coll., Oxford. Royal Sussex Regt, 1940-45. Called to the Bar, 1948. Home Office, 1948; a Private Sec. to the Prime Minister, 1955-58; Sec., Royal Commn on the Press, 1961-62; Dep. Sec., Cabinet Office, 1970-72; Dep. Sec., NI Office, March-Nov. 1972. *Recreations:* painting, gardening. *Address:* 28 Cassiobury Park Avenue, Watford, Herts. *T:* Watford 23856. *Club:* United Oxford & Cambridge University.

CAIRNS, family name of **Earl Cairns.**

CAIRNS, 5th Earl, *cr* 1878; **David Charles Cairns,** GCVO 1972 (KCVO 1969); CB 1960; Rear-Admiral; DL; Baron Cairns, 1867; Viscount Garmoyle, 1878; Her Majesty's Marshal of the Diplomatic Corps, 1962-71; Extra Equerry to the Queen, since 1972; *b* 3 July 1909; *s* of 4th Earl and Olive (*d* 1952), *d* of late J. P. Cobbold, MP; *S* father, 1946; *m* 1936, Barbara Jeanne Harrisson, *y d* of Sydney H. Burgess, Heathfield, Altrincham, Cheshire; two *s* one *d. Educ:* RNC Dartmouth. Served War of 1939-45 (despatches); Dep. Dir, Signal Dept, Admiralty, 1950, comd 7th Frigate Sqdn, 1952; HMS Ganges, 1953-54; Student Imperial Defence Coll., 1955; comd HMS Superb, 1956-57; Baghdad Pact Plans and Training Div., Admiralty, 1958; Pres., RNC Greenwich, 1958-61; retired. Pres., Navy League, 1966. DL Suffolk, 1973. *Heir: s* Viscount Garmoyle, *qv. Address:* Clopton Hall, near Woodbridge, Suffolk. *T:* Grundisburgh 248. *Club:* Turf.

CAIRNS, Rt. Hon. Sir David (Arnold Scott), PC 1970; Kt 1955; a Lord Justice of Appeal, 1970-77; *b* 5 March 1902; *s* of late David Cairns, JP, Freeman of Sunderland, and Sarah Scott Cairns; *m* 1932, Irene Cathery Phillips; one *s* two *d. Educ:* Bede Sch., Sunderland; Pembroke Coll., Cambridge (Scholar) (Hon. Fellow, 1973); Senior Optime. MA, LLB (Cantab); BSc (London); Certificate of Honour, Bar Final, 1925. Called to Bar, Middle Temple, 1926; Bencher 1958. KC 1947. Liberal Candidate at By-election, Epsom Div., 1947. Mem. of Leatherhead UDC, 1948-54; Chm., Liberal Party Commn on Trade Unions, 1948-49; Mem. of Liberal Party Cttee, 1951-53; Chm., Monopolies and Restrictive Practices Commn, 1954-56; Recorder of Sunderland, 1957-60; Comr of Assize, 1957 (Midland Circuit), May 1959 (Western Circuit), Nov. 1959 (Wales and Chester Circuit); Judge of the High Court, Probate, Divorce and Admiralty Div., 1960-70. Chairman: Statutory Cttee of Pharmaceutical Soc. of Great Britain, 1952-60; Executive of Justice (British Section of International Commn of Jurists), 1959-60; Minister of Aviation's Cttee on Accident Investigation and Licence Control, 1959-60; Govt Adv. Cttee on Rhodesian Travel Restrictions, 1968-70. *Recreations:* swimming, gardening. *Address:* Applecroft, Ashtead, Surrey. *T:* Ashtead 74132.

CAIRNS, Air Vice-Marshal Geoffrey Crerar, CBE 1970; AFC; Commander, Southern Maritime Air Region, since 1976; *b* 1926; *s* of late Dr J. W. Cairns, MD, MCh, DPH and Marion Cairns; *m* 1948, Carol, *d* of Harold Ivan Frederick Evernden, MBE; four *d. Educ:* Loretto School, Musselburgh; Cambridge Univ. Joined RAF, 1944; served: Sqdns 43 and 93, Italy; Sqdn 73, Malta, 1944-49; England 1941-51; Adjutant, Hong Kong Auxiliary Air Force; test pilot A&AEE, Boscombe Down, 1960; Jt Planning Staff, MoD, 1961; Chief Instructor, Helicopters, CFS, RAF Ternhill, 1963; ssc 1966; Supt Flying A&AEE 1968; Dir, Defence Operational Requirements Staffs, MoD, 1970; Commandant, Boscombe Down, 1972-74; ACAS (Op. Requirements), MoD, 1974-76. Group Captain, 1966; Air Commodore, 1970; Air Vice-Marshal, 1974. *Recreations:* golf, railways. *Address:* c/o Lloyds Bank, Cox and King's Branch, 6 Pall Mall, SW1.

CAIRNS, Hugh John Forster; DM; FRS 1974; Head of Imperial Cancer Research Fund Mill Hill Laboratories, since 1973; *b* 21 Nov. 1922. *Educ:* Oxford Univ. BA 1943; BM, BCh 1946; DM 1952. Surg. Registrar, Radcliffe Infirmary, Oxford, 1945; Med. Intern, Postgrad. Med. Sch., London, 1946; Paediatric Intern, Royal Victoria Infirmary, Newcastle, 1947; Chem. Pathologist, Radcliffe Infirmary, 1947-49; Virologist, Hall Inst., Melbourne, Aust., 1950-51; Virus Research Inst., Entebbe, Uganda, 1952-54; Research Fellow, then Reader, Aust. Nat. Univ., Canberra, 1955-63; Rockefeller Research Fellow, California Inst. of Technology, 1957; Nat. Insts of Health Fellow, Cold Spring Harbor, NY, 1960-61; Dir, Cold Spring Harbor Lab. of Quantitative Biology, 1963-68 (Staff Mem., 1968-); Prof of Biology (Hon.), State Univ. of New York, Stony Brook, 1968-73, Amer. Cancer Soc. Prof. 1968-73. *Address:* Imperial Cancer Research Fund Mill Hill Laboratories, Burtonhole Lane, NW7 1AD. *T:* 01-959 3236; Manor End, Partingdale Lane, NW7. *T:* 01-346 8180.

CAIRNS, Dr James Ford; MHR (ALP) for Lalor, since 1969 (for Yarra, 1955-69); *b* 4 Oct. 1914; *s* of James John Cairns and Letitia Cairns (*née* Ford); *m* 1939, Gwendolyn Olga Robb; two *s. Educ:* Melton/Sunbury State Sch.; Northcote High Sch.; Melbourne Univ. MComm and PhD (Melb.). Australian Estates Co. Ltd, 1932; Victoria Police Force, 1935. Served War, AIF, 1945. Melbourne Univ.: Sen. Tutor, Lectr, Sen. Lectr (Economic Hist.), 1946-55. Minister for Overseas Trade, 1972-74; Treasurer of Australia, 1974-75; Dep. Prime Minister, 1974-75; Minister for the Environment, Australia, 1975. *Publications:* Australia, 1951 (UK); Living with Asia, 1965; The Eagle and the Lotus,

1969; Tariffs or Planning, 1970; Silence Kills, 1970; The Quiet Revolution, 1972; numerous articles in jls and press. *Recreations:* sleeping, reading. *Address:* 21 Wattle Road, Hawthorn, Victoria 3122, Australia. *T:* 819-1929.

CAIRNS, James George Hamilton Dickson; Chief Architect and Director of Works, Home Office, since 1976; *b* 17 Sept. 1920; *s* of Percival Cairns and Christina Elliot Cairns; *m* 1944, G. Elizabeth Goodman; one *d*. *Educ:* Hillhead High Sch., Glasgow; London Polytechnic. ARIBA. Served War, Royal Corps of Signals (Intell.), 1940-46. Architects' Dept, GLC, 1946-76. Divisional Architect, Thamesmead New Town, awarded Sir Patrick Abercrombie Prize by Internat. Union of Architects, 1969. *Recreations:* golf, sailing. *Address:* Robin Wood, Birds Hill Drive, Oxshott, Surrey. *T:* Oxshott 2904. *Club:* Royal Automobile.

CAIRNS, Sir Joseph Foster, Kt 1972; JP; Lord Mayor of Belfast, 1969-72; *b* 27 June 1920; *s* of Frederick and Janette Cairns; *m* 1944, Helena McCullough; one *s* one *d*. Joined Family Business, 1935; Managing Director, J. Cairns Ltd, 1945-; Chm., Lynley Develt Co. Ltd, 1964-. Member (Unionist), Belfast Corporation, Clifton Ward, 1952-; Dep. Lord Mayor, 1964-65; Member: Senate of Northern Ireland, 1969-72; Senate, QUB, 1969-72. Contested (Unionist): Belfast Central, 1953; Oldpark, 1969. JP Belfast, 1963; High Sheriff of Belfast, 1963. *Recreations:* family life, travel. *Address:* Amaranth, Craigdarragh Road, Helens Bay, Northern Ireland. *T:* Helens Bay 3602.

CAIRNS, Julia, (Mrs Paul Davidson); writer and lecturer; Vice-President: London and Overseas Flower Arrangement Society; Society of Women Writers and Journalists; *o c* of late H. W. Akers, Oxford; *m* 1st, 1915, Frank H. James, The Royal Scots; 2nd, 1925, Capt. Paul Davidson, late 12th Royal Lancers (*d* 1942). *Educ:* Oxford. Entered journalism as a free-lance; Woman Editor of The Ideal Home, 1924; House and Home Director of Woman's Journal, 1927; Editor-in-Chief Weldons Publications, 1929-55; Home Editor, The Queen, 1956-58. President Women's Press Club of London Ltd, 1947 and 1948. *Publications:* Home-Making, 1950; How I Became a Journalist, 1960. *Recreation:* gardening. *Club:* University Women's.

CAITHNESS, 20th Earl of, *cr* 1455; **Malcolm Ian Sinclair,** ARICS; Baron Berriedale, 1455; Bt 1631; *b* 3 Nov. 1948; *s* of 19th Earl of Caithness, CVO, CBE, DSO, DL, JP; *S* father, 1965; *m* 1975, Diana Caroline, *d* of Major Richard Coke, MC. *Educ:* Marlborough; Royal Agric. Coll., Cirencester. *Heir:* kinsman Sir John Sinclair, Bt, *qv*. *Address:* Ranger's Lodge, Charlbury, Oxfordshire.

CAITHNESS, Archdeacon of; *see* Hadfield, Ven. J. C.

CAKOBAU, Ratu Sir George (Kadavulevu), GCMG 1973; GCVO 1977; OBE 1953; Governor-General of Fiji, since 1973; *b* 1911; *s* of Ratu Popi Epeli Seniloli Cakobau; *m* Adi Lelea S. Balekiwai, *d* of Vilikesa Balekiwai. *Educ:* Queen Victoria Sch.; Newington Coll., Australia; Wanganui Technical Coll., NZ. Served War, 1939-45; Captain, Fiji Military Forces. Member: Council of Chiefs, Fiji, 1938-72; Legislative Council, Fiji, 1951-70; Minister for Fijian Affairs and Local Government, 1970-71; Minister without Portfolio, 1971-72. KStJ 1973. *Address:* Government House, Suva, Fiji.

CALCUTT, David Charles, QC 1972; a Recorder of the Crown Court, since 1972; Chancellor of Diocese of Bristol and of Diocese of Exeter, since 1971; *b* 2 Nov. 1930; *s* of late Henry Calcutt, Peterborough; *m* 1969, Barbara Ann, *d* of late Vivian Walker, Stony Stratford. *Educ:* Christ Church, Oxford (Chorister); Cranleigh Sch. (Music Schol. and St Nicholas Schol.); King's Coll., Cambridge (Choral Schol.). MA, LLB, MusB. Military Service, 1949-50, Captain 1950. Stewart of Rannoch Schol. 1952, Edward Gollin Prizeman 1953, College Prizeman 1954, Cambridge. Called to Bar, Middle Temple, 1955; Garraway Rice Prizeman 1956, Harmsworth Law Schol. 1956. Dir, Edington Music Festival, 1956-64. In practice at Common Law Bar, London, and on Western Circuit, 1957-; staff of The Times, 1957-66. Governor, Cranleigh Sch., 1963-. Mem. Gen. Council of Bar, 1968-72 (Exec. Cttee, 1971-72); Dep. Chm., Somerset QS, 1970-71; Member: Crown Court Rules Cttee, 1971-77; Criminal Injuries Compensation Bd, 1977-. Mem., Legal Adv. Commn, Gen. Synod, 1973-. Dept of Trade Inspector, Cornhill Consolidated Group Ltd, 1974-77. *Recreation:* living on Exmoor. *Address:* Lamb Building, Temple, EC4; 5 Essex Court, Temple, EC4; Colebrook House, Winchester.

CALCUTTA, Archbishop of, (RC), since 1969; **His Eminence Lawrence Trevor Cardinal Picachy,** SJ; *b* 7 Aug. 1916; Indian.

Educ: St Joseph's College, Darjeeling and various Indian Seminaries. 1952-60: Headmaster of St Xavier's School, Principal of St Xavier's College, Rector of St Xavier's, Calcutta. Parish Priest of Basanti, large village of West Bengal, 1960-62; (first) Bishop of Jamshedpur, 1962-69, Apostolic Administrator of Jamshedpur, 1969-70. Cardinal, 1976. Pres., Catholic Bishops' Conf. of India, 1976- (Vice-Pres., 1972-75). *Address:* Archbishop's House, 32 Park Street, Calcutta 700016, India. *T:* Calcutta 44-4666.

CALCUTTA, Bishop of, since 1970; **Rt. Rev. Joseph Amritanand;** *b* Amritsar, 17 Feb. 1917; *m* ; one *s* one *d*. *Educ:* District Board School, Toba Tek Singh, Punjab; Forman Christian Coll., Lahore, Punjab Univ. (BA); Bishop's College, Calcutta; Wycliffe Hall, Oxford. Deacon 1941, priest 1943; Missionary-in-charge of CMS Mission Field, Gojra, 1946-48; Bishop of Assam, 1949-62; Bishop of Lucknow, 1962-70; translated, after inauguration of Church of North India, Nov. 1970; Bishop of Durgapur, 1972-74. *Address:* Bishop's House, 51 Chowringhee Road, Calcutta 700071, India. *T:* 44-5259.

CALDECOTE, 2nd Viscount *cr* 1939, of Bristol; **Robert Andrew Inskip;** DSC 1941; Chairman: Delta Metal Co., since 1972; Legal and General Assurance Society, since 1977; *b* 8 Oct. 1917; *o s* of Thomas Walker Hobart Inskip, 1st Viscount Caldecote, PC, CBE, and Lady Augusta Orr Ewing (*d* 1967), widow of Charles Orr Ewing, MP for Ayr Burghs and *e d* of 7th Earl of Glasgow; *S* father, 1947; *m* 1942, Jean Hamilla, *d* of late Rear-Adm. H. D. Hamilton; one *s* two *d*. *Educ:* Eton Coll.; King's Coll., Cambridge. BA Cantab 1939; MA 1944. RNVR, 1939-45; RNC Greenwich, 1946-47; an Asst Manager, Vickers-Armstrong Naval Yard, Walker-on-Tyne, 1947-48; Mem., Church Assembly, 1950-55; Fellow, King's Coll., and Lectr, Engineering Dept, Cambridge Univ., 1948-55; Man. Dir, English Electric Aviation, 1960-63; Dep. Man. Dir, British Aircraft Corp., 1961-67 (Dir, 1960-69); Dir, English Electric Co., 1953-69. Chairman: EDC Movement of Exports, 1965-72; Export Council for Europe, 1970-71. President: Soc. of British Aerospace Cos, 1965-66; Internat. Assoc. of Aeronautical and Space Equipment Manufacturers, 1966-68; Parliamentary and Scientific Cttee, 1966-69. Director: Consolidated Gold Fields, 1969-; Lloyds Bank, 1975-. Member: Review Bd for Govt Contracts, 1969-76; Inflation Accounting Cttee, 1974-75; Engineering Industries Council, 1975-. Chm., Design Council, 1972-. Pro-Chancellor, Cranfield Inst. of Technology, 1976-. Mem. UK Delegn to UN, 1952; Fellow, Eton Coll., 1953-72; Hon. DSc Cranfield, 1976; Hon. Fellow, SIAD, 1976; Pres., Dean Close Sch.; Governor, St Lawrence Coll. CEng, FIMechE; FIEE; MRINA. *Recreations:* sailing, shooting, golf. *Heir: s* Hon. Piers James Hampden Inskip [*b* 20 May 1947; *m* 1970, Susan Bridget, *d* of late W. P. Mellen]. *Address:* Orchard Cottage, South Harting, Petersfield, Hants. *T:* Harting 264. *Clubs:* Pratt's, Boodle's; Royal Ocean Racing, Royal Yacht Squadron.

CALDER; *see* Ritchie-Calder.

CALDER, John Mackenzie; Managing Director, John Calder (Publishers) Ltd and Calder & Boyars Ltd, since 1950; *b* 25 Jan. 1927; *e s* of James Calder, Ardargie, Forgandenny, Perthshire, and Lucianne Wilson, Montreal, Canada; *m* 1st, 1949, Mary Ann Simmonds; one *d*; 2nd, 1960, Bettina Jonic (marr. diss. 1975); one *d*. *Educ:* Gilling Castle, Yorks; Bishops College Sch., Canada; McGill Univ.; Sir George Williams Coll.; Zürich Univ. Studied political economy; subseq. worked in Calders Ltd (timber co.), Director; resigned, 1957, after takeover by Great Universal Stores; founded John Calder (Publishers) Ltd, 1950 (run as a hobby until 1957; name changed to Calder & Boyars Ltd, 1965). Organiser of literary confs for Edinburgh Festival, 1962 and 1963, and Harrogate Festival, 1969. Founded Ledlanet Nights, 1963, in Kinross-shire (four seasons per year, opera, drama, music, etc). Acquired book-selling business of Better Books, London, 1969, expanded Edinburgh, 1971. Active in fields related to the arts and on many cttees; Co-founder, Defence of Literature and the Arts Society; Chm., Fedn of Scottish Theatres, 1972-74. Contested (L): Kinross and W Perthshire, 1970; Hamilton, Oct. 1974; Prospective Parly Cand., Dunfermline. FRSA 1974. Chevalier des Arts et des Lettres, 1975. *Publications:* (ed) A Samuel Beckett Reader; (ed) Beckett at 60; (ed) The Nouveau Roman Reader; (ed) Gambit International Drama Review, etc; articles in many jls. *Recreations:* writing (several plays, stories; criticism, etc; translations); music, theatre, opera, reading, chess, lecturing, conversation; ski-ing, travelling, promoting good causes, fond of good food and wine. *Address:* c/o Calder & Boyars Ltd, 18 Brewer Street, W1. *Clubs:* Caledonian, Hurlingham; Scottish Arts, Scottish Liberal (Edinburgh).

CALDER, Air Vice-Marshal Malcolm Frederick, CB 1957; CBE 1947; Chief of Air Staff, RNZAF, since 1958; Chairman, New Zealand Chiefs of Staff Committee, 1960-62, retired; *b* 1907; *s* of late Andrew Calder; *m* 1935, Margaret Emily, *d* of Henry Mandeno, architect, Dunedin, NZ; one *s* one *d*. *Educ:* Christ Church Boys' High Sch., NZ; University Coll., Canterbury, NZ (LLB). Joined RAF, 1931; RNZAF, 1939; served War of 1939-45 in NZ and Pacific; Air Member for Personnel, Air Board, NZ, 1945-47, and 1952-53; Air Cdre 1952; NZ Senior Air Liaison Officer, London, 1954-56; served in Malaya, 1957-58. *Recreations:* fishing and golf. *Address:* Herekiekie Street, Turangi, New Zealand. *Club:* United Services (Wellington, NZ).

CALDER, Nigel David Ritchie, MA; science writer; *b* 2 Dec. 1931; *e s* of Baron Ritchie-Calder, *qv*; *m* 1954, Elisabeth Palmer; two *s* three *d*. *Educ:* Merchant Taylors' Sch.; Sidney Sussex Coll., Cambridge. Physicist, Mullard Research Laboratories, 1954-56; Editorial staff, New Scientist, 1956-66; Science Editor, 1960-62; Editor, 1962-66. Science Correspondent, New Statesman, 1959-62 and 1966-71; Chairman, Assoc. of British Science Writers, 1962-64. TV series, The Whole Universe Show, 1977. (Jtly) UNESCO Kalinga Prize for popularisation of science, 1972. *Publications:* Electricity Grows Up, 1958; Robots, 1958; Radio Astronomy, 1958; (ed) The World in 1984, 1965; The Environment Game, 1967; (ed) Unless Peace Comes, 1968; Technopolis: Social Control of the Uses of Science, 1969; The Violent Universe (TV programme and book), 1969; Living Tomorrow, 1970; The Mind of Man (TV programme and book), 1970; The Restless Earth (TV programme and book), 1972; (ed) Nature in the Round: A Guide to Environmental Science, 1973; The Life Game (TV programme and book), 1973; The Weather Machine (TV programme and book), 1974; The Human Conspiracy (TV programme and book), 1975-76; The Key to the Universe (TV programme and book), 1976; Spaceships of the Mind (TV series and book), 1978. *Recreation:* sailing. *Address:* 8 The Chase, Furnace Green, Crawley, W Sussex RH10 6HW. *T:* Crawley 26693. *Club:* Athenæum.

CALDER, Ritchie; *see* Ritchie-Calder, Baron.

CALDER-MARSHALL, Arthur; author; *b* 19 Aug. 1908; *s* of late Arthur Grotjan Calder-Marshall and Alice Poole; *m* 1934, Violet Nancy Sales; two *d*. *Educ:* St Paul's Sch.; Hertford Coll., Oxford. *Publications: novels:* Two of a Kind, 1933; About Levy, 1933; At Sea, 1934; Dead Centre, 1935; Pie in the Sky, 1937; The Way to Santiago, 1940; A Man Reprieved, 1949; Occasion of Glory, 1955; The Scarlet Boy, 1961, rev. edn 1962; *short stories:* Crime against Cania, 1934; A Pink Doll, 1935; A Date with a Duchess, 1937; *for children:* The Man from Devil's Island, 1958; Fair to Middling, 1959; Lone Wolf: the story of Jack London, 1961; *travel:* Glory Dead, 1939; The Watershed, 1947; *biography:* No Earthly Command, 1957; Havelock Ellis, 1959; The Enthusiast, 1962; The Innocent Eye, 1963; Lewd, Blasphemous and Obscene, 1972; The Two Duchesses, 1977; *autobiography:* The Magic of My Youth, 1951; *miscellaneous:* Challenge to Schools: public school education, 1935; The Changing Scene, 1937; The Book Front, ed J. Lindsay, 1947; Wish You Were Here: the art of Donald McGill, 1966; Prepare to Shed Them Now...: the biography and ballads of George R. Sims, 1968; The Grand Century of the Lady, 1976; *essays:* Sterne, in The English Novelists, ed D. Verschoyle, 1936; Films, in Mind in Chains, ed C. Day Lewis; *edited:* Tobias Smollett, Selected Writings, 1950; J. London, The Bodley Head Jack London, Vols 1-4, 1963-66; Charles Dickens, David Copperfield, 1967; Nicholas Nickleby, 1968, Oliver Twist, 1970; Bleak House, 1976; The Life of Benvenuto Cellini, 1968; Jack London, The Call of the Wild, and other stories, 1969; Jane Austen, Emma, 1970; Thomas Paine, Common Sense and the Rights of Man, 1970. *Address:* c/o Elaine Greene Ltd, 31 Newington Green, N16 9PW.

CALDERBANK, Prof. Philip Hugh; Professor of Chemical Engineering, University of Edinburgh, since 1960; *b* 6 March 1919; *s* of Leonard and Rhoda Elizabeth Calderbank; *m* 1941, Kathleen Mary (*née* Taylor); one *s* one *d*. *Educ:* Palmer's Sch., Gray's, Essex; King's Coll., London Univ. Research and Development Chemist: Ministry of Supply, 1941-44; Bakelite Ltd, 1944-47. Lecturer in Chemical Engineering Dept, University Coll., London University, 1947-53; Professor in Chem. Engineering Dept, University of Toronto, 1953-56; Senior Principal Scientific Officer, Dept of Scientific and Industrial Research, 1956-60. *Publications:* contributor: Chemical Engineering Progress; Transactions Instn of Chemical Engineers; Chemical Engineering Science. *Recreations:* reading, experimental research. *Address:* Chemical Engineering Laboratories, University of Edinburgh, Mayfield Road, Edinburgh EH9 3JL. *T:* 031-667 1011.

CALDERWOOD, Robert; Town Clerk of Manchester, since 1973; *b* 1 March 1932; *s* of Robert Calderwood and Jessie Reid (*née* Marshall); *m* 1958, Meryl Anne (*née* Fleming); three *s* one *d*. *Educ:* William Hulme's Sch., Manchester; Manchester Univ. (LLB (Hons)). Admitted solicitor, 1956; Town Clerk: Salford, 1966-69; Bolton, 1969-73. Mem., Parole Bd for England and Wales, 1971-73. *Recreations:* theatre, watching Rugby League. *Address:* 176 Brooklands Road, Sale, Cheshire M33 3PA. *T:* 061-973 3980. *Clubs:* Royal Over-Seas League; University Union (Manchester).

CALDICOTT, Hon. Sir John Moore, KBE 1963; CMG 1955; *b* 1900; *m* 1945, Evelyn Macarthur; one *s* two step *d*. *Educ:* Shrewsbury School. Joined RAF 1918. Came to Southern Rhodesia, 1925; farmed in Umvukwes District ever since. President: Rhodesia Tobacco Assoc., 1943-45; Rhodesia National Farmers' Union, 1946-48. MP for Mazoe, S Rhodesia Parliament, 1948; Minister of Agriculture and Lands, 1951, of Agriculture, Health and Public Service, 1953, of Economic Affairs, 1958-62, of The Common Market, 1962, and of Finance, until 1963, Federation of Rhodesia and Nyasaland. *Address:* 24 Court Road, Greendale, Salisbury, Rhodesia. *Club:* Salisbury (Salisbury, Rhodesia).

CALDWELL, Surg. Vice-Adm. Sir (Eric) Dick, KBE 1969; CB 1965; Executive Director, Medical Council on Alcoholism; *b* 6 July 1909; *s* of late Dr John Colin Caldwell; *m* 1942, Margery Lee Abbott. *Educ:* Edinburgh Acad.; Edinburgh Univ. MB, ChB Edinburgh 1933; LRCP, LRCSE, LRFPS(G) 1933; MD Edinburgh 1950; MRCPE 1956; FRCPE 1962; FRCP 1967. Joined Royal Navy, 1934. Served War of 1939-45 in Atlantic, Mediterranean and Pacific. Medical Specialist, RN Hosp., Hong Kong, 1947; Staff MO to Flag Officer, Malta, 1958; Sen. Med. Specialist at RN Hosp., Haslar; MO i/c of RN Hosp., Plymouth, 1963-66; Med. Dir-Gen. of Navy, 1966-69, retired. Surg. Capt. 1957; RN Consultant in Medicine, 1962; Surg. Rear-Adm. 1963; Surg. Vice-Adm. 1966. QHP 1963-69. Gilbert Blane Gold Medal, 1962; FRSocMed. CStJ. *Recreations:* golf, tennis, trying to write. *Address:* 9A Holland Park Road, Kensington, W14. *T:* 01-602 3326. *Club:* Army and Navy.

CALDWELL, Erskine; author; Editor of American Folkways, 1940-55; Member: Authors' League; American PEN; (Hon.) American Academy and Institute of Arts and Letters; *b* 17 Dec. 1903; *s* of Ira Sylvester Caldwell and Caroline Preston Bell; *m* 1st, 1925, Helen Lannigan; two *s* one *d*; 2nd, 1939, Margaret Bourke-White; 3rd, 1942, June Johnson; one *s*; 4th, 1957, Virginia Moffett Fletcher. *Educ:* Erskine Coll.; Univ. of Virginia. Newspaper reporter on Atlanta (Ga) Journal; motion picture screen writer in Hollywood; newspaper and radio correspondent in Russia. *Publications:* The Bastard, 1929; Poor Fool, 1930; American Earth, 1931; Tobacco Road, 1932; God's Little Acre, 1933; We Are the Living, 1933; Journeyman, 1935; Kneel to the Rising Sun, 1935; Some American People, 1935; You Have Seen Their Faces, 1937; Southways, 1938; North of The Danube, 1939; Trouble in July, 1940; Jackpot, 1940; Say! Is This the USA?, 1941; All-Out on the Road to Smolensk, 1942; Moscow Under Fire, 1942; All Night Long, 1942; Georgia Boy, 1943; Tragic Ground, 1944; Stories, 1945; A House in the Uplands, 1946; The Sure Hand of God, 1947; This Very Earth, 1948; Place Called Estherville, 1949; Episode in Palmetto, 1950; Call It Experience, 1951; The Courting of Susie Brown, 1952; A Lamp for Nightfall, 1952; The Complete Stories of Erskine Caldwell, 1953; Love and Money, 1954; Gretta, 1955; Gulf Coast Stories, 1956; Certain Women, 1957; Molly Cottontail, 1958 (juvenile); Claudelle Inglish, 1959; When You Think of Me, 1959; Jenny By Nature, 1961; Close to Home, 1962; The Last Night of Summer, 1963; Around About America, 1964; In Search of Bisco, 1965; The Deer at Our House (juvenile), 1966; In the Shadow of the Steeple, 1966; Miss Mamma Aimee, 1967; Writing In America, 1967; Deep South, 1968; Summertime Island, 1968; The Weather Shelter, 1969; The Earnshaw Neighborhood, 1971; Annette, 1973; Afternoons in Mid-America, 1976. *Address:* c/o McIntosh & Otis Inc., 475 Fifth Avenue, New York, NY 10017, USA. *T:* New York: MU 9-1050; (home) PO Box 4550, Hopi Station, Scottsdale, Arizona 85258, USA. *Clubs:* Phoenix Press (Phoenix, Arizona); San Francisco Press (San Francisco, Calif).

CALDWELL, Maj.-Gen. Frank Griffiths, OBE 1953 (MBE 1945); MC 1941 and Bar 1942; Director, Mabey and Johnson, since 1974; *b* 26 Feb. 1921; *s* of William Charles Francis and Violet Marjorie Kathleen Caldwell; *m* 1945, Betty, *d* of Captain Charles Palmer Buesden; one *s* one *d*. *Educ:* Elizabeth Coll., Guernsey. Commnd Royal Engrs, 1940; served Western Desert RE, 1940-43 (MC and Bar); Special Air Service NW Europe, 1944-45 (MBE); Malaya, 1951-53 (OBE); Comdr RE, 2 Div. BAOR, 1961-63; Corps Comdr RE, 1 (BR) Corps, 1967-68; Dir

Defence Operational Plans, MoD, 1970; Engineer in Chief (Army), 1970-72; Asst CGS (Operational Requirements), 1972-74. Col Comdt, RE, 1975-. Belgian Croix de Guerre, 1940, and Croix Militaire, 1945. *Recreations:* ornithology, golf. *Address:* The Eighteenth, Pond Road, Hook Heath, Woking, Surrey. *Clubs:* Army and Navy, MCC.

CALDWELL, Godfrey David; Under-Secretary, Department of Health and Social Security, 1970-75; *b* 7 Jan. 1920; *er s* of Dr J. R. Caldwell, Milnthorpe, Westmorland; *m* 1959, Helen Elizabeth, *d* of J. A. G. Barnes; one *d. Educ:* Heversham Grammar Sch., Westmorland; St Andrews Univ. (MA). Home Office, 1942; transferred to Min. of Nat. Insurance, 1945; Dept of Health and Social Security, 1968-75. *Address:* Woodside, Cartmel Fell, Windermere, Cumbria. *T:* Crosthwaite 428. *Club:* National Liberal.

CALDWELL, John Foster, CB 1952; *b* 3 May 1892; *er s* of Charles Sproule Caldwell, Solicitor, Londonderry, and Jeannie Hamilton Foster; *m* 1921, Flora, *yr d* of H. P. Grosse, AMIEE, Belfast and Portrush; one *d. Educ:* Foyle Coll., Londonderry; Trinity Coll., Dublin; King's Inns, Dublin. Called to the Bar, 1925; KC (N Ireland) 1946. First Parliamentary Draftsman to the Govt of Northern Ireland, 1945-56; Consolidator of Statute Law, N Ireland, 1956-59; former Member County Court Rules Cttee and Statute Law Cttee, N Ireland; Chief Parliamentary Counsel, Jamaica, 1959-61; Senior Legal Asst, Colonial Office, 1961-62. LLM *hc* Queen's Univ. of Belfast, 1957. *Address:* 40 Marlborough Park South, Belfast BT9 6HR. *T:* 666917.

CALDWELL, Prof. Peter Christopher, FRS 1975; Professor of Zoology (Biochemistry), University of Bristol, since 1977; *b* 25 Jan. 1927; *s* of Bernard Caldwell and Dr Margaret Joyce Caldwell, JP; *m* 1955, Phoebe-Ann, *d* of Air Chief Marshal Sir Roderic Hill, KCB, MC, AFC; two *s* three *d. Educ:* Ampleforth; Trinity Coll., Oxford (Millard Scholar; MA, DPhil). ICI Res. Fellow in Biophysics Res. Unit, UCL, 1951-54; Asst Lectr, Dept of Biophysics, UCL, 1954-55; Beit Meml Res. Fellow, 1955-57 and Johnston, Lawrence and Moseley Res. Fellow of Royal Soc., 1957-60, Marine Biol Assoc.'s Lab., Plymouth; Lectr in Zoology (Biochem.), Univ. of Bristol, 1960-66, Reader in Zoology, 1966-77. Mem. Editorial Bd, Jl of Physiology, 1973-; Mem. Council, Marine Biological Assoc., 1974-. *Publications:* sci. papers on nucleic acids, muscle contraction, intracellular pH and movt of substances across cell membranes, mainly in Jl Physiology. *Recreations:* composing, performing and listening to music; farming. *Address:* White Oak House, Youngwood Lane, Nailsea, Bristol BS19 2NS. *T:* Nailsea 2436. *Club:* Oxford and Cambridge Musical.

CALDWELL, Taylor, (Janet Miriam Taylor Caldwell), FIAL; writer; *b* Prestwich, Manchester, England, 7 Sept. 1900; Scots parentage; citizen of USA; *m* 1st, William Fairfax Combs (marr. diss.; he *d* 1972); one *d*; 2nd, Marcus Reback (*d* 1970); one *d*; 3rd, 1972, William E. Stancell (marr. diss. 1973). *Educ:* Univ. of Buffalo, Buffalo, NY. Wrote many years before publication. Formerly Sec. of Board of Special Inquiry, US Dept of Immigration and Naturalization, Buffalo, NY. Dr in lit. hum., St Bonaventure, 1977. Many awards and citations, national and international, including National Award, Nat. League of American Penwomen (gold medal), 1948, Grande Prix, Prix Chatrain, Paris, 1956, Award of Merit, Daughters of the American Revolution, 1956; McElligott Medal, Marquette Univ., Milwaukee. *Publications:* Dynasty of Death, 1938, repr. 1973; The Eagles Gather, 1939; The Earth is the Lord's, 1940; The Strong City, 1941; The Arm and the Darkness, 1942; The Turnbulls, 1943; The Final Hour, 1944; The Wide House, 1945; This Side of Innocence, 1946; There Was a Time, 1947; Melissa, 1948; Let Love Come Last, 1949; The Balance Wheel, 1951; The Devil's Advocate, 1952; Never Victorious, Never Defeated, 1954; Tender Victory, 1956; The Sound of Thunder, 1957; Dear and Glorious Physician, 1959; The Listener, 1960, (Engl. edn) The Man Who Listens, 1961; A Prologue to Love, 1962; To See the Glory, 1963; The Late Clara Beame, 1964; A Pillar of Iron, 1965; Dialogues with the Devil, 1968; Testimony of Two Men, 1968; Great Lion of God, 1970; On Growing up Tough, 1971; Captains and the Kings, 1973; Glory and the Lightning, 1974; Ceremony of the Innocent, 1976. *Recreations:* just work; occasionally gardening. *Address:* 124 Middlesex Road, Buffalo, NY 14216, USA. *Clubs:* American Legion, National League of American Penwomen (Buffalo, NY); League of Women Voters (Amherst Township, Erie County, NY); PEN (New York, NY); Women's National Republican (Washington, DC).

CALEDON, 6th Earl of, *cr* 1800; **Denis James Alexander;** Baron Caledon, 1789; Viscount Caledon, 1797; DL; *b* 10 Nov. 1920; *s* of late Lieut-Col Hon. Herbrand Charles Alexander, DSO (*b* of 5th Earl of Caledon), and of Millicent Valla, *d* of Sir Henry Bayly Meredyth, 5th Bt; *S* uncle, 1968; *m* 1st, 1943, Ghislaine Dresselhuys (marr. diss. 1948); one *d*; 2nd, 1952, Baroness Anne de Graevenitz (*d* 1963); one *s* one *d*; 3rd, 1964, Marie Elisabeth Erskine (*née* Allen). *Educ:* Eton; RMC. Major, Irish Guards; Ulster Defence Regt, 1970-. DL Co. Tyrone, 1974. *Heir: s* Viscount Alexander, *qv. Address:* Caledon Castle, Caledon, Co. Tyrone, Northern Ireland. *Club:* Turf.

CALEDONIA, Bishop of, since 1969; **Rt. Rev. Douglas Walter Hambidge,** DD; *b* London, England, 6 March 1927; *s* of Douglas Hambidge and Florence (*née* Driscoll); *m* 1956, Denise Colvill Lown; two *s* one *d. Educ:* London Univ.; London Coll. of Divinity. BD, ALCD; DD, Anglican Theol. Coll. of BC, 1970. Asst Curate, St Mark's, Dalston, 1953-56; Rector: All Saints, Cassiar, BC, 1956-58; St James, Smithers, BC, 1958-64; Vicar, St Martin, Fort St John, BC, 1964-69; Canon, St Andrew's Cathedral, Caledonia, 1965-69. *Address:* Bishop's Lodge, 208 Fourth Avenue-West, Prince Rupert, BC, Canada. *T:* 604-624-6044 or 604-624-6013.

CALGARY, Bishop of, since 1968; **Rt. Rev. Morse Lamb Goodman;** *b* Rosedale, Ont, 27 May 1917; *s* of Frederick James Goodman and Mary Mathilda Arkwright; *m* 1943, Patricia May Cunningham; three *s* one *d. Educ:* Trinity Coll., Univ. of Toronto. BA Trin., 1940; LTh Trin., 1942. Deacon, 1942, Priest, 1943, Diocese of Algoma; Asst Curate, St Paul's, Ft William, 1942-43; Incumbent, Murillo, Algoma, 1943-46; Rector, St Thomas, Ft William, 1946-53; Rector, St James, Winnipeg, 1953-60; Dean of Brandon, 1960-65; Rector, Christ Church, Edmonton, 1965-67. Conductor of Canadian Broadcasting Corporation Programme, Family Worship, 1954-68. Hon. DD: Trinity, 1961; Emmanuel and St Chad's, 1968. Companion, Order of Coventry Cross of Nails, 1974; GCKLJ. *Recreations:* fishing, walking, photography, enology. *Address:* Bishop's Court, 1029 Hillcrest Avenue SW, Calgary, Alta, Canada. *T:* 244-4587. *Clubs:* Ranchmen's (Calgary, Alta); PPCLI Officers' Mess; United Services.

CALLAGHAN, Sir Allan (Robert), Kt 1972; CMG 1945; agricultural consultant, since 1972; *b* 24 Nov. 1903; *s* of late Phillip George Callaghan and late Jane Peacock; *m* 1928, Zillah May Sampson (decd); two *s* one *d.* (and one *s* decd); *m* 1965, Doreen Rhys Draper. *Educ:* Bathurst High Sch., NSW; St Paul's Coll., Univ. of Sydney (BSc Agr. 1924); St John's Coll., Oxford (Rhodes Scholar, BSc 1926, DPhil 1928). Asst Plant Breeder, NSW, Dept of Agriculture, 1928-32; Principal, Roseworthy Agricultural Coll., South Australia, 1932-49; Asst Dir (Rural Industry) in Commonwealth Dept of War Organisation of Industry, 1943; Chm., Land Development Executive in South Australia, 1945-51; Dir of Agriculture, South Australia, 1949-59; Commercial Counsellor, Australian Embassy, Washington, DC, 1959-65; Chm., Australian Wheat Bd, 1965-71. Farrer Medal (for distinguished service to Australian Agriculture), 1954; FAIAS 1959. *Publications:* (with A. J. Millington) The Wheat Industry in Australia, 1956; numerous articles in scientific and agricultural jls on agricultural and animal husbandry matters. *Recreations:* swimming, riding, gardening. *Address:* Tralee, 22 Murray Street, Clapham, SA 5062, Australia. *T:* 276-6524.

CALLAGHAN, Sir Bede (Bertrand), Kt 1976; CBE 1968; Managing Director, Commonwealth Banking Corporation, 1965-76; Chancellor of the University of Newcastle, NSW, since 1977; *b* 16 March 1912; *s* of S. K. Callaghan and Amy M. Ryan; *m* 1940, Mary T. Brewer; three *d. Educ:* Newcastle High Sch. FBIA; FAIM. Commonwealth Bank, 1927. Mem. Board Executive Directors, IMF and World Bank, 1954-59; Gen. Man., Commonwealth Develt Bank of Australia, 1959-65; Chm., Aust. European Finance Corp. Ltd, 1971-76; Chm., Foreign Investment Review Bd, 1976-. Chm., Aust. Admin. Staff Coll., 1969-76; Mem. Council, Univ. of Newcastle, NSW, 1966-, Dep. Chancellor, 1973-77. Hon. DSc Newcastle, 1973. *Recreation:* lawn bowls. *Address:* 69 Darnley Street, Gordon, NSW 2072, Australia. *T:* (Sydney) 498-7583. *Club:* Union (Sydney).

CALLAGHAN, Rear-Adm. Desmond Noble, CB 1970; CEng, FIMechE; Director-General, National Supervisory Council for Intruder Alarms, 1971-77; *b* 24 Nov. 1915; *s* of Edmund Ford Callaghan and Kathleen Louise Callaghan (*née* Noble): *m* 1948, Patricia Munro Geddes; one *s* two *d. Educ:* RNC Dartmouth. HMS Frobisher, 1933; RNEC Keyhan, 1934; HM Ships: Royal Oak, 1937; Iron Duke, 1938; Warspite, 1939; Hereward, 1941; Prisoner of War, 1941; HMS Argonaut, 1945; HMS Glory, 1946; RNC Dartmouth, 1947; Admiralty, 1949; C-in-C Med. Staff, 1950; HMS Excellent, 1953; HMS Eagle, 1956; RN Tactical Sch., 1958; Admiralty, 1960; HMS Caledonia, 1962; Admiralty, 1965; Vice-Pres. and Pres., Ordnance Board, 1968-

71, retired 1971. FRSA. *Recreations:* Rugby, tennis, swimming. *Address:* Willand, Boyn Hill Road, Maidenhead, Berks. *T:* Maidenhead 26840. *Club:* Army and Navy.

CALLAGHAN, James; MP (Lab) Middleton and Prestwich, since Feb. 1974; *b* 28 Jan. 1927; *s* of James Callaghan and Norah Callaghan (*née* Brierley). *Educ:* Manchester Univ. (BA); London Univ. (Adv. Dip. in Educn). Lectr at St John's Coll., Manchester, 1959-74. Middleton Borough Councillor, 1971-74 (Educn, Parks, Industrial Develt, and Library Cttees). *Recreations:* sport (football coach and referee), art (painting). *Address:* 139 Hollin Lane, Middleton, Manchester M24 3LA. *T:* 061-643 8108..

CALLAGHAN, Rt. Hon. (Leonard) James, PC 1964; MP (Lab) South Cardiff, 1945-50, South-East Cardiff since 1950; Prime Minister and First Lord of the Treasury, since 1976; Leader, Labour Party, since 1976; *b* 27 March 1912; *s* of James Callaghan, Chief Petty Officer, RN; *m* 1938, Audrey Elizabeth Moulton; one *s* two *d. Educ:* Elementary and Portsmouth Northern Secondary Schs. Entered Civil Service as a Tax Officer, 1929; Asst Sec., Inland Revenue Staff Fed., 1936-47 (with an interval during the War of 1939-45, when served in Royal Navy); Parly Sec., Min. of Transport, 1947-50; Chm. Cttee on Road Safety, 1948-50; Parliamentary and Financial Sec., Admiralty, 1950-51; Chancellor of the Exchequer, 1964-67; Home Secretary, 1967-70; Sec. of State for Foreign and Commonwealth Affairs, 1974-76; Minister of Overseas Develt, 1975-76. Deleg. to Council of Europe, Strasburg, 1948-50 and 1954. Mem., Nat. Exec. Cttee, Labour Party, 1957-; Treasurer, Labour Party, 1967-76, Vice-Chm. 1973, Chm. 1974. Consultant to Police Fedn of England and Wales and to Scottish Police Fedn, 1955-64. Pres., United Kingdom Pilots Assoc., 1963-76; Hon. Pres., Internat. Maritime Pilots Assoc., 1971-76. Visiting Fellow, Nuffield Coll., Oxford, 1959-67; Hon. Fellow, 1967-. Hon. Bencher, Inner Temple, 1976. Hon. Freeman, City of Cardiff, 1974. *Publication:* A House Divided: the dilemma of Northern Ireland, 1973. *Address:* House of Commons, SW1. See also Peter Jay.

CALLAGHAN, Morley (Edward); Canadian novelist; *b* Toronto, 1903; *s* of Thomas Callaghan and Mary (*née* Dewan); *m* 1929, Lorrete Florence, *d* of late Joseph Dee; two *s. Educ:* St Michael's Coll., Univ. of Toronto (BA); Osgoode Hall Law School. Holds Hon. Doctorates. Canadian Council Prize, 1970; $50,000 Royal Bank of Canada Award, 1970. *Publications:* Strange Fugitive, 1928; Native Argosy, 1929; It's Never Over, 1930; No Man's Meat, 1931; Broken Journey, 1932; Such Is My Beloved, 1934; They Shall Inherit the Earth, 1935; My Joy in Heaven, 1936; Now That April's Here, 1937; Just Ask for George (play), 1940; Jake Baldwin's Vow (for children), 1948; The Varsity Story, 1948; The Loved and the Lost, 1951; The Man with the Coat, 1955 (MacLean's Prize, 1955); A Many Coloured Coat, 1960 (UK 1963); A Passion in Rome, 1961 (UK 1964); That Summer in Paris, 1963; Morley Callaghan, vols 1 and 2, 1964. *Recreation:* sports. *Address:* 20 Dale Avenue, Toronto, Ont., Canada.

CALLAN, Prof. Harold Garnet, FRS 1963; FRSE; MA, DSc; Professor of Natural History, St Salvator's College, St Andrews, since 1950; *b* 5 March 1917; *s* of Garnet George Callan and Winifred Edith Brazier; *m* 1944, Amarillis Maria Speranza, *d* of Dr R. Dohrn, Stazione Zoologica, Naples, Italy; one *s* two *d. Educ:* King's Coll. Sch., Wimbledon; St John's Coll., Oxford (Exhibitioner). Casberd Scholar, St John's Coll., 1937; Naples Biological Scholar, 1938, 1939. Served War of 1939-45, Telecommunications Research Establishment, 1940-45, Hon. Commission, RAFVR. Senior Scientific Officer, ARC, Inst. of Animal Genetics, Edinburgh, 1946-50. Member: Advisory Council on Scientific Policy, 1963-64; SRC, 1972-76; Council, Royal Soc., 1974-76. Trustee, British Museum (Natural History), 1963-66. Vis. Prof., Univ. of Indiana, Bloomington, USA, 1964-65; Master of United Coll. of St Salvator and St Leonard's, 1967-68. *Publications:* scientific papers, mostly on cytology and cell physiology. *Recreations:* shooting, carpentry. *Address:* 2 St Mary's Street, St Andrews, Fife. *T:* St Andrews 2311; The University, St Andrews, Fife.

CALLAN, Maj.-Gen. Michael; Director General of Ordnance Services, since 1976; *b* 27 Nov. 1925; *s* of Major John Callan and Elsie Dorothy Callan (*née* Fordham); *m* 1948, Marie Evelyn Farthing; two *s. Educ:* Farnborough Grammar Sch., Hants. rcds, jssc, psc. Enlisted Hampshire Regt, 1943; commnd 1st (KGVs Own) Gurkha Rifles (The Malaun Regt), 1944; resigned commn, 1947; re-enlisted, 1948; re-commnd, RAOC, 1949; overseas service: India, Burma, French Indo China, Netherlands East Indies, 1944-47; Kenya, 1950-53; Malaya/Singapore, 1958-61; USA, 1966-68; Hong Kong, 1970-71; Comdr, Rhine Area,

BAOR, 1975-76. Staff Coll., 1957; JSSC, 1964; RCDS, 1974. *Recreations:* golf, sailing, DIY, gardening. *Address:* Green Oaks, Prey Heath Road, Mayford, Woking GU22 0SW. *T:* Woking 62192. *Clubs:* Army and Navy; Worplesdon Golf.

CALLANDER, Lt.-Gen. Sir Colin (Bishop), KCB 1955 (CB 1945); KBE 1952; MC; *b* 13 March 1897; *y s* of late W. W. Callander, Ilminster, Som.; *m* 1923, Mary Charteris Stather Dunn; one *s* one *d. Educ:* West Buckland Sch.; RMC Sandhurst. 2nd Lieut Royal Munster Fusiliers, 1915; Leicestershire Regt 1922; Capt. 1925; Major 1936; Temp. Lt-Col 1940; Col 1944; Temp. Maj.-Gen. 1944; Maj.-Gen. 1946; Lt-Gen. 1951. Served European War, 1916-17 (wounded thrice, MC); NW Frontier, India, 1938-39 (despatches); War of 1939-45 (CB); GOC 4th Div. (Greece), 1945-46; Dir-Gen. of Military Training, 1948; GOC 2nd Div. (BAOR), 1949-51; Dir-Gen. of Military Training, 1952-54; Military Sec. to the Sec. of State for War, 1954-56; retired 1957. Col Royal Leicestershire Regt, 1954-63. *Address:* Great Maytham Hall, Rolvenden, Cranbrook, Kent. *T:* Rolvenden 436. *Club:* Army and Navy.

CALLARD, Sir Eric John, (Sir Jack Callard), Kt 1974; CEng; Chairman, British Home Stores Ltd, since 1976 (Director since 1975); *b* 15 March 1913; *s* of late F. Callard and Mrs A. Callard; *m* 1938, Pauline M. Pengelly; three *d. Educ:* Queen's Coll., Taunton; St John's Coll., Cambridge. 1st cl. Hons Mech. Sci. Tripos; BA 1935; MA 1973; Harvard Business Sch. (Adv. Management Programme, 1953). Joined ICI Ltd, 1935; seconded to Min. of Aircraft Prodn, 1942; ICI Paints Div., 1947 (Jt Man. Dir, 1955-59; Chm., 1959-64); Chairman: Deleg. Bd, ICI (Hyde) Ltd, 1959; ICI (Europa) Ltd, 1965-67; ICI Ltd, 1971-75 (Dir, 1964-75; Dep. Chm., 1967-71); Director: Pension Funds Securities Ltd, 1963-67; Imp. Metal Industries Ltd, 1964-67; Imp. Chemicals Insurance Ltd, 1966-70; Midland Bank Ltd, 1971-; Ferguson Industrial Holdings, 1975-; Commercial Union Assurance Co., 1976-. Member Council: BIM, 1964-69; Manchester Univ. Business Sch., 1964-71; Export Council for Europe, 1965-71; Member: CBI Steering Cttee on Europe, 1965-71; Cambridge Univ. Appointments Bd, 1968-71; CBI Overseas Cttee, 1969-71; Council of Industry for Management Educn, 1967-73; Appeal Cttee of British Sch. of Brussels, 1970-73; Royal Instn of GB, 1971-; Vice-President: Combustion Engnrg Assoc., 1968-75; Manchester Business Sch. Assoc., 1971- (Hon. Mem., 1966-; Pres., 1969-71); Pres., Industrial Participation Assoc., 1971- (Dep. Chm., 1967-; Chm., 1967-71). Member: Hansard Soc. Commn on Electoral Reform, 1975-76; Cttee of Inquiry into Industrial Democracy, 1976-; Equity Capital for Industry, 1976-. Trustee, Civic Trust, 1972-75; Governor, London Business Sch., 1972-75. Mem. Court, British Shippers' Council, 1972-75. FRSA 1970; FBIM 1966; Hon. FIMechE. Hon. DSc Cranfield Inst. of Technology, 1974. *Recreations:* games, fishing, fell walking. *Address:* Farthings, Jordans, Beaconsfield, Bucks.

CALLENDER, Dr Maurice Henry; Counsellor, British High Commission, Canberra, 1973-77; *b* 18 Dec. 1916; *s* of Harry and Lizbeth Callender; *m* 1941, Anne Kassel; two *s. Educ:* Univ. of Durham (MA, PhD). FSA. Commissioned: Royal Northumberland Fusiliers, 1939-41; RAF, 1941-45. Lectr, Huddersfield Technical Coll., 1945-47; Research, Univ. of Durham, 1947-49; Lectr, Bristol Univ. Extra-Mural Dept, 1949-53; MoD, 1953-62; Joint Services Staff Coll., 1959-60; Cabinet Office, 1962-64; MoD, 1964-70; Cabinet Office, 1970-73. *Publications:* Roman Amphorae, 1965; various articles in archaeological jls. *Recreations:* oil painting, golf, bridge. *Address:* 24 Glanleam Road, Stanmore, Mddx. *T:* 01-954 1435. *Clubs:* Commonwealth (Canberra); Royal Canberra Golf.

CALLEY, Sir Henry (Algernon), Kt 1964; DSO 1945; DFC 1943; DL; Owner and Manager of a stud, since 1948; *b* 9 Feb. 1914; *s* of Rev. A. C. M. Langton and Mrs Langton (*née* Calley); changed surname to Calley, 1974; unmarried. *Educ:* St John's Sch., Leatherhead. Taught at Corchester. Corbridge-on-Tyne, 1933-35; Bombay Burmah Trading Corp., 1935-36; teaching, 1936-38; Metropolitan Police Coll., and Police Force, 1938-41; Royal Air Force, 1941-48; Pilot in Bombers, Actg Wing Comdr, 1944. Mem. Wiltshire CC, 1955; Chm. Finance Cttee, 1959-68; Chm. of Council, 1968-73; Chm. Wessex Area Conservative Assoc., 1963-66. DL Wilts, 1968. *Recreation:* shooting.

CALLINAN, Sir Bernard (James), Kt 1977; CBE 1971; DSO 1945; MC 1943; Chairman and Managing Director, Gutteridge, Haskins & Davey Pty Ltd, since 1971; *b* 2 Feb. 1913; *s* of Michael Joseph Callinan and Mary Callinan (*née* Prendergast); *m* 1943, Naomi Marion Callinan (*née* Cullinan); five *s. Educ:* Univ. of Melbourne (BCE; Dip. Town and Regional Planning). FIE Aust (Pres., 1971-72; P. N. Russell Meml Medal, 1973); FICE; FRAPI; FRTPI. Lieut to Lt-Col, AIF, 1940-46. Asst

Engr, A. Gordon Gutteridge, 1934; Associate, 1946, Sen. Partner, 1948-71, Gutteridge, Haskins & Davey. Director: West Gate Bridge Authority, 1965- (Dep. Chm., 1971-); British Petroleum Co. of Aust. Ltd, 1969-. Commissioner: State Electricity Commn, 1963; Royal Commn of Inquiry, Aust. PO, 1973-74; Aust. Atomic Energy Commn, 1976-. Mem., Pontifical Commn on Justice and Peace, Rome, 1977-. Councillor, La Trobe Univ., 1964-72. Hon. Col, 4/19 Prince of Wales's Light Horse Regt, 1973. *Publications:* Independent Company, 1953; contribs to Jl Instn of Engrs, Aust., Ji Royal Soc. of Vic. *Address:* 111 Sackville Street, Kew, Vic 3101, Australia. *T:* 80.1230. *Clubs:* Melbourne, Australian, Naval and Military (Melbourne); Melbourne Cricket.

CALLMAN, Clive Vernon; His Honour Judge Callman; a Circuit Judge, since 1973, assigned to South-Eastern Circuit; *b* 21 June 1927; *o s* of Felix Callman, DMD, LDS, RCS and Edith Callman, Walton-on-Thames, Surrey; *m* 1967, Judith Helen Hines, BA, DipSocStuds (Adelaide), *o d* of Gus Hines, OBE, JP, and Hilde Hines, Springfield, Adelaide, S Aust.; one *s* one *d*. *Educ:* Ottershaw Coll.; St George's Coll., Weybridge; LSE, Univ. of London. BSc(Econ), Commercial Law. Called to the Bar, Middle Temple, 1951; Blackstone Pupillage Prizeman, 1951; practised as Barrister, London and Norwich, 1952-73; Member of South-Eastern Circuit, Central Criminal Court Bar Mess, Surrey and South London Sessions Bar Mess; Acting Dep. Chm., Co. London QS, 1971; Dep. Circuit Judge in Civil and Criminal Jurisdiction, 1971-73. Dir, Woburn Press, Publishers, 1971-73; dir of finance cos, 1961-73. Fac. Mem., Standing Cttee of Convocation, Univ. of London 1951-; Mem. Exec. Cttee, Soc. of Labour Lawyers, 1958; Chm., St Marylebone Constituency Labour Party, 1960-62. Mem. Council, Anglo-Jewish Assoc., 1956-. Editor, Clare Market Review, 1947. *Recreations:* reading, travelling, the arts. *Address:* 11 Constable Close, NW11 6UA. *T:* 01-458 3010. *Club:* Bar Yacht.

CALLOW, Robert Kenneth, FRS 1958; MA, DPhil, BSc; Member of Staff, Rothamsted Experimental Station, 1966-72; Member of Scientific Staff, Medical Research Council, 1929-66; *b* 15 Feb. 1901; 2nd *s* of late Cecil Burman Callow and Kate Peverell; *m* 1937, Nancy Helen, *d* of J. E. Newman; one *s* one *d*. *Educ:* City of London Sch.; Christ Church, Oxford. Exhibitioner, 1919, and Research Scholar, 1927, of Christ Church. Served in RAF, 1940-45; relief of Datta Khel, 1941 (despatches). Mem. of Editorial Board, Biochemical Journal, 1946-53 (Dep. Chm., 1951-53); Chm., Biological and Medical Abstracts Ltd, 1955-61; Mem. of Council, Bee Research Association, 1962-74 (Chm., 1963-68; Vice-Pres., 1974-); Visitor, Royal Instn of GB, 1970-73. *Publications:* papers (many jointly) in jls of learned societies. *Recreations:* gardening, stamp-collecting, natural history. *Address:* 39 Hendon Wood Lane, NW7 4HT. *T:* 01-959 2572.

CALNAN, Prof. Charles Dermod, MA, MB, BChir Cantab; FRCP; Director, Department of Occupational Dermatoses, St John's Hospital for Diseases of the Skin, since 1974; Consultant Dermatologist, Royal Free Hospital and St John's Hospital for Diseases of the Skin, London; *b* 14 Dec. 1917; *s* of James Calnan, Eastbourne, Sussex; *m* 1950, Josephine Gerard Keane, *d* of late Lt-Col Michael Keane, RAMC; three *s* one *d*. *Educ:* Stonyhurst Coll.; Corpus Christi Coll., Cambridge; London Hospital. 1st Cl. Hons Nat. Sci. Trip., Cambridge 1939. RAMC Specialist in Dermatology, Major, 1942-46; Marsden Prof., Royal Free Hosp., 1958; Visiting Research Associate, Univ. of Pennsylvania, 1959; Prof. of Dermatology, Inst. of Dermatology, 1960-74. WHO Cons. Adviser to Nat. Inst. of Dermatology of Thailand, 1971-. Editor: Transactions of the St John's Hosp. Dermatological Soc., 1958-75; Contact Dermatitis, 1975-. Mem. BMA; Mem. Brit. Assoc. of Dermatology. FRSocMed (Mem. Dermatological Section); Fellow Hunterian Soc. *Publications:* Atlas of Dermatology, 1974; various papers in med. and dermatological jls. *Recreations:* squash, books, theatre. *Address:* 109 Harley Street, W1.

CALNAN, Prof. James Stanislaus, FRCP; FRCS; Professor of Plastic and Reconstructive Surgery, University of London, at the Royal Postgraduate Medical School and Hammersmith Hospital, since 1970; *b* 12 March 1916; *e s* of James and Gertrude Calnan, Eastbourne, Sussex; *m* 1949, Joan (County Councillor for Great Berkhamsted and Dacorum District Councillor, 1968-, and Parish Councillor, Berkhamsted), *e d* of George Frederick and Irene Maud Williams, Roath Park, Cardiff; one *d*. *Educ:* Stonyhurst Coll.; Univ. of London at London Hosp. Med. Sch. LDS RCS 1941; MRCS, LRCP 1943; DA 1944; DTM&H 1948; MRCP (London and Edinburgh) 1948; FRCS 1949. Served War of 1939-45, F/Lt RAF, UK, France, India. RMO, Hosp. for Tropical Diseases, 1948; Sen. Lectr, Nuffield Dept of Plastic Surgery, Oxford, 1954;

Hammersmith Hospital and Royal Postgraduate Med. Sch.: Lectr in Surgery, 1960; Reader, 1965; Professor, 1970. Hunterian Prof. RCS, 1959. Vis. Prof. in Plastic Surgery, Univ. of Pennsylvania, 1959. Member: BMA; British Assoc. of Plastic Surgeons; Sen. Mem., Surgical Research Soc. Fellow, Royal Soc. of Medicine; FCST 1966. *Publications:* contribs to medical and scientific jls and chapters in books, on cleft palate, wound healing, lymphatic diseases, venous thrombosis, research methods and organisation. *Recreations:* gardening, carpentry, reading and writing. *Address:* White Haven, 23 Kings Road, Berkhamsted, Herts. *T:* Berkhamsted 2320; Royal Postgraduate Medical School, Ducane Road, W12 0HS. *T:* 01-742 2030. *See also Prof. C. D. Calnan.*

CALNE, Prof. Roy Yorke, MA, MS; FRCS; FRS 1974; Professor of Surgery, University of Cambridge, since 1965; Fellow of Trinity Hall, Cambridge, since 1965; Hon. Consulting Surgeon, Addenbrooke's Hospital, Cambridge, since 1965; *b* 30 Dec. 1930; *s* of Joseph Robert and Eileen Calne; *m* 1956, Patricia Doreen Whelan; two *s* four *d*. *Educ:* Lancing Coll.; Guy's Hosp. Med. Sch. MB, BS London with Hons (Distinction in Medicine), 1953. House Appts, Guy's Hosp., 1953-54; RAMC, 1954-56 (RMO to KEO 2nd Gurkhas); Deptl Anatomy Demonstrator, Oxford Univ., 1957-58; SHO Nuffield Orthopædic Centre, Oxford, 1958; Surg. Registrar, Royal Free Hosp., 1958-60; Harkness Fellow in Surgery, Peter Bent Brigham Hosp., Harvard Med. Sch., 1960-61; Lectr in Surgery, St Mary's Hosp., London, 1961-62; Sen. Lectr and Cons. Surg., Westminster Hosp., 1962-65; Mem., Ct of Examiners, RCS, 1970-76. Royal Coll. of Surgeons: Hallet Prize, 1957; Jacksonian Prize, 1961; Hunterian Prof., 1962; Cecil Joll Prize, 1966. Fellow Assoc. of Surgeons of Gt Brit.; Mem. Surgical Research Soc.; Corresp. Fellow, Amer. Surgical Assoc., 1972. Prix de la Société Internationale de Chirurgie, 1969. *Publications:* Renal Transplantation, 1963, 2nd edn 1967; (with H. Ellis) Lecture Notes in Surgery, 1965, 5th edn 1970; A Gift of Life, 1970; (ed and contrib.) Clinical Organ Transplantation, 1971; (ed and contrib.) Immunological Aspects of Transplantation Surgery, 1973; papers on tissue transplantation and general surgery; sections in several surgical text-books. *Recreations:* tennis, squash. *Address:* 22 Barrow Road, Cambridge. *T:* Cambridge 59831.

CALNE AND CALSTONE, Viscount; Simon Henry George Petty-Fitzmaurice; *b* 24 Nov. 1970; *s* and *heir* of Earl of Shelburne, *qv.*

CALTHORPE; *see* Anstruther-Gough-Calthorpe, and Gough-Calthorpe.

CALTHORPE, 10th Baron *cr* 1796; **Peter Waldo Somerset Gough-Calthorpe; Bt** 1728; *b* 13 July 1927; *s* of late Hon. Frederick Somerset Gough-Calthorpe and Rose Mary Dorothy, *d* of late Leveson William Vernon-Harcourt; *S* brother, 1945; *m* 1956, Saranne (marr. diss. 1971), *o d* of James Harold Alexander, Ireland. *Heir:* none. *Address:* Gansey Bay Mill, Beach Road, Port St Mary, Isle of Man.

CALVERLEY, 3rd Baron *cr* 1945; **Charles Rodney Muff;** Member of the City of Bradford Police; *b* 2 Oct. 1946; *s* of 2nd Baron Calverley and of Mary, *d* of Arthur Farrar, Halifax; *S* father, 1971; *m* 1972, Barbara Ann, *d* of Jonathan Brown, Kelbrook, nr Colne; one *s*. *Educ:* Fulneck School for Boys. *Heir: s* Hon. Jonathan Edward Muff, *b* 16 April 1975. *Address:* 10 Briarwood Grove, Wibsey, Bradford BD6 1SF, W Yorks.

CALVERT, Mrs Barbara Adamson, QC 1975; barrister-at-law; *b* 30 April 1926; *d* of Albert Parker, *qv*; *m* 1948, John Thornton Calvert, CBE; one *s* one *d*. *Educ:* St Helen's, Northwood; London Sch. of Economics (BScEcon). Called to Bar, Middle Temple, 1959; Admin. Officer, City and Guilds of London Inst., 1961; Practice at Bar, 1962-. Part-time Chm., Industrial Tribunals, London, 1974-. *Recreations:* gardening, swimming, poetry. *Address:* (home) 158 Ashley Gardens, SW1P 1HW; (chambers) 5 Essex Court, Temple, EC4Y 7AN.

CALVERT, Florence Irene; Principal, St Mary's College, University of Durham, 1975-77; *b* 1 March 1912; *d* of Ernest William Calvert and Florence Alice (née Walton). *Educ:* Univ. of Sheffield (BA, 1st Cl. Hons French and Latin, MA). Asst Language Teacher, Accrington Grammar Sch., 1936-39; Head, Modern Langs Dept, Accrington Girls' High Sch., 1939-48; Univ. of Durham: Lectr in Educn, 1948; Sen. Lectr, 1964-75. *Publications:* French Plays for the Classroom, 1951; L'Homme aux Mains Rouges, 1954; Contes, 1957; French by Modern Methods in Primary and Secondary Schools, 1965. *Address:* 7 St Mary's Close, Shincliffe, Durham DH1 2ND. *T:* Durham 65502.

CALVERT, Henry Reginald, Dr Phil; Keeper of Department of Astronomy and Geophysics in Science Museum, South Kensington, 1949-67; Keeper Emeritus, 1967-69; b 25 Jan. 1904; e s of late H. T. Calvert, MBE, DSc, of Min. of Health; m 1938, Eileen Mary Frow; two d. Educ: Bridlington Sch., East Yorks; St John's Coll., Oxford (Scholar, MA); Univ. of Göttingen, Germany (Dr Phil). 1st Cl. Hons BSc (External) London, 1925; Goldsmiths' Company's Exhibitioner, 1925. Research Physicist, ICI, 1928-30; Research Physicist, Callender's Cable & Construction Co., 1932-34. Entered Science Museum, 1934; Dep. Keeper, 1946. Ballistics research for Min. of Supply, 1940-46. Hon. Treas., British Soc. for History of Science, 1952-63. Fellow Royal Astronomical Soc. Publications: Astronomy, Globes, Orreries and other Models, 1967; Scientific Trade Cards, 1971; papers in learned journals. Recreations: chess, bridge, croquet, gardening. Address: North Point, Church Hill, Merstham, Surrey. T: Merstham 2362.

CALVERT, Louis Victor Denis; Deputy Secretary, Department of the Environment for Northern Ireland, since 1976; b 20 April 1924; s of Louis Victor Calvert, Belfast and Gertrude Cherry Hobson, Belfast; m 1949, Vivien Millicent Lawson; two s one d. Educ: Belfast Royal Academy; Queen's Univ., Belfast (BScEcon); Admin. Staff Coll., Henley-on-Thames. Served with RAF, 1943-47, navigator (F/O). Northern Ireland Civil Service, 1947-: Min. of Agriculture, 1947-56; Dep. Principal 1951; Principal, Min. of Finance, 1956-63; Min. of Health and Local Govt, 1963-65; Asst Sec. 1964; Min. of Development, 1965-73; Sen. Asst Sec. 1970; Dep. Sec. 1971; Min. of Housing, Local Govt and Planning, 1973-76. Recreations: gardening, golf, reading. Address: Department of the Environment for Northern Ireland, Stormont, Belfast 4, Northern Ireland. Club: Knock Golf.

CALVERT, Norman Hilton; Under-Secretary, Department of the Environment, since 1971; b 27 July 1925; s of Clifford and Doris Calvert; m 1st, 1949, May Yates (d 1968); one s one d; 2nd, 1971, Vera Baker. Educ: Leeds Modern Sch.; Leeds Univ.; King's Coll., Durham Univ. BA Hons 1st cl. Geography, 1950. Served Royal Signals, 1943-47: 81 (W African) Div., India, 1945-47. Min. of Housing and Local Govt: Asst Principal, 1950-55; Principal, 1956-64; Asst Sec., 1964-71; Sec., Water Resources Bd, 1964-68; Principal Regional Officer, Northern Region, 1969-71; Regional Dir, Northern Region, and Chm, Northern Econ. Planning Bd, 1971-73. Recreations: fell walking, listening to music, motoring. Address: Treetops, Roundhill Way, Cobham, Surrey. T: Oxshott 2738. Club: Royal Automobile.

CALVERT, Phyllis; actress; b 18 Feb. 1917; d of Frederick and Annie Bickle; m 1941, Peter Murray Hill (d 1957); one s one d. Educ: Margaret Morris Sch.; Institut Français. Malvern Repertory Company, 1935; Coventry, 1937; York, 1938. First appeared in London in A Woman's Privilege, Kingsway Theatre, 1939; Punch Without Judy, Embassy, 1939; Flare Path, Apollo, 1942; Escapade, St James's, 1953; It's Never Too Late, Strand, 1954; River Breeze, Phoenix, 1956; The Complaisant Lover, Globe, 1959; The Rehearsal, Globe, 1961; Ménage à Trois, Lyric, 1963; Portrait of Murder, Savoy, Vaudeville, 1963; A Scent of Flowers, Duke of York's, 1964; Present Laughter, Queen's, 1965; A Woman of No Importance, Vaudeville, 1967; Blithe Spirit, Globe, 1970; Crown Matrimonial, Haymarket, 1973; Dear Daddy, Ambassadors, 1976. Started films, 1939. Films include: Kipps, The Young Mr Pitt, Man in Grey, Fanny by Gaslight, Madonna of the Seven Moons, They were Sisters, Time out of Mind, Broken Journey, My Own True Love, The Golden Madonna, A Woman with No Name, Mr Denning Drives North, Mandy, The Net, It's Never Too Late, Child in the House, Indiscreet, The Young and The Guilty, Oscar Wilde, Twisted Nerve, Oh! What a Lovely War, The Walking Stick. TV series: Kate, 1970. Recreations: swimming, gardening, collecting costume books. Address: 99 Castelnau, SW13. T: 01-748 5365.

CALVIN, Prof. Melvin; University Professor of Chemistry, University of California, since 1971; Professor of Molecular Biology, since 1963; Director, Laboratory of Chemical Biodynamics, since 1960; Associate Director, Lawrence Berkeley Laboratory, since 1967; b 8 April 1911; s of Rose and Elias Calvin; m 1942, Marie Genevieve Jemtegaard; one s two d. Educ: Univ. of Minnesota, Minneapolis (PhD). Fellow, Univ. of Manchester, 1935-37. Univ. of California, Berkeley: Instr., 1937; Asst Prof., 1941-45; Assoc. Prof., 1945-47; Prof., 1947-71. Foreign Mem., Royal Society, 1959. Member: Nat. Acad. of Sciences (US); Royal Netherlands Acad. of Sciences and Letters; Amer. Philos. Society. Nobel Prize in Chemistry, 1961; Davy Medal, Royal Society, 1964; Virtanen Medal, 1975. Hon. Degrees: Michigan Coll. of Mining and Technology, 1955; Univ. of Nottingham, 1958; Oxford Univ., 1959; Northwestern Univ.,

1961; Univ. of Notre Dame, 1965; Brooklyn Polytechnic Inst., 1969; Rijksuniversiteit-Gent, 1970. Publications: very numerous, including (6 books): Theory of Organic Chemistry (with Branch), 1941; Isotopic Carbon (with Heidelberger, Reid, Tolbert and Yankwich), 1949; Chemistry of Metal Chelate Compounds (with Martell), 1952; Path of Carbon in Photosynthesis (with Bassham), 1957; Chemical Evolution, 1961; Photosynthesis of Carbon Compounds (with Bassham), 1962; Chemical Evolution, 1969. Address: University of California, Berkeley, Calif 94720, USA; (home) 2683 Buena Vista Way, Berkeley, Calif 94708, USA. T: 848-4036.

CALVO, Roberto Q.; see Querejazu Calvo.

CALVOCORESSI, Peter (John Ambrose); author; Publisher and Chief Executive, Penguin Books, 1973-76, Editorial Director, 1972-76; b 17 Nov. 1912; s of Pandia Calvocoressi and Irene (Ralli); m 1938, Barbara Dorothy Eden, d of 6th Baron Henley; two s. Educ: Eton (King's Scholar); Balliol Coll., Oxford. Called to Bar, 1935. RAF Intelligence, 1940-45; Wing Comdr. Trial of Major War Criminals, Nuremberg, 1945-46. Contested (L) Nuneaton, 1945. Staff of Royal Institute of International Affairs, 1949-54; Mem. Council, Royal Inst. of Internat. Affairs, 1955-70; Reader (part time) in International Relations, Univ. of Sussex, 1965-71; Member: Council, Inst. for Strategic Studies, 1961-71; Council, Inst. of Race Relations, 1970-71; UN Sub-Commn on the Prevention of Discrimination and Protection of Minorities, 1962-71; Chm., The Africa Bureau, 1963-71; Mem., Internat. Exec., Amnesty International, 1969-71; Chm., The London Library, 1970-73; Dep. Chm., N Metropolitan Conciliation Cttee, 1967-71; Dir of Chatto & Windus Ltd and The Hogarth Press Ltd, 1954-65. Publications: Nuremberg: The Facts, the Law and the Consequences, 1947; Surveys of International Affairs, vol. 1, 1947-48, 1950; vol. 2, 1949-50, 1951; vol. 3, 1951, 1952; vol. 4, 1952, 1953; vol. 5, 1953, 1954; Middle East Crisis (with Guy Wint), 1957; South Africa and World Opinion, 1961; World Order and New States, 1962; World Politics since 1945, 1968; (with Guy Wint) Total War, 1972. Recreation: tennis. Address: Guise House, Aspley Guise, Milton Keynes MK17 8HQ. T: Woburn Sands 2156; 42 William IV Street, WC2. T: 01-240 1966. Club: Garrick.

CAMBELL, Rear-Adm. Dennis Royle Farquharson, CB 1960; DSC 1940; b 13 Nov. 1907; s of Dr Archibald Cambell and Edith Cambell, Southsea; m 1933, Dorothy Elinor Downes; two d. Educ: Westminster Sch. Joined RN, 1925, HMS Thunderer Cadet Training; trained as FAA pilot, 1931; served as pilot in various naval fighter squadrons and aircraft carriers, 1932-38; of 803 Squadron, HMS Ark Royal III, 1939-40; HMS Argus, 1942; naval test pilot, 1941, 1943; Comdr, 1943; British Air Commission, USA, 1944-45; HMS Glory, 1947; Capt. of HMS Tintagel Castle, 1948; Capt., 1949; staff appointments, 1950-54; 1st Capt. of HMS Ark Royal IV, 1955-56; Director of Air Warfare, Admiralty, 1957; Rear-Adm., 1958; Flag Officer, Flying Training, 1957-60; retired, 1960. Legion of Merit (US), 1958. Address: The Old School House, Colemore, Alton, Hants.

CAMBRIDGE, family name of **Marquess of Cambridge.**

CAMBRIDGE, 2nd Marquess of, cr 1917; **George Francis Hugh Cambridge,** GCVO 1933 (KCVO 1927); Earl of Eltham, 1917; Viscount Northallerton, 1917; late Lieut Reserve Regiment 1st Life Guards and Shropshire Yeomanry; Capt. 16th Bn London Regt and RASC, TA; b London, 11 Oct. 1895; er s of 1st Marquess and Lady Margaret Evelyn Grosvenor (d 1929), 3rd d of 1st Duke of Westminster; S father, 1927; m 1923, Dorothy, 2nd d of late Hon. Osmond Hastings; one d. Royal Trustee, British Museum, 1947-73. Heir: none. Address: The Old House, Little Abington, Cambs.
See also Duke of Beaufort.

CAMBRIDGE, Sydney John Guy; HM Diplomatic Service; Counsellor, British High Commission, Nicosia, since 1975; b 5 Nov. 1928; o s of Jack and Mona Cambridge; unmarried. Educ: Marlborough; King's Coll., Cambridge (BA). Entered HM Diplomatic Service, Sept. 1952; Oriental Sec., British Embassy, Jedda, 1952-56; Foreign Office, 1956-60; First Sec., UK Delegn to United Nations, at New York, 1960-64; Head of Chancery, British Embassy, Djakarta, 1964-66; FO, 1966-70; Counsellor, British Embassy, Rome, 1970-73; Head of Financial Relations Dept, FCO, 1973-75. Recreations: mountains, music. Address: c/o Foreign and Commonwealth Office, SW1.

CAMDEN, 5th Marquess cr 1812; **John Charles Henry Pratt;** Baron Camden, 1765; Earl Camden, Viscount Bayham, 1786; Earl of Brecknock, 1812; DL, JP; Major R of O; late Scots Guards; b 12 April 1899; er s of 4th Marquess Camden, GCVO and Lady Joan Marion Nevill, CBE 1920 (d 1952), d of 3rd

Marquess of Abergavenny; *S* father, 1943; *m* 1st, 1920, Marjorie (who obtained a divorce, 1941) (*see* Marjorie, Countess of Brecknock); one *s* one *d* ; 2nd, 1942, Averil (*d* 1977), *d* of late Col Henry Sidney John Streatfeild, DSO; one *s*. *Educ:* Ludgrove, New Barnet, Herts; Eton Coll.; RMC Sandhurst. ADC to Gen. Lord Jeffreys, GOC London Dist, 1920-24. Raised and formed 45th Battery 16th Light AA Regt RA, 1938, and commanded during early part of war of 1939-45, then rejoined Scots Guards; late Hon. Col 516th LAA Regt, RA; Gold Staff at Coronation of King George VI and Queen Elizabeth, 1937. DL, JP, Kent. Conservative Peer: Younger Brother of Trinity House. Dir, Darracq Motor Engineering Co., Bayard Cars Ltd and late Dir of many cos; Dir, Nat. Sporting Club, 1937-40; Director: RAC Buildings Co. Ltd; RAC Country Club Ltd; RAC Travel Service Ltd; President: Tonbridge Area League of Mercy; Tunbridge Wells Area of RSPCA; SE Counties Agricultural Soc., 1948 (and Mem. Council); Tunbridge Wells Amateur Dramatic and Operatic Soc.; Royal Agricultural Soc. of England; Joint Pres. Royal Tunbridge Wells Civic Assoc.; Chm. Bd of Trustees, Living of King Charles-the-Martyr, Tunbridge Wells; Pres. St Pancras Almshouses; a Vice-Pres. and Mem. Cttee of Management of Royal Nat. Life-Boat Inst.; Mem. Council of Boy Scouts Assoc. for County of Kent; Hon. Pres., RAC Motor Sport Council. Late President: Women's Lying-in Hosp., Vincent Sq., SW1; Kent and Sussex Hosp., Tunbridge Wells; late Vice-Pres. Royal Northern Hospital, N7; late Trustee Kent Playing Fields Association. FMI. *Recreations:* shooting, boxing, motor-car racing, yachting, motor-boat racing; interests: farming and forestry. *Heir: s* Earl of Brecknock, *qv. Address:* Bayham Manor, Lamberhurst, Kent. *T:* Lamberhurst 500; 42 Belgrave Mews South, Belgrave Place, SW1. *T:* 01-235 5669. *Clubs:* Cavalry and Guards, Pratt's, Turf, Royal Automobile (Senior Vice-Chm., 1952), British Automobile Racing, etc, MCC, etc; Royal Yacht Squadron (Vice-Cdre 1954-65); House of Lords Yacht (Vice-Cdre); Royal Motor Yacht (Rear-Adm.); Marine Motoring Assoc. (Vice-Pres.); Royal Naval Sailing Assoc. (Hon. Mem.); Yachtsmen's Assoc. of America (Hon. Mem.), etc.

CAMDEN, John; Chairman since 1974 and Managing Director since 1966, Ready Mixed Concrete Ltd; *b* 18 Nov. 1925; *s* of late Joseph Reginald Richard John Camden and of Lilian Kate McCann; *m* 1st, 1951, Helen Demel (marr. diss. 1959); one *s* one *d* ; 2nd, 1959, Irmgard Steinbrink (marr. diss. 1971); one *d* ; 3rd, 1972, Diane Mae Yarbrough; two *d*. *Educ:* Worcester Royal Grammar Sch.; Birmingham Univ. (BSc). Royal Tank Corps and Intell. Corps, 1943-47. Joined Ready Mixed Concrete Group, 1952; Dir responsible for Group's ops in Europe, 1962. *Recreations:* golf, gardening. *Address:* Westbourn, Wentworth, Surrey.

CAME, William Gerald, CIE 1944; BSc (Bristol); retired civil engineer; *b* 8 Dec. 1889; *s* of late John Mathew and Elizabeth Bessie Came, Woodhuish Barton, Brixham, Devon; *m* 1st, 1916, Ada Coombs; one *s* one *d* ; 2nd, 1937, Gertrude Marie Farmer; one *s*. Chief Engineer and Sec. to Govt (Roads and Buildings Dept), Bihar, India, 1942-45; retired 1945; re-appointed as Chief Engineer and Secretary of the I and E Depts, 1945-48. Appointed to PWD (B and O) in 1913; previously with T. B. Cooper & Co., Civil Engineers, Bristol. Old Totnesian and an Associate of Univ. Coll., Bristol. *Address:* Somerley View, Ringwood, Hants. *T:* Ringwood 3733.

CAMERON, Hon. Lord; John Cameron, Kt 1954; DSC; LLD Aberdeen and Edinburgh; DLitt Heriot-Watt; FRSE; HRSA; FRSGS; DL; a Senator of The College of Justice in Scotland and Lord of Session since 1955; *b* 1900; *m* 1st, 1927, Eileen Dorothea (*d* 1943), *d* of late H. M. Burrell; one *s* two *d* ; 2nd, 1944, Iris, *widow* of Lambert C. Shepherd. *Educ:* Edinburgh Acad.; Edinburgh Univ. Served European War, 1918, with RNVR; Advocate, 1924; Advocate-Depute, 1929-36; QC (Scotland), 1936. Served with RNVR, Sept. 1939-44 (despatches, DSC); released to reserve, Dec. 1944. Sheriff of Inverness, Elgin and Nairn, 1945; Sheriff of Inverness, Moray, Nairn and Ross and Cromarty, 1946-48; Dean of Faculty of Advocates, 1948-55. Member: Cttee on Law of Contempt of Court, 1972-; Royal Commn on Civil Liability and Compensation for Personal Injury, 1973-. DL Edinburgh, 1953. *Address:* 28 Moray Place, Edinburgh. *T:* 031-225 7585. *Clubs:* New, Scottish Arts (Edinburgh); Highland (Inverness); Royal Forth Yacht.
See also D. B. Weir.

CAMERON, Prof. Alan Douglas Edward, FBA 1975; Anthon Professor of Latin Language and Literature, Columbia University, New York, since 1977; *b* 13 March 1938; *er s* of A. D. Cameron, Egham; *m* 1962, Averil, *o d* of T. R. Sutton, Leek; one *s* one *d*. *Educ:* St Paul's Sch. (Schol.); New Coll., Oxford (Schol.). Craven Scholar 1958; 1st cl. Hon. Mods 1959; De Paravicini Scholar 1960; Chancellor's Prize for Latin Prose 1960; 1st cl. Lit. Hum. 1961; N. H. Baynes Prize 1967; John Conington Prize 1968. Asst Master, Brunswick Sch., Haywards Heath, 1956-57; Asst Lectr, then Lectr, in Humanity, Glasgow Univ., 1961-64; Lectr in Latin, 1964-71, Reader, 1971-72, Bedford Coll., London; Prof. of Latin, King's Coll., London, 1972-77. Vis. Prof., Columbia Univ., NY, 1967-68. *Publications:* Claudian: Poetry and Propaganda at the Court of Honorius, 1970; (contrib.) Cambridge Prosopography of the Later Roman Empire, ed Jones, Morris and Martindale, 1971; Porphyrius the Charioteer, 1973; Bread and Circuses, 1974; Circus Factions, 1976; articles and reviews in learned jls. *Recreation:* the cinema. *Address:* 81 Harrow View, Harrow, Mddx. *T:* 01-427 7052; Columbia University, Morningside Heights, New York, NY 10027, USA.

CAMERON, Lt-Gen. Sir Alexander (Maurice), KBE 1952; CB 1945; MC; retired; *b* 30 May 1898; *s* of late Major Sir Maurice Alexander Cameron, KCMG; *m* 1922, Loveday (*d* 1965), *d* of Col W. D. Thomson, CMG. *Educ:* Wellington Coll. 2nd Lieut Royal Engineers, 1916. Served European War, France and Belgium (wounded, despatches, MC, 2 medals); S Persia (medal and clasp); Iraq and Kurdistan (two clasps); psc 1929. Brevet Lieut-Col, 1939; RAF Staff Coll., 1939; Brig., 1940; Maj.-Gen. 1943; SHAEF, 1944-45; Dep. QMG, 1945-48; Maj.-Gen. i/c Administration, MELF, 1948-51; GOC East African Comd, 1951-53; retired 1954; Director of Civil Defence South-Eastern Region (Tunbridge Wells), 1955-60. *Club:* Army and Navy.

CAMERON, Major Allan John, DL, JP; Vice-Lord-Lieutenant, Highland Region (Ross and Cromarty), since 1977; *b* 25 March 1917; *s* of Col Sir Donald Cameron of Lochiel, KT, CMG (*d* 1951), and of Lady Hermione Cameron, *d* of Duke of Montrose; *m* 1945, Mary Elizabeth Vaughan-Lee, Dillington, Somerset; two *s* two *d* (and one *s* decd.). *Educ:* Harrow; RMC Sandhurst. Served QO Cameron Highlanders, 1936-48; Major, Retd (POW Middle East, 1942). County Councillor, Ross-shire, 1955-75 (Chm. Educn Cttee, 1962-75); former Member: Red Deer Commn; Countryside Commn for Scotland; Mem., Broadcasting Council for Scotland. *Recreation:* curling (Past Pres. Royal Caledonian Curling Club). *Address:* Allangrange, Munlochy, Ross-shire. *T:* Munlochy 249. *Clubs:* Naval and Military; Highland (Inverness).
See also Col Sir Donald Cameron of Lochiel.

CAMERON of Lochiel, Colonel Sir Donald (Hamish), KT 1973; CVO 1970; TD 1944; JP; 26th Chief of the Clan Cameron; Lord-Lieutenant of County of Inverness, since 1971 (Vice-Lieutenant, 1963-70); Chartered Accountant; Director since 1954, Deputy Chairman, 1965-69, a Vice-Chairman since 1969, Royal Bank of Scotland; Chairman, Scotbits Securities Ltd, since 1968; Director: Culter Guard Bridge Holdings Ltd, since 1970 (Chairman, 1970-76); Scottish Widows Life Assurance Society, since 1955 (Chairman, 1964-67); *b* 12 Sept. 1910; *s* of Col Sir Donald Walter Cameron of Lochiel, KT, CMG, 25th Chief of the Clan Cameron, and Lady Hermione Emily Graham, 2nd *d* of 5th Duke of Montrose; *S* father, as 26th Chief, 1951; *m* 1939, Margaret, *o d* of Lieut-Col Hon. Nigel Gathorne-Hardy, DSO; two *s* two *d*. *Educ:* Harrow; Balliol Coll., Oxford. Joined Lovat Scouts, 1929; Major 1940; Lieut-Col 1945; Lieut-Col comdg 4/5th Bn (TA) QO Cameron Highlanders, 1955-57; Col 1957 (TARO). Hon. Colonel: 4/5th Bn QO Cameron Highlanders, 1958-67; 3rd (Territorial) Bn Queen's Own Highlanders (Seaforth and Camerons), 1967-69; 2nd Bn, 51st Highland Volunteers, 1970-75. Member (part-time): British Railways Bd, 1962-64; Scottish Railways Bd, 1964-72 (Chm. Scottish Area Bd, BTC, 1959-62); Transport Holding Co., 1962-65. Crown Estate Comr, 1957-69. Governor, Harrow Sch., 1967-. *Heir: s* Donald Angus Cameron, younger of Lochiel [*b* 2 Aug. 1946; *m* 1974, Lady Cecil Kerr, *d* of Marquess of Lothian, *qv* ; one *s* one *d*]. *Address:* Achnacarry, Spean Bridge, Inverness-shire. *T:* Gairlochy 208. *Clubs:* Boodle's, Pratt's; New (Edinburgh).
See also J. A. McL. Stewart of Ardvorlich.

CAMERON, Ellen; *see* Malcolm, E.

CAMERON, Sir (Eustace) John, Kt 1977; CBE 1970; MA Cantab; Tasmanian pastoralist, since 1946; Chancellor, University of Tasmania, since 1973; *b* 8 Oct. 1913; *s* of Eustace Noel Cameron and Alexina Maria Cameron; *m* 1934, Nancie Ailsa Sutherland; one *d*. *Educ:* Geelong Grammar Sch.; Trinity Coll., Cambridge. Served RANVR, 1942-46. ICI, 1938-41. State Pres., Liberal Party, 1948-52. Pres., Tasmanian Stockowners Assoc., 1965-68; Vice-Pres., Aust. Graziers, 1968-71. University of Tasmania: Mem. Council, 1956-; Dep. Chancellor, 1964-72. Mem. Selection Cttee, Winston Churchill Fellowship, 1965-74. *Publications:* contrib. Australian Dictionary of Biography. *Recreation:* fishing. *Address:* Lochiel, Ross, Tas 7209,

Australia. *T:* Ross 815253. *Clubs:* Tasmanian (Hobart); Launceston (Launceston).

CAMERON, Rt. Rev. Ewen Donald; Assistant Bishop, Diocese of Sydney, since 1975; *b* 7 Nov. 1926; *s* of Ewen Cameron, Balranald, NSW, and Dulce M. Cameron, Sydney, NSW; *m* 1952, Joan R., *d* of T. Wilkins, Mosman, NSW; one *s* two *d*. *Educ:* Sydney C of E Grammar Sch., N Sydney; Noore Theological Coll., Sydney. ACA (Aust.); BD (London); ThSchol (Aust. Coll. of Theol.). Public Accountancy, 1945-57. Lectr, Moore Theological Coll., 1960-63; Rector, St Stephen's, Bellevue Hill, 1963-65; Federal Secretary, CMS of Aust., 1965-72; Archdeacon of Cumberland with Sydney, 1972-75. *Address:* 3 Mildura Street, Killara, NSW 2071, Australia. *T:* 02-498-5816. *Club:* Union (Sydney).

CAMERON, Francis Ernest, MA (Oxon), FRCO (CHM), ARAM; Assistant Director, State Conservatorium of Music, Sydney, NSW, since 1968; President, Musicological Society of Australia, since 1971; *b* London, 5 Dec. 1927; *er s* of Ernest and Doris Cameron; *m* 1952, Barbara Minns; three *d*. *Educ:* Mercers' Sch.; Caerphilly Boys' Secondary Sch.; Royal Acad. of Music; University Coll., Oxford. Henry Richards Prizewinner, RAM, 1946. Organist, St Peter's, Fulham, 1943; Pianist, Canadian Legion, 1944; Organist, St Luke's, Holloway, 1945; Sub-organist, St Peter's, Eaton Square, 1945; Organist, St James-the-Less, Westminster, 1946; commissioned RASC, 1948; Organ Scholar, University Coll., Oxford, 1950; Organist: St Anne's, Highgate, 1952; St Barnabas', Pimlico, 1953; St Mark's, Marylebone Road, 1957-58; received into Roman Catholic Church, Holy Week, 1959; Choirmaster, St Aloysius, Somers Town, 1959; Master of Music, Westminster Cathedral, 1959; Visiting Organist, Church of St Thomas of Canterbury, Rainham, Kent, 1961; Organist and Choirmaster, Church of Our Lady of the Assumption and St Gregory, 1962-68. Travel for UNESCO, 1952-55; Dep. Dir of Music, LCC (subsequently GLC), 1954-68; Asst-Dir of Music, Emanuel Sch., 1954; Music Master, Central Foundation Boys' Grammar Sch., 1956; Prof. of Organ and Composition, RAM, 1959-68; *locum tenens* Dir of Music, St Felix Sch., Southwold, 1963 and 1964; Pres., "Open Score", 1946-68; inaugural Conductor, Witan Operatic Soc., 1957-58; Conductor "I Cantici," 1961-65; British Adjudicator, Fedn of Canadian Music Festivals, 1965; Conductor, Francis Cameron Chorale, 1965-68; Examr Associated Bd of Royal Schools of Music, 1965-68. *Publications:* editor (with John Steele) Musica Britannica vol. xiv (The Keyboard Music of John Bull, part I), 1960; Old Palace Yard, 1963; incidental music for film The Voyage of the New Endeavour, 1970; songs and incidental music for Congreve's Love for Love, 1972; contributor to: Church Music; Composer; The Conductor; Liturgy; Musical Times; Australian Jl of Music Education; Studies in Music. *Address:* 10 Kirkwood Street, Seaforth, NSW 2092, Australia. *T:* 949-3163.

CAMERON, George Edmund, CBE 1970; Partner, Wright Fitzsimons & Cameron, Chartered Accountants, since 1937; *b* 2 July 1911; *s* of William Cameron and Margaret Cameron (*née* Craig); *m* 1939, Winifred Audrey Brown; two *s*. *Educ:* Ballymena Academy. Chartered Accountant, 1933. Pres., Inst. of Chartered Accountants in Ireland, 1960-61. *Recreations:* golf, gardening. *Address:* Ardavon, Glen Road, Craigavad, Co. Down. *T:* Holywood 2232. *Clubs:* Ulster (Belfast); Royal County Down Golf, Royal Belfast Golf.

CAMERON, Prof. Gordon Campbell; Professor of Town and Regional Planning, University of Glasgow, since 1974; *b* 28 Nov. 1937; *s* of Archibald Arthur Cameron and Elizabeth Forsyth; *m* 1972, Brenda; one *s* one *d*. *Educ:* Quarry Bank High Sch., Liverpool; Hatfield Coll., Univ. of Durham (BA Hons). Res. Asst, Univ. of Durham, 1960-62; Univ. of Glasgow: Asst Lectr in Polit. Econ., 1962-63; Lectr in Applied Econs, 1963-68, Sen. Lectr 1968-71, Titular Prof. 1971-74. Res. Fellow, Resources for the Future, Washington, DC, and Vis. Associate Prof., Pittsburgh Univ., 1966-67; Vis. Prof., Univ. of Calif, Berkeley, 1974. Parly Boundary Comr for Scotland, 1976-. Mem., Cttee of Enquiry into Local Govt Finance (Layfield Cttee), 1974-76. Governor, Centre for Environmental Studies, London, 1975-. Editor, Urban Studies Jl, 1968-74. *Publications:* Regional Economic Development—the federal role, 1971; (with L. Wingo) Cities, Regions and Public Policy, 1974. *Recreations:* tennis, musical concerts, theatre. *Address:* 11 Ledcameroch Crescent, Bearsden, Glasgow G61 4AD. *T:* 041-942 3788.

CAMERON, Gordon Stewart, RSA 1971 (ARSA 1958); Senior Lecturer, School of Drawing and Painting, Duncan of Jordanstone College of Art, Dundee, since 1952; *b* Aberdeen, 27 April 1916; *s* of John Roderick Cameron; *m* 1962, Ellen Malcolm, *qv*. *Educ:* Robert Gordon's Coll., Aberdeen; Gray's

Sch. of Art, Aberdeen. Part-time teaching, Gray's Sch. of Art, 1945-50; engaged on anatomical illustrations for Lockhart's Anatomy of the Human Body, 1945-48; apptd Lectr in Duncan of Jordanstone Coll. of Art, 1952. Awarded Davidson Gold Medal, 1939; Guthrie Award, 1944; Carnegie Travelling Schol., 1946. Work in Public Galleries: Aberdeen, Dundee, Perth, Edinburgh, Glasgow; also in private collections in Scotland, England, Ireland and America. *Recreation:* gardening. *Address:* 7 Auburn Terrace, Invergowrie, Perthshire. *T:* Invergowrie 318.

CAMERON, James; *see* Cameron, M. J. W.

CAMERON, James Clark, CBE 1969; TD 1947; Chairman of Council, British Medical Association, since 1976; *b* 8 April 1905; *s* of Malcolm Clark Cameron, Rannoch, Perthshire; *m* 1933, Irene, *d* of Arthur Ferguson, Perth; one *s* two *d*. *Educ:* Perth Academy; St Andrews Univ. (MB, ChB). Served War of 1939-45, as Captain RAMC attached to 1st Bn, The Rifle Bde (despatches), Calais; POW, 1940. Immediate past Chm., Gen. Med. Services Cttee, and Mem. Council, BMA; Chm., Merton, Sutton and Wandsworth Med. Cttee; Member: Standing Medical Adv. Cttee; Central Health Services Council; Council for Post Grad. Med. Educn; (Chm.) Adv. Cttee on Gen. Practice; Adv. Cttee on Med. Trng; Commn of the European Communities; FRCGP. *Recreation:* medico-politics. *Address:* 201 Croydon Road, Wallington, Surrey SM6 7LT. *T:* 01-647 6123.

CAMERON, Prof. J(ames) Malcolm, MD, PhD(Glas), FRCPath, DMJ; Professor of Forensic Medicine, University of London, at The London Hospital Medical College, since 1973, and Director, Department of Forensic Medicine; Hon. Consultant: to The London Hospital, since 1967; to the Army at Home, in Forensic Medicine, since 1971; to the Royal Navy, in Forensic Medicine, since 1972; Secretary-General of the British Academy of Forensic Sciences and Editor of Medicine, Science and Law; *b* 29 April 1930; *s* of late James Cameron and Doris Mary Robertson; *m* 1956, Primrose Agnes Miller McKerrell, LCST; one *d*. *Educ:* The High Sch. of Glasgow; Univ. of Glasgow (MB, ChB, MD, PhD). Ho. Phys., Belvidere Hosp., Glasgow, 1954; Ho. Surg., Western Infirm., Glasgow, 1954-55 (Orthop. Ho. Surg., 1955); Sen. Ho. Officer in Pathology, Southern Gen. Hosp., Glasgow, 1955-56; McIntyre Clin. Res. Schol., Depts of Path. and Surgery, Glasgow Roy. Infirm., 1956-57; Registrar in Orthop. Surg., Western Infirm., Glasgow, and The Royal Hosp. for Sick Children, Glasgow, 1957-59; Registrar in Lab. Med., 1959-60, and Sen. Registrar in Path., 1960-62, Southern Gen. Hosp., Glasgow; Lectr in Path., Univ. of Glasgow, 1962. The London Hosp. Med. Coll.: Lectr in Forensic Med., 1963-65; Sen. Lectr in Forensic Med., 1965-70; Reader in Forensic Med., 1970-72. Lectr in Forensic Med. at St Bartholomew's Hosp. Med. Coll., Royal Free Hosp. Med. Sch., and Univ. Coll. Hosp. Med. Sch.; Lectr to Metropolitan Police Detective Trng Sch., SW Detective Trng Sch., Bristol, and Special Investigation Br. of RMP; Examiner in Forensic Med. to Univ. of Dublin; Convenor for Exams of Dip. in Med. Jurisp. of Honourable Soc. of Apothecaries of London; former Mem. Council, Royal Coll. of Pathologists. Member: BMA; Council, Brit. Assoc. in Forensic Med., British Acad. of Forensic Sciences (Sec. Gen.); Medico-Legal Soc. (past Vice-Pres.); Assoc. of Police Surgeons of Gt Britain (Hon. Fellow); Forensic Science Soc.; Assoc. of Clinical Pathologists; Pathological Soc. of Gt. Britain and Ire.; Hunterian Soc.; Research Defence Soc.; Soc. for Study of Addiction; Amer. Acad. of Forensic Sciences; Academic Internationalis Medicinae Legalis et Medicinae Socialis. *Publications:* scientific papers in numerous learned jls, both med. and forensic. *Recreations:* sports medicine and legal medicine. *Address:* c/o Department of Forensic Medicine, The London Hospital Medical College, Turner Street, E1 2AD. *T:* 01-247 5454, ext. 360. *Clubs:* Savage, Royal Naval Medical.

CAMERON, Prof. James Munro; University Professor, St Michaels College, University of Toronto, since 1971; *b* 14 Nov. 1910; *o s* of Alan and Jane Helen Cameron; *m* 1933, Vera Shaw; one *s* one *d*. *Educ:* Central Secondary Sch., Sheffield; Keighley Grammar Sch.; Balliol Coll., Oxford (Scholar). Tutor, Workers' Educational Assoc., 1931-32; Staff Tutor, Univ. Coll., Southampton, 1932-35; Staff Tutor, Vaughan Coll., Leicester (Dept of Adult Education, Univ. Coll., Leicester), 1935-43. Univ. of Leeds: Staff Tutor for Tutorial Classes, 1943-47; Lectr in Philosophy, 1947-60 (Sen. Lectr from 1952); Acting Head of Dept of Philosophy, 1954-55 and 1959-60; Prof. of Philosophy, 1960-67; Master of Rutherford Coll., and Prof. of Philosophy, Univ. of Kent at Canterbury, 1967-71. Vis. Prof., Univ. of Notre Dame, Indiana, 1957-58, 1965; Terry Lectr, Yale Univ., 1964-65. Newman Fellow, Univ. of Melbourne, 1968; Christian Culture Award, Univ. of Windsor, Ont, 1972. *Publications:* Scrutiny of Marxism, 1948; (trans. with Marianne Kuschnitzky)

Max Picard, The Flight from God, 1951; John Henry Newman, 1956; The Night Battle, 1962; Images of Authority, 1966; (ed) Essay on Development (1845 edn), by J. H. Newman, 1974; contribs to other books, and articles and papers in many periodicals. Address: University of St Michael's College, 81 St Mary Street, Toronto, Canada M5S 1J4.

CAMERON, Sir John; see Cameron, Hon. Lord.

CAMERON, Sir John; see Cameron, Sir E. J.

CAMERON, John Charles Finlay; Member, London Transport Executive, since 1975; b 8 Feb. 1928; s of Robert John and Nancy Angela Cameron; m 1955, Ruth Constance, d of A. D. Thompson, Sydney, NSW; two s two d. Educ: privately; University Coll., Southampton. CEng, MICE, FCIT, FIPM. Served in Royal Marines, 1946-48. Joined British Railways, Southern Region, as civil engineering draughtsman, 1948; work study assistant in British Transport Commn, 1957; Personnel and Admin. Manager of BR Workshops, 1962-68; Dir of Personnel, Rank Precision Industries, 1968; Manpower Resources Adviser to Rank Organisation, 1970; Gen. Manager, Taylor Hobson Optics, 1971; Dir and Gen. Manager, Rank Optics, 1973. Publications: papers on industrial engrg to ICE and others. Recreations: building, garden construction, music. Address: Tarrawonga, Carlton Road, South Godstone, Surrey RH9 8LE. T: South Godstone 3263.

CAMERON, Brigadier John S.; see Sorel Cameron.

CAMERON, John Taylor, QC (Scot.) 1973; b 24 April 1934; s of late John Reid Cameron, MA, formerly Director of Education, Dundee; m 1964, Bridget Deirdre Sloan; no c. Educ: Fettes Coll.; Corpus Christi Coll., Oxford; Edinburgh Univ. BA (Oxon), LLB (Edinburgh). Admitted to Faculty of Advocates, 1960. Lecturer in Public Law, Edinburgh Univ., 1960-64. Keeper of the Advocates' Library, 1977-; an Advocate-Depute, 1977-. Publications: articles in legal jls. Address: 17 Moray Place, Edinburgh EH3 6DT. T: 031-225 7695.

CAMERON, Prof. Kenneth, FBA 1976; Professor of English Language, University of Nottingham, since 1963; b Burnley, Lancs, 21 May 1922; s of late Angus W. Cameron and of E. Alice Cameron, Habergham, Burnley; m 1947, Kathleen, d of late F. E. Heap, Burnley; one s one d. Educ: Burnley Grammar Sch.; Univ. of Leeds (BA Hons, Sch. of English Language and Literature); PhD Sheffield. Served War, 1941-45; Pilot, RAF. Asst Lectr in English Language, Univ. of Sheffield, 1947-50; Nottingham University: Lectr in English Language, 1950-59; Sen. Lectr, 1959-62; Reader, 1962-63. Sir Israel Gollancz Meml Lecture, British Academy, 1976. Pres., Viking Soc., 1972-74; Hon. Dir, 1966-, Hon. Sec., 1972-, English Place-Name Soc. Gen. Editor, English Place-Name Survey, 1966-; Editor, Jl of the English Place-Name Soc., 1972-. FRHistS 1970. Hon. FilDr, Uppsala, 1977. Sir Israel Gollancz Meml Prize, British Academy, 1969. Publications: The Place-Names of Derbyshire, 1959; English Place-Names, 1961; Scandinavian Settlement in the Territory of the Five Boroughs: the place-name evidence, 1965; contribs to: Nottingham Medieval Studies; Medium Ævum; Mediaeval Scandinavia; Festschrifts, etc. Recreations: sports (supporting), home, "The Crown". Address: 292 Queens Road, Beeston, Nottingham. T: Nottingham 254503.

CAMERON, (Mark) James (Walter); journalist and author; b 17 June 1911; s of William Ernest Cameron, MA, LLB, and Margaret Douglas Robertson; m 1st, 1938, Eleanor Mara Murray (decd); one d; 2nd, 1944, Elizabeth O'Conor (marr. diss.); one s (and one step s); 3rd, 1971, Moneesha Sarkar; one step s one step d. Educ: erratically, at variety of small schools, mostly in France. Began journalism, in Dundee, 1928; after leaving Scotland joined many staffs and wrote for many publications, travelling widely as Foreign Correspt in most parts of the world; finally with (late) News Chronicle. Subseq. prod. numerous TV films, on contemporary subjects. Initiated travel series, Cameron Country, on BBC 2. Hon. Governor, Mermaid Theatre. Hon. DLitt Lancaster, 1970. Granada Award, Journalist of the Year, 1965; Granada Foreign Correspt of the Decade, 1966; Hannen Swaffer Award for Journalism, 1966. Publications: Touch of the Sun, 1950; Mandarin Red, 1955; "1914", 1959; The African Revolution, 1961; "1916", 1962; Witness in Viet Nam, 1966; Point of Departure, 1967; What a Way to Run a Tribe, 1968; An Indian Summer, 1974. Play: The Pump (radio), 1973 (Prix Italia 1973). Recreations: private life, public houses. Address: 3 Eton College Road, NW3. T: 01-586 5340. Club: Savile.

CAMERON, Marshal of the Royal Air Force Sir Neil, GCB 1976 (KCB 1975; CB 1971); CBE 1967; DSO 1945; DFC 1944; Chief of the Defence Staff, since 1977; b 8 July 1920; s of Neil and Isabella Cameron, Perth, Scotland; m 1947, Patricia Louise, d of Major Edward Asprey; one s one d. Educ: Perth Academy. Fighter and Fighter Bomber Sqdns, 1940-45; Directing Staff, Sch. of Land/Air Warfare, Old Sarum, 1945-48; Student, RAF Staff Coll., 1949; DS, RAF Staff Coll., 1952-55; CO, Univ. of London Air Sqdn, 1955-56; Personal Staff Officer, Chief of Air Staff, 1956-59; CO, RAF Abingdon, 1959-62; Imperial Defence Coll., 1963; Principal Staff Officer, Dep. Supreme Comdr, SHAPE, Paris, 1964; Asst Comdt, RAF Coll., Cranwell, 1965; Programme Evaluation Gp, MoD, 1965-66; Assistant Chief of Defence Staff (Policy), 1968-70; SASO Air Support Comd, 1970-72; Dep. Comdr, RAF Germany, 1972-73; AOC 46 Gp, RAF, 1974; Air Member for Personnel, MoD, 1974-76; Chief of the Air Staff, 1976-77. Air ADC to the Queen, 1976-77. Publications: articles in defence jls. Recreations: reading, Rugby football, defence affairs. Address: Ministry of Defence, Whitehall, SW1. Club: Royal Air Force.

CAMERON, Thomas Wright Moir, OC 1972; TD; PhD Edinburgh; HARCVS; MA Edinburgh; DSc Edinburgh; DSc BC; FRSC; Professor Emeritus of Parasitology, McGill University, Montreal; b Glasgow, 29 April 1894; e s of Hugh Cameron, Edinburgh; m Stella Blanche, y d of F. H. Hill, Oxford; one d. Educ: Allan Glen's Sch., Glasgow; Glasgow, Edinburgh, and London Univs; Royal (Dick) Veterinary Coll., Edinburgh. Commission in HLI 1914-16; RAF 1916-19; in Royal (Dick) Vet. Contingent OTC 1921-23; Major RAVC (TA) London (2nd Div.), 1923-35; McGill COTC 1939-42. Res. Schol., Edinburgh Univ., 1921-23; Min. of Agric. Res. Schol., 1921-23; Sen. Res. Asst, Inst. of Agricultural Parasitology, London, 1923-25; Lecturer and Milner Fellow, Dept of Helminthology, London Sch. of Hygiene and Tropical Medicine, 1925-29; Dir. and Founder, Inst. of Parasitology, 1932-64. Sec., Sect. of Tropical Diseases and Parasitology, Vice-President Sect. of Comparative Medicine, RSM, 1926-29; Lecturer in Helminthology, Univ. of Edinburgh and Royal (Dick) Veterinary Coll., 1929-32; Contrib. on Vet. Diseases to Bull. of Hygiene; Sec., Edin. and Can. Brs, Royal Soc. of Tropical Medicine and Hygiene. President: American Society of Parasitologists, 1949; Sect. V, RSC, 1949-50; RSC, 1957-58; Can. Society of Microbiology, 1959; Can. Society of Zoology, 1960; World Federation of Parasitologists, 1965-; Chairman, Can. Cttee, International Biological Programme; Ed., Canadian Jl Zool. Publications: Animal Diseases in Relation to Man; Internal Parasites of Domestic Animals; Principles of Parasite Control; Parasites of Man in Temperate Climates; Early History of Caribe Islands; Parasites and Parasitism; numerous papers on parasitic helminths, and on diseases of animals in relation to man. Address: 15300 Wallbrook Court, Apt 304, Silver Spring, Maryland 20906, USA.

CAMERON-RAMSAY-FAIRFAX-LUCY; see Fairfax-Lucy.

CAMERON WATT, Prof. Donald; Professor of International History in the University of London, since 1972; b 17 May 1928; s of Robert Cameron Watt, qv; m 1st, 1951, Marianne Ruth Grau (d 1962); one s; 2nd, 1962, Felicia Cobb Stanley; one step d. Educ: Rugby Sch.; Oriel Coll., Oxford. BA 1951, MA 1954; FRHistS. Asst Editor, Documents on German Foreign Policy, 1918-1945, in Foreign Office, 1951-54; Asst Lectr, Lectr, Sen. Lectr in Internat. History, LSE, 1954-66; Reader in Internat. History in Univ. of London, 1966; Editor, Survey of Internat. Affairs, Royal Inst. of Internat. Affairs, 1962-72; Rockefeller Research Fellow in Social Sciences, Inst of Advanced Internat. Studies, Washington, 1960-61; Sec., 1967, Chm., 1976-, Assoc. of Contemporary Historians; Chm., Greenwich Forum, 1974-. Mem. Editorial Bd, Political Quarterly, 1969-. Publications: Britain and the Suez Canal, 1956; (ed) Documents on the Suez Crisis, 1957; Britain looks to Germany, 1965; Personalities and Policies, 1965; (ed) Survey of International Affairs, 1961, 1966; (ed) Documents on International Affairs 1961, 1966; (ed, with K. Bourne) Studies in International History, 1967; A History of the World in the Twentieth Century, Pt I, 1967; (ed) Contemporary History of Europe, 1969; (ed) Hitler's Mein Kampf, 1969; (ed) Survey of International Affairs, 1962, 1969; (ed, with James Mayall): Current British Foreign Policy, 1970, 1971; Current British Foreign Policy, 1972, 1973; Too Serious a Business, 1975. Recreations: exploring London, cats. Address: c/o London School of Economics and Political Science, Houghton Street, WC2A 2AE. Clubs: Playboy, Players Theatre.

CAMILLERI, His Honour Sir Luigi A., Kt 1954; LLD; Chief Justice and President of the Court of Appeal, Malta, 1952-57, retired; b 7 Dec. 1892; s of late Notary Giuseppe amd Matilde (née Bonello); m 1914, Erminia, d of Professor G. Cali'; five s three d. Educ: Gozo Seminary; Royal Univ. of Malta (LLD). Called to the Bar, 1913. Consular Agent for France in Gozo,

Malta, 1919-24; Malta Legislative Assembly, 1921-24; Magistrate, 1924-30; Visitor of Notarial Acts, Chairman Board of Prison Visitors, Chairman Licensing Board, Magistrate in charge of Electoral Register, 1927-30; Judicial Bench, 1930; Royal Univ. of Malta representative on General Council of the Univ., 1933-36; Chairman Emergency Compensation Board, 1940-41; Court of Appeal, 1940-57; President Medical Council, Malta, 1959-68; Member Judicial Service Commission, 1959-62. Examiner in Criminal, Roman and Civil Law, Royal Univ. of Malta, 1931-70. Silver Jubilee Medal, 1935; Coronation Medals, 1937 and 1953. Knight of Sovereign Military Order of Malta, 1952. *Recreation:* walking. *Address:* Victoria Avenue, Sliema, Malta. *T:* Sliema 33532. *Club:* Casino Maltese (Malta).

CAMOYS, 7th Baron *cr* 1264 (called out of abeyance, 1839); **Ralph Thomas Campion George Sherman Stonor;** Chairman, Amex Bank Ltd, since 1977 (Chief Executive Officer and Managing Director, 1975-77); *b* 16 April 1940; *s* of 6th Baron Camoys and of Mary Jeanne, *d* of late Captain Herbert Marmaduke Joseph Stourton, OBE; *S* father, 1976; *m* 1966, Elisabeth Mary Hyde, *d* of Sir William Stephen Hyde Parker, 11th Bt; one *s* three *d*. *Educ:* Eton Coll.; Balliol Coll., Oxford (BA). Gen. Manager and Director, National Provincial and Rothschild (London) Ltd, 1968; Man. Director, Rothschild Intercontinental Bank Ltd, 1969. *Recreations:* the arts, shooting. *Heir:* *s* Hon. (Ralph) William (Robert Thomas) Stonor, *b* 10 Sept. 1974. *Address:* Alston Court, Nayland, Suffolk. *T:* Nayland 262651. *Club:* Boodle's.

CAMP, Jeffery Bruce, ARA 1974; artist; Lecturer, Slade School of Fine Art; *b* 1923; *s* of George Camp and Caroline Denny; *m* 1963, Laetitia Yhap. *Educ:* Edinburgh Coll. of Art. DA (Edin.). Awarded Andrew Grant post-graduate and travelling bursaries, 1944-45. Mem., London Group, 1961. One-man exhibitions: Beaux Arts Gallery, 1959, 1961, 1963; New Art Centre, 1968. Exhibitions: South London Art Gall., 1973 (retrospective); British Painting, Arts Council, Hayward Gall., 1974; Arts Council, Drawings of People, Serpentine Gall., 1975 (Chantrey Bequest purchase, 1975). *Recreation:* walking by the sea. *Address:* 78 Forthbridge Road, SW11 5NY. *T:* 01-223 5686.

CAMP, William Newton Alexander; communications consultant and author; *b* 12 May 1926; *s* of I. N. Camp, OBE, Colonial Administrative Service, Palestine, and Freda Camp; *m* 1st, 1950, Patricia Cowan (marr. diss. 1973); two *s* one *d*; 2nd, 1975, Juliet Schubart. *Educ:* Bradfield Coll.; Oriel Coll., Oxford (Classical Scholar, MA). Asst Res. Officer, British Travel and Holidays Assoc., 1950-54; Asst Sec., Consumer Adv. Council, 1954-59; Asst Sec., Gas Council, 1960-63; Public Relations Adviser, Gas Council, 1963-67; Dir of Information Services, British Steel Corp., 1967-71; Mem., British Nat. Oil Corp., 1976-; Special Adviser: milling and baking industries, 1972-; British Leyland Motor Corp., 1975; railway trades unions, 1975-76; C. A. Parsons & Co. Ltd, 1976-77; pt-time advr, British Railways Bd, 1977-. Chm., Oxford Univ. Labour Club, 1949; contested (Lab) Solihull, 1950; Mem., Southwark Borough Council, 1953-56; Press Adviser (unpaid) to Prime Minister, Gen. Election, 1970. Founder Mem., Public Enterprise Group. *Publications:* novels: Prospects of Love, 1957; Idle on Parade, 1958; The Ruling Passion, 1959; A Man's World, 1962; Two Schools of Thought, 1964; Flavour of Decay, 1967; The Father Figures, 1970; *biography:* The Glittering Prizes (F. E. Smith), 1960. *Address:* 61 Gloucester Crescent, NW1. *T:* 01-485 5110; Keeper's Cottage, Marshfield, near Chippenham, Wilts.

CAMPBELL; *see* Graham-Campbell.

CAMPBELL, family name of Duke of Argyll, of Earl of Breadalbane, of Earl Cawdor, and of Barons Campbell of Croy, Campbell of Eskan, Colgrain, Glenavy and Stratheden.

CAMPBELL OF CROY, Baron *cr* 1974 (Life Peer), of Croy in the County of Nairn; **Gordon Thomas Calthrop Campbell,** PC 1970; MC 1944, and Bar, 1945; *b* 8 June 1921; *s* of late Maj.-Gen. J. A. Campbell, DSO; *m* 1949, Nicola Elizabeth Gina Madan; two *s* one *d*. *Educ:* Wellington and Hospital. War of 1939-45: commissioned in Regular Army, 1939; RA, Major, 1942; commanded 320 Field Battery in 15 Scottish Div.; wounded and disabled, 1945. Entered HM Foreign Service, 1946; served, until 1957, in FO, UK Delegn to the UN (New York), Cabinet Office and Vienna. MP (C) Moray and Nairn, 1959-Feb. 1974; Asst Govt Whip, 1961-62; a Lord Comr of the Treasury and Scottish Whip, 1962-63; Joint Parly Under-Sec. of State, Scottish Office, 1963-64; Opposition Spokesman on Defence and Scottish Affairs, 1966-70; Sec. of State for Scotland, 1970-74. *Recreations:* music, birds. *Address:* Holme Rose, Cawdor, Nairnshire, Scotland. *T:* Croy 223. *Club:* Brooks's.

CAMPBELL OF ESKAN, Baron *cr* 1966 (Life Peer), of Camis Eskan; **John (Jock) Middleton Campbell;** Kt 1957; President, Booker McConnell Ltd, since 1967 (Chairman 1952-66); Chairman: Milton Keynes Development Corporation, since 1967; Commonwealth Sugar Exporters' Association, since 1950; Director, Commonwealth Development Corporation, since 1968; Trustee: Runnymede Trust; Chequers Trust; *b* 8 Aug. 1912; *e s* of late Colin Algernon Campbell, Colgrain, Dunbartonshire and Underriver House, Sevenoaks, Kent and of Mary Charlotte Gladys (Barrington); *m* 1st, 1938, Barbara Noel (marr. diss. 1948), *d* of late Leslie Arden Roffey; two *s* two *d*; 2nd, 1949, Phyllis Jacqueline Gilmour Taylor, *d* of late Henry Boyd, CBE. *Educ:* Eton; Exeter Coll., Oxford (Hon. Fellow, 1973). Chairman: Statesman and National Publishing Co. Ltd, 1964-77; New Towns Assoc., 1975-77; Dir, London Weekend TV Ltd, 1967-74 (Dep. Chm., 1969-73); Pres., West India Cttee, 1957-77. Mem., Community Relations Commn, 1968-77 (a Dep-Chm., 1968-71). DUniv Open, 1973. *Recreations:* reading, hitting balls, painting. *Address:* Crocker End House, Nettlebed, Oxfordshire. *T:* Nettlebed 202; 15 Eaton Square, SW1. *T:* 01-839 5133. *Clubs:* Beefsteak, Royal Commonwealth Society (West Indian), MCC, All England Lawn Tennis; Huntercombe, Portmarnock (Golf).

CAMPBELL, Sir Alan (Hugh), KCMG 1976 (CMG 1964); HM Diplomatic Service; Ambassador to Italy, since 1976; *b* 1 July 1919; *y s* of late Hugh Campbell and Ethel Campbell (née Warren); *m* 1947, Margaret Taylor; three *d*. *Educ:* Sherborne Sch.; Caius Coll., Cambridge. Served in Devonshire Regt, 1940-46. 3rd Sec., HM Foreign (now Diplomatic) Service, 1946; appointed to Lord Killearn's Special Mission to Singapore, 1946; served in Rome, 1952, Peking, 1955; UK Mission to UN, New York, 1961; Head of Western Dept, Foreign Office, 1965; Counsellor, Paris, 1967; Ambassador to Ethiopia, 1969-72; Asst Under-Sec. of State, FCO, 1972-74; Dep. Under-Sec. of State, FCO, 1974-76. Governor, Sherborne Sch., 1973-. *Recreation:* lawn tennis. *Address:* c/o Foreign and Commonwealth Office, SW1. *Clubs:* United Oxford & Cambridge University, Brooks's.

CAMPBELL, Alan Johnston, CMG 1973; retired grazier, Roma, Qld; President, Australian Country Party, Queensland, 1943-51; Federal and State Trustee, Australian Country Party, 1954-68; *b* Dubbo, NSW, 31 July 1895; *s* of Charles Campbell, Dalrymple, Scotland, and Sarah Ann Eliza (née Occleston); *m* 1965, Barbara Jane Dunn, Brisbane. *Educ:* Toowoomba Grammar Sch., Queensland. Served War, 1914-19, in 2nd Australian Light Horse Regt, in Gallipoli and Palestine. Owner of, and controlled, several sheep and cattle stations in Western Queensland from 1920 till retired in 1950, to live in Brisbane. Played active executive parts in various Grazing Industry organisations, 1922-35. Chairman: Charles Campbell & Sons Pty Ltd, of Merino Downs and Cooinda, Roma, Qld, 1933-50; The Countryman Newspaper Pty Ltd, 1947-68. Mem., for many years, Royal Society of Queensland and Australian Inst. of Internat. Affairs; directed various campaigns in grazing industry, 1929-36; Mem. Council, United Graziers Assoc. of Qld, 1929-33. Life Fellow: RGS (London), 1972; RGS (Australasia), 1956. *Publications:* The History of the Charles Campbell Clan 1781-1974; Memoirs of the Country Party 1920-74. *Recreations:* politics, photography, world travel. *Address:* Queensland Club, GPO Box 4, Brisbane, Queensland 4001, Australia. *T:* Brisbane 221.7072; (residence) 378.1477. *Clubs:* Queensland, Tattersall's, Queensland Turf, Royal Automobile (Qld) (all in Brisbane).

CAMPBELL, Alan Robertson, QC 1965; a Recorder of the Crown Court, since 1976; *b* 24 May 1917; *s* of late J. K. Campbell; *m* 1957, Vivien, *y d* of late Comdr A. H. de Kantzow, DSO, RN. *Educ:* Aldenham; Ecole des Sciences Politiques, Paris; Trinity Hall, Cambridge. Called to Bar, Inner Temple, 1939, Bencher, 1972; Western Circuit. Commissioned RA (Suppl. Res.), 1939; served France and Belgium, 1939-40; POW, 1940-45. Consultant to sub-cttee of Legal Cttee of Council of Europe on Industrial Espionage, 1965-74; Chm., Legal Res. Cttee, Soc. of Conservative Lawyers, 1968-. Member: Law Adv. Cttee, British Council, 1974-; Management Cttee, UK Assoc. for European Law, 1975-. *Publications:* (with Lord Wilberforce) Restrictive Trade Practices and Monopolies, 1956, 2nd edn, 1973; Restrictive Trading Agreements in the Common Market, 1964, and 1965 Supplement; Common Market Law, vols 1 and 2, 1969, vol. 3, 1973 and 1975 Supplements; Industrial Relations Act, 1971. *Address:* 1 Harcourt Buildings, Temple, EC4. *T:* 01-353 2214. *Clubs:* Carlton, Pratt's.

CAMPBELL, Hon. Alexander Bradshaw, PC (Canada) 1967; QC (Can) 1966; MLA; Premier, Province of Prince Edward Island, Canada, since 1966, re-elected 1970, 1974; *b* 1 Dec. 1933; *s* of Dr Thane A. Campbell and late Cecilia B. Campbell; *m* 1961,

Marilyn Gilmour; two *s* one *d. Educ:* Dalhousie Univ. (BA, LLB). Called to Bar of Prince Edward Island, 1959; practised law with Campbell & Campbell, Summerside, PEI, 1959-66. Elected MLA, 1965; Leader of Liberal Party, Dec. 1966; has served (while Premier) as Attorney-Gen., 1966-69, Minister of Development, 1969-72, Minister of Agriculture, 1972-74, and Minister of Justice, 1974-. Elder of Trinity United Church, Summerside. Hon. LLD McGill 1967. *Recreations:* curling, skiing, golf, boating. *Address:* 330 Beaver Street, Summerside, PEI, Canada. *T:* 436-2714. *Clubs:* Summerside Board of Trade, Y's Men's (Summerside).

CAMPBELL, Prof. (Alexander) Colin (Patton), FRCPath, FRCPE; Director of Studies, Royal College of Pathologists, since 1973; Procter Professor of Pathology and Pathological Anatomy, University of Manchester, 1950-73, now Professor Emeritus (formerly Dean, Faculty of Medicine and Pro-Vice Chancellor); *b* 21 Feb. 1908; *s* of late A. C. Campbell, Londonderry; *m* 1943, Hon. Elisabeth Joan Adderley, 2nd *d* of 6th Baron Norton; two *s* one *d. Educ:* Foyle Coll., Londonderry; Edinburgh Univ. MB, ChB (Hons) Edinburgh 1930; FRCPE 1939. Rockefeller Fellow and Research Fellow in Neuropathology, Harvard Univ., 1935-36; Lectr in Neuropathology, Edinburgh Univ., 1937-39; Lectr in Pathology, Edinburgh Univ., and Pathologist, Royal Infirmary, Edinburgh, 1939-50. War service, 1940-46, RAFVR (Wing-Comdr). *Publications:* papers on pathological subjects in various medical and scientific jls. *Recreations:* carpentry and cabinet-making. *Address:* The Priory House, Ascott-under-Wychwood, Oxford OX7 6AW.

CAMPBELL, Maj.-Gen. Sir (Alexander) Douglas, KBE 1956 (CBE 1945); CB 1949; DSO 1943; MC 1918; MA (Cantab); Colonel Commandant Royal Engineers, 1958-64; *b* 20 June 1899; *s* of late Colonel Alan James Campbell, DSO; *m* 1923, Patience Loveday Carlyon; three *s* one *d* (one *s* killed in action, 1945). *Educ:* Aravon Sch., Bray; Cheltenham Coll.; RMA Woolwich; Queens' Coll., Cambridge. Served European War, 1914-18, France 1918; DADFW War Office, 1933-39; War of 1939-45 (despatches); France, 1940; Asst Dir, Bomb Disposal, 1940; Chief Engr 9 Corps, N Africa, 1943; Chief Engr 1 Corps, Normandy, June 1944; Chief Engr Second Army, 1944-45; Chief Engr Fourteenth Army, June-Nov. 1945; Dep. Dir Tactical Investigation, 1945-46; Chief Engr MELF, 1947-48. E-in-C War Office, 1948-52; Vice-Adjt General to the Forces, 1952-54; Comdr Aldershot District, 1954-57, retired. Lieut Governor, Royal Hospital, Chelsea, 1957-62. Pres., Instn of Royal Engineers, 1957-61; Pres., Assoc. of Service Newspapers, 1957-74. Vice-Chm., Council of Voluntary Welfare Work, 1956-62; Member: Army Benevolent Fund Control Board, 1958-62; ATS Benevolent Fund Cttee, 1953-57 and 1959-63; Soldiers' and Airmen's Scripture Readers' Assoc. (SASRA), 1934-73. Vice-President: Officers' Christian Union, 1958-71; Sandes Soldiers' Homes; Pres., Cheltonian Soc., 1963-64; Governor and Vice-Chm., Royal Sch. for Daughters of Army Officers, 1958-74; Mem. Exec. Cttee, Gordon Boys' Sch., 1959-73; Chm., Newells and Desmoor Sch., 1968-75; Pres., Handcross Park Sch., 1976-. Dir, Taylor Woodrow Industrial Estates, 1962-65. Hon. Colonel, Queen's Univ., Belfast OTC, 1959-64. Commander USA Legion of Merit, 1946. *Address:* Green Bough Cottage, Shipley, Horsham, W Sussex. *T:* Coolham 291. *Club:* Army and Navy.

CAMPBELL, Archibald, CMG 1966; Assistant Under-Secretary of State, Ministry of Defence, 1969-74 (Assistant Secretary, 1967-69); *b* 10 Dec. 1914; *s* of Archibald Campbell and Jessie Sanders Campbell (*née* Halsall); *m* 1939, Peggie Phyllis Hussey; two *s* one *d. Educ:* Berkhamsted Sch.; Hertford Coll., Oxford. BA Oxford 1935. Barrister at Law, Middle Temple. Administrative Service, Gold Coast, 1936-46; Colonial Office, 1946; Colonial Attaché, British Embassy, Washington, 1953-56; Asst Secretary, Colonial Office, 1956-59 and 1962-67; Chief Secretary, Malta, 1959-62. *Recreations:* cricket (capped for Bucks in Minor County Competition, 1951); fishing, climbing, gardening. *Address:* Bransbury, Long Park, Chesham Bois, Bucks. *T:* Amersham 7727. *Club:* MCC.

CAMPBELL, Archibald Hunter, LLM, BCL, MA, of Lincoln's Inn, Barrister-at-Law; Regius Professor of Public Law, University of Edinburgh, 1945-72, and Dean of the Faculty of Law, 1958-64; *b* Edinburgh, 1902; *o c* of late Donald Campbell, MA. *Educ:* George Watson's Coll., Edinburgh (Dux); Univ. of Edinburgh (MA, Mackenzie Class. Schol., Ferguson Class. Schol.); University Coll., Oxford (Class. Exhibitioner). 1st Class in Hon. Mods, Lit. Hum., Jurisprudence and BCL; Sen. Demy of Magdalen Coll., 1927-28; Sen. Student of Oxford Univ., 1928; Fellow of All Souls, 1928-30 and 1936-; Stowell Civil Law Fellow, University Coll., Oxford, 1930-35; Barber Professor of

Jurisprudence, Univ. of Birmingham, 1935-45. Vice-President Society of Public Teachers of Law, 1961-62, President 1962-63. President Classical Assoc. of Scotland, 1963-. Hon. LLD Aberdeen, 1963. *Address:* 8 Braid Hills Road, Edinburgh EH10 6EZ. *Club:* New (Edinburgh).

CAMPBELL of Achalader, Brig. Archibald Pennant, DSO 1945; OBE 1939; psc 1930; retired, 1947; Ninth Chief of Baronial House of Campbell of Achalader since 1963; *b* 26 Jan. 1896; *s* of Brig.-Gen. J. C. L. Campbell of Achalader (*d* 1930); *m* 1st, 1926, Phyllis (*d* 1953), *d* of late Sir Henry Bax-Ironside, KCMG; one *d*; 2nd, 1961, Elsie, widow of Dr Howard Clapham, and *d* of late J. Thompson. *Educ:* Malvern; RMA. 2nd Lieut, RFA, 1914. Served European War, 1914-18, with RA 22nd Div. (despatches). Silver Staff Officer at Jubilee of HM King George V, 1935. GSO 2, HQ (British Troops), Egypt, 1937; Bt Lt-Col, 1939; temp. Brig., 1941; Col, 1943. Served War, 1939-45 (Egypt, UK, and NW Europe) as BGS 8 Corps Dist, CRA 47 Div., CCRA 2 Corps Dist and Comdr 8 AGRA. Served in Palestine as Comdr North Palestine Dist, 1945-46; Comdr Suez Canal South, 1946-47. Dist Comr, Boy Scouts Assoc., 1955; British Consular Agent, Moji, Japan, 1957-58. *Recreations:* shooting (big and small game), fishing, hunting. *Address:* 6 Rockley Road, South Yarra, Victoria 3141, Australia. *T:* Melbourne 248300. *Club:* Naval and Military (London).

CAMPBELL, Arnold Everitt, CMG 1966; retired as Director-General of Education, Department of Education, Wellington, New Zealand (1960-66); *b* 13 Aug. 1906; *s* of Fernly Charlwood and Mabel Annie Campbell; *m* 1934, Louise Annie Combs; one *s* two *d. Educ:* Palmerston North Boys' High Sch.; Wellington Teachers' Coll., Victoria Univ. of Wellington. Primary school teacher, 1926-28; Lecturer in Education, Victoria Univ. of Wellington, 1929-38; Director, NZ Council for Educational Research, 1939-52; Chief Inspector of Primary Schools, Dept of Education, 1953-58; Asst Director of Education, 1959. Hon. Fellow, NZ Educnl Inst., 1972. *Publication:* Educating New Zealand, 1941. *Address:* 13 Pitt Street, Wellington, New Zealand. *T:* 45-438.

CAMPBELL, Maj.-Gen. Charles Peter, CBE 1977; Engineer-in-Chief (Army), since 1977; *b* 25 Aug. 1926; *s* of late Charles Alfred Campbell and of Blanche Campbell; *m* 1949, Lucy Kitching; two *s . Educ:* Gillingham Grammar Sch.; Emmanuel Coll., Cambridge. MBIM. Commnd RE, 1945; psc 1957; DAA&QMG Trng Bde, RE, 1958-60; OC 11 Indep. Field Sqdn, RE, 1960-62; Jt Services Staff Coll., 1963; DAAG WO, 1963-65; Co. Comd, RMA Sandhurst, 1965-67; CO 21 Engr Regt, 1967-70; GSOI MoD, 1970-71; CRE 3 Div., 1971; Comd 12 Engr Bde, 1972-73; RCDS, 1974; COS HQ NI, 1975-77. *Recreations:* Rugby football referee, collecting and painting model soldiers. *Address:* c/o Lloyds Bank Ltd, Cox's & King's Branch, 6 Pall Mall, SW1Y 5NH. *Club:* Naval and Military.

CAMPBELL, Sir Clifford (Clarence), GCMG 1962; GCVO 1966; Governor-General of Jamaica, 1962-73; *b* 28 June 1892; *s* of late James Campbell, civil servant, and Blanche, *d* of John Ruddock, agriculturist; *m* 1920, Alice Esthephene, *d* of late William Jolly, planter; two *s* two *d. Educ:* Petersfield Sch.; Mico Training Coll., Jamaica. Headmaster: Fullersfield Govt Sch., 1916-18; Friendship Elementary Sch., 1918-28; Grange Hill Govt Sch., 1928-44. Member Jamaica House of Representatives (Jamaica Labour Party) for Westmoreland Western, 1944-49; Chm., House Cttee on Education, 1945-49; 1st Vice-President, Elected Members Assoc., 1945; re-elected 1949; Speaker of the House of Representatives, 1950; Senator and President of the Senate, 1962. KStJ. *Recreations:* agricultural pursuits, reading. *Address:* 8 Cherry Gardens Avenue, Kingston 8, Jamaica. *Clubs:* (Hon. Member) Caymanas Golf and Country, Ex-Services, Kingston Cricket, Liguanea, Rotary, St Andrew's, Trelawny (all in Jamaica).

CAMPBELL, Colin; *see* Campbell, A. C. P.

CAMPBELL, Sir Colin, Kt 1952; OBE 1941; Town Clerk, Plymouth, 1935-53; *b* 1891; *m* 1923, Matilda Hopwood (*d* 1955); two *d. Educ:* Burnley Grammar Sch. Town Clerk, Burnley, 1923-35. ARP Controller of Plymouth, 1939-45. *Recreation:* golf. *Address:* Reedley Hallows, Delgany, Plymouth, Devon. *T:* Plymouth 772115.

CAMPBELL, Sir Colin Moffat, 8th Bt *cr* 1667, of Aberuchill and Kilbryde, Dunblane, Perthshire; MC 1945; Chairman: James Finlay & Co. Ltd, since 1975, and associated companies; *b* 4 Aug. 1925; *e s* of Sir John Campbell, 7th Bt and Janet Moffat (*d* 1975); *S* father, 1960; *m* 1952, Mary Anne Chichester Bain, *er d* of Brigadier G. A. Bain, Sandy Lodge, Chagford, Devon; two *s* one *d. Educ:* Stowe. Scots Guards, 1943-47, Captain. Employed with James Finlay & Co. Ltd, Calcutta, 1948-58, Nairobi, 1958-71, Dir, 1971-, Dep. Chm., 1973-75. President Federation of Kenya Employers, 1962-70; Chairman: Tea Board of Kenya, 1961-71; E African Tea Trade Assoc., 1960-61, 1962-63, 1966-67. *Recreations:* gardening, racing, cards. *Heir:* s James Alexander Moffat Bain Campbell, *b* 23 Sept. 1956. *Address:* Kilbryde Castle, Dunblane, Perthshire. *T:* Dunblane 823104. *Clubs:* Boodle's; Cavalry and Guards; Western (Glasgow); Royal Calcutta Turf, Tollygunge (Calcutta); Nairobi, Muthaiga (E Africa).

CAMPBELL, Sir David, Kt 1953; MC 1918; MA, BSc, MD, LLD (Glasgow, Dublin, Liverpool, Aberdeen); DCL (Durham); FRCPG; FRSE; FRCP; Regius Professor of Materia Medica and Therapeutics, University of Aberdeen, 1930-59; Dean of the Faculty of Medicine, 1932-59; President, General Medical Council, 1949-61; *b* 6 May 1889; *m* 1921, Margaret, *o d* of Alexander Lyle of Kerse. *Educ:* Ayr Academy; Univ. of Glasgow; Johns Hopkins Univ. MA (Hons) 1911; BSc 1911; MB, ChB (Hons) 1916; MD (Hons and Bellahouston Gold Medal), 1924; LLD 1950. Captain (a/Major) RAMC (TF), 1916-19; Univ. Asst to Prof. of Materia Medica and Therapeutics, Glasgow Univ., 1919-21; Pollok Lectr in Materia Medica and Pharmacology, 1921-30; Resident Physician, 1915-16; Physician to Out-Patients, 1920-29; Asst Physician to Western Infirmary, Glasgow, 1929-30; Extra-Hon. Physician, Aberdeen Royal Infirmary, 1930-59; Rockefeller Medical Fellow in Pharmacology and Therapeutics, 1925-26. *Publications:* Handbook of Therapeutics; papers on pharmacological and therapeutic subjects in various medical and scientific jls. *Recreations:* golf, motoring. *Address:* Carskeoch, Milltimber, Aberdeenshire. *T:* Culter 733335. *Clubs:* Athenæum; Royal Northern (Aberdeen).

CAMPBELL, Donald le Strange, MC; Director: Project Services Overseas Ltd; Rolair UK Ltd; Beechdean Farms; *b* 16 June 1919; *s* of late Donald Fraser Campbell and of Caroline Campbell, Heacham, Norfolk; *m* 1952, Hon. Shona Catherine Greig Macpherson, *y d* of 1st Baron Macpherson of Drumochter; one *s* one *d*. *Educ:* Winchester Coll.; Clare Coll., Cambridge. Served War, 1939-45, Major RA (MC). EFCO Ltd, 1947-55; MEECO Ltd, 1955-61; Davy-Ashmore Ltd, 1961-67. Dep. Chairman, BNEC Latin America, 1967. *Recreations:* farming, sailing, field sports. *Address:* Bagnor Manor, Newbury, Berks RG16 8AJ. *Clubs:* Brooks's, Buck's; Royal Yacht Squadron.

CAMPBELL, Maj.-Gen. Sir Douglas; see Campbell, Sir Alexander Douglas.

CAMPBELL, Douglas Mason, QC (Scotland) 1953; Hon. Sheriff (Sheriff-Principal and Sheriff, 1958-74) of Inverness, Moray, Nairn, and Ross and Cromarty; Chairman, Workmen's Compensation and Pneumoconiosis, Byssinosis and Miscellaneous Diseases Benefit Boards; *b* 14 Nov. 1905; *s* of late David C. Campbell, Glasgow; *m* 1955, Alice Barbara Chalmers, *d* of late W. G. Chalmers Hanna, OBE, MC, CA, Edinburgh. *Educ:* Sedbergh; Worcester Coll., Oxford. BA Oxford, 1928; LLB Glasgow, 1931. Admitted to Scottish Bar, 1931. Served RA, 1940-45. Advocate-Depute, 1951-53 and 1957-58. *Recreations:* fishing, shooting, golf. *Address:* 10 Forres Street, Edinburgh EH3 6BJ. *T:* 031-225 3150. *Clubs:* United Oxford & Cambridge University; New (Edinburgh); Highland (Inverness).

CAMPBELL, Evan Roy, CBE 1958; Chairman: Rhodesia Board, Standard Bank Ltd, since 1965; Albatros Fisons Fertilizers Ltd, since 1966; Fisons Pest Control (CA) (pvt) Ltd; Central African Branch of Institute of Directors; Manica Freight Services (Rhodesia) Ltd; Standard Finance Ltd, and other companies; Director: Tanganda Tea Co. Ltd (formerly Rhodesia Tea Estates; Chairman, 1965-76); Discount Co. of Rhodesia Ltd; Messina Rhodesia Investments Ltd; M.T.D. (Mangula) Ltd; Lomagundi Smelting and Mining (Pvte) Ltd; The Messina (Rhodesia) Develt Co. Ltd, and other companies; *b* 2 Sept. 1908; *m* 1934, Norah May Vaughan; one *s* one *d*. *Educ:* St Andrew's Coll., Grahamstown, S Africa; Potchefstroom Agricultural Coll. Started farming in Umvukwes, S Rhodesia, 1931; has farmed in Inyazura since 1935. Enlisted in Rhodesia Regt, 1940; seconded to King's African Rifles (Abyssinia, Burma and India); Staff Coll., Quetta, 1944 (psc); GSO 2, 11 (E Africa) Div.; Bde Major 25 (E Africa) Infantry Bde. Rhodesia Tobacco Assoc.; Mem., 1946; Vice-Pres., 1947; Pres., 1952-58, now Life Vice-Pres.; Chm. Makoni Br., and Mem. Nat. Council, British Empire Service League, 1947; Mem., Tobacco Marketing Board, 1950; Chm., Tobacco Export Promotion Council, 1958; Chm., Gwebi Agric. Coll. Council, 1963; Pres., First Internat. Tobacco Congress; Life Vice-Pres., Manicaland Agricultural Show Society. High Comr in Great Britain for Southern Rhodesia,

1964-65. Governor, Peterhouse Sch. Farmers' Oscar for outstanding services to agriculture and British Empire Service League meritorious service medal, 1962. *Recreations:* riding, croquet, yachting. *Address:* (business) Standard Bank, Cecil Square, PO Box 373, Salisbury, Rhodesia; (private) 20 Addington Lane, Highlands, Salisbury, Rhodesia. *Clubs:* MCC; Salisbury Umtali (Rhodesia); Beira (Mozambique).

CAMPBELL, Graham Gordon; Under-Secretary, Department of Energy, since 1974; *b* 12 Dec. 1924; *s* of late Lt-Col and Mrs P. H. Campbell; *m* 1955, Margaret Rosamond Busby; one *d*. *Educ:* Cheltenham Coll.; Caius Coll., Cambridge (BA Hist.). Served War, Royal Artillery, 1943-46. Asst Principal, Min. of Fuel and Power, 1949; Private Sec. to Parly Sec., Min. of Fuel and Power, 1953-54; Principal, 1954; Asst Sec., Min. of Power, 1965; Under-Sec., DTI, 1973. *Recreations:* watching birds, music, hill-walking. *Address:* 3 Clovelly Avenue, Warlingham, Surrey CR3 9HZ. *T:* Upper Warlingham 4671.

CAMPBELL, Sir Guy (Theophilus Halswell), 5th Bt *cr* 1815; OBE 1954; MC 1941; Colonel, late 60th Rifles, El Kaimakam Bey, Camel Corps, Sudan Defence Force, and Kenya Regiment; *b* 18 Jan. 1910; *s* of Major Sir Guy Colin Campbell, 4th Bt, late 60th Rifles, and Mary Arabella Swinnerton Kemeys-Tynte, *sister* of 8th Lord Wharton; *S* father, 1960; *m* 1956, Lizbeth Webb, Bickenhall Mansions, W1; two *s*. *Educ:* St Aubyn's, Rottingdean; Eton Coll.; St Andrews Univ. War of 1939-45 (wounded); served in KOYLI, 1931-42; seconded to Camel Corps, Sudan Defence Force, 1939-47; Comd 2/7 and 7 Nuba Bns, 1943-47; Shifta Ops, Eritrea, 1946; Acting Brig., 1945, HQ SDF Group (N Africa); Palestine, 1948; Mil. Adviser to Count Folke Bernadotte and Dr Ralph Bunche of United Nations, 1948; attached British Embassy as Civil Affairs Officer, Cairo, 1948; British Mil. Mission to Ethiopia, in Ogaden Province, 1948-51; 2nd i/c 1/60th Rifles, BAOR, 1951; comd Kenya Regt (TF), 1952-56, Mau Mau ops; Head of British Mil. Mission to Libya, 1956-60; retired Aug. 1960. Col R of O, 60th Rifles. C-in-C's (MELF) Commendation, 1945; Gold Medal of Emperor Haile Selassie (non-wearable). *Recreations:* watching cricket, golf, Rugby football, polo, tennis, hockey. *Heir:* s Lachlan Philip Kemeys Campbell, *b* 9 Oct. 1958. *Clubs:* MCC, I Zingari; Royal and Ancient (St Andrews).

CAMPBELL, Maj.-Gen. Sir Hamish Manus, KBE 1963 (CBE 1958); CB 1961; *b* 6 Jan. 1905; *s* of late Major A. C. J. Campbell, Middlesex Regt and Army Pay Dept, and of Alice, *d* of late Comdr Yelverton O'Keeffe, RN; *m* 1929, Marcelle, *d* of late Charles Ortlieb, Neuchâtel, Switzerland; one *s*. *Educ:* Downside School; New Coll., Oxford. Commissioned in Argyll and Sutherland Highlanders, 1927; transferred to Royal Army Pay Corps, 1937; Lieut-Colonel and Staff Paymaster (1st Class), temp. 1945, subs. 1951; Colonel and Chief Paymaster, temp. 1954, subs. 1955; Major-General, 1959. Command Paymaster: Sierra Leone, 1940-42; Burma, 1946-48; Malta, 1953. Deputy Chief, Budget and Finance Division, SHAPE, 1954-56; Commandant, RAPC Training Centre, 1956-59; Paymaster-in-Chief, War Office, 1959-63; retired, 1963. Col Comdt, RAPC, 1963-70. *Address:* Clunie, 20 Little Knowle, Budleigh Salterton, Devon EX9 6QS. *T:* Budleigh Salterton 3818. *Club:* Army and Navy.

CAMPBELL, Harold Edward; Deputy Chairman, Stevenage Development Corporation, since 1968; Director, Co-operative Housing Centre, and South British Housing Association, since 1976; *b* 28 Feb. 1915; *s* of Edward Inkerman Campbell and Florence Annie Campbell. *Educ:* Southbury Road Elementary Sch.; Enfield Central Sch. Asst Sec., 1946-64, Sec., 1964-67, Cooperative Party; Mem., 1967-73, Dep. Chm., 1969-73, Housing Corp. Gen. Manager, Newlon Housing Trust, 1970-76; Chairman: Cooperative Planning Ltd, 1964-74; Co-Ownership Develt Soc. Ltd, 1966-76; Sutton Housing Trust, 1973- (Trustee, 1967-); Pres., Enfield Highway Cooperative Soc. Ltd, 1976- (Dir, 1965-); Dir, CWS Ltd, 1968-73. Chairman: DoE Working Party on Cooperative Housing, 1973-75; DoE Working Group on New Forms of Housing Tenure, 1976-77; Housing Assoc. Registration Adv. Cttee, 1974-; Hearing Aid Council, 1970-71. Borough Councillor, Enfield, 1959-63. *Recreations:* music, theatre, cinema. *Address:* 67A Derby Road, Enfield, Mddx EN3 4AJ. *T:* 01-804 2392. *Clubs:* Arts, Arts Theatre.

CAMPBELL, Harold Ernest, CBE 1974; Director, McLaughlin & Harvey Ltd, since 1944; *b* 28 May 1902; *s* of W. W. Campbell and Emma Campbell; *m* 1929, Marion Fordyce Wheeler; one *s* one *d*. *Educ:* Belfast Royal Academy; Trinity Coll., Dublin. MA, MAI, CEng, FICE. Asst Engr, S. Pearson & Son (Contracting Dept) Ltd, 1923-32; Civil Engr, T. J. Moran & Co. Ltd, 1932-34; McLaughlin & Harvey Ltd: Civil Engr, 1934-38; Jun. Dir, 1938-44; Chm., 1954-75. Dir, Bank of Ireland, 1960-

75; Chm., NI Airports Ltd, 1970-77; Belfast Harbour Comr, 1955-77. *Recreation:* golf. *Address:* Rockmore, Newcastle, Co. Down, N Ireland. *T:* Newcastle (Down) 22295. *Clubs:* Ulster Reform (Belfast); Royal Belfast Golf, Royal County Down Golf.
See also John Grigg.

CAMPBELL, Hugh, PhD; Career Consultant, since 1974; *b* 24 Oc● 1916; *s* of Hugh Campbell and Annie C. Campbell (*née* Spence); *m* 1946, Sybil Marian Williams, MB, ChB, *y d* of Benjamin and Sarah Williams; two *s. Educ:* University College Sch., London; St John's Coll., Cambridge (MA, PhD). Research, Dept of Colloid Science, Cambridge, 1938-45; Head of Physical Chem., Research Gp, May and Baker Ltd, 1945-61; Lectr, West Ham Techn. Coll., 1949-54; Research Manager, Chloride Electrical Storage Co. Ltd, 1961-65; Managing Dir: Alkaline Batteries Ltd, 1965-67; Electric Power Storage Ltd, 1968-71; Dir, Chloride Electrical Storage Co. Ltd, 1968-71; Industrial Advr, DTI, 1971-74. *Publications:* papers on various subjects in scientific jls. *Recreations:* skiing, theatre, travelling. *Address:* 4 The Courtyard, Barnsbury Terrace, NI 1JZ. *T:* 01-607 3834.

CAMPBELL, Ian, CEng, MIMechE, JP; MP (Lab) Dunbartonshire (West) since 1970; *b* 26 April 1926; *s* of William Campbell and Helen Crockett; *m* 1950, Mary Millar; two *s* three *d. Educ:* Dumbarton Academy; Royal Technical Coll., Glasgow (now Strathclyde Univ.). Engineer with South of Scotland Electricity Board for 17 years. Councillor, Dumbarton, 1958-70; Provost of Dumbarton, 1962-70. PPS to Sec. of State for Scotland, 1976-. *Address:* 20 McGregor Drive, Dumbarton. *T:* Dumbarton 63612.

CAMPBELL, Ian Dugald, FRCPE, FFCM; Chief Administrative Medical Officer, Lothian Health Board, since 1973; *b* Dornie, Kintail, 22 Feb. 1916; *s* of John Campbell and Margaret Campbell; *m* 1943, Joan Carnegie Osborn; one *s* two *d . Educ:* Dingwall Acad.; Edinburgh Univ. (MB, ChB 1939). FRCPE 1973, FFCM 1974. Served War, 1941-46: UK, BAOR, MEF, RAMC; final appt OC Field Amb. (Lt-Col). Med. Supt, St Luke's Hosp., Bradford, 1946-49; Asst SMO, Leeds Reg. Hosp. Bd, 1949-57; Dep. Sen. Admin. MO, S-Eastern Reg. Hosp. Bd, Scotland, 1957-72, Sen. Admin. MO, 1972-73. WHO assignments, SE Asia, 1969, 1971, 1975. *Publications:* various medical. *Recreations:* fishing, shooting, golf. *Address:* 5 Succoth Park, Edinburgh EH12 6BX. *T:* 031-337 5965. *Clubs:* New (Edinburgh); Hon. Company of Edinburgh Golfers (Muirfield); Royal Burgess Golfing Society (Barnton, Edinburgh).

CAMPBELL, Ian George Hallyburton, TD; QC 1957; Lord Chancellor's Legal Visitor, since 1963; *b* 19 July 1909; *s* of late Hon. Kenneth Campbell and Mrs K. Campbell; *m* 1949, Betty Yolande, *d* of late Somerset Maclean and *widow* of Lt-Col Allan Bruno, MBE; one adopted *s* one adopted *d. Educ:* Charterhouse, Trinity Coll., Cambridge. Barrister, Inner Temple and Lincoln's Inn, 1932. Served Artists Rifles and Rifle Brigade, 1939-45; Col 1945. Appts include: GSO2, HQ 1st Army; Chief Judicial Officer, Allied Commission, Italy; Chief Legal Officer, Military Govt, Austria (British zone). *Address:* Chancery House, Hill Brow, Liss, Hants. *T:* Liss 3141. *Clubs:* Boodle's, Brooks's.

CAMPBELL, Ian James; Scientific Adviser to Ship Department and Director of Research (Ships), Ministry of Defence, since 1976; *b* 9 June 1923; *s* of Allan and Elizabeth Campbell; *m* 1946, Stella Margaret Smith. *Educ:* George Heriot's Sch.; Edinburgh Univ. (MA). Op. Res. Sect., HQ Bomber Comd, 1943-46; Asst Lectr in Astronomy, St Andrews Univ., 1946-48; Royal Naval Scientific Service, 1948; Dept of Aeronaut. and Eng Res., Amiralty, 1948-49; Admiralty Res. Lab., 1949-59; Admiralty Underwater Weapons Estab., 1959-68; Chief Scientist, Naval Construction Res. Estab., 1969-73; Head of Weapons Dept, Admiralty Underwater Weapons Estab., 1973-76. *Publications:* papers on fluid mechanics. *Address:* Claremont, North Street, Charminster, Dorchester, Dorset. *T:* Dorchester 4270.

CAMPBELL, Ian Macdonald, CVO 1977; BSc; CEng; FICE; FCIT; Executive Member for Engineering and Research, British Railways Board, since 1977; Chairman, British Rail Engineering, since 1977; *b* 13 July 1922; *s* of late John Isdale Campbell; *m* 1946, Hilda Ann Williams; one *s* three *d. Educ:* University Coll., London. BSc(Eng). British Rail: Asst District Engr, Sheffield, 1953-57; District Engr, Kings Cross, 1957-63; Asst Civil Engr, Scottish Region, 1963-65; Chief Civil Engr, Scottish Region, Asst Gen. Man., LM Region, 1968-70; Gen. Manager, E Region, 1970-73; Exec. Dir, BR, 1973-76. Mem., Noise Adv. Council, 1976-. *Recreations:* golf, music. *Address:* 222 Marylebone Road, NW1.

CAMPBELL, Prof. Ian McIntyre, MA; Professor of Humanity, University of Edinburgh, since 1959; *b* 14 Jan. 1915; *s* of late John Campbell and Janet Donaldson; *m* 1945, Julia Margaret Mulgan; two *s* one *d. Educ:* Spier's Sch., Beith; Univ. of Glasgow; Balliol Coll., Oxford. First cl. Hons Classics, Glasgow Univ., 1936; First cl. Class. Mods, 1938. Served in Intelligence Corps, Captain, 1939-45; Hon. War Memorial Research Student, Balliol Coll., 1946; Lecturer in Humanity and Comparative Philology, Glasgow Univ., 1947-54; Prof. of Latin, Univ. Coll. of S Wales and Monmouthshire, 1954-59. *Publications:* articles and reviews in learned journals. Jt Editor of *Archivum Linguisticum*, 1949-. *Recreation:* music. *Address:* 3 McLaren Road, Edinburgh EH9 2BE. *T:* 031-667 4030.

CAMPBELL, Mrs Ian McIvor; *see* Corbet, Mrs Freda K.

CAMPBELL, Vice-Admiral Sir Ian Murray Robertson, KBE 1955; CB 1951; DSO 1942, Bar 1943; *b* 8 Aug. 1898; 2nd *s* of Brig. A. A. E. Campbell, Indian Army; *m* 1929, Marjorie Mary McCreath, Looseleigh, Tamerton Foliot, Devon; two *s.* Service in N Sea, Adriatic and Eastern Baltic, 1914-19; Captain, Naval Staff, 1940; Comd 3rd Destroyer Flotilla, HMS Milne, 1942-44; Naval Staff, and Comd HMS Jamaica, E Indies Squadron, 1945-47; Rear-Adm. 1950; Vice-Adm., 1953; Commander-in-Chief, South Atlantic Station, 1954-56; retd list, 1956. *Publication:* (jointly) The Kola Run, 1958. *Address:* Ivy Cottage, Sapperton, Glos.

CAMPBELL, Air Vice-Marshal Ian Robert, CB 1976; CBE 1964; AFC 1948; Chief of Staff, No 18 (M) Group, Strike Command, RAF, 1973-75, retired; *b* 5 Oct. 1920; *s* of late Major and of Hon. Mrs D. E. Campbell; *m* 1953, Beryl Evelyn Newbigging; one *s. Educ:* Eton; RAF Coll., Cranwell. Anti-Shipping Ops, 1940-42; POW, Italy and Germany, 1942-45; 540 Sqdn, Benson, 1946; psa 1949; PSO to C-in-C Far East, 1950; 124 (F) Wing Oldenburg, 1953; OC, RAF Sandwich, 1956; pfc 1957; OC 213 Sqdn, Bruggen, 1958; ACOS Plans HQ 2ATAF, 1959; OC, RAF Marham, 1961; MoD (Air) DASB, 1964; SASO, HQ No 1 Group, 1965; Air Attaché, Bonn, 1968; Dir of Management and Support Intell., MoD, 1970-73. *Recreations:* shooting, golf, travel. *Address:* Poulton House, Cirencester, Glos. *Clubs:* Boodle's, Royal Air Force.

CAMPBELL, Maj.-Gen. Ian Ross, CBE 1954; DSO and Bar, 1941; *b* 23 March 1900; *m* 1927, Patience Allison Russell (*d* 1961); one *d* ; *m* 1967, Irene Cardamatis. *Educ:* Wesley Coll., Melbourne; Scots Coll., Sydney; Royal Military College, Duntroon, Canberra (Graduate, 1922). Served War of 1939-45, Middle East Campaigns, Libya, Greece and Crete (DSO and bar, Cross of Kt Comdr, Greek Order of Phœnix; pow 1941-45); comd Aust. forces in Korean War, 1951-53 (CBE); Comdt, Australian Staff Coll., 1953-54; Comdt, Royal Mil. Coll. Duntroon, 1954-57; retired, 1957. Mem. Federal Exec., RSL, 1955-56. Chm., NSW Div., Aust. Red Cross Soc., 1967-74. Pres., Great Public Schs Athletic Assoc., NSW, 1966-69. *Recreation:* tennis. *Address:* 15/17 Wylde Street, Potts Point, Sydney, NSW 2011, Australia. *Clubs:* Imperial Service, Royal Sydney Golf (Sydney).

CAMPBELL, Sir Ian (Vincent Hamilton), 7th Bt *cr* 1831, of Barcaldine and Glenure; CB 1951; Assistant Under-Secretary of State, Air Ministry, 1945-55, retired 1955; *b* 1895; *e surv s* of Richard Hamilton Campbell, CIE, ICS (retd) (*d* 1923); *S* cousin, Captain Sir (Francis) Eric Dennistoun Campbell, 6th Bt, 1963; *m* 1st, Madeline (*d* 1929), *e d* of late H. Anglin Whitelocke, FRCS, Oxford; one *s* ; 2nd, Iris Constance (marriage dissolved, 1942), *d* of late Lt-Col Ronald Charles Gibb, CBE; 3rd, Agnes Louise, *e d* of late William Henry Gerhardi, and *widow* of Vsevolod Victor Watson, MBE. *Educ:* Cheltenham; Corpus Christi Coll., Oxford. Served European War, 1914-18 as Lieut The King's (Liverpool Regt); severely wounded in Battle of the Somme, 1916, and invalided from Army, May 1918. Entered Home Civil Service, 1919, as Asst Principal, Air Ministry; Priv. Sec. to Chief of Air Staff (late Marshal of the RAF Lord Trenchard), 1926-27; Private Sec. to Permanent Sec. of the Air Ministry (late Sir Walter Nicholson), 1927-30; Asst Private Sec. to successive Secs of State for Air (late Lord Thomson, late Lord Amulree, and, late Marquess of Londonderry), 1930-34; Principal, Air Ministry, 1934; Asst Sec. 1939. *Heir:* s Niall Alexander Hamilton Campbell [*b* 7 Jan. 1925; *m* 1st, 1949, Patricia Mary (marr. diss., 1956), *d* of R. Turner; 2nd, 1957, Norma Joyce, *d* of W. N. Wiggin; two *s* two *d* (including twin *s* and *d*)]. *Address:* White Rose, Hawkhurst, Kent. *T:* Hawkhurst 2268.

CAMPBELL, Sir Ilay (Mark), 7th Bt *cr* 1808, of Succoth, Dunbartonshire; *b* 29 May 1927; only *s* of Sir George Ilay Campbell, 6th Bt; *S* father, 1967; *m* 1961, Margaret Minette

Rohais, *o d* of J. Alasdair Anderson; two *d. Educ:* Eton; Christ Church, Oxford. BA 1952. Joint Scottish Agent for Messrs Christie, Manson & Woods. Pres., Assoc. for Protection of Rural Scotland; Vice-Chm., Scotland's Gardens Scheme; Scottish Rep. Nat. Art-Collections Fund. *Recreations:* heraldry, horticulture. *Heir:* none. *Address:* Lennel, Coldstream, Berwickshire. *T:* Coldstream 2254; Crarae Lodge, Inveraray, Argyll. *T:* Minard 274. *Clubs:* Turf; Puffins (Edinburgh).

CAMPBELL, James Grant, CMG 1970; Overseas Representative, Alcan International Ltd, Montreal, since 1977; Dir, subsidiary companies of Alcan Aluminium Ltd; *b* Springville, NS, Canada, 8 June 1914; *s* of John Kay Campbell and Wilna Archibald Campbell (*née* Grant); *m* 1941, Alice Isobel Dougall; one *d. Educ:* Mount Allison Univ., Canada. BSc, 1st cl. hons (Chem.). Chemical Engineer, Aluminium Co. of Canada, Arvida, Que, 1937-41; Demerara Bauxite Co. Ltd, Guyana, Gen. Supt, 1941-50; Aluminium Laboratories Ltd, London, England, 1950 (Headqrs for team investigating hydro power, bauxite and aluminium smelting in Asia, Africa and Europe); on staff of Dir of Operations, Aluminium Ltd, Montreal (concerned with world supply of raw materials for Aluminium Ltd), 1951-55; Managing Dir and Chm., Demerara Bauxite Co., Guyana, 1955-71. Mem. Bd of Regents, Mount Allison Univ., 1972. Hon. LLD Mount Allison Univ., 1966. *Recreations:* music, golf, reading. *Address:* 45 Eaton Square, SW1. *Clubs:* Travellers'; University (New York); University (Montreal).

CAMPBELL, John Davies, MBE 1957; MC 1945, and bar 1945; HM Diplomatic Service; Consul-General, Naples, since 1977; *b* 11 Nov. 1921; *s* of late William Hastings Campbell and of late The Hon. Mrs Campbell (Eugene Anne Westenra, subsequently Harbord), *d* of 14th Baron Louth; *m* 1959, Shirley Bouch; one *s* two *d. Educ:* Cheltenham Coll.; St Andrews Univ. Served War, HM Forces, 1940-46. HM Colonial Service (subseq. HMOCS), 1949-61 (despatches, 1957); HM Foreign (subseq. HM Diplomatic) Service, 1961; First Secretary, 1961; Counsellor, 1972; Counsellor (Information) Ottawa, 1972-77. *Recreations:* golf, tennis. *Address:* c/o Foreign and Commonwealth Office, Downing Street, SW1. *Clubs:* Special Forces, Royal Over-Seas League; Muthaiga Country (Nairobi); Mombasa.

CAMPBELL, Sir John Johnston, Kt 1957; General Manager, Clydesdale Bank Ltd, 1946-58, retired (Director, 1958-75); *b* 11 Dec. 1897; *s* of William Campbell, Stewarton, Ayrshire; *m* 1927, Margaret Fullarton (*d* 1967), *d* of John Brown, Dalry, Ayrshire; one *s* one *d. Educ:* Stewarton Secondary Sch. Joined service of The Clydesdale Bank at Stewarton, Ayrshire, 1913. Served with Royal Scots Fusiliers in Palestine, France, and Germany, 1916-19. London Manager, Clydesdale Bank, 1944. Pres., Institute of Bankers in Scotland, 1953-55; Chm.: Development Securities Ltd, 1958-67; Cttee of Scottish Bank Gen Managers, 1955-57. *Address:* 22 Saffrons Court, Compton Place Road, Eastbourne, E Sussex. *T:* 29271.

CAMPBELL of Canna, John Lorne; owns and farms Isle of Canna, Inner Hebrides; folklorist, editor and author; *b* 1 Oct. 1906; *s* of late Col Duncan Campbell of Inverneill and Ethel Harriet, *e d* of late John I. Waterbury, Morristown, NJ; *m* 1935, Margaret Fay (author of Folksongs and Folklore of South Uist), *y d* of late Henry Clay Shaw, Glenshaw, Pennsylvania (US); no *c. Educ:* Cargilfield; Rugby; St John's Coll., Oxford (MA 1933, DLitt, 1965). Hon. LLD, St Francis Xavier Univ., Antigonish, NS, 1953. Hon. DLitt, Glasgow Univ., 1965. *Publications:* Highland Songs of the Forty-Five, 1933; The Book of Barra (with Compton Mackenzie and Carl Hj. Borgstrom), 1936; (Ed.) Orain Ghaidhlig le Seonaidh Caimbeul, 1936; Sia Sgialachdan, Six Gaelic Stories from South Uist and Barra, 1938; Act Now for the Highlands and Islands (with Sir Alexander MacEwen), 1939; Gaelic in Scottish Education and Life, 1945; Gaelic Folksongs from the Isle of Barra (with Annie Johnston and John MacLean), 1950; Fr. Allan McDonald of Eriskay, Priest, Poet and Folklorist, 1954; Gaelic Words from South Uist and Eriskay, collected by Fr. Allan McDonald, 1958; Tales from Barra, told by the Coddy, 1960; Stories from South Uist, 1961; The Furrow Behind Me, the Autobiography of a Hebridean Crofter (trans. from tape recordings), 1962; Edward Lhuyd in the Scottish Highlands (with Prof. Derick Thomson), 1963; A School in South Uist (memoirs of Frederick Rea), 1964; Bardachd Mhgr Ailein, the Gaelic Poems of Fr. Allan McDonald, 1965; Strange Things (with Trevor H. Hall), 1968; Hebridean Folksongs (with F. Collinson), vol. i, 1969, vol. ii, 1977; Macrolepidoptera Cannae, 1970; Saoghal an Treobhaiche, 1972; (ed) A Collection of Highland Rites and Customes, 1975; contribs to various periodicals, etc. *Recreations:* entomology, sea fishing. *Address:* Isle of Canna, Scotland.

CAMPBELL, Dame Kate (Isabel), DBE 1971 (CBE 1954); Medical Practitioner; Specialist Pædiatrician, 1937-76; *b* April 1899; *d* of late Donald Campbell and late Janet Campbell (*née* Mill); unmarried. *Educ:* Hawthorn State Sch.; Methodist Ladies' Coll., Melbourne; Melbourne Univ. MB, BS, 1922; MD 1924; FRCOG 1961; Resident MO: Melbourne Hosp., 1922, Children's Hosp., 1923, Women's Hosp., 1924; Lecturer in Neo-Natal Pædiatrics, Melbourne Univ., 1927-65. Hon. Phys. to Children's Dept, Queen Victoria Hosp., Melbourne, 1926-60; Hon. Pædiatric Consultant in active practice, Queen Victoria Hospital, 1960-66; Hon. Pædiatric Consultant, 1966-; Hon. Neo-Natal Pædiatrician, Women's Hosp., Melbourne, 1945-59; First assistant in Pædiatrics, Professorial Unit, Dept of Obstetrics, Melbourne Univ., 1960-65; Gen. Med. Practice, 1927-37. Consultant to Dept of Infant Welfare, Victoria, 1961-76. Associate, Dept of Paediatrics, Monash Univ., 1971-. LLD (Hon.) 1966. *Publications:* (co-author with late Dr Vera Scantlebury Brown) Guide to the care of the young child, 1947 (last edn 1972); articles on medical subjects in Medical Journal of Australasia and Lancet. *Recreation:* theatre. *Address:* 1293 Burke Road, Kew, Melbourne, Victoria 3101, Australia. *T:* 80 2536. *Club:* Lyceum (Melbourne).

CAMPBELL, Keith Bruce, QC 1964; **His Honour Judge Campbell;** a Circuit Judge, since 1976; *b* NZ, 25 Oct. 1916; *yr s* of late Walter Henry Pearson Campbell and late Ethel Rose Campbell; *m* 1939, Betty Joan Muffett; two *s* four *d. Educ:* Christchurch Tech. High Sch. and Canterbury Univ. Coll., NZ (LLB); London Univ. (LLB). Served Army, 1939-46: in ranks of 15th/19th Hussars, BEF France, Belgium; evacuated from Dunkirk; commnd into RASC, 1941; with 1st and 8th Armies, N Africa, Italy. Called to New Zealand Bar, and to English Bar by Inner Temple, 1947; Master of the Bench, Inner Temple, 1970; a Recorder of the Crown Court, 1972-76. Gen. Council of the Bar, 1956-60, 1965-70, 1973-74; Mem., Senate of Inns of Court and Bar, 1974-75. Contested (C) Gorton Div. of Manchester, 1955; Oldham West, 1966; MP (C) Oldham West, June 1968-70. *Recreations:* boating, riding. *Address:* 1 Hare Court, Temple, EC4. *T:* 01-353 3400.

CAMPBELL, Laurence Jamieson; Headmaster, Kingswood School, Bath, since 1970; *b* 10 June 1927; *er s* of George S. Campbell and Mary P. Paterson; *m* 1954, Sheena E. Macdonald; two *s* one *d. Educ:* Hillhead High Sch., Glasgow; Aberdeen Univ., Edinburgh Univ. (MA). Lieut RA, 1945-48. Housemaster, Alliance High Sch., Kenya, 1952-56; Educn Sec., Christian Council of Kenya, 1957-62; Headmaster, Alliance High Sch., Kenya, 1963-70. Contested North Kenya Constituency, Kenya General Election, 1961. Mem. Council, Univ. of East Africa, 1963-69; Chm., Heads Assoc. of Kenya, 1965-69; Official of Kenya Commonwealth Games Team, 1970; Schoolmaster Fellow, Balliol Coll., Oxford, 1970; Chm., Overseas Appts Cttee, 1974. *Recreations:* golf, athletics, church. *Address:* Kingswood School, Bath, Avon BA1 5RG. *T:* Bath 311627. *Club:* Royal Commonwealth Society.

CAMPBELL of Airds, Brig. Lorne Maclaine, VC 1943; DSO 1940; OBE 1968; TD 1941; Argyll and Sutherland Highlanders (TA); *b* 22 July 1902; *s* of late Col Ian Maxwell Campbell, CBE; *m* 1935, Amy Muriel Jordan (*d* 1950), *d* of Alastair Magnus Campbell, Auchendarroch, Argyll; two *s. Educ:* Dulwich Coll.; Merton Coll., Oxford (Postmaster, MA). 8th Bn Argyll and Sutherland Highlanders, 1921-42, commanded 7th Bn, 1942-43, and 13th Inf. Brigade, 1943-44; BGS, British Army Staff, Washington, 1944-45; War of 1939-45: despatches four times, DSO and Bar, VC. Hon. Col 8th Bn Argyll and Sutherland Highlanders, 1954-67. Past Master of Vintners' Company (Hon. Vintner). Officer US Legion of Merit. *Address:* 95 Trinity Road, Edinburgh EH5 3JX. *T:* 031-552 6851. *Club:* New (Edinburgh).

CAMPBELL, Sir Matthew, KBE 1963; CB 1959; FRSE; Deputy Chairman, White Fish Authority, and Chairman, Authority's Committee for Scotland and Northern Ireland; *b* 23 May 1907; *s* of late Matthew Campbell, High Blantyre; *m* 1939, Isabella, *d* of late John Wilson, Rutherglen; two *s. Educ:* Hamilton Academy; Glasgow Univ. Entered CS, 1928, and after service in Inland Revenue Dept and Admiralty joined staff of Dept of Agriculture for Scotland, 1935; Principal, 1938; Assistant Sec., 1943; Under Sec., 1953; Sec., Dept of Agriculture and Fisheries for Scotland, 1958-68. *Address:* 10 Craigleith View, Edinburgh. *T:* 031-337 5168. *Club:* Royal Commonwealth Society.

CAMPBELL, Mungo, CBE 1946; MA; retired shipowner; former director, Barclays Bank Ltd, Newcastle upon Tyne; *b* 5 June 1900; 2nd *s* of late James Campbell, The Manor House, Wormley, Herts; *m* 1st, 1944, Esther McCracken (*d* 1971); one *d* decd; 2nd, 1976, Betty Kirkpatrick. *Educ:* Loretto; Pembroke Coll., Cambridge. Ministry of War Transport, 1939-46 (Dir Ship

Repair Div., 1942-46). Hon. DCL Newcastle, 1972. Comdr Order of Orange Nassau (Netherlands), 1947. *Address:* Rothley Lake House, Morpeth, Northumberland. *Clubs:* Bath; Union (Newcastle upon Tyne).

CAMPBELL, Patrick; *see* Glenavy, 3rd Baron.

CAMPBELL, Prof. Peter Nelson; Courtauld Professor of Biochemistry, and Director of the Courtauld Institute, Middlesex Hospital Medical School, London University, since 1976; *b* 5 Nov. 1921; *s* of late Alan A. Campbell and Nora Nelson; *m* 1946, Mollie (*née* Manklow); one *s* one *d. Educ:* Eastbourne Coll.; Univ. Coll., London. BSc, PhD, DSc, London; FIBiol. Research and Production Chemist with Standard Telephones and Cables, Ltd, 1942-46; PhD Student, UCL; 1946-47; Asst Lectr UCL, 1947-49; staff of Nat. Inst. for Med. Research, Hampstead and Mill Hill, 1949-54; Asst, Courtauld Inst. of Biochem., Middx Hosp. Med. Sch., 1954-57; Sen. Lectr, Middx Hosp. Med. Sch., 1957-64; Reader in Biochem., Univ. of London, 1964-67; Prof. and Head of Dept of Biochem., Leeds Univ., 1967-75. Hon. Lectr, Dept of Biochem., UCL, 1954-67. Chm., Symposium and Educn Cttees of International Union of Biochemistry. *Publications:* Structure and Function of Animal Cell Components, 1966; (ed with B. A. Kilby) Basic Biochemistry for Medical Students, 1975; ed, Essays in Biochemistry and other vols; many scientific papers in Biochem. Jl. *Recreations:* theatre, travelling, conversation. *Address:* Courtauld Institute of Biochemistry, The Middlesex Hospital Medical School, W1P 7PN. *T:* 01-636 8333.

CAMPBELL, Prof. Peter (Walter); Professor of Politics, Reading University, since 1964; *b* 17 June 1926; *o s* of late W. C. H. Campbell and of L. M. Locke. *Educ:* Bournemouth Sch.; New Coll., Oxford. 2nd class PPE, 1947; MA 1951; Research Student, Nuffield Coll., Oxford, 1947-49. Asst Lecturer in Govt, Manchester Univ., 1949-52; Lectr, 1952-60; Vice-Warden Needham Hall, 1959-60; Visiting Lectr in Political Science, Victoria Univ. Coll., NZ, 1954; Prof. of Political Economy, 1960-64, Dean, Faculty of Letters, 1966-69, Chm., Graduate Sch. of Contemporary European Studies, 1971-73, Reading University. Hon. Sec. Political Studies Assoc., 1955-58; Chm., Inst. of Electoral Research, 1959-65; Mem. Council, Hansard Soc. for Parly Govt, 1962-77; Editor of Political Studies, 1963-69; Hon. Treas., Joint Univ. Council for Social and Public Administration, 1965-69; Vice-Chm., Reading and District Council of Social Service, 1966-71; Vice-Pres., Electoral Reform Soc., 1972-. *Publications:* (with W. Theimer) Encyclopædia of World Politics, 1950; French Electoral Systems and Elections, 1789-1957, 1958; (with B. Chapman) The Constitution of the Fifth Republic, 1958. Articles in British, French and New Zealand Jls of Political Science. *Recreations:* ambling, idling, managing, meddling. *Address:* The University, Reading RG6 2AA. *T:* Reading 85123.

CAMPBELL, Sir Ralph Abercromby, Kt 1961; Chief Justice of the Bahamas, 1960-70; *b* 16 March 1906; 2nd *s* of Major W. O. Campbell, MC; *m* 1st, 1936, Joan Childers Blake (marr. diss., 1968); one *s* one *d*; 2nd, 1968, Shelagh Moore. *Educ:* Winchester; University Coll., Oxford. Barrister-at-Law, Lincoln's Inn, 1928; Western Circuit; Avocat à la Cour, Egypt, 1929; Pres. Civil Courts, Baghdad, Iraq, 1931-44; British Military Administration, Eritrea, Pres. British Military Court and Italian Court of Appeal, 1945; Resident Magistrate, Kenya, 1946; Judge of the Supreme Court, Aden, 1952 (redesignated Chief Justice, 1956)-1960. *Publications:* (Ed.) Law Reports of Kenya and East African Court of Appeal, 1950; Aden Law Reports, 1954-55; Bahamas Law Reports, 1968. *Recreations:* polo, golf, fishing. *Address:* Lomans Hill, Hartley Wintney, Hants. *T:* Hartley Wintney 3283.

CAMPBELL, Sir Robin Auchinbreck, 15th Bt *cr* 1628 (NS); *b* 7 June 1922; *s* of Sir Louis Hamilton Campbell, 14th Bt and Margaret Elizabeth Patricia, *d* of late Patrick Campbell; *S* father, 1970; *m* 1948, Rosemary (Sally), *d* of Ashley Dean, Christchurch, NZ; one *s* two *d*. Formerly Lieut (A) RNVR. *Heir: s* Louis Auchinbreck Campbell, *b* 17 Jan. 1953. *Address:* Glen Dhu, Motunau, Scargill, North Canterbury, New Zealand.

CAMPBELL, Robin Francis, DSO 1943; Director of Art, Arts Council of Great Britain, since 1969; *b* 1912; *s* of Rt. Hon. Sir Ronald Hugh Campbell, GCMG and Helen, *d* of Richard Graham; *m* 1st, 1936, Hon. Mary Hermione Ormsby Gore (marr. diss. 1945); two *s*; 2nd, 1945, Lady Mary Sybil St Clair Erskine (marr. diss. 1959); 3rd, 1959, Susan Jennifer Benson; two *s. Educ:* Wellington Coll.; New Coll., Oxford. Reuters correspondent, Berlin, Warsaw, 1936-39. Served N Africa, No 8 Commando and GHQ, Cairo, 1940-41; POW, 1941-43. Arts Council of GB, 1960-. *Address:* 6 Noel Road, N1 8HA. *T:* 01-226 1009.

CAMPBELL, Ronald Francis Boyd, MA; Director of Independent Schools Careers Organization (formerly Public School Appointments Bureau), since 1968; *b* 28 Aug. 1912; *o s* of Major Roy Neil Boyd Campbell, DSO, OBE and Effie Muriel, *y d* of Major Charles Pierce, IMS; *m* 1939, Pamela Muriel Désirée, *o d* of H. L. Wright, OBE, late Indian Forest Service; one *s* two *d. Educ:* Berkhamsted Sch.; Peterhouse, Cambridge. Asst Master, Berkhamsted Sch., 1934-39. War of 1939-45: Supplementary Reserve, The Duke of Cornwall's Light Infantry, Sept. 1939; served in England and Italy; DAQMG, HQ 3rd Div., 1943; demobilized with hon. rank of Lt-Col, 1945. Housemaster and OC Combined Cadet Force, Berkhamsted Sch., 1945-51; Headmaster, John Lyon Sch., Harrow, 1951-68. Walter Hines Page Travelling Scholarship to USA, 1960. Governor, Berkhamsted Sch., 1973. 1939-45 Star, Italy Star, Defence and Victory Medals; ERD (2 clasps). *Recreations:* sailing, fishing. *Address:* Hatch, Thursley, Godalming, Surrey. *T:* Elstead 3392. *Clubs:* Royal Cruising (Hon. Editor, Royal Cruising Club Journal and Roving Commissions), East India, Devonshire, Sports and Public Schools.

CAMPBELL, Rt. Hon. Sir Ronald Ian, PC 1950; GCMG 1947 (KCMG 1941; CMG 1932); CB 1937; Director of Royal Bank of Scotland, 1950-65 (Extra-ordinary Director, 1965-68); *b* 7 June 1890; *s* of Lieut-Col Sir Guy Campbell, 3rd Bt, and Nina, *d* of late Frederick Lehmann, 15 Berkeley Square, W1. *Educ:* Eton Coll.; Magdalen Coll., Oxford. Entered Diplomatic Service, 1914; Third Sec., Washington, 1915-20; Second and First Sec., Paris, 1920-23; Foreign Office, 1923-27; First Sec., Acting Counsellor and Counsellor, Washington, 1927-31; Counsellor, Cairo, 1931-34; Counsellor in Foreign Office, 1934-38; Minister Plenipotentiary, British Embassy, Paris, 1938-39; Minister at Belgrade, 1939-41; Minister in Washington, 1941-45; an Asst Under-Sec. of State in the Foreign Office, 1945-46; Dep. to Sec. of State for Foreign Affairs on Council of Foreign Ministers, 1945-46; British Ambassador to Egypt, 1946-50; retired, 1950. Mem., Board of Trustees for National Galleries of Scotland, 1956-66. Grand Officer of Legion of Honour. *Address:* 20 Sidegate, Haddington, East Lothian. *Clubs:* Brooks's, MCC; New (Edinburgh).
See also Sir Guy Campbell.

CAMPBELL, Ross, DSC 1944; Chairman, Atomic Energy of Canada Ltd; *b* 4 Nov. 1918; *s* of late William Marshall Campbell and of Helen Isabel Harris; *m* 1945, Penelope Grantham-Hill; two *s. Educ:* Univ. of Toronto Schs; Trin. Coll., Univ. of Toronto. BA, Faculty of Law, 1940. Served RCN, 1940-45. Joined Dept. of Ext. Affairs, Canada, 1945; Third Sec., Oslo, 1946-47; Second Sec., Copenhagen, 1947-50; European Div., Ottawa, 1950-52; First Sec., Ankara, 1952-56; Head of Middle East Div., Ottawa, 1957-59; Special Asst to Sec. of State for Ext. Aff., 1959-62; Asst Under-Sec. of State for Ext. Aff., 1962-64; Adviser to Canadian Delegns to: UN Gen. Assemblies, 1958-63; North Atlantic Coun., 1959-64; Ambassador to Yugoslavia, 1964-67, concurrently accredited Ambassador to Algeria, 1965-67; Ambassador and Perm. Rep. to NATO, 1967-73 (Paris May 1967, Brussels Oct. 1967); Ambassador to Japan, 1973-75. *Recreations:* tennis, skiing, gardening. *Address:* 275 Slater Street, Ottawa, Ont., Canada.

CAMPBELL, Ross; Deputy Chief Executive, Millbank Technical Services Ltd, since 1977 (Director 1975-77); *b* 4 May 1916; 2nd *s* of George Albert Campbell and Jean Glendinning Campbell (*née* Ross); *m* 1952, Dr Diana Stewart; one *s* two *d* (and one *d* decd). *Educ:* Farnborough Grammar Sch.; Reading Univ. CEng, FICE. Articled to Municipal Engr; Local Authority Engr, 1936-39; Air Min. (UK), 1939-44; Sqdn Ldr, RAF, Middle East, 1944-47; Air Min. (UK), 1947-52; Supt Engr, Gibraltar, 1952-55; Air Min. (UK), 1955-59; Chief Engr, Far East Air Force, 1959-62 and Bomber Comd, 1962-63; Personnel Management, MPBW, 1963-66; Chief Resident Engr, Persian Gulf, 1966-68; Dir Staff Management, MPBW, 1968-69; Dir of Works (Air), 1969-72; Under-Sec., and Dir of Defence Services II PSA, DoE, 1972-75. *Publications:* papers on professional civil engrg and trng in ICE Jl. *Recreations:* golf, tennis, music. *Address:* Caenwood, 31 Valley Road, Chorleywood, Herts. *T:* Rickmansworth 73744. *Club:* Royal Air Force.

CAMPBELL, Hon. Thane A., OC 1974; MA, LLD; Chief Commissioner, Foreign Claims Commission (Canada), 1970-74; Chief War Claims Commissioner (Canada), 1952-74; Adviser on claims under agreement with Bulgaria, 1967; *b* 7 July 1895; *s* of Alexander and Clara Tremaine Campbell; *m* 1st, 1930, Cecilia Lillian Bradshaw (*d* 1968); two *s* two *d*; 2nd, 1970, Paula Champ. *Educ:* Prince of Wales Coll., Charlottetown, PEI; Dalhousie Univ. Halifax, NS; Corpus Christi Coll., Oxford. Admitted to Bar of PEI 1927; Attorney-Gen. of PEI 1930-31 and 1935-43; Mem. of Legislative Assembly, 1931-43; Premier and Provincial Sec.-Treasurer, PEI, 1936-43; Chief Justice, Prince Edward Island, 1943-70. Chancellor, Univ. of Prince Edward Island, 1970-74. Member: Historical Sites and Monuments Bd of Canada, 1948-59; Nat. Library Adv. Council, 1949-59; Bd of Governors of: Dalhousie Coll., 1950-; St Dunstan's Univ., 1964-. Pres., Dominion Curling Assoc., 1942; Vice-Pres., Royal Caledonian Curling Club of Scotland, 1945; admitted to Curling Hall of Fame for Canada, 1975. Chm., Brier Trustees, 1963-. Holds hon. doctorates. *Address:* Box 1358, Summerside, PEI, Canada. *T:* (office) Ottawa 995-8702, (residence) 436-2556.

CAMPBELL, Sir Thomas Cockburn-, 6th Bt, *cr* 1821; Retired; *b* 8 Dec. 1918; *e s* of Sir Alexander Thomas Cockburn-Campbell, 5th Bt, and Maude Frances Lorenzo (*d* 1926), *o d* of Alfred Giles, Kent Town, Adelaide; *S* father, 1935; *m* 1944, Josephine Zoi, *e d* of Harold Douglas Forward, Curjardine, WA; one *s*. *Educ:* Melbourne C of E Grammar Sch. *Heir: s* Alexander Thomas Cockburn-Campbell [*b* 16 March 1945; *m* 1969, Kerry Ann, *e d* of Sgt K. Johnson; one *s*]. *Address:* Lot 7, Lewis Road, Forrestfield, WA 6058, Australia.

CAMPBELL, Maj.-Gen. Victor David Graham, CB 1956; DSO 1940; OBE 1946; DL; JP; *b* 9 March 1905; *s* of late Gen. Sir David G. M. Campbell, GCB; *m* 1947, Dulce Beatrix, *d* of late G. B. Collier, and *widow* of Lt-Col J. A. Goodwin. *Educ:* Rugby; RMC Sandhurst. 2nd Lieut The Queen's Own Cameron Highlanders, 1924; AQMG and DA&QMG HQ AFNEI, 1945-46; Lt-Col Comdg 1st Bn The Gordon Highlanders, 1949; Brig. Comdg 31 Lorried Infantry Brigade, 1951; Chief of Staff, HQ Scottish Command, 1954-57; psc 1938; idc 1953. DL and JP, 1962, High Sheriff, 1968, County of Devon; Chairman: Totnes RDC, 1971-72; Totnes Petty Sessional Div., 1972-75. *Address:* Beggars Bush, South Brent, South Devon.

CAMPBELL, Maj.-Gen. William Tait, CBE 1945 (OBE 1944); retired; Director, The Fairbridge Society; *b* 8 Oct. 1912; *s* of late R. B. Campbell, MD, FRCPE, Edinburgh; *m* 1942, Rhoda Alice, *y d* of late Adm. Algernon Walker-Heneage-Vivian, CB, MVO, Swansea; two *d. Educ:* Cargilfield Sch.; Fettes Coll.; RMC Sandhurst. 2nd Lieut, The Royal Scots (The Royal Regt), 1933; served War of 1939-45: 1st Airborne Div. and 1st Allied Airborne Army (North Africa, Sicily, Italy and Europe). Lieut-Col Commanding 1st Bn The Royal Scots, in Egypt, Cyprus, UK and Suez Operation (despatches), 1954-57; Col, Royal Naval War Coll., Greenwich, 1958; Brig. i/c Admin. Malaya, 1962; Maj.-Gen., 1964; DQMG, MoD (Army Dept), 1964-67; Col, The Royal Scots (The Royal Regt), 1964-74. US Bronze Star, 1945. *Recreations:* gardening, golf, shooting, fishing. *Address:* c/o Lloyds Bank Ltd (Cox's & King's Branch), 6 Pall Mall, SW1; Portland House, Ash Vale, near Aldershot, Hants GU12 5LW. *T:* Aldershot 24825. *Club:* East India, Devonshire, Sports and Public Schools.

CAMPBELL GOLDING, F.; *see* Golding, F. C.

CAMPBELL-GRAY, family name of **Lord Gray.**

CAMPBELL-JOHNSON, Alan, CIE 1947; OBE 1946; Officer of US Legion of Merit, 1947; MA Oxon; FRSA, MRI; Chairman: Campbell-Johnson Ltd, Public Relations Consultants; International Public Relations Ltd; *b* 16 July 1913; *o c* of late Lieut-Col James Alexander Campbell-Johnson and late Gladys Susanne Campbell-Johnson; *m* 1938, Imogen Fay de la Tour Dunlap; one *d* (one *s* decd). *Educ:* Westminster; Christ Church, Oxford (scholar). BA 2nd Cl. Hons Mod. Hist., 1935. Political Sec. to Rt Hon. Sir Archibald Sinclair, Leader of Parl. Lib. Party, 1937-40; served War of 1939-45, RAF; COHQ, 1942-43; HQ SACSEA (Wing Comdr i/c Inter-Allied Records Section), 1943-46. Contested (L) Salisbury and South Wilts. Div., Gen. Elections, 1945 and 1950. Press Attaché to Viceroy and Gov.-Gen. of India (Earl Mountbatten of Burma), 1947-48. Fellow Inst. of Public Relations, Pres. 1956-57. *Publications:* Growing Opinions, 1935; Peace Offering, 1936; Anthony Eden: a biography, 1938, rev. edn 1955; Viscount Halifax: a biography, 1941; Mission with Mountbatten, 1951, repr, 1972. *Recreations:* cricket, mountaineering. *Address:* 21 Ashley Gardens, Ambrosden Avenue, SW1P 1QD. *T:* 01-834 1532. *Clubs:* Brooks's, National Liberal, MCC.

CAMPBELL ORDE, Alan Colin, CBE 1943; AFC 1919; FRAeS; *b* Lochgilphead, Argyll, NB, 4 Oct. 1898; *s* of Colin Ridley Campbell Orde; *m* 1951, Mrs Beatrice McClure, *e d* of late Rev. Eliott-Drake Briscoe. *Educ:* Sherborne. Served European War, 1916-18, Flight Sub-Lieut, Royal Navy, and Flying Officer, Royal Air Force; Active service in Belgium, 1917; one of original commercial Pilots on London-Paris route with Aircraft Transport & Travel Ltd, 1919-20; Instructor and Adviser to

Chinese Govt in Peking, 1921-23; Instructor and latterly Chief Test Pilot to Sir W. G. Armstrong-Whitworth Aircraft, Ltd, Coventry, 1924-36; Operational Manager, British Airways, Ltd, 1936-39; subseq. Operations Manager, Imperial Airways Ltd; was Ops Director BOAC, during first 4 years after its inception in 1939; thereafter responsible for technical development as Development Dir until resignation from BOAC Dec. 1957. *Recreation:* reading in bed. *Address:* Smugglers Mead, Stepleton, Blandford, Dorset. *T:* Child Okeford 268. *Club:* Boodle's.

CAMPBELL-ORDE, Sir John A.; *see* Orde.

CAMPBELL-PRESTON, Hon. Mrs Angela; Chairman, 1953-74 (Director, 1945-74) Westminster Press and subsidiary companies; *b* 27 Oct. 1910; 3rd *d* of 2nd Viscount Cowdray; *m* 1st, 1930, George Antony Murray (killed in action, 1945); one *s* (*see* Duke of Atholl) (and two *s* decd); 2nd, 1950, Robert Campbell-Preston, *qv*; one *d. Educ:* home. Chm., S London Hosp. for Women, 1932-48; Chm., Lambeth Gp Hosp. Man. Cttee, 1961-64 (Vice-Chm., 1948-61); Mem., SW London Hosp. Man. Cttee, 1964-70; Sec. of various cttees of King Edward VII Hosp. Fund for London, 1942-50; Past Member: Glasgow Regional Hosp. Bd; Oban Hosps Bd of Management. Dir, Fisher's Hotel Ltd. *Recreation:* renovating houses. *Address:* 31 Marlborough Hill, NW8. *T:* 01-586 2291; Ardchattan Priory, Connel, Argyll, Scotland. *T:* Bonawe 274.

CAMPBELL-PRESTON of Ardchattan, Robert Modan Thorne, OBE 1955; MC 1943; Vice-Lieutenant, Argyll and Bute, since 1976; *b* 7 Jan. 1909; *s* of Col R. W. P. Campbell-Preston, DL, JP, of Ardchattan and Valleyfield, Fife, and Mary Augusta Thorne; *m* 1950, Hon. Angela Murray (*see* Hon. Mrs Angela Campbell-Preston); one *d. Educ:* Eton; Christ Church, Oxford (MA). Lt Scottish Horse, 1930; Lt-Col 1945. Hon. Col, Fife-Forfar Yeo./Scottish Horse, 1962-67. Member Royal Company of Archers, Queen's Body Guard for Scotland. Joint Managing Director, Alginate Industries Ltd, 1949-74. DL 1951, JP 1950, Argyllshire. Silver Star (USA), 1945. *Recreations:* shooting, fishing. *Address:* Ardchattan Priory, Connel, Argyll. *T:* Bonawe 274; 31 Marlborough Hill, NW8. *T:* 01-586 2291. *Club:* Puffin's (Edinburgh).

CAMPBELL-PURDIE, Cora Gwendolyn Jean, (Wendy); Director Bou Saada Trust (registered Charity Commissioners, December 1969) (formerly Sahara Reafforestation Committee, formed in 1965 with Reverend Austen Williams as Chairman); *b* 8 June 1925; *d* of Edmund Hamilton Campbell Purdie and Janie Theodora Williams. *Educ:* Woodford House, New Zealand. Worked with Red Cross Transport Corps in Auckland, 1943-46. English Asst at Lycées in France and Corsica, 1954-56; worked simultaneously and subseq. full-time with British timber firm in Corsica, 1954-58; FAO, Rome, on Mediterranean Reafforestation Project, Aug. 1958. Has been planting trees in N Africa, 1959 onwards; now expects at least 75 per cent success; planted: 1000 trees (given by Moroccan Min. of Agric.) in Tiznit, 1960 and again in 1961; 1000 trees (given by Algerian Min. of Agric.) planted by local agricl authorities at Bou Saada, 1964, by 1970 approx. 130,000 trees established on 260 acres; grain, fruit trees and vegetables now also grown, and bees and hens kept. Has planted many more thousands of trees (money given by: Men of the Trees; War on Want; St Martin-in-the-Fields; the Bishop of Southwark's Diocesan Fund; CORSO (New Zealand), etc). Film made of Bou Saada project, 1970; since then has travelled with film, discussing re-afforestation and forestry techniques, in Commonwealth, USA, Africa, Near and Middle East. Attended: World Food Conf., Rome, 1974; Sahel Drought Conf., Senegal, 1975. *Publications:* (in collaboration with Fenner Brockway) Woman against the Desert, 1967; contrib. The Ecologist. *Recreation:* classical music. *Address:* 84 St Paul's Road, N1. *T:* 01-359 0729.

CAMPDEN, Viscount; Anthony Baptist Noel; *b* 16 Jan. 1950; *s* and *heir* of 5th Earl of Gainsborough, *qv*; *m* 1972, Sarah Rose, *er d* of Col T. F. C. Winnington; one *s. Educ:* Ampleforth; Royal Agricultural Coll., Cirencester. *Heir: s* Hon. Henry Robert Anthony Noel, *b* 1 July 1977. *Address:* Top House, Exton, Rutland, Leics LE15 8AX. *T:* Oakham 812587; 105 Earls Court Road, W8. *T:* 01-370 5650. *Club:* Turf.
See also Sir F. S. W. Winnington, Bt.

CAMPION, Sir Harry, Kt 1957; CB 1949; CBE 1945; MA; retired as Director of Central Statistical Office, Cabinet Office, 1967; *b* 20 May 1905; *o s* of John Henry Campion, Worsley, Lancs. *Educ:* Farnworth Grammar Sch.; Univ. of Manchester. Rockefeller Foundation Fellow, United States, 1932; Robert Ottley Reader in Statistics, Univ. of Manchester, 1933-39. Dir. of Statistical Office, UN, 1946-47; Mem. of Statistical

Commission, United Nations, 1947-67; Pres.: International Statistical Institute, 1963-67; Royal Statistical Society, 1957-59; Hon. LLD, Manchester, 1967. *Publications:* Distribution of National Capital; Public and Private Property in Great Britain; articles in economic and statistical journals. *Address:* Rima, Priory Close, Stanmore, Mddx. *T:* 01-954 3267. *Club:* Reform.

CAMPION, Peter James, DPhil; FInstP; Deputy Director, National Physical Laboratory, since 1976; *b* 7 April 1926; *s* of Frank Wallace Campion and Gertrude Alice (*née* Lambert); *m* 1950, Beryl Grace Stanton, *e d* of John Stanton; one *s* one *d* (and one *s* decd). *Educ:* Westcliff High Sch., Essex; Exeter Coll., Oxford (MA, DPhil). FInstP 1964. RN, 1943. Nuffield Res. Fellow, Oxford, 1954; Chalk River Proj., Atomic Energy of Canada Ltd, 1955; National Physical Lab., Teddington, 1960-: Supt, Div. of Radiation Science, 1964; Supt, Div. of Mech. and Optical Metrology, 1974. Mem., Comité Consultatif pour les Etalons de Mesure des Rayonnements Ionisante, 1963; Chm., Sect. II, reconstituted Comité Consultatif, Mesure des radionucléides, 1970. Editor, Internat. Jl of Applied Radiation and Isotopes, 1968-71. *Publications:* A Code of Practice for the Detailed Statement of Accuracy (with A. Williams and J. E. Burns), 1973; technical and rev. papers in learned jls on neutron capture gamma rays, measurement of radioactivity, and on metrology generally. *Recreation:* winemaking. *Address:* The Hawthorns, Fee Farm Road, Claygate, Surrey. *T:* Esher 62426.

CAMPION, Sidney Ronald, OBE 1953; FRSA; FJI 1950; Author, Barrister, Journalist, Schoolmaster, Lecturer, Sculptor, and from 1940 until retirement in 1957, Head of the Press and Broadcast Division, GPO Headquarters; *b* Coalville, Leics, 30 June 1891; *e s* of Chelsea Pensioner, late Walter Campion and late Martha Robinson, Leicester; *m* 1912, Claire (*d* 1968), *y d* of late Horatio and Elizabeth Armitage, Cotebrook, Tarporley, Cheshire; one *d*; *m* 1971, Margery, *widow* of Stanley Ainsworth, Southport. *Educ:* Charnwood Street Elementary Sch., Leicester; Vaughan Working Men's Coll., Leicester; Chester Diocesan Teachers' Training Coll.; Gray's Inn; Morley Coll., London; Wimbledon School of Art; Regent Street Polytechnic School of Art; St Martin's School of Art; Southport Coll. of Art. Street newspaper seller in Leicester from 11 to 14. Worked in factories, workshops and woodmills in Leicester for three years. Assisted by late Rt Hon. J. Ramsay MacDonald, late Sir Edward Wood (Chm. Freeman Hardy & Willis, Ltd), and late Thomas Adcock, MA, was privately educated and joined editorial staff of Leicester Pioneer. Later worked on Wilmslow Express (Cheshire), Leeds Weekly Citizen, Daily Citizen, Chorley Guardian, Bradford Daily Telegraph, Daily News, London, and served as chief of the Allied (Kemsley) (now Thomson's Allied) Newspapers; Parliamentary Press Gallery staff, 1933-40; Chief Press and Broadcasting Officer to General Post Office, 1940-57. Town Councillor and Poor Law Guardian, Chorley, 1920-23; Parliamentary Labour Candidate, Oswestry, 1923; qualified as schoolmaster with First Class teaching certificate, Liverpool Univ.; admitted Gray's Inn, 1927, honours in Final and called to Bar, 1930; member South-Eastern Circuit; holder bronze medal of Royal Life Saving Society and hon. instructor in life saving; Madden Prizeman, Chester Coll. Life Member: National Union of Journalists, 1957; Newspaper Press Fund; Life Fellow RSA, 1975; Member: of Francis Bacon Society; Psychical Research Society; Society of Civil Service Authors; Cttee of Post Office Art Club of Great Britain; William Morris Society; League for Abolition of Cruel Sports; Royal National Institute for the Deaf; travelled Scandinavia, Russia (1935 and 1960), Germany, Turkey, etc. European War, 1914-18, served in RFC, RAF, IAF. *Publications:* Sunlight on the Foothills, 1941; Towards the Mountains, 1943; Reaching High Heaven, 1944; Only the Stars Remain, 1946; The World of Colin Wilson: a Biographical Study, 1962; Adventures Under the Sycamore Tree, 1964; contributor to home and overseas newspapers, magazines and periodicals, and to Central Office of Information. *Recreations:* experimenting in literary forms; picture painting, sculpture, modelling (portrait busts, etc., exhibitor: London galleries; Morden public library; Society of British Portrait Sculptors; Paris, 1963-70; Madrid, 1965; one-man exhibitions: London, 1960, Astley Hall, Chorley, Lancs, 1962; Tower Gallery, City of London, 1964); searching for the Shakespeare MSS, chess and golf. *Address:* 13 Argyle Court, Argyle Road, Southport, Merseyside PR9 9LQ. *T:* Southport 33047. *Clubs:* Press (became Life Member 1958), Paternosters.

CAMPLING, Ven. Christopher Russell; Archdeacon of Dudley and Director of Religious Education in the Diocese of Worcester, since 1976; *b* 4 July 1925; *s* of Canon William Charles Campling; *m* 1953, Juliet Marian Hughes; one *s* two *d*. *Educ:* Lancing Coll.; St Edmund Hall, Oxford (MA; Hons Theol. cl. 2); Cuddesdon Theol. Coll. RNVR, 1943-47. Deacon 1951, priest 1952; Curate of Basingstoke, 1951-55; Minor Canon

of Ely Cathedral and Chaplain of King's School, Ely, 1955-60; Chaplain of Lancing Coll., 1960-67; Vicar of Pershore with Pinvin and Wick and Birlingham, 1968-76; RD of Pershore, 1970-76. Mem., General Synod of Church of England, 1970-. *Publications:* The Way, The Truth and The Life: Vol. 1, The Love of God in Action, 1964; Vol. 2, The People of God in Action, 1964; Vol. 3, The Word of God in Action, 1965; Vol. 4, God's Plan in Action, 1965; also two teachers' volumes; Words for Worship, 1969; The Fourth Lesson, Vol. 1 1973, Vol. 2 1974. *Recreations:* music, drama, golf. *Address:* The Archdeacon's House, Dodderhill, Droitwich, Worcs WR9 0BE. *Club:* Naval.

CAMPOLI, Alfredo; violinist; *b* 20 Oct. 1906; *s* of Prof. Romeo Campoli, Prof. of Violin at Accademia di Santa Cecilia, Rome, and Elvira Campoli, dramatic soprano; *m* 1942, Joy Burbridge. Came to London, 1911; gave regular public recitals as a child; Gold Medal, London Musical Festival, 1919; toured British Isles with Melba and with Dame Clara Butt, and was engaged for series of International Celebrity Concerts at age of 15. Has played all over the world. First broadcast from Savoy Hill, 1930; has subsequently made frequent broadcasts and made many gramophone records. *Recreations:* bridge, cine-photography, table tennis, billiards, croquet. *Address:* 50 Eversley Park Road, Winchmore Hill, N21.

CAMPOS, Roberto de Oliveira, Hon. GCVO; Brazilian Ambassador to the Court of St James's, since 1975; *b* Cuiabá, Mato Grosso, 17 April 1917. *Educ:* Catholic Seminaries: Guaxupé and Belo Horizonte, Brazil (grad. Philosophy and Theol.); George Washington Univ., Washington (MA Econs); Columbia Univ., NYC (Hon. Dr). Entered Brazilian Foreign Service, 1939; Economic Counsellor, Brazil-US EDC, 1951-53; Dir 1952, Gen. Man. 1955, Pres. 1959, Nat. Economic Develt Bank; Sec. Gen., Nat. Develt Council, 1956-59; Delegate to internat. confs. incl. ECOSOC and GATT, 1959-61; Roving Ambassador for financial negotiations in W Europe, 1961; Ambassador of Brazil to US, 1961-63; Minister of State for Planning and Co-ord., 1964-67. Prof., Sch. of Econs, Univ. of Brazil, 1956-61. Mem. or past Mem., Cttees and Bds on economic develt (particularly inter-Amer. econ. develt). *Publications:* Ensaios de História Econômica e Sociologia; Economia, Planejamento e Nacionalismo; A Moeda, o Govêrno e o Tempo; A Técnica e o Riso; Reflections on Latin American Development; Do outro lado da cerca; Temas e Sistemas; Ensaios contra a maré; Política Econômica e Mitos Políticos (jtly): Trends in International Trade (GATT report); Partners in Progress (report of Pearson Cttee of World Bank); A Nova Economia Brasileira; Formas Criativas do Desenvolvimento Brasileiro; Omundo que vejo e náo desejo; techn. articles and reports on develt and internat. econs, in jls. *Address:* Brazilian Embassy, 32 Green Street, W1. *T:* 01-629 0155.

CAMPS, William Anthony; Master of Pembroke College, Cambridge, since 1970; *b* 28 Dec. 1910; *s* of P. W. L. Camps, FRCS, and Alice, *d* of Joseph Redfern, Matlock; *m* 1953, Miriam Camp, Washington, DC, *d* of Prof. Burton Camp, Wesleyan Univ., Connecticut. *Educ:* Marlborough Coll.; Pembroke Coll., Cambridge (Schol.). Fellow, Pembroke Coll., 1933; Univ. Lectr in Classics, 1939; Temp. Civil Servant, 1940-45; Asst Tutor, Pembroke Coll., 1945; Senior Tutor, 1947-62; Tutor for Advanced Students, 1963-70; Pres., 1964-70. Mem., Inst. for Advanced Study, Princeton, 1956-57; Vis. Assoc. Prof., UC Toronto, 1966; Vis. Prof., Univ. of North Carolina at Chapel Hill, 1969. *Publications:* edns of Propertius I, 1961, IV, 1965, III, 1966, II, 1967; An Introduction to Virgil's Aeneid, 1969; sundry notes and reviews in classical periodicals. *Recreations:* unremarkable. *Address:* Pembroke College, Cambridge. *T:* Cambridge 52241. *Club:* United Oxford & Cambridge University.

CAMROSE, 2nd Viscount, *cr* 1941, of Hackwood Park; **John Seymour Berry,** TD; Bt 1921; Baron 1929; Deputy Chairman (Past Chairman) of The Daily Telegraph Ltd; *b* 12 July 1909; *e s* of 1st Viscount Camrose and Mary Agnes (*d* 1962), *e d* of late Thomas Corns, 2 Bolton Street, W; *S* father, 1954. *Educ:* Eton; Christ Church, Oxford. Major, City of London Yeomanry. Served War of 1939-45, North African and Italian Campaigns, 1942-45 (despatches). MP (C) for Hitchin Division, Herts, 1941-45. Vice-Chm. Amalgamated Press Ltd, 1942-59. Younger Brother, Trinity House. *Heir:* *b* Baron Hartwell, *qv*. *Address:* Hackwood Park, Basingstoke, Hampshire. *T:* Basingstoke 64630. *Clubs:* Buck's, White's, Beefsteak, Marylebone Cricket (MCC); Royal Yacht Squadron (Trustee).

See also Earl of Birkenhead.

CANADA, Primate of All; *see* Scott, Most Rev. E. W.

CANAVAN, Dennis Andrew; MP (Lab) West Stirlingshire, since Oct. 1974; *b* 8 Aug. 1942; *s* of Thomas and Agnes Canavan; *m* 1964, Elnor Stewart; three *s* one *d. Educ:* St Columba's High Sch., Cowdenbeath; Edinburgh Univ. (BSc Hons, DipEd). Maths Teacher, 1968-70; Head of Maths Dept, St Modan's High Sch., Stirling, 1970-74; Asst Headmaster, Holy Rood High Sch., Edinburgh, 1974. Treasurer, Scottish Parly Lab. Gp; Convener, Scottish Parly Lab Gp Educn Sub-Cttee, 1976-77. Mem. Local Exec., Educnl Inst. of Scotland, 1972-74; Organising Sec., W Stirlingshire Constituency Labour Party, 1972-74; Labour Party Agent, Feb. 1974; District Councillor, 1973-74; Leader of Labour Gp, Stirling District Council, 1974; Mem. Stirling Dist Educn Sub-cttee, 1973-74; Mem. Stirlingshire Youth Employment Adv. Cttee, 1972-74. *Publications:* contribs to various jls on educn and politics. *Recreations:* walking, swimming, reading, football (Scottish Univs football internationalist, 1966-67 and 1967-68). *Address:* 15 Margaret Road, Bannockburn, Stirlingshire. *T:* Bannockburn 812581; House of Commons, SW1A 0AA. *T:* 01-219 3000. *Clubs:* Bannockburn Miners' Welfare (Bannockburn); Stirling District Labour Party (Stirling).

CANBERRA, Archbishop of, (RC), since 1967; **Most Rev. Thomas Vincent Cahill,** CBE 1972; DD, PhD; *b* 22 Feb. 1913; *s* of Patrick Cahill and Elizabeth Cavagna. *Educ:* Marist Brothers' Coll., Bendigo, Victoria, Australia; Propaganda Coll., Rome. Ordained Priest, Rome, 1935; Asst Priest, Sacred Heart Cathedral, Bendigo, Diocese of Sandhurst, Victoria, Australia, 1936-39; Secretary, Apostolic Delegation, Sydney, 1939-48; Chancellor, Diocese of Sandhurst, 1948; Bishop of Cairns, Queensland, 1948-67; appointed Archbishop of Canberra and Goulburn, 1967. *Address:* Archbishop's House, Commonwealth Avenue, Canberra, ACT 2600, Australia. *T:* Canberra 486411.

CANBERRA AND GOULBURN, Bishop of, since 1972; **Rt. Rev. Cecil Allan Warren;** *b* 25 Feb. 1924; *s* of Charles Henry and Eliza Warren; *m* 1947, Doreen Muriel Burrows. *Educ:* Sydney Univ. (BA 1950); Queen's Coll., Oxford (MA 1959). Deacon 1950, priest 1951, Dio. of Canberra and Goulburn; appointments in Diocese of Oxford, 1953-57; Canberra, 1957-63; Organising Sec. Church Society, and Director of Forward in Faith Movement, Dio. of Canberra and Goulburn, 1963-65; Asst Bishop of Canberra and Goulburn, 1965-72. *Address:* 51 Rosenthal Street, Campbell, ACT 2601, Australia. *T:* Canberra 480716. *Club:* Commonwealth (Canberra).

CANDAU, Marcolino Gomes, MD, DPH; Director-General Emeritus, World Health Organization, Geneva, since 1973; *b* Rio de Janeiro, 30 May 1911; *s* of Julio Candau and Augusta Gomes; *m* 1936; two *s*; *m* 1973, Sita Reelfs. *Educ:* Univ. of Brazil, Rio de Janeiro; Johns Hopkins Univ., USA. Various posts in Health Services of State of Rio de Janeiro, 1934-43; Asst Superintendent, Servico Especial de Saude Publica, Min. of Education and Health, 1944-47; Superintendent 1947-50; World Health Organization: Dir, Div. of Org. of Public Health Services, Geneva, 1950-51; Asst Dir-General, Dept of Advisory Services, Geneva, 1951-52; Asst Dir, Pan-American Sanitary Bureau, Dep. Reg. Dir for the Americas, Washington, 1952-53; Dir-Gen., Geneva, 1953-73. Hon. Dr of Laws: Univ. of Michigan; Johns Hopkins Univ.; Univ. of Edinburgh; The Queen's Univ. of Belfast; Seoul Univ., Korea; Royal Univ. of Malta; Hon. Dr of Medicine: Univ. of Geneva; Karolinska Inst., Stockholm; Hon. Dr: Univ. of Brazil; Univ. of Sao Paulo, Brazil; Univ. of Bordeaux; Charles Univ., Prague; Inst. of Medicine and Pharmacy, Bucharest; Univ. of Abidjan; Hon. Dr of Science: Bates Coll., Maine, USA; Univ. of Ibadan; Semmelweis Univ. of Medicine, Budapest; Univ. of Cambridge; FRCP, Hon. FRSocMed, and Hon. FRSH (all GB), and various other hon. fellowships in America and Europe; Mem., Royal Soc. of Tropical Medicine and Hygiene, GB; For. Member USSR Acad. of Med. Sciences. Mary Kingsley Medal of Liverpool Sch. of Tropical Medicine; Gold Medal of RSH, London, 1966; Harben Gold Medal, RIPH&H, London, 1973; also prizes and medals for services to public health. *Publications:* scientific papers. *Address:* Le Mas, Route du Jura, 1296 Coppet, Vaud, Switzerland.

CANDELA OUTERINO, Felix; engineer and architect; Professor, Department of Architecture, University of Illinois at Chicago, since 1971; Professor, Escuela Nacional de Arquitectura, University of Mexico, since 1953 (on leave of absence); *b* Madrid, 27 Jan. 1910; *s* of Felix and Julia Candela; *m* 1940, Eladia Martin Galan (*d* 1964); four *d*; *m* 1967, Dorothy H. Davies. *Educ:* Univ. of Madrid, Spain. Architect, Escuela Superior de Arquitectura de Madrid, 1935. Captain of Engineers, Republican Army, Spanish Civil War, 1936-39. Emigrated to Mexico, 1939; Mexican Citizen, 1941. General practice in Mexico as Architect and Contractor. Founded (with

brother Antonio) Cubiertas ALA, SA, firm specializing in design and construction of reinforced concrete shell structures. Work includes Sports Palace for Mexico Olympics, 1968. Hon. Member: Sociedad de Arquitectos Colombianos, 1956; Sociedad Venezolana de Arquitectos, 1961; International Assoc. for Shell Structures, 1962. Charles Elliot Norton Prof. of Poetry, Harvard Univ., for academic year, 1961-62; Jefferson Meml Prof., Univ. of Virginia, 1966; Andrew D. White Prof., Cornell Univ., 1969-74; Prof. Honorario, Escuela Tecnica Superior de Arquitectura de Madrid, 1969; William Hoffman Wood Prof., Leeds Univ., 1974-75. Gold Medal, Instn Structural Engineers, England, 1961; Auguste Perret Prize of International Union of Architects, 1961; Alfred E. Lindau Award, Amer. Concrete Inst., 1965. Hon. Fellow American Inst. of Architects, 1963; Hon. Corr. Member Royal Inst. of British Architects, 1963; Plomada de Oro, Soc. de Arquitectos Mexicanos, 1963; Doctor in Fine Arts (*hc*), Univ. of New Mexico, 1964; Dr Ing *hc* Univ. de Santa Maria, Caracas, 1968. *Publications:* Candela, the Shell Builder, 1962. Several articles in architectural and engineering magazines all around the world. *Address:* 1514 West Jackson Boulevard, Chicago, Illinois 60607, USA. *T:* (312) 8296029.

CANDY, Air Vice-Marshal Charles Douglas, CB 1963; CBE 1957; Air Member for Personnel, RAAF, 1966-69, retired; *b* 17 Sept. 1912; *s* of late C. H. and late Mrs Candy; *m* 1938, Eileen Cathryn Mary (*née* Poole-Ricketts); one *d.* Served War of 1939-45; Command and Staff appointments in Australia, the United Kingdom, West Africa and South-West Pacific Area; AOC North-Eastern Area, RAAF, 1946; Joint Services Staff Coll., 1947; Dept of Defence, Commonwealth of Australia, 1948-50; Director of Organisation and Staff Duties, HQ, RAAF, 1950-52; Imperial Defence Coll., 1953; SASO No. 3 Group Bomber Command, RAF, 1954-56; Deputy Chief of the Air Staff, RAAF, 1956-58 (Air Vice-Marshal, 1957); AOC Home Command, RAAF, 1958-59; Sen. Air Staff Officer, Far East Air Force, Royal Air Force, 1959-62; AOC Support Command, RAAF, 1962-66. *Recreation:* golf. *Address:* 48 Doyle Terrace, Chapman, ACT 2611, Australia. *Clubs:* Commonwealth, Royal Canberra Golf (Canberra); Royal Singapore Golf (Singapore).

CANE, Prof. Violet Rosina; Professor of Mathematical Statistics, University of Manchester, since 1971; *b* 31 Jan. 1916; *d* of Tubal George Cane and Annie Louisa Lansdell. *Educ:* Newnham Coll., Cambridge (MA, Dipl. in Math. Stats). BoT, 1940; Univ. of Aberdeen, 1941; FO, 1942; Min. of Town and Country Planning, 1946; Statistician to MRC Applied Psychol. Unit, 1948; Queen Mary Coll., London, 1955; Fellow, Newnham Coll., Cambridge, 1957; Lectr, Univ. of Cambridge, 1960. Hon. MSc Manchester, 1974. *Publications:* (contrib.) Current Problems in Animal Behaviour, 1961; (contrib.) Perspectives in Probability and Statistics, 1975; papers in Jl of Royal Stat. Soc., Animal Behaviour, and psychol jls. *Recreation:* supporting old houses. *Address:* 13/14 Little St Mary's Lane, Cambridge CB2 1RR. *T:* Cambridge 57277; Statistical Laboratory, Department of Mathematics, The University, Manchester M13 9PL.

CANET, Maj.-Gen. Lawrence George, CB 1964; CBE 1956; BE; Master General of the Ordnance, Australia, 1964-67, retired; *b* 1 Dec. 1910; *s* of late Albert Canet, Melbourne, Victoria; *m* 1940, Mary Elizabeth Clift, *d* of Cecil Clift Jones, Geelong, Victoria; one *s. Educ:* RMC Duntroon; Sydney Univ. (BE). Served War of 1939-45 with 7th Australian Div. (Middle East and Pacific). GOC Southern Command, 1960-64. Brigadier 1953; Maj.-Gen. 1957. *Address:* 37 The Corso, Isle of Capri, Surfers Paradise, Qld 4217, Australia.

CANFIELD, Cass; Senior Editor, Harper & Row, Publishers; *b* 26 April 1897; *s* of August Cass and Josephine Houghteling; *m* 1st, 1922, Katharine Emmet; two *s*; 2nd, 1938, Jane White Fuller. *Educ:* Groton Sch.; Harvard Univ. (AB); Oxford Univ. Harris, Forbes & Co. 1921-22; NY Evening Post, 1922-23; Foreign Affairs (a quarterly magazine), 1923-24; Manager, London (England) office, Harper & Bros, 1924-27; Harper & Bros, NY City, 1927; President, Harper & Bros, 1931-45; Chairman of the Board, 1945-55; Chairman Exec. Cttee, 1955-67. Served European War, 1917-18, commissioned. President National Assoc. of Book Publishers, 1932-34; Trustee, Woodrow Wilson National Fellowship Foundation; Mem. Exec. Cttee, John Fitzgerald Kennedy Library; Chairman, Governing Body, International Planned Parenthood Federation, 1966-69, now Chm. Emeritus. During War of 1939-45 with Board of Economic Warfare, Washington, DC; special advisor to American Ambassador, London, in charge of Economic Warfare Division, 1943; Director, Office of War Information, France, 1945. Albert D. Lasker Award, 1964. Hon. Phi Beta Kappa. *Publications:* The Publishing Experience, 1969; Up and Down and Around, 1972; The Incredible Pierpont Morgan, 1974; Samuel Adams' Revolution, 1976. *Address:* 10 East 53

Street, New York, NY 10022, USA. *T:* 593-7200. *Clubs:* Century Association (New York); Metropolitan (Washington).

CANHAM, Brian John; Metropolitan Stipendiary Magistrate, since 1975; *b* 27 Dec. 1930; *s* of Frederick Ernest and Nora Ruby Canham; *m* 1955, Rachel, *yr d* of late Joseph and Martha Woolley, Bank House, Longnor, Staffs; three *s* one *d*. *Educ:* City of Norwich Sch.; Queens' Coll., Cambridge. MA, LLB. Called to Bar, Gray's Inn, 1955. Army Legal Services, BAOR: Staff Captain, 1956, Major, 1958. Private practice as barrister on SE Circuit, 1963-. *Recreations:* gardening, sailing, swimming. *Address:* 4 Paper Buildings, Temple, EC4Y 7EX. *T:* 01-353 8408.

CANHAM, Bryan Frederick, MC 1943; FCIS; Director, Investment and Loans, Directorate General XVIII Credit and Investment, Commission of the European Communities, since 1976; *b* 11 April 1920; *s* of Frederick William Canham and Emma Louisa Martin; *m* 1944, Rita Gwendoline Huggett; one *s*. *Educ:* Trinity County Sch. FCIS 1968 (ACIS 1950). Served War, 1939-46: N Africa, Italy and NW Europe; Captain 1st Royal Tank Regt. Accounting and financial appts, Shell cos in Kenya, Tanzania and French W Africa, 1947-56; Controller, S Europe and N Africa, Shell Internat. Petroleum Co., 1956-60; Finance Dir, Shell Philippines and Ass. Cos, 1960-63; Finance Dir, Shell Malaysia and Ass. Cos, 1963-68; Personnel Adviser, finance and computer staff, Shell Internat. Pet. Co., 1968-73; Div. Hd, Loans, Directorate Gen. XVIII, Commn of European Communities, 1973-76. *Recreations:* reading, chess. *Address:* 25 Boulevard Prince Henri, Luxembourg. *T:* 29 152; The Old Laundry, Penshurst, Kent. *T:* Penshurst 239.

CANHAM, Erwin Dain; Editor in Chief, The Christian Science Monitor, 1964-74, now Editor Emeritus; President of The Mother Church, The First Church of Christ, Scientist, in Boston, 1966; *b* 13 Feb. 1904; *s* of Vincent Walter Canham and Elizabeth May Gowell; *m* 1st, 1930, Thelma Whitman Hart; two *d*; 2nd, 1968, Patience Mary, *yr d* of Lt-Col Robson Daltry, Bexhill-on-Sea. *Educ:* Bates Coll.; Oxford Univ. (Rhodes Scholar). Reporter, The Christian Science Monitor, 1925; covered League of Nations Assembly, Geneva, 1926-28; Correspondent at League of Nations, Geneva, 1930-32; Chief of Monitor's Washington Bureau, 1932; General News Editor in Boston, 1939; Managing Editor, 1942-45; Editor, 1945-64; Chm. Board of Directors, Federal Reserve Bank of Boston, 1963, 1964, 1965, 1966, 1967. Presidential Commission: Plebiscite Comr, N Mariana Is, April-June 1975; Resident Comr, N Mariana Is, 1976-. Awarded numerous hon. degrees by universities and colleges in the USA, from 1946 onwards. Officer, Order of Southern Cross (Brazil), 1951; Commander, Order of Orange-Nassau (Netherlands), 1952; Order of George I (Greece), 1954; Officier, Légion d'Honneur (France), 1958 (Chevalier, 1946); Grand Distinguished Service Cross of Order of Merit (German Federal Republic), 1960; Hon. Comdr, Order of British Empire (CBE), 1964. *Publications:* Awakening: The World at Mid-Century, 1951; New Frontiers for Freedom, 1954; Commitment to Freedom: The Story of the Christian Science Monitor, 1958; Man's Great Future, 1959. Co-author, The Christian Science Way of Life, 1962. *Address:* One Norway Street, Boston, Mass 02115, USA. *T:* 262-2300; (home) 242 Beacon Street, Boston, Mass 02116, USA. *T:* 247-2123. *Clubs:* Gridiron (Washington, DC); Tavern, Harvard, Saturday (Boston).

CANN, Robert John, MS London, FRCS; Surgeon Emeritus, Ear, Nose and Throat Department, Guy's Hospital; formerly Consulting Ear, Nose and Throat Surgeon, Caterham District Hospital and East Surrey Hospital, Redhill. *Educ:* London Univ. MRCS, LRCP 1924; MB, BS 1926; MS (Gold Medal, Lond.) 1930; FRCS 1949. Formerly Aural Surgeon, Evelina Hospital for Children. FRSocMed. *Address:* Wonham Cottage, Wonham Lane, Betchworth, Surrey. *T:* Reigate 42183.

CANNAN, Denis; dramatist and screenwriter; *b* 14 May 1919; *s* of late Captain H. J. Pullein-Thompson, MC, and late Joanna Pullein-Thompson (*née* Cannan); *m* 1st, 1946, Joan Ross (marr. diss.); two *s* one *d*; 2nd, 1965, Rose Evansky; he changed name to Denis Cannan, by deed poll, 1964. *Educ:* Eton. A Repertory actor, 1937-39. Served War of 1939-45, Queen's Royal Regt (despatches). Actor at Citizens' Theatre, Glasgow, 1946-48. *Publications:* plays: Max (prod. Malvern Festival), 1949; Captain Carvallo (Bristol Old Vic and St James's Theatres), 1950; Colombe (trans. from Anouilh), New Theatre, 1951; Misery Me!, Duchess, 1955; You and Your Wife, Bristol Old Vic, 1955; The Power and The Glory (adaptation from Graham Greene), Phoenix Theatre, 1956, and Phœnix Theatre, New York, 1958; Who's Your Father?, Cambridge Theatre, 1958; US (original text), Aldwych, 1966; adapted Ibsen's Ghosts,

Aldwych, 1966; One at Night, Royal Court, 1971; The Ik (adaptation and collaboration), 1975; Dear Daddy, Oxford Festival and Ambassadors, 1976 (Play of the Year award, 1976); the screenplays of several films; contribs to Times Literary Supplement. *Recreation:* loitering. *Address:* 103 Clarence Gate Gardens, Glentworth Street, NW1 6QP.

See also D . L . A . Farr .

CANNING, family name of **Baron Garvagh.**

CANNING, Victor; author; *b* 16 June 1911; *m* 1976, Mrs Adria Irving Bell. Major, RA, 1940-46. *Publications:* Mr Finchley Discovers His England, 1934; The Chasm, 1947; Golden Salamander, 1948; Forest of Eyes, 1949; Venetian Bird, 1951; House of the Seven Flies, 1952; Man from the "Turkish Slave", 1953; Castle Minerva, 1954; His Bones are Coral, 1955; The Hidden Face, 1956; Manasco Road, 1957; The Dragon Tree, 1958; Young Man on a Bicycle and other short stories, 1959; The Burning Eye, 1960; A Delivery of Furies, 1961; Black Flamingo, 1962; The Limbo Line, 1963; The Scorpio Letters, 1964; The Whip Hand, 1965; Doubled in Diamonds, 1966; The Python Project, 1967; The Melting Man, 1968; Queen's Pawn, 1969; The Great Affair, 1970; Firecrest, 1971; The Runaways, 1972; The Rainbird Pattern, 1972; Flight of the Grey Goose, 1973; The Finger of Saturn, 1973; The Painted Tent, 1974; The Mask of Memory, 1974; The Kingsford Mark, 1975; The Crimson Chalice, 1976; The Doomsday Carrier, 1976; The Circle of the Gods, 1977. *Recreations:* fishing, golf. *Address:* Lawrence Land, The Bourne, Brimscombe, Stroud, Glos. *T:* Brimscombe 4349. *Club:* Flyfishers'

CANNON, John Francis Michael; Keeper of Botany, British Museum (Natural History), since 1977; *b* 22 April 1930; *s* of Francis Leslie Cannon and Aileen Flora Cannon; *m* 1954, Margaret Joy (*née* Herbert); two *s* one *d*. *Educ:* Whitgift Sch., South Croydon, Surrey; King's Coll., Newcastle upon Tyne, Univ. of Durham (BSc 1st Cl. Hons Botany). Dept of Botany, British Museum (Nat. History), 1952, Dep. Keeper 1972. *Publications:* papers in scientific periodicals and similar pubns. *Recreations:* travel, music, gardening. *Address:* 26 Purley Bury Avenue, Purley, Surrey CR2 9JD. *T:* 01-660 3223.

CANNON, Air Vice-Marshal Leslie William, CB 1952; CBE 1945; retired; *b* 9 April 1904; *s* of late Captain W. E. Cannon, Beds, and Herts Regiment, and of Cathleen Mary Jackson, Bedford; *m* 1930, Beryl (*née* Heyworth). *Educ:* Hertford Grammar Sch.; RAF Coll., Cranwell. RAF Apprentice, 1920-23; Officer Cadet, 1923-25; Pilot Officer, No 2 (AC) Squadron, 1925-27; Flying Officer: No 441 Flight Fleet Air Arm, China Station, 1927; No 2 (AC) Squadron, 1928; Flying Instructor RAF Coll., Cranwell, 1929; F/O and Flight-Lt: Officer Engr. Course, RAF Henlow, 1929-31; Flight-Lt: Engr. Officer RAFMT Depôt, Shrewsbury, 1931-32 and RAF Coll., Cranwell, 1932-33; Engr. SO, Air HQ, India, 1933-35; Flight Comdr No 60 (B) Squdn, Kohat, India, 1935-37 (despatches); Sqdn Ldr: OC No 5 (AC) Sqdn, India, 1937; Personnel SO, HQ Training Command, 1938; Student RAF Staff Coll., Andover, 1939. Served War of 1939-45 (despatches thrice, CBE, American Silver Star): Staff Officer Directorate of Operations, Air Ministry, 1939-40; Wing Comdr: Engr. SO, HQ Bomber Command, 1940; Chief Technical Officer, No. 21 Operational Training Unit, 1941; Group Captain: Directing SO RAF Staff Coll., 1942; OC Bomber Stations in No 2 (B) Group, 1942-43. Part of 2nd TAF (England, France, Belgium, Germany); GC and Air Commodore: AO i/c Admin. HQ No 2 (B) Group, 1943-46; AOC No 85 Group, Hamburg, 1946; idc, 1947; Asst Comdt and Comdt, RAF Staff Coll., Andover, 1948-49; Director of Organisation (Establishments), 1949-51; Commander-in-Chief, Royal Pakistan Air Force, 1951-55; Director-General of Organisation, Dec. 1955-Nov. 1958, retired. At CRO, 1959. Rolls-Royce Senior Representative, India, 1960-65. *Recreations:* represented RAF at athletics, boxing, pistol shooting. *Address:* 6 Stockwells, Berry Hill, Taplow, Maidenhead, Berks SL6 0DB. *Clubs:* Royal Air Force, Victory Services; Phyllis Court (Henley-on-Thames).

CANNON, Richard Walter, CEng, FIEE, FIERE; Managing Director, Public Telecommunications, Cable and Wireless Ltd, since 1977 (Executive Director, 1973); *b* 7 Dec. 1923; *s* of Richard William Cannon and Lily Harriet Cannon (*née* Fewins); *m* 1949, Dorothy (formerly Jarvis); two *d*. *Educ:* Eltham Coll. Joined Cable and Wireless Ltd, 1941. *Publications:* telecommunications papers for IEE and IERE. *Recreations:* music, wine-making, gardening, photography. *Address:* Elm Cottage, Birch Grove, Horsted Keynes, West Sussex. *T:* Chelwood Gate 235. *Clubs:* Royal Commonwealth Society; Exiles (Twickenham, Mddx).

CANSDALE, George Soper, BA, BSc, FLS; *b* 29 Nov. 1909; *y s* of G. W. Cansdale, Paignton, Devon; *m* 1940, Margaret Sheila, *o d* of R. M. Williamson, Indian Forest Service; two *s. Educ:* Brentwood Sch.; St Edmund Hall, Oxford. Colonial Forest Service, Gold Coast, 1934-48. Superintendent to Zoological Society of London, Regent's Park, 1948-53. Inventor, SWS Filtration Unit, 1975. *Publications:* The Black Poplars, 1938; Animals of West Africa, 1946; Animals and Man, 1952; George Cansdale's Zoo Book, 1953; Belinda the Bushbaby, 1953; Reptiles of West Africa, 1955; West African Snakes, 1961; Behind the Scenes at a Zoo, 1965; Animals of Bible Lands, 1970; articles in the Field, Geographical Magazine, Zoo Life, Nigerian Field, Natural History, etc. *Recreations:* natural history, photography, sailing. *Address:* Dove Cottage, Great Chesterford, Saffron Walden, Essex CB10 1PL. *T:* Great Chesterford 274. *Club:* Royal Commonwealth Society.

CANT, Rev. Harry William Macphail; Minister of St Magnus Cathedral, Kirkwall, Orkney, since 1968; Chaplain to the Queen in Scotland since 1972; *b* 3 April 1921; *s* of late J. M. Cant and late Margaret Cant; *m* 1951, Margaret Elizabeth Loudon; one *s* two *d. Educ:* Edinburgh Acad.; Edinburgh Univ. (MA, BD); Union Theological Seminary, NY (STM). Lieut, KOSB, 1941-43; Captain, King's African Rifles, 1944-46; TA Chaplain, 7th Argyll and Sutherland Highlanders, 1962-70. Asst Minister, Old Parish Church, Aberdeen, 1950-51; Minister of Fallin Parish Church, Stirling, 1951-56; Scottish Sec., Student Christian Movt, 1956-59; Minister of St Thomas' Parish Church, 1960-68. *Publication:* Preaching in a Scottish Parish Church: St Magnus and Other Sermons, 1970. *Recreations:* angling, golf. *Address:* Cathedral Manse, Kirkwall, Orkney. *T:* Kirkwall 3312.

CANT, Rev. Canon Reginald Edward; Canon and Chancellor of York Minster since 1957; *b* 1 May 1914; 2nd *s* of late Samuel Reginald Cant; unmarried. *Educ:* Sir Joseph Williamson's Sch., Rochester; CCC, Cambridge; Cuddesdon Theological Coll. Asst Curate, St Mary's, Portsea, 1938-41; Vice-Principal, Edinburgh Theological Coll., 1941-46; Lecturer, Univ. of Durham, 1946-52 (Vice-Principal, St Chad's Coll. from 1949); Vicar, St Mary's the Less, Cambridge, 1952-57. *Publications:* Christian Prayer, 1961; part-author, The Churchman's Companion, 1964. *Address:* 3 Minster Court, York YO1 2JJ. *T:* York 25599.

CANT, Robert (Bowen); MP (Lab) Stoke-on-Trent Central since 1966; *b* 24 July 1915; *s* of Robert and Catherine Cant; *m* 1940, Rebecca Harris Watt; one *s* two *d. Educ:* Middlesbrough High Sch. for Boys; London Sch. of Economics. BSc (Econ.) 1945. Lecturer in Economics, Univ. of Keele, 1962-66. Member: Stoke-on-Trent City Council, 1953-74; Staffs CC, 1973-. Contested (Lab.) Shrewsbury, 1950, 1951. *Publication:* American Journey. *Recreation:* bookbinding. *Address:* House of Commons, SW1; (home) 119 Chell Green Avenue, Stoke-on-Trent, Staffordshire. *Club:* Chell Working Men's.

CANTERBURY, Archbishop of, since 1974; **Most Rev. and Rt. Hon. (Frederick) Donald Coggan,** PC 1961; MA; DD; *b* 9 Oct. 1909; *s* of late Cornish Arthur Coggan and late Fannie Sarah Coggan; *m* 1935, Jean Braithwaite Strain; two *d. Educ:* Merchant Taylors' School; St John's College, Cambridge; Wycliffe Hall, Oxford. Late Schol. of St John's Coll., Cambridge, 1st cl. Or. Lang. Trip. pt i, 1930; BA (1st cl. Or. Lang. Trip. pt ii) and Jeremie Sep. Prize, 1931, Naden Div. Student, 1931; Tyrwhitt Hebrew Schol. and Mason Prize, 1932; MA 1935. Asst Lectr in Semitic Languages and Literature, University of Manchester, 1931-34; Curate of St Mary Islington, 1934-37; Professor of New Testament, Wycliffe College, Toronto, 1937-44; Principal of the London College of Divinity, 1944-56; Bishop of Bradford, 1956-61; Archbishop of York, 1961-74. Chairman of the Liturgical Commission, 1960-64. President, Society for Old Testament Studies, 1967-68. Pro-Chancellor, York Univ., 1962-74; Hull Univ., 1968-74. Prelate, Order of St John of Jerusalem, 1967-. Wycliffe Coll., Toronto: BD 1941, DD (*hc*) 1944; DD (Lambeth) 1957. Hon. DD: Cambridge, 1962; Leeds, 1958; Aberdeen, 1963; Tokyo, 1963; Saskatoon, 1963; Huron, 1963; Hull, 1963; Manchester, 1972; Moravian Theol Seminary, 1976; Hon. LLD Liverpool, 1972; HHD Westminster Choir Coll., Princeton, 1966; Hon. DLitt Lancaster, 1967; STD (*hc*) Gen. Theol Seminary, NY, 1967; Hon. DCL Kent, 1975; DUniv. York, 1975; FKC, 1975. *Publications:* A People's Heritage, 1944; The Ministry of the Word, 1945; The Glory of God, 1950; Stewards of Grace, 1958; Five Makers of the New Testament, 1962; Christian Priorities, 1963; The Prayers of The New Testament, 1967; Sinews of Faith, 1969; Word and World, 1971; Convictions, 1975; contributions to Theology, etc. *Recreations:* gardening, motoring, music. *Address:* Lambeth Palace, SE1. *T:* 01-928 8282; Old Palace, Canterbury. *T:* Canterbury 63003. *Club:* Athenæum.

CANTERBURY, Dean of; *see* de Waal, Very Rev. V. A.

CANTERBURY, Archdeacon of; *see* Pawley, Ven. B. C.

CANTLAY, George Thomson, CBE 1973; Partner, Lyddon & Co., since 1941; Chairman: Coated Metals (Holdings) Ltd; Parkfield Foundries (Tees-side) Ltd; United Capitals Investment Trust Ltd; A. B. Electronic Components Ltd; Director: Newport Precision Engineering Co. Ltd; Christie-Tyler Ltd; Maple Company (Holdings) Ltd; *b* 2 Aug. 1907; *s* of G. and A. Cantlay; *m* 1934, Sibyl Gwendoline Alsop Stoker; one *s* one *d. Educ:* Glasgow High Sch. Member of Stock Exchange. Mem. Welsh Council, CBI; Vice-Pres., Welsh Region, Inst. of Directors. OStJ; FRSA. *Recreations:* music (opera), gardening. *Address:* Tyn-y-Gollen, St Mellons, Gwent CF3 9UA. *T:* Cardiff 78175; 18 Raynham, Norfolk Crescent, W2 2PG. *T:* 01-262 0098. *Clubs:* Carlton, Bath; Cardiff and County (Cardiff).

CANTLEY, Hon. Sir Joseph (Donaldson), Kt 1965; OBE 1945; **Hon. Mr Justice Cantley;** Judge of the High Court of Justice, Queen's Bench Division, since 1965; *b* 8 Aug. 1910; *er s* of Dr Joseph Cantley, Crumpsall, Manchester, and Georgina Cantley (*née* Kean); *m* 1966, Lady (Hilda Goodwin) Gerrard, *widow* of Sir Denis Gerrard. *Educ:* Manchester Grammar Sch.; Manchester Univ. Studentship and Certificate of Honour, Council of Legal Education, 1933; Barrister, Middle Temple, 1933 (Bencher 1963); QC 1954. Served throughout War of 1939-45: Royal Artillery and on Staff; 2nd Lieut Royal Artillery 1940; N Africa and Italy, 1942-45 (despatches twice); Lieut-Colonel and AAG, 1943-45. Recorder of Oldham, 1959-60; Judge of Salford Hundred Court of Record, 1960-65; Judge of Appeal, Isle of Man, 1962-65; Presiding Judge, Northern Circuit, 1970-74. Member, General Council of the Bar, 1957-61. Hon. LLD Manchester, 1968. *Recreations:* golf, music. *Address:* Royal Courts of Justice, Strand, WC2A 2LL. *Club:* Travellers'.

CAPE, Donald Paul Montagu Stewart, CMG 1977; HM Diplomatic Service; Ambassador to Laos, since 1976; *b* 6 Jan. 1923; *s* of late John Scarvell and Olivia Millicent Cape; *m* 1948, Cathune Johnston; four *s* one *d. Educ:* Ampleforth Coll.; Brasenose Coll., Oxford. Scots Guards, 1942-45. Entered Foreign Service, 1946. Served: Belgrade, 1946-49; FO, 1949-51; Lisbon, 1951-55; Singapore, 1955-57; FO, 1957-60; Bogota, 1960-61; Holy See, 1962-67; Head of Information Administration Dept, FCO, 1968-70; Counsellor, Washington, 1970-73; Counsellor, Brasilia, 1973-76. *Recreations:* riding, tennis, walking, swimming, skiing. *Address:* c/o Foreign and Commonwealth Office, SW1; Hilltop, Wonersh, Guildford, Surrey.

CAPE, Maj.-Gen. Timothy Frederick, CB 1972; CBE 1966; DSO; idc, jssc, psc; FAIM; *b* Sydney, 5 Aug. 1915; *s* of C. S. Cape, DSO, Edgecliff, NSW; *m* 1961, Elizabeth, *d* of Brig. R. L. R. Rabett; one *d. Educ:* Cranbrook Sch., Sydney; RMC Duntroon. Served with RAA, 1938-40; Bde Major Sparrow Force, Timor, 1942; GS01: (Air) New Guinea Force, 1942-43; (Ops) Melbourne, 1944; (Air) Morotai, 1945; (Ops) Japan, 1946-47; (Plans) Melbourne, 1948-49; Instructor, UK, 1950-52; Comdt, Portsea, 1954-56; Dep. Master-Gen. Ordnance, 1957-59; COS Northern Comd, Brisbane, 1961; Dir of Staff Duties, Army HQ, Canberra, 1962-63; Comdr, Adelaide, 1964; GOC Northern Comd, Brisbane, 1965-68; Master-General of the Ordnance, 1968-72; retd 1972. Chm., Nat. Disaster Relief Cttee and Mem., Nat. Council, Australian Red Cross Soc. Bronze Star (US). *Address:* 10 Scarborough Street, Red Hill, ACT 2603, Australia. *Clubs:* Melbourne, Naval and Military (Melbourne); Commonwealth (Canberra); Union (Sydney); Royal Sydney Golf.

CAPE TOWN, Archbishop of, and Metropolitan of South Africa, since 1974; **Most Rev. Bill Bendyshe Burnett,** MA; LTh; *b* 31 May 1917; *s* of Richard Evelyn Burnett and Louisa Dobinson; *m* 1945, Sheila Fulton Trollip; two *s* one *d. Educ:* Bishop's College (Rondebosch); Michaelhouse (Natal); Rhodes University College; St Paul's Theological College, Grahamstown and Queen's College, Birmingham. Schoolmaster, St John's College, Umtata, 1940; Army, 1940-45; Deacon, S Thomas', Durban, 1947; Priest, 1948; Assistant priest, St Thomas', Durban, 1947-49; Chaplain, Michaelhouse, 1950-54; Vicar of Ladysmith, 1954-57; Bishop of Bloemfontein, 1957-67; Gen. Secretary, Christian Council of S Africa, 1967-69; Asst Bishop of Johannesburg, 1967-69; Bishop of Grahamstown, 1969-74. ChStJ 1975. *Publication:* Anglicans in Natal, 1953. *Recreation:* painting. *Address:* Bishopscourt, Claremont, CP 7700, S Africa.

CAPE TOWN, Cardinal Archbishop of; His Eminence Cardinal Owen McCann, DD, PhD, BCom; Archbishop of Cape Town (RC), since 1951; Assistant at Pontifical Throne, 1960; Cardinal since 1965 (Titular Church, St Praxedes); *b* 26 June 1907. *Educ:* St Joseph's Coll., Rondebosch, CP; Univ. of Cape Town; Collegium Urbanianum de Propaganda Fide, Rome. Priest, 1935. Editor, The Southern Cross, 1940-48; Administrator, St Mary's Cathedral, Cape Town, 1948-50. Hon. DLitt Univ. of Cape Town, 1968. *Address:* Oak Lodge, Fair Seat Lane, Wynberg, CP, South Africa; Chancery Office, Cathedral Place, 12 Bouquet Street, Cape Town. *Club:* Civil Service (Cape Town).

CAPE TOWN, Bishop Suffragan of; *see* Swartz, Rt Rev. G. A.

CAPE TOWN, Dean of; *see* King, Very Rev. E. L.

CAPEL, Air Vice-Marshal Arthur John, CB 1943; DSO 1925; DFC; JP; DL; *b* 1894; *s* of late Arthur Capel, JP, Bulland Lodge, Wiveliscombe, Somerset; *m* 1934, Austin Robina, *y d* of late Charles Austin Horn, and widow of Flight Lieut H. M. Moody, MC; one *d. Educ:* Marlborough Coll.; Trinity Coll., Oxford; Royal Military Coll., Sandhurst. Was Lieut, Somerset Light Infantry; served European War, RFC and RAF, France, 1914-18 (despatches twice); Waziristan, 1924-25 (DFC, DSO); Commandant School of Army Co-operation, Old Sarum, 1936-38; at Imperial Defence Coll., 1939; War of 1939-45, served France, UK, and Middle East (despatches thrice, CB); retired from RAF Nov. 1945. JP Somerset, 1946; DL Somerset, 1952; High Sheriff of Somerset, 1952. Member Somerset County Council, 1962-64. *Address:* Bulland Lodge, Chipstable, Wiveliscombe, Somerset. *T:* Wiveliscombe 23346. *Club:* Royal Air Force.

CAPEL CURE, (George) Nigel, TD; JP; Vice Lord-Lieutenant, Essex (formerly Vice-Lieutenant), since 1958; *b* 28 Sept. 1908; *o s* of late Major George Edward Capel Cure, JP, Blake Hall, Ongar; *m* 1935, Nancy Elizabeth, *d* of late William James Barry, Great Witchingham Hall, Norwich; two *s* one *d. Educ:* Eton; Trinity Coll., Cambridge. DL and JP, 1947, High Sheriff, 1951, Essex. *Recreations:* shooting and cricket. *Address:* Blake Hall, Ongar, Essex. *T:* Ongar 2652. *Clubs:* MCC, City University.

CAPELL, family name of **Earl of Essex.**

CAPLAN, Daniel; Under-Secretary, Department of the Environment, 1970-71; *b* 29 July 1915; *y s* of Daniel and Miriam Caplan; *m* 1945, Olive Beatrice Porter; no *c. Educ:* Elem. and Secondary Schools, Blackpool; St Catharine's Coll., Cambridge. Asst Principal, Import Duties Adv. Cttee, 1938; Private Secretary to three Permanent Secretaries, Ministry of Supply, 1940; Principal, 1942; Ministry of Supply Representative and Economic Secretary to British Political Representative in Finland, 1944-45; Asst Secretary, Board of Trade, 1948; Adviser to Chancellor of Duchy of Lancaster, 1957-60; Under-Secretary, Scottish Development Dept, 1963-65; Under-Secretary, National Economic Development Office, 1966; Asst Under-Sec. of State, DEA, 1966-69; Under-Sec., Min. of Housing and Local Govt, 1969-70; Consultant to Minister for Housing for Leasehold Charges Study, 1972-73. *Publications:* People and Homes (indep. report on Landlord and Tenant Relations in England for British Property Fedn), 1975; numerous papers on religious and economic history in learned journals. *Recreations:* railways, historical research, gardening. *Address:* The Old Cottage, Whitemans Green, Cuckfield, West Sussex. *T:* Haywards Heath 54301. *Club:* Royal Automobile.

CAPLAN, Leonard, QC 1954; *b* 28 June 1909; *s* of late Henry Caplan, Liverpool; *m* 1st, 1942, Tania (*d* 1974); two *d*; 2nd, 1977, Mrs Korda Herskovits, NY. Called to the Bar, Gray's Inn, 1935; Master of the Bench, 1964; joined South Eastern Circuit; Middle Temple, 1949; served War of 1939-45, Royal Artillery (Anti-Tank); Staff Captain, 47th Div.; Staff Captain ("Q" Operations), Southern Command, engaged in D-Day Planning; passed Staff Coll., Camberley; Major, DAAG and Lt-Col, AAG, HQ Allied Land Forces, South East Asia. Conservative candidate, N Kensington, 1950-51. Chm., Coll. Hall (Univ. of London), 1958-67. Chm., Mental Health Review Tribunal, SE Region, 1960-63; Senate of Inns of Court and the Bar, 1975-77. *Publication:* (with late Marcus Samuel, MP) The Great Experiment: a critical study of Soviet Five Year Plans, 1935. *Recreation:* yachting. *Address:* 1 Pump Court, Temple, EC4. *T:* 01-353 9332; Skol, Marbella, S Spain. *Clubs:* Savage; Marbella Yacht, Bar Yacht.

CAPLAN, Philip Isaac, QC (Scot.) 1970; *b* 24 Feb. 1929; *s* of Hyman and Rosalena Caplan; *m* 1st, 1953; two *s* one *d*; 2nd, 1974, Joyce Ethel Stone; one *d. Educ:* Eastwood Sch., Renfrewshire; Glasgow Univ. (MA, LLB). Solicitor, 1952-56; called to Bar, 1957; Standing Junior Counsel to Accountant of Court. *Recreations:* reading, photography, music. *Address:* The

Green, The Causeway, Duddingston Village, Edinburgh. *T:* 031-661 4254; *Club:* University Staff (Edinburgh).

CAPLAT, Moran Victor Hingston, CBE 1968; General Administrator, Glyndebourne Festival Opera, since 1949; Secretary, Glyndebourne Festival Society; Secretary, Glyndebourne Arts Trust; *b* 1 Oct. 1916; *s* of Roger Armand Charles Caplat and Norah Hingston; *m* 1943, Diana Murray Downton; one *s* two *d* (and one *s* decd). *Educ:* privately; Royal Acad. of Dramatic Art. Actor, etc., 1934-39. Royal Navy, 1939-45. Glyndebourne: Asst to Gen. Man., 1945; Gen. Man., 1949 (title subseq. altered to Gen. Administrator). Editor, Glyndebourne Festival Programme Book. *Recreations:* gardening, sailing, travel, music (non-vocal). *Address:* The Yew Tree House, Barcombe, near Lewes, East Sussex BN8 5EF. *T:* Barcombe 202. *Clubs:* Garrick; Royal Yacht Squadron, Royal Ocean Racing, Island Sailing (Cowes).

CAPOTE, Truman; author; *b* New Orleans, USA, 30 Sept. 1924; *s* of Joseph G. Capote and Nina (*née* Faulk). *Educ:* St John's Academy and Greenwich High School (New York). O. Henry Memorial Award for short story, 1946; Creative Writing Award, Nat. Inst. of Arts and Letters, 1959. *Publications:* Other Voices, Other Rooms (novel), 1948; Tree of Night (short stories), 1949; Observations, 1949; Local Color (travel essays), 1950; The Grass Harp (novel), 1951 (dramatised, 1953); The Muses are Heard (essay), 1956; Breakfast at Tiffany's (short stories), 1958; Selected Writings, 1964; In Cold Blood, 1966; A Christmas Memory, 1966; (with H. Arlen), House of Flowers, 1968; The Thanksgiving Visitor, 1969; The Dogs Bark, 1973; short stories and articles (both fiction and non-fiction) contributed to numerous magazines. *Address:* c/o Bayouboys Ltd, 3445 Stephen Lane, Wantagh, NY 11793, USA.

CAPPER, Rt. Rev. Edmund Michael Hubert, OBE 1961; LTh (Dur.); Assistant Bishop in the Diocese of Gibraltar, since 1973; *b* 12 March 1908; *e s* of Arthur Charles and Mabel Lavinia Capper; unmarried. *Educ:* St Joseph's Academy, Blackheath; St Augustine's College, Canterbury. Deacon, 1932, Priest, 1933. Royal Army Chaplains' Dept, 1942-46 (EA); Archdeacon of Lindi and Canon of Masasi Cathedral, 1947-54; Archdeacon of Dar es Salaam, 1954-58. Provost of the Collegiate Church of St Alban the Martyr, Dar es Salaam, Tanganyika, 1957-62; Canon of Zanzibar, 1954-62; Member, Universities' Mission to Central Africa, 1936-62; Chairman, Tanganyika British Legion Benevolent Fund, 1956-62; President, Tanganyika British Legion, 1960-62; Chaplain, Palma de Mallorca, 1962-67; Bishop of St Helena, 1967-73; Chaplain of St George's, Malaga, 1973-76. *Publications:* Be Confirmed, 1960. Various missionary booklets and pamphlets. *Recreations:* swimming and walking. *Address:* c/o Barclay's Bank Ltd, 119 Waterloo Road, SE1 8UN. *Club:* Royal Commonwealth Society.

CAPRA, Frank, Legion of Merit, 1943; DSM 1945; Hon. OBE (mil.) 1946; Writer, Director and Producer of Motion Pictures; President of own producing company, Liberty Films Inc.; *b* 18 May 1897; Italian parents; *m* 1932, Lucille Rayburn; two *s* one *d. Educ:* California Institute of Technology. Col, Signal Corps, US Army; released from Army, spring of 1945. Produced and directed following pictures: Submarine, The Strong Man, Flight, Dirigible, Ladies of Leisure, Platinum Blonde, American Madness, Lady for a Day, It Happened One Night, Mr Deeds Goes to Town, Broadway Bill, Lost Horizon, You Can't Take It With You, Mr Smith Goes to Washington, Meet John Doe, Arsenic and Old Lace, It's a Wonderful Life, State of the Union, Here Comes the Groom, A Hole in the Head, Pocketful of Miracles. Member of Motion Picture Academy and of Directors' Guild. Hon. Dr Arts Temple Univ., 1971; Hon. Dr Fine Arts Carthage Coll., 1972. *Publication:* Frank Capra: the name above the title (autobiog.), 1971. *Recreations:* hunting, fishing, music. *Address:* PO Box 98, La Quinta, Calif 92253, USA.

CAPSTICK, Brian Eric, QC 1973; *b* 12 Feb. 1927; *o s* of late Eric Capstick and late Betty Capstick; *m* 1960, Margaret Harrison; one *s* one *d. Educ:* Sedbergh; Queen's Coll., Oxford (Scholar) (MA). Served HM Forces, 1945-48: 17/21st Lancers, Palestine, 1947-48. Tancred Scholar, and called to Bar, Lincoln's Inn, 1952. Dep. Chm., Northern Agriculture Tribunal, 1976. *Recreations:* shooting, reading, cooking. *Address:* (home) 71 South End Road, NW3. *T:* 01-435 3540; Blue Mill, Thropton, Northumberland; (professional) 2 Crown Office Row, Temple, EC4. *T:* 01-583 2681. *Club:* Reform.

CAPSTICK, Charles William, CMG 1972; Senior Principal Agricultural Economist, Ministry of Agriculture, Fisheries and Food, since 1968; *b* 18 Dec. 1934; *s* of William Capstick and Janet Frankland; *m* 1962, Joyce Alma Dodsworth; two *s. Educ:* King's Coll., Univ. of Durham (BSc (Hons)); Univ. of

Kentucky, USA (MS). MAFF: Asst Agric. Economist, 1961; Principal Agric. Economist, 1966; Senior Principal Agric. Economist, 1968. *Recreation:* gardening. *Address:* 7 Dellfield Close, Radlett, Herts. *T:* Radlett 7640.

CARADON, Baron (Life Peer) *cr* 1964; **Hugh Mackintosh Foot,** PC 1968; GCMG 1957 (KCMG 1951; CMG 1946); KCVO 1953; OBE 1939; *b* 8 Oct. 1907; *s* of late Rt Hon. Isaac Foot, PC; *m* 1936, Florence Sylvia Tod; three *s* one *d. Educ:* Leighton Park Sch., Reading; St John's Coll., Cambridge, Pres. Cambridge Union, 1929; Administrative Officer, Palestine Govt, 1929-37; attached to the Colonial Office, 1938-39; Asst British Resident, Trans-Jordan, 1939-42; British Mil. Administration, Cyrenaica, 1943; Colonial Secretary: Cyprus, 1943-45, Jamaica, 1945-47; Chief Sec., Nigeria, 1947-51. Acting Governor: Cyprus, 1944, Jamaica, Aug. 1945-Jan. 1946, Nigeria, 1949 and 1950. Capt.-Gen. and Gov.-in-Chief of Jamaica, 1951-57; Governor and Comdr-in-Chief, Cyprus, Dec. 1957-60; Ambassador and Adviser in the UK Mission to the UN and Permanent UK representative on Trusteeship Council, 1961-62, resigned; Minister of State for Foreign and Commonwealth Affairs and Perm. UK Rep. at the UN, 1964-70. Consultant, Special Fund of the United Nations, 1963-64. Mem., UN Expert Group on South Africa, 1964; Consultant to UN Develt Programme. Fellow, Adlai Stevenson Centre, Chicago. KStJ 1952. Hon. Fellow, St John's Coll., Cambridge, 1960. *Publication:* A Start in Freedom, 1964. *Address:* Trematon Castle, Saltash, Cornwall. *T:* Saltash 3778. *Clubs:* Travellers'; Century (New York).
See also Baron Foot, Rt Hon. Sir Dingle Foot, Rt Hon. Michael Foot.

CARBERRY, Sir John (Edward Doston), Kt 1956; Chief Justice, Jamaica, 1954-58, retired; *b* Grenada, WI, 20 Aug. 1893; *e s* of D. A. and Ruth Carberry; *m* 1920, Georgiana, *y d* of Charles Jackson; one *s* one *d. Educ:* Wesley Hall, Grenada; McGill Univ., Montreal (LLB). Served European War in 1st Bn British West Indies Regt, 1915-19. Called to Bar, Middle Temple, 1925; in practice in Jamaica until 1927, when joined Government Service as Clerk of the Courts; Resident Magistrate, 1932; Puisne Judge, Supreme Court, 1946; Senior Puisne Judge, Jamaica, 1949. *Recreation:* philately. *Address:* 8 East King's House Road, Kingston 6, Jamaica.

CARBERY, 11th Baron *cr* 1715; **Peter Ralfe Harrington Evans-Freke;** Bt 1768; *b* 20 March 1920; *o s* of Major the Hon. Ralfe Evans-Freke, MBE (*yr s* of 9th Baron) (*d* 1969), and Vera, *d* of late C. Harrington Moore; *S* uncle, 1970; *m* 1941, Joyzelle Mary, *o d* of late Herbert Binnie; three *s* two *d. Educ:* Downside School. MICE. Served War of 1939-45, Captain RE, India, Burmah. Member of London Stock Exchange, 1955-68. *Recreations:* hunting, tennis, winter sports. *Heir: e s* Hon. Michael Peter Evans-Freke [*b* 11 Oct. 1942; *m* 1967, Claudia Janet Elizabeth, *o d* of Captain P. L. C. Gurney; one *s* two *d*]. *Address:* Baskings House, Selsfield, East Grinstead, West Sussex. *T:* Sharpthorne 810761. *Clubs:* Kennel; Kildare Street and University (Dublin).

CARBERY, Dr Thomas Francis; Head of Department of Office Organisation, University of Strathclyde, since 1975; Member of Independent Broadcasting Authority (formerly Independent Television Authority), and Chairman of Scottish Committee of IBA, since 1970; *b* 18 Jan. 1925; *o c* of Thomas Albert Carbery and Jane Morrison; *m* 1954, Ellen Donnelly; one *s* two *d. Educ:* St Aloysius Coll., Glasgow; Univ. of Glasgow and Scottish Coll. of Commerce. Cadet Navigator and Meteorologist, RAFVR, 1943-47; Civil Servant, Min. of Labour, 1947-61; Sen. Lectr in Govt and Econs, Scottish College of Commerce, Glasgow, 1961-64; Sen. Lectr in Govt-Business Relations, Strathclyde Univ., 1964-75. Member: Royal Commn on Gambling, 1976-; Scottish Consumer Council, 1977-. Mem. Court 1968-71, Mem. Senate 1964-71, and 1973-, Univ. of Strathclyde. *Publication:* Consumers in Politics, 1969. *Recreations:* golf, conversation, spectating at Association football, watching television. *Address:* 32 Crompton Avenue, Glasgow G44 5TH. *T:* 041-637 0514. *Clubs:* University of Strathclyde, Glasgow Art, Ross Priory (Glasgow).

CARBONELL, William Leycester Rouse, CMG 1956; Commissioner of Police, Federation of Malaya, 1953-58, retired; *b* 14 Aug. 1912; *m* 1937; two *s. Educ:* Shrewsbury Sch.; St Catharine's Coll., Cambridge. Probationary Assistant Commissioner of Police, 1935; (title changed to) Asst Superintendent, 1938; Superintendent, 1949; Asst Commissioner, 1952: Senior, 1952; Commissioner, 1953. King's Police Medal, 1950. Perlawan Mangku Negara (PMN), Malaya, 1958. *Address:* Amery End, Tanhouse Lane, Alton, Hants.

CARCANO, Miguel Angel; Hon. KCMG; Hon. KBE; Presidente de la Academia National de la Historia, 1968-70; *b* 18 July 1889; *s* of Ramón J. Cárcano, sometime Governor of Cordoba and Ambassador, and of Ana Saenz de Zumarán; *m* Stella, *d* of Marqueses de Morra; one *s* two *d. Educ:* Faculty of Law, Univ. of Buenos Aires. Prof. of Political Economy and Admin. Law, Univ. of Buenos Aires: National Deputy, 1930-36. Minister in London on special mission for negotiation of Anglo-Argentine Treaty, 1936; Delegate Pan-American Congress, Buenos Aires, 1937; Minister of Agriculture, Industry and Commerce, Argentina, 1936-38; Ambassador of Argentina in France 1938-42, in London, 1942-46; Pres., Argentine Delegn to UN, 1946; Minister of Foreign Affairs and Worship, 1961, 1962. Member: Acad. of Letters; Acad. of Economics; Academia Nacional de la Historia; Corresp. Fellow, RHistS. Grand Cross of: Legion of Honour; Pius IX; Leopold II. Knight Comdr Order of British Empire (Hon. KBE). Knight Comdr, Order of St Michael and St George (Hon. KCMG), Knight Comdr, Order of the Crown of Italy. *Publications:* Evolución Histórica de la Tierra Pública (Premio Nacional en Letras); Organizatión de la Producción; Alberdi, su doctrina Económica, 1934; Dos Años en la Cámara, 1934; Memoria del Ministerio de Agricultura (6 vol.), 1939; Realidad de una Política, 1938; Hommage A Sarmiento, 1938; British Democracy Retains its Prestige, 1942; Victoria Sin Alas, 1949; Fortaleza de Europa, 1951; La Sexta Republica, 1958; Recuerdos del Viejo Congreso, 1960; Travesía Española, 1961; Argentina y Brasil, 1961; Saenz Peña, 1963; Churchill, Kennedy, 1967; La Presidencia de Pellegrini, 1968; Estilo de Vida Argentino, 1969; Modos de ver la Historia, 1971; La Política Internacional en la Historia Argentina (6 vols), 1973; El Mar de las Cícladas, 1974. *Address:* Centeno 3131, Buenos Aires, Argentina. *Clubs:* Athenæum; Circulo de Armas, Jockey (Buenos Aires).
See also Major Hon . J . J . Astor , Viscount Ednam .

CARD, Wilfrid Ingram, MD, FRCP; Senior Research Fellow, University Department of Medicine, Western Infirmary, Glasgow, since 1974; *b* 13 April 1908; *e s* of Henry Charles Card; *m* 1934, Hilda Margaret Brigstocke Frere (*d* 1975); one *s* two *d. Educ:* Tonbridge Sch.; St Thomas's Hospital Medical Sch. MB, BS, 1931; MD Lond. 1933; MRCP 1934; FRCP 1944, FRCPE 1953, FRCPGlas 1967. Formerly: Beit Research Fellow; Physician to Out-Patients, St Thomas' Hospital, 1939-48. Physician in Charge, Gastro-intestinal Unit, Western General Hospital, Edinburgh; Reader in Medicine, Edinburgh Univ., 1948-66; Prof. of Medicine in relation to Mathematics and Computing, Univ. of Glasgow, 1966-74; Physician to HM the Queen in Scotland, 1965-75. Member: Association of Physicians of GB; Scottish Soc. of Experimental Medicine. *Publications:* Diseases of the Digestive System; (ed) Modern Trends in Gastro-Enterology, Vols 3 and 4; contrib. to: Principles and Practice of Medicine; articles on gastro-enterological subjects in Gut, Gastro-enterology, and articles relating mathematical methods to medicine in Mathematical Biosciences, Methods of Information in Medicine, etc. *Recreation:* sailing. *Address:* Dean House, 5 East Abercromby Street, Helensburgh, Dunbartonshire. *T:* Helensburgh 2023. *Clubs:* Savile; Royal Northern Yacht (Rhu).

CARDEN, Derrick Charles, CMG 1974; HM Diplomatic Service; HM Ambassador, Sudan, since 1977; *b* 30 Oct. 1921; *s* of Canon Henry Craven Carden and Olive (*née* Gorton); *heir pres.* to Sir John Craven Carden, 7th Bt, *qv; m* 1952, Elizabeth Anne Russell; two *s* two *d. Educ:* Marlborough; Christ Church, Oxford. Sudan Political Service, 1942-54. Entered HM Diplomatic Service, 1954; Foreign Office, 1954-55; Political Agent, Doha, 1955-58; 1st Sec., Libya, 1958-62; Foreign Office, 1962-65; Head of Chancery, Cairo, 1965; Consul-General, Muscat, 1965-69; Dir, ME Centre of Arab Studies, 1969-73; Ambassador, Yemen Arab Republic, 1973-76. *Recreation:* pleasures of the countryside. *Address:* c/o Lloyds Bank, High Street, Winchester. *Club:* Vincent's (Oxford).

CARDEN, Sir Henry (Christopher), 4th Bt *cr* 1887; OBE (mil.) 1945; Regular Army Officer (17th/21st Lancers), retired; *b* 16 Oct. 1908; *o s* of Sir Frederick H. W. Carden, 3rd Bt; *S* father, 1966; *m* 1st, 1943, Jane St C. Daniell (whom he divorced, 1960); one *s* one *d* ; 2nd, 1962, Mrs. Gwyneth S. Emerson (*née* Acland), *widow* of Flt-Lt R. Emerson, Argentina. *Educ:* Eton; RMC Sandhurst. 2/Lieut, 17/21 Lancers, 1928; served Egypt and India, 1930-39. Staff Coll., 1941; comd, 2 Armoured Delivery Regt, in France, 1944-45. CO 17/21 Lancers, in Greece and Palestine, 1947-48; War Office, 1948-51; Military Attaché in Stockholm, 1951-55; retired 1956. Comdr of the Order of the Sword (Sweden), 1954. *Recreations:* most field sports and games. *Heir: s* Christopher Robert Carden [*b* 24 Nov. 1946; *m* 1972, Saimenere Rokotuibau]. *Address:* Moongrove, East Woodham, near Newbury, Berks. *Club:* Cavalry and Guards.

CARDEN, Sir John Craven, 7th Bt, *cr* 1787; *b* 11 March 1926; *s* of Capt. Sir John V. Carden, 6th Bt and Dorothy Mary, *d* of Charles Luckrart McKinnon; *S* father, 1935; *m* 1947, Isabel Georgette, *y d* of late Robert de Hart; one *d. Educ:* Eton. *Heir: cousin* Derrick Charles Carden, *qv. Address:* PO Box N7776, Lyford Cay, Nassau, Bahamas. *Club:* White's.

CARDIFF, Archbishop of, (RC), since 1961; **Most Rev. John A. Murphy,** DD; *b* Birkenhead, 21 Dec. 1905; *s* of John and Elizabeth Murphy. *Educ:* The English Coll., Lisbon. Ordained 1931; consecrated as Bishop of Appia and Coadjutor Bishop of Shrewsbury, 1948; Bishop of Shrewsbury, 1949-61. ChStJ 1974. *Address:* Archbishop's House, Westbourne Crescent, Whitchurch, Cardiff. *T:* Cardiff 66063.

CARDIFF, Auxiliary Bishop in, (RC); *see* Mullins, Rt Rev. D. J.

CARDIFF, Brig. Ereld Boteler Wingfield, CB 1963; CBE 1958 (OBE 1943); *b* 5 March 1909; *m* 1932, Margaret Evelyn, *d* of late Major M. E. W. Pope, Ashwicke Hall, Marshfield; two *d. Educ:* Eton, 2nd Lieut, Scots Guards, 1930. Served War of 1939-45: (despatches thrice); 2nd Bn Scots Guards, 201 Guards Bde; 7th Armoured Div., Western Desert. Served Italy, France, Germany, Far ELF, 1955-58; SHAPE, 1958-63. Brig. 1958; retired, Nov. 1963. Chevalier, Order of Leopold, and Croix de Guerre, 1944. *Recreations:* shooting, fishing. *Address:* Easton Court, Ludlow, Salop. *T:* Tenbury Wells 475. *Clubs:* Cavalry and Guards, White's, Pratt's.
See also R. E. B. Lloyd.

CARDIFF, Jack; film director; *b* 18 Sept. 1914; *s* of John Joseph and Florence Cardiff; *m* 1940, Julia Lily (*née* Mickleboro); three *s. Educ:* various schools, incl. Medburn Sch., Herts. Started as child actor, 1918; switched to cameras, 1928. World travelogues, 1937-39. Photographed, MOI Crown Film Unit: Western Approaches, 1942; best known films include: A Matter of Life and Death, Black Narcissus, The Red Shoes, Scott of the Antarctic, Under Capricorn, Pandora and the Flying Dutchman, African Queen, War and Peace. Started as Director, 1958. *Films include:* Sons and Lovers, My Geisha, The Lion, The Long Ships, Young Cassidy, The Mercenaries, The Liquidator, Girl on a Motorcycle, The Mutation, Ride a Wild Pony, The Prince and the Pauper, Behind the Iron Mask. Awards: Academy Award (Oscar) Photography, Black Narcissus, 1947; Golden Globe Award, 1947; Coup Ce Soir (France), 1951; Film Achievement Award, Look Magazine; BSC Award, War and Peace; New York Critics Award for best film direction, Golden Globe Award, outstanding directorial award (all for Sons and Lovers); six Academy Award nominations. Hon. Dr of Art, Rome, 1953; Hon. Mem., Assoc. Française de Cameramen, 1971. *Publication:* Autobiography, 1975. *Recreations:* tennis, cricket, painting. *Address:* 75 Woodland Rise, N10. *Club:* MCC.

CARDIGAN, Earl of; David Michael James Brudenell-Bruce; *b* 12 Nov. 1952; *s* and *heir* of 8th Marquess of Ailesbury, *qv. Educ:* Eton; Royal Agricultural Coll., Cirencester. *Address:* Leigh Hill Cottage, Savernake Forest, Marlborough, Wilts. *Club:* 1900.

CARDIGAN, Archdeacon of; *see* Evans, Ven. David E.

CARDINALE, Most Rev. Hyginus Eugene, DD, JCD; Papal Nuncio to Belgium and Luxembourg, since 1969 and to the European Economic Community, since 1970; Titular Archbishop of Nepte, since 1963; *b* 14 Oct. 1916; *s* of late Gaetano Cardinale and Uliana Cimino Cardinale. *Educ:* St Agnes Academy, Coll. Point, USA; Pontifical Roman Seminary, Rome; St Louis Theological Faculty, Naples; Pontifical Ecclesiastical Academy, Rome. Sec. of Apostolic Delegation in Egypt, Palestine, Transjordan and Cyprus, 1946-49; Auditor of Apostolic Internunciature to Egypt, 1949-52; Counsellor of Nunciature, 1952-61; Chief of Protocol of the Secretariat of State, 1961-63; Apostolic Delegate to Great Britain, Gibraltar, Malta and Bermuda, 1963-69; Special Envoy of the Holy See to the Council of Europe (Strasbourg), 1970-74. Under-Sec. of Techn. Organiz. Commn of Ecumenical Vatican Council II; Ecumenical Council Expert. Doctor of Theology, Canon Law; Diplomatic Sciences; Doctor (*hc*) Belles Lettres and Philosophy. Holds Grand Cross and is Knight Comdr in many orders. *Publications:* Le Saint-Siège et la Diplomatie, 1962; Chiesa e Stato negli Stati Uniti, 1958; La Santa Sede e il Diritto Consolare, 1963; Religious Tolerance, Freedom and Inter-Group Relations, 1966; Signs of the Times and Ecumenical Aspirations, 1967; The Unity of the Church, 1968; The Holy See and the International Order, 1976; contrib. to The Vatican and World Peace, 1969. *Address:* Avenue des Franciscains 9, 1150 Brussels, Belgium.

CARDROSS, Lord; Malcolm Harry Erskine; JP; *b* 4 July 1930; *s* and *heir* of 16th Earl of Buchan, *qv*; *m* 1957, Hilary Diana Cecil, *d* of late Sir Ivan McLannahan Power, 2nd Bt; two *s* two *d. Educ:* Eton. Sometime East India merchant. JP Westminster. *Recreation:* music. *Heir: s* Hon. Henry Thomas Alexander Erskine, *b* 31 May 1960. *Address:* 24 The Little Boltons, SW10. *Club:* Carlton.

CARDWELL, David, CB 1974; Deputy Controller, Establishments and Research B, and Chief Scientist (Army), Ministry of Defence, since 1976; *b* 27 Nov. 1920; *yr s* of George Cardwell; *m* 1948, Eileen Tonkin, *d* of late Dr F. J. Kitt; one *s* one *d. Educ:* Dulwich Coll.; City and Guilds Coll., London Univ. BSc (Eng.) London. Royal Aircraft Estab., 1942-51; Min. of Supply Headquarters, 1951-56; Military Vehicles and Engrg Estab. (formerly Fighting Vehicles Research and Development Estab.), 1956-76, Dir, 1967-76. Imperial Defence Coll., 1965. CEng, ACGI, FIMechE, MRAeS. *Recreation:* gardening. *Address:* Carn Lea, 5 Grove Road, Camberley, Surrey GU15 2DN. *T:* Camberley 22636. *Club:* Athenæum.

CARE, Henry Clifford, CB 1948; *b* 1892; *s* of William John Care and Alice Mary Allen; *m* 1923, Helen Ivy May, *d* of late Col James Cameron and Mrs M. I. Cameron, Blackheath. *Educ:* Univ. Coll. Sch., Hampstead; St John's Coll., Cambridge. Higher Div. Clerk, War Office, 1915; Principal, 1923; Asst Sec. 1937; Director of Finance (with rank of Under-Sec.), 1945-54. *Address:* Old Orchard, Little Bedwyn, Marlborough, Wilts SN8 3JP. *T:* Great Bedwyn 288.

CAREW, 6th Baron (UK) *cr* 1838; **William Francis Conolly-Carew,** CBE 1966; Baron Carew (Ireland), 1834; Bt Major retired, Duke of Cornwall's Light Infantry; *b* 23 April 1905; *e s* of 5th Baron and Catherine (*d* 1947), *o d* of late Thomas Conolly, MP, of Castletown, Co. Kildare; *S* father, 1927; *m* 1937, Lady Sylvia Maitland, CStJ, *o d* of 15th Earl of Lauderdale; two *s* two *d. Educ:* Wellington; Sandhurst. Gazetted DCLI 1925; ADC to Governor and Comdr-in-Chief of Bermuda, 1931-36. Chm., British Legion, 1963-66; Pres., Irish Grassland Assn, 1949; Br. Govt Trustee, Irish Sailors' and Soldiers' Land Trust. CStJ. *Heir: s* Hon. Patrick Thomas Conolly-Carew, Captain Royal Horse Guards, retd. [*b* 6 March 1938; *m* 1962, Celia, *d* of Col Hon. C. G. Cubitt, *qv*; one *s three d*]. *Address:* Mount Armstrong, Donadea, Naas, Co. Kildare, Ireland. *T:* Naas 68196.

CAREW, Sir Rivers (Verain), 11th Bt *cr* 1661; journalist with Irish Television, since 1967; *b* 17 Oct. 1935; *s* of Sir Thomas Palk Carew, 10th Bt, and Phyllis Evelyn (*d* 1976), *o c* of Neville Mayman; *S* father, 1976; *m* 1968, Susan Babington, *yr d* of late H. B. Hill, London; one *s* three *d* (and one *s* decd). *Educ:* St Columba's Coll., Rathfarnham, Co. Dublin; Trinity Coll., Dublin. MA, BAgr (Hort.). Asst Editor, Ireland of the Welcomes (Irish Tourist Bd magazine), 1964-67; Joint Editor, The Dublin Magazine, 1964-69. Stud farming, 1971-. *Publication:* (with Timothy Brownlow) Figures out of Mist (verse). *Recreations:* reading; music; appreciation. *Heir: s* Gerald de Redvers Carew, *b* 24 May 1975. *Address:* Killyon Manor, Hill of Down, Co. Meath, Ireland. *T:* Castlerickard 115. *Club:* Kildare Street and University (Dublin).

CAREW, Major Robert John Henry, MC; JP, DL; *b* 7 June 1888; *s* of late Col R. T. Carew, DL, of Ballinamona Park, Waterford, and Constance, *d* of Maj.-Gen. William Creagh; *m* 1st 1915, Leila Vernon (*d* 1934), *d* of late Sir Arthur V. Macan; 2nd, 1936, Dorothea Petrie (*d* 1968), *d* of late Col G. R. Townshend, RA; one *d. Educ:* Marlborough Coll.; RMC Sandhurst. Joined Royal Dublin Fus, 1908; served European War as Staff Captain and DAQMG; retired, 1920. *Recreations:* mechanical work; was Hon. Sec. of the Waterford Hunt, 1926-33. *Address:* Ballinamona Park, Waterford. *T:* Waterford 4429. *Club:* Army and Navy.

CAREW, William Desmond; *b* Sligo, Ireland, 19 Nov. 1899; *s* of Dr W. K. Carew, Colonial Medical Service; unmarried. *Educ:* Clongowes Wood Coll., Ireland; Trinity College, Dublin. 2nd Lieut Duke of Connaught's Own Lancers, Indian Army. Joined Colonial Service, 1921, and served as follows: Fiji, 1921-34; New Hebrides, 1935-40; Malaya, 1941-45 (interned by Japanese at Singapore, 1942-45); Nigeria, 1947; Fiji, 1948. Indian Gen. Service Medal, Bar 1919, Afghanistan Campaign. Puisne Judge, Supreme Court of Fiji, and Chief Justice of Tonga, 1948-55; retired, 1955. Deputy Administrator of Martial Law, Singapore, 1942. Appointed Commissioner to review salaries of Fiji Civil Service and Police Force, 1956; Judge, Court of First Instance, Gibraltar, 1961, retd, 1963. *Recreations:* fishing, golf. *Address:* 7 Donald Lane, Cambridge, New Zealand.

CAREW, William James, CBE 1937; Retired as Clerk of the Executive Council and Deputy Minister of Provincial Affairs, Newfoundland; *b* 28 Dec. 1890; *s* of late James and Mary Carew; *m* 1920, Mary Florence Channing (decd); one *s* (Titular Archbishop of Telde; Apostolic Delegate to Jerusalem and Palestine, including Israel and Syria, and Pro-Nuncio to Cyprus) three *d. Educ:* St Patrick's Hall (Christian Brothers), St John's, Newfoundland. Newspaper work, 1908-09; staff of Prime Minister's Office, 1909; Sec., 1914-34; acted as Sec. to Newfoundland Delegate to Peace Conference, 1919; Sec. of Newfoundland Delegation to Imperial Conference, 1923, 1926, 1930; Deputy Min. for External Affairs, 1932; Sec. Newfoundland Delegation to Imperial Economic Conference, Ottawa, 1932; Sec. Cttee for Celebration in Newfoundland of Coronation of King George VI, 1937; Sec. Royal Visit Cttees on occasion of visit of King George VI and Queen Elizabeth to Newfoundland, 1939. Knight Commander, Order of St Sylvester, 1976. *Recreations:* reading, fishing, walking. *Address:* 74 Cochrane Street, St John's, Newfoundland.

CAREW HUNT, Rear-Adm. Geoffrey Harry, CB 1967; Chairman, Joseph Barber & Co. Ltd; *b* 6 April 1917; *s* of late Captain Roland Cecil Carew Hunt, CMG, Royal Navy retd and Mrs Thelma Reay Carew Hunt; *m* 1st, 1939, Diana (*d* 1969), *er d* of late Rear-Adm. J. F. C. Patterson, OBE; no *c*; 2nd, 1971, Elizabeth Frances Mary Adams, 2nd *d* of late J. Hunter, MP. *Educ:* Winchester Coll. Joined RN, 1934; Midshipman on China Station, 1935-37; served in Submarines, HMS Snapper, Mediterranean and North Sea, 1939-40 (despatches twice); qualified Gunnery Officer, 1941; Home Fleet Destroyers 1942-43; HMS Diadem, Home Station, 1943-45 (despatches three times); HMS Kenya, West Indies, 1947; HMS Vanguard, Mediterranean and Home Station, 1949-50; British Naval Staff, Washington, DC, 1951-53; HMS Theseus, 1953-56; Imperial Defence Coll., 1958; HMS Defender, 1959-60; Admiralty, 1945-47, 1950-51, 1956-57, 1962-65; Admiral Commanding Reserves, 1965-68; retired from Royal Navy. *Recreations:* sailing, shooting, golf. *Address:* Mill House, Abbots Worthy, Winchester, Hants. *T:* Winchester 882115. *Clubs:* Army and Navy, MCC; Royal Naval Sailing Association.

CAREW POLE, Sir John G.; *see* Pole.

CAREY, Group Captain Alban M., CBE 1943; Chairman: Shaw & Sons Ltd, Law Publishers; Chirit Investment Co. Ltd; Maden Park Property Investment Co. Ltd; Director and Deputy Chairman, Tridant Group Printers; *b* 18 April 1906; *m* 1934, Enid Morten Bond; one *s. Educ:* Bloxham. Commissioned RAF 1929; left RAF 1946; served War of 1939-45 with RAF Coastal Command both overseas and in the UK. *Recreations:* farming, shooting, fishing, yachting. *Address:* Town Green Farm, Englefield Green, Surrey. *T:* Egham 2135. *Clubs:* Royal Air Force; Royal Air Force Yacht.

CAREY, Chapple G.; *see* Gill-Carey.

CAREY, D(avid) M(acbeth) M(oir), MA Oxon; Legal Secretary to the Archbishop of Canterbury and Principal Registrar to the Province of Canterbury since 1958; Legal Secretary to the Bishops of Ely since 1953 and Gloucester since 1957; Registrar to the Diocese of Canterbury since 1959; *b* 21 Jan. 1917; *s* of Godfrey Mohun Carey, Sherborne, Dorset, and Agnes Charlotte Carey (*née* Milligan); *m* 1949, Margaret Ruth (*née* Mills), Highfield Sch., Liphook, Hants; three *s* one *d. Educ:* Westminster Sch. (King's Scholar); St Edmund Hall, Oxford. Articled Clerk, Messrs Lee, Bolton & Lee, 1938-40. Lt-Cdr (S) RNVR, 1940-46. Qualified Solicitor, 1947; Partnership with Lee, Bolton & Lee, 1948. *Recreations:* rowing, fishing. *Address:* 1 The Sanctuary, SW1 3JT. *T:* 01-222 5381; The Queen's Stairs, Lambeth Palace, SE1 7JU. *T:* 01-928 1160; Mulberry House, Ash, Canterbury, Kent. *T:* Ash 812534. *Clubs:* Army and Navy, St Stephen's; Leander (Henley).

CAREY, Denis; producer and actor; *b* London, 3 Aug. 1909; *s* of William Denis Carey and May (*née* Wilkinson); *m* Yvonne Coulette. *Educ:* St Paul's Sch.; Trinity Coll., Dublin. First appearance as Micky in The Great Big World, Royal Court, 1921; subseq. appeared in Dublin, 1929-34, London and New York, 1935-39; Pilgrim Players, 1940-43; Glasgow Citizens' Theatre, 1943-45; Arts Council Theatre, Coventry, 1945-46; in Galway Handicap, Men without Shadows, Lyric Hammersmith, 1947. First production, Happy as Larry, Mercury, later Criterion, 1947; Georgia Story, The Playboy of the Western World, London, 1948; Assoc. Producer, Arts Theatre, Salisbury, 1948; Dir, Bristol Old Vic Company, 1949-54; London and other productions include: Two Gentlemen of Verona (from Bristol), An Italian Straw Hat, Old Vic, 1952; Henry V (from Bristol), Old Vic, 1953; The Merchant of Venice, Stratford-on-Avon, 1953; Twelfth Night, The Taming of the Shrew, Old Vic, 1954; Salad Days (from Bristol), Vaudeville, 1954; Twelfth Night, Théâtre Nat. de Belgique, Brussels, 1954; A Kind of Folly, Duchess, 1955; Follow That Girl, Vaudeville, 1960; Twelfth Night, Regent's Park, 1962. First Director, American Shakespeare Theatre, Stratford, Conn., 1955; prod Julius Cæsar, The Tempest. Director: Bristol Old Vic tour (British Council), India, Pakistan, Ceylon, 1963; The Golden Rivet, Phœnix Theatre, Dublin, 1964; Armstrong's Last Good-Night, Citizen Theatre, Glasgow, 1964; The Saints Go Cycling, Dublin Festival, 1965; African tour for British Council, 1964-65; Juno and the Paycock, Gaiety Theatre, Dublin, 1966; Hamlet, Dubrovnik Festival, Homecoming, Atelje 212, Belgrade, 1967-69; Hamlet, Kentner Theatre, Istanbul, 1968; Troilus and Cressida, Athens, USA 1969; Androcles and the Lion, Stanford, USA, 1969; Julius Caesar, Kano, Nigeria, 1974-75. Played: Teleyegin in Uncle Vanya, Royal Court, 1970; Egeus and Quince in RSC world tour of A Midsummer Night's Dream, 1972-73; Gunga Din in Chez Nous, Globe, 1974; Da in Da, Liverpool Playhouse, 1975. *Recreations:* walking and gardening. *Address:* 5 Eldon Grove, NW3. *T:* 01-435 6110

CAREY, Prof. John; Merton Professor of English Literature, Oxford University, since 1976; *b* 5 April 1934; *s* of Charles William Carey and Winifred Ethel Carey (*née* Cook); *m* 1960, Gillian Mary Florence Booth; two *s. Educ:* Richmond and East Sheen County Grammar Sch.; St John's Coll., Oxford (MA, DPhil). Harmsworth Sen. Scholar, Merton Coll., Oxford, 1957-58; Lectr, Christ Church, Oxford, 1958-59; Andrew Bradley Jun. Research Fellow, Balliol, Oxford, 1959-60; Tutorial Fellow: Keble Coll., Oxford, 1960-64; St John's Coll., Oxford, 1964-75. *Publications:* Milton, 1969; The Violent Effigy: a study of Dickens' imagination, 1973; Thackeray: Prodigal Genius, 1977; articles in Rev. of English Studies, Mod. Lang. Rev., etc. *Recreations:* swimming, gardening. *Address:* Brasenose Cottage, Lyneham, Oxon; 38 St John Street, Oxford. *T:* Oxford 54437.

CAREY, Rt. Rev. Kenneth Moir, MA; Non-stipendiary Bishop in the diocese of Moray, since 1975; *b* 6 April 1908; *s* of late Godfrey Mohun Carey and Agnes Charlotte Milligan; unmarried. *Educ:* Marlborough; Exeter Coll., Oxford; Westcott House, Cambridge. Chaplain of Oxford House, Bethnal Green, 1932-36; Curate of St Andrew's, Handsworth, Birmingham, 1936-38; Vicar of Whitworth with Spennymoor, 1939-44; Gen. Sec., Central Advisory Council of Training for the Ministry, 1944-48; Principal of Westcott House, Cambridge, 1947-61; Hon. Canon of Portsmouth Cathedral, 1956-61; Bishop of Edinburgh, 1961-75. Chaplain to the Queen, 1957-61. Hon. DD Edinburgh, 1964. *Publication:* (ed) The Historic Episcopate, 1955. *Address:* Morven, Kincraig, by Kingussie, Inverness-shire PH21 1NA.

CAREY, Lionel Mohun, TD, MA; JP; Headmaster of Bromsgrove School, 1953-71; *b* 27 Jan. 1911; 4th *s* of late G. M. Carey; *m* 1943, Mary Elizabeth Auld, MBE; two *s. Educ:* Sherborne Sch.; Corpus Christi Coll., Cambridge. Teaching Diploma Institute of Education, London, 1934. Assistant Master, Bolton Sch., Lancs., 1934-37; Christ's Hospital, 1937-53, Housemaster 1940-53. JP Sherborne. *Recreations:* walking, reading, golf, people. *Address:* Westbury Cottage, Sherborne, Dorset.

CAREY, Very Rev. Michael Sausmarez; Dean of Ely, since 1970; *b* 7 Dec. 1913; *s* of Rev. Christopher Sausmarez and Jane Robinson Carey; *m* 1945, Muriel Anne Gibbs; one *s* one *d. Educ:* Haileybury Coll.; Keble Coll., Oxford (MA 1941). Ordained, 1939, Curate St John's Waterloo Rd, SE1; Chaplain Cuddesdon Coll., 1941-43; Mission Priest, Gambia, 1943-44; Rector of Hunsdon, Herts, 1945-51; Rector of Botley, Hants, 1951-62; Archdeacon of Ely, 1962-70, and Rector of St Botolph's, Cambridge, 1965-70. Exam. Chap. to Bp of Portsmouth, 1953-59. Hon. Canon, Portsmouth, 1961-62. MA Cantab Incorp. 1967. *Recreations:* music, painting, golf. *Address:* The Deanery, Ely. *T:* Ely 2432.

CAREY, Sir Peter (Willoughby), KCB 1976 (CB 1972); Permanent Secretary, Department of Industry, since 1976; *b* 26 July 1923; *s* of Jack Delves Carey and Sophie Carey; *m* 1946, Thelma Young; three *d. Educ:* Portsmouth Grammar Sch.; Oriel Coll., Oxford; Sch. of Slavonic Studies. Served War of 1939-45: Capt., Gen. List, 1943-45. Information Officer, British Embassy, Belgrade, 1945-46; FO (German Section), 1948-51; Bd of Trade, 1953; Prin. Private Sec. to successive Presidents, 1960-64; IDC, 1965; Asst Sec., 1963-67, Under-Sec., 1967-69, Bd of Trade; Under-Sec., Min. of Technology, 1969-71; Dep. Sec., Cabinet Office, 1971-72; Dep. Sec., 1972-73, Second Permanent Sec., 1973-74, DTI; Second Permanent Sec., DoI, 1974-76. *Recreations:* music, theatre, travel. *Address:* 19 Leeward

Gardens, Wimbledon, SW19. *T:* 01-947 5530. *Club:* United Oxford & Cambridge University.

CAREY EVANS, Lady Olwen (Elizabeth), DBE 1969; *b* 3 April 1892; *d* of 1st Earl Lloyd-George of Dwyfor, PC, OM, and Margaret, GBE, *d* of Richard Owen, Mynydd Ednyfed, Criccieth; *m* 1917, Sir Thomas John Carey Evans, MC, FRCS (*d* 1947); two *s* two *d. Address:* Eisteddfa, Criccieth, Gwynedd.

CAREY-FOSTER, George Arthur, CMG 1952; DFC 1944; AFC 1941; Counsellor, HM Diplomatic (formerly Foreign) Service, 1946-68; *b* 18 Nov. 1907; *s* of George Muir Foster, FRCS, MRCP, and Marie Thérèse Mutin; *m* 1936, Margaret Aloysius Barry Egan; one *d. Educ:* Clifton Coll., Bristol. Royal Air Force, 1929-35; Reserve of Air Force Officers, 1935-39; served War of 1939-45: Royal Air Force, 1939-46 (despatches, AFC, DFC), Group Capt. Served at Foreign Office, Rio de Janeiro, Warsaw, Hanover and The Hague, 1946-68; retired, 1968. *Recreation:* wine. *Address:* Kilkeran, Castle Freke, Co. Cork. *Clubs:* Royal Air Force; Haagsche (The Hague).

CAREY JONES, Norman Stewart, CMG 1965; Director, Development Administration, Leeds University, since 1965; *b* 11 Dec. 1911; *s* of Samuel Carey Jones and Jessie Isabella Stewart; *m* 1946, Stella Myles; two *s. Educ:* Monmouth Sch.; Merton Coll., Oxford. Colonial Audit Service: Gold Coast, 1935; Northern Rhodesia, 1939; British Honduras, 1946; Kenya, 1950; Asst Financial Sec., Treasury, Kenya, 1954; Dep. Sec., Min. of Agric., Kenya, 1956; Perm. Sec., Min. of Lands and Settlement, Kenya, 1962. *Publications:* The Pattern of a Dependent Economy, 1952; The Anatomy of Uhuru, 1966; Politics, Public Enterprise and The Industrial Development Agency, 1974; articles and reviews for: Journal of Rhodes-Livingstone Inst.; E African Economics Review; Africa Quarterly; Geog. Jl. *Address:* Sandown, Rawdon, near Leeds. *Club:* Royal Commonwealth Society.

CARGILL, Ian Peter Macgillivray, MBE 1942; Vice President, Finance, International Bank for Reconstruction and Development (World Bank), since 1974; *b* 29 Sept. 1915; *s* of William Macgillivray and Ethel Mary Chestney Cargill; *m* 1st, 1934, Margaret Freeling (marr. diss. 1945); one *s*; 2nd, 1951, Inge Haure-Petersen (*d* 1965). *Educ:* Malvern Coll.; Corpus Christi Coll., Oxford. Indian CS, 1938-47; Colonial Office, 1948-50; HM Treasury, 1950-52; IBRD, 1952-. *Recreation:* golf. *Address:* 1701 North Kent Street, Arlington, Va 22209, USA. *T:* 703-524-1873. *Clubs:* Oriental, Travellers'; International (Washington, DC).

CARGILL THOMPSON, Prof. William David James, MA, PhD; Professor of Ecclesiastical History, University of London King's College, since 1976; *b* Rangoon, Burma, 17 Dec. 1930; *e s* of late William David Cargill Thompson and of Helen Mary Sutherland Cargill Thompson (*née* Reed); *m* 1966, Jennifer Anketell Williams Warren, *e d* of Rt Rev. A. K. Warren, *qv*; two *s. Educ:* Harrow Sch.; King's Coll., Cambridge (Scholar). BA 1954, MA 1959, PhD 1960; 1st Cl. Hist. Tripos Pt I 1953, Pt II 1954; Members' English Essay Prize, 1952; Lightfoot Scholar, 1955. Fellow of King's Coll., Cambridge, 1956-65, Dean, 1959-64; Lectr in History, Univ. of Sussex, 1965-69; Lectr in Ecclesiastical Hist., Univ. of London King's Coll., 1969-75, Reader, 1975-76, Dean of Faculty of Theology, 1976-78. Visiting Lectr, University Coll. of Rhodesia and Nyasaland, 1962. Commonwealth Fund Fellowship, Harvard and Huntington Library, 1957-58; Alexander von Humboldt Fellowship, Göttingen, 1964-65. Governor, Harrow Sch., 1962-; Asst Editor, Jl of Eccles. History; FRHistS 1972. *Publications:* contrib. to: Political Ideas (ed D. Thomson), 1966; Essays in Modern English Church History in Memory of Norman Sykes (ed G. V. Bennett and J. D. Walsh), 1966; Studies in Richard Hooker (ed W. S. Hill), 1972; The Dissenting Tradition (ed C. R. Cole and M. E. Moody), 1975; articles in Jl of Eccles. Hist., Jl of Theol Studies, Studies in Church History, etc. *Address:* Department of Ecclesiastical History, University of London King's College, Strand, WC2R 2LS. *T:* 01-836 5454.

CARIBOO, Bishop of, since 1974; **Rt. Rev. John Samuel Philip Snowden.** *Educ:* Anglican Theological Coll., Vancouver (LTh 1951); Univ. of British Columbia (BA 1956). Deacon 1951, priest 1952; Curate: Kaslo-Kokanee, 1951-53; Oak Bay, 1953-57; Nanaimo, 1957-60; Incumbent of St Timothy, Vancouver, 1960-64; Priest Pastoral, Christ Church Cathedral, Vancouver, 1964-66; Rector of St Timothy, Edmonton, 1966-71; Dean and Rector of St Paul's Cathedral, Kamloops, 1971-74. Domestic Chaplain to Bishop of Cariboo, 1971-73. *Address:* 360 Nicola Street, Kamloops, BC, Canada.

CARINGTON, family name of **Baron Carrington.**

CARLESS, Hugh Michael, CMG 1976; HM Diplomatic Service; Chargé d'Affaires, Buenos Aires, since 1977; *b* 22 April 1925; *s* of late Henry Alfred Carless, CIE, and of Gwendolen Patullo; *m* 1956, Rosa Maria, *e d* of Martino and Ada Frontini, São Paulo; two *s. Educ:* Sherborne; Sch. of Oriental Studies, London; Trinity Hall, Cambridge. Served in Paiforce and BAOR, 1943-47; entered Foreign (subseq. Diplomatic) Service, 1950; 3rd Sec., Kabul, 1951; 2nd Sec., Rio de Janeiro, 1953; Tehran, 1956; 1st Sec., 1957; FO, 1958; Private Sec. to Minister of State, 1961; Budapest, 1963; Civil Service Fellow, Dept of Politics, Glasgow Univ., 1966; Counsellor and Consul-Gen., Luanda, 1967-70; Counsellor, Bonn, 1970-73; Head of Latin American Dept, FCO, 1973-77. *Recreations:* mountains, history. *Address:* c/o Foreign and Commonwealth Office, SW1; 5 Bryanston Square, W1.

CARLESTON, Hadden Hamilton, CIE 1947; OBE 1944; *b* Pretoria, SA, 25 July 1904; *m* 1946, Eirene Leslie, *d* of Rev. H. L. Stevens, Torquay, S Devon; two *s* one *d. Educ:* St Olave's Sch., Southwark; Trinity Hall, Cambridge (MA). Indian Civil Service, 1927-47; Dist Magistrate of Civil and Military Station, Bangalore, 1939-43, and of various districts in Madras Presidency, including Vizagapatam, 1944-46, and The Nilgiris, 1947. Civil Liaison Officer with 19th and 25th Indian Inf. Divs, 1944. Sec. of St Cuthbert's Soc., Univ. of Durham, 1948-52; Admin. Sec., Cambridge Univ. Sch. of Veterinary Medicine, 1952-71. *Address:* 4 High Green, Great Shelford, Cambs CB2 5EG. *T:* Shelford 2096.

CARLETON, Mrs John; *see* Adam Smith, J. B.

CARLILE, Rev. Edward Wilson; Priest in Charge of Saint Michael and All Angels, Belgrave, Leicester, since 1976; *b* 11 June 1915; *s* of Victor Wilson and Elsie Carlile; *m* 1946, Elizabeth (*née* Bryant); two *s* one *d. Educ:* Epsom Coll.; King's Coll., London (BD). Chartered Accountant, 1939. Deacon, 1943; priest, 1944; Curate, All Saints, Queensbury, 1943-46; Hon. Asst Sec. of Church Army, 1946-49; Chief Sec. of Church Army, 1949-60; Vicar of St Peter's with St Hilda's, Leicester, 1960-73; Rector of Swithland, Leicester, 1973-76. *Recreations:* tennis, walking, travel, photography. *Address:* St Michael's Vicarage, 15 Portman Street, Leicester. *T:* Leicester 62184.

CARLILE, Thomas, CBE 1975; Managing Director, Babcock & Wilcox Ltd, since 1968; *b* 9 Feb. 1924; *s* of late James Love Carlile and Isobel Scott Carlile; *m* 1955, Jessie Davidson Clarkson; three *d. Educ:* Minchenden County Sch.; City & Guilds Coll., London. Joined Babcock & Wilcox Ltd, 1944; NY Office Representative, 1950-53; General Works Manager, 1961-66. Director, 1963; Managing Dir., Babcock & Wilcox (Operations) Ltd, 1966. Chm., Shipbuilding Industry Training Board, 1967-70. Pres., Engineering Employers' Fedn, 1972-74. *Address:* 8 Aldenham Grove, Radlett, Herts. *T:* Radlett 6881. *Club:* Caledonian.

CARLILL, Vice-Admiral Sir Stephen Hope, KBE 1957; CB 1954; DSO 1942; *b* Orpington, Kent, 23 Dec. 1902; *s* of late Harold Flamank Carlill; *m* 1928, Julie Fredrike Elisabeth Hildegard, *o d* of late Rev. W. Rahlenbeck, Westphalia; two *s. Educ:* Royal Naval Colleges, Osborne and Dartmouth. Lieut RN, 1925; qualified as Gunnery Officer, 1929; Commander 1937; Commanded HM Destroyers Hambledon, 1940, and Farndale, 1941-42; Captain 1942; Captain (D), 4th Destoyer Flotilla, HMS Quilliam, 1942-44 (despatches); Admiralty, 1944-46; Chief of Staff to C-in-C British Pacific Fleet, 1946-48; Captain, HMS Excellent, 1949-50; Commanded HMS Illustrious, 1950-51; Rear-Admiral, 1952; Senior Naval Member, Imperial Defence Coll., 1952-54; Vice-Admiral, 1954; Flag Officer, Training Squadron, 1954-55; Chief of Naval Staff, Indian Navy, 1955-58, retired. Representative in Ghana of West Africa Cttee 1960-66; Adviser to W Africa Cttee, 1966-67. *Recreations:* walking and gardening. *Address:* 22 Hamilton Court, Milford-on-Sea, Lymington, Hants. *T:* Milford-on-Sea 2958. *Club:* Naval and Military.

CARLISLE, 12th Earl of, *cr* 1661; **Charles James Ruthven Howard,** MC 1945; Viscount Howard of Morpeth, Baron Dacre of Gillesland, 1661; *b* 21 Feb. 1923; *o s* of 11th Earl of Carlisle, and of Lady Ruthven of Freeland, *qv*; *S* father, 1963; is *heir* to mother's barony; *m* 1945, Hon. Ela Beaumont, OStJ, *o d* of 2nd Viscount Allendale, KG, CB, CBE, MC; two *s* two *d. Educ:* Eton. Served War of 1939-45 (wounded twice, MC). Lieut late Rifle Brigade, FLAS. *Heir: s* Viscount Morpeth, *qv. Address:* Naworth Castle, Brampton, Cumbria. *T:* Brampton 2621.

CARLISLE, Bishop of, since 1972; **Rt. Rev. Henry David Halsey;** *b* 27 Jan. 1919; *s* of George Halsey, MBE and Gladys W. Halsey, DSc; *m* 1947, Rachel Margaret Neil Smith; four *d. Educ:* King's Coll. Sch., Wimbledon; King's Coll., London (BA); Wells Theol College. Curate, Petersfield, 1942-45; Chaplain, RNVR, 1946-47; Curate, St Andrew, Plymouth, 1947-50; Vicar of: Netheravon, 1950-53; St Stephen, Chatham, 1953-62; Bromley, and Chaplain, Bromley Hosp., 1962-68; Rural Dean of Bromley, 1965-66; Archdeacon of Bromley, 1966-68; Bishop Suffragan of Tonbridge, 1968-72. *Recreations:* cricket, sailing, reading, gardening, walking. *Address:* Rose Castle, Dalston, Carlisle CA5 7BZ. *T:* Raughton Head 274. *Club:* Army and Navy.

CARLISLE, Dean of; *see* Churchill, Very Rev. J. H.

CARLISLE, Archdeacon of; *see* Ewbank, Ven. W. F.

CARLISLE, Brian Apcar, CBE 1974; DSC 1945; Director, Home Oil Co. Ltd, since 1977; Oil Consultant to Lloyds Bank International, since 1975; *b* 27 Dec. 1919; 2nd *s* of Captain F. M. M. Carlisle, MC; *m* 1953, Elizabeth Hazel Mary Binnie, 2nd *d* of Comdr J. A. Binnie, RN; one *s* three *d. Educ:* Harrow Sch.; Corpus Christi Coll., Cambridge. Royal Navy, 1940-46, served in N Atlantic, Channel and Mediterranean in HMS Hood and destroyers; Sudan Political Service, 1946-54, served in Kassala, Blue-Nile and Bahr-el-Ghazal Provinces; Royal Dutch/Shell Group, 1955-74: served in India with Burmah Shell, 1960-64; Regional Co-ordinator, Middle East, 1970-74; participated in pricing negotiations with OPEC states, 1970-73. *Recreations:* gardening, crosswords, golf. *Address:* Heath Cottage, Hartley Wintney, Hants RG27 8RE. *T:* Hartley Wintney 2224.

CARLISLE, Kenneth Ralph Malcolm, TD; Director, Tribune Investment Trust Ltd; *b* 28 March 1908; *s* of late Kenneth Methven Carlisle and Minnie Marie Donner; *m* 1938, Hon. Elizabeth Mary McLaren, *d* of 2nd Baron Aberconway; one *s* three *d. Educ:* Harrow; Magdalen Coll., Oxford (BA). Binder, Hamlyn & Co., Chartered Accountants, 1931-32; Liebig's Extract of Meat Co. Ltd, Argentina, Paraguay, Uruguay, 1933-34; Liebig's Companies on Continent of Europe, 1935-37. Major, Rifle Bde, 1939-45. Distinguished Service Medal (Greece); Chevalier de l'Ordre de Leopold (Belgium), 1960. *Recreations:* all sports, including shooting, ski-ing, tennis. *Address:* (private) Laurie House, 16 Airlie Gardens, W8 7AW. *T:* 01-229 1714; Wyken Hall, Stanton, Bury St Edmunds, Suffolk. *Clubs:* Boodle's, City of London.

CARLISLE, Mark, QC 1971; a Recorder of the Crown Court, since 1976; MP (C) Runcorn, since 1964; *b* 7 July 1929; 2nd *s* of Philip Edmund and Mary Carlisle; *m* 1959, Sandra Joyce Des Voeux; one *d. Educ:* Radley Coll.; Manchester Univ. LLB (Hons) Manchester, 1952. Called to the Bar, Gray's Inn, 1953; Northern Circuit. Member Home Office Advisory Council on the Penal System, 1966-70; Joint Hon. Secretary, Conservative Home Affairs Cttee, 1965-69; Conservative Front Bench Spokesman on Home Affairs, 1969-70; Parly Under-Sec. of State, Home Office, 1970-72; Minister of State, Home Office, 1972-74. Mem., Adv. Council, BBC, 1975-. *Recreation:* golf. *Address:* 3 Bench Walk, Temple, EC4. *T:* 01-353 0431; Newstead, Mobberley, Cheshire. *T:* Mobberley 2275. *Club:* Garrick.

CARLOW, Viscount; Charles George Yuill Seymour Dawson-Damer; *b* 6 Oct. 1965; *s* and *heir* of 7th Earl of Portarlington, *qv.*

CARLYLE, Joan Hildred; Principal Lyric Soprano, Royal Opera House, Covent Garden, since 1955; *b* 6 April 1931; *d* of late Edgar James and Margaret Mary Carlyle; *m* Robert Duray Aiyar; two *d. Educ:* Howell's Sch., Denbigh, N Wales. Oscar in Ballo in Maschera, 1957-58 season; Sophie in Rosenkavalier, 1958-59; Micaela in Carmen, 1958-59; Nedda in Pagliacci (new Zeffirelli production), Dec. 1959; Mimi in La Bohème, Dec. 1960; Titania in Gielgud Production of Britten's Midsummer Night's Dream, London première, Dec. 1961; Pamina in Klemperer production of The Magic Flute, 1962; Countess in Figaro, 1963; Zdenko in Hartman production of Arabella, 1964; Sœur Angelica (new production), 1965; Desdemona in Otello, 1965, 1967; Sophie in Rosenkavalier (new production), 1966; Pamina in Magic Flute (new production), 1966; Arabella in Arabella, 1967; Marschallin in Rosenkavalier, 1968; Jenifer, Midsummer Marriage (new prod.), 1969; Donna Anna, 1970; Reiza, Oberon, 1970; Adrianna Lecouvreur, 1970; Russalka, for BBC, 1969; Elizabeth in Don Carlos, 1975. Roles sung abroad include: Oscar, Nedda, Mimi, Pamina, Zdenko, Micaela, Desdemona, Donna Anna, Arabella, Elizabeth. Has sung in Buenos Aires, Belgium, Holland, France, Monaco, Naples, Milan, Berlin, Capetown, Munich. Has made numerous recordings; appeared BBC, TV (in film). *Recreations:* gardening,

cooking, interior decorating, countryside preservation. *Address:* 44 Abbey Road, St John's Wood, NW8.

CARLYON, Thomas Symington, CMG 1968; OBE 1940; Managing Director, T. S. Carlyon & Co. Pty Ltd, since 1950; *b* Ballarat, 27 April 1902; *s* of late T. S. Carlyon, Melbourne; *m* 1950, Marie Pichoir, *d* of Edward de Launay; one *s* one *d* (by a previous *m*). *Educ:* Geelong Grammar Sch. Hotel Training, Bellevue Stratford Hotel, USA; General Manager, Hotel Australia, Sydney, 1939-40 and 1946. Member Housing and Catering Cttee, 1956 Olympic Games. Served RAAF, 1940-45 (Sqdn Leader). *Recreations:* golf, racing. *Address:* 77 Caroline Street, South Yarra, Vic. 3141, Australia. *Clubs:* Melbourne Cricket, All Racing (Victoria); Metropolitan Golf.

CARMAN, George Alfred, QC 1971; a Recorder of the Crown Court, since 1972; *b* 6 Oct. 1929; *o s* of Alfred George Carman and late Evelyn Carman; *m* 1st, 1960, Cecilia Sparrow (marr. diss. 1976); one *s*; 2nd, 1976, Frances Elizabeth Venning. *Educ:* St Joseph's Coll., Blackpool; Balliol Coll., Oxford. First Class, Final Hons Sch. of Jurisprudence, 1952. Called to the Bar (King George V Coronation Schol.) Lincoln's Inn, 1953; practised on Northern Circuit. *Address:* 5 Essex Court, The Temple, EC4; Dalhousie, Oldfield Road, Altrincham, Cheshire.

CARMICHAEL, Mrs Catherine McIntosh, (Kay); Senior Lecturer in Social Work and Social Administration, University of Glasgow, since 1974 (Lecturer, 1962); Deputy Chairman, Supplementary Benefits Commission, since 1975 (Member, 1969); *b* 22 Nov. 1925; *d* of John D. and Mary Rankin; *m* 1948, Neil George Carmichael, *qv*; one *d. Educ:* Glasgow and Edinburgh. Social worker, 1955-57; psychiatric social work, 1957-60; Dep. Dir, Scottish Probation Training Course, 1960-62. *Recreations:* reading, relaxation. *Address:* 53 Partick Hill Road, Glasgow G11 5AB. *T:* 041-334 1718.

CARMICHAEL, Sir David William G. C.; *see* Gibson-Craig-Carmichael.

CARMICHAEL, Edward Arnold; CBE 1942; FRCP; Hon. Consulting Physician, National Hospital, Queen Square; formerly Director of Neurological Research Unit and Physician National Hospital for Nervous Diseases, Queen Square, London; *b* 25 March 1896; *y s* of late Edward Carmichael, MD, Edinburgh; *m* 1927, Jeanette Marie Montgomerie; two *s. Educ:* Edinburgh Academy; Edinburgh Univ. MB, ChB, Annandale Gold Medal, 1921; FRCPE 1926, FRCP 1932. Served European War, 1914-19. President Royal Medical Society, 1921-22; Morrison Lecturer, RCP Edin., 1938; Oliver Sharpey Lecturer, 1933, Lumleian Lecturer, 1953, RCP (Lond.); Bramwell Memorial Lecturer, Edinburgh, 1963; Wall Memorial Lecturer, Washington, 1963; Visiting Professor of Neurology, Columbia Univ., New York, 1964; Visiting Scientist, Nat. Inst. of Health, Bethesda, USA, 1964-66; Visiting Professor, Montreal Neurological Inst., 1966; Visiting Professor of Neurology, Univ. of Pennsylvania, 1966-67; Milton Shy Meml Prof., Univ. of Pennsylvania, 1970; Rockefeller Foundation Travelling Fellow, 1934; Hon. Member: Society for Psychiatry and Neurology, Vienna, 1948; American Neurological Assoc., 1952; Philadelphia Neurological Society, 1967; Hon. Foreign Member, French Neurological Society, 1949; Corresp. Member German Neurological Society, 1954; President, Neurological Section, Royal Society Medicine, London, 1953-54; President EEG Society, 1963-64. Hon. DSc, Edinburgh Univ., 1963; Gold Medal, Graz Univ., 1963; Honorary Alumnus, Neurological Inst., NY, 1966. *Publications:* The Cerebrospinal Fluid (with Dr J. G. Greenfield), 1925; articles in physiological, clinical and neurological journals. *Address:* 20 Lucastes Avenue, Haywards Heath, West Sussex. *T:* Haywards Heath 54598.

CARMICHAEL, Ian (Gillett); *b* 18 June 1920; *s* of Arthur Denholm Carmichael, Cottingham, E Yorks, and Kate Gillett, Hessle, E Yorks; *m* 1943, Jean Pyman Maclean, Sleights, Yorks; two *d. Educ:* Scarborough Coll.; Bromsgrove Sch. Studied at RADA, 1938-39. Served War of 1939-45 (despatches). First professional appearance as a Robot in "RUR", by Karel and Josef Capek, The People's Palace, Stepney, 1939; stage appearances include: The Lyric Revue, Globe, 1951; The Globe Revue, Globe, 1952; High Spirits, Hippodrome, 1953; Going to Town, St Martin's, 1954; Simon and Laura, Apollo, 1954; The Tunnel of Love, Her Majesty's, 1958; The Gazebo, Savoy, 1960; Critic's Choice, Vaudeville, 1961; Devil May Care, Strand, 1963; Boeing-Boeing, Cort Theatre, New York, 1965; Say Who You Are, Her Majesty's, 1965; Getting Married, Strand, 1968; I Do! I Do!, Lyric, 1968; Birds on the Wing, O'Keefe Centre, Toronto, 1969; Darling I'm Home, S African tour, 1972; Out on a Limb, Vaudeville, 1976. Films include: (from 1955) Simon and Laura; Private's Progress; Brothers in Law; Lucky Jim; Happy is the

Bride; The Big Money; Left, Right and Centre; I'm All Right Jack; School for Scoundrels; Light Up The Sky; Double Bunk; The Amorous Prawn; Hide and Seek; Heavens Above!; Smashing Time; The Seven Deadly Sins; From Beyond the Grave. TV series include: The World of Wooster; Bachelor Father; Lord Peter Wimsey. *Recreations:* cricket, gardening, photography and reading. *Address:* c/o London Management, 235/241 Regent Street, W1A 2JT. *Club:* MCC.

CARMICHAEL, Dr James Armstrong Gordon; Chief Medical Adviser (Social Security), Department of Health and Social Security, since 1973; *b* 28 July 1913; 2nd *s* of Dr Donald Gordon Carmichael and Eileen Mona Carmichael; *m* 1936, Nina Betty Ashton (*née* Heape); two *s. Educ:* Epsom Coll.; Guy's Hospital. FRCP, MRCS. Commnd RAMC, 1935; Consultant Physician, MELF, 1953-55; Consultant Physician and Prof. of Tropical Medicine, Royal Army Medical Coll., 1957-58, retd; Hon. Colonel 1958. MO 1958, SMO 1965, Min. of Pensions and Nat. Insce; PMO, Min. of Social Security, 1967; Dep. Chief Medical Advr, DHSS, 1971-73. *Publications:* contrib. to BMJ, Jl of RAMC. *Recreation:* gardening. *Address:* Hassets, Stockton Avenue, Fleet, Hants. *T:* Fleet 4675.

CARMICHAEL, Sir John, KBE 1955; Chairman, Sidlaw Industries Ltd (formerly Jute Industries), since 1970 (Deputy Chairman, 1969, Director since 1966); Director: Fisons Ltd, since 1961 (Deputy Chairman, 1963-71); Royal Bank of Scotland Ltd, since 1966; Abbey National Building Society, since 1968; Member, Scottish Industrial Development Advisory Board, since 1972; Member, Adobe Oil and Gas Inc., Texas, since 1974; *b* 22 April 1910; *s* of late Thomas Carmichael and Margaret Doig Coupar; *m* 1940, Cecilia Macdonald Edwards; one *s* three *d. Educ:* Madras Coll., St Andrews; Univ. of St Andrews; Univ. of Michigan (Commonwealth Fund Fellow). Guardian Assurance Co., Actuarial Dept, 1935-36; Sudan Govt Civil Service, 1936-59; Member Sudan Resources Board and War Supply Dept, 1939-45; Secretary Sudan Development Board, 1944-48; Asst Financial Secretary, 1946-48; Dep. Financial Secretary, 1948-53; Director, Sudan Gezira Board, 1950-54; Chm. Sudan Light and Power Co., 1952-54; Acting Financial Secretary, then Permanent Under Secretary to Ministry of Finance, 1953-55; Financial and Economic Adviser to Sudan Government, 1955-59. Member of UK delegation to General Assembly of UN, 1959. Mem., Scottish Gas Board, 1960-70. Dep. Chm., ITA, 1960-64, Acting Chm. ITA, 1962-63; Chm., Herring Industry Bd, 1962-65; Dir, Grampian Television, 1965-72; Mem., Social and Economic Cttee, EEC, 1973-74. *Recreations:* golf, gardening. *Address:* Hayston Park, Balmullo, Fife. *T:* Balmullo 268. *Clubs:* New (Edinburgh), Honourable Company of Edinburgh Golfers; Royal and Ancient Golf (St Andrews); Augusta National Golf, Pine Valley Golf.

CARMICHAEL, Kay; see Carmichael, C. M.

CARMICHAEL, Neil George; MP (Lab) Glasgow, Kelvingrove, since 1974 (Glasgow, Woodside, 1962-74); *b* Oct. 1921; *m* 1948, Catherine McIntosh Rankin (*see* C. M. Carmichael); one *d. Educ:* Estbank Acad.; Royal Coll. of Science and Technology, Glasgow. Employed by Gas Board in Planning Dept. Past Member Glasgow Corporation. PPS to Minister of Technology, 1966-67; Jt Parly Sec., Min. of Transport, 1967-69; Parly Sec., Min. of Technology, 1969-70; Parliamentary Under-Secretary of State: DoE, 1974-75; DoI, 1975-76. *Address:* House of Commons, SW1; 53 Partick Hill Road, Glasgow G11 5AB.

CARMICHAEL-ANSTRUTHER, Sir W. E. F.; see Anstruther.

CARNAC, Rev. Sir (Thomas) Nicholas R.; see Rivett-Carnac.

CARNARVON, 6th Earl of, *cr* 1793; **Henry George Alfred Marius Victor Francis Herbert;** Baron Porchester, 1780; Lieut-Colonel 7th Hussars; *b* 7 Nov. 1898; *o s* of 5th Earl and Almina (who *m* 2nd, 1923, Lieut-Colonel I. O. Dennistoun, MVO; she *d* 1969), *d* of late Frederick C. Wombwell; *S* father, 1923; *m* 1st, 1922, Catherine (who obtained a divorce, 1936, and *m* 2nd, 1938, Geoffrey Grenfell (decd) and *m* 3rd, 1950, D. Momand), *d* of late J. Wendell, New York, and Mrs Wendell, Sandridgebury, Sandridge, Herts; one *s* one *d* ; 2nd, 1939, Ottilie (marr. diss.), *d* of Eugene Losch, Vienna. *Educ:* Eton. Owns about 4000 acres. *Publication:* No Regrets (memoirs), 1976. *Heir: s* Lord Porchester, *qv. Recreations:* racing and shooting. *Address:* Highclere Castle, near Newbury, Berks. *TA:* Carnarvon Highclere. *T:* Highclere 253204. *Clubs:* White's, Portland.

CARNE, Colonel James Power, VC 1953; DSO 1951; DL; *b* 11 April 1906; *s* of late G. N. Carne, Garras, Falmouth; *m* 1946, Mrs Jean Gibson, *widow* of Lt-Col J. T. Gibson, DSO, The Welch Regt; one *step s. Educ:* Imperial Service Coll.; Royal Military Coll., Sandhurst. Commissioned Gloucestershire Regt, 1925; seconded King's African Rifles, 1930-36; Adjutant 1st Bn Gloucestershire Regt, 1937-40. Served War of 1939-45: with KAR and on Staff, Madagascar, 1942, Burma, 1944; CO 6th and 26th Bns KAR, 1943-46. CO 5th Bn (TA) 1947-50, 1st Bn Gloucestershire Regt, 1950-51. Served Korean War of 1950-53 (DSO, VC). Freedom of Gloucester, 1953; Freedom of Falmouth, 1954. DSC (US), 1953. DL County of Gloucester, 1960. *Recreation:* fishing.

CARNEGIE, family name of **Duke of Fife** and of **Earls of Northesk** and **Southesk.**

CARNEGIE, Maj.-Gen. Robin Macdonald, OBE 1968; Chief of Staff, HQ British Army of the Rhine, since 1976; *b* 22 June 1926; *yr s* of late Sir Francis Carnegie, CBE; *m* 1955, Iona, *yr d* of Maj.-Gen. Sir John Sinclair, KCMG, CB, OBE, and of Esme Beatrice Sopwith; one *s* two *d. Educ:* Rugby. Commnd 7th Queen's Own Hussars, 1946; comd The Queen's Own Hussars, 1967-69; Comdr 11th Armd Bde, 1971-72; Student, Royal Coll. of Defence Studies, 1973; GOC 3rd Div., 1974-76. *Address:* c/o Lloyds Bank Ltd, 6 Pall Mall, SW1. *Club:* Cavalry and Guards.

CARNER, Dr Mosco; Music Critic of The Times, 1961-69; Member of the BBC Score Reading Panel, 1944-72; *b* 15 Nov. 1904; *m* 1962, Dr Elisabeth Bateman (*d* 1970); *m* 1976, Hazel, *d* of late Mr and Mrs Sebag-Montefiore. *Educ:* Vienna Univ. and Vienna Music Conservatory. Conductor at Danzig State Theatre, 1929-33. Resident in London since Autumn 1933, where active as conductor, musical author, critic and broadcaster. Music Critic of Time and Tide, 1949-62; Music Critic of The Evening News, 1957-61. Silver Medal of the Italian Government, 1964. *Publications:* A Study of 20th-Century Harmony, 1942; Of Men and Music, 1944; The History of the Waltz, 1948; Puccini, A Critical Biography, 1958, 2nd rev. edn, 1975 (Ital. edn, 1961, Japanese edn 1968); contribs to: New Oxford History of Music, 1974; 6th edn of Grove's Dictionary of Music and Musicians; Symposia on: Schubert, 1946; Schumann, 1952; The Concerto, 1952; Chamber Music, 1957; Choral Music, 1963; Alban Berg: the man and his work, 1975. *Recreations:* reading, motoring and swimming. *Address:* 14 Elsworthy Road, NW3. *T:* 01-586 1553.

CARNEY, Most Rev. James F.; *see* Vancouver, Archbishop of, (RC).

CARNEY, Admiral Robert Bostwick, Hon. CBE 1946; DSM (US), 1942 (and Gold Stars, 1944, 1946, 1955); and numerous other American and foreign decorations; United States Navy, retired; Chairman Board, Naval Historical Foundation; Director, several corporations; Corporation Consultant; *b* Vallejo, California, 26 March 1895; *s* of Robert E. and Bertha Carney; *m* 1918, Grace Stone Craycroft, Maryland; one *s* one *d. Educ:* United States Naval Acad., Annapolis, Md (BS). Served European War, 1914-18; Gunnery and Torpedo Officer aboard USS Fanning in capture of Submarine U-58 off coast of Ireland; War of 1939-45; North Atlantic, 1941-42; Commanding Officer, USS Denver, serving in Pacific, 1942-43; Chief of Staff to Admiral William Halsey (Commander, S Pacific Force), 1943-45, participating in nine battle engagements. Deputy Chief of Naval Operations, 1946-50; President of US Naval Inst., 1950-51, 1954-56; Commander Second Fleet, 1950; Commander-in-Chief, United States Naval Forces, Eastern Atlantic and Mediterranean, 1950-52; Commander-in-Chief, Allied Forces, Southern Europe (North Atlantic Treaty Organisation), 1951-53; Chief of Naval Operations, 1953-55; retired 1955. Hon. LLD, Loras Coll., 1955. *Publications:* various professional. *Recreations:* field sports, music. *Address:* 2801 New Mexico Avenue (NW), Washington, DC 20007, USA. *Clubs:* Chevy Chase Country, Alibi (Washington, DC); The Brook (NY).

CARNOCHAN, John Golder, Lay Reporter, Town and Country Planning (Scotland) Act 1972, since 1972; *b* Old Kilpatrick, 12 Sept. 1910; *s* of N. and M. G. Carnochan; *m* 1938, Helen Dewar, *y d* of A. A. and A. Ferguson, Doune; one *s.* Chartered Accountant; Entered Ministry of Food, 1942; Dep. Accountant-General, 1948; Asst Secretary, 1949; Under-Secretary, Min. of Agriculture, Fisheries and Food, 1965-70. *Address:* Hillcrest, 14 Venachar Avenue, Callander, Perthshire FK17 8JQ. *Club:* Scottish Liberal (Edinburgh).

CARNOCK, 3rd Baron, *cr* 1916, of Carnock; **Erskine Arthur Nicolson,** DSO 1918; JP; 13th Bt of Nova Scotia, *cr* 1637; Captain, RN, retired; *b* British Legation, Athens, 26 March 1884; 2nd *s* of 1st Lord Carnock and Mary Catherine (*d* 1951), *d* of Captain Arch. Rowan Hamilton, Killyleagh, Co. Down; *S* brother, 1952; *m* 1919, Katharine (*d* 1968), *e d* of 1st Baron

Roborough; one s (and one s killed in action 1942; one d decd). *Educ:* HMS Britannia; RN Staff Coll., 1913. War Staff Officer to the Light Cruiser Forces, 1914-19 (DSO, Légion d'honneur, St Anne with Swords, Crown of Italy); retired list, 1924. *Recreation:* hunting. *Heir: s* Hon. David Henry Arthur Nicolson, *b* 10 July 1920. *Address:* Beechfield Nursing Home, Harrowbeer Lane, Yelverton, South Devon.
See also Baron St Levan.

CARNWATH, Sir Andrew Hunter, KCVO 1975; DL; a Managing Director, Baring Brothers & Co. Ltd, 1955-74; Chairman, London Multinational Bank, 1971-74; *b* 26 Oct. 1909; *s* of late Dr Thomas Carnwath, DSO, Dep. CMO, Min. of Health, and Margaret Ethel (*née* McKee); *m* 1st, 1939, Kathleen Marianne Armstrong (*d* 1968); five *s* one *d*; 2nd, 1973, Joan Gertrude Wetherell-Pepper. *Educ:* Eton (King's Scholar). Served RAF (Coastal Comd Intelligence), 1939-45. Joined Baring Bros & Co. Ltd, 1928; rejoined as Head of New Issues Dept, 1945. Chm., Save and Prosper Group Ltd, 1961- (Dir, 1960-); Director: Equity & Law Life Assurance Soc. Ltd, 1955-; Scottish Agricultural Industries Ltd, 1969-75; Great Portland Estates Ltd, 1977-. Member: London Cttee, Hongkong and Shanghai Banking Corp., 1967-74; Council, Inst. of Bankers, 1955- (Dep. Chm., 1969-70, Pres., 1970-72); Cttee on Consumer Credit; Central Bd of Finance of Church of England (Chm., Investment Management Cttee), 1960-74; Chairman: Migration of Companies Adv. Panel, 1976-; Chelmsford Diocesan Bd of Finance, 1969-75 (Vice-Chm., 1967-68); Member: Council, King Edward's Hosp. Fund for London, 1962-74 (Treasurer, 1965-74; Governor, 1976-); Royal Commn for Exhibn of 1851, 1964-; Council, Friends of Tate Gall., 1962- (Treasurer, 1966-). Trustee, Imp. War Graves Endowment Fund, 1963-74, Chm., 1964-74. A Governor, Felsted Sch., 1965-; Treasurer: Essex Univ., 1973-; Victoria League, 1974-; British and Foreign Sch. Soc., 1974-. Pres., Saffron Walden Conservative Assoc. Mem., Ct of Assts, Musicians' Co., 1973-. Mem., Essex CC, 1973-77; High Sheriff, 1965, DL 1972, Essex. FIB; FRSA. *Publications:* lectures and reviews for Inst. of Bankers, etc. *Recreations:* music (playing piano, etc), pictures, travel, living in the country. *Address:* The Old Vicarage, Ugley, Bishop's Stortford, Herts. *T:* Rickling 283; 33 Grove Road, Barnes, SW13. *T:* 01-876 5338. *Club:* Athenæum.

CARO, Anthony (Alfred), CBE 1969; Sculptor; *b* 8 March 1924; *s* of Alfred and Mary Caro; *m* 1949, Sheila May Girling; two *s*. *Educ:* Charterhouse; Christ's Coll., Cambridge; Regent Street Polytechnic; Royal Acad. Schs, London. Asst to Henry Moore, 1951-53; taught part-time, St Martin's Sch. of Art, 1953-67; taught sculpture at Bennington Coll., Vermont, 1963, 1964, 1965. One-man Exhibitions: Galleria del Naviglio, Milan, 1956; Gimpel Fils, London, 1957; Whitechapel Art Gallery, London, 1963; Andre Emmerich Gallery, NY, 1964, 1966, 1968, 1970, 1972, 1973, 1974; Washington Gallery of Modern Art, Washington, DC, 1965; Kasmin Ltd, London, 1965, 1967, 1971, 1972; David Mirvish Gallery, Toronto, 1966, 1971, 1974; Galerie Bischofberger, Zurich, 1966; Kroller-Muller Museum, Holland, 1967; Hayward Gallery, London, 1969; Kenwood House, Hampstead, 1974; Galleria dell'Ariete, Milan, 1974; Watson/de Nagy Gall., Houston, 1975; Richard Gray Gall., Chicago, 1975; Lefevre Gall., London, 1976; Exhibited: First Paris Biennale, 1959 (sculpture prize); Battersea Park Open Air Exhibitions, 1960, 1963, 1966; Gulbenkian Exhibition, London, 1964; Documenta III Kassel, 1965; Primary Structures, Jewish Museum, NY, 1966; Venice Biennale, 1958 and 1966; Pittsburgh International, 1967 and 1968; Metropolitan Museum of Art, 1968; Saõ Paulo, 1969 (sculpture prize); Univ. of Pennsylvania, 1969; Everson Mus., Syracuse; Retrospective Exhibitions: Museum of Modern Art, New York, 1975; (David Bright Prize); Walker Art Gall., Minn; Mus. of Fine Arts, Houston; Mus. of Fine Arts, Boston. Given key to City of NY, 1976. Hon. DLitt East Anglia. *Relevant publications:* Anthony Caro, by R. Whelan *et al*, 1974; Anthony Caro, by W. S. Rubin, 1975. *Recreation:* listening to music while working. *Address:* 111 Frognal, Hampstead, NW3.

CARÖE, Sir (Einar) Athelstan (Gordon), Kt 1972; CBE 1958; President: Trustee Savings Banks, since 1976; President and Chairman, EEC Savings Bank Group, since 1976 (Vice-Chairman, 1973-76); Director, Norwich Union Group, since 1968; Grain Merchant and Broker, W. S. Williamson and Co., Liverpool, 1935-73; Consul for Denmark, in Liverpool, 1931-73, also for Iceland since 1947; *b* 6 Oct. 1903; *s* of Johan Frederik Caröe and Eleanor Jane Alexandra Caröe (*née* Gordon); *m* 1st, 1934, Frances Mary Lyon (*d* 1947); two *s*; 2nd, 1952, Doreen Evelyn Jane Sandland; one *s* one *d*. *Educ:* Eton Coll. (King's Scholar); Trinity Coll., Cambridge (Scholar, BA). Chairman: Liverpool Savings Bank, 1947-48; Trustee Savings Banks Assoc., 1966-76 (Dep. 1951-66); Vice-President: National Savings Cttee,

1971-; EEC Gp of Savings Banks, Brussels, 1972-. President, Liverpool Consular Corps, 1952; Chairman, Liverpool Chamber of Commerce, 1950-51. Pres., Minton Ltd, Stoke-on-Trent, 1970- (Chm. 1956-70); Chairman: Maritime Insurance Co. Ltd, Liverpool, 1951-68; Liverpool Corn Trade Assoc., 1963-67; Richards-Campbell Tiles Ltd, 1967-68. Pro-Chancellor, Liverpool Univ., 1966-75 (Dep. Treas., 1948-57; Treas., 1957-66; Pres., 1966-72); President, Lancashire County Lawn Tennis Assoc., 1953; Member Lawn Tennis Assoc. Council, 1954-66; President: Nat. Federation of Corn Trade Assocs, 1957-60; Internat. Savings Banks Inst., 1960-69 (Hon. Pres., 1969-). Hon. LLD, Liverpool, 1976. Officer, 1st Class, Order of Dannebrog, 1957 (Officer, 1945); Kt Commander, Order of Icelandic Falcon, ·1974 (Officer 1958); Comdr, Order of Crown of Belgium, 1966. King Christian X Liberty Medal, 1946; Spanish Medal, Al Merito del Ahorro, 1973. *Recreations:* lawn tennis (Lancashire doubles champion, 1933); philately (Fellow RPS(L) 1939; Roll of Distinguished Philatelists, 1972). *Address:* Anthonys Close, Caldy Road, Caldy, West Kirby, Wirral, Merseyside L48 1LP. *T:* 051-625 7089. *Clubs:* British Pottery Manufacturers (Stoke-on-Trent); Old Hall, Exchange, Palatine (Liverpool).

CAROE, Sir Olaf (Kirkpatrick), KCSI 1945 (CSI 1941); KCIE 1944 (CIE 1932); FRSL 1959; DLitt Oxon; late ICS and Officer Indian Political Service; Vice-President, Conservative Commonwealth Council, 1969 (Deputy Chairman, 1966-69); *e s* of late William Douglas Caroe and of Grace Desborough, *d* of John Rendall; *m* 1920, Frances Marion (Kaisar-i-Hind Gold Medal, 1947) (*d* 1969), *d* of late Rt Rev. A. G. Rawstorne, Bishop of Whalley; two *s*. *Educ:* Winchester; (Demy) Magdalen Coll., Oxford. Captain 4th Bn, The Queen's Regt (TF), 1914-19; entered ICS, 1919; served in Punjab till 1923, when posted to N. W. Frontier Province as Officer of Political Department; served as Deputy Commissioner, various Frontier Districts, including Peshawar, up to 1932; Chief Secretary to the Govt, of the NWFP, 1933-34; Deputy Secretary, Foreign and Political Dept, Government of India, 1934; officiated as Political Resident in the Persian Gulf, Resident in Waziristan, and as Agent to the Governor-General in Baluchistan, 1937-38 (despatches); Revenue Commissioner in Baluchistan, 1938-39; Secretary, External Affairs Dept, 1939-45; Governor North-West Frontier Province, India, 1946-47; left India Aug, 1947. Vice-Chairman Overseas League, 1951; ·visited US for British Information Services, 1952; Pres., Tibet Soc. of the UK. Lawrence of Arabia Meml Medal, Royal Soc. for Asian Affairs, 1973. *Publications:* Wells of Power, 1951; Soviet Empire, 1953 (republished 1966); The Pathans, 1958; From Nile to Indus (with Sir Thomas Rapp and Patrick Reid), 1960; Poems of Khushhal (with Sir Evelyn Howell), 1963; introd. new edn of Canbul, by Mountstuart Elphinstone, 1972; articles in The Round Table, Asian Affairs, and other journals. *Address:* Newham House, Steyning, Sussex. *T:* Steyning 812241. *Club:* Lansdowne.

CARON, Leslie (Leslie Claire Margaret, *née* Caron); film and stage actress; *b* 1 July 1931; *d* of Claude Caron and Margaret Caron (*née* Petit); *m* 1956, Peter Reginald Frederick Hall (marr. diss. 1965); one *s* one *d*; *m* 1969, Michael Laughlin (marr. diss.). *Educ:* Convent of the Assumption, Paris. With Ballet des Champs Elysées, 1947-50, Ballet de Paris, 1954. *Films include:* American in Paris, 1950; subsequently, Lili; The Glass Slipper; Daddy Long Legs; Gaby; Gigi; The Doctor's Dilemma; The Man Who Understood Women; The Subterraneans; Fanny; Guns of Darkness; The L-Shaped Room; Father Goose; A Very Special Favour; Promise Her Anything; Is Paris Burning?; Head of the Family; Madron; QB VII; Valentino. *Plays:* Orvet, Paris, 1955; Gigi, London, 1956; Ondine, London, 1961. *Recreation:* collecting antiques. *Address:* c/o Hugh J. Alexander, International Artistes Representation, 4th Floor, 235 Regent Street, W1. *T:* 01-439 8401.

CARPENTARIA, Bishop of, since 1974; **Rt. Rev. Hamish Thomas Umphelby Jamieson;** *b* 15 Feb. 1932; *s* of Robert Marshall Jamieson and Constance Marzetti Jamieson (*née* Umphelby); *m* 1962, Ellice Anne McPherson; one *s* two *d*. *Educ:* Sydney C of E Grammar Sch.; St Michael's House, Crafers (ThL); Univ. of New England (BA). Deacon 1955; Priest 1956. Mem. Bush Brotherhood of Good Shepherd, 1955-62. Parish of Gilgandra, 1957; Priest-in-Charge, Katherine, NT, 1957-62; Rector and Canon, Darwin, 1962-67; Royal Australian Navy Chaplain, 1967-74; HMAS Sydney, 1967-68; HMAS Albatross, 1969-71; Small Ships Chaplain, 1972; HMAS Cerberus, 1972-74. *Recreations:* history, music, tennis, squash. *Address:* The Bishop's House, Thursday Island, Qld 4875, Australia. *T:* Thursday Island 96.

CARPENTER; *see* Boyd-Carpenter.

CARPENTER, Very Rev. Edward Frederick; Dean of Westminster since 1974; Lector Theologiae of Westminster Abbey, 1958; *b* 27 Nov. 1910; *s* of Frederick James and Jessie Kate Carpenter; *m* Lilian Betsy Wright; three *s* one *d. Educ:* Strodes Sch., Egham; King's Coll., University of London. BA 1932, MA 1934, BD 1935, PhD 1943; AKC 1935; FKC 1951. Deacon, 1935; Priest, 1936; Curate, Holy Trinity, St Marylebone, 1935-41; St Mary, Harrow, 1941-45; Rector of Great Stanmore, 1945-51; Canon of Westminster, 1951; Treasurer, 1959-74; Archdeacon, 1963-74. Fellow of King's Coll., London University, 1954 (AKC 1935). Chairman Frances Mary Buss Foundation, 1956-; Chairman Governing Body of: North London Collegiate Sch.; Camden Sch. for Girls, 1956-; Chairman of St Anne's Soc., 1958-; Joint Chm., London Soc. of Jews and Christians, 1960-; Member, Central Religious Advisory Cttee serving BBC and ITA, 1962-67; Chairman: Recruitment Cttee, ACCM, 1967; Religious Adv. Cttee of UNA, 1969-; President: London Region of UNA, 1966-67; Modern Churchmen's Union, 1966; World Congress of Faiths, 1966. *Publications:* Thomas Sherlock, 1936; Thomas Tenison, His Life and Times, 1948; That Man Paul, 1953; The Protestant Bishop, 1956; (joint author) of Nineteenth Century Country Parson, 1954, and of History of St Paul's Cathedral, 1957; Common Sense about Christian Ethics, 1961; (jtly) From Uniformity to Unity, 1962; (jtly) The Church's Use of the Bible, 1963; The Service of a Parson, 1965; (jtly) The English Church, 1966; (jtly) A House of Kings, 1966; Cantuar: the Archbishops in their office, 1971. *Recreations:* walking, conversation, Association football. *Address:* The Deanery, Westminster, SW1. *T:* 01-222 2953.

CARPENTER, Ven. Frederick Charles; Archdeacon of the Isle of Wight, since 1977; *b* 24 Feb. 1920; *s* of Frank and Florence Carpenter; *m* 1952, Rachel Nancy, *widow* of Douglas H. Curtis. *Educ:* Sir George Monoux Grammar Sch., Walthamstow; Sidney Sussex Coll., Cambridge (BA 1947, MA 1949); Wycliffe Hall, Oxford. Served with Royal Signals, 1940-46; Italy, 1944 (despatches). Curate of Woodford, 1949-51; Assistant Master and Chaplain, Sherborne School, Dorset, 1951-62; Vicar of Moseley, Birmingham, 1962-68; Director of Religious Education, Diocese of Portsmouth, 1968-75; Canon Residentiary of Portsmouth, 1968-77. *Recreations:* music, gardening. *Address:* The Rectory, Pitts Lane, Binstead, Ryde, Isle of Wight PO33 3SU. *T:* Ryde 62890.

CARPENTER, George Frederick, ERD 1954; Assistant Under-Secretary of State, Ministry of Defence, 1971-77; *b* 18 May 1917; *s* of late Frederick and Ada Carpenter; *m* 1949, Alison Elizabeth, *d* of late Colonel Sidney Smith, DSO, MC, TD and Elizabeth Smith, Longridge, Lancs; two step *d. Educ:* Bec Sch.; Trinity Coll., Cambridge (MA). Commnd Royal Artillery (Supplementary Reserve), July 1939; War Service, 1939-46, France, 1940 and AA Comd; joined War Office, 1946; Asst Sec., 1958; Comd Sec., Northern Comd, 1961-65; Inspector of Establishments (A), MoD, 1965-71. MBIM. Silver Jubilee Medal, 1977. *Address:* 10 Park Meadow, Hatfield, Herts. *T:* Hatfield 65581. *Club:* Civil Service

CARPENTER, Rt. Rev. Harry James, Hon. DD Oxford; *b* 20 Oct. 1901; *s* of William and Elizabeth Carpenter; *m* 1940, Urith Monica Trevelyan; one *s. Educ:* Churcher's Coll., Petersfield; Queen's Coll., Oxford. Tutor of Keble Coll., Oxford, 1927; Fellow, 1930; Warden of Keble Coll., 1939-55, Hon. Fellow, 1955; Hon. Fellow, Queen's Coll., Oxford, 1955; Canon Theologian of Leicester Cathedral, 1941-55; Bishop of Oxford, 1955-70. *Publications:* (ed) Bicknell, Thirty Nine Articles, 1955; contrib. to: Oxford Dictionary of the Christian Church, ed Cross, 1957; A Theological Word Book of the Bible, ed Richardson, 1963; The Interpretation of the Bible, ed Dugmore, 1944; Jl of Theological Studies. *Address:* 1 Meadow View, Baunton, Cirencester, Glos. *T:* Cirencester 4647.

CARPENTER, John; *see* Carpenter, V. H. J.

CARPENTER, John McG. K. K.; *see* Kendall-Carpenter.

CARPENTER, Leslie; Chairman and Chief Executive, International Publishing Corporation Ltd, since 1974; *b* 26 June 1927; *s* of William and Rose Carpenter; *m* 1952, Stella Louise Bozza; one *d. Educ:* Hackney Techn. Coll. Director: Country Life, 1965; George Newnes, 1966; Odhams Press Ltd (Managing), 1968; International Publishing Corp., 1972; Reed International Ltd, 1974; Reed Publishing Holdings Ltd, 1974. *Recreations:* racing, gardening. *Address:* 22 Wickliffe Avenue, N3. *T:* 01-346 2139. *Club:* Royal Automobile.

CARPENTER, Rhys, MA Oxon, PhD, LittD; *b* Cotuit, Mass, USA, 5 Aug. 1889; *s* of William Henry Carpenter and Anna

Morgan Douglass; *m* 1918, Eleanor Houston Hill, Evanston, Ill., USA; no *c. Educ:* Columbia Univ.; Balliol Coll., Oxford. Instructor in classical archæology in Bryn Mawr Coll., Penna, USA, 1913-15; Associate, 1915-16; Associate Professor, 1916-18; Professor, 1918-55; Professor Emeritus, 1955-. Attached to the American Commission to Negotiate Peace at Paris, 1918-19, as expert on Greco-Albanian territorial problems; Annual Prof. at American Acad., Rome, 1926-27; Director, American Sch. for Classical Studies at Athens, 1927-32 and 1946-48; Professor-in-charge, Classical School, American Academy in Rome, 1939-40; Sather Professor, Univ. of California, 1944-45; Member: Hispanic Society of America, Pontifical Roman Academy of Archæology; Greek Archæological Society, German Archæological Institute, Austrian Archæological Institute, American Philosophical Society. Gold Medal, Amer. Inst. of Archaeology, 1969. *Publications:* Tragedy of Etarre, 1912; The Sunthief, and other Poems, 1914; The Plainsman, and other Poems, 1920; The Land Beyond Mexico, 1921; The Esthetic Basis of Greek Art, 1921 (2nd cd. 1959); The Greeks in Spain, 1925; The Sculpture of the Nike Temple Parapet, 1929; The Humanistic Value of Archæology, 1933; The Defenses of Acrocorinth, 1936; Folk Tale, Fiction and Saga in the Homeric Epics, 1946; Greek Sculpture: A Critical Review, 1960; Greek Art: A Study in the Evolution of Style, 1963; Discontinuity in Greek Civilization, 1966; Beyond the Pillars of Heracles, 1966; The Architects of the Parthenon, 1970; numerous articles on Greek Art in American Journal of Archæology and elsewhere. *Recreation:* archæological exploration. *Address:* Goose Walk, RD1, Chester Springs, Pa 19425, USA.

CARPENTER, Trevor Charles; Chairman, Scottish Postal Board, 1972-77; *b* 23 March 1917; *s* of late Walter Edward Carpenter and Florence Jane Carpenter, Newport, Mon.; *m* 1940, Margaret Lilian, *d* of Frederick James and May Ethel Day; one *s* five *d. Educ:* Alexandra Road Primary Sch., Newport; Newport High Sch. Exec. Officer, GPO, 1936; Higher Exec. Officer, 1947; Principal, 1951; Private Secretary to PMG, 1962; Dep. Director, Scotland, 1964; Director of Postal Personnel, GPO, 1967-70; Director of Posts, Scotland, 1970-72. *Recreations:* golf, Gaelic singing, watching Rugby football. *Address:* 26 Learmonth Terrace, Edinburgh EH4 1NZ. *T:* 031-332 8000.

CARPENTER, Maj.-Gen. (Victor Harry) John, CB 1975; MBE 1945; FCIT; Chairman of Traffic Commissioners, Yorkshire Traffic Area, since 1975; *b* 21 June 1921; *s* of Harry and Amelia Carpenter; *m* 1946, Theresa McCulloch; one *s* one *d. Educ:* Army schools; Apprentice Artificer RA; RMC Sandhurst. Joined the Army, Royal Artillery, 1936; commissioned into Royal Army Service Corps as 2nd Lieut, 1939. Served War of 1939-45 (Dunkirk evacuation, Western Desert, D-Day landings). Post-war appts included service in Palestine, Korea, Aden, and Singapore; also commanded a company at Sandhurst. Staff College, 1951; JSSC, 1960; served WO, BAOR, FARELF, 1962-71; Transport Officer-in-Chief (Army), MoD, 1971-73; Dir of Movements (Army), MoD, 1973-75. Lt-Col, 1960; Brig., 1967; Maj.-Gen., 1971. Col Comdt, RCT, 1975-. Nat. Chm., 1940 Dunkirk Veterans Assoc; President: Artificers Royal Artillery Assoc.; RCT Assoc. (formerly RASC Assoc.). *Recreation:* gardening. *Address:* Traffic Commissioners, Yorkshire Traffic Area, Hillcrest House, 386 Harehills Lane, Leeds LS9 6NF. *Club:* Royal Over-Seas League.

CARR, family name of Baron Carr of Hadley.

CARR OF HADLEY, Baron *cr* 1975 (Life Peer), of Monken Hadley; **(Leonard) Robert Carr,** PC 1963; *b* 11 Nov. 1916; *s* of late Ralph Edward and of Katie Elizabeth Carr; *m* 1943, Joan Kathleen, *d* of Dr E. W. Twining; two *d* (and one *s* decd). *Educ:* Westminster Sch.; Gonville and Caius Coll., Cambridge, BA Nat. Sci. Hons, 1938; MA 1942. FIM 1957. Joined John Dale Ltd, 1938 (Dir, 1948-55; Chm., 1958-63); Director: Metal Closures Group Ltd, 1964-70 (Dep. Chm., 1960-63 and Jt Man. Dir, 1960-63); Carr, Day & Martin Ltd, 1947-55; Isotope Developments Ltd, 1950-55; Metal Closures Ltd, 1959-63; Scottish Union & National Insurance Co. (London Bd), 1958-63; S. Hoffnung & Co., 1963, 1965-70, 1974-; Securicor Ltd and Security Services Ltd, 1961-63, 1965-70, 1974-; SGB Gp Ltd, 1974-; Prudential Assurance Co., 1976-; Mem., London Adv. Bd, Norwich Union Insurance Gp, 1965-70, 1974-76. MP (C) Mitcham, 1950-74, Sutton, Carshalton, 1974-76; PPS to Sec. of State for Foreign Affairs, Nov. 1951-April 1955, to Prime Minister, April-Dec. 1955; Parly Sec., Min. of Labour and Nat. Service, Dec. 1955-April 1958; Sec. for Technical Co-operation, 1963-64; Sec. of State for Employment, 1970-72; Lord President of the Council and Leader of the House of Commons, April-Nov. 1972; Home Secretary, 1972-74. Governor: St Mary's Hosp., Paddington, 1958-63; Imperial Coll. of Science and Technology, 1959-63 and 1976-; St Mary's Medical Sch.

Council, 1958-63; Hon. Treas., Wright Fleming Inst. of Microbiology, 1960-63. Pres., Consultative Council of Professional Management Orgns, 1976-. Duke of Edinburgh Lectr, 1976. *Publications:* (Jt) One Nation, 1950; (Jt) Change is our Ally, 1954; (Jt) The Responsible Society, 1958; (Jt) One Europe, 1965; articles in technical jls. *Recreations:* lawn tennis, music, gardening. *Address:* Monkenholt, Hadley Green, Barnet, Herts. *Club:* Brooks's.

CARR, (Albert) Raymond (Maillard); Warden of St Antony's College, Oxford, since 1968 (Sub-Warden, 1966-68); Fellow since 1964; *b* 11 April 1919; *s* of Reginald and Marion Maillard Carr; *m* 1950, Sara Strickland; three *s* one *d. Educ:* Brockenhurst Sch.; Christ Church, Oxford. Gladstone Research Exhnr, Christ Church, 1941; Fellow of All Souls' Coll., 1946-53; Fellow of New Coll., 1953-64. Director, Latin American Centre, 1964-68. Chm. Soc. for Latin American Studies, 1966-68. Prof. of History of Latin America, Oxford, 1967-68. Mem., Nat. Theatre Bd, 1968-. Corresp. Mem., Royal Acad. of History. Madrid. *Publications:* Spain 1808-1939, 1966; Latin America (St Antony's Papers), 1969; (ed) The Republic and the Civil War in Spain, 1971; The Spanish Civil War, 1971; English Fox Hunting, 1976; The Spanish Tragedy: the Civil War in Perspective, 1977; articles on Swedish, Spanish and Latin American history. *Recreation:* fox hunting. *Address:* St Antony's College, Oxford; 29 Charlbury Road, Oxford. *T:* 58136; Woolhanger Manor, Parracombe, Devon. *T:* 379.

CARR, Sir Bernard; *see* Carr, Sir F. B.

CARR, Catharine; *see* Wade, Rosalind H.

CARR, Cyril Eric; Senior Partner, Cyril Carr & Carr, Solicitors, Liverpool, since 1970; *b* 19 July 1926; *s* of late Henry Carr and of Bertha Carr; *m* 1952, Hilary; one *s* one *d. Educ:* Liverpool Coll.; St Michael's County Primary Sch.; Clifton Coll.; Bishop Ridley Coll., Canada; Upper Canada Coll.; Montreal High Sch.; Liverpool Univ. (LLB Hons 1950). Radio Security Service, Royal Signals, 1942-44 (Signalman). Qual. solicitor, 1951. Mem. Liverpool City Council (1st Liberal Mem. elected since 1939), 1962; Vice-Chm., Liberal Party Nat. Exec., 1968-72, Chm. of Liberal Party, 1972-73; Chm., Assoc. Liberal Councillors, 1971-73; contested Wavertree Div., 1964, 1966, 1970, Feb. 1974; Leader, Liberal Gp, Liverpool CC, 1962-75; Pres., Liverpool Liberal Party; Mem. Merseyside CC, 1973-77; 1st and only Chm., Liverpool Metrop. DC, 1973-74; Leader, Liverpool MDC, 1973-74, and Liverpool Met. City Council, 1974-75 (resigned leadership for health reasons). Co-Chm., Liberal Friends of Israel; Mem. NW Econ. Planning Council; Mem. Liverpool University Court and Council; Governor, Liverpool Polytechnic; Pres., Speke Boys' Club. FIArb 1974. *Recreations:* politics, Liverpool Football Club, good food and good conversation. *Address:* Yew Tree House, Yew Tree Road, Liverpool L18 3JN. *T:* 051-428 1008. *Clubs:* Reform; Racquets (Liverpool).

CARR, Prof. Denis John; Professor, Research School of Biological Sciences, Australian National University, Canberra, since 1968; *b* 15 Dec. 1915; *s* of James E. Carr and Elizabeth (*née* Brindley), Stoke-on-Trent, Staffs; *m* 1955, Stella G. M. Fawcett; no *c. Educ:* Hanley High Sch., Staffs; Manchester Univ. RAF, 1940-46. Manchester Univ.: undergraduate, 1946-49; Asst Lectr in Plant Ecology, 1949-53; Guest Research Worker at Max-Planck-Inst. (Melchers), Tübingen, 1952; Sen. Lectr in plant physiology, 1953, Reader, 1959, Melbourne; Prof. of Botany, Queen's Univ., Belfast, 1960-67. Hon. MSc Melbourne, 1958. *Publications:* Plant Growth Substances 1970, 1972; numerous papers in scientific jls. *Recreations:* research, music. *Address:* Research School of Biological Sciences, ANU Canberra, PO Box 475, ACT 2601, Australia.

CARR, Edward Hallett, CBE 1920; FBA 1956; *b* 28 June 1892. *Educ:* Merchant Taylors' Sch., London; Trinity Coll., Cambridge. Temporary Clerk Foreign Office, 1916; attached to the British Delegation to the Peace Conference, 1919; Temporary Sec. at British Embassy, Paris, for work with the Conference of Ambassadors, 1920-21; 3rd Sec. and transferred to Foreign Office, 1922; 2nd Sec. and transferred to HM Legation at Riga, 1925; transferred to Foreign Office, 1929; Asst Adviser on League of Nations Affairs, 1930-33; First Sec., 1933; resigned, 1936; Wilson Prof. of International Politics, University Coll. of Wales, Aberystwyth, 1936-47. Director of Foreign Publicity, Min. of Information, Oct. 1939-April 1940. Asst Ed. of The Times, 1941-46. Tutor in Politics, Balliol Coll., Oxford, 1953-55; Fellow, Trinity Coll., Cambridge, 1955-; Hon. Fellow, Balliol Coll., Oxford, 1966. Hon. LittD: University of Manchester, 1964; University of Cambridge, 1967; University of Sussex, 1970; Hon. Dr of Law, University of Groningen, 1964.

Publications: Dostoevsky, 1931; The Romantic Exiles, 1933; Karl Marx: A Study in Fanaticism, 1934; International Relations since the Peace Treaties, 1937; Michael Bakunin, 1937; The Twenty Years' Crisis, 1919-39, 1939; Britain: A Study of Foreign Policy from Versailles to the Outbreak of War, 1939; Conditions of Peace, 1942; Nationalism and After, 1945; The Soviet Impact on the Western World, 1946; Studies in Revolution, 1950; A History of Soviet Russia: The Bolshevik Revolution, 1917-1923, Vol. I, 1950, Vol. II, 1952, Vol. III, 1953; The Interregnum, 1923-1924, 1954; Socialism in One Country, 1924-26, Vol. I, 1958; Vol. II, 1959, Vol. III (in 2 parts), 1964; Foundations of a Planned Economy, 1926-1929, Vol. I (in 2 parts, in collaboration with R. W. Davies), 1969, Vol. II, 1971, Vol. III (2 parts), 1976; German-Soviet Relations Between the Two World Wars, 1919-39, 1951; The New Society, 1951; What is History?, 1961; 1917: Before and After, 1968. *Address:* Trinity College, Cambridge; Dales Barn, Barton, Cambs.

CARR, Dr Eric Francis, FRCP, FRCPsych; Senior Principal Medical Officer, Department of Health and Social Security, since 1976; *b* 23 Sept. 1919; *s* of Edward Francis Carr and Maude Mary Almond; *m* 1954, Janet Gilfillan; two *s* one *d. Educ:* Mill Hill Sch.; Emmanuel Coll., Cambridge. MA, MB BChir; FRCP, FRCPsych; DPM. Captain, RAMC, 1944-46. Consultant Psychiatrist: St Ebba's Hosp., 1954-60; Netherne Hosp., 1960-67; Epsom and West Park Hosps, 1967-76; Hon. Consultant Psychiatrist, KCH, 1960-76. Fellow, RSocMed. *Recreations:* reading, listening to music, cooking. *Address:* Pemberley, The Marld, Ashtead, Surrey. *T:* Ashtead 74254.

CARR, Frank George Griffith, CB 1967; CBE 1954; MA, LLB; FSA; FRAS; Associate RINA; FRInstNav; Director of the National Maritime Museum, Greenwich, SE10, 1947-66; *b* 23 April 1903; *e s* of Frank Carr, MA, LLD, and Agnes Maud Todd, Cambridge; *m* 1932, Ruth, *d* of Harold Hamilton Burkitt, Ballycastle, Co. Antrim; no *c. Educ:* Perse and Trinity Hall, Cambridge. BA 1926; LLB 1928; MA 1939. Studied at LCC Sch. of Navigation and took Yacht Master's (Deep Sea) BoT Certificate, 1927; Cambridge Univ.: Squire Law Scholar, 1922; Capt. of Boats, Trinity Hall, 1926; Pres., Law Soc., 1924; Vice-Pres., Conservative Assoc., 1925; Pres., Nat. Union of Students, 1925; Ed., The Cambridge Gownsman, 1925. Asst Librarian, House of Lords, 1929-47. Served War of 1939-45, RNVR, Lt-Comdr. Chm., Cutty Sark Ship Management Cttee, 1952-72; Mem., HMS Victory Advisory Technical Cttee, 1948-76; Vice-President: Soc. for Nautical Research; Foudroyant Trust; Internat. Sailing Craft Assocn; Governor, HMS Unicorn Preservation Soc. James Monroe Award, 1974. *Publications:* Sailing Barges, 1931; Vanishing Craft, 1934; A Yachtsman's Log, 1935; The Yachtsman's England, 1936; The Yacht Master's Guide, 1940; (jtly) The Medley of Mast and Sail, 1976; Leslie A. Wilcox, RI, RSMA, 1977; numerous articles in yachting periodicals, etc. *Recreations:* yacht cruising; nautical research. *Address:* Lime Tree House, 10 Park Gate, Blackheath, SE3. *T:* 01-852 5181. *Clubs:* Athenæum, Royal Cruising, Cruising Association; Cambridge University Cruising (Cambridge).

CARR, Sir (Frederick) Bernard, Kt 1946; CMG 1944; *b* 5 April 1893; *s* of F. W. Carr; *m* 1933, Doreen Dadds; two *d. Educ:* Whitgift. TA Artists' Rifles and Middx Regt, 1911-18; seconded Royal West African Frontier Force, 1917-18; active service, Gibraltar, Egypt, France, East Africa. Colonial Administrative Service, 1919 (Nigeria); Chief Comr, Eastern Provinces, Nigeria, 1943; retired from Colonial Service, 1949. Chief Sec., Eritrea, 1949-50. *Address:* c/o Lloyds Bank, 6 Pall Mall, SW1.

CARR, Henry Lambton, CMG 1945; MVO 1957; retired 1961; *b* 28 Nov. 1899; *e s* of Archibald Lambton and Ella Carr, Archangel; *m* 1924, Luba (*d* 1975), *d* of John George Edmund Eveleigh, London; two *s. Educ:* Haileybury Coll. Served N Russian Exped. Force (2nd Lieut), 1919. Foreign Office, 1920. HBM Passport Control Officer for Finland, 1927-41; Attaché at British Legation, Stockholm, 1941-45; Foreign Office, 1945; First Sec., HM Embassy, Copenhagen, 1955; Foreign Office, 1958. Chevalier (First Grade) of Order of Dannebrog, Denmark, 1957. *Recreation:* walking. *Address:* The Links, Forest Row, East Sussex. *T:* Forest Row 2091; c/o Barclays Bank, East Grinstead, West Sussex. *Clubs:* Royal Automobile, Danish.

CARR, Herbert Reginald Culling, MA; Headmaster, The Grammar School, Harrogate, Yorks, 1934-60; retired; *b* 16 July 1896; *s* of late Reginald Childers Culling Carr, OBE (ICS), and Enid Agnes Kenney Herbert; *m* 1927, Evelyn Dorothy Ritchie; one *d. Educ:* St Paul's Sch.; Pembroke Coll., Oxford (Open Scholar). Hons Modern History (2nd Class); Diplomas in Educn and Econs. Asst Master, Alleyn's Sch., Dulwich, 1927-31;

Headmaster, Penrith Grammar Sch., Cumberland, 1931-34. Sub-Lieut RNVR, 1915-19; Flt-Lieut RAFVR, 1940-44 (Africa Star). *Publication:* The Mountains of Snowdonia, 1925. *Recreation:* antiques. *Address:* 22 The Abbey House, Cirencester, Glos GL7 2QU. *T:* Cirencester 4442.

CARR, Air Marshal Sir John Darcy B.; *see* Baker-Carr.

CARR, Rear-Adm. Lawrence George, CB 1971, DSC 1954; Chief of Naval Staff, New Zealand, and Member of the Defence Council, 1969-72; management consultant; *b* 31 Jan. 1920; *s* of late George Henry Carr and late Susan Elizabeth Carr; unmarried. *Educ:* Wellington Technical Coll., NZ; Victoria Coll., Univ. of New Zealand. Served War: entered RNZNVR, 1941; commissioned, 1942; on loan to RN, in HM Destroyers in N Atlantic, Medit., W Af. Coast, Eng. Channel, 1941-44; HMNZS Achilles in Pacific Theatre and NZ, 1945-46; permanent Commn, RNZN, 1946. Qual. as communications specialist, 1947; served in: British Medit. Fleet, 1948; RNZN, 1949-; various appts.; in command HMNZS Kaniere, in Korea, 1953-54 (DSC); Comdr Dec. 1953; Exec. Officer, HMNZS Philomel, 1954-55; jssc, 1956; Deputy Chief of Naval Personnel, 1957-59; Qual. Sen. Officers War Coll., Greenwich, 1959-60; Captain June 1960; in command HMNZS: Philomel, 1960-62, Taranaki, 1962-64; idc 1965; Commodore, Auckland, 1966-68. Chief of Naval Personnel, Second Naval Mem., NZ Naval Bd, 1968-69. Nat. Parly Cand., Nov. 1972; Chm., Nat. Party, Pakuranga Electorate, 1976. Mem., Spirit of Adventure Trust Bd; Patron, Coastguard (NZ); first Vice-Pres., United Way. *Recreations:* golf, fishing, shooting, sailing, tennis, chess. *Address:* c/o Bank of New Zealand (Te Aro), Wellington, New Zealand; (home) 57 Pigeon Mountain Road, Half Moon Bay, Auckland, New Zealand. *T:* Howick 49692. *Clubs:* Wellington, United Service Officers (Auckland); Royal New Zealand Yacht Squadron.

CARR, Philippa; *see* Hibbert, Eleanor.

CARR, Raymond; *see* Carr, A. R. M.

CARR, Dr Thomas Ernest Ashdown, CB 1977; Senior Principal Medical Officer in charge of General Practitioner and Regional Medical Service, Department of Health and Social Security, since 1967; *b* 21 June 1915; *s* of late Laurence H. A. Carr, MScTech, MIEE, ARPS, Stockport, and late Norah E. V. Carr (*née* Taylor); *m* 1940, Mary Sybil (*née* Dunkey); one *s* two *d*. *Educ:* County High Sch. for Boys, Altrincham; Victoria Univ. of Manchester (BSc). MB, ChB 1939; FRCGP 1968; FFCM 1972; DObstRCOG. Jun. hosp. posts, Manchester and Ipswich, 1939-41; RAMC, UK and NW Europe, 1941-46; GP, Highcliffe, Hants, 1947; Mem. Hants Local Med. Cttee, 1952-55; Min. of Health: Regional Med. Officer, Southampton, 1956; Sen. Med. Officer, 1963; Principal Med. Officer, 1966. Provost of SE England Faculty 1962-64, Mem. Council 1964-66, RCGP; Mem. Exec. Cttee, Lambeth and Southwark Div., BMA, 1975-. FRSocMed. *Publications:* papers on NHS practice organisation in Medical World, Practitioner, Update, faculty jls of RCGP, Proc. of RSM. *Recreations:* playing and listening to music, skin diving, amateur cinematography, holidays abroad. *Address:* Tollgate House, 2 Pilgrims Way, Guildford, Surrey. *T:* (home) Guildford 63012, (office) 01-703 5522. *Clubs:* Civil Service; Yvonne Arnaud Theatre (Guildford).

CARR, William Compton; *b* 10 July 1918; *m*; two *s* one *d*. *Educ:* The Leys Sch., Cambridge. MP (C) Barons Court, 1959-64; PPS to Min. of State, Board of Trade, 1963; PPS to Financial Sec. to the Treasury, 1963-64. *Recreations:* reading, theatre-going, skin diving, eating, dieting.

CARR, Sir William (Emsley), Kt 1957; FRSA; Chairman: News of the World Organisation, 1960-69; News of the World Ltd, 1952-69 (now Life President of the Companies (called News International Ltd) and Consultant to the Board); Bees, Ltd, 1970-73; *b* 30 May 1912; *y s* of late Sir Emsley and Lady Carr; *m* 1938, Jean Mary Forsyth; one *s* one *d*. *Educ:* Clifton Coll.; Trinity Coll., Cambridge (BA). News of the World, 1937-. Vice-Patron, Amateur Athletic Assoc.; President: Artisan Golfers' Assoc.; Press Golfing Soc.; London Newspapers Golf Soc.; Counties Athletic Union; Vice-President: Professional Golfers' Assoc.; Llangollen Eisteddfod; Cartoonists Club. *Recreation:* sport. *Address:* Cliveden House, Cliveden Place, SW1; Bentley Wood, Halland, Sussex. *Clubs:* Buck's, Crockford's; Lucifer Golfing Society; Walton Heath Golf (Chm. 1948); Royal and Ancient Golf; Oxford and Cambridge Golfing Society.

CARR, Brig. William Greenwood, CVO 1971; DSO 1941 and Bar, 1942; DL, JP; Lieutenant of the Queen's Bodyguard of the Yeomen of the Guard, 1970-71; *b* 10 March 1901; *s* of William

Carr, DL, JP, Ditchingham Hall, Norfolk; *m* 1928, Donna Nennella, *d* of General Count Salazar, via Umbria, Rome; one *d*. *Educ:* Eton; University Coll., Oxford. Commnd in 12th Royal Lancers, 1922; Capt. and Adjt, 1925; comdg: 4th Co. of London Yeomanry, 1939; Comdg 22nd Armd Bde (8th Army), Comdg RACOCTU, Sandhurst, 1943; Brig. British Staff, GHQ, SW Pacific, 1944-45; retd 1946. Queen's Bodyguard Yeomen of the Guard: Exon, 1950; Ensign, 1954; Lieut, 1970; retired 1971. Represented England at Olympic Games (riding), 1936. JP Norfolk 1953, DL Norfolk 1961. *Recreations:* hunting, shooting, sailing. *Address:* Ditchingham Hall, Norfolk. *T:* Woodton 226; 3 Chesterfield Street, Mayfair, W1. *T:* 01-629 5725. *Clubs:* Cavalry and Guards; Royal Yacht Squadron.
See also Earl Ferrers.

CARR-ELLISON, Sir Ralph (Harry), Kt 1973; TD 1962; Chairman: Northumbrian Water Authority, since 1973; Tyne Tees Television Ltd, since 1974 (Director since 1966); Deputy Chairman, Trident Television, since 1976 (Director, since 1972); *b* 8 Dec. 1925; *s* of late Major John Campbell Carr-Ellison; *m* 1951, Mary Clare, *d* of late Major Arthur McMorrough Kavanagh, MC; three *s* one *d*. *Educ:* Eton. Served Royal Glos Hussars and 1st Royal Dragoons, 1944-49; Northumberland Hussars (TA), (Lt-Col Comdg), 1949-69; TAVR Col, Northumbrian Dist, 1969-72; Col, Dep. Comdr (TAVR), NE Dist, 1973; Chm., N of England TA&VRA, 1976-. ADC (TAVR) to HM the Queen, 1970-75. Co. Comr, Northumberland Scouts, 1958-68; Mem. Cttee of Council, Scout Assoc., 1960-67. Chm., Berwick-on-Tweed Constituency Cons. Assoc., 1959-62, Pres., 1973-77; Northern Area Cons. Assocs: Treas., 1961-66, Chm., 1966-69; Pres., 1974-; Vice Chm., Nat Union of Cons. and Unionist Assocs, 1969-71. Director, Newcastle & Gateshead Water Co., 1964-73. Governor, Swinton Conservative College, 1967-. High Sheriff of Northumberland, 1972; JP Northumberland, 1953-75. *Recreation:* Jt Master, West Percy Foxhounds, 1950-. *Address:* Hedgeley Hall, Powburn, Alnwick, Northumberland NE66 4HZ. *T:* Powburn 273; (office) Powburn 272. *Clubs:* Cavalry and Guards, Pratt's; Northern Counties (Newcastle upon Tyne).

CARR LINFORD, Alan, RWS 1955 (ARWS 1949); ARE 1946; ARCA 1946; *b* 15 Jan. 1926; *m* 1948, Margaret Dorothea Parish; one *s* one *d*. *Educ:* Royal College of Art, and in Rome. Was awarded the Prix de Rome, 1947. *Recreation:* shooting. *Address:* Midfield, Lower Green, Wimbish, Saffron Walden, Essex CB10 2XH. *T:* Radwinter 287.

CARREL, Philip, CMG 1960; OBE 1954; Committee Secretary, Overseas Relations, Institute of Chartered Accountants in England and Wales, since 1961; *b* 23 Sept. 1915; *s* of late Louis Raymond Carrel and Lucy Mabel (*née* Cooper); *m* 1948, Eileen Mary Bullock (*née* Hainworth); one *s* one *d*. *Educ:* Blundell's; Balliol. Colonial Admin. Service, 1938, Zanzibar Protectorate. EA Forces, 1940. Civil Affairs, 1941-47 (OETA); Civilian Employee Civil Affairs, GHQ MELF, 1947-49 (on secondment from Som. Prot.); Colonial Admin. Service (Somaliland Protectorate), 1947; Commissioner of Somali Affairs, 1953; Chief Sec. to the Government, Somaliland Protectorate, 1959-60. *Address:* Lych Gates, Chiltley Lane, Liphook, Hants. *T:* 722150.

CARRERAS, Sir James, Kt 1970; MBE 1945; Special Adviser to EMI Group of Companies, since 1973; *b* 30 Jan. 1909; *s* of Henry and Dolores Carreras; *m* 1927, Vera St John; one *s*. *Educ:* privately. Chm. and Chief Exec., Hammer Film Prodns Ltd, 1946-73; Director: Studio Film Laboratories Ltd; National Screen Service; Services Kinema Corp. Deputy Chairman, Royal Naval Film Corporation, 1961; Chairman, Variety International Exec. Bd, 1965. Hon. Chm. and Trustee, Friends of Duke of Edinburgh's Award Scheme; Chm., Sobell Variety Islington Trust; Dep. Chm., Police Dependents Trust; Trustee: Young Volunteer Force Foundn; Attlee Memorial Foundation; Bowles Rocks Trust Ltd. Mem. Council, Cinema and Television Benevolent Fund; Vice-Pres., The London Fedn of Boys' Clubs. Knight Grand Band, Order of African Redemption (Liberia), 1968; Grand Order of Civil Merit (Spain), 1974. *Recreation:* golf. *Address:* The White House, Bolney Avenue, Shiplake, Oxon.

CARRICK, 9th Earl of, *cr* 1748; **Brian Stuart Theobald Somerset Caher Butler;** Baron Butler (UK), 1912; Viscount Ikerrin, 1629; *b* 17 Aug. 1931; *o s* of 8th Earl of Carrick; *S* father, 1957; *m* 1951, (Mary) Belinda (marr. diss. 1976) *e d* of Major David Constable-Maxwell, TD, Bosworth Hall, near Rugby; one *s* one *d*. *Educ:* Downside. Dir., The Bowater Corp. Ltd; Chm. and Man. Dir, Ralli Brothers (Trading) Ltd; Chairman: Ralli Brothers and Coney Ltd; Maclaine Watson and Co. Ltd; Malcolm Maclaine and Co. Ltd; Duncan Fox and Co. Ltd;

Director: Nauman Gepp and Co. Ltd; Reynolds and Gibson Ltd; Kay Corporation Inc.; Van Ekris and Stoett Inc.; Ralli Hong Kong Ltd; Ralli Europe BV; Van Doon and Co. BV. Member: Council and GPC London Chamber of Commerce and Industry; Hispanic and Luzo-Brazilian Councils; Canning House Economic Affairs Council Ltd. *Heir: s* Viscount Ikerrin, *qv* . *Address:* 10 Netherton Grove, SW10. *T:* 01-352 6328. *Club:* Pratt's.

CARRICK, Edward; *see* Craig, E. A.

CARRICK, Roger John, MVO 1972; HM Diplomatic Service; Visiting Fellow, Institute of International Studies, University of California at Berkeley, 1977-78; *b* 13 Oct. 1937; *s* of John H. and Florence M. Carrick; *m* 1962, Hilary Elizabeth Blinman; two *s* . *Educ:* Isleworth Grammar Sch.; Sch. of Slavonic and East European Studies, London Univ. Served RN, 1956-58. Entered FO, 1956; SSEES, 1961; Sofia, 1962; FO, 1965; Paris, 1967; Singapore, 1971; FCO, 1973; Counsellor and Dep. Head, Personnel Ops Dept, FCO, 1976. *Recreations:* water sports, racquet games, music, reading, avoiding gardening. *Address:* c/o Foreign and Commonwealth Office, SW1A 2AH; 43 Dornden Drive, Langton Green, Tunbridge Wells, Kent TN3 0AE. *T:* Tunbridge Wells 862495. *Club:* Royal Commonwealth Society.

CARRICK, Maj.-Gen. Thomas Welsh, OBE 1959; Specialist in Community Medicine, Camden and Islington Area Health Authority (Teaching), since 1975; *b* 19 Dec. 1914; *s* of late George Carrick and late Mary Welsh; *m* 1948, Nan Middleton Allison; one *s* . *Educ:* Glasgow Academy; Glasgow Univ.; London Sch. of Hygiene and Tropical Med. MB, ChB 1937, FFCM 1972, DPH 1951, DIH 1961. House appts in medicine, surgery and urological surgery at Glasgow Royal Infirmary, 1937-38; Dep. Supt, Glasgow Royal Infirmary, 1939-40. Commissioned, RAMC, 1940. Later service appts include: Asst Dir, Army Health, 17 Gurkha Div., Malaya, 1961-63; Asst Dir, Army Health, HQ Scotland, 1964-65; Dir Army Personnel Research Establt, 1965-68; Dep. Dir, Army Health, Strategic Command, 1968-70; Prof. of Army Health, Royal Army Med. Coll., 1970; Dir of Army Health and Research, MoD, 1971-72; Comdt and Postgraduate Dean, Royal Army Medical Coll., Millbank, 1973-75, retd. Col Comdt, RAMC, 1975-. Blackham Lectr, RIPH 1977. QHS 1973. OStJ 1946. *Publications:* articles in Jl of RAMC, Army Review, Community Health. *Recreations:* gardening, walking, theatre. *Address:* 81 Lauderdale Tower, The Barbican, EC2.

CARRINGTON, 6th Baron (Ireland) *cr* 1796, (Great Britain) *cr* 1797; **Peter Alexander Rupert Carington,** PC 1959; KCMG 1958; MC 1945; Leader of the Opposition in the House of Lords, 1964-70, and since Oct. 1974; *b* 6 June 1919; *s* of 5th Baron and Hon. Sibyl Marion (*d* 1946), *d* of 2nd Viscount Colville; *S* father, 1938; *m* 1942, Iona, *yr d* of late Sir Francis McClean; one *s* two *d*. *Educ:* Eton Coll.; RMC Sandhurst. Served NW Europe, Major Grenadier Guards. Parly Sec., Min. of Agriculture and Fisheries, 1951-54; Parly Sec., Min. of Defence, Oct. 1954-Nov. 1956; High Comr for the UK in Australia, Nov. 1956-Oct. 1959; First Lord of the Admiralty, 1959-63; Minister without Portfolio and Leader of the House of Lords, 1963-64; Secretary of State: for Defence, 1970-74; for Energy, 1974; Minister of Aviation Supply, 1971-74. Chm., Cons. Party Organisation, 1972-74. Chairman, Australia and New Zealand Bank Ltd, 1967-70; Director: Barclays Bank, 1967-70, 1974-; Cadbury Schweppes Ltd, 1969-70, 1974-; Rio Tinto Zinc Corp. 1974-; Barclays Bank International, 1975-; British Metal Corp., 1965-68; Amalgamated Metal Corpn Ltd, 1969-70; Schweppes Ltd, 1968-69; Hambros Bank, 1967-70. Pres., Iran Soc., 1974-. JP 1948, DL Bucks. Fellow of Eton Coll., 1966. *Heir: s* Hon. Rupert Francis John Carington, *b* 2 Dec. 1948. *Address:* 32a Ovington Square, SW3. *T:* 01-584 1476; The Manor House, Bledlow, near Aylesbury, Bucks. *T:* Princes Risborough 3499. *Clubs:* Turf, Beefsteak, Pratt's, White's, Carlton.
See also Baron Ashcombe.

CARRINGTON, Prof. Alan, FRS 1971; Professor of Chemistry, University of Southampton, since 1967; *b* 6 Jan. 1934; *o s* of Albert Carrington and Constance (*née* Nelson); *m* 1959, Noreen Hilary Taylor; one *s* two *d*. *Educ:* Colfe's Grammar Sch.; Univ. of Southampton. BSc, MA, PhD. Univ. of Cambridge: Asst in Research, 1960; Fellow of Downing Coll., 1960; Asst Dir of Res., 1963. Tilden Lectr, Chem. Soc., 1972; Snr Fellowship, SRC, 1976. Harrison Mem. Prize, Chem. Soc., 1962; Meldola Medal, Royal Inst. of Chemistry, 1963; Marlow Medal, Faraday Soc., 1966; Corday Morgan Medal, Chem. Soc., 1967; Chem. Soc. Award in Structural Chemistry, 1970. *Publications:* (with A. D. McLachlan) Introduction to Magnetic Resonance, 1967; Microwave Spectroscopy of Free Radicals, 1974; numerous

papers on topics in chemical physics in various learned jls. *Recreations:* family, music, fishing, golf, sailing. *Address:* 46 Lakewood Road, Chandler's Ford, Hants. *T:* Chandler's Ford 5092.

CARRINGTON, Charles Edmund, MC; writer and lecturer; *b* West Bromwich, 21 April 1897; *s* of late Very Rev. C. W. Carrington; *m* 1st, 1932, Cecil Grace MacGregor (marr. diss., 1954); one *d* decd; 2nd, 1955, Maysie Cuthbert Robertson. *Educ:* Christ's Coll., New Zealand; Christ Church, Oxford. Enlisted, 1914; first commission, 1915; Capt. 5th Royal Warwickshire Regt, 1917; served in France and Italy (MC); Major TA, 1927. BA Oxford, 1921; MA 1929; MA Cambridge, 1929. Asst Master, Haileybury Coll., 1921-24 and 1926-29; Lectr, Pembroke Coll., Oxford, 1924-25; Educational Sec. to the Cambridge Univ. Press, 1929-54. Military service, 1939, France, 1940; Lt-Col Gen. Staff, 1941-45. Prof. of British Commonwealth Relations at Royal Inst. of Internat. Affairs, 1954-62; organised unofficial Commonwealth conferences, New Zealand, 1959, Nigeria, 1962; Visiting Prof., USA, 1964-65. Has served on: LCC Educn Cttee; Classical Assoc. Council; Publishers Assoc. Educational Group; Royal Commonwealth Soc. Council; Inter-Univ. Council; Overseas Migration Board, Islington Soc., etc; Chm. Shoreditch Housing Assoc., 1961-67. *Publications:* An Exposition of Empire, 1947; The British Overseas, 1950; Godley of Canterbury, 1951; Rudyard Kipling, 1955; The Liquidation of the British Empire, 1961; Soldier from the Wars Returning, 1965; (ed) The Complete Barrack-Room Ballads of Rudyard Kipling, 1973; A History of England (with J. Hampden Jackson), 1932; (under pen-name of Charles Edmonds) A Subaltern's War, 1929; T. E. Lawrence, 1935; contributor to: Camb. Hist. of the British Empire, 1959; An African Survey, 1957; Surveys of International Affairs, 1957-58 and 1959-60, etc. *Recreations:* historical studies, travel. *Address:* 56 Canonbury Park South, N1. *T:* 01-226 9486. *Club:* Travellers'.

CARROLL, Ven. Charles William Desmond; Archdeacon of Blackburn, since 1973; Vicar of Balderstone, since 1973; *b* 27 Jan. 1919; *s* of Rev. William and Mrs L. Mary Carroll; *m* 1945, Doreen Daisy Ruskell; three *s* one *d* . *Educ:* St Columba Coll.; Trinity Coll., Dublin. BA 1943; Dip. Ed. Hons 1945; MA 1946. Asst Master: Kingstown Grammar Sch., 1943-45; Rickerby House Sch., 1945-50; Vicar of Stanwix, Carlisle, 1950-59; Hon. Canon of Blackburn, 1959; Dir of Religious Education, 1959; Hon. Chaplain to Bishop of Blackburn, 1961; Canon Residentiary of Blackburn Cathedral, 1964. *Publication:* Management for Managers, 1968. *Address:* Balderstone Vicarage, Blackburn, Lancs BB2 7LL. *Clubs:* Royal Commonwealth Society; Rotary (Blackburn).

CARROLL, Maj.-Gen. Derek Raymond, OBE 1958; Driver and Operator, Family Coach Firm, since 1975; *b* 2 Jan. 1919; *er s* of late Raymond Carroll and Edith Lisle Carroll; *m* 1946, Bettina Mary, *d* of late Leslie Gould; one *s* two *d*. Enlisted TA, 1939; commnd into Royal Engineers, 1943; served Western Desert, 1941-43, Italy, 1943-44; psc 1945; various appts, 1944-66, in Germany, Sudan Defence Force, Libya, Malaya, CRE 4 Div., 1962-64; comd 12 Engr Bde, 1966-67; idc 1968; Chief Engr, BAOR, 1970-73; RARO, 1973. Bus driver, East Kent Road Car Co., 1974. Immigration Officer, Ramsgate Hoverport, 1975. *Recreation:* sailing. *Address:* c/o Barclays Bank Ltd, Wimbledon Broadway, SW19 1PU. *Club:* Royal Ocean Racing.

CARROLL, Madeleine; screen, stage, and radio actress; *d* of John Carroll, Co. Limerick, and Hélène de Rosière Tuaillon, Paris; *m* 1st, 1931, Capt. Philip Astley, MC (from whom she obtd a divorce, 1940); 2nd, 1942, Lieut Sterling Hayden, USMC (from whom she obtd a divorce, 1946); 3rd, 1946, Henri Lavorel (marr. diss.); 4th, 1950, Andrew Heiskell (marr. diss.); one *d*. *Educ:* private sch.; Birmingham Univ. (BA Hons French). Started theatrical career in touring company, playing French maid in The Lash; subsequently toured with Seymour Hicks in Mr What's his Name; became leading lady in British films as result of first screen test for The Guns of Loos; subsequently made Young Woodley, The School for Scandal, I was a Spy, and The Thirty Nine Steps; came to America in 1936 and made: The Case against Mrs Ames; The General Died at Dawn; Lloyds of London; On the Avenue; The Prisoner of Zenda; Blockade; Café Society; North-West Mounted Police; Virginia; One Night in Lisbon; Bahama Passage; My Favourite Blonde; White Cradle Inn; An Innocent Affair; The Fan. Radio appearances include the leading parts in: Cavalcade; Beloved Enemy; Romance; There's always Juliet. From 1941 until end of War, engaged exclusively in war activities.

CARRUTHERS, Alwyn Guy; Deputy Director of Statistics, Department of Employment, since 1972; *b* 6 May 1925; *yr s* of late John Sendall and of Lily Eden Carruthers, Grimsby; *m* 1950, Edith Eileen, *o d* of William and late Edith Addison Lumb; no *c. Educ:* Wintringham Grammar Sch.,, Grimsby; King's Coll., London Univ. BA First Cl. Hons in Mathematics, Drew Gold Medal and Prize, 1945. RAE, Farnborough, 1945-46; Instructor Lieut, RN, 1946-49; Rothamsted Experimental Station, 1949. Postgraduate Diploma in Mathematical Statistics Christ's Coll., Cambridge, 1951. Bd of Trade, Statistics Division: Asst Statistician, 1951; Statistician, 1954; Chief Statistician, 1962; Asst Dir, 1968; Dep. Dir, 1968-70; Head of Statistics Div., DTI, 1970-72. *Recreations:* gardening, music. *Address:* 24 Red House Lane, Bexleyheath, Kent. *T:* 01-303 4898.

CARRUTHERS, James Edwin; Under Secretary, Department of Industry, since 1977; seconded as Assistant to Chairman, British Aerospace, since 1977 (Secretary, Organising Committee, 1975-77); *b* 19 March 1928; *er s* of James and Dollie Carruthers; *m* 1955, Phyllis Williams; one *s. Educ:* George Heriot's Sch.; Edinburgh Univ. (MA; Medallist in Scottish Hist.). FSAScot. Lieut, The Queen's Own Cameron Highlanders, 1949-51, and TA, 1951-55. Air Ministry: Asst Principal, 1951; Private Sec. to DCAS, 1955; Asst Private Sec. to Sec. of State for Air, 1956; Principal, 1956; Min. of Aviation, 1960-62; Private Secretary: to Minister of Defence for RAF, 1965-67; to Parly Under Sec. of State for RAF, 1967; Asst Sec., 1967; Chief Officer, Sovereign Base Areas Admin, Cyprus, 1968-71; Dep. Chief of Public Relations, MoD, 1971-72; Private Sec. to Chancellor of Duchy of Lancaster, Cabinet Office, 1973-74; DoI, 1975-. Mem., Chorleywood UDC, 1964-65. *Recreations:* archaeology, gardening, travel. *Address:* 129 Valley Road, Chorleywood, Herts WD3 4BN. *T:* Rickmansworth 76020.

CARSE, William Mitchell, CBE 1953; *b* 23 Aug. 1899; *o s* of Robert Allison Carse, Hawkhead, Renfrewshire; *m* 1928, Helen Knox (*d* 1976), *yr d* of J. B. Beaton, Milliken Park, Renfrewshire; one *s. Educ:* Glasgow High Sch.; Glasgow Univ.; Wellington Military Coll., Madras; St John's Coll., Cambridge. Passed Examination for RMC Sandhurst, 1917; proceeded to Wellington Military Coll., Madras, 1918; gazetted to Indian Army, 1918; served in South Persia until 1920; resigned Commission; entered HM Consular Service, 1923; served in USA, Guatemala, Germany, Portuguese East Africa, Portugal and Portuguese West Africa; Consul-Gen., Loanda, Angola, 1937-39; Consul at Teneriffe, 1939; Consul-Gen. at Reykjavik, Iceland, 1943; attached to British Political Mission in Hungary, 1945-46; Consul-Gen. at Tabriz, Persia, 1946-47, and at Ahwaz Persia, 1948, Deputy High Comr for the UK in Peshawar, Pakistan, 1948-51; Consul-Gen., São Paulo, Brazil, 1951-56, retd. Appointed to Distillers Company Ltd. (Industrial Group), London, 1957. *Recreations:* yachting, riding, chess. *Address:* Little Dene, St Alban's Road, Reigate, Surrey.

CARSON, Hon. Edward; Lieutenant Life Guards; *b* 17 Feb. 1920; *yr s* of Baron Carson, a Lord of Appeal in Ordinary; *m* 1943, Heather, *d* of Lt-Col Frank Sclater, OBE, MC; one *s* one *d. Educ:* Eton; Trinity Hall, Cambridge. MP (C) Isle of Thanet Div. of Kent, 1945-53. *Address:* 5 Old Timbertop Cottages, Bethel Road, Sevenoaks, Kent. *T:* Sevenoaks 59147. *Clubs:* Wig and Pen, MCC.

CARSON, John; MP (UU) Belfast North, since Feb. 1974; Draper; *b* 1933. Member of the Orange Order; Member, Belfast District Council, (formerly Belfast Corporation), 1971-; Official Unionist Councillor for Duncairn. *Address:* House of Commons, SW1A 0AA; 15 Waterloo Park, South Belfast BT15 5HX.

CARSON, Air Cdre Robert John, CBE 1974; AFC 1964; Defence Adviser to British High Commissioner in Canada, since 1975; *b* 3 Aug. 1924; *e s* of Robert George and Margaret Etta Helena Carson; *m* 1945, Jane, *yr d* of James and Jane Bailie; three *d. Educ:* Regent House Sch., Newtownards, NI; RAF. MBIM, Mem., Inst. of Admin. Management. India, Burma, Malaya, 1945-48; Rhodesia, 1949-50; Queens Univ. Air Sqdn, 1951-52; RAF HC Examining Unit, 1952-53; AHQ Iraq, 1953-54; RAF Staff Coll., 1955; Plans, Air Min., 1956-59; 16 Sqdn, Laarbruch, Germany, 1959-62; Wing Comdr Flying, RAF Swinderby, 1962-64; Air Warfare Coll., Manby, 1964; Chief Nuclear Ops, 2ATAF Germany, 1965-67; JSSC Latimer, 1967; Chief Air Planner, UK Delegn, Live Oak, SHAPE, 1968-71; Station Comdr, RAF Leeming, 1971-73; Overseas Coll. Defence Studies, Canada, 1973-74; Air Adviser, British High Commission, Ottawa, 1974-75. Queen's Commendation (Air) 1962. *Recreations:* Rugby, tennis, golf, gardening. *Address:* 20 Meadow Drive, Scruton, near Northallerton, North Yorks. *T:* Kirkby Fleetham 656; c/o Lloyds Bank, 6 Pall Mall, SW1. *Clubs:* Royal Air Force; Rideau (Ottawa).

CARSTAIRS, Charles Young, CB 1968; CMG 1950; *b* 30 Oct. 1910; *s* of late Rev. Dr G. Carstairs, DD; *m* 1939, Frances Mary, *o d* of late Dr Claude Lionel Coode, Stroud, Glos; one *s* one *d. Educ:* George Watson's Boys' Coll., Edinburgh; Edinburgh Univ. Entered Home Civil Service, 1934, Dominions Office; transf. Colonial Office, 1935; Asst Private Sec. to Sec. of State for the Colonies, 1936; Private Sec. to Perm. Under-Sec. of State for the Colonies, 1937; Asst Sec., West India Royal Commn, 1938-39; Sec., Colonial Research Cttee, 1944-47; Administrative Sec., Development and Welfare Organisation, British West Indies, 1947-50; Sec., British Caribbean Standing Closer Assoc. Cttee, 1948-49; Dir of Information Services, Colonial Office, 1951-53, Asst Under-Sec., 1953-62; Deputy Sec., Medical Research Council, 1962-65; Under-Secretary, MPBW: Directorate-Gen., R and D, 1965-67, Construction Economics, 1967-70; Special Advr, Expenditure Cttee, House of Commons, 1971-75; on staff of clerk of the Parliaments, House of Lords, 1976-77. *Address:* St Kea, 9 Ridgegate Close, Reigate, Surrey. *T:* Reigate 44896. *Club:* Athenæum.

CARSTAIRS, Prof. George Morrison, MD; FRCPE, FRCPsych; Vice-Chancellor, University of York, 1974-Aug. 1978; working in India, from Aug. 1978; *b* Mussoorie, India, 18 June 1916; *s* of late Rev. Dr George Carstairs, DD, K-i-H, and Elizabeth H. Carstairs; *m* 1950, Vera Hunt; two *s* one *d. Educ:* George Watson's Coll., Edinburgh; Edinburgh Univ. Asst Phys., Royal Edinburgh Hosp., 1942. MO, RAF, 1942-46. Commonwealth Fellow, USA, 1948-49; Rockefeller Research Fellow, 1950-51; Henderson Res. Schol., 1951-52; Sen. Registrar, Maudsley Hosp., 1953; Scientific Staff, MRC, 1954-60; Prof. of Psychiatry, Univ. of Edinburgh, 1961-73. Dir, MRC Unit for Research on Epidemiological Aspects of Psychiatry, 1960-71. Reith Lectr, 1962. Pres., World Federation for Mental Health, 1967-71. *Publications:* The Twice Born, 1957; This Island Now, 1963; The Great Universe of Kota, 1976; chapters and articles in medical publications. *Recreations:* travel, theatre; formerly athletics (Scottish Champion 3 miler, 1937-39). *Address:* Vice-Chancellor's House, University of York, York YO1 5DD.

CARSTEN, Prof. Francis Ludwig, DPhil, DLitt Oxon; FBA 1971; Masaryk Professor of Central European History in the University of London since 1961; *b* 25 June 1911; *s* of Prof. Paul Carsten and Frida Carsten (*née* Born); *m* 1945, Ruth Carsten (*née* Moses); two *s* one *d. Educ:* Heidelberg, Berlin and Oxford Univs. Barnett scholar, Wadham Coll., Oxford, 1939; Senior Demy, Magdalen Coll., Oxford, 1942; Lectr in History, Westfield Coll., Univ. of London, 1947; Reader in Modern History, Univ. of London, 1960. Editor, Slavonic and East European Review, 1966-. *Publications:* The Origins of Prussia, 1954; Princes and Parliaments in Germany from the 15th to the 18th Century, 1959; The Reichswehr and Politics, 1918-1933, 1966; The Rise of Fascism, 1967 (rev. edn, 1970); Revolution in Central Europe, 1918-1919, 1972; Fascist Movements in Austria, 1977; ed and contributor, The New Cambridge Modern History, vol. V: The Ascendancy of France, 1961; articles in English Historical Review, History, Survey, Historische Zeitschrift, etc. *Recreations:* gardening, climbing, swimming. *Address:* 11 Redington Road, NW3. *T:* 01-435 5522.

CARSTENS, Prof. Dr Karl; Member of German Bundestag (CDU) since 1972; President of the Bundestag, since 1976; Professor of Constitutional and International Law, Cologne University, since 1960; *b* 14 Dec. 1914; *s* of Dr Karl Carstens, teacher, and Gertrud (*née* Clausen); *m* 1944, Dr Veronica Carstens(*née* Prior). *Educ:* Univs of Frankfurt, Dijon, München, Königsberg, Hamburg, Yale. Dr Laws Hamburg 1936, LLM Yale 1949. Served with Army, 1939-45; lawyer, Bremen, 1945-49; rep. of Bremen in Bonn, 1949-54; rep. of Fed. Republic of Germany to Council of Europe, Strasbourg, 1954-55; teaching at Cologne Univ., 1950-; FO, Bonn, 1955-60 (State Sec., 1960-66); Dep. Defence Minister, 1966-67; Head of Chancellor's Office, Bonn, 1968-69; Dir Research Inst., German Foreign Policy Assoc., 1969-72; Chm., Parly Opposition, 1973-76. *Publications:* Grundgedanken der amerikanischer Verfassung und ihre Verwirklichung, 1954; Das Recht des Europarats, 1956; Politische Führung—Erfahrungen im Dienst der Bundesregierung, 1971. *Address:* Bundeshaus, 53 Bonn, West Germany. *T:* Bonn 16-3330.

CARSWELL, John Patrick, CB 1977; Secretary, British Academy, since 1978; *b* 30 May 1918; *s* of Donald Carswell, barrister and author, and Catherine Carswell, author; *m* 1944, Ianthe Elstob; two *d. Educ:* Merchant Taylors' Sch; St John's Coll., Oxford (MA). Served in Army, 1940-46. Entered Min. of National Insurance, 1946. Joint Sec., Cttee on Economic and Financial Problems of Provision for Old Age (Phillips Cttee), 1953-54; Asst Sec., 1955; Principal Private Sec. to Minister of Pensions and Nat. Insurance, 1955-56; Treasury, 1961-64;

Under-Sec., Office of Lord Pres. of the Council and Minister for Science, 1964, Under-Sec., DES, 1964-74; Sec., UGC, 1974-77. *Publications:* The Prospector, 1950; The Old Cause, 1954; The South Sea Bubble, 1960; The Diary and Political Papers of George Bubb Dodington, 1965; The Civil Servant and his World, 1966; The Descent on England, 1969; From Revolution to Revolution: English Society 1688-1776, 1973; contribs to Times Literary Supplement and other periodicals. *Address:* 32 Park Village East, NW1. *T:* 01-387 3920. *Club:* Garrick.

CARTER; see Bonham-Carter and Bonham Carter.

CARTER, Arthur Herbert, JP; Council of Royal Agricultural Society of England (Vice-President); Council of Lincolnshire Agricultural Society (Chairman, 1946-47); *b* 1 June 1890; *er s* of Arthur Henry Carter, Wiggenhall, St Mary Magdalen, Norfolk; *m* 1916, Edith Mary Tindall; two *s.* Farmer and landowner in Lincolnshire and Cambridgeshire; High Sheriff Cambridgeshire and Huntingdon, 1940; Mem. Isle of Ely CC, 1922-47, Alderman 1933, resigned 1948; Council of Cambridgeshire and Isle of Ely Agricultural Society, 1923-48; Deeping Fen Drainage Board. Chairman County Civil Defence Cttee; Chairman Theatres and Cinemas Cttee; Vice-Chairman Finance Cttee; Member Holland (Lincs) War Agricultural Executive Cttee; Dep. Chairman HAEC and Chairman Labour Sub-Cttee and Housing; RASE representative on Rothamsted Trust Cttee. Freeman, City of London. *Recreations:* shooting, cricket. *Address:* The Manor House, Tydd St Giles, Wisbech, Cambs. *TA and T:* Newton 555.

CARTER, Barry Robin Octavius; Barrister-at-Law; a Recorder of the Crown Court, since 1972; *b* 20 Jan. 1928; *s* of late Stanley Noel Carter and late Winifred Margaret Carter; *m* 1959, Hermione (*née* Brock); one *s* one *d. Educ:* Sherborne; Trinity Coll., Cambridge (BA). Commnd in Royal Engrs, 1947. Called to Bar, 1953. Dep. Chm., Hampshire QS, Jan. 1971; Temp. Recorder of Salisbury, Oct. 1971. Wine Treasurer, Western Circuit, 1976-. *Recreations:* lawn tennis (Cambridge blue, 1949-51, Captain 1950); golf. *Address:* Mayles, The Drive, Cobham, Surrey. *T:* Cobham 2827; 4 Pump Court, Temple, EC4. *T:* 01-353 2656. *Clubs:* Hawks (Cambridge); Hampshire (Winchester); All England Lawn Tennis and Croquet, International Lawn Tennis of Great Britain, St George's Hill Lawn Tennis.

CARTER, Bernard Thomas; Hon. RE; artist (painter and etcher); Keeper, Pictures and Conservation, National Maritime Museum, 1974-77; *b* 6 April 1920; *s* of Cecil Carter and Ethel Carter (*née* Darby); *m* Eugenie Alexander, artist and writer; one *s. Educ:* Haberdashers' Aske's; Goldsmith's College of Art, London Univ. NDD, ATD; FRSA. RAF, 1939-46. Art lectr, critic and book reviewer, 1952-68; Asst Keeper (prints and drawings), Nat. Maritime Museum, 1968; Dep. Keeper (Head of Picture Dept), Nat. Maritime Museum, 1970. One-man exhibns in London: Arthur Jeffress Gall., 1955; Portal Gall., 1963, 1965, 1967, 1969, 1974; mixed exhibns: Royal Academy, Arts Council, British Council and galleries in Europe and USA; works in public collections, galleries abroad and British educn authorities, etc. *Publications:* Art for Young People (with Eugenie Alexander), 1958; Marine Paintings, 1977. *Recreations:* reading, listening to music, gardening, theatre. *Address:* 56 King George Street, Greenwich, SE10 8QD. *T:* 01-858 4281.

CARTER, Bruce; see Hough, R. A.

CARTER, Charles Frederick, FBA 1970; Vice-Chancellor, University of Lancaster, since 1963; *b* Rugby, 15 Aug. 1919; *y s* of late Frederick William Carter, FRS; *m* 1944, Janet Shea; one *s* two *d. Educ:* Rugby Sch.; St John's Coll., Cambridge. Friends' Relief Service, 1941-45; Lectr in Statistics, Univ. of Cambridge, 1945-51; Fellow of Emmanuel Coll., 1947-51 (Hon. Fellow, 1965-); Prof. of Applied Economics, The Queen's Univ., Belfast, 1952-59; Stanley Jevons Prof. of Political Economy and Cobden Lectr, Univ. of Manchester, 1959-63. Chairman: Science and Industry Cttee, RSA, British Assoc. and Nuffield Foundn, 1954-59; Schools' Broadcasting Council, 1964-71; Joint Cttee of the Univs and the Accountancy Profession, 1964; Adv. Bd of Accountancy Educn, 1970-76; North-West Economic Planning Council, 1965-68; Centre for Studies in Social Policy, 1972-; PO Rev. Cttee, 1976-77; NI Economic Council, 1977-; Sec.-Gen., Royal Econ. Soc., 1971-75; Member: UN Expert Cttee on Commodity Trade, 1953; Capital Investment Advisory Cttee, Republic of Ireland, 1956; British Assoc. Cttee on Metric System, 1958; Council for Scientific and Industrial Research, 1959-63; Commn on Higher Education, Republic of Ireland, 1960-67; Heyworth Cttee on Social Studies, 1963; Advisory Council on Technology, 1964-66; North Western Postal Bd, 1970-73. Pres., Manchester Statistical Soc., 1967-69; Vice-Pres., Workers' Educational Assoc.; Dir, Friends' Provident Life

Office. Joint Editor: Journal of Industrial Economics, 1955-61; Economic Journal, 1961-70. Hon. Member, Royal Irish Academy; Trustee: Joseph Rowntree Mem. Trust, 1966-; Sir Halley Stewart Trust, 1969-. Hon. DEconSc, NUI. *Publications:* The Science of Wealth, 1960, 3rd edn 1973; (with W. B. Reddaway and J. R. N. Stone) The Measurement of Production Movements, 1948; (with G. L. S. Shackle and others) Uncertainty and Business Decisions, 1954; (with A. D. Roy) British Economic Statistics, 1954; (with B. R. Williams) Industry and Technical Progress, 1957; Investment in Innovation, 1958; Science in Industry, 1959; (with D. P. Barritt) The Northern Ireland Problem, 1962, 2nd edn 1972; Wealth, 1968; (with G. Brosan and others) Patterns and Policies in Higher Education, 1971; On Having a Sense of all Conditions, 1971; (with J. L. Ford and others) Uncertainty and Expectation in Economics, 1972; articles in Economic Journal, etc. *Recreation:* gardening. *Address:* University House, Bailrigg, Lancaster LA1 4YW. *T:* Lancaster 65201. *Club:* Farmers'. *See also Prof. G. W. Carter.*

CARTER, David; see Carter, R. D.

CARTER, Sir Derrick (Hunton), Kt 1975; TD 1952; Vice-Chairman, Remploy Ltd, since 1976 (Chairman, 1972-76); *b* 7 April 1906; *s* of Arthur Hunton Carter, MD and Winifred Carter, Sedbergh; *m* 1st, 1933, Phyllis, *d* of Denis Best, Worcester; one *s* one *d*; 2nd, 1948, Madeline, *d* of Col D. M. O'Callaghan, CMG, DSO; one *d. Educ:* Haileybury Coll.; St John's Coll., Cambridge (MA). 2nd Lieut, 27th (LEE) Bn RE, TA, 1936, mobilised Aug. 1939; in AA until Dec. 1941; 1st War Advanced Class; Major RA, Dept Tank Design; comd Armament Wing of DTD, Lulworth, 1942-45 (Lt-Col). Civil Engr, Dominion Bridge Co., Montreal, 1927-28; Res. Engr, Billingham Div., ICI, 1928-33; Asst Sales Controller, ICI, London, 1933-38; Asst Sales Man., ICI, 1938-39 and 1945-47; Gen. Chemicals Div., ICI: Sales Control Man., 1947; Commercial Dir, 1951; Man. Dir, 1953; Chm., 1961; also Chm. Alkali Div., 1963; Chm. (of merged Divs as) Mond Div., 1964; retd from ICI, 1967. Chm., United Sulphuric Acid Corp. Ltd, 1967-71; Chm., Torrance & Sons Ltd, 1971-; Director: Avon Rubber Co. Ltd, 1970-; Stothert & Pitt Ltd, 1971-; BICERI Ltd, 1967-. Mem. Exec. Cttee: Gloucester Council for Small Industries in Rural Areas; Assoc. Boys' Clubs. *Recreations:* shooting, gardening. *Address:* Withington House, Withington, Cheltenham, Glos. *T:* Withington 286. *Clubs:* United Oxford & Cambridge University, Army and Navy.

CARTER, Douglas, CB 1969; Under-Secretary, Department of Trade and Industry, 1970-71; *b* 4 Dec. 1911; *3rd s* of Albert and Mabel Carter, Bradford, Yorks; *m* 1935, Alice, *d* of Captain C. E. Le Mesurier, CB, RN; three *s* one *d. Educ:* Bradford Grammar Sch.; St John's Coll., Cambridge (Scholar). First Cl. Hons, Historical Tripos Part I and Economics Tripos Part II. Wrenbury Research Scholarship in Economics, Cambridge, 1933. Asst Principal, Board of Trade, 1934; Sec., Imperial Shipping Cttee, 1935-38; Princ. BoT, 1939; Asst Sec., BoT, 1943; Chm., Cttee of Experts in Enemy Property Custodianship, Inter-Allied Reparations Agency, Brussels, 1946; Controller, Import Licensing Dept, 1949; Distribution of Industry Div., BoT, 1954; Industries and Manufacturers Div., 1957; Commercial Relations and Exports Div., 1960; Under-Sec., 1963; Tariff Div., 1965. *Publications:* articles in Bridge Magazine. *Recreations:* reading, golf, bridge, travel. *Address:* 12 Garbrand Walk, Ewell Village, Epsom, Surrey. *T:* 01-394 1316. *Clubs:* Eccentric; Walton Heath Golf.

CARTER, Hon. Sir Douglas Julian, KCMG 1977; High Commissioner for New Zealand in the United Kingdom, since 1976; *b* 5 Aug. 1908; *s* of Walter Stephen Carter and Agnes Isobel; *m* Mavis Rose Miles. *Educ:* Palmerston North High Sch.; Waitaki Boys' High Sch. Formerly, Executive Member: Federated Farmers of NZ; Primary Production Council; Pig Production Council. MP (National Party) Raglan, 1957-75; Chm., Govt Transport Cttee, 1960-70; Under Sec., Agriculture, 1966-69; Minister of Agriculture, 1972-75. *Address:* New Zealand High Commission, New Zealand House, Haymarket, SW1.

CARTER, Edward Julian, MA; ARIBA; FLA; *b* Grahamstown, South Africa, 10 June 1902; *s* of late Rev. Canon F. E. Carter; *m* 1930, Deborah Benson, *e d* of Bernard Howard, Loughton, Essex; one *s* four *d. Educ:* Lancing Coll.; Magdalene Coll., Cambridge; Architectural Assoc. Sch., London. Librarian-Editor, Royal Institute of British Architects, 1930-46. Head of Libraries Div., UN Educational, Scientific and Cultural Organisation (previously in UNESCO Preparatory Commn), 1946-57. Dir, Architectural Assoc., Bedford Square, 1961-67. Governor, Central Sch. of Art and Design, 1968-. Chairman,

Assoc. Special Libraries and Information Bureaux, 1940-45. Vice-Chairman, Soc. for Cultural Relations with USSR, 1943-45. Hon. Fellow, Library Assoc., 1962. *Publication:* The Future of London, 1962. *Address:* Upper Kilcott, Hillsley, Glos. *Club:* Athenæum.

CARTER, Edward Robert Erskine; Counsel, Bordern and Elliot, Barristers and Solicitors; *b* 20 Feb. 1923; *s* of Arthur Norwood Carter, QC, and Edith Ireland; *m* 1947, Verna Leman Andrews; two *s* two *d. Educ:* Univ. of New Brunswick; (after War) Osgoode Hall, Toronto, Ont; Univ. of New Brunswick; Univ. of New Brunswick Law Sch. (BCL 1947); Rhodes Scholar for New Brunswick, 1947; Oxford Univ. (BCL 1949). Served War with Royal Canadian Artillery, 1942-44; on loan to 7th King's Own Scottish Borderers, First British Airborne Div., 1944; PoW, Sept. 1944-April 1945. Read Law with McMillan, Binch, Wilkinson, Berry & Wright, Toronto, Ont; called to Bar of New Brunswick, 1947; Ontario 1951; associated with A. N. Carter, QC in practise of law, St John, NB, 1949-53; Legal Officer, Abitibi Power & Paper Co. Ltd, Toronto, Ont, 1953-54; joined Fennell, McLean, Seed & Carter, 1954; Partner, 1955-58. President and Chief Executive Officer: Patino Mining Corp., later Patino NV, 1958-72; Hambro Canada Ltd, 1973-75. Chm. and Dir, Advocate Mines Ltd; Director: Foodex Systems Ltd; Bank of Montreal; Hambros Ltd; Hambro Canada Ltd; Westroc Industries Ltd; Sun Alliance Insurance Co. Member, Law Soc. of Upper Canada. *Address:* (office) c/o Bordern and Elliot, 250 University Avenue, Toronto, Ontario M5H 3E9, Canada.

CARTER, Elliott (Cook), DrMus; composer; *b* New York City, 11 Dec. 1908; *m* 1939, Helen Frost-Jones; one *s. Educ:* Harvard Univ. (MA); Ecole Normale, Paris (DrMus). Professor of Greek and Maths, St John's Coll., Annapolis, 1940-42; Professor of Music: Columbia Univ., 1948-50; Yale Univ., 1960-61. *Compositions include:* First Symphony, 1942-43; Quartet for Four Saxophones, 1943; Holiday Overture, 1944; Ballet, The Minotaur, 1946-47; Woodwind Quintet, 1947; Sonata for Cello and Piano, 1948; First String Quartet, 1950-51; Sonata for Flute, Oboe, Cello and Harpsichord, 1952; Variations for Orchestra, 1953; Second String Quartet, 1960 (New York Critics' Circle Award; Pulitzer Prize; Unesco 1st Prize); Double Concerto for Harpsichord and Piano, 1961 (New York Critics' Circle Award); Piano Concerto, 1967; Concerto for Orchestra, 1970; Third String Quartet, 1971 (Pulitzer Prize); Duo for Violin and Piano, 1973-74; Brass Quintet, 1974; A Mirror on which to Dwell (song cycle), 1976; A Symphony of Three Orchestras, 1977. Member: Nat. Inst. of Arts and Letters, 1956 (Gold Medal for Music, 1971); Amer. Acad. of Arts and Sciences (Boston), 1962; Amer. Acad. of Arts and Letters, 1971; Akad. der Kunste, Berlin, 1971. Sibelius Medal (Harriet Cohen Foundation), London, 1961; Premio delle Muse, City of Florence, 1969. Holds hon. degrees. *Publication:* The Writings of Elliott Carter, 1977. *Address:* Mead Street, Waccabuc, NY 10597, USA.

CARTER, Eric Bairstow, BSc(Eng); CEng, FIMechE, FRAeS, FIProdE; retired; *b* 26 Aug. 1912; *s* of John Bolton Carter and Edith Carter; *m* 1934, Lily Roome; one *d. Educ:* Halifax Technical Coll. Workshop Supt and Lectr, Constantine Technical Coll., Middlesbrough, 1936; apptd to Air Min. (Engine Directorate), Sept. 1939; subseq. Air Min. appts to engine firms and at HQ. Asst Dir (Research and Develt, Ramjets and Liquid Propellant Rockets), Dec. 1955; Dir (Engine Prod.), 1960; Dir (Engine R&D), 1963; Dir-Gen. (Engine R&D), Min. of Technology, later MoD (Aviation Supply), 1969-72; Consultant Engineer, and Special Advr to Man. Dir, Noel Penny Turbines Ltd, 1972-77. *Address:* 27 Cherington Close, Redditch B98 0BB. *Clubs:* Civil Service; Halifax Cricket.

CARTER, Eric Stephen; Deputy Director-General, Agricultural Development and Advisory Service, since 1975; *b* 23 June 1923; *s* of Albert Harry Carter, MBE and Doris Margaret (née Mann); *m* 1948, Audrey Windsor; one *s. Educ:* Grammar Sch., Lydney; Reading Univ. BSc (Agric) 1945. Techn. Officer, Gloucester AEC, 1945-46; asst District Officer, Gloucester NAAS, 1946-49, Dist Off. 1949-57; Sen. Dist Off., Lindsey (Lincs) NAAS, 1957-63, County Agric. Off. 1963-69; Yorks and Lancs Region: Dep. Regional Dir, NAAS, 1969-71; Regional Agric. Off., ADAS, 1971-73; Regional Off. (ADAS), 1973-74; Chief Regional Off., MAFF, 1974-75. FIBiol 1974. *Publications:* contrib. press, agric. and techn. jls. *Recreations:* gardening, reading, music, countryside. *Address:* Svedala, 15 Farrs Lane, East Hyde, Luton, Beds. *T:* Harpenden 60504. *Clubs:* Farmers', Civil Service.

CARTER, Ernestine Marie, (Mrs John Waynflete Carter), OBE 1964; Associate Editor, The Sunday Times, 1968-72; *m* 1936, John Waynflete Carter, CBE (*d* 1975). *Educ:* Pape Sch.,

Savannah, Georgia; Wellesley Coll., Wellesley, Mass., USA (BA). Asst Curator of Architecture and Industrial Art, The Museum of Modern Art, New York, 1933-35, Curator, 1936-37; Specialist, Display and Exhibns Div., Min. of Information, 1939-41; US Office of War Information, London, 1941-44, in charge of exhibns and displays; Asst in Fashion Section, Britain Can Make It Exhibn, 1946; Fashion Editor, Harper's Bazaar, 1947-49; Contributor to The Observer, 1952-54; Women's Editor, The Sunday Times, 1955-68. Member: Council, Royal Coll. of Art, 1960-61; Nat. Council for Diploma in Art and Design, 1962-68; Selection Panel, Duke of Edinburgh's Award for Design, 1965-67; Council, RSA, 1976-. FRSA 1964. Hon. Dr RCA, 1976. *Publications:* Grim Glory, 1941; Flash in the Pan, 1953 (re-issued 1963); With Tongue in Chic, 1974; 20th Century Fashion: a scrapbook from 1900 to today, 1975; The Changing World of Fashion, 1977; contributor to: The Intelligent Woman's Guide to Good Taste, 1958; Saturday Book, 1961. *Recreation:* sleep. *Address:* 113 Dovehouse Street, Chelsea, SW3. *T:* 01-352 4344.

CARTER, Francis Jackson, CMG 1954; CVO 1963; CBE 1946; Under-Secretary of State of Tasmania and Clerk of Executive Council, 1953-64; also permanent head of Premier's and Chief Secretary's Department; *b* Fremantle, W Australia, 9 Sept. 1899; *s* of late Francis Henry Carter, formerly of Bendigo, Victoria; *m* 1926, Margaret Flora, *d* of late William Thomas Walker, Launceston; two *s* one *d. Educ:* Hobart High Sch.; Univ. of Tasmania. Entered Tasmanian Public Service, 1916; transferred to Hydro-Electric Dept, 1925; Asst Secretary, Hydro-Electric Commn, 1934; Secretary to Premier, 1935-39; Dep. Under-Secretary of State, 1939-53; served War of 1939-45 as State Liaison Officer to Commonwealth Dept of Home Security; Official Secretary for Tasmania in London, 1949-50; State Director for Royal Visit, 1954, 1958, 1963, and Thai Royal Visit, 1962. Executive Member, State Economic Planning Authority, 1944-55; Chairman, Fire Brigades Commn of Tasmania, 1945-70. Grand Master GL of Tasmania, 1956-59. FASA; FCIS. JP 1939. *Recreations:* music, golf and lawn bowls. *Address:* 568 Churchill Avenue, Sandy Bay, Hobart, Tasmania 7005. *T:* Hobart 5.2382. *Clubs:* Royal Automobile of Tasmania, Masonic (Hobart).

CARTER, Frank Ernest Lovell, CBE 1956 (OBE 1949); Director General of the Overseas Audit Service, 1963-71; *b* 6 Oct. 1909; *s* of Ernest and Florence Carter; *m* 1966, Gerda (née Gruen). *Educ:* Chigwell Sch.; Hertford Coll., Oxford. Served in Overseas Audit Service in: Nigeria, 1933-42; Sierra Leone, 1943; Palestine, 1944-45; Aden and Somaliland, 1946-47; Tanganyika, 1950-54; Hong Kong, 1955-59; Deputy Director in London, 1960-62. *Address:* 8 The Leys, N2 0HE. *T:* 01-458 4684. *Club:* East India, Devonshire, Sports and Public Schools.

CARTER, Prof. Geoffrey William, MA; FIEE; FIEEE; Professor of Electrical Engineering, University of Leeds, 1946-74, now Emeritus; *b* 21 May 1909; *s* of late Frederick William Carter, FRS; *m* 1938, Freda Rose Lapwood; one *s* one *d. Educ:* Rugby Sch.; St John's Coll., Cambridge. MA 1937. Student Apprentice, British Thomson-Houston Co. Ltd, Rugby, 1932-35, Research Engineer, 1935-45; University Demonstrator in Engineering Science, Oxford, 1946. *Publications:* The Simple Calculation of Electrical Transients, 1944; The Electromagnetic Field in its Engineering Aspects, 1954 (rev. edn 1967); (with A. Richardson) Techniques of Circuit Analysis, 1972; papers in Proc. IEE and elsewhere. *Recreations:* gardening, painting, winemaking. *Address:* 14 Oaklea Gardens, Leeds LS16 8BH. *T:* Leeds 673841.
See also C. F. Carter.

CARTER, Godfrey James; Parliamentary Counsel since 1972; *b* 1 June 1919; *s* of Captain James Shuckburgh Carter, Grenadier Guards (killed in action, 1918), and Diana Violet Gladys Carter (née Cavendish); *m* 1946, Cynthia Mason; three *s. Educ:* Eton (KS); Magdalene Coll., Cambridge. BA 1945, LLB 1946. War Service (Rifle Bde), Middle East, 1940-43 (twice wounded). Called to Bar, Inner Temple, 1946; Asst Parly Counsel, 1949-56; commercial dept, Bristol Aeroplane Co. Ltd, and Bristol Siddeley Engines Ltd, 1956-64; re-joined Parly Counsel Office, 1964; Dep. Counsel, 1970. *Address:* Old Bournstream House, Wotton-under-Edge, Glos. *T:* Wotton-under-Edge 3246. *Club:* Travellers'.

CARTER, James Earl, Jr; President of the United States of America, since 1977; *b* Plains, Georgia, USA, 1 Oct. 1924; *s* of James Earl Carter and Lillian (née Gordy); *m* 1946, Rosalynn Smith; three *s* one *d. Educ:* Plains High Sch.; Southwestern Coll., Georgia; Georgia Inst. of Technology; US Naval Acad. (BS); Union Coll., Schenectady, NY (post grad.). Served in US Navy submarines and battleships, 1947-53; Ensign (commissioned, 1947); Lieut 1950; retd from US Navy, 1953.

Became farmer and warehouseman, 1953, farming peanuts at Plains, Georgia. State Senator (Democrat), Georgia, 1962-66; Governor of Georgia, 1971-74. Democratic Candidate for the Presidency of the USA, 1976. *Address:* The White House, 1600 Pennsylvania Avenue NW, Washington, DC 20500, USA; PO Box 1976, Atlanta, Georgia 30301; (home) 1 Woodland Drive, Plains, Georgia 31780, USA.

CARTER, Maj.-Gen. James Norman, CB 1958; CBE 1955; *Educ:* Charterhouse; RMC Sandhurst. Commissioned The Dorset Regt, 1926; Captain, The Royal Warwickshire Regt, 1936; Lieut-Colonel, 1948; Colonel, 1950; Brigadier, 1954; Maj.-General, 1957. Asst Chief of Staff, Organisation and Training Div., SHAPE, 1955-57; Commander British Army Staff, British Joint Services Mission, Washington, 1958-60; Military Attaché, Washington, Jan.-July 1960; General Secretary, The Officers' Assoc., 1961-63. *Recreation:* golf.

CARTER, Sir John, Kt 1966; QC (Guyana) 1962; Ambassador of Guyana to China, since 1976; *b* 27 Jan. 1919; *s* of Kemp R. Carter; *m* 1959, Sara Lou (formerly Harris); two *s*. *Educ:* University of London and Middle Temple, England. Called to English Bar, 1942; admitted to Guyana (late British Guiana) Bar, 1945; Member of Legislature of Guyana, 1948-53 and 1961-64; Pro-Chancellor, Univ. of Guyana, 1962-66; Ambassador of Guyana to US, 1966-70; High Comr for Guyana in UK, 1970-76. *Recreations:* cricket, swimming. *Address:* Embassy of Guyana, No 1 Hsui Hsueh Tung Chieh, Chien Kuo Men Wai, China. *Clubs:* MCC; Georgetown (Guyana).

CARTER, John Somers; *b* 26 Feb. 1901; *s* of R. Carter. *Educ:* Edinburgh Academy; Bedford Sch.; Balliol Coll., Oxford, 1st Class Hon. Mods., 3rd Class Lit. Hum. Asst Master, Cheltenham Coll., 1924-32; Headmaster: St John's Sch., Leatherhead, 1933-47; Blundell's Sch., 1948-59. *Address:* Trelissick East, Feock, Truro, Cornwall, *T:* Devoran 862595.

CARTER, Malcolm Ogilvy, CIE 1943; MC 1918; Secretary, South-Western Regional Hospital Board, 1947-63, retired; *b* 2 July 1898; *s* of late Reginald Carter, MA, formerly Rector of Edinburgh Academy and Headmaster of Bedford Sch., and Mary Ogilvy Boyd; *m* 1921, Gwyneth Elaine, *d* of R. Platts, Bedford; one *d* ; *m* 1944, Iris Cowgill, *d* of late Rev. T. A. Thomson, Shawell, Leicester. *Educ:* Edinburgh Academy; Bedford Sch.; Balliol Coll., Oxford. RFA 1917; served in France and Belgium, 1917-18 (MC); BA (Oxon), 1920; joined ICS in Bengal, 1921; Secretary to the Board of Revenue, 1934-35; District Magistrate, Midnapore and 24 Parganas, 1935-38; Director of Land Records, Aug.-Nov. 1938; Secretary to Flood Land Revenue Commission, Bengal, 1938-40; Director of Land Records, April-July 1940; Secretary to Governor of Bengal, 1940-42; Civil Representative of the Government of Bengal with Eastern Army, 1942-43; Commissioner Chittagong Division, Bengal and Liaison Officer to XIVth Army and Third Tactical Air Force, 1943-47. FHA. *Address:* Belvedere, Leigh Woods, Bristol BS8 3PN. *Clubs:* Royal Commonwealth Society (Bristol and London); Vincent's (Oxford).

CARTER, Air Cdre North, CB 1948; DFC 1935; RAF retired; *b* 26 Nov. 1902; *s* of Lieut-Colonel G. L. Carter, CIE, Indian Army; *m* 1931, Kathleen Graham Machattie; one *s* one *d. Educ:* Wellington Coll.; RAF Coll., Cranwell. Commissioned from RAF Coll., 1922; No 5 Sqdn, India, 1923-27; RAF Depot, Iraq, 1929-32; No 56 Sqdn., North Weald, 1932-34; No 60 Sqdn., India, 1934 and 1935; RAF Staff Coll., 1936; Sqdn. Ldr., 1936; Staff Appointments, 1937-40; Wing Comdr, 1938; Commanded RAF Stations Dalcross, South Cerney, Pocklington and Castel Benito, 1941-45; Group Captain, 1946; Air Commodore, 1948; AOC Halton, 1949-50; SASO 205 Group Middle East Air Force 15, 1951-53; Provost Marshal and Chief of Air Force Police, 1953-54, retired 1954; Temp. Administrative Officer, Northern Region, Nigeria, 1955-63. *Address:* Gould's Bay, Hawkesbury River, PMB Brooklyn, NSW 2253, Australia.

CARTER, Peers Lee, CMG 1965; HM Diplomatic Service, retired; free-lance conference interpreter; *b* 5 Dec. 1916; *s* of Peers Owen Carter; *m* 1940, Joan Eleanor Lovegrove; one *s. Educ:* Radley; Christ Church, Oxford. Entered HM Foreign Service, 1939. Joined the Army in 1940; served in Africa and Europe. HM Embassy, Baghdad, 1945; First Secretary, Commissioner-General's Office, Singapore, 1951; Counsellor HM Embassy, Washington, 1958; (Temp. duty) UK Delegation to UN, New York, 1961; Head of UK Permanent Mission, Geneva, 1961; Inspector of Foreign Service Establishments, 1963-66; Chief Inspector of HM Diplomatic Service, 1966-68; Ambassador to Afghanistan, 1968-72; Ministerial Interpreter and Asst Under-Sec. of State, FCO, 1973-76. Mem., Internat. Assoc. of Conference Interpreters. Sardar-e A'ala, Afghanistan,

1971. *Recreations:* mountain walking, skiing, photography. *Address:* Holgate, Balcombe, Sussex RH17 6LL. *Clubs:* Special Forces, Travellers'.

CARTER, Peter Anthony, CMG 1970; HM Diplomatic Service, retired; *b* 16 Jan. 1914; *s* of Thomas Birchall Carter; *m* 1946, Mary Hutchison Heard; one *s* one *d. Educ:* Charterhouse; Sidney Sussex Coll., Cambridge, Metropolitan Police Office, 1936-39; Royal Tank Regt (Major), 1939-44; Colonial Office, 1947-60; Nyasaland, 1951-53; CRO, 1960-61; First Secretary, Dar-es-Salaam, 1961-64; Counsellor, Dublin, 1965-68; Head of British High Commission Residual Staff, Rhodesia, 1968-69; British High Commissioner, Mauritius, 1970-73; Senior Clerk, H of C, 1974-76. *Recreations:* golf, fishing, music. *Address:* Forth House, Beech Drive, Kingswood, Surrey.

CARTER, Raymond John; MP (Lab) Birmingham (Northfield) since 1970; Parliamentary Under-Secretary of State, Northern Ireland Office, since 1976; Electrical Engineer; *b* 17 Sept. 1935; *s* of John Carter; *m* 1959, Jeanette Hills; one *s* two *d. Educ:* Mortlake Co. Secondary Sch.; Reading Technical Coll.; Staffordshire Coll. of Technology. National Service, Army, 1953-55. Sperry Gyroscope Co.: Technical Asst, Research and Development Computer Studies, 1956-65. Electrical Engineer, Central Electricity Generating Bd, 1965-70. Mem., Gen. Adv. Council, BBC, 1974-76. Mem. Easthampstead RDC, 1963-68 (Chm. Amenity Cttee); Governor, Garth Hill Comprehensive Sch. Contested: Wokingham, Gen. Elec., 1966; Warwick and Leamington, Bye-elec., March 1968. Member: Public Accounts Cttee, 1973-74; Parly Science and Technology Cttee, 1974-76. Delegate: Council of Europe, 1974-76; WEU, 1974-76. AIEE. *Recreations:* football, athletics enthusiast, reading. *Address:* 1 Lynwood Chase, Warfield Road, Bracknell, Berkshire. *T:* Bracknell 20237.

CARTER, Air Commodore Robert Alfred Copsey, CB 1956; DSO 1942; DFC 1943; Royal Air Force, retired; *b* 15 Sept. 1910; *s* of S. H. Carter and S. Copsey; *m* 1947, Sally Ann Peters, Va, USA; two *s* one *d. Educ:* Portsmouth Grammar Sch.; RAF Coll., Cranwell. Cranwell Cadet, 1930-32; commissioned in RAF, 1932; served in India, 1933-36; grad. RAF School of Aeronautical Engineering, 1938; served in Bomber Command, 1940-45; commanded 103 and 150 Sqdns, RAF, Grimsby; grad. RAF Staff Coll., 1945; attended US Armed Forces Staff Coll., Norfolk, Va, USA, 1947; attached to RNZAF, 1950-53; comd. RAF Station, Upwood, 1953-55; SASO, RAF Transport Command, 1956-58; Director of Personal Services, Air Ministry, 1958-61; AO i/c Admin, HQ, RAF Germany, 1961-64; retired 1964. MRAeS 1960; CEng, 1966. *Address:* The Old Cottage, Castle Lane, Whaddon, Salisbury, Wilts. *Club:* Royal Air Force.

CARTER, Robert William Bernard, CMG 1964; HM Diplomatic Service, retired; *b* 1913; 3rd *s* of late William Joseph Carter and late Lucy (*née* How); *m* 1945, Joan Violet, *o d* of Theodore and Violet Magnus; one *s* two *d* (and one *d* decd). *Educ:* St Bees Sch., Cumberland; Trinity Coll., Oxford (Scholar). Asst Master, Glenalmond, Perthshire, 1936. Served with the Royal Navy, 1940-46; Lieut, RNVR. Administrative Assistant, Newcastle upon Tyne Education Cttee, 1946; Principal, Board of Trade, 1949; Trade Commissioner: Calcutta, 1952; Delhi, 1955; Accra, 1956; Principal Trade Commissioner, Colombo (Assistant Secretary), 1959; Senior British Trade Commissioner in Pakistan, 1961; Minister (Commercial), Pakistan, and Dep. High Comr, Karachi, 1967-68; Dep. High Comr, 1969-73 and Consul-Gen., 1973, Melbourne. *Recreations:* reading, travelling, collecting beer-mugs. *Address:* The Old Parsonage, Heywood, Westbury, Wilts. *T:* Westbury 822194. *Clubs:* Oriental, Naval.

CARTER, Roland; HM Diplomatic Service, Counsellor, FCO, since 1977; *b* 29 Aug. 1924; *s* of Ralph Carter; *m* 1950, Elisabeth Mary Green; one *s* two *d. Educ:* Cockburn High Sch., Leeds; Leeds Univ. Served War of 1939-45: Queen's Royal Regt, 1944; 6th Gurkha Rifles, 1945; Frontier Corps (South Waziristan and Gilgit Scouts), 1946. Seconded to Indian Political Service, as Asst Political Agent, Chilas, Gilgit Agency, 1946-47; Lectr, Zurich Univ. and Finnish Sch. of Economics, 1950-53. Joined Foreign Service, 1953: FO, 1953-54; Third Sec., Moscow, 1955; Germany, 1956-58; Second Sec., Helsinki, 1959 (First Sec., 1962); FO, 1962-67; Kuala Lumpur, 1967-69; Ambassador to People's Republic of Mongolia, 1969-71; seconded to Cabinet Office, 1971-74; Counsellor, Pretoria, 1974-77. *Publication:* Näin Puhutaan Englantia (in Finnish; with Erik Erämetsä), 1952. *Recreations:* music, linguistics, Indian studies. *Address:* c/o Lloyds Bank, St Albans, Herts.

CARTER, (Ronald) David, RDI 1975; Chairman, DCA Design Consultants Ltd; Member of the Design Council, since 1972, Deputy Chairman since 1975; *b* 30 Dec. 1927; *s* of H. Miles

Carter and Margaret Carter; *m* 1953, Theo (Marjorie Elizabeth), *d* of Rev. L. T. Towers; two *s* two *d*. *Educ:* Wyggeston Sch., Leicester; Central Sch. of Art and Design, London. Served RN, 1946-48. Appts in industry, 1951-60; Principal, David Carter Associates, 1960-75. Visiting Lectr, Birmingham Coll. of Industrial Design, 1960-65. Design Awards, 1960 and 1969; Duke of Edinburgh Prize for Elegant Design, 1967. Pres., Soc. of Industrial Artists and Designers, 1974-75; Mem., Art and Design Cttee, Council for Nat. Academic Awards, 1975-; Chm., Design Council Report on Industrial Design Educn in UK, 1977. FSIA 1967; FRSA 1975. *Recreations:* books, boats, and County Cork. *Address:* 43 Beauchamp Avenue, Leamington Spa, Warwickshire. *T:* Leamington Spa 24864. *Club:* Reform.

CARTER, His Honour Sir Walker (Kelly), Kt 1965; QC 1951; an Official Referee of the Supreme Court of Judicature, 1954-71; Chairman, Criminal Injuries Compensation Board, 1964-75; *b* 7 July 1899; *s* of late Walter Carter, CBE, and Annie Elizabeth Carter; *m* 1925, Phyllis Irene, *d* of late Edward Ernest Clarke, Bank Bldgs, Simla, India; one *d*. *Educ:* Repton Sch.; Sidney Sussex Coll., Cambridge, RFA, 1918-19. Called to Bar, Inner Temple, 1924; Bencher, 1965. RA 1939-43. Chairman, Quarter Sessions for Parts of Lindsey, 1945-67, and for Parts of Kesteven, 1961-67. *Address:* 65 Bedford Gardens, W8. *T:* 01-727 9862. *Club:* Reform.
See also J. E. Vinelott.

CARTER, Air Vice-Marshal Wilfred, CB 1963; DFC 1943; AOA, HQ Bomber Command, 1965-67; *b* 5 Nov. 1912; *s* of late Samuel Carter; *m* 1950, Margaret Enid Bray; one *s* one *d*. *Educ:* Witney Grammar Sch. RAF, 1929. Served War of 1939-45 with Bomber Command in UK and Middle East. Graduate, Middle East Centre for Arab Studies, 1945-46. Air Adviser to Lebanon, 1950-53; with Cabinet Secretariat, 1954-55; OC, RAF, Ternhill, 1956-58; Sen. RAF Dir, and later Commandant, Jt Services Staff Coll.; Asst Chief of Staff, Cento, 1960-63; Asst Commandant, RAF Staff Coll., 1963-65. Gordon Shephard Memorial Prize (for Strategic Studies), 1955, 1956, 1957, 1961, 1965, 1967. Officer, Order of Cedar of Lebanon, 1953. *Recreation:* ski-ing. *Address:* Blue Range, Macedon, Vic. 3440, Australia.

CARTER, Sir William (Oscar), Kt 1972; Consultant, Hill and Perks, Solicitors, Norwich; Partner, Bird Hill & Co., Amsterdam; *b* 12 Jan. 1905; *s* of late Oscar Carter and Alice Carter; *m* 1934, Winifred Thompson. *Educ:* Swaffham Grammar Sch.; City of Norwich Sch. Admitted Solicitor of Supreme Court of Judicature, 1931. Served War, 1940-45, RAF (Wing Comdr), UK and Middle East. Mem. Council, The Law Society, 1954-75, Vice-Pres. 1970, Pres. 1971-72; President: East Anglian Law Soc., 1952; Norfolk and Norwich Incorporated Law Soc., 1959; Internat. Legal Aid Assoc.; Mem. Council, Internat. Bar Assoc. (first Vice-Pres., 1976-). Member: County Court Rules Cttee, 1956-60; Supreme Court Rules Cttee, 1960-75; Criminal Injuries Compensation Board; Law Panel, British Council. Former Chm., Mental Health Review Tribunals for E Anglian and NE Thames RHA Areas. Director: Mann Egerton & Co. Ltd; Tibbenham Holdings Ltd. Liveryman, Worshipful Co. of Glaziers; Hon. Mem., The Fellows of American Bar Foundn. *Recreations:* swimming, walking, foreign travel. *Address:* 83 Newmarket Road, Norwich. *T:* Norwich 53772. *Clubs:* Army and Navy; Norfolk (Norwich).

CARTER, William Stovold, CMG 1970; CVO 1956; retired; Secretary, Council on Tribunals, 1970-76; *b* 10 Oct. 1915, *s* of late R. S. Carter, Bournemouth, Hants; *m* 1944, Barbara Alice Kathleen Dines; two *s* one *d*. *Educ:* Bec; Christ's Coll., Cambridge. Entered Colonial Administrative Service (Nigeria), 1939; retd as Administrative Officer, Class I (Resident), 1957. Entered Colonial Office, 1959; Asst Sec., 1965; joined Commonwealth Office, 1966; joined Foreign and Commonwealth Office, 1968; Head of Hong Kong Dept, 1965-70. *Recreation:* golf. *Address:* Broad Oak Farm, Chiddingly, near Lewes, East Sussex. *T:* Chiddingly 267.

CARTER-JONES, Lewis; MP (Lab) Eccles since 1964; industrial training adviser; *b* Gilfach Goch, S Wales, 17 Nov. 1920; *s* of Tom Jones, Kenfig Hill, Bridgend, Glam.; *m* 1945, Patricia Hylda, *d* of late Alfred Bastiman, Scarborough, Yorks; two *d*. *Educ:* Bridgend County Sch.; University Coll. of Wales, Aberystwyth; BA (Chm. Student Finance Cttee). Served War of 1939-45 (Flight Sergeant Navigator, RAF). Head of Business Studies Dept, Yale Grammar-Technical Sch., Wrexham, Denbighshire. Contested (Lab) Chester, by-election, 1956, and general election, 1959. Chairman: Anglo-Columbian Gp; Cttee for Research for Apparatus for Disabled; Parly Labour Party Disablement Gp; Possum Research Foundation; Vice-Chairman: All-Party Gp for the Chemical Industry; Parly Labour Party Aviation Gp; Disabled Income Gp (DIG);

Secretary: Indo-British Parly Gp; All-Party BLESMA Gp. Special interest, application of technology for aged and disabled; Member: Management Cttee, Inst. of Orthopaedics; Brit. Assoc. for the Retarded; Departmental Working Party on Mobility; Snowdon Cttee on Integration of Disabled in Society. Parly Adviser to RNIB. *Address:* House of Commons, SW1; Cader Idris, 5 Cefn Road, Rhosnessney, Wrexham, N Wales.

CARTIER, Rudolph; Drama Producer, Television, since 1953; also Producer Television Operas, since 1956; *b* Vienna, Austria, 17 April 1908; *s* of Joseph Cartier; *m* 1949, Margaret Pepper; two *d*. *Educ:* Vienna Academy of Music and Dramatic Art (Max Reinhardt's Master-class). Film director and Scenario writer in pre-war Berlin; came to Britain, 1935; joined BBC Television. Productions include: Arrow to the Heart, Dybbuk, Portrait of Peter Perowne, 1952; It is Midnight, Doctor Schweitzer, L'Aiglon, The Quatermass Experiment, Wuthering Heights, 1953; Such Men are Dangerous, That Lady, Captain Banner, Nineteen-Eightyfour, 1954; Moment of Truth, The Creature, Vale of Shadows, Quatermass II, The Devil's General, 1955; The White Falcon, The Mayerling Affair, The Public Prosecutor, The Fugitive, The Cold Light, The Saint of Bleecker Street, Dark Victory, Clive of India, The Queen and the Rebels, 1956; Salome, Ordeal by Fire, Counsellor-at-Law, 1957; Captain of Koepenick, The Winslow Boy, A Tale of Two Cities, Midsummer Night's Dream, 1958; Quatermass and the Pit, Philadelphia Story, Mother Courage and her Children, (Verdi's) Othello, 1959; The White Guard, Glorious Morning, Tobias and the Angel (Opera), 1960; Rashomon, Adventure Story, Anna Karenina, Cross of Iron, 1961; Doctor Korczuk and the Children, Sword of Vengeance, Carmen, 1962; Anna Christie, Night Express, Stalingrad, 1963; Lady of the Camelias, The Midnight Men, The July Plot, 1964; Wings of the Dove, Ironhand, The Joel Brand Story, 1965; Gordon of Khartoum, Lee Oswald, Assassin, 1966; Firebrand, The Burning Bush, 1967; The Fanatics, Triumph of Death, The Naked Sun, The Rebel, 1968; Conversation at Night, An Ideal Husband, 1969; Rembrandt, The Bear (Opera), The Year of the Crow, 1970; The Proposal, 1971; Lady Windermere's Fan, 1972; The Deep Blue Sea, 1973; Fall of Eagles (episodes Dress Rehearsal, End Game), 1974; Loyalties, 1976; Gaslight, 1977. Prod. Film, Corridor of Mirrors. Directed Film, Passionate Summer. Guild of Television Producers and Directors "Oscar" as best drama producer of 1957. *Recreations:* motoring, serious music, going to films or watching television, stamp-collecting. *Address:* 26 Lowther Road, Barnes, SW13.

CARTIER-BRESSON, Henri; photographer; *b* France, 22 Aug. 1908. Studied painting with André Lhote, 1927-28. Asst Dir to Jean Renoir, 1936-39; Co-founder, Magnum Photos, Paris and NY, 1947. Photographs exhibited: Mexico; Japan; Mus. of Modern Art, NY, 1947, 1968; Villa Medicis, Rome; Louvre, 1955, 1967, Grand Palais, 1970, Paris; V&A, 1969; Manege, Moscow, 1972; drawings exhibited: Carlton Gall., NY, 1975; Bischofberger Gall., Zürich, 1976; Forcalquier Gall., France, 1976. Documentary films: on hosps, Spanish Republic, 1937; (with J. Lemare) Le Retour, 1945; (with J. Boffety) Impressions of California, 1969; (with W. Dombrow) Southern Exposures, 1970. Hon. DLitt Oxon, 1975. Awards: US Camera, 1948; Overseas Press Club of America, 1949; Amer. Soc. of Magazine Photography, 1953; Photography Soc. of America, 1958; Overseas Press Club, 1954 (for Russia), 1960 (for China), 1964 (for Cuba); German Photographic Soc. *Publications:* (ed) Images à la Sauvette (The Decisive Moment), 1952; Verve, 1952; The Europeans; Moscow, 1955; From One China to the Other, 1956; Photographs by Cartier-Bresson; Flagrants Délits (The World of Henri Cartier-Bresson, 1968); (with F. Nourrissier) Vive la France, 1970; Cartier-Bresson's France, 1971; (jtly) L'Homme et la Machine, 1972 (Man and Machine, 1969) for IBM; Faces of Asia, 1972; A Propos de l'URSS, 1973 (About Russia, 1974); Henri Cartier-Bresson, 1977. *Address:* c/o Magnum Photos, 2 rue Christine, 75006 Paris, France; c/o Helen Wright, 135 East 74th Street, New York, NY 10021, USA; c/o John Hillelson, 145 Fleet Street, EC4A 2BU.

CARTLAND, Barbara (Hamilton); authoress and playwright; *d* of late Major Bertram Cartland, Worcestershire Regiment; *m* 1st, 1927, Alexander George McCorquodale (whom she divorced, 1933; he *d* 1964), of Cound Hall, Cressage, Salop; one *d*; 2nd, 1936, Hugh (*d* 1963), 2nd *s* of late Harold McCorquodale, Forest Hall, Ongar, Essex; two *s*. Published first novel at the age of twenty-one, which ran into five editions; designed and organised many pageants in aid of charity, including Britain and her Industries at British Legion Ball, Albert Hall, 1930; carried the first aeroplane-towed glider-mail in her glider, the Barbara Cartland, from Manston Aerodrome to Reading, June 1931; 2 lecture tours in Canada, 1940; Hon. Junior Commander, ATS and Lady Welfare Officer and

Librarian to all Services in Bedfordshire, 1941-49; Certificate of Merit, Eastern Command 1946; County Cadet Officer for St John Ambulance Brigade in Beds, 1943-47, County Vice-Pres. Cadets, Beds, 1948-50; organised and produced the St John Ambulance Bde Exhibn, 1945-50; Chm St John Ambulance Bde Exhibn Cttee, 1944-51; County Vice-Pres.: Nursing Cadets, Herts, 1951; Nursing Div., Herts, 1966; CC Herts (Hatfield Div.), 1955-64; Chm., St John Council, Herts; Pres. Herts Br. of Royal Coll. of Midwives, 1957. Founder, Barbara Cartland-Onslow Romany Gypsy Fund (with Earl of Onslow and Earl of Birkenhead) to Provide sites for Romany Gypsies, 1961 (first Romany Gypsy Camp at Hatfield); Dep. Pres., National Association of Health, 1965; Pres., 1966. DStJ 1972 (Mem. Chapter Gen.). *Publications: novels:* Jigsaw; Sawdust; If the Tree is Saved; For What?; Sweet Punishment; A Virgin in Mayfair; Just off Piccadilly; Not Love Alone; A Beggar Wished; Passionate Attainment; First Class Lady; Dangerous Experiment; Desperate Defiance; The Forgotten City; Saga at Forty; But Never Free; Bitter Winds; Broken Barriers; The Gods Forget; The Black Panther; Stolen Halo; Now Rough-Now Smooth; Open Wings; The Leaping Flame; Yet She Follows; Escape from Passion; The Dark Stream; After the Night; Armour against Love; Out of Reach; The Hidden Heart; Against the Stream; Again this Rapture; The Dream Within; If We Will; No Heart is Free; Sleeping Swords; Love is Mine; The Passionate Pilgrim; Blue Heather; Wings on My Heart; The Kiss of Paris; Love Forbidden; Lights of Love; The Thief of Love; The Sweet Enchantress; The Kiss of Silk; The Price is Love; The Runaway Heart; A Light to the Heart; Love is Dangerous; Danger by the Nile; Love on the Run; A Hazard of Hearts; A Duel of Hearts; A Knave of Hearts; The Enchanted Moment; The Little Pretender; A Ghost in Monte Carlo; Love is an Eagle; Love is the Enemy; Cupid Rides Pillion; Love Me For Ever; Elizabethan Lover; Desire of the Heart; The Enchanted Waltz; The Kiss of the Devil; The Captive Heart; The Coin of Love; Stars in My Heart; Sweet Adventure; The Golden Gondola; Love in Hiding; The Smuggled Heart; Love under Fire; The Messenger of Love; The Wings of Love; The Hidden Evil; The Fire of Love; The Unpredictable Bride; Love Holds the Cards; A Virgin in Paris; Love to the Rescue; Love is Contraband; The Enchanting Evil; The Unknown Heart; The Secret Fear; The Reluctant Bride; The Pretty Horse-Breakers; The Audacious Adventures; Halo for the Devil; The Irresistable Buck; Lost Enchantment; The Odious Duke; The Wicked Marquis; The Complacent Wife; The Little Adventure; The Daring Deception; No Darkness for Love; Lessons in Love; The Ruthless Rake; Journey to Paradise; The Dangerous Dandy; The Bored Bridegroom; The Penniless Peer; The Cruel Count; The Castle of Fear; The Glittering Lights; Fire on the Snow; The Elusive Earl; Moon over Eden; The Golden Illusion; No Time for Love; The Husband Hunters; The Slaves of Love; Passions in the Sand; An Angel in Hell; The Wild Cry of Love; The Blue-Eyed Witch; The Incredible Honeymoon; A Dream from the Night; Conquered by Love; Never Laugh at Love; The Secret of the Glen; The Dream and the Glory; The Proud Princess; Hungry for Love; The Heart Triumphant; The Disgraceful Duke; The Taming of Lady Lorinda; Vote for Love; The Mysterious Maid-Servant; The Magic of Love; Kiss the Moonlight; Love Locked In; The Marquis who Hated Women; Rhapsody of Love; Look Listen and Love; Duel with Destiny; The Wild Unwilling Wife; Punishment of a Vixen; The Curse of the Clan; The Outrageous Lady; A Touch of Love; The Love Pirate; The Dragon and the Pearl; The Temptation of Torilla; The Passion and the Flower; Love, Lords and Ladybirds; Love and the Loathsome Leopard; The Naked Battle; The Hell-Cat and the King; No Escape From Love. *philosophy:* Touch the Stars; *sociology:* You in the Home; The Fascinating Forties; Marriage for Moderns; Be Vivid, Be Vital; Love, Life and Sex; Look Lovely, Be Lovely; Vitamins for Vitality; Husbands and Wives; Etiquette; The Many Facets of Love; Sex and the Teenager; Charm; Living Together; Woman the Enigma; The Youth Secret; The Magic of Honey; Health Food Cookery Book; Book of Beauty and Health; Men are Wonderful; The Magic of Honey Cookbook; Food for Love; Recipes for Lovers; *biography:* Ronald Cartland, 1942; Bewitching Women; The Outrageous Queen; Polly, My Wonderful Mother, 1956; The Scandalous Life of King Carol; The Private Life of Charles II; The Private Life of Elizabeth, Empress of Austria; Josephine, Empress of France; Diane de Poitiers; Metternich; The Passionate Diplomat; *autobiography:* The Isthmus Years, 1943; The Years of Opportunity, 1947; I Search for Rainbows, 1967; We Danced All Night, 1919-1929, 1971; *verse:* Lines on Love and Life; *plays:* Blood Money; French Dressing (with Bruce Woodhouse); *revue:* The Mayfair Revue; *radio play:* The Caged Bird; *television:* Portrait of Successful Woman, 1957; This is Your Life, 1958; Success Story, 1959; Midland Profile, 1961; No Looking Back-a Portrait of Barbara Cartland, 1967; The Frost Programme, 1968; *radio:* The World of Barbara Cartland, 1970, and many other radio

and television appearances. Editor of the Common Problem, by Ronald Cartland, 1943. *Address:* Camfield Place, Hatfield, Herts. *T:* Potters Bar 42612, 42657.
See also Countess of Spencer.

CARTLAND, Sir George (Barrington), Kt 1963; CMG 1956; BA; Vice-Chancellor of the University of Tasmania, 1968-77; *b* 22 Sept. 1912; *s* of William Arthur and Margaret Cartland, West Didsbury, *m* 1937, Dorothy Rayton; two *s. Educ:* Manchester Central High Sch.; Manchester Univ.; Hertford Coll., Oxford. Entered Colonial Service, Gold Coast, 1935; served Colonial Office, 1944-49; Head of African Studies Br. and Ed. Jl of Afr. Adminis., 1945-49; Sec. London Afr. Conf., 1948; Admin. Sec., Uganda, 1949; Sec. for Social Services and Local Govt, Uganda, 1952; min. for Social Services, Uganda, 1955; Min. of Education and Labour, Uganda, 1958; Chief Sec., Uganda, 1960; Deputy Gov. of Uganda, 1961-62 (Acting Gov., various occasions, 1952-62); Registrar of Univ. of Birmingham, 1963-67. Part-time Mem., West Midlands Gas Bd, 1964-67. Chm., St John Council, Uganda, 1958-59; Pres., St John Council, Tasmania, 1969-. Dep.-Chm., Australian Vice-Chancellors' Cttee, 1975; Chm., Adv. Cttee on National Park in SW Tasmania, 1976-77. KStJ 1972; awarded Belgian medal recognising services in connection with evacuation of the Congo, 1960. *Recreations:* mountaineering, fishing. *Address:* c/o University of Tasmania, Hobart, Tasmania. *Clubs:* Athenæum; Tasmanian, Athenæum, Royal Tasmanian Yacht (all Hobart).

CARTLEDGE, Bryan George; HM Diplomatic Service; Private Secretary (Overseas Affairs) to the Prime Minister, since 1977; *b* 10 June 1931; *s* of Eric Montague George Cartledge and Phyllis (*née* Shaw); *m* 1960, Ruth Hylton Gass, *d* of John Gass; one *s* one *d. Educ:* Hurstpierpoint; St John's Coll., Cambridge. Queen's Royal Regt, 1950-51. Commonwealth Fund Fellow, Stanford Univ., 1956-57; Research Fellow, St Antony's Coll., Oxford, 1958-59. Entered HM Foreign (subseq. Diplomatic) Service, 1960; served in FO, 1960-61; Stockholm, 1961-63; Moscow, 1963-66; DSAO, 1966-68; Tehran, 1968-70; Harvard Univ., 1971-72; Counsellor, Moscow, 1972-75; Head of E European and Soviet Dept, FCO, 1975-77. *Recreations:* music, fishing. *Address:* Holly Cottage, Hellingly, Sussex; c/o Foreign and Commonwealth Office, SW1 2AH.

CARTWRIGHT, Ven. David; see Cartwright, Ven. E. D.

CARTWRIGHT, Ven. (Edward) David; Archdeacon of Winchester, Hon. Canon of Winchester Cathedral and Vicar of Sparsholt with Lainston, Hampshire, since 1973; *b* 15 July 1920; *o c* of John Edward Cartwright and Gertrude Cartwright (*née* Lusby), North Somercotes and Grimsby, Lincs; *m* 1946, Elsie Irene, *o c* of Walter and Jane Elizabeth Rogers, Grimsby; one *s* two *d. Educ:* Grimsby Parish Church Choir Sch.; Lincoln Sch.; Selwyn Coll. and Westcott House, Cambridge. 2nd Cl. Hons Hist. Tripos Pt 1, 1940; 2nd Cl. Hons Theol Tripos Pt 1, 1942; Steel Univ. Stud. in Divinity, 1941; BA 1941, MA 1945; Pres., SCM in Cambridge, 1941-42. Deacon, 1943; Priest, 1944; Curate of Boston, 1943-48; Vicar: St Leonard's, Redfield, Bristol, 1948-52; Olveston with Aust, 1952-60; Bishopston, 1960-73; Secretary, Bristol Diocesan Synod, 1967-73; Hon. Canon of Bristol Cathedral, 1970-73. Dir of Studies, Bristol Lay Readers, 1956-72; Proctor in Convocation, Mem. of Church Assembly and General Synod, 1956-73, 1975-. Member: Bristol Diocesan Bd of Finance, 1959-73; Central Bd of Finance of C of E, 1970-73. Church Commissioner, 1973; Dilapidations Legislation Commn, 1958-64; Working Party on Housing of Retired Clergy, 1972-73; Differential Payment of Clergy, 1976-77. Secretary, Bristol Council of Christian Churches, 1950-61. Anglican-Presbyterian Conversations, 1962-66; Convocations Jt Cttees on Anglican-Methodist Union Scheme, 1965. *Recreations:* book-hunting and rose-growing. *Address:* Sparsholt Vicarage, Winchester, Hants. *T:* Sparsholt 265.

CARTWRIGHT, Frederick; see Cartwright, W. F.

CARTWRIGHT, Harry, MBE 1946; MA, CEng, MIMechE, MIEE; Director, Atomic Energy Establishment, Winfrith, since 1973; *b* 16 Sept. 1919; *s* of Edwin Harry Cartwright and Agnes Alice Cartwright (*née* Gillibrand); *m* 1950, Catharine Margaret Carson Bradbury; two *s. Educ:* William Hulme's Grammar Sch., Manchester; St John's Coll., Cambridge (Schol.). 1st cl. Mechanical Sciences Tripos, 1940. Served War, RAF, 1940-46: Flt Lt, service on ground radar in Europe, India and Burma. Decca Navigator Co., 1946-47; English Electric Co., 1947-49; joined Dept of Atomic Energy, Risley, as a Design and Project Engr, 1949; Chief Engr, 1955; Dir in charge of UKAEA consultancy services on nuclear reactors, 1960-64; Dir, Water Reactors, 1964-70, and as such responsible for design and construction of Winfrith 100 MW(e) SGHWR prototype power station; Dir, Fast Reactor Systems, 1970-73. *Publications:*

various techn. papers. *Recreations:* walking, gardening. *Address:* Tabbit's Hill House, Corfe Castle, Wareham, Dorset BH20 5HZ. *T:* Corfe Castle 582. *Club:* United Oxford & Cambridge University.

CARTWRIGHT, Rev. Canon James Lawrence, FSA 1958; Canon Emeritus since 1966 (Residentiary Canon and Chancellor of Peterborough Cathedral, and Chapter Librarian, 1952-66); *b* Loughborough, 8 June 1889; *s* of James Cartwright and Harriet Macaulay Todd; *m* 1918, Ruth, *o d* of William Frederick Buck; two *d. Educ:* Loughborough Grammar Sch.; King's Coll., Cambridge. BA 1917 (2nd Class Hist. Tripos, Parts I and II); MA 1921. Admitted a Solicitor, 1911. Served European War, 1918-19, in France, Temp. 2nd Lieut Royal Sussex Regt. Deacon, 1919; Priest, 1920; Curate: St Peter's and Thorpe Acre, Loughborough, 1919-22; St John Baptist, Knighton, Leicester, 1922-25; Vicar: Christ Church, Northampton, 1925-33; Oundle with Ashton, 1933-52; Rural Dean Oundle I, 1937-52; Non-Residentiary Canon of Peterborough, 1946-52; Select Preacher, University of Cambridge, 1964. *Recreation:* reading. *Address:* 129 Park Road, Peterborough. *T:* Peterborough 68396.

CARTWRIGHT, John Cameron; MP (Lab) Greenwich, Woolwich East, since Oct. 1974; *b* 29 Nov. 1933; *s* of Aubrey John Randolph Cartwright and Jeanette Billie Billie Cartwright; *m* 1959, Iris June Tant; one *s* one *d. Educ:* Woking County Grammar School. Exec. Officer, Home Civil Service, 1952-55; Labour Party Agent, 1955-67; Political Sec., RACS Ltd, 1967-72; Director, RACS Ltd, 1972-74. Leader, Greenwich Borough Council, 1971-74. Mem., Lab Party Nat. Exec. Cttee, 1971-75 and 1976-. PPS to Sec. of State for Education and Science, 1976-. Vice-Pres., Assoc. of Metropolitan Authorities, 1974-. Trustee, Nat. Maritime Museum, 1976-. *Recreations:* do-it-yourself, watching Charlton Athletic, enrolling Labour Party members. *Address:* 17 Commonwealth Way, SE2 0JZ. *T:* 01-311 4394.

CARTWRIGHT, Rt. Hon. John Robert, CC (Canada) 1970; PC (Can.) 1967; MC 1917; Chief Justice of Canada, 1967-70; Judge, Supreme Court of Canada, 1949-70; *b* Toronto, Canada, 23 March 1895; *s* of James Strachan Cartwright, KC, MA, and Jane Elizabeth (*née* Young), Weymouth, England; *m* 1st, Jessie Carnegie, *d* of Thomas Alexander Gibson, KC, Toronto; one *d*; 2nd, Mabel Ethelwyn Tremaine, *widow* of late Brig. Arthur Victor Tremaine, CBE, CD, and *d* of George William Parmelee, LLD, DCL, of Quebec. *Educ:* Upper Canada Coll., Toronto; Osgoode Hall, Toronto. Served European War, 1914-18; enlisted Canadian Expeditionary Force, Aug. 1914; Lieut 1915; Capt. 1916; with 3rd Canadian Infantry Bn until Dec. 1915 (wounded twice); ADC to GOC 3rd Canadian Div., 1915, until demobilization in 1919; Called to bar, Ontario, 1920, with honours and Silver Medal. Appointed KC (Ont), 1933; Bencher of Law Society of Upper Canada, 1946 (Hon. Bencher, 1970); practised at Toronto with firm Smith, Rae, Greer & Cartwright. Hon. LLD: Toronto, 1959; Osgoode Hall, 1963; Queen's Univ., Kingston, Ont, 1967; York Univ., Toronto, 1969; Ottawa, 1973; Hon. DCL Bishop's Univ., Lennoxville, 1970. *Recreations:* chess and reading. *Address:* 85 Range Road, Apartment 707, Ottawa K1N 8J6, Canada. *T:* 232-1990. *Clubs:* Rideau, Country, Le Cercle Universitaire d'Ottawa (Ottawa); Toronto, Royal Canadian Military Institute (Toronto).

CARTWRIGHT, Dame Mary Lucy, DBE 1969; FRS 1947; ScD Cambridge 1949; MA Oxford and Cambridge; DPhil Oxford; Hon. LLD (Edin.) 1953; Hon. DSc: Leeds, 1958; Hull, 1959; Wales, 1962; Oxford, 1966; Fellow of Girton College, Cambridge, 1934-49, and since 1968; *b* 1900; *d* of late W. D. Cartwright, Rector of Aynhoe. *Educ:* Godolphin Sch., Salisbury, and St Hugh's Coll., Oxford. Asst Mistress Alice Ottley Sch., Worcester, 1923-24, Wycombe Abbey Sch., Bucks, 1924-27; read for DPhil, 1928-30; Yarrow Research Fellow of Girton Coll., 1930-34; Univ. Lectr in Mathematics, Cambridge, 1935-59; Mistress of Girton Coll., Cambridge, 1949-68; Reader in the Theory of Functions, Univ. of Cambridge, 1959-68, Emeritus Reader, 1968-; Visiting Professor: Brown Univ., Providence, RI, 1968-69; Claremont Graduate Sch., California, 1969-70; Case Western Reserve, 1970; Polish Acad. of Sciences, 1970; Univ. of Wales (Swansea and Cardiff), 1971; Case Western Reserve, 1971. Consultant on US Navy Mathematical Research Projects at Stanford and Princeton Universities, Jan.-May 1949. Fellow of Cambridge Philosophical Soc.; Pres. London Math. Soc., 1961-63; Pres. Mathematical Association, 1951-52. Sylvester Medal, Royal Soc., 1964; De Morgan Medal, London Mathematical Soc., 1968; Medal of Univ. of Jyväskylä, Finland, 1973. Hon. FIMA, 1972. Commandant British Red Cross Detachment, Cambridgeshire 112, 1940-44. Commander, Order of the Dannebrog. *Publications:* Integral Functions (Cambridge Tracts in Mathematics and Mathematical Physics), 1956; math. papers in various journals. *Address:* 38 Sherlock Close,

Cambridge CB3 0HP. *T:* Cambridge 52574. *See also W. F. Cartwright.*

CARTWRIGHT, Rt. Rev. Richard Fox; *see* Plymouth, Suffragan Bishop of.

CARTWRIGHT, (William) Frederick, CBE 1977; DL, MIMechE; Director, BSC (International) Ltd; a Deputy Chairman, British Steel Corporation, 1970-72; Group Managing Director, S Wales Group, British Steel Corporation, 1967-70; Chairman, The Steel Co. of Wales Ltd, 1967 (Managing Director, 1962-67); *b* 13 Nov. 1906; *s* of William Digby Cartwright, Rector of Aynhoe; *m* 1937, Sally Chrystobel Ware; two *s* one *d. Educ:* Rugby Sch. Joined Guest, Keen and Nettlefold, Dowlais, 1929; gained experience at steelworks in Germany and Luxembourg, 1930; Asst Works Manager, 1931, Tech, Asst to Managing Director, 1935, Dir and Chief Engineer, 1940, Dir and General Manager, 1943, Guest, Keen and Baldwin, Port Talbot Works; Dir and General Manager, Steel Co. of Wales, 1947; Asst Man. Dir and General Manager of the Steel Div., The Steel Co. of Wales Ltd, 1954. Pres., Iron and Steel Inst., 1960. Dir, Lloyds Bank, 1968-77 (Chm., S Wales Regional Bd, 1968-77); Director: Davy International Ltd; HTV Ltd. Dir., Develt Corp for Wales; Member: Welsh Council; Council, Univ. of Wales. Freeman of Port Talbot, 1970. DL, County of Glamorgan; High Sheriff, Glamorgan, 1961. OStJ. Hon. LLD Wales, 1968. Bessemer Gold Medal, 1958; Frederico Giolitti Steel Medal, 1960. *Recreations:* riding and yachting. *Address:* Castle-upon-Alun, St Brides Major, near Bridgend, Mid Glam. *T:* Southern-down 298. *Clubs:* Royal Ocean Racing, Royal Cruising; Royal Yacht Squadron. *See also Dame Mary Cartwright.*

CARTWRIGHT SHARP, Michael; *see* Sharp, J. M. C.

CARVELL, John Eric Maclean, CBE 1950; *b* 12 Aug. 1894; *s* of John Maclean Carvell, MBE, MRCS, and Euphemia Sarah Avery; *m* 1918, Cicely Lilian, *y d* of F. S. Garratt, Reigate, Surrey; one *d. Educ:* Berkhamsted. Served European War, 2nd Lieut Queen's Westminster Rifles, 1914; France, 1915 (twice wounded); Instructor to Portuguese Army, 1917-18; Staff Capt., HQ London District, 1918-19; Vice-Consul, Lisbon, 1919; Cadiz, 1921; Chargé d'Affaires, Port-au-Prince, 1922; Consul (Local Rank), Brest, 1925; Vice-Consul, Munich, 1929; Consul, Porto Alegre, 1932, New York, 1934; Consul-General, Munich, 1938-39; Algiers, 1942-45; Los Angeles, 1945-47; Ambassador to Ecuador, 1950-51 (Minister, 1947-50); Minister to Bulgaria, 1951-54, retd from Foreign Service, 1954.

CARVER, family name of **Baron Carver.**

CARVER, Baron *cr* 1977 (Life Peer), of Shackleford, Surrey; **Field-Marshal (Richard) Michael (Power) Carver,** GCB 1970 (KCB 1966; CB 1957); CBE 1945; DSO 1943 and Bar 1943; MC 1941; designated British Resident Commissioner in Rhodesia, 1977; Chief of the Defence Staff, 1973-76; *b* 24 April 1915; 2nd *s* of late Harold Power Carver and late Winifred Anne Gabrielle Carver (*née* Wellesley); *m* 1947, Edith, *d* of Lt-Col Sir Henry Lowry-Corry, MC; two *s* two *d. Educ:* Winchester Coll.; Sandhurst. 2nd Lieut Royal Tank Corps, 1935; War of 1939-45 (despatches twice); GSO1, 7th Armoured Div., 1942; OC 1st Royal Tank Regt, 1943; Comdr 4th Armoured Brigade, 1944; Tech. Staff Officer (1), Min. of Supply, 1947; Joint Services Staff Coll., 1950; AQMG, Allied Land Forces, Central Europe, 1951; Col GS, SHAPE 1952; Dep. Chief of Staff, East Africa, 1954 (despatches); Chief of Staff, East Africa, 1955; idc 1957; Dir of Plans, War Office, 1958-59; Comdr 6th Infty Brigade, 1960-62; Maj.-Gen. 1962; GOC, 3 Div., 1962-64, also Comdr Joint Truce Force, Cyprus, and Dep. Comdr United Nations' Force in Cyprus, 1964; Dir, Army Staff Duties, Min. of Defence, 1964-66; Lt-Gen. 1966; comd FE Land Forces, 1966-67; Gen., 1967; C-in-C, Far East, 1967-69; GOC-in-C, Southern Command, 1969-71; Chief of the General Staff, 1971-73; Field-Marshal 1973. Col Commandant: REME 1966-76; Royal Tank Regt, 1968-72; RAC, 1974-77; ADC (Gen.) 1969-72. *Publications:* Second to None (History of Royal Scots Greys, 1919-45), 1954; El Alamein, 1962; Tobruk, 1964; (ed) The War Lords, 1976. *Address:* Shackleford Old Rectory, Godalming, Surrey. *T:* Godalming 22483. *Club:* Anglo-Belgian.

CARY, family name of **Viscount Falkland.**

CARY, Sir Robert (Archibald), 1st Bt, *cr* 1955; Kt 1945; *b* 25 May 1898; *s* of Robert Cary; *m* 1924, Hon. Rosamond Mary Curzon, *d* of late Col Hon. Alfred Nathaniel Curzon and *sister* of 2nd Viscount Scarsdale, TD; one *s. Educ:* Ardingly; Royal Military Coll., Sandhurst. Served European War, 1916-18; 4th Dragoon Guards, 1916-23; Gen. Staff, Iraq, 1920; North Persia, 1921;

rejoined 4th/7th Royal Dragoon Guards, Sept. 1939, and reappointed to Gen. Staff; MP (U) Eccles, 1935-45; PPS to Civil Lord of Admiralty, 1939; PPS to Sec. of State for India, 1942-44; a Lord Commissioner of the Treasury, 1945; MP (C) Withington, Manchester, 1951-Feb. 1974; PPS to Min. of Health, 1951-52; PPS to Lord Privy Seal and Leader of the House, 1951-64. Mem. of House of Commons Select Cttee on National Expenditure, 1941. *Heir: s* Roger Hugh Cary [*b* 8 Jan. 1926; Lieut, Gren. Guards (Res.); *m* 1st, 1948, Marilda, *d* of Major P. Pearson-Gregory, MC; one *d*; 2nd, 1953, Ann Helen Katharine, *e d* of Hugh Blair Brenan; two *s* one *d*]. *Address:* Wrotham Water, Wrotham, Kent. *T:* Fairseat 822476. *Clubs:* Turf, Pratt's.

CARY, Maj.-Gen. Rupert Tristram Oliver, CB 1948; CBE 1943 (MBE 1919); DSO 1943; late Royal Corps of Signals; *b* 1896. Served European War, 1916-19, France, Belgium, India (wounded, MBE, 3 medals); Persia and Iraq, 1941-43 (despatches, CBE); signal officer Eighth Army, 1943; Maj.-Gen. 1944; Commandant Sch. of Signals, 1945-46; ADC to the King, 1946-47; Comdr of Catterick sub-district, 1946-49; retired pay, 1949.

CASALONE, Carlo D.; *see* Dionisotti-Casalone.

CASE, Air Vice-Marshal Albert Avion, CB 1964; CBE 1957 (OBE 1943); General Secretary, Hospital Saving Association, since 1969; Hon. Secretary, British Hospitals Contributory Schemes Association, since 1972; *b* Portsmouth, 5 April 1916; *s* of late Group Captain Albert Edward Case and Florence Stella Hosier Case, Amesbury, Wilts; *m* 1949, Brenda Margaret, *e d* of late A. G. Andrews, Enfield, Middx; one *s* one *d. Educ:* Imperial Service Coll. Commd RAF, 1934; Sqdn Ldr, 1940; Wing Comdr, Commanding No 202 Squadron, 1942; Group Capt., Maritime Ops HQ, ACSEA, 1945; OC, RAF, Koggala, Ceylon, 1945-46; JSSC, 1950-51; OC, RAF, Chivenor, 1953-55; OC, RAF, Nicosia, 1956-57; IDC, 1959; Air Cdre, 1959; Air Min., Dir, Operational Requirements, 1959-62; Air Vice-Marshal, 1962; AOC No 22 Group RAF, Tech. Trg Comd, 1962-66; SASO HQ Coastal Comd, 1966-68; retd. MBIM. *Recreations:* swimming (RAF blue 1946), sailing. *Address:* 25 Kewferry Road, Northwood, Middx. *Clubs:* Royal Air Force; Royal Air Force Yacht, Cruising Association.

CASE, Humphrey John; Keeper, Department of Antiquities, Ashmolean Museum, since 1973; *b* 26 May 1918; *s* of George Reginald Case and Margaret Helen (*née* Duckett); *m* 1949, Jean Alison (*née* Orr); two *s. Educ:* Charterhouse; St John's Coll., Cambridge (MA); Inst. of Archaeology, London Univ. Served War, 1939-46. Ashmolean Museum: Asst Keeper, 1949-57; Sen. Asst Keeper, 1957-69; Dep. Keeper, Dept of Antiquities, 1969-73. Vice-Pres., Prehistoric Soc., 1969-73; has directed excavations in England, Ireland and France. FSA 1954. *Publications:* in learned jls (British and foreign): principally on neolithic in Western Europe, prehistoric metallurgy and regional archaeology. *Recreations:* reading, music, swimming. *Address:* 187 Thame Road, Warborough, Oxon OX9 8DH.

CASE, Captain Richard Vere Essex, DSO 1942; DSC 1940; RD; RNR retired; Royal Naval Reserve ADC to the Queen, 1958; Chief Marine Superintendent, Coast Lines Ltd and Associated Companies, 1953-69; *b* 13 April 1904; *s* of late Prof. R. H. Case; *m* 1940, Olive May, *d* of H. W. Griggs, Preston, near Canterbury, Kent; one *s* one *d. Educ:* Thames Nautical Training Coll., HMS Worcester. Joined RNR 1920; commenced service in Merchant Service, 1920; Master's Certificate of Competency, 1928; Captain RNR, 1953; served War of 1939-45 (DSO, DSC and Bar, RD and Clasp). *Recreation:* bowls. *Address:* 5 The Serpentine, Grassendale, Liverpool L19 9DT. *T:* 051-427 1016. *Clubs:* Athenæum (Liverpool); Liverpool Cricket.

CASEY, Most Rev. Eamonn; *see* Galway and Kilmacduagh, Bishop of, (RC).

CASEY, Michael Bernard; a Deputy Chairman and Chief Executive, British Shipbuilders, since 1977; *b* 1 Sept. 1928; *s* of Joseph Bernard Casey, OBE, and late Dorothy (*née* Love); *m* 1963, Sally Louise, *e d* of James Stuart Smith; two *s* two *d. Educ:* Colwyn Bay Grammar Sch.; LSE (Scholar in Laws, 1952; LLB 1954). RAF, 1947-49. Principal, MAFF, 1961; Office of the Minister for Science, 1963-64; Asst Sec., DEA, 1967; DTI (later Dept of Prices and Consumer Protection), 1970; Under Sec., DoI, 1975-77. *Recreations:* golf, chess, bridge. *Address:* 7 Sibella Road, SW4.

CASEY, Rt. Rev. Patrick Joseph; *see* Brentwood, Bishop of, (RC).

CASEY, Dr Raymond, FRS 1970; Senior Principal Scientific Officer (Special Merit), Institute of Geological Sciences, London, since 1964; *b* 10 Oct. 1917; *s* of Samuel Gardner Casey and Gladys Violet Helen Casey (*née* Garrett); *m* 1943, Norah Kathleen Pakeman (*d* 1974); two *s. Educ:* St Mary's, Folkestone; Univ. of Reading. PhD 1958; DSc 1963. Geological Survey and Museum: Asst 1939; Asst Exper. Officer 1946; Exper. Officer 1949; Sen. Geologist 1957; Principal Geologist 1960. *Publications:* A Monograph of the Ammonoidea of the Lower Greensand, 1960-71; (ed, with P. F. Rawson) The Boreal Lower Cretaceous, 1973; numerous articles on Mesozoic palaeontology and stratigraphy in scientific press. *Recreation:* research into early Russian postal and military history (Past Pres., British Soc. of Russian Philately). *Address:* 38 Reed Avenue, Orpington, Kent. *T:* Farnborough (Kent) 51728.

CASEY, Terence Anthony, CBE 1977; General-Secretary, National Association of Schoolmasters, since 1963; President, National Federation of Professional Workers; *b* 6 Sept 1920; *s* of Daniel Casey and Ellen McCarthy; *m* 1945, Catherine Wills; two *s* three *d. Educ:* Holy Cross, near Ramsgate; Camden Coll. Teacher's Certificate; Diploma in Mod. Hist. Teaching Service, LCC, 1946-63; Headmaster, St Joseph's Sch., Maida Vale, W9, 1956-63. Pres., Nat. Assoc. of Schoolmasters, 1962-63. Member: Burnham Cttee, 1961-; Nat. Advisory Cttee on Supply and Training of Teachers; Teachers' Council Working Party; TUC Local Govt Cttee; Council, Open Univ., 1975-. Kt of the Holy Sepulchre. *Publications:* The Comprehensive School from Within, 1964; contribs to Times Educl Supplement. *Recreations:* music, opera, motoring. *Address:* Swan Court, Hemel Hempstead, Herts. *T:* Hemel Hempstead 2971. *Club:* National Liberal.

CASH, Sir Thomas James, KBE 1946; CB 1939; *b* 5 July 1888; *s* of late Thomas Cash; *m* 1929, Gladys Ann, *d* of late Charles Hopkins, Beckenham, Kent; one *s* one *d. Educ:* St Ignatius' Coll., Stamford Hill; Univ. Coll., London; Malden medal and Schol.; Hollier Scholarship in Greek; Bunnell Lewis Prizes for Latin verse. BA (Hons Classics), 1909; Fellow of University Coll., London. Barrister, Middle Temple, 1924. Entered War Office as Higher Div. Clerk, 1912; Principal, 1920; Asst Sec., 1925; Director of Finance and Assistant Under-Secretary of State, 1936; Deputy Under-Sec. of State for War, 1945-54; retired 1954. Chevalier, Legion of Honour, 1920; Comdr, Czechoslovakian Order of the White Lion, 1947. *Address:* 1 Lincoln Court, Old Avenue, Weybridge, Surrey. *T:* Weybridge 47617.

CASHEL and EMLY, Archbishop of, (RC), since 1960; **Most Rev. Thomas Morris,** DD; *b* Killenaule, Co. Tipperary, 16 Oct. 1914; *s* of James Morris and Johanna (*née* Carrigan). *Educ:* Christian Brothers Schs, Thurles; Maynooth Coll. Ordained priest, Maynooth, 1939; studied, Dunboyne Institute, 1939-41. (DD). Professor of Theology, St Patrick's Coll., Thurles, 1942-Dec. 1959, Vice-Pres., 1957-60; appointed Archbishop, 1959; consecrated, 1960. Pres., Catholic Communications Inst. Officeholder in Muintir na Tire (rural community movement). *Recreation:* reading. *Address:* Archbishop's House, Thurles, Co. Tipperary, Ireland. *T:* Thurles 242.

CASHEL, WATERFORD and LISMORE, OSSORY, FERNS and LEIGHLIN, Bishop of, since 1977; **Rt. Rev. John Ward Armstrong;** Bishop of Cashel and Emly, Waterford and Lismore, 1968-77; *b* 30 Sept. 1915; *s* of John and Elizabeth Armstrong, Belfast; *m* 1941, Doris Winifred, *d* of William J. Harrison, PC and Florence Harrison, Dublin; two *s* two *d* (and one *d* decd). *Educ:* Belfast Royal Academy; Trinity College, Dublin, BA, Respondent, 1938; Toplady Memorial Prize, Past. Theol Pr. and Abp. King's Prize (2) 1937; Biblical Greek Prize and Downes Prize (1) 1938; 1st Class Hons Hebrew, 1936 and 1937; 1st Class Divinity Testimonium, 1938; BD 1945; MA 1957 (SC). Deacon, then Priest, All Saints, Grangegorman, 1938; Hon. Clerical Vicar, Christ Church Cathedral, 1939; Dean's Vicar, St Patrick's Cathedral, 1944; Prebend. of Tassagard, St Patrick's Cathedral, 1950; Rector of Christ Church, Leeson Park, 1951; Dean of St Patrick's Cathedral, Dublin, 1958-68. Wallace Lecturer, TCD, 1954-65; Dean of Residences, University College, Dublin, 1954-63. Vice-Pres. Boys' Brigade, 1963-73. Trustee, Nat. Library of Ireland, 1964-74; Member: British Council of Churches, 1966; Anglican Consultative Council, 1971-. *Publication:* contrib. to Church and Eucharistan Ecumenical Study (Ed. Rev. M. Hurley, SJ), 1966. *Recreations:* carpentering and bird-watching. *Address:* The Palace, Kilkenny, Ireland. *T:* Kilkenny 21560. *Club:* Friendly Brothers of St Patrick (Dublin).

CASHMAN, John Prescott; Under-Secretary, Department of Health and Social Security, since 1973; *b* 19 May 1930; *s* of late

John Patrick Cashman and Mary Cashman (*née* Prescott). *Educ:* Balliol Coll., Oxford. MA (English Lang. and Lit.). Army (Intell. Corps), 1948-49. Entered Min. of Health, 1951; Principal 1957; Private Sec. to Minister, 1962-65; Asst Sec. 1965; Nuffield Foundn Trav. Fellow, 1968-69; Private Sec. to Sec. of State, 1969. *Address:* 120 Cheston Avenue, Croydon, Surrey CR0 8DD. *T:* 01-777 7255.

CASHMORE, Rt. Rev. Thomas Herbert; *b* 27 April 1892; *s* of Thomas James and Julia Cashmore; *m* 1919, Kate Marjorie Hutchinson; two *s* two *d* (and one *s* decd). *Educ:* Codrington Coll., Barbados, BWI (BA, Durham). Ordained, Barbados, for Chota Nagpur, India, 1917; SPG Missionary, Ranchi, Chota Nagpur, 1917-24; Principal St James's Coll., Calcutta, 1924-33; Vicar: St James's Parish, Calcutta, 1924-33; Holmfirth, Yorks, 1933-42; Brighouse, Yorks, 1942-46; Hon. Canon of Wakefield Cathedral, 1942-46; Canon Missioner, Diocese of Wakefield, 1946-54; Suffragan Bishop of Dunwich, 1955-67. Examining Chaplain to Bishop of St Edmundsbury and Ipswich, 1955-67. Awarded Kaisar-i-Hind (2nd Class), 1929; Defence Medal (2nd World War). *Recreation:* motoring. *Address:* Lynton, Graham Avenue, Withdean, Brighton BN1 8HA. *T:* Brighton 553005.

CASS, Edward Geoffrey, CB 1974; OBE 1951; Deputy Under-Secretary of State (Finance and Budget), Ministry of Defence, 1972-76; *b* 10 Sept. 1916; *s* of Edward Charles and Florence Mary Cass; *m* 1941, Ruth Mary Powley; four *d*. *Educ:* St Olave's; Univ. Coll., London (Scholar); The Queen's Coll., Oxford (Scholar). BSc (Econ.) London (1st Cl.) 1937; George Webb Medley Scholarship, 1938; BA Oxon. (1st Cl. PPE) 1939. Lecturer in Economics, New Coll., Oxford, 1939. From 1940 served in Min. of Supply, Treasury, Air Ministry, MoD; Private Sec. to the Prime Minister, 1949-52; Chief Statistician, Min. of Supply, 1952; Private Sec. to Min. of Supply, 1954; Imperial Defence Coll., 1958; Asst Under-Sec. of State (Programmes and Budget), 1965-72, MoD. *Address:* 60 Rotherwick Road, NW11. *T:* 01-455 1664.

CASSEL, Sir Harold (Felix), 3rd Bt *cr* 1920; TD 1975; QC 1970; **His Honour Judge Cassel;** a Circuit Judge since 1976; *b* 8 Nov. 1916; 3rd *s* of Rt Hon. Sir Felix Cassel, 1st Bt, PC, QC (*d* 1953), and Lady Helen Cassel (*d* 1947); *S* brother, 1969; *m* 1st, 1940, Ione Jean Barclay (marr. diss. 1963); three *s* one *d*; 2nd, 1963, Mrs Eileen Elfrida Smedley. *Educ:* Stowe; Corpus Christi Coll., Oxford. Served War of 1939-45, Captain, 1941, Royal Artillery. Called to Bar, Lincoln's Inn, 1946. Recorder of Great Yarmouth, 1968-71, Hon. Recorder, 1972-76. JP, Herts, 1959-62; Dep. Chm., Herts QS, 1959-62. *Recreations:* shooting, swimming, opera going. *Heir:* s Timothy Felix Harold Cassel [*b* 30 April 1942; *m* 1971, Mrs Jenifer Samuel, *d* of Kenneth Bridge Puckle; one *s* one *d*]. *Address:* 49 Lennox Gardens, SW1. *T:* 01-584 2721.

CASSELS, Field-Marshal Sir (Archibald) James (Halkett), GCB 1961 (CB 1950); KBE 1952 (CBE 1944); DSO 1944; Chief of the General Staff, Ministry of Defence, 1965-68; *b* 28 Feb. 1907; *s* of late General Sir Robert A. Cassels, GCB, GCSI, DSO; *m* 1935, Joyce, *d* of late Brig.-Gen. Henry Kirk and Mrs G. A. McL. Sceales; one *s*. *Educ:* Rugby Sch.; RMC, Sandhurst. 2nd Lieut Seaforth Highlanders, 1926; Lieut 1929; Capt. 1938; Major, 1943; Col 1946; temp. Maj.-Gen. 1945; Maj.-Gen. 1948; Lieut-Gen. 1954; Gen. 1958. Served War of 1939-45 (despatches twice): BGS 1944; Bde Comd 1944; GOC 51st Highland Div., 1945; GOC 6th Airborne Div., Palestine, 1946 (despatches); idc, 1947; Dir Land/Air Warfare, War Office, 1948-49; Chief Liaison Officer, United Kingdom Services Liaison Staff, Australia, 1950-51; GOC 1st British Commonwealth Div. in Korea (US Legion of Merit), 1951-52; Comdr, 1st Corps, 1953-54; Dir-Gen. of Military Training, War Office, 1954-57; Dir of Emergency Operations Federation of Malaya, 1957-59; PMN (Panglima Mangku Negara), 1958; GOC-in-C, Eastern Command, 1959; C-in-C, British Army of the Rhine and Comdr NATO Northern Army Group, 1960-63; Adjutant-Gen. to the Forces, 1963-64; Field-Marshal, 1968. ADC Gen. to the Queen, 1960-63. Col Seaforth Highlanders, 1957-61; Col Queen's Own Highlanders, 1961-66; Colonel Commandant: Corps of Royal Military Police, 1957-68; Army Physical Training Corps, 1961-65. Pres., Company of Veteran Motorists, 1970-73. *Recreations:* all forms of sport. *Address:* Pitearn, Alves, Forres, Moray. *Club:* Cavalry and Guards (Hon. Mem.).

CASSELS, Francis Henry, TD 1945; **His Honour Judge Cassels;** Senior Circuit Judge, Inner London Crown Court, since 1972 (Chairman, SW London Quarter Sessions, 1965-72); *b* 3 Sept. 1910; 2nd *s* of late Sir James Dale Cassels; *m* 1939, Evelyn Dorothy Richardson; one *s* one *d*. *Educ:* Sedbergh; Corpus Christi Coll., Cambridge (MA). Called to the Bar, Middle Temple, 1932. Served Royal Artillery, 1939-45. Dep. Chm.,

County of London Sessions, 1954-65. *Address:* 14 Buckingham House, Courtlands, Richmond, Surrey. *T:* 01-940 4180. *Clubs:* Royal Wimbledon Golf; Constitutional (Putney).

CASSELS, Field-Marshal Sir James; *see* Cassels, Field-Marshal Sir A. J. H.

CASSELS, Prof. James Macdonald, FRS 1959; Lyon Jones Professor of Physics, University of Liverpool, since Oct. 1960; *b* 9 Sept. 1924; *s* of Alastair Macdonald Cassels and Ada White Cassels (*née* Scott); *m* 1947, Jane Helen Thera Lawrence; one *s* one *d*. *Educ:* Rochester House Sch., Edinburgh; St Lawrence Coll., Ramsgate; Trinity College, Cambridge. BA, MA, PhD (Cantab.). Harwell Fellow and Principal Scientific Officer, Atomic Energy Research Establishment, Harwell, 1949-53. Lecturer, 1953, subseq. Senior Lecturer, University of Liverpool. Prof. of Experimental Physics, University of Liverpool, 1956-59; Visiting Prof., Cornell Univ., 1959-60. Mem. Council, Royal Soc., 1968-69. Rutherford Medal, Inst. of Physics, 1973. *Publications:* Basic Quantum Mechanics, 1970; contributions to scientific journals on atomic, nuclear and elementary particle physics. *Recreations:* fishing, walking, talking. *Address:* 14 Dudlow Court, Dudlow Nook Road, Liverpool L18 2EU. *T:* 051-722 2594.

CASSELS, John Seton; Director, Manpower Services Commission, since 1975; *b* 10 Oct. 1928; *s* of Alastair Macdonald Cassels and Ada White Cassels (*née* Scott); *m* 1956, Mary Whittington; two *s* two *d*. *Educ:* Sedbergh Sch., Yorkshire; Trinity Coll., Cambridge. Rome Scholar, Classical Archaeology, 1952-54. Entered Ministry of Labour, 1954; Secretary of the Royal Commission on Trade Unions and Employers' Associations, 1965-68; Under-Sec., NBPI, 1968-71; Managing Directors' Office, Dunlop Holdings Ltd, 1971-72; Chief Exec., Training Services Agency, 1972-75. *Address:* 10 Beverley Road, Barnes, SW13 0LX. *T:* 01-876 6270.

CASSELS, Prof. John William Scott, FRS 1963; MA, PhD; Sadleirian Professor of Pure Mathematics, Cambridge University, since 1967; Head of Department of Pure Mathematics and Mathematical Statistics, since 1969; *b* 11 July 1922; *s* of late J. W. Cassels (latterly Dir of Agriculture in Co. Durham) and late Mrs M. S. Cassels (*née* Lobjoit); *m* 1949, Constance Mabel Merritt (*née* Senior); one *s* one *d*. *Educ:* Neville's Cross Council Sch., Durham; George Heriot's Sch., Edinburgh; Edinburgh and Cambridge Univs. MA Edinburgh, 1943; PhD Cantab, 1949. Fellow, Trinity, 1949-; Lecturer, Manchester Univ., 1949; Lecturer, Cambridge Univ., 1950; Reader in Arithmetic, 1963-67. Mem. Council, Royal Society, 1970, 1971 (Sylvester Medal, 1973); Vice Pres., Internat. Mathematical Union, 1974-; Pres., London Mathematical Soc., 1976-. Dr (*hc*) Lille Univ., 1965. *Publications:* An Introduction to Diophantine Approximation, 1957; An Introduction to the Geometry of Numbers, 1959. Papers in diverse mathematical journals on arithmetical topics. *Recreations:* arithmetic (higher only), gardening (especially common vegetables). *Address:* 3 Luard Close, Cambridge CB2 2PL. *T:* 46108.

CASSIDI, Vice-Adm. Arthur Desmond; Flag Officer, Naval Air Command, since 1978; *b* 26 Jan. 1925; *s* of late Comdr Robert A. Cassidi, RN and late Clare F. (*née* Alexander); *m* 1950, Dorothy Sheelagh Marie (*née* Scott) (*d* 1974); one *s* two *d*. *Educ:* RNC Dartmouth. Qual. Pilot, 1945; CO, 820 Sqdn (Gannet aircraft), 1955; 1st Lieut HMS Protector, 1955-56; psc 1957; CO, HMS Whitby, 1959-61; Fleet Ops Officer Home Fleet, 1962-64; Asst Dir Naval Plans, 1964-67; Captain (D) Portland and CO HMS Undaunted, 1967-68; idc 1969; Dir of Naval Plans, 1970-72; CO, HMS Ark Royal, 1972-73; Flag Officer Carriers and Amphibious Ships, 1974-75; Dir-Gen., Naval Manpower and Training, 1975-77. Midshipman 1942; Sub-Lt 1944; Lieut 1945; Lt-Comdr 1953; Comdr 1956; Captain 1964; Rear-Adm. 1974; Vice-Adm. 1976. *Recreation:* country pursuits. *Address:* 15 Roupell Street, SE1 8SP. *T:* 01-928 2955.

CASSIE, Arnold Blatchford David, CBE 1955; Director of Research, Wool Industries Research Association, 1950-67, retired; *b* 17 May 1905; 3rd *s* of late D. A. Morris Cassie and late Mrs Cassie; *m* 1939, Catherine Dufour, *d* of late Surg. Capt. T. D. Halahan, OBE, RN; one *s* two *d*. *Educ:* Aberdeen Grammar Sch.; Edinburgh Univ.; Christ's Coll., Cambridge. Vans Dunlop Schol., Edin. Univ., 1926-29; Carnegie Research Schol., 1929-30; Post-grad. Research, University Coll., London, 1928-34; Scientific Officer: ICI Ltd, 1934-36, RAE, 1936-38; Chief Physicist, Wool Industries Research Assoc., 1938-50. Warner Memorial Medal 1949, Mather Lecturer 1962, Textile Institute; George Douglas Lectr, Soc. of Dyers and Colourists, 1961. Vice-Pres., Textile Institute, 1962-65; Governor, Bradford Institute of Technology, 1960-66. Hon. D.Tech. Bradford Univ., 1966.

Publications: numerous in Proc. Royal Society, Trans. Faraday Soc., Jl of Textile Inst., etc. *Recreations:* gardening, golf, music. *Address:* White Heather, Crescent Walk, Ferndown, Dorset. *T:* Ferndown 873105.

CASSIE, W(illiam) Fisher, CBE 1966; consulting civil engineer; Partner, Waterhouse & Partners, 1970-74; Professor of Civil Engineering, University of Newcastle upon Tyne (formerly King's College, University of Durham), 1943-70; *b* 29 June 1905; Scottish; *m* 1933, Mary Robertson Reid; no *c. Educ:* Grove Academy, Dundee; University of St Andrews. BSc (St Andrews), 1925. Asst Engineer, City Engineer and Harbour Engineer, Dundee; Research at University Coll., Dundee; PhD (St Andrews), 1930; first Senior Sir James Caird Scholarship in Engineering, 1930; Research and Study, University of Illinois (USA), 1930-31; MS (Ill.), 1931. Lectured at QUB, University Coll., Cardiff, UCL, 1931-40, King's Coll., Newcastle, University of Durham, 1940-70. Past Chm. Northern Counties Assoc. of Instn of Civil Engineers; Founder Chm. Northern Counties Branch Instn of Structural Engineers; Pres. Inst. Highways Engrs, 1967-68; FRSE; FICE; FIStructE; PPInstHE; Hon. LLD Dundee, 1972; Mem. Sigma XI. Bronze Medallist, Instn of Struct. Engrs; Gold badge, English Folk Dance and Song Soc. *Publications:* Structural Analysis 1947; (with P. L. Capper), Mechanics of Engineering Soils, 1949; (with J. H. Napper) Structure in Building, 1952; Fundamental Foundations, 1968; Statics, Structures and Stress, 1973; Jls of Institution of Civil Engineers, Institution of Structural Engineers, and other tech. papers. *Recreations:* photography and traditional cultures of England. *Address:* Morwick House, Beal Bank, Warkworth, Northumberland. *T:* Warkworth 292.

CASSILLIS, Earl of; Archibald Angus Charles Kennedy; *b* 13 Sept. 1956; *s* and *heir* of 7th Marquess of Ailsa, *qv. Recreations:* shooting, ski-ing, cadets and youth-work. *Address:* Cassillis House, Maybole, Ayrshire. *T:* Dalrymple 310. *Club:* New (Edinburgh).

CASSIRER, Mrs Reinhold; *see* Gordimer, Nadine.

CASSON, Sir Hugh (Maxwell), Kt 1952; RA 1970; RDI 1951; MA Cantab; RIBA, FSIA; President of the Royal Academy, since 1976; Professor of Environmental Design, Royal College of Art, 1953-75; Member Royal Danish Academy, 1954; Member: Royal Fine Art Commission, since 1960; Royal Mint Advisory Committee, since 1972; *b* 23 May 1910; *s* of late Randal Casson, ICS; *m* 1938, Margaret Macdonald Troup (*see* Margaret MacDonald Casson); three *d. Educ:* Eastbourne Coll.; St John's Coll., Cambridge. Craven Scholar, British Sch. at Athens, 1933; in private practice as architect since 1937 with late Christopher Nicholson; served War of 1939-45, Camouflage Officer in Air Ministry, 1940-44; Technical Officer Ministry of Town and Country Planning, 1944-46; private practice, Sen. Partner, Casson Conder & Partners, 1946-48; Dir. of Architecture, Festival of Britain, 1948-51. Master of Faculty, RDI, 1969-71. Trustee: British Museum (Nat. Hist.), 1976-; Nat. Portrait Gall., 1976-. Hon. Associate, Amer. Inst of Architects, 1968; Hon. Dr: RCA 1975; Southampton, 1977; Hon. LLD, Birmingham, 1977. Regular contributor as author and illustrator to technical and lay Press. *Publications:* New Sights of London (London Transport), 1937; Bombed Churches, 1946; Homes by the Million (Penguin), 1947; (with Anthony Chitty) Houses-Permanence and Prefabrication, 1947; Victorian Architecture, 1948; Inscape: the design of interiors, 1968; (with Joyce Grenfell) Nanny Says, 1972. *Recreation:* drawing. *Address:* (home) 35 Victoria Road, W8; (office) 35 Thurloe Place, SW7. *T:* 01-584 4581.

CASSON, Margaret MacDonald, (Lady Casson); Architect, Designer; Senior Tutor, School of Environmental Design, Royal College of Art, retired 1974; *b* 26 Sept. 1913; 2nd *d* of James MacDonald Troup, MD, and Alberta Davis; *m* 1938, Hugh Maxwell Casson, *q v*; three *d. Educ:* Wychwood Sch., Oxford; Bartlett Sch. of Architecture, University Coll. London; Royal Inst. of British Architecture. Office of late Christopher Nicholson, 1937-38; private practice, S Africa, 1938-39; Designer for Cockade Ltd, 1946-51; Tutor, Royal Coll. of Art, 1952; private practice as Architect and Designer for private and public buildings and interiors; also of china, glass, carpets, furniture, etc; Design consultant to various cos; Member: Design Council Index Cttees; Duke of Edinburgh's panel for Award for Elegant Design, 1962-63; Council for Design Council, 1967-73 (Chm. Panel for Design Council Awards for Consumer Goods, 1972); Three-Dimensional Design Panel of NCDAD, 1962-72 (Ext. Assessor for NCDAD, 1962-); Council of RCA, 1970; Arts Council, 1972-75; Cttee of Enquiry into Drama Training, 1973-75; Adv. Council of V&A Museum, 1975; Gardens and Park Cttee, Zoological Soc. of London, 1975; Craft Adv. Cttee, 1976-;

Bd of Governors: Wolverhampton Coll. of Art, 1964-66; West of England Coll. of Art, 1965-67; BFI, 1973- (Chm., Regional Cttee, 1976-). FSIA, Fellow RCA 1974. *Address:* 35 Victoria Road, W8 5RH. *T:* 01-937 9951.

CASTAING, J. C. de; *see* Chastenet de Castaing.

CASTERET, Norbert; Commandeur de la Légion d'Honneur, 1975 (Officier 1947); Croix de Guerre, 1917; archæologist, geologist, speleologist; *b* 19 Aug. 1897; *m* 1924, Elisabeth Martin (*d* 1940); one *s* four *d. Educ:* Lycée de Toulouse, Haute-Garonne. Bachelier; lauréat de l'Académie Française, 1934, 1936, 1938; lauréat de l'Académie des Sciences, 1935; mainteneur de l'Académie des Jeux Floraux, 1937; Grande Médaille d'Or de l'Académie des Sports, 1923; Médaille d'Or de l'Education Physique, 1947; Commandeur du Mérite de la Recherche et de l'Invention, 1956; Commandeur du Mérite sportif, 1958; Commandeur des Palmes académiques, 1964; Commandeur du Mérite National; "Oscar" du Courage Français, 1973; Médaille de Sauvetage, 1975. *Publications:* 29 Works translated into 17 languages: Dix ans sous terre (English edn: Ten Years Under the Earth); Au fond des gouffres; Mes Cavernes (English edn: My Caves); En Rampant; Exploration (English edn: Cave Men New and Old); Darkness Under the Earth; Trente ans sous terre (English edn: The Descent of Pierre Saint-Martin), etc.; contributions to L'Illustration, Illustrated London News, Geographical Magazine, etc. *Recreation:* exploring caves. *Address:* Castel Mourlon, 31800 Saint-Gaudens, France. *T:* St Gaudens 61.89.15.13.

CASTLE, family name of **Baron Castle.**

CASTLE, Baron *cr* 1974 (Life Peer), of Islington; **Edward Cyril Castle;** journalist; Member, European Parliament, since 1975; *b* 5 May 1907; *m* 1944, Barbara Anne Betts (*see* Barbara Castle). *Educ:* Abingdon and Portsmouth Grammar Schools; served on newspapers in Portsmouth, Southampton, Newcastle, 1925-31; News Editor, Manchester Evening News, 1932; Asst Editor, Daily Mirror, 1943; Asst Editor, Picture Post, 1944-50; Editor of Picture Post, 1951-52. Alderman, GLC 1964-70, Islington, 1971-. *Recreation:* gardening. *Address:* House of Lords, SW1.

CASTLE, Rt. Hon. Barbara (Anne), PC 1964; BA; MP (Lab) for Blackburn since 1955 (Blackburn East, 1950-55, Blackburn, 1945-50); *b* 6 Oct. 1911; *d* of Frank and Annie Rebecca Betts; *m* 1944, Edward Cyril Castle (now Baron Castle, *qv*) (remains known as Mrs Castle); no *c. Educ:* Bradford Girls' Grammar Sch.; St Hugh's Coll., Oxford. Elected to St Pancras Borough Council, 1937; Member Metropolitan Water Board, 1940-45; Asst Editor, Town and County Councillor, 1936-40; Administrative Officer, Ministry of Food, 1941-44; Housing Correspondent and Forces Adviser, Daily Mirror, 1944-45. Member of National Executive Cttee of Labour Party since 1950; Chairman Labour Party, 1958-59 (Vice-Chm. 1957-58). Minister of: Overseas Development, 1964-65; Transport, 1965-68; First Secretary of State and Sec. of State for Employment and Productivity, 1968-70; Sec. of State for Social Services, 1974-76. Co-Chm., Women's Nat. Commn, 1975-76. Hon. Fellow, St Hugh's Coll., Oxford, 1966. Hon. DTech: Bradford, 1968; Loughborough, 1969. *Publication:* part author of Social Security, edited by Dr Robson, 1943. *Recreations:* poetry and walking. *Address:* House of Commons, SW1.

CASTLE, Frances; *see* Blackburn, E. B.

CASTLE, Mrs G. L.; *see* Sharp, Margery.

CASTLE, Norman Henry; Chairman and Joint Managing Director, S. & W. Berisford Ltd, since Nov. 1971; Underwriting Member of Lloyds, since 1976; *b* 1 Sept. 1913; *s* of Hubert William Castle, MBE, and Elizabeth May Castle; *m* 1939, Ivy Olive Watson; one *d. Educ:* Norfolk House; Ludlow Grammar Sch. Joined Hafnia Konserves, Copenhagen, 1931; London: C. & E. Morton Ltd, 1933; Vacuum Packed Produce Ltd, 1938; Vacuum Foods Ltd, 1939. Served War of 1939-45, RAF. General Manager: A. L. Maizel Ltd, 1945; Times Foods Ltd, 1947; Director, Vacuum Foods Ltd, 1951; Managing Dir, Haigh Castle & Co, Ltd, 1956; Man. Dir, Hafnia Ham Co, Ltd, 1956; Dir, S. & W. Berisford Ltd, 1967; Man. Dir, S. & W. Berisford Ltd, 1970; Chm., Ashbourne Investments Ltd, 1976; Director: Incentive Investments Ltd, 1976; E. S. Schwab & Co. Ltd, 1976; Vice-Pres., British Importers Confedn, 1975; Pres., British Assoc. of Canned Food Importers and Distributors, 1977 (Chm., 1975-77). *Recreations:* travel, sailing. *Address:* The Penthouse, 39 Courcels, Black Rock, Brighton, E Sussex. *Clubs:* The Muscovites; Cresta Yacht (Newhaven); East Brighton Golf (Brighton).

CASTLE-MILLER, Rudolph Valdemar Thor; a Recorder of the Crown Court, 1972-75; *b* Britain, 16 March 1905; *s* of late Rudolph Schleusz-Mühlheimer, Randers, Denmark; changed name by deed poll, 1930; *m* 1939, Colleen Ruth, *d* of late Lt-Col N. R. Whitaker; one *s* one *d. Educ:* Harrow; Hertford Coll., Oxford (MA). Called to Bar, Middle Temple, 1929. Past Master, Loriners' Company, 1968. Flt Lt, Intell. Br., RAF, 1940-46. *Recreations:* motoring, travel. *Address:* 6 Wood Road, Ashill, Ilminster, Somerset TA19 9NP.

CASTLE STEWART, 8th Earl, *cr* 1800 (Ireland); **Arthur Patrick Avondale Stuart;** Viscount Stuart, 1793; Baron, 1619; Bt 1628; *b* 18 Aug. 1928; 3rd but *e surv. s* of 7th Earl Castle Stewart, MC, and Eleanor May, *er d* of late S. R. Guggenheim, New York; *S* father, 1961; *m* 1952, Edna Fowler; one *s* one *d. Educ:* Brambletye; Eton; Trinity Coll., Cambridge. Lieut Scots Guards, 1949. *Heir: s* Viscount Stuart, *qv. Address:* Stone House Farm, East Pennard, Shepton Mallet, Somerset. *T:* Ditcheat 240; Stuart Hall, Stewartstown, Co. Tyrone. *T:* Stewartstown 208. *Club:* Carlton.

CASTLEMAINE, 8th Baron *cr* 1812; **Roland Thomas John Handcock;** Major, Army Air Corps; *b* 22 April 1943; *s* of 7th Baron Castlemaine and of Rebecca Ellen, *o d* of William T. Soady, RN; *S* father, 1973; *m* 1969, Pauline Anne, *e d* of John Taylor Bainbridge. *Educ:* Campbell Coll., Belfast. *Heir: cousin* Clifford Frederick Handcock [*b* 3 Oct. 1896; *m* 1928, Margaret (decd), *d* of late Captain Philip Nicholls]. *Address:* c/o Lloyds Bank, Aldershot, Hants.

CASTLEREAGH, Viscount; Frederick Aubrey Vane-Tempest-Stewart; *b* 6 Sept. 1972; *s* and *heir* of 9th Marquess of Londonderry, *qv.*

CASTON, Geoffrey Kemp; Registrar of Oxford University, and Fellow of Merton College, Oxford, since 1972; *b* 17 May 1926; *s* of late Reginald and Lilian Caston, West Wickham, Kent; *m* 1956, Sonya, *d* of Dr J. O. Chassell, Stockbridge, Mass, USA; two *s* one *d. Educ:* St Dunstans Coll.; (Major Open Scholar) Peterhouse, Cambridge (MA). First Cl. Pt 1 History; First Cl. Pt II Law (with distinction) and Geo. Long Prize for Jurisprudence, 1950; Harvard Univ. (Master of Public Admin. 1951; Frank Knox Fellow, 1950-51). Sub-Lt, RNVR, 1945-47. Colonial Office, 1951-58; UK Mission to UN, New York, 1958-61; Dept of Techn. Co-op., 1961-64; Asst Sec., Dept of Educn and Sci. (Univs and Sci. Branches), 1964-66; Jt Sec., Schools Council, 1966-70; Under-Secretary, UGC, 1970-72. Sec., Assoc. of First Div. Civil Servants, 1956-58; Mem., Staff Side Nat. Whitley Council, 1956-58; Adv. to UK Delegn to seven sessions of UN Gen. Assembly, 1953-63; UK Rep. on UN Cttee on Non-Self-Governing Territories, 1958-60; UN Techn. Assistance Cttee, 1962-64; Mem., UN Visiting Mission to Trust Territory of Pacific Islands, 1961. Chm., SE Surrey Assoc. for Advancement of State Educn, 1962-64; UK Delegn to Commonwealth Educn Conf., Ottawa, 1964. Ford Foundn travel grants for visits to schools and univs in USA, 1964, 1967, 1970. Chairman: Planning Cttee, 3rd and 4th Internat. Curriculum Confs, Oxford, 1967, New York, 1968; Ford Foundn Anglo-American Primary Educn Project, 1968-70; Library Adv. Council (England), 1973-; Nat. Inst. for Careers Educn and Counselling, 1975-; Member: Steering Gp, OECD Workshops on Educnl Innovation, Cambridge 1969, W Germany, 1970, Illinois 1971; Vice-Chm., Educnl Res. Bd, SSRC, 1973-. Governor, Centre for Educnl Development Overseas, 1969-70. *Publications:* contribs to educl jls. *Address:* 12 Bardwell Road, Oxford.

CATCHESIDE, David Guthrie, FRS 1951; DSc London; Research Associate, Waite Agricultural Research Institute, South Australia, since 1975; *b* 31 May 1907; *s* of David Guthrie Catcheside and Florence Susanna (*née* Boxwell); *m* 1931, Kathleen Mary Whiteman; one *s* one *d. Educ:* Strand Sch.; King's Coll., University of London. Asst to Professor of Botany, Glasgow Univ., 1928-30; Asst Lecturer, 1931-33, and Lecturer in Botany, University of London (King's Coll.), 1933-36; International Fellow of Rockefeller Foundation, 1936-37; Lecturer in Botany, University of Cambridge, 1937-50; Lecturer and Fellow, Trinity Coll., Cambridge, 1944; Reader in Plant Cytogenetics, Cambridge Univ., 1950-51; Prof. of Genetics, Adelaide Univ., S. Australia, 1952-55; Prof. of Microbiology, Univ. of Birmingham, 1956-64; Prof. of Genetics, 1964-72, Dir, 1967-72, Vis. Fellow, 1973-75, Res. Sch. of Biol Scis, ANU. Research Associate, Carnegie Instn of Washington, 1958. Visiting Professor, California Inst. of Technology, 1961. Foreign Associate, Nat. Acad. of Sciences of USA, 1974. Foundation FAA, 1954; FKC 1959. *Publications:* Botanical Technique in Bolles Lee's Microtomists' Vade-Mecum, 1937-50; Genetics of Micro-organisms, 1951; Genetics of Recombination, 1977. Papers on genetics and cytology. *Address:* 16 Rodger Avenue, Leabrook, SA 5068, Australia.

CATER, Prof. Douglass; Vice Chairman, The Observer, since 1976; Director, the Aspen Institute Programme on Communications and Society, since 1970; writer and consultant, in USA, since 1968; *b* Montgomery, Ala, 24 Aug. 1923; *s* of Silas D. Cater and Nancy Chesnutt; *m* 1950, Libby Anderson; two *s* two *d. Educ:* Philip Exeter Acad. (grad.); Harvard Univ. (AB, MA). Served War, 1943-45, with OSS. Washington Editor, The Reporter (Magazine), 1950-63; Nat. Affairs Editor, 1963-64; Special Assistant: to Sec. of Army, 1951; to the President of the United States, 1964-68. Consultant to Dir, Mutual Security Agency, 1952. Visiting Professor, 1959-: Princeton Univ.; Weslyan Univ., Middletown, Conn: Stanford Univ., etc. Guggenheim Fellow, 1955; Eisenhower Exchange Fellow, 1957; George Polk Meml Award, 1961; NY Newspaper Guild, Page One Award, 1961. Mem., Delta Sigma Chi. *Publications:* (with Marquis Childs) Ethics in a Business Society, 1953; The Fourth Branch of Government, 1959; Power in Washington, 1963; The Irrelevant Man, 1970. *Address:* The Observer, 8 St Andrew's Hill, EC4V 5JA.

CATER, John Robert; Chairman, Distillers Co. Ltd, since 1976, Deputy Chairman 1975-76, Director since 1967 (Member Management Committee); *b* 25 April 1919; *s* of Sir John Cater; *m* 1945, Isobel Calder Ritchie; one *d. Educ:* George Watson's Coll., Edinburgh; Cambridge Univ. (MA). Trainee, W. P. Lowrie & Co. Ltd, 1946; James Buchanan & Co. Ltd, 1949: Dir 1950; Prodn Dir 1959; Prodn Asst, Distillers Co. Ltd, Edinburgh, 1959; Man. Dir, John Haig & Co. Ltd, 1965-70; Non-Exec. Dir, United Glass, 1969, Chm. 1972. *Recreations:* music, theatre, fishing, golf (Walker Cup team, 1955; played for Scotland, 1952-56). *Address:* 20 St James's Square, SW1Y 4JF. *T:* 01-930 1040. *Clubs:* Royal Scottish Automobile (Glasgow); Royal and Ancient (St Andrews).

CATHCART, family name of Earl Cathcart.

CATHCART, 6th Earl *cr* 1814; **Alan Cathcart,** CB 1973; DSO 1945; MC 1944; Viscount Cathcart, 1807; Baron Greenock (United Kingdom) and 15th Baron Cathcart (Scotland), 1447; Major-General; *b* 22 Aug. 1919; *o s* of 5th Earl and Vera, *d* of late John Fraser, of Cape Town; *S* father, 1927; *m* 1946, Rosemary, *yr d* of late Air Commodore Sir Percy Smyth-Osbourne, CMG, CBE; one *s* two *d. Educ:* Eton; Magdalene Coll., Cambridge. Served War of 1939-45 (despatches, MC, DSO). Adjt RMA Sandhurst, 1946-47; Regimental Adjt Scots Guards, 1951-53; Brigade Major, 4th Guards Brigade, 1954-56; Commanding Officer, 1st Battalion Scots Guards, 1957; Lt-Col comd Scots Guards, 1960; Colonel AQ Scottish Command, 1962-63; Imperial Defence Coll., 1964; Brigade Comdr, 152 Highland Brigade, 1965-66; Chief, SHAPEX and Exercise Branch SHAPE, 1967-68; GOC Yorkshire District, 1969-70; GOC and British Comdt, Berlin, 1970-73; retd. A Dep-Chm. of Cttees, House of Lords. Brigadier, Queen's Body Guard for Scotland, Royal Company of Archers. Pres., ACFA, 1975-. Cdre, RYS, 1974-. *Heir: s* Lord Greenock, *qv. Address:* 14 Eaton Mews South, SW1. *T:* 01-235 4621. *Clubs:* Brooks's; Royal Yacht Squadron (Cowes).

CATHERWOOD, Sir (Henry) Frederick (Ross), Kt 1971; Chairman: British Overseas Trade Board, since 1975; William Mallinson & Denny Mott Ltd; Wittenberg Automat Ltd; Director: John Laing & Son Ltd; The Goodyear Tyre and Rubber Co. (GB) Ltd; *b* 30 Jan. 1925; *s* of late Stuart and of Jean Catherwood, Co. Londonderry; *m* 1954, Elizabeth, *er d* of Rev. Dr D. M. Lloyd Jones, late of Westminster Chapel, London; two *s* one *d. Educ:* Shrewsbury; Clare Coll., Cambridge. Articled Price, Waterhouse & Co.; qualified as Chartered Accountant, 1951; Secretary, Laws Stores Ltd, Gateshead, 1952-54; Secretary and Controller, Richard Costain Ltd, 1954-55; Chief Executive, 1955-60; Asst Managing Director, British Aluminium Co. Ltd, 1960-62; Managing Director, 1962-64; Chief Industrial Adviser, DEA, 1964-66; Dir-Gen., NEDC, 1966-71; Managing Dir and Chief Executive, John Laing & Son Ltd, 1972-74. British Institute of Management: Mem. Council, 1961-66, 1969-; Vice-Chm., 1972; Chm., 1974-76. Member of Council: NI Development Council, 1963-64; RIIA, 1964-; BNEC, 1965-71; NEDC, 1964-71. Pres, Machine Tool Industry Res. Assoc., 1977-. Vice-Pres., 1976, Pres., 1977, Fellowship of Independent Evangelical Churches; Chm. of Council, Univs and Colls Christian Fellowship (formerly Inter-Varsity Fellowship), 1971-77 (Vice-Pres., 1976-). Trustee, Charities Aid Foundn, 1974-. Hon. DSc Aston, 1972; Hon. DSc (Econ.) QUB, 1973. *Publications:* The Christian in Industrial Society, 1964; The Christian Citizen, 1969; A Better Way, 1976. *Recreations:* music, gardening, reading. *Address:* 25 Woodville Gardens, W5; Sutton Hall, Balsham, Cambridgeshire. *Club:* United Oxford & Cambridge University.

CATHIE, Ian Aysgarth Bewley, MD, BS, MRCP, FRCPath; JP; DL; *b* London, 3 Jan, 1908; 2nd *s* of George Cathie, Ewell, Surrey, and Lilly Pickford Evans; *m* 1938, Josephine, *o d* of Joseph Cunning, FRCS, Broome Park, Betchworth, Surrey; one *s* three *d*. *Educ:* Guy's Hospital; Zürich Univ. Asst path. to Ancoats Hospital, Manchester, 1932; demonstrator in path. in Manchester Univ. and registrar in path. to Manchester Royal Inf., 1934; path. and res. Fellow in path., Christie Hospital and Holt Radium Inst., also path. to Duchess of York Hospital for Babies, Manchester, 1936. Clinical Pathologist to The Hospital for Sick Children, Great Ormond Street, London, 1938-58, retired. Pathologist in EMS, 1939; war service in RAMC, 1940-46; captured in Tobruk, POW 1942-43. Mem. Convocation, Univ. of Aston. Hon. Member, British Pædiatric Association. Lord of the Manor of Barton-on-the-Heath, Warwickshire; CC Warwicks, 1965-77 (Vice-Chm., 1973-74, Chm., 1974-76). DL Warwicks, 1974. *Publications:* Chapters in Moncrieff's Nursing and Diseases of Sick Children and (in collaboration) Garrod, Batten and Thursfield's Diseases of Children; also papers on pathology and pædiatrics in medical journals. Editor, Archives of Disease in Childhood, 1951-63. *Recreations:* gardening, hunting. *Address:* Barton House, Moreton-in-Marsh, Glos. *T:* Barton-on-the-Heath 303. *Clubs:* Chelsea Arts, Royal Automobile.

CATLEDGE, Turner; Director, The New York Times, 1968-73; *b* 17 March 1901; *s* of Lee Johnson Catledge and Willie Anna (*née* Turner); *m* 1st; two *d*; 2nd, 1958, Abby Izard. *Educ:* Philadelphia (Miss.) High Sch.; Miss. State College. BSc 1922. Neshoba (Miss.) Democrat, 1921; Resident Editor, Tunica (Miss.) Times, 1922; Man. Editor, Tupelo (Miss.) Journal, 1923; Reporter, Memphis (Tenn.) Commercial Appeal, 1923-27; Baltimore (Md) Sun, 1927-29; New York Times: City Staff, 1929; Correspondent, Washington Bureau, 1930-36; Chief Washington news Correspondent, 1936-41; Chicago Sun: Chief Correspondent, 1941-42; Editor-in-Chief, 1942-43; Nat. Correspondent, New York Times, 1943-44; Managing Editor, 1951-64; Executive Editor, 1964-68 Vice-Pres., 1968-70. Member: Pulitzer Prizes Advisory Cttee, 1955-69; AP Managing Editors Assoc., 1954-64; Advisory Board, American Press Inst.; American Soc. of Newspaper Editors (Dir., Pres. 1961); Sigma Delta Chi. Hon. DLitt Washington and Lee Univ.; Hon. Dr of Humane Letters Southwestern at Memphis; Hon. LLD: Univ. of Kentucky; Tulane Univ. *Publications:* The 168 Days (with Joseph W. Alsop, Jr), 1937; My Life and The Times, 1971. *Address:* (office) 229 West 43rd Street, New York, NY 10036, USA. *T:* 556-1234; (home) 2316 Prytania Street, New Orleans, La 70130, USA. *T:* 522-2429. *Clubs:* National Press, Gridiron (Washington); Silurians (New York); Boston (New Orleans), New Orleans Country.

CATLIN, Sir George (Edward Gordon), Kt 1970; MA, PhD; FRSL; Concerned with Atlantic Community policy, since 1925; Founder, Movement for Atlantic Union (UK); *b* 29 July 1896; *s* of late Rev. George E. Catlin, sometime Vicar of St Luke's, Kew Gardens, Surrey, and of late Mrs Catlin, *née* Orton; *m* 1925, Vera Brittain (*d* 1970); one *s* one *d*; *m* 1971, Delinda (*née* Tassi), *widow* of Lt-Comdr Victor Gates. *Educ:* Warwick; St Paul's Sch.; New Coll., Oxford (Exhibitioner in Modern History, 1914). Subsequently London Rifle Brigade. Oxford Modern History Sch. *cum laude*; Chancellor's English Essayist; *prox. accessit* Lothian Prize, 1920; Gladstone Prizeman, Matthew Arnold Memorial Prizeman, Oxford, 1921; Professor of Politics, Cornell Univ., 1924-35 (PhD Cornell); acting Head of Dept, 1928. Associated with Clarence Streit and Walter Lippmann, 1938-, and Jean Monnet, 1950-, in propaganda for Atlantic Union; draftsman of Constitution of Atlantic Inst., Paris. Foundation Lecturer: Yale Univ., 1938; Calcutta Univ., 1947; Lecturer: Peking Univ., Columbia Univ., University of California (Berkeley), Bologna, Cologne, etc.; Goethe Bicentenary Lecturer, Heidelberg Univ.; Kierkegaard Commemoration Address, University of Copenhagen, 1949; Weil Lecturer, University of N Carolina, 1957; Tagore Centenary Lecturer, Royal Society of Arts, 1961; Provost Mar Ivanios Coll., S India, 1951; Bronman Professor of Political Science, McGill Univ., 1956-60; Chairman of Dept; Walker-Ames Lecturer, University of Washington, 1964. Churchill Memorial Lectr, Fulton, Mo, 1969. Fellow and Vice-President of the World Academy of Arts and Sciences; Medallist, Soc. de l'Encouragement au Progrès (France); Vice-President and founder, Anglo-German Assoc.; Director, Investigation into Eighteenth Amendment, US Constitution, under Rockefeller Foundation, 1926; editorial writer to Yorkshire Post, 1927-28, editor of People and Freedom, and special foreign correspondent, inc. Reuters, Germany, Russia, Spanish Civil War, Italy and India; co-founder, Realist Magazine, with H. G. Wells, Arnold Bennett and others. Contested (Lab.) Brentford Div., 1931, Sunderland Div., 1935; sometime Member Executive

Cttee, Fabian Soc.; joint founder, America and British Commonwealth Assoc. (now E-SU); Technical adviser to Rt Hon. Arthur Greenwood, 1939-40; Temp. adviser to Wendell Wilkie on Presidential election campaign, 1940; Member Internat. Executive Cttee of Nouvelles Equipes Internationales (Internat. Cttee of Christian Socialist Parties) and rapporteur on European Union. Mem., FCO Liaison Cttee re US Bicentary Celebration. Vice-President: War on Want; British Atlantic Unity Cttee. Sponsor, Martin Luther King Foundn. Mem., Inst. for Strategic Studies; Mem., Adv. Council, E-SU. Draftsman of Internat. Declaration in Support of Indian Independence, 1943. LDV, 1940. Comdr, Grand Cross, Order of Merit (Germany). *Publications:* Thomas Hobbes, 1922; The Science and Method of Politics, 1926, repr. 1964; Mary Wollstonecraft's Vindication: introd., 1928; Study of the Principles of Politics, 1929, repr. 1967; Liquor Control, 1931; Preface to Action, 1934; New Trends in Socialism, ed 1935; War and Democracy, ed 1938; (ed. and introd.) Durkheim's Rules of Sociological Method, 1938; Anglo-Saxony and its Tradition, 1939; The Story of the Political Philosophers, 1939; (8th edn, published in Britain as A History of the Political Philosophers, 1950); One Anglo-American Nation: The Foundation of Anglo-Saxony, 1941; Anglo-American Union as Nucleus of World Federation, 1942; The Unity of Europe, 1945; Above All Nations (jtly), 1945; Mahatma Gandhi, 1948; What Does the West Want?, 1957; The Atlantic Community, 1959; Systematic Politics, 1962; Rabindranath Tagore centenary lectures, 1964; Political and Sociological Theory and its Applications, 1964; The Grandeur of England and the Atlantic Community, 1966; The Atlantic Commonwealth, 1969; For God's Sake, Go (autobiography), 1972; Atlanticism, 1973; Kissinger's Atlantic Charter, 1974; Détente, 1975; trans of above into various languages. *Address:* Corner Cottage, Allum Green, near Lyndhurst, Hants. *Clubs:* Pilgrims, National Liberal.

See also Rt . Hon . Shirley V. T. B. Williams.

CATLING, Hector William, MA, DPhil, FSA; Director of the British School at Athens since 1971; *b* 26 June 1924; *s* of late Arthur William Catling and Phyllis Norah Catling (*née* Vyvyan); *m* 1948, Elizabeth Anne (*née* Salter); two *s* one *d*. *Educ:* The Grammar Sch., Bristol; St John's Coll., Oxford. Casberd Exhbr, 1948, BA 1950, MA 1954, DPhil 1957. Served War, RNVR, 1942-46. At Univ.: undergrad. 1946-50, postgrad. 1950-54. Goldsmiths' Travelling Schol., 1951-53. Archaeological Survey Officer, Dept of Antiquities, Cyprus, 1955-59; Asst Keeper, Dept of Antiquities, Ashmolean Museum, Univ. of Oxford, 1959-64, Sen. Asst Keeper, 1964-71. Fellow of Linacre Coll., Oxford, 1967-71. Corresp. Mem., German Archaeological Inst., 1961; Hon. Mem., Greek Archaeological Soc., 1975. *Publications:* Cypriot Bronzework in the Mycenaean World, 1964; contribs to jls concerned with prehistoric and classical antiquity in Greek lands. *Recreation:* ornithology. *Address:* The British School at Athens, Odos Souedias 52, Athens 140, Greece; 381 Woodstock Road, Oxford.

CATLING, Sir Richard (Charles), Kt 1964; CMG 1956; OBE 1951; *b* 22 Aug. 1912; *y s* of late William Catling, Leiston, Suffolk; *m* 1951, Mary Joan Feyer (*née* Lewis) (*d* 1974). *Educ:* The Grammar School, Bungay, Suffolk. Palestine Police, 1935-48; Federation of Malaya Police, 1948-54; Commissioner of Police, Kenya, 1954-63; Inspector General of Police, Kenya, 1963-64. Colonial Police Medal, 1942; King's Police Medal, 1945. Officer Brother, OStJ, 1956. *Recreations:* fishing, sailing. *Address:* Hall Fen House, Irstead, Norfolk NR12 8XT. *Club:* East India, Devonshire, Sports and Public Schools.

CATNACH, Agnes, CBE 1952; BA; *b* 8 Dec. 1891; *d* of Charles Burney Catnach, Newcastle upon Tyne. *Educ:* Polam Hall, Darlington; Royal Holloway Coll. Headmistress of Wallasey High Sch., 1926-34, of Putney County Sch., Mayfield, 1934-51. President of Assoc. of Headmistresses, 1942-44; Chairman of Joint Cttee of Four Secondary Associations, 1944-46; Member of Secondary Schools' Examinations Council, 1946-52; Member of General Nursing Council, 1943-58. *Address:* 3 Rusper House, Michel Grove, Eastbourne, E Sussex. *T:* Eastbourne 31014.

CATO, Hon. Sir Arnott Samuel; PC (Barbados) 1976; Kt 1977; President of the Senate of Barbados, since 1976; *b* St Vincent, 24 Sept. 1912. *Educ:* St Vincent Grammar Sch. (St Vincent Scholar, 1930); Edinburgh Univ. (MB, ChB). Returned to St Vincent; Asst Resident Surgeon, Colonial Hosp., 1936-37; Ho. Surg., Barbados Gen. Hosp., 1937-41; private practice from 1941; Vis. Surgeon, Barbados Gen. Hosp., later Queen Elizabeth Hosp., and Chm. Med. Staff Cttee 1965-70. Past Pres., Barbados Br. BMA. Chm., Barbados Public Service Commn, 1972-76; (Prime Minister's Nominee) Senate of Barbados, following Gen. Election of Sept. 1976; Actg Governor Gen., 16 and 17 Nov. 1976. *Address:* Senate House, Bridgetown, Barbados.

CATO, Brian Hudson; a Recorder of the Crown Court, since 1974; Chairman: Mental Health Review Tribunal for Newcastle Regional Hospital Board, now Northern Regional Health Authority, since 1967; Industrial Tribunals, since 1975; *b* 6 June 1928; *s* of Thomas and Edith Willis Cato; *m* 1963, Barbara Edith Myles; one *s. Educ:* LEA elem. and grammar schs; Trinity Coll., Oxford; RAF Padgate. MA Oxon, LLB London. RAF, 1952-54. Called to Bar, Gray's Inn, 1952; in practice NE Circuit, 1954-. Special Lectr (part-time) in Law of Town and Country Planning, King's Coll., now Univ. of Newcastle, 1956-. Pres., N of England Medico-legal Soc., 1973-75. Freeman of City of Newcastle upon Tyne by patrimony; Mem. Plumbers', Hostmen's, Goldsmiths' and Colliers' Companies; Founder Mem., Scriveners' Co. *Recreations:* family and village life. *Address:* (chambers) 46 Grainger Street, Newcastle upon Tyne NE1 5JR. *T:* Newcastle upon Tyne 21980; (home) 10 North Jesmond Avenue, Newcastle upon Tyne NE2 3JX. *T:* Newcastle 814226; The Cottage, Front Street, Embleton, Alnwick, Northumberland NE66 3UH. *T:* Embleton 334. *Club:* Senior Common Room (Newcastle University).

CATON-THOMPSON, Gertrude, FBA 1944; Hon. LittD Cantab 1954; former Fellow of Newnham College, Cambridge; *o d* of late William Caton-Thompson and Mrs E. G. Moore. *Educ:* Miss Hawtrey's, Eastbourne; Paris. Employed Ministry of Shipping, 1915-19; Paris Peace Conference, 1919; student British School of Archæology in Egypt, 1921-26; excavated at Abydos and Oxyrhynchos, 1921-22; Malta, 1921 and 1924; Qau and Badari, 1923-25; on behalf of the British School in Egypt inaugurated the first archæological and geological survey of the Northern Fayum, 1924-26; continued work as Field Director for the Royal Anthropological Institute, 1927-28; appointed in 1928 by the British Assoc. to conduct excavations at Zimbabwe and other Rhodesian sites; Excavations in Kharga Oasis, 1930-33; South Arabia, 1937-38; Cuthbert Peek award of the Royal Geographical Society, 1932; Rivers Medallist of the Royal Anthropological Institute, 1934; Huxley medallist, 1946. Burton Medal of Royal Asiatic Society, 1954. Former Governor, Bedford Coll. for Women, and School of Oriental and African Studies, University of London; former Member: Council British Inst. of History and Archæology in East Africa. *Publications:* contributions to the Encyclopædia Britannica and various scientific journals; The Badarian Civilisation (part author), 1928; The Zimbabwe Culture, 1931 (repr. 1969); The Desert Fayum, 1935; The Tombs and Moon Temple of Hureidha, Hadramaut, 1944; Kharga Oasis in Prehistory, 1952. *Recreation:* idleness. *Address:* Court Farm, Broadway, Worcs. *Club:* English-Speaking Union.

CATTANACH, Brig. Helen, CB 1976; RRC 1963; Matron-in-Chief (Army) and Director of Army Nursing Services, Queen Alexandra's Royal Army Nursing Corps, 1973-76; *b* 21 June 1920; *d* of late Francis Cattanach and Marjory Cattanach (*née* Grant). *Educ:* Elgin Academy; trained Woodend Hospital, Aberdeen. Joined QAIMNS (R) 1945; service in India, Java, United Kingdom, Singapore, Hong Kong and Germany, 1945-52; MELF, Gibraltar and UK, 1953-57; Staff Officer, MoD, 1958-61; Inspector of Recruiting, QARANC, 1961-62; Hong Kong and UK, 1963-64; Matron: BMH Munster, 1968; Cambridge Military Hosp., Aldershot, 1969-71; Dir of Studies, QARANC, 1971-72. QHNS 1973-77. CStJ 1976 (OStJ 1971). *Recreations:* walking, race meetings, theatre. *Address:* c/o Lloyds Bank, Dorking, Surrey. *Clubs:* United Nursing Services, English-Speaking Union.

CATTELL, George Harold Bernard; Director-General, National Farmers' Union, since 1970; *b* 23 March 1920; *s* of H. W. K. Cattell; *m* 1951, Agnes Jean Hardy; three *s* one *d. Educ:* Royal Grammar Sch., Colchester. Served Regular Army, 1939-58; psc 1954; despatches, Malaya, 1957; retired as Major, RA. Asst Director, London Engineering Employers' Assoc., 1958-60; Group Industrial Relations Officer, H. Stevenson & Sons, 1960-61; Director, Personnel and Manufacturing, Rootes Motors Ltd, 1961-68; Managing Director, Humber Ltd, Chm., Hills Precision Diecasting Ltd, Chm., Thrupp & Maberly Ltd, 1965-68; Dir, Manpower and Productivity Services, Dept of Employment and Productivity, 1968-70. Member Council: Industrial Soc. 1965-; CBI, 1970-. AMN Federation of Malaya, 1958. *Recreations:* tennis, fishing. *Address:* Little Cheveney, Yalding, Kent. *T:* Hunton 365. *Clubs:* Naval and Military, Farmers', Sloane.

CATTERMOLE, Mrs James; *see* Mitchell, Dr J. E.

CATTERMOLE, Lancelot Harry Mosse, ROI 1938; painter and illustrator; *b* 19 July 1898; *s* of Sidney and Josephine Cattermole; *g s* of George Cattermole, painter in water-colours and oils; *m* 1937, Lydia Alice Winifred Coles, BA; no *c. Educ:* Holmsdale

House Sch., Worthing, Sussex; Odiham Grammar Sch., Hants. Senior Art Scholarship to Slade Faculty of Fine Art, University of London, and Central School of Arts and Crafts, London, 1923-26. Exhibitor RA, ROI, RBA, RP, etc., and Provincial Art Galleries. Signs work Lance Cattermole. *Recreations:* acting, reading and bridge. *Address:* Horizon, 17 Palmers Way, High Salvington, Worthing, W Sussex. *T:* Worthing 60436. *Club:* Army and Navy.

CATTO, family name of **Baron Catto.**

CATTO, 2nd Baron, *cr* 1936, of Cairncatto; Bt *cr* 1921; **Stephen Gordon Catto;** Chairman, Morgan Grenfell & Co. Ltd, since 1973 (a Director since 1957; Chief Executive, 1973-74); Chairman: Australian Mutual Provident Society (UK Branch); Yule Catto & Co. Ltd; Director: Australian United Corporation Holdings Ltd (Melbourne); The General Electric Co. Ltd; News International Ltd, and other companies; Member, London Advisory Committee, Hong Kong & Shanghai Banking Corporation; *b* 14 Jan. 1923; *o s* of 1st Baron Catto and Gladys Forbes, *d* of Stephen Gordon; *S* father 1959; *m* 1st, 1948, Josephine Innes (marr. diss. 1965), *er d* of G. H. Packer, Alexandria, Egypt; two *s* two *d*; 2nd, 1966, Margaret, *d* of J. S. Forrest, Dilston, Tasmania; one *s* one *d. Educ:* Eton; Cambridge Univ. Served with RAFVR, 1943-47. Member, Advisory Council, ECGD, 1959-65; part-time Mem., London Transport Bd, 1962-68. *Heir: s* Hon. Innes Gordon Catto, *b* 7 Aug. 1950. *Address:* Morgan Grenfell & Co. Ltd, 23 Great Winchester Street, EC2; Flat 6, 12 Charles Street W1X 7HB. *Clubs:* Oriental; Melbourne (Australia).

CATTON, Bruce; Senior Editor, American Heritage Magazine, since 1959 (Editor, 1954-59); *b* 9 Oct. 1899; *s* of George R. Catton; *m* 1925, Hazel Cherry; one *s. Educ:* Oberlin Coll. Newspaper Reporter in Cleveland, Boston and Washington, 1920-41. Asst Director of Information, US War Production Board, 1942-43, Director, 1944-45; Director of Information, US Dept of Commerce, 1945-47; Special Assistant, Secretary of Commerce, 1948; Asst Director of Information, US Dept of the Interior, 1950-52. Mem., Amer. Acad. of Arts and Letters. Pulitzer Prize for history, 1954; National Book Award, 1954; Presidential Medal of Freedom, 1977. Hon. degrees from various colleges and univs, inc. Oberlin, Harvard, Columbia, Michigan and Northwestern. *Publications:* The War Lords of Washington, 1948; Mr Lincoln's Army, 1951; Glory Road, 1952; A Stillness at Appomattox, 1953; U. S. Grant and the American Military Tradition, 1954; Banners at Shenandoah, 1955; This Hallowed Ground, 1956; America Goes to War, 1958; Grant Moves South, 1960; The American Heritage Picture History of the Civil War, 1960; The Coming Fury, 1961; Terrible Swift Sword, 1963; Never Call Retreat, 1965; Grant Takes Command, 1969; Waiting for the Morning Train, 1972; Gettysburg: the Final Fury, 1975. *Recreations:* virtually none, except for unadorned loafing in the north woods of Michigan every summer. *Address:* American Heritage, 10 Rockefeller Plaza, New York, NY 10020, USA. *Clubs:* Players, Century, Lotos (New York).

CAUGHEY, Sir Thomas Harcourt Clarke, KBE 1972 (OBE 1966); JP; Managing Director, since 1962, Chairman, since 1975, Smith & Caughey Ltd; *b* Auckland, 4 July 1911; *s* of James Marsden Caughey; *m* 1939, Patricia Mary, *d* of Hon. Sir George Panton Finlay; one *s* two *d. Educ:* King's Coll., Auckland. Major, Fiji Military Forces (Pacific), 1942-44. Director: S British Insurance Co. Ltd; Guardian Trust and Executors Co. of NZ. Chm., Caughey Preston Trust Bd, 1954-; Member: Eden Park Trustees; Auckland Hosps Bd, 1953-74 (Chm., 1959-74); Hosps Adv. Council, 1960-74; Vice-Pres., NZ Exec. Hosps Bds Assoc., 1960-74; Chairman: NZ MRC, 1966-71; Social Council of NZ, 1971-73. CStJ. *Recreations:* gardening, swimming. *Address:* 7 Judges Bay Road, Auckland, NZ. *Clubs:* Northern, Officers' (Auckland, NZ).

CAULCOTT, Thomas Holt; Secretary, Association of Metropolitan Authorities, since 1976; *b* 7 June 1927; *s* of late L. W. Caulcott and Doris Caulcott; *m* 1954, C. Evelyn Lowden; one *s* one *d. Educ:* Solihull Sch.; Emmanuel Coll., Cambridge. Asst Principal, Central Land Bd and War Damage Commn, 1950-53; transferred to HM Treasury, 1953; Private Sec. to Economic Sec. to the Treasury, 1955; Principal, Treasury supply divs, 1956-60; Private Sec. to successive Chancellors of the Exchequer, Sept. 1961-Oct. 1964; Principal Private Sec. to First Sec. of State (DEA), 1964-65; Asst Sec., HM Treasury, 1965-66; Min. of Housing and Local Govt, 1967-69; Civil Service Dept, 1969-70; Under-Sec., Machinery of Govt Gp, 1970-73; Principal Finance Officer, Local Govt Finance Policy, DoE, 1973-76. Harkness Fellowship, Harvard and Brookings Instn, 1960-61. *Address:* 56 Ridgway Place, SW19. *T:* 01-946 2308.

CAULFEILD, family name of **Viscount Charlemont**.

CAULFIELD, Hon. Sir Bernard, Kt 1968; **Hon. Mr Justice Caulfield**; Judge of the High Court of Justice, Queen's Bench Division, since 1968; Presiding Judge, Northern Circuit, since 1976; *b* 24 April 1914; 5th *s* of late John Caulfield and late Catherine Quinn, Haydock, Lancs; *m* 1953, Sheila Mary, *o d* of Dr J. F. J. Herbert; three *s* one *d*. *Educ:* St Francis Xavier's Coll.; University of Liverpool. LLB 1938, LLM 1940; Solicitor, 1940. Army Service, 1940-46; Home and MEF; Commnd, Dec. 1942, RAOC; released with Hon. rank of Major. Barrister-at-Law, Lincoln's Inn, 1947; joined Midland Circuit, 1949; QC 1961; Recorder of Coventry, 1963-68; Dep. Chairman QS, County of Lincoln (Parts of Lindsey), 1963-71; Leader, Midland Circuit, 1965-68; Member, General Council of Bar, 1965-68. Bencher, Lincoln's Inn, 1968. *Address:* Royal Courts of Justice, WC2A 2LL.

CAUNTER, Brigadier John Alan Lyde, CBE 1941; MC and Bar; *b* 17 Dec. 1889; *er s* of R. L. Caunter, MD, FRCS, and Mrs R. L. Caunter (*née* W. J. von Taysen); *m* 1920, Helen Margaret Napier (*d* 1942), *er d* of late Sir Walter Napier; one *s* one *d*; *m* 1945, Muriel Lilian Murphy (*née* Hicks). *Educ:* Uppingham Sch.; RMC, Sandhurst. 2nd Lieut Gloucestershire Regt, 1909; served European War, 1914-19 (MC and Bar, despatches, Brevet of Major); taken prisoner, 1914; escaped from Germany, July, 1917; operations France, Flanders, Macedonia, Turkey; Iraq Campaign, 1920-21; psc Camberley, 1923; transferred Royal Tank Corps, 1924; DAAG Rhine Army, 1925 and 1926; GSO2 Northern Command, 1927-28; DAA and QMG, N. Ireland, 1929-33; Bt. Lieut-Colonel, 1933; Lieut-Colonel, 1935; Comd 1st Bn (Light) Royal Tank Corps, 1935-39; Colonel and Temp. Brigadier 1939; Comdr 1st Army Tank Bde July-Oct. 1939; Cmdr Armoured Bde, Egypt, 1939-41; W. Desert Campaign, 1940-41, as Comdr 4th Armoured Bde (CBE, despatches); BGS, GHQ, India, 1941-43; retired 1944. Member Cornwall CC, 1952-67; Member for GB, Internat. Cttee of Internat. Game Fish Association (HQ at Fort Lauderdale, Fla, USA). *Publications:* 13 Days, 1918 (An Escape from a German Prison Camp); Shark Angling in Great Britain, 1961. *Recreations:* fishing, shooting, (present); past: Rugby football, cricket, hockey. *Address:* The Brentons, Hannafore, Looe, Cornwall. *T:* Looe 2427. *Club:* Shark Angling of Great Britain (President and Founder);(HQ at Looe).

CAUSEY, Prof. Gilbert, FRCS; retired; Sir William Collins Professor of Anatomy, Royal College of Surgeons, Professor of Anatomy, University of London, and Conservator of Hunterian Museum, 1952-70; *b* 8 Oct. 1907; 2nd *s* of George and Ada Causey; *m* 1935, Elizabeth, *d* of late F. J. L. Hickinbotham, JP, and of Mrs Hickinbotham; two *s* three *d*. *Educ:* Wigan Grammar Sch.; University of Liverpool. MB, ChB (1st Hons.), 1930; MRCS, LRCP, 1930; FRCS 1933; DSc 1964; FDSRCS 1971. Gold Medallist in Anatomy, Surgery, Medicine, and Obstetrics and Gynæcology; Lyon Jones Scholar and various prizes. Member of Anatomical and Physiological Societies. Asst Surgeon, Walton Hospital, Liverpool, 1935; Lecturer in Anatomy, University College, London, 1948; Rockefeller Foundation Travelling Fellow, 1950. John Hunter Medal, 1964; Keith Medal, 1970. *Publications:* The Cell of Schwann, 1960; Electron Microscopy, 1962; contributions to various scientific texts and journals. *Recreation:* music. *Address:* Orchard Cottage, Bodinnick-by-Fowey, Cornwall. *T:* Polruan 433.

CAUSLEY, Charles Stanley; poet; teacher; broadcaster; *b* Launceston, Cornwall, 24 Aug. 1917; *o s* of Charles Causley and Laura Bartlett. *Educ:* Launceston National Sch.; Horwell Grammar Sch.; Launceston Coll.; Peterborough Training Coll. Served on lower-deck in Royal Navy (Communications Branch), 1940-46. Literary Editor, 1953-56, of BBC's West Region radio magazines Apollo in the West and Signature. Awarded Travelling Scholarships by Society of Authors, 1954 and 1966. Mem., Arts Council Poetry Panel, 1962-66. Hon. Vis. Fellow in Poetry, Univ. of Exeter, 1973. FRSL 1958. Hon. DLitt Exeter, 1977. Awarded Queen's Gold Medal for Poetry, 1967; Cholmondeley Award, 1971. *Publications:* Hands to Dance, 1951; Farewell, Aggie Weston, 1951; Survivor's Leave, 1953; Union Street, 1957; Peninsula (ed), 1957; Johnny Alleluia, 1961; Dawn and Dusk (ed), 1962; Penguin Modern Poets 3 (with George Barker and Martin Bell), 1962; Rising Early (ed), 1964; Modern Folk Ballads (ed), 1966; Underneath the Water, 1968; Figure of 8, 1969; Figgie Hobbin, 1971; The Tail of the Trinosaur, 1973; (ed) The Puffin Book of Magic Verse, 1974; Collected Poems, 1975; The Hill of the Fairy Calf, 1976; contrib. to many anthologies of verse in Great Britain and America. *Recreations:* the theatre; European travel; the re-discovery of his native town; playing the piano with expression. *Address:* 2 Cyprus Well, Launceston, Cornwall. *T:* Launceston 2731.

CAUTE, (John) David, MA, DPhil; writer; *b* 16 Dec. 1936; *m* 1st, 1961, Catherine Shuckburgh (marr. diss. 1970); two *s*; 2nd, 1973, Martha Bates; two *d*. *Educ:* Edinburgh Academy; Wellington; Wadham Coll., Oxford. Scholar of St Antony's Coll., 1959. Spent a year in the Army in the Gold Coast, 1955-56, and a year at Harvard Univ. on a Henry Fellowship, 1960-61. Fellow of All Souls Coll., Oxford, 1959-65; Visiting Professor, New York Univ. and Columbia Univ., 1966-67; Reader in Social and Political Theory, Brunel Univ., 1967-70. Regents' Lectr, Univ. of Calif., 1974. Exec. Council, Writers' Guild, 1976. *Plays:* Songs for an Autumn Rifle, staged by Oxford Theatre Group at Edinburgh, 1961; The Demonstration, Nottingham Playhouse, 1969; Fallout, BBC Radio, 1972; The Fourth World, Royal Court, 1973; Brecht and Company, BBC TV, 1977. *Publications:* at Fever Pitch (novel), 1959 (Authors' Club Award and John Llewelyn Rhys Prize, 1960); Comrade Jacob (novel), 1961; Communism and the French Intellectuals, 1914-1960, 1964; The Left in Europe Since 1789, 1966; The Decline of the West (novel), 1966; Essential Writings of Karl Marx (ed), 1967; Fanon, 1970; The Confrontation: a trilogy, 1971 (consisting of The Demonstration (play), 1970; The Occupation (novel), 1971; The Illusion, 1971); The Fellow-Travellers, 1973; Collisions, 1974; Cuba, Yes?, 1974. *Address:* Elaine Greene Ltd, 31 Newington Green, N16 9PU.

CAUTHERY, Harold William, CB 1969; *b* 5 May 1914; *s* of Joseph Cauthery, Manchester; *m* 1938, Dorothy Constance, *d* of George E. Sawyer, Sutton Coldfield; one *s* one *d* (and one *d* decd). *Educ:* Bishop Vesey's Grammar Sch., Sutton Coldfield; Christ's College, Cambridge. Asst Inspector of Taxes, Inland Revenue, 1936; Asst Principal, Ministry of Health, 1937; Instructor-Lieut, RN, 1942-45; Principal, Ministry of Health, 1944; Asst Secretary: Ministry of Health, 1950; Ministry of Housing and Local Government, 1951; Under-Sec., Min. of Transport, 1960-66; Dep. Sec., Min. of Land and Natural Resources, 1966; Dir and Sec. and Mem., Land Commn, 1967-71; Dep. Under-Sec. of State (Air), MoD, 1971-72; Sec., Local Govt Staff Commn, 1972-74. *Publication:* Parish Councillor's Guide, 10th Edition, 1958. *Recreations:* music (piano and double bass), gardening. *Address:* Eastcote, Petworth Road, Haslemere, Surrey. *T:* Haslemere 51448. *Club:* United Oxford & Cambridge University.

CAVALCANTI, Alberto de Almeida; Film Director and Producer; *b* Rio de Janeiro, 6 Feb. 1897. *Educ:* Fine Arts Sch., Geneva (Architecture). Came into Films as an Art Director, then became Director in the French Avant-Garde Group. Came to England in 1934 and worked in the Documentary School. Back to fictional films at Ealing in 1940. Films directed in France, 1924-34: Rien que les heures, En Rade, La P'tite Lilie, Yvette, Le Capitaine Fracasse, etc. Films directed or produced in Great Britain, 1934-46: North Sea, Men of the Lightship, The Foreman Went to France, Went the Day Well, Half-Way House, Champagne Charlie, Dead of Night, The Life and Adventures of Nicholas Nickleby, They Made Me a Fugitive, The First Gentleman, For Them That Trespass. Brazilian productions: Caicara, Painel, Terra é sempre Terra and Volta Redonda; directed: Simão o Caôlho; O Canto do Mar, A Mulher de Verdade. Continental films: Brecht's Herr Puntila und sein Knecht Matti; Windrose (with Joris Ivens); Les Noces Venitiennes. Thus Spake Theodor Herzl (in Israel). Compilation, One Man and the Cinema, Parts I and II. For the Stage: Blood-wedding (in Spain); Fuente Ovejuna (in Israel); La Nuit. French TV, Les Empailles; La Visite de la Vieille-Dame. *Publication:* Filme e realidade. *Address:* 4 Villa Dufresne, 75016 Paris, France. *Club:* Garrick.

CAVALIERO, Roderick; Assistant Director General, British Council, since 1977; *b* 21 March 1928; *s* of Eric Cavaliero and Valerie (*née* Logan); *m* 1957, Mary McDonnell; one *s* four *d*. *Educ:* Tonbridge School; Hertford Coll., Oxford. Teaching in Britain, 1950-52; teaching in Malta, 1952-58; British Council Officer, 1958- (service in India, Brazil, Italy). *Publications:* Olympia and the Angel, 1958; The Last of the Crusaders, 1960. *Address:* 10 Lansdowne Road, Tunbridge Wells, Kent TN1 2NJ.

CAVALLERA, Rt. Rev. Charles; *see* Marsabit, Bishop of, (RC).

CAVAN, 12th Earl of, *cr* 1647; **Michael Edward Oliver Lambart**, TD; DL; Baron Cavan, 1618; Baron Lambart, 1618; Viscount Kilcoursie, 1647; Vice Lord-Lieutenant, Salop, since 1975; *b* 29 Oct. 1911; *o s* of 11th Earl of Cavan and Audrey Kathleen (*d* 1942), *o d* of late A. B. Loder; *S* father 1950; *m* 1947, Essex Lucy, *o d* of Henry Arthur Cholmondeley, Shotton Hall, Hadnall, Shropshire; two *d* (and one *d* decd). *Educ:* Radley College. Served War of 1939-45, Shropshire Yeomanry (despatches). Lt-Col comdg Shropshire Yeomanry, 1955-58;

Hon. Col, C Sqdn, The Queen's Own Mercian Yeomanry, TAVR, 1974-. DL Salop, 1959. *Address:* Waters Upton Manor, Wellington, Telford, Salop TF6 6PA. *T:* Great Bolas 384.

CAVANAGH, John Bryan; Dress Designer; Chairman and Managing Director, John Cavanagh Ltd, retired 1974; *b* 28 Sept. 1914; *s* of Cyril Cavanagh and Anne (*née* Murphy). *Educ:* St Paul's School. Trained with Captain Edward Molyneux in London and Paris, 1932-40. Joined Intelligence Corps, 1940, Captain (GS, Camouflage), 1944. On demobilisation, 1946, travelled throughout USA studying fashion promotion. Personal Assistant to Pierre Balmain, Paris, 1947-51; opened own business, 1952; opened John Cavanagh Boutique, 1959. Elected to Incorporated Society of London Fashion Designers, 1952 (Vice-Chm., 1956-59). Took own complete Collection to Paris, 1953; designed clothes for late Princess Marina and wedding dresses for the Duchess of Kent and Princess Alexandra. Gold Medal, Munich, 1954. *Recreations:* the theatre, swimming, travelling. *Address:* 11 Pembridge Gardens, W2.

CAVE; *see* Verney-Cave, family name of Baron Braye.

CAVE, Alexander James Edward, OFM Tertiary; MD, DSc, FRCS, FLS; Emeritus Professor of Anatomy, University of London; *b* Manchester, 13 Sept. 1900; *e s* of late John Cave and of Teresa Anne d'Hooghe; *m* 1st, 1926, Dorothy M. Dimbleby (*d* 1961); one *d*; 2nd, 1970, Catherine Elizabeth FitzGerald. *Educ:* Manchester High Sch.; Victoria University of Manchester. MB, ChB (distinction Preventive Medicine) 1923; MD (commendation) 1937; DSc, 1944; FRCS, 1959; DSc London, 1967. Senior Demonstrator (later Lecturer) in Anatomy, University of Leeds, 1924-34; Senior Demonstrator of Anatomy and Curator of Anatomical Museum, University College, London, 1934-35; Asst Conservator of Museum (1935-46), Arnott Demonstrator (1936-46) and Professor of Human and Comparative Anatomy (1941-46), Royal College of Surgeons of England; Prof. of Anatomy, St Bartholomew's Hospital Medical Coll., University of London, 1946-67, now Member Board Governors. Arris and Gale Lecturer, 1932, 1941; Hunterian Trustee; Stopford Lecturer, 1967; Morrison Watson Research Fellow, 1961-76. Late Examiner in Anatomy, University of London, Royal University of Malta, Universities of Cambridge and Ireland, Primary FRCS and English Conjoint Board; Fellow (formerly Council Mem. and Pres.), Linnean Society; Fellow (late Vice-Pres., Council Member and Silver Medallist) Zoological Society; Life-Member (late Council Mem., Hon. Secretary and Recorder, Vice-Pres.) Anatomical Soc.; Member Ray Society; Member American Assoc. of Physical Anthropologists; *Publications:* various papers on human and comparative anatomy, physical anthropology and medical history. *Address:* 18 Orchard Avenue, Finchley, N3. *T:* 01-346 3340. *Club:* Athenæum.

CAVE, Sir Charles (Edward Coleridge), 4th Bt, *cr* 1896; JP; *b* 28 Feb. 1927; *o s* of Sir Edward Charles Cave, 3rd Bt, and Betty, *o d* of late Rennell Coleridge, Salston, Ottery St Mary; *S* father 1946; *m* 1957, Mary Elizabeth, *yr d* of John Francis Gore, *qv*; four *s*. *Educ:* Eton. Lieut The Devonshire Regt, 1946-48. CC Devon, 1955-64; High Sheriff of Devonshire, 1969. JP Devon 1972. FRICS. *Heir: s* John Charles Cave, *b* 8 Sept. 1958. *Address:* Sidbury Manor, Sidmouth, Devon. *T:* Sidbury 207.

CAVE, Charles Philip H.; *see* Haddon-Cave.

CAVE, Sir Richard (Guy), Kt 1976; MC 1944; Chairman, Thorn Electrical Industries Ltd, since 1976; Director: Equity & Law Life Assurance Society Ltd; Tunnel Holdings Ltd; Tate & Lyle Ltd; *b* 16 March 1920; *s* of William Thomas Cave and Gwendolyn Mary Nichols; *m* 1957, Dorothy Gillian Fry; two *s* two *d*. *Educ:* Tonbridge; Gonville and Caius Coll., Cambridge. Joined Smiths Industries Ltd, 1946; Man. Dir, Motor Accessory Div., 1963; Chief Exec. and Man. Dir, 1968-73; Chm., 1973-76. *Recreation:* sailing. *Address:* Thamescote, Chiswick Mall, W4. *T:* 01-994 8017.

CAVE, Sir Richard (Philip), KCVO 1977 (MVO 1969); CB 1975; DL; Fourth Clerk at the Table (Judicial), House of Lords, 1965-77 and Principal Clerk, Judicial Department, House of Lords, 1959-77; Taxing Officer of Judicial Costs, House of Lords, 1957-77; Crown Examiner in Peerage Cases 1953-77; Secretary, Association of Lieutenants of Counties and Custodes Rotulorum, 1946-59, and 1964-77; Founder and President, Multiple Sclerosis Society of Great Britain and Northern Ireland (Chairman, 1953-76); a Vice-President, International Federation of Multiple Sclerosis Societies, since 1967; *b* 26 April 1912; 4th *s* of late Charles John Philip Cave and late Wilhelmina Mary Henrietta (*née* Kerr); *m* 1936, Margaret Mary, *e d* of Francis Westby Perceval; one *s*. *Educ:* Ampleforth Coll.; Trinity Coll.,

Cambridge (MA); Herts Institute of Agriculture; College of Estate Management. A Gold Staff Officer, Coronation of HM King George VI, 1937. Agent for Earl of Craven's Hamstead Marshall Estate, 1938-39. Royal Wilts Yeomanry (L. Corp.), 1939-40; The Rifle Bde (Captain; Officer i/c Cols Comdt's Office, KRRC and Rifle Bde), 1940-45. Territorial Efficiency Medal, 1946. Vice-Chm., Society for Relief of Distress, 1972; a Governor: Nuffield Nursing Homes Trust, 1969; Queen Elizabeth's Foundn for the Disabled, 1970. A Confrater of Ampleforth Abbey, 1971. DL Greater London, 1973. Gold Medal, Royal English Forestry Society, 1939; Silver Medal, RASE, 1939. KSG 1966; KCSG 1972; Kt of Honour and Devotion, SMO Malta, 1972; Kt of Justice, Sacred Military Order of Constantine of St George, 1972. *Publications:* Elementary Map Reading, 1941; articles in Atkin's Encyclopedia of Court Forms in Civil Proceedings, 1968 and 1973; Halsbury's Laws of England, 1974. *Recreations:* hill-walking, photography, collecting map postcards. *Address:* Watergate, Ham Common, Richmond, Surrey TW10 7JG. *T:* 01-940 8014. *Clubs:* Royal Commonwealth Society; University Pitt (Cambridge).

CAVE-BROWNE-CAVE, Sir Robert, 16th Bt, *cr* 1641; President of Cave & Co. Ltd, and of Seaboard Chemicals Ltd; *b* 8 June 1929; *s* of 15th Bt, and Dorothea Plewman, *d* of Robert Greene Dwen, Chicago, Ill; *S* father 1945; *m* 1954, Lois Shirley, *d* of John Chalmers Huggard, Winnipeg, Manitoba; one *s* one *d*. *Educ:* University of BC (BA 1951). *Heir: s* John Robert Charles Cave-Browne-Cave, *b* 22 June 1957. *Club:* Capilano Golf and Country (BC).

CAVELL, Rt. Rev. John K; *see* Southampton, Bishop Suffragan of.

CAVENAGH, Prof. Winifred Elizabeth, OBE 1977; PhD, BScEcon; JP; Professor of Social Administration and Criminology, University of Birmingham, 1972-77, now Emeritus; Barrister-at-Law; *d* of Arthur Speakman and Ethel Speakman (*née* Butterworth); *m* 1938, Hugh Cavenagh; one step *s*. *Educ:* London Sch. of Economics, Univ. of London; Bonn. BSc Econ (London); PhD (Birm.). Called to the Bar, Gray's Inn, 1964. With Lewis's Ltd, 1931-38; Min. of Labour, 1941-45. Univ. of Birmingham, 1946-. Birmingham: City Educn Cttee (co-opted expert), 1946-66; City Magistrate, 1949- (Dep. Chm., 1970-); Police Authority, 1970-. Governor, Birmingham United Teaching Hosps (Ministerial appt, 1958-64); W Midlands Economic Planning Council, 1967-71; Indep. Mem. of Wages Councils; Home Office Standing Advisory Cttee on Probation, 1958-67; Lord Chancellor's Standing Adv. Cttee: on Legal Aid, 1960-71; on Training of Magistrates, 1965-73. Nat. Chm., Assoc. of Social Workers, 1955-57; Council, Magistrates Assoc. (co-opted expert), 1965-. Visiting Prof., Univ of Ghana, 1971; Eleanor Rathbone Meml Lectr, 1976. *Publications:* Four Decades of Students in Social Work, 1953; The Child and the Court, 1959; Juvenile Courts, the Child and the Law, 1967; contrib. articles to: Public Administration, Brit. Jl Criminology, Justice of the Peace, Social Work To-day, etc. *Recreations:* walking, theatre, music, films. *Address:* 25 High Point, Richmond Hill Road, Edgbaston, Birmingham B15 3RU. *T:* 021-454 0109. *Club:* University Women's.

CAVENAGH-MAINWARING, Captain Maurice Kildare, DSO 1940; Royal Navy; joined Simpson (Piccadilly) Ltd, 1961; *b* 13 April 1908; *yr s* of Major James Gordon Cavenagh-Mainwaring, Whitmore Hall, Whitmore, Staffordshire; *m* Iris Mary, *d* of late Colonel Charles Denaro, OBE; one *s*. *Educ:* RN College, Dartmouth. Joint Services Staff College, 1951-52; HMS St Angelo and Flag Captain to Flag Officer, Malta, 1952-54; President, Second Admiralty Interview Board, 1955-56; Naval Attaché, Paris, 1957-60. ADC to the Queen, 1960. Retired from RN, 1960. Cross of Merit Sovereign Order, Knights of Malta, 1955; Comdr Légion d'Honneur, 1960. *Address:* 47 Cadogan Gardens, SW3. *T:* 01-584 7870; Apollo Court, St Julian's, Malta. *Club:* Naval and Military.

CAVENDISH, family name of **Baron Chesham,** of **Duke of Devonshire,** and of **Baron Waterpark.**

CAVENDISH-BENTINCK, family name of **Duke of Portland.**

CAVENDISH-BENTINCK, Victor Frederick William, CMG 1942; Chairman, Bayer (UK) Ltd; Director, NUKEM Nuklear-Chemie und-Metallurgie GmbH (Germany); *b* 18 June 1897; *s* of late Frederick Cavendish-Bentinck; *b* and *heir-pres*. to 8th Duke of Portland, *qv*; *m* 1st, 1924 (marr. diss.); one *d* (one *s* decd); 2nd, 1948, Kathleen Elsie, *yr d* of Arthur Barry, Montreal. *Educ:* Wellington Coll., Berks. Attaché HM Legation, Oslo, 1915; 2nd Lieut, Grenadier Guards, 1918; 3rd

Sec., HM Legation, Warsaw, 1919; transferred to Foreign Office, 1922; attended Lausanne Conference, 1922-23; 2nd Sec., HM Embassy, Paris, 1923; HM Legation, The Hague, 1924; transferred to Foreign Office, 1925; attended Locarno Conference, 1925; 1st Sec., HM Embassy, Paris, 1928; HM Legation, Athens, 1932; HM Embassy, Santiago, 1934; transferred to Foreign Office, 1937; Asst Under-Sec. of State, 1944; Ambassador to Poland, 1945-47; retired from Diplomatic Service, 1947. Chm. Council British Nuclear Forum. Grosses Verdienstkreuz (Germany). *Recreations:* travelling and antiques. *Address:* 21 Carlyle Square, SW3. *T:* 01-352 1258. *Clubs:* Turf, Beefsteak.

CAWDOR, 6th Earl *cr* 1827; **Hugh John Vaughan Campbell,** FRICS; Baron Cawdor, 1796; Viscount Emlyn, 1827; *b* 6 Sept. 1932; *er s* of 5th Earl Cawdor, TD, FSA, and of Wilma Mairi, *e d* of late Vincent C. Vickers; *S* father, 1970; *m* 1957, Cathryn, 2nd *d* of Maj.-Gen. Sir Robert Hinde, *qv*; two *s* three *d. Educ:* Eton; Magdalen Coll., Oxford; Royal Agricultural Coll., Cirencester. High Sheriff of Carmarthenshire, 1964. *Heir: s* Viscount Emlyn, *qv. Address:* Cawdor Castle, Nairn. *Club:* Pratt's.

CAWLEY, family name of **Baron Cawley.**

CAWLEY, 3rd Baron, *cr* 1918; **Frederick Lee Cawley,** 3rd Bt, *cr* 1906; *b* 27 July 1913; *s* of 2nd Baron and Vivienne, *d* of Harold Lee, Broughton Park, Manchester; *S* father 1954; *m* 1944, Rosemary Joan, *y d* of late R. E. Marsden; six *s* one *d. Educ:* Eton; New Coll., Oxford. BA Nat. Science (Zoology), 1935, MA 1942. Called to the Bar, Lincoln's Inn, 1938. Served War of 1939-45, Capt. RA Leicestershire Yeomanry (wounded). Mem. Woking UDC, 1949-57. Dep.-Chm. of Cttees, House of Lords, 1958-67; Mem., Jt Parly Cttees: Consolidation Bills, 1956-73; Delegated Legislation, 1972-73; Ecclesiastical, 1974. *Recreations:* gardening, shooting. *Heir: s* Hon. John Francis Cawley, *b* 28 Sept. 1946. *Address:* Bircher Hall, Leominster, Herefordshire. *T:* Yarpole 218. *Club:* Farmers'.

CAWLEY, Sir Charles (Mills), Kt 1965; CBE; Chief Scientist, Ministry of Power, 1959-67; a Civil Service Commissioner, 1967-69; *b* 17 May 1907; *s* of John and Emily Cawley, Gillingham, Kent; *m* 1934, Florence Mary Ellaline, *d* of James Shepherd, York; one *d. Educ:* Sir Joseph Williamson's Mathematical Sch., Rochester; Imperial Coll. of Science and Technology (Royal College of Sci.). ARCS, BSc (First Cl. Hons in Chem.), DIC; MSc; PhD; FRIC; DSc(London); FInstF; FRSA; Fellow, Imperial Coll. of Science and Technology. Fuel Research Station, DSIR, 1929-53. Imperial Defence Coll., 1949. A Dir, Headquarters, DSIR, 1953-59. Chm., Admiralty Fuels and Lubricants Advisory Cttee, 1957-64. Melchett Medal, Inst. of Fuel, 1968. *Publications:* Papers in various scientific and technical journals. *Address:* 8 Glen Gardens, Ferring-by-Sea, Worthing, West Sussex.

CAWLEY, Rev. Dr Frederick; Principal Emeritus, Spurgeon's College, London, since Sept. 1955 (Principal, 1950-55); *b* 8 Sept. 1884; *s* of S. R. and S. A. Cawley; *m* 1917, Mary Gold Coutts. *Educ:* Spurgeon's Coll., London; New Coll., Edinburgh. BA, BD (London); PhD (Edinburgh). Missionary: Baptist Missionary Soc., India, 1912-22 and Trinidad, West Indies, 1922-26. Baptist Minister: Falkirk, Scotland, 1926-35 and Camberwell, London, 1935-38; Penge, 1940-46. Senior Tutor, Spurgeon's Coll., London, 1938-47; Vice-Principal, 1947-50. Senator, University of London, 1951-56. *Publication:* The Transcendence of Jesus Christ, 1933. *Address:* The Tor, 30 Corstophine Road, Edinburgh EH12 6HP. *T:* 031-337 7702.

CAWSON, Prof. Roderick Anthony, MD; FDS, RCS and RCPS Glasgow; FRCPath; Professor (Hon. Consultant) and Head of Department of Oral Medicine and Pathology, Guy's Hospital Medical School since 1966; *b* 23 April 1921; *s* of Capt. Leopold Donald Cawson and Ivy Clunies-Ross; *m* 1949, Diana Hall, SRN; no *c. Educ:* King's College Sch. Wimbledon; King's College Hosp. Med. Sch. MD (London); MB, BS, BDS (Hons) (London); FDS, RCS; FDS, RCPS Glasgow; MRCPath; LMSSA. Served RAF, 1944-48; Nuffield Foundn Fellow, 1953-55; Dept of Pathology, King's Coll. Hosp., Sen. Lectr in Oral Pathology, King's Coll. Hosp. Med. Sch., 1955-62; Sen. Lectr in Oral Pathology, Guy's Hosp. Med. Sch., 1962-66. Examinerships: Pathology (BDS) London, 1965-69; Univ. of Wales, 1969-71; Dental Surgery (BDS), Glasgow, 1966-70; BChD Leeds, 1966-70; Newcastle, 1967-71; FDS, RCPS Glasgow, 1967-; BDS Lagos, 1975-. Chairman: Dental Formulary Sub-cttee (BMA); Dental and Surgical Materials Cttee, Medicines Division, 1976-; recently First Chm, Univ. Teachers' Gp (BDA). *Publications:* Essentials of Dental Surgery and Pathology 1962, 2nd edn repr. 1970; Medicine for Dental

Students (with R. H. Cutforth), 1960; (with R. G. Spector) Clinical Pharmacology in Dentistry, 1975; numerous papers, etc., in med. and dental jls. *Recreations:* reading, music, gardening (reluctantly). *Address:* 40 Court Lane, Dulwich, SE21 7DR. *T:* 01-693 5781.

CAWSTON, (Edwin) Richard, CVO 1972; Head of Documentary Programmes, BBC Television, since 1965; *b* 31 May 1923; *s* of Edwin Cawston and Phyllis, *d* of Henry Charles Hawkins; *m* 1951, Elisabeth Anne (*d* 1977), *d* of Canon R. L. Rhys; two *s. Educ:* Westminster Sch.; Oriel Coll., Oxford. Served Royal Signals, 1941-46; Captain 1945; Major and SO2 HQ Southern Comd, India, 1946. Film Editor, then Producer of original Television Newsreel, 1950-54; producer and director of major documentary films, 1955-, incl.: This is the BBC, 1959; The Lawyers, 1960; Television and the World, 1961; The Pilots, 1963; Born Chinese, 1965; Royal Family, 1969; Royal Heritage, 1977. Chm., British Acad. of Film and TV Arts, 1976 (Trustee, 1971-; Mem. Council of Management, 1959-). Awards include: British Film Acad. Award, 1959; Screenwriters Guild Award, 1961; Silver Medal, Royal TV Soc., 1961; Guild of TV Producers and Dirs Award, 1962; Italia Prize, 1962; Desmond Davis Award, 1969; Silver Satellite of AWRT, 1970. *Recreation:* making things. *Address:* Willow Cottage, Chalfont Lane, Chorleywood, Herts. *T:* Chorleywood 2333.

CAWTHRA, Rear-Adm. Arthur James, CB 1966; Admiral Superintendent, HM Dockyard, Devonport, 1964-66; *b* 30 Sept. 1911; *s* of James Herbert Cawthra, MIEE, and Margaret Anne Cawthra; *m* 1959, Adrien Eleanor Lakeman Tivy, *d* of Cecil B. Tivy, MCh, Plymouth; one *s* (and one *s* decd). *Educ:* abroad. Joined Royal Navy, 1930; Imperial Defence Course, 1956; HMS Fisgard, 1958-59; Dir Underwater Weapons, Admiralty, 1960-63. Capt. 1955; Rear-Adm. 1964. *Recreation:* sailing. *Address:* Lower Island, Blackawton, Totnes, Devon.

CAYFORD, Dame Florence Evelyn, DBE 1965; JP; Mayor, London Borough of Camden, 1969; *b* 14 June 1897; *d* of George William and Mary S. A. Bunch; *m* 1923, John Cayford; two *s. Educ:* Carlton Road Sch.; St Pancras County Secondary Sch., Paddington Technical Institute. Alderman, LCC, 1946-52; Member: LCC for Shoreditch and Finsbury, 1952-64; GLC (for Islington) and ILEA, 1964-67. Chairman: Hospital and Medical Services Cttee LCC, 1948; (Health Cttee). Division 7, 1948-49, Division 2 in 1949; Health Cttee, 1953-60; Welfare Cttee, 1965, of LCC; Metropolitan Water Bd, 1966-67 (Vice-Chm., 1965-66). Mem. Hampstead Borough Council, 1937-65 (Leader of Labour Group, 1945-58), Councillor for Kilburn until 1945, Alderman, 1945-65; Chm., LCC, 1960-61; Chairman: (Hampstead), Maternity and Child Welfare Cttee, 1941-45, Juvenile Court Panel, 1950-62; Dep. Mayoress, Camden Borough Council, 1967-68. Probation Cttee, 1959-; Leavesden Hosp. Management Cttee, 1948-63; Harben Secondary Sch., 1946-61. Member: Co-operative Political Party (ex-Chm. and Sec.); Co-operative Soc.; Labour Party; National Institute for Social Work Training, 1962-65; Min. of Health Council for Training of Health Visitors, 1962-65; Min. of Health Council for Training in Social Work, 1962-65. Chm., YWCA Helen Graham Hse, 1972-. JP, Inner London, 1941-. Freeman of Borough of Hampstead, 1961. Noble Order, Crown of Thailand, 3rd Class, 1964. *Address:* 26 Hemstal Road, Hampstead, NW6. *T:* 01-624 6181.

CAYLEY, Sir Digby (William David), 11th Bt *cr* 1661; MA; Assistant Classics Master, Stonyhurst College, since 1973; *b* 3 June 1944; *s* of Lieut-Comdr W. A. S. Cayley, RN (*d* 1964) (*g g s* of 7th Bt), and of Natalie M. Cayley, BA; *S* kinsman, 1967; *m* 1969, Christine Mary Gaunt, BA, *o d* of late D. F. Gaunt and of Mrs A. T. Gaunt, Clitheroe, Lancs; two *d. Educ:* Malvern Coll.; Downing Coll., Cambridge. Asst Classics Master, Portsmouth Grammar Sch., 1968-73. *Recreations:* Roman Imperial coinage, home improvements. *Heir: uncle* Cuthbert John Cayley [*b* 9 June 1907; *m* 1938, Cecil Lilla Iris (*d* 1972), *d* of late Adm. George Cuthbert Cayley, CB]. *Address:* Homestead, Eastham Street, Clitheroe, Lancs.

CAYLEY, Henry Douglas, OBE 1946; Director, Grindlay Brandts (Australia) Ltd, since 1974; *b* 20 Jan. 1904; *s* of late Cyril Henry Cayley, MD; *m* 1940, Nora Innes Paton, *d* of Nigel F. Paton; one *s* two *d. Educ:* Epsom Coll. Joined National Bank of India Ltd, London, 1922; Eastern Staff, 1926; Dep. Exchange Controller, Reserve Bank of India, 1939-48; rejoined National Bank of India, 1948; appointed to London Head Office, 1952; Asst Gen. Manager 1957, Dep. Gen. Manager 1960, Chief Gen. Manager 1964-69, Director 1966-72, National & Grindlays Bank Ltd; Dir, William Brandt Sons & Co. Ltd, 1965-72. *Recreations:* gardening, walking. *Address:* Virginia Lodge, Boronia Street, Bowral, NSW 2576, Australia. *Club:* Lansdowne.

CAYZER, family name of **Baron Rotherwick.**

CAYZER, Hon. Anthony; see Cayzer, Hon. M. A. R.

CAYZER, Sir James Arthur, 5th Bt, cr 1904; b 15 Nov. 1931; s of Sir Charles William Cayzer, 3rd Bt, MP, and Beatrice Eileen, d of late James Meakin and Emma Beatrice (later wife of 3rd Earl Sondes); S brother, 1943. Educ: Eton. Heir: cousin, Sir Nicholas Cayzer, qv. Address: Kinpurnie Castle, Newtyle, Angus. T: Newtyle 207. Club: Carlton.

CAYZER, Hon. (Michael) Anthony (Rathborne); shipowner; b 28 May 1920; 2nd s of 1st Baron Rotherwick; m 1952, Hon. Patricia Browne, er d of 4th Baron Oranmore and Browne, qv, and of Hon. Mrs Hew Dalrymple; three d. Educ: Eton; Royal Military Coll., Sandhurst. Commissioned Royal Scots Greys: served 1939-44 (despatches). Dep. Chairman: British & Commonwealth Shipping Co. Ltd; Union-Castle Mail Steamship Co. Ltd; Air Holdings Ltd; Chairman: British Island Airways Ltd; Servisair Ltd; Avialift Products Ltd; Britavia Ltd; Servisair (Scotland) Ltd; Castle Furnishing Services Ltd; Director: Cayzer, Irvine & Co. Ltd; Clan Line Steamers Ltd; Caledonia Investments Ltd; Overseas Containers (Holdings) Ltd; Sterling Industries Ltd; Airwork Services Ltd, British Air Transport (Holdings) Ltd; Bristow Helicopters Group Ltd; United Helicopters Ltd, and other cos. President: Inst. of Shipping and Forwarding Agents, 1963-65; Chamber of Shipping of the United Kingdom, 1967; Herts Agric. Soc., 1974; Past Vice-Pres., British Light Aviation Centre. Past Mem. Mersey Docks and Harbour Bd. Chm. Liverpool Steamship Owners Assoc., 1956-67. Trustee: Nat. Maritime Museum, 1968- (Chm., 1977-); Maritime Trust, 1975-. Address: Great Westwood, Kings Langley, Herts. T: Kings Langley 62296. Clubs: Boodle's, Royal Yacht Squadron.

CAYZER, Sir (William) Nicholas, 2nd Bt, cr 1921; Chairman of: British & Commonwealth Shipping Co. Ltd; Clan Line Steamers Ltd; Cayzer, Irvine & Co. Ltd; Caledonia Investments Ltd; Union-Castle Mail Steamship Co. Ltd and associated cos; Scottish Lion Insurance Co. Ltd; Air Holdings Ltd; b 21 Jan. 1910; s of Sir August Cayzer, 1st Bt, and Ina Frances (d 1935), 2nd d of William Stancombe, Blounts Ct, Wilts; S father, 1943; m 1935, Elizabeth Catherine, d of late Owain Williams and g d of Morgan Stuart Williams, Aberpergwm and St Donat's Castle, Glamorgan; two d. Educ: Eton; Corpus Christi Coll., Cambridge. Chm. Liverpool Steamship Owners Association, 1944-45; Pres. Chamber of Shipping of the UK, 1959; Pres. Inst. of Marine Engineers, 1963. Chm. Gen. Council of Brit. Shipping, 1959; sometime Mem. Mersey Dock and Harbour Board; sometime Mem. National Dock Labour Board. Prime Warden, Shipwrights Company, 1969. Heir: b Major Bernard Gilbert Stancomb Cayzer, b 14 March 1914. Address: The Grove, Walsham-le-Willows, Suffolk. T: Walsham-le-Willows 263; 95j Eaton Square, SW1. T: Belgravia 5551. Club: Brooks's.

CAZALET, Vice-Adm. Sir Peter Grenville Lyon, KBE 1955; CB 1952; DSO 1945, and Bar 1949; DSC 1940; retired; Chairman, Navy League, 1960-67; Vice-President Association of Royal Navy Officers; b 29 July 1899; e s of late Grenville William Cazalet and Edith Lyon; m 1928, Elise, d of late J. P. Winterbotham, Cheltenham, Glos; four s. Educ: Dulwich. Midshipman in HMS Princess Royal, 1918; Lieut 1921; Comdr 1934; Capt. 1941; Rear-Adm. 1950; Vice-Adm. 1953. Served War of 1939-45 (despatches four times); Commanded: HMS Durban, 1941-42; 23rd Destroyer Flotilla, 1944-45; HMS London, 1949; Commodore Administration, Mediterranean Fleet, 1945-46; Dep. Dir of Plans, Naval Staff, 1946-47; Commodore RN Barracks, Chatham, 1949-50; Chief of Staff to Flag Officer Central Europe, 1950-52; Allied Chief of Staff to C-in-C Mediterranean, 1953-55; Flag Officer Comdg Reserve Fleet, 1955-56; retd 1957. ADC to the King, 1950. King Haakon VII Cross, 1946. Address: 16 High Hurst Close, Newick, Lewes, East Sussex BN8 4NJ. T: Newick 2396. Club: Army and Navy.

CAZALET-KEIR, Thelma, CBE 1952; d of late W. M. Cazalet; m 1939, David (d 1969), s of Rev. Thomas Keir. Member of London County Council for East Islington, 1925-31; Alderman of County of London, 1931; contested by-election, East Islington, 1931; MP (Nat. C) East Islington, 1931-45; Parliamentary Private Secretary to Parliamentary Secretary to Board of Education, 1937-40; Parliamentary Secretary to Ministry of Education, May 1945. Member of Committee of Enquiry into conditions in Women's Services, 1942; of Committee on Equal Compensation (Civil Injuries), 1943; Chairman London Area Women's Advisory Committee, Conservative and Unionist Associations, 1943-46. Chairman Equal Pay Campaign Committee; Member Cost of Living Committee; Member Arts Council of Great Britain, 1940-49;

Member Executive Committee of Contemporary Art Society; Member Transport Users Consultative Committee for London, 1950-52. A Governor of the BBC, 1956-61. Member Committee Royal UK Beneficent Association, 1962. President Fawcett Society, 1964. Publications: From the Wings, 1967; (ed) Homage to P. G. Wodehouse, 1973. Recreations: music, lawn tennis. Address: Flat J, 90 Eaton Square, SW1. T: 01-235 7378.

CAZENOVE, Philip Henry de Lerisson, TD 1944; Major, Northamptonshire Yeomanry (retired); Stockbroker (retired); b 21 Dec. 1901; yr s of late Major Edward Cazenove; m 1942, Aurea Ethelwyn, d of C. I. L. Allix; three s one d. Educ: Eton. High Sheriff of Northants, 1949. Recreations: hunting, shooting, rackets, squash rackets, tennis, lawn tennis, golf. Address: Cottesbrooke, Northampton. T: Creaton 203. Clubs: White's, MCC, All England Lawn Tennis.

CEADEL, Eric Bertrand, MA; University Librarian, University of Cambridge, since 1967; Fellow of Corpus Christi College, Cambridge, since 1962; b London, 7 Feb. 1921; o s of late Albert Edward Ceadel, FSS, and of Bertha Margaret (née Blackall); m 1946, Pamela Mary Perkins; three s. Educ: Bec Sch., London; Christ's Coll., Cambridge (Entrance Schol.). 1st cl. hons Class. Tripos, Pts I and II; BA 1941, MA 1945; Charles Oldham Class. Schol., 1941. Suffolk Regt, then Intelligence Corps, Capt., 1941-45. A. H. Lloyd Research Schol., Christ's Coll., 1945-47; Univ. Lectr in Japanese, University of Cambridge, 1947-67; Vis Prof. of Japanese, University of Michigan, 1960, 1961; Sen. Tutor, Corpus Christi Coll., Cambridge, 1962-66; Sec., 1948-52, and Chm., 1963-65, Faculty Bd of Oriental Studies; Mem. Coun. of Senate, 1965-68; Curator in Oriental Literature, Univ. Library, Cambridge, 1954-67; Syndic of Univ. Library, 1961-67. Publications: (contrib. and ed) Literatures of the East, 1953; Classified Catalogue of Modern Japanese Books in Cambridge University Library, 1962; articles in Class. Quarterly, Asia Major and other jls. Address: 20 Porson Road, Cambridge. T: 50053.

CECIL, family name of **Baron Amherst of Hackney, Marquess of Exeter, Baron Rockley,** and **Marquess of Salisbury.**

CECIL, Lord David; see Cecil, Lord E. C. D. G.

CECIL, Lord (Edward Christian) David (Gascoyne); CH 1949; CLit 1972; Goldsmiths' Professor of English Literature, Oxford, 1948-69; Fellow of New College, Oxford, 1939-69, now Honorary Fellow; b 9 April 1902; yr s of 4th Marquess of Salisbury, KG, GCVO; m 1932, Rachel, o d of late Sir Desmond MacCarthy; two s one d. Educ: Eton; Christ Church, Oxford. Fellow of Wadham Coll., Oxford, 1924-30. Trustee of National Portrait Gallery, 1937-51. Pres., The Poetry Soc., 1947-48. Leslie Stephen Lectr, Cambridge Univ., 1935; Clark Lectr, Cambridge, 1941; Rede Lecturer, Cambridge Univ., 1955. Hon. LittD Leeds, 1950; Hon. DLit London, 1957; Hon. LLD Liverpool, 1951; St Andrews, 1951; Hon. DLitt Glasgow, 1962. Publications: The Stricken Deer, 1929; Sir Walter Scott, 1933; Early Victorian Novelists, 1934; Jane Austen, 1935; The Young Melbourne, 1939; Hardy, the Novelist, 1943; Two Quiet Lives, 1948; Poets and Story-Tellers, 1949; Lord M., 1954; The Fine Art of Reading, 1957; Max, 1964; Visionary and Dreamer: Two Poetic Painters—Samuel Palmer and Edward Burne-Jones, 1969; (ed) The Bodley Head Max Beerbohm, 1970; (ed) A Choice of Tennyson's Verse, 1971; The Cecils of Hatfield House, 1973; Library Looking-glass, 1975. Address: Red Lion House, Cranborne, Wimborne, Dorset. T: Cranborne 244. Club: Athenæum.

CECIL, Lord Martin; see Cecil, Lord W. M. A.

CECIL, Rear-Adm. Oswald Nigel Amherst; Commander British Forces, Malta, since 1975; Flag Officer, Malta, and NATO Commander South Eastern Mediterranean, since 1975; b 11 Nov. 1925; s of Comdr the Hon. Henry M. A. Cecil, OBE, RN, and the Hon. Mrs Henry Cecil; m 1951, Annette, d of Robert Barclay, Bury Hill, near Dorking, Surrey; one s. Educ: Royal Naval Coll., Dartmouth. Joined Navy, 1939; served during War, 1939-45. Comdr, 1959; Chief Staff Officer, London Div. RNR, 1959-61; in comd: HMS Corunna, 1961-63; HMS Royal Arthur, 1963-66; Captain 1966; Staff of Dep. Chief of Defence Staff (Operational Requirements), 1966-69; Captain (D) Dartmouth Trng Sqdn and in comd HMS Tenby and HMS Scarborough, 1969-71; Senior British Naval Officer, S Africa, and Naval Attaché, Capetown, as Cdre, 1971-73; Dir, Naval Operational Requirements, 1973-75; Naval ADC to the Queen, 1975; Rear-Adm. 1975. OStJ 1971. Recreations: racing, cricket, tennis. Address: The Villa Portelli, Kalkara, Malta GC. Clubs: White's, MCC.

CECIL, Robert, CMG 1959; Reader in Contemporary German History, Reading University, since 1968; Chairman, Graduate School of Contemporary European Studies, since 1976; *b* 25 March 1913; *s* of late Charles Cecil; *m* 1938, Kathleen, *d* of late Col C. C. Marindin, CBE, DSO; one *s* two *d. Educ:* Wellington Coll.; Caius Coll., Cambridge. BA Cantab. 1935, MA 1961. Entered HM Foreign Service, 1936; served in Foreign Office, 1939-45; First Sec., HM Embassy, Washington, 1945-48; assigned to Foreign Office, 1948; Counsellor and Head of American Dept, 1951; Counsellor, HM Embassy, Copenhagen, 1953-55; HM Consul-Gen., Hanover, 1955-57; Counsellor, HM Embassy, Bonn, 1957-59; Dir-Gen., British Information Services, New York, 1959-61; Head of Cultural Relations Dept, FO, 1962-67. *Publications:* Levant and other Poems, 1940; Time and other Poems, 1955; Life in Edwardian England, 1969; The Myth of the Master Race: Alfred Rosenberg and Nazi ideology, 1972; Hitler's Decision to Invade Russia, 1941, 1976; contrib. to periodicals. *Recreations:* gardening, chess, etc. *Address:* Hambledon, Hants. *T:* Hambledon 669. *Club:* Royal Automobile.

CECIL, Lord (William) Martin Alleyne; *b* 27 April 1909; 2nd *s* of 5th Marquess of Exeter, KG, CMG (*d* 1956) and *b* and *heir-pres* to 6th Marquess of Exeter, *qv*; *m* 1st, 1934, Edith Lilian De Csanady (*d* 1954); one *s*; 2nd, 1954, Lillian Jane Johnson; one *d* (and one *d* decd). *Educ:* Royal Naval Coll., Dartmouth. *Publications:* Being Where You Are, 1974; On Eagles' Wings, 1977. *Address:* 100 Mile House, PO Box 8, British Columbia, Canada. *T:* 604-395-2323.

CECIL-WRIGHT, Air Commodore John Allan Cecil, AFC, TD, AE; *b* 1886; *s* of Alfred Cecil Wright, Edgbaston; name changed by Deed Poll from Wright to Cecil-Wright, 1957; *m* 1946, Ethne Monica, *y d* of late Dr W. E. Falconar; two *s* (one of whom is by a former marriage). *Educ:* Winchester. 1st Vol. Bn Royal Warwicks Regt, 1905; served European War, 1914-19; joined RFC in 1916; Squadron Leader 605 (County of Warwick) Bomber Squadron, 1926-36; Comdt, Midland Command ATC, 1941-45; Hon. Air Cdre 605 (County of Warwick) Sq. Royal Aux. AF, 1946-55; Hon. Area Rep., RAF Benevolent Fund; Vice-Chm. (Air) Warwicks T & AFA, 1945-54. Dir, Warne Wright & Rowland, Ltd (Chm., 1920-63); Dir The Decca Navigator Co. Ltd; Mem. Birmingham City Council, 1934-39; MP (Nat. U) Erdington div. of Birmingham, 1936-45; Pres. Erdington Conservative and Unionist Assoc., 1945-55; Patron, Sutton Coldfield Cons. and U. Assoc.; Mem., Warwicks CC 1958-61; DL, Warwicks, 1933-67; Mem. Exec. Cttee, Animal Health Trust; President: Cruft's Dog Show, 1962-76; Welsh Kennel Club, 1972-; Kennel Club, 1953-73, 1976- (Chm., 1948-73, Vice-Pres., 1973-76); Alsatian League and Club of GB; Birmingham Dog Show Soc.; Vice-Pres., Nat. Canine Defence League. Pres., 605 Squadron Assoc. *Address:* 14 Richmond Court, Park Lane, Milford-on-Sea, Lymington, Hants SO4 0PT. *T:* Milford-on-Sea 2606; 33 Ennismore Gardens, SW7. *T:* 01-584 6197. *Clubs:* Royal Air Force; Kennel; Royal Lymington Yacht.

CELIBIDACHE, Sergiu; Composer and Guest Conductor to leading Orchestras all over the World; *b* Rumania, 28 June 1912; *s* of Demosthene Celibidache; *m* Maria Celibidache. *Educ:* Jassy; Berlin. Doctorate in mathematics, musicology, philosophy and Buddhist religion. Conductor and Artistic Dir, Berlin Philharmonic Orchestra, 1946-51. Member: Royal Acad. of Music, Sweden; Acad. of Music, Bologna. German Critics' Prize, 1953; Berlin City Art Prize, 1955; Grand Cross of Merit, Federal Republic of Germany, 1954. *Recreations:* skiing, water-skiing. *Address:* 79 rue Boissère, 75116 Paris, France.

CENTRAL AFRICA, Archbishop of, since 1971; **Most Rev. Donald Seymour Arden;** Bishop of Southern Malaŵi; *b* 12 April 1916; *s* of Stanley and Winifred Arden; *m* 1962, Jane Grace Riddle; two *s. Educ:* St Peter's Coll., Adelaide; University of Leeds (BA); College Resurrection, Mirfield, Deacon, 1939; Priest, 1940. Curate of: St Catherine's, Hatcham, 1939-40; Nettleden with Potten End, 1941-43; Asst Priest, Pretoria African Mission, 1944-51; Director of Usuthu Mission, Swaziland, 1951-61; Bishop of Nyasaland, 1961 (name of diocese changed, when Nyasaland was granted independence, July 1964); Bishop of Southern Malaŵi, 1971. *Publication:* Out of Africa Something New? *Recreations:* photography, farming. *Address:* Diocese of Southern Malaŵi, P/A Chilema, PO Zomba, Malaŵi. *T:* Domasi 240, 241.

CHABAN-DELMAS, Jacques Pierre Michel; Commander Légion d'Honneur; Compagnon de la Libération; Deputy, French National Assembly, Department of Gironde, since 1946; Mayor of Bordeaux, since 1947; *b* Paris, 7 March 1915; *s* of Pierre Delmas and Georgette Delmas (*née* Barrouin); *m* 1947 (2nd marr.), Mme Geoffray (*née* Marie Antoinette Iŏn) (*d*

1970); two *s* two *d*; *m* 1971, Mme Micheline Chavelet. *Educ:* Lycée Lakanal, Sceaux; Faculté de Droit, Paris; Ecole Libre des Sciences Politiques (Dip.). Licencié en droit. Journalist with l'Information, 1933. Served War of 1939-45: Army, 1939-40 (an Alpine Regt); joined the Resistance; *nom de guerre* of Chaban added (Compagnon de la Libération, Croix de Guerre); attached to Min. of Industrial Production, 1941; Inspector of Finance, 1943; Brig.-Gen., 1944; Nat. Mil. Deleg. (co-ord. mil. planning) Resistance, 1944; Inspector Gen. of Army, 1944; Sec.-Gen., Min. of Inf., 1945. Deputy for Gironde (Radical), 1946. Leader of Gaullist group (Républicans Sociaux) in Nat. Assembly, 1953-56; also Mem. Consultative Assembly of Council of Europe; Minister of State, 1956-57; Minister of Nat. Defence, 1957-58; Pres., Nat. Assembly, 1958-69; Prime Minister, June 1969-July 1972. *Publication:* L'ardeur, 1976. *Address:* 36 rue Emile Fourcand, 33000 Bordeaux, France; Mairie de Bordeaux, 33000 Bordeaux, France.

CHACKSFIELD, Air Vice-Marshal Sir Bernard, KBE 1968 (OBE 1945); CB 1961; *b* 13 April 1913; *s* of Edgar Chacksfield Ilford, Essex; *m* 1937, Myrtle, *d* of Walter Matthews, Rickmansworth, Herts; two *s* two *d* (and one *s* decd). *Educ:* Co. High Sch., Ilford; RAF, Halton; RAF Coll., Cranwell. NW Frontier, 1934-37; UK, India, Burma, Singapore, 1939-45 (OBE); Air Min., 1945-48; Western Union (NATO), Fontainebleau, 1949-51; RAF Staff Coll., 1951-53; Fighter Command, 1954-55; Director, Guided Weapons (trials), Min. of Supply, 1956-58; IDC, 1959; SASO, Tech. Trg Comd, RAF, 1960; AOC No. 22 Group RAF Technical Training Command, 1960-62; Comdt-Gen., RAF Regiment and Inspector of Ground Defence, 1963-68; retired 1968. CEng, FRAeS, 1968. Chm., Burma Star Council, 1977- (Vice-Chm., 1974-76). Order of Cloud and Banner with special rosette (Chinese), 1941. *Recreations:* scouting (HQ Comr, Air Activities, 1959-72; Chief Comr for England, 1970-77), sailing, fencing (Pres. RAF Fencing Union, 1963-68), gliding, walking, model aircraft (Pres. Soc. Model Aircraft Engrs, GB, 1965-77), modern Pentathlon (Pres., RAF Pentathlon Assoc., 1963-68), shooting (Chm. RAF Small Arms Assoc., 1963-68); swimming; youth work, amateur dramatics. *Address:* Windwhistle, Bourne End, Bucks. *T:* Bourne End 20829. *Club:* Royal Air Force.

CHADDOCK, Prof. Dennis Hilliar, CBE 1962; Professor of Engineering Design, University of Technology, Loughborough, 1966-73, retired; Professor Emeritus, 1974; Consultant Proprietor, Quorn Engineering, since 1974; *b* 28 July 1908; *m* 1937, Stella Edith Dorrington; one *s* one *d* (and one *s* decd). *Educ:* University Coll. Sch. Engineering Apprentice, Sa Adolph Saurer, Switzerland, 1927-30; Research Engineer, Morris Commercial Cars Ltd, Birmingham, 1930-32; Asst Road Motor Engineer, LMS Railway Co., Euston, 1932-41. BSc (Eng) Hons, London, 1933; MSc (Eng) London, 1938. HM Forces, 1941-46; Inspecting Officer, Chief Inspector of Armaments, 1941-43; Dep. Chief Inspecting Officer, 1943-45; Chief Design Officer, Armament Design Estabt, 1945-46; relinquished commission with rank of Lieut-Col, 1946. Superintendent, Carriage Design Branch of Armament Design Estabt, 1947-50; Imperial Defence Coll., 1951; Dep. Chief Engineer, 1952-55; Principal Superintendent, Weapons and Ammunition Div., Armament Research and Development Estabt, 1955-62; Dir of Artillery Research and Development, Ministry of Defence (Army) 1962-66. *Recreation:* model engineering. *Address:* 29 Paddock Close, Quorndon, Leics. *T:* Quorn 2607.

CHADWICK, Sir Albert (Edward), Kt 1974; CMG 1967; formerly Chairman, Gas and Fuel Corporation of Victoria; *b* 15 Nov. 1897; *s* of Andrew and Georgina Chadwick; *m* 1924, Thelma Marea Crawley; one *s* one *d. Educ:* Tungamah State Sch., Vic.; University High Sch., Vic. European War, 1914-18; served 1915-19 (MSM; despatches 1918); War of 1939-45: served RAAF, 1940-45 (Group Capt.). Engr, Robt Bryce & Co. Ltd, 1920-25; Lubricant Manager, Shell Co. of Aust. Ltd, 1925-35; Asst Gen. Man., Metropolitan Gas Co. Melbourne, 1935-51; Asst. Gen. Man., subseq. Gen. Man., Gas and Fuel Corp. of Vic., 1951-63. Chm., Overseas Telecommunications Commn (Australia), 1962-68. *Publications:* various technical and economic works. *Recreations:* golf, cricket, football, racing. *Address:* 413 Toorak Road, Toorak, Vic 3142, Australia. *T:* Melbourne 24-1163. *Clubs:* Athenæum, Victorian Amateur Turf (Melbourne); Riversdale Golf; (Pres. 1964-) Melbourne Cricket.

CHADWICK, Gerald William St John, (John Chadwick), CMG 1961; HM Diplomatic Service, retired; First Director, Commonwealth Foundation, since 1966; *b* 28 May 1915; *s* of late John F. Chadwick, Solicitor; *m* 1938, Madeleine Renée Boucheron; two *s. Educ:* Lancing; St Catharine's Coll., Cambridge (open Exhibitioner). Asst Principal, Colonial Office, 1938; transf. Dominions Office, following demobilisation, 1940;

Sec., Parl. Mission to Newfoundland, 1943; further missions to Newfoundland and Bermuda, 1946 and 1947; attended United Nations, 1949; Office of UK High Commission, Ottawa, 1949-52; Counsellor, British Embassy, Dublin, 1952-53; UK Delegn to NATO, Paris, 1954-56; Asst Sec., CRO, 1956; Asst Under-Sec. of State, CRO, 1960-66. Governor, Commonwealth Inst., 1967-. *Publications:* The Shining Plain, 1937; Newfoundland: Island into Province, 1967; International Organisations, 1969; (ed jtly) Professional Organisations in the Commonwealth, 1976; contrib. to: A Decade of the Commonwealth 1955-64, 1966; numerous reviews and articles. *Recreation:* travel. *Address:* 11 Cumberland House, Kensington Road, W8. *Clubs:* Athenæum, Royal Commonwealth Society.

CHADWICK, Rt. Rev. Graham Charles; see Kimberley and Kuruman, Bishop of.

CHADWICK, Very Rev. Henry, DD; FBA 1960; Dean of Christ Church, Oxford, since 1969; Regius Professor of Divinity and Canon of Christ Church, Oxford, 1959-69; *b* 23 June 1920; 3rd *s* of late John Chadwick, Barrister, Bromley, Kent, and Edith (*née* Horrocks); *m* 1945, Margaret Elizabeth, *d* of late W. Pemell Brownrigg; three *d*. *Educ:* Eton (King's Scholar); Magdalene Coll., Cambridge (Music Schol.). John Stewart of Rannoch Scholar, 1939. MusB. Asst Master, Wellington Coll., 1945; University of Cambridge: Fellow of Queens' Coll., 1946-58; Hon. Fellow, 1958; Junior Proctor, 1948-49. Hon. Fellow, Magdalene Coll., 1962; Fellow, Eton, 1976-. Hulsean Lecturer, 1956; Visiting Prof., University of Chicago, 1957; Gifford Lectr, St Andrews Univ., 1962-64; Burns Lectr, Otago, 1971. Editor, Journal of Theological Studies, 1954-. Member, Anglican-Roman Catholic International Commn, 1969-. Forwood Lecturer, University of Liverpool, 1961; Hewett Lecturer, Union Theological Seminary, 1962; Birkbeck Lecturer, Cambridge, 1965. For. Hon. Mem., Amer. Acad. Arts and Sciences. Hon. DD, Glasgow, Yale and Manchester; Hon. Teol Dr, Uppsala; D Humane Letters, Chicago; Correspondant de l'Académie des Inscriptions et des Belles Lettres (Institute of France). *Publications:* Origen, Contra Celsum, 1953; Alexandrian Christianity (with J. E. L. Oulton), 1954; Lessing's Theological Writings, 1956; The Sentences of Sextus, 1959; The Circle and the Ellipse, 1959; St Ambrose on the Sacraments, 1960; The Vindication of Christianity in Westcott's Thought, 1961; Early Christian Thought and the Classical Tradition, 1966; The Early Church (Pelican), 1967; The Treatise on the Apostolic Tradition of St Hippolytus of Rome, ed G. Dix (rev. edn), 1968; Priscillian of Avila, 1976. *Recreation:* music. *Address:* Christ Church, Oxford.
See also Sir John Chadwick, W. O. Chadwick, Vice-Adm. Sir A. W. R. McNicoll.

CHADWICK, John; see Chadwick, G. W. St J.

CHADWICK, John, FBA 1967; MA; LittD; Perceval Maitland Laurence Reader in Classics, University of Cambridge, since 1969; Collins Fellow, Downing College, Cambridge, since 1960; *b* 21 May 1920; *yr s* of late Fred Chadwick; *m* 1947, Joan Isobel Hill; one *s*. *Educ:* St Paul's Sch.; Corpus Christi Coll., Cambridge. Editorial Asst, Oxford Latin Dictionary, Clarendon Press, 1946-52; Asst Lectr in Classics, 1952-54, Lectr in Classics, 1954-66, Reader in Greek Language, 1966-69, Univ. of Cambridge. Corresponding Member: Deutsches Archäologisches Inst., 1957; Austrian Acad. of Scis, 1974; Acad. des Inscriptions et Belles-Lettres, Institut de France, 1975. Hon. Fellow, Athens Archaeol Soc., 1974. Hon. Dr of Philosophical Sch., University of Athens, 1958; Hon. Dr, Université Libre de Bruxelles, 1969; Hon. DLitt, Trinity Coll., Dublin, 1971. Medal of J. E. Purkyně Univ., Brno, 1966. *Publications:* (jtly) The Medical Works of Hippocrates, 1950; (jtly) Documents in Mycenaean Greek, 1956, rev. edn 1973; The Decipherment of Linear B, 1958, 2nd edn 1968 (trans. into 11 languages); The Pre-history of the Greek Language (in Camb. Ancient History), 1963; The Mycenaean World, 1976; edns of Linear B Tablets, articles in learned jls on Mycenaean Greek. *Recreation:* travel. *Address:* Downing College, Cambridge; 52 Gough Way, Cambridge. *T:* Cambridge 56864.

CHADWICK, Sir John (Edward), KCMG 1967 (CMG 1957); HM Diplomatic Service, retired; Special Adviser, Asian Development Bank, since 1973; *b* 17 Dec. 1911; *e s* of late John Chadwick; *m* 1945, Audrey Lenfestey; one *s* two *d*. *Educ:* Rugby; Corpus Christi Coll., Cambridge (MA). Dept of Overseas Trade, 1934; Asst Trade Comr, Calcutta, 1938; Eastern Group Supply Council, Simla, 1941; Commercial Secretary, Washington, 1946-48; First Sec., Tel Aviv, 1950-53; Counsellor (Commercial) Tokyo, 1953-56; Minister (Economic), Buenos Aires, 1960-62, (Commercial), Washington, 1963-67; Ambassador to Rumania, 1967-68; UK Representative to

OECD, Paris, 1969-71. Consultant, Sterling Industrial Securities, 1973. *Address:* 46 Arbrook Lane, Esher, Surrey. *Club:* Travellers'.
See also Very Rev. Henry Chadwick, W. O. Chadwick, Vice-Adm. Sir A. W. R. McNicoll.

CHADWICK, Lynn Russell, CBE 1964; sculptor since 1948; *b* 24 Nov. 1914; *s* of late Verner Russell Chadwick and Marjorie Brown Lynn; *m* 1942, Charlotte Ann Secord; one *s*; *m* 1959, Frances Mary Jamieson (*d* 1964); two *d*; *m*, Eva Reiner; one *s*. *Educ:* Merchant Taylors' Sch. Architectural Draughtsman, 1933-39; Pilot, FAA, 1941-44. Exhibitions have been held in London, in various galleries, and by the Arts Council; his works have also been shown in numerous international exhibitions abroad, including Venice Biennale, 1956. *Works in public collections:* Great Britain: Tate Gallery, London; British Council, London; Arts Council of Great Britain; Victoria and Albert Museum; Pembroke Coll., Oxford; City Art Gallery, Bristol; Art Gallery, Brighton; Whitworth Art Gallery, University of Manchester; France: Musée National D'Art Moderne, Paris; Holland: Boymans van Beuningen Museum, Rotterdam; Germany: Municipality of Recklinghausen; Staatliche Graphische Sammlung, Munich; Staatische Kunstmuseum, Duisburg; Sweden: Art Gallery, Gothenburg; Belgium: Musées Royaux des Beaux-Arts de Belgique, Brussels; Italy: Galleria D'Arte Moderna, Rome; Museo Cívico, Turin; Australia: National Gallery of SA, Adelaide; Canada: National Gallery of Canada, Ottawa; Museum of Fine Arts, Montreal; USA: Museum of Modern Art, New York; Carnegie Institute, Pittsburgh; University of Michigan; Albright Art Gallery, Buffalo; Art Institute, Chicago; Chile: Inst. de Artes Contemporáneas, Lima. *Address:* Lypiatt Park, Stroud, Glos.

CHADWICK, Owen; see Chadwick, W. O.

CHADWICK, Prof. Peter, PhD, ScD; FRS 1977; Professor of Mathematics, University of East Anglia, since 1965; *b* 23 March 1931; *s* of Jack Chadwick and Marjorie Chadwick (*née* Castle); *m* 1956, Sheila Gladys Salter, *d* of late Clarence F. Salter; two *d*. *Educ:* Huddersfield Coll.; Univ. of Manchester (BSc 1952); Pembroke Coll., Cambridge (PhD 1957, ScD 1973). Scientific Officer, then Sen. Scientific Officer, Atomic Weapons Res. Estabt, Aldermaston, 1955-59; Lectr, then Sen. Lectr, in Applied Maths, Univ. of Sheffield, 1959-65. Vis. Prof., Univ. of Queensland, 1972. Jt Exec. Editor, Qly Jl of Mechanics and Applied Maths, 1965-72. *Publications:* Continuum Mechanics, 1976; numerous papers on theoretical solid mechanics and the mechanics of continua in various learned journals and books. *Recreations:* reading, walking. *Address:* School of Mathematics and Physics, University of East Anglia, University Plain, Norwich NR4 7TJ. *T:* Norwich 56161; 8 Stratford Crescent, Cringleford, Norwich NR4 7SF. *T:* Norwich 51655.

CHADWICK, Sir R. Burton; see Burton-Chadwick.

CHADWICK, Rt. Rev. William Frank Percival; Bishop of Barking, 1959-75. *Educ:* Wadham College, Oxford; Harvard Univ., USA (Davison Scholar). Deacon, 1929, Priest, 1930, Diocese Liverpool; Curate, St Helens, 1929-34; Vicar: Widnes, 1934-38; Christ Church, Crouch End, N8, 1938-47; Barking, 1947-59. Proctor, Diocese of London, 1946, Diocese of Chelmsford, 1951; Examining Chaplain to Bishop of Chelmsford, 1951; Asst RD Barking, 1950-53, RD, Barking, 1953; Hon. Canon of Chelmsford, 1954; Pro-Prolocutor, Lower House of Canterbury, 1956; Exchange Preacher, USA, British Council of Churches, 1958; Chm., Church of England's Commn on Roman Catholic Relations, 1968-75. *Publication:* The Inner Life. *Recreation:* golf. *Address:* Harvard House, Acton, Long Melford, Suffolk. *T:* Sudbury 77015. *Club:* Royal Commonwealth Society.

CHADWICK, (William) Owen, FBA 1962; Master of Selwyn College, Cambridge, since 1956, and Regius Professor of Modern History, since 1968; *b* 20 May 1916; 2nd *s* of late John Chadwick, Barrister, Bromley, Kent, and Edith (*née* Horrocks); *m* 1949, Ruth Romaine, *e d* of B. L. Hallward, *qv*; two *s* two *d*. *Educ:* Tonbridge; St John's Coll., Cambridge. Chaplain at Wellington Coll., 1942-46; Fellow of Trinity Hall, Cambridge, 1947-56 (Dean, 1949-56); Hulsean Lecturer, 1949-50; Birkbeck Lecturer in Ecclesiastical History, 1956; Dixie Professor of Ecclesiastical History, 1958-68; Chm. Trustees, University Coll., later Wolfson Coll., Cambridge, 1965-77, Hon. Fellow 1977; Vice-Chancellor, Cambridge Univ., 1969-71. Gifford Lectr, Edinburgh Univ., 1973-74. Chm., Archbishops' Commn on Church and State, 1966-70. DD 1955. Hon. Fellow of Trinity Hall; Hon. Fellow of St John's Coll., Cambridge. Hon. Mem., American Acad. of Arts and Scis, 1977. Hon. DD: St Andrews; Oxford; Hon. DLitt: Kent; Bristol; Hon. LittD UEA; Hon. Dr

of Letters, Columbia. *Publications:* John Cassian, 1950; The Founding of Cuddesdon, 1954; From Bossuet to Newman, 1957; Western Asceticism, 1958; Creighton on Luther, 1959; Mackenzie's Grave, 1959; The Mind of the Oxford Movement, 1960; Victorian Miniature, 1960; The Reformation, 1964; The Victorian Church, part I, 1966, 3rd edn 1971; part II, 1970, 2nd edn 1972; Freedom and the Historian, 1969; The Secularization of the European Mind in the 19th Century, 1976; Acton and Gladstone, 1976; History and Catholicism, 1977; contrib. to Studies in Early British History, 1954; articles and reviews in learned journals. *Recreations:* walking, music; Cambridge XV versus Oxford, 1936-38. *Address:* Master's Lodge, Selwyn College, Cambridge.
See also Very Rev. Henry Chadwick, Sir John Chadwick, Vice-Adm. Sir A. W. R. McNicoll.

CHADWYCK-HEALEY, Sir Edward Randal, 3rd Bt, *cr* 1919; MC 1917, bar to MC 1943; *b* 23 Jan. 1898; *e s* of Sir Gerald Chadwyck-Healey, 2nd Bt, CBE, and Mary Verena, *d* of G. A. Watson, East Court, Finchampstead, Berks; *S* father 1955; *m* 1924, Rachel Margaret, TD, formerly Chief Commander, ATS, *d* of L. C. W. Phillips, Unsted Park, Godalming. *Educ:* Eton; RMA, Woolwich. Commissioned RA, 1916; served European War, 1916-18; France, RFA and RHA. Served War of 1939-45: Field Artillery (France, North Africa, Italy); Major 1942; wounded twice. Chairman of Charrington & Co. (Brewers), 1949-59. A Trustee, City Parochial Foundation, 1943-72; Prime Warden, Fishmongers' Company, 1953; President London Chamber of Commerce, 1955-57; President Freshwater Biological Assoc., 1960-; a Vice-Pres., Marine Biological Assoc., 1969-. Belgian Croix de Guerre, 1917. *Recreations:* fishing, shooting. *Heir: b* Charles Arthur Chadwyck-Healey, OBE [*b* 27 May 1910; *m* 1939, Viola, *d* of late Cecil Lubbock; three *s* two *d*]. *Address:* The Mill House, Hook, Basingstoke. *T:* Hook 2436. *Clubs:* Bath; Leander.

CHAGALL, Marc, Grand Cross Legion of Honour, 1977 (Grand Officer 1971; Commander 1965); artist; *b* Vitebsk, Russia, 7 July 1889; *m* 1915, Bella Rosenfeld (decd); one *s* one *d*; *m* 1952, Valentine Brodsky. *Educ:* Vitebsk, Russia. Left Russia, 1910, for Paris; returned to Russia, 1914; left again for Paris, 1922. Worked with Ambroise Vollard, famous art editor; left France for America, 1941; returned to France, 1948; has settled in the South of France. Has painted mural paintings besides easel pictures, ballet and theatre settings and costumes; at present working on ceramics; has done over 300 engravings. Retrospective exhibitions in the museums of London (Tate Gallery), Paris, Amsterdam, Chicago, New York, Venice, Jerusalem, and Tel Aviv, 1946-; International Prize for engraving, Biennale Venice, 1948; Erasmus Prize, 1960 (with A. Kokoschka). Salle Chagall founded in Paris Musée d'Art Moderne, 1950. *Publications:* Ma Vie, 1931; Illustrations for: Dead Souls, The Fables of La Fontaine, The Bible, The Arabian Nights, Stories from Boccaccio (verve), Burning Lights and the First Meeting, by Bella Chagall. *Address:* La Colline, Quartier les Gardettes, 06 Saint-Paul-de-Vence, AM, France.

CHAGLA, Shri Mohomedali Currim, BA (Oxon); Indian lawyer and administrator; Barrister-at-law; *b* 30 Sept. 1900; *m* 1931, Meher-un-nissa (*d* 1961), *d* of Dharsi Jivraj; two *s* one *d. Educ:* St Xavier's High Sch. and Coll., Bombay; Lincoln Coll., Oxford. Hons. Sch. of Modern History, 1922; President: Oxford Asiatic Society, 1921; Oxford Indian Majlis, 1922; called to Bar, Inner Temple, 1922; practised on Original Side of High Court, Bombay, 1922-41; Professor of Constitutional Law, Government Law Coll., Bombay, 1927-30; Hon. Secretary, Bar Council of High Court of Judicature at Bombay, 1931-41; Puisne Judge, Bombay High Court, 1941-47; Chief Justice, 1947-58. Fellow Bombay Univ.; Hon. Fellow Lincoln Coll., Oxford, 1961. Went to New York as one of India's representatives to UNO Session and fought for Cause of Indians in S Africa, 1946; Vice-Chancellor, Bombay Univ., 1947; President, Asiatic Society of Bombay, 1947-58; Chairman Legal Education Cttee, 1948; Member Law Commission, 1955-58; Shri Krishnarajendra Silver Jubilee Lecturer, 1954. Governor of Bombay, 14 Oct.-10 Dec. 1956. *Ad hoc* Judge International Court of Justice, The Hague, 1957-60; Chairman Life Insurance Corporation Enquiry Commission, 1958; Indian Ambassador to the United States, Mexico and Cuba, 1958-61; Indian High Commissioner in London and Ambassador to Ireland, 1962-63; Leader of Upper House of Parlt, India, 1964-67; Education Minister, 1963-66; Minister for External Affairs, Government of India, Nov. 1966-Sept. 1967. Member, Sikh Grievances Enquiry Commission, Sept. 1961. Leader, Indian Delegation to: Security Council for Kashmir Debate, 1964 and 1965; Commonwealth Conf., Ottawa, 1964; General Conf., UNESCO, 1964; UN General Assembly, 1967. Hon. LLD: University of Hartford, Hartford; Temple Univ., Philadelphia; Boston Univ., Boston;

Dartmouth Coll., Hanover, NH; Leningrad Univ.; Panjab Univ.; Banaras Hindu Univ. *Publications:* The Indian Constitution, 1929; Law, Liberty and Life, 1950; The Individual and the State, 1958; An Ambassador Speaks, 1962; Education and the Nation, 1966; Unity and Language, 1967; Roses in December (autobiog.), 1974. *Recreation:* bridge. *Address:* Pallonji Mansion, New Cuffe Parade, Bombay 5, India. *Club:* Willingdon (Bombay).

CHAIN, Prof. Sir Ernst (Boris), Kt 1969; FRS 1949; FRSA 1963; MA Oxon; DrPhil Berlin; PhD Cambridge; DPhil Oxon; Professor of Biochemistry, University of London at Imperial College, 1961-73, now Professor Emeritus; *b* Berlin, Germany, 19 June 1906; *s* of Dr Michael Chain, Chemist and industrialist (of Russian origin) and Margarete Eisner; *m* 1948, Dr Anne Beloff, *y d* of S. Beloff, NW3; two *s* one *d. Educ:* Luisengymnasium, Berlin; Friedrich-Wilhelm Univ., Berlin (Graduate in chemistry and physiology, 1930). Research in chemical dept of Institute of Pathology, Charité Hospital, Berlin, 1930-33; emigrated from Germany to England in 1933 because of racial persecution; research in the School of Biochemistry, Cambridge, under Sir Frederic Gowland Hopkins, OM, 1933-35; research in the Sir William Dunn School of Pathology, Oxford, since 1935. University Demonstrator and Lecturer in Chemical Pathology, University of Oxford, 1936-48; Scientific Director of International Research Centre for Chemical Microbiology, Istituto Superiore di Sanità, Rome, 1948-64. Initiated, jointly with Prof. H. W. Florey (later Lord Florey), work on penicillin that led to the remarkable curative properties of this substance; Nobel Prize for Physiology and Medicine, 1945; Harmsworth Memorial Fund, 1946; Berzelius Medal in silver of Swedish Med. Soc., 1946; Pasteur Medal of Institut Pasteur, Paris, 1946; Pasteur Medal of Société de Chimie biologique, 1946; Paul Ehrlich Centenary Prize, 1954; Gold Medal in Therapeutics, Worshipful Soc. of Apothecaries of London, 1957; Marotta Medal, Società Chimica Italiana; Carl Neuberg Medal; Hanbury Meml Medal, 1972. Heymans Meml Medal, 1974. Member Société Philomathique, Paris; Hon. Member New York Academy of Medicine; Foreign Member Accademia dei Lincei, Rome, Accademia dei XL; For. Associate, Acad. des Sciences, Inst de France; Associé Etranger, Académie Nationale de Médecine, Paris; Foreign Member, Real Acad. de Siencias, Madrid; Hon. Life Member, New York Acad. of Science; Mem., USSR Acad. of Scis, 1976. Dr hc Université de Liège, 1946, Université de Bordeaux, 1947, University of Turin, 1954, University of Paris, 1959; Albert Einstein College of Medicine, Yeshiva Univ., 1961; Universities of La Plata, Cordoba (Argentina), Montevideo (Uruguay), Brasil, 1962, Chicago, 1965, Bar-Ilan 1974, Ramat-Gan; Philadelphia College of Pharmacy. Hon. Fellow: Royal College of Physicians; Royal Society of Medicine; Institute of Biology; Weizmann Institute of Science, Rehovot, Israel; National Institute of Sciences, India; Società Chimica Italiana; Microbiological Society of Israel; Finnish Biochemical Society; Fitzwilliam Coll., Cambridge; Società delle Scienze Farmaceutiche, Milan; Deutsche Pharmazeutische Gesellschaft; Wiener Aerztegesellschaft. Commandeur de la Légion d'Honneur; Grande Ufficiale al merito della Repubblica Italiana; Grand Decoration of Honour in Gold (Austria); Order of Rising Sun, 2nd degree (Japan), 1976. *Publications:* numerous on biochemical and chemical subjects in scientific journals. *Recreation:* music. *Address:* Department of Mechanical Engineering, Imperial College of Science, Imperial Institute Road, SW7. *T:* 01-589 5111; 9 Northview, Wimbledon Common, SW19. *Club:* Athenæum.

CHAIR, S. de; *see* de Chair.

CHAKAIPA, Most Rev. Patrick; *see* Salisbury (Rhodesia), Archbishop of, (RC).

CHALDECOTT, John Anthony; Keeper, Science Museum Library, South Kensington, 1961-76; *b* 16 Feb. 1916; *o s* of Wilfrid James and Mary Eleanor Chaldecott; *m* 1940, Kathleen Elizabeth Jones; one *d. Educ:* Latymer Upper Sch., Hammersmith; Brentwood Sch.; Borough Road Coll., Isleworth; University College, London. BSc 1938, MSc 1949, PhD 1972. Meteorological Branch, RAFVR, 1939-45 (despatches). Lecturer, Acton Technical Coll., 1945-48; entered Science Museum as Asst Keeper, Dept of Physics, 1949; Deputy Keeper and Secretary to Advisory Council, 1957. Pres., British Society for the History of Science, 1972-74. FInstP. *Publications:* Science Museum handbooks; papers on the history of science. *Address:* 19 The Grove, Ratton Village, Eastbourne, E Sussex BN20 9DA.

CHALFONT, Baron, *cr* 1964 (Life Peer); **(Alun) Arthur Gwynne Jones,** PC 1964; OBE 1961; MC 1957; *b* 5 Dec. 1919; *s* of Arthur Gwynne Jones and Eliza Alice Hardman; *m* 1948, Dr Mona

Mitchell; no c. Educ: West Monmouth Sch. Commissioned into South Wales Borderers (24th Foot), 1940; served in: Burma 1941-44; Malayan campaign 1955-57; Cyprus campaign 1958-59; various staff and intelligence appointments; psc (Camberley), 1950; JSSC 1958; qual. as Russian interpreter, 1951; resigned commission, 1961, on appt as Defence Correspondent, The Times; frequent television and sound broadcasts on defence and foreign affairs, and consultant on foreign affairs to BBC Television, 1961-64; Minister of State, Foreign and Commonwealth Office, 1964-70; UK Permanent Rep. to WEU, 1969. Foreign Editor, New Statesman, 1970-71. Deputy Chairman: 20th Century Bank, 1971-72; Film & General Investments, 1971-72; Dir, IBM UK Ltd and IBM UK (Holdings) Ltd, 1973, Mem. European Adv. Council, IBM, 1973-; Director: The Actors Co., 1973-; Melo Productions, 1973-; Chairman: Nat. Envt Competition, 1972-; UNA, 1972-73; St David's Theatre Trust, 1972-; Dep. Chm., UK Commn United World Colls; President: Welsh Inst.; Hispanic and Luso Brazilian Councils, 1973-; Vice-President: European Atlantic Cttee; UK Cttee for Unicef; Member: Governing Body, Atlantic Coll.; Exec. Cttee, European Movement; Population Countdown Campaign Cttee, 1971-; IISS; RIIA; Royal Phil. Orch. Assoc. Hon. Fellow UCW Aberystwyth, 1974. Liveryman, Worshipful Co. of Paviors. Freeman, City of London. Publications: The Sword and The Spirit, 1963; contrib. The Ulster Debate, 1972; The Great Commanders, 1973; Montgomery of Alamein, 1976; contribs to The Times, Jl RUSI and other professional journals. Recreations: formerly Rugby football, cricket, lawn tennis; now music and theatre. Address: 65 Ashley Gardens, Westminster, SW1P 1QG. Clubs: Garrick, MCC, City Livery; Cardiff and County.

CHALK, Hon. Sir Gordon (William Wesley), KBE 1971; Hon. LLD; MP (Queensland), 1974-76; Deputy Premier and Treasurer, State Government of Queensland, 1965-76; Leader, Liberal Party of Australia (Queensland Div.), 1965-76; voluntarily retired; Director, several companies; b 1913; of British parentage; m 1937, Ellen Clare Grant; one s one d. Educ: Gatton Senior High Sch., Qld. Formerly: Queensland Sales Manager, Toowoomba Foundry Pty Ltd; Registered Taxation Agent. Minister for Transport, Govt of Queensland, 1957-65. Hon. LLD Queensland Univ., 1974. Address: 277 Indooroopilly Road, Indooroopilly, Qld. 4068, Australia. T: Brisbane 711598. Clubs: Tattersall's (Brisbane, Qld); Rotary International (Gatton, Qld).

CHALKER, Mrs Lynda; MP (C) Wallasey since Feb. 1974; b 29 April 1942; d of Sidney Henry James Bates and late Marjorie Kathleen Randell; m 1967, Éric Robert Chalker (marr. diss. 1973); no c. Educ: Roedean Sch.; Heidelberg Univ.; Westfield Coll., London; Central London Polytechnic. Statistician with Research Bureau Ltd (Unilever), 1963-69; Dep. Market Research Man. with Shell Mex & BP Ltd, 1969-72; Chief Exec. of Internat. Div. of Louis Harris International, 1972-74. Mem., BBC Gen. Adv. Cttee, 1975-. Jt Sec., Cons. Health and Social Services Cttee, 1975-76; Chm., Greater London Young Conservatives, 1969-70; Nat. Vice-Chm., Young Conservatives, 1970-71. Opposition Spokesman on Social Services, 1976-. Publications: (jtly) Police in Retreat (pamphlet), 1967; (jtly) Set the Party Free (pamphlet), 1969. Recreations: music, the disabled, cooking, theatre, driving. Address: House of Commons, SW1A 0AA. T: 01-219 5098.

CHALLANS, Mary; see Renault, Mary.

CHALLE, Général d'Armée Aérienne Maurice; President and Director-General, European Society of Transport and Freight, since 1969; b Le Pontet, Vaucluse, France, 5 Sept. 1905; m 1927, Madeleine Mollard; two s. Educ: Ecole Spéciale Militaire de Saint-Cyr, France. Pilot, 1925; Lieut, 1927; Captain, 1932. Ecole Supérieure de Guerre Aérienne, 1937-39. Served War of 1939-45; Sqdn Leader, with 8th Army, 1939-40; GHQ Air, 1940; Comdr, Reconnaissance Group 2/14, Avignon, Sept.-Dec. 1942; organised networks for the Resistance Movement. Lieut-Colonel 2nd Bde de Bombardement "Les Marauduers". 1945; Colonel, 1945; attached to Chief of Staff (Air), Cabinet, 1945; Deputy Chief of Staff (Air), 1946; Brig.-General (Air), Moroccan Air Command, 1949; Special Chief of Staff of Secretary of State for Air, 1951; Director, Centre d'Enseignement Supérieur Aérien and Comdr Ecole Supérieure de Guerre Aérienne, 1953; Lieut-General, Chief of Staff of Armed Forces, 1955; General, Flying Corps, 1957; Air Chief Marshal, Asst Chief of Staff of the Army, 1958; Asst C-in-C, Algeria, and Comdr 5th Aerial Region, Oct. 1958; C-in-C, Algeria, Dec. 1958. Member Conseil Supérieur de l'Air, 1958, 1960 (Secretary, 1951, 1952, 1953). Commander-in-Chief, Allied Forces Central Europe (NATO), May 1960-March 1961; led French Army revolt in Algeria, April 1961. Political prisoner, June 1961, sentenced to 15 years imprisonment; freed

1966, amnestied 1968. Grand Cross of Legion of Honour, 1960 (Grand Officer, 1952, Officer, 1945, Chevalier, 1940). War of 1939-45 (French Croix de Guerre). Holds several foreign decorations. Publication: Notre Révolte, 1968. Address: 63 avenue Raymond-Poincaré, 75116 Paris, France.

CHALLENGER, Frederick, BSc (London); PhD (Göttingen); DSc (Birmingham); CChem, FRIC; Professor of Organic Chemistry, the University, Leeds, 1930-53, Emeritus Professor, 1953; b Halifax, Yorks, 15 Dec. 1887; s of Rev. S. C. Challenger; m 1922, Esther Yates, MA (d 1969); two d. Educ: Ashville Coll., Harrogate; Derby Technical Coll.; University College, Nottingham; University of Göttingen. 1851 Exhibition Scholar, 1910-12; Asst Lecturer in Chemistry, University of Birmingham, 1912; Lecturer in Chemistry, 1915; Senior Lecturer in Organic Chemistry, University of Manchester 1920, Vice-President of Royal Institute of Chemistry, 1948-51. Hon. Governor, Ashville Coll. Publications: Aspects of the Organic Chemistry of Sulphur, 1959; numerous publications, mostly in the Journal of the Chemical Society, Biochemical Journal and Journal of Institute of Petroleum, dealing with organo-metallic compounds (particularly of bismuth), organic thiocyanates and selenocyanates, aromatic substitution, sulphur compounds of shale oil, and other heterocyclic sulphur compounds, microbiological chemistry; mechanism of biological methylation (especially by moulds) as applied to arsenic, tellurium, selenium and sulphur compounds and checked by use of compounds containing isotopic carbon; sulphonium and other compounds of sulphur in plants and animals and in metabolic disturbances (homocystinuria); reviews on the methionine-cystine relationship in mental retardation; chemical biography. Recreation: walking. Address: 19 Elm Avenue, Beeston, Nottingham. T: Nottingham 257686.

CHALLENS, Wallace John, CBE 1967 (OBE 1958); Director, Atomic Weapons Research Establishment, Aldermaston, since 1976; b 14 May 1915; s of late Walter Lincoln Challens and Harriet Sybil Challens (née Collins); m 1st, 1938, Winifred Joan Stephenson (d 1971); two s; 2nd, 1973, Norma Lane. Educ: Deacons Sch., Peterborough; University Coll., Nottingham; BSc (Hons) London. Research Dept, Woolwich, 1936; Projectile Develt Estabt, Aberporth, 1939. British Commonwealth Scientific Office, Washington, 1946; Armament Research Estabt, Fort Halstead, 1947; Atomic Weapons Research Estabt: Fort Halstead, 1954; Aldermaston, 1955-. Scientific Dir of trials at Christmas Island, 1957. Appointed: Chief of Warhead Develt, 1959; Asst Dir, 1965; Dep. Dir, 1972. FInstP 1944. US Medal of Freedom (Bronze) 1946. Recreation: golf. Address: Far End, Crossborough Hill, Basingstoke, Hampshire RG21 2AG. T: Basingstoke 64986.

CHALLIS, Dr Anthony Arthur Leonard; Director, Polymer Engineering, Science Research Council, since 1976; b 24 Dec. 1921; s of Leonard Hough Challis and Dorothy (née Busby); m 1947, L. Beryl Hedley; two d. Educ: Newcastle upon Tyne Royal Grammar Sch.; King's Coll., Univ. of Durham. 1st cl. hons BSc Chemistry; PhD. Imperial Chemical Industries: joined Billingham Div., 1946; Research Man., HOC Div., 1962; Research Dir, Mond Div., 1966; Head of Corporate Lab., 1967; Gen. Man. Planning, 1970; Sen. Vice-Pres., ICI Americas Inc., 1975-76. Mem. Science Research Council, 1973-. Mem. Court, Univ. of Stirling, 1968-74. Publications: contrib. chem. and managerial jls. Recreations: music, walking, sailing. Address: c/o Science Research Council, State House, High Holborn, WC1. Club: Royal Naval.

CHALLIS, Margaret Joan, MA; Headmistress of Queen Anne's School, Caversham, 1958-77; b 14 April 1917; d of R. S. Challis and L. Challis (née Fairbairn). Educ: Girton Coll., Cambridge. BA Hons., English Tripos, 1939, MA, 1943, Cambridge. English Mistress: Christ's Hospital, Hertford, 1940-44; Dartford Grammar School for Girls, 1944-45; Cheltenham Ladies' Coll., 1945-57. Housemistress at Cheltenham Ladies' Coll., 1949-57. Recreations: gardening, music, old churches. Address: 16 Glencairn Court, Lansdown Road, Cheltenham, Glos.

CHALMERS, George Buchanan; HM Diplomatic Service; Minister, Tehran, since 1976; b 14 March 1929; s of late George McGarvie Chalmers and of Mrs Anne Buchanan Chalmers; m 1954, Jeanette Donald Cant. Educ: Hutcheson's Grammar Sch.; Glasgow and Leiden Univs. RAF, 1950-52; FO, 1952-54; 3rd Sec., Bucharest, 1954-57; 2nd Sec., Djakarta, 1957-58; 1st Sec., Bangkok, 1958-61; FO, 1961-64; 1st Sec., Seoul, 1964-66; 1st Sec. and subseq. Commercial Counsellor, Tel Aviv, 1966-70; Dir, California Trade Drive Office, 1971; Head of Oil Dept, FCO, 1971-72; Head of S Asian Dept, FCO, 1973-75; Counsellor, Tehran, 1975-76. Recreations: ski-ing, bridge. Address: c/o Foreign and Commonwealth Office, SW1.

CHALMERS, John; General Secretary, Amalgamated Society of Boilermakers, Shipwrights, Blacksmiths and Structural Workers, since 1966; *b* 16 May 1915; *s* of John Aitken Chalmers and Alexandrina McLean; two *d* (one *s* decd). *Educ:* Clydebank Sen. Secondary Sch. Apprenticeship, Boilermaker-Plater. Trade Union Official, 1954-; Mem., Nat. Exec. Cttee, Labour Party, 1966-, Chm. 1976-77. Member: Central Arbitration Cttee, 1976-; (part-time) Org. Cttee, British Shipbuilders, 1976-. *Recreations:* reading, gardening, golf. *Address:* 23 Killingworth Drive, West Moor, Newcastle upon Tyne NE12 0ER. *T:* Newcastle upon Tyne 683246.

CHALMERS, Thomas Wightman, CBE 1957; Chief Executive, Radio Services, United Newspapers Ltd, London, 1971-75; *b* 29 April 1913; *s* of Thomas Wightman Chalmers and Susan Florence Colman. *Educ:* Bradfield Coll.; King's Coll., London. Organ Scholar, King's Coll., London, 1934-36; BSc (Engineering), 1936. Joined BBC programme staff, 1936; successively announcer, Belfast and London; Overseas Presentation Director; Chief Assistant, Light Programme, 1945, Controller, 1948-50; Director, Nigerian Broadcasting Service, 1950-56, on secondment from BBC; Controller, North Region, BBC, 1956-58; Director of the Tanganyika Broadcasting Corporation, 1958-62; Deputy Regional Representative, UN Technical Assistance Board, East and Central Africa, 1962-64; Special Asst, Overseas and Foreign Relations, BBC, 1964-71; Dir, Radio Fleet Productions Ltd, 1971-75. *Recreations:* travelling, reading and music. *Address:* 5 All Souls Place, W1.

CHALMERS, William Gordon, MC 1944; Crown Agent for Scotland, since 1974; *b* 4 June 1922; *s* of Robert Wilson Chalmers and Mary Robertson Chalmers (*née* Clark); *m* 1948, Margaret Helen McLeod; one *s* one *d*. *Educ:* Robert Gordon's Coll., Aberdeen; Aberdeen Univ. (BL). University, 1940-42 and 1947-48; served with Queen's Own Cameron Highlanders, 1942-47; Solicitor in Aberdeen, 1948-50; Procurator Fiscal Depute at Dunfermline, 1950-59; Senior Procurator Fiscal Depute at Edinburgh, 1959-63; Asst in Crown Office, 1963-67; Deputy Crown Agent, 1967-74. *Recreations:* golf, bridge. *Address:* 21 Tantallon Place, Edinburgh EH9 7NZ. *T:* 031-667 5664.

CHALMERS, William John, CB 1973; CBE 1954; Appeal Secretary, The Queen's Silver Jubilee Appeal; *b* 20 Oct. 1914; *s* of late William Chalmers and Catherine Florence (*née* Munro), Inverness; *m* 1942, Jessie Alexandra Roy, *y d* of late George Johnston McGregor and Erika Amalie (*née* Jensen), Edinburgh; one *s* one *d*. *Educ:* Inverness Royal Academy; Edinburgh University. BL 1937. Staff Commonwealth War Graves Commission, 1938; served Queen's Own Cameron Highlanders, 1939-45; Bde Major 214th Infantry Bde, 1942-43 and 1944-45 (despatches); Commonwealth War Graves Commission, 1945; Assistant Secretary, 1948-56, Sec. and Dir-Gen., 1956-75. Croix de Guerre, France, 1944; Coronation Medal, 1953. *Address:* c/o King George's Jubilee Trust, 8 Buckingham Street, WC2N 6BU. *T:* 01-839 3018; Flat 4, 194 Kennington Lane, SE11 5DL. *T:* 01-735 2552.

CHALONER, family name of Baron Gisborough.

CHALONER, Prof. William Gilbert, FRS 1976; Professor of Botany, Birkbeck College, University of London, since 1972; *b* London, 22 Nov. 1928; *s* of late Ernest J. and L. Chaloner; *m* 1955, Judith Carroll; one *s* two *d*. *Educ:* Kingston Grammar Sch.; Reading Univ. (BSc, PhD). 2nd Lt RA, 1955-56. Lectr and Reader, University Coll., London, 1956-73. Visiting Prof., Pennsylvania State Univ., USA, 1961-62; Prof. of Botany, Univ. of Nigeria, 1965-66. *Publications:* papers in Palaeontology and other scientific jls, dealing with fossil plants. *Recreations:* swimming, tennis, visiting USA. *Address:* 20 Parke Road, SW13 9NG. *T:* 01-748 4702.

CHAMBERLAIN, Rev. Elsie Dorothea, BD (London); Minister, Hutton Free Church, since 1971; President, Congregational Federation, 1973-75; *m* 1947, Rev. J. L. St C. Garrington. *Educ:* Channing Sch.; King's Coll., London (BD). Asst Minister Berkeley Street, Liverpool, 1939-41; Minister: Christ Church, Friern Barnet, 1941-46; Vineyard Congregational Church, Richmond, 1947-54; BBC Religious Dept, 1950-67; Associate Minister, The City Temple, 1968-70. 1st woman chaplain, HM Forces, 1946-47. Chm., Congregational Union of England and Wales, 1956-57. *Publications:* (ed) Lift Up Your Hearts, 1959; (ed) Calm Delight: devotional anthology, 1959; (ed) 12 Mini-Commentaries on the Jerusalem Bible, 1970. *Recreation:* music. *Address:* Greensted Rectory, Ongar, Essex. *T:* Ongar 2630.

CHAMBERLAIN, George Digby, CMG 1950; Chief Secretary, Western Pacific High Commission, 1947-52; *b* 13 Feb. 1898; *s* of Digby Chamberlain, late Knockfin, Knaresborough; *m* 1931, Kirsteen Miller Holmes; one *d* (one *s* decd). *Educ:* St Catharine's Coll., Cambridge. War Service, 1917-19, with Rifle Brigade, Lieut RARO. Asst District Commissioner, Gold Coast, 1925; Asst Principal, Colonial Office, 1930-32; Asst Colonial Secretary, Gold Coast, 1932; Asst Chief Secretary, Northern Rhodesia, 1939; Colonial Secretary, Gambia, 1943-47; Acting Governor, Gambia, July-Nov. 1943, and June-Aug. 1944; Acting High Commissioner, Western Pacific, Jan.-April, and Sept. 1951-July 1952; retired 1952. *Recreations:* shooting, fishing. *Address:* 18 Douglas Crescent, Edinburgh 12. *Club:* New (Edinburgh).

CHAMBERLAIN, Air Vice-Marshal George Philip, CB 1946; OBE 1941; RAF, retired; *b* 18 Aug. 1905; *s* of G. A. R. Chamberlain, MA, FLAS, FRICS, Enville, Staffordshire; *m* 1930, Alfreda Rosamond Kedward; one *s* one *d*. *Educ:* Denstone Coll.; Royal Air Force Coll., Cranwell. Commissioned RAF, 1925. On loan to Min. of Civil Aviation, 1947-48; Imperial Defence Coll., 1949; AOA 205 Group, MEAF, 1950; AOC Transport Wing, MEAF, 1951-52; Commandant, RAF Staff Coll., Andover, 1953-54; AO i/c A, HQ Fighter Command, 1954-57; Dep. Controller of Electronics, Min. of Supply, 1957-59, Min. of Aviation, 1959-60; Managing Director, Collins Radio Co. of England, 1961-66, non-executive director, 1967-75. *Recreations:* sailing, tennis. *Address:* Little Orchard, Adelaide Close, Stanmore, Middlesex. *Club:* Royal Air Force.

CHAMBERLAIN, Sir Henry Wilmot, 5th Bt, *cr* 1828; *b* 17 May 1899; *o s* of Sir Henry Chamberlain, 4th Bt, and Gwendolen (*d* 1928), *d* of J. Inglis Jones, Royal Horse Guards, Derry Ormond, Cardiganshire, and Lady Elizabeth Inglis Jones. *S* father 1936. *Address:* c/o Church Adams & Co., 23/25 Bell Street, Reigate, Surrey.

CHAMBERLAIN, Prof. Owen, AB, PhD; Professor of Physics, University of California, since 1958; *b* San Francisco, 10 July 1920; *s* of W. Edward Chamberlain and Genevieve Lucinda Owen; *m* 1943, Babette Cooper; one *s* three *d*. *Educ:* Philadelphia; Dartmouth Coll., Hanover, NH (AB). Atomic research for Manhattan District, 1942, transferred to Los Alamos, 1943; worked in Argonne National Laboratory, Chicago, 1947-48, and studied at University of Chicago (PhD); Instructor in Physics, University of California, 1948; Asst Professor, 1950; Associate Professor, 1954. Guggenheim Fellowship, 1957; Loeb Lecturer in Physics, Harvard Univ., 1959. Nobel Prize (joint) for Physics, 1959. Fellow American Phys. Soc.; Mem., Nat. Acad. of Sciences, 1960. *Publications:* papers in Physical Review, Physical Review Letters, Nature, Nuovo Cimento. *Address:* Department of Physics, University of California, Berkeley, California, USA.

CHAMBERLAIN, Hon. Sir (Reginald) Roderic (St Clair), Kt 1970; Judge of the Supreme Court of South Australia, 1959-71; *b* 17 June 1901; *s* of late Henry Chamberlain; *m* 1929, Leila Macdonald Haining; one *d*. *Educ:* St Peter's Coll.; Adelaide Univ. Crown Prosecutor, 1928; KC 1945; Crown Solicitor, 1952-59; Chm., SA Parole Board, 1970-75. Chm., Anti-Cancer Foundn. *Publication:* The Stuart Affair, 1973. *Recreations:* golf, bridge. *Address:* 72 Moseley Street, Glenelg South, SA 5045, Australia. *T:* 95.2036. *Clubs:* Adelaide, Royal Adelaide Golf (Adelaide).

CHAMBERLAIN, Richard, TD 1949; Master of the Supreme Court, Chancery Division, since 1964; *b* 29 Jan. 1914; *o s* of late John Chamberlain and Hilda (*née* Poynting); *m* 1938, Joan, *d* of late George and Eileen Kay; two *s* one *d*. *Educ:* Radley Coll.; Trinity Coll., Cambridge (MA). Admitted Solicitor, 1938. Served War, 1939-45: Devon Regt, TJFF, Staff Coll., Haifa. Partner, Kingsford Dorman & Co., 1948-64. Asst, Worshipful Co. of Solicitors of the City of London, 1966, Warden, 1973-74, Master, 1975. *Publication:* Asst Editor, Supreme Court Practice, 1967. *Recreations:* gardening, photography, travel, grandparental duties. *Address:* 23 Drax Avenue, Wimbledon, SW20 0EG. *T:* 01-946 4219. *Club:* Garrick.

CHAMBERLAIN, Hon. Sir Roderick; see Chamberlain, Hon Sir (Reginald) R.

CHAMBERLAIN, Ronald; Lecturer and Housing Consultant; *b* 19 April 1901; *m* Joan Smith McNeill (*d* 1950), Edinburgh; one *s* one *d*; *m* 1951, Florence Lilian Illingworth, Cricklewood. *Educ:* Owens Sch., Islington; Gonville and Caius Coll., Cambridge (MA). Formerly Secretary to National Federation of Housing Societies and (later) Chief Exec. Officer to the Miners' Welfare Commission; later engaged on administrative work for the National Service Hostels Corporation. MP (Lab) Norwood Division of Lambeth, 1945-50; Member of Middlesex County Council, 1947-52. Governor, Middlesex Hosp., 1947-74.

Recreation: tennis. *Address:* 18 Basing Hill, Golders Green, NW11. *T:* 01-455 1491.

CHAMBERLIN, Peter Hugh Girard, CBE 1974; ARA 1975; FRIBA 1959, RIBA DistTP 1963; architect and planner in private practice with Geoffry Powell and Christoph Bon, since 1952; *b* 31 March 1919; *m* 1940, Jean Bingham. *Educ:* Bedford Sch.; Pembroke Coll., Oxford; Kingston Sch. of Art. Member: Ancient Monuments Bd for England, 1976-; Central Housing Adv. Cttee, 1960-66. Governor, Thames Polytechnic, 1971-. *Planning work* includes development plans: for Barbican district in City of London; for expansion of Univ. of Leeds; for King's Coll. and New Hall, Cambridge; for Science area in Oxford; for central area of Peterborough; for new civic centre, Leicester. *Architectural commissions* include: Residential Community, Golden Lane, for City of London; Barbican redevelopment scheme for City of London (2000 flats, garages, shops, City of London Sch. for Girls, Guildhall Sch. of Music and Drama, Arts Centre with theatre for RSC, concert hall for LSO, cinema, lending library and art gallery, restaurants, etc); 13 teaching and research depts, block of lecture theatres, library, Senior Common Room, Sports Hall, hall of residence, and student flats for Univ. of Leeds; physical educn centre for Univ. of Birmingham; New Hall, Cambridge; Bousfield Sch. and Trinity Sch. for LCC; Cheltenham Grammar Sch.; industrial building in Witham, Essex, etc. *Awards* include: RIBA Bronze Medals for Bousfield Sch., Kensington, and Cooper Taber, Witham; Min. of Housing and Local Govt Medal for Golden Lane Estate; 1973 RIBA Regional Award for Chancellor's Court, Univ. of Leeds; 1974 RIBA Regional Award for St Giles' Square, Barbican; Civic Trust Commendation for St George's Fields, Univ. of Leeds. *Recreations:* travel, reading, enjoying the arts. *Address:* c/o Chamberlin, Powell & Bon, 1 Lamont Road Passage, King's Road, SW10 0HW. *T:* 01-352 2841.

CHAMBERS, Sir Paul; *see* Chambers, Sir S. P.

CHAMBERS, Prof. Robert Guy; Professor of Physics, University of Bristol, since 1964; *b* 8 Sept. 1924; *s* of A. G. P. Chambers; *m* 1950, Joan Brislee; one *d. Educ:* King Edward VI Sch., Southampton; Peterhouse, Cambridge. Work on tank armament (Ministry of Supply), 1944-46; Electrical Research Association, 1946-47; research on metals at low temperatures, Royal Society Mond Laboratory, Cambridge, 1947-57; Stokes Student, Pembroke Coll., 1950-53; PhD 1952; ICI Fellow, 1953-54; NRC Post-doctoral Fellow, Ottawa, 1954-55; University Demonstrator, Cambridge, 1955-57; Senior Lecturer, Bristol, 1958-61; Reader in Physics, Bristol, 1961-64. *Publications:* various papers in learned journals on the behaviour of metals at low temperatures. *Recreation:* star-gazing. *Address:* 123 Redland Road, Redland, Bristol BS6 6QX. *T:* 44982.

CHAMBERS, Sir (Stanley) Paul, KBE 1965; CB 1944; CIE 1941; Chairman: Liverpool & London & Globe Insurance Co. Ltd, 1968-74; London & Lancashire Insurance Co. Ltd, 1968-74; Royal Insurance Co. Ltd, 1968-74; Imperial Chemical Industries Ltd, 1960-68; Director: National Westminster Bank, Ltd, 1968-74; *b* 2 April 1904; *s* of late Philip Joseph Chambers; *m* 1st, 1926, Dorothy Alice Marion (marr. diss. 1955), *d* of late T. G. B. Copp; 2nd, 1955, Mrs Edith Pollack, 2nd *d* of late R. P. Lamb, Workington, Cumberland; two *d. Educ:* City of London Coll.; LSE (BCom 1928; MSc Econ 1934). Mem., Indian Income Tax Enquiry Cttee, 1935-36; Income Tax Adviser to Govt of India, 1937-40; Sec. and Comr, Bd of Inland Revenue, 1942-47; Chief of Finance Div., Control Commn for Germany, British Element, 1945-47; Dir, ICI Ltd, 1947; Dep. Chm., 1952-60. Dir, National Provincial Bank Ltd, 1951-69. President: Nat. Inst. of Economic and Social Res., 1955-62; British Shippers' Council, 1963-68; Inst. of Directors, 1964-68; Royal Statistical Soc., 1964-65; Advertising Assoc., 1968-70. Chm., Cttee of Inquiry into London Transport, 1953-55; Member: Cttee apptd to review organisation of Customs and Excise, Oct. 1951-Sept. 1953; Cttee on Departmental Records, June 1952-July 1954; NCB, 1956-60; Cttee of Managers, Royal Institution, 1976-. Prepared Report on Organisation of British Medical Assoc. (March 1972). A Vice-Pres., Liverpool Sch. of Tropical Medicine, 1969-74. Pro-Chancellor, Univ. of Kent, 1972-; Treasurer, Open University, 1969-75. Lectures: Jephcott, 1966; Messel Medal, 1968; (jtly) Granada Guildhall, 1968; Beveridge Memorial, 1969. Hon. DSc Bristol, 1963; Hon. LLD Liverpool, 1967; Hon. DTech Bradford, 1967; DUniv Open Univ., 1975. *Address:* 1A Frognal Gardens, Hampstead, NW3. *Clubs:* Athenæum, Reform.

CHAMBERS, Prof. William Walker, MBE 1945; William Jacks Professor of German, since 1954, and Vice-Principal, 1972-76, University of Glasgow; *b* 7 Dec. 1913; *s* of William and Agnes Chambers; *m* 1947, Mary Margaret Best; one *s* one *d. Educ:* Wishaw Public Sch.; Wishaw High Sch.; Universities of Glasgow, Paris and Munich. MA (Glasgow) 1936; L. ès L. (Paris) 1940; PhD (Munich) 1939. Served War of 1939-45 (despatches, MBE); 2nd Lieut, RA, 1941; Intelligence Staff, HQ 8th Army, North Africa, Sicily, Italy and Austria, 1942-46; Asst Lecturer in German, University of Leeds, 1946-47, Lecturer 1947-50; Prof. of Modern Languages, University College, N. Staffs, 1950-54. Chm., Conf. of Univ. Teachers of German in GB and Ireland, 1973-75; Pres., Assoc. of Univ. Teachers, 1962-63. Member: General Teaching Council for Scotland, 1973-77; Commonwealth Scholarship Commn in Britain, 1962-66. Vice-Chm., Governors, Jordanhill Coll. of Educn, 1962-67. FEIS, 1964. Verdienstkreuz Erste Klasse, 1967; Ehrensenator, Univ. of Freiburg, 1976. *Publications:* (ed) Paul Ernst, Selected Short Stories, 1953; (ed) Fouqué, Undine, 1956; (ed) Paul Ernst, Erdachte Gespräche, 1958; (with J. R. Wilkie) A Short History of the German Language, 1970. *Recreations:* gardening, music. *Address:* 45 Newlands Road, Glasgow G43 2JH. *T:* 041-632 1000.

CHAMIER, Lt-Col (Hon. Col) Richard Outram, CIE 1928; late Indian Army; *b* 24 Aug. 1888; *s* of late Maj.-General F. E. A. Chamier, CB, CIE, formerly of the Bengal Staff Corps. *Educ:* Woodcote House, Windlesham, Surrey; St Paul's Sch.; RM Coll., Sandhurst. Joined Indian Army, 1909; served European War, 1914-18, Mesopotamia; Private Secretary to the Governor of Assam, 1922, to Governor of the United Provinces, India, 1924-27. *Address:* 68 Shore Road, Warsash, near Southampton, Hants.

CHAMPERNOWNE, David Gawen, MA; FBA 1970; Professor of Economics and Statistics, Cambridge University, since 1970; Fellow of Trinity College, Cambridge, since 1959; *b* Oxford, 9 July 1912; *s* of late F. G. Champernowne, MA, Bursar of Keble Coll., Oxford; *m* 1948, Wilhelmina Dullaert; two *s. Educ:* The College, Winchester; King's Coll., Cambridge. 1st Class Maths, Pts 1 and 2; 1st Class Economics Pt 2. Asst Lecturer at London Sch. of Economics, 1936-38; Fellow of King's Coll., Cambridge, 1937-48; University Lecturer in Statistics at Cambridge, 1938-40; Asst in Prime Minister's statistical dept, 1940-41; Asst dir of Programmes, Ministry of Aircraft Production, 1941-45; Dir of Oxford Univ. Institute of Statistics, 1945-48; Fellow of Nuffield Coll., Oxford, 1945-59; Prof. of Statistics, Oxford Univ., 1948-59; Reader in Economics, Cambridge Univ., 1959-70. Editor, Economic Jl, 1971-76. *Publications:* Uncertainty and Estimation in Economics (3 vols), 1969; The Distribution of Income between Persons, 1973. *Address:* Trinity College, Cambridge; 230 Hills Road, Cambridge. *T:* Cambridge 47829.

CHAMPION, family name of **Baron Champion.**

CHAMPION, Baron, *cr* 1962, of Pontypridd (Life Peer); **Arthur Joseph Champion,** PC 1967; JP; Deputy Speaker and Deputy Chairman of Committees, House of Lords, since 1967; *b* 26 July 1897; *s* of William and Clara Champion, Glastonbury, Somerset; *m* 1930, Mary E. Williams, Pontypridd; one *d. Educ:* St John's Sch., Glastonbury. Signalman. MP (Lab.) Southern Division of Derbyshire, 1945-50, South-East Derbyshire, 1950-Sept. 1959; Parliamentary Private Secretary to Minister of Food, 1949-50, to Secretary of War, 1950-51; Joint Parliamentary Secretary, Ministry of Agriculture and Fisheries, April-Oct. 1951; Minister without Portfolio and Dep. Leader of the House of Lords, 1964-67. Formerly British Delegate to Consultative Assembly at Strasbourg; Govt appointed Director of the British Sugar Corporation, 1960-64, 1967-68. Hon. ARCVS, 1967; Hon. Mem., BVA, 1976. *Address:* 22 Lanelay Terrace, Pontypridd, Mid Glam. *T:* Pontypridd 402349.

CHAMPION, Sir Harry George, Kt 1956; CIE 1941; MA, DSc; Professor Emeritus, Oxford University, since 1959; Emeritus Fellow, St John's College, Oxford; *b* 17 Aug. 1891. *Educ:* New Coll., Oxford. BA 1912; MA 1924; DSc 1950. Joined Indian Forest Service, 1915; Conservator of Forests, United Provinces, 1938; Professor of Forestry, Oxford Univ., 1940-59. *Address:* Windrush, Boars Hill, Oxford. *T:* 735240.

CHAMPION, John Stuart, CMG 1977; OBE 1963; HM Diplomatic Service; British Resident Commissioner, Anglo/French Condominium of the New Hebrides, since 1975; *b* 17 May 1921; *er s* of Rev. Sir Reginald Champion, *qv*; *m* 1944, Olive Lawrencina, *o d* of late Lawrence Durning Holt, Liverpool; five *s* two *d. Educ:* Shrewsbury Sch.; Balliol Coll., Oxford (Schol., BA). Commnd 11 Hussars PAO, 1941-46. Colonial Service (later HMOCS), Uganda, 1946-63: District Officer; Secretariat, 1949-52; Private Sec. to Governor, 1952; Asst Financial Sec., 1956; Actg Perm. Sec., Min. of Health, 1959; Perm. Sec., Min. of Internal Affairs, 1960; retd 1963; Principal, CRO, 1963; 1st Sec., FCO, 1965; Head of Chancery, Tehran, 1968; Counsellor, Amman, 1971; FCO 1973.

Recreations: hill walking, travel, golf, music. *Address:* c/o Foreign and Commonwealth Office, SW1; Farmore, Callow, Hereford HR2 8DB. *T:* Hereford 4875. *Clubs:* Athenæum, Royal Commonwealth Society.

CHAMPION, Rev. Sir Reginald Stuart, KCMG 1946 (CMG 1944); OBE 1934; retired as Vicar of Chilham, Kent (1953-61); *b* 21 March 1895; *s* of late Philip Champion and Florence Mary Hulburd; *m* 1920, Margaret, *d* of late Very Rev. W. M. Macgregor, DD, LLD; two *s* one *d*. *Educ:* Sutton Valence Sch. Enlisted West Kent Yeomanry, 1912; Commissioned 3rd Bn E. Surrey Regt, 1913; European War, 1914-18; Occupied Enemy Territory Administration, Palestine, 1917-20; Colonial Administrative Service, 1920; District Officer, Palestine, 1920-28; Political Secretary, Aden, 1928-34; Secretary to Treaty Mission to the Yemen, 1933-34; Financial Adviser, Trans-Jordan, 1934-39; Dist Commissioner, Galilee, 1939-42; Political Mission to the Yemen, 1940; Chief Secretary, Aden, 1942-44, Gov. and C-in-C, 1944-51; retired from Colonial Service, 1951; ordained Deacon, Jan. 1952; Priest, Dec. 1952; Curate, All Saints', Maidstone, 1952. *Address:* 46 Chancellor House, Mount Ephraim, Tunbridge Wells, TN4 8BT. *T:* Tunbridge Wells 20719.
See also J. S. Champion.

CHAMPNEYS, Captain Sir Weldon D.; *see* Dalrymple-Champneys.

CHAMSON, André; Member of the French Academy; Grand Croix de la Légion d'Honneur; Grand Officier de l'Ordre du Mérite; Curator of the Petit Palais since 1945; Directeur Général des Archives de France, since 1959; International President of the Pen, 1956; *b* 6 June 1900; *s* of Jean Chamson and Madeleine Aldebert; *m* 1924, Lucie Mazauric; one *d*. *Educ:* Ecole des Chartes. Joint Curator, Palais de Versailles, 1933-39. Served War of 1939-45 (Croix de Guerre, Médaille de la Résistance); Captain, Staff of 5th Army, 1939-40; Chef de bataillon, Bde Alsace Lorraine, 1944-45. Près., Collège des Conservateurs du Musée et Domaine de Chantilly. Docteur *hc* Université Laval, Quebec. Grand Officier de l'Ordre de Léopold; Commandeur de la Couronne, Belgium; Officier of Saint Sava, Norway; Officier of Merit, Italy; Grand Officier de l'Ordre du Soleil du Pérou; Grand Officier de l'Etoile Polaire de Suède; Grand Officier de l'Ordre National de la Côte d'Ivoire. *Publications:* Roux le bandit, 1925; Les Hommes de la route, 1927; Le Crime des justes, 1928; Les Quatre Eléments, 1932; La Galère, 1938; Le Puits des miracles, 1945; Le Dernier Village, 1946; La Neige et la fleur, 1950; Le Chiffre de nos jours, 1954; Adeline Vénician, 1956; Nos Ancêtres les Gaulois, 1958; Le Rendez-vous des Espérances, 1961; Comme une Pierre qui Tombe, 1964; La Petite Odyssée, 1965; La Superbe, 1967; La Tour de Constance, 1970; Les Taillons, ou la terreur blanche, 1974; La Reconquête, 1944-45, 1975; Suite guerrière, 1976. *Address:* 35 rue Mirabeau, Paris XVIe, France. *Club:* Pen (Pres.).

CHANCE, Major Geoffrey Henry Barrington, CBE 1962; *b* 16 Dec. 1893; *s* of Ernest Chance, Burghfield, Berks; *m* 1st, 1914, Hazel Mary Louise Cadell (decd); two *d*; 2nd, 1933, Daphne Corona Wallace; one *s* one *d*. *Educ:* Eton. Engineering, 1913-14. Army, 1914-19. Qualified Chartered Accountant, 1928, practised, 1930-40; HM Treasury, 1941-45. Company director. CC, Alderman (Wilts), 1955-67; Chairman Chippenham Conservative Assoc., 1955-62; High Sheriff of Wiltshire, 1965. *Recreations:* fishing, shooting. *Address:* Braydon Hall, Minety, Malmesbury, Wilts. *T:* Minety 214.

CHANCE, Sir Hugh; *see* Chance, Sir W. H. S.

CHANCE, Ivan Oswald, CBE 1971; Chairman, Christies International Ltd, 1973-76 (Chairman, Christie, Manson and Woods Ltd, 1958-74); Consultant, since 1976; *b* 23 June 1910; *s* of Brig.-Gen. O. K. Chance, CMG, DSO, and Fanny Isabel, *d* of Sir George Agnew, 2nd Bt; *m* 1936, Pamela Violet, *d* of Everard Martin Smith. *Educ:* Eton. Joined Christie's, 1930; became a partner, 1935. Served War of 1939-45: 58 Middx AA Bn (TA), and Coldstream Guards (despatches, 1945). Chairman: Properties Cttee, Nat Trust, 1976 (Mem., Exec. Cttee, 1976-); Georgian Group. *Recreations:* travel, gardening. *Address:* 38 Belgravia Court, Ebury Street, SW1; Colby Lodge, Stepaside, Narberth, Pembrokeshire. *Clubs:* Beefsteak, Brooks's, White's; Brook (New York).

CHANCE, Kenneth Miles, DSO 1916; DL; *b* 27 Jan. 1893; *y s* of late Sir F. W. Chance, KBE; *m* 1924, D. R. Shaw; two *d*. *Educ:* Repton; Hertford Coll., Oxford. High Sheriff, Cumberland, 1949; DL Cumberland, 1961. *Recreations:* shooting, golf. *Address:* The Glebe House, Wreay, Carlisle.

CHANCE, Sir Roger (James Ferguson), 3rd Bt, *cr* 1900; MC; *b* 26 Jan. 1893; *e s* of George Ferguson Chance (2nd *s* of 1st Bt) and Mary Kathleen, *d* of Rev. Henry Stobart; *S* uncle 1935; *m* 1921, Mary Georgina, *d* of Col William Rowney, and Kate, *d* of Maj.-Gen. Fendall Currie; one *s* two *d* (and one *s* decd). *Educ:* Eton; Trinity Coll., Cambridge (MA); London University (PhD). Served European War, Aug. 1914-April 1918; Capt. and Adjutant 4th (RI) Dragoon Guards, 1916-17; Capt. 1st Batt. The Rifle Brigade, 1918 (twice wounded, despatches twice, MC); Editor, Review of Reviews, 1932-33; Press Attaché, British Embassy, Berlin, 1938; Sqdn Leader RAFVR, 1940-41. *Publications:* Until Philosophers are Kings (political philosophy), 1928; Conservatism and Wealth (with Oliver Baldwin, politics), 1929; Winged Horses (fiction), 1932; Be Absolute for Death (fiction), 1964; The End of Man (theology), 1973; Apple and Eve (a Cambridge symposium). *Heir:* *s* (George) Jeremy (ffolliott) Chance [*b* 24 Feb. 1926; *m* 1950, Cecilia Mary Elizabeth, *d* of Sir (William) Hugh (Stobart) Chance, *qv*; two *s* two *d*]. *Address:* 9 Eaton Square, SW1. *Club:* Athenæum.
See also R. T. Armstrong.

CHANCE, Sir (William) Hugh (Stobart), Kt 1945; CBE 1958; DL; *b* 31 Dec. 1896; 2nd *s* of George Ferguson Chance, Clent Grove, near Stourbridge, Worcs; *b* of Sir Roger Chance, 3rd Bt, *qv*; *m* 1st, 1926, Cynthia May (marr. diss.), *er d* of Major A. F. Baker-Cresswell, Cresswell and Harehope, Northumberland; two *s* three *d*; 2nd, 1961, Rachel Carr, *d* of late Cyril Cameron, RHA, and of Mrs Stormonth-Darling. *Educ:* Eton; Trinity Coll., Cambridge (MA). Dir, Chance Brothers Ltd, 1924-64. Served European War, 1914-18, Lieut Worcs Regt and Royal Flying Corps; Smethwick Borough Council, 1940-45; Chm. Smethwick Education Cttee, 1943-45; Worcs County Council, 1946-74, Vice-Chm., 1949-53; Chm. Education Cttee 1958-64; Pres. Assoc. of Technical Institutions, 1948-49; Chm. West Midlands Advisory Council for Further Education, 1949-61; Mem. of "Percy" Cttee on Higher Technological Education; Willis Jackson Cttee on Technical Teachers; Lord Chancellor's Cttee on Intestacy, 1951; Mem. Royal Commn. on Scottish Affairs, 1952; Pres. West Midlands Union of Conservative Associations, 1957-67. High Sheriff of Worcs, 1942; DL Worcs; Alderman Worcs CC 1953; Pres. Worcs Red Cross, 1958-67; Hon. Col (TA) Parsons Memorial Medal, 1946. *Recreation:* archery. *Address:* The Clock House, Birlingham, Pershore, Worcs WR10 3AF. *T:* Eckington 223. *Club:* Leander.
See also Bishop of Hereford.

CHANCELLOR, Alexander Surtees; Editor of The Spectator, since 1975; *b* 4 Jan. 1940; *m* 1964, Susanna Elisabeth Debenham; two *d*. *Educ:* Eton College; Trinity Hall, Cambridge. Reuters News Agency, 1964-74 (Chief Correspondent, Italy, 1968-73); ITN, 1974-75. *Recreation:* music. *Address:* The Spectator, 56 Doughty Street, WC1. *T:* 01-405 1706.

CHANCELLOR, Sir Christopher (John), Kt 1951; CMG 1948; MA; *b* 29 March 1904; *s* of late Sir John Robert Chancellor, GCMG, GCVO, GBE, DSO; *m* 1926, Sylvia Mary (OBE 1976), *e d* of Sir Richard Paget, 2nd Bt, and Lady Muriel Finch-Hatton, *d* of 12th Earl of Winchilsea and Nottingham; two *s* two *d*. *Educ:* Eton Coll.; Trinity College., Cambridge (1st class in History). Joined Reuters in 1930; Reuters' Gen. Manager and Chief Corresp in Far East with headquarters in Shanghai, 1931-39; Gen. Manager of Reuters, Ltd, 1944-59, Trustee, 1960-65; Chm. Odhams Press Ltd, 1960-61 (Vice-Chm., 1959-60); Chm. and Chief Executive, The Bowater Paper Corporation Ltd and associated cos, 1962-69. Mem. Court, London Univ., 1956-62; Chm. Exec. Cttee of The Pilgrims Soc. of Great Britain, 1958-67; Mem. Board of Regents, Memorial Univ. of Newfoundland, 1963-68; Vice-Pres., National Council of Social Service, 1959-71; Dep.-Chm., Council of St Paul's Cathedral Trust, 1954-62; Chm., Appeal and Publicity Cttee, King George VI National Memorial Fund, 1952-54; Dep.-Chm., Exec. Cttee, 1955-56. King Haakon VII Liberty Cross, 1947; Officer Order of Orange Nassau, 1950; Comdr Royal Order of Danebrog, 1951; Officer, Legion of Honour, 1951; Comdr Order of Civil Merit (Spain), 1952; Cross of Comdr Order of Phœnix, 1953; Comdr Order of Vasa, 1953; Comdr Order of Merit (Italy), 1959. *Address:* Hunstrete House, Pensford, Bristol; Hill Lodge, 14 Hillsleigh Road, W8. *Club:* Garrick.

CHANDLER, Edwin George, FRIBA, FRTPI; City Architect, City of London, since 1961; *b* 28 Aug. 1914; *e s* of Edwin and Honor Chandler; *m* 1938, Iris Dorothy, *o d* of Herbert William Grubb; one *d*. *Educ:* Selhurst Grammar Sch., Croydon. Asst Architect, Hants County Council and City of Portsmouth, 1936-39. Served in HMS Vernon, Mine Design Dept, 1940-45. Gained distinction in thesis, ARIBA, 1942, FRIBA 1961. Dep. Architect and Planning Officer, West Ham, 1945-47; City

Architect and Planning Officer, City of Oxford, 1947-61. Mem. RIBA Council, 1950-52; Mem. Univ. Social Survey Cttee, Oxford. *Publications:* Housing for Old Age, 1939; City of Oxford Development Plan, 1950. Articles contrib. to Press and professional jls. *Recreations:* landscaping, travel, swimming. *Address:* Guildhall, EC2. *T:* 01-606 3030; 36 Rouse Gardens, Alleyn Park, SE21. *T:* 01-670 4964. *Club:* Press.

CHANDLER, George, MA, PhD, FLA, FRHistS; ALAA; Director-General, National Library of Australia, since 1974; *b* 2 July 1915; *s* of W. and F. W. Chandler; *m* 1937, Dorothy Lowe; one *s*. *Educ:* Central Grammar Sch., Birmingham; Leeds Coll. of Commerce; University of London. Birmingham Public Libraries, 1931-37; Leeds Public Libraries, 1937-46; WEA Tutor Organiser, 1946-47; Borough Librarian, Dudley, 1947-50; Dep. City Librarian, Liverpool, 1950-52, City Librarian, 1952-74. Hon. Sec. Dudley Arts Club, 1948-50; Pres., Internat. Assoc. of Met. City Libraries, 1968-71; Pres. 1962-71 (Hon. Sec. 1957-62), Soc. of Municipal and County Chief Librarians; Dir, 1962-74 (Hon. Sec. 1955-62), Liverpool and District Scientific, Industrial and Research Library Advisory Council; Hon. Librarian, 1957-74 (Hon. Sec. 1950-57), Historic Soc. of Lancs and Ches; Chm., Exec. Cttee, 1965-70, President, 1971, Library Assoc.; Member: DES Library Adv. Council for England and Wales, 1965-72; British Library Organising Cttee, 1972-73; British Library Bd, 1973-74. Hon. Editor, Internat. Library Review, 1969-. Unesco expert in Tunisia, 1964. Cavalier dell'Ordine Al Merito della Repubblica Italiana, 1962; Internat. Fedn of Library Assocs Medal, 1971. *Publications:* Dudley, 1949; William Roscoe, 1953; Liverpool 1207-1957; Liverpool Shipping, 1960; Liverpool under James I, 1960; How to Find Out, 1963 (4th edn 1974); Four Centuries of Banking: Martins Bank, Vol. I, 1964, Vol. II, 1968; Liverpool under Charles I, 1965; Libraries in the Modern World, 1965; How to Find Out About Literature, 1968; Libraries in the East, 1971; Libraries, Bibliography and Documentation in the USSR, 1972; Victorian and Edwardian Liverpool and the North West, 1972; An Illustrated History of Liverpool, 1972; (ed) International Librarianship, 1972; Merchant Venturers, 1973; Victorian and Edwardian Manchester, 1974; Liverpool and Literature, 1974; (ed) International Series of Monographs on Library and Information Science; contributions to educl and library press. *Recreations:* writing, research; walking; foreign travel. *Address:* c/o National Library of Australia, Canberra, Australia.

CHANDLER, Tony John; Master of Birkbeck College, University of London, since 1977; Member, Royal Commission on Environmental Pollution, since 1973; *b* 7 Nov. 1928; *s* of Harold William and Florence Ellen Chandler; *m* 1954, Margaret Joyce Weston; one *s* one *d*. *Educ:* King's Coll., London. MSc. PhD, AKC. Lectr, Birkbeck Coll., Univ. of London, 1952-56; University Coll. London: Lectr, 1956-65; Reader in Geography, 1965-69; Prof of Geography, 1969-73; Prof. of Geography, Manchester Univ., 1973-76. Sec., Royal Meteorological Soc., 1969-73. Member: Council, NERC; Health and Safety Commn; Cttee of Experts on Major Hazards; Royal Soc. Study Gp on Pollution in the Atmosphere; Clean Air Council. *Publications:* The Climate of London, 1965; Modern Meteorology and Climatology, 1972; contribs to: Geographical Jl, Geography, Weather, Meteorological Magazine, Bulletin of Amer. Meteorological Soc., etc. *Recreations:* music, reading, travel. *Address:* 2 Gower Street, WC1E 6DP. *T:* 01-636 6930.

CHANDOS, 2nd Viscount *cr* 1954, of Aldershot; **Antony Alfred Lyttelton;** *b* 23 Oct. 1920; *s* of 1st Viscount Chandos, KG, PC, DSO, MC, and of Lady Moira (Lady Moira Lyttelton) (*d* 1976), *d* of 10th Duke of Leeds; *S* father, 1972; *m* 1949, Caroline Mary, *d* of Rt Hon. Sir Alan Lascelles, *qv*; two *s* two *d*. *Educ:* Eton; Trinity College, Cambridge (MA Hons). Served General Staff, Mediterranean, 1942-45 (despatches). Partner, Panmure Gordon & Co., 1950-75; Member of London Stock Exchange, 1950-75; Publisher, 1976-. *Heir: s* Hon. Thomas Orlando Lyttelton, *b* 12 Feb. 1953. *Address:* The Vine, Sherborne St John, Basingstoke, Hampshire. *T:* Bramley Green 227.

CHANDOS-POLE, Lt-Col John, OBE 1951; JP; Lord-Lieutenant of Northamptonshire since 1967; *b* 20 July 1909; *s* of late Brig.-Gen. Harry Anthony Chandos-Pole, CBE, DL, JP and late Ada Ismay, Heversword, Brasted, Kent; *m* 1952, Josephine Sylvia, *d* of late Brig.-Gen. Cyril Randell Crofton, CBE, Limerick House, Milborne Port, near Sherborne; two step-*d*. *Educ:* Eton; Magdalene Coll., Cambridge (MA). 2nd Lieut Coldstream Guards, 1933; ADC: to Governor of Bombay, May-Nov., 1937; to Governor of Bengal, Nov. 1937-June 1938, Oct. 1938-Feb. 1939, also to Viceroy of India, June-Oct., 1938. Served War of 1939-45: France and Belgium (wounded); Palestine, 1948 (wounded, despatches); commanded 1st Bn, Coldstream Guards, 1947-48; Guards Depot, 1948-50; 2nd Bn,

Coldstream Guards, 1950-52. Lieut-Col 1949; retired, 1953. A Member of the Hon. Corps of Gentlemen-at-Arms, 1956- (Harbinger, 1966-). DL 1965, JP 1957, Northants. KStJ 1975. *Recreations:* racing and travel. *Address:* Newnham Hall, Daventry, Northants. *T:* Daventry 2711. *Clubs:* Boodle's; Pratt's.

CHANDOS-POLE, Major John Walkelyne, DL, JP; *b* 4 Nov. 1913; *o s* of late Col Reginald Walkelyne Chandos-Pole, TD, JP, Radburne Hall; *m* 1947, Ilsa Jill, *er d* of Emil Ernst Barstz, Zürich; one *d* (one *s* decd). *Educ:* Eton; RMC, Sandhurst. Commissioned Grenadier Guards, 1933; ADC to Viceroy of India, 1938-39; retired, 1947. JP 1951, DL 1961, Derbys; High Sheriff of Derbys, 1959. *Recreation:* shooting. *Address:* Radburne Hall, Kirk Langley, Derby DE6 4LZ. *T:* Kirk Langley 246. *Clubs:* Army and Navy, Lansdowne, Pratt's; MCC; County (Derby).

CHANDRA, Ram; see Ram Chandra.

CHANDRASEKHAR, Subrahmanyan, FRS 1944; Morton D. Hull Distinguished Service Professor of Theoretical Astrophysics, University of Chicago, USA, since 1937; *b* 19 Oct. 1910; *m* 1936, Lalitha Doraiswamy. *Educ:* Presidency Coll., Madras; Trinity Coll., Cambridge (Government of Madras Research Scholar, PhD 1933, ScD 1942). Fellow of Trinity Coll., Cambridge, 1933-37. Managing Editor Astrophysical Journal, 1952-71. Nehru Memorial Lecture, India, 1968. Member: Nat. Acad. of Sciences (Henry Draper Medal, 1971); Amer. Philosophical Soc.; Amer. Acad. of Arts and Sciences (Rumford Medal, 1957). Hon. DSc Oxon 1972. Bruce Gold Medal, Astr. Soc. Pacific, 1952; Gold Medal, Royal Astronomical Soc. London, 1953; Royal Medal, Royal Society, 1962; Nat. Medal of Science (USA), 1966. *Publications:* An Introduction to the Study of Stellar Structure, 1939; Principles of Stellar Dynamics, 1942; Radiative Transfer, 1950; Hydrodynamic and Hydromagnetic Stability, 1961; Ellipsoidal Figures of Equilibrium, 1969; various papers in current scientific periodicals. *Address:* Laboratory for Astrophysics and Space Research, 933 East 56th Street, Chicago, Illinois, USA. *T:* (312) 753-8562. *Club:* Quadrangle (Chicago).

CHANNING-WILLIAMS, Maj.-Gen. John William; CB 1963; DSO 1944; OBE 1951; jssc; psc; *b* 14 Aug. 1908; *s* of late W. A. Williams, Inkpen, Berks; *m* 1936, Margaret Blatchford, *d* of late A. J. Wood, Maidenhead, Berks; three *s*. *Educ:* Trent Coll.; RMC Sandhurst. Commissioned 2nd Lieut, N. Staffs Regt, 1929. Served War of 1939-45 (despatches, DSO): BEF, France, 1939-40; Instructor, Senior Officers' School, 1942-43; GSO1, Staff Coll., Camberley, 1943-44; CO 4th Bn Welch Regt, 1944; served in France, 1944-45, India and Burma, 1945-46. Asst Instructor, Imperial Defence Coll., 1946-48; AA and QMG, 40th Inf. Div., Hong Kong, 1949-50; Colonel General Staff, HQ Land Forces, Hong Kong, 1951-52; Colonel, 1954; BGS (Operations and Plans), GHQ, MELF, 1955-58; Director of Quartering, War Office, 1960-61; Director of Movements, War Office, 1961-63; retired; Brigadier, 1957; Maj.-Gen., 1960. *Recreations:* shooting, fishing. *Address:* Hayes Well, Inkpen, Newbury, Berks.

CHANNON, Harold John, CMG 1946; DSc London, BA London; FRIC; Fellow of University College, London; *b* 7 March 1897; *s* of W. J. Channon; *m* 1925, Hilda Alice Bond, MB, BS, DPH. Mem. Commn on Higher Educn in Malaya, 1938. *Educ:* Leathersellers Company Sch.; University Coll., London. Research Asst, Bio-chemical Dept, University Coll., London, 1922-24; Beit Memorial Fellow for Medical Research, 1923-26; Asst Biochemical Dept, University Coll., London, 1925-27; Biochemist, Dept of Experimental Pathology and Cancer Research, University of Leeds, 1927-31; Prof. of Biochemistry University of Liverpool, 1932-43; Research Manager, Unilever Ltd, 1943-55. Mem. Commission on Higher Education in the Colonies; Mem. Commission on Higher Education in West Africa, 1944; Mem. of Advisory Cttee on Education in the Colonies, 1939-44. Mem. Colonial Products Council, 1956-59. *Publications:* scientific papers mainly in The Biochemical Journal. *Recreations:* gardening; fishing. *Address:* Dunwood, Southway, Sidmouth, Devon. *T:* Sidmouth 2921.

CHANNON, (Henry) Paul (Guinness); MP (C) for Southend West, since Jan. 1959; *b* 9 Oct. 1935; *o s* of late Sir Henry Channon, MP, and of late Lady Honor Svejdar (*née* Guinness), *e d* of 2nd Earl of Iveagh, KG; *m* 1963, Ingrid Olivia Georgia Guinness (*née* Wyndham); one *s* two *d*. *Educ:* Lockers Park, Hemel Hempstead; Eton Coll., Christ Church, Oxford. 2nd Lieut Royal Horse Guards (The Blues), 1955-56. Pres. of Oxford Univ. Conservative Association, 1958. Parly Private Sec. to: Minister of Power, 1959-60; Home Sec., 1960-62; First Sec. of

State, 1962-63; PPS to the Foreign Sec., 1963-64; Opposition Spokesman on Arts and Amenities, 1967-70; Parly Sec., Min. of Housing and Local Govt, June-Oct. 1970; Parly Under-Sec. of State, DoE, 1970-72; Minister of State, Northern Ireland Office, March-Nov. 1972; Minister for Housing and Construction, DoE, 1972-74; Opposition Spokesman on: Prices and Consumer Protection, March-Sept. 1974; environmental affairs, Oct. 1974-Feb. 1975. Dep. Leader, Cons. Delegn to WEU and Council of Europe, 1976-. Mem., Gen. Adv. Council to ITA, 1964-66. *Address:* 96 Cheyne Walk, SW10. *T:* 01-351 0293; Kelvedon Hall, Brentwood, Essex. *T:* Ongar 2180. *Clubs:* Buck's; White's.

CHANTLER, Philip, CMG 1963; Director of Economic Planning, Cyprus, 1969-70, Swaziland, 1970-71; *b* 16 May 1911; *s* of Tom and Minnie Chantler; *m* 1938, Elizabeth Margaret Pentney; one *d*. *Educ:* Manchester Central High Sch.; Manchester Univ.; Harvard Univ Commonwealth Fund Fellow, 1934-36; Asst Lectr in Public Admin., Manchester Univ., 1936-38; Tariffs Adviser, UK Gas Corp. Ltd, 1938-40. Served War of 1939-45: RA 1940-41; War Cabinet Secretariat, 1941-45; Economic Adviser, Cabinet Office, 1945-47; Economic Adviser, Ministry of Fuel and Power, 1947-60 (seconded as Economic Adviser, Government of Pakistan Planning Board, 1955-57); Under-Sec., Electricity Div., Min. of Power, 1961-65; Chm., North-West Economic Planning Bd, 1965-69. *Publication:* The British Gas Industry: An Economic Study, 1938. *Recreations:* gardening, cine-photography, Victorian architecture, industrial archæology, domestic odd-jobbing. *Address:* Glandore, Lyston Court, Wormelow, Hereford; Tralong Cottage, West Cork, Eire.

CHAPLAIS, Pierre Théophile Victorien Marie; Médaille de la Résistance, 1946; FBA 1973; Reader in Diplomatic in the University of Oxford, since 1957; Professorial Fellow, Wadham College, Oxford, since 1964; *b* Châteaubriant, Loire-Atlantique, France, 8 July 1920; *s* of late Théophile Chaplais and Victorine Chaplais (*née* Roussel); *m* 1948, Mary Doreen Middlemast; two *s*. *Educ:* Collège St-Sauveur, Redon, Ille-et-Vilaine; Univ. of Rennes, Ille-et-Vilaine (Licence en Droit, Licence ès-Lettres); Univ. of London (PhD). Editor, Public Record Office, London, 1948-55; Lectr in Diplomatic, Univ. of Oxford, 1955-57. *Publications:* Some Documents regarding... The Treaty of Brétigny, 1952; The War of St Sardos, 1954; Treaty Rolls, vol. I, 1955; (with T. A. M. Bishop) Facsimiles of English Royal Writs to AD 1100 presented to V. H. Galbraith, 1957; Diplomatic Documents, vol. I, 1964; English Royal Documents, King John-Henry VI, 1971; English Medieval Diplomatic Practice, Part II, 1975; articles in Bulletin of Inst. of Historical Research, English Hist. Review, Jl of Soc. of Archivists, etc. *Recreations:* gardening, fishing. *Address:* Wintles Farm House, 36 Mill Street, Eynsham, Oxford OX8 1JS. *T:* Oxford 881386.

CHAPLIN, family name of **Viscount Chaplin**.

CHAPLIN, 3rd Viscount, *cr* 1916, of St Oswalds, Blankney, in the county of Lincoln; **Anthony Freskyn Charles Hamby Chaplin;** Flight Lieutenant RAFVR; *b* 14 Dec. 1906; *er s* of 2nd Viscount and late Hon. Gwladys Alice Gertrude Wilson, 4th *d* of 1st Baron Nunburnholme; *S* father, 1949; *m* 1st, 1933, Alvilde (marr. diss., 1951; she *m* 1951, James Lees Milne), *o d* of late Lieut-Gen. Sir Tom Bridges, KCB, KCMG; one *d*; 2nd, 1951, Rosemary, *d* of 1st Viscount Chandos, KG, PC, DSO, MC; two *d*. *Educ:* Radley. Occupied with Natural History and Music. Mem. Council, Zoological Soc. of London, 1934-38, 1950-; Sec., 1952-55. Voyage to New Guinea, to collect zoological material, 1935-36. Studied musical composition in Paris with Nadia Boulanger, 1937-39. Served RAF, 1940-46. *Publications:* 3 Preludes for piano; Toccata on a fragment of D. Scarlatti for piano; Cadenza for Mozart's piano concerto in C minor k. 491; various contributions to zoological journals. *Heir:* none. *Address:* Wadstray House, Blackawton, near Totnes, S Devon.

CHAPLIN, Arthur Hugh, CB 1970; Principal Keeper of Printed Books, British Museum, 1966-70; *b* 17 April 1905; *er s* of late Rev. Herbert F. Chaplin and Florence B. Lusher; *m* 1938, Irene Marcousé. *Educ:* King's Lynn Grammar Sch.; Bedford Modern Sch.; University Coll., London. Asst Librarian: Reading Univ. 1927-28; Queen's Univ., Belfast, 1928-29; Asst Keeper, Dept of Printed Books, British Museum, 1930-52; Dep. Keeper, 1952-59; Keeper, 1959-66. Exec. Sec., Organizing Cttee of Internat. Conference on Cataloguing Principles, Paris, 1961; Mem. Council, Library Association, 1964-70; Pres., Microfilm Assoc. of GB, 1967-71. Fellow UCL, 1969. *Publications:* contributions to Jl Documentation, Library Assoc. Record, Library Quarterly, and to Cataloguing Principles and Practice (ed M. Piggott), 1954; Tradition and Principle in Library Cataloguing, 1966. *Recreations:* walking; motoring. *Address:* 44 Russell Square, WC1. *T:* 01-636 7217.

CHAPLIN, Sir Charles (Spencer), KBE 1975; producer, and actor in films; *b* London, 16 April 1889; both parents (deceased) in theatrical profession; *s* of Charles Chaplin, variety comedian and Hannah (Lily Harley), singer; *m* 1st, 1918, Mildred Harris (marr. diss.); 2nd, 1924, Lolita McMurry (Lita Grey) (marr. diss.); one *s* (and one *s* decd); 3rd, 1936, Paulette Goddard (marr. diss.); 4th, 1943, Oona, *d* of late Eugene O'Neill; three *s* five *d*. Formed his own producing organisation and built Chaplin Studios, Hollywood, California, 1918. Was a founder of United Artists' Corporation (with Mary Pickford, Douglas Fairbanks, and D. W. Griffith) with British affiliation Allied Artists. Member, American Academy of Arts and Sciences, 1970. Films Include: Shoulder Arms, The Kid, The Gold Rush, The Circus, City Lights, Modern Times, The Great Dictator, Monsieur Verdoux, Limelight (Oscar, 1973), A King in New York, A Countess from Hong Kong. Erasmus Prize, 1965; Creative Arts Award, Brandeis Univ., Mass, 1971; Hon. Oscar award, 1972. Fellow, British Acad. of Film and Television Arts, 1976. Hon. Member: AAAL, 1976; Nat. Inst. of Arts and Letters, 1976. Hon. DLitt: Oxford, 1962; Durham, 1962. Officier de l'instruction Publique, République Française; Commander, Legion of Honour, 1971. *Publications:* My Autobiography, 1964; My Life in Pictures, 1974. *Address:* c/o United Artists Ltd, 142 Wardour Street, W1.

CHAPLIN, Frederick Leslie; Chairman, F. W. Woolworth & Co. Ltd, 1961-69; Director, F. W. Woolworth, USA, 1961-69; *b* 6 Dec. 1905; *s* of late Frederick and Marion Chaplin; *m* 1934, Vera Irene Townes; two *s*. *Educ:* St Osyth's Sch., Clacton. Joined Woolworth Company, 1928; Director, 1957; Managing Dir, 1960. *Recreations:* gardening; fishing; shooting. *Address:* Links View, 5 Broad Walk, Winchmore Hill, N21. *T:* 01-886 0244.

CHAPLING, Norman Charles, CBE 1954; Managing Director, Cable and Wireless Ltd, 1951-65, retd; *b* 11 Feb. 1903; *s* of late Charles Chapling; *m* 1933, Lenora, *d* of late Ernest Hedges; one *s*. Past Man. Dir: Cable & Wireless (Mid-East) Ltd; Cable & Wireless (West Indies) Ltd; Direct West India Cable Co. Ltd; Eastern Extension Australasia & China Telegraph Co. Ltd; Eastern Telegraph Co. Ltd; Eastern Telegraph Co. (France) Ltd; Halifax & Bermudas Cable Co. Ltd; Mercury House Ltd; West Coast of America Telegraph Co. Ltd; Western Telegraph Co. Ltd. Past Dir, SA Belge de Câbles Télégraphiques. *Address:* Treveal, Mawnan Smith, Falmouth, Cornwall. *Club:* Royal Automobile.

CHAPMAN, family name of **Baron Northfield**.

CHAPMAN, (Anthony) Colin (Bruce), CBE 1970; Chairman, Group Lotus Car Cos Ltd; Designer of sports and racing cars; *b* 19 May 1928; *s* of late S. F. Kennedy Chapman; *m* 1954, Hazel Patricia Williams; one *s* two *d*. *Educ:* Stationers' Company's Sch., Hornsey; London Univ. (BSc Eng). Served as Pilot, RAF, 1950. Structural Engineer, 1951; Civil Engineer, Development engineer, British Aluminium Co., 1952. Formed own Company, Lotus Cars, manufacturing motor cars, 1955. FRSA 1968; Fellow, UCL, 1972. *Recreation:* flying. *Address:* Lotus Cars Ltd, Norwich, Norfolk NR14 8EZ. *Clubs:* British Racing Drivers, British Automobile Racing; British Racing and Sports Car.

CHAPMAN, Prof. Brian; Professor of Government, University of Manchester, since 1961, and Dean, Faculty of Economic and Social Studies, 1967-71; *b* 6 April 1923; *s* of B. P. Chapman; *m* 1972, Christina Maria, *d* of Neville and Edna O'Brien, Altrincham. *Educ:* Owen's Sch., London; Magdalen Coll. and Nuffield Coll., Oxford (DPhil, MA). Lieut, RNVR, 1942-45. Dept of Govt, University of Manchester, and Vis. Prof. at several European Univs, 1949-60; Foundn Prof. of Govt and Dir, Public Admin programme, University of W Indies, 1960-61. Mem. Council, Manchester Business School; Mem. Court, Cranfield Inst. of Technology; Vis Prof., Queen's Univ., Kingston, Ont, 1972; Vis. Prof., Univ. of Victoria, BC, 1975-76. Gen. Editor, Minerva Series. *Publications:* French Local Government, 1953; The Prefects and Provincial France, 1954; (jtly) The Life and Times of Baron Haussmann, 1956; The Profession of Government, 1959; (jtly) The Fifth Constitution, 1959; British Government Observed, 1963; The Police State, 1970; (jtly) The Resistance in Europe, 1974; (ed jtly) W.J.M.M.: Political Questions, 1974; Introduction to Government, 1977; contributions to internat. learned jls, reviews and newspapers. *Address:* Department of Government, The University, Manchester M13 9PL. *T:* 061-273 7121. *Clubs:* Naval; Manchester Business School (Manchester).

CHAPMAN, Very Rev. Clifford Thomas; Dean of Exeter since 1973; *b* 28 May 1913; *s* of late Walter and Mabel Mary Chapman; *m* 1939, Nance Kathleen, *d* of late Harold Tattersall;

one s one d. Educ: Sir Walter St John's Sch; King's College, London University (BA, BD, AKC, MTh, PhD); Ely Theological College. Deacon 1936, Priest 1937; Curate: All Saints, Child's Hill, 1936; Pinner, 1936-38; St Paul's, Winchmore Hill, 1938-39; Pinner, 1939-42; Minister of Church of Ascension Conventional District, Preston Road, Wembley, 1942-45; Vicar of Christ Church, Chelsea, 1945-50; RD of Chelsea, 1946-50; Rector of Abinger, 1950-61; Organizer of Adult Religious Educn, Dio. Guildford, 1952-61; Director of Religious Educn, 1961-63, and of Post-Ordination Training, 1958-68; Examining Chaplain to Bp of Guildford, 1953-73; Canon Residentiary and Sub-Dean of Guildford Cathedral, 1961-73; Proctor in Convocation, 1965-73. FKC 1948. Publication: The Conflict of the Kingdoms, 1951. Recreations: walking, fishing, sailing, travel, Greek and Roman antiquities. Address: The Deanery, Exeter, Devon EX1 1HT. T: Exeter 72697. Club: Royal Over-Seas League.

CHAPMAN, Colin; see Chapman, A. C. B.

CHAPMAN, Cyril Donald, QC 1965; His Honour Judge Chapman; a Circuit Judge, since 1972; b 17 Sept. 1920; s of Cyril Henry Chapman and Frances Elizabeth Chapman (née Braithwaite); m 1st, 1950, Audrey Margaret Fraser (née Gough) (marr. diss., 1959); one s; 2nd, 1960, Muriel Falconer Bristow; one s. Educ: Roundhay Sch., Leeds; Brasenose Coll., Oxford (MA). Served RNVR, 1939-45. Called to Bar, 1947; Harmsworth Scholar, 1947; North Eastern Circuit, 1947; Recorder of Huddersfield, 1965-69; of Bradford, 1969-71. Contested (C) East Leeds 1955, Goole 1964, Brighouse and Spenborough, 1966. Recreation: yachting. Address: Hill Top, Collingham, Wetherby, W Yorks. T: Collingham Bridge 2813. Club: Leeds (Leeds).

CHAPMAN, Daniel Ahmling; see Chapman Nyaho.

CHAPMAN, Francis Ian; Deputy Chairman, William Collins Sons & Co. Ltd, Publishers, since 1976; Chairman: Radio Clyde Ltd, since 1973; Harvill Press Ltd, since 1976; Hatchards Ltd, since 1976; Deben Bookshop Ltd, since 1976; b 26 Oct. 1925; s of late Rev. Peter Chapman and Frances Burdett; m 1953, Marjory Stewart Swinton; one s one d. Educ: Shawlands Academy, Glasgow. Worked in coal mines; served in RAF, 1943-47; joined Wm Collins Sons & Co. Ltd, 1947 as gen. trainee; Sales Man., 1955; Sales Dir, 1960; Jt Man. Dir, 1968-76. Director: Pan Books Ltd; Collins Liturgical Publications Ltd; Scottish Opera Theatre Royal Ltd; also numerous overseas companies of Collins. Mem. Council, Publishers' Assoc., 1963-76, 1977-; Mem. Bd, Book Develt Council, 1970-73. Publications: various articles on publishing in trade jls. Recreations: music, golf, cricket, gardening. Address: Kenmore, 46 The Avenue, Cheam, Surrey. T: 01-642 1820. Clubs: Brooks's, MCC; Royal Wimbledon Golf.

CHAPMAN, Prof. Garth; Vice Principal, Queen Elizabeth College, since 1974, and Professor of Zoology, since 1958; Dean, Faculty of Science, University of London, since 1974; b 8 Oct. 1917; o s of E. J. Chapman and Edith Chapman (née Attwood); m 1941, Margaret Hilda Wigley; two s one d. Educ: Royal Grammar Sch., Worcester; Trinity Hall, Cambridge (Major Scholar). Telecommunications Research Establishment, Ministry of Aircraft Production, 1941-45. Asst Lecturer in Zoology, Queen Mary Coll., University of London, 1945-46; Lecturer in Zoology, Queen Mary Coll., University of London, 1946-58. Vis. Prof., Univ. of California, Berkeley, 1967, Los Angeles, 1970-71. Publications: various on structure and physiology of marine invertebrates. Recreations: gardening; wood-engraving. Address: Nunns, Coxtie Green, Brentwood, Essex.

CHAPMAN, Harold Thomas, CBE 1951; FRAeS; MIMechE; formerly Director, Hawker Siddeley Group, retired 1969; b 4 Aug. 1896; 3rd s of Henry James and Elizabeth Chapman, Mornington, Wylam-on-Tyne; m 1923, Mabel Annie Graham. Educ: Rutherford Coll., Newcastle on Tyne. Served European War in RFC and RAF, 1917-19. Joined Armstrong Siddeley Motors Ltd as a Designer, 1926; Works Manager, 1936; Gen. Manager, 1945; Dir, 1946. Recreations: fishing, shooting, golfing. Address: Ty-Melyn, Rhydspence, Whitney-on-Wye, Hereford. T: Clifford 313.

CHAPMAN, John Henry Benjamin, CB 1957; b 28 Dec. 1899; s of Robert Henry Chapman and Edith Yeo Chapman (née Lillicrap); m 1929, Dorothy Rowlerson; one s one d. Educ: HM Dockyard Sch., Devonport; RNC Greenwich. Dir of Naval Construction, Admiralty, 1958-61. Dir, Fairfield S & E Co. Ltd, 1962-66; Consultant, Upper Clyde Shipbuilders, 1966-68. Mem. of Royal Corps of Naval Constructors, 1922-61; Hon. Vice-

Pres., RINA; Mem., Technical Consultative Cttee, RNLI. Address: The Small House, Delling Lane, Old Bosham, Sussex. T: Bosham 573331. Club: Bosham Sailing.

CHAPMAN, Kathleen Violet, CBE 1956; RRC 1953 (ARRC 1945); QHNS 1953-56; Matron-in-Chief, Queen Alexandra's Royal Naval Nursing Service, 1953-56, retired; b 30 May 1903; d of late Major H. E. Chapman, CBE, DL Kent, Chief Constable of Kent, and Mrs C. H. J. Chapman. Educ: Queen Anne's, Caversham. Trained St Thomas's Hospital, 1928-32. Address: Holmfield, Compton Chamberlayne, Salisbury, Wilts.

CHAPMAN, Kenneth Herbert; Managing Director, Thomas Tilling Ltd, 1967-73; Director: British Steam Specialities Ltd; Société Générale (France) Bank Ltd; Ready Mixed Concrete Ltd; Royal Worcester Ltd; Goodliffe Garages Ltd; b 9 Sept. 1908; s of Herbert Chapman and Anne Bennett Chapman (née Poxon); m 1937, Jean Martha Mahring; one s. Educ: St Peter's Sch., York. Articled Clerk, 1926; qual. Solicitor, 1931; private practice, 1931-36; joined professional staff, HM Land Registry, 1936; transf. Min. of Aircraft Prodn, 1940, Private Sec. to Perm. Sec.; transf. Min. of Supply, 1946. Joined Thomas Tilling Ltd, as Group Legal Adviser, 1948; at various times Chm. or Dir of more than 20 companies in Tilling Group. High Sheriff of Greater London, 1974. Recreations: Rugby football (Past Pres. and Hon. Treas. of RFU, mem. cttee various clubs), cricket (mem. cttee various clubs), golf. Address: Cumberland House, Thakeham, near Pulborough, Sussex RH20 3ER. T: West Chiltington 2103. Clubs: East India, Devonshire, Sports and Public Schools; West Sussex Golf; Harlequin Football.

CHAPMAN, Prof. Norman Bellamy, MA, PhD; CChem, FRIC; G. F. Grant Professor of Chemistry, Hull University, since 1956; Pro-Vice-Chancellor, 1973-76; b 19 April 1916; s of Frederick Taylor Chapman and Bertha Chapman; m 1949, Fonda Maureen Bungey; one s one d. Educ: Barnsley Holgate Grammar Sch.; Magdalene Coll., Cambridge (Entrance Scholar). 1st Cl. Parts I and II Nat. Sciences Tripos, 1937 and 1938. Bye-Fellow, Magdalene Coll., 1939-42; Univ. Demonstrator in Chemistry, Cambridge, 1945; Southampton Univ.: Lectr, 1947; Senior Lectr, 1949; Reader in Chemistry, 1955. Chm., Technical Sub-Cttee, UCCA. R. T. French Visiting Prof., Univ. of Rochester, NY, 1962-63; R. J. Reynolds Vis. Prof., Duke Univ., N Carolina, 1971. BA 1938, MA 1942, PhD 1941, Cambridge. Publications: (ed with J. Shorter) Advances in Free Energy Relationships, 1972; (ed) Organic Chemistry, Series One, vol. 2: Aliphatic Compounds (MTP Internat. Review of Science), 1973, Series Two, Vol 2, 1976; contribs to Jl Chem. Soc., Analyst, Jl Medicinal Chem., Tetrahedron, Jl Organic Chemistry, Chemistry and Industry. Recreations: music, gardening, cricket, Rugby football. Address: 61 Newland Park, Hull HU5 2DR. T: 42946.

CHAPMAN, Oscar Littleton; attorney-at-law; b Omega, Virginia, 22 Oct. 1896; s of James Jackson Chapman and Rosa Archer Blount; m 1st, 1920, Olga Pauline Edholm (d 1932); 2nd, 1940, Ann Kendrick; one s. Educ: public schs, Va.; Randolph Macon Acad., Bedford, Va.; Univ. of Denver; Westminster Law Sch. (LLB). Enlisted in US Navy, 1918, served until 1920. Served for five years as asst and chief probation officer of Juvenile Court of Denver. Admitted to law practice, 1929; Mem. of Dist of Columbia Bar: admitted to practice before Supreme Court of US, 1934. Asst-Sec. of the Interior, 1933-46; Under-Sec. of the Interior, 1946-49; Sec. of the Interior, USA, 1949-53. Active in civic, political, and veterans' affairs, both in Denver and in Washington; has served at request of President, as head of Govt div. of Red Cross, Community Fund, and War Fund drives; appointed by late President Roosevelt to Interdepartmental Cttee to coordinate Health and Welfare Services of Govt, 1935; Cttee on Vocational Education, 1936; mem. of President's Advisory Cttee on Management Improvement in Govt; director: Franklin D. Roosevelt Foundation; Harry S. Truman Library. Has received several citations for service to US. Hon. Dr of Laws; Augustana Coll., 1934; Colorado State Coll. of Education, 1940; Howard Univ., 1949, Univ. of Denver, 1951; Western State Coll. of Colorado, 1961. Mem. American Judicature Soc. and of Phi Alpha Delta Law Fraternity. Address: 1730 Pennsylvania Avenue, NW, Suite 1200, Washington, DC 20006, USA; 4975 Hillbrook Lane, Washington, DC.

CHAPMAN, Sir Robin (Robert Macgowan), 2nd Bt cr 1958; CBE 1961; TD and Bar, 1947; JP; Partner in Chapman, Hilton and Dunford, Chartered Accountants; Joint Secretary, Shields Commercial Building Society, since 1939; Chairman, Commercial Union Assurance Co. Ltd (Local Board); Director: North Eastern Investment Trust Ltd (Manager); Shields Commercial Building Society; Chairman: James Hogg & Sons

(North Shields) Ltd; John W. Pratt Ltd; Vice Lord-Lieutenant, Tyne and Wear, since 1974; *b* Harton, Co. Durham, 12 Feb. 1911; *er s* of 1st Bt and Lady Hélène Paris Chapman, JP (*née* Macgowan); *S* father, 1963; *m* 1941, Barbara May, *d* of Hubert Tonks, Ceylon; two *s* one *d*. *Educ:* Marlborough; Corpus Christi Coll., Cambridge (Exhibitioner). 1st Cl. Hons Maths, BA 1933; MA 1937. Chartered Accountant, ACA 1938; FCA 1945. Chm., Northern Counties Provincial Area Conservative Associations, 1954-57; Chm., Jarrow Conservative Association, 1957-60; Pres., Northern Soc. of Chartered Accountants, 1958-59, Mem. Cttee, 1949-60; Member: Police Authority, Co. Durham, 1955-59, 1961-65; Appeals Cttee, 1955-62; Durham Diocesan Conf., 1953-70; Durham Diocesan Synod, 1971-72; Durham Diocesan Bd of Finance, 1953-71 (Chm. 1966-70); Durham County TA, 1948-68; N England TA, 1968-74; Chm., Durham Co. Scout Council, 1972- (Scout Silver Acorn Award, 1973). Governor, United Newcastle Hospitals, 1957-64. TA Army officer, 1933-51; served War of 1939-45: RA Anti-Aircraft Command; GSO 2, 1940; CO 325 LAA regt, RA (TA), 1948-51; Hon. Col 1963; JP 1946, DL, 1952; High Sheriff of County Durham, 1960. *Recreation:* lawn tennis. *Heir: er s* David Robert Macgowan Chapman [*b* 16 Dec. 1941; *m* 1965, Maria Elizabeth de Gosztony-Zsolnay, *o d* of Dr N. de Mattyasovsky-Zsolnay, Montreal, Canada; one *s* one *d*]. *Address:* Cherry Tree House, Cleadon, near Sunderland. *T:* Boldon 7451. *Clubs:* Junior Carlton; County (Durham); Hawks (Cambridge).

CHAPMAN, Air Chief Marshal Sir Ronald I.; *see* Ivelaw-Chapman.

CHAPMAN, Roy de Courcy; Rector of Glasgow Academy, since 1975; *b* 1 Oct. 1936; *s* of Edward Frederic Gilbert Chapman and Aline de Courcy Ireland; *m* 1959, Valerie Rosemary Small; two *s* one *d*. *Educ:* Dollar Academy; St Andrews Univ. (Harkness Schol.: MA 1959); Moray House Coll. of Educn, Edinburgh. Asst Master, Trinity Coll., Glenalmond, 1960-64; Marlborough College: Asst Master, 1964-68; Head of Mod. Langs, 1968-75; OC CCF, 1969-75. *Publications:* Le Français Contemporain, 1971; (with D. Whiting) Le Français Contemporain: Passages for translation and comprehension, 1975. *Recreations:* squash, France, brewing, wine-making. *Address:* 11 Kirklee Terrace, Glasgow G12 0TH. *T:* 041-357 1776.

CHAPMAN, Hon. Sir Stephen, Kt 1966; Hon. Mr Justice **Chapman;** Judge of the High Court of Justice, Queen's Bench Division, since 1966; *b* 5 June 1907; 2nd *s* of late Sir Sydney J. Chapman, KCB, CBE, and of late Lady Chapman, JP; *m* 1963, Mrs Pauline Frances Niewiarowski, *widow* of Dmitri de Lobel Niewiarowski and *d* of late Lt-Col H. Allcard and late Mrs A. B. M. Allcard. *Educ:* Westminster; Trinity Coll., Cambridge. King's Scholar and Capt. Westminster; Entrance Scholar and Major Scholar, Trinity Coll., Cambridge; Browne Univ. Gold Medallist, 1927 and 1928; John Stuart of Rannoch Univ. Scholar, 1928; 1st Cl. Classical Tripos, Pt I, 1927, and in Pt II, 1929. Entrance Scholar, Inner Temple, 1929; Jardine student, 1931; 1st Cl. and Certificate of Honour, Bar Final, 1931; called to Bar, Inner Temple, 1931; SE Circuit, Herts-Essex Sessions; Asst Legal Adviser, Min. of Pensions, 1939-46; Prosecuting Counsel for Post Office on SE Circuit, 1947-50 (Leader, Circuit, 1962); QC 1955; Comr of Assize, Winchester, Autumn, 1961. Recorder of Rochester, 1959-61, of Cambridge, 1961-63; Judge of the Crown Court and Recorder of Liverpool, 1963-66. Dep. Chm. Herts QS, 1963. Mem. Bar Council, 1956; Hon. Treas. 1958; Vice-Chm. 1959-60. *Publications:* Auctioneers and Brokers, in Atkin's Encyclopædia of Court Forms, vol. 3, 1938; Insurance (non-marine), in Halsbury's Laws of England, 3rd edn, vol. 22, 1958; Statutes on the Law of Torts, 1962. *Recreation:* gardening. *Address:* Royal Courts of Justice, Strand, WC2; (private) 72 Thomas More House, Barbican, EC2Y 8AB. *T:* 01-628 9251; The Manor House, Ware, Herts. *T:* Ware 2123. *Club:* United Oxford & Cambridge University.

CHAPMAN, Sydney Brookes, RIBA; MRTPI; Partner, McDonald, Hamilton, Montefiore, Chartered Architects and Planning Consultants; Planning Consultant to Jones Martin Fleetwood, commercial and industrial property consultants, and to House Builders Federation; Consultant to British Property Federation; *b* 17 Oct. 1935; *m* 1976, Claire Lesley McNab (*née* Davies). *Educ:* Rugby Sch.; Manchester University. DipArch 1958; ARIBA 1960; DipTP 1961; AMTPI 1962. Nat. Chm., Young Conservatives, 1964-66 (has been Chm. and Vice-Chm. at every level of Movt); Sen. Elected Vice-Chm., NW Area of Nat. Union of C and U Assocs, 1966-70. Contested (C) Stalybridge and Hyde, 1964. MP (C) Birmingham, Handsworth, 1970-Feb. 1974; former Secretary: Conservative MPs' Local Govt Develt Cttee; All Party Animal Welfare Gp. Lectr in Arch. and Planning at techn. coll., 1964-70. Originator of nat. tree planting year, 1973 and Dir, Nat. Tree Week, 1975, 1976;

Chm., Queen's Silver Jubilee London Tree Group. RIBA: Vice-Pres., 1974-75; Chm., Public Affairs Bd, 1974-75; Mem. Council, 1972-77. *Publications:* contribs Jl Building; political booklets. *Recreation:* tree spotting. *Address:* 151/153 Gloucester Terrace, W2.

CHAPMAN-ANDREWS, Sir Edwin Arthur, KCMG 1953 (CMG 1948); OBE 1936; retired as British Ambassador at Khartoum (1956-61); *b* 9 Sept. 1903; *er s* of Arthur John Chapman-Andrews and Ada Allen, Exeter; *m* 1931, Sadie Barbara Nixon, London; two *s* two *d*. *Educ:* Hele's Sch., Exeter; University College, London (Fellow, 1952); Sorbonne; St John's Coll., Cambridge (while a probationer Vice-Consul, to study oriental languages). Probationer Vice-Consul, Levant Consular Service, 1926; Actg Vice-Consul, Port Said, Cairo and Suez, 1928-29; Actg Vice-Consul, Addis Ababa, 1930; FO, 1931-32; Vice-Consul at Kirkuk, Iraq and at Rowanduz, 1933-35; Actg Consul at Harar, 1935-36; Foreign Office, 1937; Asst Oriental Sec., Cairo, 1937-40. Hon. Commission in Royal Sussex Regt, 1940; Liaison Officer on staff of C-in-C, Middle East, with Emperor Haile Selassie; Foreign Office, 1942; Head of Personnel Dept, 1945; Inspector of Overseas Establishments, 1946; British Minister at Cairo, 1947-51; at Beirut, 1951; Ambassador, 1952. Adviser, Massey-Ferguson (Holdings) Ltd, 1962; Director: Massey-Ferguson (Export), 1964-; Mitchell Cotts (Export), 1965-73; John Carrington & Co. Ltd, 1972-. Member: Council of Lord Kitchener National Memorial Fund; British Nat. Export Council, 1965-68; Cttee for Middle East Trade (COMET), 1963-65 (Chm. 1965-68). Member Council: Anglo-Arab Assoc.; Royal Albert Hall; Royal Central Asian Soc., 1962-69. KStJ; KCSG (Papal). *Recreation:* any change of occupation handy. *Address:* 39 Brim Hill, N2. *Clubs:* Athenæum, Oriental.

CHAPMAN-MORTIMER, William Charles; author; *b* 15 May 1907; *s* of William George Chapman-Mortimer and Martha Jane McLelland; *m* 1934, Frances Statler; *m* 1956, Ursula Merits; one *d*. *Educ:* privately. *Publications:* A Stranger on the Stair, 1950; Father Goose, 1951 (awarded James Tait Black Memorial Prize, 1952); Young Men Waiting, 1952; Mediterraneo, 1954; Here in Spain, 1955; Madrigal, 1960; Amparo, 1971. *Address:* Gisebo, 56100 Huskvarna, Sweden.

CHAPMAN NYAHO, Daniel Ahmling, CBE 1961; Director: Pioneer Tobacco Co. Ltd, Ghana (Member of British-American Tobacco Group), since 1967; Standard Bank Ghana Ltd, 1970-75; *b* 5 July 1909; *s* of William Henry Chapman and Jane Atsiamesi (*née* Atriki); *m* 1941, Jane Abam (*née* Quashie); two *s* four *d* (and one *d* decd). *Educ:* Bremen Mission Schs, Gold Coast and Togoland; Achimota Coll., Ghana; St Peter's Hall, Oxford. Postgraduate courses at Columbia Univ. and New York Univ.; Teacher, Government Senior Boys' School, Accra, 1930; Master, Achimota Coll., 1930-33, 1937-46. Area Specialist, UN Secretariat, Lake Success and New York, 1946-54; Sec. to Prime Minister and Sec. of Cabinet, Gold Coast/Ghana, 1954-57; Ghana's Ambassador to USA and Permanent Representative at UN, 1957-59; Headmaster, Achimota Sch., Ghana, 1959-63; Dir, UN Div. of Narcotic Drugs, 1963-66; Ambassador (Special Duties), Min. of External Affairs, Ghana, 1967. Gen. Sec., All-Ewe Conf., 1944-46; Commonwealth Prime Ministers' Conf., 1957; Mem., Ghana delegn to the conf. of indep. African States, Accra, 1958. First Vice-Chm., Governing Council of UN Special Fund, 1959; Chairman: Mission of Indep. African States to Cuba, Dominican Republic, Haiti, Venezuela, Bolivia, Paraguay, Uruguay, Brazil, Argentina, Chile, 1958; Volta Union, 1968-69. Vice-Chm., Commn on Univ. Educn in Ghana, 1960-61. Member: Board of Management, UN Internat. Sch., New York, 1950-54, 1958-59; UN Middle East and N. Africa Technical Assistance Mission on Narcotics Control, 1963; Dir, UN Consultative Gp on Narcotics Control in Asia and Far East, Tokyo, 1964; Member: Political Cttee of Nat. Liberation Council, 1967; Board of Trustees of General Kotoka Trust Fund; Chairman: Arts Council of Ghana, 1968-69; Council of Univ. of Science and Technology, Kumasi, 1972. Darnforth Vis. Lectr, Assoc. Amer. Colls, 1969, 1970. Hon. LLD Greensboro Agric. and Techn. Coll., USA, 1958. Fellow, Ghana Acad. of Arts and Sciences. *Publications:* Human Geography of Eweland, 1946; Our Homeland—Book I: South-East Gold Coast, 1945; (Ed.) The Ewe News-Letter, 1945-46. *Recreations:* music, gardening, walking. *Address:* (Office) Tobacco House, Liberty Avenue, PO Box 5211, Accra, Ghana. *T:* 21111; (Home) 7 Ninth Avenue, Tesano, Accra, Ghana. *T:* 27180. *Clubs:* Royal Commonwealth Society (London); Accra (Ghana).

CHAPPELL, (Edwin) Philip, CBE 1976; Director, Morgan Grenfell & Co. Ltd, since 1964; a Vice-Chairman, Morgan Grenfell Holdings, since 1975; Director: Equity & Law Life Assurance; Fisons; International Computers; Guest Keen & Nettlefolds; Member London Board, Bank of New Zealand; *b* 12

June 1929; *s* of late Rev. C. R. Chappell; *m* 1962, Julia Clavering House, *d* of H. W. House, DSO, MC; one *s* three *d*. *Educ:* Marlborough Coll.; Christ Church, Oxford (MA). Joined Morgan Grenfell, 1954. Chairman: Nat. Ports Council, 1971-77; EDC for Food and Drink Manufacturing Industry, 1976-. Member: Council, Institute of Bankers, 1971; Business Educn Council, 1974; SITPRO Board, 1974-77. Governor of BBC, 1976-. *Address:* 22 Frognal Lane, NW3 7DT. *T:* 01-435 8627. *Club:* Oriental.

CHAPPELL, William; dancer, designer, producer; *b* Wolverhampton, 27 Sept. 1908; *s* of Archibald Chappell and Edith Eva Clara Blair-Staples. *Educ:* Chelsea School of Art. Studied dancing under Marie Rambert. First appearance on stage, 1929; toured Europe with Ida Rubinstein's company, working under Massine and Nijinska; danced in many ballets, London, 1929-34; joined Sadler's Wells Co., 1934, and has appeared there every season. Has designed scenery and costumes at Sadler's Wells, 1934-, and Covent Garden, 1947-, including Les Rendezvous, Les Patineurs, Giselle, Handel's Samson, and Frederick Ashton's Walk to the Paradise Garden; for many revues and London plays. Produced Lyric Revue, 1951, Globe Revue, 1952, High Spirits, Hippodrome, 1953, At the Lyric, 1953, Going to Town, St Martin's, 1954 (also arranging dances for many of these); An Evening with Beatrice Lillie, Globe, 1954 (asst prod.); Time Remembered, New, 1955; Moby Dick, Duke of York's, 1955 (with Orson Welles); The Buccaneer, Lyric, Hammersmith, 1955; Violins of St Jacques (also wrote libretto), Sadler's Wells; English Eccentrics; Love and a Bottle; Passion Flower Hotel; Travelling Light; Espresso Bongo; Living for Pleasure; Where's Charley?; appeared in and assisted Orson Wells with film The Trial; The Chalk Garden, Haymarket, 1971; Offenbach's Robinson Crusoe (1st English perf.), Camden Festival, 1973; Cockie, Vaudeville, 1973; Oh, Kay!, Westminster, 1974; National Tour, In Praise of Love, 1974; Fallen Angels, Gate Theatre, Dublin, 1975; Choreographed: Travesties, RSC Aldwych, 1974, NY, 1975; Bloomsbury, Phoenix, 1974; Directed, designed costumes and choreographed: Purcell's Fairy Queen, London Opera Centre, 1974; Donizetti's Torquato Tasso, Camden Festival, 1975; Lully's Alceste, London Opera Centre, 1975; A Moon for the Misbegotten, Dublin, 1976; The Rivals, Dublin, 1976. TV shows. Illustrator of several books. *Publications:* Studies in Ballet; Fonteyn. *Recreations:* walking, reading, cinema, painting. *Address:* 25 Rosenau Road, Battersea, SW11.

CHAPPLE, Frank Joseph; General Secretary, Electrical, Electronic, Telecommunication and Plumbing Union, since Sept. 1966; Member, General Council, TUC, since 1971; *b* Shoreditch, 1921; *m* ; two *s*. *Educ:* elementary school. Started as Apprentice Electrician; Member ETU, 1937-; Shop Steward and Branch Official; Member Exec. Council, 1958; Asst General Secretary, 1963-66. Member: National Exec. Cttee of Labour Party, 1965-71; Cttee of Inquiry into Shipping, 1967-; Royal Commn on Environmental Pollution, 1973-; Horserace Totalisator Bd, 1976-. *Recreation:* racing pigeons. *Address:* Electrical, Electronic, Telecommunications and Plumbing Union, Hayes Court, West Common Road, Bromley BR2 7AU.

CHAPPLE, Stanley; Director of Symphony and Opera, University of Washington, now Emeritus; *b* 29 Oct. 1900; *s* of Stanley Clements Chapple and Bessie Norman; *m* 1927, Barbara, *d* of late Edward Hilliard; no *c*. *Educ:* Central Foundation Sch., London. Began his musical education at the London Academy of Music at the age of 8, being successively student, professor, Vice-Principal, Principal until 1936; as a Conductor made début at the Queen's Hall, 1927, and has since conducted Symphony Orchestras in Berlin, Vienna, The Hague, Warsaw and Boston, St Louis, Washington, DC, and other American and Canadian cities. Assistant to Serge Koussevitzky at Berkshire Music Centre, 1940, 1941, 1942 and 1946; former conductor St Louis Philharmonic Orchestra and Chorus and Grand Opera Association. Hon MusDoc Colby Coll., 1947. *Address:* 18311 47th Place NE, Seattle, Washington 98155, USA.

CHAPUT DE SAINTONGE, Rev. Rolland Alfred Aimé, CMG 1953; President, Christian Audio-Visual Aid, Geneva, since 1973; *b* Montreal, Canada, 7 Jan. 1912; *s* of Alfred Edward and Hélène Jeté Chaput de Saintonge; *m* 1940, Barbara Watts; one *s* two *d*. *Educ:* Canada; USA; Syracuse Univ., NY (BA, MA); Geneva Univ. (D ès Sc. Pol.). Extra-Mural Lecturer in International Affairs: University College of the South-West, Exeter, University of Bristol, University College of Southampton, 1935-40; Staff Speaker, Min. of Information, South-West Region, 1940; served Army, 1940-46; Lieut-Col (DCLI); Asst Secretary, Control Office for Germany and Austria, 1946-48; Head of Government Structure Branch, CCG

and Liaison Officer to German Parliamentary Council, 1948-49; Head of German Information Dept, FO, 1949-58; UN High Commission for Refugees: Dep. Chief, Information and Public Relations Sect., 1960-64; Rep. in Senegal, 1964-66; Programme Support Officer, 1966-67; Chief, N and W Europe Section, 1967-68; Special Projects Officer, 1968-73. Ordained, Diocese of Quebec, 1975; admitted Community of Most Holy Sacrament, 1976. *Publications:* Disarmament in British Foreign Policy, 1935; British Foreign Policy Since the War, 1936; The Road to War and the Way Out, 1940; Public Administration in Germany, 1961. *Address:* 8 Minley Court, Somers Road, Reigate, Surrey.

CHARLEMONT, 12th Viscount *cr* 1665 (Ireland); **Richard William St George Caulfeild;** Baron Caulfeild of Charlemont, 1620 (Ireland); retired from Air Ministry, 1950; *b* 13 March 1887; 4th *s* of Henry St George Caulfeild (*d* 1943) and Jane (*d* 1924), *d* of William Goldsmith; *S* brother 1971; *m* 1914, Dorothy Laura (*d* 1961), *d* of late Frank Giles, ICS; two *d*. *Educ:* Schultz Private School, Bundaberg, Queensland. Malayan Govt Service, 1906-20; Straits Settlements Govt Service as Resident Engineer in charge construction Singapore Airport, 1931-37; Air Ministry, 1940-50; Resident Engineer, Gambia, Sierra Leone, Gold Coast, Nigeria, 1940-42; Liaison Officer, 8th and 9th US Army Air Force, 1942-45. USAAF Medal of Freedom with palm, 1945. *Recreations:* long past it. *Heir:* cousin Charles Wilberforce Caulfeild [*b* 10 March 1899; *m* 1930, Dorothy Jessie, *d* of late Albert A. Johnston]. *Address:* Lane End, Elmstead, Colchester, Essex. *T:* Wivenhoe 2826. *Club:* Royal Over-Seas League.

CHARLES, Anthony Harold, ERD; TD; MA Cantab; MB; FRCS; FRCOG; Consulting Obstetric and Gynæcological Surgeon, St George's Hospital; Consulting Surgeon, Samaritan Hospital for Women (St Mary's); Consulting Gynæcologist, Royal National Orthopædic Hospital; Hon. Gynæcologist, King Edward VII Hospital for Officers; Consulting Gynæcologist, Caterham and District Hospital; Consulting Surgeon, General Lying-in-Hospital; late Hon. Consultant in Obstetrics and Gynaecology Army; *b* 14 May 1908; 2nd *s* of H. P. Charles; *m* 1962, Rosemary Christine Hubert; three *d*. *Educ:* Dulwich; Gonville and Caius Coll., Cambridge. Examiner in Midwifery and Gynæcology: Univ. of Cambridge; Soc. of Apothecaries; RCOG; Univs of London, Hong Kong and Cairo. Past Mem., Board of Governors, St Mary's Hospital. Past President: Chelsea Clinical Soc.; Sect. of Obstetrics and Gynæcology, RSM. Late Vice-Dean, St George's Hospital Medical Sch.; late Resident Asst Surgeon and Hon. Asst Anæsthetist, St George's Hospital. Colonel AMS; late Hon. Colonel and OC, 308 (Co. of London) General Hospital, T&AVR. Hon. Surgeon to the Queen, 1957-59. Served 1939-45, Aldershot, Malta and Middle-East as Surgical Specialist; Officer-in-Charge, Surgical Division, 15 Scottish General Hospital and Gynæc. Adviser MEF. Pres., Alleyn Club. *Publications:* Women in Sport, in Armstrong and Tucker's Injuries in Sport, 1964; contributions since 1940 to Jl Obst. and Gyn., Postgrad. Med. Jl, Proc. Royal Soc. Med., Operative Surgery, BMJ. *Recreations:* golf, boxing (Middle-Weight, Cambridge *v* Oxford, 1930); Past President Rosslyn Park Football Club. *Address:* 90a Harley Street, W1. *T:* 01-935 4196; Gaywood Farm, Gay Street, Pulborough, Sussex. *Clubs:* Bath, MCC; Hawks (Cambridge).

CHARLES, Rt. Rev. Harold John; *see* St Asaph, Bishop of.

CHARLES, Jack; Director of Establishments, Greater London Council, since 1972; *b* 18 Jan. 1923; *o s* of late Frederick Walter Charles and of Alice Mary Charles; *m* 1959, Jean, *d* of late F. H. Braund, London; one *s* one *d*. *Educ:* County High Sch., Ilford. Air Min., 1939-42; RAF, 1942-46; Min. of Supply, 1947-59 (Private Sec. to Minister of Supply, 1952-54); War Office, 1959-60; UKAEA, 1960-68 (Authority Personnel Officer, 1965-68); Dep. Dir of Estabs, GLC, 1968-72. *Recreation:* gardening. *Address:* 74 Lake Rise, Romford, Essex. *T:* Romford 41464.

CHARLES, Sir John (Pendrill), KCVO 1975; MC 1945; Partner, Allen & Overy, since 1947; *b* 3 May 1914; *yr s* of late Dr Clifford Pendrill Charles and Gertrude Mary (*née* Young); *m* 1st, 1939, Mary Pamela Dudley (marr. diss.); 2nd, 1959, Winifred Marie Heath; two *d*. *Educ:* Tonbridge; Magdalene Coll., Cambridge (MA). Solicitor, 1938. Served War, 1939-45: 11th Regt (HAC) RHA; ME, Sicily and Italy. Steward, British Boxing Bd of Control, 1961-. *Recreations:* travel, fishing, sailing. *Address:* 3 Wilton Row, Belgrave Square, SW1. *T:* 01-235 5792. *Club:* White's.

CHARLES, William Travers; Fellow, Faculty of Law, Monash University, since 1976 (Special Lecturer, 1966-75); Judge of the High Court, Zambia, 1963-66; *b* Victoria, Australia, 10 Dec.

1908; *s* of William James Charles and Elizabeth Esther Charles (*née* Payne); *m* 1940, Helen Gibson Vale; one *s* one *d. Educ:* St Thomas Grammar Sch., Essendon, Victoria; University of Melbourne. Called to bar, Victoria, 1932; practised at bar, 1932-39. Served Australian Army Legal Service including Middle East, 1940-42 (Lieut-Col), seconded AAG (Discipline), AHQ Melbourne, 1942-46. Chief Magistrate and Legal Adviser, British Solomon Islands Protectorate, 1946-51; Judicial Commn, British Solomon Islands, 1951-53; Magistrate, Hong Kong, 1954-56; District Judge, Hong Kong, 1956-58; Judge of the High Court, Western Nigeria, 1958-63. *Recreations:* cricket, football, music, history. *Address:* 2 Burroughs Road, Balwyn, Vic 3103, Australia.

CHARLES-EDWARDS, Rt. Rev. Lewis Mervyn, MA, DD; *b* 6 April 1902; *s* of Dr Lewis Charles-Edwards and Lillian Hill; *m* 1933, Florence Edith Louise Barsley; one *s* one *d. Educ:* Shrewsbury School; Keble College, Oxford; Lichfield Theological College. Curate, Christ Church, Tunstall, 1925-28; St Paul, Burton on Trent, 1928-31; Pontesbury, 1931-33; Vicar, Marchington, 1933-37; Market Drayton, 1937-44; Newark on Trent, 1944-48; Rural Dean of Hodnet, 1938-44, of Newark, 1945-48; Vicar of St Martin in the Fields, London, WC2, 1948-56; Commissary to Bishop of Honduras, 1945-56; Chaplain to King George VI, 1950-52, to the Queen, 1952-56; Bishop of Worcester, 1956-70. Religious Adviser to Independent Television Authority, 1955-56. Chairman, Midland Region Religious Advisory Committee BBC, 1958-65. Member of Commission on Church and State, 1951. Chaplain and Sub-Prelate Order of St John of Jerusalem, 1965. Select Preacher, University of Cambridge, 1949; Oxford, 1964. *Publication:* Saints Alive!, 1953. *Address:* The Pant, Old Churchstoke, Montgomery, Powys SY15 6EL. *T:* Churchstoke 306. *Club:* Athenæum.

CHARLESTON, Robert Jesse; Keeper of the Department of Ceramics, Victoria and Albert Museum, 1963-76; *b* 3 April 1916; *s* of Sidney James Charleston, Lektor, Stockholms Högskola; *m* 1941, Joan Randle; one *s* one *d. Educ:* Berkhamsted Sch., Herts; New College, Oxford. Army (Major, RAPC), 1940-46; Asst, Bristol Museum, 1947; Asst Keeper, Victoria and Albert Museum, 1948; Deputy Keeper, 1959. *Publications:* Roman Pottery, 1959; (ed) English Porcelain, 1745-1850, 1965; (ed) World Ceramics, 1968; (with J. G. Ayers) The James A. de Rothschild Collection: Meissen and Oriental Porcelain, 1971; numerous articles and reviews in The Connoisseur, Jl of Glass Studies, Burlington Magazine, etc. *Recreations:* foreign travel, music. *Address:* 1 Denbigh Gardens, Richmond, Surrey. *T:* 01-940 3592.

CHARLESWORTH, Stanley; National Secretary, National Council of YMCAs, since 1975; *b* 20 March 1920; *s* of Ernest and Amy Charlesworth; *m* 1942, Vera Bridge; three *d . Educ:* Ashton under Lyne Grammar Sch.; Manchester Coll. of Commerce. YMCA: Area Sec., Community Services, 1943-52, Dep. Sec., 1952-57; Asst Regional Sec., NW Region, 1957-67, Regional Sec., 1967-75. *Recreations:* sailing, golf, walking, gardening. *Address:* National Council of YMCAs, 640 Forest Road, Walthamstow, E17 3DZ. *T:* 01-520 5599. *Club:* YMCA (Manchester).

CHARLISH, Dennis Norman; Under-Secretary and Resident Chairman, Civil Service Selection Board, since 1975; *b* 24 May 1918; *s* of Norman Charlish and Edith (*née* Cherriman); *m* 1941, Margaret Trevor, *o d* of William Trevor and Margaret Ann Williams, Manchester; one *d. Educ:* Brighton Grammar Sch.; London Sch. of Economics. Rosebery Schol., 1947; BSc (Econ) 1st class hons., 1951. Joined Civil Service as Tax Officer, Inland Revenue, 1936; Exec. Officer, Dept of Overseas Trade, 1937; Dep. Armament Supply Officer, Admty, 1941; Principal, BoT, 1949; Asst Secretary, 1959; Imperial Defence Coll., 1963; Under-Sec., BoT, 1967-69; Min. of Technology, 1969-70; Head of Establishment (Personnel) Division, DTI, 1971-74, Dept of Industry, 1974-75. *Address:* 28 Multon Road, SW18.

CHARLTON, Bobby; see Charlton, Robert.

CHARLTON, (Frederick) Noel, CB 1961; CBE 1946; Treasury Solicitor's Department; *b* 4 Dec. 1906; *s* of late Frederick William Charlton and Marian Charlton; *m* 1932, Maud Helen Rudgard; no *c. Educ:* Rugby School; Hertford Coll., Oxford Univ. (MA). Admitted a Solicitor, 1932; in private practice as Solicitor in London, 1932-39. War Service, 1939-46 (attained rank of Colonel, Gen. List). Joined Treasury Solicitor's Dept, 1946; Principal Asst Solicitor (Litigation), Treasury Solicitor's Dept, 1956-71; Sec., Lord Chancellor's Cttee on Defamation, 1971-74; Dept of Energy, 1975-77. Chairman, Coulsdon and Purley UDC, 1953-54 and 1964-65; Hon. Alderman, London

Borough of Croydon. Bronze Star (USA), 1945. *Recreations:* golf, travel. *Address:* Windyridge, 11 Hillcroft Avenue, Purley, Surrey. *T:* 01-660 2802. *Club:* Junior Carlton.
See also T. A. G. Charlton.

CHARLTON, George; artist; Member of Staff of Slade School of Art, 1919-62; examiner for General School Examinations, University of London since 1931 and Associated Examining Board since 1959; *b* 1899; *s* of James William Charlton, London; *m* 1929, Daphne, *d* of Conrad Gribble, MICE, Weybridge. Student, Slade School, 1914, at age of fifteen (Slade and Robert Ross Scholarships). Served European War, 1917-19. Senior Lecturer in charge of Slade School, 1948-49; examiner for Board of Education Art Examinations, 1932-45, 1949-50-51; member of staff of Willesden School of Art, 1949-59; exhibitor at New English Art Club from 1915, member 1925-45, 1950-, Hon. Treasurer, 1958; works purchased by Tate Gallery, Contemporary Art Society and Bradford Art Gallery; exhibitor at London, provincial and overseas galleries. Formerly Governor: Camberwell School of Art; Trent Park Coll.; Farnham School of Art, 1950-60. *Publications:* Illustration for Wolff's Anatomy for Artists; for T. F. Powys' Mr Weston's Good Wine, 1st edn; for Richard Hughes' The Spider's Palace; articles on Prof. Henry Tonks and on Prof. Frederick Brown in Dictionary of National Biography. *Address:* 40 New End Square, Hampstead, NW3.

CHARLTON, Graham; see Charlton, T. A. G.

CHARLTON, Prof. Kenneth; Professor of History of Education and Head of Department of Education, King's College, University of London, since 1972; *b* 11 July 1925; 2nd *s* of late George and Lottie Charlton; *m* 1953, Maud Tulloch Brown, *d* of late P. R. Brown, MBE and M. B. Brown; one *s* one *d. Educ:* City Grammar Sch., Chester; Univ. of Glasgow. MA 1949, MEd 1953, Glasgow. RNVR, 1943-46. History Master, Dalziel High Sch., Motherwell, and Uddingston Grammar Sch., 1950-54; Lectr in Educn, UC N Staffs, 1954-64; Sen. Lectr in Educn, Keele Univ., 1964-66; Prof. of History and Philosophy of Educn, Birmingham Univ., 1966-72. *Publications:* Recent Historical Fiction for Children, 1960, 2nd edn 1969; Education in Renaissance England, 1965; contrib. Educnl Rev., Brit. Jl Educnl Psych., Year Bk of Educn, Jl Hist. of Ideas, Brit. Jl Educnl Studies, Internat. Rev. of Educn, Trans Hist. Soc. Lancs and Cheshire, Irish Hist. Studies, Northern Hist. *Recreations:* gardening, listening to music. *Address:* King's College, Strand, WC2R 2LS.

CHARLTON, Robert, (Bobby Charlton), CBE 1974 (OBE 1969); *b* 11 Oct. 1937; *s* of Robert and Elizabeth Charlton; *m* 1961, Norma; two *d. Educ:* Bedlington Grammar Sch., Northumberland. Professional Footballer with Manchester United, 1954-73, for whom he played 751 games and scored 245 goals; FA Cup Winners Medal, 1963; FA Championship Medals, 1956-57, 1964-65 and 1966-67; World Cup Winners Medal (International), 1966; European Cup Winners medal, 1968. 100th England cap, 21 April 1970; 106 appearances for England, 1957-73. Manager, Preston North End, 1973-75. *Publications:* My Soccer Life, 1965; Forward for England, 1967; This Game of Soccer, 1967; Book of European Football, Books 1-4, 1969-72. *Recreation:* golf. *Address:* Garthollerton, Chelford Road, Ollerton, near Knutsford, Cheshire.

CHARLTON, (Thomas Alfred) Graham, CB 1970; Secretary, Trade Marks, Patents and Design Federation, since 1973; *b* 29 Aug. 1913; 3rd *s* of late Frederick William and Marian Charlton; *m* 1940, Margaret Ethel, *yr d* of A. E. Furst; three *d. Educ:* Rugby School; Corpus Christi Coll., Cambridge. Asst Principal, War Office, 1936; Asst Private Secretary to Secretary of State for War, 1937-39; Principal, 1939; Cabinet Office, 1947-49; Asst Secretary, 1949; International Staff, NATO, 1950-52; War Office, later MoD, 1952-73; Asst Under-Sec. of State, 1960-73. Coronation Medal, 1953. *Recreations:* golf, gardening. *Address:* Victoria House, Elm Road, Penn, Bucks HP10 8LQ. *T:* Penn 3195. *Club:* Anglo-Belgian.
W04624AL0070200714419, 81 Linden Avenue, Rochester, NY 14610, USA. *See also Frederick Noel Charlton.*

CHARLTON, Prof. Thomas Malcolm; Professor of Engineering, University of Aberdeen, since 1970; *b* 1 Sept. 1923; *s* of William Charlton and Emily May Charlton (*née* Wallbank); *m* 1950, Valerie McCulloch; two *s* (and one *s* decd). *Educ:* Doncaster Grammar Sch.; UC Nottingham. BSc (Eng) London, MA Cantab. Junior Scientific Officer, Min. of Aircraft Prodn, TRE, Malvern, 1943-46; Asst Engr, Merz & McLellan, Newcastle upon Tyne, 1946-54; Univ. Lectr in Engrg, Cambridge, 1954-63; Fellow, Sidney Sussex Coll., 1959-63; Prof. of Civil Engrg, Queen's Univ., Belfast, 1963-70; Dean, Faculty of Applied

Science, QUB, 1967-70. Mem., Adv. Council UDR, 1969-71. For. Mem., Finnish Acad. of Technical Sciences, 1967. FRSE 1973. *Publications:* Model Analysis of Structures, 1954, new edn 1966; Energy Principles in Applied Statics, 1959; Analysis of Statically-indeterminate Frameworks, 1961; Principles of Structural Analysis, 1969; Energy Principles in Theory of Structures, 1973; contrib. The Works of I. K. Brunel, 1976; numerous papers and articles in learned jls. *Recreations:* music, gardening, golf. *Address:* 16 Anderson Drive, Aberdeen, AB1 6TY; University of Aberdeen, Marischal College, Aberdeen AB9 1AS. *T:* Aberdeen 37918. *Club:* Royal Northern (Aberdeen).

CHARLTON, Sir William Arthur, Kt 1946; DSC; retired as General Marine Superintendent at New York, Furness Withy & Co. SS Lines, 1960; *b* 25 Feb. 1893; *s* of William and Augusta Pauline Charlton; *m* 1919, Eleanor Elcoat; two *s*. *Educ:* Blyth; Newcastle on Tyne. Master Mariner. DSC for service in N Africa landings, 1943. Younger Brother, Trinity House; Liveryman Hon. Company of Master Mariners; Fellow Royal Commonwealth Society. *Address:* Apartment 419, 81 Linden Avenue, Rochester, NY 14610, USA.

CHARNLEY, Sir John, Kt 1977; CBE 1970; DSc; FRCS; FACS; FRS 1975; Professor of Orthopædic Surgery, Manchester University, 1972-76, now Emeritus; Consultant Orthopædic Surgeon and Director of Centre for Hip Surgery, Wrightington Hospital, near Wigan, Lancs; *b* 29 Aug. 1911; *m* 1957, Jill Margaret (*née* Heaver); one *s* one *d*. *Educ:* Bury Grammar Sch., Lancs. BSc 1932; MB ChB (Manch.) 1935; FRCS 1936; DSc 1964. Hon. Cons. Orthopædic Surgeon, Manchester Royal Infirmary, 1947. Hon. Lecturer in Clinical Orthopædics, Manchester Univ., 1959; Hon. Lecturer in Mechanical Engineering, 1966, Inst. of Science and Technology, Manchester Univ. Fellow of British Orthopædic Assoc.; Hon. Member: Amer. Acad. of Orthopædic Surgeons; American, French, Belgian, Swiss, Brazilian, and French-Canadian Orthopædic Assocs; S African Medical Assoc. Gold Medal, Soc. of Apothecaries, 1971; Gairdner Foundn Internat. Award, 1973; Olof Af Acrel Medal, Swedish Surgical Soc., 1969; Cameron Prize, Univ. of Edinburgh, 1974; Albert Lasker Medical Research Award, 1974; Lister Medal, RCS, 1975. Hon. MD, Univ. of Liverpool, 1975. Freedom of Co. Borough of Bury, 1974. *Publications:* Compression Arthrodesis, 1953; The Closed Treatment of Common Fractures, 1950 (German trans., 1968); Acrylic Cement in Orthopædic Surgery, 1970. *Recreations:* other than surgery, none. *Address:* Birchwood, Moss Lane, Mere, Knutsford, Cheshire. *T:* Knutsford 2267.

CHARNLEY, William John, CB 1973; MEng, CEng, FRAeS, FRInstNav; idc; Controller, R&D Establishments and Research, Ministry of Defence, since 1977; *b* 4 Sept. 1922; *s* of George and Catherine Charnley; *m* 1945, Mary Paden; one *s* one *d*. *Educ:* Oulton High Sch., Liverpool; Liverpool Univ. MEng 1945. Aerodynamics Dept, RAE Farnborough, 1943-55; Supt. Blind Landing Experimental Unit, 1955-61; Imperial Defence Coll., 1962; Head of Instruments and Electrical Engineering Dept, 1963-65, Head of Weapons Dept, 1965-68, RAE Farnborough; Head of Research Planning, 1968-69, Dep. Controller, Guided Weapons, Min. of Technology, later MoD, 1969-72; Controller, Guided Weapons and Electronics, MoD (PE), 1972-73; Chief Scientist (RAF), 1973-77, and Dep. Controller, R&D Establishments and Res. C, MoD, 1975-77. *Publications:* papers on subjects in aerodynamics, aircraft all weather operation, aircraft navigation. *Address:* Kirkstones, Brackendale Close, Camberley, Surrey. *T:* Camberley 22547.

CHARNOCK, Henry, FRS 1976; Professor of Physical Oceanography, University of Southampton, 1966-71 and since 1978; *b* 25 Dec. 1920; *s* of Henry Charnock and Mary Gray McLeod; *m* 1946, Eva Mary Dickinson; one *s* two *d*. *Educ:* Queen Elizabeth's Grammar Sch., Municipal Techn. Coll., Blackburn; Imperial Coll., London. Staff, Nat. Inst. of Oceanography, 1949-58 and 1959-66; Reader in Physical Oceanography, Imperial Coll., 1958-59; Dir, Inst. of Oceanographic Scis (formerly Nat. Inst. of Oceanography), 1971-78. Pres., Internat. Union of Geodesy and Geophysics, 1971-75. *Publications:* papers in meteorological and oceanographic jls. *Address:* Wildcroft, Gasden Lane, Witley, Surrey. *T:* Wormley 2813.

CHARRINGTON, John Arthur Pepys; late President, Bass Charrington Ltd (formerly Chairman Charrington United Breweries Ltd from formation; previously Chairman Charrington & Co. Ltd); *b* 17 Feb. 1905; *s* of Arthur Finch Charrington and Dorothea Lethbridge; *m* 1st, Barbara Haliburton Cunard (marr. diss); three *s* two *d*; 2nd, Daphne Coleman. *Educ:* Eton; New College, Oxford. *Address:*

Netherton House, Andover, Hampshire. *T:* Linkenholt 230. *Club:* Bath.

CHARTERIS, family name of **Earl of Wemyss.**

CHARTERIS, Leslie; FRSA; author; *b* 1907; *m* 1st, Pauline Schishkin (divorced, 1937); one *d*; 2nd, Barbara Meyer (divorced, 1941); 3rd, Elizabeth Bryant Borst (divorced, 1951); 4th, Audrey Long. *Educ:* Rossall; Cambridge Univ. Many years of entertaining, but usually unprofitable, travel and adventure, and can still be had. After one or two false starts created character of "The Saint" (trans. into 15 languages besides those of films, radio, television, and the comic strip). *Publications:* Meet the Tiger, 1928; Enter the Saint; The Last Hero; Knight Templar; Featuring the Saint; Alias the Saint; She was a Lady (filmed 1938 as The Saint Strikes Back); The Holy Terror (filmed 1939 as The Saint in London); Getaway; Once More the Saint; The Brighter Buccaneer; The Misfortunes of Mr Teal; Boodle; The Saint Goes On; The Saint in New York (filmed 1938); Saint Overboard, 1936; The Ace of Knaves, 1937; Thieves Picnic, 1937; (trans., with introd.) Juan Belmonte, Killer of Bulls: The Autobiography of a Matador, 1937; Prelude for War, 1938; Follow the Saint, 1938; The Happy Highwayman, 1939; The First Saint Omnibus, 1939; The Saint in Miami, 1941; The Saint Goes West, 1942; The Saint Steps In, 1944; The Saint on Guard, 1945; The Saint Sees it Through, 1946; Call for the Saint, 1948; Saint Errant, 1948; The Second Saint Omnibus, 1952; The Saint on the Spanish Main, 1955; The Saint around the World, 1957; Thanks to the Saint, 1958; Señor Saint, 1959; The Saint to the Rescue, 1961; Trust the Saint, 1962; The Saint in the Sun, 1964; Vendetta for the Saint, 1965 (filmed 1968); The Saint on TV, 1968; The Saint Returns, 1969; The Saint and the Fiction Makers, 1969; The Saint Abroad, 1970; The Saint in Pursuit, 1971; The Saint and the People Importers, 1971; Paleneo, 1972; Saints Alive, 1974; Catch the Saint, 1975; The Saint and the Hapsburg Necklace, 1976; Send for the Saint, 1977; Supervising Editor of the Saint Magazine, 1953-67; columnist, Gourmet Magazine, 1966-68; concurrently has worked as special correspondent and Hollywood scenarist; contributor to leading English and American magazines and newspapers. *Recreations:* eating, drinking, horseracing, sailing, fishing, and loafing. *Address:* 8 Southampton Row, WC1. *Clubs:* Savage; Mensa, Yacht Club de Cannes.

CHARTERIS, Rt. Hon. Sir Martin (Michael Charles), PC 1972; GCB 1977 (KCB 1972; CB 1958); GCVO 1976 (KCVO 1962; MVO 1953); OBE 1946; Provost of Eton, since 1977; *b* 7 Sept. 1913; 2nd *s* of Hugo Francis, Lord Elcho (killed in action, 1916); *g s* of 11th Earl of Wemyss; *m* 1944, Hon. Mary Gay Hobart Margesson, *yr d* of 1st Viscount Margesson, PC, MC; two *s* one *d*. *Educ:* Eton; RMC Sandhurst. Lieut KRRC, 1936; served War of 1939-45; Lieut-Colonel, 1944. Private Secretary to Princess Elizabeth, 1950-52; Asst Private Secretary to the Queen, 1952-72; Private Secretary to the Queen and Keeper of HM's Archives, 1972-77. *Recreation:* sculpting. *Address:* Provost's Lodge, Eton College, Windsor, Berks. *T:* Windsor 66304. *Clubs:* Travellers', White's.

CHASE, Anya Seton; *see* Seton, A.

CHASE, Stuart; author; social scientist; *b* Somersworth, New Hampshire, USA, 8 March 1888; *s* of Harvey Stuart and Aaronette Rowe Chase; *m* 1st, 1914, Margaret Hatfield (divorced, 1929); one *s* one *d*; 2nd, 1930, Marian Tyler. *Educ:* Massachusetts Inst. of Technology; Harvard Univ. SB cum laude, 1910; seven years in accounting work; CPA degree from Massachusetts, 1916; four years in Government Service, ending 1921; since 1921 has been chiefly engaged in economic research and writing books and articles; some public lecturing; consulting work for government agencies, business organizations, UNESCO, etc. Member National Inst. of Arts and Letters, Phi Beta Kappa; LittD American Univ., 1949; DHL Emerson Coll., Boston, 1970; DHL New Haven Univ., 1974. *Publications:* The Tragedy of Waste, 1925; Your Money's Worth (with F. J. Schlink), 1927; Men and Machines, 1929; Prosperity: Fact or Myth?, 1929; The Nemesis of American Business, 1931; Mexico, 1931; A New Deal, 1932; The Economy of Abundance, 1934; Government in Business, 1935; Rich Land, Poor Land, 1936; The Tyranny of Words, 1938; The New Western Front, 1939; Idle Money, Idle Men, 1940; A Primer of Economics, 1941; The Road We Are Travelling, 1942; Goals for America, 1942; Where's the Money Coming From?, 1943; Democracy under Pressure, 1945; Men at Work, 1945; Tomorrow's Trade, 1945; For This We Fought, 1946; The Proper Study of Mankind, 1948 (revised, 1956); Roads to Agreement, 1951; Power of Words, 1954; Guides to Straight Thinking, 1956; Some Things Worth Knowing, 1958; Live and Let Live, 1960; American Credos, 1962; Money to Grow On, 1964; The Most Probable World,

1968; Danger-Men Talking, 1969; and many magazine articles for Harpers, Atlantic, The Saturday Review, etc. *Recreations:* tennis, ski-ing, sketching. *Address:* Georgetown, Conn 06829, USA. *Club:* Harvard (New York).

CHASTENET de CASTAING, Jacques, CBE 1938; Croix de Guerre, 1916; Grand Officier de la Légion d'Honneur, 1968; Grand Croix, Ordre du mérite, 1974; LLD Paris; historian and journalist; member of Académie française, 1956, and of Académie des Sciences morales et politiques, 1947; *b* 20 April 1893; *s* of G. Chastenet de Castaing, a French Senator; *m* 1919, Germaine Saladin; two *s. Educ:* Université de Paris. Served European War, 1914-19; Liaison officer with the American EF, 1918; French Diplomatic Service, 1919; Attaché, 1919; General Secretary, Rhineland inter-allied High Commission, 1920; Secrétaire d'Ambassade, 1921; diplomatic correspondent, L'Opinion, 1926; Editor of Le Temps, 1931; Major, French Military Mission in Egypt, 1945. *Publications:* Du Sénat, 1919; William Pitt, 1941; Godoy, 1943; Wellington, 1945; Vingt Ans d'histoire diplomatique (1920-1940), 1945; Le Siècle de Victoria, 1947; Poincaré, 1948; La France de M. Fallieres, 1949; Histoire de la IIIe République, 7 Vols, 1952-62; Elizabeth the 1st, 1953; Winston Churchill et l'Angleterre du XX Siècle, 1956; Vie quotidienne au début du règne de Victoria, 1961; L'Angleterre d'aujourd'hui, 1965; En avant vers l'Ouest, 1967; Léon Gambetta, 1968; De Pétain à de Gaulle, 1970; Cent ans de République (9 vols), 1970; Quatre Fois Vingt Ans, 1974; Une Epoque de Contestation, 1976; contribs to l'Opinion, le Figaro, la Revue de Paris, le Temps, Paris-Presse, L'Aurore, La Revue des Deux-Mondes, etc. *Address:* 14 rue d'Aumale, Paris 9e; Château de Carles, Saillans, Gironde, France. *Club:* L'Union (Paris).

CHATAWAY, Rt. Hon. Christopher John, PC 1970; Managing Director, Orion Bank, since 1974; Director: Fisons, since 1974; British Electric Traction Company, since 1974; Allied Investments, since 1974; Dorchester Hotel, since 1976; *b* 31 Jan. 1931; *m* 1st, 1959, Anna Lett (marr. diss. 1975); two *s* one *d*; 2nd, 1976, Carola Walker. *Educ:* Sherborne Sch.; Magdalen Coll., Oxford. Hons. Degree, PPE. President OUAC, 1952; rep. Great Britain, Olympic Games, 1952 and 1956; briefly held world 5,000 metres record in 1954. Junior Exec. Arthur Guinness Son & Co., 1953-55; Staff Reporter, Independent Television News, 1955-56; Current Affairs Commentator for BBC Television, 1956-59. Elected for N Lewisham to LCC, 1958-61; MP (C): Lewisham North, 1959-66; Chichester, May 1969-Sept. 1974; PPS to Minister of Power, 1961-62; Joint Parly Under-Secretary of State, Dept of Education and Science, 1962-64; Minister of Posts and Telecommunications, 1970-72; Minister for Industrial Develt, DTI, 1972-74. Treasurer, Nat. Cttee for Electoral Reform, 1976-; Treasurer, Action in Distress, 1976-. Alderman, GLC, 1967-70; Leader Educn Cttee, ILEA, 1967-69. Nansen Medal, 1960. *Publication:* (with Philip Goodhart) War Without Weapons, 1968. *Address:* 40 Addison Road, W14.

CHATER, Dr Anthony Philip John; Editor, Morning Star, since 1974; *b* 21 Dec. 1929; parents both shoe factory workers; *m* 1954, Janice (*née* Smith); three *s. Educ:* Northampton Grammar Sch. for Boys; Queen Mary Coll., London. BSc (1st cl. hons Chem.) 1951, PhD (Phys.Chem.) 1954. Fellow in Biochem., Ottawa Exper. Farm, 1954-56; studied biochem. at Brussels Univ., 1956-57; Teacher, Northampton Techn. High Sch., 1957-59; Teacher, Blyth Grammar Sch., Norwich, 1959-60; Lectr, subseq. Sen. Lectr in Phys. Chem., Luton Coll. of Technology, 1960-69; Head of Press and Publicity of Communist Party, 1969-74; Nat. Chm. of Communist Party, 1967-69. Contested (Com) Luton, Nov. 1963, 1964, 1966, 1970. Mem. Presidential Cttee, World Peace Council, 1969-. *Publications:* Race Relations in Britain, 1966; numerous articles. *Recreations:* walking, swimming, music, camping. *Address:* 8 Katherine Drive, Dunstable, Beds. *T:* Dunstable 64835.

CHATER, Maj.-Gen. Arthur Reginald, CB 1941; CVO 1966; DSO 1918; OBE 1931; *b* 7 Feb. 1896; *s* of Thomas Addison Chater and Gertrude Lockyer Peel; *m* 1954, Diana, *o d* of late Edward Charles Daubeny, and *widow* of Maj.-Gen. Archibald Maxwell Craig. *Educ:* Aldenham. Entered Royal Marines as 2nd Lieut, 1913; served with RM Brigade in Flanders, 1914 (wounded at Antwerp); Gallipoli, 1915 (despatches, French Croix de Guerre); Grand Fleet, 1916-17; was Adjt of RM Bn which landed from HMS Vindictive at Zeebrugge on 23 April 1918 (DSO, Bt Major); served in Egyptian Army, 1921-25, and Sudan Defence Forces, 1925-31; commanded Sudan Camel Corps, 1927-30; commanded Military Operations in Kordofan, 1929-30 (despatches); Senior RM Officer, East Indies Station, 1931-33; Home Fleet, 1935-36; commanded Somaliland Camel Corps, 1937-40; commanded defence of British Somaliland,

1940 (despatches, CB); Military Governor and comd Troops, British Somaliland, 1941-43; comd Portsmouth Div. Royal Marines, 1943-44; Director of Combined Operations, India and SE Asia, 1944-45; MGGS, 1945-46, comd Chatham Group, Royal Marines, 1946-48; retired pay, 1948. One of HM's Body Guard of Hon. Corps of Gentlemen-at-Arms, 1949-66 and Harbinger, 1952-66; Col Comdt Somaliland Scouts, 1948-58. Member Berkshire CC, 1955-61. *Address:* Copford Place, Copford, near Colchester, Essex. *T:* Colchester 210042. *Club:* Naval and Military.

CHATER, Nancy, CBE 1974; Headmistress, Stanley Park Comprehensive School, Liverpool, 1964-75, retired; *b* 18 July 1915; *d* of William John and Ellen Chater. *Educ:* Northampton Sch. for Girls; Girton Coll., Cambridge (Math. Schol., Bell Exhibr, MA); Cambridge Trng Coll. for Women (CertifEd). Asst Mistress, Huddersfield College Grammar Sch. for Boys, 1940-42; Asst Mistress, Fairfield High Sch. for Girls, Manchester, 1942-45; Sen. Maths Mistress, Thistley Hough High Sch., Stoke-on-Trent, 1945-49; Sen. Lectr, Newland Park Trng Coll. for Teachers, 1949-55; Dep. Head, Whitley Abbey Comprehensive Sch., Coventry, 1955-63. *Publications:* contrib. Math. Gazette. *Address:* c/o Stanley Park Comprehensive School, Priory Road, Liverpool L4 2SL. *T:* 051-263 5665. *Clubs:* Soroptomist International, Business and Professional Women's.

CHATFIELD, family name of **Baron Chatfield.**

CHATFIELD, 2nd Baron *cr* 1937, of Ditchling; **Ernle David Lewis Chatfield;** *b* 2 Jan. 1917; *s* of 1st Baron Chatfield, PC, GCB, OM, KCMG, CVO (Admiral of the Fleet Lord Chatfield), and Lillian Emma St John Matthews (*d* 1977); *S* father, 1967; *m* 1969, (Felicia Mary) Elizabeth, *d* of late Dr John Roderick Bulman, Hereford. *Educ:* RNC Dartmouth; Trinity Coll., Cambridge. ADC to Governor-General of Canada, 1940-44. *Heir:* none. *Address:* RR2, Williamstown, Ontario, Canada.

CHATT, Prof. Joseph, ScD; FRS 1961; Director, Research Unit of Nitrogen Fixation, ARC, since 1963 (in Sussex since 1964); Professor of Chemistry, University of Sussex, since 1964; *b* 6 Nov. 1914; *e s* of Joseph and M. Elsie Chatt; *m* 1947, Ethel, *y d* of Hugh Williams, St Helens, Lancs; one *s* one *d. Educ:* Nelson Sch., Wigton, Cumberland; Emmanuel Coll., Cambridge. PhD 1940; ScD 1956. Research Chemist, Woolwich Arsenal, 1941-42; Dep. Chief Chemist, later Chief Chemist, Peter Spence & Sons Ltd, Widnes, 1942-46; ICI Research Fellow, Imperial Coll., London, 1946-47; Head of Inorganic Chemistry Dept, Butterwick, later Akers, Research Laboratories, ICI Ltd, 1947-60; Group Manager, Research Dept, Heavy Organic Chemicals Div., ICI Ltd, 1961-62; Distinguished Visiting Prof. of Chemistry, Pennsylvania State Univ., 1960; Visiting Prof. of Chemistry, Yale Univ., 1963; Prof. of Inorganic Chemistry, QMC, London Univ., 1964; Royal Society Leverhulme Visiting Prof., Univ. of Rajasthan, India, 1966-67; Vis. Prof., Univ. of S Carolina, 1968. Mem. Council, Royal Soc., 1975-; Chemical Society: Mem. Council, 1952-55, 1974-76; Hon. Sec., 1956-62; Vice-Pres., 1962-65, 1972-74; Pres. Dalton Div., 1972-74; Organometallic Chem. Award, 1970; Member: Chemical Council, 1958-60; Commn on Nomenclature of Inorganic Chemistry, Internat. Union of Pure and Applied Chemistry, 1959-, Hon-Sec., 1959-63; Chm., 1976-; ARC Adv. Cttee on Plants and Soils, 1964-67; national and internat. cttees concerned with chemistry, incl. Parly and Scientific Cttee. Lectures: Tilden, 1961-62; Liversidge, 1971-72; Debye, Cornell, 1975; Nyholm, 1976-77; Arthur D. Little, MIT, 1977. Amer. Chem. Soc. Award for dist. service to Inorganic Chemistry, 1971; Chugaev Commem. Dipl. and Medal, Kurnakov Inst. of Gen. and Inorganic Chemistry, Soviet Acad. of Sciences, 1976. Hon. DSc East Anglia, 1974. *Publications:* scientific papers, mainly in Jl Chem. Soc. *Recreations:* numismatics, photography. *Address:* 28 Tongdean Avenue, Hove, East Sussex BN3 6TN. *T:* Brighton 554377.

CHATTEN, Harold Raymond Percy, CB 1975; FRINA, RCNC; Chief Executive, Royal Dockyards, Ministry of Defence, since Sept. 1975. Production Manager, HM Dockyard, Chatham, 1967-70; General Manager, HM Dockyard, Rosyth, Fife, 1970-75. MA. *Address:* Ministry of Defence (Naval), Carpenter House, Broad Quay, Bath BA1 5AB. *T:* Bath 28391, ext. 285.

CHATTERJEE, Dr Satya Saran, OBE 1971; JP; FRCP, FRCPE; Consultant Chest Physician and Physician in Charge, Department of Respiratory Physiology, Wythenshawe Hospital, Manchester, since 1959; Chairman, Overseas Doctors Association; *b* 16 July 1922; *m* 1948, Enid May (*née* Adlington); one *s* two *d. Educ:* India, UK, Sweden and USA. MB, BS; FCCP (USA). Asst Lectr, Dept of Medicine, Albany Med. Coll. Hosp., NY, 1953-54; Med. Registrar, Sen. Registrar, Dept of

Thoracic Medicine, Wythenshawe Hosp., Manchester, 1954-59. Chm., NW Conciliation Cttee, Race Relations Board, 1972-77; Mem., Standing Adv. Council on Race Relations, 1977-. President: Rotary Club, Wythenshawe, 1975-76; Indian Assoc., Manchester, 1962-71. *Publications:* research papers in various projects related to cardio/pulmonary disorders. *Address:* March, 20 Macclesfield Road, Wilmslow, Cheshire.

CHAU, Hon. Sir Sik-Nin, Kt 1960; CBE 1950; JP 1940; Chairman and General Manager, Hong Kong Chinese Bank Ltd; Chairman or Director of numerous other companies; President, Firecrackers and Fireworks Co. Ltd (Taiwan); State Trading Corporation (Far East) Ltd; *b* 13 April 1903; *s* of late Cheuk-Fan Chau, 1 Hing Hong Road, Hong Kong; *m* 1927, Ida Hing-Kwai, *d* of late Lau Siu-Cheuk; two *s. Educ:* St Stephen's Coll., Hong Kong; Hong Kong Univ.; London Univ.; Vienna State Univ. MB, BS, Hong Kong, 1923; DLO, Eng., 1925; DOMS 1926. LLD (Hon.), Hong Kong 1961. Member Medical Board, Hong Kong, 1935-41; Mem. Urban Council, 1936-41; Chm. Po Leung Kuk, 1940-41; MLC, Hong Kong, 1946-59; MEC, 1947-62. Dep. Chm., Subsid. British Commonwealth Parliamentary Assoc., Hong Kong, 1953-59. Chief Delegate of Hong Kong to ECAFE Conference in India, 1948, in Australia, 1949; Chairman ECAFE Conference in Hong Kong, 1955; Leader, Hong Kong Govt Trade Mission to Common Market countries, 1963; Asian Fair, Bangkok, 1967; first Trade Mission to USA, 1970. Fellow, Internat. Academy of Management; Pres. Indo-Pacific Cttee, 1964-67; Chairman: Hong Kong Trade Develt Council, 1966-70; Hong Kong Management Assoc., 1961-69; Fedn of Hong Kong Inds, 1959-66; Cttee for Expo '70, 1969-70; United Coll., Chinese Univ. of Hong Kong, 1959-61; Hong Kong Productivity Council, 1970-73. President, Japan Soc. of Hong Kong; Mem., Textiles Adv. Bd, 1962-74; Foreign Corresp. Nat. Ind. Conf. Bd Inc.; Member: Advisory Board to Lingnan Inst. of Business Administration; British Universities Selection Cttee, 1945-64; Council and Court of University of Hong Kong, 1945-64; Senior Member Board of Education Hong Kong, 1946-60; Chairman Hong Kong Model Housing Society; Vice-President, Hong Kong Anti-Tuberculosis Assoc.; Hon. Steward Hong Kong Jockey Club, 1974 (Steward 1946-74). Hon. President or Vice-President of numerous Assocs; Hon. Adviser of Chinese General Chamber of Commerce; Permanent Dir Tung Wah Hospital Advisory Board. Coronation Medal, 1937; Defence Medal, 1945; Coronation Medal, 1953; granted permanent title of Honourable by the Queen, 1962. *Address:* IL 3547 Hatton Road, Hong Kong. *T:* 433695.

CHAUNCY, Major Frederick Charles Leslie, CBE 1958 (OBE 1953); *b* 22 Dec. 1904; *o s* of late Col C. H. K. Chauncy, CB, CBE, Indian Army; *m* 1932, Barbara Enid Miller; one *s. Educ:* Radley; Sandhurst. Commissioned British Army, 1924; transf. IA (45th Rattray's Sikhs), 1928; transf. IPS, 1930; served Persian Gulf, NWF India, Indian States; retired 1947; re-employed under HM's Foreign Office, 1949, as Consul-General at Muscat; retired 1958; appointed by Sultan of Muscat and Oman as his Personal Adviser, 1961-70. *Recreations:* Rugby football (Sandhurst); athletics (Sandhurst, Army, England, also UK in Olympic Games). *Address:* 10 Egmont Drive, Avon Castle, Ringwood, Hants BH24 2BN. *Club:* Naval and Military.

CHAUVEL, Jean, GCMG (Hon.) 1960; GCVO (Hon.) 1957; Grand Croix de la Légion d'Honneur; Grand Croix de l'Etoile Noire; Grand Croix de Malte; Hon. DCL Internat. Oxford; *b* Paris, 16 April 1897; *s* of Ferdinand Chauvel and Mme Chauvel (*née* Derrien); *m* 1926, Diane de Warzee d'Hermalle; two *s* two *d. Educ:* Université de Paris (Licencié en Droit). Foreign Affairs, 1921-40; subsequently, consecutively, Third, Second and First Secretary, Consul-General, and Minister. Founder of Study Group, Foreign Affairs (Resistance); Delegate in France of Commn of Foreign Affairs of Algiers, 1944; acting Sec.-Gen., Foreign Affairs Commn, Algiers, 1944; Ambassador of France and Sec.-Gen. of Foreign Affairs, 1945; Perm. Representative of France at Security Council, United Nations, 1949; Ambassador of France at Berne, 1951; Delegate at Conference of Geneva, 1954; Delegate at Manila Conference, 1954; Ambassador of France and High Commissioner in Austria, 1954; Ambassador of France in London, 1955-62; Delegate at the Geneva Conference (Laos), 1961-62; Diplomatic Counsellor of Govt, 1962-63. *Publications:* Préludes, 1945; D'une eau profonde, 1948; Labyrinthe, 1950; Infidèle, 1951; Imaginaires, 1952; Clepsydre, 1958; Sables, 1963; Commentaire, 1971; L'aventure terrestre de Jean Arthur Rimbaud, 1971; Commentaire II, 1972; Commentaire III, 1973. *Address:* 123 Rue de la Tour, Paris XVIe; Le Ruluet, Combrit, Finistère. *Clubs:* Union, Union Internalliée (Paris).

CHAUVIRÉ, Yvette, Officier de la Légion d'Honneur, 1974; Commandeur des Arts et des Lettres, 1975; Officier, Ordre National du Mérite, 1972; ballerina; Artistic Director, Académie Internationale de la Danse, Paris, since 1972; *b* Paris, 22 April 1917. *Educ:* Ecole de la Danse de l'Opéra, Paris. Paris Opera Ballet, 1930; first major rôles in David Triomphant and Les Créatures de Prométhée; Danseuse étoile 1942; danced Istar, 1942; Monte Carlo Opera Ballet, 1946-47; returned to Paris Opera Ballet, 1947-49. Has appeared at Covent Garden, London; also danced in the USA, and in cities of Rome, Moscow, Leningrad, Berlin, Buenos Aires, Johannesburg, Milan, etc; official tours: USA 1948; USSR 1958, 1966, 1968; Canada 1967; Australia. Leading rôles in following ballets; Les Mirages, Lac des Cygnes, Sleeping Beauty, Giselle, Roméo et Juliette, Suite en Blanc, Le Cygne (St Saens), La Dame aux Camélias, etc. Choreographer: La Péri, Roméo et Juliette, Le Cygne. Artistic and Technical Adviser to Administrator, Paris Opera, 1963-72. Farewell performances: Paris Opera, Giselle, Nov. 1972, Petrouchka and The Swan, Dec. 1972; Berlin Opera, Giselle, 1973. *Films:* La Mort du Cygne, 1937 (Paris); Carrousel Napolitain, 1953 (Rome). *Publication:* Je suis Ballerine. *Recreations:* painting and drawing, collections of swans. *Address:* 21 Place du Commerce, Paris 75015, France.

CHAUX, Dr Victor M.; *see* Mosquera-Chaux.

CHAVAN, Yeshwantrao Balvantrao; Leader, Congress Parliamentary Party, since 1977; *b* 12 March 1913; *m* 1942, Venubai, *d* of late R. B. More, Phaltan, district Satara. *Educ:* Rajaram Coll., Kolhapur; Law Coll., Poona Univ. (BA, LLB). Took part in 1930, 1932 and 1942 Movements; elected MLA in 1946, 1952, 1957 and 1962; Parly Sec. to Home Minister of Bombay, 1946-52; Minister for Civil Supplies, Community Developments, Forests, Local Self Govt, 1952-Oct. 1956; Chief Minister: Bombay, Nov. 1956-April 1960; Maharashtra, May 1960-Nov. 1962; Defence Minister, Govt of India, 1962-66; Minister of Home Affairs, 1966-70; Minister of Finance, 1970-74; Minister of External Affairs, 1974-77. Member: Rajya Sabha, 1963-; Lok Sabha, 1963, 1967, 1971. Mem. Working Cttee of All India Congress Cttee. Hon. Doctorate: Aligarh Univ.; Kanpur Univ.; Marathwada Univ., Shivaji Univ. *Address:* 1 Racecourse Road, New Delhi 11. *T:* 376477.

CHAVASSE, Michael Louis Maude, MA; QC 1968; **His Honour Judge Chavasse;** a Circuit Judge, since 1977; *b* 5 Jan. 1923; 2nd *s* of late Bishop C. M. Chavasse, OBE, MC, DD, MA and Beatrice Cropper Chavasse (*née* Willink); *m* 1951, Rose Ethel, 2nd *d* of late Vice-Adm. A. D. Read, CB and late Hon. Rosamond Vere Read; three *d. Educ:* Dragon Sch., Oxford; Shrewsbury Sch.; Trinity Coll., Oxford (Schol). Enlisted in RAC, Oct. 1941; commnd in Buffs, 1942; served in Italy with Royal Norfolk Regt, 1943-45 (Lieut). 2nd cl. hons (Jurisprudence) Oxon, 1946. Called to Bar, Inner Temple, 1949. A Recorder of the Crown Court, 1972-77. *Publications:* (jtly) A Critical Annotation of the RIBA Standard Forms of Building Contract, 1964; (with Bryan Anstey) Rights of Light, 1959. *Recreations:* shooting, photography. *Address:* 2 Paper Buildings, Temple, EC4; Park House, Chevening, Sevenoaks, Kent. *T:* Knockholt 2271.

CHAYTOR, Sir George Reginald, 8th Bt *cr* 1831; *b* 1913; *s* of William Richard Carter Chaytor (*d* 1973) (*g s* of 2nd Bt) and Anna Laura (*d* 1947), *d* of George Fawcett; *S* cousin, Sir William Henry Clervaux Chaytor, 7th Bt, 1976. *Heir:* uncle Herbert Archibald Chaytor [*b* 1884; *m* 1911, Effie Bell, *d* of William Smith; one *s* one *d*]. *Address: 9691 Gibson Road, Chilliwack, BC, Canada.*

CHEADLE, Eric Wallers, CBE 1973; Deputy Managing Director, The Thomson Organisation Ltd, 1959-74; retired 1974 after 50 years service with the same company (Hultons/Allied Newspapers/Kemsley Newspapers/The Thomson Organization); Director: Thomson International Press Consultancy Ltd; Lancs and Cheshire County Newspapers Ltd; Macclesfield Press Ltd; Macclesfield Times and Courier Ltd; Stockport Express Ltd; Northwestern Newspaper Co. Ltd; Sporting Chronicle Publications Ltd; Thomson Withy Grove Ltd; *b* 14 May 1908; *s* of Edgar and Nellie Cheadle; *m* 1938, Pamela, *d* of Alfred and Charlotte Hulme; two *s. Educ:* Farnworth Grammar Sch. Editorial Staff, Evening Chronicle and Daily Dispatch, Manchester, 1924-30; Publicity Manager, Allied Newspapers Ltd, 1931-37; Publicity Manager-in-Chief, Allied Newspapers Group, 1938; Organiser, War Fund for the Services, 1939. Served War, RAFVR, Sqdn Ldr, 1941-46. Dir and Gen. Manager, Kemsley Newspapers Ltd, 1947-53. Mem. Council: Newspaper Publishers Assoc., 1947-; Newspaper Soc., 1959- (Pres., 1970-71); Mem., NEDC for Printing and Publishing Industry; Mem., Jt Bd for Nat. Newspaper Industry, 1965-67; Pres., Assoc. of Lancastrians in London, 1959 and 1973-74; Pres. (former Hon. Sec.), Manchester Publicity Assoc.,

1972-74 (Gold Medal, 1973); Pres., Printers' Charitable Corp., 1973-74 (Life Vice-Pres. and Chm. of Council, 1975-); Chm., Editorial Cttee, Newspaper Soc.; Mem. Bd, FIEJ/INCA (Fédération Internationale des Editeurs de Journaux et Publications), 1972-76; Member: UK Newsprint Users' Cttee; Caxton Quincentary Commem. Cttee, 1976; Hon. Life Mem., Independent Adoption Soc. *Recreations:* golf, and newspaper affairs. *Address:* The Old Church House, 172 Fishpool Street, St Albans, Herts. *T:* St Albans 59639. *Clubs:* Wig and Pen, Press, Variety, MCC.

CHECKETTS, Sqdn-Ldr David John, CVO 1969 (MVO 1966); Private Secretary to the Prince of Wales since 1970; Director: Neilson McCarthy Co.; Phoenix Lloyd Ltd; *b* 23 Aug. 1930; 3rd *s* of late Reginald Ernest George Checketts and late Frances Mary Checketts; *m* 1958, Rachel Leila Warren Herrick; one *s* three *d*. Flying Training, Bulawayo, Rhodesia, 1948-50; 14 Sqdn, Germany, 1950-54; Instructor, Fighter Weapons Sch., 1954-57; Air ADC to C-in-C Malta, 1958-59; 3 Sqdn, Germany, 1960-61; Equerry to Duke of Edinburgh, 1961-66, to the Prince of Wales, 1967-70. *Recreations:* ornithology, shooting, squash. *Address:* Church Cottage, Winkfield, Windsor, Berks. *T:* Winkfield Row 2289. *Club:* Brooks's.

CHECKLAND, Prof. Sydney George, MA, MCom, PhD; FBA 1977; Professor of Economic History, University of Glasgow, since 1957; *b* 9 Oct. 1916; *s* of Sydney Tom and Fanny Selina Savory Checkland, Ottawa; *m* 1942, Edith Olive, *d* of Robert Fraser and Edith Philipson Anthony; two *s* three *d*. *Educ:* Lisgar Collegiate Inst., Ottawa; Birmingham Univ. Associate, Canadian Bankers' Assoc., 1937; BCom 1st Cl. 1941, MCom 1946, Birmingham; PhD Liverpool, 1953; MA Cambridge, 1953; Pres. Nat. Union of Students, 1941-42. Internat. Union of Students, 1942-43. Served in British and Canadian Armies; Lieut, Gov.-Gen.'s Foot Guards, Normandy (severely wounded), Parly cand. (Commonwealth Party), Eccleshall, 1945. Asst Lecturer, Lecturer and Senior Lecturer in Economic Science, University of Liverpool, 1946-53; Univ. Lecturer in History, Cambridge, 1953-57; Lector in History, Trinity Coll., 1955-57. A Senate Assessor, and Mem. Finance Cttee, etc, Univ. Court, Glasgow, 1970-73. Member: Inst. for Advanced Study, Princeton, 1960, 1964; East Kilbride Develt Corp.; Scottish Records Advisory Council; Nat. Register of Archives (Scotland) (Chm. 1971); Economic Hist. Cttee, SSRC, 1970-72; Economic History Soc. Council, 1958- (Pres., 1977-). Chm., Bd. of Management, Urban Studies, 1970-74; Vice-Pres., Business Archives Council of Scotland. *Publications:* The Rise of Industrial Society in England, 1815-1885, 1964; The Mines of Tharsis, 1967; The Gladstones: a family biography, 1764-1851, 1971 (Scottish Arts Council Book Award); ed (with E. O. A. Checkland) The Poor Law Report of 1834, 1974; Scottish Banking, a history, 1695-1973, 1975 (Saltire Soc. Prize); The Upas Tree: Glasgow, 1875-1975, 1976; articles and reviews in economic and historical journals. *Recreations:* painting, gathering driftwood. *Address:* Number 5, The University, Glasgow G12 8QG. *T:* 041-339 1801.

CHEDLOW, Barry William, QC 1969; a Recorder of the Crown Court, since 1974; Member, Criminal Injuries Compensation Board, since 1976; *b* Macclesfield, 8 Oct. 1921; *m* Anne Sheldon, BA; one *s* one *d*. *Educ:* Burnage High Sch.; Manchester Univ. Served RAF, 1941-46: USAAF, Flying Instructor, 1942; Flt-Lt 1943. Called to Bar, Middle Temple, 1947, Bencher, 1976; Prizeman in Law of Evidence. Practises in London, Midland and Oxford Circuits. *Publications:* author and editor of various legal text-books. *Recreations:* flying (private pilot's licence), languages, sailing. *Address:* 12 King's Bench Walk, Temple, EC4. *T:* 01-583 0811; Little Kimblewick Farm, Finch Lane, Amersham, Bucks. *T:* Little Chalfont 2156.

CHEESEMAN, Eric Arthur, BSc (Econ), PhD (Med) (London); Professor of Medical Statistics, The Queen's University of Belfast, since 1961; *b* 22 Sept. 1912; 1st *s* of late Arthur Cheeseman and of Frances Cheeseman, London; *m* 1943, Henriette Edwina Woollaston; one *s*. *Educ:* William Ellis Sch.; London Univ. Mem. staff of Statistical Cttee of MRC, 1929-39. Served War of 1939-45, RA (TA); GSO3 21 Army Group, 1945. Research Statistician on staff of Statistical Research Unit of MRC and part-time lectr in Med. Statistics, London Sch. of Hygiene and Tropical Medicine, 1946-48; Lectr, later Reader, and Vice-Pres. (Finance), The Queen's Univ. of Belfast, 1948-; Prof., 1961; Dep. Dean, Faculty of Medicine, 1971-75. Statistical Adviser to Northern Ireland Hospitals Authority, 1948-73; Mem. of Joint Authority for Higher Technicological Studies, 1965-70. Consulting Statistician to Northern Ireland Tuberculosis Authority, 1950-59; Mem. of Statistical Cttee of Medical Research Council, 1950-61. Fellow Royal Statistical Soc.; Member: Statistical and Social Inquiry Soc. of Ireland; Soc.

for Social Medicine (Chm. 1976); Biometrics Soc. *Publications:* Epidemics in Schools, 1950; (with G. F. Adams) Old People in Northern Ireland, 1951; various papers dealing with medical statistical subjects in scientific journals. *Recreation:* cricket. *Address:* 43 Beverley Gardens, Bangor, Co. Down, N Ireland. *T:* Bangor 2822.

CHEESEMAN, Prof. Ian Clifford, CEng, FRAeS; Professor of Helicopter Engineering, University of Southampton, since 1970; *b* 12 June 1926; *s* of Richard Charles Cheeseman and Emily Ethel Clifford; *m* 1957, Margaret Edith Pither; one *s* two *d*. *Educ:* Andover Grammar Sch.; Imperial Coll. of Science and Technology. BSc, PhD; ARCS; FCIT. Vickers Supermarine Ltd, 1951-53; Aeroplane and Armament Estab., 1953-56; Atomic Weapons Res. Estab., 1956-58; Nat. Gas Turbine Estab., 1958-70. *Publications:* contribs to Jl RAeS, Jl CIT, Jl Sound and Vibration, Procs Phys. Soc. 'A'. *Recreations:* gardening, sailing, camping. *Address:* Four Weirs, King's Somborne, Hants. *T:* King's Somborne 246.

CHEESEMAN, John William; a Metropolitan Stipendiary Magistrate since 1972; *b* 2 Feb. 1913; *m* 1946, Lilian McKenzie; one *s*. Called to Bar, Gray's Inn, 1953. *Address:* 2 Dr Johnson's Buildings, Temple, EC4Y 7AY. *T:* 01-353 5371.

CHEETHAM, John Frederick Thomas; Secretary, Exchequer and Audit Department, since 1975; *b* 27 March 1919; *s* of late James Oldham Cheetham, MA, BCom; *m* 1943, Yvonne Marie Smith; one *s* one *d*. *Educ:* Penarth Grammar Sch.; Univ. of Wales. Entered Exchequer and Audit Dept, 1938; War Service, Royal Artillery, 1939-46; Office of Parly Comr for Administration, 1966-69; Dep. Sec., Exchequer and Audit Dept, 1973-74. *Recreations:* tennis, food and wine. *Address:* 70 Chatsworth Road, Croydon, Surrey CR0 1HB. *T:* 01-688 3740. *Club:* MCC.

CHEETHAM, Sir Nicolas (John Alexander), KCMG 1964 (CMG 1953); *b* 8 Oct. 1910; *s* of late Sir Milne Cheetham, KCMG, and late Mrs Nigel Law, CBE, DStJ; *m* 1st, 1937, Jean Evison Corfe (marr. diss. 1960); two *s*; 2nd, 1960, Lady Mabel Brooke (*née* Jocelyn). *Educ:* Eton College; Christ Church, Oxford. Entered HM Diplomatic Service, 1934; served in Foreign Office and at Athens, Buenos Aires, Mexico City and Vienna; UK Deputy Permanent Representative on North Atlantic Council, 1954-59; HM Minister to Hungary, 1959-61; Assistant Under-Secretary, Foreign Office, 1961-64; Ambassador to Mexico, 1964-68. *Publications:* A History of Mexico, 1970; New Spain, 1974. *Recreations:* travelling, shooting. *Address:* 50 Cadogan Square, SW1; 83122 Claviers, France. *Club:* Travellers'.

CHEEVER, John; writer, USA; *b* Quincy, Mass, 1912; *s* of Frederick Lincoln Cheever and Mary Liley Cheever; *m* 1941, Mary Winternitz; two *s* one *d*. *Educ:* Thayer Academy. *Publications:* novels: The Wapshot Chronicle, 1957 (Nat. Book Award for fiction); The Wapshot Scandal, 1964 (Howell's Medal for fiction); Bullet Park, 1969; World of Apples, 1973; Falconer, 1977; *short stories:* The Way Some People Live, 1943; The Enormous Radio, 1953, new edn, 1965; The Housebreaker of Shady Hill, 1958; Some People, Places and Things that will not appear in my next novel, 1961; The Brigadier and the Golf Widow, 1964. *Recreations:* practically everything excepting big game. *Address:* Cedar Lane, Ossining, New York, USA. *Club:* Century (New York).

CHEEVERS, William Harold; Director of Engineering, Granada Television, 1970-72; *b* 20 June 1918; *m* 1964, Shirley Cheevers; one *s*. *Educ:* Christ's Coll., London. Engineer, BBC Television, 1938-39. War Service, Army, PoW, 1941-45. Sen. Engr, BBC Television, 1946-54; Planning Engr, Radio-Corp. of America, in USA and Canada, 1954-55; Head of Engineering, Associated Rediffusion, 1955-60; Gen. Manager, Westward Television, Jt Man. Dir, 1963-67, Man. Dir, 1967-70; Dir, ITN News, 1967-70, and of IT Publications; also Director: Keith Prowse, 1963-70; Prowest, 1967-70; Direct Line Services, 1964-; Chm., British Regional Television Assoc., 1968-69. Fellow British Kinematograph Soc.; MInstD; MBIM; AssIEE. *Publications:* articles for most TV Jls, and Symposiums, at home and abroad. *Recreations:* boating, golf, reading. *Club:* Royal Western Yacht Club of England (Plymouth).

CHEGWIDDEN, Sir Thomas (Sidney), Kt 1955; CB 1943; CVO 1939; MA Oxon; Chevalier Légion d'Honneur, 1956; *b* 7 Feb. 1895; *s* of late Thomas Chegwidden, 8 Wimborne Road, Bournemouth; *m* 1st, 1919, Kathleen Muriel, *d* of A. O. Breeds; 2nd, 1934, Beryl Sinclair, *d* of A. H. Nicholson; one *d*. *Educ:* Plymouth Coll.; Maidstone Grammar Sch.; Worcester Coll., Oxford. RMA Woolwich, 1916; Lieut RE, 1917-18. Resigned

Commission and entered Upper Div. Civil Service, 1919; Asst Private Sec. to Dr T. J. Macnamara, Sir Montague Barlow, Mr Tom Shaw and Sir Arthur Steel-Maitland; Principal Private Sec. to Mr Oliver Stanley and Mr Ernest Brown; Under-Sec., Min. of Production, 1942-46; Civilian Dir of Studies, Imperial Defence Coll., 1946-47; Chm. of Public Services Bd and of Police Advisory Bd, S Rhodesia, 1947-53; Chm., Interim Federal Public Service Commission, Federation of Rhodesias and Nyasaland, 1953-55; Pres., Assoc. of Rhodesian Industries, 1958-61; Mem. Council, Univ. of Rhodesia, 1970-76; Fellow, Rhodesian Inst. of Management. *Publication:* The Employment Exchange Service of Great Britain (with G. Myrddin-Evans), 1934. *Address:* Lashams, Witley, Surrey GU8 5PH. *Club:* Athenæum.

CHEKE, Dudley John, CMG 1961; MA Cantab; HM Diplomatic Service, retired; *b* 14 June 1912; *s* of late Thomas William Cheke, FRIC; *m* 1944, Yvonne de Méric, *d* of late Rear-Adm. M. J. C. de Méric, MVO; two *s. Educ:* St Christopher's, Letchworth; Emmanuel Coll., Cambridge. Entered HM Consular Service, 1934; served in Japan, Manchuria, Korea, 1935-41; served 1942-43, in East Africa and Ceylon; Foreign Office, 1944-49 and 1958-61; UK delegation to OEEC, Paris, 1949-50; Commissioner-Gen.'s Office, Singapore, 1950-51; idc 1952; HM Consul-Gen., Frankfurt-am-Main, 1953-55, Osaka-Kobe, 1956-58; Mem. of Foreign Service Corps of Inspectors, 1961-63; Minister, Tokyo, 1963-67; Ambassador to the Ivory Coast, Niger and Upper Volta, 1967-70. *Recreations:* theatre, bird-watching. *Address:* Honey Farm, Bramley, Basingstoke, Hants. *Clubs:* United Oxford & Cambridge University; Union Society (Cambridge).

CHELMER, Baron *cr* 1963 (Life Peer), of Margaretting; **Eric Cyril Boyd Edwards,** Kt 1954; MC 1944; TD; JP; DL; Chairman, Provident Financial Group, since 1977; Director, NEM Group of Cos, since 1970; *b* 9 Oct. 1914; *s* of Col C. E. Edwards, DSO, MC, TD, DL, JP, and Mrs J. Edwards; *m* 1939, Enid, *d* of F. W. Harvey; one *s. Educ:* Felsted Sch. Solicitor, 1937; LLB (London) 1937. Served Essex Yeomanry, 1940-54 (MC), Lieut-Col Commanding, 1945-46. Chm., Nat. Union of Conservative Associations, 1956, Pres., 1967; Chm., Nat. Exec. Cttee of Conservative and Unionist Assoc., 1957-65; Jt Treasurer of Conservative Party, 1965-77; Chm., Conservative Party Review Cttee, 1972-73. Member: Political Cttee, Carlton Club, 1961; Cttee of Musicians' Benevolent Fund; Ralph Vaughan Williams Trust. JP Essex, 1950; DL Essex 1971. *Recreation:* "improving". *Address:* Peacocks, Margaretting, Essex; 5 John Street, Bedford Row, WC1. *Clubs:* Carlton, United and Cecil, Royal Ocean Racing.

CHELMSFORD, 3rd Viscount *cr* 1921, of Chelmsford; **Frederic Jan Thesiger;** Baron Chelmsford, 1858; Lloyd's Insurance Broker; *b* 7 March 1931; *s* of 2nd Viscount Chelmsford and of Gilian, *d* of late Arthur Nevile Lubbock; *S* father, 1970; *m* 1958, Clare Rendle, *d* of Dr G. R. Rolston, Haslemere; one *s* one *d.* Formerly Lieut, Inns of Court Regt. *Heir: s* Hon. Frederic Corin Piers Thesiger, *b* 6 March 1962. *Address:* 26 Ormonde Gate, SW3; Hazelbridge Court, Chiddingfold, Surrey.

CHELMSFORD, Bishop of, since 1971; **Rt. Rev. Albert John Trillo,** MTh; *b* 4 July 1915; *s* of late Albert Chowns and late Margaret Trillo; *m* 1942, Patricia Eva Williams; two *s* one *d. Educ:* The Quintin Sch.; King's Coll., University of London. Business career, 1931-36; University, 1936-38, BD (1st Class Hons) and AKC (1st Class Hons), 1938; MTh 1943. Asst Curate, Christ Church, Fulham, 1938-41; Asst Curate, St Gabriel's, Cricklewood (in charge of St Michael's), 1941-45; Secretary, SCM in Schools, 1945-50; Rector of Friern Barnet and Lecturer in New Testament Greek, King's Coll., London, 1950-55; Principal, Bishops' Coll., Cheshunt, 1955-63; Bishop Suffragan of Bedford, 1963-68; Bishop Suffragan of Hertford, 1968-71. Examining Chaplain to Bishop of St Edmundsbury and Ipswich, 1955-63, to Bishop of St Albans, 1963-71. Hon. Canon, Cathedral and Abbey Church at St Albans, 1958-63; Canon Residentiary, 1963-65. Fellow of King's Coll., London, 1959. Proctor in Convocation for Dean and Chapter of St Albans, 1963-64; Proctor-in-Convocation for the Clergy, 1965. Governor: Aldenham Sch., 1963-71; Harper Trust Schs, Bedford, 1963-68; Queenswood Sch., 1969-71; Forest Sch., 1976-. Chairman: Church of England Youth Council, 1970-74; Exec. Cttee, British Council of Churches, 1974-; Church of England's Commn on Roman Catholic Relations, 1975-. *Recreations:* reading and walking. *Address:* Bishopscourt, Chelmsford CM2 6BJ. *T:* Chelmsford 53053. *Club:* Royal Commonwealth Society.

CHELMSFORD, Provost of; *see* Herrick, Very Rev. R. W.

CHELSEA, Viscount; Charles Gerald John Cadogan; *b* 24 March 1937; *o s* of 7th Earl Cadogan, *qv*; *m* 1963, Lady Philippa Wallop, *d* of 9th Earl of Portsmouth, *qv*; two *s* one *d. Educ:* Eton. *Heir: s* Hon. Edward Charles Cadogan, *b* 10 May 1966. *Address:* 7 Smith Street, SW3. *T:* 01-730 2465; Marndhill, Ardington, near Wantage, Berks. *T:* East Hendred 273. *Clubs:* White's, Royal Automobile; Royal and Ancient; Royal St George's.

CHELTENHAM, Archdeacon of; *see* Evans, Ven. T. E.

CHELWOOD, Baron *cr* 1974 (Life Peer), of Lewes; **Tufton Victor Hamilton Beamish,** Kt 1961; MC 1940; DL; *b* 27 Jan. 1917; *o* surv. *s* of late Rear-Admiral T. P. H. Beamish, CB, DL; *m* 1950, Janet McMillan Stevenson (marr. diss. 1973); two *d*; *m* 1975, Mrs Pia McHenry (*née* von Roretz). *Educ:* Stowe Sch.; RMC, Sandhurst. 2nd Lieut Royal Northumberland Fusiliers, 1937; Active Service, Palestine, 1938-39; War of 1939-45 (wounded twice, despatches, MC); served in France, Belgium, 1940; Malaya, 1942; India and Burma front, 1942-43; North Africa and Italy, 1943-44; Staff Coll., Camberley, 1945 (psc). Hon. Col 411 (Sussex) Coast Regt RA (TA), 1951-57. Mem. Church of England Council on Inter-Church Relations, 1950-60. MP (C) Lewes Div. of E. Sussex, 1945-Feb. 1974. Delegate to Council of Europe and Chm. Assembly Cttee, 1951-54; Vice-Chairman: British Group Inter-Parly Union, 1952-54; Conservative and Unionist Members Cttee, 1958-74; Chm. Cons. For. Affairs Cttee, 1960-64; an Opposition defence spokesman, 1965-67; Chm., Cons. Gp for Europe, 1970-73; Jt Dep. Leader, British Delegn to European Parlt, 1973-74. Member: Monnet Action Cttee for United States of Europe, 1971-76; Council, RSPB, 1948-61 (Pres., 1967-70); Salmon and Trout Assoc.; President: Sussex Trust for Nature Conservation, 1968-; Soc. of Sussex Downsmen, 1975-. Governor, Stowe Sch. Dir of companies. DL Sussex, 1970-. Hon. Freeman, Borough of Lewes, 1970. Golden Cross of Merit, 1944; Polonia Restituta, Poland; Comdr, Order of the Phoenix, Greece, 1949; Order of the Cedar, Lebanon, 1969. Mem. of the Soc. of Authors. *Publications:* Must Night Fall?, an account of Soviet seizure of power in Eastern Europe, 1950; Battle Royal, a new account for the 700th Anniversary of Simon de Montfort's struggle against Henry III, 1965; Half Marx: a warning that democracy in Britain is threatened by a Marx-influenced Labour Party, 1971; contribs to newspapers and periodicals. *Recreations:* gardening, bird-watching, music. *Address:* Chelworth House, Chelwood Gate, Sussex. *Club:* White's.

CHENEVIX-TRENCH, Anthony, MA (Oxon); Head Master, Fettes College, Edinburgh, since 1971; *b* 10 May 1919; *s* of late C. G. Chenevix-Trench, CIE; *m* 1953, Elizabeth Chalmers, *e d* of late Capt. Sir Stewart Spicer, 3rd Bt, RN retd, and Lady Spicer, Chichester, Sussex; two *s* twin *d. Educ:* Shrewsbury Sch.; Christ Church, Oxford. Classical Schol. Christ Church, 1st Cl. Hon. Mods, De Paravicini Schol. Served War of 1939-45; joined RA 1939: seconded Indian Artillery (4th Hazara Mountain Battery, Frontier Force), 1940; served Malaya (Capt.; POW Singapore, 1942, released 1945). 1st Class Lit. Hum., and Prox. Acc., Craven and Ireland Scholarships, 1948. Asst Master, Shrewsbury Sch., 1948; Tutor in Classics, Christ Church, Oxford, 1951; House Master, Shrewsbury Sch. (Sch. House), 1952; Headmaster, Bradfield Coll., Berks, 1955-63; Head Master, Eton College, 1964-70. Mem., Robbins Cttee on Higher Education, 1961. FRSA. JP Berks, 1960-71. SBStJ (Scotland) 1974. *Recreations:* shooting and general outdoor activities. *Address:* The Lodge, Fettes College, Edinburgh EH4 1QX. *T:* 031-332 2281. *Clubs:* East India, Devonshire, Sports and Public Schools; Vincent's (Oxford).

CHENEY, Christopher Robert, FBA 1951; Professor of Medieval History, University of Cambridge, 1955-72; Fellow, Corpus Christi College, Cambridge, 1955; *b* 1906; 4th *s* of George Gardner and Christiana Stapleton Cheney; *m* 1940, Mary Gwendolen Hall; two *s* one *d. Educ:* Banbury County Sch.; Wadham Coll., Oxford (Hon. Fellow, 1968). 1st class Modern History Sch., 1928; Asst Lectr in History, University Coll., London, 1931-33; Bishop Fraser Lectr in Ecclesiastical History, University of Manchester, 1933-37; Fellow of Magdalen Coll., Oxford, 1938-45; Univ. Reader in Diplomatic, 1937-45; Joint Literary Dir of Royal Historical Society, 1938-45; Prof. of Medieval History, Univ. of Manchester, 1945-55. Hon. Fellow, Wadham Coll., Oxford. Corresp. Fellow, Mediaeval Acad. of America; Corresp. Mem., Monumenta Germaniae Historica. Hon. DLitt Glasgow, 1970. *Publications:* Episcopal Visitation of Monasteries in the 13th Century, 1931; English Synodalia of the 13th Century, 1941; Handbook of Dates, 1945; English Bishops' Chanceries, 1950; (with W. H. Semple) Selected Letters of Pope Innocent III, 1953; From Becket to Langton, 1956; (with F. M. Powicke) Councils and Synods of the English Church, Vol. II,

1964; Hubert Walter, 1967; (with M. G. Cheney) Letters of Pope Innocent III concerning England and Wales, 1967; Notaries Public in England in the XIII and XIV Centuries, 1972; Medieval Texts and Studies, 1973; Pope Innocent III and England, 1976; articles and reviews in Eng. Hist. Rev., etc. *Address:* 236 Hills Road, Cambridge. *T:* Cambridge 47765.

CHERENKOV, Prof. Pavel Alexeevich; Soviet physicist; Member of the Institute of Physics, Academy of Sciences of the USSR; *b* 27 July 1904. *Educ:* Voronezh State Univ., Voronezh, USSR. Discovered the Cherenkov Effect, 1934. Corresp. Mem., 1964-70, Academician, 1970-, USSR Acad. of Scis. Awarded Stalin Prize, 1946; Nobel Prize for Physics (joint), 1958. *Address:* Institute of Physics, Academy of Sciences of the USSR, B Kaluzhskaya 14, Moscow, USSR.

CHERKASSKY, Shura; pianist; *b* 7 Oct. 1911; *s* of late Isaac and Lydia Cherkassky; *m* 1946, Genia Ganz (marr. diss. 1948). *Educ:* Curtis Institute of Music, Pa, USA (diploma). Plays with the principal orchestras and conductors of the world and is a constant soloist at Salzburg, Vienna and Edinburgh Festivals; concerts in Asia, America, Australia and Europe. Has made numerous recordings. *Address:* c/o Ibbs & Tillett Ltd, 124 Wigmore Street, W1.

CHERMAYEFF, Serge, FRIBA, FRSA; architect; abstract painter; *b* 8 Oct. 1900; *s* of Ivan and Rosalie Chermayeff; *m* 1928, Barbara Maitland May; two *s*. *Educ:* Harrow Sch. Journalist, 1918-22; studied architecture, 1922-25; principal work in England; Studios BBC; Modern Exhibitions; Gilbey's Offices; ICI Laboratories; in Partnership: Bexhill Pavilion. Professor, Brooklyn Coll., 1942-46; Pres. and Dir, Inst. of Design, Chicago, 1946-51; Prof., Harvard Univ., 1953-62; Prof., Yale Univ., 1962-71, now Emeritus. Hon. Fellow, Assoc. of Columbian Architects. Hon. Dr of Fine Art, Washington Univ. Gold Medal, Royal Architectural Inst., Canada, 1973. *Publications:* Architecture, Art and Architectural Criticism; ARP, 1939; Community and Privacy, 1963; Shape of Community, 1970. *Address:* Box NN, Wellfleet, Mass 02667, USA.

CHERMONT, Jayme Sloan, KCVO (Hon.) 1968; Brazilian Ambassador to the Court of St James's, 1966-68, retired; *b* 5 April 1903; *s* of Ambassador E. L. Chermont and Mrs Helen Mary Chermont; *m* 1928, Zaíde Alvim de Mello Franco Chermont (decd); no *c*. *Educ:* Law Sch., Rio de Janeiro Univ. Entered Brazilian Foreign Office, 1928; served in Washington, 1930-32; Rio de Janeiro, 1932-37; London, 1937; transf. to Brazil, 1938; 1st Sec., 1941; Buenos Aires, 1943-45; transf. to Brazil, 1945; Counsellor, Brussels, 1948-50; Minister Counsellor, London (periodically Chargé d'Affaires), 1950-53; various appts, Brazilian FO, 1953-57; Consul-Gen., New York, 1957-60; Ambassador to Haiti, 1960-61; Head of Political and Cultural Depts, Brazil, 1961; Sec.-Gen., FO, 1962-63; Ambassador to Netherlands, 1963-66. Headed Brazilian Delegn to UN Gen. Assembly, 1962. Holds Orders from many foreign countries. *Recreations:* golf, chess, bridge, stamps, coins, books. *Address:* c/o Ministry of Foreign Affairs, Brasília, Brazil. *Clubs:* White's; Jockey, Country, Itanhangá Golf (Rio).

CHERNIAVSKY, Mischel; cellist; *b* Uman, South Russia, 2 Nov. 1893; became British subject, 1922; *m* 1919, Mary Rogers, Vancouver, BC; four *s* (and one *s* decd). *Educ:* privately. Studied violoncello under David Popper and Herbert Walenn. Played before the Czar, Nicholas II, when seven years old; at age of twelve performed Saint-Saëns concerto in presence of composer; toured the world with his brothers, Leo (violinist) and Jan (pianist), who with him formed the Cherniavsky Trio, 1901-23. Since 1925 has appeared in most countries of the world in recital and as soloist with orchestra. Entertained the Forces in Great Britain, 1939-42; organised concerts in Canada in aid of Mrs Churchill's Aid to Russia Fund, 1942-45; toured Union of South Africa, 1953; last public appearance in London, 1958, with Sir Thomas Beecham. *Recreations:* golf, tennis, antique collecting. *Address:* Ferme des Moines, Le Bourg-Dun, 76740 Par Fontaine-le-Dun, France. *T:* Le Havre 830014. *Club:* Dieppe Golf.

CHERRY, Prof. (Edward) Colin; Henry Mark Pease Professor of Telecommunication at Imperial College, University of London, since 1958; *b* 23 June 1914; *s* of Arthur and Margaret Cherry; *m* 1956, Heather Blanche White; two *d*. *Educ:* St Alban's; University of London. Student, with General Electric Company (Research Laboratories), 1932-36; studied for London BSc at the same time (as evening student at Northampton Polytechnic). BSc 1936, MSc 1940, DSc 1955. Research Staff of General Electric Company, 1936-45, being seconded during part of War years to Min. of Aircraft Production for radar research. Lectr,

College of Technology, Manchester, 1945-47; Reader in Telecommunication, Imperial Coll. of Science and Technology, 1949-58. Hon. ACGI. *Publications:* On Human Communication, 1957; World Communication-Threat or Promise?, 1971; numerous scientific papers on theory of electric circuits, on telecommunication principles and on the psychology of speech and hearing. *Recreations:* gardening, foreign travel, watercolour. *Address:* Combe House, Chichester Road, Dorking, Surrey. *T:* Dorking 2021.

CHESHAM, 5th Baron *cr* 1858; **John Charles Compton Cavendish,** PC 1964; *b* 18 June 1916; *s* of 4th Baron and Margot, *d* of late J. Layton Mills, Tansor Court, Oundle; *S* father, 1952; *m* 1937, Mary Edmunds, 4th *d* of late David G. Marshall, White Hill, Cambridge; two *s* two *d*. *Educ:* Eton; Zuoz Coll., Switzerland; Trinity Coll., Cambridge. Served War of 1939-45, Lieut Royal Bucks Yeomanry, 1939-42; Capt. RA (Air OP), 1942-45. JP Bucks 1946, retd. Delegate, Council of Europe, 1953-56. A Lord-in-Waiting to the Queen, 1955-59; Parly Sec., Min. of Transport, 1959-64. Chancellor, Primrose League, 1957-59. Executive Vice-Chm. Royal Automobile Club, 1966-70; Chairman: British Road Federation, 1966-72 (Vice-Pres., 1972); Internat. Road Fedn, Geneva, 1973-76; Dir, British Parking Assoc., 1972-75; Fellowship of Motor Industry, 1969-71; Hon. Sec., House of Lords Club, 1966-72; Hon. FInstHE, 1970; Hon FIRTE, 1974 (Pres., 1971-73). *Heir: s* Hon. Nicholas Charles Cavendish [*b* 7 Nov. 1941; *m* 1st, 1965, Susan Donne (marr. diss. 1969), *e d* of Dr Guy Beauchamp; 2nd, 1973, Suzanne, *er d* of late Alan Gray Byrne, Sydney, Australia; one *s*]. *Address:* South Hall, Preston Candover, near Basingstoke, Hants. *T:* Preston Candover 230. *Clubs:* Pratt's, Bath.

CHESHIRE, Geoffrey Chevalier, FBA 1945; DCL; Barrister-at-Law; Hon. Fellow of Merton College and of Exeter College, Oxford; Hon. Master of the Bench of Lincoln's Inn; Hon. LLD: Manchester University; London University; Jadavpur University, Calcutta; *b* Hartford, Ches, 27 June 1886; 2nd *s* of Walter Christopher Cheshire, Solicitor and Registrar of Northwich County Court, Ches; *m* 1st, 1915, Primrose Barstow (*d* 1962), 2nd *d* of Col T. A. A. Barstow, Seaforth Highlanders; two *s*; 2nd, 1963, Dame Mary (Kathleen) Lloyd, DBE (*d* 1972). *Educ:* Denstone Coll.; Merton Coll., Oxford. 1st Class Hon. Sch. of Jurisprudence, 1908; 2nd Cl. BCL 1910; Inns of Court Studentship, 1911. Lectr at University Coll. of Wales, Aberystwyth, 1909 and 1910; Fellow of Exeter Coll., Oxford, 1912-44; Bursar, 1919-33; All Souls Lecturer in Private International Law, 1922-33; All Souls Reader in English Law, 1933-44; Vinerian Prof. of English Law, Oxford, and Fellow of All Souls Coll., 1944-49; Mem. of Lord Chancellor's Cttee on Foreign Marriages, 1939; Deleg. to Hague Conf. on Codification of Private Internat. Law, 1951; Mem. Lord Chancellor's Cttee on Private Internat. Law, 1952-57; Mem. of the Inst. of Internat. Law, 1950-65. Served European War, Cheshire Regt, 1914-16; RFC (Kite-Balloon Section), 1916-18, Capt; Home Guard, 1940. *Publications:* Investigation of Charges in the RAF, 1919; Modern Real Property, 1925, 10th edn 1967, 12th edn by E. H. Burn 1976; Private International Law, 1935, 9th edn by P. M. North, 1974; (with C. H. S. Fifoot) The Law of Contract, 1945, 9th edn (ed M. P. Furmston), 1976; International Contracts, 1948; (Gen. Ed.) Stephen's Commentaries, 19th edn; The Private International Law of Husband and Wife, 1963. *Address:* Laundry Cottage, Empshott, Liss, Hants.

See also Group Capt. G. L. Cheshire.

CHESHIRE, Group Captain (Geoffrey) Leonard, VC 1944; DSO 1940; DFC 1941; RAF retired; *b* 7 Sept. 1917; *s* of Geoffrey Chevalier Cheshire, *qv*; *m* 2nd, 1959, Susan Ryder, *qv*; one *s* one *d*. *Educ:* Stowe Sch.; Merton Coll., Oxford. 2nd Class Hon. Sch. of Jurisprudence, 1939; OU Air Sqdn, 1936; RAFVR, 1937; Perm. Commn RAF, 1939; trained Hullavington; served War of 1939-45 (VC, DSO, DFC, two Bars to DSO); joined 102 Sqdn, 1940; Flying Officer, 1940; posted 35 Sqdn, 1941; Wing Comdr, Commanding 76 Sqdn, 1942; comd RAF Station, Marston Moor, 1943; 617 Sqdn, 1943; HQ Eastern Air Command, South-East Asia, 1944; British Joint Staff Mission, Washington, 1945; retired 1946; official British observer at dropping of Atomic Bomb on Nagasaki, 1945. Founder of Cheshire Foundation Homes (140 Homes for the disabled in 35 countries); Co-founder of Mission for the Relief of Suffering. Hon. LLD Liverpool, 1973. *Publications:* Bomber Pilot, 1943; Pilgrimage to the Shroud, 1956; The Face of Victory, 1961. *Relevant publications:* Cheshire, VC, by Russell Braddon; No Passing Glory, by Andrew Boyle; New Lives for Old, by W. W. Russell. *Recreations:* photography, tennis. *Address:* Cavendish, Suffolk. *Clubs:* Royal Air Force; Queen's (Hon. Life Mem.).

CHESHIRE, Mrs Geoffrey Leonard; *see* Ryder, Susan.

CHESHIRE, Air Chief Marshal Sir Walter (Graemes), GBE 1965 (CBE 1949); KCB 1959 (CB 1955); idc; psa; Member, Commonwealth War Graves Commission, 1968-74, Vice-Chairman, 1970-74; *b* 21 March 1907; *s* of late John F. Cheshire, Beckenham, Kent; *m* 1940, Mary, *d* of late Col E. W. Chance, OBE, TD; two *s*. *Educ:* Ipswich Sch.; Downing Coll., Cambridge. Commnd into RAF, 1926; Sqdn Ldr, 1937; RAF Staff Coll., 1938; various appts, Bomber Command; Air Attaché, Moscow; on staff HQ, ACSEA, 1939-45; AOC French Indo-China, 1945-46; idc 1949; AOC Gibraltar, 1950-52; Comdt RAF Staff Coll., Andover, 1952-53; Air Officer in charge of Administration, HQ 2nd TAF, 1953-55; AOC No 13 Group, Fighter Command, 1955-57; RAF Instructor at Imperial Defence Coll., 1957-59; AOC, RAF Malta, and Dep. C-in-C (Air), Allied Forces, Mediterranean, 1959-61; Mem. for Personnel, Air Council, 1961-64; Air ADC to the Queen, 1963-65; Air Mem. for Personnel, Min. of Defence, 1964-65; retired, 1965. *Address:* 30 Courtenay Place, Belmore Lane, Lymington, Hants. *Club:* Royal Air Force.

CHESTER, Bishop of, since 1974; **Rt Rev. Hubert Victor Whitsey**; *b* 21 Nov. 1916; *s* of Samuel and Rachel Whitsey, Blackburn, Lancs; *m* 1950, Jean Margaret Bellinger; two *s* one *d*. *Educ:* Queen Elizabeth's Grammar Sch., Blackburn; Technical Coll., Blackburn; St Edmund Hall, Oxford (MA); Westcott House, Cambridge. Midland Bank, 1933-39. Royal Regt Artillery (TA), 1938-46 (Lt Col 1945). Asst Curate, Chorley, Lancs, 1949-51; Vicar: Farington, Lancs, 1952-55; St Thomas, Halliwell, Bolton, 1955-60; Asst Rural Dean, Bolton, 1957-60; Vicar: All Saints and Martyrs, Langley, Manchester, 1960-68; Downham, Lancs, 1968-71; Hon. Canon, Manchester Cathedral, 1963, Emeritus, 1968; Bishop Suffragan of Hertford, 1971-74. *Recreations:* idleness, practicality. *Address:* Bishop's House, Chester.

CHESTER, Archdeacon of; see Williams, Ven. H. L.

CHESTER, Sir (Daniel) Norman, Kt 1974; CBE 1951; MA; Warden of Nuffield College, Oxford, 1954-Oct. 1978; Official Fellow of Nuffield College, 1945-54; *b* 27 Oct. 1907; *s* of Daniel Chester, Chorlton-cum-Hardy, Manchester; *m* 1936, Eva, *d* of James H. Jeavons. *Educ:* Manchester Univ. BA Manchester, 1930, MA 1933; MA Oxon, 1946. Rockefeller Fellow, 1935-36, Lecturer in Public Administration, 1936-45, Manchester Univ.; Mem. of Economic Section, War Cabinet Secretariat, 1940-45. Editor of jl of Public Administration, 1943-66. Mem. Oxford City Council, 1952-74. Chairman: Oxford Centre for Management Studies, 1965-75; Police Promotion Examinations Bd, 1969-; Cttee on Association Football, 1966-68; Football Grounds Improvement Trust, 1975-; Vice-Pres. (ex-Chm.), Royal Inst. of Public Administration; Past Pres., Internat. Political Science Assoc. Hon. LittD Manchester, 1968. Corresp. Mem., Acad. des Sciences Morales et Politiques, Institut de France, 1967. Chevalier de la Légion d'Honneur, 1976. *Publications:* Public Control of Road Passenger Transport, 1936; Central and Local Government: Financial and Administrative Relations, 1951; The Nationalised Industries, 1951; (ed) Lessons of the British War Economy, 1951; (ed) The Organization of British Central Government, 1914-56; (with Nona Bowring) Questions in Parliament, 1962; The Nationalisation of British Industry, 1945-51, 1975; articles in learned journals. *Address:* 136 Woodstock Road, Oxford. *Club:* Reform.

CHESTER, Dr Peter Francis, FInstP; Director, Central Electricity Research Laboratories, since 1973; Chairman, SRC Energy Round Table, since 1975; a Member, Science Research Council, since 1976; *b* 8 Feb. 1929; *s* of late Herbert and of Edith Maud Chester (*née* Pullen); *m* 1953, Barbara Ann Collin; one *s* four *d*. *Educ:* Gunnersbury Grammar Sch.; Queen Mary College, London. BSc 1st Physics 1950; PhD London 1953. Post-doctoral Fellow, Nat. Research Council, Ottawa, 1953-54; Adv. Physicist, Westinghouse Res. Labs, Pittsburgh, 1954-60; Head of Solid State Physics Section, CERL, 1960-65; Head of Fundamental Studies Section, CERL, 1965-66; Res. Man., Electricity Council Res. Centre, 1966-70; Controller of Scientific Services, CEGB NW Region, 1970-73; Vice-Pres., Inst. of Physics, 1972-76. Mem. Science Board, SRC, 1972-75. A Dir, Fulmer Res. Inst., 1976-. *Publications:* original papers in solid state and low temperature physics. *Address:* Central Electricity Research Laboratories, Kelvin Avenue, Leatherhead, Surrey KT22 7SE.

CHESTER, Prof. Theodore Edward, CBE 1967; D.jur, MA (Econ) Manchester; Diploma in Commerce; Senior Research Fellow and Emeritus Professor, University of Manchester; Professor of Social Administration, 1955-75; Member, Council of Manchester Business School, since 1964; *b* 28 June 1908; *m* 1940, Mimi; one *s*. Teaching and research in law and administration, 1931-39. Service with HM Forces, 1940-45. Asst Man. in London city firm, 1946-48; Acton Soc. Trust: Senior Research Worker, 1948-52; Dir, 1952-55; Dean, Faculty of Economic and Social Studies, Univ. of Manchester, 1962-63. Research work into problems of large-scale Administration in private and public undertakings including the hosp. and educn service in Britain and comparative studies abroad as well as into the problems of training managers and administrators. Vis. Prof. at many foreign univs and institutions, notably in the United States, Western Europe, and Australia, 1959-; Kenneth Pray Vis. Prof., Univ. of Pa, 1968; first Kellogg Vis. Prof., Washington Univ., St Louis, 1969 and 1970. Mem. Summer Fac., Sloan Inst. of Health Service Admin, Cornell Univ., 1972-. Ford Foundn Travelling Fellowships, 1960, 1967. WHO Staff Training Programme, 1963-; UN Res. Inst. for Economic and Social Studies, 1968. Member: National Selection Cttee for the recruitment of Sen. Hospital Administrative Staff, 1956-66; Advisory Cttee on Management Efficiency in the Health Service, 1959-65; Cttee of Inquiry into recruitment, training and promotion of clerical and administrative staffs in the Hospital Service, 1962-63; Programme Cttee of Internat. Hosp. Fedn and Chm. study group into problems of trng in hosp. admin, 1959-65; Pres. Corp of Secs, 1956-66; Trng Couns for Social Workers and Health Visitors, 1963-65; Cttee on Technical Coll. Resources, 1964-69; Adviser: Social Affairs Div., OECD, 1965-66; Turkish State Planning Org. on Health and Welfare Problems, 1964. Broadcasts on social problems in Britain and abroad. Golden Needle of Honour, Austrian Hosp. Dirs Assoc., 1970. *Publications:* (for Acton Soc. Trust) Training and Promotion in Nationalised Industry, 1951; Patterns of Organisation, 1952; Management under Nationalization, 1953; Background and Blueprint: A Study of Hospital Organisation under the National Health Service, 1955; The Impact of the Change (co-author), 1956; Groups, Regions and Committees, 1957; The Central Control of the Service, 1958; (with H. A. Clegg): The Future of Nationalization, 1953; Wage Policy and the Health Service, 1957; Post War Growth of Management in Western Europe, 1961; Graduate Education for Hospital Administration in the United States: Trends, 1969; The British National Health Service, 1970; The Swedish National Health Service, 1970; Organisation for Change: preparation for reorganisation, 1974 (OECD); Editor and contrib. Amer. Coll. Hosp. Administrators; regular contribs to scientific and other jls. *Recreations:* travel, music, swimming, detective stories. *Address:* Lisvane, 189 Grove Lane, Hale, Altrincham, Cheshire. *T:* 061-980 2828.

CHESTER JONES, Prof. Ian, DSc; Professor of Zoology, University of Sheffield, since 1958; *b* 3 Jan. 1916; *s* of late H. C. Jones; *m* 1942, Nansi Ellis Williams; two *s* one *d*. *Educ:* Liverpool Institute High Sch. for Boys; Liverpool Univ. BSc 1938; PhD 1941; DSc 1958. Served in Army, 1941-46. Commonwealth Fund Fellow, Harvard Univ., 1947-49. Senior Lecturer in Zoology, Univ. of Liverpool, 1955. Chm., Soc. for Endocrinology, 1966 (Sir Henry Dale medal, 1976). Dr de l'Université de Clermont (*hc*), 1967. *Publications:* The Adrenal Cortex, 1957; Integrated Biology, 1971; General, Comparative and Clinical Endocrinology of the Adrenal Cortex, 1976. *Address:* Department of Zoology, University of Sheffield S10 2TN.

CHESTERFIELD, Archdeacon of; see Cleasby, Ven. T. W. I.

CHESTERFIELD, Arthur Desborough, CBE 1962; Vice-Chairman, Woolwich Equitable Building Society, since 1976 (Director since 1966); Director: RoyWest Banking Corporation Ltd, since 1965 (Chairman, 1972-77); Trust Corporation of Bahamas Ltd, since 1967 (Chairman, 1972-77); Singer & Friedlander (Holdings) Ltd, since 1967 (Chairman, 1967-76); Singer & Friedlander Ltd, since 1967 (Chairman, 1967-76); Clifford Property Co. Ltd, since 1973; *b* 21 Aug. 1905; *s* of Arthur William and Ellen Harvey Chesterfield; *m* 1932, Betty, *d* of John Henry Downey; two *s* three *d*. *Educ:* Hastings Grammar Sch. Entered Westminster Bank Ltd, 1923; Joint Gen. Manager, 1947; Chief Gen. Manager, 1950-65, retired; Director, Nat. Westminster Bank, 1963-69, Local Dir, Inner London, 1969-74. Member: Export Guarantees Adv. Council, 1952-63; Nat. Savings Cttee, 1954-67; Chm., City of London Savings Cttee, 1962-72. FIB (Mem. Council, 1950-65). *Recreations:* music, gardening. *Address:* Coaters, Shirleys, Ditchling, Sussex. *T:* Hassocks 3514.

CHESTERMAN, Sir Clement (Clapton), Kt 1974; OBE 1919; Consulting Physician in Tropical Diseases, retired; *b* 30 May 1894; 5th *s* of late W. T. Chesterman, Bath, and Elizabeth Clapton; *m* 1917, Winifred Lucy, *d* of late Alderman F. W. Spear; three *s* two *d*. *Educ:* Monkton Combe Sch.; Bristol Univ.

MD London 1920; DTM and H, Cantab, 1920; FRCP 1952. Served European War, 1914-18 (despatches, OBE): Capt. RAMC (SR), 1917-19, Middle East. Medical Missionary, Belgian Congo, 1920-36; MO and Secretary, Baptist Missionary Soc., 1936-48. Lecturer in Tropical Medicine, Middlesex Hospital Medical Sch., 1944; Lecturer in Tropical Hygiene, University of London Institute of Education, 1956. Member Commn Royale Belge pour la Protection des Indigènes; Mem. Colonial Advisory Medical Cttee; Past Vice-Pres. Royal Society Tropical Medicine and Hygiene; Pres. Hunterian Society, 1967-68; Hon. Mem. Belgian Royal Society of Tropical Medicine. Occasional broadcasts on Medical Missions and Tropical Diseases. Hon. FRAM, 1972. Serbian Red Cross Medal, 1915; Chevalier, Ordre Royal du Lion, 1938. *Publications:* In the Service of Suffering, 1940; A Tropical Dispensary Handbook (7th edn), 1960; articles in Transactions of Royal Society of Tropical Medicine and Hygiene, British Encyclopædia of Medical Practice, etc. *Recreation:* golf. *Address:* 7 Parsifal Road, NW6 1UG. *T:* 01-435 6475. *Clubs:* Royal Commonwealth Society; Highgate Golf.

CHESTERMAN, Sir Ross, Kt 1970; MSc, PhD; DIC; Warden of Goldsmiths' College (University of London), 1953-74; Vice-Master of the College of Craft Education, since 1960 (Dean, 1958-60); *b* 27 April 1909; *s* of late Dudley and Ettie Chesterman; *m* 1938, Audrey Mary Horlick; one *s* one *d. Educ:* Hastings Grammar Sch.; Imperial College of Science, London (scholar). Acland English Essay Prizeman, 1930; 1st class hons BSc (Chem.), 1930; MSc 1932; Lecturer in Chemistry, Woolwich Polytechnic; PhD 1937; Science master in various grammar schools; Headmaster, Meols Cop Secondary Sch., Southport, 1946-48. Chief County Inspector of Schools, Worcestershire, 1948-53. Educnl Consultant to numerous overseas countries, 1966-73. Ford Foundation Travel Award to American Univs, 1966. Chairman: Standing Cttee on Teacher Trng; Nat. Council for Supply and Trng of Teachers Overseas, 1971; Adv. Cttee for Teacher Trng Overseas, FCO (ODA), 1972-74. Fellow *hc* of Coll. of Handicraft, 1958. Liveryman and Freeman of Goldsmiths' Co., 1968. *Publications:* The Birds of Southport, 1947; chapter in The Forge, 1955; chapter in Science in Schools, 1958; Teacher Training in some American Universities, 1967; scientific papers in chemical journals; articles in educational periodicals. *Recreations:* music, painting, travel. *Address:* Greenacre, 27 Greenhill Road, Otford, Sevenoaks, Kent TN14 5RR.

CHESTERS, Prof. Charles Geddes Coull, OBE 1977; BSc, MSc, PhD; FRSE; FLS; FInstBiol; Professor of Botany, University of Nottingham, 1944-69, now Emeritus Professor; *b* 9 March 1904; *s* of Charles and Margaret Geddes Chesters; *m* 1928, Margarita Mercedes Cathie Maclean; one *s* one *d. Educ:* Hyndland Sch.; Univ. of Glasgow. Lecturer in Botany, 1930, Reader in Mycology, 1942, Univ. of Birmingham. Chairman: Educn and other Cttees, Associated Exam. Bd; Jt Cttee, HNC Applied Biol. *Publications:* scientific papers on mycology and microbiology, mainly in Trans. British Myc. Soc., Ann. Ap. Biol., Jl Gen. Microb. *Recreations:* photography and collecting fungi. *Address:* Grandage Cottages, Quenington, near Cirencester, Glos GL7 5DB.

CHESTERS, Dr John Hugh, OBE 1970; FRS 1969; Consultant, since 1971; *b* 16 Oct. 1906; 2nd *s* of Rev. George M. Chesters; *m* 1936, Nell Knight, Minnesota, USA; three *s* one *d. Educ:* High Pavement Sch., Nottingham; King Edward VII Sch., Sheffield; Univ. of Sheffield. BSc Hons Physics, 1928; PhD 1931; DSc Tech 1945; Hon. DSc 1975. Metropolitan-Vickers Research Schol., Univ. Sheff., 1928-31. Robert Blair Fellowship, Kaiser-Wilhelm Inst. für Silikatforschung, Berlin, 1931-32; Commonwealth Fund Fellowship, Univ. of Illinois, 1932-34; United Steel Cos Ltd: in charge of Refractories Section, 1934-45; Asst Dir of Research, 1945-62; Dep. Dir of Research, United Steel Cos Ltd, 1962-67, Midland Group, British Steel Corporation, 1967-70; Dir, Corporate Labs, BISRA, 1970-71. President: Brit. Ceramic Soc., 1951-52; Inst. of Ceramics, 1961-63; Iron and Steel Inst., 1968-69; Inst. of Fuel, 1972-73. Foreign Associate, Nat. Acad. of Engineering, USA, 1977. Iron and Steel Inst., Bessemer Gold Medal, 1966; John Wilkinson Gold Medal, Staffs Iron and Steel Inst., 1971; American Inst. Met. Eng: Robert Hunt Award, 1952; Benjamin Fairless Award, 1973. FInstF, FIM, FICeram; Fellow, Amer. Ceramic Soc. *Publications:* Steelplant Refractories, 1945, 2nd edn 1957; Iron and Steel, 1948; Refractories: production and properties, 1973; Refractories for Iron- and Steelmaking, 1974; numerous articles in Jl of Iron and Steel Inst., Trans Brit. Cer. Soc., Jl Amer. Cer. Soc., Jl Inst. of Fuel, etc. *Recreations:* foreign travel, fishing. *Address:* 21 Slayleigh Lane, Sheffield S10 3RF. *T:* Sheffield 301257.

CHESTERTON, Elizabeth Ursula, OBE 1977; architect and town planner; *b* 12 Oct. 1915; *d* of Maurice Chesterton, architect, and Dorothy (*née* Deck). *Educ:* King Alfred Sch.; Queen's Coll., London; Architectural Assoc. Sch. of Architecture, London. AA Dipl. (Hons) 1939; ARIBA 1940; DistTP 1968; FRTPI 1967 (AMTPI 1943). Asst County Planning Officer, E. Suffolk CC, 1940-47; Develt Control Officer, Cambs CC Planning Dept, 1947-51; Mem. Staff: Social Res. Unit, Dept of Town Planning, UCL, 1951-53; Architectural Assoc. Sch. of Architecture, 1954-61. Member: Council, Architectural Assoc., 1964-67; Royal Fine Art Commn, 1970-; Historic Buildings Council, 1973-. *Publications:* (jtly) Report on Local Land Use for the Dartington Hall Trustees, 1957; The Historic Core of King's Lynn: study and plan, 1964; North West Solent Shore Estates Report, 1969; Snowdon Summit Report for Countryside Commn, 1974; The Crumbles, Eastbourne, for Chatsworth Settlement, 1976; Aldeburgh, Suffolk, for Aldeburgh Soc., 1976. *Recreations:* narrow boat owner; gardening; travel. *Address:* The Studio, Money's Yard, The Mount, Hampstead, NW3 6SZ. *T:* 01-435 0666.

CHESTERTON, Sir Oliver (Sidney), Kt 1969; MC 1943; Partner in Chesterton & Sons, Chartered Surveyors, London; Chairman, Woolwich Equitable Building Society, since 1976 (Vice-Chairman, 1969-76); Director: Property Growth Assurance, since 1972; London Life Association, since 1975; *b* 28 Jan. 1913; *s* of Frank and Nora Chesterton; *m* 1944, Violet Ethel Jameson; two *s* one *d. Educ:* Rugby Sch. Served War of 1939-45, Irish Guards. Vice-Chm., Council of Royal Free Med. Sch., 1964-; Crown Estate Comr, 1969-. Past Pres., Royal Instn of Chartered Surveyors, Hon. Sec., 1972-; Pres., Commonwealth Assoc. Surveying and Land Economy, 1969-77; first Master, Chartered Surveyors' Co., 1977-78. Governor, Rugby Sch., 1972-. *Recreations:* golf, fishing, National Hunt racing. *Address:* 7 York House, Kensington Church Street, W8. *Clubs:* White's; Rye Golf.

CHESWORTH, Donald Piers; Warden, Toynbee Hall, since 1977; Chairman, Mauritius Salaries Commission, since 1973; Director, Notting Hill Social Council, since 1967; *b* 30 Jan. 1923; *s* of Frederick Gladstone Chesworth and Daisy Radmore. *Educ:* King Edward VI Sch., Camp Hill, Birmingham; London Sch. of Economics. War of 1939-45: Nat. Fire Service (Mem. Nat. Exec. Fire Brigades Union, 1941-42); also Royal Air Force. Chm., Nat. Assoc. of Labour Student Organisations, 1947; Student and Overseas Sec., Internat. Union of Socialist Youth, 1947-51. Contested (Lab) elections: Warwick and Leamington, 1945; Bromsgrove, 1950 and 1951; Mem. LCC (Kensington N Div.), 1952-65 (Whip and Mem., Policy Cttee); Labour Adviser: Tanganyika Govt (and Chm., Territorial Minimum Wages Bd), 1961-62; Mauritius Govt (and Chm., Sugar Wages Councils), 1962-65; Mem. Economics Br., ILO, Geneva, 1967; Co-opted Mem., ILEA Educn Cttee, 1970-74 (Chm., Res. Section; Vice-Chm., Appt Head Teachers Section); Alderman, Royal Borough of Kensington and Chelsea, 1971-. Chm., Assoc. for Neighbourhood Councils, 1972-74. Member: Council and Exec., War on Want, 1965- (Chm., 1967, 1968, 1970-74); Exec. Bd, Voluntary Cttee on Overseas Aid and Develt, 1969-; Nat. Cttee, UK Freedom from Hunger Campaign, 1969-; S Metropolitan Conciliation Cttee, Race Relations Bd, 1975-77; Chm., World Development Political Action Trust, 1971-75; Trustee: UK Bangladesh Fund, 1971-72; Campden Charities, 1971-; Internat. Extension Coll., 1972-. Treas., Brit. Bangladesh Soc., 1973-. Mem. Bd of Visitors, Hewell Grange Borstal, 1950-52; Chm. Managers Mayford Home Office Approved Sch., 1952-58. Chairman of Governors: Isaac Newton Sch., N Kensington, 1971-; Paddington Sch., 1972-; Mem., Ct of Governors, LSE, 1973-. *Publications:* Report Tanganyika Territorial Minimum Wages Board, 1961; Reports Mauritius Sugar Wages Councils, 1962-65; Reports Mauritius Salaries Commission, 1973-75; contrib. Statutory Wage Fixing in Developing Countries (ILO), 1968; contrib. Internat. Labour Review. *Recreation:* travel. *Address:* 13 Ashburn Gardens, SW7 4DG. *T:* 01-370 2097. *Clubs:* Royal Commonwealth Society; Stella Clavisque (Mauritius).

CHETWODE, family name of **Baron Chetwode.**

CHETWODE, 2nd Baron *cr* 1945, of Chetwode; **Philip Chetwode;** Bt, 1700; *b* 26 March 1937; *s* of Capt. Roger Charles George Chetwode (*d* 1940; *o s* of Field Marshal Lord Chetwode, GCB, OM, GCSI, KCMG, DSO) and Hon. Molly Patricia Berry, *d* of 1st Viscount Camrose (she *m* 2nd, 1942, 1st Baron Sherwood, from whom she obtained a divorce, 1948, and *m* 3rd, 1958, Sir Richard Cotterell, 5th Bt, *qv*); *S* grandfather, 1950; *m* 1967, Mrs Susan Dudley Smith; two *s* one *d. Educ:* Eton. Commissioned Royal Horse Guards, 1956-66. *Heir: s* Hon. Roger Chetwode, *b* 29 May 1968. *Address:* Crowood House, Ramsbury, Wilts. *T:* Ramsbury 242. *Club:* White's.

CHETWYN, Robert; *b* 7 Sept. 1933; *s* of Frederick Reuben Suckling and Eleanor Lavinia (*née* Boffee). *Educ:* Rutlish, Merton, SW; Central Sch. of Speech and Drama. First appeared as actor with Dundee Repertory Co., 1952; subseq. in repertory at Hull, Alexandra Theatre, Birmingham, 1954; Birmingham Repertory Theatre, 1954-56; various TV plays, 1956-59; 1st prodn, Five Finger Exercise, Salisbury Playhouse, 1960; Dir of Prodns, Opera Hse, Harrogate, 1961-62; Artistic Dir, Ipswich Arts, 1962-64; Midsummer Night's Dream, transf. Comedy (London), 1964; Resident Dir, Belgrade (Coventry), 1964-66; Assoc. Dir, Mermaid, 1966, The Beaver Coat, three one-act plays by Shaw; There's a Girl in My Soup, Globe, 1966 and Music Box (NY), 1967; A Present for the Past, Edinburgh Fest., 1966; The Flip Side, Apollo, 1967; The Importance of Being Earnest, Haymarket, 1968; The Real Inspector Hound, Criterion, 1968; What the Butler Saw, Queens, 1968; The Country Wife, Chichester Fest., 1968; The Bandwaggon, Mermaid, 1968 and Sydney, 1970; Cannibal Crackers, Hampstead, 1969; When We are Married, Strand, 1970; Hamlet, in Rome, Zurich, Vienna, Antwerp, Cologne, then Cambridge (London), 1971; Parents Day, Globe, 1972; Restez Donc Jusq'au Petit Dejeuner, Belgium, 1973; Who's Who, Fortune, 1973; At the End of the Day, Savoy, 1973; Chez Nous, Globe, 1974; Qui est Qui, Belgium, 1974; The Doctor's Dilemma, Mermaid, 1975; Getting Away with Murder, Comedy, 1976; Private Lives, Melbourne, 1976; It's All Right If I Do It, Mermaid, 1977; A Murder is Announced, Vaudeville, 1977. Has directed for BBC TV. *Publication:* (jtly) Theatre on Merseyside (Arts Council report), 1973. *Recreations:* tennis, films, gardening. *Address:* 1 Wilton Court, Eccleston Square, SW1V 1PH.

CHETWYND, family name of Viscount Chetwynd.

CHETWYND, 10th Viscount *cr* 1717 (Ireland); **Adam Richard John Casson Chetwynd;** Baron Rathdown, 1717 (Ireland); with Colonial Mutual Life Assurance Society Ltd, Salisbury, Rhodesia, since 1968, Unit Manager, since 1972, Agency Manager, Johannesburg, since 1975; *b* 2 Feb. 1935; *o s* of 9th Viscount and of Joan Gilbert, *o c* of late Herbert Alexander Casson, CSI, Ty'n-y-coed, Arthog, Mer; *S* father, 1965; *m* 1966, Celia Grace (marr. diss. 1974), *er d* of Comdr Alexander Robert Ramsay, DSC, RNVR, Fasque, Borrowdale, Salisbury, Rhodesia; twin *s* one *d*. *Educ:* Eton. 2nd Lieut Cameron Highlanders, 1954-56. Freeman, Guild of Air Pilots and Air Navigators. *Recreations:* shooting, flying. *Heir: s* Hon. Adam Douglas Chetwynd, *b* 26 Feb. 1969. *Address:* c/o Ouvry and Co., 53 Romney Street, SW1.

CHETWYND, Sir Arthur (Ralph Talbot), 8th Bt *cr* 1795; President and General Manager, Chetwynd Films Ltd, Toronto, Canada, since 1950; *b* Walhachin, BC, 28 Oct. 1913; *o s* of Hon. William Ralph Talbot Chetwynd, MC, MLA (*d* 1957) (*b* of 7th Bt), and of Frances Mary, *d* of late James Jupe; *S* uncle, 1972; *m* 1940, Marjory May McDonald, *er d* of late Robert Bruce Lang, Vancouver, BC, and Glasgow, Scotland; two *s*. *Educ:* Vernon Preparatory School, BC; University of British Columbia (Physical Education and Recreation). Prior to 1933, a rancher in interior BC; Games Master, Vernon Prep. School, BC, 1933-36, also Instructor, Provincial Physical Education and Recreation; Chief Instructor, McDonald's Remedial Institute, Vancouver, 1937-41; Director of Remedial Gymnastics, British Columbia Workmen's Compensation Board, 1942; RCAF, 1943-45; Associate in Physical and Health Education, Univ. of Toronto, also Publicity Officer, Univ. of Toronto Athletic Assoc., 1946-52. *Recreations:* golf, swimming, badminton, squash. *Heir: er s* Robin John Talbot Chetwynd [*b* 21 Aug. 1941; *m* 1967, Heather Helen, *d* of George Bayliss Lothian; one *s* one *d*]. *Address:* 402-95 Thorncliffe Park Drive, Toronto, Ontario M4H 1L7. *T:* (416) 423-0367. *Clubs:* Naval and Military; Albany, Empire of Canada (Pres., 1974-75), Board of Trade, Board of Trade Golf and Country (all in Toronto).

CHETWYND, George Roland, CBE 1968; Member, BSC (Industry) Ltd; Chairman, Cleveland Area Health Authority, since 1977; *b* 14 May 1916; *s* of George Chetwynd and Anne Albrighton. *Educ:* Queen Elizabeth Grammar Sch., Atherstone; King's Coll., London University. BA Hons History, 1939; Postgraduate Scholarship; enlisted Royal Artillery, 1940; commissioned Army Educational Corps, 1942. MP (Lab) Stockton-on-Tees, 1945-62; Parliamentary Private Secretary to Minister of Local Government and Planning, 1950-51 (to Chancellor of Duchy of Lancaster, 1948-50); Director: North East Development Council, 1962-67; Northern and Tubes Group, BSC, 1968-70; Board Member, BSC, 1970-76. Delegate to Consultative Assembly, Council of Europe, 1952-54; Member: NATURE Conservancy, 1952-62; General Advisory Council, ITA, 1964; North-East Advisory Cttee for Civil Aviation, 1964; Northern Economic Planning Council, 1964-;

Board, BOAC, 1966-74; Northern Industrial Develt Bd, 1972-; Vice-Chm., Northern RHA, 1973-76; Dep. Chm., 1967-70, Chm., 1970-71, Land Commn; Chm., Council, BBC Radio Cleveland, 1976-. Chm. of Governors, Queen Mary's Hosp., Roehampton, 1952. Freedom of Borough of Stockton-on-Tees, 1968. *Recreations:* walking, sea fishing. *Address:* The Briars, Thorpe Larches, Sedgefield, Stockton-on-Tees, Cleveland. *T:* Stillington 336.

CHETWYND-TALBOT, family name of **Earl of Shrewsbury and Waterford.**

CHETWYND-TALBOT, Richard Michael Arthur; *see* Talbot.

CHEVELEY, Stephen William, OBE 1946; farmer; with Cheveley & Co., Agricultural Consultant, since 1959; *b* 29 March 1900; *s* of George Edward Cheveley and Arabella Cheveley; *m* 1926, Joan Hardy; two *s* one *d*. *Educ:* Leeds Modern Sch.; Leeds Univ. (BSc 1922; MSc). Served War, HAC, 1917-18. Min. of Agric. Scholarship, Farm Costings Res., 1922-23. British Sulphate of Ammonia Fedn, 1924-26; ICI Ltd, 1927-59; Chm., ICI Central Agricultural Control, 1952-59; Man. Dir, Plant Protection Ltd, 1945-51. Min. of Agric., Technical Develt Cttee, 1941-46; Chm., Foot and Mouth Res. Inst., 1950-58. Governor, Wye Coll., 1963-76; Chm., Appeal Cttee, Centre for European Agric. Studies, 1973-75. Chm., Farmers' Club, 1956. Master, Worshipful Co. of Farmers, 1961. *Publications:* Grass Drying, 1937; Out of a Wilderness, 1939; A Garden Goes to War, 1940; (with O. T. W. Price) Capital in UK Agriculture, 1956. *Recreations:* farming, fishing, painting. *Address:* Dunorlan Farm, Tunbridge Wells, Kent. *T:* Tunbridge Wells 26632. *Clubs:* Athenaeum, Farmers'.

CHEVRIER, Hon. Lionel, CC (Canada) 1967; PC (Can.); QC (Can.); Member, Legal Firm of Geoffrion, Prud'homme, Chevrier, Cardinal, Marchessault, Mercier & Greenstein, 500 Place d'Armes, Montreal; *s* of late Joseph Elphège Chevrier and late Malvina DeRepentigny; *m* 1932, Lucienne, *d* of Thomas J. Brulé, Ottawa; three *s* three *d*. *Educ:* Cornwall College Institute; Ottawa Univ.; Osgoode Hall. Called to bar, Ontario, 1928; KC 1938; called to Bar, Quebec, 1957. MP for Stormont, Canada, 1935-54; MP for Montreal-Laurier, 1957-64. Dep. Chief Government Whip, 1940; Chm., Special Parly Sub-Cttee on War Expenditures, 1942; Parliamentary Asst to Minister of Munitions and Supply, 1943; Minister of Transport, 1945-54; Pres., St Lawrence Seaway Authority, 1954-57; Minister of Justice, 1963-64; High Commissioner in London, 1964-67. Delegate, Bretton Woods Conf., 1945; Chm., Canadian Delegn, UN General Assembly, Paris, 1948; Pres., Privy Council, Canada, 1957. Comr-Gen. for State Visits to Canada, 1967; Chairman: Canadian Economic Mission to Francophone Africa, 1968; Mission to study Canadian Consular Posts in USA, 1968; Seminar to study river navigation for Unitar, Buenos Aires, 1970. Hon. degrees: LLD: Ottawa, 1946; Laval, 1952; Queen's, 1956; DCL, Bishops', 1964. *Publication:* The St Lawrence Seaway, 1959. *Recreations:* walking and reading. *Address:* 500 Place d'Armes, Montreal 126, Canada.

CHEW, Victor Kenneth, TD 1958; Keeper, Department of Physics, Science Museum, London, since 1970; *b* 19 Jan. 1915; *yr s* of Frederick and Edith Chew. *Educ:* Christ's Hospital; Christ Church, Oxford (Scholar). 1st class, Final Honours School of Natural Science (Physics), 1936; BA (Oxon) 1936, MA 1964. Asst Master, King's Sch., Rochester, 1936-38; Winchester Coll., 1938-40. Served War: Royal Signals, 1940-46. Asst Master, Shrewsbury Sch., 1946-48 and 1949-58; Lecturer in Education, Bristol Univ., 1948-49. Entered Science Museum as Asst Keeper, 1958; Deputy Keeper and Sec. to Advisory Council, 1967. *Publications:* official publications of Science Museum. *Recreations:* choral singing, mountain walking, photography. *Address:* Flat 24, Andrewes House, Barbican, EC2Y 8AX.

CHEWTON, Viscount; James Sherbrooke Waldegrave; *b* 8 Dec. 1940; *e s* of 12th Earl Waldegrave, *qv*. *Educ:* Eton Coll.; Trinity Coll., Cambridge. *Address:* 47 Linden Gardens, W2; West End Farm, Chewton Mendip, Bath. *Clubs:* Brooks's, Beefsteak.

CHEYNE, Major Sir Joseph (Lister Watson), 3rd Bt *cr* 1908; OBE 1976; Curator, Keats Shelley Memorial House, Rome; *b* 10 Oct. 1914; *e s* of Sir Joseph Lister Cheyne, 2nd Bt, MC, and Nelita Manfield (*d* 1977), *d* of Andrew Pringle, Borgue; *S* father, 1957; *m* 1st, 1938, Mary Mort (marr. diss. 1955; she *d* 1959), *d* of late Vice-Adm. J. D. Allen, CB; one *s* one *d*; 2nd, 1955, Cicely, *d* of T. Metcalfe, Padiham, Lancs; two *s* one *d*. *Educ:* Stowe Sch.; Corpus Christi Coll., Cambridge. Major, The Queen's Westminsters (KRRC), 1943; Italian Campaign. 2nd Sec. (Inf.), British Embassy, Rome, 1968, 1st Sec., 1971, 1st Sec. (Inf.),

1973-76. *Heir: s* Patrick John Lister Cheyne [*b* 2 July 1941; *m* 1968, Helen Louise Trevor, *yr d* of Louis Smith, Southsea; one *s* two *d*]. *Address:* Leagarth, Fetlar, Shetland; 7 Via Delle Terme Deciane, Rome, Italy. *T:* Rome 5778835.

CHEYSSON, Claude, Officer Legion of Honour 1962; Croix de Guerre (5 times); European Commissioner (Development) since 1973; Member, Board of Le Monde, since 1969; *b* 13 April 1920; *s* of Pierre Cheysson and Sophie Funck-Brentano; *m* 1969, Danièle Schwarz; one *s* one *d* (and two *s* one *d* by former marrs). *Educ:* Coll. Stanislas, Paris; Ecole Polytechnique; Ecole Nationale d'Administration. Escaped from occupied France, 1943; Tank Officer, Free French Forces, France and Germany, 1944-45. Liaison Officer with German authorities, Bonn, 1948-52; Political Adviser to Viet Nam Govt, Saigon, 1952-53; Personal Adviser: to Prime Minister of France, Paris, 1954-55; to French Minister of Moroccan and Tunisian Affairs, 1956; Sec.-Gen., Commn for Techn. Cooperation in Africa, Lagos, Nairobi, 1957-62; Dir-Gen., Sahara Authority, Algiers, 1962-66; French Ambassador in Indonesia, 1966-69; Pres., Entreprise Minière et Chimique, 1970-73. Grand Officer, Nat. Orders of Cameroun, Lebanon, Togo, Tunisia, Upper Volta; Comdr, Nat. Orders of Central African Rep., Indonesia, Lebanon and Mali; US Presidential Citation. Dr *hc* Univ. of Louvain. *Publications:* articles on develt policies and 3rd World. *Recreation:* ski-ing. *Address:* Commission of the European Communities, 200 rue de la Loi, Brussels 1040, Belgium. *T:* 7358040.

CHIANG, Yee, BSc; LHD; DLit; FRSA; FAAS; Professor of Chinese, Columbia University, USA, 1970-72; now Emeritus Professor; *b* 19 May 1903; *s* of Chiang Ho-an and Tsai Hsiang-Lin. *Educ:* Nat. South-Eastern Univ., Nanking. Teacher of Chemistry in two different middle schools; Lecturer in Chemistry at National Chi-Nan Univ.; soldier in the Chinese Army for one year; Asst Editor of a daily newspaper at Hangchow in Chekiang province; District Governor of four districts, Kiukiang, Yushan, Tangtu, and Wuhu in Kiangsi and Anhui provinces; Lecturer in Chinese at Sch. of Oriental Studies, London Univ., 1935-38; in charge of Chinese Section at Wellcome Historical Medical Museum, 1938-40. Designed the décor and costumes for the Sadler's Wells Ballet, The Birds, 1942; Curator of Chinese Ethnology, Peabody Museum, Salem, Massachusetts, USA, 1956-; Ralph Waldo Emerson Fellow in Poetry, Harvard Univ., 1958-59; Vis. Prof. of Chinese, ANU, 1972-73. Mem. Sub-Cttee on New Art Center for Univ. of Virginia, 1962; Senior Specialist, East-West Center, 1967. Hon. LHD Hofstra; Hon. LittD ANU; Hon. DArt, Rider; Hon. DLitt Hong Kong. *Publications:* a Book of poems in Chinese, 1935; The Chinese Eye, 1935; The Silent Traveller in Lakeland, 1937; Chinese Calligraphy, 1938; The Silent Traveller in London, 1938; Birds and Beasts, 1939; Chinpao and the Giant Panda, 1939; The Silent Traveller in Wartime, 1939; A Chinese Childhood, 1940; The Silent Traveller in the Yorkshire Dales, 1941; Lo Cheng, the Boy who wouldn't keep still, 1941; Chinpao at the Zoo, 1941; The Men of the Burma Road, 1942; The Story of Ming, 1943; The Silent Traveller in Oxford, 1944; Dabbitse, 1944; Yebbin, 1947; The Silent Traveller in Edinburgh, 1948; The Silent Traveller in New York, 1950; Chinese Painting, 1953; The Silent Traveller in Dublin, 1955; The Silent Traveller in Paris, 1956; The Silent Traveller in Boston, 1959; The Silent Traveller in San Francisco, 1964; Chinese Ch'an Poetry, 1966; The Silent Traveller in Japan, 1971; China Revisited, 1977; contributed many articles to various English and American papers and magazines. *Recreations:* calligraphy, painting, walking, travelling and climbing. *Address:* c/o W. W. Norton Co., 500 Fifth Avenue, New York, NY 10036, USA; c/o Methuen & Co. Ltd, 11 New Fetter Lane, EC4.

CHIANG KAI-SHEK, Madame (Mayling Soong Chiang); Chinese sociologist; *y d* of C. J. Soong; *m* 1927, Generalissimo Chiang Kai-Shek (*d* 1975). *Educ:* Wellesley Coll., USA. LHD, John B. Stetson Univ., Deland, Fla, Bryant Coll., Providence, RI, Hobart and William Smith Colls, Geneva, NY; LLD, Rutgers Univ., New Brunswick, NJ, Goucher Coll., Baltimore, MD, Wellesley Coll., Wellesley, Mass, Loyola Univ., Los Angeles, Cal., Russell Sage Coll., Troy, NY, Hahnemann Medical Coll., Philadelphia, Pa, Wesleyan Coll., Macon, Ga, Univ. of Michigan, Univ. of Hawaii; Hon. FRCS. First Chinese woman appointed Mem. Child Labor Commn; Inaugurated Moral Endeavor Assoc.; established schools in Nanking for orphans of Revolutionary Soldiers; former Mem. Legislative Yuan; served as Sec.-General of Chinese Commission on Aeronautical Affairs; Member Chinese Commission on Aeronautical Affairs; Director-General of the New Life Movement and Chairman of its Women's Advisory Council; Founder and Director: National Chinese Women's Assoc. for War Relief; National Assoc. for Refugee Children; Chinese Women's Anti-Aggression League; Huashing Children's Home;

Cheng Hsin Medical Rehabilitation Center for Post Polio Crippled Children. Chm., Fu Jen Catholic University. Governor, Nat. Palace Museum. Frequently makes inspection tours to all sections of Free China where personally trained girl workers carry on war area and rural service work; accompanies husband on military campaigns; first Chinese woman to be decorated by National Govt of China. Recipient of highest military and Civil decorations; Hon. Chm., British United Aid to China Fund, China; Hon. Chm., Soc. for the Friends of the Wounded; Hon. President, American Bureau for Medical Aid to China; Patroness, International Red Cross Commn; Hon. President, Chinese Women's Relief Assoc. of New York; Hon. Chairman, Canadian Red Cross China Cttee; Hon. Chairman, Board of Directors, India Famine Relief Cttee; Hon. Mem., New York Zoological Soc.; Hon. Pres., Cttee for the Promotion of the Welfare of the Blind; Life Mem., San Francisco Press Club and Associated Countrywomen of the World; Mem., Phi Beta Kappa, Eta Chapter; first Hon. Member, Bill of Rights Commemorative Society; Hon. Member, Filipino Guerrillas of Bataan Assoc. Medal of Honour, New York City Federation of Women's Clubs; YWCA Emblem; Gold Medal, New York Southern Soc.; Chi Omega Nat. Achievement Award for 1943; Gold Medal for distinguished services, National Institute for Social Sciences; Distinguished Service Award, Altrusa Internat. Assoc.; Churchman Fifth Annual Award, 1943; Distinguished Service Citation, All-American Conf. to Combat Communism, 1958; Hon. Lieut-Gen. US Marine Corps. *Publications:* China in Peace and War, 1939; China Shall Rise Again, 1939; This is Our China, 1940; We Chinese Women, 1941; Little Sister Su, 1943; Ten Eventful Years, for Encyclopædia Britannica, 1946; Album of Reproduction of Paintings, vol. I, 1952, vol. II, 1962; The Sure Victory, 1955; Madame Chiang Kai-Shek Selected Speeches, 1958-59; Madame Chiang Kai-shek Selected Speeches, 1965-66; Album of Chinese Orchid Paintings, 1971; Album of Chinese Bamboo Paintings, 1972; Album of Chinese Landscape Paintings, 1973; Album of Chinese Floral Paintings, 1974. *Address:* Shihlin, Taipei, Taiwan.

CHIASSON, Most Rev. Donat; *see* Moncton, Archbishop of, (RC).

CHIBNALL, Albert Charles, FRS 1937; PhD (London); ScD (Cantab); Fellow of Clare College, Cambridge; Fellow of the Imperial College of Science and Technology, London; *b* 28 Jan. 1894; *s* of G. W. Chibnall; *m* 1st, 1931 (wife *d* 1936); two *d*; 2nd, 1947, Marjorie McCallum Morgan, DPhil, Fellow of Clare Hall; one *s* one *d*. *Educ:* St Paul's Sch.; Clare Coll., Cambridge; Imperial Coll. of Science and Technology; Yale Univ., New Haven, Conn. 2nd Lieut, ASC 1914; Capt., 1915; attached RAF, 1917-19, served Egypt and Salonika. Huxley Medal, 1922; Imperial Coll. Travelling Fellow, 1922-23; Seessel Fellow, Yale Univ., 1923-24; Hon. Asst in Biochemistry, University Coll., London, 1924-30; Asst Prof. 1930-36, Prof. 1936-43, Emeritus Prof. 1943, of Biochemistry, Imperial Coll.; Sir William Dunn Prof. of Biochemistry, Univ. of Cambridge, 1943-49. Silliman Lectr, Yale Univ., 1938; Bakerian Lectr, Royal Society, 1942. Hon. Mem., Biochem. Soc.; Vice-Pres., Bucks Record Soc. Hon. DSc St Andrews, 1971. *Publications:* Protein Metabolism in the Plant, 1939; Richard de Baden and the University of Cambridge, 1315-1340, 1963; Sherington, fiefs and fields of a Buckinghamshire village, 1965; papers in scientific journals on plant biochemistry. *Address:* 6 Millington Road, Cambridge. *T:* Cambridge 53923. *Club:* Athenæum.

CHICHESTER, family name of **Marquess of Donegall.**

CHICHESTER, 9th Earl of, *cr* 1801; **John Nicholas Pelham;** Bt 1611; Baron Pelham of Stanmer, 1762; *b* (posthumous) 14 April 1944; *s* of 8th Earl of Chichester (killed on active service, 1944) and Ursula (she *m* 2nd, 1957, Ralph Gunning Henderson; marr. diss. 1971), *o d* of late Walter de Pannwitz, de Hartekamp, Bennebroek, Holland; *S* father, 1944; *m* 1975, Mrs June Marijke Hall. *Recreations:* music, flying. *Heir: kinsman* Richard Anthony Henry Pelham, *b* 1st Aug. 1952. *Address:* Little Durnford Manor, Salisbury, Wilts.

CHICHESTER, Bishop of, since 1974; **Rt. Rev. Eric Waldram Kemp,** MA Oxon, DD; *b* 27 April 1915; *o c* of Tom Kemp and Florence Lilian Kemp (*née* Waldram), Grove House, Waltham, Grimsby, Lincs; *m* 1953, Leslie Patricia, 3rd *d* of late Rt Rev. K. E. Kirk, sometime Bishop of Oxford; one *s* four *d*. *Educ:* Brigg Grammar Sch., Lincs; Exeter Coll., Oxford; St Stephen's House, Oxford. Deacon 1939; Priest 1940; Curate of St Luke, Southampton, 1939-41; Librarian of Pusey House, Oxford, 1941-46; Chaplain of Christ Church Oxford, 1943-46; Actg Chap., St John's Coll., Oxford, 1943-45; Fellow, Chaplain, Tutor, and Lectr in Theology and Medieval History, Exeter Coll., Oxford, 1946-69; Dean of Worcester, 1969-74. Exam.

Chaplain: to Bp of Mon, 1942-45; to Bp of Southwark, 1946-50; to Bp of St Albans, 1946-69; to Bp of Exeter, 1949-69; to Bp of Lincoln, 1950-69. Proctor in Convocation for University of Oxford, 1949-69. Bp of Oxford's Commissary for Religious Communities, 1952-69; Chaplain to the Queen, 1967-69. Canon and Prebendary of Caistor in Lincoln Cathedral, 1952; Hon. Provincial Canon of Cape Town, 1960-; Bampton Lecturer, 1959-60. FRHistS 1951. *Publications*: (contributions to) Thy Household the Church, 1943; Canonization and Authority in the Western Church, 1948; Norman Powell Williams, 1954; Twenty-five Papal Decretals relating to the Diocese of Lincoln (with W. Holtzmann), 1954; An Introduction to Canon Law in the Church of England, 1957; Life and Letters of Kenneth Escott Kirk, 1959; Counsel and Consent, 1961; The Anglican-Methodist conversations: A Comment from within, 1964; (ed) Man: Fallen and Free, 1969. Contrib. to English Historical Review, Jl of Ecclesiastical History. *Recreations:* music, travel. *Address:* The Palace, Chichester, W Sussex. *T:* Chichester 782161. *Club:* National Liberal.

CHICHESTER, Dean of; *see* Holtby, Very Rev. R. T.

CHICHESTER, Archdeacon of; *see* Eyre, Ven. R. M. S.

CHICHESTER, Sir (Edward) John, 11th Bt *cr* 1641; *b* 14 April 1916; *s* of Comdr Sir Edward George Chichester, 10th Bt, RN, and Phyllis Dorothy, *d* of late Henry F. Compton, Minstead Manor, Hants; *S* father, 1940; *m* 1950, Hon. Mrs Anne Rachel Pearl Moore-Gwyn, *widow* of Capt. Howel Moore-Gwyn, Welsh Guards, and *d* of 2nd Baron Montagu of Beaulieu and of Hon. Mrs Edward Pleydell-Bouverie; two *s* three *d. Educ:* Radley; RMC Sandhurst. Commissioned RSF, 1936. Patron of one living. Served throughout War of 1939-45. Was employed by ICI Ltd, 1950-60. A King's Foreign Service Messenger, 1947-50. Formerly Capt., Royal Scots Fusiliers and Lieut RNVR. *Heir: s* James Henry Edward Chichester, *b* 15 Oct. 1951. *Address:* Battramsley Lodge, Boldre, Lymington, Hants. *Club:* Naval.

CHICHESTER-CLARK, family name of **Baron Moyola.**

CHICHESTER-CLARK, Sir Robert, (Sir Robin Chichester-Clark), Kt 1974; Director: Berndtson International; Alfred Booth and Co.; management consultant; *b* 10 Jan. 1928; *s* of late Capt. J. L. C. Chichester-Clark, DSO and Bar, DL, MP, and Mrs C. E. Brackenbury; *m* 1st, 1953, Jane Helen Goddard (marr. diss. 1972); one *s* two *d*; 2nd, 1974, Caroline, *d* of Anthony Bull, *qv*; two *s. Educ:* Royal Naval Coll.; Magdalene Coll., Cambridge (BA Hons Hist. and Law). Journalist, 1950; Public Relations Officer, Glyndebourne Opera, 1952; Asst to Sales Manager, Oxford Univ. Press, 1953-55. MP (UU) Londonderry City and Co., 1955-Feb. 1974; PPS to Financial Secretary to the Treasury, 1958; Asst Government Whip (unpaid), 1958-60; a Lord Comr of the Treasury, 1960-61; Comptroller of HM Household, 1961-64; Chief Opposition Spokesman on N Ireland, 1964-70, on Public Building and Works, 1965-70; Minister of State, Dept of Employment, 1972-74. Hon. FIWM 1972. *Recreation:* fishing. *Club:* Carlton. *See also Baron Moyola.*

CHIEF RABBI; *see* Jakobovits, Rabbi Dr Immanuel.

CHIEPE, Hon. Gaositwe Keagakwa Tibe, PMS 1975; MBE 1962; FRSA; Minister for Mineral Resources and Water Affairs, since 1977; *b* 20 Oct. 1922; *d* of late T. Chiepe. *Educ:* Fort Hare, South Africa (BSc, EdDip); Bristol Univ., UK (MA (Ed)). Asst Educn Officer, 1948-53; Educn Officer and Schools Inspector, 1953-62; Sen. Educn Officer, 1962-65; Dep. Dir of Educn, 1965-67; Dir of Educn, 1968-70; Diplomat, 1970-; High Comr to UK and Nigeria, 1970-74; Ambassador: Denmark, Norway, Sweden, France and Germany, 1970-74; Belgium and EEC, 1973-74 Minister of Commerce and Industry, 1974-77. Member: Botswana Society; Botswana Girl Guide Assoc.; Internat. Fedn of University Women. Hon. LLD Bristol, 1972. FRSA 1973. *Recreations:* gardening, a bit of swimming (in Botswana), reading. *Address:* Ministry of Mineral Resources and Water Affairs, Private Bag 0018, Gabarone, Botswana. *Club:* Notwane (Botswana).

CHILCOTT, C. M.; *see* Fordyce, C. M.

CHILD, Christopher Thomas; National President, Bakers' Union, 1968-77; *b* 8 Jan. 1920; *s* of late Thomas William and Penelope Child; *m* 1941, Lilian Delaney; two *s* one *d. Educ:* Robert Ferguson Sch., Carlisle; Birmingham Coll. of Food and Domestic Science. Apprenticed baker, 1936-41; gained London City and Guilds final certificates in Breadmaking, Flour Confectionery and Bakery Science, 1951, and became Examiner in these subjects for CGLI. Full-time trade union official in

Birmingham, 1958. Chairman: Nat. Council Baking Education; Nat. Joint Apprenticeship Council for Baking. Mem., Industrial Training Bd, Food, Drink and Tobacco, 1968-; Vice-Pres., EEC Food Group; Mem., EEC Cttees on Food Products, Vocational Training, and Food Legislation; Sec., Jt Bakers' Unions of England, Scotland and Ireland. *Recreations:* fishing, gardening, climbing in English Lake District. *Address:* 200 Bedford Road, Letchworth, Herts SG6 4EA. *T:* Letchworth 72170.

CHILD, Clifton James, OBE 1949; MA, PhM, FRHistS; Administrative Officer, Cabinet Office Historical Section, 1969-76, retired; *b* Birmingham, 20 June 1912; *s* of late Joseph and Georgina Child; *m* 1938, Hilde Hurwitz; two *s. Educ:* Moseley Grammar Sch.; Universities of Birmingham, Berlin and Wisconsin. Univ. of Birmingham: Entrance Schol., 1929; Kenrick Prizeman, 1930; BA 1st class hons, 1932; Francis Corder Clayton Research Schol., 1932-34; MA 1934. Univ. of Wisconsin: Commonwealth Fund Fellow, 1936-38; PhM 1938. Educn Officer, Lancs Community Council, 1939-40. Joined Foreign Office, 1941; Head of American Section, FO Research Dept, 1946-58; African Section, 1958-62; Dep. Librarian and Departmental Record Officer, 1962; Librarian and Keeper of the Papers, FO, 1965-69; Cabinet Office, 1969-76. FRHistS 1965. *Publications:* The German-Americans in Politics, 1939; (with Arnold Toynbee and others) Hitler's Europe, 1954; contribs to learned periodicals in Britain and US. *Recreations:* gardening, foreign travel. *Address:* Westcroft, Westhall Road, Warlingham, Surrey. *T:* Upper Warlingham 2540.

CHILD, Sir (Coles John) Jeremy, 3rd Bt *cr* 1919; actor; *b* 20 Sept. 1944; *s* of Sir Coles John Child, 2nd Bt, and Sheila (*d* 1964), *e d* of Hugh Mathewson; *S* father, 1971; *m* 1971, Deborah Jane (*née* Snelling) (marr. diss. 1976); one *d. Educ:* Eton; Univ. of Poitiers (Dip. in Fr.). Trained at Bristol Old Vic Theatre Sch., 1963-65; Bristol Old Vic, 1965-66; repertory at Windsor, Canterbury and Colchester; Conduct Unbecoming, Queen's, 1970; appeared at Royal Court, Mermaid and Bankside Globe, 1973; Oh Kay, Westminster, 1974; *films include:* Privilege, 1966; Play Dirty, 1967; Oh What a Lovely War!, 1967; The Breaking of Bumbo, 1970; TV series: Father, Dear Father, The Glittering Prizes, Plays for Britain, Wings, Backs to the Land. *Recreations:* travel, squash, swimming, photography. *Address:* 48 Sydney Street, SW3. *T:* 01-351 1498. *Club:* Roehampton.

CHILD, Sir Jeremy; *see* Child, Sir C. J. J.

CHILD, Ven. Kenneth; Archdeacon of Sudbury since 1970; Rector of Great and Little Thurlow with Little Bradley since 1969; *b* 6 March 1916; *s* of late James Child, Wakefield; *m* 1955, Jane, *d* of late G. H. B. Turner and of Mrs Turner, Bolton; one *s* two *d. Educ:* Queen Elizabeth's School, Wakefield; University of Leeds (BA); College of the Resurrection, Mirfield. Deacon 1941, Priest 1942, Manchester; Curate of St Augustine, Tonge Moor, 1941-44; Chaplain to the Forces, 1944-47; Vicar of Tonge Moor, 1947-55; Chaplain of Guy's Hospital, 1955-59; Rector of Newmarket, 1959-69; Rural Dean of Newmarket, 1963-70. Proctor in Convocation, 1964-; Hon. Canon of St Edmundsbury, 1968-. Hon. CF, 1947. *Publications:* Sick Call, 1965; In His Own Parish, 1970. *Recreation:* travel. *Address:* Great Thurlow Vicarage, Haverhill, Suffolk. *T:* Thurlow 209. *Club:* Subscription Rooms (Newmarket).

CHILD-VILLIERS; *see* Villiers.

CHILDS, Rt. Rev. Derrick Greenslade; *see* Monmouth, Bishop of.

CHILDS, Hubert, CMG 1951; OBE 1943; *b* 6 July 1905; 3rd *s* of late Dr W. M. Childs, first Vice-Chancellor of the University of Reading. *Educ:* Oakham Sch.; University College, Oxford. Colonial Administrative Service, Nigeria, 1928-46; Sierra Leone, 1946-58. On Military service, 1941-46. Chief Comr, Protectorate, Sierra Leone, 1950-58. UK Plebiscite Administrator for Southern Cameroons, 1960-61. *Address:* Brown's Gate, Bucklebury, Reading, Berks.

CHILDS, Leonard, CBE 1961 (OBE 1946); DL; JP; Chairman, Great Ouse River Authority, 1949-74; *b* April 1897; *s* of Robert R. Childs, Grove House, Chatteris; *m* 1924, Mary M., *d* of John Esson, MIMinE, Aberdeen; three *s. Educ:* Wellingborough. Served European War, 1914-18, in Royal Flying Corps and Artists' Rifles. County Councillor, Isle of Ely, 1922 (Chairman, 1946-49); Custos Rotulorum, 1952-65; High Sheriff, Cambs and Hunts, 1946; DL Cambs, 1950; JP Isle of Ely, 1932. *Recreation:* shooting. *Address:* South Park Street, Chatteris, Cambridgeshire. *T:* Chatteris 2204.

CHILE, BOLIVIA AND PERU, Bishop of, since 1977; **Rt. Rev. Colin Frederick Bazley;** *b* 27 June 1935; *s* of Reginald Samuel Bazley and Isabella Davies; *m* 1960, Barbara Helen Griffiths; three *d. Educ:* Birkenhead School; St Peter's Hall, Oxford (MA); Tyndale Hall, Bristol. Deacon 1959, priest 1960; Assistant Curate, St Leonard's, Bootle, 1959-62; Missionary of S American Missionary Society in Chile, 1962-69; Rural Dean of Chol-Chol, 1962-66; Archdeacon of Temuco, 1966-69; Assistant Bishop for Cautin and Malleco, Dio. Chile, Bolivia and Peru, 1969-75; Assistant Bishop for Santiago, 1975-77. *Recreations:* football (Liverpool supporter) and fishing on camping holidays. *Address:* Iglesia Anglicana, Casilla 675, Santiago, Chile. *T:* 292158.

CHILSTON, 3rd Viscount *cr* 1911, of Boughton Malherbe; **Eric Alexander Akers-Douglas;** Baron Douglas of Baads, 1911; *b* 17 Dec. 1910; *s* of 2nd Viscount and Amy (*d* 1962), *d* of late J. R. Jennings-Bramly, RHA; *S* father, 1947; *m* 1955, Marion (*d* 1970), *d* of late Capt. William Charles Howard, RE. *Educ:* Eton; Trinity Coll., Oxford. Formerly Flight Lieut RAFVR. *Publications:* part author, Survey of International Affairs, 1938 Vol. III, Hitler's Europe, Realignment of Europe (Royal Institute of International Affairs); Chief Whip: The Political Life and Times of A. Akers-Douglas, 1st Viscount Chilston, 1961; W. H. Smith, 1965. *Heir: cousin* Alastair George Akers-Douglas, [*b* 6 Sept. 1946; *m* 1971, Juliet Lovett; two *s*]. *Address:* Chilston Park, Maidstone, Kent. *T:* Lenham 214. *Club:* Brooks's.

CHILTON, Air Marshal Sir (Charles) Edward, KBE 1959 (CBE 1945); CB 1951; RAF (retired); Consultant and Director, IBM (Rentals) UK; *o s* of J. C. Chilton; *m* 1st, 1929, Betty Ursula (*d* 1963), 2nd *d* of late Bernard Temple Wrinch; one *s*; 2nd, 1964, Joyce Cornforth. Royal Air Force general duties branch; Air Commodore, 1950; Air Vice-Marshal, 1954; Air Marshal, 1959. Dep. Air Officer i/c Administration, Air Command, SE Asia, 1944; AOC Ceylon, 1946; Imperial Defence Coll., 1951; AOC Gibraltar, 1952; Asst Chief of the Air Staff (Policy), 1953-54; SASO, HQ Coastal Command, 1955; AOC Royal Air Force, Malta, and Dep. Comdr-in-Chief (Air), Allied Forces Mediterranean, 1957-59; AOC-in-C, Coastal Command and Maritime Air Commander Eastern Atlantic Area, and Commander Maritime Air, Channel and Southern North Sea, 1959-62. Specialist navigator (Air Master navigator certificate) and Fellow (Vice-Pres. 1949-51, 1959-61, 1963-65), Royal Institute of Navigation. Pres. RAF Rowing Club, 1956; Vice-Adm. and Hon. Life Mem. RAF Sailing Assoc.; Hon. Vice-Pres. RAF Swimming Assoc. MInstD. Grand Cross of Prince Henry the Navigator (Portugal), 1960. *Address:* 11 Charles House, Phyllis Court Drive, Henley-on-Thames, Oxon. *Clubs:* Royal Air Force; (Vice-Patron) Royal Gibraltar Yacht; Phyllis Court (Henley).

CHILTON, Donovan; retired as Keeper, Department of Electrical Engineering and Communications, Science Museum, London (1960-74); *b* 24 Feb. 1909; 5th *s* of Percy Chilton and Ada Grace Ryall; *m* 1937, Jane Margaret Saunders; two *s* (one *d* decd). *Educ:* Latymer Upper Sch.; Royal College of Science (Royal Scholar); University of Göttingen, Germany. BSc 1931; ARCS 1930; DIC 1931. Works physicist, Ilford Ltd, 1932-38; entered Science Museum, 1938; Dep. Keeper, 1949; Keeper, 1960-74. Air Ministry, Meteorological Office, 1939-45. FInstP. *Address:* 33 Park Avenue, Hutton, Brentwood, Essex CM13 2QL. *T:* Brentwood 210775.

CHILTON, Brig. Sir Frederick Oliver, Kt 1969; CBE 1963 (OBE 1957); DSO 1941 and bar 1944; Chairman, Repatriation Commission, Australia, 1958-70; *b* 23 July 1905. *Educ:* Univ. of Sydney (BA, LLB). Solicitor, NSW, 1929. Late AIF; served War of 1939-45, Libya, Greece, New Guinea and Borneo (despatches, DSO and bar); Controller of Joint Intelligence, 1946-48; Asst Sec., Dept of Defence, Australia, 1948-50; Dep. Sec., 1950-58. *Address:* Clareville Beach, NSW, Australia. *Clubs:* Melbourne, Union, Naval and Military (Melbourne); Imperial Service (Sydney).

CHILVER, Amos Henry, MA, DSc; Vice-Chancellor, Cranfield Institute of Technology, since 1970; Chairman, Universities' Computer Board, since 1975; Director: SKF (UK) Ltd, since 1972; English China Clays Ltd, since 1973; De La Rue Company, since 1973; National Westminster Bank, South-East Region, since 1975; Delta Metal Co., since 1977; *b* 30 Oct. 1926; *e s* of Amos H. Chilver and Annie E. Mack; *m* 1959, Claudia, *o d* of Sir Wilfrid Grigson; three *s* two *d. Educ:* Southend High Sch.; Bristol Univ. (Albert Fry Prize 1947). FBIM 1976; Fellow, Fellowship of Engineering, 1977. Structural Engineering Asst, British Railways, 1947; Asst Lecturer, 1950, Lecturer, 1952, in Civil Engineering, Bristol Univ.; Demonstrator, 1954, Lectr,

1956, in Engineering, Cambridge Univ.; Fellow of Corpus Christi Coll., Cambridge, 1958-61; Chadwick Prof. of Civil Engineering, UCL, 1961-69. Director: Centre for Environmental Studies, 1967-69; Node Course (for civil service and industry), 1974-75; Chm., RAF Trng and Educn Adv. Cttee., 1976-; Member: Ferrybridge Enquiry Cttee, 1965; Management Cttee, Inst. of Child Health, 1965-69; ARC, 1967-70 and 1972-75; SRC, 1970-74; Beds Educn Cttee, 1970-74; Planning and Transport Res. Adv. Council, 1972-; Cttee for Ind. Technologies, 1972-76; ICE Special Cttee on Educn and Trng, 1973 (Chm.); CNAA, 1973-76; Royal Commn on Environmental Pollution, 1976-; Adv. Council for Applied R&D, 1977-. Telford Gold Medal, ICE, 1962. *Publications:* Problems in Engineering Structures (with R. J. Ashby), 1958; Strength of Materials (with J. Case), 1959; Thin-walled Structures (ed), 1967; papers on structural theory in engineering journals. *Address:* Cayley Lodge, Cranfield, Bedford MK43 0SX. *T:* Bedford 750111; 2 Hampstead Square, NW3. *T:* 01-435 0675. *Clubs:* Athenæum, United Oxford & Cambridge University.

CHILVER, Elizabeth Millicent, (Mrs R. C. Chilver); Principal of Lady Margaret Hall, Oxford, since 1971; *b* 3 Aug. 1914; *o d* of late Philip Perceval Graves and late Millicent Graves (*née* Gilchrist); *m* 1937, Richard Clementson Chilver, *qv. Educ:* Benenden Sch., Cranbrook; Somerville Coll., Oxford (Hon. Fellow, 1977). Journalist, 1937-39; temp. Civil Servant, 1939-45; Daily News Ltd, 1945-47; temp. Principal and Secretary, Colonial Social Science Research Council and Colonial Economic Research Cttee, Colonial Office, 1948-57; Director, Univ. of Oxford Inst. of Commonwealth Studies, 1957-61; Senior Research Fellow, Univ. of London Inst. of Commonwealth Studies, 1961-64; Principal, Bedford Coll., Univ. of London, 1964-71, Fellow, 1974. Mem. Royal Commn on Medical Education, 1965-68. Trustee, British Museum, 1970-75; Mem. Governing Body, SOAS, Univ. of London, 1975-. Médaille de la Reconnaissance française, 1945. *Publications:* articles on African historical and political subjects. *Address:* 108 Clifton Hill, NW8. *T:* 01-624 2702.

CHILVER, Prof. Guy Edward Farquhar, MA, DPhil; Professor of Classical Studies, University of Kent at Canterbury, 1964-76, now Emeritus Professor; *b* 11 Feb. 1910; *er s* of late Arthur Farquhar Chilver and late Florence Ranking; *m* 1st, 1945, Sylvia Chloe (marr. diss. 1972), *d* of late D. P. Littell; 2nd, 1973, Marie Elizabeth, *d* of W. J. Powell. *Educ:* Winchester; Trinity Coll., Oxford. Harmsworth Sen. Scholar, Merton Coll., 1932-34. Queen's Coll., Oxford: Fellow and Prælector in Ancient History, 1934-63; Dean, 1935-39; Sen. Tutor, 1948-63; Emeritus Fellow, 1964-; Dep. Vice-Chancellor, Kent Univ., 1966-72, Dean of Humanities, 1964-74. Min. of Food, 1940-45; British Food Mission, Washington, 1943-45. Member Hebdomadal Council, Oxford Univ., 1949-63; Visiting Prof., University of Texas, 1963; Vice-Pres., Society for Promotion of Roman Studies, 1964-. *Publications:* Cisalpine Gaul, 1941; trans. (with S. C. Chilver), and annotated, Unesco History of Mankind, Vol. II, 1965; articles in learned journals. *Recreation:* bridge. *Address:* Oak Lodge, Boughton, near Faversham, Kent. *T:* Boughton 246. *Clubs:* Reform; Kent and Canterbury (Canterbury).

See also R. C. Chilver, B. Davidson.

CHILVER, Richard Clementson, CB 1952; *b* 1912; *yr s* of Arthur Farquhar Chilver; *m* 1937, Elizabeth Chilver, *qv. Educ:* Winchester; New Coll., Oxford. HM Civil Service, 1934-72 (Under-Secretary 1946, Deputy Secretary, 1955); Administrative Director, Insurance Technical Bureau, 1972-76. *Address:* 108 Clifton Hill, NW8. *T:* 01-624 2702.

See also Prof. G. E. F. Chilver, B. Davidson.

CHINA, William Edward, CBE 1959; MA, ScD, FIBiol; DipAgric Cantab; FRES; Keeper, Department of Entomology, British Museum (Natural History), 1955-61; Deputy Chief Scientific Officer, 1957-61; *b* 7 Dec. 1895; 2nd *s* of William Edwin China, London; *m* 1922, Lita Frances Gaunt, *d* of late A. R. Gaunt, Birmingham; one *s* twin *d. Educ:* Battersea Polytechnic; Trinity Hall, Cambridge (Open Scholar 1914). Entered British Museum as Asst, 1922; Asst Keeper, 1927; Dep. Keeper, 1944; Keeper, 1955. World authority on Hemiptera. Scientific Controller, International Trust, 1959-70, and Sec., International Commn, 1962-70, on Zoological Nomenclature. Foreign Mem. Soc. pro Faun. Flor. Fennica; Corresponding Mem. Entomological Soc. of Egypt. Served in France in Special Brigade (Poison Gas), RE, 1915-17; in 52 Squadron (Observer), RAF, 1918. Home Guard, 1940-45. *Publications:* over 200 scientific papers on the structure, taxonomy, evolution and zoogeography of the insect order Hemiptera. *Recreation:* gardening. *Address:* Chy-an-Cloam, Gwelenys Road, Mousehole, Penzance, Cornwall TR19 6PY. *T:* Mousehole 516.

CHIONA, Most Rev. James; *see* Blantyre, Archbishop of, (RC).

CHIPIMO, Elias Marko; Chairman, Standard Bank Zambia Ltd, since 1976 (Deputy Chairman, 1975); *b* 23 Feb. 1931; *s* of Marko Chipimo, Zambia (then Northern Rhodesia); *m* 1959, Anna Joyce Nkole Konie; four *s* three *d. Educ:* St Canisius, Chikuni, Zambia; Munali; Fort Hare Univ. Coll., SA; University Coll. of Rhodesia and Nyasaland. Schoolmaster, 1959-63; Sen. Govt Administrator, 1964-67; High Comr for Zambia in London, and Zambian Ambassador to the Holy See, 1968-69; Perm. Sec., Min. of Foreign Affairs, 1969. Chairman: Zambia Stock Exchange Council, 1970-72; Zambia Nat. Bldg Soc., 1970-71; Dep. Chm., Development Bank of Zambia Ltd, 1973-75; Dir, Zambia Airways Corp., 1975-. Pres., Lusaka Branch, Zambia Red Cross, 1970-75; Mem., Zambia Univ. Council, 1970-76; Dir, Internat. Sch. of Lusaka, 1970-76. Cllr, Lusaka City Council, 1974. *Publication:* Our Land and People, 1966. *Recreations:* rose gardening, reading, general literature, linguistics, philosophy, politics, economics, discussions, chess. *Address:* PO Box 2238, Lusaka, Zambia.

CHIPP, David Allan; Editor in Chief of The Press Association since 1969; *b* 6 June 1927; *s* of late Thomas Ford Chipp and of Isabel Mary Ballinger; unmarried. *Educ:* Geelong Grammar Sch., Australia; King's Coll., Cambridge (MA). Served with Middlesex Regt, 1944-47; Cambridge, 1947-50. Joined Reuters as Sports Reporter, 1950; Correspondent for Reuters: in SE Asia, 1953-55; in Peking, 1956-58; various managerial positions in Reuters, 1960-68; Editor of Reuters, 1968. *Recreations:* coaching rowing; listening to Wagner. *Address:* Mile House, Ibstone, Bucks. *T:* Turville Heath 348. *Clubs:* Garrick; Leander (Henley-on-Thames).

CHIPPERFIELD, Geoffrey Howes; Under Secretary, Department of the Environment, since 1976; *b* 20 April 1933; *s* of Nelson Chipperfield and Eleanor Chipperfield; *m* 1959, Gillian James; two *s. Educ:* Cranleigh; New Coll., Oxford. Called to the Bar, Gray's Inn, 1955. Joined Min. of Housing and Local Govt, 1956; Harkness Fellow, Inst. of Govtl Studies, Univ. of Calif, Berkeley, 1962—63; Principal Private Sec., Minister of Housing, 1968—70; Sec., Greater London Develt Plan Inquiry, 1970-73. *Recreations:* reading, gardening. *Address:* Bridge House West, Sea Wall, Dymchurch, Kent. *Club:* United Oxford & Cambridge University.

CHIRAC, Jacques René; President, Rassemblement des Français pour la République, since 1976; Mayor of Paris, since 1977; *b* Paris, 29 Nov. 1932; *s* of François Chirac and Marie-Louise (née Valette); *m* 1956, Bernadette Chodron de Courcel; two *s. Educ:* Lycée Carnot and Lycée Louis-le-Grand, Paris; Ecole Nationale d'Administration. Diploma of Inst. of Polit. Studies, Paris, and of Summer Sch., Harvard Univ., USA. Served Army in Algeria. Auditor, Cour des Comptes, 1959; Head Dept: Sec.-Gen. of Govt, 1962; Private Office of Georges Pompidou, 1962-67; Counsellor, Cour des Comptes, 1965; State Sec.: Employment Problems, 1967-68; Economy and Finance, 1968-71; Minister for Parly Relations, 1971-72; Minister for Agriculture and Rural Development, 1972-74; Home Minister, March-May 1974; Prime Minister, 1974-76; Sec.-Gen., UDR, Dec. 1974-June 1975. Deputy from Corrèze, elected 1967, 1968, 1973 and 1976 (UDR), and Pres., Gen. Council of Corrèze, 1970. Holds several civil and military awards, etc. *Publication:* a thesis on development of Port of New Orleans, 1954. *Address:* 57 rue Boissière, Paris 16e, France.

CHIRICO, Giorgio de; Italian artist; painter, theatrical designer and writer; *b* Greece, 10 July 1888; *s* of Evaristo and Gemma de Chirico; *m* Isabella Far. *Educ:* Polytechnic Institute, Athens; Academy of Fine Arts, Munich. During early career as a painter in Italy and Paris, began series of Italian townscapes; launched metaphysical School, Italy, 1917; has designed scenery and costumes for ballet and operatic productions; other work includes murals, lithographs, book illustrations, designs etc. Known for his compositions of horses, gladiators, archaeological subjects, scenes of Greek mythology, portraits, still life. Since 1968, he has carried out his characteristic subjects in sculpture. Hon. RBA 1949. *Publications:* Hebdomeros, 1929; (with Isabella Far) Commedia dell' arte moderna, 1945, and other volumes of art criticism; Memorie della mia vita, 1945. *Address:* Piazza di Spagna 31, Rome, Italy.

CHISHOLM, Archibald Hugh Tennent, CBE 1946; MA; *b* 17 Aug. 1902; 2nd *s* of late Hugh Chisholm and Mrs Chisholm (née Harrison), Rush Park, Co. Antrim; *m* 1939, Josephine, *e d* of J. E. Goudge, OBE, ICS; one *s* two *d. Educ:* Westminster; Christ Church, Oxford. Wall Street Journal of NY, 1925-27; The British Petroleum Co. (then Anglo-Persian/Anglo-Iranian Oil Co.), Iran and Kuwait, 1928-36 and London, 1945-72. Editor of

The Financial Times, 1937-40; Army, 1940-45 (despatches twice, CBE). FZS; FInstPet. Chevalier, Légion d'Honneur. *Publication:* The First Kuwait Oil Concession Agreement: a Record of the Negotiations, 1911-1934, 1975. *Address:* The Old School House, Durrus, Co. Cork, Ireland. *T:* Durrus 10. *Clubs:* Athenæum, Bath, MCC; Cork and County.

CHISHOLM, Sir Henry, Kt 1971; CBE 1965; MA, FCA; Chairman, Corby Development Corporation (New Town), 1950-76; Director, Philips Electronic Holdings Ltd, since 1974; *b* 17 Oct. 1900; *e s* of late Hugh Chisholm and of Eliza Beatrix Chisholm (née Harrison); *m* 1st, 1925, Eve Hyde-Thomson; one *s* ; 2nd, 1940, Audrey Viva Hughes (née Lamb); two *s* ; 3rd, 1956, Margaret Grace Crofton-Atkins (née Brantom). *Educ:* Westminster (Schol.); Christ Church, Oxford (Scholar). 2nd Mods, 2nd Lit. Hum., BA 1923, MA 1960. Manager, Paris Office, Barton Mayhew & Co., Chartered Accountants, 1927-32; Partner, Chisholm Hanke & Co., Financial Consultants, 1932-38; Overseas Mills Liaison Officer, Bowater Group, 1938-44; Dir, Bowater-Lloyd (Newfoundland) Ltd, 1940-44; Mem. and Chm. of Departmental Cttees on Organisation of Naval Supply Services, Admiralty, 1942-45; Dir and Financial Controller, The Metal Box Co. Ltd, 1945-46; Joint Managing Dir, A. C. Cossor Ltd, 1947-60; Chm. Ada (Halifax) Ltd, 1961-74. Mem. Adv. Council, Industrial Estates Ltd (Nova Scotia), 1968-75. Mem., Monopolies Commn, 1966-69. Pres., London Flotilla, RNVSR, 1947-53 (Vice-Pres., 1975-); Chm., Whitley Council for New Towns Staff, 1961-75; a Governor of Westminster Sch., 1954-; Founder Mem. British Institute of Management. *Recreations:* sailing, gardening, travel. *Address:* Scott's Grove House, Chobham, Woking, Surrey. *T:* Chobham 8660. *Clubs:* Athenæum, Royal Automobile, Naval (Hon. Life Mem.), Royal Yacht Squadron, Royal Ocean Racing, Royal London Yacht.

CHISHOLM, Prof. Michael Donald Inglis; Professor of Geography, University of Cambridge, since 1976; Professorial Fellow, St Catharine's College, Cambridge, since 1976; *b* 10 June 1931; *s* of M. S. and A. W. Chisholm; *m* 1959, Edith Gretchen Emma (née Hoof); one *s* two *d. Educ:* St Christopher Sch., Letchworth; St Catharine's Coll., Cambridge (MA). MA Oxon. Nat. Service Commn, RE, 1950-51. Deptl Demonstrator, Inst. for Agric. Econs, Oxford, 1954-59; Asst Lectr, then Lectr in Geog., Bedford Coll., London, 1960-64; Vis. Sen. Lectr in Geog., Univ. of Ibadan, 1964-65; Lectr, then Reader in Geog., Univ. of Bristol, 1965-72; Prof. of Economic and Social Geography, Univ. of Bristol, 1972-76. Associate, Economic Associates Ltd, consultants, 1965-; Mem. SSRC, and Chm. of Cttees for Human Geography and Planning, 1967-72; Mem., Local Govt Boundary Commn for England, 1971-. Mem. Council, Inst. of British Geographers, 1961 and 1962, Junior Vice-Pres., 1977. Gill Memorial Prize, RGS, 1969. Geography Editor for Hutchinson Univ. Lib., 1973-. *Publications:* Rural Settlement and Land Use: an essay in location, 1962; Geography and Economics, 1966; (ed jtly) Regional Forecasting, 1971; (ed jtly) Spatial Policy Problems of the British Economy, 1971; Research in Human Geography, 1971; (ed) Resources for Britain's Future, 1972; (jtly) Freight Flows and Spatial Aspects of the British Economy, 1973; (jtly) The Changing Pattern of Employment, 1973; (ed jtly) Studies in Human Geography, 1973; (ed jtly) Processes in Physical and Human Geography: Bristol Essays, 1975; Human Geography: Evolution or Revolution?, 1975; papers in Farm Economist, Oxford Econ. Papers, Trans Inst. British Geographers, Geography, Applied Statistics, Area, etc. *Recreations:* gardening, swimming, theatre, opera, interior design. *Address:* Department of Geography, Downing Place, Cambridge CB2 3EN.

CHISHOLM, Roderick Æneas, CBE 1946; DSO 1944; DFC and bar; AE; ARCS; BSc; *b* 23 Nov. 1911; *s* of Edward Consitt Chisholm and Edith Maud Mary Cary Elwes; *m* 1945, Phillis Mary Sanchia, *d* of late Geoffrey A. Whitworth, CBE; one *s* two *d. Educ:* Ampleforth Coll.; Imperial Coll. of Science and Technology, London. AAF, 1932-40; Royal Air Force, 1940-46 (Air Cdre). Hon. Treasurer, Georgian Group. *Publication:* Cover of Darkness, 1953. *Address:* 19 Tedworth Square, Chelsea, SW3.

CHISWELL, Rt. Rev. Peter; *see* Armidale, Bishop of.

CHITNIS, family name of Baron Chitnis.

CHITNIS, Baron *cr* 1977 (Life Peer), of Ryedale, N Yorks; **Pratap Chidamber Chitnis;** Chief Executive and Director, Joseph Rowntree Social Service Trust, since 1975 (Secretary, 1969-75); *b* 1 May 1936; *s* of late Chidamber N. Chitnis and Lucia Mallik; *m* 1964, Anne Brand; one *s* decd. *Educ:* Penryn Sch.; Stonyhurst Coll.; Univs of Birmingham (BA) and Kansas (MA). Admin. Asst, Nat. Coal Board, 1958-59; Liberal Party

Organisation: Local Govt Officer, 1960-62; Agent, Orpington Liberal Campaign, 1962; Trng Officer, 1962-64; Press Officer, 1964-66; Head of Liberal Party Organisation, 1966-69. Member: Community Relations Commn, 1970-77; BBC Immigrants Programme Adv. Cttee, 1972-77. *Publications:* Local Government Handbook, 1960; (ed) Liberal Election Agents Handbook, 1962. *Address:* Beverley House, Shipton Road, York. *T:* York 25744.

CHITTY, Letitia, MA (Cantab), FRAeS, MICE; *b* 15 July 1897; *d* of Herbert Chitty, FSA and Mabel Agatha Bradby. *Educ:* mostly privately and Newnham Coll., Cambridge. Maths Tripos Part I, 1917; Mech. Science Tripos 1921. Associate of Newnham Coll. 1927-43 and 1958-70. Air Ministry, 1917-19; Airship Stressing Panel, 1922; Bristol Aeroplane Co., 1923-24; Asst to Prof. R. V. Southwell, 1926-32; Airship Analysis, 1933; Asst then Lectr, Civil Engrg, Imperial Coll., 1934-62; work on arch dams for Instn of Civil Engineers and Construction Industry Research and Information Assoc., 1962-69. Telford Gold Medal, ICE, 1969. Fellow, Imp. Coll. of Science and Technology, 1971. FRAeS 1934; AMICE 1947. *Publications:* Abroad: an Alphabet of Flowers, 1948; technical contributions (mostly in collaboration) to Aero R. and M., Proc. Royal Society, Phil. Mag., RAeS Journal and Journal of ICE. *Address:* Flat 9, Imperial Court, 6 Lexham Gardens, W8. *T:* 01-370 1706.

CHITTY, Margaret Beryl, CMG 1977; HM Diplomatic Service; Head of Commonwealth Co-ordination Department, Foreign and Commonwealth Office, since 1975; *b* 2 Dec. 1917; *d* of Wilfrid and Eleanor Holdgate; *m* 1949, Keith Chitty, FRCS (*d* 1958). *Educ:* Belvedere Sch. (GPDST), Liverpool; St Hugh's Coll., Oxford (BA, MA). Dominions Office, 1940; Private Sec. to Parly Under-Sec. of State, 1943-45; Principal, 1945; CRO, 1947-52; First Sec., Commonwealth Office, 1958; UK Mission to UN, New York, 1968-70; FCO, 1970-71; Dep. British High Comr in Jamaica, 1971-75. *Address:* 16 Chapel Road, Stanford-in-the-Vale, Faringdon, Oxon SN7 8LE. *T:* Stanford-in-the-Vale 461. *Club:* United Oxford & Cambridge University.

CHITTY, Susan Elspeth, (Lady Chitty); author; *b* 18 Aug. 1929; *d* of Rudolph Glossop and Mrs E. A. Hopkinson; *m* 1951, Sir Thomas Willes Chitty, Bt, *qv*; one *s* three *d*. *Educ:* Godolphin Sch., Salisbury; Somerville Coll., Oxford. Mem. editorial staff, Vogue, 1952-53; subseq. journalist, reviewer, broadcaster and lecturer. *Publications: novels:* Diary of a Fashion Model, 1958; White Huntress, 1963; My Life and Horses, 1966; *biographies:* The Woman who wrote Black Beauty, 1972; The Beast and the Monk, 1975; Charles Kingsley and North Devon, 1976; *non-fiction:* (with Thomas Hinde) On Next to Nothing, 1976; (with Thomas Hinde) The Great Donkey Walk, 1977; *edited:* The Intelligent Woman's Guide to Good Taste, 1958; The Puffin Book of Horses, 1975. *Recreations:* riding, travel. *Address:* Bow Cottage, West Hoathly, Sussex RH19 4QF. *T:* Sharpthorne 810269.

CHITTY, Sir Thomas Willes, 3rd Bt *cr* 1924; author (as Thomas Hinde); *b* 2 March 1926; *e s* of Sir (Thomas) Henry Willes Chitty, 2nd Bt, and Ethel Constance (*d* 1971), *d* of S. H. Gladstone, Darley Ash, Bovingdon, Herts; *S* father, 1955; *m* 1951, Susan Elspeth (*see* S. E. Chitty); one *s* three *d*. *Educ:* Winchester; University Coll., Oxford. Royal Navy, 1944-47. Shell Petroleum Co., 1953-60. Granada Arts Fellow, Univ. of York, 1964-65; Visiting Lectr, Univ. of Illinois, 1965-67; Vis. Prof., Boston Univ., 1969-70. *Publications: novels:* Mr Nicholas, 1952; Happy as Larry, 1957; For the Good of the Company, 1961; A Place Like Home, 1962; The Cage, 1962; Ninety Double Martinis, 1963; The Day the Call Came, 1964; Games of Chance, 1965; The Village, 1966; High, 1968; Bird, 1970; Generally a Virgin, 1972; Agent, 1974; Our Father, 1975; *non-fiction:* (with wife, as Susan Hinde) On Next to Nothing, 1976; (with Susan Chitty) The Great Donkey Walk, 1977; *anthology:* Spain 1963. *Heir: s* Andrew Edward Willes Chitty, *b* 20 Nov. 1953. *Address:* Bow Cottage, West Hoathly, Sussex RH19 4QF.

CHIVERS, Edgar Warren, CB 1963; BSc; Director, Royal Armament Research and Development Establishment, 1962-67; *b* 7 Dec. 1906; *s* of E. Norton Chivers and Rose Chivers (*née* Warren); *m* 1934, Ruth, *d* of Rev. W. Simons; one *s* one *d*. *Educ:* Hampton Grammar Sch.; Queen Mary Coll., University of London. Joined Research Dept, Woolwich (War Office), 1928; Air Defence Experimental Establishment, 1931-40; Radar Research and Development Establishment, 1940-53; Supt of Ground Radar, 1947; Royal Radar Establishment, 1953-54; Head of Ground Radar Dept, 1953; Min. of Supply, Dir of Atomic Weapons (Development and Production), 1954-56; War Office, Royal Armament Research and Development Establt, 1956-; Head of Guided Weapons and Electronics, 1956; Dep. Dir, 1957. *Publications:* various in technical journals.

Recreations: gardening, music, bee-keeping. *Address:* Huckleberry, High Hurstwood, Uckfield, E Sussex.

CHLOROS, Prof. Alexander George; Professor of Comparative Law, University of London, King's College, since 1966; Director of the Centre of European Law, King's College, since 1974; *b* Athens, 15 Aug. 1926; *yr s* of late George Chloros and of Pipitsa Chloros (*née* Metaxas, now Salti), Athens; *m* 1st, 1951, Helen Comninos, London (*d* 1956); one *d*: 2nd, 1965, Jacqueline Destouche, Marseilles; one *d*. *Educ:* Varvakeion Model Sch., Athens; University Coll., Oxford. BA Oxon 1951; MA Oxon 1955; LLD London 1972. Asst Lectr in Law, 1951-54, and Lectr in Law, 1954-59, University Coll. of Wales, Aberystwyth; Lectr in Laws, Univ. of London, King's Coll., 1959-63; Reader in Comparative Law, Univ. of London, 1963-66. Hayter Scholar, Inst. of Comparative Law, Belgrade, Yugoslavia, 1963-64; Vice-Dean, Internat. Univ. of Comparative Sciences, Luxembourg, 1962-66; Dean of the Faculty of Laws, King's Coll., London, 1971-74; Adviser to Seychelles Government, for: recodification and reform of Code Napoléon, 1973; recodification and reform of Commercial Code, 1975. Visiting Professor: (Professeur associé), Faculty of Law, Univ. of Paris I, 1974-75; Uppsala Univ., 1976. Member: Soc. of Public Teachers of Law; UK Cttee on Comparative Law, Inst. Advanced Legal Studies; Brit. Inst. Internat. and Comparative Law; UK deleg. and Vice-Pres., Council of Europe Sub-Cttee on Fundamental Legal Concepts; UK deleg., Conf. of European Law Faculties, Council of Europe, Strasbourg, 1968; Leader of UK delegn to 2nd Conf., 1971, Pres., and 1st Vice-Pres., 3rd Conf., 1974, Pres., Organising Cttee of 4th Conf.; exch. Lecturer, Faculty of Law, Univ. of Leuven, Belgium; Director: Brit. Council scheme for foreign lawyers; Student Exchange Scheme with Univ. of Aix-en-Provence; UK deleg. representing Cttee of Vice-Chancellors and Principals at Preparatory Cttee, European Inst. in Florence, and UK Mem., Prov. Academic Cttee. Corresp. Mem., Acad. of Athens, 1976. Associate Mem., Internat. Acad. of Comparative Law, 1976. Medal of Univ. of Zagreb, Yugoslavia, 1972. Gen. Editor, European Studies in Law, 1976-. *Publications:* Ed. Vol. IV (Family Law) and contributor to Internat. Encyc. of Comparative Law, Max Planck Inst. of Internat. and For. Law, Hamburg; Ch. 2 in Graveson, Law and Society, 1967; Yugoslav Civil Law, 1970; ed., A Bibliographical Guide to the Law of the United Kingdom, the Channel Is. and Isle of Man, 2nd edn, 1973; ed jtly (with K. H. Neumayer) Liber Amicorum Ernst J. Cohn, 1975; Codification in a Mixed Jurisdiction, 1977; contrib. various British and foreign learned periodicals on Comparative Law and legal philosophy. *Recreations:* photography, swimming, travel, European history, coins, icons. *Address:* Faculty of Laws, King's College, Strand, WC2R 2LS. *T:* 01-836 5454. *Clubs:* Athenæum, Royal Commonwealth Society; Fondation Universitaire (Brussels).

CHOLMELEY, Francis William Alfred F.; *see* Fairfax-Cholmeley.

CHOLMELEY, John Adye, FRCS; Surgeon, Royal National Orthopædic Hospital, 1948-70, Hon. Consultant Surgeon, since 1970; Chairman of Joint Examining Board for Orthopædic Nursing; *b* 31 Oct. 1902; *s* of Montague Adye Cholmeley and Mary Bertha Gordon-Cumming; unmarried. *Educ:* St Paul's Sch.; St Bartholomew's Hosp. MRCS, LRCP 1926; MB, BS London 1927; FRCS 1935; Resident appts St Bart's Hosp, 1928-30; Asst MO: Lord Mayor Treloar Cripples' Hosp., Alton, 1930-32; Alexandra Orth. Hosp., Swanley, 1933-34; Resident Surg. and Med. Supt, Country Br., Royal Nat. Orth. Hosp., Stanmore, 1940-48 (Asst Res. Surg., 1936-39); former Orthopædic Surg., Clare Hall Hosp., Neasden Hosp. Mem. Internat. Soc. of Orthopædic Surgery and Trauma (Société Internationale de Chirurgie Orthopédique et de Traumatologie, SICOT); FRSocMed (Pres. Orthopædic Sect., 1957-58); Fellow Brit. Orth. Assoc. *Publications:* articles on orthopædic subjects, particularly tuberculosis and poliomyelitis in med. jls. *Address:* 14 Warren Fields, Valencia Road, Stanmore, Mddx. *T:* 01-954 6920.

CHOLMELEY, Sir Montague (John), 6th Bt *cr* 1806; Captain, Grenadier Guards; *b* 27 March 1935; *s* of 5th Bt and Cecilia, *er d* of W. H. Ellice; *S* father, 1964; *m* 1960, Juliet Auriol Sally Nelson; one *s* two *d*. *Educ:* Eton. Grenadier Guards, 1954-64. *Heir: s* Hugh John Frederick Sebastian Cholmeley, *b* 3 Jan. 1968. *Address:* Church Farm, Burton le Coggles, Grantham, Lincs. *T:* Corby Glen 329. *Clubs:* White's, Cavalry and Guards.

CHOLMONDELEY, family name of **Marquess of Cholmondeley,** and of **Baron Delamere.**

CHOLMONDELEY, 6th Marquess of, *cr* 1815; **George Hugh Cholmondeley,** GCVO 1977; MC 1943; DL; Bt 1611; Viscount

Cholmondeley, 1661; Baron Cholmondeley of Namptwich (Eng.), 1689; Earl of Cholmondeley, Viscount Malpas, 1706; Baron Newborough (Ire.), 1715; Baron Newburgh (Gt Brit.), 1716; Earl of Rocksavage, 1815; late Grenadier Guards; Lord Great Chamberlain of England since 1966; *b* 24 April 1919; *e s* of 5th Marquess of Cholmondeley, GCVO, and Sybil (CBE 1946), *d* of Sir Edward Albert Sassoon, 2nd Bt; *S* father, 1968; *m* 1947, Lavinia Margaret, *d* of late Colonel John Leslie, DSO, MC; one *s* three *d. Educ:* Eton; Cambridge Univ. Served War of 1939-45: 1st Royal Dragoons, in MEF, Italy, France, Germany (MC). Retd hon. rank Major, 1949. DL Chester, 1955. *Heir: s* Earl of Rocksavage, *qv. Address:* Cholmondeley Castle, Malpas, Cheshire. *T:* Cholmondeley 202. *Clubs:* Turf, Cavalry and Guards.

CHOLMONDELEY CLARKE, Marshal Butler; Master of the Supreme Court of Judicature (Chancery Division), since 1973; *b* 14 July 1919; *s* of Major Cecil Cholmondeley Clarke and Fanny Ethel Carter; *m* 1947, Joan Roberta Stephens; two *s. Educ:* Aldenham. Admitted a solicitor, 1943; Partner, Burton Yeates & Hart, Solicitors, London, WC2, 1946-72. Pres., City of Westminster Law Soc., 1971-72; Mem. Council, Law Soc., 1966-72; Chm., Family Law Cttee, 1970-72; Chm., Legal Aid Cttee, 1972; Chancery Procedure Cttee, 1968-72; Ecclesiastical Examiner, Dio. London; Trustee, United Law Clerks' Soc.; Mem. Council, Inc. Soc. The Church Lads' Brigade. *Recreations:* reading, photography. *Address:* 25 Moore Street, SW3 2QW. *Club:* Turf.

CHOMSKY, Prof. (Avram) Noam, PhD; Institute Professor, Massachusetts Institute of Technology, since 1976 (Ferrari P. Ward Professor of Modern Languages and Linguistics, 1966-76); *b* Philadelphia, 7 Dec. 1928; *s* of late William Chomsky and of Elsie Simonofsky; *m* 1949, Carol Doris Schatz; one *s* two *d. Educ:* Central High Sch., Philadelphia; Univ. of Pennsylvania (PhD). Massachusetts Institute of Technology: Asst Prof., 1955-58; Associate Prof., 1958-61; Prof. of Modern Langs, 1961-66. Res. Fellow, Harvard Cognitive Studies Center, 1964-65. Vis. Prof., Columbia Univ., 1957-58; Nat. Sci. Foundn Fellow, Inst for Advanced Study, Princeton, 1958-59; Linguistics Soc. of America Prof., Univ. of Calif, LA, 1966; Beckman Prof., Univ. of Calif, Berkeley, 1966-67; Lectures: Shearman, UCL, 1969; John Locke, Oxford, 1969; Bertrand Russell Meml, Cambridge 1971; Nehru Meml, New Delhi, 1972. Member: Nat. Acad. of Scis; Amer. Acad of Arts and Scis; Linguistics Soc. of America; Amer. Philosophical Assoc.; Amer. Acad. of Political and General Sci.; Assoc. Symbolic Logic; Aristotelian Soc., GB; Corresp. Mem., British Acad., 1974. Fellow, Amer. Assoc. for Advancement of Science. Mem., Council, Internat. Confedn for Disarmament and Peace, 1967. Hon. DLitt London, 1967; Hon. DHL: Chicago, 1967; Loyola Univ., Chicago, 1970; Swarthmore Coll., 1970; Bard Coll., 1971; Delhi, 1972; Massachusetts, 1973. *Publications:* Syntactic Structures, 1957; Current Issues in Linguistic Theory, 1964; Aspects of the Theory of Syntax, 1965; Cartesian Linguistics, 1966; Topics in the Theory of Generative Grammar, 1966; Language and Mind, 1968; (with Morris Halle) Sound Pattern of English, 1968; American Power and the New Mandarins, 1969; At War with Asia, 1970; Problems of Knowledge and Freedom, 1971; Studies on Semantics in Generative Grammar, 1972; For Reasons of State, 1973; The Backroom Boys, 1973; Peace in the Middle East?, 1974; (with Edward Herman) Bains de Sang, 1974; Reflections on Language, 1975; The Logical Structure of Linguistic Theory, 1975; Essays on Form and Interpretation, 1977. *Recreation:* gardening. *Address:* Department of Linguistics, Massachusetts Institute of Technology, Massachusetts Avenue, Cambridge, Mass 02139, USA. *T:* 617-253-7819.

CHOPE, Robert Charles; His Honour Judge Chope; a Circuit Judge (formerly Judge of County Courts), since 1965; *b* 26 June 1913; *s* of Leonard Augustine and Ida Florence Chope; *m* 1946; one *s* two *d. Educ:* St Paul's Sch.; University Coll., London. Called to Bar, Inner Temple, 1938. Served Royal Artillery, 1939-45. Dep. Chm., Cornwall QS, 1966-71. *Address:* 12 King's Bench Walk, Temple, EC4; Carclew House, Perranarworthal, Truro, Cornwall.

CHORLEY, family name of **Baron Chorley.**

CHORLEY, 1st Baron *cr* 1945, of Kendal; **Robert Samuel Theodore Chorley,** QC 1961; JP; *b* Kendal, 1895; *e s* of late R. F. Chorley; *m* Katharine Campbell, *d* of late Edward Hopkinson, DSc; two *s* one *d. Educ:* Kendal Sch.; Queen's Coll., Oxford (Hastings Exhibitioner, Robert Herbert prize, MA). During European War served in Foreign Office; Cheshire Regt (HS), and Min. of Labour; called to Bar, 1920 (certificate of Honour); Pres. Hardwicke Soc., 1921-22; Tutor at the Law Society's School of Law, 1920-24; Lectr in Commercial Law, 1924-30; Sir

Ernest Cassel Prof. of Commercial and Industrial Law in the Univ. of London, 1930-46; Dean of Faculty of Laws, London Univ., 1939-42; temporarily employed in Home Office, 1940-41; Acting Asst Sec., Min. of Home Security, 1941; Dep. Regional Comr for Civil Defence, NW Region, 1942-44; Chm. of Westmorland QS, 1944-68. Contested (Lab) Northwich Div., 1945. Lord in Waiting to the King, 1946-50. Member: Hobhouse Cttee (National Parks), 1945; Parly Delegn to India, 1945; Mocatta Cttee (Indorsements on Cheques), 1955. Former Mem. Council and Vice-Chm., National Trust; Hon. Sec. of Council for Preservation of Rural England, 1935-67, a Vice-Pres., 1969-; Pres., Fell Rock Climbing Club of English Lake District, 1935-37. Assoc. of University Teachers: Mem. Coun. and Exec. Cttee, 1938-; Vice-Pres., 1945-47; Pres., 1947; Hon. Gen. Sec., 1953-65; President: Nat. Council for the Abolition of the Death Penalty, 1945-48; Sheffield and Peak District Branch, CPRE, 1946-75; Friends of the Lake District, 1961-69 (Vice-Pres., 1946-56 and 1969-); Fire Service Research and Training Trust, 1946-73; Pres., Holiday Fellowship, 1947-57; a Vice-Pres. of Howard League for Penal Reform, 1948-; Chm., Inst. for Study and Treatment of Delinquency, 1950-56 (Pres., 1956-72); Pres., British Mountaineering Council, 1950-53; Pres., Ethical Union, 1950-54; Pres., Soc. of Public Teachers of Law, 1954-55; Vice-Pres., Alpine Club, 1956-58; Pres., Haldane Soc., 1957-72; Pres., Commons and Footpaths Preservation Soc., 1961-75. Hon. Fellow: Inst. of Bankers, 1960; LSE 1970. *Publications:* (jointly) Leading Cases in Mercantile Law; (jointly) Shipping Law; Law of Banking; (jointly) Leading Cases in the Law of Banking; (ed.) Arnould's Law of Marine Insurance (13th, 14th and 15th edns); General Editor Modern Law Review, 1937-71; various articles in the Law Quarterly Review, Modern Law Review, and elsewhere. *Recreations:* gardening, mountaineering and travel. *Heir: s* Hon. Roger Richard Edward Chorley, *qv. Address:* The Rookery, Stanmore, Mddx; House of Lords, SW1. *Club:* Alpine.

CHORLEY, Charles Harold, CB 1959; Second Parliamentary Counsel, 1968-69; *b* 10 June 1912; *o s* of late Arthur R. Chorley; *m* 1941, Audrey, *d* of R. V. C. Ash, MC; two *d. Educ:* Radley; Trinity Coll., Oxford. Called to Bar (Inner Temple), 1934. Joined Office of Parliamentary Counsel, 1938; one of the Parliamentary Counsel, 1950-68. *Address:* Paddock Wood, Tisbury, Salisbury, Wilts. *T:* Tisbury 325.

CHORLEY, Prof. Richard John; Professor of Geography, University of Cambridge, since 1974; *b* 4 Sept. 1927; *s* of Walter Joseph Chorley and Ellen Mary Chorley; *m* 1965, Rosemary Joan Macdonald More; one *s* one *d. Educ:* Minehead Grammar Sch.; Exeter Coll., Oxford. MA (Oxon), ScD (Cantab). Lieut, RE, 1946-48. Fulbright Schol., Columbia Univ., 1951-52; Instructor: in Geography, Columbia Univ., 1952-54; in Geology, Brown Univ., 1954-57; Cambridge Univ.: Demonstrator in Geography, 1958-62; Lectr in Geography, 1962-70, Reader, 1970-74. British rep. on Commn on Quantitative Techniques of Internat. Geographical Union, 1964-68; Dir, Madingley Geog. Courses, 1963-. Gill Meml Medal of RGS, 1967. First Hon. Life Mem., British Geomorphological Res. Gp, 1974. *Publications:* co-author of: The History of the Study of Landforms, Vols I and II, 1964, 1973; Atmosphere, Weather and Climate, 1968; Network Analysis in Geography, 1969; Physical Geography, 1971; co-editor of: Frontiers in Geographical Teaching, 1965; Models in Geography, 1967; editor of: Water, Earth and Man, 1969; Spatial Analysis in Geomorphology, 1972; Directions in Geography, 1973; contribs to: Jl of Geology, Amer. Jl of Science, Bulletin of Geolog. Soc. of Amer., Geog. Jl, Geol. Magazine, Inst. of Brit. Geographers, etc. *Recreation:* gardening. *Address:* 76 Grantchester Meadows, Newnham, Cambridge CB3 9UL.

CHORLEY, Hon. Roger Richard Edward, FCA; Partner in Coopers & Lybrand, Chartered Accountants, since 1967; *b* 14 Aug. 1930; *er s* and *heir* of 1st Baron Chorley, *qv*; *m* 1964, Ann, *d* of late A. S. Debenham; two *s. Educ:* Stowe Sch.; Gonville and Caius Coll., Cambridge (BA). Expedns to Himalayas, 1954 (Rakaposhi), 1957 (Nepal); joined Cooper Brothers & Co. (later Coopers & Lybrand), 1955; New York office, 1959-60; Pakistan (Indus Basin Project), 1961; Hon. Sec., Climbers Club, 1963-67; seconded to Nat. Bd for Prices and Incomes as accounting adviser, 1965-68; Mem. Management Cttee, Mount Everest Foundn, 1968-70; Hon. Treas., Alpine Club, 1968- (Vice-Pres., 1975-); Mem. Finance Cttee, National Trust, 1970-; Mem. Finance Act 1960 Tribunal, 1974-; Mem. Royal Commn on the Press, 1974-77. *Recreations:* mountains (Past Pres. CU Mountaineering Club), travel. *Address:* 69 Bedford Gardens, W8 7EF. *Clubs:* Reform, Alpine.

CHOWDHURY, Abu Sayeed; President of Bangladesh, 1972-73; unanimously elected President of Republic of Bangladesh from April 1973, for five year term, resigned December 1973; Foreign Minister of Bangladesh, 1975; *b* 31 Jan. 1921; *s* of late Abdul

Hamid Chowdhury (formerly Speaker, the then East Pakistan Assembly); *m* 1948, Khurshid Chowdhury; two *s* one *d. Educ:* Presidency Coll.; Calcutta Univ. (MA, BL). Called to the Bar, Lincoln's Inn, 1947. Gen.-Sec., Presidency Coll. Union, 1941-42; Pres. British Br. of All India Muslim Students' Fedn, 1946; Mem., Pakistan Delegn to Gen. Assembly of the UN, 1959; Advocate-Gen., E Pakistan, 1960; Mem., Constitution Commn, 1960-61; Judge, Dacca High Court, July 1961-72; Chm., Central Bd for Develt of Bengali, 1963-68; Leader, Pakistan Delegn to World Assembly of Judges and 4th World Conf. on World Peace through Law, Sept. 1969; Vice-Chancellor, Dacca Univ., Nov., 1969-72, in addition to duties of Judge of Dacca High Court; Mem., UN Commn on Human Rights, 1971; Ambassador-at-large for Govt of Bangladesh, designated by Bangladesh Govt as High Comr for UK and N Ireland, 1971, and Head of the Bangladesh Missions at London and New York, April 1971-11 Jan. 1972; Chancellor, all Bangladesh Univs, 1972-73. Special Rep. of Bangladesh, 1973-75; Leader, Bangladesh Delegns: Conf. on Humanitarian Law, Geneva, 1974, 1975 (Chm., Drafting Cttee); World Health Assemblies, Geneva, 1974, 1975; Internat. Labour Confs, Geneva, 1974, 1975 (Chm., Human Resources Cttee); Confs on Law of the Sea, Caracas, 1974, Geneva, 1975; Gen. Conf. Internat. Atomic Energy Agency, Vienna, 1974; Non-aligned Foreign Ministers' Conf., Lima, 1975; UN Special Session, Sept., 1975, NY; 30th Session of Gen. Assembly, UN, 1975; Islamic Foreign Ministers' Conf., Jeddah, 1975; led goodwill missions to: Saudi Arabia, Egypt, Syria, Lebanon and Algeria, 1974; Turkey, 1975. Minister of Shipping and Ports, 8-21 Aug. 1975. Hon. Fellow, Open Univ. Hon. Deshikottama Viswabharati (Shantiniketan), India, 1972; Hon. Dr Laws Calcutta, 1972. *Recreations:* reading, gardening. *Address:* 2 Paper Buildings, Temple, EC4. *T:* 01-353 9119. *Clubs:* Royal Over Seas League, Royal Commonwealth Society; Golf (Geneva); (Hon.) Rotarian, Rotary (Dacca).

CHRIMES, Prof. Stanley Bertram, MA, PhD, LittD; Professor of History and Head of Department of History, University College, Cardiff, 1953-74, now Emeritus; Director, University College, Cardiff, Centenary History Project, since 1975; Deputy Principal, 1964-66; Dean of Faculty of Arts, 1959-61; *b* 23 Feb. 1907; *yr s* of late Herbert Chrimes and Maude Mary (*née* Rose); *m* 1937, Mabel Clara, *o d* of late L. E. Keyser. *Educ:* Purley County Sch., Surrey; King's Coll., London (Lindley Student, BA, MA); Trinity Coll., Cambridge (Research Studentship, Senior Rouse Ball Student, PhD, LittD). Lectr, 1936, Reader, 1951, in Constitutional History, University of Glasgow. Temp. Principal, Ministry of Labour and National Service, 1940-45. Alexander Medal, Royal Hist. Society, 1934. *Publications:* English Constitutional Ideas in the XVth century, 1936 (American repr. 1965, 1976); (translated) F. Kern's Kingship and Law in the Middle Ages, 1939 (repr. 1948, 1956; paperback edn 1970); (ed and trans.) Sir John Fortescue's De Laudibus Legum Anglie, 1942 (repr. 1949); English Constitutional History, 1948 (4th rev. edn 1967; edn in Japan, 1963); (ed) The General Election in Glasgow, February 1950, 1950; An Introduction to the Administrative History of Mediæval England, 1952 (3rd rev. edn 1966); Some Reflections on the Study of History, 1954; (ed and cont. 7th edn) Sir W. Holdsworth's History of English Law, Vol. I, 1957; (ed, with A. L. Brown) Select Documents of English Constitutional History, 1307-1485, 1961; Lancastrians, Yorkists, and Henry VII, 1964 (2nd rev. edn 1966); King Edward I's Policy for Wales, 1969; ed (with C. D. Ross and R. A. Griffiths) and contrib., Fifteenth-Century England, studies in politics and society, 1972; Henry VII, 1972, repr. 1977; articles and reviews in Trans Royal Hist. Soc., English Historical Review, Law Quarterly Review, etc. *Address:* 24 Cwrt-y-vil Road, Penarth, South Glamorgan.

CHRIST CHURCH, Dublin, Dean of; *see* Salmon, Very Rev. T. N. D. C.

CHRIST CHURCH, Oxford, Dean of; *see* Chadwick, Very Rev. H.

CHRISTCHURCH, Bishop of, since 1966; **Rt. Rev. William Allan Pyatt**, MA; *b* Gisborne, NZ, 4 Nov. 1916; *e s* of A. E. Pyatt; *m* 1942, Mary Lilian Carey; two *s* one *d. Educ:* Gisborne High Sch.; Auckland Univ.; St John's Coll., Auckland; Westcott House, Cambridge. BA 1938 (Senior Sch. in History); MA 1939. Served War of 1939-45: combatant service with 2 NZEF; Major, 2 IC 20 NZ Armd Regt 1945. Ordained, 1946; Curate, Cashmere, Staffs, 1946-48; Vicar: Brooklyn, Wellington, NZ, 1948-52; Hawera, 1952-58; St Peter's, Wellington, 1958-62; Dean of Christchurch, 1962-66. Mem. Council, Canterbury Univ., NZ, 1973. *Publications:* contribs to NZ Jl of Theology. *Recreations:* Rugby referee; political comment on radio; work among alcoholics. *Address:* Bishopscourt, 100 Park Terrace, Christchurch, NZ. *T:* 62.653. *Club:* Canterbury Officers (Christchurch).

CHRISTENSEN, Arent Lauri, (A. Lauri Chris); Norwegian painter and etcher; *b* 30 April 1893; *m* 1933, Hjordis Charlotte Lohren (Lill Chris), painter. *Educ:* The Royal Drawing Sch., Oslo. Began career as etcher and painter in Oslo; later travelled in the South, especially in Provence and Italy, and made a series of decorative landscape-etchings, which were exhibited in several countries; his interest in classic antiquity-especially the Grecian and Egyptian culture- inspired him to make various figure-compositions with incidents from the life in the antiquity and from Homer's Iliad; these compositions have been exhibited throughout Europe and America. Decorated Asker High Sch. with wall-paintings. Invented a new graphic method Chrisgrafia. The following museums have bought his works: British Museum, Victoria and Albert Museum, National Galleriet, Oslo, New York Free Arts Library Museum, Bibliothèque Nationale, Paris, Brooklyn Museum, Brooklyn, etc; Mem. of the Soc. of Graphic Art, London, 1926. *Address:* Villa Chriss, Fjeldstadvn 16, Nesbru, Norway.

CHRISTENSEN, Christian Neils, CBE 1970; ERD; *b* 10 Dec. 1901; *s* of C. N. Christensen, Liverpool; *m* 1928, Elsie Florence Hodgson; one *s* one *d*. Shipping and forwarding, 1915-19; Man. Dir, Ex-Army Transport Ltd, 1919-39; army service, France, N Africa, Sicily, Italy, 1939-45 (Lt-Col, despatches twice; Officer, Legion of Merit, USA, 1944); Man. Dir, North Western Transport Services Ltd and Dir, Transport Services (BTC) Ltd, 1945-49; Road Haulage Executive: Eastern Divisional Man., 1950-55; Midland Divisional Man., 1955-63; Man. Dir, British Road Services Ltd, and Chm., BRS (Contracts) Ltd, 1963-68; Chm., Road Air Cargo Express (International) Ltd, 1968-71, retired. FCIT. *Recreation:* gardening. *Address:* Ellesmere, 22 Greensleeves Avenue, Broadstone, Dorset, BH18 8BL. *T:* Broadstone 4501.

CHRISTENSEN, Eric Herbert, CMG 1968; Secretary-General, President's Office, Permanent Secretary, Ministry of External Affairs, and Secretary to the Cabinet, The Gambia, since 1967; also Head of the Public Service since 1967; *b* 29 Oct. 1923; *s* of George Vilhelm Christensen and Rose Fleury; *m* 1951, Diana, *d* of Rev. J. Dixon-Baker; four *s* three *d*. Teacher, St Augustine's Sec. Sch., Bathurst, 1941-43; Military Service, W African Air Corps (RAF), Bathurst, 1944-45; Clerk, The Secretariat, Bathurst, 1946-47; Head of Chancery, then Vice-Consul, French Consulate, Bathurst, 1947-60; acted as Consul on several occasions; Attaché, Senegalese Consulate-Gen., Bathurst, 1961-65, acted as Consul-Gen. on several occasions; Asst Sec. (Ext. Affairs), Gambia Govt, 1965; Principal Asst Sec., Prime Minister's Office, Bathurst, 1966-67. Foreign decorations include: Grand Officer, Order of the Brilliant Star of China (Taiwan), 1966; Officer, Order of Merit of Islamic Republic of Mauritania, 1967; Officer, Nat. Order of Republic of Senegal, 1967; Knight Commander's Cross, Badge and Star, Order of Merit of Federal Republic of Germany, 1968; Order of Republic of Nigeria, 1970; Order of Diplomatic Merit, Republic of Korea, 1970, and also those from Egypt, Republic of Guinea and Republic of Liberia. *Recreations:* reading, photography, philately, chess. *Address:* 6 Kent Street, Banjul, The Gambia. *T:* (office) Banjul 662, (home) Serekunda 2222.

CHRISTENSEN, Jens; Commander First Class, Order of the Dannebrog; Ambassador of Denmark to the Court of St James's, since Sept. 1977; *b* 30 July 1921; *s* of Christian Christensen and Sophie Dorthea Christensen; *m* 1950, Tove (*née* Jessen); one *s* two *d*. *Educ:* Copenhagen Univ. (MPolSc 1945). Joined Danish Foreign Service, 1945; Head of Section, Econ. Secretariat of Govt, 1947; Sec. to OECD Delegn in Paris, 1949 and to NATO Delegn, 1952; Hd of Sect., Min. of Foreign Affairs, 1952, Actg Hd of Div., 1954; Chargé d'Affaires *a .i.* and Counsellor of Legation, Vienna, 1957; Asst Hd of Econ.-Polit. Dept, Min. of For. Affairs, 1960; Dep. Under-Sec., 1961; Under-Sec. and Hd of Econ.-Polit. Dept, 1964-71; Hd of Secretariat for Europ. Integration, 1966; Ambassador Extraord. and Plenipotentiary, 1967; State Sec. for Foreign Econ. Affairs, 1971. Knight Grand Cross: Order of Icelandic Falcon; Order of Northern Star, Sweden; Order of St Olav, Norway. *Address:* Royal Danish Embassy, 55 Sloane Street, SW1X 9SR. *T:* 01-235 1255.

CHRISTIAN, Clifford Stuart, CMG 1971; consultant in environmental matters; *b* 19 Dec. 1907; *s* of Thomas William and Lilian Elizabeth Christian; *m* 1933, Agnes Robinson; four *d*. *Educ:* Univ. of Queensland (BScAgr); Univ. of Minnesota (MS). Officer-in-charge: Northern Australia Regional Survey Section, 1946-50; Land Research and Regional Survey Section, CSIRO, 1950-57; Chief, Div. of Land Research, CSIRO, 1957-60; Mem. Executive, CSIRO, 1960-72. Farrer Memorial Medal, 1969. FAIAS; FWA; Fellow, Aust. Acad. of Technological Sciences. Hon. DScAgr Queensland, 1976. *Publications:* chapter contribs to books; articles in various pubns mainly concerning natural resources. *Recreation:* photography. *Address:* 6 Baudin Street, Forrest, ACT 2603, Australia. *T:* 73.1742. *Club:* Commonwealth (Canberra).

CHRISTIAN, Prof. John Wyrill, FRS 1975; Professor of Physical Metallurgy, Oxford University, since 1967; Fellow of St Edmund Hall, Oxford, since 1963; *b* 9 April 1926; *e s* of John Christian and Louisa Christian (*née* Crawford); *m* 1949, Maureen Lena Smith; two *s* one *d. Educ:* Scarborough Boys' High Sch.; The Queen's Coll., Oxford. BA 1946, DPhil 1949, MA 1950. Pressed Steel Co. Ltd Research Fellow, Oxford University, 1951-55; Lectr in Metallurgy, 1955-58; George Kelley Reader in Metallurgy, 1958-67. Visiting Prof.: Univ. of Illinois, 1959; Case Inst. of Technology, USA, 1962-63; MIT and Stanford Univ., 1971-72. Rosenhain medallist of Inst. of Metals, 1969. *Publications:* Metallurgical Equilibrium Diagrams (with others), 1952; The Theory of Transformations in Metals and Alloys, 1965; (Editor) Structure Reports (Metals), 1962-64, (Brit. Editor) Acta Metallurgica, 1967-75; Progress in Materials Science, 1970-; Jl Less Com. Metals, 1976-; papers in various scientific jls. *Address:* 27 Linton Road, Oxford. *T:* Oxford 58569.

CHRISTIAN, Prof. Reginald Frank; Professor of Russian, St Andrews University, since 1966; *b* Liverpool, 9 Aug. 1924; *s* of late H. A. Christian and late Jessie Gower (*née* Scott); *m* 1952, Rosalind Iris Napier; one *s* one *d. Educ:* Liverpool Inst.; Queen's Coll., Oxford (Open Scholar; MA). Hon. Mods Class. (Oxon), 1943; 1st cl. hons Russian (Oxon), 1949. Commnd RAF, 1944; flying with Atlantic Ferry Unit and 231 Sqdn, 1943-46. FO, British Embassy, Moscow, 1949-50; Lectr and Head of Russian Dept, Liverpool Univ., 1950-55; Sen. Lectr and Head of Russian Dept, Birmingham Univ., 1956-63; Vis. Prof. of Russian, McGill Univ., Canada, 1961-62; Prof. of Russian, Birmingham Univ., 1963-66; Exchange Lectr, Moscow, 1964-65. Mem. Univ. Ct, 1971-73, Associate Dean, Fac. of Arts, 1972-73, Dean, Fac. of Arts, 1975-, St Andrews Univ. Pres., British Univs Assoc. of Slavists, 1967-70; Member, Internat. Cttee of Slavists, 1970-75. *Publications:* Korolenko's Siberia, 1954; (with F. M. Borras) Russian Syntax, 1959, 2nd rev. edn, 1971; Tolstoy's War and Peace: a study, 1962; (with F. M. Borras) Russian Prose Composition, 1964, 2nd rev. edn, 1974; Tolstoy: a critical introduction, 1969; numerous articles and reviews in Slavonic and E European Review, Slavonic and E European Jl, Mod. Languages Review, Survey, Forum, Birmingham Post, Times Lit. Supp., etc. *Recreations:* tennis, squash, fell-walking, violin. *Address:* The Roundel, St Andrews, Fife. *T:* St Andrews 3322; Scioncroft, Knockard Road, Pitlochry, Perthshire. *T:* Pitlochry 2993.

CHRISTIANSEN, Michael Robin; bookseller; *b* 7 April 1927; *e s* of Arthur and Brenda Christiansen; *m* 1st, 1948, Kathleen Lyon (marr. diss.); one *s* one *d* ; 2nd, 1961, Christina Robinson; one *s* one *d. Educ:* Hill Crest, Frinton; St Luke's, Conn., USA. Reporter, Daily Mail, 1943; Royal Navy, 1945-47; Chief Sub-Editor: Daily Mail, 1950; Daily Mirror, 1956; Dep. Editor, Sunday Pictorial, 1960; Asst Editor, Daily Mirror, 1961-64; Editor, Sunday Mirror, 1964-72; Dep. Editor, Daily Mirror, 1972-74, Editor, 1975. *Recreations:* golf, coarse cricket. *Address:* 2 Armstrong Close, Danbury, Essex.

CHRISTIANSON, Alan, CBE 1971; MC 1945; Deputy Chairman, South of Scotland Electricity Board, 1967-72; retired; *b* 14 March 1909; *s* of Carl Robert Christianson; *m* 1936, Gladys Muriel Lewin, *d* of William Barker; two *d. Educ:* Royal Grammar Sch., Newcastle upon Tyne; FCA, CompIEE. Served as Major, RA, 1939-45: comd Field Battery, 1943-45. Central Electricity Bd, 1934-48; Divisional Sec., British Electricity Authority, SW Scotland Div., 1948-55; Dep. Sec., S of Scotland Electricity Bd, 1955-62; Chief Financial Officer, 1962-65; Gen. Man., Finance and Administration, 1965-67. *Recreation:* golf. *Address:* Tynedale, Lennox Drive East, Helensburgh, Dunbartonshire. *T:* Helensburgh 4503.

CHRISTIE, Ann Philippa; *see* Pearce, A. P.

CHRISTIE, Charles Henry; Warden of St Edward's School, Oxford, since 1971; *b* 1 Sept. 1924; *s* of late Lieut-Comdr C. P. Christie and Mrs C. S. Christie; *m* 1950, Naida Joan Bentley; one *s* three *d. Educ:* Westminster Sch. (King's Scholar); Trinity Coll., Cambridge (Exhibitioner). Served 1943-46, RNVR (despatches, 1945). Trinity Coll., Cambridge, 1946-49; Asst Master, Eton Coll., 1949-57; Under Master and Master of Queen's Scholars, Westminster Sch., 1957-63; Headmaster, Brighton Coll., 1963-71. *Address:* The Warden's House, St Edward's School, Oxford. *T:* Oxford 55241.

CHRISTIE, George William Langham; Chairman, Glyndebourne Productions Ltd; *b* 31 Dec. 1934; *o s* of John and Audrey Mildmay Christie; *m* 1958, Patricia Mary Nicholson; three *s* one *d. Educ:* Eton. Asst to Sec. of Calouste Gulbenkian Foundation, 1957-62. Chm. of Glyndebourne Productions, 1956-, and of other family companies. *Address:* Glyndebourne, Lewes, E Sussex. *T:* Ringmer 812250.

CHRISTIE, Prof. Ian Ralph, FBA 1977; Professor of Modern British History, University College London, since 1966, and Chairman of the History Department, since 1975; *b* 11 May 1919; *s* of John Reid Christie and Gladys Lilian (*née* Whatley). *Educ:* privately; Worcester Royal Grammar Sch.; Magdalen Coll., Oxford, 1938-40 and 1946-48 (MA). Served War, RAF, 1940-46. University Coll. London: Asst Lectr in Hist., 1948; Lectr, 1951; Reader, 1960; Dean of Arts, 1971-73. Jt Literary Dir, Royal Hist. Soc., 1964-70, Mem. Council, 1970-74. Mem. Editorial Bd, History of Parliament Trust, 1973-. *Publications:* The End of North's Ministry, 1780-1782, 1958; Wilkes, Wyvill and Reform, 1962; Crisis of Empire: Great Britain and the American Colonies, 1754-1783, 1966; (ed) Essays in Modern History selected from the Transactions of the Royal Historical Society, 1968; Myth and Reality in late Eighteenth-century British Politics, 1970; (ed) The Correspondence of Jeremy Bentham, vol. 3, 1971; (with B. W. Labaree) Empire or Independence, 1760-1776, 1976; (with Lucy M. Brown) Bibliography of British History, 1789—1851, 1977; contrib. to jls. *Recreation:* walking. *Address:* 10 Green Lane, Croxley Green, Herts. *T:* Rickmansworth 73008. *Club:* Royal Commonwealth Society.

CHRISTIE, John Arthur Kingsley; Under-Secretary, Ministry of Agriculture, Fisheries and Food, 1970-75; *b* 8 Feb. 1915; *s* of Harold Douglas Christie and Enid Marian (*née* Hall); *m* 1951, Enid Margaret (*née* Owen); one *s* two *d. Educ:* Rugby Sch.; Magdalen Coll., Oxford. BA (1st cl. Hon. Mods, 1st cl. Litt. Hum.). Asst Principal, Min. of Agriculture, 1937-41; Sub-Lt, RNVR, 1941-45; Asst Private Sec. to Lord President of the Council, 1945-47; Min. of Agriculture: Principal, 1947-52; Asst Sec., 1952-70. *Recreations:* music, travel. *Address:* 43 Brittains Lane, Sevenoaks, Kent. *T:* Sevenoaks 53356.

CHRISTIE, John Belford Wilson; Sheriff of Tayside, Central and Fife (formerly Perth and Angus) at Dundee, since Nov. 1955; *b* 4 May 1914; *o s* of late J. A. Christie, Advocate, Edinburgh; *m* 1939, Christine Isobel Syme, *o d* of late Rev. J. T. Arnott; four *d. Educ:* Merchiston Castle Sch.; St John's Coll., Cambridge; Edinburgh Univ. Admitted to Faculty of Advocates, 1939. Served War of 1939-45, in RNVR, 1939-46. Sheriff-Substitute of Western Div. of Dumfries and Galloway, 1948-55. Mem., Parole Bd for Scotland, 1967-73; Mem., Queen's Coll. Council, Univ. of St Andrews, 1960-67; Mem. Univ. Court, 1967-75, and Hon. Lectr, Dept of Private Law, Univ. of Dundee. Hon.LLD Dundee, 1977. *Recreations:* curling, golf. *Address:* Annsmuir Farm, Ladybank, Fife. *T:* Ladybank 480. *Clubs:* New (Edinburgh); Royal and Ancient (St Andrews).

CHRISTIE, John Rankin; Deputy Master and Comptroller of the Royal Mint, since 1974; *b* 5 Jan. 1918; *s* of Robert Christie and Georgina (*née* Rankin); *m* 1941, Constance May Gracie; one *s* two *d. Educ:* Ormskirk Gram. Sch.; London Sch. of Economics. War Office, 1936-39; Min. of Supply, 1939; Royal Artillery, 1943-47; Min. of Supply, 1947-54; Air Ministry, 1954; Private Sec. to Ministers of Supply, 1955-57; Asst Sec., 1957; British Defence Staffs, Washington, 1962-65; Under-Sec., Min. of Aviation, 1965-67, Min. of Technology, 1967-70, Min. of Aviation Supply, 1970-71; Asst Under-Sec. of State, MoD, 1971-74. *Recreations:* travel, bird-watching. *Address:* Twitten Cottage, East Hill, Oxted, Surrey. *T:* Oxted 3047.

CHRISTIE, John Traill; Principal of Jesus College, Oxford, 1950-67, Hon. Fellow, 1967; Assistant Master, Westminster School, 1967-69; *b* 1899; 4th *s* of late C. H. F. Christie, DL, JP; *m* 1933, Lucie Catherine, *o d* of late T. P. Le Fanu, CB; two *d. Educ:* Winchester; Trinity Coll., Oxford (Scholar). 1st Class Class. Mods, 1920; 1st Class Lit. Hum., 1922. Sixth Form Master, Rugby Sch., 1922-28; Fellow and Tutor, Magdalen Coll., Oxford, 1928-32; Headmaster of Repton Sch., 1932-37; Headmaster of Westminster Sch., 1937-49. *Recreation:* walking. *Address:* Great Henny, Sudbury, Suffolk. *Club:* Athenæum.

CHRISTIE, Julie (Frances); actress; *b* 14 April 1940; *d* of Frank St John Christie and Rosemary Christie (*née* Ramsden). *Educ:* Convent; Brighton Coll. of Technology; Central Sch. of Speech and Drama. *Films:* Crooks Anonymous, 1962; The Fast Lady, 1962; Billy Liar, 1963; Darling, 1964 (Oscar, NY Film Critics Award, Br. Film Academy Award, etc); Young Cassidy, 1964; Dr Zhivago, 1965 (Donatello Award); Fahrenheit 451, 1966;

Far from the Madding Crowd, 1966; Petulia, 1967; In Search of Gregory, 1969; The Go-Between, 1971; McCabe and Mrs Miller, 1972; Don't Look Now, 1973; Shampoo, 1974. Motion Picture Laurel Award, Best Dramatic Actress, 1967; Motion Picture Herald Award, Best Dramatic Actress, 1967. *Address:* c/o ICM Ltd, 22 Grafton Street, W1. *T:* 01-629 8080.

CHRISTIE, Ronald Victor, MD (Edin.); MSc (McGill); DSc (London); FACP; FRCP(C); FRCP; Professor of Medicine and Chairman of the Department, McGill University, 1955-64; now Emeritus Professor; Dean of the Faculty of Medicine, 1964-68; formerly Director Medical Professorial Unit and Physician, St Bartholomew's Hospital; Professor of Medicine, University of London, 1938-55; *b* 1902; *s* of late Dr Dugald Christie, CMG; *m* 1933, Joyce Mary Ervine (*d* 1967); one *s* one *d. Educ:* in China and later at George Watson's Coll.; Edinburgh Univ. House Physician and House Surg., Royal Infirmary, Edinburgh; Asst in Medicine, Rockefeller Institute for Medical Research, NY; Asst in Dept of Pathology, Freiburg Univ.; Research Associate, McGill Univ. Clinic, Royal Victoria Hosp.; Montreal; Asst Dir of the Med. Unit and Asst Physician, London Hosp. Harveian Orator, RCP, 1969. Hon. FRCPEd; Hon. ScD, Dublin, 1962; Hon. DSc, Edinburgh, 1970; Hon. LLD Otago, 1975. *Publications:* papers in medical and scientific journals. *Address:* Box 11147, 1055 W Georgia, Vancouver, BC V6E 3P3, Canada.

CHRISTIE, Hon. Sir Vernon (Howard Colville), Kt 1972; Speaker of the Legislative Assembly, Victoria, 1967-73; MLA (L) for Ivanhoe, Victoria, 1955-73; *b* Manly, NSW, 17 Dec. 1909; *s* of C. Christie, Sydney; *m* 1936, Joyce, *d* of F. H. Hamlin; one *s* two *d*. Chm. Cttees, Legislative Assembly, 1956-61, 1965-68; Director: Australian Elizabethan Theatre Trust, 1969-; Australian Ballet Foundn; Vice-Pres., Qld Ballet; Pres., Aust. Flying Art Sch. Hon. Life Mem., Victoria Br., CPA. AASA; FCIS; AFAIM. *Recreations:* bowls, sailing, music, ballet and the arts, conservation, fly fishing. *Address:* Gray Street, Redlands Bay, Queensland 4165, Australia. *Clubs:* Queensland, Royal Queensland Yacht Squadron.

CHRISTIE, Walter Henry John, CSI 1948; CIE 1946; OBE 1943; *b* 17 Dec. 1905; *s* of late H. G. F. Christie and Mrs L. M. Christie (*née* Humfrey); *m* 1934, Elizabeth Louise, *d* of late H. E. Stapleton; two *s* two *d. Educ:* Eton (KS, Newcastle Medallist); King's Coll., Cambridge (Winchester Reading Prize). Joined Indian Civil Service, 1928 and served in Bengal and New Delhi; Joint Private Sec. to the Viceroy, 1947; Adviser in India to Central Commercial Cttee, 1947-52; Vice-Chm., British India Corp. Ltd, 1952-58; Commonwealth Develt Finance Co. Ltd, 1959-68; Adviser, E African Develt Bank, 1969-70. Pres., Upper India Chamber of Commerce, 1955-56; Vice-Pres., Employers' Federation of India, 1956; Pres., UK Citizens Assoc., 1957; Steward, Indian Polo Assoc., 1951. *Publications:* contribs to Blackwood's Magazine. *Address:* Quarry Ridge, Oxted, Surrey. *Clubs:* East India, Devonshire, Sports and Public Schools; Achilles.

CHRISTIE, Sir William, KCIE 1947 (CIE 1941); CSI 1945; MC; retired as Chairman, Bailey Meters & Controls Ltd Croydon and Cornhill Insurance Co. Ltd; former Director, Thomas Tilling Ltd; *b* 29 Feb. 1896; *s* of late Rev. Alexander Mackenzie Christie; *m* Marjorie Haughton, 2nd *d* of late Henry Hall Stobbs; one *s* one *d. Educ:* Perth Acad., Perth; Bell Baxter Sch., Cupar, Fife; St Andrews Univ.; Clare Coll., Cambridge. Served Royal Scots, 1914-19 (MC). Joined Indian Civil Service, 1920; Finance Sec., UP, 1938-44; Chief Sec., UP, 1944-45; Chief Comr, Delhi, 1945-47. *Address:* Davan House, The Woodlands, Gerrards Cross, Bucks. *T:* Gerrards Cross 82246. *Club:* Caledonian.

CHRISTIE, Sir William, Kt 1975; MBE 1970; JP; Lord Mayor of Belfast, 1972-75; a Company Director; *b* 1 June 1913; *s* of Richard and Ellen Christie, Belfast; *m* 1935, Selina (*née* Pattison); one *s* two *d* (and one *s* decd). *Educ:* Ward Sch., Bangor, Northern Ireland. Belfast City Councillor, 1961; High Sheriff of Belfast, 1964-65; Deputy Lord Mayor, 1969; Alderman, 1973-77. JP Belfast, 1951; DL Belfast, 1977. Salvation Army Order of Distinguished Auxiliary Service, 1973. *Recreations:* travel, walking, boating. *Address:* 96 Warren Road, Donaghadee, Co. Down, BT21 0PQ.

CHRISTISON, Gen. Sir (Alexander Frank) Philip, 4th Bt *cr* 1871; GBE 1948 (KBE 1944); CB 1943; DSO 1945; MC (and Bar); DL; *b* 17 Nov. 1893; 2nd *s* of Sir Alexander Christison, 2nd Bt, and Florence (*d* 1949), *d* of F. T. Elworthy; *S* half-brother, 1945; *m* 1st, 1916, Betty (*d* 1974), *d* of late Rt Rev. A. Mitchell, Bishop of Aberdeen and Orkney; (one *s* killed in action in Burma, 7 March 1942) two *d* (and one *d* decd); 2nd, 1974, Vida Wallace Smith, MBE. *Educ:* Edinburgh Academy; Oxford Univ. (BA); Hon. Fellow, University Coll., Oxford, 1973. 2nd

Lieut Cameron Highlanders, 1914; Capt. 1915; Bt Major, 1930; Bt Lt-Col 1933; Lt-Col Duke of Wellington's Regt, 1937; Col 1938; comd Quetta Bde, 1938-40; Comdt Staff Coll., Quetta, 1940-41; Brig. Gen. Staff, 1941; Maj.-Gen. 1941; Lt-Gen. 1942; Gen. 1947; comd XXIII and XV Indian Corps, 1942-45; Temp. Comdr 14th Army, 1945; C-in-C, ALFSEA, 1945; Allied Comdr Netherland East Indies, 1945-46; GOC-in-C Northern Command, 1946; GOC-in-C Scottish Command and Governor of Edinburgh Castle, 1947-49; ADC Gen. to the King, 1947-49; retired pay, 1949. Col, The Duke of Wellington's Regt, 1947-57; Col, 10th Princess Mary's Own Gurkha Rifles, 1947-57; Hon. Col, 414 Coast Regt Royal Artillery, 1950-57. Chm., Alban Timber Ltd. President: Scottish Unionist Party, 1957-58; Army Cadet Force, Scotland; Vice-President: Burma Star Assoc.; Officers' Assoc.; Chairman: Scottish Salmon Angling Fedn, 1969; Lodge Trust for Ornithology, 1969; Clarsach Soc. DL Roxburghshire, 1956. FSA Scot, 1957. Chinese Order of Cloud and Banner with Grand Cordon, 1949. *Publications:* Birds of Northern Baluchistan, 1940; The Birds of Arakan (with Aubrey Buxton), 1946. *Heir:* none. *Recreations:* ornithology (MBOU), Celtic languages, field sports. *Address:* The Croft, Melrose, Roxburghshire. *T:* Melrose 2456. *Club:* New (Edinburgh).

CHRISTMAS, Arthur Napier, CEng, FIEE, FRAeS; Chief Scientific Officer and Director of Materials Quality Assurance, Ministry of Defence, 1971-74, retired; *b* 16 May 1913; *s* of Ernest Napier and Florence Elizabeth Christmas; *m* 1940, Betty Margaret Christmas (*née* Bradbrook); one *s* one *d. Educ:* Holloway Sch.; Northampton Technical Coll., London (BSc (Hons)). BEAIRA, 1934-37; Post Office Research Station, 1937-46; Prin. Scientific Officer, Min. of Supply, 1946-51; Sec., British Washington Guided Missile Cttee, 1951-54; Sen. Prin. Scientific Officer, Armament Research and Develt Estabt, 1954-59; DCSO, 1959; Dir, Guided Weapons Research and Techniques, Min. of Aviation, 1959-62; Dir for Engrg Develt, European Launcher Develt Org., 1962-67; Prin. Supt, Royal Armament Research and Develt Estabt, 1967-71. *Recreations:* sailing, mountain walking, music. *Address:* Old Farm Cottage, Itchenor, Sussex. *T:* Birdham 512224. *Clubs:* Itchenor Sailing, Island Sailing, Chichester Cruiser Racing.

CHRISTODOULOU, Anastasios; Secretary, The Open University, since 1969; *b* Cyprus, 1 May 1932; *s* of Christodoulos and Maria Haji Yianni; *m* 1955, Joan P. Edmunds; two *s* two *d. Educ:* St Marylebone Grammar Sch.; The Queen's Coll., Oxford (MA). Colonial Administrative Service, Tanganyika (Tanzania), 1956-62; served as District Commissioner and Magistrate. Univ. of Leeds Administration, 1963-68: Asst Registrar, 1963-65; Dep. Sec., 1965-68. *Recreations:* sport, music, bridge; international and Commonwealth relations. *Address:* Croylands, Church Road, Aspley Heath, Milton Keynes MK17 8TG. *T:* Woburn Sands 582591. *Club:* Royal Commonwealth Society.

CHRISTOFAS, Kenneth Cavendish, CMG 1969; MBE 1944; Director General in the Secretariat of the Council of Ministers of the European Communities, since 1973; *b* 18 Aug. 1917; *o s* of late Edward Julius Goodwin and of Lillian Christofas (*step-s* of late Alexander Christofas); *m* 1948, Jessica Laura (*née* Sparshott); two *d. Educ:* Merchant Taylors' Sch.; University Coll., London (Fellow, 1976). Served War of 1939-45 (MBE): commissioned in The Queen's Own Royal West Kent Regt, 1939; Adjt 1940; Staff Capt. 1941; DAAG 1942; Staff Coll., Quetta, 1944; AAG 1944; GSO1, War Office, 1946. Resigned from Army with Hon. rank of Lieut-Col and joined Sen. Br. of HM Foreign Service, 1948 (HM Diplomatic Service after 1965); served in Foreign Office, 1948-49 and 1951-55; Rio de Janeiro, 1949-51; Rome, 1955-59 and as Dep. Head of UK Delegn to European Communities, Brussels, 1959-61; seconded to CRO for service as Counsellor in the British High Commn, Lagos, 1961-64 and to Colonial Office as Head of Economic Dept, 1965-66; on sabbatical year at Univ. of London, 1964-65; Counsellor in Commonwealth Office, then in FCO, 1966-69; Minister and Dep. Head of UK Delegn to EEC, 1969-72 (acting Head, March-Oct. 1971); Cabinet Office, on secondment, 1972-73. Order of Polonia Restituta (Poland), 1944. *Recreations:* railways and motoring. *Address:* Rue de la Loi 170, 1040 Brussels, Belgium. *T:* 736.7900; 3 The Ridge, Bolsover Road, Eastbourne, Sussex BN20 7JE. *T:* Eastbourne 22384. *Clubs:* East India, Devonshire, Sports and Public Schools; Cercle Royal Gaulois (Brussels).

CHRISTOFF, Boris; opera singer (bass); *b* Plovdiv, near Sofia, Bulgaria, 18 May 1919; *s* of Kyryl and Rayna Teodorova; *m* Franca, *d* of Raffaello de Rensis. *Educ:* Univ. of Sofia (Doctor of Law). Joined Gussla Choir and Sofia Cathedral Choir as soloist. Obtained scholarship, through King Boris III of Bulgaria, to study singing in Rome under Riccardo Stracciari; made concert début at St Cecilia Academy in Rome, 1946 and operatic début,

1946; Covent Garden début, 1950, as Boris Godunov and Philip II; subsequently has appeared at all leading European and American opera houses; American début, Metropolitan Opera House, 1950; as Boris Godunov, San Francisco, 1956. Principal rôles include: Boris Godunov, King Philip, Galitzky, Konchak, Don Quixote, Ivan the Terrible, Ivan Susanin, Mephistopheles, Moses, Don Basilio, Pizarro, Simon Boccanegra. Has made numerous recordings, including opera and songs, winning many prix du disque; these include particularly the complete lyric works of the five great Russian composers. Hon. Mem. Théâtre de l'Opéra, Paris, Mem. La Scala, Milan. Holds foreign decorations. Commendatore della Repubblica Italiana. *Address:* Via Bertoloni 1, Rome, Italy.

CHRISTOPHER, Anthony Martin Grosvenor; General Secretary, Inland Revenue Staff Federation, since 1976; *b* 25 April 1925; *s* of George Russell Christopher and Helen Kathleen Milford Christopher (*née* Rowley); *m* 1962, Adela Joy Thompson. *Educ:* Cheltenham Grammar Sch.; Westminster Coll. of Commerce. Articled Pupil, Agric. Valuers, Gloucester, 1941-44; RAF, 1944-48; Inland Revenue, 1948-57; Asst Sec. 1957-60, Asst Gen. Sec. 1960-74, Jt Gen. Sec. 1975, Inland Revenue Staff Fedn; Mem. TUC General Council, 1976-. Mem., Tax Reform Cttee, 1974-. Dir, Civil Service Building Soc., 1958-; Mem. Bd, Civil Service Housing Assoc., 1958-. Chm., Nat. Assoc. for Care and Resettlement of Offenders, 1973-; Mem., Home Sec.'s Adv. Council for Probation and After-care, 1967-77; Mem., Inner London Probation and After-care Cttee, 1966-; Chm., Alcoholics Recovery Project, 1970-76; Mem., Home Sec.'s Working Party on Treatment of Habitual Drunken Offenders, 1969-71. *Publication:* (jtly) Policy for Poverty, 1970. *Recreations:* gardening, books, music, study of early English porcelain. *Address:* 19 Arkwright Road, Sanderstead, Surrey. *T:* 01-657 4001.

CHRISTOPHER, Sir George Perrin, Kt 1946; Member of Council, Chamber of Shipping, since 1927; *b* 1890; married. Formerly held the following positions: Dir, Peninsular & Oriental Steam Navigation Co.; Chm., Hain Steamship Co. Ltd; Chm. and Man. Dir, Union-Castle Mail Steamship Co. Ltd; Mem. General Cttee of Lloyd's Register of Shipping; Mem. Exec. Council of Shipping Federation Ltd; Mem. Gen. Council, King George's Fund for Sailors; Mem. Cttee, HMS Worcester. Chm. Tramp Shipping Administrative Cttee, 1939, and London Gen. Shipowners' Soc., 1939; Dir of Commercial Services, Ministry of War Transport, 1941-45 (Dep.-Dir, 1939-41); Pres. of the Chamber of Shipping of the United Kingdom, 1948-49 (Vice-Pres., 1947-48); Jt Vice-Chm. of General Council of British Shipping, 1947-49; Liveryman Worshipful Co. of Shipwrights. *Address:* Trencrom, Raglan Road, Reigate, Surrey. *T:* Reigate 42530.

CHRISTOPHERS, Brevet Col Sir (Samuel) Rickard, Kt 1931; CIE 1915; OBE 1918; FRS 1926; MB; IMS retired; *b* 27 Nov. 1873; *s* of Samuel Hunt Christophers, Liverpool; *m* 1902, Elsie Emma (*d* 1963), *d* of FitzRoy Sherman; one *s* one *d*. Member Malaria Commission, Royal Society and Colonial Office, 1898-1902; joined Indian Medical Service, 1902; Officer in Charge Central Malaria Bureau, India, 1910-22; Director Central Research Inst., Kasauli, India, 1922-32; KHP 1927-30; Professor of Malarial Studies, Univ. of London; Leverhulme Fellow, MRC, in charge Experimental Malaria Unit at the London School of Hygiene and Tropical Medicine, 1932-38. Buchanan Medal of Royal Society, 1952. *Publications:* Practical Study of Malaria; Reports to the Malaria Committee of the Royal Society; various publications on malaria, kalaazar and medical zoology, etc. *Address:* c/o Lloyds Bank Ltd, Cox's and King's Branch, PO Box 220, 6 Pall Mall, SW1Y 5NH; Cluanie House, 18 Ridgeway, Broadstone, Dorset.

CHRISTOPHERSON, Sir Derman (Guy), Kt 1969; OBE 1946; FRS 1960; DPhil (Oxon) 1941; MICE, FIMechE; Vice-Chancellor and Warden of Durham University since 1960; *b* 6 Sept. 1915; *s* of late Derman Christopherson, Clerk in Holy Orders, formerly of Blackheath, and Edith Frances Christopherson; *m* 1940, Frances Edith, *d* of late James and Martha Tearle; three *s* one *d*. *Educ:* Sherborne Sch.; University Coll., Oxford (Hon. Fellow, 1977). Henry Fellow at Harvard Univ., 1938; Scientific Officer, Research and Experiments Dept, Ministry of Home Security, 1941-45; University Demonstrator, Cambridge Univ. Engineering Dept, 1945, Lecturer, 1946; Professor of Mechanical Engineering, Leeds Univ., 1949-55; Prof. of Applied Science, Imperial Coll. of Science and Technology, 1955-60. Fellow of Magdalene Coll., Cambridge, 1945, Bursar, 1947. Mem. Council of Institution of Mechanical Engineers, 1950-53; Clayton Prize, Instn of Mechanical Engineers, 1963. Chairman: Cttee of Vice-Chancellors and Principals, 1967-70; Central Council for Educn and Training in

Social Work, 1971-; CNAA (Chm., Educn Cttee), 1966-74; Board of Washington New Town Develt Corp., 1964-; Science Research Coun., 1965-70. Mem. Council, Royal Soc., 1975. Fellow, Imperial Coll. of Science and Technology, 1966; Hon. Fellow, Magdalene Coll., Cambridge, 1969. Hon. DCL: Kent, 1966; Newcastle, 1971; Hon DSc: Aston, 1967; Sierra Leone, 1970; Hon. LLD: Leeds, 1969; Royal Univ. of Malta, 1969. *Publications:* The Engineer in The University, 1967; The University at Work, 1973; various papers in Proc. Royal Soc., Proc. IMechE, Jl of Applied Mechanics, etc. *Recreation:* chess. *Address:* Durham University, Old Shire Hall, Old Elvet, Durham DH1 3HP. *Club:* Athenæum.

CHRISTOPHERSON, Harald Fairbairn; Commissioner of Customs and Excise since 1970; *b* 12 Jan. 1920; *s* of late Captain H. Christopherson, MN, and of Mrs L. G. L. Christopherson (*now* Christensen); *m* 1947, Joyce Winifred Emmett; one *s* two *d*. *Educ:* Heaton Grammar Sch., Newcastle upon Tyne; King's Coll., Univ. of Durham (BSc and DipEd). Served in RA, 1941-46, Captain 1945. Teacher and lecturer in mathematics, 1947-48. Entered administrative class, Home CS, Customs and Excise, 1948; seconded to Trade and Tariffs Commn, W Indies, 1956-58; Asst Sec., 1959; seconded to Treasury, 1965-66; Under Sec., 1969. *Recreations:* music, travel. *Address:* 57a York Road, Sutton, Surrey SM2 6HN. *T:* 01-642 2444.

CHRISTY, Ronald Kington, CB 1965; HM Chief Inspector of Factories, 1963-67; *b* 18 Aug. 1905; *s* of William and Edna Christy; *m* 1931, Ivy, *y d* of W. Hinchcliffe, Whitchurch, Salop; one *s* one *d*. *Educ:* Strand Sch.; King's Coll., Univ. of London. Appointed HM Inspector of Factories, 1930; HM Superintending Inspector of Factories, 1953-59; HM Dep. Chief Inspector of Factories, 1959-63. Mem., Nuclear Safety Advisory Cttee, 1963-67. *Recreations:* gardening, travelling. *Address:* 6 Tyne Walk, Bembridge, IoW. *T:* Bembridge 2255.

CHUBB, family name of **Baron Hayter.**

CHUBB, Prof. Frederick Basil, MA, DPhil, LittD; Professor of Political Science, Dublin University, Trinity College, since 1960; *b* 8 Dec. 1921; *s* of late Frederick John Bailey Chubb and Gertrude May Chubb, Ludgershall, Wilts; *m* 1946, Margaret Gertrude, *d* of late George Francis and Christina Englert; no *c*. *Educ:* Bishop Wordsworth's Sch., Salisbury; Merton Coll., Oxford. BA 1946; MA Oxon; MA Dublin; DPhil Oxon 1950; LittD Dublin 1976. Lecturer in Political Science, Trinity Coll., Dublin, 1948; Fellow in Polit. Sci., 1952; Reader in Polit. Sci., 1955; Bursar, 1957-62. Vice-Pres. Inst. of Public Administration, 1958; Chm., Comhairle na n-Ospidéal, 1972; Chm., Employer-Labour Conf., 1970; MRIA 1969. *Publications:* The Control of Public Expenditure, 1952; (with D. E. Butler (ed) and others) Elections Abroad, 1959; A Source Book of Irish Government, 1964; (ed with P. Lynch) Economic Development and Planning, 1969; The Government and Politics of Ireland, 1970; Cabinet Government in Ireland, 1974; articles in learned jls. *Recreation:* fishing. *Address:* 19 Clyde Road, Ballsbridge, Dublin 4. *T:* 684625.

CHUBB, John Oliver, CMG 1976; HM Diplomatic Service; Counsellor, Foreign and Commonwealth Office, since 1973; *b* 21 April 1920; *s* of Clifford Chubb and Margaret Chubb (*née* Hunt); *m* 1945, Mary Griselda Robertson; one *s* two *d*. *Educ:* Rugby; Oxford (MA). Served War, Scots Guards, 1940-46. Joined Diplomatic Service, 1946; Beirut, 1947; Bagdad, 1948-49; Canal Zone, 1950-52; Cyprus, 1953; FO, 1954-56; Tokyo, 1957-61; FO, 1961-63; Hong Kong, 1964-66; FO, 1967. *Recreations:* reading, spectator sports, golf, gardening, sailing. *Address:* 42 Clifton Hill, NW8 0QG. *T:* 01-624 2794. *Clubs:* Athenæum, MCC; Berkshire Golf, Senior Golfers' Society.

CHUNG, Kyung-Wha, Korean Order of Merit; concert violinist; *b* 26 March 1948; *d* of Chun-Chai Chung and Won-Sook (Lee) Chung. *Educ:* Juilliard Sch. of Music, New York. Moved from Korea to New York, 1960; 7 years' study with Ivan Galamian, 1960-67; New York début with New York Philharmonic Orch., 1967; European début with André Previn and London Symphony Orch., Royal Festival Hall, London, 1970. First prize, Leventritt Internat. Violin Competition, NY, 1967. *Recreations:* sleeping, eating, reading, swimming. *Address:* c/o Harrison Parrott, 22 Hillgate Street, W8. *T:* 01-229 9166.

CHURCH, Brig. Sir Geoffrey Selby, 2nd Bt *cr* 1901; CBE 1940; MC; DL, JP; *b* 11 Jan. 1887; 2nd *s* of Sir William Selby Church, Bt, KCB, and Sybil Constance, *d* of Charles John Bigge, Linden, Northumberland; *S* father, 1928; *m* 1st, 1913, Doris Louise (*d* 1917), *d* of late Sir W. Somerville, KBE; 2nd, 1920, Helene Elizabeth (*d* 1962), *d* of John L. Trayner, Mich., USA; no *c*. *Educ:* Winchester; University Coll., Oxford. Sheriff of Herts,

1936; JP 1927, DL 1931, Herts. ADC (Additional) to King George VI, 1941-51. *Recreations:* outdoor sports. *Heir:* none. *Address:* St Michaels, Hatfield, Herts. *T:* Hatfield 62115. *Club:* United Oxford & Cambridge University.

CHURCH, Prof. Ronald James H.; *see* Harrison-Church.

CHURCHER, Maj.-Gen. John Bryan, CB 1952; DSO 1944, Bar 1946; retired; Director and General Secretary, Independent Stores Association, 1959-71; *b* 2 Sept. 1905; *s* of late Lieut-Col B. T. Churcher, Wargrave, Berks, and Beatrice Theresa Churcher; *m* 1937, Rosamond Hildegarde Mary, *y d* of late Frederick Parkin, Truro Vean, Truro, Cornwall; one *s* two *d. Educ:* Wellington Coll., Berks; RMC Sandhurst. Commissioned DCLI, 1925; Lieut, 1927; Capt. KSLI, 1936; Staff Coll., 1939; served War of 1939-45 (despatches, DSO and Bar); commanded: 1 Bn Hereford Regt, 1942-44; 159 Inf. Bde, 1944-46; 43 Div., 1946; Northumbrian Dist., 1946; 2 Div., 1946; 3 Div., 1946-47; 5 Div., 1947-48; Brig., Imperial Defence Coll., 1948; BGS, Western Command, 1949-51; Chief of Staff, Southern Comd, 1951-54; GOC, 3rd Inf. Div., 1954-57; Dir of Military Training at the War Office, 1957-59; retired, 1959. ADC to King George VI, 1949-52; ADC to the Queen to 1952. *Address:* Tudor Barn, Stanway, near Colchester, Essex. *T:* Colchester 210294. *Club:* Army and Navy.

CHURCHILL; *see* Spencer-Churchill.

CHURCHILL, 3rd Viscount *cr* 1902; **Victor George Spencer;** Baron 1815; *b* 31 July 1934; *s* of 1st Viscount Churchill, GCVO, and late Christine Sinclair (who *m* 3rd, Sir Lancelot Oliphant, KCMG, CB); *S* half-brother, 1973. *Educ:* Eton; New Coll., Oxford (MA). Lieut, Scots Guards, 1953-55. Morgan Grenfell & Co. Ltd, 1958-74. Investment Manager, Central Board of Finance of the Church of England and Charities Official Investment Fund, 1974. *Heir* (to Barony only): Richard Harry Ramsay Spencer, *b* 11 Oct. 1926. *Address:* 6 Cumberland Mansions, George Street, W1.

CHURCHILL, Diana (Josephine); actress, stage and screen; *b* Wembley, 21 Aug. 1913; *d* of Joseph H. Churchill, MRCS, LRCP and Ethel Mary Nunn; *m* Barry K. Barnes (*d* 1965); *m* 1976, Mervyn Johns. *Educ:* St Mary's Sch., Wantage; Guildhall Sch. of Music (scholarship). First professional appearance in Champion North, Royalty, 1931; subsequently in West End and in Repertory. Old Vic Season, 1949-50, New Theatre, as Rosaline in Love's Labour's Lost, Miss Kate Hardcastle in She Stoops to Conquer, Lizaveta Bogdanovna in A Month in the Country and Elise in The Miser; High Spirits, London Hippodrome, 1953; The Desperate Hours, London Hippodrome, 1955; Hamlet, Stratford-on-Avon Festival, 1956; Lady Fidget in The Country Wife, Royal Court Theatre, 1956; The Rehearsal, Globe Theatre, 1961; The Winter's Tale, Cambridge, 1966; The Farmer's Wife, Chichester, 1967; Heartbreak House, Chichester, later Lyric, 1967. Has also appeared in several films. *Address:* c/o Al. Parker Ltd, 50 Mount Street, W1.

CHURCHILL, Hon. Gordon, PC (Canada); DSO 1945; ED; QC; Canadian barrister, retired; *b* Coldwater, Ont, 8 Nov. 1898; *s* of Rev. J. W. and Mary E. Churchill; *m* 1922, Mona Mary, *d* of C. W. McLachlin, Dauphin, Man.; one *d. Educ:* Univ. of Manitoba. MA 1931, LLB 1950. Served European War, 1916-18, France; served War of 1939-45 (DSO), commanded First Canadian Armoured Carrier Regt, NW Europe. Principal of a Manitoba High Sch., 1928-38; Mem. Manitoba Legislature, 1946-49; called to Manitoba Bar, 1950; Member Federal Parlt for Winnipeg South Centre, 1951-68, retired; Federal Minister: for Trade and Commerce, 1957-60; of Veterans' Affairs, 1960-63; of National Defence, Feb.-April 1963. Hon. LLD Winnipeg 1976. *Recreation:* golf. *Address:* 202-140 Douglas Street, Victoria, BC, Canada.

CHURCHILL, John (George Spencer); mural and portrait, townscape, landscape painter; sculptor, lecturer and author since 1932; *b* 31 May 1909; *s* of John Strange Spencer Churchill and Lady Gwendoline Bertie; *m* 1st, 1934, Angela Culme Seymour; one *d*; 2nd, 1941, Mary Cookson; 3rd, 1953, Kathlyn Tandy (*d* 1957); 4th, 1958, Lullan Boston. *Educ:* Harrow School; Pembroke Coll., Oxford; Royal Coll. of Art; Central Sch. of Art; Westminster Sch. of Art; Ruskin Sch. of Art, Oxford; private pupil of Meninsky, Hubbard, Nicholson and Lutyens. Stock Exchange, 1930-32. Served War, Major GSO, RE, 1939-45. Mural and portrait, townscape and landscape paintings in England, France, Spain, Portugal, Italy, Switzerland, Belgium and America, 1932-76. Lectr in America, 1961-69. *Work includes:* incised relief carving on slate and cement cast busts, in Marlborough Pavilion at Chartwell,

Westerham, Kent (National Trust), 1949; reportage illustrations and paintings of Spanish Revolution, 1936, and Evacuation of BEF from Dunkirk, 1940 (in Illustrated London News). Mem., Soc. of Mural Painters. *Publications:* Crowded Canvas, 1960; A Churchill Canvas, 1961 (USA), serialised in Sunday Dispatch and Atlantic Monthly, USA; contrib. illustr.: Country Life, Connoisseur, etc. *Recreations:* music, travel. *Address:* (professional) Oscar Court, 17 Tite Street, SW3 4JR. *T:* 01-352 2352; (domicile) Apartement Churchill, Grimaud 83360, France. *T:* 94.43.21.31. *Clubs:* Press, Curzon House; Cincinatti (Washington, DC, USA).

CHURCHILL, Very Rev. John Howard; Dean of Carlisle, since 1973; *b* 9 June 1920; *s* of John Lancelot and Emily Winifred Churchill; *m* 1948, Patricia May, *d* of late John James and Gertrude May Williams; one *s* two *d. Educ:* Sutton Valence Sch.; Trinity Coll., Cambridge (Exhibitioner); Lincoln Theological Coll. BA 1942, MA 1946. Deacon, 1943; priest, 1944; Asst curate: St George, Camberwell, 1943-48; All Hallows', Tottenham, 1948-53; Chaplain and Lectr in Theology, King's Coll., London, 1953-60; Vicar of St George, Sheffield, 1960-67; Lectr in Education, Univ. of Sheffield, 1960-67; Canon Residentiary of St Edmundsbury, 1967-73; Director of Ordinands and Clergy Training, Diocese of St Edmundsbury and Ipswich, 1967-73. Lady Margaret Preacher, Univ. of Cambridge, 1969; Proctor in Convocation, 1970-. *Publications:* Prayer in Progress, 1961; Going Up: a look at University life, 1963. *Recreation:* walking. *Address:* The Deanery, Carlisle CA3 8TZ. *T:* Carlisle 23335.
See also A . E . C . Green .

CHURCHILL, Maj.-Gen. Thomas Bell Lindsay, CB 1957; CBE 1949; MC; *b* 1 Nov. 1907; 2nd *s* of late Alec Fleming Churchill, of PWD, Ceylon and Hong Kong, and late Elinor Elizabeth (*née* Bell); *m* 1934, Gwendolen Janie (*d* 1962), *e d* of late Lewis Williams, MD; one *s* one *d*; *m* 1968, Penelope Jane Ormiston (marr. diss. 1974). *Educ:* Dragon Sch., Oxford; Magdalen Coll. Sch., Oxford; RMC Sandhurst. Gained Prize Cadetship to RMC Sandhurst, 1926; Prize for Mil. Hist., 1927. 2nd Lieut, Manchester Regt, 1927; Burma Rebellion, 1930-31 (despatches, MC); Adjt, 1931-34; instructor in interpretation of air photographs, RAF Sch. of Photography, 1934-39; Company Comdr, France, 1939-40; GSO1 Commandos, Sicily and Salerno Landings, 1943; comd 2nd Commando Bde, Italy, Jugoslavia, Albania, 1943-44; comd 11th and 138th Inf Bdes, Austria, 1945-46; Zone Comdr, Austria, 1947-49; DDPS, War Office, 1949-51; student, Imperial Def. Coll., 1952; Brig. i/c Admin, HQ Western Comd, 1953-55; Maj.-Gen. i/c Admin., GHQ, Far ELF, 1955-57; Vice-Quartermaster-Gen. to the Forces, 1957-60; Deputy Chief of Staff, Allied Land Forces, Central Europe, 1960-62, retd. Col The Manchester Regt, 1952-58; Col The King's Regt (Manchester and Liverpool). 1958-62. Pres., Commando Assoc. and Chm. Trustees, Commando Benevolent Fund; Chm., Assoc. of Veterans of Jugoslavia, 1974-; a Vice-Pres., British-Jugoslav Soc., 1975-. Partisan Star with Gold Wreath (Yugoslavia), 1970. *Publications:* Manual of Interpretation of Air Photographs, 1939; articles to Yorks Archæolog. Jl, 1935, to Army Quarterly and to Jl of RUSI. *Recreations:* genealogy, heraldry; fine arts. *Address:* Lower Minchingdown Farm, Black Dog, near Crediton, Devon. *T:* Witheridge 474.

CHURCHILL, Winston Spencer; MP (C) Stretford (Lancs) since 1970; author; journalist; *b* 10 Oct. 1940; *s* of late Randolph Frederick Edward Spencer Churchill, MBE and of Mrs Averell Harriman, *e d* of 11th Baron Digby, KG, DSO, MC, TD; *m* 1964, Mary Caroline d'Erlanger, *d* of late Sir Gerard d'Erlanger, CBE, Chairman of BOAC; two *s* two *d*; *g s* of Baroness Spencer-Churchill, *qv. Educ:* Eton; Christ Church, Oxford (MA). Correspondent in: Yemen, Congo and Angola, 1964; Borneo and Vietnam, 1966; Middle East, 1967; Czechoslovakia, 1968; Nigeria, Biafra and Middle East, 1969. Correspondent of The Times, 1969-70. Lecture tours of the US and Canada, 1965, 1969, 1971, 1973, 1975. Contested Gorton Div. of Manchester in Bye-election, Nov. 1967. PPS to Minister of Housing and Construction, 1970-72, to Minister of State, FCO, 1972-73; Sec., Cons. Foreign and Commonwealth Affairs Cttee, 1973-; Opposition front-bench spokesman on Defence, 1976-. Sponsored Motor Vehicles (Passenger Insce) Act 1972. Pres., Trafford Park Indust. Council, 1971. Trustee, Nat. Benevolent Fund for the Aged, 1973; Governor, English-Speaking Union, 1975. Hon. LLD, Westminster Coll., USA. *Publications:* First Journey, 1964; (with late Randolph Churchill) Six Day War, 1967. *Recreations:* tennis, sailing, ski-ing. *Address:* Broadwater House, Chailey, Sussex. *Clubs:* White's, Buck's; St James's (Manchester).

CHURSTON, 4th Baron cr 1858; Richard Francis Roger Yarde-Buller; Bt 1790; VRD; Lieut-Comdr RNVR, retired; b 12 Feb. 1910; er s of 3rd Baron and Jessie (who m 2nd, 1928, Theodore William Wessel), o d of Alfred Smither; S father, 1930; m 1st, 1933, Elizabeth Mary (from whom he obtained a divorce, 1943, and who m 1943, Lieut-Col P. Laycock; she d 1951), 2nd d of late W. B. du Pre; one s one d; 2nd, 1949, Mrs Jack Dunfee. Educ: Eton Coll. Heir: s Hon. John Francis Yarde-Buller [b 29 Dec. 1934; m 1973, Alexandra, d of A. Contomichalos; one s one d]. Address: Woodcote, St Andrew, Guernsey, Channel Isles. Club: Royal Yacht Squadron.
See also Earl Cadogan, Sir G. A. Lyle, Bt.

CHUTE, Marchette; author; b 16 Aug. 1909; d of William Young Chute and Edith Mary Pickburn; unmarried. Educ: Univ. of Minnesota (BA). Doctor of Letters: Western Coll., 1952; Carleton Coll., 1957; Dickinson Coll., 1964. Mem., American Acad. of Arts and Letters. Outstanding Achievement Award, Univ. of Minnesota, 1958; co-winner of Constance Lindsay Skinner Award, 1959. Publications: Rhymes about Ourselves, 1932; The Search for God, 1941; Rhymes about the Country, 1941; The Innocent Wayfaring, 1943; Geoffrey Chaucer of England, 1946; Rhymes about the City, 1946; The End of the Search, 1947; Shakespeare of London, 1950; An Introduction to Shakespeare, 1951 (English title: Shakespeare and his Stage); Ben Jonson of Westminster, 1953; The Wonderful Winter, 1954; Stories from Shakespeare, 1956; Around and About, 1957; Two Gentle Men: the Lives of George Herbert and Robert Herrick, 1959; Jesus of Israel, 1961; The Worlds of Shakespeare (with Ernestine Perrie), 1963; The First Liberty: a history of the right to vote in America, 1619-1850, 1969; The Green Tree of Democracy, 1971; Rhymes About Us, 1974; various articles in Saturday Review, Virginia Quarterly Review, etc. Recreations: walking, reading, talking. Address: 450 East 63rd Street, New York, NY 10021, USA. T: Templeton 8-8920. Clubs: Royal Society of Arts; PEN, Renaissance Society of America, Society of American Historians (New York).

CHWATT, Professor Leonard Jan B.; see Bruce-Chwatt.

CHYNOWETH, David Boyd; County Treasurer, South Yorkshire County Council, since 1973; b 26 Dec. 1940; s of Ernest and Blodwen Chynoweth; m 1968, Margaret Slater; two d. Educ: Simon Langton Sch., Canterbury; Univ. of Nottingham (BA). IPFA. Public Finance posts with Derbs CC, 1962 and London Borough of Ealing, 1965; Asst County Treas., Flints CC, 1968; Dep. County Treas., West Suffolk CC, 1970. Recreations: sailing, photography. Address: County Offices, Regent Street, Barnsley, S Yorks S70 2DX. T: Barnsley 86141. Club: Royal Over-Seas League.

CILENTO, Sir Raphael West, Kt 1935; MD, BS (Adelaide); DTM&H (England); (life) FRSanI (London); FRHistSoc, Queensland; Director-General of Health and Medical Services, Queensland, Australia, 1934-45; Hon. Professor of Tropical and Social Medicine, University of Queensland, 1937-45; Barrister Supreme Court, Queensland, since 1939; b 2 Dec. 1893; s of Raphael Ambrose Cilento and Frances Ellen Elizabeth West; m 1920, Phyllis Dorothy, d of late C. T. McGlew; three s three d. Educ: Adelaide High Sch.; Prince Alfred Coll., South Australia; Univ. of Adelaide. Colonial Medical Service (Federated Malay States), 1920-21; Duncan and Lalcaca medals, London Sch. of Tropical Medicine, 1922; Dir, Australian Inst. of Tropical Medicine, Townsville, North Queensland, 1922-28; Dir of Public Health, New Guinea, 1924-28; Rep. (Brit.) League of Nations Mission on Health Conditions in the Pacific with Dr P. Hermant (French rep.), 1928-29; Dir for Tropical Hygiene, Commonwealth of Australia, and Chief Quarantine Officer (General) NE Div., 1928-34, Brisbane, Qld; Pres., Royal Society Qld, 1933-34; Chm., State Nutritional Advisory Board, 1937; Pres., Med. Board of Qld, 1939; Assessor, Med. Assessment Tribunal, 1940; Senior Administrative Officer, Commonwealth Dept of Health, Canberra, ACT; Mem., Army Medical Directorates Consultative Cttee, 1941-45; Chm., National Survey, Health of Coal Miners, Australia, 1945; UNRRA Zone Dir, British occupied area Germany, Maj.-Gen., with assimilated status, BAOR, 1945-46; Dir, Div. of Refugees, 1946, of Div. of Social Activities, 1947-50, UN, NY. Pres., Royal Hist. Soc. of Queensland, 1934-35, 1943-44, 1953-68; Pres., Nat. Trust of Queensland, 1967-71. Publications: Malaria, 1924; White Man in the Tropics, 1925; Factors in Depopulation; NW Islands of the Mandated Territory of New Guinea, 1928; Health Problems in the Pacific, 1929; Anne Mackenzie Oration, 1933; Second Sir Herbert Maitland Oration, 1937; Tropical Diseases in Australasia, 1940 (and 1942); Blueprint for the Health of a Nation, 1944. Recreations: international affairs, reading history. Address: Altavilla, 56 Glen Road, Toowong, Queensland 4066, Australia. Clubs: Johnsonian (Brisbane); Australasian Pioneers

(Sydney).
See also Sean Connery.

CITRINE, family name of Baron Citrine.

CITRINE, 1st Baron cr 1946, of Wembley; Walter McLennan Citrine, PC 1940; GBE 1958 (KBE 1935); Comp. IEE; b Liverpool, 22 Aug. 1887; m 1913, Doris Slade (d 1973); two s. Mersey District Sec. of Electrical Trades Union, 1914-20; Pres., Fed. Engineering and Shipbuilding Trades, Mersey District, 1917-18; Sec., 1918-20; Asst Gen. Sec., Electrical Trades Union, 1920-23; Asst Sec., TUC, 1924-25, Gen. Sec., 1926-46; Mem., Nat. Coal Board, 1946-47; Chm., Miners' Welfare Commn, 1946-47. Pres., Internat. Fed. of Trade Unions, 1928-45; Dir, Daily Herald (1929) Ltd, 1929-46; Mem., Nat. Production Advisory Council, 1942-46 and 1949-57; Past Mem., Reconstruction Jt Advisory Council; Treasury Consultative Council; Visiting Fellow, Nuffield Coll., 1939-47; Trustee of Imperial Relations Trust, 1937-49; Nuffield Trust for the Forces, 1939-46; Mem. of Cinematograph Films Council, 1938-48; Exec. Cttee of Red Cross, and St John War Organisation, 1939-46; Chm. of Production Cttee on Regional Boards (Munitions), 1942; Mem., Royal Commission on W Indies, 1938; Pres., British Electrical Development Assoc., 1948-52; Chm. Central Electricity Authority, 1947-57; Pres., Electrical Research Assoc., 1950-52 and 1956-57; Pres. (1955) and Mem. of Directing Cttee, Union Internationale des Producteurs et Distributeurs d'Energie Electrique; Part-time Mem., Electricity Council, 1958-62. Part-time Mem. of UK Atomic Energy Authority, 1958-62. Hon. LLD, Manchester. Publications: ABC of Chairmanship; The Trade Union Movement of Great Britain; Labour and the Community; I Search for Truth in Russia, 1936 and 1938; My Finnish Diary; My American Diary, 1941; In Russia Now, 1942; British Trade Unions, 1942; Men and Work, 1964; Two Careers, 1967, etc. Heir: s Hon. N. A. Citrine, qv. Address: Gorse Cottage, Berry Head, Brixham, Devon. T: Brixham 51091.

CITRINE, Hon. Norman Arthur, LLB; solicitor in general practice; author, editor, lecturer; b 27 Sept. 1914; e s and heir of 1st Baron Citrine, qv; m 1939, Kathleen Alice Chilvers; one d. Educ: University Coll. Sch., Hampstead; Law Society's Sch., London. Admitted solicitor of Supreme Court (Hons) 1937; LLB (London), 1938. Served War of 1939-45, Lieut RNVR, 1940-46. Legal Adviser to Trades Union Congress, 1946-51; entered general legal practice, 1951. Publications: War Pensions Appeal Cases, 1946; Guide to Industrial Injuries Acts, 1948; Trade Union Law, 1950, 3rd edn, 1968; Editor, ABC of Chairmanship, 1952-. Recreations: boating, engineering, painting, carpentry. Address: Gorse Cottage, Berry Head, Brixham, Torbay, Devon. T: Brixham 51091.

CIVIL, Alan; Principal Horn, BBC Symphony Orchestra, since 1966; b 13 June 1928; m Shirley Jean Hopkins; three s two d. Educ: Northampton, various schools. Principal Horn, Royal Philharmonic Orchestra, 1953-55; Philharmonia Orchestra, 1955-66. Guest Principal, Berlin Philharmonic Orchestra; international horn soloist; Prof. of Horn, Royal Coll. of Music, London; composer; founder of Alan Civil Horn Trio. Member: London Wind Soloists; London Wind Quintet; Music Group of London. Recreations: brewing, gardening, Baroque music. Address: Downe Hall, Downe, Kent. T: Farnborough (Kent) 52982. Club: Savage.

CLAGUE, Col Sir (John) Douglas, Kt 1971; CBE (mil.) 1946 (OBE (mil.) 1943); MC 1942; QPM 1968; CPM 1966; TD 1954; JP; b 13 June 1917; 2nd s of Alfred Ernest and Hannah Clague, Isle of Man; m 1947, Margaret Isolin Cowley; one s two d. Educ: King William's College, Isle of Man. Served War, 1939-46, in the Far East: Hong Kong, China, India, Burma, Siam, finishing with rank of Colonel. Since 1947 involved in business and politics, Hong Kong; Chm., Hutchison International Ltd Group of Cos, 1952-76. Unofficial Mem., Exec. Council of Hong Kong, 1961-74. JP Hong Kong, 1952. Commendatore dell' Ordine al Merito della Republica Italiana, 1969. Recreations: golf, swimming, racing. Address: Ballamacleog, 26 Middle Gap Road, Hong Kong. T: Hong Kong 96129. Clubs: Junior Carlton, The Royal Commonwealth Society; Royal and Ancient (St Andrews); Sunningdale Golf; MCC; Hong Kong, Royal Hong Kong Jockey (Steward) (Hong Kong).

CLAIR, René; writer and film director; Member of the French Academy, since 1960; Commandeur de la Légion d'Honneur; b 11 Nov. 1898; m 1928, Bronia Perlmutter; one s. Hon. LLD Cambridge, 1956; Hon. Dr RCA, 1967. Films include: Paris qui dort, 1923; Entr'acte, 1924; Un chapeau de paille d'Italie, 1927; Sous les Toits de Paris, 1930; Le Million, 1931; A Nous la Liberté, 1932; Quartorze Juillet, 1933; Le Dernier Milliardaire,

1934; The Ghost Goes West, 1935; Flame of New Orleans, 1940; I Married a Witch, 1942; It Happened Tomorrow, 1943; Le Silence est d'Or, 1946; La Beauté du Diable, 1949; Les Belles de Nuit, 1952; Les Grandes Manœvres, 1955; Porte des Lilas, 1956; Tout l'Or du Monde, 1961; Les Fêtes Galantes, 1965. *Publications:* Adams (Star Turn), 1926; La Princesse de Chine, 1951; Réflection faite (Reflection on the Cinema), 1951; Comédies et Commentaires, 1959; Discours de Reception à l'Académie Française, 1962; Cinéma d'hier et d'aujourd'hui (Cinema Yesterday and Today), 1970; L'Etrange Ouvrage des Cieux, 1971; Jeux du hasard (short stories), 1976. *Address:* 11 bis Avenue de Madrid, 92200 Neuilly sur Seine, France.

CLAMAGERAN, Alice Germaine Suzanne; Director, School of Social Workers, Centre Hospitalier Universitaire de Rouen, 1942-73; President, International Council of Nurses, 1961-65; *b* 5 March 1906; *d* of William Clamageran, shipowner at Rouen and of Lucie Harlé. *Educ:* Rouen. Nursing studies: Red Cross School of Nurses, Rouen; Ecole Professionnelle d'Assistance aux Malades, Paris. Tutor, Red Cross Sch. for Nurses, Rouen, 1931-42 (leave, for course in Public Health at Florence Nightingale Internat. Foundn, London, 1934-35). War service (6 months), 1939-40. President: Bd of Dirs, Fondation Edith Seltzer (Sanatorium Chantoiseau, Briançon) for Nurses, Social Workers and Medical Auxiliaries; Assoc. Médico-Sociale Protestante de Langue Française; Hon. Pres. Nat. Assoc. of Trained Nurses in France. Médaille de Bronze de l'Enseignement Technique, 1960; Officier dans l'Ordre de la Santé Publique, 1961; Chevalier, Légion d'Honneur, 1962. *Address:* Hautonne, 27310 Bourg-Achard, France.

CLANCARTY, 8th Earl of, *cr* 1803; **William Francis Brinsley Le Poer Trench;** Baron Kilconnel, 1797; Viscount Dunlo, 1801; Baron Trench (UK), 1815; Viscount Clancarty (UK), 1823; Marquess of Heusden (Kingdom of the Netherlands), 1818; author; *b* 18 Sept. 1911; 5th *s* of 5th Earl of Clancarty and of Mary Gwatkin, *d* of late W. F. Rosslewin Ellis; *S* half-brother, 1975; *m* 1st, 1940, Diana Joan (marr. diss. 1947), *yr d* of Sir William Younger, 2nd Bt; 2nd, 1961, Mrs Wilma Dorothy Millen Belknap (marr. diss. 1969), *d* of S. R. Vermilyea, USA; 3rd, 1974, Mrs Mildred Alleyn Spong (*d* 1975); 4th, 1976, May, *widow* of Commander Frank M. Beasley, RN and *o d* of late E. Radonicich. *Educ:* Nautical Coll., Pangbourne. Founder President of Contact International. *Publications:* (as Brinsley Le Poer Trench): The Sky People, 1960; Men Among Mankind, 1962; Forgotten Heritage, 1964; The Flying Saucer Story, 1966; Operation Earth, 1969; The Eternal Subject, 1973; Secret of the Ages, 1974. *Recreations:* Ufology, travel, walking. *Heir:* nephew Nicholas Power Richard Le Poer Trench, *b* 1 May 1952. *Address:* 6 Lyall Street, Belgravia, SW1. *Clubs:* Brooks's, Buck's.

CLANFIELD, Viscount; Ashton Robert Gerard Peel; *b* 16 Sept. 1976; *s* and *heir* of 3rd Earl Peel, *qv*.

CLANMORRIS, 7th Baron (Ireland), *cr* 1800; **John Michael Ward Bingham;** *b* 3 Nov. 1908; *o s* of 6th Baron Clanmorris; *S* father, 1960; *m* 1934, Madeleine Mary, *d* of late Clement Ebel, Copyhold Place, Cuckfield, Sussex; one *s* one *d*. *Educ:* Cheltenham Coll.; France and Germany. *Publications:* as John Bingham: My Name is Michael Sibley, 1952; Five Roundabouts to Heaven, 1953; The Third Skin, 1954; The Paton Street Case, 1955; Marion, 1958; Murder Plan Six, 1958; Night's Black Agent, 1960; A Case of Libel, 1963; A Fragment of Fear, 1965; The Double Agent, 1966; I Love, I Kill, 1968; Vulture in the Sun, 1971; The Hunting Down of Peter Manuel, 1974; God's Defector, 1976; The Marriage Bureau Murders, 1977. *Heir: s* Hon. Simon John Ward Bingham [*b* 25 Oct. 1937; *m* 1971, Gizella Maria, *d* of Sandor Zverkó; one *d*]. *Address:* 24 Abingdon Villas, W8. *Club:* Press.
See also Hon. Charlotte Bingham.

CLANWILLIAM, 6th Earl of, *cr* 1776; **John Charles Edmund Carson Meade;** Bt 1703; Viscount Clanwilliam, Baron Gilford, 1766; Baron Clanwilliam (UK), 1828; Major Coldstream Guards (retired); *b* 6 June 1914; *o s* of 5th Earl of Clanwilliam; *S* father, 1953; *m* 1948, Catherine, *y d* of late A. T. Loyd, Lockinge, Wantage, Berks; six *d*. *Educ:* Eton; RMC Sandhurst. Adjt, 1939-42; Staff Coll., Haifa, 1942; Bde Major, 201 Guards Motor Brigade, 1942-43; Bde Major, 6 Guards Tank Brigade, 1944; Command and Gen. Staff Sch., Fort Leavenworth, USA, 1944; served in Middle East and France (despatches twice); retd, 1948. HM Lieutenant for Co. Down, 1962-75, HM Lord-Lieutenant, 1975. *Heir: cousin* John Herbert Meade [*b* 27 Sept. 1919; *m* 1956, Maxine, *o d* of late J. A. Hayden-Scott; one *s* two *d*]. *Address:* Montalto, Ballynahinch, Co. Down. *T:* Ballynahinch 2296. *Clubs:* Carlton, Pratt's.

CLAPHAM, Prof. Arthur Roy, CBE 1969; FRS 1959; MA, PhD Cantab; FLS; Professor of Botany in Sheffield University, 1944-69, Professor Emeritus 1969; Pro-Vice-Chancellor, 1954-58, Acting Vice-Chancellor, 1965; Member of the Nature Conservancy, 1956-72 (Chairman, Scientific Policy Committee, 1963-70); Chairman, British National Committee for the International Biological Programme; President, Linnean Society, 1967-70; *b* 24 May 1904; *o s* of George Clapham, Norwich; *m* 1933, Brenda North Stoessiger; one *s* two *d* (and one *s* decd). *Educ:* City of Norwich Sch.; Downing Coll., Cambridge (Foundation Scholar). Frank Smart Prize, 1925; Frank Smart Student, 1926-27; Crop Physiologist at Rothamsted Agricultural Experimental Station, 1928-30; Demonstrator in Botany at Oxford Univ., 1930-44. Mem., NERC, 1965-70; Trustee, British Museum (Natural History), 1965-75. Hon. LLD Aberdeen, 1970; Hon. LittD, Sheffield, 1970. Linnean Gold Medal (Botany), 1972. *Publications:* (with W. O. James) The Biology of Flowers, 1935; (with T. G. Tutin and E. F. Warburg) Flora of the British Isles, 1952, 1962; Excursion Flora of the British Isles, 1959, 1968; (with B. E. Nicholson) The Oxford Book of Trees, 1975; various papers in botanical journals. *Address:* The Parrock, Arkholme, Carnforth, Lancs. *T:* Hornby 21206.

CLAPHAM, Brian Ralph; His Honour Judge Clapham; a Circuit Judge since 1974; *b* 1 July 1913; *s* of Isaac Clapham and Laura Alice Clapham (*née* Meech); *m* 1961, Margaret Warburg; two *s*. *Educ:* Tonbridge Sch.; Wadham Coll., Oxford; University Coll., London (LLB; LLM 1976). Called to Bar, Middle Temple, 1936; SE Circuit. Contested (Lab): Tonbridge, 1950; Billericay, 1951, 1955; Chelmsford, 1959. Councillor, Tonbridge and Southborough UDCs, 1947-74; Chm., Tonbridge UDC, 1959-60. *Recreations:* walking and talking. *Address:* 10 Bounds Oak Way, Southborough, Tunbridge Wells, Kent. *T:* Tunbridge Wells 31969.

CLAPHAM, Sir Michael (John Sinclair), KBE 1973; Chairman: Imperial Metal Industries Ltd, since 1974; BPM Holdings Ltd, since 1974; Deputy Chairman, Lloyds Bank Ltd, since 1974; *b* 17 Jan. 1912; *s* of late Sir John Clapham, CBE and Lady Clapham, Cambridge; *m* 1935, Hon. Elisabeth Russell Rea, *d* of 1st Baron Rea of Eskdale; three *s* one *d*. *Educ:* Marlborough Coll.; King's Coll., Cambridge (MA). Apprenticed as printer with University Press, Cambridge, 1933-35; Overseer and later Works Man., Percy Lund Humphries & Co. Ltd, Bradford, 1935-38; joined ICI Ltd as Man., Kynoch Press, 1938; seconded, in conseq. of developing a diffusion barrier, to Tube Alloys Project (atomic energy), 1941-45; Personnel Dir, ICI Metals Div., 1946; Midland Regional Man., ICI, 1951; Jt Man. Dir, ICI Metals Div., 1952; Chm. 1959; Dir, ICI, 1961-74, Dep. Chm. 1968-74; served as Overseas Dir; Dir, ICI of Austr. & NZ Ltd, 1961-74; Director: Imp. Metal Industries Ltd, 1962-70; Lloyds Bank Ltd, 1971-; Grindlay's Bank Ltd, 1975-. Dep. Pres., 1971-72, Pres., 1972-74, CBI. Member: IRC, 1969-71; Standing Adv. Cttee on Pay of Higher Civil Service, 1968-71; Review Body on Doctors' and Dentists' Remuneration, 1968-70; Birmingham Educn Cttee, 1949-56; W Mids Adv. Coun. for Techn., Commercial and Art Educn, and Regional Academic Bd, 1952; Life Governor, Birmingham Univ., 1955 (Mem. Coun., 1956-61); Member: Court, Univ. of London, 1969-; Govt Youth Service Cttee (Albermarle Cttee), 1958; CNAA, 1964-77 (Chm., 1971-77); NEDC, 1971-. Hon. DSc Aston, 1973. *Publications:* Printing, 1500-1730, in The History of Technology, Vol. III, 1957; Multinational Enterprises and Nation States, 1975; various articles on printing, personnel management and education. *Recreations:* sailing, canal boating, cooking. *Address:* 26 Hill Street, W1X 7FU. *T:* 01-499 1240. *Clubs:* Royal Yacht Squadron, Royal Cruising.
See also B. D. Till.

CLAPPEN, Air Commodore Donald William, CB 1946; RAF retired; *b* 30 June 1895; 2nd *s* of late E. S. Clappen and of Mrs F. Clappen, Westcliff-on-Sea; *m* 1917, Kathleen Mary Broughton Knight; one *s*. *Educ:* St John's Coll., Westcliff-on-Sea; Hurstpierpoint; University Coll., London. Joined Bleriot Aviation Co. as apprentice, 1911; flying pupil, 1912, gaining Pilot's Certificate No 591 Aug. 1913, on Bleriot Monoplane; Flying Instructor, Hendon, until outbreak of war; joined 1st Bn London Scottish (14th Bn Territorials), 1914; Commission Royal Flying Corps, 1916 (despatches); subsequently RAF, 1918; passed University and Engineer Course, 1922; various appointments including two overseas tours, Iraq prior to outbreak of war. Middle East, 1939-42; Officer Commanding RAF Cosford, near Wolverhampton, 1942-43; Senior Engineer Officer, Army Co-operation Command, 1943; Senior Air Staff Officer HQ 24 Gp, 1943-44; Air Officer Commanding RAF Station, St Athan, Wales, 1944-46; Senior Technical Staff Officer, HQ Bomber Command, 1946; retd 1949. *Recreations:*

tennis, winter sports (ski-ing), forestry, cine-photography. *Address:* Three, The Garth, Great Missenden, Bucks. *T:* Great Missenden 4667. *Clubs:* Royal Air Force; Ski Club of Gt. Britain.

CLARE, Ernest Elwyn S.; *see* Sabben-Clare.

CLARE, Herbert Mitchell N.; *see* Newton-Clare.

CLARENDON, 7th Earl of, 2nd *cr* 1776; **George Frederick Laurence Hyde Villiers;** a Managing Director, Seccombe Marshall and Campion Ltd, since 1962; *b* 2 Feb. 1933; *o s* of Lord Hyde (*d* 1935) and Hon. Marion Féodorovna Louise Glyn, Lady Hyde (*d* 1970), *er d* of 4th Baron Wolverton; *S* grandfather, 1955; *m* 1974, Jane Diana, *d* of E. W. Dawson; one *s*. Page of Honour to King George VI, 1948-49; Lieut RHG, 1951-53. *Heir: s* Lord Hyde, *qv*. *Address:* 8 Chelsea Square, SW3 6LF. *T:* 01-352 6338.

CLARFELT, Jack Gerald; Managing Director and Deputy Chairman, FMC Ltd, since 1975; *b* 7 Feb. 1914; *s* of Barnett Clarfelt and Rene (*née* Frankel); *m* 1948, Baba Fredman; one *s* one *d*. *Educ:* Grocers' Co. Sch.; Sorbonne. Practised as Solicitor in own name, 1938-40; Man. Dir, Home Killed Meat Assoc., 1940-43 and 1945-54; Queen's Royal Surreys, 1943-45; Man. Dir, Fatstock Marketing Corp., 1954-60; Chm., Smithfield & Zwanenberg Gp Ltd, 1960-75; Dir, Macpherson Train & Co. Ltd, 1975-. *Recreations:* golf, swimming. *Address:* 37A Queen's Grove, St Johns Wood, NW8 6HN. *T:* 01-722 3345. *Clubs:* City Livery, Farmers'.

CLARINGBULL, Sir (Gordon) Frank, Kt 1975; BSc, PhD, FGS, FInstP, FMA; Director, British Museum (Natural History), 1968-76; *b* 21 Aug. 1911; *s* of William Horace Claringbull and Hannah Agnes Cutting; *m* 1st, 1938, Grace Helen Mortimer (*d* 1953); one *s* one *d*; 2nd, 1953, Enid Dorothy Phyllis, *d* of late William Henry Lambert. *Educ:* Finchley Grammar Sch.; Queen Mary Coll., Univ. of London (Fellow 1967). British Museum (Natural Hist.): Asst Keeper, 1935-48; Princ. Scientific Officer, 1948-53; Keeper of Mineralogy, 1953-68. Explosives res., Min. of Supply, 1940-43; special scientific duties, War Office, 1943-45. Mineralogical Soc.: Gen. Sec., 1938-59; Vice-Pres, 1959-63; Pres., 1965-67; For. Sec., 1967-71, Managing Trustee, 1969-77; Gemmological Assoc.: Vice-Pres., 1970-72, Pres., 1972-. Mem., Standing Commn on Museums and Galleries, 1976-. *Publications:* Crystal Structures of Minerals (with W. L. Bragg); papers in journals of learned societies on mineralogical and related topics. *Recreations:* craftwork, gardening, photography. *Address:* Padfield House, West Bradley, Glastonbury, Somerset BA6 8LS. *T:* Baltonsborough 557. *Club:* Athenæum.

CLARK; *see* Chichester-Clark.

CLARK, family name of Baron Clark.

CLARK, Baron *cr* 1969 (Life Peer); **Kenneth Mackenzie Clark,** OM 1976; CH 1959; KCB 1938; CLit 1974; FBA 1949; Chancellor of University of York since 1969; *b* 13 July 1903; *o s* of late Kenneth McKenzie Clark and Margaret Alice McArthur; *m* 1927, Elizabeth Martin; (*d* 1976); two *s* one *d*. *Educ:* Winchester; Trinity College, Oxford (Hon. Fellow, 1968). Worked for two years with Mr Bernard Berenson, Florence; Keeper of Dept of Fine Art, Ashmolean Museum, Oxford, 1931-33; Director of National Gallery, 1934-45; Surveyor of the King's Pictures, 1934-44; Director of Film Div., later Controller, Home Publicity, Ministry of Information, 1939-41; Slade Professor of Fine Art, Oxford, 1946-50, and October 1961-62; Prof. of the History of Art, Royal Academy. Chairman Arts Council of Great Britain, 1953-60; Chairman of the ITA, 1954-57. Former Trustee, British Museum. Prof. of Art History, RA, 1977-. Member: Conseil Artistique des Musées Nationaux; Amer. Academy; Swedish Academy; Spanish Academy; Florentine Acad.; French Acad., 1973; Institut de France. Hon. Mem., American Inst. of Architects. Hon. Degrees from Universities: Oxford, Cambridge, London, Glasgow, Liverpool, Sheffield, York, Warwick, Bath, Columbia (NY), Brown (Rhode Island). Hon. FRIBA; Hon. FRCA. Serena Medal of British Academy (for Italian Studies), 1955; Gold Medal and Citation of Honour New York University; US Nat. Gall. of Arts Medal, 1970; Gold Medal, Academie des Beaux-Arts. HRSA. Comdr, Legion of Honour, France; Comdr, Lion of Finland; Order of Merit, Grand Cross, 2nd Cl., Austria. *Publications:* The Gothic Revival, 1929; Catalogue of Drawings of Leonardo da Vinci in the collection of His Majesty the King at Windsor Castle, 1935; One Hundred Details in the National Gallery, 1938; Leonardo da Vinci, 1939, new edn 1967; Last Lectures by Roger Fry, edited with an introduction, 1939; L. B. Alberti on Painting, 1944; Constable's Hay Wain, 1944; (Introduction to)

Praeterita, 1949; Landscape into Art, 1949; Piero della Francesca, 1951; Moments of Vision, 1954; The Nude, 1955; Looking, 1960; Ruskin Today, 1964; Rembrandt and the Italian Renaissance, 1966; A Failure of Nerve, 1967; Civilisation, 1969; Looking at Pictures, 1972; (jtly) Westminster Abbey, 1972; The Artist Grows Old (Rede Lecture), 1972; The Romantic Rebellion, 1973; Another Part of the Wood (autobiog.), 1974; Henry Moore Drawings, 1974; The Drawings by Sandro Botticelli for Dante's Divine Comedy, 1976; The Other Half (autobiog.), 1977; Animals and Men, 1977. Numerous TV programmes, 1965-68; TV series: *Civilisation,* 1969; *Romantic versus Classic Art,* 1973. *Address:* The Garden House, Castle Road, Saltwood, Hythe, Kent.
See also Hon. A. K. M. Clark.

CLARK, Rt. Rev. Alan Charles; *see* East Anglia, Bishop of, (RC).

CLARK, Hon. Alan Kenneth McKenzie; MP (C) Plymouth Sutton, since Feb. 1974; historian; *b* 13 April 1928; *s* of Baron Clark, *qv*; *m* 1958, Caroline Jane Beuttler; two *s*. *Educ:* Eton; Christ Church, Oxford (MA). Household Cavalry (Training Regt), 1946; RAuxAF, 1952-54. Barrister, Inner Temple, 1955. Mem., Inst. for Strategic Studies, 1963. Mem., RUSI. *Publications:* The Donkeys, A History of the BEF in 1915, 1961; The Fall of Crete, 1963; Barbarossa, The Russo-German Conflict, 1941-45, 1965; Aces High: the war in the air over the Western Front 1914-18, 1973; (ed) A Good Innings: the private papers of Viscount Lee of Fareham, 1974. *Address:* Town Farm, Bratton-Clovelly, Devon. *T:* Bratton-Clovelly 252; Saltwood Castle, Hythe, Kent. *T:* Hythe 67190. *Club:* Brooks's.

CLARK, Albert William; Metropolitan Magistrate since 1970; *b* 23 Sept. 1922; *s* of William Charles Clark and Cissy Dorothy Elizabeth Clark; *m* 1951, Frances Philippa, *d* of Dr Samuel Lavington Hart, Tientsin; one *s* one *d*. *Educ:* Christ's Coll., Finchley. War service, 1941-46, Royal Navy. Called to Bar, Middle Temple, 1949; Clerk of Arraigns, Central Criminal Court, 1951-56; Clerk to the Justices, E Devon, 1956-70; Dep. Chm., Inner London QS, 1971; Dep. Circuit Judge, 1972. *Recreations:* fly-fishing, walking, etc. *Address:* Coombe Cottage, Renfrew Road, Kingston Hill, Surrey. *T:* 01-942 8100.

CLARK, Alec Fulton Charles, CB 1960; Under-Secretary, Scottish Home and Health Department (retired); *b* 17 Dec. 1898; *yr s* of Charles and Mary Clark; *m* 1926, Mary, *er d* of David and Janet Watson; one *s* one *d*. *Educ:* Dunfermline High Sch.; Edinburgh Univ.; Lincoln Coll., Oxford. Asst Principal, Ministry of Agriculture and Fisheries, 1925; Principal, Ministry of Agriculture and Fisheries, 1934; Principal, Scottish Home Dept, 1939; Asst Sec. in Scottish Home Dept, 1942; promoted Under-Sec., 1953; retd 1963. *Recreation:* music. *Address:* 22 Warrender Park Terrace, Edinburgh EH9 1EF. *T:* 031-229 1020.

CLARK, Sir Andrew Edmund James, 3rd Bt *cr* 1883; MBE 1941; MC; QC 1943; *b* 18 July 1898; *o s* of Sir James Clark, 2nd Bt, CB, CMG, and Lilian Margaret, 2nd *d* of Robert Hopkins, Tidmarsh Manor, Berks; *S* father, 1948; *m* 1st, 1921, Angelica (*d* 1922), *d* of James Taylor, Strensham, Worcs; 2nd, 1924, Adeline Frances, *o d* of late Col A. D. Derviche-Jones, DSO; two *d*. *Educ:* Eton. 2nd Lieut Regular Army, RFA, 1916; served France and Belgium, 1916-18 (MC); Order of St John of Jerusalem; retd, 1921. Called to Bar, Inner Temple, 1928, Lincoln's Inn, 1930; called up for service with Regular Army, 1939-45; Lieut-Col and Hon. Brigadier RARO. Bencher of Inner Temple, 1951; conducted Crichel Down Inquiry, 1954. *Publications:* The Way of Lucifer; God's Children; Selected Poems. *Recreations:* shooting, fishing, gardening. *Heir:* none. *Address:* 45 Victoria Road, Kensington, W8. *T:* 01-937 7008. *Clubs:* Boodle's, MCC.

CLARK of Herriotshall, Arthur Melville, MA (Hons); DPhil; DLitt; FRSE; FRSA; Reader in English Literature, Edinburgh University, 1946-60; *b* 20 Aug. 1895; 4th *s* of late James Clark and Margaret Moyes McLachlan, Edinburgh. *Educ:* Stewart's Coll., Edinburgh; Edinburgh Univ. (Sibbald Bursar and Vans Dunlop Scholar); Oriel Coll., Oxford (Scholar); MA First Class Hons and twice medallist, DLitt Edinburgh; DPhil Oxford. Lectr in English Language and Literature, Reading, 1920; Tutor to Oxford Home Students, 1921; Sec. of Oxford Union Soc., 1923; Pres. of Speculative Soc., 1926-29; Lectr in English Literature, Edinburgh Univ., 1928-46; Dir of Studies, Edinburgh Univ., 1931-47; Editor of Edinburgh University Calendar, 1933-45; External Examiner in English, St Andrews Univ., 1939-43, and Aberdeen Univ., 1944-46. Pres. of Scottish Arts Club, 1948-50. Pres. of Edinburgh Scott Club, 1957-58. Exhibitor RSA, SSA; Dir, Scottish Students' Song Book Cttee Ltd. Knight's Cross, Order of Polonia Restituta, 1968.

Publications: The Realistic Revolt in Modern Poetry, 1922; A Bibliography of Thomas Heywood (annotated), 1924; Thomas Heywood, Playwright and Miscellanist, 1931; Autobiography, its Genesis and Phases, 1935; Spoken English, 1946; Studies in Literary Modes, 1946; Two Pageants by Thomas Heywood, 1953; Sonnets from the French, and Other Verses, 1966; Sir Walter Scott: The Formative Years, 1969; contribs to Encyc. Brit., Collier's Encyc., Encyc. of Poetry and Poetics, Cambridge Bibl. of Eng. Lit., Library, Mod. Lang. Review, Classical Review, etc. *Recreations:* walking, pastel-sketching. *Address:* 3 Woodburn Terrace, Edinburgh EH10 4SH. *T:* 031-447 1240; Herriotshall, Oxton, Berwickshire. *Clubs:* New, Scottish Arts (Edinburgh); Union Society (Oxford).

CLARK, Charles Joseph, (Joe); MP (Progressive C) Rocky Mountain Constituency, since 1972; Leader of HM's Loyal Opposition, in House of Commons of Canada, since 1976; *b* 5 June 1939; *s* of Charles and Grace Clark; *m* 1973, Maureen McTeer (she retained her maiden name); one *d*. *Educ:* High River High Sch.; Univ. of Alta (BA History); Univ. of Alberta (MA Polit. Sci.). Journalist, Canadian Press, Calgary Herald, Edmonton Jl, High River Times, 1964-66; Prof. of Political Science, Univ. of Alberta, Edmonton, 1966-67; Exec. Asst to Hon. Robert L. Stanfield, Leader of HM's Loyal Opposition, 1967-70. Hon. LLD New Brunswick, 1976. *Recreations:* riding, reading, walking, film going. *Address:* Stornoway, 541 Acacia Avenue, Ottawa, Ont, Canada. *T:* 996-5084.

CLARK, Col Charles Willoughby, DSO 1918; OBE 1945; MC 1916; DL; *b* 6 April 1888; *m* 1916; one *s* (one *d* decd). *Educ:* Atherstone Grammar Sch. Apprentice, Alfred Herbert Ltd, Coventry, 1904; Dir, 1934 (Chm. 1958-66). Served European War, 1914-18, France, Machine Gun Corps, Royal Tank Corps (MC, DSO, despatches twice). Chm. Coventry Conservative Assoc., 1945-48; Pres. Coventry Chamber of Commerce, 1951-53; Chm. Manufacturers' Section Cttee of Machine Tool Trades Assoc., 1946-55. Mem. Bd of Trade Machine Tool Advisory Council, 1957-66. Freeman of the City of London. Fellow Royal Commonwealth Society; FInstD; Mem. Inst of Export. DL Warwickshire, 1965. *Recreations:* shooting and fishing. *Address:* Flat 41, Regency House, Newbold Terrace, Leamington Spa, Warwickshire. *T:* Leamington Spa 24004; Brooklands Close, Ablington, near Bibury, Glos. *T:* Bibury 326. *Club:* Royal Automobile.

CLARK, Colin Grant, MA, DLitt (Oxon); Research Fellow, Monash University, Melbourne, Australia; Director of Institute for Research in Agricultural Economics, Oxford, 1953-69; Fellow of the Econometric Society; *b* 2 Nov. 1905; *s* of James Clark, merchant and manufacturer, Townsville and Plymouth; *m* 1935, Marjorie Tattersall; eight *s* one *d*. *Educ:* Dragon Sch.; Winchester; Brasenose Coll., Oxford; MA 1931, DLitt 1971; MA Cantab 1931; took degree in chemistry; Frances Wood Prizeman of the Royal Statistical Soc., 1928; Asst to late Prof. Allyn Young of Harvard; worked on the New Survey of London Life and Labour, 1928-29, and Social Survey of Merseyside, 1929-30; on Staff of Economic Advisory Council, Cabinet Offices, 1930-31; University Lectr in Statistics, Cambridge, 1931-37. Contested (Lab): North Dorset, 1929; Wavertree (Liverpool), 1931; South Norfolk, 1935. Visiting Lectr at Univs of Melbourne, Sydney, and Western Australia, 1937-38. Under-Sec. of State for Labour and Industry, Dir of Bureau of Industry, and Financial Adviser to the Treasury, Qld, 1938-52. Hon. ScD, Milan; Hon. DEcon, Tilburg. *Publications:* The National Income, 1924-31, 1932; (with Prof. A. C. Pigou) Economic Position of Great Britain, 1936; National Income and Outlay, 1937; (with J. G. Crawford) National Income of Australia, 1938; Critique of Russian Statistics, 1939; The Conditions of Economic Progress, 1940 (revised edns 1951 and 1957); The Economics of 1960, 1942; Welfare and Taxation, 1954; Australian Hopes and Fears, 1958; The Real Product of Soviet Russia, 1960; Taxmanship, 1964; (with Miss M. R. Haswell) The Economics of Subsistence Agriculture, 1964; Economics of Irrigation, 1967; Population Growth and Land Use, 1967; Starvation or Plenty?, 1970; The Value of Agricultural Land, 1973; other pamphlets and numerous articles in Economic periodicals. *Recreations:* walking, gardening. *Address:* Mannix College, Monash University, Clayton, Victoria 3168, Australia. *Club:* Johnsonian (Brisbane).

CLARK, David Allen Richard; *b* 18 July 1905; *s* of David Richard Clark and Sarah Ann Clark (*née* Clark); *m* 1932, Mary Kathleen, *y d* of Samuel Finney and Mary Ellen Finney (*née* Bagnall), Burslem, Stoke-on-Trent; three *s*. *Educ:* West Felton, Oswestry, C of E Sch.; Oswestry Boys' High Sch.; Oswestry Technical Coll.; Faculty of Technology, Manchester Univ. Stoney Prizeman, 1930; BScTech 1931; MScTech 1932. Apprentice fitter and turner, GWR Co., Oswestry Works, 1921-

27; Asst, Surveyor's Office, Oswestry RDC, 1929; Draughtsman, Sentinel Steam Wagon Co. Ltd., Shrewsbury, 1930; Part-time Lectr, Manchester Coll. of Technology, 1931-32; Lectr, Heanor Mining and Technical Coll., 1932-36; Senior Lectr, Kingston-upon-Thames Technical Coll., 1936-39; Head of Engineering Dept, Luton Technical Coll., 1939-47; Principal, Constantine Technical Coll., Middlesbrough, 1947-55; Principal, Nottingham Regional Coll. of Technology, 1955-65. CEng, FIMechE. *Publications:* Materials and Structures, 1941; Advanced Strength of Materials, 1951; articles in technical and educational journals. *Recreation:* collection of old English pottery and porcelain. *Address:* 50 Manor Drive, Upton, Wirral, Merseyside.

CLARK, David (George); *b* 19 Oct. 1939; *s* of George and Janet Clark; *m* 1970, Christine Kirkby; one *d*. *Educ:* Manchester Univ. (BA(Econ), MSc). Forester, 1956-57; Laboratory Asst in Textile Mill, 1957-59; Student Teacher, 1959-60; Student, 1960-63; Pres., Univ. of Manchester Union, 1963-64; Trainee Manager in USA, 1964; University Lecturer, 1965-70. Contested Manchester (Withington), Gen. Elec. 1966; MP (Lab) Colne Valley, 1970-Feb. 1974; contested Colne Valley, Oct. 1974; Opposition spokesman on Agriculture and Food, 1973-74. Prospective Parly Cand. (Lab) for South Shields. *Publications:* The Industrial Manager, 1966; various articles on Management and Management Education. *Recreations:* fell-walking, ornithology. *Address:* 15 New Lane, Skelmanthorpe, Huddersfield, West Yorks. *Clubs:* Golcar Socialist, Honley Socialist, Slaithwaite Working Men's (all Yorks).

CLARK, David S.; *see* Stafford-Clark.

CLARK, Desmond; *see* Clark, John Desmond.

CLARK, Mrs Edward; *see* Lutyens, Elisabeth.

CLARK, Sir Fife; *see* Clark, Sir T. F.

CLARK, Lt-Gen. Findlay; *see* Clark, Lt-Gen. S. F.

CLARK, (Francis) Leo, QC 1972; **His Honour Judge Leo Clark;** a Circuit Judge, since 1976; *b* 15 Dec. 1920; *s* of Sydney John Clark and Florence Lilian Clark; *m* 1st, 1957, Denise Jacqueline Rambaud; one *s*; 2nd, 1967, Dr Daphne Margaret Humphreys. *Educ:* Bablake Sch.; St Peter's Coll., Oxford (MA). Called to Bar, Lincoln's Inn, 1947. Dep. Chm., Oxford County QS, 1970; a Recorder of the Crown Court, 1972-76. *Recreations:* tennis, travel. *Address:* Loudwater House, Loudwater, Rickmansworth, Herts. *T:* Rickmansworth 76895. *Clubs:* Hurlingham; Union (Oxford); Moor Park Golf.

CLARK, Sir George Anthony, 3rd Bt *cr* 1917; DL; Captain Reserve of Officers, Black Watch, 1939-64; Senator, N Ireland Parliament, 1951-69; *b* 24 Jan. 1914; *e s* of Sir George Ernest Clark, 2nd Bt and Norah Anne (*d* 1966), *d* of W. G. Wilson, Glasgow; *S* father 1950; *m* 1949, Nancy Catherine, 2nd *d* of George W. N. Clark, Carnabane, Upperlands, Co. Derry; one *d*. *Educ:* Canford. DL Belfast, 1961. *Recreations:* golf, tennis. *Heir:* *b* Colin Douglas Clark, MC, MA [*b* 20 July 1918; *m* 1946, Margaret Coleman, *d* of late Maj.-Gen. Sir Charlton Watson Spinks, KBE, DSO, and *widow* of Major G. W. Threlfall, MC; one *s* two *d*]. *Address:* Tullygirvan House, Ballygowan, Newtownards, Co. Down, Northern Ireland BT23 6NR. *T:* Ballygowan 267. *Clubs:* Bath; Ulster (Belfast); Royal Ulster Yacht (Bangor, Co. Down).

CLARK, Sir George (Norman), Kt 1953; DLitt; MA; Hon. LLD, Aberdeen; Hon. LitD, Utrecht; Hon. DLitt, Durham, Sheffield, Hull, Columbia; Hon. LittD, Dublin and Cambridge; Hon. Fellow: Trinity College, Dublin, 1953; Trinity College, Cambridge, 1955; Balliol and Oriel Colleges, Oxford, 1957; All Souls College, Oxford, 1975; Trustee, British Museum, 1949-60; Member, University Grants Committee, 1951-58; President of the British Academy, 1954-58; President, Northamptonshire Record Society, 1958-65; *b* 27 Feb. 1890; *s* of late J. W. Clark, CBE, JP; *m* 1919, Barbara, *e d* of W. B. Keen; one *s* one *d*. *Educ:* Bootham Sch.; Manchester Grammar Sch.; Balliol Coll., Oxford; Brakenbury Scholar, 1908. 1st Cl. Lit. Hum., 1911; 1st Cl. Modern History, 1912; Fellow of All Souls Coll., 1912; 2nd Lieut Post Office Rifles, Aug. 1914; served in France; retd with rank of Capt., 1920; Fellow and Lectr of Oriel Coll., 1919-31; Tutor, 1922; Librarian, 1930; joined staff of English Historical Review, 1919; Editor, 1920-25; Joint Editor, 1925-26 and 1938-39; Univ. Lectr in Modern History, 1927-31; Proctor, 1929-30; Chichele Prof. of Economic History and Fellow of All Souls Coll., 1931-43; Regius Prof. of Modern History and Fellow of Trinity Coll., Cambridge, 1943-47; Provost of Oriel Coll., Oxford, 1947-57, retd. Fellow of All Souls Coll., Oxford, 1961-

75. Creighton Lectr, London Univ., 1948; Ford's Lectr, Oxford Univ., 1949-50; Murray Lectr, Glasgow Univ., 1952; Wiles Lectr, Queen's Univ., Belfast, 1956; Donnellan Lectr, Trinity Coll., Dublin, 1960; Whidden Lectr, McMaster Univ., 1960; Leslie Stephen Lectr, Cambridge Univ., 1965. FBA 1936; FRCP (Hon.) 1965. Mem., Royal Danish Acad. of Sciences; Foreign Mem., Royal Netherlands Academy of Sciences; Foreign Hon. Mem., American Acad. of Arts and Sciences and Amer. Historical Assoc. Comdr Order of Orange-Nassau. *Publications:* The Dutch Alliance and the War against French Trade, 1923; (with F. W. Weaver) Churchwarden's Accounts of Marston, etc, 1925; The Seventeenth Century, 1929; The Later Stuarts, 1934; Science and Social Welfare in the Age of Newton, 1937; Guide to English Commercial Statistics (1696-1782), 1938; (with W. J. M. van Eysinga) The Colonial Conferences between England and the Netherlands, 2 vols, 1940, 1951; The Wealth of England, 1946; Early Modern Europe, 1957; War and Society in the Seventeenth Century, 1958; The Campden Wonder, 1959; History of the Royal College of Physicians, 2 vols, 1964-66; English History, a survey, 1971. *Address:* 7 Ethelred Court, Headington, Oxford OX3 9DA. *T:* Oxford 61028. *Club:* Athenæum.

CLARK, Sir (Gordon Colvin) Lindesay, AC 1975; KBE 1968; CMG 1961; MC; BSc; MME; Mining Engineer and Company Director, Australia; *b* 7 Jan. 1896; *s* of late Lindesay C. Clark, Launceston, Tas.; *m* 1922, Barbara J., *d* of A. C. Walch; one *s* two *d. Educ:* Church of England Grammar Sch., Launceston, Tasmania; Universities of Tasmania and Melbourne. Deputy-Controller of Mineral Production, Dept of Supply, Australia, 1942-44. Chairman: Western Mining Corp. Ltd, 1952-74 (Dir, 1974-); Central Norseman Gold Corp. NL, 1952-74; Gold Mines of Kalgoorlie (Aust.) Ltd, 1952-74; BH South Ltd, 1956-74 (Dir, 1974-); Alcoa of Australia Ltd, 1961-70, Dep. Chm. 1970-72; Director: Broken Hill Associated Smelters Pty Ltd, 1944-67; North Broken Hill Ltd, 1953-71; Beach Petroleum NL, 1964-72. Pres., Australasian Inst. of Mining and Metallurgy, 1959. Hon. DEng, Melbourne Univ., 1961; Hon. LLD, Monash Univ., 1975. Australasian Inst. of Mining and Metallurgy Medal, 1963; Kernot Meml Medal, Melbourne Univ., 1964. *Recreation:* golf. *Address:* (business) City Mutual Building, 459 Collins Street, Melbourne, Victoria 3001, Australia. *T:* 67.7556; (private) 8 Moralla Road, Kooyong, Victoria 3144, Aust. *T:* 20.2675. *Clubs:* Melbourne; Australian (Melbourne); Tasmanian (Hobart); Weld (Perth).

CLARK, Grahame; *see* Clark, J. G. D.

CLARK, Henry Maitland; wine merchant with IDV Ltd; Assistant Controller, Council for Small Industries in Rural Areas; *b* 11 April 1929; *s* of Major H. F. Clark, Rockwood, Upperlands, Co. Londonderry; *m* 1972, Penelope Winifred Tindal; two *d. Educ:* Shrewsbury Sch.; Trinity Coll., Dublin; Trinity Hall, Cambridge. Entered Colonial Service and appointed District Officer, Tanganyika, 1951; served in various Districts of Tanganyika, 1951-59; resigned from Colonial Service, 1959. MP (UU) Antrim North (UK Parliament), Oct. 1959-1970; Chm. Conservative Trade and Overseas Devel Sub-Cttee; Member: British Delegation to Council of Europe and WEU, 1962-65; Advisory Council Food Law Res. Centre, Univ. of Brussels; Exec. Cttee, Lepra (British Leprosy Relief Assoc.); Select Cttee on Overseas Aid and Develt, 1969-70; Grand Jury, Co. Londonderry, 1970. A Commonwealth Observer, Mauritius General Election, 1967. Vice-Pres., Dublin Univ. Boat Club. *Recreations:* rowing coach, sailing, shooting, golf, collecting old furniture. *Address:* Rockwood, Upperlands, Co. Derry, Northern Ireland. *T:* Maghera 237; Old Vicarage, Swallowcliffe, Salisbury, Wilts. *T:* Tisbury 334. *Clubs:* Royal Commonwealth Society, Carlton; Leander; University (Dublin); Royal Portrush Golf.

See also H. W. S. *Clark.*

CLARK, (Henry) Wallace (Stuart), MBE 1970; DL; Director, Wm Clark & Sons, Linen Manufacturers, since 1972; Chairman, Everbond Interlinings, London, since 1969; *b* 20 Nov. 1926; *s* of Major H. F. Clark, MBE, JP, RA, Rockwood, Upperlands, and Sybil Emily (*née* Stuart); *m* 1957, June Elisabeth Lester Deane; two *s. Educ:* Shrewsbury School. Lieut, RNVR, 1945-47 (bomb and mine disposal). District Comdt, Ulster Special Constabulary, 1955-70; Major, Ulster Defence Regt, 1970-. Foyle's Lectr, USA tour, 1964. Led Church of Ireland St Columba commemorative curragh voyage, Derry to Iona, 1963. DL 1962, High Sheriff 1969, Co. Londonderry. *Publications:* (jtly) North and East Coasts of Ireland, 1957; (jtly) South and West Coasts of Ireland, 1962, 2nd edn 1970; Guns in Ulster, 1967; Rathlin Disputed Island, 1972; Sailing Round Ireland, 1976; numerous newspaper and magazine articles. *Recreations:* sailing, shooting, travel, country pursuits. *Address:* Gorteade

Cottage, Upperlands, Co. Londonderry, N Ireland. *T:* Maghera 42737. *Clubs:* Royal Cruising, Irish Cruising (Cdre 1962).

See also H. M. *Clark.*

CLARK, Most Rev. Howard Hewlett, CC (Canada) 1970; DD; Chancellor, University of Trinity College, Toronto, since 1972; *b* 23 April 1903; *s* of Douglass Clark and Florence Lilian Hewlett; *m* 1935, Anna Evelyn Wilson; one *s* three *d. Educ:* University of Toronto; Trinity College, Toronto. BA 1932. Christ Church Cathedral, Ottawa: Curate 1932. Priest-in-Charge, 1938, Rector 1939-54, Canon 1941; Dean of Ottawa, 1945; Bishop of Edmonton, 1954, Archibishop of Edmonton, 1959-61; Primate of Anglican Church of Canada, 1959-70; Metropolitan and Archbishop of Rupert's Land, 1961-69; Episcopal Canon of St George's Collegiate Church, Jerusalem, 1964-70. DD (*jure dignitatis*) Trinity College, Toronto, 1945; subsequently awarded numerous honorary doctorates in divinity and in civil law, both in Canada and abroad. *Publication:* The Christian Life According to the Prayer Book, 1957. *Address:* 252 Glenrose Avenue, Toronto, Ont M4T 1K9, Canada.

CLARK, Ian Robertson; Member, British National Oil Corporation; *b* 18 Jan. 1939; *s* of Alexander Clark and Annie Dundas Watson; *m* 1961, Jean Scott Waddell Lang; one *s* one *d. Educ:* Dalziel High Sch., Motherwell. FCCA, IPFA, FRVA. Trained with Glasgow Chartered Accountant; served in local govt, 1962-76. *Publications:* contribs to professional and religious periodicals. *Recreations:* theology, general reading, walking. *Address:* 48 Auchingramont Road, Hamilton, Lanarks. *Club:* Caledonian.

CLARK, James McAdam, CVO 1972; MC 1944; HM Diplomatic Service, retired; *b* 13 Sept. 1916; *er s* of late James Heriot Clark of Wester Coltfield, and late Ella Catherine McAdam; *m* 1946, Denise Thérèse, *d* of late Dr Léon Dufournier, Paris; two *d. Educ:* Edinburgh Univ. BSc (Hons) Tech. Chemistry, 1938. Asst Lectr, Edinburgh Univ., 1938-39. Served Royal Artillery, 1939-46 (MC), rank of Capt.; Royal Mil. Coll. of Science, 1945-46 (pac). Min. of Fuel and Power, 1947-48. Entered Foreign (now Diplomatic) Service, 1948; FO, 1948-50; Head of Chancery, Quito, 1950-53; FO, 1953-56; Head of Chancery, Lisbon, 1956-60; Counsellor, UK Rep. to and Alternate Gov. of Internat. Atomic Energy Agency, Vienna, 1960-64; Head of Scientific Relations Dept, FO, 1964-66; Counsellor on secondment to Min. of Technology, 1966-70; Consul-Gen., Paris, 1970-77. Officer Order of Christ of Portugal, 1957. *Publications:* a number of poems and articles. *Recreations:* golf, sailing, music, disputation. *Address:* Hill Lodge, Aldeburgh, Suffolk. *Clubs:* Travellers'; Aldeburgh Yacht, Aldeburgh Golf.

CLARK, John, OBE 1969; TD 1942; Chartered Surveyor; Partner in J. M. Clark & Partners, since 1925; *b* 11 June 1903; *s* of J. M. Clark, Haltwhistle, and Mrs Clark (*née* Jackson); *m* 1928, Audrey Irwin; one *s* three *d. Educ:* Oundle. Served 4th Bn, Royal Northumberland Fusiliers, 1922-43; retd as Lt-Col. President: Chartered Land Agents Soc., 1956; Royal Instn of Chartered Surveyors, 1969. *Recreation:* shooting. *Address:* Featherstone Castle, Haltwhistle, Northumberland. *Clubs:* National; Northern Counties (Newcastle upon Tyne).

CLARK, Sir John (Allen), Kt 1971; Chairman and Chief Executive, The Plessey Company Ltd, since 1970; *b* 14 Feb. 1926; *e s* of late Sir Allen Clark and Lady (Jocelyn) Clark, *d* of late Percy and Madeline Culverhouse; *m* 1952, Deirdre Kathleen (marr. diss. 1962), *d* of Samuel Herbert Waterhouse and Maeve Murphy Waterhouse; one *s* one *d*; *m* 1970, Olivia, *d* of H. Pratt and of Mrs J. A. Day; twin *s* one *d. Educ:* Harrow; Cambridge. Received early industrial training with Metropolitan Vickers and Ford Motor Co.; spent over a year in USA, studying the electronics industry. Served War of 1939-45; commissioned RNVR. Asst to Gen. Manager, Plessey International Ltd, 1949; Dir and Gen. Man., Plessey (Ireland) Ltd, and Wireless Telephone Co. Ltd, 1950; appointed to main board, The Plessey Co. Ltd, 1953; Gen. Man., Plessey Components Group, 1957; Man. Dir, 1962-70, and Dep. Chm., 1967-70, The Plessey Co. Ltd. Director: International Computers Ltd, 1968; Banque Nationale de Paris Ltd, 1976-. Pres., Telecommunication Engineering and Manufacturing Assoc., 1964-66, 1971-73; Vice-President: Inst. of Works Managers; Engineering Employers' Fedn. Member: Nat. Defence Industries Council; Engineering Industries Council, 1975-. CompIEE; FIM. Order of Henry the Navigator, Portugal, 1973. *Recreations:* golf, shooting. *Address:* The Plessey Co. Ltd, Millbank Tower, SW1. *T:* 01-834 9641. *Club:* Bath.

See also Michael W. *Clark.*

CLARK, Prof. J(ohn) Desmond, CBE 1960; PhD, DSc; FBA 1961; FSA 1952; FRSSAf 1959; Professor of Anthropology, University of California, Berkeley, USA, since 1961; b London, 10 April 1916; s of late Thomas John Chown Clark and Catharine (née Wynne); m 1938, Betty Cable, d of late Henry Lea Baume and late Frances M. S. (née Brown); one s one d. Educ: Monkton Combe Sch.; Christ's Coll., Cambridge. PhD in Archaeology (Cambridge), 1950; ScD Cantab 1975. Dir, Rhodes-Livingstone Museum, Livingstone, N Rhodesia, 1938-61. Has conducted excavations in Southern, East and Equatorial Africa, the Sahara, Ethiopia, Syria, 1938-. Military Service in East Africa, Abyssinia, The Somalilands and Madagascar, 1941-46. Founder Mem. and Sec., N Rhodesia Nat. Monuments Commn, 1948-61. Corr. Mem. Scientific Coun. for Africa South of the Sahara, 1956-64, etc. Fellow, Amer. Acad. of Arts and Sciences, 1965. Huxley Medal, RAI, 1974. Comdr, Nat. Order of Senegal, 1968. Publications: The Prehistoric Cultures of the Horn of Africa, 1954; The Prehistory of Southern Africa, 1959; The Stone Age Cultures of Northern Rhodesia, 1960; Prehistoric Cultures of Northeast Angola and their Significance in Tropical Africa, 1963; (ed) Proc. 3rd Pan-African Congress on Pre-history, 1957; (comp.) Atlas of African Pre-history, 1967; (ed, with W. W. Bishop) Background to Evolution in Africa, 1967; Kalambo Falls Prehistoric Site, vol. I, 1969, vol. II, 1973; The Prehistory of Africa, 1970; contribs to learned journals on prehistoric archaeology. Recreations: rowing, walking, photography. Address: 1941 Yosemite Road, Berkeley, Calif. 94707, USA. T: 525/4519 Area Code 415. Club: Royal Commonwealth Society.

CLARK, Sir John (Douglas), 4th Bt cr 1886; b 9 Jan. 1923; s of Sir Thomas Clark, 3rd Bt and of Ellen Mercy, d of late Francis Drake; S father, 1977; m 1969, Anne, d of Angus and Christina Gordon, Aberfawn, Beauly, Inverness-shire. Educ: Gordonstoun School; Edinburgh University. Entered firm of T. & T. Clark, Publishers, Edinburgh, 1953; Partner, 1958; retired through ill-health. Recreations: golf, chess, bibliography, jazz. Heir: b Francis Drake Clark [b 16 July 1924; m 1958, Mary, d of late John Alban Andrews, MC, FRCS; one s]. Address: 23 Wester Coates Avenue, Edinburgh EH12 5LS. T: 031-337 1913.

CLARK, Prof. (John) Grahame (Douglas), CBE 1971; FBA 1951; MA, PhD, ScD (Cantab); Master of Peterhouse, since 1973 (Fellow, since 1950); b 28 July 1907; s of Lt-Col Charles Douglas Clark and Maude Ethel Grahame Clark (née Shaw); m 1936, Gwladys Maude (née White); two s one d. Educ: Marlborough Coll.; Peterhouse, Cambridge. Served War of 1939-45, RAFVR, in Photographic Interpretation, 1941-43, and Air Historical Br., 1943-45. Research Student, 1930-32, and Bye-Fellow, 1933-35, of Peterhouse; Faculty Asst Lectr in Archæology, Cambridge, 1935-46, and Univ. Lectr, 1946-52; Disney Prof. of Archæology, Cambridge, 1952-74; Head of Dept of Archæology and Anthropology, Cambridge, 1956-61 and 1968-71. Lectures: Munro, in Archæology, Edinburgh Univ., 1949; Reckitt, British Acad. 1954; Dalrymple in Archæology, Glasgow Univ., 1955; G. Grant MacCurdy, Harvard, 1957; William Evans Vis. Prof., Univ. of Otago, NZ, 1964; Commonwealth Vis. Fellow, Australia, 1964; Hitchcock Prof., Univ. of California, Berkeley, 1969; Leverhulme Vis. Prof., Uppsala, 1972. Member: Ancient Monuments Board, 1954-77; Royal Commn on Historical Monuments, 1957-69; a Trustee, BM, 1975-; Pres., Prehistoric Soc., 1958-62; Vice-Pres., Soc. of Antiquaries, 1959-62. Hon. Editor, Proceedings Prehistoric Soc., 1935-70. Hon. Corr. Mem., Royal Soc. Northern Antiquaries, Copenhagen, 1946, and of Swiss Prehistoric Soc., 1951; Fellow, German Archæological Inst., 1954; Hon. Member: RIA, 1955; Archæol. Inst. of America, 1977; Foreign Member: Finnish Archæological Soc., 1958; Amer. Acad. of Arts and Sciences (Hon.) 1961; Royal Danish Acad. of Sciences and Letters, 1964; Royal Netherlands Acad. of Sciences, 1964; For. Fellow, Royal Society of Sciences, Uppsala, 1964; For. Associate, Nat. Acad. of Sciences, USA, 1974; Royal Soc. of Humane Letters, Lund, 1976. Hon. DLitt: Sheffield, 1971; National Univ. of Ireland, 1976; Uppsala, 1977. Hodgkins Medal, Smithsonian Institution, 1967; Viking Medal, Wenner-Gren Foundn, 1971; Lucy Wharton Drexel Gold Medal, Museum, Univ. of Pennsylvania, 1974. Comdr, Order of the Danebrog, 1961. Publications: The Mesolithic Settlement of Northern Europe, 1936; Archæology and Society 1939, 1947 and 1957; Prehistoric England, 1940, 1941, 1945, 1948, 1962; From Savagery to Civilization, 1946; Prehistoric Europe, The Economic Basis, 1952; Excavations at Star Carr, 1954; The Study of Prehistory, 1954; World Prehistory, An Outline, 1961; (with Stuart Piggott) Prehistoric Societies, 1965; The Stone Age Hunters, 1967; World Prehistory, a new outline, 1969; Aspects of Prehistory, 1970; The Earlier Stone Age Settlement of Scandinavia, 1975; numerous papers in archæological journals. Recreations: gardening, travel, contemporary art. Address: The Master's

Lodge, Peterhouse, Cambridge. T: Cambridge 50256. Club: United Oxford & Cambridge University.

CLARK, Sir John S.; see Stewart-Clark.

CLARK, Leo; see Clark, F. L.

CLARK, Leonard, OBE 1966; poet and author; retired HM Inspector of Schools; b 1 Aug. 1905; m Jane, d of William Mark Callow, New Cross, and Annie Maria Callow (née Graham); one s one d. Educ: Monmouth Sch.; Normal Coll., Bangor. Teacher in Glos and London, 1922-28, 1930-36; Asst Inspector of Schools, Bd of Educn, 1936-45; HM Inspector of Schools, Min. of Educn (later DES), 1945-70; worked in SW, E and W Ridings, and Metropolitan Divisions; visits to Germany, Malta, Mauritius. Home Guard (Devon Regt), 1940-43. Consultant on Poetry for Seafarers' Educn Service, 1940-54; Mem., Literature Panel, Arts Council of GB, 1965-69. Mem., Westminster Diocesan Schools Commn, 1970-76; Adviser for Secondary Schools, Diocese of London, 1970-72. Liveryman of Haberdashers' Co., 1965; Freeman, City of London, 1965. Hon. Life Mem., NUT, 1970. FRSL 1953; Hon. ALAM 1972. (Jtly) International Who's Who in Poetry Prize, 1972. Kt, Order of St Sylvester, 1970. Publications: Poems, 1925; (ed) The Open Door: anthology of verse for juniors, 1937; Passage to the Pole, 1944; (ed) The Kingdom of the Mind: essays and addresses of Albert Mansbridge, 1945; (ed) Alfred Williams: his life and work, 1945; Rhandanim, 1945; XII Poems, 1948; The Mirror (poems), 1948; English Morning (poems), 1953; Walter de la Mare, a checklist, 1956; Sark Discovered, 1956, rev. edn 1972; (ed) Andrew Young: prospect of a poet, 1957; (trans. jtly) Edmond de Goncourt, The Zemganno Brothers, 1957; Selected Poems, 1958; (ed) Quiet as Moss, 36 poems by Andrew Young, 1959; Walter de la Mare: a monograph, 1960; (ed) Collected Poems of Andrew Young, with bibliographical notes, 1960; (comp.) Drums and Trumpets: poetry for the youngest, 1962; Green Wood (autobiography), 1962; Daybreak (poems), 1963; When They Were Children, 1964; (comp.) Common Ground: an anthology for the young, 1964; Who Killed the Bears?, 1964; Andrew Young, 1964; (comp.) All Things New: anthology, 1965; (comp.) The Poetry of Nature, 1965; A Fool in the Forest (autobiography), 1965, paperback 1977; The Year Round (poems), 1965; Robert Andrew Tells a Story, 1965; Robert Andrew and the Holy Family, 1965; Robert Andrew and Tiffy, 1965; Robert Andrew by the Sea, 1965; Robert Andrew and the Red Indian Chief, 1966; Robert Andrew and Skippy, 1966; Robert Andrew in the Country, 1966; Fields and Territories (poems), 1967; Prospect of Highgate and Hampstead, 1967; Grateful Caliban (autobiography), 1967; Flutes and Cymbals: an anthology for the young, 1968; (ed) Sound of Battle, 1969; (introd) Life in a Railway Factory by Alfred Williams, 1969; Near and Far (poems), 1969; Here and There (poems), 1969; (ed jtly) The Complete Poems of Walter de la Mare, 1970; (ed) Longmans Poetry Library (64 titles), 1970; Walking With Trees (poems), 1970; (comp.) Poems by Children, 1970; All Along Down Along, 1971; Singing in the Streets (poems), 1972; Secret as Toads (poems), 1972; Poems of Ivor Gurney (comp.), 1973; Mr Pettigrew's Harvest Festival, 1974; Great and Familiar (anthology), 1974; Complete Poems of Andrew Young (comp.), 1974; The Hearing Heart (poems), 1974; Tribute to Walter de la Mare (with Edmund Blunden), 1974; Mr Pettigrew's Train, 1975; The Broad Atlantic (poems), 1975; Four Seasons (poems), 1976; Mr Pettigrew and the Bell Ringers, 1976; Collected Poems and Verses for children, 1976; The Inspector Remembers (autobiog.), 1976; Winter to Winter (poems), 1977; contrib. poems and articles to learned jls in GB and USA. Recreations: gardening, music, book collecting, writing. Address: 50 Cholmeley Crescent, Highgate, N6 5HA. T: 01-348 0092. Clubs: Highgate Literary, MCC.

CLARK, Leslie Joseph, CBE 1977; BEM 1942; Special Adviser on the international gas industry to the Chairman of British Gas, since 1975; Chairman, Northern Gas Region (formerly Northern Gas Board), 1967-75; b 21 May 1914; s of Joseph George Clark and Elizabeth (née Winslow); m 1940, Mary M. Peacock; one s one d. Educ: Stationers' Company's Sch.; King's Coll., London, BSc(Eng), 1st Cl. Hons, 1934; MSc 1948. Engineer, Gas Light & Coke Co., then North Thames Gas Board. Chief Engineer, North Thames Gas Board, 1962-65 (pioneered work for development of sea transp. of liquefied natural gas, 1954-63), Dep. Chm., 1965-67. Pres., Instn of Gas Engineers, 1965-66; Pres., IGU, 1973-76 (Vice.-Pres., 1970-73). Fellow, Fellowship of Engineering. CEng, FICE, FIMechE, FIGasE, FInstF, MIEE, AMIChemE. Founder Fellow, Fellowship of Engineering, 1976. Publications: technical papers to Instns of Gas Engineers and Mech. Engrs, Inst. of Fuel, World Power Conf., Internat. Gas Union, etc. Recreations: model engineering, walking, photography, music. Address:

Hillway, New Ridley Road, Stocksfield, Northumberland. *T:* Stocksfield 2339. *Club:* Anglo-Belgian.

CLARK, Sir Lindesay; *see* Clark, Sir G. C. L.

CLARK, Marjorie, (Pen-name, Georgia Rivers); journalist, writer of fiction; *b* Melbourne; *d* of George A. and Gertrude M. Clark. *Educ:* Milverton Girls' Grammar Sch. *Publications:* Jacqueline, 1927; Tantalego, 1928; The Difficult Art, 1929; She Dresses for Dinner, 1933; 12 full-length serials, numerous short stories and articles. *Recreation:* music. *Address:* Flat 5, 8 Hepburn Street, Hawthorn, Victoria 3122, Australia. *Club:* PEN (Melbourne Centre).

CLARK, Gen. Mark Wayne, DSC (US); DSM (3 Oak Leaf Clusters) (US Army); DSM (US Navy); US Army, retired; President Emeritus, The Citadel, Military College of South Carolina (President, 1954-65); *b* Madison Barracks, New York, USA, 1 May 1896; *s* of Col Charles Carr and Rebecca Clark; *m* 1st, 1924, Maurine Doran (*d* 1966); one *s* (one *d* decd); 2nd, 1967, Mrs Mary Millard Applegate, Muncie, Ind. *Educ:* United States Mil. Acad. (BS 1917); Infantry Sch. (grad. 1925); Comd and Gen. Staff Sch. (grad. 1935); Army War Coll. (grad. 1937). Served European War, 1917-18 (wounded); Dep. Chief of Staff, Civilian Conservation Corps, 1936-37; Mem. Gen. Staff Corps, March-June 1942; Chief of Staff for Ground Forces, May 1942; C-in-C Ground Forces in Europe, July 1942; led successful secret mission by submarine to get information in N Africa preparatory to Allied invasion, 1942; Comdr Fifth Army in Anglo-American invasion of Italy, 1943, capture of Rome, June 1944; Commanding Gen. 15th Army Group, Dec. 1944; Gen., 1945; US High Commissioner and Comdg Gen. US Forces in Austria, 1945-47; dep. US Sec. of State, 1947; sat in London and Moscow with Council of Foreign Ministers negotiating a treaty for Austria, 1947; Comdg Gen. 6th US Army, HQ San Francisco, 1947-49; Chief, US Army Field Forces, Fort Monroe, Virginia, 1949-52; 1952-53: Comdr-in-Chief, United Nations Command; C-in-C, Far East; Commanding Gen., US Army Forces in the Far East; Governor of the Ryukyu Islands. Thanks of US House of Representatives, 1945. Hon. KCB 1955; Hon. KBE 1944. Hon. DCL Oxford, 1945; many other awards and honours, both American and foreign. *Publications:* Calculated Risk, 1950; From the Danube to the Yalu, 1954. *Recreations:* fishing, hunting, golfing and hiking. *Address:* 17 Country Club Drive, Charleston, South Carolina 29412, USA. *T:* 795-5333.

CLARK, Michael Lindsey, PPRBS; sculptor; *b* 1918; *s* of P. Lindsey Clark, *qv*; *m* 1942, Catherine Heron; five *s* three *d.* *Educ:* Blackfriars Sch.; City of London Art School. ARBS 1949; FRBS 1960; Pres., RBS, 1971-76. Otto Beit Medal for Sculpture, 1960 and Silver Medal, 1967, RBS. *Address:* Flat 1, Plas Newydd, Hill Road, Beacon Hill, Hindhead, Surrey.

CLARK, Michael William, CBE 1977; Deputy Chairman and Deputy Chief Executive, Plessey Co. Ltd, since 1976 (Managing Director, 1970-76); *b* 7 May 1927; *yr s* of late Sir Allen Clark and late Lady (Jocelyn Anina Marie Louise) Clark (*née* Emerson Culverhouse); *m* 1955, Shirley (*née* MacPhadyen) (*d* 1974); two *s* two *d. Educ:* Harrow. 1st Foot Guards, Subaltern, 1945-48. Ford Motor Co., 1948-49; Bendix Aviation (USA), 1949-50; Plessey Co. Ltd, 1950- (Exec. Dir, 1951; formed Electronics Div., 1951; Main Bd Dir, 1953); formed Plessey (UK) Ltd (Chm. and Man. Dir, 1962; Dir responsible for Corporate Planning, 1965, Man. Dir, Telecommunications Gp, 1967, and for Home Groups, 1969); formed Plessey Electronics Systems Ltd, 1976. Member: Council, BIM; Council, Inst. of Dirs; Nat. Electronics Council; Ct of Univ. of Essex; EDC for Electronics Industry. Comp. IEE, 1964; Comp. IERE, 1965. *Publications:* various articles. *Recreations:* fishing, forestry. *Address:* Braxted Park, Witham, Essex. *Club:* Boodle's. *See also Sir J. A. Clark.*

CLARK, Percy, CBE 1970; Director of Information, Labour Party, since 1964; *b* 18 May 1917; *s* of Perceval Harold Clark and Grace Lilian Clark; *m* 1st, 1941, Nan Dalgleish (*d* 1970); two *s* two *d;* 2nd, 1972, Doreen Stainforth. Early career in newspapers: owner South Lancs News Agency, 1936-47. Labour Party: Publications Officer, 1947; Regional Publicity Dir, 1957; Dep. Dir, Information, 1960. MIPR. *Recreation:* music. *Address:* 1 Strutton Court, Great Peter Street, SW1P 2HH. *T:* 01-222 5836. *Club:* MCC.

CLARK, Philip Lindsey, DSO; FRBS; sculptor; *b* 1889; *m* 1917, Truda Mary Calnan (*d* 1952); six *s*; *m* 1962, Monica Mary Hansford. *Educ:* Douglas House Sch., Cheltenham. Studied sculpture at the Royal Academy Schs, London; served European War, 1914-18, Artists' Rifles, Royal Sussex Regt, rank of Capt. (despatches, DSO); War of 1939-45, Cameronians (Scottish

Rifles), RAF Regt and RNVR, 1940-45. First exhibited sculpture at Royal Academy, 1920; Paris Salon, 1921. *Works:* The Cameronians (Scottish Rifles) War Memorial (1914-18), Glasgow; St Saviour's (Southwark) War Memorial, Boro High Street; sculpture on Belgian Soldiers' Memorial (1914-18), Kensal Green, awarded Palm of Order of Crown of Belgium, 1932; sculpture in wood, stone and bronze works in Westminster Cathedral, Aylesford Priory, English Martyrs Church, Wallasey, and in and on many other churches and public buildings. *Address:* Flat 2, 6 Douglas Avenue, Exmouth, Devon. *T:* Exmouth 3570.
See also M. L. Clark.

CLARK, Ramsey; lawyer, New York City, since 1970; *b* Dallas, Texas, 18 Dec. 1927; *s* of late Thomas Campbell Clark, Associate Justice, US Supreme Court, and of Mary Ramsey; *m* 1949, Georgia Welch, Corpus Christi, Texas; one *s* one *d. Educ:* Public Schs, Dallas, Los Angeles, Washington; Univ. of Texas (BA); Univ. of Chicago (MA, JD). US Marine Corps, 1945-46. Admitted to: State Bar of Texas, 1951; Bar of Supreme Court of US, 1956; Bars of the District of Columbia, and of New York. Member: Federal Bar Assoc.; Amer. Bar Assoc.; Amer. Judicature Soc. Engaged private practice of law, Dallas, 1951-61; Asst Attorney Gen., Lands Div., Dept of Justice, 1961-65. Dep. Attorney Gen. of the US, 1965-67, Attorney Gen., 1967-69. Adjunct Professor: Howard Univ., 1969-72; Brooklyn Law Sch., 1973-. *Publication:* Crime in America, 1970. *Address:* 37 West 12th Street, New York, NY 10011, USA.

CLARK, His Honour Reginald, QC 1949; Judge of Clerkenwell, Middlesex, County Court Circuit 41, 1955-66, retired; *b* 18 March 1895; *y s* of J. T. Clark, Manchester; *m* 1923, Joan Marguerite, *y d* of R. Herbert Shiers, Bowdon, Ches.; three *d. Educ:* Trinity Hall, Cambridge. Called to Bar, Lincoln's Inn, 1920; Northern Circuit, 1920-23; practised Rangoon Bar, 1924-41; Judge, High Court, Madras, 1944; resigned from Madras High Court, 1948. Chm., N Midland District Valuation Board, Coal Nationalisation Act, 1948-49; Chm., Road and Rail Appeal Tribunal, 1949. Comr of Assize, North-Eastern, Western and South-Eastern Circuits, 1949; a County Court Judge, Circuit 58, Ilford, etc, 1950-55. Served in TF, European War, 1914-18, Gallipoli and France. Served in Army in Burma and India, 1942-44. *Recreations:* fishing and golf. *Address:* 4 Trumpeters House, Old Palace Yard, Richmond, Surrey. *T:* 01-940 2829. *Club:* East India, Devonshire, Sports and Public Schools.

CLARK, Sir Robert (Anthony), Kt 1976; DSC 1944; Chairman, Hill Samuel & Co. Ltd, since 1974; Chief Executive, Hill Samuel Group Ltd, since 1976; a Director, Bank of England, since 1976; Chairman, Industrial Development Advisory Board, since 1973; *b* 6 Jan. 1924; *yr s* of John Clark and Gladys Clark (*née* Dyer); *m* 1949, Andolyn Marjorie Lewis; two *s* one *d. Educ:* Highgate Sch.; King's Coll., Cambridge. Served War, Royal Navy, 1942-46 (DSC). Partner with Slaughter and May, Solicitors, 1953; became a director of merchant bankers, Philip Hill, Higginson, Erlangers Ltd (now known as Hill Samuel & Co. Ltd), 1961-. *Recreations:* reading, music. *Address:* Munstead Wood, Godalming, Surrey. *T:* Godalming 7867; Hill Samuel & Co. Ltd, 100 Wood Street, EC2P 2AJ. *T:* 01-628 8011. *Clubs:* Pratt's, Travellers'.

CLARK, Very Rev. Robert James Vodden; Dean of Edinburgh, 1967-76; Canon of Edinburgh Cathedral, 1962, Hon. Canon 1976; Rector of St Leonard's, Lasswade, Midlothian, since 1969; *b* 12 April 1907; *s* of Albert Arther Clark and Bessie Vodden; *m* 1934, Ethel Dolina McGregor Alexander; one *d. Educ:* Dalry Normal Practising Episcopal Church Sch.; Edinburgh; Church Army Coll.; Coates Hall Theol. Coll. Ordained, 1941. Men's Social Dept, Church Army, 1926; varied work in homes for men; special work in probation trng home under Home Office, 1934-39; St Paul and St George, Edinburgh, 1941-44; Rector, St Andrew's, Fort William, 1944-47; seconded to Scottish Educn Dept as Warden-Leader of Scottish Centre of Outdoor Trng, Glenmore Lodge, 1947-49; Curate i/c St David's, Edinburgh, 1949-54; Rector of Christ Church, Falkirk, 1954-69. Mem., Royal Highland and Agric. Soc. *Recreations:* mountaineering (Mem., Scottish Mountaineering Club); photography (Mem., Esk Valley Camera Club). *Address:* St Leonard's Rectory, Dobbie's Road, Lasswade, Midlothian EH18 1LR.

CLARK, Lt-Gen. (Samuel) Findlay, CBE 1945; CD 1950; MEIC; MCSEE; PEng; *b* 17 March 1909; *m* 1937, Leona Blanche Seagram. *Educ:* Univ. of Manitoba (BScEE); Univ. of Saskatchewan (BScME). Lieut, Royal Canadian Signals, 1933. Assoc. Prof. of Elec. and Mechan. Engrg (Capt.) at RMC Kingston, 1938. Overseas to UK, Aug. 1940 (Major); Comd 5th Canadian Armd Div. Sigs Regt (Lt-Col), 1941. GSO1 Can. Mil.

HQ, London, 1942; Staff Course, Camberley, England (Col), 1942-43; CSO, HQ 2nd Canadian Corps until end of War (Brig. 1943). Dep. Chief of Gen. Staff, 1945; Imperial Defence Coll., 1948; Canadian Mil. Observer on Western Union Mil. Cttee; Maj.-Gen. 1949; Canadian Mil. Rep. NATO, London, 1949; Chm., Joint Staff. CALE, London, 1951; QMG of Canadian Army, 1951; GOC Central Comd, 1955; CGS, Sept. 1958-61. Chm., Nat. Capital Commission, 1961-67. Past Col Comdt, Royal Canadian Corps of Signals; Hon. Lt-Col, 744 Comm. Sqn. FRCGS. Legion of Merit (USA), 1945; Comdr Order of Orange Nassau (Netherlands), 1945. OStJ. *Recreations:* fishing, shooting. *Address:* 3180 Midland Road, Victoria, BC, Canada. T: 592 4338. *Club:* Union (Victoria).

CLARK, Ven. Sidney Harvie, MA; Archdeacon of Stow, 1967-75 and Vicar of Hackthorn and Rector of Cold Hanworth, 1967-75; *b* 26 July 1905; *s* of John Harvie Clark and Minnie Young Hunter, Glasgow and Chiswick, London; *m* 1936, Sheilah Marjorie, *d* of late Dr G. C. L. Lunt, Bishop of Salisbury; one *s* one *d* (one *d* decd). *Educ:* St Paul's Sch., London; Jesus Coll. and Westcott House, Cambridge. Deacon, 1930; Priest, 1931; Curate, St Mary's, Gateshead, Co. Durham, 1930-34; St Mary's, Portsea, 1934-36; Rector, Jarrow-on-Tyne, 1936-40; St John's, Edinburgh, 1940-47; Rector of Wishaw, 1947-48; Archdeacon of Birmingham, 1947-67; Vicar of Harborne, 1948-67. *Recreations:* walking, camping. *Address:* Stow House, Skillington, Grantham, Lincs NG33 5HQ. T: Buckminster 447. *Club:* Royal Commonwealth Society.

CLARK, Stuart Ellis; *b* 6 Feb. 1899; *s* of Robert and Susanah Clark, Dartford, Kent; *m* 1st, 1923, Mabel Olive Winspear (*d* 1932); one *s*; 2nd, 1935, Joan Bulley. *Educ:* Wilson's Sch. Acting Sec., Southern Rly Co., 1944; Asst Docks and Marine Manager, Southern Rly Co., Southampton Docks, 1947; Sec., Docks Executive, 1948; Sec., Docks and Inland Waterways Board of Management, British Transport Commission, 1950-55. *Recreations:* golf, swimming. *Address:* Knapp Cottage, Wambrook, near Chard, Somerset. T: Chard 2442.

CLARK, Terence Joseph; HM Diplomatic Service; Counsellor (Press and Information), Bonn, since 1976; *b* 19 June 1934; *s* of Joseph Clark and Mary Clark; *m* 1960, Lieselotte Rosa Marie Müller; two *s* one *d*. *Educ:* Thomas Parmiter's, London. RAF (attached to Sch. of Slavonic Studies, Cambridge), 1953-55; Pilot Officer, RAFVR, 1955. HM Foreign Service, 1955; ME Centre for Arab Studies, 1956-57; Bahrain, 1957-58; Amman, 1958-60; Casablanca, 1961-62; FO, 1962-65; Asst Polit. Agent, Dubai, 1965-68; Belgrade, 1969-71; Hd of Chancery, Muscat, 1972-73; Asst Hd of ME Dept. FCO, 1974-76. *Recreations:* aquatic sports, amateur dramatics. *Address:* c/o Foreign and Commonwealth Office, SW1A 2AH; 33 Lovelace Road, West Dulwich, SE21.

CLARK, Sir (Thomas) Fife, Kt 1965; CBE 1949; Consultant; formerly Director General, Central Office of Information; *b* 1907; *m*; two *s* one *d*. *Educ:* Middlesbrough High Sch. (North Riding Scholar). Reporter, sub-editor, Parly lobby corresp. and diplomatic correspondent, Westminster Press provincial newspapers, 1924-39; Public Relations and Principal Press Officer, Min. of Health, 1939-49; Controller, Home Publicity, COI, 1949-52; Adviser on Govt Public Relations and Adviser on Public Relations to Prime Ministers Sir Winston Churchill and Sir Anthony Eden, 1952-55; as Dir Gen, COI, 1954-71, responsible on behalf of FCO for organisation of British Pavilions at World Exhibitions in Brussels, 1958, Montreal, 1967 and Osaka, 1970; acted as Chief Officer, Nov. 1956-March 1957, to first Cabinet Minister, Dr Charles Hill, to co-ordinate Govt inf. services home and overseas. Consultant on External Relations to Crown Agents for Overseas Govts and Administrations, 1971-75, and to Trident Television Gp of Cos, 1976-. First Pres., Internat. Public Relations Assoc., 1955-57; Fellow and Past Pres., Inst. of Public Relations (President's Medal, 1967); Pres., Civil Service Horticultural Fedn, 1959-70. Mem., Coun. of Management, Brighton Arts Festival, 1966-. *Publication:* The Central Office of Information, 1971. *Address:* Wave Hill, Nevill Road, Rottingdean, Sussex. T: Brighton 33020. *Club:* Athenæum.

CLARK, Wallace; *see* Clark, H. W. S.

CLARK, William Donaldson; Vice-President for External Relations, International Bank for Reconstruction and Development (World Bank), since 1974 (Director, External Relations, 1973-74); *b* 28 July 1916; *y s* of John McClare Clark and Marion Jackson; unmarried. *Educ:* Oundle Sch.; Oriel Coll., Oxford (MA). 1st class Hons Mod. Hist., Gibbs Prize.

Commonwealth Fellow and Lectr in Humanities, Univ. of Chicago, 1938-40; Min. of Information, and Brit. Inf. Services, Chicago, 1941-44; Press Attaché, Washington, 1945-46; London Editor, Encyclopædia Britannica, 1946-49; Diplomatic Corresp., Observer, 1950-55; Public Relations Adviser to Prime Minister, 1955-56; toured Africa and Asia for BBC and Observer, 1957; Editor of "The Week" in Observer, 1958-60; Dir, Overseas Development Inst., 1960-68; Dir of Information and Public Affairs, IBRD, 1968-73. Frequent broadcasts and television appearances, including original Press Conference series (BBC), and Right to Reply (ATV). *Publications:* Less than Kin: a study of Anglo-American relations, 1957; What is the Commonwealth?, 1958; Number 10 (novel and (with Ronald Miller) play), 1966; Special Relationship (novel), 1968. *Recreations:* writing, talking, travel. *Address:* (office) World Bank, Washington, DC 20433, USA; (home) 3407 Rodman Street NW, Washington, DC 20008, USA. T: 363-0499; The Mill, Cuxham, Oxford. T: Watlington 2381; Biniparell, Menorca, Baleares, Spain. *Clubs:* Athenæum, Savile; Athletic (Washington).

CLARK, William Gibson; MP (C) Croydon South, since 1974 (E Surrey, 1970-74); *b* 18 Oct. 1917; *m* 1944, Irene Dorothy Dawson Rands; three *s* one *d*. *Educ:* London. Mem. Association of Certified Accountants, 1941. Served in Army, 1941-46 (UK and India), Major. Mem. Wandsworth Borough Council, 1949-53 (Vice-Chm. Finance Cttee). Contested (C) Northampton, 1955; MP (C) Nottingham South, 1959-66. Opposition Front Bench Spokesman on Economics, 1964-66; Chm., Select Cttee on Tax Credits, 1973. Jt Deputy Chm., Conservative Party Organisation, 1975- (Jt Treasurer, 1974-75). Hon. Nat. Dir, Carrington £2 million Appeal, 1967-68. *Recreations:* tennis, gardening. *Address:* The Clock House, Box End, Bedford. T: Bedford 852361; 3 Barton Street, SW1. T: 01-222 5759. *Clubs:* Junior Carlton (Dep. Chm.), Buck's.

CLARK HUTCHISON; *see* Hutchison.

CLARK-KENNEDY, Archibald Edmund, MD (Cantab); FRCP; Fellow of Corpus Christi College, Cambridge, since 1919; Physician to the London Hospital, 1928-58; Dean of the London Hospital Medical College, 1937-53; *s* of late Rev. A. E. Clark-Kennedy (RN retired), Rector of Ewhurst, Surrey; *m* 1918, Phyllis, *d* of late Charles Howard Jeffree, Howard Lodge, Clapham Park; one *s* one *d*. *Educ:* Wellington Coll.; Corpus Christi Coll., Cambridge (exhibitioner, scholar). 1st class hons in Natural Science Tripos. Lieut, Queen's Royal West Surrey Regt (5th Territorial Bn), Aug. 1914; served as a combatant officer in India, then in Mesopotamia with IEF, D; returned to England, 1917; obtained diploma of MRCS and LRCP; commd in RAMC, 1918; served in France as MO to 158th Army RFA Bde. MRCP 1922; FRCP 1930. *Publications:* Stephen Hales, DD, FRS, an Eighteenth Century Biography, 1929; Medicine (two vols): Vol. I, The Patient and his Disease, 1947; Vol. II, Diagnosis, Prognosis and Treatment; Medicine in its Human Setting, 1954; Patients as People, 1957; Human Disease (a Pelican medical book), 1957; How to Learn Medicine, 1959; Clinical Medicine, The Modern Approach, 1960; The London: A Study in the Voluntary Hospital System (two vols): Vol. I, The First Hundred Years, 1740-1840, 1962; Vol. II, The Second Hundred Years, 1840-1948, 1963; Edith Cavell, Pioneer and Patriot, 1965; Man, Medicine and Morality, 1969; Attack the Colour! the Royal Dragoons in the Peninsula and at Waterloo, 1975; papers in medical and scientific journals. *Recreations:* mountaineering, sailing, hunting. *Address:* 7 Maitland House, Barton Road, Cambridge. T: Cambridge 52323.

CLARKE, Prof. Alan Douglas Benson, CBE 1974; Professor of Psychology, University of Hull, since 1962; *b* 21 March 1922; *s* of late Robert Benson Clarke and late Mary Lizars Clarke; *m* 1950, Dr Ann Margaret (*née* Gravely); two *s*. *Educ:* Lancing Coll.; Univs of Reading and London. 1st cl. hons BA Reading 1948; PhD London 1950; FBPsS. Reading Univ., 1940-41 and 1946-48. Sen. Psychol., 1951-57 and Cons. Psychol., 1957-62, Manor Hosp., Epsom. Dean of Faculty of Science, 1966-68, and Pro-Vice-Chancellor 1968-71, Univ. of Hull. Rapporteur, WHO Expert Cttee on Organization of Services for Mentally Retarded, 1967; Mem. WHO Expert Adv. Panel on Mental Health, 1968-; Maudsley Lectr, Royal Medico-Psychol Assoc., 1967; Chm., Trng Council for Teachers of Mentally Handicapped, 1969-74; Hon. Vice-Pres., Nat. Assoc. for Mental Health, 1970-; President, Internat. Assoc. for Sci. Study of Mental Deficiency, 1973-76, Hon. Vice-Pres., 1976-; Editor, Brit. Jl Psychol., 1973-; Mem. Editorial Bds of other jls; Mem., Personal Social Services Council, 1973-; Mem., DHSS/SSRC Working Gp on Transmitted Deprivation, 1974-. Hon. Life Mem., Amer. Assoc. on Mental Deficiency, 1975 (Research award, 1977, with Ann M. Clarke). Pres., BPsS, 1977-78. *Publications* (with Ann M.

Clarke): Mental Deficiency: the Changing Outlook, 1958, 3rd edn 1974; Mental Retardation and Behavioural Research, 1973; Early Experience: myth and evidence, 1976; numerous in psychol and med. jls. *Address:* 55 Newland Park, Hull HU5 2DR. *T:* Hull 444141.

CLARKE, Arthur Charles; *b* 16 Dec. 1917; *s* of Charles Wright Clarke and Norah Mary Willis; *m* 1953, Marilyn Mayfield (marr. diss. 1964). *Educ:* Huish's Grammar Sch., Taunton; King's Coll., London (BSc); FKC 1977. HM Exchequer and Audit Dept, 1936-41. Served RAF, 1941-46. Instn of Electrical Engineers, 1949-50. Techn. Officer on first GCA radar, 1943; originated communications satellites, 1945. Chm., British Interplanetary Soc., 1946-47, 1950-53. Asst Ed., Science Abstracts, 1949-50. Since 1954 engaged on underwater exploration on Gt Barrier Reef of Australia and coast of Ceylon. Extensive lecturing, radio and TV in UK and US. Unesco, Kalinga Prize, 1961; Acad. of Astronautics, 1961; World Acad. of Art and Science, 1962; Stuart Ballantine Medal, Franklin Inst., 1963; Westinghouse-AAAS Science Writing Award, 1969; Amer. Inst. of Aeronautics and Astronautics Aerospace Communications Award, 1974; Nebula Award, 1974; John Campbell Award, 1974; Hugo Award, 1974. *Publications:* non-fiction: Interplanetary Flight, 1950; The Exploration of Space, 1951; The Young Traveller in Space, 1954 (publ. in USA as Going into Space); The Coast of Coral, 1956; The Making of a Moon, 1957; The Reefs of Taprobane, 1957; Voice Across the Sea, 1958; The Challenge of the Spaceship, 1960; The Challenge of the Sea, 1960; Profiles of the Future, 1962; Voices from the Sky, 1965; (with Mike Wilson): Boy Beneath the Sea, 1958; The First Five Fathoms, 1960; Indian Ocean Adventure, 1961; The Treasure of the Great Reef, 1964; Indian Ocean Treasure, 1964; (with R. A. Smith) The Exploration of the Moon, 1954; (with Editors of Life) Man and Space, 1964; (ed) The Coming of the Space Age, 1967; The Promise of Space, 1968; (with the astronauts) First on the Moon, 1970; Report on Planet Three, 1972; (with Chesley Bonestell) Beyond Jupiter, 1973; The View from Serendip, 1977; *fiction:* Prelude to Space, 1951; The Sands of Mars, 1951; Islands in the Sky, 1952; Against the Fall of Night, 1953; Childhood's End, 1953; Expedition to Earth, 1953; Earthlight, 1955; Reach for Tomorrow, 1956; The City and the Stars, 1956; Tales from the White Hart, 1957; The Deep Range, 1957; The Other Side of the Sky, 1958; Across the Sea of Stars, 1959; A Fall of Moondust, 1961; From the Ocean, From the Stars, 1962; Tales of Ten Worlds, 1962; Dolphin Island, 1963; Glide Path, 1963; Prelude to Mars, 1965; The Nine Billion Names of God, 1967; (with Stanley Kubrick) novel and screenplay, 2001: A Space Odyssey, 1968; The Lost Worlds of 2001, 1972; Of Time and Stars, 1972; The Wind from the Sun, 1972; Rendezvous with Rama, 1973; The Best of Arthur C. Clarke, 1973; Imperial Earth, 1975; papers in Electronic Engineering, Wireless World, Wireless Engineer, Aeroplane, Jl of British Interplanetary Soc., Astronautics, etc. *Recreations:* diving, photography, table-tennis. *Address:* 25 Barnes Place, Colombo 7, Sri Lanka. *T:* Colombo 94255; c/o David Higham Associates, 5 Lower John Street, Golden Square, W1R 3PE. *Clubs:* Arts, British Sub-Aqua.

CLARKE, Brig. Arthur Christopher L. S.; *see* Stanley-Clarke.

CLARKE, Arthur Grenfell, CMG 1953; *b* 17 Aug. 1906; *m* 1934, Rhoda McLean Arnott. *Educ:* Mountjoy Sch., Dublin; Dublin Univ. Appointed Cadet Officer, Hong Kong, 1929; entered service of Hong Kong Government, 1929; interned in Stanley Camp during Japanese occupation; Financial Sec., 1952-62; retired, 1962. *Address:* Foxdene, Brighton Road, Foxrock, Co. Dublin. *T:* 894368.

CLARKE, Captain Arthur Wellesley, CBE 1946; DSO 1943; RN; *b* 16 April 1898; *s* of late Capt. Sir Arthur W. Clarke, KCVO, KBE, and Lady Clarke; *m* 1926, Kate Cicely Lance; one *s.* *Educ:* Merton Court Prep. Sch.; RN Colls Osborne and Dartmouth; Emmanuel Coll., Cambridge (6 months 1919). Midshipman, 1914; Lieut 1918; Comdr 1933; Capt. 1939; retired list, 1948 and re-employed at Admiralty. Served at sea throughout European War, 1914-18; Dardanelles, 1915 (despatches); Battle of Jutland, 1916; Atlantic and North Sea convoys. Between wars qualified as Navigating and Staff Officer; served at sea including in command at home and abroad; Asst Sec., Cttee of Imperial Defence, 1933-36. War of 1939-45: War Cabinet office, 1940, and later Addtl Naval Attaché, USA; commanded HMS Sheffield, Atlantic, North Russian and Malta convoys, N African landings and Barents Sea battle, 1941-43; Chief of Staff to Governor and C-in-C Malta, and later Naval Liaison Officer to Comdr, 8th Army, 1943; Chief of Staff to Head of Brit. Admty Delegn USA, 1944-46; comd HMS Ocean, 1946-48; Chief of Naval Information, Admty, 1948-57. Vice-President: King George's Fund for Sailors; Younger Brother, Trinity

House. Officer, Legion of Merit (USA), 1946. *Recreation:* gardening. *Address:* 16 Yarborough Road, Southsea, Hants. *T:* Portsmouth 24539. *Clubs:* Naval (Hon. Mem.); Royal Navy 1765-85.

CLARKE, Sir Ashley; *see* Clarke, Sir H. A.

CLARKE, Rev. Basil Fulford Lowther; Hon. Canon of Christ Church, Oxford, since 1970; *b* 6 March 1908; *s* of late Rev. W. K. L. Clarke; *m* 1939, Eileen Noël Coates; one *s* two d. *Educ:* St John's Sch., Leatherhead; St John's Coll., Durham (BA 1930; MA 1933); Cuddesdon Theological Coll. Deacon 1932; Priest 1933. Curate of: St Andrew's, Coulsdon, Surrey, 1932-35; St Mary's, Monmouth, 1935-38; St James's, Watford, 1938-39; SS Philip and James's, Oxford, 1939-44; Vicar of Knowl Hill, Berks, 1944-74. Member: Exec. Cttee, Council for Places of Worship, 1972; Adv. Bd for Redundant Churches, 1969; Westminster Abbey Arch. Adv. Panel, 1973. *Publications:* Church Builders of the 19th Century, 1938; Lesson Notes on the Prayer Book, 1943; My Parish Church, 1943; Clement Joins the Church, 1944; Anglican Cathedrals outside the British Isles, 1958; The Building of the 18th Century Church, 1963; (with Sir John Betjeman) English Churches, 1964; Parish Churches of London, 1966. *Recreations:* visiting churches, and research in connexion with them. *Address:* 220 Henley Road, Caversham, Reading, Berks. *T:* Reading 471750.

CLARKE, Charles Edward, CBE 1960; Directing Actuary, Government Actuary's Department, 1970-74; *b* 8 July 1912; *s* of late Edward James Clarke and late Lucy Ann Clarke (*née* Hunniball); *m* 1941, Ethel Arbon; two *s.* *Educ:* Thetford Grammar School. FIA 1940. Entered Govt Actuary's Dept, 1929. *Publication:* Social Insurance in Britain, 1950. *Recreations:* walking, travel, photography, do-it-yourself jobs at home. *Address:* 14 Ashmere Avenue, Beckenham, Kent. *T:* 01-658 1360. *Club:* Reform.

CLARKE, Sir (Charles Mansfield) Tobias, 6th Bt *ct* 1831; *b* Santa Barbara, California, 8 Sept. 1939; *e s* of Sir Humphrey Orme Clarke, 5th Bt, and Elisabeth (*d* 1967), *d* of Dr William Albert Cook; *S* father, 1973; *m* 1971, Charlotte, *e d* of Roderick Walter. *Educ:* Eton; Christ Church, Oxford (MA); Sorbonne; New York Graduate Business School. Vice Pres., Bankers Trust Company, New York. *Recreations:* travel, photography, fox hunting; Pres., Bibury Cricket Club; Vice-Pres., Bibury Association Football Club. *Heir:* half *b* Orme Roosevelt Clarke [*b* 30 Nov. 1947; *m* 1971, Joanna Valentine, *d* of John Barkley Schuster, TD]. *Address:* 80 Campden Hill Road, W8 7AA. *T:* 01-937 6213; The Church House, Bibury, Glos. *T:* Bibury 225. *Clubs:* Boodle's, Pratt's; Pilgrims; Jockey (Paris); The Brook, Racquet & Tennis (New York).

CLARKE, Cyril Alfred Allen, MA; Headmaster, Holland Park Secondary School, 1957-71; *b* 21 Aug. 1910; *s* of late Frederick John Clarke; *m* 1934, Edna Gertrude Francis; three *s.* *Educ:* Langley Sch., Norwich; Culham Coll. of Educn; Birkbeck Coll., Univ. of London; King's Coll., Univ. of London. Entered London Teaching Service, 1933; Royal Artillery, 1940-46; Staff Officer (Major) in Educn Br. of Mil. Govt of Germany, 1945-46; Asst Master, Haberdashers' Aske's Hatcham Boys' Sch., 1946-51; Headmaster: Isledon Sec. Sch., 1951-55; Battersea Co. Sec. Sch., 1955-57. Chm. Governors, Langley Sch. FRSA. *Recreations:* photography, reading. *Address:* 22 Manor Drive North, New Malden, Surrey. *T:* 01-337 4223.

CLARKE, Prof. Sir Cyril (Astley), KBE 1974 (CBE 1969); FRS 1970; MD, ScD, FRCP, FRCOG; Emeritus Professor and Hon. Nuffield Research Fellow, Department of Genetics, University of Liverpool (Professor of Medicine, 1965-72, Director, Nuffield Unit of Medical Genetics, 1963-72, and Nuffield Research Fellow, 1972-76); Consultant Physician, United Liverpool Hospitals (David Lewis Northern, 1946-58, Royal Infirmary since 1958) and to Broadgreen Hospital since 1946; *b* 22 Aug. 1907; *s* of Astley Vavasour Clarke, MD, JP, and Ethel Mary Clarke, *d* of H. Simpson Gee; *m* 1935, Frieda (Féo) Margaret Mary, *d* of Alexander John Campbell Hart and Isabella Margaret Hart; three *s.* *Educ:* Wyggeston Grammar Sch., Leicester; Oundle Sch.; Gonville and Caius Coll., Cambridge; Guy's Hosp. (Schol.). 2nd Class Hons, Natural Science Tripos Pt I; MD Cantab 1937; ScD Cantab 1963. FRCP 1949; FRCOG 1970; FRACP 1973; FRCPI 1973; FRSA 1973; FFCM 1974; FACP 1976; Fellow Ceylon Coll. of Physicians 1974; FRCPE 1975. House Phys., Demonstr in Physiology and Clin. Asst in Dermatology, Guy's Hosp., 1932-36. Life Insurance practice, Grocers' Hall, EC2, 1936-39. Served, 1939-46, as Med Specialist, RNVR: HM Hosp. Ship Amarapoora (Scapa Flow and N Africa), RNH Seaforth and RNH Sydney. After War, Med. Registrar, Queen Elizabeth Hosp., Birmingham. Visiting

Prof. of Genetics, Seton Hall Sch. of Med., Jersey City, USA, 1963; Lumleian Lectr, RCP, 1967; Ingleby Lectr, Univ. of Birmingham, 1968; Foundn Lectr, RCPath, 1971; Inaugural Faculty Lecture, Univ. of Leeds, 1972; P. B. Fernando Meml Lecture, Colombo, 1974; Marsden Lecture, Royal Free Hosp., 1976. Examr in Med., Dundee Univ., 1965-69. Pres., RCP, 1972-77 (Censor, 1967-69, Sen. Censor, 1971-72, Dir, Med. Services Study Unit, 1977-); Pres. Liverpool Med. Instn, 1970-71; Member: MRC Working Party, 1966; Sub-Cttee of Dept of Health and Social Security on prevention of Rhesus hæmolytic disease, 1967 (Chm., 1973-); Bd of Governors, United Liverpool Hosps, 1969; Assoc. of Hungarian Medical Socs, 1973; Pres., Harveian Soc.; Governor and Councillor, Bedford Coll., 1974, Chm. of Council, 1975. Chm., Cockayne Trust Fund, Natural History Museum, 1974-. Hon. Fellow, Caius Coll., Cambridge, 1974. Hon. DSc: Edinburgh, 1971; Leicester, 1971; East Anglia, 1973; Birmingham, Liverpool and Sussex, 1974; Hull, 1977. Gold Medal in Therapeutics, Worshipful Soc. of Apothecaries, 1970; James Spence Medal, Brit. Paediatric Assoc., 1973; Addingham Medal, Leeds, 1973; John Scott Medal and Award, Philadelphia, 1976; Fothergillian Medal, Med. Soc., 1977. *Publications:* Genetics for the Clinician, 1962; (ed) Selected Topics in Medical Genetics, 1969; Human Genetics and Medicine, 1970, 2nd edn, 1977; (ed) Rhesus Hæmolytic Disease: selected papers and extracts, 1975; many contribs med. and scientific jls, particularly on prevention of Rhesus hæmolytic disease and on evolution of mimicry in swallowtail butterflies. *Recreations:* small boat sailing, breeding swallowtail butterflies. *Address:* Nuffield Unit of Medical Genetics, The University, Crown Street, PO Box 147, Liverpool, L69 3BX. *T:* 051-709 6022; High Close, Thorsway, Caldy, Merseyside L48 2JJ. *T:* 051-625 8811. *Clubs:* Athenæum; Oxford and Cambridge Sailing Society (Pres., 1975-77); West Kirby Sailing, Royal Mersey Yacht; United Hospitals Sailing (Pres.).

CLARKE, Denzil Robert Noble; Chairman, British-American Tobacco Co. Ltd, 1966-70 (Director, 1954-70; Vice-Chairman, 1962); Director, Sun Life Assurance Society, since 1966; *b* 9 July 1908; *er s* of late R. T. Clarke, ICS, LLD and late Mrs M. M. G. Clarke (*née* Whyte); *m* 1942, Ismay Elizabeth, *e d* of late Lt-Col Hon. R. M. P. Preston, DSO; one *s* two *d. Educ:* Stonyhurst Coll. Articled Clerk, Singleton Fabian & Co., Chartered Accountants, 1926; ACA 1932; FCA 1960. Joined British-American Tobacco Co. Ltd, 1932. War service, 1941-45; Far East; Lt-Col 1944. *Recreations:* gardening, tennis. *Address:* Puffins, South Drive, Wokingham, Berks. *T:* Wokingham 780975. *Clubs:* Special Forces, Army and Navy.
    See also Maj.-Gen. D. A. B. Clarke.

CLARKE, Maj.-Gen. Desmond Alexander Bruce, CB 1965; CBE 1961 (OBE 1944); *b* 15 July 1912; *yr s* of late R. T. Clarke, ICS, LLD, Weybridge and late Mrs R. T. Clarke (*née* Whyte), Loughbrickland, Co. Down; *m* Madeleine, 2nd *d* of Rear-Adm. Walter Glyn Petre, DSO, Weybridge; three *s* two *d. Educ:* Stonyhurst Coll.; RMA Woolwich. Commissioned RA, 1932. Served War of 1939-45 (OBE; despatches 4 times); Middle East, India, France, Germany; AA and QMG, 59 (Staffs) Div., 1943; AA and QMG, 43 (Wessex) Div., Dec. 1944. Brig. i/c Administration, Southern Command, 1960-62; Dir of Personal Services, War Office, 1962-64; Dir of Personal Services (Army), Min. of Defence, 1964-66; retd Oct. 1966. Chevalier, Order of the Crown (Belgium), 1945; Croix de Guerre (Belgium), 1945. *Address:* Vine Ridge, Hannington, Hants.
    See also D. R. N. Clarke.

CLARKE, Edward, QC 1960; **His Honour Judge Clarke;** a Circuit Judge (Judge of the Central Criminal Court), since 1964; *b* 21 May 1908; *s* of William Francis Clarke; *m* 1948, Dorothy May, *d* of Thomas Leask, Richmond, Surrey; three *s* one *d. Educ:* Sherborne Sch.; King's Coll., London. Called to Bar, Lincoln's Inn, 1935. Served War, 1943-46 in France, Belgium, Holland and Germany, Lieut-Col, Judge Advocate-General's Staff. Bencher, 1955, Treasurer, 1973, Lincoln's Inn; Dep. Chm., Herts Quarter Sessions, 1956-63; Dep. Chm., London Quarter Sessions, 1963-64. FKC, 1965. President: King's Coll. London Assoc., 1972-73; Old Shirburnian Soc., 1975-76. *Publications:* (with Derek Walker Smith) The Life of Sir Edward Clarke; Halsbury's Laws of England (Criminal Law). *Recreations:* lawn tennis, criminology. *Address:* Central Criminal Court, EC4; 2 Addisland Court, Holland Villas Road, W14. *T:* 01-603 8140. *Clubs:* Garrick, MCC.

CLARKE, Edwin (Sisterson), MD, FRCP; Director, Wellcome Institute for the History of Medicine, since 1973; *b* Felling-on-Tyne, 18 June 1919; *s* of Joseph and Nellie Clarke; *m* 1st, 1949, Margaret Elsie Morrison; two *s*; 2nd, 1958, Beryl Eileen Brock; one *d. Educ:* Jarrow Central Sch.; Univ. of Durham Med. Sch. (MD); Univ. of Chicago Med. Sch. (MD). Neurological

Specialist, RAMC, 1946-48; Nat. Hosp., Queen Square, 1950-51; Postgrad. Med. Sch. of London, 1951-58; Lectr in Neurology and Consultant Neurologist to Hammersmith Hosp., 1955-58; Asst Sec. to Wellcome Trust, 1958-60; Asst Prof., History of Medicine, Johns Hopkins Hosp. Med. Sch., 1960-62; Vis. Assoc. Prof., History of Medicine, Yale Univ. Med. Sch., 1962-63; Med. Historian to Wellcome Historical Med. Library and Museum, 1963-66; Sen. Lectr and Head of Sub-Dept of History of Medicine, University Coll. London, 1966-72, Reader, 1972-73. *Publications:* (jtly) The Human Brain and Spinal Cord, 1968; (ed) Modern Methods in the History of Medicine, 1971; (jtly) An Illustrated History of Brain Function, 1972; articles in jls dealing with neurology and with history of medicine. *Address:* Wellcome Institute for History of Medicine, Wellcome Building, Euston Road, NW1. *T:* 01-387 4477; Fewcott House, Fewcott, near Bicester, Oxon.

CLARKE, Elizabeth Bleckly, CVO 1969; MA; JP; Headmistress, Benenden School, Kent, 1954-Dec. 1975; *b* 26 May 1915; *d* of Kenneth Bleckly Clarke, JP, MRCS, LRCP, Cranborne, Dorset, and Dorothy Milborough (*née* Hasluck). *Educ:* Grovely Manor Sch., Boscombe, Hants; St Hilda's Coll., Oxford, 1933-37. BA 1936, BLitt and MA 1940. Asst Mistress, The Grove Sch., Hindhead, 1937-39; Benenden Sch., 1940-47; called to the Bar, Middle Temple, 1949; Vice-Principal, Cheltenham Ladies' Coll., 1950-54. JP, County of Kent, 1956. *Recreations:* walking, gardening. *Address:* The Old Oast, Stream Lane, Hawkhurst, Kent TN18 4RD. *T:* Hawkhurst 2566. *Club:* English-Speaking Union.

CLARKE, Sir Ellis (Emmanuel Innocent), TC 1969; GCMG 1972 (CMG 1960); Kt 1963 (but does not use the title within Republic of Trinidad and Tobago); President of Trinidad and Tobago, since 1976 (Governor General and C-in-C, 1973-76); *b* 28 Dec. 1917; *o c* of late Cecil Clarke and of Mrs Elma Clarke; *m* 1952, Eyrmyntrude (*née* Hagley); one *s* one *d. Educ:* St Mary's Coll., Trinidad (Jerningham Gold Medal); London Univ. (LLB 1940); Gray's Inn. Private practice at Bar of Trinidad and Tobago, 1941-54; Solicitor-Gen., Oct. 1954; Dep. Colonial Sec., Dec. 1956; Attorney-Gen., 1957-62; Trinidad and Tobago Perm. Rep. to UN, 1962-66; Ambassador: to United States, 1962-72; to Mexico, 1966-72; Rep. on Council of OAS, 1967-72. Chm. of Bd, British West Indian Airways, 1968-72. KStJ 1973. *Address:* President's House, Port of Spain, Trinidad. *Clubs:* Queen's Park Cricket (Port of Spain); Arima Race (Trinidad); Tobago Golf (President, 1969-75).

CLARKE, Sir Frederick (Joseph), Kt 1967; Governor of St Lucia, 1967-73; *b* 21 May 1912; 2nd *s* of late R. G. H. Clarke; *m* 1944, Phyliss (*née* Lunn), *o c* of Henry and Elizabeth Lunn, Bosthill, Tamworth; one *s* two *d* (and one *s* decd). *Educ:* St Vincent Grammar Sch.; School of Medicine, Edinburgh. LRCPE, LRCSE, LRFPS (G) 1944. General Medical Practice, Peterborough, Northants, 1945; District Medical Officer, St Lucia, 1946, CMO, St Lucia, 1961. Retired from Civil Service, Sept. 1963. Private Practice, 1963-67. Speaker of the Legislative Council, St Lucia, 1964-67. KStJ 1968. *Recreations:* cricket, bridge, gardening. *Address:* PO Box 391, Castries, St Lucia, West Indies. *Clubs:* Rotary, Press (St Lucia), St Lucia Cricket.

CLARKE, Geoffrey, RA 1976 (ARA 1970); ARCA; artist and sculptor; *b* 28 Nov. 1924; *s* of John Moulding Clarke and Janet Petts; two *s. Educ:* Royal College of Art (Hons). Exhibitions: Gimpel Fils Gallery, 1952, 1955; Redfern Gallery, 1965. Works in public collections: Victoria and Albert Museum; Tate Gallery; Arts Council; Museum of Modern Art, NY; etc. Prizes for engraving: Triennial, 1951; London, 1953, Tokyo, 1957. Commissioned work includes: iron sculpture, Time Life Building, New Bond Street; cast aluminium relief sculpture (1000 sq. ft), Castrol House, Marylebone Road; mosaics, Liverpool Univ. Physics Block and Basildon New Town; stained glass windows for new Treasury, Lincoln Cathedral; bronze sculpture (80 ft high), Thorn Electric Building, Upper St Martin's Lane; relief sculpture on Canberra and Oriana; 3 (70 ft high) stained glass windows, high altar, cross and candlesticks (10 ft high cast silver), the flying cross and crown of thorns, all in Coventry Cathedral; sculpture, Nottingham Civic Theatre; UKAEA Culham; Westminster Bank, Bond Street; Univs of Liverpool, Exeter, Cambridge, Oxford, Manchester and Lancaster; screens in Royal Military Chapel, Birdcage Walk. Further work at Chichester, Newcastle, Manchester, Plymouth, Ipswich, Canterbury, Taunton, Winchester, St Paul, Minnesota, Newcastle Civic Centre, Wolverhampton, Leicester, Churchill Coll., Aldershot, Suffolk Police HQ, All Souls, W1. *Address:* Stowe Hill, Hartest, Bury St Edmunds, Suffolk. *T:* Hartest 319.

CLARKE, Gerald Bryan, CMG 1964; ISO 1954; Secretary to the Cabinet and Secretary to the Prime Minister, Rhodesia, 1955-70, retired; *b* Gwelo, Rhodesia, 1 Nov. 1909; *s* of Francis Joseph Clarke and Margaret Shiel; *m* 1946, Eleanor, *widow* of B. C. Catella; one *s* one *d* (and one step *s*). *Educ:* St George's Coll., Salisbury, Rhodesia. Joined Southern Rhodesian Civil Service, 1927; Treasury, 1927-40. Served War, 1940-45: S Rhodesia Armoured Car Regt, E Africa and Abyssinia; Pretoria Regt, 6th SA Armoured Div., Italy. Chief Clerk, Treasury, 1945-48; Asst Sec., Public Services Board, 1948; Under-Sec., Cabinet Office, 1950. Attended Constitutional Confs on HMS Tiger, Dec. 1966, and HMS Fearless, 1968, as Mem. of Rhodesian Delegn. Comr of Oaths, Rhodesia. Coronation Medal, 1952; Independence Decoration, 1970. *Recreation:* rearing trees. *Address:* Dromara, Chamakowa Road, PO Box 45, Juliasdale, Inyanga District, Rhodesia. *T:* Juliasdale 129-21715. *Club:* Umtali (Umtali).

CLARKE, Guy Hamilton, CMG 1959; HM Ambassador to Nepal, 1962-63, retired; *b* 23 July 1910; 3rd *s* of late Dr and Mrs Charles H. Clarke, Leicester. *Educ:* Wyggeston Grammar Sch., Leicester; Trinity Hall, Cambridge. Probationer Vice-Consul, Levant Consular Service, Beirut, 1933; transf. to Ankara, 1936; Corfu, 1940; Adana, 1941; Baltimore, 1944; has since served at: Washington, Los Angeles (Consul 1945), Bangkok, Jedda, Kirkuk (Consul 1949), Bagdad, Kirkuk (Consul-Gen. 1951); Ambassador to the Republic of Liberia, 1957-60, and to the Republic of Guinea, 1959-60; Mem. United Kingdom Delegation to United Nations Gen. Assembly, New York, 1960; HM Consul-General, Damascus, Feb. 1961, and Chargé d'Affaires there, Oct. 1961-Jan. 1962. *Address:* 73 Duchess Drive, Newmarket, Suffolk.

CLARKE, Very Rev. (Harold George) Michael, MA 1925; FRSA; *b* 1898; *s* of George Herbert Clarke, then second master of Hymer's Coll., Hull; *m* 1923, Katharine Beryl, *d* of late Barry Edward Girling, Algiers; two *s* one *d*. *Educ:* St Paul's Sch. (scholar); Trinity Coll., Cambridge (scholar). Served with 2nd Field Company RE in France, 1918. 1st Class Hons Mathematical Tripos, Pt 1, 1919, 2nd Class Hons History Tripos, Pt 2, 1921. Deacon, 1938; Priest, 1939. Asst Master at Winchester Coll., 1921-32; Headmaster of Rossall Sch., 1932-37; Headmaster of Repton Sch., 1937-44; Rector of Holy Trinity, St Marylebone, 1945-51. Chm., Standing Joint Cttee Public and Preparatory Schs, 1940-43; lectured in Canada, 1945, at invitation of Canadian Council of Churches; one of founders, and till 1961 Governor, of Administrative Staff Coll., Greenlands, Henley-on-Thames; Chm., Marriage Welfare Cttee of Family Welfare Assoc., 1948-51; Advisory Sec. to Bishop of London on Religious Drama, 1949-51; Rural Dean of St Marylebone, 1950-51; Provost of Birmingham, 1951-61. Master of the Glovers' Company, 1960. Chm. Home Cttee, SPG, 1961-64. Rector of Westonbirt with Lasborough, and Chaplain to Westonbirt Sch., 1961-68. Sub-Warden, Servants of Christ the King, 1963-70; Chaplain to Haberdashers' Co., 1970. *Address:* Flint Cottage, Chipperfield, Herts.
See also F. I. Kilvington.

CLARKE, Sir (Henry) Ashley, GCMG 1962 (KCMG 1952; CMG 1946); GCVO 1961; Member: General Board, Assicurazioni Generali of Trieste, since 1964; Council, British School at Rome, since 1962; Vice-Chairman, Venice in Peril Fund, since 1970; *b* 26 June 1903; *e s* of H. R. H. Clarke, MD; *m* 1st, 1937, Virginia (marr. diss. 1960), *d* of Edward Bell, New York; 2nd, 1962, Frances, *d* of John Molyneux, Worcs. *Educ:* Repton; Pembroke Coll., Cambridge. Entered Diplomatic Service, 1925; 3rd Sec., Budapest and Warsaw; 2nd Sec., Constantinople, FO and Gen. Disarmament Conf, Geneva; 1st Sec., Tokyo; Counsellor, FO; Minister, Lisbon and Paris; Deputy Under-Sec., FO; Ambassador to Italy, 1953-62, retd. London Adviser, Banca Commerciale Italiana, 1962-71; Sec.-Gen., Europa Nostra, 1969-70. Governor: BBC, 1962-67; Brit. Inst. of Recorded Sound, 1964-67; Member: Exec. Cttee, Keats-Shelley Assoc., 1962-71; D'Oyly Carte Trust, 1964-71; Governing Body, Royal Acad. of Music, 1967-73; Adv. Council, V&A Mus., 1969-73; Nat. Theatre Bd, 1962-66; Chairman: Italian Art and Archives Rescue Fund, 1966-70; Royal Acad. of Dancing, 1964-69. Hon. Dr of Political Science, Genoa, 1956; Hon. Academician, Accademia Filarmonica Romana, 1962; Hon. Fellow: Pembroke Coll., Cambridge, 1962; Ancient Monuments Soc., 1969; Royal Acad. of Music, 1971; Ateneo Veneto, 1973. Pietro Torta Prize, 1974 and Bolla Award, 1976 (for conservation in Venice). Knight Grand Cross of the Order of Merit of the Republic of Italy; Knight Grand Cross, Order of St Gregory the Great, 1976. *Recreation:* music. *Address:* Fondamenta Bonlini 1113, Dorsoduro, Venice, Italy. *Clubs:* Athenæum, Garrick.

CLARKE, Sir Henry O.; *see* Osmond-Clarke.

CLARKE, Hilton Swift; Chairman, Atlantic International Bank Ltd, since 1973; *b* 1 April 1909; *yr s* of Frederick Job Clarke; *m* 1934, Sybil Muriel, *d* of late C. J. C. Salter; one *s*. *Educ:* Highgate School. FIB. Bank of England, 1927-67. Director: Charterhouse Group Ltd (Chm. Charterhouse Japhet Ltd, 1971-73); United Dominions Trust Ltd; Guthrie Corp. Ltd; Bank of Scotland Ltd (London Bd); Astley & Pearce Ltd. Freeman, City of London, 1973. Hon. FRCGP 1975. *Recreation:* gardening. *Address:* Hedges, Peaslake, Guildford, Surrey. *T:* Dorking 730757. *Club:* Royal Fowey Yacht.

CLARKE, James Samuel, MC 1943 and Bar 1944; Under-Secretary and Principal Assistant Solicitor, Inland Revenue, since 1970; *b* 19 Jan. 1921; *s* of James Henry and Deborah Florence Clarke; *m* 1949, Ilse Cohen; two *d*. *Educ:* Reigate Grammar Sch.; St Catharine's Coll., Cambridge (MA). Army Service, 1941-45: Royal Irish Fusiliers; served 1st Bn N Africa and Italy; Major 1943. Called to Bar, Middle Temple, 1946. Entered Legal Service (Inland Rev.), 1953; Sen. Legal Asst, 1958; Asst Solicitor, 1965. *Recreations:* gardening, sailing, skiing. *Address:* Engadine, Balcombe Road, Horley, Surrey. *T:* Horley 2577. *Club:* National Liberal.

CLARKE, Jonathan Dennis; a Recorder of the Crown Court, since 1972; Partner in firm of Townsends, solicitors, since 1959; *b* 19 Jan. 1930; *e s* of late Dennis Robert Clarke, Master of Supreme Court, and of Caroline Alice (*née* Hill); *m* 1956, Susan Margaret Elizabeth, *o d* of late Comdr Arthur Howard Ashworth, RN (retd) and of Mrs Doreen Ruthven Ashworth (*née* Ruthven-Smith); one *s* three *d*. *Educ:* Kidstones Sch.; University Coll. London. Admitted Solicitor, 1956; Mem. Council, Law Soc., 1964-; Sec., Nat. Cttee of Young Solicitors, 1962-64; Mem., Matrimonial Causes Rule Cttee, 1967-; Mem. Legal Studies Bd, CNAA, 1968-75; Governor, College of Law, 1970-. *Recreation:* sailing. *Address:* West Lodge, Westlecot Road, Swindon, Wilts. *T:* Swindon 27695. *Clubs:* Junior Carlton; Island Sailing.

CLARKE, Kenneth Harry; MP (C) Rushcliffe Division of Nottinghamshire since 1970; *b* 2 July 1940; *e c* of Kenneth Clarke, Nottingham; *m* 1964, Gillian Mary Edwards; one *s* one *d*. *Educ:* Nottingham High Sch.; Gonville and Caius Coll., Cambridge (BA, LLB). Chm., Cambridge Univ. Conservative Assoc., 1961; Pres., Cambridge Union, 1963; Chm., Fedn Conservative Students, 1963. Called to Bar, Gray's Inn 1963; practising Mem., Midland Circuit, 1963-. Research Sec., Birmingham Bow Group, 1965-66; contested Mansfield (Notts) in General Elections of 1964 and 1966. PPS to Solicitor General, 1971-72; an Asst Govt Whip, 1972-74 (Govt Whip for Europe, 1973-74); a Lord Comr, HM Treasury, 1974. Mem., Parly delegn to Council of Europe and WEU, 1973-74; Sec., Cons. Parly Health and Social Security Cttee, 1974; Opposition Spokesman on: Social Services, 1974-76; Industry, 1976-. *Publications:* pamphlets published by Bow Group, 1964-. *Recreations:* modern jazz music; watching Association Football. *Address:* House of Commons, SW1.

CLARKE, Marshal Butler C.; *see* Cholmondeley Clarke.

CLARKE, Prof. Martin Lowther; *b* 2 Oct. 1909; *s* of late Rev. William Kemp Lowther Clarke; *m* 1942, Emilie de Rontenay Moon, *d* of late Dr R. O. Moon; two *s*. *Educ:* Haileybury Coll.; King's Coll., Cambridge. 1st class Classical Tripos, Parts I and II; Craven Scholar; Browne Medallist; Chancellor's Medallist; Craven Student. Asst, Dept of Humanity, Edinburgh Univ., 1933-34; Fellow of King's Coll., Cambridge, 1934-40; Asst Lecturer in Greek and Latin, University Coll., London, 1935-37. Foreign Office, 1940-45. Lecturer, 1946-47, and Reader, 1947-48, in Greek and Latin, University Coll., London; Prof. of Latin, University Coll. of North Wales, 1948-74, Vice-Principal, 1963-65, 1967-74. *Publications:* Richard Porson, 1937; Greek Studies in England, 1700 to 1830, 1945; Rhetoric at Rome, 1953; The Roman Mind, 1956; Classical Education in Britain, 1500-1900, 1959; George Grote, 1962; Bangor Cathedral, 1969; Higher Education in the Ancient World, 1971; Paley, 1974. *Address:* Lollingdon House, Cholsey, Wallingford OX10 9LS. *T:* Cholsey 651389.

CLARKE, Mary; Editor, Dancing Times, since 1963; *b* 23 Aug. 1923; *d* of Frederick Clarke and Ethel Kate (*née* Reynolds); unmarried. *Educ:* Mary Datchelor Girls' School. London Corresp., Dance Magazine, NY, 1943-55; London Editor, Dance News, NY, 1955-70; Asst Editor and Contributor, Ballet Annual, 1952-63; joined Dancing Times as Asst Editor, 1954. *Publications:* The Sadler's Wells Ballet: a history and an appreciation, 1955; Six Great Dancers, 1957; Dancers of Mercury: the story of Ballet Rambert, 1962; (with Clement Crisp) Ballet, an Illustrated History, 1973; (with Clement Crisp)

Making a Ballet, 1974; (with Clement Crisp) Introducing Ballet, 1976; ed (with David Vaughan) Encyclopedia of Dance and Ballet, 1977; contrib. Encycl. Britannica; has reviewed for Sunday Times, Observer, Guardian. *Recreations:* walking, reading, eating. *Address:* 11 Danbury Street, Islington, N1 8LD. *T:* 01-226 9209. *Club:* Gautier.

CLARKE, Very Rev. Michael; *see* Clarke, Very Rev. H. G. M.

CLARKE, Rear-Adm. Noel Edward Harwood, CB 1959; *b* 21 Oct. 1904; *s* of Henry Trevisa Clarke and Margaret Evelyn Sale; *m* 1942, Katherine Miller, *d* of Harman Visger, France Lynch, near Stroud; two *s. Educ:* RN Colleges, Osborne and Dartmouth. RNEC Keyham, 1923-27; HMS Marlborough, 1927-29; HMS Kent, 1930-33; HMS Cairo, 1933-34; HM Dockyard, Portsmouth, 1934-36; HMS Sheffield, 1936-39; Admty, 1939-41; HMS Cumberland, 1942-43; HMS Excellent, 1943-47; HM Dockyard, Singapore, 1947-49; Admty, 1949-52; HM Dockyard, Gibraltar, 1952-56; Admty, 1957; Dir of Fleet Maintenance, Admty, 1958; Command Engineer Officer and Chief Staff Officer (Technical), on staff of C-in-C, Portsmouth, Nov. 1958-July 1960, retd; worked with Nat. Economic Development Office, 1963-68. *Recreation:* golf. *Address:* Seamark House, St Helens, Isle of Wight. *T:* Bembridge 2866. *Club:* Royal Naval and Royal Albert Yacht (Portsmouth).

CLARKE, Norman; Secretary and Registrar, Institute of Mathematics and its Applications, since 1965; *b* 21 Oct. 1916; *o s* of late Joseph Clarke and of Ellen Clarke, Oldham; *m* 1940, Hilda May Watts; two *d. Educ:* Hulme Grammar Sch., Oldham; Univ. of Manchester (BSc). FInstP, FIMA. Pres., Manchester Univ. Union, 1938-39. External Ballistics Dept, Ordnance Bd, 1939-42; Armament Res. Estabt, Br. for Theoretical Res., 1942-45; Dep. Sec., Inst. Physics, 1945-65; Hon. Sec., Internat. Commn on Physics Educn, 1960-66. Southend-on-Sea County Borough Council: Mem., 1961-74; Alderman, 1964-74; Chm. of Watch Cttee, 1962-69 and of Public Protection Cttee, 1969-; Vice-Chm., Essex and Southend-on-Sea Jt Police Authority, 1969-; Member: Essex CC, 1973-; Southend-on-Sea Borough Council, 1974- (Mayor, 1975-76). *Publications:* papers on physics educn; editor and contributor: A Physics Anthology: (with S. C. Brown) International Education in Physics; Why Teach Physics; The Education of a Physicist; contributor: A Survey of the Teaching of Physics in Universities (Unesco); Metrication. *Recreations:* music, boating, cricket, gastronomy. *Address:* 106 Olive Avenue, Leigh-on-Sea, Essex SS9 3QE. *T:* Southend-on-Sea 558056; Institute of Mathematics and its Applications, Maitland House, Warrior Square, Southend-on-Sea, Essex SS1 2JY. *T:* Southend-on-Sea 612177.

CLARKE, Norman Eley; Under Secretary, Director of Establishments and Personnel (Departmental), Department of Health and Social Security, since 1976; *b* 11 Feb. 1930; *s* of Thomas John Laurence Clarke and May (*née* Eley); *m* 1953, Pamela Muriel Colwill; three *s* one *d. Educ:* Hampton Grammar Sch. Grade 5 Officer, Min. of Labour and National Service, 1948-56; Asst Principal, National Assistance Bd, 1957-61 (Private Sec. to Chm., 1960-61); Principal, Nat. Asstnce Bd, subseq. Min. of Social Security, and DHSS, 1961-69; Private Sec. to Minister without Portfolio, Jan.-June 1970; Principal, DHSS, 1970-71; Asst Sec., 1971-75; Under Sec., Dir of Estabts and Personnel (HQ), Jan.-Sept. 1976. *Recreations:* reading, tennis, watching Queens Park Rangers, talking. *Address:* Winton, Guildford Lane, Woking, Surrey. *T:* Woking 64453.

CLARKE, Prof. Patricia Hannah, DSc; FRS 1976; Professor of Microbial Biochemistry, University College, University of London, since 1974; *b* 29 July 1919; *d* of David Samuel Green and Daisy Lilian Amy Willoughby; *m* 1940, Michael Clarke; two *s. Educ:* Howells Sch., Llandaff; Girton Coll., Cambridge (BA). DSc London. Armament Res. Dept, 1940-44; Wellcome Res. Labs, 1944-47; National Collection of Type Cultures, 1951-53; Lectr, Dept of Biochemistry, UCL, 1953; Reader in Microbial Biochemistry, 1966. Hon. Gen. Sec., Soc. for General Microbiology, 1965-70; Mem., CNAA, 1973-. *Publications:* Genetics and Biochemistry of Pseudomonas (ed with M. H. Richmond), 1975; papers on genetics, biochemistry and enzyme evolution in Jl of Gen. Mcrobiol. and other jls. *Address:* Department of Biochemistry, University College London, Gower Street, WC1E 6BT. *T:* 01-387 7050.

CLARKE, Paul (Henry Francis); His Honour Judge Paul Clarke; a Circuit Judge since 1974; *b* 14 Oct. 1921; *s* of Dr Richard Clarke, FRCP, Clifton, Bristol; *m* 1955, Eileen Sheila, *d* of Lt-Col J. K. B. Crawford, Clifton Coll.; two *s* one *d. Educ:* Clifton Coll.; Exeter Coll., Oxford (MA). Served War, Gloucester Regt and Royal Engineers, 1940-46. Called to Bar, Inner Temple, 1949, practising as Barrister from Guildhall Chambers, Bristol, 1949-74. *Address:* Saffron Close, Chudleigh, Devon TQ13 0EE.

CLARKE, Peter, PhD, CChem, FRIC, FInstPet; Director, Robert Gordon's Institute of Technology, Aberdeen, since 1970; *b* 18 March 1922; *er s* of Frederick John and Gladys May Clarke; *m* 1947, Ethel Jones; two *s. Educ:* Queen Elizabeth's Grammar Sch., Mansfield; University Coll., Nottingham (BSc). Industrial Chemist, 1942; Sen. Chemistry Master, Buxton Coll., 1947; Lectr, Huddersfield Technl Coll., 1949; British Enka Ltd, Liverpool, 1956; Sen. Lectr, Royal Coll. of Advanced Tech., Salford, 1962; Head of Dept of Chemistry and Biology, Nottingham Regional Coll. of Technology, 1963; Vice-Principal, Huddersfield Coll. of Technology, 1965-70. Chm., Assoc. of Principals of Colleges (Scotland); Pres., Aberdeen Business and Professional Club. Burgess of Guild, City of Aberdeen, 1973. *Publications:* contribs to Jl of Chem. Soc., Chemistry and Industry. *Recreations:* gardening, swimming. *Address:* Tulloch Lodge, West Cults, Aberdeenshire AB1 9ES.

CLARKE, Major Peter Cecil, CVO 1969; Chief Clerk, Duchy of Lancaster, and Extra Equerry to HRH Princess Alexandra, the Hon. Mrs Angus Ogilvy; *b* 9 Aug. 1927; *s* of late Captain E. D. Clarke, CBE, MC, Binstead, Isle of Wight; *m* 1950, Rosemary Virginia Margaret Harmsworth, *d* of late T. C. Durham, Appomattox, Virginia, USA; one *s* two *d. Educ:* Eton; RMA, Sandhurst. 3rd The King's Own Hussars and 14th/20th King's Hussars, 1945-64. Seconded as Asst Private Secretary to HRH Princess Marina, Duchess of Kent, 1961-64; Comptroller, 1964-68; Comptroller to HRH Princess Alexandra, 1964-69. *Recreations:* golf, fishing. *Address:* 6 Gordon Place, W8. *T:* 01-937 0356. *Clubs:* Cavalry and Guards, MCC.

CLARKE, Peter James; Secretary of the Forestry Commission, since 1976; *b* 16 Jan. 1934; *s* of Stanley Ernest Clarke and Elsie May (*née* Scales); *m* 1966, Roberta Anne, *y d* of Robert and Ada Browne; one *s* one *d. Educ:* Enfield Grammar Sch.; St John's Coll., Cambridge (MA). Exec. Officer, WO, 1952-62 (univ., 1957-60), Higher Exec. Officer, 1962; Sen. Exec. Officer, Forestry Commn, 1967, Principal 1972; Principal, Dept of Energy, 1975. *Recreations:* gardening, amateur dramatics. *Address:* 5 Murrayfield Gardens, Edinburgh EH12 6DG. *T:* 031-337 3145.

CLARKE, Reginald Arnold, CMG 1962; OBE 1960; DFC 1945; Director of Personnel, International Bank for Reconstruction and Development, Washington, DC, since 1970 (Assistant Director of Administration, 1964-70); *b* 6 May 1921; *s* of late John Leonard Clarke; *m* 1949, Dorithea Nanette Oswald; three *s* one *d. Educ:* Doncaster Grammar Sch. Royal Air Force, 1939-46; Provincial Administration, Nigeria, 1947-52; Financial Secretary's Office, Nigeria, 1952-57; Federal Ministry of Finance, Nigeria, 1957, Permanent Sec., 1958-63, retd. *Recreations:* tennis, tennis, bridge. *Address:* c/o Midland Bank, Gosforth, Cumbria; 8104 Hamilton Spring Road, Bethesda, Maryland 20034, USA. *Club:* Royal Air Force Reserves.

CLARKE, Robin Mitchell, MC 1944; JP; Manager, Crawley, Commission for the New Towns, since 1962; *b* 8 Jan. 1917; *e s* of Joseph and Mary Clarke; *m* 1946, Betty Mumford; twin *s* and *d. Educ:* Ruckholt Central Sch., Leyton. Middleton and St Bride's Wharf, Wapping, 1932-34; Town Clerk's Office, City of Westminster, 1935-40. War of 1939-45: 12th Regt, RHA (HAC) and 142 (Royal Devon Yeomanry) Fd Regt, RA; Major, 1944; served Sicily and Italy (wounded, despatches, MC). Town Clerk's Office, Westminster, 1946-48; Crawley Development Corporation, 1948-62. ACIS 1949; FCIS 1959 (Mem. Nat. Council, 1968-; Senior Vice-Pres., 1977). Commandant, C Div., Sussex Special Constabulary, 1962-71. Chm., W Sussex Indust. Savings Cttee, 1975-. JP Crawley, 1971. *Address:* Hillcrest, 40 Mount Close, Pound Hill, Crawley, Sussex. *T:* Pound Hill 2266.

CLARKE, Roger Simon Woodchurch, JP; Chairman, The Imperial Tobacco Co. Ltd, 1959-64; *b* 29 June 1903; *s* of late Charles S. Clarke, Tracy Park, Wick, Bristol; *m* 1936, Nancy Lingard, *d* of late William Martin, formerly of St Petersburg; no *c. Educ:* RN Colleges, Osborne and Dartmouth. Joined The Imperial Tobacco Co., 1922; Dir, 1944-68. Pro-Chancellor, Bristol Univ., 1975-. JP Bristol, 1964. Hon. LLD Bristol, 1975. *Address:* The Little Priory, Bathwick Hill, Bath. *T:* Bath 5388.

CLARKE, Major Sir Rupert William John, 3rd Bt *cr* 1882; MBE 1943; late Irish Guards; Director: National Bank of Australasia, since 1955; Conzinc Riotinto of Australia Ltd, since 1962; Austiran Ltd, since 1976; Chairman: Unifed Distillers Co. since 1960; Cadbury Schweppes Australia Ltd (formerly Schweppes (Australia)); Victory Reinsurance Co. of Australia; King Ranch Australia Pty Ltd; Bain Dawes Australia Ltd; *b* 5 Nov. 1919; *s* of 2nd Bt and Elsie Florence (who *m* 2nd, 1928, 5th Marquess of Headfort), *d* of James Partridge Tucker, Devonshire; *S* father, 1926; *m* 1947, Kathleen, *d* of P. Grant Hay, Toorak, Victoria,

Australia; two *s* one *d* (and one *s* decd). *Educ:* Eton; Magdalen Coll., Oxford (MA). Served War of 1939-45 (despatches, MBE). Chm., Vict. Amateur Turf Club. *Heir:* s Rupert Grant Alexander Clarke, *b* 12 Dec. 1947. *Address:* Bolinda Vale, Clarkefield, Vic 3430, Australia; Richmond House, 56 Avoca Street, South Yarra, Vic 3141. *Clubs:* Cavalry and Guards, Lansdowne; Melbourne, Athenæum, Australian (Melbourne); Union (Sydney); Queensland (Brisbane).

CLARKE, Samuel Harrison, CBE 1956; MSc; Hon. MIFireE; *b* 5 Sept. 1903; *s* of Samuel Clarke and Mary Clarke (*née* Clarke); *m* 1928, Frances Mary Blowers (*d* 1972); one *s* two *d*; *m* 1977, Mrs Beryl N. Wood; two step *d*. *Educ:* The Brunts Sch., Mansfield; University Coll., Nottingham (MSc London). Forest Products Res. Laboratory of DSIR, 1927; Fire Research Div., Research and Experiments Dept, Ministry of Home Security, 1940; Dir of Fire Research, DSIR, and Fire Offices Cttee, 1946-58; Dir of Fuel Research Station, DSIR, 1958; Dir, Warren Spring Laboratory, DSIR, 1958-63; Careers Officer, Min. of Technology, 1963-67 (DSIR, 1964-65). Mem. Stevenage Development Corporation, 1962-71; Chm., Herts Assoc. for Care and Resettlement of Offenders, 1974-. *Publications:* papers in scientific and technical jls. *Recreations:* exchanging ideas, painting. *Address:* 35 Lonsdale Court, Lonsdale Road, Stevenage, Herts SG1 5EL.

CLARKE, Stanley George, CBE 1975; Chief Inspector of the Prison Service, 1971-74; Member, Prisons Board, 1971-74; *b* Dunfermline, 5 May 1914; *s* of Stanley and Catherine Clarke; *m* 1940, Mary Preston Lewin; one *s* one *d*. *Educ:* Sutton High Sch., Plymouth (school colours: cricket, Rugby, soccer). Civil Service Clerk: Dartmoor Prison, 1931; Lowdham Grange Borstal, 1933; North Sea Camp, 1935; Borstal Housemaster: Portland, 1937; North Sea Camp, 1939. Served War, 1941-45 (despatches): Sqdn Ldr, RAF. Borstal Housemaster: Hollesley Bay Colony, 1945; Gaynes Hall, 1946. Dep. Governor, Manchester Prison, 1947; Governor: Norwich Prison, 1949; Nottingham Prison, 1952; Eastchurch Prison, 1955; Liverpool Prison, 1959. Asst Dir of Prisons, in charge of North Region, 1964; Asst Controller, Prison Dept, 1970. *Recreations:* cricket, tennis, motoring. *Address:* 17 Grundy's Lane, Malvern Wells, Worcs.

CLARKE, Mrs Stella Rosemary, JP; a Governor of the BBC, since 1974; *b* 16 Feb. 1932; *m* 1952, Charles Nigel Clarke; four *s* one *d*. *Educ:* Cheltenham Ladies' Coll.; Trinity Coll. Dublin. Long Ashton RDC: Councillor, Chm. Council, Housing and Public Health Cttees, 1955-73; Mem., Wood Spring Dist Council, 1973-; co-opted Mem., Somerset CC, Social Services and Children's Cttee, 1957-73. Chm., Project for Girls at Risk, Bristol, 1971-. Purchased and restored Theatre Royal, Bath, with husband, 1974-76. JP Bristol, 1968. *Recreations:* family and the variety of life. *Address:* Gatcombe Court, Flax Bourton, near Bristol BS19 1PX. *T:* Long Ashton 3141.

CLARKE, Brig. Terence Hugh, CBE 1943; *b* 17 Feb. 1904; *e s* of late Col Hugh Clarke, AM, Royal Artillery, and of Mrs Hugh Clarke, Bunces, Kennel Ride, Ascot; *m* 1928, Eileen Armistead, Hopelands, Woodville, NZ; two *d*. *Educ:* Temple Grove; Haileybury Coll.; RMA Sandhurst. 2nd Lieut Glos Regt, 1924; served India, 1924-27; China, 1928; India, 1928-31, in IA Ordnance Corps; England, 1931-33, Glos Regt; transferred to RAOC, 1933; Norway, 1940 (despatches); DDOS 1st Army, 1942, as Brig. (despatches, CBE); DDOS 2nd Army, 1944; Normandy to Luneberg, Germany (despatches); comd RAOC Training Centre, 1946; DDOS Southern Command, 1948-50; retired from Army, 1950, to enter industry as a Dir of public and private companies. MP (C) Portsmouth West, 1950-66; Parly Cand. (C) Portsmouth West, 1966, 1970. *Recreations:* capped six times for the Army at Rugby and boxed heavyweight for Army; sailing, ski-ing and horse racing. *Address:* Hollybank House, Emsworth, Hants PO10 7UE. *T:* Emsworth 2256.

CLARKE, Col Thomas Cecil Arthur, DSO 1941; OBE 1945; MIMechE; late Royal Tank Regt; Secretary Royal Armoured Corps War Memorial Benevolent Fund, and Royal Tank Regt Assoc. and Benevolent Fund, 1951-62; *b* 24 Nov. 1898; *s* of Cecil Clarke, Hampstead; *m* 1932, Dorothy Leslie-Spinks, Bournemouth; one *s* one *d*. *Educ:* Dover Coll.; RMC Sandhurst. In Regular Army from 1917; served European War, 1917-19 (wounded); War of 1939-45 (DSO, OBE, despatches thrice, wounded); commanded 46th (Liverpool Welsh) RT Regt; retired 1951. *Address:* 8 The Pines, The Avenue, Branksome, Poole, Dorset.

CLARKE, Thomas Ernest Bennett, OBE 1952; screenwriter; *b* 7 June 1907; 2nd *s* of late Sir Ernest Michael Clarke; *m* 1932, Joyce Caroline Steele; one *d* (one *s* decd). *Educ:* Charterhouse; Clare Coll., Cambridge. Staff writer on Answers, 1927-35;

editorial staff Daily Sketch, 1936; subsequently free-lance journalist. Wrote screen-plays of films: Johnny Frenchman, Hue and Cry, Against the Wind, Passport to Pimlico, The Blue Lamp, The Magnet, The Lavender Hill Mob (Academy and Venice Awards), The Titfield Thunderbolt, The Rainbow Jacket, Who Done It?, Barnacle Bill, A Tale of Two Cities, Gideon's Day, The Horse Without a Head. Other screen credits include For Those in Peril, Halfway House, Champagne Charlie (lyrics), Dead of Night, Train of Events, Encore, Law and Disorder, Sons and Lovers, A Man Could Get Killed. *Play:* This Undesirable Residence. *Publications:* Go South-Go West, 1932; Jeremy's England, 1934; Cartwright Was a Cad, 1936; Two and Two Make Five, 1938; What's Yours?, 1938; Mr Spirket Reforms, 1939; The World Was Mine, 1964; The Wide Open Door, 1966; The Trail of the Serpent, 1968; The Wrong Turning, 1971; Intimate Relations, 1971; This is Where I Came In (autobiog.), 1974; The Man Who Seduced a Bank, 1977. *Recreations:* racing, gardening. *Address:* Tanners Mead, Oxted, Surrey. *T:* Oxted 2183.

CLARKE, Sir Tobias; *see* Clarke, Sir C. M. T.

CLARKE, William Malpas, CBE 1976; Director General and Deputy Chairman, Committee on Invisible Exports, since 1976 (Director, 1966-76); *b* 5 June 1922; *o s* of late Ernest and Florence Clarke; *m* 1st, 1946, Margaret, *y d* of late Reginald Braithwaite and of Lilian Braithwaite; two *d*; 2nd, 1973, Faith Elizabeth, *d* of Lionel and late Florence Dawson. *Educ:* Audenshaw Grammar Sch.; Univ. of Manchester. Served Royal Air Force, 1941-46; Flying Instructor, 1942-44; Flight-Lieut, 1945. Editorial Staff, Manchester Guardian, 1948-55; The Times: Asst City Editor, 1955-57; City Editor, 1957-62; Financial and Industrial Editor, 1962-66; Editor, The Banker, March-Sept. 1966, Consultant 1966-76; Consultant, Euromoney, 1977-. Director: Grindlays Bank Ltd; Grindlay Brandts Ltd; Swiss Reinsurance Co (UK) Ltd; UK Provident Instn; Cincinnati Milacron Ltd; Trade Indemnity Co. Ltd; Euromoney Publications; Romney Trust Ltd; City Communications Orgn (Dep. Chm.). Mem. Council, RIIA. *Publications:* The City's Invisible Earnings, 1958; The City in the World Economy, 1965; Private Enterprise in Developing Countries, 1966; (ed, as Director of Studies) Britain's Invisible Earnings, 1967; The World's Money, 1970. *Recreations:* books, opera. *Address:* 37 Park Vista, Greenwich, SE10. *T:* 01-858 0979. *Club:* Reform.

CLARKE HALL, Denis; architect in private practice; President, Architectural Association, 1958-59; Chairman, Architects Registration Council of the UK, 1963-64; *b* 4 July 1910; *m* 1936, Mary Garfitt; one *s* two *d*. *Educ:* Bedales. Has had his own practice, 1937-. Holds AA Dip. *Publications:* articles in technical journals. *Address:* Moorhouse, Iping, Midhurst, W Sussex.

CLARKE HALL, Lady, (Edna); artist; *d* of late Rev. B. Waugh, founder of the NSPCC; *m* 1898, Sir W. Clarke Hall (*d* 1932); two *s*. *Educ:* The Slade Sch. (Slade Scholarship). Drawings, water-colours, etchings and lithographs. Represented at the Tate Gallery, British, Victoria and Albert and Fitzwilliam Museums and Manchester City Art Gallery. Exhibition, d'Offay Couper Gallery, London, 1971. *Publications:* Poems, 1926; Facets, 1930. *Address:* Upminster Common, Essex.

CLARKE TAYLOR, Air Vice-Marshal James; *see* Taylor, Air Vice-Marshal J. C.

CLARKSON, Prof. Brian Leonard, PhD; Professor of Vibration Studies, since 1966, and Director, Institute of Sound and Vibration Research, since 1967, University of Southampton; *b* 28 July 1930; *s* of L. C. Clarkson; *m* 1953, Margaret Elaine Wilby; three *s* one *d*. *Educ:* Univ. of Leeds (BSc, PhD). FRAeS; Fellow, Soc. of Environmental Engineers; FInst Acoustics. George Taylor Gold Medal, RAeS, 1963. Dynamics Engineer, de Havilland Aircraft Co., Hatfield, Herts, 1953-57; Sir Alan Cobham Research Fellow, Dept of Aeronautics, Univ. of Southampton, 1957-58; Lectr, Dept of Aeronautics and Astronautics, Univ. of Southampton, 1958-66. Sen. Post Doctoral Research Fellow, Nat. Academy of Sciences, USA, 1970-71 (one year's leave of absence from Southampton). Sec., Internat. Commn on Acoustics, 1975-. *Publications:* author of sections of two books: Technical Acoustics, vol. 3 (ed Richardson) 1959; Noise and Acoustic Fatigue in Aeronautics (ed Mead and Richards), 1967; technical papers on Jet Noise and its effect on Aircraft Structures, Jl of Royal Aeronautical Soc., etc. *Recreations:* walking, gardening, travelling, lazing in the sun. *Address:* Tanglewood, 58 Chalk Hill, West End, Southampton SO3 3DB. *T:* West End 3524; Institute of Sound and Vibration Research, The University, Southampton SO9 5NH. *T:* Southampton 559122.

CLARKSON, Derek Joshua, QC 1969; **His Honour Judge Clarkson;** a Circuit Judge, since 1977; *b* 10 Dec. 1929; *o s* of Albert and Winifred Charlotte Clarkson (*née* James); *m* 1960, Peternella Marie-Luise Ilse Canenbley; one *s* one *d. Educ:* Pudsey Grammar Sch.; King's Coll., Univ. of London. LLB (1st cl. Hons) 1950. Called to Bar, Inner Temple, 1951; Nat. Service, RAF, 1952-54 (Flt Lt). In practice as Barrister, 1954-77; Prosecuting Counsel to Post Office on North-Eastern Circuit, 1961-65; Prosecuting Counsel to Inland Revenue on North-Eastern Circuit, 1965-69; Recorder of Rotherham, 1967-71; Recorder of Huddersfield, 1971; a Recorder of the Crown Court, 1972-77. Mem., Gen. Council of the Bar, 1971-73. *Recreations:* walking, book collecting, dialect study. *Address:* 26 Cornwall Road, Harrogate, Yorks. *T:* Harrogate 4673. *Clubs:* Reform; Leeds (Leeds).

CLARKSON, Prof. Geoffrey Peniston Elliott, PhD; Dean, College of Business Administration, Northeastern University, Boston, since 1977; Visiting Professor, Sloan School of Management, Massachusetts Institute of Technology, since 1975; *b* 30 May 1934; *s* of George Elliott Clarkson and Alice Helene (*née* Manneberg); *m* 1960, Eleanor M. (*née* Micenko); two *d. Educ:* Carnegie-Mellon Univ., Pittsburgh, Pa (BSc, MSc, PhD). Asst Prof., Sloan Sch. of Management, MIT, 1961-65, Associate Prof., 1965-67. Vis. Ford Foundn Fellow, Carnegie-Mellon Univ., 1965-66; Vis. Prof., LSE, 1966-67; Nat. Westminster Bank Prof. of Business Finance, Manchester Business Sch., Univ. of Manchester, 1967-77. Dir of and consultant to public and private manufng and financial services cos, 1969-. *Publications:* Portfolio Selection: a simulation of trust investment, USA 1962 (Ford Dissertation Prize, 1961); The Theory of Consumer Demand: a critical appraisal, USA 1963; Managerial Economics, 1968; (with B. J. Elliott) Managing Money and Finance, 1969 (2nd edn 1972). *Recreations:* fishing, sailing, reading. *Address:* College of Business Administration, Northeastern University, Boston, Mass 02115, USA. *Clubs:* Royal Automobile, Crockfords.

CLASEN, Andrew Joseph, Hon. GCVO 1968; Grand Cross, Adolphe Nassau; Commander Order of the Oaken Crown; Grand Cross: Order of Orange Nassau; Iceland Falcon; Luxembourg Ambassador in London, 1955-71 (Minister, 1944-55); *b* 5 Sept. 1906; *yr s* of late Bernard Clasen and Claire Duchscher; *m* 1944, Joan Mary Lowe; one *s* one *d. Educ:* Beaumont Coll.; Univs of Oxford, London and Aix-la-Chapelle. DrIng, BSc; ARSM; Hon. FIC. Acting Sec.-Gen. Luxembourg Foreign Affairs Ministry, Consul-Gen., Chargé d'Affaires, 1940-44. Luxembourg Delegate to Red Cross, UNRRA, European Council, UN, NATO and WEU. Grand Officer, Order of Tunisian Republic. *Address:* The Manor House, Rotherfield, Sussex. *Club:* Turf.

CLATWORTHY, Robert, RA 1973 (ARA 1968); sculptor; *b* 1 Jan. 1928; *s* of E. W. and G. Clatworthy; *m* 1954, Pamela Gordon (marr. diss.); two *s* one *d. Educ:* Dr Morgan's Grammar Sch., Bridgwater. Studied West of England Coll. of Art, Chelsea Sch. of Art, The Slade. Teacher, West of England Coll. of Art, 1967-71. Visiting Tutor, RCA, 1960-72; Mem., Fine Art Panel of Nat. Council for Diplomas in Art and Design, 1961-72; Governor, St Martin's Sch. of Art, 1970-71; Head of Dept of Fine Art, Central Sch. of Art and Design, 1971-75. Exhibited: Hanover Gall., 1954, 1956; Waddington Galls, 1965; Holland Park Open Air Sculpture, 1957; Battersea Park Open Air Sculpture, 1960, 1963; Tate Gallery, British Sculpture in the Sixties, 1965; British Sculptors 1972, Burlington House; Basil Jacobs Fine Art Ltd, 1972. Work in Collections: Arts Council, Contemporary Art Soc., Tate Gallery, Victoria and Albert Museum, Greater London Council. *Address:* 15 Park Street, SE1.

CLAUDE, Prof. Albert; Director, Laboratoire de Biologie Cellulaire et Cancérologie, since 1970; Director Emeritus, Institut Jules Bordet, Brussels; Professor, Catholic University of Louvain; *b* Longlier, 23 Aug. 1899. *Educ:* Univ. of Liège. Joined Rockefeller Inst., now Rockefeller Univ., 1929; Adjunct Prof., 1972-; Dir, Institut Jules Bordet, 1949-71; Vis. Res. Prof., Johnson Res. Foundn, 1967-. Awarded (jtly with Prof. Christian de Duve and Prof. George Emil Palade) Nobel Prize for Medicine or Physiology, 1974 (he carried out initial work and they developed his findings). *Address:* Laboratoire de Biologie Cellulaire, rue des Champs Elysées 62, 1050 Brussels, Belgium.

CLAXTON, Rt. Rev. Charles Robert, MA, DD; Assistant Bishop, Diocese of Exeter since 1971; *b* 16 Nov. 1903; *s* of Herbert Bailey and Frances Ann Claxton; *m* 1930, Agnes Jane Stevenson; two *s* two *d. Educ:* Monkton Combe Sch.; Weymouth Coll.; Queen's Coll., Cambridge. Deacon, 1927; Priest, 1928; Curate, St John's, Stratford, E15, 1927-29; St John, Redhill,

1929-33; St Martin-in-the-Fields, 1944-46; Vicar Holy Trinity, Bristol, 1933-38; Hon. Canon of Bristol Cathedral, 1942-46; Hon. Chaplain to Bishop of Bristol, 1938-46; Hon. Chaplain to Bishop of Rochester, 1943-46; Rector of Halsall, near Ormskirk, Lancs, 1948-59; Suffragan Bishop of Warrington, 1946-60; Bishop of Blackburn, 1960-71. *Recreation:* golf. *Address:* St Martins, Budleigh Salterton, Devon. *T:* Budleigh Salterton 2193.

CLAXTON, John Francis, CB 1969; Deputy Director of Public Prosecutions 1966-71; *b* 11 Jan. 1911; *s* of late Alfred John Claxton, OBE, and Dorothy Frances O. Claxton (*née* Roberts); *m* 1937, Norma Margaret Rawlinson; no *c. Educ:* Tonbridge Sch.; Exeter Coll., Oxford (BA). Called to Bar, 1935. Joined Dept of Dir of Public Prosecutions, 1937; Asst Dir, 1956-66. *Recreations:* model making, gardening. *Address:* The White Cottage, Lock Road, Marlow, Bucks. *T:* Marlow 2744.

CLAXTON, Maj.-Gen. Patrick Fisher, CB 1972; OBE 1946; General Manager, Regular Forces Employment Association, since 1971; *b* 13 March 1915; *s* of late Rear-Adm. Ernest William Claxton and Kathleen O'Callaghan Claxton, formerly Fisher; *m* 1941, Jóna Gudrún Gunnarsdóttir; two *d. Educ:* Sutton Valence Sch.; St John's Coll., Cambridge (BA). Served GHQ, India, 1943-45; Singapore, 1945-46; WO, 1946-48; British Element Trieste Force, 1949-51; HQ, BAOR, 1952-54; RASC Officers' Sch., 1955-56; Amphibious Warfare HQ and Persian Gulf, 1957-58; Col, WO, 1959-60; Brig., WO, 1961-62; DST, BAOR, 1963-65; CTO, BAOR, 1965-66; Comdt, Sch. of Transport, and ADC to the Queen, 1966-68; Transport Officer-in-Chief (Army), 1969-71, retired; Col. Comdt, RCT, 1972-. FCIT. *Address:* The Lodge, Beacon Hill Park, Hindhead, Surrey. *T:* Hindhead 4437. *Club:* MCC.

CLAY, Charles John Jervis; Deputy Chairman, International Commodities Clearing House Ltd, since 1975 (Director since 1952; Managing Director, 1971-75); *b* 19 March 1910; *s* of late Arthur J. Clay and Bridget Clay (*née* Parker-Jervis); *m* 1935, Patricia Agnes, *d* of late James and Dorothy Chapman; one *s* two *d. Educ:* Eton; New College, Oxford; Pitmans Business College. Served War, 1939-45, Rifle Bde (Officer), and PoW (despatches). Anthony Gibbs & Sons Ltd, 1933-70 (Man. Dir, 1952-70); Dir, R. J. Rouse & Co. Ltd, 1961-74; Dir-Gen., Accepting Houses Cttee, 1971-76. Chairman: Anton Underwriting Agencies Ltd, 1958-76; Wool Testing Services International Ltd, 1961-74; Automated Real-Time Investments Exchange Ltd, 1972-; London Bd, National Mutual Life Assoc. of Australasia Ltd, 1969-; Quality Control International Ltd, 1974-; Mem. London Cttee, Ottoman Bank, 1955-; Dir, A. P. Bank Ltd, 1977-. Member: Public Works Loans Bd, 1958-70; ECGD Adv. Council, 1965-70. Mem. Executive Cttee, BBA, 1973-76; Mem. Council, CBI, 1972-76. *Publications:* Modern Merchant Banking, 1976; papers and speeches on Commodity Futures Trading and Clearing. *Recreations:* sailing, archery, gardening. *Address:* Lamberts, Hascombe, Godalming, Surrey. *T:* Hascombe 240. *Clubs:* Brooks's, MCC.

CLAY, Sir Charles Travis, Kt 1957; CB 1944; Hon. LittD; FSA; FBA 1950; Librarian, House of Lords, 1922-56; *b* 30 July 1885; *y s* of late John William Clay of Rastrick House, Yorks; *m* 1913, Hon. Violet (*d* 1972), 2nd *d* of late Lord Robson; three *d. Educ:* Harrow; Balliol Coll., Oxford; 1st Class History. Asst private sec. to Marquess of Crewe at Colonial Office, 1909-10, and at India Office, 1910-14; Asst Librarian, House of Lords, 1914-22; Lieut Devon Yeo.; Major, Territorial Army Reserve; served European War (despatches twice, DAQMG). Pres., Yorks Archæological Soc., 1953-56. *Address:* 30 Queen's Gate Gardens, SW7. *T:* 01-584 0205. *Club:* Brooks's.

CLAY, Sir Henry Felix, 6th Bt *cr* 1841; consultant to McLellan and Partners, Consulting Engineers; *b* 8 Feb. 1909; *s* of Sir Felix Clay, 5th Bt, and Rachel, *er d* of Rt Hon. Henry Hobhouse; *S* father, 1941; *m* 1933, Phyllis Mary, *yr d* of late R. H. Paramore, MD, FRCS; one *s* two *d. Educ:* Gresham's Sch.; Trinity Coll., Cambridge. *Heir: s* Richard Henry Clay [*b* 2 June 1940; *m* 1963, Alison Mary, *o d* of Dr J. Gordon Fife; three *s* two *d*]. *Address:* 18 Kensington Park Gardens, W11 3HT. *Club:* United Oxford & Cambridge University.

CLAY, John Lionel, TD 1961; **His Honour Judge Clay;** a Circuit Judge, since 1977; *b* 31 Jan. 1918; *s* of Lionel Pilleau Clay and Mary Winifred Muriel Clay; *m* 1952, Elizabeth, *d* of Rev. Maurice and Lady Phyllis Ponsonby; one *s* three *d. Educ:* Harrow Sch.; Corpus Christi Coll., Oxford (MA). Served War of 1939-45 (despatches): in 1st Bn Rifle Bde, N Africa (8th Army), Italy, 1941-44; Instr, Infantry Heavy Weapons Sch., 1944-45; 1st Bn Rifle Bde, Germany, 1945-46. London Rifle Bde Rangers (TA); Major, 2nd i/c Bn and 23 SAS (TA), 1948-60. Called to the Bar, Middle Temple, 1947; a Recorder of the Crown Court,

1975-76. Chm., Horserace Betting Levy Appeal Tribunal for England and Wales, 1974-77. *Recreations:* gardening, fishing, shooting. *Address:* Newtimber Place, Hassocks, Sussex BN6 9BU. *T:* Hurstpierpoint 833104.

CLAY, John Martin; Deputy Chairman, Hambros Bank Ltd, since 1972 (Director, since 1961); Director, Bank of England, since 1973; *b* 20 Aug. 1927; *s* of late Sir Henry Clay and Gladys Priestman Clay; *m* 1952, Susan Jennifer, *d* of Lt-Gen. Sir Euan Miller, *qv*; four *s. Educ:* Eton; Magdalen Coll., Oxford. Mem., Commonwealth Develt Corp., 1970-. FBIM 1971. *Recreation:* sailing. *Address:* Farningham House, Farningham, Dartford, Kent. *T:* Farningham 862266. *Club:* Royal Thames Yacht.

CLAY, Gen. Lucius DuBignon; US Army (retd); Senior Partner, Lehman Brothers, 1963-73; Director, Chase International Investment Corp., 1963-72; Chairman, Continental Can Company, 1950-62; *b* 23 April 1897; *s* of Alexander Stephen and Francis White Clay; *m* 1918, Marjorie McKeown; two *s. Educ:* USMA, West Point, New York. Instructor, Officers' Training Camp, 1918-19; Engr Sch. of Application, 1919-20; Asst Prof. Mil. Science and Tactics, Alabama Poly. Inst., 1920-21; Constr Quartermaster and Post Engr Ft Belvoir, Va, 1921-24; Instr Dept Civil Engr, USMA, 1924-27; 11th Engrs Canal Zone, Field Mapping, 1927-30; Asst to Dist Engr Pittsburgh, in charge Construction Lock and Dam No. 2, Allegheny River, 1930-33; Asst to Chief of Engrs in River and Harbor Sec., 1933-37; Consultant on Devel. of Water Resources to Nat. Power Corp., Philippine Commonwealth, 1937-38; in charge constr. of Denison Dam, 1938-40; Asst to Administrator Civil Aeronautics Admin. on Airport Program, 1940-41; Dir of Matériel, ASF, 1942-44; commanded Normandy Base, 1944; Dep. Dir War Mobilization and Reconversion, 1945; Dep. Mil. Gov. of Germany, 1945-47; C-in-C, European Comd, and Military Governor of US Zone of Germany, 1947-49; retired, 1949. Personal Representative of the President, with rank of Ambassador, in Berlin, Aug. 1961-May 1962. Numerous hon. degrees, civic hons, medals, foreign decorations. Trustee: Presbyterian Hosp. of NY. *Publication:* Decision in Germany, 1950. *Recreations:* fishing, golf. *Address:* 633 Third Avenue, New York, NY 10017, USA. *Clubs:* Army and Navy (Washington DC); University, Links, Pinnacle, Blind Brook (all NY); Bohemian (San Francisco).

CLAYDEN, Rt. Hon. Sir (Henry) John, PC 1963; Kt 1958; *b* 26 April 1904; *s* of Harold William and Florence Hilda Clayden; *m* 1948, Gwendoline Edith Lawrance. *Educ:* Diocesan Coll., Capetown; Charterhouse; Brasenose Coll., Oxford. Called to Bar, Inner Temple, 1926; Advocate, South Africa, 1927; practised Johannesburg. Served War with S African Engineer Corps and SA Staff Corps, 1940-45. Apptd KC 1945; Judge, Supreme Court of South Africa, Transvaal Provincial Div., 1946-55, 1964-65. Judge of Federal Supreme Court, 1955; Chief Justice, Federation of Rhodesia and Nyasaland, Dec. 1960-April 1964. Chm., Industrial Tribunals, 1967-77. Chm. Southern Rhodesia Capital Commission, 1955; Federal Delimitation Commission, 1958; Hammarskjöld Accident Commission, 1962. Acting Gov.-Gen., Federation of Rhodesia and Nyasaland, May-June 1961. Hon. LLD Witwatersrand. *Address:* 8 Walton Street, SW3. *T:* 01-589 1300. *Clubs:* Athenæum; Rand Salisbury (Rhodesia).

CLAYSON, Christopher William, CBE 1974 (OBE 1966); Chairman, Scottish Council for Postgraduate Medical Education, 1970-74, retired; *b* 11 Sept. 1903; *s* of Christopher Clayson and Agnes Lilias Montgomerie Hunter; *m* Elsie Webster Breingan. *Educ:* George Heriot's Sch.; Edinburgh University. MB, ChB 1926; DPH 1929; MD (Gold Medal) Edinburgh 1936; FRCPE 1951; FRCP 1967. Physician: Southfield Hosp., Edinburgh, 1931-44; Edinburgh City Hosp., 1939-44; Lectr in Tuberculosis Dept, Univ. of Edinburgh, 1939-44; Med. Supt, Lochmaben Hosp., 1944-48; Consultant Phys. in Chest Medicine, Dumfries and Galloway, 1948-68; retd from clinical practice, 1968. Served on numerous Govt and Nat. Health Service cttees, 1948-; Chm., Scottish Licensing Law Cttee, 1971-73. Pres., RCPE, 1966-70; Mem., Scottish Soc. of Physicians; Mem., Thoracic Soc.; Hon. FACP 1968; Hon. FRACP 1969; Hon. FRCPGlas 1970; Hon. FRCGP 1971. *Publications:* various papers on tuberculosis problem in leading medical jls. *Recreations:* gardening, fishing. *Address:* Cockiesknowe, Lochmaben, Lockerbie, Dumfriesshire. *T:* Lochmaben 231. *Clubs:* Caledonian; New (Edinburgh).

CLAYSON, Sir Eric (Maurice), Kt 1964; DL; Director: BPM Holdings Ltd; ATV Network Ltd, since 1966; Birmingham Regional Board, Lloyds Bank Ltd; Chairman, Birmingham Area Board, Sun Alliance & London Insurance Group Ltd; *b* 17 Feb. 1908; *yr s* of late Harry and Emily Clayson; *m* 1933,

Pauline Audrey Wright; two *s. Educ:* Woodbridge Sch. Chartered Accountant, 1931; Birmingham Post & Mail Group Ltd: Dir, 1944-74; Man. Dir, 1947; Jt Man. Dir, 1957; Chm., 1957-74; Director: Associated TV Ltd, 1964-75; Sun Alliance & London Insurance Group, 1965-75. President: Birmingham Publicity Assoc., 1948-49 (Chm., 1947-48); W Midlands Newspaper Soc., 1949-50; The Newspaper Soc., 1951-52 (Hon. Treasurer, 1956-60); Birmingham Branch, Incorporated Sales Managers' Assoc., 1953-54; Birmingham and Midland Inst., 1967-68. Vice-Pres., Fédération Internationale des Editeurs de Journaux et Publications, 1954-67. Chairman: Exec. Cttee, British Industries Fair, 1956-57; Midlands Regular Forces Resettlement Cttee, 1961-70 (Mem., 1958-70). Director: The Press Assoc. Ltd, 1959-66 (Chm., 1963-64); Reuters Ltd, 1961-66. Member: Council, Birmingham Chamber of Commerce, 1951- (Vice-Pres., 1953-54, Pres., 1955-56); Gen. Council of the Press, 1953-72; BBC Midland Regional Adv. Council, 1954-57; W Midland Regional Economic Planning Council, 1965-68. Governor, The Royal Shakespeare Theatre, Stratford-upon-Avon, 1963- (Mem. Exec. Council, 1963-74); Life Governor, Birmingham Univ., 1956-, Mem. Council, 1959-71; Mem. Convocation, Univ. of Aston in Birmingham, 1967-. President: Radio Industries Club of the Midlands, 1965-69; Midland Counties Golf Assoc., 1960-62; Vice-Pres., Professional Golfers' Assoc., 1959-. Guardian, Standard of Wrought Plate in Birmingham, 1969-. DL West Midlands, 1975. *Recreation:* reading newspapers. *Address:* The Poor's Piece, Linthurst Road, Barnt Green, Birmingham B45 8JJ. *T:* 021-445 1209.

CLAYTON, Sir Arthur Harold, 11th Bt of Marden, *cr* 1732; DSC 1945; Lt-Comdr RNR; *b* 14 Oct. 1903; *s* of Sir Harold Clayton, 10th Bt, and Leila Cecilia (*d* 1976), *d* of Francis Edmund Clayton; *S* father, 1951; *m* 1st, 1927, Muriel Edith (*d* 1929), *d* of late Arthur John Clayton; 2nd, 1931, Alexandra Andreevsky (marr. diss. 1954); one *s* one *d*; 3rd, 1954, Dorothy (Jill) (*d* 1964), *d* of Arthur John Greenhalgh; 4th, 1965, Diana Bircham, *d* of late Charles Alvery Grazebrook. *Educ:* Haileybury Coll. In business in London, 1923-41, 1946-50. Served War of 1939-45, RNVR, 1941-46 (despatches, DSC). *Recreations:* short and long distance sailing. *Heir: s* David Robert Clayton [*b* 12 Dec. 1936; *m* 1911, Julia Louise, *d* of late C. H. Redfearn; one *s*]. *Address:* Colonsay Kingswear, Dartmouth, Devon. *T:* Kingswear 243. *Clubs:* Royal Naval Sailing Association Portsmouth; Royal Yachting Association; Brixham Yacht (Brixham); Royal Dart Yacht (Kingswear); Shore Line (Lifeboat).

CLAYTON, Prof. Frederick William; Professor of Classics, 1948-75, and Public Orator, 1965-73, University of Exeter; *b* 13 Dec. 1913; *s* of late William and Gertrude Clayton, Liverpool; *m* 1948, Friederike Luise Büttner-Wobst; two *s* two *d. Educ:* Liverpool Collegiate Sch.; King's Coll., Cambridge. Members' Essay Prizes (Latin and English), Porson Prize, Browne Medal, 1933; Craven Scholar in Classics, 1934; Chancellor's Medal for Classics, 1935; Fellow of King's Coll., 1937. Served War of 1939-45: Intelligence Corps, 1940-42; RAF, India, 1942-45. *Publications:* The Cloven Pine, 1942; various articles. *Address:* Halwill, Clydesdale Road, Exeter, Devon. *T:* Exeter 71810.
See also G. Clayton.

CLAYTON, Air Marshal Sir Gareth (Thomas Butler), KCB 1970 (CB 1962); DFC 1940, and Bar, 1944; Air Secretary, Ministry of Defence, 1970-72, retired; *b* 13 Nov. 1914; *s* of Thomas and Katherine Clayton; *m* 1938, Elisabeth Marian Keates; three *d. Educ:* Rossall Sch. Entered RAF, 1936; served in various Bomber and Fighter Squadrons, 1936-44; RAF Staff Coll., 1944; Air Attaché, Lisbon, 1946-48; various command and staff appts, 1948-58; idc 1959; Air Ministry, 1960-61; Air Officer Commanding No. 11 Group, RAF, 1962-63; Chief of Staff, Second Allied Tactical Air Force, Germany, 1963-66 Dir-Gen., RAF Personal Services, 1966-69; Chief of Staff, HQ RAF Strike Command, 1969-70. A Vice-Pres., RAFA (Vice-Chm., 1974-). *Recreation:* fishing. *Address:* c/o Lloyds Bank Ltd, 263 Tottenham Court Road, W1. *Clubs:* Royal Air Force, Pathfinder.

CLAYTON, Prof. George; Newton Chambers Professor of Applied Economics, University of Sheffield, since 1967; *b* 15 July 1922; *s* of late William Clayton and Gertrude Alison Clarke Clayton; *m* 1948, Rhiannon Jones, JP; two *s* two *d. Educ:* Liverpool Collegiate Sch.; King's Coll., Cambridge. Univ. of Liverpool: Asst Lectr, 1947-50; Lectr, 1950-57; Sen. Lectr, 1957-60 and 1961-63; Sen. Simon Res. Fellow, Univ. of Manchester, 1960-61; Prof. and Head of Dept of Econs, UCW Aberystwyth, 1963-67. Member: Council, Royal Econ. Soc., 1965-68; (part-time) East Midland Gas Bd, 1967-70; Crowther Cttee on Consumer Credit, 1968-70; Scott Cttee on Property Bonds and Equity-linked Insce, 1970-72. Chm., British, Canadian and Amer. Mission to British Honduras, 1966; Econ. Adviser: Govt

of Tanzania, 1965-66; Govt of Gibraltar, 1973-. Chm., Assoc. of Univ. Teachers of Economics. *Publications:* (contrib.) A New Prospect of Economics, ed G. L. S. Shackle, 1956; (contrib.) Banking in Western Europe, ed R. S. Sayers, 1959; Insurance Company Investment, 1965; Problems of Rail Transport in Rural Wales: Two Case Studies, 1967; Monetary Theory and Monetary Policy in the 1970s, 1971; British Insurance, 1971; articles in Econ. Jl, etc. *Recreations:* tennis, sailing, theatre, fell walking. *Address:* 58 Endcliffe Vale Road, Sheffield S10 3EW. *T:* Sheffield 664836. *Club:* Hawks (Cambridge).
See also Prof. F. W. Clayton.

CLAYTON, Jack; film director; *b* 1921; *m* Christine Norden (marr. diss.); *m* Katherine Kath (marr. diss.). Entered film industry, 1935. Served War of 1939-45, RAF Film Unit. Production Manager: An Ideal Husband; Associate Producer: Queen of Spades; Flesh and Blood; Moulin Rouge; Beat the Devil; The Good Die Young; I am a Camera; Producer and Director: The Bespoke Overcoat, 1955; The Innocents, 1961; Our Mother's House, 1967; Director: Room at the Top, 1958; The Pumpkin Eater, 1964; The Great Gatsby, 1974. *Address:* c/o Romulus Films Ltd, Brook House, Park Lane, W1.

CLAYTON, John Pilkington, MVO 1975; MA, MB, BChir; Apothecary to HM Household at Windsor since 1965; Surgeon Apothecary to HM Queen Elizabeth the Queen Mother's Household at the Royal Lodge, Windsor, since 1965; Senior Medical Officer: Eton College since 1965 (MO, 1962-65); Royal Holloway College since 1962 (MO, 1953-62); Divisional Surgeon, St John's Ambulance Brigade, since 1955; *b* 13 Feb. 1921; *s* of late Brig.-Gen. Sir Gilbert Clayton, KCMG, KBE, CB, and Enid, *d* of late F. N. Thorowgood. *Educ:* Wellington Coll.; Gonville and Caius Coll., Cambridge; King's Coll. Hospital. RAFVR, 1947-49; Sqdn Ldr 1949. Senior Resident, Nottingham Children's Hosp., 1950. MO, Black and Decker Ltd, 1955-70. *Address:* Town End House, Eton College, Windsor. *T:* Windsor 62257.

CLAYTON, Prof. Keith Martin; Professor of Environmental Sciences, University of East Anglia, since 1967; *b* 25 Sept. 1928; *s* of Edgar Francis Clayton and Constance Annie (*née* Clark); *m* 1st, 1950 (marr. diss. 1976); three *s* one *d*; 2nd, 1976. *Educ:* Bedales Sch.; Univ. of Sheffield (MSc). PhD London. Demonstrator, Univ. of Nottingham, 1949-51. Served RE, 1951-53. Lectr, London Sch. of Economics, 1953-63; Reader in Geography, LSE, 1963-67; Univ. of E Anglia: Founding Dean, Sch. of Environmental Scis, 1967-71; Pro-Vice-Chancellor, 1971-73; Dir, Centre of E Anglian Studies, 1974-; Vis. Professor, State Univ. of New York at Binghamton, 1960-62. Member: Natural Environment Res. Council, 1970-73; UGC, 1973-. *Publications:* Editor and publisher, Geo Abstracts, 1960-. *Recreations:* gardening, sailing. *Address:* 100 Pottergate, Norwich, Norfolk NR2 1EQ. *T:* Norwich 23394.

CLAYTON, Lucie; see Kark, Evelyn F.

CLAYTON, Michael Thomas Emilius, CB 1976; OBE 1958; *b* 15 Sept. 1917; *s* of Lt-Col Emilius Clayton, OBE, RA and Irene Dorothy Constance (*née* Strong); *m* 1942, Mary Margery Pate; one *d*. *Educ:* Bradfield College, Berks. Attached War Office, 1939 and Ministry of Defence, 1964-76. *Recreations:* philately, country pursuits generally. *Address:* Hillside Cottage, Marshwood, Bridport, Dorset. *T:* Hawkchurch 452.

CLAYTON, Richard Henry Michael, (William Haggard); writer; *b* 11 Aug. 1907; *o s* of late Rev. Henry James Clayton and late Mabel Sarah Clayton (*née* Haggard); *m* 1936, Barbara, *e d* of late Edward Sant, Downton, Wilts; one *s* one *d*. *Educ:* Lancing; Christ Church, Oxford. Indian Civil Service, 1931-39; Indian Army, 1939-46 (GSO1 1943); BoT, 1947-69 (Controller of Enemy Property, 1965-69). *Publications:* Slow Burner, The Telemann Touch, 1958; Venetian Blind, 1959; Closed Circuit, 1960; The Arena, 1961; The Unquiet Sleep, 1962; The High Wire, 1963; The Antagonists, 1964; The Hard Sell, The Powder Barrel, 1965; The Power House, 1966; The Conspirators, The Haggard Omnibus, 1967; A Cool Day For Killing, 1968; The Doubtful Disciple, Haggard For Your Holiday, 1969; The Hardliners, 1970; The Bitter Harvest, 1971; The Protectors, 1972; The Little Rug Book (non-fiction), 1972; The Old Masters, 1973; The Kinsmen, 1974; The Scorpion's Tail, 1975; Yesterday's Enemy, 1976; The Poison People, 1977. *Recreations:* golf, gardening. *Address:* Yew Tree Cottage, Farnborough Street, Farnborough, Hants. *Club:* Travellers'.

CLAYTON, Vice-Adm. Richard Pilkington; Controller of the Navy, since 1976; *b* July 1925; *s* of Rear-Adm. John Wittewronge Clayton and Florence Caroline Schuster. *Educ:* Horris Hill, Newbury; RNC Dartmouth. Midshipman, HMS Cumberland, 1942-43; various destroyers, 1944; Home Fleet destroyers, 1944-46; HMS Comus, Far East, 1946-49; Trng Sqdn destroyers, 1949-53; HMS Striker, Suez, 1956; psc 1957; comd HMS Puma, 1958-59; Admty, 1959-61; HMS Lion, 1962-64; MoD, 1964-66; Captain of Dockyard, Gibraltar, 1967-68; comd HMS Kent and HMS Hampshire, 1968-69; MoD, 1970-72; Flag Officer Second Flotilla, 1973-74; Sen. Naval Mem., Directing Staff, RCDS, 1975. Lt-Comdr 1953; Comdr 1958; Captain 1964; Rear-Adm. 1973. *Recreation:* winter sports. *Address:* Château de Roaix, 84 Roaix, France. *Clubs:* Ski Club of Great Britain; Royal Naval and Royal Albert Yacht (Portsmouth).

CLAYTON, Robert James, CBE 1970 (OBE 1960); CEng, FIEE, FInstP, FRAeS, FIERE, FIEEE; Technical Director, The General Electric Co. Ltd, since 1968; Director of a number of GEC operating companies; member of a number of government and industry committees on electronics, particularly research; *b* 30 Oct. 1915; *m* 1949, Joy Kathleen King; no *c*. *Educ:* Cambridge Univ. (MA). GEC Research Labs, 1937; Manager, GEC Applied Electronics Labs, 1955; Dep. Dir, Hirst Research Centre, 1960; Man. Dir, GEC (Electronics), 1963; Man. Dir, GEC (Research), 1966. Mem. Council, 1964-68, Chm. of Electronics Div., 1968-69, Vice-Pres., 1970-73, Dep. Pres., 1974-75, Pres., 1975-76, IEE. Vis. Prof., Electrical Engrg Dept, Imperial Coll. of Science and Technology. *Publications:* papers in Proc. IEE. *Recreations:* theatre, music. *Address:* Drumness, Church Road, Stanmore, Mddx. *T:* 01-954 0329. *Club:* United Oxford & Cambridge University.

CLAYTON, Prof. Sir Stanley (George), Kt 1974; MD, MS London; FRCP; FRCS; FRCOG; FKC 1976; Professor of Obstetrics and Gynæcology, King's College Hospital Medical School, 1967-76, now Emeritus; Hon. Consulting Surgeon: King's College Hospital; Queen Charlotte's Hospital; Chelsea Hospital for Women; *b* 13 Sept. 1911; *s* of Rev. George and Florence Clayton; *m* 1936, Kathleen Mary Willshire; one *s* one *d*. *Educ:* Kingswood Sch.; King's Coll. Hosp. Med. Sch. Qualified, 1934; FRCS 1936; Sambrooke Schol., Jelf Medal, Hallett Prize. Surg. EMS; Major RAMC. Obstetric Surg., Queen Charlotte's Hosp., 1946; Surg., Chelsea Hosp. for Women, 1953; Obstetric and Gynæcological Surg., King's Coll. Hosp., 1947-63; Prof. of Obst. and Gyn., Postgrad. Inst. of Univ. of London, 1963-67. Vice-Pres., RCOG, 1971, Pres., 1972-75; Mem. Council, RCS, 1975 (Chm., Adv. Cttee on Distinction Awards, 1976). Pres., Nat. Assoc. of Family Planning Doctors, 1974-76; Vice-Pres., FPA, 1976. Examiner, Univs of London, Oxford, Cambridge, Birmingham, Dublin, Wales and RCOG. Editor, Jl of Obstetrics and Gynaecology, 1963-75. Hon. Fellow, Amer. Assoc. of Obstetrics and Gynaecology, 1975; Hon. FCOG (SA); Hon. Fellow, S Atlantic Assoc. of Obst. and Gyn., 1973; For. Mem., Belgian Soc. of Obst. and Gyn., 1965; Beecham Lectr, Inst. of Obst. and Gyn., 1973. *Publications:* Pocket Gynaecology, 1948, 8th edn 1976; Pocket Obstetrics, 8th edn 1976; jointly: Queen Charlotte's Text-Book, 11th edn 1965; Ten Teachers' Obstetrics, 12th edn 1972; Ten Teachers' Gynaecology, 12th edn 1971; British Obstetric and Gynæcological Practice, 3rd edn 1964; contrib. Encyclopædia Britannica, 1974; articles in med. jls. *Address:* Fir Tree Lodge, Fir Tree Road, Leatherhead, Surrey.

CLAYTON, Stanley James; Town Clerk of the City of London since 1974; *b* 10 Dec. 1919; *s* of late James John Clayton and late Florence Clayton; *m* 1955, Jean Winifred, *d* of Frederick Etheridge; one *s* one *d*. *Educ:* Ensham Sch.; King's Coll., London (LLB). Served War of 1939-45, commnd RAF. Admitted Solicitor 1958. City of Westminster, 1938-52; Camberwell, 1952-60; Asst Solicitor, Holborn, 1960-63; Deputy Town Clerk: Greenwich, 1963-65; Islington, 1964-69; City of London, 1969-74. Comdr, Order of Dannebrog (Denmark); holds other foreign orders. *Address:* Redriff, 215 East Dulwich Grove, SE22 8SY. *T:* 01-693 1019.

CLEALL, Ven. Aubrey Victor George; Archdeacon of Colchester, 1959-69, now Archdeacon Emeritus; *b* 9 Dec. 1898; *s* of late George and Cecilia Cleall, Crewkerne, Somerset. *Educ:* Selwyn Coll., Cambridge; Wells Theological Coll. BA 1922, MA 1926, Cambridge; MA (*ad eund.*) 1947, TCD. Deacon, 1924; Priest, 1925; Curate of Crewkerne, 1924-28; Vicar of Waltham Abbey, 1929-59. Diocesan Inspector of Schools (Chelmsford Dio.), 1932-46. Saint Antholin's Lecturer (City of London), 1937-57. Officiating CF, 1940-46; Comd 6th Cadet Bn, The Essex Regt (Actg Major TARO), 1942-44. Rural Dean of Chigwell, 1946-59; Hon. Canon of Chelmsford Cathedral, 1949-59; Rector of Wickham St Paul with Twinstead, 1959-63. Member: Convocation of Canterbury and Church Assembly, 1965-69; Essex County Education Cttee, 1951-59 and 1961-67. Governor, Colchester Royal Grammar Sch., 1963-67. *Address:* 189 Seaside, Eastbourne, E Sussex BN22 7NP. *T:* Eastbourne 639816.

CLEALL, Charles; HM Inspector of Schools, since 1972; b 1 June 1927; s of Sydney Cleal and Dorothy Bound; m 1953, Mary, yr d of G. L. Turner, Archery Lodge, Ashford, Mddx; two d . Educ: Hampton Sch.; Univ. of London (BMus); Univ of Wales (MA); Jordanhill Coll. of Educn, Glasgow. ADCM, GTCL, FRCO(CHM), LRAM, HonTSC. Command Music Adviser, RN, 1946-48; Prof., TCL, 1949-52; Conductor, Morley Coll. Orch., 1949-51; Organist and Choirmaster, Wesley's Chapel, City Road, EC4, 1950-52; Conductor, Glasgow Choral Union, 1952-54; BBC Music Asst, Midland Region, 1954-55; Music Master, Glyn County Sch., Ewell, 1955-66; Conductor, Aldeburgh Festival Choir, 1957-60; Organist and Choirmaster: St Paul's, Portman Sq., W1, 1957-61; Holy Trinity, Guildford, 1961-65; Lectr in Music, Froebel Inst., 1967-68; Adviser in Music, London Borough of Harrow, 1968-72; Warden, Music in Education Section, ISM, 1971-72. Internat. Composition Prizeman of Cathedral of St John the Divine, NY; Limpus Fellowship Prizeman of RCO. Publications: Voice Production in Choral Technique, 1955 (2nd edn, 1970); The Selection and Training of Mixed Choirs in Churches, 1960; Music and Holiness, 1964; Plainsong for Pleasure, 1969. Recreations: learning anything; correspondence; etymology; indexing; post codes; thought. Address: 29 Colthill Circle, Milltimber, Aberdeen AB1 0EH.

CLEARY, Denis Mackrow, CMG 1967; HM Diplomatic Service, retired; b 20 Dec. 1907; s of late Francis Esmonde Cleary and late Emmeline Marie Cleary (née Mackrow); m 1st, 1941, Barbara Wykeham-George (d 1960); 2nd, 1962, Mary Kent (née Dunlop), widow of Harold Kent; one step-d. Educ: St Ignatius Coll. and St Olave's Sch.; St John's Coll., Cambridge (Major Schol.). 1st Class Hons Pts I and II, Math. Tripos; BA 1930; MA 1934. Asst Principal, India Office, 1931; Principal, 1937; seconded to Min. of Home Security, 1940-44; Dep. Principal Officer to Regional Commissioner, Cambridge, March 1943-Sept. 1944; seconded to Foreign Office (German Section) as Asst Sec., 1946-49; transferred to CRO and posted to Delhi as Counsellor, 1949-51; Dep. High Commissioner, Wellington, 1955-58; Mem. of British Delegn to Law of the Sea Conf., Geneva, 1960; Dep. High Comr, Nicosia, 1962-64; Head of Atlantic Dept, Commonwealth Office, 1964-68 (Mem., Cttee for Exports to the Caribbean, 1965-67); retd 1968; re-employed in Internat. Div., DHSS, 1968-72; UK Delegate to Public Health Cttees, Council of Europe, 1968-72; Chm., Council of Europe Med. Fellowships Selection Cttee, 1972-74. Recreations: gardening, walking. Address: High Gate, Burwash, East Sussex TN19 7LA. T: Burwash 882712.

CLEARY, Jon Stephen; novelist, screen writer; b 22 Nov. 1917; s of Matthew Cleary and Ida (née Brown); m 1946, Constantine Lucas; two d. Educ: Marist Brothers' Sch., Randwick, NSW. Variety of jobs, 1932-40; served with AIF, 1940-45; freelance writer, 1945-48; journalist with Australian News and Information Bureau: London, 1948-49; New York, 1949-51; subseq. full-time writer. Publications: These Small Glories (short stories), 1946; You Can't See Round Corners, 1947; The Long Shadow, 1949; Just Let Me Be, 1950; The Sundowners, 1952; The Climate of Courage, 1953; Justin Bayard, 1955; The Green Helmet, 1957; Back of Sunset, 1959; North from Thursday, 1960; The Country of Marriage, 1962; Forest of the Night, 1963; A Flight of Chariots, 1964; The Fall of an Eagle, 1964; The Pulse of Danger, 1966; The High Commissioner, 1967; The Long Pursuit, 1967; Season of Doubt, 1968; Remember Jack Hoxie, 1969; Helga's Web, 1970; Mask of the Andes, 1971; Man's Estate, 1972; Ransom, 1973; Peter's Pence, 1974; The Safe House, 1975; A Sound of Lightning, 1976; High Road to China, 1977; Vortex, 1977. Recreations: cricket, squash rackets, reading. Address: c/o Wm Collins Sons & Co. Ltd, 14 St James's Place, SW1.

CLEARY, Rt. Rev. Joseph Francis; Auxiliary Bishop of Birmingham, (RC), and Titular Bishop of Cresima, since 1965; b 4 Sept. 1912; s of William Cleary and Ellen (née Rogers). Educ: Dublin; Oscott Coll., Sutton Coldfield. Ordained Priest 1939. Asst, St Chad's Cathedral, 1939-41; Archbishop's Sec., 1941-51; Parish Priest, SS Mary and John's, Wolverhampton, 1951-; Diocesan Treasurer, 1963-65; Provost of Diocesan Chapter, 1966-. Address: Presbytery, Snow Hill, Wolverhampton WV2 4AD. T: Wolverhampton 21676.

CLEARY, Sir Joseph Jackson, Kt 1965; b 26 Oct. 1902; s of Joseph Cleary, JP; m 1945, Ethel McColl. Educ: Holy Trinity C of E Sch., Anfield, Liverpool; Skerry's Coll., Liverpool. Alderman, 1941, JP, 1927 for Liverpool; Lord Mayor of Liverpool, 1949-50. Contested East Toxteth Div., Liverpool, March 1929 and May 1929; West Derby, Oct. 1931; MP (Lab) Wavertree Div. of Liverpool, Feb.-Oct. 1935. Lecture tour to Forces in Middle East, 1945. Freeman, City of Liverpool, 1970.

Recreations: football (Association), tennis. Address: 115 Riverview Heights, Liverpool L19 0LQ. T: 051-427 2133.

CLEASBY, Ven. Thomas Wood Ingram; Archdeacon of Chesterfield, since 1963; Rector of Morton, Derby, since 1970; b 27 March 1920; s of T. W. Cleasby, Oakdene, Sedbergh, Yorks, and Jessie Brown Cleasby; m 1st, 1956, Olga Elizabeth Vibert Douglas (d 1967); one s one d (and one d decd); 2nd, 1970, Monica, e d of Rt Rev. O. S. Tomkins, qv; one d. Educ: Sedbergh Sch., Yorks; Magdalen Coll., Oxford; Cuddesdon Coll., Oxford. BA, MA (Hons Mod. History) 1947. Commissioned, 1st Bn Border Regt, 1940; served 1st Airborne Div., 1941-45, Actg Major. Ordained, Dio. Wakefield, 1949 (Huddersfield Parish Church). Domestic Chaplain to Archbishop of York, 1952-56; Anglican Chaplain to Univ. of Nottingham, 1956-63; Vicar of St Mary and All Saints, Chesterfield, 1963-70. Recreations: fell-walking, bird-watching, gardening, fishing. Address: Morton Rectory, Derby DE5 6GU. T: Tibshelf 2402.

CLEAVER, Leonard Harry, FCA; JP; Director: A. W. Phillips Ltd; Outersport Ltd; b 27 Oct. 1909; s of late Harry Cleaver, OBE, JP; m 1938, Mary Richards Matthews; one s. Educ: Bilton Grange and Rugby. Chartered Accountant: articled Agar, Bates, Neal & Co., Birmingham; Sec. and Chief Accountant, Chance Bros Ltd, 1935-51; Partner, Heathcote & Coleman, 1951-59. MP (C) Yardley Div. of Birmingham, 1959-64; PPS to Parly Sec. to Min. of Housing and Local Govt, 1963-64; contested Yardley Div. of Birmingham, 1964, 1966. Member: Smethwick Nat. Savings Cttee, 1939-45; Birmingham Probation Cttee, 1955-73; Central Council, Probation and After-Care Cttees for England and Wales, 1966-73; Governor, Yardley Educnl Foundn, 1968-73. JP Birmingham, 1954. City Councillor, Yardley Ward, 1966-70. Recreations: Rugby football and fishing. Address: The Long House, Calf Lane, Chipping Campden, Glos GL55 6JQ. T: Evesham 840870.

CLEAVER, Air Vice-Marshal Peter (Charles), CB 1971; OBE 1945; Secretary, Cranfield Institute of Technology, since 1973; b 6 July 1919; s of William Henry Cleaver, Warwick; m 1948, Jean, d of J. E. B. Fairclough, Ledbury; two s. Educ: Warwick Sch.; Coll. of Aeronautics (MSc). Staff Coll., Haifa, 1945; HM Asst Air Attaché, Bucharest, 1947-49; Coll. of Aeronautics, Cranfield, 1950-52; Structural Research, RAE Farnborough, 1952-55; Min. of Supply, 1955-57; HQ FEAF, 1957-60; Maintenance Comd, 1960-63; OC, Central Servicing Develt Estabt, 1963-64; Air Officer Engineering, HQ Flying Trg Comd, 1964-65; idc 1966; Air Officer Engineering: HQ FEAF, 1967-69; Air Support Command, 1969-72; retired 1972. CEng, FRAeS. Recreations: shooting, gardening. Address: Willow House, Watling Street, Little Brickhill, Milton Keynes MK17 9LS. Club: Royal Air Force.

CLEE, Sir Charles (Beaupré Bell), Kt 1947; CSI 1946; CIE 1938; b 5 Feb. 1893; s of J. B. B. Clee; m 1931, Rosemary Margaret Meredydd, d of late H. P. M. Rae; one s. Educ: Cambridge Univ. Nominated to Indian Civil Service, 1919, after serving with Suffolk Regt during European War; arrived India, 1919; Asst Collector and Magistrate, Bombay; Acting Dir of Information, 1924; Sec., Indian Tariff Board, 1925; Dep. Sec. to Govt Finance Dept, Bombay, 1928; Officiating Sec. to Govt, Home and Ecclesiastical Dept, Bombay, 1932; Officiating Sec. to Govt Finance Dept, 1933; Collector and Magistrate, 1935; Officiating Sec. to Govt Finance Dept, Bombay, 1936; Sec. to Govt Finance Dept, Sind, 1936; Officiating Chief Sec., 1938; Fin. Sec., 1939; Chief Sec. to Govt of Sind, 1940; Revenue Comr for Sind, 1943; retired, 1950. Recreations: shooting, cricket, golf. Address: c/o Lloyds Bank Ltd, Cox's & King's Branch, 6 Pall Mall, SW1.

CLEESE, John Marwood; writer and actor; b 27 Oct. 1939; s of Reginald and Muriel Cleese; m 1968, Connie Booth; one d . Educ: Clifton Sports Acad.; Downing College, Cambridge (MA). Started making jokes professionally, 1963; started on British television, 1966; series have included: The Frost Report, 1966-67; At Last the 1948 Show, 1967; Monty Python's Flying Circus, 1969-; Fawlty Towers, 1975-. Hon. LLD St Andrews, 1971. Recreations: gluttony, sloth. Address: c/o David Wilkinson, 8 Waterloo Place, SW1.

CLEGG, Sir Alec, (Alexander Bradshaw Clegg), Kt 1965; Chief Education Officer, West Riding County Council, 1945-74, retired; b 13 June 1909; s of Samuel and Mary Clegg, Sawley, Derbs; m 1940, Jessie Coverdale Phillips, West Hartlepool; three s. Educ: Long Eaton Gram. Sch.; Bootham Sch., York; Clare Coll., Cambridge (BA); London Day Training Coll.; King's Coll., London (MA), FKC 1972. Asst Master, St Clement Danes Gram. Sch., London, 1932-36; Admin. Asst Birmingham Educn Cttee, 1936-39; Asst Educn Officer, Ches CC, 1939-42; Dep.

Educn Officer, Worcs CC, 1942-45; West Riding, Jan.-Sept. 1945. Chm. of Governors, Centre for Information and Advice on Educational Disadvantage, 1976-. Hon LLD Leeds, 1972; Hon DLitt Loughborough, 1972. Chevalier de l'ordre de L'Etoile Noire, 1961. *Publications:* The Excitement of Writing, 1964, USA 1972; (with B. Megson) Children in Distress, 1968; (ed) The Changing Primary School, 1972. *Address:* Saxton, Tadcaster, N Yorks. *T:* Barkston Ash 288.

CLEGG, Sir Alexander Bradshaw; *see* Clegg, Sir Alec.

CLEGG, Brian George Herbert; Chairman, Northern Region of British Gas Corporation, since 1975; *b* 10 Dec. 1921; *s* of Frederic Bradbury Clegg and Gladys Butterworth; *m* 1st, 1949, Iris May Ludlow; one *s* one *d*; 2nd, 1976, Anne Elizabeth Robertson. *Educ:* Manchester Grammar Sch.; Trinity Coll., Cambridge (Open Math. Schol., MA). FIS, FIM, CEng, FIGasE, MBIM. Sci. Officer, Min. of Supply, 1942 (Hon. Flt-Lt); Statistician, Liverpool Gas Co., 1946; Market and Operational Res. Man., Southern Gas Bd, 1957; Commercial Man., Southern Gas Bd, 1961; Dep. Dir of Marketing, Gas Council, 1968; Dir of Marketing, British Gas Corp., 1972. *Publications:* numerous articles and papers on marketing and fuel matters. *Recreations:* swimming, ice-skating, ski-ing. *Address:* Norgas House, Killingworth, PO Box 1GB, Newcastle upon Tyne NE99 1GB. *T:* Newcastle upon Tyne 683000.

CLEGG, Sir Cuthbert (Barwick), Kt 1950; TD; JP; *b* 9 Aug. 1904; *s* of Edmund Barwick Clegg, DL, JP, Shore, Littleborough, Lancs; *m* 1930, Helen Margaret, *y d* of Arthur John Jefferson, MD; one *s*. *Educ:* Charterhouse; Trinity Coll., Oxford (MA). Pres., British Employers Confederation, 1950-52; JP Lancs, 1946, Sheriff, 1955; Sheriff of Westmorland, 1969; Major (retired), Duke of Lancaster's Own Yeomanry. Member: Cotton Industry Working Party, 1946; Cotton Manufacturing Commission, 1947-49; Anglo-American Council on Productivity, 1948-52; Economic Planning Bd, 1949-53; British Productivity Council, 1952-54; Leader, UK Cotton Industry Mission to India, Hong Kong and Pakistan, 1957. Hon. Life Governor, The Cotton, Silk and Man-Made Fibres Research Association (Pres., 1962-67); President: UK Textile Manufacturers' Assoc., 1960-69; Overseas Bankers' Club, 1966-67; Inst. of Bankers, 1968-69. Chm., Martins Bank Ltd, 1964-69; Dir, Barclays Bank Ltd, 1968-75; Dep. Chm., Barclays Bank Trust Co. Ltd, 1969-76; Vice-Chm., Halifax Building Soc., 1971-76 (Dir, 1960-76). *Address:* Willow Cottage, Arkholme, Carnforth, Lancs. *T:* Hornby 21205. *Club:* Bath.

CLEGG, Professor Edward John, MD, PhD; FIBiol; Regius Professor of Anatomy, University of Aberdeen, since 1976; *b* 29 Oct. 1925; *s* of Edward Clegg and Emily Armistead; *m* 1958, Sheila Douglas Walls; two *d* (and one *d* decd). *Educ:* High Storrs Grammar Sch., Sheffield; Univ. of Sheffield (MB, ChB Hons 1948, MD 1964). PhD Liverpool, 1957; FIBiol 1974. RAMC, 1948-50 and RAMC (TA), 1950-61; Major, RAMC (RARO). Demonstr, Asst Lectr and Lectr in Anatomy, Univ. of Liverpool, 1952-63; Lectr, Sen. Lectr and Reader in Human Biology and Anatomy, Univ. of Sheffield, 1963-77. MO, British Kangchenjunga Expedn, 1955; Sci. Mem., Chogolungma Glacier Expedn, 1959; Leader, WHO/IBP Expedn, Simien Mountains, Ethiopia, 1967. *Publications:* The Study of Man: an introduction to human biology, 1968 (2nd edn 1977); papers on anatomy, endocrinology and human biology. *Recreations:* mountaineering, fishing, sailing, music. *Address:* c/o Department of Anatomy, Marischal College, Aberdeen AB9 1AS. *T:* 0224 40241, ext. 233M. *Clubs:* Alpine; Wayfarers (Liverpool).

CLEGG, Hugh Anthony, CBE 1966; MA, MB Cantab; Hon. MD (TCD); Hon. DLit QUB; FRCP; retired; *b* 19 June 1900; *s* of Rev. John Clegg and Gertrude, *d* of John Wilson; *m* 1932, Baroness Kyra Engelhardt, *o d* of late Baron Arthur Engelhardt, Smolensk, Russia; one *s* one *d*. *Educ:* Westminster Sch. (King's Schol.); Trinity Coll., Cambridge (Westminster Exhibr, Senior Schol., in Nat. Science); St Bartholomew's Hospital. 1st Class Hons Part 1 Nat. Sci. Tripos; House Physician at St Bartholomew's Hosp.; House Physician at Brompton Hosp. for Diseases of the Chest; Medical Registrar, Charing Cross Hosp.; Sub-editor, British Medical Journal, 1931-34; Deputy Editor, 1934-46; Editor, 1947-65; Dir, Office for Internat. Relations in Med., RSM, 1967-72; Founder and Editor, Tropical Doctor, a jl of med. practice in the Tropics, 1971-72. Hon. Fellow: American Medical Assoc.; Alpha Omega Alpha Honor Med. Soc. Late Chm., UNESCO Cttee on Co-ordination of Abstracting in the Medical and Biological Sciences. Initiator and Sec., First World Conf. on Med. Educn, London, 1953, and Ed. of its Proceedings, 1954; Editor, Medicine a Lifelong Study (Proceedings of the Second World Conf. on Med. Educn, Chicago, 1959). Vice-Pres., L'Union Internationale de la Presse Médicale, and Pres. of its Third Congress, 1957; Member: Med. Panel, British Council to 1965; Council, World Medical Assoc., 1957-61 (Chm., Cttee on Medical Ethics and author of first draft of code of ethics on human experimentation, subsequently modified as Declaration of Helsinki); RCP Cttees on air pollution and health, and smoking tobacco and health, 1969-77. Gold Medal of BMA, 1966. *Publications:* What is Osteopathy? (jointly), 1937; Brush up your Health, 1938; Wartime Health and Democracy, 1941; contributed medical terms Chambers's Technical Dictionary, 1940; How to Keep Well in Wartime (Min. 'of Information), 1943; Medicine in Britain (British Council), 1944; revised Black's Medical Dictionary, 1940-44; Advisory Editor medical section of Chambers's Encyclopædia. *Recreation:* reading reviews of the books I should like to read but haven't the time to. *Address:* 42 Cloncurry Street, Fulham, SW6 6DU.

CLEGG, Prof. Hugh Armstrong; Professor of Industrial Relations, University of Warwick, since 1967; *b* 22 May 1920; *s* of late Rev. Herbert Hobson Clegg and of Mabel (*née* Duckering); *m* 1941, Mary Matilda (*née* Shaw); two *s* two *d*. *Educ:* Kingswood Sch., Bath; Magdalen Coll., Oxford. Served War, 1940-45; Official Fellow, Nuffield Coll., Oxford, 1949-66; Emeritus Fellow, 1966-. Chm., Civil Service Arbitration Tribunal, 1968-71; Dir, Industrial Relations Res. Unit, SSRC, 1970-74; Member: Royal Commn on Trade Unions and Employers' Assocs, 1965-68; Cttee of Inquiry into Port Transport Industry, 1964-65; Ct of Inquiry into Seamen's Dispute, 1966-67; Nat. Board for Prices and Incomes, 1966-67; Ct of Inquiry into Local Authorities' Manual Workers' Pay Dispute, 1970; Council, Conciliation and Arbitration Service, 1974-. *Publications:* Labour Relations in London Transport, 1950; Industrial Democracy and Nationalisation, 1951; The Future of Nationalisation (with T. E. Chester), 1953; General Union, 1954; Wage Policy in the Health Service (with T. E. Chester), 1957; The Employers' Challenge (with R. Adams), 1957; A New Approach to Industrial Democracy, 1960; Trade Union Officers (with A. J. Killick and R. Adams), 1961; General Union in a Changing Society, 1964; A History of British Trade Unions (with A. Fox and A. F. Thompson), Vol. I, 1964; The System of Industrial Relations in Great Britain, 1970; How to run an Incomes Policy and Why we made such a Mess of the Last One, 1971; Workplace and Union (with I. Boraston and M. Rimmer), 1975; Trade Unionism under Collective Bargaining, 1976. *Recreations:* walking, beer. *Address:* 48 Amherst Road, Kenilworth, Warwicks. *T:* Kenilworth 54825.

CLEGG, Walter; MP (C) North Fylde since 1966; *b* 18 April 1920; *s* of Edwin Clegg; *m* 1951, Elise Margaret Hargreaves. *Educ:* Bury Grammar Sch.; Arnold Sch., Blackpool; Manchester Univ. Law Sch. Articled to Town Clerk, Barrow-in-Furness, 1937. Served in Royal Artillery, 1939-46 (commnd 1940). Qualified as Solicitor, 1947; subsequently in practice. Lancashire CC, 1955-61. Opposition Whip, 1967-69; a Lord Comr, HM Treasury, 1970-72; Vice-Chamberlain, HM Household, 1972-73, Comptroller, 1973-74; an Opposition Whip, March-Oct. 1974. Chm., Cons. NW Members Group; Vice-Chm., Assoc. of Conservative Clubs, 1969-71; Hon. Sec., Cons. Housing and Local Govt Cttee, 1968-69; Pres., Cons. NW Area Clubs; Mem. Exec., 1922 Cttee, 1975-76, Hon. Treasurer, 1976-. *Recreations:* fishing, shooting, reading. *Address:* Beech House, Raikes Road, Little Thornton, near Blackpool, Lancs. *T:* Thornton 2131. *Club:* Carlton.

CLEGG-HILL, family name of **Viscount Hill.**

CLELAND, William Paton, FRCP, FRCS, FACS; Surgeon, Brompton Chest Hospital, since 1948; Hon. Thoracic Surgeon, King's College Hospital; Senior Lecturer in Thoracic Surgery, Royal Postgraduate Medical School, since 1949; Civilian Consultant in Thoracic Surgery to the RN; Adviser in Thoracic Surgery to the Department of Health and Social Security; *b* 30 May 1912; *o s* of late Sir John Cleland, CBE; *m* 1940, Norah, *d* of George E. Goodhart; two *s* one *d*. *Educ:* Scotch Coll., Adelaide; Univ. of Adelaide, S Australia. MB, BS (Adelaide). Resident appts, Royal Adelaide and Adelaide Children's Hosps, 1935-36; MRCP 1939; House Physician and Resident Surgical Officer, Brompton Chest Hosp., 1939-41. Served in EMS as Registrar and Surgeon, 1939-45. FRCS 1946. Consulting Thoracic Surg., 1948-; Dir, Dept of Surgery, Cardio-Thoracic Inst., Brompton Hosp. Member: Assoc. Thoracic Surgeons of Gt Brit. and Ire.; Thoracic Soc.; British Cardiac Soc.; FRSocMed. Comdr, Order of Lion of Finland; Comdr, Order of Icelandic Falcon. *Publications:* (jt author) Medical and Surgical Cardiology, 1969; chapters on thoracic surgery in British Surgical Practice, Diseases of the Chest (Marshall and Perry), Short Practice of Surgery (Bailey and Love), and Operative Surgery (Rob and Rodney Smith); articles on pulmonary and cardiac surgery in medical literature. *Recreations:* fishing, sailing, farming, photography. *Address:* 50 Shrewsbury House, Cheyne Walk, Chelsea, SW3 5LW. *T:* 01-352 6530.

CLEMENS, Clive Carruthers, MC 1946; HM Diplomatic Service; Deputy Consul-General, Johannesburg, since 1974; *b* 22 Jan. 1924; British; *s* of late M. B. Clemens, Imperial Bank of India, and late Margaret Jane (*née* Carruthers); *m* 1947, Philippa Jane Bailey; three *s. Educ:* Blundell's Sch.; St Catharine's Coll., Cambridge. War Service 1943-46: commissioned in Duke of Cornwall's Light Infantry; served in India and Burma, 1944-45. Entered HM Foreign Service and apptd to FO, 1947; Third Sec., Rangoon, 1948; Third (later Second) Sec., Lisbon, 1950; FO, 1953; First Sec., Budapest, 1954; Brussels, 1956; Seoul, 1959; FO, 1961; Strasbourg (UK Delegn to Council of Europe), 1964; Counsellor, Paris, 1967; Principal British Trade Comr, Vancouver, 1970-74. *Recreations:* birdwatching, photography. *Address:* c/o Foreign and Commonwealth Office, SW1.

CLEMENT, David James; Deputy Secretary, Department of Finance, Northern Ireland, since 1975; *b* 29 Sept. 1930; *s* of James and Constance Clement; *m* 1958, Margaret Stone; two *s* one *d. Educ:* Chipping Sodbury Grammar Sch.; Univ. of Bristol (BA). IPFA. Internal Audit Asst, City of Bristol, 1953-56; Accountancy/Audit Asst, 1956-60, Chief Accountancy Asst, 1960-65, City of Worcester; Dep. Chief Finance Officer, Runcorn Develt Corp., 1965-68; Chief Finance Officer, Antrim and Ballymena Develt Commn, 1968-72; Asst Sec., Dept of Finance, NI, 1972-75. *Recreations:* lawn tennis, Association football, contract bridge, philately. *Address:* Department of Finance, Stormont, Belfast BT4 3SW. *T:* Belfast 63210.

CLEMENT, David Morris, CBE 1971; FCA, IPFA; Member, National Coal Board, 1969-76; Chairman, NCB (Ancillaries) Ltd, since 1973; *b* 6 Feb. 1911; 2nd *s* of Charles William and Rosina Wannell Clement, Swansea; *m* 1938, Kathleen Mary, *o d* of Ernest George Davies, ACA, Swansea; one *d. Educ:* Bishop Gore's Grammar Sch., Swansea. Mem. Inst. Chartered Accountants, 1933. A. Owen John & Co., Swansea, and Sissons Bersey Gain Vincent & Co., London, Chartered Accts, 1928-35; ICI Ltd, Lime Gp, 1935-40; Chloride Electrical Storage Co. Ltd, 1941-46; National Coal Board: Sec., North Western Div., 1946-49; Chief Acct, Northern and Durham Divs, 1950-55; Dep Dir-Gen. of Finance, 1955-61; Dir-Gen. of Finance, 1961-69. Chm., Public Corporations Finance Gp, 1975-76. Member: Council, CIPFA; Council, CGLI. *Recreations:* golf, photography. *Address:* 19 The Highway, Sutton, Surrey. *T:* 01-642 3626. *Clubs:* Royal Automobile, Directors'.

CLEMENT, John Handel; Under-Secretary, Welsh Office, since 1971 and Director, Industry Department, since 1976; *b* 24 Nov. 1920; *s* of late William Clement and Mary Hannah Clement; *m* 1946, Anita Jones; one *d* (and one *d* decd). *Educ:* Pontardawe Grammar Sch. RAF, 1940-46, Flt Lt (despatches). Welsh Board of Health: Clerical Officer, 1938; Exec. Officer, 1946; Higher Exec. Officer, 1948; Sen. Exec. Officer, 1956; Principal, Welsh Office, Min. of Housing and Local Govt, 1960, Asst Sec., 1966. Private Sec. to Sec. of State for Wales, 1966. Sec., Council for Wales, 1955-59; Chm., Welsh Planning Bd, 1971-. *Recreations:* Welsh Rugby, fishing. *Address:* 6 St Brioc Road, Heath, Cardiff. *T:* Cardiff 64192.

CLÉMENT, René; Chevalier de la Légion d'Honneur; Officier des Arts et des Lettres; film director since 1945; *b* Bordeaux, France, 18 March 1913; *m* 1940, Bella Guritch. *Educ:* in decorative and fine arts and architecture, Paris. Bataille du rail, 1946 (mise en scène and international jury prizes, Cannes); Les Maudits, 1947 (film d'aventures prize, Cannes); Walls of Malapaga, 1948 (mise en scène prize, Cannes; Oscar, 1950, Hollywood); Château de verre, 1950; Jeux interdits (Lion d'or, 1952, Venice; British award; Oscar, 1952, Hollywood, etc); Monsieur Ripois, 1954 (mise en scène prize, Cannes); Gervaise, 1956 (Critics prize, Venice; British award; Press prize, New York; 10 Best Direction in World, Tokyo, etc); Sea Wall, 1958; Quelle joie de vivre, 1960; Le jour et l'Heure, 1963; Les Félins, 1964; Is Paris Burning?, 1966; Le Passager de la Pluie, 1969; La Maison sous les arbres, 1971; La Course du lièvre à travers champs, 1972. *Publication:* (with C. Audry) Bataille du rail, 1947. *Recreations:* antiques, painting, music. *Address:* 91 Avenue Henri Martin, 75016 Paris, France. *T:* Trocadéro 30-93; 10 Avenue de St Roman, Monte Carlo. *T:* 30-59-35.

CLEMENTI, Air Vice-Marshal Cresswell Montagu, CB 1973; CBE 1968 (OBE 1946); *b* 30 Dec. 1918; *s* of late Sir Cecil Clementi, GCMG and Lady Clementi, MBE; *m* 1940, Susan, *d* of late Sir Henry Pelham, KCB and Hon. Lady Pelham; two *s* one *d. Educ:* Winchester; Magdalen Coll., Oxford (MA).

Commnd in RAFVR, 1938; served War of 1939-45 as pilot in Bomber Comd and Air Armament specialist; CO, No 214 (FMS) Sqdn, 1946-48; RAF Staff Coll., 1949; Air Min. (Bomber Ops Directorate), 1950-52; Wing Comdr i/c Flying, RAF Sylt, Germany, 1953-54; jssc, Latimer, 1955; Directing Staff, 1955-57; attended nuclear weapons trials at Christmas Island, 1958; comd RAF Stn Bassingbourn, 1958-61; Gp Capt. Ops/Plans/Trng, Near East Air Force, Cyprus, 1961-63; idc 1964; Dir of Air Staff Plans, MoD (Air Force Dept), 1965-67; AOC No 19 Gp, RAF Mount Batten, Plymouth, 1968-69; Senior RAF Mem., RCDS (formerly IDC), 1969-71; AOA, Air Support Comd, RAF Upavon, Jan.-Aug. 1972; AOA, Strike Comd. 1972-74; retired 1974. Administrator, The Richmond Fellowship, 1974-76. Mem., Court of Assistants, Mercers' Co., 1973-, Master, 1977-78. *Recreations:* walking, riding, travel. *Address:* 8 Chiswick Staithe, W4 3TP. *T:* 01-995 9532. *Club:* Royal Air Force.

CLEMENTS, Clyde Edwin, CMG 1962; OBE 1958; Director: C. E. Clements & Co. Pty Ltd, since 1926; C. E. Clements (Holdings) Ltd; President, Clements Peruana SA; *b* 2 Aug. 1897; *e s* of late Edwin Thomas Clements and late Mrs Clements; *m* 1919, Doris Gertrude Garrett; one *d. Educ:* Devonport Grammar Sch., Tasmania; Queen's Coll., Hobart, Tas. Served European War, 1914-18. Vice-Pres. Young Christian Workers, 1943-66; Dir Young Christian Workers Co-operative Soc. Ltd, 1948-62. Pres. Austr. AA, 1956-57; Mem. Bd, Austr. Nat. Travel Assoc., 1956-57; Mem. Bd, Tourist Develt Authority of Victoria, 1958-69; Vice-Pres. (OTA) World Touring Organization, 1958. Mem. Board of Management, Sir Colin MacKenzie Sanctuary, Healesville, Vic, 1962. Hon. Consul of Peru. *Recreations:* golf, angling. *Address:* 11 Cosham Street, Brighton, Vic 3186, Australia. *T:* 92.3974. *Clubs:* Royal Automobile of Victoria (Vice-Pres. 1942-44, 1952-53; Pres. 1955-62); RACV Country; Victoria Golf; West Brighton (Vic).

CLEMENTS, Sir John (Selby), Kt 1968; CBE 1956; FRSA; Actor, Manager, Producer; *b* 25 April 1910; *s* of late Herbert William Clements, Barrister-at-Law, and Mary Elizabeth (*née* Stephens); *m* 1st, 1936, Inga Maria Lillemor Ahlgren (marr. diss. 1946); 2nd, 1946, Dorothy Katharine (*see* Kay Hammond), *d* of late Sir Guy Standing, KBE, and Dorothy Frances Plaskitt. *Educ:* St Paul's Sch.; St John's Coll., Cambridge. British Actors' Equity: Mem. Council, 1948, 1949; Vice-Pres., 1950-59; Trustee, 1958. Member: Arts Council Drama Panel, 1953-58; Council, RADA, 1957-. First stage appearance, Out of the Blue, Lyric, Hammersmith, 1930; subsequently appeared in: She Stoops to Conquer, Lyric; The Beaux' Stratagem, Royalty, 1930; The Venetian, Little, 1931; Salome, Gate Theatre, 1931; many Shakespearian parts under management of late Sir Philip Ben Greet; founded The Intimate Theatre, Palmers Green, London, 1935, and ran it as weekly repertory theatre until 1940, directing most of and appearing in nearly 200 plays; produced Yes and No, Ambassadors, 1937; appeared in: Skylark, Duchess, 1942; They Came to a City, Globe, 1943; (also produced) Private Lives, Apollo, 1944; (with Old Vic Co.) played Coriolanus, Petruchio and Dunois, New, 1947-48; appeared in Edward My Son, Lyric, 1948-49; as Actor-Manager-Producer, has presented and played in: The Kingmaker; Marriage à la Mode, St James's, 1946; The Beaux' Stratagem, Phoenix and Lyric, 1949-50; Man and Superman, New and Princes, 1951; (also author) The Happy Marriage, Duke of York's, 1952-53; Pygmalion, St James's 1953-54; The Little Glass Clock, Aldwych, 1954-55; personal management of Saville Theatre, 1955-57, where presented and played in: The Shadow of Doubt; The Wild Duck, 1955-56; The Rivals, 1956; The Seagull; The Doctor's Dilemma; The Way of the World, 1956-57; Adviser on Drama to Associated Rediffusion Ltd, 1955-56, where produced films including: A Month in the Country; The Wild Duck; played in: (also co-presented and directed) The Rape of the Belt, Piccadilly, 1957-58; (also presented) Gilt and Gingerbread, Duke of York's, 1959; The Marriage-Go-Round, Piccadilly, 1959-60; produced Will You Walk a Little Faster?, Duke of York's, 1960; played in: J. B., Phœnix, 1961; The Affair, Strand, 1961; The Tulip Tree, Haymarket, 1962; Old Vic American tour, 1962; played in: (also co-presented and directed) The Masters, Savoy, 1963; Robert and Elizabeth, Lyric, 1964. Director, Chichester Festival Theatre, 1966-73; 1966 season, presented: The Clandestine Marriage; (also played in) The Fighting Cock (subseq. Duke of York's); The Cherry Orchard; (also played) Macbeth; 1967 season, directed: The Farmer's Wife; (also played Shotover) Heartbreak House (subseq. Lyric); presented: The Beaux' Stratagem; An Italian Straw Hat; 1968 season, presented: The Unknown Soldier and His Wife; The Cocktail Party (subseq. Wyndham's); (played Prospero) The Tempest; The Skin of our Teeth; 1969 season, presented: The Caucasian Chalk Circle; (also directed and played in) The Magistrate (subseq. Cambridge); The Country Wife; (also played Antony) Antony and Cleopatra; 1970 season, presented: Peer Gynt; Vivat! Vivat!

Reginal; (also directed) The Proposal; Arms and the Man; The Alchemist; 1971 season presented: (also directed and played in) The Rivals; (also played in) Dear Antoine (subseq. Piccadilly); Caesar and Cleopatra; Reunion in Vienna; 1972 Season, presented: The Beggar's Opera; (also directed and played in) The Doctor's Dilemma; 1973 Season, presented: (also directed and played in) The Director of the Opera; (also directed) Dandy Dick; dir, Waters of the Moon, Chichester, 1977; dir and played in, The Case in Question, Haymarket, 1975; entered films, 1934; films include: Things to Come; Knight Without Armour; South Riding; Rembrandt; The Four Feathers; Convoy; Ships With Wings; Undercover; They Came to a City; Train of Events; The Silent Enemy; The Mind Benders; Oh What a Lovely War!. *Address:* Rufford Court, 109 Marine Parade, Brighton, E Sussex BN2 1AT. *T:* Brighton 63026. *Club:* Garrick.

CLEMENTS, Julia; *see* Seton, Lady, (Julia).

CLEMENTS, Rt. Rev. Kenneth John; *b* 21 Dec. 1905; *s* of John Edwin Clements and Ethel Evelyn Clark; *m* 1935, Rosalind Elizabeth Cakebread; one *s* two *d. Educ:* Highgate Sch., London; St Paul's Coll., University of Sydney. BA (Hons) 1933; ThD 1949. Registrar, Diocese of Riverina, 1933-37; Rector of: Narrandera, NSW, 1937-39; Tumbarumba, NSW, 1939-43; Gunning, NSW, 1943-44; Director of Studies, Canberra Grammar Sch., Canberra, ACT, 1945; Registrar Diocese of Canberra and Goulburn, 1946-56; Archdeacon of Goulburn, 1946-56; Asst Bishop of Canberra and Goulburn, 1949-56; Bishop of Grafton, NSW, 1956-61; Bishop of Canberra and Goulburn, 1961-71; retired, 1971. *Address:* Mons School Road, Buderim, Qld 4551, Australia.

CLEMENTS, Richard Harry; Editor of Tribune, since 1961; *b* 11 Oct. 1928; *s* of Harry and Sonia Clements; *m* 1952, Bridget Mary MacDonald; two *s. Educ:* King Alfred Sch., Hampstead; Western High Sch., Washington, DC; Regent Street Polytechnic. Middlesex Independent, 1949; Leicester Mercury, 1951; Ed., Socialist Advance (Labour Party Youth paper), 1953; industrial staff, Daily Herald, 1954; joined Tribune, 1956. *Publication:* Glory without Power: a study of trade unions, 1959. *Recreation:* woodwork. *Address:* Tribune Publications Ltd, 24 St John Street, EC1. *T:* 01-253 2994.

CLEMINSON, James Arnold Stacey, MC 1945; Chairman, since 1977, and Chief Executive, since 1973, Reckitt & Colman Ltd; *b* 31 Aug. 1921; *s* of Arnold Russel Cleminson and Florence Stacey; *m* 1950, Helen Juliet Measor; one *s* two *d . Educ:* Rugby Sch. Served War, 1940-46, mainly in Parachute Regt. Reckitt & Colman, 1946-: Overseas Co., 1946; Dir, Reckitt & Colman Overseas, 1957; Chm., Food and Wine Div., Norwich, 1970. Mem., Food EDC, 1976-; Dep. Pres., Food Manufrs Fedn, 1977-. Chm., Council of Endeavour Trng; Trustee, Airborne Forces Security Fund. *Recreations:* hunting, shooting, tennis, golf, fishing. *Address:* Loddon Hall, Hales, Norfolk. *Clubs:* Queen's; Aldeburgh.

CLEMITSON, Rear-Adm. Francis Edward, CB 1952; retired; *b* 9 Nov. 1899; *s* of William David and Helen Louisa Clemitson; *m* 1933, Kathleen Farquhar Shand; two *d. Educ:* Christ's Hospital. Entered Royal Navy as Cadet, 1917; Lieut (E), 1921; Commander (E), 1933; Capt. (E), 1943; Rear-Adm. (E), 1949; Deputy Engineer-in-Chief of the Fleet (Admin.), Admiralty, 1950-53; retired Oct. 1953. *Recreations:* tennis, golf, philately. *Address:* Tanhurst, Bramley, Surrey. *T:* Bramley 3148.

CLEMITSON, Ivor Malcolm; MP (Lab) Luton East since Feb. 1974; *b* 8 Dec. 1931; *s* of Daniel Malcolm Clemitson and Annie Ellen Clemitson; *m* 1960, Janet Alicia Meeke; one *s* one *d. Educ:* Harlington Primary Sch.; Luton Grammar Sch.; London Sch. of Economics (BScEcon); Bishops Theol College. Deacon 1958, Priest 1959. Curate: St Mary's (Bramall Lane), Sheffield, 1958-61; Christ Church, Luton, 1962-64; Industrial Chaplain, Dio. St Albans, 1964-69; Dir of Industrial Mission, Dio. Singapore, 1969-70; Research Officer, National Graphical Assoc., 1972-74. *Recreations:* watching football, theatre, travel. *Address:* 49 Marlborough Road, Luton, Beds. *T:* Luton 419198.

CLEMO, George Roger, DSc; FRS 1937; FIC; Professor of Organic Chemistry, King's College, University of Durham, 1925-54, Professor Emeritus, 1954; Director of Department of Chemistry, 1932-54. *Educ:* University Coll., Exeter; Queen's Coll., Oxford. Late asst to Prof. W. H. Perkin at Oxford; was in charge of the Research Department of the British Dyestuffs Corporation, Manchester. *Address:* Cherryburn, Mickley, Stocksfield, Northumberland NE43 7DD.

CLEMOES, Prof. Peter Alan Martin, PhD (Cantab); FRHistS; Elrington and Bosworth Professor of Anglo-Saxon, Cambridge University, since 1969; Official Fellow of Emmanuel College, Cambridge, 1962-69, Professorial Fellow since 1969; Fellow, Queen Mary College, London University, since 1975; *b* 20 Jan. 1920; *o s* of Victor Clemoes and Mary (*née* Paton); *m* 1956, Jean Elizabeth, *yr d* of Sidney Grew; two *s. Educ:* Brentwood Sch.; Queen Mary Coll., London; King's Coll., Cambridge. BA London (1st Cl. Hons English) 1950; Soley Student, King's Coll., Cambridge, 1951-53; Research Fellow, Reading Univ., 1954-55; PhD Cambridge 1956. Lectr in English, Reading Univ., 1955-61; Lectr in Anglo-Saxon, Cambridge Univ., 1961-69; Coll. Lectr in English, 1963-69 and Dir of Studies in English, 1963-65; Tutor, 1966-68; Asst Librarian, 1963-69. Mem., Council of Early English Text Soc., 1971-. Founder and Chief Editor, Anglo-Saxon England, 1972-. *Publications:* The Anglo-Saxons, Studies... presented to Bruce Dickins (ed and contrib.), 1959; General Editor of Early English Manuscripts in Facsimile (Copenhagen), 1963-74, and co-editor of vol. XIII, 1966, vol. XVIII, 1974; Rhythm and Cosmic Order in Old English Christian Literature (inaug. lecture), 1970; England before the Conquest: Studies... presented to Dorothy Whitelock (co-ed and contrib.), 1971; textual and critical writings, especially on the works of Ælfric. *Address:* 14 Church Street, Chesterton, Cambridge. *T:* Cambridge 58655.

CLERK, Sir John Dutton, 10th Bt *cr* 1679; CBE 1966; VRD; FRSE 1977; JP; Lord-Lieutenant of Midlothian since 1972 (Vice-Lieutenant, 1965-72); Cdre RNR; retd; *b* 30 Jan. 1917; *s* of Sir George James Robert Clerk, 9th Bt, and Hon. Mabel Honor (*d* 1974), *y d* of late Col Hon. Charles Dutton and *sister* of 6th Baron Sherborne, DSO; *S* father, 1943; *m* 1944, Evelyn Elizabeth Robertson; two *s* two *d. Educ:* Stowe. Brig., Queen's Body Guard for Scotland, Royal Company of Archers, 1973. JP 1955, DL 1956, Midlothian. *Heir:* s Robert Maxwell Clerk [*b* 3 April 1945; *m* 1970, Felicity Faye, *yr d* of George Collins, Bampton, Oxford; one *s* one *d*]. *Address:* Penicuik House, Penicuik, Midlothian, Scotland. *T:* Penicuik 74318. *Clubs:* Royal Over-Seas League; New (Edinburgh).

CLERKE, Sir John Edward Longueville, 12th Bt *cr* 1660; Captain Royal Wilts Yeomanry, RAC, TA; *b* 29 Oct. 1913; *s* of late Francis William Talbot Clerke, *e s* of 11th Bt, and Albinia Mary, *er d* of Edward Henry Evans-Lombe (she *m* 3rd, 1923, Air Chief Marshal Sir Edgar Rainey Ludlow-Hewitt, GCB, GBE, CMG, DSO, MC); *S* grandfather, 1930; *m* 1948, Mary, *d* of Lt-Col I. R. Beviss Bond, Prosperity, Natal, S Africa and The Old Rectory, North Newnton, Marlborough, Wilts; one *s* two *d. Heir:* s Francis Ludlow Longueville Clerke, *b* 25 Jan. 1953. *Address:* Westbrook House, Bromham, Chippenham, Wilts.

CLEVELAND, Archdeacon of; *see* Southgate, Ven. J. E.

CLEVELAND, (James) Harlan; Director, Program in International Affairs, Aspen Institute for Humanistic Studies, since 1974; *b* 19 Jan. 1918; *s* of Stanley Matthews Cleveland and Marian Phelps (*née* Van Buren); *m* 1941, Lois W. Burton; one *s* two *d. Educ:* Phillips Acad., Andover, Mass; Princeton Univ.; Oxford Univ. Farm Security Admin., Dept of Agric., 1940-42; Bd of Econ. Warfare (subseq. Foreign Econ. Admin.), 1942-44; Exec. Dir Econ. Sect., 1944-45, Actg Vice-Pres., 1945-46, Allied Control Commn, Rome; Mem. US Delegn, UNRRA Council, London, 1945; Dept Chief of Mission, UNRRA Italian Mission, Rome, 1946-47; Dir, UNRRA China Office, Shanghai, 1947-48; Dir, China Program, Econ. Coop. Admin., Washington, 1948-49; Dept Asst Adminstr, 1949-51; Asst Dir for Europe, Mutual Security Agency, 1952-53; Exec. Ed., The Reporter, NYC, 1953-55, Publ., 1955-56; Dean, Maxwell Sch. of Citizenship and Pub. Affairs, Syracuse Univ., 1956-61; Asst Sec. for Internat. Orgn Affairs, State Dept, 1961-65; US Ambassador to NATO, 1965-69; Pres., Univ. of Hawaii, 1969-74. Holds hon. degrees and foreign orders; US Medal of Freedom, 1946. Woodrow Wilson Award, Princeton Univ. *Publications:* The Obligation of Power, 1966; NATO: the transatlantic bargain, 1970; The Future Executive, 1972; (ed jtly) The Art of Overseasmanship, 1957; (jtly) The Overseas Americans, 1960; (ed) The Promise of World Tensions, 1961; (ed jtly) The Ethic of Power, 1962; (ed jtly) Ethics and Bigness, 1962. *Address:* Aspen Institute for Humanistic Studies, PO Box 2820, Princeton, NJ 08540, USA. *Clubs:* Century (NY); International (Washington); Waikiki Yacht (Honolulu); Mid Pacific (Lanikai, Hawaii).

CLEVERDON, (Thomas) Douglas (James); publisher and radio producer; *b* 17 January 1903; *er s* of Thomas Silcox Cleverdon, Bristol; *m* 1944, Elinor Nest, *d* of Canon J. A. Lewis, Cardiff; two *s* one *d* (and one *s* decd). *Educ:* Bristol Grammar Sch.; Jesus Coll., Oxford. Bookseller, and publisher of fine printing, Bristol, 1926-39. Free-lance acting and writing for BBC West Region, 1935-39; joined BBC (Children's Hour), 1939; W Regional Features Producer, 1939-43; Features Producer, London, 1943, until retirement in 1969; now free-lance producer. Devised and co-produced BBC Brains Trust, 1941. BBC War Corresp. in Burma, 1945; from 1947, mainly concerned with productions for Third Programme including radio works by Max Beerbohm, J. Bronowski, Bill Naughton, George Barker, David Gascoyne, Ted Hughes, David Jones, Stevie Smith, Henry Reed, Dylan Thomas (Under Milk Wood), Peter Racine Fricker, Elizabeth Poston, Humphrey Searle and other poets and composers. Directed first stage prods of Under Milk Wood, in Edinburgh and London, 1955, and in New York, 1957. Directed: Poetry Festivals, Stratford-upon-Avon, 1966-67, and 1969-70; Cheltenham Festival of Literature, 1971. Compiled exhibition of paintings, engravings and writings of David Jones, NBL, 1972. Co-Publisher, Clover Hill Edns (illustrated by contemporary engravers), 1964-. *Publications:* Engravings of Eric Gill, 1929; Growth of Milk Wood, 1969; (ed) Sixe Idyllia of Theocritus, 1971; (ed) Under Milk Wood (Folio Soc.), 1972; (ed) Verlaine, Femmes: Hombres, 1972. *Recreations:* book-collecting; visual arts. *Address:* 27 Barnsbury Square, N1. *T:* 01-607 7392. *Clubs:* Savile, Double Crown.

CLEVERLEY FORD, Rev. Preb. Douglas William; Chaplain to the Queen since 1973; Senior Chaplain to the Archbishop of Canterbury, since 1975; *b* 4 March 1914; *yr s* of late Arthur James and Mildred Ford; *m* 1939, Olga Mary, *er d* of Dr Thomas Bewley Gilbart-Smith; no *c. Educ:* Great Yarmouth Grammar Sch.; Univ. of London. BD, MTh, ALCD (1st cl.). Deacon 1937, Priest 1938. London Coll. of Divinity: Tutor, 1937-39; Lectr, 1942-43 and 1952-58; Lectr, Church Army Trng Coll., 1953-60. Curate of Bridlington, Yorks, 1939-42; Vicar of Holy Trinity, Hampstead, 1942-55; Vicar of Holy Trinity with All Saints Church, South Kensington, 1955-74; Hon. Dir, Coll. of Preachers, 1960-73; Rural Dean of Westminster, 1965-74; Prebendary of St Paul's Cathedral, 1968-; Provincial Canon of York, 1969-. Chm., Queen Alexandra's House, Kensington Gore, 1966-74; Mem. Governing Body, Westminster City Sch. and United Westminster Schs, 1965-74; Hon. Life Governor: British and Foreign Bible Soc., 1948; Church's Ministry among the Jews. *Publications:* An Expository Preacher's Notebook, 1960; The Christian Faith Explained, 1962; A Theological Preacher's Notebook, 1962; A Pastoral Preacher's Notebook, 1965; A Reading of St Luke's Gospel, 1967; Preaching at the Parish Communion, Vol. 1 1967, Vol. 2 1968, Vol. 3 1969; Preaching Today, 1969; Preaching through the Christian Year, 1971; Praying through the Christian Year, 1973; Have You Anything to Declare?, 1973; Preaching on the Special Occasions, 1974; Preaching at the Parish Communion (Series III), 1975; New Preaching on the Old Testament, 1976; New Preaching from the Old Testament, 1977; contrib. Churchman's Companion 1967, Expository Times. *Recreations:* maintenance of country cottage and garden, music, languages. *Address:* Lambeth Palace, SE1 7JU; Rostrevor, Lingfield, Surrey RH7 6BZ. *Club:* Athenæum.

CLEWES, Howard Charles Vivian; novelist; *b* York, 27 Oct. 1912; British parentage; *m* 1946, Renata Faccincani; one *d. Educ:* Merchant Taylors' Sch. Various advertising agents, 1931-37. Served War of 1939-45, infantry company Comdr Green Howards, then Major G2; Chief Press and Information Officer, Milan, Italy, 1945-47. Professional novelist, resident Florence, Rome, London, 1948-. *Publications:* (in UK, USA, etc) Dead Ground, 1946; The Unforgiven, 1947; The Mask of Wisdom, 1948; Stendhal, 1949; Green Grow the Rushes, 1950; The Long Memory, 1951; An Epitaph for Love, 1952; The Way the Wind Blows, 1954; Man on a Horse, 1964; *plays:* Quay South, 1947; Image in the Sun, 1955; *films:* The Long Memory, Steel Bayonet, The One that Got Away, The Day They Robbed the Bank of England, Mutiny on the Bounty, The Holiday, Up from the Beach, William the Conqueror, The Novice, The 40 Days of Musa Dagh, etc. *Recreations:* writing, fishing. *Address:* Wildwood, North End, NW3. *T:* 01-455 7110.

CLEWS, Michael Arthur; Master of the Supreme Court Taxing Office, since 1970; *b* Caudebec, France, 16 Sept. 1919; *s* of late Roland Trevor Clews and late Marjorie (*née* Baily); *m* 1947, Kathleen Edith, *d* of late Adam Hollingworth, OBE, JP, and Gertrude (*née* Bardsley); three *c. Educ:* Epworth Coll., Rhyl; Clare Coll., Cambridge (MA). Served in Indian Army (Major, RA and V Force), 1940-46. Solicitor, 1953; Partner, W. H. House & Son, and Knocker & Foskett, Sevenoaks, 1957-70. *Address:* The Red House, Hever, Edenbridge, Kent. *T:* Edenbridge 713520.

CLIBBORN, Donovan Harold, CMG 1966; HM Diplomatic Service, retired; *b* 2 July 1917; *s* of Henry Joseph Fairley Clibborn and Isabel Sarah Jago; *m* 1st, 1940, Margaret Mercedes Edwige Nelson (*d* 1966); one *s* two *d*; 2nd, 1973, Victoria Ondiviela Garvi. *Educ:* Ilford High Sch.; St Edmund Hall,

Oxford (MA). Laming Travelling Fellow, Queen's Coll., Oxford, 1938-40. Entered Consular Service, 1939; Vice-Consul, Genoa, 1939-40. Army Service, 1940-45: Intelligence Corps and Royal Signals, Western Desert, Sicily, Italy, NW Europe (despatches); Major, 1944. Foreign Office, 1945-46; Consul, Los Angeles, 1946-48; Foreign Office, 1948-50; 1st Sec. (UK High Commn, India), Madras, 1950-52; 1st Sec. (Information), Rio de Janeiro, 1952-56; 1st Sec. (Commercial), Madrid, 1956-60; Consul (Commercial), Milan, 1960-62; Counsellor (Economic), Tehran, 1962-64; Counsellor, Rio de Janeiro, 1964-66; Consul-General, Barcelona, 1966-70; Ambassador, El Salvador, 1971-75. *Recreations:* reading, music. *Address:* Calle de Dr Moragas 188, Attico 1A, Santa Maria de Barberá, Prov. Barcelona, Spain.

CLIBURN, Van, (Harvey Lavan Cliburn Jr); Pianist; *b* Shreveport, La, 12 July 1934; *o c* of Harvey Lavan Cliburn and Rildia Bee (*née* O'Bryan). *Educ:* Kilgore High Sch., Texas; Juilliard Sch. of Music, New York. Made début in Houston, Texas, 1947; subsequently has toured extensively in United States and Europe. Awards include first International Tchaikovsky Piano Competition, Moscow, 1958, and every US prize, for pianistic ability. *Recreation:* swimming. *Address:* c/o Hurok Concerts, 1370 Avenue of the Americas, New York City, NY 10019, USA; 455 Wilder Place, Shreveport, La 71104, USA.

CLIFFORD, family name of **Baron Clifford of Chudleigh.**

CLIFFORD OF CHUDLEIGH, 13th Baron *cr* 1672; **(Lewis) Hugh Clifford,** OBE 1962; DL; Count of The Holy Roman Empire; farmer and landowner; President: Devon Branch, Country Landowners Association, 1973-75; Devon Branch, Royal British Legion; *b* 13 April 1916; *o s* of 12th Baron and Amy (*d* 1926), *er d* of John A. Webster, MD; *S* father, 1964; *m* 1945, Hon. Katharine Vavasseur Fisher, 2nd *d* of 2nd Baron Fisher; two *s* two *d. Educ:* Beaumont Coll.; Hertford Coll., Oxford (BA). 2nd Lieut, Devonshire Regt, 1935. Served War of 1939-45: North Africa; Major, 1941 (prisoner of war, escaped). Retd, 1950. Lieut-Col, 1959; Col, 1961. ADC(TA), 1964-69. Hon. Col, The Royal Devon Yeomanry/1st Rifle Volunteers, RAC, T&AVR (formerly the Devonshire Territorials, RAC), 1968-71; Dep. Hon. Col, The Wessex Yeomanry, 1971-72, Hon. Col D Sqdn, 1972-. Pres., Devon Co. Agricultural Assoc., 1973-74. DL Devon, 1964. *Recreations:* shooting, sailing. *Heir:* s Hon. Thomas Hugh Clifford [*b* 17 March 1948. Commnd Coldstream Guards, 1967, retired 1977 (Captain)]. *Address:* (seat) Ugbrooke Park, Chudleigh, South Devon TQ13 0AD; Morella, Montrose, Vic, Australia. *Clubs:* Army and Navy; Royal Yacht Squadron.

CLIFFORD, Clark McAdams; Senior Partner, Clifford, Warnke, Glass, McIwain & Finney, since 1969; *b* 25 Dec. 1906; *s* of Frank Andrew Clifford and Georgia (*née* McAdams); *m* 1931, Margery Pepperell Kimball; three *d. Educ:* Washington Univ., St Louis (LLB). Served US Naval Reserve, 1944-46 (Naval Commendation Ribbon). Practised law in St Louis, 1928-43; specialised in trial cases, corporation and labour law; Special Counsel to President of US, 1946-50; Senior Partner, Clifford & Miller, 1950-68; Secretary of Defense, USA, 1968-69. Director, Phillips Petroleum Co. Trustee, Washington Univ., St Louis. Medal of Freedom with Distinction, USA, 1969. *Recreation:* golf. *Address:* 815 Connecticut Avenue, Washington, DC 20006, USA.

CLIFFORD, Sir (Geoffrey) Miles, KBE 1949 (OBE 1939); CMG 1944; ED; Médaille de la Résistance Française avec Rosette; *b* 1897; *m* 1st, 1920, Ivy Dorothy ("Peta") (decd), *y d* of Arthur Robert Eland, Thrapston, Northants; no *c*; 2nd, Mary, *e d* of late Thomas Turner, Shelbyville, Ill., USA. *Educ:* privately. Served European War (France and Flanders), 1914-18; Army of the Rhine, 1919-20. Comd Nigerian European Defence Force, 1938-40 (Special Duty, 1941-42). Entered Colonial Administrative Service (Nigeria), 1921; Acting Resident, Adamawa, 1934-37; Principal Asst Sec., 1938-41; seconded as Colonial Sec., Gibraltar, 1942-44; Senior Resident, Nigeria, 1944; Chm. Salaries Commn, Cyprus, 1945; attached CO, 1946; Governor and C-in-C of Falkland Islands, 1946-54. Chief Warden, Westminster, 1954-57; Mem., LCC, 1955-58; Hon. Organiser, Mental Health Research Fund; Dir, Leverhulme Trust, 1956-65; Cttee of Management, Trans-Antarctic Expedition; Mem., Antarctic Sub-Cttee, International Geophysical Year; Chm., British National Cttee on Antarctic Research; a Vice-Pres., RGS, 1956-62; St Paul's Cathedral Trust Council; a Trustee of Toc H; Vice-Pres., African Medical and Research Foundn; Life Gov., Imperial Cancer Research Fund; Trustee, McIndoe Memorial Research Unit; Mem., Management Cttee (co-opted), Inst. of Basic Med. Sciences; Hon. Treasurer, Soc. for Health Educn; Mem., Porritt Working Party on Med. Aid to Developing Countries and Chm. Anglo-Amer. Conf. on same theme; Chm. Planning Cttee, Chelsea

Group of Post-graduate Hospitals; Chm. Cttee of Management, Inst. Latin American Studies, London Univ.; Mem. Council Voluntary Service Overseas. Chairman: Nigerian Electricity Supply Corp.; United Nigeria Group. Fellow, UCL; Mem. Ct of Patrons, RCS; Chm., Conf. of Foundations, Ditchley, 1966; a Gov., United Westminster Schs. Hon. FRCS; Hon. FDS, RCS. *Publications*: A Nigerian Chiefdom; Notes on the Bassa-Komo Tribe; book reviews and occasional contribs to the Press. *Address*: Orchards, Brenchley, Kent. *Clubs*: Athenæum; Antarctic (Hon. Mem.).

CLIFFORD, Graham Douglas, CMG 1964; FCIS; Director, The Institution of Electronic and Radio Engineers, 1937-78; *b* 8 Feb. 1913; *s* of John William Clifford and Frances Emily Reece; *m* 1937, Marjory Charlotte Willmot; two *d* (one *s* decd). *Educ*: London schs and by industrial training. Molins Machine Co. Ltd, 1929; Columbia Graphophone Co. Ltd, 1931; American Machinery Co. Ltd, 1934. Secretary: Radio Trades Exam. Bd, 1942-65 (Hon. Mem. 1965); Nat. Electronics Council, 1961-. Managing Editor of The Radio and Electronic Engineer and Electronics Rev. Hon. Mem., Assoc. of Engineers and Architects, Israel, 1966; Hon. Treasurer, UK Cttee for the Gandhi Centenary, 1969; Hon. Sec. and Governor, Nehru Meml Trust. Comdr, Order of Merit, Research and Invention, France, 1967. *Publications*: A Twentieth Century Professional Institution, 1960; (ed) Nehru Memorial Lectures, 1973; contribs to various technical journals. *Recreations*: photography, genealogy, music, but mainly work. *Address*: 45 West Park Lane, West Worthing, W Sussex. *T*: Worthing 41423. *Club*: Royal Automobile.

CLIFFORD, Prof. James Lowry; William Peterfield Trent Professor of English, Columbia University, 1964-69 (Professor of English, 1946-69), now Emeritus Professor; President, Lichfield Johnson Society, 1958-59; *b* Evansville, Ind., USA, 24 Feb. 1901; *s* of George S. and Emily Orr Clifford; *m* 1940, Virginia Iglehart; two *s* one *d*. *Educ*: Wabash Coll. (AB); Massachusetts Inst. of Tech. (BS); Columbia Univ. (PhD). Manager, Young Car Co., Evansville, Indiana, 1926-28; English Master, Evans Sch., Tucson, Ariz., 1929-32; Graduate student, Columbia Univ., 1932-35; Travelling Fellow, Columbia Univ., 1935-36; Dept of English, Lehigh Univ., Bethlehem, Pa, 1938-44, Instructor to Associate Prof.; Associate Prof. of English, Barnard Coll., 1944-46; Guggenheim Fellowship, 1951-52 and 1965-66. Mem. Gen. Advisory Editorial Cttee, Yale Boswell Edition and Yale Edition of the Works of Samuel Johnson, also Mem. Adv. Cttee, Wesleyan Univ. Fielding Edn. Pres., Amer. Soc. for Eighteenth Century Studies, 1972-73; Hon. Vice-Pres., Johnson Soc. of London; Hon. Mem., The Johnson Club, London and Johnson Soc., Oslo, Norway; Mem., The Johnsonians, NY. Hon. LittD Evansville Coll., 1955; Hon. LHD: Wabash Coll., 1956; Indiana Univ., 1963; Lehigh Univ., 1972. Phi Beta Kappa. PEN; FRSL 1956; FRSA 1970. *Publications*: Hester Lynch Piozzi (Mrs Thrale), 1941; Dr Campbell's Diary (edn), 1947; Pope and his Contemporaries (ed with Louis A. Landa), 1949; Johnsonian Studies, 1887-1950: a Survey and Bibliography, 1951 (rev. edn 1970); Young Samuel Johnson, 1955; Eighteenth Century English Literature: Modern Essays in Criticism (ed), 1959; Biography as an Art (ed), 1962; Smollett's Peregrine Pickle (ed), 1964; Man versus Society in 18th Century Britain (ed), 1968; From Puzzles to Portraits: problems of a literary biographer, 1970; Editor, Johnsonian News Letter, 1940-; various other editions for the Augustan Reprint Soc., and articles in scholarly jls; Festschrift, English Writers of the Eighteenth Century, ed J. H. Middendorf, 1971. *Recreations*: baseball, music and theatre. *Address*: 25 Claremont Avenue, New York, NY 10027, USA. *T*: New York-Monument 3-2233.

CLIFFORD, Sir Miles; see Clifford, Sir G. M.

CLIFFORD, Rev. Paul Rowntree, MA; President, Selly Oak Colleges, Birmingham, since 1965; *b* 21 Feb. 1913; *s* of Robert and Harriet Rowntree Clifford; *m* 1947, Marjory Jean Tait; one *s* one *d*. *Educ*: Mill Hill Sch.; Balliol Coll., Oxford; Mansfield and Regents Park Colls, Oxford. MA (Oxon) 1939. West Ham Central Mission, London: Asst Minister, 1938-43; Supt Minister, 1943-53; McMaster Univ., Hamilton, Canada: Asst Prof. of Homiletics and Pastoral Theology, 1953-59; Dean of Men and Chm. of Dept of Religion, 1959-64; Prof. of Religion, 1964-65. *Publications*: The Mission of the Local Church, 1953; The Pastoral Calling, 1959; Now is the Time, 1970; Interpreting Human Experience, 1971; The Death of the Dinosaur, 1977; articles in Jl of Religion, Metaphysical Review, Dialogue, Canadian Jl of Theology, Scottish Jl of Theology, Foundations, Religious Studies. *Recreations*: golf, gardening. *Address*: President's House, Selly Oak Colleges, Birmingham B29 6LE. *T*: 021-472 2462. *Club*: Reform.

CLIFFORD, Sir Roger (Charles Joseph Gerrard), 6th Bt *cr* 1887; Manager Rod Weir & Co. Ltd, Waikanae Stock and Station Agents; *b* 28 May 1910; *s* of Charles William Clifford, *d* 1939 (3rd *s* of 1st Bt) and Sicele Agnes (*d* 1948), *d* of Sir Humphrey de Trafford, 2nd Bt; *S* brother, 1970; *m* 1st, 1934, Henrietta Millicent Kiver (*d* 1971); two *s* one *d*; 2nd, 1973, Gretchen Patrice Pollock. *Educ*: Beaumont College, Old Windsor; Harper Adams Agricultural College. *Heir*: *er s* Roger Joseph Clifford [*b* 5 June 1936; *m* 1968, Joanna Theresa, *d* of C. J. Ward, Christchurch, NZ; one *d*]. *Address*: 17 Kotare Street, Waikanae, New Zealand.

CLIFFORD, William Henry Morton, CB 1972; CBE 1966; Legal Consultant, Civil Service College, since 1974; *b* 30 July 1909; *s* of Henry Edward Clifford, FRIBA, Glasgow, and Margaret Alice, *d* of Dr William Gibson, Campbeltown, Argyll; *m* 1936, Katharine Winifred, *d* of Rev. H. W. Waterfield, Temple Grove, Eastbourne; one *s* two *d*. *Educ*: Tonbridge Sch.; Corpus Christi Coll., Cambridge. Admitted a solicitor, 1936. Entered Solicitor's Department, GPO, 1937. Served in Army, 1939-45: Major GS, Army Council Secretariat, WO, 1944-45. Transferred to Solicitor's Office, Min. of National Insurance, 1945; Assistant Solicitor, Min. of Pensions and Nat. Insurance (later Min. of Social Security), 1953; Solicitor, DHSS (formerly Min. of Social Security), 1968-74. *Recreations*: reading, listening to music (especially opera), genealogy, walking, sailing. *Address*: Woodbrook, 9 Lake Road, Tunbridge Wells, Kent. *T*: Tunbridge Wells 21612.

CLIFFORD-TURNER, Raymond; Senior Partner, Clifford-Turner, solicitors; *b* 7 Feb. 1906; *s* of Harry Clifford-Turner, solicitor; *m* 1933, Zoë Vachell; one *s* two *d*. *Educ*: Rugby Sch.; Trinity Coll., Cambridge. Solicitor, 1930; Partner, Clifford-Turner & Co., 1931. Wing Commander, RAFVR. *Recreations*: golf, racing. *Address*: 86 Eaton Place, SW1. *T*: 01-235 2443; Childown, Stonehill Road, Chertsey, Surrey. *Clubs*: Portland; Berkshire; Swinley.
See also Hon. A. G. Berry.

CLIFT, Richard Dennis; HM Diplomatic Service; Counsellor on secondment to Northern Ireland Office, since 1977; *b* 18 May 1933; *s* of late Dennis Victor Clift and of Helen Wilmot Clift (*née* Evans); *m* 1957, Barbara Mary Travis; three *d*. *Educ*: St Edward's Sch., Oxford; Pembroke Coll., Cambridge. BA 1956. FO, 1956-57; Office of British Chargé d'Affaires, Peking, 1958-60; British Embassy, Berne, 1961-62; UK Delegn to NATO, Paris, 1962-64; FO, 1964-68; Head of Chancery, British High Commn, Kuala Lumpur, 1969-71; FCO, 1971-73; Counsellor (Commercial), Peking, 1974-76; Canadian Nat. Defence Coll., 1976-77. *Recreations*: sailing, walking. *Address*: c/o Foreign and Commonwealth Office, SW1A 2AL. *Club*: Royal Automobile.

CLIFTON, Bishop of (RC), since 1974; **Rt. Rev. Mervyn Alban Newman Alexander, DD**; *b* London, 29 June 1925; *s* of William Paul Alexander and Grace Evelyn Alexander (*née* Newman). *Educ*: Bishop Wordsworth School, Salisbury; Prior Park College, Bath; Gregorian University, Rome (DD 1951). Curate at Pro-Cathedral, Clifton, Bristol, 1951-63; RC Chaplain, Bristol University, 1953-67; Parish Priest, Our Lady of Lourdes, Weston-super-Mare, 1967-72; Auxiliary Bishop of Clifton and Titular Bishop of Pinhel, 1972-74; Vicar Capitular of Clifton, 1974. *Address*: St Ambrose, Leigh Woods, Bristol BS8 3PW. *T*: Bristol 33072.

CLIFTON, Henry Talbot de Vere; *b* 16 Dec. 1907; *s* of late John Talbot Clifton and late Violet Mary (author, Mrs John Talbot Clifton). *Educ*: Christ Church, Oxford. Lord of the Manor of Anstey; Lord of the Manor of Lytham. Owner of Kildalton Castle, Islay, Scotland. *Publications*: Gleams Britain's Day, Dielma and other poems. *Recreations*: racing, fishing, music, horses, dogs.

CLIFTON, Leon James Thomas; Under-Secretary, Department of Trade and Industry (formerly Ministry of Technology), 1967-72, retired; *b* 17 May 1912; *s* of William Clifton and Helen Florence Clifton (*née* Holloway); *m* 1937, Doris Camp; one *s* one *d*. *Educ*: Fulham Central. Air Min., 1929; Min. of Aircraft Production, 1940; Min. of Supply, 1946; Min. of Aviation, 1959 (Dir of Contracts, 1960-67). *Recreations*: bowls, gardening. *Address*: 9 Evans Gardens, Hunstanton, Norfolk. *T*: Hunstanton 2057.

CLIFTON, Lt-Col Peter Thomas, DSO 1945; DL; JP; Clerk of the Cheque and Adjutant, HM Body Guard of Honourable Corps of Gentlemen at Arms, since 1973; *b* 24 Jan. 1911; *s* of Lt-Col Percy Robert Clifton, CMG, DSO, TD, Clifton Hall, Nottingham; *m* 1st, 1934, Ursula (marr. diss. 1936), *d* of Sir

Edward Hussey Packe; 2nd, 1948, Patricia Mary Adela (who *m* 1935, Robert Cobbold, killed in action 1944), *d* of Major J. M. Gibson-Watt, Doldowlod, Radnorshire; two *d. Educ:* Eton; RMC Sandhurst. 2nd Lieut Grenadier Guards, 1931; served War of 1939-45: France, 1939-40; Italy, 1944-45; Lt-Col 1944; Palestine, 1945-47. Mem. HM Body Guard of Hon. Corps of Gentlemen at Arms, 1960-. DL Notts 1954; JP Notts 1952-59, Hants 1964. *Address:* Dummer House, Basingstoke, Hants. *T:* Dummer 306. *Clubs:* Cavalry and Guards, White's; Royal Yacht Squadron.
See also *J. D. Gibson-Watt.*

CLIFTON-BROWN, Anthony George, TD; late Major RA; formerly Director: Royal Exchange Assurance; Westminster Bank Ltd; Westminster Foreign Bank Ltd; Bank of New South Wales (London Board); one of HM Lieutenants for City of London, 1950-60; *b* 11 Feb. 1903; *y s* of late Edward Clifton-Brown; *m* 1st, 1930, Delia Charlotte (*d* 1947), *y d* of late George Edward Wade; three *d*; 2nd, 1949, Phyllis Adrienne McCulloch, (Bridget) (*d* 1977), *d* of late Francis Harvey, Dublin. *Educ:* Eton; Trinity Coll., Cambridge. Mem. of Court of Assistants, Merchant Taylors' Company (Master, 1945-46; First Upper Warden, 1955-56); Sheriff of the City of London, 1957-58; Alderman of Broad Street Ward, 1950-60. Chm., Management Cttee, Royal London Homœopathic Hosp., 1948-61. Commendatore of Order of Merit of Italian Republic. *Address:* Via del Moro 7, 00153 Rome, Italy.

CLIFTON-BROWN, Lt-Col Geoffrey Benedict; *b* 25 July 1899; *m* 1927, Robina Margaret, *d* of late Rowland Sutton; two *s* (one *d* decd). *Educ:* Eton; RMC Sandhurst. 2nd Lieut 12th Lancers, 1918; Major, 1935; Lt-Col, 1940; served with 12th Lancers in France and Belgium, 1939-40, evacuated Dunkirk (despatches). MP (C) Bury St Edmunds Div. of West Suffolk, 1945-50. *Address:* The Old Rectory, Cockfield, Bury St Edmunds, Suffolk. *T:* Cockfield Green 217.

CLINTON, 22nd Baron *cr* 1299 (title abeyant 1957-65); **Gerard Nevile Mark Fane Trefusis;** landowner; *b* 7 Oct. 1934; *s* of Capt. Charles Fane (killed in action, 1940); assumed by deed poll, 1958, surname of Trefusis in addition to patronymic; *m* 1959, Nicola Harriette Purdon Coote; one *s* two *d. Educ:* Gordonstoun. Took seat in House of Lords, 1965. Mem., Prince of Wales's Councils, 1968-. *Recreations:* shooting, fishing, forestry. *Heir: s* Hon. Charles Patrick Rolle Fane Trefusis, *b* 21 March 1962. *Address:* Heanton Satchville, near Okehampton, North Devon. *T:* Dolton 224, *Club:* Boodle's.

CLINTON, David Osbert F.; *see* Fynes-Clinton.

CLINTON, (Francis) Gordon, FRCM; FBSM; Hon. RAM; ARCM; baritone; Member, Board of Professors, Royal College of Music, since 1975; Chorus Master, City of Birmingham Symphony Orchestra Chorus, since 1974; *b* 19 June 1912; *s* of Rev. F. G. Clinton, Broadway, Worcs; *m* 1939, Phyllis Jarvis, GRSM, ARCM; two *s* one *d. Educ:* Evesham Grammar Sch.; Bromley Sch. for Boys. Open Schol. RCM, 1935; Vicar Choral, St Paul's Cathedral, 1937-49; served War of 1939-45 in RAF; demobilised as Flt-Lieut. Appearances at over 2,000 major concerts and festivals, 1946-; joined staff, RCM, 1949; Principal, Birmingham Sch. of Music, 1960-74. Examr to Associated Board, 1956-. Tours of America, Canada, Europe, Africa, Australasia, Far East (singing, adjudicating, lecturing). *Recreations:* sport, wild-life. *Address:* 42 Pembroke Croft, Hall Green, Birmingham. *T:* 021-744 3513.

CLINTON-THOMAS, Robert Antony, CBE 1965; British Consul, Ostend, since 1973; *b* 5 April 1913; *s* of late Brig. R. H. Thomas, CSI, DSO, and Lady Couchman; *m* 1949, Betty Maria Clocca. *Educ:* Haileybury; Peterhouse, Cambridge (MA). Indian Civil Service, 1937-47; Foreign Office, 1947-49; 1st Sec. and Consul, Manila, 1949-53; Head of Chancery, HM Embassy, Tripoli, 1953-56; FO, 1956-57; Counsellor and Head of Chancery, HM Embassy, Addis Ababa, 1957-59; Counsellor and Head of Chancery, Political Office with the Near East Forces, Cyprus, 1959-61; Political Adviser to the C-in-C Middle East Comd, Aden, 1961-62; Counsellor, HM Embassy, Oslo, 1962-65; FCO (formerly FO), 1965-70; Consul-Gen., Antwerp, 1970-73. *Address:* British Consulate, Ostend, Belgium.

CLISSITT, William Cyrus, OBE 1968; TD; JP; Editor, Evening Express, Liverpool, 1928-54; Secretary of the Press Council, 1960-68; *o s* of late Cyrus Thomas Clissitt, JP, Newport, Mon; *b* 1898; *m* 1923, Antoinette Mary (marr. diss. 1972), *e d* of late Joseph Herbert Canning, OBE, JP (Knight of Papal Order of St Gregory), Newport, Mon; one *s* two *d.* Editor Torbay Herald, Torquay, 1924; active service with Artists' Rifles OTC, European War, 1914-18; and Royal Artillery, 1939-45 (Lt-Col);

commanded Sudan Artillery in the rank of Kaimakam; inaugurated Weekly Wireless Talks on Sport for BBC at Cardiff, 1923; Founder Mem. Guild of British Newspaper Editors; selected Military Mem. West Lancs T & AFA; Hon. Col 626 (Liverpool Irish) HAA Regt RA, TA, 1950-55. JP Liverpool. *Publications:* Knowsley Hall; numerous newspaper articles on wide variety of subjects. *Recreation:* aerophilately. *Address:* 150 Stow Hill, Newport, Gwent. *T:* Newport 65516.

CLITHEROE, 1st Baron *cr* (June) 1955, of Downham; Bt *cr* 1945 (succeeded to Btcy Sept. 1955); **Ralph Assheton,** PC 1944; KCVO 1977; KStJ; FSA; JP; DL; Lord-Lieutenant of Lancashire, 1971-76 (Vice-Lieutenant, 1956-71); High Steward of Westminster since 1962; *b* 24 Feb. 1901; *o s* of Sir Ralph Assheton, 1st Bt; *m* 1924, Hon. Sylvia Benita Frances Hotham, FRICS, FLAS, *d* of 6th Baron Hotham; two *s* one *d. Educ:* Eton (Oppidan Schol.); Christ Church, Oxford (MA). Called to Bar, Inner Temple, 1925; MP (Nat. U) Rushcliffe Div. of Notts, 1934-45; City of London, 1945-50; Blackburn West, 1950-55. Parly Sec., Min. of Labour and Min. of National Service, 1939-42; Parly Sec., Min. of Supply, 1942-43; Financial Sec. to the Treasury, 1943-44; Chm. Conservative Party Organisation, 1944-46; Chm. Public Accounts Cttee, 1948-50; Chm. Select Cttee on Nationalised Industries, 1951-53; Mem. Royal Commission on West Indies, 1938-39. Chm., Borax (Holdings) Ltd, 1958-69 (Dir, 1947-); Deputy Chairman: (Jt) National Westminster Bank Ltd until 1971 (formerly a Dep. Chm. National Provincial Bank); John Brown & Co. Ltd until 1971; Director: The Mercantile Investment Trust Ltd (Chm. 1958-71); Coutts & Co., 1955-71; formerly Director: Tube Investments Ltd (Dep. Chm.); Rio Tinto Zinc; Tanganyika Concessions Ltd; and other cos. Pres., NW of England and IoM TAVR, 1973-75. DL 1955, JP 1934, Lancashire; Mem. Council, Duchy of Lancaster, 1956-77. *Heir: s* Hon. Ralph John Assheton [*b* 3 Nov. 1929; *m* 1961, Juliet, *d* of Christopher Hanbury; two *s* one *d. Educ:* Eton; Christ Church (Scholar), Oxford (MA)]. *Address:* 17 Chelsea Park Gardens, SW3. *T:* 01-352 4020; Downham Hall, Clitheroe, Lancs. *T:* Chatburn 210. *Clubs:* Carlton, Royal Automobile, MCC.
See also *Sir W. M. J. Worsley, Bt.*

CLITHEROW, Rt. Rev. Richard George, MA Cantab; *b* 1 Oct, 1909; *s* of H. G. Clitherow, MRCS, and Elizabeth Willis Clitherow; *m* 1941, Diana, *d* of H. St J. Durston; two *s* one *d. Educ:* Dulwich College; Corpus Christi College, Cambridge; Wells Theological College. Asst Curate, St Augustine, Bermondsey, 1936-40. Chaplain to the Forces, 1940-46 (despatches). Canon Residentiary, Guildford Cathedral, 1946-58; Bishop Suffragan of Stafford, 1958-74. *Recreations:* fishing and gardening. *Address:* 37 Fairbanks Walk, Swynnerton, Stone, Staffs.

CLIVE, Nigel David, CMG 1967; OBE 1959; MC 1944; TD; Adviser to Secretary-General of OECD, since 1970; *b* 13 July 1917; *s* of late Horace David and Hilda Mary Clive; *m* 1949, Maria Jeanne Tambakopoulou. *Educ:* Stowe; Christ Church, Oxford (Scholar). Commissioned 2nd Mddx Yeomanry, 1939; served in Middle East and Greece. Joined Foreign Office, 1946; served Athens, 1946-48; Jerusalem, 1948; FO, 1948-50; Baghdad, 1950-53; FO, 1953-58; Tunis, 1958-62; Algiers, 1962-63; FO, 1964-65; Head of Information Research Dept, FCO (formerly FO), 1966-69. *Recreations:* reading, travel. *Address:* 60 Elm Park Road, SW3. *T:* 01-352 2969; 20 rue de l'Abbé de l'Epée, 75005 Paris, France. *T:* 325-1105. *Clubs:* Brooks's, MCC.

CLOAKE, John Cecil, CMG 1977; HM Diplomatic Service; Ambassador to Bulgaria, since 1976; *b* 2 Dec. 1924; *s* of late Dr Cecil Stedman Cloake, Wimbledon, and Maude Osborne Newling; *m* 1956, Margaret Thomure Morris, Washington, DC, USA; one *s. Educ:* King's Coll. Sch., Wimbledon; Peterhouse, Cambridge. Served in Army, 1943-46 (Lieut RE). Foreign Office, 1948; 3rd Sec., Baghdad, 1949, and Saigon, 1951; 2nd Sec., 1952; FO, 1954; Private Sec. to Permanent Under-Sec., 1956, and to Parly Under-Sec., 1957; 1st Sec., 1957; Consul (Commercial), New York, 1958; 1st Sec., Moscow, 1962; FO, 1963; DSAO, 1965; Counsellor, 1966; Head of Accommodation Dept, 1967; Counsellor (Commercial), Tehran, 1968-72; Fellow, Centre for International Studies, LSE, 1972-73; Head of Trade Relations and Exports Dept, FCO, 1973-76. *Recreations:* gardening, painting, architecture, local history, genealogy. *Address:* c/o Foreign and Commonwealth Office, SW1. *Club:* Travellers'.

CLODE, Dame (Emma) Frances (Heather), DBE 1974 (CBE 1969; OBE 1955; MBE 1951); Chairman, Women's Royal Voluntary Service, 1971-74; *b* 12 Aug. 1903; *d* of Alexander and Florence Marc; *m* 1927, Colonel Charles Clode (then Captain in

Royal Norfolk Regt); one *s. Educ:* privately. Joined WRVS, 1939; served in Cambridge, 1940-45; WRVS Headquarters, 1945; Vice-Chm. 1967. CStJ 1973. *Address:* 1 Willow Close, Pershore, Worcs WR10 1JN. *Club:* Lansdowne.

CLOGHER, Bishop of, since 1973; **Rt. Rev. Robert William Heavener;** *b* 28 Feb. 1906; *s* of Joseph and Maria Heavener; *m* 1936, Ada Marjorie, *d* of Rev. Chancellor Thomas Dagg; one *s* one *d. Educ:* Trinity Coll., Dublin (MA). Ordained, 1929; Curate, Clones; Diocesan Curate, 1930; Curate-in-charge, Lack, 1933-38; Rector, Derryvullen N, 1938-46; Rector, Monaghan, 1946-73; Rural Dean, 1946. Examining Chaplain and Canon of Clogher, 1951-62; Canon of St Patrick's Cathedral, Dublin, 1962-68; Archdeacon of Clogher, 1968-73. OCF, 1938-43; Member of Staff of Command Welfare Officer, NI District, 1938-43. *Publications:* Co. Fermanagh, 1940 (a short topographical and historical account of NI); Diskos, 1970 (a collection of material for Adult Education). *Recreations:* tennis, rare book collecting. *Address:* The See House, Thornfield, Fivemiletown, Co. Tyrone. *T:* Fivemiletown 265. *Club:* Friendly Brother House (Dublin).

CLOGHER, Bishop of, (RC), since 1970; **Most Rev. Patrick Mulligan;** *b* 9 June 1912; *s* of James and Mary Martin. *Educ:* St Macartan's, Monaghan; Maynooth. Prof., St Macartan's, 1938; Bishop's Sec., 1943; Headmaster, Clones, 1948; Headmaster, St Michael's, Enniskillen, 1957; Parish Priest of Machaire Rois and Vicar General and Archdeacon, 1966. *Publications:* contribs to IER, JLAS, Seanchas Clochair. *Address:* Bishop's House, Monaghan, Ireland. *T:* Monaghan 19.

CLORE, Sir Charles, Kt 1971; President, Sears Engineering Ltd; Chairman: Sears Holdings Ltd; British Shoe Corporation Ltd; Lewis's Investment Trust Ltd; Selfridges Ltd; Sears Industries Inc.; Scottish Motor Traction Co. Ltd; Mappin & Webb Ltd; Princes Investments Ltd; *b* 26 Dec. 1904; *m* 1943, Francine Rachel Halphen (marr. diss.); one *s* one *d. Educ:* London. Is also Dir of a number of other public companies engaged in commercial and industrial enterprises. *Address:* 22 Park Street, Park Lane, W1Y 4AE. *T:* 01-499 3821.

CLOSE, Roy Edwin, CBE 1973; Director General, British Institute of Management, since 1976; *b* 11 March 1920; *s* of Bruce Edwin and Minnie Louise Close; *m* 1947, Olive Joan Forty; two *s. Educ:* Trinity Grammar Sch., N London. Served Army, 1939-46; SAS, 1943-46 (Captain). Editorial Staff, The Times; Asst Editor, The Times Review of Industry, 1949-56; Executive, Booker McConnell GP; Dir, Bookers Sugar Estates, 1957-65; Directing Staff, Admin. Staff Coll., Henley, 1965; Industrial Adviser, NEDO, 1966-69; Industrial Dir, NEDO, 1969-73; MSc Univ. of Aston in Birmingham, 1973; Chm., Univ. of Aston Management Centre; Dean of Faculty of Management, 1973-76. *Publications:* various articles on industrial, economic subjects. *Recreations:* squash, swimming, walking, reading, listening to music. *Address:* 5 Chester Mews, SW1. *T:* 01-235 3879; Cathedral Cottage, North Elmham, Norfolk. *Clubs:* Reform, Special Forces.

CLOSE-SMITH, Charles Nugent, TD 1953; Underwriting Member of Lloyd's (Deputy Chairman, 1970); *b* 7 July 1911; 2nd *s* of Thomas Close Smith, Boycott Manor, Buckingham, and Mary Morgan-Grenville, *d* of 11th Baroness Kinloss; *m* 1946, Elizabeth Vivien, *d* of late Major William Kinsman, DSO, Dublin; three *s. Educ:* Eton; Magdalene Coll., Cambridge. Entered Lloyd's, 1932; 2nd Lt, Royal Bucks Yeomanry, 1938. Served War of 1939-45 France and Burma (despatches); retd as Lt-Col, RA. Chairman Lloyd's Non-Marine Underwriters Assoc., 1965; elected to Committee of Lloyd's, 1967-70. *Recreation:* horticulture. *Address:* The Heymersh, Britford, Salisbury, Wilts. *T:* Salisbury 6760. *Clubs:* Boodle's, Gresham.

CLOSS, Prof. August, MA, DPhil; Professor of German and Head of German Department, University of Bristol, 1931-64, now Emeritus; Dean of the Faculty of Arts, 1962 and 1963; *b* 9 Aug. 1898; 4th *s* of late A. Closs; *m* 1931, Hannah Margaret Mary (*d* 1953), novelist and art-critic, *d* of late Robert Priebsch, Prof. and Medievalist at UCL; one *d. Educ:* Berlin, Vienna, Graz, London. Lectured at Sheffield Univ., 1929-30; at University Coll., London, 1930-31. Guest-Prof. at univs of Amsterdam, Ghent, Berlin, Heidelberg, Frankfurt A/M, Bern, Vienna, Rome, Florence, etc, and in the USA at Univs of Columbia, Princeton, Yale, California and at Canadian and Indian Univs. Hon. Fellow Hannover Univ.; Korresp. Mitglied der Deutschen Akademie; Membre Corresp. de l'Institut International des Arts et des Lettres (Zürich); Fellow of PEN. FRSL. Comdr, Cross of Order of Merit, West Germany, Austrian Cross of Merit *Litteris et Artibus. Publications:* Medieval Exempla: (Dame World) Weltlohn, 1934; The Genius

of the German Lyric, 1938 (enlarged 2nd edn 1962, paperback edn 1965); German Lyrics of the Seventeenth Century, 1940, 1947; Hölderlin, 1942, 1944; Tristan und Isolt, 1944, 1974; Die Freien Rhythmen in der deutschen Dichtung, 1947; Novalis-Hymns to the Night, 1948; Die neuere deutsche Lyrik vom Barock bis zur Gegenwart, 1952, 1957; Deutsche Philologie im Aufriss; Woge im Westen, 1954; Medusa's Mirror; Reality and Symbol, 1957; The Harrap Anthology of German Poetry, 1957, new edn 1969; Reality and Creative Vision in German Lyrical Poetry (Symposium), 1963; Introductions to German Literature (4 vols), 1967; Twentieth Century German Literature, 1969, 2nd edn 1971; The Sea in the Shell, 1977; (ed) Briefwechsel, 1977; contribs to Times Literary and Educ. Supplements, German Life and Letters, Modern Lang. Rev., Euphorion, Reallexikon, Deutsches Literatur-Lexikon, Aryan Path, Germanistik, Universitas, and American journals. *Recreations:* music, collecting first editions. *Address:* 40 Stoke Hill, Stoke Bishop, Bristol BS9 1EX. *T:* Bristol 682244. *Club:* University of Bristol.

CLOTHIER, Cecil Montacute, QC 1965; a Recorder (formerly Recorder of Blackpool), since 1965; Judge of Appeal in the Isle of Man, since 1972; *b* 28 Aug. 1919; *s* of Hugh Montacute Clothier, Liverpool; *m* 1943, Mary Elizabeth, *o d* of late Ernest Glover Bush; one *s* two *d. Educ:* Stonyhurst Coll.; Lincoln Coll., Oxford (BCL, MA). Served 1939-46, 51 (Highland) Div.; British Army Staff, Washington, DC; Hon. Lt-Col Royal Signals. Called to Bar, Inner Temple, 1950, Bencher, 1973. A Legal Assessor to Gen. Medical and Gen. Dental Councils; Mem., Royal Commn on NHS, 1976-. *Address:* Goldsmith Building, Temple, EC4Y 7BL. *T:* 01-353 7881.

CLOTWORTHY, Stanley Edward, CBE 1959; Chairman, Alcan Aluminium (UK) Ltd, 1969-74; *b* 21 June 1902; *s* of Joseph and Fanny Kate Clotworthy; *m* 1927, Winifred Edith, *d* of J. Mercer Harris; one *s* one *d. Educ:* Peter Symonds Sch., Winchester; University Coll., Southampton. Student apprenticeship with B. T. H. Ltd, Rugby, 1923-26; Macintosh Cable Co., Liverpool, 1926-27; Alcan Industries Ltd (formerly Northern Aluminium Co.), 1927-67. Pro-Chancellor, Southampton Univ., 1972-. Hon. DSc Southampton, 1969. *Recreations:* shooting, gardening. *Address:* Kemano, Warreners Lane, St George's Hill, Weybridge, Surrey. *T:* Weybridge 42904.

CLOUDSLEY-THOMPSON, Prof. John Leonard, MA, PhD (Cantab), DSc (London); FRES, FLS, FZS, FIBiol, FWA; Professor of Zoology, Birkbeck College, University of London, since 1972 (Reader 1971-72); *b* Murree, India, 23 May 1921; *s* of Dr Ashley George Gyton Thompson, MA, MD (Cantab), DPH, and Muriel Elaine (*née* Griffiths); *m* 1944, Jessie Anne Cloudsley, MCSP, DipBS, LCAD; three *s. Educ:* Marlborough Coll.; Pembroke Coll., Cambridge. War of 1939-45: commissioned into 4th Queen's Own Hussars, 1941; transf. 4th Co. of Lond. Yeo. (Sharpshooters); N Africa, 1941-42 (severely wounded); Instructor (Capt.), Sandhurst, 1943; rejoined regt for D Day, Caen Offensive, etc, 1944 (Hon. rank of Capt. on resignation). Lectr in Zoology, King's Coll., Univ. of London, 1950-60; Prof. of Zoology, Univ. of Khartoum, and Keeper, Sudan Nat. Hist. Museum, 1960-71. Nat. Science Foundn Sen. Res. Fellow, Univ. of New Mexico, Albuquerque, USA, 1969. Took part in: Cambridge Iceland Expedn, 1947; Expedn to Southern Tunisia, 1954; univ. expedns with his wife to various parts of Africa, 1960-73, incl. Trans-Sahara crossing, 1967. Liveryman, Worshipful Co. of Skinners, 1952-. Royal African Soc's Medal, 1969. Editor, Jl of Arid Environments (assisted by wife). *Publications:* Biology of Deserts (ed), 1954; Spiders, Scorpions, Centipedes and Mites, 1958 (2nd edn 1968); Animal Behaviour, 1960; Rhythmic Activity in Animal Physiology and Behaviour, 1961; Land Invertebrates (with John Sankey), 1961; Life in Deserts (with M. J. Chadwick), 1964; Desert Life, 1965; Animal Conflict and Adaptation, 1965; Animal Twilight, 1967; Microecology, 1967; Zoology of Tropical Africa, 1969; The Temperature and Water Relations of Reptiles, 1971; Desert Life, 1974; Terrestrial Environments, 1975; Insects and History, 1976; Evolutionary Trends in the Mating of Arthropoda, 1976; (ed jtly) Environmental Physiology of Animals, 1976; Man and the Biology of Arid Zones, 1977; The Water and Temperature Relations of Woodlice, 1977; The Desert, 1977; Animal Migration, 1978; Ecology, Adaptation and Biological Rhythm, 1978; contribs to Encyclopædia Britannica, Encyclopedia Americana; shorter monographs and children's books; many scientific articles in learned jls, etc. *Recreations:* music (especially opera), photography, travel. *Address:* Department of Zoology, Birkbeck College, Malet Street, WC1E 7HX; (permanent) c/o National Westminster Bank Ltd, 62 Victoria Street, SW1E 6QE; (home) Flat 9, 4 Craven Hill, W2 3DS; Little Clarkes, Little Sampford, Saffron Walden, Essex CB10 2SA.

CLOUGH, (John) Alan, CBE 1972; MC 1945; Deputy Chairman since 1970, and Chief Executive since 1977, British Mohair Spinners Ltd; *b* 20 March 1924; *s* of John Clough and late Yvonne (*née* Dollfus); *m* 1st, 1949, Margaret Joy Catton (marr. diss.); one *s* two *d*; 2nd, 1961, Mary Cowan Catherwood; one *s* one *d*. *Educ:* Marlborough Coll.; Leeds Univ. HM Forces, Queen's Bays, 1942-47, N Africa and Italy (Captain); TA Major, Yorkshire Hussars, 1947-55. Director: Robert Clough (Keighley) Holdings Ltd; Smith (Allerton) Ltd; Keighley Fleece Mills Co. Ltd; Jeremiah Ambler Ltd, 1970-; Christopher Waud Ltd, 1970-; Worsted Spinners Fedn, 1964-; Crofton Yarns Ltd, 1968-; Stork Brothers Ltd; Jeremiah Ambler (Ulster) Ltd. Mayor, Co. of Merchants of Staple of England, 1969-70. Chm., Wool Industries Res. Assoc., 1967-69; Chm., Wool Textile Delegn, 1969-72; Member: Wool Textile EDC, 1967-72; Jt Textile Cttee, NEDO, 1972-74; President: Comitextil (Co-ordinating Cttee for Textile Industries in EEC), Brussels, 1975-77 (Vice-Pres., 1974-75); British Textile Confedn, 1974-77. CompTI 1975. *Recreations:* fishing, gardening, travel. *Address:* Spitalcroft Green, Knaresborough, N Yorks. *T:* Harrogate 863232; Glen Lodge, Glen, Co. Donegal, Ireland. *Club:* Boodle's.

CLOUGH, Prunella; painter; *b* 1919; *d* of Eric Clough Taylor, poet and civil servant, and Thora Clough Taylor. *Educ:* privately; Chelsea Sch. of Art. Exhibited at Leger Gallery, 1947; Roland Browse & Delbanco, 1949; Leicester Galleries, 1953; Whitechapel Gallery, 1960; Grosvenor Gallery, 1964, 1968; Graves Art Gallery, Sheffield, 1972; New Art Centre, 1975; Serpentine Gallery, 1976. City of London Midsummer Prize, 1977. *Address:* 65 Moore Park Road, SW6.

CLOUSTON, Air Cdre (retd) Arthur Edmond, CB 1957; DSO 1943; DFC 1942; AFC and Bar, 1939; RAF retd; *b* 7 April 1908; *s* of R. E. Clouston, mining engineer, Motueka, Nelson, NZ; *m* 1937, Elsie, *d* of late S. Markham Turner, Farnborough, Hants; two *d*. *Educ:* Rockville Sch.; Bainham Sch. Joined Royal Air Force, 1930. Record Flight, London-Capetown-London, 1937 (Seagrave Trophy); Record Flight, London-NZ-London, 1938 (Britannia Trophy). Served War of 1939-45 (DFC, DSO), engaged in Research Test Flying, Fighter Comd, Coastal Comd; AOC, Singapore, 1954-57; Comdt, Aeroplane and Armament Experimental Establishment, Boscombe Down, Amesbury, 1957-60. Group Capt. 1947; Air Cdre 1954. *Publication:* The Dangerous Skies (autobiography), 1954. *Address:* Wings, Constantine Bay, Padstow, Cornwall.

CLOUTMAN, Air Vice-Marshal Geoffrey William, FDSRCS; QHDS 1976; Director of Dental Services, Royal Air Force, since 1977; *b* 1 April 1920; *s* of Rev. Walter Evans Cloutman and Dora Cloutman; *m* 1949, Sylvia Brown; three *d*. *Educ:* Cheltenham Grammar Sch.; Queen Mary Coll., and The London Hosp., Univ. of London. LDSRCS 1942, FDSRCS 1954. House Surg., London Hosp.; joined RAFVR, 1942; War Service, UK and India; specialisation in preventive dentistry, 1948-; dental hygiene trng; oral surgery appts, 1955-73: RAF Hosps, Fayid, Akrotiri, Aden, Wegberg, Wroughton, Uxbridge; Principal Dental Off., Strike Comd, 1973. *Publications:* papers in Brit. Dental Jl and Dental Practitioner. *Recreations:* English church music, cricket, Rugby. *Address:* 56 Moor Lane, Rickmansworth, Herts. *T:* Rickmansworth 72697. *Club:* Royal Air Force.

CLOVER, Robert Gordon, TD 1951; QC 1958; JP; **His Honour Judge Clover;** a Circuit Judge (formerly Judge of County Courts), since 1965; *b* 14 Nov. 1911; *m* 1947, Elizabeth Suzanne (*née* McCorquodale); two *s*. *Educ:* Lancing Coll.; Exeter Coll., Oxford. MA, BCL Oxford. Called to Bar, Lincoln's Inn, 1935. Served in RA, 1939-45 (despatches, 1944). Practised on Northern Circuit, 1935-61; Recorder of Blackpool, 1960-61; Dep. Comr for purposes of Nat. Insurance Acts, 1961-65; Dep. Chm., Bucks QS, 1969-71; Chm., Marlow Magistrates Court, 1972. JP Bucks, 1969. *Address:* The Garth, Marlow, Bucks. *T:* Marlow 4170.

CLOWES, Col Henry Nelson, CVO 1977; DSO 1945; OBE 1953; Lieutenant of Hon. Corps of Gentlemen-at-Arms, since 1976; *b* 21 Oct. 1911; *yr s* of late Major E. W. Clowes, DSO, Bradley Hall, Ashbourne, Derbs; *m* 1941, Diana Katharine, MBE, *er d* of late Major Basil Kerr, DSC; one *s*. *Educ:* Eton; Sandhurst. Served in Scots Guards, 1931-57: Adjt RMA Sandhurst, 1940-41; psc 1942; Bde Major 4th Inf. Bde, 1942-44; comd 2nd Bn Scots Guards, 1944-46; jssc 1947; cmd 1st Bn Scots Guards, 1947-50; War Office (AG4), 1950-52; AAG Scottish Comd, 1952-54; Lt-Col comdg Scots Guards, 1954-57; retired 1957. Mem. Her Majesty's Body Guard, 1961; Clerk of the Cheque and Adjt, 1966; Standard Bearer, 1973-76. *Recreations:* shooting, fishing. *Address:* 30 Burnsall Street, SW3 3SU. *T:* 01-352 9565. *Clubs:* Cavalry and Guards, Pratt's, Shikar.

CLOWES, Maj.-Gen. Norman, CBE 1943; DSO 1918; MC; ADC to the King, 1946-49; retired Sept. 1949; *b* 7 Oct. 1893; *s* of late Albert Clowes, Warwick, Queensland; *m*; one *s*. *Educ:* Toowoomba Grammar Sch.; RMC Duntroon. Commissioned Australian Staff Corps, 1914; served with AIF, 1914-18, in Egypt, Gallipoli, France, Belgium; Grad. Staff Coll., Camberley, 1920; exchange duty Indian Army, 1927-30; transf. British Army, 1931; Comdg 1st Bn Manchester Regt, 1937-39, served during Palestine Rebellion, 1937-38. Col, 1939; Brig. 1941; temp. Maj.-Gen. 1943. Despatches 5 times; Croix de Guerre, France; Medal of Freedom, USA. *Address:* Tanglin, Harefield Road, Middleton-on-Sea, Sussex.

CLOYNE, Bishop of, (RC), since 1957; **Most Rev. John J. Ahern;** *b* 31 Aug. 1911; *s* of James Ahern and Ellen Mulcahy. *Educ:* St Colman's Coll., Fermoy; St Patrick's Coll., Maynooth; Irish Coll., Rome. Ordained, 1936. Prof. at St Colman's Coll., Fermoy, 1940-44; St Patrick's Coll., Maynooth, 1946-57. *Address:* Bishop's House, Cobh, Co. Cork, Ireland.

CLUCAS, Sir Kenneth (Henry), KCB 1976 (CB 1969); Permanent Secretary, Department of Prices and Consumer Protection, since 1974; *b* 18 Nov. 1921; *o s* of late Rev. J. H. Clucas; *m* 1960, Barbara, *e d* of Rear-Adm. R. P. Hunter, USN (Retd), Washington, DC; two *d*. *Educ:* Kingswood Sch.; Emmanuel Coll., Cambridge. Royal Signals, 1941-46 (despatches). Joined Min. of Labour as Asst Principal, 1948; 2nd Sec. (Labour), British Embassy, Cairo, 1950; Principal, HM Treasury, 1952; Min. of Labour, 1954; Private Sec. to Minister, 1960-62; Asst Sec., 1962; Under-Sec., 1966-68; Sec., Nat. Bd for Prices and Incomes, 1968-71; First Civil Service Comr and Dep. Sec., CSD, 1971-73; Dep. Sec., DTI, 1974. *Address:* Cariad, Knoll Road, Godalming, Surrey. *T:* Godalming 6430. *Club:* Athenæum.

CLUTTERBUCK, Vice-Adm. Sir David Granville, KBE 1968; CB 1965; *b* Gloucester, 25 Jan. 1913; *m* 1937, Rose Mere Vaile, Auckland, NZ; two *d*. Joined RN, 1929. Served War of 1939-45 (despatches twice): navigating officer of cruisers HMS Ajax, 1940-42, HMS Newfoundland, 1942-46 (present Japanese surrender at Tokyo). Subsequently commanded destroyers Sluys and Cadiz; Naval Attaché at British Embassy, Bonn; Capt. (D) of Third Training Squadron in HMS Zest, Londonderry, 1956-58; commanded cruiser HMS Blake; Chief of Staff to C-in-C Home Fleet and C-in-C Allied Forces Eastern Atlantic, 1963-66; Rear-Adm., 1963; Vice-Adm. 1966; Dep. Supreme Allied Comdr, Atlantic, 1966-68. Administrative Dir, Business Graduates Assoc. Ltd, 1969-. *Address:* 29 Elvaston Place, SW7. *Club:* Army and Navy.

CLUTTERBUCK, Edmund Harry Michael, OBE 1957; Deputy Chairman, Scottish & Newcastle Breweries Ltd; *b* 22 July 1920; *s* of Maj.-Gen. W. E. Clutterbuck, *qv*; *m* 1945, Anne Agatha Woodsend; one *s* three *d*. *Educ:* Winchester Coll.; New Coll., Oxford (MA). HM Forces, 1940-46. Joined William Younger & Co. Ltd, 1947; Dir, Scottish Brewers Ltd, 1955; Scottish & Newcastle Breweries Ltd: Dir, 1960; Techn. Man. Dir, 1965; Jt Man. Dir, 1970; Dep. Chm., 1973; Director: Scottish American Mortgage Co., 1962; Scottish Eastern Investment Trust, 1965; Scottish Widows' Fund, 1965; Pres., European Brewery Convention, 1971; Member: Heriot-Watt Univ. Court, 1959; Herring Industry Bd, 1963; White Fish Authority, 1973; Dep. Chm., Royal Inst. of Internat. Affairs (Scottish Br.), 1969. *Recreations:* music, fishing, shooting, travel, languages. *Address:* Greystane, 4 Kinellan Road, Edinburgh EH12 6ES. *T:* 031-337 6027. *Club:* New (Edinburgh).

CLUTTERBUCK, Maj.-Gen. Richard Lewis, CB 1971; OBE 1958; Lecturer in Politics, University of Exeter, since 1972; *b* London, 22 Nov. 1917; *s* of late Col L. St J. R. Clutterbuck, OBE, late RA, and late Mrs I. J. Clutterbuck; *m* 1948, Angela Muriel Barford; three *s*. *Educ:* Radley Coll.; Pembroke Coll., Cambridge. MA Cantab (Mech. Scis); PhD (Econ. and Pol.), London Univ., 1971. Commd in RE, 1937; War Service: France, 1940; Sudan and Ethiopia, 1941; Western Desert, 1941-43; Italy, 1944; subseq. service in: Germany, 1946 and 1951-53; Italy, 1946; Palestine, 1947; Malaya, 1956-58; Christmas Island (Nuclear Trials), 1958; USA, 1961-63; Singapore, 1966-68. Instructor, British Army Staff Coll., 1953-56; Instructor, US Army Staff Coll., 1961-63; idc 1965; Chief Engr, Far East Land Forces, 1966-68; Engr-in-Chief (Army), 1968-70; Chief Army Instructor, Royal Coll. of Defence Studies, 1971-72, retired. Col Comdt, RE, 1972-77. FICE. *Publications:* Across the River (as Richard Jocelyn), 1957; The Long Long War, 1966; Protest and the Urban Guerrilla, 1973; Riot and Revolution in Singapore and Malaya, 1973; Living with Terrorism, 1975; Guerillas and Terrorists, 1977; contribs to British and US jls. *Address:* Department of Politics, University of Exeter, Exeter. *Clubs:* Royal Commonwealth Society, Army and Navy.

WW—16

CLUTTERBUCK, Maj.-Gen. Walter Edmond, DSO 1943; MC; *b* 17 Nov. 1894; *s* of E. H. Clutterbuck, JP, Hardenhuish Park, Chippenham, Wilts; *m* 1919, Gwendolin Atterbury (*d* 1975), *o d* of H. G. Younger, JP, Benmore, Argyllshire; one *s* three *d. Educ:* Horris Hill; Cheltenham Coll.; RMC Sandhurst. Commissioned Royal Scots Fusiliers, 1913; served European War, 1914-19, France, Gallipoli, Egypt, Palestine, and S Russia (wounded twice, MC and bar, Crown of Italy, 1914 Star and clasp, despatches twice); Bt Lt-Col 1939; War of 1939-45 commanded: 1st Royal Scots Fusiliers, 1939-40; 10th Inf. Bde, 1940-41; 1st Div., 1941-43, N Africa and Pantellaria (DSO, Legion of Honour); an Inf. Div. Home Forces, 1943. Chief of British Military Mission to Egypt, 1945-46; retired pay, 1946. *Recreations:* hunting, fishing, shooting. *Address:* Hornby Castle, Bedale, N Yorks. *T:* Old Catterick 579. *Club:* Naval and Military.
See also E. H. M. Clutterbuck.

CLUTTON, Rafe Henry, FRICS; Partner in Cluttons, Chartered Surveyors, London, since 1955; *b* 13 June 1929; *s* of Robin John Clutton and Rosalie Muriel (*née* Birch); *m* 1954, Jill Olwyn Evans; four *s* one *d. Educ:* Tonbridge Sch., Kent. FRICS 1959. Director, Legal & General Assurance Soc. Ltd, 1972-. Member: National Theatre Bd, 1976-; Salvation Army London Adv. Bd, 1971-. Governor, Royal Foundn of Grey Coat Hosp., 1967-. *Recreations:* occasional sailing and perpetual gardening. *Address:* Fairfield, North Chailey, Sussex. *T:* Newick 2431. *Clubs:* Royal Thames Yacht, City of London.

CLUTTON-BROCK, Arthur Guy; independent social worker, 1965-72, retired; *b* 5 April 1906; *s* of late Henry Alan Clutton-Brock and late Rosa Clutton-Brock; *m* 1934, Francys Mary Allen; one *d. Educ:* Rugby Sch.; Magdalene Coll., Cambridge (Hon. Fellow, 1973). Cambridge House, 1927; Rugby House, 1929; Borstal Service, 1933; Principal Probation Officer for the Metropolitan Police Court District, 1936; Head of Oxford House, 1940; Christian Reconstruction in Europe, 1946; Agricultural Labourer, 1947; Agriculturalist at St Faith's Mission, 1949; Field Worker of African Development Trust, 1959-65; deported from Rhodesia by rebel regime, 1971. Treasurer, Cold Comfort Farm Soc., 1966. *Publications:* Dawn in Nyasaland, 1959; Cold Comfort Confronted, 1973. *Address:* Gelli Uchaf, Llandyrnog, Clwyd LL16 4HR.

CLUVER, Eustace Henry, ED; MA; DM, ChB Oxon; DPH London; FRSH; Emeritus Professor of Medical Education, University of the Witwatersrand, Johannesburg, SA, since 1963; *b* 28 Aug. 1894; *s* of late Dr F. A. Cluver, Stellenbosch; *m* 1929, Eileen Ledger; three *d. Educ:* Victoria Coll., Stellenbosch; Hertford Coll., Oxford (Rhodes scholar). 1st class Final Hon. Sch. of Physiology, 1916. Elected to a Senior Demyship at Magdalen Coll., 1917; King's Coll. (Burney Yeo Scholarship, 1918). Served European War, 1914-18 (Capt. S Af. Med. Corps, BEF, France); War of 1939-45 (Col Dir of Pathology, S Af. Med. Corps). Prof. of Physiology, Univ. of the Witwatersrand, Johannesburg, 1919-26; Sec. for Public Health and Chief Health Officer for the Union of South Africa, 1938-40; Dir of S African Inst. for Med. Research and Prof. of Preventive Medicine, Univ. Witwatersrand, 1940-59. LLD (*hc*) Witwatersrand, 1974. KStJ. *Publications:* Public Health in South Africa, 1934 (Textbook), 6th edn 1959; Social Medicine, 1951; Medical and Health Legislation in the Union of South Africa, 1949, 2nd edn 1960; papers in scientific and medical journals. *Address:* Mornhill Farm, Walkerville, Transvaal, South Africa.

CLWYD, 2nd Baron *cr* 1919; **John Trevor Roberts;** Bt, 1908; Assistant Secretary of Commissions, Lord Chancellor's Department of House of Lords, 1948-61; *b* 28 Nov. 1900; *s* of 1st Baron and Hannah (*d* 1951), *d* of W. S. Caine, MP; *S* father, 1955; *m* 1932, Joan de Bois, *d* of late Charles R. Murray, Woodbank, Partickhill, Glasgow; one *s* one *d. Educ:* Gresham's Sch.; Trinity Coll., Cambridge. BA 1922. Barrister, Gray's Inn, 1930. JP County of London, 1950. *Recreation:* fishing. *Heir: s* Hon. (John) Anthony Roberts [*b* 2 Jan. 1935; *m* 1969, Geraldine, *yr d* of C. E. Cannons, Queanbeyan, NSW; three *s*]. *Address:* 15 Aubrey Road, W8. *T:* 01-727 7911; Trimmings, Gracious Street, Selborne, Hants.

CLWYD, Ann, (Ann Clwyd Roberts); journalist and broadcaster; Welsh Correspondent, The Guardian; Vice-Chairman, Welsh Arts Council, since 1975; *b* 21 March 1937; *d* of Gwilym Henri Lewis and Elizabeth Ann Lewis; *m* 1963, Owen Dryhurst Roberts, Editor, News and Current Affairs, BBC Wales. *Educ:* Halkyn Primary Sch.; Holywell Grammar Sch.; The Queen's Sch., Chester; University Coll., Bangor. Student-teacher, Hope Sch., Flintshire, 1955-56; BBC Studio Manager, 1958-63; freelance reporter, producer. Member: Welsh Hospital Board, 1970-74; Arts Council of Gt Britain, 1975-; Mem., Cardiff Community Health Council, 1975-. Member: Nat. Union of Journalists; TGWU. Contested (Lab): Denbigh, 1970; Gloucester, Oct. 1974. Member: Royal Commn on NHS, 1976-; Mental Health Tribunal for Wales. Mem. working party: report, Organisation of Out-Patient Care, for Welsh Hosp. Bd; Bilingualism in the Hospital Service; Mem., Labour Party Study Gp, People and the Media. Mem., Civic Trust for Wales. Governor, UC Aberystwyth. *Publications:* articles in New Statesman, Labour Weekly. *Recreations:* committees and shredding paper, sailing. *Address:* 1 Lon Werdd, St Fagans, Cardiff. *T:* Cardiff 593492.

CLYDE, James John, QC (Scot.) 1971; *b* 29 Jan. 1932; *s* of Rt Hon. Lord Clyde; *m* 1963, Ann Clunie Hoblyn; two *s. Educ:* Edinburgh Academy; Corpus Christi Coll., Oxford (BA); Edinburgh Univ. (LLB). Called to Scottish Bar, 1959; Advocate-Depute, 1973-74. Contested (C) Dundee East, 1974. Chancellor to Bishop of Argyll and the Isles, 1972-. Mem., Scottish Valuation Adv. Council, 1972-; Chm., Med. Appeal Tribunal, 1974-. *Publications:* (ed jtly) Armour on Valuation, 3rd edn, 1961, 4th edn, 1971. *Recreations:* music, golf, walking. *Address:* 9 Heriot Row, Edinburgh EH3 6HU. *T:* 031-556 7114. *Club:* New (Edinburgh).

CLYDESMUIR, 2nd Baron *cr* 1948, of Braidwood; **Ronald John Bilsland Colville,** KT 1972; CB 1965; MBE 1944; TD; Lord High Commissioner to the General Assembly, Church of Scotland, 1971 and 1972; Lord-Lieutenant, Lanarkshire, since 1963; Lieutenant, Royal Company of Archers, Queen's Body Guard for Scotland; *b* 21 May 1917; *s* of 1st Baron Clydesmuir, PC, GCIE, TD, and Agnes Anne (*d* 1970), CI 1947, Kaisar-i-Hind Gold Medal; *S* father, 1954; *m* 1946, Joan Marguerita, *d* of Lt-Col E. B. Booth, DSO, Darver Castle, Co. Louth; two *s* two *d. Educ:* Charterhouse; Trinity Coll., Cambridge. Served in The Cameronians (Scottish Rifles), 1939-45 (MBE, despatches). Commanded 6/7th Bn The Cameronians, TA, 1953-56. Director: Colvilles Ltd, 1958-70; British Linen Bank (Dep. Governor, 1966-71); Bank of Scotland (Dep. Governor, 1971-72, Governor, 1972-); Scottish Provident Instn, 1954-; Scotbits Securities Ltd, 1960-; The Scottish Western Investment Co., 1965-; BSC Strip Mills Div., 1970-73; Caledonian Offshore Co. Ltd, 1971-; Barclays Bank, 1972-; Chm., North Sea Assets Ltd, 1972-. Chm., Exec. Cttee, Scottish Council (Development and Industry); President: Scottish Council of Physical Recreation, 1964-72; Scottish Br., National Playing Fields Assoc.; Chm., Council, Territorial, Auxiliary and Volunteer Reserve Assocs, 1969-73, Pres., 1974-; Chm., Lanarkshire T&AFA, 1957-63, Pres. 1963-68; Pres. Lowland TA&VRA. Hon. Colonel: 6th/7th (Territorial) Bn, The Cameronians (Scottish Rifles), 1967-71; 52 Lowland Volunteers, T&AVR, 1970-75. Chm., Scottish Outward Bound Assoc. DL Lanarkshire, 1955, Vice-Lieut, 1959-63. Hon. LLD Strathclyde, 1968; Hon. DSc Heriot-Watt, 1971. *Recreations:* shooting, fishing. *Heir: s* Hon. David Ronald Colville, *b* 8 April 1949. *Address:* Langlees House, Biggar, Lanarkshire. *T:* Biggar 20057. *Clubs:* Caledonian; New (Edinburgh).
See also Capt. N. E. F. Dalrymple Hamilton.

COAD, Maj.-Gen. Basil Aubrey, CB 1953; CBE 1950; DSO 1944 (Bar 1945); DL; *b* 27 Sept. 1906; *s* of late Engineer-Capt. H. J. Coad, RN, and late Mrs E. M. Coad; *m* 1st, 1935, Janet Octavia (*d* 1954); no *c*; 2nd, 1955, Mrs Clare Henley; one *d. Educ:* Felsted; RMC Sandhurst. Commissioned into Wilts Regt, 1926; served in India, 1926-28; Shanghai, 1929-30; Adjutant 2nd Bn Wilts Regt, 1934-37; Palestine, 1935-36; Adjt 4th Bn Wilts Regt, 1937-39; comd 5th Bn Dorsetshire Regt, 1942-44; Comdr 130 Infantry Bde, 1944-46; Staff Coll., 1946; comd 2nd Bn Wilts Regt, Dec. 1946-48; formed and comd 27 Infantry Bde, 1948-51; Hong Kong, 1949-50; Korea, 1950-51; Comdr 2nd Infantry Div., 1951-54; Pres., Regular Commissions Board, Westbury, Wilts, 1954-57, retired. Col The Wilts Regt (Duke of Edinburgh's), 1954-59; Col The Duke of Edinburgh's Royal Regt (Berks and Wilts), 1959-64. DL Wilts 1963. Officer, US Legion of Merit, 1954; American Silver Star, 1950. *Recreation:* gardening. *Address:* Nursteed House, Devizes, Wilts. *Club:* Army and Navy.

COADY, Aubrey William Burleton, CMG 1959; Chairman, Electricity Commission of NSW, 1959-75 (Member since 1950); *b* Singleton, NSW, 15 June 1915; *s* of W. A. Coady, Belmont; *m* 1964, Phyllis K., *d* of late G. W. Mathews. *Educ:* Newcastle High Sch.; Sydney Univ. (BA, BEc). Under-Sec. and Comptroller of Accounts, NSW Treasury, 1955-59. *Address:* 42 Rickard Avenue, Mosman, NSW 2088, Australia.

COAKER, Maj.-Gen. Ronald Edward, CB 1972; CBE 1963; MC 1942; *b* 28 Nov. 1917; *s* of late Lieut-Col Vere Arthur Coaker, DSO, and Cicely Annie Coaker (*née* Egerton), Richard's Hill,

Battle, Sussex; *m* 1946, Constance Aimée Johanna, *d* of Francis Newton Curzon, Lockington Hall, Derby; one *s* two *d*. *Educ:* Wellington; RMC, Sandhurst. 2nd Lieut IA (Skinner's Horse), 1937; served War of 1939-45, Middle East, Italy and Burma; transf. 17th/21st Lancers, 1947; Lt-Col 1954; GSO1, 7th Armoured Div., 1954-56; comd 17th/21st Lancers, 1956-58; Col GS to Chief of Defence Staff, 1958-60; Brig. 1961; Commandant RAC Centre, 1961-62; Dir of Defence Plans (Army), 1964-66; Assistant Chief of Staff (Intelligence), SHAPE, 1967-70; Dir of Military Operations, MoD, 1970-72. Maj.-Gen. 1966; retired 1972. Col 17th/21st Lancers, 1965-75. DL Rutland 1973. *Recreations:* agriculture, field sports, bridge, tennis. *Address:* Seaton Old Rectory, Uppingham, Rutland LE15 9HU. *T:* Morcott 276; Estate Office, Lockington, Derby DE7 2RH. *T:* Kegworth 2226. *Club:* Cavalry and Guards.

COALES, Prof. John Flavell, CBE 1974 (OBE 1945); FRS 1970; Professor of Engineering (Control), Cambridge University, 1965-74, now Emeritus; Fellow of Clare Hall, 1964-74, now Emeritus; *b* 14 Sept. 1907; *s* of John Dennis Coales and Marion Beatrice Coales (*née* Flavell); *m* 1936, Mary Dorothea Violet, *d* of Rev. Guthrie Henry Lewis Alison; two *s* two *d*. *Educ:* Berkhamsted Sch.; Sidney Sussex Coll., Cambridge (MA). Admty Dept of Scientific Res., 1929-46; Res. Dir, Elliott Bros (London) Ltd, Engrg Dept, Cambridge Univ.: Asst Dir of Res., 1953; Lectr, 1956; Reader in Engrg, 1958; Prof., 1965. Part-time Mem., E Electricity Bd, 1967-73. Mackay Vis. Prof. of Electrical Engrg, Univ. of Calif., Berkeley, 1963. Internat. Fedn of Automatic Control: MEC, 1957; Vice-Pres., 1961; Pres., 1963. Brit. Conf. on Automation and Computation: Gp B Vice-Chm., 1958; Chm., 1960. UK Automation Council: Chm. Res. and Develt Panel, 1960-63; Chm. For. Relations Panel, 1960-64; Vice-Chm., 1961-63; Chm., 1963-66. Instn of Electrical Engrs: Mem. Council, 1953-55, 1964-77; Chm., Measurement Section, 1953; Chm., Control and Automation Div., 1965, etc; Vice-Pres., 1966-71; Pres., 1971-72. Council of Engineering Institutions: Vice-Chm., 1974; Chm., 1975 (Mem. Council for Envtl Sci. and Engrg, 1973-); World Environment and Resources Council, Pres., 1973-74. Pres., Soc. of Instrument Technology, 1958. Past Member, Gen. Bd and Exec. Cttee of Nat. Physical Laboratory; Member: Adv. Council, RMCS, 1963-73; Educn Adv. Cttee for RAF, 1967-76; Trng and Educn Adv. Cttee of RAF, 1976-; Court of Cranfield Inst. of Technology, 1970-; Governing Body, Nat. Inst. of Agric. Engrg, 1970-75; Envtl Design and Engrg Res. Cttee, DoE Bldg Res. Estab., 1973-; British Council Sci. Adv. Cttee, 1973-75; Engrg and Bldgs Bd, ARC, 1973-77; British Library Adv. Council, 1975-. Governor: Hatfield Coll. of Technology, 1951-68; Hatfield Polytechnic, 1969-70 (Hon. Fellow, 1971-). CEng, FICE, FIEE (Pres., IEE, 1971-72), FIEEE, FIAgrE, FInstP; Founder Fellow, Fellowship of Engineering, 1976; Hon. Mem., Inst. of Measurement and Control, 1971. Hon. DSc City Univ. 1970; Hon. DTech Loughborough, 1977. Harold Hartley Medal, 1971. *Publications:* (ed) Automatic and Remote Control (Proc. First Congr. of Internat. Fedn of Automatic Control), 1961; original papers on radio direction finding, radar, information theory, magnetic amplifiers, automatic control, automation and technical education. *Recreations:* mountaineering, farming, gardening. *Address:* 4 Latham Road, Cambridge CB2 2EQ. *Clubs:* Athenæum, Alpine.

COATE, Maj.-Gen. Sir Raymond Douglas, KBE 1967; CB 1966; *b* 8 May 1908; *s* of Frederick James and Elizabeth Anne Coate; *m* 1939, Frances Margaret Varley; two *s*. *Educ:* King Edward's Sch., Bath; RMC Sandhurst. Commissioned into Devonshire Regt, 1928; transferred to Royal Army Pay Corps, 1937; Paymaster-in-Chief, 1963-67; Col Comdt RAPC, 1970-74. Chm., Officers' Widows' Branch, SSAFA, 1969-; Financial Sec., Friends of the Elderly and Gentlefolks' Help, 1969-. *Address:* 18 Roehampton Close, SW15 5LU.

COATES, Edith, OBE 1977; Principal Dramatic Mezzo-Soprano, Royal Opera, Covent Garden, 1947; *b* Lincoln, 31 May 1908; *d* of Percy and Eleanor Coates, Leeds; *m* 1933, Harry Powell Lloyd. *Educ:* Trinity Coll. of Music, London. Principal Mezzo, Sadler's Wells, 1935 (Carmen, Delilah, Azucena, Ortrud, Amneris, etc); Principal Mezzo, Covent Garden, 1937 (first appearance there under Sir Thomas Beecham, and in The Ring under Furtwängler, in Coronation season and 1938, 1939); Sadler's Wells, New Theatre and Provinces, singing many roles during War of 1939-45 and in Germany after war. Created role of Auntie in Britten's Peter Grimes, Sadler's Wells, 1945, and afterwards sang it at Paris Opera, Monnaie, Brussels and Covent Garden; has sung over 60 roles in opera; many oratorios, Royal Albert Hall, BBC and Provinces; many concerts and broadcasts; sang title role at Covent Garden in Tchaikowsky's Queen of Spades under Kleiber, 1950-51; sang in first English performances of Berg's Wozzeck, 1952; sang in first

performance of Tippett's Midsummer Marriage, Covent Garden, 1955, Janacek's Jenufa, Covent Garden, 1956, and John Gardner's Moon and Sixpence, Sadler's Wells, 1957; played in Candide (Hillman-Bernstein after Voltaire), Saville, 1959; Countess in Queen of Spades, Covent Garden, 1961; sang in first performances of Grace Williams' Opera, The Parlour, Welsh National Opera, Cardiff, 1966; English Opera Group, 1963, 1965, 1967. Hon. FTCL. *Recreations:* reading, walking. *Address:* Montrose, Cross Lane, Findon, Worthing, West Sussex. *T:* Findon 2040. *Club:* Lansdowne.

COATES, Sir Ernest (William), Kt 1973; CMG 1970; State Director of Finance and Permanent Head of Victoria Treasury, Australia, since 1959; *b* 30 Nov. 1916; *s* of Thomas Atlee Coates; *m* 1st, 1943, Phyllis E. Morris (*d* 1971); one *s* three *d*; 2nd, 1974, Patricia Ann, *d* of late C. A. Fisher, Herts. *Educ:* Ballarat High Sch.; Univ. of Melbourne. Member: Bd of State Savings Bank of Victoria, 1960-; Nat. Debt Commn, Australia, 1963-; Australian Universities Commn, 1968-. *Recreations:* golf, music. *Address:* 64 Molesworth Street, Kew, Victoria 3101, Australia. *T:* 86 8226. *Clubs:* Melbourne, Athenæum (Melbourne); Green Acres Golf, Lorne Golf.

COATES, Brig. Sir Frederick (Gregory Lindsay), 2nd Bt *cr* 1921; *b* 19 May 1916; *o* *s* of Sir William Frederick Coates, 1st Bt, Belfast, N Ireland; *S* father, 1932; *m* 1940, Joan Nugent, *d* of late Maj.-Gen. Sir Charlton Spinks, KBE, DSO; one *s* two *d*. *Educ:* Eton; Sandhurst. Commissioned Royal Tank Regt, 1936; Served War of 1939-45, North Africa and NW Europe. Min. of Supply, 1947-53; Asst Military Attaché, Stockholm, 1953-56; British Joint Services Mission, Washington, 1956-58; Comdt, RAC School of Tank Technology, 1958-61; Asst Dir of Fighting Vehicles, and Col GS, War Office and MoD, 1961-66; Brig., British Defence Staff, Washington, DC, 1966-69; Mil. Dep. to Head of Defence Sales, 1969-71; retired 1971. *Heir:* *s* David Charlton Frederick Coates [*b* 16 Feb. 1948; *m* 1973, Christine Helen, *d* of Lewis F. Marshall; one *s*]. *Address:* Launchfield, Briantspuddle, Dorchester, Dorset DT2 7HN. *Clubs:* Royal Yacht Squadron; RMYC; PYC; Island Sailing; RAC Yacht.

COATES, Prof. Geoffrey Edward, MA, DSc; Professor of Chemistry, University of Wyoming, since 1968; *b* 14 May 1917; *er* *s* of Prof. Joseph Edward Coates, OBE; *m* 1951, Winifred Jean Hobbs; one *s* one *d*. *Educ:* Clifton Coll.; Queen's Coll., Oxford. Research Chemist, Magnesium Metal Corp., 1940-45; Univ. of Bristol: Lecturer in Chemistry, 1945-53; Sub-Warden of Wills Hall, 1946-51; Prof. of Chemistry, Univ. of Durham, 1953-68. *Publications:* Organo-metallic Compounds (monograph), 1956, new edns 1960, 1967; Principles of Organometallic Chemistry, 1968; papers in scientific journals. *Address:* Chemistry Department, University of Wyoming, Laramie, Wyoming 82071, USA. *Club:* Royal Commonwealth Society.

COATES, John Francis, OBE 1955; FRINA; Deputy Director, Ship Design, Ministry of Defence, since 1977; *b* 30 March 1922; *s* of Joseph Edward Coates and Ada Maria Coates; *m* 1954, Jane Waymouth; two *s*. *Educ:* Clifton Coll.; Queen's Coll., Oxford (MA 1946). RCNC; FRINA 1969. Entered RCNC, 1943; Constructor: Chatham Dockyard, 1951; Naval Construction Res. Estabt, Dunfermline, 1953; Ship Dept, MoD, 1957; Chief Constructor, Fleet Maintenance, 1964; Hd of Forward Design, Ship Dept, 1970; RCDS, 1971; Supt, Naval Construction Res. Estabt, Dunfermline, 1974. *Recreation:* nautical research. *Address:* Sabinal, Lucklands Road, Bath BA1 4AU. *T:* Bath 23696.

COATES, Michael Arthur, FCA; Senior Partner, Price Waterhouse & Co., since 1975; *b* 12 May 1924; *yr* *s* of Joseph Michael Smith Coates, OBE, Elmfield, Wylam, Northumberland, and late Lillian Warren Coates (*née* Murray); *m* 1st, 1952, Audrey Hampton Thorne (marr. diss. 1970); one *s* two *d*; 2nd, 1971, Sally Rogers (*née* Thorne). *Educ:* Uppingham Sch. Admitted Mem., Inst. of Chartered Accountants, 1951. Served RA, mainly in ME and Italy, 1942-47. Articled with Price Waterhouse & Co., Newcastle, 1942; returned to Price Waterhouse, 1947; transf. to London, 1954; Partner, Price Waterhouse & Co., 1959-, Dep. Sen. Partner, 1974-75; Chm., Price Waterhouse Internat. Manpower Cttee, 1971-74; Mem., Policy Cttee, 1974-. *Recreations:* diverse, including music, modern painting, antiques, gardens, reading, railways, photography. *Address:* The Old Rectory, Avon Dassett, Leamington Spa, Warwicks. *T:* Farnborough (Banbury) 472; 20 Wilton Crescent, SW1. *T:* 01-235 4423.

COATES, Patrick Devereux; *b* 30 April 1916; *s* of late H. H. H. Coates, OBE, and late Mrs F. J. Coates; *m* 1946, Mary Eleanor, *e* *d* of late Capt. Leveson Campbell, DSO, RN and Mrs Campbell; one *s* one *d*. *Educ:* Trinity Coll., Cambridge. Entered

Consular Service and served at Peking, Canton and Kunming, 1937-41; attached to Chinese 22nd Div. in Burma (despatches) and to Chinese forces in India, 1941-44; Actg Chinese Sec. to HM Embassy in China, 1944-46; 1st Sec., Foreign Office, 1946-50; transf. to Min. of Town and Country Planning, 1950; Asst Sec., Min. of Housing and Local Govt, 1955; Asst Under-Sec. of State, Dept of Economic Affairs, 1965-68, Min. of Housing and Local Govt, 1968-70, Dept of the Environment, 1970-72. Hon. Vis. Fellow, SOAS, Univ. of London, 1973-76. *Recreations:* Chinese studies, getting into the fresh air. *Address:* Lewesland Cottage, Barcombe, near Lewes, Sussex BN8 5TG. *T:* Barcombe 400407.

COATES, Reginald Charles; Professor of Civil Engineering in the University of Nottingham since 1958; Deputy Vice-Chancellor, University of Nottingham, 1966-69; *b* 28 June 1920; *s* of Wilfrid and Margaret Anne Coates; *m* 1942, Doris Sheila (*née* Sharrad); two *s* one *d*. *Educ:* New Mills Grammar Sch.; The Herbert Strutt Sch., Belper, Derbyshire; University Coll., Nottingham. Served War of 1939-45, Corps of Royal Engineers. Lectr in Civil Engineering, University Coll., Nottingham, 1946, Senior Lectr in Civil Engineering, University of Nottingham, 1953. Member: Council, Instn of Civil Engineers, 1969-72 (Vice-Pres., 1975-); Sheffield Regional Hosp. Bd, 1971-74; Nottingham Univ. Hosp. Man. Cttee, 1970-74 (Vice-Chm.); Notts AHA (Vice-Chm.), 1974-75; Research Cttee, Construction Industry Research and Information Assoc., 1973-; Adv. Cttee, Books for Overseas, British Council, 1974-; CNAA Cttee for Science and Technology, 1975-; Construction and Housing Res. Adv. Council, DoE, 1976-. *Publications:* (with M. G. Coutie and F. K. Kong) Structural Analysis, 1972; occasional articles in technical press. *Recreations:* cooking and idling. *Address:* University of Nottingham, Nottingham.

COATES, Sir Robert E. J. C. M.; *see* Milnes Coates.

COATS, Sir Alastair Francis Stuart, 4th Bt, *cr* 1905; *b* 18 Nov. 1921; *s* of Lieut-Col Sir James Stuart Coats, MC, 3rd Bt and Lady Amy Coats (*d* 1975), *er d* of 8th Duke of Richmond and Gordon; *S* father, 1966; *m* 1947, Lukyn, *d* of Capt. Charles Gordon; one *s* one *d*. Served War of 1939-45, Coldstream Guards (Capt.). *Heir:* *s* Alexander James Coats, *b* 6 July 1951. *Address:* Birchwood House, Durford Wood, Petersfield, Hants. *T:* Liss 2254.
See also Viscount Ednam.

COBB, Richard Charles, FBA 1967; Professor of Modern History, University of Oxford, since 1973; Fellow of Worcester College, Oxford; *b* 20 May 1917; *s* of Francis Hills Cobb, Sudan Civil Service, and Dora Cobb (*née* Swindale); *m* 1963, Margaret Tennant; three *s* one *d*. *Educ:* Shrewsbury Sch.; Merton Coll., Oxford. Postmastership in History, Merton, 1934. HM Forces, 1942-46. Research in Paris, 1946-55; Lectr in History, UCW Aberystwyth, 1955-61; Sen. Simon Res. Fellow, Manchester, 1960; Lectr, University of Leeds, 1962; Fellow and Tutor in Modern History, Balliol Coll., 1962-72, Hon. Fellow, 1977; Reader in French Revolutionary History, Oxford, 1969-72. Vis. Prof. in the History of Paris, Collège de France, 1971. Lectures: Raleigh, British Academy, 1974; Zaharoff, Oxford, 1976. Chevalier des Palmes Académiques, 1956; Officier de l'Ordre National du Mérite, 1977. *Publications:* L'armée révolutionnaire à Lyon, 1952; Les armées révolutionnaires du Midi, 1955; Les armées révolutionnaires, vol. 1, 1961, vol. 2, 1963; Terreur et Subsistances, 1965; A Second Identity: essays on France and French history, 1969; The Police and the People: French Popular Protest 1789-1820, 1970; Reactions to the French Revolution, 1972; Paris and its Provinces 1792-1802, 1975; A Sense of Place, 1975; Tour de France, 1976. *Address:* Worcester College, Oxford. *Club:* Gridiron (Oxford).

COBB, Rear-Adm. Robert, CBE 1953 (OBE 1941); retired; *b* 18 Sept. 1900; *s* of late Lieut-Col Cobb; *m* 1930, Honor, *d* of late Sir C. Aubrey Smith; one *s* one *d*. *Educ:* All Saints, Bloxham; RN Colls, Osborne and Dartmouth. Joined Osborne, 1914; Midshipman, 1917; Comdr (E), 1934; Asst Naval Attaché, Europe, 1935-37; Capt. (E), 1944; Rear-Adm. (E), 1951; retired list 1954. War of 1939-45 (despatches twice, OBE). With British Council, 1954-59. *Address:* Hill Farm Cottage, 18 Highlands Road, Fareham, Hants. *T:* Fareham 80286.

COBB, Timothy Humphry, MA; *b* 4 July 1909; *s* of Humphry Henry Cobb and Edith Muriel (*née* Stogdon); *m* 1952, Cecilia Mary Josephine, *d* of W. G. Chapman; two *s* one *d*. *Educ:* Harrow; Magdalene Coll., Cambridge. Asst Master, Middlesex Sch., Concord, Mass, USA, 1931-32; Bryanston Sch., Blandford, Dorset, 1932-47, Housemaster, Head of Classics, Estate Bursar; Headmaster of King's Coll., Budo, Kampala, Uganda, 1947-58; formerly Sec., Uganda Headmasters' Association; Headmaster,

Dover College, 1958-73. *Publication:* Certificate English Language Practice, 1958. *Recreations:* music, railway photography, producing plays. *Address:* Parkgate Farm, Framlingham, Woodbridge, Suffolk. *Clubs:* MCC, Royal Commonwealth Society.

COBBAN, James Macdonald, CBE 1971; TD; MA; DL; JP; Headmaster of Abingdon School, 1947-70; *b* 14 Sept. 1910; *s* of late A. M. Cobban, MIStructE, Scunthorpe, Lincs; *m* 1942, Lorna Mary (*d* 1961), *er d* of late G. S. W. Marlow, BSc, FRIC, barrister-at-law, Sydenham; four *d* (one *s* decd). *Educ:* Pocklington Sch.; Jesus Coll., Cambridge (Scholar); Univ. of Vienna. Classical Tripos, Part I, 1931, Part II, 1932; Sandys Student, 1932: Thirlwall Medallist and Gladstone Prizeman, 1935; MA, Cambridge; MA, Oxford (Pembroke Coll.). Asst Master, King Edward VI Sch., Southampton, 1933-36; Class. Sixth Form Master, Dulwich Coll., 1936-40, 1946-47. Intelligence Corps (TA), 1941; GSO3, Directorate of Mil. Intelligence, 1941; Intermediate War Course, Staff Coll., 1943; DAQMG, Combined Ops HQ, 1943; Staff Officer, CCG, 1944 (Lt-Col 1945). Rep. Diocese of Oxford on Gen. Synod, 1970-; Chm., Abingdon Co. Bench, 1964-74; Member: Cttee GBA, 1972- (Dep. Chm., 1976-); Direct Grant Schs Jt Cttee, 1966- (Chm., 1975-); Cttee, GBGSA, 1976-; Council, Ind. Schs Careers Orgn, 1972-; Cttee, United Soc. Christian Lit., 1974-; Thames Valley Police Authority, 1973-; Vale of White Horse DC, 1973-76; Governor: Stowe Sch., 1970-; Wellington Coll., 1970-; Sch. of St Helen and St Katharine, 1954- (Chm., 1958-67); Abingdon Coll. of Further Education, 1974-. JP Berks, 1950, Oxon, 1974; DL Berks, 1966, Oxon, 1974. *Publications:* Senate and Provinces, 78-49 BC, 1935; (in collaboration) Civis Romanus, 1936; Pax et Imperium, 1938; Church and School, 1963. *Address:* The Old Vicarage, Steventon, Oxon OX13 6SJ. *T:* Abingdon 831444.

COBBETT, David John, TD 1973; ERD 1962; Export Director (Special Projects), British Railways Board, since 1977; *b* 9 Dec. 1928; *m* 1952, Beatrix Jane Ogilvie Cockburn; three *s*. *Educ:* Royal Masonic Sch. FCIT. Gen. Railway admin. and managerial positions, 1949-67; Divl Movements Manager, Liverpool Street, 1967; Divl Manager, Norwich (British Railways Bd), 1968-70; Asst Managing Dir, Freightliners Ltd, 1970-73; Dep. Gen. Manager, British Railways Bd Scottish Region, 1973; Gen. Manager, British Railways Scottish Region, 1974-76; Chm., British Transport Ship Management, Scotland, 1974-76; Gen. Manager, BR Eastern Region, 1976-77. Bt Col, Royal Corps of Transport (RARO), 1974. *Recreations:* military matters, historical reading, games. *Address:* The Grange, Strensall, York YO3 8XA. *T:* York 490334.

COBBOLD, family name of **Baron Cobbold.**

COBBOLD, 1st Baron *cr* 1960, of Knebworth; **Cameron Fromanteel Cobbold,** KG 1970; PC 1959; GCVO 1963; DL; Lord Chamberlain of HM Household, 1963-71; Chancellor of the Royal Victorian Order, 1963-71; Governor of Bank of England, 1949-61; one of HM Lieutenants for the City of London; *b* 14 Sept. 1904; *s* of late Lt-Col Clement Cobbold; *m* 1930, Lady (Margaret) Hermione (Millicent) Bulwer-Lytton, *er d* of 2nd Earl of Lytton, KG, PC, GCSI, GCIE; two *s* one *d*. *Educ:* Eton; King's Coll., Cambridge. Entered Bank of England as Adviser, 1933; Exec. Dir, 1938; Dep. Governor, 1945. A Permanent Lord in Waiting to the Queen, 1971-. Chm., Hertfordshire Playing Fields Assoc.; Vice-Pres., British Heart Foundn (Pres. to 1976); Chm., Middlesex Hosp. Board of Governors and Med. Sch. Council, 1963-74. High Sheriff of County of London for 1946-47. Hon. Fellow Inst. of Bankers, 1961; Fellow of Eton, 1951-67; Steward of the Courts, Eton, 1973-. Chm. Malaysia Commission of Enquiry, 1962. Hon. LLD, McGill Univ., 1961. Hon. DSc (Econ.), London Univ., 1963. DL Herts, 1972. *Heir:* *s* Hon. David Antony Fromanteel Lytton-Cobbold [*b* 14 July 1937; assumed by deed poll, 1960, the additional surname of Lytton; *m* 1961, Christine Elizabeth, 3rd *d* of Major Sir Dennis Frederic Bankes Stucley, 5th Bt, *qv*; three *s* one *d*]. *Address:* Lake House, Knebworth, Herts. *T:* Stevenage 812310.

COBHAM, 11th Viscount *cr* 1718; **John William Leonard Lyttelton;** Bt 1618; Baron Cobham 1718; Lord Lyttelton, Baron of Frankley 1756 (renewed 1794); Baron Westcote (Ire.) 1776; Partner of Hagley Hall Farms, since 1976; *b* 5 June 1943; *e s* of 10th Viscount Cobham, KG, PC, GCMG, GCVO, TD, and of Elizabeth Alison Viscountess Cobham, *d* of J. R. Makeig-Jones, CBE; *S* father, 1977; *m* 1974, Penelope Ann, *e d* of Roy Cooper, Moss Farm, Ollerton, near Knutsford, Cheshire. *Educ:* Eton; Christ's College, New Zealand; Royal Agricultural College, Cirencester. *Recreations:* cricket, shooting. *Heir:* *b* Hon. Christopher Charles Lyttelton [*b* 23 Oct. 1947; *m* 1973, Tessa

Mary, *d* of late Col A. G. J. Readman, DSO]. *Address:* Hagley Hall, near Stourbridge, West Midlands DY9 9LG. *T:* Hagley 5823; 20 Kylestrome House, Cundy Street, Ebury Street, SW1. *T:* 01-730 5756. *Club:* MCC.

COBHAM, Barony of; (abeyant).

COBHAM, Ven. John Oldcastle, MA; Archdeacon of Durham and Canon Residentiary of Durham Cathedral, 1953-69, now Archdeacon Emeritus; Licence to Officiate Diocese of St Edmundsbury and Ipswich, since 1969; *b* 11 April 1899; *s* of late Ven. John Lawrence Cobham; *m* 1934, Joan (*d* 1967), *d* of late Rev. George Henry Cobham; no *c. Educ:* St Lawrence Coll., Ramsgate; Tonbridge Sch.; Corpus Christi Coll., Cambridge; Univ. of Marburg; Westcott House, Cambridge; Académie Goetz. Served in Royal Field Artillery, 1917-19; Curate at St Thomas', Winchester, 1926-30; Vice-Principal of Westcott House, Cambridge, 1930-34; Principal of The Queen's Coll., Birmingham, 1934-53; Vicar of St Benet's, Cambridge, 1940-45; Recognised Lectr, Dept of Theology, Birmingham Univ., 1946-53; Hon. Canon, Derby Cathedral, 1950-53. Chaplain to the Forces (EC), 1943-45. Select Preacher: Univ. of Cambridge, 1933 and 1940; Univ. of Birmingham, 1938; Univ. of Oxford, 1952-53; Examining Chaplain to the Bishop of Durham, 1953-66, to the Bishop of Wakefield, 1959-68. Member: Liturgical Commn, 1955-62; Archbishop of Canterbury's Commn on Roman Catholic Relations, 1964-69. George Craig Stewart Memorial Lecturer, Seabury-Western Theological Seminary, Evanston, Ill., 1963. *Publications:* Concerning Spiritual Gifts, 1933; co-translator of K. Barth in Revelation, a Symposium, 1937; contributor to: The Parish Communion, 1937; No Other Gospel, 1943; The Significance of the Barmen Declaration for the Oecumenical Church, 1943; DNB 1931-40 (E. C. Hoskyns), 1949; Theological Word Book of the Bible, 1950. *Recreation:* sketching. *Address:* Sands House, 5 Church Close, Aldeburgh, Suffolk IP15 5DY. *T:* Aldeburgh 2803.

COBURN, Prof. Kathleen; OC 1974; Professor of English, Victoria College, University of Toronto, 1953-74, now Emeritus; author; *b* 1905; *d* of Rev. John Coburn and Susannah Coburn. *Educ:* University of Toronto (MA); Oxford University (BLitt). Imperial Order of the Daughters of the Empire (IODE) Travelling Scholarship, 1930-31. Formerly Lectr, Asst Prof., and Assoc. Prof. of English, Victoria College, University of Toronto. University Women's Internat. Senior Fellowship, 1948-49; John Simon Guggenheim Memorial Fellowship, 1953-54, renewed, 1957-58; Commonwealth Visiting Fellowship (Univ. of London), 1962-63. FRSC 1958. Rose Mary Crawshay Prize for English Literature (Brit. Acad.), 1959. Hon. Fellow, St Hugh's Coll., Oxford, 1970; Hon. Fellow, Champlain Coll., Trent Univ., Ont., 1972; Corresp. FBA, 1973. DHL Haverford, 1972; Hon. LLD, Queen's Univ., Kingston, Ontario, 1964; Hon. DLitt: Trent Univ., 1972; Cambridge, 1975. *Publications:* The Philosophical Lectures of S. T. Coleridge, 1949; Inquiring Spirit, 1951; The Letters of Sara Hutchinson, 1954; The Notebooks of S. T. Coleridge, vol. i, 1957, vol. ii, 1961, vol. iii, 1973; Coleridge: A Collection of Critical Essays, 1967; The Self-Conscious Imagination (Riddell Meml Lectures), 1972; Discourse, Royal Institution, 1972; general editor, The Collected Coleridge, 1968. *Address:* Victoria College, Toronto, Canada.

COCHRAN, William; PhD, MA; FRS 1962; Professor of Natural Philosophy, University of Edinburgh, since 1975; *b* 30 July 1922; *s* of James Cochran and Margaret Watson Cochran (*née* Baird); *m* 1953, Ingegerd Wall; one *s* two *d. Educ:* Boroughmuir Sch., Edinburgh; Edinburgh Univ. Asst Lectr, Edinburgh Univ., 1943-46; Demonstrator and Lectr, Univ. of Cambridge, 1948-62; Reader in Physics, Univ. of Cambridge, 1962-64. Fellow of Trinity Hall, Cambridge, 1951-64; Prof. of Physics, Univ. of Edinburgh, 1964-75. Research fellowships abroad, 1950-51, 1958-59, 1970. Guthrie medallist, Inst. Physics and Phys. Soc., 1966. *Publications:* Vol. III of The Crystalline State (with Prof. H. Lipson), 1954, new edn 1966; Dynamics of Atoms in Crystals, 1973. *Recreations:* Scots verse, family history. *Address:* Department of Physics, The University, The King's Buildings, Edinburgh EH9 3JZ; 71 Clermiston Road, Edinburgh.

COCHRANE, family name of **Earl of Dundonald** and **Baron Cochrane of Cults.**

COCHRANE OF CULTS, 3rd Baron *cr* 1919; **Thomas Charles Anthony Cochrane;** *b* 31 Oct. 1922; *s* of 2nd Baron Cochrane of Cults, DSO, and Hon. Elin Douglas-Pennant (*d* 1934), *y d* of 2nd Baron Penrhyn; *S* father, 1968. *Educ:* privately. *Heir: b* Hon. (Ralph Henry) Vere Cochrane [*b* 20 Sept. 1926; *m* 1956, Janet Mary Watson, *d* of late Dr W. H. W. Cheyne; two *s*]. *Address:* Balgownie, 18 Cliff Terrace, Buckie, Banffshire.

COCHRANE, Lord; Iain Alexander Douglas Blair Cochrane; *b* 17 Feb. 1961; *s* and *heir* of 14th Earl of Dundonald, *qv.*

COCHRANE, Sir Desmond Oriel Alastair George Weston, 3rd Bt *cr* 1903; Consul-General of Ireland to the Republics of Syria and The Lebanon since 1949; *b* 22 Oct. 1918; 2nd *s* of Sir Ernest Cochrane, 2nd Bt, and Elsa, *y d* of Erwin Schumacher; *S* father, 1952; *m* 1946, Yvonne, *o c* of late Alfred Bey Sursock and of Donna Maria Sursock; three *s* one *d. Educ:* Eton. Served War of 1939-45; Staff Captain: Northern Command, 1941; War Office, AG 12, 1942; GHQ Middle East Forces (Mil. Sec. Branch), 1943; Military Sec. to GOC 9th Army, 1944. *Heir: s* Henry Mark Sursock Cochrane [*b* 23 Oct. 1946; *m* 1969, Hala, *d* of Fuad Es Said; one *s* one *d*]. *Address:* Maison Sursock, Beyrouth, Lebanon. *Club:* Carlton.

COCHRANE, Maj.-Gen. James Rupert, CB 1951; CBE 1947; retired; *b* 28 Nov. 1904; *s* of Brig.-Gen. J. K. Cochrane, CMG; *m* 1937, Hilary, *d* of H. W. Standen, Westways, Sevenoaks; one *s* one *d. Educ:* Charterhouse; RMA Woolwich. Commissioned Royal Artillery, 1925; Staff Coll., Camberley, 1939; Imperial Defence Coll., 1948. Served War of 1939-45 (despatches): in NW Europe, Italy and Middle East, on Staff and Commanding 191 (Herts and Essex) Yeomanry Fd Regt. Chief of Staff, HQ British troops in Palestine and Transjordan, 1945-47 (despatches). Commanded HAA Regt, 1947; Chief of Staff, HQ East Africa Command, 1949-52; Comd 51 (U) AA Brigade, 1952-53; Deputy Chief of Staff HQ Allied Land Forces, Central Europe, 1953-56; Principal Staff Officer to Deputy Supreme Allied Commander (Viscount Montgomery), Allied Powers in Europe, 1956-58; retired, 1959. *Recreation:* fishing. *Address:* Plestor House, Selborne, Alton, Hants. *Club:* Army and Navy.

COCHRANE, Air Chief Marshal Hon. Sir Ralph (Alexander), GBE 1950 (KBE 1945); KCB 1948; AFC 1919; FRAeS; *b* 24 Feb. 1895; *y s* of 1st Baron Cochrane of Cults; *m* 1930, Hilda Frances Holme Wiggin; two *s* one *d. Educ:* Osborne and Dartmouth. Entered Navy, 1912; transferred to newly created Airship branch 1915 and to RAF 1919; served in Egypt and Iraq, 1920-23, and at Aden, 1928-29; on the directing staff RAF Staff Coll., Andover, 1930-31, and at Air Ministry, 1932-33; Imperial Defence Coll., 1934. Seconded to New Zealand Govt to advise on air defence and became first Chief of the Air Staff of the Royal New Zealand Air Force, 1936-39. ADC to the King, 1939-40. Held various appointments covering intelligence and training, 1939-42; commanded Nos 3 and 5 Bomber Groups, 1942-45; AOC-in-C Transport Command, 1945-47; AOC-in-C Flying Training Command, 1947-50; Vice-CAS, Air Ministry, 1950-52; retd Nov. 1952. Air ADC to the King, 1949; ADC to the Queen, 1952. Joint Man. Dir Atlantic Shipbuilding Co., 1953-56; Rolls Royce Ltd, 1956-61; Chairman: RJM Exports Ltd, 1962; Cochrane's of Oxford Ltd, 1970. RUSI Gold Medal Essay, 1935; Edward Busk Meml Prize, RAeS, 1948; Triennial Award of Merit, InstT, 1958-61. *Address:* Grove Farmhouse, Shipton-under-Wychwood, Oxford OX7 6DG. *T:* 830253. *Clubs:* Brooks's, Royal Air Force.

COCHRANE, Dr Robert Greenhill, CMG 1969; MD, FRCP, DTM&H; Regional Leprosy Officer, Shinyanga Region, Tanzania, 1969-72; Medical Superintendent, Kola Ndoto Leprosarium, Tanzania, 1969-72; retired; *b* 11 Aug. 1899; *s* of Dr Thomas Cochrane and Grace Hamilton Cochrane (*née* Greenhill); *m* 1st, 1927, Ivy Gladys Nunn (*d* 1966); two *s* one *d* ; 2nd, 1968, Dr Martha Jeane Shaw. *Educ:* Sch. for Sons of Missionaries, Blackheath (now Eltham Coll.); Univ. of Glasgow; St Bartholomew's Hosp., London; London Sch. of Tropical Medicine. Med. Sec., BELRA (now LEPRA), 1928-33; Med. Supt, Leprosy Hosp., Chingleput, S India, 1933-44 and 1948-51; Dir, Leprosy Campaign and Dir of Leprosy Research, Madras State, India, 1941-51; Dir and Prin. Prof. of Medicine and Dermatology, and Dir, Rural Medicine, Christian Med. Coll., Vellore, S India, 1944-48; Adviser in Leprosy to Min. of Health, London, 1951-65; Vis. Med. Officer, Homes of St Giles, E Hanningfield, Essex, 1951-66; Tech. Med. Adviser, Amer. Leprosy Mission, Inc., 1953-64; Dir, Leprosy Study Centre, London, 1953-65; Med. Supt, Leprosy Hosp., Vadathorasalur, S Arcot, Madras, 1966-68. Pres., Internat. Leprosy Assoc., 1963-68, since when Pres. Emeritus. Kaisar-i-Hind gold medal (India), 1935. *Publications:* A Practical Textbook of Leprosy, 1947; Leprosy in Theory and Practice, 1959 (3rd edn 1973); Biblical Leprosy, A Suggested Interpretation, 1961; contribs to Internat. Jl of Leprosy, Leprosy Review. *Address:* 606 Swede Street, Norristown, Pa 19401, USA. *Club:* Royal Commonwealth Society.

COCKAYNE, Dame Elizabeth, DBE 1955; Chief Nursing Officer, Ministry of Health, 1948-58, retired; *d* of William and Alice Cockayne, Burton-on-Trent. *Educ:* Secondary Sch.,

Burton-on-Trent, and privately. Gen. Hospital Training, Royal Infirmary, Sheffield; Fever Training, Mount Gold Hospital, Plymouth; Midwifery Training, Maternity Hospital, Birmingham. Former experience includes: Supervisor of Training Sch., LCC; Matron of West London Hosp., St Charles' Hosp., Royal Free Hosp. *Recreation:* gardening. *Address:* Rushett Cottage, Little Heath Lane, Cobham, Surrey.

COCKBURN, Claud; journalist; *b* 12 April 1904; *s* of Henry Cockburn, CB, and Elizabeth Stevenson; *m* 1940, Patricia Arbuthnot; three *s*. *Educ:* Berkhamsted Sch.; Keble Coll., Oxford; Universities of Budapest and Berlin. Travelling Fellow of The Queen's College, Oxford; Correspondent of The Times in New York and Washington, 1929-32; Editor, The Week, 1933-46; Diplomatic and Foreign Correspondent, the Daily Worker, 1935-46; since 1953 has written principally for Punch, New Statesman and Private Eye; Atlantic Monthly, 1968-; weekly columnist, Irish Times. *Publications:* High Low Washington, 1933; Reporter in Spain, 1936; Beat the Devil, 1952; Overdraft on Glory, 1955; (autobiog.) In Time of Trouble, 1956; Nine Bald Men, 1956; Aspects of History, 1957; (autobiog.) Crossing the Line, 1958; (autobiog.) View from the West, 1961; (autobiog.) I, Claud, 1967; Ballantyne's Folly, 1970; Bestseller, 1972; The Devil's Decade, 1973; Jericho Road, 1974; Union Power: the growth and challenge in perspective, 1976. *Recreation:* travel. *Address:* Brook Lodge, Youghal, County Cork, Ireland.

COCKBURN, Prof. Forrester, MD; FRCPE; Samson Gemmell Professor of Child Health, University of Glasgow, since 1977; *b* 13 Oct. 1934; *s* of Forrester Cockburn and Violet E. Bunce; *m* 1960, Alison Fisher Grieve; two *s*. *Educ:* Leith Acad.; Univ. of Edinburgh (MD). DCH Glasgow. FRCPE 1971. Med. trng, Royal Infirmary of Edinburgh, Royal Hosp. for Sick Children, and Simpson Memorial Maternity Pavilion, Edinburgh, 1959-63; Huntingdon Hertford Foundn Res. Fellow, Boston Univ., Mass, 1953-55; Nuffield Sen. Res. Fellow, Univ. of Oxford, 1965-66; Wellcome Trust Sen. Med. Res. Fellow, Univ. of Edin. and Simpson Meml Maternity Pavilion, 1966-71; Sen. Lectr, Dept of Child Life and Health, Univ. of Edin., 1971—77. *Publications:* Neonatal Medicine, 1974; contrib. Foetal and Neonatal Nutrition. *Recreations:* sailing, fishing. *Address:* University Department of Child Health, Royal Hospital for Sick Children, Yorkhill, Glasgow G38SJ. *T:* 041-339 8888.

COCKBURN, Sir John (Elliot), 12th Bt of that Ilk, *cr* 1671; Managing Director, Cellar Management Ltd; *b* 7 Dec. 1925; *s* of Lieut-Col Sir John Cockburn, 11th Bt of that Ilk, DSO and of Isabel Hunter, *y d* of late James McQueen, Crofts, Kirkcudbrightshire; *S* father, 1949; *m* 1949, Glory Patricia, *er d* of N. Mullings; three *s* two *d*. *Educ:* RNC Dartmouth; Royal Agricultural Coll., Cirencester. Served War of 1939-45, joined RAF, July 1944. *Recreation:* reading. *Heir: s* Charles Christopher Cockburn, *b* 19 Nov. 1950. *Address:* 48 Frewin Road, SW18. *Club:* Naval and Military.

COCKBURN, Sir Robert, KBE 1960 (OBE 1946); CB 1953; PhD, MSc, MA; Senior Research Fellow, Churchill College, Cambridge, 1970-77; Chairman, National Computing Centre, 1970-77; *b* 31 March 1909; 2nd *s* of late Rev. R. T. Cockburn, Columba Manse, Belford, Northumberland; *m* 1935, Phyllis Hoyland; two *d*. *Educ:* Southern Secondary Sch. and Municipal Coll., Portsmouth; London Univ. BSc 1928, MSc 1935, PhD 1939, London; MA Cantab 1973. Taught Science at West Ham Municipal Coll., 1930-37; research in communications at RAE Farnborough, 1937-39; in radar at TRE Malvern, Worcs, 1939-45; in atomic energy at AERE Harwell, 1945-48; Scientific Adviser to Air Min., 1948-53; Princ. Dir of Scientific Research (Guided Weapons and Electronics), Ministry of Supply, 1954-55; Deputy Controller of Electronics, Ministry of Supply, 1955-56; Controller of Guided Weapons and Electronics, Ministry of Supply, 1956-59; Chief Scientist of Ministry of Aviation, 1959-64; Dir, RAE, Farnborough, 1964-69. Chairman: Television Adv. Cttee for Posts and Telecommunications, 1971-; BBC Engineering Adv. Cttee, 1973-. Hon. Fellow, RAeS, 1970. Congressional Medal for Merit, 1947. *Publications:* scientific papers. *Recreation:* sailing. *Address:* 21 Fitzroy Road, Fleet, Hants. *T:* Fleet 5518. *Clubs:* Athenæum; Royal Air Force Yacht.

COCKBURN-CAMPBELL, Sir Thomas; see Campbell.

COCKCROFT, Dr Janet Rosemary, OBE 1975; Deputy Chairman, Bottoms Mill Co. Ltd, Todmorden, since 1974 (Director, since 1961); *b* 26 July 1916; *er d* of late Major W. G. Mowat, MC, TD, JP, of Buchollie, Lybster, Caithness, Scotland, and late Mary Mowat; *m* 1942, Peter Worby Cockcroft; two *s* one *d*. *Educ:* Glasgow Univ. MB, ChB 1938. Ho. Surg. and Ho. Phys., Glasgow Royal Infirmary, 1938-39; GP, 1939-43; Asst MOH, Co. of Caithness, 1943-46; MO, Maternity and Child Welfare, Halifax, 1950-53; Part-time MOH, WRCC, 1953-67; MO, Family Planning Assoc., 1947-75 (Halifax and Sowerby Bridge Clinics); MO, British Red Cross, Halifax, 1960-66; Chairman: N Midlands FPA Doctors' Gp, 1966-68; Halifax FPA Clinic, 1963-75. Mem., Food Additives and Contaminants Cttee, MAFF, 1972-; Chm., Consumers' Cttees for England and Wales and for GB, MAFF, 1975-; Vice-Pres., 1969-70, Pres., 1970-72, Nat. Council of Women of GB; Vice-Pres., Internat. Council of Women, 1973-76; UK Rep., UN Status of Women Commn, 1973-; Mem., BBC Northern Adv. Council, 1975-. Elder, United Reformed Church, 1973-. *Recreations:* travel, reading. *Address:* Dalemore, Savile Park, Halifax, W Yorks HX1 3EA. *T:* Halifax 52621. *Club:* Naval and Military.

COCKCROFT, John Hoyle; MP (C) Nantwich since Feb. 1974; *b* 6 July 1934; *s* of Lionel Fielden Cockcroft and Jenny Hoyle; *m* 1971, Tessa Fay Shepley; two *d*. *Educ:* Trearddur House; Oundle; St John's Coll., Cambridge. BA Hons History and Econs 1958; Pres., Cambridge Union, 1958. Royal Artillery, 1953-55. Feature Writer and Investment Analyst, Financial Times, 1959-61; Economist, GKN, 1962-67; seconded to Treasury, 1965-66; Econ. Leader-writer, Daily Telegraph, 1967-74. *Publications:* Why England Sleeps, 1971; A History of Guest Keen and Nettlefolds. *Recreations:* walking, reading, swimming, entertaining. *Address:* The Cottages, Great Gransden, Cambs. *Club:* Farmers'.

COCKCROFT, Dr Wilfred Halliday; Vice-Chancellor, The New University of Ulster, since 1976; *b* 7 June 1923; *s* of Wilfred Cockcroft and Bessie Halliday; *m* 1949, Barbara Rhona Huggan; two *s*. *Educ:* Keighley Boys' Grammar Sch.; Balliol Coll., Oxford (Williams Exhibnr, 1941, Hon. Scholar, 1946). MA, DPhil Oxon; FIMA. Technical Signals/Radar Officer, RAF, 1942-46. Asst Lectr, Univ. of Aberdeen, 1949, Lectr 1950; Lectr, Univ. of Southampton, 1957, Reader 1960; G. F. Grant Prof. of Pure Mathematics, Univ. of Hull, 1961; Vis. Lectr and Prof., Univs of Chicago, Stanford, State Univ. of NY, 1954, 1959, 1967. University Grants Committee: Mem., 1973-76; Mem., Math. Sciences Subcttee, 1967-72, Chm. 1973-76; Chm., Educn Subcttee, 1973-76; Mem., Management and Business Studies Subcttee, and Educnl Technology Subcttee, 1973-76. Chairman: Nuffield Maths Project Consultative Cttee, 1963-71; Specialist Conf. on Maths in Commonwealth Schs, Trinidad, 1968; SRC Maths Subcttee, 1969-73 (Mem. 1964-68). Member: SRC Science Bd, 1969-73; Council, London Math. Soc., 1973-76; Council, Inst. of Maths and its Applications, 1974-; Computer Bd for Univs and Res. Councils, 1975-76. *Publications:* Your Child and Mathematics, 1968; Complex Numbers, 1972. *Recreations:* swimming, tennis, sketching, bad piano playing. *Address:* The New University of Ulster, Coleraine, Northern Ireland. *T:* Coleraine 4141.

COCKER, Prof. Ralph, CBE 1968; MB, ChB, LDS (Victoria University Manchester), FRCS, FDSRCS; Professor Emeritus of Dental Surgery in the University of London, ex-Director of Dental Studies, and Sub-Dean, King's College Hospital Medical School, University of London, 1947-73, Consultant Dental Surgeon and ex-Director of Dental Department, King's College Hospital, 1947-73, Hon. Consultant Dental Surgeon, since 1973; *b* 18 April 1908; *er s* of Frank Barlow Cocker and Mary Wildman; *m* 1942, Margaret (*née* Jacques); one *s* two *d*. *Educ:* William Hulme's Grammar Sch., Manchester; Manchester Univ. Preston Prize and Medallist, Manchester Univ., 1930. Private Practice, 1930-36; Asst Hon. Dental Surg., Manchester Dent. Hosp., 1933-36; Lectr in Clin. Dental Surg., Manchester Univ., 1936-45; Industrial Health Service (ICI Ltd), 1940-45; Lectr in Periodontia, Manchester Univ., 1945-47; Actg Cons. Dental Surg., Manchester Royal Infirmary, 1945-47; Past Examr in Dental Surgery, Univs of Manchester, London, Birmingham, Bristol, Sheffield, St Andrews; Chm. Bd of Examrs for Statutory Exam. (GDC), 1964-73; Member: Bd of Faculty, RCS, 1955-71 (Vice-Dean, 1964-65) and Examr to Coll. for Dipl. and Final Fellowship in Dental Surgery; Standing Dental Adv. Cttee of Dept. of Health and Social Security, 1963-74 (Vice-Chm. 1965-74); GDC, 1963-74 (Chm., Educn Cttee, 1970-74, Chm. Central Examining Bd for Dental Hygienists, 1967-74); Sec., Odontolog. Section, RSM, 1961-63 (Vice-Pres. 1970-73); Mem., Dental Educn Adv. Coun. of Gt Brit., 1947-73 (Chm., 1956-57; Treas., 1957-73; Sec., 1967-73); Mem. and Chm., Assoc. of British Dental Hospitals, 1947-73; Mem., Dental Industry Standards Cttee (BSI); Founder Mem., King's Coll. Hosp. Med. Sch. Council and King's Coll. Hosp. Bd of Govs, 1948-73; Mem. Bd of Dental Studies, London Univ., 1948-73 (Chm., 1966-71); Adviser in Dental Surgery to Dept. of Health and Social Security, 1968-74; Temp. Adviser, WHO, 1970-72. *Recreations:* mountaineering, ski-ing, photography, ornithology. *Address:* 10 Oaks Avenue, Gipsy Hill, SE19 1QY. *T:* 01-670 4068; Charing Kent, 2437. *Club:* Alpine.

COCKER, Sir William Wiggins, Kt 1955; OBE 1946; JP; MA; LLD; Director of Cocker Chemical Co. Ltd; President, British Tar Products Ltd; a Lloyd's Underwriter; b 17 Oct. 1896; s of Wiggins Cocker, Accrington; m 1922, Mary Emma Bowker, Accrington (d 1965); one s one d; m 1970, Mrs Rhoda Slinger, Accrington. Freedom of Borough of Accrington, 1958. Address: 384 Clifton Drive North, St Annes-on-Sea, Lancs.

COCKERAM, Eric (Paul); JP; Chairman, Watson Prickard Ltd; b 4 July 1924; er s of Mr and Mrs J. W. Cockeram; m 1949, Frances Irving; two s two d. Educ: The Leys Sch., Cambridge. Served War, 1942-46: Captain The Gloucestershire Regt; "D Day" landings (wounded and discharged). MP (C) Bebington, 1970-Feb. 1974. PPS: to Minister for Industry, 1970-72; to Minister for Posts and Telecommunications, 1972; to Chancellor of Exchequer, 1972-74. Mem., Select Cttee on Corporation Tax, 1971. Chm., Liverpool Stores Cttee, 1960-68; Prospective Parly Cand. (C), Ludlow. Pres., Menswear Assoc. of Britain, 1964-65. Mem., Bd of Governors, United Liverpool Hosps, 1965-74; Chm., Liverpool NHS Exec. Council, 1970. Director: Liverpool Building Soc.; TSB (Mid-Lancs and Merseyside); Member of Lloyd's. Liveryman, Worshipful Co. of Glovers. Freeman: City of London; City of Springfield, Ill. JP, City of Liverpool, 1960. Recreations: bridge, shooting, country walking. Address: Fairway Lodge, Links Hey Road, Caldy, Wirral, Cheshire L48 1NB. T: 051-625 1100. Clubs: Carlton, Royal Automobile; Lyceum, Exchange (Liverpool).

COCKERELL, Sir Christopher (Sydney), Kt 1969; CBE 1966; MA; FRS 1967; Consultant, British Hovercraft Corporation, since 1973; Chairman, Ripplecraft Co. Ltd, since 1950; Joint Managing Director, Wavepower Ltd, since 1974; b 4 June 1910; s of late Sir Sydney Cockerell; m 1937, Margaret Elinor Belsham; two d. Educ: Gresham's; Peterhouse, Cambridge (Hon. Fellow, 1974). Pupil, W. H. Allen & Sons, Bedford, 1931-33; Radio Research, Cambridge, 1933-35; airborne and navigational equipment research and development, Marconi Wireless Telegraph Co. Ltd, 1935-50; inventor of and engaged on hovercraft since 1953; Consultant (hovercraft), Ministry of Supply, 1957-58. Consultant, Hovercraft Development Ltd, 1958-70 (Dir, 1959-66). Foundn Pres., Internat. Air Cushion Engrg Soc., 1969-71 (Vice-Pres., 1971-); Pres., UK Hovercraft Soc., 1971-; Member, Min. of Technology's Adv. Cttee for Hovercraft, 1968-69. A Trustee of National Portrait Gallery, 1967-. Hon. Fellow: Swedish Soc. of Aeronautics, 1963; Soc. of Engineers, 1966; Manchester Inst. of Sci. and Tech., 1967; Downing Coll., Cambridge, 1969. Hon. Mem., Southampton Chamber of Commerce, 1967. Hon. DSc: Leicester, 1967; Heriot-Watt, 1971; London, 1975; Hon. Dr RCA, 1968. Hon. Freeman, Borough of Ramsgate, 1971. Viva Shield, Worshipful Co. of Carmen, 1961; RAC Diamond Jubilee Trophy, 1962. Thulin Medal, Swedish Soc. of Aeronautics, 1963; Howard N. Potts Medal, Franklin Inst., 1965; Albert Medal, RSA, 1966; Churchill Medal, Soc. of Engineers, 1966; Royal Medal, Royal Soc., 1966; Mitchell Memorial Medal, Stoke-on-Trent Assoc. of Engineers, 1967; Columbus Prize, Genoa, 1968; John Scott Award, City of Philadelphia, 1968; Elmer A. Sperry Award, 1968; Gold Medal, Calais Chamber of Commerce, 1969; Bluebird Trophy, 1969. Recreations: antiquities, gardening, fishing. Address: 16 Prospect Place, Hythe, Hants SO4 6AU.

COCKERELL, Sydney (Morris); FSA; bookbinder; Senior Partner of D. Cockerell & Son since 1946; b 6 June 1906; er s of late Douglas Cockerell and Florence Arundel; m 1931, Elizabeth Lucy Cowlishaw; one s two d. Educ: St Christopher Sch., Letchworth. Partnership with Douglas Cockerell, 1924. Vis. Lectr, Sch. of Library, Archive and Information Studies, UCL, 1945-76. Assisted with repair and binding of Codex Sinaiticus Manuscript at British Museum, 1934; has repaired and bound many early and medieval manuscripts including Codex Bezae Book of Cerne, Book of Deer, Thornton Romances, Fitzwilliam Virginal Book, Handel's Conducting Score of Messiah, and repaired and treated, amongst others, papers of Wordsworth, Milton, Tennyson, Isaac Newton, Captain Cook's First Circumnavigation of the Globe; designed and made numbers of tooled bindings, including Rolls of Honour for House of Lords, House of Commons, Book of RAF at Church of St Clement Danes (10 vols), Newfoundland Book of Rembrance, Lectern Bible for Chichester Cathedral, tooled bindings for collectors and exhibition. Revived and developed craft of marbling paper; designed and made tools and equipment for binding and marbling. Visited Ceylon, Ethiopia, Italy, Canada, Tunisia, Portugal, USA and Greece to advise on book conservation. Member Technical Committees for: British Standards; Nat. Maritime Mus.; care of Lincoln Magna Carta, Lincoln Cathedral. Hon. Mem. Soc. of Scribes and Illuminators, 1956; Fellow International Institute for Conservation of Historic and Artistic Works, 1959; Master, Art Workers Guild, 1961.

Pres., Double Crown Club, 1976-77. Publications: Marbling Paper, 1934; Appendix to Bookbinding and the Care of Books, 1943, revised and repr. 1973; The Repairing of Books, 1958; contributor to: The Calligrapher's Handbook, 1956; Encyclopædia Britannica, 1963. Recreation: keeping the house up and the weeds down. Address: Riversdale, Grantchester, Cambridge. T: Trumpington 2124.

COCKERILL, Geoffrey Fairfax; Under-Secretary, Department of Education and Science, since 1972; b 14 May 1922; e s of Walter B. Cockerill and Mary W. Cockerill (née Buffery); m 1959, Janet Agnes Walters, JP, MA, d of Archibald J. Walters, MBE, and Elsie Walters; two s. Educ: Humberstone Foundation Sch., Cleethorpes; UC Nottingham. BA 1947. Royal Artillery, 1941-45 (Actg Captain). Cadet, Min. of Labour, 1947; entered Min. of Educn, 1952; Principal, 1954; Private Sec. to last Minister of Educn and Secs of State for Educn and Science, 1963-65; Asst Sec., 1964; Sec., Public Schools Commn, 1966-68; Jt Sec., Schools Council for Curriculum and Examinations, 1970-72. Recreations: gardening, photography, towpath cycling. Address: 31 Upper Brighton Road, Surbiton, Surrey. T: 01-399 0125. Club: Royal Commonwealth Society.

COCKERTON, Rev. John Clifford Penn; Principal, St John's College and Cranmer Hall, Durham, since 1970; b 27 June 1927; s of late William Penn Cockerton and Eleanor Cockerton; m 1974, Diana Margaret Smith, d of Mr and Mrs W. Smith, Upper Poppleton, York. Educ: Wirral Grammar Sch.; Univ. of Liverpool; St Catherine's Society, Oxford; Wycliffe Hall, Oxford. Asst Master, Prenton Secondary Sch., 1949-51; Deacon 1954; Priest 1955; Asst Curate, St Helens Parish Church, 1954-58; Tutor 1958-60, Chaplain 1960-63, Cranmer Hall, Durham; Vice-Principal, St John's Coll., Durham, 1963-70. Examining Chaplain to Bishop of Durham, 1971-73. Recreation: music. Address: St John's College, Durham. T: Durham 69113. Club: Royal Commonwealth Society.

COCKETT, Frank Bernard, MS, FRCS; Consultant Surgeon to St Thomas' Hospital since 1954; Hon. Surgeon, Florence Nightingale Hospital, London, since 1960; b Rockhampton, Australia, 22 April 1916; s of late Rev. Charles Bernard Cockett, MA, DD; m 1945, Felicity Ann (d 1958), d of Col James Thackeray Fisher, DSO, Frieston, near Grantham, Lincs; one s two d; m 1960, Dorothea Anne Newman; twin s. Educ: Bedford Sch.; St Thomas's Hosp. Med. Sch. BSc (1st Cl. Hons), 1936; MRCS, LRCP 1939; MB, BS (London) 1940; FRCS (English) 1947; MS (London) 1953. Sqdn Ldr (Surgical Specialist) RAFVR, 1942-46; Surgical Registrar, St Thomas' Hosp., 1947-48; Resident Asst Surg., St Thomas' Hosp., 1948-50; Senior Lecturer in Surgery, St Thomas's Hosp. Med. Sch., 1950-54. Fellow Assoc. of Surgs of Gt Brit.; Mem. European Soc. of Cardiovascular Surgery. Publications: The Pathology and Surgery of the Veins of the Lower Limb, 1956; several contribs to Operative Surgery (ed. C. G. Rob and Rodney Smith), 1956; various papers in medical and surgical journals. Recreations: sailing, tennis, squash, gardening, collecting marine paintings. Address: 61 Harley Street, W1. T: 01-580 3612; 14 Essex Villas, Campden Hill, Kensington, W8. T: 01-937 9883. Clubs: Little Ship; Island Sailing.

COCKEY, Air Cdre Leonard Herbert, CB 1945; Royal Air Force (retired); b 1893; s of late Rev. H. A. Cockey, Oldland Vicarage, Glos; m 1942, Eileen Anne, d of James A. Hogan, Tipperary; one s two d. Educ: Bristol Univ. Served European War, 1914-18 (French Croix de Guerre avec Palme, 1916). Qualified RAF Staff Coll. and idc. Served War of 1939-45 in Bomber Command and Southern Rhodesia; retired, 1945. Address: Sprayside, Banks Road, Sandbanks, Dorset. T: Canford Cliffs 707485. Club: Royal Air Force.

COCKFIELD, Sir (Francis) Arthur; Kt 1973; Chairman, Price Commission, 1973-77; Managing Director and Chairman Executive Management Committee, Boots Pure Drug Co. Ltd, 1961-67, retired; b 28 Sept. 1916; 2nd s of late Lieut C. F. Cockfield and Louisa (née James); m Aileen Monica Mudie, Choreographer. Educ: Dover County; London Sch. of Economics (LLB, BSc (Econ.)). Called to Bar, Inner Temple, 1942. Home Civil Service, Inland Revenue, 1938; Asst Sec. to Board of Inland Revenue, 1945; Commissioner of Inland Revenue, 1951-52; Dir of Statistics and Intelligence to Board of Inland Revenue, 1945-52; Finance Dir, Boots Pure Drug Co. Ltd, 1953-61. Mem., NEDC, 1962-64; Advr on Taxation Policy to Chancellor of Exchequer, 1970-73. Mem., Court of Governors, Univ. of Nottingham, 1963-67. Pres., Royal Statistical Soc., 1968-69. Hon. Fellow, LSE, 1972. Address: Connaught House, Mount Row, Berkeley Square, W1. Club: Reform.

COCKIN, Rt. Rev. George Eyles Irwin; Rector of Bainton, Diocese of York, since 1969; Assistant Bishop, Diocese of York, since 1969; Rural Dean of Harthill, since 1973; *b* 15 Aug. 1908; *s* of late Charles Irwin Cockin, Solicitor, and Judith Cockin. *Educ:* Repton; Leeds University (BA); Lincoln Theological College. Tutor, St Paul's College, Awka, Nigeria, 1933-40; Supervisor, Anglican Schools, E Nigeria, 1940-52. Deacon, 1953, Priest, 1954; Curate, Kimberworth, Rotherham, 1953-55; Sen. Supervisor, Anglican Schools, E Nigeria, 1955-58; Canon, All Saints Cathedral, Onitsha, 1957; first Bishop of Owerri, 1959-69. *Address:* The Rectory, Bainton, Driffield, North Humberside. *T:* Middleton-on-the-Wolds 377.

COCKING, Prof. John Martin, MA; Leverhulme Emeritus Research Fellow, since 1975; Fellow, since 1965 and Emeritus Professor, since 1975, King's College, University of London; *b* 9 Nov. 1914; *s* of Matthew Maddern Bottrell Cocking and Annie Cocking; *m* 1941, May Parsons Wallis; one *s. Educ:* Penzance County Sch. for Boys; King's Coll., London; Sorbonne; British Institute in Paris. BA (Hons) French, 1935; Teacher's Diploma (London), 1936; Diplôme d'Etudes Universitaires (Sorbonne), 1937; MA (London), 1939. Lecturer in English Literature, British Institute in Paris, 1937-38, Lecturer in English and Asst to the Dir, 1938-39; Asst Lecturer in French, King's Coll., London, 1939-46 (including 5 years' absence on war service in the Army); Lecturer in French, 1946-52, Prof. of French Lang. and Literature, 1952-75, King's Coll., London. Officier de l'ordre national du mérite (France), 1973. *Publications:* Marcel Proust, 1956; articles in journals and reviews. *Address:* Trevecca, Ludgvan, Penzance, Cornwall TR20 8EZ. *T:* Cockwells 538.

COCKRAM, Ben, CMG 1948; OBE 1944; Jan Smuts Professor of International Relations, University of the Witwatersrand, 1961-70, Emeritus Professor, since 1971; *b* 1903; *s* of B. B. Cockram, St Helier's, Jersey, Channel Islands; *m* 1928, Doris Mary Holdrup; one *d. Educ:* Victoria Coll.; Taunton's Sch.; Queen's Coll., Oxford. BA (London); MA (Oxon); PhD (Michigan, USA). Asst Principal, Dominions Office, 1926; Private Sec. to Parly and Permanent Under-Secs of State, 1929-34; Principal, 1934-39; Political Sec. to UK High Comr in Union of S Africa, 1939-44; Counsellor, British Embassy, Washington, DC, 1944-49; Asst Sec., CRO, 1949-51; Dep. High Comr for the UK in Australia, 1952-54, and Acting High Comr, May-Oct. 1952; Dir of Information, CRO, 1954-57, Dir of Information Services, 1957-62. Adviser to UK delegs to Assembly and Council of League of Nations, 1935, 1936, 1937 and 1938, to Brussels Conference, on Far East, 1936, to San Francisco Conference, 1945, to Councils of UNRRA and FAO, to Peace Conference, Paris, 1946, the Assembly, Security, Economic and Social, and Trusteeship Councils of UN, 1946, 1947 and 1948; to Unesco Conferences, Paris, 1958 and 1960. Mem. of Far Eastern Commission on Japan, 1946-48; Mem. UK Delegation to Commonwealth Educational Conferences: at Oxford, 1959; at Delhi, 1962; Leader, UK Delegations to Unesco Confs on SE Asia, at Bangkok, 1960; on Latin America, at Santiago, Chile, 1961; on Africa, at Paris, 1962. South African Rep. at Nuclear Proliferation Conf., Toronto, 1966. *Publications:* Seen from South Africa, 1963; Problems of Southern Africa, 1964; The Conduct of British Foreign Policy, 1964; Rhodesia and UDI, 1966; The Population Problem and International Relations, 1970. *Recreation:* swimming. *Address:* 198 Main Road, Muizenberg, CP, South Africa.

COCKRAM, Sir John, Kt 1964; Director since 1952, General Manager, 1941-73, The Colne Valley Water Company; Director since 1970, Chairman since 1971, Rickmansworth and Uxbridge Valley Water Co.; *b* 10 July 1908; *s* of Alfred John and Beatrice Elizabeth Cockram; *m* 1937, Phyllis Eleanor, *d* of Albert Henning; one *s* two *d. Educ:* St Aloysius Coll., Highgate. Chartered Accountant. Member: Herts CC, 1949-74 (Chm. 1961-65); Thames Conservancy, 1954-74; Exec. Cttee, British Waterworks Assoc., 1948-74 (Pres., 1957-58); Water Companies Assoc., 1950- (Chm.); Central Advisory Water Cttee, 1955-74; Thames Water Authy, 1973-76. Life Governor, Haileybury. *Recreations:* fishing, gardening. *Address:* Rebels' Corner, The Common, Chorleywood, Hertfordshire. *Clubs:* Bath, MCC.

COCKS, family name of Baron Somers.

COCKS, Sir Barnett; see Cocks, Sir T. G. B.

COCKS, Rt. Rev. Francis William; see Shrewsbury, Bishop Suffragan of.

COCKS, Rt. Hon. Michael Francis Lovell, PC 1976; MP (Lab) Bristol South since 1970; Parliamentary Secretary to the Treasury and Government Chief Whip, since 1976; *b* 19 Aug.

1929; *s* of Dr H. F. Lovell Cocks; *m* 1954, Janet Macfarlane; two *s* two *d. Educ:* Bristol University. Various posts in education from 1954; Lectr, Bristol Polytechnic, 1968. Contested (Lab): Bristol West, 1959; South Gloucestershire, 1964, 1966. An Asst Govt Whip, 1974-76. *Recreations:* swimming, listening to music, reading. *Address:* House of Commons, SW1.

COCKS, Sir (Thomas George) Barnett, KCB 1963 (CB 1961); OBE 1949; Clerk of the House of Commons, 1962-73, retired; *b* 1907; *m* 1952, Iris Mary Symon (*née* Coltman); one *s* one step *d. Educ:* Blundells Sch.; Worcester Coll., Oxford. Clerk in the House of Commons, from 1931; temporarily attached Min. of Home Security, 1939. Hon. Sec. and later a Trustee of the History of Parliament; Mem., Assoc. of Secretaries-General of Parliaments, 1959-73; Pres., Governing Bd, Internat. Centre of Parliamentary Documentation, Geneva, 1972; Chm., Westminster Pastoral Foundn Nat. Council. *Publications:* The Parliament at Westminster, 1949; (with Strathearn Gordon) A People's Conscience, 1952; The European Parliament, 1973; Mid-Victorian Masterpiece, 1977. Editor: Erskine May's Parliamentary Practice, 15th, 16th, 17th and 18th edns; Council of Europe Manual of Procedure, seven edns. *Address:* 13 Langford Green, SE5 8BX. *T:* 01-274 5448.

COCKSHUT, Mrs Gillian; see Avery, G. E.

CODRINGTON, Sir Christopher William Gerald Henry, 2nd Bt *cr* 1876; *b* 6 Oct. 1894; *s* of late Sir Gerald William Henry Codrington, 1st Bt, and Lady Edith Sybil Henrietta Denison (*d* 1945), *d* of 1st Earl of Londesborough; *S* father, 1929; *m* 1st, 1921, Joan (*d* 1961), 2nd *d* of T. Reginald Hague-Cook; one *s*; 2nd, 1963, Henrietta Desirée Moutray Read, *d* of late Major Beresford Moutray Read. *Educ:* Uppingham. Joined 19th Royal Hussars, 1914; served with 19th Hussars in France, 1914-18 (wounded); High Sheriff for Co. of Glos, 1938. *Recreations:* cricket, shooting, hunting. *Heir: s* Simon Francis Bethel Codrington [*b* 14 Aug. 1923; *m* 1959, Pamela Joy Halliday, *d* of Major G. W. B. Wise, MBE; three *s*. Late Coldstream Guards]. *Address:* Castle Grove, Bampton, Tiverton, Devon.

CODRINGTON, John Ernest Fleetwood, CMG 1968; *b* 1919; *s* of late Stewart Codrington; *m* 1951, Margaret, *d* of late Sir Herbert Hall Hall, KCMG; three *d. Educ:* Haileybury; Trinity Coll., Cambridge. Served RNVR, 1940-42: HMS Enchantress, HMS Vanity; Royal Marines, 1942-46: 42 (RM) Commando; Colonial Administrative Service, 1946: Gold Coast (later Ghana), 1947-58; Nyasaland, 1958-64; Financial Sec., Bahamas, 1964-70; Bahamas Comr in London, 1970-73, acting High Comr, 1973-74; Financial Sec., Bermuda, 1974-77. *Recreation:* sailing. *Address:* Chequers Close, Lymington, Hants. *Clubs:* Army and Navy; Royal Lymington Yacht.

CODRINGTON, Kenneth de Burgh; Professor Emeritus of Indian Archæology in University of London (Institute of Archæology and School of Oriental and African Studies); *o s* of late Col H. de B. Codrington, IA; *m* 1927, Philippa Christine, *y d* of late E. V. Fleming, CB; one *s* one *d. Educ:* Sherborne Sch.; Cadet Coll., Wellington, India; Corpus Christi Coll., Cambridge; Wadham Coll., Oxford. Indian Army, 33rd QVO Light Horse, 1917; invalided, 1921; BA 1921; MA 1926. RAF Educational Staff, Cranwell, 1922; Prof. of Archæology and Fellow of the Graduate Sch., Univ. of Cincinnati, USA, 1925-26; Hon. Lecturer, University Coll., London and School of Oriental and African Studies, 1931; appointed Prof., 1948. Mem. Cttee of Management, Inst. of Archæology, 1944-67; Keeper, Indian Section, Victoria and Albert Museum, South Kensington, until 1948. London Division RNVR, 1924-39; Commander (S) retd, 1946. Joined J. Hackin, Dir of the French Archæological Delegation in Afghanistan, 1940. Catalogued and hung Burlington Fine Arts Club Exhibn of Indian Art (with Laurence Binyon), 1930; organised Tagore Society's Exhibn of Indian Art, London, 1944; Mem. Selection and Hanging Cttee, Royal Academy Exhibn of Art of India and Pakistan, Burlington House, 1947. Served on Councils of the Royal Asiatic Soc., Royal Anthropological Inst., and Museums Assoc.; Hon. Fellow, School of Oriental and African Studies. Chm., Civil Service Retirement Fellowship, SE Kent. Served on County Youth Cttee (Training). *Publications:* Ancient India, 1926; rev. edn of Vincent Smith's History of Indian Fine Art, 1930; An Introduction to the Study of Medieval Indian Sculpture, 1929; An Introduction to the Study of Islamic Art in India (India Soc.), 1934; The Wood of the Image, 1934; Cricket in the Grass, 1959; Birdwood and the Arts of India (Birdwood Lecture, RSA), 1969; papers on art, archæology and anthropology. *Address:* Rose Cottage, Appledore, Kent. *T:* Appledore 388.

CODRINGTON, Sir William (Alexander), 8th Bt *cr* 1721; in command with Gulf Oil Marine; *b* 5 July 1934; *e s* of Sir William

Richard Codrington, 7th Bt, and Joan Kathleen Birellu, *e d* of Percy E. Nicholas, London, NW; *S* father, 1961. *Educ:* St Andrew Coll., S Africa; S African Naval Coll., General Botha. Joined Merchant Navy, 1952; joined Union Castle Mail Steamship Co., 1960; Master Mariner's Certificate of Competency, 1961. Joined Gulf Oil, 1973. *Recreation:* sailing. *Heir: b* Giles Peter Codrington, *b* 28 Oct. 1943. *Address:* 99 St James Drive, Wandsworth Common, SW17. *Club:* Royal Southern Yacht.

CODRON, Michael Victor; theatrical producer; *b* 8 June 1930; *s* of I. A. Codron and Lily (*née* Morganstern). *Educ:* St Paul's Sch.; Worcester Coll., Oxford (BA). Mem. council, English Stage Company; Director, Hampstead Theatre; Governor, Mermaid Theatre. Productions include: Share My Lettuce, Breath of Spring, 1957; Dock Brief and What Shall We Tell Caroline?, The Birthday Party, Valmouth, 1958; Pieces of Eight, 1959; The Wrong Side of the Park, The Caretaker, 1960; Three, Stop It Whoever You Are, One Over the Eight, The Tenth Man, Big Soft Nellie, 1961; Two Stars for Comfort, Everything in the Garden, Rattle of a Simple Man, 1962; Next Time I'll sing to You, Private Lives (revival), The Lovers and the Dwarfs, Cockade, 1963; Poor Bitos, The Formation Dancers, Entertaining Mr Sloane, 1964; Loot, The Killing of Sister George, Ride a Cock Horse, 1965; Little Malcolm and his Struggle against the Eunuchs, The Anniversary, There's a Girl in my Soup, Big Bad Mouse, 1966; The Judge, The Flip Side, Wise Child, The Boy Friend (revival), 1967; Not Now Darling, The Real Inspector Hound, 1968; The Contractor, Slag, The Two of Us, The Philanthropist, 1970; The Foursome, Butley, A Voyage Round my Father, The Changing Room, 1971; Veterans, Time and Time Again, Crown Matrimonial, My Fat Friend, 1972; Collaborators, Savages, Habeas Corpus, Absurd Person Singular, 1973; Knuckle, Flowers, Golden Pathway Annual, The Norman Conquests, John Paul George Ringo... and Bert, 1974; A Family and A Fortune, Alphabetical Order, A Far Better Husband, Ashes, Absent Friends, Otherwise Engaged, Stripwell, 1975; Funny Peculiar, Treats, Donkey's Years, Confusions, Teeth 'n' Smiles, Yahoo, 1976; Dusa, Stas, Fish & Vi, Just Between Ourselves, Oh, Mr Porter, Breezeblock Park, The Bells of Hell, The Old Country, 1977. *Recreation:* collecting Caroline memorabilia. *Address:* c/o 117 Regent Street, W1. *Club:* Garrick.

COE, Denis Walter; Assistant Director, Middlesex Polytechnic, since 1974; *b* 5 June 1929; *s* of James and Lily Coe, Whitley Bay, Northumberland; *m* 1953, Margaret Rae, *d* of William F. Chambers, Middlesbrough; three *s* one *d. Educ:* Bede Trng Coll., Durham; London Sch. of Economics. Teacher's Certificate, 1952; BSc (Econ.) 1960; MSc (Econ.) 1966. National Service in RAF, 1947-50; Junior and Secondary Schoolmaster, 1952-59; Dep. Headmaster, Secondary Sch., 1959-61; Lectr in Govt, Manchester Coll. of Commerce, 1961-66. Contested (Lab) Macclesfield, 1964; MP (Lab) Middleton, Prestwich and Whitefield, 1966-70; Parly deleg. to Council of Europe and WEU, 1968-70. Dean of Students, NE London Polytechnic, 1970-74. Chm., Nat. Bureau for Handicapped Students, 1975-. Mem. Governing Council, Nat. Youth Theatre, 1968-. *Recreations:* music, drama, walking. *Address:* 7E Hollycroft Avenue, NW3.

COFFER, David Edwin, CBE 1973 (OBE 1963); General Secretary, The Royal British Legion, since 1959; *b* 18 Sept. 1913; *s* of David Gilbertson Coffer and Florence Ellen Gard; *m* 1947, Edith Mary Moulton; three *d. Educ:* Colfe Grammar Sch. *Address:* 74 Ridgeway Drive, Bromley, Kent BR1 5DQ. *T:* 01-857 5483. *Clubs:* Royal Over-Seas League, Kennel.

COFFEY, Christopher, JP; *b* 8 Dec. 1902; *s* of Bernard and Thirza Coffey; *m* 1922, Doris May Coffey (*née* Scott); four *s* two *d. Educ:* St Catherine's, Sheffield. Employed in Railway Industry, Traffic Grade; NUR Trade Union Sec. (Branch); Nat. Conf. Sec.; Approved Soc. Branch Sec.; District Council Pres.; represented NUR at TUC and Labour Party Annual Conference, 1918-49; City Councillor, Nottingham, 1945-, Lord Mayor, 1953-54; JP 1947; Alderman, 1954; Hon. Alderman, 1975; Labour Party Organising Sec., 1949-53. *Recreations:* fishing, football (soccer). *Address:* 55 Glapton Road, Nottingham. *T:* 865818.

COFFEY, John Nimmo; Stipendiary Magistrate, Greater Manchester (sitting at Manchester), since 1975; a Recorder of the Crown Court, since 1972; *b* 20 Feb. 1929; *s* of Samuel Coffey, DSc, FRIC, and Ruth (*née* Stevenson); *m* 1953, Anne Hesling Bradbury, LLB, JP; three *d. Educ:* Stockport Grammar Sch.; Victoria Univ. of Manchester (LLB). Called to Bar, Gray's Inn, 1951. *Recreations:* sailing, music, gardening. *Address:* 9 Highfield Park, Heaton Mersey, Stockport, Cheshire. *T:* 061-432 4185.

COFFIN, Cyril Edwin; Director General, Food Manufacturers' Federation, since 1977; *b* 29 June 1919; *o s* of late Percy Edwin and Helena Constance Coffin; *m* 1947, Joyce Mary, *d* of C. R. Tobitt, Castle Hedingham; one *s* one *d* (and one *d* decd). *Educ:* King's Coll. Sch., Wimbledon; King's Coll., Cambridge (MA). Enlisted Royal Artillery, 1939; transf. Royal Scots, 1940; commnd RIASC, 1941. Temp. Asst Princ., Burma Office, 1946; Asst Princ., Min. of Food, 1947; Princ., 1948; jssc 1950; Asst, Sec., Min. of Agric., Fisheries and Food, 1957; seconded to Office of Minister for Science, 1963; Alternate UK Governor, Internat. Atomic Energy Agency, 1964. Under-Secretary: Min. of Technology, 1966, later DTI; Dept of Prices and Consumer Protection, 1974-77. *Recreations:* music, learning languages. *Address:* 54 Cambridge Avenue, New Malden, Surrey. *T:* 01-942 0763. *Club:* Union (Cambridge).

COGGAN, Most Rev. and Rt. Hon. F. Donald; *see* Canterbury, Archbishop of.

COGHILL, John Percival, CBE 1951; Foreign Service, retired; Minister to Republic of Honduras, 1954-55; *b* 29 Nov. 1902; *s* of Percy de Geiger Coghill and Dr Agnes Irene Sinclair Coghill. *Educ:* Loretto Sch.; Cheltenham Coll.; Emmanuel Coll., Cambridge. Served at various Foreign Service posts in China. *Recreation:* walking. *Club:* Royal Commonwealth Society.

COGHILL, Sir (Marmaduke Nevill) Patrick (Somerville), 6th Bt *cr* 1778; TD 1947; DL Herts; Lieut-Col RA (TA), retd; *b* 18 March 1896; *s* of 5th Bt and Elizabeth Hildegarde Augusta, *d* of late Col Thomas Henry Somerville, Drishane, Skibbereen; *S* father, 1921. *Educ:* Haileybury. Joined RA 1915; served in France until Armistice and afterwards in Turkey and Iraq; Commanded 86th (Hertfordshire Yeomanry), Fd Regt RA TA, 1939-41, and served in Middle East, 1941-45 (despatches). Col, Arab Legion, Jordan, 1952-56. Order of Istiqlal, 2nd Class, Jordan, 1956. OStJ 1957. *Heir: b* Prof. Nevill Henry Kendal Aylmer Coghill, *qv. Address:* Savran House, Aylburton, Lydney, Glos.

COGHILL, Prof. Nevill Henry Kendal Aylmer, MA; Merton Professor of English Literature, Oxford, 1957-66; Fellow and Tutor in English Literature, Exeter College, Oxford, 1925-57; Emeritus Fellow: Exeter College, Oxford, 1957; Merton College, Oxford, 1966; *b* 19 April 1899; 2nd *s* of Sir Egerton Bushe Coghill, 5th Bt, and Elizabeth Hildegarde Augusta, *d* of late Col Thomas Henry Somerville, Drishane, Skibbereen; *heir-pres.* to Sir Patrick Coghill, 6th Bt, *qv; m* 1927, Elspeth Nora (marr. diss. 1933), *d* of Dr Harley, Inchture, Perthshire; one *d. Educ:* Haileybury; Exeter Coll., Oxford. Stapeldon Scholar (History), Exeter Coll., Oxford, 1916. Served European War, from 1917; 2nd Lieut RFA (BSF), 1918-19. Research Fellow, Exeter Coll., 1924, Official Fellow, 1925, and Tutor in English Literature; Sub-Rector, 1940-45; Dean of Degrees, 1940; Clark Lecturer, Trinity Coll., Cambridge, 1959. Mem. Oxford University Drama Commission, 1945; Dir, Friends of OUDS, 1940-47; produced: A Midsummer Night's Dream, Haymarket, 1945; Pilgrim's Progress, Covent Garden, 1951; Dr Faustus, University Theatre, Oxford, 1966; jt dir, Dr Faustus (film), 1967. FRSL 1950. Governor of Shakespeare Memorial Theatre, Stratford-upon-Avon, 1956. Pres., Poetry Soc., 1964-66. Hon. DLitt, Williams Coll., Mass, 1966; Hon. LLD St Andrews, 1971. Has broadcast on Chaucer, Langland, etc. *Play:* (with Martin Starkie) Canterbury Tales, Phœnix Theatre, 1968. *Publications:* The Pardon of Piers Plowman (Gollancz Mem. Lecture, Br. Acad., 1945); Visions from Piers Plowman, 1949; The Poet Chaucer, 1949; The Canterbury Tales (in modern English), 1951; Geoffrey Chaucer, 1956; Shakespeare's Professional Skills, 1964; Troilus and Criseyde (in modern English), 1971; (ed) A Choice of Chaucer's Verse, 1972; Chaucer's Idea of What is Noble, 1972. *Recreations:* producing Shakespearian and other plays; music, etc. *Address:* Savran House, Aylburton, near Lydney, Glos. *T:* Lydney 2240; c/o Merton College, Oxford. *Club:* Travellers'.

COGHILL, Sir Patrick; *see* Coghill, Sir M. N. P. S.

COGMAN, Very Rev. Frederick Walter; Dean of Guernsey since 1967; Rector of St Peter Port, Guernsey, since 1976; *b* 4 March 1913; *s* of William Frederick Cogman and Mabel Cozens; *m* 1940, Rose Hélène Mauger; one *s* one *d. Educ:* Rutlish Sch., Merton; King's Coll., London. Asst Priest, Upton-cum-Chalvey, Slough, 1938-42; Chaplain and Housemaster, St George's Sch., Harpenden, 1942-48; Rector of St Martin, Guernsey, 1948-76. *Recreations:* music, painting. *Address:* The Deanery, Guernsey. *T:* Guernsey 38303.

COHEN, His Honour Arthur; *see* Cohen, His Honour N. A. J.

COHEN, Sir B. N. W.; *see* Waley-Cohen.

COHEN, Sir Edward, Kt 1970; Director; Solicitor; Consultant, Paveys, Melbourne, Australia; Chairman: E Z Industries Ltd; Electrolytic Zinc Co. of Australasia Ltd; Commercial Union Assurance Co. of Australia Ltd; Commercial Union Properties (Australia) Pty Ltd; Derwent Metals Pty Ltd; Emu Bay Railway Co. Ltd; CUB Fibre Containers Pty Ltd; Carlton & United Breweries Ltd; former Vice-Chairman, Herald and Weekly Times Ltd; Director: Associated Pulp & Paper Mills Ltd; Michaelis Bayley Ltd; and other cos; *m* 1939, Meryl D. Fink; one *s. Educ:* Scotch Coll., Melbourne; (Exhibnr in Greek and Roman History) Ormond Coll., Univ. of Melbourne (LLB). Served, 1940-45: AIF, 2/12 Fd Regt, 9th Div. Artillery, Captain 1942. Past Member: Faculty of Law of Melbourne Univ., Council of Legal Education, and Bd of Examiners. Chm., Pensions Cttee of Melbourne Legacy, 1959-; Mem. Council Law Inst. of Victoria, 1959-68, Pres. 1965-66. *Address:* 19 Russell Street, Toorak, Victoria 3142, Australia; (office) 390 Lonsdale Street, Melbourne, Victoria 3000, Australia. *Clubs:* Naval and Military, Victoria Racing, Royal Automobile (all in Melbourne).

COHEN, George Cormack; Sheriff-Substitute of the Lothians and Peebles at Edinburgh, 1955-66; *b* 16 Dec. 1909; *s* of J. Cohen and Mary J. Cormack, Melfort House, Bearsden, Dunbartonshire; *m* 1939, Elizabeth, *d* of James H. Wallace, Malvern; one *s* one *d. Educ:* Kelvinside Academy, Glasgow; Glasgow Univ. MA 1930, LLB 1934, Admitted to Scottish Bar, 1935; Sheriff-Substitute of Caithness at Wick, 1944-51; of Ayr and Bute at Kilmarnock, 1951-55. *Recreations:* travel, gastronomy, philately, gardening. *Address:* Sandlewood, Hadlow Park, Tonbridge, Kent. *T:* Hadlow 513. *Club:* Royal Automobile.

COHEN, Sir Jack, Kt 1965; OBE 1951; JP; Alderman, Borough of Sunderland, 1935-74, and Councillor, 1929; Mayor, 1949-50; *b* 2 Nov. 1896; *s* of Samuel Cohen, Sunderland; *m* 1921, Kitty, *d* of Abraham Sinclair, Glasgow; one *s* one *d.* Served European War, 1914-18. JP Sunderland, 1939. *Address:* 16 Barnes Park Road, Sunderland, Tyne and Wear SR4 7PE. *T:* Sunderland 226593.

COHEN, Prof. John, PhD; Professor of Psychology, University of Manchester, since 1952; *b* 20 Jan. 1911; *s* of Joseph and Rebecca Cohen, Tredegar, Mon.; *m* 1st, 1939; one *s* one *d*; 2nd, 1955, Rosemarie Loss; three *s. Educ:* Tredegar Elementary and County Schs.; University Coll., London (MA, PhD). Research at: University Coll., London, 1933-40; Institute of Experimental Psychology, Oxford, 1940. RAC, 1940-41; attached to Offices of War Cabinet and Central Statistical Office, 1941-48; Joint Sec., Expert Cttee on Work of Psychologists and Psychiatrists in the Services, 1942-45; Mem., Working Party on Recruitment and Training of Nurses, 1946-47; Tech. Sec., Internat. Preparatory Commn for World Congress on Mental Health, 1948; Mem., Inter-professional Advisory Cttee to World Fedn for Mental Health, 1949-52; Consultant to UNESCO, 1948, 1950, 1967; Lectr in Psychology, Univ. of Leeds, 1948-49; Prof. of Psychology, Univ. of Jerusalem, 1949-51; Lectr in Psychology, Birkbeck Coll., Univ. of London, 1951-52. Mem. of Council, Brit. Psychological Soc., 1956-59. Hon. MA (Manchester), FBPsS 1943. Fellow, World Academy of Art and Science; Corr. Mem., Centre de Recherches de Psychologie Comparative. Member: Internat. Editorial Bd of Medikon; Editorial Cttee of IKON Revue Internationale de Filmologie; Adv. Bd, Internat. Soc. for Study of Time. *Publications:* Human Nature, War and Society, 1946; Report on Recruitment and Training of Nurses, 1948; co-editor: Human Affairs, 1937; Educating for Democracy, 1939; co-author: Risk and Gambling, 1956; Humanistic Psychology, 1958; Chance, Skill and Luck, 1960; Readings in Psychology (ed) 1964; Behaviour in Uncertainty, 1964; Human Robots in Myth and Science, 1966; A New Introduction to Psychology, 1966; Psychological Time in Health and Disease, 1967; Psychology: An Outline for the intending Student (ed), 1967; Causes and Prevention of Road Accidents (with B. Preston), 1968; (with I. Christensen) Information and Choice, 1970; Elements of Child Psychology, 1970; Homo Psychologicus, 1971; Psychological Probability, 1972; Everyman's Psychology, 1973; numerous papers in psychological, medical, psychiatric and other learned jls. *Recreations:* travel, music. *Address:* Department of Psychology, The University, Manchester. *T:* 061-273 3333.

COHEN, Sir John (Edward), Kt 1969; Founder of Tesco Stores (Holdings) Limited and associated companies; First Life President since 1969 (formerly Chairman); *b* 6 Oct. 1898; *m* 1924, Sarah Fox; two *d. Educ:* Rutland Street LCC Sch. Served with RFC, 1917-19, France, Egypt, Palestine. Commenced in business on own account, 1919. Master, Worshipful Company of Carmen, 1976-77. FGI. *Recreations:* bridge, world travel.

Address: 22 Cumberland Terrace, Regent's Park, NW1. *Clubs:* Royal Automobile, City Livery.

COHEN, John Michael, FRSL 1957; critic and translator; *b* 5 Feb. 1903; *s* of late Arthur Cohen and Elizabeth (*née* Abrahams); *m* 1928, Audrey Frances Falk; four *s. Educ:* St Paul's Sch.; Queens' Coll., Cambridge. After short spell in publishing, joined family manufacturing business, 1925-40; war-time Schoolmaster, 1940-46; writing and translating from that date. *Publications: translations:* Don Quixote, 1950; Rousseau's Confessions, 1953; Rabelais, 1955; Life of Saint Teresa, 1957; Montaigne's Essays, 1958; Pascal's Pensées, 1961; Bernal Diaz, The Conquest of New Spain, 1963; The Spanish Bawd, 1964; Zarate, The Discovery and Conquest of Peru, 1968; The Four Voyages of Christopher Columbus, 1969; Sent off the Field, 1974; *criticism and biography:* Robert Browning, 1952; History of Western Literature, 1956; Life of Ludwig Mond, 1956; Poetry of This Age, 1959 (2nd, revised edn, 1966); Robert Graves, 1960; English Translators and Translations, 1962; The Baroque Lyric, 1963; En tiempos difiiles (a study of the new Cuban poetry), 1971; J. L. Borges, 1974; Journeys down the Amazon, 1975; *anthologies:* Penguin Book of Comic & Curious Verse, 1952; More Comic & Curious Verse, 1956; Penguin Book of Spanish Verse, 1956; Yet More Comic & Curious Verse, 1959; Latin American Writing Today, 1967; Writers in the New Cuba, 1967; A Choice of Comic and Curious Verse, 1975; *dictionaries:* (with M. J. Cohen) Penguin Dictionary of Quotations, 1960; (with M. J. Cohen) Penguin Dictionary of Modern Quotations, 1971; other translations. *Recreations:* meditation; listening to music; gardening. *Address:* Knappswood, Upper Basildon, Reading, Berks. *T:* Upper Basildon 282.

COHEN, Comdr Kenneth H. S., CB 1954; CMG 1946; RN; European Adviser to United Steel Companies, 1953-66; Vice-President: European League for Economic Co-operation, since 1972; Franco-British Society, since 1972 (Chairman, 1967-72); *b* 15 March 1900; *s* of late Herman Cohen, Barrister-at-Law, Inner Temple; *m* 1932, Mary Joseph, *d* of late Ernest Joseph, CBE, FRIBA; one *s* one *d. Educ:* Elstree Sch.; Eastbourne Coll. "Special Entry" RN Cadet, 1918, Midshipman, HMS Iron Duke; specialised in Torpedo Duties, 1926; RN Staff Coll., 1932; retired (Lt-Comdr), 1935; appointed HMS President, 1939; Comdr 1940. Attached Foreign Office, 1945. Councillor, RIIA, 1963-75. Officier de la Légion d'Honneur; Croix de Guerre avec palmes (France); Legion of Merit, Degree of Officer (USA); Officier de la Couronne (Belgium); Order of the White Lion (Czechoslovakia); Commandeur de l'Etoile Noire (France), 1960. *Publications:* articles in national press on problems of European integration. *Address:* 33 Bloomfield Terrace, SW1. *T:* 01-730 3228. *Club:* Garrick.

COHEN, Laurence Jonathan, FBA 1973; Fellow and Praelector in Philosophy, Queen's College, Oxford, since 1957; *b* 7 May 1923; *s* of Israel and Theresa Cohen; *m* 1953, Gillian Mary Slee; three *s* one *d. Educ:* St Paul's Sch., London; Balliol Coll., Oxford (MA 1947). Served War: Naval Intell. in UK and SEAC, 1942-45, and Lieut (Sp.) RNVR. Asst in Logic and Metaphysics, Edinburgh Univ., 1947; Lectr in Philosophy, St Andrews Univ. at Dundee, 1950; Commonwealth Fund Fellow in Logic at Princeton and Harvard Univs, 1952-53. Visiting Lectr, Hebrew Univ. of Jerusalem, 1952; Visiting Prof.: Columbia Univ., 1967; Yale Univ., 1972. Sec., Internat. Union of History and Philosophy of Science (Div. of Logic Methodology and Philosophy of Science), 1975-; Pres., British Soc. for Philosophy of Science, 1977-. *Publications:* The Principles of World Citizenship, 1954; The Diversity of Meaning, 1962; The Implications of Induction, 1970; The Probable and the Provable, 1977; articles in British, Belgian, Dutch, French, Israeli and US philosophical jls. *Recreations:* gardening; work for Council for Protection of Rural England. *Address:* Sturt House, East End, North Leigh, Oxfordshire.

COHEN, Hon. Leonard Harold Lionel; Director-General, Accepting Houses Committee, since 1976; barrister-at-law; *b* 1 Jan. 1922; *s* of Rt Hon. Lord Cohen, PC (Life Peer), and Adelaide, Lady Cohen (*née* Spielmann); *m* 1949, Eleanor Lucy Quixano Henriques; two *s* one *d. Educ:* Eton Coll.; New Coll., Oxford (MA). War Service, Rifle Bde (wounded), Captain, 1941-45. Called to Bar, Lincoln's Inn, 1948; practised at Chancery Bar, 1949-61. Dir, M. Samuel & Co. Ltd (subseq. Hill Samuel & Co. Ltd), 1961-76; Man. Dir, S. Hoffnung & Co. Ltd, 1975-; Chm., United Services Trustee, 1976-. Master of the Skinners' Co., 1971-72. Hon. Col, 39th (City of London) Signal Regt (V), 1973-. *Recreations:* shooting, golf, reading, opera. *Address:* 57 Bedford Gardens, W8 7EF. *T:* 01-229 6401. *Club:* White's.

COHEN, Dr Louis; Executive Secretary, Institute of Physics, since 1966; *b* 14 Oct. 1925; *s* of late Harry Cohen and Fanny Cohen (*née* Abrahams); *m* 1948, Eve G. Marsh; one *s* two *d*. *Educ:* Manchester Central High Sch.; Manchester Univ.; Imperial Coll., London. BSc, PhD, FInstP. Research Physicist, Simon-Carves Ltd, 1953-63; Research Manager, Pyrotenax Ltd, 1963-66. Hon. Sec., Council of Science and Technology Insts, 1969-; Treasurer, European Physical Soc., 1968-73; Corresp. Mem., Manchester Literary and Philosophical Soc., 1963. FRSA. *Publications:* papers and articles on physics and related subjects. *Recreations:* cooking, books, music, the theatre. *Address:* 9 Limewood Close, W13 8HL. *T:* 01-997 2001.

COHEN, Myrella, QC 1970; **Her Honour Judge Myrella Cohen;** a Circuit Judge, since 1972; *b* 16 Dec. 1927; *d* of Samuel and Sarah Cohen, Manchester; *m* 1953, Lt-Col Mordaunt Cohen, TD; one *s* one *d*. *Educ:* Manchester High Sch. for Girls; Colwyn Bay Grammar Sch.; Manchester Univ. (LLB 1948). Called to the Bar, Gray's Inn, 1950. Recorder of Hull, 1971. *Address:* c/o Crown Court, Moot Hall, Newcastle upon Tyne NE1 1RT.

COHEN, Nat; Director: EMI Films Ltd (retired 1977 as Chairman and Chief Executive); EMI Film Productions Ltd; EMI Film & Theatre Corporation Ltd; *b* 1906. Entered film industry, 1930. *Films produced include:* Carry On Sergeant, and 12 other Carry On films; A Kind of Loving; Billy Liar; Darling; Far From the Madding Crowd; Murder on the Orient Express. *Address:* EMI Films Ltd, 142 Wardour Street, W1V 4AE. *T:* 01-437 0444.

COHEN, Lt-Col Nathan Leslie, TD 1949; JP; *b* 13 Jan. 1908; *s* of Reuben and Maud Cohen; unmarried. *Educ:* Stockton-on-Tees Grammar Sch.; Clifton Coll. In private practice as a Solicitor until 1939; called to the Bar, Lincoln's Inn, 1954. War Service, Aug. 1939-May 1945. Senior Legal Officer (Lt-Col), Military Govt, Carinthia, Austria, 1945-49; Pres. of Sessions Courts, Malaya, 1949-57; Justice of the Special Courts, Cyprus, 1958-59; Judge of HM Court of Sovereign Base Areas of Akrotiri and Dhekalia, Cyprus, 1960-67; Adjudicator under Immigration Appeals Act, 1970-71. Vice-President: Northern Area, British Legion; Cleveland Co. British Red Cross Soc.; Pres., St John Ambulance Assoc., Stockton. JP Stockton-on-Tees, 1967. Diamond Jubilee Medal (Johore), 1955; Colonial Police Medal, 1956. *Recreations:* travelling, shooting, reading. *Address:* 35 Richmond Road, Stockton-on-Tees, Cleveland. *Club:* Royal Over-Seas League.

COHEN, His Honour (Nathaniel) Arthur (Jim), JP; County Court Judge, Circuit No 38, 1955-56, Circuit No 43, 1956-60, Circuit No 56, 1960-70, retired; *b* 19 Jan. 1898; 2nd *s* of late Sir Benjamin Arthur Cohen, KC, and Lady Cohen; *m* 1st, 1927, Judith Luard (marr. diss.); two *s*; 2nd, 1936, Joyce Collingridge. *Educ:* Rugby; CCC, Oxford (BA). Served European War, 1916-19, Royal Navy. Called to Bar, Inner Temple, 1923. War of 1939-45; recalled to RN and placed on Emergency List with rank of Commander. Legal Adviser to UNRRA, 1946-49; Dep. Chm., Foreign Compensation Commn, 1950-55. JP Surrey, 1958. *Recreations:* golf, music. *Address:* Bay Tree Cottage, Crockham Hill, Edenbridge, Kent. *Club:* United Oxford & Cambridge University.

COHEN, Percy, CBE 1936; Joint Director, Conservative Research Department, 1948-59; *b* London, 25 Dec. 1891; *e s* of late M. Cohen; *m* 1917, Rosa Abrams (*d* 1973); one *s* one *d*. *Educ:* Central Foundation Sch., London. Entered service of Conservative Central Office, 1911; Head of Library and Information Dept, 1928-48. Served first European War, France. Worked in 12 General Elections; Editor, Constitutional Year Book, 1929-39; Editor, Notes on Current Politics, 1942-59. Sec. to several post-war problems Cttees, 1944-45. *Publications:* British System of Social Insurance, 1932; Unemployment Insurance and Assistance in Britain, 1938; (ed) Conservative Election Handbook, 1945; (ed) Campaign Guide, 1950, 1951, 1955 and 1959. *Recreation:* walking. *Address:* 115 Grove Hall Court, St John's Wood, NW8. *T:* 01-286 2489. *Club:* Constitutional.

COHEN, Reuben K.; *see* Kelf-Cohen.

COHEN, Sir Rex (Arthur Louis), KBE 1964 (OBE 1944); Chairman, Barclaytrust Property Management Ltd; Director: Barclays Bank Trust Co.; Tribune Investment Trust; *b* 27 Nov. 1906; *s* of Rex David Cohen, Condover Hall, Shrewsbury; *m* 1932, Nina Alice Castello; one *d*. *Educ:* Rugby Sch.; Trinity Coll., Cambridge (BA). Served KSLI, 1938-45. Past Mem., BoT Cttee for Consumer Protection. Past Chairman: Lewis's Investment Trust Group, 1958-65 (Joint Man. Dir, 1945); NAAFI, 1961-63; Higgs & Hill Ltd, 1966-72; Meat and Livestock Commn, 1967-72. Officer, Order of Orange Nassau (Netherlands), 1944. *Recreations:* racing, horse breeding, shooting. *Address:* Ruckmans Farm, Oakwood Hill, near Dorking, Surrey. *T:* Oakwood Hill 255. *Clubs:* White's; Jockey (Newmarket).

COHEN, Dr Richard Henry Lionel, CB 1969; Chief Scientist, Department of Health and Social Security, 1972-73, retired; *b* 1 Feb. 1907; *y s* of Frank Lionel and Bertha Hendelah Cohen; *m* 1934, Margaret Clarkson Deas; one *s*. *Educ:* Clifton Coll.; King's Coll., Cambridge; St Bartholomew's Hospital. Miscellaneous hosp. appts, 1940-46; MRC, 1948-62; Dep. Chief Med. Off., MRC, 1957-62; Dept of Health and Social Security (formerly Min. of Health), 1962-73. *Club:* Reform.

COHEN, Prof. Robert Donald, MD, FRCP; Professor of Metabolic Medicine, London Hospital Medical College, University of London, since 1974; *b* 11 Oct. 1933; *s* of Dr Harry H. and Ruby Cohen; *m* 1961, Dr Barbara Joan Boucher; one *s* one *d*. *Educ:* Clifton Coll.; Trinity Coll., Cambridge. MA, MD (Cantab). Hon. Cons. Physician, London Hosp., 1967; Chm., Editorial Bd, Clinical Science and Molecular Medicine, 1973-74; Dir, Academic Unit of Metabolism and Endocrinology, London Hosp. Med. Coll., 1974; Chairman: Adv. Cttee on the Application of Computing Science to Medicine and the Nat. Health Service, 1976-77; DHSS Computer R&D Cttee, 1977. *Publications:* Clinical and Biochemical Aspects of Lactic Acidosis (with H. F. Woods), 1976; papers in Clin. Sci. and Molecular Med., BMJ, Lancet. *Address:* The London Hospital, Whitechapel Road, E1 1BB. *T:* 01-247 5454.

COHEN, Ruth Louisa, CBE 1969; MA; Principal, Newnham College, Cambridge, 1954-72; University Lecturer in Economics, Cambridge, 1945-74; Governor, Hebrew University of Jerusalem; *b* 10 Nov. 1906; *d* of late Walter Samuel Cohen and late Lucy Margaret Cohen. *Educ:* Hayes Court, Kent; Newnham Coll., Cambridge. Commonwealth Fund Fellow, Stanford and Cornell Univs., USA, 1930-32; Research Officer, Agricultural Economics Research Inst., Oxford, 1933-39; Fellow of Newnham Coll., Cambridge, 1939-54; Min. of Food, 1939-42; Board of Trade, 1942-45. Lay Mem., Gen. Medical Council, 1961-76. City Cllr, Cambridge, 1973-. *Publications:* History of Milk Prices, 1936; Economics of Agriculture, 1939; articles in Economic Journal, etc. *Address:* 25 Gough Way, Cambridge. *T:* Cambridge 62699. *Club:* University Women's.

COHEN, Stanley; MP (Lab) Leeds (South East) since 1970; *b* 31 July 1927; *s* of Thomas and Teresa Cohen; *m* 1954, Brenda P. Rafferty; three *s* one *d*. *Educ:* St Patrick's and St Charles' Schools, Leeds. Served in Royal Navy, 1947-49. Employed in Clothing Industry, 1943-47 and 1949-51; Clerical Officer with British Railways, 1951-70. Mem. Leeds City Council, 1952-; elected Alderman, 1968. Parly Candidate (Lab) Barkston Ash County Constituency, 1966. PPS to Minister of State, DES, 1976-. Mem., Duke of Edinburgh's Commonwealth Study Conf. to Australia, 1968. *Recreations:* walking, camping, driving. *Address:* 164 Ring Road, Halton, Leeds LS15 7AE. *T:* Leeds 649568. *Clubs:* Crossgates Recreational; Irish Centre (Leeds).

COHEN, Prof. Sydney, FRCPath; Professor of Chemical Pathology, Guy's Hospital Medical School, since 1965; *b* Johannesburg, SA, 18 Sept. 1921; *s* of Morris and Pauline Cohen; *m* 1950, June Bernice Adler; one *s* one *d*. *Educ:* King Edward VIIth Sch., Johannesburg; Witwatersrand and London Univs. MD, PhD. Lectr, Dept of Physiology, Witwatersrand Univ., 1947-53; Scientific Staff, Nat. Inst. for Med. Research, London, 1954-60; Reader, Dept of Immunology, St Mary's Hosp. Med. Sch., 1960-65. Mem., MRC, 1974-76; Chm., Tropical Med. Research Bd, MRC, 1974-76; Mem. Governing Cttee, Nat. Biological Standards Bd, 1976-77; Chm., WHO Scientific Gp on Immunity to Malaria, 1976-. Nuffield Dominion Fellow in Medicine, 1954; Founder Fellow, RCPath, 1964. *Publications:* (with late E. H. Sadun) Immunity to Parasitic Infections, 1976; papers on protein metabolism, immunology and parasitic diseases in sc. jls. *Recreations:* golf, gardening, forestry. *Address:* 3 Greenaway Gardens, NW3 7DJ. *T:* 01-435 1195. *Club:* Royal and Ancient (St Andrews).

COHN, Prof. Norman, MA (Oxon); DLitt (Glasgow); FRHistS; author and historian; Astor-Wolfson Professor, University of Sussex, since 1973; *b* London, 12 Jan. 1915; *yr s* of late August Cohn and Daisy Reimer; *m* 1941, Vera (*née* Broido); one *s*. *Educ:* Gresham's Sch., Holt (Scholar); Christ Church, Oxford (Scholar). 1st Class in Honour Sch. of Medieval and Mod. Languages, 1936. Served in HM Forces, 1940-46. Lectr in French, Glasgow Univ., 1946-51; Prof. of French, Magee Univ. Coll., 1951-60; King's Coll., Durham Univ., 1960-63; Professorial Fellow and Dir, Columbus Centre, Sussex Univ.,

1966-73; Hugh Le May Fellow, Rhodes Univ., 1950. Fellow, Center for Advanced Study in the Behavioral Sciences, Stanford, Calif, 1966. Vis. Fellow, Center for Humanities, Wesleyan Univ., Conn, 1971; Fellow, Netherlands Inst. for Advanced Study, 1975-76. *Publications:* Gold Khan and other Siberian legends, 1946; The Pursuit of the Millennium, 1957 (revised edns 1961, 1970); Warrant for Genocide, 1967 (revised edn 1970; Anisfield-Wolf Award in Race Relations); Europe's Inner Demons, 1975; *contributor to:* Millennial Dreams in Action (ed. Thrupp), 1962; Caste and Race (ed. de Reuck and Knight), 1967, and to reviews and learned jls; General Editor, Columbus Centre's Studies in the Dynamics of Persecution and Extermination. *Recreations:* walking, travel, looking at pictures. *Address:* 61 New End, NW3. *T:* 01-435 5755. *Club:* Athenæum.

COHN, Prof. Paul Moritz; Professor of Mathematics in the University of London, at Bedford College, since 1967; *b* Hamburg, 8 Jan. 1924; *o c* of late James Cohn and late Julia Cohn (*née* Cohen); *m* 1958, Deirdre Sonia Sharon; two *d. Educ:* Trinity Coll., Cambridge. BA 1948, MA, PhD 1951. Chargé de Recherches, Univ. de Nancy, 1951-52; Lectr, Manchester Univ., 1952-62; Reader, London Univ., at Queen Mary Coll., 1962-67. Visiting Prof.: Yale Univ., 1961-62; Univ. of California (Berkeley), 1962; Univ. of Chicago, 1964; State Univ. of New York (Stony Brook), 1967; Rutgers Univ., 1967-68; Univ. of Paris, 1969; Tulane Univ., 1971; Indian Inst. of Technology, Delhi, 1971; Univ. of Alberta, 1972; Carleton Univ., Ottawa, 1973; Technion, Haifa, 1975. Sec., London Mathematical Soc., 1965-67; Mem. Council, London Math. Soc., 1968-71, 1972-75. Lester R. Ford Award (Mathematical Assoc. of America), 1972; Senior Berwick Prize, London Mathematical Soc., 1974. *Publications:* Lie Groups, 1957; Linear Equations, 1958; Solid Geometry, 1961; Universal Algebra, 1965 (trans foreign langs); Free Rings and their Relations, 1971; Algebra, vol. I, 1974, vol. II, 1977; Skewfield Constructions, 1977; papers on algebra in various mathematical periodicals. *Address:* Department of Mathematics, Bedford College, Regent's Park, NW1 4NS. *T:* 01-486 4400.

COIA, Jack Antonio, CBE 1967; LLD 1970; BArch; FRIBA 1941; RSA 1962; MRTPI; architect; Commissioner, Royal Fine Art Commission for Scotland, since 1969; *b* 17 July 1898; *m* 1939, Eden Bernard; three *d. Educ:* St Aloysius Coll.; Glasgow Sch. of Art; Strathclyde Univ. Works include: immense contribution to RC Church Architecture in Scotland, 1936- (St Anne's Church, Glasgow); Catholic Pavilion, Post Office and Industry North Pavilion for the Empire Exhibition, Glasgow, 1938; Shipbuilding and Railways Section for the Festival of Britain Exhibition, Glasgow, 1951. Senior Partner of Gillespie Kidd and Coia whose works include: Flats at East Kilbride (Saltire Award 1953); and among several awards: from Civic Trust, Bellshill Maternity Hospital, 1962, Old Persons Housing and Home at Dumbarton, 1969; from RIBA: Bronze Medal and Regional Awards for Architecture in Scotland: St Bride's Church, East Kilbride, Church of Our Lady of Good Counsel, Dennistoun, 1966, St Peter's College at Cardross, 1967, Halls of Residence, The Lawns, Cottingham, for Hull University, 1968. Pres., Royal Incorpn of Architects in Scotland, 1967-68. Royal Gold Medal for Architecture, 1969. *Recreation:* golf. *Clubs:* Glasgow Art (Glasgow); Scottish Arts (Edinburgh).

COKAYNE, family name of **Baron Cullen.**

COKE, family name of **Earl of Leicester.**

COKE, Viscount; Edward Douglas Coke; *b* 6 May 1936; *s* and *heir* of 6th Earl of Leicester, *qv*; *m* 1962, Valeria Phyllis, *e d* of late L. A. Potter; two *s* one *d. Educ:* St Andrew's, Grahamstown, CP, S Africa. *Recreations:* skiing, sailing, shooting. *Heir: s* Hon. Thomas Edward Coke, *b* 6 July 1965. *Address:* Burnham Norton, King's Lynn, Norfolk. *T:* Burnham Market 495. *Clubs:* Farmers'; Norfolk (Norwich).

COKE, Dorothy Josephine, RWS 1943 (ARWS 1935); artist; an official war artist, 1940, Women's Services subjects; *d* of Joseph Charles Coke and Edith Mary Price. *Educ:* The Slade School. Mem. of the New English Art Club. *Address:* 11 Eley Crescent, Rottingdean, Brighton, E Sussex.

COKE, Gerald Edward, CBE 1967; JP; DL; *b* 25 Oct. 1907; *o s* of late Major the Hon. Sir John Coke, KCVO, and late Hon. Mrs Coke; *m* 1939, Patricia, *e d* of late Rt Hon. Sir Alexander Cadogan, PC, OM, GCMG, KCB; two *s* one *d* (and one *s* decd). *Educ:* Eton; New Coll., Oxford (MA). Served War of 1939-45, Lieut-Col. Treas., Bridewell Royal Hosp. (King Edward's Sch., Witley), 1946-72; Chm., Glyndebourne Arts Trust, 1955-75; Dir, Royal Acad. of Music, 1957-74; Dir, Royal Opera House, Covent Garden, 1958-64; a Governor, BBC, 1961-66. Director:

Rio Tinto-Zinc Corp., 1947-75 (Dep. Chm. 1962-66; Chm. Rio Tinto Co., 1956-62); S. G. Warburg & Co., 1945-75; United Kingdom Provident Instn, 1952-74. JP 1952, DL 1974, Hants. Hon. FRAM 1968. *Address:* Jenkyn Place, Bentley, Hants. *T:* Bentley 3118. *Club:* Brooks's.

COKER, Peter Godfrey, RA 1972 (ARA 1965); ARCA 1953; *b* 27 July 1926; *m* 1951, Vera Joyce Crook; one *s. Educ:* St Martin's Sch. of Art; Royal Coll. of Art (Royal Schol.). Brit. Inst. Schol., 1954. Arts Council Award to Artists, 1976. One-man Exhibitions: Zwemmer Gall., 1956, 1957, 1959. 1964, 1967; Magdalene Street Gall., Cambridge, 1968; Stone Gall., Newcastle, 1969; Thackeray Gall., London, 1970, 1972, 1974, 1975, 1976. Retrospective Exhibitions: Minories, Colchester, 1972; Victoria Gall., Bath, 1972; Morley Gall., London, 1973; Mappin Art Gall., Sheffield, 1973. Represented in Group Exhibitions: Tate Gall., 1958; Jordan Gall., Toronto, 1958; Northampton, 1960; Europaisches Forum, Alpbach, Austria, 1960; Neue Galerie, Linz, 1960; RCA, 1952-62; Painters in E Anglia, Arts Council, 1966; Bicentenary Exhibn, Royal Acad., 1768-1968, 1968; British Painting 1900-1960, Sheffield and Aberdeen, 1975-76. Works in permanent collections: Arts Council; Contemp. Art Soc., GB; Contemp. Art Soc., Wales; Chantrey Bequest; Nat. Portrait Gall.; V&A; Stedelijk Museum Ostend; Rugby Library and Museum; Chelmsford and Essex Museum; Art Galls and Mus. of Carlisle, Ipswich, Leicester, Rochdale; Art Galls of Bath (Victoria), Batley, Birmingham, Coventry (Herbert), Kettering, Leeds City, Sheffield City, Southport (Atkinson); RCA; RA; Educn Cttees of Nottingham, Essex, Derbyshire, Lancs, ILEA; Liverpool Univ. *Publication:* Etching Techniques, 1976. *Recreation:* music. *Address:* The Red House, Mistley, Manningtree, Essex. *T:* Manningtree 2179.

COLAHAN, Air Vice-Marshal William Edward, CBE 1973; DFC 1945; AOC and Commandant, RAF College Cranwell, since 1975; *b* 7 Aug. 1923; *er s* of Dr W. E. and Dr G. C. J. Colahan; *m* 1949, Kathleen Anne Butler; one *s* two *d. Educ:* Templeton High Sch., S Africa; Univ. of Cape Town. S African Air Force, 1941-46; service in Italy, France (Temp. Captain); Royal Air Force, 1947-: Flt-Lt 1947; Sqdn Ldr 1952; psa 1957; Wing Comdr 1959; jssc 1962; Gp Captain 1965; Air Cdr 1970; idc 1970; Air Comdr Malta, 1971-73; Air Vice-Marshal 1973; ACAS (Operations), 1973-75. *Recreation:* shooting. *Address:* Northbeck House, Scredington, Lincs. *T:* Sleaford 2489. *Club:* Royal Air Force.

COLBECK-WELCH, Air Vice-Marshal Edward Lawrence, CB 1961; OBE 1948; DFC 1941; Royal Air Force, retired; *b* 29 Jan. 1914; *s* of Major G. S. M. Colbeck-Welch, MC, Collingham, Yorks; *m* 1938, Doreen, *d* of T. G. Jenkin, Sliema, Malta; one *s* two *d. Educ:* Leeds Grammar Sch. Commnd RAF, 1933; No. 22 Sqdn, RAF, 1934-37; CFS Instructor Course, 1937; Flying Instr RAuxAF Sqdns, 1937-39; Staff duties, 1940; OC No. 29 Night Fighter Sqdn, 1941-42; Staff Coll., 1942; Staff duties, 1943-44; Staff duties in 2nd TAF and OC No. 139 (Bomber) Wing, 1944-45; Air Min. Dep. Dir Air Defence, 1945-47; Staff duties in USA, 1947-50; OC Fighter Stations (2), 1950-53; Air Min. Personnel Staff duties, 1954-55; student, idc 1956; Comdt Central Fighter Estab., 1957-58; SASO, HQ No 13 (F) Group, 1959; SASO, HQ Fighter Comd RAF, 1960-63. *Recreation:* sailing. *Address:* La Cote au Palier, St Martin, Jersey, CI. *Clubs:* Royal Air Force, Royal Automobile; Royal Air Force Yacht, Royal Channel Islands Yacht, St Helier Yacht.

COLBERT, Claudette; stage and film actress; *b* Paris, 13 Sept. 1905; *d* of Georges Chauchoin and Jeanne Loew; *m* 1st, Norman Foster (marr. diss.); 2nd, Dr Joel J. Pressman (*d* 1968). Went to America, 1908. First appearances: New York Stage, 1925; London stage, 1928. Returned to Broadway stage, 1958-60. After success on Broadway, entered films, 1929. *Plays include:* Wild Westcotts, The Marionette Man, We've Got to Have Money, The Cat Came Back, Leah Kleschna, High Stakes, A Kiss in the Taxi, The Ghost Train, The Pearl of Great Price, The Barker, The Mulberry Bush, La Gringa, Within the Law, Fast Life, Tin Pan Alley, Dynamo, See Naples and Die, The Marriage-Go-Round. *Films include:* For the Love of Mike, The Lady Lies, Manslaughter, The Smiling Lieutenant, Sign of the Cross, Cleopatra, Private Worlds, Maid of Salem, It Happened One Night (Academy Award, 1934), The Gilded Lily, I Met Him in Paris, Bluebeard's Eighth Wife, Zaza, Midnight, Drums Along the Mohawk, Skylark, Remember the Day, Palm Beach Story, No Time for Love, So Proudly We Hail, Without Reservations, The Secret Heart, The Egg and I, Sleep My Love, Three Came Home, The Secret Fury, The Planter's Wife, Destiny, Versailles, Parrish. *Address:* Bellerive, St Peter, Barbados, West Indies.

COLCHESTER, Suffragan Bishop of, since 1966; **Rt. Rev. Roderic Norman Coote,** DD; *b* 13 April 1915; *s* of late Comdr B. T. Coote and late Grace Harriet (*née* Robinson); *m* 1964, Erica Lynette, *d* of late Rev. E. G. Shrubbs, MBE; one *s* two *d. Educ:* Woking County Sch.; Trinity Coll., Dublin. Curate Asst, St Bartholomew's, Dublin, 1938-41; Missionary Priest in the Diocese of Gambia and the Rio Pongas, 1942; Bishop of Gambia and the Rio Pongas, 1951-57; Suffragan Bishop of Fulham, 1957-66; Archdeacon of Colchester, 1969-72. Member, General Synod of Church of England, 1969-72. *Recreations:* tennis, squash; piano (composer and broadcaster); Irish Champion 120 yds Hurdles. *Address:* The Bishop's House, 32 Inglis Road, Colchester, Essex.

COLCHESTER, Archdeacon of; *see* Roxburgh, Ven. J. W.

COLCHESTER, Rev. Halsey Sparrowe, CMG 1968; OBE 1960; MA Oxon; Vicar of Bollington, Cheshire, since 1976; *b* 5 March 1918; *s* of late Ernest Charles Colchester; *m* 1946, Rozanne Felicity Hastings Medhurst, *d* of late Air Chief Marshal Sir Charles Medhurst, KCB, OBE, MC; four *s* one *d. Educ:* Uppingham Sch.; Magdalen Coll., Oxford. Served Oxf. and Bucks Lt Inf., 1940-43; 2nd SAS Regt, 1944-46 (despatches); Captain. Joined Diplomatic Service, 1947; FO 1948-50; 2nd Sec., Istanbul, 1950-54; FO 1954-56; Consul, Zürich, 1956-60; 1st Sec., Athens, 1960-64; FO 1964-68; Counsellor, Paris, 1968-72; retired from Diplomatic Service, 1972; Ordinand at Cuddesdon Theological Coll., 1972-73; Curate, Minchinhampton, Glos, 1973-76. Deacon, 1973; Priest, 1974. *Recreations:* walking, theatre-going, wild flowers. *Address:* Bollington Vicarage, near Macclesfield, Cheshire. *T:* Bollington 73162.

COLCHESTER, Trevor Charles, CMG 1958; *b* London, 18 April 1909; *s* of Charles Colchester; *m* 1937, Nancy Joan Russell; one *d. Educ:* Corpus Christi Coll., Cambridge (MA). Colonial Service, 1931-64; in Kenya, Zanzibar, and Northern Rhodesia. Sec. to Cabinet, Kenya, 1954-57; Permanent Sec., Kenya, 1957-61. Sec., Commonwealth Assoc. of Architects, 1964-74. Hon. FRIBA 1975. *Recreations:* conservation, gardening. *Address:* Plomesgate, Aldeburgh, Suffolk.

COLDRICK, Albert Percival, OBE 1974; FCIT 1972; Member, Industrial Tribunal, since 1975; Chairman: National Health Service SE Thames Appeals Tribunal, since 1974; Executive Committee, Industrial Participation Association; *b* 6 June 1913; *s* of Albert Percival and Florence Coldrick; *m* 1938, Esther Muriel Blades; three *s. Educ:* Britannia Bridge Elementary Sch.; Wigan Mining and Technical College. Railway Controller, 1933-47; Transport Salaried Staffs' Assoc.: full-time Officer, 1948-62; Sen. Asst Sec., 1962-66; Asst Gen. Sec., 1967; Gen. Sec., 1968-73. Mem., General Council, TUC, 1968-73. Mem., Midlands and West Region Rlys Bd, 1975-77. Jt Editor, International Directory of the Trade Union Movement, 1977. *Recreations:* reading, walking, photography. *Address:* 10 Murray Avenue, Bromley, Kent. *T:* 01-464 4089.

COLDSTREAM, Sir George (Phillips), KCB 1955 (CB 1949); KCVO 1968; QC 1960; *b* 20 Dec. 1907; *s* of late Francis Menzies Coldstream; *m* 1st, 1934, Mary Morna (marr. diss. 1948), *o d* of Major A. D. Carmichael, Meigle, Perthshire; one *d* (and one *d* decd); 2nd, Sheila Hope, *widow* of Lt-Col J. H. H. Whitty, DSO, MC. *Educ:* Rugby; Oriel Coll., Oxford. Called to the Bar, Lincoln's Inn, 1930. Bencher, 1954; Asst to Parly Counsel to Treasury, 1934-39; Legal Asst, Lord Chancellor's Office, 1939-44; Dep. Clerk of the Crown, 1944-54; Clerk of the Crown in Chancery and Permanent Sec. to the Lord Chancellor, 1954-68. Member: Royal Commn on Assizes and Quarter Sessions, 1967-70; Top Salaries Review Body, 1971-. Chm., Council of Legal Educn, 1970-73. Hon. LLD Columbia Univ., 1966. *Address:* The Gate House, Seaford, East Sussex. *T:* Seaford 892801. *Clubs:* Athenæum; Royal Cruising.

COLDSTREAM, Prof. John Nicolas, FSA; FBA 1977; Professor of Aegean Archaeology, Bedford College, University of London, since 1975; *b* 30 March 1927; *s* of Sir John Coldstream and Phyllis Mary Hambly; *m* 1970, Imogen Nicola Carr. *Educ:* Eton; King's College, Cambridge (Class. Tripos, BA 1951, MA 1956). FSA 1964. Nat. Service, Buffs and HLI (Egypt and Palestine), 1945-48. Asst Master, Shrewsbury Sch., 1952-56; Temp. Asst Keeper, Dept of Greek and Roman Antiquities, BM, 1956-57; Macmillan Student, British Sch. at Athens, 1957-60; Bedford College, London: Lectr, 1960-66; Reader, 1966-75. Mem., Managing Cttee, British Sch. at Athens, 1966-. Chm., Nat. Organizing Cttee, XI Internat. Congress of Classical Archaeol., London, 1978. Editor, Annual of the British School at Athens, 1968-73. *Publications:* Greek Geometric Pottery, 1968; (with G. L. Huxley) Kythera: Excavations and Studies, 1972; Knossos: The Sanctuary of Demeter, 1973; Geometric

Greece, 1977; articles in British and foreign classical and archaeological journals. *Recreations:* music, travel. *Address:* 180 Ebury Street, SW1.

COLDSTREAM, Sir William (Menzies), Kt 1956; CBE 1952; painter; Slade Professor of Fine Art, at University College, University of London, 1949-75; Vice-Chairman, Arts Council of Great Britain, 1962-70 (Member, 1953); Fellow of University College, London; Senior Fellow, Royal College of Art; *b* 28 Feb. 1908; *yr s* of George Probyn Coldstream, MB, CM, and Lilian Mercer Tod; *m* 1st, 1931, Nancy Culliford Sharp (marr. diss. 1942); two *d*; 2nd, 1961, Monica Mary Hoyer, *d* of A. E. Monrad Hoyer; one *s* two *d. Educ:* privately; Slade Sch. of Fine Art, University Coll., London. Member: London Artists Assoc., 1931; London Group, 1933; work represented in exhibitions of: World's Fair, NY, 1938; British Art Since Whistler, Nat. Gallery, 1939; UN Internat. Exhibition, Paris, 1946; Retrospective Exhibition, South London Gallery, 1962; Painting and Sculpture of a Decade, Tate Gallery, 1964 (represented). Pictures in the collections of: Tate Gallery, National Gallery of Canada, National Museum of Wales, Ashmolean Museum, Imperial War Museum, Arts Council, British Council, Bristol Art Gallery, etc. Works purchased by Contemporary Art Soc. and Chantrey Bequest, 1940. In association with Claude Rogers and Victor Pasmore founded the Sch. of Drawing and Painting, Euston Road, 1937. Served War of 1939-45 with RE; official War Office Artist, Middle East and Italy, 1943-45. Trustee of National Gallery, 1948-55, 1956-63; Trustee of Tate Gallery, 1949-55, 1956-63; a Dir of Royal Opera House, Covent Garden, 1957-62; Chairman: Art Panel of Arts Council, 1953-62; Nat. Adv. Council on Art Education, 1958-71; British Film Institute, 1964-71; Hon. DLitt: Nottingham, 1961; Birmingham, 1962; Hon. DEd CNAA, 1975. *Address:* University College London, Gower Street, WC1. *T:* 01-387 7050. *Clubs:* Athenæum, MCC. *See also J. W. D. Margetson.*

COLE, family name of **Baron Cole** and of **Earl of Enniskillen.**

COLE, Baron *cr* 1965, of Blackfriars (Life Peer); **George James Cole,** GBE 1973; Chairman, Unilever Ltd, 1960-70 (Director, 1948; Vice-Chairman, 1956); Vice-Chairman, Unilever NV, 1960-70; Chairman, Leverhulme Trust; *b* 3 Feb. 1906; *s* of late James Francis Cole; *m* 1940, Ruth, *d* of late Edward Stanley Harpham; one *s* one *d. Educ:* Raffles Inst., Singapore. Joined a Lever Brothers Ltd subsidiary, The Niger Co. Ltd (later merged into The United Africa Co. Ltd), 1923; various positions in London and Africa till 1939 when appointed Controller for British West Africa; Staff of Resident Minister, W Africa, as Commercial Mem. at Supply Centre, 1941; Director: The United Africa Co. Ltd, 1945-63 (Joint Man. Dir, 1952-55); Taylor Woodrow (West Africa) Ltd, 1947-55; Finance Corp. for Industry Ltd, 1965-73; Chm., Palm Line Ltd, 1952-55 (Dir, 1949); on European Continent for Unilever Ltd, 1955; Chm., Rolls-Royce (1971) Ltd, 1970-72; Chm., Govt Advisory Cttee on Appointment of Advertising Agents, 1962-70; Pres., Advertising Assoc., 1970-73; Mem. Council: RIIA; Royal African Society; UK South Africa Trade Assoc.; Vice-Pres., Hispanic Council; Vice-Pres., Luso-Brazilian Council; Mem. Internat. Adv. Cttee, Chase Manhattan Bank, 1965-73; FRSA; FZS; Corresp. Emeritus, The Conf. Bd (New York). Comdr, Order of Orange Nassau, 1963. *Address:* 50 Victoria Road, W8. *T:* 01-937 9085. *Clubs:* Athenæum, Hurlingham.

COLE, Viscount; Andrew John Galbraith Cole; pilot, and company director; Captain Irish Guards, 1965; *b* 28 April 1942; *s* and *heir* of 6th Earl of Enniskillen, *qv*; *m* 1964, Sarah, *o d* of Maj.-Gen. J. Keith-Edwards, CBE, DSO, MC, Nairobi; three *d. Educ:* Eton. *Address:* c/o Williams & Glyn's Bank Ltd, 9 Pall Mall, SW1.

COLE, (Alexander) Colin, MVO 1977; TD 1972; Windsor Herald of Arms since 1966 (Fitzalan Pursuivant of Arms Extraordinary, 1953; Portcullis Pursuivant of Arms, 1957); *b* 16 May 1922; *er s* of late Capt. Edward Harold Cole, and of Blanche Ruby Lavinia (*née* Wallis); *m* 1944, Valerie, *o d* of late Capt. Stanley Walter Card; four *s* three *d. Educ:* Dulwich; Pembroke Coll. Cambridge; Brasenose Coll., Oxford. BCL Oxon; MA Oxon. Served War of 1939-45, Capt. Coldstream Guards. Barrister-at-law (Inner Temple), 1949. One of the Court of Assistants of the Hon. Artillery Company; Major, 6th (Volunteer) Bn, Queen's Regt, 1971-73, Lt-Col RARO (Brevet, 1973). Mem. Court of Common Council of City of London (Castle Baynard Ward), 1964-; Sheriff, City of London, 1976-77. Freeman of City of London, Freeman and Liveryman, Scriveners' and Basketmakers Companies of London. Fellow Heraldry Soc. (Mem. Council); Hon. Heraldic Adviser, Monumental Brass Soc.; Sec., College of Arms Trust; Registrar and Librarian, College of Arms, 1967-74. Officer of Arms attendant, Imperial Soc. of Knights Bachelor. FSA (London). OStJ. *Publications:* articles on heraldry and kindred subjects in their appropriate journals; illus. Visitations of London (1568) and Wiltshire (1623) (Harleian Soc.). *Recreations:* art, archæology, architecture, parenthood and wine-bibbing. *Address:* College of Arms, Queen Victoria Street, EC4. *T:* 01-248 1188; Holly House, Burstow, Surrey. *Clubs:* Cavalry and Guards, City Livery.

COLE, Prof. Boris Norman, BSc(Eng) (London), PhD (Birmingham), WhSch, CEng, FIMechE; Professor of Mechanical Engineering and Head of Department of Mechanical Engineering, University of Leeds, since 1962; *b* 8 Jan. 1924; *s* of James Edward Cole and Gertrude Cole; *m* 1945, Sibylle Duijts; two *s* one *d. Educ:* King Edward's Sch., Birmingham. Apprenticed to Messrs Belliss and Morcom Ltd, Engineers, Birmingham. Dept of Mech. Engrg, Univ. of Birmingham: Lectr, 1949-55; Sen. Lectr, 1955-58; Reader, 1958-62; Chm. of Faculty Bd of Applied Sciences, Birmingham Univ., 1955-57 and 1959-62. Member: Smethwick Co. Borough Educn Cttee, 1957-60; Engrg Materials Res. Requirements Bd, 1974-, and various other govt cttees; Governor, Engrg Industries Training Bd, Leeds Training Centre, 1967-. Prizewinner, IMechE, 1953 and 1962. *Publications:* numerous in fields of solid and fluid mechanics and in engineering education. *Recreations:* walking, music, social history of engineering. *Address:* 399 Gledhow Lane, Leeds LS7 4NQ. *T:* Leeds 621306.

COLE, Charles Woolsey, MA, LHD, PhD, ScD, LittD, LLD; President Emeritus, Amherst College; *b* 8 Feb. 1906; *s* of Bertha Woolsey Dwight and Charles Buckingham Cole; *m* 1st, 1928, Katharine Bush Salmon (decd); two *d*; 2nd, 1974, Marie Greer Donahoe. *Educ:* Montclair (New Jersey) High Sch.; Amherst Coll., Amherst, Mass; Columbia Univ., NY, Univ. Fellow, Columbia, 1928-29; Instr History, Columbia Coll., 1929-35; Travelling Fellow of Social Science Research Council in Paris, 1932-33; Assoc. Prof. Economics, Amherst Coll., 1935-37; Prof. Economics, Amherst Coll., 1937-40; Prof. Hist. in graduate faculty, Columbia, 1940-46; Pres., Amherst Coll., 1946-60. Vice-Pres., Rockefeller Foundn, 1960-61; US Ambassador to Chile, 1961-64. Chief, Service Trades Branch, Office of Price Administration, Washington, DC, 1942; Regional Price Exec., New York Office of Price Administration, 1942-43; Columbia's Navy Sch. of Military Govt and Administration in addition to lecturing at Army Sch. of Mil. Govt in Charlottesville, Va, 1943-45; Vis. Lectr in Economics at Yale Univ., New Haven, Conn., 1938-39. Trustee, Merrill Trust. Grand Cross, Order of Merit (Chile); Grand Officer, Order of Morazán (Honduras). *Publications:* French Mercantalist Doctrines Before Colbert, 1931; Colbert and a Century of French Mercantilism, 1939; Economic History of Europe (with S. B. Clough), 1941; French Mercantilism, 1683-1700, 1943; (with C. J. H. Hayes and M. Baldwin) History of Europe, 1949; History of Western Civilization, 1967; (with H. W. Bragdon and S. P. McCutchen): A Free People: the United States in the Formative Years, 1970; A Free People: the United States in the Twentieth Century, 1970; History of a Free People, 1973; edited Macmillan Career Books. *Recreation:* fly fishing for trout. *Address:* The Highlands, Seattle, Washington 98177, USA. *Clubs:* Century, Anglers' (New York); University (Seattle), Seattle Golf.

COLE, Claude Neville David, CBE 1977; JP; Chief Executive and Managing Director, Thomson Regional Newspapers Ltd, since 1972; Director: The Thomson Organisation Ltd (Executive Board), since 1973; Press Association (Chairman, 1976-77, 1977-78); Reuters Ltd, since 1976; Member, Press Council, since 1976; *b* 4 June 1928; 2nd *s* of late W. J. Cole and of Mrs M. J. Cole; *m* 1951, Alma Gwlithyn Williams; one *s* one *d* (one *s* decd). *Educ:* Royal Masonic School; Harvard Business Sch. Journalist: Merthyr Express; South Wales Echo; Daily Graphic (Manchester); Daily Sketch (London); Daily Recorder; Empire News (Cardiff); Editor, Western Mail, Cardiff, 1956-59; Managing Director (now Director): Western Mail and Echo Ltd, 1959-67; Newcastle Chronicle and Journal Ltd, 1967-69; Asst Man. Dir and Editorial Dir, Thomson Regional Newspapers Ltd, 1969-72. Director: Scotsman Publications Ltd; Press Consultancy Services Ltd; Welsh Nat. Opera Co. Ltd, 1960-71; Chairman: F. J. Glindon Ltd; Celtic Press Ltd; Thomson International Press Consultancy Ltd. Chm., Cole Cttee on Recruitment of Nurses in Wales, 1961-63; Chm., Working Party on Welsh Tourism, 1963-64; Member: Court of Governors of Univ. of Wales, 1962-; Council of Univ. of Wales, 1962-; Council of Welsh National Sch. of Medicine, 1964-67; Governing Body of Cardiff Coll. of Music and Drama, 1963-67; Council of Cardiff New Theatre Trust, 1964-67; Welsh Nat. Theatre Cttee; Aberfan Disaster Fund, 1966-67; Welsh Hospitals Bd, 1962-67. Vice-Patron, Coun. for Wales, Brit. Empire and Commonwealth Games. Pres., Tenovus. OStJ.

Publications: This and Other Worlds (poems), 1975; Meeting Places and other poems, 1977. *Recreations:* two of the three R's. *Address:* 71 Ashley Gardens, Westminster, SW1. *T:* 01-828 1792. *Clubs:* East India, Devonshire, Sports and Public Schools, Lansdowne; County (Cardiff).

COLE, Colin; *see* Cole, A. C.

COLE, Sir David (Lee), KCMG 1975 (CMG 1965); MC 1944; HM Ambassador to Thailand, since 1973; *b* 31 Aug. 1920; *s* of late Brig. D. H. Cole, CBE, LittD, and Charlotte Cole (*née* Wedgwood); *m* 1945, Dorothy (*née* Patton); one *s. Educ:* Cheltenham Coll.; Sidney Sussex Coll., Cambridge. MA (1st Cl. Hons History). Served Royal Inniskilling Fusiliers, 1940-45. Dominions Office, 1947; seconded to Foreign Office for service with UK Delegn to UN, New York, 1948-51; First Sec., Brit. High Commn, New Delhi, 1953-56; Private Sec. to Rt Hon. the Earl of Home (Sec. of State for Commonwealth Relations and Lord President of the Council), 1957-60; Head of Personnel Dept, CRO, 1961-63; British Dep. High Comr in Ghana, 1963-64; British High Comr in Malawi, 1964-67; Minister (Political), New Delhi, 1967-70; Asst Under-Sec. of State, FCO, 1970-73. *Recreation:* watercolour painting. *Address:* c/o Foreign and Commonwealth Office, SW1. *Club:* Travellers'.

COLE, Maj.-Gen. Eric Stuart, CB 1960; CBE 1945; retired; Consultant Director, Granger Associates Ltd, Weybridge; *b* 1906; *s* of John William Cole; *m* 1941, Doris Cole. Served Palestine, 1936-39; War of 1939-45 in Italy, France, Greece (despatches, CBE); Maj.-Gen., 1958; Dir of Telecommunications, War Office, 1958-61. Col Comdt Royal Corps of Signals, 1962-67. Pres., Radio Soc. of GB, 1961. *Address:* 28 Royal Avenue, Chelsea, SW3. *Clubs:* Army and Navy, MCC, Roehampton.

COLE, Frank; *see* Cole, (George) Francis.

COLE, George; actor on stage, screen, radio and television; *b* 22 April 1925; *m* 1st, 1954, Eileen Moore (marr. diss. 1966); one *s* one *d*; 2nd, 1967, Penelope Morrell; one *s* one *d. Educ:* Surrey County Council Secondary Sch., Morden. Made first stage appearance in White Horse Inn, tour and London Coliseum, 1939; Cottage to Let, Birmingham, 1940; West End and on tour, 1940-41; subseq. West End plays included Goodnight Children, New, 1942; Mr Bolfry, Playhouse, 1943. Served in RAF, 1943-47. Returned to stage in Dr Angelus, Phoenix, 1947; The Anatomist, Westminster, 1948; Mr Gillie, Garrick, 1950; A Phoenix too Frequent and Thor with Angels, Lyric, Hammersmith, 1951; Misery Me, Duchess, 1955; Mr Bolfry, Aldwych, 1956; Brass Butterfly, Strand, 1958; The Bargain, St Martin's, 1961; The Sponge Room and Squat Betty, Royal Court, 1962; Meet Me on the Fence (tour), 1963; Hedda Gabler, St Martin's, 1964; A Public Mischief, St Martin's, 1965; Too True To Be Good, Strand, 1965; The Waiting Game, Arts, 1966; The Three Sisters, Royal Court, 1967; Doubtful Haunts, Hampstead, 1968; The Passionate Husband, 1969; The Philanthropist, Mayfair, 1971; Country Life, Hampstead, 1973; Déjà Revue, New London, 1974; Motive (tour), 1976; Banana Ridge, Savoy, 1976. *Films include:* Cottage to Let, 1941; Morning Departure, Laughter in Paradise, Scrooge, Top Secret, 1949-51; Will Any Gentleman?, The Intruder, 1952; Happy Ever After, Our Girl Friday, 1953; Belles of St Trinian's, 1954; Quentin Durward, 1955; The Weapon, It's a Wonderful World, The Green Man, 1956; Blue Murder at St Trinian's, Too Many Crooks, Don't Panic Chaps, The Bridal Path, 1957-59; The Pure Hell of St Trinian's, Cleopatra, Dr Syn, 1961-62; One Way Pendulum, Legend of Dick Turpin, 1964; Great St Trinian's Train Robbery, 1965; The Green Shoes, 1969; Vampire Lovers, 1970; Girl in the Dark, 1971; The Blue Bird, 1975. TV Series include Life of Bliss (also radio), A Man of our Times, Don't Forget to Write. *Address:* Donnelly, Newnham Hill Bottom, Nettlebed, Oxon.

COLE, George Francis, (Frank); Chairman: Crane's Screw (Holdings) Ltd, since 1975; James Cooke & Son Ltd, since 1976; Director, Clarkson Head Harris Ltd; *b* 3 Nov. 1918; *m* 1940, Gwendoline Mary Laver; two *s* one *d. Educ:* Manchester Grammar Sch. Dir and Gen. Manager, Clarkson Engineers Ltd, 1944-53; Gen. Man., Ariel Motors Ltd (BSA Group), 1953-55; Dir, then Man. Dir, Vono Ltd, 1955-67. Past Chairman: Grovewood Products Ltd; Portways Ltd; R. & W. H. Symington Holdings Ltd; National Exhibition Centre Ltd; Past Director: Duport Ltd; Shipping Industrial Holdings Ltd. Pres., Birmingham Chamber of Commerce and Industry, 1968-69. Leader of Trade Missions to West Germany, Yugoslavia, Romania and Hungary. FBIM; Life Governor, Birmingham Univ.; Liveryman of City of London. Radio and Television appearances. *Publications:* press articles on economics, exports, etc. *Recreations:* tennis, oil painting. *Address:* Tudor Cottage, Barston, Solihull, West Midlands. *T:* Hampton-in-Arden 2724.

COLE, Dr Herbert Aubrey, CMG 1967; Controller, Fisheries Research and Development, Ministry of Agriculture, Fisheries and Food, 1972-74; *b* 24 Feb. 1911; *s* of Edwin Aubrey Cole, Farmer; *m* 1936, Elizabeth Lloyd; two *s* one *d. Educ:* Friars Sch., Bangor, N Wales; Univ. Coll. of N Wales. Entire career in Fishery Research, Min. of Agric., Fisheries and Food, Dir of Fishery Research, 1958-72. *Publications:* numerous articles in learned jls. *Recreation:* gardening. *Address:* Forde House, Moor Lane, Hardington Mandeville, Yeovil, Somerset BA22 9NW. *T:* West Coker 2090.

COLE, Humphrey John Douglas; Chief Economic Adviser, Departments of the Environment and Transport, since 1976; *b* 30 Jan. 1928; *s* of late G. D. H. Cole and of Dame Margaret I. Cole, *qv* ; *m* 1955, Hilda Annette Robinson; two *s* one *d. Educ:* Winchester Coll.; Trinity Coll., Cambridge. Research, Oxford Inst. of Statistics, 1950-61; Head, Economic Indicators and Foreign Trade, OECD Statistics Div., 1961-66; Dept of Economic Affairs: Senior Economic Adviser (Regional), 1966-67; Asst Dir of Economics, 1967-69; Dir of Economics, Min. of Technology, 1969-70; Dir of Econs (Urban and Highways), DoE, 1970-72; Dir Gen., Econs and Resources, DoE, 1972-74. *Publications:* articles in Bulletin of Inst. of Statistics, 1950-61. *Recreations:* walking, family. *Address:* 3 The Mead, W13. *T:* 01-997 8285.

COLE, John Sydney Richard, QC (Somaliland); MA; Barrister-at-Law; Senior Lecturer, Law School, University of Dublin, since 1966; *b* 24 Jan. 1907; *o s* of late Rev. R. Lee Cole, MA, BD, Dublin; *m* 1st, 1931, Doreen Mathews (*d* 1966); one *s* one *d* ; 2nd, 1968, Mrs Deirdre Gallet. *Educ:* Methodist Coll., Belfast; Cork Gram. Sch.; Trinity Coll., Dublin (Scholar and Moderator). AIArb. Master, Royal Coll., Mauritius, 1930-36; Education Officer, Nigeria, 1936-40; Crown Counsel, Nigeria, 1940-46; Attorney-Gen., Bahamas, 1946-51; Somaliland Protectorate, 1951-56; Attorney-Gen. and Minister for Legal Affairs, Tanganyika, 1956-61; retired, 1961. English Legal Draftsman to Government of Republic of Sudan, 1962-65. Reid Prof. of Penal Legislation, Univ. of Dublin, 1965-66. *Publication:* (with W. N. Denison) Tanganyika-the Development of its Laws and Constitution, 1964; Irish Cases on the Law of Evidence, 1972; Irish Cases on Criminal Law, 1975. *Recreations:* walking, swimming. *Address:* 2 Rus in Urbe, Glenageary, Dublin. *T:* 801993. *Club:* Kildare Street and University (Dublin).

COLE, Leslie Barrett, MA, MD Cantab, FRCP; Hon. Consultant Physician, Addenbrooke's Hospital, Cambridge; Fellow of King's College, Cambridge, 1949-66; Dean of Post Graduate Medical School, University of Cambridge, 1957-65; *b* 1898; *s* of Samuel Barrett Cole and Annie Gammon; *m* 1927, Mary, *d* of late Surg. Capt. H. W. Finlayson, DSO; three *s. Educ:* Leighton Park Sch.; King's Coll., Cambridge (Exhibitioner). Served European War, 1916-18, RFA, India and Mesopotamia; RAMC 1939-41, BEF France. St Thomas's Hosp. (Medical Registrar and Resident Asst Physician; Mead Medal and Toller Prize); formerly Physician: W Suffolk Hosp.; Papworth Hosp. Assessor, MD Cttee, Univ. of Cambridge, 1958-65; Late Examiner: Medicine for MRCP and to Univs of Oxford, Cambridge and Bristol, also Conjoint Board; in Pharmacology, to Univ. of Cambridge; in Pathology to Conjoint Board. Royal College of Physicians: Councillor, 1950; Censor, 1960-62; Sen. Censor and Sen. Vice-Pres., 1964-65. Hon. Lt-Col RAMC. *Publications:* Dietetics in General Practice, 1939; numerous contribs to medical journals on cardiology, diabetes and general medical subjects and on tetanus to Quart. Jl of Medicine, Index of Treatment, British Encyclopædia of Medical Practice and Surgery of Modern Warfare. *Recreations:* riding, sailing. *Address:* 57 De Freville Avenue, Cambridge. *T:* Cambridge 50836. *Club:* Athenæum.

COLE, Dame Margaret Isabel, DBE 1970 (OBE 1965); author and lecturer; *b* Cambridge, 1893; *d* of Prof. J. P. Postgate, LittD, Prof. of Latin, Univ. of Liverpool, and Edith Allen; *m* 1918, G. D. H. Cole (*d* 1959); one *s* two *d. Educ:* Roedean Sch., Brighton; Girton Coll., Cambridge (1st class Hons Classical Tripos). Classical Mistress, St Paul's Girls' Sch., 1914-16; Asst Sec., Labour Research Dept, 1917-25; Lectr for Univ. Tutorial Classes, London, 1925-49, Cambridge, 1941-44; Contributor to Evening Standard, New Statesman, Guardian, Listener, Socialist Commentary, etc; Hon. Sec., New Fabian Research Bureau, 1935-39; of Fabian Soc., 1939-53; Chm., 1955; Pres., 1963-; Mem., LCC Education Cttee, 1943-65; Alderman, 1952-65; Chm., Further Education Cttee, 1951-60 and 1961-65; Mem., ILEA Educn Cttee, 1965-67; Vice-Chm., Further and

Higher Education Sub-Cttee, 1965-67. *Publications:* The Bolo Book (with G. D. H. Cole), 1923; Twelve Studies in Soviet Russia (ed), 1932; Roads to Success (ed), 1936; Women of To-Day, 1937; Marriage Past and Present, 1938; Books and the People, 1938; Democratic Sweden (ed.), 1938; Evacuation Survey (ed), 1940; Our Soviet Ally (ed), 1943; Beatrice Webb: a Memoir, 1945; Our Partnership (part Editor), 1948; Makers of the Labour Movement, 1948; The Webbs and Their Work (ed), 1949; Growing up into Revolution, 1949; The Diaries of Beatrice Webb (ed), 1952; Robert Owen of New Lanark, 1953; The Diaries of Beatrice Webb II (ed), 1956; Servant of the County, 1956; The Story of Fabian Socialism, 1961; Life of G. D. H. Cole, 1971; also detective novels and works on politics, etc, jointly with late G. D. H. Cole, for many years. *Recreations:* reading, looking at own and other countries. *Address:* 4 Ashdown, Cliveden Court, W13 8DR. *T:* 01-997 8114. *Clubs:* Arts Theatre, English-Speaking Union.
See also H. J. D. Cole.

COLE, Prof. Monica M.; Professor of Geography, since 1964 and Director of Research in Geobotany, Terrain Analysis and related Resource Use, Bedford College, University of London; *b* 5 May 1922; *d* of William Henry Parnall Cole and Dorothy Mary Cole (*née* Thomas). *Educ:* Wimbledon County Grammar Sch.; Bedford Coll., Univ. of London. Research Asst, Min. of Town and Country Planning, Cambridge, 1944-45; Postgrad. study, Univ. of London, 1945-46; Lectr in Geography: Univ. of Capetown, 1947; Univ. of Witwatersrand, 1948-51, Univ. of Keele, 1951-64. Assoc. Prof., Univ. of Idaho summer sch., 1952; Vis. Lectr, Univs of Queensland, Melbourne, and Adelaide, 1960. Mem. British delegn Internat. Geographical Congress in: Washington, 1952; Rio de Janeiro, 1956; London, 1964; New Delhi, 1968; Montreal, 1972. Research: vegetation/soils/geomorphology: S Africa, 1948-51; Brazil, 1956, 1965; Central and E Africa, 1959; Australia, 1960, 1962, 1963, 1965, 1966, 1967, 1968; Venezuela, 1964; Southern Africa, 1967, 1968; plant indication of mineralization: Australia, Africa, Brazil, UK, 1964-73; remote sensing for terrain analysis: Australia, UK, 1970-76. *Publications:* The Transvaal Lowveld, 1956; South Africa, 1961, 1966; contribs to Geograph. Jl, Geography, Trans. Inst. Brit. Geographers, S African Geograph. Jl, Trans. Instn Mining and Metallurgy, Proc. Royal Soc., Jl Applied Ecology, ESRO, Jl Biogeography. *Recreations:* painting, photography, tennis, squash, walking, climbing. *Address:* Bedford College, Regent's Park, NW1.

COLE, Norman John, VRD; *b* 1 June 1909; *s* of Walter John Cole and Maud Mary (*née* Thomas); *m* 1935, Margaret Grace, *d* of Arthur James Potter, Buxton, Derbyshire; one *s* two *d. Educ:* St John's Coll., Southsea. Served abroad War of 1939-45, with Royal Navy; RNVR, 1934-54 (Lt-Comdr). Formerly held offices in Conservative Associations in Barnet Vale and Potters Bar. Mem. of Potters Bar Urban District Council, 1947-48. MP (L and C) South Division of Bedfordshire, 1951-66; sponsored Private Member's Bill which became Children and Young Persons (Amendment) Act, 1952. Has served for many years on numerous youth, health, welfare and church cttees. *Recreations:* formerly Association football, cricket, tennis, rowing. *Address:* Derwent House, 30 Warwick Road, New Barnet, Herts. *T:* 01-449 5076.

COLE, Richard Raymond Buxton; solicitor; Recorder of the Crown Court, since 1976; *b* 11 June 1937; *s* of Raymond Buxton Cole, DSO, TD, DL, and Edith Mary Cole; *m* 1962, Sheila Joy Rumbold; one *s* one *d. Educ:* Dragon School, St Edward's, Oxford. Admitted as Solicitor 1960; Partner in Cole & Cole Solicitors, Oxford, 1962-. Mem. Governing Body, Dragon Sch., 1975-. Chm., Burford Parish Council, 1976-. *Recreations:* sport, gardening. *Address:* Tanners Close, Burford, Oxon. *T:* Burford 3102. *Clubs:* MCC; Frewen (Oxford).

COLE, Ven. Ronald Berkeley; Archdeacon of Leicester since 1963 (of Loughborough, 1953-63); *b* 20 Oct. 1913; *s* of James William and Florence Caroline Cole; *m* 1943, Mabel Grace Chapman; one *s* one *d. Educ:* Bishop's Coll., Cheshunt. Registrar, London County Freehold and Leasehold Properties Ltd, 1934-40. Deacon, 1942; Priest, 1943; Curate, Braunstone, Leicester, 1942-48; Succentor, Leicester Cathedral, 1948-50; Vicar of St Philip, Leicester, 1950-73. Hon. Chaplain, 1949-53, Examining Chaplain, 1956-, to Bishop of Leicester. DLitt Geneva Theol. Coll., 1972. *Recreations:* gardening, motoring. *Address:* 41 Morland Avenue, Leicester LE2 2PF. *T:* Leicester 706698.

COLE, William Charles, MVO 1966; DMus, FRAM, FRCM; FRCO; The Master of the Music at the Queen's Chapel of the Savoy since 1954; Member Council, Royal College of Organists, since 1960 (Hon. Treasurer since 1964; President, 1970-72);

Hon. Secretary, Royal Philharmonic Society, since 1969; Member, Central Music Library Committee, since 1964, Chairman 1973; *b* 9 Oct. 1909; *s* of Frederick George Cole and Maria (*née* Fry), Camberwell, London; *m* 1st, Elizabeth Brown Caw (*d* 1942); three *d*; 2nd, Winifred Grace Mitchell; one *s*. *Educ:* St Olave's Grammar Sch.; RAM. Organist and Choirmaster, Dorking Parish Church, 1930; Music Master, Dorking County Sch., 1931; served War of 1939-45, in Air Ministry; Hon. Musical Dir, Toynbee Hall, 1947-58; Prof. of Harmony and Composition, and Lectr in History of Music, Royal Academy of Music, 1945-62; Royal Academy of Dancing: Lectr, 1948-62; Chm. Music Cttee, 1961-68; Mem. Exec. Council, 1965-68; Mem., Grand Council, 1976-; Conductor: People's Palace Choral Soc., 1947-63; Leith Hill Musical Festival, 1954-77; Sec., Associated Bd of Royal Schools of Music, 1962-74. President: Surrey County Music Assoc., 1958-76; The London Assoc. of Organists, 1963-66. Member: Governing Cttee, Royal Choral Soc., 1972- (Chm., Music Cttee, 1975-); Exec. Cttee, Musicians' Benevolent Fund, 1972-. Mem. Education Cttee, Surrey CC, 1951-62. *Publications:* Rudiments of Music, 1951; chapter on Development of British Ballet Music, in The Ballet in Britain, 1962; The Form of Music, 1969; articles in various musical jls and in various learned jls on stained glass. *Recreation:* stained glass. *Address:* Packways, Hindhead, Surrey. *T:* Hindhead 4917. *Club:* Garrick.

COLE, Maj.-Gen. William Scott, CB 1949; CBE 1946; Army Officer, retired; *b* 29 March 1902; *s* of late William Scott Cole; *m* 1st, 1948, Kathleen Winifred Coleing (marr. diss. 1970); one *d*; 2nd, 1971, Alice Rose Pitts, *widow* of Dr G. T. Pitts. *Educ:* Victoria Coll., Jersey; RMA Woolwich. Commissioned into the Corps of Royal Engineers, 1921. Served War of 1939-45; Temp. Brig., 1943; Substantive Col, 1945; Subs. Brig., 1951; temp. Maj.-Gen., 1955; Subs. Maj.-Gen., 1956; retd 1958. *Club:* Army and Navy.

COLE-HAMILTON, John, CBE 1954; DL; *b* 15 Oct. 1899; *s* of late Col A. R. Cole-Hamilton; *m* 1930, Gladys Cowie; one *s* two *d*. *Educ:* Royal Academy, Irvine. Served European War, 1914-19, with RFC and RAF. Major, Home Guard, 1942. DL for County of Ayr, 1951. *Address:* Beltrim House, Kilwinning, Ayrshire.

COLEBROOK, Philip Victor Charles, CEng, AMIChemE; Managing Director of Pfizer Ltd since 1958; Chairman and Managing Director of the Pfizer Group 1961-69; Vice-President, Pfizer International, since 1967; Managing Director: Calor Gas Holding Company, since 1969; Imperial Continental Gas Association, since 1973 (Director, 1971); *b* 8 March 1924; *s* of Frederick Charles Colebrook and Florence Margaret (*née* Cooper); *m* 1946, Dorothy Ursula Kemp; one *s* three *d*. *Educ:* Andover Grammar Sch.; Guildford Technical Coll.; Battersea Polytechnic, London. Served War of 1939-45, RNVR. Joined Pfizer as Works and Production Manager, 1952; appointed Dir, Pfizer Ltd, 1956. Mem., NHS Affairs Cttee, Assoc. of the British Pharmaceutical Industry, 1963-67. Trustee and Mem. of Steering Cttee, Univ. of Kent at Canterbury, 1964-65. *Publication:* Going International, 1972. *Recreations:* sailing, skiing, golf. *Address:* Kestrels, Easterton, Wilts. *Clubs:* Royal Automobile; Royal Cinque Ports Yacht.

COLECLOUGH, Peter Cecil; Chairman, Howard Machinery Ltd, since 1969 (Director since 1950); Director: National Westminster Bank (Chairman SE Region); NCR Ltd; *b* 5 March 1917; *s* of late Thomas James Coleclough and of Hilda Emma (*née* Ingram); *m* 1944, Pamela Beresford (*née* Rhodes); two *s*. *Educ:* Bradfield. Served War, Cheshire Yeomanry, 1939; commnd into Roy. Warwickshire Regt, 1940; served until 1946. Mem., FBI/CBI Council, 1962-72; Chm., E Region, CBI, 1971-72; Mem., FBI Mission to Sudan, 1962; Leader, OECD/BIAC Investment Gp to Ceylon, 1968 and 1969; Chm., Meat and Livestock Commn, 1971-74; Pres., Agricl Engrs Assoc., 1971-72; Pres., Royal Warrant Holders Assoc., 1971-72; Mem., Intervention Bd for Agricl Produce, 1972-74; Chm., Appeals and Management Cttee, S Essex Medical Educn and Research Trust, 1969-75 (Patron, 1975-). *Recreation:* fishing. *Address:* Longlands Hall, Stonham Aspal, Stowmarket, Suffolk IP14 6AR. *T:* Stonham 242. *Club:* Bath.

COLEGATE, Raymond; Member, Civil Aviation Authority, since 1974; Head, Economic Department, since 1975; *b* 31 Aug. 1927; *s* of Ernest William and Violet Colegate; *m* 1961, Sally Healy; one *s* one *d*. *Educ:* County Sch. for Boys, Gravesend; LSE. BA London (Hons History). Joined BoT, 1949; seconded to Central Statistical Office, 1952-53; Asst Private Sec. to President, 1955-56; seconded to Treasury, 1957-59; seconded to EFTA Secretariat, Geneva and Brussels, 1960-64; CRE Dept, BoT, 1964-67; Aviation Dept, BoT/DTI, 1967-72; Head,

Economic Policy and Licensing Div., CAA, 1972-75. *Publications:* all anonymous. *Recreations:* music, travel, thinking. *Address:* 40 Lebanon Park, Twickenham TW1 3DG. *T:* 01-892 2325.

COLEMAN, Arthur Percy; Deputy Director and Secretary to the Board of Trustees, British Museum (Natural History), since 1976 (Museum Secretary, 1965-76); *b* 8 Feb. 1922; *s* of late Percy Coleman and Gladys May Coleman (*née* Fisher); *m* 1948, Peggy (*née* Coombs); two *d*. *Educ:* Wanstead Co. High Sch.; Bristol Univ. War Service in 1st King George V Own Gurkha Rifles, 1943-47; Min. of Public Building and Works, 1948-61; HM Treasury, 1961-64. *Recreations:* flowering shrubs, wild life, golf. *Address:* The Orchard, Vicarage Road, Coopersale, Epping, Essex. *T:* Epping 74180.

COLEMAN, Bernard; HM Diplomatic Service; Consul-General, Bilbao, since 1976; *b* 3 Sept. 1928; *s* of William Coleman and Ettie Coleman; *m* 1950, Sonia Dinah (*née* Walters); two *d*. *Educ:* Alsop High Sch., Liverpool. HM Forces (RAEC), 1946-48. Entered Foreign (later Diplomatic) Service, 1950; FO, 1950-53; Lima, 1953-56; Detroit, 1956-59; Second Secretary (Information): Montevideo, 1959-62; Caracas, 1962-64; First Sec. (Inf.), Caracas, 1964-66; FCO, 1967-69; First Sec. (Inf.), Ottawa, 1969-73; FCO, 1973-74; seconded to DTI, 1974-75. *Recreations:* golf, reading, walking, travel. *Address:* c/o Foreign and Commonwealth Office, SW1; Anlyn, Milford Road, Elstead, Surrey. *Club:* Royal Commonwealth Society.

COLEMAN, Prof. Donald Cuthbert, FBA 1972; Professor of Economic History, Cambridge University, since 1971; Fellow of Pembroke College, Cambridge; *b* 21 Jan. 1920; *s* of Hugh Augustus Coleman and Marian Stella Agnes Cuthbert; *m* 1954, Jessie Ann Matilda Child (*née* Stevens). *Educ:* Haberdashers' Aske's, Hampstead (now Elstree); London Sch. of Economics, Univ. of London. BSc(Econ), PhD. Worked in London, in insurance, 1937-39; admitted LSE, 1939. Served War, in Army, 1940-46: commissioned Royal Warwickshire Regt, 1941; transf. RA, 1942; active service in N Africa, Italy and Greece. Returned to LSE, 1946; BSc(Econ), 1st Cl. Hons. 1949; Leverhulme Research Studentship, 1949-51; PhD 1951. Lectr in Industrial History, LSE, 1951-58; Reader in Economic History, 1958-69; Prof. of Economic History, 1969-71. Visiting Associate Prof. of Economics, Yale Univ., 1957-58. English Editor, Scandinavian Economic History Review, 1952-61; Editor, Economic History Review, 1967-73. FRHistS. *Publications:* The British Paper Industry, 1495-1860, 1958; Sir John Banks: Baronet and Businessman, 1963; Courtaulds: an economic and social history (2 vols), 1969; What Has Happened to Economic History? (Inaug. Lect.), 1972; Industry in Tudor and Stuart England, 1975; The Economy of England 1450-1750, 1977; (with A. H. John) Trade, Government and Economy in Pre-Industrial England, 1977; numerous articles in: Economic History Review, Economica, etc. *Recreations:* music, cricket, coarse gardening. *Address:* Over Hall, Cavendish, Sudbury, Suffolk. *T:* Glemsford 280325.

COLEMAN, Donald Richard; MP (Lab) Neath since 1964; a Lord Commissioner, HM Treasury, since 1974; *b* 19 Sept. 1925; *s* of late Albert Archer Coleman and of Winifred Marguerite Coleman; *m* 1949, Phyllis Eileen (*née* Williams) (*d* 1963); one *s*; *m* 1966, Margaret Elizabeth Morgan; one *d*. *Educ:* Cadoxton Boys' Sch., Barry; Cardiff Technical Coll. Laboratory Technician, Welsh National Sch. of Medicine, Cardiff, 1940-42; Central Tuberculosis Laboratory, Cardiff, 1942-46; Sen. Technician, Swansea Technical Coll., 1946-50; University Coll., Swansea, 1950-54; Metallurgist, Research Dept, Steel Co. of Wales Ltd, Abbey Works, Port Talbot, 1954 until election to Parliament. PPS to Minister of State for Wales (later Secretary of State for Wales), 1967-70; an Opposition Whip, 1970-74. *Address:* Penderyn, 18 Penywern Road, Bryncoch, Neath, West Glamorgan. *T:* Neath 4599.

COLEMAN, Laurence Vail; Director Emeritus, American Association of Museums, since 1958; *b* 19 Sept. 1893; *s* of Thaddeus Vail Coleman and Kate Pratt; *m* 1917, Martine Weeks (decd); three *s*; *m* 1939, Susannah Armstrong. *Educ:* B. S. College of City of New York, 1915; MA Yale Univ., 1919; grad. work, Harvard Univ., 1919. Research Asst, NY State Commn on Ventilation, 1915; Asst in public health, American Museum Natural History, 1916; Asst in Zoology, Peabody Museum Natural History, 1917; US Army, 1918; Chief of Exhibits, American Museum Natural History, 1919-21; Dir, Safety Inst. America, 1921-23; Exec. Sec., American Assoc. of Museums, 1923-26; Dir, 1927-58. Trustee, Edward MacDowell Assoc., 1939-47; Hill-Stead Museum Trust, Connecticut, 1946-49; Mem. Executive Cttee, Internat. Museums Office, Paris, 1930-36; Educational Advisory Cttee, Pan-American Union,

1929-34; Jt Cttee on Materials for Research of American Council of Learned Societies and Social Science Research Council, 1931-40; Nat Cttee of USA on Intellectual Co-operation of the League of Nations, 1932-46; Cttee on Conservation of Cultural Resources, of National Resources Planning Board, 1941-43; US Nat. Cttee of Internat. Council of Museums, 1948-51. Hon. Fellow, The Museums Assoc. (British); Fellow, Rochester Museum Assoc.; Mid-west Museums Conf., USA; Charter Mem., Nat. Trust for Historical Preservation. Surveys of Museums in: USA, 1924 and 1932-34; Europe, 1927 and 1938; South America, 1928 and 1937; Canada, 1942. Received Alumni Service Medal, 1933, and Townsend Harris Medal, 1944, of College of City of New York; Distinguished Service Award of American Assoc. of Museums, 1940. *Publications:* Manual for Small Museums, 1927; Museums in South America, 1929; Historic House Museums, 1933; The Museum in America (3 vols), 1939, repr. 1970; College and University Museums, 1942; Company Museums, 1942; Museum Buildings (vol. 1), 1950; (with Beardsley Ruml) Manual of Corporate Giving, 1952; contribs to educational magazines in US and Europe. *Address:* 3801 Connecticut Avenue NW, Washington, DC 20008, USA. *Clubs:* Cosmos (Emeritus Mem.) (Washington); Lake Placid (NY State).

COLEMAN, Terry, (Terence Francis Frank); reporter and author; *b* 13 Feb. 1931; *s* of J. and D. I. B. Coleman; *m* 1954, Lesley Fox-Strangeways Vane; two *d*. *Educ:* 14 schs. LLB London. Formerly: Reporter, Poole Herald; Editor, Savoir Faire; Sub-editor, Sunday Mercury, and Birmingham Post; Reporter and then Arts Corresp., The Guardian, 1961-70, Chief Feature Writer, 1970-74; Special Writer with Daily Mail, 1974-76; Chief Feature Writer, The Guardian, 1976-, writing mainly political interviews. *Publications:* The Railway Navvies, 1965 (Yorkshire Post prize for best first book of year); A Girl for the Afternoons, 1965; (with Lois Deacon) Providence and Mr Hardy, 1966; The Only True History: collected journalism, 1969; Passage to America, 1972; (ed) An Indiscretion in the Life of an Heiress (Hardy's first novel), 1976; The Liners, 1976; Airship, 1978. *Recreations:* cricket, opera, circumnavigation (once). *Address:* The Guardian, Farringdon Road, EC1. *T:* 01-278 2332. *Clubs:* National Liberal; MCC.

COLEMAN, Rt. Rev. William Robert, DD; Professor of Humanities, York University, Toronto; *b* Ulverton, Quebec, 16 Aug. 1917; *s* of Rev. Stanley Harold Coleman and Mary Ann Coleman (*née* Armstrong); *m* 1947, Mary Elizabeth Charmes, *er d* of Thomas Summers and Marion Wilson; one *s* two *d*. *Educ:* St Mary's Collegiate Inst.; Brantford Collegiate Inst.; University Coll. and Wycliffe Coll. (BD); Univ. of Toronto (MA); Union Theological Seminary, New York (STM); Univs of Cambridge and Edinburgh. Deacon, 1942; Priest, 1943; Curate, Church of the Epiphany, Sudbury, Ont., 1942-43; Priest-in-charge, 1943-45; post-graduate study, 1945-47; Prof. of Religious Philosophy and Ethics, Wycliffe Coll., 1947-50; Dean of Divinity and Harold Prof., Bishop's Coll., Lennoxville, Quebec, 1950-52; Principal, Huron Coll., London, Ont., 1952-61; Bishop of Kootenay, 1961-65. FRSA, London. DD Wycliffe Coll., 1951. DD (Hon.) Huron Coll., 1961; DD (Hon.) Trinity Coll., Toronto, 1962. *Publications:* contributed to: In Such an Age (ed W. C. Lockhart), 1951; The Church in the Sixties (ed. P. Jefferson), 1962. *Address:* 25 Four Winds Drive, Apartment 903, Downsview, Ontario, Canada.

COLERAINE, 1st Baron *cr* 1954, of Haltemprice; **Richard Kidston Law,** PC 1943; High Steward of Kingston-upon-Hull; *b* Helensburgh, 27 Feb. 1901; *y s* of late Rt Hon. Andrew Bonar Law and Annie Pitcairn Robley; *m* 1929, Mary Virginia, *y d* of late A. F. Nellis, Rochester, NY; two *s*. *Educ:* Shrewsbury Sch.; St John's Coll., Oxford. Travelled in Asia Minor, India, Canada, United States, and South America; editorial staff, Morning Post, 1927; New York Herald-Tribune, 1928; Philadelphia Public Ledger, 1929; MP (U) SW Hull, 1931-45; (C) South Kensington Div., Nov. 1945-Feb. 1950; Haltemprice Div. of Kingston-on-Hull, 1950-54. Financial Sec., War Office, 1940-41; Parly Under-Sec. of State, Foreign Office, 1941-43; Minister of State, 1943-45; Minister of Education, 1945. Leader, UK Delegn Hotsprings Conf. on Food and Agriculture, 1943. Mem., Medical Research Council, 1936-40; Mem., Industrial Health Research Board, 1936-40; Chm. of Council of British Socs for Relief Abroad, 1945-49-54; Chm., Nat. Youth Employment Council, 1955-62; Chm., Central Transport Consultative Cttee, 1955-58; Chm., Mansfield House Univ. Settlement, 1953-66; Hon. Treas., British Sailors Soc., 1955-74; Chm., Marshall Scholarship Commn, 1956-65; Chm., Standing Advisory Cttee on Pay of Higher Civil Service, 1957-61. Chm., Royal Postgraduate Medical Sch. of London, 1958-71, Fellow 1972. Hon. LLD New Brunswick, 1951. *Publications:* The Individual and the Community in Ernest Barker's The Character of

England, 1947; Return from Utopia, 1950; For Conservatives Only, 1970. *Recreations:* sailing, walking. *Heir: s* Hon. (James) Martin (Bonar) Law [*b* 8 Aug. 1931; *m* 1st, 1958, Emma Elizabeth (marr. diss, 1966), *o d* of late Nigel Richards and of Mrs H. C. C. Batten; two *d*; 2nd, 1966, Patricia, *yr d* of Maj.-Gen. Ralph Farrant, *qv*; one *s* two *d*]. *Address:* Mill Cottage, Swallowcliffe, Salisbury; 43b Sloane Street, SW1.

COLERIDGE, family name of **Baron Coleridge.**

COLERIDGE, 4th Baron *cr* 1873, of Ottery St Mary; **Richard Duke Coleridge,** KBE 1971 (CBE 1951; OBE 1944); DL; Captain Royal Navy, retired; *b* 24 Sept. 1905; *e s* of 3rd Baron Coleridge and Jessie Alethea Mackarness (*d* 1957); *S* father, 1955; *m* 1936, Rosamund, *er d* of Admiral Sir W. W. Fisher, GCB, GCVO; two *s*. *Educ:* RNC Osborne and Dartmouth. Entered RN, 1919; RN Staff Course, 1938; invalided off Med. station and retd, 1939; rejoined, 1940, Offices of War Cabinet and of Minister of Defence, with appt to GQG Vincennes, France; War Cabinet Office in London, July 1940-May 1941; Jt Staff Mission, Washington, May 1941; Brit. Jt Staff and Combined Chiefs of Staff, 1942-45, and attended the Confs of Washington, Quebec (1942 and 1943), Cairo, Malta and Yalta; Council of Foreign Ministers, London Conf., Sept. 1945; UN Assembly in London, Jan. 1946; Mil. Staff Cttee of UN, New York, 1946-48; Brit. Jt Services Mission in Washington, 1948, and also Chief Staff Officer to Marshal of the RAF Lord Tedder (Chm. of Brit. Chiefs of Staff Cttee and Brit. Rep. on Standing Gp of NATO, 1950-51); rep. Brit. Chiefs of Staff on Temp. Cttee of Council of NATO, in Paris, 1951; attended Lisbon Conf., 1952; Exec. Sec., NATO, 1952-70. Chairman: Devon and Exeter Savings Bank, 1971-75; SW Trustee Savings Bank, 1975-. DL Devon 1973. US Legion of Merit. *Heir: s* Hon. William Duke Coleridge, Major Coldstream Guards, retired [*b* 18 June 1937; *m* 1962, Everild (Judy), *o d* of Lt-Col and Mrs Beauchamp Hambrough, Wisper's Farm, Nairobi; one *s* two *d*]. *Address:* The Chanter's House, Ottery St Mary, S Devon. *T:* Ottery St Mary 2417. *Club:* Army and Navy.

COLERIDGE, Lady (Marguerite) Georgina; *b* 19 March 1916; *d* of 11th Marquess of Tweeddale; *m* 1941, Arthur Coleridge, *yr s* of John Duke Coleridge; one *d*. *Educ:* home, abroad as a child. Joined National Magazine Co.: Circulation Dept, 1937; Advertisement Dept., 1938; joined Country Life, 1945; Editor of Homes and Gardens, 1949-63; Chm., Inst. of Journalists (London District), 1954, Fellow 1970; Chm., Women's Press Club, 1959 (Pres., 1965-67). Dir, Country Life Ltd, 1962-74; Dir, George Newnes Ltd, 1963-69; Publisher: Homes and Gardens; Woman's Journal, 1969-71; Ideal Home, 1970-71; Dir, Special Projects, IPC Women's Magazines, 1971-74; Consultant: IPC Women's Magazines, 1974-; Public Relations Counsel Ltd, 1974-. Mem., Internat. Assoc. of Women and Home Page Journalists, 1968-74; Associate, Women in Public Relations, 1972-; Associate Mem., Ladies Jockeys Assoc. of GB, 1973-; Founder Mem., Media Soc. Ltd (Inst. of Journalists Foundn), 1973-76; Pres., Captive Women's Luncheon Club, 1966-. Freeman, Worshipful Co. of Stationers and Newspapermakers, 1973. *Publications:* Grand Smashional Pointers (book of cartoons), 1934; I Know What I Like (clichés), 1959. *Recreations:* racing, detective stories, cooking; nothing highbrow. *Address:* 33 Peel Street, W8 7PA. *T:* 01-727 7732.

COLES, Captain (RNR retired) Arthur Edward, RD (with clasp); Commodore, Orient Line, retired; *b* 2 July 1902; *s* of late Arthur Coles, FCIS, and Ella May Coles; *m* 1940, Dorothy Blanche, *widow* of G. A. Griffin; no *c*. *Educ:* King Edward's Sch., Bath, Somerset. Cadet in Macandrew's Line, 1918. Joined RNR as probationary Sub-Lieut, 1927; joined Orient Line, 1928. Served Royal Navy, 1938-46; War of 1939-45 (despatches thrice, 1940; Dieppe, 1942; Normandy, 1944): HMS Malaya, 1939; Fleet Mine-sweepers; 9th Flotilla, 1941-42, 18th Flotilla, 1943-44; HMS Lochinvar (Trg Comdr), 1945-46. In command Orient Line ships, 1951-62. Younger Brother of Trinity House, 1951-. *Recreations:* motoring, photography. *Address:* Engleberg, 80 Dagger Lane, West Bromwich, West Midlands B71 4BS. *T:* 021-553 0827. *Club:* Birmingham.

COLES, Sir Arthur (William), Kt 1960; *b* 6 Aug. 1892; *s* of George and Elizabeth Coles; *m* 1919, Lilian Florence Knight; two *s* three *d* (and one *s* decd). *Educ:* State Sch.; Geelong Coll. Served European War, 1914-18: 6th Bn, 1914, Gallipoli and France; commissioned, 1916; wounded thrice. Original partner in retail firm of G. J. Coles & Co., 1919; Dir and Gen. Man. on formation of Company, 1921; Managing Dir, 1931-44. JP 1934; Mem. Melbourne City Council, 1933-44; Lord Mayor of Melbourne, 1938-39-40; MP, Henty, Vic., 1940, resigned, 1946. Mem. Commonwealth War Workers Housing Trust, 1941-45; Chairman: Commonwealth War Damage Commn, 1942-48;

Commonwealth Rationing Commn, 1942-50; Austr. Nat. Airlines Commn, 1946-50; British Commonwealth Pacific Airlines, 1946-50; Geelong Coll. Council, 1939-69; Austr. Trustees, Northcote Trust Fund, 1952-75. Vice-Chm., Trusts Corp. of Presbyterian Church of Vic., 1957-77; Mem., Commonwealth Immigration Planning Council, 1948-68; Part-time Mem. of Executive, CSIRO, 1956-65; Mem. Advisory Council, CSIRO, 1965-70; Australian Delegations to Commonwealth Agricultural Bureaux: Quinquennial Conf., London, 1960; Leader Delegn, 1965. *Recreation:* golf. *Address:* 48 Irving Road, Toorak, Victoria 3142, Australia. *T:* 20-6030. *Clubs:* Athenæum, Peninsula Country Golf (both in Victoria, Australia).
See also Sir E . B . *Coles* , Sir G . J . *Coles* , Sir K . F . *Coles* , Sir N . C . *Coles* .

COLES, Prof. Bryan Randell, DPhil; FInstP; Professor of Solid State Physics, Imperial College, University of London, since 1966; *b* 9 June 1926; *s* of Charles Frederick Coles and Olive Irene Coles; *m* 1955, Merivan Robinson; two *s*. *Educ:* Canton High Sch., Cardiff; Univ. of Wales, Cardiff (BSc); Jesus Coll., Univ. of Oxford (DPhil). FInstP 1972. Lectr in Metal Physics, Imperial Coll., London, 1950; Res. Fellow, Carnegie Inst. of Technol., Pittsburgh, 1954-56. Vis. Prof., Univ. of Calif, San Diego, 1962 and 1969. Vice-Pres., Inst. of Physics, 1968-72; Mem. Physics Cttee, SRC, 1972-76 (Chm. 1973-76). Chm. Bd of Dirs, Taylor & Francis Ltd (Scientific Publishers), 1976-. *Publications:* Electronic Structures of Solids (with A. D. Caplin), 1976; papers on structure, electrical properties, superconductivity and magnetic properties of metals and alloys in Philosoph. Magazine, Advances in Physics, Jl of Physics. *Recreations:* music, natural history, theatre. *Address:* 61 Courtfield Gardens, SW5. *T:* 01-373 3539.

COLES, Sir Edgar (Barton), Kt 1959; Director, G. J. Coles & Co. Ltd, Melbourne; *b* St James, Vic, 3 June 1899; *s* of George Coles, Horsham, Vic.; *m* Mabel Irene (*see* Dame Mabel Coles); one *s* two *d*. *Educ:* Scotch Coll., Launceston, Tasmania. Bank of NSW, 1916-19; G. J. Coles & Co.: joined, 1919; Sec., 1921-34; Dir, 1930-; Joint Managing Dir, 1940-44; Sole Managing Dir, 1944-61, Controlling Managing Dir, 1961-67, and Deputy Chm., 1958-61; Vice-Chm., 1961-63; Chm., 1963-68. Pres., Retail Traders Assoc. of Vic, 1946-48 and 1951-54. Pres., Australian Council of Retailers, 1952-54; Councillor of Royal Agricultural Soc., 1957-. *Recreations:* golf, photography. *Address:* Hendra, Mt Eliza, Vic 3930, Australia. *T:* Mt Eliza 71291; 236 Bourke Street, Melbourne, Vic 3000, Australia. *Clubs:* Athenæum (Melbourne); Victoria Racing; Victoria Amateur Turf; Melbourne Cricket; Lawn Tennis Assoc. of Victoria; Peninsula Golf.
See also Sir A . W . *Coles* , Sir G . J . *Coles* , Sir K . F . *Coles* , Sir N . C . *Coles* .

COLES, Sir George (James), Kt 1957; CBE 1942; Founder and Director, G. J. Coles & Co.; *b* 28 March 1885; *s* of George Coles, Horsham, and Elizabeth Coles (*née* Scouler); *m* 1920, Margaret Gertrude, *d* of C. Herbert; one *s* three *d* (and one *d* decd). *Educ:* Beechworth Grammar Sch. Served War as L-Corp. 60th Bn AIF, 1916-18. Founded G. J. Coles and Co., 1914; Man. Dir, 1923-31; Chm., 1923-56. *Publication:* Chain Store Economics, 1927. *Recreations:* golf, bowls. *Address:* 28 St George's Road, Toorak, Vic 3142, Australia. *T:* 24-4901. *Clubs:* Athenæum (Melbourne); Peninsula Country Golf.
See also Sir A . W . *Coles* , Sir E . B . *Coles* , Sir K . F . *Coles* , Sir N . C . *Coles* .

COLES, Gerald James Kay, QC 1976; a Recorder of the Crown Court, since 1972; *b* 6 May 1933; *o s* of James William Coles and Jane Elizabeth Coles; *m* 1958, Kathleen Yolande, *e d* of Alfred John Hobson, FRCS, and Kathleen Elizabeth Hobson; three *s*. *Educ:* Coatham Sch., Redcar; Brasenose Coll., Oxford; Harvard Law Sch., Harvard Univ. Meritorious Award, Hastings Schol., Queen's Coll., Oxford, 1949; Akroyd Open Schol. 1950; BA 1954, BCL 1955, Oxon; Westengard Schol., Harvard Law Sch., 1955; LLM 1956. Called to Bar, Middle Temple, 1957; practised at Bar, London and NE Circuit, 1957-; Prosecuting Counsel to Inland Revenue, 1971-76. *Recreations:* music, theatre, photography. *Address:* The Old Rectory, Sessay, Thirsk, N Yorks. *T:* Hutton Sessay 218; (chambers) 5 King's Bench Walk, Temple, EC4Y 7DN. *T:* 01-353 2882/4; 2 Park Square, Leeds LS1 2NE. *T:* Leeds 33277/8/9. *Clubs:* Junior Carlton; Leeds (Leeds).

COLES, Sir Kenneth (Frank), Kt 1957; Director: G. J. Coles & Co. Ltd (Deputy Chairman, 1945-76; Chairman, 1956-63); Australian Oil and Gas Corp.; *b* 19 April 1896; *s* of George and Elizabeth Coles; *m* 1925, Marjorie Evelyn Tolley; one *s* two *d*. Entered G. J. Coles & Co. Ltd, 1920; appointed London

Manager, 1926; State Manager for NSW, 1933. Pres., Internat. Soc. for Welfare of Crippled, 1957-60. *Recreation:* golf. *Address:* 83 Victoria Road, Bellevue Hill, Sydney, Australia. *T:* 36 4728. *Clubs:* Royal Sydney Golf (Sydney); Elanora Country.
See also Sir A . W . *Coles* , Sir E . B . *Coles* , Sir G . J . *Coles* , Sir N . C . *Coles* .

COLES, Dame Mabel Irene, DBE 1971 (CBE 1965); President: Royal Women's Hospital, Melbourne, 1968-72; Australian Women's Liberal Club, since 1965; Director, Asthma Foundation of Victoria, 1965; *d* of late E. Johnston; *m* 1927, Sir Edgar Coles, *qv*; one *s* two *d*. Associated with Royal Women's Hosp. for 25 years; Chairman: Ladies Cttee for (two) $1,000,000 appeals; (two) Door Knock Appeals; Asthma Ladies' Appeal Cttee; Patroness: Family Planning Assoc. of Vic.; Rheumatism and Arthritis Assoc. of Vic.; 3Rs Assoc.; Frankston Musical Soc., National Theatreites; Trustee, Mayfield Centre. *Recreations:* dogs, horses, walking. *Address:* Hendra, Williams Road, Mount Eliza, Vic. 3930, Australia. *Clubs:* Alexandra, Peninsula Country (Melbourne).

COLES, Norman, CB 1971; Consultant; Director, Laser Engineering Ltd, since 1975; *b* 29 Dec. 1914; *s* of Fred and Emily Coles; *m* 1947, Una Valerie Tarrant; five *s*. *Educ:* Hanson High Sch., Bradford; Royal College of Science; City and Guilds Coll. Head, Armament Dept, RAE, 1959; Dir Gen. Equipment Research and Development, Min. of Aviation, 1962; Dep. Controller: of Aircraft (RAF), Min. of Technology, 1966-68; of Guided Weapons, Min. of Technology, 1968-69; Dep. Chief Adviser (Research and Studies), MoD, 1969-71; Dep. Controller, Establishments and Research, MoD, 1971-75. *Recreations:* carpentry, crossword puzzles. *Address:* Shottery, 3 Kingsley Avenue, Camberley, Surrey. *T:* Camberley 22953.

COLES, Sir Norman (Cameron), Kt 1977; Chairman, G. J. Coles & Co. Ltd, Melbourne, since 1968; *b* 10 Sept. 1907; *s* of George Coles and Annie Cameron Coles; *m* 1932, Dorothy Verna Deague; one *s* one *d*. *Educ:* Launceston C of E Grammar Sch., Tas; Trinity Grammar Sch., Kew, Vic. AASA, FCIS. Joined G. J. Coles & Co. Ltd, Australia, 1924: Company Secretary, 1933; Director, 1949; Finance Dir, 1963-67; Man. Dir, 1967-75. *Recreations:* golf, gardening. *Address:* (office) G. J. Coles & Co. Ltd, 236 Bourke Street, Melbourne, Vic 3000, Australia. *T:* 66-6048; (home) 28 Somers Avenue, Malvern, Vic 3144, Australia. *Clubs:* Athenæum (Melbourne); Melbourne Cricket, Victoria Racing, Peninsula Golf (all Victoria).
See also Sir A . W . *Coles* , Sir E . B . *Coles* , Sir G . J . *Coles* , Sir K . F . *Coles* .

COLES, Air Marshal Sir William (Edward), KBE 1967 (CBE 1952); CB 1963; DSO 1944; DFC and Bar; AFC; Member of Council, Royal Air Force Benevolent Fund and Royal Air Force Association, since 1975; *b* 1913; *s* of late George Frederick Coles, Shenington, Banbury; *m* 1945, Eileen Marjorie, *d* of Ernest Wilberforce Hann; two *s*. *Educ:* Tysoe Secondary Sch. Entered Royal Air Force, 1938; served in 216, 233 and 117 Squadrons, Middle East, N Africa, Italy, Burma and European theatres, 1939-44; RAF Staff Coll., 1945; Air Min., 1946-48; Empire and Central Flg Sch., 1948-50; Comd RAF Middleton St George, 1950; Chief Instr CFS, 1951-53; Sen. RAF Liaison Officer and Air Advisor to UK High Comr in Austr., 1953-55; HQ, Flg Trg Comd, 1956; idc 1957; SASO, HQ No 3 Bomber Gp, RAF Mildenhall, Suffolk, 1957-60; AOC No 23 Gp, RAF Flg Trg Comd, 1960-63; Dir-Gen. of Personal Services (RAF), Min. of Defence, 1963-66; AOC-in-C, RAF Technical Training Comd, 1966-68. Controller, RAF Benevolent Fund, 1968-75. DFC (US) 1944. *Recreations:* golf, winter sports. *Address:* 3 Walpole Road, Surbiton, Surrey. *T:* 01-399 4625; Top Farm House, Shenington, Banbury, Oxon. *Club:* Royal Air Force.

COLEY, (Howard William) Maitland; Stipendiary Magistrate for Wolverhampton (formerly South Staffordshire), since 1961; *b* 14 July 1910; *s* of late W. Howard Coley; *m* 1940, Cecile Muriel (from whom he obtained a divorce, 1966), *d* of C. C. H. Moriarty, CBE; one *d*; *m* 1968, Jill Barbour-Simpson; one *s*. *Educ:* Rugby; Christ's Coll., Cambridge. Called to Bar, Middle Temple, 1934. Served RAF, 1940-45. Recorder of Wenlock, 1946; Recorder of Burton upon Trent, 1956-61; Dep. Chm., Staffordshire QS, 1959-71; Dep. Circuit Judge, 1972. *Recreations:* golf, sailing. *Address:* New House Farm, Mamble, near Kidderminster, Worcs. *T:* Clows Top 236.

COLFOX, Sir (William) John, 2nd Bt *cr* 1939; JP; DL; *b* 25 April 1924; *yr* and *o surv. s* of Sir (William) Philip Colfox, 1st Bt, MC, and Mary (Frances) Lady Colfox (*d* 1973); *S* father, 1966; *m* 1962, Frederica Loveday, *d* of Adm. Sir Victor Crutchley, *qv*; two *s* three *d*. *Educ:* Eton. Served in RNVR, 1942-46, leaving as Lieut. Qualified Land Agent, 1950. JP Dorset, 1962, High

Sheriff of Dorset, 1969, DL Dorset, 1977. *Recreation:* outdoor sports. *Heir: s* Philip John Colfox, *b* 27 Dec. 1962. *Address:* Symondsbury House, Bridport, Dorset. *T:* Bridport 22956.

COLGATE, Dennis Harvey, MM 1944; Registrar of Family Division of Supreme Court since 1975; *b* 9 Oct. 1922; *s* of Charles William and Marjorie Colgate; *m* 1961, Kathleen (*née* Marquis); one *d. Educ:* Varndean Sch., Brighton; Univ. Coll. of South West, Exeter; King's Coll., London (LLB). HM Forces, 1942-47; Principal Probate Registry, 1947-64 (Estabt Officer 1959-64); District Probate Registrar of High Court, Manchester, 1964-75. Consulting Editor, Tristram and Coote's Probate Practice. *Publications:* (ed jtly) Rayden on Divorce, 7th edn 1958 and 8th edn 1960; (ed jtly) Atkin's Court Forms (Probate), 2nd edn 1974. *Recreations:* walking, camping, do-it-yourself. *Address:* 10 Frogmore Close, Hughenden Valley, High Wycombe, Bucks HP14 4LN. *T:* Naphill 2659.

COLGRAIN, 3rd Baron *cr* 1946, of Everlands; **David Colin Campbell;** a Managing Director, Antony Gibbs Holdings Ltd, since 1954; *b* 24 April 1920; *s* of 2nd Baron Colgrain, MC, and of Margaret Emily, *d* of late P. W. Carver; *S* father, 1973; *m* 1st, 1945, Veronica Margaret (marr. diss. 1964), *d* of late Lt-Col William Leckie Webster, RAMC; one *s* one *d*; 2nd, 1973, Mrs Sheila M. Hudson. *Educ:* Eton; Trinity Coll., Cambridge. Served War of 1939-45, 9th Lancers. Manager, Nat. and Grindlays Bank Ltd, India and Pakistan, 1945-49; joined Antony Gibbs and Sons Ltd, 1949. Treas., Central Council for the Disabled. *Heir: s* Hon. Alastair Colin Leckie Campbell, *b* 16 Sept. 1951. *Address:* Flat 4, 51 Winchester Street, SW1.

COLHOUN, Prof. John; Barker Professor of Cryptogamic Botany, University of Manchester, since 1960; Dean, Faculty of Science, 1974 and 1975; Pro-Vice-Chancellor, since 1977; *b* 15 May 1913; *yr s* of late James Colhoun and Rebecca Colhoun, Castlederg, Co. Tyrone; *m* 1949, Margaret, *e d* of late Prof. Gilbert Waterhouse, FRGS, and Mary Elizabeth, *e d* of Sir Robert Woods; three *d. Educ:* Edwards Sch., Castlederg, Co. Tyrone; The Queen's Univ. of Belfast; Imperial Coll. of Science, London Univ. BSc, MAgr (Belfast), PhD, DSc (London), MSc (Manchester), DIC. Min. of Agriculture for Northern Ireland: Research Asst, 1939-46; Senior Scientific Officer, 1946-50; Principal Scientific Officer, 1951-60. The Queen's Univ., Belfast: Asst Lecturer in Agricultural Botany, 1940-42; Asst Lectr 1942-45, Jun. Lectr 1945-46, Lectr 1946-54, Reader 1954-60, in Mycology and Plant Pathology. Warden of Queen's Chambers, 1942-49. FLS 1955. FIBiol 1963. Pres., British Mycological Soc., 1963; Chm., Fedn of British Plant Pathologists, 1968. Jt Editor, Phytopathologische Zeitschrift, 1973-. *Publications:* Diseases of the Flax Plant, 1947; Club Root Disease of Crucifers caused by *Plasmodiophora Bassicae* Woron, 1958; numerous papers in Annals of Applied Biology, Annals of Botany, Trans Brit. Mycological Soc., Nature, Phytopath. Z. *Address:* 12 Southdown Crescent, Cheadle Hulme, Cheshire. *T:* 061-485 2084. *Clubs:* Athenæum, Farmers'.

COLIN, Rt. Rev. Gerald Fitzmaurice; *see* Grimsby, Bishop Suffragan of.

COLLAR, Prof. (Arthur) Roderick, CBE 1964; FRS 1965; MA, DSc, CEng; FAIAA, FCASI; Sir George White Professor of Aeronautical Engineering, University of Bristol, 1945-73, now Emeritus; Pro-Vice-Chancellor, 1967-70 (Vice-Chancellor 1968-69); *b* 22 Feb. 1908; *s* of late Arthur Collar, JP, and Louie Collar; *m* 1934, Winifred Margaret Moorman; two *s. Educ:* Simon Langton Sch., Canterbury; Emmanuel Coll., Cambridge (Scholar). Aerodynamics Dept, Nat. Physical Laboratory, 1929-41; Structural and Mechanical Engineering Dept, Royal Aircraft Establishment, 1941-45. Pres., Royal Aeronautical Soc., 1963-64; Chairman: Aeronautical Research Council, 1964-68; Chm. Council, Rolls-Royce Technical Coll.; Mem. Adv. Council, Royal Military Coll. of Science, Shrivenham (Chm., 1970-76). Member: Clifton Coll. Council; Council, Royal Society, 1971-73; Bd of Governors, United Bristol Hosps, 1968-74; Academic Adv. Council, Cranfield Inst. of Technology, 1970-75; SW Regional Hosp. Bd, 1969-74. Founder Fellow, Fellowship of Engineering, 1976. Liveryman, Guild of Air Pilots and Air Navigators. Hon. LLD Bristol, 1969; Hon. DSc: Bath, 1971; Cranfield, 1976. R38 Memorial Prize (joint), 1932; George Taylor Gold Medal, 1947; Orville Wright Prize, 1958; J. E. Hodgson Prize, 1960; Gold Medal, RAeS, 1966, Hon. FRAeS 1973. *Publications:* Elementary Matrices (joint), 1938; (joint ed.) Hypersonic Flow; numerous papers in technical press. *Recreations:* sport (onlooker), poetry, music. *Address:* 12 Rockleaze, Bristol BS9 1NE. *T:* Bristol 681491. *Clubs:* Royal Commonwealth Society; Bristol Savages.

COLLARD, Douglas Reginald, OBE 1976; HM Diplomatic Service, retired; Director, Anglo-Arab Association, since 1976; Resident Director, Arab British Centre; *b* 7 April 1916; *s* of late Hebert Carthew Collard and late Mary Ann (*née* Pugh); *m* 1947, Eleni Alkmini Kiortsi (marr. diss. 1969), Greece; two *s* three *d. Educ:* Wallasey Grammar Sch.; privately. Army Service, 1940-46 (despatches); UNRRA, Greece, 1946-47; Asst Commercial Adviser, British Econ. Mission to Greece, 1947; Consul, Patras, Greece, 1947-52; Develt Div., Beirut, 1952-54; 2nd Sec. (Commercial); Khartoum, 1954-56; Copenhagen, 1958-61; FCO, 1956-58 and 1967-69; 1st Sec. (Commercial): Tripoli, 1961-65; Lahore, 1965-67; Montevideo, 1969-71; 1st Sec., later Counsellor (Commercial), Algiers, 1971-73; Consul-Gen., Bilbao, 1973-76. *Recreations:* reading, walking, 16th century Spanish history. *Address:* 21 Collingham Road, SW5 0NU. *T:* 01-373 8417. *Club:* Reform.

COLLARD, Prof. Patrick John, MD, FRCP; JP; Professor of Bacteriology and Director of Department of Bacteriology and Virology, University of Manchester, since 1962; *b* 22 April 1920; *s* of Rupert John Collard; *m* 1st, 1948, Jessie Robertson (marr. diss. 1955); one *s* one *d*; 2nd, 1956, Kathleen Sarginson; one *s* one *d. Educ:* St Bartholomew's Medical Coll., Univ. of London. Qualified MB, BS, 1942; MD 1951. House Appts, 1942-44. RAMC, 1944-48. Registrar, Westminster Hospital, 1948-50; Lectr, Guy's Hosp. Med. Sch., 1950-54; Prof. of Bacteriology, University Coll., Ibadan, Nigeria, 1954-62. FRCP 1972. JP. *Publications:* The Development of Microbiology, 1976; papers in: BMJ, Lancet, Jl Soc. Gen. Microbiol., Jl of Hygiene, West African Med. Jl, etc. *Recreations:* talking, reading, playing chess, silver-smithing. *Address:* 9 Holmewood Court, Ballbrook Avenue, Didsbury, Manchester M20 0AB. *T:* 061-445 3479. *Club:* Athenæum.

COLLETT, Rear-Adm. George Kempthorne, CB 1957; DSC 1942; *b* 25 Jan. 1907; *s* of William George and Ruth Lilian Collett; *m* 1937, Rongnye, *e d* of Sir Charles A. Bell, KCIE, CMG; one *s* one *d. Educ:* RNC Osborne and Dartmouth. Comdr, 1939; Liaison Officer with Gen. de Gaulle, 1940; Executive Officer, HMS Trinidad, 1941-42; Staff Officer, Home Fleet, 1942-44; Naval Asst to First Sea Lord, 1944-45; CO, HMS Cardigan Bay, 1946-48; Min. of Supply, 1948-50; Joint Services Staff Coll., 1950-52; CO, HMS Bermuda, 1952-54; Vice Naval Deputy, SHAPE, Paris, 1955-57; retd 1958. Legion of Honour (officer), 1945. *Recreation:* gardening. *Address:* Coombe Farm, Churt, Farnham, Surrey. *T:* Headley Down 712533. *Club:* Army and Navy.

COLLETT, Sir Ian (Seymour), 3rd Bt *cr* 1934; *b* 5 Oct. 1953; *s* of David Seymour Collett (*d* 1962), and of Sheila Joan Collett, *o d* of late Harold Scott; *S* grandfather, 1971. *Educ:* Lancing College, Sussex. *Recreations:* fishing, sailing, cricket, shooting. *Heir: uncle* Christopher Collett [*b* 10 June 1931; *m* 1959, Christine Anne, *o d* of late Oswald Hardy Griffiths; two *s* one *d*]. *Address:* 11 Collingham Gardens, SW5. *T:* 01-373 6807. *Clubs:* Hurlingham, MCC, Flyfishers'.

COLLETT, Sir (Thomas) Kingsley, Kt 1968; CBE 1956; formerly Director, Adams Bros & Shardlow Ltd (Creative Printers), London and Leicester, retired 1971; *b* 7 March 1905; 6th *s* of late Sir Charles Collett, 1st Bt, Bromley, Kent (Lord Mayor of London, 1933-34); *m* 1930, Beatrice Olive, *d* of late Thomas H. Brown, Bickley, Kent. *Educ:* Bishop's Stortford Coll. Mem., City of London Territorial Auxiliary and Volunteer Reserve Assoc. Forces Association. HM Lieut for City of London, 1958-76. Freeman, City of London, 1930; Liveryman, Worshipful Co. of Distillers, 1934 (Master, 1960-61); Mem., Ct of Common Coun., City of London (Ward of Bridge), 1945-; Chairman: City of London Freemen's Sch. Cttee, 1949-52; Port of London Health Authority, 1953; City Lands Cttee and Chief Commoner, 1955; Special Cttee, 1956-66; Policy and Parly Cttee, 1967-70. Corp. of London Rep. on Bd of Port of London Authority, 1959-67; Mem., Pollution Control Cttee, PLA; Chm., Lord Mayor's Appeal Cttee; Kennedy Mem. Fund, 1964; Churchill Fund, 1965; Vice-Chm., Lord Mayor's Appeal Cttee: cleaning St Paul's Cath, 1963-64; Attlee Meml Fund, 1967. Governor, Royal Hospitals; Chm., Governing Council, Bishop's Stortford Coll., 1964-76. Chm., East India and Sports Club, 1959-66. Chevalier, Mil. Order of Christ (Portugal), 1956. *Recreations:* gardening, golf, shooting. *Address:* Fairfax Cottage, Wilderness Road, Chislehurst, Kent. *Club:* East India, Devonshire, Sports and Public Schools.

COLLEY, Thomas, MB, ChB (Victoria); MRCS, LRCP, FRCSE; DOMS; Emeritus Cons. Ophthalmologist, Wessex Regional Hospital Board; late Director of Ophthalmology to West Dorset Group of Hospitals; late Hon. Surgeon to Weymouth and Dorset County Royal Eye Infirmary; late Hon. Ophthalmic Surgeon to

Dorset County Hospital, Dorchester and Weymouth and District Hospital; Ophthalmic Surgeon to EMS Hospital, Portwey, Weymouth (War Years); late Cons. Oculist to the Dorset CC and Weymouth Education Committee; *b* Dec. 1894; *s* of Thomas and Esther Colley, Preston; *m* Eleanor Mary, *e d* of late Rev. D. J. Thomas, OBE, MA, JP; two *d*. *Educ:* privately; Manchester Univ. (Dumville Surgical Prize, Medical Clinical Prize); Edinburgh University. House appointments Royal Infirmary, Manchester, Central Branch Royal Infirmary, Manchester, Hospital for Sick Children, Great Ormond Street, London, Royal London Ophthalmic Hospital (Moorfields). Chm., W Dorset Group Med. Adv. Cttee, 1948-54; Member: Med. Adv. Cttee to SW Metropolitan Regional Hosp. Bd, 1949-51, (Mem., Med. Adv. Cttee of Western Area, 1948-53); W Dorset Group Hospitals Management Cttee, 1948-61. FRSM (Mem. of Council, Section of Ophthalmology, 1938-42); Mem. of Ophthalmological Soc., BMA, etc. *Publications:* papers in medical journals. *Recreation:* philately. *Address:* 9 Westbury Court Road, Westbury-on-Trym, Bristol. *T:* 622683.

COLLICK, Percy Henry; Assistant General Secretary, Associated Society of Locomotive Engineers, 1940-57 (Organising Secretary, 1934-40). Contested (Lab) Reigate Division of Surrey, 1929 and 1931; MP (Lab) West Birkenhead, 1945-50, Birkenhead, 1950-64. General Purposes Cttee, TUC, 1930-34; National Executive, Labour Party, 1944; Joint Parly Sec., Min. of Agriculture, 1945-47. Mem. Council, Royal College of Veterinary Surgeons, 1949-53. Hon. Freeman of Birkenhead, 1965. *Address:* 142 Hendon Way, NW2.

COLLIER, family name, Monkswell Barony.

COLLIER, Air Vice-Marshal Sir (Alfred) Conrad, KCB 1947 (CB 1943); CBE 1941; retired as Chief Executive, Guided Weapons Division, English Electric Aviation Ltd, 1960; *b* 16 Nov. 1895; *m* 1st, 1920, G. M. C. Luis (*d* 1961); two *s* one *d*; 2nd, 1963, Kathleen, *d* of late Joseph Donaghy, JP, Londonderry. *Educ:* Sherborne Sch. 2nd Lieut 9th King's Own (RL) Regt, 1914; RFC, 1915 with subsequent continuous service in RFC and RAF; Air Attaché, Moscow, 1934-37; Dep. Dir of Plans, Air Min., 1938; Dir of Allied Air Co-operation, Air Min., 1940; Head of Air Section, British Military Mission to Moscow, 1941; Air Officer i/c Administration, AHQ, India, 1942-43; Deputy AOC-in-C Transport Comd, 1943-45; AOC No. 3 Group, Bomber Comd, 1946; Dir-Gen. of Technical Services, Min. of Civil Aviation, 1946-47; Air Vice-Marshal, 1946; Controller of Technical and Operational Services, Min. of Civil Aviation, 1947, resigned, 1948. A Governor, National Hospitals for Nervous Diseases, 1961-64. DL Kent, 1952-64. FRAeS. Order of White Lion, 2nd Class (Czechoslovakia); Grand Officer, Order of Orange Nassau (Netherlands); Officer, Legion of Honour, and Croix de Guerre (France). *Address:* c/o Lloyds Bank Ltd, Walton-on-Thames, Surrey. *Club:* Travellers'.

COLLIER, Andrew James, CB 1976; Deputy Secretary, Department of Health and Social Security, since 1973; *b* 12 July 1923; *s* of Joseph Veasy Collier and Dorothy Murray; *m* 1950, Bridget, *d* of George and Edith Eberstadt, London; two *d*. *Educ:* Harrow; Christ Church, Oxford. Served Army, 1943-46. Entered HM Treasury, 1948; Private sec. to: Sir Henry Wilson Smith, 1950; Sir Leslie Rowan, 1951; Chancellors of the Exchequer, 1956-59; Asst Sec., 1961; Under-Sec., 1967; Under-Secretary: Civil Service Dept, 1968-71; DHSS, 1971-73. *Address:* 82 Old Church Street, SW3. *T:* 01-352 5150. *Club:* Athenæum.

COLLIER, Air Vice-Marshal Sir Conrad; *see* Collier, Sir A. C.

COLLIER, Kenneth Gerald; Consultant on teacher education overseas, since 1975; *b* 1910; *m* 1938, Gwendoline Halford; two *s*. *Educ:* Aldenham Sch.; St John's Coll., Cambridge. MA 1935; Diploma in Education (Oxon) 1945. Technical translation, Stockholm, 1931-32; Schoolmaster, 1933-41; Royal Ordnance Factories, 1941-44; Physics Master, Lancing Coll., 1944-49; Lectr, St Luke's Coll., Exeter, 1949-59; Principal, College of the Venerable Bede, Durham, 1959-75. Editor, Education for Teaching, 1953-58. Chm., Assoc. Teachers in Colls and Depts of Education, 1964-65. Vis. Prof. of Education, Temple Univ., Philadelphia, 1965, 1968. Seconded to Nat. Council for Educational Technology, 1971. *Publications:* The Science of Humanity, 1950; The Social Purposes of Education, 1959; New Dimensions in Higher Education, 1968; (ed) Innovation in Higher Education, 1974; (ed) Values and Moral Development in Higher Education, 1974; (contrib.) Sixth Form Citizens, 1950; Religious Faith and World Culture (New York), 1951; articles in educational and other jls. *Recreations:* local history; music; the film. *Address:* 4 Branksome Road, Norwich, Norfolk NR4 6SN. *T:* Norwich 57035. *Club:* Royal Over-Seas League.

COLLIER, Prof. Leslie Harold, MD, DSc; FRCPath; Director, Lister Institute of Preventive Medicine, Vaccines and Sera Laboratories, Elstree, Herts, since 1974; *b* 9 Feb. 1921; *s* of late Maurice Leonard Collier and Ruth (*née* Phillips); *m* 1942, Adeline Barnett; one *s*. *Educ:* Brighton Coll.; UCH Med. Sch. (MD). DSc London 1968; MRCP; FRCPath 1975. House Phys., UCH, 1943; served RAMC, 1944-47; Asst Pathologist, St Helier Hosp., Carshalton, 1947; Lister Inst. of Preventive Medicine, 1948-: Head, Dept of Virology, 1955-74; Dep. Dir, 1968-74. Hon. Dir, MRC Trachoma Unit, 1957-73. Chibret Gold Medal, Ligue contre le Trachome, 1959; Luys Prize, Soc. de Médecine de Paris, 1963. *Publications:* papers in med. and scientific jls. *Recreations:* various. *Address:* Brontë Cottage, 89 South End Road, NW3 2RJ. *T:* 01-794 6331.

COLLIER, Dr William Adrian Larry; general practitioner in Hackney, since 1970; *b* 25 Nov. 1913; *s* of Hon. Gerald Collier, 2nd *s* of 2nd Baron Monkswell, and Lily Anderson; *S* uncle as 4th Baron Monkswell, 1964; disclaimed title, 7 April 1964; *m* 1945, Helen (*née* Dunbar, now Mrs Kemp); two *s*; *m* 1951, Nora Selby; one *s* one *d*. *Educ:* Fellowship Sch.; Odenwald Schule; Summerhill; Univs of Queensland, Edinburgh, London and Cambridge. IB 1937; MB, ChB Edinburgh 1943; DPH London 1947, PHLS (Trainee), 1947-50. Mem., Halstead UDC, 1954-67; Essex CC, 1958-61. GP, Halstead, Essex, 1951-69. Member: Amenity Cttee, Nat. Assoc. River Authorities, 1970-72; Council, Forest School Camps; Council, Centreprise 1973. *Publications:* World Index of Imprints used on Tablets and other Solid Dose Forms, 1964, 6th edn (now known as IMPREX), 1977; contribs to Lancet, Pharmaceutical Journal, Drug Intelligence and Clinical Pharmacy (washington DC). *Recreations:* swimming, camping, kids, local government, Essex River Authority. *Heir:* (*to disclaimed barony*); *s* Gerard Collier, *b* 28 Jan. 1947. *Address:* 54 Amhurst Road, Hackney, E8. *T:* 01-985 5839.

COLLIER-WRIGHT, John Hurrell, CBE 1966; Member, British Transport Docks Board, 1974-77; *b* 1 April 1915; *s* of John Robert Collier Collier-Wright and Phyllis Hurrell Walters; *m* 1940, Pauline Beatrice Platts; three *s* (and one *s* decd). *Educ:* Bradfield Coll.; Queen's Coll., Oxford (MA). FCIT. Traffic Apprentice, LNER, 1936-39. Served War of 1939-45, RE, France, Iraq and Iran (Lt-Col; US Legion of Merit). East African Railways and Harbours, 1946-64; Chief Commercial Supt; joined British Transport Docks Bd, 1964; Chief Commercial Man., 1964-70; Asst Man. Dir, 1970-72; Dep. Man. Dir, 1972-77; Dir, British Transport Advertising, 1966-77. *Recreations:* fishing, architecture, music. *Address:* Laurel Cottage, 71 Main Street, Mursley, Bucks MK17 0RT. *Clubs:* United Oxford & Cambridge University; Nairobi (Kenya).

COLLIGAN, John Clifford, CBE 1963 (OBE 1957); Director-General, Royal National Institute for the Blind, 1950-72; Secretary, British Wireless for the Blind Fund, since 1950; Hon. Treasurer and Life Member, World Council for the Blind, since 1969 (British Representative, 1954-69); *b* 27 Oct. 1906; *s* of John and Florence Colligan, Wallasey, Cheshire; *m* 1st, 1934, Ethel May Allton (*d* 1948); one *s* one *d*; 2nd, 1949, Frances Bird. *Educ:* Liscard High Sch., Wallasey. Dep. Sec., National Institute for the Blind, 1945-49. *Publications:* The Longest Journey, 1969; various articles on blind welfare. *Recreations:* fishing, gardening. *Address:* 3 Jonathans, Dene Road, Northwood, Mddx. *T:* Northwood 21988.

COLLIN, Maj.-Gen. Geoffrey de Egglesfield, CB 1975; MC 1944; MBIM; *b* 18 July 1921; *s* of late Charles de Egglesfield Collin and Catherine Mary Collin; *m* 1949, Angela Stella (*née* Young); one *s* three *d*. *Educ:* Wellington Coll., Crowthorne, Berks. Served War of 1939-45: commissioned as 2nd Lt, RA, 1941; in India and Burma, 1942-45. Qualified as Army Pilot, 1946; attended Staff Coll., Camberley, 1951; Instructor at RMA, Sandhurst, 1954-56; served Kenya, 1956-58; Instructor at Staff Coll., Camberley, 1960-62; comd 50 Missile Regt, RA, 1962-64; CRA, 4th Div., 1966-67; attended Imperial Defence College, London, 1968; Comdt, Royal School of Artillery, 1969-71; Maj.-Gen. RA, HQ BAOR, 1971-73; GOC North East District, York, 1973-76; retired 1976. Col Comdt, RA, 1976-. *Recreations:* fishing, ornithology, music, photography. *Address:* c/o Lloyds Bank, 6 Pall Mall, SW1. *Club:* Army and Navy.

COLLINGS, Maj.-Gen. Wilfred d'Auvergne, CB 1946; CBE 1941; *b* Guernsey, 8 Aug. 1893; 5th *s* of C. d'Auvergne Collings, MD, and Laura Josephine Williams; *m* 1928, Nancy Draper Bishop; two *s* one *d*. *Educ:* Elizabeth Coll., Guernsey; RMC Sandhurst. Commissioned ASC 1914. Served in France, Gallipoli and Mesopotamia, 1914-18 (despatches twice); seconded for service with Egyptian Army, 1923-24 and Sudan Defence Force, 1925-30; on active service in Palestine, 1937-39;

Dep. Dir of Supplies and Transport, Western Desert Force, 1940, British Forces in Greece, 1941, Eighth Army, 1941; Dir of Supplies and Transport, Persia and Iraq Force, 1942-43, 21st Army Group, 1944-45, and British Army of the Rhine, 1945-46; retired 1948. Chief of Supply and Transport Div., UN Relief and Works Agency in the Near East, 1949-53. Maj.-Gen. 1944. Commander, Order of Leopold II (Belgium); MC of Greece, Croix de Guerre of France and Belgium. *Address:* La Verdure, Clifton, St Peter Port, Guernsey. *Club:* Army and Navy.

COLLINGWOOD, Adrian Redman, CBE 1975; TD 1953; Chairman of the Eggs Authority since 1971; *b* Driffield, Yorks, 26 Feb. 1910; *s* of Bernard Joseph Collingwood and Katherine Mary Collingwood; *m* 1939, Dorothy Strong; two *d*. *Educ:* Hull Technical College. FIB. Served War of 1939-45, E Yorks Regt (50th Div.) (Major; despatches, 1944); wounded in Western Desert; POW for a year, then escaped by means of tunnel. Midland Bank: Asst Man., Whitefriargate Branch, Hull, 1947-51; Branch Supt, 1951-55; Gen. Manager's Asst, 1955-59; Gen. Manager (Agriculture), 1959-66; retd from bank, 1971. *Publications:* lectures. *Recreations:* previously rugger, cricket, tennis; now golf, bridge, gardening. *Address:* Flat 6, Burrells, 25 Court Downs Road, Beckenham, Kent. *T:* 01-650 2265. *Clubs:* Farmers'; Rugby (Rugby); (Chm.) Langley Park Golf.

COLLINGWOOD, Rt. Rev. Mgr. Canon Cuthbert; retired; *b* 26 May 1908; *s* of late Austin Vincent Collingwood. *Educ:* St Edmund's College, Ware. Ordained by His Eminence Cardinal Bourne, 1934; Chaplain of Westminster Cathedral and Asst Master of Ceremonies, 1934-44, Master of Ceremonies, 1945-49; Editor of Westminster Cathedral Chronicle, 1940-45; Private Sec. to HE Cardinal Griffin, 1944-47; Administrator of Westminster Cathedral, 1947-54; Canon of Metropolitan Chapter of Westminster, 1948-73, Hon. Canon, 1973; Parish Priest of Staines, 1954-73. Privy Chamberlain to HH the Pope, 1946, Domestic Prelate, 1968. Chm. of Catholic Truth Soc., 1948-71; Pres. of Metropolitan and City Catholic Police Guild, 1948-73. *Address:* 7 Overton Court, Overton Park Road, Cheltenham, Glos GL50 3BW. *T:* Cheltenham 59239.

COLLINGWOOD, Lt-Gen. Sir George; *see* Collingwood, Lt-Gen. Sir R. G.

COLLINGWOOD, John Gildas, CEng, FIChemE; Director: Unilever Ltd, 1965-77; Unilever NV, 1965-77; Head of Research Division of Unilever Ltd, 1961-77; *b* 15 June 1917; *s* of Stanley Ernest Collingwood and Kathleen Muriel (*née* Smalley); *m* 1942, Pauline Winifred (*née* Jones); one *s* one *d*. *Educ:* Wycliffe Coll., Stonehouse, Glos. University Coll. London (BSc). English Charcoal, 1940-41; British Ropeway Engrg Co, 1941-44; De Havilland Engines, 1944-46; Olympia Oil and Cake Mills Ltd, 1946-49; British Oil and Cake Mills Ltd, 1949-51; Mem., UK Milling Group of Unilever Ltd, 1951-60; Dir, Advita Ltd, 1951-60; Dir, British Oil & Cake Mills Ltd, 1955-60. Instn of Chemical Engrs: Mem. Research Cttee, 1963-68; Mem. Council, 1964-67. Mem. Council of Univ. of Aston, 1971- (Chm., Academic Advisory Cttee, 1964-71); Mem., Research Cttee, CBI, 1970-71; Member: Council for Scientific Policy, 1971-72; Council, British Nutrition Foundn, 1970-; Food Standards Cttee, 1972-; Royal Commn on Environmental Pollution, 1973-. Hon. DSc, Aston, 1966; Fellow, University Coll. London, 1970. *Recreations:* sailing, music. *Address:* 54 Downs Road, Coulsdon, Surrey. *T:* Downland 54817.

COLLINGWOOD, Lawrance Arthur, CBE 1948; *b* 14 March 1887; *s* of J. H. Collingwood; *m* 1914, Anna Koenig, St Petersburg, Russia; two *s* two *d*. *Educ:* Westminster Abbey Choir Sch.; Exeter Coll., Oxford; St Petersburg Conservatoire. For 50 years associated with work for EMI (HMV); for 25 years associated with work of The Old Vic and Sadler's Wells, first as repetiteur, then conductor; musical dir of Sadler's Wells Opera Co., 1940-47. *Address:* Annalac, Rynachulig, Killin, Perthshire, Scotland.

COLLINGWOOD, Lt-Gen. Sir (Richard) George, KBE 1959 (CBE 1951); CB 1954; DSO 1944; *b* 7 Oct. 1903; 4th *s* of Col C. G. Collingwood, Lilburn Tower and Glanton Pyke, Northumberland. *Educ:* RN Colls Osborne and Dartmouth; RMC Sandhurst. Entered Cameronians, 1923; Brigadier, 1944; served in Middle East and Burma. GOC 52 Lowland Division and Lowland District, Oct. 1952-55; Maj.-Gen. 1953; GOC, Singapore District, 1957-58; GOC-in-C, Scottish Command, 1958-61; Gov. of Edinburgh Castle, 1958-61; retired, 1961. Col, The Cameronians (Scottish Rifles), 1964-68. A Mem. of the Jockey Club (Steward, 1960). Knight Grand Cross, Order of the Sword (Sweden), 1964. *Recreations:* hunting, shooting, racing. *Address:* Abbey Lands, Alnwick, Northumberland. *T:* Alnwick 2220. *Club:* Boodle's.

COLLINGWOOD, Brig. Sydney, CMG 1957; CBE 1945; MC 1917; retired; *b* 10 July 1892; *s* of late Sir William Collingwood, KBE, MICE, JP, Dedham Grove, near Colchester, Essex; *m* 1st, 1915, Charlotte Annie (decd), *d* of Colonel James Charles Oughterson, late 18th Royal Irish, Greenock; two *s* one *d*; 2nd, 1940, Eileen Mary, *widow* of late Major W. D. G. Batten, 3rd Gurkha Rifles, and *d* of A. Willson, Waldegrave Park, Twickenham. *Educ:* Liverpool Coll.; Royal Military Academy. 2nd Lieut, RA, 1912. Served European War, 1914-18. Major, 1930; Bt Lieut-Col 1934; Col, 1938; Brig., 1940; BGS, Southern Command, 1940-42; DDPS, War Office, 1942-46; retd, 1946. Regional Dir, Southern Region, Imperial War Graves Commission (Headquarters, Rome), 1946-57. Croix de Guerre, 1917. *Recreation:* rural preservation. *Address:* The Croft, Dedham, Colchester, Essex. *Club:* Naval and Military.

COLLINS, Brig. Arthur Francis St Clair, CBE 1940 (OBE 1918); MC; *b* 10 March 1892; *s* of late Dr A. H. Collins, Edinburgh; one *d*. *Educ:* Bedford Sch. 3rd Bn Beds Regt, 1911-13; ASC 1913; Temp. Capt., 1914; Adjt, 1917-18; Acting Major, 1918-19; Adjt, 1927-28; Major, 1933; Lt-Col, 1939; Temp. Col, 1940; Col, 1943; Brig., 1941-46; served France and Belgium, 1914-21 (despatches twice, 1914 Star, MC, OBE); Germany and Upper Silesia, 1919-21; India, 1926; Shanghai, 1927; BEF France, 1939-40 and 1945 (CBE); retired pay, 1946; AMIME 1933. *Recreations:* Rugby, tennis, golf, rowing. *Address:* 17 Ingles Road, Folkestone, Kent. *Club:* Army and Navy.

COLLINS, Basil Eugene Sinclair; Managing Director, Cadbury Schweppes Ltd, since 1974; *b* 21 Dec. 1923; *s* of Albert Collins and Pauline Alicia (*née* Wright); *m* 1942, Doris Slott; two *d*. *Educ:* Great Yarmouth Grammar School. Accountant, L. Rose & Co. Ltd, 1945, Sales Man. 1955; Export Dir, Schweppes (Overseas) Ltd, 1958; Group Admin Dir, Schweppes Ltd, 1964, Chm. of Overseas Gp 1968; Chm. of Overseas Gp, Cadbury Schweppes Ltd, 1969, Dep. Man. Dir 1972. Royal College of Nursing: Chm., Finance and General Purposes Cttee, 1970; Hon. Treasurer, 1970; Chm., Develt Trust, 1971; Vice-Pres., 1972. Fellow Inst. of Dirs, 1974; FZS 1975; FBIM 1976. *Recreations:* music, languages, travel, English countryside. *Address:* Clive House, Connaught Place, W2 2EX. *T:* 01-262 1212; Wyddial Parva, Buntingford, Herts SG9 0EL. *Club:* Carlton.

COLLINS, Bernard John, CBE 1960; town planner, retired; Controller (formerly Director) of Planning and Transportation, Greater London Council, 1969-74; *b* 3 July 1909; *s* of late John Philip and Amelia Bounevialle Collins; *m* 1937, Grete Elisabeth, *e d* of H. A. Piehler; one *s* three *d*. *Educ:* Ampleforth. Served Royal Artillery, 1939-45, North Africa (despatches) and Italy. Ryde Memorial Prizeman, RICS, 1937. President: Town Planning Inst., 1957-58; International Fedn of Surveyors, 1967-69; Mem. Bureau, Internat. Fedn for Housing and Planning, 1962-66; Vice-Pres., 1968-73, Sen. Vice-Pres., 1973-74, Pres., 1974-75, RICS; Mem. Board of Governors, Coll. of Estate Management, 1959-69; Vice-Chm. of Executive, Town and Country Planning Assoc., 1951-62; Chm., Assoc. of County Planning Officers, 1954-58; County Planning Officer, Middx, 1947-62; Sec. and Chief Exec. Commn for the New Towns, 1962-64; Dir of Planning, GLC, 1964-69; responsible for preparation of Greater London Develt Plan, 1969. Chairman, Technical Panel: Conf. on London and SE Regional Planning, 1964-74; Greater London and SE Regional Sports Council, 1966-74; advised on reorganisation of planning system, City of Jerusalem, 1971. Described by William Hickey of Daily Express as probably the world's top town planner. Pres. Honoraire, Fédération Internationale des Géomètres, 1970-; Hon. Mem., Deutscher Verein für Vermessungswesen (German Soc. of Surveyors), 1965-; Membre d'honneur, Union Belge des Géomètres-experts Immobiliers, 1976-. *Publications:* Development Plans Explained (HMSO), 1951; Middlesex Survey and Development Plan, 1952; numerous addresses, articles and papers on town planning. *Address:* Foxella, Matfield, Kent TN12 7ET. *Club:* Athenæum.

COLLINS, Sir Charles Henry, Kt 1947; CMG 1941; *b* 10 Feb. 1887; *s* of late C. H. Collins, Torquay; *m* 1913, Florence E. Campkin (*d* 1968); one *d* (one *s* and one *d* decd). *Educ:* King's Coll., Univ. of London. BA 1909. Entered Ceylon Civil Service, 1910; Dep. Chief Sec., 1940; Acting Financial Sec. in 1935, 1936, 1937, 1940, and 1943; Acting Chief Sec. in 1944, 1945 and 1947; adviser to govt on changes in administration and procedure in connection with introduction of new constitution, 1946; retired, 1948. *Publications:* Public Administration in Ceylon, 1951; Public Administration in Hong Kong, 1952. *Recreations:* historical and archæological studies. *Address:* Devoncroft, Clandon Road, West Clandon, Guildford, Surrey GU4 7TL. *T:* Guildford 222542. *Club:* Royal Commonwealth Society.

COLLINS, Sir David (Charles), Kt 1975; CBE 1969; Chairman: Normalair-Garrett Ltd, since 1968; Normalair-Garrett (Holdings) Ltd, since 1968; Westland Helicopters Ltd, 1968-76; Director: British Hovercraft Corporation Ltd; Westland Aircraft Ltd; Westland Engineers Ltd and other associated Westland Cos; *b* 23 Jan. 1908; *s* of Richard and Margaret Collins; *m* 1936, Dorothy Bootyman. *Educ:* grammar schs and Technical Coll. Qualified as Chartered Mechanical Engr. Student Apprentice, then Design Staff, Gloster Aircraft Ltd, 1928; Production Engr, Blackburn Aircraft Ltd, 1933; Fairey Aviation Ltd: Chief Planning Engr, 1941; Dep. Man., 1943; Man., 1946; joined Westland Aircraft Ltd as Works Dir, 1951; Dep. Man. Dir, 1959; Man. Dir, 1965; Chief Exec. and Chm. subsidiary cos, 1968; Chm., 1970-77. Council Member: CBI, 1966-76; Soc. of British Aerospace Cos Ltd. CEng, FIMechE, FIProdE, FRAeS. Founder Fellow, Fellowship of Engineering. Hon. DSc Bath, 1976. *Recreations:* golf, fishing. *Address:* Little Gables, Redwood Road, Sidmouth, Devon EX10 9AB. *T:* Sidmouth 6756. *Club:* Honiton Golf.

COLLINS, Sir Geoffrey Abdy, Kt 1952; *b* 5 June 1888; *y s* of Philip George and Susan Kate Collins; *m* 1936, Joan Mary, 2nd *d* of Albert Edward and Margaret Alice Ratcliffe; one *s* four *d*. *Educ:* Rugby; Christ's Coll., Cambridge (BA, LLB). Admitted solicitor, 1913. Served European War, 1914-18, in The Rifle Brigade (Capt.). Member: Royal UK Beneficent Assoc. Cttee, 1926-54 (Chm., 1950-54); Council of The Law Society, 1931-56, Pres., 1951-52. Past Master, Tylers and Bricklayers Co. *Address:* Mullion, 20 Ballard Estate, Swanage, Dorset. *T:* Swanage 2030.

COLLINS, Henry Edward, CBE 1948; Consulting Mining Engineer; Director, Inter-Continental Fuels Ltd; *b* 4 Oct. 1903; *s* of James Collins; *m* 1934, Cecilia Harris (*d* 1975); no *c*. *Educ:* Rotherham Grammar Sch.; Univ. of Sheffield (MEng). Sen. Lectr in Mining, Univ. of Sheffield, 1935-38; Manager, Rossington Main Colliery, Doncaster, 1939-42; Agent, Markham Colliery, Doncaster, 1942-44; Chief Mining Agent, Doncaster Amalgamated Collieries Ltd, 1944-45; Dir Coal Production, CCG, 1945-47; British Chm., UK/US Coal Control Gp, Germany (later Combined Coal Control Gp), 1947-50; Production Dir, Durham Div., NCB, 1950-56; Dir-Gen. of Reconstruction, NCB, 1956-57; Board Mem. for Production, NCB, 1957-67; Consultant to NCB, 1967-69. Mem., Govtl Cttee on Coal Derivatives, 1959-60; Chairman: NCB Opencast Executive, 1961-67; NCB Brickworks Executive, 1962-67; Whittlesea Central Brick Co. Ltd, 1966-67; Field Research Steering Cttee, Min. of Power, 1964-67; Past Director: Omnia Concrete Sales Ltd; Bradley's (Concrete) Ltd; Powell Duffryn Technical Services Ltd; Member: Minister of Power's Adv. Council on Research and Develt, 1963-67; Min. of Power Nat. Jt Pneumoconiosis Cttee, 1964-67; Safety in Mines (Adv.) Bd; Mining Qualifications Bd, 1962-69. Pres., Inst. of Mining Engineers, 1962. *Publications:* numerous papers on mining engineering subjects. *Address:* Rising Sun, 22a West Side, Wimbledon Common, SW19 4UF. *T:* 01-946 3949. *Club:* Athenæum.

COLLINS, Vice-Adm. Sir John (Augustine), KBE 1951; CB 1940; RAN retired; *b* Deloraine, Tasmania, 7 Jan. 1899; *s* of Michael John Collins, MD; *m* 1930, Phyllis Laishley, *d* of A. J. McLachlan; one *d*. *Educ:* Royal Australian Naval Coll. Served European War with Grand Fleet and Harwich Force, 1917-18; thereafter in various HM and HMA Ships abroad and in Australian waters; Squadron Gunnery Officer, HMA Squadron; Liaison Officer for visit of Duke and Duchess of York to Australia; in command HMAS Anzac; staff course; Asst Chief of Naval Staff, Australia; Capt. HMAS Sydney (CB), 1939-41; Asst Chief of Staff to C-in-C, China, 1941 (despatches); Cdre comdg China Force, 1942 (Comdr of Order of Orange Nassau); Capt. HMAS Shropshire, 1943-44; Cdre comdg HM Australian Sqdn (wounded), 1944-46; idc 1947; Chief of Naval Staff and First Naval Mem., Australian Commonwealth Naval Bd, Melbourne, 1948-55; Australian High Comr to New Zealand, 1956-62. Officer of Legion of Merit (US); Royal Humane Society's Certificate for Saving Life at Sea. *Publication:* As Luck Would Have It, 1965. *Recreation:* golf. *Address:* 13 Dumaresq Road, Rose Bay, Sydney, NSW 2029, Australia. *Club:* Royal Sydney Golf.

COLLINS, John Ernest Harley, MBE 1944; DSC 1945 and Bar 1945; DL; Chairman of Morgan Grenfell Holdings Ltd and Guardian Royal Exchange Assurance since 1974; *b* 24 April 1923; *o s* of late G. W. Collins, Taynton, Glos; *m* 1946, Gillian, *e d* of 2nd Baron Bicester; one *s* one *d*. *Educ:* King Edward's Sch., Birmingham; Birmingham Univ. Royal Navy, 1941-46. Morgan Grenfell & Co. Ltd, 1946, Dir 1957. Director: Royal Exchange Assce, 1957; Rank Hovis McDougall Ltd; Charter Consolidated

Ltd; Debenture Corp. Ltd; National Bank of Australasia; Chm. United Services Trustee, 1968-76. DL Oxon, 1975; High Sheriff, Oxon, 1975. *Recreations:* most outdoor sports. *Address:* Tusmore Park, Bicester, Oxon. *T:* Fritwell 209. *Clubs:* Brooks's, White's, Pratt's.

COLLINS, (John) Martin, QC 1972; a Recorder of the Crown Court, since 1972; *b* 24 Jan. 1929; *s* of John Lissant Collins and Marjorie Mary Collins; *m* 1957, Daphne Mary, *d* of George Martyn Swindells, Prestbury; two *s* one *d*. *Educ:* Uppingham Sch.; Manchester Univ. (LLB). Called to Bar, Gray's Inn, 1952. Dep. Chm., Cumberland QS, 1969-72. *Address:* 2 Pump Court, Temple, EC4; Pott Hall, Pott Shrigley, Macclesfield, Cheshire. *Clubs:* Athenæum, Bath.

COLLINS, Maj.-Gen. Joseph Clinton, CB 1953; CBE 1951 (OBE 1946); *b* 8 Jan. 1895; British; *m* 1925, Eileen Patricia Williams; two *d*. *Educ:* London Hosp. Served European War, 1914-18, France and Belgium, 1914; Surgeon Probationer, RNVR, 1915-16; Lieut, RAMC, 1917; Egyptian Army, 1923-33; DDMS, BAOR, 1946-49; DMS Far ELF, 1949-51; DMS Northern Command, 1951-53; KHS 1951-54; Dir Medical Services, BAOR, 1953-Dec. 1954, retired. CStJ 1948. 3rd Class Order of Nile. *Address:* c/o Williams & Glyn's Bank Ltd, Whitehall, SW1.

COLLINS, Gen. (retd) J(oseph) Lawton, DSM 1942 (Oak Leaf Cluster, 1943, 1944, 1953); Silver Star, 1943 (Army Oak Leaf Cluster, and Navy Gold Star, 1944); Legion of Merit, 1943 (Oak Leaf Cluster, 1945); Bronze Star Medal, 1944; Director, Chas Pfizer & Co. Inc., 1957-69; Vice-Chairman, Pfizer International Subsidiaries 1957-72; *b* New Orleans, La, 1 May 1896; *s* of Jeremiah Bernard Collins and Catherine Lawton; *m* 1921, Gladys Easterbrook; one *s* two *d*. *Educ:* Louisiana State Univ.; US Military Academy. 2nd Lieut, Infantry, 1917; 22nd Infantry, Fort Hamilton, NY, until Jan. 1918; graduated Inf. Sch. of Arms, Fort Sill, Oklahoma, 1918; went overseas and took command of bn of 18th Inf., Coblenz, 1919; Asst Chief of Staff, Plans and Training Div., American Forces in Germany, until 1921; Instr, US Mil. Acad., 1921-25; graduated: Inf. Sch., Fort Benning, Ga, 1926; Advanced Course, Field Artillery Sch., Fort Sill, Oklahoma, 1927; Instr, Inf. Sch., 1927-31; student, Comd and Gen. Staff Sch., Fort Leavenworth, Kansas, 1931-33; with 23rd Bde (Philippine Scouts), Fort William McKinley, and Asst Chief of Staff, Mil. Intell., Philippine Div., until 1936; Student: Army Industrial Coll., 1936-37; Army War Coll., 1937-38; Instr there, 1938-40. Served War of 1939-45; Office of Sec., War Dept Gen. Staff, 1940-41; Chief of Staff, VII Army Corps, 1941; Chief of Staff, Hawaiian Dept, 1941; Comdg Gen., 25th Inf. Div. in Guadalcanal ops, New Georgia Campaign, 1942-43; comd VII Army Corps, European Theater, for Invasion of France, 1944; and subseq. campaigns to end of hostilities, 1945; Dep. Comdg Gen. and Chief of Staff, HQ, Army Ground Forces, 1945; Dir of Information, War Dept, 1945; Dep. Chief of Staff, US Army, 1947, and Vice Chief of Staff (upon creation of that post), 1948; Chief of Staff, US Army, 1949-53; US Rep., Standing Group, NATO and US Mem. Mil. Cttee, 1953-56; US Special Rep. in Viet Nam with personal rank Ambassador, Nov. 1954-May 1955. Holds hon. degrees. Army of Occupation Medal, Germany, European War, 1914-18, and War of 1939-45; American Defense Service Medal; Asiatic-Pacific Medal; European-African-Middle Eastern Campaign Ribbon. (In addition to above US decorations) Hon. CB (British) 1945; Order of Suvorov, 2nd Class, twice (Russian); Croix de Guerre with Palm, Legion of Honor, Degree of Grand Officer (French); Order of Leopold II, Grand Officer Croix de Guerre with Palm (Belgian). *Address:* 4000 Massachusetts Avenue, NW, Washington, DC 20016, USA. *T:* 362-0971. *Clubs:* Army and Navy (Washington, DC); Chevy Chase (Md).

COLLINS, Rear-Adm. Kenneth St Barbe, CB 1959; OBE 1945; DSC 1942; *b* 9 June 1904; *s* of late Charles Bury Collins, Col RE and late Ethel St Barbe; *m* 1932, Helen Mary Keen; one *s* one *d*. *Educ:* Lydgate House Sch., Hunstanton, Norfolk; RN Colls Osborne and Dartmouth. Midshipman, HMS Warspite, 1922, Vimiera, 1923; Sub-Lt, HMS Fitzroy, 1925; Lt and Lt-Comdr surveying ships, 1927-37; Seaplane Carrier, HMS Albatross, 1939; (as Comdr) Staff of Allied Naval Expeditionary Force, North Africa, 1942; staff of Allied Naval Expeditionary Force, Europe, 1943; surveying, 1947-54; Hydrographer of the Navy, 1955-60; Rear-Adm., 1957; retd 1960. Consultant to the Survey and Mapping Branch of Dept of Mines and Technical Surveys, Ottawa, 1960-63. *Address:* The Old Parsonage, Bentley, near Farnham, Surrey. *T:* Bentley 3227.

COLLINS, Canon Lewis John; Canon since 1948, and Treasurer since 1970, of St Paul's Cathedral (Chancellor, 1948-53; Precentor, 1953-70); *b* 23 March 1905; *s* of Arthur Collins and

Hannah Priscilla; m 1939, Diana Clavering Elliot; four s. Educ: Cranbrook Sch.; Sidney Sussex Coll. and Westcott House, Cambridge. Curate of Whitstable, 1928-29; Chaplain, Sidney Sussex Coll., Cambridge, 1929-31; Minor Canon of St Paul's Cathedral, 1931-34; a Dep. Priest-in-Ordinary to HM the King, 1931-34, Priest-in-Ordinary, 1934-35; Vice-Principal, Westcott House, Cambridge, 1934-37; Chaplain RAFVR, 1940-45; Dean of Oriel Coll., Oxford, 1938-48; Fellow Lecturer and Chaplain, 1937-48. Chairman: Campaign for Nuclear Disarmament, 1958-64; Martin Luther King Foundn, 1969-73; President: Christian Action, 1959- (Chairman, 1946-73); Internat. Defence and Aid Fund, 1964-. Order of Grand Companion of Freedom, Third Div., Zambia, 1970; Commander, Order of the Northern Star, Sweden, 1976. Publications: The New Testament Problem, 1937; A Theology of Christian Action, 1949; Faith Under Fire, 1966; contributor, Three Views of Christianity, 1962. Address: 2 Amen Court, EC4. T: 01-248 3747.

COLLINS, Martin; see Collins, J. M.

COLLINS, Michael; Director, National Air and Space Museum, Smithsonian Institution, since 1971; former NASA Astronaut; Command Module Pilot, Apollo 11 rocket flight to the Moon, July 1969; b Rome, Italy, 31 Oct. 1930; s of Maj.-Gen. and Mrs James L. Collins, Washington, DC, USA; m 1957, Patricia M. Finnegan, Boston, Mass; one s two d. Educ: St Albans Sch., Washington, DC (grad.). US Mil. Academy, West Point, NY (BSc); advanced through grades to Colonel; Harvard Business Sch. (AMP), 1974. Served as an experimental flight test officer, Air Force Flight Test Center, Edwards Air Force Base, Calif; he was one of the third group of astronauts named by NASA in Oct. 1963; served as backup pilot for Gemini 7 mission; as pilot with John Young on the 3-day 44-revolution Gemini 10 mission, launched 18 July 1966, he shared record-setting flight (successful rendezvous and docking with a separately launched Agena target vehicle; he also completed two periods of extravehicular activity); subseq. assigned as Command Module Pilot for the third manned Apollo flight, and was in orbit 20 July 1969, when Neil Armstrong and Edwin Aldrin landed on the Moon. Asst Sec. of State for Public Affairs, US, 1970-71. Maj. Gen. Air Force Reserve. Dir, AF Historical Foundn; Member Bd of Governors: St Albans Sch.; Nat. Space Club; Nat. Aviation Club; Mem. Bd of Trustees, Theodore Von Karman Meml Foundn Inc.; Mem., General Thomas D. White USAF Space Trophy Cttee; Member: Soc. of Experimental Test Pilots; Internat. Acad. of Astronautics of Internat. Astronautical Fedn; Washington Inst. of Foreign Affairs. FAIAA; Fellow, Amer. Astronautical Soc. Member, Order of Daedalians. Hon. degrees from: Stonehill Coll.; St Michael's Coll.; Northeastern Univ.; Southeastern Univ. Further awards include Presidential Medal of Freedom, NASA; DSM; Exceptional Service Medal; Air Force: DSM; Astronaut Wings; DFC. Publications: Carrying the Fire (autobiog.), 1974; Flying to the Moon and Other Strange Places (for children), 1976. Recreations: fishing, handball. Address: National Air and Space Museum, Smithsonian Institution, Washington, DC 20560, USA. Club: Cosmos.

COLLINS, Miss Nina; see Lowry, Mrs N. M.

COLLINS, Norman Richard; Director, Associated Television Corporation Ltd (formerly Deputy Chairman); former Director: ATV Network Ltd; Independent Television News Co.; Independent Broadcasting Services Ltd; Governor, Sadler's Wells Foundation; Chairman: Central School of Speech and Drama; Loch Ness Investigation Bureau; b 3 Oct. 1907; s of late Oliver Norman Collins; m 1931, Sarah Helen, d of Arthur Francis Martin; one s two d. Educ: William Ellis Sch., Hampstead. At Oxford Univ. Press, 1926-29; Asst Literary Editor, News-Chronicle, 1929-33; Dep. Chm., Victor Gollancz Ltd, publishers, 1934-41. Controller Light Programme, BBC, 1946-47; late Gen. Overseas Service Dir, BBC; Controller Television, BBC, 1947-50, resigned. Governor, British Film Inst., 1949-51; Governor, Atlantic Inst, 1965-69; Member: Council, English Stage Co.; Exec. Cttee, Nat. Book League, 1965-69. General Comr of Taxes, 1967-. President: Appeals Cttee, Nat. Playing Fields Assoc., 1967-69; Adoption Cttee for Aid to Displaced Persons, 1962-70; Radio Industries Club, 1950; Pitman Fellowship, 1957; Regent Advertising Club, 1959-66. Chm., Age Action Year, 1976. Publications: The Facts of Fiction, 1932; Penang Appointment, 1934; The Three Friends, 1935; Trinity Town, 1936; Flames Coming Out of the Top, 1937; Love in Our Time, 1938; "I Shall not want", 1940; Anna, 1942; London belongs to Me, 1945 (TV series, 1977); Black Ivory, 1947; Children of the Archbishop, 1951; The Bat That Flits, 1952; The Bond Street Story, 1958; The Governor's Lady, 1968; The Captain's Lamp (play), 1938. Address: Mulberry House, Church Row, NW3. Clubs: Carlton, Turf, MCC.

COLLINS, Pauline; actress (stage and television); b Exmouth, Devon, 3 Sept. 1940; d of William Henry Collins and Mary Honora Callanan; m John Alderton, qv; two s one d. Educ: Convent of the Sacred Heart, Hammersmith, London; Central Sch. of Speech and Drama. Stage: 1st appearance in A Gazelle in Park Lane, Theatre Royal, Windsor, 1962; 1st London appearance in Passion Flower Hotel, Prince of Wales, 1965; The Erpingham Camp, Royal Court, 1967; The Happy Apple, Hampstead, 1967, and Apollo, 1970; Importance of Being Earnest, Haymarket, 1968; The Night I chased the Women with an Eel, 1969; Come As You Are (2 parts), New, 1970; Judies, Comedy, 1974; Engaged, National Theatre, Old Vic, 1975; Confusions, Apollo, 1976; television, 1962-: series: Upstairs Downstairs; No Honestly; P. G. Wodehouse. Address: c/o Chartwell Artists Ltd, 3 Hill Street, W1.

COLLINS, Peter G., RSA 1974 (ARSA 1966); painter in oil; lecturer, Duncan of Jordanstone College of Art, Dundee; b Inverness, 21 June 1935; s of E. G. Collins, FRCSE; m 1959, Myra Mackintosh; one s one d. Educ: Fettes Coll., Edinburgh; Edinburgh Coll. of Art. Studied in Italy, on Andrew Grant Major Travelling Scholarship, 1957-58. Work in permanent collections: Aberdeen Civic; Glasgow Civic; Scottish Arts Council. Recreations: music and procrastination. Address: Royal Scottish Academy, The Mound, Edinburgh; 28 Baxter Park Terrace, Dundee.

COLLINS, Prof. Philip Arthur William; Professor of English, University of Leicester, since 1964; Head of Department of English, 1971-76; Public Orator, since 1975; b 28 May 1923; er s of Arthur Henry and Winifred Nellie Collins; m 1st, 1952, Mildred Lowe (marr. diss. 1963); 2nd, 1965, Joyce Dickins; two s one d. Educ: Brentwood Sch.; Emmanuel Coll., Cambridge (Sen. Schol.). MA 1948. Served War (RAOC and Royal Norfolk Regt), 1942-45. Leicester: Staff Tutor in Adult Educn, 1947; Warden, Vaughan Coll., 1954; Sen. Lectr in English, 1962-64; Prof., 1964. Visiting Prof.: Univ. of California, Berkeley, 1967; Columbia, 1969; Victoria Univ., NZ, 1974. Sec., Leicester Theatre Trust Ltd, 1963-; Member: Drama Panel, Arts Council of Gt Britain, 1970-75; National Theatre Bd, 1976-. Many overseas lecture-tours; performances, talks and scripts for radio and television. Publications: James Boswell, 1956; (ed) English Christmas, 1956; Dickens and Crime, 1962; Dickens and Education, 1963; The Canker and the Rose (Shakespeare Quater-centenary celebration) perf. Mermaid Theatre, London, 1964; The Impress of the Moving Age, 1965; Thomas Cooper the Chartist, 1969; A Dickens Bibliography, 1970; Dickens's Bleak House, 1971; (ed) Dickens, the Critical Heritage, 1971; (ed) A Christmas Carol: the public reading version, 1971; Reading Aloud: a Victorian Métier, 1972; (ed) Dickens's Public Readings, 1975; Dickens's David Copperfield, 1977; contrib. to: Encyclopaedia Britannica, Dickensian, Essays and Studies, Notes and Queries, Listener, Review of English Studies, TLS. Recreations: theatre, theatricals, music. Address: 26 Knighton Drive, Leicester LE2 3HB. T: Leicester 706026.

COLLINS, Stuart Verdun, CB 1970; retired; Chief Inspector of Audit, Department of the Environment (formerly Ministry of Housing and Local Government), 1968-76; b 24 Feb. 1916; m 1st, 1942, Helen Simpson (d 1968); two d; 2nd, 1970, Joan Mary Walmsley (widow); one step s two step d. Educ: Plymouth Coll. Entered Civil Service as Audit Assistant in the District Audit Service of the Ministry of Health, 1934; appointed District Auditor for the London Audit District, 1958. IPFA, FBCS. Recreations: golf, do-it-yourself, sailing. Address: Kemendine, Court Wood, Newton Ferrers, Devon.

COLLINS, Brig. Thomas Frederick James, CBE 1945 (OBE 1944); JP; DL; b 9 April 1905; s of Capt. J. A. Collins and Emily (née Truscott); m 1942, Marjorie Morwenna, d of Lt-Col T. Donnelly, DSO; one d. Educ: Haileybury; RMC, Sandhurst. Gazetted to Green Howards, 1924; Staff College, 1938. Served War of 1939-45 (despatches twice, OBE, CBE): France, 1940, NW Europe, 1944-45. Retired, with rank of Brig., 1948. Essex County Council: CC, 1960; Vice-Chm., 1967; Chm., 1968-71. JP 1968, DL 1969, Essex. Comdr, Order of Leopold II (Belgium), 1945. Recreation: shooting. Address: Ashdon Hall, Saffron Walden, Essex. T: Ashdon 232. Club: Army and Navy.

COLLINSON, Prof. Patrick, PhD; FRHistS, FAHA; Professor of History, University of Kent at Canterbury, since 1976; b 10 Aug. 1929; s of William Cecil Collinson and Belle Hay (née Patrick); m 1960, Elizabeth Albinia Susan Selwyn; two s two d. Educ: King's Sch., Ely; Pembroke Coll., Cambridge (Exhibnr 1949, Foundn Scholar 1952; BA 1952, 1st Cl. Hons Hist. Tripos Pt II; Hadley Prize for Hist., 1952). PhD London, 1957; FRHistS 1967; FAHA 1974. University of London: Postgrad. Student, Royal Holloway Coll., 1952-54; Res. Fellow, Inst. of

Hist. Res., 1954-55; Res. Asst, UCL, 1955-56; Lectr in Hist., Univ. of Khartoum, 1956-61; Asst Lectr in Eccles. Hist., King's Coll., Univ. of London, 1961-62, Lectr, 1962-69 (Fellow 1976); Prof. of Hist., Univ. of Sydney, 1969-75. Ford's Lectr in Eng. Hist., Univ. of Oxford, 1978-79. *Publications:* The Elizabethan Puritan Movement, 1967 (USA 1967); articles and revs in Bull. Inst. Hist. Res., Eng. Hist. Rev., Hist., Jl Eccles. Hist., Studies in Church Hist., TLS. *Recreations:* mountains, fishing, music, gardening. *Address:* 73 Beaconsfield Road, Canterbury, Kent. *T:* Canterbury 55121.

COLLINSON, Richard Jeffreys Hampton; His Honour Judge Collinson; a Circuit Judge, since 1975; *b* 7 April 1924; *s* of Kenneth Hampton Collinson and Edna Mary Collinson; *m* 1955, Gwendolen Hester Ward; two *s* two *d. Educ:* Heath Grammar Sch., Halifax; Wadham Coll., Oxford (BCL, MA). Sub-Lieut, RNVR, 1944-46. Called to Bar, Middle Temple, 1950; Northern Circuit. Councillor, then Alderman, Wallasey County Borough Council, 1957-74, Leader of Council, 1965-72. *Address:* Merehaven, 2 Mere Lane, Wallasey, Merseyside L45 3HY. *T:* 051-639 5818.

COLLIS, John Stewart; author; *b* 16 Feb. 1900; *s* of W. S. Collis and Edith (*née* Barton), Irish; *m* 1929, Eirene Joy; two *d*; *m* 1974, Lady Beddington-Behrens. *Educ:* Rugby Sch.; Balliol Coll., Oxford (BA). FRSL. *Publications:* include: Shaw, 1925; Forward to Nature, 1927; Farewell to Argument, 1935; The Sounding Cataract, 1936; An Irishman's England, 1937; While Following the Plough, 1946; Down to Earth, 1947 (Heinemann Foundation Award); The Triumph of the Tree, 1950; The Moving Waters, 1955; Paths of Light, 1959; An Artist of Life, 1959; Marriage and Genius, 1963; The Life of Tolstoy, 1969; Bound upon a Course (autobiog.), 1971; The Carlyles, 1972; The Vision of Glory, 1972; The Worm Forgives the Plough, 1973; Christopher Columbus, 1976. *Recreation:* tennis. *Address:* Park House, Abinger Common, Dorking, Surrey. *T:* Dorking 730412.

COLLISON, family name of **Baron Collison.**

COLLISON, Baron (Life Peer) *cr* 1964, of Cheshunt; **Harold Francis Collison,** CBE 1961; Chairman, Supplementary Benefits Commission, 1969-75; *b* 10 May 1909; *m* 1946, Ivy Kate Hanks.*Educ:* The Hay Currie LCC Sch.; Crypt Sch., Gloucester. Firstly, worked in a commercial office in London; farm worker in Glos, 1934-53. National Union of Agricultural Workers (later Nat. Union of Agricultural and Allied Workers): District Organiser in Gloucester and Worcs, 1944; Nat. Officer, 1946; General Secretary, 1953-69. Mem., TUC Gen. Coun., 1953-69, Chm., 1964-65; Chm., Social Insce and Industrial Welfare Cttee of TUC, 1957-69. President: Internat. Fedn of Plantation, Agricultural and Allied Workers, 1960-76; Assoc. of Agriculture, 1976-; Member: Coun. on Tribunals, 1959-69; Nat. Insce Adv. Cttee, 1959-69; Governing Body of ILO, 1960-69; Pilkington Cttee on Broadcasting, 1960-62; Central Transport Consultative Cttee, 1962-70; Agric. Adv. Council, 1962; Adv. Cttee on Agricultural Educn, 1963; Royal Commn on Trades Unions and Employers' Assocs, 1965-68; Home-Grown Cereals Authority, 1965-; Industrial Health Adv. Cttee; Economic Develt for Agriculture; Industrial Consultative Cttee, Approach to Europe; Overseas Labour Consultative Cttee; Agric. Productivity Cttee, British Productivity Council; Chairman: Land Settlement Assoc., 1977- (Vice-Chm., 1964-74); Agric. Apprenticeship Council, 1968-74; Mem., N Thames Gas Board (part-time), 1961-72. *Recreations:* gardening, chess. *Address:* Honeywood, 163 Old Nazeing Road, Broxbourne, Herts. *T:* Hoddesdon 63597.

COLLISON, Lewis Herbert, TD; MA; Headmaster of Liverpool College, 1952-70; *b* 30 July 1908; *s* of late Mr and Mrs W. H. Collison; *m* 1934, Edna Mollie Ivens; two *d. Educ:* Mill Hill Sch.; St John's Coll., Cambridge. Asst Master of Sedbergh Sch., 1931-40; Major in King's Own Royal Regt, 1940-45; Housemaster of Sedbergh Sch., 1946-52. Mem. Council, University of Liverpool, 1963-69. JP Liverpool, 1958-70. *Recreations:* pottery, sailing. *Address:* Ithaca, Boat Dyke Lane, Upton, Norfolk NR13 6BL. *Club:* Hawks (Cambridge).

COLMAN, Anthony David, QC 1977; barrister-at-law; *b* 27 May 1938; *s* of Solomon Colman and Helen Colman; *m* 1964, Angela Glynn; two *d. Educ:* Harrogate Grammar Sch.; Trinity Hall, Cambridge (MA). Called to the Bar, Gray's Inn, 1962. *Publication:* 2nd edn, Mathew's Practice of the Commercial Court (1902), 1967. *Recreations:* cricket, opera, gardening, the 17th Century, Sifnos. *Address:* 4 Essex Court, Temple, EC4Y 9AJ. *T:* 01-353 6771.

COLMAN, David Stacy, MA; retired; *b* Broughty Ferry, Angus, 1 May 1906; *yr s* of Dr H. C. Colman; *m* 1934, Sallie Edwards (*d*

1970). *Educ:* Shrewsbury Sch.; Balliol Coll., Oxford (Scholar). 1st Class Hon. Mods, 1926; 1st Class Lit. Hum., 1928. Asst Master at Shrewsbury Sch., 1928-31 and 1935-36; Fellow of Queen's Coll., Oxford and Praelector in Classics and Ancient History, 1931-34; Headmaster, C of E Grammar Sch., Melbourne, 1937-38; Shrewsbury School: Asst Master, 1938-66; Master of Day Boys, 1949-61; Librarian, 1961-66. Mem Council, Soc. for Promotion of Roman Studies, 1958-61, Classical Assoc., 1961-64. *Publication:* Sabrinae Corolla: The Classics at Shrewsbury School under Dr Butler and Dr Kennedy, 1950. *Address:* 19 Woodfield Road, Shrewsbury SY3 8HZ. *T:* 53749. *Clubs:* National Liberal; Leander; Salop (Shrewsbury).

COLMAN, Elijah Alec, JP; Chairman: E. Alec Colman Group of Companies; Langham Life Assurance Co. Ltd; Datakeep Ltd; *b* Tipton, Staffs, 7 Jan. 1903; *s* of Abraham and Leah Colman; *m* 1956, Eileen Amelia Graham; no *c. Educ:* Tipton Green Coun. Sch., Staffs. Dir of numerous charitable organisations; concerned with rehabilitation of refugees throughout the world; Chm., British Friends of Bar-Ilan Univ.; Exec. Mem., Jt Palestine Appeal; Dep. Chm., Anglo-Israel Chamber of Commerce. Mem. Ct, Patternmakers Co. JP Inner London, 1962. Hon. PhD, Bar-Ilan Univ., 1974. *Recreations:* reading, philosophy. *Clubs:* East India, Devonshire, Sports and Public Schools, City Livery, Royal Automobile.

COLMAN, Sir Michael (Jeremiah), 3rd Bt *cr* 1907; *b* 7 July 1928; *s* of Sir Jeremiah Colman, 2nd Bt, and Edith Gwendolyn Tritton; *S* father, 1961; *m* 1955, Judith Jean Wallop, *d* of Vice-Adm. Sir Peveril William-Powlett, *qv*; two *s* three *d. Educ:* Eton. Director: Reckitt & Colman Ltd; Waterer's Sons & Crisp Ltd. Capt., Yorks Yeomanry, RARO, 1967. *Recreations:* farming, shooting. *Heir:* *s* Jeremiah Michael Powlett Colman, *b* 23 Jan. 1958. *Address:* Malshanger, Basingstoke, Hants. *T:* Basingstoke 780241; Tarvie, Bridge of Cally, Blairgowrie, Perthshire. *T:* Strathardle 264. *Club:* Cavalry and Guards.

COLOMBO, Archbishop of, (RC), since 1977; **Most Rev. Nicholas Marcus Fernando,** STD; *b* 6 Dec. 1932. *Educ:* St Aloysius Seminary, Colombo; Universitas Propaganda Fide, Rome. BA (London); STD (Rome). Chairman, Episcopal Commission for Seminaries, Sri Lanka. *Address:* Archbishop's House, Colombo 8, Sri Lanka. *T:* 95471.

COLOMBO, Emilio; President of the European Parliament, since 1977; *b* Potenza, Italy, 11 April 1920. *Educ:* Rome Univ. Deputy: Constituent Assembly, 1946-48; Italian Parliament (Christian Democrat), 1948-; Under-Secretary: of Agriculture, 1948-51; of Public Works, 1953-55; Minister: of Agriculture, 1955-58; of Foreign Trade, 1958-59; of Industry and Commerce, 1959-60, March-April 1960, July 1960-63; of the Treasury, 1963-70, Feb.-May 1972, 1974-76; Prime Minister, 1970-72; Minister of State for UN Affairs, 1972-73; Minister of Finance, 1973-74. European Parliament: Mem., 1976-; Chm., Political Affairs Cttee, 1976-77. Formerly Vice-Pres., Italian Catholic Youth Assoc. *Address:* Camera dei Deputati, Rome, Italy; Via Aurelia 239, Rome, Italy.

COLQUHOUN, Maj.-Gen. Sir Cyril (Harry), KCVO 1968 (CVO 1965); CB 1955; OBE 1945; late Royal Artillery; Secretary of the Central Chancery of the Orders of Knighthood, 1960-68; Extra Gentleman Usher to the Queen since 1968; *b* 1903; *s* of late Capt. Harry Colquhoun; *m* 1930, Stella Irene, *d* of late W. C. Rose, Kotagiri, India, and Cheam, Surrey; one *s*. Served War of 1939-45 (despatches, OBE); Palestine, 1946-48 (despatches); Comdr, 6th, 76th and 1st Field Regiments; CRA 61st Div., 1945; CRA 6th Airborne Div., 1947-48; CRA 1st Infantry Div., 1949-50; Comdt, Sch. of Artillery, 1951-53; GOC 50th (Northumbrian) Infantry Div. (TA), and Northumbrian District, 1954-56; GOC Troops, Malta, 1956-59; retired 1960. Col Commandant: Royal Artillery, 1962-69; Royal Malta Artillery, 1962-70. *Recreations:* gardening, shooting. *Address:* Longwalls, Shenington, Banbury, Oxon OX15 6NQ. *T:* Edgehill 246. *Club:* Army and Navy.

COLQUHOUN, Rev. Canon Frank, MA; Canon Residentiary of Norwich Cathedral, since 1973, Vice-Dean since 1974; *b* 28 Oct. 1909; *s* of Rev. R. W. Colquhoun; *m* 1st, 1934, Dora Gertrude Hearne Slater; one *s* one *d*; 2nd, 1973, Judy Kenney. *Educ:* Warwick Sch.; Durham Univ. LTh 1932, BA 1933, MA 1937, Durham. Deacon, 1933; Priest, 1934; Curate, St Faith, Maidstone, 1933-35; Curate, New Malden, Surrey, 1935-39; Vicar, St Michael and All Angels, Blackheath Park, SE3, 1939-46; Editorial Sec., Nat. Church League, 1946-52; Priest-in-Charge, Christ Church, Woburn Square, WC1, 1952-54; Vicar of Wallington, Surrey, 1954-61; Canon Residentiary of Southwark Cathedral, 1961-73; Principal, Southwark Ordination Course, 1966-72. Editor, The Churchman, 1946-53.

Publications: Harringay Story, 1954; Your Child's Baptism, 1958; The Gospels, 1961; Total Christianity, 1962; The Catechism, 1963; Lent with Pilgrim's Progress, 1965; Christ's Ambassadors, 1965; (ed) The Living Church in the Parish, 1952; (ed) Parish Prayers, 1967; (ed) Hard Questions, 1967; Preaching through the Christian Year, 1972; Strong Son of God, 1973; Preaching at the Parish Communion, 1974; Contemporary Parish Prayers, 1975. *Recreations:* writing, listening to music. *Address:* 27 The Close, Norwich NR1 4DZ. *T:* Norwich 28506.

COLQUHOUN of Luss, Captain Sir Ivar (Iain), 8th Bt *cr* 1786; JP; DL; Hon. Sheriff (formerly Hon. Sheriff Substitute); Chief of the Clan; Grenadier Guards; *b* 4 Jan. 1916; *s* of Sir Iain Colquhoun, 7th Bt, and Geraldine Bryde (Dinah) (*d* 1974), *d* of late F. J. Tennant; *S* father, 1948; *m* 1943, Kathleen, 2nd *d* of late W. A. Duncan and of Mrs Duncan, 53 Cadogan Square, SW1; one *s*. one *d* (and one *s* decd). *Educ:* Eton. JP 1951, DL 1952, Dunbartonshire. *Heir: s* Malcolm Rory Colquhoun, Younger of Luss, *b* 20 Dec. 1947. *Address:* Camstraddan, Luss, Dunbartonshire; Eilean da Mheinn, Crinan, Argyllshire; 37 Radnor Walk, SW3. *Clubs:* White's, Royal Ocean Racing. *See also Duke of Argyll.*

COLQUHOUN, Ms Maureen Morfydd; MP (Lab) Northampton North, since Feb. 1974; *b* 12 Aug. 1928; *m* 1949, Keith Colquhoun; two *s* one *d*. Councillor: Shoreham UDC, 1965-74; Adur District Council, 1973-; County Councillor, West Sussex, 1973-. *Recreations:* walking, camping. *Address:* 16 King's Walk, Shoreham-by-Sea, West Sussex BN4 5LG. *T:* Shoreham-by-Sea 3854.

COLSTON, Michael; Chairman and Managing Director, Charles Colston Group Ltd, since 1969; *b* 24 July 1932; *s* of Sir Charles Blampied Colston, CBE, MC, DCM, FCGI and Lady (Eliza Foster) Colston, MBE; *m* 1st, 1956, Jane Olivia Kilham Roberts (marr. diss.); three *d*; 2nd, 1977, Judith Angela Briggs. *Educ:* Ridley Coll., Canada; Stowe; Gonville and Caius Coll., Cambridge. Joined 17th/21st Lancers, 1952; later seconded to 1st Royal Tank Regt for service in Korea. Founder Dir Charles Colston Group Ltd (formerly Colston Appliances Ltd) together with late Sir Charles Colston, 1955; Chm. and Man. Dir, Colston Appliances Ltd, 1969-76. Chairman: Tallent Engineering Ltd, 1969; ITS Rubber Ltd, 1969; Dishwasher Develt Council, 1970-75; Vice-Chm., Assoc. Manufrs of Domestic Electrical Appliances, 1975. Member Council: Inst. of Directors (Chm., Thames Valley Br.); British Electrotechnical Approvals Bd. *Recreations:* fishing, shooting, tennis; founder Cambridge Univ. Water Ski Club. *Address:* Ewelme Park, Nettlebed, Oxfordshire. *T:* Nettlebed 641279.

COLT, Sir Edward (William Dutton), 10th Bt *cr* 1694; MB, MRCP; Consultant in Endocrinology, St Barnabas Hospital, Bronx, New York; Assistant Attending Physician, St Luke's Hospital, New York; Associate in Clinical Medicine, Columbia University, New York; *b* 22 Sept. 1936; *s* of Major John Rochfort Colt, North Staffs Regt (*d* 1944), and of Angela Miriam Phyllis (*née* Kyan; she *m* 1946, Capt. Robert Leslie Cock); *S* uncle, 1951; *m* 1966, Jane Caroline (marr. diss. 1972), *d* of James Histed Lewis, Geneva and Washington, DC. *Educ:* Stoke House, Seaford; Douai Sch.; University Coll., London. Lately: Medical Registrar, UCH; House Physician, Brompton Hosp. Mem., BMA. FACP. *Recreations:* the arts, skiing, lawn tennis, jogging. *Heir:* none. *Address:* 240 E 82nd Street, Apt 20A, New York, NY 10028, USA; c/o Cock, 11 Stafford Road, Seaford, East Sussex.

COLTART, James Milne; Chairman: Scottish Television Ltd, 1969-75 (Managing Director, 1957-61, Deputy Chairman, 1961-69); Highland Printers Ltd, since 1959; Deputy Chairman: The Thomson Organisation Ltd, 1964-76 (Managing Director, Thomson Newspapers Ltd, 1959-61); Thomson Television (International) Ltd, since 1962; The Scotsman Publications Ltd, since 1962 (Managing Director, 1955-62); Director, Thomson Printers Ltd and various other newspaper and television companies in Britain and overseas; Chairman of Trustees, The Thomson Foundation, since 1969 (Trustee since 1962); *b* 2 Nov. 1903; *s* of Alexander Coltart and Alice Moffat; *m* 1927, Margaret Shepherd (*d* 1956); one *s*; *m* 1961, Mary Fryer; one *s* one *d*. *Educ:* Hamilton Cres., Glasgow. Accountant: Ioco Rubber Co. Ltd, 1926; Weir Housing Co. Ltd, 1927; Dir and Sec., Marr Downie & Co. Ltd, 1937; Man. Dir, Reid Bros Ltd, 1939; Asst Gen. Manager, Scottish Daily Express, 1950; Gen. Manager, Evening Citizen Ltd, 1955. Hon. LLD Strathclyde Univ., 1967. *Recreations:* golf, fishing. *Address:* (business) 16th Floor, International Press Centre, Shoe Lane, EC4. *T:* 01-353 6718; Manor Cottage, Smithwood Common, Cranleigh, Surrey. *T:* Ewhurst 3633.

COLTHURST, Sir Richard La Touche, 9th Bt *cr* 1744; *b* 14 Aug. 1928; *er s* of Sir Richard St John Jefferyes Colthurst, 8th Bt, and Denys Maida Hanmer West (*d* 1966), *e d* of Augustus William West; *S* father, 1955; *m* 1953, Janet Georgina, *d* of L. A. Wilson-Wright, Coolcarrigan, Co. Kildare; three *s* one *d*. *Educ:* Harrow; Peterhouse, Cambridge (MA). Underwriting Mem. of Lloyd's. Liveryman of Worshipful Company of Grocers. *Recreations:* forestry, cricket, tennis, swimming. *Heir: s* Charles St John Colthurst [*b* 21 May 1955. *Educ:* Eton; Magdalene Coll., Cambridge]. *Address:* Blarney Castle, County Cork, Eire. *T:* Cork 85210; Wheatlands, Crockham Hill, Kent TN8 6ST. *T:* Crockham Hill 260. *Clubs:* City University, MCC.

COLTON, Cyril Hadlow, CBE 1970; Consultant, Courtaulds Ltd, since 1967; *b* 15 March 1902; *yr s* of Albert Edward Colton and Kate Louise; *m* 1932, Doree Beatrice Coles; one *s* two *d*. *Educ:* Reigate Grammar School. Man-made fibres industry from 1921: Fabrique de Soie Artificiel de Tubize, 1921; British Celanese Ltd, 1923: Dir, 1945; Chm., 1964; Pres., 1968; Courtaulds Ltd, 1957: Marketing Dir, 1962-67; Dir, Samuel Courtauld Ltd, 1959-64; Dir, Courtaulds SA, 1962-68. Chm., Rayon Allocation Cttee, 1940-49; Member: Council, British Rayon Research Assoc., 1946-61; BoT Utility Cloth Cttee, 1950-52; BoT Mission to Middle East, 1954; Pres., Textile Inst., 1954-55. Chairman: British Man-Made Fibres Fedn, 1967-75; British Man-Made Fibres Producers Cttee, 1965-72; Silk and Man-Made Fibres Users Assoc., 1968-70; BSI Textile Div., 1969-72; Pres., Bureau International pour la Standardisation de la Rayonne et des Fibres Synthetiques, 1969-72; Vice-Pres., Cttee Internat. des Fibres Synthetiques, 1969-72; Pres., British Display Soc., 1966-; Mem. Council, Cotton, Silk and Man-Made Fibres Research Assoc. (Shirley Inst.), 1969-72; Dep. Chm., Textile Council, 1967-72; Mem., Crowther Cttee on Consumer Credit, 1968-71. CompTI; FRSA; FInstM. Liveryman, Worshipful Co. of Weavers. *Address:* Appin House, Cobham, Surrey. *T:* Cobham 4477. *Club:* English-Speaking Union.

COLTON, Gladys M.; Head Mistress, City of London School for Girls, 1949-72; *b* 1909; *er d* of William Henry Colton. *Educ:* Wycombe High Sch.; University Coll., London. BA Hons, History; Postgrad. DipEd, London. Asst Mistress: Slepe Hall, St Ives, 1932-37; Beaminster Grammar Sch., 1937-41; Senior History Mistress, Ealing Girls' Grammar Sch., 1941-49. Mem. Governing Body, City of London Coll., 1957-62. Mem., St Bartholomew's Hosp. Nurse Educn Cttee, 1962-72. FRSA 1953 (Mem. Council, 1969-73). *Recreations:* music, gardening. *Address:* Four Winds, Westleton, Saxmundham, Suffolk. *T:* Westleton 402. *Club:* English-Speaking Union.

COLUMBIA, BRITISH, Metropolitan of the Ecclesiastical Province of; *see* New Westminster, Archbishop of.

COLUMBIA, BRITISH, Bishop of, since 1970; **Rt. Rev. Frederick Roy Gartrell;** *b* 27 March 1914; *s* of William Frederick Gartrell and Lily Martha Keeble; *m* 1940, Grace Elizabeth Wood; three *s* one *d*. *Educ:* McMaster Univ. (BA); Wycliffe Coll. (LTh, BD). Deacon, 1938; Priest, 1939. Curate, St James the Apostle, Montreal, 1938; Rector, All Saints', Noranda, PQ, 1940; Senior Asst, St Paul's, Bloor Street, Toronto, 1944; Rector, St George's, Winnipeg, Manitoba, 1945; Archdeacon of Winnipeg, 1957; Rector, Christ Church Cathedral, Ottawa, and Dean of Ottawa, 1962-69. DD (*hc*): Wycliffe Coll., Toronto, 1962; St John's Coll., Winnipeg, 1965. *Recreation:* golf. *Address:* 1794 Barrie, Victoria V8N 2W7, BC, Canada.

COLVILLE, Lt-Col David Chaigneau, DSO 1940; MC; Queen's Messenger, 1946-63, retd; late Oxfordshire and Bucks LI; *b* 4 July 1898; *y s* of late Robert Frederick Steuart Colvill, Coolock, Co. Dublin, and Sophia Maconchy; *m* 1954, Kathleen, *widow* of Paul Boissier. *Educ:* Winchester; RMC Sandhurst. 2nd Lieut, Oxon and Bucks Light Infantry, 1916; Capt., 1925; Major, 1938; Temp. Lt-Col, 1940; served European War, France, 1917-18 (wounded, MC); N Russia, 1919; India and Burma, 1926-35 (India General Service Medal with Clasp, Burma, 1931); BEF, France and Belgium, 1939-40 (wounded, DSO); commanded 1st Bn (43rd Light Infantry), 1940-42; BLA, Normandy and Belgium, 1944-45; retired, 1946. *Address:* Jacobs, Boxford, Suffolk CO6 5NZ. *Club:* Naval and Military.

COLVILLE, family name of Viscount Colville of Culross and of Baron Clydesmuir.

COLVILLE OF CULROSS, 4th Viscount *cr* 1902; **John Mark Alexander Colville,** 14th Baron (Scot.) *cr* 1604; 4th Baron (UK) *cr* 1885; *b* 19 July 1933; *e s* of 3rd Viscount and Kathleen Myrtle, OBE 1961, *e d* of late Brig.-Gen. H. R. Gale, CMG, RE, Bardsey, Saanichton, Vancouver Island; *S* father, 1945; *m* 1st,

1958, Mary Elizabeth Webb-Bowen (marr. diss. 1973); four s; 2nd, 1974, Margaret Birgitta, Viscountess Davidson, o d of Maj.-Gen. C. H. Norton, qv. Educ: Rugby; New Coll., Oxford (MA). Lieut Grenadier Guards Reserve. Barrister-at-law, Lincoln's Inn, 1960. Minister of State, Home Office, 1972-74. Mem., Royal Company of Archers (Queen's Body Guard for Scotland). Hon. Mem., Rating and Valuation Assoc. Heir: s Master of Colville, qv. Address: Worlingham Hall, Beccles, Suffolk. T: Beccles 713191; Fawsyde, Kinneff, Inverbervie, Kincardineshire, Scotland. T: Catterline 208.
See also Baron Carrington.

COLVILLE, Master of; Hon. Charles Mark Townshend Colville; b 5 Sept. 1959; s and heir of 4th Viscount Colville of Culross, qv . Educ: Rugby. Address: Rookyards, Spexhall, near Halesworth, Suffolk. T: Ilketshall 318.

COLVILLE, Sir Cecil; see Colville, Sir H. C.

COLVILLE, Maj.-Gen. Edward Charles, CB 1955; DSO 1944, Bar, 1945; JP; DL; retired; b 1 Sept. 1905; s of late Admiral Hon. Sir Stanley Colville, GCB, GCMG, GCVO, and of The Lady Adelaide Colville (d 1960), d of 4th Earl Clanwilliam, GCB, KCMG, RM; m 1934, Barbara Joan Denny; two d. Educ: Marlborough; Sandhurst. ADC to Governor-Gen., Canada, 1932-34; Brigade Comd, 1944-46 (despatches); Military Adviser to UK High Comr, Canada, 1946-47; Comd Inf. Bde, TA, 1949-52; BGS, HQ Northern Army Group, 1952-54; Chief of Staff, Far East Land Forces, 1954-55; Comdr 51st Highland Div., 1956-59; retired, 1959. JP West Sussex, 1960; DL West Sussex, 1962. Address: Old Bartons, Stoughton, near Chichester, West Sussex. T: Compton 278. Club: Army and Navy.
See also Sir A. B. C. Edmonstone, Bt.

COLVILLE, Sir (Henry) Cecil, Kt 1962; MS (Melbourne), FRACS; private surgical practice, Melbourne; b 27 Aug. 1891; s of John William Colville and Mary Newman; m 1916, Harriet Elizabeth Tatchell; two d. Educ: Melbourne Church of England Grammar Sch. MB, BS (Melbourne) 1914; MS (Melbourne) 1920; FRACS 1931. War service, RAMC and AAMC, 1915-17. Pediatric Surg., Alfred Hospital, Melbourne, 1924-51. Pres., Federal Council of BMA, 1955-62; Pres. AMA, 1962-64. Address: 1045 Burke Road, Hawthorn, Vic 3123, Australia. T: Melbourne 82-5252. Club: Naval and Military.

COLVILLE, Sir John (Rupert), Kt 1974; CB 1955; CVO 1949; Director: Hill, Samuel and Co.; Coutts and Co.; Grindlays Bank; Provident Life Association; Deputy Chairman, London Committee, Ottoman Bank; Chairman: Thames Valley Broadcasting; Eucalyptus Pulp Mills Ltd; b 28 Jan. 1915; s of late Hon. George Colville and Lady Cynthia Colville; m 1948, Lady Margaret Egerton (see Lady Margaret Colville); two s one d. Educ: Harrow; Trinity Coll., Cambridge. Page of Honour to King George V, 1927-31. 3rd Sec., Diplomatic Service, 1937; Asst Private Sec. to Mr Neville Chamberlain, 1939-40; to Mr Winston Churchill, 1940-41 and 1943-45, and to Mr Clement Attlee, 1945. Served War of 1939-45, Pilot, RAFVR, 1941-44. Private Sec. to Princess Elizabeth, 1947-49; 1st Sec., British Embassy, Lisbon, 1949-51; Counsellor, Foreign Service, 1951; Joint Principal Private Sec. to the Prime Minister, 1951-55. Hon. Fellow, Churchill Coll., Cambridge, 1971. Officier, Légion d'Honneur. Publications: Fools' Pleasure, 1935; contrib. to Action This Day-Working with Churchill, 1968; Man of Valour, 1972; Footprints in Time, 1976; The New Elizabethans, 1977. Address: The Old Rectory, Stratfield Saye, Reading, Berks. T: Turgis Green 203. Clubs: White's, Pratt's.

COLVILLE, Lady Margaret; b 20 July 1918; d of 4th Earl of Ellesmere and Violet, Countess of Ellesmere; m 1948, Sir John Rupert Colville, qv; two s one d. Served War of 1939-45 in ATS (Junior Subaltern). Lady in Waiting to the Princess Elizabeth, Duchess of Edinburgh, 1946-49. Address: The Old Rectory, Stratfield Saye, Reading, Berks. T: Turgis Green 203.
See also Duke of Sutherland.

COLVIN, Howard Montagu, CBE 1964; FBA 1963; MA; Fellow of St John's College, Oxford, since 1948, Librarian since 1950, Tutor in History since 1957; Reader in Architectural History, Oxford University, since 1965; Member: Historic Buildings Council for England, since 1970; Royal Commission on Ancient and Historical Monuments of Scotland, since 1977; Royal Fine Art Commission, 1962-72; Royal Commission on Historical Monuments, 1963-76; b 15 Oct. 1919; s of late Montagu Colvin; m 1943, Christina Edgeworth, d of late H. E. Butler, Prof. of Latin at University Coll., London; two s. Educ: Trent Coll.; University Coll., London (Fellow, 1974). Served in RAF, 1940-46 (despatches); Asst Lecturer, Dept of History, University Coll., London, 1946-48. Hon. FRIBA. Publications: The White

Canons in England, 1951; A Biographical Dictionary of English Architects 1660-1840, 1954; (General Editor and part author) The History of the King's Works, 6 Vols, 1963-; A History of Deddington, 1963; Catalogue of Architectural Drawings in Worcester College Library, 1964; Architectural Drawings in the Library of Elton Hall (with Maurice Craig), 1964; (ed with John Harris) The Country Seat, 1970; Building Accounts of King Henry III, 1971; A Biographical Dictionary of British Architects 1600-1840, 1978; articles on mediæval and architectural history in Archaeological Journal, Architectural Review, etc. Address: 50 Plantation Road, Oxford. T: Oxford 57460.

COLVIN, John Horace Ragnar, CMG 1968; HM Diplomatic Service; Foreign and Commonwealth Office, since 1974; b Tokyo, 18 June 1922; s of late Adm. Sir Ragnar Colvin, KBE, CB and of Lady Colvin; m 1st, 1948, Elizabeth Anne Manifold (marr. diss., 1963); one s one d; 2nd, 1967, Moranna Sibyl de Lerisson Cazenove; one s one d. Educ: RNC Dartmouth; University of London. Royal Navy, 1935-51. Joined HM Diplomatic Service, 1951; HM Embassies, Oslo, 1951-53 and Vienna, 1953-55; British High Commn, Kuala Lumpur, 1958-61; HM Consul-General, Hanoi, 1965-67; Ambassador to People's Republic of Mongolia, 1971-74. Address: The Old Parsonage, Pamber Heath, near Basingstoke, Hants. T: Silchester 253. Club: Brooks's.

COLVIN, Brigadier Dame Mary Katherine Rosamond, DBE 1959 (OBE 1947); TD; Extra Lady in Waiting to the Princess Royal, 1964-65 (Lady in Waiting, 1962-64); b 25 Oct. 1907; d of Lt-Col F. F. Colvin, CBE. Commissioned 1939; Commanded Central Ordnance Depot, ATS Gp, Weedon, Northants, 1943-44; subsequently held staff appointments in Military Government, Germany; Comdt WRAC Sch. of Instruction, 1948-51; Asst Dir, WRAC, HQ. Scottish Comd, 1951-54; Inspector of Recruiting (Women's Services), War Office, 1954-56; Dep. Dir, WRAC, HQ Eastern Command, 1956-57; Dir of the Woman's Royal Army Corps, 1957-61. Hon. ADC to the Queen, 1957-61, retd. Address: Pasture House, North Luffenham, Oakham, Rutland LE15 8JU.

COLWYN, 3rd Baron, cr 1917; **Ian Anthony Hamilton-Smith;** Bt 1912; Dental Surgeon since 1966; b 1 Jan. 1942; s of 2nd Baron Colwyn and Miriam Gwendoline, d of Victor Ferguson; S father 1966; m 1964, Sonia Jane, d of P. H. G. Morgan, The Eades, Upton-on-Severn; one s one d. Educ: Cheltenham Coll.; Univ. of London. BDS London 1966; LDS, RCS 1966. Recreations: Rugby Union, motoring, music. Heir: s Hon. Craig Peter Hamilton-Smith, b 13 Oct. 1968. Address: Yew Tree Cottage, Dumbleton, near Evesham, Worcs. T: Ashton-under-Hill 383; (practice): Painswick House, Cheltenham, Glos; 23 Wimpole Street, W1.

COLYER, Air Marshal Douglas, CB 1942; CMG 1958; DFC 1918; MA; b 1 March 1893; y s of Henry Charles Colyer, HM Customs, and Charlotte, d of Owen Hill, Greenhithe, Kent; m Violet (d 1977), d of Charles Zerenner. Educ: St Dunstan's Coll. and St Catharine's Coll., Cambridge. 2nd Lieut Lincolnshire Regt, 1915; transf. to RFC, 1916; permanent commission in Royal Air Force, 1919; Air Adviser, Latvian Govt, 1930-31; Air Attaché Paris, Madrid, Lisbon, 1936-40; RAF Mem., Combined Chiefs of Staff, Washington, 1945-46; Civil Air Attaché, Paris, 1947-52; Civil Aviation Representative, Western Europe, 1952-60; retd, 1960. Officer of Legion of Honour, 1938; Order of Polonia Restituta, 2nd Class, 1941; Commander of Legion of Merit (USA), 1946; Grand Officer, Order of Orange-Nassau (Holland), 1946. Address: c/o National Westminster Bank, Cambridge.

COLYER, John Stuart, QC 1976; b 25 April 1935; s of Stanley Herbert Colyer, MBE, and late Louisa (née Randle); m 1961, Emily Warner, o d of Stanley Leland Dutrow and Mrs Dutrow, Blue Ridge Summit, Pa, USA; two d. Educ: Dudley Grammar Sch.; Shrewsbury; Worcester Coll., Oxford (Open History Scholarship; BA 1955, MA 1961). 2nd Lieut RA, 1954-55. Called to the Bar, Middle Temple, 1959; Instructor, Univ. of Pennsylvania, Philadelphia, 1959-60, Asst Prof., 1960-61; practised English bar, Midland and Oxford Circuit (formerly Oxford Circuit), 1961-; Lectr (Law of Landlord and Tenant), Council of Legal Educn, 1970-. Publications: (ed jtly) Encyclopaedia of Forms and Precedents (Landlord and Tenant), vol. XI, 1965, vol. XII, 1966; A Modern View of the Law of Torts, 1966; articles in Conveyancer. Recreations: entertaining my children; opera; cultivation of cacti and of succulents (esp. Lithops); gardening generally; travel. Address: 11 King's Bench Walk, Temple, EC4. T: 01-353 2484. Club: Wig and Pen.

COLYER-FERGUSSON, Sir James Herbert Hamilton, 4th Bt, *cr* 1866; *b* 10 Jan. 1917; *s* of Max Christian Hamilton Colyer-Fergusson (*d* on active service, 1940) and Edith Jane (*d* 1936), singer, *d* of late William White Miller, Portage la Prairie, Manitoba; *S* grandfather, 1951. *Educ:* Harrow; Balliol Coll., Oxford. BA 1939; MA 1945. Formerly Capt., The Buffs; served War of 1939-45 (prisoner-of-war, 1940). Entered service of former Great Western Railway Traffic Dept, 1947, later Operating Dept of the Western Region of British Rlys. Personal Asst to Chm. of British Transport Commission, 1957; Passenger Officer in SE Division of Southern Region, BR, 1961; Parly and Public Correspondent, BR Bd, 1967; Deputy to Curator of Historical Relics, BRB, 1968. Retired. *Heir:* none. *Address:* 61 Onslow Square, SW7. *Club:* Bath.
See also Sir Basil Goulding, Bt, Viscount Monckton of Brenchley.

COLYTON, 1st Baron, *cr* 1956, of Farway and of Taunton; **Henry Lennox d'Aubigné Hopkinson,** PC 1952; CMG 1944; *b* 3 Jan. 1902; *e s* of late Sir Henry Lennox Hopkinson, KCVO; *m* 1st, 1927, Alice Labouisse (*d* 1953), *d* of Henry Lane Eno, Bar Harbor, Maine, USA; one *s*; 2nd, 1956, Mrs Barbara Addams, *d* of late Stephen Barb, New York. *Educ:* Eton Coll.; Trinity Coll., Cambridge (BA History and Modern Languages Tripos). Entered Diplomatic Service, 1924; 3rd Sec., Washington, 1924; 2nd Sec., Foreign Office, 1929; Stockholm, 1931; Asst Private Sec. to Sec. of State for Foreign Affairs, 1932; Cairo, 1934; 1st Sec., 1936; Athens, 1938; War Cabinet Secretariat, 1939; Private Sec. to Permanent Under-Sec. for Foreign Affairs, 1940; Counsellor, Office of Minister of State in the Middle East, 1941; Minister Plenipotentiary, Lisbon, 1943; Dep. Brit. High Comr in Italy, 1944-46. Resigned from Foreign Service to enter politics, 1946; Head of Conservative Parly Secretariat and Jt Dir, Conservative Research Dept, 1946-50; MP (C) Taunton Div. of Somerset, 1950-56; Sec. for Overseas Trade, 1951-52; Minister of State for Colonial Affairs, 1952-Dec. 1955; Mem., Consultative Assembly, Council of Europe, 1950-52; Delegate, General Assembly, United Nations, 1952-55; Chairman: Anglo-Egyptian Resettlement Board, 1957-60; Joint East and Central African Board, 1960-65; Tanganyika Concessions Ltd, 1966-72. Royal Humane Society's Award for saving life from drowning, 1919. OStJ 1959. Grand Cross, Order of Prince Henry the Navigator (Portugal), 1972; Dato, Order of the Stia Negara (Brunei), 1972; Commander, Order of the Zaire (Congo) 1971. *Heir:* s Hon. Nicholas Henry Eno Hopkinson [*b* 18 Jan. 1932; *m* 1957, Fiona Margaret, *o d* of Sir Torquil Munro, *qv*; two *s*]. *Address:* Résidence Mirabeau, Apt 1107, 2 avenue des Citronniers, Monte Carlo, Monaco. *Clubs:* Buck's, White's, Beefsteak; Monte Carlo.

COMAY, Michael; Fellow, Leonard Davis Institute for International Affairs, Jerusalem; Associate General Chairman, Chaim Weizmann Centenary; *b* Cape Town, 17 Oct. 1908; *s* of Alexander and Clara Comay; *m* 1935, Joan Solomon; one *s* one *d*. *Educ:* Univ. of Cape Town (BA, LLB). Barrister, 1931-40. Served with S African Army, Western Desert and UK, 1940-45 (Major). Settled Palestine as representative S African Zionist Fedn, 1945; Adviser, Political Dept Jewish Agency, 1946-48; Dir, British Commonwealth Div., Israel Foreign Min., 1948-51; Asst Dir-Gen., Israel For. Min., 1951-53 and 1957-59; Minister, then Ambassador to Canada, 1953-57; Perm. Rep. and Ambassador of Israel to UN, 1960-67; Political Adviser to For. Minister and Ambassador-at-Large, 1967-70; Ambassador of Israel to the Court of St James's, 1970-73. *Recreations:* walking, painting. *Address:* 47 Harav Berlin Street, Jerusalem, Israel.

COMBE, Air Vice-Marshal Gerard, CB 1946; retired; *b* 15 Feb. 1902; 3rd *s* of late Percy Combe, Cobham, Surrey; *m* 1930, Brenda Mary, *er d* of Capt. Hugh Bainbridge, Killeen, Bournemouth; two *s*. *Educ:* King's College Sch.; RAF Coll., Cranwell. Flying duties in No 31 Sqdn India (NWFP), 1922-26; on return to UK in 1926 specialised in Armament; Armament Staff duties until 1932; Flying duties in No 30 Sqdn, Iraq, 1932-33 (Barzan Operations, Northern Kurdistan); Staff Coll. (psc), 1934; Armament and Chemical Warfare duties, 1935-38; commanded No 52 (Bomber) Sqdn, 1939; Armament Staff duties, Advanced Air Striking Force, 1939-40 (despatches). During 1941-45: Vice-Pres. (Air) Ordnance Board; Chief Superintendent Chemical Defence Experimental Station, Porton; Dir of Armament Development (MAP); Dir-Gen. of Armament, Air Ministry, 1945-47; Senior Air Staff Officer, RAF, HQ MEAF, 1947-49; Pres. of The Ordnance Board, 1950-51; AOA, HQ Maintenance Command, 1951-52; Air Officer Commanding, No 41 Group, 1953-55, retd 1955. United States Legion of Merit, Degree of Commander, 1946. *Recreation:* sailing. *Address:* Woodpeckers Cottage, Brockenhurst, Hants. *T:* Brockenhurst 3360. *Club:* Royal Lymington Yacht.

COMBERMERE, 5th Viscount, *cr* 1826; **Michael Wellington Stapleton-Cotton;** Bt 1677; Baron Combermere, 1814; Lecturer in Biblical and Religious Studies, University of London, Department of Extra-Mural Studies, since 1972; *b* 8 Aug. 1929; *s* of 4th Viscount Combermere and Constance Marie Katherine (*d* 1968), *d* of Lt-Col Sir Francis Dudley W. Drummond, KBE; *S* father, 1969; *m* 1961, Pamela Elizabeth, *d* of Rev. R. G. Coulson; one *s* two *d*. *Educ:* Eton; King's Coll., Univ. of London. Palestine Police, 1947-48; Royal Canadian Mounted Police, 1948-50; Short-service commn as gen. duties Pilot, RAF, 1950-58, retd as Flt-Lt; Sales Rep., Teleflex Products Ltd, 1959-62; read Theology, KCL, 1962-67 (BD, MTh). *Heir:* s Hon. Thomas Robert Wellington Stapleton-Cotton, *b* 30 Aug. 1969. *Address:* 46 Smith Street, SW3. *T:* 01-352 1319. *Club:* Royal Automobile.

COMBS, Sir Willis (Ide), KCVO 1974; CMG 1962; HM Diplomatic Service, retired; *b* Melbourne, 6 May 1916; *s* of Willis Ide Combs, Napier, New Zealand; *m* 1942, Grace Willis; two *d*. *Educ:* Dannevirke High Sch.; Victoria Coll., NZ; St John's Coll., Cambridge. Served in HM Forces, 1940-46. Apptd Mem. Foreign Service, 1947; transf. to Paris as 2nd Sec. (Commercial), Dec. 1947; 1st Sec., Nov. 1948; transf. to Rio de Janeiro, as 1st Sec., 1951; to Peking as 1st Sec. and Consul, 1953 (Chargé d'Affaires, 1954); Foreign Office, 1956; to Baghdad as Counsellor (Commercial), 1959; Diplomatic Service Inspector, 1963; Counsellor, British Embassy, Rangoon, 1965; Asst Under-Sec. of State, FCO, 1968; Ambassador to Indonesia, 1970-75. *Address:* Sunset, Wadhurst Park, Wadhurst, East Sussex. *Club:* United Oxford & Cambridge University.

COMFORT, Alexander; medical biologist; poet and novelist; Senior Fellow, Institute for Higher Studies, Santa Barbara, California, since 1975; *b* 10 Feb. 1920; *s* of late Alexander Charles and Daisy Elizabeth Comfort; *m* 1st 1943, Ruth Muriel Harris (marr. diss. 1973); one *s*; 2nd, 1973, Jane Tristram Henderson. *Educ:* Highgate Sch.; Trinity Coll., Cambridge (Robert Styring Scholar Classics, and Senior Scholar, Nat. Sciences); London Hospital (Scholar). 1st Cl. Nat. Sc. Tripos, Part I, 1940; 2nd Cl. Nat. Sc. Tripos, 1st Div. (Pathology), 1941; MRCS, LRCP 1944; MB, BCh Cantab 1944; MA Cantab 1945; DCH London 1945; PhD London 1949 (Biochemistry); DSc London 1963 (Gerontology). Refused military service in war of 1939-45. Lectr in Physiology, London Hospital Medical Coll., 1948-51; Hon. Research Associate, Dept of Zoology, 1951-73, and Dir of Research, Gerontology, 1966-73, UCL; Clin. Lectr, Dept Psychiatry, Stanford Univ., 1974-; Prof., Dept of Pathol., Univ. of Calif Sch. of Med., Irvine, 1976-. Pres., Brit. Soc. for Research on Ageing, 1967. *Publications:* The Silver River, 1937; No Such Liberty (novel), 1941; Into Egypt (play), 1942; France and Other Poems, 1942; A Wreath for the Living (poems), 1943; Cities of the Plain (melodrama), 1943; The Almond Tree (novel), 1943; The Powerhouse (novel), 1944; Elegies, 1944; The Song of Lazarus (poems, USA), 1945; Letters from an Outpost (stories), 1947; Art and Social Responsibility (essays), 1947; The Signal to Engage (poems), 1947; Gengulphus (play), 1948; On this side Nothing (novel), 1948; First Year Physiological Technique (textbook), 1948; The Novel and Our Time (criticism), 1948; Barbarism and Sexual Freedom (essays), 1948; Sexual Behaviour in Society (social psychology), 1950; The Pattern of the Future (broadcast lectures), 1950; Authority and Delinquency in the Modern State (social psychology), 1950; And all but He Departed (poems), 1951; A Giant's Strength (novel), 1952; The Biology of Senescence (textbook), 1956; Darwin and the Naked Lady (essays), 1961; Come Out to Play (novel), 1961; Haste to the Wedding (poems), 1961; Are you Sitting Comfortably? (songs), 1962; Sex and Society (social psychology), 1963; Ageing, the Biology of Senescence (textbook), 1964; The Koka Shastra (translation), 1964; The Process of Ageing (science), 1965; Nature and Human Nature (science), 1966; The Anxiety Makers (med. history), 1967; The Joy of Sex (counselling), 1973; More Joy (counselling), 1974; A Good Age, 1976; I and That: notes on the Biology of Religion, 1978; Poems, 1978. *Address:* 683 Oak Grove Drive, Santa Barbara, Calif 93108, USA.

COMFORT, Anthony Francis; HM Diplomatic Service, retired; *b* Plymouth, 12 Oct. 1920; *s* of Francis Harold Comfort and Elsie Grace (*née* Martin); *m* 1948, Joy Margaret Midson; two *s* one *d*. *Educ:* Bristol Grammar Sch.; Oriel Coll., Oxford. Entered Foreign Service, 1947; 2nd Sec. (Commercial), Athens, 1948-51; Consul, Alexandria, 1951-53; 1st Sec. (Commercial), Amman, 1953-54; Foreign Office, 1954-57; seconded to Colonial Office, 1957-59; 1st Sec. (Commercial), Belgrade, 1959-60; 1st Sec. and Consul, Reykjavik, 1961-65; Inspector of Diplomatic Establishments, 1965-68, retired 1969. *Recreations:* walking, gardening. *Address:* Garliford, Bishop's Nympton, South Molton, Devon.

COMFORT, Dr Charles Fraser, OC; CD; RCA; artist and author; Emeritus Director, National Gallery of Canada, 1965; *b* Edinburgh, 22 July 1900; *m* 1924, Louise Chase, Winnipeg; two *d. Educ:* Winnipeg Sch. of Art and Art Students' League, New York. Cadet Officer, Univ. of Toronto Contingent of Canadian OTC, 1939; Commnd Instr in Infantry Weapons, 1940; Sen. Canadian War Artist (Army) Major, 1942-46 (UK, Italy and NW Europe). Head of Dept of Mural Painting, Ontario Coll. of Art, 1935-38; Associate Prof., Dept of Art and Archaeology, Univ. of Toronto, 1946-60 (Mem. staff, 1938); Dir, Nat. Gall. of Canada, 1959. Gold Medal and cash award, Great Lakes Exhibn, Albright Gall., Buffalo, NY, 1938; has travelled widely in Europe; Royal Society Fellowship to continue research into problems of Netherlandish painting, 1955-56; studied under Dr William Heckscher of Kunsthistorisch Inst., Utrecht. *Works include:* landscape painting and portraiture (oils and water colour); mural paintings and stone carvings in many public buildings. Pres., Royal Canadian Academy of Arts, 1957-60; Past Pres. and Charter Mem., Canadian Soc. of Painters in Water Colour; Past Pres. and Charter Mem., Canadian Group of Painters; Mem., Ontario Soc. of Artists. Dr of Laws *hc*, Mount Allison Univ., 1958. Medaglia di benemerenza culturale (Italy), 1963; Univ. of Alberta National Award in painting and related arts, 1963. Centennial Decoration, 1967; OC 1972. *Publications:* Artist at War, 1956 (Toronto); contrib. to Royal Commission Studies Report on National Development in the Arts, Letters and Sciences, Vol. II, 1951; contrib. various art and literary publications. *Address:* 28 Boulevard Alexandre Taché, Hull, PQ, Canada.

COMINO, Demetrius, OBE 1963; President, Dexion-Comino International Ltd, 1973 (Chairman, 1947-73); *b* Australia, 4 Sept. 1902; *s* of John and Anna Comino, Greek origin, naturalized British; *m* 1935, Katerina Georgiadis; one *d. Educ:* University Coll., London. BSc 1st cl. hons Engrg 1923. Student Apprentice with The British Thompson Houston Co. Ltd, Rugby, until 1926; started own business, Krisson Printing Ltd, 1927; started present company, 1947. FRSA 1971; FBIM; Fellow, UCL, 1971. Golden Cross, King George I (Greece), 1967. *Publications:* contribs to official jl of Gk Chamber of Technology and to New Scientist. *Recreations:* thinking; preparing a book on basic unifying concepts and an educational foundation on the basis of these concepts. *Address:* Silver Birches, Oxford Road, Gerrards Cross, Bucks. *T:* Gerrards Cross 83170.

COMMAGER, Henry Steele, MA Oxon; MA Cantab; Professor of American History, Amherst College, since 1956; Professor of History, Columbia University, 1938-56; Hon. Professor, University of Santiago de Chile; *b* 25 Oct. 1902; *s* of James W. Commager and Anna Elizabeth Dan; *m* 1928; Evan Carroll; one *s* two *d. Educ:* Univ. of Chicago; Univ. of Copenhagen. AB, Univ. of Chicago, 1923; MA, 1924; PhD, 1928; Scholar Amer-Scand. Foundation, 1924-25; taught History New York Univ., 1926-29; Prof. of History, 1929-38. Lectr on American History, Cambridge Univ., 1942-43; Hon. Fellow, Peterhouse; Pitt Prof. of Amer. Hist., Cambridge Univ., 1947-48; Lectr, Salzburg Seminar in Amer. Studies, 1951; Harold Vyvyan Harmsworth Prof. of American History, Oxford Univ., 1952; Gotesman Lectr, Upsala Univ., 1953; Special State Dept lectr to German Univs, 1954; Zuskind Prof., Brandeis Univ., 1954-55; Prof., Univ. of Copenhagen, 1956; Visiting Prof., Univ. of Aix-Provence, summer 1957; Lectr, Univ. of Jerusalem, summer 1958; Commonwealth Lectr, Univ. of London, 1964; Harris Lectr, Northwestern Univ., 1964; Visiting Prof., Harvard, Chicago, Calif, City Univ. NY, Nebraska, etc. Editor-in-Chief, The Rise of the American Nation; Consultant, Office War Information in Britain and USA; Mem. US Army War Hist. Commn; Mem. Historians Commn on Air Power; special citation US Army; Consultant US Army attached to SHAEF, 1945. Trustee; American Scandinavian Foundation; American Friends of Cambridge Univ. Mem. of the Amer. Acad. of Arts and Letters, USA (Gold Medal for History, 1972). Hon degrees: EdD Rhode I; LittD: Washington, Ohio Wesleyan, Pittsburgh, Marietta, Hampshire Coll., 1970; Adelphi Coll., 1974; DLitt: Cambridge, Franklin-Marshall, W Virginia, Michigan State; LHD: Brandeis, Puget Sound, Hartford, Alfred; LLD: Merrimack, Carleton; Dickinson Coll., 1967; Franklin Pierce Coll., 1968; Columbia Univ., 1969; Ohio State, 1970; Wilson Coll., 1970; W. C. Post Coll., 1974; Alassa Univ., 1974; DHL: Maryville Coll., 1970; Univ. of Mass, 1972. Knight of Order of Dannebrog (Denmark), 1957 (1st cl.). *Publications:* Theodore Parker, 1936; Growth of the American Republic, 1930, 2 vols 1939; sub-ed (with S. E. Morison) Documents of American History, 1934, 9th edn 1974; Heritage of America (with A. Nevins), 1939; America: Story of a Free People (with A. Nevins), 1943, new edn 1966; Majority Rule and Minority Rights, 1944; Story of the Second World War, 1945; ed

Tocqueville, Democracy in America, 1947; ed America in Perspective, 1947; ed The St Nicholas Anthology, 1947; The American Mind, 1950; The Blue and the Gray, 2 vols 1950; Living Ideas in America, 1951; Robert E. Lee, 1951; Freedom, Loyalty, Dissent, 1954 (special award, Hillman Foundation); Europe and America since 1942 (with G. Bruun), 1954; Joseph Story, 1956; The Spirit of Seventy-Six, 2 vols (with R. B. Morris); Crusaders for Freedom; History: Nature and Purpose, 1965; Freedom and Order, 1966; Search for a Usable Past, 1967; Was America a Mistake?, 1968; The Commonwealth of Learning, 1968; The American Character, 1970; The Use and Abuse of History, 1972; Britain Through American Eyes, 1974; The Defeat of America, 1974; Essays on the Enlightenment, 1974; edited: Atlas of American Civil War; Winston Churchill, History of the English Speaking Peoples; Why the Confederacy Lost the Civil War; Major Documents of the Civil War; Theodore Parker, an Anthology; Immigration in American History; Lester Ward and the Welfare State; The Struggle for Racial Equality; Joseph Story, Selected Writings and Judicial Opinions; Winston Churchill, Marlborough, 1968. *Recreation:* music. *Address:* Amherst College, Mass 01002, USA; (summer) Linton, Cambs, England. *Clubs:* Savile, Lansdowne (London); Century, Lotos (New York); St Botolph (Boston); (former Pres.) PEN (American Centre).

COMPSTON, Nigel Dean, MA, MD, FRCP; Consulting Physician: Royal Free Hospital, since 1954; Royal Masonic Hospital, since 1960; St Mary Abbot's Hospital, 1957-73; King Edward VII Hospital for Officers, since 1965; *b* 21 April 1918; *s* of George Dean Compston and Elsie Muriel Robinson; *m* 1942, Diana Mary (*née* Standish); two *s* one *d. Educ:* Royal Masonic Sch.; Trinity Hall, Cambridge; Middlesex Hospital. BA Cantab 1939; MRCS, LRCP 1942; MB, BCh Cantab 1942; MRCP 1942; MA, MD Cantab 1947; FRCP 1957. RAMC, 1942-47 (Temp. Lt-Col). Research Fellow, Middlesex Hosp. Medical Sch., 1948-51; E. G. Fearnsides Scholar, Cambridge, 1951; Mackenzie Mackinnon Research Fellow, RCP, 1951; Asst Prof. Medicine, Middlesex Hosp., 1952-54; Treasurer, RCP, 1970 (formerly Asst Registrar). Examiner: Pharmacology and Therapeutics, Univ. of London, 1958-63, Medicine, 1968; Medicine, RCP, 1965-; Medicine, Univ. of Cambridge, 1971-. Vice-Dean, Royal Free Hosp. Sch. of Medicine, 1968-70; Mem. Bd of Governors, The Royal Free Hosp., 1963-74. Hon. Editor Proc. RSM, 1966-70. *Publications:* Multiple Sclerosis (jtly), 1955; Recent Advances in Medicine (jtly), 1964, 1968. Contributions to learned jls. *Recreations:* ski-ing, golf. *Address:* Puckstye Cottage, Holtye Common, Cowden, Kent. *T:* Cowden 789; 149 Harley Street, W1. *T:* 01-935 4444. *Clubs:* Highgate Golf, Royal Ashdown Forest Golf.

COMPSTON, Vice-Adm. Sir Peter (Maxwell), KCB 1970 (CB 1967); *b* 12 Sept. 1915; *s* of Dr G. D. Compston; *m* 1st, 1939, Valerie Bocquet (marr. diss); one *s* one *d*; 2nd, 1953, Angela Brickwood. *Educ:* Epsom Coll. Royal Navy, 1937; specialised in flying duties. Served 1939-45, HMS Ark Royal, Anson, Vengeance; HMCS Warrior, 1946; HMS Theseus, 1948-50 (despatches); Directorate of RN Staff Coll., 1951-53; Capt. 1955; in comd HMS Orwell and Capt. 'D' Plymouth, 1955-57; Imperial Defence Coll., 1958; Naval Attaché, Paris, 1960-62; in comd HMS Victorious, 1962-64; Rear-Adm., Jan. 1965; Chief of British Naval Staff and Naval Attaché, Washington, 1965-67; Flag Officer Flotillas, Western Fleet, 1967-68; Dep. Supreme Allied Comdr, Atlantic, 1968-70, retired. Member: Cttee of Management, RNLI; Cttee, Royal Humane Soc. *Recreations:* theatre, country life. *Address:* Holmwood, Stroud, near Petersfield, Hants. *Clubs:* Army and Navy; Seaview Yacht (Seaview, Isle of Wight).

COMPTON, family name of **Marquess of Northampton**.

COMPTON, Earl; Spencer Douglas David Compton; *b* 2 April 1946; *s* and *heir* of 6th Marquess of Northampton, *qv*; *m* 1st, 1967, Henriette Luisa Maria (marr. diss. 1973), *o d* of late Baron Bentinck; one *s* one *d*; 2nd, 1974, Annette Marie (marr. diss. 1977), *er d* of C. A. R. Smallwood; 3rd, 1977, Hon. Mrs Rosemary Dawson-Damer. *Educ:* Eton. *Heir:* s Lord Wilmington, *qv. Address:* Castle Ashby, Northampton. *T:* Yardley Hastings 232. *Club:* Turf.

COMPTON, Denis Charles Scott, CBE 1958; professional cricketer, retired 1957; Sunday Express Cricket Correspondent, since 1950; BBC Television Cricket Commentator, since 1958; *b* 23 May 1918; *m* 1st; one *s*; 2nd; two *s*; 3rd, 1975, Christine Franklin Tobias; one *d. Educ:* Bell Lane Sch., Hendon. First played for Middlesex, 1936. First played for England *v* New Zealand, 1937; *v* Australia, 1938; *v* West Indies, 1939; *v* India, 1946; *v* S Africa, 1947. Played in 78 Test matches; made 123 centuries in first-class cricket. Association football: mem. of

Arsenal XI; England XI, 1943; Editor, Denis Compton's Annual, 1950-57. *Publications:* Playing for England, 1948; Testing Time for England, 1948; In Sun and Shadow, 1952; End of an Innings, 1958; Denis Compton's Test Diary, 1964. *Recreation:* golf. *Address:* Royds House, Mandeville Place, W1M 6AE. *T:* 01-935 7733. *Clubs:* MCC; Wanderers (Johannesburg).

COMPTON, Sir Edmund (Gerald), GCB 1971 (KCB 1965, CB 1948); KBE 1955; MA; Chairman, English Local Government Boundary Commission, since 1971; *b* 30 July 1906; *er s* of late Edmund Spencer Compton, MC, Pailton House, Rugby; *m* 1934, Betty Tresyllian, 2nd *d* of late Hakewill Tresyllian Williams, DL, JP, Churchill Court, Kidderminster; one *s* four *d.* *Educ:* Rugby (Scholar); New Coll., Oxford (Scholar); 1st Class Lit. Hum., 1929; Hon. Fellow 1972. Entered Home Civil Service, 1929; Colonial Office, 1930; transf. to HM Treasury, 1931; Private Sec. to Financial Sec. to Treasury, 1934-36; seconded to Min. of Aircraft Production as Private Sec. to Minister, 1940; Min. of Supply, 1941; Asst Sec., HM Treasury, 1942, Under-Sec., 1947, Third Sec., 1949-58; Comptroller and Auditor General, Exchequer and Audit Dept, 1958-66; Parly Comr for Administration, 1967-71, and in NI, 1969-71. Chairman: Irish Sailors and Soldiers Land Trust, 1946-; Central Bd of Finance of C of E, 1965-73; Milbern Trust, 1968-; Governing Body, Rugby Sch., 1969-72; BBC Programmes Complaints Commn, 1972-; Governing Body, Royal Acad. of Music. Hon. FRAM 1968. *Recreation:* music. *Address:* 53 Evelyn Gardens, SW7. *T:* 01-370 3220. *Clubs:* Athenæum, Boodle's.

COMPTON, Eric Henry, CVO 1954; Retired Commissioner, New Zealand Police; *b* 14 March 1902; *s* of William Henry Compton and Harriet Compton (*née* Morgon); *m* 1925, Nona Audrey Muriel Cole; five *s* one *d.* *Educ:* Hastings High Sch., NZ. Joined NZ Police Force, 1923; Detective Sergt, 1939, Chief Detective, 1946, Sub-Insp., 1952, Asst Comr, 1952, Comr, 1953; retired on superannuation, 1956. Chm., British Sailors' Soc., Wellington, 1952-; Dep. Chm., NZ British Sailors' Soc., 1952-; Management Cttee, Christian Business Men's Assoc., 1951; Hon. Sec., NZ Fellowship of Peruvian Bible Schs. Lady Godley Medal 1919; Coronation Medal 1953. *Recreation:* bowls (indoor). *Address:* 69 Churchill Avenue, Palmerston North, New Zealand. *T:* 81-645.

COMPTON, Fay, CBE 1975; *b* London, 18 Sept. 1894; *d* of Edward Compton and Virginia Bateman; *m* 1st, Harry Gabriel Pélissier (*d* 1913); one *s*; 2nd, Lauri de Freece (*d* 1921); 3rd, 1922, Leon Quartermaine (marr. diss., 1942; he died 1967); 4th, 1942, Ralph Champion Shotter (marr. diss., 1946). *Educ:* Leatherhead Court, Surrey. First appearance on stage, 1911; America, 1914; London music-hall stage (Coliseum), 1939. Has played Titania, Ophelia, Calpurnia, Paulina, and other Shakespearean parts, and had many successes in leading rôles of great variety, including: name part in Mary Rose, 1920 and 1926; Fanny Grey in Autumn Crocus, Lyric, 1931 (subsequently on tour); Dorothy Hilton in Call it a Day, Globe, 1935-37 (subsequently touring in the same part); Mary in Family Portrait, on tour 1940, and Strand, 1948 (Ellen Terry Award); Ruth in Blithe Spirit, Piccadilly, 1941-42; Martha Dacre in No Medals, Vaudeville, 1944-46; name part in Candida, Piccadilly, 1947; Gina Ekdal in The Wild Duck, St Martin's, 1948, etc. Old Vic Company, 1953-54 (having first appeared at Edinburgh Festival of 1953 with the Company): Gertrude in Hamlet; Countess of Rossillion in All's Well That Ends Well; Constance of Bretagne in King John; Volumnia in Coriolanus; Juno in The Tempest. Lady Bracknell in The Importance of Being Earnest, Old Vic, 1959; visited USA, 1959, playing lead in God and Kate Murphy; Comtesse de la Brière in What Every Woman Knows, Old Vic, 1960; Acted, Chichester Festival Theatre, 1962, 1963; A Month in the Country, Guildford (Yvonne Arnaud), 1965. Film career began 1917; has appeared in several notable films including, more recently, The Story of Esther Costello; Town on Trial; The Virgin and the Gipsy; has broadcast, and first appeared on television, 1952, since when has played numerous important rôles in plays and serials (including The Forsyte Saga, 1967). *Publication:* Rosemary: Some Remembrances, 1926. *Address:* 19 Albany Villas, Hove, East Sussex.

COMPTON, Michael Graeme; Keeper of Exhibitions and Education, Tate Gallery, since 1970; *b* 29 Sept. 1927; *s* of Joseph Nield Compton, OBE, and Dorothy Margaret Townsend Compton; *m* 1952, Susan Paschal Benn; two *d.* *Educ:* Courtauld Institute, London (BA Hons History of Art). Asst to Director, Leeds City Art Gallery and Templenewsam, 1954-57; Keeper of Foreign Schools, Walker Art Gallery, Liverpool, 1957-59; Dir, Ferens Art Gall., Hull, 1960-65; Asst Keeper, Modern Collection, Tate Gall., 1965-70. Member: Art Panel, Arts Council; Fine Arts Adv. Cttee, British Council. *Publications:* Optical and Kinetic Art, 1967; Pop Art, 1970; (jtly) Catalogue of Foreign Schools, Walker Art Gallery, 1963; articles in art jls, exhibn catalogues. *Address:* Court Hayes, Wolf's Hill, Oxted, Surrey RH8 0QT.

COMPTON, Robert Herbert K.; *see* Keppel-Compton.

COMPTON, Air Vice-Marshal William Vernon C.; *see* Crawford-Compton.

COMPTON MILLER, Sir John (Francis), Kt 1969; MBE (mil.) 1945; TD; MA Oxon; Barrister-at-Law; Senior Registrar, The Family Division (formerly Probate, Divorce and Admiralty Division), 1964-72 (Registrar, 1946-64), retired 1972; *b* 11 May 1900; 3rd *s* of Frederic Richard Miller, MD and Effie Anne, *d* of Samson Rickard Stuttaford; *m* 1st, 1925, Alice Irene Mary (*d* 1931), *er d* of John Scales Bakewell; one *s*; 2nd, 1936, Mary, *e d* of Rev. Alexander MacEwen Baird-Smith; one *s* one *d.* *Educ:* St Paul's Sch.; New Coll., Oxford. Called to Bar, Inner Temple, 1923; went the Western Circuit, practised Criminal, Common Law, Probate and Divorce Courts. Major, Inns of Court Regt, TA, 1936. A Deputy Judge Advocate, United Kingdom and North West Europe. Examiner, Council of Legal Education, 1951-64. UK Rep., Council of Europe Sub-Cttee on Registration of Wills. *Publications:* I tried my hand at Verse, 1968; Further Verse, 1970. *Recreations:* painting, versing, heraldic art. *Address:* 2 Crown Office Row, Temple, EC4. *T:* 01-583 1352. *Club:* Garrick.

COMYN, James, QC 1961; a Recorder, and Honorary Recorder of Andover, since 1972; *b* Co. Dublin, 8 March 1921; *o s* of late James Comyn, QC, Dublin and late Mary Comyn; *m* 1967, Anne, *d* of late Philip Chaundler, MC, Biggleswade, and of Mrs Chaundler, Cambridge; one *s* one *d.* *Educ:* Oratory Sch.; New Coll., Oxford (MA). Ex-Pres. of Oxford Union. Inner Temple, 1942; called to Irish Bar, 1947. Recorder of Andover, 1964-71. Master of the Bench, Inner Temple, 1968-; Mem. and Chm., Bar Council, 1973-74. A Governor of the Oratory Sch., 1964. Owner of the "Clareville" herd of pedigree Aberdeen-Angus and the "Beaufield" herd of pedigree Herefords. *Publication:* Their Friends at Court, 1973. *Recreations:* farming, golf. *Address:* Queen Elizabeth Building, Temple, EC4. *T:* 01-583 7837; Belvin, Tara, Co. Meath, Ireland. *T:* Navan 25111. *Clubs:* Athenæum, Royal Dublin Society.

CONAN DOYLE, Air Comdt Dame Jean (Lena Annette), (Lady Bromet), DBE 1963 (OBE 1948); Director of the Women's Royal Air Force, 1963-66, retired; *b* 21 Dec. 1912; *d* of late Sir Arthur Conan Doyle and Lady Conan Doyle (*née* Jean Leckie); *m* 1965, Air Vice-Marshal Sir Geoffrey Bromet, *qv.* *Educ:* Granville House, Eastbourne. Joined No 46 (Co. of Sussex) ATS, RAF Company, Sept. 1938; commnd in WAAF, 1940; served in UK, 1939-45; commnd in RAF, 1949; Comd WRAF Admin Officer: BAFO, Germany, 1947-50; HQ Tech. Trg. Comd, 1950-52 and 1962-63; Dep. Dir, 1952-54 and 1960-62; OC, RAF Hawkinge, 1956-59; Inspector of the WRAF, 1954-56 and 1959-60. Hon. ADC to the Queen, 1963-66. A Governor, Star and Garter Home, 1968-. *Address:* 72 Cadogan Square, SW1; Home Green, Littlestone-on-Sea, New Romney, Kent. *Clubs:* Naval and Military, Royal Air Force.

CONANT, James Bryant, Hon. CBE 1948; PhD; Author and Educational Consultant, in US, since 1965; President Emeritus, Harvard University; *b* 26 March, 1893; *s* of James Scott Conant and Jennet Orr Bryant; *m* 1921, Grace Thayer Richards; two *s.* *Educ:* Roxbury Latin Sch.; Harvard, AB, 1913, PhD, 1916; Instructor in Chemistry, Harvard, 1916-17; Lieut Sanitary Corps, USA, 1917; Major, Chemical Warfare Service, 1918; Asst Prof., Harvard, 1919-25; Assoc. Prof., 1925-27; Sheldon Emery Prof., Organic Chemistry, 1928-33; Chm., Dept of Chemistry, 1931-33; Pres., 1933-53, retired. US High Commissioner, 1953-55, Ambassador, 1955-57, Federal Republic of Germany. *Hon. degrees:* LLD: Chicago, 1933, New York, 1934, Princeton, 1934, Yale, 1934, Amherst, 1935, Coll. of Charleston, 1935, Coll. of William and Mary, 1936, Williams, 1938, Dartmouth, 1938, Tulane, 1939, Calif, 1940, Pa, 1940, Bristol (England), 1941, Queen's, 1941, Jewish Theol Seminary, 1951, NC, 1945, Toronto, 1945, Baylor, Ill., State of New York, 1947, Northeastern, Mass, 1948, Michigan, Yeshiva, Wesleyan, 1949, Swarthmore Coll., 1950, Jewish Theol Seminary, 1951, Birmingham (England), 1954; Harvard, Edinburgh, and Michigan State Univs, 1955, Leeds, 1956; New Hampshire, 1966; LHD, Boston, 1934; ScD: Columbia, Stevens Inst., Tufts Coll., 1934, Wisconsin, 1935, Cambridge (England), 1941, McGill, 1945, Free Univ. of Berlin, 1954; DCL: Oxford (England), 1936, Colgate, 1952; LittD: Algiers, 1944, Hamilton Coll., 1947; DSc: London, 1946 Lyons (France), 1947,

Canterbury University Coll., NZ, 1951; FEIS 1947; admitted to Univ. of Adelaide *ad eundem gradum,* 1951. Lectures: Univ. of Calif, 1924; Sachs, Teachers' Coll., 1945; Terry, Yale, 1946; Stafford-Little, Princeton, 1957; Godkin, Harvard, 1958; Stimpson, Goucher Coll., 1951; Page Barbour, Univ. Va, 1952, Stevenson, LSE, 1952; Morrow, Smith Univ., 1959; Inglis, Harvard, 1959; Pollack, Harvard, 1959; Jefferson, Univ. of Calif, 1960. Research Associate California Technical, 1927. Mem. Educational Policies Commn of NEA, 1941-46, 1947-50, 1957-63; Chairman: National Defence Research Cttee and Dep. Dir, Office of Scientific Research and Development, 1941-46; Steering Cttee for Manhattan Dist charged with production of atomic bombs, 1942-45; Gen. Advisory Cttee of AEC, 1947-52. Member: Nat. Acad. of Sciences; Amer. Chem. Soc.; Mass. Historical Soc.; Amer. Acad. of Arts and Sciences, Amer. Philosophical Soc.; Nat. Science Foundation, 1950-53; Science Advisory Cttee, 1951-53. For. Member: Royal Society; Royal Institute of Chemistry; RSE; Hon. FCS; awarded Chandler Medal, Columbia Univ., 1932; Nichols Medal, 1932; Priestley Medal, Amer. Chem. Soc., 1944; Medal of Merit with Oak Leaf Cluster, 1948; Woodrow Wilson Award for Distinguished Service, 1959; Presidential Medal of Freedom, 1963; Great Living American Award, 1965; Sylvanus Thayer Award, 1965; Arches of Science Award, 1967; Atomic Pioneer Award, 1970. Hon. Fellow, Emmanuel Coll., Cambridge. Comdr, Legion of Honor. *Publications:* Practical Chemistry (with N. H. Black); Organic Chemistry; Chemistry of Organic Compounds; Our Fighting Faith, 1942; On Understanding Science, 1947; Education in a Divided World, 1948 (Gleichkeit der Chancen, 1955); Fundamentals of Organic Chemistry (with A. H. Blatt), 1950; Science and Common Sense, 1951; Modern Science and Modern Man, 1952; Education and Liberty, 1953; The Citadel of Learning, 1956; Germany and Freedom, 1958; The American High School Today, 1959; The Child, The Parent, and the State, 1959; Education in the Junior High School Years, 1960; Slums and Suburbs, 1961; Thomas Jefferson and the Development of American Public Education, 1962; The Education of American Teachers, 1963; Two Modes of Thought, 1964; Shaping Educational Policy, 1964; The Comprehensive High School, 1967; Scientific Principles and Moral Conduct, 1967; My Several Lives, 1970; Editor: Vols II and IX Organic Syntheses; Harvard Case Histories in Experimental Science; papers in scientific journals on researches in organic chemistry. *Address:* (home) 200 East 66th Street, New York, NY 10021. *Clubs:* Athenæum; Tavern, Harvard; Century, Chemists, Harvard (New York); Cosmos (Washington).

CONANT, Sir John (Ernest Michael), 2nd Bt *cr* 1954; farmer and landowner, since 1949; *b* 24 April 1923; *s* of Sir Roger Conant, 1st Bt, CVO, and of Daphne, Lady Conant, *d* of A. E. Learoyd; *S* father, 1973; *m* 1950, Periwinkle Elizabeth, *d* of late Dudley Thorp, Kimbolton, Hunts; two *s* two *d* (and one *s* decd). *Educ:* Eton; Corpus Christi Coll., Cambridge (BA Agric). Served in Grenadier Guards, 1942-45; at CCC Cambridge, 1946-49. Farming in Rutland, 1950-; High Sheriff of Rutland, 1960. *Recreations:* fishing, shooting, tennis. *Heir: s* Simon Edward Christopher Conant, *b* 13 Oct. 1958. *Address:* Lyndon Hall, Oakham, Rutland LE15 8TU. *T:* Manton 275. *Club:* Farmers'.

CONCANNON, John Dennis; MP (Lab) Mansfield, since 1966; Minister of State, Northern Ireland Office, since 1976; *b* 16 May 1930; *m* 1953, Iris May Wilson; two *s* two *d. Educ:* Rossington Sec. Sch. Coldstream Guards, 1947-53; Mem. Nat. Union of Mineworkers, 1953-66; Branch Official, 1960-65. Mem., Mansfield Town Council, 1962-66. Asst Govt Whip, 1968-70; Opposition Whip, 1970-74; Vice-Chamberlain, HM Household, 1974; Parly Under-Sec. of State, NI Office, 1974-76. *Recreations:* cricket, basket-ball. *Address:* 69 Skegby Lane, Mansfield, Notts. *T:* Mansfield 27235.

CONDLIFFE, John Bell, MA, DSc, LLD, LittD; retired; Consultant, Stanford Research Institute, Menlo Park, 1959-74; Professor of Economics, 1940-58, now Emeritus, University of California, Berkeley; *b* Melbourne, Australia, 23 Dec. 1891; *s* of Alfred B. and Margaret Condliffe; *m* 1916, Olive Grace, *d* of Charles Mills; two *s* one *d. Educ:* Canterbury Coll., University of NZ; Gonville and Caius Coll., Cambridge (Sir Thomas Gresham Research Student). Prof. of Economics, Canterbury Coll., 1920-26; Research Sec., Institute of Pacific Relations, 1927-31; Visiting Prof. of Economics, Univ. of Mich, 1930-31; Economic Intelligence Service, League of Nations, 1931-36; Univ. Prof. of Commerce, LSE, 1936-39; Associate-Dir, Div. of Economics and History, Carnegie Endowment for International Peace, 1943-48; Research Associate, Institute of International Studies, Yale Univ., 1943-44; Fulbright Research Scholar, Cambridge Univ., 1951; Consultant, Reserve Bank of New Zealand, 1957; Adviser, National Council of Applied Economic Research, New Delhi, 1959-60; Henry E. Howland Memorial

Prize, 1939; Wendell L. Willkie Memorial Prize, 1950; Sir James Wattie Prize, 1972. FRSA, 1949; Fellow Amer. Assoc. for the Advancement of Science, 1953. Gold Cross, Royal Order of Phœnix (Greece), 1954. *Publications:* The Life of Society, 1922; A Short History of New Zealand, 1925; Problems of the Pacific, 1928; New Zealand in the Making, 1930 (rev. edn, 1959); Problems of the Pacific, 1929, 1930; China To-day-Economic, 1933; World Economic Survey, 1931-32, 1932-33, 1933-34, 1934-35, 1935-36, 1936-37; The Reconstruction of World Trade, 1940; Agenda for a Post-War World, 1942; The Common Interest in International Economic Organization (with A. Stevenson), 1944; The Commerce of Nations, 1950; Point Four and the World Economy, 1950; The Welfare State in New Zealand, 1958; Foreign Aid Re-examined, 1963; The Development of Australia, 1964; Foresight and Enterprise, 1965; Economic Outlook for New Zealand, 1969; Te Rangi Hiroa: the life of Sir Peter Buck, 1971; Defunct Economists, 1974; articles in journals, etc. *Address:* 1641 Canyonwood Court No 1, Walnut Creek, Calif 94595, USA. *Clubs:* Bohemian (San Francisco); Faculty (Berkeley); Cosmos (Washington).

CONDON, Denis David, OBE 1964; Senior Representative at Lloyd's of London for Neilson McCarthy, Consultants, 1968-75; *b* 23 Oct. 1910; *s* of Capt. D. Condon and Mrs A. E. Condon; *m* 1933, Mary Marson; one *d. Educ:* Paston Grammar Sch., North Walsham, Norfolk. Journalist until 1939. War Service with Royal Artillery, UK and Burma (Major). Joined India Office, 1946; CRO, 1947; served India, Ceylon, Australia, Nigeria; Head of News Dept, CO, 1967-68. *Recreations:* fishing, bird-watching, gardening. *Address:* Rose Cottage, Weir, Dulverton, Somerset. *T:* Dulverton 309. *Clubs:* Gymkhana (Delhi); Australasian Pioneers (Sydney).

CONEY, Rev. Canon Harold Robert Harvey, MA Oxon; *b* 28 Oct. 1889; *s* of John Harvey and Hope Josephine Coney; *m* 1925, Edith Mary Carpenter; three *s* one *d. Educ:* Keble Coll., Oxford; Cuddesdon Coll. Formerly an Architect; served in France, 1915-17, Civil Service Rifles (despatches); Meritorious Service Medal, 1916; deacon, 1920; priest, 1921; Curate of Bermondsey, 1920-23; Warden of Caius Coll. Mission, Battersea, 1923-28; Vicar of Felkirk, 1928-37; Canon Missioner of Wakefield Cathedral, 1937-40; Champney Lecturer in Christian Evidence, 1937-40; Campden Lecturer, Wakefield Cathedral, 1937-40; Rector of Thornhill, Dewsbury, 1940-61 and Rural Dean of Dewsbury, 1947-61; Hon. Canon of Wakefield Cathedral, 1937-61, Canon Emeritus, 1961; Curate of Coonamble, NSW, Australia, 1961-63; Permission to officiate, Bath and Wells, 1963-69, Brisbane, 1969-75. *Recreation:* laughing. *Address:* Ellesborough Manor, Butler's Cross, near Aylesbury, Bucks.

CONGLETON, 8th Baron *cr* 1841; **Christopher Patrick Parnell;** Bt 1766; *b* 11 March 1930; *s* of 6th Baron Congleton (*d* 1932) and Hon. Edith Mary Palmer Howard (MBE 1941) (she *m* 2nd, 1946, Flight Lieut A. E. R. Aldridge, who died 1950), *d* of late R. J. B. Howard and late Lady Strathcona and Mount Royal; *S* brother, 1967; *m* 1955; Anna Hedvig, *d* of G. A. Sommerfelt, Oslo, Norway; two *s* three *d. Educ:* Eton; New Coll., Oxford. *Heir: s* Hon. John Patrick Christian Parnell, *b* 17 March 1959. *Address:* Ebbesbourne Wake, Salisbury, Wilts.

CONLAN, Bernard; MP (Lab) Gateshead (East) since 1964; Engineer; *b* 24 Oct. 1923; *m* ; one *d. Educ:* Manchester Primary and Secondary Schs. Mem., AEU, 1940-, Officer, 1943-. City Councillor, Manchester, 1954-66. Joined Labour Party, 1942; contested (Lab) High Peak, 1959. A Vice-Chm., Parly Lab. Party Trade Union Gp, 1974-. *Address:* House of Commons, SW1; 33 Beccles Road, Sale, Cheshire.

CONN, Prof. John Farquhar Christie, DSc; CEng; FRINA; John Elder Professor of Naval Architecture, University of Glasgow, 1957-73; *b* 5 July 1903; *s* of Alexander Aberdein Conn and Margaret Rhind Wilson; *m* 1935, Doris Maude Yeatman; one *s* one *d. Educ:* Robert Gordon's Coll., Aberdeen; Glasgow Univ. Apprenticeship at Alexander Hall and Co. Ltd, Aberdeen, 1920-25; employed in several shipyards; Scientific staff, Ship Div., National Physical Laboratory, 1929-44; Chief Naval Architect, British Shipbuilding Research Association, 1945-57. Hon. Vice-Pres., RINA. *Publications:* various papers in Trans. of Royal Instn of Naval Architects and other learned societies. *Recreations:* music, reading. *Address:* 14 Elm Walk, Bearsden, Glasgow G61 3BQ. *T:* 041-942 4640.

CONNALLY, John Bowden; lawyer; *b* 27 Feb. 1917; *s* of John Bowden Connally and Lela (*née* Wright); *m* 1940, Idanell Brill; two *s* one *d. Educ:* Univ. of Texas (LLB). Served US Navy, 1941-46. Pres. and Gen. Manager, KVET radio stn, 1946-49; Admin. Asst to Lyndon Johnson, 1949; employed with Powell, Wirtz & Rauhut, 1950-52; Attorney to Richardson & Bass, oil merchants, 1952-61; Sec. US Navy, 1961; Governor of Texas, 1962-68; Secretary of the Treasury, USA, 1971-72. Member: President's Adv. Cttee on Exec. Organisation, 1969-70; President's Foreign Intelligence Adv. Bd, 1972-74 and 1976-; US Adv. Cttee on reform of Internat. Monetary System, 1973-74; Partner, Vinson Elkins, 1972-; Director: Gibraltar Savings Assoc., 1972-; First City National Bank of Houston 1972-; Falconbridge Nickel Mines, 1973-; First City Bancorporation of Texas, 1974-; Justin Industries Inc., 1975-; Greyhound Corporation, 1977-; The Methodist Hospital, 1977-. *Address:* c/o Vinson Elkins, First City National Bank Building, Houston, Texas 77002, USA.

CONNELL, Sir Charles (Gibson), Kt 1952; Consultant, Connell & Connell, WS, 10 Dublin Street, Edinburgh; *b* 11 March 1899; *s* of late Sir Isaac Connell, SSC, and Mary Jane (*née* Gibson); *m* 1927, Constance Margaret Weir (*d* 1976); one *s* one *d. Educ:* Melville Coll., Edinburgh; Edinburgh Univ. 2nd Lieut RFA, 1917-19. WS 1923; BL Edinburgh, 1923. JP City of Edinburgh, 1933. Secretary: Royal Scottish Agricultural Benevolent Instn, 1935-66; Scottish Agricultural Arbiters Assoc., 1935-66; Chm., Dominion & General Trust Ltd; Dir, The Edinburgh Building Soc.; Life Governor, Melville Coll. Trust. Member: Nature Conservancy, 1961-73 (Chm., Scottish Cttee, 1961-72); Council, Soc. for Promotion of Nature Conservation; Council for Nature; Dept Cttee on Registration of Title to Land in Scotland, 1963; Chm., Scottish Wildlife Trust; Hon. Vice-Pres., Selborne Soc. Pres., Scottish Unionist Assoc., 1944-45 (Joint Hon. Sec., 1938-54); Hon. Pres., Scottish Ornithologists Club; Trustee, Scottish Country Life Museums Trust. Hon. LLD Dundee, 1976. *Publications:* Ed 3rd, 4th and 5th Edns (1961) of Connell on the Agricultural Holdings (Scotland) Acts. *Recreations:* wildlife conservation, gardening. *Address:* 12 Abbotsford Park, Edinburgh EH10 5DZ. *T:* 031-447 2026. *Clubs:* Caledonian, New (Edinburgh).

CONNELL, Charles Percy; Puisne Judge, Kenya Colony, 1951-64, retired; *b* 1 Oct. 1902; *s* of late C. R. Connell, Barrister-at-Law and late K. Adlard; *m* 1946, Mary O'Rourke. *Educ:* Charterhouse; New Coll., Oxford (Hons, Jurisprudence). Called to Bar, Lincoln's Inn, 1927. Joined Kenya Judicial Service, 1938 (Resident Magistrate). Served War of 1939-45 (8th Army Clasp and war medals); commissioned King's African Rifles, 1941; British Military Administration (Legal and Judicial), Eritrea and Tripolitania, 1942-46. Acting Puisne Judge, Kenya, 1950, retired 1964. *Recreations:* tennis, cricket and trout fishing. *Address:* c/o National Westminster Bank, 14 Sloane Square, SW1.

CONNELL, John MacFarlane; Member of Management Committee, The Distillers Company Ltd, since 1971; *b* 29 Dec. 1924; *s* of late John Maclean Connell and Mollie Isobel MacFarlane; *m* 1949, Jean Matheson Sutherland Mackay, *d* of late Major George Sutherland Mackay and Christine Bourne; two *s. Educ:* Stowe; Christ Church, Oxford. Joined Tanqueray, Gordon & Co. Ltd, 1946, Export Dir 1954, Man. Dir 1962-70; Dir, Distillers Co. Ltd, 1965; Chm., Gin Rectifiers and Distillers Assoc., 1968-71. Pres., Royal Warrant Holders Assoc., 1975. *Recreations:* golf, shooting. *Address:* 20 St James's Square, SW1Y 4JF. *T:* 01-930 1040. *Club:* Royal and Ancient (St Andrews).

CONNELL, Dame Ninette; *see* de Valois, Dame Ninette.

CONNELL, Philip Henry; Physician, The Bethlem Royal Hospital and The Maudsley Hospital, since 1963; *b* 6 July 1921; *s* of George Henry Connell and Evelyn Hilda Sykes; *m* 1st, 1948, Marjorie Helen Gilham; two *s*; 2nd, 1973, Cecily Mary Harper. *Educ:* St Paul's Sch.; St Bartholomew's Hosp., London. MD, BS, MRCS, FRCP, FRCPsych, DPM (academic). St Stephen's Hosp., Fulham Road, 1951-53; Bethlem Royal and Maudsley Hosps, 1953-57; Cons. Psychiatrist, Newcastle Gen. Hosp. and Physician i/c Child Psychiatry Unit, Newcastle Gen. Hosp. in assoc. with King's Coll., Durham Univ., and Assoc. Phys., Royal Victoria Infirm., 1957-63. Extensive nat. and internat. work on drug addiction and dependence (incl. work for WHO, Council of Europe and CENTO), and on maladjusted and psychiatrically ill children and adolescents. Mem. numerous adv. cttees, working parties, etc; Pres., Soc. for Study of Addiction, 1973-76; Chm., Inst. for Study of Drug Dependence; Mem. Council, RCPsych. Mem., editorial bds, various jls. *Publications:* Amphetamine Psychosis (monograph), 1958; (ed jtly) Cannabis and Man, 1975; numerous chapters in books, papers in sci. jls and proc. sci. confs. *Recreations:* theatre, bridge, tennis. *Address:* 25 Oxford Road, Putney, SW15 2LG. *T:* 01-788 1416; 21 Wimpole Street, W1M 7AD. *T:* 01-636 2220. *Club:* Athenæum.

CONNELLY, Marc; playwright; *b* 13 Dec. 1890; *s* of Patrick Joseph Connelly and Mabel Louise Fowler Cook. *Educ:* Trinity Hall, Washington, PA. Member of Authors' League of America (Past Pres.) and of National Inst. of Arts and Letters (Past Pres.). Prof. of Playwriting, Yale (retired). LittD (Hon.) Bowdoin. *Publications:* Plays: The Wisdom Tooth, The Green Pastures (awarded Pulitzer Prize, 1930), and others; co-author: Dulcy, Merton of the Movies, Beggar on Horseback, To the Ladies, Farmer Takes a Wife, and others; several musical comedies; A Souvenir from Qam (novel), 1965; Voices Offstage (memoirs), 1968; contributor of verse, articles and fiction to magazines, including Coroner's Inquest (awarded O. Henry short-story prize). *Address:* 25 Central Park West, New York City, NY, USA. *TA:* Marconel NY. *T:* Circle 7-2147. *Clubs:* Savage; Players' (New York).

CONNELLY, Thomas John; *b* 24 Dec. 1925; *s* of William and Jane Connelly; *m* 1952, Naomi Shakow; one *s* one *d. Educ:* Priory St Elementary Sch., Colchester; Ruskin Coll.; Lincoln Coll., Oxford. BA 1955. Research Officer: Amalgamated Soc. of Woodworkers, 1955-63; G&MWU, 1963-66; Adviser, Industrial Relations Prices and Incomes Bd, 1966-68; various posts, finally as Chief Officer, Race Relations Bd, 1968-77; apptd Chief Executive, Commn for Racial Equality, 1977, but withdrew from appt. *Publication:* The Woodworkers 1860-1960, 1960. *Recreations:* reading, walking. *Address:* 4 Grena Gardens, Richmond, Surrey. *T:* 01-940 0471.

CONNER, Cyril, JP; *b* 26 Feb. 1900; *m* 1st, 1930, Mary Stephanie Douglass; two *d*; 2nd, 1946, Margaret Isobel Hunt (*née* Murison); one *d* (one step *s* adopted). *Educ:* Haileybury; Merton Coll., Oxford. MA Greats and Law. Commn in RGA 1918. Called to Bar, Inner Temple, and practised at Common Law Bar, London, 1924-38; Arbitrator for Milk Marketing Board, 1934-38; BBC Dir for NE England, 1938; Head of BBC's Commonwealth and Foreign Relations, 1941-60, except Jan.-July 1953, when BBC Controller for Northern Ireland. Mem., Administrative Council of European Broadcasting Union, 1951-60. Delegate to Commonwealth Broadcasting Confs, 1946, 1952, 1956, 1960. Chm. of Frances Martin Coll., London, 1950 and 1951. Dep. Chm., West Sussex QS, 1963-71; JP West Sussex, 1963-. Chm., Rent Assessment Cttee for Surrey and Sussex, 1966-73. Company Director, 1973-. *Publications:* contributions to Juridical Review and other legal journals. *Address:* Lovehill House, Trotton, near Rogate, West Sussex. *T:* Midhurst 3665. *Clubs:* Athenæum, Special Forces.

CONNER, Rearden; (pen-name of **Patrick Reardon Connor**), MBE 1967; novelist and short-story writer; *b* 19 Feb. 1907; *s* of John and Bridie Connor; *m* 1942, Malinka Marie Smith; no *c. Educ:* Christian Brothers Schs; Presentation Coll., Cork. Worked in Min. of Aircraft Production, during War, in Research and Development of Equipment. Carried on in this field, after war, in Min. of Supply, and later in Min. of Aviation and Min. of Technology. Critic of fiction, The Fortnightly, 1935-37, also on Books of the Month; Reader of fiction for Cassell, 1948-56. Work has been included in: Best Short Stories Anthology (twice); Pick of To-Day's Short Stories; Whit Burnett anthology (USA), Stories of the Forties. *Publications:* Shake Hands with The Devil, 1933 (Literary Guild Selection in USA; filmed, 1958); Rude Earth, 1934; Salute to Aphrodite, 1935 (USA); I am Death, 1936; Time to Kill, 1936 (USA); Men Must Live, 1937; The Sword of Love, 1938; Wife of Colum, 1939; The Devil Among the Tailors, 1947; My Love to the Gallows, 1949; Hunger of the Heart, 1950; The Singing Stone, 1951; The House of Cain, 1952; (under *pseudonym* Peter Malin): To Kill is My Vocation, 1939; River, Sing Me a Song, 1939; Kobo the Brave, 1950. *Recreations:* listening to music; going to the theatre. *Address:* 4 Hastings Drive, Hunstanton, Norfolk. *T:* Hunstanton 2372.

CONNERY, Sean, (Thomas Connery); actor; *b* 25 Aug. 1930; *s* of Joseph and Euphamia Connery; *m* 1st, 1962, Diane (marr. diss. 1974), *d* of Sir Raphael West Cilento, *qv*, and Lady Cilento; one *s* (and one step *d*); 2nd, 1975, Micheline Roquebrune. Served Royal Navy. Dir, Tantallon Films Ltd, 1972-. Has appeared in films: No Road Back, 1956; Action of the Tiger, 1957; Another Time, Another Place, 1957; Hell Drivers, 1958; Tarzan's Greatest Adventure, 1959; Darby O'Gill and the Little People, 1959; On the Fiddle, 1961; The Longest Day, 1962; The Frightened City, 1962; Woman of Straw, 1964; The Hill, 1965; A Fine Madness, 1966; Shalako, 1968; The Molly Maguires, 1968; The Red Tent (1st Russian co-production), 1969; The Anderson Tapes, 1970; The Offence, 1973; Zardoz, 1973; Ransom, 1974; Murder on the Orient Express, 1974; The Wind and the Lion, 1975; The Man Who Would Be King, 1975; Robin and Marian, 1976; *as James Bond:* Dr No, 1963; From Russia With Love, 1964; Goldfinger, 1965; Thunderball, 1965; You

Only Live Twice, 1967; Diamonds are Forever, 1971. *Recreations:* oil painting, golf, reading, cooking. *Address:* c/o ICM Ltd, 22 Grafton Street, W1.

CONNOLLY, Sir Willis (Henry), Kt 1971; CBE 1962; Chairman, State Electricity Commission of Victoria, 1956-71; *b* 25 Nov. 1901; *s* of Joseph John Connolly and Adelaide May Connolly (*née* Little); *m* 1927, Mary Milton Clark; one *s* one *d. Educ:* Benalla High Sch. (Matriculation Cert.); Univ. of Melbourne (BEE, BCom). Whole Career spent with SEC of Victoria, 1921-71: Engr and Manager, Electricity Supply, 1937-49; Asst to Gen. Manager, 1949-51; Asst Gen. Manager, 1951-56. Pres. Victoria Inst. of Colleges, 1967-74. Chm., Aust. Nat. Cttee, World Energy Conf., 1958- (Pres., World Energy Conf., 1962-68); Past Pres., Electricity Supply Assoc. of Australia; former Chm., Electrical Research Bd; Mem., Faculty of Engineering, Univ. of Melbourne. Kernot Meml Medal, 1957; "The Australasian Engineer" Award, 1960; Peter Nicol Russell Meml Medal, 1968. Hon. Mem. Australasian Inst. of Mining and Metallurgy, 1970. Hon. DEng Monash, 1967; Hon. DEd, Victoria Inst. of Colleges, 1974. *Recreations:* tennis (a Vice-Pres., LTA of Victoria); photography, music, reading. *Address:* 16 Monkstadt Street, St Kilda, Victoria 3182, Australia. *T:* 91 2670. *Clubs:* Australian, Melbourne, Rotary (all in Melbourne).

CONNOR, Bishop of, since 1969; **Rt. Rev. Arthur Hamilton Butler,** MBE 1944; DD; MA; *b* 8 March 1912; *s* of George Booker and Anne Maude Butler; *m* 1938, Betty (*d* 1976), *d* of Seton Pringle, FRCSI; one *s. Educ:* Friars School, Bangor; Trinity Coll., Dublin. Curate: Monkstown, Dublin, 1935-37; Christ Church, Crouch End, N8, 1937; Holy Trinity, Brompton, SW3, 1938-39. Army, 1939-45: Chaplain, 2nd DCLI, 1939-43; Senior Chaplain, 1st Div., 1943-45. Incumbent of Monkstown, 1945-58; Bishop of Tuam, Killala and Achonry, 1958-69. *Recreations:* golf, fishing. *Address:* Bishop's House, 22 Deramore Park, Belfast BT9 5JU. *T:* Belfast 668442. *Clubs:* Ulster (Belfast); University, Royal Irish Yacht (Dublin).

CONNOR, Patrick Reardon; *see* Conner, Rearden.

CONOLLY-CAREW, family name of **Baron Carew.**

CONQUEST, (George) Robert (Acworth), OBE 1955; writer; *b* 15 July 1917; *s* of late Robert Folger Westcott Conquest and Rosamund, *d* of H. A. Acworth, CIE; *m* 1st, 1942, Joan Watkins (marr. diss. 1948); two *s*; 2nd, 1948, Tatiana Mihailova (marr. diss. 1962); 3rd, 1964, Caroleen, *d* of C. A. Macfarlane, Castle Eden. *Educ:* Winchester; Magdalen Coll., Oxford. MA Oxon 1972; DLitt 1974. Oxf. and Bucks LI, 1939-46; Foreign Service, 1946-56; Fellow, LSE, 1956-58; Fellow, Univ. of Buffalo, 1959-60; Literary Editor, The Spectator, 1962-63; Fellow, Columbia Univ., 1964-65; Fellow, Woodrow Wilson International Center, 1976-77; Fellow, Hoover Instn, 1977-. FRSL 1972. *Publications:* Poems, 1955; A World of Difference, 1955; (ed) New Lines, 1956; Common Sense About Russia, 1960; Power and Policy in the USSR, 1961; Courage of Genius, 1962; Between Mars and Venus, 1962; (ed) New Lines II, 1963; (with Kingsley Amis) The Egyptologists, 1965; The Great Terror, 1968; Arias from a Love Opera, 1969; The Nation Killers, 1970; Lenin, 1972, etc. *Address:* 28 Shawfield Street, SW3. *T:* 01-352 2334. *Club:* Travellers'.

CONRAN, (George) Loraine, FMA; Director, Manchester City Art Galleries, 1962-76; *b* 29 March 1912; *o s* of Col George Hay Montgomery Conran; *m* 1st, 1938, Jacqueline Elspeth Norah Thullier O'Neill Roe (marr. diss. 1970); one *s* one *d* (and one *d* decd); 2nd, 1970, Elizabeth Margaret Johnston; one *d. Educ:* RNC Dartmouth. Museum and Art Gallery, Birmingham, 1935; Walker Art Gallery, Liverpool, 1936; Southampton Art Gallery, 1938; Curator, The Iveagh Bequest, Kenwood, 1950. Pres., Museums Assoc. (Hon. Sec., 1959-64); Hon. Sec., Contemporary Art Soc., 1959-65. Chm., Jt Cttee of Museums Assoc. and Carnegie UK Trust; Member: British Nat. Cttee, Internat. Council of Museums, 1959-71; Ct, RCA. Hon. MA Manchester, 1973. Served War of 1939-45 (despatches). *Address:* 9 Church Wood Road, Manchester M20 0TZ. *T:* 061-445 7133. *Club:* Athenæum.

CONRAN, Terence Orby; Chairman: Habitat Design Holdings Ltd, since 1971; Habitat America Holdings Inc.; Habitat Europe Ltd; Director: Conran Ink; The Neal Street Restaurant; The Creative Business; Conran Associates; *b* 4 Oct. 1931; *m*; two *s*; *m* 1963, Caroline Herbert; two *s* one *d. Educ:* Bryanston, Dorset. Chm., Conran Holdings Ltd, 1965-68; Jt Chm., Ryman Conran Ltd, 1968-71. Mem., Royal Commn on Environmental Pollution, 1973-76. RSA Presidential Medal for Design Management to Conran Group; RSA Presidential Award for Design Management to Habitat Designs Ltd, 1975. *Publications:*

The House Book, 1974; The Kitchen Book, 1977. *Recreations:* gardening, cooking. *Address:* Barton Court, Kintbury, Newbury, Berks. *T:* Kintbury 200.

CONROY, Sir Diarmaid (William), Kt 1962; CMG 1960; OBE 1955; TD 1946; QC (Gibraltar) 1953; (Kenya) 1956; Chairman, Industrial Tribunals (Southampton), since 1974; President, Industrial Tribunals for England and Wales, 1965-74; *b* 22 Dec. 1913; *m* 1939, Alice Lilian Elizabeth Craig; one *s* two *d. Educ:* Mount St Mary's; Gray's Inn. Practised at Bar, 1935-39; served War, 1939-46, with London Irish Rifles (Major, wounded); Crown Counsel, N Rhodesia, 1946; Legal Draftsman, N Rhodesia, 1949; Attorney-Gen., Gibraltar, 1952; Permanent Sec. of Ministry of Legal Affairs, Solicitor-Gen. and Dep.-Speaker, Kenya, 1955-61; Chief Justice, N Rhodesia, 1961-65. *Recreations:* sailing, fishing. *Address:* 26 Ward Avenue, Cowes, Isle of Wight PO31 8AY. *T:* Cowes 5949. *Club:* Royal London Yacht (Cowes).

CONS, Hon. Derek; Hon. Mr Justice Cons; Judge of Supreme Court of Hong Kong, since 1972; *b* 15 July 1928; *s* of Alfred Henry Cons and Elsie Margaret (*née* Neville); *m* 1952, Mary Roberta Upton Wilkes. *Educ:* Rutlish; Birmingham Univ. (LLB (Hons)). Called to Bar, Gray's Inn, 1953. RASC (2nd Lieut), 1946-48. Magistrate, Hong Kong, 1955-62; Principal Magistrate, Hong Kong, 1962-66; District Judge, Hong Kong, 1966-72. *Recreations:* golf, sailing. *Address:* The Supreme Court, Hong Kong; Mulberry Mews, Church Street, Fordingbridge, Hants. *Clubs:* Bramshaw Golf (Hants); Hong Kong, Royal Hong Kong Yacht, Shek O Country (Hong Kong).

CONSTABLE, Sir Robert Frederick S.; *see* Strickland-Constable.

CONSTANT, Antony; Group Management Development Executive, the Delta Metal Co. Ltd; *b* 1918; *s* of Frederick Charles and Mary Theresa Constant; *m* 1947, Pamela Mary Pemberton; one *s. Educ:* Dover Coll.; King's Coll., Cambridge. Asst master, Oundle Sch., 1939-45; Staff of Dir of Naval Intelligence, Admiralty, 1940-44; Educational Adviser to the Control Commission, Germany, 1945. Asst Master, and Asst House Master of School House, Rugby Sch., 1945-49; Rector of Royal Coll., Mauritius, 1949-53; Dir of Studies, RAF Coll., Cranwell, 1953-59; Educational Adviser to the Ministry of Defence and Chm. of Joint-Services Working Party, 1959-62; joined Delta Group of Companies, 1963, as Head of Training Dept. Mem. Bd for Postgraduate Studies, and Mem. Faculty Bd, Management Centre, Univ. of Aston, 1973-77. *Publications:* various papers on historical geography. *Recreations:* ornithology, sailing. *Address:* Delta Metal Co. Ltd, Management Development Office, Great Tindal Street, Ladywood, Birmingham B16 8DR.

CONSTANTINE, Air Chief Marshal Sir Hugh (Alex), KBE 1958 (CBE 1944); CB 1946; DSO 1942; Co-ordinator, Anglo-American Community Relations, Ministry of Defence (Air), 1964-77; *b* 23 May 1908; *s* of Fleet Paymaster Henry Constantine, RN, and Alice Louise Squire; *m* 1937, Helen, *d* of J. W. Bourke, Sydney, Australia; one *d. Educ:* Christ's Hosp.; Royal Air Force Coll., Cranwell. Pilot Officer in RAF, 1927; 56 (F) Sqdn, 1928-29; Flying Instructor, RAF Coll., 1930-31; CFS Instructor, 1932-33 and 1936-37; No 1 Armoured Car Co. (Iraq), 1934-36 (Palestine, despatches); Sqdn Ldr, 1936; 214 Bomber Sqdn, 1936-38; graduated Staff Coll., Andover, 1940; served in Bomber Comd, 1940-45 (despatches, four times); Gp Capt. 1941; comd RAF Elsham Wolds, 1942; SASO No 1 (B) Gp, 1944; Dep. SASO Bomber Comd; Air Vice-Marshal, Jan. 1945, and commanded No 5 (B) Group Bomber Command; Chief Intelligence Officer, BAFO and Control Commission, Germany, 1946; idc, 1947; SASO, 205 Gp (Egypt), 1948-49; Dir of Intelligence, Air Min., 1950-51; AO i/c A, Fighter Comd, 1952-54; AOC No 25 Group, Flying Training Command, 1954-56; Deputy Chief of Staff (Plans and Operations), SHAPE, NATO, 1956-59; AOC-in-C, Flg Trg Comd, 1959-61; Commandant, Imperial Defence Coll., 1961-64. Air Marshal, 1958; Air Chief Marshal, 1961. Governor, Christ's Hospital, 1963. Order of Polonia Restituta (2nd Class), 1945. *Recreations:* Rugby (English Trial, 1934), Eastern Counties, RAF and Leicester; golf. *Address:* 4 Chester Row, SW1. *T:* 01-730 0700. *Club:* Royal Air Force.

CONSTANTINE, Sir Theodore, Kt 1964; CBE 1956; AE 1945; DL; *b* 15 March 1910; *er s* of Leonard and Fanny Louise Constantine; *m* 1935, Sylvia Mary, *y d* of Wallace Henry Legge-Pointing; one *s* one *d. Educ:* Acton Coll. Personal Asst to Chm. of public company, 1926-28; Executive in industry, 1928-38; Managing Dir of public company subsidiary, 1938-39. Served War of 1939-45, Auxiliary Air Force. Resumed pre-war

Directorships, Oct. 1945. Dir of Industrial Holding Company, 1956-59; Chm. of Public Companies, 1959-68. Organisational work for Conservative Party as Constituency Chm., Area Chm., Mem. Nat. Exec. Cttee, Policy Cttee, Nat. Advisory Cttee on Publicity. Chm., Nat. Union Cons. and Unionist Assocs, 1967-68. Trustee, Sir John Wolstenholme Charity; Master, Worshipful Co. of Coachmakers, 1975; Freeman of City of London. High Sheriff of Greater London, 1967; DL Greater London, 1967. *Recreations:* (now spectator) motor racing, power boats. *Address:* Hunters Beck, Uxbridge Road, Stanmore, Mddx. *T:* 01-954 0624. *Clubs:* Carlton, Royal Automobile; British Automobile Racing.

CONSTANTINE, Prof. Tom, CEng, FICE, FIMunE; Professor of Civil Engineering since 1967, Chairman of Civil Engineering Department since 1969, and Pro-Vice-Chancellor since 1975, Salford University; *b* 10 Sept. 1926; *s* of Arthur Constantine and Jane Alice Constantine (*née* Fenton); *m* 1949, Mary Moss; one *s* one *d*. *Educ:* Haslingden Grammar Sch.; Burnley Technical Coll.; Manchester Univ. BSc (Eng) London Univ., PhD Manchester. Asst Experimental Officer, Road Research Lab., 1946-48; Engineering Asst, City of Bradford, 1948-50; Asst Engineer, Oldham County Borough, 1950-52; Sen. Asst Engineer, St Helens Co. Borough, 1952-55; Lectr in Civil Engineering: Univ of Manchester, 1955-61; Univ. of Newcastle upon Tyne, 1961-66; Visiting Prof. and Research Engr, Univ. of California, 1964; Sen. Lectr in Civil Engrg, Univ. of Sheffield, 1966-67. Mem., SRC Civil Engrg and Transport Cttee and Chm. Transport Sub-Cttee. IMunE: Bronze Medals, 1956 and 1963; Rees Jeffreys Prizeman, 1961; ICE: Crampton Prizeman, 1963. *Publications:* Passenger Transport Integration, Pilot Study, Sheffield Area, Vols I and 2, 1966; numerous technical papers in Fluid Mechanics and Transport Engrg and Planning. *Recreations:* gardening, music, running. *Address:* 12 Rawlinson Road, Southport, Merseyside PR9 9LU. *T:* 35321.

CONTI, Rt. Rev. Mario Joseph; *see* Aberdeen, Bishop of, (RC).

CONWAY, Most Rev. Dominic J.; *see* Elphin, Bishop of, (RC).

CONWAY, Hugh Graham, CBE 1964; *b* 25 Jan. 1914; *s* of G. R. G. Conway; *m* 1937, Eva Gordon Simpson; two *s*. *Educ:* Merchiston Castle Sch., Edinburgh; Cambridge Univ. Joined aircraft industry, 1938; Man. Dir, Bristol Engine Division, Rolls Royce Ltd, 1964-70; Dir, Rolls-Royce Ltd, 1966-70, Rolls-Royce (1971) Ltd, 1971; Gp Managing Dir, Gas Turbines, Rolls-Royce Ltd, 1970-71. Member: Decimal Currency Board, 1967-71; Design Council, 1971- (Dep. Chm., 1972-76). *Publications:* Engineering Tolerances, 1948; Fluid Pressure Mechanisms, 1949; Landing Gear Design, 1958; Bugatti, 1963; Grand Prix Bugatti, 1968. *Recreation:* vintage motoring. *Address:* 33 Sussex Square, W2.

CONYNGHAM, family name of Marquess Conyngham.

CONYNGHAM, 7th Marquess *cr* 1816; Frederick William Henry Francis Conyngham; Baron Conyngham, 1781; Viscount Conyngham, 1789; Earl Conyngham, Viscount Mount Charles, 1797; Earl of Mount Charles, Viscount Slane, 1816; Baron Minster (UK), 1821; late Captain Irish Guards; *b* 13 March 1924; *e s* of 6th Marquess Conyngham and Antoinette Winifred (*d* 1966), *er d* of late J. W. H. Thompson; *S* father, 1974; *m* 1st, 1950, Eileen Wren (marr. diss. 1970), *o d* of Capt. C. W. Newsam, Ashfield, Beauparc, Co. Meath; three *s*; 2nd, 1971, Mrs Elizabeth Anne Rudd. *Educ:* Eton. *Heir: s* Earl of Mount Charles, *qv. Address:* Slane Castle, Co. Meath, Eire; Bifrons, near Canterbury. *Club:* Boodle's.

COOK, Prof. Alan Hugh, FRS 1969; Jackson Professor of Natural Philosophy, Cambridge University, since 1972; *b* 2 Dec. 1922; *s* of late Reginald Thomas Cook, OBE, and of Ethel Cook; *m* 1948, Isabell Weir Adamson; one *s* one *d*. *Educ:* Westcliff High Sch. for Boys; Corpus Christi Coll. Cambridge. MA, PhD, ScD. Admty Signal Estabt, 1943-46; Research Student, then Res. Asst, Dept of Geodesy and Geophysics, Cambridge, 1946-51; Metrology Div., Nat. Physical Laboratory, Teddington, 1952. Vis. Fellow, Jt Inst. for Laboratory Astrophysics, Boulder, Colorado, 1965-66; Supt, Standards (subseq. Quantum Metrology) Div., Nat. Physical Laboratory, 1966-69; Prof. of Geophysics, Univ. of Edinburgh, 1969-72. FInstP; FRSE 1970; Foreign Fellow, Acad. Naz. dei Lincei, 1971. Pres., RAS, 1977-. C. V. Boys Prize, Inst. of Physics, 1967. *Publications:* Gravity and the Earth, 1969; Global Geophysics, 1970; Interference of Electromagnetic Waves, 1971; Physics of the Earth and Planets, 1973; many contribs learned jls on gravity, artificial satellites, precise measurement, fundamental constants of physics and astronomy. *Recreations:* amateur theatre, travel, painting. *Address:* Cavendish Laboratory, Madingley Road, Cambridge

CB3 0HE. *T:* Cambridge 66477; King's College, Cambridge. *T:* Cambridge 50411; 8 Wootton Way, Cambridge CB3 9LX. *T:* Cambridge 56887.

COOK, Air Vice-Marshal Albert Frederick, CBE 1955 (OBE 1946); *b* 26 Aug. 1901; *s* of Charles Neville Cook, Dun Laoghaire, Co. Dublin; *m* 1st, 1929, Cecil Phyllis (*d* 1967), *d* of Lionel McEnnery, Dublin; two *d*; 2nd, 1969, Penelope, *d* of late K. B. Anderson, Weybridge. *Educ:* Kingstown Sch.; Royal College of Surgeons, Dublin. LRCP, LRCS, Ireland, 1924; DPH 1935. Joined RAF, 1925; seconded to Transjordan Frontier Force, 1928-30; served War of 1939-45 (despatches): Middle East, France and Germany; Principal Medical Officer, BAFO, Germany, 1949-51; PMO, Flying Trg Comd, 1951-55; PMO, Bomber Comd, 1955-56. QHP 1956; PMO, MEAF, 1957-59; retired, 1959. *Address:* Crown Cottage, Worplesdon, Surrey. *Club:* Royal Air Force.

COOK, Alexander Edward, CMG 1955; *b* 3 April 1906; *s* of Edward Arthur Cook and M. J. Cook (*née* Wreford); *m* 1936, Ethel Catherine Margaret (*née* Mayo); one *s* two *d*. *Educ:* Imperial Service Coll., Windsor; Pembroke Coll., Cambridge. Entered Colonial Service as a Cadet, Nigeria, 1928; Asst District Officer, District Officer, Asst Sec.; Financial Sec., Gibraltar, 1945; Financial Sec., Eastern Region, Nigeria, 1953; Permanent Sec., Ministry of Finance, Eastern Region, Nigeria, 1954; retired 1956; Mem., British Caribbean Federal Capital Commn, 1956. Attached Fed. Govt of UK of Libya as Economic Adviser, under auspices of UN Tech. Assistance Admin., 1959-60. *Recreations:* fishing and golf. *Address:* The White Cottage, Whitby Road, Milford-on-Sea, near Lymington, Hants. *T:* Milford-on-Sea 3526. *Clubs:* United Oxford & Cambridge University, Royal Over-Seas League.

COOK, (Alfred) Melville, MusDoc, FRCO; Organist and Choirmaster of the Metropolitan United, Toronto, since 1967; Member, Music Faculty (Organ), McMaster University, since 1974; *b* 18 June 1912; *s* of Harry Melville and Vera Louis Cook; *m* 1944, Marion Weir Moncrieff; no *c*. *Educ:* King's Sch., Gloucester. Chorister, 1923-28, Asst Organist, 1932-37, Gloucester Cathedral. Organist and Choirmaster: All Saints, Cheltenham, 1935-37; Leeds Parish Church, 1937-56. MusDoc Durham, 1940. Served War in RA, 1941-46. Organist and Master of the Choristers, Hereford Cathedral, 1956-66. Conductor, Three Choirs Festival, Hereford, 1958, 1961, 1964; Conductor, Hereford Choral Soc., 1957-66. Organist and Choirmaster, All Saints', Winnipeg; Conductor of the Winnipeg Philharmonic Choir, Canada, 1966. *Recreations:* walking, swimming. *Address:* Metropolitan United Church, 51 Bond Street, Toronto, Canada.

COOK, Arthur Herbert, FRS 1951; DSc, PhD, FRIC; Director, Brewing Industry Research Foundation, Nutfield, Surrey, 1958-71 (Assistant Director, 1949-58), retired 1971; *b* London, 10 July 1911; *s* of Arthur Cook, London. *Educ:* Owen's Sch., Islington, London; Universities of London (Imperial Coll. of Science and Technology) and Heidelberg. Joined staff of Imperial Coll., 1937; Asst Prof. and Reader in the University, 1947-49. Hon. DSc Heriot-Watt. *Publications:* (with late Prof. F. Mayer) Chemistry of the Natural Colouring Matters. Numerous articles, mainly in Journal of Chemical Soc. Editor, The Chemistry and Biology of Yeasts, 1958; Barley and Malt: Biology, Biochemistry, Technology, 1962. *Recreations:* gardening, photography. *Address:* Merrylands, Lympstone, Devon. *T:* Exmouth 71426. *Club:* Athenæum.

COOK, Bernard Christopher Allen, CMG 1958; OBE 1945; *b* 20 July 1906; *s* of late Sir Edward Cook, CSI, CIE; *m* 1933, Margaret Helen Mary, *d* of Rt Rev. C. E. Plumb, DD; two *d* (and one *s* decd). *Educ:* Radley Coll. (Open Scholarship); Brasenose Coll., Oxford (Open Scholarship). ICS 1929; held various posts in UP; Govt of India: Finance and Commerce Cadre, 1938; Custodian of Enemy Property, 1939-41; Actg Joint Sec., Finance Dept, and Mem. Central Legislative Assembly, 1946; Indian Trade Comr, London, 1946-47; Foreign Service, 1947; Control Commn, Germany (currency reform), 1948-49; Political Adviser, Asmara, 1949-51; First Sec. (Commercial), Paris, 1951-53; Counsellor (Commercial), Rangoon, 1953-57; Counsellor (Commercial), HBM Embassy, Mexico City, 1957-59; HM Consul-General, Barcelona, 1959-66; retired, 1966; re-employed, 1967-69. *Address:* 11 Priory Court, Granville Road, Eastbourne BN20 7ED. *Club:* Oriental.

COOK, Brian Francis, FSA; Keeper of Greek and Roman Antiquities, British Museum, since 1976; *b* 13 Feb. 1933; *yr s* of late Harry Cook and Renia Cook; *m* 1962, Veronica Dewhirst. *Educ:* St Bede's Grammar Sch., Bradford; Univ. of Manchester (BA); Downing Coll. and St Edmund's House, Cambridge

(MA); British Sch. at Athens. FSA 1971. Dept of Greek and Roman Art, Metropolitan Museum of Art, New York: Curatorial Asst, 1960; Asst Curator, 1961; Associate Curator, 1965-69; Asst Keeper, Dept of Greek and Roman Antiquities, BM, 1969-76. *Publications:* Inscribed Hadra Vases in the Metropolitan Museum of Art, 1966; Greek and Roman Art in the British Museum, 1976; articles and revs on Greek, Etruscan and Roman antiquities in Brit. and foreign periodicals. *Recreations:* reading, gardening. *Address:* 4 Belmont Avenue, Barnet, Herts. *T:* 01-440 6590. *Club:* Challoner.

COOK, Brian Hartley K.; *see* Kemball-Cook.

COOK, Charles Alfred George, MC 1945; GM 1945; FRCS; Consultant Ophthalmic Surgeon: Guy's Hospital, 1954-73; Moorfields Eye Hospital, 1956-73; Teacher of Ophthalmology, University of London (Guy's Hospital and Institute of Ophthalmology), 1955-73; *b* 20 Aug. 1913; *s* of late Charles F. Cook and Beatrice Grist; *m* 1939, Edna Constance Dobson; one *s* one *d*. *Educ:* St Edward's Sch., Oxford; Guy's Hospital. MRCS LRCP, 1939; DOMS (Eng.), 1946; FRCS, 1950. Capt. and Major RAMC, 1939-45. Moorfields Eye Hospital: Clinical Asst, 1946-47; Ho. Surg., 1948-49; Sen. Resident Officer, 1950; Chief Clin. Asst, 1951-55. Sen. Registrar, Eye Dept, Guy's Hospital, 1951-55; Moorfields Research Fellow, Inst. of Ophthalmology, 1951-58; Ophthalmic Surg., West Middlesex Hospital, 1954-56. Mem., Court of Examrs, RCS; Examr for DOMS, RCP and RCS; Examr Brit. Orthoptic Board; Sec., Ophthalmological Soc. of UK, 1956-57; Vice-Dean, Inst. of Ophthalmology, 1959-62. Governor, Royal Normal Coll. for Blind. Mem. Ct, Co. of Spectacle Makers. Freeman, City of London. *Publications:* (ed) S. Duke Elder, Embryology, vol. 3, 1963; (contrib.) Payling, Wright and Symers, Systematic Pathology, 1966; (jt) May and Worth, Diseases of the Eye, 1968; articles in Brit. Jl of Ophthalmology, Trans Ophthalmological Soc., Jl of Pathology and other Med. Jls. *Recreations:* swimming, reading; an interest in all outdoor recreations. *Address:* 13 Clarence Terrace, Regents Park, NW1. *T:* 01-723 5111. *Clubs:* Athenæum, Garrick.

COOK, Air Vice-Marshal Eric, DFC 1945; Bursar and Fellow, Hughes Hall, Cambridge, since 1975; *b* 30 April 1920; *s* of late Thomas Cook and Sara Elizabeth Cook (*née* Hunnam); *m* 1953, Thelma, *o d* of late Alfred and Isabelle Pentland Withnell, Chorley, Lancs; one *s*. *Educ:* Sunderland Technical Coll. MA Cantab. Served War, Bomber Command Sqdns, 1940-45 (despatches twice). Command, MEAF VIP Sqdn, 1951; Staff, HQ Transport Comd, 1953; Sqdn Comdr, Training Comd, 1955-57; Sen. Personnel Staff Officer, MEAF, 1959-60; Chief Instr, Jet Provost Wing, 1961; Sen. Air Staff Officer, Ghana Air Force, 1963; AOA, RAF Germany, 1968-71; Dir of Flying Training, 1971-72; Dir-Gen. RAF Training, 1972-75. *Recreations:* ball games, outdoor activities, music. *Address:* Hawkwood, Madeley Court, Hemingford Grey, Cambridgeshire. *T:* St Ives 63647. *Clubs:* Royal Air Force, MCC.

COOK, Eric William; Foreign and Commonwealth Office, since 1977; *b* 24 Feb. 1920; *s* of Ernest Gordon Cook and Jessie (*née* Hardy); *m* 1949, Pauline Elizabeth Lee; one *s*. *Educ:* various private estabts. RAF, 1940-46. GPO, 1947-49; FO (later FCO), 1949-; Consul, Belgrade, 1961-64; Vice-Consul, Leopoldville, 1964-65; Consul, Cleveland, Ohio, 1967-69; also served at Rome, Moscow, Peking and Djakarta; Consul Gen., Adelaide, 1974-76. *Recreations:* music, writing and photography. *Address:* 11 St Ann's Court, Nizells Avenue, Hove, East Sussex. *T:* Brighton 776100.

COOK, Vice-Adm. Eric William L.; *see* Longley-Cook.

COOK, Sir Francis Ferdinand Maurice, 4th Bt, *cr* 1886; *b* 21 Dec. 1907; *s* of Sir H. F. Cook, 3rd Bt, and Hon. Mary Hood, *e d* of 2nd Viscount Bridport; *S* father, 1939, also as Visconde de Monserrate in Portugal; *m* 1937, Joan Loraine Ashton-Case (marr. diss., 1942), *d* of late Hon. Mrs Herbert Eaton; one *s*; *m* 1951, Jane Audrey Nott (marr. diss., 1956), *er d* of Mrs Turnbull and step *d* of late Lieut-Comdr S. G. L. Turnbull, RN (retd); one *d*; *m* 1956, Mrs Bridget Brenda Polland (*née* Lynch), *d* of Thomas David Lynch. *Educ:* Bradfield Coll., Berks, and privately. Musician, composer, organist; reconstructive scientist on mediums and methods of the old masters. FRSA; Member: Chelsea Art Soc., 1938-; Royal Cornish Soc., Truro; Jersey Artists' Group; St Ives Soc. of Artists, Cornwall; Assoc. Mem., Royal Soc. of British Artists, 1938-48; Patron and Mem., British Picture Restorers Assoc. Gold Medallist, 1934. Exhibited works at RA, RBA, London Portrait Soc., London Group, etc., and provinces. Represented in the permanent collections Walker Art Gall., Liverpool, Manchester, Northampton. *Recreation:* architecture. *Heir: s* Christopher Wymondham Rayner Herbert

Cook [*b* 24 March 1938; *m* 1975, Mrs Margaret Miller, *d* of late John Murray (one *s* one *d* of previous marriage)]. *Address:* Le Coin, La Haule, St Aubin, Jersey, CI. *T:* Jersey Central 41234; (Studio) The Studio, Augres Galleries, Augres, Trinity, Jersey, CI. *T:* Jersey Central 63333. *Clubs:* Arts, Royal Automobile; Victoria (St Helier).

COOK, Francis John Granville, MA Cantab; Headmaster of Campbell College, Belfast, 1954-71; *b* 28 Jan. 1913; *o s* of late W. G. Cook and Nora Braley; *m* 1942, Jocelyn McKay, *d* of late John Stewart, Westholm, Dunblane, Perthshire; one *s* two *d*. *Educ:* Wyggeston Sch.; Downing Coll., Cambridge. Historical Tripos, Law Tripos; Squire Scholar; Tancred Studentship, Lincoln's Inn. Asst Master, Rossall Sch., 1937; served War, 1940-46, with Royal Navy; Headmaster of Junior Sch., Rossall Sch., 1949-54. *Recreations:* gardening, fishing, savouring retirement. *Address:* Greenhead of Troquhain, Balmaclellan, Castle Douglas, Kirkcudbrightshire. *T:* Corsock 653. *Clubs:* Naval.

COOK, Frank Patrick; Member, Commission for Local Administration in England; *b* 28 March 1920; *o c* of Frank Cook, FRCS, FRCOG and Edith Harriet (*née* Reid); *m* 1st, 1945, Rosemary Eason (marr. diss. 1975); two *s* one *d*; 2nd, 1975, Margaret Rodgers, 2nd *d* of Dr J. W. Rodgers, PhD. *Educ:* Rugby; Trinity Hall, Cambridge (Open Schol.); LSE (Personnel Management). Royal Marines, 1939-46; Courtaulds Ltd, 1946-56; Nat. Coal Board, 1956-61; Venesta Ltd, 1961-64; Principal, British Transport Staff Coll., 1964-69; First Chief Exec., English Tourist Board, 1970-74; Local Ombudsman, 1974-. A Vice-Pres., Inst. of Personnel Management, 1965-67; Mem., Nat. Nursing Staff Cttee, 1967-72; Mem., Brighton and Lewes HMC, 1972-74; a Vice-Pres., Royal Coll. of Nursing, 1973-; Mem., Ombudsman Adv. Bd, Internat. Bar Assoc., 1975-; Mem. Exec. Cttee, Fawcett Soc., 1975-. *Publications:* Shift Work, 1954; articles on personnel management. *Address:* 5 Malton Way, Clifton, York. *Club:* Naval and Military.

COOK, George Steveni L.; *see* Littlejohn Cook.

COOK, Sir Halford; *see* Cook, Sir P. H.

COOK, Harold James; a Metropolitan Stipendiary Magistrate, since 1975; *b* 25 Jan. 1926; *s* of Harold Cook and Gwendoline Lydia (*née* List); *m* 1952, Mary Elizabeth (*née* Edwards); one *s*. *Educ:* The John Lyon Sch., Harrow; Edinburgh Univ. RN, 1943-47. Civil Service, 1947-52. Called to the Bar, Gray's Inn, 1952; Dep. Chief Clerk, Bow Street, and later Thames, Magistrates' Courts, 1952-54; Inner London QS, 1955; Dep. Clerk to Justices, Gore Div., Mddx, 1956-60; Clerk to Justices, Highgate Div., 1961, and also Barnet and South Mymms Divs, 1968. *Publications:* contrib. legal jls.

COOK, Rt. Rev. Henry George; Co-ordinator of Historical Programs, Government of Northwest Territories, since 1974; *b* Walthamstow, London, England, 12 Oct. 1906; *s* of Henry G. Cook and Ada Mary Evans; *m* 1935, Opal May Thompson, Sarnia, Ont, *d* of Wesley Thompson and Charity Ellen Britney; two *s* one *d*. *Educ:* Ingersoll Collegiate Inst., Ont; Huron Coll. (LTh); Univ. of Western Ont, London, Canada (BA). Deacon, 1935, Priest, 1936; Missionary at Fort Simpson, 1935-43; Canon of Athabasca, 1940-43; Incumbent S Porcupine, Ont., 1943-44; Archdeacon of James Bay, 1945-48; Principal, Bp Horden Sch., Moose Factory, 1945-48; Mem., Gen Synod Exec., 1943-47; Supt of Indian Sch. Admin., 1948-62; Bishop Suffragan of the Arctic, 1963-66, of Athabasca, 1966-70 (the area of Mackenzie having been part first of one diocese and then of the other, constituted an Episcopal District, 1970); Bishop of Mackenzie, 1970-74. RCN(R) Chaplain, 1949-56. Hon. DD Huron Coll. and Univ. of Western Ont. 1946. *Recreations:* fishing, coin collecting, model carving. *Address:* Box 158, Yellowknife, Northwest Territories, Canada.

COOK, Cdre Henry Home; *b* 24 Jan. 1918; Director: Ellerman City Liners Ltd, Camomile Street, London, since 1973; C. Gold Associates Ltd, since 1974; *o s* of George Home Cook, Edinburgh; *m* 1943, Theffania, *yr d* of A. P. Saunders, Gerrards Cross; two *s* two *d*. *Educ:* St Lawrence Coll., Ramsgate; Pangbourne College. Entered RN as Paymaster Cadet, 1936; Comdr 1955; Captain 1963; Cdre 1970. Naval Sec. to Vice-Adm. Sir Guy Sayer, 1953-59; Sqdn Supply Officer, 1st S/m Sqdn, 1959; Comdr, RNC Greenwich, 1961; Naval Attaché, Ankara, 1964; Dir of Public Relations (RN), 1966; Defence Adviser to British High Comr, and Head of British Defence Liaison Staff, Ottawa, 1970-72; retired, 1973. ADC to HM the Queen, 1971-72. FInstAM 1973. DipCAM 1975. *Recreations:* fencing, swimming, sailing. *Address:* Ramblers Cottage, Layters Green, Chalfont St Peter, Bucks. *T:* Gerrards Cross 83724. *Club:* Army and Navy.

COOK, Rear-Adm. James William Dunbar, CB 1975; Head of Personnel and Administration Ocean Inchcape Ltd, since 1975; *b* 12 Dec. 1921; *s* of James Alexander Cook, Pluscarden, Morayshire; *m* 1949, Edith May Williams; one *s* two *d. Educ:* Bedford Sch.; HMS Worcester. CO, HM Ships Venus, Dido and Norfolk; Sen. British Naval Officer, S Africa, 1967-69 (as Cdre); Dir RN War College, 1969-71; Asst Chief of Naval Staff (Ops), 1973-75; retired from RN, 1975. Comdr 1957; Captain 1963; Rear-Adm. 1973; jssc 1958; sowc 1970. *Recreations:* golf, gardening. *Address:* Springways Cottage, Farnham Lane, Haslemere, Surrey. *T:* Haslemere 3615. *Club:* Army and Navy.

COOK, Dr John Barry; Headmaster of Christ College, Brecon, since 1973; *b* 9 May 1940; *er s* of Albert Edward and Beatrice Irene Cook, Gloucester; *m* 1964, Vivien Margaret Roxana Lamb, *o d* of Victor and Marjorie Lamb, St Albans; two *s* one *d. Educ:* Sir Thomas Rich's Sch., Gloucester; King's Coll., Univ. of London (BSc 1961, AKC 1961); Guy's Hosp. Med. Sch. (PhD 1965). Guy's Hospital Medical School: Biophysics research, 1961-64; Lectr in Physics, 1964-65; Haileybury College: Asst Master, 1965-72; Senior Science Master and Head of Physics Dept, 1967-72. Mem., Governing Body of Church in Wales. *Publications:* (jtly) Solid State Biophysics, 1969; Multiple Choice Questions in A-level Physics, 1969; Multiple Choice Questions in O-level Physics, 1970; papers in Nature, Molecular Physics, Internat. Jl of Radiation Biology, Jl of Scientific Instruments, Educn in Science, Conference and Trends in Education. *Recreation:* all sports. *Address:* Headmaster's House, Christ College, Brecon, Powys LD3 8AG. *T:* Brecon 3359.

COOK, John Edward E.; *see* Evan-Cook.

COOK, John Gilbert, CVO 1970; CBE 1963; HM Treasury Valuer, 1950-69, retd; *b* 16 May 1911; *s* of late John Andrew Cook; *m* 1st, 1937, Doreen Violet Mary Harrington (*d* 1973); two *s* two *d*; 2nd, 1973, Hilda Joan (Bunty) Plewman (*née* Braggins). *Educ:* Bedford Sch. Articled to Sir H. Trustram Eve, 1929-32. FRICS. *Recreations:* Rugby football (English International and Barbarian; Captain of Bedford, 1936-39), golf, cricket. *Address:* Sleepers, 6 Highfield Road, Overstrand, Norfolk. *T:* Overstrand 561. *Clubs:* MCC, Pathfinder; Royal Cromer Golf.

COOK, Prof. John Manuel, FSA; FBA 1974; Professor of Ancient History and Classical Archæology, Bristol University, 1958-76 (formerly Reader); *b* 11 Dec. 1910; *s* of late Rev. C. R. Cook; *m* 1939, Enid May (*d* 1976), *d* of Dr W. A. Robertson; two *s*; *m* 1977, Nancy Easton Law, MA, *widow* of Ralph Hamilton Law. *Educ:* Marlborough; King's Coll., Cambridge. Sir William Browne's Medal for Greek Ode, 1933; Members' Latin Essay Prize, 1933; Augustus Austen Leigh Student in King's Coll., 1934; Asst in Humanity and Lectr in Classical Archæology, Edinburgh Univ., 1936-46; Dir of British Sch. of Archæology at Athens, 1946-54; Dean, Faculty of Arts, 1966-68, Pro-Vice-Chancellor, 1972-75, Bristol Univ. C. E. Norton Lectr of the Archaeological Inst. of America, 1961-62; Visiting Prof., Yale Univ., 1965; Gray Memorial Lectr, Cambridge, 1969; Geddes-Harrower Prof., Univ. of Aberdeen, 1977. Served in Royal Scots, Force 133, and HQ Land Forces, Greece. *Publications:* The Greeks in Ionia and the East, 1962; (with W. H. Plommer) The Sanctuary of Hemithea at Kastabos, 1966; The Troad, an archaeological and historical study, 1973; chapters in: Cambridge Ancient History; Cambridge History of Iran. *Address:* 8 Dalrymple Crescent, Edinburgh EH9 2NU.

COOK, Joseph, FRIC; Consultant, Millbank Technical Services Ordnance Ltd, since 1977 (Managing Director, 1974-77, on secondment from Ministry of Defence); *b* 7 April 1917; *y s* of Joseph Cook, MBE, JP, and Jane Cook (*née* Adams), Cumberland; *m* 1950, Betty, *d* of James and Elizabeth Barlow, Standish, Lancs; two *d. Educ:* Whitehaven Grammar Sch.; Univ. of Liverpool (BSc, DipEd). RAF, 1939-40. Posts in Ministries of Supply, Aviation, Technology and Defence 1941-59; Dir, ROF Burghfield, 1959-65; Gp Dir, Ammunition Factories, 1966; Dir Gen. (Prodn), ROF, 1966-74. *Recreations:* swimming, golf. *Address:* Abbots-wood, Bramley Road, Pamber End, near Basingstoke, Hants. *T:* Basingstoke 850304.

COOK, Melville; *see* Cook, Alfred Melville.

COOK, Norman Charles, BA; FSA, FMA; Hon. Curator, Wells Museum, Somerset, since 1972; *b* 24 Jan. 1906; *s* of George and Emily Cook; *m* 1934, Dorothy Ida Waters; one *s* one *d. Educ:* Maidstone Grammar Sch. Maidstone Museum, 1924-37; Morven Institute of Archaeological Research, Avebury, 1937-39; Curator, Southampton Museum, 1947-50; Director: Guildhall Museum, 1950-71; Museum of London, 1970-72.

Hon. Sec., 1954-59, Pres., 1964-65, Museums Assoc. Vice-Pres., Soc. of Antiquaries, 1967-. *Recreation:* archæology. *Address:* 8 Cathedral Green, Wells, Somerset BA5 2UE.

COOK, Peter Edward; writer; entertainer; *b* 17 Nov. 1937; *s* of Alexander and Margaret Cook; *m* 1st, 1964, Wendy Snowden; two *d*; 2nd, 1973, Judy Huxtable. *Educ:* Radley Coll.; Pembroke Coll., Cambridge (BA). Part-author and appeared in: *revues:* Pieces of Eight, 1958; One Over the Eight, 1959; Beyond the Fringe, 1959-64 (London and New York); Behind the Fridge, 1971-72 (Australia and London); Good Evening, 1973-75 (US); *television:* Not Only but Also (four series, BBC), 1965-71. *Films:* The Wrong Box, 1965; Bedazzled, 1967; Monte Carlo or Bust, 1969; The Bed-Sitting Room, 1970; The Rise and Rise of Michael Rimmer, 1971. *Publication:* Dud and Pete: The Dagenham Dialogues, 1971. *Recreations:* gambling, gossip, golf. *Address:* c/o Wright & Webb, 10 Soho Square, W1. *T:* 01-734 9641.

COOK, Sir (Philip) Halford, Kt 1976; OBE 1965; Ambassador and Special Labour Adviser in Europe, Australian Permanent Mission, Geneva, since 1973; *b* 10 Oct. 1912; *s* of Rev. R. Osborne Cook and May Cook; *m* 1945, Myra V., *d* of M. A. Dean; one *s* one *d. Educ:* Wesley Coll., Melbourne; Queen's Coll., Univ. of Melbourne; University Coll., Univ. of London; Columbia and Kansas Univs, USA. MA Melbourne, 1938; PhD Kansas, 1941. FBPsS 1943; FAPsS 1968, Hon. FAPsS 1972. Lectr, Industrial Relations, Univ. of Melbourne, 1945-46, Lectr, Indust. Admin, 1947-50; Professional Staff, Tavistock Inst. of Human Relations, London, 1950-51; Asst Sec., 1952-63, First Asst Sec., 1963-68, Sec., 1968-72, Aust. Dept of Labour and Nat. Service. Chm., Governing Body, ILO, 1975-76. Fellow, Queen's Coll., Univ. of Melbourne, 1972. *Publications:* Theory and Technique of Child Guidance, 1944; Productivity Team Technique, 1951; articles in jls on psychology and on indust. relations. *Recreations:* reading and travel. *Address:* Australian Permanent Mission, 56 rue de Moillebeau, 1211 Geneva 19, Switzerland. *T:* Geneva 34 62 00. *Club:* Athenæum (Melbourne).

COOK, Reginald, FCA; Chairman, South Wales Electricity Board, since 1977; Member, Electricity Council, since 1977; *b* 29 Dec. 1918; *s* of Harold Cook and Gwendolyn Cook, Birmingham; *m* 1945, Constance Irene Holt, Norden, Lancs; one *s* one *d. Educ:* Rochdale High Sch.; Manchester Univ. (BA); Admin. Staff Coll. Served War, 1939-46; Staff Captain, RA. Local Govt Service with Corporations of Manchester, West Bromwich and York, 1946-52; Midlands Electricity Board: accountancy posts, 1952-59; Chief Accountant, 1959-69; Exec. Mem., 1964-69; Dep. Chm., S Wales Electricity Bd, 1969-77. MBIM. Gold Medal, IMTA, 1949. *Recreations:* countryside activities, gardening, golf, bridge. *Address:* Heppleshaw, Itton, Chepstow, Gwent. *T:* Shirenewton 265.

COOK, Brig. Richard Arthur, CBE 1961; *b* 26 May 1908; *m* 1940, Sheila Mary Ostell Prosser; two *s. Educ:* St Paul's; RMA, Woolwich. Commissioned, Royal Artillery, 1928. Posted to India, 1933. Served War of 1939-45 in India and Burma: Staff Coll., 1941; Regimental Comd, 1943; Joint Services Staff Coll., 1947; Col, 1948; Col Administrative Plans, GHQ, MELF, 1948-51; CRA (Brig.) 16th Airborne Div., 1954-56; NATO Defence Coll., 1957; BGS, Southern Command, 1958-61; retired from Army, 1961. *Address:* Drove End House, West Grimstead, near Salisbury, Wilts. *T:* Farley 205. *Club:* Army and Navy.

COOK, Robert Finlayson, (Robin F. Cook); MP (Lab) Edinburgh Central, since Feb. 1974; *b* 28 Feb. 1946; *s* of Peter Cook, schoolmaster and Christina Cook (*née* Lynch); *m* 1969, Margaret K. Whitmore, medical consultant; two *s. Educ:* Aberdeen Grammar Sch.; Univ. of Edinburgh. MA Hons English Lit. Tutor-Organiser with WEA, 1970-74. Chm., Scottish Assoc. of Labour Student Organisations, 1966-67; Sec., Edinburgh City Labour Party, 1970-72; Mem., Edinburgh Corporation, 1971-74, Chm. Housing Cttee, 1973-74. Member: Tribune Group; Council of Europe. *Recreations:* eating, reading, talking. *Address:* c/o House of Commons, SW1A 0AA. *T:* 01-219 5120. *Club:* Abbotsford (Edinburgh).

COOK, Prof. Robert Manuel, FBA 1976; Laurence Professor of Classical Archaeology, University of Cambridge, 1962-76; *b* 4 July 1909; *s* of Rev. Charles Robert and Mary Manuel Cook; *m* 1938, Kathleen, *d* of James Frank and Ellen Hardman Porter. *Educ:* Marlborough Coll.; Cambridge Univ. Walston Student, Cambridge Univ., 1932; Asst Lectr in Classics, Manchester Univ., 1934; Lectr, 1938; Sub-warden, St Anselm's Hall, Manchester, 1936-38; Laurence Reader in Classical Archaeology, Cambridge Univ., 1945, Ord. Mem., German Archaeological Inst., 1953. *Publications:* Corpus Vasorum

Antiquorum, British Museum 8, 1954; Greek Painted Pottery, 1960, 2nd edn 1972; The Greeks till Alexander, 1962; (with Kathleen Cook) Southern Greece: an archaeological guide, 1968; Greek Art, 1972. *Address:* 15 Wilberforce Road, Cambridge CB3 0EQ. *T:* Cambridge 52863.
See also Prof. J. M. Cook.

COOK, Robin; see Cook, R. F.

COOK, William Birkett, MA; Master of Magdalen College School, Oxford, since 1972; *b* 30 Aug. 1931; *e s* of William James and Mildred Elizabeth Cook, Headington, Oxford; *m* 1958, Marianne Ruth, *yr d* of late A. E. Taylor, The Schools, Shrewsbury; one *s* one *d* (and one *d* decd). *Educ:* Dragon Sch.; Eton (King's Schol.); Trinity Coll., Cambridge (Schol.). National Service, 1950-51 (commnd in RA). Porson Prizeman, 1953; 1st cl. Classical Tripos Pt I, 1953, Pt II, 1954; Henry Arthur Thomas Student, 1954; MA Oxon by incorporation, 1972. Asst Master, Shrewsbury Sch., 1955-67, and Head of Classical Faculty, 1960-67; Headmaster of Durham Sch., 1967-72. *Recreations:* music, gardening. *Address:* Magdalen College School, Oxford. *T:* Oxford 42191.

COOK, Sir William (Richard Joseph), KCB 1970 (CB 1951); Kt 1958; FRS 1962; Chairman, Marconi International Marine Co., 1971-75; Director: Rolls-Royce (1971) Ltd, 1971-76; Buck & Hickman Ltd, since 1970; GEC-Marconi Electronics Ltd, since 1972; *b* 10 April 1905; *s* of John Cook; *m* 1929, Grace (*née* Purnell); one *d* ; *m* 1939, Gladys (*née* Allen); one *s* one *d*. *Educ:* Trowbridge High Sch.; Bristol Univ. Entered CS, 1928; various scientific posts in Research Estabs of WO and Min. of Supply, 1928-47; Dir of Physical Research, Admiralty, 1947-50; Chief of Royal Naval Scientific Service, 1950-54; Deputy Dir, Atomic Weapons Research Establishment, Aldermaston, 1954-58; Mem. for Reactors, Atomic Energy Authority, 1961-64 (Mem. for Development and Engineering, 1959-61, for Engineering and Production, 1958-59); Dep. Chief Scientific Adviser, Ministry of Defence, 1964-67; Chief Adviser (Projects and Research) MoD, 1968-70. Hon. DSc: Strathclyde, 1967; Bath, 1975. *Address:* Adbury Springs, Newbury, Berks. *T:* Newbury 40409. *Club:* Athenæum.

COOKE, (Alfred) Alistair, KBE (Hon.) 1973; journalist and broadcaster; *b* 20 Nov. 1908; *s* of Samuel Cooke and Mary Elizabeth Byrne; *m* 1st, 1934, Ruth Emerson; one *s* ; 2nd, 1946, Jane White Hawkes; one *d*. *Educ:* Blackpool Grammar Sch.; Jesus Coll., Cambridge (Scholar); Yale Univ.; Harvard. Founded Cambridge University Mummers, 1928; First Class, English Tripos, 1929; Second Class, 1930. Editor, The Granta, 1931; Commonwealth Fund Fellow, 1932-34. BBC Film Critic, 1934-37; London Correspondent for NBC, 1936-37; Commentator on American Affairs for BBC, 1938-; Special Correspondent on American Affairs, The London Times, 1938-40; American Feature Writer, The Daily Herald, 1941-43; UN Correspondent of the Manchester Guardian (which changed name to Guardian, 1959), 1945-48; Chief Correspondent in US of The Guardian, 1948-72. Master of ceremonies: Ford Foundation's television programme, Omnibus, 1952-61; UN television programme, International Zone, 1961-67; Masterpiece Theatre, 1971-. Wrote and narrated, America: a personal history of the United States, BBC TV, 1972-73 (Peabody Award for meritorious services to broadcasting, 1972; Writers' Guild of GB award for best documentary of 1972; Dimbleby Award, Soc. of Film and TV Arts, 1973; four Emmy awards of (US) Nat. Acad. of TV Arts and Sciences, 1973). Hon. LLD: Edinburgh, 1969; Manchester, 1973; Hon. LittD St Andrews, 1975. Peabody Award for internat. reporting, 1952; Benjamin Franklin Medal, RSA, 1973; Howland Medal, Yale Univ., 1977. *Publications:* (ed) Garbo and the Night Watchmen, 1937, repr. 1972; Douglas Fairbanks: The Making of a Screen Character, 1940; A Generation on Trial: USA v Alger Hiss, 1950; Letters from America, 1951; Christmas Eve, 1952; A Commencement Address, 1954; (ed) The Vintage Mencken, 1955; Around the World in Fifty Years, 1966; Talk about America, 1968; Alistair Cooke's America, 1973; Six Men, 1977. *Recreations:* golf, photography, music, travel. *Address:* 1150 Fifth Avenue, New York City; Nassau Point, Cutchogue, Long Island, NY, USA. *Clubs:* Athenæum; Royal and Ancient (St Andrews); National Press (Washington); Players (New York); San Francisco Golf.

COOKE, Alistair; see Cooke, Alfred A.

COOKE, Rear-Adm. Anthony John; Senior Naval Member, Directing Staff, Royal College of Defence Studies, since 1975; *b* 21 Sept. 1927; *s* of Rear-Adm. John Ernest Cooke, *qv* ; *m* 1951, Margaret Anne, *d* of Frederick Charles Hynard; two *s* three *d* . *Educ:* St Edward's Sch., Oxford. Entered RN 1945; specialised in navigation, 1953; Army Staff Coll., 1958; Sqdn Navigating

Officer, HMS Daring, Second Destroyer Sqdn, 1959-61; Staff Navigating Officer to Flag Officer, Sea Trng, 1961; Comdr 1961; Directorate of Naval Ops and Trade, 1961-63; i/c HMS Brighton, 1964-66; Directorate of Navigation and Tactical Control, 1966; Captain 1966; Captain of Dockyard and Queen's Harbourmaster, Singapore, 1967-69; Captain 1st Destroyer Sqdn, Far East, later Divnl Comdr 3rd Div. Western Fleet, i/c HMS Galatea, 1969-71; Dir, Royal Naval Staff Coll., 1971-73; Cdre Clyde i/c Clyde Submarine Base, 1973-75; Rear-Adm. 1976. *Recreation:* philately. *Address:* Chalkhurst, Eynsford, Kent. *T:* Farningham 862789.

COOKE, Dr Arthur Hafford, MBE 1946; Warden of New College, Oxford, since 1976; *b* 13 Dec. 1912; *er s* of late Sydney Herbert Cooke and Edith Frances (*née* Jee); *m* 1939, Ilse (*d* 1973), *d* of late Prof. Hans Sachs; two *s* . *Educ:* Wyggeston Grammar Sch., Leicester; Christ Church, Oxford (MA, DPhil). Research Lectr, Christ Church, 1939. Radar research for Admiralty, 1940-45. Fellow of New Coll., Oxford, 1946-76; University Lectr in Physics, 1944-71; Reader in Physics, 1971-76. Member: Gen. Bd of the Faculties, 1962-72 (Vice- Chm., 1969-71); Hebdomadal Council, 1969-. *Publications:* articles in scientific jls on magnetism and low temperature physics. *Address:* New College, Oxford. *T:* Oxford 48451.

COOKE, Prof. Brian Ernest Dudley; Professor of Oral Medicine and Oral Pathology, University of Wales, Dean of Welsh National School of Medicine Dental School and Consultant Dental Surgeon to University Hospital of Wales, since 1962; *b* 12 Jan. 1920; *e s* of Charles Ernest Cooke and Margaret Beatrice Wood; *m* 1948, Marion Neill Orkney Hope; one *s* one *d*. *Educ:* Merchant Taylors' Sch.; London Univ. LDSRCS 1942; LRCP, MRCS 1949; FDSRCS 1952; MDSU London 1959; MRCPath 1965, FRCPath 1974. Served RNVR (Dental Br.), 1943-46. Nuffield Dental Fellow, 1950-52; Trav. Nuffield Fellow, Australia, 1964. Lectr 1952-57, Reader in Dental Med. 1958-62, Guy's Hosp. Dental School. Rep. Univ. of Wales on Gen. Dental Council, 1964-; Mem. Bd of Faculty of Dental Surgery, RCS England, 1964-72 (Vice-Dean 1971-72); Chm., Dental Educn Adv. Council, GB, 1975- (Mem. 1962-); Adviser in Dental Surgery to Welsh Hosp. Bd, 1962-74; Civilian Consultant in Dental Surgery to RN, 1967-. Hon. Adviser, Editorial Bd, British Jl of Dermatology, 1967-76. Mem., S Glamorgan AHA, 1974-76. Mem. Bd of Governors: United Cardiff Hosps, 1965-71; HMC (Cardiff) Univ. Hosp. of Wales, 1971-74. Vice-Provost, Welsh Nat. Sch. of Medicine, 1974-76. Examr in Dental Surgery and Oral Pathology, Liverpool, Manchester and London Univs; Examr for Primary Fellowship in Dental Surgery, RCS, 1967-73. Hon. Mem., Pierre Fauchard Acad., 1967. Charles Tomes Lectr, RCS, 1963; Guest Lectr, Students' Vis. Lectrs Trust Fund, Witwatersrand Univ., 1967. Pres., Section of Odontology, RSocMed, 1975. Cartwright Prize and Medal, RCS, 1955; Chesterfield Prize and Medal, St John's Hosp. for Diseases of Skin, 1955. *Publications:* (jtly) Oral Histopathology, 1959, 2nd edn 1970; scientific contribs to medical and dental jls. *Recreations:* various. *Address:* 4 Mill Place, Lisvane, Cardiff. *T:* Cardiff 756110.

COOKE, Cecil; see Cooke, R. C.

COOKE, Sir Charles (Arthur John), 11th Bt, *cr* 1661; *b* 12 Nov. 1905; *yr s* of 10th Bt and Lady Mildred Adelaide Cecilia Denison; *S* father, 1964; *m* 1932, Diana, *o d* of late Maj.-Gen. Sir Edward Maxwell Perceval, KCB, DSO, JP; one *s* one *d*. *Educ:* Wellington Coll.; RMC Sandhurst. Served War of 1939-45, 4/7th Dragoon Guards, France (prisoner, 1940). Capt., 1945, Major, 1952, 4/7th Dragoon Guards; retired from Army, 1953. *Recreations:* shooting and fishing. *Heir: s* David William Perceval Cooke [*b* 28 April 1935; *m* 1959, Margaret Frances, *d* of Herbert Skinner, Knutsford, Cheshire; three *d*]. *Address:* 15 Esplanade, Fowey, Cornwall.

COOKE, Charles Fletcher F.; see Fletcher-Cooke.

COOKE, Christopher Herbert, CIE 1946; *b* 29 May 1899; *s* of late F. J. Cooke, ICS (retired); *m* 1929, Beryl Gourley Ainsley; one *s* one *d*. *Educ:* Clifton; Christ Church, Oxford (MA). Indian Civil Service (United Provinces), 1922; Joint Magistrate, Collector, Settlement Officer, 1922-39; Revenue Sec., Finance Sec., Settlement Commissioner, 1939-44; Commissioner, Lucknow Division, 1945-47; retired from ICS, 1947; Settlement Commissioner for Forest Reserves, Ghana, 1951-57. *Recreation:* golf. *Address:* Redholme, Great Missenden, Bucks. *T:* Great Missenden 2580.

COOKE, Cynthia Felicity Joan, CBE 1975; RRC 1969; Matron-in-Chief, Queen Alexandra's Royal Naval Nursing Service, 1973-76; *b* 11 June 1919; *d* of late Frank Alexander Cooke,

MBE, and of Ethel May (*née* Buckle). *Educ:* Rosa Bassett Sch. for Girls; Victoria Hosp. for Children, Tite Street, Chelsea; RSCN, 1940; University Coll. Hosp., London, SRN, 1942; Univ. of London, Sister Tutor Diploma, 1949. Joined QARNNS, 1943; served in: Australia, 1944-45; Hong Kong, 1956-58; Malta, 1964-66. HMS: Collingwood, Gosling, Goldcrest; RN Hospitals: Chatham, Plymouth, Haslar. Principal Tutor, Royal Naval School of Nursing, 1967-70; Principal Matron, RN Hosp., Haslar, 1970-73. QHNS 1973-76. CStJ 1975. *Address:* 3 Glebe Court, Fleet, Hampshire. *T:* Fleet 28893.

COOKE, George William, CBE 1975; FRS 1969; Chief Scientific Officer, Agricultural Research Council, since 1975; *b* 6 Jan. 1916; *s* of late William Harry Cooke and late Sarah Jane Cooke (*née* Whittaker); *m* 1944, Elizabeth Hannah Hill; one *s* one *d*. *Educ:* Loughborough Grammar Sch.; University Coll., Nottingham. BSc (Chem.) London Univ., 1937, PhD London, 1940. Awarded Min. of Agric. Research Schol., tenable at Rothamsted Experimental Station, 1938; apptd Scientific Officer there, 1941, and Prin. Sc. Officer, 1951; Head of Chemistry Dept, 1956-75; Deputy Dir, 1962-75 (acting Dir, 1972-73). Chm., Agriculture Group of Soc. of Chem. Industry, 1956-58; President: Fertiliser Soc., London, 1961-62; British Soc. of Soil Science, 1976-78. Lectures: Amos Meml, East Malling Res. Station, 1967; Francis New Meml, Fertiliser Soc., 1971; Clive Behrens, Univ. of Leeds, 1972-73; Scott Robertson Meml, QUB, 1973. For. Mem., Lenin All-Union Acad. of Agric. Scis, USSR, 1972. Research Medal of Royal Agricultural Soc., 1967. *Publications:* Fertilizers and Profitable Farming, 1960; The Control of Soil Fertility, 1967; Fertilizing for Maximum Yield, 1972; many papers in scientific jls on soil science, crop nutrition and fertilizers. *Recreations:* boats, canoes. *Address:* 33 Topstreet Way, Harpenden, Herts. *T:* Harpenden 2899. *Club:* Farmers'.

COOKE, Gilbert Andrew, FCA; Group Managing Director, C. T. Bowring & Co. Ltd, since 1976; *b* 7 March 1923; *s* of Gilbert N. Cooke and Laurie Cooke; *m* 1949, Katherine Margaret Mary McGovern; one *s* one *d*. *Educ:* Bournemouth Sch. FCA 1950. Sen. Clerk, chartered accountants, 1950-54; Bowmaker Ltd: Chief Accountant, 1955; Dir, 1968; Man. Dir, 1968; Dep. Chm. and Chief Exec., 1972; Dir, C. T. Bowring & Co. Ltd, 1969. Chm., Finance Houses Assoc., 1972-74. *Recreations:* music, reading. *Address:* Kilmarth, Onslow Road, Burwood Park, Walton-on-Thames, Surrey. *T:* Walton-on-Thames 40451.

COOKE, Rev. Canon Greville (Vaughan Turner), MA, MusB Cantab; FRAM; FSA; Canon Emeritus, Peterborough Cathedral, since 1956; Composer, Author, Poet, Broadcaster; Adjudicator at Musical Festivals; *b* 14 July 1894; *s* of William Turner Cooke, Chief Clerk of Central Office of Royal Courts of Justice, London, and Adeline Hannah, *d* of David Johnson, MD. *Educ:* Hamilton House, Ealing; Royal Academy of Music (Schol., Exhibitioner, Prizewinner); Christ's Coll., Cambridge (Stewart of Rannoch Schol., 1913, Organ Schol.); Ridley Hall, Cambridge (Theol. Studentship); ARAM 1913; BA 1916; MusBac 1916; MA 1920. Ordained, 1918; Curate, Tavistock, 1918, Ealing, 1920; Dep. Minor Canon of St Paul's Cathedral, 1920-21; Vicar of Cransley, Northants, 1921-56; Rector of Buxted, 1956-71. Canon Non-residentiary of Peterborough Cathedral, 1955. Prof., Royal Academy of Music, 1925-59, FRAM 1927; FSA 1962. Mem., Athenæum, 1931-53. Dir of Music, London Day Training Coll. Examiner for LRAM Diploma, Associated Board Exams, 1927; Lectr for London Univ., Royal Institution of Great Britain, League of Arts, Music Teachers' Association, Sussex Archæological Soc. (Mem. Council), London Appreciation Soc., RSCM, RSA, Shell-Mex, IBM. *Publications:* The Theory of Music, 1928; Art and Reality, 1929; Tonality and Expression, 1929; Poems, 1933; Cransley Broadcast Sermons, 1933; The Light of the World, 1949 (USA 1950, paperback 1965); A Chronicle of Buxted, 1960 (paperback 1965); The Grand Design, 1964; Thus Saith the Lord: a Biblical anthology, 1967; Jenny Pluck Pears, 1972; musical publications include: *orchestral:* Prelude for Strings; *songs:* Three Songs; Day-dreams; The Shepherdess; Bereft; Eileen Aroon; But Yesterday; Your Gentle Care; My Heaven; Weep you no more; The Bells of Heaven; Shepherd Boy's Song; *choral:* Nobody Knows; Deep River; Jillian of Berry; Oh, to be in England; How can I help England; Claribel; Oh, Hush Thee My Baby; Cobwebs; *anthems:* Drop, Slow Tears; Let us with a gladsome mind; This Joyful Eastertide; Bread of the World; Lo! God is Here; *pianoforte:* High Marley Rest; Time Keepers; Meadowsweet; La Petite; Pets' Corner; Up the Ladder; A Day at the Sea; Bargain Basement; Reef's End; Cormorant Crag: Song Prelude; Whispering Willows; Haldon Hills; In the Cathedral; Gothic Prelude; *violin and piano:* High Marley Rest; *'cello and piano:* Sea Croon. Composer of several Hymns and contributor to Hymns Ancient and Modern, 1950, BBC Hymn Book, Baptist Hymn Book, Methodist Hymn Book, etc. *Address:* Waveney, West Close, Middleton-on-Sea, West Sussex.

COOKE, Jean Esme Oregon, RA 1972 (ARA 1965); (professional name Jean E. Cooke); Lecturer in Painting, Royal College of Art, 1964-74; *b* 18 Feb. 1927; *d* of Arthur Oregon Cooke, Grocer, and of Dorothy Emily Cooke (*née* Cranefield); *m* 1953, John Randall Bratby (marr. diss.); *qv*; three *s* one *d*. *Educ:* Blackheath High Sch.; Central Sch. of Arts and Crafts, Camberwell; City and Guilds; Goldsmiths' Coll. Sch. of Art; Royal Coll. of Art. NDD in Sculpture, 1949. Pottery Workshop, 1950-53. Purchase of self-portrait, 1969, and portrait of John Bratby (called Lilly, Lilly on the Brow), 1972, by Chantry Bequest; portraits of Dr Egon Wellesz and Dr Walter Oakshott for Lincoln Coll., Oxford; portrait of Mrs Bennett, Principal, for St Hilda's Coll., Oxford, 1976. One-man shows: Establishment Club, 1963; Leicester Gall., 1964; Bear Lane Gall., Oxford, 1965; Arun Art Centre, Arundel; Ashgate Gall., Farnham; Moyan Gall., Manchester; Bladon Gall., Hampshire, 1966; Lane Gall., Bradford, 1967; Gallery 66, Blackheath, 1967; Motley Gall., Lewisham, 1968; Phoenix, Suffolk, 1970; New Grafton Gall., 1971; Ansdell Gall., 1974; Woodlands Gall., Blackheath, 1976; J. K. Taylor Gall., Cambridge. Works exhibited: Furneaux Gall., 1968; Upper Grosvenor Gall., 1968; Ashgate Gall., 1973; Agnews, 1974; Gall. 10, Richmond Hill, 1974; Leonie Jonleigh Gall., 1976; Dulwich Coll. Picture Gall., 1976; British Painting 1952-77, Royal Acad., 1977. *Recreations:* gardening, biology, swimming, walking. *Address:* 7 Hardy Road, Blackheath, SE3. *T:* 01-858 6288. *Club:* Chelsea Arts.

COOKE, Rear-Adm. John Ernest, CB 1955; CEng, FIMechE; Royal Navy, retired; *b* 1899; *s* of Arthur Cockerton Cooke; *m* 1923, Kathleen Mary (*d* 1976), *d* of Walter James Haward; one *s* one *d*. *Educ:* Owen's Sch. Entered Royal Navy, 1915; served War of 1939-45, HMS Furious and HMS Anson; Capt., 1946; Manager of the Engineering Dept, HM Dockyard, Malta, 1950-53; Rear-Adm., 1953; Manager of the Engineering Dept, HM Dockyard, Portsmouth, 1954-57; retired. General Manager, Production, Messrs Bailey (Malta) Ltd, 1959-61. *Address:* Kells, Glen Dale, Rowlands Castle, Hants. *Clubs:* Royal Commonwealth Society; Union, Malta Sports (Malta). *See also A . J . Cooke.*

COOKE, Sir John F.; *see* Fletcher-Cooke.

COOKE, Kenneth; *see* Cooke, R. K.

COOKE, Randle Henry, MVO 1971; *b* 26 April 1930; *o s* of Col H. R. V. Cooke, Dalicote Hall, Bridgnorth, Salop and Mrs E. F. K. Cooke, Brodawel, Tremeirchion, N Wales; *m* 1961, Clare Bennett; one *s* one *d*. *Educ:* Heatherdown, Ascot; Eton College. 2nd Lieut, 8th King's Royal Irish Hussars, 1949; served Korea, 1950-53 with Regt and USAF (POW); ADC to GOC 7th Armoured Div., 1955; Regimental Adjt, 1957; Instructor, RMA Sandhurst, 1960; Sqdn Comdr, Queen's Royal Irish Hussars, Malaya, Borneo and Germany, 1963; GSO3 (SD), HQ 1st Div., 1965. Equerry to the Duke of Edinburgh, 1968-71; Private Sec. to Lord Mayor of London, 1972-74. *Recreations:* equitation and most things to do with water. *Address:* Traboyack House, Straiton, Maybole, Ayrshire KA19 7NH. *T:* Straiton 225. *Club:* Cavalry and Guards.

COOKE, (Richard) Kenneth, OBE 1945; Metropolitan Stipendiary Magistrate since 1970; a Recorder of the Crown Court, since 1972; *b* 17 March 1917; *s* of Richard and Beatrice Mary Cooke; *m* 1945, Gwendoline Mary Black; no *c*. *Educ:* Sebright Sch., Wolverley; Birmingham Univ. Admitted Solicitor (Hons), 1939; Birmingham Law Soc. Prizeman. Sqdn Leader, RAFVR, 1939-45. Solicitor in private practice specialising in Magistrates' Courts, 1945-52; Clerk: to Prescot and St Helens Justices, 1952-57; to Rotherham County Borough and WR Justices, 1957-64; to Bradford City Justices, 1964-70. Mem. Council, Magistrates' Assoc., 1973- (Vice-Chm. Legal Cttee; Hon. Sec. Inner London Branch). Reader, Rochester Dio., 1970-. *Publications:* contribs to Criminal Law Review, Justice of the Peace and Local Govt Review, etc. *Recreations:* fishing, choral singing, sampling bin ends. *Address:* 8 St Paul's Square, Church Road, Bromley, Kent. *T:* 01-464 6761.

COOKE, Robert (Gordon), MA (Oxon); MP (C) Bristol West, since March 1957; *b* 29 May 1930; *er s* of Robert V. Cooke, *qv*; *m* 1966, Jenifer Patricia Evelyn, *yr d* of Evelyn Mansfield King, *qv*; one *s* one *d*. *Educ:* Harrow; Christ Church, Oxford. Pres., Oxford Univ. Conservative Assoc., 1952; Editor, Oxford Tory, 1952-53. Councillor, City and Co. of Bristol, 1954-57; contested Bristol SE at Gen. Election, 1955. Parliamentary Private Secretary to: Minister of State, Home Office, 1958-59; Minister of Health, 1959-60; Minister of Works, 1960-62; introduced: Fatal Accidents Act, 1959; Historic Buildings Bill, 1963; Motorways Commn Bill, 1968; Owner Occupiers Under-occupied Housing Bill, 1973 and 1974. State Dept Foreign

Leader Visitor in USA, 1961. Chairman: Cons. Broadcasting and Communications Cttee, 1962-64, 1973-76; Arts and Heritage Cttee of Cons. Party, 1970- (Vice-Chm., 1959-62 and 1964-70); House of Commons Administration Cttee, 1974-; a Commissioner, 1976; Vice-Chm., Media Cttee, 1976-; Member: Services Cttee, House of Commons, 1967-; Select Cttee on Wealth Tax (Chm. Nat. Heritage Sub-Cttee); Jt Cttee, Broadcasting Proceedings of Parlt; Parly delegn to Brazil, 1975; Council of Europe, Athens, 1976; Historic Buildings Council for England; Historic Houses Cttee, BTA. Trustee, Primrose League. Director, Westward Television, 1970-. Clerk, Parish Meeting of Athelhampton. FRSA. *Publications:* West Country Houses, 1957; Government and the Quality of Life, 1974. *Recreations:* architecture, building, gardening. *Address:* Athelhampton, Dorchester, Dorset. *T:* Puddletown 363. *Clubs:* Carlton, Pratt's, Farmer's, Royal Automobile, Garrick, MCC.

COOKE, Brig. Robert Thomas, CBE 1943; psc†; *b* 23 Jan. 1897; *o s* of Capt. Robert George Cooke and Sarah Louisa, *d* of Thomas Connolly, Dundalk, Co. Louth; *m* 1922, Löie Howard, *d* of Frank Shawcross-Smith, Buxton, Derbyshire; two *d*. *Educ:* Warwick Sch.; RMC Sandhurst; Staff Coll., Camberley. 2nd Lieut ASC, 1915; Capt., 1926; Bt Major, 1937; Major, 1938; Lieut-Col, 1940; Col, 1942; Brig., 1943. Served France, Belgium, Egypt and Syria, 1914-19 (severely wounded twice). Staff Coll. 1930-31; Staff Appointments: Aldershot Command, 1932-34; Southern Command, 1934-36; Active Service, Palestine Rebellion, 1937-38; GSO2, War Office, 1938-40. AA&QMG, Narvik, March 1940; AA&QMG 54 Div., July 1940; AQMG (ops) Eastern Command, 1941; DQMG 1st Army, Aug. 1942; DQMG, AFHQ, N Africa, Dec. 1942; DA&QMG 9 Corps BNAF, March 1943; Brig. "Q" 15 Army Group, July 1943; DA&QMG 5 Army, Italy, Sept. 1943; Brig. i/c Administration, HQ L of C 21st Army Group, Nov. 1943-Feb. 1945; Col i/c Admin S Wales District, 1945-46; Brig. "Q" GHQ, Middle East, 1946-47; Brig. i/c Administration, British Troops in Egypt, 1947; invalided out of Army as result of war wounds, 1949. Croix de Guerre, 1944. *Recreations:* hunting, golf, tennis. *Address:* 35 Egerton Road, Queen's Park, Bournemouth, Dorset. *T:* Bournemouth 33851; c/o Lloyds Bank Ltd, Bournemouth, Dorset.

COOKE, Robert Victor, FRCS 1929; Sheriff of Bristol, 1971-72; retired from National Health Service, 1967, when Senior Surgeon: Bristol Royal Hospital; Bristol Homoeopathic Hospital; Tetbury and Almondsbury District Hospitals; *b* Berkeley, Glos, 17 May 1902; *e s* of John Cooke and Rose Eva (*née* O'Neill); *m* 1st, 1929, Elizabeth Mary (*d* 1964), MD, MRCP, *d* of Hugh Gordon Cowie, MD, Banff, Scotland; two *s*; 2nd, 1970, Dr Mavis Coutts. *Educ:* Lydney Grammar Sch., Glos; Bristol Univ.; Bristol Gen. Hosp. (ChM 1930); Middlesex Hosp.; Guy's Hosp. House appointments in Bristol and London; Asst to Prof. of Surgery, Univ. of Wales, 1929-33; Hon. Asst Surgeon, Bristol Gen. Hosp. and Bristol Children's Hosp., 1933-. Royal College of Surgeons: Mem. Council, 1949-75; Mem. Court of Examiners; Hunterian Prof.; Vice-Pres., Central Consultants and Specialists Cttee, 1969-71). British Medical Association: Mem.; Pres., Section of Surgery, Oxford, 1963; Pres., 1967-68. Pres., Proctological and Surgical Sections, RSM. Formerly Examiner in Surgery, Univs of Glasgow, Birmingham, Wales, Bristol, Oxford, Liverpool, Lahore, Cairo, Khartoum, Nairobi, Ceylon, Hong Kong. Lectures: A. B. Mitchell Meml, Belfast, 1966; Bradshaw, RCS, 1970; (first) De Silva Meml, Colombo, 1970; Sheen Meml, 1975. Mem., Bd of Governors, Bristol Royal Hosp. Hon. Secretary: Bristol Medico-Chirurgical Soc., 1935-46; Moynihan Chirurgical Club, 1950-59; Pres., Anchor Soc., 1971-72. FRSM; Fellow, Assoc. of Surgeons of Great Britain and Ireland. Liveryman, Soc. of Apothecaries of London. Hon. MD 1967. Cecil Joll Award, RCS, 1963; Lawrence Abel Cup, BMA, 1965. *Publications:* papers on intravenous pyelography, blood vessel injuries, goitre surgery, surgery of colon and biliary tract; chapter on intestinal resection and anastomosis in Textbook of British Surgery, 1956. *Recreations:* golf, gardening (FRHS, and Mem. Iris, Rose and Delphinium Socs); Antiquary (Collector of English furniture; Mem., Bristol and Glos Archaeological Soc.). *Address:* Litfield House, Clifton Down, Bristol BS8 3JU. *T:* Bristol 36363.
See also Robert Gordon Cooke.

COOKE, Rt. Hon. Sir Robin (Brunskill), Kt 1977; PC 1977; PhD; Judge, Court of Appeal of New Zealand, since 1976; *b* 9 May 1926; *s* of Philip Brunskill Cooke and Valmai Digby Gore; *m* 1952, Phyllis Annette Miller; three *s*. *Educ:* Wanganui Collegiate Sch.; Victoria University Coll., Wellington (LLM); Gonville and Caius Coll., Cambridge (MA, PhD). Trav. Scholarship in Law, NZ, 1950; Fellow, Gonville and Caius Coll., Cambridge, 1952 (Yorke Prize, 1954). Called to the Bar, Inner Temple, 1954; practised at NZ Bar, 1955-72; QC 1964; Judge of

Supreme Court, 1972. Chm., Commn of Inquiry into Housing, 1970-71. *Publications:* (ed) Portrait of a Profession (Centennial Book of NZ Law Society), 1969; articles in Law Qly Rev. and NZ Law Jl. *Recreations:* running, golf. *Address:* 4 Homewood Crescent, Karori, Wellington, New Zealand. *T:* 768-059. *Clubs:* United Oxford & Cambridge University; Wellington, Wellington Golf (NZ).

COOKE, (Roland) Cecil, CMG 1959; CBE 1952; Director of Exhibitions, Central Office of Information, 1946-61, retired; *b* 28 June 1899; *m* 1924, Doris Marjorie, *d* of Reginald Fewings. Architectural Asst, LCC, 1921; Dir of Publicity, Catesbys, Ltd, 1935; Dir of Exhibitions Div., Ministry of Information, 1945. Dir of Exhibitions, Festival of Britain, 1949-51; Dir, Festival Gardens Co., 1951; Dir of Exhibitions, British Government Pavilion, Brussels, 1958; UK representative, International Jury, Brussels Exhibition, 1958. Comr Gen., British Pavilion, Seattle World's Fair. *Publications:* contrib. to periodicals and press, illustrated stories for children, political and strip cartoons. *Recreation:* painting. *Address:* Greenbanks, Fairmile Lane, Cobham, Surrey. *T:* Cobham 2557.

COOKE, Rupert C.; *see* Croft-Cooke.

COOKE, Hon. Sir Samuel Burgess Ridgway, Kt 1967; Hon. Mr Justice Cooke; Judge of the High Court of Justice, Queen's Bench Division, since 1967; Chairman of the Law Commission, since 1973; *b* 16 March 1912; *o s* of Samuel and Jessie Lennox Cooke; *m* 1st, Isabel Nancy, *d* of late E. F. Bulmer, Adams Hill, Hereford; 2nd, Diana, *d* of late George Witherby, Burley, Hants. *Educ:* Gonville and Caius Coll., Cambridge (schol.). 1st Class Hons Classical Tripos Pt I, 1932, 1st cl. Hons, Law Tripos Pt II, 1934; Pres., Cambridge Union Soc., 1934. Cholmeley Schol., Lincoln's Inn; called to Bar (cert. of honour), 1936; Asst to Parly Counsel to Treasury, 1938-45; Parly Counsel, 1945-46; private practice, 1946; Jun. Counsel to Min. of Lab. and Nat. Service, 1950-60; QC 1960. Bencher of Lincoln's Inn; Mem., Senate of the Four Inns of Court, 1966-68; Vice-Chm., Statute Law Cttee, 1973-. *Address:* 3 Well Road, Hampstead, NW3. *T:* 01-435 1282; Rectory Farm, Plumpton, Northants. *T:* Blakesley 271.

COOKE, Tom Harry; Editor-in-Chief and Director of St Regis Newspapers Ltd (publishers of the Bolton Evening News and the Lancashire Journal Series of weekly papers), since 1965; *b* 26 March 1923; *er s* of Tom Cooke and Dorothy Cooke; *m* 1952, Jean Margaret Taylor; four *d*. *Educ:* Bacup and Rawtenstall Grammar Sch. Served RAF, 1942-47. Journalist on weekly, evening and morning papers in Lancs, 1939-51; Parly and Lobby Corresp. with Kemsley (now Thomson) Newspapers, 1951-59; Asst Editor, Evening Telegraph, Blackburn, 1959-64; Dep. Editor, The Journal, Newcastle upon Tyne, 1964-65. Pres., Guild of Brit. Newspaper Editors, 1975-76; Mem., Press Council, 1976-; Management Mem., Newspapers Mutual Insce Soc. *Recreations:* music, esp. opera; travel, reading. *Address:* (home) 2 Hill Side House, Hill Side, Bolton BL1 5DT. *T:* Bolton 492170; (office) Mealhouse Lane, Bolton BL1 1DE. *T:* Bolton 22345.

COOKE, William Peter; Head of Banking Supervision, Bank of England, since 1976; *b* 1 Feb. 1932; *s* of late Douglas Edgar Cooke, MC (Chief Educn Officer for Bucks) and of Florence May (*née* Mills); *m* 1957, Maureen Elizabeth, *er d* of late Dr E. A. Haslam-Fox; two *s* two *d*. *Educ:* Royal Grammar Sch., High Wycombe; Kingswood Sch., Bath; Merton Coll., Oxford (MA). Entered Bank of England, 1955; Bank for Internat. Settlements, Basle, 1958-59; Personal Asst to Man. Dir, IMF, Washington, DC, 1961-65; Sec., City Panel on Takeovers and Mergers, 1968-69; First Dep. Chief Cashier, Bank of England, 1970-73; Adviser to Governors, 1973-76. Chairman: City EEC Cttee, 1973-; Group of Ten Cttee on Banking Regulations and Supervisory Practices at BIS, Basle, 1977-. *Recreations:* music, golf, travel. *Address:* Heathside, Fulmer Way, Gerrards Cross, Bucks. *Club:* Overseas Bankers.

COOKSLEY, Clarence Harrington, CBE 1973; QPM 1969; DL; one of HM Inspectors of Constabulary, 1975-77; *b* 16 Dec. 1915; *e s* of late Clarence Harrington Cooksley and Elsie Cooksley, Nottingham; *m* 1940, Eunice May White, Nottingham; two *s*. *Educ:* Nottingham. Joined Nottinghamshire Constabulary, 1938. Served Duke of Wellington's Regt and Dep. Asst Provost Marshal, Special Investigation Branch, Royal Corps of Military Police, 1942-46. Dir. of Dept of Law, Police Coll., Bramshill, 1961; Dep. Chief Constable of Hertfordshire, 1961-63; Chief Constable: Northumberland County Constabulary, 1963-69; Northumberland Constabulary, 1969-74; Northumbria Police, 1974-75. DL Northumberland 1971. OStJ 1966. *Address:* 32 Callerton Court, Ponteland, Newcastle upon Tyne.

COOKSON, Prof. Richard Clive, FRS 1968; MA, PhD, FRIC; Professor of Chemistry in the University of Southampton since 1957; *b* 27 Aug. 1922; *s* of late Clive Cookson; *m* 1948, Ellen Fawaz; two *s*. *Educ:* Harrow Sch.; Trinity Coll., Cambridge. BA 1944; MA, PhD Cantab 1947. Research Fellow, Harvard Univ., 1948; Research Div. of Glaxo Laboratories Ltd, 1949-51; Lectr, Birkbeck Coll., London Univ., 1951-57. Fellow, Winchester Coll., 1970. *Publications:* papers, mainly in Jl Chem. Soc. *Address:* Chemistry Department, The University, Southampton SO9 5NH. *T:* 559122.

COOKSON, Roland Antony, CBE 1974 (OBE 1946); Director, Lead Industries Group Ltd (until 1967 known as Goodlass Wall & Lead Industries Ltd), since 1948 (a Managing Director, 1952, Chairman 1962-73); Chairman, Consett Iron Co. Ltd, 1966-67 (Director 1955; Acting Chairman 1964); Director of Lloyds Bank Ltd since 1964 (Chairman, Northern Regional Board); *b* 12 Dec. 1908; *s* of late Bryan Cookson; *m* 1st, 1931, Rosamond Gwladys (*d* 1973), *er d* of late Sir John S. Barwick, 2nd Bt; one *d*; 2nd, 1974, Dr Anne Aitchison, *widow* of Sir Stephen Charles de Lancey Aitchison, 3rd Bt. *Educ:* Harrow; Magdalen Coll., Oxford. Vice-Chm., Northern Regional Board for Industry, 1949-65; Mem., Northern Economic Planning Council, 1965-68; Pres., Tyneside Chamber of Commerce, 1955-57; Chm., Northern Regional Council, CBI, 1970-72 (Vice-Chm., 1968-70); Mem., Port of Tyne Authority, 1968-74. Mem., Court and Council, Univ. of Newcastle upon Tyne; Chm., Careers Adv. Board, Univs of Newcastle upon Tyne and Durham, 1962-73. Hon. DCL Newcastle, 1974. *Recreations:* music, fishing, shooting. *Address:* Howden Dene, Corbridge, Northumberland. *T:* Corbridge 2422. *Clubs:* Brooks's; Northern Counties (Newcastle upon Tyne).
See also Sir Richard Barwick, Bt.

COOLEY, Sir Alan (Sydenham), Kt 1976; CBE 1972; Secretary, Department of Productivity, since 1977; *b* 17 Sept. 1920; *s* of Hector William Cooley and Ruby Ann Cooley; *m* 1949, Nancie Chisholm Young; four *d*. *Educ:* Geelong Grammar Sch.; Melbourne Univ. (BEngSc). Cadet Engr, Dept of Supply, 1940-43; Engrg Rep., London, 1951-52; Manager, Echuca Ball Bearing Factory, 1953-55; Supply Rep., Washington, 1956-57; Manager, Small Arms Factory, Lithgow, 1958-60; Dept of Supply: First Asst Sec. (Management Services and Planning), 1961-62; Controller-Gen. (Munitions Supply), 1962-66; Sec., 1966-71; Chm., Australian Public Service Bd, 1971-77. *Recreations:* golf, fishing. *Address:* Department of Productivity, Anzac Park West Building, Constitution Avenue, Canberra, ACT 2600, Australia. *T:* 48 2743. *Clubs:* Commonwealth (Canberra); Melbourne, Melbourne Cricket (Vic).

COOLS-LARTIGUE, Sir Louis, Kt 1968; OBE 1955; Governor of Dominica since November 1967; *b* 18 Jan. 1905; *s* of Theodore Cools-Lartigue and Emily (*née* Giraud); *m* 1932, Eugene (*née* Royer); two *s* four *d*. *Educ:* Convents, St Lucia and Dominica; Dominica Grammar Sch. Clerk, Dominica Civil Service, 1924; Chief Clerk to Administrator and Clerk of Councils, 1932; Colonial Treas., Dominica, 1940, St Vincent, 1945; Asst Administrator, St Lucia, 1949; Chief Sec., Windward Is, 1951, retd, 1960 on abolition of office; performed duties of Governor's Dep., Windward Is, over fifty times; Speaker of Legislative Council, Dominica, 1961-67; Speaker of House of Assembly, Dominica, March-Oct. 1967. KStJ 1975. *Recreations:* tennis, swimming. *Address:* Government House, Roseau, Dominica, West Indies.

COOMBE, Michael Rew; 2nd Junior Treasury Counsel at the Central Criminal Court, since 1975; a Recorder of the Crown Court, since 1976; *b* 17 June 1930; *s* of John Rew Coombe and Phyllis Mary Coombe; *m* 1961, Elizabeth Anne Hull; two *s* one *d* (and one *s* decd). *Educ:* Berkhamsted; New Coll., Oxford. MA (Eng. Lang. and Lit.). Called to Bar, Middle Temple, 1957. 2nd Prosecuting Counsel to the Inland Revenue at Central Criminal Court and 5 Courts of London Sessions, 1971; 2nd Counsel to the Crown at Inner London Sessions, Sept. 1971; 1st Counsel to the Crown at Inner London Crown Court, 1974; 4th Junior Treasury Counsel at Central Criminal Court, 1974. *Recreations:* theatre, antiquity, art and architecture, printing. *Address:* 112 Lupus Street, SW1V 4AJ. *T:* 01-828 8742; 2 Harcourt Buildings, Temple, EC4Y 9DB. *T:* 01-353 2112.

COOMBS, Derek Michael; Managing Director and Joint Chairman, S&U Stores Ltd, since 1975 (Joint Managing Director, 1970-75); Director, Metalrax Holdings Ltd, since 1975; political journalist; *b* 12 Aug. 1931; *s* of late Clifford and Mary Coombs; *m* 1959, Patricia O'Toole; one *s* one *d*. *Educ:* Rydal Prep. Sch.; Bromsgrove. Dir, S&U Stores Ltd, 1960 (also of subsids). MP (C) Birmingham, Yardley, 1970-Feb. 1974. Successfully introduced unsupported Private Member's Bill for

relaxation of Earnings Rule, 1972, establishing parly record for a measure of its kind; pioneered new Cons. rate scheme for Oct. 1974 Gen. Election. *Publications:* numerous articles on home, economic and foreign affairs. *Recreations:* hunting, ski-ing, tennis, theatre, collecting paintings. *Address:* 14 Chester Street, SW1. *T:* 01-235 8765; Shottery Grange, Cottage Lane, Shottery, Stratford-on-Avon, Warwicks. *T:* Stratford-on-Avon 5249.

COOMBS, Herbert Cole, AC 1975; MA, PhD; FAA; FAHA; FASSA; Visiting Fellow, Centre for Resource and Environmental Studies, Australian National University, since 1976; *b* 24 Feb. 1906; *s* of Francis Robert Henry and Rebecca Mary Coombs; *m* 1931, Mary Alice Ross; three *s* one *d*. *Educ:* Univ. of Western Australia, Perth, WA (MA); LSE (PhD). Asst Economist, Commonwealth Bank of Australia, 1935; Economist to Commonwealth Treasury, 1939; Mem., Commonwealth Bank Board, 1942; Dir of Rationing, 1942; Dir-Gen. of Post-War Reconstruction, 1943; Governor, Commonwealth Bank of Australia, 1949-60; Chm., Commonwealth Bank Board, 1951-60; Governor and Chm. of Board, Reserve Bank of Australia, 1960-68; Chancellor, ANU, 1968-76. Chairman: Australian Elizabethan Theatre Trust, 1954-68; Australian Council for Arts, 1968-74; Australian Council for Aboriginal Affairs, 1968-76; Royal Commn on Australian Govt Admin, 1974-76. Hon. LLD: Melbourne; ANU; Sydney; Hon. DLitt WA; Hon. Fellow LSE, 1961. *Publication:* Other People's Money, 1971. *Recreations:* golf, squash, theatre-going. *Address:* 119 Milson Road, Cremorne, NSW 2090, Australia.

COOMBS, Ven. Peter Bertram; Archdeacon and Borough Dean of Wandsworth, since 1975; *b* 30 Nov. 1928; *s* of Bertram Robert and Margaret Ann Coombs; *m* 1953, Catherine Ann (*née* Buckwell); one *s* one *d*. *Educ:* Reading Sch.; Bristol Univ. (MA 1960); Clifton Theological Coll. Curate, Christ Church, Beckenham, 1960-64; Rector, St Nicholas, Nottingham, 1964-68; Vicar, Christ Church, New Malden, 1968-75; Rural Dean of Kingston upon Thames, 1970-75. *Recreations:* walking, sketching. *Address:* 68 Wandsworth Common North Side, SW18 2QX. *T:* 01-874 5766.

COOMBS, Prof. Robert Royston Amos, ScD; FRS 1965; FRCPath 1969; Quick Professor of Biology, and Head, Immunology Division, Department of Pathology, University of Cambridge, since 1966; Fellow of Corpus Christi College, since 1962; *b* 9 Jan. 1921; *s* of Charles Royston Amos and Edris Owen Amos (formerly Coombs); *m* 1952, Anne Marion Blomfield; one *s* one *d*. *Educ:* Diocesan Coll., Cape Town; Edinburgh and Cambridge Univs. BSc, MRCVS Edinburgh 1943; PhD Cambridge 1947; Stringer Fellow, King's Coll., Cambridge, 1947. Asst Director of Research, Dept of Pathology, University of Cambridge, 1948; Reader in Immunology, University of Cambridge, 1963-66. Hon. FRCP 1973; Hon. MD Linköping Univ. 1973. *Publications:* (with Anne M. Coombs and D. G. Ingram) Serology of Conglutination and its relation to disease, 1960; (ed with P. G. H. Gell) Clinical Aspects of Immunology, 1963; numerous scientific papers on immunology. *Recreation:* retreat to the country. *Address:* 6 Selwyn Gardens, Cambridge. *T:* Cambridge 52681.

COONEY, Raymond George Alfred, (Ray Cooney); actor, author, director, theatrical producer; *b* 30 May 1932; *s* of Gerard Cooney and Olive (*née* Clarke); *m* 1962, Linda Dixon; two *s*. *Educ:* Alleyn's Sch., Dulwich. First appeared in Song of Norway, Palace, 1946; toured in Wales, 1954-56; subseq. played in: Dry Rot and Simple Spymen, Whitehall; Mousetrap, Ambassador; Charlie Girl, Adelphi; Not Now Darling (film); Not Now Comrade (film). Productions (some jointly) include: Thark (revival); Doctor at Sea; The Queen's Highland Servant; My Giddy Aunt; Move Over Mrs Markham; The Mating Game; Lloyd George Knew My Father; That's No Lady-That's My Husband; Say Goodnight to Grandma; Two and Two Make Sex; At the End of the Day; Why Not Stay for Breakfast?; A Ghost on Tiptoe; My Son's Father; The Sacking of Norman Banks; The Bedwinner; The Little Hut; Springtime for Henry; Saint Joan; The Trials of Oscar Wilde; The Dame of Sark; Jack the Ripper; There Goes the Bride (and played leading role, Ambassadors, 1974); Ipi Tombi; What's a Nice Country Like US Doing In a State Like This?; Some of My Best Friends Are Husbands; Banana Ridge; Fire Angel. *Publications:* (with H. and M. Williams) Charlie Girl, 1965; *plays:* (with Tony Hilton) One for the Pot, 1961; Chase Me Comrade, 1964; (with Tony Hilton) Stand by your Bedouin, 1966; (with John Chapman) Not Now Darling, 1967; (with John Chapman) My Giddy Aunt, 1968; (with John Chapman) Move Over Mrs Markham, 1969; (with Gene Stone) Why Not Stay for Breakfast?, 1970; (with John Chapman) There Goes the Bride, 1973. *Recreations:* tennis, swimming, golf. *Address:* Duke of York's Theatre, St Martins Lane, WC2. *T:* 01-836 9831. *Club:* Dramatists'.

COOP, Sir Maurice (Fletcher); Kt 1973; Consultant, Dunlop Holdings Ltd; Solicitor; *b* 11 Sept. 1907; *s* of George Harry and Ada Coop; *m* 1948, Elsie Hilda Brazier. *Educ:* Epworth Coll., Rhyl; Emmanuel Coll., Cambridge (BA). Admitted Solicitor of Supreme Court, 1932. Sec., Dunlop Rubber Co. Ltd, 1948-68; Dir, Dunlop Rubber Co. Ltd, 1966-70. Chm., Standing Adv. Cttee to Govt on Patents, 1972-74. *Recreations:* Association football, cricket. *Address:* 39 Hill Street, Berkeley Square, W1X 7FG. *T:* 01-499 3484. *Club:* United Oxford & Cambridge University.

COOPER, family name of Viscount Norwich and Baron Cooper of Stockton Heath.

COOPER; see Ashley-Cooper.

COOPER OF STOCKTON HEATH, Baron *cr* 1966, of Stockton Heath (Life Peer); **John Cooper**, MA; General Secretary and Treasurer, National Union of General and Municipal Workers, 1962-73; National Water Council, since 1973; *b* 7 June 1908; *s* of late John Ainsworth Cooper and of Annie Lily Cooper (*née* Dukes); *m* 1934, Nellie Spencer (marr. diss. 1969); three *d* ; *m* 1969, Mrs Joan Rogers. *Educ:* Stockton Heath Council Sch.; Lymm Grammar Sch., Cheshire. Employed Crosfields Soap Works, Warrington, 1924-28; NUGMW, 1928-73, District Sec., Southern Dist, 1944-61; Chm., 1952-61. Member: Manchester CC, 1936-42; LCC, 1949; Alderman, 1952-53; London Labour Party Executive; MP (Lab) Deptford, 1950-51; PPS to Sec. of State for Commonwealth Relations, 1950-51. Member: NEC Labour Party, 1953-57; TUC Gen. Council, 1959-73 (Pres., TUC, 1970-71). Chm., British Productivity Council, 1965-66; Mem., Thames Conservancy, 1955-74. Governor various instns, etc. MA Oxon. Prix de la Couronne Française, 1970. *Address:* 23 Kelvin Grove, Chessington, Surrey. *T:* 01-397 3908.

COOPER, Very Rev. Alan; see Cooper, Very Rev. W. H. A.

COOPER, Sqdn Ldr Albert Edward, MBE 1946; formerly: Managing Director, Dispersions Ltd; Director, Ault & Wiborg International Ltd; *b* 23 Sept. 1910; *s* of Albert Frederick Smith and Edith Alice Cooper, Withernsea, Yorks; *m* 1933, Emily Muriel, *d* of William John Nelder, Launceston; one *d*. *Educ:* London Coll. for Choristers; Australia. Entered politics, 1935, when elected to Ilford Borough Council; Chairman: Electricity and Lighting Cttees; Education (Finance) and Legal and Parliamentary Cttees; Alderman, 1947. Served War of 1939-45; enlisted in RAF, 1940, and served as navigator in Coastal Command. Contested (C) Dagenham, Gen. Election, 1945; MP (C) Ilford South, 1950-66, 1970-Feb. 1974; PPS to President of the Board of Trade, 1952-54. *Recreations:* cricket, swimming, bridge, and motoring. *Address:* 156 Park West, W2.

COOPER, Rev. Albert Samuel; Moderator, Free Church Federal Council, 1973-74; *b* 6 Nov. 1905; *s* of Samuel and Edith Cooper; *m* 1936, Emily, *d* of Hugh and Emily Williams; one *s* one *d*. *Educ:* Birkenhead Inst.; London Univ. (external student; BA Hons Philosophy); Westminster Coll., Cambridge (DipTheol); Fitzwilliam House, Cambridge (BA Theol Tripos, MA). Ordained 1936. Pastoral charges: St Columba's Presbyterian Church, Grimsby, 1936-41; Blundellsands Presbyt. Ch., Liverpool, 1941-44; St Columba's Presbyt. Ch., Cambridge, 1944-60; St Columba's Presbyt. (later United Reformed) Ch., Leeds, 1960-72, retd 1972. Free Church Chaplain, Fulbourn Mental Hosp., Cambridgeshire, 1950-60. Moderator, Presbyt. Ch. of England, 1968-69. *Recreation:* walking. *Address:* 10 Thorpe Bank, Rock Ferry, Birkenhead, Merseyside L42 4NP. *T:* 051-645 0418.

COOPER, Andrew Ramsden, CBE 1965; Industrial Consultant, since 1966; Member for Operations and Personnel, Central Electricity Generating Board, 1959-66; *b* 1 Oct. 1902; *s* of Mary and William Cooper, Rotherham, Yorks. *Educ:* Rotherham Grammar Sch.; Sheffield Univ. Colliery Engineer, Yorks and Kent, 1916-28; Chief Electrical Engineer, Pearson & Dorman Long, 1928; Personal Asst to G. A. Mower, London, 1935; joined Central Electricity Board Operation Dept, NW England and N Wales, 1936; transf. to HQ, 1937; Operation Engineer, SE and E England, 1942; Chief Operation Engineer to Central Electricity Board, 1944; Controller, Merseyside and N Wales Div. (Central Electricity Authority), 1948-52; NW Div., 1952-54; N West, Mersyside and N Wales Div., 1954-57; Mem. and Regional Dir, CEGB, 1957-59. Inventor, ARCAID Deaf/Blind Conversation Machine; Pres., Electrical Industries Benevolent Assoc., 1964-65; Mem., GB-USSR Cultural Relations Cttee. Faraday Lectr, 1952-53. MEng; CEng; FIEE; MRI; FInstF; FIEEE; Fellow, Fellowship of Engineering, 1977. Pres., CIGRE, 1966-72. Bernard Price Meml Lectr, S African Inst. of Electr. Engrg, 1970; Meritorious Service Award, Power Engrg Soc. of America, 1972; Donor, Power/Life Award, Power Engrg Soc. Hon. Mem., Batti-Wallahs Assoc. Hon. MEng Liverpool Univ., 1954. *Publications include:* Load Dispatching, with Special Reference to the British Grid System (a paper receiving John Hopkinson Award, 1948, and Willans Medal, 1952, IEE). *Recreations:* golf, music, writing, broadcasting. *Address:* 4 Exeter House, Putney Heath, SW15. *T:* 01-788 5544. *Clubs:* Savile, Electrical Industries; Royal Wimbledon Golf.

COOPER, Beryl Phyllis, QC 1977; a Recorder of the Crown Court, since 1977; *b* 24 Nov. 1927; *o c* of Charles Augustus Cooper and Phyllis Lillie (*née* Burrows), 80 South Cliff Tower, Eastbourne, Sussex. *Educ:* Surbiton High Sch.; Univ. of Birmingham (BCom 1960). Called to the Bar, Gray's Inn, 1960. Hosp. Adminstr, Royal Free Hosp., 1951-57. Formerly: Councillor, St Pancras Metrop. Bor. Council; Mem., Homeopathic Hosp. Cttee; Mem., Bd of Visitors, Wandsworth Prison. Conservative Parly Candidate, Stepney, 1966; Founder Mem., Bow Gp (former Sec. and Council Mem.). Member: Cripps Cttee, Women and the Law; Home Office Cttee on Criminal Statistics (Perks Cttee); Housing Corp., 1976-. *Publications:* pamphlets for CPC; articles on social, criminal and local govt matters. *Recreations:* travel, swimming, golf. *Address:* 42 Great Brownings, College Road, Dulwich, SE21 7HP. *T:* 01-670 7012; 2 Dr Johnson's Buildings, Temple, EC4Y 7AY. *T:* 01-353 5371. *Clubs:* English-Speaking Union; Royal Eastbourne Golf.

COOPER, Sir Charles (Eric Daniel), of Woollahra, 5th Bt, *cr* 1863; *b* 5 Oct. 1906; *s* of Sir Daniel Cooper, 4th Bt, and Lettice Margaret, *y d* of 1st Viscount Long; *S* father 1954; *m* 1st, 1931, Alice Estelle (*d* 1952), *y d* of late William Manifold, Victoria, Australia; 2nd, 1953, Mary Elisabeth, *e d* of Capt. J. Graham Clarke, Frocester Manor, Glos; two *s*. *Educ:* Harrow; RMC Sandhurst. Lieut 1st The Royal Dragoons, 1926; Capt., 1935; Major, 1945. Served War of 1939-45. *Recreations:* hunting and shooting. *Heir: s* William Daniel Charles Cooper, *b* 5 March 1955. *Address:* Heywood Manor, Boldre, Lymington, Hants. *T:* Brockenhurst 2163. *Club:* Cavalry and Guards.

COOPER, Lady Diana, (Diana, Viscountess Norwich); 3rd *d* of 8th Duke of Rutland, KG (*d* 1925), and Violet Lindsay (*d* 1937); *m* 1919 (as Lady Diana Manners) A. Duff Cooper, 1st Viscount Norwich (*cr* 1952), PC, KCMG, DSO (*d* 1954); one *s* (*see* 2nd Viscount Norwich). Nurse at Guy's Hospital during European War, 1914-18. Took leading part in Max Reinhardt's play, The Miracle, that showed, on and off, for 12 years in London and provincial towns, in USA (New York and all the great cities), and on the Continent (Prague, Buda-Pest, Vienna, Dortmund, Salzburg). Pres., Order of Charity. *Publications:* The Rainbow Comes and Goes, 1958; The Light of Common Day, 1959; Trumpets from the Steep, 1960. *Address:* 10 Warwick Avenue, W2; Le Marget-gallerie des Pâtres, Uzès, Gard, France.

COOPER, Douglas; Art Historian and Critic; Slade Professor of Fine Art, Oxford University, 1957-58; Flexner Lecturer, Bryn Mawr, 1961; *b* London, 20 Feb. 1911. *Educ:* various European Univs. Dep.-Dir, Monuments and Fine Arts Branch, Control Commn for Germany, 1944-46; Lectr, Courtauld Institute of Art. Chevalier de la Légion d'Honneur. *Publications:* Letters of Van Gogh to Emile Bernard, 1937; The Road to Bordeaux, 1940; Paul Klee, 1949; Turner, 1949; Juan Gris, 1949; Leger, 1949; Degas Pastels, 1954; Catalogue of the Courtauld Collection, 1954; Van Gogh Water Colours, 1955; Toulouse-Lautrec, 1956; Graham Sutherland, 1961; De Staël, 1962; Picasso: Les Déjeuners, 1962; Picasso: Theatre, 1968; The Cubist Epoch, 1971; Braque: The Great Years, 1973; Juan Gris: catalogue raisonné, 1976. *Address:* Monte Carlo Star, Monte Carlo.

COOPER, Sir Francis Ashmole, (Sir Frank), 4th Bt *cr* 1905; Chairman, Ashmole Investment Trust Ltd, 1969-74; *b* 9 Aug. 1905; *s* of Sir Richard Ashmole Cooper, 2nd Bt, and Alice Elizabeth (*d* 1963), *d* of Rev. E. Priestland, Spondon; *S* brother, 1970; *m* 1933, Dorothy F. H., *d* of Emile Deen, Berkhamsted, and Maggie Louise Deen; one *s* three *d*. *Educ:* Lancing Coll.; King's Coll., Cambridge (MA); University Coll., London (PhD). Joined Cooper, McDougall and Robertson Ltd, 1926; on leave to University College, 1931-36; Technical Director, 1940-62; retired, 1962. *Recreation:* yachting. *Heir: s* Richard Powell Cooper [*b* 13 April 1934; *m* 1957, Angela Marjorie, *e d* of Eric Wilson, Norton-on-Tees; one *s* two *d*]. *Address:* La Bastide de la Maraouro, 06490 Tourrettes sur Loup, France. *Clubs:* Carlton, Royal Thames Yacht; Royal Motor Yacht (Sandbanks, Poole).

COOPER, Sir Frank, KCB 1974 (CB 1970); CMG 1961; Permanent Under Secretary of State, Ministry of Defence, since 1976; *b* 2 Dec. 1922; *s* of late V. H. Cooper, Fairfield,

Manchester; *m* 1948, Peggie, *d* of F. J. Claxton; two *s* one *d.* *Educ:* Manchester Grammar Sch.; Pembroke Coll., Oxford (Hon. Fellow, 1976). War of 1939-45: Pilot, Royal Air Force, 1941-46. Asst Principal, Air Ministry, 1948; Private Secretary: to Parly Under-Sec. of State for Air, 1949-51; to Permanent Under-Sec. of State for Air, 1951-53; to Chief of Air Staff, 1953-55; Asst Sec., Head of the Air Staff, Secretariat, 1955-60; Dir of Accounts, Air Ministry, 1961-62; Asst Under-Sec. of State, Air Min., 1962-64, Min. of Defence, 1964-68; Dep. Under-Sec. of State, Min. of Defence, 1968-70; Dep. Sec., CSD, 1970-73; Permanent Under-Sec. of State, NI Office, 1973-76. Commodore, Civil Service Sailing Assoc., 1976. *Recreations:* tennis, sailing. *Address:* Delafield, Camden Park Road, Chislehurst, Kent. *Club:* Athenæum.

COOPER, Wing-Comdr Geoffrey; President: Raydel Ltd (a property company in Nassau, Bahamas); Estate Developers Ltd; Land Title Clearance Ltd; *b* 18 Feb. 1907; *s* of Albert Cooper, Leicester, and Evelyn J. Bradnam, Hastings; *m* 1951, Mrs Tottie Resch, Blanc Pignon, Jersey, CI. *Educ:* Wyggeston Gram. Sch., Leicester; Royal Grammar School, Worcester. Accountancy, business management. Auxiliary Air Force, 1933; Imperial Airways, 1939. Served Royal Air Force 1939-45, Pilot (mentioned in despatches). MP (Lab) for Middlesbrough West Div., 1945-51. *Publications:* Cæsar's Mistress (exposé of BBC and nationalisation); articles in England, Bahamas and USA on civil aviation, business management and government methods. *Recreations:* portrait and landscape painting, swimming, tennis, horse riding. *Address:* PO Box 4305, Nassau, Bahamas. *Club:* Royal Air Force.

COOPER, George A.; Marketing and Business Consultant, Thames Television Ltd, since 1977 (Director, 1968; Managing Director, 1974-77); Chairman, Independent Television Publications Ltd, since 1971; *b* 9 Oct. 1915; *s* of late Joseph Cooper; *m* 1944, Irene Burns; one *d.* Exec. with internat. publishing gp; served War of 1939-45, Royal Artillery (Captain); Exec., Hulton Press, 1949-55; Director: ABC Television Ltd, 1955-77; Independent Television News, 1976-77; Chm., Network Programme Cttee of Independent Television, 1975-77. *Recreations:* golf, walking. *Address:* 43 Rivermill, 151 Grosvenor Road, SW1V 3JN. *T:* 01-821 9305. *Clubs:* Royal Automobile, Thirty.

COOPER, George Edward; Chairman, North Thames Gas Region (formerly North Thames Gas Board), 1970-77; Part-time Member, British Gas Corporation, 1973-77; *b* 25 Jan. 1915; *s* of H. E. Cooper and R. A. Jones, Wolverhampton; *m* 1941, Dorothy Anne Robinson; one *s. Educ:* Wolverhampton Municipal Grammar Sch. Wolverhampton and Walsall Corp., 1933-40. Served War, 1940-45, with RA in Middle East (Bimbashi Sudan Defence Force), Captain. Qualified as Accountant, Inst. of Municipal Treasurers and Accountants, 1947; Hemel Hempstead Development Corp., 1948-50; W Midlands Gas Bd (finally Dep. Chm.), 1950-70. IPFA (FIMTA 1965); CIGasE 1968. OStJ 1976. *Recreations:* photography, geology, golf. *Address:* 2 Whichert Close, Beaconsfield, Bucks. *Club:* City Livery.

COOPER, Maj.-Gen. George Leslie Conroy, MC 1953; Chief of Staff, United Kingdom Land Forces, since 1978; *b* 10 Aug. 1925; *s* of Lt-Col G. C. Cooper and Mrs Y. V. Cooper, Bulmer Tye House, Sudbury; *m* 1957, Cynthia Mary Hume; one *s* one *d. Educ:* Downside Sch.; Trinity Coll., Cambridge. Commnd 1945; served with Bengal Sappers and Miners, 1945-48; Korea, 1952-53; psc 1956; jssc 1959; Instructor, RMA Sandhurst, 1959-62 and Staff Coll., Camberley, 1964; GSO1, 1st Div., 1964-66; CRE, 4th Div., 1966-68; MoD, 1968-69; Comdr, 19th Airportable Bde, 1969-71; Royal Coll. of Defence Studies, 1972; Dep. Dir Army Trng, 1973-74; GOC SW District, 1974-75; Dir, Army Staff Duties, MoD, 1976-78. *Recreations:* ski-ing, sailing, tennis, shooting, gardening. *Address:* c/o Barclays Bank Ltd, 3-5 King Street, Reading, Berks. *Club:* Army and Navy.

COOPER, Sir Gilbert (Alexander), Kt 1972; CBE 1964; ED 1943; MLC, Bermuda, 1968-72, retired; *b* 31 July 1903; *s* of Alexander Samuel and Laura Ann Cooper. *Educ:* Saltus Grammar Sch., Bermuda; McGill Univ., Canada (BCom). Mem., Corp. of Hamilton, Bermuda, 1946-72; Mayor of Hamilton, 1963-72. Mem., House of Assembly, 1948-68 (Chm. House Finance Cttee, 1959-68). *Recreations:* music, painting, sailing, swimming. *Address:* Shoreland, Pembroke, Bermuda. *T:* 5-4189. *Clubs:* Royal Bermuda Yacht, Royal Hamilton Amateur Dinghy, Bermuda Police.

COOPER, Harold H.; *see* Hinton-Cooper.

COOPER, Henry, OBE 1969; company director since 1972; *b* 3 May 1934; *s* of Henry William Cooper and late Lily Nutkins; *m* 1960, Albina Genepri; two *s. Educ:* Athelney Street Sch., Bellingham. Professional boxer, 1954-71. *Film:* Royal Flash, 1975. *Publication:* Henry Cooper: an autobiography, 1972. *Recreation:* golf. *Address:* 36 Brampton Grove, NW4.

COOPER, James Lees; President and Publisher, The Globe and Mail, Toronto, 1963-74; Director, The Globe and Mail Ltd; *b* Darwen, Lancs, 6 March 1907; *s* of James William and Alice (Lees) Cooper; *m* 1930, Ruby Smith; one *d. Educ:* Darwen Grammar Sch. Articled to Darwen News as journalist; worked as reporter, Ashton-under-Lyne; Allied Newspapers, Manchester, and Daily Express, London. War Correspondent, 1941-45: Malta Convoys, Western Desert, Madagascar, Sicily, Italy campaigns. First staff correspondent in Canada for Daily Express, 1947-55; Chief of New York Bureau, 1955-57; organized Overseas Edn of Globe and Mail and its printing and distribution by The Times of London (first overseas edn of a Canadian newspaper), 1958; returned to Canada as Asst to Editor and Publisher, 1959. Dir, Imperial Trust, Montreal; Hon. Chm., Canadian Section, Commonwealth Press Union; led Canadian delegn to Commonwealth Press Union Quinquennial Conf., 1970, in Gibraltar, Malta, Cyprus and Scotland. *Address:* 140 King Street West, Toronto 1, Ont, Canada. *T:* 361 5100.

COOPER, Joan Davies, CB 1972; National Institute for Social Work, since 1976; *b* 12 Aug. 1914; *d* of late Valentine Holland Cooper and of Wynnefred Louisa Cooper; unmarried. *Educ:* Fairfield High Sch., Manchester; University of Manchester (BA). Asst Dir of Educn, Derbyshire CC, 1941; Children's Officer, E Sussex CC, 1948; Chief Inspector, Children's Dept, Home Office, 1965-71; Dir, Social Work Service, DHSS, 1971-76. Mem., SSRC, 1973-76. Chm., Inst. Child Psychology; Vice Pres., Nat. Children's Bureau. FRAI. *Recreation:* gardening. *Address:* The Garden House, Paine's Twitten, Lewes, East Sussex. *T:* Lewes 2604. *Club:* University Women's.

COOPER, Prof. John Philip, DSc; FRS 1977; FIBiol; Director, Welsh Plant Breeding Station, University College of Wales, Aberystwyth, since 1975; *b* Buxton, Derbyshire, 16 Dec. 1923; *o s* of Frank Edward and Nora Goodwin Cooper; *m* 1951, Christine Mary Palmer; one *s* three *d. Educ:* Stockport Grammar Sch.; Univ. of Reading (BSc 1945, PhD 1953, DSc 1964); FitzWilliam House, Cambridge (DipAgrSc 1946). Scientific Officer, Welsh Plant Breeding Station, 1946-50; Lectr, Univ. of Reading, 1950-54; Plant Geneticist, 1950-59, and Head of Dept of Develtl Genetics, Welsh Plant Breeding Station, 1959-75. Consultant, FAO Headquarters, Rome, 1956; Nuffield Royal Society Bursary, CSIRO, Canberra, 1962; Visiting Professor: Univ. of Kentucky, 1965; Univ. of Khartoum, 1975. *Publications:* (ed, with P. F. Wareing) Potential Crop Production, 1971; (ed) Photosynthesis and Productivity in Different Environments, 1975; various papers on crop physiology and genetics in sc. jls. *Recreations:* gardening, walking. *Address:* Bronsiriol, Bryn-y-mor, Aberystwyth, Dyfed. *T:* Aberystwyth 617644. *Club:* Farmers'.

COOPER, Joseph; Pianist and Broadcaster; *b* 7 Oct. 1912; *s* of Wilfrid Needham and Elsie Goodacre Cooper; *m* 1st, 1947, Jean (*d* 1973), *d* of late Sir Louis Greig, KBE, CVO; no *c*; 2nd, 1975, Carol, *d* of Charles and Olive Borg. *Educ:* Clifton Coll. (music schol.); Keble Coll., Oxford (organ schol.). MA (Oxon), ARCM (solo piano). Studied piano under Egon Petri, 1937-39. Served War, in RA, 1939-46. Solo pianist debut, Wigmore Hall, 1947 (postponed, Oct. 1939, owing to War); concerto debut, Philharmonia Orchestra, 1950; BBC debut Promenade Concerts Royal Albert Hall, 1953. Since then has toured in: British Isles, Europe, Africa, India, Canada. Many solo piano records. Chm., BBC TV prog., Face The Music, 1971-77. Liveryman, Worshipful Co. of Musicians, 1963-; Mem., Music Panel of Arts Council (and Chm. piano sub-cttee), 1966-71; Trustee, Countess of Munster Musical Trust, 1975-. Governor, Clifton College. Ambrose Fleming award, Royal Television Soc., 1961; Music Trades Assoc. Record Award, 1976. *Publications:* Hidden Melodies, 1975, 1976, 1977; Arrangement of Vaughan Williams Piano Concerto for 2 pianos (in collab. with composer). *Recreations:* walking, architecture. *Address:* Trocks Mill Cottage, Mill Hill, Barnes Common, SW13. *T:* 01-876 8529. *Club:* Garrick.

COOPER, Joshua Edward Synge, CB 1958; CMG 1943; retired from the Foreign Office; *b* 3 April 1901; *e s* of late Richard E. Synge Cooper and Mary Eleanor, *y d* of William Burke; *m* 1934, Winifred, *d* of Thos F. Parkinson; two *s. Educ:* Shrewsbury; Brasenose Coll., Oxford; King's Coll., London. Civil Service, 1925; Trans. Air Min. (attached FO), 1936; returned to FO, 1943; retired, 1961. *Publications:* Russian Companion, 1967;

Four Russian Plays, 1972. *Address:* Kingsfield, Cobbler's Hill, Great Missenden, Bucks. *T:* Great Missenden 2400.

COOPER, Maj.-Gen. Kenneth Christie, CB 1955; DSO 1945; OBE 1943; psc; idc; retired; *b* 18 Oct. 1905; 4th *s* of E. C. Cooper; *m* 1933, Barbara Harding-Newman; one *s* one *d. Educ:* Berkhamsted Sch. 2nd Lieut, Royal Tank Corps, 1927; India, 1930-34; Adjt, 6 RTR, Egypt, 1935-38; Staff Coll., 1939; Bde Major, 23 Armd Bde, 1939-40; CO Fife and Forfar Yeomanry, 1941-42; GSO1, 9 Corps, N Africa, 1942-43; BGS, AFHQ, N Africa-Italy, 1943-44; Comdr, 7 Armoured Bde, 1945-46; Brig., Royal Armoured Corps, N Comd, 1947-48; Chief of Staff, West Africa Comd, 1948-50; idc 1951; Asst Comdt, Staff Coll., 1952-53. GOC 7th Armoured Div., Dec. 1953-March 1956; Chief of Staff to the Comdr-in-Chief Allied Forces, Northern Europe, 1956-59; retired, 1959. *Recreations:* Rugby, hockey, lawn tennis, shooting. *Address:* West End House, Donhead St Andrew, Shaftesbury, Dorset. *Club:* Army and Navy.

COOPER, Prof. Kenneth Ernest; Emeritus Professor of Bacteriology, Bristol University, 1968; *b* 8 July 1903; *s* of E. Cooper; *m* 1930, Jessie Griffiths; no *c. Educ:* Tadcaster Grammar Sch.; Leeds Univ. BSc 1925, PhD 1927 Leeds; LRCP MRCS 1936; FIBiol. Leeds University: Research Asst in Chemotherapy, 1928-31; Research Asst in Bacteriology, 1931-36; Lectr in Bacteriology, 1936-38; Bristol University: Lectr in Bacteriology, 1938-46; Reader in Bacteriology, 1946-50; Prof. of Bacteriology, 1951-68; Dep. Dean of the Faculty of Science, 1955-58. Hon. Gen. Sec. of Soc. for Gen. Microbiology, 1954-60, Hon. Treas., 1961-68, Hon. Mem., 1969. *Publications:* numerous papers in medical, chemical and bacteriological journals. *Recreations:* golf, chess. *Address:* Fairfield, Clevedon Road, Tickenham, Clevedon, Avon BS21 6RB. *T:* Nailsea 2375.

COOPER, Prof. Leon N., PhD; Thomas J. Watson, Sr, Professor of Science, Brown University, Providence, RI, since 1974; Director, Center for Neural Studies; *b* NYC, 28 Feb. 1930; *s* of Irving Cooper and Anna Cooper (*née* Zola); *m* 1969, Kay Anne Allard; two *d. Educ:* Columbia Univ. (AB 1951, AM 1953, PhD 1954). Nat. Sci. Foundn post-doctoral Fellow, and Mem., Inst. for Advanced Study, 1954-55; Res. Associate, Univ. of Illinois, 1955-57; Asst Prof., Ohio State Univ., 1957-58; Associate Prof., Brown Univ., 1958-62, Prof., 1962-66, Henry Ledyard Goddard Prof., 1966-74. Consultant, various governmental agencies, industrial and educational organizations. Lectr, Summer Sch., Varenna, Italy, 1955; Visiting Professor: Brandeis Summer Inst., 1959; Bergen Internat. Sch. Physics, Norway, 1961; Scuola Internazionale di Fisica, Erice, Italy, 1965; Ecole Normale Supérieure, Centre Universitaire Internat., Paris, 1966; Cargèse Summer Sch., 1966; Radiation Lab., Univ. of Calif. at Berkeley, 1969; Faculty of Scis, Quai St Bernard, Paris, 1970, 1971; Brookhaven Nat. Lab., 1972. Alfred P. Sloan Foundn Res. Fellow, 1959-66; John Simon Guggenheim Meml Foundn Fellow, 1965-66. Fellow: Amer. Physical Soc.; Amer. Philosoph. Soc.; Amer. Acad. of Arts and Sciences; Nat. Acad. of Sciences. Comstock Prize, Nat. Acad. of Scis, 1968; (jtly) Nobel Prize for Physics, 1972. Hon. DSc: Columbia, 1973; Sussex, 1973; Illinois, 1974; Brown, 1974; Gustavus Adolphus Coll., 1975; Ohio State Univ., 1976. *Publications:* Introduction to the Meaning and Structure of Physics, 1968; The Physicist's Conception of Nature, 1973; contrib. The Many Body Problem, 1963; contrib. to numerous jls incl. Physics Rev., Amer. Jl Physics. *Recreations:* music, theatre, skiing. *Address:* 31 Summit Avenue, Providence, RI 02906, USA. *T:* (401)-421-1181; Physics Department, Brown University, Providence, RI 02912, USA. *T:* (401)-863-2172. *Club:* University (Providence, RI).

COOPER, Dr Leslie Hugh Norman, OBE 1973; FRS 1964; CChem, FRIC, FIBiol, FGS; formerly Deputy Director, Marine Biological Laboratory, Plymouth, retired 1972; *b* 17 June 1905; *s* of Charles Herbert Cooper and Annie Cooper (*née* Silk), Austral, Woodland Park, Prestatyn, Clwyd; *m* 1935, Gwynedd Daloni Seth Hughes, Bryngwynt, Bangor, Gwynedd; four *s* one *d. Educ:* John Bright Grammar Sch., Llandudno; University Coll. of North Wales, Bangor. PhD 1927, DSc 1938, Univ. of Wales. Chemist, Rubber Research Assoc., 1927-29; Chemist, Imperial Chemical Industries, 1929-30; Chemist at the Marine Biological Laboratory, Plymouth, engaged on the study of the physics and chemistry of the ocean as a biological environment, 1930-72; continuing research in quaternary oceanography at Plymouth. Hon. DSc Exon, 1974. *Publications:* numerous papers on oceanography. *Address:* 2 Queens Gate Villas, Lipson, Plymouth PL4 7PN. *T:* Plymouth 61174.

COOPER, Louis Jacques B.; *see* Blom-Cooper.

COOPER, Prof. Malcolm McGregor, CBE 1965; Emeritus Professor, University of Newcastle upon Tyne, since 1972; *b* Havelock North, New Zealand, 17 Aug. 1910; *s* of Laurence T. Cooper, farmer, and Sarah Ann Cooper; *m* 1937, Hilary Mathews, Boars Hill, Oxford; three *d. Educ:* Napier Boys High Sch., NZ; Massey Agricultural Coll., Palmerston North, NZ; University Coll., Oxford. BAgrSc (NZ), 1933; Rhodes Scholarship, 1933; Oxford, 1934-37; Diploma Rural Econ., 1935; BLitt in Agric. Economics, 1937. Returned to NZ 1937; Mem. of Staff, Dept of Scientific and Industrial Research, till 1940, when appointed Lecturer in Dairy Husbandry at Massey Agric. Coll. Served War of 1939-45, with NZ Mil. Forces, 1941-46; in Italy with 2 NZ Div. in an Infantry battalion, 1943-45; rank of Major on demobilisation; returned to Massey as Head of Dept of Dairy Husbandry, 1946; Prof. of Agriculture, Univ. of London, 1947-54; Prof. of Agriculture and Rural Economy, and Dean, Fac. of Agriculture, Univ. of Newcastle upon Tyne, 1954-72; Pro-Vice-Chancellor, Univ. of Newcastle upon Tyne, 1971-72. Nat. Res. Coordinator, Instituto Nacional Investigaciones Agrarias, Spain, 1972-75. President: British Grassland Soc., 1958-59; British Soc. of Animal Production, 1972-73; formerly Member: Nature Conservancy Council; Agricultural Advisory Council; Advisory Board, Pig Industry Development Authority; Agricultural Research and Advisory Cttee for Government of Sudan; Scientific Advisory Panel of the Minister of Agriculture; Agricultural Cttee of UGC; Chm., Beef Recording Assoc. (UK) Ltd. FRSE 1956, Hon. FRASE 1969. Massey Ferguson Award for services to agriculture, 1970. Hon DSc Massey Univ., NZ, 1972. *Publications:* (in collaboration) Principles of Animal Production (New Zealand), 1945; Beef Production, 1953; Competitive Farming, 1956; Farm Management, 1960; Grass Farming, 1961; Sheep Farming, 1965; (with M. B. Willis) Profitable Beef Production, 1972; technical articles on agricultural topics. *Recreations:* Rugby football (Rugby Blue, 1934, 1935 and 1936; Capt. OURFC 1936, and Sec. 1935; capped for Scotland, 1936); summer sports, reading, farming. *Address:* Holme House, Lesbury, Alnwick, Northumberland. *Club:* Farmers'.

COOPER, Margaret Jean Drummond; Chief Education Officer, General Nursing Council for England and Wales, since 1974; *b* 24 March 1922; *d* of Canon Bernard R. Cooper and A. Jean Cooper (*née* Drackley). *Educ:* School of St Mary and St Anne, Abbots Bromley; Royal College of Nursing. SRN, SCM, RNT. Nursing trng and early posts, Leicester Royal Infirmary, 1941-47; Midwifery trng, General Lying-in Hosp., SW1 and Coventry and Warwicks Hosp.; Nurse Tutor, Middlesex Hosp., 1953-55; Principal Tutor: General Hosp., Northampton, 1956-63; Addenbrooke's Hosp., Cambridge, 1963-68; Principal, Queen Elizabeth Sch. of Nursing, Birmingham, 1968-74. Chm., General Nursing Council for England and Wales, 1971-74 (Mem., 1965 and 1970). *Recreations:* birds, books, buildings. *Address:* General Nursing Council, 17 Portland Place, W1A 1BA; 28 Lambert Cross, Saffron Walden, Essex CB10 2DP.

COOPER, Martin Du Pré, CBE 1972; Music Editor of the Daily Telegraph, 1954-76; *b* 17 Jan. 1910; *s* of late Cecil Henry Hamilton Cooper, sometime Dean of Carlisle, and late Cecil Stephens; *m* 1940, Mary, *d* of late Lieut-Col Douglas Stewart, DSO, and late Mabel Elizabeth Ponsonby; one *s* three *d. Educ:* Winchester; Oxford (BA). Studied music in Vienna, 1932-34, with Egon Wellesz; Asst Editor, Royal Geographical Soc. Journal, 1935-36; Music Critic: London Mercury, 1934-39; Daily Herald, 1945-50; The Spectator, 1946-54; joined music staff of Daily Telegraph, 1950; Editor of Musical Times, 1953-56. Pres., Critics' Circle, 1959-60. Mem., Editorial Bd of New Oxford History of Music, 1960-. Hon. FTCL; Hon. RAM 1976. *Publications:* Gluck, 1935; Bizet, 1938; Opéra Comique, 1949; French Music from the death of Berlioz to the death of Fauré, 1950; Russian Opera, 1951; Les Musiciens anglais d'aujourd'hui, 1952; Ideas and Music, 1966; Beethoven-the Last Decade, 1970. *Address:* 34 Halford Road, Richmond, Surrey.

COOPER, Sir Patrick Graham Astley, 6th Bt *cr* 1821; Director, Crendon Concrete Co. Ltd, Long Crendon, since 1973; *b* 4 Aug. 1918; *s* of late Col C. G. A. Cooper, DSO, RA and I. M. M. A. Cooper, Abergeldie, Camberley, Surrey; *S* cousin, Sir Henry Lovick Cooper, 5th Bt, 1959; *m* Audrey Ann Jervoise, *d* of late Major D. P. J. Collas, Military Knight of Windsor; one *s. Educ:* Marlborough Coll. Qualified RICS, 1949; Sen. Asst Land Comr, Min. of Agric., Fisheries and Food, 1950-59. Joined Crendon Concrete Co. Ltd, 1959. Served 1939-40, Gunner, RA, 52 AA Bde TA (invalided out). *Recreations:* golf, tennis. *Heir: s* Alexander Paston Astley Cooper [*b* 1 Feb. 1943; *m* 1974, Minnie Margaret, *d* of Charles Harrison]. *Address:* Monkton Cottage, Monks Risborough, Aylesbury, Bucks. *T:* Princes Risborough 4210. *Club:* Farmers'.

COOPER, Robert George; Chairman, Northern Ireland Fair Employment Agency, since 1976; Member: Equal Opportunities

Commission for Northern Ireland, since 1976; Northern Ireland Standing Advisory Commission on Human Rights, since 1976; *b* 24 June 1936; *er s* of William Hugh Cooper and Annie (*née* Pollock); *m* 1974, Patricia, *yr d* of Gerald and Shiela Nichol, Belfast; one *s*. *Educ:* Foyle Coll., Londonderry; Queen's Univ., Belfast (LLB). Industrial Relations, International Computers Ltd, Belfast, 1958-65; Asst Sec., Engineering Employers' Fedn, NI, 1965-67, Sec. 1967-72; Gen. Sec., Alliance Party of Northern Ireland, 1972-73. Member (Alliance): West Belfast, NI Assembly, 1973-75; West Belfast, NI Constitutional Convention, 1975-76; Minister, Manpower Services, NI, 1974. *Address:* Lynwood, 104 Bangor Road, Holywood, Co. Down, N Ireland. *T:* Holywood 2071.

COOPER, Ronald Cecil Macleod; Under-Secretary, Department of Trade, since 1973; *b* 8 May 1931; *s* of Cecil Redvers Cooper and Norah Agnes Louise Cooper (*née* Macleod); *m* 1st, 1953, June Bicknell (marr. diss. 1967); 2nd, 1967, Christine Savage; one *s* two *d*. *Educ:* Royal Grammar Sch., Newcastle upon Tyne; St Edmund Hall, Oxford (MA). Asst Principal, Min. of Supply, 1954-59; Principal, Min. of Aviation, 1959-62. On loan to European Launcher Develt Org., Paris, 1962-67; Asst Sec., Min. of Technology, 1968-70; Dept of Trade and Industry, 1970-73. *Recreations:* music, reading. *Address:* Marlboro, 9 Kingsway, Chalfont St Peter, Bucks SL9 8NS. *T:* Gerrards Cross 82781. *Club:* United Oxford & Cambridge University.

COOPER, Sidney G.; *see* Grattan-Cooper.

COOPER, Sidney Pool; Head of Public Services, British Museum, 1973-76; *b* 29 March 1919; *s* of late Sidney Charles Henry Cooper and Emily Lilian Baptie; *m* 1940, Denise Marjorie Peverett; two *s* one *d*. *Educ:* Finchley County Sch.; Northern Polytechnic (BSc); University Coll. London (MSc). Laboratory of the Government Chemist, 1947; Asst Keeper, National Reference Library of Science and Invention, British Museum, 1963; Dep. Keeper, NRLSI, 1969. *Recreations:* gardening, golf. *Address:* 98 King's Road, Berkhamsted, Herts. *T:* Berkhamsted 4145. *Clubs:* Civil Service, City Glee.

COOPER, Wilfred Edward S.; *see* Shewell-Cooper.

COOPER, William, (Harry Summerfield Hoff); novelist; Personnel Adviser to Millbank Technical Services, since 1976; *b* 1910; married; two *d*. Assistant Commissioner, Civil Service Commission, 1945-58; Personnel Consultant to: UKAEA, 1958-72; CEGB, 1958-72; Commn of European Communities, 1972-73; Asst Dir, Civil Service Selection Bd, 1973-75; Mem. Bd of Crown Agents, 1975-77. *Publications:* (as H. S. Hoff) Trina, 1934; Rhéa, 1935; Lisa, 1937; Three Marriages, 1946; (as William Cooper) Scenes from Provincial Life, 1950; The Struggles of Albert Woods, 1952; The Ever-Interesting Topic, 1953; Disquiet and Peace, 1956; Young People, 1958; C. P. Snow (British Council Bibliographical Series, Writers and Their Work, No 115) 1959; Prince Genji (a play), 1960; Scenes from Married Life, 1961; Memoirs of a New Man, 1966; You Want The Right Frame of Reference, 1971; Shall We Ever Know?, 1971; Love on the Coast, 1973; You're Not Alone, 1976. *Address:* 22 Kenilworth Court, Lower Richmond Road, SW15. *Club:* Savile.

COOPER, Maj.-Gen. William Frank, CBE 1971; MC 1945; Deputy Quarter-Master-General, 1973-76; retired 1976; *b* 30 May 1921; *s* of Allan Cooper, Officer of Indian State Railways, and Margaret Cooper; *m* 1945, Elisabeth Mary Finch; one *s* one *d*. *Educ:* Sherborne Sch.; RMA Woolwich. Commnd in RE, 1940; served N Africa and Italy (MC; despatches 1944); Malaya, 1956-58 (despatches); S Arabia, 1963-65 (OBE); Chief Engr FARELF, 1968-70; Dep. Dir Army Staff Duties, MoD, 1970-72; Dir, Mil. Assistance Office, 1972-73. *Recreations:* tennis, golf, birdwatching, theatre. *Address:* c/o Lloyds Bank Ltd, High Street, Guildford, Surrey. *Club:* Army and Navy.

COOPER, Very Rev. (William Hugh) Alan; Honorary Assistant to the Bishop of Karachi, since 1977; *b* 2 June 1909; *s* of William and Ethel Cooper; *m* 1940, Barbara (*née* Bentall); one *s* two *d*. *Educ:* King's Coll. Sch., Wimbledon; Christ's Coll., Cambridge; St John's Hall, London. Curate of Lee, 1932-36; Holy Trinity, Cambridge, 1936-38; CMS Missionary and Diocesan Missioner of Dio. Lagos, 1938-41; Curate of Farnham, 1941-42; Rector of Ashtead, 1942-51; Vicar of St Andrew, Plymouth, 1951-62; Preb. of Exeter Cathedral, 1958-62; Provost of Bradford, 1962-77. *Address:* Holy Trinity Cathedral Vicarage, PO Box 3939, Karachi 4, Pakistan; 1 Barton Wood Road, New Milton, Hants BH25 7BH.

COOPER, Prof. Sir William M.; *see* Mansfield Cooper.

COOPER-KEY, Sir Neill, Kt 1960; *b* 26 April 1907; *er s* of late Captain E. Cooper-Key, CB, MVO, Royal Navy; *m* 1941, Hon. Lorna Harmsworth, *er d* of 2nd Viscount Rothermere, *qv*; one *s* one *d*. *Educ:* RNC, Osborne, Dartmouth. Served War of 1939-45, Irish Guards. Consultant and Dir of cos, formerly Vice-Chm., Associated Newspapers Group Ltd (Dir, 1944-72). Mem., Cttee of Management, RNLI, 1957-67. MP (C) Hastings, 1945-70. *Clubs:* Carlton, White's.
See also Sir James G. Le N. King.

COORAY, Edmund Joseph, CMG 1955; OBE 1952; Officier, Légion d'Honneur, 1961; Chairman, Browns Group, Colombo; *b* 16 Nov. 1907; 2nd *s* of M. E. Cooray, Wadduwa, Ceylon; *m* 1933, Eileen de S. Wijeyeratne; two *s* two *d*. *Educ:* St Joseph's Coll., Colombo, Ceylon; University of London (BA Hons 1927; LLB Hons 1930; LLM 1931). Barrister-at-Law, Lincoln's Inn, 1931; passed Ceylon Civil Service Examination, 1931 (1st in order of merit); served in Ceylon Civil Service, 1931-53; Senator, Ceylon, 1955-61; Minister of Justice, 1960. *Recreations:* tennis, gardening. *Address:* 14 Dawson Road, Colombo 5, Sri Lanka. *T:* Colombo 88203. *Club:* 80 (Colombo).

COORAY, His Eminence Thomas Benjamin, Cardinal, OMI; BA, PhD, DD; Archbishop of Colombo (RC), 1947-76, now Archbishop Emeritus; *b* 28 Dec. 1901. *Educ:* St Joseph's Coll., Colombo; Univeristy Coll., Colombo; The Angelicum, Rome. Created Cardinal, 1965; Member, Pontifical Commn for Canon Law. *Address:* Cardinal's Residence, Tewatta, Ragama, Sri Lanka.

COOTE, Captain Sir Colin (Reith), Kt 1962; DSO 1918; journalist; Managing Editor of the Daily Telegraph and Morning Post 1950-64 (deputy editor, 1945-50); *er s* of late Howard Coote. *Educ:* Chilverton Elms, Dover; Rugby; Balliol Coll., Oxford. BA 1914. Served European War, 1914-18 (wounded and gassed). MP (CL) Isle of Ely Division, 1917-22. Legion of Honour, 1958. *Publications:* Italian Town and Country Life, 1925; In and About Rome, 1926; Maxims and Reflections of The Rt Hon. Winston Churchill, 1948; (with R. H. Mottram) Through Five Generations: The History of the Butterley Company, 1950; (with P. D. Bunyan) Sir Winston Churchill: A Self-Portrait, 1954; A Companion of Honour: The Story of Walter Elliot, 1965; Editorial, 1965; The Government We Deserve, 1969; The Other Club, 1971. *Address:* 16 Bigwood Road, NW11.

COOTE, John Oldham; Captain, RN; Director-General, Film Production Association, since 1976; *b* 13 Aug. 1921; *o s* of Frederick S. and Edith F. Coote; *m* 1944, Sylvia Mary (*née* Syson); three *d*. *Educ:* Felsted. Royal Navy 1940-60 (despatches 1944). Joined Beaverbrook Newspapers, 1960 (Vice-Chm., and Man. Dir, 1968-74); Gen. Manager, Sunday Express, 1963; Managing Dir and Gen. Manager, Evening Standard, 1965; Dep. Chm. and Gp Man. Dir, Beaverbrook Newspapers Ltd, 1974-75. *Recreations:* sailing, golf. *Address:* 47 Caversham Street, SW3. *Clubs:* Garrick, Royal Yacht Squadron.

COOTE, Rear-Adm. Sir John Ralph, 14th Bt, *cr* 1621; CB 1957; CBE 1946; DSC; RN retired; *b* 10 Jan. 1905; *s* of Sir Ralph Coote, 13th Bt, and Alice (*d* 1975), *y d* of late Thomas Webber of Kellyville, Queen's Co.; *S* father 1941; *m* 1927, Noreen Una, JP Wilts 1950, *o d* of late Wilfred Tighe of Rossanagh, Ashford, Co. Wicklow; two *s*. *Educ:* Royal Naval Colls, Osborne and Dartmouth. Retired 1958. *Heir:* *s* Christopher John Coote [*b* 22 Sept. 1928; *m* 1952, Anne Georgiana, *d* of Lt-Col Donald Handford, Guyers House, Corsham, Wilts; one *s* one *d*]. *Address:* Monkton House, near Melksham, Wilts. *T:* Melksham 702286.

COOTE, Rt. Rev. Roderic Norman; *see* Colchester, Suffragan Bishop of.

COPAS, Most Rev. Virgil; *see* Kerema, Archbishop of, (RC).

COPE, David Robert, MA; Headmaster of Dover College, since 1973; *b* 24 Oct. 1944; *yr s* of Dr C. L. Cope; *m* 1966, Gillian Margaret Peck; one *s* two *d*. *Educ:* Winchester Coll. (Scholar); Clare Coll., Cambridge (Scholar). 1st Cl. Hons Hist. Tripos Part II, 1965; BA 1965; MA 1972. Asst Master, Eton Coll., 1965-67; Asst British Council Representative (Cultural Attaché), Mexico City, 1968-70; Asst Master, Bryanston Sch., 1970-73. *Recreations:* music, foreign travel. *Address:* Dover College, Dover, Kent CT17 9RX. *T:* Dover 205969.

COPE, Prof. F(rederick) Wolverson, DSc, FGS, CEng, FIMinE; Consultant Geologist; Professor of Geology and Head of Geology Department, University of Keele, 1950-76; *b* 30 July 1909; *e s* of late Fred and Ida Mary Cope (*née* Chappells),

Macclesfield; *m* 1st, 1935, Ethel May Hitchens, BSc (*d* 1961); one *s* two *d* ; 2nd, 1962, Evelyn Mary Swales, BA, AKC, *d* of late John Frederick and Ada Mary Swales, Kingston-upon-Hull; one *d*. *Educ:* The King's Sch., Macclesfield; Univs of Manchester (DSc 1946) and London. Brocklehurst Scholar, 1928; John Dalton Prize, 1930; BSc with First Class Honours in Geology, 1931; MSc, Mark Stirrup Scholar, Manchester, 1932. Demonstrator in Geology, Bedford Coll., Univ. of London, 1933-34; Daniel Pidgeon Fund, Geol. Soc. of London, 1937; Prin. Geologist in Geological Survey of GB, 1934-50; Murchison Award of Geol. Soc. of London, 1948; Vis. Prof. of Geology, Univ. of Pisa, 1964. FGS 1934; CEng 1968; FIMinE 1969. *Publications:* The North Staffordshire Coalfields, in Coalfields of Great Britain (ed by late Sir Arthur Trueman), 1954; Geology Explained in the Peak District, 1976; various research publications mainly in the fields of stratigraphy and palaeontology. *Recreations:* landscape sketching, cars, ornithology, Italy. *Address:* 6 Boley Drive, Clacton-on-Sea, Essex CO15 6LA. *T:* Clacton-on-Sea 21829.

COPE, James Francis, MP; Speaker of the Australian House of Representatives, 1973-75; *b* 26 Nov. 1907; *s* of G. E. Cope; *m* 1931, Myrtle Irene, *d* of S. J. Hurst; one *d*. *Educ:* Crown Street Public Sch., NSW. Hon. Treaurer, NSW Br., Aust. Glass Workers' Union; Delegate to Federal Council, 1953-55. MHR (Lab) for divs of: Cook, 1955; Watson, 1955-69; Sydney, 1969-. *Recreations:* billiards, horse racing, cricket, football. *Address:* Parliament House, Canberra, ACT 2601, Australia. *T:* Canberra 726383.

COPE, John Ambrose; MP (C) South Gloucestershire since Feb. 1974; *b* 13 May 1937; *s* of George Cope, MC, FRIBA, Leicester; *m* 1969, Djemila Lovell Payne, *d* of Col P. V. L. Payne, Martinstown, Dorset and Mrs Tanetta Blackden, Selborne; two *d*. *Educ:* Oakham Sch., Rutland. FCA. Commnd RA and RE, Nat Service and TA. Conservative Research Dept, 1965-67; Personal Asst to Chm. of Conservative Party, 1967-70; contested (C) Woolwich East, 1970; Special Asst to Sec. of State for Trade and Industry, 1972-74. Secretary: Cons. Parly Finance Cttee; Cons. Parly Smaller Business Cttee; Parly Gp for Concorde. *Publication:* (with Bernard Weatherill) Acorns to Oaks (Policy for Small Business), 1967. *Recreation:* woodwork. *Address:* House of Commons, SW1; Bluegates, Berkeley, Glos. *Clubs:* St Stephen's; Tudor House (Chipping Sodbury).

COPE, John Wigley, MA, MB, BChir Cantab, FRCS; Retired; formerly Surgeon in charge Ear, Nose and Throat Department, St Bartholomew's Hospital; *b* 1 Nov. 1907; *o s* of J. J. Cope, Widney Manor, Warwicks; *m* 1937, Muriel Pearce Brown, Reading; two *s* one *d*. *Educ:* King Edward's Sch., Birmingham; Trinity Coll., Cambridge; St Bartholomew's Hosp., London. Demonstrator in Anatomy, St Bartholomew's Med. Coll., 1935. Served with RAFVR (Med. Branch) as Aural Specialist, 1940-45 (Sqdn-Ldr). Aural Surgeon, Royal Waterloo Hosp., 1946; Surgeon, Royal National Throat, Nose and Ear Hosp., 1946. Dean, St Bartholomew's Hosp. Med. Coll., 1962-68. Pres., Section of Otology, RSM, 1970-71 (formerly Sec.). *Recreations:* shooting, rock-climbing, gardening, golf. *Address:* Owls Hatch Cottage, Seale, near Farnham, Surrey. *T:* Runfold 2456.

COPE, Maclachlan Alan Carl S.; *see* Silverwood-Cope.

COPELAND, Mrs Roy; *see* Bracewell, J. W.

COPEMAN, Harold Arthur; Under-Secretary, HM Treasury, 1972-76; *b* 27 Jan. 1918; *s* of H. W. M. and G. E. Copeman; *m* 1948, Kathleen (Kay) Gadd; one *s*. *Educ:* Manchester Grammar Sch.; The Queen's Coll., Oxford. BA, 1st Cl. Hons in PPE, 1939. Served War, Army: Cheshire Regt, RA (Instructor in gunnery) and Ordnance Board (Applied Ballistics Dept), 1940-45. HM Treasury, 1946-76. Vis. Fellow, Warwick Univ., 1976. *Recreations:* music, cricket, squash, photography. *Address:* The Limes, Avon Dassett, Leamington Spa, Warwicks. *T:* Farnborough (Banbury) 245.

COPISAROW, Alcon Charles, DSc; FInstP; CEng; FIEE; Non-Executive Director, British Leyland, since 1976; Lay Member, Press Council, since 1975; General Commissioner for Income Tax, since 1975; *b* 25 June 1920; *o s* of late Dr Maurice Copisarow, Manchester; *m* 1953, Diana, *y d* of Ellis James Castello, MC, Bucklebury, Berks; two *s* two *d*. *Educ:* Manchester Central Grammar Sch.; University of Manchester; Imperial Coll. of Science and Technology; Sorbonne, Paris. Council of Europe Research Fellow. Served War, 1942-47; Lieut RN, 1943-47; British Admiralty Delegn, Washington, 1945. Home Civil Service, 1946-66; Office of Minister of Defence, 1947-54. Scientific Counsellor, British Embassy, Paris, 1954-60. Dir, Forest Products Research Laboratory, Dept of Scientific

and Industrial Research, 1960-62; Chief Technical Officer, Nat. Economic Development Council, 1962-64; Chief Scientific Officer, Min. of Technology, 1964-66, Head of Internat. Div., 1964-65, Head of Electrical, Chemical Plant and Materials Industries Div., 1965-66; Dir and Vice-Pres., McKinsey & Co. Inc., 1966-76. Chairman: Commonwealth Forest Products Conf., Nairobi, 1962; CENTO Conf. on Investment in Science, Teheran, 1963; Cttee for Research on Dental Materials and Equipment, 1966; Member: Scientific Manpower Cttee, Advisory Council on Scientific Policy, 1963-64; Econ. Develt Cttees for Electronics Industry, 1963-64, and for Heavy Electrical Industry, 1966-67; Trop. Prod. Adv. Cttee, 1965-66; Cabinet (Official) Cttees. Mem. Bd of Governors, English-Speaking Union, 1976-. Hon. FTCL. *Address:* The White House, Denham, Bucks. *Clubs:* Athenæum, MCC.

COPLAND, Aaron; American composer; *b* Brooklyn, NY, 14 Nov. 1900; *s* of Harris M. Copland and Sarah Mittenthal; unmarried. *Educ:* Boys' High Sch., Brooklyn, NY; studied music privately; Fontainebleau Sch. of Music, France; Paris (with Nadia Boulanger). Guggenheim Fellow, 1925, 1926. Lecturer on music, New School for Social Research, NY, 1927-37; organised Copland-Sessions Concerts, which presented American music, 1928-31; tour of Latin-American countries, as pianist, conductor and lecturer in concerts of American music, 1941 and 1947; Charles Eliot Norton Prof. of Poetry, Harvard Univ., 1951-52. *Principal works:* Symphony for Organ and Orchestra, 1924; First Symphony (orch.), 1928; Short Symphony (No. II), 1933; El Salon Mexico (orch.), 1936; Billy the Kid (ballet), 1938; Piano Sonata, 1941; Lincoln Portrait (speaker and orch.), 1942; Rodeo (ballet), 1942; Sonata for Violin and piano, 1943; Appalachian Spring (ballet, Pulitzer Prize), 1944; Third Symphony, 1946; Clarinet Concerto, 1948; Piano Quartet, 1950; Twelve Poems of Emily Dickinson, 1950; The Tender Land (Opera), 1954; Symphonic Ode (1929, rev. 1955); Piano Fantasy, 1957; Orchestral Variations 1958; Nonet, 1960; Connotations for Orchestra, 1962; Dance Panels, 1962; Music for a Great City, 1964; Emblems for Symphonic Band, 1964; Inscape for Orchestra, 1967; Duo for flute and piano, 1971; Three Latin-American Sketches, 1972; various film scores. Pres., American Acad. Arts and Letters, 1971; Member: National Institute of Arts and Letters; American Academy of Arts and Sciences; President of the Edward MacDowell Assoc., 1962; American Soc. of Composers, Authors and Publishers; Hon. Mem., Accademia Santa Cecilia, Rome; Hon. Mem., RAM, 1959; Hon. Dr of Music, Princeton Univ., 1956, Harvard Univ., 1961; Hon. Dr of Humane Letters, Brandeis Univ., 1957. FRSA 1960. Presidential Medal of Freedom, Washington, 1964; Howland Prize, Yale Univ., 1970; Haendel Medallion, NY, 1970; Chancellor's Medal, Syracuse Univ., 1975; Creative Arts Award, Brandeis Univ., 1975. *Publications:* What to listen for in music, 1939 (revised 1957); Our New Music, 1941; Music and Imagination, 1952; Copland on Music, 1960; The New Music 1900-1960, 1968. *Address:* c/o Boosey and Hawkes, 30 West 57 Street, New York, USA. *Clubs:* Harvard, Century Association (New York).

COPLAND, Very Rev. Charles McAlester; Provost of St John's Cathedral, Oban, since 1959; *b* 5 April 1910; *s* of Canon Alexander Copland and of Violet Williamina Somerville McAlester; *m* 1946, Gwendoline Lorimer Williamson; two *d*. *Educ:* Forfar Academy; Denstone Coll.; Corpus Christi Coll., Cambridge (MA); Cuddesdon College. Curate, Peterborough Parish Church, 1934-38; Mission Priest, Chanda, CP, India, 1938-53 (Head of Mission, 1942-53); Canon of Nagpur, 1952; Rector, St Mary's, Arbroath, 1953-59; Canon of Dundee, 1953. *Recreations:* formerly Rugby football, athletics; rifle shooting (shot for Cambridge, for Scotland 1932-76). *Address:* The Rectory, Oban, Argyll. *T:* Oban 2323.

COPLAND SIMMONS, Rev. F. P.; *see* Simmons.

COPLESTON, Ernest Reginald, CB 1954; Secretary, Committee of Enquiry into the Governance of the University of London, 1970-72; *b* 16 Nov. 1909; *s* of F. S. Copleston, former Chief Judge of Lower Burma; *m* Olivia Green. *Educ:* Marlborough Coll.; Balliol Coll., Oxford. Inland Revenue Dept, 1932; Treasury, 1942; Under-Sec., 1950; Dep. Sec., 1957-63, Sec., 1963-69, UGC; retired. *Address:* Holland Hill, Bulmer, Sudbury, Suffolk. *T:* Twinstead 356.

COPLESTON, Rev. Frederick Charles, SJ; MA Oxon, DPhil Rome, Gregorian Univ.; FBA 1970; Principal of Heythrop College, University of London, 1970-74; Emeritus Professor of University of London, 1974; Dean, Faculty of Theology, 1972-74; *b* 10 April 1907; *s* of F. S. Copleston, former Chief Judge of Lower Burma, and N. M. Little. *Educ:* Marlborough Coll.; St John's Coll., Oxford (Hon. Fellow, 1975). Entered Catholic

Church, 1925; Soc. of Jesus, 1930; ordained 1937. Prof. of History of Philosophy: Heythrop Coll., Oxford, 1939-70, and Univ. of London, 1972-74; Gregorian Univ., Rome, 1952-68; Dean of Faculty of Theology, Univ. of London, 1972-74; Visiting Professor: Univ. of Santa Clara, Calif., 1974-75; Univ. of Hawaii, 1976. *Publications:* Friedrich Nietzsche, Philosopher of Culture, 1942, new edn 1975; St Thomas and Nietzsche, 1944; Arthur Schopenhauer, Philosopher of Pessimism, 1946; A History of Philosophy (vol. 1, Greece and Rome, 1946; revised 1947; vol. 2, Augustine to Scotus, 1950; vol. 3, Ockham to Suárez, 1953; vol. 4, Descartes to Leibniz, 1958; vol. 5, Hobbes to Hume, 1959; vol. 6, Wolff to Kant, 1960; vol. 7, Fichte to Nietzsche, 1963; vol. 8, Bentham to Russell, 1966; vol. 9, Maine de Biran to Sartre, 1975); Medieval Philosophy, 1952; Existentialism and Modern Man, 1948; Aquinas (Pelican), 1955; Contemporary Philosophy, 1956, rev. edn 1972; A History of Medieval Philosophy, 1972; Religion and Philosophy, 1974; Philosophers and Philosophies, 1976; articles in learned journals. *Address:* Campion Hall, Oxford OX1 1QS. *T:* Oxford 40861.

COPLESTONE-BOUGHEY, John Fenton; His Honour Judge Coplestone-Boughey; a Circuit Judge (formerly Judge of the County Courts), since 1969; *b* 5 Feb. 1912; *o s* of late Comdr A. F. Coplestone-Boughey, RN; *m* 1944, Gilian Beatrice, *e d* of late H. A. Counsell, Appleby; one *s* one *d. Educ:* Shrewsbury School; Brasenose Coll., Oxford (Open Exhibitioner, Matthew Arnold Prizeman). Inner Temple, Entrance Scholar 1934, Barrister 1935. Legal Assistant, Min. of Health, 1937-40. Royal Artillery, 1940-46; Advanced Class, Military Coll. of Science, 1945. Chester Chronicle & Associated Newspapers, Ltd: Dir, 1947-56; Dep. Chm., 1956-65. Chairman, Nat. Insurance Tribunals (SW London), 1951-69; Referee, Nat. Service and Family Allowances Acts, 1957-69. Battersea etc Hospital Management Cttee: Member 1960-69, Chairman 1969-74; Mem., Wandsworth etc AHA, 1973-. Governor, St Thomas' Hosp., 1971-74; Special Trustee, St George's Hospital, 1974-. Mem. Council, Queen's Coll., London, 1976-. *Publications:* contrib. to Halsbury's Laws of England. *Recreations:* walking, travel. *Address:* 82 Oakley Street, SW3. *T:* 01-352 6287. *Club:* Athenæum.

COPLEY, John (Michael Harold); Resident Producer, Royal Opera, Covent Garden, since 1972; *b* 12 June, 1933; *s* of Ernest Harold Copley and Lilian Forbes. *Educ:* King Edward's, Five Ways, Birmingham; Sadler's Wells Ballet Sch.; Central Sch. of Arts and Crafts, London (Dip. with Hons in Theatre Design). Appeared as the apprentice in Britten's Peter Grimes for Covent Garden Opera Co, 1950; stage managed: both opera and ballet companies at Sadler's Wells, in Rosebery Avenue, 1953-57; also various musicals, plays, etc, in London's West End, incl. The World of Paul Slickey and My Fair Lady. Joined Covent Garden Opera Co.: Dep. Stage Manager, 1960; Asst Resident Producer, 1963; Associate Resident Producer, 1966. *Productions include:* at Covent Garden: Suor Angelica, 1965; Cosi fan Tutte, 1968; Orpheo ed Euridice, 1969; Le Nozze di Figaro, 1971; Don Giovanni, 1973; La Bohème, 1974; Faust, 1974; L'elisir d'amore, 1975; Benvenuto Cellini, 1976; Ariadne auf Naxos, 1976; at London Coliseum (for Sadler's Wells, subseq. English Nat. Opera): Carmen, Il Seraglio, Il Trovatore, La Traviata, Mary Stuart; Rosenkavalier, La Belle Hélène, 1975; Werther, 1977; Macbeth, Athens Festival; Lucia, Netherlands Opera; Lucia, Opera National de Belge; La Clemenza di Tito and L'Infedelta delusa, for Wexford Festival; Lucia, Dallas Civic Opera, Texas and Chicago Lyric Opera; Madame Butterfly, Greek Nat. Opera, 1976; Fidelio, Nozze di Figaro, Rigoletto, Magic Flute, Jenufa, Ariadne auf Naxos and Madame Butterfly for Australian Opera; La Traviata and Falstaff for Welsh National Opera Co; Acis and Galatea for English Opera Group (also seen in Stockholm, Paris, Montreal EXPO '67). Sang as soloist in Bach's St John Passion, Bremen, Germany, 1965; appeared as Ferdy in John Osborne's play, A Patriot for Me, at Royal Court Theatre, 1965. Co-directed (with Patrick Garland) Fanfare for Europe Gala, Covent Garden, 3 Jan. 1973. *Recreation:* cooking. *Address:* 9D Thistle Grove, SW10 9RR.

COPP, Darrell John Barkwell; General Secretary, Institute of Biology, since 1951; *b* 25 April 1922; *s* of J. J. H. Copp and L. A. Hoad; *m* 1944, Margaret Henderson; two *s* one *d. Educ:* Taunton's Sch., Southampton; Southampton Univ. (BSc). FIBiol. Scientific Officer, Admty Signals Estabt, 1942-45; Asst Sec., British Assoc. for Advancement of Science, 1947-51. Sec., Council for Nature, 1958-63; originator and co-ordinator of first National Nature Week, 1963. Jt Hon. Sec., Parly and Scientific Cttee, 1976-. Hon. MTech Bradford, 1975. *Publications:* reports and reviews in scientific jls. *Recreations:* mountain walking, renovating country cottages. *Address:* Duke's Mount, Woldingham, Surrey. *T:* Woldingham 2374.

COPP, Prof. (Douglas) Harold, OC 1971; MD, PhD; FRS 1971; FRSC; FRCP(C); Professor and Head of Department of Physiology, University of British Columbia, Canada, since 1950; *b* 16 Jan. 1915; *s* of Charles J. Copp and Edith M. O'Hara; *m* 1939, Winnifred A. Thompson; three *d. Educ:* Univ. of Toronto, Canada (BA, MD); Univ. of California, Berkeley, Calif (PhD); British Columbia College of Physicians and Surgeons (Lic.). Asst Prof. of Physiology, Calif, 1945-50. Co-ordinator, Health Scis, Univ. of British Columbia, 1976-77. Vice-Pres., Acad. of Sci., 1977-78. FRSC 1959 (Mem. Council, 1973-75, 1977-); FRCP(C) 1974. Hon. LLD: Queen's Univ., Kingston, Ont, 1970; Univ. of Toronto, 1970; Hon. DSc: Univ. of Ottawa, 1973; Acadia Univ., 1975. *Recreation:* gardening. *Address:* 4755 Belmont Avenue, Vancouver V6T 1A8, British Columbia, Canada. *T:* Vancouver 224-3793.

COPP, John Sidney, MBE 1943; solicitor, retired 1976; part-time Member, Monopolies and Mergers Commission, since 1975; *b* 10 Nov. 1915; *s* of Sidney Alfred Copp and Mary (*née* Vickery); *m* 1948, Wendy Muriel Atkins; two *s* two *d. Educ:* Blundells. Solicitor, 1938; private practice, 1938-39. War service, RE, 1939-46 (Lt-Col 1944). Joined Imperial Chemical Industries Ltd, 1946; Solicitor to ICI, 1965-76, retd. *Recreations:* gardening, opera going and record collecting. *Address:* Heathwood, Willey Lane, Caterham, Surrey CR3 6AR. *T:* Caterham 42500.

COPPEL, Dr Elias Godfrey, CMG 1965; QC (at the Bar of Victoria and Tasmania); *b* 7 Oct. 1896; *s* of Albert Coppel; *m* 1925, Marjorie Jean Service (*d* 1970); two *s* (and one *s* decd). *Educ:* Melbourne Grammar Sch.; Melbourne Univ. Served European War, 1st Australian Imperial Force, France, 1915-19. Admitted to the Bar, 1922; LLD 1936; KC 1945. Acting Justice, Supreme Court, Victoria, 1950-52; Acting Justice, Supreme Court, Tasmania, 1956 and 1958; Warden of Convocation, University of Melbourne, 1950-59; Mem. of University Council, 1959-67. *Publication:* The Law Relating to Bills of Sale, 1935. *Address:* 14 Ailsa Avenue, East Malvern, Victoria 3145, Australia.

COPPLESON, Sir Lionel (Wolfe), Kt 1969; Chairman, Managing Director and Director of Companies; retd as Chairman of Custom Credit Corporation Group, but remained on Boards, 1969; *b* Wee Waa, NSW, 29 May 1901; *s* of Albert and Siba Coppleson; *m* 1st, 1929, Edith Maude, *d* of Alfred Bamford; one *s* one *d*; 2nd, 1972, Marjorie Florence, *d* of Stephen Simpson. *Educ:* Sydney Grammar Sch. Joined Coppleson Ltd (merchants), Wee Waa, 1918; Manager, 1924; estab. Finance Construction Ltd, builders, Sydney, 1927; acquired George Ward Pty Ltd, roofing engrs, 1930; estab. George Ward Pty Ltd, Melbourne, 1933; apptd Special Distributor for John Lysaght Ltd in NSW and Vic, 1938; estab. 3 factories for war supplies, 1940; apptd to advise John Lysaght Ltd, England, 1946; estab. George Ward Distributors Pty Ltd, also George Ward Pty Ltd Registered Master Builders, 1947; estab. Wilkins Servis Pty Ltd, washing machine manufrs (Chm.), 1948; Chairman: Inter Copper NL; United Nickel Ltd; Foundation Dep. Chm.: Custom Credit Corp. Ltd, 1953; Nat. & Gen. Ins. Co. Ltd, 1954; Custom Life Assce Co. Ltd, 1957; First Nat. Reinsurance of Aust. Ltd and Custom Factors Ltd, 1958; Chm., 1962: Custom Credit Group of Cos; Addenbrooke Pty Ltd; Copanco Pty Ltd; Bamford Services Pty Ltd; Cokeson Pty Ltd; Foundation Pres.: Inst. of Urology, Sydney, 1964; Aust. Kidney Foundation, 1968. Mem. cttee for appeals, various organisations, etc. *Recreations:* played: football, cricket, tennis, golf, bowls, snooker; swimming and life-saving (surf) champion; racing, trotting, boxing, horticulture, orchid growing, agricultural shows. *Address:* Addenbrooke, 21 Cranbrook Road, Bellevue Hill, NSW 2023, Australia. *T:* 36 6475. *Clubs:* Newcastle, Royal Prince Alfred Yacht, Australian Golf, Royal Motor Yacht, Pioneers, Australian Jockey, American National, Tattersalls (all in NSW); Stock Exchange (Melbourne).

COPPLESTONE, Frank Henry; Managing Director, Southern Television, since 1976; Director: Independent Television News Ltd, since 1977; Independent Television Publications Ltd, since 1976; *b* 26 Feb. 1925; 2nd *s* of late Rev. Frank T. Copplestone; *m* 1950, Margaret Mary (*d* 1973), *d* of late Edward Walker; three *s. Educ:* Truro Sch.; Nottingham Univ. (BA). Royal Horse Artillery, 1943-47. Pres., Univ. of Nottingham Union, 1952-53; Pres., Nat. Union of Students, 1954-56; Internat. Research Fellow, 1956-58; Regional Officer, Independent Television Authority, 1958-62; Head of Regional Services, ITA, 1962-63; Head of Programme Services, ITA, 1963-67; Controller, ITV Network Programme Secretariat, 1967-73; Dir, ITV Programme Planning Secretariat, 1973-75. *Recreations:* sailing, reading, music. *Address:* Little Thatches, Ashley, Kings Somborne, Stockbridge, Hants. *T:* Kings Somborne 248; 4 West Street,

Polruan, Cornwall. *Clubs:* Savile, Sportsman; Royal Southern Yacht, Royal Fowey Yacht, Fowey Gallants Sailing.

COPPOCK, Prof. John Terence, FBA 1975; FRSE 1976; Ogilvie Professor of Geography, University of Edinburgh, since 1965; *b* 2 June 1921; *s* of late Arthur Coppock and of Valerie Margaret Coppock (*née* Phillips); *m* 1953, Sheila Mary Burnett; one *s* one *d. Educ:* Penarth County Sch.; Queens' Coll., Cambridge. MA (Cantab), PhD (London). Civil Servant: Lord Chancellor's Dept, Min. of Works, Board of Customs and Excise, 1938-47. Served War, Army (commissioned Welch Regt, 1941), 1939-46. Cambridge Univ., 1947-50. University Coll. London (Dept of Geography): successively, Asst Lecturer, Lecturer, Reader, 1950-65. Mem., Scottish Sports Council, 1976-. *Publications:* The Changing Use of Land in Britain (with R. H. Best), 1962; An Agricultural Atlas of England and Wales, 1964, 2nd edn 1976; Greater London (ed, with H. C. Prince), 1964; An Agricultural Geography of Great Britain, 1971; Recreation in the Countryside: a Spatial Analysis (with B. S. Duffield), 1975; Spatial Dimensions of Public Policy (ed, with W. R. D. Sewell), 1976; An Agricultural Atlas of Scotland, 1976; numerous papers: mainly in geographical, but also historical, planning and agricultural periodicals, mainly on theme of rural land use in Great Britain. *Recreations:* listening to music, natural history. *Address:* 57 Braid Avenue, Edinburgh EH10 6EB. *T:* 031-447 3443.

COPSON, Prof. Edward Thomas, MA Oxford, DSc Edinburgh, FRSE; Emeritus Professor of Mathematics, St Andrews University; *b* 21 Aug. 1901; *s* of late T. C. Copson; *m* 1931, Beatrice Mary, *er d* of late Prof. Sir Edmund Whittaker, FRS; two *d. Educ:* King Henry VIII Sch., Coventry; St John's Coll., Oxford. Lecturer, University of Edinburgh, 1922-29; St Andrews, 1930-34; Asst Prof., RNC, Greenwich, 1934-35; Prof. of Mathematics, University Coll., Dundee, 1935-50; Regius Prof. of Mathematics, St Andrews Univ., 1950-69. Keith Prize, Royal Society of Edinburgh, 1939-41. Master of St Salvator's Coll., St Andrews, 1954-57. Hon. LLD St Andrews, 1971. *Publications:* The Theory of Functions of a Complex Variable, 1935; The Mathematical Theory of Huygens' Principle (with Prof. Bevan Baker), 1939; Asymptotic Expansions, 1965; Metric Spaces, 1968; Partial Differential Equations, 1975; papers in various mathematical periodicals. *Address:* 42 Buchanan Gardens, St Andrews, Fife. *T:* St Andrews 2708. *Club:* Royal and Ancient (St Andrews).

CORAH, Sir John (Harold), Kt 1952; Chairman, N. Corah & Sons Ltd, Leicester, 1954-64 (Deputy Chairman, 1924-54); *b* 25 Dec. 1884; *s* of Alfred Corah of Scraptoft Hall, Leicestershire; *m* 1st, 1913, Vivienne Woodhouse (*d* 1942); one *d*; 2nd, 1951, Edmée Pattera. *Educ:* Marlborough. JP 1924; High Sheriff of Leicestershire, 1933; Dep. Chm., County Bench, 1942-51. *Recreations:* sailing and cruising. *Address:* Gayhurst, Fernside Lane, Sevenoaks, Kent. *T:* Sevenoaks 56501. *Club:* Royal Motor Yacht (Sand Banks, Dorset).

CORBET, Mrs Freda (Kunzlen), (Mrs Ian McIvor Campbell), BA; JP; *b* 1900; *d* of James Mansell; *m* 1925, William Corbet (*d* 1957); *m* 1962, Ian McIvor Campbell (*d* 1976). *Educ:* Wimbledon County Sch.; University Coll., London. Called to Bar, Inner Temple, 1932. MP (Lab) NW Camberwell, later Peckham Div. of Camberwell, 1945-Feb. 1974. Awarded Freedom of Southwark, 1974. JP, Co. London, 1940. *Address:* 39 Gravel Road, Bromley, Kent.

CORBET, Lieut-Col Sir John (Vincent), 7th Bt, *cr* 1808; MBE 1946; DL; JP; RE (retired); *b* 27 Feb. 1911; *s* of Archer Henry Corbet (*d* 1950) and Anne Maria (*d* 1951), *d* of late German Buxton; *S* kinsman, Sir Gerald Vincent Corbet, 6th Bt, 1955; *m* 1st, 1937, Elfrida Isobel Francis; 2nd, 1948, Doreen Elizabeth Stewart (*d* 1964), *d* of Arthur William Gibbon Ritchie; 3rd, 1965, Annie Elizabeth Lorimer, MBE, MSc, Dunedin, NZ. *Educ:* Shrewsbury Sch.; RMA; Magdalene Coll., Cambridge. BA 1933, MA 1972. 2nd Lieut, RE, 1931; served North-West Frontier, India, 1935, and War of 1939-45 in India, Burma and Malaya (despatches, MBE); Lieut-Col, 1953; retd 1955. DL County of Salop, 1961; JP 1957; High Sheriff of Salop, 1966; CC Salop (Chm., Highways Transport Cttee). OStJ; Mem., Church Assembly, later General Synod, 1960-75; Mem. Board of Visitors, Stoke Heath Borstal. *Address:* Acton Reynald, near Shrewsbury, Salop. *T:* Clive 259. *Club:* Royal Thames Yacht.

CORBET, Air Vice-Marshal Lancelot Miller, CB 1958; CBE 1944; RAF retired; *b* Brunswick, Vic, Australia, 19 April 1898; *s* of late John Miller and late Ella Beatrice Corbet, Caulfield, Vic, Australia; *m* 1924, Gwenllian Elizabeth, *d* of late Thomas Powell and late May Maria Bennett, Claremont, Western Australia; one *s. Educ:* Melbourne High Sch.; Scotch Coll.,

Melbourne; Melbourne Univ. (MB, BS 1922). RMO, Perth (WA) Hospital, 1922-23, Perth Children's Hospital 1923; Hon. Asst Anæsthetist, Perth Hospital, 1931; Clinical Asst to Out-Patient Surgeon, Perth Hospital, 1931-32. Was Major AAMC; commanded 6th Field Hygiene Sect., 1930-32; entered RAF 1933; served in UK and India, 1933-37; Principal MO, W Africa, 1941-43; Principal MO, Transport Command, RAF, 1943-45; Principal MO, Malaya, 1945-46; Principal MO, British Commonwealth Air Forces, Japan, 1946-48; OC, RAF Hospital, Nocton Hall, 1949-52; Principal MO, HQBF, Aden, 1952-54; Principal MO, 2nd Tactical Air Force, 1954-56; Dep. Dir-Gen. of Medical Services, Air Ministry, 1956-58, retired. KStJ. *Recreations:* lacrosse, tennis, squash, golf, etc. *Address:* 24 Hensman Street, South Perth, WA 6151, Australia. *T:* Perth 67-3025. *Club:* Naval and Military (Perth, West Australia).

CORBETT, family name of **Baron Rowallan.**

CORBETT, Ven. Charles Eric; Archdeacon of Liverpool since 1971. *Educ:* Jesus College, Oxford (BA 1939, MA 1943); Wycliffe Hall, Oxford. Deacon 1940, priest 1941, St Asaph; Curate of Gresford, 1940-44; CF, 1944-47; Curate of Eglwys-Rhos, 1947-49; Rector of Harpurhey, 1949-54; Vicar of St Catherine's, Wigan, 1954-61; Vicar of St Luke, Farnworth, 1961-71. Rural Dean of Farnworth, 1964-71. *Address:* 20 Garth Drive, Liverpool L18 6HW.

CORBETT, Captain Hugh Askew, CBE 1968; DSO 1945; DSC 1943; RN; Warden of University Centre, Cambridge University, since 1969; *b* 25 June 1916; *s* of late Rev. F. St John Corbett, MA, FRSL, FRHistS, St Georges-in-the-East, London and late Elsie L. V. Askew; *m* 1945, Patricia Nancy, *d* of Thomas Patrick Spens, OBE, MC; three *s. Educ:* St Edmund's Sch., Canterbury. Joined Royal Navy, 1933; commanded HMS: Wheatland, 1943-45 (Lieut); Cæsar as Capt. (D), 8th Destroyer Sqdn, 1961-63; HMS Fearless, 1965-67 (Capt.); Head of Naval Manpower Future Policy Div., 1967-69. Imp. Def. Coll., 1960. MBIM 1967. *Address:* Holly Cottage, 3 Clare Road, Cambridge. *T:* Cambridge 57735.

CORBETT, Prof. John Patrick, MA; Professor of Philosophy, University of Bradford, 1972-76; *b* 5 March 1916; *s* of E. S. H. and K. F. Corbett; *m* 1st, 1940, Nina Angeloni; two *s*; 2nd, 1968, Jan Adams; two *d. Educ:* RNC, Dartmouth; Magdalen Coll., Oxford. Lieut, RA, 1940; POW in Germany, 1940-45. Fellow of Balliol, 1945-61; Prof. of Philosophy, Univ. of Sussex, 1961-72; Jowett Lectr in Philosophy. Council of Europe Fellow, 1957; Visiting Lectr, Yale Univ., 1958; NATO Fellow, 1960; Vis. Prof., Univ. of Toronto, 1968. *Publications:* Europe and the Social Order, 1959; Ideologies, 1965. *Address:* Banquet House Farm, Barkisland, Halifax, West Yorks.

CORBETT, Prof. Peter Edgar; Yates Professor of Classical Art and Archaeology in the University of London (University College), since 1961; *b* 19 June 1920; 2nd *s* of Ernest Oliver Corbett and Margaret Edgar. *Educ:* Bedford Sch.; St John's Coll., Oxford. Royal Artillery, 1940-41, RAFVR, 1942-45. Thomas Whitcombe Greene Scholar, and Macmillan Student of British School at Athens, 1947-49; Asst Keeper in Dept of Greek and Roman Antiquities, British Museum, 1949-61. Lectr in Classics, Univ. of Calif, Los Angeles, 1956. *Publications:* The Sculpture of the Parthenon, 1959; (with A. Birchall) Greek Gods and Heroes, 1974; articles in Jl of Hellenic Studies, Hesperia, Annual of Brit. School at Athens, BM Quarterly, Bulletin of the Inst. of Classical Studies. *Address:* University College, Gower Street, WC1E 6BT.

CORBETT, Robin; MP (Lab) Hemel Hempstead since Oct. 1974; *b* 22 Dec. 1933; *s* of Thomas Corbett and Marguerite Adele Mainwaring; *m* 1970, Val Hudson; one *d. Educ:* Holly Lodge Grammar Sch., Smethwick. Newspaper and magazine journalist, 1950-69; Editorial Staff Develt Exec., IPC Magazines, 1969-72; Sen. Lab. Adviser, IPC Magazines, 1972-74. Mem. Nat. Union of Journalists Nat. Exec. Council, 1965-69. Mem. Agricultural Sub-Cttee, Labour Party Nat. Exec. Cttee. *Recreations:* visiting North Wales; pottering. *Address:* 96 Piccotts End, Hemel Hempstead, Herts. *T:* Hemel Hempstead 52866. *Clubs:* Press; Chipperfield Working Men's; Hemel Hempstead Cricket.

CORBETT, Rupert Shelton, MA, MChir Cantab; FRCS; retired 1961; *b* 11 Feb. 1893; 2nd *s* of late Henry Shelton Corbett. *Educ:* Diocesan Coll., South Africa; Stubbington House, Hampshire; Cambridge Univ.; St Bartholomew's Hosp., London. MRCS, LRCP 1917; FRCS; MA Cantab 1922; BCh 1922; MB 1923; MChir 1927; formerly: Surgeon, St Bartholomew's Hosp.; Surgeon, St Andrew's Hosp., Dollis Hill; Consulting Surgeon, Chalfonts and Gerrards Cross Hosp.; Examiner in Surgery,

Universities of Cambridge and London; Mem. of Examining Board, Royal Coll. of Surgeons; Mayo Lectr, Ann Arbor, USA, 1955; First Gordon-Watson Memorial Lectr, 1958; Mem. Council, Assoc. of Surgeons of Great Britain and Ireland, 1957-59; Pres., Chiltern Medical Soc., 1960-61. Chm., Jersey District Nursing Assoc. Central Cttee, 1971-. Vice-President: Jersey Branch, Royal Commonwealth Soc.; St John Ambulance Assoc., Jersey. OStJ 1977 (SBStJ 1971). *Publications:* contributions in British Surgical Practice; various articles in med. jls. *Address:* Katrina, Beaumont Hill, St Peter, Jersey. *T:* Central 20065.

CORBETT, Lt-Gen. Thomas William, CB 1941; MC and Bar; psc; *b* 2 June 1888; *m* 1st, 1915, Flora Margaret McDonell (*d* 1951); 2nd, 1952, S. N. E., *widow* of Lt-Col H. H. C. Withers, DSO, RE; one *d*. Served with Hodson's Horse and 2nd Royal Lancers: 2nd Lieut, Indian Army, 1908; Captain, 1915; Bt Major, 1919; Major, 1922; Bt Lt-Col, 1930; Lt-Col, 1933; Col, 1935; Maj.-Gen., 1940; served European War, 1914-19 (MC); a Corps Comdr, Middle East, 1942; CGS, Middle East, 1942; retired, 1943. *Recreation:* painting. *Address:* Panthill, Barcombe, E Sussex. *T:* Barcombe 305. *Club:* Hurlingham.

CORBETT, Lt-Col Uvedale, DSO 1944; *b* 12 Sept. 1909; *s* of Major C. U. Corbett, Stableford, Bridgnorth, Shropshire; *m* 1st, 1935, Veronica Marian Whitehead (marr. diss., 1952); two *s* one *d*; 2nd, 1953, Mrs Patricia Jane Walker. *Educ:* Wellington (Berks); RMA, Woolwich. Commissioned Royal Artillery, 1929; relinquished command 3rd Regt RHA 1945; retired. MP (C) Ludlow Div. of Shropshire, 1945-51. *Address:* Shobdon Court, Leominster, Herefordshire. *T:* Kingsland 260. *Club:* Army and Navy.

CORBETT ASHBY, Dame Margery (Irene), DBE 1967; LLD Hon. President, International Alliance of Women; Hon. President, British Commonwealth League; *b* 1882; *d* of C. H. Corbett of Woodgate, Danehill, Sussex, and Marie, *d* of George Gray, Tunbridge Wells; *m* 1910, Arthur Brian Ashby, barrister, Inner Temple; one *s*. *Educ:* Home; Newnham Coll., Cambridge. Sec. to the National Union of Suffrage Societies on leaving college; lectured on education and land questions from Liberal platforms; Liberal candidate, 1918, 1922, 1923, 1924, 1929 General Elections; 1937 and 1944 by-elections; substitute delegate for UK to Disarmament Conference, 1931-35; travelled and lectured all over Europe, in India, Pakistan, Near East, United States and Canada, speaking in English, French, and German. *Recreations:* gardening and travelling. *Address:* Wickens, Horsted Keynes, West Sussex. *T:* Chelwood Gate 264. *Club:* University Women's.

CORBETT-WINDER, Col John Lyon, OBE 1949; MC 1942; JP; Lord-Lieutenant of Powys, since 1974 (of Montgomeryshire, 1960-74); *b* 15 July 1911; *o s* of Major W. J. Corbett-Winder, Vaynor Park, Berriew, Montgomery (Lord Lieutenant of Montgomeryshire, 1944-50); *m* 1944, Margaret Ailsa, *d* of Lt-Col J. Ramsay Tainsh, CBE, VD; one *s* two *d*. *Educ:* Eton; RMC Sandhurst. 2nd Lieut, 60th Rifles, 1931; Lt-Col, 1942. Served War of 1939-45, Western Desert and N Africa, 1939-43 (despatches twice); Commanded: 44 Reconnaissance Regt; 1st Bn 60th Rifles; GSO1 Infantry Directorate, WO, 1944-47; commanded 2nd Bn 60th Rifles, Palestine, 1947-48 (despatches); AAG, HQ Southern Command, 1948-51; GSO1, HQ 53 Welsh Inf. Div., 1952-55; Col Gen. Staff, SHAPE Mission to Royal Netherlands Army, 1955-57; Dep. Mil. Sec., HQ, BAOR, 1957-58; retd 1958; RARO, 1958-69. Mem., Parly Boundary Commn for Wales, 1963-. Pres., TA & VR Assoc. for Wales, 1977-. JP Powys (formerly Montgomeryshire), 1959. Commander, Order of Orange Nassau, 1958. KStJ 1970 (CStJ 1966). *Recreations:* gardening, forestry, shooting. *Address:* Vaynor Park, Berriew, Welshpool, Powys. *T:* Berriew 204.

CORBIN, Maurice Haig Alleyne; Hon. Mr Justice Corbin; Justice of Appeal, Supreme Court, Trinidad and Tobago, since 1972; *b* 26 May 1916; *s* of L. A. Corbin; *m* 1943, Helen Jocelyn Child; one *s* two *d*; *m* 1968, Jean Barcant. *Educ:* Harrison Coll., Barbados; Queen's Royal Coll., Trinidad. Solicitor, 1941; appointed Magistrate, Trinidad, 1945; called to the Bar, Middle Temple, 1949; Crown Counsel, 1953; Registrar, Supreme Court, 1954; Puisne Judge, Supreme Court, 1957-72. *Recreation:* tennis. *Address:* 6 Antigua Drive, Federation Park, Trinidad, West Indies. *Club:* Queen's Park Cricket (Port of Spain, Trinidad).

CORBY, George Arthur; Director of Services and Deputy Director General, Meteorological Office, since 1976; *b* 14 Aug. 1917; *s* of Bertie John Corby and Agnes May (*née* Dale); *m* 1951, Gertrude Anne Nicoll; one *s* one *d*. *Educ:* St Marylebone Grammar Sch.; Univ. of London (BSc Special Maths 1st Cl.).

Architect's Dept. LCC, 1936-42; entered Met. Office, 1942; Flt Lt, RAFVR, 1943; Sqdn Leader, Dep. Chief Met. Officer, ACSEA, 1945-46; Sen. Met. Off., Northolt Airport, 1947-53; research, 1953-73; Dep. Dir for Communications and Computing, 1973-76. Vice-Pres., Royal Meteorol. Soc., 1975-77. *Publications:* official scientific pubns and res. papers on mountain airflow, dynamical meteorol., and numerical forecasting. *Recreations:* music, photography. *Address:* 4 Ardwell Close, Crowthorne, Berks. *T:* Crowthorne 3695.

CORCORAN, Percy John; His Honour Judge Corcoran; a Circuit Judge (formerly County Court Judge), since 1970; *b* 26 Nov. 1920; *s* of Michael Joseph and Sarah Corcoran, Macclesfield, S Australia; *m* 1949, Jean, JP, MSc, LCST; one *s* one *d*. *Educ:* Christian Brothers' Coll., Adelaide. Royal Australian Air Force, 1941-47. Called to Bar, Gray's Inn, 1948; practised as Barrister, 1948-70; Deputy Judge Advocate, 1953-57; Asst Recorder: Blackpool, 1959-70; Blackburn, 1962-70; Chm., Mental Health Tribunal, NW Area, 1962-70. Pres., Caterham District Scout Council. *Recreations:* golf, walking, music. *Address:* 18 Stanstead Road, Caterham, Surrey. *T:* Caterham 42423.

CORDEAUX, Lt-Col John Kyme, CBE 1946; *b* 23 July 1902; *yr s* of late Col E. K. Cordeaux, CBE; *m* 1928, Norah Cleland (who obtained a divorce, 1953); one *s* (and one *s* decd); *m* 1953, Mildred Jessie Upcher. *Educ:* Royal Naval Colleges Osborne and Dartmouth. Served Royal Navy 1916-23; transf. Royal Marines (Lieut), 1923; RN Staff Coll., 1937. Served War, 1939-46; Naval Intelligence Div., 1939-42; Major, 1940; Actg Lieut-Col 1941; temp. Col, 1942; seconded to Foreign Office, 1942-46; Lieut-Col 1946. Contested (C), Bolsover Div. of Derbyshire, 1950 and 1951; prospective Conservative Candidate, North Norfolk Div., 1952-53; MP (C), Nottingham Central, 1955-64; promoted, as Private Member's Bill, Landlord and Tenant Act, 1962. Commander, Order of Orange-Nassau (Netherlands), 1944; Commander, Order of Dannebrog (Denmark), 1945; Haakon VII Liberty Cross (Norway), 1946. *Publication:* Safe Seat (novel), 1967. *Recreations:* Association football; cricket. *Address:* 11 Hyde Park Gardens, W2.

CORDEIRO, His Eminence Cardinal Joseph; *see* Karachi, Archbishop of, (RC).

CORDINGLEY, Maj-Gen. John Edward, OBE 1959; Controller, Royal Artillery Institution, since 1975; Chairman, Board of Management, Royal Artillery Charitable Fund, since 1977; *b* 1 Sept. 1916; *s* of Air Vice-Marshal Sir John Cordingley, KCB, KCVO, CBE, and late Elizabeth Ruth Carpenter; *m* 1st, 1940, Ruth Pamela (marr. diss. 1961), *d* of late Major S. A. Boddam-Whetham; two *s*; 2nd, 1961, Audrey Helen Anne, *d* of late Maj-Gen. F. G. Beaumont-Nesbitt, CVO, CBE, MC; two step *d*. *Educ:* Sherborne; RMA, Woolwich. 2nd Lieut RA, 1936; served War of 1939-45, Europe and India. Brigade Comdr, 1961-62; Imperial Defence Coll., 1963; Dir of Work Study, Min. of Defence (Army), 1964-66; Dep. Dir, RA, 1967-68; Maj-Gen., RA, BAOR, 1968-71, retired. Col Comdt, RA, 1973-. Bursar, Sherborne Sch., 1971-74. Fellow, Inst. of Work Study Practitioners, 1965; MBIM, 1966. *Recreations:* golf and gardening. *Address:* Church Farm House, Rotherwick, Basingstoke, Hants RG27 9BG. *T:* Hook 2734. *Clubs:* Army and Navy; Senior Golfers, Royal Saint George's.

CORDLE, John Howard; Chairman, E. W. Cordle & Son Ltd since 1968 (Managing Director, 1946-68); *b* 11 Oct. 1912; *s* of late Ernest William Cordle; *m* 1st, 1938 (marr. diss., 1956); three *s* (one *d* decd); 2nd, 1957 (marr. diss. 1971), *e d* of Col A. Maynard, OBE; one *s* four *d*. *Educ:* City of London Sch. Served RAF (commissioned), 1940-45. Member: Archbishops of Canterbury and York Commission on Evangelism, 1945-46; Church Assembly, 1946-53; Oxford Trust of Churches Patronage Board, 1947-. Mem. of Lloyd's, 1952; Mem. Founders Livery Company and Freeman of City of London, 1956. Director: Amalgamated Developers Ltd; Presswork Ltd. Prospective Parly Cand. (C) NE Wolverhampton, 1949; contested (C) Wrekin Div., 1951; MP (C) Bournemouth E and Christchurch, Oct. 1959-1974; Bournemouth E, 1974-77; Chairman: West Africa Cttee, Conservative Commonwealth Council; Mem., Ecclesiastical Cttee; Member UK Delegation to: Council of Europe, Strasbourg, 1974- (Vice-Chm., Parly and Public Relations Cttee); WEU, Paris, 1974-. Life Governor: St Mary's and St Paul's Coll., Cheltenham; Epsom Coll.; Mem. Court of University of Southampton. Gold Staff Officer, Coronation, 1953. Grand Band, Order of the Star of Africa (Liberia), 1964. *Recreations:* shooting, tennis, golf, gardening. *Address:* Malmesbury House, The Close, Salisbury, Wilts. *T:* Salisbury 27027. *Clubs:* Carlton, National, English-Speaking Union, Royal Commonwealth Society.

COREN, Alan; Editor of Punch, since 1978; *b* 27 June 1938; *s* of Samuel and Martha Coren; *m* 1963, Anne Kasriel; one *s* one *d*. *Educ:* East Barnet Grammar Sch.; Wadham Coll., Oxford (Open scholar; BA); Yale; Univ. of California, Berkeley. Asst Editor, Punch, 1963-66, Literary Editor 1966-69, Dep. Editor 1969-77. TV Critic, The Times, 1971-; Columnist: Daily Mail, 1972-76; Evening Standard, 1977-; regular contributor to: Sunday Times, Atlantic Monthly, Listener, TLS, Observer, Tatler. Commonwealth Fellowship, 1961-63. Rector, St Andrews Univ., 1973-76. *Publications:* The Dog It Was That Died, 1965; All Except the Bastard, 1969; The Sanity Inspector, 1974; The Bulletins of Idi Amin, 1974; Golfing For Cats, 1975; The Further Bulletins of Idi Amin, 1975; The Lady From Stalingrad Mansions, 1977; The Peanut Papers, 1977; The Arthur Westerns (for children), 1976-78. *Recreations:* bridge, broadcasting. *Address:* 26 Ranulf Road, NW2.

CORFIELD, Sir Conrad Laurence, KCIE 1945 (CIE 1937); CSI 1942; MC; ICS (retired); *s* of late Rev. Egerton Corfield, MA, Rector of Finchampstead, Berks; *m* 1922, Phyllis Betha (*d* 1932), *d* of late L. P. E. Pugh, KC; one *s* one *d*; *m* 1961, Mrs Sylvia Daunt (*d* 1977), widow of Lt-Col C. O'B. Daunt, OBE, MC, Central India Horse. *Educ:* St Lawrence; St Catharine's Coll., Cambridge. Capt. 1st Cambridgeshire Regt; served European War, France; joined ICS 1920; Asst Comr Punjab; Asst Private Sec. to the Viceroy, 1921-22; joined Political Dept 1925; served in Kathiawar, Baluchistan, Rajputana, Central India, and Hyderabad; Vice-Pres., Rewa State Council, 1933-34; Joint Sec., Political Dept, Simla, 1934-38; Officiating Political Sec., June-Sept. 1937; Resident at Jaipur, 1938-40; officiating Resident for Rajputana, May-Oct. 1939; Resident for the Punjab States, 1941-45; Political Adviser to the Viceroy as Crown Representative, 1945-47. Governor and Vice-Pres., St Lawrence Coll. Chm., Wokingham Div. Conservative Assoc., 1950-54 (Pres. 1954-62). Chm. Wessex Area, 1960-63; former Chairman: Yateley Industries for Disabled Girls, 1954-64; St John Council for Berks, 1944-62; St Crispin's Sch., Wokingham, 1954-67; Finchampstead Parish Council, 1955-61. CStJ. *Publication:* The Princely India I Knew, 1975. *Recreations:* (past) Captain, Cambridge Univ. Hockey, 1919-20; English Hockey International, 1920; gardening. *Address:* High Ground, Finchampstead, Wokingham, Berks RG11 3SE. *T:* Eversley 733239. *Club:* Travellers'.

CORFIELD, Rt. Hon. Sir Frederick (Vernon), PC 1970; Kt 1972; QC 1972; *b* 1 June 1915; *s* of late Brig. F. A. Corfield, DSO, OBE, IA, and M. G. Corfield (née Vernon); *m* 1945, Elizabeth Mary Ruth Taylor; no *c. Educ:* Cheltenham Coll. (Scholar); RMA, Woolwich. Royal Artillery, 1935; 8th Field Regt, RA, India, 1935-39; served War of 1939-45; Actg Captain and Adjutant, 23rd Field Regt, BEF, 3rd Div., 1939; 51st (Highland) Div., 1940 (despatches); prisoner of war, Germany, 1940-45. Called to Bar, Middle Temple, 1945 (Middle Temple Scholarship); JAG's Branch, WO, 1945-46; retired, 1946; farming, 1946-56. MP (C) South Gloucester, 1955-Feb. 1974; Jt Parly Sec., Min. of Housing and Local Govt, 1962-64; Minister of State, Board of Trade, June-Oct. 1970; Minister of Aviation Supply, 1970-71; Minister for Aerospace, DTI, 1971-72. Mem., British Waterways Bd, 1974-. *Publications:* Corfield on Compensation, 1959; A Guide to the Community Land Act, 1976. *Recreations:* gardening, fishing. *Address:* Wordings Orchard, Sheepscombe, near Stroud, Glos.; 2 Paper Buildings, Temple, EC4.

CORFIELD, Kenneth George; Deputy Chairman and Managing Director, Standard Telephones & Cables Ltd, since 1969; Chairman, Standard Telephones and Cables (Northern Ireland), since 1974; Senior Officer, International Telephone and Telegraph Corporation (UK), since 1974; Vice-President, ITT Europe Inc., since 1967; *b* 27 Jan. 1924; *s* of Stanley Corfield and Dorothy Elizabeth (née Manson); *m* 1960; one *d. Educ:* South Staffs Coll. of Advanced Technology. CE, FIMechE, FInstBM. Management Develt, ICI Metals Div., 1946-50; Man. Dir, K. G. Corfield Ltd, 1950-60; Exec. Dir, Parkinson Cowan, 1960-66. Chm., EDC for Ferrous Foundries Industry, 1975-. Mem., Adv. Council, Science Museum, 1975-. President: TEMA, 1974-; BAIE, 1975-. CompIEE 1974. DUniv Surrey, 1976. *Recreations:* hunting, shooting, photography. *Address:* 14 Elm Walk, Hampstead, NW3 7UP.

CORI, Prof. Carl Ferdinand; Biochemist at Massachusetts General Hospital, Harvard Medical School, Boston, Mass, since 1967; Professor of Biochemistry, Washington University School of Medicine, St Louis, Mo, 1931-67; *b* Prague, Czechoslovakia, 5 Dec. 1896; *s* of Carl Cori and Maria Lippich; went to US, 1922; naturalised, 1928; *m* 1920, Gerty T. (*d* 1957), *d* of Otto Radnitz; one *s*; *m* 1960, Anne Fitz-Gerald Jones. *Educ:* Gymnasium, Trieste, Austria; (German) University of Prague (MD). Asst in Pharmacology, University of Graz, Austria, 1920-21; Biochemist State Inst. for Study of Malignant Disease, Buffalo, NY, 1922-31. Mem. Nat. Acad. of Sciences, Royal Society etc. Hon. ScD: Western Reserve, 1946, Yale, 1946, Boston Univ., 1948, Cambridge, 1949; Brandeis, 1965; Gustavus Adolphus Coll., 1965; Washington Univ., 1966; St Louis Univ., 1966; Monash, 1966; Granada, 1967; Univ. of Trieste, 1971. Shared Nobel Prize in Medicine and Physiology, 1947. Mid-West Award, 1946; Squibb Award, 1947; Sugar Research Foundation Award, 1947 and 1950; Willard Gibbs Medal, 1948. *Publications:* articles in scientific journals. *Address:* Enzyme Research Laboratory, Massachusetts General Hospital, Fruit Street, Boston, Mass 02114, USA.

CORISH, Brendan; TD Wexford since 1945; Member of Council of State since 1964; *m* 1949; three *s. Educ:* Christian Brothers' Sch., Wexford. Vice-Chm. of Labour Party, Republic of Ireland, 1946-49; Party Chm., 1949-53; Parly Party Whip, 1947-54; Parly Sec. to Minister for Local Govt and Defence, 1948-51; Minister for Social Welfare, 1954-57; Party Leader, 1960-77; Tanaiste (Deputy Prime Minister) and Minister for Health and Social Welfare, 1973-77. *Address:* Leinster House, Kildare Street, Dublin 2, Ireland.

CORK, Bishop of, (RC), since 1952; **Most Rev. Cornelius Lucey;** and Ross, Bishop of, since 1954; *b* Windsor, Co. Cork. *Educ:* Maynooth; Innsbruck. Priest, 1927. Co-Founder and Pres., Christus Rex Soc. for priests; Founder and Superior, La Sociedad de Santo Toribio (missionary and welfare organisation for the barriadas of Peru). *Address:* Bishop's House, Cork, Eire.

CORK AND ORRERY, 13th Earl of, *cr* 1620; **Patrick Reginald Boyle;** Baron Boyle of Youghall, 1616; Viscount Dungarvan, 1620; Viscount Kinalmeaky, Baron Boyle of Bandon Bridge and Baron Boyle of Broghill (Ireland), 1628; Earl of Orrery, 1660; Baron Boyle of Marston, 1711; writer, artist and broadcaster; *b* 7 Feb. 1910; *s* of Major Hon. Reginald Courtenay Boyle, MBE, MC (*d* 1946), and Violet (*d* 1974), *d* of late Arthur Flower; *S* uncle, 12th Earl of Cork and Orrery, 1967; *m* 1952, Dorothy Kate, *o d* of late Robert Ramsden, Meltham, Yorks. *Educ:* Harrow Sch.; Royal Military College, Sandhurst. Royal Ulster Rifles, 1930-33; Capt. London Irish Rifles, Royal Ulster Rifles (TA), 1935-38. Served War of 1939-45 with Royal Ulster Rifles, Burma Rifles, Cameronians (Scottish Rifles) in Special Force (Chindits) (severely wounded) and Parachute Regt. Now Hon. Major, late Army Air Corps. Dep. Chm. of Cttees, House of Lords; Vice-Pres., British Cancer Council. Hereditary Life Governor, Christian Faith Soc. FRSA 1947. *Publications:* (author and illustrator) Sailing in a Nutshell, 1935; (jointly) Jungle, Jungle, Little Chindit, 1946. Contribs to the Hibbert Jl. *Recreations:* sailing, oil-painting, gardening. *Heir:* *b* Hon. John William Boyle, DSC [*b* 12 May 1916; *m* 1943, Mary Leslie, *d* of late Gen. Sir Robert Gordon Finlayson, KCB, CMG, DSO; three *s*]. *Address:* Flint House, Heyshott, Midhurst, W Sussex. *Clubs:* Royal Thames Yacht; Cork and County (Cork).

CORK, CLOYNE, and ROSS, Bishop of, since 1957; **Rt. Rev. Richard Gordon Perdue;** *b* 13 Feb. 1910; *s* of Richard Perdue; *m* 1943, Evelyn Ruth Curry, BA; two *d. Educ:* Trinity Coll., Dublin. BA 1931; MA and BD 1938. Deacon 1933, priest 1934, Dublin. Curate of Drumcondra with N Strand, 1933-36; Rathmines, 1936-40; Incumbent of Castledermot with Kinneagh, 1940-43; Roscrea, Diocese of Killaloe, 1943-54; Archdeacon of Killaloe and Kilfenora, 1951-54; Examining Chaplain to Bishop of Killaloe, 1951-54; Bishop of Killaloe, Kilfenora, Clonfert and Kilmacduagh, 1953-57. *Address:* The Palace, Bishop Street, Cork.

CORK, Kenneth Russell, FCA; Senior Partner, W. H. Cork, Gully & Co., Chartered Accountants, since 1946; *b* 21 Aug. 1913; *s* of William Henry Cork and Maud Alice (née Nunn); *m* 1937, Nina Lippold; one *s* one *d. Educ:* Berkhamsted. ACA 1937, FCA 1946. Enlisted HAC, 1938; called up, 1939; served in North Africa and Italy, 1939-45 (rank Lt-Col). Common Councilman, City of London, 1951-70; Alderman, City of London (Ward of Tower), 1970; Sheriff, City of London, 1975-76; Liveryman, Worshipful Co. of Horners, Mem. Court, 1970. Chm., Plantation Holdings Ltd, 1977-; Director: Ladbroke Group Ltd; Richard Costain Ltd. Chairman: EEC Bankruptcy Convention Adv. Cttee to Dept Trade, 1973; Insolvency Law Review Cttee, 1977. Chairman: NI Finance Corpn, 1974-76; NI Develt Agency, 1976-77, Hon. Consultant, 1977-. Mem., Cttee to Review the Functioning of Financial Institutions, 1977-. Pres., Inst. of Credit Management Ltd. Governor, Royal Shakespeare Theatre, 1967- (Chm., 1975-); Dir, Shakespeare Theatre Trust Ltd (Chm. 1967-75); Dir, City Arts Trust Ltd. Treas., Royal Concert, 1970. FRSA 1970. *Recreations:* sailing, photography, painting. *Address:* Cherry Trees, Grimms Lane,

Great Missenden, Bucks. *T:* Great Missenden 2628. *Clubs:* Royal Thames Yacht, City Livery, Gresham; Hardway Sailing (Gosport); Bosham Sailing.

CORKERY, Michael; First Senior Prosecuting Counsel to the Crown, at the Central Criminal Court, since 1977; *b* 20 May 1926; *o s* of late Charles Timothy Corkery and of Nellie Marie Corkery; *m* 1967, Juliet Shore Foulkes, *o d* of late Harold Glyn Foulkes; one *s* one *d*. *Educ:* The King's Sch., Canterbury. Commissioned in Welsh Guards, 1945; served until 1948. Called to Bar, Lincoln's Inn, 1949, Bencher 1973; Mem., South Eastern Circuit; 3rd Junior Prosecuting Counsel to the Crown at the Central Criminal Court, 1959; 1st Junior Prosecuting Counsel to the Crown, 1964; 5th Senior Prosecuting Counsel to the Crown, 1970; 3rd Sen. Prosecuting Counsel, 1971; 2nd Sen. Prosecuting Counsel, 1974. *Recreations:* shooting, sailing. *Address:* 5 Paper Buildings, Temple, EC4.

CORLEY, Sir Kenneth (Sholl Ferrand), Kt 1972; Chairman and Chief Executive, Joseph Lucas (Industries) Ltd, 1969-73; *b* 3 Nov. 1908; *s* of late S. W. Corley and late Mrs A. L. Corley; *m* 1937, Olwen Mary Yeoman; one *s* one *d*. *Educ:* St Bees, Cumberland. Joined Joseph Lucas Ltd, 1927; Director, 1948. Pres., Birmingham Chamber of Commerce, 1964. Governor, Royal Shakespeare Theatre; Life Governor, Birmingham Univ.; Pres., Soc. of Motor Mfrs and Traders, 1971; Chm., British Industry Roads Campaign, 1972-. Chevalier, Légion d'Honneur, 1975. *Recreations:* fell-walking, bee-keeping, theatre. *Address:* 34 Dingle Lane, Solihull, West Midlands B91 3NG. *T:* 021-705 1597; Yewtree, Wasdale, Cumbria. *T:* Wasdale 285. *Club:* Royal Automobile.

CORLEY, Michael Early Ferrand; His Honour Judge Corley; a Circuit Judge (formerly County Court Judge), since 1967; *b* 11 Oct. 1909; *s* of Ferrand Edward Corley, late of Christian College, Madras, and Elsie Maria Corley. *Educ:* Marlborough; Oriel Coll., Oxford. Called to Bar, 1934. War Service, RNVR, 1940-46. *Address:* 3 Brockley Grove, Hutton, Brentwood, Essex.

CORMACK, John; Fisheries Secretary, Department of Agriculture and Fisheries for Scotland, since 1976; *b* 27 Aug. 1922; *yr s* of late Donald Cormack and of Anne Hunter Cormack (*née* Gair); *m* 1947, Jessie Margaret Bain; one *s* one *d* (and one *d* decd). *Educ:* Royal High Sch., Edinburgh. Served RAPC, 1941-46; Captain, 1946. Entered Department of Agriculture for Scotland, 1939: Principal, 1959; Private Sec. to Sec. of State for Scotland, 1967-69; Asst Sec., 1969; Under Sec., 1976. *Recreations:* golf, music. *Address:* 57 Craigmount Avenue North, Edinburgh EH12 8DN. *T:* 031-334 5420. *Club:* Royal Commonwealth Society.

CORMACK, Sir Magnus (Cameron), KBE 1970; Senator for Victoria; President of the Senate, 1971-74; *b* Caithness, Scotland, 12 Feb. 1906; *s* of William Petrie Cormack and Violet McDonald Cameron; *m* 1935, Mary Gordon Macmeiken; one *s* three *d*. *Educ:* St Peter's Sch., Adelaide, S Aust. Farmer and Grazier. Served War, 1940-44; Aust. Imperial Forces, SW Pacific Area, Major. Pres., Liberal Party Organisation, 1947-49; Senator for Victoria, 1951-53 and 1962-. *Recreation:* deep sea sailing. *Address:* 7 Market Court, Portland, Victoria 3305, Australia. *Clubs:* Australian, Naval and Military (Melbourne, Victoria); Hamilton (Victoria).

CORMACK, Patrick Thomas; MP (C) Staffordshire South West, since 1974 (Cannock, 1970-74); *b* 18 May 1939; *s* of Thomas Charles and Kathleen Mary Cormack, Grimsby; *m* 1967, Kathleen Mary McDonald; two *s*. *Educ:* St James' Choir School and Havelock School, Grimsby; Univ. of Hull (BA Hons English and History). Second Master, St James' Choir School, Grimsby, 1961-66; Company Education and Training Officer, Ross Group Ltd, Grimsby, 1966-67; Assistant Housemaster, Wrekin College, Shropshire, 1967-69; Head of History, Brewood Grammar School, Stafford, 1969-70. Member: Grants Cttee; Historic Churches Preservation Trust; Executive, Commons, Footpaths and Open Spaces Preservation Soc; All Party Heritage Cttee (founder Sec.); Heritage in Danger (Vice-Chm.). *Publication:* Heritage in Danger, 1976. *Recreations:* fighting philistines, walking, visiting old churches. *Address:* Somerford Grange, Brewood, Stafford; 1a Heathview Gardens, Roehampton SW15. *Club:* Constitutional.

CORNBERG, Mrs Sol; *see* Gaskin, Catherine.

CORNELL, Ward MacLaurin; Agent General for Ontario in the United Kingdom since 1972; *b* London, Ont, 4 May 1924; *m* Georgina Saxon; three *s* two *d*. *Educ:* Pickering Coll.; Univ. of Western Ontario. Lectr in English and History, Pickering Coll.,

Ont, 1949-54; Vis. Lectr, Conestoga Coll.; Gen. Manager, Broadcast Div. (Radio), Free Press Printing Co., 1954-67; Pres., Ward Cornell Ltd, Creative Projects in Communications, 1967-72. *Recreations:* reading, tennis, travelling. *Address:* (office) Ontario House, 13 Charles II Street, SW1Y 4QS. *T:* 01-930 6404; (home) Flat 6, 12 Reeves Mews, W1. *Clubs:* London, Lambs, London Hunt and Country, Celebrity (all Canada).

CORNER, Edred John Henry, CBE 1972; FRS 1955; FLS; Professor of Tropical Botany, University of Cambridge, 1966-73, now Emeritus; *b* 12 Jan. 1906; *s* of late Edred Moss Corner and Henrietta Corner (*née* Henderson); *m* 1953, Helga Dinesen Sondergoord; one *s* two *d* (by 1st *m*). *Educ:* Rugby Sch. Asst Dir, Gardens Dept, Straits Settlements, 1929-45; Principal Field Scientific Officer, Latin America, Unesco, 1947-48; Lecturer in Botany, Cambridge, 1949-59; Reader in Plant Taxonomy, 1959-65; Fellow, Sidney Sussex Coll., Cambridge, 1959-73. Member: American Mycological Soc.; Brit. Mycological Soc.; French Mycological Soc.; Fellow, American Assoc. for the Advancement of Science; Corr. Member: Botanical Soc. of America; Royal Netherlands Botanical Soc.; Hon. Mem., Japanese Mycological Soc. Mem., Governing Body of Rugby Sch., 1959-75. Darwin Medal, Royal Soc., 1960; Patron's Medal, RGS, 1966; Gold Medal, Linnean Soc. of London, 1970; Victoria Medal of Honour, RHS, 1974. *Publications:* Wayside Trees of Malaya (2 vols), 1940 and 1952; A Monograph of Clavaria and allied genera, 1950; Life of Plants, 1964; Natural History of Palms, 1966; Monograph of Cantharelloid Fungi, 1966; Boletus in Malaysia, 1972; Seeds of Dicotyledons, 2 vols, 1976. *Address:* 91 Hinton Way, Great Shelford, Cambs CB2 5AH. *T:* Shelford 2167.

CORNER, Frank Henry; Secretary of Foreign Affairs, New Zealand, since 1973; *b* 17 May 1920; *y s* of Charles William Corner, Napier, NZ, and Sybil Corner (*née* Smith); *m* 1943, Lynette Robinson; two *d*. *Educ:* Napier Boys' High Sch.; Victoria Univ. of Wellington. MA, 1st cl. History; James Macintosh and Post-graduate Scholar. External Affairs Dept, NZ, and War Cabinet Secretariat, 1943; 1st Sec., NZ Embassy, Washington, 1948-51; Sen. Counsellor, NZ High Commn, London, 1952-58; Dep. Sec. NZ Dept of External Affairs, 1958-62; Perm. Rep. (Ambassador) to UN, 1962-67; Ambassador of NZ to USA, 1967-72; Permanent Head of Prime Minister's Dept, 1973-75. Mem., NZ Delegn to Commonwealth Prime Ministers' Meetings, 1944, 1946, 1951-57, 1973, 1975; Deleg. to UN Gen. Assembly, 1949-52, 1955, 1960-68, 1973, 1974; NZ Rep. to UN Trusteeship Council, 1962-66 (Pres., 1965-66; Chm., UN Vis. Mission to Micronesia, 1964); NZ Rep. on UN Security Coun., 1966; Adviser, NZ Delegn: Paris Peace Conf., 1946; Geneva Conf. on Korea, 1954; numerous other internat. confs as adviser or delegate. *Recreations:* music, walking, gardening. *Address:* (private) 26 Burnell Avenue, Wellington 1, NZ. *T:* 737-022; (office) Parliament Building, Wellington 1. *T:* 736-678.

CORNER, George Washington; Editor, American Philosophical Society, Philadelphia, Pennsylvania, since 1977; *b* 12 Dec. 1889; *s* of George Washington Corner, Jr, and Florence Elmer (*née* Evans); *m* 1915, Betsy Lyon Copping (*d* 1976), *d* of Rev. Bernard Copping and Cora (*née* Lyon); one *s* (one *d* decd). *Educ:* Boys' Latin Sch., Baltimore; Johns Hopkins Univ., Baltimore (AB 1909, MD 1913). Asst in Anatomy, Johns Hopkins Univ., 1913-14; Resident House Officer, Johns Hopkins Hosp., 1914-15; Asst Prof. of Anatomy, University of Calif., 1915-19; Associate Prof. of Anatomy, Johns Hopkins, 1919-23; Prof. of Anatomy, Univ. of Rochester, 1923-40; Dir, Dept of Embryology, Carnegie Instn of Washington, Baltimore, 1940-55; Historian, Rockefeller Inst., New York, 1956-60; Exec. Officer, Amer. Philosophical Soc., 1960-77. George Eastman Visiting Prof., Oxford, and Fellow, Balliol Coll., 1952-53; Vicary Lectr, RCS, 1936; Vanuxem Lectr, Princeton, 1942; Terry Lectr, Yale, 1944. Passano Award, 1958. Member: United States National Academy of Sciences (Vice-Pres., 1953-57); American Philosophical Soc. (Vice-Pres. 1953-56). Hon. Fellow Royal Society, Edinburgh; Foreign Mem., Royal Society, London. Dr (*hc*) Catholic Univ., Chile, 1942; Hon. DSc: Rochester, 1944; Boston, 1948; Oxford, 1950; Chicago, 1958; MA (by decree) Oxford, 1952; Hon. ScD Thomas Jefferson Univ., 1971; Hon. LLD: Tulane 1955; Temple, 1956; Johns Hopkins, 1975; Hon. DMedScience, Woman's Med. Coll., 1958; Hon. LittD Pa, 1965. *Publications:* Anatomical Texts of Earlier Middle Ages, 1927; Anatomy (a history), 1930; Hormones in Human Reproduction, 1942; Ourselves Unborn, 1944; ed The Autobiography of Benjamin Rush, 1948; Anatomist at Large, 1958; George Hoyt Whipple and His Friends, 1963; Two Centuries of Medicine, 1965; History of the Rockefeller Institute, 1965; Doctor Kane of the Arctic Seas, 1972; numerous articles on histology, embryology, physiology of reproduction, history of medicine.

Recreation: travel. *Address:* American Philosophical Society, 104 South Fifth Street, Philadelphia, Pa 19106, USA. *Clubs:* Tudor-Stuart (Baltimore); Franklin Inn (Philadelphia); Century (NY).

CORNER, Philip; Director General of Quality Assurance, Ministry of Defence Procurement Executive, since 1975; *b* 7 Aug. 1924; *s* of late William Henry Corner and of Dora (*née* Smailes); *m* 1948, Nora Pipes; no *c*. *Educ:* Dame Allan's Boys' Sch., Newcastle upon Tyne; Bradford Technical Coll.; RNEC Manadon; Battersea Polytechnic. BScEng (London); CEng, MIMechE, MIEE. Short Bros (Aeronautical Engrs), 1942-43; Air Br., RN, Sub-Lieut RNVR, 1944-46; LNER Co., 1946-47; Min. of Works, 1947-50; Min. of Supply, 1950; Ministry of Defence: Dir of Guided Weapons Prodn, 1968-72; Dir of Quality Assurance (Technical), 1972-75. *Recreations:* gardening, listening to music. *Address:* 97 Dartnell Park Road, West Byfleet, Weybridge, Surrey KT14 6QE.

CORNFORD, Sir (Edward) Clifford, KCB 1977 (CB 1966); Chief of Defence Procurement, Ministry of Defence, since 1977; *b* 6 Feb. 1918; *s* of John Herbert Cornford; *m* 1945, Catherine Muir; three *s* three *d*. *Educ:* Kimbolton Sch.; Jesus Coll., Cambridge (BA). Joined RAE, 1938. Operational Research with RAF, 1939-45. Guided Weapons Res. at RAE, 1945-60; jssc 1951; Head of Guided Weapons Dept, RAE, 1956-61; Min. of Defence: Chm., Def. Res. Policy Staff, 1961-63; Asst Chief Scientific Adviser, 1963-64; Chief Scientist (Army), Mem. Army Board, Ministry of Defence, 1965-67; Chm. Programme Evaluation Group, MoD, 1967-Jan. 1968 Dep. Chief Adviser (Research and Studies), MoD, 1968-69; Controller of Guided Weapons and Electronics, Min. of Technology, later Min. of Aviation Supply and MoD (Procurement Executive), 1969-72; Ministry of Defence (PE): Controller (Policy), 1972-74; Dep. Chief Exec., 1974-75; Chief Exec. and Permanent Under Sec. of State, 1975-77. FRAeS. *Publications:* on aeronautical subjects in jls of learned socs and technical publications. *Recreation:* travelling. *Address:* Beechurst, Shaftesbury Road, Woking, Surrey. *T:* 68919. *Club:* Athenæum.

CORNFORTH, Sir John (Warcup), Kt 1977; CBE 1972; FRS 1953; DPhil; Royal Society Research Professor, University of Sussex, since 1975; *b* 7 Sept. 1917; *er s* of J. W. Cornforth, Sydney, Aust.; *m* 1941, Rita, *d* of W. C. Harradence; one *s* two *d*. *Educ:* Sydney High Sch.; Universities of Sydney and Oxford. BSc Sydney 1937; MSc Sydney, 1938; 1851 Exhibition Overseas Scholarship, 1939-42; DPhil Oxford, 1941; scientific staff of Med. Research Coun., 1946-62; Dir, Shell Research, Milstead Lab. of Chem. Enzymology, 1962-75. Assoc. Prof. in Molecular Sciences, Univ. of Warwick, 1965-71; Vis. Prof., Univ. of Sussex, 1971-75. Lectures: Pedler, Chem. Soc., 1968-69; Andrews, Univ. of NSW, 1970; Max Tishler, Harvard Univ., 1970; Robert Robinson, Chem. Soc., 1971-72; Pacific Coast, 1973. Corday-Morgan Medal and Prize, Chem. Soc., 1953; (with G. J. Popjak) CIBA Medal, Biochem. Soc., 1965; Flintoff Medal, Chem. Soc., 1966; Stouffer Prize, 1967; Ernest Guenther Award, Amer. Chem. Soc., 1969; (with G. J. Popjak) Davy Medal, Royal Soc., 1968; Prix Roussel, 1972; (jtly) Nobel Prize for Chemistry, 1975; Royal Medal, Royal Soc., 1976. For. Hon. Mem., Amer. Acad., 1973; Corresp. Mem., Aust. Acad., 1977. Hon. DSc: ETH Zürich, 1975; Oxford, Warwick, Dublin and Liverpool, 1976; Aberdeen, Hull and Sussex, 1977. Hon. Fellow, St Catherine's Coll., Oxford, 1976. Has been deaf since boyhood. *Publications:* numerous papers on organic chemical and biochemical subjects. *Recreations:* lawn tennis, chess, gardening. *Address:* Saxon Down, Cuilfail, Lewes, East Sussex BN7 2BE.

CORNISH, Jack Bertram; HM Civil Service; Under-Secretary, since 1976; Department of Health and Social Security, since 1961; *b* 26 June 1918; *s* of Bertram George John Cornish and Nora Jarmy; *m* 1946, Mary Milton; three *d*. *Educ:* Price's Grammar Sch., Fareham; Cotham Grammar Sch., Bristol. Admiralty, 1937-61: London, Bath, Plymouth, Singapore. Supply Ships in Singapore and Newfoundland, 1941 and 1942. *Recreations:* music, painting, gardening. *Address:* 146 Ladwell, Hursley, Winchester, Hants. *T:* Hursley 75257.

CORNISH, Prof. Ronald James; Consultant, Allott & Lomax, Sale, Cheshire, since 1970; *b* Exeter, Devon, 30 Dec. 1898; *s* of William Henry Cornish and Eva Maud Eliza (*née* Horrell); *m* 1927, Edith Oliver Oliver; twin *d*. *Educ:* Hele's Sch., Exeter; Exeter Sch., Exeter; Manchester Univ. RGA, 1917-19; engineer, Messrs Mather & Platt, Ltd, Manchester, 1922-25; Manchester University: Asst Lecturer, 1925-29; Lecturer, 1929-34; Head of Dept of Municipal Engineering, 1934-53; Prof. of Municipal Engineering, 1953-61; Prof. Emeritus, 1966; seconded, Jan.-June 1960, as Prof. of Engineering in University Coll. of Ibadan, Nigeria; Prof. of Civil Engineering, Indian Institute of

Technology, Hauz Khas, New Delhi, 1961-66; Head of Civil Engrg Dept, Malta Coll. of Arts, Science and Technology, 1966-70. FICE (Ex-Mem. Council); FIStructE (Ex-Mem. Council, Hon. Librarian, 1972-74, Lewis E. Kent award, 1974); MIMechE; FIMunE; FIE (Ind.). Hon. FIPHE; FRSH (Ex-Mem. Council). *Publications:* papers in Proc. Royal Soc., Philosophical Magazine, Jls of Engineering Instns, etc. *Address:* 20 Oakdene Road, Marple, Stockport SK6 6PJ. *T:* 061-427 2768.

CORNISH, William Herbert, CB 1955; Receiver for the Metropolitan Police District, 1961-67; *b* 2 Jan. 1906; *s* of late Rev. Herbert H. Cornish and Susan Emerson; *m* 1938, Eileen May Elizabeth Cooney; two *d*. *Educ:* Wesley Coll., Dublin; Trinity Coll., Dublin. Scholar, 1st Cl. Moderator with Large Gold Medal in Modern History and Political Science. Entered Home Office, 1930; Asst Sec., 1942; Asst Under-Sec. of State, 1952-60. *Recreations:* gardening and music. *Address:* 2 Tormead, Dene Road, Northwood, Mddx. *T:* Northwood 21933.

CORNISH, Prof. William Rodolph; Professor of English Law, London School of Economics, University of London, since 1970; *b* 9 Aug. 1937; *s* of Jack R. and Elizabeth E. Cornish, Adelaide, S Australia; *m* 1964, Lovedy E. Moule; one *s* two *d*. *Educ:* Univs of Adelaide (LLB) and Oxford (BCL). Lectr in Law, LSE, 1962-68; Reader in Law, Queen Mary Coll., London, 1969-70. *Publications:* The Jury, 1968; (Jt Editor) Sutton and Shannon on Contracts, 1970; articles etc in legal periodicals. *Address:* 23 Broadhinton Road, SW4.

CORNOCK, Maj.-Gen. Archibald Rae, CB 1975; OBE 1968; Director of Army Quartering, 1973-75; *b* 4 May 1920; *s* of Matthew Cornock and Mrs Mary Munro MacRae; *m* 1951, Dorothy Margaret Cecilia; two *d*. *Educ:* Coatbridge. MBIM 1965. Interpreter in German, French and Hungarian. NW Frontier, 1940-42; Burma, 1942-43; transf. Royal Indian Navy, 1943; Burma (Arakan), 1944-46; Gordon Highlanders, 1947-50; transf. RAOC, 1950; psc 1954; GSO2 Intelligence, 1955-57; DAQMG Northern Army Gp, 1959-61; comd 16 Bn RAOC, 1961-64; SEATO Planning Staff, Bangkok, 1964; Defence Attaché, Budapest, 1965-67; Comdt 15 Base Ordnance Depot, 1967; DDOS Strategic Comd, 1968-70; Brig. Q (Maint.), MoD, 1970-72; Dir of Clothing Procurement, 1972. Col Comdt, RAOC, 1976-. *Recreations:* sailing, opera, languages, golf. *Address:* 20 Claremont, 14 St Johns Avenue, Putney Hill, SW15 2AB. *T:* 01-789 5892. *Clubs:* Royal Thames Yacht, Army and Navy; Highland Brigade.

CORNWALL, Archdeacon of; see Young, Ven. Peter Claude.

CORNWALL, Ian Wolfran, PhD London; Reader in Human Environment, University of London, 1965-74; *b* 28 Nov. 1909; *s* of Lt-Col J. W. Cornwall, CIE, IMS, and Effie E. C. (*née* Sinclair), *d* of Surg.-Gen. D. Sinclair, IMS; *m* 1st, 1937, Anna Margareta (*née* Callear) (*d* 1967); two *s*; 2nd, 1974, Mary L. Reynolds (*née* Miller). *Educ:* private sch.; Wellington Coll., Berks; St John's Coll., Cambridge (BA). Teaching, clerking, pharmaceutical manufacturing, selling, 1931-39; Postal and Telegraph Censorship, Press Censorship, MOI, 1939-45. London Univ. Inst. of Archaeology: Student, 1945-47 (Diploma, 1947); Secretary, 1948-51. University teacher and researcher, 1951-74, retd. (PhD London, 1952). Life Mem., Geologists' Assoc. Henry Stopes Memorial Medal, Geologists' Assoc., 1970. *Publications:* Bones for the Archaeologist, 1956; Soils for the Archaeologist, 1958; The Making of Man, 1960 (Carnegie Medal of Library Assoc.); The World of Ancient Man, 1964; Hunter's Half Moon (fiction), 1967; Prehistoric Animals and their Hunters, 1968; Ice Ages, 1970. Contribs to specialist jls. *Recreations:* geology, gardening, photography. *Address:* Cherry Lodge, Longueville Road, St Saviour, Jersey, CI.

CORNWALL, Gen. Sir J. H. M.; see Marshall-Cornwall.

CORNWALL, Rt. Rev. Nigel Edmund, CBE 1955; Assistant Bishop, Diocese of Winchester, and Canon Residentiary of Winchester Cathedral, 1963-73; *b* 13 Aug. 1903; *s* of late Alan Whitmore Cornwall, priest, sometime Archdeacon of Cheltenham; *m* 1959, Mary, *d* of Rev. C. R. Dalton. *Educ:* Marlborough Coll; Oriel Coll., Oxford. BA, 3rd class History, 1926; MA 1930. Cuddesdon Theological Coll., 1926-27; Deacon, Diocese of Durham, 1927; Curate, St Columba's, Southwick, Sunderland, 1927-30; Priest, Durham, 1928; Chaplain to Bishop of Colombo, 1931-38; Curate, St Wilfred's, Brighton, 1938-39; Missionary Priest of Diocese of Masasi, 1939-49; Headmaster, St Joseph's Coll., Chidya, 1944-49; Bishop of Borneo, 1949-62. Commissary to Bishop of Kuching, in England, 1963-. *Address:* 4 Cedar Court, Christchurch Road, Winchester.

CORNWALL-JONES, Brig. Arthur Thomas, CMG 1949; CBE 1945 (OBE 1943); *b* 21 July 1900; *s* of Rev. E. Cornwall-Jones (sometime Canon of Aberdeen); *m* 1929, Marie Evelyn Joan, *d* of late Lieut-Col R. H. Hammersley-Smith, CBE; four *s. Educ:* Trinity Coll., Glenalmond. IA, 1920-47; 2nd Bn 5th Royal Gurkha Rifles (FF); Asst Sec. Offices of War Cabinet and Minister of Defence, 1939-41 and 1943-44; Sec. Middle East Defence Cttee, 1941-43; British Sec. Combined Chiefs of Staff, 1944-46; Senior Asst Sec. (Military) of the Cabinet, 1946-50. British Army since Aug. 1947 (Gen. List, Supernumerary); retired pay, 1950. Served with British, Australian and Pakistan Administrative Staff Colls and Philippine Executive Academy, 1950-68. US Legion of Merit (Comdr) 1946. *Address:* Snowball Hill, Russells Water, Henley-on-Thames, Oxon. *T:* Nettlebed 309.

CORNWALL-LEGH, C. L. S.; *see* Legh.

CORNWALLIS, family name of **Baron Cornwallis.**

CORNWALLIS, 2nd Baron, *cr* 1927, of Linton, Kent, in County of Kent; **Wykeham Stanley Cornwallis,** KCVO 1968; KBE 1945; MC; DL; Lord Lieutenant of Kent and Custos Rotulorum, 1944-72; HM's Lieutenant for City and County of Canterbury, 1944-72; one of HM's Lieutenants for City of London; President: Whitbread Fremlin's Ltd; Isherwood, Foster & Stacey; former Director: Royal Insurance Co. (Chairman, London Board; Local Director and Chairman, Kent Board); Barclays Bank (Local Director Maidstone and Canterbury Districts); Director, Whitbread Investment Co.; former Chairman, Albert E. Reed & Co.; *b* 14 March 1892; *s* of 1st Baron and Mabel (*d* 1957), *d* of O. P. Leigh, Belmont Hall, Cheshire; *S* father, 1935; *m* 1st, 1917, Cecily Etha Mary (*d* 1943), *d* of Sir James Walker, 3rd Bt of Sand Hutton; one *s* (one *d* decd); 2nd, 1948, Esmé Ethel Alice (*d* 1969), *widow* of Sir Robert Walker, 4th Bt, Sand Hutton. *Educ:* Eton; RMC Sandhurst. Served European War, 1914-18, Royal Scots Greys and General Staff, France and Belgium (wounded, despatches, MC). Hon. Colonel: 5th Bn The Buffs, E Kent Regt, 1956-67; 415 Coast Regt RA (TA), 1935-56; 8th Bn (Territorial), The Queen's Regt, 1967-68. Pro-Chancellor, Univ. of Kent at Canterbury, 1962-72. President: Inst. of Packaging, 1961-64; (former) Kent County Boy Scouts Assoc.; Kent County Playing Fields Assoc.; Kent County Agricultural Soc.; Kent Assoc. of Workmen's Clubs; Kent Squash Raquets Assoc.; Marden and District Commercial Fruit Show; Vice-Pres., Kent Co. Royal British Legion; Patron: Kent Assoc. of Boys' Clubs; Folkestone Race Course; Vice-Patron: Kent County Society; Assoc. of Men of Kent and Kentish Men; Life Vice-Pres. and formerly Trustee of MCC (Pres. 1948); Trustee RASE; Kent County Council: Vice-Chm., 1931-35; Chm., 1935-36, late Alderman; Chm. Kent War Agricultural Executive Cttee, 1939-46; DL, JP Kent; former Vice-Pres., SE District T&AVR. Hon. DCL Univ. of Kent at Canterbury, 1968.Freeman, City of London. Hon. Freeman, Borough of Maidstone. Provincial Grand Master, Masonic Province of East Kent (Past Provincial Grand Master, Kent and West Kent). Grand Master's Order of Service to Masonry. Edward Hardy Gold Medal, for service to County of Kent. KStJ. Knight Comdr, Order of Dannebrog (Denmark); Knight, Order of Mark Twain (USA). *Recreations:* Kent Cricket XI, 1919-26 (Captain, 1924-25-26). *Heir: s* Hon. Fiennes Neil Wykeham Cornwallis, *qv. Address:* Ashurst Park, Tunbridge Wells, Kent TN3 0RD. *T:* Fordcombe 212; Dundurn House, St Fillans, Perthshire. *Clubs:* Cavalry and Guards, Devonshire, MCC (Pres. 1948); (Patron) Kent County (Maidstone), etc.
See also Major Sir F. William S. Steel, Bt.

CORNWALLIS, Hon. Fiennes Neil Wykeham, OBE 1963; DL; Chairman, Magnet and Planet Building Society, since 1977 (Director, 1975, and Deputy Chairman, 1975-77); *b* 29 June 1921; *s* and *heir* of 2nd Baron Cornwallis, *qv; m* 1st, 1942, Judith Lacy Scott (marr. diss. 1948); one *s* (one *d* decd); 2nd, 1951, Agnes Jean Russell Landale; one *s* three *d. Educ:* Eton. Served War, Coldstream Guards, 1940-44. Farmer, 1945. Pres., British Agricultural Contractors Assoc., 1952-54; Pres., Nat. Assoc. of Agricultural Contractors, 1957-63. Director: Checkers Ltd; Checkers Growers Ltd; County Quality (Promotion and Marketing) Ltd; Northinvest Ltd; Planet Building Soc., 1968 (Chm. 1971-75). DL Kent, 1976. *Recreation:* fishing. *Address:* Ruck Farm, Horsmonden, Tonbridge, Kent. *T:* Brenchley 2267; 25B Queen's Gate Mews, SW7. *T:* 01-589 1167. *Clubs:* Brooks's, Farmers'.

CORNWELL, David John Moore, (John le Carré); writer; *b* 19 Oct. 1931; *s* of Ronald Thomas Archibald Cornwell and Olive (*née* Glassy); *m* 1954, Alison Ann Veronica Sharp (marr. diss. 1971); three *s; m* 1972, Valerie Jane Eustace; one *s. Educ:* Sherborne; Berne Univ.; Lincoln Coll., Oxford. Taught at Eton, 1956-58. Mem. of HM Foreign Service, 1960-64. *Publications:* Call for the Dead, 1961 (filmed as The Deadly Affair, 1967); A Murder of Quality, 1962; The Spy Who Came in from the Cold, 1963; The Looking-Glass War, 1965; A Small Town in Germany, 1968; The Naïve and Sentimental Lover, 1971; Tinker, Tailor, Soldier, Spy, 1974; The Honourable Schoolboy, 1977. *Address:* John Farquharson Ltd, Bell House, Bell Yard, WC2A 2JR.

CORRIE, John Alexander; MP (C) Bute and North Ayr, since Feb. 1974; *b* 29 July 1935; *s* of John Corrie and Helen Brown; *m* 1965, Jean Sandra Hardie; two *d. Educ:* Kirkcudbright Acad.; George Watson's Coll.; Lincoln Agric. Coll., NZ. Farmed in NZ, 1955-59, in Selkirk, 1959-65 and in Kirkcudbright, 1965-. Lectr for British Wool Marketing Bd and Agric. Trng Bd, 1966-74; Mem. Cttee, National Farmers Union, 1964-74 (Vice-Chm. Apprenticeship Council, 1971-74); Nuffield Scholar in Agriculture, 1972. District Officer, Rotary International, 1973-74 (Community service). Nat. Chm., Scottish Young Conservatives, 1964; contested (C) North Lanark, 1964 and Central Ayr, 1966; opposition spokesman on educn in Scotland, Oct. 1974-75; an Opposition Scottish Whip, 1975-76 (resigned over Devolution); Mem. European Parlt, 1975-76 and 1977- (Mem. Cttees of Agriculture, Reg. Develt and Transport). *Recreations:* shooting, fishing, riding, tennis, golf, curling, water ski-ing, bridge. *Address:* Park of Tongland, Kirkcudbright DG6 4NE, Scotland. *T:* Ringford 232; 30 Morpeth Terrace, SW1; Carlung Farm, West Kilbride, Ayrshire. *Clubs:* Beefsteak, Annabel's; Caledonian (Edinburgh).

CORRIE, W(allace) Rodney, CB 1977; Chairman, North West Economic Planning Board, since 1969, and Regional Director (NW), Department of the Environment, since 1971; *b* 25 Nov. 1919; *o c* of late Edward and Mary Ellen Corrie; *m* 1952, Helen Margaret (*née* Morice), *widow* of Flt-Lt A. H. E. Kahn; one *s* one *d. Educ:* Leigh Grammar School; Christ's Coll., Cambridge (BA 1941, MA 1944). Served Royal Signals, 1940-46 (despatches). Entered Civil Service, Min. of Town and Country Planning, 1947; Min. of Housing and Local Govt, 1951; Asst Secretary, 1961; Assistant Under-Secretary of State, DEA, 1969; Under-Secretary: Min. of Housing and Local Govt, 1969; Dept of the Environment, 1970. *Recreations:* fell-walking, exploring byways. *Address:* Windgather, Wainwright Road, Altrincham, Cheshire WA14 4BS.

CORRY; *see* Lowry-Corry, family name of Earl of Belmore.

CORRY, Sir James Perowne Ivo Myles, 3rd Bt, *cr* 1885; a Vice-President of King George's Fund for Sailors; The Royal Alfred Merchant Seamen's Society, and of Royal Merchant Navy School; *b* 10 June 1892; *s* of 2nd Bt and Charlotte, *d* of late J. Collins; *S* father, 1926; *m* 1st, 1921, Molly Irene (marr. diss., 1936), *y d* of late Major O. J. Bell; one *s* two *d;* 2nd, 1946, Cynthia, *widow* of Capt. David Polson, and *o d* of late Capt. F. H. Mahony and Mrs Francis Bliss; one *d. Educ:* Eton; Trinity Coll., Cambridge. *Heir: s* Lt-Comdr William James Corry, RN retd [*b* 1924; *m* 1945, Diana (*née* Lapsley); four *s* two *d*]. *Address:* Dunraven, Fauvic, Jersey, CI. *Clubs:* Lansdowne, Leander.

CORTAZZI, Henry Arthur Hugh, CMG 1969; Deputy Under-Secretary of State, Foreign and Commonwealth Office, since 1975; *b* 2 May 1924; *m* 1956, Elizabeth Esther Montagu; one *s* two *d. Educ:* Sedbergh Sch.; St Andrews and London Univs. Served in RAF, 1943-47; joined Foreign Office, 1949; Third Sec., Singapore, 1950-51; Third/Second Sec., Tokyo, 1951-54; FO, 1954-58; First Sec., Bonn, 1958-60; First Sec., later Head of Chancery, Tokyo, 1961-65; FO, 1965-66; Counsellor (Commercial), Tokyo, 1966-70; Royal Coll. of Defence Studies, 1971-72; Minister (Commercial), Washington, 1972-75. *Publications:* trans. from Japanese, Genji Keita: The Ogre and other stories of the Japanese Salarymen, 1972; The Guardian God of Golf and other humorous stories, 1972. *Recreations:* Japanese studies, the arts including antiques. *Address:* c/o Foreign and Commonwealth Office, SW1; (home) 8 Browning Close, Randolph Avenue, W9 1BW. *T:* 01-286 8904. *Club:* Army and Navy.

CORTLANDT, Lyn, BA; FIAL, FRSA; artist, United States; *d* of late Graf Karl Gustav von Lubieński and late Mrs Elinor Ernestine (Thiel) Cortlandt. *Educ:* Los Angeles: Chouinard and Jepson Art Insts; New York: Art Students' League of NY; Art Sch. of Pratt · Inst.; Columbia Univ. Sch. of Painting and Sculpture; Hans Hofmann Sch. of Fine Arts; China Inst. in America followed by private instruction. Phi Beta Kappa, Phi Kappa Phi. National exhibitions in USA include: Pennsylvania Academy of Fine Arts, National Academy of Design, Brooklyn

Museum and many others; also numerous exhibitions in Europe, India, Japan, S America. Represented in Collections: Metropolitan Museum of Art, New York; Museum of Fine Arts, Boston; Fogg Museum of Art; Art Inst. of Chicago; Brooklyn Museum; Baltimore Museum of Art; Cincinnati Art Museum; Springfield Museum of Fine Arts, Mass; Musée National d'Art Moderne, Paris, France; Stedelijk Museum, Amsterdam, Netherlands; New York Public Library, Boston Public Library; and other important public and private collections. Titles of Major Paintings: Echo Through the Ages; Corridors of Time; Towards Tomorrow; Doorway in the Distance; Voyage to Yesterday; The Force of Destiny; Discovery; Stardust to Stardust; The Earliest Time; The Spark of Life. Toured extensively in Brazil and Argentina by invitation, 1963. Solo exhibitions, Museums in São Paulo, Buenos Aires, etc, 1964-65. Radio: Moderator, Panel Forums on Art Subjects. Lectured on Contemporary Art and on various National Ideologies, in foreign countries. Member: Allied Artists of America; The Painters' and Sculptors' Soc. of NJ; Creative Club; Philadelphia Water Color Club; Internat. Platform Assoc.; Amer. Acad. of Political and Social Science; Acad. of Political Science; Center for the Study of Democratic Institutions; Amer. Judicature Soc.; UN/USA; Nat. Trust for Historic Preservation; Nat. Soc. of Literature and the Arts; Knight of Mark Twain; Comitato Internazionale: Centro Studi e Scambi Internazionali; Accademia Internazionale Leonardo da Vinci; New York Zoological Soc. Adv. Mem., Marquis Biographical Library Soc., etc. Recipient of numerous awards. CSSI Medal of Honor. *Recreations:* reading, music, travel, tennis. *Address:* 1070 Park Avenue, New York, NY 10028, USA. *T:* Atwater 9-6370. *Clubs:* Pen and Brush; Le Cercle d'Or.

CORVEDALE, Viscount; Benedict Alexander Stanley Baldwin; *b* 28 Dec. 1973; *s* and *heir* of 4th Earl Baldwin of Bewdley, *qv*.

CORY, (Charles) Raymond; Chairman, John Cory & Sons Ltd, since 1965; Vice-Chairman, British Transport Docks Board, since 1969 (Member, since 1966); Chairman, South Glamorgan Area Health Authority, since 1974; *b* 20 Oct. 1922; *s* of Charles and Ethel Cory; *m* 1946, Vivienne Mary Roberts, Kelowna, BC, Canada; three *d*. *Educ:* Harrow; Christ Church, Oxford. Served, RNVR, Ord. Seaman to Lieut, 1942-46. Chm., Finance Cttee, Representative Body of the Church in Wales, 1975-; Pres., Cardiff Chamber of Commerce, 1959-60. *Publication:* A Century of Family Shipowning, 1954. *Recreations:* skiing, sailing, country. *Address:* The Old Vicarage, Llanblethian, Cowbridge, South Glamorgan. *T:* Cowbridge 2251. *Club:* Cardiff and County.

CORY, Sir Clinton James Donald, 4th Bt, *cr* 1919; *b* 1 March 1909; 2nd *s* of Sir Donald Cory, 2nd Bt, shipowner of Llandaff, Glam, and Gertrude, *d* of Henry Thomas Box; *S* brother, 1941; *m* 1935, Mary, *o d* of Dr A. Douglas Hunt, Park Grange, Derby; one *s*. *Educ:* Brighton Coll.; abroad. *Recreations:* shooting, fishing, gardening. *Heir: s* Clinton Charles Donald Cory, *b* 13 Sept. 1937. *Address:* 18 Cloisters Road, Letchworth, Herts SG6 3JS. *T:* Letchworth 77206.

CORY, Raymond; see Cory, C. R.

CORY-WRIGHT, Sir Richard (Michael), 4th Bt *cr* 1903; *b* 17 Jan. 1944; *s* of Capt. A. J. J. Cory-Wright (killed in action, 1944), and of Susan Esterel (who *m* 2nd, 1949, late Lt-Col J. E. Gurney, DSO, MC), *d* of Robert Elwes; *S* grandfather, 1969; *m* 1976, Veronica, *o d* of James Bolton. *Educ:* Eton; Birmingham Univ. *Heir:* Michael Cory-Wright [*b* 5 March 1920; *m* 1954, Elizabeth, *d* of late Major J. A. Morrison, DSO]. *Address:* The Old Oak, Water Lane, Oxton, Southwell, Notts NG25 0SH.

CORYTON, Air Chief Marshal Sir (William) Alec, KCB 1950 (CB 1942); KBE 1945; MVO 1919; DFC 1922; RAF retired; *b* 16 Feb. 1895; 3rd *s* of late William Coryton, Pentillie Castle, Cornwall; *m* 1925, Philippa Dorothea, *e d* of late Daniel Hanbury, Castle Malwood, Lyndhurst, *g d* of Sir Thomas Hanbury of La Mortola, Italy; three *d*. *Educ:* Eton; Cambridge. Rifle Brigade; wounded, 1915; RAF 1917; Flying Instructor to the Duke of York, 1919 (MVO); India N-WF 1920 (DFC); Dir of Operations (Oversea), Air Ministry, 1938-41 (CB); AOC Bomber Group, 1942-43; Air Ministry, 1943-44, Asst Chief of the Air Staff (Operations); Air Comdr, Third Tactical Air Force, and Bengal, Burma, SEAC, 1944-45 (KBE); Controller of Supplies (Air) Min. of Supply, 1946-50; Chief Exec. Guided Weapons, Min. of Supply, 1950-51; retired list, 1951. Managing Dir Engine Div., Bristol Aeroplane Co. Ltd 1951; Chm. and Man. Dir Bristol Aero-Engines, Ltd, 1955; Dep. Chm. (Resident in Bristol), Bristol Siddeley Engines Ltd, 1950-64, retired. *Address:* Two Leas, Langton-Matravers, Dorset BH19 3EU. *See also Sir Michael Nall, Bt.*

COSBY, Brig. Noel Robert Charles, CIE 1945; MC; Indian Army, retired; *b* 26 Dec. 1890; *s* of Robert Parkyn Cosby; *m* 1st, 1938, May Margrit Kellersberger (*d* 1942), Berne, Switzerland; no *c*; 2nd, 1960, Margaret Esther Remon Bunting. *Educ:* HMS Worcester, Greenhithe, Kent, for competitive entry to RN. Commissioned Indian Army, Jan. 1915 and posted 5th Royal Gurkhas FF in Egypt; served Turkish attack on Suez Canal, 1915; Gallipoli, May-Dec. 1915 (evacuated wounded, despatches twice, MC); Mesopotamia, 1917-19 (despatches); almost continuous service on NW Frontier, India, regimentally and with Frontier Corps, 1921-45; Mohmand Ops, 1935 (despatches); Waziristan Ops, 1939-40 (wounded, despatches); retired 1945 after four years as Inspector-Gen. Frontier Corps with rank of Brig. *Recreation:* gardening. *Address:* Houmet Herbé, Alderney, CI.

COSGRAVE, Liam; Member of Dail Eireann since 1943; *b* April 1920; *s* of late William T. Cosgrave; *m* 1952, Vera Osborne; two *s* one *d*. *Educ:* Synge Street Christian Brothers; Castleknock College, Dublin; King's Inns. Served in Army during Emergency. Barrister-at-Law, 1943; Senior Counsel, 1958. Chairman Public Accounts Committee, 1945; Parliamentary Secretary to Taoiseach and Minister for Industry and Commerce, 1948; Minister for External Affairs, 1954-57; Leader, Fine Gael Party, 1965-77; Taoiseach (Head of Govt of Ireland), 1973-77. Leader first delegation from Ireland to the UN Assembly. Hon. LLD Duquesne Univ., Pittsburg, Pa, and St John's Univ., Brooklyn, 1956. Knight Grand Cross of Pius IX. Hon. LLD: de Paul Univ., Chicago, 1958; NUI, 1974; Dublin Univ., 1974. *Address:* Leinster House, Kildare Street, Dublin 12.

COSLETT, Air Marshal Sir (Thomas) Norman, KCB 1963 (CB 1960); OBE 1942; CEng, FIMechE; idc; psc; *b* 8 Nov. 1909; *s* of Evan Coslett; *m* 1938, Audrey Garrett. *Educ:* Barry Grammar Sch.; Halton; Cranwell. Dep. Dir of Engineering Plans, Air Ministry, 1954; Senior Technical Staff Officer, HQ Coastal Command, 1957; Commandant, No 1 School of Technical Training, 1958-61; AOC No 24 Group, 1961-63; AOC-in-C, RAF Maintenance Command, 1963-66. Air Cdre, 1957; Air Vice-Marshal, 1962; Air Marshal, 1963; retired, 1966. Dir, Flight Refuelling (Holdings) Ltd, 1966-. *Recreation:* farming. *Address:* c/o A R 8b, Adastral House, Theobald's Road, WC1; 28 Lower Park, Putney Hill, SW15.

COSSLETT, Dr Vernon Ellis, FRS 1972; Reader in Electron Physics, University of Cambridge, 1965-75, now Emeritus; Fellow of Corpus Christi College, Cambridge, since 1963; *b* 16 June 1908; *s* of Edgar William Cosslett and Anne Cosslett (*née* Williams); *m* 1st, 1936, Rosemary Wilson (marr. diss. 1940); 2nd, 1940, Anna Joanna Wischin (*d* 1969); one *s* one *d*. *Educ:* Cirencester Grammar Sch.; Bristol Univ. BSc Bristol 1929; PhD Bristol 1932; MSc London 1939; ScD Cambridge 1963. Research at: Bristol Univ., 1929-30; Kaiser-Wilhelm Institut, Berlin, 1930-31; University Coll., London, 1931-32; Research Fellow, Bristol Univ., 1932-35; Lectr in Science, Faraday House, London, 1935-39; Research (part-time), Birkbeck Coll., London, 1936-39; Keddey-Fletcher-Warr Research Fellow of London Univ. (at Oxford), 1939-41; Lectr in Physics, Electrical Laboratory, Oxford Univ., 1941-46; ICI Fellow, Cavendish Laboratory, Cambridge, 1946-49; Lectr in Physics, Univ. of Cambridge, 1949-65. Past Pres., Royal Microscopical Soc.; Past Vice-Pres., Inst. of Physics; Past Pres., Assoc. of Univ. Teachers. Hon. DSc Tübingen, 1963; Hon. MD Gothenburg, 1974. *Publications:* Introduction to Electron Optics, 1946 (1951); Practical Electron Microscopy, 1951; X-ray Microscopy (with W. C. Nixon), 1960; Modern Microscopy, 1966; many scientific papers. *Recreations:* gardening, mountain walking, listening to music. *Address:* 31 Comberton Road, Barton, Cambridge. *T:* Comberton 2428.

COSTAIN, Albert Percy; MP (C) Folkestone and Hythe since 1959; *b* 5 July 1910; *s* of William Percy Costain and Maud May Smith; *m* 1933, Joan Mary, *d* of John William Whiter; one *s* one *d*. *Educ:* King James, Knaresborough; Coll. of Estate Management. Production Dir on formation of Richard Costain Ltd, 1933; Chm., Richard Costain Ltd, 1966-69; Chm., Pre-stressed Concrete Development Group, 1952. London Treasurer, National Children's Home, 1950-60. FIOB Author of Home Safety Act, 1961; Parliamentary Private Secretary: to Minister of Public Bldg and Works, 1962-64; to Minister of Technology, 1970; to Chancellor of Duchy of Lancaster, 1970-72; to Sec. of State for the Environment, 1972-74. Member: Cttee of Public Accts, 1961-64, 1974-; Estimates Cttee, 1960-61, 1965-70, 1974-; Estimates Sub-Cttee on Building and Natural Resources, 1965-; Chairmen's Panel, House of Commons, 1975-. Joint Vice-Chm., Conservative Party Transport Cttee, 1964. Jt Sec., Conservative Housing and Local Govt Cttee, 1964-65, Jt

Vice-Chm., 1965-66; All Party Tourists and Resorts Cttee: Sec., 1964-66; Vice-Chm., 1966-69; Chm., 1970-71; Vice-Chm., Conservative Party Arts, Public Building and Works Cttee, 1965-70; Chm., Cons. Party Horticulture Cttee, 1976. *Recreations:* sailing, golf. *Address:* Inwarren, Kingswood, Surrey. *T:* Mogador 2443; 2 Albion Villas, Folkestone, Kent CT20 1RP. *Clubs:* Carlton; Walton Heath Golf.

COSTAIN, Noel Leslie, OBE 1964; Director of Works, University of Sheffield, since 1964; *b* 11 Jan. 1914; *s* of George Wesley Costain and Minnie Grace Pinson; *m* 1945, Marie José Elizabeth (*née* Bishton); two *d*. *Educ:* King Edward's Sch., Five Ways, Birmingham; Univ. of Birmingham (BSc). CEng, MICE, FINucE. Engineer with Sir R. MacAlpine & Sons, 1937-38; Epsom and Ewell BC, 1939; Air Min., Directorate-Gen. of Works; Section Officer, Orkneys and Shetlands, 1940-43; Prin. Works Officer, Sierra Leone, 1944-46; Superintending Engr, Air Ministry, 1946-51; RAF Airfield Construction Br.: Cmdg 5352 Wing, Germany, and OC, RAF Church Lawford, 1951-54; Superintending Engr, Works Area, Bristol, 1954-58; Chief Engr, MEAF, 1958-60; Chief Resident Engr, BMEWS, Fylingdales, 1960-63. Vice-Chm., Yorkshire Univs Air Squadron Cttee. Mem. Council, Instn of Nuclear Engineers, 1965; Vice-Pres., 1969; President, 1972-76. Governor, Wm Rhodes Sch., Chesterfield. *Recreations:* travel, gardening. *Address:* Tapton Grange, Tapton, Chesterfield S43 1QQ. *T:* Chesterfield 34332. *Club:* International Sporting.

COSTANZI, Edwin J. B.; *see* Borg-Costanzi.

COSTAR, Sir Norman (Edgar), KCMG 1963 (CMG 1953); *b* 18 May 1909. *Educ:* Battersea Grammar School; Jesus Coll., Cambridge. Asst Principal, Colonial Office, 1932; Private Sec. to Permanent Under Sec., Dominions Office, 1935; served in UK High Commissioner's Offices, Australia, 1937-39, New Zealand, 1945-47. Principal, 1938; Asst Sec., 1946. Dep. High Commissioner, Ceylon, 1953-57; Asst Under-Sec., Commonwealth Relations Office, 1958-60; Dep. High Commissioner in Australia, 1960-62; High Commissioner: Trinidad and Tobago, 1962-66; Cyprus, 1967-69. Adjudicator, Immigration Appeals, 1970-. *Club:* United Oxford & Cambridge University.

COSTELLO, Gordon John; Chief Accountant of the Bank of England, since 1975; *b* 29 March 1921; *s* of late Ernest James Costello and Hilda May Costello; *m* 1946, Joan Lilian Moore; two *s* one *d*. *Educ:* Varndean Sch. Served War, 1939-45 (RA). Bank of England, 1946; worked in various Departments; Asst Chief Accountant, 1964; Asst Sec., 1965; Dep. Sec., 1968; Dep. Chief Cashier, 1970. *Recreations:* music, travel, walking, tennis. *Address:* 26 Peacock Lane, Brighton, Sussex BN1 6WA. *T:* Brighton 552344.

COSTIGAN, Rev. John, SJ; MA; Superior, St Aloysius, Oxford, since 1971; *b* Feb. 1916. *Educ:* Stonyhurst; Oxford. Joined the Soc. of Jesus, 1934; ordained, 1949. Rector of: Beaumont Coll., 1958-64; St Aloysius' Coll., Glasgow, 1964-70. *Address:* St Aloysius, 25 Woodstock Road, Oxford OX2 6HA.

COSTLEY-WHITE, Cyril Grove, CMG 1953; Historical Section, India Office Library and Records, since 1968; *b* 30 Oct. 1913; *s* of late Very Rev. H. Costley-White, DD; *m* 1st, 1938, Elizabeth Delmore (marr. diss. 1955); two *s* one *d*; 2nd, 1955, Elisabeth Marianne, *d* of late Rev. Noel Braithwaite Chard and of late Lady Janet Chard; two *s*. *Educ:* Eton; Balliol Coll., Oxford. Joined Colonial Office (after competitive examination), 1937; transferred, 1940, to Dominions Office. Served on Staff of UK High Commissioner in Canada, 1941-44, and New Zealand, 1944-46; Deputy United Kingdom High Commissioner in Ceylon, 1949-50; Asst Sec., CO (formerly CRO), 1951-68; retd 1968 and re-employed as a disestablished officer. *Address:* 129a Ashley Gardens, SW1. *T:* 01-828 8159.

COTES, Peter, (Sydney Arthur Boulting); author, lecturer, play producer, film and television director; *e s* of Arthur Boulting and Rose Bennett; *m* 1st, 1938, Myfanwy Jones (marr. diss.); 2nd, 1948, Joan Miller. *Educ:* Taplow; Italia Conti and privately. Was for some years an actor; made theatrical debut, Portsmouth Hippodrome, in the arms of Vesta Tilley. Formed own independent play-producing co. with Hon. James Smith, 1949, presented Rocket to the Moon, St Martin's Theatre, and subsequently produced, in association with Arts Council of Great Britain, notable seasons in Manchester and at Embassy and Lyric Theatres, Hammersmith. Founded: New Lindsey, 1946; New Boltons, 1951. West-End Productions include: Pick Up Girl, 1946; The Animal Kingdom, 1947; The Master Builder, 1948; Miss Julie, 1949; Come Back, Little Sheba, 1951; The Father, 1951; The Biggest Thief in Town, 1951; The Mousetrap, 1952; The Man, 1952; A Pin to see the Peepshow, Broadway, 1953; Happy Holiday, 1954; Hot Summer Night, 1958; Epitaph for George Dillon (Holland), 1959; The Rope Dancers, 1959; Girl on the Highway, 1960; A Loss of Roses, 1962; The Odd Ones, 1963; Hidden Stranger, Broadway, 1963; What Goes Up...!, 1963; So Wise, So Young, 1964; Paint Myself Black, 1965; The Impossible Years, 1966; Staring at the Sun, 1968; Janie Jackson, 1968; The Old Ladies, 1969; Look, No Hands!, 1971. Films: The Right Person; Two Letters; Jane Clegg; Waterfront; The Young and the Guilty; has prod. and adapted numerous plays for BBC Television and ITV; was Sen. Drama Dir, AR-TV, 1955-58; producing stage plays and films, 1959-60; Supervising Producer of Drama Channel 7, Melbourne, 1961; produced and adapted plays for Anglia TV, 1964; produced first TV series of P. G. Wodehouse short stories, on BBC; wrote George Robey centenary TV Tribute, BBC Omnibus series, 1969; wrote and dir. in One Pair of Eyes series, BBC TV, 1970; has written and narrated many productions for radio incl. Back into the Light, The Prime Minister of Mirth, Mervyn Peake. FRSA; Member: Theatrical Managers' Assoc.; Medico-Legal Soc.; Our Society; Guild of Drama Adjudicators. *Publications:* No Star Nonsense, 1949; The Little Fellow, 1951; A Handbook of Amateur Theatre, 1957; George Robey, 1972; The Trial of Elvira Barney, 1976; Circus, 1976; Origin of a Thriller, 1977; JP, 1977. *Recreations:* walking, writing letters, criminology. *Address:* 27 Cathcart Road, SW10. *T:* 01-352 4252. *Club:* Savage.

COTILL, John Atrill T.; *see* Templeton-Cotill.

COTRUBAS, Ileana, (Mme Manfred Ramin); opera singer; *b* Rumania, *d* of Vasile and Maria Cotrubas; *m* 1972, Manfred Ramin. *Educ:* Conservatorul Ciprian Porumbescu, Bucharest. Opera and concert engagements all over Europe, N America and Japan. Permanent guest at Royal Opera House, Covent Garden; Member, Vienna State Opera; also frequently sings in Scala, Milan, Munich, Berlin, Paris, Chicago. Main operatic roles: Susanna, Pamina, Gilda, Traviata, Manon, Tatyana, Mimi, Melisande. Has made numerous recordings. *Address:* c/o Royal Opera House, Covent Garden, WC2.

COTT, Hugh Bamford, ScD Cantab, DSc Glasgow; FRPS, FZS; Fellow of Selwyn College, Cambridge, since 1945; *b* 6 July 1900; *s* of late Rev. A. M. Cott, Ashby Magna; *m* 1928, Joyce Radford; one *s* one *d*. *Educ:* Rugby Sch.; RMC, Sandhurst; Selwyn Coll., Cambridge. Joined 1st Bn the Leics Regt; served in Ireland, 1919-21. 2nd class, Nat. Sciences Tripos, Pt I, 1925. Carried out zoological expeditions to SE Brazil, 1923; Lower Amazon, 1925-26; Zoological Society's Expedition to the Zambesi, 1927, Canary Islands, 1931, Uganda, 1952, Zululand, 1956, Central Africa, 1957; Lecturer in Hygiene, Bristol Univ., 1928-32; Asst and Lecturer in Zoology, Glasgow Univ., 1932-38; Strickland Curator and Lectr in the University of Cambridge, 1938-67; Lectr, 1945-67, and Dean, 1966-67, of Selwyn Coll., Cambridge. Founder Member, Soc. Wildlife Artists. War of 1939-45: Mem. Advisory Cttee on Camouflage, 1939-40; Capt. and Major (RE) MEF; served Western Desert, 1941 (despatches); Chief Instructor, Middle East Camouflage Sch., 1941-43; GSO 2 (Cam) Mountain Warfare Trg Centre, 1943-44. *Publications:* Adaptive Coloration in Animals, 1940; Zoological Photography in Practice, 1956; Uganda in Black and White, 1959; Looking at Animals: a zoologist in Africa, 1975; various scientific papers on adaptive coloration, feeding habits of tree frogs, camouflage, edibility of birds, ecology of crocodiles, etc published in Trans and Proc. of Zool Soc. London, Proc. R. Ent. Soc. London, Photographic Jl, Engineers' Jl etc. *Recreations:* travel, pen drawing, photography. *Address:* Denebanks, Netherbury, Bridport, Dorset. *T:* Netherbury 348.

COTTENHAM, 8th Earl of, *cr* 1850; **Kenelm Charles Everard Digby Pepys;** Bt 1784 and 1801; Baron Cottenham, 1836; Viscount Crowhurst, 1850; *b* 27 Nov. 1948; *s* of 7th Earl of Cottenham and Lady Angela Isabel Nellie Nevill, *d* of 4th Marquess of Abergavenny; *S* father, 1968; *m* 1975, Sarah, *d* of Captain S. Lombard-Hobson, CVO, OBE, RN. *Educ:* Eton. *Heir:* kinsman Charles Donald Leslie Pepys [*b* 25 Sept. 1909; *g g s* of 1st Earl of Cottenham; *m* 1941, Hon. Pamela Sophia Nadine Stonor, *d* of 5th Baron Camoys]. *See also Baron McGowan*.

COTTER, Lt-Col Sir Delaval James Alfred, 6th Bt, *cr* 1763; DSO 1944; late 13th/18th Royal Hussars; *b* 29 April 1911; *s* of 5th Bt and Ethel Lucy (*d* 1956), *d* of Alfred Wheeler; *S* father, 1924; *m* 1st, 1943, Roma (marr. diss., 1949), *widow* of Sqdn Ldr K. A. K. MacEwen and *o d* of late Adrian Rome, Dalswinton Lodge, Salisbury, SR; two *d*; 2nd, 1952, Mrs Eveline Mary Paterson, *widow* of Lieut-Col J. F. Paterson, OBE, and *d* of late E. J. Mardon, ICS (retired). *Educ:* Malvern Coll; RMC, Sandhurst.

Served War of 1939-45 (DSO); retired, 1959. JP Wilts, 1962-63. *Heir: n* Patrick Laurence Delaval Cotter [*b* 21 Nov. 1941; *m* 1967, Janet, *d* of George Potter, Barnstaple; one *s* two *d*]. *Address:* Green Lines, 1 Werne Courtney, Blandford Forum, Dorset. *Club:* Cavalry and Guards.

COTTERELL, Geoffrey; author; *b* 24 Nov. 1919; *yr s* of late Graham Cotterell and of Millicent (*née* Crews). *Educ:* Bishops Stortford College. Served War of 1939-45, Royal Artillery, 1940-46. *Publications:* Then a Soldier, 1944; This is the Way, 1947; Randle in Springtime, 1949; Strait and Narrow, 1950; Westward the Sun, 1952 (repr. 1973); The Strange Enchantment, 1956 (repr. 1973); Tea at Shadow Creek, 1958; Tiara Tahiti, 1960 (filmed 1962, screenplay with Ivan Foxwell); Go, said the bird, 1966; Bowers of Innocence, 1970; Amsterdam, the life of a city, 1972. *Recreation:* golf. *Address:* 2 Fulbourne House, Blackwater Road, Eastbourne, Sussex. *Clubs:* Savage, Cooden Beach Golf.

COTTERELL, Lt-Col Sir Richard (Charles Geers), 5th Bt, *cr* 1805; CBE 1965; Lord Lieutenant and Custos Rotulorum for County of Hereford, 1945-57; a Forestry Commissioner (unpaid), 1945-64; *b* 1 June 1907; *s* of Sir J. R. G. Cotterell, 4th Bt, and Lady Evelyn Amy Gordon Lennox, *e d* of 7th Duke of Richmond and Gordon; *S* father, 1937; *m* 1st, 1930, Lady Lettice Lygon (marr. diss. 1958), *e d* of 7th Earl Beauchamp; two *s* two *d*; 2nd, 1958, Patricia Lady Sherwood, *d* of 1st Viscount Camrose. *Educ:* Eton; Sandhurst. Entered Royal Horse Guards, 1927; retd on to Reserve of Officers, 1932; entered Shropshire Yeo., 1935; Major, 1937; commanded 76th Shropshire Yeomanry Medium Regt RA in Middle East and Italy, 1943-45 (despatches). Chm., Wye River Authority, 1968-74. JP 1938. *Heir: s* John Henry Geers Cotterell [*b* 8 May 1935; *m* 1959, Vanda Alexandra Clare Bridgewater; three *s* one *d*]. *Address:* Garnons, Hereford. *T:* Bridge Sollers 232. *Club:* White's.
    See also Viscount Camrose, Baron Chetwode, Sir Terence Falkiner, C. E. A. Hambro, Baron Sinclair.

COTTERILL, Kenneth William, CMG 1976; Deputy Head, Export Credits Guarantee Department; *b* 5 June 1921; *s* of William and Ada May Cotterill; *m* 1948, Janet Hilda Cox; one *d*. *Educ:* Sutton County Sch.; London School of Economics, BSc (Econ). Served War in Royal Navy, 1941-46. After the war, joined ECGD; Principal, 1956; Asst Sec., 1966; Under Sec., 1970; Dep. Head of Dept, 1976. *Recreations:* reading, walking, gardening. *Address:* 15 Minster Drive, Croydon CR0 5UP. *T:* 01-681 670.

COTTESLOE, 4th Baron (UK) *cr* 1874; **John Walgrave Halford Fremantle,** GBE 1960; TD; Bt 1821; Baron of Austrian Empire, *cr* 1816; *b* 2 March 1900; *s* of 3rd Baron Cottesloe, CB and Florence (*d* 1956), *d* of Thomas Tapling; *S* father 1956; *m* 1st, 1926, Lady Elizabeth Harris (marr. diss., 1945), *o d* of 5th Earl of Malmesbury; one *s* one *d*; 2nd, 1959, Gloria Jean Irene Dunn; one *s* two *d*. *Educ:* Eton; Trinity Coll., Cambridge. BA (Hons) Mechanical Sciences 1921; MA 1924. Served as OC 251 (Bucks) AA Battery RA (TA), 1938-39; GSO 1 att. 2nd Armoured Division, 1940; Senior Military Liaison Officer to Regional Commissioner, NE Region, 1940-41; GSO 1 (Technical) AA Command, 1941-42; Commanding Officer, 20 LAA Regt RA, 1942-44; GSO 1 (Radar) War Office, 1944-45. Mem. LCC, 1945-55. Chairman: Thomas Tapling & Co. Ltd; Yiewsley Engineering Co. Ltd; Vice-Chm., PLA, 1956-67. Chairman: Tate Gallery, 1959-60; Arts Council of Gt Britain, 1960-65; South Bank Theatre Bd (from inception), 1962-; Adv. Council and Reviewing Cttee on Export of Works of Art, 1954-72; Heritage in Danger, 1973-; Royal Postgrad. Med. Sch., 1949-58 (Fellow); NW Met. Reg. Hosp. Bd, 1953-60; Hammersmith and St Mark's Hospital, 1968-74; Northwick Park Hosp. Adv. Cttee, 1970-74; a Governor, King Edward's Hosp. Fund for London. Chairman: British Postgraduate Medical Fedn, 1958-72; Nat. Rifle Assoc., 1960-72; Vice-Chm., City Parochial Foundn; Pres., Hospital Saving Assoc., 1973-; Hon. Sec. Amateur Rowing Assoc., 1932-46; a Steward of Henley Royal Regatta; Pres., Leander, 1957-62. Fomer DL County of London (later Greater London). *Recreations:* rowed in winning crews in Oxford and Cambridge Boat Race, 1921 and 1922 and in Grand Challenge Cup, Henley, 1922; Captain of English VIII at Bisley and has shot in English VIII on 37 occasions and won Match Rifle Championship six times, with many other first prizes for long-range shooting. *Heir: s* Comdr Hon. John Tapling Fremantle, (RN retd) [*b* 22 Jan. 1927; *m* 1958, Elizabeth Ann, *d* of Lieut-Col Henry Shelley Barker, Walcote House, Walcote, Rugby; one *s* two *d*]. *Address:* 21 Lyndhurst Road, Hampstead, NW3 5NX. *T:* 01-435 6626; Folly, Winsford Hill, Somerset. *Clubs:* Travellers', Leander.

COTTON, Bernard Edward, CBE 1976; Chairman and Chief Executive, Samuel Osborn & Co. Ltd, since 1969; *b* 8 Oct. 1920; *s* of Hugh Harry Cotton and Alice Cotton; *m* 1944, Stephanie Anne, *d* of Rev. A. E. and Mrs Furnival; three *s*. *Educ:* Sheffield City Grammar Sch.; Sheffield Univ. Served Army, 1939-45, latterly as Lieut, Worcs Yeomanry (53rd Airlanding Light Regt RA). Joined Round Oak Steelworks, Brierley Hill, 1949, Sales Man., 1954-57; Gen. Man., Samuel Osborn (Canada) Ltd, Montreal, 1957-63; Sales Dir, Samuel Osborn & Co. Ltd, 1963-69, Man. Dir 1969. Chm., Yorks and Humberside Reg. Econ. Planning Council, 1970-; Pres., Yorks and Humberside Develt Assoc., 1973-. Chm., BIM Working Party on Employee Participation, 1975. Vice-Chm. Governors, Sheffield Polytechnic; Mem. Council, Sheffield Univ. Searcher, Cutlers' Co. in Hallamshire. *Recreations:* gardening and other quiet pursuits. *Address:* 2 Moorbank Road, Sheffield S10 5TR. *T:* Sheffield 303082; Flat No 1, The Manor House, Lympstone, Devon. *T:* Exmouth 5120. *Clubs:* Cavalry and Guards; The Club (Sheffield).

COTTON, Christopher P.; *see* Powell-Cotton.

COTTON, Prof. H., MBE 1918; DSc; *b* 17 June 1889; *s* of John Thomas and Sophia Cotton; *m* 1915, Lilian Hall; one *s*. *Educ:* Manchester Univ., resident at Hulme Hall. Asst Lecturer in Electrical Engineering and in Physics at Technical Coll., Huddersfield; Lecturer in Electrical Engineering at Technical Sch., St Helens; Lecturer at University Coll., Nottingham; Emeritus Prof. of Electrical Engineering at Nottingham Univ.; retired 1954; three years in France with the Meteorological Section RE during the war; practical training in Electrical Engineering at the Hanley Power Station and with the Westinghouse Electrical Co. Ltd. *Publications:* Electricity Applied to Mining; Mining Electrical Engineering; Design of Electrical Machinery; Advanced Electrical Technology; Electrical Transmission and Distribution; Electric Discharge Lamps; Principles of Illumination; Applied Electricity; Vector and Phasor Analysis of Electric Fields and Circuits; Basic Electrotechnology; contributor to Journal of Institution of Electrical Engineers, World Power, Electrician, Electrical Review and Electrical Times. *Recreation:* music. *Address:* St George's Lodge, Cherry Tree Road, Woodbridge, Suffolk. *T:* 3081.

COTTON, Henry; *see* Cotton, T. H.

COTTON, John Anthony; His Honour Judge Cotton; a Circuit Judge, since 1973; *b* 6 March 1926; *s* of Frederick Thomas Hooley Cotton and Catherine Mary Cotton; *m* 1960, Johanna Aritia van Lookeren Campagne; three *s* two *d*. *Educ:* Stonyhurst Coll.; Lincoln Coll., Oxford. Called to the Bar, Middle Temple, 1949; Dep. Chm., W Riding of Yorks QS, 1967-71; Recorder of Halifax, 1971; a Recorder and Hon. Recorder of Halifax, 1972-73. *Recreation:* golf. *Address:* 81 Lyndhurst Road, Sheffield S11 9BJ. *T:* Sheffield 585569.

COTTON, Sir John Richard, KCMG 1969 (CMG 1959); OBE 1947; retired from HM Diplomatic Service, 1969; Adjudicator, Immigration Appeals; *b* 22 Jan. 1909; *s* of late J. J. Cotton, ICS, and late Gigia Ricciardi Arlotta; *m* 1937, Mary Bridget Connors, Stradbally, County Waterford, Ireland; three *s*. *Educ:* Wellington Coll.; RMC, Sandhurst (prize Cadet and King's India Cadet). Commissioned 1929; 8th King George's Own Light Cavalry (IA), 1930-34; transferred to Indian Political Service, 1934; served in: Aden, Abyssinia (Attaché HM Legation, 1935), Persian Gulf, Rajputana, Hyderabad, Kathiawar, Baroda, New Delhi (Dep. Sec. Political Dept). Transferred to HM Foreign Service, 1947; served in Karachi (First Sec.), 1947-48, Foreign Office, 1949-51, Madrid (Counsellor [Commercial] HM Embassy), 1951-54; Consul-Gen., Brazzaville, 1954-55, Leopoldville, 1955-57; Counsellor (Commercial), HM Embassy, Brussels, 1957-62. Consul-Gen., São Paulo, Brazil, 1962-65; Ambassador to Congo Republic (Kinshasa), and to Burundi, 1965-69. *Recreations:* golf, photography. *Address:* Lansing House, Hartley Wintney, Hants. *T:* Hartley Wintney 2681. *Club:* Army and Navy.

COTTON, Leonard Thomas, MCh; FRCS; Surgeon, King's College Hospital, since 1957; Surgeon, Queen Victoria Hospital, East Grinstead, and St Luke's Nursing Home for the Clergy; Vice Dean, King's College Hospital Medical School, 1976, Dean Elect 1977; *b* 5 Dec. 1922; *s* of Edward Cotton and Elizabeth (*née* Webb); *m* 1946, Frances Joanna Bryan; one *s* two *d*. *Educ:* King's College Sch., Wimbledon; Oriel Coll., Oxford; King's Coll. Hospital. MRCS, LRCP 1946; BM, BCh Oxon 1946; FRCS 1950; MCh Oxon 1957. House Surgeon, King's College Hospital, 1946; Resident Surgical Officer, Royal Waterloo Hospital, 1947; Resident Surgical Officer, Weymouth and

District Hospital, 1948; National Service, Surgical Specialist RAMC, 1949-51; Senior Registrar and Registrar, King's College Hospital, 1951-57; Surgical Tutor, King's Coll. Hospital Medical Sch., 1957-65. FRSM; Member: Surgical Research Soc., Assoc. of Surgeons; Vascular Surgical Soc.; Ct of Examiners, RCS. Hunterian Prof., RCS. *Publications:* (ed) Hey Groves' Synopsis of Surgery; co-author, short text-book of Surgery; contributions to medical journals. *Recreations:* gardening, reading, squash. *Address:* 126 College Road, SE19. *T:* 01-670 7156; Private Wing, King's College Hospital, Denmark Hill, SE5. *T:* 01-274 8670; 22 Harley Street, W1. *T:* 01-637 0491.

COTTON, Michael James, ARIBA, MRTPI; Deputy Chairman and Managing Director, Millbank Technical Services and Deputy Secretary, Crown Agents, since 1974; Chairman, Millbank Technical Services (Ordnance), since 1975; *b* 22 Dec. 1920; *s* of Clifford Cotton and Mildred L. (*née* Palmer); *m* 1945, Dorsey Jane (*née* Thomas); one *d.* *Educ:* School of Architecture and Dept of Civic Design, Liverpool University. War Service, 1940-46, Royal Marines 42 Commando (Captain). Asst Town Planner, Staffs CC, 1949-50; Architect Planner, Stevenage Development Corp., 1950-52; Asst Town Planner, Fedn of Malaya, 1952-54; Architect and Sen. Architect, Public Works Dept, Singapore, 1954-59; Sen. Architect, Directorate of Works, WO, 1959-64; Chm. Joint Post Office/MPBW R&D Group, 1964-66; Chief Architect, Scottish Office, 1966-67; Asst Dir Overseas Services, MPBW, 1967-69; Dir of Defence Services II, MPBW, later DoE, 1969-72; Dir, Home Estate Management, DoE, 1972-74. *Recreation:* golf. *Address:* Applecroft, Stoatley Rise, Haslemere, Surrey. *T:* Haslemere 51823. *Club:* Arts.

COTTON, (Thomas) Henry, MBE 1946; late Flight Lieutenant RAFVR (invalided, 1943); golfer; golf manager, Sotogrande Second Course, since 1975; Professional Golf Correspondent of Golf Illustrated; Director and Founder Golf Foundation for development of youthful golfers; Golf Course Architect: Abridge, Felixstowe, Canons Brook, Ampfield, Megève and Deauville (France), Penina, Val de Lobo and Golf de Monte Gorda, Algarve (Portugal), Castle Eden Golf Club, Eaglescliffe, Stirling, Gourock, Windmill Hill, Bletchley, Sene Valley, Folkestone, Campo de Lagoa, Madeira, Ely, Cambs, etc; *b* Holmes Chapel, Cheshire, 26 Jan. 1907; *m* 1939, Mrs Maria Isabel Estanguet Moss. *Educ:* Alleyn's Sch. Played in first Boys' Golf Championship, 1921; asst at Fulwell, 1924; Rye, 1925; Cannes, 1926; professional Langley Park, 1927; Waterloo, Brussels, 1933; Ashridge, 1936; won Kent Professional Championship, 1926-27-28-29-30; Belgian Open, 1930, 1934, 1938; Dunlop Tournament, 1931, 1932, 1953, runner-up, 1959; News of the World Tournament, 1932 and 1939; British Open, 1934, 1937 and 1948 (1934 was First British win for 11 years); Italian Open, 1936; German Open, 1937-38-39; Silver King Tournament, 1937; Czechoslovak Open, 1937-38; Harry Vardon Trophy, 1938; Daily Mail £2000 Tournament, 1939; Penfold Tournament, 1939 and 1954; News Chronicle Tournament, 1945; Star Tournament, 1946; Prof. Golfers' Assoc. Match Play Champion, 1946; French Open Champion, 1946 and 1947; Vichy Open Champion, 1946; represented Great Britain v America, 1929, 1937, 1947, 1953; Ryder Cup Team Capt., 1939, 1947 and 1953; Spalding Tournament, 1947; visited USA in 1929, 1931, 1947, 1948, 1956 and 1957; visited Argentine 1929, 1948, 1949 and 1950; lowest record round in Open Championships (65). Collected over £70,000 for Red Cross and other war charities in 130 matches organised by himself. Golf Manager, Penina Golf Hotel, Portugal, 1968-75. Hon. Life Mem., Professional Golf Assoc. Vice-Pres., National Golf Clubs Advisory Bureau. *Publications:* Golf, 1932; This Game of Golf, 1948; My Swing, 1952; (Henry Cotton's) My Golfing Album, 1960; Henry Cotton Says, 1962; Studying the Golf Game, 1964; The Picture World of Golf, 1965; Golf in the British Isles, 1969; A History of Golf, 1973. *Recreations:* painting, motoring, photography. *Address:* Club de Golf, Sotogrande, Cadiz, Spain.

COTTON, William Frederick, OBE 1976; JP; Controller, BBC 1, since 1977; *b* 23 April 1928; *s* of William Edward (Billy) Cotton and Mabel Hope; *m* 1st, 1950, Bernadine Maud (*née* Sinclair); three *d*; 2nd, 1965, Ann Corfield (*née* Bucknall); one step *d.* *Educ:* Ardingly College. Jt Man. Dir, Michael Reine Music Co., 1952-56; BBC-TV: Producer, Light Entertainment Dept, 1956-62; Asst Head of Light Entertainment, 1962-67; Head of Variety, 1967-70; Head of Light Entertainment Gp, 1970-77. JP Richmond, 1976. *Recreations:* squash, golf, motor racing. *Address:* 19 Model Cottages, East Sheen, SW14 7PH. *T:* 01-878 2430.

COTTON, STAPLETON-, family name of **Viscount Combermere.**

COTTRELL, Sir Alan (Howard), Kt 1971; FRS 1955; Master of Jesus College, Cambridge, since 1974; Vice-Chancellor, University of Cambridge, since 1977; *b* 17 July 1919; *s* of Albert and Elizabeth Cottrell; *m* 1944, Jean Elizabeth Harber; one *s.* *Educ:* Moseley Grammar Sch.; University of Birmingham. BSc 1939; PhD 1942. Lectr in Metallurgy, University of Birmingham, 1943-49; Prof. of Physical Metallurgy, University of Birmingham, 1949-55; retired March 1955. Deputy Head of Metallurgy Division, Atomic Energy Research Establishment, Harwell, Berks, 1955-58; Goldsmiths' Prof. of Metallurgy, Cambridge Univ., 1958-65; Dep. Chief Scientific Adviser (Studies), Min. of Defence, 1965-67, Chief Adviser, 1967; Dep. Chief Scientific Advr to HM Govt, 1968-71, Chief Scientific Advr, 1971-74. Part-time Mem., UKAEA, 1962-65; Member: Adv. Council on Scientific Policy, 1963-64; Central Adv. Council for Science and Technology, 1967-; Exec. Cttee, British Council, 1974-; Adv. Council, Science Policy Foundn, 1976-. A Vice-Pres., Royal Society, 1964, 1976, 1977. Fellow Royal Swedish Academy of Sciences; Hon. Fellow, Christ's Coll., Cambridge, 1970 (Fellow, 1958-70). Foreign Hon. Mem., American Academy of Arts and Sciences, 1960; Foreign Associate, Nat. Acad. of Sciences, USA, 1972; Hon. Mem., Amer. Soc. for Metals, 1972 (Fellow 1975); Foreign Associate, Nat. Acad. of Engrng, USA, 1976; Hon. Mem., Metals Soc., 1977. Hon. DSc: Columbia Univ., 1965; Newcastle Univ., 1967; Liverpool Univ., 1969; Manchester, 1970; Warwick, 1971; Sussex, 1972; Bath, 1973; Strathclyde, 1975; Cranfield, 1975; Aston, 1975. Rosenhain Medallist of the Inst. of Metals; Hughes Medal, 1961, Rumford Medal, 1974, Royal Society; Inst. of Metals (Platinum) Medal, 1965; Réaumur Medal, Société Française de Métallurgie, 1964; James Alfred Ewing Medal, ICE, 1967; Holweck Medal, Société Française de Physique, 1969; Albert Sauveur Achievement Award, Amer. Soc. for Metals, 1969; James Douglas Gold Medal, Amer. Inst. of Mining, Metallurgical and Petroleum Engrs, 1974; Harvey Science Prize, Technion Israel Inst., 1974; Acta Metallurgica Gold Medal, 1976; Guthrie Medal and Prize, Inst. of Physics, 1977. *Publications:* Theoretical Structural Metallurgy, 1948, 2nd edn 1955; Dislocations and Plastic Flow in Crystals, 1953; The Mechanical Properties of Matter, 1964; Theory of Crystal Dislocations, 1964; An Introduction to Metallurgy, 1967; Portrait of Nature, 1975; scientific papers to various learned journals. *Recreation:* music. *Address:* The Master's Lodge, Jesus College, Cambridge. *T:* Cambridge 53310. *Club:* Athenæum.

COTTRELL, Thomas Edward; Managing Director and Chief Executive Officer, Texaco Ltd, since 1973; *b* 30 July 1920; *s* of O. P. Cottrell and Alva T. Cottrell; *m* 1942, Laura; four *d.* *Educ:* Colgate Univ., Hamilton, NY. BA Philosophy and Econs. Sales Management positions with Texaco Inc. in New England, the South, San Francisco and New York, 1946-69; Dep. Man. Dir, Regent Oil Co. Ltd, UK, 1969; Vice-Pres., Texaco Europe Ltd, Brussels, 1969-70; Gen. Man., International Sales, Texaco Inc., US, 1970-71; Asst to Sen. Vice-Pres. Sales Exec. Staff, 1971-73. *Recreations:* golf, fishing. *Address:* Flat 12, Hans Court, Hans Road, SW3 1RY. *T:* 01-584 7608. *Clubs:* Roehampton; Wentworth Golf.

COTTS, Sir Crichton Mitchell; *see* Cotts, Sir R. C. M.

COTTS, Sir (Robert) Crichton Mitchell, 3rd Bt, *cr* 1921; *b* 22 Oct. 1903; *yr s* of Sir William Dingwall Mitchell Cotts, 1st Bt, KBE, MP (*d* 1932), and Agnes Nivison (*d* 1966), 2nd *d* of late Robert Sloane; *S* brother, 1964; *m* 1942, Barbara, *o d* of late Capt. Herbert J. A. Throckmorton, Royal Navy; two *s* three *d.* *Heir:* *s* Richard Crichton Mitchell Cotts, *b* 26 July 1946. *Address:* Valley Farm, Clopton, near Woodbridge, Suffolk.

COUCHMAN, Dame Elizabeth (May Ramsay), DBE 1961 (OBE 1941); JP; BA; *b* 1878; *d* of late Archibald Tannock and Elizabeth Ramsay Tannock; *m* 1917, Claude Ernest Couchman (decd). *Educ:* University of Western Australia (BA). President, Australian Women's National League, 1927-45; Mem., Australian Broadcasting Commission, 1932-42; Senior Vice-Pres., Royal Commonwealth Soc., 1950-61; office-bearer in many educational, patriotic and social-service organisations. Life Member: National Council of Women (Vic); Liberal Party (Vic). *Publications:* articles in the press on Liberal politics and current topics. *Club:* Australian Women's Liberal (Melbourne).

COUCHMAN, Adm. Sir Walter (Thomas), KCB 1958 (CB 1954); CVO 1953; OBE 1939; DSO 1942; *b* 1905; *s* of Malcolm Edward Couchman, CSI, and Emily Elizabeth Ranking; *m* 1st, 1937, Phyllida Georgina Connellan (marr. diss. 1965); one *s* two *d*; 2nd, 1965, Mrs Hughe Hunter Blair (*d* 1972), *widow* of Lieut-Col D. W. Hunter Blair; 3rd, 1972, Mrs Daphne Harvey, *widow* of Captain E. H. N. Harvey, RN. *Educ:* RN Colleges Osborne and Dartmouth. Specialised in Naval Aviation, 1928; Staff Coll.,

1935; Comdr 1938; Captain 1942; qualified Naval Pilot; comd HMS Glory, 1946; Dir of Naval Air Org. and Trg, Admty, 1947; Flag Officer Flying Trg, 1951; Rear-Adm., 1952; Flag Officer, Aircraft Carriers, 1954; Deputy Controller of Supplies (Air), Ministry of Supply, 1955-56; Vice-Adm. 1956; Flag Officer Air (Home), 1957-60; Adm. 1959; Vice-Chief, Naval Staff, Admiralty, 1960. *Address:* The Old Vicarage, Bulmer, Sudbury, Suffolk.

COUGHTRIE, Thomas, CBE 1958; Chairman, Bruce Peebles Industries Ltd, and Bruce Peebles Ltd, Edinburgh, 1961-67; *b* 28 Oct. 1895; *m* 1918, Mary Morrison; one *s* two *d. Educ:* Royal Coll. of Science, Glasgow. Founded Belmos Co. Ltd, Elect. Engrs, 1919 (merged with Bruce Peebles & Co. Ltd, Edinburgh, 1961); Mem. Royal Fine Art Commn for Scotland, 1962-67; Chm. Valuation Appeals Cttee, Co. Lanark, 1956-71; Director: Ailsa Investment Trust Ltd; Alva Investment Trust Ltd, 1958-63. Chm., Greentower Farms Ltd. JP Lanark, 1959. Hon. LLD Glasgow, 1959; Hon. DSc Heriot-Watt, 1968. *Recreations:* golf, gardening, reading. *Address:* Orchard House, Crossford, Carluke, Lanarkshire. *T:* Crossford 203. *Clubs:* Athenæum, East India, Devonshire, Sports and Public Schools; Western (Glasgow).

COULL, Prof. Alexander, PhD; FRSE; FICE, FIStructE; Regius Professor of Civil Engineering, University of Glasgow, since 1977; *b* 20 June 1931; *s* of William Coull and Jane Ritchie (*née* Reid); *m* 1962, Frances Bruce Moir; one *s* two *d. Educ:* Peterhead Acad.; Univ. of Aberdeen (BScEng, PhD). FRSE 1971; FICE 1972, FIStructE 1973; FASCE 1972. Res. Asst, MIT, USA, 1955; Struct. Engr, English Electric Co. Ltd, 1955-57; Lectr in Engrg, Univ. of Aberdeen, 1957-62; Lectr in Civil Engrg, Univ. of Southampton, 1962-66; Prof. of Struct. Engrg, Univ. of Strathclyde, 1966-76. *Publications:* Tall Buildings, 1967; Fundamentals of Structural Theory, 1972; author or co-author of 80 res. papers in scientific jls. *Recreations:* golf, watching sport. *Address:* 11 Blackwood Road, Milngavie, Glasgow G62 7LB. *T:* 041-956 1655. *Club:* Buchanan Castle Golf (Drymen).

COULSHAW, Rev. Leonard, CB 1949; MC 1917; FKC; *b* 24 Feb. 1896; *s* of late Percy Dean Coulshaw and late Alice Maud Hatt; *m* 1932, Yvonne Cecilia Joan, *d* of Rev. C. Hanmer-Strudwick, Rector of Slawston, Leics; no *c. Educ:* Southend-on-Sea High Sch. for Boys; King's Coll., London; Ely Theological Coll. Served European War, 1914-18, Essex Regiment, 1914-20 (MC, despatches); left Army with rank of Captain. Ordained, 1923; Curate, St Andrew's, Romford, Essex; commissioned as Chaplain, RN, 1927; served in HMS Cyclops, 1927-29; RN Barracks, Portsmouth, 1929; HMS Iron Duke, 1929-30; HMS Effingham (Flagship East Indies Station), 1930-32; Royal Hospital Sch., Holbrook, 1932-34; Senior Chaplain HMS Ganges, 1934-37; HMS Royal Sovereign, 1937 (present at Coronation Review, Spithead); HMS Revenge, 1937. Chaplain Royal Naval Hospital, Malta, 1937-40; RM Depot, Lympstone, 1940-42; Senior Chaplain, RN Base, Lyness, 1942-44; Chaplain HM Dockyard, Sheerness, 1944-46; RM Barracks, Portsmouth, 1946-47; Chaplain of the Fleet and Archdeacon of the Royal Navy, 1948-52; KHC, 1948-52; QHC, 1952; Vicar of: West End, Southampton, 1952-54; Frensham, 1954-65. *Address:* 4 Ashurst Court, Alverstoke, Gosport, Hants PO12 2TZ. *T:* Gosport 82467.

COULSHED, Dame (Mary) Frances, DBE 1953 (CBE 1949); TD 1951; Brigadier, Women's Royal Army Corps, retired; *b* 10 Nov. 1904; *d* of Wilfred and Maud Coulshed. *Educ:* Parkfields Cedars, Derby; Convent of the Sacred Heart, Kensington. Served War of 1939-45 (despatches); North-West Europe, 1944-45, with General Headquarters Anti-Aircraft Troops and at Headquarters Lines of Communications; Deputy Dir, Anti-Aircraft Command, 1946-50; Dep. Dir, War Office, July-Dec. 1950; ADC to the King, 1951, to the Queen, 1951-54; Dir, WRAC, 1951-Sept. 1954. Order of Leopold I of Belgium with palm, Croix de Guerre with palm, 1946. *Address:* 815 Endsleigh Court, Upper Woburn Place, WC1.

COULSON, Mrs Ann Margaret; Assistant Director, North Worcestershire College, since 1976; Member, Independent Broadcasting Authority, since 1976; *b* 11 March 1935; *d* of Sidney Herbert Wood and Ada (*née* Mills); *m* 1958, Peter James Coulson; two *s* one *d. Educ:* The Grammar Sch., Chippenham, Wilts; UCL (BScEcon); Univ. of Manchester (DSA); Wolverhampton Technical Teachers' Coll. (CertEd). AMBIM. Hosp. Admin, 1956-62; Lectr in Econs and Management, Bromsgrove Coll. of Further Educn, 1968-76. Elected to City of Birmingham Dist Council, 1973; special interest in Social Services. *Recreations:* cooking, family camping and sailing. *Address:* 81 Westhill Road, Kings Norton, Birmingham B38 8TG. *T:* 021-458 2230.

COULSON, (James) Michael; Barrister-at-Law; Deputy Chairman, Northern Agricultural Land Tribunal, since 1967; a Chairman of Industrial Tribunals, since 1968; *b* 23 Nov. 1927; *s* of William Coulson, Wold Newton Hall, Driffield, E Yorks; *m* 1st, 1955, Dilys Adair Jones (marr. diss.); one *s*; 2nd, 1977, Barbara Elizabeth Islay, *d* of Dr Roland Moncrieff Chambers. *Educ:* Fulneck Sch., Yorks; Merton Coll., Oxford; Royal Agricultural Coll., Cirencester. Served E Riding Yeomanry (Wenlocks Horse); Queen's Own Yorks Yeomanry (Major). Called to Bar, Middle Temple, 1951; Mem. North Eastern Circuit. Former Mem., Tadcaster RDC. Sometime Sec. Bramham Moor and York and Ainsty Point to Point Race Meetings. MP (C) Kingston-upon-Hull North, 1959-64; Mem., Executive Cttee, Conservative Commonwealth Council; Parliamentary Private Sec. to the Solicitor-Gen., 1962-64. Asst Recorder of Sheffield, 1965-71; Dep. Chm., N Riding of Yorks QS, 1968-71. *Recreations:* hunting, reading, travel. *Address:* The Tithe Barn, Wymondham, Melton Mowbray, Leics; 5 King's Bench Walk, Temple, EC4. *Club:* Cavalry and Guards.

COULSON, Sir John Eltringham, KCMG 1957 (CMG 1946); President, Hampshire Branch, British Red Cross Society, since 1972; Secretary-General of EFTA, 1965-72, retired; *b* 13 Sept. 1909; *er s* of H. J. Coulson, Bickley, Kent; *m* 1944, Mavis Ninette Beazley; two *s. Educ:* Rugby; Corpus Christi Coll., Cambridge (Hon. Fellow 1975). Entered Diplomatic Service in 1932. Served in Bucharest, Min. of Econ. Warfare, War Cabinet Office, Foreign Office and Paris. Sometime Dep. UK representative to UN, New York; Asst Under-Sec., Foreign Office, 1952-55; Minister British Embassy, Washington, 1955-57; Asst to Paymaster-Gen., 1957-60; Ambassador to Sweden, 1960-63; Dep. Under-Sec. of State, Foreign Office, 1963-65; Chief of Administration of HM Diplomatic Service, Jan.-Sept. 1965. Director: Atlas Copco (GB); Sheerness Steel Co. *Recreations:* fishing, golf. *Address:* The Old Mill, Selborne, Hants. *Club:* Brooks's.

COULSON, Prof. John Metcalfe; Professor of Chemical Engineering, University of Newcastle upon Tyne (formerly University of Durham), 1954-75 (on leave of absence to Heriot-Watt University, 1968-69), now Emeritus; *b* 13 Dec. 1910; *m* 1943, Clarice Dora Scott (*d* 1961); two *s*; *m* 1965, Christine Gould; one *d. Educ:* Clifton Coll.; Christ's Coll., Cambridge; Imperial Coll. Royal Arsenal, Woolwich, 1935-39; Asst Lectr, Imperial Coll., 1939; Ministry of Supply (Royal Ordnance Factories), 1939-45; Lectr in Chem. Engineering, Imperial Coll., 1945-52; Reader, 1952-54. Hon. DSc Heriot-Watt, 1973. Davis Medal, ICE, 1973. *Publications:* Chemical Engineering Vol. I and Vol. II (with Prof. J. F. Richardson), 1954 and 1955, 3rd edn 1977; contrib. Instn of Chem. Eng, Chem. Eng Science, etc. *Recreations:* chess, photography. *Address:* 2 Rosedale, Pannal, Harrogate, N Yorks.

COULSON, Michael; *see* Coulson, J. M.

COULSON, Maj.-Gen. Samuel M.; *see* Moore-Coulson.

COULTER, Robert, MC 1945; Controller BBC Scotland, 1973-75; *b* 15 June 1914; *s* of John and Margaret Coulter, Glasgow; *m* 1940, Flora Macleod Bell; no *c. Educ:* Irvine Royal Academy; Glasgow Univ. MA Hons English Lit. and Lang. 1st Bn Royal Scots Fusiliers, India, UK, Madagascar and Burma, 1939-46 (Major). Principal English Master, Ayr Grammar Sch., 1946-48; Educn Administration, Belfast, 1948-53; BBC Northern Ireland, 1953-67: radio and TV producer; TV organiser; Asst Head of Programmes; Dir of Television, Uganda, 1967-69; Head of Programmes, BBC Scotland, 1969-73. *Recreations:* swimming, bad golf, good company. *Address:* 18 Knockmore Park, Bangor, Co. Down, N Ireland.

COULTHARD, Alan George Weall; a Recorder of the Crown Court, since 1972; Hon. Recorder of Borough of Llanelli, since 1975; Chairman, Medical Appeals Tribunal for Wales, since 1976; *b* Bournemouth, 20 Jan. 1924; *s* of late George Robert Coulthard and Cicely Eva Coulthard (*née* Minns); *m* 1948, Jacqueline Anna, *d* of late Dr T. H. James, Fishguard; two *s* two *d. Educ:* Watford Grammar Sch. Pilot, RAF, 1941-46 (Flt-Lt); 1st Officer, BOAC, 1946-48; Pilot and Staff Officer, RAF, 1948-58. Called to Bar, Inner Temple, 1959; practised at Bar, Swansea, 1959-; Asst Recorder, 1970. Contested (L) Pembrokeshire, 1964. Mem. Exec. Cttee, Swansea Festival of Music and the Arts, 1969-; Pres., Swansea Festival Patrons' Assoc., 1974-. BBC sound and TV broadcasts, 1960-. *Recreations:* music, fast motor cars, ornithology, country life. *Address:* 130 Eaton Crescent, Swansea SA1 4QR. *T:* Swansea 59126, 52988. *Club:* Ffynone (Swansea). *See also* C. W. Coulthard.

COULTHARD, Air Vice-Marshal Colin Weall, CB 1975; AFC 1953 (Bar 1958); FRAeS; *b* 27 Feb. 1921; *s* of late Wing Comdr George Robert Coulthard and Cicely Eva Coulthard (*née* Minns); *m* 1st, 1941, Norah Ellen Creighton (marr. diss.); one *s* two *d*; 2nd, 1957, Eileen Pamela (*née* Barber); one *s*. *Educ:* Watford Grammar Sch.; De Havilland Aeronautical Tech. Sch. Commissioned RAF, 1941; Fighter Pilot, 1942-45 (dispatches, 1945); HQ Fighter Comd, 1948-49; RAF Staff Coll., 1950; OC 266 Sqn, Wunstorf, 1952-54, DFLS, CFE, 1955; OC Flying, 233(F) OCU, 1956-57; OC AFDS, CFE, 1957-59; HQ Fighter Comd, 1959-60; Stn Cdr, Gutersloh, 1961-64; MoD, 1964-66; SOA, AHQ Malta, 1966-67; DOR 1(RAF), MoD, 1967-69; Air Attaché, Washington, DC, 1970-72; Mil. Dep. to Head of Defence Sales, MoD, 1973-75, retired 1976. FRAeS 1975. *Recreations:* walking, shooting, motor sport. *Address:* Fiddlers, Old Truro Road, Goonhavern, Truro TR4 9NN. *T:* Zelah 312. *Club:* Royal Air Force.
See also *A . G . W . Coulthard* .

COULTHARD, William Henderson, CBE 1968; MSc, CEng, FIMechE, FRPS; Deputy Director, Royal Armament Research and Development Establishment, 1962-74; *b* 24 Nov. 1913; *s* of William and Louise Coulthard, Flimby, Cumberland; *m* 1942, Peggie Frances Platts Taylor, Chiselhurst; one *d* (one *s* decd). *Educ:* Flimby, Workington Schs; Armstrong Coll., University of Durham. Mather Schol., University of Durham, 1932. Linen Industry Research Assoc., 1934; Instrument Dept, Royal Aircraft Estabt, 1935; Air Ministry HQ, 1939; Sqdn Ldr RAFVR, 1944; Official German Translator, 1945; Air Photography Div., RAE, 1946; Supt, later Dep. Dir, Fighting Vehicles Research and Development Estabt, 1951. *Publications:* Aircraft Instrument Design, 1951; Aircraft Engineer's Handbook, 1953; (trans.) Mathematical Instruments (Capellen), 1948; (trans.) Gyroscopes (Grammel), 1950; articles in technical journals. *Recreations:* art history (Diploma in History of Art, London Univ., 1964); languages. *Address:* Argyll, Francis Close, Ewell, Surrey. *T:* 01-337 4909.

COUNSELL, Hazel Rosemary; barrister-at-law; a Recorder of the Crown Court, since 1976; *b* 7 Jan. 1931; *d* of Arthur Henry Counsell and Elsie Winifred Counsell. *Educ:* Clifton High Sch.; Switzerland; Univ. of Bristol (LLB). Called to the Bar, Gray's Inn, 1956; Western Circuit, 1956-. Legal Dept, Min. of Labour, 1959-62. Governor, Colston Girls Sch. *Recreations:* flying, reading, swimming, travel. *Address:* Albion Chambers, Bristol 1; The Penthouse, Wallcroft, Durdham Park, Bristol 6. *T:* Bristol 22144. *Clubs:* Bristol Flying, Wessex Flying.

COUNSELL, John William, OBE 1975; Managing Director of the Theatre Royal, Windsor, since 1938; *b* 24 April 1905; *s* of Claude Christopher Counsell and Evelyn Counsell (*née* Fleming); *m* 1939, Mary Antoinette Kerridge; twin *d*. *Educ:* Sedbergh Sch.; Exeter Coll., Oxford. Mem. of the OUDS, 1923-26; formerly engaged as a tutor. First appearance on professional stage, Playhouse, Oxford, 1928; two tours of Canada with Maurice Colbourne in Shavian Repertory, 1928-29; leading juvenile, Northampton and Folkestone Repertory Cos, 1929-30; Stage Manager for Baliol Holloway's production of Richard III, New, 1930; Stage Dir, Scenic Artist and eventually Producer, Oxford Repertory Company, 1930-33; Producer and Joint Man.-Dir, Windsor Repertory Company, 1933-34; Lover's Leap, Vaudeville, 1934; toured as Tubbs in Sweet Aloes, 1936; toured S Africa in The Frog, 1936-37; refounded Windsor Repertory Co., 1938. Called to the Colours as Territorial reservist, 1940; served in N Africa, France and Germany, 1942-45; Mem. planning staff of SHAEF; demobilised, 1945, rank of Lieut-Col. Resumed direction of Theatre Royal, Windsor. Has, in addition, produced: Birthmark, Playhouse, 1947; Little Holiday, 1948; Captain Brassbound's Conversion, Lyric, Hammersmith, 1948; The Man with the Umbrella, Duchess, 1950; Who Goes There!, Vaudeville, 1951; His House in Order, 1951; Waggon Load of Monkeys, Savoy, 1951; For Better for Worse, Comedy, 1952; Anastasia, St James's, 1953; Grab Me a Gondola, Lyric, 1956; Three Way Switch, Aldwych, 1958; How Say You?, Aldwych, 1959. *Publications:* Counsell's Opinion (autobiography), 1963; Play Direction: a practical viewpoint, 1973. *Recreations:* gardening, photography. *Address:* 3 Queen's Terrace, Windsor, Berks. *T:* Windsor 65344. *Club:* Green Room.

COUNSELL, Paul Hayward; His Honour Judge Counsell; a Circuit Judge since 1973; *b* 13 Nov. 1926; twin *s* of Frederick Charles Counsell and Edna Counsell; *m* 1959, Joan Agnes Strachan; one *s* two *d*. *Educ:* Colston Sch., Bristol; Queen's Coll., Oxford (MA). Served RAF, 1944-48. Admitted Solicitor, 1951; called to Bar, Inner Temple, 1962. Northern Rhodesia: Crown Solicitor, 1955-56; Crown Counsel, 1956-61; Resident Magistrate, 1958; Dir of Public Prosecutions, 1962-63; Solicitor General, 1963-64; QC 1963; Acting Attorney General, 1964;

Solicitor-General, Zambia, 1964, MLC 1963-64. In chambers of Lord Hailsham, Temple, 1965-73; Dep. Circuit Judge, 1971-73. Chm., Industrial Tribunal, 1970-73. *Recreation:* model engineering. *Address:* c/o Hitchin County Court, Station House, Nightingale Road, Hitchin, Herts. *T:* Hitchin 50011.

COUPER, Sir (Robert) Nicholas (Oliver), 6th Bt *cr* 1841; *b* 9 Oct. 1945; *s* of Sir George Robert Cecil Couper, 5th Bt, and of Margaret Grace, *d* of late Robert George Dashwood Thomas; *S* father, 1975; *m* 1972, Curzon Henrietta, *d* of Major George Burrell MacKean, DL, JP. *Educ:* Eton; RMA, Sandhurst. Major, Blues and Royals; retired, 1975. Now working with Savills as an estate agent. *Heir: cousin* Jonathan Every Couper, *b* 26 Feb. 1931. *Address:* 5 Parthenia Road, SW6. *Club:* Cavalry and Guards.

COUPLAND, Prof. Rex Ernest; Professor of Human Morphology, University of Nottingham, since 1967; Hon. Consultant, Regional Hospital Board, since 1970; *b* 30 Jan. 1924; *s* of Ernest Coupland, company dir; *m* 1947, Lucy Eileen Sargent; one *s* one *d*. *Educ:* Mirfield Grammar Sch.; University of Leeds. MB, ChB with honours, 1947; MD with distinction, 1952; PhD 1954; DSc 1970. House appointments, Leeds General Infirmary, 1947; Demonstrator and Lecturer in Anatomy, University of Leeds, 1948, 1950-58; Asst Prof. of Anatomy, University of Minnesota, USA, 1955-56; Prof. of Anatomy, Queen's Coll., Dundee, University of St Andrews, 1958-67. Medical Officer, RAF, 1948-50. FRSE 1960. Member: Biological Research Board of MRC, 1964-70; Med. Adv. Bd, Crippling Diseases Foundn, 1971-75; Chm., MRC Non-Ionizing Radiations Cttee, 1970-; Pres., Anat. Soc. GB and Ireland, 1976-78. *Publications:* The Natural History of the Chromaffin Cell, 1965; (ed jtly) Chromaffin, Enterochromaffin and Related Cells, 1976; papers in jls of anatomy, physiology, endocrinology, pathology and pharmacology on endocrine and nervous systems; chapters on: Anatomy of the Human Kidney, in Renal Disease (ed Black), 1962, 1968, 1973; The Chromaffin System, in Catecholamines (ed Blaschko and Muscholl), 1973; The Blood Supply of the Adrenal Gland, in Handbook of Physiology, 1974; The Adrenal Medulla, in The Cell in Medical Science (ed Beck and Lloyd), 1976; Endocrinal System, in Textbook of Human Anatomy (ed W. J. Hamilton), 1976; Asst Editor, Gray's Anatomy (ed Davies), 1967. *Recreations:* shooting, gardening. *Address:* Olive Quill, Nottingham Road, Ravenshead, near Nottingham. *T:* Blidworth 3518.

COURAGE, Edward Raymond, CBE 1964; *b* 29 Sept. 1906; *er s* of Raymond Courage; *m* 1948, Hermione Mary Elizabeth, *er d* of Lt-Col Sir John Reynolds, 2nd Bt, MBE; one *s*. *Educ:* Eton; Trinity Coll., Cambridge. High Sheriff of Northants, 1953-54. *Recreations:* racing, shooting, fishing. *Address:* Edgcote, Banbury, Oxfordshire; 31 Abbotsbury House, Abbotsbury Road, W14. *Clubs:* Garrick, Jockey.

COURAGE, Richard Hubert, JP; DL; *b* 23 Jan. 1915; *s* of Raymond Courage and Mildred Frances Courage (formerly Fisher); *m* 1941, Jean Elizabeth Agnes Watson (*d* 1977), *d* of late Sir Charles Cuningham Watson, KCIE, CSI, ICS; two *s* (and one *s* decd). *Educ:* Eton. Served War of 1939-45: Northants Yeomanry, 1939-46, Major (despatches). Director: Courage Ltd, 1948-75 (Chm., 1959-75); Imperial Group Ltd, 1972-75; Norwich Union Insce Group; Chm., London Adv. Bd, Norwich Union Insce Gp, 1975- (Dir, 1964-). Chm. Governors, Brentwood Sch., Essex. JP Essex, 1955; DL Essex, 1977. *Recreations:* yachting and shooting. *Address:* Fitzwalters, Shenfield, Essex. *T:* Brentwood 220191.

COURATIN, Rev. Canon Arthur Hubert; Sixth Canon and Chapter Librarian, Durham Cathedral, 1962-74, Canon Emeritus since 1974; Examining Chaplain to Bishop of Southwark since 1959; *b* 1902; *s* of Arthur Louis and Marian Couratin. *Educ:* Dulwich Coll.; Corpus Christi Coll., Oxford (Scholar); S Stephen's House, Oxford. 1st Cl. Classical Moderations; 2nd Cl. Literae Humaniores; 2nd Cl. Hons Sch. of Theology; BA 1925; MA 1927. Deacon, 1926; priest, 1927; Asst Curate, S Saviour's, Roath, 1926-30 (in charge of S Francis', Roath, 1927-30); Vice-Principal, Queen's Coll., Birmingham, 1930; Asst Curate, S Stephen's, Lewisham (in charge of Church of the Transfiguration, Lewisham), 1930-35; Chaplain, S Stephen's House, Oxford, 1935-36, Vice-Principal, 1936, Principal, 1936-62; Junior Chaplain, Merton Coll., Oxford, 1936-39. Hon. Canon of Christ Church, 1961-62. *Address:* 7 Pimlico, Durham DH1 4QW. *T:* Durham 64767.

COURCEL, Baron de; (Geoffroy Chodron de Courcel); Grand Officier, Légion d'Honneur, 1969; Compagnon de la Libération, 1943; Croix de Guerre, 1939-45; Secretary-General, Ministry of Foreign Affairs, France, 1973-76; *b* Tours, Indre-et-Loire, 11

Sept. 1912; *s* of Louis Chodron de Courcel, Officer, and Alice Lambert-Champy; *m* 1954, Martine Hallade; two *s*. *Educ:* Stanislas Coll.; University of Paris. DenDr, LèsL, Dip. Ecole des Sciences Politiques. Attaché, Warsaw, 1937; Sec., Athens, 1938-39; Armée du Levant, 1939; joined Free French Forces, June 1940; Chef de Cabinet, Gén. de Gaulle, London, 1940-41; Captain 1st Spahis marocains Regt, Egypt, Libya and Tunisia, 1941-43; Dep.-Dir of Cabinet, Gén de Gaulle, Algiers, 1943-44; Mem. Conseil de l'Ordre de la Libération, 1944; Regional Comr for Liberated Territories, 1944; in charge of Alsace-Lorraine Dept, Min. of Interior, 1944-45; Counsellor, 1945; in Min. of Foreign Affairs: Dep. Dir Central and N European Sections, 1945-47; First Counsellor, Rome, 1947-50; Minister Plen., 1951; Dir Bilateral Trade Agreements Section, 1951; Dir African and ME Section, 1953; Dir Gen., Polit. and Econ. Affairs, Min. of Moroccan and Tunisian Affairs, 1954; Perm. Sec., Nat. Defence, 1955-58; Ambassador, Perm. Rep. to NATO, 1958; Sec.-Gen. Présidence de la République, 1959-62; Ambassador to London, 1962-72. Ambassadeur de France, 1965; Hon. DCL Oxon, 1970; Hon. LLD Birmingham, 1972. MC (Great Britain) 1943; Grand Cross of Royal Victorian Order (Hon. GCVO), 1950, etc. *Publication:* L'influence de la Conférence de Berlin de 1885 sur le droit Colonial International, 1936. *Recreations:* shooting, swimming. *Address:* 7 rue de Médicis, 75006 Paris, France; La Ravinière, Fontaines en Sologne, 41250 Bracieux, France.

COURCY; *see* de Courcy.

COURNAND, André Frédéric, MD; Professor Emeritus of Medicine, Columbia University College of Physicians and Surgeons, New York, since 1964 (Professor of Medicine, 1951-60); *b* Paris, 24 Sept. 1895; *s* of Jules Cournand and Marguérite Weber; *m* 1st, Sibylle Blumer (*d* 1959); three *d* (one *s* killed in action, 1944); 2nd, 1963, Ruth Fabian (*d* 1973); 3rd, 1975, Beatrice Berle. *Educ:* Sorbonne, Paris. BA Faculté des Lettres, 1913; PCB Faculté des Sciences, 1914; MD Faculté de Médecine, 1930. Interne des Hôpitaux de Paris, 1925-30. Came to US in 1930; naturalized American Citizen since 1941. Director, Cardio-Pulmonary Laboratory, Columbia University Division, Bellevue Hospital; Visiting Physician, Chest Service, Bellevue Hospital, 1952. Member: American Physiological Soc.; Assoc. of Amer. Physicians; National Acad. of Sciences (USA), 1958; Hon. Member: British Cardiac Soc.; Swedish Soc. Internal Medicine; Swedish Cardiac Soc.; Soc. Médicale des Hôpitaux, Paris; Foreign Mem., Académie Royale de Médecine de Belgique, 1970; Foreign Member: Académie des Sciences, Institut de France, 1957; Académie Nationale de Médecine, Paris, 1958. Laureate: Andreas Retzius Silver Medal of Swedish Soc. Internal Medicine, 1946; Award, US Public Health Assoc., 1949. Croix de Guerre (1914-18) France, three stars; Commandeur de la Légion d'Honneur, 1970 (Officier, 1957). Nobel Prize for Medicine and Physiology (jointly), 1956; Jimenez Diaz Fondacion Prize, 1970; Trudeau Medal, 1971. Doctor (*hc*): University of Strasburg, 1957; University of Lyons, 1958; Université libre de Bruxelles 1959; University of Pisa, 1961; University of Birmingham, 1961; Gustaphus Adolphus, Coll., Minnesota, 1963; University of Brazil, 1965; Columbia Univ., 1965; Univ. of Nancy, 1968. *Publications:* Cardiac Catheterization in Congenital Heart Disease, 1949; L'Insuffisance cardiaque chronique, 1950; Shaping the Future, 1974; numerous articles on human physiopathology of lungs and heart. *Recreations:* Groupe de la Haute Montagne du Club Alpin Français, 1929, and American Alpine Club. *Address:* 1361 Madison Avenue, New York, NY 10028, USA. *T:* Atwater 9-4456. *Club:* Century Association (New York).

COURT, Hon. Sir Charles (Walter Michael), Kt 1972; OBE 1946; MLA (Liberal Party) for Nedlands, since 1953; Premier of Western Australia, since 1974; also Treasurer, and Minister co-ordinating Economic and Regional Development, since 1974; *b* Crawley, Sussex, 29 Sept. 1911; *s* of late W. J. Court, Perth; *m* 1936, Rita M., *d* of L. R. Steffanoni; five *s*. *Educ:* Leederville and Rosalie State Schs; Perth Boys' Sch. Chartered Accountant, 1933; Partner, Hendry, Rae & Court, 1938-70. Served AIF, 1940-46; Lt-Col. State Registrar, Inst. Chartered Accountants in Aust. (WA Br.), 1946-52, Mem. State Council, 1952-55. Dep. Leader, 1957-59, 1971-72, and Leader, 1972-74, of Opposition, WA; Minister, Western Australia: for Industrial Development and the NW, 1959-71; for Railways, 1959-67; for Transport, 1965-66. Chm., Adv. Cttee under WA Prices Control Act, 1948-52; Pres., WA Band Assoc., 1954-59. Hon. Colonel: WA Univ. Regt, 1969-75; SAS Regt, 1976-. FCA; FCIS; FASA. Hon. LLD Univ. of WA, 1969. Manufacturers' Export Council Award, 1969; James Kirby Award, Inst. of Production Engrs, 1971. *Publications:* many professional papers on accountancy, and papers on economic and resource development. *Recreations:* music, yachting. *Address:* 46 Waratah Avenue, Nedlands, WA 6009, Australia. *Clubs:* Commercial Travellers Association, Nedlands Rotary, Lions.

COURT, Emeritus Prof. Seymour Donald Mayneord, CBE 1969; MD; FRCP; *b* 4 Jan. 1912; *s* of David Henry and Ethel Court; *m* 1939, Dr Frances Edith Radcliffe; two *s* one *d*. *Educ:* Adams Grammar Sch., Wem; Birmingham Univ (MB, ChB, 1936; MD 1947); FRCP 1956. Resident Hosp. appts Birmingham Gen. Hosps, and Hosp. for Sick Children, London, 1936-38; Paediatric Registrar, Wander Scholar, Westminster Hosp., 1938-39; Physician, EMS, 1939-46; Nuffield Fellow in Child Health, 1946-47; Reader in Child Health, University of Durham, 1947-55; James Spence Prof. of Child Health, Univ. of Newcastle upon Tyne, 1955-72, Emeritus Professor, 1972. Chm., Child Health Services Cttee for Eng. and Wales, 1973-76. Pres., British Paediatric Assoc., 1973-76. *Publications:* (jointly) Growing Up in Newcastle upon Tyne, 1960; (ed) The Medical Care of Children, 1963; (ed jointly) Paediatrics in the Seventies, 1972; (jointly) The School Years in Newcastle upon Tyne, 1974; contributions to special jls and text books on respiratory infection in childhood. *Recreations:* walking, natural history, poetry. *Address:* Innocks, Cottles Lane, Turleigh, Bradford on Avon, Wilts. *T:* Bradford on Avon 3880.

COURTENAY, family name of **Earl of Devon**.

COURTENAY, Lord; Hugh Rupert Courtenay; Associate with Messrs Stratton & Holborow, Chartered Surveyors and Chartered Land Agents, Exeter; *b* 5 May 1942; *o s* of 17th Earl of Devon, *qv*; *m* 1967, Dianna Frances, *er d* of J. G. Watherston, Jedburgh, Roxburghshire; one *s* three *d*. *Educ:* Winchester; Magdalene Coll., Cambridge (BA). ARICS. *Recreations:* riding, hunting, shooting. *Heir:* s Hon. Charles Peregrine Courtenay, *b* 14 Aug. 1975. *Address:* The Stables House, Powderham, near Exeter, Devon. *T:* Starcross 370. *Club:* University Pitt (Cambridge).

COURTENAY, Sir Harrison; *see* Courtenay, Sir W. H.

COURTENAY, Thomas Daniel, (Tom Courtenay); actor; *b* 25 Feb. 1937; *s* of Thomas Henry Courtenay and late Annie Eliza Quest; *m* 1973, Cheryl Kennedy. *Educ:* Kingston High Sch., Hull; University Coll., London. RADA, 1958-60; started acting professionally, 1960; Old Vic, 1960-61: Konstantin Treplieff, Poins, Feste and Puck; Billy Liar, Cambridge Theatre, June 1961-Feb. 1962 and on tour; Andorra, National Theatre (guest), 1964; The Cherry Orchard, and Macbeth, Chichester, 1966; joined 69 Theatre Co., Manchester, 1966: Charley's Aunt, 1966; Hamlet (Edinburgh Festival), 1968; She Stoops to Conquer, Garrick, 1969; Charley's Aunt, Apollo, 1971; Time and Time Again, Comedy, 1972 (Variety Club of GB Stage Actor Award, 1972); The Norman Conquests, Globe, 1974; The Fool, Royal Court, 1975; Otherwise Engaged, NY, 1977. Began acting in films, 1962. *Films:* The Loneliness of the Long Distance Runner; Private Potter; Billy Liar; King and Country (Volpi Cup, 1964); Operation Crossbow; King Rat; Dr Zhivago; The Night of the Generals; The Day the Fish Came Out; A Dandy in Aspic; Otley; One Day in the Life of Ivan Denisovitch; Catch Me a Spy. Has appeared on Television. Best Actor Award, Prague Festival, 1968; TV Drama Award (for Oswald in Ghosts), 1968. *Recreations:* listening to music (mainly classical and romantic); watching sport (and occasionally taking part in it, in a light-hearted manner). *Address:* Barnes, SW13. *Clubs:* Savile, Garrick.

COURTENAY, Hon. Sir (Woldrich) Harrison, KBE 1973 (OBE 1950); LLD; QC 1974; Speaker, House of Representatives, Belize, (formerly British Honduras), 1963-74 (of Legislative Assembly, 1961-63); Chancellor of Anglican Diocese, since 1956, Registrar since 1946; Barrister-at-Law; *b* Belize City, 15 July 1904; *s* of William and Sarah Courtenay; *m* 1929, Josephine Robinson; three *s* one *d*. *Educ:* Belize High Sch., British Honduras; Lincoln's Inn, London. Mem. Civil Service, Belize (British Honduras Secretariat), 1920-37; acted on several occasions as Clerk of Legislative and Exec. Councils, and as Head of Educn Dept, 1930; Sec.-Accountant, British Honduras Govt Marketing Agency, 1925-33; also Sec. of Stann Creek Develt Bd. Left for UK, Nov. 1933, to read for the Bar; called to Bar, Lincoln's Inn, 1936; returned to British Honduras and resumed duty, July 1936; resigned, 1937, and entered into private practice; admitted Solicitor of Supreme Court, Belize, 1937; Magistrate, Belize, 1938-41. Was for many years Diocesan Sec. and Mem. Synod, 1926-, Dio. Brit. Honduras; Diocesan Treas.; and Sec.-Treas., Bd of Governors of St Hilda's Coll. (Elected) MLC, 1945-54; MEC, 1947-54; Past Mem., Electricity Bd; also served on several other Bds and Cttees. British Honduras rep. to Conf. on Closer Assoc. of the BWI, Montego Bay, 1947, also to 2nd and 3rd WI confs; Leader of first delegn from Legislative Council to Colonial Office on Constitutional Reform and Economic Develt, 1947. Member: Standing Closer Assoc. Cttee, which prod. first Federal Constitution, 1948-51;

Brit. Section, Caribbean Commn, 1948-52; Alternate Mem., 1952-55; BWI Regional Economic Cttee, 1951-54; Council of University Coll. of the WI; Finance and General Purposes Cttee, Bd of Extra-Mural Studies, and Bd of Inst. of Social and Economic Research, 1948-58; Chm., constitutional Reform Commn, 1949-51; Fiscal Revision Cttee, 1952-53. Representative: at Installation of Princess Alice as Chancellor of University Coll. of WI, 1950; CPA Confs, NZ 1950 and Canada 1952; on visits to Australia, Canada, Jamaica, etc, 1950-52; for visit of the Queen and the Duke of Edinburgh to Jamaica, 1953; to Sugar Conf., Grenada, 1950, and Trade Promotion Conf., Trinidad, 1954; (for BWI) on UK delegn to Conf. of Commonwealth Finance Ministers, Sydney, 1954; Chm., BWI Regional Parly Conf., Jamaica, 1952; Chm. and Constitutional Adviser to United Front Political delegn to London for constitutional talks, 1960; Chm., NEDC, 1962-66; Constitutional Adviser to Political delegn to London for constitutional talks, 1963; Adviser, British Honduras delegn to tripartite confs on Anglo-Guatemalan Dispute, and with Mediator in the dispute, 1962-67. Hon. LLD (Univ. of WI), 1972; Hon. Citizen of San Juan, Puerto Rico, 1948. *Recreations:* travel, reading, music. *Address:* Cloverleaf Park, Northern Highway, (PO Box 636) Belize. *Club:* Royal Commonwealth Society (West Indian).

COURTNEIDGE, Dame Cicely, DBE 1972 (CBE 1951); *b* Sydney, NSW, 1 April, 1893; *d* of late Robert Courtneidge and Rosaline May Adams; *m* Jack Hulbert, *qv.* First appearance on stage, Prince's Theatre, Manchester, 1901; on London stage, Apollo, 1907; appeared in variety theatres with great success, from 1916; has made popular broadcasts; Gaiety Theatre, New York, 1925; commenced film career, 1929; *Films include:* Ghost Train; Jack's The Boy; Aunt Sally; Soldiers of the Queen; The L-shaped Room; Wrong Box; Things are Looking Up; Imperfect Gentleman; *Revues include:* Little Revue; House That Jack Built; Folly to be Wise; By the Way; Over the Moon; *Plays include:* Hide and Seek, Hippodrome. 1937; Under Your Hat, Palace, 1938; Full Swing, Palace, 1942; Under the Counter, Phoenix, 1945, New York, 1947, Australia, 1947-48; Her Excellency, Hippodrome, 1949; Gay's the Word, Saville, 1951; The Bride and the Bachelor, Duchess, 1956; Fool's Paradise, Apollo, 1959; The Bride Comes Back, Vaudeville, 1960; High Spirits, Savoy, 1964; Dear Octopus, Haymarket, 1967; Move Over Mrs Markham, Vaudeville, 1971. *Publication:* autobiography: Cicely, 1953. *Address:* c/o Herbert de Leon (Management) Ltd, Fielding House, 13 Bruton Street, W1X 8JY.

COURTNEY, Comdr Anthony Tosswill, OBE 1949; RN; author and lecturer; Managing Director, New English Typewriting School Ltd, since 1969; *b* 16 May 1908; *s* of Basil Tosswill Courtney and Frances Elizabeth Courtney (*née* Rankin); *m* 1st, 1938, Elisabeth Mary Cortlandt Stokes (*d* 1961); no *c*; 2nd, 1962, Lady (Elizabeth) Trefgarne (marr. diss. 1966); 3rd, 1971, Mrs Angela Bradford. *Educ:* Royal Naval Coll., Dartmouth. Midshipman, HMS Ramillies, 1925; world cruise in HMS Renown with the Duke and Duchess of York, 1927; Sub-Lieut HMS Cornwall, 1930; Lieut HMS Malaya, 1931-33; qualified as Interpreter in Russian after language study in Bessarabia, 1934; qualified in Signals and W/T at Signal Sch., Portsmouth, 1935; served at Admiralty and on staff of C-in-C, Plymouth, 1936; Flag Lieut to Rear-Adm. comdg Third Cruiser Sqdn, Mediterranean Fleet, 1937-39; Staff of Adm. comdg 3rd Battle Squadron and N Atlantic Escort Force, 1939-41; Naval Mission in Russia, 1941-42; Flag Lieut and Signals Officer to Adm. comdg Aircraft Carriers, 1943; Staff of Adm. comdg S Atlantic Station, 1944; Staff of Rear-Adm., Gibraltar, 1945; Intelligence Div., Naval Staff, Admiralty, 1946-48; Chief Staff Officer (Intelligence) Germany, 1949-51; qualified as Interpreter in German; Intelligence Div., Naval Staff, Admiralty, 1952-53; retd with rank of Comdr, 1953. Entered business as Export Consultant (ETG Consultancy Services), until 1965. Contested (C) Hayes and Harlington, 1955. MP (C) Harrow East, 1959-66. Vice-Chm. Conservative Navy Cttee, 1964. Chm. Parliamentary Flying Club, 1965; Mem. Exec. Council, Monday Club. *Publication:* Sailor in a Russian Frame, 1968. *Recreations:* shooting, music, fishing. *Address:* Mulberry House, Urchfont, Devizes, Wilts. *T:* Chirton 357. *Club:* White's.

COURTNEY, Group Captain Ivon Terence, CBE 1919; RAF (retired); *b* 14 Oct. 1885; *y s* of late William McDougall Courtney, Stormonstown, Co. Dublin; *m* 1915, Emily Lilian (*d* 1964), *y d* of Alfred Campbell Courtney, Danesfield, Clontarf, Co. Dublin; one *s. Educ:* Tonbridge; Rossall. Commissioned Royal Marine Light Infantry, 1904; seconded to Naval Wing, RFC, 1912 for flying duty and to RNAS, 1914; permanently transferred to RAF, 1919; retired list, 1932. *Address:* National Westminster Bank, 26 Haymarket, SW1.

COURTNEY, Victor Desmond, JP; Member Federal Immigration Planning Council, 1951-56; Trustee Soldiers' Dependants Appeal Fund (WA); *b* Raymond Terr., NSW, 1894; *m* 1937, Thela, *d* of late John Richards, Perth; one *d.* Has been all his life in journalism, and has contributed to a number of Australian papers. Man. Dir Western Press Ltd and associated companies until he disposed of his interests in Dec. 1954; now author and publisher, and Dir, Craft Print Ltd. *Publications;* Random Rhymes, 1941; Cold is the Marble, 1948; All I May Tell, 1956; Life of J. J. Simons, 1961; Perth and All This!, 1962; As We Pass By, 1963. *Recreations:* motoring, swimming. *Address:* 45 North Beach Road, North Beach, Western Australia. *Clubs:* Reelers, Perth Football, Royal Automobile, National Football League (WA).

COURTOWN, 9th Earl of, *cr* 1762; **James Patrick Montagu Burgoyne Winthrop Stopford;** Baron Courtown (Ire.), 1758; Viscount Stopford, 1762; Baron Saltersford (GB), 1796; *b* 19 March 1954; *s* of 8th Earl of Courtown, OBE, TD, DL, and of Patricia, 3rd *d* of Harry S. Winthrop, Auckland, NZ; *S* father, 1975. *Educ:* Eton College; Berkshire Coll. of Agriculture. *Heir:* *b* Hon. Jeremy Neville Stopford, *b* 22 June 1958. *Address:* Beechshade, Cambridge Road, Beaconsfield, Bucks.

COUSIN, Prof. David Ross; Emeritus Professor of Philosophy, University of Sheffield; *b* 28 Jan. 1904; *s* of John William Cousin and Marion Miller Young; *m* 1930, Beatrice Elizabeth Connell; three *s. Educ:* Merchiston Castle Sch., Edinburgh; The Queen's Coll., Oxford (BA). Class. Mods 1925; Lit Hum 1927; Philosophy, Politics and Economics, 1928. Asst, Dept of Logic, University of Glasgow, 1928; Lecturer, 1930; Senior Lecturer, 1948. Board of Trade (temp. Principal), 1941-45. Prof. of Philosophy, Univ. of Sheffield, 1949-69; Dean of Faculty of Arts, 1958-61. Vis. Prof., Dept of Philosophy, Univ. of Edinburgh, Oct.-Dec., 1974. *Publications:* contributions to learned jls. *Address:* 16 Cobden Crescent, Edinburgh EH9 2BG.

COUSINS, Rt. Hon. Frank, PC 1964; Chairman, Community Relations Commission, 1968-70; *b* Bulwell, Notts, 8 Sept. 1904; *m* 1930, Annie Elizabeth Judd; two *s* two *d. Educ:* King Edward Sch., Doncaster. Mem. Institute of Transport; Organiser, Rd Transport Section, TGWU, 1938; Nat. Officer (Rd Tr. Section), 1944; Nat. Sec. (Rd Tr. Section), 1948; Asst Gen. Sec. TGWU, 1955; General Secretary, TGWU, 1956-69 (seconded, as Minister of Technology, Oct. 1964-July 1966). MP (Lab) Nuneaton, Jan. 1965-Dec. 1966. Elected Mem., Gen. Council of TUC, 1956-69. Member: British Transport Jt Consultative Council, 1955-63; Min. of Labour Nat. Jt Advisory Council, 1956; Exec. Council Internat. Transport Workers Federation, 1956 (Pres., 1958-60, 1962-64); Colonial Labour Advisory Cttee, 1957-62; London Travel Cttee, 1958-60; Political Economy Club, 1957; Council for Scientific and Industrial Research, 1960-64; National Economic Development Council; Central Advisory Council for Science and Technology, 1967-; Nat. Freight Corp., 1968-73; Governor, Nat. Inst. of Economic and Social Research, 1958; Chm., Central Training Council, 1968-. *Recreations:* gardening, reading. *Address:* Ramsfold Cottage, Roundhurst, Blackdown, near Haslemere, Surrey.
See also *J . P . Cousins .*

COUSINS, John Peter; Director of Manpower and Industrial Relations, National Economic Development Office, since 1975; *b* 31 Oct. 1931; *s* of Rt Hon. Frank Cousins, *qv* ; *m* 1976; Pauline Cousins (*née* Hubbard); three *d . Educ:* Doncaster Central Sch. Motor engineering apprentice, 1947-52; RAF Engineering, 1952-55; BOAC cabin crew and clerical work, 1955-63; Full Time Official, TGWU, 1963-75, Nat. Sec., 1966-75. Mem., Transport and Local Govt Cttees, TUC; UK Deleg., ILO; International Transport Workers Federation: Member: Aviation Sect.; Local Govt Cttee; Chemical Cttee; Civil Aviation Cttee; Mem. Industrial Training Bds. Member: Countryside Commn, 1972-; New Towns Commn, 1975-; Sandford Cttee to review National Parks in England and Wales, 1972-73. *Recreations:* hill walking, trout fishing, 17th and 18th century music. *Address:* 58 Casterbridge Road, Blackheath, SE3. *T:* 01-856 7638.

COUSINS, Norman; Editor, Saturday Review, 1940-71, and since 1975; *b* 24 June 1915; *s* of Samuel and Sara Cousins; *m* 1939, Ellen Kopf; four *d. Educ:* Teachers Coll., Columbia Univ. Educational Editor, New York Evening Post, 1935-36; Managing Editor, Current History Magazine, 1936-39 (World War II edn, USA); Editor: World Magazine, 1972-73; Saturday Review/World, 1973-74. Chm., Conn Fact-Finding Commission on Education, 1948-51. Vice-Pres. PEN Club, American Center, 1952-55; National Press and Overseas Press Clubs; Lectr for US Dept of State; co-Chm., National Cttee for a Sane Nuclear Policy, 1957-63. Pres. United World Federalists, 1952-54 (Hon. Pres., 1955-). Pres., World Assoc. of World

Federalists, 1965-. Chairman: Nat. Educational Television, 1969-70; Nat. Programming Council for Public Television; Mem. Bd of Directors: The Charles F. Kettering Foundn; The Samuel H. Kress Foundn; Educational Broadcasting Corp.; US Govt Rep. at dedication Nat. Univ., Addis Ababa, 1962; co-Chm., Citizens' Cttee for a Nuclear Test-Ban Treaty, 1963; Chm., Cttee for Culture and Intellectual Exchange, for International Co-operation Year, 1965; US Presidential Rep. at Inauguration of Pres. of Philippines, 1966; US Govt Rep. at Internat. Writers Conf., Finland, 1966. Chm. Mayor's Task Force on Air Pollution, NYC, 1966-. Holds various hon. degrees. Awards include: Benjamin Franklin Award for Public Service in Journalism, 1956; Eleanor Roosevelt Peace Award, 1963; Overseas Press Club Award for best interpretation of foreign affairs in magazine writing, 1965; Family of Man Award, 1968; Carr Van Anda Award for Enduring Contribs to Journalism, Ohio Univ., 1971; Peace Medal of UN, 1971; Nat Arts Club Gold Medal for Literature, 1972; Univ. of Missouri Honor Award for Conspicuous Contribs to Journalism, 1972; Drexel Univ. Distinguished Achievement Award, 1972; Irita Van Doren Book Award, 1972. *Publications:* The Good Inheritance, 1941; (ed) A Treasury of Democracy, 1941; Modern Man is Obsolete, 1945; (ed jtly) Poetry of Freedom, 1946; Talks with Nehru, 1951; Who Speaks for Man?, 1953; Saturday Review Treasury (ed. sup.), 1957; In God We Trust (ed), 1958; March's Thesaurus (ed. sup.), 1958; Dr Schweitzer of Lambaréné, 1960; In Place of Folly, 1961; Present Tense, 1967; The Improbable Triumvirate, 1972. *Recreations:* music (especially organ), sports, reading, chess. *Address:* (office) 488 Madison Avenue, NYC 10022, USA; (home) 160 Silvermine Road, New Canaan, Conn 06840, USA. *Clubs:* Coffee House, Century (New York).

COUSINS, Philip; Under Secretary, HM Treasury, since 1974; *b* 5 Feb. 1923; *s* of Herbert and Ella Cousins; *m* 1948, Ruby Laura Morris; two *d*. *Educ:* Royal Liberty School, Romford. Served in Royal Air Force, 1943-47. Joined Treasury, 1949. *Address:* 102 Philbeach Gardens, SW5. *T:* 01-373 6164.

COUSTEAU, Jacques-Yves; Commandeur, Légion d'Honneur; Croix de Guerre with Palm; Officier du Mérite Maritime; Chevalier du Mérite Agricole; Officier des Arts et des Lettres; marine explorer; *b* 11 June 1910; *s* of Daniel and Elizabeth Cousteau; *m* 1937, Simone Melchior; two *s*. *Educ:* Stanislas, Paris; Navy Academy, Brest. Lt de vaisseau, War of 1939-45. Was partly responsible for invention of the Aqualung, 1943, a portable breathing device for divers. Established Undersea Research Group, 1946; Founder and President: Campagnes Océanographiques Françaises, 1950; Centre d'Etudes Marines Avancées, 1952; since 1951 has made annual oceanographic expdns on his ship Calypso, and has made film records of his undersea expdns since 1942; took part in making of the Bathyscaphe; promoted Conshelf saturation dive programme, 1962-65. Dir, Musée Océanographique, Monaco, Feb. 1957-; Gen. Sec., Internat. Commn for Scientific Exploration of the Mediterranean Sea, 1966. For. Assoc. Mem., Nat. Acad. Scis, USA, 1968; Corresp. Mem., Hellenic Inst. of Marine Archaeology, 1975. Hon. DSc: California 1970; Brandeis 1970. Gold Medal, RGS, 1963; Pott's Medal, Franklin Inst., 1970; Gold Medal Grand Prix d'Océanographie Albert Ier, 1971; Grande Médaille d'Or, Soc. d'encouragement au Progrès, 1973; Award of New England Aquarium, 1973; Prix de la couronne d'or, 1973; Polena della Bravura, 1974; Gold Medal "Sciences", 1974. *Publications:* Par 18 mètres de fond, 1946; La Plongée en Scaphandre, 1950; (with Frederic Dumas) The Silent World, 1953 (New York and London), first published in English, then in other languages (film awarded Oscar for best documentary feature film of 1956; Grand Prix, Gold Palm, Festival Cannes, 1956); (ed with James Dugan) Captain Cousteau's Underwater Treasury, 1960 (London); The Living Sea, 1963 (London); World Without Sun, 1965 (film awarded Oscar, 1966); (with P. Cousteau) The Shark, 1970; with P. Diolé: Life and Death in a Coral Sea, 1971; Diving for Sunken Treasure, 1971; The Whale: mighty monarch of the sea, 1972; Octopus and Squid, 1973; Galapagos, Titicaca, the Blue Holes: three adventures, 1973; The Ocean World of Jacques Cousteau (20 vol encyclopedia), 1973; Diving Companions, 1974; Dolphins, 1975; articles in National Geographical Magazine, 1952-66. *Films:* The Golden Fish, awarded Oscar for best short film, 1960; TV films and series: The Undersea World of Jacques Cousteau, 1967; South to Fire and Ice, The Flight of Penguins, Beneath the Frozen World, Blizzard at Hope Bay, Life at the end of the world, 1973. *Address:* Oceanographic Institute, Fondation Albert Ier, Prince de Monaco, Monaco. *Clubs:* Club des Explorateurs (Paris); Club Alpin Sous Marin; Yacht Club de France.

COUTTS; *see* Money-Coutts.

COUTTS, David Burdett M.; *see* Money-Coutts.

COUTTS, Frederick, CBE 1967; General of The Salvation Army, 1963-69; *b* 21 Sept. 1899; British; *m* 1st, 1925, Bessie Lee (*d* 1967); one *s* three *d*; 2nd, 1969, Olive Gatrall. *Educ:* Leith Academy and Whitehill. RFC, 1917-18. Officer, The Salvation Army, 1920. Literary Sec. to the General, 1952. Training Principal, International Training Coll., 1953-57; Territorial Comdr, Eastern Australia, 1957-63. *Publications:* The Timeless Prophets, 1944; He had no Revolver, 1944; The Battle and the Breeze, 1945; Portrait of a Salvationist, 1955; Jesus and Our Need, 1956; The Call to Holiness, 1957; Essentials of Christian Experience, 1969; The Better Fight: the history of the Salvation Army 1914-1946, 1973; No Discharge in This War, 1975; No Continuing City, 1976. *Recreation:* reading. *Address:* 3 Dubrae Close, St Albans, Herts. *T:* St Albans 59655.

COUTTS, Prof. John Archibald; Professor of Jurisprudence in the University of Bristol, 1950-75, now Emeritus; Pro-Vice Chancellor, 1971-74; *b* 29 Dec. 1909; *e s* of Archibald and Katherine Jane Coutts; *m* 1940, Katherine Margaret Alldis; two *s*. *Educ:* Merchant Taylors', Crosby; Downing Coll., Cambridge (MA, LLB). Barrister Gray's Inn, 1933; lectured in Law: University Coll., Hull, 1934-35; King's Coll., London, 1935-36; Queen's Univ., Belfast, 1936-37; Trinity Coll., Dublin, 1937-50; Prof. of Laws, University of Dublin, 1944-50. Fellow, Trinity College, Dublin, 1944-50. Visiting Professor: Osgoode Hall Law Sch., Toronto, 1962-63; Univ. of Toronto, 1970-71, 1975-76. *Publications:* The Accused (ed); contributions to legal journals. *Address:* 22 Hurle Crescent, Clifton, Bristol BS8 2SZ. *T:* Bristol 36984.

COUTTS, Thomas Gordon, QC (Scotland) 1973; *b* 5 July 1933; *s* of Thomas Coutts and Evelyn Gordon Coutts; *m* 1959, Winifred Katherine Scott, BSc, MA; one *s* one *d*. *Educ:* Aberdeen Grammar Sch.; Aberdeen Univ. (MA, LLB). Admitted Faculty of Advocates, 1959; Standing Junior Counsel to Dept Agric. (Scot.), 1965; Chm. Industrial Tribunals, 1972. *Recreations:* golf, stamp collecting. *Address:* 6 Heriot Row, Edinburgh EH3 6HU. *Club:* New (Edinburgh).

COUTTS, Sir Walter (Fleming), GCMG 1962 (KCMG 1961; CMG 1953); Kt 1961; MBE 1949; Director, The Farmington Trust, since 1971; Director: Inchcape (East Africa) Ltd; Assam Investments; Chairman, Grindlays (Commercial) Holdings, since 1974; *b* Aberdeen, 30 Nov. 1912; *s* of late Rev. John William Coutts, MA, DD, and Mrs R. Coutts, Crieff; *m* 1942, Janet Elizabeth Jamieson, CStJ, 2nd *d* of late A. C. Jamieson and of Mrs M. E. Jamieson, Welwyn, Herts; one *s* one *d*. *Educ:* Glasgow Academy; St Andrews Univ.; St John's Coll., Cambridge. MA St Andrews, 1934. District Officer Kenya, 1936; Secretariat Kenya, 1946; District Commissioner, 1947; Administrator, St Vincent, 1949; Minister for Education, Labour and Lands, Kenya, 1956-58, Chief Sec., 1958-61; Special Commissioner for African Elections, Feb. 1955; Governor of Uganda, Nov. 1961-Oct. 1962; Governor-Gen. and C-in-C, Uganda, 1962-63. Sec. to Dulverton Trust, 1966-69; Asst Vice-Chancellor (Administration), Univ. of Warwick, 1969-71. Chm., Pergamon Press, 1972-74. KStJ. *Recreation:* gardening. *Address:* 6 Stanmore Gardens, Mortimer, Berks. *T:* Mortimer 332860.

COUVE DE MURVILLE, Maurice; Commandeur de la Légion d'Honneur; Ambassadeur de France; Deputy, French National Assembly, Paris 8ème Arrondissement, since 1973; Chairman, Foreign Affairs Committee of the National Assembly, since 1973; *b* 24 Jan. 1907; *m* 1932, Jacqueline Schweisguth; three *d*. *Educ:* Paris Univ. Inspecteur des finances, 1930; directeur des finances extérieures, 1940; membre du Comité français de la libération nationale (Alger), 1943; représentant de la France, Conseil consultatif pour l'Italie, 1944; Ambassador in Rome, 1945; directeur général des affaires politiques, Ministère des Affaires Etrangères, 1945-50; Ambassador in Egypt, 1950-54; French Permanent Rep., NATO, Sept. 1954-Jan. 1955; Ambassador in the US, 1955-56; Ambassador of France to the Federal Republic of Germany, 1956-58; Ministre des Affaires Etrangères, 1958-68, de l'Economie et des Finances, June-July 1968; Prime Minister of France, 1968-69. *Publication:* Une Politique étrangère 1958-69, 1973. *Address:* 44 rue du Bac, 75007 Paris, France.

COUZENS, Kenneth Edward, CB 1976; Second Permanent Secretary (Overseas Finance), HM Treasury, since 1977; *b* 29 May 1925; *s* of Albert Couzens and May Couzens (*née* Biddlecombe); *m* 1947, Muriel Eileen Fey; one *s* one *d*. *Educ:* Portsmouth Grammar Sch.; Caius Coll., Cambridge. Inland Revenue, 1949-51; Treasury, 1951-68, and 1970-; Civil Service Dept, 1968-70. Private Sec. to Financial Sec., Treasury, 1952-55, and to Chief Sec., 1962-63; Asst Sec., 1963-69; Under-Secretary: CSD, 1969-70; Treasury, 1970-73; Dep. Sec., Incomes Policy and Public Finance, 1973-77. *Address:* Coverts Edge, Woodsway, Oxshott, Surrey. *T:* Oxshott 3207.

COVEN, Major Edwina Olwyn, JP; stores consultant, freelance journalist and broadcaster, since 1960; *b* 23 Oct. 1921; *d* of Sir Samuel Instone, DL, and Lady (Alice) Instone; *m* 1951, Frank Coven, *qv*. *Educ:* Queen's Coll., London; St Winifred's, Ramsgate; Lycée Victor Duruy, Paris; Marlborough Gate Secretarial Coll., London (1st Cl. Business Diploma). Volunteered for Mil. Service, Private ATS; commnd ATS (subseq. WRAC); Army Interpreter (French); served UK and overseas, incl. staff appts, Plans and Policy Div., Western Union Defence Org. and NATO, Directorate Manpower Planning, WO, 1942-56. 1959-: Children's Writer, Fleetway Publications; Gen. Features Writer, National Magazine Co.; Reporter, BBC Woman's Hour; performer and adviser, children's and teenage progs, ITV. Chm., Davbro Chemists, 1967-71; Mem., Women's Adv. Cttee (Clothing and Footwear Sub-Cttee), BSI, 1971-73. JP Inner London, North Westminster, 1965-72 (Dep. Chm., 1971-72); JP City of London Commn, 1969 (Dep. Chm., 1971-); Mem., Central Council Probation and After-Care Cttee, 1971; Chm., City of London Probation and After-Care Cttee, 1971-77. Dowgate Ward, City of London: elected to Court of Common Council, 1972-; elected Alderman, 1973 and 1974; Deputy, 1975-. Freedom, City of London, 1967; Mem., Guild of Freemen, City of London, 1971; Freeman, Loriners Co., 1967; Liveryman, Spectacle Makers Co., 1972. Member: Council, WRAC Assoc., 1973-; Associated Speakers, 1975-; Bd of Governors, City of London Sch., 1972-; Bd of Governors, City of London Sch. for Girls, 1972- (Dep. Chm., 1976-); Royal Soc. of St George, 1972-. *Publication:* Tales of Oaktree Kitchen, 1959 (2nd edn 1960; adapted for ITV children's educnl series). *Recreations:* looking after much-loved husband and homemaking generally; lawn tennis; watching a variety of spectator sports. *Address:* 22 Cadogan Court, Draycott Avenue, SW3 3BX. *T:* 01-589 8286. *Clubs:* Queen's, Hurlingham; Devonshire (Eastbourne).

COVEN, Frank; London and European Director, The Nine Television Network of Australia, since 1974; *b* 26 April 1910; *s* of Isaac L. Coven and Raie Coven; *m* 1951, Edwina Coven (*née* Instone), *qv*; *Educ:* The Perse, Cambridge; France and Germany. Studied film prodn, UFA and EFA Studios, Berlin. TA (Ranks), 1938; War Service, 1939-45 (commnd 1941). Film admin and prodn, Gaumont British Studios, 1932; Studio Manager, Gainsborough Pictures, 1935; TV prodn, BBC/Daily Mail, 1937-38; Jt Dep. Organiser, Daily Mail Ideal Home Exhibition (radio, television, special features), 1945; Manager, Public Relations, Associated Newspapers, 1949; interviews, Wimbledon tennis commentaries, children's series "Write it Yourself" BBC TV, 1949-54 (subseq. ITV); TV Adviser, Bd of Associated Newspapers, 1953, Associated Rediffusion, 1954; London Rep., Television Corporation Ltd, Sydney, and Herald-Sun Pty, Melbourne, 1954; Dir, Compagnie Belge Transmarine SA and Imperial Stevedoring Co. SA, 1959; Head of Publicity and Promotions, Associated Newspapers, 1961; 1962: Dir, Associated Newspapers Gp; Dir, Bouverie Investments Ltd; Managing Director: Northcliffe Developments Ltd; Frank Coven Enterprises Ltd, presenting (with John Roberts) plays in London, incl. The Professor, How's the World Treating You? and, with London Traverse Theatre Co., works by Saul Bellow and others, 1964-69; Gen. Man., United Racecourses Ltd (Epsom, Sandown Park, Kempton Park), 1970, Man. Dir 1970, Vice-Chm. 1972. Mem., Royal Soc. of St George, 1972. *Publications:* various Daily Mail Guides to Television Development in UK. *Recreations:* lawn tennis, swimming, study of varied media (current affairs). *Address:* 22 Cadogan Court, Draycott Avenue, SW3 3BX. *T:* 01-589 8286. *Clubs:* Savage, Hurlingham, Queen's; Devonshire (Eastbourne).

COVENEY, Prof. James; Professor of Modern Languages, University of Bath, since 1969; *b* 4 April 1920; *s* of James and Mary Coveney; *m* 1955, Patricia Yvonne Townsend; two *s*. *Educ:* St Ignatius Coll., Stamford Hill, London; Univ. of Reading (BA, 1st Cl. hons French, 1950); Univ. of Strasbourg (Dr Univ 1953). Served War of 1939-45: private, The Welch Regt, 1940; Commnd in Queen's Own Royal West Kent Regt; served subsequently in RAF and US Naval Air Service; demobilized as Flt-Lt (Pilot), RAF. Univ. of Strasbourg: French Govt Research Scholar, 1950-51; Lecteur d'Anglais, 1951-53; Vis. Lectr, Collège de l'Europe Libre, Strasbourg, 1951-53; Lectr in French, Univ. of Hull, 1953-58; Asst Dir of Exams (Mod. Langs), Civil Service Commn, 1958-59; Translator, lang. service, UNO Secretariat, New York, 1959-61; Interpreter/Translator NATO Secretariat, on Staff of C-in-C, Allied Forces Eastern Atlantic Area, 1961-64; Sen. Lectr and Head of Mod. Langs,

Univ. of Bath, 1964-68; Jt Dir, Centre for European Ind. Studies, Univ. of Bath, 1969-75; Language Training Consultant to McKinsey & Co. Inc., management consultants, 1969-74; Lexicography Adviser to Longman Gp Ltd, 1973-76. Vis. Prof. of Mod. Langs, University Coll. at Buckingham, 1974-; Vis. Prof., Ecole Nationale d'Administration, Paris, 1975-. Member: Conseil du Comité de Strasbourg de l'Alliance Française, 1951-53; Assoc. Internat. des Traducteurs de Conférence, 1967; Conf. Internat. Permanente des Directeurs des Instituts Universitaires de Traducteurs et Interprètes, 1971 (Chm. 1974-75); Nat. Council for Modern Languages, 1972-75 (Sec. 1972-74); Jt Sec., Assoc. of Univ. Profs of French, 1973-. Mem., Anglo-French Permanent Mixed Cultural Commn, 1973-. Governor, Bell Educnl Trust, 1972. Corresp. Mem., Académie des Sciences, Agriculture, Arts et Belles Lettres, Aix-en-Provence, 1975; Member: Cttee of Management, British Inst. in Paris, 1975-; Council, Fédération Britannique de l'Alliance Française, 1976-; Comité de Patronage, Centre Charles Maubras, Aix-en-Provence, 1976. FRSA 1974. *Publications:* La Légende de l'Empereur Constant, 1955; (jtly) Glossary of French and English Management Terms, 1972; International Organization Documents for Translation from French, 1972; (jtly) Le français pour l'ingénieur, 1974; (jtly) Glossary of German and English Management Terms; articles in British, French and American periodicals. *Address:* 40 Westfield Close, Bath, Avon. *T:* Bath 316670. *Club:* Carlton.

COVENTRY, family name of **Earl of Coventry.**

COVENTRY, 11th Earl of, *cr* 1697; **George William Coventry;** Viscount Deerhurst, 1697; *b* 25 Jan. 1934; *o s* of 10th Earl and Hon. Nesta Donne Philipps, *e d* of 1st Baron Kylsant; *S* father, 1940; *m* 1st, 1955, Marie Farquhar-Medart (marr. diss. 1963): one *s*; 2nd, 1969, Ann (marr. diss. 1975), *d* of F. W. J. Cripps, Bickley, Kent. *Educ:* Eton; RMA, Sandhurst. *Heir:* *s* Viscount Deerhurst, *qv*.
See also Earl of Harrowby.

COVENTRY, Bishop of, since 1976; **Rt. Rev. John Gibbs;** *b* 15 March 1917; *s* of late A. E. Gibbs, Bournemouth; *m* 1943, G. Marion, *d* of late W. J. Bishop, Poole, Dorset; one *s* one *d*. *Educ:* Univ. of Bristol; Western Coll., Bristol; Lincoln Theological Coll. BA (Bristol); BD (London). In the ministry of the Congregational Church, 1943-49. Student Christian Movement: Inter-Collegiate Sec., 1949-51; Study Sec. and Editor of Student Movement, 1951-55. Curate of St Luke's, Brislington, Bristol, 1955-57; Chaplain and Head of Divinity Dept, Coll. of St Matthias, Bristol, 1957-64, Vice-Principal, 1962-64; Principal, Keswick Hall Coll. of Education, Norwich, 1964-73; Examining Chaplain to Bishop of Norwich, Hon. Canon of Norwich Cathedral, 1968-73; Bishop Suffragan of Bradwell, 1973-76. Member, Durham Commn on Religious Education, 1967-70; Chairman: C of E Children's Council, 1968-71; C of E Bd of Educn Publications Cttee, 1971-, Education and Community Cttee, 1974-76. *Recreations:* music, sailing, bird watching. *Address:* Bishop's House, 23 Davenport Road, Coventry, W Midlands CV5 6PW.

COVENTRY, Archdeacon of; *see* Bridges, Ven. P. S. G.

COVENTRY, Provost of; *see* Williams, Very Rev. Harold C. N.

COVENTRY, Rev. John Seton, SJ; Master, St Edmund's House, Cambridge, since 1976; *b* 21 Jan. 1915; *yr s* of late Seton and Annie Coventry, Barton-on-Sea, Hants. *Educ:* Stonyhurst; Campion Hall, Oxford. MA Oxon 1945. Entered Society of Jesus, 1932; ordained, 1947; Prefect of Studies, Beaumont, 1950; Rector, Beaumont, 1956-58; Provincial, English Province of Soc. of Jesus, 1958-64; Lectr in Theology, Heythrop Coll., 1965-76. *Publications:* Morals and Independence, 1946; The Breaking of Bread, 1950; Faith Seeks Understanding, 1951; The Life Story of the Mass, 1959; The Theology of Faith, 1968; Christian Truth, 1975. *Address:* St Edmund's House, Cambridge CB3 0BN. *T:* Cambridge 50398.

COWAN, Prof. Charles Donald, MA Cantab, PhD London; Professor of the History of South-East Asia in the University of London since 1961; Director, School of Oriental and African Studies, London, since 1976; *b* London, 18 Nov. 1923; *s* of W. C. Cowan and Minnie Ethel (*née* Farrow); *m* 1st, 1945, Mary Evelyn, *d* of Otto Vetter, Perth, WA (marr. diss. 1960); two *d*; 2nd, 1962, Daphne Eleanor, *d* of Walter Rishworth Whittam, Rangoon. *Educ:* Kilburn Grammar Sch.; Peterhouse, Cambridge. Served Royal Navy, 1941-45. Lecturer in History, Raffles Coll., Singapore, 1947-48, and University of Malaya, 1948-50; Lectr in the History of South-East Asia, Sch. of Oriental and African Studies, University of London, 1950-60. Visiting Prof. of South-East Asian History, Cornell Univ., 1960-

61. *Publications:* Nineteenth Century Malaya, 1961; (ed) The Economic Development of South-East Asia, 1964; (ed) The Economic Development of China and Japan, 1964; (with P. L. Burns) Sir Frank Swettenham's Malayan Journals, 1975; (with O. L. Wolters) Southeast Asian History and Historiography, 1976. *Address:* School of Oriental and African Studies, University of London, WC1.

COWAN, Sir Christopher (George) Armstrong, Kt 1958; JP; *b* 6 April 1889; *s* of late William James Cowan and Frances Isabella Cowan, Wood Green, London; *m* 1912, Bertha Lydia Caroline, *d* of late James and Emma Ross; one *s* (and one *s* decd). *Educ:* Merchant Taylors' Sch. Barrister-at-Law, Middle Temple, 1927; SE Circuit, Surrey and S London Sessions. Mem. Ruislip-Northwood Urban Dist Council, 1936-49. Mddx CC: Councillor, 1937, Alderman, 1951-58, Vice-Chm., 1955-56, Chm., 1956-57; Alderman, 1961-65; High Sheriff, Mddx, 1960; JP, 1942; Chm. Uxbridge Bench, 1947-64 (Dep.-Chm. 1944-47). Ex-Member: Standing Jt Cttee; Magistrates' Courts Cttee; Advisory Cttee; Agricultural Wages Cttee; NW Home Counties Regional Advisory Water Cttee, 1945-58, 1961-65; Northwood and Pinner Hosp. Bd, 1936-48 (Chm.). Member: Harefield and Northwood Group Hosp. Management Cttee, 1948-63; NW Metrop. Reg. Hosp. Bd, 1957-63; Chm. Nat. Assistance Tribunals, 1934-49; Chm. Cowan Brothers (Stratford) Ltd until 1968. *Address:* Kiln Farm, Northwood, Mddx. *T:* Northwood 21122.

COWAN, Brig. Colin Hunter, DL; Chief Executive, Cumbernauld Development Corporation, since 1970; *b* 16 Oct. 1920; *s* of late Lt-Col S. Hunter Cowan, DSO and Mrs Jean Hunter Cowan; *m* 1949, Elizabeth Williamson, MD; two *s* one *d*. *Educ:* Wellington Coll.; RMA Woolwich; Trinity Coll., Cambridge (MA). MICE. Comd Engineer Regt, 1960-63; Defence Adviser, UK Mission to the UN, 1964-66; Brigadier Engineer Plans, MoD (Army), 1968-70. DL Dunbartonshire, 1973. *Recreations:* music, photography. *Address:* Hillcroft, Dullatur by Glasgow GS8 0AW. *T:* Cumbernauld 23242. *Club:* Army and Navy.

COWAN, Maj.-Gen. David Tennant, CB 1945; CBE 1945; DSO 1942, Bar 1944; MC; Indian Army (retired); late RARO; *b* 8 Oct. 1896; *s* of Charles Thomas and Kate Cowan; *m* 1st, 1920, Anne Elliot Dunlop (*d* 1973); one *d* (one *s* killed in action); 2nd, 1973, Frances Elisabeth Newall, *widow* of Lt-Col F. H. A. Stables. *Educ:* Reading; Glasgow Univ. 2nd Lieut Argyll and Sutherland Highlanders, 1915; Capt. 1920; Bt Major, 1933; Major, 1934; Bt Lt-Col 1938; Lt-Col 1940; Brig. 1941; Maj.-Gen. 1942. Served European War, 1914-18 with 2nd Bn, The Argyll and Sutherland Highlanders (despatches, MC); 3rd Afghan War; Waziristan Ops, 1919-20 (despatches) and 1937 (despatches). 6th Gurkha Rifles, 1917-40; Staff Coll., Quetta, 1927-28; Chief Instructor, Indian Military Academy, 1932-34; Comdt 1/6 Gurkha Rifles, 1939-40; DDMT GHQ, India, 1941; Offg DMT, GHQ, India, 1941-42. War of 1939-45 in Burma (despatches, DSO and bar, CBE, CB). GOC 17th Indian Div., 1942-45, and British and Indian Div., British Commonwealth Occupation Force, Japan, 1945-46. Retd 1947, RARO 1948. Commandant, Devon Army Cadet Force, 1948-58. Chm. Approved Sch., Devon, 1951-60; Sec. (part-time) Assoc. of Managers of Approved Schs, 1963-73. DL Devon, 1953-63. Hon. Commandant Empire Village, VIth British Empire and Commonwealth Games, Wales, 1958. *Recreations:* games, fishing. *Address:* Ridgecoombe, Penton Grafton, Andover, Hants SP10 0RR. *Club:* Army and Navy.

COWAN, William Graham, MBE 1943; Managing Director, J. H. Carruthers & Co. Ltd, since 1950; *b* 29 April 1919; *s* of William Cowan, WS, Edinburgh, and Dorothy Isobel Horsbrugh; *m* 1960, Karen Wendell Hansen, Crestwood, NY; two *s* one *d*. *Educ:* Edinburgh Academy; Cambridge Univ. (MA). CEng, FIMechE, FSIAD, FRSA. Served 1940-46, Royal Engrs and Gen. Staff, Africa, Italy (Lt-Col). Asst Man. Dir, North British Locomotive Co. Ltd, 1947-50; Mem. Exec. Cttee, Scottish Council (Develt and Industry), 1972-74; Pres., Scottish Engrg Employers' Assoc., 1972. Mem., Design Council, 1974- (Chm., Scottish Cttee, 1976-); Mem., Scottish Transport Group, 1977-. *Recreation:* industrial archæology. *Address:* Bryans, Jackton, East Kilbride. *T:* East Kilbride 20012. *Clubs:* Caledonian, New (Edinburgh).

COWANS, Harry Lowes; MP (Lab) Newcastle Central, since Nov. 1976; *b* 1932; *m* Margaret; one *s* three *d*. Was a Technician Officer, Signals and Telecommunications Dept, British Rail. Branch Sec., NUR; Mem. Exec. Cttee, Labour Party Northern Region. Member: Gateshead Metropolitan DC (Chm., Housing Cttee); Tyne and Wear Metropolitan CC (Mem. Management, Finance and Transport Cttees). *Address:* House of Commons,

SW1A 0AA; 4 Station Cottages, Elysium Lane, Bensham, Gateshead NE8 2XH.

COWARD, David John, CMG 1965; OBE 1962; Registrar General, Kenya, since 1955; *b* 21 March 1917; *s* of late Robert J. Coward, Exmouth, Devon; *m* 1954, Joan, *d* of late Reginald Frank, Doncaster; three *d*. *Educ:* Exmouth Grammar Sch. and Law Society's Sch. of Law. Admitted a solicitor, 1938. Joined RN as a rating at outbreak of war, 1939; commissioned, 1941; demobilized as Lieut-Comdr (S) RNVR, 1947. ADC to Governor of Trinidad, 1947. Joined Colonial Legal Service, 1948, Asst Registrar Gen., Kenya; Dep. Registrar Gen., 1952; Registrar Gen., Official Receiver and Public Trustee, 1955. Acted as Permanent Sec. for Justice and Constitutional Affairs, 1963-64. Served in Kenya Police Reserve, 1949-63, latterly as Senior Superintendent i/c Nairobi Area. Colonial Special Constabulary Medal, 1954. *Recreation:* golf. *Address:* PO Box 40,231, Nairobi, Kenya. *T:* Nairobi 20660. *Clubs:* Naval; Nairobi and Limuru Country (Kenya).

COWARD, Richard Edgar; Director General, Bibliographic Services Division, British Library, since 1975; *b* 1927; *s* of Edgar Frank Coward and Jean (*née* McIntyre); *m* 1949, Audrey Scott Lintern; one *s* two *d*. *Educ:* Richmond Grammar Sch., Surrey. FLA. Member: Adv. Cttee on BBC Archives, 1976-; Library Adv. Council (England), 1976-. *Address:* 12 Marylebone Mews, W1. *T:* 01-486 7316.

COWBURN, Norman; Chief General Manager, Britannia Building Society, since 1970; *b* 5 Jan. 1920; *s* of Harold and Edith Cowburn; *m* 1945, Edna Margaret Heatley; two *s* one *d*. *Educ:* Queen Elizabeth's Grammar Sch., Blackburn. FCIS, FBS. Burnley Building Soc., 1936. Served War, 1940-46. Burnley Building Soc., 1946; Leek and Westbourne Building Soc., 1954 (re-named Britannia Building Soc., Dec. 1975). *Recreations:* golf, gardening. *Address:* Greywoods, Birchall, Leek, Staffs. *T:* Leek 383214.

COWDEROY, Brenda; National General Secretary, Young Women's Christian Association of Great Britain, 1971-77; *b* 27 June 1925; *o c* of late Frederick Cowderoy and of Evelyn Cowderoy (*née* Land). *Educ:* Surbiton High Sch.; St Hugh's Coll., Oxford (MA). Called to Bar, Gray's Inn, 1949. John Lewis Partnership: Asst Legal Adviser, 1954-56; Head of Legal Dept, 1956-70. *Recreations:* history of art, golf. *Address:* 26 Rossetti Road, Birchington, Kent.

COWDRAY, 3rd Viscount, *cr* 1917; Weetman John Churchill Pearson, TD; Bt, *cr* 1894; Baron, *cr* 1910; Captain, Sussex Yeomanry; Chairman, S. Pearson & Son Ltd, since 1954; *b* 27 Feb. 1910 (twin); *s* of 2nd Viscount and Agnes Beryl (*d* 1948), *d* of Lord Edward Spencer Churchill; *S* father, 1933; *m* 1st, 1939, Lady Anne Bridgeman (from whom he obtained a divorce, 1950), *d* of 5th Earl of Bradford; one *s* two *d*; 2nd, 1953, Elizabeth Georgiana Mather, 2nd *d* of A. H. M. Jackson; one *s* two *d*. *Educ:* Eton; Christ Church, Oxford. Parliamentary Private Sec. to Under-Sec. of State for Air, 1941-42. *Recreations:* polo, shooting, fishing. *Heir:* s. Hon. Michael Orlando Weetman Pearson [*b* 17 June 1944; *m* 1977, Ellen, *yr d* of late Hermann Erhardt]. *Address:* Cowdray Park, Midhurst, West Sussex. *T:* Midhurst 2461; Dunecht, Skene, Aberdeenshire. *T:* Lyne of Skene 244. *Clubs:* Cavalry and Guards, White's.
    See also Duke of Atholl, Viscount Blakenham, Hon. Mrs Angela Campbell-Preston, Baron Cranworth.

COWDREY, (Michael) Colin, CBE 1972; Executive: Barclays Bank International; Whitbread & Co. Ltd; Director, Whitbread Fremlins; *b* 24 Dec. 1932; *s* of Ernest Arthur Cowdrey and Kathleen Mary Cowdrey (*née* Taylor); *m* 1956, Penelope Susan Cowdrey (*née* Chiesman); three *s* one *d*. *Educ:* Homefield, Sutton, Surrey; Tonbridge; Brasenose Coll., Oxford. Cricket: 5 years Tonbridge Sch. XI (Capt., 1949-50); Public Schs (Lord's) (Capt. 1950); (3 years) Oxford XI (Capt. 1954); Kent Cap, 1951 (Captain, 1957-71); 117 appearances for England, 1954-75; Capt. 23 times; 11 Overseas Tours; 107 centuries in first class cricket, of which 23 were Test centuries; on retirement in 1975, held record for most runs and most catches in Test Matches. Runner-up Amateur Rackets Title, Queen's Club, 1953 and Doubles, 1965. Member: Council, Australia Soc.; Winston Churchill Memorial Trust. Freeman, City of London, 1962. *Publications:* Cricket Today, 1961; Time for Reflection, 1962; Tackle Cricket This Way, 1969; The Incomparable Game, 1970; MCC: the Autobiography of a Cricketer, 1976. *Recreation:* golf. *Address:* Kentish Border, Limpsfield, Surrey. *T:* Limpsfield Chart 2377. *Club:* MCC.

COWDRY, Rt. Rev. Roy Walter Frederick; Assistant Bishop of Port Elizabeth, since 1970; Rector of St Cuthbert's, Port

Elizabeth, since 1964; *b* 28 April 1915; *s* of Frederick William Thomas Cowdry and Florence Emma (*née* Roberts); *m* 1964, Elizabeth Melene, *d* of Rt Rev. B. W. Peacey; two *s*. *Educ:* King's Coll., London. Deacon, 1941; Priest, 1942. Asst Curate: St Nicholas, Perivale, 1941-44; Christ Church, Ealing, 1944-50; Domestic Chaplain to Archbishop of Cape Town, 1950-58; Asst Bishop of Cape Town, 1958-61; Bishop Suffragan of Cape Town, 1961-64; Asst Bishop of Grahamstown, 1965-70. Chaplain, Cape Town Gaol, 1951-57. Chaplain, OStJ, 1961. *Address:* St Cuthbert's Rectory, 24 Westbourne Road, Port Elizabeth 6001, S Africa. *T:* 332526. *Club:* Port Elizabeth.

COWE, (Robert George) Collin; Fellow and Senior Bursar, Magdalen College, Oxford, since 1970; *b* 24 Sept. 1917; *s* of Peter and Annie Cowe, Berwick-upon-Tweed; *m* 1943, Gladys May, *d* of William Greenwood Wright and Jessie Wright, Bingley, Yorks; one *d*. *Educ:* The Duke's Sch., Alnwick; The Grammar Sch., Berwick-upon-Tweed; Edinburgh Univ. MA (Hons Classics) 1939; MA Oxon, 1970. Served Royal Regiment of Artillery, Field Branch, 1939-46; Major, RA, 1944-46. National Coal Board, 1947-70; Private Sec. to Chm., 1947-49; Principal Private Sec. to Chm., 1949-52; Sec., East Midlands Div., 1952-55; Staff Dir, North-Eastern Div., 1955-58; Dep.-Sec. to NCB, 1958-59; Sec., 1960-67; Man. Dir, Associated Heat Services Ltd (associate co. of NCB), 1967-69. *Recreations:* riding, swimming. *Address:* Brookside Cottage, Brook End, Chadlington, Oxford OX7 3NF. *T:* Chadlington 373.

COWELL, Frank Richard, CMG 1952; BA, BSc (Econ), PhD London; retired Civil Servant; Secretary United Kingdom National Commission for UNESCO, 1946-58; *b* 16 Nov. 1897; *s* of William Frank Cowell and E. A. Pearce; *m* 1927, Lilian Margaret (*d* 1970), *d* of Rev. A. E. Palin; two *s*. *Educ:* Roan Sch., Greenwich; King's Coll., London; London Sch. of Economics. BA 1919, BSc (Econ) 1927. Rockefeller Foundation Fellow in the Social Sciences, 1929-31; PhD 1938. Served in HM Stationery Office, 1921-39; Foreign Office, 1939-46. Dep. Sec. Gen. British Council, May-Nov. 1940; served on British Mission to French National Cttee, 1940-43. *Publications:* Brief Guide to Government Publications, 1938; Cicero and the Roman Republic, 1948, 6th edn (Penguin), 1972; History, Civilization and Culture, 1952; Culture, 1959; Everyday Life in Ancient Rome, 1961, 7th edn 1972; Revolutions of Ancient Rome, 1962; Values in Human Society, 1970; The Dominance of Rome, 1970; The Athenæum: Club and Social Life 1824-1974, 1975; Leibniz, 1978. *Address:* Crowdleham House, Kemsing, Kent. *T:* Sevenoaks 61192. *Club:* Athenæum.
See also J . R . Cowell.

COWELL, John Richard; Secretary, Royal Horticultural Society, since 1975; *b* 30 April 1933; *er s* of Frank Richard Cowell, *qv*; *m* 1972, Josephine Suzanne Elizabeth, *d* of I.A.F. Craig, Burneston, Yorks; two *s* one *d*. *Educ:* Westminster Sch.; Trinity Coll., Cambridge (MA). Secretariat: London Chamber of Commerce, 1957-58; Royal Horticultural Soc., 1958-. *Recreations:* gardening, fishing. *Address:* Crowdleham House, Kemsing, Sevenoaks, Kent. *T:* Sevenoaks 61192. *Club:* Athenæum.

COWEN, Alan Biddulph, CMG 1961; OBE 1945; retired as Deputy Chairman of Standards Association of Rhodesia and Nyasaland; *b* 26 Sept. 1896; *m*; two *s*. *Educ:* St John's Coll., Johannesburg, S Africa; Sch. of Mines and Technology. Formerly Chm., Southern Rhodesian Electricity Supply Commission; Mem. of Federal Power Board. CEng; FIEE; F(SA)IEE. *Address:* 325 Main Road, Eastcliff, Hermanus, Cape Province, S Africa.

COWEN, John David, MC 1943; TD 1944; MA; FSA; Director, Barclays Bank Ltd, 1965-74; *b* 16 Nov. 1904; *e s* of John Edward Cowen, Minsteracres, Northumberland; *m* 1944, Rhoda Susan Harris; one *s* two *d*. *Educ:* Rugby (scholar); Hertford Coll., Oxford (scholar). Final Law Soc. Exams (Hons), 1931. Entered Barclays Bank Ltd, 1931; Gen. Manager (Staff), 1948-49; Gen. Manager, 1950-65. Fellow, Inst. of Bankers (Mem. Council, 1950-59); Chairman: Inter-Bank Cttee on Electronics, 1955-61; Inter-Bank Working Party on Negotiating Machinery in Banking, 1965-67. Joined Northumberland Hussars Yeomanry, 1929; Major, 1942; served in North Africa, Sicily (despatches), France and Germany. Dir, Newcastle upon Tyne and Gateshead Gas Co., 1934-47 (Chm. 1947). Mem., Standing Commn on Museums and Galls, 1966-73; Governor, Museum of London, 1965-67; Vice-Pres., Soc. of Antiquaries of London (Treasurer, 1964-71); Pres., The Prehistoric Soc., 1966-70; Pres. Soc. of Antiquaries of Newcastle upon Tyne, 1966-68 (Hon. Curator, 1933-39, 1947-48); Hon. Mem. German Archaeolog. Inst.; Hon. DCL (Durham), 1961. *Publications:* articles in banking and archaeological jls (Brit. and foreign). *Recreations:* prehistory,

travel. *Address:* Over Court, Bisley, near Stroud, Glos GL6 7BE. *T:* Bisley 209; 35 Argyll Road, W8 7DA. *T:* 01-937 2127. *Club:* Athenæum.

COWEN, Sir Zelman, Kt 1976; CMG 1968; QC (Aust.) 1971; Governor-General of Australia, since Dec. 1977; *b* 7 Oct. 1919; *s* of late Bernard and of Sara Cowen; *m* 1945, Anna Wittner; three *s* one *d*. *Educ:* Scotch Coll., Melbourne; University of Melbourne; Oxford Univ. BA 1939, LLB 1941, LLM 1942, Melbourne; BCL, MA 1947, DCL 1968, Oxford. Lieut, RANVR, 1941-45. Called to Bar, Gray's Inn, 1947; called to Vic (Aust.) Bar, 1951, Queensland Bar, 1971. Victorian Rhodes Schol., 1941; Vinerian Schol., Oxford Univ., 1947. Fellow and Tutor, Oriel Coll., Oxford, 1947-50; Prof. of Public Law and Dean of Faculty of Law, University of Melbourne, 1951-66; Dominion Liaison Officer to Colonial Office (UK), 1951-66; Prof. Emer., University of Melbourne, 1967; Vice-Chancellor and Professor, Univ. of New England, Armidale, NSW, 1967-70; Vice-Chancellor, Qld Univ., 1970-77. Vis. Professor: University of Chicago, 1949; Harvard Univ., 1953-54 and 1963-64; Fletcher Sch. of Law and Diplomacy, 1954 and 1964; University of Utah, 1954; University of Ill, 1957-58; Washington Univ., St Louis, 1959; Tagore Law Prof., Univ. of Calcutta, 1975. Mem., Social Science Res. Coun. of Aust., 1952-; For. Hon. Mem., Amer. Acad. of Arts and Sciences, 1965. Broadcaster on radio and TV on nat. and internat. affairs; Mem. and Chm., Victorian State Adv. Cttee of Australian Broadcasting Commn (at various times during 1950's and 1960's); Mem., Chief Justice's Law Reform Cttee, 1951-66; President: Asthma Foundn of Victoria, 1963-66; Adult Educn Assoc. of Australia, 1968-70; Aust. Inst. of Urban Studies, 1973. Mem., Club of Rome, 1973; Mem., Law Reform Commn, Australia, 1976-; Chm., Aust. Vice-Chancellors' Cttee, 1977-78. Mem. Board: Governors, Hebrew Univ. of Jerusalem, 1969-; Directors, Australian Opera, 1969; Internat. Assoc. for Cultural Freedom, 1970; Chm. Bd of Governors, Utah Foundn, 1975; Trustee, Queensland Univ. Overseas Foundn, 1976. FRSA 1971; FASSA 1972; FACE 1972. Hon. LLD: Hong Kong, 1967; Queensland, 1972; Melbourne, 1973. *Publications:* (ed jtly) Dicey's Conflict of Laws, 1949; Australia and the United States: Some Legal Comparisons, 1954; (with P. B. Carter) Essays on the Law of Evidence, 1956; American-Australian Private International Law, 1957; Federal Jurisdiction in Australia, 1959; (with D. M. da Costa) Matrimonial Causes Jurisdiction, 1961; Sir John Latham and other papers, 1965; British Commonwealth of Nations in a Changing World, 1965; Isaac Isaacs, 1967; The Private Man, 1969; Faces of Liberty, 1977; articles and chapters in legal works in UK, US, Canada, Germany, Australia. *Recreations:* swimming, music, theatre. *Address:* Government House, Canberra, ACT 2600, Australia. *Clubs:* Queensland (Brisbane); University (Sydney).

COWERN, Raymond Teague, RA 1968 (ARA 1957); RWS; RE; ARCA; RWA; painter, etcher and draughtsman; *b* 12 July 1913; *s* of George Dent Cowern and Elsie Ellen Teague; *m* Margaret Jean Trotman; one *s* two *d*. *Educ:* King Edward's Grammar Sch., Aston, Birmingham. Studied Central Sch. of Art, Birmingham, Royal Coll. of Art, London. Worked with Sakkarah Expedition of the Oriental Institute of Chicago; Rome Scholar in Engraving, 1937-39; commissioned by Pilgrim Trust Scheme for Recording Britain. Served in the Army, 1940-46. Principal, Brighton Coll. of Art, 1958-70; Associate Dir, and Dean of Faculty of Art and Design, Brighton Polytechnic, 1970-74. Represented by work at British Museum and in public collections Glasgow, Liverpool, Birmingham, Oxford, Cambridge, Bristol and museums abroad. *Address:* 41 Irish Street, Whitehaven, Cumbria CA28 7BY.

COWEY, Brig. Bernard Turing Vionnée, DSO 1945; OBE 1976; DL; *b* 20 Nov. 1911; *s* of late Lt-Col R. V. Cowey, DSO, RAMC and late Mrs B. A. Cowey (*née* Blancke); *m* 1947, Margaret Heath Dean (*née* Godwin). *Educ:* Wellington; RMC Sandhurst. Commnd The Welch Regt, 1931; served War of 1939-45: N Africa, 1939-41 (despatches 1941); psc 1941; India, 1942-43; Burma, 1944-45; CO 2 Yorks and Lancs, 1944; CO 2 Welch, 1945-47; Co. Comdr RMA Sandhurst, 1947-49; Chief Instructor, Staff Coll., Quetta, 1952-53; CO 1 Welch, 1953-56; Comd (Brig.) 9 Indep. Armd Bde Gp TA, 1956 and 148 Inf. Bde Gp TA, 1956-58; Inspector of Intelligence, 1961-63; retd 1963. Sec., Notts T&AFA, 1965-67; TAVR Council (formerly TA Council): Dep. Sec., 1967-72; Sec., 1973-75. DL Notts, 1973. Regional Sec., British Field Sports Soc., 1976-. *Recreations:* Rugby football (played for Wales, Barbarians and Army, 1934-35; Chm., Army Rugby Union Referees Soc., 1963-73); Arab horses (Hon. Show Dir, Arab Horse Show, 1968-). *Address:* Trent Hills Farm, Flintham, Newark, Notts. *T:* 063-68 5274. *Clubs:* Army and Navy, British Sportsman's.

COWGILL, Bryan; Managing Director, Thames Television, since 1977; *b* 27 May 1927; *m* 1966, Jennifer E. Baker; two *s. Educ:* Clitheroe Grammar School. Marine, subseq. Lieut, 3rd Royal Marine Commando Bde, SE Asia, 1943-47. Copy boy, then reporter, then feature writer with Lancashire Evening Post and Preston Guardian Group, 1942-50; edited local newspaper, Clitheroe, 1950-55; joined BBC TV as Outside Broadcasts prodn asst, 1955; produced Sportsview and Grandstand, 1957-63; Head of BBC Sport, 1963; Head of TV Outside Broadcasts Group, 1972; Controller, BBC1, 1974-77; Dir, News and Current Affairs, BBC, 1977. *Recreation:* golf. *Address:* Thames Television House, 306-316 Euston Road, NW1 3BB. *T:* 01-387 9494.

COWIE, Hon. Lord; William Lorn Kerr Cowie; a Senator of the College of Justice in Scotland, since 1977; *b* 1 June 1926; *s* of late Charles Rennie Cowie, MBE and Norah Slimmon Kerr; *m* 1958, Camilla Henrietta Grizel Hoyle; two *s* two *d. Educ:* Fettes Coll.; Clare Coll., Cambridge; Glasgow Univ. Sub-Lieut RNVR, 1944-47; Cambridge, 1947-49; Glasgow Univ., 1949-51; Mem., Faculty of Advocates, 1952; QC (Scotland) 1967. *Address:* 20 Blacket Place, Edinburgh EH9 1RL. *T:* 031-667 8238.

COWIE, Mervyn Hugh, CBE 1960; ED 1954; Financial Director, African Medical and Research Foundation (Flying Doctor Services), since 1972; *b* 13 April 1909; *s* of Capt. Herbert Hugh Cowie, JP; *m* 1st, 1934, Erica Mary Beaty (*d* 1956); two *s* one *d*; 2nd, 1957, Valori Hare Duke; one *s* one *d. Educ:* Brighton; Brasenose Coll., Oxford. Hon. Game Warden, 1932-; Mem. Nairobi District Council, 1932-36; KAR, Reserve of Officers, 1932-38 (3rd and 5th Battalions); Kenya Regt, 1939; served War of 1939-45; Abyssinia, Middle East, Madagascar (retd Lieut-Col). MLC Kenya, 1951-60; Dir of Manpower, Mau-Mau Emergency, 1953-56. Founder and Dir, Royal National Parks of Kenya, 1946-66. Vice-Pres. E African Tourist Travel Assoc., 1950-65; Mem. Nat. Parks Commn, Internat. Union for Conservation of Nature, 1959-66; Hon. Trustee, Uganda Nat. Parks, 1950-; Vice-Pres., Fauna Preservation Soc., London; Trustee, East African Wild Life Soc. TV and Radio (BBC Natural History Section). Editor, Royal Nat. Parks of Kenya Annual Reports, 1946-65. Lectures (tours USA and Britain). FCA; FZS. Gold Medal, San Diego Zool Soc., 1972. Order of the Golden Ark, Netherlands, 1975. *Publications:* Fly Vulture, 1961; I Walk with Lions (USA), 1964; African Lion, 1965. Contributor to International Journals and Conferences. *Recreations:* big game photography, mountaineering, flying and wild life conservation. *Address:* PO Box 55549, Mbagathi, Nairobi, Kenya. *T:* Langata 891060. *Clubs:* Shikar; Explorer's (New York); Muthaiga Country (Nairobi); Nairobi Rotary (Past Pres.); Mountain Club of Kenya.

COWIE, William Lorn Kerr; *see* Cowie, Hon. Lord.

COWLES, Virginia, OBE 1947; writer; *b* USA, 24 Aug. 1912; *d* of Florence Wolcott Jaquith and Edward Spencer Cowles; *m* 1945, Aidan M. Crawley, *qv*; two *s* one *d. Educ:* privately. Newspaper correspondent, 1937-41 and 1943-45; Special Asst to the American Ambassador, American Embassy, London, 1942-43. *Publications:* Looking for Trouble, 1941; How America is Governed, 1944; No Cause for Alarm, 1949; Winston Churchill: The Era and the Man, 1953; Edward VII and His Circle, 1956; The Phantom Major, 1958; The Great Swindle, 1960; The Kaiser, 1963; 1913: The Defiant Swan Song, 1967; The Russian Dagger, 1969; The Romanovs, 1971; The Rothschilds, 1973. *Recreation:* politics. *Address:* 19 Chester Square, SW1. *T:* 01-730 3030.

COWLES-VOYSEY, Charles, FRIBA, retired; *b* 24 June 1889; *e s* of Charles Francis Annesley Voysey, FRIBA, architect; *m* 1912, Dorothea Denise Cowles; no *c. Educ:* private sch.; University Coll., London. Architect for: Worthing Civic Centre; White Rock Pavilion, Hastings; the Guildhall, Cambridge; Watford Town Hall; Bromley (Kent), Town Hall Extensions; Bridgeton Halls, Glasgow; Municipal Offices, High Wycombe; Kingsley Hall, Bow; Bognor Regis Municipal Offices; Hampshire County Council Offices, Winchester, and other public buildings and private houses; Consulting Architect to various local authorities. *Recreation:* landscape painting. *Address:* 2 Bunkers Hill, NW11 6XA. *T:* 01-455 7274. *Club:* Athenæum.

COWLEY, 7th Earl *cr* 1857; **Garret Graham Wellesley;** Baron Cowley, 1828; Viscount Dangan, 1857; Vice-President, and Senior Investment Manager, Trust Department, Bank of America, San Francisco, since 1974; *b* 30 July 1934; 3rd *s* of 4th Earl Cowley (*d* 1962) and of Mary (Elsie May), Countess Cowley; *S* nephew, 1975; *m* 1st, 1961, Elizabeth Suzanne Lennon (marr. diss. 1966), S Carolina; one *s* one *d*; 2nd, 1968,

Isabelle O'Bready, Quebec, Canada. *Educ:* Univ. of S California (BSc Finance 1957); Harvard Univ. (MBA 1962). Investment Research Analyst: Wells Fargo Bank, San Francisco, 1962-64; Dodge & Cox, San Francisco, 1964-66; Asst Head, Investment Research Dept, Wells Fargo Bank, 1966-67; Vice-Pres., Investment Counsel, Thorndike, Doran, Paine & Lewis, Los Angeles, 1967-69; Vice-Pres., Exec. Cttee Mem., Securities, Real Estate and Company Acquisition Advisor, Shareholders Capital Corp., Los Angeles, 1969-74. Served US Army Counter Intelligence Corps, primarily in France, 1957-60. *Heir: s* Viscount Dangan, *qv. Address:* 124 Waldo Avenue, Piedmont, California 94611, USA. *T:* 415-547-6929. *Club:* Harvard (San Francisco).

COWLEY, Rev. Canon Colin Patrick; Rector of Wonston, Winchester, 1955-71; Canon of Winchester, 1950-55, Hon. Canon, 1955; Canon Emeritus, 1971; *b* 3 Aug. 1902; *er s* of Rev. H. G. B. Cowley; *m* 1930, Dorothea Minna Pott, 69 Victoria Road, Kensington, W8; three *d. Educ:* Winchester; Hertford Coll., Oxford. Curate at St Mary's, Bridport, 1926-28; Curate at St Mary Abbots, Kensington, 1928-35; Rector of Shenfield, Essex, 1935-50. Chaplain to the Forces, 1940-45. *Recreations:* golf and walking. *Address:* Cheriton Lodge, 42 Cheriton Road, Winchester, Hants.

COWLEY, Denis Martin; AE 1945; QC 1965; a Recorder of the Crown Court, since 1974; Deputy Senior Judge, Sovereign Base Areas, Cyprus; *b* 30 Jan. 1919; *s* of late Sir William Percy Cowley, CBE; *m* 1940, Margaret Hazel, *d* of Hugo Teare, Ramsey, Isle of Man; one *s* two *d. Educ:* Radley Coll.; Exeter Coll., Oxford (MA (Hons Jurisprudence)). Served RAFVR, 1939-45. Called to Bar, Inner Temple, 1946; Bencher, 1972. Midland and Oxford Circuit. *Recreations:* shooting, sailing. *Address:* 2a Huntingdon Drive, The Park, Nottingham. *T:* 42948; Ellan Vannin, The Quay, Castletown, Isle of Man. *T:* Castletown 3532; Francis Taylor Buildings, Temple, EC4. *T:* 01-353 9942. *Club:* United Oxford & Cambridge University.

COWLEY, Maj.-Gen. John Cain, CB 1971; Paymaster-in-Chief and Inspector of Army Pay Services, Ministry of Defence, 1967-72, retired; joined de Zoete and Bevan, Stockbrokers, 1972; *b* 17 July 1918; *er s* of late Philip Richard and Eleanor Cowley, Ballaquane, Peel, Isle of Man; *m* 1948, Eileen Rosemary, *d* of late George Percival Stewart, Aigburth, Liverpool; three *s. Educ:* Douglas School, Isle of Man. War of 1939-45: commissioned, RAPC, 1940; served: Palestine, Western Desert, Italy, France, Belgium, Holland, Germany. Dep. Asst Adj.-Gen., Middle East, 1949-51; GSOI, with Permanent Under Sec., War Office, 1952-54; West African Frontier Force, 1956-59; Dep. Paymaster-in-Chief: War Office, 1960-63; BAOR, 1963-65; Chief Paymaster, Eastern Command, 1965-67. Capt. 1946, Maj. 1953, Lt-Col 1955, Col. 1960, Brig. 1963, Maj.-Gen. 1967; psc, 1948; jssc, 1955; Administrative Staff Coll., 1960. Col Comdt, RAPC, 1974-. *Recreations:* shooting, fishing, ornithology. *Address:* The Old Post Office, Nuthurst, Horsham, West Sussex. *T:* Lower Beeding 266. *Clubs:* Army and Navy, Flyfishers'.

COWLEY, Lt-Gen. Sir John Guise, GC (AM 1935); KBE 1958 (CBE 1946; OBE 1943); CB 1954; late RE; Chairman, Polamco Ltd, since 1976; *b* 20 Aug. 1905; *s* of Rev. Henry Guise Beatson Cowley, Fourgates, Dorchester, Dorset; *m* 1941, Irene Sybil, *d* of Percy Dreuille Millen, Berkhamsted, Herts; one *s* three *d. Educ:* Wellington Coll.; RMA Woolwich. 2nd Lieut RE 1925; Capt. 1936; Major 1940; Lieut-Col 1941; Brig. 1943; Maj.-Gen. 1953; Lieut-Gen. 1957. Served War of 1939-45, Middle East, Italy, and North-West Europe (despatches four times, OBE). Chief of Staff, HQ, Eastern Command, 1953-56; Vice-QMG, 1956-57; Controller of Munitions, Ministry of Supply, 1957-60; Master-Gen. of the Ordnance, War Office, 1960-62; retd, 1962. Col Commandant: Royal Pioneer Corps, 1961-67; Royal Engineers, 1961-70. Chairman: Bowmaker Ltd, 1962-71; Wilverley Securities Ltd, 1970-73; Keith and Henderson Ltd, 1973-76; Director: British Oxygen Ltd, 1962-76; Alastair Watson Ltd, 1962-70; C. T. Bowring and Co. Ltd, 1969-71. Governor, Wellington Coll., 1960-76, Vice-Pres. and Chm. of Governors, 1969-76; Chairman of Governors: Eagle House Sch., 1968-76; Bigshotte Sch., 1968-76; Governor, Brockenhurst Sixth Form Coll., 1969-. Knight Comdr Order of Orange Nassau (Netherlands). FRSA. *Recreations:* golf, bridge. *Address:* Whitemoor, Sandy Down, Boldre, Lymington, Hants. *T:* Brockenhurst 3369. *Club:* Army and Navy.

COWLEY, Kenneth Martin, CMG 1963; OBE 1956; Secretary, Oversea Services Pensioners Association; *b* 15 May 1912; *s* of late Robert Martin Cowley, OBE, and late Mabel Priscilla Cowley (*née* Lee); *m* 1948, Barbara (*née* Tannahill); one *s* (and one step *s*). *Educ:* Merchant Taylors' Sch., Crosby; Exeter Coll., Oxford. District Officer, Kenya, 1935-44; Asst Sec., 1944-46;

District Comr, 1946-49; Actg Native Courts Officer, 1949-53; Sec. for African Affairs, 1953-56; Provincial Commissioner, Southern Province, Kenya, 1956-63 (despatches, 1957); Sec., Kenya Regional Boundaries and Constituencies Commns, 1962; Sen. Administrative Manager, Express Transport Co. Ltd, Kenya, 1963-70. *Recreation:* natural history. *Address:* Grasmere, 38 Wellington Avenue, Fleet, Hants. *T:* Fleet 5990. *Clubs:* East India, Sports and Public Schools; Nairobi (Kenya).

COWLING, Richard John, ARICS; Deputy Chief Valuer, Inland Revenue Valuation Office, 1972-74; *b* 2 Feb. 1911; *s* of Sydney George and Madge Prentice Cowling, late of East Grinstead; *m* 1936, Doris Rosa, *o d* of Albert James Puttock, Guildford; one *s*. *Educ:* Skinners' Company's Sch. Articles and private practice as a surveyor, 1928-35; War Office Lands Branch, 1936; Inland Revenue Valuation Office, 1937. TA Commission, Green Howards, 1942. *Recreations:* golf, bridge, sailing. *Address:* 18 Gateways, Epsom Road, Guildford, Surrey GU1 2LF. *T:* Guildford 73473.

COWLING, Thomas George, FRS 1947; Professor of Applied Mathematics, Leeds University, 1948-70, now Professor Emeritus; *b* 17 June 1906; *s* of George and Edith Eliza Cowling; *m* 1935, Doris Moffatt; one *s* two *d*. *Educ:* Sir George Monoux Sch., Walthamstow; Oxford Univ. Teacher of mathematics, Imperial Coll. of Science, University Coll., Swansea, University Coll., Dundee, Manchester Univ., and at University Coll., Bangor (Prof. of Mathematics, 1945-48). Gold Medallist, Royal Astronomical Soc., 1956, Pres., 1965-67. Hon. Fellow, Brasenose Coll., Oxford, 1966. Halley Lectr, Oxford Univ., 1969. *Publications:* (with S. Chapman) The Mathematical Theory of Non-Uniform Gases, 1939; Molecules in Motion, 1950; Magneto-hydrodynamics, 1957, 2nd edn 1976; also a number of papers, chiefly astronomical and gas-theoretic. *Recreation:* gardening. *Address:* 19 Hollin Gardens, Leeds LS16 5NL. *T:* 785342.

COWPER, Brig. Anthony William, CBE 1964 (OBE 1945); company director; *b* 10 May 1913; *s* of Walter Taylor Cowper, solicitor, Southgate, London, and West Burton, Yorks; *m* 1949, Margaret Mary, *d* of Clarence W. Fry, Upminster, Essex; no *c*. *Educ:* Merchant Taylors' Sch. Joined Christie's, Fine Art Auctioneers, 1932. Commissioned from TA (HAC) into West Yorks Regt, Nov. 1939; War Service in India, Burma, Ceylon and Singapore, 1940-45 (OBE). Granted regular commn, 1947; served overseas almost continuously (mainly Far East) in Regtl and Staff appts (despatches, Malayan Emergency, 1954); Col 1961; Brig. 1965; Defence Adviser to British High Comr in Malaysia, 1967; retd 1969. Freeman of City of London. *Recreations:* fly fishing, small boat sailing, antiques, Far East affairs. *Address:* 97 Kingsway Gardens, 38 Kings Park Road, Perth, West Australia 6005. *T:* 213373.

COWPER, Sir Norman (Lethbridge), Kt 1967; CBE 1958; *b* 15 Sept. 1896; *yr s* of Cecil Spencer de Grey Cowper; *m* 1925, Dorothea Huntly, *d* of Hugh McCrae; three *d*. *Educ:* Sydney Grammar Sch.; University of Sydney (BA, LLB). Served War of 1939-45, 2nd AIF, Lt.-Col. Solicitor, Supreme Court of NSW, 1923. Partner, Allen, Allen & Hemsley, 1924-70. Dir, Australian Inst. of Polit. Science, 1932-69; Mem. Council, Australian National Univ., 1955-74; Mem. Board of Trustees, Sydney Grammar Sch., 1935-75 (Chm., 1951-75); Chm., Council on New Guinea Affairs, 1965. *Publications:* occasional articles: Australian Quarterly, Australian Outlook, Australian Dictionary of Biography. *Recreations:* reading, gardening. *Address:* Wivenhoe, Millewa Avenue, Wahroonga, Sydney, Australia. *T:* 48 2336. *Club:* Australian (Sydney).

COWPERTHWAITE, David Jarvis; Under-Secretary, Scottish Home and Health Department, since 1974; *b* 14 Sept. 1921; *s* of J. J. Cowperthwaite and Mrs J. W. B. Cowperthwaite (*née* Jarvis); *m* 1944, Patricia Stockdale; two *d*. *Educ:* Edinburgh Academy; Exeter Coll., Oxford (MA). Nigerian Admin. Service, 1942-48; joined Home Civil Service (Scottish Home Dept), 1948. *Recreations:* cricket, golf. *Address:* 69 Northumberland Street, Edinburgh EH3 6JG. *T:* 031-557 0215.
See also Sir J . J . Cowperthwaite .

COWPERTHWAITE, Sir John James, KBE 1968 (OBE 1960); CMG 1964; International Adviser to Jardine Fleming & Co. Ltd, Hong Kong, since 1972; Financial Secretary, Hong Kong, 1961-71; *b* 25 April 1915; *s* of late John James Cowperthwaite and Jessie Wemyss Barron Jarvis Cowperthwaite; *m* 1941, Sheila Mary, *d* of Alexander Thomson, Aberdeen; one *s*. *Educ:* Merchiston Castle Sch.; St Andrews Univ; Christ's Coll., Cambridge. Entered Colonial Administrative Service, Hong Kong, 1941; seconded to Sierra Leone, 1942-45. *Address:* 25 South Street, St Andrews, Fife. *T:* St Andrews 4759. *Clubs:*

Royal Hong Kong Jockey, Royal Hong Kong Golf; Royal and Ancient.
See also D . J . Cowperthwaite .

COWTAN, Maj.-Gen. Frank Willoughby John, CBE 1970 (MBE 1947); MC 1942 and Bar, 1945; *b* 10 Feb. 1920; *s* of late Air Vice-Marshal F. C. Cowtan, CB, CBE, KHS and late Mrs N. A. Cowtan (*née* Kennedy); *m* 1949, Rose Isabel Cope; one *s* one *d*. *Educ:* Wellington Coll.; RMA Woolwich. 2nd Lieut Royal Engineers, 1939; served War of 1939-45, BEF, N Africa, Italy, NW Europe (Captain); Palestine, Kenya, Middle East, 1945-50 (Major); psc 1951; Middle East, UK, BAOR, 1952-58; Liaison Officer to US Corps of Engrs, USA, 1958-60 (Bt Lt-Col); CO 131 Parachute Engr Regt, 1960-62; CO Victory Coll., RMA Sandhurst, 1962-65 (Lt-Col); Comd 11 Engr Bde, BAOR, 1965-67 (Brig.); ndc (Canada) 1967-68; Dir of Quartering (Army), 1968-70; Dep. QMG, MoD(AD), 1970-71; Comdt, RMCS, 1971-75, retired. Hon. Col 131 Indep. Para. Sqn RE (V); Col Comdt RE, 1977. *Recreations:* golf, shooting, wildfowling, sailing, travel, languages. *Address:* Rectory Cottage, Coleshill, Swindon, Wilts. *Club:* Army and Navy.

COX; see Roxbee Cox.

COX, Albert Edward; His Honour Judge Edward Cox; a Circuit Judge, since 1977; *b* 26 Sept. 1916; *s* of Frederick Stringer Cox; *m* 1962, Alwyn Winifred Cox, JP. Admitted Solicitor, 1938. A Recorder of the Crown Court, 1972-77. Pres., London Criminal Courts Solicitors' Assoc., 1967-68; Mem., Parole Board, 1971-75. *Address:* 38 Carlton Hill, NW8 0JY. *Club:* Hurlingham.

COX, Anthony; see Cox, J. A.

COX, Anthony Wakefield, CBE 1972; FRIBA, AADip; Partner in Architects' Co-Partnership since 1939; *b* 18 July 1915; *s* of late William Edward Cox, CBE, and of Elsie Gertrude Wakefield; *m* 1943, Susan Babington Smith, ARIBA, AADip; two *d*. *Educ:* Mill Hill Sch.; Architectural Association Sch. of Architecture, London. RIBA Journal, 1938-39; Sir Alexander Gibb & Partners, ordnance factories and hostels, 1940-42. Served War: Royal Engineers, Western Europe and India, 1943-46; Hertfordshire CC Schools, 1946-47; reabsorbed in Architects' Co-Partnership, 1947; part-time teaching AA Sch. of Architecture, 1948-54; Mem. Council: Architectural Assoc., 1956-64 (Pres. 1962-63); RIBA, 1967-72; Member: Bd of Educn, RIBA, 1967-73; Royal Fine Art Commn, 1970-. Hon. Sec., Highgate Cemetery Trust, 1977-. *Works include* Depts of: Chemistry at Univ. of Leicester and University Coll., London; Chemistry and Biochemistry at Imperial Coll. of Science and Technology; buildings for: Inst. of Psychiatry, London; the Maudsley Hosp., London. Jt Editor of Focus, 1938-39. *Recreations:* reading, listening, looking, making. *Address:* 5 Bacon's Lane, Highgate, N6. *T:* 01-340 2543.

COX, Prof. Archibald; Carl M. Loeb University Professor, Harvard University; *b* 17 May 1912; *s* of Archibald Cox and Frances Bruen (*née* Perkins); *m* 1937, Phyllis Ames; one *s* two *d*. *Educ:* St Paul's Sch., Concord; Harvard Univ. AB 1934, LLB 1937. Admitted to Mass Bar, 1937. Gen. practice with Ropes, Gray, Best, Coolidge & Rugg, 1938-41; Office of Solicitor-Gen., US Dept of Justice, 1941-43; Assoc. Solicitor, Dept of Labor, 1943-45; Lectr on Law, Harvard, 1945-46, Prof. of Law, 1946-61; Solicitor-Gen., US Dept of Justice, 1961-65; Williston Prof. of Law, Harvard Law Sch., 1965-76. Pitt Prof., Univ. of Cambridge, 1974-75. Co-Chm., Constrn Industry Stablizn Commn, 1951-52; Chm., Wage Stablzn Bd, 1952; Mem. Bd Overseers, Harvard, 1962-65. Special Watergate Prosecutor, 1973. Hon. LLD: Loyola, 1964; Cincinnati, 1967; Rutgers, Amherst, Denver, 1974; Harvard, 1975; Michigan, 1976. *Publications:* Cases on Labor Law, 8th edn 1977; (jtly) Law and National Law or Policy, 1960; Civil Rights, the Constitution and the Courts, 1967; The Warren Court, 1968; The Role of the Supreme Court in American Government, 1976; miscellaneous articles. *Address:* Glezen Lane, Wayland, Mass 01778, USA; (office) Harvard Law School, Cambridge, Mass 02138. *T:* 1-617-495-3133. *Clubs:* Somerset (Boston, Mass); Century Association (New York).

COX, Brian Robert Escott, QC 1974; a Recorder of the Crown Court, since 1972; *b* 30 Sept. 1932; *yr s* of late George Robert Escott Cox; *m* 1st, Vivienne Snape (marr. diss.); one *s* two *d*; 2nd, 1969, Noelle Gilormini; one *s* one *d*. *Educ:* Rugby Sch.; Oriel Coll., Oxford (BA, MA). Called to Bar, Lincoln's Inn, 1954. Midland and Oxford Circuit. *Address:* 1 King's Bench Walk, Temple, EC4. *T:* 01-353 8436.

COX, Sir Christopher (William Machell), GCMG 1970 (KCMG 1950; CMG 1944); *b* 17 Nov. 1899; *e s* of late A. H. Machell

Cox, Chevin Close, St Audries, Somerset. *Educ:* Clifton Coll.; Balliol Coll., Oxford. 2nd Lieut RE (Signals), 1918; 1st class Classical Moderations; 1st class Lit Hum, 1923; War Memorial Student, Balliol Coll., 1923-24; Craven Fellow, Oxford Univ., and Senior Demy, Magdalen Coll., 1924-26; archæological exploration in Turkey, 1924, 1925, 1926, 1931; Fellow of New Coll., Oxford, 1926-70, Hon. Fellow, 1970. Sub-Warden, 1931; Dean, 1934-36; visited Africa, 1929; Persia, 1936; Dir of Education, Anglo-Egyptian Sudan, and Principal of Gordon Coll., Khartoum, 1937-39; Mem. of Governor-General's Council, 1938-39; Educational Adviser to the Sec. of State for the Colonies, 1940-61; Educational Adviser: Dept of Technical Co-operation, 1961-64; ODM, 1964-70. Pres., Education Sect., British Assoc., 1956. Hon. DLit Belfast, 1961; Hon. LLD: Hong Kong, 1961; Chinese Univ. of Hong Kong, 1969; Hon. LLD Leeds, 1962; Hon. DCL Oxford, 1965. *Publications:* Monumenta Asiae Minoris Antiqua, Vol. V (with A. Cameron), 1937; occasional papers. *Address:* New College, Oxford. *Club:* Athenæum.

COX, Prof. David Roxbee, PhD; FRS 1973; Professor of Statistics, Imperial College of Science and Technology, since 1966; Head of Department of Mathematics, 1970-74; *b* 15 July 1924; *s* of S. R. Cox, Handsworth, Birmingham; *m* 1948, Joyce (*née* Drummond), Keighley, Yorks; three *s* one *d. Educ:* Handsworth Grammar Sch., Birmingham; St John's Coll., Cambridge (MA). PhD Leeds, 1949. Posts at Royal Aircraft Establishment, 1944-46; Wool Industries Research Assoc., 1946-50; Statistical Laboratory, Cambridge, 1950-55; Visiting Prof., University of N Carolina, 1955-56; Reader in Statistics, Birkbeck College, 1956-60; Professor of Statistics, 1961-66. For. Hon. Mem., Amer. Acad. of Arts and Sciences, 1974. Editor of Biometrika, 1966-. *Publications:* Statistical Methods in the Textile Industry, 1949 (jt author); Planning of Experiments, 1958; Queues, 1961 (jt author); Renewal Theory, 1962; Theory of Stochastic Processes, 1965 (jt author); Statistical Analysis of Series of Events, 1966 (jt author); Analysis of Binary Data, 1970; Theoretical Statistics, 1974 (jt author); papers in Jl of Royal Statistical Society, Biometrika, etc. *Address:* Imperial College, SW7. *T:* 01-589 5111.

COX, Dennis George; Under-Secretary (Industrial Relations), Department of Employment, 1971-74; a Deputy Chairman, Central Arbitration Committee, since 1977; *b* 23 Feb. 1914; *s* of George and Amelia Cox; *m* 1938, Victoria Barraclough; two *s. Educ:* University College Sch.; Queens' Coll., Cambridge. Royal Navy, 1942-45; served with Netherlands and Norwegian navies, Lieut RNVR. Entered Min. of Labour, 1936; Asst Sec. 1966; Regional Controller, SW Region. *Recreations:* gardening, fishing. *Address:* 133a Ashley Gardens, Thirleby Road, SW1P 1HN. *T:* 01-828 5901; Church Cottage, Laughton, Lewes, East Sussex. *T:* Ripe 382. *Club:* Army and Navy.

COX, Edward; *see* Cox, A. E.

COX, Sir (Ernest) Gordon, KBE 1964; TD; FRS 1954; FRIC; FInstP; DSc; Secretary of the Agricultural Research Council, 1960-71; *b* 24 April 1906; *s* of Ernest Henry Cox and Rosina Ring; *m* 1st, 1929, Lucie Grace Baker (*d* 1962); one *s* one *d* ; 2nd, 1968, Prof. Mary Rosaleen Truter, DSc, *d* of Dr D. N. Jackman. *Educ:* City of Bath Boys' Sch.; University of Bristol. Research Asst, Davy-Faraday Laboratory, Royal Institution, 1927; Chemistry Dept, Univ. of Birmingham, 1929-41 (Reader in Chemical Crystallography, 1940); Prof. of Inorganic and Structural Chemistry, University of Leeds, 1945-60; commissioned in Territorial Army, 1936; special scientific duties, War Office, 1942-44; attached to HQ staff of 21 Army Group, France and Germany, as Technical Staff Officer, Grade I, 1944-45. Vice-Pres., Institute of Physics, 1950-53; Mem. Agric. Research Council, 1957-60. Hon. DSc: Newcastle, 1964; Birmingham, 1964; Bath, 1973; East Anglia, 1973; Hon. LLD Bristol, 1969; Hon. ARCVS, 1972. *Publications:* numerous scientific papers in jls of various learned societies, chiefly on the crystal structures of chemical compounds. *Recreations:* music, gardening, natural history. *Address:* 117 Hampstead Way, NW11 7JN. *T:* 01-455 2618. *Clubs:* Athenæum, English-Speaking Union, Lansdowne.
See also *P . A . Cox* .

COX, Sir Geoffrey (Sandford), Kt 1966; CBE 1959 (MBE 1945); Chairman: Upitn Inc., USA; London Broadcasting Co., since 1977; Deputy Chairman, Independent Television Publications Ltd; *b* 7 April 1910; *s* of Sandford Cox, Wellington, NZ, and Mary Cox (*née* MacGregor); *m* 1935, Cecily Barbara Talbot Turner; two *s* two *d. Educ:* Southland High Sch., New Zealand; Otago Univ., New Zealand (MA); Rhodes Scholar, 1932-35; Oriel Coll., Oxford (BA). Reporter, Foreign and War Corresp. News Chronicle, 1935-37, Daily Express, 1937-40. Enlisted New

Zealand Army, 1940; commissioned, Dec. 1940; served in 2 New Zealand Div., Greece, Crete, Libya, Italy; Major, Chief Intelligence Officer, Gen. Freyberg's staff (despatches twice). First Sec. and Chargé d'Affaires, NZ Legation, Washington, 1943; NZ Rep., first UNRRA Conf., 1943; Political Corresp., News Chronicle, 1945; Asst Editor, News Chronicle 1954. Regular Contributor, BBC radio and TV, 1945-56; Editor and Chief Exec., Independent Television News, 1956-68; founded News at Ten, 1967; Dep. Chm., Yorkshire Television, 1968-71; Chm., Tyne Tees Television, 1971-74. Trustee, Internat. Broadcast Inst. TV Producers' Guild Award Winner, 1962; Fellow, Royal TV Soc.; Silver Medal, 1963; Fellow, British Kinematograph and TV Soc. *Publications:* Defence of Madrid, 1937; The Red Army Moves, 1941; The Road to Trieste, 1946. *Recreations:* fishing, golf. *Club:* Garrick.

COX, Sir (George) Trenchard; *see* Cox, Sir Trenchard.

COX, Sir Gordon; *see* Cox, Sir E. G.

COX, Harry Bernard, CBE 1956; Deputy Chairman, Thos Wyatt Nigeria Ltd, since 1967; Consultant, Knight, Frank & Rutley, since 1967; *b* 29 Nov. 1906; *e* surv. *s* of Rev. Charles Henry Cox, BSc; *m* 1955, Joan, *e d* of P. Munn, Brighton; one *s* one *d. Educ:* Upholland Grammar Sch.; Keble Coll., Oxford. Colonial Administrative Service, Nigeria, 1930; Dir of Commerce and Industries, Nigeria, 1949; Acting Development Sec., Nigeria, 1953-54; Acting Commissioner for Nigeria, 1955; Principal Sec. to the Commissioner for Nigeria in the United Kingdom, 1955. John Holt & Co. (Liverpool) Ltd, 1958; Chm., John Holt (Nigeria) Ltd, 1962. Leader, Westminster Chamber of Commerce Mission to Nigeria, 1974. *Address:* 10 Moore Street, SW3 2QN. *T:* 01-584 2035. *Club:* Oriental.

COX, Major Horace B. T.; *see* Trevor Cox.

COX, Ian Herbert, CBE 1952; MA; FGS; FRGS; FZS; *b* 20 Feb. 1910; *e s* of late Herbert Stanley Cox and Elizabeth Dalgarno; *m* 1945, Susan Mary, *d* of late Lieut Comdr N. G. Fowler Snelling and *widow* of Flt Lieut D. S. S. Low; two *s* two *d. Educ:* Oundle; Magdalene Coll., Cambridge (Exhibnr). Geologist, Oxford Univ. Hudson Straits Expedition, 1931; research, Dept of Geology, Cambridge, 1932-36; with BBC 1936-39; served War of 1939-45 (Comdr, RNVR); BBC 1946; Science Corresp., London Press Service, 1947-48; Dir of Sc., Festival of Britain Office, 1948-51; Shell Internat. Pet. Co., 1952-70 (Hd Sc. and Develt TR Div., Convener Shell Grants Cttee); Mem. Council: RGS, 1953-57, 1959-62; Overseas Develt Inst., 1966-74; British Assoc. for the Advancement of Science, 1960-73 (Gen. Treasurer, 1965-70); Chelsea Coll., Univ. of London, 1968-74; Mem. Management Cttee, Scott Polar Research Inst., 1955-57; Vice-Pres., Geol. Soc., 1966-68; Mem., Bd of Governors, and Vice-Pres., Exec. Cttee, European Cultural Foundn (Amsterdam); Corresp. Member: Agric. Typology Commn; Internat. Geographical Union; Mem. Court, RCA. Pres., Arctic Club, 1961. *Publications:* papers on geology and palæontology of the Arctic; (ed) The Queen's Beasts, 1953; The Scallop, 1957; monographs in World Land Use Survey. *Recreations:* working with wood and stone; gardening. *Address:* Shepherd's House, The Sands, Farnham, Surrey. *T:* Runfold 2080. *Club:* Athenæum.

COX, (James) Anthony; His Honour Judge Anthony Cox; a Circuit Judge, since 1976; *b* 21 April 1924; *s* of Herbert Sidney Cox and Gwendoline Margaret Cox; *m* 1950, Doris Margaret Fretwell; three *s* one *d. Educ:* Cotham Sch., Bristol; Bristol Univ. LLB Hons 1948. War Service, Royal Marines (Lieut), 1943-46. Called to Bar, Gray's Inn, 1949; a Recorder of the Crown Court, 1972-76. *Recreations:* cricket, sailing, the arts. *Address:* Haldruhay, Newton Ferrars, South Devon. *Clubs:* MCC; Bristol (Bristol); Royal Western Yacht (Plymouth).

COX, Sir John (William), Kt 1951; CBE 1946; Member, 1930-68, and Speaker of the House of Assembly, Bermuda, 1948-68; *b* 29 April 1900; *s* of Henry James and Ellen Augusta Cox; *m* 1926, Dorothy Carlyle, *d* of J. D. C. Darrell; three *s. Educ:* Saltus Grammar Sch., Bermuda. Merchant; Partner of the firm of Pearman, Watlington & Co., Hamilton, Bermuda, General and Commission Merchants. Comdr, Royal Netherlands Order of Orange Nassau, 1956. *Address:* The Grove, Devonshire Parish, Bermuda. *T:* 2-0303. *Clubs:* Royal Bermuda Yacht, Royal Hamilton Amateur Dinghy, Mid Ocean (Bermuda).

COX, Air Vice-Marshal Joseph, CB 1957; OBE 1950; DFC 1940; retired; *b* 25 Oct. 1904; *m* 1933, Dorothy Thomas; one *d. Educ:* Peter Symond's Sch., Winchester, Hants. Commissioned, RAF, 1928; various appts at home and abroad, 1929-39. War of 1939-45: Examining Officer (flying), Central Flying Sch., 1939-40;

comd No 15 (Bomber) Sqdn, June-Dec. 1940; Chief Instructor No 33 Service Flying Training Sch., Canada, 1941-42; commanded No 31 Bombing and Gunnery Sch., Canada, 1942-43; commanded No 12 Advanced (Pilot) Flying Unit, and Stn Comdr RAF Spitalgate (Grantham), 1943-45. Comd No 8302 Air Disarmament Wing in Germany, 1945-46; comd RAF Fuhlsbuttel (Hamburg), 1946-48; Senior Personnel Staff Officer, HQ Maintenance Comd, 1948-51; Stn Comdr RAF Finningley, 1951-52; AOC, RAF, Ceylon, 1952-55; Senior Air Staff Officer, Flying Training Command, 1955-58; retired, 1958. *Recreations:* tennis, swimming, cricket, (in younger days) soccer, hockey, squash, badminton, water polo, riding. *Address:* Pippins, 19 Highmoor Road, Caversham, Reading, Berks RG4 7BL. *T:* 472761. *Clubs:* MCC, Royal Air Force, Royal Air Force Reserves; Adastrian Cricket.

COX, Dr Leonard Bell, CMG 1968; Consulting Neurologist since 1927; *b* 29 Aug. 1894; *s* of Rev. Edward Thomas Cox and Isabella Bell; *m* 1925, Nancy Compson Trumble; one *d* (and one *d* decd). *Educ:* Wesley Coll., Melbourne; Melbourne Univ. MB, BS Melbourne 1916; MRCPE 1919; MD Melbourne 1920; FRACP 1938. Hon. and Consulting Neurologist, Alfred Hosp., Melbourne, 1934-; Cons. Neurologist, Queen Victoria Hosp., 1948. Served European War, 1914-18, Capt. AAMC, 1917; War of 1939-45, Wing Comdr, Consultant in Neurology to RAAF. Foundation Pres., Aust. Assoc. of Neurologists, 1950. Chairman: Trustees of Nat. Gallery of Victoria, 1957-65; Nat. Gallery and Cultural Centre Building Cttee, 1957-64; Member: Commonwealth Research Adv. Cttee, 1948; Felton Bequests Cttee, 1958-; Nat. Soc. of Victoria, 1976. *Publications:* Ars Vivendi, 1942; (jt) Human Torulosis, 1946; The National Gallery of Victoria, 1861-1968: a search for a collection, 1970; articles on neurology and neuropathology in med. jls. *Recreations:* Chinese art, country gardening. *Address:* Folly Farm, Falls Road, Olinda, Vic 3788, Australia. *T:* 751-1101. *Clubs:* Melbourne, Melbourne Cricket (Melbourne).

COX, Dame Marjorie (Sophie), DBE 1950 (CBE 1943; OBE 1937); *b* 13 Dec. 1893; Fellow of University College, London; retired; *d* of late Albert and Amelia Cox, Trowbridge, Wilts. *Educ:* University Coll., London. BA London. Entered Civil Service as temp. clerk in 1915 and became established through Lytton examination in 1921; Mem. Beveridge Cttee on Social Security; Dep. Sec. Min. of Pensions (later of Pensions and National Insurance), 1946-54. *Recreation:* reading. *Address:* 10 The Paragon, Wannock Lane, Willingdon, Eastbourne, East Sussex. *T:* Polegate 4159.

COX, Norman Ernest, CMG 1973; MA; HM Diplomatic Service; Ambassador to Mexico, since 1977; *b* 28 Aug. 1921; *s* of late Ernest William Cox and late Daisy Beatrice (*née* Edmonds); *m* 1945, Maruja Margarita (*née* Cruz); one *s* one *d*. *Educ:* Lycée Français de Madrid; King's Coll., London. Tax Officer, Inland Revenue, 1938-41; Army, Intell. Corps, 1941-45: Gibraltar, 1942-45; Attaché, Madrid, 1945-47; FO, 1947-50; 2nd Sec., Sofia, 1950-52; 2nd Sec., Montevideo, 1952-54; FO, 1954-57; Dep. Regional Information Officer for SE Asia, Singapore, 1957-60; FO, 1960-62: Laos Conf., Geneva, 1961; Sec. to UK Conf. Delegn to ECSC, Luxemburg, 1962-63; 1st Sec. (Commercial), Madrid, 1963-66; Counsellor (Information), Mexico, Regional Information Officer for Central American Republics, PRO to Duke of Edinburgh for 1968 Olympics, 1966-68; Counsellor (Commercial), Moscow, 1969-72; Inst. of Latin American Studies, London Univ., 1972-73; Diplomatic Service Inspector, 1973-74; Ambassador to Ecuador, 1974-77. *Recreations:* swimming, walking, climbing, travelling; archaeology, history, linguistics, comparative religion. *Address:* c/o Foreign and Commonwealth Office, SW1. *Club:* Royal Automobile.

COX, Patricia Ann; Under Secretary, Scottish Education Department, since 1976; *b* 25 May 1931; *d* of Sir (Ernest) Gordon Cox, *qv*. *Educ:* Leeds Girls' High Sch.; Newnham Coll., Cambridge (MA). Asst Principal, Dept of Health for Scotland, 1953; Principal: SHHD, 1959-62; HM Treasury, 1962-65; SHHD, 1965-67; Asst Sec., Scottish Educn Dept, 1967. *Publication:* Sandal Ash (novel for children), 1950. *Recreations:* opera, archaeology, needlework, walking. *Address:* 2 Gloucester Place, Edinburgh EH3 6EF. *T:* 031-225 6370.

COX, Peter Denzil John H.; *see* Hippisley-Cox, P. D. J.

COX, Peter Richmond, CB 1971; Deputy Government Actuary, 1963-74; *b* 3 Sept. 1914; *s* of Richard R. Cox, Civil Servant, and Nellie (*née* Richmond); *m* 1971, Faith Blake Schenk. *Educ:* King's Coll. Sch., Wimbledon. Entered Government Actuary's Dept, 1933. Qualified as Fellow, Institute of Actuaries, 1939. Joint Hon. Sec., Institute of Actuaries, 1962-64 (Vice-Pres.,

1966-68). Pres., Eugenics Soc., 1970-72. Chm., CS Insurance Soc., 1973-. Silver Medal, Inst. of Actuaries, 1975. *Publications:* Demography, 1950 (5 edns); (with R. H. Storr-Best) Surplus in British Life Assurance, 1962; (ed jtly) Population and Pollution, 1972; Resources and Population, 1973; Population and the New Biology, 1974; Equalities and Inequalities in Education, 1975; various papers on actuarial and demographic subjects. *Recreations:* music, painting, gardening. *Address:* The Level House, Mayfield, East Sussex TN20 6BW. *T:* Mayfield 2217. *Club:* Actuaries.

COX, Philip (Joseph), DSC 1943; QC 1967; a Recorder, and Honorary Recorder of Northampton, since 1972; *b* 28 Sept. 1922; *s* of Joseph Parriss Cox, Rugby; *m* 1951, Margaret Jocelyn Cox, *d* of R. C. H. Cox, Purley, Surrey; one *s* one *d*. *Educ:* Rugby Sch; Queens' Coll., Cambridge. RNVR, 1942-46 (Lieut). Called to Bar, Gray's Inn, 1949; Bencher, 1972; practised at Bar, Birmingham, 1949-67. Mem. County Court Rules Cttee, 1962-68; Dep. Chm., Northants QS, 1963-71; Dep. Chm., Warwicks QS, 1966-71; Leader, Midland and Oxford Circuit, 1975-; Mem. Senate, Inns of Court and Bar, 1974-. Legal Assessor to Disciplinary Cttee, RCVS, 1969-; Chm., Cttee of Enquiry into London Smallpox Outbreak, 1973. Pres., Edgbaston Liberal Assoc., 1974. *Recreations:* sailing, golf, gardening, reading. *Address:* (home) 40 George Road, Edgbaston, Birmingham B15 1PL. *T:* 021-454 2656; (chambers) 1 King's Bench Walk, Temple, EC4. *Clubs:* Naval; Birmingham; Royal Cruising, Bar Yacht.

COX, Richard Charles, MBE 1961; Counsellor, HM Diplomatic Service; Deputy Secretary General, Cento, since 1975; *b* 27 May 1920; *s* of Charles Victor Cox and Marjorie Eleanor Cox (*née* Fox); *m* 1941, Constance (*née* Goddard); one *s*. *Educ:* Gravesend Grammar Sch. Served War of 1939-45, RAF; released with rank of Sqdn Leader, 1946. Entered Colonial Office, 1937; Dominions Office, 1946; High Commn, Colombo, 1949-52; Second Sec., Calcutta, 1953-54; CRO, 1954-56; First Sec., Bombay, 1956-59; CRO, 1960-63; First Sec., Valletta, 1964-68; FCO, 1968-72; NI Office, 1972-74. *Recreations:* swimming, gardening, watching Rugby football. *Address:* The Old Forge, Hartley, Kent. *T:* Longfield 2035. *Club:* Travellers'.

COX, Sir Robert; *see* Cox, Sir W. R.

COX, Ronald; Director-General, Greater Glasgow Passenger Transport Executive, 1973-77; *b* St Helens, Lancs, 3 Feb. 1916; *s* of Frederick Nisbet Cox and Annie Cox; *m* 1941, Edna Frances Heaton; one *s* one *d*. *Educ:* Higher Grade Boys' Sch., St Helens, Lancs (Oxford Univ. Cert., 6 credits); Trainee Transport Officer, St Helens Corp. Transport (Endorsed Cert. in Commerce, NC Engrg). Served War, Flt Lt (Tech.), RAF Transport Command, 1940-46. Sen. Traffic Officer, St Helens Corp. Transport, 1946-48; Traffic Supt, Salford City Transport, 1948-53; Dep. Engr and Gen. Manager, Rochdale Corp. Transport, 1953-54, Engr and Gen. Manager, 1954-62; Gen. Manager, Bournemouth Corp. Transport, 1962-64; Transport Manager, Edinburgh Corp. Transport, 1964-73. RSA Dip. (prizewinner transport subjects); MIRTE, MInstT, FCIT. *Recreation:* sailing. *Address:* Wendover, Castlelaw Road, Colinton, Edinburgh EH13 0DN. *T:* 031-441 1715; 6 Stonehanger Court, Salcombe, Devon. *T:* Salcombe 3456.

COX, Roy Arthur, FCA, FCMA, FCIS, FBS, JDipMA; Director since 1976 and Chief General Manager since 1970, Alliance Building Society; *b* 30 Nov. 1925; *s* of J. W. Arthur Cox; *m* 1951; one *s* one *d*. *Educ:* Isleworth Grammar Sch. JDipMA; FCA 1953; FCMA 1957; FCIS 1970; FBS 1971. War Service, 1944-47. Wells & Partners, Chartered Accountants, 1942-49; Colombo Commercial Co. Ltd, 1950-61; Urwick, Orr & Partners, Management Consultants, 1961-65; Alliance Building Society: Sec., 1965; Gen. Man., 1967. Dir, Southern Bd, Legal & General Assurance Soc. Ltd, 1972-. Building Societies Association: Chm., S Eastern Assoc., 1972-74; Mem. Council, 1973-; Chm., Gen. Purposes and Public Relations Cttee, 1975-77. Mem., Royal Commn on Distribution of Income and Wealth, 1974-. *Recreations:* golf, bridge. *Address:* Parsonage House, Henfield, West Sussex. *T:* Henfield 2588.

COX, Thomas Michael; MP (Lab) Wandsworth, Tooting, since 1974 (Wandsworth Central, 1970-74); a Lord Commissioner of the Treasury, since 1977; *b* London, 1930. *Educ:* state schools; London Sch. of Economics. Electrical worker. Former Mem., Fulham Borough Council; contested (Lab) GLC elections, 1967; contested (Lab) Stroud, 1966. An Asst Govt Whip, 1974-77. Member: ETU; Co-operative Party. *Address:* House of Commons, SW1.

COX, Thomas Richard Fisher, CMG 1955; Bursar, St Andrew's College, Dublin, since 1962; *b* 21 Feb. 1907; *s* of late Rev. James Fisher Cox; *m* 1st, 1933, Doreen Alice Rae; one *s* two *d*; 2nd, 1968, Rowena Mary Figgis; three *s. Educ:* Portora Royal Sch.; TCD; University Coll., Oxford. Provincial Admin., Uganda, 1930; acted as Sec. for African Affairs, 1949-50; Chm. Languages Board, Uganda, 1950-60; Provincial Comr, Uganda, 1950-61. *Publications:* articles in Uganda Jl and Jl of African Admin. *Recreations:* golf, gardening; formerly boxing (boxed for Oxford Univ. *v* Cambridge Univ., 1930). *Address:* 21 Hyde Park, Dalkey, Co. Dublin. *T:* 804596.

COX, Sir Trenchard, Kt 1961; CBE 1954; MA; FRSA (Vice-President 1964-68); FMA; FSA; Director and Secretary, Victoria and Albert Museum, 1956-66; *b* 31 July 1905; *s* of late William Pallett Cox and Marion Beverley; *m* 1935, Mary Désirée (*d* 1973), *d* of late Sir Hugh Anderson, Master of Gonville and Caius Coll., Cambridge. *Educ:* Eton; King's Coll., Cambridge. Worked as volunteer at the National Gallery and Brit. Museum (Dept of Prints and Drawings), 1929-32; spent a semester at the University of Berlin in the Dept of Arts, 1930; Asst to the Keeper, Wallace Collection, 1932-39; seconded for war-time duties, to Home Office, 1940-44; Dir of Birmingham Museum and Art Gallery, 1944-55. Member: Ancient Monuments Board for England, 1959-69; Standing Commn on Museums and Galleries, 1967-. People's Warden, St Martin-in-the Fields, 1968. Hon. DLitt Birmingham, 1956. Chevalier, Légion d'Honneur, 1967. *Publications:* The National Gallery, a Room-to-Room Guide, 1930; Jehan Foucquet, Native of Tours, 1931; part editor of the Catalogue to the Exhibition of French Art at Burlington House, Jan.-March 1932; The Renaissance in Europe, 1933; A General Guide to the Wallace Collection, 1933; A Short Illustrated History of the Wallace Collection and its Founders, 1936; David Cox, 1947; Peter Bruegel, 1951; Pictures: a Handbook for Curators, 1956. *Recreations:* reading, play-going, travelling. *Address:* 33 Queen's Gate Gardens, SW7. *T:* 01-584 0231. *Clubs:* Athenæum, Beefsteak.

COX, Maj.-Gen. William Reginald, CB 1956; DSO 1945; Director Territorial Army, Cadets and Home Guard, 1958-60, retired; *b* 13 June 1905; *s* of late Major W. S. R. Cox; *m* 1947, Dorothy Irene Cox; no *c. Educ:* Wellington Coll. Commissioned KSLI, 1925; Adjutant, 2nd Bn, 1931-34; Staff Coll., Camberley, 1938; served War of 1939-45: Bde Major 114 Inf. Bde, 1940; Instr, Staff Coll., Camberley, 1941; GSO 1 Northern Comd, York, 1942; comd 1 Worcs. Regt, 1942-43; GSO 1, 21 Army Gp, 1943-44; comd 7 Green Howards, 1944; 131 Lorried Inf Bde, 1944; 129, 146 and 31 Inf. Bdes, 1945-47; BGS Western Comd, 1948; idc 1949; DAG, GHQ, MEF, 1950-52; Dep. Dir Infty, War Office, 1952-54; Chief of Staff, Southern Command, 1954-55; GOC 53rd (Welsh) Div., TA, and Mid-West District, 1955-58. Col, KSLI, 1957-63. Order of White Lion of Czechoslovakia (3rd Cl.); Military Cross of Czechoslovakia, 1945. *Recreations:* tennis, golf. *Address:* c/o National Westminster Bank, Salisbury, Wilts. *Club:* Naval and Military.

COX, Sir (William) Robert, KCB 1976 (CB 1971); Chief Executive (Second Permanent Secretary), Property Services Agency, Department of the Environment, since 1974; *b* 2 Jan. 1922; *s* of late William Robert and Berthe Marie Cox, Winchester; *m* 1948, Elizabeth Anne Priestley Marten; one *s* one *d. Educ:* Peter Symonds' Sch., Winchester; Christ's Coll., Cambridge. Foreign Office (German Sect.), 1946; Min. of Town and Country Planning, 1950; Min. of Housing and Local Govt, 1952-69 (Under-Sec., 1965); Asst Under-Sec. of State, Office of Sec. of State for Local Govt and Regional Planning, 1969-70; Dep. Under-Sec. of State, Home Office, and Dir-Gen. of Prison Service, 1970-73; Dep. Chief Exec. III, Property Services Agency, DoE, 1974. Member: UN Cttee on Crime Prevention and Control, 1972-74; Bureau of the European Cttee on Crime Problems, 1972-73. *Recreation:* music. *Address:* 2 Marsham Street, SW1. *Club:* Athenæum.

COX, William Trevor; *see* Trevor, W.

COXETER, Harold Scott Macdonald, FRS 1950; PhD Cambridge, 1931; Professor of Mathematics, University of Toronto, since 1948; *b* 9 Feb. 1907; *s* of Harold Samuel Coxeter and Lucy (*née* Gee); *m* 1936, Hendrina Johanna Brouwer, The Hague; one *s* one *d. Educ:* King Alfred Sch., London; St George's Sch., Harpenden; Trinity Coll., Cambridge. Entrance Scholar, Trinity Coll., 1926; Smith's Prize, 1931. Fellow Trinity Coll., Cambridge, 1931-36; Rockefeller Foundation Fellow, Princeton, 1932-33; Procter Fellow, Princeton, 1934-35; Asst Prof., 1936-43, Associate Prof., 1943-48, University of Toronto. Visiting Professor: Notre Dame, 1947; Columbia Univ., 1949; Dartmouth Coll., 1964; Univ. of Amsterdam, 1966; Univ. of Edinburgh, 1967; Univ. of E Anglia, 1968; ANU, 1970; Univ. of

Sussex, 1972; Univ. of Utrecht, 1976; Calif. Inst. of Technology, 1977. Editor Canadian Jl of Mathematics, 1948-57. President: Canadian Mathematical Congress, 1965-67; Internat. Mathematical Congress, 1974. Foreign Mem., Koninklijke Nederlandse Akademie van Wetenschappen, 1975. Hon. LLD: Alberta, 1957; Trent, 1973; Hon. DMath Waterloo, 1969; Hon. DSc Acadia, 1971. *Publications:* Non-Euclidean Geometry, 1942 and 1965; Regular Polytopes, 1948, 1963 and 1973; The Real Projective Plane, 1949, 1955 and 1959; (with W. O. J. Moser) Generators and Relations, 1957, 1964 and 1972; Introduction to Geometry, 1961 and 1969; Projective Geometry, 1964 and 1974; (with S. L. Greitzer) Geometry Revisited, 1967; Twelve Geometric Essays, 1968; Regular Complex Polytopes, 1974; (with W. W. Rouse Ball) Mathematical Recreations and Essays, 12th edn, 1974; various mathematical papers. *Recreations:* music, travel. *Address:* 67 Roxborough Drive, Toronto M4W 1X2, Canada.

COXWELL-ROGERS, Maj.-Gen. Norman Annesley, CB 1944; CBE 1943 (OBE 1933); DSO 1940; *b* 29 May 1896; *s* of late Henry Annesley Coxwell-Rogers, Asst Inspector-General Royal Irish Constabulary, Dowdeswell, Glos, and late Mary Georgina, *d* of Edmund Waller, Dundrum and Bray, Co. Dublin; *m* 1928, Diana Coston; one *s* one *d. Educ:* Cheltenham Coll.; Royal Military Academy, Woolwich. 2nd Lieut Royal Engineers, 1915; service at home, Gibraltar and India; served France and Belgium, 1915-18 (wounded, despatches twice); NW Frontier, Mohmand Operations, 1933, served as Field Engineer in charge of construction of Gandab Road (OBE, despatches); Mohmand Operations, 1935, as CRE (Bt Lieut-Col); War of 1939-45, BEF, France, Sept. 1939-June 1940, N Africa, Sicily, and Italy, 1943, Chief Engineer Allied Armies in Italy (despatches twice, DSO, CBE, CB, Legion of Merit (USA)); Colonel, 1941; Maj.-Gen. 1943; retired pay, 1946. Col Comdt RE, 1956-61. *Recreation:* field sports. *Address:* Rossley Manor, near Cheltenham, Glos. *T:* Andoversford 233. *Club:* Naval and Military.

COYNE, James E.; Canadian banker; *b* Winnipeg, 17 July 1910; *s* of James Bowes Coyne and Edna Margaret Coyne (*née* Elliott); *m* 1957, Meribeth Stobie; one *s* one *d. Educ:* University of Manitoba (BA); University of Oxford (BCL). RCAF (Flying Officer), 1942-44. Admitted to the Bar, Manitoba, 1934; solicitor and barrister in Manitoba, 1934-38; Financial Attaché, Canadian Embassy, Washington, DC, 1941; Mem. War-time Prices and Trade Board, Ottawa, 1942 (Dep.-Chm.). Bank of Canada, Ottawa: Asst to the Governors, 1944-49; Deputy-Governor, 1950-54; Governor, 1955-61. *Address:* 29 Ruskin Row, Winnipeg, Manitoba, Canada.

COZENS, Brig. Dame (Florence) Barbara, DBE 1963; RRC 1958; *b* 24 Dec. 1906; *d* of late Capt. A. Cozens, S Staffs. *Educ:* Seabury Sch., Worthing. Nurse Training: the Nightingale Sch., St Thomas' Hosp., London, 1928-32. Joined QAIMNS, 1933. Served War of 1939-45, England and Continent. Lieut-Col 1954; Col 1958; Brig. 1960; Matron-in-Chief and Dir of Army Nursing Services, 1960-64, retd; Chief Nursing Officer to St John Ambulance Brigade, 1965-72. Col Commandant, QARANC, 1966-69. DStJ 1972. *Recreation:* gardening. *Address:* 174 Old Dover Road, Canterbury, Kent. *Club:* United Nursing Services.

COZENS, Air Cdre Henry Iliffe, CB 1946; AFC 1939; RAF retired; *b* 13 March 1904; *m* 1956, Gillian Mary, *o d* of Wing Comdr O. R. Pigott, Wokingham, Berks; one *s* two *d. Educ:* St Dunstan's Coll.; Downing Coll., Cambridge. MA 1934. Commissioned in RAF, 1923; Mem. of British Arctic Air Route Expedition, 1930-31. Served War of 1939-45 (AFC, CB). idc 1947. *Address:* Horley Manor, Banbury, Oxon. *Club:* Royal Air Force.

COZZENS, James Gould; US author; *b* Chicago, USA, 19 Aug. 1903; *s* of Henry William Cozzens and Bertha Wood; *m* 1927, Bernice Baumgarten. *Educ:* Kent Sch., Connecticut; Harvard University. *Publications:* Confusion, 1924; Michael Scarlett, 1925; Cockpit, 1928; The Son of Perdition, 1929; SS San Pedro, 1931; The Last Adam, 1933; Castaway, 1934; Men and Brethren, 1936; Ask Me Tomorrow, 1940; The Just and the Unjust, 1942; Guard of Honour, 1949; By Love Possessed, 1958; Children and Others, 1965; Morning, Noon and Night, 1968; A Flower in her Hair, 1974; A Rope for Dr Webster, 1976. *Recreation:* writing. *Address:* PO Box 2372, Stuart, Florida 33494, USA.

CRABB, Rt. Rev. Frederick Hugh Wright; *see* Athabasca, Bishop of.

CRABBE, Kenneth Herbert Martineau, TD; Wedd Durlacher Mordaunt & Co.; *b* 4 Nov. 1916; *m* 1940, Rowena Leete; one *s. Educ:* Stowe Sch. Member, Stock Exchange, London, 1937-;

Mem. Council, The Stock Exchange, 1963- (Dep. Chm., 1970-73). Commnd TA, 1937; psc; Major. *Recreations:* golf, fishing, shooting, painting. *Address:* Spandrels Walliswood, Ockley, Surrey RH5 5RJ. *T:* Oakwood Hill 275. *Clubs:* Boodle's, Ski Club of Great Britain; West Sussex Golf.

CRABBE, Mrs Pauline, (Mrs Joseph Benjamin), OBE 1969; JP; Secretary, London Brook Advisory Centres, since Nov. 1971; *b* 1 April 1914; *y d* of Cyril and Edith Henriques, Kingston, Jamaica; *m* 1st, 1936, Geoffrey Henebery (marr. diss. 1948); one *d*; 2nd, 1949, Neville Crabbe (marr. diss. 1960); one *s*; 3rd, 1969, Joseph Benjamin; three step *s*. *Educ:* Highgate Convent; London Academy of Music and Drama; London Univ. (extra-mural course in Psychology). Actress and broadcaster, 1945-53; secretarial work with British Actors' Equity and WEA, 1953-56; then with Old People's Welfare and London Council of Social Service, 1956-57; Welfare Sec. and Dep. Gen. Sec. to Nat. Council for Unmarried Mother and her Child, 1957-69; Conciliation Officer for Race Relations Bd, 1969-71. Founder Mem., Haverstock Housing Trust for Fatherless Families, 1966; Mem. Bd, Housing Corp., 1968-75; Member: Community Relations Commn, 1972-77; Standing Adv. Council on Race Relations, 1977-. Radio and TV broadcaster and panellist. JP London, 1967. FRSA 1972. *Publications:* articles and book reviews in social work jls. *Recreations:* entertaining, walking, indoor gardening, the theatre and the arts. *Address:* 27 Elgin Court, Elgin Avenue, W9 2NU. *T:* 01-289 0824. *Club:* Magistrates' Association.
See also Sir Cyril Henriques.

CRABBE, Reginald James Williams, FIA, FSS; Managing Director, 1956-74, and Chairman, since 1967, Provident Life Association of London Ltd; Chairman: United Standard Insurance Co. Ltd, since 1967; Vigilant Assurance Co. Ltd, since 1970; Deputy Chairman, Cope & Timmins Ltd, since 1971 (Chairman 1975-77); *b* 22 June 1909; *e s* of late Harry James and Annie Martha Crabbe; *m* 1948, Phyllis Maud Smith; two *d*. *Educ:* Chigwell Sch., Essex. Entered National Mutual Life Assurance Soc., 1926; FIA 1933; joined Provident Life as Asst Actuary, 1935. Chm., Life Offices' Assoc., 1965, 1966. *Publication:* (with C. A. Poyser, MA, FIA) Pension and Widows' and Orphans' Funds, 1953. *Recreations:* reading, gardening, music, art. *Address:* Fairways, 166 Lower Green Road, Esher, Surrey. *T:* Esher 62219.

CRABBIE, Mrs (Margaret) Veronica, CBE 1977; Member, Secretary of State for Scotland's Consultative Council on Social Work, since 1977; *b* 26 Nov. 1910; *d* of late Sir Christopher Nicholson Johnston (Lord Sands, Senator of the College of Justice, Scotland), and Lady Sands; *m* 1938, John Patrick Crabbie; two *s* one *d*. *Educ:* St Denis Sch., Edinburgh; Queen Margaret's Sch., Escrick, York. Chairman: Edinburgh Home for Mothers and Infants, 1951-66; Walpole Housing Assoc., 1969-72; Scottish Council for the Unmarried Mother and her Child, 1966-72; WRVS, Scotland, 1972-77. *Recreation:* curling. *Address:* 17 Ravelston Dykes, Edinburgh EH4 3JE. *T:* 031-332 4489. *Club:* New (Edinburgh).

CRABTREE, Jonathan; a Recorder of the Crown Court, since 1974; barrister-at-law; *b* 17 April 1934; *s* of Charles H. Crabtree and Elsie M. Crabtree; *m* 1957, Caroline Ruth Keigwin (*née* Oliver) (marr. diss. 1976); two *s* three *d*. *Educ:* Bootham; St John's Coll., Cambridge (MA, LLB). Called to Bar, Gray's Inn, 1958. *Recreations:* cricket, cooking. *Address:* 7 Upper Price Street, York YO2 18J. *T:* York 22825.

CRABTREE, Prof. Lewis Frederick, PhD, FRAeS; Sir George White Professor of Aeronautical Engineering, University of Bristol, since 1973; *b* 16 Nov. 1924; *m* 1955, Averil Joan Escott; one *s* one *d*. *Educ:* Univ. of Leeds; Imperial Coll. of Science and Technology; Cornell Univ., USA. BSc (Mech Eng) Leeds, 1945; DIC (Aeronautics), 1947; PhD (Aero Eng), Cornell, 1952. Air Engr Officer, RNVR, 1945-46. Grad. apprentice, Saunders-Roe Ltd, E Cowes, IoW, 1947-50; ECA Fellowship, Grad. Sch. of Aero. Engrg, Cornell Univ., 1950-52; Aerodynamics Dept, RAE, Farnborough, 1953-73; Head of: Hypersonics and High temperature Gasdynamics Div., 1961-66; Low Speed Aerodynamics Div., 1966-70; Propulsion Aerodynamics and Noise Div., 1970-73. Visiting Prof., Cornell Univ., 1957. AFAIAA; *Publications:* Elements of Hypersonic Aerodynamics, 1965; contributor to: Incompressible Aerodynamics, 1960; Laminar Boundary Layers, 1963; articles chiefly in Jl RAeS, Aeron. Quart., Jl Aeron. Sci., Jahrbuch der WGLR, and Reports and Memos of ARC. *Address:* Queen's Building, The University, Bristol. *T:* Bristol 24161.

CRACKNELL, William Martin; Chief Executive, Glenrothes Development Corporation, since 1976; *b* 24 June 1929; *s* of John Sidney Cracknell and Sybil Marian (*née* Wood); *m* 1962, Gillian Goatcher; two *s* two *d*. *Educ:* St Edward's School, Oxford; RMA Sandhurst. Regular Army Officer, Royal Green Jackets, 1949-69; British Printing Industries Fedn, 1969-76. *Address:* Alburne Knowe, Orchard Drive, Glenrothes, Fife. *T:* Glenrothes 752413.

CRACROFT, Air Vice-Marshal Peter Dicken, CB 1954; AFC 1932; *b* 29 Nov. 1907; *s* of Lt-Col H. Cracroft, Bath; *m* 1932, Margaret Eliza Sugden Patchett; two *s*. *Educ:* Monkton Combe Sch., Bath. Commissioned RAF 1927; Fleet Air Arm, 1928-31; Central Flying Sch. Instructors' Course, 1931; Flying Instructor, Leuchars, 1931-35; Adjt HMS Courageous, 1936-37; Chief Flying Instructor, Oxford Univ. Air Sqdn, 1937-39; RAF Stn Mount Batten, 1939-40; Air Staff, Coastal Command, 1940-41; OC RAF Station, Chivenor, 1941-43; SASO 19 Gp (later 17 Gp), 1933-44; OC 111 Op. Trg Unit, Bahamas, 1944-45; SASO HQ Air Comd, SE Asia, Mil. Gov. Penang, 1945; AOC Bombay, 1945-46; SASO, HQ 19 Gp, 1946-48; RAF Dir and CO, Jt Anti-Submarine Sch., Londonderry, 1948-50; Sen. Air Liaison Officer, S Africa, 1950-52; AOC 66 Gp, Edinburgh, 1952-53; Senior Air Staff Officer, Headquarters Coastal Command, 1953-55; AOC Scotland and 18 Group, 1955-58; retired from RAF, Dec. 1958. *Recreations:* tennis, fishing, shooting. *Address:* Alderney House, Burton Bradstock, Bridport, Dorset DT6 4NQ. *Club:* Royal Air Force.

CRADOCK, Percy, CMG 1968; HM Ambassador to the German Democratic Republic, since 1976; *b* 26 Oct. 1923; *m* 1953, Birthe Marie Dyrlund. Served Foreign Office, 1954-57; First Sec., Kuala Lumpur, 1957-61, Hong Kong, 1961, Peking, 1962; Foreign Office, 1963-66; Counsellor and Head of Chancery, Peking, 1966-68; Chargé d'Affaires, Peking, 1968-69; Head of Planning Staff, FCO, 1969-71; Under-Sec., Cabinet Office, 1971-75. *Address:* c/o Foreign and Commonwealth Office, SW1. *Club:* Reform.

CRADOCK-HARTOPP, Sir J. E.; *see* Hartopp.

CRAFT, Professor Ian Logan, FRCS; Professor of Obstetrics and Gynaecology, Royal Free Hospital, London, since 1976; *b* 11 July 1937; *s* of Reginald Thomas Craft and Lois Mary (*née* Logan); *m* 1959, Jacqueline Rivers Symmons; two *s*. *Educ:* Owens Sch., London; Westminster Med. Sch., Univ. of London (MB, BS). FRCS 1966; MRCOG 1970. Sen. Registrar, Westminster Hosp. Teaching Gp (Westminster Hosp. and Kingston Hosp.), 1970-72; Sen. Lectr and Consultant, Inst. of Obstetrics and Gynaecology, Queen Charlotte's Hosp., London, 1972-76. FRSocMed. *Publications:* contrib. BMJ, Lancet and other medical jls. *Recreations:* art, music, ornithology, sports of most types. *Address:* 12 Coval Gardens, East Sheen, SW14 7DG. *T:* 01-876 5461, (office) 01-794 0500, ext. 3859.

CRAFT, Prof. Maurice, PhD; Goldsmiths' Professor of Education in the University of London, and Head of Department of Advanced Studies in Education, Goldsmiths' College, London, since 1976; *b* 4 May 1932; *er s* of Jack and Polly Craft, London; *m* 1957, Alma, *y d* of Elio and Dinah Sampson, Dublin; two *d*. *Educ:* LCC Elem. Sch. and Colfe's Grammar Sch., SE13; LSE, Univ. of London (BSc Econ); Sch. of Education, Trinity Coll., Univ. of Dublin (HDipEd); Inst. of Education, Univ. of London (AcadDipEd); Dept of Sociology, Univ. of Liverpool (PhD 1972). 2/Lt RAOC (Nat. Service), 1953-55. Asst Master, Catford Secondary Sch., SE6, 1956-60; Princ. Lectr and Head of Dept of Sociology, Edge Hill Coll. of Education, Ormskirk, Lancs, 1960-67; Sen. Lectr in Education, i/c Advanced Courses, Univ. of Exeter, 1967-73; Sub-Dean, Faculty of Educn, 1969-73; Prof. of Education, and Chairman, Centre for the Study of Urban Education, La Trobe Univ., Melbourne, 1973-75. *Publications:* Urban Education—A Dublin Case Study, 1973; School Welfare Provision in Australia, 1977; (ed) Family, Class and Education: a Reader, 1970; (ed jtly) Linking Home and School, 1967 (2nd edn, 1972); (ed jtly) Guidance and Counselling in British Schools, 1969 (2nd edn, 1974); contrib. to numerous books and to the following jls: Internat. Review of Educn, Social and Econ. Admin., Educn for Teaching, Higher Educn Jl, New Society, Administration, Studies. *Recreations:* music, walking. *Address:* Goldsmiths' College, University of London, New Cross, SE14 6NW. *T:* 01-692 7171 (ext. 228).

CRAGG, Rt. Rev. (Albert) Kenneth, DPhil; Hon. Canon of Canterbury; Reader in Religious Studies, University of Sussex, and Assistant Bishop, Diocese of Chichester, since 1974; *b* 8 March 1913; *yr s* of Albert and Emily Cragg; *m* 1940, Theodora Melita, *yr d* of John Wesley Arnold; three *s* (one *d* decd). *Educ:* Blackpool Grammar Sch.; Jesus Coll., Oxford; Tyndale Hall, Bristol. BA Oxon 2nd Cl. Hons Mod. Hist., 1934; MA Oxon

1938; DPhil 1950. Ellerton Theol. Essay Prize, Oxford, 1937; Green Moral Philos. Prize, Oxford, 1947. Deacon, 1936; Priest, 1937; Curate, Higher Tranmere Parish Church, Birkenhead, 1936-39; Chaplain, All Saints', Beirut, Lebanon, 1939-47; Warden, St Justin's House, Beirut, 1942-47; Asst Prof. of Philos., Amer. University of Beirut, 1942-47; Rector of Longworth, Berks, 1947-51; Sheriff's Chap., Berks, 1948; Prof. of Arabic and Islamics, Hartford Seminary, Conn, USA, 1951-56; Rockefeller Travelling Schol., 1954; Res. Canon, St George's Collegiate Church, Jerusalem, 1956-61; Fellow, St Augustine's Coll., Canterbury, 1959-60, Sub-Warden, 1960-61, Warden, 1961-67; Examng Chaplain to Archbishop of Canterbury, 1961-67; Asst Bishop to Archbishop in Jerusalem, 1970-74. Select Preacher: Cambridge, 1961; Dublin, 1962; Oxford, 1974. Proctor in Convocation, Canterbury, 1965-68; Visiting Prof., Union Theological Seminary, New York, 1965-66; Lectr, Faculty of Divinity, Cambridge, 1966; Jordan Lectr, Sch. of Oriental and African Studies, University of London, 1967; Vis. Prof., University of Ibadan, Nigeria, 1968; Bye-Fellow, Gonville and Caius Coll., Cambridge, 1968-74. Editor, The Muslim World Quarterly, 1952-60. *Publications:* The Call of the Minaret, 1956; Sandals at the Mosque, 1959; The Dome and the Rock, 1964; Counsels in Contemporary Islam, 1965; Christianity in World Perspective, 1968; The Privilege of Man, 1968; The House of Islam, 1969; Alive to God, 1970; The Event of the Qur'ān, 1971; The Mind of the Qur'ān, 1973; The Wisdom of the Sufis, 1976; The Christian and Other Religion, 1977; translated: City of Wrong, 1959; The Theology of Unity, 1965; A Passage to France, 1976; The Hallowed Valley, 1977; Contributor: Journal of World History, 1957; Religion in the Middle East, 1969. *Address:* 174 Osborne Road, Brighton BN1 6LS. *T:* Brighton 501896; University of Sussex, Falmer, Brighton BN1 9RH.
See also Ven. H. W. Cragg.

CRAGG, Ven. Herbert Wallace, MA; Archdeacon of Bromley since 1969; Vicar of Christ Church, Beckenham, since 1957; Hon. Canon of Rochester since 1963; *b* 18 Nov. 1910; *s* of Albert and Emily Cragg; *m* 1938, Elsie Emery; three *d. Educ:* Tyndale Hall, Bristol; St John's Coll., Durham. LTh 1932, BA 1933, MA 1938. Curate: St Mary, Kirkdale, Liverpool, 1933-37; Cheadle Parish Church, Cheshire, 1937-38; Vicar: The Saviour, Blackburn, 1938-44; St James, Carlisle, 1944-57. Hon. Canon of Carlisle, 1956-57; Proctor in Convocation for Carlisle, 1951-57; for Rochester, 1959-69. *Publications:* The Sole Sufficiency of Jesus Christ, 1961; The Holy Spirit and the Christian Life, 1962; The Encouragement of the Believer, 1964; Victory in the Christian Life, 1964. *Address:* Christ Church Vicarage, 61 Hayes Lane, Beckenham, Kent BR3 2RE.
See also Rt Rev. A. K. Cragg.

CRAGG, James Birkett; Professor of Environmental Science, University of Calgary, Alberta, since 1976; *b* 8 Nov. 1910; *s* of late A. W. Cragg, N Shields; *m* 1937, Mary Catherine Macnaughtan (marr. diss. 1968); five *s* (one *d* decd); *m* Jean Moore. *Educ:* private sch.; Tynemouth High Sch.; Durham Univ. BSc King's Coll., University of Durham, 1933; DThPT, 1934; MSc, 1937; DSc Newcastle, 1965. Demonstrator, Physiology Dept, Manchester Univ., 1935; Asst Lecturer, and later Lecturer, in Zoology, University Coll. of North Wales, 1937; seconded to Agricultural Research Council, 1942; Scientific Officer, ARC Unit of Insect Physiology, 1944; Reader in Zoology, Durham Colls, in University of Durham, 1946; Prof. of Zoology, University of Durham, 1950-61; Dir, Merlewood Research Station (Nature Conservancy, NERC), Grange-over-Sands, Lancs, 1961-66; Dir, Environmental Sciences Centre, and Prof. of Biology, 1966-72; Killam Meml Prof., 1966-76, Vice-Pres. (Academic), 1970-72, Univ. of Calgary, Alberta. Former Chairman: Commn for Ecology; Internat. Union for Conservation of Nature; Convenor, Internat. Biological Programme PT Cttee; Mem., Internat. Biological Programme Cttees; Consultant, Ford Foundation, 1965. Commonwealth Prestige Fellow (New Zealand), 1964. *Publications:* papers in scientific periodicals; formerly Editor, Advances in Ecological Research. *Recreation:* books. *Address:* 3312 Underhill Drive, Calgary, Alberta T2N 4E7, Canada. *Club:* Athenæum.

CRAGG, Rt. Rev. Kenneth; *see* Cragg, Rt. Rev. A. K.

CRAGGS, Prof. James Wilkinson, BSc, PhD; Professor of Engineering Mathematics, University of Southampton, since 1967; *b* 3 Feb. 1920; *s* of Thomas Gibson Craggs and Margaret (née Wilkinson); *m* 1946, Mary Baker; two *s* one *d. Educ:* Bede Collegiate Sch., Sunderland; University of Manchester. BSc 1941, PhD 1948, Manchester; PhD Cambridge, 1953. Junior Lectr, Royal Military Coll. of Science, 1941-45; Asst Lectr, University of Manchester, 1947-49; Lecturer, Queen's Coll., Dundee, 1951-52; King's Coll., Newcastle upon Tyne: Lectr,

1952-56; Senior Lecturer, 1956-60; Reader in Mathematics, 1960-61; Prof. of Mathematics, University of Leeds, 1961-63; Prof. of Applied Mathematics, Melbourne Univ., 1963-67. *Publications:* contrib. learned journals regarding the mechanics of solids and fluids. *Recreation:* Methodist lay preacher. *Address:* University of Southampton, Highfield, Southampton.

CRAGGS, Prof. John Drummond, MSc, PhD, FInstP; Professor of Electronic Engineering, University of Liverpool, since 1955; *b* 17 May 1915; *s* of Thomas Lawson Craggs and Elsie Aidrienne Roberts; *m* 1941, Dorothy Ellen Margaret Garfitt; two *d. Educ:* Huddersfield Coll.; University of London. Research Student, King's Coll., London Univ., 1937-38; Metropolitan-Vickers High Voltage Research Laboratory, Manchester, 1938-48; University of California, Radiation Laboratory, 1944-45; apptd Sen. Lectr, 1948, and, later, Reader, Dept of Electrical Engineering, University of Liverpool. A Pro-Vice-Chancellor, Liverpool Univ., 1969-72. *Publications:* Counting Tubes, 1950 (with S. C. Curran); Electrical Breakdown of Gases, 1953 (with J. M. Meek); High Voltage Laboratory Technique, 1954 (with J. M. Meek); papers in various professional jls. *Address:* Stone Cottage, Newton-cum-Larton, West Kirby, Wirral, Merseyside. *T:* 051-625 5055.

CRAIB, Douglas Duncan Simpson, CBE 1974; DL; farmer and company director, since 1937; Chairman, Electricity Consultative Council for North of Scotland Area, since 1971; Board Member: North of Scotland Hydro Electric Board, since 1971; Potato Marketing Board of Great Britain, since 1968; *b* 5 April 1914; *s* of Peter Barton Salsbury Simpson and Helen Duncan; changed name by deed poll, 1930; *m* 1939, Moyra Louise Booth; one *s* one *d. Educ:* Aberdeen Grammar Sch.; Dundee High School. Commerce, 1934. Captain, 7th Bn Seaforth Highlanders, 1939-42. Chm. of Dirs, Royal Highland and Agric. Soc. of Scotland, 1967-69 (Hon. Sec. and Hon. Treas., 1970-74); Chm., Highland Agric. Exec. Cttee, 1970-72; Mem., Scottish Agric. Develt Council, 1972-; Governor: N of Scotland Coll. of Agriculture, 1970-; Rowett Res. Inst., Aberdeen, 1973-; Trustee, The MacRobert Trusts, Scotland, 1970-. FRAgSs 1971. DL Moray 1974. *Address:* Stynie House, Fochabers, Morayshire. *T:* Fochabers 231. *Club:* Farmers'.

CRAIG, family name of Viscount Craigavon.

CRAIG, Albert James Macqueen, CMG 1975; HM Diplomatic Service; Ambassador to Syria, since 1976; *b* 13 July 1924; *s* of James Craig and Florence Morris; *m* 1952, Margaret Hutchinson; three *s* one *d. Educ:* Liverpool Institute High Sch.; Univ. of Oxford. Queen's Coll., Oxford (Exhibr), 1942; 1st cl. Hon. Mods Classics, 1943 (Hon. Schol.); Army, 1943-44; 1st cl. Oriental Studies (Arabic and Persian), 1947; Sen. Demy, Magdalen Coll., 1947-48; Lectr in Arabic, Durham Univ., 1948-55; seconded to FO, 1955 as Principal Instructor at Middle East Centre for Arab Studies, Lebanon; joined Foreign Service substantively, 1956; served: FO, 1958-61; HM Political Agent, Trucial States, 1961-64; 1st Sec., Beirut, 1964-67; Counsellor and Head of Chancery, Jedda, 1967-70; Supernumerary Fellow, St Antony's Coll., Oxford, 1970-71; Head of Near East and N Africa Dept, FCO, 1971-75; Dep. High Comr, Kuala Lumpur, 1975-76. *Address:* c/o Foreign and Commonwealth Office, SW1. *Club:* Travellers'.

CRAIG, Very Rev. Archibald Campbell, MC 1918; DD (Hon.); *b* 3 Dec. 1888; *yr s* of Rev. Alexander McRae Craig; *m* 1950, Mary Isobel Laidlaw, *d* of Rev. John Laidlaw; no *c. Educ:* Kelso High Sch.; Edinburgh Univ.; New Coll., Edinburgh. Served European War, 1914-18, 13th Royal Scots and Intelligence Corps, 1914-19. Pastorates in Galston and Glasgow, 1921-30; Chaplain to University of Glasgow, 1930-39; Sec. to the Churches' Commission on International Friendship and Social Responsibility, 1939-42; Gen. Sec., British Council of Churches, 1942-46; Asst Leader, Iona Community, 1946-47; Lecturer in Biblical Studies, Glasgow Univ., 1947-57. Moderator of the Gen. Assembly of the Church of Scotland, May 1961-62. Hon. DD: Edinburgh, 1938; Glasgow, 1961; Dublin, 1961. *Publications:* University Sermons, 1937; Preaching in a Scientific Age (Warrack Lectures), 1954; God Comes Four Times, 1957. *Recreation:* gardening. *Address:* St John's, Doune, Perthshire. *T:* Doune 386.

CRAIG, Mrs Barbara Denise, MA Oxon; Principal of Somerville College, Oxford, since 1967; *b* 22 Oct. 1915; *o d* of John Alexander Chapman and Janie Denize (née Callaway); *m* 1942, Wilson James Craig; no *c. Educ:* Haberdashers' Aske's Girls' Sch., Acton; Somerville Coll., Oxford. Craven Fellow, 1938; Goldsmiths' Sen. Student, 1938; Woolley Fellow in Archæology of Somerville Coll., 1954-56. Temp. Asst Principal, Mins of Supply and Labour, 1939-40; Asst to Prof. of Greek, Aberdeen

Univ., 1940-42; Temp. Asst Principal, Min. of Home Security, 1942; Temp. Principal, Min. of Production, 1943-45. Unofficial work as wife of British Council officer in Brazil, Iraq, Spain, Pakistan, 1946-65; from 1956, archæological work on finds from British excavations at Mycenae. *Recreations:* bird-watching (Mem. Brit. Ornithologists' Union); walking. *Address:* Somerville College, Oxford. *T:* Oxford 55880. *Club:* University Women's.

CRAIG, Charles (James); opera singer (tenor); *b* 3 Dec. 1920; *s* of James and Rosina Craig; *m* 1946, Dorothy Wilson; one *s* one *d.* *Educ:* in London. Protégé of Sir Thomas Beecham; Principal Tenor with Carl Rosa Opera Co., 1953-56; joined Sadler's Wells Opera Co., 1956. Appears regularly at Internat. Opera Houses, incl. Covent Garden, Milan, Rome, Vienna, Paris, Berlin, Buenos Aires, etc; repertoire of 48 operas, incl. Otello, Aida, Turandot, Norma, Andrea Chenier, Die Walküre, Götterdämmerung, Lohengrin, etc. Concerts, TV and radio, and records. International Opera Medal Award, 1962. *Recreations:* motoring, cooking. *Address:* Whitfield Cottage, Whitfield, Northants.

CRAIG, Clifford, CMG 1951; radiologist; *b* 3 Aug. 1896; *s* of Dr W. J. Craig, Box Hill, Victoria, Australia; *m* 1927, Edith Nance Bulley; two *s* one *d. Educ:* Scotch Coll., Melbourne; University of Melbourne. MB, BS, 1924; MD Melbourne, 1926; MS Melbourne, 1930; FRACS 1930; DDR 1954. Surgeon Superintendent, Launceston General Hospital, 1926-31; Hon. Surgeon, Launceston General Hospital, 1932-41; Surgeon Superintendent, 1941-51. Pres., Tasmanian Branch, BMA, 1941; Mem. Federal Council, BMA, 1941-47. Pres. Rotary International, Launceston, 1950; Pres., Medical Council, Tasmania, 1954-66; Chairman, Tasmanian Cancer Cttee; President: Nat. Trust of Aust. (Tasmania), 1963-72; Aust. Cancer Soc., 1970-73. Served European War, 1914-18, 1st AIF (Palestine), 1916-18; War of 1939-45, RAAF, 1940-45. *Publications:* The Engravers of Van Diemen's Land, 1961; Old Tasmanian Prints, 1964; History of the Launceston General Hospital, 1963; (jtly) Early Colonial Furniture in New South Wales and Van Diemen's Land, 1972; A Bibliographical Study of the Van Diemen's Land 'Pickwick Papers', 1973; articles in medical jls. *Recreations:* Cricket Blue, Melbourne Univ.; tennis, golf. *Address:* 21 High Street, Launceston, Tasmania 7250, Australia. *T:* 24182. *Clubs:* Launceston (Launceston); Naval and Military (Melbourne).

CRAIG, Air Vice-Marshal David Brownrigg, OBE 1967; Assistant Chief of Air Staff (Operations), Ministry of Defence, since 1975; *b* 17 Sept. 1929; *s* of Major Francis Brownrigg Craig and Mrs Olive Craig; *m* 1955, Elisabeth June Derenburg; one *s* one *d. Educ:* Radley Coll.; Lincoln Coll., Oxford (MA). Commnd in RAF, 1951; OC RAF Cranwell, 1968-70; ADC to the Queen, 1969-71; Dir, Plans and Ops, HQ Far East Comd, 1970-71; OC RAF Akrotiri, 1972-73. Gp Captain 1968; Air Cdre 1972; Air Vice-Marshal 1975. *Recreations:* fishing, shooting, golf. *Address:* Heathfield, Firbank Lane, Woking, Surrey GU21 1QS. *T:* Woking 72585. *Club:* Royal Air Force.

CRAIG, Prof. David Parker, FRS 1968; FAA 1969; FRIC; Professor of Chemistry, Australian National University, since 1967; *b* 23 Dec. 1919; *s* of Andrew Hunter Craig, Manchester and Sydney, and Mary Jane (*née* Parker); *m* 1948, Veronica, *d* of Cyril Bryden-Brown, Market Harborough and Sydney; three *s* one *d. Educ:* Sydney Church of England Grammar Sch.; University of Sydney; University Coll., London. MSc (Sydney) 1941, PhD (London) 1950, DSc (London) 1956. Commonwealth Science Scholar, 1940. War Service: Capt., Australian Imperial Force, 1941-44. Lectr in Chemistry, University of Sydney, 1944-46; Turner and Newall Research Fellow, 1946-49, and Lectr in Chemistry, University Coll., London, 1949-52; Prof. of Physical Chemistry, Univ. of Sydney, 1952-56; Prof. of Chemistry, University Coll., London, 1956-67, Vis. Prof., 1968-; Firth Vis. Prof., Univ. of Sheffield, 1973; Vis. Prof. University Coll., Cardiff, 1975-. Pres. Sydney University Union, 1955; Fellow of University Coll., London, 1964-. *Publications:* original papers on chemistry in scientific periodicals. *Address:* Research School of Chemistry, Australian National University, Box 4 PO Canberra, ACT 2600, Australia. *Club:* Athenæum.

CRAIG, Douglas, OBE 1965; Director: Sadler's Wells Theatre, since 1970; Opera and Drama School, Royal College of Music, since 1976; *b* 26 May 1916; *m* 1955, Dorothy Dixon; two *d. Educ:* Latymer Upper Sch.; St Catharine's Coll., Cambridge (MA). FRCM, FRSA. Winchester Prize, Cambridge, 1938. Intell. Corps, 1940-46, Major 1944. Baritone, Sadler's Wells Opera and elsewhere, 1946-; Artistic Dir, Opera for All, 1949-65; Stage Dir, Glyndebourne, 1952-55; Asst Gen. Man., Glyndebourne, 1955-59; Producer, Royal Coll. of Music, 1958-;

Freelance Opera Producer, 1959-; Dep. Dir, London Opera Centre, 1965-66; Administrator, Welsh Nat. Opera, 1966-70. *Publication:* (ed) Delius: Koanga (opera), 1975. *Recreation:* travel. *Address:* 43 Park Road, Radlett, Herts WD7 8EG. *T:* Radlett 7240. *Club:* Oxford and Cambridge Music.

CRAIG, Edward Anthony, (works also under name of Edward Carrick), FRSA; writer and lecturer, designer for film and theatre; independent film art director; *b* 3 Jan. 1905; *s* of late Edward Gordon Craig, CH; *m* 1960, Mary, *d* of late Lieut-Col H. A. Timewell, OBE. Studied art, the theatre and photography in Italy, 1917-26; has discovered numerous documents of great value to the history of the theatre; Art Dir to the Welsh Pearson Film Co., 1928-29; Art Dir for Associated Talking Pictures, 1932-36; Supervising Art Dir, Criterion Film, 1937-39; established AAT Film Sch., 1937; Art Dir to the Crown Film Unit (Ministry of Information), 1939-46; Executive Art Dir, Independent Producers (Rank), 1947-49; wood-engravings, oil paintings, and scene designs exhibited at: the St George's Gallery, 1927 and 1928; at the Redfern Gallery, 1929, 1931, 1938; The Grubb Group, 1928-38; also in the principal Galleries of Canada and North America; designer of scenes and costumes for numerous London productions and at Stratford-upon-Avon, 1949. *Official Purchasers:* the British Museum; Victoria and Albert Museum; Metropolitan Museum, New York; Yale Univ., USA; The University, Austin, Texas. *Publications:* Designing for Moving Pictures, 1941; Meet the Common People, 1942; Art and Design in British Films, 1948; Designing for Films, 1949; Gordon Craig, The Story of his Life, 1968; (in Italian) Fabrizio Carini Motta, 1972, Polish trans., 1977. *Illustrations:* The Georgics of Virgil, 1931, etc; books of verse by John Keats, Edith Sitwell, Edmund Blunden, W. H. Davies, etc. *Recreations:* books and music. *Address:* Cutlers Orchard, Bledlow, Aylesbury, Bucks HP17 9PA.

CRAIG, Elizabeth Josephine; Cookery Expert, People's Friend, etc; lecturer; *b* 16 Feb. 1883; *d* of late Rev. John Mitchell Craig, The Manse, Memus, Forfar, Angus, and Katherine Nichol; *m* 1919, A. E. Mann (*d* 1973), American War Correspondent and broadcaster; no *c. Educ:* George Watson's Ladies' Coll., Edinburgh. Editor of Woman's Life, 1915-18; Freelance from then onward, contrib. to daily, weekly, and monthly periodicals. Mem. Inst. Hygiene (MIH); Fellow of the Cookery and Food Association (FCFA); FRSA; Chevalière de Corteaux de Champagne; Dame de la Chaine des Rôtisseurs. *Publications:* Cooking with Elizabeth Craig, 1932, new edn 1961; (with A. Simon) Madeira, Wine, Cakes and Sauce, 1933; Entertaining with Elizabeth Craig, 1933; Standard Recipes, 1934; Economical Cookery, 1934; Wine in the Kitchen, 1934; Family Cookery, 1935; Woman, Wine and a Saucepan, 1936; Bubble and Squeak, 1936; Keeping House with Elizabeth Craig, 1936; Tested Recipes (boxed cards), 1936; The Housewife's Monthly Calendar, 1936; Cookery, 1937; Gardening, 1937; Housekeeping, 1937; Needlecraft, 1937; 1000 Household Hints, 1937; 1500 Everyday Menus, 1937; Simple Housekeeping, 1938; Simple Gardening, 1938; Enquire Within: the happy housewife's ABC, 1938; Cooking in Wartime, 1940; Practical Gardening, 1952; Court Favourites, 1953; Waterless Cookery, 1954; Beer and Vittels, 1955; The Scottish Cookery Book, 1956; Family Cookery, 1957, new edn 1971; Instructions to Young Cooks, 1957; Scandinavian Cooking, 1958; A Cook's Guide to Wine, 1959; Cottage Cheese and Yogurt, 1960; Banana Dishes, 1962; Cooking Continental, 1965; What's Cooking in Scotland, 1965; The Art of Irish Cooking, 1969; The Business Woman's Cook Book, 1970; (ed) The Potluck Cookery Book by T. Campbell, 1962; (ed) Around the World on a Salad Bowl by V. Bennett and C. Kahman, 1963; (ed) Sunset: the Penguin salad book, 1965. *Recreations:* gardening, travelling. *Address:* St Catherine's, Botesdale, Diss, Norfolk. *T:* Botesdale 434. *Clubs:* Pen, Parrot, Arts Theatre.

CRAIG, Hamish M.; see Millar-Craig.

CRAIG, Norman; Assistant Under-Secretary of State, Ministry of Defence, since 1972; *b* 15 May 1920; *s* of George Craig, OBE; *m* 1st, 1946, Judith Margaret Newling (marr. diss. 1957); one *s*; 2nd, 1960, Jane Hudson; two *s* one *d. Educ:* Penarth County Sch.; Cardiff Univ. Army Service, Royal Sussex Regt, 1940-47. Board of Trade, 1948; Min. of Supply, 1953; Private Sec. to Minister, 1959-60; Sec. to Cttee of Inquiry into Aircraft Industry, 1964-65. Course at IDC, 1968. *Address:* 51 Hayes Lane, Beckenham, Kent. *T:* 01-650 7916.

CRAIG, Rev. Prof. Robert; Principal and Vice-Chancellor since 1970, Principal and Professor of Theology since 1969, University of Rhodesia; *b* 22 March 1917; *s* of late John Craig, stone-mason, and late Anne Peggie, linen-weaver; *m* 1950, Olga Wanda, *d* of late Michael and of Helena Strzelec; one *s* one *d.*

Educ: Fife CC schs; St Andrews Univ.; Union Theol Seminary, NY. MA (Ordinary) 1938, BD with distinction in Systematic Theology 1941, PhD 1950, St Andrews; STM *magna cum laude* Union Theol Seminary 1948. Pres., Students' Rep. Council, Chm. Union Debating Soc., Berry Schol. in Theology, St Andrews Univ., 1941; Asst Minister, St John's Kirk, Perth, 1941-42, ordained 1942; Chaplain (4th class), Army, 1942-47: infantry bns, NW Europe, 1944-45 (despatches, France, 1944); Egypt, Syria, Palestine, 1945-47; HCF 1947. Hugh Black Fellow and Instructor in Systematic Theology, Union Theol Seminary, 1947-48; Dep. Leader, Iona Community, Scotland, 1948-49; Natal Univ.: Prof. of Divinity, 1950-57; College Dean, Adviser of Students and personal rep. of Principal and Vice-Chancellor, 1953-54; Prof. of Religion, Smith Coll., Mass, 1958-63; UC Rhodesia and Nyasaland: Prof. of Theology, 1963; Dean, Faculty of Arts, 1965; Vice-Principal, 1966; Actg Principal, 1967 and 1969. External Examiner: Rhodes, S Africa Univs, 1950-58; McGill, Boston, Natal, Cape Town Univs, 1959-. Vis. Lectr, Ecumenical Inst., Bossey, Switz., 1955; John Dewey Mem. Lectr, Vermont Univ., 1961; Ainslie Mem. Lectr, Rhodes Univ., 1965. Brit. Council Commonwealth Interchange Fellow, Cambridge Univ., 1966. Hon. DD St Andrews, 1967; Hon. Fellow, Rhodesian Instn of Engineers, 1976. *Publications:* The Reasonableness of True Religion, 1954; Social Concern in the Thought of William Temple, 1963; Religion: Its Reality and Its Relevance, 1965; The Church: Unity in Integrity, 1966; Religion and Politics: a Christian view, 1972; On Belonging to a University, 1974. *Recreations:* the cinema, theatre, contemporary and recent history, light classical music, listening and talking to people. *Address:* The University of Rhodesia, Box 2702, Salisbury, Rhodesia. *T:* Salisbury 36635. *Club:* Kate Kennedy (St Andrews).

CRAIG, Thomas Rae, CBE 1969 (OBE 1945); TD; DL; retired; Deputy Governor, The Bank of Scotland, 1972-77; *b* 11 July 1906; *s* of Sir John Craig, CBE, and Jessie Craig (*née* Sommerville); *m* 1931, Christina Gay (*née* Moodie); three *s* one *d. Educ:* Glasgow Academy; Lycée Malherbe, Caen, Normandy. Served War of 1939-45: Lt-Col 6th Cameronians; AA and QMG 52nd (Lowland) Div. Dir of Colvilles Ltd, 1935; Man. Dir, 1958; Dep. Chm., 1961; Chm. and Man. Dir, 1965-68. Mem. Bd, BSC, 1967-72. Formerly Dir of companies. Member: Convocation of Strathclyde Univ.; Court of Glasgow Univ.; BR (Scottish) Bd (formerly Scottish Railways Bd), 1966-77. DL Dunbartonshire, 1973. Hon. LLD: Strathclyde, 1968; Glasgow, 1970. *Recreation:* farming. *Address:* Invergare, Rhu, Dunbartonshire. *T:* Rhu 427. *Clubs:* Naval and Military; Royal Scottish Automobile (Glasgow).

CRAIG, Rt. Hon. William, PC (N Ire.) 1963; MP (VUP) Belfast East, since Feb. 1974; Member (UUUC), for East Belfast, Northern Ireland Constitutional Convention, 1975-76; Founder and Leader: Ulster Vanguard, Northern Ireland, since 1972; Vanguard Unionist Party, since 1973; *b* 2 Dec. 1924; *s* of late John Craig and Mary Kathleen Craig (*née* Lamont); *m* 1960, Doris Hilgendorff; two *s Educ:* Dungannon Royal Sch.; Larne Grammar Sch.; Queen's Univ., Belfast. Served War of 1939-45, Royal Air Force, 1943-46. Qualified as solicitor, 1952. MP (U) Larne Div. of Antrim, NI Parliament, 1960-73; Mem. (Vanguard Unionist Progressive), N Antrim, NI Assembly, 1973-75. Chief Whip, Parliament of Northern Ireland, 1962-63; Minister of Home Affairs, 1963-64, and 1966-68; Minister of Health and Local Government, 1964; Minister of Development, 1965-66. Member: Council of Europe; WEO. *Recreations:* travel, motoring, shooting. *Address:* 23 Annadale Avenue, Belfast, Northern Ireland BT7 3JJ. *T:* Belfast 644096. *Club:* Royal North of Ireland Yacht (Cultra, Belfast).

CRAIGAVON, 3rd Viscount *cr* 1927, of Stormont, Co. Down; **Janric Fraser Craig;** Bt 1918; *b* 9 June 1944; *s* of 2nd Viscount Craigavon; *S* father, 1974. *Educ:* Eton; King's Coll., London Univ. (BA). ACA. *Heir:* none. *Address:* Flat 13, 65 Courtfield Gardens, SW5 0NQ. *T:* 01-373 9834.

CRAIGEN, James Mark; MP (Lab and Co-op) Glasgow Maryhill since Feb. 1974; *b* 2 Aug. 1938; *e s* of James Craigen, MA and Isabel Craigen; *m* 1971, Sheena Millar. *Educ:* Shawlands Academy, Glasgow; Strathclyde University. MLitt, Heriot-Watt, 1974. MBIM. Compositor, 1954-61. Industrial Relations Asst, Scottish Gas Bd, 1963-64; Head of Organisation and Social Services at Scottish TUC, 1964-68; Asst Sec., and Industrial Liaison Officer, Scottish Business Educn Council, 1968-74. Glasgow City Councillor, 1965-68, Magistrate, 1966-68; JP Glasgow, 1966-75; Mem. Scottish Ambulance Service Bd, 1966-71; Mem. Police Adv. Bd for Scotland, 1970-74; PPS to Sec. of State for Scotland, 1974-76. Mem., UK Delegn to Council of Europe Assembly, 1976-. Mem. General and Municipal Workers Union. *Address:* 38 Downie Grove, Edinburgh EH12 7AX; House of Commons, SW1A 0AA.

CRAIGIE, Dr Hugh Brechin, CBE 1965; Principal Medical Officer, Mental Health Division, Scottish Home and Health Department, retired; *b* 19 May 1908; *s* of late Hugh Craigie; *m* 1st, 1933, Lillia Campbell (*d* 1958), *d* of Dr George Campbell Murray; three *s* ; 2nd, 1962, Eileen (MBE 1950), *d* of F. S. Lyons. *Educ:* Manchester Grammar Sch.; Manchester Univ. House Physician, Manchester Royal Infirmary, 1931-32; Asst Medical Officer, Monsall Fever Hosp., Manchester, 1932-33; Senior Medical Officer, County Mental Hosp., Lancaster, 1933-46; Dep. Med. Supt, County Mental Hosp., Whittingham, 1946; HM Senior Medical Commissioner, General Board of Control for Scotland, 1947. Served War of 1939-45 (despatches), RAMC (Hon. Lieut-Col). *Publications:* various papers on psychiatry. *Address:* Belmont Cottage, Gullane, East Lothian.

CRAIGIE, James, OBE 1946; FRS 1947; MB, ChB, PhD, DPH; LLD St Andrews 1950; *b* 25 June 1899; *s* of James Craigie and Frances Stewart McHardy; *m* 1929, Margaret Kerr Scott Fotheringham; two *d. Educ:* Perth Acad.; University of St Andrews. Asst Medical Officer, Murray Royal, Perth, 1923; Asst in Bacteriology, University of St Andrews, 1927; Research Associate, Connaught Laboratories, Toronto, 1931, Research Mem., 1943; successively Lecturer in Epidemiology, 1932, Associate Prof. of Virus Infections, 1940, Prof. of Virus Infections, 1946, and Sec., 1935-45, at the Sch. of Hygiene, University of Toronto. Mem. of Scientific Staff, Imperial Cancer Research Fund, 1947-64; Mem., Joint United States-Canadian Commission (Rinderpest), 1942-46; Pres., Soc. of American Bacteriologists, 1946; FRS Canada, 1946; United States of America Typhus Commission Medal, 1946; Medal of Freedom, 1947; Stewart Prize (BMA), 1950. *Publications:* on bacteriology, virus diseases, typhoid phage-typing and experimental oncology. *Address:* 24 Inveralmond Drive, Edinburgh EH4 6JX.

CRAIGIE, John Hubert, OC 1967; FRS 1952; *b* 8 Dec. 1887; *s* of John Yorston Craigie and Elizabeth Mary Pollock; *m* 1926, Miriam Louise, *d* of Allen R. Morash and Clara Louise (*née* Smith). *Educ:* Harvard Univ. (AB); University of Minnesota (MSc); University of Manitoba (PhD). Dalhousie Univ., 1914. Served European War, 1914-18, Canadian Expeditionary Force, 1915-18; Indian Army, 1918-20. Canada Dept of Agriculture: Plant Pathologist, 1925-27; Senior Plant Pathologist, 1927-28; Officer-in-Charge (of Laboratory), Dominion Laboratory of Plant Pathology, Winnipeg, 1928-45; Associate Dir, Science Service, Canada Dept of Agriculture, Ottawa, 1945-52; retired 1952. Hon. DSc: University of British Columbia, 1946; University of Manitoba, 1959; Hon. LLD: University of Saskatchewan, 1948; Dalhousie Univ., 1951. *Publications:* papers in scientific journals. *Address:* 479 Kensington Avenue, Ottawa 3, Canada. *T:* 722-1511.

CRAIGMYLE, 3rd Baron, *cr* 1929, of Craigmyle; **Thomas Donald Mackay Shaw;** Director of Inchcape & Co. Ltd; Chairman: Craigmyle & Co. Ltd; Claridge Mills Ltd; *b* 17 Nov. 1923; *s* of 2nd Baron and Lady Margaret Cargill Mackay (*d* 1958), *e d* of 1st Earl of Inchcape; *S* father, 1944; *m* 1955, Anthea Esther Christine, *y d* of late E. C. Rich; three *s* three *d. Educ:* Eton; Trinity Coll., Oxford (MA). Served RNVR, 1943-46. FRSA. *Publication:* (ed with J. Gould) Your Death Warrant?, 1971. *Recreations:* Scottish country dancing and piping. *Heir:* s Hon. Thomas Columba Shaw, *b* 19 Oct. 1960. *Address:* 18 The Boltons, SW10 9SY; Scottas, Knoydart, Inverness-shire PH41 4PL. *Clubs:* Caledonian; Royal Thames Yacht; Bengal (Calcutta).
See also W. B. Dean.

CRAIGTON, Baron, *cr* 1959 (Life Peer); **Jack Nixon Browne,** PC 1961; CBE 1944; *b* 3 Sept. 1904; *m* 1950, Eileen Nolan, *d* of late Henry Whitford Nolan, London. *Educ:* Cheltenham Coll. Served War of 1939-45, RAF (Balloon Command), Actg Group Capt. Contested (C) Govan Div., Glasgow, in 1945; MP (C) Govan Div., 1950-55; MP (C) Craigton Div. of Glasgow, 1955-Sept. 1959; Parly Private Sec. to Sec. of State for Scotland, 1952-April 1955; Parly Under-Sec., Scottish Office, April 1955-Oct. 1959; Minister of State, Scottish Office, Nov. 1959-Oct. 1964. City of Westminster Chamber of Commerce (formerly Westminster Chamber of Commerce): Mem., General Purposes Cttee, 1948; Mem., Exec. Cttee, 1950; Chm., 1954; Pres., 1966-. Chm., United Biscuits (Holdings) Ltd, 1967-72. Trustee, World Wildlife Fund (British Nat. Appeal), 1965-; Vice-Chm., Fauna Preservation Soc., 1970-; Chairman: Cttee for Environmental Conservation, 1972-; All-Party Conservation Cttee of both Houses of Parliament, 1972-; Fedn of Zoological Gardens, 1975. *Recreation:* gardening. *Address:* Friary House, Friary Island, Wraysbury, near Staines, Mddx. *T:* Wraysbury 2213. *Club:* Buck's.

CRAM, Alastair Lorimer, MC 1945; Appellate Judge, Supreme Court of Appeal, Malawi, 1964-68, retired; in private practice at Scots Bar, Edinburgh; *b* 25 Aug. 1909; *m* 1951, Isobel Nicholson; no *c. Educ:* Perth Academy; Edinburgh University (LLB). Solicitor, 1933; private practice, 1935-39; admitted Scots Bar, 1946. Served in HM Army, 1939-48: POW, successful escapes; RA, SAS, Intelligence Corps, Counsel War Crimes Group NW Europe, Major; GSO 2. Resident Magistrate, Kenya, 1948; Actg Puisne Judge, 1953-56; Sen. Resident Magistrate, Kenya, 1956; Temp. Puisne Judge, 1958-60; Puisne Judge, High Court of Nyasaland, 1960; acting Chief Justice and (briefly) Governor-General, Malawi, 1965; Legal Dept, Scottish Office, 1971-74. Athlete, climber, and traveller: in Alps, 1930-60, and Himalayas, 1960 and 1963; in African, Asian and South American deserts, 1940-66; in Amazon basin and Peruvian Andes, 1966; in Atlas Mts, 1971. *Publications:* Editor, Kenya Law Reports, 1952-56; contribs law reports, legal and mountaineering jls. *Recreations:* shooting, sound-recordings, photography (still and cine), orchid-collecting, languages. *Address:* 5 Upper Dean Terrace, Edinburgh. *T:* 031-332 5441. *Clubs:* Alpine; Scottish Mountaineering (Edinburgh).

CRAMER, Hon. Sir John (Oscar), Kt 1964; FREI; QRV; MHR (L) for Bennelong, New South Wales, 1949-74; Senior Partner, Cramer Brothers, real estate auctioneers; Managing Director, Higgins (Buildings) Ltd; *b* Quirindi, NSW, 18 Feb. 1897; *s* of J. N. Cramer, Quirindi; *m* 1921, Mary (Dame Mary Cramer, *qv*), *d* of William M. Earls; two *s* two *d. Educ:* state public schs; business coll. Mayor of North Sydney, 1940-41; Member: Sydney County Council, 1935- (Chm., 1946-49); Statutory Cttee on Public Works, 1949-56 (Chm., 1955-56); Executive Building Industry Congress of New South Wales; Executive of Liberal Party of Australia, NSW Division (a founder of Provisional Exec.). Minister for the Army, 1956-63. *Recreation:* bowls. *Address:* Unit 7, 47a Shirley Road, Wollstonecraft, NSW 2065, Australia. *T:* 43 5007. *Club:* Rotary.

CRAMER, Dame Mary (Theresa), DBE 1971; Past President of the Mater Hospital Auxiliary, Sydney, New South Wales, Australia; *d* of William M. Earls; *m* 1921, Hon. Sir John (Oscar) Cramer, *qv*; two *s* two *d.* Has been for many years in public life and interested in charitable activities; was closely associated with the Red Cross movement; during War of 1939-45 she was the first area officer of Women's Aust. Nat. Services on the North Shore. *Address:* Unit 7, 47a Shirley Road, Wollstonecraft, NSW 2065, Australia.

CRAMOND, Ronald Duncan; Under-Secretary, Scottish Development Department, since 1973; *b* 22 March 1927; *s* of Adam and Margaret Cramond; *m* 1954, Constance MacGregor; one *s* one *d. Educ:* George Heriot's Sch.; Edinburgh Univ. (MA). Sen. Medallist History 1949. MBIM 1970. Commnd Royal Scots, 1950. Entered War Office, 1951; Private Sec. to Parly Under-Sec. of State, Scottish Office, 1956; Principal, Dept of Health for Scotland, 1957; Mactaggart Fellow (Applied Econs), Glasgow Univ., 1962; Haldane Medallist in Public Admin, 1964; Asst Sec., Scottish Develt Dept, 1966. *Publication:* Housing Policy in Scotland, 1966. *Recreations:* golf, hill walking, Rugby refereeing. *Address:* c/o Scottish Development Department, New St Andrews House, Edinburgh EH1 3SZ. *Club:* Royal Commonwealth Society.

CRAMOND, Dr William Alexander, OBE 1960; Principal and Vice-Chancellor of Stirling University, since 1975; *b* 2 Oct. 1920; *er s* of William James Cramond, MBE and of May Battisby, Aberdeen; *m* 1949, Bertine J. C. Mackintosh, MB, ChB, Dornoch; one *s* one *d. Educ:* Robert Gordon's Coll., Aberdeen; Aberdeen Univ. MB, ChB, MD, FRCPsych, FANZCP, FRACP, DPM. Physician Supt, Woodilee Mental Hosp., Glasgow, 1955-61; Dir of Mental Health, S Australia, 1961-65; Prof. of Mental Health, Univ. of Adelaide, 1963-71; Principal Medical Officer in Mental Health, Scottish Home and Health Dept, 1971-72; Dean of Faculty of Medicine and Prof. of Mental Health, Univ. of Leicester, 1972-75. *Publications:* papers on psychosomatic medicine and on care of dying in Brit. Jl Psychiat., Lancet, BMJ. *Recreations:* walking, reading, theatre. *Address:* c/o Stirling University, Stirling FK9 4LA.

CRAMP, Prof. Rosemary Jean; Professor of Archaeology, University of Durham, since 1971; *b* 6 May 1929. *Educ:* St Anne's Coll., Oxford (MA, BLitt). Lectr, St Anne's Coll., Oxford, 1950-55; Lectr, Durham Univ., 1955, Sen. Lectr, 1966. Member: Ancient Monuments Board for England, 1974-; Royal Commn on Ancient and Historical Monuments of Scotland, 1975-. *Publications:* contribs in the field of Early Monasticism, Anglo-Saxon Sculpture and Northern Archaeology. *Address:* Department of Archaeology, University of Durham, 46 Saddler Street, Durham DH1 3NU. *T:* Durham 64466.

CRAMPTON SMITH, Alec; *see* Smith, Alexander C.

CRANBORNE, Viscount; Robert Michael James Cecil; *b* 30 Sept. 1946; *s* and *heir* of 6th Marquess of Salisbury, *qv*; *m* 1970, Hannah Ann, *er d* of Lt-Col William Joseph Stirling of Keir; two *s* one *d. Educ:* Eton; Oxford. Prospective Parly Cand. (C), South Dorset, 1976. *Heir: s* Hon. Robert Edward William Cecil, *b* 1970. *Address:* The Lodge House, Hatfield Park, Hertfordshire.

CRANBROOK, 4th Earl of, *cr* 1892; **John David Gathorne-Hardy,** CBE 1955; Viscount Cranbrook, 1878; Baron Medway, 1892; DL, JP Suffolk; Hon. MA Cantab; Member, East Suffolk County Council, 1934-74 (Chairman, 1950-57); *b* 15 April 1900; *e s* of 3rd Earl and Lady Dorothy Boyle, *y d* of 7th Earl of Glasgow; *S* father, 1915; *m* 1st, 1926, Bridget (who obtained a divorce 1930), *o d* of late Rupert D'Oyly Carte; 2nd, 1932, Fidelity, OBE 1972, JP Suffolk, *o d* of late Hugh E. Seebohm; two *s* three *d. Educ:* Eton; RMA, Woolwich. Gunner RFA, 1918-19; Lieut, RFA, 1921-32; Alderman LCC, 1928-30; Parliamentary Private Sec. to HM First Commissioner of Works (Earl Peel), 1927-28; Deputy Regional Commissioner for Eastern Civil Defence Region, 1940-45. Chm., East Anglian Regional Hosp. Bd, 1947-59. Hon. Air Cdre 3619 (Suffolk) Fighter Control Unit, RAuxAF, 1950-61. Trustee, British Museum (Natural History), 1963-73; Mem., Nature Conservancy, 1967-72. KStJ. *Heir: s* Lord Medway, *qv. Address:* Red House Farm, Great Glemham, Saxmundham, Suffolk. *T:* Rendham 424.

CRANE, Prof. Francis Roger; Professor of Law, Queen Mary College, University of London, since 1965; *b* 19 Dec. 1910; *m* 1938, Jean Berenice Hadfield; two *s* one *d. Educ:* Highgate Sch.; University Coll., London. LLB 1933; Solicitor, 1934, Clifford's Inn Prize. Lecturer in Law; King's Coll. and private practice, 1935-38; Lecturer in Law, University of Manchester, 1938-46; Prof. of Law, University of Nottingham, 1946-52; Prof. of English Law, King's Coll., London, 1952-65; Dean of the Faculty of Law, QMC, London, 1965-76. University of London: Mem. Senate, 1969-71, 1973-; Chm. Academic Council, 1975-; Mem. Court, 1975-. Visiting Professor: Tulane Univ., 1960; University of Khartoum, 1963; Dean of the Faculty of Law and Visiting Prof., University of Canterbury (New Zealand), 1964; Vis. Professor: Univ. of Melbourne, 1972; Monash Univ., 1972. Served War of 1939-45: Royal Corps of Signals, Major, 1944. Pres., Soc. of Public Teachers of Law, 1975-76. FKC 1976. *Publications:* (jointly) A Century of Family Law, 1957; articles and notes in legal periodicals. *Address:* 10 Myddelton Park, Whetstone, N20 0HX. *T:* 01-445 4642.

CRANE, Sir Harry (Walter Victor), Kt 1966; OBE 1949; JP; Industrial Relations Consultant since 1965; *b* 12 Feb. 1903; *s* of William and Ann Crane; *m* 1930, Winefride Mary, *d* of Thomas and Lucy Wing; one *s. Educ:* Nottingham. Engineer Fitter. NUGMW: District Officer, 1934; Nat. Officer, 1943; District Sec., 1957; retd from Union service, 1965. Member: Catering Commn, 1950-52; Catering Hygiene Cttee, 1949-52; Food Hygiene Adv. Coun.; Workers' Travel Assoc. (now Galleon World Travel Assoc.) Management Cttee, 1960-; (pt-time) E Midlands Electricity Bd, 1965-73; Milk Marketing Bd, 1966-72. Director (part-time), Transport Holding Co., Ministry of Transport, 1966-73. Hon. Pres., Galleon World Travel, 1973-. Chairman: Labour Party Conference Arrangements Cttee, 1954-65; Industrial Injuries Advisory Council, 1967-73; Sec. or Chm. of Joint Industrial Councils during Trade Union career. FREconS 1944. JP 1961. *Recreations:* swimming, gardening, reading. *Address:* Riverain, 22 Cliff Drive, Radcliffe-on-Trent, Nottingham. *T:* Radcliffe-on-Trent 2683. *Clubs:* Royal Commonwealth Society, Civil Service.

CRANE, Morley Benjamin, FRS 1947; Hon. FLS; VMH; formerly Deputy Director and Head of Pomology Department of the John Innes Horticultural Institution; *b* 17 March 1890. *Publications:* (with Sir Daniel Hall) The Apple, 1933; (with W. J. C. Lawrence) The Genetics of Garden Plants, 4th edn 1952; many research papers on origin, genetics and breeding of cultivated fruits and plants. *Address:* Plovers Dip, Fishponds Way, Haughley, Suffolk.

CRANE, Prof. William Alfred James, MD; FRCP, FRCPGlas, FRCPath; Joseph Hunter Professor of Pathology, University of Sheffield, since 1965; Dean of Sheffield Medical School, since 1976; Hon. Consultant Pathologist, since 1959; Hon. Director of Cancer Research, since 1968; *b* 27 June 1925; *s* of late William Crane and Margaret McGechie; *m* 1952, Yvonne Elizabeth Dann; one *s* one *d. Educ:* Univ. of Glasgow (MB ChB, MD Hons and Bellahouston Gold Medal). FRCPath 1971 (MRCPath 1963); FRCPGlas 1972 (MRCPGlas 1965); FRCP

1975 (MRCP 1967). RAMC, 1948-50; Hansen Scholar and Lectr, Univ. of Glasgow, 1951-56; Asst Prof., Univ. of Chicago, 1956-57; Lectr in Pathology, Univ. of Glasgow, 1957-59; Sen. Lectr in Pathology, Univ. of Sheffield, 1959-64; Associate Prof., Univ. of Chicago, 1962. Mem., MRC Bd, 1970-76; Mem. Council, RCPath, 1970-73; Sec., Path. Soc. of GB and Ire., 1969-74. Hon. Mem., Dutch Path. Soc., 1976. *Publications:* papers in scientific and med. jls on endocrinology and hypertension. *Recreations:* gardening, music. *Address:* 56 Stumperlowe Crescent Road, Fulwood, Sheffield S10 3PR.

CRANKSHAW, Edward, TD; FRSL; writer; Correspondent on Soviet Affairs for The Observer, 1947-68; *b* 3 Jan. 1909; *s* of Arthur and Amy Crankshaw; *m* 1931, Clare, *d* of late E. A. Carr. *Educ:* Bishop's Stortford Coll. Commissioned 4th Bn Queen's Own Royal West Kent Regt (TA), 1936; GSO1 attached Brit. Mil. Mission, Moscow, 1941-43. Ehrenkreuz für Wissenschaft und Kunst, 1st Class (Austria). *Publications:* Joseph Conrad: Aspects of the Art of the Novel, 1936; Vienna: the Image of a Culture in Decline, 1938; Britain and Russia, 1945; Russia and the Russians, 1947; Russia by Daylight, 1951; The Forsaken Idea: a study of Viscount Milner, 1952; Gestapo: Instrument of Tyranny, 1956; Russia without Stalin, 1956; Krushchev's Russia, 1959; The Fall of the House of Habsburg, 1963; The New Cold War: Moscow v. Pekin, 1963; Krushchev: a Biography, 1966; Maria Theresa, 1969; The Habsburgs, 1971; Tolstoy: the making of a novelist, 1974; The Shadow of the Winter Palace: the drift to revolution, 1825-1917, 1976 (Yorkshire Post Prize, 1976; Heinemann Award, 1977); *novels:* Nina Lessing, 1938; What Glory?, 1939; The Creedy Case, 1954; many translations from German and French, incl. five plays by Ernst Toller; contribs to many periodicals and symposia in UK and USA. *Recreations:* fishing, music. *Address:* Church House, Sandhurst, Kent. *T:* 293. *Club:* Brooks's.

CRANLEY, Viscount; Rupert Charles William Bullard Onslow; *b* 16 June 1967; *s* and *heir* of 7th Earl of Onslow, *qv*.

CRANMER, Philip, FRCO; Secretary, Associated Board of the Royal Schools of Music, since 1974; *b* 1 April 1918; *s* of Arthur Cranmer and Lilian Phillips; *m* 1939, Ruth Loasby; one *s* three *d*. *Educ:* Wellington; Christ Church, Oxford (BMus, MA). Asst Music Master, Wellington Coll. 1938-40; served RA, 1940-46; Major, Education Officer, Guards Div., 1946; Dir of Music, King Edward's Sch., Birmingham, 1946; Staff Accompanist, Midland Region, BBC, 1948; Lectr in Music, Birmingham Univ., 1950; Hamilton Harty Prof. of Music, Queen's Univ., Belfast, 1954-70; Prof. of Music, Univ. of Manchester, 1970-74. Pres., Incorporated Soc. of Musicians, 1971; Gen. Editor, Eulenberg Miniature Score edn, 1976-. FRCO 1947. Hon. RAM 1967; FRMCM 1974; FRCM 1976. Chevalier de l'Ordre de Léopold II, 1947; Croix de Guerre Belge, 1947. *Publication:* The Technique of Accompaniment, 1970. *Recreation:* squash. *Address:* 14 Bedford Square, WC1B 3JG.

CRANSTON, Prof. Maurice (William); Professor of Political Science at the London School of Economics, since 1969; seconded as Professor of Political Science, European University Institute, since 1978; *b* 8 May 1920; *o c* of William Cranston and Catherine Harris; *m* 1958, Baroness Maximiliana von und zu Fraunberg; two *s*. *Educ:* London Univ.; St Catherine's, Oxford (MA, BLitt). Lecturer (part-time) in Social Philosophy, London Univ., 1950-59; Reader (previously Lecturer) in Political Science at London Sch. of Economics, 1959-69. Visiting Prof. of Government: Harvard Univ., 1965-66; Dartmouth Coll., USA, 1970-71; Univ. of British Columbia, 1973-74; Univ. of California, 1976; Ecole des Hautes Etudes, Paris, 1977. Pres., Institut International de Philosophie Politique, 1976-; Vice-Pres. de l'Alliance Française en Angleterre, 1964-. Literary Adviser to Methuen Ltd, 1959-69. FRSL. Foreign Hon. Mem., Amer. Acad. of Arts and Sciences, 1970-. *Publications:* Freedom, 1953; Human Rights Today, 1954 (revised edn 1962); John Locke: a biography, 1957 (James Tait Black Memorial Prize); Jean-Paul Sartre, 1962; What Are Human Rights? (New York), 1963, 2nd rev. edn (London), 1973; Western Political Philosophers (ed), 1964; A Glossary of Political Terms, 1966; Rousseau's Social Contract, 1967; Political Dialogues, 1968; La Quintessence de Sartre (Montreal), 1969; Language and Philosophy (Toronto), 1969; The New Left (ed), 1970; Politics and Ethics, 1972; The Mask of Politics, 1973. *Recreation:* walking. *Address:* Badia Fiesolana, San Domenico di Fiesole 50016, Italy. *T:* (55) 477931. *Club:* Garrick.

CRANSTON, Prof. William Ian; Professor of Medicine, St Thomas's Hospital Medical School, since 1964; *b* 11 Sept. 1928; *s* of Thomas and Margaret Cranston; *m* Pamela Isabel Pearson; four *s*. *Educ:* High Sch. for Boys, Glasgow; Aberdeen Grammar Sch.; Boys' High Sch., Oswestry; University of Aberdeen, FRCP London 1965 (MRCP 1952); MB, ChB (Hons), 1949; MD Aberdeen 1957; MA Oxon. 1962. Royal Infirmary, Aberdeen: House Physician, 1949-50; Medical Registrar, 1952-53; Asst in Medical Unit, St Mary's Hospital, Paddington, 1953-56; 1st Asst in Dept of Regius Prof. of Med., Radcliffe Inf., Oxford, 1961-64. Mem., Med. Res. Soc. *Recreations:* reading, gardening, painting. *Address:* St Thomas's Hospital Medical School, Albert Embankment, Westminster Bridge, SE1.

CRANSTONE, Bryan Allan Lefevre; Curator, Pitt Rivers Museum, Oxford, since 1976; *b* 26 Feb. 1918; *s* of late Edgar Arnold Cranstone and late Clarice Edith Cranstone; *m* 1941, Isabel May, *d* of W. Gough-Thomas; one *s*. *Educ:* Bootham Sch., York; St Catharine's Coll., Cambridge (MA). Hampshire Regt, 1939-46. Asst Keeper, Dept of Ethnography, BM, 1947-69; field work, New Guinea, 1963-64; Dep. Keeper, Dept of Ethnography, BM (later Museum of Mankind), 1969-76. Vis. Lectr, University Coll., London, 1955-71. Fellow, Linacre Coll., Oxford, 1976. *Publications:* Melanesia: a short ethnography, 1961; The Australian Aborigines, 1973; (with D. C. Starzecka) The Solomon Islanders, 1974; articles in learned jls and encyclopaedias. *Address:* Pitt Rivers Museum, Parks Road, Oxford OX1 3PP.

CRANSWICK, Rt. Rev. Geoffrey Franceys, BA, ThD; *b* 10 April 1894; *s* of late Canon E. G. Cranswick, Sydney; *m* 1927, Rosamund Mary, 3rd *d* of late Blews Robotham, The Knoll, Littleover, Derby; one *s*. *Educ:* The King's Sch., Parramatta; Church of England Grammar Sch., N Sydney; University of Sydney (BA 1916); Ridley Hall, Cambridge. Tutor, Moore Theological Coll., Sydney, 1916; Travelling Sec., Australian Student Christian Movement, 1918; Curate, Parish Church, West Ham, 1920; Missionary CMS, Bengal, India, 1923, as Principal of King Edward's Sch., Chapra, Bengal; Organising Sec. CMS in Canterbury, Rochester and Chichester Dioceses, 1938; India Sec. at HQ CMS, 1938-43; Chm., India Cttee, Conference of British Missionary Socs, 1941; Bishop of Tasmania, 1944-63, retd. UNA Vice-Patron (Tasmania). *Recreations:* bowls, gardening. *Address:* 142 Davey Street, Hobart, Tasmania 7000, Australia.

CRANWORTH, 3rd Baron, *cr* 1899; **Philip Bertram Gurdon;** Lieutenant, Royal Wiltshire Yeomanry; *b* 24 May 1940; *s* of Hon. Robin Gurdon (killed in action, 1942) and Hon. Yoskyl Pearson (she *m* 2nd, 1944, as his 2nd wife, Lieut-Col. Alistair Gibb, and 3rd, 1962, as his 2nd wife, 1st Baron McCorquodale of Newton, PC, KCVO), *d* of 2nd Viscount Cowdray; *S* grandfather, 1964; *m* 1968, Frances Henrietta Montagu Douglas Scott, *d* of late Lord William Scott and of Lady William Scott, Beechwood, Melrose; two *s* one *d*. *Educ:* Eton; Magdalene Coll., Cambridge. *Heir:* *s* Hon. Sacha William Robin Gurdon, *b* 12 Aug. 1970. *Address:* Grundisburgh Hall, Woodbridge, Suffolk IP13 6TW.
See also Earl of Aboyne, *C. M. T. Smith-Ryland*.

CRATHORNE, 2nd Baron *cr* 1959; **Charles James Dugdale;** Bt 1945; consultant and lecturer in Fine Art; *b* 12 Sept. 1939; *s* of 1st Baron Crathorne, PC, TD, and Nancy, OBE (*d* 1969), *d* of Sir Charles Tennant, 1st Bt; *S* father, 1977; *m* 1970, Sylvia Mary, *yr d* of Brig. Arthur Herbert Montgomery, OBE, TD; one *s* one *d*. *Educ:* Eton College; Trinity Coll., Cambridge. MA Cantab (Fine Arts). Impressionist and Modern Painting Dept, Sotheby & Co., 1963-66; Assistant to the President, Parke-Bernet, New York, 1966-69; James Dugdale & Associates, London, Independent Fine Art Consultancy Service, 1969-. Director, Radio Tees, 1975-. Annual lecture tours to America, 1970-. *Publications:* Edouard Vuillard, 1967; (co-author) Tennant's Stalk, 1973; contribs to Apollo and The Connoisseur. *Recreations:* photography, travel, collecting, shooting, fishing, golf, Royal Tennis. *Heir:* *s* Hon. Thomas Arthur John Dugdale, *b* 30 Sept. 1977. *Address:* Crathorne House, Yarm, Cleveland. *T:* Hutton Rudby 700431; 14 Bedford Gardens, W8. *T:* 01-727 9833. *Clubs:* White's, Queen's; Royal Company of Edinburgh Golfers (Edinburgh).

CRAUFURD, Sir Robert (James), 9th Bt *cr* 1781; Member of the London Stock Exchange; *b* 18 March 1937; *s* of Sir James Gregan Craufurd, 8th Bt and of Ruth Marjorie, *d* of Frederic Corder; *S* father, 1970; *m* 1964, Catherine Penelope, *yr d* of late Captain Horatio Westmacott, Torquay; three *d*. *Educ:* Harrow; University College, Oxford. Elected Member of the London Stock Exchange, 1969. *Recreations:* gardening, local history, music and Commonwealth coins. *Address:* Brightwood, Aldbury, Tring, Herts.

CRAVEN, family name of **Earl of Craven.**

CRAVEN, 7th Earl of, *cr* 1801; **Thomas Robert Douglas Craven;** Viscount Uffington, 1801; Baron Craven, 1665; *b* 24 Aug. 1957; *e s* of 6th Earl of Craven and of Elizabeth (*née* Johnstone-Douglas); *S* father, 1965. *Heir: b* Hon. Simon George Craven, *b* 16 Sept. 1961. *Address:* The Dower House, Hamstead Marshall, Newbury, Berks.

CRAVEN, Archdeacon of; *see* Rogers, Ven. D. A.

CRAVEN, Prof. Avery O., LLD (Hon.), LittD (Hon.); Professor of History, The University of Chicago, 1927-54; now Emeritus Professor; *b* 1886; *s* of Oliver and Mary Pennington Craven; *m* 1936, Georgia Watson; one *d. Educ:* Simpson Coll (AB), University of Chicago (PhD); Harvard Univ. (MA). MA Cambridge, 1952. Instructor, Simpson Coll., 1908-11; Asst Prof., College of Emporia, 1920-23; Associate Professor: Michigan State Coll., 1924-25; University of Ill, 1925-27; University of Chicago, 1927; Prof. of History, University of Sydney (Australia), 1948-49; Prof. of American History and Institutions, Cambridge, 1952-53. Hon. DHL: Wayne State Univ.; Purdue Univ. *Publications:* Soil Exhaustion as a factor in History of Virginia and Maryland, 1925; Edmond Ruffin, Southerner, 1931; The Repressible Conflict, 1936; Democracy in American Life, 1938; The Coming of the Civil War, 1942; The United States, Experiment in Democracy, 1947; Civil War in the Making, 1959; An Historian and the Civil War, 1964; Ending of the Civil War, 1968; Reconstruction, 1969; Rochel of Old Louisiana, 1975. *Address:* Dune Acres, RFD3, Chesterton, Indiana, USA. *T:* Chesterton 4722. *Club:* Quadrangle (Chicago, Ill).

CRAVEN, Marjorie Eadon, RRC 1941 (1st Class); *b* 21 March 1895; *yr d* of late John Alfred Craven and Susannah Eadon Craven, Sheffield, Yorks. *Educ:* Roedean Sch. SRN; SCM; RNT; Diploma in Nursing, Leeds Univ.; Health Visitor. Mem. St John VAD, 1915-17; Leeds Gen. Infirmary, 1917-26; studied nursing administration: Bedford Coll., London, Royal College of Nursing, 1926; Teachers' Coll., Columbia Univ., NY City, 1927-28. Matron, West London Hospital, 1929-38 and 1947-53; Matron and Principal Matron, TANS, 1939-44; Matron-in-Chief, British Red Cross Soc. and Joint Cttee, Order of St John and BRCS, 1953-62, retd. Vice-Pres., W. L. H. Nurses' League; Vice-Pres., National Florence Nightingale Memorial Cttee. Officer (Sister) Order of St John, 1957. Florence Nightingale Medal, 1961. *Recreation:* music. *Address:* 5 Pembroke Close, Grosvenor Crescent, SW1X 7ET; Green Finches, 33 North Park, Gerrards Cross, Bucks SL9 8AT. *T:* Gerrards Cross 82349. *Clubs:* VAD Ladies', St John House.

CRAVEN, Air Marshal Sir Robert Edward, KBE 1970 (OBE 1954); CB 1966; DFC 1940; *b* 16 Jan. 1916; *s* of Gerald Craven, Port Elizabeth, S Africa, and Edith Craven, York; *m* 1940, Joan Peters; one *s* one *d. Educ:* Scarborough Coll. MN, 1932-37; Pilot Officer, RAF, 1937; 201, 210, 228 Sqdns, 1937-41; RAF Staff Coll., 1942; Staff Appts: Coastal Command, 1942 (despatches thrice); Directing Staff, RAF Staff Coll., 1944; HQ, Mediterranean and Middle East, Cairo, 1945; CO Eastleigh, Kenya, 1946; RN Staff Coll., 1948; Directing Staff, Joint Services Staff Coll., 1949; Standing Group, NATO Washington, 1951; RAF St Eval, 1954; Directing Staff, RAF Staff Coll., 1957; Group Capt. 1957; CO RAF Lyneham, 1959; Director, Personal Services, RAF, 1961; Air Cdre 1961; Air Officer Admin., Transport Comd, 1964; Air Vice-Marshal, 1965; SASO, Flying Training Comd, 1967-68, Training Comd, 1968-69; Commander, Maritime Air Forces, 1969-72, retired. Order of Menelik (Ethiopia), 1955. *Recreations:* fishing, antique furniture restoration and reproduction. *Address:* Letcombe House, Letcombe Regis, Oxon. *Club:* Royal Air Force.

CRAWFORD, 29th Earl of, *cr* 1398, and **BALCARRES,** 12th Earl of, *cr* 1651; **Robert Alexander Lindsay,** PC; Lord Lindsay of Crawford, before 1143; Lord Lindsay of Balcarres, 1633; Lord Balniel, 1651; Baron Wigan (UK), 1826; Baron Balniel (Life Peer), 1974; Premier Earl of Scotland; Head of House of Lindsay; Chairman, Lombard North Central; Director: National Westminster Bank; Sun Alliance and London Insurance Group; Chairman, Historic Buildings Council for Scotland; *b* 5 March 1927; *er s* of 28th Earl of Crawford and 11th of Balcarres, KT, GBE, and of Mary, 3rd *d* of late Lord Richard Cavendish, PC, CB, CMG; *S* father, 1975; *m* 1949, Ruth Beatrice, *d* of Leo Meyer-Bechtler, Zürich; two *s* two *d*. *Educ:* Eton; Trinity College, Cambridge. Served with Grenadier Guards, 1945-49. MP (C) Hertford, 1955-74, Welwyn and Hatfield, Feb.-Sept. 1974; Parliamentary Private Secretary: to Financial Secretary of Treasury, 1955-57; to Minister of Housing and Local Government, 1957-60; Minister of State for Defence, 1970-72; Minister of State for Foreign and Commonwealth Affairs, 1972-74. President, Rural District

Councils Assoc., 1959-65; Chm., National Association for Mental Health, 1963-70. *Heir: s* Lord Balniel, *qv*. *Address:* 107 Frognal, NW3. *T:* 01-435 3342.

CRAWFORD, Brig. Alastair Wardrop Euing; *b* 1896; *s* of Col E. R. Crawford, DL, of Auchentroig, Buchlyvie; *m* 1924, Helena Beatrice (*d* 1977), *d* of Adm. Sir Charles Dundas of Dundas, KCMG; one *s* two *d. Educ:* Glenalmond; RMC Sandhurst. Served European War, 1916-18; 2nd Lieut Royal Scots Greys, 1916; retired as Major, 1937. Recalled, 1939; Lt-Col Comdg 43rd Reconnaissance Regt, RAC, 1942-43; served in NW Europe, 1944-46, with HQ VIII Corps (despatches), Brig., 1945; retired, 1946. Mem. of Queen's Body Guard for Scotland (Royal Company of Archers), 1949. DL 1947-65, JP 1951-65. Vice-Lieut, 1964-65, Stirlingshire. *Recreations:* shooting, hunting. *Address:* La Fougeraie, Archirondel, Gorey, Jersey, CI. *T:* East 52504. *Clubs:* Cavalry and Guards, English-Speaking Union; New, Royal Caledonian Hunt (Edinburgh); Stirling and County.

CRAWFORD, Sir (Archibald James) Dirom, Kt 1957; Hon. Treasurer Western Area Conservative and Unionist Association since 1959 (President, 1956-59; Chairman, 1951-56); *b* 1899; *s* of Malcolm M. Crawford and Ethel Elizabeth Crawford, *d* of Andrew Wernicke; unmarried. *Educ:* Winchester; RMC Sandhurst. Served as Subaltern, 6th Inniskilling Dragoons, then RARO; invalided out of Service, 1939. Chairman: Bridgwater Div. Conservative and Unionist Assoc., 1948-51; Somerset County Federation of Conservative and Unionist Assocs, 1950-51. Pres., Somerset County Cttee, British Legion, Dec. 1957-(Hon. Treasurer, 1953-57). *Address:* Park House, Over Stowey, Bridgwater, Somerset. *T:* Nether Stowey 269. *Club:* Cavalry and Guards.

CRAWFORD, David Gordon; HM Diplomatic Service; Ambassador to Qatar, Arabian Gulf, since 1974; *b* 10 June 1928; *m* 1953, Anne Sturgeon Burns; one *s* three *d. Educ:* Ashford Grammar School, Kent; London School of Economics. Served HM Forces, 1947-55. Joined Diplomatic Service, 1956; FO, 1956; MECAS, 1957-59; Taiz, 1959; Bahrain, 1959-62; FO, 1962-64; First Sec., New York, 1964-67; First Sec. and Head of Chancery, Amman, 1967-69; Consul-Gen., Oman, 1969-71; Head of Accommodation and Services Dept, FCO, 1971-74. *Address:* c/o Foreign and Commonwealth Office, SW1.

CRAWFORD, Sir Dirom; *see* Crawford, Sir A. J. D.

CRAWFORD, Douglas; *see* Crawford, G. D.

CRAWFORD, Brig. Sir Douglas Inglis, Kt 1964; CB 1952; DSO 1945; TD 1942; Lord-Lieutenant, Metropolitan County of Merseyside, since 1974; Vice-Chairman, United Biscuits, 1962-74; Chairman, D. S. Crawford Ltd; *b* 22 March 1904; *e s* of Archibald Inglis and Mary Forsyth Crawford; unmarried. *Educ:* Uppingham; Magdalene Coll., Cambridge. Served War of 1939-45 in Field Artillery; Comd 87 (Field) Army Group RA (TA), 1947-51; Chm., W Lancs T&AFA, 1951-66; Dir, Royal Insurance Co. Ltd, 1951-74. DL Lancs, 1951; High Sheriff of the County Palatine of Lancaster, 1969-70. Hon. LLD Liverpool, 1976. KStJ 1974. *Recreation:* shooting. *Address:* Fernlea, Mossley Hill, Liverpool L18 8BP. *T:* Allerton 2013. *Clubs:* White's, Boodle's; Royal and Ancient, Hon. Company of Edinburgh Golfers.

CRAWFORD, Sir Ferguson; *see* Crawford, Sir W. F.

CRAWFORD, Sir Frederick, GCMG 1961 (KCMG 1953; CMG 1951); OBE 1945; *b* 9 March 1906; *s* of James Mansfield Crawford, MD, Hull; *m* 1st, 1936, Maimie Alice (*d* 1960), *d* of John Harold Green, London and Cape Town; two *s*; 2nd, 1962, Clio, *widow* of Vasso Georgiadis, Uganda, and *d* of Jean Colocotronis, Athens. *Educ:* Hymers Coll., Hull; Balliol Coll., Oxford (BA). Colonial Civil Service; Cadet, Tanganyika, 1929; Asst District Officer, 1931; District Officer, 1941; seconded E African Governors' Conference, 1942-43 and 1945-46; Exec. Officer, Economic Control Board, Tanganyika, 1944-45. Economic Sec., N Rhodesia, 1947; Dir of Development, N Rhodesia, 1948-50. Governor and Comdr-in-Chief, Seychelles, 1951-53; Dep. Governor of Kenya, 1953-56; Governor of Uganda, 1956-Oct. 1961; Resident Director in Rhodesia: BSA Co., 1961-65; Anglo-American Corp. of SA Ltd, 1965-74. Retired. KStJ 1958. *Publication:* Review of the Northern Rhodesia Development Plan, 1948. *Recreations:* fishing, golf. *Address:* 89A Route de Florissant, Geneva, Switzerland. *Clubs:* Brooks's; Royal and Ancient Golf (St Andrews).

CRAWFORD, (George) Douglas; MP (SNP) Perth and East Perthshire since Oct 1974; Director, Polecon Co., since 1970; *b* 1 Nov. 1939; *s* of Robert and Helen Crawford; *m* 1964, Joan

Burnie; one s one d. Educ: Glasgow Academy; St Catharine's Coll., Cambridge (MA). Features Editor, Business, 1961-63; Industrial Corresp., Glasgow Herald, 1963-66; Editor, Scotland Magazine, 1966-70. Recreations: hill-walking, playing piano and clavichord, watching cricket. Address: 43 Coates Gardens, Edinburgh EH12 5LF. T: 031 337 1470. Clubs: Savile; Scottish Arts, Press (Edinburgh).

CRAWFORD, Hon. Sir George (Hunter), Kt 1972; Judge of the Supreme Court of Tasmania since 1958; b 12 Dec. 1911; s of Frederick Charles Crawford and Ruby Priscilla (née Simpson); m 1936, Helen Zoë, d of Dr Bruce Arnold Anderson (d 1976); two s one d. Educ: East Launceston State Sch.; Launceston Church Grammar Sch.; Univ. of Tasmania (LLB). Barrister and Solicitor, 1934-58; Mem. Cttee, Northern Law Society, 1946-58 (Vice-Pres. 1957-58). Served (including War): AMF, 1929-40; AIF, 1940-44, Lt-Col. Councillor, Northern Br., Royal Soc. of Tasmania, 1954-72 (Chm., 1957-58 and 1966-68); Mem. Cttee, Tasmanian Historical Res. Assoc., 1960-62 (Chm., 1961-62); Mem. Bd, Launceston Church Grammar Sch., 1946-71 (Chm., 1958-65); Mem. Bd, Cradle Mountain-Lake St Clair Nat. Park; Mem. Adv. Cttee, Cradle Mountain, 1956-71; Pres., N Tasmania Branch, Roy. Commonwealth Soc., 1974-76. Col Comdt, Royal Regt of Australian Artillery, in Tasmania Command, 1972. Recreations: music, historical research. Address: 7 Beulah Gardens, Launceston, Tasmania 7250, Australia. T: Launceston 317390. Clubs: Tasmanian (Hobart); Naval, Military and Air Force (Hobart); Launceston, Northern (Launceston).

CRAWFORD, Maj.-Gen. George Oswald, CB 1956; CBE 1944; Director of Ordnance Services, War Office, 1958-61; b 1902; s of late Col Arthur Gosset Crawford, Nailsworth, Glos; m Sophie Cecilia (d 1974), d of J. C. Yorke, JP, Langton, Dwrbach, Pembs; two s one d; m 1974, Ella Brown. Educ: Bradfield; RMC. 2nd Lieut Glos Regt, 1922; transf. RAOC 1928. Served CMF, 1942-45; Lieut-Col 1942; Brig. 1943; Dep. Dir of Ordnance Services, Western Command, 1947-51; DDOS, Southern Command, 1951-55; ADC to the Queen, 1954-55; Maj.-Gen. 1955; Inspector, Royal Army Ordnance Corps, 1955-57; Commandant Mechanical Transport Organisation, Chilwell, 1957-58; Col Comdt RAOC, 1960-66. Address: Gwyers, Dinton, Wilts.
See also Wilson Stephens.

CRAWFORD, Hugh Adam, RSA 1958 (ARSA 1938); Painter; b 28 Oct. 1898; s of John Cummings and Agnes Crawford; m 1934, Kathleen Mann, ARCA, d of late Archibald and Rosamond Mann, Old Coulsdon, Surrey; two s (one d decd). Educ: Garelochhead Public Sch.; Glasgow Sch. of Art. Served in European War, 1915-19. Dipl. Glasgow Sch. of Art, 1923; studied in London, 1923-25. Runner-up, Prix de Rome, 1926. Lectr, 1926, Head of Drawing and Painting Dept, 1936, Glasgow Sch. of Art; Head of Gray's Sch. of Art, Aberdeen, 1948; Princ., Duncan of Jordanstone Coll. of Art, Dundee, 1953. Commissions include portraits of: Lord Strathclyde; Lord Hughes; Sir Hector Maclennan; Sir Patrick Dolan; Sir Alexander King, etc.; also portraits for War Records. Publications: contribs to Scottish Library Review of criticisms of books on art. Recreation: study of magnetism. Address: Carronmor, Blanefield, Stirlingshire. T: Blanefield 512. Clubs: Savile, Chelsea; Scottish Arts (Edinburgh); Art (Glasgow).

CRAWFORD, James, CBE 1956; Full-time Member National Coal Board, 1957-62 (Part-time Member, 1956-57), retired; Member, General Council of Trades Union Congress, 1949-57; Chairman, British Productivity Council, 1955-56; b Maybole, 1 Aug. 1896; s of late James Crawford; m 1st, 1929, Mary McInnes (d 1944), d of James McGregor; two s; 2nd, 1945, Agnes Crosswhaite, d of William Sheal; one s. Educ: Cairn Sch.; Carrick Academy, Maybole. Served European War, 1914-18, 6th Highland Light Infantry, and 2nd and 10th Cameronians. Mem. of Glasgow City Council, 1930-38; Magistrate, 1935-38. Contested (Lab.) Kilmarnock Div. of Ayr and Bute, 1935; Mem. Advisory Council, Dept of Scientific and Industrial Research, 1950-55; Gen. Pres., National Union of Boot and Shoe Operatives, 1944-57. Recreation: bowls. Address: 118 Northampton Road, Earls Barton, Northampton. T: Northampton 810282.

CRAWFORD, Sir John (Grenfell), Kt 1959; CBE 1954; MEc (Sydney); FAIAS; Chancellor, Australian National University, since 1976; Senior Agricultural Adviser to World Bank, Washington, since 1967; Director, Australia-Japan Economic Research Project; b 4 April 1910; s of Henry and Harriet Crawford, Sydney; m 1935, Jessie Anderson Morgan; one d. Educ: Sydney Univ.; Harvard Univ.; Research Fellow, University of Sydney, 1933-35; Lectr, Agricultural Economics,

University of Sydney (Part-time), 1934-41; Commonwealth Fund Fellow, USA, 1938-40; Economic Adviser, Rural Bank of NSW, 1935-43; Director, Commonwealth Bureau of Agricultural Economics, 1945-50; Sec., Dept of Commerce and Agriculture, 1950-56; Sec., Dept of Trade, Commonwealth of Australia, 1956-60; resigned from Civil Service, 1960. Dir and Prof. of Economics, Research Sch. of Pacific Studies, Australian National Univ., 1960-67, and Fiscal Adviser to the Univ.; Vice-Chancellor, ANU, 1968-73; Chancellor, Univ. of Papua and New Guinea, 1972-75. Vice-Chm., Commonwealth Cttee of Economic Enquiry, 1962-64, 1966-67. Mem. World Bank Economic Mission to India, 1964-65; Chairman: Technical Adv. Cttee to Consultative Gp of Internat. Agricultural Res., 1971-76; Australian Develt Adv. Board, to 1977. Pres., ANZAAS, 1967-68 (Medallist, 1971). Hon. DSc Newcastle, NSW, 1966; Hon. DEc New England, NSW, 1969; Hon. LLD: Tasmania, 1971; Papua New Guinea, 1975; ANU, 1976; Hon. DSc Econ Sydney, 1972. Publications: Australian National Income (with Colin Clark), 1938; Australian Trade Policy 1942-66: A Documentary History, 1968; A Commission to Advise on Assistance to Industries (report to Aust. Govt), 1973; articles in Economic Record, Journal of Public Administration, Australian Outlook; several edited books on Australian Economic Affairs and several published lectures on trade and educn policy. Recreations: tennis, reading. Address: 32 Melbourne Avenue, Deakin, ACT 2000, Australia. Clubs: Commonwealth (Canberra); Union (Sydney); Melbourne (Melbourne).

CRAWFORD, Maj.-Gen. John Scott, CB 1945; CBE 1940; CEng, FIMechE; b 6 Feb. 1889; s of John Paton Crawford; m 1916, Amy Middleton-Andrews; two s. Educ: Liverpool Coll.; Campbell Coll., Belfast. RASC 1915-28; RAOC, 1928-39. Dir of Mechanization on formation of Ministry of Supply; Dep. Dir-Gen. of Tanks and Transport, and in 1943, Dep. Dir-Gen. of Armaments Production. Mem. of Council SMM & T (Vice-Pres., 1948-50; Hon. Treas. 1953-57). Mem. Inst. Engineering Inspection (Pres. 1953-54). Pres. Rubber Research Assoc., 1952-54. Vice-Pres. Liverpool Coll., Mem. Court of Worshipful Co. of Carmen, Master, 1957-58. Comdr, Order of Leopold II (Belgium), 1963. Recreations: golf, fishing. Address: 11 Glenmore House, Richmond Hill, Surrey. T: 01-940 1225. Club: Royal Automobile.

CRAWFORD, Captain John Stuart, DSO 1940; OBE 1970; Royal Navy, retired; HM Consul, Tromsö, Norway, 1956-70, retired; b 24 March 1900; s of late John Crawford, MD, BS, and late Christian Patricia Blackstock; m 1927, Katherine Macdonald; one d (and one s decd). Educ: Dollar Academy; RNC, Osborne and Dartmouth. Midshipman, 1916-18; HMS Valiant; Lieut, 1920; Lieut-Comdr, 1928; Comdr, 1934; Capt., 1940. Naval Attaché Angora, 1946-48; retired list, 1950. County Civil Defence Officer, Northants, 1951; Asst Commissioner of Police (in charge of Marine Police Branch), Malaya, 1951-55. Younger Brother of Trinity House, 1961-. Address: The Gardens, West Stafford, Dorchester, Dorset. Club: Naval and Military.

CRAWFORD, Michael; actor since 1955; b 19 Jan. 1942. Educ: St Michael's Coll., Bexley; Oakfield Sch., Dulwich. In orig. prodn of Britten's Noyes Fludde and of Let's Make an Opera; subseq. stage appearances: Travelling Light, 1965; The Anniversary, 1966; No Sex Please, We're British, Strand, 1971; Billy, Drury Lane, 1974; Same Time, Next Year, Prince of Wales, 1976. Films include: Soap Box Derby; Blow Your Own Trumpet; Two Left Feet; The War Lover; Two Living, One Dead; The Knack, 1964; A Funny Thing Happened on the Way to the Forum, 1965; The Jokers, How I Won the War, 1966; Hello Dolly, 1968; The Games, 1969; Hello and Goodbye, 1970; Alice in Wonderland, 1972. Numerous radio broadcasts and TV appearances, incl. own TV series, Some Mothers Do 'Ave 'Em. Address: c/o Michael Linnit Ltd, Globe Theatre, Shaftesbury Avenue, W1. T: 01-439 4371.

CRAWFORD, Peter John, QC 1976; a Recorder of the Crown Court, since 1974; b 23 June 1930; s of William Gordon Robertson and Doris Victoria Robertson (née Mann, subseq. Crawford); m 1955, Jocelyn Lavender; two s two d. Educ: Berkhamsted Sch.; Brasenose Coll., Oxford (MA). Called to Bar, Lincoln's Inn, 1953. Mem., Paddington Borough Council, 1962-65; Chm., W London Family Service Unit, 1972-. Recreation: sailing. Address: 13 King's Bench Walk, Temple, EC4Y 7EN. T: 01-353 7204.

CRAWFORD, (Robert) Norman, CBE 1973; Divisional Head, Northern Ireland Development Agency, since 1976; b 14 June 1923; s of Wm Crawford and Annie Catherine (née Rexter); m 1948, Jean Marie Patricia (née Carson); one s five d. Educ: Foyle Coll., Londonderry; Queen's Univ., Belfast (BComSc). FCA.

Sec./Accountant, John McNeill Ltd, 1948-60; Dep. Man. Dir, McNeill Group Ltd, 1960-66, Man. Dir 1966-68; Chm., N Ireland Transport Holding Co., 1968-75. Pres., N Ireland Chamber of Commerce and Industry, 1966-67; Chairman: N Ireland Regional Bd, BIM, 1966-69; Nature Reserves Cttee, 1967-; NI Outward Bound Assoc., 1969-76; R. N. Crawford & Co., Merchant Bank Facilities, 1968-. Member Senate, Queen's University, Belfast. *Address:* 10 Fort Road, Helens Bay, Bangor, Co. Down. *T:* Helens Bay 3661. *Clubs:* Ulster Reform (Belfast); Kildare Street and University (Dublin).

CRAWFORD, Sir (Robert) Stewart, GCMG 1973 (KCMG 1966; CMG 1951); CVO 1955; HM Diplomatic Service, retired; *b* 27 Aug. 1913; *s* of late Sir William Crawford, KBE, head of W. S. Crawford Ltd, advertising agents; *m* 1938, Mary Katharine, *d* of late Eric Corbett, Gorse Hill, Witley, Surrey; three *s* one *d* (and one *s* decd). *Educ:* Gresham's Sch., Holt; Oriel Coll., Oxford. Home Civil Service (Air Ministry), 1936; Private Sec. to Chief of Air Staff, 1940-46; Asst Sec., Control Office for Germany and Austria, 1946; Foreign Office, 1947; Counsellor, British Embassy, Oslo, 1954-56; Counsellor, later Minister, British Embassy, Baghdad, 1957-59; Dep. UK Delegate to OEEC Paris, 1959-60; Asst Under Sec., Foreign Office, 1961-65; Political Resident, Persian Gulf, 1966-70; Dep. Under-Sec. of State, FCO, 1970-73. Chm., Cttee on Broadcasting Coverage, 1973-74; Mem., BBC Gen. Adv. Council, 1976-. *Recreations:* opera, gardening. *Address:* 5a Manchester Street, W1; Ruperts Elm, Northfield End, Henley-on-Thames, Oxon. *T:* Henley 4702. *Club:* United Oxford & Cambridge University.

CRAWFORD, Prof. Sir Theodore, (Sir Theo), Kt 1973; Professor of Pathology in the University of London, 1948-77, Professor Emeritus, 1977; Director of Pathological Services, St George's Hospital and Medical School, 1946-77; *b* 23 Dec. 1911; *s* of late Theodore Crawford and late Sarah Mansfield; *m* 1st, 1938, Margaret Donald Green, MD (*d* 1973); two *s* three *d* ; 2nd, 1974, Priscilla Leathley Chater. *Educ:* St Peter's Sch., York; Glasgow Academy; Glasgow Univ. BSc, 1932; MB, ChB, 1935; FRFPS, 1938; MD 1941; Bellahouston Gold Medal (Glasgow Univ.), 1941; MRCP 1960; FRCP Glas 1962; FRCPath 1963, FRCP 1964; Hall Tutorial and Research Fellow, 1936-38. Asst Physician, Glasgow, Royal Hosp. for Sick Children, 1936-38; Lecturer in Pathology (Glasgow Univ.), 1939-46. Served War of 1939-45, Major RAMC, 1941-45. Mem. of the Medical Research Council, 1960-64 (and Mem. Cell Board, 1974-); Registrar, Coll. of Pathologists, 1963-68; Consultant Adviser in Pathology to Dept of Health and Social Security and Chm. of its Central Pathology Cttee, 1969-. Royal Society of Medicine (Pres. Section of Pathology, 1961-62). Pres., Royal Coll. of Pathologists, 1969-72 (Vice-Pres., 1968-69); Mem., Pathological Soc. of Great Britain, etc.; Chm., Scientific Cttee, British Empire Cancer Campaign, 1969- (Hon. Sec., 1955-67; Hon. Sec. of the Campaign, 1967-70). Member: Council Epsom Coll., 1949-71; Standing Medical Advisory Cttee, Health Services Council, 1964-69; Cttee on Safety of Medicines, 1969- (Vice-Chm., 1976-); Army Pathology Adv. Cttee, 1970-75; DHSS Cttee on Smoking and Health, 1973-. *Publications:* (ed) Modern Trends in Pathology, 1967; Pathology of Ischaemic Heart Disease, 1977; scientific papers in Lancet, British Medical Journal, British Journal of Surgery, Archives of Disease in Childhood, British Journal of Opthalmology, Journal of Pathology and Bacteriology, etc. *Recreations:* horticulture, growing trees, hill walking, music. *Address:* 51 Whitelands House, Cheltenham Terrace, King's Road, SW3 4QZ. *T:* 01-730 4428; St George's Hospital, SW1. *T:* 01-235 7727; Garrien, Strathlachlan, Strachur, Argyll. *T:* Strachur 205. *Club:* Hanstown.

CRAWFORD, Sir (Walter) Ferguson, KBE 1958 (OBE 1921); CMG 1950; *b* 11 April 1894; *s* of H. F. Crawford, Melbourne, Vic., Australia; *m* 1927, Marjorie Vivienne Shirley; one *s* one *d*. *Educ:* Sydney Grammar Sch., Sydney, NSW; Sydney Univ.; New Coll., Oxford, NSW Rhodes Scholar, 1915. Served European War, 1914-18, in Argyll and Sutherland Highlanders, 1915-18 (despatches). Irak Political Service, 1919-21; Sudan Political Service, 1921-44; Governor Northern Province, Sudan, 1942-44; Palestine Govt Liaison Officer, 1944-46; Head of British Middle East Development Div. (Foreign Office), 1946-60. Dir-Gen., Middle East Assoc., 1960-64. *Recreation:* golf. *Address:* Baidland, Shant Lane, Churt, Surrey.

CRAWFORD, Vice-Adm. Sir William (Godfrey), KBE 1961; CB 1958; DSC 1941; *b* 14 Sept. 1907; *s* of late H. E. V. Crawford, Wyld Court, Axminster, and late Mrs M. E. Crawford; *m* 1939, Mary Felicity Rosa, *d* of late Sir Philip Williams, 2nd Bt; three *s* one *d*. *Educ:* RN Coll., Dartmouth. Lieut RN, 1929; specialised in gunnery, 1932; Lieut-Comdr, 1937; Gunnery Officer, HMS Rodney, 1940-42; Comdr Dec. 1941; Exec. Officer, HMS Venerable, 1944-46; Capt. 1947; in comd HMS Pelican and 2nd

Frigate Flotilla, Med., 1948-49; Dep.-Dir RN Staff Coll., 1950-52; in comd HMS Devonshire, 1952-53; in comd RN Coll., Dartmouth, 1953-56; Rear-Adm. 1956; Imperial Defence Coll., 1956-58; Flag Officer, Sea Training, 1958-60; Vice-Adm. 1959; Comdr British Navy Staff and Naval Attaché Washington, 1960-62; retired list, 1963. Dir, Overseas Offices, BTA, 1964-72. *Recreations:* sailing, fishing. *Address:* Toller House, Toller Porcorum, Dorchester, Dorset. *T:* Maiden Newton 461. *Clubs:* Naval and Military; Cruising (Naval Member).

CRAWFORD, William Neil Kennedy Mellon, VRD 1955; Senior Partner, Davidson Smith, Wighton & Crawford, CA, Edinburgh; Partner, Turquands Barton Mayhew & Co., Edinburgh; Chairman, Amalgamated Quarries (Scotland) Ltd; Director, Robb Caledon Shipbuilders Ltd; *b* 8 Jan. 1910; *s* of Robert Crawford, MINA, MIES, and Flora Crawford (*née* Mellon); *m* 1939, Alison Gordon Lawrie, *d* of R. D. Lawrie, Edinburgh; two *d*. *Educ:* St Andrew's Coll., Dublin; George Watson's Coll., Edinburgh. Qual. Chartered Accountant, 1933; commenced practice in Edinburgh. Service with RNVR, 1939-46; subseq. RNR (now Captain). Pres., Edinburgh Chamber of Commerce. Past Pres., Inst. Chartered Accountants of Scotland, 1973-74. MStJ 1972. *Address:* (home) Seaforth, Primrosebank Road, Edinburgh EH5 3JJ. *T:* 031-552 3806; (office) 18 Ainslie Place, Edinburgh EH3 6AX. *T:* 031-226 4161. *Clubs:* English-Speaking Union, Naval; New, Bruntsfield Links Golfing Society (Edinburgh).

CRAWFORD-COMPTON, Air Vice-Marshal William Vernon, CB 1965; CBE 1957; DSO 1943, Bar 1945; DFC 1941, Bar, 1942; RAF retired, 1969; *b* 2 March 1915; *s* of William Gilbert Crawford-Compton; *m* 1949, Chloe Clifford-Brown; two *d*. *Educ:* New Plymouth High Sch., New Zealand. Joined RAF, 1939; served War of 1939-45 (DFC and Bar, DSO and Bar); 11 Group and 2nd TAF Group Capt., 1955; SASO, 11 (Fighter) Group; Student, Imperial Defence Coll., 1961; Air Officer in Charge of Administration, Near East Air Force, 1962-63; SASO 1963-66. Air Vice-Marshal, 1963. Legion of Honour (France); Croix de Guerre (France); Silver Star (USA). *Recreations:* golf, tennis, fishing. *Address:* Church Farm House, Yapton, Arundel, West Sussex BN18 0EP.

CRAWLEY, Aidan Merivale, MBE; President, London Weekend Television, 1971-73; *b* 10 April 1908; *s* of late Canon A. S. Crawley; *m* 1945, Virginia Cowles, *qv*; two *s* one *d*. *Educ:* Harrow; Oxford. Journalist, 1930-36; Educational Film Producer, 1936-39. AAF, 601 Sqdn, 1936-40; Asst Air Attaché, Ankara, Belgrade (resident Sofia), May 1940-May 1941; joined 73 (F) Sqdn, Egypt; shot down July 1941; prisoner until May 1945. MP (Lab) Buckingham Div. of Bucks, 1945-51; Parliamentary Private Sec. to successive Secs of State for the Colonies, 1945 and 1946-47; Parliamentary Under-Sec. of State for Air, 1950-51; resigned from the Labour Party, 1957; MP (C) West Derbyshire, 1962-67; Editor-in-Chief, Independent Television News Ltd, 1955-56; making television documentaries for BBC, 1956-60; Chm., London Weekend Television, 1967-71; Mem. Monckton Commission on Federation of Rhodesia and Nyasaland, 1960. Pres., MCC, 1973. *Publications:* Escape from Germany, 1956; De Gaulle: A Biography, 1969; The Rise of Western Germany 1945-72, 1973. *Recreation:* cricket; Co-Founder and President, Haig Nat. Village Cricket Championship, 1971. *Address:* 19 Chester Square, SW1. *T:* 01-730 3030. *Club:* White's.

CRAWLEY, Mrs Aidan Merivale; *see* Cowles, Virginia.

CRAWLEY, Charles William; Hon. Fellow of Trinity Hall, 1971; University Lecturer in History, 1931-66; Vice-Master of Trinity Hall, Cambridge, 1950-66, Emeritus Fellow, 1966; *b* 1 April 1899; *s* of Charles Crawley, barrister of Lincoln's Inn, and Augusta, *d* of Rt Rev. Samuel Butcher, Bishop of Meath; *m* 1930, Kathleen Elizabeth, *d* of Lieut-Col H. G. Leahy, OBE, RA; four *s* one *d*. *Educ:* Winchester (Scholar); Trinity Coll., Cambridge (Scholar). Fellow of Trinity Hall, 1924-66. Asst Tutor, 1927, Acting Senior Tutor, 1940, Senior Tutor, 1946-58. *Publications:* The Question of Greek Independence, 1821-1833, 1930, repr. 1973; (ed) New Cambridge Modern History, Vol. IX, 1965; John Capodistrias: unpublished documents, 1970; Trinity Hall: the history of a Cambridge College, 1350-1975, 1976. *Address:* 1 Madingley Road, Cambridge. *T:* 52849. *Club:* Athenæum.

CRAWLEY, Desmond John Chetwode, CMG 1964; CVO 1961; HM Diplomatic Service, retired; *b* 2 June 1917; *s* of late Lieutenant-Colonel C. G. C. Crawley, OBE and late Agnes Luke; *m* 1945, Daphne Lesley, *y d* of late Sir Vere Mockett, MBE, and late Ethel Norah Gaddum Tomkinson; two *s* one *d*. *Educ:* King's Sch., Ely; Queen's Coll., Oxford. Entered Indian

Civil Service, serving in Madras Presidency, 1939; entered Indian Political Service, serving in Baluchistan, 1946; entered Commonwealth Relations Office, 1947, and served in London, Calcutta, and on loan to the Foreign Office in Washington; Principal Private Secretary to Sec. of State for Commonwealth Relations, 1952-53; British Dep. High Commissioner in Lahore, Pakistan, 1958-61; Imperial Defence Coll., 1962; British High Commissioner in Sierra Leone, 1963-66; Ambassador to Bulgaria, 1966-70; Minister to Holy See, 1970-75. Coronation Medal, 1953. Grand Cross, Order of St Gregory the Great (Holy See), 1973. *Address:* 35 Chartfield Avenue, SW15. *T:* 01-788 9529. *Club:* United Oxford & Cambridge University.

CRAWLEY, John Cecil, CBE 1972 (MBE 1944); Chairman of Trustees of Visnews, since 1976; *b* 1909; *s* of John and Kathleen Crawley; *m* 1933, Constance Mary Griffiths; two *d. Educ:* William Ellis Sch. War Service, Army, 1939-45. Journalism: Reynolds, 1927; Central News Agency, 1928; National Press Agency, 1929; Press Secretaries, 1933; BBC: Sub-Editor, 1945; Foreign Correspondent, New York, 1959-63; Foreign News Editor, 1963-67; Editor of News and Current Affairs, 1967-71; Chief Asst to Dir-Gen., BBC, 1971-75. *Recreations:* walking, bird-watching. *Address:* 157 Clarence Gate Gardens, NW1. *T:* 01-723 6876.

CRAWLEY-BOEVEY, Sir Thomas (Michael Blake), 8th Bt *cr* 1784; Editor, Which?, since 1976; *b* 29 Sept. 1928; *er s* of Sir Launcelot Valentine Hyde Crawley-Boevey, 7th Bt, and Elizabeth Goodeth (*d* 1976), *d* of Herbert d'Auvergne Innes, late Indian Police; *S* father, 1968; *m* 1957, Laura Coelingh; two *s. Educ:* Wellington Coll.; St John's Coll., Cambridge (BA 1952, MA 1956). 2nd Lieut, Durham Light Infantry, 1948. With Shipping Agents, 1952-61; with Consumers' Association, 1961-; Editor, Money Which?, 1968-76. *Recreations:* gardening, bicycling, bee-keeping. *Heir: er s* Thomas Hyde Crawley-Boevey, *b* 26 June 1958. *Address:* 41 Thornhill Road, N1. *T:* 01-607 5575.

CRAWSHAW, 4th Baron, *cr* 1892; **William Michael Clifton Brooks,** Bt, *cr* 1891; *b* 25 March 1933; *s* of 3rd Baron and Sheila (*d* 1964), *o d* of late Lieut-Col P. R. Clifton, CMG, DSO; *S* father, 1946. *Educ:* Eton; Christ Church, Oxford. Jt Master, Oxford Univ. Drag Hounds, 1952-53. Treasurer, Loughborough Div. Conservative Assoc., 1954-58; County Commissioner, Leics Boy Scouts, 1958-. Pres., Leics Assoc. of the Disabled; Chm., Quorn Hunt Cttee, 1971-. Lord of the Manor of Long Whatton. Patron of the Living of Shepshed. *Heir: b* Hon. David Gerald Brooks [*b* 14 Sept. 1934; *m* 1970, Belinda Mary, *d* of George Burgess, Melbourne, and of Mrs J. P. Allen, Coleman's Hatch, Sussex; one *d. Educ:* Eton; Royal Agricultural College, Cirencester]. *Address:* Whatton, Loughborough, Leics. *TA:* Kegworth. *T:* Hathern 225. *Clubs:* Boodle's, MCC.

CRAWSHAW, Sir (Edward) Daniel (Weston), Kt 1964; QC (Aden) 1949; *b* 10 Sept. 1903; British; *m* 1942, Rosemary Treffry; one *s* two *d* (and one *s* decd). *Educ:* St Bees Sch.; Selwyn Coll., Cambridge. Solicitor, Supreme Court of Judicature, England, 1929; Barrister-at-Law, Gray's Inn, 1946; Solicitor, Northern Rhodesia, 1930-32; Colonial Legal Service, Tanganyika, 1933-39; Zanzibar, 1939-47; Attorney-Gen., Aden, 1947-52; Puisne Judge, Tanganyika, 1952-60; Justice of Appeal, Court of Appeal for Eastern Africa, 1960-65. Commissioner, Foreign Compensation Commission, 1965-75. Brilliant Star of Zanzibar, 1947; Coronation Medal, 1953. *Recreation:* golf. *Address:* 1 Fort Road, Guildford, Surrey. *T:* Guildford 76883. *Clubs:* Royal Over-Seas League; County (Guildford).

CRAWSHAW, Philip, CBE 1959 (MBE 1948); Director-General, Royal Over-Seas League, since 1959; *b* 25 Nov. 1912; twin *s* of R. Crawshaw; *m* 1947, June Patricia, *d* of E. D. K. Mathews; two *d. Educ:* Repton. Travelling Sec., Over-Seas League, 1936; Asst Sec., 1940; Sec., 1946; Sec.-Gen., 1956. *Address:* Over-Seas House, St James's, SW1. *T:* 01-493 5051; 73 Albert Drive, Wimbledon, SW19. *T:* 01-788 1494.

CRAWSHAW, Lt-Col Richard, OBE 1958; TD 1958; MA, LLB; DL; Barrister-at-Law; MP (Lab) Toxteth Division of Liverpool since 1964; *b* 25 Sept. 1917; *s* of Percy Eli Lee Crawshaw and Beatrice Lavinia (*née* Barritt); *m* 1960, Audrey Frances Lima; no *c. Educ:* Pendleton Gram. Sch.; Tatterford Sch.; Pembroke Coll., Cambridge (MA); London Univ. (LLB). Clerk, 1931-33; Engineer, 1933-36; Theological Student, 1936-39; Royal Artillery and Parachute Regt, 1939-45; Pembroke Coll., Cambridge, 1945-47; called to Bar, Inner Temple, 1948; Northern Circuit. Liverpool City Council, 1948-65. Commanded 12/13th Bn, The Parachute Regt, TA, 1954-57. Mem., Speaker's Panel of Chairmen, 1971-. Estd world non-stop walking record of 255.8 miles, 1972; estd world non-stop

walking record (literally non-stop) of 231 miles, 1974. DL Merseyside, 1970. *Recreations:* climbing, walking, free fall parachuting and youth activities. *Address:* The Orchard, Aintree Lane, Liverpool L10 8LE. *T:* 051-526 7886.

CRAWSHAY, Col Sir William (Robert), Kt 1972; DSO 1945; ERD; TD; DL; *b* 27 May 1920; *o s* of late Captain J. W. L. Crawshay, MC, Caversham Park, Oxon, and of Hon. Mrs. George Egerton, Brussels; *m* 1950, Elisabeth Mary Boyd Reynolds, *d* of Lt-Col Guy Reynolds, late 9 Lancers, Penpergwm Lodge, Abergavenny. *Educ:* Eton. Served Royal Welch Fus.(SR), 1939-46; SOE 1944 (DSO, despatches twice); TA, 1947-62, Parachute Regt, Welch Regt, SW Brigade. ADC to HM the Queen, 1966-71. Hon. Col, 3rd RRW (V) Bn, 1970-. Mem., Arts Council of GB, 1962-74; Chairman: Welsh Arts Council, 1968-74; Council, University Coll. of Cardiff, 1966; Member: Council and Court, Univ. of Wales, 1967; Welsh Council, 1966-69, 1970-; Vice-Pres., 1973- (Mem., Council and Court, 1966-), Nat. Museum of Wales. Pres., Royal British Legion, Wales Area, 1974-. Mem., Crafts Adv. Council, 1974-. Hon. LLD, Univ. of Wales, 1975. DL Glamorgan, 1964, Monmouthshire, 1970, Gwent, 1974. Chevalier, Légion d'honneur, 1956; Croix de Guerre (France) with Palms twice, 1944, 1945. KStJ 1969. *Address:* Llanfair Court, Abergavenny, Gwent. *Clubs:* White's; Cardiff and County (Cardiff).

CREAGH, Maj.-Gen. Edward Philip Nagle, CB 1954; retired; *b* 29 Feb. 1896; *s* of late P. W. Creagh, Fermoy, Co. Cork and Mrs S. H. Creagh; *m* 1927, Ethel Frances Montgomery (*d* 1973); one *s* one *d. Educ:* St Augustine's Coll., Ramsgate; University Coll. of Cork, NUI. MB, BCh 1917; MRCP 1931. Commissioned RAMC, 1917; Captain 1918; Major 1929; Lt-Col 1943; Col 1948; Brig., 1951; Maj.-Gen., 1953; QHP 1953. War of 1939-45 (despatches). Retired, Feb. 1956. Col Comdt, RAMC, 1956-63. *Recreations:* amateur rider (up to 1927); trout fishing, golf. *Address:* Old Vicarage, Thriplow, near Royston, Cambs. *T:* Fowlmere 272.

CREAGH, Maj.-Gen. Sir Kilner Rupert B.; see Brazier-Creagh.

CREAMER, Amos Albert, DFC 1943; Public Trustee, since 1975; *b* 6 May 1917; *s* of late Amos and Anne Creamer; *m* 1946, Margaret Lloyd; one *s* one *d. Educ:* Owens Sch.; King's Coll., London. 1st class Hons LLB 1939. Entered Treasury, 1935, Inland Revenue, 1936. Served in RAF, Bomber and Training Comds (Sqdn Ldr), 1941-46. Entered Min. of Works, 1946; Asst Sec., 1956; Under-Sec., 1965; Under-Sec., Treasury, 1967, Civil Service Dept, 1968-75. *Address:* 5 Wildcroft Gardens, Edgware, Mddx.

CREAMER, Brian; Physician, St Thomas' Hospital, London, and Senior Lecturer in Medicine, St Thomas's Hospital Medical School, since 1959; Hon. Consultant in Gastroenterology to the Army, since 1970; *b* 12 April 1926; *s* of L. G. Creamer and late Mrs Creamer, Epsom; *m* 1953, Margaret Holden Rees; two *s* one *d. Educ:* Christ's Hosp.; St Thomas' Hosp. MB, BS Hons London, 1948; MD London, 1952; FRCP 1966 (MRCP 1950); Research Asst, Mayo Clinic, Rochester, USA, 1955-56. Sir Arthur Hurst Memorial Lectr, 1968; Watson Smith Lectr, RCP, 1971. Member: British Soc. of Gastroenterology; Assoc. of Physicians of GB and NI. *Publications:* (ed) Modern Trends in Gastroenterology, vol. 4, 1970; (ed) The Small Intestine, 1974; contributions to med. jls. *Recreations:* painting, gardening, and listening to music. *Address:* Tetherdown, Oxshott Rise, Cobham, Surrey KT11 2RN. *T:* Cobham 3994.

CREAN, Hon. Frank; MHR for Melbourne Ports, since 1951; *b* Hamilton, Vic, 28 Feb. 1916; *s* of J. Crean; *m* 1946, Mary, *d* of late A. E. Findlay; three *s. Educ:* Hamilton High Sch.; Melbourne High Sch.; Melbourne Univ. BA Hons; BCom. DPA; FASA. Income Tax Assessor, 1934-45. MLA: for Albert Park, Vic, 1945-47; for Prahran, 1949-51; Mem. Exec., Federal Parly Labour Party, 1956-72, Dep. Leader, 1975-76; Mem., Jt Parly Cttee on Public Accounts, 1952-55; Treasurer, Commonwealth of Australia, 1972-74; Minister for Overseas Trade, 1974-75, also Deputy Prime Minister, 1975. Chm., Council of Adult Educn, 1947-74. *Publication:* (with W. J. Byrt) Government and Politics in Australia, 1972. *Address:* Parliament House, Canberra, ACT 2600, Australia; 106 Harold Street, Middle Park, Vic 3206.

CREASEY, Lt-Gen. Timothy May, CB 1975; OBE 1966; GOC Northern Ireland, since 1977; *b* 21 Sept. 1923; *s* of late Lt-Col G. M. Creasey and late Phyllis Creasey, *d* of Vice-Adm. F. C. B. Robinson, RN; *m* 1951, Ruth Annette, *y d* of Major J. I. H. Friend, OBE, MC, DL, JP, Northdown, Kent; one *s* one *d* (and one *s* decd). *Educ:* Clifton Coll. Commissioned Baluch Regt, IA, 1942. Served War: Far East, Italy, Greece, 1942-45. Transf. to

Royal Norfolk Regt, 1946; Instructor, Sch. of Infantry, 1951-53; Bde Major, 39th Infantry Bde, Kenya and Ireland, 1955-56; Instr, Army Staff Coll., 1959-61; Instr, RMA, Sandhurst, 1963-64; commanded: 1 Royal Anglian, Aden and BAOR, 1965-67; 11th Armoured Bde, 1969-70; Student, IDC, 1971; Comdr, Sultan's Armed Forces, Oman, 1972-75; Dir of Infantry, 1975-77. Dep. Col, Royal Anglian Regt, 1976-; Colonel Commandant: The Queen's Div., 1977-; Small Arms Sch. Corps, 1977-. Jordanian Order of Independence, 1st class, 1974; Order of Oman, 2nd class, 1975. *Recreations:* shooting, golf. *Address:* c/o Grindlays Bank Ltd, 13 St James's Square, SW1. *Clubs:* MCC, Army and Navy.

CREASY, Sir Gerald Hallen, KCMG 1946 (CMG 1943); KCVO 1954; OBE 1937; *b* 1 Nov. 1897; *y s* of Leonard and Ellen Maud Creasy; *m* 1925, Helen Duff, *y d* of Reginald B. Jacomb; one *s* one *d. Educ:* Rugby. On Military Service (RA), 1916-19; entered Colonial Office, 1920; Chief Sec. to the West African Council, 1945-47; Governor and C-in-C, Gold Coast, 1947-49; Governor and C-in-C, Malta, 1949-54, retired 1954. GCStJ 1970 (KStJ 1949). LLD (*hc*) Royal University of Malta, 1954. *Address:* 2 Burlington Court, Eastbourne, East Sussex. *T:* Eastbourne 27147.

CREASY, Leonard Richard, CB 1972; OBE 1961; CEng, FICE, FIStructE; civil engineer in private practice since 1974; *b* 21 Dec. 1912; *s* of William and Ellen Creasy; *m* 1937, Irene Howard; one *s* one *d. Educ:* Wimbledon Technical Coll. BSc(Eng) London. Served War, RE, E Africa, 1944-46. Service in Industry, 1928-34; HM Office of Works, Asst Engr, 1935; Min. of Works, Suptg Engr, 1959; MPBW: Dir, Civil Engrg, 1966; Dir, Central Services, 1968; Dir of Civil Engrg Develt, Dept of the Environment, 1970-73. Concerned with Inquiries into disasters at Aberfan, Ronan Point and Brent, and with design of Radio Towers, London and Birmingham; Plant House, Royal Botanical Gardens, Edinburgh; Wind Tunnels, Bedford NAE; and other structures. Bronze Medal, Reinforced Concrete Assoc.; Manby and Telford Premiums, Instn Civil Engrs; Pres., Instn Struct. Engrs, 1973 (Bronze Medal and Certif. of Merit of the Instn). *Publications:* Pre-stressed Concrete Cylindrical Tanks, 1961; James Forrest Lecture, 1968; many other papers on civil and structural engrg projects and engrg economics. *Recreations:* music, opera, languages. *Address:* 5 The Oaks, Epsom, Surrey KT18 5HH. *T:* Epsom 22361.

CREDITON, Bishop Suffragan of, since 1974; **Rt. Rev. Philip John Pasterfield;** *b* 1920; *s* of Bertie James Pasterfield and Lilian Bishop Pasterfield (*née* Flinn); *m* 1948, Eleanor Maureen, *d* of William John Symons; three *s* one *d. Educ:* Denstone Coll., Staffs; Trinity Hall, Cambridge (MA); Cuddesdon Coll., Oxford. Army Service, 1940-46; commnd in Somerset Light Infantry. Deacon 1951, Priest 1952. Curate of Streatham, 1951-54; Vicar of West Lavington, Sussex, and Chaplain, King Edward VII Hosp., Midhurst, 1954-60; Rector of Woolbeding, 1955-60; Vicar of Oxton, Birkenhead, 1960-68; Rural Dean of Birkenhead, 1966-68; Canon Residentiary and Sub Dean of St Albans, 1968-74; Rural Dean of St Albans, 1972-74. *Recreations:* ornithology, music, cricket, fishing. *Address:* 10 The Close, Exeter EX1 1EZ. *T:* Exeter 73509.

CREE, Brig. Gerald Hilary, CBE 1946; DSO 1945; Colonel, The Prince of Wales's Own Regiment of Yorkshire, 1960-70; *b* 23 June 1905; *s* of late Maj.-Gen. Gerald Cree; *m* 1945, Joan Agnes, *d* of late Lt-Col W. R. Eden, RA; one *d. Educ:* Kelly Coll.; RMC Sandhurst. Commissioned, The West Yorks Regt; 1924; King's African Rifles, 1931-36; comd 2nd Bn West Yorks Regt, 1942-44; 1st Bn 1946-48; Comdr 25 (East African) Infantry Bde, 1944-45 and Brig. 1953. Served Palestine, East Africa, Abyssinia, Western Desert, Iraq, Burma, 1938-45. Commander 127 (East Lancs) Infantry Brigade (TA), 1953-56; Col, The West Yorks Regt, 1956-57, Col, PWO Regt of Yorkshire, 1960-70, retd. *Address:* Yetson House, Ashprington, Totnes, Devon. *Club:* Naval and Military.

CREED, Albert Lowry, MA; *b* 16 July 1909; *s* of Rev. Albert H. Creed; *m* 1943, Joyce Marian (*née* Hunter), Leeds; two *s* one *d. Educ:* Kingswood Sch.; Downing Coll., Cambridge. MA Cantab 1931. Asst Master: Stretford Grammar Sch., 1932-35; Bishop's Stortford Coll., 1935-39; Housemaster, Christ's Hospital, 1939-42; Headmaster: Staveley-Netherthorpe Grammar Sch., 1942-46; Truro Sch., Cornwall, 1946-59; Kingswood Sch., 1959-70; Volunteer with Botswana Min. of Educn, 1973-74. Chm., West Cornwall Hospital Management Cttee, 1957-59; Vice-Pres., Methodist Conf., 1962-63; a Dir, The Methodist Recorder. Pres., Kingswood Old Boys' Assoc., 1975-76. *Address:* Trevor House, Langford, near Lechlade, Glos. *T:* Filkins 392. *Club:* Royal Commonwealth Society.

CREEGGAN, Rt. Rev. Jack Burnett; *b* 10 Nov. 1902; *s* of Alfred Henry Creeggan and Mary Laura (*née* Sheffield); *m* 1931, Dorothy Jarman (*née* Embury); one *s* one *d. Educ:* Deseronto (Ont) Public and High Schs; Queen's Univ. (BA); Bishop's Univ. (LST). Priest, 1928; served in many parishes in Dio. Ontario; Canon, St George's Cathedral, Kingston, Ont, 1952; Archdeacon of: Ontario, 1953; Frontenac, 1962; Kingston, 1969; Bishop of Ontario, 1970-74. Prolocutor, Lower House, Provincial Synod of Ont., 1963. Hon. DCL, Bishop's Univ., Lennoxville, PQ, 1971. *Recreations:* curling, golf. *Address:* Apt 304, 67 Sydenham Street, Kingston, Ontario K7L 3H2, Canada. *T:* 542-5319.

CREESE, Nigel Arthur Holloway; Headmaster, Melbourne Grammar School, since 1970; *b* 4 June 1927; *s* of late H. R. Creese; *m* 1951, Valdai (*née* Walters); two *s* two *d. Educ:* Blundell's Sch.; Brasenose Coll., Oxford. Assistant Master: Bromsgrove Sch., 1952-55; Rugby Sch., 1955-63; Headmaster, Christ's Coll., Christchurch, NZ, 1963-70. *Address:* Melbourne Church of England Grammar School, Domain Road, South Yarra, Victoria 3141, Australia.

CREIGHTMORE, Peter Beauchamp; Master of Supreme Court, Queen's Bench Division, since 1975; *b* 15 Jan. 1928; *s* of Maximilian Louis Creightmore, MRCS, LRCP and Mary Arnell Beauchamp; *m* 1957, June Patricia, *d* of Harold William Hedley, Captain Suez Canal Co. (Pilote Major), and Gwendoline Pugh; one *s* one *d. Educ:* Geelong Grammar Sch. (H. H. Whittingham Student, 1945); Worcester Coll., Oxford (MA). O/Sig, RNVR, 1952, commnd 1955. Called to Bar, Inner Temple, 1954; Oxford, later Oxford and Midland, Circuit. *Recreations:* narrow-boating; music. *Address:* Owletts House, Ashurst Wood, Sussex.

CREIGHTON, Prof. Donald Grant, CC (Canada) 1967; University Professor, University of Toronto, since 1967; Professor of History since 1945, and Chairman, Department of History, 1955-59, University of Toronto; *b* 1902; 2nd *s* of late Rev. William B. Creighton and of Laura Harvie; *m* 1926, Luella Sanders Browning Bruce; one *s* one *d. Educ:* Victoria Coll., University of Toronto; Balliol Coll., Oxford. Univ. Lectr, Dept of History, Univ. of Toronto, 1927; John Simon Guggenheim Memorial Fellowship, 1940-41; Rockefeller Fellowship, 1944-45; Nuffield Travelling Fellowship, 1951-52. Chm., Canadian Cttee, Encyclopedia Americana, 1956-63; Commonwealth Mem., Monckton Advisory Commn on Central Africa, 1959; Member: Ontario Adv. Cttee on Confedn, 1965-; Historic Sites and Monuments Bd of Canada, 1958-. Sir John A. Macdonald Prof., 1965. Fellow, Royal Soc. of Canada, 1946; Pres., Canadian Historical Assoc., 1956-57; Corresponding Member: Royal Historical Soc., 1966; British Acad., 1974. Tyrrell Medal, Royal Soc. Canada, 1951; Governor-General's Medal for Academic Non-fiction, 1952 and 1955; Univ. of British Columbia's Medal for Biography, 1955; National Award in Letters, Univ. of Alberta, 1957. Molson Prize, awarded by Canada Council, 1964. Hon. LLD: Univs of New Brunswick, 1949; Queen's, Kingston, Ontario, 1956; Saskatchewan, 1957; British Columbia, 1959; St Francis Xavier, 1967; Victoria, BC, 1967; Dalhousie, 1970; Toronto, 1974; Hon. DLitt: Manitoba, 1957; McGill, 1959; Laurentian, 1970; Meml Univ., Newfoundland, 1974. *Publications:* The Commercial Empire of the St Lawrence, 1937; Dominion of the North: A History of Canada, 1944; John A. Macdonald: The Young Politician, 1952; John A. Macdonald: The Old Chieftain, 1955; The Story of Canada, 1959, 2nd edn, 1971; The Road to Confederation, 1964; Canada's First Century, 1970; Towards the Discovery of Canada, 1972; Canada: the heroic beginnings, 1974; The Forked Road: Canada, 1939-1957, 1977. *Address:* 15 Princess Street, PO Box 225, Brooklin, Ont, Canada. *Clubs:* Athenæum; Arts and Letters, University (Toronto).

CREIGHTON, Harold Digby Fitzgerald; Chairman, 1967-75, Editor, 1973-75, The Spectator; *b* 11 Sept. 1927; *s* of late Rev. Digby Robert Creighton and Amy Frances Creighton; *m* 1964, Harriett Mary Falconer Wallace, *d* of late A. L. P. F. Wallace of Candacraig, Strathdon; four *d. Educ:* Haileybury. National Service, Army (Lieut), India and ME, 1945-48. Consolidated Tin Smelters, Penang, 1950-52; Dir, machine tool companies, London, 1952-63; Chm., Scottish Machine Tool Corp. Ltd, Glasgow, 1963-68. *Recreations:* celebration, convivial conversation, reading. *Address:* 11c Mount Street, W1. *Club:* Beefsteak.

CREMIN, Cornelius Christopher; Chairman, Irish delegation to 3rd UN Conference on the Law of the Sea, since 1973; *b* 6 Dec. 1908; 2nd *s* of D. J. Cremin and Ann (*née* Singleton), Kenmare, Co. Kerry; *m* 1935, Patricia Josephine (decd), Killarney; one *s* three *d* ; *m* 1974, Dr Mary Eta Murphy, Beare Island. *Educ:*

National Univ. of Ireland. BComm 1930; MA (Classics) 1931. Travelling studentship (Classics), NUI, 1931-34; Brit. Sch. at Athens and Rome, 1932; Dipl. in Class. Archaeol., Oxford, 1934; 3rd Sec., Dept of External Affairs, 1935; 1st Sec., Irish Legation, Paris, 1937-43; Chargé d'Affaires, Berlin, 1943-45; Chargé d'Affaires, Lisbon, 1945-46; Couns., Dept of External Affairs, Dublin, 1946-48; Asst Sec., 1948-50; Minister to France, March-Sept. 1950; Ambassador to France, 1950-54; Head of Irish Delegn, OEEC, 1950-54, and Vice-Chm. of OEEC Council (official), 1952-54; Ambassador to the Holy See, 1954-56; Sec. of the Dept of External Affairs, Dublin, 1958-62; Irish Ambassador to Britain, 1963-64 (and 1956-58); Irish Permanent Representative at UN, 1964-74. LLD *hc* National Univ. of Ireland, 1965. Grand Officer of the Legion of Honour, 1954; Knight Grand Cross of the Order of Pius, 1956; Grand Cross of Merit (Fed. Germany), 1960. *Recreations:* golf, boating. *Address:* Tuosist, Killarney, Ireland.

CREMONA, His Honour John Joseph; Chief Justice of Malta and President of the Constitutional Court, Court of Appeal and Court of Criminal Appeal, since 1971; Judge, European Court of Human Rights, since 1965; Emeritus Professor, University of Malta, since 1965; *b* 6 Jan. 1918; *s* of late Dr Antonio Cremona, KM, MD and Anne (*née* Camilleri); *m* 1949, Marchioness Beatrice Barbaro of St George; one *s* two *d*. *Educ:* Malta Univ. (BA 1936, LLD *cum laude* 1942); Rome Univ. (DLitt 1939); London Univ. (BA 1st Cl. Hons 1946, PhD in Laws 1951). DrJur Trieste, 1972. Crown Counsel, 1947; Lectr in Constitutional Law, Malta Univ., 1947-65, Prof. of Criminal Law, 1959-65; Attorney-Gen., 1957-64; Vice-Pres., Constitutional Court and Court of Appeal, 1965-71; sometime Actg Governor General and Actg Pres., Republic of Malta. Member: Cttee of Experts of Human Rights and Cttee on State Immunity, Council of Europe, Strasbourg; Scientific Council, Revue des Droits de l'Homme, Paris; Patronage Cttee, Europäische Grundrechte Zeitschrift, Strasbourg; Scientific Council Centro Internazionale per Protezione dei Diritti dell' Uomo, Pesaro, Italy; delegate and rapporteur, internat. confs. FRHistS; Fellow *ex titulo*, Internat. Acad. of Legal Medicine and Social Medicine; Hon. Fellow, LSE; Hon. Mem., Real Acad. de Jurisprudencia y Legislacion, Madrid. Kt Comdr, Order of Merit, Italy, 1968; Kt, SMOM Malta, 1966; KSG, 1972; Kt Comdr, Constantine St George, 1971. *Publications:* The Treatment of Young Offenders in Malta, 1956; The Malta Constitution of 1835, 1959; The Doctrine of Entrapment in Theft, 1959; The Legal Consequences of a Conviction, 1962; The Constitutional Development of Malta, 1963; From the Declaration of Rights to Independence, 1965; Human Rights Documentation in Malta, 1966; articles in French, German, Italian and American law jls. *Recreation:* gardening. *Address:* Chambers of the Chief Justice, Republic Street, Valletta, Malta. *T:* 23281; 5 Victoria Gardens, Sliema. *T:* 33203.

CRESPI, (Caesar) James; a Recorder of the Crown Court, since 1973. *Educ:* Trinity Hall, Cambridge (BA). Called to the Bar, Middle Temple, 1951, South Eastern Circuit. *Address:* 5 Paper Buildings, Temple, EC4Y 7HB. *T:* 01-353 7811. *Club:* Garrick.

CRESPIN, Régine; Chevalier de la Légion d'Honneur, 1972; soprano singer; *b* 23 Feb.; *d* of Henri Crespin and Marguerite (*née* Meirone); *m* 1962, Lou Bruder, French novelist, critic, poet, translator. *Educ:* Nîmes; Conservatoire National, Paris (Baccalauréat). Has been working at the Opera, Paris, from 1951, in all the famous opera houses of Europe and all over the world, giving concerts, recitals, etc. Chevalier de l'Ordre National du Mérite, 1965; Comdr des Art et des Lettres, 1974. *Recreations:* sea, sun, sleep, books, theatre; and my dog! *Address:* 3 Avenue Frochot, 75009 Paris, France.

CRESSWELL, William Foy, CBE 1956; Senior Official Receiver in Bankruptcy, 1948-56; *b* 2 Nov. 1895; *s* of Edward Cresswell and Annie Maria (*née* Foy); *m* 1922, Olive May Barham; two *d*. *Educ:* Portsmouth Secondary Sch. Entered Civil Service as Boy Clerk, 1911. Served with Hon. Artillery Company 2nd Inf. Bn in France, Italy and Austria, 1916-19. Appointed to Bankruptcy Department, Board of Trade, 1921; Asst Official Receiver, High Court, 1931; Official Receiver, Swansea and district, 1934; Official Receiver, Bradford, Yorks, 1936; recalled to London to assist with BoT War Damage Insurance Schemes, 1941. Retired, Dec. 1956. *Recreations:* walking, gardening, the open air. *Address:* 27 Sullington Gardens, Worthing, West Sussex. *T:* Findon 2065.

CRESSWELL, Jack Norman; Deputy Chairman of Lloyd's, 1972, 1974; *b* 20 April 1913; *s* of late Sydney and Dora Creswell; *m* 1938, Lilian Jane (Jean) Maxwell; two *s*. *Educ:* Highgate School. Served War, 1942-46, 2nd Household Cavalry Regt; Captain and Adjt, The Life Guards, 1945-46. Member of Lloyd's, 1946;

Mem. Cttee, 1969-72, 1974; Mem. Cttee Lloyd's Underwriters Non-Marine Assoc., 1968-74, Chm. 1973. Director: R. W. Sturge (Motor Underwriting) Ltd; J. Besso, Roden & Co. Ltd. *Recreations:* photography, family croquet. *Address:* Lullington Court, near Polegate, E Sussex. *T:* Alfriston 870548. *Clubs:* Cavalry and Guards, City of London.

CRESWELL, Sir Michael Justin, KCMG 1950 (CMG 1952); Ambassador to Argentine Republic, 1964-69; retired; *b* 21 Sept. 1909; *s* of late Col Edmund William Creswell, RE; *m* 1st, 1939, Elizabeth Colshorn; one *s*; 2nd, 1950, Baroness C. M. thoe Schwartzenberg; one *s*. *Educ:* Rugby; New Coll., Oxford. Laming Travelling Fellow, Queen's Coll., Oxford, 1932. Entered Foreign Service, 1933; 3rd Sec., Berlin, 1935-38; 2nd Sec., Madrid, 1939-44, Athens, 1944; Foreign Office, 1944-47; Counsellor, Tehran, 1947-49; Singapore, 1949-51; Minister, British Embassy, Cairo, 1951-54; Ambassador to Finland, 1954-58; Senior Civilian Instructor, Imperial Defence Coll., 1958-60; Ambassador to Yugoslavia, 1960-64. Chm., Surrey Amenity Council, 1974-; Member: Waverley DC, 1974-; Surrey CC, 1977-. *Recreations:* travel, wild life. *Address:* Copse Hill, Ewhurst, near Cranleigh, Surrey. *T:* Ewhurst 311.

CRESWICK, Sir Alexander Reid, (Sir Alec Creswick), Kt 1974; company director and pastoralist, Australia; Chairman, Victoria Racing Club Committee, since 1969 (Member, 1959); *b* 1912; *s* of late H. F. Creswick; *m* 1st, Claudia, *d* of C B. Palmer; two *s*; 2nd, Diana Bingham Meeks, *d* of Anthony Hordern; two *d*. *Educ:* Melbourne Church of England Grammar Sch.; St John's Coll., Oxford. Served War of 1939-45, Australian Army Service Corps. Past Pres.: Victoria Polo Assoc.; Equestrian Fedn of Aust. Formerly: Master of Melbourne Hounds; Manager of Aust. Olympic Equestrian Teams: Rome, Stockholm, Montreal. Life Mem., Council of Royal Agricultural Soc. of Victoria. Director, Carlton and United Breweries Ltd. *Address:* Allanvale, Avenel, Victoria 3664, Australia; c/o 414 Collins Street, Melbourne, Vic. 3000, Australia. *Clubs:* Jockey (Newmarket, Eng.); VRC, Melbourne (Melbourne).

CRESWICK, Harry Richardson, MA; Librarian Emeritus of Cambridge University; *b* 1902; *m* Agnes Isabel, *d* of late J. W. Stubbings. *Educ:* Barnet Grammar Sch.; Trinity Coll., Cambridge. On staff of University Library, Cambridge, 1926-38; Deputy Librarian, Bodleian Library, Oxford 1939-45; Bodley's Librarian and Student of Christ Church, 1945-47; Librarian of Cambridge Univ. and Professorial Fellow of Jesus Coll., 1949-67, Emeritus Fellow, 1976. Hon. LittD, Trinity Coll., Dublin. *Address:* Gifford, East Lothian, Scotland.

CREW, Air Vice-Marshal Edward Dixon, CB 1973; DSO 1944 and Bar 1950; DFC 1941 and Bar 1942; FRAeS 1972; Planning Inspectorate, Department of the Environment, since 1973; *b* 24 Dec. 1917; *er s* of F. D. Crew, MB, MRCS, LRCP; *m* 1945, Virginia Martin; one *s*. *Educ:* Felsted Sch.; Downing Coll., Cambridge (MA). Commissioned RAFVR, 1939; served War of 1939-45: night fighter sqdns; 604 sqdn, 85 Sqdn; Comd 96 Sqdn; permanent commission, 1945. Malayan Emergency, Comd No 45 Sqdn, 1948-50; on exchange, RCAF, 1952-54; CFE, 1954-56; Comd RAF Brüggen, Germany, 1959-62; Comdr, Air Forces Borneo, 1965-66; AOC Central Reconnaissance Estabt, 1968; Dep. Controller, Nat. Air Traffic Services, 1969-72; various Air Staff jobs at Air Min. and MoD; retd 1973. *Recreations:* shooting, tennis. *Address:* c/o National Westminster Bank Ltd, 10 Benet Street, Cambridge. *Club:* Royal Air Force.

CREWE, Albert V., PhD; Professor, Department of Physics and the Enrico Fermi Institute since 1963 (Assistant Professor, 1956-59; Associate Professor, 1959-63), Dean of Physical Sciences Division, since 1971, University of Chicago; *b* 18 Feb. 1927; *m* 1949, Doreen Patricia Blunsdon; one *s* three *d*. *Educ:* Univ. of Liverpool (BS, PhD). Asst Lectr, 1950-52, Lectr, 1952-55, Univ. of Liverpool; Div. Dir, Particle Accelerator Division, Argonne National Laboratory, 1958-61; Dir, Argonne National Laboratory, 1961-67. Member: Nat. Acad. of Sciences; Amer. Acad. of Arts and Sciences. Named Outstanding New Citizen by Citizenship Council of Chicago, 1962; received Immigrant's Service League's Annual Award for Outstanding Achievement in the Field of Science, 1962; Illinois Sesquicentennial Award, 1968; Industrial Research Award, 1970; Distinguished Award, Electron Microscope Soc. of America, 1976. *Publications:* Research USA (with J. J. Katz), 1964; contribs to: Proc. Royal Soc.; Proc. Phys. Soc.; Physical Review; Science; Physics Today; Jl of Applied Physics; Reviews of Scientific Instruments, etc. *Address:* 63 Old Creek Road, Palos Park, Illinois, USA. *T:* Gibson 8-8738. *Clubs:* Cosmos (Washington DC); Quadrangle, Wayfarers' (Chicago).

CRIBB, Air Cdre Peter Henry, CBE 1957; DSO 1942, and Bar, 1944; DFC 1941; JP; Chairman, Capricorn Investments Pty Ltd; *b* 28 Sept. 1918; *s* of late Charles B. Cribb and Mrs Ethel Cribb; *m* 1949, Vivienne Janet, *yr d* of Col S. T. J. Perry, MC, TD, DL, Oxton, Birkenhead, Ches; three *s. Educ:* Bradford Grammar Sch.; Prince Henry's Sch., Otley. Flt Cadet, RAF Coll., 1936-38; Flying duties in Bomber Comd, 1938-45 (Comd No. 582 Sqdn, RAF Little Staughton); Comdg RAF Salbani, RAF Peshawar, India and Staff No. 1 Indian Gp, 1945-47; OC 203 Sqdn, 1947, and HQ Staff, 1950, Coastal Comd; RAF Staff Coll., Bracknell, 1951; Asst Dir Tech. Intell., Air Min., 1951-53; Gp Capt. Plans and Policy, HQ Bomber Comd, 1953-57; 2nd TAF, Germany (OC Oldenburg, Ahlhorn and Gutersloh), 1957-60; Air Min., Dep. Dir Air Staff Briefing, 1959-61, Dir, 1961-62; SASO, Air Forces, Middle East, 1962-63; IDC, 1964; Deputy to Asst Chief of Defence Staff (Joint Warfare), MoD 1965-66; retired, 1966. Administrative Manager, Goldsworthy Mining Ltd, 1966-68. Associate Fellow, Australian Inst. of Management, 1969; State Pres., Ryder-Cheshire Foundn for Relief of Suffering, 1970. Man. Sec., Lake Karrinyup Country Club. JP Western Australia, 1968. *Recreations:* sailing, fishing. *Address:* 193 Lockhart Street, Como, Western Australia 6152, Australia. *Clubs:* Royal Air Force; Royal Freshwater Bay Yacht (Perth).

CRICHTON, family name of **Earl of Erne.**

CRICHTON, Viscount; John Henry Michael Ninian Crichton; *b* 19 June 1971; *s* and *heir* of Earl of Erne, *qv.*

CRICHTON, Sir Andrew Maitland-Makgill-, Kt 1963; Director, P&OSN Co., since 1957; Vice-Chairman, Port of London Authority, 1967-76 (Member, 1964-67); *b* 28 Dec. 1910; *s* of Lt-Col D. M.-M.-Crichton, Queen's Own Cameron Highldrs, and Phyllis (*née* Cuthbert); *m* 1948, Isabel, *d* of Andrew McGill, Sydney, NSW. *Educ:* Wellington Coll. Joined Gray, Dawes & Co., 1929; transf. India to Mackinnon Mackenzie & Co. (Agents of BI Co. and for P & O on Indian Continent and in parts of Far East), 1931. Joined IA, 1940; DDM (Shipping), Col, at GHQ India, 1944. Mackinnon Mackenzie, Calcutta, 1945-48; P&O Co., UK (Gen. Manager, 1951); Chm., Overseas Containers Ltd, 1965-73; Director: Julian S. Hodge & Co. Ltd; Hodge Group Ltd; Standard Chartered Group; Bain Dawes Gp (Insce) Ltd; Amalgamated Tin Mines of Nigeria. Chairman: Nat. Assoc. Port Employers, 1958-65; EDC for GPO, 1965-70; Vice-Chm., British Transport Docks Bd, 1963-68; Member: Baltic Exchange; Nat. Freight Corp., 1969-73; Court of The Chartered Bank; Police Council for GB (Arbitrator); Industrial Arbitration Bd. FRSA; FCIT (a past Vice-Pres.). *Recreations:* golf, music. *Address:* 55 Hans Place, Knightsbridge, SW1. *T:* 01-584 1209; The Mill House, Earl Soham, Suffolk. *T:* Earl Soham 330. *Clubs:* City of London, Caledonian.
See also Maj.-Gen. Edward Maitland-Makgill-Crichton.

CRICHTON, David George, MVO 1968; British Consul-General, Nice, 1970-74; *b* 31 July 1914; *e s* of late Col Hon. Sir George Crichton, GCVO; *m* 1941, Joan Fenella, *d* of late Col D. W. Cleaver; one *s* one *d. Educ:* Eton. Worked as journalist, Reading and Manchester, and on Daily Telegraph, Paris and London, 1933-39; served War of 1939-45 in Derbyshire Yeomanry (despatches); Major 1944; entered Foreign Service, 1946; served in Belgrade, Singapore, Alexandria, Miami, La Paz and Santiago. *Address:* Résidence Bois Joli, 06-Cap d'Ail, France. *Club:* Boodle's.

CRICHTON, Maj.-Gen. Edward Maitland-Makgill-, OBE 1948 (MBE 1945); GOC 51st Highland Division, 1966-68, retired; *b* 23 Nov. 1916; *s* of Lt-Col D. E. Maitland-Makgill-Crichton, Queen's Own Cameron Highlanders and Phyllis (*née* Cuthbert); *m* 1951, Sheila Margaret Hibbins, Bexhill-on-Sea; three *s. Educ:* Bedford Sch.; RMC SAndhurst. 2nd Lieut Queen's Own Cameron Highlanders, 1937; Adjt 5th Bn Cameron Highlanders, 1939; served with 5th Cameron Highlanders and 51 (Highland) Div., N Africa, Sicily, Normandy, NW Europe, 1940-45; GSO 1, HQ British Commonwealth Occupation Force, Japan, 1946-47; Mobilisation Br., WO 1948-50; 1st Bn Cameron Highlanders, Tripoli and Canal Zone, 1950-52; Jt Services Staff Coll., 1953; GSO 1, 3rd Inf. Div. (UK Strategic Reserve), Canal Zone, Egypt, UK and Suez, 1953-57; with 1st Bn Cameron Highlanders, Aden, 1957; comd 1st Liverpool Scottish, 1958-61; Comdr 152 (Highland) Inf. Bde, 1962-64; Dep. Dir Army Staff Duties, MoD, 1965-66. *Recreations:* shooting, golf, gardening, fishing. *Address:* Clive House, Letham, Angus. *T:* Letham 391. *Club:* Army and Navy.
See also Sir Andrew Maitland-Makgill-Crichton.

CRICHTON, Hon. Sir (John) Robertson (Dunn), Kt 1967; **Hon. Mr Justice Crichton;** Judge of the High Court of Justice, Queen's Bench Division, since 1967; *b* 2 Nov. 1912; *s* of Alexander Cansh and Beatrice Crichton, Wallasey, Ches; *m* 1944, Margaret Vanderlip, *d* of Col Livingston Watrous, Washington, DC, and Nantucket, Mass, USA; two *s* one *d. Educ:* Sedbergh Sch.; Balliol Coll., Oxford. Called to the Bar, Middle Temple, 1936; Bencher, 1959. Served War of 1939-45, RA (TA). KC 1951; QC 1952. Recorder of Blackpool, 1952-60; Judge of Appeal of the Isle of Man, 1956-60; Recorder of Manchester and Judge of Crown Court at Manchester, 1960-67. *Recreations:* gardening, painting. *Address:* Royal Courts of Justice, Strand, WC2; Hempfield, Dunham Massey, Altrincham, Cheshire. *T:* 061-928 6101. *Club:* United Oxford & Cambridge University.

CRICHTON, Col Walter Hugh, CIE 1941; MB, ChB Edinburgh 1919; DPH London 1934; IMS (retired); *b* 24 July 1896; *m* 1920, Dorothy Martindale, Trinity, Edinburgh; one *s* one *d.* Apptd Indian Medical Service, 1920; Foreign Political Dept, 1930; Vice-Consul, Seistan, Persia; Agency Surgeon Kurram Valley, NWFP, 1932; MOH, Simla, 1934; Chief Health Officer, Delhi Prov., 1936; on active service Paiforce, 1941; ADMS, Basra, 1942; Mil. Gov., CMF, 1943; Dir PH Mil. Gov., 21 Army Group, BLA, 1944-45; Dir Public Health, CP and Behar, 1945-47; MOH Kent Co. Dists, 1948-50; Chief WHO Mission, Korea, 1950; PH Administrator WHO East Med. Region, until 1956; ACMO Norfolk; Freeman Naples City, 1944; Cross of Merit (1st Class) Order of Malta, 1944; Kt Comdr Order of Orange-Nassau, 1946. *Address:* Carousel, Polstead Heath, near Colchester CO6 5BA. *T:* Hadleigh (Suffolk) 2374. *Club:* Naval and Military.

CRICHTON-BROWN, Sir Robert, Kt 1972; CBE 1970; TD 1974; *b* Melbourne, 23 Aug. 1919; *s* of late L. Crichton-Brown, Sydney; *m* 1941, Norah Isabelle, *d* of late A. E. Turnbull; one *s* one *d. Educ:* Sydney Grammar Sch. Served War, 1939-45, BEF; Major, Royal Artillery and Gen. Staff, France, Iceland, India, Burma (despatches twice). Exec. Chm. and Man. Dir, Edward Lumley Ltd; Chm. and Man. Dir, The Security & General Insurance Co. Ltd; Chairman: Security Life Assurances Ltd; Clarke Chapman (Aust.) Pty Ltd (John Thompson (Aust.) Pty Ltd); WestHam Dredging Co. Pty Ltd; Ham-Dredging (Aust.) Pty Ltd; Vice-Chm., Rothmans of Pall Mall (Aust.) Ltd; Director: The Commercial Banking Co. of Sydney Ltd; H. C. Sleigh Ltd. Fed. Pres., Inst. of Dirs in Australia (Chm., NSW Br.). Dir, Royal Prince Alfred Hosp.; Pres., Postgrad. Med. Res. Foundn; Mem., Finance Cttee, Royal Australasian Coll. of Physicians. Area Pres., E Metropolitan Area, Scout Assoc. of Australia (NSW Br.). Underwriting Mem. of Lloyd's, 1946. *Address:* 11 Castlereagh Street, Sydney, NSW 2000, Australia. *Clubs:* Royal Yacht Squadron; Australian (Sydney); Cruising Yacht Club of Australia, Royal Sydney Yacht Squadron, Royal Prince Alfred Yacht.

CRICHTON-MILLER, Donald, TD; MA; *b* 1906; *s* of late Hugh Crichton-Miller, MA, MD, FRCP; *m* 1931, Monica, *d* of late B. A. Glanvill, JP, Bromley, Kent; two *s* one *d. Educ:* Fettes Coll. Edinburgh; Pembroke Coll., Cambridge (Exhibitioner). Played Rugby Football for Cambridge and Scotland; Asst Master: Monmouth Sch., 1929-31; Bryanston Sch., 1931-34; Stowe Sch., 1934-36; Head Master: Taunton Sch., Somerset, 1936-45; Fettes Coll., 1945-58; Stowe Sch., 1958-63. Carried out education surveys in Pakistan, 1951, and Malta, 1956. HM Comr, Queen Victoria Sch., Dunblane. *Recreations:* games and sports of various kinds. *Address:* Westridge House, Compton, Berks.

CRICHTON-STUART, family name of **Marquess of Bute.**

CRICK, Alan John Pitts, OBE 1956; Political and Economic Adviser to Commercial Union Assurance Company, since 1973; *b* 14 May 1913; *er s* of Owen John Pitts Crick and Margaret Crick (*née* Daw), late of Minehead, Somerset; *m* 1941, Norah (*née* Atkins); two *d. Educ:* Latymer Upper Sch.; King's Coll., London Univ. (MA); Heidelberg Univ. (Dr.phil). Vice-Consul, British Consulate-Gen., Free City of Danzig, 1938-39. Served War, Army, 1939-46: commissioned, 1940; Egypt and Libya, 1941-43, HQ Eighth Army; NW Europe, 1944-46 (despatches); Major, GSO2, Intell., SHAEF; HQ 21 Army Group and HQ BAOR. Min. of Defence Jt Intell. Bureau, 1946-63; jssc, 1948; British Jt Services Mission, Washington, 1953-56; Asst Dir, Jt Intell. Bureau, 1957-63; idc, 1960; Counsellor, British Embassy, Washington, 1963-65; Asst Sec., Cabinet Office, 1965-68; Def. Intell. Staff, MoD, 1968-73; Director of Economic Intelligence, MoD, 1970-73. *Recreations:* travel, antiquarian interests, books. *Address:* 71 London Road, Tunbridge Wells, Kent. *T:* Tunbridge Wells 26000; Condat sur Trincou, 24530 Champagnac-de-Belair, France. *Club:* Naval and Military.
See also R . Pitts Crick.

CRICK, Prof. Bernard, BSc (Econ.), PhD (London); Professor of Politics, Birkbeck College, University of London, since 1971; *b* 16 Dec. 1929; *s* of Harry Edgar and Florence Clara Crick. *Educ:* Whitgift Sch.; University Coll., London. Research student, LSE, 1950-52; Teaching Fellow, Harvard, 1952-54; Asst Prof., McGill, 1954-55; Vis. Fellow, Berkeley, 1955-56; Asst Lectr, later Lectr, later Sen. Lectr, LSE, 1957-65; Prof. of Political Theory and Institutions, Sheffield Univ., 1965-71. Jt Editor, Political Quarterly, 1966-. Joint Sec., Study of Parlt Gp, 1964-68. Hon. Vice Pres., Politics Assoc. Council of the Hansard Soc., 1962-. *Publications:* The American Science of Politics, 1958; In Defence of Politics, 1962, 2nd edn 1964 (trans. German, Japanese, Spanish, Italian); The Reform of Parliament, 1964, 2nd edn 1968; (ed) Essays on Reform, 1967; (ed with W. A. Robson) Protest and Discontent, 1970; (ed) Machiavelli: The Discourses, 1971; Political Theory and Practice, 1972; (ed with W. A. Robson) Taxation Policy, 1973; Basic Forms of Government, 1973; Crime, Rape and Gin, 1975. *Recreations:* polemicising, book- and theatre-reviewing, hill-walking. *Address:* Flat 5, 9 Clydesdale Road, W11. *T:* 01-727 5524.

CRICK, Francis Harry Compton, FRS 1959; BSc London, PhD Cantab; J. W. Kieckhefer Distinguished Professor, The Salk Institute, since 1977; *b* 8 June 1916; *e s* of late Harry Crick and late Annie Elizabeth (*née* Wilkins); *m* 1st, 1940, Ruth Doreen Dodd (divorced, 1947); one *s*; 2nd, 1949, Odile Speed; two *d*. *Educ:* Mill Hill Sch.; University Coll., London; Caius Coll., Cambridge (Hon. Fellow, 1976). Scientist in Admiralty, 1940-47; Strangeways Laboratory, Cambridge, 1947-49; MRC Lab. of Molecular Biology, Cambridge, 1949-77; Brooklyn Polytechnic, NY, USA, 1953-54. Vis. Lectr Rockefeller Inst., NY, USA, 1959; Vis. Prof., Chemistry Dept, Harvard, 1959; Fellow, Churchill Coll., Cambridge, 1960-61; Vis. Biophysics Prof., Harvard, 1962; Non-resident Fellow, Salk Inst. for Biological Studies, San Diego, 1962-73; Ferkauf Foundn Visiting Prof., Salk Inst., 1976-77; Fellow, UCL, 1962; For. Hon. Mem., Amer. Acad. of Arts and Sciences, 1962; Hon. Mem., Amer. Soc. Biological Chem., 1963; Hon. MRIA, 1964; Hon. Fellow, Churchill Coll., Cambridge, 1965; FAAAS 1966; Hon. FRSE, 1966; For. Associate, US Nat. Acad. of Sciences, 1969; Mem., German Acad. of Science, Leopoldina, 1969; For. Mem., American Philos. Soc., Philadelphia, 1972; Hon. Mem., Hellenic Biochem. and Biophys. Soc., 1974. Lectures: Bloor, Rochester, USA, 1959; (with J. D. Watson) Warren Triennial Prize, Boston, USA, 1959; Korkes Meml, Duke Univ., 1960; Herter, Johns Hopkins Sch. of Medicine, USA, 1960; Franklin Harris, Mount Zion Hosp., 1962; Holme, London, 1962; Henry Sidgewick Meml, Cambridge, 1963; Harveian, London, 1963; Graham Young, Glasgow, 1963; Robert Boyle, Oxford, 1963; James W. Sherrill, Scripps Clinic, 1964; Elisha Mitchel Meml, N Carolina, 1964; Vanuxem, Princeton, 1964; Charles West, London, 1964; William T. Sedgwick Meml, MIT, 1965; A. J. Carlson Meml, Chicago, 1965; Failing, Univ. of Oregon, 1965; Robbins, Pomona Coll., 1965; Telford Meml, Manchester, 1965; Kinnaird, Regent St Polytechnic, 1965; John Danz, Univ. of Washington, 1966; Sumner, Cornell, 1966; Royal Society Croonian, 1966; Cherwell-Simon Meml, Oxford, 1966; Genetical Soc. Mendel, 1966; Rickman Godlee, UCL, 1968; Shell, Stanford Univ., 1969; Evarts A. Graham Meml, Washington Univ., St Louis Missouri; Gehrmann, Illinois Univ., 1973; Cori, Buffalo, NY, 1973; Jean Weigle Meml, Calif Inst. of Technology, 1976; John Stauffer Distinguished, Univ. of Southern Calif, 1976; Smith Kline and French, Univ. of Calif, SF, 1977. Lasker Award (jointly), 1960; Prix Charles Léopold Mayer, French Académies des Sciences, 1961; Research Corp. Award (with J. D. Watson), 1961; Gairdner Foundation Award, Toronto, 1962; Nobel Prize for Medicine (jointly), 1962; Royal Medal, Royal Soc., 1972; Copley Medal, Royal Soc., 1976. *Publications:* Of Molecules and Men, 1966; papers and articles on molecular and cell biology in scientific journals. *Recreation:* conversation, especially with pretty women. *Address:* The Salk Institute for Biological Studies, PO Box 1809, San Diego, Calif 92112, USA; 337 Longden Lane, Calif 92075, USA.

CRICK, R(onald) Pitts, FRCS, DOMS; Senior Ophthalmic Surgeon, King's College Hospital, since 1950; Recognised Teacher in the Faculty of Medicine, University of London, since 1960; Chairman, Ophthalmic Post-Graduate Training, SE Thames Regional Health Authority, since 1972; *b* 5 Feb. 1917; *yr s* of Owen J. Pitts Crick and Margaret Daw, Minehead, Som; *m* 1941, Jocelyn Mary Grenfell Robins, *yr d* of Leonard A. C. Robins and Geraldine Grenfell, Hendon; four *s* one *d*. *Educ:* Latymer Upper Sch., London; King's Coll. and (Science School.) King's Coll. Hosp. Med. Sch., Univ. of London. MRCS, LRCP 1939. Surgeon, MN, 1939-40; Surg. Lieut, RNVR, 1940-46. Ophthalmic Registrar, King's Coll. Hosp., 1946-48; DOMS 1946. Surgical First Asst, Royal Eye Hosp., 1947-50; Ophth. Surg., Epsom County Hosp., 1948-49; Ophth. Registrar,

Belgrave Hosp. for Children, 1948-50; Ophth. Surg., Sevenoaks Hosp., 1948-50; Sen. Ophthalmic Surg., Royal Eye Hosp., 1950-69; Ophthalmic Surg., Belgrave Hosp. for Children, 1950-66. Examr to RCS for Diploma in Ophthalmology, 1961-68. FRCS, 1950. Hon. Ophth. Surg., Royal London Soc. for the Blind, 1954-57. FRSocMed, Vice-Pres. Ophthalmological Section, 1964, and Mem. Council Ophthalmolog. Section, 1953-54 and 1956-58. Member: Ophthalmolog. Soc. of the UK; Faculty of Ophthalmologists; Oxford Ophthalmolog. Congress; Southern Ophthalmolog. Soc. (Vice-Pres., 1969; Pres., 1970); Chm., Internat. Glaucoma Assoc., 1975; Charter Mem., Internat. Glaucoma Congress, USA, 1977-. *Publications:* Cardiovascular Affections, Ateriosclerosis and Hypertension (Section in Systematic Ophthalmology, ed A. Sorsby), 1950 and 1958; A Short Text Book of Opthalmology, 1975; medical and opthalmic contribs to Brit. Jl Ophthalmology, BMJ, Jl RN Med. Service, Trans Ophthalmolog. Soc. of the UK, etc. *Recreations:* walking, motoring, sailing. *Address:* Private Consulting Rooms, King's College Hospital, SE5. *T:* 01-274 8570; Pembroke House, Sevenoaks, Kent. *T:* Sevenoaks 53633. *Clubs:* Royal Automobile; Royal Motor Yacht.
  See also A. J. P. Crick.

CRIDLAND, Charles Elliot Tapscott; Vice-Chairman, The Aero Group, 1969-70; *b* Glos, 21 July 1900; *s* of S. L. Cridland; *m* 1st, 1923, Kathleen (*d* 1957), *d* of Capt. Bell, Cheltenham; two *d*; 2nd, 1948, Joan Gardiner, *d* of late G. A. McLennan and Mrs E. Coy. *Educ:* Trent Coll., Long Eaton; Faraday House Engineering Coll., London. Chm. and Managing Director: Rye & Co., Lincoln, 1927-30; Eclair Doors Ltd, 1937-47; Aldis Bros Ltd, 1946-57; Automatic Changers Ltd, 1956-57; Chairman: Hawkes & Snow (Curtaincraft) Ltd, 1949-63; Portable Balers Ltd, 1953-61; Aero Heat Treatment Ltd, 1947-69; Hard Coating Ltd, 1951-69; Chisholm, Gray and Co. Ltd, 1956-69; Aerotaps Ltd, 1958-69; Aerocoldform Ltd, 1956-69; Broadstone Ballvalve Co. Ltd, 1959-69; Bendz Ltd, 1962-69; Quality Machined Parts, Ltd, 1964-69; Kinsman Ltd, 1965-69. Vice-Chm., Mercian Builders Merchants Ltd, 1965-67. Dir, A. D. Foulkes Ltd, 1958-65. Mem. Org. Cttee, Birmingham Productivity Assoc., 1955-63. Chm. Organisation Cttee, National Farmers' Union, Glos Branch, 1946; Chm., Steel Rolling Shutter Assoc., 1945-46. Scientific Instrument Manufacturers' Assoc. of Gt Brit. Ltd: Mem. Council, 1949-57, Vice-Pres., 1953 and 1957, Pres., 1954-56; Chm., Transport Users' Consultative Cttee, W Midlands Area, 1960-69; Mem., Central Transport Consultative Cttee, 1963-69. Mem. Court of Assistants, The Worshipful Co. of Scientific Instrument Makers, 1955; elected Master, 1956 and 1957; Freeman, City of London, 1955. *Ex-officio* Mem. Bd of Govs, Faraday House Engrg Coll., 1961-63; Vice-Pres. and Hon. Treas. Faraday House Old Students Assoc., 1960, Pres. 1962-63. Served War, RAF, 1918-19. *Recreations:* golf (played for Warwicks and Glos), and farming. *Address:* c/o National Westminster Bank Ltd, Prospect Hill, Douglas, Isle of Man.

CRIPPS, family name of **Baron Parmoor.**

CRIPPS, Anthony L.; *see* Cripps, M. A. L.

CRIPPS, Sir Cyril Thomas, Kt 1971; MBE 1944; Chairman, Pianoforte Supplies Ltd, Simplex Works, Roade, Northampton, since 1919; *b* 21 April 1892; *s* of Ernest Henry and Emmeline Harriet Cripps; *m* 1913, Amy Elizabeth Humphrey; one *s* two *d*. *Educ:* Archbishop Sumner's Memorial Sch., Kennington, London. Chairman, Northampton Rural District Council, 1961-74 (elected RDC, 1950; Vice-Chm., 1954); County Alderman, Northamptonshire County Council, 1963-74 (elected CC, 1954). Hon. LLD, Nottingham Univ., 1961. *Address:* Three Ways, Roade, Northampton.

CRIPPS, Dame Isobel, GBE 1946; *b* 25 Jan. 1891; 2nd *d* of late Harold William Swithinbank, FRGS, DL, JP, RN, Denham Court, Bucks; *m* 1911, Rt Hon. Sir Stafford Cripps, PC, CH, FRS, QC (*d* 1952); one *s* three *d*. FRSA. Special Grand Cordon of Order of Brilliant Star, 1st class, China, 1946; Award of Nat. Cttee of India in celebration of Internat. Women's Year, 1976. *Address:* Greyholme, Minchinhampton, Stroud, Glos GL6 9HS. *T:* Brimscombe 3089.
  See also J. S. Cripps.

CRIPPS, John Stafford, CBE 1968; Chairman, Countryside Commission, 1970-77; *b* 10 May 1912; *s* of late Rt Hon. Sir Stafford Cripps, PC, CH, FRS, QC, and Isobel (*see* Dame Isobel Cripps); *m* 1st, 1936, Ursula (marr. diss. 1971), *d* of late Arthur C. Davy; four *s* two *d*; 2nd, 1971, Ann Elizabeth Farwell. *Educ:* Winchester; Balliol Coll., Oxford. 1st Class Hons Politics, Philosophy and Economics (Modern Greats). Editor, The Countryman, 1947-71. Filkins Parish Councillor; Witney Rural District Councillor, 1946-74; Chairman: Rural District

Councils' Association, 1967-70; Rural Cttee of Nat. Council of Social Service; Member: Oxfordshire Planning Cttee, 1948-69; W Oxfordshire Technical Coll. Governors, 1951-70; South East Economic Planning Council, 1966-73; Nature Conservancy, 1970-73; Exec. Cttee, CPRE, 1963-69; Inland Waterways Amenity Advisory Council, 1968-73; Defence Lands Cttee, 1971-73; Water Space Amenities Commn, 1977-. Prepared report on Accommodation for Gypsies, 1976. *Address:* Filkins, Lechlade, Glos. *TA:* Filkins. *T:* Filkins 209. *Club:* Farmers'.

CRIPPS, (Matthew) Anthony Leonard, CBE 1971; DSO 1943; TD 1947; QC 1958; a Recorder, since 1972 (Recorder of Nottingham, 1961-71); Master of the Bench, Middle Temple, since 1965; Hon. Judge of Court of Arches, since 1969; *b* 30 Dec. 1913; *s* of late Major Hon. L. H. Cripps; *m* 1941, Dorothea Margaret (Surrey CC 1965-67), *d* of G. Johnson Scott, Ashby-de-la-Zouch; three *s. Educ:* Eton; Christ Church, Oxford; Combined Army and RAF Staff Coll., 1944-45. Royal Leicestershire Regt, TA, 1933. Served War of 1939-45: Norway, Sweden, Finland, Iceland, N Africa, Italy, Egypt, 1939-44 (Capt. to Lt-Col); Staff Officer, Palestine and Syria, 1944-46. Barrister-at-law, Middle Temple, 1938, Inner Temple, 1961, and Hong Kong, 1974. Chairman: Disciplinary Cttees, Milk Marketing Bd, 1956-, Potato and Egg Marketing Bds, 1956-67; Isle of Man Govt Commn on Agricultural Marketing, 1961-62; Home Sec.'s Adv. Cttee on Service Candidates, 1966- (Dep. Chm., 1965); Nat. Panel, Approved Coal Merchants Scheme, 1972-; Nat. Panel, Approved Solid Fuel Distributors Scheme. Member: Agricultural Wages Bd, 1964-67; Northumberland Cttee of Inquiry into Foot and Mouth Disease, 1968-69; Cttee of Inquiry, Export of Live Animals for Slaughter, 1973-74. Chm., Billbrook Finance Ltd; Dir, Caledonian African Investment Trust (Pty) Ltd (S Africa). Chm., Alpine Sun for British Children. *Publications:* Agriculture Act 1947, 1947; Agriculture Holdings Act, 1948, 1948; (ed) 9th edn, Cripps on Compulsory Purchase: Powers, Procedure and Compensation, 1950; legal articles, especially on agricultural matters, for Law Jl and Encyclopaedia Britannica. *Recreations:* family life and gardening. *Address:* Alton House, Felbridge, East Grinstead, Sussex. *T:* 23238; 1 Harcourt Buildings, Temple EC4. *T:* 01-353 9421. *Clubs:* Brooks's, Lansdowne; United Services (Nottingham).

CRISHAM, Air Vice-Marshal William Joseph, CB 1953; CBE 1944; RAF, retired; *b* 19 Nov. 1906; Served War of 1939-45; Nos 13 and 23 Sqdns; Central Fighter Establishment, 1950-53; No 12 Group Fighter Command, 1953-56; RAF Levant MEAF, 1956-58; RAF Germany (2nd TAF), 1958-61; retired 1961. *Club:* Royal Air Force.

CRISP, Prof. Dennis John, ScD; FRS 1968; Professor in Department of Marine Biology, University College of North Wales, since 1962; Hon. Director, Natural Environment Research Council Unit of Marine Invertebrate Biology, since 1965; *b* 29 April 1916; *m* 1944, Ella Stewart Allpress; one *s* one *d. Educ:* St Catharine's Coll., Cambridge. Research Asst, Dept of Colloid Science, Univ. of Cambridge, 1943-46; ICI (Paints Div.), i/c of Marine Paints Res. Stn, Brixham, Devon, 1946-51; Dir, Marine Science Laboratories, University Coll. of N Wales, 1951-70. *Publications:* (ed) Grazing in Terrestrial and Marine Environments, 1964; (ed) 4th European Marine Biology Symposium Volume (1969), 1971; papers in Proc. Royal Soc., Jl Marine Biol. Assoc., Jl Experimental Biology, Jl Animal Ecology, etc. *Recreations:* travel, photography. *Address:* Craig y Pîn, Llandegfan, Menai Bridge, Gwynedd. *T:* Menai Bridge 712775.

CRISP, Sir (John) Peter, 4th Bt *cr* 1913; *b* 19 May 1925; *o s* of Sir John Wilson Crisp, 3rd Bt, and Marjorie (*d* 1977), *d* of F. R. Shriver; *S* father, 1950; *m* 1954, Judith Mary, *d* of late H. E. Gillett; three *s* one *d. Educ:* Westminster. *Heir: s* John Charles Crisp, *b* 10 Dec. 1955. *Address:* Hollyhocks, Cranleigh, Surrey. *T:* Cranleigh 3969.

CRISP, Prof. Leslie Finlay; Professor of Political Science, Australian National University, since 1950; Member since 1974, Chairman, since 1975, Board of Commonwealth Banking Corporation; Member, Board of University Cooperative Bookshops Pty Ltd, Sydney, since 1972; *b* Melbourne, 19 Jan. 1917; *s* of Leslie Walter and Ruby Elizabeth Crisp; *m* 1940, Helen Craven Wighton; one *s* two *d. Educ:* St Peter's Coll., Adelaide; St Mark's Coll., Univ. of Adelaide (MA); Balliol Coll., Oxford (Rhodes Schol., MA). Australian Public Service, 1940-50: Dir-Gen., Dept of Post-War Reconstruction, 1949-50. Chm., Canberra Hosp. Bd, 1951-55; Mem., Prime Minister's Cttee on Future of Nat. Library and Archives, 1956; Chm., Prime Minister's Cttee on Integration of Data Bases, 1973-74. *Publications:* Parliamentary Government of the Commonwealth

of Australia, 1949; Australian Federal Labour Party, 1955; Ben Chifley, 1961; Australian National Government, 1965; Peter Richard Heydon 1913-1971, 1972, etc. *Recreation:* golf. *Address:* 47 Stonehaven Crescent, Deakin, Canberra, ACT 2600, Australia. *T:* 813828. *Clubs:* National Press (Canberra); Royal Canberra Golf.

CRISP, Hon. Sir (Malcolm) Peter, Kt 1969; retired; a Justice of the Supreme Court of Tasmania, 1952-71; Senior Puisne Judge, 1968-71; *b* Devonport, Tasmania, 21 March 1912; *s* of late T. M. Crisp, Burnie, (legal practitioner), and Myrtle May (*née* Donnelly); *m* 1935, Edna Eunice (*née* Taylor); two *d. Educ:* St Ignatius Coll., Riverview, Sydney; Univ. of Tasmania (LLB). Admitted legal practitioner, Tas, 1933; Crown Prosecutor, 1940. Served AIF, 1940-46 (in Australia, UK and Borneo, 2/1 Tank Attack Regt and Staff appts; rank of Colonel on discharge). Crown Solicitor, 1947-51; Solicitor-Gen. and KC, 1951. Lecturer in Law of Real Property, Univ. of Tasmania, 1947-52; Mem. Univ. Council, 1948-55; Chairman: State Library Bd, 1956-; Council, Nat. Library of Aust., 1971 (Mem., 1960-71); President, Library Assoc. of Aust., 1963-66; Australian Adv. Council on Bibliographical Services, 1973-; Royal Commissioner, Fluoridation of Public Water Supplies, 1966-68. *Recreations:* cruising, angling. *Address:* 10 Anglesea Street, Hobart, Tasmania. *T:* Hobart 235639. *Clubs:* Tasmanian, Royal Yacht Club of Tasmania (Hobart).

CRISP, Sir Peter; *see* Crisp, Sir (John) P.

CRISP, Hon. Sir Peter; *see* Crisp, Hon. Sir M. P.

CRITCHETT, Sir Ian (George Lorraine), 3rd Bt *cr* 1908; BA Cantab; *b* 9 Dec. 1920; *s* of Sir Montague Critchett, 2nd Bt, and Innes, 3rd *d* of late Col F. G. A. Wiehe, The Durham Light Infantry; *S* father, 1941; *m* 1st, 1948, Paulette Mary Lorraine (*d* 1962), *e d* of Col H. B. Humfrey; 2nd, 1964, Jocelyn Daphne Margret, *e d* of Comdr C. M. Hall, Higher Boswarva, Penzance, Cornwall; one *s* one *d. Educ:* Harrow; Clare Coll., Cambridge. RAFVR, 1942-46. Joined Foreign Office, 1948; 3rd Sec. (Commercial), at Vienna, 1950-51; 2nd Sec. (Commercial) at Bucharest, 1951-53; 2nd Sec. at Cairo, 1956. *Heir: s* Charles George Montague Critchett, *b* 2 April 1965. *Address:* Uplands Lodge, Pains Hill, Limpsfield, Surrey. *Clubs:* Travellers', Pratt's, MCC.

CRITCHLEY, Julian Michael Gordon; MP (C) Aldershot, since 1974 (Aldershot and North Hants, 1970-74); writer and journalist; *b* 8 Dec. 1930; *s* of Dr Macdonald Critchley, *qv*; *m* 1955, Paula Joan Baron (divorced 1965); two *d*; *m* 1965, Mrs Heather Goodrick; one *s* one *d. Educ:* Shrewsbury; Sorbonne; Pembroke Coll., Oxford (MA). MP (C) Rochester and Chatham, 1959-64; contested Rochester and Chatham, 1966. Chm. of the Bow Group, 1966-67. Vice-Chm., Cons. Party Broadcasting Cttee; Chm., Cons. Party Media Cttee, 1976-. Delegate to WEU and Council of Europe; Chm., WEU Defence Cttee. Pres., Atlantic Assoc. of Young Political Leaders, 1968-70. *Publications:* (with O. Pick) Collective Security, 1974; (with O. Pick) Détente, 1977; various Bow Group and CPC pamphlets. *Recreations:* watching boxing, the country, reading military history. *Address:* The Brewer's House, 18 Bridge Square, Farnham, Surrey. *Clubs:* Coningsby; Oxford Union Society.

CRITCHLEY, Macdonald, CBE 1962; MD, ChB 1st Class Hons (Bristol), FRCP; MD (Zürich) *hc*; D en M (Aix-Marseille) *hc*; FACP (hon.). Consulting Neurologist; *s* of Arthur Frank and Rosina Matilda Critchley; *m* 1st, Edna Auldeth Morris (decd); two *s*; 2nd, Eileen Hargreaves. *Educ:* Christian Brothers Coll.; Univ. of Bristol (Lady Haberfield Scholarship in Medicine, Markham Skerritt Prize for Original Research). Goulstonian Lectr, RCP, 1930; Hunterian Prof., RCS, 1935; Royal Coll. of Physicians: Bradshaw Lectr, 1942; Croonian Lectr, 1945; Harveian Orator, 1966; Pres., World Fedn of Neurology, 1965-73; Hon. Consulting Neurologist, King's Coll. Hosp.; Hon. Consulting Physician, National Hosp., Queen Square; formerly Dean, Inst. of Neurology; Neurological Physician, Royal Masonic Hosp.; formerly Neurologist to Royal Hosp. and Home for Incurables, Putney. Consulting Neurologist to Royal Navy, 1939-77; Long Fox Lectr, Univ. of Bristol, 1935; William Withering Lectr, Univ. of Birmingham, 1946; Tisdall Lectr, Univ. of Manitoba, 1951; Semon Lectr, Univ. of London, 1951; Sherrington Lectr, Univ. of Wisconsin; Orator, Medical Soc. of London, 1955. Pres. Harveian Soc., 1947. Hunterian Orator, 1957; Doyne Memorial Lectr, 1961; Wartenberg Lectr, 1961; Victor Horsley Memorial Lectr, 1963; Honyman Gillespie Lectr, 1963; Schorstein Lectr, 1964; Hughlings Jackson Lectr and Medallist, RSM, 1964; Gowers Lectr and Medallist, 1965; Veraguth Gold Medallist, Bern, 1968; Sam T. Orton Award for

work on Dyslexia, 1974; Arthur Hall Memorial Lectr, 1969; Rickman Godlee Lectr, 1970; Cavendish Lectr, 1976. Pres. Assoc. of British Neurologists, 1962-64; Second Vice-Pres., RCP, 1964; Mem., GMC, 1957-73. Hon. Fellow, Pan-African Assoc. of Neurological Scis; Hon. Mem., RSM; Hon. Corresp. Mem. Académie de Médecine de France, Norwegian Academy of Science and Letters, Royal Academy of Medicine, Barcelona, and Neurological Socs of France, Switzerland, Holland, Turkey, Uruguay, US, Canada, Australia, Brazil, Argentine, Germany, Chile, Spain, Roumania, Norway, Czechoslovakia, Greece, Italy, Bulgaria, Hungary, Peru, Poland and Sweden. Visiting Prof., Univs of: Istanbul, 1949; California, 1950 and 1964; Hawaii, 1966. Master, Worshipful Soc. of Apothecaries, 1956-57. Served European War, 1917-18; Surgeon Captain RNVR, 1939-46. *Publications:* Mirror Writing; Neurology of Old Age; Observations on Pain; Language of Gesture; Shipwreck-survivors; Sir William Gowers; The Parietal Lobes; The Black Hole; Developmental Dyslexia; Aphasiology; The Dyslexic Child; Silent Language; (ed jtly) Music and the Brain, 1976; various articles on nervous diseases. *Address:* Private Consulting Room, National Hospital, Queen Square, WC1. *T:* 01-837 3611. *Clubs:* Athenæum, Garrick.
See also J. M. G. Critchley.

CRITCHLEY, Thomas Alan, JP; Assistant Under-Secretary of State, Home Office, 1972-76; *b* 11 March 1919; *y s* of Thomas Critchley and Annie Louisa Darvell; *m* 1942, Margaret Carol Robinson; one *s* two *d. Educ:* Queen Elizabeth's Grammar Sch., Barnet. Entered Civil Service, 1936. Served War, 1940-46 (commnd in RAOC). Asst Principal, Home Office, 1947; Principal, 1948; Cabinet Office, 1954-56; Principal Private Sec., to Home Secretary, 1957-60; Asst Sec., 1958; Sec., Royal Commn on Police, 1960-62; Sec. to Lord Denning's Enquiry into the Profumo Affair, 1963; Sec. of the Gaming Board for Great Britain, 1971-72; Director (and Mem.), Uganda Resettlement Board, 1972-74; leader, enquiry into UK Immigrants Adv. Service, 1976; Vice-Chm., WRVS, 1977-. JP Middlesex 1977. *Publications:* The Civil Service Today, 1951; A History of Police in England and Wales, 1967 (Amer. edn, 1972); The Conquest of Violence, 1970; (with P. D. James) The Maul and the Pear Tree, 1971; contributor to: The Police We Deserve, 1973, and various jls. *Recreations:* reading, gardening, mountain walking. *Address:* 26 Temple Fortune Lane, NW11. *T:* 01-455 4894. *Club:* Reform.

CROAN, Thomas Malcolm; Sheriff of Grampian, Highland and Islands (formerly Aberdeen, Kincardine and Banff) at Banff and Peterhead, since 1969; *b* 7 Aug. 1932; *s* of John Croan and Amelia Sydney; *m* 1959, Joan Kilpatrick Law; one *s* three *d. Educ:* St Joseph's Coll., Dumfries; Edinburgh University. MA 1953; LLB 1955. Admitted to Faculty of Advocates, 1956; Standing Junior Counsel, to Scottish Develt Dept, 1964-65 and (for highways work) 1967-69; Advocate Depute, 1965-66. *Recreations:* sailing, reading. *Address:* Belvedere, Sandyhill Road, Banff. *T:* Banff 5861.

CROCKER, Antony James Gulliford, CB 1973; Under-Secretary, Family Support Division, Department of Health and Social Security, since 1974; *b* 28 Oct. 1918; *s* of late Cyril James Crocker and Mabel Kate Crocker; *m* 1st, 1943, E. S. B. Dent; 2nd, 1949, Nancy Wynell, *d* of late Judge Gamon and Eleanor Margaret Gamon; two *s* one *d. Educ:* Sherborne Sch. (Scholar); Trinity Hall, Cambridge (Major Scholar, MA). Served War, 1939-46, Dorsetshire Regt (Major). Asst Princ. 1947, Princ. 1948, Min. of Nat. Insurance. Sec., Nat. Insce Advisory Cttee, 1955-56; Asst Sec., Min. of Pensions and Nat. Insce, 1956; Under-Secretary; War Pensions Dept, 1964 (Min. of Social Security, 1966-68); Supplementary Benefits Commn, 1968; Tax Credits Div., 1972; New Pensions Scheme, 1974. *Recreations:* horticulture, philately. *Address:* Wealdover, Guildown Avenue, Guildford, Surrey. *T:* 66555. *Club:* United Oxford & Cambridge University.

CROCKER, Peter Vernon; His Honour Judge Crocker; a Circuit Judge, since 1974; *b* 29 June 1926; *s* of Walter Angus Crocker and Fanny Victoria Crocker (*née* Dempster); *m* 1950, Nancy Kathleen Sargent. *Educ:* Oundle; Corpus Christi Coll., Cambridge (BA). Called to Bar, Inner Temple, 1949. *Recreations:* gardening, tennis, swimming. *Address:* The Park Farm, Snow Hill, Crawley Down, Sussex RH10 3EE. *T:* Copthorne 712061. *Club:* United Oxford & Cambridge University.

CROCKER, Walter Russell, CBE 1955; Australian diplomat, retired 1970; Lieutenant-Governor of South Australia, since 1973; *b* 25 March 1902; *e s* of late Robert Crocker and Alma Bray, Parnaroo, SA; *m* 1950, Claire (marr. diss. 1968), *y d* of F. J. Ward, Headmaster of Prince Alfred Coll., Adelaide, and

widow of Dr John Gooden, Physicist; two *s. Educ:* University of Adelaide; Balliol Coll., Oxford; Stanford University, USA. Entered Colonial Administrative Service (Nigeria), 1930; transf. to League of Nations, 1934, and to ILO (Asst to Dir-Gen). Served War, 1940-45 (Lt-Col, Croix de Guerre avec palme, Ordre royal du Lion, Belgium). Farming at Parnaroo, 1946; UN Secretariat (Chief of Africa Sect.), 1946-49; Prof. of Internat. Relations, Aust. Nat. Univ., 1949-52; Actg Vice-Chancellor, 1951; High Commissioner for Australia to India, 1952-55; Ambassador of Australia to Indonesia, 1955-57; High Comr to Canada, 1957-58; High Comr for Australia to India and Ambassador to Nepal, 1958-62; Amb. of Australia to the Netherlands and Belgium, 1962-65; Ambassador to Ethiopia and High Commissioner to Kenya and Uganda, 1965-67; Ambassador to Italy, 1967-70. Hon. Colonel, Royal South Australia Regt, 1977-. L'Ordre royal du Lion (Belgium), 1945; Cavaliere di Gr. Croce dell'Ordine al Merito (Italy), 1970; Order of Malta, 1975. *Publications:* The Japanese Population Problem, 1931; Nigeria, 1936; On Governing Colonies, 1946; Self-Government for the Colonies, 1949; Can the United Nations Succeed?, 1951; The Race Question as a factor in International Relations, 1955; Nehru, 1965; Australian Ambassador, 1971. *Recreations:* gardening, walking, music; previously ski-ing, tennis. *Address:* Government House, Adelaide, South Australia. *Clubs:* United Oxford & Cambridge University, Reform; Adelaide.

CROCKFORD, Brig. Allen Lepard, CBE 1955 (OBE 1945); DSO 1943; MC 1916; TD 1942; late Hon. Colonel RAMC 54 and 56 Division (TA); *b* 11 Sept. 1897; *s* of late J. A. V. Crockford, West Worthing, Sussex; *m* 1924, Doris Ellen Brookes-Smith; one *s* two *d. Educ:* Gresham's Sch.; King's Coll., Cambridge; St Thomas's Hosp. Glos Regt, BEF (Capt.; wounded), 1915-19. BA Cantab, 1920; MA 1926; MB, BCh Cantab, 1922; Gen. Practice, 1924-39; RAMC (TA): served with 43rd, Guards Armoured, 46th and 56th Divs, BNAF and CMF (Col), 1939-45; Gen. Practice, 1945-46; Medical Sec., St Thomas's Hosp. Medical Sch., London, SE1, 1946-64. Col (TA), ADMS, 56 Armoured Div., 1947; Brig. (TA); DDMS AA Comd, 1949; KHS 1952; QHS 1952-57; OStJ 1954. *Recreations:* reading, gardening. *Address:* Holly Cottage, Humshaugh, Hexham, Northumberland NE46 4AG. *T:* Hexham 81298. *Club:* Royal Ocean Racing.

CROFT, family name of **Baron Croft.**

CROFT, 2nd Baron *cr* 1940, of Bournemouth; **Michael Henry Glendower Page Croft;** Bt 1924; *b* 20 Aug. 1916; *s* of 1st Baron Croft, PC, CMG, and Hon. Nancy Beatrice Borwick (*d* 1949), *y d* of 1st Baron Borwick; *S* father, 1947; *m* 1948, Lady Antoinette Fredericka Conyngham (*d* 1959), *o d* of 6th Marquess Conyngham; one *s* one *d. Educ:* Eton; Trinity Hall, Cambridge (BA). Served War of 1939-45, Capt. RASC. Called to the Bar, Inner Temple, 1952. Director: Henry Page & Co. Ltd, 1946-57; Ware Properties Ltd, 1958-65. Mem. Exec. Cttee, Contemporary Arts Soc., 1960-68 and 1970- (Hon. Sec., 1971-76, Hon. Treasurer, 1976-). FRSA. OStJ. *Heir:* s Hon. Bernard William Henry Page Croft [*b* 28 Aug. 1949. *Educ:* Stowe; Univ. of Wales, Cardiff. BScEcon]. *Address:* 8 Hereford Square, SW7; Croft Castle, near Leominster, Herefordshire. *Clubs:* Athenæum, Bath.

CROFT, Sir Bernard Hugh (Denman), 13th Bt *cr* 1671; *b* 24 Aug. 1903; *s* of Sir Hugh Matthew Fiennes Croft, 12th Bt, and Lucy Isabel, *e d* of Frederick Taylor, Terrible Vale, near Uralla, NSW; *S* father, 1954; *m* 1931, Helen Margaret, *d* of H. Weaver; three *s* two *d. Educ:* Armidale Sch., NSW. Rep. NSW Rugby Union in NZ, 1928. *Recreations:* football, tennis, golf. *Heir:* s Owen Glendower Croft [*b* 26 April 1932; *m* 1959, Sally, *d* of Dr T. M. Mansfield, Brisbane, Queensland; one *s* one *d*]. *Address:* Salisbury Court, Uralla, NSW 2358, Australia. *T:* Uralla 24.

CROFT, Ivor John; painter in oils; Head of Home Office Research Unit, since 1972; *b* 6 Jan. 1923; *s* of Oswald Croft and Doris (*née* Phillips). *Educ:* Westminster Sch.; Christ Church, Oxford (MA); Inst. of Education, Univ. of London (MA); LSE. Temp. jun. admin. officer, FO, 1942-45; asst teacher, LCC, 1949-51; Inspector, Home Office Children's Dept, 1952-66; Sen. Research Officer, Home Office Research Unit, 1966-72. Governor, ILEA Secondary Schs, 1959-68. Mem. Exec. Cttee, English Assoc., 1966-77 (Hon. Treas. 1972-75). Group shows, 1958, 1963, 1967, 1968, 1969, 1973; one-man shows, 1970, 1971. *Publications:* contrib. various learned jls. *Clubs:* Athenæum, Reform.

CROFT, (John) Michael, OBE 1971; Director, National Youth Theatre, since 1956; *b* 8 March 1922. *Educ:* Plymouth Grove Elem. Sch. and Burnage Gram. Sch., Manchester; Keble Coll.,

Oxford (BA Hons). War Service in RAF and RN, 1940-45. After short career as actor, took up teaching, 1949; Asst English Master, Alleyn's Sch., 1950-55 (prod. series of Shakespeare plays with large schoolboy cos); founded Youth Theatre with group from Alleyn's Sch., 1956; this grew rapidly into nat. organisation with provincial branches; rep. Gt Brit. at Paris Festival, 1960 and W Berlin Festival, 1961; appeared at Old Vic, 1965. Also Dir Shakespeare for leading cos in Belgium and Holland, 1960-65; founded Dolphin Theatre Co., Shaw Theatre, 1971; productions include: Devil's Disciple, 1971; Romeo and Juliet, 1972; Nat. Youth Theatre Productions include: Zigger Zagger, Strand, 1968, Berlin Festival, 1968, Holland Festival, 1970; Little Malcolm and his Struggle, Holland Festival, 1968; Fuzz, Berlin Festival, 1970. *Publications:* (novel) Spare the Rod, 1954; (travel book) Red Carpet to China, 1958. *Recreations:* sport, travel. *Address:* 74 Bartholomew Road, NW5. *Club:* Savile.

CROFT, Sir John William Graham, 4th Bt *cr* 1818; Lieutenant late RHA; *b* 30 May 1910; *s* of late William Graham Croft, 4th *s* of 2nd Bt, and Marjorie, *d* of late Rev. T. G. S. Hall; *S* uncle, 1930. *Educ:* Stowe. Heir: cousin Major John Archibald Radcliffe Croft [*b* 27 March 1910; *m* 1953, Lucy Elizabeth Jupp; one *s*]. *Address:* Rayham Farm, Whitstable, Kent CT5 3DZ.

CROFT, Michael; *see* Croft, J. M.

CROFT, Col Noel Andrew Cotton, DSO 1945; OBE 1970; MA Oxon; Essex Regiment; retired; *b* 30 Nov. 1906; *s* of late Rev. Canon R. W. Croft, MA; *m* 1952, Rosalind, 2nd *d* of late Comdr A. H. de Kantzow, DSO, RN; three *d. Educ:* Lancing Coll.; Stowe Sch.; Christ Church, Oxford; Sch. of Technology, Manchester. Cotton Trade, 1929-32; Mem. British Trans-Greenland Expedition, 1933-34; ADC to Maharajah of Cooch Behar, India, 1934-35; Second-in-Command, Oxford Univ. Arctic Expedition to North-East Land, 1935-36; Ethnological Exped. to Swedish Lapland, 1937-38; Sec. to Dir of Fitzwilliam Museum, Cambridge, 1937-39. Served War of 1939-45, Capt. 1939; WO Mission to Finno-Russian War, 1939-40; Bde Intelligence Officer Independent Companies, Norwegian Campaign, 1940; Combined Ops, 1940-41; Major, 1941; Asst Mil. Attaché, Stockholm, 1941-42; sea or parachute ops in Tunisia, Corsica, Italy, France, and Denmark, 1943-45; Lieut-Col 1945; Asst Dir Scientific Research, War Office, 1945-49; WO Observer on Canadian Arctic Exercise "Musk-Ox", 1945-46, and on NW Frontier Trials, India, 1946-47; attached Canadian Army, 1947-48. GSO1, War Office, 1949-51; Liaison Officer HQ Continental Army, USA, 1952-54; comd The Infantry Junior Leaders Bn, 1954-57; Comdt Army Apprentices Sch., Harrogate, 1957-60; Comdt, Metropolitan Police Cadet Corps, 1960-71. Chm., Women's Transport Service (FANY). Corresp. Fellow, Arctic Inst. of North America; Chm., Reindeer Council of UK. Polar Medal (clasp Arctic, 1935-36), 1942; Back Award, RGS, 1946. *Publications:* (with A. R. Glen) Under the Pole Star, 1937; Polar Exploration, 1939. *Recreations:* mountaineering, ski-ing, sailing, photography. *Address:* River House, Strand-on-the-Green, W4. *T:* 01-994 6359. *Clubs:* Alpine, Hurlingham, Special Forces.

CROFT, Roy Henry Francis; Under Secretary, Finance and Economic Appraisal Division, Department of Industry, since 1976; *b* 4 March 1936; *s* of late William Henry Croft and Dorothy Croft; *m* 1961, Patricia Ainley; one *s* two *d . Educ:* Isleworth Grammar Sch.; Christ's Coll., Cambridge (MA). BoT, 1959; Treasury, 1961-62; DEA, 1964-67; Private Sec. to Pres. Bd of Trade, 1967-70; Cabinet Office, 1970-72; Civil Aviation Div., Dept of Trade, 1973-76. *Address:* Abell House, John Islip Street, SW1P 4LN. *T:* 01-211 6473.

CROFT, Stanley Edward, TD 1951; Associate, Abbey Life Assurance Company; formerly HM Diplomatic Service; *b* 18 Oct. 1917; *s* of Edward John and Alice Lucy Croft; *m* 1950, Joan Mary Kaye; four *s* two *d. Educ:* Portsmouth Grammar School. TA, 1939; served War of 1939-45, RA, Middle East, Aden, Italy, Germany. Min. of Labour, 1935; Admty, 1937-39 and 1946-47; transf. to Diplomatic Service, 1947; Vice-Consul, Barcelona, 1950; 2nd Sec., Lahore, 1951; Washington, 1955; Madrid, 1956; 1st Sec., FO, 1960; Consul, Geneva, 1961; FO and CRO, 1965-70; Consul-Gen., Madrid, 1970; Counsellor and Consul-Gen., Luanda, 1974-77. *Recreations:* swimming, tennis, camping, fishing, carpentry. *Address:* South Lodge, Ruxbury Road, Chertsey, Surrey. *Club:* Royal Commonwealth Society.

CROFT-COOKE, Rupert, BEM (mil.); novelist, playwright, biographer, writer of books on travel, food and wine, circus, gypsies; *b* Edenbridge, Kent, 20 June 1903; *s* of late Hubert Bruce Cooke, London Stock Exchange, and late Lucy, *d* of Dr Alfred Taylor. *Educ:* Tonbridge Sch.; Wellington Coll., Salop (now Wrekin Coll.). Founded and edited weekly, La Estrella,

Argentina, 1923-24; antiquarian bookseller, 1929-31; Lecturer in English Institute Montana, Zugerberg, Switzerland, 1931, etc. Joined Intelligence Corps, 1940; served Madagascar campaign (BEM (mil.)), 1942; commnd 3rd (Queen Alexandra's Own) Gurkha Rifles, 1943; Capt. (Field Security Officer) Poona Dist, 1944; Instr, Intell. Sch., Karachi, 1945; FSO, Delhi Dist, 1945-46. Book Critic, The Sketch, 1947-53. *Publications:* four early books of poems; Twenty Poems from the Spanish of Becquer, 1926; Some Poems, 1929; Troubadour, 1930; Banquo's Chair (play), 1930; Give him the Earth, 1930; Tap Three Times (play), 1931; Night Out, 1932; Cosmopolis, 1932; Release the Lions, 1933; Picaro, 1934; Shoulder the Sky, 1934; Deliberate Accident (play), 1934; Blind Gunner, 1935; Crusade, 1936; God in Ruins, 1936; Kingdom Come, 1937; The World is Young, 1937; Rule, Britannia, 1938; Darts, 1938; Pharaoh with his Wagons, 1938; How to get more out of Life, 1938; Same Way Home, 1939; Major Road Ahead (ed), 1939; Glorious, 1940; Octopus, 1946; Ladies Gay, 1946; The Circus Book (ed), 1947; Rudyard Kipling (English Novelists Series), 1948; Wilkie, 1948; Brass Farthing, 1950; Three Names for Nicholas, 1951; Cities, 1951; The Sawdust Ring, 1951; Nine Days with Edward, 1952; Harvest Moon, 1953; A Few Gypsies, 1955; Fall of Man, 1955; Sherry, 1955; Seven Thunders, 1956 (film, 1957); Port, 1957; Barbary Night, 1958; Smiling Damned Villain; Thief, 1960; English Cooking; Madeira, 1961; Wine and Other Drinks, 1962; Bosie, 1963; Clash by Night (film), 1963; Paper Albatross, 1965; The Gorgeous East, 1965; Feasting with Panthers, 1967; The Ghost of June, 1968; The Sound of Revelry, 1969; Wolf from the Door, 1969; Exotic Food, 1969; Exiles, 1970; Under the Rose Garden, 1971; While the Iron's Hot, 1971; The Unrecorded Life of Oscar Wilde, 1972; Nasty Piece of Work, 1973; autobiographical series, The Sensual World: The Man in Europe Street, 1939; The Circus has no Home, 1940; The Moon in My Pocket, 1948; The Life for Me, 1953; The Blood-Red Island, 1953; The Verdict of You All, 1955; The Tangerine House, 1956; The Gardens of Camelot, 1958; The Quest for Quixote, 1959; The Altar in the Loft, 1960; The Drums of Morning, 1961; The Glittering Pastures, 1962; The Numbers Came, 1963; The Last of Spring; The Wintry Sea, 1964; The Purple Streak, 1966; The Wild Hills, 1966; The Happy Highways, 1967; The Licentious Soldiery, 1971; The Dogs of Peace, 1973; The Caves of Hercules, 1974; The Long Way Home, 1975; The Green Green Grass, 1977. *Address:* c/o Grindlay's Bank Ltd, 13 St James's Square, SW1Y 4LF.

CROFT-MURRAY, Edward, CBE 1966; Keeper, Department of Prints and Drawings, British Museum, 1954-72; *b* Chichester, 1 Sept. 1907; *s* of Bernard Croft-Murray; *m* 1960, Rosemary Jill Whitford-Hawkey; one *d. Educ:* Lancing Coll.; Magdalen Coll., Oxford. Asst Keeper, Dept of Prints and Drawings, Brit. Museum, 1933; Dep. Keeper, 1953. Served War, 1939-46: Admiralty, 1939-40; Civilian Officer, Military Intelligence, War Office, 1940-43; Major, Allied Control Commission (Monuments and Fine Arts Section), Italy and Austria, 1943-46. Trustee, Cecil Higgins Museum, Bedford; Member: (Rep. Oxford Univ.), Brit. Instn Fund; Council for Places of Worship; Whitworth Art Gall., Manchester; Benton Fletcher Collection, Fenton Hse (Nat. Trust); Musicians' Union; Painter-Stainers' Co., 1971. Advisor on Musical Instruments to Messrs Christie. FSA 1940. *Publications:* Venetian Drawings of the XVII and XVIII Centuries, at Windsor Castle (with Sir Anthony Blunt), 1957; Catalogue of British Drawings in the British Museum, Vol. I (with Paul Hulton), 1960; Decorative Painting in England, 1537-1837, Vol. I, 1962, Vol. II, 1971; papers in Archaeologia, Apollo, Burlington Magazine, Country Life and Walpole Society. *Recreations:* music (especially that of the XVIIIth and early XIXth century); study of wall-painting in England. *Address:* 4 Maids of Honour Row, Richmond Green, Surrey. *T:* 01-940 2548; Croft Castle, near Leominster, Herefordshire. *Clubs:* Athenæum, Beefsteak.

CROFTON, family name of Baron Crofton.

CROFTON, 6th Baron *cr* 1797; **Charles Edward Piers Crofton;** Bt 1758; *b* 27 April 1949; *s* of 5th Baron Crofton and of Ann, *e d* of Group Captain Charles Tighe, Ballina Park, Co. Wicklow; *S* father, 1974; *m* 1976, Maureen Jacqueline, *d* of S. J. Bray, Taunton, Somerset. Heir: *b* Hon. Guy Patrick Gilbert Crofton [*b* 17 June 1951; commissioned 9/12 Royal Lancers, 1971]. *Address:* 132 Lathom Road, E6.

CROFTON, Denis Hayes, OBE 1948 (MBE 1943); retired Home and Indian Civil Servant; Member, Panel of Inspectors, Department of the Environment, since 1969; Chairman, Tunbridge Wells and District Branch, Civil Service Retirement Fellowship, since 1972; *b* 14 Dec. 1908; *s* of late Richard Hayes Crofton, Colonial Civil Service and Mabel Annie Crofton (*née* Smith); *m* 1933, Alison Carr, *d* of late Andrew McClure and

Ethel McClure; three *s* one *d. Educ:* Tonbridge Sch.; Corpus Christi Coll., Oxford (Class. Mods, Lit. Hum., MA). Indian Civil Service, 1932; served in Bihar; subdivisional Magistrate, Giridih, 1934, Jamshedpur, 1935; Under-Sec. to Govt of Bihar, Polit. and Appt Depts, 1936; Under-Sec. to Govt of India, Dept of Labour, 1939; Private Sec. to Indian Mem., Eastern Gp Supply Council, 1941; Dist Mag. and Collector, Shahabad, Bihar, 1942; Sec. to Gov. of Bihar, 1944; apptd to Home Civil Service, 1947; Principal, Min. of Fuel and Power, Petroleum Div. 1948; Asst Sec., Petroleum Div. and Chm., OEEC Oil Cttee, Paris, 1950-53; Asst Sec., Monopolies and Restrictive Practices Commn, 1953; Asst Sec., Min. of Fuel and Power, Electricity Div., 1956; Petroleum Div., 1961; Accountant General and Under-Secretary for Finance, 1962-68. *Recreations:* reading, gardening. *Address:* Tile Barn House, 147 Hadlow Road, Tonbridge, Kent. *T:* Tonbridge 353445. *Club:* Royal Commonwealth Society.

CROFTON, Sir John Wenman, Kt 1977; retired; Professor of Respiratory Diseases and Tuberculosis, University of Edinburgh, 1952-77; *b* 1912; *s* of Dr W. M. Crofton; *m* 1945, Eileen Chris Mercer; two *s* three *d. Educ:* Tonbridge; Sidney Sussex Coll., Cambridge; St Thomas's Hosp. Medical qualification, 1936; War of 1939-45, RAMC; France, Middle East, Germany. Lecturer in Medicine, Postgraduate Medical Sch. of London, 1947-51, Senior Lecturer, 1951; Part-time Tuberculosis Unit, Medical Research Council, Brompton Hosp., 1947-50; Dean of Faculty of Medicine, 1964-66, and Vice-Principal, 1969-70, Univ. of Edinburgh. Vice-Pres., 1972-73, Pres., 1973-76, RCPE. Weber-Parkes Prize, RCP, 1966. *Publications:* (jt author) Respiratory Diseases, 1969, 2nd edn 1975; contributor to BMJ, Lancet, Thorax, etc. *Recreations:* conversation, family life, mountains. *Address:* 7 Pentland Avenue, Colinton, Edinburgh EH13 0HZ. *T:* 031-441 3730. *Club:* University Staff (Edinburgh).

CROFTON, Sir Malby (Sturges), 5th Bt *cr* 1838 (orig. *cr* 1661); Partner, Messrs Fenn & Crosthwaite; Member of the London Stock Exchange, 1957-75; *b* 11 Jan. 1923; *s* of Sir Malby Richard Henry Crofton, 4th Bt, DSO and Bar, and Katharine Beatrix Pollard; *S* father, 1962. *Educ:* Eton (King's Scholar); Trinity Coll., Cambridge (scholar). Served with Life Guards, 1942-46, in Middle East and Italy. Member: Kensington Borough Council, 1962, Leader, 1968-; GLC, 1970-73; ILEA, 1970-73; Ealing N, GLC, 1977-; Leader, GLC Scrutiny Cttee, 1977-. *Recreations:* tennis, swimming, motoring, planting trees, farming. *Heir:* kinsman Henry Edward Melville Crofton [*b* 15 Aug. 1931; *m* 1955, Brigid, twin *d* of Gerald K. Riddle; two *s* one *d*]. *Address:* 17 Launceston Place, W8; Longford House, Co. Sligo, Eire.

CROFTON, Sir Patrick Simon, 7th Bt *cr* 1801; *b* 2 Dec. 1936; *o s* of Major Morgan G. Crofton (*d* 1947); *S* grandfather, 1958; *m* 1967, Mrs Lene Eddowes, *d* of Kai Augustinus, Copenhagen, and Mrs R. Tonnesen, Port Elizabeth, SA; one *d. Educ:* Eton Coll. 2nd Lieut Welsh Guards, 1955-57. Entered Steel Industry, 1957; became Public Relations Consultant, 1961. Joint Managing Dir, Crofton Mohill Holdings Ltd; Dir, Blair Eames Suslak, Sir Patrick Crofton Ltd, Advertising Agents; Managing Dir, Sir Patrick Crofton Developments Ltd. *Recreations:* skiing, motoring, music, political argument. *Heir:* uncle Hugh Denis Crofton, *b* 10 April 1937. *Clubs:* Cavalry and Guards, East India, Devonshire, Sports and Public Schools.

CROKER, Edgar Alfred; Secretary and Chief Executive of the Football Association, since 1973; *b* 13 Feb. 1924; *m* 1952, Kathleen Mullins; one *s* two *d. Educ:* Kingston Technical Coll. Served War: Flt Lieut, RAF, 1942-46. Flt Lieut, RAFVR, 1947-55. Professional footballer: Charlton Athletic, 1947-51; Headington United, 1951-56. Sales Dir, Douglas Equipment, 1956-61; Chairman and Managing Dir, Liner-Croker Ltd, 1961-73; Chairman, Liner Concrete Machinery Co. Ltd, 1971-73. King's commendation for brave conduct, 1946. *Recreations:* golf, tennis, soccer, bridge, squash. *Address:* South Court, The Park, Cheltenham, Glos. *T:* Cheltenham 27618. *Clubs:* Sportsman; New (Cheltenham).

CROLL, Hon. David Arnold, QC; BA, LLB; Senator; *b* Moscow, 12 March 1900; *s* of Hillel and Minnie Croll; *m* 1925, Sarah Levin; three *d. Educ:* public schs and Patterson Collegiate Institute, Windsor; Osgoode Hall, Toronto; University of Toronto. Emigrated to Canada with family, 1906, settling at Windsor, Ont; first and only commercial venture operation of news-stand, which greatly facilitated secondary education; after high school and course articled to solicitor; graduation from Osgoode Hall law sch. followed by practice at Windsor, 1925-30; presently senior partner in Croll and Croll, Windsor, Ont., and Croll and Godfrey, Toronto, Ont. Mayor of Windsor, Ont., 1930-34, 1939-40; Mem. for Windsor-Walkerville, Ont.

Legislature, 1934-44; late Minister of Labour, Public Welfare and Municipal Affairs for the Province of Ont.; was youngest and first Jewish Cabinet Minister and first Jewish Senator, in Canada. Mem. of House of Commons for Toronto Spadina, 1945-55 when appointed to Senate. Served War of 1939-45, with Canadian Army overseas, enlisting as Private in Sept. 1939 and discharged in rank of Col in Sept. 1945. *Recreations:* golf and the more strenuous sports. *Address:* Toronto-Dominion Centre, Box 192, Suite 3503, Toronto, Ont, Canada M5K 1H6. *Club:* Primrose (Toronto).

CROLY, Brig. Henry Gray, CBE 1958; JP; Secretary, Wolfenden Committee on Voluntary Organisations, since 1974; *b* 7 June 1910; *s* of late Lt-Col W. Croly, DSO, late RAMC, Ardvarna, Tralee; *m* 1939, Marjorie Rosanne, *er d* of late Major J. S. Knyvett, late R Warwickshire Regt, Clifford Manor Road, Guildford; two *s* two *d. Educ:* Sherborne Sch.; RMA Woolwich. 2nd Lieut RA, 1930; served in India: Mohmand Ops, 1935; Waziristan, 1936-37 (despatches); served War of 1939-45, mostly India and Burma; GSO1, British Mil. Mission to France, 1946-47; 2nd-in-Comd 26 Medium Regt RA, 1947-48; jssc 1949; GSO1, WO, 1950-51; Col GS, SHAPE, 1952; OC 26 Field Regt Suez Canal Zone, 1953-55; Dep. Sec., Chiefs of Staff Cttee, 1955-58; UK Nat. Mil. Rep. to SHAPE, 1959-61; retd 1962. Sec., Health Visitor Trng Council and Council for Trng in Social Work, 1963-66; Asst Sec. of Commns, Lord Chancellor's Office, 1966-74. JP Surrey, 1968. *Recreations:* golf, gardening, reading. *Address:* Heatherwood, Lower Bourne, Farnham, Surrey. *T:* Farnham 4851. *Clubs:* Army and Navy, MCC; Hankley Common Golf.

CROMARTIE, 4th Earl of *cr* 1861; **Roderick Grant Francis Mackenzie,** MC 1945; TD 1964; JP; DL; CC; Major Seaforth Highlanders, retired; Viscount Tarbat of Tarbat, Baron Castlehaven and Baron MacLeod of Leod, *cr* 1861; *b* 24 Oct. 1904; *er* surv. *s* of Lt-Col Edward Walter Blunt-Mackenzie, DL (*d* 1949) and Countess of Cromartie, (3rd in line); *S* mother, 1962, having discontinued use of surname of Blunt, for himself and son, and reverted to Mackenzie; *m* 1st, 1933, Mrs Dorothy Downing Porter (marr. diss. 1945), *d* of Mr Downing, Kentucky, USA; two *d*; 2nd, 1947, Olga (Mendoza) (marr. diss. 1962), *d* of late Stuart Laurance, Paris; one *s*; 3rd, 1962, Lilias Richard, MB, ChB, *d* of Prof. (James) Walter MacLeod, *qv. Educ:* Charterhouse; RMC Sandhurst. Commissioned to 1st Bn Seaforth Highlanders in Ireland, 1924; transferred to 2nd Bn Seaforth Highlanders, in India, 1925; seconded to Nigeria Regt of RWAFF, 1928-29; rejoined 2nd Seaforth Highlanders, 1930; Operations North-West Frontier, India, 1930-31; in France in 1940 with 4th Seaforth Highlanders (MC). Sec., Scottish Peers Assoc., House of Lords. JP Ross and Cromarty, 1937, DL Ross and Cromarty, 1976; CC Ross and Cromarty, 1963-77 (Vice-Convener, 1970-71, Convener, 1971-75); Hon. Sheriff (formerly Hon. Sheriff Substitute); Convener, Ross and Cromarty District Council, 1975-77. FSAScot. *Heir: s* Viscount Tarbat, *qv. Address:* Castle Leod, Strathpeffer, Ross and Cromarty, Scotland. *Clubs:* Army and Navy, Pratt's.

CROMARTIE, (Ronald) Ian (Talbot); HM Diplomatic Service; Counsellor, British Embassy, Bonn, since 1972; *b* 27 Feb. 1929; *s* of late Ronald Duncan Cromartie and of Mrs Margaret Talbot Cromartie; *m* 1962, Jennifer Frances, *er d* of late Captain Ewen Fairfax-Lucy and Mrs Margaret Fairfax-Lucy; two *s* one *d. Educ:* Sherborne; Clare Coll., Cambridge (MA, PhD). Scientific research at Univs of Cambridge and Tübingen, 1950-58; Univ. Demonstrator in Organic Chemistry, Cambridge, 1958-60. Entered Foreign (later Diplomatic) Service, 1961; served in: FO, 1961-62; Saigon, 1962-64; FO, 1964-67; UK Disarmament Delegn, Geneva, 1967-69; FCO, 1969-72. *Publications:* papers in Jl of Chem. Soc. and other scientific periodicals. *Recreations:* walking, sailing, shooting. *Address:* British Embassy, Bonn, BFPO 19; 61 Ashley Gardens, SW1. *Club:* United Oxford & Cambridge University.

CROMBIE, Alistair Cameron, MA, BSc, PhD; Fellow of Trinity College, Oxford, since 1969; Lecturer in History of Science, University of Oxford, since 1953; *b* 4 Nov. 1915; 2nd *s* of William David Crombie and Janet Wilamina (*née* Macdonald); *m* 1943, Nancy Hey; three *s* one *d* (and one *s* decd). *Educ:* Geelong Grammar Sch.; Trinity Coll., Melbourne Univ.; Jesus Coll., Cambridge. Zoological Lab., Cambridge, 1941-46; Lectr in History and Philosophy of Science, University Coll., London, 1946-53, nominated Reader, resigned; Technischen Hochschule, Aachen, 1948; Vis. Prof., Univ. of Washington, 1953-54; All Souls Coll., Oxford, 1954-69; Princeton Univ., 1959-60; Council of Science Museum, London, 1962-66; Guest Vis., Australian Univs, 1963; Brit. Nat. Cttee for History of Science, 1963-69; Visiting Professor: Tokyo Univ. (guest of Japan Soc. for Promotion of Sci.), 1976; All-India Inst. of Med. Scis, and guest of Indian Nat. Sci. Acad., 1976. Editor: Brit. Jl Philos. Sci., 1949-54; Hist. Sci., 1961-; Dir, Oxford Univ. Symp. Hist. Sci., 1961; Pres., Brit. Soc. Hist. Sci., 1964-66; Pres., Internat. Acad. Hist. Sci., 1968-71; Member: Internat. Acad. Hist. Med.; Academia Leopoldina; FRHistS. Galileo Prize, 1969. *Publications:* Augustine to Galileo, 1952, 3rd edn 1970; Robert Grosseteste and the Origins of Experimental Science, 1953, 3rd edn 1971; Scientific Change, 1963; The Mechanistic Hypothesis and the Scientific Study of Vision, 1967; contrib. Annals of Sci., Brit. Jl Hist. Sci., EHR, Isis, Jl Animal Ecol., Physis, Proc. Royal Soc. Lond., Rev. de Synthèse, TLS, Dict. Sci. Biogr., Encyc. Brit., New Cambridge Modern Hist., etc. *Recreations:* literature, travel, landscape gardening. *Address:* Orchard Lea, Boars Hill, Oxford. *T:* Oxford 735692. *Clubs:* Athenæum, Brooks's.

CROMBIE, Prof. Leslie, FRS 1973; FRIC; Sir Jesse Boot Professor of Organic Chemistry, University of Nottingham, since 1969; *b* 10 June 1923; *s* of Walter Leslie Crombie and Gladys May Crombie (*née* Clarkson); *m* 1953 Winifred Mary Lovell Wood; two *s* two *d*. *Educ:* King's Coll., London. PhD. DSc. Admiralty Chemical Lab., Portsmouth Naval Dockyard, 1941-46. Lectr, Imperial Coll., London, SW7, 1950-58; Reader in Organic Chemistry, King's Coll., London Univ., 1958-63; Prof. of Organic Chemistry, University Coll. (Univ. of Wales), Cardiff, 1963-69. Tilden Lectr, Chem. Soc., 1970; Simonsen Lectr, 1975; Hugo Muller Lectr, 1977; Pres., Perkin Div. of Chem. Soc., 1976-78. *Publications:* many original papers in learned chemical jls, especially those of Chem. Soc., London. *Recreation:* gardening. *Address:* 153 Hillside Road, Bramcote, Beeston, Nottingham. *T:* 259412. *Club:* Athenæum.

CROMER, 3rd Earl of, *cr* 1901; **George Rowland Stanley Baring;** Viscount, *cr* 1898; Baron, *cr* 1892; KG 1977; PC 1966; GCMG 1974 (KCMG 1971); MBE (Mil) 1945; Adviser to Baring Brothers & Co. Ltd; Chairman: London Multinational Bank Ltd; IBM (UK) Ltd; Director: Shell Transport & Trading Co. Ltd; P & O Steam Navigation Co. Ltd; Imperial Group Ltd; Compagnie Financière de Suez; *b* 28 July 1918 (known as Viscount Errington) (King George V stood sponsor); *os* of 2nd Earl of Cromer, PC, GCB, GCIE, GCVO, and Lady Ruby Elliot, 2nd *d* of 4th Earl of Minto; *S* father, 1953; *m* 1942, Hon. Esmé Harmsworth, 2nd *d* of Viscount Rothermere, *qv*; two *s* (one *d* decd). *Educ:* Eton; Trinity Coll., Cambridge. Page of Honour to King George V, 1931-35; to Queen Mary at Coronation, 1937. Private Sec. to Marquess of Willingdon representing HM Govt on missions to: Argentina, Uruguay and Brazil, 1938; New Zealand and Australia, 1940. Joined staff, Baring Brothers & Co. Ltd., 1938. Served War of 1939-45, Grenadier Guards; passed Staff Coll., Camberley; NW Europe (despatches, MBE); demobilised, 1945, Lt-Col. Rejoined Baring Brothers & Co. Ltd., 1945; sent on secondment to: J. P. Morgan & Co.; Kidder Peabody & Co.; Morgan Stanley & Co.; Chemical Bank (all of New York City); Man. Dir., Baring Brothers & Co. Ltd, 1948-61; Director: Daily Mail & General Trust Ltd; Anglo-Newfoundland Develt Co. Ltd; Royal Insurance Co. Ltd; Liverpool London & Globe Insurance Co. Ltd; Lewis Investment Trust Ltd; Harris & Partners Ltd (Toronto) (Hon. Chm., 1967-70). Mem., Inter-Parly Mission to Brazil, 1954; Econ. Minister and Head of UK Treasury and Supply Delegn, Washington, 1959-61; UK Exec. Dir, IMF, IBRD, IFC, 1959-61; Governor, Bank of England, 1961-66; Dir, Bank for International Settlements, Basle 1961-66; UK Governor: IBRD, IFC, IDA, 1963-66; Senior Partner and Man. Dir, Baring Brothers & Co. Ltd, 1967-70; Chm., IBM (UK) Ltd, 1967-70; Dir, Union Carbide Corpn (NY), 1967-70; Chairman: Accepting Houses Cttee, 1967-70; OECD High Level Cttee on Capital Movements, 1967-70. HM Ambassador, Washington, 1971-74. HM Lieutenant, City of London 1961-; Dep. Lieutenant, Kent, 1968-. Chm., Churchill Meml Trust; Dep Chm., The Queen's Silver Jubilee Appeal Council, 1977. Hon LLD New York Univ., 1966. *Heir: s* Viscount Errington, *qv*. *Address:* 88 Leadenhall Street, EC3A 3DT. *T:* 01-588 2830. *Clubs:* Brooks's, Beefsteak, MCC; Royal Yacht Squadron (Cowes), Brook (NY), Metropolitan (Washington).

CROMPTON, Air Cdre Roy Hartley, OBE 1962; Course Director, Home Defence College, Easingwold, York, since 1976; *b* 24 April 1921; *er s* of Frank and Ann Crompton, Bedford; *m* 1961, Rita Mabel Leslie; one *s* one *d*. *Educ:* Bedford Sch.; University Coll., London (BA Hons). MBIM. Flying Trng, S Africa, 1942; India and Burma, 1944-45; Air Min., 1946-48; Adjt No 604 Sqdn RAuxAF, 1949-51; psc 1952; Sqdn Comdr No 211 AFS, 1952-54; Dirg Staff OATS, 1954-56; PSO to C-in-C Fighter Comd, 1956-59; OC Flying No 5 FTS, 1959-61; jssc 1962; Chiefs of Staff Secretariat, 1962-64; Stn Comdr No 1 FTS, 1965-67; sowc 1967; Dep. Dir Defence Policy Staff, 1968-70; Gp Dir RAF Staff Coll., 1970; Project Officer, Nat. Defence Coll.,

1970-71; AOC and Comdt, Central Flying Sch., RAF, 1972-74. Dir of Studies, then Directing Staff, Home Defence Coll., York, 1974-76. *Publications:* contrib. RAF Quarterly. *Recreations:* cricket, tennis, golf, music, horticulture. *Address:* Sharnford Lodge, Huby, York YO6 1HT. *T:* Easingwold 810454. *Clubs:* Royal Air Force, MCC.

CROMPTON-INGLEFIELD, Col Sir John (Frederick), Kt 1963; TD; DL; Chairman, Inglefield Group of Companies; *b* 1904; *e s* of Adm. Sir F. S. Inglefield, KCB, DL; *m* 1926, Rosemary, *d* of Adm. Sir Percy Scott, 1st Bt, KCB, KCVO, LLD; three *d*. *Educ:* RN Colls Osborne and Dartmouth. Retired from Royal Navy, 1926. Derbyshire Yeomanry (Armoured Car Co.), Lieut 1936, Major 1939. Served War of 1939-45, with 1st Derbyshire Yeo. and 79th Armoured Div. (despatches) Africa and Europe. Lt-Col Comdg Derbyshire Yeo, 1950-53; Bt Col 1954; Hon. Col, Leics and Derbyshire Yeo., 1962-70. Chm. W Derbyshire Conservative and Unionist Assoc., 1951-66; Vice-Chm., 1957-64, Chm., TA, Derbyshire, 1964-69. CC 1932-55, JP 1933, DL 1953, and High Sheriff, 1938, Derbyshire. OStJ. *Recreation:* shooting. *Address:* 15 Beaufort Gardens, SW3. *T:* 01-589 0650. *Club:* Cavalry and Guards.

CROMWELL, 6th Baron *cr* 1375 (called out of abeyance 1923); **David Godfrey Bewicke-Copley;** Partner in Mullens & Co. since 1960; *b* 29 May 1929; *s* of 5th Baron Cromwell, DSO, MC, and of Lady Cromwell (Freda Constance, *d* of Sir F. W. B. Cripps, DSO); *S* father, 1966; *m* 1954, Vivian Penfold, *y d* of H. de L. Penfold, Isle of Man; two *s* two *d*. *Educ:* Eton; Magdalene Coll., Cambridge. Called to the Bar, Inner Temple, 1954. Mem. London Stock Exchange, 1956-; Second Govt Broker, 1973-. *Heir: s* Hon. Godfrey John Bewicke-Copley, *b* 4 March 1960. *Address:* The Manor House, Great Milton, Oxfordshire. *T:* Great Milton 230.

CRONIN, Archibald Joseph, MD (Glasgow), MRCP, DPH London; novelist; *b* 19 July 1896; *s* of Patrick Cronin and Jessie Montgomerie; *m* Agnes Mary Gibson, MB, ChB; three *s*. *Educ:* Glasgow Univ. Served European War, Surgeon Sub-Lieut, RNVR; graduated MB, ChB, with hons, 1919; Physician to Out-Patients Bellahouston War Pensions Hospital; Medical Superintendent Lightburn Hospital, Glasgow; general practice South Wales, 1921-24; Medical Inspector of Mines for Great Britain, 1924; MD (hons) 1925; Report on First-Aid Conditions in British Coal Mines, 1926, published by HM Stationery Dept, also Report on Dust Inhalation in Hæmatite Mines; practised medicine in London, 1926-30; in 1930 decided to give up medicine, follow natural bent and devote himself to literature; first novel, Hatter's Castle, published in 1931, was instantaneous success; first play, Jupiter Laughs, produced 1940. Hon. DLitt: Bowdoin Univ.; Lafayette Univ. *Publications:* Hatter's Castle, 1931; Three Loves, 1932; Grand Canary, 1933; The Stars Look Down, 1935; The Citadel, 1937; The Keys of the Kingdom, 1942; The Green Years, 1944; Shannon's Way, 1948; The Spanish Gardener, 1950; Adventures in Two Worlds, 1952; Beyond this Place, 1953; Crusader's Tomb, 1956; The Northern Light, 1958; The Judas Tree, 1961; A Song of Sixpence, 1964; A Pocketful of Rye, 1969; The Minstrel Boy, 1975; The Lady with Carnations, 1976; Creator of Dr Finlay's Casebook. *Recreations:* golf, tennis, gardening, fishing. *Address:* Champ-Riond, Baugy sur Clarens, Vaud, Switzerland. *Clubs:* Pilgrims, University, Links (New York).
See also V. A. P. Cronin.

CRONIN, John Desmond, FRCS; MP (Lab) Loughborough since 1955; Consultant Surgeon; *b* 1 March 1916; *s* of John Patrick Cronin and Beatrice Cronin (*née* Brooks); *m* 1941, Cora, *d* of Rowland Mumby-Croft; one *s* two *d*. *Educ:* London Univ. MRCS, LRCP 1939; MB, BS (London) 1940; FRCS 1947. House Surgeon, St Bartholomew's Hosp., 1939-40; Surgeon EMS, Royal Free Hosp., 1941-42. Served RAMC, 1942-46, France, Germany and Burma campaigns; Surgical Specialist, Major (Actg Lt-Col 1945). Asst Orthopædic Surgeon, Prince of Wales's Hosp., 1947-51; Orthopædic Surgeon, French Hosp., 1948-. Vice-Chm., North St Pancras Labour Party, 1950. Member LCC, 1952-55. Opposition Whip, House of Commons, 1959-62. Director: Racal Electronics Ltd, 1965-; Knight Wegenstein Ltd, 1969-70. Officier, Légion d'Honneur, 1967 (Chevalier, 1960). *Publications:* contributions to British Med. Journal and Proceedings Royal Soc. Medicine, and to the national press; Report on the Medical Services of Malta (pub. Central Office of Information, Govt of Malta). *Recreations:* yacht racing, shooting, riding, tennis, squash racquets, cooking. *Address:* 14 Wimpole Street, W1. *T:* 01-580 2460. *Club:* Hurlingham.

CRONIN, Vincent Archibald Patrick; author; *b* 24 May 1924; *s* of Archibald Joseph Cronin, *qv*; *m* 1949, Chantal, *d* of Comte

Jean de Rolland; two s three d. *Educ:* Ampleforth; Harvard; Trinity Coll., Oxford. Rifle Bde, 1943-45. *Publications:* The Golden Honeycomb, 1954; The Wise Man from the West, 1955; The Last Migration, 1957; A Pearl to India, 1959; The Letter after Z, 1960; Louis XIV, 1964; Four Women in Pursuit of an Ideal, 1965; The Florentine Renaissance, 1967; The Flowering of the Renaissance, 1970; Napoleon, 1971; Louis and Antoinette, 1974; trans., Giscard d'Estaing, Towards a New Democracy, 1977. *Address:* 44 Hyde Park Square; W2 2JT.

CRONNE, Prof. Henry Alfred; Professor of Medieval History in the University of Birmingham, 1946-70, now Emeritus Professor; Dean of the Faculty of Arts, 1952-55; *b* 17 Oct. 1904; *o c* of late Rev. James Kennedy Cronne, Portaferry, Co. Down, N Ireland; *m* 1936, Lilian Mey, *er d* of E. F. Seckler, Bishops Tawton, Barnstaple; one d. *Educ:* Campbell Coll., Belfast; Queen's Univ. of Belfast; Balliol Coll., Oxford; Inst. of Historical Research. MA Belfast; MA Oxon; MA Birmingham, *jure officii.* Asst Lecturer in History, QUB, 1928-31; Lecturer in Medieval History, King's Coll., London, 1931, and subsequently Lecturer in Palaeography and Reader in Medieval History. War of 1939-45, served in Home Guard and Somerset Special Constabulary. *Publications:* Bristol Charters, 1378-1499, 1946; (ed with Charles Johnson) Regesta Regum Anglo-Normannorum, Vol. II, 1100-1135, 1956, (ed with R. H. C. Davis), Vol. III, 1135-1154, 1968, and Vol. IV, Facsimiles and Diplomatic, 1135-54, 1969; The Reign of Stephen, 1970; contribs to historical jls. *Recreations:* writing, drawing. *Address:* Winswood Cottage, Cheldon, Chulmleigh, N Devon. *T:* Chulmleigh 567.

CROOK, family name of **Baron Crook.**

CROOK, 1st Baron *cr* 1947, of Carshalton, Surrey; **Reginald Douglas Crook;** Member, General Practice Finance Corporation, 1966-76; *b* 2 March 1901; *s* of Percy Edwin Crook; *m* 1922, Ida G. Haddon; one s. *Educ:* Strand Sch. Local Govt Service; Organising Sec. of Poor Law Officers' Union and Ed., Poor Law Gazette, 1920-24; Gen. Sec., Min. of Labour Staff Assoc., 1925-51, and Ed., Civil Service Argus, 1929-51; Sec., Fedn of Min. of Labour Staff, 1944-51; Mem., National Whitley Council for Civil Service, 1925-51; Mem., Min. of Labour Departmental Whitley Council, 1925-51; Hon. Sec., Labour Parliamentary Assoc., 1945-47; a Dep. Chm. of Cttees, House of Lords, 1949-75; Mem., Ecclesiastical Cttee of Parliament, 1949-75; Chm. of Interdeptl Cttee of Enquiry as to Optical Services, appointed by Min. of Health, 1949-52; Mem., Parl. Delegn to Denmark, 1949; Deleg. to Finland, 1950; Mem., Police Wages Council, 1951; Chm., National Dock Labour Board, 1951-65, also Chm., National Dock Labour Board (Nominees) Ltd and Chm., National Dock Labour Board Pensions Trustees Ltd; Delegate, United Nations General Assembly, 1950; Mem., United Nations Administrative Tribunal, 1951-71, Vice-Pres., 1952-71; Mem., UK Goodwill Mission to 350th Anniversary of Virginia, 1957; President: (also Fellow) Brit. Assoc. of Industrial Editors, 1953-61; Assoc. of Optical Practitioners, 1951- (Pres., 1959-); Cystic Fibrosis Research Foundation Trust; The Pre-Retirement Assoc.; Sutton Talking Newspaper, 1975-; Vice-Pres., Royal Soc. for the Prevention of Accidents; Vice-Pres. and Fellow, Inst. of Municipal Safety Officers. Member: Inst. of Neurology; London Electricity Board, 1967-72; Chm., London Electricity Consultative Council, 1967-72. Master, Worshipful Co. of Spectacle Makers, 1963-65; an Apothecary, 1951-, and Freeman, 1948-, of City of London. Warden, 1968, Senior Warden, 1971, Master, 1972, Guild of Freemen of City of London. JP Surrey. KStJ 1955. Mem. Chapter-Gen. of St John, 1957-. *Heir: s* Hon. Douglas Edwin Crook [*b* 19 Nov. 1926; *m* 1954, Ellenor Rouse; one s one d]. *Address:* Breedene, Princes Avenue, Carshalton, Surrey. *T:* 01-643 2620.

CROOK, Arthur Charles William; Consultant to Times Newspapers, since 1974; Editor, The Times Literary Supplement, 1959-74; *b* 16 Feb. 1912; *m* 1948, Sarita Mary Vivien Bushell (marr. diss.); one s two d. Editorial staff of The Times; Asst Editor, The Times Literary Supplement, 1951-59. *Recreation:* theatre. *Address:* 70 Regent's Park Road, NW1. *T:* 01-722 8446. *Club:* Garrick.

CROOK, Eric Ashley, FRCS; Consulting Surgeon; *b* 25 April 1894; *s* of Thomas Ashley and Emma Daisy Crook; *m* 1924, Elizabeth Grace Garratt; one s one d. *Educ:* Winchester; New Coll., Oxford (MA, MCh). FRCS 1922. Cons. Surgeon: Charing Cross Hosp., Gordon Hosp., Putney Hosp., Royal Masonic Hosp. Served European War, 1914-18, Surg. Lieut, RN. *Address:* Silver Mist, Harmans Cross, Swanage, Dorset. *See also* W. H. C. Frend.

CROOK, Dr Joseph Mordaunt; Reader in Architectural History, Bedford College, University of London, since 1975; *b* 27 Feb. 1937; *e s* of late Austin Mordaunt Crook and Irene Woolfenden; *m* 1st, 1964, Margaret, *o d* of late James Mulholland; 2nd, 1975, Susan, *o d* of late F. H. Mayor. *Educ:* Wimbledon Coll.; Brasenose Coll., Oxford. BA (1st cl. Mod. Hist.) 1958; DPhil 1961, MA 1962, Oxon; FSA 1972. Research Fellow: Inst. of Historical Res., 1961-62; Bedford Coll., London, 1962-63; Warburg Inst., London, 1970-71; Asst Lectr, Univ. of Leicester, 1963-65; Lectr, Bedford Coll., London, 1965-75. Member: Exec. Cttee, Soc. Architect. Historians of Gt Britain, 1964-; RIBA Drawings Cttee, 1969-75; Exec. Cttee, Georgian Gp, 1970-; Exec. Cttee, Victorian Soc., 1970-; Historic Buildings Council, DoE, 1974-. Editor, Architectural History, 1967-75; Adv. Editor, British Studies Monitor, 1974-. *Publications:* (contrib.) Concerning Architecture, 1967; The Greek Revival, 1968; (contrib.) The Country Seat, 1970; (ed) Eastlake, A History of the Gothic Revival, 1970; Victorian Architecture: A Visual Anthology, 1971; The British Museum, 1972; (contrib.) The Age of Neo Classicism, 1972; The Greek Revival: Neo-Classical Attitudes in British Architecture 1760-1870, 1972; (ed) Emmet, Six Essays, 1972; (ed) Kerr, The Gentleman's House, 1972; (jtly) The History of the King's Works, Vol. VI, 1782-1851, 1973 (Hitchcock Medallion, 1974); The Reform Club, 1973; (contrib.) The Building of Early America, 1976; (contrib.) Seven Victorian Architects, 1976; numerous articles in Architect. History, Architect. Review, Country Life, History Today, Jl Royal Soc. Arts, RIBA Jl, TLS, etc. *Recreation:* strolling. *Address:* 47 Kelly Street, NW1. *T:* 01-485 9012. *Club:* Reform.

CROOK, Kenneth Roy; HM Diplomatic Service; Ambassador to Afghanistan, since 1976; *b* 30 July 1920; *s* of Alexander Crook, Prescot, Lancs, and Margaret Kay Crook; *m* 1943, Freda Joan Vidler; two d. *Educ:* Prescot Grammar Sch., Lancs; Skerry's Coll., Liverpool. Appointed to: Board of Trade, 1937; Min. of War Transport, 1939. Royal Navy, 1941-46. Board of Trade, 1946-49; Commonwealth Relations Office, 1949; Second Sec., Canberra, 1951-54; First Sec., Madras, 1956-59; Deputy High Commissioner: Peshawar, W Pakistan, 1962-64; Dacca, E Pakistan, 1964-67; Counsellor, FCO, 1967; Head of Information Research Dept, FCO, 1969-71; Governor, Cayman Is, 1971-74; Canadian Nat. Defence Coll., 1974-75; Head of Science and Technology Dept, FCO, 1975-76. *Recreations:* walking, gardening, golf. *Address:* c/o Foreign and Commonwealth Office, SW1; 16 Burntwood Road, Sevenoaks, Kent. *T:* Sevenoaks 52774.

CROOK, Brig. Paul Edwin, CBE 1965 (OBE 1946); DSO 1957; Welfare Officer, Lincolnshire Police, since 1971; *b* 19 April 1915; *s* of late Herbert Crook and Christine Crook, Lyme Regis; *m* 1st, 1944, Joan (marr. diss. 1967), *d* of late William Lewis; one d; 2nd, 1967, Betty, *o d* of late John William Wyles. *Educ:* Uppingham Sch.; Emmanuel Coll., Cambridge. BA 1936, MA 1956. Commnd into QORWK Regt, 1935; served: India and Palestine, 1937-39; War of 1939-45, Africa, NW Europe, Burma; Chief Civil Affairs Officer (Col), Netherlands East Indies, 1946; comd 3rd Bn The Parachute Regt, 1954-57; Suez Ops, 1956; comd Army Airborne Trng and Develt Centre, 1959-62; Comdr and Chief of Staff, Jamaica Defence Force, 1962-65; Security Ops Advisor to High Comr for Aden and S Arabia, 1965-67; Comdr, Rhine Area, 1969-70. Col, 1959; Brig., 1963; retired 1971. ADC to The Queen, 1965. Hon. Col, 16 Ind. Co. Parachute Regt (VR), 1974-. Bronze Star (US), 1945. *Recreations:* cricket, golf, jazz. *Address:* The Old Chapel, Glentworth, Lincolnshire DN21 5DH. *T:* Hemswell 268. *Clubs:* Naval and Military; MCC; Jamaica (W Indies).

CROOKENDEN, Maj.-Gen. George Wayet Derek; Fellow and Senior Bursar, Peterhouse, Cambridge, since 1975; *b* 11 Dec. 1920; *o s* of Lt-Col John Crookenden and Iris Margherita Gay; *m* 1948, Elizabeth Mary Angela Bourke; one s one d. *Educ:* Winchester Coll.; Christ Church, Oxford. Commnd Royal Artillery, 1941. GSO1, SHAPE, 1961-62; CO, 19 Field Regt, RA, 1962-64; Comdr, 7 Artillery Bde, 1964-67; Exercise Controller, CICC (West), 1969-71; Chief, British Commanders-in-Chief Liaison Mission, 1971-72; C of S, Contingencies Planning, SHAPE, 1972-75. Col Comdt, RA, 1977-. *Address:* c/o Lloyds Bank Ltd, 95-97 Regent Street, Cambridge CB2 1BQ. *Club:* Army and Navy.

CROOKENDEN, Lt-Gen. Sir Napier, KCB 1970 (CB 1966); DSO 1945; OBE 1954; Lieutenant, HM Tower of London, since 1975; *b* 31 Aug. 1915; 2nd *s* of late Col Arthur Crookenden, CBE, DSO; *m* 1948, Patricia Nassau, *d* of 2nd Baron Kindersley, CBE, MC, and of Nancy Farnsworth, *d* of Dr Geoffrey Boyd; two s two d. *Educ:* Wellington Coll.; RMC, Sandhurst. Commissioned, Cheshire Regt, 1935; Bde Major, 6th Airlanding Bde, 1943-44; CO, 9th Bn, The Parachute Regt,

1944-46; GSO1 (Plans) to Dir of Ops, Malaya, 1952-54; Comdr, 16th Parachute Bde, 1960-61; idc 1962; Dir, Land/Air Warfare MoD (Army Dept), 1964-66; Commandant, RMCS, Shrivenham, 1967-69; GOC-in-C, Western Comd, 1969-72. Col, The Cheshire Regt, 1969-71; Col Comdt, The Prince of Wales Div., 1971-74. A Trustee, Imperial War Museum, 1973-. Chm., SS&AFA, 1974-. *Publication:* Dropzone Normandy, 1976. *Address:* Sissinghurst Place, Cranbrook, Kent TN17 2JP. *T:* Sissinghurst 263. *Clubs:* Army and Navy; Ski Club of Great Britain.

CROOKS, James, CVO 1958; FRCS; Hon. Consulting Ear, Nose and Throat Surgeon, The Hospital for Sick Children, Great Ormond Street; *b* 2 Oct. 1901; *s* of James amd Margaret Crooks, Loanhead, Midlothian; *m* 1st, 1931, Irene G. Heath (whom he divorced 1950); two *d*; 2nd, 1970, Caroline A. Woollcombe. *Educ:* University, Edinburgh; Royal Infirmary, Edinburgh; St Bartholomew's Hospital, London. MB, ChB, Edinburgh 1923; FRCS 1928. House Surgeon, Royal Infirmary, Edinburgh, 1924; House Physician, Casualty Officer, Resident Medical Supt, Surgical Registrar, The Hospital for Sick Children, 1924-31, Chm. Med. Cttee, 1950-53; Chm., Building Cttee, 1948-67. Kirk-Duncanson Research Scholar in USA, Vienna, Paris, Copenhagen, 1929-31; Fellow Royal Society of Medicine; Mem. Royal Medical Society Edinburgh; Hon. Mem. Brit. Paed. Assoc. *Publications:* The Ear, Nose and Throat in Garrod, Batten and Thursfield's Diseases of Children; Accessory Nasal Sinusitis in Childhood, 1936; Chronic Running Ear in Childhood, 1938; Tonsils and Adenoids: evaluation of removal in 50 Doctors' children; (with S. E. T. Cusdin) Suggestions and Demonstration Plans for Hospitals for Sick Children, 1947. *Recreations:* painting, sailing. *Address:* Meadow Farm, Ringshall, near Berkhamsted, Herts. *T:* Little Gaddesden 2295.

CROOKS, Air Vice-Marshal Lewis M.; *see* Mackenzie Crooks.

CROOKS, Very Rev. Samuel Bennett, TD 1964; SCF 1963; Dean of Belfast since 1970; *b* 20 Jan. 1920; 3rd *s* of Rev. S. B. Crooks, Rector of St Stephen's, Belfast; *m* 1945, Isabel Anne (*née* Kennedy), Belfast; one *s* one *d*. *Educ:* Down High Sch., Downpatrick, Co. Down; Trinity Coll. Dublin. BA 1943, MA 1947. Dean's Vicar, 1943-47, Vicar Choral, 1947-49, Minor Canon, 1952-61, Belfast Cathedral. Rector of St John's, Orangefield, Belfast, 1949-63; Rural Dean of Hillsborough, 1953-63; Rector of Lurgan, 1963-70; Archdeacon of Dromore, 1964-70. Chaplain to the Houses of Parliament, 1970-74. ChStJ 1976. *Address:* The Deanery, 5 Deramore Drive, Belfast BT9 5JQ. *T:* Belfast 660980.

CROOM, Sir John (Halliday), Kt 1975; TD 1946; FRCP, FRCPE; Chairman, Scottish Council for Postgraduate Medical Education, since 1974; *b* 2 July 1909; *s* of David Halliday Croom and Eleanor Addey Blair Cunynghame; *m* 1940, Enid Valerie Samuel, actress (known as Valerie Tudor); one *s* one *d*. *Educ:* Trinity Coll., Glenalmond; Gonville and Caius Coll., Cambridge; Univ. of Edinburgh. BA Cantab, MB, ChB Edin.; FRCPE 1940 (MRCPE 1936), FRCP 1972, FFCM 1972. Served War, RAMC (Lt-Col), France, ME, Malta, Italy, 1939-45 (despatches). Consultant Phys.: Royal Infirmary, Edinburgh, 1946-74; Chalmers Hosp., Edin., 1960-66. Royal Coll. of Phys., Edin.: Sec., Councillor and Vice-Pres., 1950-70; Pres., 1970-73. Principal MO, Standard Life Ass. Co., 1946-; Med. Adviser: Royal Bank of Scotland, 1965-; Northern Lighthouse Bd, 1952-; Hon. Cons. Phys. to Army in Scotland, 1970-75. Chairman: Scottish Cttee of Action on Smoking and Health, 1972-; Scientific Adv. Gp, 1975-, and Cancer Programme Planning Gp, 1976- of Planning Council, Scotland; Scottish Health Services Scientific Council, 1972-75; Chm., Edinburgh Crematorium Bd, 1972-. Has served on numerous NHS cttees. Hon. FRACP 1972; Hon. FACP 1973. *Publications:* several articles in sci. jls. *Recreations:* racing, fishing, golf. *Address:* 18 Succoth Avenue, Edinburgh EH12 6BU. *T:* 031-337 2033. *Clubs:* Army and Navy; New (Edinburgh); Hon. Company of Edinburgh Golfers.

CROOM-JOHNSON, Hon. Sir David Powell, Kt 1971; DSC 1944; VRD 1953; **Hon. Mr Justice Croom-Johnson;** Judge of Queen's Bench Division, High Court of Justice, since 1971; *b* 28 Nov. 1914; 3rd *s* of late Hon. Sir Reginald Powell Croom-Johnson, sometime a Judge of the High Court, and late Lady (Ruby) Croom-Johnson; *m* 1940, Barbara Douglas, *y d* of late Erskine Douglas Warren, Toronto; one *d*. *Educ:* The Hall, Hampstead; Stowe Sch.; Trinity Hall, Cambridge (MA). RNVR (London Div.) 1936-53; served with Royal Navy, 1939-46; Lt-Comdr RNR (retired). Called to Bar, Gray's Inn, 1938; Western Circuit; Master of the Bench, 1964; Member: Gen. Council of the Bar, 1958-62; Senate of Inns of Court, 1966-70. QC 1958; Recorder of Winchester, 1962-71; Judge of Courts of Appeal, Jersey and Guernsey, 1966-71. Vice-Chm., Home Office Cttee

on Mentally Abnormal Offenders, 1972-75. Mem., Council, Oakdene Sch., 1956-; Chm., Knightsbridge Assoc., 1965-71. *Recreations:* books, music. *Address:* Royal Courts of Justice, WC2. *Clubs:* Garrick, Royal Automobile.
See also H. P. Croom-Johnson.

CROOM-JOHNSON, Henry Powell, CMG 1964; CBE 1954 (OBE 1944); TD 1948; *b* 15 Dec. 1910; *e s* of late Hon. Sir Reginald Croom-Johnson, sometime Judge of High Court, and of late Lady (Ruby) Croom-Johnson; *m* 1947, Jane, *er d* of late Archibald George Mandry; two *s*. *Educ:* Stowe Sch.; Trinity Hall, Cambridge. Asst Master, Bedford Sch., 1932-34. Joined staff of British Council, 1935. Served with Queen's Westminsters and King's Royal Rifle Corps, 1939-46 (staff Sicily, Italy, Greece; Lt-Col). Rejoined British Council, 1946: Controller Finance Div., 1951; Controller European Div., 1956; Representative in India, 1957-64; Controller, Overseas Div. B, 1964; Asst Dir-Gen., 1966-72, retired 1973. *Recreations:* climbing, books, music. *Address:* 3a Ravenscourt Square, W6. *T:* 01-748 3677; The Cottage, Hillesden, Buckingham. *T:* Steeple Claydon 391. *Club:* Savile.
See also Sir D. P. Croom-Johnson.

CROOME, (John) Lewis, CMG 1957; *b* 10 June 1907; *s* of John and Caroline Croome; *m* 1st, 1931, Honoria Renée Minturn (*née* Scott; as Honor Croome, Editorial Staff of The Economist) (*d* 1960); four *s* one *d* (and one *s* decd); 2nd, 1961, Pamela Siola, *o d* of Lt-Col Tyrrel Hawker, Hurstbourne Priors, Hants; one *s*. *Educ:* Henry Thornton Sch., Clapham; London Sch. of Economics. Imperial Economic Cttee, 1931-39; Ministry of Food, 1939-48; Deputy (later Head), British Food Mission, Ottawa, 1942-46; HM Treasury (Central Economic Planning Staff), 1948-51; Min. of Food, 1951-54; UK Delegation to OEEC, Paris, 1954-57; Ministry of Agriculture, Fisheries and Food, 1957-58; Chief Overseas Relations Officer, UKAEA, 1958-72, retired. *Recreations:* painting, gardening. *Address:* Pearmain, Ruxley, Claygate, Surrey. *T:* Esher 62597.

CROOT, Sir (Horace) John, Kt 1965; CBE 1962; Member and Medical Chairman, Pensions Appeal Tribunals, since 1970; *b* 14 Oct. 1907; *s* of Horace Croot, LDS, RCS and Winifred Croot; *m* 1st, 1944, Ruth Martyn; 2nd, 1955, Irene Linda Louvain Burley; no *c*. *Educ:* Haileybury; Guy's Hosp. Med. Sch. MRCS, LRCP and MB, BS (London), 1930. Resident Posts, Guy's Hospital etc, 1930-32; medical practice, Hong Kong and Canton, 1932-36; Surgeon, Chinese Maritime Customs, 1935-36; post-grad. study, London, FRCS, 1938. Lt-Col RAMC, 1940-46, mainly India and Burma (despatches), 1944. Sen. Lectr in Surgery, Univ. of Bristol, and Hon. Consultant Surgeon, United Bristol Hosps, 1946-50; Prof. of Surgery, Univ. of E Africa, 1951-58; Mem., Legislative Council, Uganda, 1955-61; Minister of Health and Labour, Uganda, 1958-61; Sen. Consultant Surgeon, Mulago Hosp., Kampala, 1961-69. Pres., Assoc. of Surgeons of E Africa, 1956 and 1962. *Address:* 29 Knole Wood, Devenish Road, Sunningdale, Berks. *T:* Ascot 23651.

CROSBIE, William, RSA 1973; artist; *b* Hankow, China, 31 Jan. 1915; *s* of Archibald Shearer Crosbie, marine engineer, and Mary Edgar, both Scottish; *m* 1st, 1944, M. G. McPhail (decd); one *d* (and one *d* decd); 2nd, 1975, Margaret Anne Roger. *Educ:* Chinese Tutor; Renfrew primary sch.; Glasgow Academy; Glasgow Sch. of Art, Glasgow Univ. (4 yrs under Forrester Wilson). Haldane Travelling Schol., 1935, for 3 yr period of study in British Schs in Athens, Rome and Paris (Beaux Arts); studied history and theory of techniques, in Beaux Arts and Sorbonne, and finally took a post-grad. qualif. in these (continues to acquire craftsmanship); passed into studio of Fernand Leger, Paris, and remained until war declared. Served War of 1939-45: ambulance service, WVS driving pool, and at sea. Has exhibited, on average, every two yrs, 1946-; principally one-man exhibns: Glasgow, Edinburgh, London, etc; also in USA, Brussels, Hamburg, etc. *Works in:* Kelvingrove Galls, Glasgow; Scottish provincial galls; Sydney State Gall., Australia; Wellington, NZ; Royal collection, UK, etc; also in many private collections. *Recreation:* sailing. *Address:* Studio, 12 Ruskin Lane, Glasgow G12 8EA. *T:* 041-334 4573. *Club:* Glasgow Art.

CROSFIELD, Very Rev. George Philip Chorley; Provost of St Mary's Cathedral, Edinburgh, since 1970; *b* 9 Sept. 1924; *s* of James Chorley Crosfield and Marjorie Louise Crosfield; *m* 1956, Susan Mary Jullion (*née* Martin); one *s* two *d*. *Educ:* George Watson's Coll., Edinburgh; Selwyn Coll., Cambridge. Royal Artillery, 1942-46 (Captain). Priest, 1952; Asst Curate: St David's, Pilton, Edinburgh, 1951-53; St Andrew's, St Andrews, 1953-55; Rector, St Cuthbert's, Hawick, 1955-60; Chaplain, Gordonstoun School, 1960-68; subseq. Canon and Vice Provost, St Mary's Cathedral, Edinburgh. *Recreations:* walking, reading, carpentry. *Address:* 8 Lansdowne Crescent, Edinburgh, EH12 5EQ. *T:* 031-225 2978.

CROSS, family name of **Viscount Cross** and **Baron Cross of Chelsea.**

CROSS, 3rd Viscount, *cr* 1886; **Assheton Henry Cross;** late Lieut Scots Guards; *b* 7 May 1920; *e s* of 2nd Viscount and Maud Evelyn (who *m* 2nd, 1944, Guy Hope Coldwell (*d* 1948), Stoke Lodge, Ludlow, Salop; she *d* 1976), *d* of late Maj.-Gen. Inigo Jones, CVO, CB, Kelston Park, Bath; *S* father, 1932; *m* 1952, Patricia Mary (marr. diss., 1957; she *m* 1960, Comdr G. H. H. Culme-Seymour), *e d* of E. P. Hewetson, JP, The Craig, Windermere, Westmorland; two *d* ; *m* 1972, Mrs Victoria Webb (marr. diss. 1977). *Educ:* Shrewsbury; Magdalene Coll., Cambridge. *Heir:* none. *Club:* Cavalry and Guards.

CROSS OF CHELSEA, Baron *cr* 1971 (Life Peer), of the Royal Borough of Kensington and Chelsea; **(Arthur) Geoffrey (Neale) Cross,** PC 1969; Kt 1960; a Lord of Appeal in Ordinary, 1971-75; Chairman, Appeals Committee, Takeover Panel, since 1976; *b* 1 Dec. 1904; *e s* of late Arthur George Cross and Mary Elizabeth Dalton; *m* 1952, Joan, *d* of late Major Theodore Eardley Wilmot, DSO, and *widow* of Thomas Walton Davies; one *d.* *Educ:* Westminster; Trinity College, Cambridge. Craven Scholar, 1925. Fellow of Trinity College, 1927-31, Hon. Fellow, 1972; called to the Bar, Middle Temple, 1930, Master of the Bench, 1958, Reader, 1971; QC 1949. Chancellor of the County Palatine of Durham, 1959. A Judge of the High Court of Justice, Chancery Div., 1960-69; a Lord Justice of Appeal, 1969-71. *Publications:* Epirus, 1932; (with G. R. Y. Radcliffe) The English Legal System (6th edn 1977). *Address:* The Bridge House, Leintwardine, Craven Arms, Salop. *T:* Leintwardine 205.
See also Sir A . R . N . Cross .

CROSS, Alexander Galbraith, MA, MD, FRCS; Ophthalmic Surgeon; lately Dean of the Medical School, St Mary's Hospital; Civilian Consultant in Ophthalmology, RN, since 1946; Consultant Surgeon, Moorfields Eye Hospital, 1947-73; Consultant Ophthalmic Surgeon, St Mary's Hospital, 1946-73; Consultant Ophthalmic Surgeon, Royal National Throat, Nose, and Ear Hospital, 1954-73; Ophthalmic Surgeon, St Dunstan's, 1946-77; Hon. Consultant Ophthalmologist, Royal National Institute for the Blind, since 1968; *b* 29 March 1908; *er s* of late Walter Galbraith Cross and Mary Stewart Cross, Wimbledon; *m* 1939, Eileen Longman, twin *d* of late Dr H. B. Corry, Liss, Hants; one *d.* *Educ:* King's Coll. Sch.; Gonville and Caius Coll., Cambridge; St Mary's Hosp., London (University Scholar). Meadows Prize, 1932, Broadbent and Agnes Cope Prizes, 1933, Cheadle Gold Medallist, 1933, St Mary's Hospital. House Phys. and House Surg., St Mary's, 1933-35; House Surg. and Sen. Res. Officer, Moorfields Eye Hosp., 1937-39; Opthalmic Surgeon: West Middlesex Hosp., 1938-48; Tite Street Children's Hosp., 1939-48; Princess Beatrice Hosp., 1939-47; Royal Masonic Hosp., 1961-71. Wing Comdr, RAFVR, 1941-46 and Adviser in Ophthalmology, South-East Asia Air Forces. Examiner in Fellowship and in Diploma of Ophthalmology for RCS and in Ophthalmology for Univ. of Bristol; Recognised Teacher of Ophthalmology, University of London. Co-opted Mem. Council RCS, 1963-68. Mem. Bd of Governors: St Mary's Hosp., 1951-60; Moorfields Eye Hosp., 1962-65 and 1968-75. Mem. Paddington Group Hosp. Management Cttee, 1952-60. Pres. Ophthalmological Soc. of UK, 1975-77 (Sec. 1949-51; Vice-Pres., 1963-66); Member: RSocMed (Sec. 1951, Ophthalmic Section, Vice-Pres., 1960); BMA (Sec. 1948, Ophthalmic Section, Vice-Pres., 1957). Chm., Opthalmic Gp Cttee, 1963-71; Mem. Council, Faculty of Ophthalmologists, 1963-65, Vice-Pres. 1964, Pres. 1968-71; Dean, Inst. of Ophthalmology, 1967-75 (Deputy Dean, 1966-67); Mem., Orthoptists Bd 1970, Vice-Chm. 1971, Chm. 1972-75. *Publications:* 12th Edn, May and Worth's Diseases of the Eye; articles in British Jl of Ophthalmology, the Lancet, and other med. jls, dealing with ophthalmology. *Recreations:* gardening, lawn tennis, golf, squash racquets. *Address:* 92 Harley Street, W1. *T:* 01-580 3614; 4 Cottenham Park Road, Wimbledon, SW20. *T:* 01-946 3491.

CROSS, Alexander Urquhart, TD 1959; JP; Lord Provost of Perth, 1972-75; *b* 24 Dec. 1906; *m* 1936; one *s* one *d.* *Educ:* Univ. of Glasgow (MA). Owner of private school, 1931-70 (except war years, 1939-45). JP 1972, DL 1972-75, Perth. OStJ 1975. *Address:* 6 Craigie Road, Perth. *T:* Perth 25013.

CROSS, Sir (Alfred) Rupert (Neale), Kt 1973; FBA 1967; Vinerian Professor in the University of Oxford since Oct. 1964; *b* 15 June 1912; *s* of Arthur George Cross and Mary Elizabeth (*née* Dalton); *m* 1937, Aline Heather Chadwick; no *c.* *Educ:* Worcester Coll. for the Blind; Worcester Coll., Oxford (Hon.

Fellow, 1972). DCL 1958. Solicitor, 1939; Hon Master of the Bench, Middle Temple, 1972. Tutor, Law Soc., 1945-48; Fellow of Magdalen Coll., Oxford, 1948-64, Hon. Fellow 1975; Visiting Prof., Univ. of Adelaide, 1962, and Sydney, 1968. Hon. LLD: Edinburgh, 1973; Leeds, 1975. *Publications:* Evidence (4th edn), 1974; Precedent in English Law (3rd edn), 1977; (with P. Asterley Jones) Introduction to Criminal Law (7th edn), 1972; Cases in Criminal Law (5th edn), 1973; (with Nancy Wilkins) An Outline of the Law of Evidence (4th edn), 1975; The English Sentencing System, 1971, 2nd edn 1975; Punishment, Prison and the Public (Hamlyn Lectures), 1971; Statutory Interpretation, 1976; articles in Law Quarterly Review, Modern Law Review and Criminal Law Review. *Recreation:* chess. *Address:* All Souls College, Oxford. *T:* Oxford 22251.
See also Baron Cross of Chelsea.

CROSS, Dr Barry Albert, FRS 1975; Director, ARC Institute of Animal Physiology, since 1974; Warden of Leckhampton, Corpus Christi College, Cambridge, since 1975; *b* 17 March 1925; *s* of Hubert Charles and Elsie May Cross; *m* 1949, Audrey Lilian Crow; one *s* two *d.* *Educ:* Reigate Grammar Sch.; Royal Veterinary Coll. London, MRCVS, BSc (Vet Sci); St John's Coll. Cambridge, BA Hons, MA, PhD. ScD 1964. ICI Research Fellow, Physiological Lab., Cambridge, 1949-51, Gedge Prize 1952; Demonstrator, Zoological Lab., Cambridge, 1951-55; Lectr, 1955-58; Rockefeller Fellow at UCLA, 1957-58; Lectr, Dept. of Anatomy, Cambridge 1958-67; Supervisor in Physiology at St John's Coll., 1955-67; Fellow, Corpus Christi Coll., Cambridge, 1962, and Tutor for Advanced Students, 1964-67; WHO Consultant, Geneva 1964; Prof. and Head of Dept of Anatomy, Univ. of Bristol, 1967-74, and Chm., Sch. of Preclinical Studies, 1969-73. Lectures: Share Jones, RCVS, 1967; Charnock Bradley, Edinburgh Univ., 1968; Glaxo, 1975; Keith Entwhistle, Cambridge, 1976; Sir John McFadyean, London Univ., 1976. Member: Council, Anatomical Soc., 1968-73 (Vice Pres. 1973-74); Council, Assoc. for Study of Animal Behaviour, 1959-62, 1973-75 (Asst Editor 1952-58); Cttee, Soc. for Study of Fertility, 1961-65 (Mem. Editorial Bd 1962-); Cttee, Physiological Soc., 1971-75 (Chm. 1974-75); Internat. Soc. for Neuroendocrinology (Vice-Pres., 1972-75, Pres., 1976-); Mem. Farm Animals Welfare Adv. Cttee, MAFF, 1975-. FIBiol. 1975. Chevalier, Order of Dannebrog, 1968; Comdr d'honneur de l'Ordre du Bontemps de Médoc et des Graves, 1973. *Publications:* sci. papers on neuroendocrine topics in various biol. jls. *Recreations:* gardening, travel, cinephotography. *Address:* 6 Babraham Road, Cambridge. *T:* Cambridge 48368. *Club:* Athenæum.

CROSS, Beverley; playwright; *b* 13 April 1931; *s* of George Cross, theatrical manager, and Eileen Williams, actress; *m* 1st, 1955, Elizabeth Clunies-Ross (marr. diss.); two *d* ; 2nd, 1965, Gayden Collins (marr. diss.); one *s* ; 3rd, 1975, Maggie Smith, *qv. Educ:* Nautical Coll., Pangbourne; Balliol Coll., Oxford. Mem. Shakespeare Memorial Theatre Company, 1954-56; then began writing plays. One More River, Duke of York's, 1959; Strip the Willow, Arts, Cambridge, 1960 (Arts Council Drama Award for both, 1960); The Singing Dolphin, Oxford, 1960; The Three Cavaliers, Birmingham Rep., 1960; Belle, or The Ballad of Dr Crippen, Strand, 1961; Boeing-Boeing, Apollo, 1962; Wanted On Voyage, Marlowe, Canterbury, 1962; Half A Sixpence, Cambridge, London, 1963; Jorrocks, New, London, 1966; The Owl on the Battlements, Nottingham, 1971; Catherine Howard, York, 1972; The Great Society, Mermaid, 1974; Hans Andersen, Palladium, 1974. *Libretti:* The Mines of Sulphur, Sadler's Wells, 1965; All the King's Men, 1969; Victory, Covent Garden, 1970; The Rising of the Moon, Glyndebourne, 1970. *Screen plays of:* Jason and the Argonauts, 1962; The Long Ships, 1963; Genghis Khan, 1965; Half A Sixpence, 1966; (with Carlo Lizzani) Mussolini: Ultimo Atto, 1973; Sinbad and the Eye of the Tiger, 1977. *Television plays:* The Nightwalkers, 1960; The Dark Pits of War, 1960; Catherine Howard, 1969; March on, Boys!, 1975; A Bill of Mortality, 1975. *Directed:* Boeing-Boeing, Sydney, 1964; The Platinum Cat, Wyndham's, 1965. *Publications:* Mars in Capricorn, 1955; The Nightwalkers, 1956; Plays For Children, 1960. *Recreations:* rough shooting, fishing. *Address:* c/o Curtis Brown Ltd, 1 Craven Hill, W2 3EW. *T:* 01-262 1011. *Clubs:* MCC, Dramatists.

CROSS, Clifford Thomas, CB 1977; Commissioner, Customs and Excise, since 1970; *b* 1 April 1920; *o s* of late Arthur and Helena Cross; *m* 1942, Ida Adelaide Barker; one *s* two *d.* *Educ:* Latymer Upper Sch., Hammersmith; Univ. of London (LLB). Joined Inland Revenue, 1939; Customs and Excise, 1946; Asst Sec. 1959; Comr 1970. *Recreations:* squash rackets, bonsai culture, watching television, etc. *Address:* Monkton Combe, 10 Drake Road, Westcliff-on-Sea, Essex. *T:* 01-626 1515.

CROSS, Rt. Rev. David Stewart; see Doncaster, Bishop Suffragan of.

CROSS, Frederick Victor, CMG 1949; Director: Navcot Shipping Holdings; Sitmar Line (London) Ltd; Navigation & Coal Trade Co. Ltd; Alva Shipping (Holdings) Ltd; Alva Star Shipping Co. Ltd; *b* 19 April 1907; *m* 1932, Gwendoline Horton; one *s* one *d. Educ:* RNC Greenwich. INA scholarship, 1927. Shipping Attaché, British Embassy, Washington, DC, 1946-49; Asst Sec., MoT, 1949-51. Officer: Order of Orange Nassau, 1947; Order of the Crown of Belgium, 1948. *Address:* 21 Durham Avenue, Bromley, Kent.

CROSS, Hannah Margaret, (Mrs E. G. Wright); barrister-at-law; *b* 25 April 1908; *o d* of late F. J. K. Cross and Eleanor Mary Cross (*née* Phillimore); *m* 1936, Edmund Gordon Wright, Barrister-at-Law (*d* 1971); one *s* one *d. Educ:* Downe House Sch.; St Hilda's Coll., Oxford. BA 1929. Called to Bar, Lincoln's Inn, 1931; first woman Mem. of Gen. Council of Bar, 1938-45; Civil Defence, 1939-45. *Address:* The Quay House, Sidlesham, near Chichester, West Sussex. *T:* Sidlesham 258.

CROSS, James Richard, (Jasper), CMG 1971; Under-Secretary, Coal Division, Department of Energy (formerly Department of Trade and Industry), since 1973; *b* 29 Sept. 1921; *s* of J. P. Cross and Dinah Cross (*née* Hodgins); *m* 1945, Barbara Dagg; one *d. Educ:* King's Hosp., Dublin; Trin. Coll., Dublin. Scholar, First Cl. Moderatorship Economics and Polit. Science. RE (Lieut). Asst Principal, Bd of Trade, 1947; Private Sec. to Parly Sec., 1947-49; Principal, 1950; Trade Commissioner: New Delhi, 1953-56; Halifax, 1957-60; Winnipeg, 1960-62; Asst Sec., 1962; Sen. Trade Comr, Kuala Lumpur, 1962-66; Bd of Trade, 1966-67; Under Sec., 1968; Sen. British Trade Comr, Montreal, 1968-70 (kidnapped by terrorists and held for 59 days, Oct.-Dec. 1970); Under-Sec., Export Planning and Develt Div., DTI, 1971-73; Sec., British Overseas Trade Bd, 1972. *Recreations:* theatre, bridge, the New Forest. *Address:* 10 Wykeham Place, Lymington, Hants.

CROSS, Joan, CBE 1951; opera singer; *b* Sept. 1900. *Educ:* St Paul's Girls' Sch. Principal soprano, Old Vic and Sadler's Wells, 1924-44; Dir of Opera, Sadler's Wells, 1941-44; subsequently Principal, National Sch. of Opera (Ltd), Morley Coll., London, resigned. *Address:* Brook Cottage, Yoxford, Saxmundham, Suffolk.

CROSS, Air Chief Marshal Sir Kenneth (Brian Boyd), KCB 1959 (CB 1954); CBE 1945; DSO 1943; DFC 1940; *b* 4 Oct. 1911; *s* of Pembroke H. C. Cross and Mrs Jean Cross; *m* 1945, Brenda Megan, *d* of Wing-Comdr F. J. B. Powell; two *s* one *d. Educ:* Kingswood Sch., Bath. Pilot Officer, RAF, 1930; Flying Badge, 1931; 25 Fighter Sqdn, 1931; Flying Officer, 1932; Flying Instructor, No 5 FTS Sealand and Cambridge Univ. Air Sqdn, 1934; Flt Lt 1935; Sqdn Ldr 1938; commanded No 46 Fighter Sqdn UK, Norway, 1939-40; Wing Comdr 1940; posted Middle East, 1941; Actg Group Capt. 1941; Actg Air Commodore, 1943; Director Overseas Operations, Air Ministry, 1944; Imperial Defence Coll., 1946; reverted Group Capt., 1946; Group Capt. Operations HQ BAFO Germany, 1947; OC Eastern Sector Fighter Command, 1949; Dir of Weapons, Air Ministry, 1952; subs. Air Cdre, 1953; Dir of Ops, Air Defence, 1954-Dec. 1955; Air Vice-Marshal, 1956; AOC No 3 (Bomber) Group, 1956-59; Air Marshal, 1961; AOC-in-C, Bomber Comd, 1959-63; Air Chief Marshal, 1965; AOC-in-C, Transport Comd, 1963-66, retd, 1967. Director: Suffolk Branch, 1968, London Branch, 1974, British Red Cross Soc. Norwegian War Cross, 1941; USA Legion of Merit, 1944; French Legion of Honour, 1944; French Croix de Guerre, 1944; Dutch Order of Orange Nassau, 1945. *Recreations:* Rugby football and golf (colours RAF). *Address:* 12 Callow Street, Chelsea, SW3. *Club:* Royal Air Force.

CROSS, Prof. Kenneth William, MB, DSc, FRCP; Professor of Physiology, London Hospital Medical College since 1960; Hon. Physiologist to The London Hospital; *b* 26 March 1916; *s* of late George Cross, Ealing; *m* 1942, Joyce M. Wilson (*née* Lack, *d* 1970); one step *d*; *m* 1970, Dr Sheila R. Lewis. *Educ:* St Paul's Sch.; St Mary's Hospital Medical Sch. Qualified, 1940; House appointments in St Mary's Hospital Sector; graded Physician EMS Amersham Emergency Hosp. 1945; Friends' Ambulance Unit, China, 1946-47. Lecturer in Physiology, 1947, Reader, 1952, St Mary's Hosp. *Publications:* contrib. to Journal of Physiology. *Address:* 22 Highgate Heights, Shepherd's Hill, N6 5RF. *T:* 01-340 1035.

CROSS, Brig. Lionel Lesley, CBE 1950; *b* 7 June 1899; *yr s* of Charles Frederick Cross, FRS, and Edith, *d* of Maj.-Gen. Charles Stainforth, CB; *m* 1940, Rose Blanche Margaret (*d*

1976), *d* of Sir Robert Taylor, Kytes, Herts; no *c. Educ:* Wellington Coll.; RMA Woolwich. Commissioned RFA, 1918; France and Belgium, 1918. Adjutant Bucks and Berks Yeo. Artillery, 1925-29; retd 1929. Rejoined Army, 1939; Staff Capt. RA 1939; France and Belgium, 1940; Major 1941; Lieut-Col 1942; Asst Dir of Public Relations, War Office, 1942-46; Brig. 1946; Dep. Dir of Public Relations, War Office, 1946-50; Chief of Public Information, SHAPE, 1954-58 (Dep., 1951-54); retired, 1958. Sec., CPU, 1959-70. *Recreations:* racing, bridge. *Addresss:* 15 Cedar House, Marloes Road, W8. *T:* 01-937 0112. *Club:* Army and Navy.

CROSS, Mrs Margaret Natalie; see Smith, Maggie.

CROSS, Prof. Robert Craigie, CBE 1972; MA Glasgow, MA Oxford; Regius Professor of Logic, since 1953, Vice-Principal, 1974-77, University of Aberdeen; *b* 24 April 1911; *s* of Matthew Cross and Margaret Dickson; *m* 1943, Peggy Catherine Elizabeth Vernon; two *d. Educ:* Glasgow Univ.; Queen's Coll., Oxford. MA 1st Cl. Hons Classics, Glasgow, 1932; 1st Cl. Hons Classical Mods, Oxford, 1934; 1st Cl. Lit. Hum., Oxford, 1936. Fellow and Tutor in Philsophy, Jesus Coll., Oxford, 1938; served War, 1941-45, Navy and Admiralty; Senior Tutor, Jesus Coll., Oxford, 1948-53. Trustee, Scottish Hospital Endowments Research Trust, 1968-; Mem., University Grants Cttee, 1965-74; Mem., North Eastern Regional Hospital Bd, 1958-65. *Publications:* (with A. D. Woozley) Plato's Republic: A Philosophical Commentary, 1964; contributions to learned jls. *Address:* 14 Westfield Terrace, Aberdeen. *T:* 22470.

CROSS, Sir Rupert; see Cross, Sir A. R. N.

CROSSE, Rev. Frank Parker; Rector of Upton Magna, Shrewsbury, 1960-67; *b* 24 Oct. 1897; *s* of Edmund Francis Crosse and Margaret Laidlaw Selby; *m* 1925, Isabel McIver McIntyre; two *d. Educ:* St Bees; RMC Sandhurst. Commissioned Regular Army, South Staffs Regt, 1916 (MC). Priest 1924; Vicar, Christ Church, Derry Hill, Wilts, 1926; Private Chaplain to Marquess of Lansdowne, 1927; Vicar, St Aldhelm's, Branksome, Bournemouth, 1931; Dean and Archdeacon of Grahamstown, 1934-44; Rector of Barlborough, 1944-51; Rector of Morton, Derby, 1951-60; Custos, Denstone Coll., 1955-71; Canon of Derby Cathedral, 1956-60. Vice-Provost and Senior Chaplain (Midland Div.) Woodard Schs, 1962-70. *Publication:* Intercessions in Time of War, 1939. *Address:* 24 Preston Trust Homes, Preston, Telford, Salop. *T:* Kinnersley 3669.

CROSSE, Gordon; composer; *b* 1 Dec. 1937; *s* of Percy and Marie Crosse; *m* 1965, Elizabeth Bunch. *Educ:* Cheadle Hulme Sch.; St Edmund Hall, Oxford; Accad. di S Cecilia, Rome. Music Fellow, Essex Univ., 1969-74; Composer in residence, King's Coll., Cambridge, 1974-76. *Operas:* Purgatory, 1966; The Grace of Todd, 1967; The Story of Vasco, 1970; Potter Thompson, 1973; *other compositions:* Concerto da Camera, 1962; Meet My Folks, 1963; "Symphonies", 1964; Second Violin Concerto, 1970; Memories of Morning: Night, 1972; Ariadne, 1973; Symphony 2, 1975; much other orchestral, vocal and chamber music. *Address:* Brant's Cottage, Wenhaston, Halesworth, Suffolk.

CROSSFIELD, Robert Sands, OBE 1967; DL; JP; *b* 21 May 1904; *s* of Robert and Ellen Louise Crossfield, Ulverston; *m* 1929, Miriam, *d* of Rev. W. H. Wicks; no *c. Educ:* Earnseat Sch., Arnside; Millhill Sch., London. Director of a number of family private limited companies, now retired. Interested many years in local govt: Mem. Westmorland CC, 1940; CA, 1958-74; Chm. of Council, 1952-70. High Sheriff of Westmorland, 1970-71; JP 1945, DL 1971, Cumbria (formerly Westmorland). *Recreations:* golf, motoring. *Address:* Brantfell, Arnside, Cumbria. *T:* Arnside 761244. *Club:* Old Millhillians.

CROSSLAND, Anthony, FRCO; Organist and Master of the Choristers, Wells Cathedral, since 1971; *b* 4 Aug. 1931; *s* of Ernest Thomas and Frances Elizabeth Crossland; *m* 1960, Barbara Helen Pullar-Strecker; one *s* two *d. Educ:* Christ Church, Oxford. MA. Mus (Oxon), FRCO (CHM), ARCM. Asst Organist: Christ Church Cathedral, Oxford, 1957-61; Wells Cathedral, 1961-71. *Recreations:* music, reading, photography. *Address:* 15 Vicars' Close, Wells, Somerset. *T:* Wells (Somerset) 73526.

CROSSLAND, Prof. Bernard, MSc (London); PhD (Bristol); DSc (Nottingham); MRIA; FIMechE; FIProdE; FIW; Professor and Head of Department of Mechanical Engineering, The Queen's University, Belfast, since 1959; *b* 20 Oct. 1923; *s* of R. F. Crossland and K. M. Rudduck; *m* 1946, Audrey Elliott Birks; two *d. Educ:* Simon Langton's, Canterbury. Apprentice,

Rolls Royce Ltd, 1940-41; Nottingham Univ., 1941-43; Technical Asst, Rolls Royce, 1943-45; Asst Lectr, Lectr and then Senior Lectr in Mechanical Engineering, Univ. of Bristol, 1946-59. Chm., Youth Careers Guidance Cttee, N Ireland, 1975; Mem., N Ireland Training Council, 1964-76, 1977-. George Stephenson and Thomas Hawksley Medals, IMechE. *Publications:* An Introduction to the Mechanics of Machines, 1964; various papers on fatigue of metals and effect of very high fluid pressures on properties of materials; strength of thick-walled vessels, explosive welding, friction welding, and design. *Recreations:* sailing, walking. *Address:* Ashby Institute, Stranmills Road, Belfast BT9 5AH; The Queen's University, Belfast BT7 1NN. *T:* Belfast 45133. *Club:* Athenæum.

CROSSLAND, Sir Leonard, Kt 1969; Chairman: Eaton Ltd (UK), since 1972; Ford Motor Co. Ltd, 1968-72; Sedgeminster Technical Developments Ltd, since 1974; *b* 2 March 1914; *s* of Joseph and Frances Crossland; *m* 1st, 1941, Rhona Marjorie Griffin; two *d*; 2nd, 1963, Joan Brewer. *Educ:* Penistone Grammar Sch. Purchase Dept, Ford Motor Co. Ltd, 1937-39. Royal Army Service Corps, 1939-45. Ford Motor Co. Ltd: Purchase Dept. 1945-54; Chief Buyer, Tractor and Implement Dept, 1954-57; Chief Buyer, Car and Truck Dept, 1957-59; Asst Purchase Manager, 1959-60; Purchase Manager, 1960-62; Exec. Dir, Supply and Services, 1962-66; Dir, Manufacturing Staff and Services, 1966; Asst Man. Dir, 1966-67; Man. Dir, 1967; Dep. Chm., 1967; Chm., Autolite Motor Products Ltd; Director: Henry Ford & Son Ltd, Cork; Eaton Corp. (US), 1974-. *Recreations:* shooting, fishing, golf. *Address:* Abbotts Hall, Great Wigborough, Colchester, Essex. *T:* Peldon 456. *Clubs:* City Livery, Royal Automobile, British Racing Drivers', American.

CROSSLAND, Prof. Ronald Arthur; Professor of Greek, University of Sheffield, since 1958; *b* 31 Aug. 1920; *s* of late Ralph Crossland, BSc, and late Ethel Crossland (*née* Scattergood). *Educ:* Stanley Road Elementary Sch., Nottingham; Nottingham High Sch.; King's Coll., Cambridge. Major Scholar in Classics, King's Coll., Cambridge, 1939-41 and 1945-46. National Service in Royal Artillery, 1941-45. Henry Fellow, Berkeley Coll., Yale Univ., 1946-47; Instructor in Classics, Yale Univ., 1947-48; Senior Student of Treasury Cttee for Studentships in Foreign Languages and Cultures (for research in Hittite Philology and Linguistics), 1948-51; Hon. Lectr in Ancient History, University of Birmingham, 1950-51; Lecturer in Ancient History, King's Coll., University of Durham, Newcastle upon Tyne, 1951-58. Harris Fellow of King's Coll., Cambridge, 1952-56. Vis. Prof., Univ. Texas, 1962; Collitz Vis. Prof., Univ. Michigan, 1967. Pres., South Shields Archaeological and Historical Soc., 1976-77. *Publications:* (with A. Birchall) Bronze Age Migrations in the Aegean, 1973; chapter, Immigrants from the North, in Cambridge Ancient History, rev. edn, 1967; Teaching Classical Studies, 1976; articles in Trans Philological Soc., Archivum Linguisticum, Studia Balcanica, Past and Present. *Recreations:* music, travel. *Address:* 103 Vernon Crescent, Ravenshead, Notts NG15 9BP. *T:* (private) Blidworth 5124; (office) Sheffield 78555.

CROSSLEY, family name of **Baron Somerleyton.**

CROSSLEY, Sir Christopher John, 3rd Bt *cr* 1909; Lieutenant-Commander Royal Navy, retired; *b* 25 Sept. 1931; *s* of late Lt-Comdr Nigel Crossley, RN (*s* of late Eric Crossley, OBE, 2nd *s* of 1st Bt); *S* great uncle (Sir Kenneth Crossley, OBE, 2nd *s* of 1st Bt); *S* great uncle (Sir Kenneth Crossley, OBE), 1957; *m* 1959, Carolyne Louise (marr. diss. 1969), *d* of late L. Grey Sykes; two *s*; *m* 1977, Lesley, *e d* of late Dr K. A. J. Chamberlain. *Educ:* Canford Sch. Entered Royal Navy, 1950. *Recreations:* royal tennis, squash. *Heir:* *s* Nicholas John Crossley, *b* 10 Dec. 1962. *Address:* 54 Rosebank Wharf, Holyport Road, Fulham, SW6.

CROSSLEY, Prof. Eric Lomax; Professor of Dairying, University of Reading, 1947-68, now Professor Emeritus; *b* 15 Sept. 1903; British; *m* 1933, Janet Hircombe Sutton; one *s*. *Educ:* Nottingham High Sch.; High Pavement Sch., Nottingham; University Coll., Nottingham. Research work bacteriology and biochemistry at University Coll., Nottingham and Nat. Inst. for Research in Dairying, Shinfield, Reading, 1923-25; Advisory Dairy Bacteriologist, Min. of Agriculture, at Harper Adams Agricultural Coll., Newport, Salop, 1925-29; Chief scientific and technical adviser, dir of laboratories, Aplin & Barrett Ltd, Yeovil, Som and associated Cos, 1929-47. Has been engaged in scientific investigation (particularly bacteriology) of milk processing and manufacture of dairy and other food products. Part-time Consultant, FAO. President: Soc. Dairy Technology, 1953-54; Internat. Commn for Dried and Condensed Milks, 1960-65; Inst. of Food Science and Technology, 1967-69. Technical Mission to Peru, ODM, 1970. Gold Medal, Soc. of Dairy Technol., 1975. *Publications:* The United Kingdom Dairy Industry; original papers in scientific journals. *Recreations:* entomology and music. *Address:* Cliffdene, Shooters Hill, Pangbourne, Berks. *T:* Pangbourne 2967.

CROSSLEY, Geoffrey Allan, CMG 1974; HM Diplomatic Service; Minister to the Holy See, since 1978; *b* 11 Nov. 1920; *s* of Thomas Crossley and Winifred Mary Crossley (*née* Ellis); *m* 1945, Aline Louise Farcy; two *s* one *d*. *Educ:* Penistone; abroad; Gonville and Caius Coll., Cambridge (Scholar). Served War of 1939-45: Min. of Supply, 1941-; Foreign Office, 1942-; in Algeria and France. Foreign Service, 1945-: Second Sec., Paris, 1945-48; FO, 1948-49; Alternate UK Deleg. on UN Balkans Commn, Greece, 1949-52; Dep. Regional Inf. Officer with Commissioner-Gen. for SE Asia, Singapore, 1952-55; FO, 1955-57; Consulate-Gen., Frankfurt, for Saar Transition from France to Germany, 1957-59; Political Office, NE Command, Cyprus (later in charge), 1959-61; Head of Chancery, Berne, 1961-65; on secondment to Min. of Overseas Development, as Head of W and N African Dept, 1965-67; Dep. High Comr, Lusaka, 1967-69; Counsellor, Oslo, 1969-73; Ambassador to Colombia, 1973-78. *Recreations:* tennis, squash, ski-ing, swimming, water-skiing, hacking, painting, music. *Address:* c/o Foreign and Commonwealth Office, SW1.

CROSSLEY, Harry; Chief Executive, Derbyshire County Council, since 1974; *b* 2 Sept. 1918; *s* of late Percy Crossley and Nellie McMinnies Crossley, Burnley, Lancs; *m* 1949, Pamela, *e d* of late Ald. E. A. C. Woodcock, Kettering, Northants; two *s*. *Educ:* Burnley Grammar Sch. Solicitor. LAM RTPI. War service, RA, attached Indian Army (Major), 1939-46. Private practice and local govt service as solicitor; Derbyshire CC: Dep. Clerk of Peace and of CC, 1960-69; Clerk of Peace and of CC, 1969-74. Clerk to Derbyshire Lieutenancy, 1969-; Sec., Lord Chancellor's Adv. Cttee for Derbyshire, 1969-. Clerk, Peak Park Planning Bd, 1969-74. *Publications:* articles for legal and local govt jls. *Recreations:* golf, tennis, hockey, gardening. *Address:* Alpine, Bracken Lane, Holloway, Matlock DE4 5AS. *T:* Dethick 382. *Club:* Royal Automobile.

CROSSLEY, Wing-Comdr Michael Nicholson, DSO 1940; OBE 1946; DFC; Fighter Command; farming in South Africa since 1955; *b* 29 May 1912; *s* of late Major E. Crossley, OBE; *m* 1957, Sylvia Heyder (*d* 1975); one *s* two *d*. *Educ:* Eton Coll.; Munich. Commissioned in RAF, 1935. *Recreation:* golf. *Address:* Loughrigg, White River 1240, E Transvaal, S Africa. *Club:* Rand (Johannesburg).

CROSSMAN, Douglas Peter, TD 1944; DL; Chairman, Huntingdon Steeplechases Ltd; Director, National Westminster Bank (Outer London); *b* 25 Sept. 1908; *s* of late Percy Crossman, Gt Bromley Hall, Colchester; *m* 1st, 1932, Monica, *d* of late C. F. R. Barnett; two *s* one *d*; 2nd, 1939, Jean Margaret, *d* of late Douglas Crossman, Cokenach, Royston. *Educ:* Uppingham; Pembroke Coll., Cambridge. Commission Warwicks Yeomanry, 1934-45. Chairman: Mann Crossman Paulin Ltd, 1961-65; Watney Mann Ltd, 1965-70. President: Licensed Victuallers' Sch., 1958; Shire Horse Soc., 1958; Beer and Wine Trade Benev., 1960; Licensed Victuallers' Nat. Homes, 1963; Hunts Agricultural Soc., 1965; Chairman: Govs, Dame Alice Owen's Sch., 1951-65; Hunts Conservative Assoc., 1954-61; Eastern Area, Nat. Union of Conservative Party, 1965; Nat. Union of Conservative Party, 1969. Master, Brewers' Co., 1950. Chairman, Brewers' Soc., 1968, 1969. DL Huntingdonshire, 1958. Master: Essex and Suffolk Foxhounds, 1938-40; Cambridgeshire Foxhounds, 1947-49. *Recreations:* hunting, shooting, fishing, gardening. *Address:* Tetworth Hall, Sandy, Beds. *T:* Gamlingay 212. *Club:* Cavalry and Guards.

CROSTHWAIT, Timothy Leland, CMG 1964; MBE 1944; HM Diplomatic Service, retired; *b* 5 Aug. 1915; *s* of Lt-Col L. G. Crosthwait, Survey of India; *m* 1959, Anne Marjorie, *d* of Col T. M. M. Penney. *Educ:* Wellington Coll.; Peterhouse, Cambridge (MA). Appointed to Indian Civil Service, 1937; Asst Private Sec. to Viceroy, 1942-44; Air Min., 1948-55; Commonwealth Relations Office, 1955; British Deputy High Commissioner in Ceylon, 1957-61; Asst Sec., CRO, 1961-63; British High Commissioner, Zanzibar, 1963-64; British Deputy High Commissioner, Malta, 1965-66; British High Commissioner, Guyana, 1966-67; Ambassador, Malagasy Republic, 1970-75. *Address:* 39 Eaton Terrace, SW1. *T:* 01-730 9553. *Club:* United Oxford & Cambridge University.

CROSTHWAITE, Cecil, MBE 1943; TD 1942 and 3 bars; JP; Lord-Lieutenant and Custos Rotolorum of Cleveland, since 1974; *b* 1909; *o s* of late Sir William Crosthwaite; *m* Norah Mahoney Bowden, twin *d* of late Frank W. Bowden; one *s* two *d* (and one *s* decd). *Educ:* Windermere; Uppingham. Served 50

Divl Sigs TA, 1929-39; 23 Divl Sigs TA, 1939-40; SO Northern Comd HQ, 1940-41; GSO WO, 1941-46; rep. Chamber of Commerce NR TA Assoc., 1947-65. Chm., Seahorse Securities Ltd, Tees Towing Co. Ltd, British Marine Mutual Insce Assoc. Ltd, British Tugowners' Assoc., 1957-61; Co-Founder, European Tugowners' Assoc., 1961 (Chm., 1975-); Dep. Chm., Lyon & Lyon Gp of Companies and Tees & Hartlepool Port Authority, 1969; Dir other shipping, transport and construction companies. French Vice-Consul, 1968; Mem. N of England Air Adv. Cttee, 1964; Vice-Pres., N of England TA&VRA, 1975; Pres., St John Council, Cleveland. DL NR Yorks, 1963; JP Cleveland, 1974. KStJ 1974. *Recreations:* (some continuous, others as opportunity permits) hatha yoga, horticulture, sculpture, music. *Address:* Langbaurgh Hall, Great Ayton, North Yorkshire; Cleveland Buildings, Queen's Square, Middlesbrough, Cleveland TS2 1NX. *Clubs:* Carlton; Cleveland (Middlesbrough).

CROSTHWAITE, Sir (Ponsonby) Moore, KCMG 1960 (CMG 1951); *b* 13 Aug. 1907; *o s* of late P. M. Crosthwaite, MICE, and late Agnes Alice, *y d* of J. H. Aitken, Falkirk, Stirlingshire. *Educ:* Rugby; CCC, Oxford. Laming Fellowship, Queen's Coll., 1931. Entered Diplomatic Service, 1932; has served in Bagdad, Moscow, Madrid, Athens and Foreign Office; Deputy UK Representative to United Nations, New York, 1952-58; Ambassador to the Lebanon, 1958-63; Ambassador to Sweden, 1963-66. *Recreations:* travel, the arts. *Address:* 17 Crescent Grove, SW4. *Club:* Athenæum.

CROSTHWAITE-EYRE, Sir Oliver (Eyre), Kt 1961; Verderer of New Forest, 1948-74; Chairman: Eyre & Spottiswoode Ltd, 1961-73; Associated Book Publishers Ltd, 1963-73; 1900 Club, 1960-73; *b* 14 Oct. 1913; *e s* of Major J. S. Crosthwaite-Eyre and Dorothy Muriel Eyre; *m* 1939, Maria Alexandra Puthon; two *s* three *d*. *Educ:* Downside; Trinity Coll., Cambridge. Served War of 1939; enlisted private, 1940; commissioned, April 1940; served Norway, Middle East, and NW Europe (despatches). MP (C) New Forest Div. of Hants, 1950-68 (New Forest and Christchurch Div., 1945-50). DL Southampton, 1954. *Address:* Blenmans House, 12 Yellow Wood Lane, PO Chisipite, Salisbury, Rhodesia. *Club:* Salisbury (Rhodesia).

CROUCH, David (Lance); MP (C) Canterbury since 1966; Director: David Crouch & Co. Ltd; Pfizer Ltd; Burson-Marsteller Ltd; *b* 23 June 1919; *s* of late Stanley Crouch and Rosalind Kate Crouch (*née* Croom); *m* 1947, Margaret Maplesden, *d* of Major Sydney Maplesden Noakes, DSO and Norah Parkyns Maplesden Noakes (*née* Buckland), Shorne, Kent; one *s* one *d*. *Educ:* University Coll. Sch. Served in City of London Yeomanry (TA), 1938-39; served War of 1939-45, Royal Artillery: Major 1943; attached RAF Staff (GSO2), 1944-45. Joined British Nylon Spinners Ltd, 1946; ICI Ltd, 1950; Dir of Publicity, Internat. Wool Secretariat, 1962-64. Formed own co., David Crouch & Co. Ltd, as international marketing and public relations consultants (Chairman, 1964-). Contested (C) West Leeds, 1959. Chairman: Anglo-Egyptian Parly Gp; All-Party Gp for the Chemical Industry; Member: Select Cttee for Nationalized Industries, 1966-74; Public Accounts Cttee, 1974-. Trustee, Theatres Trust, 1977-. Member: SE Thames RHA; Soc. of Chemical Industry; Council Univ. of Kent; Council, RSA, 1974- (Fellow, 1971). *Recreations:* cricket, tennis, golf. *Address:* 3 Tufton Court, Tufton Street, SW1; Barton Manor, Westmarsh, Canterbury, Kent.

CROUT, Dame Mabel, DBE 1965; JP; Alderman, London Borough of Greenwich, 1964-71; *b* 6 Jan. 1890. Member of Woolwich Borough Council, 1919-64 (Mayor, 1936-37); Mem. of London Borough of Greenwich, 1964-71. JP, London, 1920-. Mem. of London County Council, 1949-55. Freeman of Woolwich, 1959. *Address:* 112 Strongbow Crescent, Eltham, SE9. *T:* 01-850 3444.

CROWDER, F(rederick) Petre, QC 1964; MP (C) Ruislip-Northwood since 1950; a Recorder (formerly Recorder of Colchester), since 1967; Barrister-at-Law; *b* 18 July 1919; *s* of late Sir John Ellenborough Crowder; *m* 1948, Hon. Patricia Stourton, *d* of 25th Baron Mowbray, MC (also 26th Baron Segrave and 22nd Baron Stourton); two *s*. *Educ:* Eton; Christ Church, Oxford. Served War of 1939-45; joined Coldstream Guards, 1939, and served in North Africa, Italy, Burma; attained rank of major. Contested North Tottenham, 1945. Called to the Bar, Inner Temple, 1948, Master of the Bench, 1971. South Eastern Circuit; North London Sessions. Recorder of Gravesend, 1960-67; Herts QS: Dep. Chm., 1957-63; Chm., 1963-71. PPS to Solicitor-Gen., 1952-54; PPS to Attorney General, 1954-62. *Address:* 2 Harcourt Buildings, Temple, EC4. *T:* 01-353 2112; (residence) 8 King's Bench Walk, Temple, EC4. *T:* 01-353 6997; Aston Dene, Aston, near Stevenage, Herts. *Clubs:* Carlton, Pratt's, Turf.

CROWE, Brian Lee; Head of Planning Staff, Foreign and Commonwealth Office, since 1976; *b* 5 Jan. 1938; *s* of Eric Crowe and Virginia Crowe; *m* 1969, Virginia Willis; two *s*. *Educ:* Sherborne; Magdalen Coll., Oxford (1st Cl. Hons PPE). Joined FO, 1961; served: Moscow, 1962-64; London, 1965-67; Aden, 1967; Washington, 1968-73; Bonn, 1973-76. *Recreations:* winter sports, tennis, riding. *Address:* 137 Rosendale Road, SE21. *T:* 01-761 2610.

CROWE, Sir Colin Tradescant, GCMG 1973 (KCMG 1963; CMG 1956); HM Diplomatic Service, retired; *b* 7 Sept. 1913; *s* of late Sir Edward Crowe, KCMG; *m* 1938, Bettina Lum. *Educ:* Stowe Sch.; Oriel Coll., Oxford. Served at HM Embassy, Peking, 1936-38 and 1950-53; Shanghai, 1938-40; HM Embassy, Washington, 1940-45; Foreign Office, 1945-48, 1953-56; UK Delegn to OEEC, Paris, 1948-49; HM Legation, Tel Aviv, 1949-50; Imperial Defence Coll., 1957; Head, British Property Commn, Cairo, 1959; British Chargé d'Affaires, Cairo, 1959-61; Deputy UK Representative to the UN, New York, 1961-63; Ambassador to Saudi Arabia, 1963-64; Chief of Administration, HM Diplomatic Service, 1965-68; High Comr in Canada, 1968-70; UK Permanent Rep. to UN, 1970-73. Supernumerary Fellow, St Antony's Coll., Oxford, 1964-65. Dir, Grindlay's Bank Ltd, 1976-. Chm., Marshall Aid Commemoration Commn, 1973-. Chm. Council, Cheltenham Ladies Coll., 1974-; Mem., Coll. Cttee, University Coll., London, 1976-. *Address:* Pigeon House, Bibury, Glos. *Club:* Travellers'.

CROWE, Gerald Patrick, QC 1973; a Recorder of the Crown Court, since 1976; *b* 3 April 1930; *y s* of Patrick Crowe and Ethel Maud Crowe (*née* Tooth); *m* 1954, Catherine Mary, *d* of Joseph and Rose Murphy, Newry, N Ireland. *Educ:* St Francis Xavier's Coll.; Liverpool Univ. (LLB). Called to Bar, Gray's Inn, 1952; practised Northern Circuit. *Recreations:* golf, fishing. *Address:* The Spinney, Long Hey Road, Caldy, Cheshire. *T:* 051-625 8848; Goldsmith Building, Temple, EC4Y 7BL.

CROWE, Prof. Percy Robert, BSc Econ. (London); PhD (Glasgow); MA (Manchester); Professor in Geography, University of Manchester, 1953-71, Emeritus Professor, since 1972; a Pro-Vice-Chancellor, 1968-71; *b* 2 March 1904; *m* 1931, Margaret D. J. Robertson; two *s* one *d*. *Educ:* Henry Thornton Sch., Clapham, London; London Sch. of Economics and Political Science. Asst to Lecturer in Geography, Glasgow Univ., 1925-28; Commonwealth Fund Fellow, 1928-30; Lectr in Geography, Glasgow Univ., 1928-47; Technical Officer, Meteorological Office, 1939-41; Commission in RAF 1944-45; Reader in Geography, University of London, and Head of Geography Dept, Queen Mary Coll., 1947-53. *Publications:* Concepts in Climatology, 1971; articles in geographical and meteorological jls. *Recreations:* hill walking, chess. *Address:* 239 Bramhall Lane South, Bramhall, Cheshire. *T:* 061-439 1134.

CROWE, Prof. Ralph Vernon, FRIBA; Professor of Architecture and Head of Department, School of Architecture, The University, Newcastle upon Tyne, since 1976; *b* 30 Sept. 1915; *s* of Sidney John Crowe and Sarah Emma (*née* Sharp); *m* 1943, Nona Heath Eggington; two *s* one *d*. *Educ:* Westminster City Sch.; Architectural Assoc., London (MA, AA Dipl. Hons); Sch. of Planning and Res. for Reg. Develt. FRIBA 1939; MRTPI 1946. War Service, 1941-45: Captain, RE. Govt Architect and Planning Officer, Govt of Barbados, BWI, 1947-50; teaching, Arch. Assoc., 1950-52; Basildon New Town, 1952-53; LCC, 1953-58; County Architect: Shropshire, 1958-66; Essex, 1966-76. *Publications:* contribs to professional and tech. jls. *Recreations:* music (flute), hill walking, chess. *Address:* c/o The School of Architecture, The University, Newcastle upon Tyne NE1 7RU. *T:* Newcastle upon Tyne 28511.

CROWE, Dame Sylvia, DBE 1973 (CBE 1967); landscape architect in private practice since 1945; *b* 1901; *d* of Eyre Crowe; unmarried. *Educ:* Berkhamsted; Swanley Hort. Coll. Designed gardens, 1927-39. Served FANY and ATS, 1939-45. Since 1945, private practice as landscape architect has included: work as consultant to: Harlow and Basildon New Town Corporations; Bough Beech and Empingham reservoirs; Central Electricity Generating Board, for Trawsfynydd and Wylfa Nuclear Power Stations; Forestry Commission; reclamation of land after 1952 floods and design of public gardens at Mablethorpe and Sutton on Sea; gardens for Oxford Univ., various Colls and Commonwealth Inst., London; Sec., Internat. Federation Landscape Architecture, 1948-59; Vice-Pres., 1964; Pres., Inst. Landscape Architects, 1957-59; Chm., Tree Council, 1974-76. Hon. FRIBA, 1969; Hon. FRTPI, 1970. Hon. DLitt Heriot-Watt, 1976. *Publications:* Tomorrow's Landscape, 1956; Garden Design, 1958; The Landscape of Power, 1958; Landscape of Roads, 1960; Forestry in the Landscape, 1966. *Recreations:* walking and gardening. *Address:* 182 Gloucester Place, NW1 6DS. *T:* 01-723 9968.

CROWLEY, Sir Brian Hurtle, Kt 1969; MM; Chairman, 1962-74 (Member 1944-74), Australian Jockey Club Committee; *m* 1922, Dorothy, *d* of L. Sweet; one *s* two *d*. *Educ*: Scots College, Sydney. Served with Aust. Imperial Forces, 1916-19. *Address*: 3 Bedford Crescent, Collaroy, NSW 2097, Australia. *Clubs*: Union, Australian, Elanora Country (all Sydney).

CROWLEY, Rear-Adm. George Clement, CB 1968; DSC 1942, and Bar 1944; Official Fellow and Domestic Bursar of Corpus Christi College, Oxford University, 1969-75; *b* 9 June 1916; *s* of Charles Edmund Lucas Crowley and Beatrice Cicely Crowley; *m* 1948, Una Margaret Jelf; two *s*. *Educ*: Pangbourne Coll. Cadet, HMS Frobisher, 1933; served in China and New Zealand, 1934-39; served War of 1939-45, destroyers; comdg HMS Walpole, 1943-45; comdg HMS Tenacious, 1945-46 (despatches); RN Staff Course, 1947; Staff appts, 1948-53; Exec. Off., HMS Newfoundland, 1953-55; Drafting Comdr, Chatham, 1955-57; Asst Dir Plans, 1957-59; Capt. (D) 7th Destroyer Sqdn, 1959-61; CO New Entry, Trng Estab. HMS Raleigh, 1961-63; Capt. of Fleet to Flag Off. C-in-C Far East Fleet, 1963-64; Staff of Jt Exercise Unison, 1964-65; Staff of Defence Operational Analysis Estab., W Byfleet, 1965-66; Director-General, Naval Personal Services, 1966-68. Capt. 1957; Rear-Adm. 1966. *Recreations*: fishing, tennis, gardening. *Address*: Windrush, Shroton, Blandford, Dorset.

CROWLEY, Thomas Michael, CMG 1970; Assistant Secretary, Ministry of Defence, since 1971; *b* 28 June 1917; *s* of late Thomas Michael Crowley; *m* 1965, Eicke Laura, *d* of late Carl Jensen; one *s*. *Educ*: Forres Acad.; Aberdeen Univ. Entered Civil Service in 1940; Assistant Secretary: Min. of Technology, 1953-70; DTI, 1970; Min. of Aviation Supply, 1970-71. *Address*: c/o Ministry of Defence, St Giles Court, 1-13 St Giles High Street, WC2H 8LD.

CROWLEY-MILLING, Air Marshal Sir Denis, KCB 1973; CBE 1963; DSO 1943; DFC 1941, Bar 1942; Controller, RAF Benevolent Fund, since 1975; *b* 22 March 1919; *s* of T. W. and G. M. Crowley-Milling (*née* Chinnery); *m* 1943, Lorna Jean Jeboult (*née* Stuttard); two *d* (one *s* decd). *Educ*: Malvern Coll., Worcs. RAF Volunteer Reserve, 1937-39; served with Fighters and Fighter Bombers, Nos 615, 242, 610 and 181 Sqdns, 1939-44; Air Ministry Operational Requirements, 1945-47; OC No 6 Sqdn, Middle East, 1947-50; Personal Staff Officer C-in-C Fighter Comd, 1950-52; Wing Comdr Flying, RAF Odiham, 1952-54; Directing Staff, RAF Staff Coll., Bracknell, 1954-57; Flying Coll., RAF Manby, 1957-58; Plans Staff Fighter Comd, 1958-59; Group Capt. Operations Central Fighter Establishment, 1959-62; Station Comdr, RAF Leconfield, 1962-64; AOC RAF Hong Kong, 1964-66; Dir Operational Requirements, MoD (Air), 1966-67; Comdr, RAF Staff and Principal Air Attaché, Washington, 1967-70; AOC No 38 Gp, RAF Odiham, 1970-72; AOC 46 Gp RAF Upavon, 1973; UK Rep., Perm. Mil. Deputies Gp, Cento, 1974-75. *Recreations*: golf and shooting. *Address*: c/o Barclays Bank Ltd, 46 Park Lane, W1A 4EE. *Club*: Royal Air Force.

CROWSON, Richard Borman; HM Diplomatic Service; Counsellor for Hong Kong Affairs, British Embassy, Washington, since 1977; *b* 23 July 1929; *s* of Clarence Borman Crowson and late Cecilia May Crowson (*née* Ramsden); *m* 1960, Sylvia Cavalier (marr. diss. 1974); one *s* one *d*. *Educ*: Downing Coll., Cambridge (MA). FCIS. HMOCS, Uganda, 1955-62; Foreign Office, 1962-63; First Sec. (Commercial), Tokyo, 1963-68; Dep. High Commissioner, Barbados, 1968-70; FCO, 1970-75; Counsellor (Commercial and Aid), Jakarta, 1975-77. *Recreations*: music, drama, travel. *Address*: c/o Foreign and Commonwealth Office, SW1; 67 Crofton Road, Orpington, Kent. *T*: Orpington 30781. *Club*: Royal Commonwealth Society.

CROWTHER, Edward, CBE 1951; Chairman, Northern Gas Board, 1949-62, retired; *b* 7 Oct. 1897; *er s* of John Henry Crowther, Wallasey, Ches; *m* 1927, Gwyneth Ethel, *er d* of R. T. Lewis, Stoke-on-Trent; one *d*. *Educ*: Wallasey Grammar Sch.; Liverpool Univ. (Master of Engineering). Various appts in gas industry; Gen. Manager, Chief Engineer and Dir of Newcastle upon Tyne and Gateshead Gas Co. immediately prior to nationalisation of gas industry; Pres., Instn of Gas Engineers, 1948-49. Hon. FICE. *Publications*: contribs to technical literature of gas industry. *Recreation*: golf. *Address*: c/o Mr R. Gallop, 40 Mayfield Gardens, Walton on Thames, Surrey KT12 5PP.

CROWTHER, Eric (John Ronald), OBE 1977; Metropolitan Magistrate, since 1968; *b* 4 Aug. 1924; *s* of Stephen Charles Crowther, company secretary, and Olive Beatrix Crowther (*née* Selby); *m* 1959, Elké Auguste Ottilie Winkelmann; one *s* one *d*. *Educ*: University College Sch., Hampstead. Royal Navy, 1943-

47 (Medit. Area of Ops). Awarded Tancred Studentship in Common Law, 1948; Called to Bar, Lincoln's Inn, 1951; winner of Inns of Court Contest in Advocacy, 1951; Lectr and Student Counsellor, British Council, 1951-; Lecturer on Elocution and Advocacy for Council of Legal Educn, 1955-; Dir of Studies, Post-Final Gps, Council of Legal Educn, 1975-. Joined Inner Temple *ad eundem*, 1960. Practised at Criminal Bar, 1951-68. Formerly Member: SE Circuit; Surrey and S London Sessions; Mddx Sessions, Central Criminal Court. Editor, Commonwealth Judicial Jl. *Recreations*: travel, transport, the theatre, debating, student welfare. *Address*: 21 Old Buildings, Lincoln's Inn, WC2.

CROWTHER, Francis Harold; retired from Diplomatic Service, 1966; *b* Umtali, Southern Rhodesia, 25 May 1914; *s* of A. D. Crowther; *m* 1952, Mary Eleanor, *d* of F. G. Forman; two *d*. *Educ*: Plumtree Sch., Southern Rhodesia; Univ. of Cape Town; Christ Church, Oxford. Entered Consular Service, Japan, 1938; served in Japan, India, Ceylon, Singapore, Indochina, Korea, Foreign Office, Yugoslavia, Morocco, Mozambique and the Netherlands. *Address*: 59 Sloane Gardens, SW1.

CROWTHER, (Joseph) Stanley; MP (Lab) Rotherham, since June 1976; *b* 30 May 1925; *s* of Cyril Joseph Crowther and Florence Mildred (*née* Beckett); *m* 1948, Margaret Royston; two *s*. *Educ*: Rotherham Grammar Sch.; Rotherham Coll. of Technology. Royal Signals, 1943-47. Journalist: Rotherham Advertiser, 1941-43 and 1947-50; Yorkshire Evening Post, 1950-51; freelance, 1951-. Mem., Rotherham Borough Council, 1958-59, 1961-76; Mayor of Rotherham, 1971-72, 1975-76; Chm., Yorkshire and Humberside Develt Assoc., 1972-76; Exec. Mem., Town and Country Planning Assoc., 1973-. *Recreations*: walking, singing, listening to jazz. *Address*: 15 Clifton Crescent South, Rotherham S65 2AR. *T*: Rotherham 64559. *Clubs*: Central Labour, Eastwood View Working Men's (Rotherham).

CROWTHER, Sir William (Edward Lodewyk Hamilton), Kt 1964; CBE 1955; DSO 1919; VRD; FRACP; medical practitioner; President of Medical Council of Tasmania, 1953-54; *b* 9 May 1887; *s* of Edward L. Crowther, MD; *m* 1915, Joyce Nevett Mitchell, Tunallock, NSW; one *s*. *Educ*: Ormond Coll.; University of Melbourne. Late CO 5th Field Ambulance AIF (despatches, wounded, DSO, 1914-15 star, two medals). Pres., Tasmanian Br., BMA, 1934-42. Hon. Consulting Physician, Hobart Gen. Hosp. Halford Oration, 1933; Archibald Watson Memorial Lecture, 1951; Roentgen Oration, 1953. Hon. Advisor, Australian Bibliography Library Bd, State Library of Tasmania, 1965. *Publications*: series on the extinct Tasmanian race and on history of medicine in Tasmania, to scientific journals. *Recreations*: yachting, historical research. *Address*: 190 Macquarie Street, Hobart, Tasmania 7000. *Club*: Tasmanian (Hobart).

CROWTHER-HUNT, family name of **Baron Crowther-Hunt**.

CROWTHER-HUNT, Baron *cr* 1973 (Life Peer), of Eccleshill in the West Riding of the County of York; **Norman Crowther Crowther-Hunt**, PhD; Fellow and Lecturer in Politics, Exeter College, Oxford, since 1952; *b* 13 March 1920; *s* of late Ernest Angus Hunt, and of Florence Hunt, Bradford, Yorks; *m* 1944, Joyce, *d* of late Rev. Joseph Stackhouse, Walsall Wood, Staffs; three *d*. *Educ*: Wellington Road Council Sch.; Belle Vue High Sch., Bradford; Sidney Sussex Coll., Cambridge. Exhibitioner, 1939-40, Open Scholar, 1945-47, Sidney Sussex Coll.; MA 1949; PhD 1951. Served RA, 1940-45; War Office (GSO3), 1944-45. First Cl. Hist. Tripos, 1946 and 1947; Res. Fellow, Sidney Sussex Coll., 1949-51; Commonwealth Fund Fellow, Princeton Univ., USA, 1951-52. Domestic Bursar, Exeter Coll., 1954-70. Deleg., Oxford Univ. Extra-Mural Delegacy, 1956-70; Vis. Prof., Michigan State Univ., 1961. Constitutional Adviser to the Govt, March-Oct. 1974; Minister of State: DES, 1974-76; Privy Council Office, 1976. Member: Cttee on the Civil Service (Fulton Cttee), 1966-68 (Leader of Management Consultancy Group); Commn on the Constitution, 1969-73 (principal author of the Memorandum of Dissent); Civil Service Coll. Adv. Council, 1970-74. Mem. Council, Headington Sch., Oxford, 1966-74. Hon. DLitt Bradford, 1974. *Publications*: Two Early Political Associations, 1961; (ed) Whitehall and Beyond, 1964; (ed) Personality and Power, 1970. *Recreations*: playing tennis, squash and the piano; broadcasting. Cambridge Univ. Assoc. Football XI, 1939-40. *Address*: 14 Apsley Road, Oxford. *T*: Oxford 58342; Exeter College, Oxford. *T*: Oxford 44681.

CROXTON-SMITH, Claude; President, Institute of Chartered Accountants in England and Wales, June 1970-71; *b* 24 Aug. 1901; *m* 1928, Joan Norah Bloss Watling; two *d*. *Educ*: Dulwich Coll.; Gonville and Caius Coll., Cambridge. The Sales Staff, Anglo American Oil Co. Ltd, 1924-31; Articled Clerk, Inst. of

Chartered Accountants in England and Wales, 1932-36; Chartered Accountant, 1936-39. Served War of 1939-45, RAOC (Major). Chartered Accountant in Public Practice (Bristol), 1946-. *Recreations:* walking, reading. *Address:* 5 Wanscow Walk, Henleaze, Bristol BS9 4LE. *T:* Bristol 627673. *Club:* Bristol (Bristol).

CROYDON, Bishop Suffragan of, since 1977; **Rt. Rev. Geoffrey Stuart Snell;** Archdeacon of Croydon; Archbishop's Representative with HM Forces; *b* 25 Oct. 1920; *s* of Charles James and Ellen Snell; *m* 1948, Margaret Lonsdale Geary; two *s* one *d*. *Educ:* Exeter School; St Peter's College, Oxford (MA 2nd cl. Hons PPE). Called to the Bar, Inner Temple, 1957. UK Civil Service, 1937-39. Served Army, 1939-46, Major, Supplies and Transport. University, 1946-49; Overseas Admin. Civil Service, 1950-54; Managing Governor, Gabbitas-Thring Educational Trust, 1954-61. Deacon and priest, Church of England, 1962; Fellow, Central College of the Anglican Communion, Canterbury, 1964-67; Founder/Director, Christian Organisations Research and Advisory Trust, 1968-75, of Africa, 1975-77. *Publication:* Nandi Customary Law, 1955. *Recreations:* music, travel. *Address:* 52 Selhurst Road, S Norwood SE25 5QD. *T:* 01-684 4832. *Clubs:* East India, Devonshire Sports, and Public Schools; United Kenya (Nairobi).

CROYDON, Archdeacon of; *see* Croydon, Suffragan Bishop of.

CROZIER, Brian Rossiter; Director and co-founder, Institute for the Study of Conflict, since 1970; Editor, Conflict Studies, 1970-75; *b* 4 Aug. 1918; *s* of R. H. Crozier and Elsa (*née* McGillivray); *m* 1940, Mary Lillian Samuel; one *s* three *d*. *Educ:* Lycée, Montpellier; Peterborough Coll., Harrow; Trinity Coll. of Music, London. Music and art critic, London, 1936-39; reporter-sub-editor, Stoke-on-Trent, Stockport, London, 1940-41; aeronautical inspection, 1941-43; sub-editor: Reuters, 1943-44; News Chronicle, 1944-48; and writer, Sydney Morning Herald, 1948-51; corresp., Reuters-AAP, 1951-52; features editor, Straits Times, 1952-53; leader writer and corresp., Economist, 1954-64; commentator, BBC English, French and Spanish overseas services, 1954-66; Chm., Forum World Features, 1965-74. *Publications:* The Rebels, 1960; The Morning After, 1963; Neo-Colonialism, 1964; South-East Asia in Turmoil, 1965 (3rd edn 1968); The Struggle for the Third World, 1966; Franco, 1967; The Masters of Power, 1969; The Future of Communist Power (in USA: Since Stalin), 1970; De Gaulle, vol. 1 1973, vol. 2 1974; A Theory of Conflict, 1974; The Man Who Lost China (Chiang Kai-shek), 1976; Security and the Myth of 'Peace', 1976; contrib. jls in many countries. *Recreations:* swimming, taping stereo, powerful cars. *Address:* (home) 112 Bridge Lane, Temple Fortune, NW11 9JS. *T:* 01-458 3109; (office) 12-12a Golden Square, W1R 3AF. *T:* 01-439 7381. *Clubs:* Travellers', Royal Automobile.

CROZIER, Eric John; writer and theatrical producer; *b* 14 Nov. 1914; *s* of John and Ethel Mary Crozier, London; *m* 1st, 1936, Margaret Johns (marriage dissolved, 1949); two *d*; 2nd, 1950, Nancy Evans. *Educ:* University Coll. Sch., London; Royal Academy of Dramatic Art; British Institute, Paris. Play producer for BBC Television Service, 1936-39. Produced plays and operas for Sadler's Wells Opera, Stratford-on-Avon Memorial Theatre, Glyndebourne Opera and other theatres, 1944-46. Closely associated with Benjamin Britten as producer or author of his operas, 1945-51, and was co-founder with him of The English Opera Group, 1947, and The Aldeburgh Festival of Music and the Arts, 1948. *Publications:* Christmas in the Market Place (adapted from French of Henri Ghéon), 1944; (with Benjamin Britten) Albert Herring, a comic opera in three acts, 1947; Saint Nicolas, a cantata, 1948; Let's Make an Opera, an entertainment for children, 1949; The Life and Legends of Saint Nicolas, 1949; Noah Gives Thanks, a play, 1950; (with E. M. Forster and Benjamin Britten) Billy Budd, an opera in four acts, 1951; opera translations include: The Bartered Bride, Otello, Falstaff, La Traviata, Idomeneo. *Recreation:* listening to music. *Address:* Church Field Cottage, Great Glemham, Saxmundham, Suffolk. *T:* Rendham 471.

CRUDDAS, Maj.-Gen. Ralph Cyril, CB 1953; DSO and Bar, 1943; retired; *b* 26 Aug. 1900; 2nd and *o surv. s* of late Rev. W. S. Cruddas and late Catharine, *d* of J. H. Peter-Hoblyn; *m* 1940, Edwina Marjorie Clare, 2nd *d* of Sir Charles Hanson, 2nd Bt; three *d*. *Educ:* Cheltenham Coll.; Royal Military College, Sandhurst. 2nd Lieut DCLI, 1919; Private Sec. to the Governor of Assam, 1933-35; served War of 1939-45, in Middle East, Italy and NW Europe; commanded 7th Battalion Oxford and Bucks Light Infantry, 1941-43; commanded: Cyrenaica District, 1947-48; Tactical Wing Sch. of Infantry, 1948-49; 133 Infantry Brigade, 1949-51; GOC Land Forces, Hong Kong, 1951-54;

retired 1955. *Address:* Springfield House, Nunney, near Frome, Somerset. *T:* Nunney 309.

CRUDDAS, Rear-Adm. Thomas Rennison, CB 1974; Deputy Controller Aircraft B, Procurement Executive, Ministry of Defence, 1973-76; retired; *b* 6 Feb. 1921; *s* of late Thomas Hepple Wheatley Cruddas, MBE, and Lily (*née* Rennison); *m* 1943, Angela Elizabeth Astbury; one *s* one *d*. *Educ:* Queen Elizabeth Grammar Sch., Darlington; RN Engineering College, Keyham. Joined RN 1938; RNEC, 1939-42. Served War, 1939-45: in Mediterranean and E Indies, in HM Ships Unicorn and Valiant. HMS Cardigan Bay, 1948-50; specialised Aero. Engrg, 1950; RNAY Donibristle, 1951-53; Comdr, 1953; HMS Ark Royal, 1953-55; RNAY Fleetlands, 1956-58; Admty, 1958-61; Staff of Flag Officer Aircraft Carriers, 1961-63; Captain, 1963; Asst Dir Ship Production, 1964-66; service with USN, Washington, DC, as Programme Manager UK Phantom Aircraft, 1967-69; Command Engr Officer, Staff FONAC, 1970-72; Rear-Adm. Engineering, Naval Air Comd, 1972. MIMechE, FRAeS. *Recreations:* golf, horticulture. *Address:* Beeches Close, Bishop's Waltham, Hants. *T:* Bishop's Waltham 2335. *Club:* Corhampton Golf.

CRUFT, John Herbert; Music Director, Arts Council of Great Britain, since 1965; *b* 4 Jan. 1914; *er s* of late Eugene and Winifred Cruft; *m* 1938, Mary Margaret Miriam, *e d* of late Rev. Pat and Miriam McCormick; two *s*. *Educ:* Westminster Abbey Choir Sch.; Westminster Sch.; Royal College of Music (K. F. Boult Conducting Scholar). Oboist in BBC Television, London Philharmonic and Suisse Romande Orchestras, 1936-40. Served with Royal Corps of Signals, 1940-46. London Symphony Orchestra: Oboist, 1946-49; Sec., 1949-59. British Council: Dir of Music Dept, 1959-61; Dir of Drama and Music Dept, 1961-65. FRCM, Hon. RAM. *Address:* 7 Phene Street, Chelsea, SW3.

CRUICKSHANK, Andrew John Maxton, MBE 1945; actor; *b* 25 Dec. 1907; *m* 1939, Curigwen Lewis; one *s* two *d*. *Educ:* Aberdeen Grammar Sch.; LLD St Andrews. With Baynton Shakespearean Company, 1929; appeared in Richard of Bordeaux, New York, 1934; Mary Tudor, London Playhouse, 1935; Lysistrata, Gate, 1936; Macbeth, Old Vic, 1937 (Mem. of Old Vic Company, 1937-40). Served Royal Welch Fus., and GS, 1940-45. Spring 1600, Lyric, Hammersmith, 1945-46; The White Devil, Duchess, 1947; The Indifferent Shepherd, Criterion, 1949; Memorial Theatre, Stratford (Parts included Wolsey, Kent and Julius Caesar), 1950; St Joan, Cort Theatre, New York, 1951; Dial M for Murder, Westminster Theatre, 1952; Dead on Nine, Westminster, 1955; The House by the Lake, Duke of York's, 1956; Inherit The Wind, 1960; Look Homeward Angel, 1960; The Lady From the Sea, Queen's, 1961; The Master Builder, Ashcroft Theatre, Croydon, 1963; Alibi for a Judge, Savoy, 1965; Lloyd George Knew my Father, Savoy, 1973; When We Dead Awaken, Haymarket Leicester, 1975. Has appeared in many films, also in radio and on television; TV series, Dr Finlay's Casebook; author of play, Games, 1975. *Address:* 33 Carlisle Mansions, Carlisle Place, SW1. *Club:* Garrick.

CRUICKSHANK, Charles Greig, MA, DPhil; FRHistS; author; *b* 10 June 1914; *s* of late George Leslie Cruickshank, Fyvie; *m* 1943, Maire Kissane; three *s*. *Educ:* Aberdeen Grammar Sch.; Aberdeen Univ.; Hertford Coll., Oxford; Edinburgh Univ. Min. of Supply, 1940-46; BoT, 1946-51; Trade Comr, Ceylon, 1951-55 (economic mission to Maldive Is, 1953); Canada, 1955-58; Sen. Trade Comr, NZ, 1958-63; Exec. Sec., Commonwealth Econ. Cttee, 1964-66; Dir, Commodities Div., Commonwealth Secretariat, 1967-68; BoT (Regional Export Dir, London and SE), 1969-71; Inspector, FCO, 1971-72; CAA, 1972-73; Asst Sec., DTI, 1973. *Publications:* Elizabeth's Army, 1966; Army Royal, 1969; The English Occupation of Tournai, 1971; (jtly) A Guide to the Sources of British Military History, 1971; The German Occupation of the Channel Islands (official history), 1975; Greece 1940-41, 1976; The V-Mann Papers, 1976; The Tang Murders, 1976; The Fourth Arm: psychological warfare, 1938-45, 1977; The Ebony Version, 1977; contrib. to English Historical Review, Army Quarterly, History Today, Punch, etc. *Recreation:* golf. *Address:* 15 McKay Road, Wimbledon Common, SW20 0HT. *T:* 01-947 1074. *Club:* Royal Wimbledon Golf.

CRUICKSHANK, Herbert James, CBE 1969; CEng, MIMechE; FIOB; *b* 12 July 1912; *s* of late James William Cruickshank and of Dorothy Adeline Cruickshank; *m* 1939, Jean Alexandra Payne; no *c*. *Educ:* Charlton Central Sch.; Regent Street Polytechnic (Schol.). Bovis Ltd: Staff Trainee, 1931; Plant and Labour Controller, 1937; Gilbert-Ash Ltd: (formed within Bovis Gp), 1945; Director, 1949; Civil Engineering Works in Nyasaland, 1949-55; Managing Dir, UK, 1960-63; Chm. and

Man. Dir, 1964; Dir, Bovis Holdings, 1964-72; Group Man. Dir, 1966, Dep. Chm. 1970-72. Member: Metrication Bd, 1969-73; SE Thames RHA. *Recreations:* singing, photography, sketching. *Address:* 45 Bidborough Ridge, Tunbridge Wells, Kent. *T:* Tunbridge Wells 27270. *Clubs:* Oriental, MCC.

CRUICKSHANK, Prof. John; Professor of French, University of Sussex, since 1962; *b* Belfast, N Ireland, 18 July 1924; *s* of Arthur Cruickshank, parliamentary reporter, and Eva Cruickshank (*née* Shummacher); *m* 1st, 1949, Kathleen Mary Gutteridge; one *s*; 2nd, 1972, Marguerite Doreen Penny. *Educ:* Royal Belfast Academical Institution; Trinity Coll., Dublin. Awarded Mod. Lang. Sizarship, TCD, 1943; Cryptographer in Mil. Intell., 1943-45; 1st class Moderatorship in Mod. Langs (French and German) and 2nd class Moderatorship (Mental and Moral Science), TCD, 1948; Lecteur d'Anglais, Ecole Normale Supérieure, Paris, 1948-49; Asst Lectr in French and German, Univ. of Southampton, 1951; Sen. Lectr in French, Univ. of Southampton, 1961. Mem., UGC, 1970-77. *Publications:* Albert Camus and the Literature of Revolt, 1959; Critical Readings in the Modern French Novel, 1961; The Novelist as Philosopher, 1962; Montherlant, 1964; (ed) French Literature and Its Background: vols 1-6, 1968-70; Benjamin Constant, 1974; articles in: French Studies; Modern Language Review; Essays in Criticism; Chicago Review; Symposium; London Magazine; Times Literary Supplement, etc. *Recreations:* bird-watching, painting in oils, watching cricket. *Address:* Woodpeckers, East Hoathly, Sussex BN8 6QL. *T:* Halland 364.

CRUICKSHANK, Flight-Lieut John Alexander, VC 1944; late RAF; with Grindlay's Bank Ltd, London, 1952-76; retired; *b* 20 May 1920; *s* of James C. Cruickshank, Aberdeen, and Alice Bow, Macduff, Banffshire; *m* 1955, Marian R. Beverley, Toronto, Canada. *Educ:* Aberdeen Grammar Sch.; Daniel Stewart's Coll., Edinburgh. Entered Commercial Bank of Scotland, 1938; returned to banking, 1946. Mem. of Territorial Army and called for service, Aug. 1939, in RA; transferred to RAF 1941 and commissioned in 1942; all RAF service was with Coastal Command. ADC to Lord High Commissioner to the Gen. Assembly of the Church of Scotland, 1946-48. *Address:* 2 Greenbank Crescent, Edinburgh EH10 5SG. *T:* 031-447 5924.

CRUICKSHANK, John Merrill, CMG 1951; OBE 1937; *b* 4 Sept. 1901; *s* of J. P. and J. E. Cruikshank (*née* Crombie); *m* 1930, Elaine Strong; one *s*. *Educ:* McGill Univ. (MD, CM, DPH). Colonial Medical Service; Surgeon, Bahamas, 1928-30; Chief Medical Officer, Bahamas, 1930-40; DMS Bahamas Military Forces, 1939-41; RCAF, 1941-46; Asst Medical Adviser, Colonial Office, 1946-48; Insp.-Gen., S Pacific Health Service, and DMS, Fiji, 1948-56; WHO Area Representative for S Pacific, 1956-59. Subseq. Dir, Medical Services, Belmont, Calif; retd. Certificate Tropical Medicine, London; Fellow: Amer. Coll. Surgeons; Amer. Coll. Physicians; Royal Sanitary Inst. OStJ 1950. *Publications:* articles in medical journals. *Recreation:* electronics. *Address:* 401-33 Avenue SW, Calgary, Alberta T2S 0S8, Canada. *T:* 2436691. *Club:* Corona.

CRUMP, Maurice, CBE 1959; *b* 13 Jan. 1908; *s* of William Hamilton Crump and Jean Morris Alan Crump (*née* Esplen); *m* 1946, Mary Arden, *d* of Austin Stead, Montreal, PQ, Canada. *Educ:* Harrow; Oxford. Called to Bar, Inner Temple, 1931, practised Western Circuit. RAF Reserve, 1929-35; recommissioned RAF Volunteer Reserve, 1940; served War of 1939-45, as pilot, 1940-45; Capt. in Command on North Atlantic Return Ferry, 1944-45. In Dept of Dir of Public Prosecutions, 1945; Asst Dir, 1951-58, Deputy Dir, 1958-66. *Recreations:* flying, travelling. *Address:* Dorval, Punta de la Mona, Almuñecar, P. de Granada, Spain. *Clubs:* United Oxford & Cambridge University, Royal Air Force.

CRUMP, Rt. Rev. William Henry Howes; *b* London, Ontario, Canada, 13 March 1903; *m* 1932, Betty Margaret Dean Thomas; one *s* one *d*. *Educ:* London, Ontario; University of Western Ontario; Huron College; Trinity College, Toronto. Ordained Deacon, 1926; Curate, Wawanesa, Manitoba, 1926; Priest, 1927. Rector: Glenboro, Manitoba, 1927; Holland, Manitoba, 1931; Boissevain, Manitoba, 1933; St Aidan's, Winnipeg, 1933-44; Christ Church, Calgary, 1944-60; Canon of St Paul, Diocese of Calgary, 1949; Bishop of Saskatchewan, 1960-71. *Address:* Pinethorpe, RR No 2, Whitby, Ont, Canada.

CRUMP, William Maurice Esplen; *see* Crump, Maurice.

CRUSE, Rt. Rev. John Howard, MA; *b* 15 Feb. 1908; *s* of George Thomas Cruse; *m* 1942, Ethne, *d* of Winslow Sterling-Berry, MB; no *c*. *Educ:* Roborough Sch.; Jesus Coll., Cambridge; Wycliffe Hall, Oxford, 2nd Class Economics Tripos, 2nd Class Theological Tripos, MA, Jesus Coll. Curate of St John, Southall,

1932; Curate of Christ Church, Folkestone, 1934; Vicar of St Paul's, South Harrow, 1936; Vicar of Holy Trinity, Cambridge, 1942 (Chaplain to the Cambridge Pastorate); Exam. Chaplain to Bishop of Sodor and Man; Proctor in Convocation, 1948; Provost of Sheffield, 1949; Bishop Suffragan of Knaresborough, 1965-72. *Publication:* Marriage, Divorce and Repentance, 1949. *Recreations:* fishing and sailing. *Address:* Flat 2, 28 York Place, Harrogate, N Yorks.

CRUTCHLEY, Brooke, CBE 1954; Printer of the University of Cambridge, 1946-74; Fellow of Trinity Hall, 1951-73, Emeritus Fellow, 1977 (Vice-Master, 1966-70); *b* 31 July 1907; *yr s* of late Ernest Tristram Crutchley, CB, CMG, CBE, and Anna, *d* of James Dunne; *m* 1936, Diana, *d* of late Lt-Col Arthur Egerton Cotton, DSO, and Beryl Marie (who *m* 2nd, John Lee Booker); two *s* one *d*. *Educ:* Shrewsbury; Trinity Hall, Cambridge. Editorial Staff of Yorkshire Post, 1929-30; Asst Univ. Printer at Cambridge, 1930-45; Secretary's Dept of the Admiralty, 1941-45. Pres., Inst. of Printing, 1972-74. *Address:* 2 Courtyards, Little Shelford, Cambs. *T:* Shelford 2389. *Club:* Double Crown.

CRUTCHLEY, Adm. Sir Victor Alexander Charles, VC 1918; KCB 1946 (CB 1945); DSC 1918; RN retired; DL; *b* 2 Nov. 1893; *s* of late Percy Edward Crutchley and late Hon. Frederica Louisa, 2nd *d* of 3rd Baron Southampton; *m* 1930, Joan Elizabeth Loveday, *y d* of late William Coryton, Pentillie Castle, Cornwall, and late Mrs William Coryton; one *s* one *d*. *Educ:* Osborne and Dartmouth. Served European War in HMS Centurion, Battle of Jutland; in HMS Brilliant in attempt to block Ostend Harbour, 22-23 April 1918 (DSC); in HMS Vindictive in similar attempt, 9-10 May 1918 (VC, Croix de Guerre); commanded HMS Diomede, New Zealand; Senior Officer, First Minesweeping Flotilla, 1935-36; Capt. Fishery Protection and Minesweeping Flotilla, 1936-37; commanded HMS Warspite, 1937-40; Commodore RN Barracks, Devonport, 1940-42; commanded Australian Naval Squadron, 1942-44; Flag Officer Gibraltar, 1945-47; retired, 1947, as Adm. DL Dorset, 1957. Chief Comdr Legion of Merit (USA), 1944; Polonia Restituta, 1942. *Address:* Mappercombe Manor, Nettlecombe, Bridport, Dorset DT6 3SS.
See also Sir William John Colfox, Bt.

CRUTTWELL, Mrs Geraldine; *see* McEwan, Geraldine.

CRUTTWELL, Hugh (Percival); Principal of Royal Academy of Dramatic Art since 1966; *b* 31 Oct. 1918; *s* of Clement Chadwick Cruttwell and Grace Fanny (*née* Robin); *m* 1953, Geraldine McEwan, *qv*; one *s* one *d*. *Educ:* King's Sch., Bruton; Hertford Coll., Oxford. *Address:* 8 Ranelagh Avenue, Barnes, SW13. *T:* 01-878 0695.

CRYER, George Robert; MP (Lab) Keighley, since Feb. 1974; Parliamentary Under-Secretary of State, Department of Industry, since 1976; *b* 3 Dec. 1934; *m* 1963, Ann (*née* Place); one *s* one *d*. *Educ:* Salt High Sch., Shipley; Hull Univ. BSc Econ Hons, Certif. Educn. Secondary Sch. Teacher, Hull, 1959, Bradford, 1961 and Keighley, 1962; Asst Personnel Officer, 1960; Dewsbury Techn. Coll., 1963; Blackburn Coll. of Technology, 1964-65; Keighley Techn. Coll., 1965-74. Contested (Lab) Darwen Div. of Lancs, 1964; Labour Councillor, Keighley Borough Council, 1971-74. *Publications:* Steam in the Worth Valley, Vol. 1 1969, Vol. 2 1972. *Recreation:* working on Worth Valley Railway. *Address:* Holyoake, Providence Lane, Oakworth, Keighley, W Yorks. *T:* Haworth 42595. *Club:* Workers Union Social (Keighley).

CUBBON, Sir Brian Crossland, KCB 1977 (CB 1974); Permanent Under Secretary of State, Northern Ireland Office, since 1976; *b* 9 April 1928; *m* 1956, Elizabeth Lorin Richardson; three *s* one *d*. *Educ:* Bury Grammar Sch.; Trinity Coll., Cambridge. Entered Home Office, 1951; Cabinet Office, 1961-63; Private Sec. to Home Sec., 1968-69; Under Sec., 1969; Cabinet Office, 1971-75 (Dep. Sec., 1972); Dep. Sec., Home Office, 1975-76. *Address:* c/o Northern Ireland Office, Great George Street, SW1P 3AJ. *Club:* United Oxford & Cambridge University.

CUBBON, Maj.-Gen. John Hamilton, CB 1962; CBE 1958 (OBE 1940); DL; *b* 15 March 1911; *s* of Joseph Cubbon; *m* 1951, Amelia Margaret Yates; two *s* one *d*. *Educ:* St Bees Sch.; RMC Sandhurst. 2nd Lieut Ches Regt, 1931; Commanded: 1st Bn The Parachute Regt, 1946-49; 1st Bn The Ches Regt, 1951-54; 18th Infantry Bde, Malaya, 1956-57. Maj.-Gen. 1960; GOC SW Dist, 1960-63; GOC Land Forces, Middle East Command, 1963-65. DL Devon, 1969. *Recreation:* sailing. *Address:* The Hayes, Harpford, Sidmouth, Devon.

CUBITT, family name of **Baron Ashcombe.**

CUBITT, Hon. (Charles) Guy, CBE 1973; DSO 1943; TD; DL; *b* 13 Feb. 1903; 3rd *surv. s* of 2nd Baron Ashcombe, CB; *m* 1927, Rosamond Mary Edith, *d* of Sir Montagu Cholmeley, 4th Bt; one *s* two *d. Educ:* Eton; RMC Sandhurst. Lt-Col Surrey Yeomanry (despatches, DSO); Hon. Col Surrey Yeomanry, 1951. Life-Pres., The Pony Club, 1971; Pres., BHS, 1952; Chm., Royal Internat. Horse Show. High Sheriff of Surrey, 1955; Surrey County Council, 1955 (Alderman, 1965-72); DL Surrey, 1956. *Address:* Dormers, Tetbury, Glos GL8 8HA. *T:* Tetbury 52423. *Club:* Cavalry and Guards.
See also Baron Carew, H. G. Cubitt.

CUBITT, Hugh Guy, CBE 1977; FRICS; JP; Director, National Westminster Bank (Chairman, Outer London Region) and other companies; Partner, Cubitt & West (Estate Agents and Surveyors); *b* 2 July 1928; *s* of Col Hon. (Charles) Guy Cubitt, *qv; m* 1958, Linda Ishbel, *d* of late Hon. Angus Campbell, CBE; one *s* two *d. Educ:* RNC Dartmouth and Greenwich. Lieut RN, 1949; served in Korea, 1949-51; Flag Lieut to Adm., BJSM Washington, 1952 and to C-in-C Nore, 1953; retd 1953. Qual. Chartered Auctioneer and Estate Agent, 1958; FRICS 1970. Partner: Rogers Chapman & Thomas, 1958-67; Cubitt & West, 1962-. Mem. Westminster City Council, 1963-; Chairman: Highways Cttee, 1968-71; Town Planning Cttee, 1971-72; Leader of Council, 1972-77; Alderman, 1974-77; Lord Mayor and dep. High Steward of Westminster, 1977-78. Hon. Treas., London Boroughs Assoc., 1974-77. Mem. Home Office Cttee on London Taxicab Trade (Stamp Cttee), 1967-70. JP Surrey, 1964; Dep. Chm., Dorking PSD, 1974-. Liveryman, Needlemakers' Co. *Recreations:* country sports, travel, photography. *Address:* Chapel House, West Humble, Dorking, Surrey. *T:* Dorking 2994. *Clubs:* Boodle's, MCC.

CUBITT, James William Archibald, MBE 1945; FRIBA; architect, sculptor; Senior Partner of James Cubitt and Partners, London, Nigeria, Malaya, since 1948; *b* 1 May 1914; *s* of James Edward and Isabel Margaret Cubitt; *m* 1st, 1939, Ann Margaret Tooth (marr. diss. 1947); one *s* one *d*; 2nd, 1950, Constance Anne (*née* Sitwell) (marr. diss. 1972); one *s*; 3rd, 1973, Eleni Collard (*née* Kiortsis). *Educ:* Harrow; Brasenose Coll., Oxford; Architectural Association Sch. of Architecture. BA Oxon 1935; ARIBA 1940; FRIBA 1955. Army, 1940-45. In private practice as architect from 1948. Main works in England: exhibition and shop design; schools for Herts CC, W Riding CC, LCC, Leeds Corporation. Has also designed many public buildings, schools, offices and private houses in Ghana; now works in Nigeria, Brunei and Libya. Architect for the Universities of Libya and Nigeria. Chm., Mortimer and Burghfield Local Labour Party, 1974-. Writes articles and reviews. Council of Architectural Assoc., 1960- (Pres., 1965-66). Sculpture: one-man show, John Whibley Gallery, March 1962; Burgos Gallery, New York, March 1966. *Address:* 25 Gloucester Place, W1. *T:* 01-935 0288.

CUCKNEY, John Graham; Senior Crown Agent and Chairman of the Crown Agents for Oversea Governments and Administrations, since 1974; Chairman: Millbank Technical Services, since 1974; Port of London Authority, since 1977; Director, Abbey Capital Property Group (Australia), since 1974; *b* 12 July 1924; *s* of late Air Vice-Marshal E. J. Cuckney, CB, CBE, DSC; *m* 2nd, 1960, Muriel, *d* of late Walter Scott Boyd. *Educ:* Shrewsbury; St Andrews Univ. (MA). War Service, Royal Northumberland Fusiliers, 1942-46. Attached War Office (Civil Asst, Gen. Staff), 1949-57; Chm. and Dir of various industrial and financial cos, 1957-72, including: Man. Dir, Standard Industrial Gp, 1966-70; Chairman: Mersey Docks and Harbour Board, 1970-72; Standard Industrial Trust, 1966-70; Director: Lazard Bros & Co., 1964-70; J. Bibby & Sons, 1970-72; Dep. Chm., Stanley Gibbons International, 1974-76; Chief Executive (Second Perm. Sec.), Property Services Agency, DoE, 1972-74. Independent Mem., Railway Policy Review Cttee, 1966-67; special Mem., Hops Marketing Bd, 1971-72; Chm., EDC for Building, 1976-. *Address:* 4 Millbank, SW1P 3JD. *Clubs:* Athenæum, Travellers'.

CUDLIPP, family name of **Baron Cudlipp.**

CUDLIPP, Baron *cr* 1974 (Life Peer), of Aldingbourne, W Sussex; **Hugh Cudlipp,** Kt 1973; OBE 1945; Chairman: International Publishing Corporation Ltd, 1968-73 (Deputy Chairman, 1964-68); International Publishing Corporation Newspaper Division, 1970-73; Deputy Chairman (editorial), Reed International Board, 1970-73; Director, Associated Television Ltd, 1956-73; *b* 28 Aug. 1913; *s* of William Cudlipp, Cardiff; *m* 2nd, 1945, Eileen Ascroft (*d* 1962); 3rd, 1963, Jodi, *d* of late John L. Hyland, Palm Beach, Fla, and Mrs D. W. Jones, Southport. *Educ:* Howard Gardens Sch., Cardiff. Provincial

newspapers in Cardiff and Manchester, 1927-32; Features Ed., Sunday Chronicle, London, 1932-35; Features Ed., Daily Mirror, 1935-37; Ed., Sunday Pictorial, 1937-40. Military Service, 1940-46; CO, British Army Newspaper Unit, CMF, 1943-46. Ed., Sunday Pictorial, 1946-49; Managing Ed., Sunday Express, 1950-52; Editorial Dir, Daily Mirror and Sunday Pictorial, 1952-63; Joint Managing Dir, Daily Mirror and Sunday Pictorial, 1959-63; Chm., Odhams Press Ltd, 1961-63; Chm., Daily Mirror Newspapers Ltd, 1963-68. Mem., Royal Commn on Standards of Conduct in Public Life, 1974-76. *Publications:* Publish and be Damned!, 1955; At Your Peril, 1962; Walking on the Water, 1976. *Address:* The Dene, Hook Lane, Aldingbourne, West Sussex. *Clubs:* Garrick; Royal Southern Yacht.

CUDLIPP, Michael John; Director of Information, National Enterprise Board, since 1975; *b* 24 April 1934; *o s* of late Percy Cudlipp and Mrs Gwendoline May Cudlipp; *m* 1957, Margaret Susannah Rees (marr. diss. 1975); one *d. Educ:* Tonbridge Sch., Kent. Trainee reporter, feature writer, gossip columnist, sub-editor, South Wales Echo, Cardiff, 1953-57; Sub-editor, Evening Chronicle, Manchester (various freelance jobs on daily and Sunday newspapers in Manchester), 1957-58; News Editor and Asst Editor (News), Sunday Times, 1958-67; Asst Editor (Night), Jt Man. Editor and sen. Dep. Editor, The Times, 1967-73; Chief Editor, London Broadcasting Co., 1973-74; Consultant on Public Relations to NI Office (temp. Civil Servant with rank of Under-Sec.), 1974-75. Consultant on newspaper economics, manning, labour relations and budgeting. *Recreations:* reading, the arts, Welsh Rugby football. *Address:* c/o Barclays Bank Ltd, Bedford Row Branch, 54A Theobalds Road, WC1X 8NR.

CUDLIPP, Reginald; Director, Anglo-Japanese Economic Institute, London, since 1961; *b* Cardiff, 11 Dec. 1910; *s* of William Cudlipp, Cardiff; *m* 1945, Rachel Joyce Braham. *Educ:* Cardiff Technical Coll. Began journalistic career on Penarth News, Glamorgan; Sub-Ed., Western Mail, Cardiff; joined News of the World Sub-Editorial Staff, 1938; served War, 1940-46; rejoined News of the World and became Special Correspondent in USA, 1946-47; Features Ed., 1948-50, Dep. Ed., 1950-53, Ed., 1953-59; Dir, News of the World Ltd, 1955-60. Extensive industrial tours and on-the-spot economic study of Japan regularly, 1962-. Member: Japan Soc.; RSAA; RSA; RIIA; Royal Commonwealth Soc. Editor, Japan (quarterly review and monthly survey), and special publications on the Japanese scene. Lecturer and writer on Japan's past, present and future; also first-hand research on developing nations and economic co-operation, especially in Africa and Asia. *Publications:* numerous contribs to newspapers and periodicals, on Japan and Anglo-Japanese affairs. *Recreations:* music, travel, and reading, writing and talking about Japan. *Address:* 342 Grand Buildings, Trafalgar Square, WC2. *T:* 01-930 5567.

CUDMORE, Derek George, CBE 1972 (OBE 1970); HM Overseas Civil Service, retired; *b* 9 Nov. 1923; *s* of late Harold Thomas Cudmore and of Winifred Laura Cudmore; *m* 1952, Vera Beatrice (*née* Makin); no *c. Educ:* Regent Street Polytechnic; Slough Grammar Sch. Served War, Royal Navy, 1942-46 (Lt RNVR). Joined Colonial Service as Administrative Officer, 1947; Nigeria and Southern Cameroons, 1947-56; Northern Rhodesia, 1956-57. Consecutively Dist. Comr, Sen. Asst. Sec. and Dep. Financial Sec., British Solomon Islands, 1957-67; Asst Resident Comr, Gilbert and Ellice Islands, 1967-71; Governor, BVI, 1971-74; Development Officer, Kingdom of Tonga, 1975-77. *Recreations:* golf, travel, sailing. *Address:* Perhams, Honiton, Devon. *Clubs:* Royal Over-Seas League; Nuku'alofa.

CULHANE, Rosalind, (Lady Padmore), MVO 1938; OBE 1949; Treasury Welfare Adviser, 1943-64; *y d* of late F. W. S. Culhane, MRCS, LRCP, Hastings, Sussex; *m* 1964, Sir Thomas Padmore, *qv.* Joined Treasury in 1923 and attached to office of Chancellor of Exchequer; Asst Private Sec. to Mr Chamberlain, 1934, Sir John Simon, 1937, Sir Kingsley Wood, 1940. *Address:* 39 Cholmeley Crescent, N6. *T:* 01-340 6587.

CULLEN OF ASHBOURNE, 2nd Baron *cr* 1920; **Charles Borlase Marsham Cokayne,** MBE 1945; Major, Royal Signals; *b* 6 Oct. 1912; *e s* of 1st Baron and Grace Margaret (*d* 1971), *d* of Rev. Hon. John Marsham; *S* father, 1932; *m* 1942, Valerie Catherine Mary (marr. diss. 1947), *o d* of late W. H. Collbran; one *d*; *m* 1948, Patricia Mary, *er d* of late Col S. Clulow-Gray and late Mrs Clulow-Gray, formerly of Clare Priory, Suffolk. *Educ:* Eton. Served War of 1939-45 (MBE). Amateur Tennis Champion, 1947, 1952. One of HM Lieutenants, City of London, 1976-. *Heir:* *b* Hon. Edmund Willoughby Marsham Cokayne [*b* 18 May 1916; *m* 1943, Janet Manson, *d* of late William Douglas Watson and of Mrs Lauritson, Calgary].

Address: 75 Cadogan Gardens, SW3. *T:* 01-589 1981. *Clubs:* MCC, Queen's.

CULLEN, Prof. Alexander, OBE 1960; DSc(Eng); FRS 1977; FIEE, FIEEE, FInstP, FCGI; Pender Professor of Electrical Engineering, University College London, since 1967; *b* 30 April 1920; *s* of Richard and Jessie Cullen, Lincoln; *m* 1940, Margaret, *er d* of late Alexander Lamb, OBE; two *s* one *d. Educ:* Lincoln Sch.; City and Guilds Coll., London. Staff of Radio Dept, RAE Farnborough, working on development of radar, 1940-46; Lectr in Electrical Engineering, University Coll., London, 1946-55 (title of Reader conferred 1955); Prof. of Electrical Engineering, University of Sheffield, 1955-67. Kelvin premium of IEE, 1952; Extra premium of IEE, 1953 (with Prof. H. M. Barlow and Dr A. E. Karbowiak); Radio Sect. premium of IEE, 1954; Ambrose Fleming premium of IEE, 1956 (with J. C. Parr), 1975 (with Dr J. R. Forrest); Duddell premium of IEE, 1957 (with Dr H. A. French); Electronics and Communications Sect. premium of IEE, 1959. Member: Brit. Nat. Cttee, URSI; Davy Faraday Laboratory Cttee, Bd of Managers, Royal Instn. Fellow, Fellowship of Engineering, 1977. *Publications:* Microwave Measurements (jointly with Prof. H. M. Barlow), 1950; a number of papers on electromagnetic waves and microwave measurement techniques in IEE proceedings and elsewhere. *Recreations:* music and reading. *Address:* Dept of Electronic and Electrical Engineering, University College London, Torrington Place, WC1.

CULLEN, Douglas; see Cullen, W. D.

CULLEN, James Reynolds; *b* 13 June 1900; *s* of Rev. James Harris Cullen, London Missionary Society; *m* 1931, Inez, *e d* of M. G. Zarifi, MBE; one *s* two *d. Educ:* Weimar Gymnasium; Tonbridge Sch.; Balliol Coll., Oxford (Scholar). Hertford Schol., 1919; Craven Schol., 1920; 1st class Hon. Mods, 1920; 2nd class Lit. Hum. 1922; MA 1925. Asst Master, Winchester Coll., 1922-30; archæological expeditions to Asia Minor, 1925, and Mytilene, 1930; Dir of Education, Cyprus, 1930-45; Dir of Education, Uganda, 1945-52; Asst Master, Oundle Sch., 1953-60, Cranbrook and Benenden Schs, 1960-68. *Address:* Weathercock House, Hawkhurst, Kent TN18 4QA. *Club:* Royal Commonwealth Society.

CULLEN, Raymond; Chairman, The Calico Printers' Association Ltd and subsidiaries, 1964-68; *b* 27 May 1913; *s* of late John Norman Cullen and Bertha (*née* Dearden); *m* 1940, Doris, *d* of A. W. Paskin; two *d. Educ:* King's Sch., Macclesfield; St Catharine's Coll., Cambridge (Scholar, MA). Joined The Calico Printers' Assoc. Ltd Commn Printing, 1934; transf. overseas, 1938; service in India and China. Dir, W. A. Beardsell & Co. (Private) Ltd, Madras, 1946 (Chm. and Man. Dir, 1949-55); Chm. and Man. Dir, Mettur Industries Ltd, 1949-55; Chm. and Man. Dir, Marshall Fabrics Ltd, 1955-62; Director: Calico Printers' Assoc. Ltd, 1962-68; Barclays Bank Ltd Manchester Local Bd, 1965-69. Member: Textile Coun., 1967-69; Coun., Inst. of Directors, 1967-69; NW Economic Planning Coun., 1968-69; Governor, Manchester Grammar Sch. *Recreations:* fishing, golf (Pres., Cheshire Union of Golf Clubs). *Address:* Cranford, Ladybrook Road, Bramhall, Cheshire. *T:* 061-485 3204. *Clubs:* East India, Devonshire, Sports and Public Schools; St James's (Manchester).

CULLEN, William Douglas, QC (Scotland) 1973; *b* 18 Nov. 1935; *s* of late Sheriff K. D. Cullen and Mrs G. M. Cullen; *m* 1961, Rosamond Mary Downer; two *s* two *d. Educ:* Dundee High Sch.; St Andrews Univ. (MA); Edinburgh Univ. (LLB). Called to the Scottish Bar, 1960. *Publication:* The Faculty Digest Supplement 1951-60, 1965. *Recreations:* gardening, natural history. *Address:* 62 Fountainhall Road, Edinburgh EH9 2LP. *T:* 031-667 6949. *Club:* New (Edinburgh).

CULLINGFORD, Rev. Cecil Howard Dunstan, MA; FRSA; *b* 13 Sept. 1904; *s* of Francis James and Lilian Mabel Cullingford; *m* 1st, 1933, Olive Eveline (*d* 1971), *d* of Lt-Col P. H. Collingwood, Clifton, Bristol; one *s* one *d* ; 2nd, 1972, Penelope Wood-Hill, *e d* of Dr H. Wood-Hill, Beccles. *Educ:* City of London Sch.; Corpus Christi Coll., Cambridge (Foundation Scholar). 1st Class Hons in Classical Tripos, Parts 1 and 2, and Historical Tripos, Part 2. VIth Form Master, Brighton Coll., 1928-32; Vice-Principal, Clifton Theological Coll., 1932-34; Chaplain of Oundle Sch., 1935-46. Army Chaplain, 1939-45; Guards Armoured Div., 1939-43; Staff Chaplain, 21st Army Group, 1943-44; Senior Chaplain, 79th Armoured Div., 1944-45. Headmaster of Monmouth Sch., 1946-56; Lectr in Naval History at Britannia, RNC Dartmouth, 1957-60; Chaplain: St John's Sch., Leatherhead, 1960-64; St Michael's Sch., Limpsfield, 1964-67; Vicar of Stiffkey with Morston, 1967-72; Rural Dean of Beccles, 1973-76. Pres., Silleren Ski Club, 1966;

Vice-Pres., Wessex Cave Club; Hon. Member: Cave Res. Group of GB; British Speleological Assoc.; British Cave Res. Assoc. *Publications:* Exploring Caves, 1951; (ed) British Caving: an Introduction to Speleology, 1953 (2nd edn 1961); (ed) A Manual of Caving Techniques, 1969; The Thornhill Guide to Caving, 1976; (ed) The Science of Speleology, 1976. *Recreations:* hockey, pot-holing, music, archæology. *Address:* The Staithe, Beccles, Suffolk. *T:* Beccles 712182.
See also E. C. M. Cullingford.

CULLINGFORD, Eric Coome Maynard, CMG 1963; *b* 15 March 1910; *s* of Francis James and Lilian Mabel Cullingford; *m* 1938, Friedel Fuchs; two *s* one *d. Educ:* City of London Sch.; St Catharine's Coll., Cambridge (Exhibitioner). Entered Ministry of Labour as Third Class Officer, 1932; Principal, 1942. Served with Manpower Div. of CCG, 1946-50. Asst Sec., Min. of Labour, 1954. Labour Attaché, Bonn, 1961-65, 1968-72. Regional Controller, Eastern and Southern Region, Dept of Employment and Productivity, 1966-68; retired 1973. *Publication:* Trade Unions in West Germany, 1976. *Address:* Oaklands, 21 Furze Field, Oxshott, Surrey.
See also Rev. C. H. D. Cullingford.

CULLINGWORTH, Prof. (John) Barry; Chairman and Professor, Department of Urban and Regional Planning, University of Toronto, since 1977; Visiting Professor, University of Strathclyde; *b* 11 Sept. 1929; *s* of Sidney C. and Winifred E. Cullingworth; *m* 1951, Betty Violet (*née* Turner); one *s* two *d. Educ:* High Pavement Sch., Nottingham; Trinity Coll. of Music, London; London Sch. of Economics. Research Asst, Asst Lectr and Lectr, Univ. of Manchester, 1955-60; Sen. Lectr and Reader, Univ. of Glasgow, 1963-66; Dir, Centre for Urban and Regional Studies, Univ. of Birmingham, 1966-72. Dir, Planning Exchange, Scotland, 1972-75; Official Historian, Cabinet Office, 1971-75. Vice-Chm., Scottish Housing Adv. Cttee; Chairman: Cttee on Community Facilities in Expanding Towns (Report, The Needs of New Communities, 1967); Cttee on Unfit Housing in Scotland (Report, Scotland's Older Houses, 1967); Cttee on Allocation of Council Houses (Report, Council Housing: Purposes, Procedures and Practices, 1968); former Chm., Adv. Cttee on Rent Rebates and Rent Allowances. Vice-Pres., Housing Centre Trust. FRSA 1974; Hon. MRTPI. *Publications:* Housing Needs and Planning Policy, 1960; Housing in Transition, 1963; Town and Country Planning in England and Wales, 1964, 6th edn 1976; English Housing Trends, 1965; Housing and Local Government, 1966; Scottish Housing in 1965, 1967; A Profile of Glasgow Housing, 1968; (with V. Karn) Ownership and Management of Housing in New Towns, 1968; Housing and Labour Mobility, (Paris) 1969; Problems of an Urban Society (3 vols), 1973; Reconstruction and Land Use Planning, 1975. *Address:* Department of Urban and Regional Planning, 230 College Street, Toronto, Canada. *Club:* Reform.

CULLIS, Prof. Charles Fowler; Professor of Physical Chemistry since 1967 and Head of Chemistry Department since 1973, City University, London; *b* 31 Aug. 1922; 2nd *s* of late Prof. C. G. Cullis, Prof. of Mining Geology, Univ. of London, and Mrs W. J. Cullis (*née* Fowler); *m* 1958, Marjorie Elizabeth, *er d* of late Sir Austin Anderson and of Lady Anderson; two *s* two *d. Educ:* Stowe Sch. (Open Schol.); Trinity Coll., Oxford. BA 1944, BSc 1st Cl. Hons Chem. 1945, DPhil 1948, MA 1948, DSc 1960; FRIC 1958. ICI Research Fellow in Chem., Oxford, 1947-50; Lectr in Phys. Chem., Imperial Coll., London, 1950-59; Sen. Lectr in Chem. Engrg and Chem. Tech., Imperial Coll., 1959-64; Reader in Combustion Chemistry, Univ. of London, 1964-66. Vis. Prof., College of Chem., Univ. of California, Berkeley, 1966; Vis. Scientist, CSIRO, Sydney, 1970. Mem. Council, Chem. Soc., 1969-72, 1975-; Member: Chem. Soc. Library Bd, 1970-; Chem. Soc. Publications Bd, 1976-; Hon. Sec., Brit. Sect. of Combustion Inst., 1969-74; Mem., Rockets Sub-cttee, 1968-73, and of Combustion Sub-cttee, 1969-72, Aeronautical Research Council; Member: Navy Dept Fuels and Lubricants Adv. Cttee (Fire and Explosion Hazards Working Gp), 1967-; Safety in Mines Research Adv. Bd, 1973-; Scientific Editor, Internat. Union of Pure and Applied Chem., 1976-. Joseph Priestley Award, Chem. Soc., 1974. *Publications:* numerous sci. papers in Proc. Royal Soc., Trans Faraday Soc., Jl Chem. Soc., etc, mainly concerned with chemistry of combustion reactions. *Recreations:* music, travel. *Address:* Chieveley, Black Hill, Lindfield, Sussex RH16 2HF. *T:* Lindfield 2188; Chemistry Department, City University, St John Street, EC1V 4PB. *T:* 01-253 4399, ext. 367. *Clubs:* Athenæum, United Oxford & Cambridge University.
See also M. F. Cullis.

CULLIS, Michael Fowler, CVO 1955; Adviser on relations with non-governmental bodies, Foreign and Commonwealth Office, since 1974; *b* 22 Oct. 1914; *s* of late Prof. Charles Gilbert Cullis, Imperial Coll. of Science and Technology, London Univ., and

late Winifred Jefford Cullis (née Fowler); m Catherine Robertson, Arbroath, Scotland; no c. Educ: Wellington Coll. (scholar); Brasenose Coll., Oxford (Hulme Scholar). MA, classics. Law (Lincoln's Inn), and journalism, 1938-39. Military Intelligence, Gibraltar, 1939-40; served Min. of Economic Warfare (London, Spain and Portugal), 1940-44; joined FO as head of Austrian Section, 1945; Political Adviser on Austrian Treaty negotiations (London, Moscow, Vienna, Paris, New York), 1947-50; Special Asst, Schuman Plan, 1950; First Sec., British Embassy, Oslo, 1951-55; Regional (Information) Counsellor for the five Nordic countries, British Embassy, Copenhagen, 1955-58; Dep. Gov. of Malta, 1959-61; Sen. Research Associate, Atlantic Institute, Paris, 1962-65; writing, lecturing, etc, at various European centres, 1965-66; Dir, Arms Control and Disarmament Res., FO, then FCO, 1967-74. Chevalier (1st cl.) Order of Dannebrog, 1957. *Recreations:* music, Siciliana, chess. *Address:* County End, Bushey Heath, Herts. *T:* 01-950 1057. *Club:* Athenæum.
See also C. F. Cullis.

CULLITON, Hon. Edward Milton; Chief Justice of Saskatchewan, since 1962; b Grand Forks, Minnesota, USA, 9 April 1906; s of John J. Culliton and Katherine Mary Kelly, Canadians; m 1939, Katherine Mary Hector. *Educ:* Primary educn in towns in Saskatchewan; Univ. of Saskatchewan. BA 1926, LLB 1928. Practised law in Gravelbourg, Sask., 1930-51. Served War: Canadian Armed Forces (active, overseas, Judges' Advocate Br.), 1941-46. MLA for Gravelbourg, 1935-44, re-elected, 1948; Mem. Opposition until 1951; Provincial Sec., 1938-41; Minister without portfolio, 1941-44. Apptd Judge of Court of Appeal for Sask., 1951. Chm., Sask. Jubilee Cttee, 1952-55. Univ. of Sask.: Mem. Bd of Governors, 1955-61; Chancellor, 1963-69; Mem. Bd, Can. Nat. Inst. for the Blind, 1955- (Pres. Sask. Div., 1962-); Chm., Adv. Bd, Martha House (unmarried mothers), 1955-; Chm., Sask. Revision of Statutes Cttee, 1963-65, and again 1974 until completion 1975-76. Mem., Knights of Columbus, 1930-; Hon. DCL, Saskatchewan, 1962. Kt Comdr of St Gregory (Papal) 1963. *Recreations:* golf, curling (McDonald Brier Trustee); interested in football. *Address:* (residence) 1303-1830 College Avenue, Regina, Saskatchewan S4P 1C2, Canada. *T:* 569-1758. (office) The Court House, 2425 Victoria Avenue, Regina, Sask. S4P 3E4, Canada. *T:* 565-5412 (area code: 306). *Clubs:* Wascana Country, Wascana Curling, Assiniboia, United Services Institute (all Regina, Sask.).

CULLWICK, Prof. Ernest Geoffrey, OBE 1946; Captain (L) RCN(R), retired; MA, DSc, FIEE, FRSE; Watson-Watt Professor of Electrical Engineering in the University of Dundee, 1967-73 (University of St Andrews, Queen's College, Dundee, 1949-67); now Professor Emeritus; b Wolverhampton, 24 May 1903; s of late Herbert Ernest Cullwick and Edith Ada Ascough; m 1929, Mamie Ruttan, o d of G. B. Boucher, Peterborough, Ontario; one s one d. *Educ:* Wolverhampton Grammar Sch.; Downing Coll., Cambridge (Mathematical Scholar, Foundation Scholar in Engineering). Mathematical and Mechanical Sciences Tripos, Industrial Bursar of the Royal Exhibition of 1851; with British Thomson Houston Co. and Canadian General Electric Co.; Asst Prof. of Electrical Engineering, Univ. of British Columbia, Vancouver, 1928-34; Lectr in Electrical Engineering, Military Coll. of Science, Woolwich, 1934-35; Associate Prof. of Electrical Engineering, Univ. of British Columbia, 1935-37; Prof. and Head of Dept of Electrical Engineering, Univ. of Alberta, Edmonton, 1937-46; Dir of Electrical Engineering, RCN, 1942-47; Dir, Electrical Research Div. Defence Research Board, Ottawa, 1947-49. Dean: Faculty of Applied Science, Univ. of St Andrews, 1955-60, 1965-67; Fac. of Engineering and Applied Science, Univ. of Dundee, 1967-71. Coun., Royal Soc. of Edinburgh, 1958-61; Chm. Scottish Centre IEE, 1961-63. Life Mem., Engineering Inst. of Canada. *Publications:* The Fundamentals of Electromagnetism, 1939; Electromagnetism and Relativity, 1957; technical, scientific and educational papers. *Recreations:* genealogy, bookbinding, philately. *Address:* 20 Riverdale, River, Dover, Kent.

CULME-SEYMOUR, Comdr Sir Michael; see Seymour.

CULSHAW, John (Royds), OBE 1966; author and producer; b 28 May 1924; s of Percy Ellis Culshaw and late Dorothy Royds Culshaw. *Educ:* King George V Sch., Southport, Lancs. RNAS (Fleet Air Arm), Lieut, 1942-46. The Decca Record Co. Ltd (Classical Recordings), 1946-54; Capitol Records Inc., Hollywood, USA, 1954-56; The Decca Record Co. Ltd (Manager, Classical Recordings), 1956-67; Head of Music Programmes, BBC TV, 1967-75. Mem. Arts Council and Chm., Music Panel, 1975-77. Vienna Philharmonic Orchestra: Nicolai Medal, 1959; Schalk Medal, 1967. *Publications:* Sergei Rachmaninov, 1949; The Sons of Brutus, 1950; A Century of Music, 1951; A Place of Stone, 1952; Ring Resounding, 1967;

Reflections on Wagner's Ring, 1976. Contributor: The Gramophone, Saturday Review (USA), High Fidelity (USA), etc. *Recreation:* flying. *Address:* 16 Arlington Avenue, N1. *T:* 01-359 2837.

CULVER, Roland Joseph; actor; b 31 Aug. 1900; s of Edward Culver and Florence Tullege; m 1st, 1934, Daphne Rye (marr. diss.); two s; 2nd, 1947, Nan Hopkins. *Educ:* Highgate Coll.; Royal Academy of Dramatic Art. First appearance on stage, Hull Rep. Theatre, as Paul, in Peter and Paul, 1925; first London appearance, Century Theatre, with Greater London Players, 1925; there followed continuous parts in plays in West End theatres. Played Lieut-Comdr Rogers, in French Without Tears, Criterion, Nov. 1936 until 1939; Ford, in Believe It or Not, New, 1940; Viscount Goring, in An Ideal Husband, Westminster, 1943; George Wayne, in Another Love Story, Phoenix, 1944. First English actor to go to Hollywood after end of 1939-45 War; on returning to England appeared as Ronald Knight, MA, in Master of Arts, Strand, 1949; Oscar, in Who is Sylvia?, Criterion, 1950; William Collyer, in The Deep Blue Sea, Duchess, 1952; prod revival of Aren't We All?, Haymarket, 1953. First appearance on New York stage at Coronet, 1953, as Philip, in The Little Hut; Simon Foster in Simon and Laura, Strand, London, 1954; Stanley Harrington in Five Finger Exercise, Comedy Theatre, London, 1958, New York and US tour, 1959-61; Sir Richard Conyngham, PC, MP, in Shout for Life, Vaudeville, 1963; Dr Parker in Carving a Statue, Haymarket, 1964; Lebedyev in Ivanov, Phœnix, 1965, New York and United States tour 1966; Getting Married, Strand, 1967; Hay Fever, Duke of York's, 1968; His, Hers and Theirs, Apollo, 1969; My Darling Daisy, Lyric, 1970; Trelawny, Prince of Wales, 1972; The Bedwinner, Royalty, 1974; Polonius, in Hamlet, Nat. Theatre, 1975; Agamemnon in Troilus and Cressida, Nat. Theatre, 1976. Wrote and appeared in his own play, A River Breeze, 1956. Has appeared on BBC TV and ITV; since 1972 various television plays and serials including: Wives and Daughters; Cranford; The Pallisers (as The Duke of Omnium). Entered films, 1931, and has appeared in numerous successful pictures. *Films include:* French without Tears, On Approval, The First of the Few, Secret Mission, To Each His Own, Down to Earth, Emperor Waltz, Trio, Quartette. *Publication:* A River Breeze (play), 1957. *Recreations:* painting, golf, hacking and writing. *Address:* The Old School, Fawley Green, Henley-on-Thames, Oxon RG9 6HZ. *T:* Henley 3778. *Clubs:* Garrick, Green Room.

CUMBER, John Alfred, CMG 1966; MBE 1954; TD; HM Overseas Civil Service, retired; Director-General, Save the Children Fund, since 1976; b 30 Sept. 1920; s of A. J. Cumber, FRIBA, AMICE; m 1945, Margaret Anne Tripp. *Educ:* Richmond County Sch.; LSE. Served War of 1939-45 (Major). Joined Colonial Service, 1947; served Kenya: District Officer, 1947; District Comr, 1950; Senior District Comr, 1960; Senior Asst Sec., 1961-63; Administrator of the Cayman Islands, 1964-68; Comr in Anguilla, 1969. *Recreations:* art, photography, music, swimming. *Address:* Hillside Cottage, Bickleigh, near Tiverton, Devon EX16 8RF.

CUMBERBATCH, Arthur Noel, CMG 1953; CBE 1942 (MBE 1933); Minister (Commercial), Cairo, 1948-54, retired from Foreign Service, 1954; b 25 Dec. 1895. *Educ:* King's Coll. Sch.; Paris. Served European War, 1914-18 (despatches). Employed in Commercial Secretariat, Athens, 1920; Asst to the Commercial Sec., Athens, 1931; Commercial Secretary, Athens, 1934. Served, later, in Cairo, Tehran and again in Athens. *Address:* 64 Chesterfield House, Chesterfield Gardens, W1. *T:* 01-493 7148.

CUMBERLEGE, Geoffrey Fenwick Jocelyn, DSO 1917; MC 1918; b 18 April 1891; 3rd s of late Henry Mordaunt and Blanche Cumberlege, Walsted Place, Lindfield, Sussex; m 1927, Vera Gladys, 3rd d of Major Sir A. D. Gibbons, 7th Bt; three s one d. *Educ:* Charterhouse; Worcester Coll., Oxford; MA. Hon. Fellow Worcester Coll., Oxford; Hon. DCL, Durham, 1953. Served France, 1915-18, Italy, 1918-19 (Croce di Guerra); substantive Capt. in Oxford and Bucks LI, Oct. 1917 (DSO, MC, despatches thrice); Manager of Oxford University Press in India, 1919-27, in USA, 1927-34. Publisher to the Univ. of Oxford, 1945-56. *Address:* Idlehurst, Birch Grove, Horsted Keynes, Sussex. *T:* Chelwood Gate 224. *Clubs:* United Oxford & Cambridge University; Royal Bombay Yacht (Bombay).

CUMBERLEGE, Julia Frances, JP; Lay Member, Press Council, since 1977; b 27 Jan. 1943; d of Dr L. U. Camm and late M. G. G. Camm; m 1961, Patrick Francis Howard Cumberlege; three s. *Educ:* Convent of the Sacred Heart, Tunbridge Wells. Mem., East Sussex AHA, 1977-. Member: Lewes DC, 1966- (Leader, 1977-); East Sussex CC, 1974-. JP East Sussex, 1973. *Recreations:* tennis, gardening, music. *Address:* Vuggles Farm, Newick, Lewes, Sussex. *T:* Barcombe 400453.

CUMING, Frederick George Rees, RA 1974 (ARA 1969); ARCA 1954; NDD 1948; NEAC 1960; painter; *b* 16 Feb. 1930. *Educ:* University School, Bexley Heath; Sidcup Art School; Royal College of Art. Has exhibited in many galleries, London, New York, etc. Work purchased by official bodies, including: Ministry of Works, RA, Kent Education Cttee, Scunthorpe Art Gallery, Scunthorpe Education Cttee. *Address:* 36 Earlsfield Road, Hythe, Kent.

CUMING, Mariannus Adrian, CMG 1962; Chairman, Cuming Smith & Co. Ltd, Melbourne, since 1945, and formerly associated fertiliser companies; formerly Director: Broken Hill Pty Co. Ltd and subsidiaries; Imperial Chemical Industries of Australia and New Zealand Ltd; *b* 26 Nov. 1901; *s* of J. Cuming, Melbourne; *m* 1926, Wilma Margaret, *d* of W. C. Guthrie; three *s* one *d. Educ:* Melbourne Grammar Sch.; Melbourne Univ. (BSc); Imperial Coll., London (Dip.). Dir, Alfred Hospital, Melbourne, 1945-76. *Recreations:* golf, fishing. *Address:* 29 Stonnington Place, Toorak, Vic 3142, Australia. *T:* Melbourne 20 5319. *Clubs:* Australian, Melbourne, Royal Melbourne Golf (Melbourne); Weld (Perth).

CUMINGS, Sir Charles (Cecil George), KBE 1951; *b* 30 March 1904; *s* of late Capt. C. E. G. Cumings and E. M. Cumings, OBE; *m* 1942, Enid Gethen; one *s* one *d. Educ:* St Andrew's Coll. and Rhodes University Coll., Grahamstown, S Africa; New Coll., Oxford. Called to the Bar, Inner Temple, 1927; Sudan Political Service, 1927-30; Legal Dept, Sudan Govt, 1930; Advocate-Gen., 1943; Chief Justice, 1945; Legal Sec., 1947-54. Lectr in Law, Rhodes Univ., 1953-55. Resident Dir in Africa, British South Africa Company, 1957-59. *Recreation:* tennis. *Address:* c/o Mr A. R. Taylor, 16 Shumack Street, Weetangera, Canberra, ACT 2614, Australia.

CUMMING; *see* Gordon-Cumming.

CUMMING, Sir Duncan (Cameron), KBE 1953 (CBE 1946); CB 1948; *b* 10 Aug. 1903; *s* of late Dr R. Cumming; *m* 1930, Nancy Acheson Houghton (*d* 1971); one *d. Educ:* Giggleswick; Caius Coll., Cambridge. Sudan Political Service, 1925; Chief Administrator, Cyrenaica (Brig.), 1942; Chief Civil Affairs Officer, Middle East (Maj.-Gen.), 1945-48. Governor, Kordofan Province, Sudan, 1949. Deputy Civil Sec., Sudan Government, 1950-51; Chief Administrator of Eritrea, 1951-52. Man. Dir, BOAC Associated Companies Ltd, 1955-59; BOAC Adviser on African Affairs, 1959-64. Pres., Soc. for Libyan Studies, 1969-74; Royal Geographical Society: Hon. Treasurer, 1971-74; Pres., 1974-77; Member: Mt Everest Foundn, 1971-77; British Inst., E Africa. KStJ. *Address:* 22A Wimbledon Park Road, SW18 1LT. *Club:* Athenæum.

CUMMING, Lt-Col Malcolm Edward Durant, CB 1961; OBE 1945; attached War Office, 1934-65; *b* 27 Sept. 1907. *Educ:* Eton; Royal Military Coll., Sandhurst. Served with 60th Rifles, 1927-34. *Recreations:* fishing and rural interests generally. *Address:* c/o Lloyds Bank Ltd, Cox & King's Branch, 6 Pall Mall, SW1. *Club:* Greenjackets.

CUMMING, Lt-Col Sir Ronald Stuart, Kt 1965; TD; Chairman, Distillers Company Ltd, 1963-67 (Dir 1946-67); *b* April 1900; *s* of John F. Cumming, OBE, DL, JP, Aberlour, Banffshire; *m* 1924, Mary, OBE 1953, *d* of late Col Wm Hendrie, Hamilton, Ont; two *d. Educ:* Uppingham; Aberdeen Univ. Grenadier Guards, 1918-19; Dir, John Walker & Sons Ltd, 1931-39; Joint Man. Dir, James Buchanan & Co. Ltd, 1939-46; served Seaforth Highlanders (TA), 1939-45; Man. Dir, James Buchanan & Co. Ltd, 1946-51; Chm., Booth's Distilleries Ltd, 1953-63; Chm., John Walker & Sons Ltd, 1957-63; Chm. Council, Scotch Whisky Assoc., 1961-67. Hon. LLD Strathclyde, 1967. *Recreations:* fishing, shooting, golf. *Address:* Sourden Brae, Rothes, Morayshire. *Clubs:* Boodle's; New (Edinburgh).

CUMMING, Roualeyn Charles Rossiter, CIE 1942; KPM 1940; *b* 2 Nov. 1891; *e s* of Roualeyn Charles Cumming, Calne, Wilts; *m* 1st, 1916, Pauline Grace (*d* 1952), *y d* of Edward Hagarty Parry, Stoke Poges; 2nd, 1958, Eileen Mary, *née* Steel (*d* 1975), *widow* of Comdr E. D. Michell, DSC, RN. *Educ:* St Paul's Sch. Entered Indian Police, 1911; Personal Asst to Chief Comr of Assam, 1914-16; Political Officer, NE Frontier, India, 1926-30; Deputy Inspector-Gen. of Police, Assam, 1935-37; Inspector Gen. of Police and Joint Sec. in Home Dept, Govt of Assam, 1937-46. *Recreation:* golf. *Address:* Post Mead, Bishop's Waltham, Hampshire. *Club:* East India, Devonshire, Sports and Public Schools.

CUMMING, William Richard, CVO 1954; Chairman, Public Lending Right Committee, Australia Council, since 1976; *b* 15 Oct. 1911; *e s* of late George Cumming, Coorparoo, Qld; *m* 1939, Evelyn Joyce, *o d* of late George Paul, Epping, NSW; one *s* one *d. Educ:* Gregory Terr., Brisbane; Univs of Queensland and Sydney. BA Queensland, LLB, DipPubAd Sydney. Admitted to NSW Bar, 1941. Enlisted in AIF and served War of 1939-45 with AAPC, Major. Adviser, Federal Taxation Dept, 1947-51; Prime Minister's Dept, Australia: Senior Exec. Officer, 1951-55, Asst Secretary, 1955-60, and 1966-70; Official Sec., Australian High Commissioner's Office, London, 1960-66, 1970-73 (various periods); Acting Deputy High Commissioner, 1965-66, 1972-73; Cultural Counsellor, Aust. High Commn, London, 1973-74; Consultant, Australia Council, 1974-76. Extra Gentleman Usher to the Queen, 1962-66, 1971-74; Dir, Royal Visits, ACT, 1953-54, 1956, 1957-58; Dir-Gen., Australia, Royal Visit, 1959. Secretary: Commonwealth Literary Fund, 1955-60, 1967-70; Commonwealth Historic Memorials Cttee, 1955-60, 1967-70; Commonwealth Art Advisory Bd, 1955-60, 1967-70; Commonwealth Assistance to Australian Composers, 1967-70; Council, Australian Nat. Gallery, 1968-70; Official Sec., Australian High Commn, London, 1970-73. Member: Council, Nat. Library of Australia, 1967-70; Council, Australian Inst. of Aboriginal Studies, 1969-70. *Recreations:* collecting antiques and Australian art, motoring. *Address:* 2 Eric Street, Wahroonga, NSW 2076, Australia. *Clubs:* Oriental; University (Sydney).

CUMMING-BRUCE, Rt. Hon. Sir (James) Roualeyn Hovell-Thurlow-, PC 1977; Kt 1964; MA; **Rt. Hon. Lord Justice Cumming-Bruce;** a Lord Justice of Appeal, since 1977; Judge of the Restrictive Practices Court, since 1968; *b* 9 March 1912; *s* of 6th Baron Thurlow and Grace Catherine, *d* of Rev. Henry Trotter; *m* 1955, Lady (Anne) Sarah Alethea Marjorie Savile, *d* of 6th Earl of Mexborough; two *s* one *d. Educ:* Shrewsbury; Magdalene Coll., Cambridge (Hon. Fellow, 1977). Barrister, Middle Temple, 1937 (Harmsworth Scholar); Master of the Bench, 1959; Treasurer, 1975. Served War of 1939-45 (Lt-Col RA). Chancellor of Diocese of Ripon, 1954-57; Recorder of Doncaster, 1957-58; Recorder of York, 1958-61; Junior Counsel to the Treasury (Common Law), 1959-64; Judge of the High Court, Family Div. (formerly Probate, Divorce and Admiralty Div.), 1964-77; Presiding Judge, North Eastern Circuit, 1971-74. *Address:* 1 Mulberry Walk, Chelsea, SW3. *T:* 01-352 5754. *Clubs:* Pratt's, United Oxford & Cambridge University.
See also Baron Thurlow.

CUMMINGS, Constance, CBE 1974; actress; *b* Seattle, USA; *d* of Kate Cummings and Dallas Vernon Halverstadt; *m* 1933, Benn Wolfe Levy, MBE (*d* 1973); one *s* one *d. Educ:* St Nicholas Girls Sch., Seattle, Washington, USA. Began stage work, 1932; since then has appeared in radio, television, films and theatre; joined National Theatre Co., 1971. Plays include: The Petrified Forest; Return to Tyassi; Goodbye, Mr Chips; The Good-Natured Man; St Joan; Romeo and Juliet; The Taming of the Shrew; Lysistrata; The Rape of the Belt; JB; Who's Afraid of Virginia Woolf?; Justice is a Woman; Fallen Angels; A Delicate Balance; Hamlet; National Theatre: Coriolanus, Amphitryon 38, 1971; A Long Day's Journey into Night, 1972; The Cherry Orchard, The Bacchae, 1973; Children, Mermaid, 1974; The Circle, 1974-75; Stripwell, Royal Court, 1975. Has appeared Albert Hall, performing with orchestra Peter and the Wolf and Honegger's Jeanne d'Arc au Bûcher. Mem., Arts Council, 1965-71; Chm., Young People's Theatre Panel, 1966-70. *Recreations:* anthropology and music. *Address:* 68 Old Church Street, SW3. *T:* 01-352 0437.

CUNARD, Major Sir Guy (Alick), 7th Bt *cr* 1859; Licensed Trainer for Steeple Chases and Hurdle Races; *b* 2 Sept. 1911; *s* of Captain Alick May Cunard (*d* 1926) (*s* of William Samuel Cunard, *g s* of 1st Bt) and Cecil Muriel (*d* 1964), *d* of late Guy St Maur Palmes, Lingcroft, York; *S* brother, 1973; unmarried. *Educ:* Eton; RMC, Sandhurst. Gazetted 16/5th Lancers, 1931; transferred to 4/7th Royal Dragoon Guards, 1933; Captain, 1939; Major, 1946; active service France and Belgium, 1940, and Western Desert; retired, 1949. *Recreations:* steeplechasing, point-to-pointing, hunting, cricket. *Heir:* none. *Address:* The Garden House, Wintringham, Malton, N Yorks. *T:* Rillington 286.

CUNDIFF, Major Frederick William; Director: Chesters Brewery Co. Ltd; National Gas and Oil Engine Co.; *s* of late Sir William Cundiff. MP (C) Rusholme Div. of Manchester, 1944-45; Withington Div. of Manchester, 1950-51. *Address:* Grenaway, Chelford Road, Prestbury, Macclesfield, Cheshire SK10 4PT.

CUNEO, Terence Tenison; portrait and figure painter, ceremonial, military and engineering subjects; *b* 1 Nov. 1907; *s* of Cyrus Cuneo and Nell Marion Tenison; *m* 1934, Catherine Mayfield Monro, *yr d* of Major E. G. Monro, CBE; one *d. Educ:*

Sutton Valence Sch.; Chelsea and Slade. Served War of 1939-45: RE, and as War Artist; special propaganda paintings for Min. of Information, Political Intelligence Dept of FO, and War Artists Advisory Cttee; representative of Illustrated London News, France, 1940. Royal Glasgow Inst. of Fine Arts; Pres. of Industrial Painters Group; Exhibitor, RA, RP, ROI Paris Salon (Hon. Mention, 1957). Has painted extensively in North Africa, South Africa, Rhodesia, Canada, USA, Ethiopia and Far East; one-man exhibition, Underground Activities in Occupied Europe, 1941; one-man exhibitions: RWS Galleries, London, 1954 and 1958; Sladmore Gall., 1971, 1972, 1974. Best known works include: Meml Paintings of El Alamein and The Royal Engineers, King George VI at The Royal Artillery Mess, Woolwich, King George VI and Queen Elizabeth at The Middle Temple Banquet, 1950; Meml Painting of The Rifle Brigade, 1951; Visit to Lloyd's of Queen Elizabeth II with the Duke of Edinburgh to lay Foundation Stone of Lloyd's New Building, 1952; Queen's Coronation Luncheon, Guildhall, The Duke of Edinburgh at Cambridge, 1953; Portraits of Viscount Allendale, KG, as Canopy Bearer to Her Majesty, 1954; Coronation of Queen Elizabeth II in Westminster Abbey (presented to the Queen by HM's Lieuts of Counties), 1955; Queen's State Visit to Denmark, Engineering Mural in Science Museum, 1957; Queen Elizabeth II at RCOG, 1960; Queen Elizabeth II at Guildhall Banquet after Indian Tour, 1961; Equestrian Portrait of HM the Queen as Col-in-Chief, Grenadier Guards, 1963; Garter Ceremony, 1964; first official portraits of Rt Hon. Edward Heath, 1971, of Field Marshal Viscount Montgomery of Alamein, 1972; HM the Queen as Patron of Kennel Club, 1975. *Publications:* (autobiog.) The Mouse and his Master, 1977; articles in The Studio, The Artist. *Recreations:* writing, sketching, travel, riding. *Address:* 201 Ember Lane, East Molesey, Surrey. *T:* 01-398 1986. *Club:* Junior Carlton.

CUNINGHAME, Sir John Christopher Foggo M.; *see* Montgomery Cuninghame, Sir J. C. F.

CUNINGHAME, Sir William Alan Fairlie-, 15th Bt *cr* 1630; MC; BE (Sydney); retired as Research Officer, National Standards Laboratory, Sydney; *b* 31 Jan. 1893; *s* of 13th Bt and Georgiana Maud, *d* of late Edward Hardman Macartney; *S* brother, 1939; *m* 1929, Irene Alice (*d* 1970), *d* of late Henry Margrave Terry; one *s*. *Educ:* Sydney Univ. Served European War, 1915-19 (MC). Res. Officer, Metrology Div., Commonwealth Scientific and Industrial Res. Orgn, 1943-58. *Heir: s* William Henry Fairlie-Cuninghame [*b* 1 Oct. 1930; *m* 1972, Janet Menzies, *d* of late Roy Menzies Saddington; one *s*]. *Address:* 62 Farrer Brown Court, Nuffield Village, Castle Hill, NSW 2154, Australia.

CUNLIFFE, family name of **Baron Cunliffe.**

CUNLIFFE, 3rd Baron *cr* 1914; of Headley; **Roger Cunliffe,** RIBA; AMBIM; Partner, SCP, since 1973; *b* 12 Jan. 1932; *s* of 2nd Baron and Joan Catherine Lubbock; *S* father, 1963; *m* 1957, Clemency Ann Hoare; two *s* one *d. Educ:* Eton; Trinity Coll., Cambridge (MA); Architectural Association (AA Dipl.); Open Univ. With various architectural firms in UK and USA, 1957-65; Associate, Robert Matthew, Johnson-Marshall & Partners, 1966-69; Dir, Architectural Assoc., 1969-71. Mem., Urban Motorways Cttee, 1969-72. Governor: Lancing Coll., 1967-; Goldsmiths' Coll., 1972-. *Publications:* (with Leonard Manasseh) Office Buildings, 1962; contrib. various professional jls. *Recreations:* photography, skiing, taxonomy. *Heir: s* Hon. Henry Cunliffe, *b* 9 March 1962. *Address:* 1 Hurst Avenue, N6 5TX.

CUNLIFFE, Prof. Barrington Windsor; Professor of European Archaeology, Oxford University, and Fellow of Keble College, since 1972; *b* 10 Dec. 1939. *Educ:* Portsmouth; St John's Coll., Cambridge (MA, PhD). Lecturer, Univ. of Bristol, 1963-66; Prof. of Archæology, Univ. of Southampton, 1966-72. Mem., Ancient Monuments Bd for England, 1976-. FSA. *Publications:* Fishbourne, a Roman Palace and its Garden, 1971; Roman Bath Discovered, 1971; The Cradle of England, 1972; The Making of the English, 1973; The Regni, 1973; Iron Age Communities in Britain, 1974; Rome and the Barbarians, 1975; contribs to several major excavation reports and articles to Soc. of Antiquaries, and in other learned jls. *Recreation:* mild self-indulgence. *Address:* Keble College, Oxford.

CUNLIFFE, Christopher Joseph; His Honour Judge Christopher Cunliffe; a Circuit Judge (formerly County Court Judge), since 1966; *b* 28 Feb. 1916; *s* of Lt-Col E. N. Cunliffe, OBE, RAMC, Buckingham Crescent, Manchester, and Harriet Cunliffe (*née* Clegg); *m* 1942, Margaret Hamer Barber; two *d. Educ:* Rugby Sch.; Trinity Hall, Cambridge. BA 1937. Called to the Bar, Lincoln's Inn, 1938. Legal Cadet, Br. North Borneo Civil

Service. 1939-40. Served RAFVR, 1941-46; Intelligence, Judge Advocate General's Branch. Practised on Northern Circuit, 1946; Dep. Coroner, City of Liverpool, 1953; Chairman: National Insurance Tribunal, Bootle, 1956-; Mental Health Review Tribunal for SW Lancs and W Ches, 1961-. *Recreations:* golf, gardening.

CUNLIFFE, Sir David Ellis, 9th Bt *cr* 1759; *b* 29 Oct. 1957; *s* of Sir Cyril Henley Cunliffe, 8th Bt and of Lady Cunliffe (Eileen, *d* of Frederick William and Nora Anne Parkins); *S* father, 1969. *Heir: b* Andrew Mark Cunliffe, *b* 17 April 1959. *Address:* 17 Gurney Court Road, St Albans, Herts.

CUNLIFFE, Hon. Geoffrey; *b* 26 Aug. 1903; 2nd *s* of 1st Baron . Cunliffe and Edith Boothby (later Dowager Baroness Cunliffe, *d* 1965); *m* 1st, 1922, Patrick Sidney (*d* 1940), *o d* of late Robert B. Frend, Ardsallagh, Co. Tipperary; one *s* (and *er s* killed in action, 1945); 2nd, 1941, Gavrelle (marr. diss. 1947), *d* of William Arthur Thomas, and *widow* of Christopher Hobhouse; one *s* one *d* ; 3rd, 1947, Barbara Waring, *d* of late Dr J. A. Gibb, Maidstone, Kent. *Educ:* Eton; Trinity Coll., Cambridge. Controller of Aluminium, Min. of Supply and Min. of Aircraft Production, 1939-41; Mem., Industrial and Export Council, Board of Trade, 1941; Dir of Office Machinery, BoT, 1941-42; Dep. Chm. and Man. Dir, British Aluminium Co. Ltd, 1947-59; Man. Dir of Norcros Ltd, 1959-63. A Dep. Pres., British Standards Instn, 1964-70 (Chm. Finance Cttee, 1959-61; Pres. of the Instn, 1961-63; Chm. Gen. Council, 1961-64). *Address:* Poyntzfield House, by Conon Bridge, Ross-shire.

CUNLIFFE, Prof. Marcus Falkner; Professor of American Studies, University of Sussex, since 1965; *b* 5 July 1922; *s* of Keith Harold and Kathleen Eleanor Cunliffe; *m* 1st, 1949, Mitzi Solomon (marr. diss. 1971), NY; one *s* two *d* ; 2nd, 1971, Lesley Hume. *Educ:* Oriel Coll., Oxford. Commonwealth Fund Fellow, Yale Univ., 1947-49; Lectr in American Studies, 1949-56, Sen Lectr, 1956-60, Prof. of Amer. Hist. and Instns, 1960-64, Univ. of Manchester. Fellow, Center for Advanced Study in the Behavioral Sciences, Stanford, Calif., 1957-58; Vis. Prof. in American History, Harvard Univ., 1959-60; Vis. Prof., Michigan Univ., 1973; Fellow, Woodrow Wilson Internat. Centre, Washington DC, 1977-78. Member: Massachusetts Historical Soc.; Soc. of American Historians. Hon. Dr Humane Letters, Univ. of Pennsylvania, 1976. *Publications:* The Literature of the United States, 1954; George Washington: Man and Monument, 1958; The Nation Takes Shape, 1789-1837, 1959; Soldiers and Civilians: The Martial Spirit in America, 1775-1865, 1968; American Presidents and the Presidency, 1969; (ed with R. Winks) Pastmasters: some essays on American historians, 1969; The Ages of Man, 1971; (ed) The Times History of Our Times, 1971; (ed) Sphere History of Literature, Vols 8 and 9 (American Literature), 1974-75; The Age of Expansion 1848-1917, 1974; Monarchy and the Americans, 1978; (ed) The Divided Loyalist: Crèvecoeur's America, 1978. *Recreation:* the pursuit of happiness. *Address:* 19 Clifton Terrace, Brighton BN1 3HA. *T:* Brighton 25164.

CUNLIFFE, Captain Robert Lionel Brooke, CBE 1944; Royal Navy, retired; *b* 15 March 1895; *s* of Col Foster Cunliffe and Mrs Cunliffe (*née* Lyon); *m* 1st, 1926, Barbara Eleanor Cooper (*d* 1970); three *d* ; 2nd, 1971, Christina Cooper. *Educ:* RN Colls Osborne and Dartmouth. Comdr 1930; Capt. 1936; commanded HMS Milford, 1938-39; RNC Dartmouth, 1939-42; Commodore, Dover, 1942; commanded HMS Illustrious, 1942-44 (despatches); Cdre, RN Barracks, Devonport, 1944-46; Retd, 1946. Naval Asst to UK High Comr, Canada, 1946-48. Grand Officer Order of Leopold II, Belgium, 1948. *Recreations:* cricket, shooting. *Address:* The Garden House, Pakenham, Bury St Edmunds, Suffolk. *T:* Pakenham 30236. *Club:* Army and Navy.

See also Baron Sackville .

CUNLIFFE, Stella Vivian; Director of Statistics, Home Office, 1972-77; *b* 12 Jan. 1917; *d* of Percy Cunliffe and Edith Blanche Wellwood Cunliffe. *Educ:* privately, then Parsons Mead, Ashtead; London School of Economics (BScEcon). Danish Bacon Co, 1939-44; Voluntary Relief Work in Europe, 1945-47; Arthur Guinness Son and Co. Ltd, 1947-70; Head of Research Unit, Home Office, 1970-72. Pres., Royal Statistical Soc., 1975-77. *Recreations:* work with youth organisations; gardening; prison after-care. *Address:* 69 Harriotts Lane, Ashtead, Surrey. *T:* Ashtead 72343.

CUNLIFFE, His Honour Thomas Alfred; a Circuit Judge (formerly County Court Judge), 1963-75; *b* 9 March 1905; *s* of Thomas and Elizabeth Cunliffe, Preston; *m* 1938, Constance Isabella Carden; one *s* one *d. Educ:* Lancaster Royal Grammar Sch.; Sidney Sussex Coll., Cambridge (Classical Scholar). Inner

Temple: Profumo Prize, 1926; Paul Methven Prize, 1926. Called to the Bar, Inner Temple, 1927; Yarborough Anderson Scholar, 1927. Practised Northern Circuit, 1927-63; Dep. Chm., Lancs County Quarter Sessions, 1961-63; Recorder, Barrow-in-Furness, 1962-63. RAFVR (Squadron Leader), 1940-45. *Recreations:* music, gardening. *Address:* 39 Dee Park Road, Gayton, Wirral, Merseyside L60 3RG.

CUNLIFFE-JONES, Rev. Prof. Hubert, DD (Hon.); Professor of Theology, University of Manchester, 1968-73, now Professor Emeritus; *b* Strathfield, Sydney, NSW, Australia, 30 March 1905; *s* of Rev. Walter and Maud Cunliffe-Jones; *m* 1933, Maude Edith Clifton, BSc, DipEd Sydney; two *s* two *d. Educ:* Newington Coll., Sydney; Sydney and Oxford Univs; Camden Coll., Sydney; Mansfield Coll., Oxford. Congregational Minister, Warrnambool, Vic., Australia, 1928-29; Travelling Sec., Australian SCM 1929-30; Congregational Minister, Witney, Oxon, 1933-37; Tutor in Systematic Theology, Yorks United Independent Coll., Bradford, 1937-47; Principal Yorks United Independent Coll., Bradford, 1947-58; Associate Principal, Northern Congregational Coll., Manchester, 1958-66; Prof., History of Doctrine, Univ. of Manchester, 1966-68 (Lectr, 1958-66). Chm. of the Congregational Union of England and Wales, 1957-58. Hon. DD Edinburgh, 1956. *Publications:* The Holy Spirit, 1943; The Authority of the Biblical Revelation, 1945; Deuteronomy, 1951; Jeremiah, 1960; Technology, Community and Church, 1961; Christian Theology since 1600, 1970; articles in Theology, Expository Times, etc. *Recreation:* drama. *Address:* 5 Wood Road, Manchester M16 9RB.

CUNLIFFE-LISTER, family name of **Baroness Masham of Ilton** and **Earl of Swinton.**

CUNLIFFE-OWEN, Sir Dudley (Herbert), 2nd Bt, *cr* 1920; Managing Director: Palace Hotel & Casino Ltd; Palace Entertainments Ltd, since 1965; *b* 27 March 1923; 2nd (but *o* surv.) *s* of Sir Hugo Cunliffe-Owen, 1st Bt and Helen Elizabeth Cunliffe-Owen (*d* 1934), *d* of James Oliver, New York; *S* father 1947; *m* 1st, 1947, Mary Maud (*d* 1956), *e d* of R. R. Redgrave; 2nd, 1956, Hon. Juliana Eveline Nettlefold (*née* Curzon) (marr. diss., 1962), 3rd *d* of 2nd Viscount Scarsdale, TD; one *d*; 3rd, 1964, Jean, *o d* of late Surg. Comdr A. N. Forsyth, RN; one *s* one *d. Educ:* RN Coll., Dartmouth. Served War, 1939-46 (despatches); Lieut Royal Navy; retired 1947. *Recreation:* yachting. *Heir: s* Hugo Dudley Cunliffe-Owen, *b* 16 May 1966. *Address:* Eyreton House, Quarterbridge, Douglas, Isle of Man. *T:* Douglas 4545. *Club:* Royal Thames Yacht.

CUNNANE, Most Rev. Joseph; *see* Tuam, Archbishop of, (RC).

CUNNINGHAM, Gen. Sir Alan Gordon, GCMG 1948; KCB 1941 (CB 1941); DSO 1918; MC 1915; LLD; *b* 1 May 1887; *s* of Prof. D. J. Cunningham, FRS, and Elizabeth Cumming Browne; *m* 1951, Margery, *widow* of Sir Harold Edward Snagge, KBE. *Educ:* Cheltenham; Royal Military Academy, Woolwich. First commission, 1906; served European War, France, 1914-18; Brigade Major and Gen. Staff Officer 2nd Grade (despatches 5 times, DSO and MC); Gen. Staff Officer, Straits Settlements, 1919-21; passed Naval Staff Coll., 1925; Brevet Lt-Col 1928; Instructor, Machine Gun Sch., 1928-31; Lt-Col 1935; Imperial Defence Coll., 1937; Comdr Royal Artillery, 1st Div., 1937-38; Maj.-Gen., 1938; Comdr 5th Anti-Aircraft Div. TA, 1938; commanded 66th, 9th and 51st Divs, 1940; GOC East Africa Forces, 1940-41; GOC-in-C 8th Imperial Army in Middle East, 1941; Commandant Staff College, Camberley, 1942; Lt-Gen. 1943; GOC Northern Ireland, 1943-44; GOC-in-C Eastern Command, 1944-45; Gen., 1945; High Commissioner and C-in-C for Palestine, 1945-48; Col Commandant Royal Artillery, 1944-54. Pres., Council of Cheltenham Coll., 1951-63. Comdr American Legion of Merit, 1945; Brilliant Star of Zanzibar (1st class), 1941; Ordre de la Couronne (1st Class), Belgium, 1950; Order of Menelik (1st Class), 1954, etc. *Recreations:* gardening, fishing. *Club:* Army and Navy.

CUNNINGHAM, Alexander Alan; A Vice President, General Motors, since 1976; *b* Bulgaria, 7 Jan. 1926; naturalised citizen, US; *m* 1955, Dorothy Ilene; one *s* three *d. Educ:* General Motors Inst., Michigan. BSc (Industrial Engrg) 1951. Served War of 1939-45, navigation electronics radar specialist, RAF. General Motors: Jun. Process Engr, Frigidaire Div., 1951; Asst to Frigidaire Man., NY, Gen. Motors Overseas Ops, 1952; Prodn Planning Technician for Adam Opel AG, Germany, 1953; Exec. Asst to Man. Dir, GM Ltd, London, 1956; Master Mechanic, Gen. Motors do Brasil, 1957, Works Man. 1958; Works Man., Gen. Motors Argentina SA, 1962; Man. Dir, Gen. Motors do Brasil, 1963; Man., Adam Opel's Bochum plant, 1964; Asst Gen. Manufrg Man., Adam Opel AG, 1966, Gen. Manufrg Man. 1969; Man. Dir, Adam Opel AG, 1970; Gen. Dir,

European Organisations, Gen. Motors Overseas Corp., 1974-76. *Address:* General Motors Corporation, 767 Fifth Avenue, New York 10022, USA. *T:* (212) 486-2400.

CUNNINGHAM, Air Cdre Alexander Duncan, CB 1941; CBE 1919 (OBE 1919); late RAF; *b* 18 July 1888; *m* 1918, Hilda Carter (*d* 1954); *m* 1965, Mrs Gladys Way, September Cottage, Bourne End. Served European War, 1914-19 (despatches, OBE, CBE); Air Commodore, 1933; retired list, 1938. Re-employed, 1939-45 (despatches), Air Vice-Marshal, 1940. *Address:* c/o Ministry of Defence (Air), Whitehall, SW1.

CUNNINGHAM, Sir Charles (Craik), GCB 1974 (KCB 1961; CB 1946); KBE 1952; CVO 1941; Director, Securicor Ltd, since 1971; *b* Dundee, 7 May 1906; *s* of late Richard Yule Cunningham, Abergeldie, Kirriemuir, and Isabella Craik; *m* 1934, Edith Louisa Webster; two *d. Educ:* Harris Acad., Dundee; University of St Andrews. Entered Scottish Office, 1929; Private Sec. to Parliamentary Under Sec. of State for Scotland, 1933-34; Private Sec. to Sec. of State for Scotland, 1935-39; Asst Sec., Scottish Home Dept, 1939-41; Principal Asst Sec., 1941-42; Dep. Sec., 1942-47; Sec., 1948-57; Permanent Under-Sec. of State, Home Office, 1957-66; Dep. Chm., UKAEA, 1966-71; Chm., Radiochemical Centre Ltd, 1971-74. Chm., Uganda Resettlement Bd, 1972-73. Mem., Nat. Radiological Protection Bd, 1971-74; Vice-Pres. and Trustee, Royal Inst. Public Admin. Hon. LLD St Andrews, 1960. *Address:* Bankside, Peaslake, Surrey GU5 9RL. *T:* Dorking 730402. *Clubs:* Reform; New (Edinburgh).

CUNNINGHAM, George, BA, BSc; MP (Lab) Islington South and Finsbury, since 1974 (South West Islington, 1970-74); *b* 10 June 1931; *s* of Harry Jackson Cunningham and Christina Cunningham, Dunfermline; *m* 1957, Mavis, *d* of Harold Walton; one *s* one *d. Educ:* Dunfermline High Sch.; Blackpool Grammar Sch.; Univs of Manchester and London. Nat. Service in Royal Artillery (2nd Lieut), 1954-56; on staff of Commonwealth Relations Office, 1956-63; 2nd Sec., British High Commn, Ottawa, 1958-60; Commonwealth Officer of Labour Party, 1963-66; Min. of Overseas Development, 1966-69; Overseas Development Inst., 1969-70. Contested (Lab) Henley Div. of Oxfordshire, 1966. *Publications:* (Fabian pamphlet) Rhodesia, the Last Chance, 1966; (ed) Britain and the World in the Seventies, 1970; The Management of Aid Agencies, 1974. *Address:* 28 Manor Gardens, Hampton, Middlesex. *T:* 01-979 6221.

CUNNINGHAM, Prof. George John, MBE 1945; Professor and Chairman, Department of Academic Pathology, Virginia Commonwealth University, Richmond, since 1974; Conservator of Pathological Collection, Royal College of Surgeons; Consultant Pathologist to South East and South West Regional Health Authorities; *b* 7 Sept. 1906; *s* of George S. Cunningham and Blanche A. Harvey; *m* 1957, Patricia Champion, Brisbane, Australia. *Educ:* Royal Belfast Academical Institution; Dean Close Sch., Cheltenham; St Bartholomew's Hospital Medical Coll. MRCS, LRCP, 1931; MB, BS London, 1933; MD London, 1937; FRCPath 1964. Asst Pathologist, Royal Sussex County Hosp., Brighton, 1934-42. War Service, RAMC, Middle East and Italy (temp. Lt-Col). Senior Lectr in Pathology, St Bartholomew's Hosp., London, 1946-55; Sir William Collins Prof. of Pathology, Univ. of London, at RCS, 1955-68; Prof. of Pathology, Medical Coll. of Virginia, and Chief Laboratory Service, McGuire VA Hosp., Richmond, 1968-74. Dorothy Temple Cross Travelling Fellow in America, 1951-52; Vis. Prof., New York State Univ., 1961; Vis. Prof., Cairo Univ., 1963. Past Pres., Assoc. Clin. Path., Internat. Acad. of Pathology, Quekett Microscopical Club. Freeman, City of London. *Publications:* chap. on Gen. Pathology of Malignant Tumours in Cancer, Vol. 2, 1957; chap. on Microradiography, in Tools of Biological Research, Vol. 2, 1960; and several articles on Pathology, in medical press. *Recreation:* golf. *Address:* 300 West Franklin Street, Apartment 1203-E, Richmond, Va 23220, USA. *T:* 804 643-1012. *Clubs:* National Liberal; Surrey County Cricket; Royal Blackheath Golf; Downtown (Richmond, Va).

CUNNINGHAM, Sir Graham, KBE 1946; Kt 1943; LLB London; FSGT; *b* 19 May 1892; *s* of Daniel Cunningham and Charlotte Eliza Galetti; *m* 1st, 1924, Marjorie Minshaw Harris (decd); two *s* one *d*; 2nd, 1934, Olive St John Williams (*d* 1958); 3rd, 1958, Edith Ellen Smith. *Educ:* Bancrofts Sch., Woodford Wells, Essex. Chm., 1935-61 (Managing Dir, 1929-60) Triplex Safety Glass Company, Ltd; Chm. Shipbuilding Advisory Cttee, 1946-60; Mem. Economic Planning Bd, 1947-61; Dep. Chm. Royal Commission on the Press, 1961-62. Crown Governor, Dep. Chm. and Hon. Fellow, Imperial Coll. of Science and Technology; Past Pres. Soc. of British Gas Industries (1956); Past Pres., Soc. Glass Technology; Dep. Dir-Gen. Children's

Overseas Reception Board, 1940; Dir of Claims, War Damage Commission, 1941; Chief Executive and Controller-Gen. Munitions Production, Ministry of Supply, 1941-46; Chm., Scrap Steel Investigation Cttee, 1946; US Medal of Freedom with Silver Bar, 1945; Chm. Dollar Exports Board, 1949. Liveryman of the Coach Makers and Harness Makers Company; Past Master, Curriers Company; Past Master, Glaziers Company. *Recreation:* gardening. *Address:* Woolmers, Mannings Heath, near Horsham, W Sussex. *T:* Horsham 3809. *Club:* Junior Carlton.

CUNNINGHAM, Lt-Gen. Sir Hugh (Patrick), KBE 1975 (OBE 1966); Deputy Chief of Defence Staff (Operational Requirements), since 1976; *b* 4 Nov. 1921; *s* of late Sir Charles Banks Cunningham, CSI; *m* 1955, Jill, *d* of J. S. Jeffrey, East Knoyle; two *s* two *d*. *Educ:* Charterhouse. 2nd Lieut, RE, 1942; served War of 1939-45, India, New Guinea, Burma; Greece, 1950-51; Egypt, 1951-53; Instructor, Sch. of Infantry, 1955-57, RMA Sandhurst, 1957-60; Cameroons, 1960-61; CRE 3 Div., Cyprus and Aden, 1963-66; comd 11 Engr Bde, BAOR, 1967-69; comd Mons OCS, 1969-70; Canada, 1970-71; GOC SW District, 1971-74; ACGS (OR), 1974-75. Col, Queen's Gurkha Engineers (formerly Gurkha Engrs), 1976-; Col Comdt, RE, 1976-. *Recreations:* bird-watching, opera, golf. *Address:* Little Leigh, East Knoyle, Salisbury, Wilts. *Clubs:* Athenæum, Army and Navy, MCC.

CUNNINGHAM, Rt. Rev. Jack; *b* 1 Sept. 1926; *s* of James and Kathleen Eleanor Cunningham; *m* 1962, Marjorie Elizabeth Davies. *Educ:* Queen Elizabeth Gram. Sch., Wakefield, Yorks; Edinburgh Theological Coll. (GOE). RAF, 1945-48; Theological Coll., 1949-52; Curate, St Mark with St Barnabas, Coventry, 1952-58; Vicar: St Thomas, Longford, Coventry, 1958-62; St Alban, Coventry, 1962-67; Priest-in-Charge, St Michael, Kitwe, Zambia, 1967-71; Bishop of Central Zambia, 1971-77. *Recreations:* golf, mountaineering. *Address:* c/o USPG, 15 Tufton Street, Westminster, SW1P 3QQ.

CUNNINGHAM, Group Captain John, CBE 1963 (OBE 1951); DSO 1941; DFC; Chief Test Pilot for de Havilland Aircraft Co., since 1946; Executive Director, Hawker Siddeley Aviation, since 1963; *b* 27 July 1917; *s* of late A. G. Cunningham and of E. M. Cunningham. *Educ:* Whitgift. Apprenticed to De Havilland Aircraft Co., Hatfield, 1935-38; employed, 1938-Aug. 1939, with De Havillands, Light Aircraft Development and Test Flying. Called up Aug. 1939; joined AAF, 1935; commanded 604 Sqdn, 1941-42; Staff job, 1942-43; commanded 85 Sqdn, 1943-44 (DSO and two bars, DFC and bar); Group Capt. Night Operations HQ 11 Group, 1944. International Record Flight, 16 Oct. 1957: London to Khartoum direct; distance 3,064 statute miles in 5 hrs 51 mins, by Comet 3; average speed 523 statute mph. Derry and Richards Memorial Medal of Guild of Air Pilots and Air Navigators for 1965. *Address:* Hawker Siddeley Aviation, Hatfield Aerodrome, Herts.

CUNNINGHAM, Dr John A.; MP (Lab) Whitehaven, Cumberland, since 1970; Parliamentary Under-Secretary of State, Department of Energy, since 1976; *b* 4 Aug. 1939; *s* of Andrew Cunningham; *m* 1964, Maureen; one *s* two *d*. *Educ:* Jarrow Grammar Sch.; Bede Coll., Durham Univ. Hons Chemistry, 1962; PhD Chemistry, 1966. Formerly: Research Fellow in Chemistry, Durham Univ.; School Teacher; Trades Union Officer. Mem., Parly Select Cttee on Science and Technology, 1970-. PPS to Rt Hon. James Callaghan, 1974-76. *Recreations:* golf, squash, gardening, classical and folk music, reading, listening to other people's opinions. *Address:* House of Commons, SW1.

CUNNINGHAM, Robert Kerr, PhD; FRIC; Chief Natural Resources Adviser, Ministry of Overseas Development, since 1976; *b* 7 June 1923; *s* of John Simpson Cunningham and Agnes Stewart Cunningham; *m* 1947, Jean Sinclair (*née* Brown); one *s* one *d*. *Educ:* Bathgate Acad., Scotland; Edinburgh Univ. (BSc); London Univ. (PhD). FRIC 1964. Served War, RAF, 1942-46. Science Teacher, W Lothian County Educn Cttee, 1947-50; Science Lectr and Chemist, Govt of Bahamas, 1950-55; Colonial Res. Fellowship, Rothamsted Experimental Stn, 1955-56; Res. Off., W African Cocoa Res. Inst., Gold Coast and Ghana, 1956-60; Principal Scientific Off., Rothamsted Experimtl Stn, 1960-64; Prof. of Chemistry and Soil Science, Univ. of WI, Trinidad, 1964-67; Adviser on Res. and Nat. Resources, Min. of Overseas Develt, 1967-76. *Publications:* many scientific papers dealing mainly with soil chem. and plant nutrition in jls; several reports on organisation of R&D in developing countries; (co-author) reports on Brit. and internat. aid in natural resources field. *Recreations:* walking, reading, golf. *Address:* 35 Clarence Road, Harpenden, Herts AL5 4AH. *T:* Harpenden 4203. *Club:* Royal Air Force.

CUNNINGHAME GRAHAM of Gartmore, Adm. Sir Angus (Edward Malise Bontine), KBE 1951 (CBE 1944); CB 1947; JP; Lord Lieutenant of Dunbartonshire, 1955-68; Keeper of Dumbarton Castle, since 1955; *b* 1893; *s* of Comdr C. E. F. Cunninghame Graham, MVO, Royal Navy; *m* 1924, Mary Patricia, *d* of late Col Lionel Hanbury, CMG; one *s* one *d*. *Educ:* Osborne and Dartmouth. HM Yacht Victoria and Albert, 1914; served in Grand Fleet, 1914-18; SNO West River, China, 1936-38; Capt. of HM Signal Sch., 1939-41; Capt. of HMS Kent, 1941-43; Commodore Royal Naval Barracks, Chatham, 1943-45; ADC to King George VI; Rear-Adm, 1945; Rear-Adm. Comdg 10th Cruiser Squadron, and 2nd in Comd Home Fleet, 1945-46; Flag Officer, Scotland, 1950-51, and Admiral Superintendent, Rosyth, 1947-51; Vice-Adm. 1948; retd list, 1951; Adm., 1952. A Captain in Royal Company of Archers (Queen's Body Guard for Scotland), 1969-. Hon. Sheriff 1959. Vice-President: RNLI; Earl Haig Fund, Scotland; Trustee for National Library of Scotland; Commissioner of Queen Victoria Sch. A Vice-Pres. National Trust for Scotland. DL Dunbartonshire, 1952-55. JP 1955. *Address:* Ardoch, Cardross, Dunbartonshire, Scotland. *T:* Dumbarton 62905. *Clubs:* Naval and Military; Royal Yacht Squadron (Naval Member); New (Edinburgh).

See also Baron Polwarth.

CUNYNGHAME, Sir (Henry) David St Leger Brooke Selwyn, 11th Bt (of Milncraig), *cr* 1702; *b* 7 Feb. 1905; *s* of Lieut-Col Sir Percy Francis Cunynghame, 10th Bt, OBE, DL, JP, and Maud Albinia Margaret (*d* 1948), *o d* of Major Selwyn-Payne, Badgeworth Court, Gloucester; *S* father, 1941; *m* 1941, Hon. Pamela Margaret Stanley, *qv*; three *s*. *Educ:* Eton. Formerly Mem., Board of Dirs of various British Motion Picture Producing and Distributing Companies. Served as Sqdn Ldr; RAFVR during War of 1939-45. *Heir: s* Andrew David Francis Cunynghame [*b* 25 Dec. 1942; *m* 1972, Harriet Ann, *d* of C. T. Dupont, Montreal]. *Address:* 15 Madeline Road, SE20. *T:* 01-778 7740. *Club:* Athenæum.

CUNYNGHAME, Sir James Ogilvy B.; *see* Blair-Cunynghame.

CURE, (George) Nigel C.; *see* Capel Cure.

CURIE, Eve, (Mrs Henry R. Labouisse), writer and journalist; *b* Paris, 6 Dec. 1904; *d* of late Marie and Pierre Curie; *m* 1954, Henry Richardson Labouisse, *qv*. *Educ:* by governesses, generally Polish; Sévigné College; Bachelor of Science and Bachelor of Philosophy. Accompanied her mother in her tour of the US 1921; devoted several years to the study of the piano and gave her first concert in 1925 in Paris; later she took up musical criticism and under a pseudonym acted for several years as musical critic of the weekly journal Candide; after the death of her mother in 1934 she collected and classified all the papers, manuscripts, and personal documents left by Mme Curie and went to Poland in 1935 to obtain material as to Mme Curie's youth; wrote Mme Curie's biography; went to America again in 1939 and has gone several times since on lecture tours; was a co-ordinator of the women's war activities at the Ministry of Information in Paris at the beginning of the war, until she went on a lecture tour in the USA; came back to Paris 2 May 1940; after the French capitulation went to live in London for six months, then to America for her third lecture tour; Vichy Govt deprived her of French citizenship in April 1941; in 1942, travelled, as a war correspondent to the battlefronts of Libya, Russia, Burma, China; enlisted in the Fighting French corps, Volontaires Françaises, 1943, as a private; received basic training in England; 2nd Lieut 1943; 1st Lieut 1944. Co-publisher of Paris-Presse, an evening paper in Paris, 1944-49. Special Adviser to the Sec. Gen. of NATO, Paris, Aug. 1952-Nov. 1954. *Publications:* Madame Curie (in US), 1937 (trans. into 32 langs); Journey Among Warriors, 1943. *Recreation:* swimming. *Address:* 1 Sutton Place South, New York, NY 10022, USA.

CURLE, Sir John (Noel Ormiston), KCVO 1975 (CVO 1956); CMG 1966; Director of Protocol, Hong Kong, since 1976; *b* 12 Dec. 1915; *s* of Major W. S. N. Curle, MC, Melrose, Scotland; *m* 1st, 1940, Diana Deane; one *s* one *d*; 2nd, 1948, Pauline, *widow* of Capt. David Roberts; one step *s* two step *d*. *Educ:* Marlborough; New Coll., Oxford. 1st Class Hons, MA, Laming Travelling Fellow of Queen's Coll. Diplomatic Service, 1939; Irish Guards, 1939; War Cabinet Secretariat, 1941-44. Has served in Lisbon, Ottawa, Brussels, Stockholm (Counsellor), Athens (Counsellor); Boston (Consul-Gen., 1962-66); Ambassador to: Liberia, 1967-70 and Guinea, 1968-70; the Philippines, 1970-72; Vice Marshal of Diplomatic Corps, 1972-75; retired 1975. Liveryman, Masons Company. *Recreations:* skiing (represented Oxford *v* Cambridge, and British Univs *v* Swiss Univs), polo. *Address:* Appletree House, near Aston-le-

Walls, Daventry, Northants NN11 6UG. *T:* Chipping Warden 211; Government Secretariat, Hong Kong. *Clubs:* Cavalry and Guards, Beefsteak; Hong Kong.

CURLEWIS, His Honour Judge Sir Adrian (Herbert), Kt 1967; CVO 1974; CBE 1962; retired as Judge of the District Court, New South Wales, Australia, (1948-71); *b* 13 Jan. 1901; *s* of late Judge Herbert R. Curlewis and late Ethel Turner, Authoress; *m* 1928, Beatrice Maude Carr; one *s* one *d. Educ:* Sydney Church of England Grammar Sch.; Univ. of Sydney. Called to Bar of NSW, 1927. Served War of 1939-45, Capt. 8 Div. AIF, Malaya. President: Surf Life Saving Assoc. of Australia, 1933-75; International Surf Life Saving Council, 1956-71; Patron, World Life Saving, 1971-74; Chairman: Australian Outward Bound Trust (Founder and Past Pres.), 1956-; National Fitness Council, New South Wales, 1948-71; National Co-ordinator, Duke of Edinburgh's Award in Australia, 1958-73; Pres., Royal Humane Soc. (NSW), 1968-. Youth Policy Adv. Cttee to NSW Government, 1961-63. Chm. and Royal Commissioner on various Government Enquiries. *Recreations:* surfing, gardening. *Address:* 5 Hopetoun Avenue, Mosman, NSW 2088, Australia. *T:* 969-8365. *Clubs:* University (Sydney); Elanora Country (NSW).

CURRALL, Alexander, CB 1970; CMG 1965; Managing Director, (Posts), Post Office, 1972-77; *b* 30 Jan. 1917; *s* of late R. T. Currall, Edinburgh; *m* 1940, Madeleine Crombie Saunders; one *s. Educ:* George Watson's Coll., Edinburgh; Edinburgh Univ. Min. of Supply, 1939-40; Royal Artillery and Indian Artillery, 1940-46. Successively in Min. of Supply, Min. of Materials and Board of Trade, concerned mainly with internat. economic negotiations, excepting the period 1950-54, when responsible for public trading in non-ferrous metals, and 1954-55, when holding a Commonwealth Fellowship for travel and study in USA. Seconded to Foreign Office as Dep. Consul-Gen., New York, and Dir of British Industrial Development Office, 1960-62; Minister (Commercial), British High Commn, Ottawa, 1962-66; Under-Secretary: Board of Trade, 1966-67; DEA, 1967-68; Dir, Dept for Nat. Savings, 1968-72. Manager, Royal Instn, 1972-75, 1977-. *Address:* 5 Spencer Hill, SW19 4PA. *Clubs:* Caledonian, City of London.

CURRAN, Sir Charles (John), Kt 1974; Director-General of the BBC, 1969-Sept. 1977, then Consultant to BBC Board of Governors on international broadcasting matters until 31 Dec. 1978; Managing Director and Chief Executive, Visnews, since 1978; *b* 13 Oct. 1921; *s* of Felix Curran and Alicia Isabella (*née* Bruce); *m* 1949, Silvia Meyer; one *d. Educ:* Wath-on-Dearne Gram. Sch., S Yorks; Magdalene Coll., Cambridge. Indian Army, 1941-45. Producer, Home Talks, BBC, 1947-50; Asst Editor, Fishing News, 1950-51; BBC, 1951-, including appts as Canadian Rep., 1956-59 and Sec., 1963-66; Dir of External Broadcasting, 1967-69. Pres., European Broadcasting Union, 1973-78; Mem., Exec. Cttee, British Council, 1973-; Mem., 'The Tablet' Trust, 1976-. Hon. DLitt City, 1977. *Recreation:* formerly refereeing coarse Rugby, now enjoying music. *Address:* Visnews Ltd, Cumberland Avenue, NW10 7EH. *T:* 01-965 7733. *Clubs:* Athenæum, United Oxford & Cambridge University.

CURRAN, Desmond, CBE 1961; FRCP; Lord Chancellor's Medical Visitor, 1967-75; Hon. Consulting Psychiatrist, St George's Hospital, since 1967; formerly Professor of Psychiatry, St George's Hospital Medical School, University of London, 1961-67, now Emeritus Professor; Civil Consultant in Psychological Medicine to the Royal Navy, 1946-67; *b* 14 Feb. 1903; *s* of late J. P. Curran; *m* 1938, Marguerite (*née* Gothard); two *s. Educ:* Wellington Coll.; Trinity Coll., Cambridge; St George's Hosp.; Johns Hopkins Hosp., Baltimore. MB, BChir Cambridge, 1928; MRCP 1928, FRCP 1937; MRCS, LRCP 1927; DPM London 1930; House jobs, St George's, 1927-28; HP, Bethlem, 1928-29; RMO and Registrar, Maida Vale Hosp. for Nervous Diseases, 1929-30; Intern, Phipps Clinic, Baltimore, 1930-31; AMO, Maudsley Hosp., 1931-34 (and late part-time). Rockefeller Travelling Fellowship, 1930-31; Gaskell Gold Medal Psychological Medicine, 1933. Consultant Psychiatrist: St George's Hosp., 1934-67; Maida Vale Hosp. for Nervous Diseases, 1934-46. War of 1939-45: Consultant in Psychological Medicine to Royal Navy (Temp. Surg. Capt. RNVR), 1939-46. Croonian Lecturer, RCP 1948. President: Psychiatric Section, RSM, 1951-52; Royal Med. Psychological Assoc., 1963-64. Member: (Franklin) Deptl Cttee on Punishments, Prisons and Borstals, etc, 1948-51; (Wolfenden) Deptl Cttee on Homosexuality and Prostitution, 1954-57; (Representative RCP), Gen. Med. Council, 1961-67. Examiner in Psychiatry: RCP; Univs of London, Edinburgh, Newcastle; NUI. Distinguished Fellow, Amer. Psychiatric Assoc., 1966. Hon. FRCPsych, 1972. *Publications:* (jointly) Psychological Medicine, 8th edn 1976; articles and papers in medical text

books and journals. *Recreation:* golf. *Address:* 51 Cottesmore Court, Stanford Road, W8 5QW. *T:* 01-937 4763. *Clubs:* Athenæum, United Oxford & Cambridge University.

CURRAN, Harry Gibson, CMG 1953; *b* 1901; *s* of late James P. and Jessie M. Curran; *m* 1962, Betty, *d* of Harold Beazley. *Educ:* Royal Naval College, Dartmouth; University College, Oxford (MA). Served War of 1939-45, Middle East (despatches). Treasury Representative, South Asia, 1950-53; Canada, 1953-56; Head of Economic Mission, Ecuador, 1956-58; Representative World Bank, India, 1959-61; Dep. Dir, European Office, World Bank, 1961-66. *Address:* Fairmile, St Mark's Avenue, Salisbury, Wilts. *Club:* Travellers'.

CURRAN, Rt. Hon. Sir Lancelot (Ernest), PC (N Ireland) 1957; Kt 1964; BA, LLB (QUB); Lord Justice of Appeal, Supreme Court of Judicature, Northern Ireland, 1956-75; *b* 8 March 1899; 4th *s* of late Miles Curran, Myrtlefield Park, Belfast; *m* 1st, 1924, Doris Lee; two *s* (one *d* decd); 2nd, 1976, Mrs Margaret P. Curran. *Educ:* Royal Belfast Academical Institution. Barrister, King's Inns, 1923; QC (NI) 1943; Bencher, Inn of Court of N Ireland, 1946. MP Carrick Div., Co. Antrim, NI Parlt, April 1945 (re-elected June 1945)-1949; Parly Sec., Min. of Finance and Chief Whip, 1945. Served European war, 1917-18, RFC and RAF; War of 1939-45, Major, Army. Lecturer in Contract and Tort, Queen's Univ., Belfast; Chm. Court of Referees and Dep. Umpire under Unemployment Pensions Acts, 1926-45; Senior Crown Prosecutor for Co. Down; Attorney-Gen., NI, 1947-49; Judge of High Courts of Justice, NI, 1949-56. *Recreation:* golf. *Address:* Rock Cottage, Tullyard, Co. Down. *T:* Drumbo 600. *Club:* Royal Co. Down Golf.

CURRAN, Prof. Robert Crowe, MD; FRSE 1962; Leith Professor of Pathology, Birmingham University, since 1966; Hon. Consultant Pathologist to the United Birmingham Hospitals; *b* 28 July 1921; *s* of John Curran and Sarah Crowe, Netherton, Wishaw, Lanarkshire; *m* 1947, Margaret Marion Park; one *s* one *d. Educ:* Glasgow Univ. MB, ChB 1943, MD 1956; FRCPath 1967; FRCP 1969. RAMC, 1945-47. Lectr in Pathology, Glasgow Univ., 1950-55. Sen. Lectr and Cons. Pathologist, Sheffield Univ., 1955-58; Prof. of Pathology, St Thomas's Hospital Medical Sch., 1959-66; Chm., Division of Pathological Studies, Birmingham, 1968-74. Registrar, Royal Coll. of Pathologists, 1968-73. *Publications:* Colour Atlas of Histopathology, 1966, 1972; The Pathological Basis of Medicine, 1972; Gross Pathology—a Colour Atlas, 1974; scientific papers on structure and disorders of connective tissue, etc. *Recreations:* golf, music. *Address:* 12 Hintlesham Avenue, Edgbaston, Birmingham B15 2PH.
See also Sir S. C. Curran.

CURRAN, Sir Samuel (Crowe), Kt 1970; FRS 1953; FRSE 1947; Principal and Vice-Chancellor, University of Strathclyde, since 1964; *b* 23 May 1912; *s* of John Curran, Kinghorn, Fife, and Sarah Owen Crowe, Ballymena, Ulster; *m* 1940, Joan Elizabeth, *yr d* of Charles William Strothers and Margaret Beatrice (*née* Millington); three *s* one *d. Educ:* Glasgow Univ.; St John's Coll., Cambridge (Hon. Fellow 1971). DSc Glasgow 1950; MA; BSc, PhD Glasgow, 1937; Cavendish Laboratory, 1937-39; PhD Cantab, 1941; RAE, 1939-40; Min. of Aircraft Production and Min. of Supply, 1940-44; Manhattan Project (Min. of Supply), Univ. of California, 1944-45 (Invention of Scintillation Counter, 1944). Researches in nuclear physics. Natural Philosophy, Glasgow Univ. 1945-55; UK Atomic Energy Authority, 1955-58; Chief Scientist, AWRE, Aldermaston, Berks, 1958-59. Principal, Royal Coll. of Science and Technology, Glasgow, 1959-64. Pres., Scottish Soc. for the Mentally Handicapped, 1954-. Member: Council for Scientific and Industrial Research, 1962-65; Science Research Council, 1965-68; Adv. Council on Technology, 1965-70; Chairman: Adv. Cttee on Med. Research, 1962-75; Adv. Bd on Relations with Univs, 1966-70; Dep. Chm., Electricity Council, 1977-; Mem. Council, Royal Society of Edinburgh, 1961-64; Mem., Scottish Econ. Planning Council, 1965-68; Chief Scientific Adviser to the Sec. of State for Scotland, 1967-; Mem., Oil Develt Council for Scotland, 1973-. Director: Scottish Television, 1964-; Hall Thermotank Ltd, 1969-76; Cetec Systems Ltd, 1965-77; Internat. Res. and Develt Co. Ltd, 1970-; Gen. Steels Div., BSC, 1970-73. Hon. Pres., Scottish-Polish Cultural Assoc., 1972-. FRCPS (Hon.) 1964; Hon. LLD: Glasgow, 1968; Aberdeen, 1971; Hon. ScD Lodz, 1973. Freeman, Motherwell and Wishaw, 1966. DL Glasgow, 1969. St Mungo Prize, 1976. Comdr, St Olav (Norway), 1966; Officer of Polonia Restituta, 1970; Comdr, Order Polish People's Republic, 1976. *Publications:* (with J. D. Craggs) Counting Tubes, 1949; Luminescence and the Scintillation Counter, 1953; Alpha, Beta and Gamma Ray Spectroscopy, 1964; (jt) Energy Resources and the Environment, 1976; papers on nuclear researches and education in Proc. Royal Soc.,

London, Proc. Royal Soc. Edinburgh, Philosophical Magazine, Physical Review, Nature, etc. *Recreation:* golf. *Address:* University of Strathclyde, Royal College, George Street, Glasgow G1 1XW. *Clubs:* Caledonian; Royal Scottish Automobile (Glasgow).
See also R. C. Curran.

CURREY, Rear-Adm. Edmund Neville Vincent, CB 1960; DSO 1944; DSC 1941; *b* 1 Oct. 1906; *s* of Dr and Mrs E. F. N. Currey, Lismore, Co. Waterford, Ireland; *m* 1941, Rosemary Knight; one *d*. *Educ:* Royal Naval Colls, Osborne and Dartmouth. Joined RNC Osborne 1920; served in submarines and destroyers as junior officer; served War of 1939-45; commanded HM ships Wrestler, Escapade and Musketeer; Comdr, 1942; Capt., 1949; subsequently served with British Naval Mission to Greece; Naval Asst to Adm. Commanding Reserves; in command of HMS Bermuda; Naval Asst to Second Sea Lord; Rear-Adm., 1958; Chief of Staff to C-in-C, Portsmouth, 1958-61, retired. Polish Gold Cross of Merit, with swords, 1943. *Recreation:* golf. *Address:* 11 George Street, Bathwick Hill, Bath, Avon. *T:* Bath 63743.

CURREY, Rear-Adm. Harry Philip, CB 1956; OBE 1941; *b* 18 Sept. 1902; *s* of Hon. H. L. Currey; *m* 1928, Rona Gwenllian Harkness; one *s* one *d*. *Educ:* RN Colls Osborne and Dartmouth. Served War of 1939-45: Western Approaches, GHQ, Cairo, E Indies Stn, Eastern Fleet, Mediterranean, British Pacific Fleet. Admty, 1945-47; Capt. of Dockyard, HM Dockyard, Devonport, 1948-50; HMS Bermuda, 1951-53; Flag Officer, Gibraltar and Adm. Supt, HM Dockyard, Gibraltar, 1953-56; retired, 1956. Mem. Cttee, RUKBA. *Recreations:* fishing, gardening. *Address:* Pond Cottage, Newton Valence, near Alton, Hants GU34 3RB. *T:* Tisted 281. *Club:* Naval and Military.

CURREY, Ronald Fairbridge, MC, MA, Hon. LLD; *b* 23 Oct. 1894; *s* of late Hon. H. L. Currey and Ethelreda (*d* 1942), *d* of late C. A. Fairbridge; *m* 1924, Dorothy White; three *s*. *Educ:* Diocesan Coll., Rondebosch; S Andrews Coll., Grahamstown; Rhodes Univ. Coll., Grahamstown; Trinity Coll., Oxford; Rhodes Scholar, 1912. Served 1914-18, Argyll and Sutherland Highlanders (attached Black Watch), France and Belgium (MC and Bar); Asst Master, Rugby Sch., 1920-21; S Andrews Coll., Grahamstown, 1922-26; Joint Headmaster, Ridge Preparatory Sch., Johannesburg, 1927-30; Rector of Michaelhouse, Balgowan, Natal, 1930-38; Headmaster of S Andrews Coll., Grahamstown, S Africa, 1939-55; Headmaster, Ruzawi Sch., Marandellas, S Rhodesia, 1956-61; Lectr in Classics, Rhodes Univ., Grahamstown, until 1965. *Publications:* (with others) Coming of Age-Studies in South African Politics, Economics, and Citizenship, 1930; Some Notes on The Future of the South African Church Schools, 1942; Rhodes: a Biographical Footnote, 1946; (with others) The South African Way of Life, 1953; S Andrews College, 1855-1955, 1955; Rhodes University, 1904-1970, 1970. *Address:* 34 Hill Street, Grahamstown, South Africa.

CURRIE, Prof. Alastair Robert, FRCP, FRCPE, FRCP Glasgow, FRSE; Professor of Pathology, Edinburgh University, since April 1972; Pathologist, Royal Infirmary of Edinburgh; Consultant Pathologist, Lothian Health Board; *b* 8 Oct. 1921; *s* of late John Currie and of Margaret Mactaggart; *m* 1949, Jeanne Marion Clarke, MB, ChB; three *s* two *d*. *Educ:* High Sch. and Univ. of Glasgow. BSc 1941; MB, ChB Glasgow, 1944; MRCPE 1947, FRCPE 1957; MCPath 1963; FRCPath 1965; FRCP Glasgow, 1964; FRSE 1964; MRCP 1966; FRCP 1971; FRCSE 1973. RAMC 1944-49; Lectr in Pathology, Univ. of Glasgow 1947-54; Sen. Lectr in Pathology, Univ. of Glasgow, and Cons. Pathologist, Royal Infirmary, Glasgow, 1954-59; Head, Div. of Pathology, Imperial Cancer Research Fund, London, 1959-62; Regius Prof. of Pathology, Univ. of Aberdeen, 1962-72. Chairman: Standing Adv. Cttee on Laboratory Services, 1968-72; Biomedical Res. Cttee, 1975-; Member: MRC, 1964-68 and 1976- (Chm., Cell Biology and Disorders Bd, 1977-); Scottish NE Regional Hosp. Bd, 1966-71; Scientific Cttee, 1969-, Exec. Cttee and Grand Council, 1977-, Cancer Res. Campaign; Scottish Health Services Council, 1969-72; Chief Scientist's Cttee, Scottish Home and Health Dept, 1974-; Court, Edinburgh Univ., 1976-. *Publications:* papers in scientific and med. jls. *Recreations:* reading, gardening. *Address:* 42 Murrayfield Avenue, Edinburgh EH12 6AY. *T:* 031-337 3100. *Club:* Athenæum.

CURRIE, Sir George (Alexander), Kt 1960; retired as Vice-Chancellor, University of New Zealand (May 1952-Dec. 1961); *b* Banffshire, Scotland, 13 Aug. 1896; *s* of George Currie, farmer, and Mary Currie; *m* 1923, Margaret, *d* of Alexander Smith; two *s*. *Educ:* University of Aberdeen (BscAg, DSc). War

Service, Gordon Highlanders, 1915-18. Manager, Salter Estate Co. Ltd, N Queensland, 1923-26; Scientific Officer, Dept Agric., Queensland, 1926-29; Principal Research Officer, Council for Scientific and Industrial Research, Australia, 1929-39; Prof. of Agriculture, University of Western Australia, 1939-40; Vice Chancellor, Univ. of Western Australia, 1940-52. Chm. Commn on Higher Educn for Papua and New Guinea, 1963-64. Hon. LLD: Aberdeen, 1948; Melbourne, 1954; Dalhousie, Canada, 1958; Papua, New Guinea, 1967. Hon. DLitt, University of Western Australia, 1952. *Publications:* The Origins of CSIRO, 1901-26, 1966; some 20 bulletins, pamphlets and articles on scientific research; articles on univ. educn and admin. *Address:* 20 Chermside Street, Canberra, ACT 2600, Australia.

CURRIE, George Boyle Hanna, MBE 1946; *b* 19 Dec. 1905; *s* of late Very Rev. William John Currie, BA, DD; *m* 1933, Stephanie Maud Evelyn Costello; two *s* two *d*. *Educ:* Campbell Coll., Belfast; Trinity Coll., Dublin (BA, MA, LLB). Called to Bar, Middle Temple, 1932; Northern Circuit, 1932; Councillor, Wirral UDC, 1934-50 (Chm. Council, 1938); contested (C) East Flintshire, 1950 and 1951; MP (UU) North Down, 1955-70. Served War, 1939-46 (MBE 1946); RAFVR (Sqdn Ldr). Mem., Council for Arab-British Understanding, 1970-71. *Recreations:* salmon fishing, golf. *Address:* (chambers) Queen Insurance Building D, Queen Avenue, 13 Castle Street, Liverpool L2 4UE. *T:* 051-236 5072; (residence) 1 Pump Court, Temple, EC4. *T:* 01-583 1594; Wyncote, Roscote Close, Lower Village, Heswall, Wirral, Merseyside. *T:* Heswall 1444. *Club:* County (Downpatrick).

CURRIE, Sir James, KBE 1967 (OBE 1950); CMG 1958; retired from HM Diplomatic Service, 1967; *b* 6 May 1907; *o s* of Charles Howat Currie and Rebecca Ralston, Glasgow; *m* 1945, Daisy Mowat; one *s*. *Educ:* Glasgow Academy; Glasgow Univ.; Balliol Coll., Oxford; London School of Economics. Did not take up appt at UCL, 1931; William Hollins & Co. Ltd, 1931-34; National Milk Publicity Council, 1934-39; Ministry of Economic Warfare, 1939. Commercial Secretary: Rio de Janeiro, 1941; Ankara, 1944; First Secretary (Commercial), Istanbul, 1945; Santiago, Chile, 1947; Commercial Counsellor, Washington, 1949; Commercial Counsellor and Consul-General, Copenhagen, 1952; Consul-General: São Paulo, 1956; Johannesburg, 1962. Commonwealth Foundn, 1967; Community Relations Commn, 1970; London Council of Univ. of Witwatersrand. *Publications:* Professional Organisations in the Commonwealth, 1970; reviews for TLS, The Times and other jls. *Recreations:* fishing and golf. *Address:* Juniper House, Tostock, Bury St Edmunds, Suffolk. *Club:* Reform.

CURRIE, (Joseph) Austin; Member (SDLP), for Fermanagh and South Tyrone, Northern Ireland Constitutional Convention, 1975-76; *b* 11 Oct. 1939; *s* of John Currie and Mary (*née* O'Donnell); *m* 1968, Anne Ita Lynch; two *s* two *d*. *Educ:* Edendork Sch.; St Patrick's Academy, Dungannon; Queen's Univ., Belfast (BA). MP (Nat) Tyrone, Parlt of N Ireland, 1964-72; Mem. (SDLP), Fermanagh and S Tyrone, NI Assembly, 1973-75; Minister of Housing, Planning and Local Govt, 1974. *Address:* Tullydraw, Donaghmore, Co. Tyrone.

CURRIE, Piers William Edward, MC 1945; Deputy Master, Court of Protection, since 1971; *b* 26 Feb. 1913; *e c* of late P. A. Currie, OBE and Mrs L. A. Currie; *m* 1956, Ella Rosaleen, *y c* of late Rev. W. and Mrs Bennett-Hughes; no *c*. *Educ:* Rugby Sch.; Brasenose Coll., Oxford (MA). Solicitor, admitted Dec. 1939. Served War, 1940-45, in 4th Regt RHA. Sen. Legal Asst, Nat. Coal Bd, 1946-53; Asst Sec., 1953-55; Sec., W Midlands Divisional Bd, 1955-60; Sec. and Legal Adviser, 1960-62; Dep. Sec., NCB, 1962-67. Legal Adviser, Land Commission, 1967-71. *Recreations:* church affairs, gardening, natural history. *Address:* The White House, Trimingham, Norfolk NR11 8HP. *Club:* United Oxford & Cambridge University.

CURRIE, Rear-Adm. Robert Alexander, CB 1957; DSC 1944, bar 1945; DL; *b* 29 April 1905; 5th *s* of John Currie, Glasgow, and Rachel Thomson, Dundee; *m* 1944, Lady (Edith Margaret) Beevor, *widow* of Sir Thomas Beevor, 6th Bt, and *d* of Frank Agnew, Eccles, Norfolk; one step *s* (*see* Sir Thomas Beevor, 7th Bt) three step *d*. *Educ:* RN Colleges, Osborne and Dartmouth. Specialised in Gunnery, 1930. Served War, 1939-45: HMS Hood; HMS Warspite, 2nd Battle of Narvik; Plans Division, Admiralty; Convoy Escort Comdr; Assault Gp Comdr, Far East; Captain RN, 1945; Captain (D) Fifth Flotilla, 1948-49; idc 1950; Director, Royal Naval Staff Coll., 1951-52; Comdg Officer, HMS Cumberland, 1953; Rear-Adm., 1954; Chief of Staff to Chairman, British Joint Service Mission, Washington, DC, 1954-57; retired, 1957. Member: Cttee of Enquiry into the Fishing Industry, 1958-60; W Suffolk County Council, 1962-74. DL, Suffolk, 1968. King Haakon VII Liberty Cross, Norway,

1945. *Recreations:* shooting, fishing, painting. *Address:* Thorpe Morieux Hall, near Bury St Edmunds. *T:* Cockfield Green 276.

CURRIE, Sir Walter Mordaunt Cyril, 5th Bt, *cr* 1846; Member of the Performing Right Society; *b* 3 June 1894; *s* of 4th Bt and Bertha (*d* 1951), *d* of T. A. Mitford Freeman; *S* father, 1941. *Educ:* Sherborne. Served European War, 1915-16, with RAOC. *Publications:* Some 25 lyrics and part songs, 2 cantatas; choral symphony, Odysseus; Nativity Play, The Three Kings, music by C. Armstrong Gibbs. *Address:* Chasefield Cottage, Wickham Bishops, Witham, Essex.

CURRY, Dr Alan Stewart; Controller, Forensic Science Service, Home Office, since 1976; *b* 31 Oct. 1925; *s* of late Richard C. Curry and of Margaret Curry; *m* 1973, J. Venise Hewitt; one *s* (by previous marriage). *Educ:* Arnold Sch., Blackpool; Trinity Coll., Cambridge (Scholar). MA, PhD, CChem, FRIC, FRCPath. Served War of 1939-45 with RAF. Joined Home Office Forensic Science Service, 1952; served in NE Region, 1952-64; Dir, Nottingham Forensic Sci. Lab., 1964-66; Dir, Home Office Central Research Estabt, Aldermaston, 1966-76. Pres., Internat. Assoc. of Forensic Toxicologists, 1969-75; UN Consultant in Narcotics; Hon. Consultant in Forensic Toxicology to RAF. Hon. Mem., Belg. Pharmaceutical Soc. *Publications:* Poison Detection in Human Organs, 1962 (3rd edn 1976); Advances in Forensic and Clinical Toxicology, 1973; (ed, with wife) The Biochemistry of Women, Clinical Concepts; Methods for Clinical Investigation, 1974; (ed) Methods of Forensic Sciences, Vols 3 and 4; many papers in med. and sci. jls. *Recreations:* sailing, amateur radio. *Address:* Home Office, Horseferry House, Dean Ryle Street, SW1P 2AW. *T:* 01-211 4367. *Clubs:* Athenæum, Civil Service, Safari.

CURRY, Thomas Peter Ellison, QC 1966, 1973; *s* of Maj. F. R. P. Curry; *m* 1950, Pamela Joyce, *d* of late Group Capt. A. J. Holmes, AFC, JP; two *s* two *d. Educ:* Tonbridge; Oriel Coll., Oxford. BA 1948; MA 1951. Served War of 1939-45; enlisted 1939; commnd, 1941; 17th Indian Div., India and Burma, 1941-45. War Office, 1946. Called to Bar, Middle Temple, 1953. QC 1966. Solicitor, 1968; partner in Freshfields, Solicitors, 1968-70; returned to Bar; re-appointed QC 1973. Rep. Army, Oxford and Sussex at Squash Racquets (described as fastest mover in squash, 1947; triple blue, Oxford; twice cross country winner); World Student Games (5000 m), 1947; British Steeplechase champion 1948, Olympic Games, 1948. Served on AAA Cttee of Inquiry, 1967. Holder of French certificate as capitaine-mécanicien for mechanically propelled boats. *Publications:* (Joint Editor) Palmer's Company Law, 1959; (Joint Editor) Crew on Meetings, 1966, 1975. *Recreations:* work, gardening. *Address:* Rickhurst Farm, Dunsfold, Surrey. *T:* Dunsfold 356.

CURSON, Bernard Robert, CMG 1967; HM Diplomatic Service, retired; *b* 14 Nov. 1913; *e s* of late Robert and Mabel Curson; *m* 1949, Miriam Olive Johnson, Lynchburg, Virginia; one *s . Educ:* University Coll. Sch. Asst Private Sec. to Sec. of State for India, 1943-44, and 1945-46; Mem., UK Delegn to UN Assembly, 1946, 1947, 1948; Private Sec. to Sec. of State for Commonwealth Relations, 1948-50; Office of High Comr, Ceylon, 1950-52; Mem., UK Delegn to UN Wheat Conf., Geneva, 1956; Mem., UK Delegn to Colombo Plan Consultative Cttee, Wellington, 1956, and Saigon, 1957; British Information Services, Canada, 1958-64; Consul-Gen., Atlanta, USA, 1970-73. *Address:* 3804 Peachtree Road, NE, Atlanta, Ga 30319, USA. *Club:* Travellers'.

CURTIN, Rt. Rev. Mgr. Canon Jeremiah John, DD; Priest-Director and Ecclesiastical Adviser, Universe Enquiry Bureau, since 1953; Canon of Southwark Diocesan Chapter, 1958; Domestic Prelate to HH Pope John XXIII, 1961, Protonotary Apostolic, 1972; *b* Sileby, Leics, 19 June 1907; *e s* of late Jeremiah John Curtin and Mary Bridget Curtin (*née* Leahy). *Educ:* Battersea Polytechnic; Wimbledon Coll.; St Joseph's Coll., Mark Cross; St John's Seminary, Wonersh; Gregorian Univ., Rome. BA London 1927; DD Rome 1933 (Gregorian Univ.). Priest, 1931; Prof. of Philosophy and Theology, St John's Seminary, Wonersh, 1933-48; Vice-Rector, 1947-48; Parish Priest, St Paul's, Hayward's Heath, 1948-56; Parish Priest, Our Lady of Ransom, Eastbourne, 1956-61; Rector, Pontificio Collegio Beda, Rome, 1961-72. *Recreations:* archæology, music. *Address:* 48 Castle Street, Farnham, Surrey GU9 7JQ. *T:* Farnham 4659. *Club:* Athenæum.

CURTIS, Colin Hinton Thomson, CVO 1970; ISO 1970; Chairman, Metropolitan Public Abattoir Board, since 1971; Member, Queensland Meat Industry Authority, since 1972; *b* 25 June 1920; *s* of A. Curtis, Brisbane; *m* 1943, Anne Catherine Drevesen; one *s. Educ:* Brisbane Grammar School. RANR Overseas Service, 1940-45. Sec. and Investigation Officer to

Chm., Sugar Cane Prices Board, 1948-49; Asst Sec. to Central Sugar Cane Prices Board, 1949; Sec. to Premier of Queensland, 1950-64; Mem., Qld Trade Missions to SE Asia, 1963 and 1964; Asst Under-Sec., Premier's Dept, 1961-64; Assoc. Dir and Dir of Industrial Development, 1964-66; Under-Sec., Premier's Dept and Clerk of Exec. Council, 1966-70; State Dir, Royal Visit, 1970; Agent-General for Queensland in London, 1970-71. *Recreations:* squash, yachting, swimming. *Address:* 117 Carlton Terrace, Manly, Qld 4179, Australia. *Clubs:* RSL Memorial, Cricketers, Tattersalls, Royal Queensland Yacht, Rugby League (Queensland).

CURTIS, Prof. David Roderick, FRS 1974; FAA 1965; Professor of Pharmacology, John Curtin School of Medical Research, Australian National University, since 1973; *b* 3 June 1927; *s* of E. D. and E. V. Curtis; *m* 1952, Lauris Sewell; one *s* one *d. Educ:* Univ. of Melbourne; Australian National Univ. MB, BS Melbourne 1950, PhD ANU 1957. Dept of Physiology, John Curtin Sch., ANU: Research Scholar, 1954-56; Research Fellow, 1956-57; Fellow, 1957-59; Sen. Fellow, 1959-62; Professorial Fellow, 1962-66; Prof. of Pharmacology, 1966-68; Prof. of Neuropharmacology, 1968-73. Vis. Prof., Dept of Physiology, Downstate Med. Center, NY, 1959-60. *Publications:* papers in fields of neurophysiology, neuropharmacology in Jl Physiology, Jl Neurophysiol., Brain Research, Exper. Brain Research, etc. *Recreation:* tennis. *Address:* 7 Patey Street, Campbell, Canberra City, ACT 2601, Australia. *T:* Canberra (062) 48-5664: John Curtin School of Medical Research, Australian National University, PO Box 334, ACT 2601. *T:* Canberra (062) 49-2757.

CURTIS, Sir (Edward) Leo, Kt 1965; Lord Mayor of Melbourne, Australia, 1963-64 and 1964-65; *b* London, 13 Jan. 1907; *m* 1938, Elvira Lillian Prahl. Joined Melbourne City Council, Dec. 1955; retired March 1975. Past President of Retail Traders Association of Victoria. *Address:* 5 Kenley Court, Toorak, Vic. 3142, Australia. *Clubs:* Athenæum, Kelvin (Melbourne); various sporting.

CURTIS, Most Rev. Ernest Edwin, CBE 1976; Priest-in-charge of St Mary, Whitwell, diocese of Portsmouth, since 1976; Hon. Assistant Bishop of Portsmouth, since 1976; *b* 24 Dec. 1906, *s* of Ernest John and Zoe Curtis; *m* 1938, Dorothy Anne Hill (*d* 1965); one *s* one *d; m* 1970, Evelyn Mary Josling. *Educ:* Sherborne; Foster's Sch.; Royal College of Science, London. BSc (hons Chem.) London, 1927; ARCSc 1927; Dipl. Educn, London, 1928. Asst Master, Lindisfarne Coll., Westcliff, 1928-31; Wells Theol Coll., 1932-33; Asst Curate, Holy Trinity, Waltham Cross, 1933-36; Chaplain i/c parishes Rose Hill and Bambous, and Principal, St Paul's Theol Coll., Mauritius, 1937-44; Missions to Seamen Chaplain, Port Louis, 1944; Priest i/c St Wilfrid, Portsmouth, 1945-47; Vicar, All Saints, Portsmouth, and Chaplain, Royal Portsmouth Hospital, 1947-55; Priest i/c St Agatha, Portsmouth, 1954-55; Vicar, St John Baptist, Locks Heath, 1955-66; Warden of Readers, Dio. Portsmouth, 1956-66; Rural Dean of Alverstoke, 1964-66; Bishop of Mauritius and Seychelles, 1966-72; of Mauritius, 1973-76; Archbishop of the Indian Ocean, 1973-76. *Recreations:* walking, hill-climbing, piano. *Address:* Whitwell Vicarage, Ventnor, Isle of Wight PO38 2QT.

CURTIS, Brig. Francis Cockburn, CBE 1945; MA; MIEE; Fellow Emeritus, Trinity Hall, Cambridge, since 1961; *b* 2 May 1898; *s* of late Lieut-Col J. G. C. Curtis, Oxford and Bucks Light Infantry, Walmer, Kent; *m* 1933, Dorothy Joan Grant; two *s* one *d. Educ:* Bedales Sch.; RMA, Woolwich; King's Coll., Cambridge. Commissioned RE 1917; served in Flanders (despatches), Iraq and Palestine; transferred to Royal Signals, 1923; served on General Staff in War Office and Aldershot Command, and in Home Office (ARP Dept), and Office of the Lord Privy Seal; OC 38th (Welsh) Divisional Signals, 1940-41; Army Council Secretariat (Secretary Standing Cttee on Army Administration), 1941; Joint Planning Staff, 1942; Colonel 1943; Dep. Director of Military Operations, 1943-44; Director of Post-Hostilities Plans, War Office, 1944; Brigadier, General Staff (Plans and Ops), GHQ, MELF, 1945-48; Director for European Inter-Allied Planning, War Office, 1948-51; retired 1951; Fellow and Bursar, Trinity Hall, Cambridge, 1952-59; Treasurer, 1959-61. *Recreation:* fishing. *Address:* 16 Marlborough Court, Cambridge CB3 9BQ. *T:* Cambridge 50664. *Club:* Naval and Military.

CURTIS, John S.; *see* Sutton Curtis.

CURTIS, Sir Leo; *see* Curtis, Sir E. L.

CURTIS, Michael Howard; Executive Aide to HH The Aga Khan; Director, Nation Printers and Publishers, Nairobi,

Kenya, since 1959, Chairman, 1976-77; *b* 28 Feb. 1920; *e s* of Howard and Doris May Curtis; *m* 1st, 1947, Barbara Winifred Gough; two *s* two *d* ; 2nd, 1961, Marian Joan Williams. *Educ:* St Lawrence Coll.; Sidney Sussex Coll., Cambridge (MA). Eastern Daily Press, Norwich, 1945; News Chronicle: Leader Writer, 1946; Dep. Editor, 1952; Editor, 1954-57; Dir, News Chronicle Ltd, 1954-57; Personal Aide to HH The Aga Khan, 1957-59. *Address:* La Vieille Maison, Villemetrie, 60300 Senlis, France. *Clubs:* Garrick, East India, Devonshire, Sports and Public Schools; Muthaiga (Nairobi).

CURTIS, Percy John, CB 1960; CBE 1955; Secretary, Exchequer and Audit Department, 1955-63; *b* 3 Oct. 1900; *s* of J. H. Curtis, Trimdon, Co. Durham; *m* 1st, 1924, Dorothy Hilda Ford Hayes (*d* 1954); one *s*; 2nd, 1958, Joyce Irene Potter. *Educ:* Rye Grammar Sch. Entered Exchequer and Audit Dept, 1920. *Address:* 2 Rigault Road, SW6. *T:* 01-736 4072. *Club:* Reform.

CURTIS, Peter; see Lofts, Norah.

CURTIS, Philip; His Honour Judge Curtis; a Circuit Judge (formerly a Judge of County Courts), since 1969; *b* 29 April 1908; *s* of James William and Emma Curtis; *m* 1937, Marjorie Lillian Sharp; two *s* one *d. Educ:* St Mary's RC, Denton, Lancs; Manchester Grammar; Brasenose Coll., Oxford. Called to the Bar, Gray's Inn, 1944. *Address:* Mottram Hall Farm, Mottram St Andrew, near Macclesfield, Cheshire. *T:* Prestbury 49509.

CURTIS, Richard Herbert, QC 1977; a Recorder of the Crown Court, since 1974. *Educ:* Oxford univ. (BA). Called to Bar, Inner Temple, 1958. *Address:* 3 Fountain Court, Birmingham. *T:* 021-236 5854.

CURTIS, Richard James Seymour, OBE 1962; *b* 22 Oct. 1900; *s* of late Sir George Curtis, KCSI, ICS, and of late Lady Curtis, OBE, La Frégate, Dinard, France; *m* 1929, Mary Margaret, *o d* of late Rev. and Mrs H. J. Boyd, St Paul's Vicarage, St Leonards-on-Sea; one *s* one *d. Educ:* Haileybury; King's Coll., Cambridge; University of Caen. Hons degree in History, Cambridge, 1922. Appointed Assistant Anglais at Lycée Corneille, Rouen, by Board of Education, Oct. 1922; Asst Master, Hurst Court, Sept. 1923, Partner, 1926, Headmaster, 1933-61. Incorporated Assoc. of Preparatory Schools (Vice-Chm. IAPS, 1946; Chm. 1957). Asst Sec. and Sec., Common Entrance Examination Board, 1961-67. Mem. Hastings Borough Council, 1952-61; President Soc. of Schoolmasters, 1962. *Publications:* (with A. R. Slater) Latin and French Revision Papers, 1948. Translator of The Revolutionaries, by Louis Madelin; Russia Unveiled, by Panait Istrati; Murder Party, by Henry Bordeaux; The Corsairs of St Malo, by Dupont. *Address:* The Wychert, Haddenham, Bucks. *T:* Haddenham 291136.

CURTIS, Very Rev. Wilfred Frank; Provost of Sheffield, since 1974; *b* 24 Feb. 1923; *s* of W. A. Curtis, MC and Mrs M. Curtis (*née* Burbidge); *m* 1951, Muriel (*née* Dover); two *s* two *d. Educ:* Bishop Wordsworth's Sch., Salisbury; King's Coll., London (AKC). Served in RA, 1942-47; Major 1946. London Univ., 1947-52; Curate of High Wycombe, 1952-55; staff of Church Missionary Soc., 1955-74: Area Sec., Devon and Cornwall, 1955-65; Adviser in Rural Work, 1957-65; SW Regional Sec., 1962-65; Home Sec., 1965-74. Vice-Pres., Church Missionary Soc., 1977; Mem., General Synod, 1977. *Recreations:* walking, photography, nature study. *Address:* The Cathedral, Sheffield S1 1HA. *T:* Sheffield 25367; Cathedral Vicarage, 2 Cherry Tree Road, Sheffield S11 9AA. *T:* 54029. *Club:* Sheffield.

CURTIS, Wilfred Harry, CB 1953; CBE 1950; *b* 23 May 1897; retired as Assistant Under-Secretary of State, War Office, 1958. *Educ:* Summerleaze, Harptree, Somerset. JP County of London, 1950-58. *Address:* Ashton, Dunsfold, Surrey. *T:* Dunsfold 384.

CURTIS, Sir William (Peter), 7th Bt *cr* 1802; *b* 9 April 1935; *s* of Sir Peter Curtis, 6th Bt, and of Joan Margaret, *d* of late Reginald Nicholson; *S* father, 1976. *Educ:* Winchester College; Trinity College, Oxford (MA); Royal Agricultural College, Cirencester. *Heir: cousin* Major Edward Philip Curtis, 16th/5th The Queen's Royal Lancers [*b* 25 June 1940. *Educ:* Bradfield; RMA Sandhurst]. *Address:* Little Manor, near Bishop's Waltham, Hants.

CURTIS BROWN, Spencer; *b* 1906; *s* of A. Curtis Brown and Caroline Lord; *m* 1928, Jean, *d* of Rev. W. Watson, DD; one *d. Educ:* Harrow; Magdalene Coll., Cambridge (History Exhibitioner), Personal Adviser to General Sikorski, Polish Prime Minister, 1941-43; Intelligence Corps (Special Services); assisted in reorganizing book trade in liberated countries, 1945; Chm., Curtis Brown Ltd, London, literary agents, 1945-1968; served on various Government Cttees concerned with book

distribution. *Publications:* (jt author) The Dark Side of the Moon, 1946; biographical introduction to Elizabeth Bowen's Pictures and Conversations, 1975. *Recreation:* listening to other people. *Club:* Travellers'.

CURTIS-RALEIGH, Nigel Hugh; His Honour Judge Curtis-Raleigh; a Circuit Judge (formerly Judge of County Courts), since 1966; *b* 8 Nov. 1914; *s* of late Capt. H. T. R. Curtis-Raleigh; *m* 1964, Jean Steadman, MB, DPM; five *s. Educ:* Wellington; Queen's Coll., Oxford (History Exhibitioner, Kitchener Scholar). Called to the Bar, Middle Temple (Harmsworth Law Scholar), 1939. Served HAC, 1939-40. *Recreations:* music, chess, poker.

CURTISS, Air Vice-Marshal John Bagot; Commandant, RAF Staff College, since 1977; *b* 6 Dec. 1924; *s* of Major E. F. B. Curtiss; *m* 1946, Peggy Drughorn Bowie; three *s* one *d . Educ:* Radley Coll.; Wanganui Collegiate Sch., NZ; Worcester Coll., Oxford. Served War: Oxford Univ. Air Sqdn, 1942-43; Bomber Comd, 1944-45; Transport Comd, 1945-49; Training Comd, 1950-53; Fighter Comd, 1953-64; Dir, RAF Staff Coll., 1967-69; Gp Capt Ops, HQ Strike Comd, 1972-74; SASO, HQ 11 Gp, 1974-75; Dir-Gen. Organisation, RAF, 1975-77. *Recreations:* squash, sailing; Pres. RAF Cricket Assoc., 1976. *Address:* c/o Coutts & Co., 1 Old Park Lane, W1Y 4BS. *Clubs:* MCC, Royal Air Force; Royal Lymington Yacht.

CURZON; see Roper-Curzon.

CURZON, family name of Earl Howe and Viscount Scarsdale.

CURZON, Sir Clifford (Michael), Kt 1977; CBE 1958; Hon. DMus; FRAM; Pianist; *b* 18 May 1907, of British parents; *m* 1931, Lucille Wallace (*d* 1977), American harpsichordist; two adopted *s. Educ:* Royal Academy of Music (Thalberg Scholar and Potter Exhibitioner); studied under Prof. Chas Reddie at Royal Academy of Music, Schnabel (Berlin), Katherine Goodson, and Landowska and Boulanger (Paris); concert tours in England, Europe and USA; in 1936 and 1938 toured Europe under the auspices of the British Council; Soloist at the Royal Philharmonic, BBC and Promenade Concerts, etc.; also Colonne and Société Philharmonique Concerts, Paris. 1st performance of Alan Rawsthorne's Piano Concerto No 2, commnd by Arts Council for Festival of Britain, 1951. Formed (with Szigeti, Primrose and Fournier) the Edinburgh Festival Piano Quartet, 1952. American Tours, 1948-70, including solo appearances with New York Philharmonic Orchestra under Bruno Walter, the Philadelphia Orchestra, Pittsburgh and Toronto Orchestras, etc.; Soloist Holland Festival, 1953; Zürich Festival, 1953; tour of Continent as soloist with BBC Symphony Orchestra under Sir Malcolm Sargent, 1954; Soloist Bergen and Munich Festivals, 1954. Soloist Beethoven Festival, Bonn, Salzburg, Edinburgh and Prades Festivals. Hon. DMus Leeds, 1970; Hon. DLitt Sussex, 1973. *Recreations:* gardening and swimming. *Address:* The White House, Millfield Place, Highgate, N6 6JP. *T:* 01-340 5348; The Close, Glenridding, Cumbria.

CURZON, Leonard Henry, CB 1956; *b* 4 Jan. 1912; *s* of late Frederick Henry Curzon; *m* 1935, Greta, *e d* of late Willem and Anny van Praag; one *s. Educ:* Sir Walter St John's Sch.; Jesus Coll., Cambridge (Scholar, BA, LLB). Civil Servant, 1934-72: Import Duties Adv. Cttee; Air Ministry, Ministries of Aircraft Production, Supply, Aviation and Defence. Later on staff of Monopolies and Mergers Commn. IDC 1947. *Address:* 69 Christchurch Mount, Epsom, Surrey. *T:* Epsom 22732.

CUSACK, Henry Vernon, CMG 1955; CBE 1947; HM Overseas Civil Service (retired); Deputy Director General of the Overseas Audit Service, 1946-55; *b* 26 June 1895; 2nd *s* of late Edward Cusack, Bray, Co. Wicklow, and of Constance Louisa Vernon, *e d* of late Col Vernon, DL, JP, Clontarf Castle, Dublin; unmarried. *Educ:* Aravon Sch., Ireland. Served European War, 1914-19 (General Service and Victory medals), France, Belgium and North Russia, as Captain, RASC, attached RGA; entered Colonial Audit Service, 1920; Asst Auditor: Sierra Leone, 1920-22, Nigeria, 1922-28; Sen. Asst Auditor, Nyasaland, 1928-33; Asst Director, Central Office, Colonial Audit Dept London, 1933-37; Auditor, Gold Coast, 1937-46; a Governor of the King's Hospital Sch., Dublin (Chm., 1964-69). FRGS. Coronation Medal, 1953. *Address:* Kildare Street and University Club, 17 St Stephen's Green, Dublin 2. *T:* Dublin 62975. *Clubs:* Naval and Military; Kildare Street and University (Dublin); Royal St George Yacht (Dun Laoghaire, Co. Dublin).

CUSACK, Hon. Sir Ralph Vincent, Kt 1966; Hon. Mr Justice Cusack; Judge of the High Court of Justice (Queen's Bench Division) since 1966; *b* 13 April 1916; *s* of late His Honour John Cusack, KC, and late Dora, *d* of R. Winder, Solicitor;

unmarried. *Educ:* King's Coll. Sch.; University of London; and in Italy. LLB 1939; Barrister, Gray's Inn, 1940; Bencher, 1966. Served in Army, 1940-46; Staff Capt., HQ Eastern Command, 1943-44; Dep. Asst Military Secretary (Major), War Office, 1944-46. Freeman, City of London, 1949; Member General Council of the Bar, 1953-57, 1960-64; QC 1960; Recorder of Gloucester, 1961-64; of Wolverhampton, 1964-66; Comr of Assize, South Eastern Circuit, July 1965; Leader of the Oxford Circuit, 1964-66. Deputy Chairman, Berkshire Quarter Sessions, 1962-68. Mem., 1974-76, Vice-Chm., 1975-76, Parole Bd. *Address:* 221 Ashley Gardens, Westminster, SW1P 1PA. *T:* 01-834 5610; Royal Courts of Justice, Strand, WC2. *Clubs:* Athenæum, Garrick.

CUSDEN, Victor Vincent, OBE 1943; *b* 26 Jan. 1893; *s* of James Cusden and Elizabeth Susan Wakelyn; *m* 1927, Aimée Louise Charlotte Pauwels; one *s* (one *d* decd). *Educ:* Christ's Hospital. Interned during war at Ruhleben Camp, Germany, where studied for Consular Service; granted Civil Service Certificate as a Probationer Vice-Consul in the Consular Service, 1919; appointed to Salonica, 1919; transferred to Antwerp, 1920; acting Vice-Consul at Charleroi, 1920-21; given substantive rank of Vice-Consul, 1921; acting Consul-General at Antwerp, 1921-22-23; acting Vice-Consul at Ghent, 1921; transferred to Valparaiso, 1924; acting Consul-General at Valparaiso, 1924-25 and 1927; transferred to Barcelona, 1928; acting Consul-General at Barcelona in 1928, 1929 and 1930; acting Consul at Malaga, 1929; in charge of Consulate General at Dakar, 1930; Consul at Nantes, 1930 (did not proceed); Consul-General at Dakar, 1931; at Loanda, 1941; Izmir (Smyrna), Turkey, 1946-51; Retired, 1951. Coronation Medal, 1937. *Address:* Mayfield, Avisford Park Road, Walberton, Arundel, W Sussex BN18 0AP.

CUSDIN, Sidney Edward Thomas, OBE 1946; DSc (Hong Kong); FRIBA, AADip; Consultant to Firm of Cusdin, Burden and Howitt, Architects; *b* 28 July 1908; *s* of Sidney Herbert Cusdin, London; *m* 1936, Eva Eileen (Peggy), *d* of F. P. Dorizzi, London; no *c. Educ:* Municipal School of Arts and Crafts, Southend-on-Sea, Essex; Architectural Assoc., London. AA Holloway Scholarship, 1927; Fifth Year Travelling Studentship, 1929; joined staff of Stanley Hall & Easton and Robertson: British Pavilions at Brussels Internat. Exhibition and Johannesburg Exhibition; elected Member of AA Council, 1937, and worked on RIBA Cttees. Served War of 1939-45, RAF, on staff of HQ, No. 26 Group (despatches twice, OBE). Re-joined firm of Easton & Robertson, 1946 (firm later known as Easton & Robertson, Cusdin, Preston and Smith, until 1965 when this partnership was dissolved). Pres. AA, 1950-51; Mem. Council RIBA, 1950-51. Awarded Henry Saxon Snell Prize and Theakston Bequest, 1950; Principal works: London: Development of the Hosp. for Sick Children, Great Ormond Street, British Postgraduate Medical Fedn, and London Univ., Inst. of Child Health; Medical Coll. of St Bartholomew's Hosp., New Hostel and Labs; Middlesex Hosp. Medical Sch.; New Sch. Buildings and Astor Coll.; National Inst. for Medical Research Develt, Mill Hill; Cambridge: Dept of Engineering, New Workshops and Laboratories; Univ. Chemistry Laboratories; United Cambridge Hosps, Addenbrooke's Hosp., Hills Rd, New Develt; MRC, extension of Lab. of Molecular Biology; Harlow: Princess Alexandra Hosp.; Belfast: Queen's Univ. of Belfast, Inst. of Clin. Science; Royal Victoria Hosp. Develt; Royal Belfast Hosp. for Sick Children, alterations and additions; Malaya: plans for Develt of Univ. of Malaya; Hong Kong; plans for develt of Univ. of Hong Kong; Cons. Architect for: Queen Elizabeth Hosp., Hong Kong (awarded RIBA Bronze Medal); Faculty of Medicine, Univ. of Riyad, Saudi Arabia; Cons. Architect to The Imperial Cancer Research Fund, London. Chm., British Consultants Bureau, 1972-74. *Publications:* (with James Crooks) Suggestions and Demonstration Plans for Hospitals for Sick Children, 1947. *Recreations:* theatre, travel, fishing; spending time in believing that "WS" was Shakespeare. *Address:* 27 Devonshire Close, W1N 1LG. *T:* 01-637 1891; 34 Ringshall, Little Gaddesden, near Berkhamsted, Herts. *Clubs:* Savile, Royal Air Force, The Sette of Odd Volumes.

CUSHING, David Henry, DPhil; FRS 1977; Deputy Director, Fisheries Research, England and Wales, since 1974; *b* 14 March 1920; *s* of W. E. W. Cushing and Isobel (*née* Batchelder); *m* 1943, Diana R. C. Antona-Traversi; one *d. Educ:* Duke's Sch., Alnwick; Newcastle upon Tyne Royal Grammar Sch.; Balliol Coll., Oxford (MA, DPhil). RA, 1940-45; 1st Bn, Royal Fusiliers, 1945-46. Fisheries Lab., 1946-. *Publications:* The Arctic Cod, 1966; Fisheries Biology, 1968 (USA); Detection of Fish, 1973; Fisheries Resources and their Management, 1974; Marine Ecology and Fisheries, 1975. *Address:* 198 Yarmouth Road, Lowestoft, Suffolk. *T:* Lowestoft 65569.

CUSHION, Air Vice-Marshal Sir William Boston, KBE 1947 (CBE 1942; OBE 1927); CB 1944; RAF, retired; *b* 30 Jan. 1891; *s* of late William Cushion, Surlingham, Norwich; *m* 1917, Esther Jane Kenyon-Spooner; two *d. Educ:* Gresham's Sch., Holt; Faraday House, London, WC1. 2nd Lieut Manchester Regt, 1914; attached Royal Flying Corps, 1915; served France, 1915-18; permanent commission, Royal Air Force, 1919, as Flight Lieut; Sqdn Leader, 1921; served India, 1922-27. Wing Comdr, 1930; Iraq, 1933-35; Group Capt., 1937; Air Commodore, 1940; Temp. Air Vice-Marshal, 1942; late Director-General of Equipment, Air Ministry; British Overseas Airways Corp., retired, 1956. *Address:* 146 Rivermead Court, SW6. *T:* 01-736 4687. *Club:* Hurlingham.

CUST, family name of **Baron Brownlow.**

CUSTANCE, Michael Magnus Vere, CB 1959; *b* 3 Jan. 1916; *e s* of late Mrs Arthur Long (Marjorie Bowen, novelist); *m* ; one *s* one *d. Educ:* St Paul's (schol.); The Queen's Coll., Oxford (open hist. schol., BA Hons, 1st cl., Mod. Hist., 1937). Asst Principal, Board of Trade, 1938; Ministry of Shipping, 1939; Royal Air Force, 1941-45; Principal, Ministry of War Transport, 1943; Asst Sec., Min. of Transport, 1948; Under-Sec., Min. of Transport and Civil Aviation, 1956; Dep. Sec., Min. of Transport and Civil Aviation, 1958; in Ministry of Aviation, 1959-63; in Ministry of Transport, 1963-66; in Min. of Social Security, later DHSS, 1966-75; Chief Advr to Supplementary Benefits Commn, 1968-75. IDC (1952 Course). *Address:* The Patch, Lodsworth, Petworth, Sussex. *Club:* Royal Commonwealth Society.

CUTCLIFFE, (Dorothy) Margaret; Regional Nursing Officer, North East Thames Regional Health Authority, since 1974; *b* 19 Aug. 1922; *d* of late Albert Edward Cutcliffe and Agnes Marguerite Cutcliffe. *Educ:* Holmewood Sch., N12; University Coll. Hosp.; The London Hosp. and South London Hosp. SRN 1946, SCM 1948; Dip in Nursing (London Univ.), 1957. Ward Sister, University Coll. Hosp., 1948; Asst Matron, St George's Hosp., SW1, 1959; Dep. Matron, The London Hosp., E1, 1961; Matron, St James Hosp., SW12, 1966; Chief Nursing Officer, SW London Gp HMC, 1971. *Recreations:* music, bird watching. *Address:* Flat 25, 74 Wimbledon Park Road, SW18 5SH. *T:* 01-870 5599.

CUTFORTH, Maj.-Gen. Sir Lancelot Eric, KBE 1958 (CBE 1949; OBE 1945); CB 1953; Chairman: London Area Transport Users' Consultative Committee, 1964-72; London Transport Passengers Committee, 1970-71; *b* 14 Aug. 1899; *s* of G. H. Cutforth; *m* 1925, Vera Reffell; two *d. Educ:* St Peter's Sch., York; Royal Military Academy, Woolwich. 2nd Lieut RA, 1918; AAG, War Office, 1941; DDOS 1942; DOS, HQ BAOR, 1946; DDOS, War Office, 1948; DOS, MELF, 1951; Maj.-Gen., 1951; Inspector, RAOC, War Office, 1953-55; Director of Ordnance Services, War Office, 1955-58, retired: Colonel Comdt RAOC, 1957-65; Director-General of Inspection, Ministry of Supply, 1958-60; Asst Master-Gen. of Ordnance (Inspection), WO, 1960-62. *Address:* Glade, Earleydene, Ascot, Berks SL5 9JY. *T:* Ascot 20923. *Club:* Army and Navy.

CUTHBERT, Lady, (Betty Wake), CBE 1946 (OBE 1943); OStJ 1944; *d* of Guy Shorrock and Emma Wake; *m* 1928, Vice-Adm. Sir John Cuthbert, *qv*; no *c.* Joined Auxiliary Fire Service, London, as driver, 1938; Fire Staff, Home Office, 1941; Chief Woman Fire Officer, National Fire Service, 1941-46. Nat. Chm., Girls' Venture Corps, 1946-67 (Pres. 1967). Mem., Hampshire CC, 1967-74. *Address:* Ibthorpe Manor Farm, Hurstbourne Tarrant, Andover, Hants.

CUTHBERT, Vice-Adm. Sir John (Wilson), KBE 1957 (CBE 1945); CB 1953; *b* 9 April 1902; *s* of William Cuthbert, Glasgow; *m* 1928, Betty Wake, *d* of Guy Shorrock (*see* Lady Cuthbert); no *c. Educ:* Kelvinside Acad.; RN Colleges. Midshipman, 1919; Commander, 1936; Captain, 1941; Rear-Adm., 1951; Vice-Adm., 1954. Commanded: HMS Glasgow, 1942; Ajax, 1944-46; Vengeance, 1949-50; Joint Planning Staff, London, 1942-44; Deputy Controller Admiralty, 1951-53; Flag Officer Flotillas, Home Fleet, 1953-54. Admiral Commanding Reserves, 1955-56; Flag Officer, Scotland, 1956-58. Retired List, 1958. Member Royal Company of Archers (Queen's Body Guard for Scotland). *Address:* Ibthorpe Manor Farm, Hurstbourne Tarrant, near Andover, Hants. *T:* Hurstbourne Tarrant 237. *Club:* Naval and Military.

CUTHBERTSON, Sir David (Paton), Kt 1965; CBE 1957; MD, DSc Glasgow; FRSE, FRCPE; Hon. Senior Research Fellow in Pathological Biochemistry, Glasgow University, and Hon. Consultant in the Biochemical Department of the Royal Infirmary, Glasgow; late Director Rowett Research Institute,

1945-65; *b* 9 May 1900; *s* of John Cuthbertson, MBE, Kilmarnock; *m* 1928, Jean Prentice, *d* of late Rev. Alexander P. Telfer, MA, Tarbet, Dunbartonshire; two *s* one *d. Educ:* University of Glasgow. BSc 1921; MB, ChB, 1926; DSc, 1931; MD, 1937. Bellahouston Gold Medallist. 2nd Lieut (temp.) Royal Scots Fusiliers, 1919. Lecturer in Pathological Biochemistry and Clinical Biochemist, Royal Infirmary and University of Glasgow, 1926-34; Grieve Lecturer in Physiological Chemistry, University of Glasgow, 1934-45; Arris and Gale Lecturer Royal College of Surgeons, 1942. Lieut-Col and Zone Medical Advisor (No. 1) Glasgow Home Guard, 1941-43; seconded to Administrative Headquarters, Medical Research Council, 1943-45. Consultant Director Commonwealth Bureau of Animal Nutrition, 1945-65; Hon. Consultant in Physiology and Nutrition to the Army, 1946-65. Member: UK Agricultural Mission to Canada, 1950; Tech. Cttee, Scottish Agricultural Improvement Council, 1951-64; Advisory Cttee on Pesticides and other Toxic Chemicals, 1966-71. Chairman: General and Organising Cttees, 9th International Congress of Animal Production, 1966; ARC Tech. Cttee on Nutrient Requirements of Livestock, 1959-65. President: International Union of Nutritional Sciences, 1960-66 (Hon. Pres., 1972-); Sect. I (1953) and Sect. M (1958) of British Assoc.; Nutrition Soc., 1962-65; British Soc. of Animal Production, 1966-67. Scientific Governor, British Nutrition Foundn, 1968-76 (Hon. Pres., 1976-). Baxter Lectr, American Coll. of Surgeons, 1959. Hon. Member: American Institute of Nutrition; Society Biochemistry, Biophysics et Microbiol. Fenniae; British Soc. of Animal Production; British Nutrition Soc. Hon. DSc Rutgers, 1958; Hon. LLD: Glasgow, 1960; Aberdeen, 1972; Dr *hc* Zagreb, 1969. Hon. FRCSE 1967; Hon. FRCPath 1970; Hon. FRCPS Glas; Hon. FIFST 1972. *Publications:* papers on Physiology of Protein Nutrition and Metabolism and on Metabolic Response to Injury, Ruminant Digestion, etc. *Recreations:* water-colour painting and golf. *Address:* Glenavon, 11 Willockston Road, Troon, Ayrshire. *T:* Troon 312028. *Club:* Athenæum.

CUTHBERTSON, Prof. Joseph William, DSc, FIM, MIEE; retired as Cripps Professor of Metallurgy, University of Nottingham (1954-66), now Emeritus Professor; *b* 27 Feb. 1901; *s* of late William Edward Cuthbertson, MRCS, LRCP, and late Kathleen Cuthbertson; *m* 1933, Milly Beatrix Nelson; no *c. Educ:* Manchester Grammar Sch., University of Manchester. Asst, ultimately Senior Lecturer, Dept of Metallurgy, Manchester Univ., 1929-44; seconded to Ministry of Supply, 1942-46; Asst Director of Research, Tin Research Institute, 1944-54. *Publications:* numerous scientific papers, progress reviews, and articles on metallurgy and electro-metallurgy. *Recreations:* motoring, gardening. *Address:* Flat 1, Belvedere, The Esplanade, Grange-over-Sands, Cumbria LA11 7HH. *T:* Grange-over-Sands 3344.

CUTLER, Sir (Arthur) Roden, VC; KCMG 1965; KCVO 1970; CBE 1957; Governor of New South Wales, since 1966; acts as Administrator of the Commonwealth of Australia when Governor General is absent. *b* 24 May 1916; *s* of Arthur William Cutler and Ruby Daphne (*née* Pope); *m* 1946, Helen Gray Annetta (*née* Morris); four *s. Educ:* Sydney High Sch.; University of Sydney (BEc). Public Trust Office (NSW), 1935-42; War of 1939-45 (VC). State Secretary, RSS & AILA (NSW), 1942-43; Mem., Aliens Classification and Adv. Cttee to advise Commonwealth Govt, 1942-43; Asst Dep. Dir, Security Service, NSW, 1943; Asst Comr Repatriation, 1943-46; High Comr for Australia to New Zealand, 1946-52; High Comr for Australia to Ceylon, 1952-55; HM's Australian Minister to Egypt, 1955-56; Secretary General, SEATO Conference, 1957; Chief of Protocol, Dept of External Affairs, Canberra, 1957-58; State President of RSL, formerly RSSAILA (ACT), 1958; Australian High Comr to Pakistan, 1959-61; Australian Representative to Independence of Somali Republic, 1960; Australian Consul-General, New York, 1961-65; Ambassador to the Netherlands, 1965. Delegate to UN General Assembly, and Australian Rep., Fifth Cttee. 1962-63-64. Hon. Col, Royal New South Wales Regt, 1966; Hon. Col, Sydney Univ. Regt, 1966; Hon. Air Cdre 22 Squadron RAAF. Hon. LLD, Univ. of Sydney; Hon. DSc: Univ. of New South Wales; Univ. of Newcastle. KStJ 1965. *Recreations:* swimming, shooting, yachting. *Address:* Government House, Sydney, NSW 2000, Australia.

CUTLER, Hon. Sir Charles (Benjamin), KBE 1973; ED 1960; Deputy Premier, 1972-76, Minister for Local Government, 1972-76, and Minister for Tourism, 1975-76, New South Wales; *b* Forbes, NSW, 20 April 1918; *s* of George Hamilton Cutler and Elizabeth Cutler; *m* 1943, Dorothy Pascoe (OBE 1976); three *s* one *d. Educ:* rural and high schs, Orange, NSW. MLA for Orange, NSW, 1947; Leader of Country Party (NSW), 1959; Dep. Premier and Minister for Educn, 1965. Hon. DLitt

Newcastle Univ., NSW, 1968. *Recreation:* golf. *Address:* 52 Kite Street, Orange, NSW 2800, Australia. *T:* 62-6418. *Clubs:* Royal Automobile, Imperial Service (Sydney); Orange Golf.

CUTLER, Horace Walter, OBE 1963; Member of Greater London Council for Harrow West since 1964, Leader of the Council, since 1977; *b* London, N16, 28 July 1912; *s* of Albert Benjamin and Mary Ann Cutler; *m* 1957, Christiane, *d* of Dr Klaus Muthesius; one *s* three *d* (and one *s* of previous marriage). *Educ:* Harrow Grammar Sch.; Hereford. Served War of 1939-45: RNVR, 1941-46, Lieut. Harrow Borough Council: elected 1952; Chm. Planning Cttee, 1954; Chm. Housing Cttee, 1955-58; Dep. Mayor, 1958; Alderman, 1959; Mayor, 1959-60; Leader of Council, 1961-65; Chm., Gen. Purposes Cttee, 1962-65; Middlesex CC: elected, 1955; Vice-Chm., Estates and Housing Cttee, 1957; Chm. Planning Cttee, 1961-65; Dep. Leader of CC, 1962; Leader, 1963-65; Greater London Council: Dep. Leader of Opposition, 1964-67 and 1973-74; Dep. Leader, 1967-73; Leader of Opposition, 1974-77; Chm. Housing Cttee, 1967-70; Policy and Resources Cttee, 1970-73. Member: Milton Keynes New City Develt Corp.; Central Housing Adv. Cttee, Min. of Housing and Local Govt, 1967-74; Nat. Housing and Town Planning Exec. Cttee, 1967-74 (Vice-Chm., London Region, 1968); Dir, S Bank Theatre Bd; Member: Arts Council; Nat. Theatre Bd, 1975-. Contested (C) Willesden East, 1970; Pres., Harrow West Conservative Assoc., 1964- (Chm., 1961-64). Freeman of Harrow. *Recreations:* golf, ski-ing, classical music, travel. *Address:* Hawkswood, Hawkswood Lane, Gerrards Cross, Bucks. *T:* Fulmer 3182. *Club:* Constitutional.

CUTLER, Sir Roden; *see* Cutler, Sir A. R.

CUTT, Rev. Samuel Robert; Minor Canon of St Paul's, since 1971; Succentor of St Paul's and Warden of the College of Minor Canons, since 1974; part-time Lecturer, Theological Department of King's College, London, since 1973; Priest in Ordinary to the Queen, since 1975; *b* 28 Nov. 1925; *s* of Robert Bush Cutt and Lilian Elizabeth Cutt (*née* Saint); *m* 1972, Margaret Eva (*d* 1975), *yr d* of Norman and Eva McIntyre. *Educ:* Skegness Grammar Sch.; Selwyn Coll., Cambridge; Cuddesdon Coll., Oxford. BA Cantab 1950, MA 1954. Deacon 1953, Priest 1954. Asst Curate, St Aidan, West Hartlepool, 1953-56; Tutor for King's Coll. London at St Boniface Coll., Warminster, 1956-59; Sub-Warden for KCL at St Boniface Coll., 1959-65; Lectr and Tutor of Chichester Theol Coll., 1965-71; Priest Vicar of Chichester Cath., 1966-71. *Recreations:* walking, music, biographical studies, heraldry, cooking. *Address:* 6 Amen Court, EC4M 7BU. *T:* 01-248 1943.

CUTTELL, Rev. Canon Colin, OBE 1977; Vicar of All Hallows, Barking-by-the-Tower, Guild Church of Toc H, 1963-76; *b* 24 Sept. 1908; *s* of late Maurice John Cuttell, Cheltenham, Glos, and Blanche Vickers; unmarried. *Educ:* Bishop's Univ., Lennoxville (BA; STM 1968). Deacon, 1937; Priest, 1938. Missioner of Wabamun, Canada, 1937-42; Domestic Chaplain to the Archbishop of Quebec, 1942-43; Chaplain to the Forces, 1943-44; Priest Vicar, Southwark Cathedral, 1945-49; Bishop of Southwark's Chaplain for Industrial Relations, 1948-63; Commissary for Bishop of Qu'Appelle, 1951; Founder and Senior Chaplain, S London Industrial Mission, 1950. Canon Residentiary and Librarian of Southwark Cathedral, 1954-63. Acting Chaplain, Lincoln Coll., Oxford. Sabbatical year, 1960; Acting Provost, Southwark, 1961. Field Commissioner, Toc H, 1962; Deputy Admin. Padre, Toc H, 1963. Editor of Over the Bridge, 1948. *Publication:* Ministry Without Portfolio, 1962. *Recreations:* swimming, sketching, walking. *Address:* Home Farm Lodge, Everlands, Sevenoaks, Kent.

CUTTS, Rt. Rev. Richard Stanley; *see* Argentina and Eastern South America, Bishop in.

CYRIAX, James Henry, MD; Visiting Professor in Orthopaedic Medicine, University of Rochester, New York, USA, since 1975; *b* 27 Oct. 1904; *s* of Edgar Ferdinand Cyriax, MD, and Anna Kellgren, LRCP; *m* 1947, Patricia Jane McClintock; three *s* one *d. Educ:* University College Sch., London; Gonville and Caius Coll., Cambridge; St Thomas's Hosp., London. LRCP 1929, MD 1938, MRCP 1954. Orthopaedic Physician, St Thomas' Hosp., London, 1947-69. Civil Consultant: Min. of Aviation; BA. First Fellow., British Assoc. of Manipulative Medicine; Patron, Irish Soc. of Orthopaedic Medicine; Président d'Honneur, Societé française de Medicine Orthopédique; Hon. Member: Norwegian Soc. of Manual Medicine; Swedish Soc. of Manual Medicine; North American Acad. of Manipulative Medicine; Purkyne Med. Soc. of Czechoslovakia. Freeman, City of London; Liveryman, Worshipful Co. of Apothecaries. *Publications:* Textbook of Orthopaedic Medicine (two vols), 1947, vol. I, 7th edn, 1978, vol. II, 8th edn, 1977; Cervical

Spondylosis, 1971; The Slipped Disc, 1970, 2nd edn 1975; Manipulation: past and present, 1975; contrib. BMJ, Lancet, Jl of Bone and Joint Surgery. *Recreation:* sailing. *Address:* 32 Wimpole Street, W1M 7AE. *T:* 01-580 3167; Clarence Cottage, Park Village West, NW1. *T:* 01-387 4778. *Clubs:* Savile; Faculty (Rochester, NY, USA).

CZIFFRA; Pianist; *b* Budapest, Hungary; *m* 1942, Madame Soleyka Cziffra; one *s. Educ:* Conservatoire of Music Franz Liszt, Budapest. Has given recitals and taken part in concerts at the Festival Hall, London, and throughout the world: USA, Canada, France, Israel, Benelux, Italy, Switzerland, Japan, S America, also BBC and BBC Television, London. Records for HMV: Liszt, Grieg, Tchaikowski, Beethoven, Schumann, paraphrases by G. Cziffra, etc. Founded, 1968, biennial Concours International de Piano, Versailles, for young pianists; Founder, with son, Festival of La Chaise Dieu; undertook the creation, in the Chapelle Royale Saint Frambourg, Senlis, of an Auditorium Franz Liszt and an Academy of Music of the same name, 1973; Pres., Fondation Cziffra, 1975-. Chevalier de la Légion d'Honneur, 1973. Comdr, Ordre des Arts et des Lettres, 1975. *Address:* 4 rue Saint Pierre, 60300 Senlis, France.

D

d'ABREU, Francis Arthur, ERD 1954; Surgeon, since 1946, Consultant Surgeon, since 1969, Westminster Hospital; Surgeon, 1950-69, now Emeritus, Hospital of St John and St Elizabeth; Surgeon to Jockey Club and National Hunt Committee, since 1964, and to Horserace Betting Levy Board; *b* 1 Oct. 1904; *s* of Dr John Francis d'Abreu and Teresa d'Abreu; *m* 1945, Margaret Ann Bowes-Lyon; one *s* two *d. Educ:* Stonyhurst Coll.; Birmingham Univ. MB, ChB Birmingham 1929; MRCS, LRCP 1929; FRCS, 1932; ChM Birmingham 1935. House Surgeon, Gen. Hosp., Birmingham, 1929; Res. Surgical Officer, Gen. and Queen's Hosps, Birmingham, 1930-34; Surg. Registrar, St Bartholomew's Hosp., London, and Westminster Hosp., 1934-39. Formerly: Examiner to Soc. of Apothecaries; Examiner to Univs of Cambridge and London; Mem., Ct of Examiners, RCS. Lieut RAMC (Supp. Reserve), 1939. Served War of 1939-45: Major, RAMC, 1939, Lt-Col 1942-45. Kt of Magistral Grace, Sov. and Mil. Order of Malta; Kt Comdr, Order of St Gregory (Holy See), 1977. *Publications:* contrib. to various medical jls. *Recreations:* ski-ing, squash, tennis. *Address:* 36 Cumberland Terrace, Regent's Park, NW1. *Club:* Hurlingham.

DACCA, Archbishop of, (RC), since 1967; **Most Rev. Theotonius A. Ganguly,** CSC, DD, PhD; *b* Hashnabad, Dacca, Bengal, 18 Feb. 1920; *s* of Nicholas K. Ganguly. *Educ:* Little Flower Seminary, Dacca, Bengal; St Albert Seminary, Ranchi, India. PhD Notre Dame Univ., USA, 1951. Priest, 1946; Mem. of Congregation of Holy Cross, 1951; Prof., Notre Dame Coll., Dacca, 1952-60; Principal, Notre Dame Coll., 1960; Auxiliary Bishop of Dacca, 1960; Coadjutor Archbishop of Dacca, 1965. *Address:* Archbishop's House, PO Box 3, Dacca 2, Bangladesh. *T:* Dacca 242379.

DACIE, Prof. Sir John (Vivian), Kt 1976; FRS 1967; MD, FRCP; Professor of Haematology, Royal Post-graduate Medical School of London, University of London, 1957-77, now Emeritus; *b* 20 July 1912; British; *s* of John Charles and Lilian Maud Dacie, Putney; *m* 1938, Margaret Kathleen Victoria Thynne; three *s* two *d. Educ:* King's Coll. Sch., Wimbledon; King's Coll., London: King's Coll. Hospital, London. MB, BS London 1935; MD 1952; MRCP 1936; FRCP 1956; MD (Hon.): Uppsala, 1961; Marseille, 1977; FRCPath (Pres., 1973-75); Pres., RSM, 1977-. Various medical appointments, King's Coll. Hospital, Postgraduate Medical Sch. and Manchester Royal Infirmary, 1936-39. Pathologist, EMS, 1939-42; Major, then Lieut-Col, RAMC, 1943-46. Senior Lecturer in Clinical Pathology, then Reader in Haematology, Postgraduate Medical Sch., 1946-56. *Publications:* Practical Haematology, 1950, 2nd edn, 1956, 5th edn (jointly), 1975; Haemolytic Anaemias, 1954, 2nd edn, Part I, 1960, Part II, 1962, Parts III and IV, 1967; various papers on anaemia in medical journals. *Recreations:* music, entomology, gardening. *Address:* 10 Alan Road, Wimbledon, SW19. *T:* 01-946 6086.

da COSTA, Harvey Lloyd, CMG 1962; QC Jamaica 1959; Attorney-at-Law; Attorney-General of the West Indies, 1959-62; *b* 8 Dec. 1914; *s* of John Charles and Martha da Costa. *Educ:*

Calabar High Sch., Jamaica; St Edmund Hall (Sen. Exhibnr; Rhodes Schol.), Oxford. BA (Hons) London; MA, BLitt Oxon. Practised at Chancery Bar, 1950-52; Crown Counsel, Jamaica, 1952-54; Sen. Crown Counsel, Jamaica, 1954-56; Asst Attorney-Gen., Jamaica, 1956-59. *Recreations:* swimming, tennis. *Address:* 15 Hollywood Road, SW10.

da COSTA, Sergio Corrêa, GCVO; Brazilian Permanent Representative to United Nations in New York, since 1975; *b* 19 Feb. 1919; *s* of Dr I. A. da Costa and Lavinia Corrêa da Costa; *m* 1943, Zazi Aranha; one *s* two *d. Educ:* Law Sch., Univ. of Brazil; post grad. UCLA; Brazilian War Coll. Career diplomat; Sec. of Embassy, Buenos Ayres, then Washington, 1944-48; Acting Deleg., Council of OAS, Wash., 1946-48; Inter-American Econ. and Social Coun., Washington, 1946-48; Dep. Head, Economic Dept, Min. of Ext. Relations, 1952; Actg Pres., Braz. Nat. Techn. Assistance Commn, 1955-58; Minister-Counsellor, Rome, 1959-62; Permanent Rep. to FAO, Rome, 1960; Mem., Financial Cttee of FAO, 1962-63; Ambassador to Canada, 1962-65; Asst Sec.-Gen. for Internat. Organizations at Min. Ext. Relations, 1966; Sec.-Gen., Min. of Ext. Relations, 1967-68; Ambassador to UK, 1968-75. Grand Officer: Military Order of Aeronautical Merit, Brazil, 1967; Order of Naval Merit, Brazil, 1967; Grand Cross of Victorian Order (Hon. GCVO), Gt Britain, 1968; also numerous Grand Crosses, etc, of Orders, from other countries, 1957-. *Publications:* (mostly in Brazil): As 4 Coroas de Pedro I, 1941; Pedro I e Metternich, 1942; Diplomacia Brasileira na Questao de Leticia, 1943; A Diplomacia do Marechal, 1945; Every Inch a King-A biography of Pedro I, Emperor of Brazil, 1950 (NY 1964, London 1972). *Recreations:* reading, writing, boating. *Address:* 998 Fifth Avenue, New York, NY 10028, USA. *Clubs:* White's, Travellers' (London); Rideau, Country (Ottawa); Circolo della Caccia (Rome).

DACRE, Baroness (27th in line), *cr* 1321; **Rachel Leila Douglas-Home;** *b* 24 Oct. 1929; *er* surv. *d* of 4th Viscount Hampden, CMG (*d* 1965) (whose Barony of Dacre was called out of abeyance in her favour, 1970) and of Leila Emily, *o d* of late Lt-Col Frank Evelyn Seely; *m* 1951, Hon. William Douglas-Home, *qv*; one *s* three *d. Heir: s* Hon. James Thomas Archibald Douglas-Home, *b* 16 May 1952. *Address:* Drayton House, East Meon, Hants.

da CUNHA, John Wilfrid, JP; **His Honour Judge da Cunha;** a Circuit Judge (formerly Judge of County Courts), since 1970; *b* 6 Sept. 1922; 2nd *s* of Frank C. da Cunha, MD, DPH, and Lucy (*née* Finnerty); *m* 1953, Janet, MB, ChB, JP, *d* of Louis Savatard, (Hon.) MSc, LSA, and Judith Savatard, MB, BS; one *s* four *d. Educ:* Stonyhurst Coll., Lancs; St John's Coll., Cambridge. MA Cantab 1954. Served 1942-47, 23rd Hussars (RAC) and Judge Advocate Gen. (War Crimes), Hon. Major. Called to Bar, Middle Temple, 1948; Northern Circuit. Chm., Local Appeal Tribunal, Min. of Social Security (Wigan), 1964-69. Asst Recorder, Oldham County Borough QS, 1966-70; Chm., Industrial Tribunals, 1966-70; Dep. Chm., Lancs County QS, 1968-71. Comr, NI (Emergency Provisions) Act, 1973; Member: Appeals Tribunal; Parole Bd, 1976-. JP Lancs 1968. *Recreations:* gardening, pottering. *Address:* Beech Cottage, Mobberley, Knutsford, Cheshire. *T:* Mobberley 3320. *Club:* Manchester.

DAENIKER, Dr Armin; Swiss Ambassador to the Court of St James's, 1957-63, retired; *b* 24 Feb. 1898; *m* 1938; no *c. Educ:* Universities of Zürich, Berne, Geneva, London Sch. of Economics (doctor juris utriusque, Zürich). Vice-Consul, Riga, 1927; Shanghai, 1930; Swiss Chargé d'Affaires, Tokio, 1933, Teheran, 1936; Head of Administrative Div., Federal Political Dept, Berne, 1946; Swiss Minister, New Delhi, 1948, and concurrently in Bangkok, 1950; Swiss Minister, Stockholm 1952; Swiss Mem., Neutral Nations Commn for Repatriation of Prisoners of War in Korea, 1953-54; Swiss Minister to the Court of St James's, 1955; Mem. Council, Swiss Winston Churchill Foundation. *Address:* Villa Sonnenhof, 2 Jolimontstrasse, Berne, Switzerland.

D'AETH, Rev. Narbrough Hughes, CB 1951; CBE 1943; Licentiate to Officiate, Diocese of Bath and Wells, 1976; *b* 17 Jan. 1901; *s* of late Capt. Reginald Hughes D'Aeth and late Lady Nina Hughes D'Aeth; *m* 1934, Mary Colbeck, *d* of late E. W. Davis; three *d. Educ:* Royal Naval Colls, Osborne and Dartmouth. Served European War, 1914-18, with Grand Fleet, 1917-19; transferred to RAF, 1920; Malta, 1922; China, 1926-28; British Arctic Air Route Expedn in E Greenland, 1930-31; Polar Medal, 1932; Aden, 1934-36; War of 1939-45 in UK and N Africa (despatches thrice, CBE); AOC, RAF, Malta, 1949-52; AO i/c Administration at Headquarters, Technical Training Command, 1952-54; Senior Air Staff Officer, Headquarters,

Home Command, 1954-56. Group Capt., 1941; Air Commodore, 1943; Air Vice Marshal, 1950; retired, 1956. Lincoln Theological Coll., 1956-57. Ordained Deacon, Dec. 1957; Curate, St John the Baptist, Crowthorne, Dec. 1957-59; Rector: East Langdon with Guston, Kent, 1959-60; Flinders Islands, 1960-67; Priest-in-Charge, Midland and Swan Parishes, Perth, 1967-71; Licentiate to Officiate: dio. of Perth, 1971-72; dio. of Exeter, 1972-76. American Legion of Merit, 1945; Czechoslovak Medal of Merit, 1945. *Address:* Knowlton Cottage, 11 Exmoor Way, Minehead, Somerset TA24 8AZ.

DAGGETT, William Ingledew; late Senior Ear, Nose and Throat Surgeon to King's College Hospital; Consulting Ear, Nose and Throat Surgeon to Leatherhead Hospital and St Luke's Hostel for Clergy; late Chairman King's College Hospital Group Medical Committee; late Brigadier RAMC; Consultant in Otolaryngology to Army; *b* 2 Oct. 1900; *s* of Dr H. Ingledew Daggett, Boroughbridge; *m* 1928, Eileen Hilda (marr. diss., 1947), *d* of Col T. W. Simpson; no *c. Educ:* Sedbergh (Exhibitioner); Caius Coll., Cambridge (Scholar, 1st Class Hons Nat. Sci. Tripos); King's Coll. Hosp. (Scholar), MA, MB, BChir Cantab; FRCS; recognised teacher University of London. *Publications:* in medical and surgical journals. *Address:* 15 Devonshire Close, W1. *T:* 01-580 5366. *Club:* Bath.

DAHL, Rev. Canon Murdoch Edgcumbe; Canon Theologian of St Albans Cathedral, since 1968; *b* 11 March 1914; *s* of Oscar Horace and Edith Gladys Dahl; *m* 1940, Joan, *d* of Daniel Charles and Edith Marion Woollaston; three *s. Educ:* Royal Grammar Sch., Newcastle upon Tyne; Armstrong Coll. (subsq. King's Coll.), Newcastle upon Tyne; St John's Coll., Durham. BA 1936, MA 1956, Durham. Deacon 1937; Priest 1938. Curate of: St Paul, Astley Bridge, 1937-39; Fallowfield, 1939-43; Harpenden, 1943-49; Vicar of Arlesey and Rector of Astwick, 1949-51; Minister, St Oswald's, Croxley Green, 1951-56; Vicar of Great with Little Hormead and Rector of Wyddial, 1956-65; Examining Chaplain to Bishop of St Albans, 1959-; Hon. Canon of St Albans, 1963-65, Canon Residentiary, 1965-68. *Publications:* Resurrection of the Body, 1962; Sin Streamlined, 1966; The Christian Materialist, 1968. *Address:* 2 Sumpter Yard, St Albans, Herts AL1 1BY. *T:* St Albans 61744.

DAHL, Roald; writer; *b* 13 Sept. 1916; *s* of Harald Dahl and Sofie Magdalene Hesselberg; *m* 1953, Patricia Neal; one *s* three *d* (and one *d* decd). *Educ:* Repton. Public Schools Exploring Soc. expedn to Newfoundland, 1934; Eastern Staff of Shell Co., 1934-39, served in Dar-es-Salaam; RAF flying trng, Nairobi and Habbanyah, 1939-40; No 80 Fighter Sqdn, Western Desert, 1940 (wounded); Greece, 1941; Syria, 1941; Asst Air Attaché, Washington, 1942-43; Wing Comdr, 1943; British Security Co-ordination, N America, 1943-45. Edgar Allan Poe Award, Mystery Writers of America, 1954 and 1959. *Publications:* Over to You (short stories), 1945; Sometime Never (A Fable for Supermen), 1948; Someone Like You (short stories), 1953; Kiss Kiss (short stories), 1960; Switch Bitch (short stories), 1974; *children's books:* (with Walt Disney) The Gremlins, 1943; James and the Giant Peach, 1962; Charlie and the Chocolate Factory, 1964; The Magic Finger, 1966; Fantastic Mr Fox, 1970; Charlie and the Great Glass Elevator, 1972; Danny, the Champion of the World, 1975; The Wonderful Story of Henry Sugar and Six More, 1977; *play:* The Honeys, 1955; *screenplays:* You Only Live Twice, 1967; Chitty Chitty Bang Bang, 1968; Willy Wonka and the Chocolate Factory, 1971; contrib. New Yorker, Harper's Magazine, Atlantic Monthly, Saturday Evening Post, Colliers, etc. *Recreations:* gaming, cultivating orchids (phalaenopsis only), drinking fine wine, collecting paintings, furniture and antique objects of all kinds. *Address:* Gipsy House, Great Missenden, Bucks HP16 0PB. *T:* Great Missenden 2757. *Club:* Curzon House.

DAHL, Robert Henry, TD 1950; MA Oxford; Head Master of Wrekin College, 1952-71; *b* 21 April 1910; *y s* of Murdoch Cameron Dahl, London, and Lilian May Edgcumbe; *m* 1936, Lois Helen Allanby; three *s. Educ:* Sedbergh Sch.; Exeter Coll., Oxford. Asst Master (Modern Langs) at Merchant Taylors' Sch., 1934-38. Asst Master and Housemaster at Harrow Sch., 1938-52. Served War of 1939-45: Intelligence Corps, Middle East, 1941-43; Major, 1943; Political Intelligence Dept of Foreign Office, 1943-46. FRSA 1969. *Publication:* Joint Editor, Selections from Albert Schweitzer, 1953. *Recreations:* golf, music. *Address:* Fermain, Wood Close, Tostock, Bury St Edmunds, Suffolk.

DAHRENDORF, Prof. Ralf, PhD, DrPhil; FBA 1977; Director, London School of Economics and Political Science, since 1974; *b* Hamburg, 1 May 1929; *s* of Gustav Dahrendorf and Lina Dahrendorf (*née* Witt); *m* 1954, Vera Banister; three *d. Educ:* several schools, including Heinrich-Hertz Oberschule,

Hamburg; studies in philosophy and classical philology, Hamburg, 1947-52; DrPhil 1952; postgrad. studies at London Sch. of Economics, 1952-54; Leverhulme Research Schol., 1953-54; PhD 1956. Habilitation, and University Lecturer, Saarbrücken, 1957; Fellow at Center for Advanced Study in the Behavioural Sciences, Palo Alto, USA, 1957-58; Prof. of Sociology, Hamburg, 1958-60; Vis. Prof. Columbia Univ., 1960; Prof. of Sociology, Tübingen, 1960-64; Vice-Chm., Founding Cttee of Univ. of Konstanz, 1964-66; Prof of Sociology, Konstanz, 1966-69; Parly Sec. of State, Foreign Office, W Germany, 1969-70; Mem., Commn of European Communities, Brussels, 1970-74. Member: Hansard Soc. Commn on Electoral Reform, 1975-76; Royal Commn on Legal Services, 1976-; Commn to Review Functioning of Financial Instns, 1977-. Senator, Max-Planck Gesellschaft, 1975-; Trustee, Ford Foundn, 1976-. Vis. Prof. at several Europ. and N American univs. Reith Lecturer, 1974. Hon. Fellow: LSE; Imperial Coll. Hon. MRIA 1974; Fellow, St Antony's Coll., Oxford, 1976. Foreign Hon. Mem., Amer. Acad. of Arts and Sciences, 1975-; FRSA 1977. Hon. DLitt Reading, 1973; Hon. LLD: Manchester, 1973; Wagner Coll., NY, 1977; Hon. DHL Kalamazoo Coll., 1974; Hon. DSc: Ulster, 1973; Bath, 1977; DUniv Open, 1974; Hon. LittD Dublin, 1975; Hon. Dr Univ. Catholique de Louvain, 1977. Journal Fund Award for Learned Publication, 1966. Grand Croix de l'Ordre du Mérite du Sénégal, 1971; Grosses Bundesverdienstkreuz mit Stern und Schulterband (Federal Republic of Germany), 1974; Grand Croix de l'Ordre du Mérite du Luxembourg, 1974; Grosses goldenes Ehrenzeichen am Bande für Verdienste um die Republik Österreich (Austria), 1975; Grand Croix de l'Ordre de Léopold II (Belgium), 1975. *Publications include:* Marx in Perspective, 1953; Industrie- und Betriebssoziologie, 1956 (trans. Italian, Spanish, Dutch, Japanese, Chinese); Soziale Klassen und Klassenkonflikt, 1957 (Class and Class Conflict, 1959; also trans. French, Italian, Spanish, Finnish, Japanese); Homo Sociologicus, 1959 (trans. English, Italian, Portuguese, Finnish); Die angewandte Aufklärung, 1963; Gesellschaft und Demokratie in Deutschland, 1965 (Society and Democracy in Germany, 1966; also trans. Italian); Pfade aus Utopia, 1967 (Uscire dall'Utopia, 1971); Essays in the Theory of Society, 1968; Konflikt und Freiheit, 1972; Plädoyer für die Europäische Union, 1973; The New Liberty, 1975 (trans. German). *Address:* London School of Economics and Political Science, Houghton Street, Aldwych, WC2A 2AE. *T:* 01-405 7686. *Clubs:* PEN, Reform, Political Economy.

DAICHES, David, MA Edinburgh; MA, DPhil Oxon; PhD Cantab; FRSL; Professor of English, University of Sussex, 1961-77, and Dean of the School of English Studies, 1961-68; *b* 2 Sept. 1912; *s* of Rabbi Dr Salis Daiches and Flora Daiches (*née* Levin); *m* 1937, Isobel J. Mackay (*d* 1977); one *s* two *d. Educ:* George Watson's Coll., Edinburgh; Edinburgh Univ. (Vans Dunlop Schol., Elliot Prize); Balliol Coll., Oxford (Elton Exhibnr). Asst in English, Edinburgh Univ., 1935-36; Andrew Bradley Fellow, Balliol Coll., Oxford, 1936-37; Asst Prof. of English, Univ. of Chicago, 1939-43; Second Sec., British Embassy, Washington, 1944-46; Prof. of English, Cornell Univ., USA, 1946-51; University Lecturer in English at Cambridge, 1951-61; Fellow of Jesus Coll., Cambridge, 1957-62. Visiting Prof. of Criticism, Indiana Univ., USA, 1956-57; Elliston Lectr, University of Cincinnati, Spring 1960; Whidden Lectr, Mcmaster Univ., Canada, 1964; Hill Foundation Visiting Prof., Univ. of Minnesota, Spring 1966; Ewing Lectr, Univ. of California, 1967; Carpenter Memorial Lectr, Ohio Wesleyan Univ., 1969. Fellow, Centre for the Humanities, Wesleyan Univ., Middletown, Conn, 1970. Hon. Fellow, Sunderland Polytechnic, 1977. Hon. LittD, Brown Univ; Docteur *hc* Sorbonne; Hon. DLitt Edinburgh. *Publications:* The Place of Meaning in Poetry, 1935; New Literary Values, 1936; Literature and Society, 1938; The Novel and the Modern World, 1939 (new edn, 1960); Poetry and the Modern World, 1940; The King James Bible: A Study of its Sources and Development, 1941; Virginia Woolf, 1942; Robert Louis Stevenson, 1947; A Study of Literature, 1948; Robert Burns, 1950 (new edn 1966); Willa Cather: A Critical Introduction, 1951; Critical Approaches to Literature, 1956; Two Worlds (autobiog.), 1956; Literary Essays, 1956; John Milton, 1957; The Present Age, 1958; A Critical History of English Literature, 1960; George Eliot's Middlemarch, 1963; The Paradox of Scottish Culture, 1964; (ed) The Idea of a New University, 1964; English Literature (Princeton Studies in Humanistic Scholarship), 1965; More Literary Essays, 1968; Some Late Victorian Attitudes, 1969; Scotch Whisky, 1969; Sir Walter Scott and his World, 1971; A Third World (autobiog.), 1971; (ed) The Penguin Companion to Literature: Britain and the Commonwealth, 1971; Robert Burns and his World, 1971; (ed with A. Thorlby) Literature and Western Civilization, vol. I, 1972, vols II and V, 1973, vols III and IV, 1975; vol. VI, 1976; Charles Edward Stuart: the life and

times of Bonnie Prince Charlie, 1973; Robert Louis Stevenson and his World, 1973; Was, 1975; Moses, 1975; James Boswell and his World, 1976; Scotland and the Union, 1977; Gen. Editor, Studies in English Literature, 1961-. *Recreations:* talking, music. *Address:* Philpstoun House, by Linlithgow, West Lothian.
See also L. H. Daiches.

DAICHES, Lionel Henry, QC (Scot) 1956; *b* 8 March 1911; *s* of late Rev. Dr. Salis Daiches, Edinburgh, and Mrs Flora Daiches; *m* 1947, Dorothy Estelle Bernstein (marr. diss. 1973); two *s*. *Educ:* George Watson's Coll., Edinburgh; Edinburgh Univ. (MA, LLB). Pres., Edinburgh Univ. Diagnostic Soc., 1931; Convener of Debates, Edinburgh Univ. Union, 1933; Editor, The Student, 1933. Served 1940-46 in N Stafford Regt and Major, JAG Branch in N Africa and Italy, including Anzio Beach-head. Admitted Scots Bar, 1946. Standing Junior Counsel to Board of Control, Scotland, 1950-56; Sheriff-Substitute of Lanarkshire at Glasgow, 1962-67. Contested (L) Edinburgh South, 1950. *Publication:* Russians at Law, 1960. *Recreations:* walking and talking. *Address:* 10 Heriot Row, Edinburgh. *T:* 031-556 4144. *Clubs:* Puffin's, Scottish Arts (Edinburgh); RNVR (Scotland).
See also D. Daiches.

DAIN, Rt. Rev. Arthur John; Assistant Bishop, Diocese of Sydney, since 1965; *b* 13 Oct. 1912; *s* of Herbert John Dain and Elizabeth Dain; *m* 1939, Edith Jane Stewart, MA, *d* of Dr Alexander Stewart, DD; four *d*. *Educ:* Wolverhampton Gram. Sch.; Ridley Coll., Cambridge. Missionary in India, 1935-40; 10th Gurkha Rifles, 1940-41; Royal Indian Navy, 1941-47; Gen. Sec., Bible and Medical Missionary Fellowship, formerly Zenana Bible and Medical Mission, 1947-59; Overseas Sec., British Evangelical Alliance, 1950-59; Federal Sec., CMS of Australia, 1959-65; Hon. Canon of St Andrew's Cathedral, 1963. *Publications:* Mission Fields To-day, 1956; Missionary Candidates, 1959. *Recreation:* sport. *Address:* 3 Mitchell Place, 4 Mitchell Road, Darling Point, NSW 2027, Australia. *T:* 328 7940.

DAINTON, Sir Frederick (Sydney), Kt 1971; FRS 1957; MA, BSc Oxon, PhD, ScD Cantab; Chairman, University Grants Committee, since 1973; *b* 11 Nov. 1914; *y s* of late George Whalley and Mary Jane Dainton; *m* 1942, Barbara Hazlitt, PhD, *o d* of late Dr W. B. Wright, Manchester; one *s* two *d*. *Educ:* Central Secondary Sch., Sheffield; St John's Coll., Oxford; Sidney Sussex Coll., Cambridge. Open Exhibitioner, 1933; Casberd Prizeman, 1934, Casberd Scholar, 1935, Hon. Fellow 1968, St John's Coll., Oxford; Goldsmiths' Co. Exhibitioner, 1935, 1st class Hons Chemistry, 1937, University of Oxford; Research Student, 1937, Goldsmiths' Co. Senior Student, 1939, University Demonstrator in Chemistry, 1944, H. O. Jones Lecturer in Physical Chemistry, 1946, University of Cambridge. Fellow, 1945, Praelector, 1946, Hon. Fellow 1961, St Catharine's Coll., Cambridge. Prof. of Physical Chemistry, University of Leeds, 1950-65; Vice-Chancellor, Nottingham Univ., 1965-70; Dr Lee's Prof. of Chemistry, Oxford University, 1970-73. Vis. Prof., Univ. Toronto, 1949; Tilden Lectr, 1950, Faraday Lectr, 1973, Chem. Soc.; Peter C. Reilly Lectr, Univ. of Notre Dame, Ind., USA, 1952; Arthur D. Little Visiting Prof., MIT, 1959; George Fisher Baker Lectr, Cornell Univ., 1961; Boomer Lectr, Univ. of Alberta, 1962. Chm., Cttee on Swing away from Science (report published as Enquiry into the Flow of Candidates in Science and Technology into Higher Education, Cmnd 3541, 1968). Chairman: Assoc. for Radiation Research, 1964-66; Nat. Libraries Cttee, 1968-69; Adv. Cttee on Sci. and Tech. Information, 1966-70; Adv. Bd for Res. Councils, 1972-73; British Cttee, Harkness Fellowship, 1977- (Mem., 1973-). President: Faraday Soc., 1965-67; Chemical Soc., 1977; Assoc. for Science Education, 1967; Library Assoc., 1977. Member: Council for Scientific Policy, 1965- (Chm. 1969-72); Central Advisory Council for Science and Technology, 1967-70; Trustee, Natural Hist. Museum, 1974-. Foreign Member: Swedish Acad. of Sci., 1968; Amer. Acad. of Arts and Scis, 1972; Acad. of Scis, Göttingen, 1975. Sylvanus Thompson Medal, British Institute of Radiology, 1958; Davy Medal, Royal Soc., 1969. Hon. ScD: Lódź, 1966; Dublin, 1968; Hon. DSc: Bath Univ. of Technology, 1970; Loughborough Univ. of Technology, 1970; Heriot-Watt, 1970; Warwick, 1970; Strathclyde, 1971; Exeter, 1971; QUB, 1971; Manchester, 1972; E Anglia, 1972; Leeds, 1973; McMaster, 1975; Uppsala, 1977; Hon. LLD: Nottingham, 1970; Aberdeen, 1972. *Publications:* Chain Reactions, 1956; papers on physico-chemical subjects in scientific jls. *Recreations:* walking, colour photography. *Address:* University Grants Committee, 14 Park Crescent, W1N 4DH. *T:* 01-636 7799; Fieldside, Water Eaton Lane, Oxford OX5 2PR. *T:* Kidlington 5132. *Club:* Athenæum.

DAINTREE JOHNSON, Harold; *see* Johnson, H. D.

DAKERS, Mrs Andrew; *see* Lane, Jane.

DAKERS, Lionel Frederick, FRCO; Director, Royal School of Church Music (Special Commissioner, 1958-72), since 1972; Examiner to the Associated Board of the Royal Schools of Music, since 1958; *b* Rochester, Kent, 24 Feb. 1924; *o s* of Lewis and Ethel Dakers; *m* 1951, Mary Elisabeth, *d* of Rev. Claude Williams; four *d*. *Educ:* Rochester Cathedral Choir Sch. Studied with H. A. Bennett, Organist of Rochester Cathedral, 1933-40, with Sir Edward Bairstow, Organist of York Minster, 1943-45, and at Royal Academy of Music, 1947-51. Organist of All Saints', Frindsbury, Rochester, 1939-42. Served in Royal Army Educational Corps, 1943-47. Cairo Cathedral, 1945-47; Finchley Parish Church, 1948-50; Asst Organist, St George's Chapel, Windsor Castle, 1950-54; Asst Music Master, Eton Coll., 1952-54; Organist of Ripon Cathedral, 1954-57; Conductor Ripon Choral Soc. and Harrogate String Orchestra, 1954-57; Hon. Conductor, Exeter Diocesan Choral Association, 1957; Lectr in Music, St Luke's Coll., Exeter, 1958-70; Organist and Master of the Choristers, Exeter Cathedral, 1957-72; Conductor: Exeter Musical Soc., 1957-72; Exeter Chamber Orchestra, 1959-65. President: Incorporated Assoc. of Organists, 1972-75; London Assoc. of Organists, 1976-; Mem. Council, Royal Coll. of Organists, 1967- (Pres., 1976-). Sec., Cathedral Organists' Assoc., 1972. Chm., Organs Adv. Cttee of Council for Care of Churches of C of E, 1974. ARCO, 1944; FRCO, 1945; ADCM, 1952; BMus Dunelm, 1951; ARAM 1955; FRAM, 1962; FRSCM 1969; Fellow, St Michael's Coll., Tenbury, 1973. Hon. Fellow, Westminster Choir Coll., USA, 1975. Compositions: church music, etc. *Publications:* Church Music at the Crossroads, 1970; A Handbook of Parish Music, 1976. *Recreations:* book collecting, gardening, continental food, travel. *Address:* Addington Palace, Croydon CR9 5AD. *T:* 01-654 7676. *Clubs:* Athenæum, Savage.

DAKIN, Dorothy Danvers; Headmistress, The Red Maids' School, Bristol, since 1961; *b* 22 Oct. 1919; *d* of Edwin Lionel Dakin, chartered civil engr and Mary Danvers Dakin (*née* Walker), artist. *Educ:* Sherborne Sch. for Girls; Newnham Coll., Cambridge. MA Geography. 2nd Officer WRNS (Educn), 1943-50; Housemistress, Wycombe Abbey Sch., 1950-60. President: West of England Br., Assoc. of Headmistresses, 1969-71; Assoc. of Headmistresses of Girls' Boarding Schs, 1971-73; Girls' Schs Assoc. (Independent and Direct Grant), 1973-75; Chm., Jt Council, Independent Schs Information Service, 1977-. *Recreations:* fencing, painting, travel, embroidery. *Address:* The Red Maids' School, Westbury-on-Trym, Bristol. *T:* Bristol 626131. *Club:* Soroptimist International (Bristol).

DALDRY, Sir Leonard (Charles), KBE 1963 (CBE 1960); Chairman, St Loye's College for the Disabled, Exeter, since 1969; *b* 6 Oct. 1908; *s* of Charles Henry Daldry; *m* 1938, Joan Mary (*d* 1976), *d* of John E. Crisp; no *c*; *m* 1976, Monica Mary, *d* of late G. E. Benson and of Helen Benson, Moretonhampstead, Devon; one *s*. Joined Barclays Bank DCO 1929. Local Dir in W Africa at Lagos, 1952. Assoc. Inst. of Bankers, 1936. Mem. Nigerian Railway Corp., 1955-60; Special Mem., Nigerian House of Reps, 1956-59; Senator, Federal Legislature, Nigeria, 1960-61; Chm., Nigeria Bd, Barclays Bank DCO, 1961-63. *Recreation:* croquet. *Address:* Prospect House, Budleigh Salterton, Devon. *Club:* Athenæum.

DALE, Jim; actor, singer, composer, lyricist; *b* 15 Aug. 1935; *m* 1957, Patricia Joan Gardiner; three *s* one *d*. *Educ:* Kettering Grammar School. Music Hall comedian, 1951; singing, compèring, directing, 1951-61; films, 1965-, include: Lock Up Your Daughters, The Winter's Tale, The Biggest Dog in the World, National Health, Adolf Hitler-My Part in his Downfall, Joseph Andrews, Pete's Dragon, Bloodshy. Joined Frank Dunlop's Pop Theatre for Edinburgh Festival, 1967-68; National Theatre, 1969-71: main roles in National Health, Love's Labour's Lost, Merchant of Venice, Good-natured Man, Captain of Kopenick; also appeared at Young Vic in Taming of the Shrew, Scapino (title rôle and wrote music); title rôle in musical The Card, 1973; Compère of Sunday Night at the London Palladium, 1973-74; Scapino (title rôle), Broadway, 1974-75 (Drama Critics' and Outer Circle Awards for best actor; Tony award nomination for best actor). Composed film music for: The Winter's Tale, Shaliko, Twinky, Georgy Girl (nominated for Academy Award), Joseph Andrews. *Recreation:* escapology. *Address:* 26 Pembridge Villas, W11. *T:* 01-229 3678.

DALE, Sir William (Leonard), KCMG 1965 (CMG 1951); International legal consultant; Visiting Fellow, Cambridge University Centre of International Studies; Director of Studies, Government Legal Officers Course; *b* 17 June 1906; *e s* of late

Rev. William Dale, Rector of Preston, Yorks; *m* 1966, Mrs Gloria Spellman Finn, Washington, DC; one *d. Educ:* Hymers Coll., Hull; London (LLB); Barrister, Gray's Inn, 1931. Asst Legal Adviser, Colonial and Dominions Offices, 1935; Min. of Supply, 1940-45; Dep. Legal Adviser, Colonial and Commonwealth Relations Offices, 1945; Legal Adviser, United Kingdom of Libya, 1951-53; Legal Adviser: Min. of Educn, 1954-61; CRO, subseq. CO, 1961-66. Special Asst to the Law Officers, 1967-68; Gen. Counsel, UNRWA, Beirut, 1968-73. *Publications:* Law of the Parish Church, 1932 (5th edn, 1975); Legislative Drafting: a new approach, 1977; contributions to journals. *Recreation:* music (except Wagner). *Address:* Colwood Manor East, Bolney, Sussex. *T:* Warninglid 306; Lamb Building, Temple, EC4. *Club:* Travellers'.

DALGARNO, Prof. Alexander, PhD; FRS 1972; Professor of Astronomy, since 1967, Chairman of Department of Astronomy, 1971-76, Associate Director of Centre for Astrophysics, since 1973, Harvard University; Member of Smithsonian Astrophysical Observatory, since 1967; *b* 5 Jan. 1928; *s* of William Dalgarno; *m* 1st, 1957, Barbara Kane (marr. diss. 1972); two *s* two *d*; 2nd, 1972, Emily Izsák. *Educ:* Southgate Grammar Sch.; University Coll., London (Fellow 1976). BSc Maths, 1st Cl. Hons London, 1947; PhD Theoretical Physics London, 1951; AM Harvard, 1967. The Queen's University of Belfast: Lectr in Applied Maths, 1952; Reader in Maths, 1956; Dir of Computing Lab, 1960; Prof. of Quantum Mechanics, 1961; Prof. of Mathematical Physics, 1966-67; Acting Dir, Harvard Coll. Observatory, 1971-73. Chief Scientist, Geophysics Corp. of America, 1962-63. Editor, Astrophysical Journal Letters, 1973-. Fellow, Amer. Acad. of Arts and Sciences, 1968; Corresp. Mem., Internat. Acad. Astronautics, 1972. *Publications:* numerous papers in scientific journals. *Recreations:* squash, books. *Address:* c/o Harvard College Observatory, 60 Garden Street, Cambridge, Mass 02138, USA.

DALGETTY, James Simpson, MA, LLB; Solicitor to Secretary of State for Scotland and Solicitor in Scotland to HM Treasury, 1964-71; *b* 13 Aug. 1907; *s* of late Rev. William Dalgetty and Elizabeth Reid Dalgetty (*née* Simpson); *m* 1936, Mary Macdonald; one adopted *d. Educ:* George Watson's Coll., Edinburgh; Edinburgh Univ. Legal Asst, Dept of Health for Scotland, 1937; Asst Solicitor, 1944; Asst solicitor, Office of Solicitor to Sec. of State for Scotland, 1946; Senior Legal Draftsman to Govt of Nyasaland, and acting Solicitor-Gen., 1962-64. *Recreations:* photography, travel, reading. *Address:* Glenora, Marine Parade, North Berwick. *T:* North Berwick 3112.

DALGLISH, Captain James Stephen, CVO 1955; CBE 1963; *b* 1 Oct. 1913; *e s* of late Rear-Adm. Robin Dalglish, CB; *m* 1939, Evelyn Mary, *e d* of late Rev. A. Ll. Meyricke, formerly Vicar of Aislaby, near Whitby; one *s* one *d. Educ:* RN Coll., Dartmouth. Commanded HMS Aisne, 1952-53; HM Yacht Britannia, 1954, HMS Woodbridge Haven and Inshore Flotilla, 1958-59; HMS Excellent, 1959-61; HMS Bulwark, 1961-63; jssc 1950; idc 1957; retired from RN, 1963. Welfare Officer, Metropolitan Police, 1963-73. *Recreations:* gardening, painting. *Address:* Park Hall, Aislaby, Whitby, North Yorks. *T:* Sleights 213.

DALHOUSIE, 16th Earl of, *cr* 1633; **Simon Ramsay,** KT 1971; GBE 1957; MC 1944; LLD; Baron Ramsay, 1619; Lord Ramsay, 1633; Baron Ramsay (UK), 1875; Lord Chamberlain to the Queen Mother, 1965; Lord-Lieutenant of Angus, since 1967; Chancellor, Dundee University, since 1977; *b* 17 Oct. 1914; 2nd *s* of 14th Earl (*d* 1928) and Lady Mary Adelaide Heathcote Drummond Willoughby (*d* 1960), *d* of 1st Earl of Ancaster; *S* brother, 1950; *m* 1940, Margaret Elizabeth, *d* of late Brig.-Gen. Archibald and Hon. Mrs Stirling of Keir; three *s* two *d. Educ:* Eton; Christ Church, Oxford. Served TA, Black Watch, 1936-39; embodied, 1939. MP (C) for County of Angus, 1945-50; Conservative Whip, 1946-48 (resigned). Governor-General, Fedn of Rhodesia and Nyasaland, 1957-63. Hon. LLD: Dalhousie, 1952; Dundee, 1967. *Heir: s* Lord Ramsay, *qv. Address:* Brechin Castle, Brechin. *T:* Brechin 2176; Dalhousie Castle, Bonnyrigg, Midlothian; 5 Margaretta Terrace, SW3. *T:* 01-352 6477. *Club:* White's.
See also Maj.-Gen. Sir G. F. Johnson, Earl of Scarbrough.

DALI, Salvador (Felipe Jacinto); Spanish painter; stage-designer; book-illustrator; writer; interested in commercial art and films; *b* Figueras, Upper Catalonia, 11 May 1904; *s* of Salvador Dali, notary and Felipa Dome (Doménech); *m* 1935, Gala (*née* Elena Diaranoff); she *m* 1st, Paul Eluard. *Educ:* Academy of Fine Arts, Madrid; Paris. First one-man show, Barcelona, 1925; became prominent Catalan painter by 1927; Began surrealist painting in Paris, 1928; first one-man show, Paris, Nov. 1929; first one-man show, New York, Nov. 1933. Visited United States, 1934, 1939, 1940; lectured in Museum of Modern Art, New York, 1935; later, came to London; first visited Italy, 1937. Designer of scenery and costumes for ballet, etc., also of film scenarios. Has held exhibitions of paintings in many American and European Cities; Exhibition of jewels, London, 1960; major exhibition, Rotterdam, 1970. *Publications:* Babaouo (ballet and film scenarios), 1932; Secret Life of Salvador Dali, 1942; Hidden Faces (novel), 1944; Fifty Secrets of Magic Craftsmanship, 1948; Diary of a Genius, 1966; The Unspeakable Confessions of Salvador Dali, 1976. *Address:* Hotel St Regis, 5th Avenue, and 55th Street, New York, NY 10022, USA; Port-Lligat, Cadaqués, Spain.

DALITZ, Prof. Richard Henry, FRS 1960; Royal Society Research Professor at Oxford University, since 1963; *b* 28 Feb. 1925; *s* of Frederick W. and Hazel B. Dalitz, Melbourne, Australia; *m* 1946, Valda (*née* Suiter) of Melbourne, Australia; one *s* three *d. Educ:* Scotch Coll., Melbourne; Univ. of Melbourne; Trinity Coll., Univ. of Cambridge, PhD Cantab, 1950. Lecturer in Mathematical Physics, Univ. of Birmingham, 1949-55; Research appointments in various Univs, 1953-55; Reader in Mathematical Physics, Univ. of Birmingham, 1955-56; Prof. of Physics, Univ. of Chicago, 1956-66. Maxwell Medal and Prize, Institute of Physics and the Physical Soc., 1966; Bakerian Lectr and Jaffe Prize, The Royal Soc., 1969; Hughes Medal, The Royal Soc., 1975. *Publications:* Strange Particles and Strong Interactions, 1962 (India); Nuclear Interactions of the Hyperons, 1965 (India); numerous papers on theoretical physics in various British and American scientific jls. *Recreations:* mountain walking, travelling. *Address:* 1 Keble Road, Oxford OX1 3NP; All Souls College, Oxford.

DALKEITH, Earl of; Richard Walter John Montagu Douglas Scott; *b* 14 Feb. 1954; *s* and *heir* of 9th Duke of Buccleuch, *qv. Educ:* Eton; Christ Church, Oxford. A Page of Honour to HM the Queen Mother, 1967-69. *Address:* Eildon Hall, Melrose, Roxburghshire. *T:* St Boswells 2705.

DALLARD, Berkeley Lionel Scudamore, CMG 1948; JP; chartered accountant; *b* Waikari, Christchurch, New Zealand, 27 Aug. 1889; *s* of Geo. Joseph Dallard, Settler, born Tewkesbury, England, and Saria Maria, born Cheltenham, England; *m* 1915, Agnes Rowan Inglis; three *d. Educ:* Waikari Public Sch.; Rangiora High Sch.; Victoria University Coll. Entered Civil Service, NZ, 1907; served in Stamp Office, Audit Office, Board of Trade, Public Service Commissioner's Office (Asst Public Service Commr, 1929), Justice Dept; Controller Gen. of Prisons, and Chief Probation Officer, NZ, 1925-49; Under Sec. for Justice and Registrar Gen., NZ, 1934-49, retd, 1949. Govt Mem. of Govt Service Tribunal, 1949-60, retd. City Councillor, Wellington, 1949-62. Chairman: Wellington Hospital Board, 1962-66; Combined Purchasing Cttee for NZ Hosps, 1963-71. *Publications:* miscellaneous brochures on Criminology and Law. *Address:* 94 Upland Road, Kelburn, Wellington, NZ. *TA* and *T:* Wellington 759209. *Clubs:* (Past Pres.) Savage, (Past Pres.) Rotary (Wellington, NZ).

DALLEY, Christopher Mervyn, CMG 1971; MA Cantab; CEng; Chairman of Oil Exploration Holdings Ltd and Viking Jersey Equipment Ltd, since 1973; *b* 26 Dec. 1913; *er s* of late Christopher Dalley; *m* 1947, Elizabeth Alice, *yr d* of Lt-Gen. Sir James Gammell, KCB, DSO, MC; one *s* three *d. Educ:* Epsom Coll., Surrey; Queens' Coll., Cambridge. Served in RN, 1939-45 (Lt-Comdr). Joined British Petroleum Co., 1946; joined Iranian Oil Operating Companies in Iran 1954: Asst Gen. Managing Dir, 1958; joined Iraq Petroleum Co. and associated companies, 1962; Man. Dir. 1963; Chm., 1970-73. Pres., Inst. of Petroleum, 1970; Mem. Council, World Petroleum Congress, 1970. Mem., Governing Body, Royal Medical Foundn (Epsom Coll.), 1970. Order of Homoyoun (Iran), 1963. *Address:* Mead House, Woodham Walter, near Maldon, Essex. *T:* Danbury 2404; 6 Godfrey Street, SW3. *T:* 01-352 8260. *Club:* Athenæum.

DALLING, Sir Thomas, Kt 1951; FRCVS, FRSE; lately Veterinary Consultant with the United Nations Food and Agriculture Organisation; *b* 23 April 1892. *Educ:* George Heriot's Sch., Edinburgh; Royal (Dick) Veterinary College. MRCVS 1914; Fitzwygram and Williams Memorial Prizes. Served with RAVC in France, 1916-18 (despatches), Major. Joined Staff of Glasgow Veterinary Coll., 1919, and later became Chief Investigator of Animal Diseases Research Assoc.; Veterinary Superintendent, Wellcome Physiological Research Laboratories, 1923; Prof. of Animal Pathology, University of Cambridge, 1937 (MA); Dir, Ministry of Agriculture and Fisheries Laboratories, Weybridge, 1942; Chief Veterinary Officer, Ministry of Agriculture and Fisheries, 1948-52; Hon. FRCVS, 1951; Hon. degrees: DSc Belfast, 1951; LLD Glasgow, 1952; DSc Bristol, 1952; LLD Edinburgh, 1959. Dalrymple-

Champneys Cup and Medal, 1935; John Henry Steele Memorial Medal in gold, 1950; Thomas Baxter Prize, 1951. Hon. Associate Royal Coll. of Veterinary Surgeons (Mem. Council, 1938-57; Pres., 1949-50, 1950-51; Vice-Pres., 1951-52, 1952-53); late Mem. Agricultural Research Council. *Publications:* many veterinary and scientific articles. *Address:* 77 Howdenhall Road, Edinburgh EH16 6PW.

DALMENY, Lord; Harry Ronald Neil Primrose; *b* 20 Nov. 1967; *s* and *heir* of 7th Earl of Rosebery, *qv.*

DALRYMPLE, family name of Earl of Stair.

DALRYMPLE, Viscount; John David James Dalrymple; *b* 4 Sept. 1961; *s* and *heir* of 13th Earl of Stair, *qv.*

DALRYMPLE, Sir Hew (Fleetwood) Hamilton-, 10th Bt, *cr* 1697; CVO 1974; late Major, Grenadier Guards; Vice-Lieutenant of East Lothian, since 1973; Managing Director (Commercial Operations), Scottish & Newcastle Breweries; Director: Scottish American Investment Company; Stewart Unit Trust Managers; *b* 9 April 1926; *er s* of Sir Hew (Clifford) Hamilton-Dalrymple, 9th Bt, JP; *S* father, 1959; *m* 1954, Lady Anne-Louise Mary Keppel, 3rd *d* of 9th Earl of Albemarle, *qv;* four *s. Educ:* Ampleforth. Ensign and Adjutant, Queen's Body Guard for Scotland (Royal Company of Archers). Pres., E Lothian County Scout Council. DL East Lothian, 1964. *Heir: e s* Hew Richard Hamilton-Dalrymple [*b* 3 Sept. 1955. *Educ:* Ampleforth; Corpus Christi Coll., Oxford]. *Address:* Leuchie, North Berwick, East Lothian. *T:* North Berwick 2903. *Club:* Cavalry and Guards.

DALRYMPLE, Ian Murray, FRSA; Film Producer, Writer and Director; *b* 26 Aug. 1903; *s* of late Sir William Dalrymple, KBE, LLD; *m* 2nd, Joan Margaret, *d* of late James Douglas Craig, CMG, CBE; one *s* and one *d* of previous marriage and two *s. Educ:* Rugby Sch.; Trinity Coll., Cambridge (Editor of The Granta, 1924-25). Executive Producer, Crown Film Unit, Min. of Information, 1940-43; subseq. op. through Wessex Film Productions Ltd and Ian Dalrymple (Advisory) Ltd. Chm. Brit. Film Acad., 1957-58. Film Editor, 1927-35. Screen writer, 1935-39, films including The Citadel, South Riding, Storm in a Teacup, The Lion Has Wings. Produced for Crown Film Unit; Fires Were Started, Western Approaches, Coastal Command, Ferry Pilot, Close Quarters, Wavell's 30,000, Target for To-Night, London Can Take It, etc. Independent productions: The Woman in the Hall, Esther Waters, Once a Jolly Swagman, All Over The Town, Dear Mr Prohack, The Wooden Horse, Family Portrait, The Changing Face of Europe (series), Royal Heritage, Raising a Riot, A Hill in Korea. Commissioned productions include: The Heart of the Matter, The Admirable Crichton, A Cry from the Streets, Bank of England (Educational Films), The Boy and the Pelican. Film Adviser, Decca Ltd, 1967-68. Supervising Film Projects, Argo Record Co. Ltd (Div. of Decca Ltd), 1969. Prod Chaucer's Tale, 1970. *Address:* 3 Beaulieu Close, Cambridge Park, Twickenham TW1 2JR.

DALRYMPLE-CHAMPNEYS, Captain Sir Weldon, 2nd Bt, *cr* 1910; CB 1957; MA, DM, BCh, DPH Oxon; Fellow and former Member of Council (Milroy Lecturer, 1950), Royal College of Physicians, London; Captain, Grenadier Guards (retired); Deputy Chief Medical Officer, Ministry of Health, 1940-56; President: Section of Epidemiology and Public Health, Royal Society of Medicine, 1943-45; Section of Comparative Medicine, 1954-55; Section of History of Medicine, 1957-59; Vice-President Emeritus, Royal Society of Health; Fellow and Ex-Chairman, Royal Veterinary College; Member of Council, Animal Health Trust; President, Federation of Civil Service Photographic Societies; President Hæmophilia Society; *b* 7 May 1892; *o surv. s* of Sir Francis Henry Champneys, 1st Bt, and Virginia Julian (*d* 1922), *o d* of late Sir John Warrender Dalrymple, 7th Bt, of North Berwick; *S* father, 1930; *m* 1st, 1924, Anne, OBE 1948 (*d* 1968), *d* of late Col A. Spencer Pratt, CB, CMG, Broom Hall, Kent; 2nd, 1974, Norma (Hon. Research Fellow, Somerville Coll., Oxford), *widow* of A. S. Russell and *d* of late Col R. Hull Lewis. *Educ:* Oriel Coll., Oxford (Hon. Fellow, 1967). Served European War, 1914-19 (wounded); Senior Asst MOH, Willesden UDC; Hon. Physician to the King, 1941-44; Lord of the Manor of Stanwick (Northants); assumed additional surname of Dalrymple by deed poll, 1924. Ex-Chm., Vegetable Drugs Cttee, Ministry of Supply. Past Pres., Joint Food and Agriculture Organisation/World Health Organisation Expert Cttee on Brucellosis. Corresp. Mem., Sociedad Peruana de Salud Publica. Hon. ARCVS. Hon. Diploma, Amer. Veterinary Epidemiological Soc. *Publications:* Reports to Ministry of Health on the Accommodation for the Sick provided at certain Public Schools for Boys in England, 1928; Undulant Fever, 1929; Bovine Tuberculosis in Man, with

special reference to infection by milk, 1931; The Supervision of Milk Pasteurising Plants, 1935; Undulant Fever, a Neglected Problem (Milroy Lectures, Royal College of Physicians), 1950; Brucella Infection and Undulant Fever in Man, 1960; also numerous articles in scientific journals. *Recreations:* yachting, swimming, travelling, photography, etc. *Heir:* none. *Address:* 39 Ritchie Court, 380 Banbury Road, Oxford. *T:* Oxford 58171. *Club:* Athenæum.

DALRYMPLE HAMILTON, Captain North Edward Frederick, CVO 1961; MBE 1953; DSC 1943; DL; Royal Navy; *b* 17 Feb. 1922; *s* of Admiral Sir Frederick Dalrymple-Hamilton, KCB; *m* 1949, Hon. Mary Colville, *d* of 1st Baron Clydesmuir, PC, GCIE, TD; two *s. Educ:* Eton. Entered Royal Navy, 1940; Comdr 1954; Captain 1960. Comdg Officer HMS Scarborough, 1958; Executive Officer, HM Yacht Britannia, 1959; Captain (F) 17th Frigate Squadron, 1963; Dir of Naval Signals, 1965; Dir, Weapons Equipment Surface, 1967; retd, 1970. Brig., Royal Company of Archers, Queen's Body Guard for Scotland. DL Ayrshire, 1973. *Address:* Lovestone House, Bargany, Girvan, Ayrshire KA26 9RF. *T:* Old Dailly 227. *Clubs:* Pratt's; New (Edinburgh).

DALRYMPLE-HAY, Sir James Brian, 6th Bt, *cr* 1798; estate agent; Partner, Whiteheads, Estate Agents, since 1967; *b* 19 Jan. 1928; *e s* of Lt-Col Brian George Rowland Dalrymple-Hay (*d* on active service, 1943) and Beatrice (*d* 1935), *d* of A. W. Inglis; *S* cousin, 1952; *m* 1958, Helen Sylvia, *d* of late Stephen Herbert Card and of Molly M. Card; three *d. Educ:* Hillsbrow Preparatory Sch., Redhill; Blundell's Sch., Tiverton, Devon. Royal Marine, 1946-47; Lieut Royal Marine Commando, 1947-49; Palestine Star, 1948. Estate Agent and Surveyor's Pupil, 1949; Principal, 1955-67. *Recreations:* cricket, Rugby football, swimming. *Heir: b* John Hugh Dalrymple-Hay [*b* 16 Dec. 1929; *m* 1962, Jennifer, *d* of late Brig. Robert Johnson, CBE; one *s*]. *Address:* The Red House, Church Street, Warnham, near Horsham, W Sussex.

DALRYMPLE-SMITH, Captain Hugh, RN (retired); *b* 27 Sept. 1901; *s* of late Arthur Alexander Dalrymple-Smith and late Mary Glover; *m* 1939, Eleanor Mary Hoare; two *s* one *d. Educ:* Ovingdean; Osborne; Dartmouth. Midshipman, 1917; Ronald Megaw Prize for 1921-22; qualified gunnery 1925, advanced course, 1928. Capt. 1941 (despatches); Admiralty Operations Div., 1942-43; commanding HMS Arethusa, including Normandy landings, 1943-45 (despatches). Naval Attaché, Nanking, 1946-48; commanding HMS King George V, 1948-49. Retired, Dec. 1950, and recalled as Actg Rear-Adm.; Chief of Staff to C-in-C Allied Forces, Northern Europe, 1951-53; retired as Captain. Dir, Television Audience Measurement Ltd, 1958-66. *Recreation:* painting. *Address:* Dale Cottage, Bridge Street, Wickham, Hants PO17 5JE. *T:* Wickham 833103.

DALRYMPLE-WHITE, Sir Henry Arthur Dalrymple, 2nd Bt, *cr* 1926; DFC 1941 and Bar 1942; *b* 5 Nov. 1917; *o s* of Lt-Col Sir Godfrey Dalrymple-White, 1st Bt, and late Hon. Catherine Mary Cary, *d* of 12th Viscount Falkland; *S* father 1954; *m* 1948, Mary (marr. diss. 1956), *o d* of Capt. Robert H. C. Thomas; one *s. Educ:* Eton; Magdalene Coll., Cambridge; London Univ. Formerly Wing Commander RAFVR. Served War of 1939-45. *Heir: s* Jan Hew Dalrymple-White, *b* 26 Nov. 1950. *Address:* c/o Brown, Shipley Ltd, Founders Court, Lothbury, EC2.

DALTON, Sir Alan (Nugent Goring), Kt 1977; CBE 1969; Deputy Chairman, English China Clays Ltd, since 1968; Managing Director, English Clays, Lovering & Pochin & Co. Ltd, since 1961; *b* 26 Nov. 1923; *s* of Harold Goring Dalton and Phyllis Marguerite (*née* Ash). *Educ:* Shendish Prep. Sch., King's Langley; King Edward VI Sch., Southampton. Fellow, Inst. of Dirs; FBIM; FRSA. *Recreations:* sailing, painting, reading. *Address:* English China Clays Ltd, John Keay House, St Austell, Cornwall.

DALTON, Alfred Hyam, CB 1976; Deputy Chairman, Board of Inland Revenue, since 1973 (Commissioner of Inland Revenue since 1970); *b* 29 March 1922; *m* 1946, Elizabeth Stalker; three *d. Educ:* Merchant Taylors' Sch., Northwood; Aberdeen Univ. Served War, REME, 1942-45 (despatches). Entered Inland Revenue, 1947; Asst Sec., 1958; Sec. to Board, 1969. *Recreation:* bridge. *Address:* 10 Courtmead Close, Burbage Road, SE24 9HW. *T:* 01-733 5395. *Club:* Reform.

DALTON, Maj.-Gen. Sir Charles (James George), Kt 1967; CB 1954; CBE 1949 (OBE 1941); *b* 28 Feb. 1902; *s* of late Maj.-Gen. James Cecil Dalton, Col Comdt, RA, and late Mary Caroline, *d* of late Gen. Sir George Barker, GCB; *m* 1936. Daphne, *d* of Col Llewellyn Evans, and late Mrs F. A. Macartney; one *s* two *d* (and one *s* decd). *Educ:* Aysgarth Sch., Yorks; Cheltenham

Coll.; RMA Woolwich. Commissioned, RA, 1921; Staff Coll., Camberley, 1935-36; served in Egypt and India, 1922-39; staff appts in India and Burma, 1939-45 (CRA 26 Ind. Div., BGS 33 Ind. Corps, CRA 14 Ind. Div.); served with CCG, 1946; War Office (Brig. AG Coordination), 1946-49; Comdr 8 AA Bde, 1949-51; Services Relations Adviser to UK High Comr Control Commn for Germany, 1951-54; Dir of Manpower Planning, War Office, 1954-57, retired. Capt. 1934, Major 1939, Lt-Col 1946, Col 1947, Brig. 1951, Maj.-Gen. 1954. Col Comdt RA, 1960-65. Dir-Gen. of Zoological Soc. of London, 1957-67. High Sheriff of Yorks 1972. CStJ. *Recreations:* shooting and fishing. *Address:* The Hutts, Grewelthorpe, Ripon, North Yorks. *T:* Kirkby Malzeard 355. *Club:* Army and Navy.

DALTON, Maj.-Gen. John Cecil D'Arcy, CB 1954; CBE 1948; Vice Lord-Lieutenant North Yorkshire, since 1977; *b* 2 Mar. 1907; *yr s* of late Maj.-Gen. J. C. Dalton, Col Comdt RA, and of late Mrs Dalton; *m* 18 July 1942, Pamela Frances, *d* of late Brig.-Gen. W. H. E. Segrave, DSO; two *s*. *Educ:* Cheltenham Coll.; RMA Woolwich, 2nd Lieut RA, 1926; psc 1939; served War of 1939-45; France and Flanders, 1940; N Africa, 1942-43; NW Europe, 1944. COS, British Commonwealth Forces, Korea, 1952-54; Maj.-Gen., 1958; Maj.-Gen. i/c Administration, Gen. HQ, Far East Land Forces, 1957-59; Dir of Quartering War Office, 1959-60; Vice-Quartermaster-Gen., War Office, 1960-62, retired 1962. CC N Riding Yorks, 1964-70, DL North Riding Yorks, 1967, High Sheriff, Yorkshire, 1970-71. *Address:* Hauxwell Hall, Leyburn, North Yorks. *Club:* Army and Navy.

DALTON, Vice-Adm. Sir Norman (Eric), KCB 1959 (CB 1956); OBE 1944; *b* 1 Feb. 1904; *s* of late William John Henry Dalton, Portsmouth; *m* 1927, Teresa Elizabeth, *d* of late Richard Jenkins, Portsmouth; one *s* one *d*. *Educ:* RN Colls Osborne and Dartmouth. Joined RN, 1917; Capt. 1946; Rear-Adm. 1954; Vice-Adm. 1957. Deputy Engineer-in-Chief of the Fleet, 1955-57; Engineer-in-Chief of the Fleet, 1957-59; Dir-Gen. of Training, 1959-60; retired 1960. *Address:* New Lodge, Peppard Lane, Henley-on-Thames, Oxon. *T:* Henley 5552. *Club:* Army and Navy.

DALTON, Peter Gerald Fox, CMG 1958; *b* 12 Dec. 1914; *s* of late Sir Robert (William) Dalton, CMG; *m* 1944, Josephine Anne Helyar; one *s* one *d*. *Educ:* Uppingham Sch.; Oriel Coll., Oxford. HM Embassy, Peking 1937-39; HM Consulate-Gen., Hankow, 1939-41; HM Embassy, Chungking, 1941-42; Foreign Office, 1942-46; HM Legation, Bangkok, 1946; HM Embassy, Montevideo, 1947-50; Foreign Office, 1950-53; Political Adviser, Hong Kong, 1953-56; Foreign Office, 1957-60; HM Embassy, Warsaw, 1960-63; HM Consul-General: Los Angeles, 1964-65; San Francisco, 1965-67; Minister, HM Embassy, Moscow, 1967-69; retd from HM Diplomatic Service, 1969. *Address:* Rotherdale Cottage, Fir Toll Road, Mayfield, Sussex. *T:* Mayfield 3421.

DALTON, Philip Neale; Vice President, Immigration Appeal Tribunal, since 1970; *b* 30 June 1909; *o s* of late Sir Llewelyn Dalton, MA; *m* 1947, Pearl, *d* of Mark Foster, Kenya; one *s* two *d*. *Educ:* Downside Sch.; Trinity Coll., Cambridge. Barrister-at-law. Inner Temple, 1933; Resident Magistrate, Ghana, 1937; military service, 1939-45; Crown Counsel, Ghana, 1945-51; Solicitor-Gen., Fiji, 1951-53; Attorney-Gen., British Solomon Islands, and Legal Adviser, Western Pacific High Commission, 1953-56; Attorney-Gen., Zanzibar, 1957-63; Puisne Judge, Kenya, 1963-69. Order of the Brilliant Star (second class) Zanzibar, 1963. *Recreations:* cricket, golf. *Address:* Spring Lane, Aston Tirrold, Oxon. *Clubs:* Royal Commonwealth Society; Nairobi (Nairobi).

DALY, Most Rev. Cahal Brendan; *see* Ardagh and Clonmacnois, Bishop of, (RC).

DALY, Harry John, CMG 1966; FRACP 1946; FFARCS 1949; FFARACS; Retired Anæsthetist; *b* 3 Aug. 1893; *s* of Henry and Victoria Daly, both Irish; *m* 1921, Jean Edmunds, Sydney. *Educ:* St Ignatius Coll., Sydney, Australia, MB, ChM Sydney, 1918; FFARACS Melbourne 1952. Gen. Practice, Haberfield NSW; Specialist Anæsthetist, Sydney, 1929; Hon. Consulting Anæsthetist to Lewisham, Sydney and St Vincent's Hospitals. Dean, Faculty of Anæsthetists, RACS, 1954. Hon. Member: Royal Society of Medicine; Liverpool Soc. Anæsthetists, 1935. Orton Medallion, RACS, 1969. Hon. FRACS, 1973. *Publications:* numerous scientific articles in med. jls, 1932-56. *Recreations:* fishing, gardening. *Address:* 8 The Parapet, Castlecrag, NSW 2068, Australia. *T:* 955957. *Club:* Royal Sydney Golf.

DALY, Rt. Rev. John Charles Sydney; Assistant to the Bishop of Coventry, 1968-75, and Vicar of Bishop's Tachbrook, 1970-75; *b*

13 Jan. 1903; *s* of S. Owen Daly. *Educ:* Gresham's Sch., Holt; King's Coll., Cambridge; Cuddesdon Coll., Oxford. Curate, St Mary's Church, Tyne Dock, South Shields, 1926-29; Vicar, Airedale with Fryston, Yorks, 1929-35; Bishop of Gambia, 1935-51; Bishop of Accra, 1951-55; Bishop in Korea, 1955-65, of Taejon (Korea), 1965-68; Priest-in-charge of Honington with Idlicote and Whatcote, 1968-70. *Address:* Rye Croft, Honington, Shipston-on-Stour, Warwicks. *T:* Shipston-on-Stour 62140.

DALY, Lawrence; General Secretary, National Union of Mineworkers, since 1968; *b* 20 Oct. 1924; *s* of James Daly and late Janet Taylor; *m* 1948, Renée M. Baxter; four *s* one *d*. *Educ:* primary and secondary schools. Glencraig Colliery (underground), 1939; Workmen's Safety Inspector, there, 1954-64. Part-time NUM lodge official, Glencraig, 1946; Chm., Scottish NUM Youth Committee, 1949; elected to Scottish Area NUM Exec. Cttee, 1962; Gen. Sec., Scottish NUM, 1964; National Exec., NUM, 1965. *Publications:* (pamphlets): A Young Miner Sees Russia, 1946; The Miners and the Nation, 1968. *Recreations:* literature, politics, folk-song. *Address:* 222 Euston Road, NW1. *T:* 01-387 7631. *Club:* Jewel Miners' (Edinburgh).

DALY, Dame Mary Dora, DBE 1951 (CBE 1949; OBE 1937); Victorian President of Catholic Welfare Organisation since 1941; Federal President, Australian Association of Ryder-Cheshire Foundations; *b* Cootamundra, NSW; *d* of late T. P. MacMahon, Darling Point, Sydney; *m* 1923, Dr John J. Daly, Melbourne; one *s* one *d*. *Educ:* Loreto Abbey, Ballarat, Vic. War of 1939-45; Mem. of finance and advisory cttees, Australian Comforts Fund; Mem. executive cttees, Lord Mayor of Melbourne's appeals for food for Britain, toys for Britain, Victorian Government fat for Britain drive. Member: National Council, Aust. Red Cross Soc.; Executive and Council (1936-), Victorian Div., Red Cross Soc.; Council, Nat. Heart Foundn of Australia (Victorian Div.); Council and Executive, Ryder-Cheshire Foundn (Victoria); Victorian Council Girl Guides Assoc., 1954; Anti-Cancer Council (Victoria); Council, Order of the British Empire Assoc., Victoria; Lady Mayoress's (Melbourne) Cttee for Metropolitan Hosps and charities; Patron: Nat. Boys Choir; Yooralla Hosp. Sch., for Crippled Children (Pres., DMD Cttee); Austral Salon for advancement of music, literature and fine arts. Pres., Australian Catholic Relief, Archdiocese of Melbourne, 1966-75. Comr for Affidavits, State of Victoria. Cross, Pro Ecclesia et Pontifice, 1952. *Publications:* Marie's Birthday Party, 1934; Cinty, 1961; Timmy's Christmas Surprise, 1967; Holidays at Hillydale, 1974; articles in several magazines. *Recreations:* music, reading, gardening. *Address:* 6 Henry Street, Kew, Vic 3101, Australia; Finavarra, Stevens Street, Queenscliff, Victoria.

DALY, Michael de Burgh, MA, MD, ScD Cambridge; MRCP; Professor of Physiology in the University of London, at St Bartholomew's Hospital Medical College, since 1958; *b* 7 May 1922; *s* of late Dr Ivan de Burgh Daly, CBE, FRS; *m* 1948, Beryl Esmé, *y d* of late Wing Commander A. J. Nightingale; two *s*. *Educ:* Loretto Sch., Edinburgh; Gonville and Caius Coll., Cambridge; St Bartholomew's Hospital. Nat. Science Tripos. Part I, 1943, Part II, 1944, Physiology. House-physician, St Bartholomew's Hospital, 1947; Asst Lecturer, 1948-50, and Lecturer, 1950-54, in Physiology, University Coll., London. Rockefeller Foundation Travelling Fellowship in Medicine, 1952-53; Locke Research Fellow of Royal Soc., 1954-58; Vis. Prof. of Physiology, Univ. of NSW, 1966; Vis. Lectr, Swedish Univs, 1961. Mem., Adv. Panel for Underwater Personnel Res., MoD. Former Co-Editor of Journal of Physiology. FRSM. Member: Soc. of Experimental Biol.; Physiological Soc. Schafer Prize in Physiology, University Coll., London, 1953; Thruston Medal, Gonville and Caius Coll., 1957; Sir Lionel Whitby Medal, Cambridge Univ., 1963. *Publications:* contributor to Winton and Bayliss' Human Physiology, to Starling's Principles of Human Physiology; papers on the integrative control of respiration and the cardiovascular system in Journal of Physiology; contrib. to film on William Harvey and the Circulation of the Blood. *Recreation:* model engineering. *Address:* 7 Hall Drive, Sydenham, SE26 6XL. *T:* 01-778 8773.

DALY, Lt-Gen. Sir Thomas (Joseph), KBE 1967 (CBE 1953; OBE 1944); CB 1965; DSO 1945, Chief of the General Staff, Australia, 1966-71; *b* 19 March 1913; *s* of late Lt-Col T. J. Daly, DSO, VD, Melbourne; *m* 1946, Heather, *d* of late James Fitzgerald, Melbourne; three *d*. *Educ:* St Patrick's Coll., Sale; Xavier Coll., Kew, Vic; RMC, Duntroon. 3rd LH, 1934; attached for training 16/5 Lancers, India, 1938; Adj, 2/10 Aust. Inf. Bn, 1939; Bde Major, 18 Inf. Bde, 1940; GSO2 6 Aust. Div., 1941; GSO1 5 Aust. Div., 1942; Instructor, Staff Sch. (Aust.), 1944; CO 2/10 Inf. Bn, AIF, 1944; Instr, Staff Coll., Camberley,

UK, 1946; Joint Services Staff Coll., Latimer, 1948; Dir of Mil. Art, RMC Duntroon, 1949; Dir of Infantry, AHQ, 1951; Comd 28 Brit. Commonwealth Inf. Bde, Korea, 1952; Dir, Ops and Plans, AHQ, 1953; IDC, London, 1956; GOC Northern Command, Australia, 1957-60; Adjt Gen., 1961-63; GOC, Eastern Command, Australia, 1963-66. Col Comdt, Royal Australian Regt, and Pacific Is Regt, 1971-75. Vice-Chm., Associated Securities Ltd, 1971-76; Director: Jennings Industries Ltd, 1974-; Fruehauf Trailers (Aust.) Ltd; Associated Merchant Bank (Singapore), 1975-77. Mem., Nat. Council, Australian Red Cross, 1972-75; Chm., Bd of Trustees, Australian Nat. War Memorial, 1974 (Mem., 1972-74); Councillor, Royal Agricl Soc. of NSW, 1972-. Legion of Merit (US), 1953. *Recreations:* golf, tennis, cricket, ski-ing. *Address:* 16 Victoria Road, Bellevue Hill, NSW 2023, Australia. *Clubs:* Australian (Sydney); Naval and Military (Melbourne); Royal Sydney Golf, Melbourne Cricket, Ski Club of Australia.

DALYELL, Tam; MP (Lab) West Lothian, since 1962; *b* 9 Aug. 1932; *s* of late Gordon and Eleanor Dalyell; *m* 1963, Kathleen, *o d* of Baron Wheatley, *qv*; one *s* one *d. Educ:* Eton; King's Coll., Cambridge; Moray House Teachers' Training Coll., Edinburgh. Trooper, Royal Scots Greys, 1950-52; Teacher, Bo'ness High Sch., 1956-60. Contested (Lab) Roxburgh, Selkirk, and Peebles, 1959. Dep.-Director of Studies on British India ship-school, Dunera, 1961-62. Member Public Accounts Cttee, House of Commons, 1962-66; Secretary, Labour Party Standing Conference on the Sciences, 1962-64; PPS to Minister of Housing, 1964-65; Chairman: Parly Labour Party Education Cttee, 1964-65; Parly Labour Party Sports Group, 1964-74; Parly Lab. Party Foreign Affairs Gp, 1974-75; Vice-Chairman: Parly Labour Party Defence and Foreign Affairs Gps, 1972-74; Scottish Labour Group of MPs, 1973-75; Parly Lab. Party, Nov. 1974-; Sub-Cttee on Public Accounts; Member: European Parlt, 1975-; European Parlt Budget Cttee, 1976-; European Parlt Energy Cttee; Member: House of Commons Select Cttee on Science and Technology, 1967-69; Liaison Cttee between Cabinet and Parly Labour Party, 1974-76; Council, National Trust for Scotland; PPS to late R. H. S. Crossman, MP, 1964-70. Mem. Scottish Council for Devlt and Industry Trade Delegn to China, Nov. 1971. Political columnist, New Scientist. *Publications:* The Case of Ship-Schools, 1960; Ship-School Dunera, 1963; Devolution: end of Britain, 1977. *Recreations:* tennis, swimming. *Address:* The Binns, Linlithgow, Scotland. *T:* Philipstoun 255.

DALZELL-PAYNE, Brig. Henry Salusbury Legh, CBE 1973; Chief of Staff HQ 1 (BR) Corps, since 1976; *b* 1929; *s* of Geoffrey Legh Dalzell-Payne; *m* 1963, Serena Helen, *d* of Col Clifford White Gourlay, MC, TD; two *d. Educ:* Cheltenham; RMA Sandhurst. Commissioned, 7th Hussars, 1949; Major, Sultan of Muscat's Armed Forces, 1959-60; Staff Coll., Camberley, 1961; BM HQ Armd Brigade Gp, 1962-64; Queen's Own Hussars, 1964-65; Instructor, Staff Coll., Camberley, 1966; Comd 3rd Dragoon Guards, 1967-69; Gen. Staff, Mil. Ops, MoD, 1970-72; student, RCDS, 1973; Comdr, 6th Armoured Brigade, 1974-75. *Club:* Cavalry and Guards.

DALZIEL, Dr Keith, FRS 1975; University Lecturer in Biochemistry, University of Oxford, since 1963; Fellow of Wolfson College since 1970; *b* 24 Aug. 1921; *s* of late Gilbert and Edith Dalziel; *m* 1945, Sallie Farnworth; two *d. Educ:* Grecian Street Central Sch., Salford; Royal Techn. Coll., 1st cl. hons BSc London 1944; PhD London; MA Oxon. Lab. Technician, Manchester Victoria Meml Jewish Hosp., 1935-44, Biochemist 1944-45; Asst Biochemist, Radcliffe Infirmary, Oxford, 1945-47; Res. Asst, Nuffield Haematology Res. Fund, Oxford, 1947-58; Rockefeller Trav. Fellowship in Medicine, Nobel Inst., Stockholm, 1955-57; Sorby Res. Fellow of Royal Soc., Sheffield Univ., 1958-63; Vis. Prof. of Biochemistry, Univ. of Michigan, 1967. Member: Editorial Bds, European Jl of Biochemistry and Biochimica Biophysica Acta, 1971-74; Enzyme Chem. and Technol. Cttee, SRC, 1974. *Publications:* sci. papers in Biochem. Jl, European Jl of Biochemistry, etc. *Recreations:* music, golf. *Address:* Department of Biochemistry, South Parks Road, Oxford. *T:* Oxford 59214; 25 Hampden Drive, Kidlington, Oxford. *T:* Kidlington 2623.

DAMER; see Dawson-Damer.

DAMERELL, Derek Vivian; Governor and Chief Executive, BUPA, since 1974; *b* 4 Aug. 1921; *s* of William James Damerell (Lt-Col), MBE and Zoe Damerell; *m* 1942, Margaret Isabel Porritt; two *s* three *d. Educ:* ISC; Edinburgh Univ.; Harvard Business Sch. Parent Bd, BPB Industries, 1953-64; Regional Dir, Internat. Wool Secretariat, 1965-73. Governor, Nuffield Nursing Homes Trust; Dir, The Medical Centre; Chm. and Founder, Independ. Hosp. Gp. Council, Internat. Fedn of

Voluntary Health Service Funds; Mem. Bd of Governors, Assoc. Internat. de la Mutualité. *Recreations:* sailing (jt founder, BCYC, 1947); travel. *Address:* Stodham Park, Liss, Hants. *T:* Liss 2316. *Clubs:* various yacht.

DAMMERS, Very Rev. Alfred Hounsell; Dean of Bristol, since 1973; *b* 10 July 1921; *s* of late B. F. H. Dammers, MA, JP; *m* 1947, Brenda Muriel, *d* of late Clifford Stead; two *s* two *d. Educ:* Malvern Coll. (Schol.); Pembroke Coll., Cambridge (Schol., MA); Westcott House, Cambridge. Served RA (Surrey and Sussex Yeo.), 1941-44. Asst Curate, Adlington, Lancs, 1948; Asst Curate, S Bartholomew's, Edgbaston, Birmingham, and Lectr at Queen's Coll., Birmingham, 1950; Chaplain and Lectr at S John's Coll., Palayamkottai, S India, 1953; Vicar of Holy Trinity, Millhouses, Sheffield, and Examining Chaplain to Bishop of Sheffield, 1957; Select Preacher at Univ. of Cambridge, 1963; Select Preacher at Univ. of Oxford, 1975; Chairman, Friends of Reunion, 1965; Canon Residentiary and Director of Studies, Coventry Cathedral, 1965. Founder and Central Correspondent, The Life Style Movement, 1972. Companion, Community of the Cross of Nails, 1975. *Publications:* Great Venture, 1958; Ye Shall Receive Power, 1958; All in Each Place, 1962; God is Light, God is Love, 1963; AD 1980, 1966. *Recreations:* travel (home and abroad); walking, candle making, sailing. *Address:* The Deanery, 20 Charlotte Street, Bristol BS1 5PZ. *T:* Bristol 22443.

DANCE, Brian David, MA; Headmaster, St Dunstan's College, Catford, since 1973; *b* 22 Nov. 1929; *s* of late L. H. Dance and of Mrs M. G. Dance (*née* Shrivelle); *m* 1955, Chloe Elizabeth, *o d* of J. F. A. Baker, *qv*; two *s* two *d. Educ:* Kingston Grammar Sch.; Wadham Coll., Oxford. BA 1952, MA 1956. Asst Master, Kingston Grammar Sch., 1953-59; Sen. History Master: Faversham Grammar Sch., 1959-62; Westminster City Sch., 1962-65; Headmaster: Cirencester Grammar Sch., 1965-66; Luton Sixth Form Coll., 1966-73. Cambridge Local Examination Syndicate, 1968-73; Headmasters' Assoc. Council, 1968-76 (Exec. Cttee, 1972-76, Hon. Legal Sec. 1975-76). *Publications:* articles in: Times Educnl Supp.; Headmasters' Assoc. 'Review'. *Recreations:* most ball games (especially cricket and Rugby football), music, philately. *Address:* Headmaster's House, St Dunstan's College, Catford SE6 4TY. *T:* 01-690 1277. *Club:* East India, Devonshire, Sports and Public Schools.

DANCKWERTS, Rt. Hon. Sir Harold Otto, PC 1961; Kt 1949; a Lord Justice of Appeal, 1961-69; *b* 23 Feb. 1888; *s* of William Otto Danckwerts, KC, and Mary Caroline Lowther; *m* 1st, 1918, Florence Mary Pride (*d* 1969); one *s* one *d*; 2nd, 1969, Ella Hamilton Marshall, Glasgow. *Educ:* Winchester Coll.; Balliol Coll., Oxford (MA); Harvard Univ., USA. Called to Bar, Lincoln's Inn, 1913 (Certificate of Honour), Bencher, 1941, Treasurer, 1962. Mobilised as Lance Corp. and a farrier, Aug. 1914; during European War, 1914-19, served with E Riding of Yorkshire Yeomanry and Machine Gun Corps (Captain) (despatches); Tutor to Law Society, 1914-23; Reader to Law Society, 1923-41; Junior Counsel to Treasury and Board of Trade in Chancery matters and Junior Counsel to Attorney-General in Charity matters, 1941-49; Judge of the High Court of Justice (Chancery Division), 1949-61. *Address:* 4 Stone Buildings, Lincoln's Inn, WC2A 3XT. *Club:* Kennel.

DANCKWERTS, Prof. Peter Victor, GC 1940; MBE 1943; FRS 1969; FIChemE; Shell Professor of Chemical Engineering, Cambridge University, 1959-77, now Emeritus; Fellow of Pembroke College, Cambridge, 1959-77; *b* 14 Oct. 1916; *s* of late Vice-Adm. V. H. Danckwerts and Joyce Danckwerts; *m* 1960, Lavinia, *d* of Brig.-Gen. D. A. Macfarlane. *Educ:* Winchester Coll.; Balliol Coll., Oxford; Massachusetts Inst. of Technology. BA (chemistry) Oxon, 1938; SM (Chemical Engineering Practice), MIT, 1948; MA Cantab 1948. RNVR, 1940-46. Commonwealth Fund Fellow, MIT, 1946-48; Demonstrator and Lecturer, Dept of Chemical Engineering, Cambridge Univ., 1948-54; Deputy Director of Research and Development, Industrial Group, UK Atomic Energy Authority, 1954-56; Prof. of Chemical Engineering Science, Imperial College of Science and Technology, 1956-59. MIChemE 1955 (President, 1965-66). For. Hon. Mem., Amer. Acad. of Arts and Scis, 1964. E. V. Murphree Award, ACS, 1973. *Address:* The Abbey House, Abbey Road, Cambridge. *T:* Cambridge 57275.

DANCY, John Christopher, MA; Principal, Saint Luke's College of Education, Exeter, 1972-78; Professor of Education, University of Exeter, from Oct. 1978; *b* 13 Nov. 1920; *e s* of Dr J. H. Dancy and late Dr N. Dancy; *m* 1944, Angela Bryant; two *s* one *d. Educ:* Winchester (Scholar); New Coll., Oxford (Scholar, MA). 1st Class, Classical Hon. Mods., 1940; Craven Scholar, 1946; Gaisford Greek Prose Prize, 1947; Hertford Scholar, 1947;

Arnold Historical Essay Prize, 1949. Served in Rifle Brigade, 1941-46; Capt. GSO(3)I, 30 Corps, 1945; Major, GSO(2)I, 1 Airborne Corps, 1945-46. Lecturer in Classics, Wadham Coll., 1946-48; Asst Master, Winchester Coll., 1948-53; Headmaster of Lancing Coll., 1953-61; Master, Marlborough Coll., 1961-72. Member, Public Schools' Commission, 1966-68. *Publications:* Commentary on 1 Maccabees, 1954; The Public Schools and the Future, 1963; Commentary on Shorter Books of Apocrypha, 1972. *Address:* Saint Luke's College, Exeter EX1 2LU. *T:* Exeter 52221; 7 Baring Crescent, Exeter EX1 1TL.

DANE, William Surrey, CBE 1953; MC; Patron, The Association of Independent Hospitals (Chairman, 1960-63; President, 1963-69); Member Board of Governors, Hospital for Sick Children, Great Ormond Street, for 24 years (Vice-Chairman 1957-67); Member Committee of Management, Institute of Child Health, University of London, 1955-67; Member Council, Charing Cross Hospital Medical School, 1956-67; Life Vice-President Printers' Charitable Corporation; Hon. Vice-President Lloyd Memorial (Printers) Convalescent Home (President, 1950-61); a Vice-Chairman and Managerial Consultant of Odhams Press Ltd, printers and publishers of Long Acre, WC2, 1959-March 1961 (Joint Managing Director, 1947-57, Managing Director, 1958); Chairman, Daily Herald, 1949-60; Member, General Advisory Council of the BBC, 1956-62; *b* 1892; *e s* of James Surrey Dane, Adelaide, SA; *m* 1919, Dorothy Mary, *d* of late Rev. W. A. Armstrong, MA, Funtington Vicarage, near Chichester; one *s* two *d*. Served European War, 1914-19, Captain and Adjt, Seaforth Highlanders (despatches, MC); during War of 1939-45 was a Director at Min. of Information, 1939, and Min. of Supply, 1941-45. *Address:* Apple Porch, Peaslake, near Guildford. Surrey. *T:* Dorking 730235.

DANGAN, Viscount; Garret Graham Wellesley; *b* 30 March 1965; *s* and *heir* of 7th Earl Cowley, *qv*.

DANIEL, Adm. Sir Charles (Saumarez), KCB 1948 (CB 1945); CBE 1941; DSO 1939; *b* 23 June 1894; *s* of late Lieut-Colonel C. J. Daniel, CBE, DSO; *m* 1919, Marjory Katharine (*d* 1958), *d* of Arthur C. Wilson, MB, ChB, Formby; one *d*; *m* 1963, Mrs Pares Wilson, The Manor House, Little Shelford, Cambridge. *Educ:* Southcliffe Sch., Filey; RN Colleges, Osborne and Dartmouth. HMS Orion, Home Fleet and Grand Fleet, 1912-18 (despatches, Jutland, 1914-15 Star, 2 medals); specialised in Signals and Wireless, 1918; Commander, 1928; Experimental Commander HM Signal Sch., 1928-30; passed RN and RAF Staff Colleges, 1931-32; Commander HMS Glorious, 1933-34; Captain, 1934; passed Imperial Defence Coll., 1935; Plans Div., Admiralty, for Joint Planning Cttee, 1936-38; Captain D 8th Destroyer Flotilla, 1938-40, European War (DSO); Director of Plans, Naval Staff, Admiralty, 1940-41 (CBE); In Command HMS Renown, 1941-43; Rear-Adm. 1943. Flag Officer, Combined Operations, 1943; Vice-Adm. (Admin.) British Pacific Fleet, Rear-Adm. Commanding 1st Battle Squadron, British Pacific Fleet, 1944-45 (CB); Third Sea Lord and Controller of the Navy, 1945-49 (KCB); Vice-Adm. 1946; Commandant Imperial Defence Coll., 1949-51; Admiral 1950; retired list, 1952. Chairman, Television Advisory Cttee, 1952-62. A Director of Blaw Knox Ltd, 1953-66. *Address:* The Manor House, Little Shelford, Cambridge. *T:* Shelford 3253.

DANIEL, Gerald Ernest, FCA, IPFA, FRVA; County Treasurer, Nottinghamshire County Council, since 1974; Director, Horizon Midlands Ltd, since 1975; *b* 7 Dec. 1919; *s* of Ernest and Beata May Daniel; *m* 1942, Ecila Roslyn Dillow; one *s* one *d*. *Educ:* Huish's Grammar Sch., Taunton. Served War, 1939-46, Somerset LI. Various appts in Borough Treasurers' Depts at Taunton, Bexhill and Scunthorpe, 1935-50; Cost and machine accountant, subseq. Chief Accountant, City Treasury, Bristol, 1950-60; Dep. Borough Treasurer, Reading, 1960-64; Borough Treasurer, West Bromwich, 1965-68; City Treasurer, Nottingham, 1968-74. Pres., Nottingham Soc. of Chartered Accountants, 1976; Vice-Pres., Assoc. of Public Service Finance Officers, 1977; Mem. Council, CIPFA, 1971-77. *Recreations:* gardening, music. *Address:* County Hall, West Bridgford, Nottingham NG2 7QP. *T:* Nottingham 863366; 242 Melton Road, Edwalton, Nottingham. *T:* Nottingham 231025.

DANIEL, Prof. Glyn Edmund, MA, LittD; Fellow of St John's College, Cambridge, since 1938; Disney Professor of Archæology, University of Cambridge, since 1974 (Lecturer, 1948-74); *b* 23 April 1914; *o s* of John Daniel and Mary Jane (*née* Edmunds); *m* 1946, Ruth, *d* of late Rev. R. W. B. Langhorne, Exeter. *Educ:* Barry County Sch.; University College, Cardiff; St John's Coll., Cambridge (Scholar; BA 1st Class Hons with Distinction, Archaeological and Anthropological Tripos). Strathcona Student, 1936; Allen Scholar, 1937; Wallenberg Prizeman, 1937; Research

Fellowship, St John's Coll., 1938; PhD 1938; MA 1939. Intelligence Officer, RAF, 1940-45; in charge Photo Interpretation, India and SE Asia, 1942-45 (despatches); Wing Comdr, 1943. Faculty Asst Lectr in Archaeology, 1945-48; Steward of St John's Coll., 1946-55; Leverhulme Research Fellow, 1948-50. Lecturer: Munro, Archaeology, Edinburgh Univ., 1954; Rhys, British Acad., 1954; O'Donnell, Edinburgh Univ., 1956; Josiah Mason, Birmingham Univ., 1956; Gregynog University College, Wales, 1968; Ballard-Matthews, University Coll. of North Wales, 1968; George Grant MacCurdy, Harvard, 1971. Visiting Prof., Univ. Aarhus, 1968; Ferrens Prof., Univ. Hull, 1969. Pres., South Eastern Union of Scientific Socs, 1955. LittD 1962. President: Bristol and Gloucestershire Archaeological Soc., 1962-63; RAI, 1977-. Hon. Mem. Istituto Italiano di Preistoria e Protostoria, Corresponding Fellow, German Archaeological Institute, Corresponding Mem., Jutland Archaeological Soc. Editor, Ancient Peoples and Places, and of Antiquity, since 1958. Director: Anglia Television, Ltd; Antiquity Publications Ltd; Cambridge Arts Theatre. FSA 1942. Knight (First Class) of the Dannebrog, 1961. *Publications:* The Three Ages, 1942; A Hundred Years of Archaeology, 1950; The Prehistoric Chamber Tombs of England and Wales, 1950; A Picture Book of Ancient British Art (with S. Piggott), 1951; Lascaux and Carnac, 1955; ed Myth or Legend, 1955; Barclodiad y Gawres (with T. G. E. Powell), 1956; The Megalith Builders of Western Europe, 1958; The Prehistoric Chamber Tombs of France, 1960; The Idea of Prehistory, 1961; The Hungry Archaeologist in France, 1963; New Grange and the Bend of the Boyne (with late S. P. O'Riordain), 1964; (ed with I. Ll. Foster), Prehistoric and Early Wales, 1964; Man Discovers his Past, 1966; The Origins and Growth of Archaeology, 1967; The First Civilisations, 1968; Archaeology and the History of Art, 1970; Megaliths in History, 1973; (ed jtly) France before the Romans, 1974; A Hundred and Fifty Years of Archaeology, 1975; Cambridge and the Back-Looking Curiosity: an inaugural lecture, 1976; and articles in archaeological journals. *Recreations:* travel, walking, swimming, food, wine, writing detective stories (The Cambridge Murders, 1945; Welcome Death, 1954). *Address:* The Flying Stag, 70 Bridge Street, Cambridge. *T:* 56082; La Marnière, Zouafques-par-Tournehem, 62890 France. *T:* Calais 35.61.40. *Club:* United Oxford & Cambridge University.

DANIEL, Sir Goronwy Hopkin, KCVO 1969; CB 1962; DPhil Oxon; Principal, Aberystwyth University College, since 1969; Vice-Chancellor, University of Wales, since 1977; *b* Ystradgynlais, 21 March 1914; *s* of David Daniel; *m* 1940, Lady Valerie, *d* of 2nd Earl Lloyd George; one *s* two *d*. *Educ:* Pontardawe Secondary Sch.; Amman Valley County Sch.; University College of Wales, Aberystwyth; Jesus Coll., Oxford. Fellow of University of Wales; Meyricke Scholar, Jesus Coll.; Oxford Institute of Statistics, 1937-40; Lecturer, Dept of Economics, Bristol Univ., 1940-41; Clerk, House of Commons, 1941-43; Ministry of Town and Country Planning, 1943-47; Ministry of Fuel and Power, Chief Statistician, 1947-55; Under-Sec., Coal Div., 1955-62, Gen. Div., 1962-64; Permanent Under-Sec. of State, Welsh Office, 1964-69. Chm., British Nat. Conf. on Social Welfare, 1970; Pres., West Wales Assoc. for the Arts, 1971-; Member: Welsh Language Council, 1974-; Gen. Adv. Council, BBC, 1974-. Dir, Commercial Bank of Wales, 1972-. Chairman: Home-Grown Timber Adv. Cttee, 1974-; Cttee on Water Charges in Wales, 1974-75. *Publications:* papers in statistical, fuel and power, and other journals. *Recreations:* country pursuits, sailing. *Address:* Plas Penglais, Aberystwyth, Dyfed. *T:* Aberystwyth 3583. *Clubs:* Travellers'; Royal Welsh Yacht.

DANIEL, Henry Cave; *b* 16 Aug. 1896; *s* of late H. T. Daniel, Manor House, Stockland, Bridgwater; *m* 1931, Barbara, *d* of late Mrs Blain, King's Barrow, Wareham, Dorset; one *s* one *d*. *Educ:* Eton; RMC, Sandhurst. Joined 17th Lancers, 1914, and served European War, 1914-18, with that regiment, retiring in 1920. Rejoined Army, 1939, and served War of 1939-45, in France and England until invalided out in 1941. High Sheriff of Somerset, 1949. *Recreations:* hunting and shooting. *Address:* The Old Mill, Sparkford, Yeovil, Som. *T:* North Cadbury 427. *Clubs:* Cavalry and Guards; Somerset County (Taunton).

DANIEL, (John) Stuart, QC 1961; *b* 17 Feb. 1912; *s* of Walter John Daniel and Nena Nithsdale Newall. *Educ:* Haileybury; Merton Coll., Oxford. Called to Bar, Middle Temple, 1937. Member, Lands Tribunal, 1967-76. *Address:* Paradise Cottage, Great Wratting, Haverhill, Suffolk. *T:* Thurlow 328. *Club:* Garrick.

DANIEL, Norman Alexander, CBE 1974 (OBE 1968); PhD; British Council Representative, Egypt, and Cultural Counsellor, British Embassy, Cairo, since 1973; *b* 8 May 1919; *s* of George

Frederick Daniel and Winifred Evelyn (*née* Jones); *m* 1941, Marion Ruth, *d* of Harold Wadham Pethybridge; one *s*. *Educ:* Frensham Heights Sch.; Queen's Coll., Oxford (BA); Edinburgh Univ. (PhD). Asst Dir, British Inst., Basra, 1947; British Council Asst Representative: Baghdad, 1948; Beirut, 1952; Edinburgh, 1953; Dir, Brit. Inst., Baghdad, 1957; Dep. Rep., Brit. Council, Scotland, 1960; Brit. Council Rep., Sudan, 1962; Vis. Fellow, University Coll., Cambridge, 1969-70; Dir, Visitors Dept, Brit. Council, London, 1970; Cultural Attaché, Cairo, 1971. *Publications:* Islam and the West: the making of an image, 1958 (3rd edn 1966); Islam, Europe and Empire, 1966; The Arabs and Mediaeval Europe, 1975; The Cultural Barrier, 1975; (contrib.) History of the Crusades, vol. 5 (USA, in progress); contrib. to learned jls. *Recreations:* gardening, mediaeval history, history of intercultural relations. *Address:* Landmark, Flimwell, Wadhurst, East Sussex TN5 7PA. *T:* Flimwell 325.

DANIEL, Prof. Peter Maxwell, MA, MB, BCh Cambridge; MA, DM Oxon; DSc London; FRCP; FRCS; FRCPath; FRCPsych; FInstBiol; Senior Research Fellow, Department of Applied Physiology and Surgical Science, Institute of Basic Medical Sciences, Royal College of Surgeons; Professor of Neuropathology, University of London, at the Institute of Psychiatry, Maudsley Hospital, 1957-76; Hon. Consultant Neuropathologist, the Bethlem Royal and Maudsley Hospitals, 1956-76; *b* 14 Nov. 1910; *s* of Peter Daniel, FRCS, surgeon to Charing Cross Hospital, and Beatrice Laetitia Daniel. *Educ:* Westminster Sch.; St John's Coll., Cambridge; New Coll., Oxford. Hon. Consultant Pathologist, Radcliffe Infirmary, 1948-56; Senior Research Officer, University of Oxford, 1949-56; Hon. Consultant in Neuropathology to the Army at Home, 1952-76. John Hunter Medal and Triennial Prize, 1946-48, and Erasmus Wilson Lectr, 1964, RCS. Editorial Board of: Jl of Physiology, 1958-65; Jl of Neurology, Neurosurgery and Psychiatry, 1953-64; Journal of Neuroendocrinology, 1966-; Brain, 1974-76. President: British Neuropathological Society, 1963-64; Neurological Section, RSM, 1970-71; Harveian Soc. London, 1966 (Trustee, 1971-); Mem. Council: Royal Microscopical Soc., 1968-72; Neonatal Soc., 1959-61; Assoc. of British Neurologists, 1966-69; Section of Hist. of Med., RSM, 1973-; Mem. Council, Osler Club, 1972-. Member: Bd of Govs, Bethlem Royal and Maudsley Hosps, 1966-75; Council, Charing Cross Hosp. Medical Sch., 1972-. Chairman: Academic Bd, Inst. of Psychiatry, 1966-70; Central Academic Council, British Postgrad. Med. Fedn, 1975-. *Publications:* (Jointly) Studies of the Renal Circulation, 1947; The Hypothalamus and Pituitary Gland; papers in various medical and scientific journals. *Address:* 5 Seaforth Place, Buckingham Gate, SW1E 6AB. *T:* 01-834 3087. *Clubs:* Athenæum, Garrick, Savage, Green Room.

DANIEL, Reginald Jack, OBE 1958; CEng, FRINA, FIMarE; RCNC; Director-General Ships and Head of Royal Corps of Naval Constructors since 1974; also Senior Ministry of Defence Representative, Bath; *b* 27 Feb. 1920; *o s* of Reginald Daniel Daniel and Florence Emily (*née* Woods); *m* 1st, Joyce Earnshaw (marr. diss.); two *s*; 2nd, 1977, Elizabeth, *o d* of George Mitchell, Long Ashton, Som. *Educ:* Royal Naval Engineering Coll., Keyham; Royal Naval Coll., Greenwich. Grad., 1942; subseq. engaged in submarine design. Served War of 1939-45; Staff of C-in-C's Far East Fleet and Pacific Fleet, 1943-45. Atomic Bomb Tests, Bikini, 1946; Admty, Whitehall, 1947-49; Admty, Bath, Aircraft Carrier Design, 1949-52; Guided Missile Cruiser design, 1952-56; Nuclear and Polaris Submarine design, 1956-65; IDC, 1966; Materials, R&D, 1967-68; Head of Forward Design, 1968-70; Deputy Director, Submarine Design and Production, 1970-74. Fellow, Fellowship of Engineering, 1976. *Publications:* Parsons Meml Lecture, 1976; papers for RINA, etc. *Recreations:* gardening, motoring, music. *Address:* Meadowland, Cleveland Walk, Bath BA2 6JU. *Clubs:* Royal Commonwealth Society; Bath and County.

DANIEL, Stuart; *see* Daniel, J. S.

DANIELL, Brig. Averell John, CBE 1955; DSO 1945; *b* 19 June 1903; *s* of late Lt-Col Oswald James Daniell, QO Royal West Kent Regt, and late May Frances Drummond Daniell (*née* Adams); *m* 1934, Phyllis Kathleen Rhona Grove-Annesley; two *s* one *d*. *Educ:* Wellington Coll.; RM Acad., Woolwich. Commissioned, Royal Field Artillery, 1923; Captain, RA, 1936; Major, 1940; Lt-Col, 1943. Served War of 1939-45; Middle East, Iraq, Burma. Col, 1948; Brig., 1952; retired, 1955. Administrative Officer, Staff Coll., Camberley, 1955-61. Colonel Commandant, Royal Artillery, 1956-66. *Address:* Oak Lodge, Hythe, Kent. *T:* Hythe 66494.

DANIELL, Sir Peter (Averell), Kt 1971; TD 1950; DL; Senior Government Broker, 1963-73; *b* 8 Dec. 1909; *s* of R. H. A. Daniell and Kathleen Daniell (*née* Monsell); *m* 1935, Leonie M.

Harrison; two *s* one *d*. *Educ:* Eton Coll.; Trinity Coll., Oxford (MA). Joined Mullens & Co., 1932, Partner, 1945; retd 1973. Served KRRC, 1939-45, Middle East and Italy. DL Surrey 1976. *Recreations:* shooting, fishing, golf. *Address:* Glebe House, Buckland, Surrey. *T:* Betchworth 2320. *Clubs:* Brooks's, Alpine.

DANIELL, Ralph Allen, CBE 1965 (OBE 1958); HM Diplomatic Service, retired; *b* 26 Jan. 1915; 2nd *s* of late Reginald Allen Daniell; *m* 1943, Diana Lesley (*née* Tyndale); one *s* three *d*. *Educ:* Lancing Coll.; University Coll., Oxford. Appointed to Board of Trade, 1937. Joined HM Forces, 1942; served with Royal Tank Regt in North Africa and Italian campaigns, 1943-45. Appointed to HM Foreign Service as First Sec., 1946; Mexico City, 1946; Rome, 1949; Foreign Office, 1951; Helsinki, 1953; Counsellor, 1958; Washington, 1958; New York, 1959; Cairo, 1962; Wellington, 1967; Consul-Gen., Chicago, 1972-74. *Address:* The Old Forge, Poulner, Ringwood, Hants BH24 1TY.

DANIELL, Roy Lorentz, CBE 1957; Barrister-at-Law; Charity Commissioner, 1953-62; *s* of late Edward Cecil Daniell, Abbotswood, Speen, Bucks; *m* 1936, Sheila Moore-Gwyn, *d* of late Maj. Moore-Gwyn, Clayton Court, Liss, Hants. *Educ:* Gresham's Sch., Holt; New Coll., Oxford. *Address:* Common Side, Russell's Water, Henley on Thames, Oxon. *T:* Nettlebed 696. *Club:* United Oxford & Cambridge University.

DANIELLI, Prof. James Frederic, FRS 1957; PhD, DSc, MIBiol; Professor, Worcester Polytechnic Institute, since 1974; *b* 13 Nov. 1911; *s* of James Frederic Danielli; *m* 1937, Mary Guy; one *s* one *d*. *Educ:* Wembley County Sch.; London, Princeton and Cambridge Univs. Commonwealth Fund Fellow, 1933-35; Beit Medical Research Fellow, 1938-42; Fellow of St John's Coll., Cambridge, 1942-45; Physiologist to Marine Biological Assoc., 1946; Reader in Cell Physiology, Royal Cancer Hospital, 1946-49; Prof. of Zoology, King's Coll., London, 1949-62; Chm., Dept of Biochemical Pharmacology, Univ. of Buffalo, 1962-65; Provost for Faculty of Natural Sciences and Mathematics, 1967-69; Dir, Center for Theoretical Biol., 1965-74, and Asst to Pres., 1969-72, State Univ. of NY at Buffalo (formerly Univ. of Buffalo, NY). *Publications:* Permeability of Natural Membranes (with H. Davson), 1943; Cell Physiology and Pharmacology, 1950; Cytochemistry: a critical approach, 1953; Editor: Journal of Theoretical Biology; Internat. Review of Cytology; Progress in Surface and Membrane Science. *Address:* Worcester Polytechnic Institute, Worcester, Mass 01609, USA; Tangnefedd, Dinas Cross, Dyfed, Wales.

DANIELS, David Kingsley, CBE 1963 (OBE 1945); retired as Secretary-General, Royal Commonwealth Society (1958-67); *b* 17 Feb. 1905; *y s* of late E. Daniels and Anne M. Daniels; unmarried. *Educ:* Kent Coll., Canterbury; St Edmund Hall, Oxford. Colonial Administrative Service, Tanganyika, 1928; King's African Rifles, 1940; Chief Staff Officer, Military Admin., Somalia, 1941 (despatches); Senior Civil Affairs Officer, Reserved Areas, Ethiopia, 1943-45 (OBE); Chief Secretary (Colonel), Military Administration, Malaya, 1945-46; Principal Asst Secretary, Singapore, 1947-49; Under Secretary, Singapore, 1950-52; Dep. Chief Secretary, Federation of Malaya, 1952-55; Director, Malayan Students Dept in UK, 1956-58. *Address:* Little Oaten, 28 Oaten Hill, Canterbury, Kent. *T:* Canterbury 63029. *Clubs:* Royal Commonwealth Society, MCC.

DANIELS, George, FSA, FBHI; author, watch maker, horological consultant; *b* 19 Aug. 1926; *s* of George Daniels and Beatrice (*née* Cadou); *m* 1964, Juliet Anne (*née* Marryat); one *d*. *Educ:* elementary. 2nd Bn E Yorks Regt, 1944-47. Started professional horology, 1947; restoration of historical watches, 1956-; hand watch making to own designs, 1969-. FSA 1976; FBHI 1951. Worshipful Co. of Clockmakers: Liveryman, 1968; Jun. Warden, 1977; Renter Warden, 1978; Asst Hon. Surveyor. Arts, Sciences and Learning Award, City Corporation, London, 1974; Victor Kullberg Medal, Stockholm Watch Guild, 1977. *Publications:* Watches (jtly), 1965 (3rd edn 1978); English and American Watches, 1967; The Art of Breguet, 1975 (2nd edn 1978); (jtly) Clocks and Watches of the Worshipful Company of Clockmakers, 1975; Sir David Salomons Collection, 1978. *Recreations:* vintage cars, fast motorcycles, opera, Scotch whisky. *Address:* 34 New Bond Street, W1A 2AA.

DANIELS, Harold Albert; *b* 8 June 1915; *s* of Albert Pollikett Daniels and Eleanor Sarah Maud Daniels (*née* Flahey); *m* 1946, Frances Victoria Jerdan; one *s*. *Educ:* Mercers' Sch.; Christ's Coll., Cambridge. BA 1937; Wren Prize 1938; MA 1940. Asst Principal, Post Office, 1938; Admiralty, 1942; Post Office, 1945; Principal, 1946; Asst Sec., 1950; Under-Sec., 1961; Min. of Posts and Telecommunications, 1969. Asst Under Sec. of State, Home Office, 1974-76. *Address:* Lyle Court Cottage, Bradbourne Road, Sevenoaks, Kent. *T:* Sevenoaks 54039.

DANIELS, Prof. Henry Ellis; Professor of Mathematical Statistics, University of Birmingham, since 1957; *b* 2 Oct. 1912; *s* of Morris and Hannah Daniels; *m* 1950, Barbara Edith Pickering; one *s* one *d. Educ:* Sciennes Sch., Edinburgh; George Heriot's Sch., Edinburgh; Edinburgh Univ.; Clare Coll., Cambridge. MA Edinburgh 1933, BA Cantab 1935, PhD Edinburgh 1943. Statistician, Wool Industries Research Assoc., 1935-47; Ministry of Aircraft Production, 1942-45; Lecturer in Mathematics, University of Cambridge, 1947-57; Fellow, King's Coll. Cambridge, 1975-76. Pres., Royal Statistical Soc., 1974-75; Fellow Inst. of Mathematical Statistics; elected Mem. Internat. Statistical Inst., 1956. Guy Medal (Silver) Royal Statistical Society. *Publications:* papers in Journal of the Royal Statistical Society, Annals of Mathematical Statistics, Biometrika, etc. *Recreations:* playing the piano, repairing watches. *Address:* 253 Northfield Road, Kings Norton, Birmingham B30 1EB. *T:* 021-458 1467.

DANIELS, Jeffery; Director, Geffrye Museum, London, since 1969; *b* 13 July 1932; *s* of John Henry and Edith Mary Daniels. *Educ:* Milford Haven Grammar Sch.; Balliol Coll., Oxford. Read Modern History; MA Oxon. Heal & Son Ltd, 1953-56; Teaching (ILEA), 1956-69. Mem., Internat. Consultative Cttee for Mostra di Sebastiano Ricci, Udine, 1976; Hon. Sec., London Fedn of Museums and Art Galls. Member: AICA; Assoc. of Art Historians. *Publications:* Architecture in England, 1968; Biography and catalogue raisonné of Sebastiano Ricci, 1976; contrib. to: The Times, The Connoisseur, Apollo, Art and Artists, The Burlington Magazine; Art News (USA). *Recreations:* opera, ballet, Venice. *Address:* 5 Edith Grove, Chelsea, SW10 0JZ. *T:* 01-352 7692. *Clubs:* Society of Authors, Motor Sports.

DANILOVA, Alexandra, lecturer, teacher and choreographer; *b* Pskoff, Russia, 20 Nov. 1906; *d* of Dionis Daniloff and Claudia Gotovzeffa; *m* 1st, 1931, Giuseppe Massera (*d* 1936); 2nd, 1941, Kazimir Kokic (marr. annulled, 1949). *Educ:* Theatrical Sch., Petrograd. Maryinski Theatre, Leningrad, 1923-24; Diaghileff Company, 1925-29; Waltzes from Vienna, 1931; Colonel de Basil Company, 1933-37; Prima Ballerina, Ballet Russe de Monte Carlo, 1938-58. Teacher (on Faculty) of School of American Ballet. Guest artist Royal Festival Hall, London, 1955; Ballerina in Oh Captain (Musical), New York, 1958. With own Company has toured West Indies, Japan, Philippines, USA, Canada and S Africa. Capezio Award (for outstanding services to Art of the Dance), 1958; Guest Choreographer Metropolitan Opera House, Guest Teacher and Choreographer, Germany (Krefeld Festival of Dance) and Amsterdam, 1959-60; Choreographed Coppelia for La Scala di Milano, 1961; Lecture performances throughout US; Guest Choreographer, Washington Ballet, 1962-64. *Recreations:* needlework, ping-pong, gardening. *Address:* Apartment 2 P, Carnegie House, 100 West 57 Street, New York, NY 10019, USA; RFD 2, Church Road, Lakewood, New Jersey, USA.

DANINOS, Pierre; French Author; *b* Paris, 26 May 1913; *m* 1st, 1942, Jane Marrain; one *s* two *d*; 2nd, 1968, Marie-Pierre Dourneau. *Educ:* Lycée Janson de Sailly, Paris. Began to write for newspapers, 1931; reporter for French press in England, USA, etc. Liaison agent with British Army, Dunkirk, 1940. Published first book in Rio de Janeiro, 1940; returned to France, 1941, from South America, Chronicler for Le Figaro. *Publications:* Les Carnets du Bon Dieu (Prix Interallié 1947); L'Eternel Second, 1949; Sonia les autres et moi (Prix Courteline, 1952) (English trans., Life with Sonia, 1958); Les Carnets du Major Thompson, 1954 (English trans., Major Thompson Lives in France, 1955); Le Secret du Major Thompson, 1956 (English trans., Major Thompson and I, 1957); Vacances à Tous Prix, 1958; Un certain Monsieur Blot, 1960 (English trans., 1961); Le Jacassin, 1962; Snobissimo, 1964; Le 36ème dessous, 1966; Le Major Tricolore, 1968; Ludovic Morateur, 1970; Le Pyjama, 1972; Les Touristocrates, 1974; Made in France, 1977. *Recreations:* tennis, ski-ing, collecting British hobbies. *Address:* 81 rue de Grenelle, Paris 7e, France.

DANKS, Sir Alan (John), KBE 1970; Chairman, (NZ) University Grants Committee, 1966-77; *b* 9 June 1914; *s* of T. E. Danks; *m* 1943, Loma Beryl Hall (*née* Drabble). *Educ:* West Christchurch High Sch.; Univ. of Canterbury, NZ. Teaching profession, 1931-43; Economics Dept of Univ. of Canterbury, 1943-66; Prof., 1962; Pro-Vice Chancellor of Univ. of Canterbury, 1964. Hon. LLD Canterbury, 1973. *Address:* 116 Upland Road, Wellington, New Zealand. *Club:* Wellington, NZ.

DANKWORTH, Mrs C. D.; *see* Laine, Cleo.

DANKWORTH, John Philip William, CBE 1974; ARAM 1969; musician; *b* 20 Sept. 1927; British; *m* 1960, Cleo Laine, *qv*; one *s* one *d. Educ:* Monoux Grammar Sch. Studied Royal Academy of Music, 1944-46. Closely involved with post-war development of British jazz, 1947-60; formed large jazz orchestra, 1953. Composed works for combined jazz and symphonic musicians including: Improvisations (with Matyas Seiber, 1959); Escapade (commissioned by Northern Sinfonia Orch., 1967); Tom Sawyer's Saturday, for narrator and orchestra (commissioned by Farnham Festival), 1967; String Quartet, 1971; Piano Concerto (commissioned by Westminster Festival, 1972). Many important film scores (1964-) including: Saturday Night and Sunday Morning, Darling, The Servant, Morgan, Accident; other works include Palabras, 1970. *Recreations:* driving, household maintenance. *Address:* The Old Rectory, Wavendon, Milton Keynes MK17 8LT. *Club:* Ronnie Scott's.

DANN, Howard Ernest, CBE 1965; Director, Snowy Mountains Engineering Corporation, 1970-74, and Commissioner, Snowy Mountains Hydro-Electric Authority, 1967-74; *b* 27 April 1914; *m* 1946, Marjorie Bush; two *s. Educ:* Brighton Grammar Sch. (Dux); University of Melbourne (BMechE). AIF, 1940-44; Major RAEME. Supt. Engineer, Electric Authority of NSW, 1946-50; Member Commonwealth and States Snowy River Cttee, 1946-49 (NSW Representative, Techn. Cttee); Chief Engineer Investigations, Snowy Mountains Hydro-Electric Authority, prior to Associate Comr, Snowy Mountains Hydro-Electric Authority, 1959-67. FIEAust, MASCE. *Publications:* papers in journals of Instn of Engrs (Australia) and American Society of Civil Engineers. *Recreation:* golf. *Address:* 20 Attunga Place, Cooma North, NSW 2630, Australia. *T:* 2-1539.

DANN, Mrs Jill; *b* 10 Sept. 1929; *d* of Harold Norman Cartwright and Marjorie Alice Thornton; *m* 1952, Anthony John Dann; two *s* two *d* (and one *s* decd). *Educ:* Solihull High Sch. for Girls, Malvern Hall; Birmingham Univ. (LLB); St Hilda's Coll., Oxford (BCL). Called to the Bar, Inner Temple, 1952. Mayoress of Chippenham, 1964-65. Church Commissioner, 1968-; Member: General Synod of Church of England, and of its Standing Cttee, 1971-; Crown Appointments Commn, 1977-. *Recreations:* reading, sport. *Address:* Harnish Mead, 30 Hardenhuish Lane, Chippenham, Wilts SN14 6HN. *T:* Chippenham 3142.

DANN, Rt. Rev. Robert William; Co-Adjutor Bishop, Diocese of Melbourne, since 1969; *b* 28 Sept. 1914; *s* of James and Ruth Dann; *m* 1949, Yvonne (*née* Newnham); one *s* two *d. Educ:* Trinity Coll., Univ. of Melbourne. BA Hons Melbourne 1946. Deacon, 1945; Priest, 1946. Dir of Youth and Religious Education, Dio. Melbourne, 1946; Incumbent: St Matthew's, Cheltenham, 1951; St George's, Malvern, 1956; St John's, Footscray, 1961; Archdeacon of Essendon, 1961; Dir of Evangelism and Extension, Dio. Melbourne, 1963. *Address:* 8 Stanley Grove, Canterbury, Victoria 3126, Australia. *T:* 826714. *Club:* Royal Automobile of Victoria (Melbourne).

[*See supplementary pages.*

DANNATT, Sir Cecil, Kt 1961; OBE 1943; MC 1917; FIEE; MIMechE; Director, Associated Electrical Industries, 1954-63, retired (Vice-Chairman, 1960-62); *b* 21 Sept. 1896; *s* of late Mark and Hannah Dannatt; *m* 1925, Winifred Ethel Flear; two *s. Educ:* Burton-on-Trent Grammar Sch.; Durham Univ. DSc University of Durham, 1936. Research Engineer, 1921-40; Prof. of Electrical Engineering, Birmingham Univ., 1940-44. Managing Director Metropolitan-Vickers Electrical Co., 1954-60. *Publications:* Electrical Transmission and Interconnection, 1926; prize papers, IEE. *Recreation:* golf. *Address:* The Willows, Oxshott, Surrey. *T:* Oxshott 2424. *Club:* Royal Automobile.

DANNATT, Prof. (James) Trevor, ARA 1977; FRIBA; Senior Partner, Trevor Dannatt & Partners, Architects; Professor of Architecture, Manchester University, since 1975; *b* 15 Jan. 1920; *s* of George Herbert and Jane Ellen Dannatt; *m* 1953, Joan Howell Davies; one *s* one *d. Educ:* Colfes Sch.; Sch. of Architecture, Regent Polytechnic (Dip. Arch.). Professional experience in office of Jane B. Drew and E. Maxwell Fry, 1943-48; Architects Dept, LCC (Royal Festival Hall Gp), 1948-52; commenced private practice, 1952. Vis. Prof., Washington Univ., St Louis, 1976. Assessor for national and international architectural competitions. Editor, Architects' Year Book, 1945-62. Architectural work includes private houses, housing, school, university and welfare buildings, conservation and restoration. Won internat. competition for conference complex in Riyadh, Saudi Arabia, 1974. *Publications:* Modern Architecture in Britain, 1959; Trevor Dannatt: Buildings and Interiors 1951-72, 1972; contribs to Architectural Rev., Architects' Jl, and various foreign journals. *Recreations:* the arts, including architecture. *Address:* 8 St Mary's Grove, N1. *T:* 01-486 6844. *Club:* Travellers'.

DANNAY, Frederic; co-author with late Manfred B. Lee, under pseudonym of Ellery Queen. Visiting Professor at University of Texas, 1958-59. *Publications:* Roman Hat Mystery, 1929; French Powder Mystery, 1930; Dutch Shoe Mystery, 1931; Greek Coffin Mystery, Egyptian Cross Mystery, 1932; American Gun Mystery, Siamese Twin Mystery, 1933; Chinese Orange Mystery, Adventures of Ellery Queen, 1934; Spanish Cape Mystery, 1935; Halfway House, 1936; Door Between, 1937; Devil to Pay, Four of Hearts, Challenge to the Reader, 1938; Dragon's Teeth, 1939; New Adventures of Ellery Queen, 1940; 101 Years' Entertainment, 1941; Calamity Town, The Detective Short Story (a bibliography), Sporting Blood, 1942; There Was an Old Woman, Female of the Species, 1943; Misadventures of Sherlock Holmes, Best Stories from Ellery Queen's Mystery Magazine, 1944; Case Book of Ellery Queen, Murderer Is a Fox, Rogues' Gallery, 1945; The Queen's Awards (1946), To the Queen's Taste, 1946; The Queen's Awards (1947), Murder By Experts, 1947; 20th Century Detective Stories, The Queen's Awards (1948), Ten Days' Wonder, 1948; The Queen's Awards (1949), Cat of Many Tails, 1949; The Queen's Awards (Fifth Series), Literature of Crime, Double, Double, 1950; Origin of Evil, Queen's Quorum, The Queen's Awards (Sixth Series), 1951; Calendar of Crime, King is Dead, The Queen's Awards (Seventh Series), 1952; Scarlet Letters, The Queen's Awards (Eighth Series), 1953; Glass Village, Ellery Queen's Awards (Ninth Series), 1954; QBI: Queen's Bureau of Investigation, Ellery Queen's Awards (Tenth Series), 1955; Inspector Queen's Own Case, Ellery Queen's Awards (Eleventh Series), 1956; In the Queens' Parlor, Ellery Queen's Awards (Twelfth Series), 1957; The Finishing Stroke, Ellery Queen's 13th Annual, 1958; Ellery Queen's 14th Mystery Annual, 1959; Ellery Queen's 15th Mystery Annual, 1960; Ellery Queen's 16th Mystery Annual, 1961; Quintessence of Queen, To Be Read Before Midnight, 1962; Player on the Other Side, Ellery Queen's Mystery Mix, 1963; And On the Eighth Day, Double Dozen, 1964; Queens Full, The Fourth Side of the Triangle, Ellery Queen's 20th Anniversary Annual, 1965; Ellery Queen's Crime Carousel, Study in Terror, 1966; Poetic Justice, Ellery Queen's All-Star Line-up, Face to Face, 1967; Ellery Queen's Mystery Parade, QED: Queen's Experiments in Detection, House of Brass, 1968; Cop Out Minimysteries, Ellery Queen's Murder Menu, 24th Mystery Annual, 1969; The Last Woman in His Life, Ellery Queen's Grand Slam, 1970; A Fine and Private Place, Ellery Queen's Headliners, 26th Mystery Annual, The Golden 13, 1971; Ellery Queen's Mystery Bag, 1972; Ellery Queen's Crookbook, 1974; Ellery Queen's Murdercade, 1975; (ed) Ellery Queen's Christmas Hamper, 1975; Ellery Queen's Crime Wave, 1976; Four Men Called John, Ellery Queen's Searches and Seizures, 1977; Co-author with late Manfred B. Lee, under pseudonym of Barnaby Ross; *publications:* Tragedy of X, Tragedy of Y, 1932; Tragedy of Z, Drury Lane's Last Case, 1933. All four Barnaby Ross publications reissued as by Ellery Queen, 1940-46. Co-author with late Manfred B. Lee, of Ellery Queen, Jr juvenile mysteries and of Radio and Television Programs (Adventures of Ellery Queen). Co-editor with late Manfred B. Lee, of 21 collections of short stories by Dashiell Hammett, Stuart Palmer, John Dickson Carr, Margery Allingham, Roy Vickers, O. Henry, Erle Stanley Gardner, Lawrence Treat, Edward D. Hoch, Michael Gilbert, Stanley Ellin and Julian Symonds. Co-editor with late Manfred B. Lee, of Ellery Queen's Mystery Magazine (37th year of publication). Under author's name of Daniel Nathan; *publication:* The Golden Summer, 1953. The following address is for all names (Frederic Dannay, Ellery Queen, Barnaby Ross, Daniel Nathan). *Address:* 29 Byron Lane, Larchmont, New York 10538, USA.

DANTER, Harold Walter Phillips; *b* 31 March 1886; *s* of late Lieut-Col F. W. Danter, VD, RE, JP, Gerrards Cross, Bucks; unmarried. *Educ:* Christ's Hospital, Hertford, London, and West Horsham. Clerk in the Bank of England, 1904-14. Held commission in 5th East Surrey Regt, 1908-10. Student at Lichfield Theological Coll., 1914-16; Deacon, 1916; Priest, 1917. Work with Church Army, BEF, France, 1918-19. Curate: St Paul's, Stafford, 1917-19; Holy Trinity, Woolwich, 1919-21; SS Mary and John, Oxford, 1921-28; Vicar of Pattishall, Northants, 1928-33; Rural Dean, Brackley III deanery, 1933-53; Vicar of Brackley, 1933-56; Non-residentiary Canon of Peterborough Cathedral, 1955-56; Canon Emeritus of Peterborough Cathedral, 1956-58. Received into the Roman Catholic Church, March 1958. *Publication:* The Hill of Daydreams (Poems), 1917. *Recreation:* general interest in art and literature. *Address:* 32 Thorncliffe Road, Oxford. *T:* Oxford 55598.

DAR-ES-SALAAM, Archbishop of, (RC), since 1969; HE Cardinal Laurean Rugambwa; *b* Bukongo, 12 July 1912; *s* of Domitian Rushubirwa and Asteria Mukaboshezi. *Educ:* Rutabo, Rubya Seminary; Katigondo Seminary; Univ. of Propaganda, Rome (DCL 1951). Priest 1943; Bishop of Rutabo, 1952-60; Cardinal 1960; Bishop of Bukoba, 1960-69. Member: Knights of Columbus; Knights of St Peter Claver. Hon. Dr of Laws: Notre Dame, 1961; St Joseph's Coll., Philadelphia, 1961; Rosary Hill Coll., Buffalo, 1965; Hon. DHL New Rochelle, 1961; Hon. Dr Civil and Canon Law, Georgetown Univ. (Jesuits), 1961; Giving of the Scroll, Catholic Univ. of America, 1961. *Address:* Archbishop's House, PO Box 167, Dar-es-Salaam, Tanzania, East Africa.

DAR-ES-SALAAM, Bishop of; *see* Tanzania, Archbishop of.

DARBISHIRE, David Harold, JP; Chairman, FMC Ltd, since 1975; *b* 23 Oct. 1914; *s* of H. D. Darbishire and Hester E. Bright (*g d* of Rt Hon. John Bright, MP); *m* 1939, Phebe Irene Lankester; three *d*. *Educ:* Sidcot; Wye Agric. Coll. (Wye DipAgric). Farmer; Vice-Pres., NFU, 1971-74. Mem., Metrication Bd, 1970-77. *Recreations:* hunting, fishing. *Address:* Manor Farm, Wormleighton, Leamington Spa CV33 0XW. *Club:* Farmers'.

DARBOURNE, John William Charles, CBE 1977; RIBA; Partner, Darbourne & Darke, Architects and Landscape Planners, since 1961; *b* 11 Jan. 1935; *s* of late William Leslie Darbourne and Violet Yorke; *m* 1960, Noreen Fifield; one *s* three *d*. *Educ:* Battersea Grammar Sch.; University Coll., London Univ. (BA Hons Arch. 1958). Harvard (MLA). RIBA 1960; AILA. Asst Architect in private practice, 1958-60; Post-grad. study in landscape arch. and planning, Harvard, 1960, completed degree course, 1964; estabd own practice with Geoffrey Darke (following successful entry in national architect. competition), 1961; practice moved to Richmond, 1963, and steadily grew to undertake several large commns, particularly public housing, 1966-. Involved in professional and local cttees, and national confs. *Recreations:* working late, the piano; latterly tennis and squash and now the obsessive folly of golf. *Address:* 10 Dynevor Road, Richmond, Surrey. *T:* 01-940 2241.

DARBY, Rt. Rev. Harold Richard; *see* Sherwood, Bishop Suffragan of.

DARBY, Henry Clifford, OBE 1946; LittD 1960; FBA 1967; Professor of Geography in the University of Cambridge, 1966-76; Fellow of King's College, Cambridge; *b* 7 Feb. 1909; *s* of Evan Darby, Resolven, Glamorgan; *m* 1941, Eva Constance Thomson; two *d*. *Educ:* Neath County Sch.; St Catharine's Coll., Cambridge. 1st Class Geographical Tripos, Parts I, 1926, II, 1928; PhD 1931; MA 1932. Lecturer in Geography, University of Cambridge, 1931-45; Ehrman Fellow, King's Coll., Cambridge, 1932-45; Intelligence Corps, 1940-41 (Capt.); Admiralty, 1941-45; John Rankin Prof. of Geography, University of Liverpool, 1945-49; Prof. of Geography, University Coll. London, 1949-66; Leverhulme Research Fellow, 1946-48; Visiting Prof. Univ. of Chicago, 1952, Harvard Univ., 1959, 1964-65, and Univ. of Washington, 1963; Mem. Council, English Place-Name Soc., 1953-; Mem., Royal Commission on Historical Monuments (England), 1953-; Mem., National Parks Commn, 1958-63; Mem., Water Resources Board, 1964-68. Pres. Institute of British Geographers, 1961; Pres., Section E British Assoc., 1963; Chm., British National Cttee for Geography, 1973-. Hon. Member: Croatian Geog Soc., 1957; Royal Netherlands Geog. Soc., 1958; RGS, 1976; Hon. Fellow, St Catharine's Coll., Cambridge, 1960. Victoria Medal, RGS, 1963. Daly Medal, American Geog. Soc., 1963. Hon. LHD Chicago, 1967; Hon. LittD Liverpool, 1966; Hon. DLitt: Durham, 1970; Hull, 1975; Ulster, 1977. *Publications:* An Historical Geography of England before AD 1800 (Editor, and Contributor), 1936; The Cambridge Region (Editor and Contributor), 1938; The Medieval Fenland, 1940; The Draining of the Fens, 3rd edn, 1968; The University Atlas (with H. Fullard), 16th edn, 1974; The Library Atlas (with H. Fullard), 10th edn, 1973; The New Cambridge Modern History Atlas (with H. Fullard), 1970; General Editor and Contributor, The Domesday Geography of England, 7 vols, 1952-77; (ed and contrib.) A New Historical Geography of England, 1973; articles in geographical and historical journals. *Address:* 60 Storey's Way, Cambridge. *T:* Cambridge 54745.

DARBY, Peter Howard, CBE 1973; QFSM 1970; Chief Officer of the London Fire Brigade, since 1977; *b* 8 July 1924; *s* of William Cyril Darby and Beatrice Colin; *m* 1948, Ellen Josephine Glynn; one *s* one *d*. *Educ:* City of Birmingham Coll. of Advanced Technology. Fire Brigades: Dep. Ch. Officer, Suffolk and Ipswich FB, 1963; Chief Officer, Nottingham FB, 1966; Chief

Officer, Lancashire FB, 1967; County Fire Officer, Greater Manchester FB, 1974; Regional Fire Comdr (No 10) NW Region, 1974-76; Regional Fire Adviser (No 5) Greater London Region, 1977. Pres., Chief and Asst Chief Fire Officers' Assoc., 1975-76; Fire Adviser, Assoc. of Metropolitan Authorities, 1975; Mem. Bd, Fire Service Coll., 1977; Mem. Adv. Council, Central Fire Brigades, 1977; Adviser, Nat. Jt Council for Local Authority Fire Brigades, 1977. *Recreations:* fell-walking, golf, fishing, sailing. *Address:* London Fire Brigade Headquarters, 8 Albert Embankment, SE1 7PB. *T:* 01-582 3811. *Club:* KSC.

D'ARCY, Surgeon Rear-Adm. Thomas Norman, CB 1953; CBE 1950; retired; *b* 12 Feb. 1896; *s* of Dr S. A. D'Arcy, Rosslea, County Fermanagh, Ireland; *m* 1922, Eleanor Lennox Broadbent, Port Said; two *s* two *d. Educ:* Royal School, Cavan; RCS Dublin. Qualified, 1919; Surgeon Probationer RNVR, 1915-18; Surgeon Lieut RN, 1919; Surgeon Lieut-Comdr 1925; Surgeon Comdr 1930; Surgeon Capt. 1943; Surgeon Rear-Adm., 1951; Medical Officer in Charge, RN Hospital, Plymouth, and Command Medical Officer, 1951-54. KHS 1951; QHS 1952-54. CStJ 1953. Gilbert Blane medal, 1929. *Publications:* surgical articles to Jl of RN Medical Service (Co-Editor, 1946-47). *Recreations:* hockey (old Irish International), fishing. *Address:* South Wind, Witley, Surrey. *T:* Godalming 5751.

DARCY DE KNAYTH, Baroness (18th in line), *cr* 1332; **Davina Marcia Ingrams** (*née* Herbert); *b* 10 July 1938; *d* of late Squadron Leader Viscount Clive (*d* on active service, 1943), and of Vida, *o d* of late Capt. James Harold Cuthbert, DSO, Scots Guards (she *m* 2nd, 1945, Brig. Derek Schreiber, MVO (*d* 1972)); *S* to father's Barony, 1943; *m* 1960, Rupert George Ingrams (*d* 1964), *s* of late Leonard Ingrams and of Mrs Ingrams; one *s* two *d. Heir: s* Hon. Caspar David Ingrams, *b* 5 Jan. 1962. *Address:* Camley Corner, Stubbings, Maidenhead, Berks.

D'ARCY HART, P. M.; see Hart, P. M. D.

DARELL, Brig. Sir Jeffrey (Lionel), 8th Bt, *cr* 1795; MC 1945; *b* 2 Oct. 1919; *s* of late Lt-Col Guy Marsland Darell, MC (3rd *s* of 5th Bt); *S* cousin, 1959; *m* 1953, Bridget Mary, *e d* of Maj.-Gen. Sir Allan Adair, 6th Bt, *qv*; one *s* two *d. Educ:* Eton; RMC, Sandhurst. Commissioned Coldstream Guards, July 1939; served War of 1939-45: ADC to GOC-in-C, Southern Comd, 1942; Bde Major, Guards Bde, 1953-55; Officer Comdg 1st Bn Coldstream Guards, 1957-59; GSO1, PS12, War Office, 1959; College Comdr RMA Sandhurst, 1961-64; Comdg Coldstream Guards, 1964-65; Comdr, 56 Inf. Brigade (TA), 1965-67; Vice-Pres., Regular Commns Bd, 1968-70; Comdt, Mons OCS, 1970-72; MoD, 1972-74; retd 1974. ADC to HM the Queen, 1973-74. *Recreations:* normal. *Heir: s* Guy Jeffrey Adair Darell, *b* 8 June 1961. *Address:* 55 Green Street, W1. *T:* 01-629 3860; Denton Lodge, Harleston, Norfolk. *T:* Homersfield 206. *Club:* Cavalry and Guards.

DARESBURY, 2nd Baron, *cr* 1927, of Walton, Co. Chester; **Edward Greenall,** Bt, *cr* 1876; late Life Guards; *b* 12 Oct. 1902; *o* surv. *s* of 1st Baron Daresbury, CVO, and late Frances Eliza, OBE 1945, *d* of Capt. Wynne-Griffith, 1st Royal Dragoons; *S* father 1938; *m* 1st 1925, Joan Madeline (*d* 1926), *d* of Capt. Robert Thomas Oliver Sheriffe, of Goadby Hall, Melton Mowbray; 2nd, 1927, Josephine (*d* 1958), *y d* of Brig.-Gen. Sir Joseph Laycock, KCMG, DSO; one *s* ; 3rd, 1966, Lady Helena Hilton Green (*née* Wentworth-Fitzwilliam) (*d* 1970), 4th *d* of 7th Earl Fitzwilliam. *Educ:* Wixenford; Eton. *Heir: s* Hon. Edward Gilbert Greenall [*b* 27 Nov. 1928; *m* 1952, Margaret Ada, *y d* of late C. J. Crawford and of Mrs Crawford, Wayside, St Andrews; three *s* one *d*]. *Address:* Altavilla, Askeaton, Co. Limerick, Eire. *T:* Rathkeale 138.

DARGIE, Sir William Alexander, Kt 1970; CBE 1969 (OBE 1960); FRSA 1951; artist; portrait, figure and landscape painter; Chairman, Commonwealth Art Advisory Board, Prime Minister's Department, 1969-73 (Member, 1953-73); *b* 4 June 1912; *s* of Andrew and Adelaide Dargie; *m* 1937, Kathleen, *d* of late G. H. Howitt; one *s* one *d. Educ:* Melbourne, and in studio of A. D. Colquhoun. Official War Artist (Capt.) with AIF in Middle East, Burma, New Guinea, India, 1941-46. Dir, National Gallery of Victoria Art Schs, 1946-53. Member: Interim Council of Nat. Gallery Canberra, 1968-72; Nat. Capital Planning Cttee, Canberra, 1970-73; Aboriginal Arts Adv. Cttee, 1970-72; Trustee: Native Cultural Reserve, Port Moresby, Papua-New Guinea, 1970-73; Museum of Papua-New Guinea, 1970-73. Archibald Prize for portraiture, 1941, 1942, 1945, 1946, 1947, 1950, 1952, 1956; Woodward Award, 1940; McPhillimy Award, 1940; McKay Prize, 1941. Painted portrait of The Queen for Commonwealth of Aust., 1954; the Duke of Gloucester, 1947; the Duke of Edinburgh for City of Melbourne, 1956. Portraits of

Sir Macfarlane Burnet, Sir William Ashton, Sir Lionel Lindsay, acquired for Commonwealth Nat. Collection. Rep. in public and private collections in Aust., NZ, England and USA. One-man exhibition, Leger Galls, London, 1958. Exhibits with RA and Royal Soc. of Portrait Painters. *Publication:* On Painting a Portrait, 1956. *Recreations:* books, chess, tennis. *Address:* 19 Irilbarra Road, Canterbury, Victoria 3126, Australia. *T:* 836 3396 Melbourne. *Clubs:* Melbourne, Savage (Melbourne).

DARKIN, Maj.-Gen. Roy Bertram, CBE 1969; Commander Base Organisation RAOC, 1971-73, retired; *b* 3 Sept. 1916; *s* of late Bertram Duncan and of late Isobel Doris Darkin, Aylsham, Norfolk; *m* 1945, Louise Margaret, *d* of late Francis Charles Sydney Green and late Lilian Green, Buckden, Hunts; no *c. Educ:* Felsted School. Commnd Baluch Regt, IA, 1940; war service, NW Frontier, Iraq, Persia (despatches); psc 1943; G2 HQ ALFSEA service, Burma; DAQMG India Office, 1945; transf. RAOC, 1946; Sen. Instructor, RAAOC Sch., Melbourne, 1952-54; DAQMG HQ Aldershot District, 1954-55; jssc 1955; AA&QMG Land Forces, Hong Kong, 1960-62; AAG (Col) MoD, 1962-65; Sen. Provision Officer, COD Bicester, 1965-66; Dir of Ordnance Services, FARELF (Brig.), 1966-69; Dep. Dir Ordnance Services MoD, 1969-71. Hon. Col, RAOC, T&AVR, 1971-73; Col Comdt, RAOC, 1975-. MBIM. *Recreations:* travel, golf, philately. *Address:* c/o Lloyd's Bank Ltd, 75 Castle Street, Farnham, Surrey. *Clubs:* Army and Navy, MCC; Hankley Common Golf.

DARLING, family name of **Barons Darling** and **Darling of Hillsborough.**

DARLING, 2nd Baron, *cr* 1924, of Langham; **Robert Charles Henry Darling;** DL; Major retired, Somerset Light Infantry; *b* 15 May 1919; *s* of late Major Hon. John Clive Darling, DSO; *S* grandfather, 1936; *m* 1942, Bridget Rosemary Whishaw, *d* of Rev. F. C. Dickson; one *s* two *d. Educ:* Wellington Coll.; RMC Sandhurst. Retired, 1955. Chief Exec., Royal Bath and West and Southern Counties Soc. DL Somerset 1972, Avon 1974. *Recreations:* fishing, gardening. *Heir: s* Hon. Robert Julian Henry Darling [*b* 29 April 1944; *m* 1970, Janet, *yr d* of Mrs D. M. E. Mallinson, Richmond, Yorks; one *s* one *d*]. *Address:* Puckpits, Limpley Stoke, Bath, Avon. *T:* Limpley Stoke 2146.

DARLING OF HILLSBOROUGH, Baron *cr* 1974 (Life Peer), of Crewe; **George Darling,** PC 1966; Journalist; *b* 1905; *s* of F. W. Darling, Co-operative shop asst; *m* 1932, Dorothy, *d* of T. W. Hodge, farmer; one *s* one *d. Educ:* Elementary Sch., Crewe; Liverpool and Cambridge Univs. MP (Co-op and Lab), Hillsborough Div. of Sheffield, 1950-Feb. 1974; Minister of State, BoT, 1964-68. Engineer; market research executive; newspaper reporter; BBC Industrial Correspondent, 1945-49; author. Pres., Inst. of Trading Standards Admin. *Recreation:* gardening. *Address:* 17 Amersham Road, Beaconsfield, Bucks. *T:* Beaconsfield 3352.

DARLING, Prof. Arthur Ivan, CBE 1971; Professor of Dental Medicine, University of Bristol, since 1959 (of Dental Surgery, 1947-59); Director of Dental Studies in the University of Bristol since 1947; Hon. Director, Dental Unit of MRC since 1961; *b* 21 Nov. 1916; *s* of John Straughan Darling and Henrietta Jeffcoat; *m* 1948, Kathleen Brenda Pollard; one *s* three *d. Educ:* Whitley Bay and Monkseaton Grammar Sch.; King's Coll., Univ. of Durham, LDS Dunelm, 1937, BDS Dunelm, 1938; Parker Brewis Research Fellow, 1938-41; MDS Dunelm, 1942; LRCP, MRCS 1947; FDSRCS 1948; DDSc Dunelm 1957; FFDRCSI 1964; FRCPath 1967. Lecturer: in Operative Dental Surgery, 1941, in Oral Anatomy, 1943, in Dental Materia Medica, 1945, University of Durham; Dean of Med. Faculty, Univ. of Bristol, 1963-66; Pro-Vice-Chancellor, Univ. of Bristol, 1968-72. Mem., Avon AHA (Teaching); Vice-Dean, Bd of Dental Faculty, RCS, 1977-. *Publications:* scientific papers on professional subjects in journals. *Recreations:* fishing and music. *Address:* 7 Rylestone Grove, Bristol BS9 3UT.

DARLING, Rev. Charles Brian Auchinleck, CMG 1949; MA Cantab; *b* 5 March 1905; *s* of late Ven. James George Reginald Darling, sometime Archdeacon of Suffolk and Norah Lilian Loxdale Auchinleck; *m* 1939, Rachel Middleton Lankester, *d* of Capt. Cyril Lankester Paul, RA; one *s* one *d. Educ:* Framlingham Coll.; Jesus Coll., Cambridge. Colonial Admin. Service, 1928, Gold Coast Colony; seconded Colonial Office, 1939; Principal, Dominions Office, 1940-45; Asst Chief Secretary: East African Governors' Conference, 1945; East Africa High Commission, 1948; retd 1951; ordained, 1952; retd 1966. *Recreation:* fly-fishing. *Address:* Fallow Hill, Bromeswell, Woodbridge, Suffolk. *T:* Eyke 222.

DARLING, Hon. Sir Clifford, Kt 1977; MP (Bahamas); Minister of Labour and National Insurance, Commonwealth of the Bahamas; *b* Acklins Island, 6 Feb. 1922; *s* of Charles and Aremelia Darling. *Educ:* Acklins Public Sch.; several public schs in Nassau. Became taxi-driver (Gen. Sec. Bahamas Taxicab Union for 8 yrs, Pres. for 10 yrs). An early Mem., Progressive Liberal Party; MHA for Englerston; Senator, 1964-67; Dep. Speaker, House of Assembly, 1967-69; Minister of State, Oct. 1969; Minister of Labour and Welfare, Dec. 1971. Past Chm., Tourist Advisory Bd; instrumental in introd. of a comprehensive Nat. Insce Scheme in the Bahamas, Oct. 1974. Member: Masonic Lodge; Acklins, Crooked Is and Long Cays Assoc. *Address:* C. H. Bain Building, POB 1525, Nassau, Bahamas.

DARLING, Maj.-Gen. Douglas Lyall, CB 1968; DSO 1943 and Bar, 1945; MC 1941 and Bar, 1942; GOC 53 (Welsh) Division (TA)/Wales District, Dec. 1963-May 1968, retired; *b* 3 Oct. 1914; *s* of late George Kenneth Darling, CIE; *m* 1953, Elizabeth Anne Forsyth; two *d. Educ:* Eton; Sandhurst. Commissioned into Rifle Bde, 1934. Served War of 1939-45 with Rifle Bde, and commanded 7th Bn The Rifle Bde, 1942-45. Comd Eaton Hall OCTU, 1945-48; GSO1, Plans, Min. of Defence, 1952-53; School of Infantry, 1954-55. GSO1, Staff Coll., 1956-58; Comd 133 Infantry Brigade, 1959-61; Imperial Defence Coll., 1962-63; Chief, British Commanders-in-Chief Mission to the Soviet Forces in Germany, 1963. *Recreations:* hunting, combined training and horse trials, sailing. *Address:* Darley House, Hullavington, Chippenham, Wilts. *T:* Hullavington 241. *Clubs:* Army and Navy; Royal Channel Islands Yacht.
See also General Sir K. T. Darling.

DARLING, Sir Frank F.; *see* Fraser Darling.

DARLING, Gerald Ralph Auchinleck, RD 1967; QC 1967; MA; Lieutenant-Commander, retired; *b* 8 Dec. 1921; *er s* of late Lieut-Col R. R. A. Darling and Moira Moriarty; *m* 1954, Susan Ann, *d* of late Brig. J. M. Hobbs, OBE, MC; one *s* one *d. Educ:* Harrow Sch. (Reginald Pole Schol.); Hertford Coll., Oxford (Baring Schol., Kitchener Schol.; MA 1948). Served with RNVR, 1940-46: Fleet Fighter Pilot, N Africa, Sicily, Salerno landings, Malta convoys; Test Pilot, Eastern Fleet; Chief Test Pilot, British Pacific Fleet; RNR until 1967. Called to Bar, Middle Temple, 1950 (Harmsworth Law Schol.), Bencher, 1972; Barrister, Northern Ireland, 1957; QC Hong Kong 1968. Panel of Lloyd's Arbitrators in Salvage Cases, 1967, Panel of Wreck Commissioners, 1967. Freeman of City of London, 1968. *Publication:* (contrib.) 3rd edn Halsbury's Laws of England (Admiralty and Ship Collisions). *Recreations:* fly fishing, shooting. *Address:* Crevenagh House, Omagh, Northern Ireland; Queen Elizabeth Building, Temple, EC4. *T:* 01-353 5728. *Clubs:* Naval and Military; Tyrone County (Omagh).

DARLING, Henry Shillington, CBE 1967; Director-General, International Centre for Agricultural Research in Dry Areas, since 1977; *b* 22 June 1914; *s* of late J. S. Darling, MD, FRCS, and Marjorie Shillington Darling, BA, Lurgan, N Ireland; *m* 1940, Vera Thompson Chapman, LDS, Belfast; one *s* two *d. Educ:* Watts' Endowed Sch.; Greenmount Agric. Coll., N Ireland; Queen's Univ., Belfast; Imp. Coll. Tropical Agriculture, Trinidad. BSc (1st Hons), 1938, BAgr (1st Hons) 1939, MAgr 1950, Belfast; AICTA 1942; PhD London, 1959. Middle East Anti-Locust Unit, Iran and Arabia, 1942-44; Research Dir., Dept of Agriculture: Uganda, 1944-47; Sudan, 1947-49; Faculty of Agriculture, University Coll., Khartoum, 1949-54; Head of Hop Research Dept, Wye Coll., London Univ., 1954-62; Prof. of Agriculture and Dir of Inst. for Agric. Research, Ahmadu Bello Univ., Zaria, Nigeria, 1962-68; Dep. Vice-Chancellor, Ahmadu Bello Univ., 1967-68; Principal, Wye College, Univ. of London, 1968-77. Technical Adviser, Parly Select Cttee for Overseas Develt, 1970-71. Chairman: Agricultural Panel, Intermediate Technology Develt Gp; British Council Agricl Adv. Panel; Member: Senate and Collegiate Council, London Univ. (Chm., Senate European Studies Cttee), and other univ. cttees; Council, Royal Veterinary Coll.; Council, Ahmadu Bello Univ. Exec. Cttee, and Acad. Policy Cttee, Inter-Univ. Council for Higher Educn Overseas (also Chm., W African Gp and Mem., working parties and gps); Kent Educn Cttee; Exec. Cttee East Malling Res. Station; Council S and E Kent Productivity Assoc. Pres., Agricultural Sect., British Assoc., 1971-72. Technical Adviser: Tear Fund; Methodist Missionary Soc.; Pres., Inter-Collegiate Christian Fellowship, 1971-72. FInstBiol 1968. Hon. DSc Ahmadu Bello Univ., 1968. Order of the Hop, 1959. *Publications:* many papers in jls and reports dealing with applied biology, entomology, agricultural science and rural development in the Third World. *Recreations:* reading, walking, Christian dialogue. *Address:* 2 Tudor End, Kennington, Ashford, Kent. *Clubs:* Athenæum, Farmers'; Samaru (Nigeria).

DARLING, James Carlisle S.; *see* Stormonth Darling.

DARLING, Sir James Ralph, Kt 1968; CMG 1958; OBE 1953; MA Oxon; MA (Hon.) Melbourne; DCL (Hon.) Oxon; FACE; Headmaster, Geelong Church of England Grammar School, Corio, Victoria, Australia, 1930-61; *b* 18 June 1899; *s* of late Augustine Major Darling and Jane Baird Nimmo; *m* 1935, Margaret Dunlop, *er d* of late John Dewar Campbell; one *s* three *d. Educ:* Repton Sch.; Oriel Coll., Oxford. 2nd Lieut Royal Field Artillery, 1918-19, France and Germany; Asst Master Merchant Taylors' Sch., Crosby, Liverpool, 1921-24; Asst Master Charterhouse Sch., Godalming, 1924-29; in charge of Public Schs Empire Tour to NZ, 1929; Hon. Sec. Headmasters' Conference of Australia, 1931-45, Chm., 1946-48; Member: Melbourne Univ. Council, 1933-71; Commonwealth Univs Commission, 1942-51; Commonwealth Immigration Advisory Council, 1952-68; Australian Broadcasting Control Board, 1955-61. President: Australian Coll. of Educn, 1959-63 (Hon. Fellow 1970); Australian Road Safety Council, 1961-70; Chairman: Australian Expert Gp on Road Safety, 1970-71; Australian Frontier Commission, 1962-71 (President, 1971-73); Australian Broadcasting Commission, 1961-67; Commonwealth Immigration Publicity Council, 1962-71; Pres., Elizabethan Trust. Hon. LLD Melbourne, 1973. *Publications:* The Education of a Civilized Man, 1962; Timbertop (with E. H. Montgomery), 1967. *Address:* 3 Myamyn Street, Armadale, Victoria 3143, Australia. *T:* 20.6262. *Clubs:* Australian (Sydney); Melbourne (Melbourne).

DARLING, Gen. Sir Kenneth (Thomas), GBE 1969 (CBE 1957); KCB 1963 (CB 1957); DSO 1945; Commander-in-Chief, Allied Forces, Northern Europe, 1967-69, retired; *b* 17 Sept. 1909; *s* of late G. K. Darling, CIE; *m* 1941, Pamela Beatrice Rose Denison-Pender. *Educ:* Eton; Royal Military College, Sandhurst. Commissioned 7th Royal Fusiliers, 1929; jssc 1946; idc 1953. Served NW Europe, 1944-45: Comd 5th Parachute Bde, 1946; Comd Airborne Forces Depot, 1948; Comd 16th Parachute Bde, 1950; Brig. A/q 1st (Br) Corps, 1954; Chief of Staff 1st (Br) Corps, 1955; Chief of Staff 2nd Corps, 1956. Dep. Dir of Staff Duties (D), WO, 1957-58; GOC Cyprus District and Dir of Ops, 1958-60; Dir of Infantry, 1960-62; GOC 1st (Br) Corps, 1962-63; GOC-in-C, Southern Command, 1964-66. Colonel: The Royal Fusiliers (City of London Regt), 1963-68; The Royal Regt of Fusiliers, 1968-74; Col Comdt, The Parachute Regt, 1965-67. ADC Gen., 1968-69. *Recreation:* riding. *Address:* Vicarage Farmhouse, Chesterton, Bicester, Oxon. *T:* Bicester 2092. *Club:* Army and Navy.
See also Maj.-Gen. D. L. Darling.

DARLINGTON, Rear-Adm. Sir Charles (Roy), KBE 1965; BSc; Director of the Naval Education Service and Head of Instructor Branch, Royal Navy, Oct. 1960-Oct. 1965, retired; on staff of Haileybury, 1965-75; *b* 2 March 1910; *o s* of C. A. Darlington, Newcastle under Lyme, Staffs; *m* 1935, Nora Dennison Wright, Maulds Meaburn, Westmorland; one *s* one *d. Educ:* Orme Sch., Newcastle under Lyme; Manchester Univ. (BSc). Double First in Maths 1931; Sen. Maths Master, William Hulme's Gram. Sch., 1937-40. Entered Royal Navy, 1941 (Instructor Lieut); served in: HM Ships Valiant and Malaya during War, and later in HM Ships Duke of York, Implacable, Vanguard and Tyne. On Staff of C-in-C Home Fleet, 1954-55, as Fleet Meteorological Officer; for various periods in Admty, HMS Excellent and HMS Collingwood. Rear-Adm. 1960. *Recreations:* cricket, hill-walking, mathematics and trying to avoid ignorance of the arts, and particularly of history. *Address:* 11 Freestone Road, Southsea, Hants. *T:* Portsmouth 25974.

DARLINGTON, Cyril Dean, DSc; FRS 1941; Sherardian Professor of Botany, University of Oxford, 1953-71, now Emeritus; Keeper, Oxford Botanic Garden, 1953-71; Fellow of Magdalen College, 1953-71; Hon. Fellow, 1971; *b* 19 Dec. 1903; *m* Margaret Upcott; one *s* three *d* (and one *s* decd); 2nd, Gwendolen Harvey (*née* Adshead). *Educ:* St Paul's Sch.; Wye Coll. Rockefeller Fellow in Pasadena, 1932, in Kyoto, 1933. Royal Medal of Royal Society, 1946; Pres. Genetical Soc., 1943-46. Pres. Rationalist Press Assoc., 1948; Dir, John Innes Horticultural Institution, 1939-53; Fellow of Wye Coll. For. Mem. Acc. Lincei and Royal Danish Academy of Sciences. Joint Founder of Heredity, 1947. *Publications:* Chromosomes and Plant Breeding, 1932; Recent Advances in Cytology, 3rd edn 1965; Evolution of Genetic Systems, 1939, 1958; The Conflict of Science and Society, 1948; The Facts of Life, 1953; Chromosome Botany and the Origins of Cultivated Plants, 1956, 3rd edn 1973; Darwin's Place in History, 1959; Genetics and Man, 1964; The Evolution of Man and Society, 1969; The Little Universe of Man, 1977; (jointly): The Handling of Chromosomes, 1942, 6th edn 1976; Chromosome Atlas of Flowering Plants, 1945, 1956; The Elements of Genetics, 1949; Genes, Plants and People,

1950; edited: Teaching Genetics, 1963; Chromosomes Today, 1966-72. *Recreation:* gardening. *Address:* Botany School, Oxford; Pin Farm Cottage, South Hinksey, Oxon.

DARLINGTON, William Aubrey, CBE 1967; MA; author, journalist, and dramatist; dramatic critic of the Daily Telegraph, 1920-68; Member, Editorial Staff of the Daily Telegraph; *b* Taunton, 20 Feb. 1890; *o s* of late Thomas Darlington, HMIS Board of Education; *m* Marjorie (*d* 1973), *y d* of late Sydney Sheppard; one *d. Educ:* Shrewsbury; St John's Coll., Cambridge (Classical Scholar); Honours in Classics and in English Literature. Was a schoolmaster 1913-14; during war, held commission in 7th Northumberland Fusiliers (TF); began contributing to Punch and other periodicals in 1916; took up journalism as profession in 1919, being asst editor and afterwards editor of The World; joined staff of the Daily Telegraph as dramatic critic, 1920; for many years Mem. of Advisory Cttee for Diploma in Dramatic Art, London Univ.; Lecturer on Playwriting at East London Coll., London Univ., 1926-27; Pres., Critics' Circle, 1930; London Theatre Correspondent of New York Times, 1939-60. *Publications:* novels: Alf's Button; Wishes Limited; Egbert; Alf's Carpet; Mr Cronk's Cases; Alf's New Button; *theatre books:* Through the Fourth Wall; Literature in the Theatre; Sheridan; J. M. Barrie; The Actor and his Audience; The World of Gilbert and Sullivan; Six Thousand and One Nights; Laurence Olivier; *autobiography:* I Do What I Like; *plays:* Alf's Button; Carpet Slippers; Marcia Gets Her Own Back; The Key of the House; English version of A Knight Passed By, by Jan Fabricius; burlesque version of The Streets of London. *Recreation:* golf. *Address:* Monksdown, Bishopstone, Sussex. *T:* Seaford 892657. *Club:* Garrick.

DARNLEY, 10th Earl of, *cr* 1725; **Peter Stuart Bligh;** Baron Clifton of Leighton Bromswold, 1608; Baron Clifton of Rathmore, 1721; Viscount Darnley, 1723; late Major, Dragoon Guards; *b* 1 Oct. 1915; *s* of 9th Earl and Daphne Rachel, *d* of late Hon. Alfred Mulholland; *S* father 1955. *Educ:* Eton; Royal Military College, Sandhurst. Served War of 1939-45 (prisoner). *Heir:* half-brother Hon. Adam Ivo Stuart Bligh [*b* 8 Nov. 1941; *m* 1965, Susan Elaine, *y d* of late Sir Donald Anderson; one *s* one *d*]. *Address:* Puckle Hill House, Shorne, Gravesend, Kent.

DARNLEY-THOMAS, Mrs John; see Hunter, Rita.

DART, Raymond Arthur; United Steelworkers of America Professor of Anthropology, The Institutes for the Achievement of Human Potential, Philadelphia, since 1966; Emeritus Professor since 1959, Professor of Anatomy, 1923-58, and Dean of the Faculty of Medicine, 1925-43, University of the Witwatersrand, Johannesburg; *b* Toowong, Brisbane, Australia, 4 Feb. 1893; *s* of Samuel Dart and Eliza Anne Brimblecombe; *m* 1936, Marjorie Gordon Frew, Boksburg, Transvaal; one *s* one *d. Educ:* Ipswich Grammar Sch., Queensland (Scholarship holder); University of Queensland (Scholarship holder and Foundation scholar); graduated BSc (Hons) 1913; MSc 1915; Sydney Univ., 1914-17; graduated MB, ChM (Hons) 1917; MD 1927; Demonstrator of Anatomy and Acting Principal of St Andrew's Coll., Sydney, 1917; House Surgeon at Royal Prince Alfred Hospital, Sydney, 1917-18; Capt., AAMC, Australia, England, France, 1918-19; Senior Demonstrator of Anatomy, University Coll., London, 1919-20; Fellow of Rockefeller Foundation, 1920-21; Senior Demonstrator of Anatomy and Lecturer in Histology, University Coll., London, 1921-22; Capt., SAMC, 1925; Major, 1928; Lieut-Col Reserve Officers, 1940; Pres. of Anthropological Section SAAAS, 1926 (Gold Medal, 1939); Vice-Pres., SAAAS, 1952; Vice-Pres. of Anthropological Section, BAAS, Johannesburg, 1929; Mem. of International Commission on Fossil Man since 1929; Fellow of Royal Society of South Africa, 1930, and Mem. of Council, 1938, Vice-Pres. 1938-39, 1939-40, 1950-51; Mem. Board, SA Institute for Medical Research, 1934-48; Mem. SA Med. Council, 1935-48, Executive Cttee, 1940-48; Mem. SA Nursing Council from its inception in 1944 until 1951; Mem. Medical Advisory Cttee, SA Council for Scientific and Industrial Research, 1946-48; Pres. Anthropological Section, First Pan-African Congress of Prehistory, 1947-51; guest-lecturer at The Viking Fund Seminar, New York, and public lecturer of The Lowell Inst., Boston, 1949; Inaugural Lecturer, John Irvine Hunter Memorial, Univ. of Sydney, NSW, 1950; Woodward Lecturer, Yale Univ., USA, 1958; Inaugural Van Riebeeck Lecturer; R. J. Terry Meml Lectr, Washington Univ. Sch. of Medicine, St Louis, 1971. SA Broadcasting Corp., 1959. Pres. SA Archaeological Soc., 1951; Pres. SA Assoc. for Advancement of Science, Bulawayo, S Rhodesia, 1953; Vice-Pres., Fourth Pan-African Congress of Prehistory, 1959-62; Pres. SA Museums Assoc., 1961-62; Vice-Pres., Assoc. Scientific and Technical Socs of S Africa, 1961-62, 1962-63, Pres., 1963-64; Pres. SA Soc. of Physiotherapy, 1961-

68, Hon. Life Vice-Pres., 1968-; Mem., Internat. Primatological Cttee, 1963-; Mem., Municipal Library Advisory Cttee, Johannesburg, 1964-. Coronation Medal, 1953; Sen. Capt. Scott Memorial Medal, SA Biological Soc., 1955; Viking Medal and Award for Physical Anthropology, Wenner-Gren Foundation of New York, 1957; Simon Biesheuvel Medal (Behavioural Sciences), 1963; Gold Medal, SA Nursing Assoc., 1970; Silver Medal, SA Medical Assoc., 1972. Hon. DSc: Natal, 1956; Witwatersrand, 1964; La Salle, 1968. Fellow Odontological Soc. of SA, 1937; Fellow Institute of Biology, 1964; For. Fellow, Linnaean Soc., 1974. Raymond Dart Lectureship in Institute for Study of Man in Africa, estab. 1964; Museums of Man and Science, Johannesburg, initiated 1966, Board of Governors, 1968. Hon. Life Member: Dental Assoc. of South Africa, 1958, Medical Assoc. of South Africa, 1959, Anatomical Society of Great Britain and Ireland, 1961, Anatomical Soc. of Southern Africa, 1970, S African Nursing Assoc., 1970; Archaeological Soc. of SA, 1973. *Publications:* Racial Origins, chapter in The Bantu-speaking Tribes of South Africa, 1937; chapters on genealogy and physical characters, in Bushmen of the Southern Kalahari, 1937; (ed) Africa's Place in the Human Story, 1954; The Oriental Horizons of Africa, 1955; Adventures with the Missing Link, 1959; Africa's Place in the Emergence of Civilisation, 1960; Beyond Antiquity, 1965; over 250 articles on anthropological, archaeological, neurological and comparative anatomical subjects in scientific and lay periodicals. *Recreations:* swimming, music. *Address:* 20 Eton Park, Eton Road, Sandhurst, Johannesburg, South Africa. *T:* 45.4241. *Clubs:* Associated Scientific and Technical, Country (Johannesburg).

DARTMOUTH, 9th Earl of, *cr* 1711; **Gerald Humphry Legge;** Baron Dartmouth, 1682; Viscount Lewisham, 1711; *b* 26 April 1924; *s* of 8th Earl of Dartmouth, CVO, DSO; *S* father, 1962; *m* 1948, Raine (marr. diss. 1976), *d* of late Alexander McCorquodale; three *s* one *d. Educ:* Eton. Served War, 1943-45, Coldstream Guards, Italy (despatches). FCA 1951. Dir, Rea Bros Ltd, Bankers, 1958. Hon. LLD Dartmouth Coll., USA, 1969. *Heir: s* Viscount Lewisham, *qv. Address:* The Manor House, Chipperfield, King's Langley, Herts. *Clubs:* Buck's, Bath.

See also Baron Herschell.

DARVALL, Sir (Charles) Roger, Kt 1971; CBE 1965; Director: Australia New Guinea Corporation Ltd; Longman Australia Pty Ltd; H. C. Sleigh Ltd; Munich Reinsurance Company of Australia Ltd; Australian Eagle Insurance Co. Ltd; Electrolux Pty Ltd; L. M. Ericsson Pty Ltd; Grosvenor International (Australia) Holdings Pty Ltd; Penguin Books Australia Ltd; *b* 11 Aug. 1906; *s* of late C. S. Darvall; *m* 1931, Dorothea M., *d* of late A. C. Vautier; two *d. Educ:* Burnie, Tasmania. FASA. Gen. Manager, Australia & New Zealand Bank Ltd, Melbourne, 1961-67. *Recreations:* motoring, gardening, outdoors. *Address:* 2 Martin Court, Toorak, Vic 3142, Australia. *T:* 24-4647. *Clubs:* Athenæum, Melbourne, Australian (Melbourne).

DARVALL, Frank Ongley, CBE 1954; retired from HM Diplomatic Service, 1970; a Governor, Sulgrave Manor; Member Council of Haileybury and Imperial Service College; *b* 16 April 1906; 5th *s* of late R. T. Darvall and Annie E. Johnson, Reading; *m* 1931, Dorothy, *er d* of Harry Edmonds and late Jane Quay, NY City; one *s* decd. *Educ:* Dover Coll.; Reading (BA); London (BA, PhD); Columbia (MA). President Nat. Union of Students, 1927-29; Commonwealth Fund Fellow, 1929-31; Assoc. Sec. for Internat. Studies, Internat. Students Service, 1931-32; Dir, Geneva Students Internat. Union, 1933. Lecturer in Economics and History, Queen's Coll., Harley Street, 1933-36; Director Research and Discussion, English-Speaking Union, 1936-39; Dep. Director American Div., Ministry of Information, 1939-45; British Consul, Denver, 1945-46; 1st Secretary HM Embassy, Washington, 1946-49; Vice-Chairman Kinsman Trust, 1949-56; Editor, The English-Speaking World, 1950-53; Director-General, English-speaking Union of the Commonwealth, 1949-57; Chairman, Congress of European-American Assoc., 1954-57. European Editor, World Review, 1958-59. Hon. Dir, UK Cttee, Atlantic Congress, 1959; Attached British High Commn, Cyprus, 1960-62; Dir, British Information Services, Eastern Caribbean, 1962-66; attached, British Consulate-Gen., Barcelona, 1966; Consul, Boston, 1966-68; FCO (formerly CO), 1968-70. Dean of Academics, Alvescot Coll., 1970-71, Vice-Pres., 1971-72. Contested (L) Ipswich, 1929, King's Lynn, 1935, Hythe bye-election, 1939. Extension Lecturer and Tutorial Classes Tutor, Cambridge and London Universities, 1933-39. *Publications:* Popular Disturbances and Public Order in Regency England, 1934; The Price of European Peace, 1937; The American Political Scene, 1939. *Address:* c/o Lloyds Bank Ltd, 46 Victoria Street, SW1. *Club:* Travellers'.

DARVALL, Sir Roger; *see* Darvall, Sir C. R.

DARWEN, 2nd Baron, *cr* 1946, of Heys-in-Bowland; **Cedric Percival Davies;** Publisher; President, Independent Publishers' Guild, since 1973; *b* 18 Feb. 1915; *e s* of 1st Baron and M. Kathleen Brown; *S* father 1950; *m* 1934, Kathleen Dora, *d* of George Sharples Walker; three *s* one *d. Educ:* Sidcot; Manchester Univ. BA Hons English Lit. and Language, Manchester, 1947. Engaged in Cotton Industry, 1932-40. On staff of school for Maladjusted Children, 1942-44. Manchester Univ., 1944-48, Teaching Diploma, 1948. Warden of Letchworth Adult Education Centre, 1948-51; Secretary to Training and Education Dept of National Assoc. for Mental Health, 1951-53; Founded Darwen Finlayson Ltd, Publishers, 1954, Chm., and Man. Dir, 1954-73; Dep. Editor of John O'London's, 1959-62. Chm., Hollybank Engineering Co. Ltd., 1957-70. *Publications:* designed and ed, Illustrated County History Series. *Recreations:* sailing, painting, cinéphotography. *Heir: s* Hon. Roger Michael Davies, [*b* 28 June 1938; *m* 1961, Gillian Irene, *d* of Eric G. Hardy, Bristol; two *s* three *d*]. *Address:* White Lodge, Sandelswood End, Beaconsfield, Bucks. *T:* Beaconsfield 3355.

DARWENT, Very Rev. Frederick Charles; Dean of Aberdeen and Orkney, since 1973; *b* Liverpool, 20 April 1927; *y s* of Samuel Darwent and Edith Emily Darwent (*née* Malcolm); *m* 1949, Edna Lilian, *o c* of David Waugh and Lily Elizabeth Waugh (*née* McIndoe); twin *d. Educ:* Warbreck Sch., Liverpool; Ormskirk Grammar Sch., Lancs; Wells Theological Coll., Somerset. Followed a Banking career, 1943-61 (War service in Far East with Royal Inniskilling Fusiliers, 1945-48). Deacon 1963; priest 1964, Diocese of Liverpool; Curate of Pemberton, Wigan, 1963-65 (in charge of St Francis, Kitt Green, 1964-65); Rector of: Strichen, 1965-71; New Pitsligo, 1965-; Fraserburgh, 1971-; Canon of St Andrew's Cathedral, Aberdeen, 1971. Hon. LTh, St Mark's Inst. of Theology, 1974. *Recreations:* amateur stage (acting and production), music (especially jazz); paddle steamers. *Address:* St Peter's Rectory, Fraserburgh, Aberdeenshire AB4 5PJ. *T:* Fraserburgh 2158. *Clubs:* Rotary International; Club of Deer (Aberdeens).

DARWIN, Henry Galton, CMG 1977; MA; Deputy Legal Adviser, Foreign and Commonwealth Office, since 1976; *b* 6 Nov. 1929; *s* of late Sir Charles Darwin, KBE, FRS; *m* 1958, Jane Sophia Christie; three *d. Educ:* Marlborough Coll.; Trinity Coll., Cambridge. Called to Bar, Lincoln's Inn, 1953. Asst Legal Adviser, FO, 1954-60 and 1963-67; Legal Adviser, British Embassy, Bonn, 1960-63; Legal Counsellor: UK Mission to UN, 1967-70; FCO, 1970-73; a Dir-Gen., Legal Service, Council Secretariat, European Communities, Brussels, 1973-76. *Publications:* contribs in Report of a Study Group on the Peaceful Settlement of International Disputes, 1966 and International Regulation of Frontier Disputes, 1970; notes in British Yearbook of International Law and American Jl of International Law. *Address:* 30 Hereford Square, SW7. *T:* 01-373 1140. *Club:* Athenæum.

DARYNGTON, 2nd Baron, *cr* 1923, of Witley; **Jocelyn Arthur Pike Pease;** *b* 30 May 1908; *s* of 1st Baron Daryngton, PC and Alice (*d* 1948), 2nd *d* of Very Rev. H. Mortimer Luckock, sometime Dean of Lichfield; *S* father 1949. *Educ:* Eton; privately; Trinity Coll., Cambridge (MA). Member Inner Temple, 1932. *Heir:* none. *Address:* The Street, Monks Eleigh, near Ipswich, Suffolk.

DAS, Sudhi Ranjan; Chairman, Board of Directors of the Statesman Ltd, since 1968; *b* 1 Oct. 1894; *e s* of late Rakhal Chandra Das; *m* 1919, Swapana, 2nd *d* of late Rai Bahadur S. B. Majumdar; two *s* one *d. Educ:* Tagores Sch., Santiniketan; Bangabasi Coll., Calcutta; University Coll., London. Graduated Calcutta Univ., 1915; LLB London 1st class 1st, 1918; called to Bar, Gray's Inn, 1918; joined Calcutta Bar, 1919; Lecturer University Law College; Additional Judge, Calcutta High Court, 1942; Puisne Judge, Calcutta High Court, 1944; Chief Justice of East Punjab High Court, 1949; Judge, Federal Court of India, 1950; Judge, Supreme Court of India, 1950-56; Chief Justice of India, 1956-59. Vice-Pres., Indian Council for Cultural Relations, 1964-65. Mem., Univ. Grants Commn, 1962-. Vice-Chancellor, Visva-Bharati (University founded by Dr Rabindra Nath Tagore), 1959-65. Editor, Mulla's Transfer of Property Act. LLD *hc* : Calcutta Univ., 1957; Allahabad Univ., 1958; Dr *hc* Visva-Bharati, 1966. Fellow of University Coll., London, 1961. *Publications:* Amader Santiniketan; Amader Gurudeva; Jä Deklechi Jä Payechi; Smaraner Tulikäi. *Address:* Swapanpuri, Kalimpong, West Bengal, India.

DASH, Sir Roydon Englefield Ashford, Kt 1945; DFC; Hon. LLD London; FRICS; Chairman of the Stevenage Development Corporation, 1953-62; *b* 3 March 1888; *s* of late Roland Ashford Dash, FSI; *m* 1933, Joan Pritchett Harrison. *Educ:* Haileybury Coll., Herts. Chief Valuer, Board of Inland Revenue, retired 1951. *Recreations:* golf and motoring. *Address:* 52 The Shimmings, Boxgrove Road, Guildford, Surrey.

DASHWOOD, Sir Francis (John Vernon Hereward), 11th Bt, *cr* 1707; (Premier Baronet of Great Britain); *b* 7 Aug. 1925; *s* of Sir John Lindsay Dashwood, 10th Bt, CVO, and Helen Moira Eaton; *S* father, 1966; *m* 1957, Victoria Ann Elizabeth Gwynne de Rutzen (*d* 1976); one *s* three *d* ; *m* 1977, Marcella, *widow* of Jack Frye, CBE. *Educ:* Eton; Christ Church, Oxford; Harvard Business Sch., USA. BA 1948, MA 1953. Foreign Office, 1944-45. Aluminium Company of Canada Ltd, 1950-51; EMI Ltd, 1951-53. Member of Buckinghamshire County Council, 1950-51; Member Lloyd's, 1956. Contested (C) West Bromwich, 1955, Gloucester, 1957. High Sheriff Bucks, 1976. *Heir: s* Edward John Francis Dashwood, *b* 25 Sept. 1964. *Address:* West Wycombe Park, Buckinghamshire. *T:* High Wycombe 23720. *Club:* Brooks's.

DASHWOOD, Sir Richard (James), 9th Bt *cr* 1684, of Kirtlington Park; *b* 14 Feb. 1950; *s* of Sir Henry George Massy Dashwood, 8th Bt, and of Susan Mary, *er d* of late Major V. R. Montgomerie-Charrington, Hunsdon House, Herts; *S* father, 1972. *Educ:* Maidwell Hall Preparatory Sch.; Eton College. Commissioned 14/20th King's Hussars, 1969; T&AVR, 1973-. *Heir:* uncle John Arthur Dashwood [*b* 17 July 1910; *m* 1952, Patricia Maud, *o d* of Frederick Burrows]. *Address:* Ledwell Cottage, Sandford St Martin, Oxfordshire OX5 4AN. *T:* Great Tew 267. *Club:* Cavalry and Guards.

da SILVA, John Burke, CMG 1969; HM Diplomatic Service, retired; Adviser, Commercial Union Assurance Co., since 1973; *b* 30 Aug. 1918; *o s* of late John Christian da Silva; *m* 1st, 1940, Janice Margaret (decd), *d* of Roy Mayor, Shrewsbury, Bermuda; one *d* ; 2nd, 1963, Jennifer Jane, *yr d* of late Capt. the Hon. T. T. Parker, DSC, RN, Greatham Moor, Hants; one *s* two *d. Educ:* Stowe Sch.; Trinity Coll., Cambridge (MA). Served Army, 1940-46: Major, Intell. Corps (despatches). Control Commission, Germany, 1946-50; Foreign Office, 1951; 2nd Sec., Rome, 1954; Consul, Hamburg, 1956; FO, 1958; 1st Sec., Bahrein, 1960; on Staff of C-in-C, Middle East, Aden, 1963; Counsellor, Washington, 1966; FCO, 1969-73. Chm., Governors, Virginia Water Junior Sch., 1973-. *Recreation:* Oriental Art. *Address:* Copse Close, Virginia Water, Surrey. *T:* Wentworth 2342. *Club:* Bath.

DATE, William Adrian, CBE 1973; Chairman, Grenada Public Service Board of Appeal; Member: Judicial and Legal Services Commission, West Indies Associated States; Grenada Development Corporation; *b* 1 July 1908; *er s* of James C. Date; *m* 1933, Dorothy MacGregor Grant; two *d. Educ:* Queen's Royal Coll., Trinidad; Grenada Boys' Secondary Sch.; Lodge Sch., Barbados; Middle Temple, London. Magistrate and District Govt Officer, St Lucia, 1933-39; Crown Attorney, St Vincent, 1939-44; Legal Draughtsman, Jamaica, 1944-47; Chief Secretary, Windward Islands, 1947-50; Puisne Judge of the Supreme Court of the Windward and Leeward Islands, 1950-56; Puisne Judge, British Guiana, 1956-64, retd. Vice-Pres., Grenada Building and Loan Assoc.; Dir, Grenada Co-op Bank. *Recreations:* golf, tennis, bridge. *Address:* PO Box 133, St George's, Grenada, West Indies.

DAUBE, Prof. David, FBA 1957; MA, DCL, PhD, Dr jur; Director of the Robbins Hebraic and Roman Law Collections and Professor-in-Residence at the School of Law, University of California, Berkeley, since 1970; Visiting Professor of History, University of Constance, since 1966; Emeritus Regius Professor, Oxford University, since 1970; Member, Academic Board, Institute of Jewish Studies, London, since 1953; *b* Freiburg, 8 Feb. 1909; 2nd *s* of Jakob Daube; *m* 1936 (marr. diss., 1964); three *s. Educ:* Berthold-gymnasium, Freiburg; Universities of Freiburg, Göttingen and Cambridge. Fellow of Caius Coll., 1938-46, Hon. Fellow, 1974; Lecturer in Law, Cambridge, 1946-51; Professor of Jurisprudence at Aberdeen, 1951-55; Regius Prof. of Civil Law, Oxford Univ., and Fellow of All Souls Coll., 1955-70; Senior Fellow, Yale Univ., 1962; Delitzsch Lecturer, Münster, 1962; Gifford Lecturer, Edinburgh, for 1962 and 1963 (lectures delivered, 1963-64); Olaus Petri Lecturer, Uppsala, 1963; Ford Prof. of Political Science, Univ. of California, Berkeley, 1964; Riddell Lectr, Newcastle, 1965; Gray Lectr, Cambridge, 1966; Lionel Cohen Lectr, Jerusalem, 1970. Pres., Classical Assoc. of GB, 1976-77. Corresp. Mem., Akad. Wiss., Göttingen, 1964, Bayer. Akad. Wiss., Munich, 1966; Hon. Mem. Royal Irish Acad., 1970; Fellow: Amer. Acad. of Arts and Sciences, 1971; World Acad. of Art and Sci., 1975; Hon. Fellow, Oxford Centre for Postgraduate Hebrew Studies, 1973. Hon.

LLD: Edinburgh 1960; Leicester 1964; Dr *hc* Paris 1963; Hon. DHL Hebrew Union Coll., 1971; Dr *jur hc* Munich, 1972. *Publications:* Studies in Biblical Law, 1947; The New Testament and Rabbinic Judaism, 1956; Forms of Roman Legislation, 1956; The Exodus Pattern in the Bible, 1963; The Sudden in the Scriptures, 1964; Collaboration with Tyranny in Rabbinic Law, 1965; He that Cometh, 1966; Roman Law, 1969; Civil Disobedience in Antiquity, 1972; Ancient Hebrew Fables, 1973; (ed) Studies in memory of F. de Zulueta, 1959; (with W. D. Davies) Studies in honour of C. H. Dodd, 1956, and articles. *Address:* School of Law, University of California, Berkeley, Calif 94720, USA.

DAULTANA, Mumtaz Mohammad Khan; Ambassador of Pakistan to the Court of St James's since 1972; *b* 23 Feb. 1916; *o s* of Nawab Ahmadyar Daultana; *m* 1943, Almas Jehan; one *s* one *d*. *Educ:* St Anthony's Sch., Lahore; Government Coll., Lahore (BA (Hons)); Corpus Christi Coll., Oxford (MA); Called to Bar, Middle Temple, 1940; 1st cl. 1st position in Bar exam. Mem., All India Muslim League, 1942-; unopposed election as Mem. Punjab Legislative Assembly, 1943; Gen. Sec., Punjab Muslim League, 1944; Sec., All India Muslim League Central Cttee of Action, 1945; Elected Member: Punjab Assembly, 1946; Constituent Assembly of India, 1947; Constituent Assembly, Pakistan, 1947; Finance Minister, Punjab, 1947-48; Pres., Punjab Muslim League, 1948-50; Chief Minister of Punjab, 1951-53; Finance Minister, West Pakistan, 1955-56; Defence Minister, Pakistan, 1957; Pres., Pakistan Muslim League, 1967-72. Elected Member: Nat. Assembly of Pakistan, 1970; Constitution Cttee of Nat. Assembly, 1972. *Publications:* Agrarian Report of Pakistan Muslim League, 1950; Thoughts on Pakistan's Foreign Policy, 1956; Kashmir in Present Day Context, 1965. *Recreations:* music, squash. *Address:* Pakistan Embassy, Lowndes Square, SW1X 9JN; 8 Durand Road, Lahore, Pakistan. *T:* 52459 (Lahore), 512387 (Karachi). *Clubs:* United Oxford & Cambridge University, Travellers'; Gymkhana (Lahore).

DAUNT, Maj.-Gen. Brian, CB 1956; CBE 1953; DSO 1943; late RA; *b* 16 March 1900; *s* of Dr William Daunt, Parade House, Hastings; *m* 1938, Millicent Margaret, *d* of Capt. A. S. Balfour, Allermuir House, Colinton, Edinburgh; two *d* (one *s* decd). *Educ:* Tonbridge; RMA, Woolwich. Commissioned RA, 1920; served NW Frontier, India, 1929-30; War of 1939-45; France, 1940, as 2 i/c Regt; CO Anti-Tank Regt, 1941; Italy, as CO 142 Field Regt, RA, Royal Devon Yeo., 1943 (DSO); CRA: 1st Armoured Div., 1944; 46 Div., 1944; 10 Indian Div., 1946; Italy, 1945 (despatches). Has had various Brigadier's appts. Commandant Coast Artillery Sch. and Inspector Coast Artillery, 1950-53; General Officer Commanding Troops, Malta, 1953-Nov. 1956; retired, 1957; Controller, Home Dept, British Red Cross Society, 1957-66. Col Comdt RA, 1960-65. CStJ 1966. *Recreations:* shooting, fishing, gardening. *Address:* Blackstone House, Sotwell, near Wallingford, Oxon OX10 0PX. *T:* Wallingford 37060. *Club:* Army and Navy.

DAUNT, Patrick Eldon; Principal Administrator, Directorate for Education and Training, Commission of European Communities, since 1974; *b* 19 Feb. 1925; *s* of Dr Francis Eldon Daunt and Winifred Doggett Daunt (*née* Wells); *m* 1958, Jean Patricia, *d* of Lt-Col Percy Wentworth Hargreaves and of Joan (*née* Holford); three *s* one *d*. *Educ:* Rugby Sch.; Wadham Coll., Oxford. BA, 1st Cl. Hons Lit. Hum., 1949, MA 1954, Oxon. Housemaster, Christ's Hosp., 1959; Headmaster, Thomas Bennett Comprehensive Sch., Crawley, 1965. Chm., Campaign for Comprehensive Educn, 1971-73. *Publication:* Comprehensive Values, 1975. *Recreation:* family life. *Address:* Avenue des Cactus 29, 1150 Brussels, Belgium. *T:* Brussels 770-64-12.

DAVENPORT, Rear-Adm. Dudley Leslie, CB 1969; OBE 1954; *b* 17 Aug. 1919; *s* of late Vice-Adm. R. C. Davenport, CB, Catherington, Hants; *m* 1950, Joan, *d* of late Surg. Comdr H. Burns, OBE; two *s*. *Educ:* RNC, Dartmouth. Naval Cadet, 1933; Midshipman, 1937; served in Destroyers, Mediterranean and Atlantic, 1939-45; commanded HMS Holmes, 1945 and HMS Porlock Bay, 1946; served in HMS Sheffield, 1947-48; at HMS Ganges, 1949-51; Naval Staff Course, 1951; Naval Instructor, Indian Defence Services Staff Coll., 1951-53; comd HMS Virago, 1954-55; NATO Defence Course, 1955-56; Comdr RN Barracks, Chatham, 1956-57; Captain, 1957; Staff of Admiral Comdg Reserves, 1958-60; Captain Inshore Flotilla Far East, 1960-62; Director Naval Officers Appointments (Seaman Officers), 1962-64; comd HMS Victorious, 1964-66; Rear-Admiral, 1967; Flag Officer, Malta, 1967-69; retd, 1969. *Recreations:* golf, gardening. *Address:* Rose Cottage, Halnaker, Chichester, Sussex. *T:* Halnaker 210. *Club:* Army and Navy.

DAVENPORT, Lt-Col Sir Walter Henry B.; *see* Bromley-Davenport.

DAVENPORT-HANDLEY, David John, OBE 1962; JP; DL; Chairman, Clipsham Quarry Co., since 1947; *b* 2 Sept. 1919; *s* of John Davenport-Handley, JP; *m* 1943, Leslie Mary Goldsmith; one *s* one *d*. *Educ:* RNC Dartmouth. RN retd 1947. Chm., Rutland and Stamford Conservative Assoc., 1952-65; Treasurer, East Midlands Area Conservative Assoc., 1965-71, Chm. 1971-77; Vice-Chm., Nat. Union of Conservative & Unionist Assocs, 1977-. Governor, Swinton Conservative Coll., 1973-77; Chairman: Board of Visitors, Ashwell Prison, 1955-73; Governors, Casterton Community Coll., 1960-; Trustee, Oakham Sch., 1970-. JP 1948, High Sheriff 1954, DL 1962, Vice-Lieutenant 1972, Rutland; DL Leicestershire 1974. *Recreations:* gardening, shooting. *Address:* Clipsham Hall, Oakham, Rutland, Leics. *T:* Castle Bytham 204. *Club:* English-Speaking Union.

DAVENTRY, 2nd Viscount, *cr* 1943; **Robert Oliver Fitz Roy,** Captain RN; retired; *b* 10 Jan. 1893; *er s* of late Captain Rt Hon. Edward Algernon Fitz Roy, MP and of 1st Viscountess Daventry, CBE; *S* mother, 1962; *m* 1916, Grace Zoë, *d* of late Claude Hume Campbell Guinness; four *d* (and one *d* decd). *Educ:* Royal Naval Colleges, Osborne, Dartmouth. Joined Royal Navy, 1906; Captain, 1936. Served European War, 1914-18; served War of 1939-45: comd HMS Rodney (despatches). High Sheriff, Rutland, 1956-57. *Heir: b* Hon. John Maurice Fitz Roy Newdegate, Commander RN retired [*b* 20 March 1897; *m* 1919, Lucia Charlotte Susan, OBE, *d* of Sir Francis Newdigate Newdegate, GCMG; one *s* two *d*]. *Address:* 82 Swan Court, SW3. *T:* 01-352 7200. *Club:* Carlton.
   See also Sir *Geoffrey Bates* , Bt , *F . H . M . FitzRoy Newdegate* .

DAVEY, David Garnet, OBE 1949; MSc, PhD; Research Director of Pharmaceuticals Division, Imperial Chemical Industries Ltd, 1969-75; *b* 8 Aug. 1912; *y s* of I. W. Davey, Caerphilly, Glamorgan; *m* 1938, Elizabeth Gale; one *s* two *d*. *Educ:* University Coll., Cardiff (1st cl. Hons Zoology; MSc 1935); Gonville and Caius Coll., Cambridge (PhD 1938); Harvard Univ. Med. Sch. (Research Fellow). Inst. of Animal Pathology, Univ. of Cambridge, 1938; Lectr, University Coll., Cardiff, 1939-40; Min. of Supply (Radar), 1941; joined ICI 1942; Biological Research Manager, Pharmaceuticals Div., 1957-69. Pres., European Soc. for Study of Drug Toxicity, 1964-69; Member: MRC, 1971-75; Cttee on Review of Medicines, 1975-; Sub-cttee on Toxicity, Clinical Trials, and Therapeutic Efficacy, Cttee on Safety of Medicines, 1976-. Chalmers Gold Medal, Royal Soc. Tropical Medicine and Hygiene, 1947; Therapeutics Gold Medal, Apothecaries Soc., 1947. *Publications:* contribs to Annals Trop. Med.; Trans Royal Soc. Tropical Medicine and Hygiene; British Med. Bulletin; Proc. European Soc. for Study of Drug Toxicity, etc. *Recreation:* gardening. *Address:* The Heyes, 49 Heyes Lane, Alderley Edge, Cheshire. *T:* Alderley Edge 2415.

DAVEY, Francis, MA; Headmaster of Merchant Taylors' School since 1974; *b* 23 March 1932; *er s* of Wilfred Henry Davey, BSc and Olive (*née* Geeson); *m* 1960, Margaret Filby Lake, MA Oxon, AMA, *o d* of Harold Lake, DMus Oxon, FRCO; one *s* one *d*. *Educ:* Plymouth Coll.; New Coll., Oxford (Hon. Exhibr); Corpus Christi Coll., Cambridge (Schoolmaster Fellow Commoner). 1st cl. Class. Hon. Mods 1953, 2nd cl. Lit. Hum. 1955, BA 1955, MA 1958. RAF, 1950-51; Classical Upper Sixth Form Master, Dulwich Coll., 1955-60; Head of Classics Dept, Warwick Sch., 1960-66; Headmaster, Dr Morgan's Grammar Sch., Bridgwater, 1966-73. *Publications:* articles in Enciclopedia dello Spettacolo and Classical Review. *Recreations:* Rugby, swimming, gardening, travel. *Address:* Merchant Taylors' School, Sandy Lodge, Northwood, Mddx HA6 2HT. *T:* Northwood 21850. *Clubs:* East India, Devonshire, Sports and Public Schools; Union (Oxford).

DAVEY, Geoffrey Wallace; a Recorder of the Crown Court, since 1974; *b* 16 Oct. 1924; *s* of late Hector F. T. Davey and Alice M. Davey; *m* 1964, Joyce Irving Steel; two *s* one *d*. *Educ:* Queen Elizabeth Grammar Sch., Faversham; Wadham Coll., Oxford (MA). Called to Bar, Lincoln's Inn, 1954; admitted Ghana Bar, 1957; resumed practice NE Circuit, 1970. *Recreations:* golf, cooking, carpentry. *Address:* 22 Brompton Road, Northallerton, N Yorkshire. *T:* Northallerton 5943; 19 Baker Street, Middlesbrough, Cleveland. *T:* Middlesbrough 211310; 5 King's Bench Walk, Temple, EC4.

DAVEY, Idris Wyn; Under-Secretary, Welsh Office, 1972-77; *b* 8 July 1917; 2nd *s* of late S. Davey and M. Davey, Blaina, Mon; *m* 1943, Lilian Lloyd-Bowen; two *d*. *Educ:* Nantyglo Grammar

Sch.; Cardiff Technical Coll.; London Univ. (BSc). Admiralty, 1940-47; Welsh Bd of Health: Asst Principal, 1948; Principal, 1951; Sec. Local Govt Commn for Wales, 1959-62; Welsh Office: Asst Sec. (in Min. of Housing and Local Govt), 1962; Establishment Officer, 1966-72; Under-Sec., 1972; seconded as Sec. and Mem., Local Govt Staff Commn for Wales and NHS Staff Commn for Wales, 1972-73. *Recreations:* watching Rugby football, gardening. *Address:* 4 Southgate Road, Pennard, Gower, West Glam.

DAVEY, Jocelyn; *see* Raphael, Chaim.

DAVEY, Keith Alfred Thomas, CB 1973; Solicitor and Legal Adviser, Department of the Environment, since 1970; *b* 1920; *s* of W. D. F. Davey; *m* 1949, Kathleen Elsie, *d* of Rev. F. J. Brabyn; one *s* one *d*. *Educ:* Cambridge and County High Sch.; Fitzwilliam House, Cambridge (MA). Served War of 1939-45, Middle East (Captain). Called to the Bar, Middle Temple, 1947. Principal Asst Solicitor, DHSS, 1968-70. *Recreations:* looking at churches, reading history, keeping cats and dogs. *Address:* 165 Shelford Road, Trumpington, Cambridge CB2 2ND. *Club:* Athenæum.

DAVEY, Roy Charles; Headmaster, King's School, Bruton, 1957-72; *b* 25 June 1915; *s* of William Arthur Davey and Georgina (*née* Allison); *m* 1940, Kathleen Joyce Sumner; two *d*. *Educ:* Christ's Hospital; Brasenose Coll., Oxford (Open Scholar). Asst Master, Weymouth Coll., 1937-40. War Service, Royal Artillery, 1940-46. Senior Master, 1946-49, Warden, 1949-57, The Village Coll., Impington. Vice Chm. Governors, St Hugh's Sch., Faringdon. FRSA. *Recreations:* poetry, botany, gardening, games. *Address:* Fir Trees, Buckland Newton, Dorchester, Dorset DT2 7BI. *T:* Buckland Newton 262. *Club:* East India, Devonshire, Sports and Public Schools.

DAVEY, Prof. Thomas Herbert, OBE 1941; *b* 30 June 1899; *s* of Rev. Charles Davey, DD, Belfast, N Ireland; *m* 1935, Irene Margaret Cottom; one *s*. *Educ:* Royal Belfast Academical Institution; Queen's Univ., Belfast. War service, 1917-18; MB, BCh, BAO Belfast, 1925; MD 1934; Liverpool School of Tropical Medicine, 1929; Professor of Tropical Diseases of Africa, Liverpool School of Tropical Medicine, and Director of Sir Alfred Lewis Jones Research Laboratory, Freetown, Sierra Leone, 1938; Prof. of Tropical Hygiene, Liverpool School of Tropical Medicine, Liverpool Univ., 1945-61, now emeritus. *Publications:* (with Dr W. P. H. Lightbody) Control of Disease in the Tropics, 1956; Blacklock and Southwell's Guide to Human Parasitology, 1957. *Recreation:* gardening. *Address:* 87 Belmont Church Road, Belfast BT4 3FG. *T:* Belfast 658691.

DAVEY, William, PhD; FRIC; President, Portsmouth Polytechnic, since 1969; *b* Chesterfield, Derbyshire, 15 June 1917; *m* 1941, Eunice Battye; two *s*. *Educ:* University Coll., Nottingham; Technical Coll., Huddersfield. BSc, PhD (London, external). Chemist: ICI Scottish Dyes, 1940; Boots, 1941; Shell, 1942-44. Lectr and Sen. Lectr in Organic Chemistry, Acton Techn. Coll., 1944-53; Head of Dept of Chemistry and Biology, The Polytechnic, Regent Street, London, W1, 1953-59; Principal, Coll. of Technology, Portsmouth, 1960-69. FRSA, FRIC, FBIM. *Publications:* Industrial Chemistry, 1961; numerous original papers in: Jl Chem. Soc., Inst. Petroleum, Jl Applied Chem. *Recreations:* motoring, foreign travel. *Address:* 67 Ferndale, Waterlooville, Portsmouth PO7 7PH. *T:* Waterlooville 3014.

DAVID, Mrs Elizabeth, OBE 1976; 2nd *d* of Rupert Sackville Gwynne, MP, and Hon. Stella Ridley; *m* 1944, Lt-Col Ivor Anthony David (marr. diss., 1960). Chevalier du Mérite Agricole (France), 1977. *Publications:* A Book of Mediterranean Food, 1950; French Country Cooking, 1951; Italian Food, 1954; Summer Cooking, 1955; French Provincial Cooking, 1960; English Cooking, Ancient and Modern: vol. I, Spices, Salt and Aromatics in the English Kitchen, 1970; English Bread and Yeast Cookery, 1977. *Address:* c/o Penguin Books Ltd, Harmondsworth, Middlesex.

DAVID, Richard (William), CBE 1967; formerly Publisher to the University, Cambridge University Press; Fellow of Clare Hall, Cambridge; *b* 28 Jan. 1912; *e s* of Rev. F. P. and Mary M. David, Winchester; *m* 1935, Nora, *o surv d* of G. B. Blakesley, Ashby-de-la-Zouch; two *s* two *d*. *Educ:* Winchester Coll. (Scholar); Corpus Christi Coll., Cambridge (Scholar). Joined editorial staff, CUP, 1936. Served RNVR, 1940-46, in Mediterranean and Western Approaches; qualified navigator, 1944; Lt-Comdr, 1945. Transferred to London Office of CUP, 1946; London Manager, 1948-63; Sec. to the Syndics of the Press, 1963-70. Member of Council of Publishers Assoc., 1953-63; Chairman of Export Research Cttee, 1956-59; President, 1959-61.

Publications: The Janus of Poets, 1935; Love's Labour's Lost (The Arden Edition of Shakespeare), 1951; Shakespeare in the Theatre, 1978; journal articles on the production of Shakespeare plays, and on botanical subjects, especially Carex. *Recreations:* music, botanising, fly-fishing. *Address:* 41 Barton Road, Cambridge; Cove, New Polzeath, Wadebridge, Cornwall.

DAVID, Robin (Robert) Daniel George, QC 1968; DL; His Honour Judge David; a Circuit Judge (formerly Chairman, Cheshire Quarter Sessions), since 1968; *b* 30 April 1922; *s* of late Alexander Charles Robert David and Edrica Doris Pole David (*née* Evans); *m* 1944, Edith Mary David (*née* Marsh); two *d*. *Educ:* Christ Coll., Brecon; Ellesmere Coll., Salop. War Service, 1943-47, Captain, Royal Artillery. Called to Bar, Gray's Inn, 1949; joined Wales and Chester Circuit, 1949. Dep. Chairman, Cheshire QS, 1961; Dep. Chairman, Agricultural Land Tribunal (Wales), 1965-68; Commissioner of Assize, 1970; Mem., Parole Bd for England and Wales, 1971-74. DL Cheshire 1972. *Recreations:* caravanning, boating. *Address:* (home) Hallowsgate House, Kelsall, Cheshire. *T:* Kelsall 51456; (chambers) 4 Paper Buildings, Temple, EC4. *T:* 01-353 8408, 01-353 0196; (chambers) 40 King Street, Chester. *T:* Chester 23886.

DAVIDSON, family name of **Viscount Davidson.**

DAVIDSON, 2nd Viscount *cr* 1937, of Little Gaddesden; **John Andrew Davidson;** *b* 22 Dec. 1928; *er s* of 1st Viscount Davidson, PC, GCVO, CH, CB, and of Frances Joan, Viscountess Davidson, *qv*; *S* father, 1970; *m* 1st, 1956, Margaret Birgitta (marr. diss. 1974), *o d* of Maj.-Gen. C. H. Norton, *qv*; four *d* (including twin *d*); 2nd, 1975, Mrs Pamela Dobb (*née* Vergette). *Educ:* Westminster School; Pembroke College, Cambridge (BA). Served in The Black Watch and 5th Bn KAR, 1947-49. Director: Strutt & Parker (Farms) Ltd, 1960-75; Lord Rayleigh's Farms Inc., 1960-75; Member of Council: CLA, 1965-75; RASE, 1973; Chm., Management Committee, Royal Eastern Counties Hospital, 1966-72; Mem., East Anglia Economic Planning Council, 1971-75. *Recreations:* music, gardening. *Heir:* *b* Hon. Malcolm William Mackenzie Davidson [*b* 28 Aug. 1934; *m* 1970, Mrs Evelyn Ann Carew Perfect, *yr d* of William Blackmore Storey; one *s* one *d*]. *Address:* The Old Rectory, Stonham Aspal, Stowmarket, Suffolk. *T:* Stonham 515.

DAVIDSON, Dowager Viscountess; Frances Joan Davidson; Baroness (Life Peer), *cr* 1963, under title of **Baroness Northchurch;** DBE 1952 (OBE 1920); *y d* of 1st Baron Dickinson, PC, KBE; *m* 1919, 1st Viscount Davidson, PC, GCVO, CH, CB (*d* 1970); two *s* two *d*. MP (U) Hemel Hempstead Division of Herts, 1937-Sept. 1959. *Recreations:* gardening, walking. *Address:* 16 Lord North Street, Westminster, SW1. *T:* 01-222 2167.

DAVIDSON, Alan Eaton, CMG 1975; author; HM Diplomatic Service, retired; *b* 30 March 1924; *s* of William John Davidson and Constance (*née* Eaton); *m* 1951, Jane Macatee; three *d*. *Educ:* Leeds Grammar Sch.; Queen's Coll., Oxford. 1st class hons Class. Mods. and Greats. Served in RNVR (Ordinary Seaman, later Lieut) in Mediterranean, N Atlantic and Pacific, 1943-46. Member of HM Foreign Service, 1948; served at: Washington, 1950-53; The Hague, 1953-55; FO, 1955-59; First Secretary, British Property Commission, and later Head of Chancery, British Embassy, Cairo, 1959-61; Head of Chancery and Consul, Tunis, 1962-64; FO, 1964; Counsellor, 1965; Head, Central Dept, FO, 1966-68; Head of Chancery, UK Delegn to NATO, Brussels, 1968-71; seconded, as Vis. Fellow, Centre for Contemporary European Studies, Univ. of Sussex, 1971-72; Head of Defence Dept, FCO, 1972-73; Ambassador to Vientiane, 1973-75. *Publications:* Seafish of Tunisia and the Central Mediterranean, 1963; Snakes and Scorpions Found in the Land of Tunisia, 1964; Mediterranean Seafood, 1972; The Role of the Uncommitted European Countries in East-West Relations, 1972; Fish and Fish Dishes of Laos, 1975; Seafood of South East Asia, 1976; North Atlantic Sea Food, 1978. *Address:* 45 Lamont Road, World's End, SW10. *T:* 01-352 4209.

DAVIDSON, Alfred Edward; international lawyer; Director, Channel Tunnel Study Group, 1960-70; Counsel to Wilmer, Cutler & Pickering, Attorneys at Law, 1972-75; *b* New York, 11 Nov. 1911; *s* of Maurice Philip Davidson and Blanche Reinheimer; *m* 1934, Claire H. Dreyfuss. *Educ:* Harvard Univ. (AB); Columbia Law Sch. (LLB). Advocate, Bar of New York, 1936; of Dist of Columbia, 1972; Asst to Gen. Counsel, US Dept of Labour, Wash., 1938-40; review section, Solicitor's Office, 1940-41; Legis. Counsel, Office of Emergency Management, in Exec. Office of President, 1941-43; Asst Gen. Counsel, Lend-Lease Admin. (later Foreign Economic Admin.), 1943-45; Gen. Counsel, 1945-; Gen. Counsel, UNRRA, Nov. 1945; Counsel, Preparatory Commn for Internat. Refugee Org., 1947; Dir,

European Headqrs of UNICEF, 1947-51; Advisor, Office of Sec.-Gen. of UN, 1951-52; Gen. Counsel, UN Korean Reconstr. Agency, 1952-54; Exec. Asst to Chm., Bd of Rio Tinto of Canada, 1955-58; Vice-Pres., Gen. Counsel, Techn. Studies, 1957-70, 1975-; European Representative, Internat. Finance Corp., 1970-72. Dir, Gen. Counsel, Construction Capital Co., 1964-69. Hon. Chm., Democratic Party Cttee, France. Co-Founder, Assoc. for Promotion of Humor in Internat. Affairs; Co-Chm., Bipartisan Cttees on Medicare Overseas and Absentee Voting; Dir, Assoc. of American Residents Overseas. *Publications:* contribs. various periodicals and newspapers. *Recreations:* tennis, bridge, chess, reading. *Address:* 5 rue de la Manutention, 75116 Paris, France. *Clubs:* Queen's, Lansdowne (London); Standard (France).

DAVIDSON, Arthur; MP (Lab) Accrington since 1966; Parliamentary Secretary, Law Officers' Department, since 1974; *b* 7 Nov. 1928. *Educ:* Liverpool Coll.; King George V Sch., Southport; Trinity Coll., Cambridge. Served in Merchant Navy. Barrister, Middle Temple, 1953. Trinity Coll., Cambridge, 1959-62; Editor of the Granta. Contested (Lab) Blackpool S, 1955, and Preston N, 1959. PPS to Solicitor-General, 1968-70; Chm., Home Affairs Gp, Parly Labour Party, 1971-74. Mem. Council, Consumers' Association, 1970-74. Chm., House of Commons Jazz Club, 1973-. *Recreations:* lawn tennis, ski-ing, theatre, modern jazz; formerly Member Cambridge Univ. athletics team. *Address:* House of Commons, SW1. *Clubs:* AEF, Free Gardeners (Accrington).

DAVIDSON, Basil Risbridger, MC 1945; author and historian; *b* 9 Nov. 1914; *s* of Thomas and Jessie Davidson; *m* 1943, Marion Ruth Young; three *s*. Served War of 1939-45 (despatches twice, MC, US Bronze Star, Jugoslav Zasluge za Narod); British Army, 1940-45 (Balkans, N Africa, Italy); Temp. Lt-Col demobilised as Hon. Major. Editorial staff of The Economist, 1938-39; The Star (diplomatic correspondent, 1939); The Times (Paris correspondent, 1945-47; chief foreign leader-writer, 1947-49); New Statesman (special correspondent, 1950-54); Daily Herald (special correspondent, 1954-57); Daily Mirror (leader-writer, 1959-62). Vis. Prof., Univ. of Ghana, 1964; Regents' Lectr, Univ. of California, 1971; Montagu Burton Vis. Prof. of Internat. Relations, Edinburgh Univ., 1972. A Vice-Pres., Anti-Apartheid Movement, 1969-. Freeman of City of Genoa, 1945. Hon. DLitt Ibadan, 1975. Haile Selassie African Research Award, 1970; Medalha Amílcar Cabral, 1976. *Publications: novels:* Highway Forty, 1949; Golden Horn, 1952; The Rapids, 1955; Lindy, 1958; The Andrassy Affair, 1966; *non-fiction:* Partisan Picture, 1946; Germany: From Potsdam to Partition, 1950; Report on Southern Africa, 1952; Daybreak in China, 1953; The New West Africa (ed.), 1953; The African Awakening, 1955; Turkestan Alive, 1957; Old Africa Rediscovered, 1959; Black Mother, 1961; The African Past, 1964; Which Way Africa?, 1964; The Growth of African Civilisation: West Africa AD 1000-1800, 1965; Africa: History of a Continent, 1966; A History of East and Central Africa to the late 19th Century, 1967; Africa in History: Themes and Outlines, 1968; The Liberation of Guiné, 1969; The Africans, An Entry to Cultural History, 1969; Discovering our African Heritage, 1971; In the Eye of the Storm: Angola's People, 1972; Black Star, 1974; Can Africa Survive?, 1975. *Address:* c/o Barclays Bank Ltd, PO Box 175, EC4P 4DR.

DAVIDSON, Brian, CBE 1965; *b* 14 Sept. 1909; *o s* of late Edward Fitzwilliam Davidson and late Esther Davidson (*née* Schofield); *m* 1935, Priscilla Margaret, *d* of late Arthur Farquhar and Florence Chilver; one *s* one *d* (and one *s* decd). *Educ:* Winchester Coll. (Scholar); New Coll., Oxford (Scholar). Gaisford Prize for Greek Verse; 1st class Honour Mods.; 2nd class LitHum; President, Oxford Union Society; President OU Conservative Assoc.; BA 1932. Cholmeley Student Lincoln's Inn; Barrister-at-Law, 1933; Law Society Sheffield Prize; Solicitor, 1939; Air Ministry and Ministry of Aircraft Production, 1940. With Bristol Aeroplane Co., 1943-68: Business Manager, 1946; Director, 1950-68; Director, Bristol Siddeley Engines Ltd, 1959-68. Solicitor with Gas Council, later British Gas Corp., 1969-75. Member: Monopolies Commission, 1954-68; Gloucestershire CC (and Chairman Rating Valuation Appeals Cttee), 1953-60; Cttee Wine Society, 1966-. *Recreations:* fox-hunting, sailing (represented Oxford Univ.), Scottish country dancing, bridge. *Address:* Sands Court, Dodington, Avon BS17 6SE. *T:* Chipping Sodbury 313077.
See also Prof. G. E. F. Chilver, R. C. Chilver.

DAVIDSON, Charles Kemp, QC (Scot.) 1969; Procurator to the General Assembly of the Church of Scotland, since 1972; *b* Edinburgh, 13 April 1929; *s* of Rev. Donald Davidson, DD, Edinburgh; *m* 1960, Mary, *d* of Charles Mactaggart, Campbeltown, Argyll; one *s* two *d*. *Educ:* Fettes Coll.,

Edinburgh; Brasenose Coll., Oxford; Edinburgh Univ. Admitted to Faculty of Advocates, 1956; Vice-Dean, 1977-; Keeper, Advocates' Library, 1972-76. *Address:* 22 Dublin Street, Edinburgh EH1 3PP. *T:* 031-556 2168.

DAVIDSON, Hon. Sir Charles (William), KBE 1964 (OBE 1945); retired; *b* 14 Sept. 1897; *s* of Alexander Black Davidson and Marion Perry; *m* 1929, Mary Gertrude Godschall Johnson; one *s* two *d*. *Educ:* Townsville Grammar Sch., Townsville. Served European War, 1914-18: 42 Bn AIF, 1916-19; Lieut; France (wounded); served War of 1939-45: 42 Bn AIF, 1939-44; Lt-Col; Hon. Colonel 42 Inf. Bn, 1955. Dairy farmer, 1921-25; sugar farming from 1925. MHR for Capricornia (Queensland), 1946-49, and for Dawson (Queensland), 1949-63, retired; Postmaster-General, 1956-63; Minister for Navy, 1956-58; Dep. Leader, Parliamentary Country Party, 1958-63. *Recreations:* bowls, golf, fishing, gardening. *Address:* 439 Brisbane Corso, Yeronga, Brisbane, Qld 4104, Australia. *T:* Brisbane 48.4264. *Clubs:* United Service, Masonic (Brisbane); Mackay Civic.

DAVIDSON, Francis, CBE 1961; Finance Officer, Singapore High Commission, London, 1961-71; *b* 23 Nov. 1905; *s* of James Davidson and Margaret Mackenzie; *m* 1937, Marial Mackenzie, MA; one *s* one *d*. *Educ:* Millbank Public Sch., Nairn; Nairn Academy. Commercial Bank of Scotland Ltd, 1923-29; Bank of British West Africa Ltd, 1929-41; Colonial Service (Treasury), 1941-61; retired from Colonial Service, Nov. 1961, as Accountant-General of Federation of Nigeria. *Recreation:* philately. *Address:* Woolton, Nairn, Scotland. *T:* Nairn 52187. *Club:* Royal Over-Seas League.

DAVIDSON, Howard William, CMG 1961; MBE 1942; *b* 30 July 1911; *s* of late Joseph Christopher Davidson, Johannesburg, and Helen, *d* of James Forbes; *m* 1st, 1941, Anne Elizabeth, *d* of late Captain R. C. Power; one *d*; 2nd, 1956, Dorothy (marr. diss. 1972), *d* of late Sir Wm Polson, KCMG; one *step s. Educ:* King Edward VII Sch., Johannesburg; Witwatersrand Univ.; Oriel Coll., Oxford (1st cl. Greats 1934). Cadet, Colonial Admin. Service, Sierra Leone, 1935; District Commissioner, 1942; Dep. Fin. Secretary, 1949; Fin. Secretary, Fiji, 1952; Fin. Secretary, N Borneo, 1958; State Financial Secretary and Member Cabinet, Sabah, Malaysia, 1963-64; Financial Adviser, 1964-65; Member of Inter-Governmental Cttee which led to establishment of new Federation of Malaysia; retired, 1965. Inspector (part-time) Min. of Housing and Local Government, 1967-70. Consultant with Peat, Marwick Mitchell & Co, to report on finances of Antigua, 1973. Appointed PDK (with title of Datuk) in first Sabah State Honours List, 1963. *Recreations:* cricket, gardening, fishing. *Address:* Glebe Cottage, Tillington, Petworth, West Sussex. *Clubs:* East India, Devonshire, Sports and Public Schools; Sussex County Cricket.

DAVIDSON, Ian Douglas, CBE 1957; *b* 27 Oct. 1901; *s* of Rev. John Davidson, JP, and Elizabeth Helen (*née* Whyte); *m* 1st, 1936, Claire Louise (*d* 1937), *d* of E. S. Gempp, St Louis, Missouri; one *d*; 2nd, 1938, Eugenia, *d* of late Marques de Mohernando and Lorenza, Marquesa de Mohernando; one *d. Educ:* King William's Coll. Royal Dutch Shell Group of Companies, 1921-61; President: Mexican Eagle Oil Co., 1936-47; Cia Shell de Venezuela, 1953-57; Canadian Shell Ltd, 1957-61. Order of St Mark (Lebanon), 1957; Orden del Libertador (Venezuela), 1957. *Address:* 494 Avenue Road, Toronto, Ontario M4V 2J5, Canada. *Clubs:* Caledonian (London); Toronto, York (Toronto); Links (NY).

DAVIDSON, Ian Thomas Rollo, QC 1977; a Recorder of the Crown Court, since Dec. 1974; *b* 3 Aug. 1925; *s* of late Robert Davidson and of Margaret Davidson; *m* 1954, Gyöngyi, *d* of Prof. Cs. Anghi; one *s* one *d. Educ:* Fettes Coll.; Corpus Christi Coll., Oxford (Schol.). MA, Lit. Hum. Royal Armoured Corps, 1943-47, Lieut Derbs Yeomanry. Called to Bar, Gray's Inn, 1955. Asst Lectr, University Coll., London, 1959-60; Deputy Recorder, Nottingham, 1971. *Recreations:* music, golf, photography. *Address:* 28A Queen's Avenue, N10 3NR. *T:* 01-444 6592.

DAVIDSON, Ivor Macaulay; Director-General Engines, Procurement Executive, Ministry of Defence, since 1974; *b* 27 Jan. 1924; *s* of late James Macaulay and Violet Alice Davidson; *m* 1948, Winifred Lowes; four *s* one *d. Educ:* Bellahouston Sch.; Univ. of Glasgow. Royal Aircraft Establishment, 1943; Power Jets (R&D) Ltd, 1944; attached RAF, 1945; National Gas Turbine Establishment, 1946: Dep. Dir, 1964; Dir, 1970-74. *Publications:* numerous, scientific and technical. *Recreations:* music, gardening. *Address:* Monksway, Pirbright Road, Farnborough, Hants. *T:* Farnborough 44686.

DAVIDSON, James, MB, ChB, FRCP Edinburgh; FSAScot.; late Senior Lecturer on Pathology, University of Edinburgh and Consultant Pathologist to the Edinburgh Southern Hospitals and The Royal Victoria and Associated Hospitals; *b* 3 Feb. 1896; *s* of James Davidson and Isabella Slater Shaw; *m* 1927, Constance Ellen Cameron; two *d. Educ:* University of Edinburgh. House Physician, Royal Infirmary, Edinburgh; Tutor in Clinical Medicine, University of Edinburgh; Lecturer on Morbid Anatomy and Senior Asst to Prof. of Pathology, University of Edinburgh; Senior Pathologist to Royal Infirmary, Edinburgh; Asst to Prof. of Medical Jurisprudence, University of Edinburgh; Lecturer on Forensic Medicine, London Hospital Medical Coll.; Director of Metropolitan Police Laboratory, Hendon, NW9. *Publications:* various papers on subjects dealing with Pathology and Forensic Science; (joint) text-book, Practical Pathology, 1938. *Recreations:* gardening, golf and fishing. *Address:* Linton Muir, West Linton, Peebles-shire. *Club:* New (Edinburgh).

DAVIDSON, James Alfred, OBE 1971; British High Commissioner, Brunei, since 1974; *b* 22 March 1922; *s* of Lt-Comdr A. D. Davidson and Mrs (Elizabeth) Davidson; *m* 1955, Daphne (*née* While); two *d,* and two step *s. Educ:* Christ's Hospital; RN Coll., Dartmouth. Royal Navy, 1939-60 (war Service Atlantic, Mediterranean and Far East); commanded HM Ships Calder and Welfare; Comdr 1955; retd 1960. Holds Master Mariner's Cert. of Service. Called to the Bar, Middle Temple, 1960. Joined CRO (later FCO) 1960; served Port of Spain, Phnom Penh (periods as Chargé d'Affaires 1970 and 1971); Dacca (Chargé d'Affaires, later Dep. High Comr, 1972-73). Visiting Scholar, University of Kent, 1973-74. *Recreations:* usual. *Address:* c/o Foreign and Commonwealth Office, SW1; Little Frankfield, Seal Chart, Kent. *T:* Sevenoaks 61600. *Club:* Army and Navy.

DAVIDSON, James Duncan Gordon, MVO 1947; Chief Executive, Royal Highland and Agricultural Society of Scotland, since 1970; *b* 10 Jan. 1927; *s* of Alastair Gordon Davidson and M. Valentine B. Davidson (*née* Osborne); *m* 1st, 1955, Catherine Ann Jamieson; one *s* two *d* ; 2nd, 1973, Janet Stafford. *Educ:* RN Coll., Dartmouth; Downing Coll., Cambridge. Active List, RN, 1944-55. Subseq. farming, and political work; contested (L) West Aberdeenshire, 1964; MP (L) West Aberdeenshire, 1966-70. Introduces Country Focus, Grampian TV. MBIM; MIEx. *Recreations:* family, farming, skiing. *Address:* Tillychetly, Alford, Aberdeenshire. *T:* Alford 2246.

DAVIDSON, James Patton; Deputy Chairman and Managing Director, Clyde Port Authority, since 1976; *b* 23 March 1928; *s* of Richard Davidson and Elizabeth Ferguson Carnichan; *m* 1953, Jean Stevenson Ferguson Anderson; two *s* . *Educ:* Rutherglen Acad.; Glasgow Univ. (BL). Mil. service, commissioned RASC, 1948-50. Clyde Navigation Trust, 1950; Asst Gen. Manager, 1958. Clyde Port Authority: Gen. Manager, 1966; Managing Dir. 1974. Chairman: Ardrossan Harbour Co.; Clydeport Stevedoring Services Ltd; Clyde Container Services Ltd; S. & H. McCall Transport (Glasgow) Ltd; Scotway Haulage Ltd; Scotway Joinery Services Ltd; R. & J. Strang Ltd; Rhu Marina Ltd; Nat. Assoc. of Port Employers, 1974—. FCIT. *Recreations:* golf, reading. *Address:* 25 Stewarton Drive, Cambuslang. Glasgow G72 8DF. *T:* 041-641 3346; Clyde Port Authority, 16 Robertson Street, Glasgow G2 8DS. *T:* 042-221 8733. *Clubs:* Oriental; Royal Scottish Automobile (Glasgow); Cambuslang Golf; Troon Golf.

DAVIDSON, Prof. John Frank, FRS 1974; Professor of Chemical Engineering, University of Cambridge, since 1975; *b* 7 Feb. 1926; *s* of John and Katie Davidson; *m* 1948, Susanne Hedwig Ostberg; one *s* one *d. Educ:* Heaton Grammar Sch., Newcastle upon Tyne; Trinity Coll., Cambridge. MA, PhD, ScD; CEng, FIChemE, MIMechE. 1st cl. Mech. Scis Tripos, Cantab, 1946, BA 1947. Engrg work at Rolls Royce, Derby, 1947-50; Cambridge Univ.: Research Fellow, Trinity Coll., 1949; research, 1950-52; Univ. Demonstrator, 1952; Univ. Lectr, 1954; Steward of Trinity Coll., 1957-64; Reader in Chem. Engrg, Univ. of Cambridge, 1964-75. Visiting Professor: Univ. of Delaware, 1960; Univ. of Sydney, 1967. Mem., Flixborough Ct of Inquiry, 1974-75. Pres., IChemE, 1970-71. Founder Fellow, Fellowship of Engineering, 1976. For. Associate, Nat. Acad. of Engrg, US, 1976. *Publications:* (with D. Harrison): Fluidised Particles, 1963; Fluidization, 1971. *Recreations:* hill walking, gardening, mending cars and other domestic artefacts. *Address:* 5 Luard Close, Cambridge CB2 2PL. *T:* Cambridge 46104.

DAVIDSON, Maj.-Gen. Kenneth Chisholm, CB 1948; MC; psc; late Infantry; *b* 4 July 1897; *m* 1934, Diana Blanche Wilson; one

s one *d. Educ:* Newbury Grammar Sch. 2nd Lieut Gordon Highlanders, 1915; served European War, 1914-19 (wounded twice); War of 1939-45, Persia and Iraq Force (despatches), Sicily (despatches), Italy (despatches). Lieut-Col, 1942; Col, 1942; Brig., 1947; actg Maj.-Gen., 1946; retired pay, 1949 (with hon. rank of Maj.-Gen.). *Address:* Rooklands, Tangley, near Andover, Hants. *T:* Chute Standen 612.

DAVIDSON, Sir (Leybourne) Stanley (Patrick), Kt 1955; FRSE; Professor of Medicine, University of Edinburgh, 1938-59, retired; Physician to the Queen in Scotland, 1952-61, an Extra Physician to HM in Scotland, since 1961; *b* 3 March 1894; 2nd *s* of late Sir L. F. W. Davidson; *m* Isabel Margaret, *e d* of late Hon. Lord Anderson; no *c. Educ:* Cheltenham Coll.; Trinity Coll., Cambridge; Edinburgh Univ.; BA (Cambridge), MB, ChB 1919, Edinburgh Univ., 1st class hons, MD, awarded gold medal for thesis; MD Oslo; FRCP (London), 1940; FRCP (Edinburgh), 1925. Pres., 1953-56; LLD (Edinburgh Univ.) 1962. Regius Prof. of Medicine, University of Aberdeen, 1930-38; Sen. Phys. Royal Infirmary, Aberdeen, 1932-38, etc. Hon. Physician to King George VI in Scotland, 1947-52. Hon. LLD Aberdeen, 1970. *Publications:* Pernicious Anæmia, monograph (with Prof. G. L. Gulland), 1930; A Textbook of Medical Treatment (with D. M. Dunlop and Stanley Alstead), 1963; The Principles and Practice of Medicine (with Staff of Edinburgh Univ. Dept of Medicine), 1963; Human Nutrition and dietetics (with R. Passmore), 1963; articles in medical journals. *Recreations:* tennis, golf, fishing, shooting. *Address:* 28 Barnton Gardens, Davidson's Mains, Edinburgh EH4 6AE. *Club:* New (Edinburgh).

DAVIDSON, Mrs Paul; see Cairns, Julia.

DAVIDSON, Roger Alastair McLaren, CMG 1947; Secretary of the Scottish Universities Entrance Board, 1953-66; *b* 6 Feb. 1900; *s* of late Rev. R. S. Davidson, The Manse, Kinfauns, Perthshire; *m* 1928, Elsie Stuart, *d* of late J. A. Y. Stronach, Edinburgh; one *s* one *d. Educ:* Fettes Coll., Edinburgh; University of Edinburgh. Served European War, 1914-18, 2nd Lieut Royal Highlanders, 1918-19; entered Colonial Education Service, 1924; Nigeria, 1924-37; Asst Dir of Education, Tanganyika, 1937-40; seconded to Colonial Office, 1941-43; Asst Dir of Education, Southern Provinces, Nigeria, 1943-44; Dir of Education, Nigeria, 1944-51; Inspector-Gen. of Education, Nigeria, 1951-53. *Address:* Longrigg, St Andrews. *T:* 2345. *Club:* Royal and Ancient (St Andrews).

DAVIDSON, Air Vice-Marshal Sinclair Melville, CBE 1968; Secretary, The Institution of Electronic and Radio Engineers, since 1977; *b* 1 Nov. 1922; *s* of late James Stewart Davidson and Ann Sinclair Davidson (*née* Cowan); *m* 1944, Jean Irene, *d* of late Edward Albert Flay; one *s* (and one *s* decd). *Educ:* Bousfield Sch., Kensington; RAF Cranwell; RAF Techn. College. CEng, FIERE. War service with 209, 220 and 53 Sqdns RAF, 1941-45 (despatches); Staff RAF Coastal and Fighter Comds, 1946-53; Air Staff, Egypt, Iraq and Cyprus, 1954-55; psa 1956; Air Staff, Air Min., 1957-60; jssc 1960; Dirg Staff, RAF Staff Coll., Bracknell, 1961-63; Asst Comdt, RAF Locking, 1963-64; Chm. Jt Signal Bd (Middle East), 1965; Chief Signal Officer and Comd Electrical Engr, Near East Air Force, 1966-67; idc 1968; Dir of Signals (Air), MoD, 1969-71; AO Wales and Stn Comdr, RAF St Athan, 1972-74; Asst Chief of Defence Staff (Signals), 1974-77. *Address:* Moy Cottage, Fielden Lane, Crowborough, Sussex. *T:* Crowborough 4724. *Club:* Royal Air Force.

DAVIDSON, Sir Stanley; see Davidson, Sir L. S. P.

DAVIDSON, William Bird; a Deputy Chairman, National Westminster Bank Ltd, 1973-76 (Director and Chief Executive, 1970-72); Chairman, Lombard North Central, 1973-76; Director, Allied London Properties Ltd, since 1976; *b* 18 May 1912; 2nd *s* of late J. N. Davidson; *m* 1941, Christina M. Ireton; two *s. Educ:* Queen Elizabeth Grammar Sch., Penrith. War Service, Royal Artillery, 1939-45. Entered Nat. Provincial Bank, 1929; Jt Gen Manager, 1961; Chief Gen. Manager, 1967-68; Dir, 1968; Dir and Jt Chief Executive, Nat. Westminster Bank, 1968-70. FIB. *Recreation:* golf. *Address:* Rose Cottage, 9 Starrock Road, Coulsdon, Surrey. *T:* Downland 53687.

DAVIDSON-HOUSTON, Major Aubrey Claud; portrait painter since 1952; *b* 2 Feb. 1906; *s* of late Lt-Col Wilfred Bennett Davidson-Houston, CMG, and Annie Henrietta Hunt; *m* 1938, Georgina Louie Ethel (*d* 1961), *d* of late Capt. H. S. Dobson; one *d. Educ:* St Edward's Sch., Oxford; RMC, Sandhurst; Slade Sch. of Fine Art. 2nd Lieut, Royal Sussex Regt, 1925; ADC to Governor of Western Australia, 1927-30; Nigeria Regt, RWAFF, 1933-37; PoW (Germany), 1940-45; Sch. of Infty, 1946-47; MS Branch, WO, 1948-49; retd, 1949. Slade Sch. of

Fine Art, 1949-52 (diploma). *Portraits include:* The Queen, for RWF; The Duke of Edinburgh, for 8th King's Royal Irish Hussars, for Duke of Edinburgh's Royal Regt, and for the House of Lords; Queen Elizabeth, The Queen Mother, for Black Watch of Canada; The Prince of Wales, for Royal Regt of Wales; The Princess Royal, for WRAC; The Duke of Gloucester, for Royal Inniskilling Fusiliers, for Scots Guards and for Trinity House; The Duchess of Kent for ACC; also portraits for Lincoln Coll. and Keble Coll., Oxford, and for Selwyn Coll., Cambridge; also for a number of other regts and for City Livery cos, schools, etc. A Governor, St Edward's School, Oxford. *Address:* Hillview, West End Lane, Esher, Surrey. *T:* Esher 64769; 4 Chelsea Studios, 412 Fulham Road, SW6. *T:* 01-385 2569. *Clubs:* Buck's, Naval and Military, MCC.

DAVIE, Alan, CBE 1972; painter, poet, jazz musician and designer of jewellery; *b* 1920. *Educ:* Edinburgh Coll. of Art. Gregory Fellowship, Leeds Univ., 1956-59. One-man exhibitions, since 1946, in GB, USA and most European countries. Work represented in exhibitions: 4th Internat. Art Exhibn, Japan; Pittsburgh Internat.; Documenta II & III, Kassel, Germany; British Painting 1700-1960, Moscow; Salon de Mai, Paris; Peggy Guggenheim Collection; ROSC Dublin; Peter Styvesant Collection; British Painting and Sculpture 1960-1970, Washington; III Bienal de Arte Coltejer, Colombia; British Painting, Hayward Gall., 1974; One-man exhbn, Edinburgh Fest., 1972. Works in Public Collections: Tate Gall., Belfast, Bristol, Durham, Edinburgh, Hull, Leeds, Manchester, Newcastle, Wakefield; Boston, Buffalo, Dallas, Detroit, Yale New Haven, Phoenix, Pittsburgh, Rhode Island, San Francisco; Ottawa, Adelaide, Sydney, Auckland, São Paulo, Tel Aviv, Venice, Vienna, Baden-Baden, Bochum, Munich, Amsterdam, Eindhoven, The Hague, Rotterdam, Oslo, Basle, Stockholm, Gothenburg and Paris. First public recital of music, Gimpel Fils Gall., 1971. Prize for Best Foreign Painter, VII Bienal de São Paulo, 1963. *Relevant publication:* Alan Davie (ed Alan Bowness), 1967. *Address:* Gamels Studio, Rush Green, Hertford.

DAVIE, Rev. Sir (Arthur) Patrick; *see* Ferguson Davie.

DAVIE, Cedric Thorpe, OBE 1955; FRAM; Master of Music, since 1945, and Professor of Music, since 1973, University of St Andrews; composer (especially for film, theatre, radio); *b* 30 May 1913; *s* of Thorpe and Gladys Louise Davie; *m* 1937, Margaret Russell Brown (*d* 1974); two *s. Educ:* High Sch. of Glasgow; Royal Scottish Academy of Music; Royal Academy of Music; Royal College of Music. Member: Scottish Arts Council, 1965-74; Arts Council of Great Britain, 1968-74. FRAM, 1949. Hon. Mem., Royal Scottish Acad., 1977. Hon. LLD Dundee, 1969. *Publications:* Musical Structure and Design, 1949; Oxford Scottish Song Book, 1969; Robert Burns: writer of songs, 1975; articles and reviews in learned jls. *Recreations:* eating and drinking; travel Northwards in search of sunshine. *Address:* 5 North Street, St Andrews, Fife. *T:* St Andrews 3950.

DAVIE, Prof. Donald Alfred; Olive H. Palmer Professor in the Humanities, Stanford University, California, since 1974; *b* 17 July 1922; *s* of George Clarke Davie and Alice (*née* Sugden); *m* 1945, Doreen John; two *s* one *d. Educ:* Barnsley Holgate Gram. Sch.; St Catharine's Coll., Cambridge (Hon. Fellow, 1973). BA 1947; PhD 1951. Served with Royal Navy, 1941-46 (Sub-Lieut RNVR). Lecturer in Dublin Univ., 1950-57; Fellow of Trinity Coll., Dublin, 1954-57; Visiting Prof., University of Calif., 1957-58; Lecturer, Cambridge Univ., 1958-64; Fellow of Gonville and Caius Coll., Cambridge, 1959-64; George Elliston Lecturer, University of Cincinnati, 1963; Prof. of Literature, University of Essex, 1964-68, and Pro-Vice-Chancellor, 1965-68; Prof. of English, Stanford Univ., 1968-74. Clark Lectr, Trinity Coll., Cambridge, 1976. Fellow, Amer. Acad. of Arts and Scis, 1973. *Publications:* poetry: Brides of Reason, 1955; A Winter Talent, 1957; The Forests of Lithuania, 1959; A Sequence for Francis Parkman, 1961; Events and Wisdoms, 1964; Essex Poems, 1969; Six Epistles to Eva Hesse, 1970; Collected Poems, 1972; The Shires, 1975; In the Stopping Train, 1977; criticism and literary history: Purity of Diction in English Verse, 1952; Articulate Energy, 1957, 2nd edn 1976; The Heyday of Sir Walter Scott, 1961; Ezra Pound: Poet as Sculptor, 1965; Introduction to The Necklace by Charles Tomlinson, 1955; Thomas Hardy and British Poetry, 1972; Pound, 1976; anthologies: The Late Augustans, 1958; (with Angela Livingstone) Modern Judgements: Pasternak, 1969; Augustan Lyric, 1974. *Recreations:* verse-translation; literary politics; travel. *Address:* 989 Cottrell Way, Stanford, Calif 94305, USA. *Clubs:* Athenæum, Savile; Union (Cambridge).

DAVIE, Sir Paul (Christopher), Kt 1967; Chairman, Council and General Development Services Ltd, since 1971; *b* 30 Sept. 1901;

s of Charles Christopher Davie and Beatrice Paulina Mabel (*née* Walrond); *m* 1938, Betty Muriel, *d* of late Captain Ronald Henderson, MP for Henley div. of Oxfordshire, 1924-32, of Studley Priory, Oxon.; one *s* one *d. Educ:* Winchester; New Coll., Oxford. Called to Bar, Lincoln's Inn, 1925; 2nd Asst Legal Advisor, Home Office, 1936; Asst Legal Advisor, 1947. Remembrancer, City of London, 1953-67. Chm., Nat. Deaf Children's Soc., 1970-74. *Publications:* Silicosis and Asbestosis Compensation Schemes, 1932; Joint Managing Ed., Encyclopædia of Local Government Law and Administration, 1934. *Recreations:* history, gardening. *Address:* The Old Rectory, Bentley, Hants. *T:* Bentley 3128. *Club:* Travellers'.

DAVIE, Prof. Ronald, PhD; FBPsS; Professor of Educational Psychology, Department of Education, University College, Cardiff, since 1974; *b* 25 Nov. 1929; *s* of late Thomas Edgar Davie and Gladys (*née* Powell); *m* 1957, Kathleen, *d* of William Wilkinson, Westhoughton, Lancs; one *s* one *d. Educ:* King Edward VI Grammar Sch., Aston, Birmingham; Univ. of Reading (BA 1954); Univ. of Manchester (PGCE and Dip. Deaf Educn 1955); Univ. of Birmingham (Dip. Educnl Psych. 1960); Univ. of London (PhD 1970). FBPsS 1973. Teacher, schs for normal and handicapped children, 1955-60; Co. Educnl Psychologist, IoW, 1961-64; Nat. Children's Bureau, London: Sen. Res. Officer, 1964; Dep. Dir, 1968; Dir of Res., 1972. Co-Dir, Nat. Child Develt Study, 1968-; Pres., Links Assoc., 1977-; Chairman: Trng and Educn. Cttee, Nat. Assoc. Mental Health, 1969-72; Working Gp rep. nat. vol. orgs concerned with handicapped children, 1971-74; Assoc. for Child Psychol. and Psychiatry, 1972-73 (Hon. Sec. 1965-70); Working Gp rep. professional assocs in S Wales concerned with children, 1974-; Working Party, Children Appearing Before Juvenile Courts, Children's Reg. Planning Cttee for Wales, 1975-77; Develt Psychol. Section, Brit. Psychol. Soc., 1975-77 (Treas. 1973-75). Member: Council of Management, Nat. Assoc. Mental Health, 1969-; Working Party, Children at Risk, DHSS, 1970-72; Educn and Employment Cttee, Nat. Deaf Children's Soc., 1972-; Management Cttee, Craig y Parc Sch., 1974-76; Local Authority Social Services Res. Liaison Gp, DHSS, 1975-77; Cttee, Welsh Br., Assoc. for Child Psychol. and Psychiatry, 1975-; Chief Scientist's Res. Cttee, DHSS, 1977-; Bd of Assessors, Therapeutic Educn, 1975-. *Publications:* (co-author) 11,000 Seven-Year Olds, 1966; Directory of Voluntary Organisations concerned with Children, 1969; Living with Handicap, 1970; From Birth to Seven, 1972; chapters in books and papers in sci. and other jls on educn, psychol., child care and health. *Recreations:* photography, antique furniture, Rugby, athletics. *Address:* 26 Archer Road, Penarth, South Glam CF6 2HJ. *T:* Penarth 703248.

DAVIES, family name of **Barons Darwen, Davies, Davies of Leek** and **Davies of Penrhys.**

DAVIES; *see* Edmund-Davies.

DAVIES; *see* Llewelyn-Davies.

DAVIES, 3rd Baron, *cr* 1932, of Llandinam; **David Davies,** MA; CEng, MICE, MBA; Chairman, Welsh National Opera and Drama Company, since 1975; *b* 2 Oct. 1940; *s* of 2nd Baron and Ruth Eldrydd (*d* 1966), 3rd *d* of Major W. M. Dugdale, CB, DSO; *S* father (killed in action), 1944; *m* 1972, Beryl, *d* of W. J. Oliver, Harborne, Birmingham; one *s* one *d. Educ:* Eton; King's Coll., Cambridge. *Heir: s* Hon. David Daniel Davies, *b* 23 Oct. 1975. *Address:* Plas Dinam, Llandinam, Powys.

DAVIES OF LEEK, Baron *cr* 1970 (Life Peer), of Leek, Staffordshire; **Harold Davies,** PC 1969; Member, Executive Committee, Inter-Parliamentary Union, since 1975; *b* 31 July 1904; *m* Jessie Elizabeth Bateman, BSc, London; one *d. Educ:* Lewis Grammar Sch., Pengam, Glam. Trained for teaching; Schoolmaster and Tutor in Adult Education; several lecture tours in USA and Canada; Lecturer to various organisations and Labour Movement. MP (Lab) Leek Div. of Staffs, 1945-70; formerly Member several Parliamentary Cttees; Joint Parliamentary Secretary, Ministry of Social Security, 1966-67 (Ministry of Pensions and National Insurance, 1965-66). Special Envoy of (Prime Minister) on Peace Mission to Hanoi, 1965. FRGS. *Publications:* various Press articles on Social and Educational Problems, etc.; numerous writings and pamphlets on Far East, SE Asia, etc. *Recreations:* was keen on all sports and played most of them, now interested in foreign affairs (Far East), agriculture, education, economic affairs. *Address:* 81 Trentham Road, Longton, Stoke-on-Trent, Staffs. *T:* Stoke-on-Trent 39976; 77 Montpelier Rise, NW1. 02-455 8015.

DAVIES OF PENRHYS, Baron *cr* 1974 (Life Peer), of Rhondda; **Gwilym Elfed Davies;** *b* 9 Oct. 1913; *s* of David Davies and

Miriam Elizabeth (*née* Williams); *m* 1940, Gwyneth Rees, *d* of Daniel and Agnes Janet Rees; two *s* one *d*. *Educ:* Tylorstown Boys' Sch. Branch Official Tylorstown Lodge, NUM, 1935-59. Member Glamorgan CC, 1954-61. Chairman Local Government Cttee, 1959-61. MP (Lab) Rhondda East, Oct. 1959-Feb. 1974; PPS to Minister of Labour, 1964-68, to Minister of Power, 1968. Part-time Mem., S Wales Electricity Bd, 1974-. Freeman, Borough of Rhondda, 1975. *Recreations:* Rugby football and cricket. *Address:* Maes-y-Ffrwd, Ferndale Road, Tylorstown, Rhondda, Glam. *T:* Ferndale 730254.

DAVIES, Air Commodore Adolphus Dan, CB 1953; CBE 1947; psa; *b* 14 Oct. 1902; *m* 1925, Kathleen Hobbs (*d* 1969); one *d*. Cranwell, 1921-23; Air Ministry, Dep. Directorate War Organisation, 1938; Commanded Scampton, Bomber Command, 1943; Fiskerton, Bomber Command, 1944; Air Ministry, Directorate Gen. of Manning, 1944; Air Officer Commanding Royal Air Force, Hong Kong, 1948; Air Cdre 1949; Air Officer in charge of Administration, Coastal Command, 1951-54; retired Aug. 1954. *Address:* 22 Ravenswood Park, Northwood, Mddx. *T:* Northwood 24290.

DAVIES, Air Marshal Alan Cyril, CB 1974; CBE 1967; Deputy C-in-C, RAF Strike Command, since 1977; *b* 31 March 1924; *s* of Richard Davies, Maidstone; *m* Julia Elizabeth Ghislaine Russell; two *s* (and one *s* decd). Enlisted RAF, 1941; commnd 1943; comd Joint Anti-Submarine School Flight, 1952-54; comd Air Sea Warfare Development Unit, 1958-59; comd No 201 Sqdn, 1959-61; Air Warfare Coll., 1962; Dep. Dir, Operational Requirements, MoD, 1964-66; comd RAF Stradishall, Suffolk, 1967-68; idc 1969; Dir of Air Plans, MoD, 1969-72; ACAS (Policy), MoD, 1972-74; Dep. COS (Ops and Intell.), HQ Allied Air Forces Central Europe, 1974-77. *Address:* R3 Section, Lloyds Bank Ltd, 6 Pall Mall, SW1. *Club:* Royal Air Force.

DAVIES, Albert John; Chief Agricultural Officer, Agricultural Development and Advisory Service, Ministry of Agriculture, Fisheries and Food, since 1971; *b* 21 Jan. 1919; *s* of David Daniel Davies and Annie Hilda Davies; *m* 1944, Winnifred Ivy Caroline Emberton; one *s* one *d*. *Educ:* Amman Valley Grammar Sch.; UCW Aberystwyth. BSc Hons agric. 1940. FIBiol. Adv. Staff, UCW Aberystwyth, 1940-41; Asst Techn. Adviser, Montgomeryshire War Agricultural Cttee, 1941-44; Farm Supt, Welsh Plant Breeding Stn, 1944-47; Nat. Agricultural Adv. Service: Crop Husbandry Adviser Wales, 1947-51; Grassland Husbandry Adviser Wales, 1951-57 and E Mids, 1957-59; Dep. Dir Wales, 1959-64; Regional Dir SW Region, 1964; Chief Farm Management Adviser, London Headquarters, 1964-67; Sen. Agric. Adviser, 1967-68; Dep. Dir, 1968-71. *Publications:* articles in learned jls and agric. press. *Recreations:* golf, Rugby, gardening. *Address:* Cefncoed, 38A Ewell Downs Road, Ewell, Surrey. *T:* 01-393 0069. *Club:* Farmers'.

DAVIES, (Albert) Meredith; Conductor: Royal Choral Society, since 1972; Leeds Philharmonic Society, since 1975; Guest Conductor, Royal Opera House, Covent Garden, and Sadler's Wells; also BBC; *b* 30 July 1922; 2nd *s* of Reverend E. A. Davies; *m* 1949, Betty Hazel, *d* of late Dr Kenneth Bates; three *s* one *d*. *Educ:* Royal College of Music; Stationers' Company's Sch.; Keble Coll., Oxford; Accademia di S. Cecilia, Rome. Junior Exhibitioner, RCM, 1930; Organist to Hurstpierpoint Coll., Sussex, 1939; elected Organ Scholar, Keble Coll., 1940. Served War of 1939-45, RA, 1942-45. Conductor St Albans Bach Choir, 1947; Organist and Master of the Choristers, Cathedral Church of St Alban, 1947-49; Musical Dir, St Albans Sch., 1948-49; Organist and Choirmaster, Hereford Cathedral, and Conductor, Three Choirs' Festival (Hereford), 1949-56; Organist and Supernumerary Fellow of New Coll., Oxford, 1956; Associate Conductor, City of Birmingham Symphony Orchestra, 1957-59; Dep. Musical Dir, 1959-60; Conductor, City of Birmingham Choir, 1957-64; Musical Dir, English Opera Group, 1963-65; Musical Dir, Vancouver Symphony Orchestra, 1964-71; Chief Conductor, BBC Trng Orchestra, 1969-72. *Address:* 8 Averill Street, W6 8EB.

DAVIES, Hon. Sir (Alfred William) Michael, Kt 1973; **Hon. Mr Justice Michael Davies;** a Judge of the High Court of Justice, Queen's Bench Division, since 1973; *b* 29 July 1921; *er s* of Alfred Edward Davies, Stourbridge; *m* 1947, Margaret, *y d* of Robert Ernest Jackson, Sheffield; one *s* three *d*. *Educ:* King Edward's Sch., Birmingham; University of Birmingham (LLB). Called to Bar, Lincoln's Inn, 1948, Bencher 1972; QC 1964; Dep. Chm. Northants QS, 1962-71; Recorder of: Grantham, 1963-65; Derby, 1965-71; Crown Court, 1972-73. Leader of Midland Circuit, 1968-71, Jt Leader of Midland and Oxford Circuit, 1971-73. Chm. Mental Health Review Tribunal, for Birmingham Area, 1965-71; Comr of Assize (Birmingham), 1970; Chancellor, Dio. of Derby, 1971-73; Mem., Gen. Council

of the Bar, 1968-72. Chm., Hospital Complaints Procedure Cttee, 1971-73. *Recreations:* golf and the theatre. *Address:* Royal Courts of Justice, WC2. *Club:* Garrick.

DAVIES, Alun B. O.; *see* Oldfield-Davies.

DAVIES, Very Rev. Alun Radcliffe; Dean of Llandaff, since 1977; *b* 6 May 1923; *s* of Rev. Rhys Davies and Jane Davies; *m* 1952, Winifred Margaret Pullen; two *s* one *d*. *Educ:* Cowbridge Grammar Sch.; University Coll., Cardiff (BA 1945); Keble Coll., Oxford (BA 1947, MA 1951); St Michael's Coll., Llandaff. Curate of Roath, 1948-49; Lecturer, St Michael's Coll., Llandaff, 1949-53; Domestic Chaplain to Archbishop of Wales, 1952-57, to Bishop of Llandaff, 1957-59; Chaplain RNR, 1953-60; Vicar of Ystrad Mynach, 1959-75; Chancellor of Llandaff Cathedral, 1969-71; Archdeacon of Llandaff, 1971-77; Residentiary Canon of Llandaff Cathedral, 1975-77. *Address:* The Deanery, The Cathedral Green, Llandaff, Cardiff. *T:* Cardiff 561545.

DAVIES, Sir Alun Talfan, Kt 1976; QC 1961; MA; LLB; barrister-at-law; a Recorder, and Honorary Recorder of Cardiff, since 1972; Judge of the Courts of Appeal, Jersey and Guernsey, since 1969; *b* Gorseinon, 22 July 1913; *s* of late Rev. W. Talfan Davies, Presbyterian Minister, Gorseinon; *m* 1942, Eiluned Christopher, *d* of late Humphrey R. Williams, Stanmore, Middx; one *s* three *d*. *Educ:* Gowerton Gram. Sch.; Aberystwyth Univ. Coll. of Wales (LLB), Hon. Professorial Fellow, 1971; Gonville and Caius Coll., Cambridge (MA, LLB). Called to the Bar, Gray's Inn, 1939; Bencher, 1969-. Practised on Wales and Chester circuit. Contested (Ind.) University of Wales (by-elec.), 1943; contested (L): Carmarthen Div., 1959 and 1964; Denbigh, 1966. Mem. Court of University of Wales and of Courts and Councils of Aberystwyth and Swansea University Colls. Recorder: of Merthyr Tydfil, 1963-68; of Swansea, 1968-69; of Cardiff, 1969-71; Dep. Chm., Cardiganshire QS, 1963-71. Mem., Commn on the Constitution, 1969-73. Pres., Court of Nat. Eisteddfod of Wales, 1977-. Dep. Chm., Commercial Bank of Wales, 1973- (Dir, 1971-); Vice-Chm., HTV Ltd. Chm. Trustees, Aberfan Fund (formerly Aberfan Disaster Fund), 1969-. Hon LLD Wales: Aberystwyth, 1973. *Address:* 10 Park Road, Penarth, South Glam. *T:* Penarth 701341; 5 King's Bench Walk, Temple, EC4. *T:* 01-353 4713. *Clubs:* Reform; Cardiff and County (Cardiff); Bristol Channel Yacht (Swansea).

DAVIES, Prof. Anna Elbina; Professor of Comparative Philology, Oxford University, since 1971; Fellow of Somerville College, Oxford, since 1971; *b* Milan, 21 June 1937; *d* of Augusto Morpurgo and Maria (*née* Castelnuovo); *m* 1962, John Kenyon Davies; no *c*. *Educ:* Liceo-Ginnasio Giulio Cesare, Rome; Univ. of Rome. Dott.lett. Rome, 1959; Libera docente, Rome, 1963; MA Oxford, 1964. Asst in Classical Philology, Univ. of Rome, 1959-61; Junior Research Fellow, Center for Hellenic Studies, Harvard Univ., 1961-62; Univ. Lectr in Classical Philology, Oxford, 1964-71; Fellow of St Hilda's Coll., Oxford, 1966-71, Hon. Fellow, 1972. Visiting Professor: Univ. of Pennsylvania, 1971; Yale Univ., 1977; Collitz Prof. of Ling. Soc. of America, Univ. of South Florida, 1975. Pres., Philological Soc., 1976-. *Publications:* Mycenaeae Graecitatis Lexicon, 1963; articles and reviews on comparative and classical philology in Italian, German, British and American jls. *Address:* 22 Yarnells Hill, Oxford. *T:* Oxford 47099; Somerville College, Oxford.

DAVIES, Rear-Adm. Anthony, CB 1964; CVO 1972; Royal Navy, retired; *b* 13 June 1912; *s* of James Arthur and Margaret Davies; *m* 1940, Lilian Hilda Margaret, *d* of Admiral Sir H. M. Burrough, *qv*; two *s* two *d*. *Educ:* Royal Naval College, Dartmouth. Midshipman, HMS Danae, 1930-32; Sub-Lieut, HMS Despatch, 1934; Lieut, HMS Duncan, 1935-37; Gunnery course, 1938; HMS Repulse, 1939; HMS Cossack 1940-41; Lieut-Comdr, HMS Indefatigable, 1943-45; Comdr, HMS Triumph, 1950; HMS Excellent, 1951-54; Capt., HMS Pelican, 1954-55; Dep. Dir, RN Staff Coll., 1956-57; Far East Fleet Staff, 1957-59; Dep. Dir, Naval Intelligence, 1959-62; Head of British Defence Liaison Staff, Canberra, Australia, 1963-65. Warden, St George's House, Windsor Castle, 1966-72. *Address:* Barn House, Aldbourne, Marlborough, Wilts. *T:* Aldbourne 418.

DAVIES, Rt. Hon. Sir Arthian; *see* Davies, Rt Hon. Sir (William) Arthian.

DAVIES, Prof. Arthur; Reardon-Smith Professor of Geography, University of Exeter, 1948-71; Deputy Vice-Chancellor, University of Exeter, 1969-71; Dean of the Faculty of Social Studies, 1961-64; *b* 13 March 1906; *s* of Richard Davies, Headmaster, and Jessie Starr Davies, Headmistress; *m* 1933, Lilian Margaret Morris; one *d*. *Educ:* Cyfarthfa Castle Sch.; University Coll. of Wales, Aberystwyth, 1st cl. Hons in

Geography and Anthropology, 1927; MSc Wales 1930; Fellow, University of Wales, 1929-30, Asst Lecturer in Geography, Manchester Univ., 1930-33; Lecturer in Geography, Leeds Univ., 1933-40. Served War of 1939-45, RA 1940-45, Normandy (despatches twice, Major); Mem., High Mil. Tribunal of Hamburg, 1945. *Publications:* Yugoslav Studies, Leplay Soc., London, 1932; Polish Studies, Leplay Soc., London, 1933; contrib. to Encyclopaedia Britannica and geographical and historical learned journals. *Recreations:* gardening and architecture. *Address:* Morlais, Winslade Park, Clyst St Mary, Devon. *T:* Topsham 3296.

DAVIES, Brian Meredith; see Davies, J. B. M.

DAVIES, Bryan; MP (Lab) Enfield North since Feb. 1974; *b* 9 Nov. 1939; *s* of George William and Beryl Davies; *m* 1963, Monica Rosemary Mildred Shearing; two *s* one *d*. *Educ:* Redditch High Sch.; University Coll., London; Inst. of Education; London Sch. of Economics. BA Hons History London, Certif. Educn, BScEcons London. Teacher, Latymer Sch., 1962-65; Lectr, Middlesex Polytechnic at Enfield, 1965-74. Member: Select Cttee on Public Expenditure, 1975-; Select Cttee on Overseas Develt, 1975-. Mem., MRC, 1977-. *Recreations:* playing cricket, squash, tennis; reading non-modern poetry; going to the theatre. *Address:* 21 Briscoe Road, Hoddesdon, Herts. *T:* Hoddesdon 66427. *Clubs:* Winchmore Hill Cricket, Enfield Highway Workingmen's.

DAVIES, Bryn; Member, Welsh Council, since 1965; Member, General Council, Wales Trades Union Congress, since 1974; Development Commissioner, since 1975; *b* 22 Jan. 1932; *s* of Gomer and Ann Davies; *m* 1956, Esme Irene Gould; two *s*. *Educ:* Cwmlai School, Tonyrefail. Served HM Forces (RAMC), 1949-51; Forestry Commn, 1951-56; South Wales and Hereford Organiser, Nat. Union of Agricultural Workers, 1956-. *Recreations:* cricket and Rugby football. *Address:* 36 Hall Drive, North Cornelly, Bridgend, Mid Glamorgan. *T:* Bridgend 740426. *Clubs:* Tonyrefail Rugby; Glamorgan CC.

DAVIES, Caleb William, CMG 1962; MRCS; LRCP; FFCM; DPH; Regional Specialist in Community Medicine, since 1974 (Acting Regional Medical Officer, 1977), South Western Regional Health Authority; *b* 27 Aug. 1916; *s* of Caleb Davies, KIH, MB, ChB, and Emily (*née* Platt); *m* 1939, Joan Heath; three *s* one *d*. *Educ:* Kingswood Sch., Bath; University Coll. and University Coll. Hosp. Med. Sch., London; Edinburgh Univ.; London Sch. of Hygiene and Tropical Med. Kenya: MO, 1941; MOH, Mombasa, 1946; Tanganyika: Sen. MO, 1950; Asst Dir of Med. Services, 1952; Uganda: Dep. Dir of Medical Services, 1958; Permanent Sec. and Chief Medical Officer, Ministry of Health, 1960; retired 1963; South-Western Regional Hosp. Bd: Asst SMO, 1963-66; Principal Asst SMO, 1966-74. *Recreations:* tennis, swimming, photography. *Address:* Thorncliffe, 7 The Batch, Saltford, near Bristol BS18 3EN. *T:* Saltford 3522.

DAVIES, Carlton Griffith, CMG 1953; MC 1915; *b* 2 Aug. 1895; *o* surv. *s* of late Walter Davies, MBE, Calcutta and Ealing; *m* 1926, Florence Evelyn, *y d* of late Robert MacSymon, Greenock and Liverpool; two *s* (and one *s* and one *d* decd). *Educ:* Rugby Sch.; Exeter Coll., Oxford. Served European War, 1914-19, London Regt (The Queen's), and Machine-Gun Corps (MC, despatches). Asst District Comr, Sudan Political Service, 1920; Comr, Gezira Area, 1930; Asst Civil Sec., 1935-36; Asst Financial Sec., 1936-40; seconded to Sudan Defence Force, 1940-41 (despatches). Governor, Upper Nile Province, 1941-45; Sudan Agent in London, 1951-55. 4th Class Order of the Nile (Egypt), 1930; Officer of the Order of Leopold (Belgium), 1949. *Recreations:* golf, sailing and gardening. *Address:* Three Lanes End Farm, Wisborough Green, Billingshurst, West Sussex RH14 0EF. *T:* Wisborough Green 375. *Clubs:* Royal Over-Seas League, Royal Commonwealth Society.

DAVIES, Ven. Carlyle W.; see Witton-Davies.

DAVIES, Christopher Evelyn K.; see Kevill-Davies.

DAVIES, (Claude) Nigel (Byam); *b* 2 Sept. 1920; unmarried. *Educ:* Eton. Studied at Aix en Provence University, 1937, and at Potsdam, 1938. PhD London (archaeology). Entered Sandhurst, 1939, and later commissioned Grenadier Guards. Served Middle East, Italy and Balkans, 1942-46. Formerly Managing Dir of Windolite Ltd from 1947. MP (C) Epping Div. of Essex, 1950-51. *Publications:* Los Señoríos Independientes del Imperio Azteca, 1968; Los Mexicas: Primeras Pasos Hacia el Imperio, 1973; The Aztecs, 1973. *Recreation:* travel. *Club:* Carlton.

DAVIES, Cyril James; County Treasurer, Tyne and Wear County, since 1973; *b* 24 Aug. 1923; *s* of James and Frances

Davies; *m* 1948, Elizabeth Leggett; two *s* two *d*. *Educ:* Heaton Grammar Sch. CIPFA, ACIS, FRVA. Served RN, Fleet Air Arm, 1942-46. City Treasurer's Dept, Newcastle upon Tyne, 1946-: Dep. City Treas., 1964; City Treas., 1969; Treas., Tyne and Wear Co., with additional management responsibility for leisure services, incl. arts and theatres, 1973-. Treasurer: Theatre Royal, Newcastle; Empire Theatre, Sunderland; Northumbria Tourist Bd. Mem. Adv. Council, Scottish Opera; Chm., Finance Cttee, Northern Sinfonia Orch. *Recreations:* theatre, walking, music. *Address:* 4 Mitchell Avenue, Jesmond, Newcastle upon Tyne NE2 3LA. *T:* Newcastle upon Tyne 815196. *Club:* Naval.

DAVIES, Dr David; Editor of Nature, since 1973; *b* 11 Aug. 1939; *s* of Trefor Alun and Kathleen Elsie Davies; *m* 1968, Joanna Rachel Peace; one *s* two *d*. *Educ:* Nottingham High Sch.; Peterhouse, Cambridge. MA, PhD. Res. Scientist, Dept of Geophysics, Cambridge, 1961-69; Rapporteur, Seismic Study Gp of Stockholm Internat. Peace Res. Inst. (SIPRI), 1968-73. Leader, Seismic Discrimination Gp, MIT Lincoln Laboratory, 1970-73. *Publications:* Seismic Methods for Monitoring Underground Explosions, 1968; numerous scientific papers. *Recreations:* orchestral and choral conducting. *Address:* 32 St Margaret's Passage, SE13. *T:* 01-852 4447.

DAVIES, David Arthur; Secretary-General, World Meteorological Organization, Geneva, Switzerland, since 1955; *b* 11 Nov. 1913; *s* of Garfield Brynmor Davies and Mary Jane Davies (*née* Michael); *m* 1938, Mary Shapland; one *s* two *d*. *Educ:* University of Wales (MSc) (1st cl. Hons Maths; 1st cl. Hons Physics). Technical Officer, Meteorological Office, 1936-39. War Service, RAF, 1939-47 (despatches). Principal Scientific Officer, Met. Office, 1947-49; Dir, E African Met. Dept, Nairobi, 1949-55; Pres. World Meteorological Organization Regional Assoc. for Africa, 1951-55. Hon. Member: Amer. Meteorological Soc., 1970; Hungarian Meteorol Soc., 1975. FInstP. Dr *hc* Univ. Bucharest, 1970. Eötvös Lorand, Univ. of Budapest, 1976. *Publications:* various meteorological papers and articles. *Recreation:* music. *Address:* Chemin des Rojalets, Coppet, Vaud, Switzerland. *T:* (022) 76 18 26. *Club:* Anglo-Belgian.

DAVIES, David Cyril, BA, LLB; Headmaster, Crown Woods School, since 1971; *b* 7 Oct. 1925; *s* of D. T. E. Davies and Mrs G. V. Davies, JP; *m* 1952, Joan Rogers, BSc; one *s* one *d*. *Educ:* Lewis Sch., Pengam; UCW Aberystwyth, Asst Master, Ebbw Vale Gram. Sch., 1951-55; Head, Lower Sch., Netteswell Bilateral Sch., 1955-58; Sen. Master and Dep. Headmaster, Peckham Manor Sch., 1958-64; Headmaster: Greenway Comprehensive Sch., 1964-67; Woodberry Down Sch., 1967-71. *Recreations:* reading, Rugby and roughing it. *Address:* 9 Plaxtol Close, Bromley, Kent. *T:* 01-464 4187.

DAVIES, Sir David (Henry), Kt 1973; first Chairman, Welsh Development Agency, since 1976; General Secretary, Iron and Steel Trades Confederation, 1967-75; *b* 2 Dec. 1909; British; *m* 1934, Elsie May Battrick; one *s* one *d* (and one *d* decd). *Educ:* Ebbw Vale, Mon. Organiser, 1950, Asst. Gen. Sec., 1953-66, Iron and Steel Trades Confederation. Chm., Jt Adv. Cttee on Safety and Health in the Iron and Steel Industry, 1965-67; Vice-Chm., Nat. Dock Labour Bd, 1966-68; Hon. Treas. WEA, 1962-69 (Mem. Central Coun. and Central Exec. Cttee, 1954-69); Hon. Treas., British Labour Party, 1965-67 (Chm., 1963; Mem. Nat. Exec., 1954-67); Hon. Sec., Brit. Sect., Internat. Metalworkers Federation, 1960-; Member: Ebbw Vale UDC, 1945-50; Royal Institute of International Affairs, 1954-; Iron and Steel Operatives Course Adv. Cttee, City and Guilds of London Institute Dept of Technology, 1954-68; Iron and Steel Industry Trng Bd, 1964-; Constructional Materials Gp, Economic Development Cttee for the Building and Civil Engrg Industries, 1965-68; Iron and Steel Adv. Cttee, 1966-; English Industrial Estates Corporation, 1971-; Vice-Pres., European Coal and Steel Community Consultative Cttee, 1975- (Pres., 1973-74). Governor: Ruskin Coll., Oxford, 1954-68; Iron and Steel Industry Management Trng Coll., Ashorne Hill, Leamington Spa, 1966-. Mem. TUC Gen. Coun., 1967-75. *Address:* 82 New House Park, St Albans, Herts. *T:* St Albans 56513.

DAVIES, D(avid) H(erbert) Mervyn, MC 1944; TD 1946; QC 1967; Barrister-at-law; *b* 17 Jan. 1918; *s* of Herbert Bowen Davies and Esther Davies, Llangunnor, Carms; *m* 1951, Zita Yollanne Angelique Blanche Antoinette, 2nd *d* of Rev. E. A. Phillips, Bale, Norfolk. *Educ:* Swansea Gram. Sch. Solicitor, 1939 (Daniel Reardon Prize, Travers Smith Schol.). Commissioned Welch Regt (TA), 1936; served War of 1939-45, 18th Bn Welch Regt and 2nd London Irish Rifles, Africa, Italy and Austria. Called to Bar, Lincoln's Inn, 1947; Bencher, 1974; Bar Council, 1972; Mem., Senate of Inns of Court, 1975.

Publication: The Copyright Act 1956, 1957. *Address:* 5 New Square, Lincoln's Inn, WC2. *T:* 01-405 6430; 7 Stone Buildings, Lincoln's Inn, WC2. *T:* 01-242 8061.

DAVIES, David Hywel, MA, PhD, FIEE; Assistant Chief Scientific Adviser (Projects), Ministry of Defence, since 1976; *b* 28 March 1929; *s* of John and Maggie Davies; *m* 1961, Valerie Elizabeth Nott; one *s* two *d*. *Educ:* Cardiff High Sch.; Christ's Coll., Cambridge. Radar Research Estabt, 1956; Head of Airborne Radar Group, RRE, 1970; Head of Weapons Dept, Admty Surface Weapons Estabt, 1972. *Publications:* papers on electronics, radar and remote sensing, in Proc. IEE, etc. *Recreations:* do-it-yourself, photography, knots. *Address:* 15 Denison Close, Malvern, Worcs WR14 2EU. *T:* Malvern 3330.

DAVIES, (David John) Denzil; MP (Lab) Llanelli since 1970; Minister of State, HM Treasury, since 1976; *b* 9 Oct. 1938; *s* of G. Davies, Conwil Elfed, Carmarthen; *m* 1963, Mary Ann Finlay, Illinois; one *s* one *d*. *Educ:* Queen Elizabeth Grammar Sch., Carmarthen; Pembroke Coll., Oxford. Bacon Scholar, Gray's Inn, 1961; BA (1st cl. Law) 1962; Martin Wronker Prize (Law), 1962. Teaching Fellow, Univ. of Chicago, 1963; Lectr in Law, Leeds Univ., 1964; called to Bar, Gray's Inn, 1964. Member: Select Cttee on Corporation Tax, 1971; Jt Select Cttee (Commons and Lords) on Delegated Legislation, 1972; Public Accounts Cttee, 1974-; PPS to the Secretary of State for Wales, 1974-76. *Address:* House of Commons, SW1.

DAVIES, Sir David (Joseph), Kt 1969; Chairman, Wales Tourist Board, 1965-70; *b* 30 Aug. 1896; *s* of David and Catherine Davies; *m* 1924, Eleanor Irene Davies (*née* Bowen); one *s*. *Educ:* Maesteg Higher Grade and Bridgend County Schools. Served in Welch Regt, 1915-19, Acting Captain. Mem. Court, University Coll., Cardiff, 1959-76; Mem. Court and Council, National Museum of Wales, 1961-73. *Address:* 28 Queen Anne Square, Cardiff CF1 3ED. *T:* Cardiff 22695. *Club:* Cardiff and County (Cardiff).

DAVIES, David Lewis, DM; Medical Director, Alcohol Education Centre; *b* 16 April 1911; *s* of late Harry Davies and the late Anne Davies; *m* 1945, Celia Marjorie Rapport, MB, FFA RCS; three *s*. *Educ:* Manchester Grammar Sch.; St John's Coll., Oxford (Scholar). BA Oxford (1st Cl. Hons Physiology), 1933; BM, BCh 1936; DPMEng 1943; MA 1944; DM 1948; MRCP 1964; FRCP 1970; FRCPsych 1971. RAMC (Temp. Major), 1942-46. Physician, Bethlem Royal and Maudsley Hosp., 1948, now Emeritus; Dean, Institute of Psychiatry, University of London, 1950-66. Mem., Adv. Cttee on Alcoholism to DHSS; Chairman: Attendance Allowance Bd, 1976-; Soc. for Study of Addiction. Patron, The Helping Hand Orgn. Hon. Mem., Venezuelan Psychiatric Association, 1964. *Publications:* (ed jtly) Psychiatric Education, 1964; (ed jtly) Studies in Psychiatry, 1968; papers on psychiatric subjects in med. jls. Chapters in Louis Wain: the man who drew cats, 1968. Wrote script and commentary for film, Victorian Flower Paintings, 1967. *Recreations:* gardening, travel. *Address:* 152 Harley Street, W1N 1HH. *T:* 01-935 2477; 8 Tollgate Drive, College Road, SE21. *T:* 01-693 9380.

DAVIES, Prof. David Richard Seaborne, MA Cantab; LLB Wales; JP; Dean of the Faculty of Law, University of Liverpool, 1946-71, Professor of the Common Law, 1946-71, now Emeritus, Public Orator, 1950-55, Pro-Vice Chancellor, 1956-60, Warden of Derby Hall, 1947-71; *b* 26 June 1904; *er s* of late David S. and Claudia Davies, Pwllheli. *Educ:* Pwllheli Gram. Sch.; University Coll., Aberystwyth; St John's Coll., Cambridge. (McMahon and Strathcona Studentships). First Class Hons LLB (Wales); Law Tripos, 1927 (Class I, Div. I); Yorke Prize, Cambridge Univ., 1928; Lecturer, and later Reader, in English Law in University of London at London Sch. of Economics, 1929-45; Nationality Div., Home Office, 1941-45; Sec. of the Naturalization (Revocation) Cttee, 1944-48; Member: Oaksey Departmental Cttee on Police Conditions, 1948-49; Standing Cttee on Criminal Law Revision, 1959-72; Chm., Departmental Cttee on Agricultural Diploma Education in Wales, 1956; MP (L) Caernarvon Boroughs, April-July 1945. Pres., Soc. of Public Teachers of Law, 1960-61. Lucien Wolf Memorial Lecturer, 1952. British delegate, SEATO Universities Conference, Pakistan, 1961. Cooley Lecturer, University of Mich., 1962. BBC (Wales) Annual Lecture, 1967. Examiner for many Universities, The Law Society, the Civil Service, etc. Chm., Liverpool Licensing Planning Cttee, 1960-63. Pres., Nat. Eisteddfod of Wales, 1955, 1973, 1975. Pres., Student Council, Univ. of Wales and UCW Aberystwyth; Hon. Life Pres., Liverpool Univ. Legal Soc.; Hon. Life Mem., Univ. Guild of Undergraduates; former Governor: Liverpool College; Rydal School; Life Pres., Liverpool Univ. RFC; Vice-Pres., London Welsh RFC; Pres., Pwllheli Sports Club. JP Liverpool, later

Caernarvonshire (Gwynedd); High Sheriff of Caernarvonshire, 1967-68. *Publications:* articles in Law Quarterly Review, Modern Law Review, Nineteenth Century, The Annual Survey of English Law, 1930-41. Journal of the Soc. of Public Teachers of Law, etc. *Recreation:* gardening. *Address:* Y Garn, Pwllheli, N Wales. *T:* Pwllheli 2109.

DAVIES, David Ronald, MB, BS, FRCS; Surgeon, University College Hospital, London, 1946-75; *b* Clydach, Swansea, 11 May 1910; 3rd *s* of late Evan Llewelyn and Agnes Jane Davies; *m* 1940, Alice Christine, 2nd *d* of Rev. John Thomson; three *s*. *Educ:* University Coll. and University Coll. Hosp., London. MRCS, LRCP 1934; MB BS London, 1934; FRCS, 1937. House appts at UCH, Asst, Surgical Unit, UCH, 1937-39; Asst Surg. EMS at UCH and Hampstead Gen. Hosp., 1939-41; served RAMC, Surgical Specialist and Officer-in-Charge Surgical Div., 1941-46; Surgeon: Queen Mary's Hospital, Roehampton, 1947-69; Harrow Hosp., 1946-69. Mem., BMA. Fellow: University Coll. London; Assoc. of Surgeons; RSocMed; British Assoc. of Urological Surgeons; Internat. Assoc. of Urologists. *Publications:* The Operations of Surgery (with A. J. Gardham); various papers on surgical subjects. *Address:* 15 Camden Square, NW1 9UY; Newland Farm, Withypool, Somerset. *T:* Exford 352. *Club:* Oriental.

DAVIES, Denzil; *see* Davies, David J. D.

DAVIES, Donald, OBE 1973; Board Member, National Coal Board, since 1973; *b* 13 Feb. 1924; *s* of late Wilfred Lawson Davies and Alwyne Davies; *m* 1948, Mabel (*née* Hellyar); two *d*. *Educ:* Ebbw Vale Grammar Sch.; UC Cardiff (BSc). CEng, FIMinE. Colliery Man., 1951-55; Gp Man., 1955-58; Dep. Prodn Man., 1958-60; Prodn Man., 1960-61; Area Gen Man., 1961-67; Area Dir, 1967-73. *Recreations:* golf, walking. *Address:* Wendy Cottage, Dukes Wood Avenue, Gerrards Cross, Bucks SL9 7LA. *T:* Gerrards Cross 85083.

DAVIES, Duncan Sheppey; Chief Scientist, Department of Industry, since 1977; *b* 20 April 1921; *o s* of Duncan S. Davies and Elsie Dora, Liverpool; *m* 1944, Joan Ann Frimston, MA; one *s* three *d*. *Educ:* Liverpool Coll.; Trinity Coll., Oxford (Minor Scholar). MA, BSc, DPhil. Joined ICI Dyestuffs Div., 1945; Research Dir, Gen. Chemicals Div., 1961; first Dir, ICI Petrochemical and Polymer Lab., 1962; Dep. Chm., Mond Div., 1967; Gen. Manager, Research, ICI, 1969-77. Member: SRC, 1969-73; SRC/SSRC, 1973-; Adv. Bd for Res. Councils, 1977-; Swann Manpower Working Gp, 1964-66; Council, Liverpool Univ., 1967-69; Council, QEC London, 1975-. Vis. Prof., Imperial Coll., 1968-70; Vis. Fellow, St Cross Coll., Oxford, 1970. Vis. Prof. Fellow, UC Swansea, 1974-. DUniv. Stirling, 1975. Castner Medal, SCI, 1967. *Publications:* (with M. C. McCarthy) Introduction to Technological Economics, 1967; The Humane Technologist, 1976; various papers in pure and applied chemistry jls. *Recreations:* music, writing. *Address:* 29 North Grove, Highgate, N6. *T:* 01-340 9498. *Clubs:* Athenæum, United Oxford & Cambridge University.

DAVIES, Ednyfed Hudson, BA (Wales); MA (Oxon); Chairman, Wales Tourist Board, since 1976; *b* 4 Dec. 1929; *s* of Rev. E. Curig Davies and Enid Curig (*née* Hughes); *m* 1972, Amanda Barker-Mill, *d* of Peter Barker-Mill and Elsa Barker-Mill; two *d*. *Educ:* Friars Sch., Bangor; Dynevor Grammar Sch., Swansea; University College of Swansea; Balliol Coll., Oxford. Called to the Bar, Gray's Inn, 1976. Lecturer in Dept of Extra-Mural Studies, University of Wales, Aberystwyth, 1957-61; Lecturer in Political Thought, Welsh Coll. of Advanced Technology, Cardiff, 1961-66. MP (Lab) Conway, 1966-70. Part-time TV and Radio Commentator and Interviewer on Current Affairs, 1962-66; on full-time contract to BBC presenting Welsh-language feature programmes on overseas countries, 1970-76. *Address:* Wales Tourist Board, Llandaff, Cardiff CF5 2YZ. *T:* Cardiff 567701; Farrar's Building, Temple, EC4. *T:* 01-583 9241. *Club:* Cardiff and County (Cardiff).

DAVIES, Edward Gwynfryn, CBE 1970; JP; DL; Member, Forestry Commission, 1959-73, and Chairman, National Committee for Wales, 1963-73; *b* 28 Nov. 1904; *o s* of Edward and Anne Davies; *m* 1932, Sarah Annie Adams; two *s*. *Educ:* Cwmavon Elementary Sch., Port Talbot. Mining Industry, 1918-21; Steel Industry, 1921-69; Trade Unionist, 1928-. Mem., Glamorgan CC, 1945-74 (Alderman, 1953-74, Chm., 1969-70); Glamorgan Representative: Glamorgan River Authy, 1956-74; Univ. Cts of Wales, 1957-74; Standing Jt Cttee, later S Wales Police Authy, 1963-74; Welsh Jt Educn Cttee, 1956-74; Glamorgan Magistrates Cts, 1970-74; Mem., Mid-Glamorgan HMC, 1948-69. JP Port Talbot, 1948 (Dep. Chm., Port Talbot Borough Magistrates, 1968-); DL Glamorgan 1972. Chm., Urdd Gobaith Cymru, Cwmavon, 1939-74, Hon. Life Pres., 1975;

initiated into Gorsedd of Bards, 1967. Pres., S Glamorgan Welsh Congregational Union, 1970-71. *Recreations:* gardening, local history, music. *Address:* Min-y-Gors, Heol-y-Graig, Cwmavon, Port Talbot, W Glam. *T:* Cwmavon 342.

DAVIES, (Edward) Hunter; author and journalist; Editor, Sunday Times Magazine, since 1975; *b* Renfrew, Scotland, 7 Jan. 1936; *s* of late John Hunter Davies and Marion (*née* Brechin); *m* 1960, Margaret Forster, *qv;* one *s* two *d* . *Educ:* Creighton Sch., Carlisle; Carlisle Grammar Sch.; University Coll., Durham. BA 1957, DipEd 1958; Editor of Palatinate. Reporter: Manchester Evening Chronicle, 1958-59; Sunday Graphic, London, 1959-60; Sunday Times, 1960-: Atticus, 1965-67; Chief Feature Writer, 1967; Editor, Look pages, 1970; Editor, Scene pages, 1975. *Television:* The Playground (play), 1967; The Living Wall, 1974; George Stephenson, 1975. *Publications:* Here We Go, Round the Mulberry Bush, 1965 (filmed, 1968); The Other Half, 1966; (ed) The New London Spy, 1966; The Beatles, 1968; The Rise and Fall of Jake Sullivan, 1970; (ed) I Knew Daisy Smuten, 1970; A Very Loving Couple, 1971; Body Charge, 1972; The Glory Game, 1972; A Walk Along the Wall, 1974; George Stephenson, 1975; The Creighton Report, 1976. *Recreations:* football—playing and watching; walking. *Address:* 11 Boscastle Road, NW5. *T:* 01-485 3785. *Club:* Dartmouth Park Football.

DAVIES, Elidir (Leslie Wish), FRIBA, FRSA; Chartered Architect in private practice; *b* 3 Jan. 1907; *yr s* of late Rev. Thomas John Landy Davies and Hetty Boucher (*née* Wish); *m* Vera (*née* Goodwin) (*d* 1974). *Educ:* privately; Colchester Sch.; Bartlett Sch. of Architecture, University of London (under Prof. Albert Richardson). Min. of Supply Air Defence, 1939-44; Min. of Town and Country Planning, London and Wales, 1944-47; University Lectr and Cons. to Argentinian and Uruguay Govts on planning and low cost housing, 1947-49; private practice (Devereux and Davies); rebuilding of Serjeants' Inn, Fleet Street; Royal Vet. Coll., London Univ. (Research and Field Labs); King's Coll. Sch., Wimbledon (Jun. Sch. and Sci. Labs); St James's Hosp., Balham (Out-patients' and other Depts); St Benedict's Hosp. (Hydrotherapy Dept), 1950-61. West Indies: 5-year Hospital progr. for Trinidad (incl. new gen. and maternity hosps, trg schs, specialist depts, and hosp. services). Cons. Arch. Hosps to Govts of Guiana, Barbados and Grenada, 1957-63. Private practice (Elidir L. W. Davies & Partners). Architect to: St David's Coll., Lampeter, restoration and new bldgs; London Borough of Camden; Central Library, Shaw Theatre and arts centre; Mermaid Theatre; Dynevor Castle, Carmarthen, Wales; new arts centre for drama and films; Chigwell Central Public Library; church work: The Temple, White Eagle Lodge, Hants; rebuilding of Wren's church, St Michael Paternoster Royal; Cons. Architect to: St David's Trust, Welsh Nat. Arts Theatre Centre, Cardiff; Govt Offices, Century House, Waterloo; BP Offices, 100 Euston Road; private houses and housing developments in London and the country. Chm., Soc. of Theatre Consultants, 1969-71; Mem. of Exec., Assoc. of British Theatre Technicians, 1965-71. Bronze Medal, RIBA, 1953. *Publications:* lectures and articles; contrib. to pubn relating to hospital architecture. *Recreations:* theatre, travel, sailing, visual arts. *Address:* 100 Wigmore Street, W1. *T:* 01-486 3841; Hesmonds Oast, East Hoathly, Sussex. *Clubs:* Garrick, Art Workers' Guild.

DAVIES, Elwyn, MA; Hon. LLD Wales; MSc, PhD Manchester; President, National Library of Wales, since 1977; (Treasurer, 1959-64; Vice-President, 1970-77); Chairman: Library Advisory Council (Wales), since 1972; Wales Regional Library Scheme, since 1973; Welsh Folk Museum, since 1974; *b* 20 Sept. 1908; *e s* of late Rev. Ben Davies, Llandeilo, Carms; *m* 1940, Margaret, *o d* of late Matthew Henry Dunlop, Bury, Lancs; no *c. Educ:* Llandysul and Llandeilo Grammar Schs; Universities of Wales (Aberystwyth Coll.) and Manchester. Asst Lectr and Lectr in Geography, University of Manchester, 1934-45, seconded Intelligence Div. Naval Staff, 1941-45; Sec. to the Council, University of Wales, Sec. of the University Press Board and the Board of Celtic Studies, 1945-63; Sec. University Bd for Training Colls, 1945-48, and Univ. Educn Bd, 1948-49; Sec., Univ. Extension Bd, 1945-61; Permanent Sec., Welsh Dept, Min. of Educn, 1963-64; Sec. for Welsh Educn, DES, 1964-69. A Governor: National Museum of Wales, 1957- (Mem. Council, 1959-); University College of Wales, Aberystwyth, 1965- (Mem. Council, 1965-); Univ. of Wales, 1966-. Member: Bd of Celtic Studies, Univ. of Wales, 1972-; Local Govt Boundary Commn for Wales, 1974-; Adv. Council, British Library, 1975-. Mem. Pilkington Cttee on Broadcasting, 1960-62. Mem. Standing Commission on Museums and Galleries, 1960-64. Hon. Fellow, UC Cardiff, 1970. *Publications:* Cyfarwyddiadau i Awduron (A Guide for Authors), 1954; (ed) A Gazetteer of Welsh Place-Names, 1957-75; (ed) Celtic Studies in Wales, 1963; (ed with Alwyn D. Rees) Welsh Rural Communities, 1960; papers in anthropological and geographical periodicals. *Recreations:* watching Rugby football and cricket, walking. *Address:* Butts Field, Tenby, Dyfed SA70 8AQ.

DAVIES, Emlyn Glyndwr, MSc; Chief Scientific Officer, Controller, Forensic Science Service, Home Office, 1974-76; *b* 20 March 1916; *yr s* of late William and Elizabeth Davies; *m* 1940, Edwina, *d* of late Lemuel and Alice Morgan, Blaengarw; two *s. Educ:* Bargoed Grammar Sch.; Maesycwmmer Grammar Sch.; University Coll of Wales, Aberystwyth (MSc). Asst Master, Ardwyn Sch., 1939-42; Ministry of Supply, 1942-44; Forensic Science Laboratory, Cardiff, 1944-58; Director, Forensic Science Laboratories: Nottingham, 1958-59; Preston, 1959-63; Forensic Science Adviser, Home Office, 1963-74. Pres., Forensic Science Soc., 1975-77. *Publications:* contribs to scientific jls. *Recreation:* Rugby football. *Address:* 14 Church Hill Close, Llanblethian, Cowbridge, S Glamorgan CF7 7JH. *T:* Cowbridge 2234.

DAVIES, Emrys Thomas, HM Diplomatic Service; Commercial Counsellor, British Embassy, Peking, since 1976; *b* 8 Oct. 1934; *s* of Evan William Davies and Dinah Davies (*née* Jones); *m* 1960, Angela Audrey May; one *s* two *d* . *Educ:* Parmiters Foundation Sch.; assorted universities. RAF, 1953-55. Sch. of Oriental and African Studies, London Univ., 1955-56. Served Peking, 1956-59; FO, 1959-60; Bahrain, 1960-62; FO, 1962-63; Asst Political Adviser to Hong Kong Govt, 1963-68; First Sec., British High Commn, Ottawa, 1968-71; FCO, 1972-76. *Address:* c/o Foreign and Commonwealth Office, SW1A 2AH; 25 Old Deer Park Gardens, Richmond, Surrey. *Club:* Royal Commonwealth Society.

DAVIES, Ernest Albert John; journalist, author; *b* London, 18 May 1902; *s* of late Alderman Albert Emil Davies; *m* 1st, 1926, Natalie Rossin, New York (marr. diss. 1944; she *d* 1955); two *s* one *d* ; 2nd, 1944, Peggy Yeo (*d* 1963); one *d. Educ:* Wycliffe Coll.; London Univ. (Diploma in Journalism). Managing Editor, Traffic Engineering and Control, 1960-76; Managing Editor, Antique Finder, 1962-72; Editor Clarion, 1929-32; Associate Editor, New Clarion, 1932. Served on Fabian Soc. Exec., 1940; Gov. National Froebel Foundation, 1938-40. With British Broadcasting Corporation, 1940-45, and its North American Service Organiser, 1944-45. Contested (Lab) Peterborough, 1935; MP (Lab) Enfield Division of Middx, 1945-50, East Enfield, 1950-59. Parl. Private Sec. to Min of State, 1946-50; Parliamentary Under-Sec. of State, Foreign Office, 1950-51. Chm. Transport Group Parliamentary Labour Party, 1945-50 and 1951-59; Jt Chm. Parliamentary Roads Study Group, 1957-59. Mem. Select Cttee on Nationalised Industries, 1952-59, Chm. British Yugoslav Soc., 1957-; Mem., Exec. Cttee, European-Atlantic Gp, 1958-65 (Vice-Pres., 1966-). Mem. British Delegation to Gen. Assembly, UN, 1947, 1948-49 and 1950; Dep. Leader British Deleg. to UN Conf. on Freedom of Information, 1948; Mem. British Deleg. to London Conf. 1950; Leader UK Deleg., Economic Commn for Europe, Geneva, 1950; UK Representative at Foreign Ministers' Deputies' Four Power Talks, Paris, 1951. Vice-Chm., British Parking Assoc., 1969-71, 1976-77 (Pres., 1977-; Hon. Sec. 1971-76; Mem. Council, 1968-); Hon. FInstHE. Managing Dir, Printerhall Ltd. Orden de la Liberación de España, Republican Govt, 1960; Ordenom Jugoslovenske Zvezde sa zlatnim vencem (Yugoslavia), 1976. *Publications:* How Much Compensation, 1935; National Capitalism, 1939; The State and the Railways, 1940; American Labour, 1943; British Transport, 1945; National Enterprise, 1946; Problems of Public Ownership, 1952; (ed) Roads and Their Traffic, 1960; Transport in Greater London, 1962; (ed) Traffic Engineering Practice, 1963, new edn 1968; Contrib. Encyclopaedia Britannica. *Address:* 6f Observatory Gardens, Kensington, W8 7HY. *T:* 01-937 4769. *Clubs:* Wig and Pen, National Liberal.

DAVIES, Dr Ernest Arthur, JP; Management Selection Consultant, MSL; *b* 25 Oct. 1926; *s* of Daniel Davies and Ada (*née* Smith), Nuneaton; *m* 1st, 1956, Margaret Stephen Tait Gatt (marr. diss. 1967), *d* of H. Gatt, Gamesley, near Glossop; no *c* ; 2nd, 1972, Patricia, *d* of S. Bates, Radford, Coventry. *Educ:* Coventry Jun. Techn. Coll.; Westminster Trng Coll., London; St Salvator's Coll., University of St Andrews; St John's Coll., Cambridge. PhD Cantab 1959; MInstP 1959. RAF Aircraft Apprentice, 1942-43 (discharged on med. grounds). Westminster Trng Coll., 1946-48; Teacher, Foxford Sch., Coventry, 1948-50; University of St Andrews, 1950-54 (1st cl. hons Physics, Neil Arnott Prize, Carnegie Schol.); subseq. research in superconductivity, Royal Society Mond Lab., Cambridge; AEI Research Scientist, 1957-63; Lectr in Physics, Faculty of Technology, University of Manchester, 1963-66. MP (Lab) Stretford, 1966-70; Parliamentary Private Secretary to: PMG (Mr Edward Short), Nov.-Dec. 1967; Foreign Secretary

(Mr George Brown), Jan.-Mar. 1968; Foreign and Commonwealth Sec. (Mr Michael Stewart), 1968-69; Jt Parly Sec., Min. of Technology, 1969-70. Co-Vice-Chm., Parly Labour Party's Defence and Services Group; Mem., Select Cttee on Science and Technology, 1966-67, 1967-68, 1968-69; Parly Deleg. to 24th Gen. Assembly of UN (UK Rep. on 4th Cttee). Councillor: Borough of Stretford, 1961-67; Borough of Southwark, 1974-; JP Lancs, 1962. *Publications:* contribs to Proc. Royal Society, Jl of Physics and Chem. of Solids. *Recreations:* reading, walking. *Address:* 7 Langford Green, Champion Hill, Camberwell, SE5. *T:* 01-274 9612.

DAVIES, Rev. Ernest William; Rector of Piddlehinton, 1957-64; Rural Dean of Bere Regis, 1961-64; retired; *b* 23 May 1901; *s* of late Ernest James Davies; *m* 1928, Winifred Lancashire, Hythe, Kent; two *s* two *d. Educ:* Dulwich Coll.; St John's Coll., Oxford (Classical Scholar); 1st Class Hon. Mods 1922, 2nd Class Lit. Hum., 1924, BA 1924, MA 1927, Oxford Univ. Diploma in Education, 1934. Ordained priest, 1955. Headmaster, King's Sch., Rochester, 1935-57. *Address:* Weyside Cottage, Upwey, Weymouth, Dorset. *T:* Upwey 2011.

DAVIES, Eryl Oliver, MA, BLitt (Oxon); HM Chief Inspector of Schools (Wales), since 1972; *b* 5 Dec. 1922; 2nd *s* of late John Edwyn Davies and Elisabeth Oliver Davies, Taimawr, Merthyr Tydfil; *m* 1952, Dr Joyce Crossley, Bradford; one *s* one *d. Educ:* Cyfarthfa Castle, Merthyr; Jesus Coll., Oxford. Served War, 1942-46: commissioned South Wales Borderers; served 2nd Bn KSLI, in Normandy (despatches), and War Office, Directorate of Infantry (Major). Asst Master, Bradford Grammar Sch., 1948; HM Inspector, Welsh Dept, Min. of Educn, 1956; Staff Inspector, 1967; Asst Sec., Welsh Office, 1970. Member: Sch. Broadcasting Council of the UK; Schools Council; Open Univ. Adv. Cttee for Wales. *Publications:* articles and poetry in literary jls. *Recreations:* reading, walking. *Address:* 203 Cyncoed Road, Cardiff. *T:* Cardiff 752047. *Club:* National Liberal.

DAVIES, Rev. Canon George Colliss Boardman, DD; Proctor in Convocation, Diocese of Worcester, 1964-75; Canon Residentiary of Worcester, 1963-77, Vice Dean, 1970-74 and Treasurer, 1970-77; *b* 7 Dec. 1912; *y s* of late Ven. George Middlecott Davies and Berta Mary, *d* of late Admiral F. R. Boardman, CB; *m* 1951, Edith Mavis, *d* of late J. D. Maitland-Kirwan; one *d. Educ:* Monkton Combe Sch.; St Catharine's Coll., Cambridge, 2nd cl. Historical Tripos pt 1, 1934; MA 1938; BD 1947; DD 1951; Curate of Woking, 1937-39; permission to officiate Diocese of Ely, 1939-40; Rector of St Clement with St Edmund and St George, Colegate, Norwich, 1940-42; Rector of North Tamerton, 1942-51; Rector of Kingham, 1951-56; Beresford Prof. of Ecclesiastical History, Trinity Coll. Dublin, 1956-63, and Professor of Pastoral Theology, 1960-63; Canon and Treasurer of St Patrick's Cathedral, Dublin, 1962-63. Mem. Gen. Synod of Ch. of Ireland, 1961-63. Commissary to Bp of Kimberley and Kuruman, 1968-76; Dir, Post Ordination Studies, and Examining Chaplain to Bp of Worcester, 1971-75. Mem., Exec. Cttee, CMS, 1964-73. Governor: Malvern Girls' Coll., 1968-; Dean Close, Cheltenham, 1974-. Trinity Coll., Dublin, MA and DD (*ad eund*), 1959. *Publications:* The Early Cornish Evangelicals, 1951; Henry Phillpotts, Bishop of Exeter, 1954; Men for the Ministry: The History of the London College of Divinity, 1963. Contribs to The Church Quarterly Review, The Churchman. *Address:* 53 Blenheim Drive, Oxford. *T:* Oxford 56297. *Club:* Royal Commonwealth Society.

DAVIES, George Francis, CMG 1962; Chairman, Davies Brothers Ltd, since 1954; *b* 26 Jan. 1911; *yr s* of late C. B. Davies, CBE, MIEA, and late Ruby A. Davies; *m* 1935, Margaret Ingles; one *s* three *d. Educ:* Clemes Coll., Hobart, Tasmania. Gen. Man., Davies Brothers Ltd, 1940; Director: Commercial Broadcasters Pty Ltd (Chm., 1950-); Australian Newsprint Mills Ltd, 1954-; Tasmanian Television Ltd; Tasmanian Containers Pty Ltd, 1959-. Dir, National Heart Foundation of Australia, 1961. Trustee: Tasmanian Museum and Art Gallery, 1955- (Chm., 1962-); Winston Churchill Memorial Trust, 1968-; Perpetual Trustees and Natural Executors Ltd, 1968-. *Recreations:* golf, fishing, racing. *Address:* 391 Sandy Bay Road, Hobart, Tasmania 7005. *T:* 25.1141. *Clubs:* Tasmanian, Athenæum (Hobart); Launceston (Launceston).

DAVIES, George Peter H.; *see* Humphreys-Davies.

DAVIES, Gwen F.; *see* Ffrangcon-Davies.

DAVIES, (Gwilym) E(dnyfed) Hudson; *see* Davies, Ednyfed H.

DAVIES, Gwilym Prys; Partner, Morgan Bruce & Nicholas, Solicitors, Cardiff, Pontypridd and Porth, since 1957; Special Adviser to the Secretary of State for Wales, since 1974; *b* 8 Dec. 1923; *s* of William and Mary Matilda Davies; *m* 1951, Llinos Evans; three *d. Educ:* Towyn Sch., Towyn, Merioneth; University College of Wales, Aberystwyth. Served RN, 1942-46. Faculty of Law, UCW, Aberystwyth, 1946-52; President of Debates, Union UCW, 1949; President Students' Rep. Council, 1950; LLB 1949; LLM 1952. Admitted Solicitor, 1956. Contested (Lab) Carmarthen, 1966. Member: Welsh Council, 1967-69; Welsh Adv. Cttee, ITA, 1966-69; Working Party on 4th TV Service in Wales, Home Office and Welsh Office, 1975-; Chm., Welsh Hosps Bd, 1968-74; Mem., Adv. Gp, Use of Fetuses and Fetal Material for Res., DHSS and Welsh Office, 1972. OStJ. *Publications:* A Central Welsh Council, 1963; Y Ffermwr a'r Gyfraith, 1967. *Address:* Lluest, 78 Church Road, Tonteg, Pontypridd, Mid Glam. *T:* Newtown Llantwit 2462.

DAVIES, Rev. Gwynne Henton; Principal, Regent's Park College, Oxford, 1958-72; *b* 19 Feb. 1906; *m* 1935, Annie Bronwen (*née* Williams); two *d. Educ:* Perse Sch., Cambridge; University College of South Wales, Cardiff; Oxford; Marburg/Lahn, Germany. Minister West End Baptist Church, London, W6, 1935-38; Tutor Bristol Baptist Coll., 1938-51; special Lecturer in Hebrew, University of Bristol, 1948-51; (First) Prof. of Old Testament Studies, Faculty of Theology, Durham Univ., 1951-58; Select Preacher to the Universities of Cambridge and Oxford. OT Editor, The Teachers' Commentary (revised 7th edn), 1955. Secretary, Society for Old Testament Study, 1946-62 (President, 1966); Vice-Pres., Baptist Union of GB and Ireland, 1970-71, Pres., 1971-72. OT Lecture, Pantyfedwen Foundn, 1975. Hon. DD: Glasgow, 1958; Stetson, 1965. *Publications:* (with A. B. Davies) The Story in Scripture, 1960; Exodus, 1967; Who's Who in the Bible, 1970; Deuteronomy, in Peake's Commentary on the Bible, rev. edn, 1962; 20 articles in The Interpreter's Bible Dictionary, 1962; The Ark in the Psalms, in Promise and Fulfilment (ed F. F. Bruce), 1963; essay in R. Goldman's Breakthrough, 1968; Genesis, in The Broadman Bible Commentary, 1969; Gerhard von Rad, in O.T. Theology in Contemporary Discussion (ed R. Laurin). *Address:* Headlands, Broad Haven, Haverfordwest, Dyfed SA62 3JP. *T:* Haverfordwest 83339.

DAVIES, Handel, CB 1962; MSc; CEng; FRAeS; FAIAA; Technical Director, British Aircraft Corporation, since 1969; *b* 2 June 1912; *m* 1942, Mary Graham Harris. *Educ:* Aberdare Grammar Sch.; University of Wales. Royal Aircraft Establishment and Ministry of Aircraft Production, 1936-47; Head of Aerodynamics Flight Division, RAE, 1948-52. Chief Superintendent, Aeroplane and Armament Experimental Establishment, Boscombe Down, 1952-55; Scientific Adviser to Air Ministry, 1955-56; Dep. Director-General, then Director-General, Scientific Research (Air), Ministry of Supply, 1957-59; Dep. Director, RAE, Farnborough, 1959-63. Dep. Controller of Aircraft, (R&D), Ministry of Aviation, 1963-67, Ministry of Technology, 1967-69. Pres., RAeS, 1977-78. Gold Medal, RAeS, 1974. *Publications:* papers in Reports and Memoranda of Aeronautical Research Council and in Journal of Royal Aeronautical Society. *Recreation:* sailing. *Address:* British Aircraft Corporation Ltd, Weybridge, Surrey KT13 0RN; Keel Cottage, Woodham Road, Horsell, Woking, Surrey. *T:* Woking 4192. *Clubs:* Naval and Military; Royal Air Force Yacht (Hamble).

DAVIES, Harold Haydn, CB 1956; MC 1917; Chairman Welsh Board of Health, 1952-57; retired; *b* 27 Dec. 1897; *s* of late John Davies, Ammanford, and London; *m* 1926, Cecilia, *er d* of late Morgan Michael, Pontardulais, Glam.; one *s* one *d. Educ:* London; Pembroke Coll., Cambridge. Asst Secretary (Dep. Establishment Officer) Ministry of Housing and Local Govt, 1951; Ministry of Health, 1921-51. Gazetted to Royal Northumberland Fusiliers, 1917; served European War, 1914-18; BEF, France, 1917-18 (MC; prisoner of war, March 1918). Vice Chm., Holloway Sanatorium Hospital Gp, 1958-68; Mem., NW Surrey Hospital Management Cttee, 1968-74. OStJ 1957. *Address:* Woodlands, Coombe Park, Kingston Hill, Surrey. *T:* 01-546 2030.

DAVIES, Hector Leighton, CBE 1941; JP, DL; *b* Sebastapol, near Griffithstown, Mon. 18 April 1894; *e s* of late Sir John Cecil Davies, CBE, of the Mount, Gowerton, and later Stelvio, Newport, Mon; *m* 1924, Miss Ballantyne Poulton le Fylde; one *s* one *d. Educ:* Malvern Coll.; Technical Education, Swansea and Germany. Chm., Swansea Pilotage Authority; Past President of Council of Iron and Steel Institute; Past Chairman: Swansea Employment Cttee; Welsh Bd of Industry; Industrial Estates Management Corporation of Wales; S Wales Regional Industrial Advisory Cttee of National Savings Movement; Industrial

Welfare Society. JP 1927; DL Glam 1956. *Address:* Cobwebs, Penmaen, Gower, Glam. *Clubs:* Royal Automobile; Bristol Channel Yacht (Swansea).

DAVIES, Humphrey; *see* Davies, Morgan Wynn Humphrey.

DAVIES, Hunter; *see* Davies, E. H.

DAVIES, Rev. Canon Hywel Islwyn, BA; PhD; Rector of Collyweston, 1969-76; Rural Dean of Barnack, 1973-76; *b* 14 Feb. 1909; *s* of Rev. H. J. Davies and Mary Davies, Loughor, Swansea; *m* 1st, 1940, Beti Lewis Beynon (decd); one *d*; 2nd, 1956, Glenys Williams. *Educ:* Gowerton Grammar Sch.; University of Wales; Gonville and Caius Coll., Cambridge; St Michael's Coll., Llandaff. BA 1st Class Philosophy, 1932 Pierce Scholar; PhD University of Cambridge; Lord Rhondda Scholar, 1936. Ordained, 1936; Curacy, Merthyr Tydfil; Lecturer, 1940, Tutor 1942, St David's Coll., Lampeter; Vicar, Llanstephan, Carms, and Tutor, Trinity Coll., Carmarthen, 1945; Director Adult Education, Diocese of St David's, 1946; Examining Chaplain Bishop of Monmouth; Vicar Llanbadarn Fawr and Lecturer, University College of Wales, Aberystwyth, 1947; Vicar of Llanelly and Canon of St David's Cathedral, 1950; Dean of Bangor, 1957-61; Head of Dept of Religion and Philosophy, Univ. of Ife, 1961-69, Prof. 1966-69, Mem. Univ. Council and Dean of Faculty of Arts, 1963-69. Examining Chaplain to Archbishop of Wales and to Bishop of Bangor, 1957. Public Preacher: Dio. Lagos, Ibadan, and N Nigeria; Examining Chaplain to Bishops of Ibadan and Northern Nigeria; Canon, St James's Cathedral, Ibadan, 1966, Canon Emeritus 1969. Governor, Immanuel Theological Coll., Ibadan. Examiner: Univ. of Ibadan; Univ. of Lagos. Mem. Adv. Panel, W African Sch. Certificate. *Publications:* various, in philosophical, theological, Welsh, English, and African journals. *Recreation:* Celtic Bygones. *Address:* 39 Ambergate Road, Liverpool L19 9AU. *T:* 051-427 4689. *Club:* Royal Commonwealth Society.

DAVIES, Ian Leonard, MA; CEng, FIEE; Director, Admiralty Underwater Weapons Establishment, since 1975; *b* 2 June 1924; *s* of late H. Leonard Davies and of Mrs J. D. Davies; *m* 1951, Hilary Dawson, *d* of late Rear-Adm. Sir Oswald Henry Dawson, KBE; two *s* two *d. Educ:* Barry County Sch.; St John's Coll., Cambridge. Mechanical Sciences Tripos, 1944, and Mathematical Tripos Pt 2, 1949. Telecommunications Research Estabt, 1944; Blind Landing Experimental Unit, 1946. TRE (later the Royal Radar Establishment), 1949-69; Imperial Defence Coll., 1970; Asst Chief Scientific Adviser (Projects), MoD, 1971-72; Dep. Controller Electronics, 1973, Dep. Controller Air Systems (D), 1973-75, MoD(PE). Mem. Council, IEE, 1974-77 (Chm.), Electronics Div. Bd, 1975-76). *Publications:* papers on information theory, radar, and lasers. *Recreations:* music, sailing, walking. *Address:* 15 Bincleaves Road, Weymouth, Dorset. *T:* Weymouth 5891. *Club:* Athenæum.

DAVIES, Ifor; MP (Lab) Gower since Oct. 1959; *b* 9 June 1910; *s* of Jeffrey and Elizabeth Jane Davies; *m* 1950, Doreen Griffiths; one *s* one *d. Educ:* Gowerton; Swansea Technical; Ruskin Coll., Oxford. Oxford Diploma, Economics and Politics. Accountant, 1931-39; Personnel Officer, ICI, 1942-47; Ministry of Labour, Statistics Dept, 1947-48; Personnel Officer, Aluminium Wire and Cable Co. Ltd, 1948-59; Opposition Whip (Welsh), 1961-64; a Lord Commissioner of the Treasury and Govt Whip, 1964-66; Parly Under-Sec. of State, Welsh Office, 1966-69; Sec., Welsh Labour Gp, 1960-66; Chm., Welsh Parly Party, 1970-71. Executive Member South Wales District, WEA, 1950-60; Secretary Gowerton Welsh Congregational Chapel, 1948; Hon. Secretary Gower Constituency Labour Party, 1948-59; Member Glamorgan County Council, 1958-61; President: S Wales and Mon Br., Urban District Councils Assoc., 1970-; Gower Soc., 1971-; Chm. Council, University Coll. of Swansea, 1971-; Chairman: Welsh Grand Cttee, 1971-; Welsh Labour Gp MPs, 1973-; Mem., Speaker's Panel of Chairmen. *Recreations:* walking and listening to music. *Address:* Ty Pentwyn, Three Crosses, Swansea, W Glam. *T:* Gowerton 2222.

DAVIES, Iforwyn Glyndwr; Formerly Senior Principal Medical Officer, Ministry of Health; QHP 1957-59; *b* 11 June 1901; *s* of Richard and Margaret Davies, Porth, South Wales; *m* 1930, Lillian May, *d* of Evan James, Cardiff, South Wales; one *s. Educ:* The County Sch., Porth; University College, Cardiff; St Bartholomew's Hospital, London. MRCS, LRCP, 1923; MB, BS London, 1924; MD London, 1944; MRCP, 1926; FRCP, 1954. Formerly: Tuberculosis Physician, City of Nottingham, 1933; Deputy MOH, City and County of Bristol, 1937; Lecturer in Public Health, University of Bristol, 1937; Dep. Director, Preventive Medicine Laboratories; Prof., of Public Health,

University of Leeds, 1947, also Medical Officer of Health and School Medical Officer, City of Leeds. *Publications:* Text-Book: Modern Public Health for Medical Students, 1955 (2nd edn, 1963); contrib. to Lancet, Medical Officer, Public Health. *Recreation:* music. *Address:* Amberley, Well Meadows, Shaw, Newbury, Berks. *T:* Newbury 42055.

DAVIES, Ven. Ivor Gordon; Archdeacon of Lewisham, since 1972; Proctor in Convocation, since 1965; *b* 21 July 1917; *m* 1946, Kristine Wiley, SRN; one *s* two *d. Educ:* University of Wales (BA); Oxford; London (BD). Deacon 1941, Priest 1942, Llandaff; Curate of St Paul's, Cardiff, 1941-44; CF 1944-47; Curate of St John the Baptist, Felixstowe, 1947-49; Vicar of St Thomas', Ipswich, 1950-57; Residentiary Canon of Southwark Cathedral and Diocesan Missioner, 1957-72; Dean of Lewisham, 1970-72. *Address:* 2 St Austell Road, Lewisham Hill, SE13. *T:* 01-852 3649.

DAVIES, Jack Gale Wilmot, OBE 1946; Executive Director of the Bank of England, 1969-76; *b* 10 Sept. 1911; *s* of Langford George Davies, MD, BCh, MRCS, LRCP, and Lily Barnes Davies; *m* 1949, Georgette O'Dell (*née* Vanson); one *s. Educ:* Tonbridge Sch.; St John's Coll., Cambridge. Nat. Institute of Industrial Psychol., 1935-39. Regimental service, The Middlesex Regt, 1940-42; Chief Psychologist, Directorate for Selection of Personnel, War Office, 1942-46. Bureau of Personnel, UN Secretariat, 1946-48; Secretariat, Human Factors Panel, Cttee on Industrial Productivity, 1948-49; Staff Training Section, UN Secretariat, 1950-52; Secretary, Cambridge Univ. Appointments Board, 1952-68; Asst to the Governor, Bank of England, 1968. Dir, Portals Holdings Ltd, 1976-. FBPsS 1946. Fellow St John's Coll., Cambridge, 1959-68. Hon. DLitt City, 1976. *Publications:* articles in Occupational Psychology and similar journals. *Recreations:* cricket, golf, music. *Address:* 31 Wingate Way, Cambridge. *Clubs:* Royal Automobile, MCC.

DAVIES, Rev. Jacob Arthur Christian; Deputy Director, Agricultural Operations Division, FAO, since 1975; *b* 24 May 1925; *s* of Jacob S. Davies and Christiana; *m* Sylvia Onikeh Cole; two *s* two *d. Educ:* Univ. of Reading (BSc 1950); Selwyn Coll., Cambridge; Imperial Coll. of Tropical Agriculture. Permanent Secretary, Min. of Agriculture and Natural Resources, 1961-63; Chief Agriculturist, 1962-67; Project Co-manager, UNDP, FAO, 1967-69; Chm., Public Service Commn, 1969-71; Ambassador to USA, 1971-72; High Comr for Sierra Leone in London, 1972-74; Non-resident Ambassador to Denmark, Sweden and Norway, 1972-74. *Recreations:* philately, sports. *Address:* Agricultural Operations Division, FAO, Viale delle Terme di Caracolla, Rome, Italy.

DAVIES, (James) Brian Meredith, MD, DPH, FFCM; Director of Social Services, City of Liverpool, since 1971; Hon. Lecturer in (Preventive) Paediatrics, University of Liverpool, since 1964; *b* 27 Jan. 1920; *s* of late Dr G. Meredith Davies and Caroline Meredith Davies; *m* 1944, Charlotte (*née* Pillar); three *s. Educ:* Bedford Sch.; Medical Sch., St Mary's Hosp., London Univ. MB, BS (London) 1943 MD (London) 1948, DPH 1948, MFCM 1972, FFCM 1974. Various hosp. appts. Served War, RAMC, Captain, 1944-47. Asst MOH, Lancashire CC, 1948-50; Dep. MOH, City of Oxford, 1950-53; Clin. Asst (infectious Diseases), United Oxford Hosps, 1950-53; Dep. MOH, City of Liverpool, 1953-69. Chm., Liverpool div., BMA, 1958-59; Chm. Bd of Governors, William Rathbone Staff Coll., Liverpool, 1961-; Council of Europe Fellowship, to study Elderly: in Finland, Sweden, Norway and Denmark, 1964 (report awarded special prize); Mem. Public Health Laboratory Service Bd, 1966-71. Teaching Gp of Soc. of Community Med. (Sec. of Gp, 1958-72, Pres. Gp, 1972-73). Dir Personal Health and Social Services, City of Liverpool, 1969-71; Governor, Occupational Therapy Coll., Huyton, Liverpool, 1969-; Dir of MERIT (Merseyside Industrial Therapy Services Ltd), 1970-75; Mem. Council, Queen's Inst. of District Nursing, 1971-; Assoc. of Dirs of Social Services: Chm., NW Br., 1971-73; Mem. Exec. Council, 1973-; Pres. 1976-77; Mem. Exec. Cttee of Central Council for the Disabled, 1973-76; Adviser to Social Services Cttee of Assoc. of Metropolitan Authorities, 1974-; Member: RCP Cttee on Rheumatism and Rehabilitation, 1974-; DES Cttee of Enquiry into Special Educn for Disabled Children, 1975-; Exec. Cttee, Liverpool Personal Services Soc., 1973. Pres., Merseyside Ski Club, 1970-77. Mem. Council, Prospect Hall Coll., 1974; Chm., Bd of Governors, William Rathbone Staff Coll., Liverpool, 1961-75. *Publications:* Community Health, Preventative Medicine and Social Services, 1975; Community Health and Social Services, 1976; numerous papers on Public Health, Physically and Mentally Handicapped and various social services, in scientific and other jls. *Recreations:* skiing, golf, fishing, gardening, music. *Address:* Tree Tops, Church Road, Thornton Hough, Wirral, Merseyside. *T:* 051-336 3435 (office

051-227 3911). *Clubs:* Royal Over-Seas League; Royal Birkdale Golf (Southport).

DAVIES, Dame Jean; *see* Lancaster, Dame J.

DAVIES, John; *see* Davies, L. J.

DAVIES, John Alun Emlyn; retired 1977; *b* 4 May 1909; *s* of Robert Emlyn and Mary Davies; *m* 1941, Elizabeth Boshier; three *s. Educ:* Ruabon Grammar Sch.; Trinity Coll., Cambridge (Scholar). BA 1st cl. Pts I and II, History Tripos. Called to Bar, Lincoln's Inn, 1936. Served War of 1939-45: DAA&QMG 2nd Parachute Bde, 1943; DAAG 1st Airborne Div., 1944. Joined BoT, 1946; Asst Solicitor, 1963; Principal Asst Solicitor, DTI, 1968-72; Asst Solicitor, Law Commn, 1972-74; part-time Asst, Law Commn, 1974-77. Asst Sec. to Jenkins Cttee on Company Law, 1959-62. *Recreations:* gardening, walking. *Address:* 29 Crescent Road, Sidcup, Kent. *T:* 01-300 1421. *Club:* Reform.

DAVIES, Rt. Hon. John (Emerson Harding), PC 1970; MBE 1946; MP (C) Knutsford since 1970; Director, Hill Samuel Group, 1969-70 and since 1974; *s* of Arnold Thomas Davies, FCA, and Edith Minnie (*née* Harding); *m* 1943, Vera Georgina Bates; one *s* one *d. Educ:* St Edward's Sch., Oxford. Enlisted RASC, 1939; Commissioned 2nd Lieut, RASC, 1940; G2 (Tech.) Combined Ops Experimental Establishment (COXE), 1945-46. Joined Anglo-Iranian Oil Co., 1946; served in Stockholm, London and Paris, 1946-55; General Manager, Markets, 1956-60; Director BP Trading, 1960; Vice-Chairman and Managing Director, Shell Mex and BP, 1961-65; Director-General, CBI, 1965-69. Minister of Technology, July-Oct. 1970; Sec. of State for Trade and Industry and Pres., Bd of Trade, 1970-72; Chancellor of the Duchy of Lancaster, 1972-74; Opposition Front Bench Spokesman on Foreign and Commonwealth Affairs, 1976-. Member: NEDC, 1964-72; Nat. Joint Advisory Council, Dept of Employment and Productivity (formerly Min. of Labour), 1965-69; British Productivity Council, 1965-69; British National Export Council, 1966-69; Council of Industrial Design, 1966-70; Public Schools Commission, 1966-68. Governor: St Edward's Sch., Oxford; Windlesham House School Trust; Pres., Incorporated Soc. of Prep. Schools, 1974-. DUniv Essex, 1967; Hon. DTech Loughborough, 1972. FCA 1960 (ACA 1939); FRSA 1964; JDipMA 1965. *Recreations:* travel and music. *Address:* 4 St Barnabas Villas, SW8. *Clubs:* Oriental, Hurlingham, Beefsteak.

DAVIES, Rev. John Gordon, MA, DD; Edward Cadbury Professor of Theology and Head of Department of Theology, University of Birmingham, since Oct. 1960; Director of Institute for Study of Worship and Religious Architecture, University of Birmingham, since 1962; *b* 20 April 1919; *s* of late A. G. Davies and of Mrs Davies, Chester; *m* 1945, Emily Mary Tordoff; one *s* two *d. Educ:* King's Sch., Chester; Christ Church, Oxford; Westcott House, Cambridge. Curate of Rotherhithe, Dec. 1942-Sept. 1948; Univ. of Birmingham: Asst Lecturer in Theology, 1948-50; Lecturer, 1950-57; Senior Lecturer, 1957-59; Reader, 1959-60; Dean of Faculty of Arts, 1967-70. BA Oxon., 1942; MA 1945; BD 1946; DD 1956; MA (Official) Birmingham, 1952; Hon. DD St Andrews, 1968. Hereditary Freeman, City of Chester; Brother of Ancient and Worshipful Company of Skinners and Felt Makers. Bampton Lecturer, 1958. Hon. Canon, Birmingham, 1965. Hon. Mem., Guild for Religious Architecture, USA. Conover Memorial Award, New York, 1967. *Publications:* The Theology of William Blake, 1948 (USA 1966); The Origin and Development of Early Christian Church Architecture, 1952 (USA 1953); Daily Life in the Early Church: Studies in the Church Social History of the First Five Centuries, 1952 (reprinted 1955); Daily Life of Early Christians, 1953; Social Life of Early Christians, 1954; The Spirit, the Church, and the Sacraments, 1954; La Vie quotidienne des premiers chrétiens, 1956; Members One of Another; Aspects of Koinonia, 1958; He Ascended into Heaven: A Study in the History of Doctrine (Bampton Lectures, 1958), 1958; Der Heilige Geist, die Kirche und die Sakramente, 1958; The Making of the Church, 1960; Intercommunion, 1961; The Architectural Setting of Baptism, 1962; Holy Week, A Short History, 1963; The Early Christian Church, 1965; A Select Liturgical Lexicon, 1965; La Chiesa delle Origini, 1966; Worship and Mission, 1966; As Origens do Cristianismo, 1967; Dialogo con el Mundo, 1967; The Secular Use of Church Buildings, 1968; Liturgiskt Handlexikon, 1968; Every Day God: encountering the Holy in World and Worship, 1973; Christians, Politics and Violent Revolution, 1976; co-author: An Experimental Liturgy, 1958; translator: Essays on the Lord's Supper, 1958; The Eucharistic Memorial Vol. I, 1960, Vol. II, 1961; Mission in a Dynamic Society, 1968. Editor, A Dictionary of Liturgy and Worship, 1972; Worship and Dance, 1975; Contributor to: Becoming a Christian, 1954; The Teachers' Commentary, 1955; The Concise

Encyclopædia of Living Faiths, 1959; Making the Building Serve the Liturgy, 1962; The Modern Architectural Setting of the Liturgy, 1964; A Manual for Holy Week, 1967; Preface to Christian Studies, 1971; Journal of Theological Studies; Journal of Hellenic Studies; Vigiliae Christianae; Harvard Theological Review; Encyclopædia Britannica, etc. *Recreation:* cooking. *Address:* 28 George Road, Edgbaston, Birmingham B15 1PJ. *T:* 021-454 6254.

DAVIES, John Howard Gay; Editorial Director, Thomson Regional Newspapers Ltd; *b* 17 Jan. 1923; *er s* of late E. E. Davies, Nicholaston Hall, Gower, Glamorgan; *m* 1st, 1948, Eira Morgan (marr. dissolved, 1953); 2nd, 1955, Betty Walmsley; one *s. Educ:* Bromsgrove Sch.; Wadham Coll., Oxford. Welsh Guards, 1942-46 (despatches). Western Mail, 1950-52; Daily Telegraph, 1952-55; Deputy Editor, Western Mail, 1955-58; an Assistant Editor, Sunday Times, 1958-62; Exec. Assistant to Editorial Director, Thomson Newspapers Ltd, 1962-64; Editor, Western Mail, 1964, 1965. Mem., British Cttee, IPI. *Address:* 41 Chartfield Avenue, SW15. *T:* 01-788 8685.

DAVIES, J(ohn) R(obert) Lloyd, CMG 1953; Principal, Training Services Agency, since 1973; *b* 24 March 1913; *o s* of late J. R. and Mrs Davies, Muswell Hill; *m* 1943, Margery, *o d* of late Major and Mrs McClelland, Nottingham; one *s* one *d. Educ:* Highgate Sch.; Oriel Coll., Oxford. Joined staff of Ministry of Labour, 1936; Private Secretary to Sir Thomas Phillips, 1940. Served War of 1939-45: Royal Navy; Lieut RNVR; service in Far East; Dep. Labour Attaché, HM Embassy, Washington, 1945-47; Asst Secretary, Ministry of Labour, London, Oct. 1947; Labour Attaché, HM Embassy, Paris, 1956-60; Asst Sec., Dept of Employment, 1960-72; Counsellor (Labour), HM Embassy, Washington, DC, 1972-73. *Recreations:* music, geology and reading. *Address:* 35 Grange Gardens, Pinner, Middx HA5 5QD. *Club:* United Oxford & Cambridge University.

DAVIES, Prof. John Tasman, PhD, DSc London; MA, ScD Cantab; Professor of Chemical Engineering and Head of Department, University of Birmingham, since 1960; *b* 1 May 1924; *m* 1948, Ruth Batt; two *s. Educ:* Boys' High Sch., Christchurch, NZ; Canterbury University Coll.; London Univ. MA Cantab. 1955; PhD London 1949; DSc London 1955; ScD Cantab 1967. Worked with Sir Eric Rideal, FRS, Royal Institution London, 1946-48; Research Associate and Bristol-Myers Fellow, Stanford Univ., Calif. (USA) (worked with late Prof. J. W. McBain, FRS), 1948-49; Beit Mem. Fellow for Medical Research, Royal Instn and KCL, 1949-52; Lectr in: Chemistry, KCL, 1952-55; Chemical Engineering, Cambridge Univ., 1955-60. Overseas guest lecturer at Gordon Conference on Surface Activity, USA, 1956. Visiting Prof., University of Minnesota, 1963. Member: UN Consultative Commn to Indian Inst. of Petroleum, 1967-71; UNESCO Advisory Group on Petroleum Technology, Arab States, 1967; (part-time) West Midlands Gas Board, 1968-72. Member Sigma-Xi, 1949 (USA), FIChemE. *Publications:* (with Sir Eric Rideal, FRS) Interfacial Phenomena, 1961; The Scientific Approach, 1965, 2nd edn 1973; Turbulence Phenomena, 1972; many on Surface Phenomena and Chemical Engineering. *Address:* Department of Chemical Engineering, The University, Birmingham B15 2TT. *T:* 021-472 1301.

DAVIES, Joseph Marie, QC 1962; **His Honour Judge J. M. Davies;** a Circuit Judge (formerly Judge of County Courts), since 1971; *b* 13 Jan. 1916; *s* of Joseph and Mary Davies, St Helen's; *m* 1948, Eileen Mary (*née* Dromgoole); two *s* two *d. Educ:* Stonyhurst Coll.; Liverpool Univ. Called to Bar, Gray's Inn, Nov. 1938; practice in Liverpool. Recorder of Birmingham, 1970-71; Cumberland Co. QS: Dep. Chm., 1956-63, 1970-71; Chm., 1963-70. Served War of 1939-45; The King's Regt, Nov. 1939-Dec. 1941; RIASC and Staff Allied Land Forces, SE Asia, 1942-46. *Address:* 4 Elm Grove, Eccleston Park, Prescot, Lancs. *T:* 051-426 5415. *Clubs:* Athenæum (Liverpool); Union (Birmingham); Cumberland County.

DAVIES, Kenneth; *see* Davies, S. K.

DAVIES, Kenneth Arthur, CMG 1952; OBE 1946; *b* 28 Jan. 1897; *s* of William and Alice Davies; *m* 1932, Edna Myfanwy, *d* of Rev. T. Rowlands; one *s. Educ:* Pontypridd Grammar Sch.; University Coll., Wales, Aberystwyth; Trinity Coll., Cambridge. Served European War, 1914-18, with RFA in France and Belgium, 1916-19; 1st Class Hons Geology BSc, University Coll., Aberystwyth. Research Scholar, 1923-26; Fellow of University of Wales, 1926; MSc 1925; PhD (Cantab.), 1928. Field Geologist, Govt of Uganda, 1929; Senior Geologist, 1936; Director, Geological Survey, 1939, retired 1951. Adviser on Mineral Development to Uganda Govt, 1952-54 and 1965;

Commonwealth Geological Liaison Officer, 1954. Dep.-Dir Overseas Geological Surveys, 1957-65. Adviser to United Nations, 1966. Fellow, Geological Society, 1928; FIMM 1950. Murchison Medallist, Geological Society, 1954. *Publications:* various on Stratigraphy of Central Wales and graptolites in British Geological journals, and on African Geology in British and American journals. *Recreation:* gardening. *Address:* Park Cottage, Somerset Road, SW19.

DAVIES, Sir Lancelot Richard B.; *see* Bell Davies.

DAVIES, (Lewis) John, QC 1967; a Recorder of the Crown Court, since 1974; *b* 15 April 1921; *s* of William Davies, JP, and Esther Davies; *m* 1956, Janet Mary Morris; one *s* two *d. Educ:* Pontardawe Grammar Sch.; University College of Wales, Aberystwyth; Trinity Hall (Common Law Prizeman, 1943; Scholar, 1943-44), Cambridge. LLB Wales 1942 (1st cl.); BA Cantab (1st cl.); LLB Cantab (1st cl.). Asst Principal, HM Treasury, 1945-46; Senior Law Lecturer, Leeds Univ., 1946-48; Administrative Asst, British Petroleum, 1949-52. Called to the Bar, Middle Temple, 1948, Bencher, 1973; Mem., Bar Council, 1969-71; Mem., Senate, 1976-. *Recreations:* gardening, golf. *Address:* Old Manor Cottage, 24 Park Road, Teddington, Mddx. *T:* 01-977 3975. *Club:* Travellers'.

DAVIES, Lewis Mervyn, CMG 1966; OBE 1962; Secretary for Security, Hong Kong, since 1973; *b* 5 Dec. 1922; *s* of late Rev. Canon L. C. Davies; *m* 1st, 1950, Ione Podger (*d* 1973); one *s*; 2nd, 1975, Mona A. Birley; two step *s. Educ:* St Edward's Sch., Oxford. Served with Fleet Air Arm, 1941-46: Lieut A, RNVR. District Commissioner, Gold Coast, 1948; Western Pacific: Senior Asst Secretary, 1956-62; Financial Secretary, 1962-65; Chief Secretary, 1965-70; Deputy Governor, Bahamas, 1970-73. Lay Canon, Cathedral Church of St Barnabas, Honiara, 1965-70. Commandeur de l'Ordre National du Mérite, 1966. *Recreations:* sailing, tennis. *Address:* c/o Government Secretariat, Lower Albert Road, Hong Kong.

DAVIES, Lloyd; *see* Davies, J. R. L.

DAVIES, Col Lucy Myfanwy, CBE 1968 (OBE 1962); Deputy Controller Commandant, WRAC, since 1967; *b* 8 April 1913; *d* of late Col A. M. O. Anwyl-Passingham, CBE, DL, JP, and late Margaret Anwyl-Passingham; *m* 1955, Major D. W. Davies, TD, RAMC (*d* 1959); no *c. Educ:* Francis Holland Graham Street Sch. Driver FANY, 1939; commnd ATS, 1941; served in Egypt, 1945-48; Asst Director, WRAC Middle East (Cyprus), 1957-59; Comdt WRAC Depot, 1961-64; Dep. Director WRAC, 1964-68; retired, 1968. An underwriting Member of Lloyd's, 1971-. OStJ 1938. *Recreations:* travel, racing, reading. *Address:* 6 Elm Place, SW7. *T:* 01-373 5731. *Clubs:* Curzon House; Sandown Park, Lingfield Park.

DAVIES, Marcus John A.; *see* Anwyl-Davies.

DAVIES, Meredith; *see* Davies, Albert Meredith.

DAVIES, Mervyn; *see* Davies, D. H. M.

DAVIES, Hon. Sir Michael; *see* Davies, Hon. Sir A. W. M.

DAVIES, Michael John, CMG 1961; OBE 1957; Secretary, Imperial College of Science and Technology, and Clerk to the Governing Body, since 1962; *b* 7 Oct. 1918; *y s* of late David Alexander Davies; *m* 1949, Elizabeth Eve Burridge; two *s* one *d. Educ:* Diocesan Coll., Cape Town; University of Cape Town; Trinity Coll., Oxford. (MA) as a Rhodes Scholar. Appointed to Colonial Service in Tanganyika, as an Administrative Officer, 1940. Private Secretary to the Governor, 1943-47; seconded to the Colonial Office, 1947-49. Assistant Special Representative for Tanganyika at Trusteeship Council of United Nations, 1958 and 1959; Minister: for Constitutional Affairs in Tanganyika, 1959; for Security and Immigration, 1959-60; for Information Services, 1960-61 (until date of Self Government in Tanganyika, May 1st). Acting Chief Secretary May-Aug., 1960; retired from HM Overseas Civil Service, 1962. Médaille de la Belgique Reconnaissante (for services to Belgian Refugees), 1961. *Recreations:* watching Rugby football (Welsh International, 1938 and 1939); playing golf; gardening. *Address:* Lanrick, Cross-in-Hand, Sussex. *T:* Heathfield 3499.

DAVIES, Prof. (Morgan Wynn) Humphrey, LLM, MSc; CEng, FIEE; Professor of Electrical Engineering, Queen Mary College, University of London, since 1956; Dean of Engineering, University of London, since 1976; *b* 26 Dec. 1911; *s* of late Richard Humphrey Davies, CB; *m* 1944, Gwendolen Enid, *d* of late Canon Douglas Edward Morton, Camborne, Cornwall; one *s. Educ:* Hill Crest, Swanage; Westminster Sch.; University

College of N Wales, Bangor; Charlottenburg Technische Hochschule, Berlin. Grad. Apprentice with Metropolitan-Vickers, 1933; Lecturer in Electrical Engineering, University of Wales, 1935-42; Commonwealth Fellow, MIT, 1938-39; University Lecturer in Electrical Engineering, College of Technology, Manchester, 1943; Education Officer to Instn of Electrical Engineers, 1944-47; Lecturer, 1947, and University Reader, 1952, in Electrical Engineering, Imperial Coll., University of London, 1947-56. Member: Council, IEE, 1948-51, 1958-61 (Chm., Science and Gen. Div. 1964-65). Council, City & Guilds of London Inst., 1952-; Engineering Adv. Cttee, BBC, 1965-71; Computer Bd for Univs and Res. Councils, 1968-71; Council, Univ. of Wales, Bangor, 1976-; Chm., Bd of Univ. of London Computer Centre, 1968-. *Publications:* Power System Analysis (with J. R. Mortlock), 1952; papers in Proc. of Instn of Electrical Engineers. *Recreation:* travel. *Address:* Church Bank, Beaumaris, Anglesey. *Club:* Athenæum.

DAVIES, Nigel; *see* Davies, Claude N. B.

DAVIES, Oswald, CBE 1973; DCM 1944; JP; Chairman and Chief Executive, Fairclough Construction Group Ltd (formerly Leonard Fairclough Ltd), since 1965; *b* 23 June 1920; *s* of George Warham Davies and Margaret (*née* Hinton); *m* 1942, Joyce Davies; one *s* one *d. Educ:* Central Schs, Sale; Manchester Coll. of Technology. FBIM, FIHE, FIOB, FFB. Joined Leonard Fairclough Ltd at age of 15 years and became Agent/Engineer at 18. Served War of 1939-45: Sapper, bomb disposal squad, RE, Europe and ME, from 1940 (DCM (ME) 1944); returned to Europe, where involved with his unit in clearance of waterways, port, docks and bridge reconstruction. On release, Contracts Manager, area office, Stafford; then steel works near Chester. Dir, 1948, Jt Man. Dir, 1951, Leonard Fairclough Ltd. JP 1969. *Recreations:* gardening, Rugby football, sport. *Address:* Dingle Bank, Church Road, Lymm, Cheshire WA13 0QD. *T:* Lymm 2701.

DAVIES, Oswald Vaughan L.; *see* Lloyd-Davies.

DAVIES, P(eter) Maxwell; freelance composer; conductor; *b* 8 Sept. 1934. *Educ:* Leigh Grammar Sch.; Manchester Univ.; Royal Manchester Coll. of Music. MusB (Hons), 1956. Studied with Goffredo Petrassi in Rome (schol. 1957); Harkness Fellow, Grad. Music Sch., Princetown Univ., NJ, 1962. Dir of Music, Cirencester Grammar Sch., 1959-62; Lecture tours in Europe, Australia and New Zealand, 1965; Visiting Composer, Adelaide Univ., 1966; Co-Dir, with Harrison Birtwistle, of Pierrot Players, 1967-70; Dir, The Fires of London, 1971; has conducted many concerts with these ensembles in Britain and abroad. Series for Schools Broadcasts, BBC Television. *Publications:* Trumpet Sonata, 1955; Five Pieces for Piano, 1956; St Michael Sonata, for 17 Wind Instruments, 1957; Alma Redemptoris Mater for 6 Wind Instruments, 1957; Five Motets for Soprano, Contralto, Tenor and Bass soli, double Choir and Instruments, 1959; Prolation for Orchestra, 1959; Ricercar and Doubles on 'To Many a Well', 1959; O Magnum Mysterium, 1960 (Instrumental parts); Four Carols from O Magnum Mysterium for unaccompanied chorus, 1960; Fantasia on O Magnum Mysterium for organ, 1960; Te Lucis Ante Terminum, 1961; String Quartet, 1961; First Fantasia on an In Nomine of John Taverner, 1962 (commissioned by BBC); Leopardi Fragments, 1962; Sinfonia, 1962; The Lord's Prayer for SATB choir, 1962; Four Carols, 1962; Five Little Pieces for Piano Solo, 1962-64; Veni Sancte Spiritus for Soprano, Contralto and Bass soli, mixed Chorus and small Orchestra, 1963; Second Fantasia on John Taverner's In Nomine for Orchestra, 1964; Shakespeare Music for Chamber Ensemble, 1964; Ecce Manus Tradentis for mixed Chorus and Instruments, 1965; Seven in Nomine for Instruments, 1963-65; The Shepherd's Calender for Young Singers and Instrumentalists, 1965; Revelation and Fall for Soprano solo and Instruments, 1965; Shall I Die For Mannis Sake?, Carol for Soprano and Alto Voices and Piano, 1966; Five Carols for Soprano and Alto Voices, unaccompanied, 1966; Hymnos for Clarinet and Piano, 1967; Antechrist for Chamber Ensemble, 1967; L'Homme Armé for Chamber Ensemble, 1968; Fantasia and Two Pavans (Purcell, real. Davies), 1968-69; Eight Songs for a Mad King, 1969; St Thomas Wake—Foxtrot for Orchestra (commnd by City of Dortmund), 1969; Worldes Blis, 1969; Eram Quasi Agnus, 1969; Cauda Pavonis, 1969; Solita for flute solo, 1969; opera, Taverner, 1970; Hymn to St Magnus, 1972; Stone Litany, 1973; Ave Maris Stella for Chamber Ensemble, 1975; The Blind Fiddler for Soprano and Chamber Ensemble, 1976; opera, The Martyrdom of St Magnus, 1977; A Mirror Whitening Light, 1977; film score, The Devils, 1971. *Address:* c/o Boosey & Hawkes, PO Box 1BR, W1.

DAVIES, Rhys, OBE 1968; novelist and short story writer; *b* 9 Nov. 1903; *s* of Thomas R. and Sarah A. Davies. *Educ:* Porth

Co. Sch. *Publications:* The Withered Root, 1927; A Pig in a Poke, 1931; Count Your Blessings, 1932; The Red Hills, 1932; Love Provoked, 1933; Honey and Bread, 1935; The Things Men Do, 1936; A Time to Laugh, 1937; My Wales, 1937; Jubilee Blues, 1938; Under the Rose, 1940; Tomorrow to Fresh Woods, 1941; A Finger in Every Pie, 1942; The Story of Wales, 1943; The Black Venus, 1944; The Trip to London, 1946; The Dark Daughters, 1947; Boy With a Trumpet, 1949; Marianne, 1951; The Painted King, 1954; No Escape (play), 1954; Collected Stories, 1955; The Perishable Quality, 1957; The Darling of Her Heart, 1958; Girl Waiting in the Shade, 1960; The Chosen One, 1967; Print of a Hare's Foot, 1969; Nobody Answered the Bell, 1971; Honeysuckle Girl, 1975; contributions to numerous British and American periodicals. *Recreations:* theatre; living in London; cultivating ruined characters. *Address:* c/o Curtis Brown Ltd, 1 Craven Hill, W2 3EW.

DAVIES, Rt. Rev. Robert Edward; *see* Tasmania, Bishop of.

DAVIES, Prof. Robert Ernest, FRS 1966; University of Pennsylvania: Benjamin Franklin Professor of Molecular Biology, since 1970 (Professor of Biochemistry: School of Medicine, 1955-62; Graduate School of Medicine, 1962-70); Member, Institute for Environmental Medicine, School of Medicine, since 1970; Chairman, Department of Animal Biology, School of Veterinary Medicine, 1962-73; Chairman, Graduate Group Committee on Molecular Biology, 1962-72; *b* 17 Aug. 1919; *s* of William Owen Davies and Stella Davies; *m* 1961, Helen C. (*née* Rogoff); two *step s*. *Educ:* Manchester Grammar Sch.; Univ. of Manchester and Univ. of Sheffield. BSc(Chem.) Manchester, 1941; MSc Manchester 1942; PhD Sheffield 1949; DSc Manchester 1952; MA Oxon 1956; MA Penn 1971. Temp. Asst Lectr in Chemistry, Univ. of Sheffield. Half-time research (Ministry of Supply), Chemical Defence Research Dept), 1942; Full-time research on temp. staff, Medical Research Unit for Research in Cell Metabolism, 1945. Apptd to Estab. Staff of MRC, 1947; Hon. Lectr in Biochemistry, Univ. of Sheffield, 1948-54. Vis. Prof., Pharmakologisches Inst., Univ. Heidelberg, March-May 1954. *Publications:* very many: in chemistry, biochemistry, physiolog. and biology journals concerning secretion, muscle contraction, kidneys, etc. *Recreations:* mountaineering, caving, underwater swimming, white water boating. *Address:* Department of Animal Biology, School of Veterinary Medicine, University of Pennsylvania, Pa 19174, USA. *T:* (office) 215 243-7861; 7053 McCallum Street, Philadelphia, Pa 19119, USA. *Clubs:* Fell and Rock-climbing Club of the English Lake District; Cave Diving Group; Manchester Univ. Mountaineering.

DAVIES, Robert Henry, MBE 1962; DFC 1943; HM Diplomatic Service; Counsellor, HM Embassy, Paris, since 1976; *b* 17 Aug. 1921; *s* of John and Lena Davies; *m* 1st, 1945, Marion Ainsworth (marr. diss. 1973); one *s* one *d*; 2nd, 1973, Maryse Deuson. *Educ:* John Bright County Sch., Llandudno. RAF, 1940-46; flew with S African Air Force, N Africa, 1942-43. Joined Min. of Food, 1946; transf. to CRO, 1954; served in India, 1954-57 and Canada, 1959-62; HM Diplomatic Service, 1965; served in Brussels, 1967-70; Consul-Gen. and Counsellor (Admin), Moscow, 1973-75; FCO, 1975-76. *Recreations:* golf, birdwatching, reading. *Address:* c/o Foreign and Commonwealth Office, King Charles Street, SW1A 2AH. *Club:* Bramley Golf.

DAVIES, Prof. Rodney Deane, DSc, PhD, FInstP, FRAS; Professor of Radio Astronomy, University of Manchester, since 1976; *b* 8 Jan. 1930; *s* of Holbin James Davies and Rena Irene (*née* March), Mallala, S Australia; *m* 1953, Valda Beth Treasure; one *s* two *d* (and one *s* decd). *Educ:* Adelaide High Sch.; Univ. of Adelaide (BSc Hons, MSc); Univ. of Manchester (PhD, DSc). Research Officer, Radiophysics Div., CSIRO, Sydney, 1951-53; Univ. of Manchester: Asst Lectr, 1953-56; Lectr, 1956-67; Reader, 1967-76. Visiting Astronomer, Radiophysics Div., CSIRO, Australia, 1963. Member: Internat. Astronomical Union, 1958; Org. Cttee and Working Gps of various Commns; Council, Royal Astronomical Soc., 1972-75 (Vice-Pres. 1973-75); Bd and various panels and cttees of Astronomy Space and Radio Bd and Science Bd of Science Research Council; British Nat. Cttee for Astronomy, 1974-77. *Publications:* Radio Studies of the Universe (with H. P. Palmer), 1959; Radio Astronomy Today (with H. P. Palmer and M. I. Large), 1963; The Crab Nebula (co-ed with F. G. Smith), 1971; numerous contribs to Monthly Notices of RAS and internat. jls on the galactic and extragalactic magnetic fields, structure and dynamics of the Galaxy and nearby external galaxies, using radio spectral lines. *Recreations:* cricket, gardening, fell-walking. *Address:* University of Manchester, Nuffield Radio Astronomy Laboratories, Jodrell Bank, Macclesfield, Cheshire SK11 9DL. *T:* Lower Withington 321.

DAVIES, Roy Dicker Salter, CBE 1967; a Chief Inspector of Schools, Department of Education and Science, 1958-68, retired; *b* 24 March 1906; *yr s* of Ernest Salter Davies, CBE, and Evelyn May Lile. *Educ:* Tonbridge Sch.; Magdalen Coll., Oxford (MA). Served RE, 1939-40, RA, 1940-45. Appointed HM Inspector of Schools, 1934; Staff Inspector, 1951. Mem., Departmental Cttee on Adult Educn, 1969-73. *Recreations:* watching Rugby football; cricket. *Address:* Wick House, Stogumber, Taunton, Somerset. *T:* Stogumber 422.

DAVIES, Rev. Rupert Eric; Warden, John Wesley's Chapel, Bristol, since 1976; *b* 29 Nov. 1909; *s* of Walter Pierce and Elizabeth Miriam Davies; *m* 1937, Margaret Price Holt; two *s* two *d*. *Educ:* St Paul's Sch.; Balliol Coll. (Class. Scholar), Oxford; Wesley House, Cambridge; Univ. of Tübingen, Germany. First cl. in Honour Mods, Classics, 1930; second cl. in Lit. Hum., 1932; first cl. in Theology, Pt II, 1934 (Wesley House); trav. schol. in Germany, 1934-35; BD (Cantab) 1946. Chaplain, Kingswood Sch., Bath, 1935-47; Methodist Minister, Bristol, 1947-52 and 1973-76; Tutor, Didsbury Coll., Bristol, 1952-67; Principal, Wesley Coll., Bristol, 1967-73. Pres., Methodist Conf., 1970-71. Select Preacher to Univs of: Cambridge, 1962; Oxford, 1969; Mem. Exec. Cttee, World Methodist Council, 1956-76; Mem., Anglican-Methodist Unity Commn, 1965-68; World Council of Churches: Faith and Order Commn, 1965-75; Deleg. to Fourth Assembly, 1968. *Publications:* The Problem of Authority in the Continental Reformers, 1946; Catholicity of Protestantism (ed), 1950; Approach to Christian Education (ed), 1956; John Scott Lidgett (ed), 1957; The Church in Bristol, 1960; Methodists and Unity, 1962; Methodism, 1963; History of the Methodist Church in Great Britain (ed), vol. I, 1965; We Believe in God (ed), 1968; Religious Authority in an Age of Doubt, 1968; A Christian Theology of Education, 1974; What Methodists Believe, 1976. *Recreations:* golf, theatre. *Address:* 6 Elmtree Drive, Bishopsworth, Bristol. *T:* Bristol 631457.

DAVIES, Ryland; opera singer; tenor; *b* 9 Feb. 1943; *s* of Gethin and Joan Davies; *m* 1966, Anne Elizabeth Howells, *qv*. *Educ:* Royal Manchester College of Music (Fellow, 1971) (studied with Frederic R. Cox, OBE). Début as Almaviva in The Barber of Seville, Welsh Nat. Opera, 1964; Glyndebourne Fest. Chorus, 1964-66: soloist rôles incl.: Belmonte in Il Seraglio, Ferrando in Cosi Fan Tutte, Flamand in Capriccio; rôles with Welsh Nat. Opera incl., Tamino in The Magic Flute, and with Scottish Opera, Ferrando; Sadler's Wells Opera: Almaviva, also Essex in Britten's Gloriana; Royal Opera: Hylas in The Trojans, Don Ottavio in Don Giovanni, Ferrando, Cassio in Otello, Ernesto in Don Pasquale, Lysander in A Midsummer Night's Dream, Almaviva. Overseas venues incl. Salzburg, as Cassio; S Francisco and Chicago, as Ferrando, also Paris; début NY Met., 1975, Ferrando and Almaviva; Vienna, Missa Solemnis; Bruxelles Opera, Werther. Concert works in UK incl.: Messiah, Saul, Beethoven's Ninth Symphony, Christ on the Mount of Olives, Verdi's Requiem, Dream of Gerontius, Dvorak's St Ludmila; concert perfs in USA incl. Messiah and Die Fledermaus. Many recordings, incl.: Il Seraglio, The Trojans, Saul, Cosi Fan Tutte, Thérèse, Monteverdi Madrigals, Idomeneo, Haydn's The Seasons, Messiah, L'oracolo-Leone, Judas Maccabaeus. *Recreations:* antiques, art, cinema, sport. *Address:* Milestone, Broom Close, Esher, Surrey. *T:* Esher 64527.

DAVIES, Mrs Ryland; *see* Howells, Anne.

DAVIES, Sam; *see* Davies, Stanley Mason.

DAVIES, (Stanley) Kenneth, CBE 1951; Chairman: Wire Ropes Ltd, Wicklow; Wesdore Ltd, Cardiff; *b* 25 April 1899; 2nd *s* of late Sir John Davies, CBE, JP; *m* 1938, Stephanie Morton; one *s* one *d*. *Educ:* Christ Coll., Brecon; Blundell's; Royal Military Academy, Woolwich. Commnd RA, 1918; served France and Germany, 1918-19. Chairman and Managing Director: George Elliot & Co. Ltd; Bridgwater Wire Ropes Ltd; Somerset Wire Co. Ltd; Terrells Wire Ropes Ltd; Yacht and Commercial Rigging Co. Ltd; Hartlepool Wire Rope Co.; Excelsior Ropes Ltd (for varying periods between 1929 and 1960, when they were incorp. in British Ropes Ltd, now Bridon Ltd, or in GKN Ltd). Founder Member, Cardiff Aeroplane Club, 1929. Private pilot's licence, 1931-61. Formed Cambrian Air Services Ltd, 1935, Managing Director, 1935-51. Member Cttee Royal Aero Club of United Kingdom, 1935 (Vice-Chm., 1948-51, Chm. 1952-58, Vice-Pres., 1958-); Member Board British European Airways Corporation, 1951-67; Dep. Chairman BEA Helicopters Ltd, 1965-67; Chairman Welsh Advisory Council for Civil Aviation, 1948-60; Chairman Cardiff Airport Consultative Cttee, 1956-63; Member Welsh Cttee of Arts Council of Great Britain, 1954-67; Member Consultative Cttee, Sadler's Wells Trust, 1962-;

Chairman of Contemporary Art Society of Wales, 1966-72; Liveryman of the Guild of Air Pilots and Air Navigators; Vice-President, FAI (Federation Aeronautique Internationale), rep. UK; Member Cttee, Dublin Theatre Festival, 1967; Mem. Ct of Governors, National Theatre of Wales. Life Member: Iron & Steel Institute; S Wales Inst. of Engineers; Royal Agricultural Society; Royal Dublin Society. FRSA; FCIT. Coronation medal, 1953. *Recreations:* aviation and gastronomy (Vice-Pres., Internat. Wine and Food Society). *Address:* Killoughter, Ashford, Co. Wicklow. *T:* Wicklow 4126; Collingdon Road, Cardiff. *T:* 21693. *Clubs:* Athenæum, Brooks's, Turf, Royal Automobile; County (Cardiff); Kildare Street and University (Dublin); Bristol Channel Yacht (Swansea).

DAVIES, Stanley Mason, (Sam Davies), CMG 1971; Consultant, Vickers Ltd (Medical) and other international medical firms, since 1977; *b* 7 Feb. 1919; *s* of late Charles Davies, MBE and Constance Evelyn Davies; *m* 1943, Diana Joan (*née* Lowe); three *d. Educ:* Bootle Grammar School. War Service, UK and W Europe, 1939-46; Royal Army Dental Corps, 1939-41 (Sgt); Corps of Royal Engineers, 1941-46 (Staff Captain). Clerical Officer, Min. of Labour, 1936; Exec. Officer, Inland Revenue, 1938; Higher Exec. Officer, Min. of Pensions, 1946-53; Min. of Health, 1953-68; Asst Sec., DHSS, 1968-75; Under Sec., Industries and Exports Div., DHSS, 1975-76. FSAScot. Croix de Guerre (France), 1944. *Recreations:* reading, archæology, philately. *Address:* 31 Leverstock Green Road, Hemel Hempstead, Herts. *T:* Hemel Hempstead 54312. *Club:* Savile.

DAVIES, Stuart Duncan, CBE 1968; FRAeS, BSc; Past President, Royal Aeronautical Society, 1972-73 (President, 1971-72); *b* 5 Dec. 1906; *s* of William Lewis Davies and Alice Dryden Duncan; *m* 1935, Ethel Rosalie Ann Radcliffe; one *d. Educ:* Westminster City Sch.; London Univ. (BSc Eng.). Vickers (Aviation) Ltd, 1925-31; Hawker Aircraft Ltd, 1931-36; A. V. Roe and Co. Ltd, 1938-55, Chief Designer, 1945-55; with Dowty Group Ltd, 1955-58, as Managing Director of Dowty Fuel System Ltd; Technical Director: Hawker Siddeley Aviation Ltd, 1958-64; Dowty Rotol Ltd, 1965-72. British Gold Medal for Aeronautics, 1958. *Address:* Glenwood, Nightingales, West Chiltington, West Sussex. *T:* West Chiltington 3512.

DAVIES, Thomas Glyn, CBE 1966; *b* 16 Aug. 1905; *s* of Thomas Davies, Gwaelod-y-Garth, Cardiff; *m* 1935, Margaret Berry; one *d. Educ:* Pontypridd Grammar Sch.; Univ. of Wales, Cardiff (MA). Asst Master, Howard Gardens High Sch., Cardiff, 1927-37; Warden, Educational Settlement, Pontypridd, 1937-43; Director of Education: Montgomeryshire, 1943-58; Denbighshire, 1958-70, retd. Mem. ITA, later IBA, 1970-75. Member: Court and Council, UC Bangor; Court, UC Cardiff. *Recreations:* travel, music. *Address:* 42 Park Avenue, Wrexham, Clwyd. *T:* Wrexham 52697.

DAVIES, Trevor Arthur L.; *see* Lloyd Davies.

DAVIES, Walter, OBE 1966; Secretary-General of The British Chamber of Commerce for Italy since 1961; *b* 7 Dec. 1920; *s* of late William Davies and late Frances Poole; *m* 1947, Alda, *d* of Tiso Lucchetta, Padua; two *d. Educ:* St Margaret's Higher Grade Sch., Liverpool; Liverpool Coll. of Commerce. Served War: RA, 1940-41; Scots Guards, 1942-47. Commendatore dell'Ordine al Merito della Repubblica Italiana, 1967. *Recreations:* good food, good company, fishing, motoring. *Address:* Via G. Dezza 27, 20144, Milan, Italy. *T:* Milan 4694391. *Club:* British American (Milan).

DAVIES, Wilfred Horace; Director: Cable & Wireless Ltd, 1968; Nigerian External Telecommunications Ltd, 1969-73; Sierra Leone External Telecommunications Ltd, 1969-74; East African External Telecommunications Co. Ltd, 1969-74; Oceanic Wireless Network Inc. Philippines, 1973; Eastern Telecommunications Philippines Inc., 1974; Chairman: Cable & Wireless Systems Ltd (Hong Kong), 1973; Asiadata Ltd (Hong Kong), 1973; Fiji Telecommunications Ltd, 1976; Trustee, Cable & Wireless Pension Funds, 1962; *b* 7 March 1917; *s* of late Gerald Edward Davies and Editha Lucy (*née* Sweet-Escott); *m* 1st, Helen Rose Gillam; one *s* one *d*; 2nd, Eva Nancy Berry; two *s. Educ:* Aldenham Sch. Cable & Wireless Ltd, 1935: Asst Staff Manager, 1957; Dep. Staff Manager, 1961; Staff Manager, 1962; Dir, 1968. MBIM. *Recreations:* golf, gardening. *Address:* (office) Mercury House, Theobalds Road, WC1. *T:* 01-242 4433; (home) Hartrow, Sleepers Hill, Winchester, Hants. *T:* Winchester 3758. *Clubs:* Royal Commonwealth Society, Exiles.

DAVIES, Rt. Hon. Sir (William) Arthian, PC 1961; Kt 1952; DL; a Lord Justice of Appeal, 1961-74; *b* 10 May 1901; *s* of late Arthian Davies; *m* 1933, Mary Bailey, *d* of late Henry Liptrot; one *d. Educ:* Dulwich; Trinity Coll., Oxford (MA). Barrister,

1925; QC 1947; sometime Exr and Asst Reader to Council of Legal Education and Gresham Lecturer in Law; Junior Counsel to Ministry of Labour and National Service, 1934-47; Recorder of Merthyr Tydfil, 1946-49, Chester, 1949-52. JP (Bucks), 1948; DL 1967; Dep. Chairman Quarter Sessions: Co. Cardigan, 1949-52; Bucks, 1951-61, Chm. 1961-71. Bencher, Inner Temple, 1952; Judge of High Court of Justice, Probate, Divorce, and Admiralty Division, 1952-59; Judge of High Court of Justice, Queen's Bench Div., 1959-61. Dep. Chairman Parliamentary Boundary Commn for Wales, 1958-61; Chairman Home Office Cttee on Matrimonial Proceedings in Magistrates' Courts, 1958. Hon. Fellow, Trinity Coll., Oxford, 1969. *Address:* Ballinger Lodge, Great Missenden, Bucks.

DAVIES, William Llewellyn M.; *see* Monro Davies.

DAVIES, William Rupert R.; *see* Rees-Davies.

DAVIES, William Tudor, CBE 1963 (OBE 1960); FREconS; FBIM; JP; Barrister at Law and Economist; Independent Chairman and Adviser of Trade Associations; Adviser on industrial legislation and conciliation and international cartels; *b* Nantyglo, Gwent; *o s* of John Pritchard Davies; *m* 1937, Iva Mary, *yr d* of Philip Kyle, OBE. *Educ:* University of Wales, Aberystwyth; University of Bristol; University of Manchester. BA 1st Class Honours; 1st Class Diplomas in Theory and Practice of Education; Founder Member, Fellow and Hon. Life Member, British Institute of Management; Research Medallist, University of Bristol; Post-Graduate Research, University of Manchester; Post-Graduate Research, University of Cambridge; Lecturer in Economics; Editorial staff Manchester Guardian; Parliamentary candidate, 1922 and 1923; Editorial staff Financial News; Chairman of Joint Cttee of Building and Civil Engineering Industries set up under Control of Employment Act, 1939; Independent Chairman of Joint Industrial Council of Distributive Trades; Chairman of Wages Councils; Chairman, Reinstatement in Civil Employment Tribunals; Member: Further Education and Training Tribunal; London Conscientious Objectors' Tribunal, 1940-60; Chairman of National Insurance Tribunals; Independent Chairman of the National Conciliation Board for the Co-operative Service; Chairman of Boards of Inquiry under Ministry of Labour; Independent Chairman Local Appeal Boards; Independent Chairman Joint Cttee of North Wales Coal Industry; Chairman, Road Transport Inquiries under Road Traffic Acts, 1961, and Compulsory Purchase orders; Hearing Appeals from Licensing Authorities and Public Inquiries, Ministry of Transport; Member Isle of Man Traffic Tribunal; Commissioner of Inquiry in Nigeria for Secretary of State for the Colonies; Barrister and Solicitor of Supreme Court, Federation of Nigeria, etc. *Publications:* National Essay Prize on The Creation of an International Police Force (Welsh National Eisteddfod, Caernarvon, 1921); The Rationalisation of Industry, 1928; The Economic Task, 1931; The Economics of Plenty, 1934; Trade Associations and Industrial Co-ordination, 1938-39; Personnel Management and Essential Work Orders, 1944; National Insurance, Law of Tribunals, 1950. *Recreations:* golf, walking. *Address:* 2 Harcourt Buildings, Temple, EC4. *T:* 01-353 7202; Sunhaven, 35 Links Avenue, Gidea Park, Essex. *T:* Romford 41026. *Club:* National Liberal.

DAVIES, Dr Wyndham Roy; *b* 3 June 1926; *s* of late George Edward Davies, LLB, Llangadock, Carms, and of Ellen Theresa (*née* Merris), Treaford Hall, Birmingham. *Educ:* King Edward's, Birmingham; Birmingham and London Universities. LRCP 1948; MB, ChB, 1949; DPH 1958; DIH 1959. House Surgeon, General Hospital, Birmingham, 1949; Receiving Room Officer, Children's Hospital, Birmingham, 1949; Resident Medical Officer, Little Bromwich Hospital, Birmingham, 1950. Entered RN, 1950; HMS Surprise, 1950-51; HMS St Angelo, 1951-53; Squadron Medical Officer, 4th Destoyer Sqdn, Home Fleet, 1953-54; Research Assistant, St George's Hospital Medical Sch. (MRC), 1955; Admiralty Medical Board and HMS Dauntless (WRNS), 1956-57; stood by building of HMS Albion, HMS Malcolm, 1957; HMS Glory, 1957; London School of Hygiene and Tropical Medicine, 1958; RN Medical Sch., 1958-59; habitability trials, HMS Centaur and HMS Bulwark, 1959-60; Joint Services Amphib. Warfare Centre, 1960-63; qual. shallow water diver, 1960; Chemical Defence Exper. Establishment, 1963; retired as Surgeon Lieut-Comdr, 1963. Adopted Prospective Parliamentary Candidate for Birmingham Perry Barr Div., 1963; MP (C) Perry Barr Div. of Birmingham, 1964-66. Joint Secretary, Party Educn and Sci. Cttee, 1965-66; Vice-President, Birmingham Cons. and Unionist Assoc., 1965-71. Dir, Medical Economic Res. Inst., 1968-. Hon. Medical Adviser, British Sub-Aqua Club, 1959-66; Hon. Medical Adviser, British Safety Council, 1962-64; Governor, Royal Humane Society, 1962-; Chairman Organizing Cttee, World

Congress of Underwater Activities, 1962; Cttee, Poole and Dorset Adventure Centre, 1961-64; Island Comdr for Sea Scouts, Malta, 1951-53; ADC, Boy Scouts, City of Westminster, 1957-62; Founder Member Old Edwardians BP Guild, 1948-; Hon. Secretary, Houses of Parliament BP Guild, 1964-66. Medical Officer British Schools Exploring Society Exped. to Labrador, 1958; Medical Commn on Accident Prevention, 1963-70; Founder, Society for Underwater Technology; BMA Rep., 1968-70, 1972-; Exec. Council, Monday Club, 1965-69; Chairman: Health Cttee, 1965-69; University Liaison Cttee, 1967-68. Mem., Medical Cttee, SW Metropolitan Reg. Hosp. Bd, 1972-. Dir, Brit. Cellular Therapy Soc., 1974-; Mem., Deutsch Gesellschaft für Zelltherapie, 1972-. Editor, Fellowship for Freedom in Medicine Bulletin, 1972-. *Publications:* Expired Air Resuscitation, 1959; Skin Diving, 1959; Collectivism or Individualism in Medicine, 1965; Reforming the National Health Service, 1967; The Pharmaceutical Industry, A Personal Study, 1967; Health—or Health Service?, 1972; articles in The Practitioner and Physiological Journal. *Recreations:* all sports on, in or under water, travel, exploring, painting. *Clubs:* Carlton; British Schools Exploring.

DAVIES-SCOURFIELD, Brig. Edward Grismond Beaumont, CBE 1966 (MBE 1951); MC 1945; General Secretary, National Association of Boys Clubs, since 1973; *b* 2 Aug. 1918; 3rd *s* of H. G. Davies-Scourfield and Helen (*née* Newton); *m* 1945, Diana Lilias (*née* Davidson); one *s* one *d*. *Educ:* Winchester Coll.; RMC Sandhurst. Commnd into KRRC, 1938; served War of 1939-45 (despatches 1945); psc; commanded: 3rd Green Jackets (Rifle Bde), 1960-62; Green Jackets Bde, 1962-64; British Jt Services Trng Team (Ghana), 1964-66; British Troops Cyprus and Dhekelia Area, 1966-69; Salisbury Plain Area, 1970-73; retd 1973. *Recreations:* hunting, shooting, tennis, reading, walking. *Address:* Old Rectory Cottage, Medstead, Alton, Hants. *T:* Alton 62133. *Club:* Army and Navy.

d'AVIGDOR-GOLDSMID, Maj.-Gen. Sir James (Arthur), 3rd Bt *cr* 1934; CB 1975; OBE 1955; MC 1944; *b* 19 Dec. 1912; *yr s* of Sir Osmond d'Avigdor-Goldsmid, 1st Bt, and Alice Lady d'Avigdor-Goldsmid; *S* brother, 1976; unmarried. *Educ:* Harrow; RMC, Sandhurst. 2nd Lieut 4th/7th Royal Dragoon Guards, 1932. Served War of 1939-45, France and Germany (wounded). Commanded: 4th/7th Royal Dragoon Guards, 1950-53; 20th Armoured Brigade Group, 1958-61; Director, Royal Armoured Corps, War Office, subseq. Ministry of Defence, 1962-65; President, Regular Commissions Board, Feb.-Sept. 1965; Director TA and Cadets, 1966-68; Col of 4th/7th Royal Dragoon Guards, 1963-73; Chm., SE TA&VRA; Hon. Col The Mercian Yeomanry, T&AVR, 1972-77. MP (C) Lichfield and Tamworth, 1970-Sept. 1974; Mem., Select Cttee on Estimates, 1971-74. Chairman, Racecourse Security Services Ltd. Member: Horserace Betting Levy Bd, 1974-77; Council, Winston Churchill Meml Trust. Comr Royal Hosp. Chelsea, 1972. *Heir:* none. *Address:* 101 Mount Street, W1. *T:* 01-499 1989. *Clubs:* Cavalry and Guards (Chm.), Turf, Jockey.

DAVIGNON, Viscount Etienne; Ambassador of HM the King; Member of the Commission of the European Communities, since 1977 (with responsibility for internal market, customs union and industrial affairs); *b* Budapest, 4 Oct. 1932; *m* 1959, Françoise de Cumont; one *s* two *d*. *Educ:* University of Louvain (LLD). Diplomat; Head of Office of Minister for Foreign Affairs, Belgium, 1963; Political Director, Ministry for Foreign Affairs, Belgium, 1969; Chm., Gov. Board, Internat. Energy Agency, 1974. *Recreations:* tennis, golf, skiing. *Address:* 200 rue de la Loi, 1049 Brussels, Belgium. *T:* 735.80.40.

DAVIN, Daniel Marcus, (Dan Davin), MBE 1945; Oxford Academic Publisher, 1974-78; Deputy Secretary to Delegates of the Oxford University Press, 1974-78; *b* 1 Sept. 1913; *s* of Patrick and Mary Davin; *m* 1939, Winifred Kathleen Gonley; three *d*. *Educ:* Marist Brothers Sch., Invercargill, NZ; Sacred Heart Coll., Auckland; Otago Univ. (MA); Balliol Coll., Oxford (First in Greats, 1939, MA 1945). Served War: Royal Warwickshire Regt, 1939-40; 2 NZEF, 1940-45; served in Greece and Crete (wounded 1941); Intell. GHQ, ME, 1941-42; NZ Div., N Africa and Italy, 1942-45 (despatches thrice, MBE). With Clarendon Press, 1945-78. Fellow of Balliol Coll., 1965-; FRSA. *Publications:* novels: Cliffs of Fall, 1945; For the Rest of Our Lives, 1947; Roads from Home, 1949; The Sullen Bell, 1956; No Remittance, 1959; Not Here, Not Now, 1970; Brides of Price, 1972; *short stories:* The Gorse Blooms Pale, 1947; Breathing Spaces, 1975; *miscellaneous prose:* Introduction to English Literature (with John Mulgan), 1947; Crete (Official History), 1953 (Wellington, War Hist. Br., Dept of Internal Affairs); Writing in New Zealand: The New Zealand Novel (Parts One and Two, with W. K. Davin), 1956; Katherine Mansfield in Her Letters, 1959; Closing Times (Recollections of Julian Maclaren-

Ross, W. R. Rodgers, Louis MacNeice, Enid Starkie, Joyce Cary, Dylan Thomas, Itzik Manger), 1975; *editions:* New Zealand Short Stories, 1953; English Short Stories of Today: Second Series, 1958; Katherine Mansfield, Selected Stories, 1963. *Recreations:* gardening, walking, talking. *Address:* 103 Southmoor Road, Oxford. *T:* Oxford 57311. *Club:* Travellers'.

DAVIS; see Lovell-Davis.

DAVIS, Alfred George Fletcher H.; see Hall-Davis.

DAVIS, Andrew Frank; Artistic Director and Chief Conductor, Toronto Symphony Orchestra, since 1975; *b* 2 Feb. 1944; *m* 1970, Felicity Mary Vincent. *Educ:* Watford Grammar Sch.; King's Coll., Cambridge (MA, BMus); Accademia di S Cecilia, Rome. Assistant Conductor, BBC Scottish Symphony Orchestra, 1970-72; Asst Conductor, New Philharmonia Orchestra, 1973-77; Principal Guest Conductor, Royal Liverpool Philharmonic Orchestra, 1974-77. *Recreations:* kite flying, the study of mediaeval stained glass. *Address:* 1 Leighton Road, NW5.

DAVIS, Anthony Ronald William James, JP; Editor, Middle East Construction, since 1975; *b* 26 July 1931; *e s* of Donald William Davis, Barnes and Mary Josephine Davis (*née* Nolan-Byrne), Templeogue Mill, Co. Dublin; *m* 1960, Yolande Mary June, *o d* of Patrick Leonard, retd civil engr; one *s* two *d* (and one *d* decd). *Educ:* Hamlet of Ratcliffe and Oratory; Regent Street Polytechnic. Joint Services School for Linguists on Russian course as National Serviceman (Army), 1953-55; Architectural Asst, Housing Dept, Mddx County Architect's Dept, 1956-58; Sub-Editor, The Builder, 1959; Editor: Official Architecture and Planning, 1964-70; Building, 1970-74; Dir, The Builder, subseq. Building, 1974-77; Member Board: Architecture and Planning Publications Ltd, 1966; Building (Publishers) Ltd, 1972. Mem. Council, Modular Soc., 1970. JP Berkshire, 1973. *Publications:* contribs to various, architectural and technical. *Recreations:* collecting porcelain, music and dreaming. *Address:* 8 Blake Close, Dowles Green, Wokingham, Berks. *T:* Wokingham 785046. *Clubs:* Savage, Architecture.

DAVIS, Anthony Tilton, MA; JP; Head Master, Reading School, since 1966; *b* 14 Aug. 1931; *o s* of John and late Evelyn Davis; unmarried. *Educ:* St Bartholomew's Grammar Sch., Newbury; Reading Univ.; St John's Coll., Cambridge (Scholar). 1st class hons Class. Tripos Part I, 1954; 1st class hons (with distinction in Ancient History) Class. Tripos Part II, 1955. Sub-Lieut, RNVR, 1955-57. Asst Master and Classical Sixth Form Master, Harrow Sch., 1957-66 (Head of Latin, 1964-66). Pres., St John Ambulance Brigade (West Berks), 1972-; Member: Thames Valley Police Authority, 1972-; Court of Reading Univ., 1972-. JP Reading, 1971. *Publications:* Sallust, Catiline, 1967; articles and reviews in Greece and Rome and Didaskalos. *Recreations:* cricket (Captain, Berks CCC, 1960-70); music, water colours, ski-ing. *Address:* The Head Master's Lodge, Reading School, Reading, Berks. *T:* Reading 81886.

DAVIS, Archibald William; *b* 20 May 1900; *s* of late G. W. Davis, Crayford, Kent; *m* 1930, Eunice, *d* of late W. Pidd, Westwood, Coventry (*d* 1975); one *s*. *Educ:* Bablake Sch., Coventry; University College, London; Balliol Coll., Oxford; Emmanuel Coll., Cambridge. Entered HM Levant Consular Service, 1922; served at Consular posts in Iran, Turkey, Syria and Iraq; Political Officer, Aleppo (N Syria), 1941-42, with rank of Lt-Col; HM Consul-General, Basra, Iraq, 1946-49; Seville, Spain, 1950-53; retired 1953. *Address:* Rowanduz, Mendip Edge, Bleadon Hill, Weston-super-Mare, Avon. *T:* Bleadon 812830.

DAVIS, Bette; Actress; *b* Lowell, Mass. *Educ:* Cushing Academy, Ashburnham, Mass. Stage experience in Wild Duck, Broken Dishes, Solid South; entered films, 1930. Pictures she has appeared in: Dangerous (Academy Award of 1935 won 1936); The Petrified Forest, The Golden Arrow, 1936; Marked Woman, Kid Galahad, It's Love I'm After, That Certain Woman, 1937; Jezebel (Academy Award of 1938 won 1939); The Sisters, 1938; Dark Victory, Juarez, The Old Maid, Private Lives of Elizabeth and Essex, 1939; All This and Heaven Too, 1940; The Letter, The Great Lie, The Bride came COD, The Man who came to Dinner, The Little Foxes, 1941; In This our Life, Watch on the Rhine, Old Acquaintance, 1942; Mr Skeffington; The Corn is Green; A Stolen Life; Deception; Winter Meeting; June Bride; The Story of a Divorce; All about Eve; Another Man's Poison; The Star; The Virgin Queen; Wedding Breakfast; The Scapegoat, Pocketful of Miracles; Whatever Happened to Baby Jane?; Dead Image; Where Love Has Gone; Hush... Hush, Sweet Charlotte; The Nanny; The Anniversary; Connecting Rooms; Bunny O'Hare; Madam Sin; The Game; Burnt Offerings, 1977. Life Achievement Award,

Amer. Film Institute, 1977. *Publication:* The Lonely Life, 1963. *Relevant Publication:* Mother Goddam by Whitney Stine, 1975 (footnotes by Bette Davis). *Recreations:* swimming and horseback riding. *Address:* c/o Gottlieb, Schiff, Ticktin, Fabricant & Sternklar, PC, 555 Fifth Avenue, New York, NY 10017, USA.

DAVIS, Sir Charles (Sigmund), Kt 1965; CB 1960; Second Counsel to the Speaker, House of Commons, since 1974; *b* London, 22 Jan. 1909; *y s* of late Maurice Davis (*b* Melbourne, Australia) and Alfreda Regina Davis; *m* 1940, Pamela Mary, *er d* of late J. K. B. Dawson, OBE, and Phyllis Dawson; two *d. Educ:* Trinity Coll., Cambridge. Double 1st Cl. Hons, Law Tripos; Sen. Schol., Exhibitioner and Prizeman of Trinity, 1927-30; MA 1934. Called to the Bar, Inner Temple (Studentship and Certif. of Honour), 1930, and in Sydney Australia, 1931; practised as barrister in London, 1931-34; entered Legal Branch, Ministry of Health, 1934; held legal posts in various public offices, 1938-46 (Corporal, Home Guard, 1940-45); Asst Solicitor, Min. of Agric. and Fisheries, 1946-55; Prin. Asst Solicitor, MAFF, 1955-57; Legal Adviser and Solicitor, MAFF, and Forestry Commission, 1957-74, retired. *Recreations:* music (LRAM, ARCM) and much else. *Address:* 38 Kenilworth Avenue, SW19 7LW.

DAVIS, Mrs Chloë Marion, OBE 1975; Chairman, Consumer Affairs Group of National Organisations, since 1973; Member: Council on Tribunals since 1970; Consumer Consultative Committee to EEC, 1973-76; Consumer Standards Advisory Committee of British Standards Institution since 1965 (Chairman 1970-73); Executive Committee, Housewife's Trust, 1970-77; *b* Dartmouth, Devon, 15 Feb. 1909; *d* of Richard Henry Pound and Mary Jane Chapman; *m* 1928, Edward Thomas Davis, printer and sometime writer; one *s. Educ:* limited formal, USA and England. Various part-time voluntary social and public services from 1929; Birth Control Internat. Information Centre, 1931-38; voluntary activity in bombing etc emergencies, also cookery and domestic broadcasting during War of 1939-45; information service for Kreis Resident Officers, Control Commn for Germany, Berlin, 1946-48; regional Citizens Advice Bureaux office, London Council of Social Service, 1949-55; Sen. Information Officer to Nat. Citizens Advice Bureaux Council, 1956-69. Nat. House-Building Council, 1973-76. *Recreations:* reading present history in the morning in newspapers and past history in books in the evening; gardening, walking, talking with friends. *Address:* Auberville Cottage, 246 Dover Road, Walmer, Kent CT14 7NP. *T:* Deal 4038.

DAVIS, Clinton; *see* Davis, S. C.

DAVIS, Colin (Rex), CBE 1965; Musical Director, Royal Opera House, Covent Garden, since Sept. 1971; Principal Guest Conductor: Boston Symphony Orchestra, since 1972; London Symphony Orchestra, since 1974; *b* 25 Sept. 1927; *s* of Reginald George and Lillian Davis; *m* 1949, April Cantelo (marr. diss., 1964); one *s* one *d*; *m* 1964, Ashraf Naini; three *s. Educ:* Christ's Hospital; Royal College of Music. Orchestral Conductor, Freelance wilderness, 1949-57; Asst Conductor, BBC Scottish Orchestra, 1957-59. Conductor, Sadler's Wells, 1959, Principal Conductor, 1960-65, Musical Director, 1961-65; Chief Conductor, BBC Symphony Orchestra, 1967-71, Chief Guest Conductor, 1971-75. Artistic Director, Bath Festival, 1969. Conducted at: Metropolitan Opera House, New York, 1969, 1970, 1972; Bayreuth Fest., 1977. *Recreations:* anything at all. *Address:* Royal Opera House, Covent Garden, WC2.

DAVIS, Brig. Cyril Elliott, CBE 1941; *b* 15 March 1892; *y s* of late O. J. H. Davis, Ford Park, Plymouth, Devon; *m* 1st, 1918, Fay (*d* 1957), *y d* of Leathes Prior, Eaton, Norwich; two *s*; 2nd, 1958, Helen, *widow* of Rev. T. V. Garnier, OBE. *Educ:* Alton Sch.; Plymouth Coll. Regular Commission in ASC, 1912, from 3rd DCLI (SR); served European War, 1914-18, France, Belgium, Greek Macedonia, Serbia, Bulgaria, European Turkey, Egypt, Palestine (1914 Star and Clasp, BWM and Victory Medal); Palestine Campaign, 1937 (Palestine Gen. Service Medal); Lieut-Col 1939 and posted to Singapore. Temp. Col 1940; Col 1941; Dep. Dir of Supplies and Transport, Malaya Command (acting Brig.), 1941; transferred to S Western Pacific Command, Java, Jan. 1942; Ceylon, March 1942; retired April 1946. A General Comr of Income Tax, 1958-67. King George V Jubilee Medal, 1935; Comdr Order of Leopold II (Belgium), 1951. *Address:* The White House, Exford, Minehead, Somerset TA24 7PP. *T:* Exford 412.

DAVIS, David; *see* Davis, William Eric.

DAVIS, Prof. Derek Russell, MD, FRCP; Norah Cooke Hurle Professor of Mental Health, University of Bristol, since 1962; *b* 20 April 1914; *s* of late Edward David Darelan Davis, FRCS, and of Alice Mildred (*née* Russell); *m* 1939, Marit, *d* of Iver M. Iversen, Oslo, Norway; one *s* one *d. Educ:* Stowe Sch., Buckingham; Clare Coll., Cambridge (major entrance and foundn schol.); Middlesex Hosp. Med. Sch. MA, MD; FRCP. Ho. Phys., Mddx Hosp., 1938; Addenbrooke's Hosp., Cambridge, 1939; Asst Physician, Runwell Hosp., 1939; Mem. Scientific Staff, MRC, 1940; Lectr in Psychopathology, Univ. of Cambridge, 1948; Reader in Clinical Psychology, 1950; Dir, Med. Psychology Research Unit, 1958; Consultant Psychiatrist, United Cambridge Hosps, 1948; Editor, Quarterly Jl of Experimental Psychology, 1949-57. Visiting Prof., Univ. of Virginia, 1958. Fellow, Clare Coll., Cambridge, 1961. Dean of Medicine, Univ. of Bristol, 1970-72. Mem., Avon AHA (Teaching), 1974-; Pres., Fedn of Mental Health Workers, 1972. Adolf Meyer Lectr, Amer. Psychiatric Assoc., 1967. FRCPsych, FBPsS. *Publications:* An Introduction to Psychopathology (3rd edn), 1972; many articles in scientific and med. jls. *Recreations:* Ibsen studies, theatre. *Address:* 9 Clyde Road, Bristol BS6 6RJ. *T:* Bristol 34744.

DAVIS, (Ernest) Howard, CMG 1969; OBE 1960; Deputy Governor, Gibraltar, since 1971; *b* 22 April 1918; *m* 1948, Marie Davis (*née* Bellotti); two *s. Educ:* Christian Brothers Schs, Gibraltar and Blackpool; London Univ. (BA 1st cl. hons). Gen. Clerical Staff, Gibraltar, 1936-46; Asst Sec. and Clerk of Councils, 1946-54; seconded Colonial Office, 1954-55; Chief Asst Sec., Estabt Officer and Public Relations Officer, Gibraltar, 1955-62; Director of Labour and Social Security, 1962-65; Financial and Development Secretary, 1965-71; Acting Governor, various periods, 1971-77. *Recreations:* cricket, gardening. *Address:* 8 Mount Road, Gibraltar. *T:* A.70358.

DAVIS, Francis John, CMG 1970; OBE 1966; Chairman of Commission, Commonwealth Serum Laboratories, 1967-75; *b* 13 April 1900; *s* of Albert Henry Davis and Caroline Billing; *m* 1933, Thelma Doris Cox. *Educ:* State Schools, Victoria. Member of Parliament of Australia for Deakin, Vic, Dec. 1949-Nov. 1966 (Liberal). *Recreations:* travelling, walking, reading. *Address:* 5a/12 Marine Parade, St Kilda, Victoria 3182, Australia. *T:* 94-6164.

DAVIS, Godfrey Rupert Carless, FSA; Secretary, Royal Commission on Historical Manuscripts, since 1972; *b* 22 April 1917; *s* of late Prof. Henry William Carless Davis and Rosa Jennie Davis (*née* Lindup); *m* 1942, Dorothie Elizabeth Mary Loveband; one *s* two *d. Educ:* Highgate Sch.; Balliol Coll., Oxford (MA, DPhil). Rome Scholar in Ancient History, 1938. Army Service, 1939-46, Devon Regt and Intell. Corps, Captain 1942. Dept of MSS, British Museum: Asst Keeper, 1947; Dep. Keeper, 1961-72. FRHistS 1954 (Treas. 1967-74); FSA 1974. *Publications:* Medieval Cartularies of Great Britain, 1958; Magna Carta, 1963; contrib. British Museum Cat. Add. MSS 1926-1950 (6 vols); learned jls. *Address:* 214 Somerset Road, SW19 5JE. *T:* 01-946 7955.
See also R. H. C. Davis.

DAVIS, Harold Sydney, FRCP; Consultant Physician: Royal Free Hospital, London, since 1954; King Edward VII Hospital, Windsor, since 1945; Hampstead General Hospital since 1946; Florence Nightingale Hospital, London, since 1947; Hon. Physician to the Queen, T&AVR, 1967-68; *b* 6 Aug. 1908; *s* of Harold Adamson Davis and Edith May Davis, Jamaica, WI; *m* 1940, Molly, *d* of Herbert Percy Stimson, London; one *d. Educ:* Jamaica Coll., WI; Dulwich Coll., London; Gonville and Caius Coll., Cambridge; Charing Cross Hosp., London (Exhibr). BA 1930, MB, BChir 1935, MA 1936, Cantab.; LRCP, MRCS 1933; MRCP 1936; FRCP 1954. Held usual resident appts in various London hosps, 1933-39. Commissioned into RAMC, March 1939 (Lieut); seconded as Physician, Ashridge Hosp. (EMS), 1940. OC 308 (Co. London) Gen. Hosp. RAMC/AER, 1964 (Col). Examr in Medicine, London Univ.; Lectr in Medicine, Royal Free Hosp. Sch. of Medicine, London Univ., 1962; Mem. Bd of Govs, Royal Free Hosp., 1963. Pres., Eagle Ski Club, 1960-63. *Publications:* contrib. learned jls. *Recreation:* ski-mountaineering. *Address:* Fingest Hill Cottage, near Henley-on-Thames, Oxon. *T:* Turville Heath 275; 90a Harley Street, W1. *T:* 01-935 8033. *Clubs:* Bath, Ski Club of Gt Britain (Vice-Pres. 1964), Kandahar Ski.

DAVIS, Howard; *see* Davis, E. H.

DAVIS, Air Chief Marshal Sir John (Gilbert), GCB 1968 (KCB 1964; CB 1953); OBE 1945; psc 1946; idc 1955; RAF, retired; Lieutenant-Governor and Commander-in-Chief of Jersey, 1969-74; *b* 24 March 1911; *e s* of late John Davis, Whitby, Yorks; *m*

1937, Doreen, *d* of Arthur Heaton, Hinckley, Leics; one *s* one *d*. *Educ:* Whitby Grammar Sch.; Queens' Coll., Cambridge, MA 1937. First Commnd RAF, 1934; served Bomber Sqdns 142 and 57, 1934-36; Instructor No 10 Flying Training Sch., 1936-37; Navigation Staff duties, 1938-39; served war of 1939-45 on anti-submarine duties in Mediterranean, Iceland, Azores, UK. Instructor RAF Staff Coll., 1948-50; Gp Captain Plans HQ MEAF, 1951-53; Dir of Plans, Air Ministry, 1955-58; SASO, Bomber Command HQ, 1958-59; Air Officer Commanding No 1 Group, Bomber Command, 1959-61; Air Officer Commanding Malta, and Dep. Comdr-in-Chief (Air), Allied Forces Mediterranean, 1961-63; Air Mem. for Supply and Organisation, MoD, 1963-66; Air Officer Commanding-in-Chief: Flying Trng Comd, 1966-68; Trng Comd, 1968-69. Air ADC to the Queen, 1967-69. KStJ 1969. *Recreations:* ornithology, fishing, golf. *Address:* The Stone House, Ruswarp, near Whitby, North Yorks. *Clubs:* Royal Air Force; Union Society (Cambridge).

DAVIS, Sir John (Gilbert), 3rd Bt *cr* 1946; Vice-President, Abitibi Paper Co. Ltd, Toronto, since 1976; *b* 17 Aug. 1936; *s* of Sir Gilbert Davis, 2nd Bt, and of Kathleen, *d* of Sidney Deacon Ford; *S* father, 1973; *m* 1960, Elizabeth Margaret, *d* of Robert Smith Turnbull; one *s* two *d*. *Educ:* Oundle School; Britannia RNC, Dartmouth. RN, 1955-56. Joined Spicers Ltd, 1956; emigrated to Montreal, Canada, 1957; joined Inter City Papers and progressed through the company until becoming Pres., 1967; transf. to parent co. in 1976. Director: Milmont Fibreboard; Val Mar Swimming Pools; Hilroy; Canada Envelope; Inter City Papers; Canadian Arthritis Soc. *Recreations:* sports, golf, tennis, squash; music, reading. *Heir: s* Richard Charles Davis, *b* 11 April 1970. *Address:* 70 York Mills Road, Toronto, Ont M2P 1B7, Canada. *T:* 222-4916. *Clubs:* Donalda (Toronto); Badminton and Squash (Montreal); Kanawaki Golf; Seigniory (Montebello).

DAVIS, Sir John (Henry Harris), Kt 1971; President, since 1977, The Rank Organisation Ltd, Subsidiary and Associated Cos (Chief Executive, 1962-74; Chairman, 1962-77); Joint President, Rank Xerox, since 1972 (formerly Joint Chairman); Chairman: The Children's Film Foundation Ltd; National Centre of Films for Children; Director, Eagle Star Insurance Co. Ltd; *b* 10 Nov. 1906; *s* of Sydney Myering Davis and Emily Harris; *m* 1926, Joan Buckingham; one *s*; *m* 1947, Marion Gavid; two *d*; *m* 1954, Dinah Sheridan (marr. diss. 1965); *m* 1976, Mrs Felicity Rutland. *Educ:* City of London Sch. British Thomson-Houston Group, 1931-38. Joined Odeon Theatres (predecessor of The Rank Organisation); Chief Accountant, Jan. 1938; Sec., June 1938; Jt Managing Dir, 1942; Man. Dir, 1948-62 and Dep. Chm., 1951-62, The Rank Organisation Ltd. Chm., Southern Television Ltd, 1968-76. Trustee, Westminster Abbey Trust (Chm., fund raising cttee, Westminster Abbey Appeal, 1973). Pres., The Advertising Assoc., 1973-76. FCIS 1939. Commandeur de l'Ordre de la Couronne (Belgium), 1974; KStJ. Hon. DTech Loughborough, 1975. *Recreations:* farming, gardening, reading, travel, music. *Address:* Crowhurst Place, Lingfield, Surrey RH7 6LY. *Club:* Royal Automobile.

DAVIS, Leslie Harold Newsom, CMG 1957; *b* 6 April 1909; *s* of Harold Newsom Davis and Aileen Newsom Davis (*née* Gush); *m* 1950, Judith Anne, *d* of L. G. Corney, CMG; one *s* two *d*. *Educ:* Marlborough; Trinity Coll., Cambridge. Apptd to Malayan Civil Service, 1932; Private Sec. to Governor and High Comr, 1938-40; attached to 22nd Ind. Inf. Bde as Liaison Officer, Dec. 1941; interned by Japanese in Singapore, 1942-45; District Officer, Seremban, 1946-47; British Resident, Brunei, 1948; Asst Adviser, Muar, 1948-50; Sec. to Mem. for Education, Fed. of Malaya, 1951-52. Mem. for Industrial and Social Relations, 1952-53; Sec. for Defence and Internal Security, Singapore, 1953-55; Permanent Sec., Min. of Communications and Works, Singapore, 1955-57; Special Rep., Rubber Growers' Assoc. in Malaya, 1958-63. *Recreation:* golf. *Address:* Berrywood, Heyshott, near Midhurst, West Sussex. *Club:* United Oxford & Cambridge University.

DAVIS, Leslie John, MD Ed.; FRCP London, Edinburgh and Glasgow; Professor Emeritus, University of Glasgow, 1961; Hon. Consulting Physician, Glasgow Royal Infirmary; *b* 1899; *s* of late John Davis; *m* 1938, Marjorie Adelaide, *yr d* of late Arthur Cleveland. *Educ:* University Coll. Sch.; Edinburgh Univ. Served at sea, 1918; MB, ChB, Edinburgh 1924; House Surgeon, Royal Infirmary, Edinburgh, 1925; Research Student, London Sch. of Tropical Medicine, 1926; Asst Bacteriologist, Wellcome Tropical Research Laboratories, 1927-30; Prof. of Pathology, Hong-Kong Univ., 1931-39; Dir, Medical Laboratory, Bulawayo, 1939-40; Asst and later Lecturer, Dept of Medicine, Edinburgh Univ.; Temp. Asst Physician, Royal Infirmary, Edinburgh, and later Physician, Municipal Hospitals,

Edinburgh, 1940-45; Muirhead Prof. of Medicine, University of Glasgow, 1945-61; Consulting Physician to the Royal Navy, 1954-61. *Publications:* The Megaloblastic Anaemias (with A. Brown), 1953; numerous contribs to medical and scientific journals mainly on pathological and haematological subjects. *Recreations:* fishing, model engineering. *Address:* Norton Brook, Yarmouth, Isle of Wight. *T:* Yarmouth 474. *Club:* Royal Solent Yacht.

DAVIS, Madeline; Regional Nursing Officer, Oxford Regional Health Authority, since 1973; *b* 12 March 1925; *d* of late James William Henry Davis, JP, and Mrs Edith Maude Davis; *m* 1977, Comdr William Milburn Gibson, RN. *Educ:* Haberdashers' Aske's Hatcham Girls' Sch.; Guy's Hosp. (SRN); British Hosp. for Mothers and Babies, Woolwich; Bristol Maternity Hosp. (SCM). Ward Sister, then Dep. Night Supt, Guy's Hosp., 1949-53; Asst Matron, Guy's Hosp., 1953-57; Admin. Sister then Dep. Matron, St Charles' Hosp., London, 1957-61; Asst Nursing Officer, 1962-68, Chief Regional Nursing Officer, 1968-73, Oxford Regional Hosp. Bd. Mem., Central Midwives Board. *Publication:* (with Mrs R. Sanders) article (Scheduling of Student Nurses with the Aid of a Computer) in The Hospital. *Recreations:* village community work, theatre, golf. *Address:* Cherry Holt, Middle Street, Islip, Oxon. *T:* Kidlington 4741. *Club:* North Oxford Golf.

DAVIS, Sir Maurice, Kt 1975; OBE 1953; **Hon. Chief Justice Davis;** Chief Justice of the West Indies Associated States Supreme Court, and of Supreme Court of Grenada, since 1975; *b* St Kitts, 30 April 1912; *m* Kathleen; one *s* five *d*. QC 1965. Pres., St Kitts Bar Assoc., 1968-75. Mem. Legislature, St Kitts, 1944-57; Mem., Exec. Council, St Kitts; Dep. Pres., Gen. Legislative Council, and Mem., Fed. Exec. Council, Leeward Is. *Recreations:* cricket, football. *Address:* Supreme Court, Grenada, West Indies.

DAVIS, Dr Michael; Director of Nuclear Energy and Electricity, Commission of European Communities, Brussels, since 1973; *b* 9 June 1923; *s* of William James Davis and Rosaline Sarah (*née* May); *m* 1951, Helena Hobbs Campbell, *e d* of Roland and Catherine Campbell, Toronto. *Educ:* UC Exeter (BSc); Bristol Univ. (PhD). FIMM, FInstP. Radar Officer, Flagship, 4th Cruiser Sqdn, British Pacific Fleet, Lieut (Sp. Br.) RNVR, 1943-46 (despatches). Res. Fellow, Canadian Atomic Energy Project, Toronto Univ., 1949-51; Sen. Sci. Officer, Services Electronics Res. Lab., 1951-55; subseq. UKAEA: Commercial Dir and Techn. Adviser, 1956-73. Chm., OECD Cttee on World Uranium Resources, 1969-73; Dir, NATO Advanced Study Inst., 1971; advised NZ Govt on Atomic Energy, 1967. *Publications:* (ed jtly) Uranium Prospecting Handbook, 1972; papers in various sci. jls. *Recreation:* sculpture. *Address:* 200 Rue de la Loi, 1049 Brussels, Belgium. *T:* 735-00-40. *Club:* United Oxford & Cambridge University.

DAVIS, Michael McFarland; Director for Wales, Property Services Agency, Department of the Environment, since 1972; *b* 1 Feb. 1919; 2nd *s* of Harold McFarland and Gladys Mary Davis; *m* 1942, Aline Seton Butler; three *d*. *Educ:* Haberdashers' Aske's, Hampstead. Entered Air Ministry, 1936. Served War, RAF, 1940-45 (PoW, 1942-45). Private Sec. to Chiefs and Vice-Chiefs of Air Staff, 1945-49, and to Under-Secretary of State for Air, 1952-54; Harvard Univ. Internat. Seminar, 1956; Student, IDC, 1965; Command Sec., FEAF, 1966-69; on loan to Cabinet Office (Central Unit on Environmental Pollution), 1970; transf. to Dept of Environment, 1971. Delegate to UN Conf. on Human Environment, Stockholm, 1972. *Recreations:* doing up old things, travel, music, wine. *Address:* 35 Church Road, Whitchurch, Cardiff. *T:* Cardiff 614444.

DAVIS, Morris Cael, CMG 1970; MD, FRACP; Consultant Physician, 110 Collins Street, Melbourne; *b* 7 June 1907; *s* of David and Sarah Davis; *m* 1933, Sophia Ashkenasy (*d* 1966); two *s*. *Educ:* Melbourne High Sch.; Univ. of Melbourne. MB, BS (1st cl. hons) Melbourne, 1930; MD 1932; MRCP 1938; FRACP 1946. Univ. of Melbourne: Prosector in Anatomy, 1927; Beaney Schol. in Pathology, 1932-33; Lectr in Pathology, 1933; Lectr in Medicine, Dental Faculty, 1940-63; Bertram Armytage Prize for Med. Res., 1934 and 1942; Fulbright Smith Mundt Schol., 1953-54. Alfred Hosp., Melbourne: Acting Pathologist, 1933-35; Physican to Out-Patients, 1938-46; Phys. to In-Patients, 1946-67; Cons. Phys., 1967-; Foundn Chm., Cardiovascular Diagnostic Service, 1959-67; Dir and Founder, Dept of Visual Aids, 1954-67; Chm. Drug Cttee, 1960-67. Med. Referee, Commonwealth Dept of Health. Travelled Nuffield Sponsorship, 1954; Litchfield Lectr, Oxford Univ., 1954; Hon. Consultant, Dental Hosp., Melbourne, 1946-. Mem., Curricular Planning Cttee, RMIT; Hon. Pres., Medico-Clerical Soc. of Victoria. Pres., Victorian Friends of Hebrew Univ., Jerusalem,

1953-64; Federal Pres., Australian Friends Hebrew Univ., 1964; Alternate Governor, Hebrew Univ., 1961-63. Founder, Australian Medical Assoc. Arts Group, Pres. 1959-; Pres., Bezalel Fellowship of Arts. Vice-Pres., Aust. Kidney Foundn Appeal, 1971; Mem., Epworth Hosp. Appeal Cttee, 1975-76. *Publications:* papers on medicine, medical philosophy and medical educn in Australian Med. Jl, Australian Dental Jl, student jls. *Recreations:* ceramics, painting, music, book collecting, garden. *Address:* 177 Finch Street, Glen Iris, Vic. 3146, Australia. *T:* Melbourne 509.2423. *Clubs:* University House, Australian American Association, Australian American Club, National Gallery Society (Melbourne).

DAVIS, Nathanael Vining; Chairman of the Board and Chief Executive Officer, since 1972, Director since 1947, Alcan Aluminium Limited (President, 1947-72); *b* 26 June 1915; *s* of Rhea Reineman Davis and Edward Kirk Davis; *m* 1941, Lois Howard Thompson; one *s* one *d. Educ:* Harvard Coll.; London Sch. of Economics. With Alcan group since 1939 with exception of 3 years on active duty with US Navy. *Address:* Box 6090, Montreal, Quebec, Canada H3C 3H2. *T:* 877-2340. *Clubs:* Mount Royal, St James's (Montreal); University, The Links (New York); Somerset (Boston); The Country Club (Brookline, Mass).

DAVIS, Prof. Norman, MBE 1945; FBA 1969; Merton Professor of English Language and Literature, University of Oxford, since 1959; *b* Dunedin, NZ, 16 May 1913; *s* of James John and Jean Davis; *m* 1944, Magdalene Jamieson Bone; no *c. Educ:* Otago Boys' High Sch., Dunedin; Otago Univ.; Merton Coll., Oxford. MA NZ 1934; BA Oxon 1936, MA 1944; NZ Rhodes Scholar, 1934. Lecturer in English, Kaunas, Lithuania, 1937; Sofia, Bulgaria, 1938. Government service mainly abroad, 1939-46. Lecturer in English Language, Queen Mary Coll., University of London, 1946; Oriel and Brasenose Colls., Oxford, 1947; Oxford Univ. Lectr in Medieval English, 1948; Prof. of English Language, University of Glasgow, 1949. Hon. Dir of Early English Text Soc., 1957-. Jt Editor, Review of English Studies, 1954-63. R. W. Chambers Meml Lecturer, UCL, 1971. *Publications:* Sweet's Anglo-Saxon Primer, 9th edn 1953; The Language of the Pastons (Sir Israel Gollancz Memorial Lecture, British Academy, 1954), 1955; Paston Letters (a selection), 1958; Beowulf facsimile ed. Zupitza, 2nd edn 1959; English and Medieval Studies (ed with C. L. Wrenn), 1962; The Paston Letters (a selection in modern spelling), 1963; Glossary to Early Middle English Verse and Prose (ed J. A. W. Bennett and G. V. Smithers), 1966; rev. edn, Tolkien-Gordon: Sir Gawain, 1967; Non-Cycle Plays and Fragments (EETS), 1970; Paston Letters and Papers of the Fifteenth Century, Part I, 1971, Part II, 1977; reviews and articles in jls. *Address:* Merton College, Oxford.

DAVIS, Prof. Ralph, FBA 1973; Professor of Economic History, University of Leicester, since 1964, Pro-Vice-Chancellor, since 1976; *b* 30 April 1915; *s* of Ernest Alfred and Emily Davis; *m* 1949, Dorothy Easthope; two *s* one *d. Educ:* London School of Economics (1946-50). Lectr and Reader in Economic History, Univ. of Hull, 1950-64. Trustee, Nat. Maritime Museum, 1968-75. *Publications:* Rise of the English Shipping Industry, 1962; Twenty-one-and-a-half Bishop Lane, 1962; Aleppo and Devonshire Square, 1967; Rise of the Atlantic Economies, 1973; many articles in jls, etc. *Address:* Department of Economic History, University of Leicester, Leicester LE1 7RH.

DAVIS, Prof. Ralph Henry Carless, FBA 1975; Professor of Medieval History, University of Birmingham, since 1970; Editor of History since 1968; *b* 7 Oct. 1918; *s* of late Prof. Henry William Carless Davis and Rosa Jennie Davis; *m* 1949, Eleanor Maud Megaw; two *s. Educ:* Leighton Park Sch.; Balliol Coll., Oxford. Friends' Ambulance Unit, 1939-45. Asst Master, Christ's Hosp., Horsham, 1947-48; Lectr, University Coll., London, 1948-56; Fellow and Tutor, Merton Coll., Oxford, 1956-70; Mem. Hebdomodal Council, Oxford Univ., 1967-69. *Publications:* The Mosques of Cairo, 1944; (ed) The Kalendar of Abbot Samson of Bury St Edmunds, 1954; A History of Medieval Europe, 1957; King Stephen, 1967; (ed with H. A. Cronne) Regesta Regum Anglo-Normannorum, vol. iii, 1968, vol. iv, 1969; The Normans and their Myth, 1976; articles in historical and archæological jls. *Recreations:* travel, archæology, architecture. *Address:* 56 Fitzroy Avenue, Harborne, Birmingham B17 8RJ. *T:* 021-427 1711.
See also G. R. C. Davis.

DAVIS, Sir Rupert C. H.; see Hart-Davis.

DAVIS, S(tanley) Clinton; MP (Lab) Hackney Central since 1970; Parliamentary Under-Secretary of State, Department of Trade, since 1974; *b* 6 Dec. 1928; *s* of Sidney Davis; *m* 1954, Frances Jane Clinton Davis (*née* Lucas); one *s* three *d. Educ:* Hackney Downs Sch.; Mercers' Sch.; King's Coll., London University. LLB 1950; admitted Solicitor 1953. Mem. Exec. Council, Nat. Assoc. of Labour Student Organisations, 1949-50. Councillor, London Borough of Hackney, 1959; Mayor of Hackney, 1968. Contested (Lab): Langstone Div. of Portsmouth, 1955; Yarmouth, 1959 and 1964. *Recreations:* golf, Association football, reading biographical histories. *Address:* Essex Lodge, 354 Finchley Road, Hampstead, NW3. *T:* 01-435 4976.

DAVIS, Terence Anthony Gordon, (Terry Davis); motor industry manager; *b* 5 Jan. 1938; *s* of Gordon Davis and Gladys (*née* Avery), Stourbridge, West Midlands; *m* 1963, Anne, *d* of F. B. Cooper, Newton-le-Willows, Lancs; one *s* one *d. Educ:* King Edward VI Grammar Sch., Stourbridge, Worcestershire; University Coll. London (LLB); Univ. of Michigan, USA (MBA). Company Executive, 1962-71. Joined Labour Party, 1965; contested (Lab) Bromsgrove, Gen. Election, 1970, By-election 1971, Gen. Elections Feb. and Oct. 1974; MP (Lab) Bromsgrove, May 1971-Feb. 1974; contested (Lab) Birmingham, Stechford, March 1977. Member, Assoc. of Scientific, Technical and Managerial Staffs. Member, Yeovil Rural District Council, 1967-68. *Address:* 48 Western Road, West Hagley, Stourbridge, West Midlands.

DAVIS, William; Editor of High Life, inflight magazine of British Airways; *b* 6 March 1933; *m* 1967, Sylvette Jouclas. *Educ:* City of London Coll. On staff of Financial Times, 1954-59; Editor, Investor's Guide, 1959-60; City Editor, Evening Standard, 1960-65 (with one year's break as City Editor, Sunday Express); Financial Editor, The Guardian, 1965-68; Editor, Punch, 1968-77. Dir, City Arts Trust. Broadcaster and lecturer. *Publications:* Three Years Hard Labour: the road to devaluation, 1968; Merger Mania, 1970; Money Talks, 1972; Have Expenses, Will Travel, 1975; It's No Sin to be Rich, 1976. *Recreations:* drinking wine, travelling, thinking about retirement. *Address:* c/o 23 Tudor Street, EC4Y 0HR. *T:* 01-583 9199. *Clubs:* Garrick, Hurlingham.

DAVIS, William Eric, (Professionally known as **David Davis**), MBE 1969; MA Oxon; LRAM, ARCM; *b* 27 June 1908; *s* of William John and Florence Kate Rachel Davis; *m* 1935, Barbara de Riemer; one *s* two *d. Educ:* Bishop's Stortford Coll.; The Queen's Coll., Oxford (MA). Schoolmaster, 1931-35; joined BBC as mem. of Children's Hour, 1935. Served with RNVR Acting Temp. Lieut, 1942-46. BBC, 1946-70; Head of Children's Hour, BBC, 1953-61; Head of Children's Programmes (Sound), BBC, 1961-64; Producer, Drama Dept, 1964-70, retired; *Publications:* various songs, etc. including: Lullaby, 1943; Fabulous Beasts, 1948; Little Grey Rabbit Song Book, 1952; *poetry:* A Single Star, 1973; various speech recordings, including The Tales of Beatrix Potter. *Recreations:* children, cats, growing roses. *Address:* 18 Mount Avenue, W5 2RG. *T:* 01-997 8156. *Club:* Garrick.

DAVIS, Hon. William Grenville, QC (Can.); Premier of Ontario, Canada, and President of the Council, Ontario, since 1971; Leader, Progressive Conservative Party; lawyer (former partner in law firm, Brampton); *b* Brampton, Ont., 30 July 1929; *s* of Albert Grenville and Vera M. Hewetson; *m* 1953, Helen MacPhee (*d* 1962), *d* of Neil MacPhee, Windsor, Ontario; *m* 1963, Kathleen Louise, *d* of Dr R. P. Mackay, California; two *s* three *d. Educ:* Brampton High Sch.; University Coll., Univ. of Toronto (BA); Osgoode Hall Law Sch. (grad. 1955). Called to Bar of Ontario, 1955. Elected Mem. (C) Provincial Parlt (MPP) for Peel Riding, 1959, 1963, Peel North Riding, 1967, 1971, Brampton Riding, 1975. Mem., Select Cttee to examine and study admin. and exec. problems of Govt of Ontario, 1960-63; 2nd Vice-Chm., Hydro-Electric Power Commn of Ontario, Dec. 1961-Nov. 1962; Minister of Educn, Oct. 1962-March 1971; also Minister of Univ. Affairs, 1964-71. Holds hon. doctorates in Law from six Ontario Univs: Wilfrid Laurier, W Ontario, Toronto, McMaster, Queen's, Windsor; Cert. of Merit, Edinboro Univ., Pa, USA. Amer. Transit Assoc. Man of the Year, 1973. *Publications:* Education in Ontario, 1965; The Government of Ontario and the Universities of the Province (Frank Gerstein Lectures, York Univ.), 1966; Building an Educated Society 1816-1966, 1966; Education for New Times, 1967. *Address:* Office of the Premier of Ontario, Parliament Buildings, Toronto, Ont., Canada; 61 Main Street South, Brampton, Ontario. *Clubs:* Kiwanis, Albany (both in Ont.); Freemasons.

DAVIS, William Herbert, TD; BSc; CEng, FIMechE, FIProdE; Director, Military Contracts and Government Affairs, Leyland Cars, since 1976; *b* 27 July 1919; *s* of William and Dora Davis; *m* 1945, Barbara Mary Joan (*née* Sommerfield); one *d. Educ:* Waverley Grammar Sch.; Univ. of Aston in Birmingham (BSc).

Austin Motor Co.: Engr Apprentice, 1935-39; Mech. Engr and Section Leader, Works Engrs, 1946-51; Supt Engr, 1951; Asst Production Manager, 1954; Production Manager, 1956; Dir and Gen. Works Manager, 1958. British Motor Corp. Ltd: Dir of Production, 1960; Dep. Managing Dir (Manufacture and Supply), 1961; Dep. Managing Dir, British Leyland (Austin-Morris Ltd), 1968; Chairman and Chief Executive, Triumph Motor Co. Ltd, 1970; Managing Dir, Rover Triumph BLUK Ltd, 1972; Dir (Manufacture) British Leyland Motor Corporation, 1973. MIPlantE, FBIM, FIWM, SME(USA). *Recreations:* riding, motoring, photography; interests in amateur boxing. *Address:* Arosa, The Holloway, Alvechurch, Worcs. *T:* Redditch 66187.

DAVIS, Most Rev. William Wallace; *b* 10 Dec. 1908; *s* of Isaac Davis and Margaret Dixon; *m* 1933, Kathleen Aubrey Acheson (*d* 1966); two *s* two *d* ; *m* 1968, Helen Mary Lynton. *Educ:* Bishop's Univ., Lennoxville, PQ. BA 1931, BD 1934; Deacon, 1932; Priest, 1932; Curate, St Matthew's, Ottawa, 1932-36; Rector, Coaticook, PQ, 1936-38; Rector, St Matthew's, Quebec, 1938-52; Archdeacon of Quebec, 1947-52; Dean of Nova Scotia, and Rector of the Cathedral Church of All Saints, Halifax, NS, 1952-58; Bishop Coadjutor of Nova Scotia, 1958-63; Bishop of Nova Scotia, 1963; Archbishop of Nova Scotia and Metropolitan of Ecclesiastical Province of the Atlantic, Canada, 1972-75. DD University of King's Coll., Halifax, 1954; Hon. DCL Bishop's Univ., Lennoxville, PQ, 1960; Hon. LLD St Francis Xavier Univ., Nova Scotia. *Address:* Apt 712, 1465 Baseline Road, Ottawa, Ont K2C 3L8, Canada.

DAVIS, Adm. Sir William (Wellclose), GCB 1959 (KCB 1956; CB 1952); DSO 1944, and Bar, 1944; DL; *b* 11 Oct. 1901; *s* of late W. S. Davis, Indian Political Service; *m* 1934, Lady Gertrude Elizabeth Phipps, 2nd *d* of 3rd Marquis of Normanby; two *s* two *d. Educ:* Summerfields, Oxford; Osborne and Dartmouth Naval Colls. Midshipman, 1917; Lieut, 1921; Comdr, 1935; Capt., 1940; Rear-Adm., 1950; Acting Vice-Adm. and Vice-Adm., 1953; Adm. 1956, Dep. Dir of Plans and Cabinet Offices, 1940-42; commanded HMS Mauritius, 1943-44; Dir of Under Water Weapons, Admiralty, 1945-46; Imperial Defence Coll., 1947; Chief of Staff to C-in-C Home Fleet, 1948-49. The Naval Sec., Admiralty, 1950-52; Flag Officer 2nd in Command Mediterranean, 1952-54; Vice-Chief of the Naval Staff, Admiralty, 1954-57; Comdr-in-Chief, Home Fleet, and NATO Comdr-in-Chief, Eastern Atlantic Area, 1958-60; First and Principal Naval ADC to the Queen, 1959-60, retired. Vice-Pres., King George's Fund for Sailors; Member: Royal Institution of GB (Vice-Pres.); Royal United Service Institution; European-Atlantic Group (Vice-Pres.); British Atlantic Cttee; Pres., Gloucestershire Outward Bound; Treasurer, Friends of Gloucester Cathedral; Mem., St Helena Assoc. DL Glos 1963. *Recreations:* fishing, shooting. *Address:* Coglan House, Longhope, Glos. *T:* Longhope 830282. *Clubs:* Naval and Military; Ends of the Earth.

DAVIS-GOFF; *see* Goff, Sir E. W. D.

DAVIS-RICE, Peter; Regional Nursing Officer, North Western Regional Health Authority, since 1973; *b* 1 Feb. 1930; *s* of Alfred Davis-Rice and Doris Eva (*née* Bates); *m* 1967, Judith Anne Chatterton; one *s* two *d. Educ:* Riley High Sch., Hull; Royal Coll. of Nursing, Edinburgh; Harefield Hosp., Mddx; City Hosp., York. SRN; British Tuberculosis Assoc. Cert.; AMBIM; NAdmin(Hosp)Cert. Staff Nurse, Charge Nurse, St Luke's Hosp., Huddersfield, 1954-57; Theatre Supt, Hull Royal Infirmary, 1957-62; Asst Matron (Theatres), Walton Hosp., Liverpool, 1962-66; Matron, Billinge Hosp., Wigan, 1966-69; Chief Nursing Officer, Oldham and District HMC, 1969-73. *Publications:* contrib. Nursing Times. *Recreations:* badminton, tennis, do-it-yourself. *Address:* Riencourt, 185 Frederick Street, Oldham OL8 4DH. *T:* 061-624 2485.

DAVISON, family name of **Baron Broughshane.**

DAVISON, Arthur Clifford Percival, CBE 1974; FRAM 1966; Musical Director and Conductor: Little Symphony of London, since 1964; Virtuosi of England, since 1970; *b* Montreal, Canada; *s* of Arthur Mackay Davison and Hazel Edith Smith; *m* 1950, Barbara June, *d* of Sir William Hildred, *qv* ; one *s* two *d. Educ:* Conservatory of Music, McGill Univ.; Conservatoire de Musique, Montreal; Royal Associated Board Scholar at Royal Acad. of Music, London; later studies in Europe. Dir and Dep. Leader, London Philharmonic Orch., 1962-64; Guest Conductor, Royal Danish Ballet, 1964; Asst Conductor, Bournemouth Symphony Orch., 1965-66. Guest Conductor of Orchestras: London Philharmonic; London Symphony; New Philharmonia; Royal Philharmonic; BBC Orchs; Birmingham Symphony; Bournemouth Symphony; Ulster; Royal Liverpool

Philharmonic; New York City Ballet; CBC Radio and Television Orchs; Royal Danish. Founder of Arthur Davison Concerts for Children, 1966; Dir and Conductor, Nat. Youth Orch. of Wales, 1966-; Conductor and Lectr, London Univ., Goldsmiths' Coll., 1971-; Governor and Guest Lectr, Welsh Coll. of Music and Drama, 1973-. Tour of Europe recorded for BBC TV. Hon. Master of Music, Univ. of Wales, 1974. EMI/CFP award for sale of half a million classical records, 1973. *Publications:* various articles in musical jls. *Recreations:* reading, theatre-going, fishing, boating on Thames, antiques. *Address:* 23 The Bridle Road, Purley, Surrey CR2 3JB. *T:* 01-660 2932. *Clubs:* Savage, Royal Over-Seas League.

DAVISON, Ian Frederic Hay, FCA; Managing Partner, Arthur Andersen & Co., Chartered Accountants, London, since 1966; *b* 30 June 1931; *s* of Eric Hay Davison, FCA, and Inez Davison; *m* 1955, Maureen Patricia Blacker; one *s* two *d. Educ:* Dulwich Coll.; LSE (BScEcon); Univ. of Mich. ACA 1956, FCA 1966. Institute of Chartered Accountants: Mem. Cttee, London and Dist Soc., 1965-72; Mem., Technical Adv. Cttee, 1971-75; Mem. Council, 1975-; Mem., Auditing Practices Cttee, 1973-; Mem., Inflation Accounting Steering Gp, 1975-. Indep. Mem., NEDC for Bldg Industry, 1971-; Mem., Price Commn, 1977-. Dept of Trade Inspector, London Capital Securities, 1975-77. London Borough of Greenwich: Councillor and Alderman, 1961-73; Chm., Housing Cttee, 1968-70; Chm., London Boroughs Jt Computer Cttee, 1968-71. Governor, Greenwich Theatre, 1968- (Chm., 1968-74). *Recreations:* theatre, music, squash, ski-ing. *Address:* 53 Lee Road, Blackheath, SE3 9RT. *T:* 01-852 8506. *Clubs:* Carlton, Arts, MCC.

DAVISON, John A. B.; *see* Biggs-Davison.

DAVISON, Ralph, OBE 1970; QPM 1962; DL; Chief Constable of Cleveland Constabulary (formerly Teesside Constabulary), 1968-76, retired; *b* 25 March 1914; *s* of Ralph Dixon Davison and Elizabeth (*née* Bulmer), Saltburn, Yorks; *m* 1939, Joyce, *d* of George Smith and Winifred (*née* Elstob), Spennymoor, Co. Durham; one *s* one *d. Educ:* Sir William Turner's Sch., Redcar. School Teacher, 1932; Liverpool City Police, 1934-56; Chief Constable, Middlesbrough, 1956-68. County Director, St John Ambulance Assoc., Cleveland, 1974. Coronation Medal, 1953; Police Long Service and Good Conduct Medal, 1956. DL Cleveland 1975. CStJ 1974 (SBStJ 1965). *Recreations:* photography, music, gardening, philately. *Address:* Esk Mill, Castleton, near Whitby, N Yorks. *T:* Castleton 626.

DAVISON, William Norris; His Honour Judge Davison; a Circuit Judge (formerly a County Court Judge), since 1971; *b* 20 Aug. 1919; *s* of late Dr W. H. Davison; *m* 1947, Margaret, *d* of late G. H. Bettinson; one *s* two *d. Educ:* King Edward's High School, Birmingham; Trinity College, Dublin. RNVR, 1939-43; Royal Indian Naval Volunteer Reserve, 1943-46. Called to the Bar (Middle Temple), 1949; practised Midland Circuit, 1949-71. *Recreation:* collecting. *Address:* Kilsby, Llanwrtyd Wells, Powys LD5 4TL. *T:* Llanwrtyd Wells 281.

DAVITT, Cahir; President of the High Court, Eire, 1951-66, retired (Hon. Mr Justice Davitt); *b* 15 Aug. 1894; *s* of Michael Davitt and Mary Yore; *m* 1925, Sarah Gertrude Lynch; four *s* one *d. Educ:* O'Connell Sch. and University Coll., Dublin, BA, NUI, 1914; LLB, 1916; Barrister, King's Inns, Dublin, 1916, Bencher, 1927. Judge of the Dail Courts, 1920-22; Judge-Advocate Gen., Irish Free State Defence Forces, 1922-26; Temp. Judge, Circuit Court, 1926-27; Circuit Judge, City and County of Dublin, 1927-45; (Puisne) Judge of the High Court, 1945-51. Mem. of Judiciary Cttee, 1923-24, to advise Irish Free State Executive in relation to the establishment of Courts of Justice under the IFS Constitution; Chairman: Civil Service Compensation Board, 1929-66; Commission of Inquiry into Derating, 1930; Med. Bureau of Road Safety, 1969-74. President: Irish Rugby Football Union, 1936-37; Irish Squash Rackets Assoc., 1936. *Recreation:* golf. *Address:* 88 Lower Churchtown Road, Dublin 14. *T:* 981831. *Clubs:* Milltown Golf, Fitzwilliam Lawn Tennis (Dublin).

DAVSON, Sir Geoffrey Leo Simon, 2nd Bt; *see* Glyn, Sir Anthony, 2nd Bt.

DAVY, Brig. George Mark Oswald, CB 1945; CBE 1943; DSO 1941; US Legion of Merit; Gold Cross of Merit with Swords, Poland; Sculptor; Painter of horses in oils and of landscapes and seascapes in watercolours; Vice-President, Chelsea Art Society; Associate Member, National Society of Painters, Sculptors and Printmakers; *b* 22 Sept. 1898; *s* of late Capt. G. C. H. Davy; *m* 1932, Isabel Gwendolen (*d* 1970), *d* of late E. Alan Hay, Bengeo House, Hertford; one *s.* European War, 1914-18, France and Belgium: RFA and RHA; transferred to 3rd Hussars, 1931; Staff

Coll., Camberley, 1932-33; Bde Major, 150 Inf. Bde, 1935-36; Company Comdr RMC, Sandhurst, 1937-38; Naval Staff Coll., Greenwich, 1939; France and Belgium, 1939-40; Western Desert, 1940-41; Greece, April 1941; commanded 3rd and 7th Armoured Bdes in Desert, 1941; Director of Military Operations GHQ, Middle East, 1942-44; Dep. Asst Chief of Staff (Operations), AFHQ Algiers, 1944; commanded Land Forces Adriatic, 1944-45; War Office representative with the Polish Forces, 1945-47; retd 1948; recommissioned for military service, 1956; retd again 1959. *Publication:* The Seventh and Three Enemies, 1953. *Recreation:* fishing. *Address:* Jordanstone, by Alyth, Perthshire. *Club:* Cavalry and Guards.

DAVY, Humphrey Augustine A.; *see* Arthington-Davy.

DAWBARN, Simon Yelverton, CMG 1976; HM Diplomatic Service; Consul-General, Montreal, since 1975; *b* 16 Sept. 1923; *s* of Frederic Dawbarn and Maud Louise Mansell; *m* 1948, Shelby Montgomery Parker; one *s* two *d*. *Educ:* Oundle Sch.; Corpus Christi Coll., Cambridge. Served in HM Forces (Reconnaissance Corps), 1942-45. Reckitt & Colman (Overseas), 1948-49. Joined Foreign Service, 1949. Foreign Office, 1949-53; Brussels, 1953; Prague, 1955; Tehran, 1957; seconded to HM Treasury, 1959; Foreign Office, 1961; Algiers, 1965; Athens, 1968; FCO, 1971-75. Head of W African Dept and concurrently non-resident Ambassador to Chad, 1973-75. *Address:* c/o Foreign and Commonwealth Office, SW1. *Club:* Travellers'.

DAWE, Donovan Arthur; Principal Keeper, Guildhall Library, London, 1967-73, retired; *b* 21 Jan. 1915; *s* of late Alfred Ernest and Sarah Jane Dawe, Wallington, Surrey; *m* 1946, Peggy Marjory Challen; two *d*. *Educ:* Sutton Grammar Sch. Associate, Library Assoc., 1938. Entered Guildhall Library as junior assistant, 1931. Served with Royal West African Frontier Force in Africa and India, 1941-46. Freeman of City of London and Merchant Taylors' Company, 1953. FRHistS 1954. *Publications:* Skilbecks; drysalters 1650-1950, 1950; 11 Ironmonger Lane: the story of a site in the City of London, 1952; The City of London: a select book list, 1972; contribs professional literature, Connoisseur, Musical Times, Genealogists' Magazine, etc. *Recreations:* the countryside, local history, musicology. *Address:* 46 Green Lane, Purley, Surrey CR2 3PJ. *T:* 01-660 4218.

DAWES, Charles Ambrose William, MC 1942; Member of Lloyd's since 1950; Fruit Farmer since 1961; Vice Chairman, East Kent Packers, since 1974 (Director since 1972); *b* 30 March 1919; *s* of Edwyn Sandys Dawes and Joan Prideaux (*née* Selby); *m* 1940, Mary Neame Finn; one *s* three *d*. *Educ:* Stowe. Joined W. A. Browne & Co., Chartered Accountants, 1938. 2nd Lieut (TA), 97th (Kent Yeomanry) Field Regt, RA, 1939; served in France and Middle East, 1939-42; RA Training Regt, Cromer, 1943-46; Captain, 1942. Joined J. B. Westray & Co. Ltd, 1946: Director, 1949; joined New Zealand Shipping Co. Ltd, 1953: Director, 1955; Dep. Chairman, 1961; Chairman, 1966-70. Dir, 1966-72, Dep. Chm., 1971-72, P&OSN Co. Director: Australian and New Zealand Banking Group Ltd, 1971-76; Mercantile & General Reinsurance Co. Ltd, 1963-; Bain Dawes Group Ltd, 1970-72; Shepherd Neame Ltd, Brewers, Faversham, 1974-. Hon. Treasurer, King George's Fund for Sailors, 1977- (Dep. Chm., 1970-76); Mem. Gen. Council, Barnardo's, 1973-. *Recreations:* shooting, gardening. *Address:* Mount Ephraim, near Faversham, Kent. *T:* Boughton 310. *Clubs:* Farmers', City of London.

DAWES, Edgar Rowland, CMG 1958; Vice-Chairman Australian Broadcasting Commission, 1945-67; Governor, Adelaide Festival of Arts, since 1965; Member of Board: Royal Adelaide Hospital; Queen Elizabeth Hospital; *b* 28 Nov. 1902; *s* of George and Gertrude Dawes, Norwood, SA; *m* 1926, Adeline Melba Hurcombe (decd); one *s* one *d*; *m* 1966, Patricia M., *d* of W. Henderson. *Educ:* Public and High Sch., Norwood; Adelaide Univ. Secretary, Australian Society of Engineers, 1926-39; MHA, SA, 1929-32; Director Industries Corp., 1935-39; Member Board, Inst. Medical and Veterinary Sciences, 1935-. Area Management Board (Govt Appt), Min. of Munitions, 1939-45; also Asst Controller, Gun Ammunition; Controller, Ordnance Production and Chief Technical Officer. Member first Council of National Univ., Canberra, 1953-57; Commonwealth Govt Delegate to UNSCAT Conference, Geneva, 1963. Director of private companies (Engineering), 1945-. Chm. and Comr, Charitable Funds, SA, 1967-; Dep. Chm., Inst. of Med. and Veterinary Science (IMVS), SA, 1967. *Recreations:* fishing and boating. *Address:* 18 St Georges Avenue, Glandore, SA 5037, Australia. *T:* 93.2673. *Club:* Naval and Military.

DAWES, Prof. Geoffrey Sharman, FRS 1971; Director of Nuffield Institute for Medical Research, Oxford, since 1948; *b* 21 Jan. 1918; *s* of Rev. W. Dawes, Thurlaston Grange, Derbyshire; *m* 1941, Margaret Monk; two *s* two *d*. *Educ:* Repton Sch.; New Coll., Oxford. BA 1939; BSc 1940; BM, BCh 1943; DM 1947. Rockefeller Travelling Fellowship, 1946; Fellow, Worcester Coll., Oxford, 1946; University Demonstrator in Pharmacology, 1947; Foulerton Research Fellow, Royal Society, 1948. Governor of Repton, 1959, Chm., 1971-. A Vice-Pres., Royal Society, 1976, 1977. FRCOG, FRCP. Max Weinstein Award, 1963; Gairdner Foundation Award, 1966. *Publications:* Foetal and Neonatal Physiology, 1968; various publications in physiological and pharmacological journals. *Recreation:* fishing. *Address:* 8 Belbroughton Road, Oxford. *T:* Oxford 58131.

DAWICK, Viscount; Alexander Douglas Derrick Haig; *b* 30 June 1961; *s* and *heir* of 2nd Earl Haig, *qv*.

DAWNAY, family name of Viscount Downe.

DAWNAY, Lt-Col Christopher Payan, CBE 1946; MVO 1944; *s* of late Maj.-Gen. Guy P. Dawnay, CB, CMG, DSO, MVO, and Mrs Cecil Dawnay; *m* 1939, Patricia, *d* of Sir Hereward Wake, 13th Bt, CB, CMG, DSO; two *s* two *d*. *Educ:* Winchester; Magdalen Coll., Oxford. With Dawnay Day & Co. Ltd, Merchant Bankers, 1933-39 and 1946-50. War service with Coldstream Guards and in various staff appointments, 1939-45. Partner Edward de Stein & Co., Merchant Bankers, 1951-60; Director Lazard Bros & Co. Ltd, 1960-74; Chairman: Guardian Assurance Co., 1967-68; Guardian Royal Exchange Assurance Co., 1970-74. One of HM Lieutenants, City of London. US Legion of Merit. *Recreations:* fishing, shooting. *Address:* Longparish House, Andover, Hants. *T:* Longparish 204. *Club:* Brooks's.
See also Captain O. P. Dawnay.

DAWNAY, Hon. George William ffolkes, MC 1944; DL; Coldstream Guards; Director, Barclays Bank Ltd, since 1956; Local Advisory Director, Barclays Bank Ltd, Norwich; *b* 20 April 1909; *s* of 9th Viscount Downe, CMG and Dorothy, *o c* of Sir William ffolkes, 3rd Bt; *m* 1945, Rosemary Helen (*d* 1969), *d* of late Lord Edward Grosvenor and of late Lady Dorothy Charteris; two *s* two *d*. *Educ:* Eton. DL Norfolk, 1961. *Address:* Hillington Hall, King's Lynn, Norfolk. *T:* Hillington 304.

DAWNAY, Captain Oliver Payan, CVO 1953; Partner in Grieveson, Grant & Co., Stockbrokers; *b* 4 April 1920; *s* of late Maj.-General Guy Payan Dawnay, CB, CMG, DSO, MVO; *m* 1st, 1944, Lady Margaret Dorothea Boyle (marr. diss. 1962), *y d* of 8th Earl of Glasgow, DSO; two *s* one *d*; 2nd, 1963, Hon. Iris Irene Adele Peake, *e d* of 1st Viscount Ingleby, PC; one *d*. *Educ:* Eton; Balliol Coll., Oxford. Parliamentary and Press section, Ministry of Economic Warfare, 1939-40. Served War of 1939-45: Coldstream Guards, 1940-46; Adjt 1st Batt., 1943-44; seconded to Foreign Office, Conference Dept, 1945-46; demobilised, as Captain, 1946. Messrs Dawnay Day and Co., Merchant Bankers, 1946-50. Private Secretary and Equerry to Queen Elizabeth the Queen Mother, 1951-56; Extra Equerry, 1956-62. *Address:* Flat 5, 32 Onslow Square, SW7; Wexcombe House, Marlborough, Wilts. *Clubs:* Brooks's, MCC.
See also Lt-Col C. P. Dawnay.

DAWNAY, Vice-Adm. Sir Peter, KCVO 1961 (MVO 1939); CB 1958; DSC 1944; DL; Royal Navy, retired; an Extra Equerry to the Queen since 1958; *b* 14 Aug. 1904; *s* of Maj. Hon. Hugh and Lady Susan Dawnay; *m* 1936, Lady Angela Montagu-Douglas-Scott, *d* of 7th Duke of Buccleuch; one *s* one *d*. *Educ:* Osborne and Dartmouth. Legion of Merit (USA). In command HMS Saintes and 3rd Destroyer Flotilla, 1950-51; in command HMS Mercury (HM Signal Sch.), 1952-53; in command HMS Glasgow, 1954-56. Deputy Controller of the Navy, Admiralty, 1956-58; Flag Officer, Royal Yachts, 1958-62; retired, 1962. High Sheriff, Hants, 1973; DL Hants 1975. *Address:* Hattingley House, Hattingley, Alton, Hampshire GU34 5NQ. *T:* Alton 62294. *Club:* White's.

DAWOOD, Nessim Joseph; Arabist and Middle East Consultant; Managing Director, The Arabic Advertising and Publishing Co. Ltd, London, since 1958; Director: Contemporary Translations Ltd, London, since 1962; Bradbury Wilkinson (Graphics) Ltd, 1975; *b* Baghdad, 27 Aug. 1927; 4th *s* of late Yousef Dawood, merchant, and Muzli (*née* Tweg); *m* 1949, Juliet, 2nd *d* of M. and N. Abraham, Baghdad and New York; three *s*. *Educ:* The American Sch. and Shamash Sch., Baghdad; Iraq State Scholar in England, UC Exeter, 1945-49; Univ. of London, BA (Hons). FIL 1959. Has written and spoken radio and film commentaries.

Publications: The Muqaddimah of Ibn Khaldun, 1967 (US, 1969); Penguin Classics: The Thousand and One Nights, 1954; The Koran, 1956, 16th edn 1977; Aladdin and Other Tales, 1957; Tales from The Thousand and One Nights, 1973; contribs to specialised and technical English-Arabic dictionaries; translated numerous technical publications into Arabic. *Recreation:* going to the theatre. *Address:* Berkeley Square House, Berkeley Square, W1X 5LE. *T:* 01-409 0953. *Club:* Hurlingham.

DAWS, Dame Joyce (Margaretta), DBE 1975; FRCS, FRACS; Surgeon, Queen Victoria Memorial Hospital, Melbourne, Victoria, Australia; Thoracic Surgeon, Prince Henry's Hospital, Melbourne, since 1975; President, Victorian Branch Council, Australian Medical Association, 1976; *b* 21 July 1925; *d* of Frederick William Daws and Daisy Ethel Daws. *Educ:* Royal School for Naval and Marine Officers' Daughters, St Margaret's, Mddx; St Paul's Girls' Sch., Hammersmith; Royal Free Hosp., London. MB, BS (London) 1949; FRCS 1952, FRACS. Ho. Surg., Royal Free Hosp.; SHMO, Manchester Royal Infirmary; Hon. Surg., Queen Victoria Meml Hosp., Melb., 1958; Asst Thoracic Surg., Prince Henry's Hosp., Melb., 1967. Hon. Sec., Victorian Br., AMA, 1974. *Recreations:* opera, ballet, theatre, desert travel, swimming. *Address:* 26 Edwin Street, Heidelberg West, Victoria 3081, Australia. *T:* 454411. *Club:* Lyceum (Melb.).

DAWSON, Alistair Benedict, QC 1976; *b* 21 March 1922; 4th *s* of late Alexander Thomson Dawson and Isobel Margaret Dawson, Portelet House, Jersey. *Educ:* Stonyhurst Coll.; Balliol Coll., Oxford (MA 1947); Scots Coll. and Gregorian Univ., Rome. Served with 102 Medium Regt, RA, N Africa and Italy, 1943-45 (Lieut). Called to Bar, Middle Temple, 1951. Captain, HQRA 56 (London) Div., TA, 1952-57. Editor, Estates Gazette Digest, 1965-74. *Recreations:* gardening, cooking, music. *Address:* 2 Paper Buildings, Temple, EC4Y 7ET. *T:* 01-353 5835; 59 Westcroft Square, W6 0TA. *T:* 01-748 4914.

DAWSON, Anthony Michael, MD, FRCP; Physician to the Royal Household since 1974; Physician: St Bartholomew's Hospital, since 1965; King Edward VII Hospital for Officers, since 1968; King Edward VII Convalescent Home for Officers, Osborne, since 1975; *b* 8 May 1928; *s* of Leslie Joseph Dawson and Mabel Jayes; *m* 1956, Barbara Anne Baron Forsyth, *d* of late Thomas Forsyth, MB, ChB; two *d*. *Educ:* Wyggeston Sch., Leicester; Charing Cross Hosp. Med. Sch. MB, BS 1951, MD 1959, London; MRCP 1954, FRCP 1964. Jun. appts, Charing Cross Hosp., Brompton Hosp., Royal Postgrad. Med. Sch., Central Middlesex Hosp., 1951-57; MRC and US Public Health Res. Fellow, Harvard Med. Sch. at Massachusetts Gen. Hosp., 1957-59; Lectr and Sen. Lectr in Medicine, Royal Free Hosp. Med. Sch., 1959-65. Hon. Sec., Assoc. of Physicians of Gt Britain and Ireland, 1973. *Publications:* contrib. med. books and jls. *Recreation:* music. *Address:* Flat 4, Stone House, 9 Weymouth Street, W1. *T:* 01-636 4121. *Club:* Royal Automobile.
See also J. L. Dawson.

DAWSON, Christopher William, CMG 1947; *b* 31 May 1896; *s* of Rev. H. Dawson, MA, and Tertia Dean; *m* 1924, Jill, *d* of Prof. R. G. McKerron, Aberdeen Univ.; no *c*. *Educ:* Dulwich Coll.; Brasenose Coll., Oxford. Joined East Surrey Regt, 1915; served in India (NW Frontier) and Mesopotamia; demobilised with rank of Captain, 1919. Joined Malayan Civil Service 1920 and served in various parts of Malaya until 1942. Called to Bar, Gray's Inn, 1929. Secretary for Defence Malaya, 1941-42; interned by Japanese in Singapore, 1942-45; Chief Secretary and Officer Administering the Govt, Sarawak, 1946-50; retired, 1950; Deputy Chief Secretary, British Administration, Eritrea, 1951-52. President: British Assoc. of Malaya, 1957-58; Sarawak Assoc., 1962. *Address:* 17 Oaklands Court, Chichester, W Sussex. *T:* Chichester 80638.

DAWSON, Sir (Hugh Halliday) Trevor, 3rd Bt *cr* 1920; Executive Director, Arbuthnot Latham & Co. Ltd, Merchant Bankers, since 1965; Chairman, Arbuthnot Securities Ltd, since 1976; *b* 6 June 1931; *s* of Sir Hugh Trevor Dawson, 2nd Bt, CBE, and of Vera Anne Loch, *d* of late Sir Frederick Loch Halliday, CIE, MVO; *S* father, 1976; *m* 1955, Caroline Jane, *d* of William Antony Acton, *qv*; two *s*. *Educ:* Harrow; RMA, Sandhurst. Joined Scots Guards, 1949; Major 1960; retired 1961. *Recreations:* racing, shooting. *Heir:* *s* Hugh Michael Trevor Dawson, *b* 28 March 1956. *Address:* 31 Eaton Square, SW1; Scrope Manor, Froxfield, Wiltshire. *Clubs:* White's, Pratt's, Cavalry and Guards, Bath, Buck's, Turf, City of London, Royal Aero, MCC; Bembridge Sailing (IoW).

DAWSON, John Alexander, CBE 1942; FICE; *b* 24 March 1886; *s* of Alexander Dawson, Aberdeen; *m* Margaret, er *d* of late Alexander M. Cruickshank, Bloemfontein, SA; two *s* one *d*. *Educ:* Robert Gordon's Coll., Aberdeen; Aberdeen and Glasgow Universities, BSc (Engineering) Glasgow. Entered Admiralty as Asst Civil Engineer, 1912; served at Portsmouth, Admiralty, Ostend (1919) and Rosyth; transferred to Air Ministry, 1921; served at Air Ministry, Inland Area, Singapore, Coastal Command; Chief Engineer Air Defence of Great Britain; Chief Engineer Bomber Command; Dep. Director of Works, 1938; Director of Works, Air Ministry, 1940-48; Chief Resident Engineer, London Airport, 1948-54, retired 1954. *Address:* Belle Causey, Barnstaple, North Devon. *T:* Barnstaple 71112. *Club:* Saunton Golf.

DAWSON, John Leonard, MB, MS; FRCS; Surgeon to HM Royal Household, since 1975; Surgeon: King's College Hospital, since 1964; Bromley Hospital, since 1967; King Edward VII Hospital for Officers, since 1975; *b* 30 Sept. 1932; *s* of Leslie Joseph Dawson and Mabel Annie Jayes; *m* 1958, Rosemary Brundle; two *s* one *d*. *Educ:* Wyggeston Boys' Grammar Sch., Leicester; King's College Hosp., Univ. of London. MB, BS 1955, MS 1964; FRCS 1958. Served RAMC, 1958-60. Nuffield Scholarship, Harvard Univ., 1963-64. Examiner in Surgery, Univ. of London and Soc. of Apothecaries, 1968-. *Publications:* contribs to surgical text-books and jls on surgery of the liver, gall-bladder and stomach. *Recreations:* squash, tennis, skiing, gardening, reading. *Address:* 107 Burbage Road, Dulwich, SE21 7AF. *T:* 01-733 3668. *See also A. M. Dawson.*

DAWSON, Ven. Peter; Archdeacon of Norfolk, since 1977; *b* 31 March 1929; *s* of Leonard Smith and Cicely Alice Dawson; *m* 1955, Kathleen Mary Sansome; one *s* three *d*. *Educ:* Manchester Grammar School; Keble Coll., Oxford (MA); Ridley Hall, Cambridge. Nat. service, Army, 1947-49; University, 1949-52; Theological College, 1952-54. Asst Curate, St Lawrence, Morden, Dio. Southwark, 1954-59; Vicar of Barston, Warwicks, Dio. Birmingham, 1959-63; Rector of St Clement, Higher Openshaw, Dio. Manchester, 1963-68; Rector of Morden, Dio. Southwark, 1968-77, and Rural Dean of Merton, 1975-77. *Recreation:* gardening. *Address:* 11 Cringleford Chase, Colney Lane, Cringleford, Norwich NR4 7RS. *T:* Norwich 58183.

DAWSON, Richard Leonard Goodhugh, MB, FRCS; Plastic Surgeon: Mount Vernon Centre for Plastic Surgery, Northwood, since 1953; Northwick Park Hospital, and Edgware General Hospital, since 1970; *b* 24 Aug. 1916; *s* of L. G. Dawson and Freda Hollis; *m* 1945, Betty Marie Freeman-Mathews; two *s*. *Educ:* Bishop's Stortford Coll., Herts; University Coll., London; University College Hospital. MRCS, LRCP 1939; MB London 1940; FRCS 1947; BS London 1948. Royal Army Medical Corps, 1941-46; service in England and Far East (4 years); POW in Japanese hands, 1942-45. Member, British Assoc. Plastic Surgeons (President, 1974). *Publications:* Chapters in Operative Surgery, 1957; numerous contributions to Lancet, BMJ, British Journal Plastic Surgery and other journals. *Recreations:* squash, golf, gardening. *Address:* (office) 100 Harley Street, W1. *T:* 01-935 0066; (home) Tara, Colley Hill Lane, Hedgerley, Bucks. *T:* Fulmer 2697.

DAWSON, Sir Trevor; *see* Dawson, Sir H. H. T.

DAWSON, Air Chief Marshal Sir Walter Lloyd, KCB 1954 (CB 1945); CBE 1943; DSO 1948; *b* 6 May 1902; *s* of late W. J. Dawson, Sunderland; *m* 1927, Elizabeth Leslie (*d* 1975), *d* of late D. V. McIntyre, MA, MB, ChB; one *s* one *d*. Station Comdr St Eval, Coastal Command, 1942-43; Dir, Anti-U-Boat Operations, 1943; Dir of Plans, 1944-46; AOC Levant, 1946-48; Commandant, School of Land/Air Warfare, Old Sarum, 1948-50; idc, 1950-51 (RAF Instructor); Asst Chief of the Air Staff (Policy), 1952-53; Deputy Chief of Staff (Plans and Operations), SHAPE, 1953-56; Inspector-General of RAF, 1956-57; Air Member for Supply and Organisation, 1958-60, retired. Chm., Handley Page, 1966-69 (Vice-Chm., 1964-66). Dir, Southern Electricity Bd, 1961-72. *Address:* Woodlands, Heathfield Avenue, Sunninghill, Berks. *Club:* Royal Air Force.

DAWSON, Wilfred; Director, Driver and Vehicle Licensing, Department of Transport, since 1976; *b* 11 Jan. 1923; *s* of Walter and Ivy Dawson; *m* 1944, Emily Louise Mayhew; two *d*. *Educ:* Riley High Sch., Hull. Civil Service: Air Min., 1939-49; Min. of Town and Country Planning, 1949; Principal, Min. of Housing and Local Govt, 1963; Asst Sec., DoE, 1970; Under-Sec., DoE, 1974-76. *Recreations:* walking, woodworking. *Address:* 12 Woollacott Drive, Caswell, Swansea, West Glamorgan.

DAWSON-DAMER, family name of **Earl of Portarlington**.

DAWSON-MORAY, Edward Bruce, CMG 1969; *b* 30 June 1909; *s* of late Alwyn Bruce Dawson-Moray and late Ada (*née* Burlton); *m* 1st, 1933, Ursula Frances (*née* Woodbridge) (marr. diss.); one *s* one *d*; 2nd Beryl Barber. *Educ:* Cranbrook Sch.; University of London (BA Hons). Housemaster, Chillon Coll., Switzerland, 1938-42. British Legation, Berne, 1942; 3rd Secretary, 1944; 3rd Secretary and Vice-Consul, Rome, 1947-48; Consul: Leopoldville, 1948-50; Detroit, 1950-51; 1st Secretary and Consul, Rangoon, 1952-54; Information Officer and Consul, Naples, 1954-56; Foreign Office, 1956-60; Consul, Casablanca, 1960-63; Chief Establishment Officer, Diplomatic Wireless Service, 1963-69; Principal, Civil Service Dept, 1969-74; retired. Advr, Pre-retirement training, CSD. Senior Editor, Foreign Office List, 1957-60. *Recreations:* literature, photography, opera, travel. *Address:* 2 Pennypiece, Cleeve Road, Goring-on-Thames, Reading, Berks RG8 9BY. *T:* Goring-on-Thames 3314. *Club:* Phyllis Court (Henley).

DAWTRY, Sir Alan, Kt 1974; CBE 1968 (MBE (mil.) 1945); TD 1948; Chairman: Sperry Rand Ltd, since 1977; Sperry Rand (Ireland) Ltd, since 1977; *b* 8 April 1915; *s* of Melancthon and Kate Nicholas Dawtry, Sheffield; unmarried. *Educ:* King Edward VII Sch., Sheffield; Sheffield Univ. (LLB). Admitted Solicitor, 1938; Asst Solicitor, Sheffield, 1938-48; Deputy Town Clerk, Bolton, 1948-52; Deputy Town Clerk, Leicester, 1952-54; Town Clerk, Wolverhampton, 1954-56; Chief Exec. (formerly Town Clerk), Westminster City Council, 1956-77; Hon. Sec., London Boroughs Assoc.; Mem. Council of Management, Architectural Heritage Fund. Served War of 1939-45: Commissioned RA; Campaigns France, North Africa, Italy (MBE, despatches twice); released with rank of Lt-Col. Member: Metrication Bd, 1969-74; Clean Air Council, 1960-75. Pres., Soc. of Local Authority Chief Execs, 1975-76. FBIM 1975. Foreign Orders: The Star (Afghanistan); Golden Honour (Austria); Leopold II (Belgium); Rio Branco (Brazil); Merit (Chile); Legion of Honour (France); Merit (W Germany); the Phœnix (Greece); Merit (Italy); Homayoun (Iran); The Rising Sun (Japan); the Star (Jordan); African Redemption (Liberia); Oaken Crown (Luxembourg); Loyalty (Malaysia); the Right Hand (Nepal); Orange-Nassau (Netherlands); the Two Niles (Sudan); the Crown (Thailand); Zaire (Zaire). *Address:* 806 Collingwood House, Dolphin Square, SW1. *T:* 01-828 6759.

DAY, Prof. Alan Charles Lynn; Professor of Economics, London School of Economics, University of London, since 1964; *b* 25 Oct. 1924; *s* of Henry Charles Day, MBE, and Ruth Day; *m* 1962, Diana Hope Bocking; no *c*. *Educ:* Chesterfield Grammar Sch.; Queens' Coll., Cambridge. Asst Lecturer, then Lecturer, LSE, 1949-54; Economic Adviser, HM Treas., 1954-56; Reader in Economics, London Univ., 1956-64. Ed., National Inst. Econ. Review, 1960-62; Econ. Correspondent, The Observer, intermittently, 1957-. Economic Adviser on Civil Aviation, BoT, later Dept of Trade and Industry, 1968-72; Economic Adviser, Civil Aviation Authority, 1972-. Member: Council, Consumers' Assoc., 1963-; Board, British Airports Authority, 1965-68; SE Region Econ. Planning Council, 1966-69; Home Office Cttee on the London Taxicab Trade, 1967-70; Layfield Cttee on Local Govt Finance, 1974-76. British Acad. Leverhulme Vis. Prof., Graduate Inst. for International Studies, Geneva, 1971. Governor, LSE, 1971-. *Publications:* The Future of Sterling, 1954; Outline of Monetary Economics, 1956; The Economics of Money, 1959; (with S. T. Beza) Wealth and Income, 1960. *Address:* 2 Regent Square, WC1. *T:* 01-837 7950; 11 Christchurch Hill, NW3. *T:* 01-435 4584. *Club:* Reform.

DAY, Bernard Maurice; Assistant Under-Secretary of State (Operational Requirements), Ministry of Defence, since 1976; *b* 7 May 1928; *s* of M. J. Day and Mrs M. H. Day; *m* 1956, Ruth Elizabeth Stansfield; two *s* one *d*. *Educ:* Bancroft's Sch.; London School of Economics (BScEcon). Army service, commnd RA, 1946-48. British Electric Traction Fedn, 1950-51; Asst Principal, Air Ministry, 1951; Private Sec. to Air Mem. for Supply and Organisation, 1954-56; Principal, 1956; Cabinet Secretariat, 1959-61; Asst Sec., 1965; Sec., Meteorological Office, 1965-69; Estabt Officer, Cabinet Office, 1969-72; Head of Air Staff Secretariat, MoD, 1972-74; Asst Under Sec. of State, MoD, 1974; Civilian Staff Management, 1974-76. *Recreation:* squash. *Address:* Burfield, Farmleigh Grove, Burwood Park, Walton-on-Thames, Surrey KT12 5BU. *T:* Walton-on-Thames 27416. *Club:* Royal Commonwealth Society.

DAY, Derek Malcolm, CMG 1973; HM Diplomatic Service; Ambassador in Addis Ababa, since 1975; *b* 29 Nov. 1927; *s* of late Mr and Mrs Alan W. Day; *m* 1955, Sheila Nott; three *s* one *d*. *Educ:* Hurstpierpoint Coll.; St Catharine's Coll., Cambridge. Royal Artillery, 1946-48; St Catharine's Coll., 1948-51. Entered HM Foreign Service, Sept. 1951; Third Sec., British Embassy, Tel Aviv, 1953-56; Private Sec. to HM Ambassador, Rome,

1956-59; Second, then First Sec., FO, 1959-62; First Sec., British Embassy, Washington, 1962-66; First Sec., FO, 1966-67; Asst Private Sec. to Sec. of State for Foreign Affairs, 1967-68; Head of Personnel Operations Dept, FCO, 1969-72; Counsellor, British High Commn, Nicosia, 1972-75. *Recreations:* golf, gardening, and the family. *Address:* c/o Foreign and Commonwealth Office, SW1; Falconhurst, Lingfield, Surrey. *T:* Lingfield 832538. *Club:* United Oxford & Cambridge University.

DAY, Graham; *see* Day, J. G.

DAY, James Wentworth; FRSA; author, journalist and publicist; Chairman and Managing Director of News Publicity Ltd; *b* Marsh House, Exning, Suffolk, 21 April 1899; *s* of late J. T. Wentworth Day, Lacies Court, Abingdon, Berks, and Martha Ethel Staples of Landwade Hall, Exning and Wicken; *m* 1943, Marion Edith, *d* of late Hamish McLean, Mount Hutt Estates, S Island, NZ, and of Mrs Hamish McLean, Christchurch, NZ; one *d*. *Educ:* Newton Coll.; Cambridge. Served European War, 1917-18; Daily Express, Publicity Manager, 1923; Asst Editor Country Life, 1925; acting Editor of the Field, 1930-31; Dramatic Critic, Sunday Express, 1932, and Editor of English Life; as Personal Representative of Lady Houston, 1933-34, was on exec. of Houston-Mount Everest flight, negotiated purchase of Saturday Review (editor, 1934), conducted High Tory campaign in nine bye-elections. Editor, Illustrated Sporting and Dramatic News, 1935-36-37; Propaganda Adviser to Egyptian Government, 1938-39; Publicity Adviser to Anglo-Turk Relief Cttee, 1940; War Correspondent in France, 1940, and with minesweepers; Near East Correspondent to BBC, 1941. Invalided out, 1943; fought press and parly campaign against extravagance and injustices of War Agricl Exec. Cttee system, which led to release of 17,000 acres of govt controlled farms in E Anglia and setting up of Land Appeal Tribunals; drafted Amendment to Pests Act 1954, which made it criminal offence to spread myxomatosis. Dir-Gen., 1100th Anniversary Festival, Bury St Edmunds. Contested (C) Hornchurch Div. of Essex, 1950 and 1951. Editor, East Anglia Life, 1962-66; Country Correspondent, Daily Mail. Member Society of Authors; Member Inst. of Journalists; owns a large part of Adventurers' Fen and a few good Old Masters, mainly of the Wentworth family. Founded Essex Wildfowlers' Assoc., 1924; Hon. Life Mem., Wildfowlers' Assoc. of GB and Ireland. *Publications:* The Lure of Speed, 1929; The Life of Sir Henry Segrave, 1930; Speed, the Life of Sir Malcolm Campbell, 1931; My Greatest Adventure (for Sir Malcolm Campbell), 1932; Kaye Don—the Man, 1934; The Modern Fowler, 1934; A Falcon on St Paul's, 1935; King George V as a Sportsman, 1935; Sporting Adventure, 1937; The Dog in Sport, 1938; Sport in Egypt, 1939; Farming Adventure, 1943; Harvest Adventure, 1945; Gamblers' Gallery, 1948; Wild Wings, 1949; Coastal Adventure, 1949; Inns of Sport, 1949; Marshland Adventure, 1950; Broadland Adventure, 1951; The New Yeomen of England, 1952; Rural Revolution, 1952; The Modern Shooter, 1953; Norwich and the Broads, in quest of the Inn, 1953; The Wisest Dogs in the World, 1954; A History of the Fens, 1954; Ghosts and Witches, 1954; They Walk the Wild Places, 1956; Poison on the Land, 1957; The Angler's Pocket Book, 1957; The Dog Lover's Pocket Book, 1957; Lady Houston, DBE—The Woman Who Won the War, 1958; A Ghost Hunter's Game Book, 1958; Newfoundland—The Fortress Isle, 1959; HRH Princess Marina, Duchess of Kent (The First Authentic Life Story), 1962; The Queen Mother's Family Story, 1967; Portrait of the Broads, 1967; In Search of Ghosts, 1969; Rum Owd Boys, 1975. Edited Best Sporting Stories (anthology). Contributions to Great Georgians; The English Counties; 50 Great Ghost Stories, 1966; 50 Great Horror Stories, 1969; Treasures of Britain (Readers Digest), 1968; Essex Ghosts, 1974, etc; has broadcast and written many articles on politics, the Near East, field sports, natural history, agriculture, dogs, flying, motoring, racing, shipping, etc, in the leading newspapers and journals. *Recreations:* taking the Left Wing intelligentsia at its own valuation; shooting (especially wildfowling), riding, fishing, sailing, natural history, and old furniture. *Address:* Ingatestone, Essex. *T:* Ingatestone 3035. *Clubs:* United Oxford & Cambridge University, Press, 1900.

DAY, John King, TD; MA, BSc; Principal, Elizabeth College, Guernsey, CI, 1958-71; *b* Ipoh, Perak, FMS, 27 Oct. 1909; *s* of Harold Duncan Day, Mining Engineer, and Muriel Edith Day; *m* 1935, Mary Elizabeth Stinton, *er d* of late Tom Stinton, Headmaster of the High Sch., Newcastle-under-Lyme; three *s*. *Educ:* Stamford Sch.; Magdalen Coll., Oxford. Demy 1928-32. Honour School of Natural Science (Chemistry) Class 2. Assistant Master, Kendal Sch., Westmorland, 1932; Asst Master and Housemaster, Gresham's Sch., 1933-57. Served Royal Norfolk Regt (7th Bn) and Military College of Science, 1939-45. *Recreations:* walking, fishing and sketching. *Address:* Sunnyside

Cottage, Hunworth Green, Melton Constable, Norfolk. *T:* Holt 3435.

DAY, (Judson) Graham; Professor of Business Studies, Dalhousie University, Halifax, Nova Scotia, since 1977; *b* 3 May 1933; *s of* Frank Charles Day and Edythe Grace (*née* Baker); *m* 1958, Leda Ann (*née* Creighton); one *s* two *d* . *Educ:* Queen Elizabeth High Sch., Halifax, NS; Dalhousie Univ., Halifax, NS (LLB). Private practice of Law, Windsor, Nova Scotia, 1956-64; Canadian Pacific Ltd, Montreal and Toronto, 1964-71; Cammell Laird Shipbuilders Ltd, Birkenhead, Eng., 1971-75; Dep. Chm., Organising Cttee for British Shipbuilders and Dep. Chm. and Chief Exec. designate, British Shipbuilders, 1975-76. Member: Nova Scotia Barristers' Soc.; Law Soc. of Upper Canada; Canadian Bar Assoc. *Recreations:* reading; lakeside chalet in Canada. *Address:* School of Business Administration, Dalhousie University, Halifax, Nova Scotia B3H 4H6, Canada.

DAY, Lance Reginald; Keeper, Science Museum Library, since 1976; *b* 2 Nov. 1927; *s of* late Reginald and of Eileen Day; *m* 1959, Mary Ann Sheahan; one *s* two *d*. *Educ:* Sherrardswood Sch., Welwyn Garden City; Alleyne's Grammar Sch., Stevenage; Northern Polytechnic and University Coll., London (MSc). Res. Asst, Science Museum Library, 1951-64, Asst Keeper 1964-73; Dep. Keeper, Science Museum, Dept of Chemistry, 1973-74; Keeper, Science Museum, Dept of Communications and Electrical Engrg, 1974-76. Sec., Nat. Railway Museum Cttee, 1973-75; Hon. Sec., Newcomen Soc., 1973-. *Publications:* reviews and articles. *Recreation:* music. *Address:* 10 Russellcroft Road, Welwyn Garden City, Herts. *T:* Welwyn Garden 22387.

DAY, Robin; Television Journalist; *b* 24 Oct. 1923; *s of* late William and Florence Day; *m* 1965, Katherine Mary, *d of* R. I. Ainslie, DSO, QC, Perth, WA; two *s*. *Educ:* Bembridge, Sch.; St Edmund Hall, Oxford. Military service, 1943-47; commd RA, 1944. Oxford, 1947-51: Union debating tour of American universities, 1949; President Union, 1950; BA Hons (Jurisprudence), 1951. Middle Temple: Blackstone Entrance Scholar, 1951; Harmsworth Law Scholar, 1952-53; called to Bar, 1952. British Information Services, Washington, 1953-54; free-lance broadcasting and journalism, 1954-55; BBC Talks Producer (radio), 1955; Newscaster and Parliamentary Correspondent, Independent TV News, 1955-59; Guild of TV Producers' Merit Award, Personality of the Year, 1957; columnist in News Chronicle, 1959; joined BBC TV programme Panorama, 1959; Introducer of Panorama, 1967-72. Mem., Phillimore Cttee on Law of Contempt, 1971-74. (L) Hereford, 1959. Richard Dimbleby Award for factual television, 1974. *Publications:* Television: A Personal Report, 1961; The Case for Televising Parliament, 1963; Day by Day: a dose of my own hemlock, 1975. *Recreations:* reading, talking, ski-ing. *Address:* c/o BBC TV Studios, Lime Grove, W12. *Club:* Garrick.

DAYMOND, Douglas Godfrey; Civil Service Commissioner, since 1975; *b* 23 Nov. 1917; *s of* Samuel Kevern and Minnie Daymond; *m* 1945, Laura Vivien (*née* Selley); one *s* one *d*. *Educ:* Saltash Grammar Sch; London Univ. LLB Hons 1947. Called to Bar, Gray's Inn, 1952. Inland Revenue, 1935; Customs and Excise, 1939; War Service with Royal Engineers in Egypt, Greece and Crete, POW 1941-45; Inland Revenue, 1947; Asst Sec., Royal Commn on Taxation, 1951-55; Sec., Tithe Redemption Commn, 1959-60; Dep. Dir, CS Selection Bd, 1970; Under-Sec., Civil Service Dept, 1973. *Recreations:* gardening, theatre, music. *Address:* 55 Salisbury Road, Farnborough, Hants GU14 7AG. *T:* Farnborough (Hants) 42517; Flat 73, Fort Picklecombe, near Millbrook, Cornwall. *Club:* Royal Commonwealth Society.

DAYSH, Prof. George Henry John, CBE 1973; BLitt Oxon; DCL; Deputy Vice-Chancellor of University of Newcastle upon Tyne and Professor of Geography in the University, 1963-66; Emeritus Professor, since Oct. 1966 (Professor of Geography, King's College, University of Durham, Newcastle upon Tyne, 1943-63; Sub Rector, King's College, 1955-63); *b* 21 May 1901; *s* of Alfred John Daysh and Margaret (*née* Campbell); *m* 1927, Sheila Guthrie (*d* 1971), *er d of* Dr A. F. A. Fairweather; one *s* one *d*. *Educ:* Eggars Grammar Sch.; University College, Reading; Wadham Coll., Oxford. Housemaster, Pocklington Sch., E. Yorks, 1924-27; Lecturer in Geography, Bedford Coll., University of London, 1927-29; Lecturer-in-charge, Dept of Geography, 1930-38, Reader of Geography, 1938-43, King's Coll., Newcastle upon Tyne. Seconded for special duties with Dist Comr for special area of Cumberland, 1938; Senior Research Officer, Ministry of Town and Country Planning, 1943-45. Member of Exec. of NE Development Board, 1934-39, Vice-President NE Industrial and Development Assoc.; Chairman Research Cttee of NEIDA; Secretary Commn on Ports of International Geographic Union, 1947-51; Chairman

University of Durham Matriculation and Sch. Examination Board, 1953-63. Part-time Member Northern Gas Board, 1956-70. Chairman, Newcastle upon Tyne Hospital Management Cttee, 1968-71. Visiting Prof. Fouad I Univ., 1951. Chairman, Triennial Grants Cttee, University College of Sierra Leone, 1960. Consultant to Cumberland Development Council, 1966-69. Chm., Tyne Tees Television, 1968-71; Dep. Chm., Trident Television Ltd, 1970-72; Dir, Solway Chemicals Ltd. Hon. DCL (Newcastle), 1964. FRSA; FRGS (Victoria Medal 1972). *Publications:* Southampton-Points in its Development, 1928; A Survey of Industrial Facilities of the North-East Coast, 1936 (rev., 1940 and 1949); West Cumberland with Alston-a Survey of Industrial Facilities, 1938 (revised 1951); (ed) Studies in Regional Planning, 1949; (ed) Physical Land Classification of North-East England, 1950; (with J. S Symonds) West Durham, 1953; (ed) A Survey of Whitby, 1958; contribs to Geographical Journal, Geography, Economic Geography, Geographical Review, etc. *Recreations:* gardening, field sports. *Address:* 2 Dunkirk Terrace, Corbridge, Northumberland. *T:* Corbridge-on-Tyne 2154.

DEACON, Lt-Col Edmund Henry; JP; DL; *b* 1902; *s of* late Col E. Deacon, DL, Sloe House, Halstead, Essex; *m* 1927, Betty, *d of* late Brig.-Gen. J. E. C. Livingstone-Learmonth, CMG, DSO; one *d*. *Educ:* Wellington; Trinity Coll., Cambridge; Master Newmarket and Thurlow Hounds, 1934-42. Joint Master East Essex Hounds, 1947-50. Commanding 15 Bn Essex Home Guard, 1952; Chairman of Governors of Felsted Sch., 1952-65. DL 1953, JP 1954, Essex. *Address:* Brick House, Steeple Bumpstead, Haverhill, Suffolk. *Club:* Cavalry and Guards.

DEACON, Sir George (Edward Raven), Kt 1971; CBE 1954; FRS 1944; FRSE 1957; FRAS; FRGS; DSc; Director, National Institute of Oceanography, 1949-71; Foreign Member, Swedish Royal Academy of Sciences, 1958; *b* 21 March 1906; *m* 1940, Margaret Elsa Jeffries (*d* 1966); one *d*. *Educ:* City Boys' Sch., Leicester; King's Coll., London. FKC. Vis. Prof. of Chemistry of the Environment, KCL, 1974. Served on Scientific Staff of the Discovery Cttee, in England and in the Royal Research Ships William Scoresby and Discovery II, 1927-39. Hon. DSc: Liverpool, 1961; Leicester, 1970. Polar Medal, 1942; Alexander Agassiz Medal, US National Academy of Sciences, 1962; Royal Medal, Royal Soc., 1969; Founder's Medal, RGS, 1971; Scottish Geographical Medal, 1972. Hon. Member, Royal Society of New Zealand, 1964; President, Royal Institute of Navigation, 1961-64; Vice-President, RGS, 1965-70. *Publications:* Oceanographical papers in the Discovery Reports, etc. *Address:* Flitwick House, Milford, Surrey. *T:* Godalming 5929.

DEACON ELLIOTT, Air Vice-Marshal Robert, CB 1967; OBE 1954; DFC 1941 (2 mentions); Bursar, Civil Service College, Sunningdale Park, since 1969; *b* 20 Nov. 1914; British; *m* 1948, Grace Joan Willes, Leamington Spa; two *s* one *d*. *Educ:* Northampton. 72 Fighter Sqdn (Dunkirk and Battle of Britain), 1939-41; HQ Fighter Comd, 1942-43; 84 Group 2 ATAF, 1944-46; Air Ministry (OR 5), 1946-48; OC Flying Wing and OC 26 APC in Cyprus, 1948-51; HQ Fighter Comd, Head of Admin. Plans, 1951-54; Army Staff Coll., on Directing Staff, 1954-56; CO, RAF Leconfield, 1956-57; CO, RAF Driffield, 1957-58; Air University USAF, Maxwell AFB, USA, 1958-61; Commandant, Officer and Aircrew Selection Centre, 1962-65; AOC, RAF Gibraltar, 1965-66; AOC, RAF Malta, and Dep. C-in-C (Air), Allied Forces Mediterranean, 1966-68, retd. *Recreations:* squash rackets, shooting, photography. *Address:* Park House, Sunningdale Park, Ascot, Berks. *T:* Ascot 23178. *Club:* Royal Air Force.

DEADMAN, Ronald; Editor, Teachers' World, 1968-76; Member of the Press Council, 1969-75; *s of* Thomas Deadman and Margaret Healey; *m* 1952, Joan Evans; no *c*. *Educ:* Hinguar Street Sch., Shoeburyness; Oakley Coll., Cheltenham. Served RAF, 1937-45. Teaching, 1950-66; Features Editor, The Teacher, 1966-67; Editor, Everyweek, 1967-68. *Publications:* Enjoying English, Bk 1, 1966; Bk 2, 1968; Bk 3 (Contrasts), 1971; Bk 4 (Perception), 1972; (novels for children): The Happening, 1968; Wanderbodies, 1972; The Pretenders, 1972; (ed, short stories) The Friday Story, 1966; Words in Your Ear, vols 1 and 2, 1972; Going My Way, vols 1, 2 and 3, 1973; (with Arthur Razzell) Ways of Knowing, 1977; contribs to New Statesman, The Times, British Clinical Jl, Guardian, BBC, Where magazine, Education and Training. *Recreation:* brooding. *Address:* Flat 1, Dawley House, 91 Uxbridge Road, Ealing, W5. *T:* 01-579 7224.

DEAKIN, Maj.-Gen. Cecil Martin Fothergill, CB 1961; CBE 1956; *b* 20 Dec. 1910; *m* 1934, Evelyn, *e d of* late Sir Arthur Grant, Bt of Monymusk, Aberdeenshire; one *s* one *d*. *Educ:* Winchester Coll. Commissioned into Grenadier Guards, 1931.

Served with Regt NW Europe, 1944-45 (despatches). Commanded: 2nd Bn Grenadier Guards, 1945-46; 1st Bn, 1947-50; 32nd Guards Bde, 1953-55; 29th Infantry Bde, 1955-57 (Suez Expedition, despatches); Brigadier, General Staff, War Office, 1957-59; Director of Military Training, 1959; GOC 56th London Div., TA, 1960; Director Territorial Army, Cadets and Home Guard, 1960-62; Commandant of the JSSC, Latimer, 1962-65. Director, Mental Health Foundn, 1967. President, Grenadier Guards Assoc. *Recreations:* numerous. *Address:* Stocks Farm House, Beenham, Berks. *Club:* Royal Yacht Squadron.
See also Sir A. B. C. Edmonstone, Bt.

DEAKIN, Rt. Rev. Thomas Carlyle Joseph Robert Hamish; *see* Tewkesbury, Bishop Suffragan of.

DEAKIN, Sir William, Kt 1975; DSO 1943; MA; Warden of St Antony's College, Oxford, 1950-68, retired; Hon. Fellow, 1969; *b* 3 July 1913; *e s* of Albert Witney Deakin, Aldbury, Tring, Herts; *m* 1st, 1935, Margaret Ogilvy (marr. diss. 1940), *d* of late Sir Nicholas Beatson Bell, KCSI; two *s*; 2nd, 1943, Livia Stela, *d* of Liviu Nasta, Bucharest. *Educ:* Westminster Sch.; Christ Church, Oxford. 1st Class, Modern History, 1934; Amy Mary Preston Read Scholar, 1935. Fellow and Tutor, Wadham Coll., Oxford, 1936-49; Research Fellow, 1949; Hon. Fellow, 1961. Served War of 1939-45; with Queen's Own Oxfordshire Hussars, 1939-41; seconded to Special Operations, War Office, 1941; led first British Military Mission to Tito, May 1943. First Secretary, HM Embassy, Belgrade, 1945-46. Russian Order of Valour, 1944; Chevalier de la Légion d'Honneur, 1953; Grosse Verdienstkreuz, 1958; Yugoslav Partisan Star (1st Class), 1969. *Publications:* The Brutal Friendship, 1962; The Embattled Mountain, 1971. *Address:* Le Castellet, Var, France. *Clubs:* White's, Brooks's.

DEAKINS, Eric Petro; MP (Lab) Waltham Forest, Walthamstow, since 1974 (Walthamstow West, 1970-74); Parliamentary Under-Secretary of State, Department of Health and Social Security, since 1976; *b* 7 Oct. 1932; *er s* of late Edward Deakins and Gladys Deakins. *Educ:* Tottenham Grammar Sch.; London Sch. of Economics. BA (Hons) in History, 1953. Executive with FMC (Meat) Ltd, 1956; General Manager, Pigs Div., FMC (Meat) Ltd, 1969. Parly Under-Sec. of State, Dept of Trade, 1974-76. *Publication:* A Faith to Fight For, 1964. *Recreations:* writing, cinema, squash, football. *Address:* House of Commons, SW1. *T:* 01-219 5158.

DEAN, (Arthur) Paul; MP (C) Somerset North since 1964; Company Director; *b* 14 Sept. 1924; *s* of Arthur Percival Dean and Jessie Margaret Dean (*née* Gaunt); *m* 1957, Doris Ellen Webb. *Educ:* Ellesmere Coll., Shropshire; Exeter Coll., Oxford (MA, BLitt). Former President Oxford Univ. Conservative Assoc. and Oxford Carlton Club. Served War of 1939-45, Capt. Welsh Guards; ADC to Comdr 1 Corps BAOR. Farmer, 1950-56. Resident Tutor, Swinton Conservative Coll., 1957; Conservative Research Dept, 1957-64, Assistant Director from 1962; a Front Bench Spokesman on Health and Social Security, 1969-70; Parly Under-Sec. of State, DHSS, 1970-74. Formerly, Member Governing Body of Church in Wales. *Publications:* contributions to political pamphlets. *Recreation:* fishing. *Address:* Richmonte Lodge, East Harptree, near Bristol; House of Commons, SW1. *Clubs:* St Stephen's; Bath and County; Keynsham Conservative.

DEAN, Barbara Florence; Headmistress, Godolphin and Latymer School, Hammersmith, since 1974; *b* 1 Sept. 1924; *d* of Albert Sidney and Helen Catherine Dean. *Educ:* North London Collegiate Sch.; Girton Coll., Cambridge (MA); London Inst. of Educn (Teachers' Dipl.). Asst History Mistress, Roedean Sch., 1947-49; Godolphin and Latymer School: Asst History Mistress and Head of Dept, 1949-70; Deputy Headmistress, 1970-73. *Address:* 9 Stuart Avenue, Ealing, W5 3QJ. *T:* 01-992 8324.

DEAN, Basil, CBE 1947 (MBE 1918); Governing Director of B. D. Enterprises Ltd, since 1939, and of Basil Dean Productions, Ltd, 1926-64; Organised and was First Controller of Liverpool Repertory Theatre (The Playhouse) until 1913; Cheshire Regt, 1914; Captain, 1916; Director Entertainment Navy and Army Canteen Board, 1917; Joint Managing Director of Drury Lane Theatre, 1924-25; Managing Director of ReandeaN Co., St Martin's Theatre, London, 1919-25; founded and was first Chairman and Joint Managing Director Associated Talking Pictures, Ltd, ATP Studios, Ltd (re-named Ealing Studios), and their subsidiary companies, 1929-36; General European Representative of the Radio Keith Orpheum Corporation (USA); Chairman and Managing Director of Radio Keith Orpheum, Ltd, 1930-32; Shute Lecturer, Liverpool Univ., 1932-33; Director of National Service Entertainment, 1941; founder

and director-general of Entertainments National Service Assoc. (ENSA), 1939; Director of Entertainments Navy, Army, and Air Force Institutes, 1939; produced Flecker's Hassan (musical score by Delius), His Majesty's, 1923; A Midsummer Night's Dream, Drury Lane, 1924; other productions include The Skin Game, 1920; A Bill of Divorcement, 1921; Loyalties, 1922; The Constant Nymph, 1926; Young Woodley, 1928; The Circle of Chalk, 1929; Autumn Crocus, 1931; Call it a Day, 1935; When we are Married, 1938; Johnson over Jordan, 1939; The Diary of a Nobody, 1954; Who Cares?, 1956; Touch It Light, 1958; devised and presented Cathedral Steps before St Paul's Cathedral, and Coventry Cathedral, 1942, Salute to the Red Army, for Ministry of Information, Albert Hall, 1943; re-produced Hassan for South African National Theatre, 1950 and for Dublin Drama Festival, 1960. Mem. of Council, and Chm. Finance and Gen. Purposes Cttee, RADA, until 1972. *Publications:* various plays and pamphlets, including Marriages are made in Heaven (Manchester, 1908); Mother to be, Effie (Manchester, 1909); The Love Cheats (London, 1910); (with Barry Jackson) Fifinella (London, 1919); part author (with Margaret Kennedy) of Come with Me, 1928; (with George Munro), Murder Gang, 1933; The Actor and his Workshop, 1922; The Theatre in Emergency, 1939; The Theatre in Reconstruction, 1945; wrote official history of ENSA (The Theatre at War), 1956; *dramatisations:* The Constant Nymph (with Margaret Kennedy), 1926; Beau Geste (with P. C. Wren, 1928); Sleeveless Errand (with Norah James), 1933; The Heart of the Matter (with Graham Greene), 1949; The Diary of a Nobody (original book of George and Weedon Grossmith), 1954; *autobiography:* Vol 1, Seven Ages, 1970; Vol 2, Mind's Eye, 1973. *Address:* 102 Dorset House, Gloucester Place, NW1. *T:* 01-935 6154. *Club:* Garrick.
See also J. J. Dean, W. B. Dean.

DEAN, Brenda; Secretary, SOGAT Manchester Branch, since 1972; *b* 29 April 1943; *d* of Hugh Dean and Lillian Dean. *Educ:* St Andrews Junior Sch., Eccles; Stretford High Sch. for Girls. Admin. Sec., SOGAT, 1959-72. Member: Printing and Publishing Trng Bd, 1974-; Women's National Commn, 1975-; Supplementary Benefits Commn, 1976-; Price Commn, 1977-. *Recreations:* driving, reading, relaxing, thinking! *Address:* 32 Woodley Avenue, Thornton, Cleveleys, Lancs. *T:* Cleveleys 77997.

DEAN, (Charles) Raymond, QC 1963; **His Honour Judge Dean;** a Circuit Judge (formerly Judge of County Courts), since 1971; *b* 28 March 1923; *s* of late Joseph Irvin Gledhill Dean and late Lilian Dean (*née* Waddington); *m* 1948, Pearl Doreen (*née* Buncall); one *s* one *d*. *Educ:* Hipperholme Grammar Sch.; The Queen's Coll., Oxford (1941-42 and 1945-47). RAF Flying Duties, 1942-45 (Flt Lieut). BA (Jurisprudence) 1947, MA 1948; called to Bar, Lincoln's Inn, 1948; Deputy Chairman, West Riding QS, 1961-65; Recorder: of Rotherham, 1962-65; of Newcastle upon Tyne, 1965-70; of Kingston-upon-Hull, 1970-71. *Recreations:* fishing, motoring, reading, Rugby Union (now non-playing), golf. *Address:* 34 Oakwood Lane, Leeds, West Yorks. *T:* Leeds 655266. *Club:* Leeds.

DEAN, Col Donald John, VC 1918; OBE 1961; TD; DL; JP; *b* 1897; *m* 1923, Marjorie, *d* of late W. R. Wood; one *s* one *d*. Served European War, 1914-18 (despatches, VC); War of 1939-45 (despatches). JP 1951, DL 1957, Kent. Comdr Royal Danish Order of the Dannebrog. *Address:* 1 Park Avenue, Sittingbourne, Kent ME10 1QX.

DEAN, Eric Walter, CB 1968; CBE 1958; retired; *b* 5 March 1906; *s* of late Thomas W. Dean, London; *m* 1935, Joan Mary, *d* of late L. A. Stanley, Folkestone; one *d*. *Educ:* Forest Sch.; Exeter Coll., Oxford. Called to Bar, Inner Temple, 1931. Solicitors Dept, Board of Trade, 1935-58; Asst Solicitor, 1947-61; Principal Asst Solicitor, 1961-68, retired. *Recreations:* music, horse-racing. *Address:* 18 The Beeches, Brighton BN1 5LS. *T:* Brighton 509777. *Club:* Bath.

DEAN, Frederick Harold, CB 1976; Judge Advocate General since 1972; *b* 5 Nov. 1908; *o c* of late Frederick Richard Dean and Alice Dean (*née* Baron), Manchester; *m* 1st, 1939, Gwendoline Mary Eayrs Williams (marr. diss., 1966; she *d* 1975); 3rd *d* of late Rev. W. Williams, Kingsley, Staffs; one *s* one *d*; 2nd, 1966, Sybil Marshall Dennis (*d* 1977), *o c* of late Col F. B. M. Chatterton, CMG, CBE. *Educ:* Manchester Grammar Sch.; Manchester Univ. LLB 1930; LLM 1932. Called to Bar, Middle Temple, 1933. Practised on Northern Circuit, 1934-40 and 1945-50. Served in RAFVR, 1940-45 in UK, Iraq, Egypt and E Africa (Sqdn Ldr). AJAG, 1950; DJAG: Far East, 1954-57 and 1962-65; Middle East, 1958-61; Germany, 1967-68; Vice Judge Advocate General, 1968-72. *Publication:* Bibliography of the History of Military and Martial Law (in composite vol.,

Guide to the Sources of British Military History, 1971). *Recreations:* travel, walking, music, reading. *Address:* The Old Farmhouse, Lower Street, Quainton, Aylesbury, Bucks HP22 4BL. *T:* Quainton 263. *Club:* Athenæum.

DEAN, Sir John (Norman), Kt 1957; *b* 13 Dec. 1899; *s* of late George Dean; *m* 1st, 1935, Charlotte Helen Audrey (*d* 1973), *d* of late Thomas Atkinson Walker; one *s*; 2nd, 1974, Isabel Bothwell-Thomson. *Educ:* Felsted; King's Coll., London University. BSc London (Hons Chemistry). Flying Officer, RNAS and RAF, 1916-19. Chairman: The Telegraph Construction and Maintenance Co. Ltd, 1954-61; Submarine Cables Ltd, 1960-63; Asst to President, General Cable Corporation of New York, USA, 1964-69, retd. ARIC; FIRI; Comp. IEE. *Publications:* various, to technical and scientific bodies. *Recreation:* gardening. *Address:* Kiln Ridge, Ide Hill, Sevenoaks, Kent TN14 6JH. *T:* Ide Hill 245. *Club:* Army and Navy.

DEAN, Joseph Jabez; MP (Lab) Leeds West, since Feb. 1974; *b* 1923. Engineer; formerly Shop Steward, AUEW. Formerly Leader, Manchester City Council. PPS to Minister of State, CSD, 1974-77. *Address:* House of Commons, SW1A 0AA.

DEAN, Joseph (Jolyon); His Honour Judge Joseph Dean; a Circuit Judge, South Eastern Circuit, since 1975; *b* 26 April 1921; *s* of Basil Dean, *qv*; *m* 1962, Jenefer Mills; one *s* two *d*. *Educ:* Elstree Sch.; Harrow Sch.; Merton Coll., Oxford (MA Classics and Law). 51st (Highland) Div., RA, 1942-45. Called to the Bar, Middle Temple, 1947; Bencher 1972. *Publication:* Hatred, Ridicule or Contempt, 1953 (paperback edns 1955 and 1964). *Recreation:* domestic maintenance. *Address:* The Hall, West Brabourne, Ashford, Kent. *T:* Sellindge 2267; 4 Brick Court, Temple, EC4.
See also Winton Dean.

DEAN, Sir Maurice (Joseph), KCB 1957 (CB 1946); KCMG 1949; *b* 16 Sept. 1906; *y s* of late W. J. Dean, Purley, Surrey; *m* 1943, Anne, *d* of W. F. Gibson, Cardiff; one *s* one *d*. *Educ:* St Olave's; Trinity Coll., Cambridge. Mathematical Tripos Part I, 1926; Part II, 1928; Mayhew Prize. Asst Principal, Air Ministry, 1929; Asst Under-Secretary of State, 1943; Deputy Secretary, Control Office for Germany and Austria, 1946; Deputy Under-Secretary of State, Foreign Office (German Section), 1947-48; Deputy Secretary, Ministry of Defence, 1948-52; Third Secretary, HM Treasury, 1952; Second Secretary, Board of Trade, 1952-55; Permanent Under-Secretary of State, Air Ministry, 1955-63; a Second Secretary, HM Treasury, Nov. 1963-64; Joint Permanent Under-Secretary of State, Dept of Education and Science, April-Oct. 1964; Permanent Secretary, Ministry of Technology, 1964-66. Dir, British Printing Corp., 1966-71. Co-opted, Member Cambridge Univ. Appointments Board, 1957-60; Member Cambridge Univ. Women's Appointments Board, 1963-76. Chairman, London Advisory Board, Salvation Army, 1968-76. Visiting Prof., Dept of Administration, Strathclyde Univ., 1966-76. Councillor, Bedford Coll., Univ. of London, 1972-76. Hon. LLD Strathclyde, 1970. *Address:* 27 Bathgate Road, SW19. *T:* 01-946 0290. *Clubs:* United Oxford & Cambridge University; Royal Wimbledon (Golf).
See also P. A. R. Brown.

DEAN, Sir Patrick (Henry), GCMG 1963 (KCMG 1957; CMG 1947); Chairman, Cambridge Petroleum Royalties, since 1975; Director, Taylor Woodrow, since 1969; International Adviser, American Express, since 1969; Director, Ingersoll-Rand Holdings, since 1971; Director of Governing Body: Rugby School, since 1972; English-Speaking Union, since 1972; *b* 16 March 1909; *o s* of late Professor H. R. Dean and Irene, *d* of Charles Arthur Wilson; *m* 1947, Patricia Wallace, *y d* of late T. Frame Jackson; two *s*. *Educ:* Rugby Sch.; Gonville and Caius Coll., Cambridge. Classical Scholar, Gonville and Caius Coll., 1928; First Class Hons, Classical Tripos Part I; Law Tripos Parts 1 and 2, 1929-32; Fellow of Clare Coll., Cambridge, 1932-35; called to the Bar, 1934; Barstow Law Scholar, Inns of Court, 1934; practised at Bar, 1934-39; Asst Legal Adviser, Foreign Office, 1939-45; Head of German Political Dept, FO, 1946-50; Minister at HM Embassy, Rome, 1950-51; Senior Civilian Instructor at Imperial Defence Coll., 1952-53; Asst Under-Secretary of State, Foreign Office, 1953-56; Dep. Under-Secretary of State, Foreign Office, 1956-60; Permanent Representative of the United Kingdom to the United Nations, 1960-64; Ambassador in Washington, 1965-69. Mem., Departmental Cttee to examine operation of Section 2 of Official Secrets Act, 1971. Hon. Fellow, Clare Coll. and Gonville and Caius Coll., Cambridge, 1965. Hon. Bencher, Lincoln's Inn, 1965. Hon. LLD Lincoln Wesleyan Univ., 1961, Chattanooga Univ., 1962, Hofstra Univ., 1964, Columbia Univ., 1965,

University of South Carolina, 1967, College of William and Mary, 1968. KStJ 1971. *Publications:* various articles and notes in the Law Quarterly Review. *Recreations:* mountains, walking, shooting. *Address:* 5 Bentinck Mansions, Bentinck Street, W1. *T:* 01-935 0881. *Club:* Brooks's.
See also Rt. Hon. Sir E. W. Roskill.

DEAN, Paul; *see* Dean, A. P.

DEAN, Dr Paul; Director, National Physical Laboratory, since 1977 (Deputy Director, 1974-76); *b* 23 Jan. 1933; *s* of late Sydney and Rachel Dean; *m* 1961, Sheila Valerie Gamse; one *s* one *d*. *Educ:* Hackney Downs Grammar Sch.; Queen Mary Coll., Univ. of London. BSc, PhD; FInstP, FIMA. National Physical Laboratory: Sen. Sci. Officer, 1957; Principal Sci. Officer, 1963; Sen. Principal Sci. Officer (Individual Merit), 1967; Head of Central Computer Unit, 1967; Supt, Div. of Quantum Metrology, 1969; Under-Sec., DoI (Head of Space and Air Res. and R&D Contractors Divs), 1976-77. *Publications:* numerous papers and articles in learned jls. *Recreations:* chess, music. *Address:* 39 Banstead Road South, Sutton, Surrey SM2 5LG.

DEAN, Rt. Rev. Ralph Stanley; Theological Consultant, Christ Church, Greenville, SC, since 1973; *b* London, 1913; *m* 1939, Irene Florence, *er d* of late Alfred Bezzant Wakefield. *Educ:* Roan Sch., Greenwich; Wembley County Sch.; London Coll. of Divinity, BD London 1938; ALCD 1938; MTh 1944. Deacon 1938; Priest 1939; Curate of St Mary, Islington, 1938-41; Curate-in-charge, St Luke, Watford, 1941-45; Chaplain and Tutor, London Coll. of Divinity, 1945-47, Vice-Principal, 1947-51; Principal, Emmanuel Coll., Saskatoon, Canada, 1951-56; Incumbent of Sutherland and Hon. Canon of Saskatoon, 1955-56; Bishop of Cariboo, 1957; Anglican Executive Officer, 1964-69; Archbishop of Cariboo and Metropolitan of British Columbia, 1971-73. Episcopal Secretary, Lambeth Conference, 1968. Hon. DD: Wycliffe Coll., Toronto, 1953; Emmanuel Coll., Saskatoon, 1957; Anglican Theolog. Coll., Vancouver, 1965; Huron Coll., Ont, 1965; Hon. STD, Hartford Coll., Conn, 1966. *Publications:* In the Light of the Cross, 1961; article on Anglican Communion, Encyclopædia Britannica. *Address:* Christ Church, Greenville, South Carolina 29601, USA.

DEAN, Raymond; *see* Dean, C. R.

DEAN, Dr William John Lyon, OBE 1959; Chairman, Herring Industry Board, since 1971 (Member, since 1963); *b* 4 Nov. 1911; *s* of William Dean, Lossiemouth; *m* 1938, Ellen Maud Mary, *d* of Charles Weatherill, CBE; two *s* one *d*. *Educ:* Elgin Academy; Aberdeen Univ. (MB, ChB). Served RAF, 1935-43. Gen. med. practice, 1943-66. Provost of Lossiemouth, 1949-58; Chm., Jt CC of Moray and Nairn, 1964-71; Mem. NE Regional Hosp. Bd, 1947-58. Member: Cttee for Scotland and Northern Ireland White Fish Authority, 1954-; White Fish Authority, 1963-. *Publication:* Safety at Sea in Fishing Vessels, 1969 (FAO/ILO/WHO). *Recreation:* fishing (lobster, salmon, trout). *Address:* 6 Ravelston Heights, Edinburgh EH4 3LX. *T:* 031-332 9172. *Club:* New (Edinburgh).

DEAN, Winton (Basil), FBA 1975; author and musical scholar; *b* Birkenhead, 18 March 1916; *e s* of Basil Dean, *qv*, and Esther, *d* of A. H. Van Gruisen; *m* 1939, Hon. Thalia Mary Shaw, 2nd *d* of 2nd Baron Craigmyle; one *s* one adopted *d* (and two *d* decd). *Educ:* Harrow; King's Coll., Cambridge (MA). Translated libretto of Weber's opera Abu Hassan (Arts Theatre, Cambridge) 1938. Served War of 1939-45: in Admiralty (Naval Intelligence Div.), 1944-45. Member: Music Panel, Arts Council, 1957-60, Cttee of Handel Opera Society (London), 1955-60; Council, Royal Musical Assoc., 1965- (Vice-Pres., 1970-). Ernest Bloch Prof. of Music, University of California (Berkeley), 1965-66. Ed, with Sarah Fuller, Handel's opera Julius Caesar (Barber Inst. of Fine Arts, Birmingham), 1977. Hon. RAM 1971. *Publications:* The Frogs of Aristophanes (trans. of choruses to music by Walter Leigh), 1937; Bizet (Master Musicians), 1948 (3rd rev. edn, 1975); Carmen, 1949; Introduction to the Music of Bizet, 1950; Franck, 1950; Hambledon v Feathercombe, the Story of a Village Cricket Match, 1951; Handel's Dramatic Oratorios and Masques, 1959; Shakespeare and Opera (Shakespeare in Music), 1964; Georges Bizet, His Life and Work, 1965; Handel and the Opera Seria, 1969; Beethoven and Opera (in The Beethoven Companion), 1971; ed, Handel, Three Ornamented Arias, 1976; (ed) E. J. Dent, The Rise of Romantic Opera, 1976; contributed to Grove's Dictionary of Music and Musicians (5th edn) and to musical periodicals and learned journals. *Recreations:* cricket, shooting; naval history. *Address:* Hambledon Hurst, Godalming, Surrey. *T:* Wormley 2644.
See also J. J. Dean.

DEANE, family name of **Baron Muskerry.**

DEANE, Major Donald Victor, CIE 1947; CBE 1959 (OBE 1941); RE (retired); Consultant to International Nickel Ltd, 1961-73; *b* 19 Oct. 1902; *s* of late V. M. Deane, Braiswick, Colchester, Essex; *m* 1929, Dorothy Doreen Cuerden; two *d. Educ:* Gresham's Sch., Holt; RMA, Woolwich. Commissioned into RE, 1922; proceeded to India, 1925; selected for special employment in Indian Mints, 1932; Mint Master, Calcutta, 1938. Retired from Army, 1947. Senior Master of the Indian Govt Mints, 1947-57, retired. 1939-45 Star; India General Service, Silver Jubilee, War, and India Service medals. *Recreation:* golf. *Address:* Tara, Fauvic, Jersey, CI. *T:* Jersey Central 53272. *Club:* Royal Jersey Golf.

DEANE, Phyllis Mary; Reader in Economic History, University of Cambridge, since 1971; Fellow of Newnham College since 1961; *b* 13 Oct. 1918; *d* of John Edward Deane and Elizabeth Jane Brooks; single. *Educ:* Chatham County Sch.; Hutcheson's Girls' Grammar Sch., Glasgow; Univ. of Glasgow. MA Hons Econ. Science Glasgow 1940; MA Cantab; FRHistS. Carnegie Research Scholar, 1940-41; Research Officer, Nat. Inst. of Econ. and Social Research, 1941-45; Colonial Research Officer, 1946-48; Research Officer: HM Colonial Office, 1948-49; Cambridge Univ. Dept of Applied Econs, 1950-61; Lectr, Faculty of Econs and Politics, Univ. of Cambridge, 1961-71. Vis. Prof., Univ. of Pittsburgh, 1969. Editor, Economic Jl, 1968-75. *Publications:* (with Julian Huxley) The Future of the Colonies, 1945; The Measurement of Colonial National Incomes, 1948; Colonial Social Accounting, 1953; (with W. A. Cole) British Economic Growth 1688-1959, 1962; The First Industrial Revolution, 1965; papers and reviews in econ. jls. *Recreations:* walking, gardening. *Address:* 4 Stukeley Close, Cambridge CB3 9LT.

DEANE-DRUMMOND, Maj.-Gen. Anthony John, CB 1970; DSO 1960; MC 1942 and Bar, 1945; Director, Paper and Paper Products Industry Training Board, since 1971; *b* 23 June 1917; *s* of late Col J. D. Deane-Drummond, DSO, OBE, MC; *m* 1944, Mary Evangeline Boyd; four *d. Educ:* Marlborough Coll.; RMA, Woolwich. Commissioned Royal Signals, 1937. War Service in Europe and N Africa; POW, Italy, 1941 (escaped, 1942); Staff Coll., 1945; Bde Major, 3rd Parachute Bde, 1946-47; Instructor, Sandhurst, 1949-51 and Staff Coll., 1952-55; CO, 22 Special Air Service Regt, 1957-60; Bde Comdr, 44 Parachute Bde, 1961-63; Asst Comdt, RMA, Sandhurst, 1963-66; GOC 3rd Division, 1966-68; ACDS (Operations), 1968-70, retired 1971. Col Comdt, Royal Corps of Signals, 1966-71. *Publications:* Return Ticket, 1951; Riot Control, 1975. *Recreations:* gliding (Pilot, British Team, 1958, 1960, 1963, 1965; British Gliding Champion, 1957). *Address:* c/o Williams & Glyn's Bank Ltd, Lombard Street, EC3. *Club:* Army and Navy.

DEANS, Rodger William, CB 1977; Solicitor to Secretary of State for Scotland and Solicitor in Scotland to HM Treasury, since 1971; *b* 21 Dec. 1917; *s* of Andrew and Elizabeth Deans, Perth; *m* 1943, Joan Radley; one *s* one *d. Educ:* Perth Academy; Edinburgh Univ. Qual. Solicitor in Scotland, 1939. Served in RA and REME, 1939-46 (Major); Mil. Prosecutor, Palestine, 1945-46; Procurator Fiscal Depute, Edinburgh, 1946-47; entered Office of Solicitor to Sec. of State for Scotland, 1947; Scottish Office: Legal Asst, 1947-50; Sen. Legal Asst, 1951-62; Asst Solicitor, 1962-71. *Recreations:* mountaineering, curling, golfing, etc. *Address:* 25 Grange Road, Edinburgh EH9 1UQ. *T:* 031-667 1893. *Clubs:* Royal Commonwealth Society; Scottish Arts (Edinburgh).

DEARBERGH, Geoffrey Frederick; Registrar in Bankruptcy of High Court; Clerk of the Restrictive Practices Court; *b* 15 March 1924; *s* of Tom and Blanche Dearbergh; *m* 1954, Elizabeth Mary Bryant; two *d. Educ:* Winchester College. Served in Army (60th Rifles), 1942-47. Called to Bar, Inner Temple, 1948. *Address:* 10 Pembroke Road, W8 6NT. *T:* 01-602 5888.

DEARE, Ronald Frank Robert; Counsellor (Overseas Development), British Embassy, Washington, and Alternate Executive Director of the World Bank, since 1976; *b* 9 Oct. 1927; *s* of late Albert Victor Deare and of Lilian Deare; *m* 1952, Iris Mann; one *s. Educ:* Wellington Sch., Somerset. RAF Service, 1945-48. CO 1948; Second Sec., UK Commn, Singapore, 1959; CO, 1962; Dept of Technical Cooperation, 1963; Principal, Min. of Overseas Develt, 1965; Private Sec. to Minister of Overseas Develt, 1971; Asst Sec., 1973. *Recreations:* reading, gardening. *Address:* c/o British Embassy, 3100 Massachusetts Avenue, Washington, DC 20008, USA; 10 Fairford Close, Haywards Heath, West Sussex RH16 3EF. *T:* Haywards Heath 50590.

DEARING, Ronald Ernest; Deputy Secretary, Department of Industry, since 1976; *b* 27 July 1930; *s* of E. H. A. Dearing and M. T. Dearing (*née* Hoyle); *m* 1954, Margaret Patricia Riley; two *d. Educ:* Doncaster Grammar Sch.; Hull Univ. (BScEcon); London Business Sch. (Sloan Fellow). Min. of Labour and Nat. Service, 1946-49; Min. of Power, 1949-62; HM Treasury, 1962-64; Min. of Power, Min. of Technology, DTI, 1965-72; Regional Dir, N Region, DTI, 1972-74, and Under-Sec., DTI later Dept of Industry, 1972-76. MBIM. *Recreations:* cricket, chess, gardening. *Address:* 15 Embercourt Road, Thames Ditton, Surrey.

DEARNLEY, Christopher Hugh, MA (Oxon), BMus, FRCO; Organist of St Paul's Cathedral since 1968; *b* 11 Feb. 1930; 3rd *s* of Rev. Charles Dearnley; *m* 1957, Bridget (*née* Wateridge); three *s* one *d. Educ:* Cranleigh Sch., Surrey; Worcester Coll., Oxford. Organ Scholar, Worcester Coll., Oxford, 1948-52. Asst Organist, Salisbury Cathedral, and Music Master, the Cathedral Sch., Salisbury, 1954-57; Organist and Master of the Choristers, Salisbury Cathedral, 1957-67. Pres., Incorporated Assoc. of Organists, 1968-70; Chm., Friends of Cathedral Music, 1971-. *Publications:* The Treasury of English Church Music, Vol. III, 1965; English Church Music 1650-1750, 1970. *Recreations:* sketching, bicycling, gardening. *Address:* 5 Amen Court, EC4.

DEARNLEY, Gertrude, MD, BS London; FRCOG; Gynæcological Surgeon, retired; *d* of late Rev. T. W. Dearnley, MA Oxon. *Educ:* Liverpool High Sch.; London (Royal Free Hospital) School of Medicine for Women. *Recreation:* gardening. *Address:* Mill Cottage, Ewood, Newdigate, Surrey. *T:* Newdigate 286.

DEAS, (James) Stewart, MA, BMus, Hon. FTCL; James Rossiter Hoyle Professor of Music in the University of Sheffield, 1948-68, Emeritus Professor, since 1969; Dean of the Faculty of Arts, University of Sheffield, 1955-58; *b* 19 June 1903; *e s* of John Mackenzie Deas, Asst Keeper HM General Register House, Edinburgh and Elizabeth Bryce Cooper; *m* 1936, Hilda Jamieson; one *s* two *d. Educ:* George Watson's Coll.; Edinburgh Univ. MA 1924, BMus 1929, Bucher Scholar, 1926-30, in Berlin and Basle. Studied with Sir Donald Tovey and Felix Weingartner. Conductor Edinburgh Opera Co., 1931-33; music critic, Glasgow Evening Times, 1934-35; Director of South African Coll. of Music and Prof. of Music, University of Cape Town, 1935-38; war service Foreign Office and BBC; music critic, The Scotsman, London, 1939-44, Edinburgh (Editorial Staff), 1944-48; Conductor Edinburgh Chamber Orchestra, 1946-48; Member BBC Scottish Music Advisory Cttee, 1947-48; Member Council, Programme Cttee, Edinburgh International Festival, 1946-48; has been Guest Conductor of various orchestras including Hallé, London Symphony, Royal Philharmonic, BBC Scottish, Cape Town Municipal and Hovingham Festival. Conductor, Sheffield Chamber Orchestra, 1951-68; Chairman, Sheffield Bach Society, 1959-63. Contributor, weekly music page, Country Life, 1966-73. *Publications:* In Defence of Hanslick, 1940, 2nd edn 1973; Or Something, 1941; contrib. Felix Weingartner, 1976; articles in Music and Letters and other periodicals. *Address:* 1 The Slade, Froxfield, near Petersfield, Hants. *T:* Hawkley 346. *Clubs:* Savile, Arts.

DEAVIN, Stanley Gwynne, CBE 1971 (OBE 1958); FCA; Chartered Accountant; Chairman, North Eastern Gas Board, 1966-71, retired (Dep. Chairman, 1961-66); *b* 8 Aug. 1905; *s* of Percy John Deavin and Annie (*née* Crayton); *m* 1934, Louise Faviell; one *s* one *d. Educ:* Hymer's Coll., Hull. Firm of Chartered Accountants, 1921-33; Secretary and Accountant, Preston Gas Co., 1933-49; North Western Gas Board: Secretary, 1949-61; Member Board, 1960-61. OStJ. *Recreations:* cricket, Rugby football, theatre. *Address:* 50 Hookstone Drive, Harrogate, North Yorks. *T:* Harrogate 884301. *Clubs:* Royal Automobile; Yorks County Cricket.

DeBAKEY, Prof. Michael Ellis, MD, MS; President, Baylor College of Medicine, since 1969 (Professor of Surgery and Chairman of Department of Surgery since 1948, Chief Executive Officer, 1968-69, Baylor University College of Medicine; Vice-President for Medical Affairs, Baylor University, 1968-69); Surgeon-in-Chief, Ben Taub General Hospital, Houston, Texas; Director: Cardiovascular Research and Training Center, Methodist Hospital (Houston), since 1968; National Heart and Blood Vessel Research and Demonstration Center; Consultant in Surgery to various Hospitals etc., in Texas, and to Walter Reed Army Hospital, Washington, DC; *b* 7 Sept. 1908; *s* of Shaker Morris and Raheija Zerba DeBakey; *m* 1936, Diana Cooper (*d* 1972); four *s. Educ:* Tulane Univ., New Orleans, La, USA (Distinguished Alumnus of Year, 1974). Residency in New Orleans, Strasbourg, and Heidelberg, 1933-36; Instructor, Dept of Surgery, Tulane Univ., 1937-40; Asst Prof. of Surgery, 1940-46; Associate Prof. of Surgery, 1946-48. Colonel Army of US (Reserve). In Office of Surgeon-General, 1942-46, latterly Director Surgical Consultant Div. (Meritorious Civilian Service Medal, 1970). Chairman, President's Commission on Heart Disease, Cancer and Stroke, 1964; US Chm., Task for Mechanical Circulatory Assistance, Jt US-USSR Cttee, 1974; has served on governmental and university cttees, etc., concerned with public health, research and medical education. Mem. Adv. Editorial Bds: Coeur, 1969-; Biomedical Materials and Artificial Organs, 1971-. Member and Hon. Member of medical societies, including: American Assoc. for Thoracic Surgery (Pres. 1959); Hon. Fellow, RCS, 1974; International Cardiovascular Society (Pres. 1959); BMA (Hon. Foreign Corresp. Member 1966); Royal Society Med., London; Acad. of Medical Sciences, USSR; US—China Physicians Friendship Assoc., 1974. Has received numerous awards from American and foreign medical institutions, and also honorary doctorates; Hektoen Gold Medal, Amer. Med. Assoc., 1970. *Publications:* The Blood Bank and the Technique and Therapeutics of Transfusions, 1942; (with B. M. Cohen) Buerger's Disease, 1962; A Surgeon's Diary of a Visit to China, 1974; The Living Heart, 1977; contributions to standard textbooks of medicine and surgery, Current Therapy, and many symposia; Editor, Year Book of General Surgery, etc.; numerous articles in medical journals. *Recreations:* hunting, music. *Address:* Baylor College of Medicine, 1200 Moursund Avenue, Houston, Texas 77030, USA. *T:* 797-9353; 5323 Cherokee, Houston, Texas 77005, USA. *Clubs:* Cosmos, University Federal (Washington, DC); River Oaks Country (Houston, Texas).

de BEER, Esmond Samuel, CBE 1969; FBA 1965; FSA, FRSL, FRHistSoc; historical scholar, specialising in seventeenth-century English history; engaged in editing John Locke correspondence; *b* 1895; *s* of I. S. de Beer and Emily, *d* of Bendix Hallenstein, Dunedin, NZ. *Educ:* Mill Hill Sch.; New Coll., Oxford (MA); University College, London (MA). Studied under late Sir Charles Firth. A Trustee, National Portrait Gallery, 1959-67. Independent Member, Reviewing Cttee on Export of Works of Art, 1965-70. Fellow University College, London, 1967. Hon. Fellow, New Coll., Oxford; Hon. DLitt (Durham, Oxford); Hon. LittD (Otago). Hon. Vice-Pres., the Historical Association; Pres., Hakluyt Society, 1972- (Hon. Vice-Pres., 1966). *Publications:* first complete edition of Diary of John Evelyn, 195; (ed) The Correspondence of John Locke, vols I, II, III and IV, 1976-77; articles and reviews in learned periodicals, etc. *Address:* 31 Brompton Square, SW3 2AE. *T:* 01-584 5687. *Club:* Athenæum.

DEBENHAM, Sir Gilbert Ridley, 3rd Bt, *cr* 1931; *b* 28 June 1906; 2nd *s* of Sir Ernest Ridley Debenham, 1st Bt, JP; *S* brother, Sir Piers Debenham, 2nd Bt, 1964; *m* 1935, Violet Mary, *e d* of late His Honour Judge (George Herbert) Higgins; three *s* one *d*. *Educ:* Eton; Trinity Coll., Cambridge. *Heir:* *s* George Andrew Debenham [*b* 10 April 1938; *m* 1969, Penelope Jane, *d* of John David Armishaw Carter; one *s* one *d*]. *Address:* Tonerspuddle Farm, Dorchester, Dorset.

DEBENHAM TAYLOR, John, CMG 1967; OBE 1959; TD 1967; HM Diplomatic Service; Foreign and Commonwealth Office, since 1973; *b* 25 April 1920; *s* of John Francis Taylor and Harriett Beatrice (*née* Williams); *m* 1966, Gillian May James; one *d*. *Educ:* Aldenham School. Eastern Counties Farmers Assoc. Ltd, Ipswich and Great Yarmouth, 1936-39. Commd in RA (TA), Feb. 1939; served War of 1939-46 in Finland, Middle East, UK and SE Asia (despatches, 1946). Foreign Office, 1946; Control Commn for Germany, 1947-49; 2nd Sec., Bangkok, 1950; Actg Consul, Songkhla, 1951-52; Vice-Consul, Hanoi, 1952-53; FO, 1953-54; 1st Sec., Bangkok, 1954-56; FO, 1956-58; Singapore, 1958-59; FO, 1960-64; Counsellor, 1964; Counsellor: Kuala Lumpur, 1964-66; FCO (formerly FO), 1966-69; Washington, 1969-72; Paris, 1972-73. *Recreations:* walking, reading, history. *Address:* c/o Foreign and Commonwealth Office, SW1. *Clubs:* Travellers', Naval and Military.

de BOER, Anthony Peter; Chairman, Attock Oil Co., since 1974; Director: Tarmac Ltd, since 1971; Steel Brothers Holdings Ltd since 1971; Tomatin Distillers Co. Ltd, since 1971; Chloride Group, since 1976; National Bus Co., since 1969; Chairman: Keep Britain Tidy Group, since 1969; British Road Federation, since 1972; *b* 22 June 1918; *s* of Goffe de Boer and Irene Kathleen (*née* Grist), *m* 1942, Pamela Agnes Norah Bullock; one *s*. *Educ:* Westminster School. Served War of 1939-45: RE (AA), 1939-40; Indian Army, 6th Gurkha Rifles, 1940-43; RIASC, 1944-46; Major 1944. Joined Royal Dutch/Shell Gp, 1937: served in China, Sudan, Ethiopia, Egypt, Palestine, 1946-58; Area Co-ordinator, Africa and Middle East, 1959-63; Chm., Shell Trinidad, 1963-64; Man. Dir, Marketing, Shell Mex & BP,

1964-67. Mem. Bd, British Travel Assoc., 1965-67; Dep. Chm., Wm Cory & Son, 1968-71; Dep. Chm., Associated Heat Services Ltd, 1969-76; Director: British Transport Advertising, 1973-; Internat. Road Fedn, 1974-; Mem. Council, Sussex Univ., 1969-; Chm., Indep. Schools Careers Org; Pres., Fuel Luncheon Club, 1967-69; Dir, Brighton and Hove Albion Football Club, 1969-72. Freeman, City of London; Liveryman, Coach Makers' and Coach Harness Makers' Co. FBIM 1970 (Mem. Council 1974). *Recreations:* football, racing, theatre. *Address:* Halletts Barn, Ditchling Common, Hassocks, Sussex. *T:* Hassocks 2442. *Clubs:* Garrick, East India, Devonshire, Sports and Public Schools.

de BONO, Dr Edward Francis Charles Publius; Lecturer in Medicine, Department of Investigative Medicine, University of Cambridge, since 1976; Director of The Cognitive Research Trust, Cambridge, since 1971; *b* 19 May 1933; *s* of late Prof. Joseph de Bono, CBE and of Josephine de Bono; *m* 1971, Josephine Hall-White; two *s*. *Educ:* St Edward's Coll., Malta; Royal Univ. of Malta; Christ Church, Oxford (Rhodes Scholar). BSc, MD Malta; DPhil Oxon; PhD Cantab. Research Asst, Dept of Regius Prof. of Medicine, Univ. of Oxford, 1958-60; Jun. Lectr in Med., Oxford, 1960-61; Asst Dir of Res., Dept of Investigative Medicine, Cambridge Univ., 1963-76. Research Associate: also Hon. Registrar, St Thomas' Hosp. Med. Sch., Univ. of London; Harvard Med. Sch., and Hon. Consultant, Boston City Hosp., 1965-66. *Publications:* The Use of Lateral Thinking, 1967; The Five-Day Course in Thinking, 1968; The Mechanism of Mind, 1969; Lateral Thinking: a textbook of creativity, 1970; The Dog Exercising Machine, 1970; Technology Today, 1971; Practical Thinking, 1971; Lateral Thinking for Management, 1971; Beyond Yes and No, 1972; Children Solve Problems, 1972; Eureka!: an illustrated history of inventions from the wheel to the computer, 1974; Teaching Thinking, 1976; The Greatest Thinkers, 1976; Wordpower, 1977; The Happiness Purpose, 1977; The Case of the Disappearing Elephant, 1977; contribs to Nature, Lancet, Clinical Science, Amer. Jl of Physiology, etc. *Recreations:* polo, travel, toys, thinking. *Address:* Cranmer Hall, Fakenham, Norfolk. *Club:* Athenæum.

DEBRÉ, Michel Jean-Pierre; Deputy from La Réunion, French National Assembly, since 1963, re-elected 1967, 1968, 1973; *b* 15 Jan. 1912; *s* of Prof. Robert Debré and Dr Jeanne Debré (*née* Debat-Ponsan); *m* 1936, Anne-Marie Lemaresquier; four *s*. *Educ:* Lycée Louis-le-Grand; Faculté de Droit de Paris (LLD); Ecole Libre des Sciences Politiques; Cavalry Sch., Saumur. Auditeur, Conseil d'Etat, 1934; French Army, 1939-44; Commissaire de la République, Angers region, 1944-45; Saar Economic Mission, 1947; Secretary-General for German and Austrian Affairs, 1948. Senator from Indre et Loire, 1948, re-elected 1955; Minister of Justice, 1958-59; Prime Minister, 1959-62; Minister of Economic Affairs and Finances, 1966-68; Minister for Foreign Affairs, 1968-69; Minister for National Defence, 1969-73. Member Union des Démocrats pour la Vème République. Officer Légion d'Honneur, Croix de Guerre, Rosette of Résistance, Free French Medal, Medal of Escaped Prisoners. *Publications:* Refaire la France 1944; Demain la Paix, 1945; La Mort de l'Etat Républicain, 1948; La République et son Pouvoir, 1950; La République et ses Problèmes, 1951; Ces Princes qui nous Gouvernent, 1957; Au Service de la Nation, 1963; Jeunesse, quelle France te faut-il?, 1965; Une certaine idée de la France, 1972. *Recreation:* equitation. *Address:* 18 rue Spontini, Paris 16e, France.

de BROGLIE, 7th Duc; Louis Victor de Broglie; Member of the Institut de France, Académie Française since 1944, Académie des Sciences since 1933; Professor, Faculté des Sciences, Paris, since 1932; Foreign Member Royal Society (London) since 1953; *b* Dieppe, 15 Aug. 1892; *s* of Victor, Duc de Broglie; *S* brother, Duc Maurice, 1960; unmarried. *Educ:* Lycée Janson de Sailly, Paris. Licencié ès Lettres, 1910; Licencié ès Sciences, 1913; served Radio-télégraphie Militaire, 1914-19; Docteur ès Sciences, 1924; Maître de Conférences, Faculté des Sciences, Paris, 1928. Permanent Sec., Académie des Sciences, 1942-75. Nobel Prize for Physics, 1929. *Publications:* Thèse de doctorat sur la théorie des Quanta, 1924; nombreux mémoires, articles, livres sur la physique, en particulier sur la théorie de Quanta et la mécanique ondulatoire et sur la philosophie des sciences. *Address:* 94 Perronet, 92 Neuilly-sur-Seine, France. *T:* Maillot 76.09.

de BROKE; *see* Willoughby de Broke.

de BRUYNE, Dirk, Knight, Order of Netherlands Lion, 1976; Managing Director, Royal Dutch/Shell Group of Companies, since 1971; President, Royal Dutch Petroleum Co., The Hague, since 1977 (Managing Director, 1974-77); *b* Rotterdam, Netherlands, 1 Sept. 1920; *s* of Dirk E. de Bruyne and Maria van

Alphen, Rotterdam; *m* 1945,Geertje Straub; one *s* one *d. Educ:* Erasmus Univ., Rotterdam (Grad. Econ.). Joined Royal Dutch/Shell Gp of Companies, 1945: served in: The Hague, 1945-55; Indonesia, 1955-58; London, 1958-60 (Dep. Gp Treasurer); The Hague, 1960-62 (Finance Manager); Italy, 1962-65 (Exec. Vice-Pres., Shell Italiana); London, 1965-68 (Regional Co-ordinator: Oil, Africa); Germany, 1968-70 (Pres., Deutsche Shell); Dir of Finance, Shell Petroleum Co. Ltd, 1970; Director: Shell Transport & Trading Co. Ltd, 1971-74; Shell Canada Ltd, 1977-; Chm., Shell Oil Co., USA, 1977-. *Recreations:* swimming, reading. *Address:* Shell Centre, SE1 7NA. *T:* 01-934 3868; 10 Kingston House, Princes Gate, SW7; De Schouwenburgh, Stoeplaan 9, Wassenaar, Netherlands. *Clubs:* Dutch (London); De Witte (The Hague).

de BRUYNE, Dr Norman Adrian, FRS 1967; Chairman, Techne Inc., since 1973 (President, 1967-73); *b* 8 Nov. 1904; *s* of Pieter Adriaan de Bruyne and Maud de Bruyne (*née* Mattock); *m* 1940, Elma Lilian Marsh; one *s* one *d. Educ:* Lancing Coll.; Trinity Coll., Cambridge. MA 1930, PhD 1930. Fellow of Trinity Coll., Cambridge, 1928-44. Managing Director: Aero Research Ltd, 1934-48; Ciba (ARL) Ltd, 1948-60; Techne (Cambridge) Ltd, 1964-67. Dir, Eastern Electricity Bd, 1962-67. Awarded Simms Gold Medal, RAeS, 1937. FInstP 1944; FRAeS 1955; Fellow, Fellowship of Engineering, 1976. *Recreation:* inventing. *Address:* 3700 Brunswick Pike, Princeton, New Jersey 08540, USA. *T:* 609-452 9275.

de BUNSEN, Sir Bernard, Kt 1962; CMG 1957; MA Oxon; Principal of Chester College, Chester, 1966-71; *b* 24 July 1907; *s* of late L. H. G. de Bunsen, and late Victoria de Bunsen (*née* Buxton); *m* 1975, Joan Allington Harmston, MBE. *Educ:* Leighton Park Sch.; Balliol Coll., Oxford. Schoolmaster, Liverpool Public Elementary Schools, 1930-34; Asst Director of Education, Wiltshire CC, 1934-38; HM Inspector of Schools, Ministry of Education, 1938-46; Director of Education, Palestine, 1946, until withdrawal of British administration, 1948; Professor of Education, Makerere University College, East Africa, 1948, acting Principal, Aug. 1949, Principal, 1950-64, Hon. Fellow, 1968. Vice-Chancellor of University of East Africa, 1963-65; Chairman: Africa Educational Trust, 1967-; Archbishops' Working Party on Future of Theological Colleges, 1967-68; Africa Bureau, 1971-; Vice-Pres., The Anti-Slavery Soc., 1975-. Hon LLD St Andrews, 1963. *Address:* 3 Prince Arthur Road, NW3. *T:* 01-435 3521.

DE BUTTS, Brig. Frederick Manus, CMG 1967; OBE 1961 (MBE 1943); DL; *b* 17 April 1916; *s* of late Brig. F. C. De Butts, CB, DSO, MC, and K. P. M. O'Donnell; *m* 1944, Evelyn Cecilia, *d* of Sir Walter Halsey, 2nd Bt; one *s* one *d. Educ:* Wellington Coll.; Oriel Coll., Oxford. Commissioned into Somerset LI, 1937. Served War of 1939-45, in Middle East, Italy, France and Germany. Staff Coll., 1944; Joint Services Staff Coll., 1954; Bt Lieut-Colonel, 1957; Commanded 3rd Bn Aden Protectorate Levies, 1958-60; Bde Colonel, Light Infantry, 1961-64; Comdr, Trucial Oman Scouts, 1964-67; HQ Home Counties District, Shorncliffe, Kent, 1967-68; Defence Attaché, Cairo, 1968-71; retired 1971; employed on contract as COS (Brig.), MoD, United Arab Emirates, 1971-73; Hon. Brig. 1973. Mem., Dacorum DC, 1976-. County Chm., Hertfordshire Scouts, 1973-76, County Comr, 1976-; Governor, Abbot's Hill School, 1971- (Chm., 1975-). DL Herts 1975. *Recreations:* tennis, sailing, riding, shooting. *Address:* The Old Vicarage, Great Gaddesden, Hemel Hempstead, Herts. *T:* Hemel Hempstead 62129.

DEBY, John Bedford; a Recorder of the Crown Court, since 1977; *b* 19 Dec. 1931; *s* of Reginald Bedford Deby and Irene (*née* Slater). *Educ:* Winchester Coll.; Trinity Coll., Cambridge (MA). Called to the Bar, Inner Temple, 1954. *Address:* 11 Britannia Road, Fulham, SW6 2HJ. *T:* 01-736 4976. *Club:* The Club (Sheffield).

de CANDOLE, Eric Armar Vully, CMG 1952; CBE 1950; MA; Sudan Political Service (retired); *b* 14 Sept. 1901; *e s* of late Rev. Armar Corry Vully de Candole, Rector of Ayot Saint Lawrence, Hertfordshire and late Edith Hodgson; *m* 1932, Marian Elizabeth Pender, *d* of Maj. H. Constable Roberts, DSO, MVO; three *s. Educ:* Colet Court; Aldenham Sch.; Worcester Coll., Oxford (Exhibitioner). Hons, Modern History, 1923, BA 1924, MA 1946. Joined Sudan Political Service, 1923; served in Education Dept as Tutor, Gordon Coll., 1923-27; Acting Warden, 1927-28; Berber, Khartoum and Darfur Provinces as Dist Comr and Magistrate, 1928-36; Resident, Dar Masalit, 1936-44; Bimbashi, SADF, 1940-44; Dep.-Governor, Northern Province, 1944-46; seconded to British Military Administration as Chief Secretary, Cyrenaica, 1946-48; Chief Administrator, Somalia, 1948; Chief Administrator, Cyrenaica, 1948-49;

HBM's Resident in Cyrenaica, 1949-51. With Kuwait Oil Co. Ltd, 1952-66. Order of the Nile, Egypt (4th class), 1934; Order of Istiqlal, Libya (1st class), 1954. *Publications:* articles on Middle East. *Recreations:* gardening, riding and travel. *Address:* Shootwood, Burley, Hants. *T:* Burley 2330. *Club:* Travellers'.

de CARDI, Beatrice Eileen, OBE 1973; retired 1973, but continuing archæological research in Lower Gulf countries; *b* 5 June 1914; *d* of Edwin Count de Cardi and Christine Berbette Wurrflein. *Educ:* St Paul's Girls' Sch.; University Coll. London (BA). Secretary (later Asst), London Museum, 1936-44; Personal Asst to Representative of Allied Supplies Exec. of War Cabinet in China, 1944-45; Asst UK Trade Comr: Delhi, 1946; Karachi, 1947; Lahore, 1948-49; Asst Sec. (title changed to Sec.), Council for British Archæology, 1949-73. Archæological research: in Kalat, Pakistan Baluchistan, 1948; in Afghanistan, 1949; directed excavations: in Kalat, 1957; at Bampur, Persian Baluchistan, 1966; survey in Ras al-Khaimah (then Trucial States), 1968; Middle East lecture tour for British Council, 1970; survey with RGS's Musandam Expedn (Northern Oman), 1971-72; directed archæological research projects: in Qatar, 1973-74; in Central Oman, 1974-76; survey in Ras al Khaimah, 1977. Winston Churchill Meml Trust Fellowship for work in Oman, 1973. FSA 1950 (Vice-Pres., 1976). *Publications:* Excavations at Bampur, a third millennium settlement in Persian Baluchistan, 1966; (contrib.) Vol. 51, Pt 3, Anthropological Papers of the American Museum of Natural History, 1970; contribs to Antiquity, Iran, Pakistan Archæology, East and West, Jl of Oman Studies. *Recreations:* archæological fieldwork, travel, cooking. *Address:* 1a Douro Place, Victoria Road, W8 5RW. *T:* 01-937 9740.

de CHAIR, Somerset; *b* 22 Aug. 1911; *s* of late Admiral Sir Dudley de Chair, Governor of NSW; *m* 1st, 1932, Thelma Arbuthnot (marr. diss. 1950); one *s* (and one *s* decd); 2nd, 1950, Carmen Appleton (*née* Bowen) (marr. diss. 1958); two *s*; 3rd, 1958, Mrs Margaret Patricia Manlove (*née* Field-Hart) (marr. diss. 1974); one *d*; 4th, 1974, Juliet, Marchioness of Bristol, *o d* of 8th Earl Fitzwilliam, DSC. *Educ:* King's Sch., Paramatta, New South Wales; Balliol Coll., Oxford. MP (Nat C) for S. West Norfolk, 1935-45; Parliamentary Private Secretary to Rt Hon. Oliver Lyttelton MP, Minister of Production, 1942-44; MP (C) South Paddington, 1950-51. 2nd Lieut Supp. Res. RHG, 1938; served with Household Cavalry in the Middle East, during Iraqi and Syrian campaigns (wounded), IO to 4th Cavalry Bde, 1940-41; Captain GS (I), 1942; Chairman National Appeal Cttee of UN Assoc., and member of National Exec., 1947-50. *Publications:* The Impending Storm, 1930, and Divided Europe, 1931 (on International situation); Peter Public, 1932 (a political extravaganza); Enter Napoleon, 1935 (a novel); Red Tie in the Morning (a novel), 1937; The Golden Carpet (Iraq Campaign), 1943; The Silver Crescent (Syrian Campaign), 1943; A Mind on the March, 1945; Editor of Napoleon's Memoirs (2 vols), 1945; edited and translated Supper at Beaucaire by Napoleon, 1945; The First Crusade (edited and translated from Gesta Francorum), 1946; The Teetotalitarian State (a novel), 1947; The Dome of the Rock (a novel), 1948; The Millennium (poems), 1949; Julius Caesar's Commentaries (new edn), 1952; The Story of a Lifetime (novel), 1954; The Waterloo Campaign, 1957; Editor of Admiral de Chair's memoirs, The Sea is Strong, 1961; Bring Back the Gods (novel), 1962; Collected Verse, 1970; Friends, Romans, Concubines (novel), 1973; The Star of the Wind (novel), 1974. *Address:* St Osyth Priory, St Osyth, Essex; Farm of the Running Waters, Kortright, Delaware County, New York, USA. *Club:* Carlton.

DECIES, 6th Baron *cr* 1812; **Arthur George Marcus Douglas de la Poer Beresford;** Ex-Flying Officer, RAFVR (DFC, USA); *b* 24 April 1915; *s* of 5th Baron Decies and Helen Vivien (*d* 1931), *d* of late George Jay Gould; *S* father, 1944; *m* 1937, Ann Trevor (*d* 1945); *m* 1945, Mrs Diana Galsworthy; one *s* two *d. Heir: s* Hon. Marcus Hugh Tristram de la Poer Beresford [*b* 5 Aug. 1948; *m* 1970, Sarah Jane (marr. diss. 1974), *o d* of Col Basil Gunnell, New Romney, Kent]. *Address:* Château de Betouzet, Andrein, 64 Sauveterre de Béarn, France.

de CLIFFORD, 26th Baron *cr* 1299; **Edward Southwell Russell,** OBE 1955; TD; psc; Colonel (retired) REME; *b* 30 Jan. 1907; *o s* of 25th Baron and Evelyn Victoria Anne, *d* of Walter Robert Chandler [she *m* 2nd, 1913, Capt. Arthur Roy Stock (*d* 1915); 3rd, George Vernon Tate, MC]; *S* father, 1909; *m* 1st, 1926, Dorothy Evelyn Meyrick (marr. diss. 1973); two *s*; 2nd, 1973, Mina Margaret, *o d* of George Edward Sands and Comtesse Sands de Sainte Croix. *Educ:* Eton; Engineering Coll. of London Univ. *Heir: s* Hon. John Edward Southwell Russell [*b* 8 June 1928; *m* 1959, Bridget Jennifer, *yr d* of Duncan Robertson, Llangollen, Denbs]. *Address:* The Birches, Silvington, Cleobury Mortimer, Kidderminster, Worcs.
See also His Honour Judge T. Elder-Jones.

de COURCY, family name of Baron Kingsale.

de COURCY, Kenneth Hugh; *b* 6 Nov. 1909; 2nd *s* of late Stephen de Courcy of Co. Galway and Hollinwood Mission, and late Minnie de Courcy; *m* 1950, Rosemary Catherine (marr. diss. 1973), *o d* of late Comdr H. L. S. Baker, OBE, RN (retired), Co. Roscommon, Eire; two *s* two *d*. *Educ:* King's College Sch. and by travelling abroad. 2nd Lieut, 3rd City of London Regt (Royal Fusiliers) TA (Regular Army Candidate), 1927. 2nd Lieut Coldstream Guards (Supplementary Reserve), 1930; Lieut and resigned, 1931; Hon. Secretary to late Sir Reginald Mitchell-Banks' unofficial cttee on Conservative policy, 1933; 1934, formed with late Earl of Mansfield, late Viscount Clive, late Lord Phillimore, and with Sir Victor Raikes, KBE, Imperial Policy Group and was Hon. Secretary 1934-39; travelled as Group's chief observer of Foreign Affairs in Europe and America, 1935-39; special visit of enquiry to Mussolini, Doctor Beneš, Dr Schuschnigg, 1936; to King Boris of Bulgaria, etc., 1938; to Italy and King Boris, 1939-40; FCO released 45 secret reports from 1936-40 to PRO, 1972; adviser on War Intelligence to United Steel Companies Ltd, 1944-45. Formerly published monthly serial memoranda on Foreign Affairs and Strategy, (1938-); Proprietor of: Intelligence Digest; The Weekly Review, 1951-; Director of Ringrone Newspapers Ltd, 1966-68. Editor: Bankers Digest, 1969-72; Special Office Brief, 1974-; World Charts and Graphs, 1976-. Trustee, Marquis de Verneuil Trust, 1971-. Lord of the Manors of Stow-on-the-Wold and Maugersbury, Glos. Hon. Citizen of New Orleans, La, USA, 1950. *Publications:* Review of World Affairs (23 vols since 1938); various articles on Strategy and Foreign Affairs. *Recreation:* climbing. *Address:* Yeomans Cottage, Longborough, Glos.

DE COURCY-IRELAND, Lt-Col Gerald Blakeney, MVO 1917; MC 1916; The Worcestershire Regt; *b* 1895; *m* 1924, Helen Beresford, *e d* of late John Stapleton-Martin, MA, barrister-at-law, and late Mrs Stapleton-Martin, Wood Hall, Norton, Worcester; one *d*. *Educ:* Sherborne; Clare Coll., Cambridge. Temp. 2nd Lieut King's Royal Rifle Corps, 1914; temp. Lieut 1915; temp. Captain, 1916; Acting Major, 1917; Adjutant, 9th Service Batt., 1918; relinquished Commission, 1920; Lieut The Worcestershire Regt, 1916; Captain, 1925; Major, 1938; retired pay, 1946, with hon. rank of Lt-Col. *Recreation:* shooting. *Address:* Greathed Manor, Ford Manor Road, Dormansland, Lingfield, Surrey RH7 6PA. *T:* Lingfield 833558.

de COURCY-IRELAND, Patrick Gault; Head of Training Department and Director of Diplomatic Service Language Centre, Foreign and Commonwealth Office, since 1976; *b* 19 Aug. 1933; *s* of late Lawrence Kilmaine de Courcy-Ireland and Elizabeth Pentland Gault; *m* 1957, Margaret Gallop; one *s* three *d*. *Educ:* St Paul's Sch.; Jesus Coll., Cambridge (MA). HM Forces (2nd Lieut), 1952-54. Joined Foreign Service, 1957; Student, ME Centre for Arab Studies, 1957-59; Third, later Second Sec., Baghdad, 1959-62; Private Sec. to HM Ambassador, Washington, 1963; Consul (Commercial), New York, 1963-67; UN (Polit.) Dept, 1967-69; Asst Head of Amer. Dept, 1969-71; First Sec. and Hd of Chancery, Kuwait, 1971-73; Asst Hd of SW Pacific Dept, 1973-76. *Recreations:* reading, opera. *Address:* Foreign and Commonwealth Office, SW1A 2AH. *Clubs:* Hurlingham, MCC.

de COURCY LING, John; HM Diplomatic Service; Counsellor, HM Embassy, Paris, since 1974; *b* 14 Oct. 1933; *s* of Arthur Norman Ling and Veronica de Courcy; *m* 1959, Jennifer Haynes; one *s* three *d*. *Educ:* King Edward's Sch., Edgbaston; Clare Coll., Cambridge. 2nd Lieut, Royal Ulster Rifles, 1956. FO, 1959; 2nd Sec., Santiago, 1963-66; 1st Sec., Nairobi, 1966-69; Chargé d'Affaires, Chad, 1973. *Recreations:* sailing, ski-ing. *Address:* c/o Foreign and Commonwealth Office, SW1A 2AL; Horton Lodge, Horton, Berks. *T:* Colnbrook 2136. *Clubs:* Travellers'; Union Interallée (Paris).

DEDIJER, Vladimir, DJur, MA Oxon; Order of Liberation, of Yugoslavia, etc.; Yugoslav Author; *b* 4 Feb. 1914; *m* 1944, Vera Krizman; one *s* two *d* (and two *s* decd). *Educ:* Belgrade Univ. Served War from 1941, Tito's Army, Lieut-Colonel; Yugoslav Delegate to Peace Conference, Paris, 1946, and to UN General Assemblies, 1945, 1946, 1948, 1949, 1951, 1952. Member Central Cttee, League of Communists of Yugoslavia, 1952-54, when expelled (defended right of M Djilas to free speech, 1954; sentenced to 6 months on probation, 1955). Prof. of Modern History, Belgrade Univ., 1954-55. Simon Senior Fellow, Manchester Univ., 1960; Research Fellow, St Antony's Coll., Oxford, 1962-63; Research Associate, Harvard Univ., 1963-64; Visiting Prof.: Cornell Univ., 1964-65; MIT, 1969; Brandeis, 1970; Michigan, 1971, 1973, 1974. Hon. Fellow, Manchester Univ. President International War Crimes Tribunal, 1966.

Member, Serbian Acad. of Science. *Publications:* Partisan Diary, 1945; Notes from the United States, 1945; Paris Peace Conference, 1948; Yugoslav-Albanian Relations, 1949; Tito, 1952; Military Conventions, 1960; The Beloved Land, 1960; Road to Sarajevo, 1966; The Battle Stalin Lost, 1969; History of Jugoslavia, 1972. Contrib. to Acta Scandinavica. *Address:* Gorkičeva 16, 61.000 Ljubljana, Yugoslavia. *T:* 61-729.

de DUVE, Prof. Christian René Marie Joseph, Grand Cross Order of Leopold II 1975; Professor of Biochemistry, Catholic University of Louvain, since 1951; President, International Institute of Cellular and Molecular Pathology, Brussels, since 1975; Andrew W. Mellon Professor at Rockefeller University, New York, since 1962; *b* England, 2 Oct. 1917; *s* of Alphonse de Duve and Madeleine Pungs; *m* 1943, Janine Herman; two *s* two *d*. *Educ:* Jesuit Coll., Antwerp; Catholic Univ. of Louvain; Med. Nobel Inst., Stockholm; Washington Univ., St Louis. MD 1941, MSc 1946, Agrégé de l'Enseignement Supérieur 1945, Louvain. Lectr. Med. Faculty, Catholic Univ. of Louvain, 1947-51. Vis. Prof. at various univs. Mem. editorial and other bds and cttees; mem. or hon. mem. various learned socs, incl. For. Assoc. Nat. Acad. of Scis (US) 1975. Holds hon. degrees. Awards incl. Nobel Prize in Physiol. or Med., 1974. *Publications:* numerous scientific. *Recreations:* tennis, ski-ing, bridge. *Address:* Le Pré St Jean, 5 rue de Weert, 5988 Nethen, Belgium. *T:* (010)-866628; 80 Central Park West, New York, NY 10023, USA. *T:* (212)-724-8048.

DEE, Philip Ivor, CBE 1946 (OBE 1943); FRS 1941; MA Cantab; Professor of Natural Philosophy at University of Glasgow, 1943-72, now Professor Emeritus; *b* Stroud, Glos, 8 April 1904; *s* of Albert John Dee, Stroud; *m* 1929, Phyllis Elsie Tyte; two *d*. *Educ:* Marling Sch., Stroud; Sidney Sussex Coll., Cambridge (Scholar). Stokes Student at Pembroke Coll., Cambridge, 1930-33; Lecturer in Physics at Cavendish Laboratory and Fellow of Sidney Sussex Coll., Cambridge, 1934-43; Superintendent, Tele-communications Research Establishment, Ministry of Aircraft Production, 1939-45. Advisory Council DSIR, 1947-52. Hughes Medal of Royal Society, 1952. *Publications:* scientific papers in Proceedings of Royal Society, etc. *Address:* Speedwell, Buchanan Castle Estate, Drymen, Stirlingshire. *T:* Drymen 283.

DEED, Basil Lingard, OBE 1946; TD; MA; Headmaster of Stamford School, 1947-68; *b* 1909; *s* of late S. G. Deed, Maldon; *m* 1937, Elizabeth Mary, *d* of late S. P. Cherrington, Berkhamsted; four *d*. *Educ:* Haileybury Coll.; Peterhouse, Cambridge. 2nd Class Classical Tripos Part I; 1st class Classical Tripos Part II. Asst Master, Berkhamsted School, 1931-37; Asst Master, Shrewsbury Sch., 1937-47; served War of 1939-45, mostly on General Staff; Lt-Col MEF, 1943; Italy, 1944-45. Councillor (Ind.) Oxfordshire CC, 1972-. *Address:* Bendor, Warborough, Oxon. *T:* Warborough 8514. *Clubs:* National Liberal; Blackwater Sailing.

DEEDES, Maj.-Gen. Charles Julius, CB 1968; OBE 1953; MC 1944; *b* 18 Oct. 1913; *s* of General Sir Charles Deedes, KCB, CMG, DSO; *m* 1939, Beatrice Murgatroyd, Brockfield Hall, York; three *s*. *Educ:* Oratory Sch.; Royal Military Coll., Sandhurst. Served War of 1939-45 (despatches); Asst Military Secretary, GHQ Middle East, 1945; Officer Comdg Glider Pilot Regt, 1948; GSO1 War Office, 1950; Officer Comdg 1st Bn KOYLI, 1954 (despatches); Colonel General Staff, War Office, 1956; Comd 146 Infantry Brigade (TA), 1958; Deputy Director, MoD, 1962; C of S, HQ Eastern Comd, 1965; C of S, HQ Southern Comd, 1968. Colonel of the KOYLI, 1966-68. Dep. Colonel, The Light Infantry (Yorks), 1968-72. Military Cross (Norway), 1940. *Recreations:* riding, tennis. *Address:* Lea Close, Brandsby, York. *T:* Brandsby 239.

DEEDES, Rt. Hon. William Francis, PC 1962; MC 1944; DL; Editor, The Daily Telegraph, since Dec. 1974; *b* 1 June 1913; *s* of William Herbert Deedes; *m* 1942, Evelyn Hilary Branfoot; two *s* three *d*. *Educ:* Harrow. MP (C) Ashford Div. of Kent, 1950-Sept. 1974; Parliamentary Sec., Ministry of Housing and Local Government, Oct. 1954-Dec. 1955; Parliamentary Under-Sec., Home Dept., 1955-57; Minister without Portfolio, 1962-64. DL, Kent, 1962. *Address:* New Hayters, Aldington, Kent. *T:* Aldington 269. *Club:* Junior Carlton.

DEEGAN, Joseph William, CMG 1956; CVO 1954; KPM; Inspector-General of Colonial Police, 1966-67; *b* 8 Feb. 1899; *s* of John and Sarah Deegan; *m* 1926, Elinor Elsie Goodson; one *s* two *d*. *Educ:* St Paul's and St Gabriel's Schs, Dublin. Army, 1919-25 (seconded to King's African Rifles, 1922-25); Tanganyika Police, 1925-38; Uganda Police, 1938-56 (Commissioner of Police, 1950-56); Dep. Inspector-Gen. of Colonial Police, 1956-61, 1963-65. Colonial Police Medal, 1942; King's Police Medal, 1950. *Address:* Tuffshard, Cuckmere Road, Seaford, East Sussex. *T:* Seaford 4180.

DEER, Arthur Frederick, CMG 1973; Director: The Mutual Life and Citizens' Assurance Co Ltd, Australia, since 1956 (General Manager, 1955-74); Bowater-Scott Ltd; Dow Chemical (Aust.) Ltd; Glass Containers Ltd; *b* 15 June 1910; *s* of Andrew and Maude Deer; *m* 1936, Elizabeth Christine, *d* of G. C. Whitney; one *s* three *d. Educ:* Sydney Boys' High Sch.; Univ. of Sydney (BA, LLB, BEc). Admitted to Bar of NSW, 1934. The Mutual Life and Citizens' Assurance Co Ltd: joined Company, 1930; apptd Manager for S Australia, 1943, and Asst to Gen. Manager, 1954. Chm., Life Offices' Assoc. for Australasia, 1960-61, 1967-68; Pres., Australian Insurance Inst., 1966. Chm., Cargo Movement Co-ordination Cttee, NSW, 1974-; Mem., Admin. Review Council, Aust. Fellow, Senate of Univ. of Sydney, 1959- (Chm. Finance Cttee of the Univ., 1960-). Nat. Pres., Australia-Britain Soc.; Chm., Salvation Army Sydney Adv. Bd. *Recreations:* golf, tennis. *Address:* 1179 Pacific Highway, Turramurra, NSW 2074, Australia. *T:* 44 2912. *Clubs:* Australian, Union, University, Athenæum, Avondale, Elanora, Royal Sydney Golf (all in Australia).

DEER, Mrs Olive G.; Member of Grimsby Borough Council, 1964-67; *b* Grimsby, 31 July 1897; *m* 1916, George Deer, OBE (*d* 1974); one *s* one *d. Educ:* Barcroft Street Sch., Cleethorpes, Lincs. Member: Min. of Labour Exchange Cttees, 1921-45; Bd of Guardians, 1922-25; Bracebridge Mental Hosp. Cttee, 1933-47; Lincoln City Council, 1945-49; Sheffield Regional Hosp. Bd, 1948-50; Bd of Nat. Hosp., Queen Square, 1950; S Eastern Metrop. Regional Hosp. Bd, 1957. Dir, 1940-50, Chm., 1946-48, Lincoln Co-operative Soc. Alderman, LCC, 1952-58; Councillor, LCC (Shoreditch and Finsbury), 1958-64. Chm. LCC Welfare Cttee, 1955-62; Chm. of the London County Council, 1962-63. *Address:* Medina, Carlton Road, Manby, Louth, Lincs. *T:* S Cockerington 386.

DEER, Prof. William Alexander, MSc Manchester, PhD Cantab; FRS 1962; FGS; Professor of Mineralogy and Petrology, Cambridge University, 1961-Sept. 1978; Master of Trinity Hall, Cambridge, 1966-75; *b* 26 Oct. 1910; *s* of William Deer; *m* 1939, Margaret Marjorie (*d* 1971), *d* of William Kidd; two *s* one *d* ; *m* 1973, Rita Tagg. *Educ:* Manchester Central High Sch.; Manchester Univ.; St John's Coll., Cambridge. Graduate Research Scholar, 1932, Beyer Fellow, 1933, Manchester Univ.; Strathcona Studentship, St John's Coll., Cambridge, 1934; Petrologist on British East Greenland Expedition, 1935-36; 1851 Exhibition Senior Studentship, 1938; Fellow, St John's Coll., Cambridge, 1939; served War of 1939-45, RE, 1940-45. Murchison Fund Geological Soc. of London, 1945 (Murchison Medal, 1974); Junior Bursar, St John's Coll., 1946; Leader NE Baffin Land Expedition, 1948; Bruce Medal, Royal Society of Edinburgh, 1948; Tutor, St John's Coll., 1949; Prof. of Geology, Manchester Univ., 1950-61; Fellow of St John's Coll., Cambridge, 1961-66, Hon. Fellow, 1969; Vice-Chancellor, Cambridge Univ., 1971-73. Percival Lecturer, Univ. of Manchester, 1953; Joint Leader East Greenland Geological Expedition, 1953; Leader British East Greenland Expedition, 1966. Trustee, British Museum (Natural History), 1967-75. President: Mineralogical Soc., 1967-70; Geological Soc., 1970-72; Member: NERC, 1968-71; Marshall Aid Commemoration Commn, 1973-. *Publications:* papers in Petrology and Mineralogy. *Recreation:* gardening. *Address:* Streading, Church Street, Great Shelford, Cambs.

DEERHURST, Viscount; Edward George William Coventry; *b* 24 Sept. 1957; *s* and *heir* of 11th Earl of Coventry, *qv.*

de FARIA, Antonio Leite, Hon. GCVO 1973; Grand Cross of Christ (Portugal), 1949; Portuguese Ambassador to the Court of St James's, 1968-73; retired; *b* 23 March 1904; *s* of Dr Antonio B. Leite de Faria and Dona Lucia P. de Sequeira Braga Leite de Faria; *m* 1926, Dona Herminia Cantilo de Faria; two *s. Educ:* Lisbon University (Faculty of Law). Attaché to Min. of Foreign Affairs, 1926; Sec. to Portuguese Delegn, League of Nations, 1929-30; 2nd Sec., Rio de Janeiro, 1931, Paris, 1933, Brussels, 1934; 1st Sec., London, 1936; Counsellor, London, 1939; Minister to Exiled Allied Govts, London, 1944; Minister to The Hague, 1945; Dir Gen., Political Affairs, and Acting Sec. Gen., Min. of Foreign Affairs, 1947; Ambassador: Rio de Janeiro, 1950; NATO, 1958; Paris, 1959; Rome (Holy See), 1961; London, 1968. Holds many foreign decorations. *Address:* Rua da Horta Seca 11, Lisboa. *T:* 32 25 38; Casa do Bom Retiro, S Pedro de Azurem, Guimarães. *T:* 40408.

de FERRANTI, Basil Reginald Vincent Ziani; Deputy Chairman, Ferranti Ltd; Chairman, Economic and Social Committee of the European Communities, since 1976 (Member, 1973); *b* 2 July 1930; *yr s* of Sir Vincent de Ferranti, *qv* ; *m* 1st, 1956, Susan Sara, *d* of late Christopher and of Lady Barbara Gore; three *s* ; 2nd, 1964, Simone, *d* of late Col and of Mrs H. J. Nangle; one *d* ;

3rd, 1971, Jocelyn Hilary Mary, *d* of Wing Comdr and Mrs A. T. Laing. *Educ:* Eton; Trinity Coll., Cambridge. Served 4th/7th Royal Dragoon Guards, 1949-50. Man., Domestic Appliance Dept, Ferranti Ltd, 1954-57. Contested Exchange Div. of Manchester, Gen. Election, 1955; MP (C) Morecambe and Lonsdale Div. of Lancaster, Nov. 1958-Sept. 1964. Dir of overseas operations, Ferranti Ltd, 1957-62; Parliamentary Sec., Ministry of Aviation, July-Oct. 1962. Dep. Man. Dir, Internat. Computers and Tabulators, Sept. 1963 until Managing Dir, 1964; Dir, International Computers Ltd until 1972. Pres., British Computer Soc., 1968-69; Chm., UK Automation Council, 1968-70. Member of Council: Instn of Electrical Engineers, 1962-65; Cheltenham Coll., 1959-66. Hon. DSc City, 1970. *Publications:* contrib. Brit. Computer Soc. Jl, Proc. IFIP, Proc. Royal Instn of GB. *Recreations:* ski-ing, sailing. *Address:* Ferranti Ltd, Millbank Tower, Millbank, SW1. *T:* 01-834 6611; 19 Lennox Gardens, SW1. *Club:* Royal Yacht Squadron.
See also S. B. J. Z. de Ferranti.

de FERRANTI, Sebastian Basil Joseph Ziani; Chairman, Ferranti Ltd, since 1963 (Managing Director, 1958-75; Director 1954); *b* 5 Oct. 1927; *er s* of Sir Vincent de Ferranti, *qv* ; *m* 1953, Mona Helen, *d* of T. E. Cunningham; one *s* two *d. Educ:* Ampleforth. 4th/7th Dragoon Guards, 1947-49. Brown Boveri, Switzerland, and Alsthom, France, 1949-50. President: Electrical Research Assoc., 1968-69; BEAMA, 1969-70; Centre for Educn in Science, Educn and Technology, Manchester and region, 1972-. Chm., Internat. Electrical Assoc., 1970-72. Mem., Nat. Defence Industries Council, 1969-. Trustee, Tate Gallery, 1971-. Lectures: Granada, Guildhall, 1966; Royal Instn, 1969; Louis Blériot, Paris, 1970; Faraday, 1970-71. Hon. DSc: Salford Univ., 1967; Cranfield Inst. of Technology, 1973. Hon. Fellow, Univ. of Manchester Inst. of Science and Technology. *Address:* Kerfield House, Knutsford, Cheshire. *Clubs:* Cavalry and Guards, Pratt's.
See also B. R. V. Z. de Ferranti.

de FERRANTI, Sir Vincent Ziani, Kt 1948; LLD (*hc*); DEng (*hc*); FIEE; Chairman, Ferranti Ltd, 1930-63; *b* 16 Feb. 1893; *s* of Dr Sebastian Ziani de Ferranti, FRS and Gertrude Ruth Ince; *m* 1919, Dorothy H. C. Wilson; two *s* three *d. Educ:* Repton. Served European War, 1914-19, Royal Engineers, Capt. (MC); War of 1939-45, Major Comdg Field Coy. RE, France, 1939-40. Lieut-Col Comdg 63rd County of Lancs Bn Home Guard, 1940-44. Hon. Col 123 Field Engr Regt RE, TA, 1948-57. Chm., International Executive Council, and British National Cttee, World Power Conference, 1950-62; Brit. Electrical and Allied Mfctrs Assoc.: Chm. 1938-39, Vice-Pres. 1946-57, Pres. 1957-59; Pres. Instn of Electrical Engineers, 1946-47; Pres. British Electrical Power Convention, 1949-50; Pres. Television Soc., 1954-57. *Address:* Henbury Hall, Macclesfield, Cheshire. *T:* Macclesfield 22400. *Club:* Athenæum.
See also B. R. V. Z. and S. B. J. Z. de Ferranti.

de FISCHER-REICHENBACH, Henry-Béat, Dr jur.; Swiss Ambassador to the Court of St James's, 1964-66; *b* 22 July 1901; *s* of Henry B. de Fischer-Reichenbach, bailiff-delegate of the Sov. Order of Malta in Switzerland, and Caroline Falck-Crivelli; *m* 1949, Madeleine de Graffenried; three *d. Educ:* Stella Matutina Jesuit Coll., Feldkirch; Universities of Fribourg, Munich, Paris and Berne. Entered Federal Political Dept, Berne, 1929; Attaché, Swiss Legation, The Hague, 1931; Second Secretary, Buenos-Aires and Montevideo, 1933; First Secretary: Warsaw, 1939; Bucharest, 1940; Chargé d'affaires successively Riga, Kowno, Reval, Helsinki, 1940; Counsellor: Bucharest, 1941; Cairo and Beirut, 1947; Minister: Cairo, 1949; Ethiopia, 1952; Lisbon, 1954; Ambassador, Vienna, 1959-64. Mem. Board of Patrons, C. G. Jung Inst., Zürich, 1969-. President: Fondation pour l'histoire des Suisses à l'étranger; Swiss Assoc., Knights of Malta; Comité exécutif international pour l'assistance aux Lépreux de l'Ordre de Malte; Pres., European Anti-leprosy Assoc., 1972-73; Fedn Européenne des Assocs contre la Lepre, 1972-73. *Publications:* Contributions à la connaissance des relations suisses-égyptiennes, 1956; Dialogue luso-suisse, 1960 (Camões Prize, 1961); The Swiss presence in the United Kingdom during the 18th Century, 1967; L'étonnante épopée des Suisses dans les Iles britanniques de l'époque de César au Marché Commun, 1977. *Recreations:* history, architecture, psychology. *Address:* Le Pavillon, Thunplatz 52, Berne. *T:* 44.15.09; Clos Soleil, Vufflens-le-Château, Vaud, Switzerland. *Clubs:* Travellers'; Grande Société (Berne).

de FONBLANQUE, Maj.-Gen. Edward Barrington, CB 1948; CBE 1945; DSO 1944; *b* 29 May 1895; *s* of Lester Ramsay de Fonblanque and Constance Lucy Kerr; *m* 1934, Elizabeth Sclater; two *s* one *d. Educ:* Rugby. Joined Royal Artillery 1914; served European War, 1914-18 (despatches); Instructor Equitation Sch., Weedon, 1921-25; Capt., Royal Horse

Artillery, 1923-31; Instructor, Staff Coll., Quetta, 1934-38; Commanded B/O Battery RHA, 1938-39; Commanded 2 RHA, 1939-40; GSO 1, 2 Div., 1940; CRA 45 Div., 1940-41; Chief of Staff 10 Corps and 10 Army, 1941-43 (despatches); CCRA 5 Corps, 1944-45; Chief of Staff I Corps, 1946; Chief Administrative Officer, Control Commission Germany, 1947; ADC to the King, 1947; Comdr, Salisbury Plain District, 1948-51; retired, 1951. Asst Comr, Civil Defence, Malaya, 1951; Inspector-Gen., Federal Home Guard, Malaya, 1952-58. Col Comdt, RA 1952; Representative Col Comdt 1959; retd 1960. Comdr, Legion of Merit. *Recreation:* sailing. *Address:* The Cottage, Bank, near Lyndhurst, Hants. *T:* Lyndhurst 2214; c/o Lloyds Bank, 6 Pall Mall, SW1.

de FRANCIA, Prof. Peter Laurent; Professor, School of Painting, Royal College of Art, London, since 1973; *b* 25 Jan. 1921; *s* of Fernand de Francia and Alice Groom. *Educ:* Academy of Brussels; Slade Sch., Univ. of London. Canadian Exhibition Commn, Ottawa, 1951; American Museum, Central Park West, NY, 1952-53; BBC, Television, 1953-55; Teacher, St Martin's Sch., London, 1955-63; Tutor, Royal College of Art, 1963-69; Principal, Dept of Fine Art, Goldsmiths Coll., 1969-72. *Publication:* Fernand Léger, 1969. *Address:* 44 Surrey Square, SE17 2JX. *T:* (home) 01-703 8361; (office) 01-584 5020.

de FREITAS, Rt. Hon. Sir Geoffrey Stanley, PC 1967; KCMG 1961; MP (Lab) Kettering since 1964; Vice-President, European Parliament, since 1975; President, North Atlantic Assembly, since 1976; Barrister-at-law, Lincoln's Inn (Cholmeley Schol.); Director, Laporte Industries, since 1968; *b* 7 April 1913; *s* of Sir Anthony Patrick de Freitas, OBE, and Maud, *d* of Augustus Panton Short; *m* 1938, Helen Graham, *d* of Laird Bell, Hon. KBE, Hon. LLD Harvard, of Illinois, USA; three *s* one *d*. *Educ:* Haileybury (Governor); Clare Coll., Cambridge (Hon. Fellow); Yale Univ. (Mellon Fellow). Pres. of Cambridge Union, 1934. Shoreditch Borough Council (Lab), 1936-39; Bar Council, 1939. RA 1939, RAF, 1940-45. MP (Lab) Central Nottingham, 1945-50, Lincoln, 1950-61; Parliamentary Private Sec. to Prime Minister, 1945-46; Under-Sec. of State for Air, 1946-50; Under-Sec. of State, Home Office, 1950-51; Shadow Minister of Agriculture, 1960-61; Mem. Privileges Cttee, 1964-67; Chm., Select Cttee on Overseas Develt, 1974-. British High Comr in Ghana, 1961-63; designated (1963) British High Comr in East African Federation when formed; British High Comr in Kenya, 1963-64. Pres., Assembly of Council of Europe, 1966-69; Delegate: to UN, 1949 and 1964; to Council of Europe, 1951-54 and 1965-69 (Leader of UK Delegn); to N Atlantic Assembly, 1970- (founder Mem. 1955; Leader of the UK Delegn). Chairman: Gauche Européenne, 1966-; Labour Cttee for Europe, 1965-72; Attlee Foundn, 1967-76; Party's Defence Cttee, 1964-71, 1974-76; Soc. of Labour Lawyers, 1955-58; Vice-Chairman: Nature Conservancy, 1954-58; British Council, 1964-68; Churches Social Responsibility Cttee, 1956-61; Council: Churchill Trust, 1967-77; Agricultural Cooperative Association, 1964-69. Farmed at Bourn, Cambs, 1953-69. *Recreations:* the countryside; formerly games and athletics (full blue CUAC). *Address:* 11 Trumpington Road, Cambridge. *T:* Cambridge 58477; House of Commons, SW1. *T:* 01-219 4571, 01-799 3770. *Clubs:* Reform, Garrick, Guild of Air Pilots (Liveryman); Hawks (Cambridge).

DE FREYNE, 7th Baron *cr* 1851; **Francis Arthur John French;** Knight of Malta; *b* 3 Sept. 1927; *s* of 6th Baron and Victoria (*d* 1974), *d* of Sir J. Arnott, 2nd Bt; *S* father 1935; *m* 1954, Shirley Ann, *o c* of late D. R. Pobjoy; two *s* one *d*. *Educ:* Ladycross, Glenstal. *Heir: s* Hon. Fulke Charles Arthur John French, *b* 21 April 1957. *Club:* Kildare Street and University (Dublin).

de GALE, Sir Leo (Victor), GCMG 1974; CBE 1969; Governor-General of Grenada since 1974; *b* 28 Dec. 1921; 3rd *s* of late George Victor and late Marie Leonie de Gale, Grenada; *m* 1953, Brenda Mary Helen (*née* Scott), Trinidad; five *s* two *d*. *Educ:* Grenada Boys' Secondary Sch.; Sir George Williams Univ., Canada. Dip. Accountancy, Dip. Business Admin, Qual. Land Surveyor. Served with 1st Canadian Survey Regt, 1940-45. Co-founder firm de Gale & Rapier, Auditors, 1949. Dir, Brit. Red Cross Br., Grenada, 1960-65; Chm. and Mem., Grenada Breweries Ltd, 1964-74; Dep. Chm., Grenada Banana Soc., 1965-69; Chm. Bd of Governors, Grenada Boys' Secondary Sch., 1960-65; Mem., West Indies Associated States Judicial and Legal Service Commn, 1970-73. *Recreations:* golf, fishing, reading. *Address:* Governor-General's House, Grenada. *T:* 2401 and 2954. *Clubs:* St George's Men's (Grenada); Grenada Yacht.

de GEX, Maj.-Gen. George Francis, CB 1964; OBE 1949; Director, Royal Artillery, 1964-66, retired; *b* 23 April 1911; *s* of late Brig.-Gen. F. J. de Gex, CB, CMG; *m* 1946, Ronda Marianne, *d* of late C. F. Recaño; one *d*. *Educ:* Wellington Coll.,

Berks; Trinity Hall, Cambridge (MA). 2nd Lieut RA 1931; served War of 1939-45: BEF, 1940 (despatches); NW Europe, 1944. Lt-Col 1953; Col 1954; Brig. 1959; Comd 1 AGRA, 1958-59; DMS(B), War Office, 1959-60. Comdr Artillery, Northern Army Group, 1961-64. Col Comdt, RA 1967-76. DSC (USA), 1945. *Recreation:* shooting. *Address:* Hyde House, Pilton, Shepton Mallet, Somerset. *Club:* Army and Navy.

de GREY, family name of **Baron Walsingham.**

de GREY, Roger, RA 1969 (ARA 1962); Principal, City and Guilds of London Art School, since 1973; *b* 18 April 1918; *s* of Nigel de Grey, CMG, OBE, and Florence Emily Frances (*née* Gore); *m* 1942, Flavia Hatt (*née* Irwin); two *s* one *d*. *Educ:* Eton Coll.; Chelsea Sch. of Art. Served War of 1939-45: Royal West Kent Yeomanry, 1939-42; RAC, 1942-45 (US Bronze Star, 1945). Lecturer, Dept of Fine Art, King's Coll., Newcastle upon Tyne, 1947-51; Master of Painting, King's Coll., 1951-53; Senior Tutor, later Reader in Painting, Royal Coll. of Art, 1953-73. Treasurer, RA, 1976. Pictures in the following public collections: Arts Council; Contemporary Arts Society; Chantrey Bequest; Queensland Gallery, Brisbane; Manchester, Carlisle, Bradford and other provincial galleries. Hon. ARCA, 1959. *Address:* City and Guilds of London Art School, 124 Kennington Park Road, SW11 4DJ; 5 Camer Street, Meopham, Kent. *T:* 2327.

de GUINGAND, Maj.-Gen. Sir Francis W., KBE 1944 (CBE 1943; OBE 1942); CB 1943; DSO 1942; Chairman: Rothmans of Pall Mall (UK); Carreras Ltd, 1967-68, and other Cos; Director and International Director of the Rothmans Group; *b* 28 Feb. 1900; *s* of late Francis J. de Guingand; *m* 1942, Arlie R., *widow* of Major H. D. Stewart, West Yorks Regt (marr. diss., 1957); one *d*. *Educ:* Ampleforth Coll.; RMC, Sandhurst. Joined W Yorks Regt, 1919; seconded to KAR, 1926-31; OC Troops Nyasaland, 1930-31; Adjt 1st Bn W Yorks Regt, 1932-34; Staff Coll., Camberley, 1935-36; Mil. Asst to Sec. of State for War (Mr Hore-Belisha), 1939-40; Dir Mil. Intell., Middle East, 1942; Chief of Staff: 8th Army, 1942-44; 21st Army Group, 1944-45; retd pay, 1947. DSM (USA); CL of M (USA); Legion of Honour (France); Croix de Guerre (France); Order of Kutuzov 1st Grade (Russia); Order of Orange Nassau (Dutch). *Publications:* Operation Victory, 1947; African Assignment, 1953; Generals at War, 1964. *Recreations:* shooting, fishing, golf, sailing. *Address:* c/o Carreras Ltd, 27 Baker Street, W1; Residence Château Mont Joli, Boulevard Metropole, 06400 Cannes, France. *Clubs:* Army and Navy, Royal Automobile, White's; Rand, Country (Johannesburg).

de HAVILLAND, Olivia Mary, (Mme. P. P. Galante); actress; *b* Tokyo, Japan, 1 July 1916; *d* of Walter Augustus de Havilland and Lilian Augusta (*née* Ruse) (parents British subjects); *m* 1st, 1946, Marcus Aurelius Goodrich (marr. diss., 1953); one *s*; 2nd, 1955, Pierre Paul Galante; one *d*. *Educ:* in California; won scholarship to Mills Coll., but career prevented acceptance. Played Hermia in Max Reinhardt's stage production of Midsummer Night's Dream, 1934. *Legitimate theatre* (USA): Juliet in Romeo and Juliet, 1951; Candida, 1951 and 1952; A Gift of Time, 1962. Began film career 1935, Midsummer Night's Dream. Nominated for Academy Award, 1939, 1941, 1946, 1948, 1949; Acad. Award, 1946, 1949; New York Critics' Award, 1948, 1949; San Francisco Critics' Award, 1948, 1949; Women's National Press Club Award for 1950; Belgian Prix Femina, 1957; British Films and Filming Award, 1967. *Important Films:* The Adventures of Robin Hood, 1938; Gone With the Wind, 1939; Hold Back the Dawn, 1941; Princess O'Rourke, 1943; To Each His Own, 1946; The Dark Mirror, 1946; The Snake Pit, 1948; The Heiress, 1949; My Cousin Rachel, 1952; Not as a Stranger, 1955; The Ambassador's Daughter, 1956; Proud Rebel, 1957; The Light in the Piazza, 1961; Lady in a Cage, 1963; Hush... Hush, Sweet Charlotte, 1965; The Adventurers, 1969; Pope Joan, 1971; Airport '77, 1976. Also TV 1966, 1967, 1971. US lecture tours, 1971, 1972, 1973, 1974, 1975, 1976. Pres. of Jury, Cannes Film Festival, 1965. Took part in narration of France's Bicentennial Gift to US, Son et Lumière, A Salute to George Washington, Mount Vernon, 19 May 1976; read excerpts from Thomas Jefferson at BiCentennial Service, American Cathedral in Paris, 4 July 1976. Amer. Legion Humanitarian Medal, 1967. *Publication:* Every Frenchman Has One, 1962. *Address:* 75764 Paris, Cedex 16, France.

de HAVILLAND, Maj.-Gen. Peter Hugh, CBE 1945; DL; *b* 29 July 1904; *s* of late Hugh de Havilland, JP, CA, The Manor House, Gt Horkesley, Essex; *m* 1930, Helen Elizabeth Wrey (*d* 1976), *d* of late W. W. Otter-Barry, Horkesley Hall, Essex; two *s*. *Educ:* Eton; RMA, Woolwich. 2nd Lieut, RA, 1925; Lieut RHA, 1933-36; Adjt 84th (East Anglian) Field Bde, RA (TA),

1936-38; served War of 1939-45 (despatches thrice, CBE); France, Middle East, N Africa, NW Europe; Brig. i/c Administration, 1 Corps, 1945-47; Dep. Regional Comr, Land Schleswig Holstein, 1948; Dep. Head, UK Deleg. Five Power Military Cttee, 1949; UK Mil. Rep., SHAPE, 1951; Chief of Staff, Northern Comd, 1953-55, retd 1955. DL Essex, 1962. Comdr Order of Leopold II, 1945. *Recreations:* shooting, flying. *Address:* Horkesley Hall, Colchester. *T:* Great Horkesley 259. *Club:* Army and Navy.

DEHN, Conrad Francis, QC 1968; Barrister; a Recorder of the Crown Court, since 1974; *b* London, 24 Nov. 1926; *o s* of late C. G. Dehn, Solicitor and Cynthia (*née* Fuller: Francyn the painter); *m* 1954, Sheila, *y d* of late W. K. Magan; two *s* one *d. Educ:* Charterhouse (Sen. Exhibr); Christ Church, Oxford (Holford Exhibr). Served RA, 1945-48; 2nd Lieut 1947. Lord Justice Holker Jun. Schol., Gray's Inn, 1949; Slade Exhibn, Christ Church, 1950; 1st cl. hons PPE Oxon. 1950, MA 1952; Holt Schol., Gray's Inn, 1951; Lord Justice Holker Sen. Exhibn, Gray's Inn, 1952; Pres., Inns of Court Students Union, 1951-52. WEA Tutor, 1951-55. Called to Bar, Gray's Inn, 1952; Bencher, 1977. Mem. Governing Body, United Westminster Schs, 1953-57. *Publication:* contrib. to Ideas, 1954. *Recreations:* reading, walking. *Address:* 38 Camberwell Grove, SE5; Fountain Court, Temple, EC4 9DH. *T:* 01-353 7356. *Club:* Reform.

de HOGHTON, Sir (Henry Philip) Anthony (Mary), 13th Bt *cr* 1611; *b* 19 April 1919; *e s* of Sir Cuthbert de Hoghton, 12th Bt, JP, and Helen (*d* 1943), *o d* of late Major Duncan Macdonald of Glencoe; *S* father 1958. *Educ:* Beaumont; Magdalen Coll., Oxford. *Heir:* half-*b* Richard Bernard Cuthbert de Hoghton [*b* 26 Jan. 1945. *Educ:* Ampleforth; McGill Univ.; Birmingham Univ.]. *Address:* Hoghton Tower, Hoghton, Lancs. *T:* Hoghton 452.

DE-JA-GOU; *see* Gowda, Deve Javare.

de JONG, Major Nicholas Charles Callard; Director, Pitney Bowes Ltd, since 1973; *b* 15 Oct. 1911; *s* of David de Jong, Wallasey, Cheshire and Jessie Florence de Jong (*née* Callard), Totnes, Devon; *m* 1937, Olwen May East, Milford Haven; one *d. Educ:* Queen Elizabeth's, Crediton; Techn. Coll., Cardiff; University of South Wales. BSc(Eng) 1st cl. hons (London); CEng, MICE, FIMechE, FIEE. L. G. Mouchell & Co. Ltd, Bridge design and building, 1932-34; entered GPO service by open competition, 1934; served in various grades and places, incl.: Telephone Man., Preston, 1953-57; Controller, N Ire., 1957-61; overseas consultancy work in W Indies and Cyprus; various posts in Engrg Dept of PO: Dep. Engr-in-Chief, 1966; Dir of Mechanisation and Buildings, 1967-73. Officer, Order of Orange Nassau, 1946; Bronze Star (USA), 1946. *Recreations:* boats, golf, travel. *Address:* 33 Mount Avenue, Westcliff-on-Sea, Essex SS0 8PS. *T:* Southend 75824.

DEKKER, Wisse; Director, Philips Lamp, since 1976; Chairman, 1973-76 and Managing Director, 1972-76, Philips Electronic & Associated Industries Ltd; *b* 26 April 1924; *m* 1946, Helena Brouwer; one *s* one *d. Educ:* Holland. Joined US Forces (101) Airborne Div., 1944; volunteered for Dutch Army, 1945; served with 42nd Royal Marine Comd, 1945; Lieut Special Services, Malaysia and Indonesia, 1945-48. Joined Philips, 1948; served in South East Asia and Holland until 1966 when transf. to Japan as Pres., Philips Far East Gp of Companies. Vis. Prof., Univ. of Strathclyde Business Sch., 1973-76. FBIM. *Recreations:* golf, sailing. *Address:* Arundel Great Court, 8 Arundel Street, WC2R 3DT. *T:* 01-836 4360. *Clubs:* Buck's; Royal Thames Yacht, Wentworth.

De la BÈRE, Sir Rupert, 1st Bt, *cr* 1953; KCVO 1953; Kt 1952; President, Proprietors of Hay's Wharf Ltd and other Companies; Alderman of City of London for Ward of Tower; *b* 16 June 1893; *s* of Lillian Margaret and Reginald De la Bère; *m* 1919, Marguerite (*d* 1969), *e d* of late Sir John Humphery; two *s* three *d. Educ:* Tonbridge Sch. Captain East Surrey Regt; served European War 1914-18, India, Mesopotamia, Egypt; seconded to RFC and RAF; graduated at Aboukir, Egypt. MP (C) Evesham Div. of Worcs, 1935-50, South Worcs, 1950-55; Sheriff of City of London, 1941-42; Lord Mayor of London, 1952-53. KStJ 1953. Knight Comdr, Order of the Dannebrog (Denmark), 1954; Knight Comdr Order of the North Star (Sweden), 1954. *Heir:* s Cameron De la Bère [*b* 12 Feb. 1933; *m* 1964, Clairemonde, *o d* of Casimir Kaufmann, Geneva; one *d*]. *Recreations:* aviation and squash racquets. *Address:* Crowborough Place, Crowborough, East Sussex. *T:* Crowborough 103. *Club:* Carlton.

DELACOMBE, Maj.-Gen. Sir Rohan, KCMG 1964; KCVO 1970; KBE 1961 (CBE 1951; MBE 1939); CB 1957; DSO 1944; Governor of Victoria, Australia, 1963-74; Administrator of the Commonwealth of Australia on four occasions; *b* 25 Oct. 1906; *s* of late Lieut-Col Addis Delacombe, DSO, Shrewton Manor, near Salisbury; *m* 1941, Eleanor Joyce (CStJ), *d* of late R. Lionel Forster, JP, Egton Manor, York; one *s* one *d. Educ:* Harrow; RMC Sandhurst. 2nd Lieut The Royal Scots, 1926; served Egypt, N China, India and UK, 1926-37; active service Palestine, 1937-39 (despatches, MBE); France, Norway, Normandy, Italy, 1939-45; Lieut-Col comd 8th Bn and 2nd Bn The Royal Scots, 1943-45; GSO1, 2nd Infantry Div., Far East, 1945-47; Colonel GS, HQ, BAOR, 1949-50; Brig. Comd 5 Inf. Bde, 1950-53, Germany; Dep. Mil. Sec., War Office, 1953-55; Maj.-Gen. 1956. Col The Royal Scots, 1956-64; GOC 52 Lowland Div. and Lowland District, 1955-58; GOC Berlin (Brit. Sector) 1959-62. Mem. Queen's Body Guard for Scotland, Royal Company of Archers, 1957. KStJ, 1963; Freeman, City of Melbourne, 1974. Hon. Col 1st Armoured Regt (Australian Army), 1963-74; Hon. Air Cdre RAAF. LLD *hc* Melbourne; LLD *hc* Monash. *Recreations:* normal. *Address:* Shrewton Manor, near Salisbury, Wilts. *T:* Shrewton 253. *Clubs:* Army and Navy, MCC.

DELACOURT-SMITH, family name of **Baroness Delacourt-Smith of Alteryn.**

DELACOURT-SMITH OF ALTERYN, Baroness *cr* 1974 (Life Peer), of Alteryn, Gwent; **Margaret Delacourt-Smith;** *b* 1916; *d* of Frederick James Hando; *m* 1939, Charles Smith (subsequently Lord Delacourt-Smith, PC) (*d* 1972); one *s* two *d. Educ:* Newport High School for Girls; St Anne's College, Oxford (MA). *Address:* 56 Aberdare Gardens, NW6 3QD.

de LACRETELLE, Jacques; French Writer; Member of Académie Française, since 1936; *b* 14 July 1888; *m* 1933, Yolande de Naurois; three *c*. First book published in 1920; Prix Femina, 1922; Grand Prix du roman de l'Académie Française, 1927. *Publications:* La Vie inquiète de Jean Hermelin, 1920; Silbermann, 1922; La Bonifas, 1925; Histoire de Paola Ferrani, 1929; Amour nuptial, 1929; Le Retour de Silbermann, 1930; Les Hauts Ponts (4 vols), 1932-35; L'Ecrivain public, 1936; Croisières en eaux troubles, 1939; Le Demi-Dieu ou le voyage en Grèce, 1944; Le Pour et le Contre, 1946; Une visite en été (play), 1952; Deux cœurs simples, 1953; Tiroir secret, 1959; Les Maîtres et les Amis, 1959; Grèce que j'aime, 1960; La Galerie des amants, 1963; L'Amour sur la place, 1964; Talleyrand, 1964; Racine, 1970; Portraits d'autrefois, figures d'aujourd'hui 1973; Journal de bord, 1974; Les Vivants et leur ombre, 1977; translation of Precious Bane by Mary Webb and Wuthering Heights by Emily Brontë. *Address:* 49 rue Vineuse, 75016 Paris, France. *T:* 553-79.87.

DELAFONS, John; Under Secretary, Department of the Environment, since 1972; *b* 14 Sept. 1930; *m* 1957, Sheila Egerton; four *d. Educ:* Ardingly; St Peter's College, Oxford. Asst Principal, Min. of Housing and Local Govt, 1953; Harkness Fellowship, Harvard, 1959-60; Principal, 1959-66; Principal Private Sec. to Minister, 1965-66; Assistant Sec., 1966-72. *Address:* 14 Inglis Road, W5 3RN. *T:* 01-992 5440.

de la LANNE-MIRRLEES, Robin Ian Evelyn Stuart; *see* Mirrlees.

de la MARE, Sir Arthur (James), KCMG 1968 (CMG 1957); KCVO 1972; HM Diplomatic Service, retired; Business consultant, since 1975; Chairman, Anglo-Thai Society, since 1976; *b* 15 Feb. 1914; *s* of late Walter H. de la Mare, Trinity, Jersey, Channel Islands, and late Laura Vibert Syvret; *m* 1940, Katherine Elisabeth Sherwood; three *d. Educ:* Victoria Coll., Jersey; Pembroke Coll., Cambridge. Joined HM Foreign Service, 1936. HM Vice-Consul: Tokyo, 1936-38; Seoul, Korea, 1938-39; USA 1942-43; First Sec., Foreign Service, 1945; HM Consul, San Francisco, 1947-50; HM Embassy, Tokyo, 1951-53; Counsellor, HM Foreign Service, 1953-63; Head of Security Dept, Foreign Office, 1953-56; Counsellor, HM Embassy, Washington, 1956-60; Head of Far Eastern Dept, Foreign Office, 1960-63; Ambassador to Afghanistan, 1963-65; Asst Under-Sec. of State, Foreign Office, 1965-67; High Comr in Singapore, 1968-70; Ambassador to Thailand, 1970-73. *Recreations:* gardening, golf. *Address:* The Birches, Onslow Road, Burwood Park, Walton-on-Thames, Surrey KT12 5BB. *Clubs:* Oriental, Royal Commonwealth Society; Tokyo (Tokyo, Japan).

de la MARE, Prof. Peter Bernard David, MSc NZ; PhD London; DSc London; FRSNZ; Professor of Chemistry and Head of Chemistry Department, University of Auckland, New Zealand, since 1967; *b* 3 Sept. 1920; *s* of late Frederick Archibald and of Sophia Ruth de la Mare, Hamilton, NZ; *m* 1945, Gwynneth

Campbell, *yr d* of late Alexander and Daisy Gertrude Jolly, Hastings, NZ; two *d. Educ:* Hamilton High Sch., Hamilton, NZ; Victoria University Coll. (University of NZ); University Coll., London. BSc NZ, 1941; MSc NZ, 1942; PhD London, 1948; DSc London, 1955. Agricultural Chemist, NZ Govt Dept of Agriculture, 1942-45; Shirtcliffe Fellow (University of NZ) at University Coll. London, 1946-48; University Coll. London: Temp. Asst Lecturer, 1948; Lecturer, 1949; Reader, 1956; Prof. of Chemistry, Bedford Coll., University of London, 1960-67. FRSNZ 1970. *Publications:* (with J. H. Ridd) Aromatic Substitution-Nitration and Halogenation, 1959; (with W. Klyne) Progress in Stereochemistry 2, 1958, 3, 1962; (with R. Bolton) Electrophilic Addition to Unsaturated Systems, 1966; Electrophilic Halogenation, 1976; scientific papers and reviews. *Recreations:* cricket, chess, table tennis, etc. *Address:* Chemistry Department, University of Auckland, Auckland, New Zealand.

de la MARE, Richard Herbert Ingpen; President, Faber & Faber (Publishers) Ltd, since 1971 (Chairman, Faber & Faber Ltd, 1960-71); Chairman, Faber Music Ltd, 1966-71; *b* 4 June 1901; *e s* of late Walter John de la Mare, OM, CH, and Constance Elfrida Ingpen; *m* 1930, Amy Catherine (*d* 1968), *er d* of late Rev. S. A. Donaldson, DD, Master of Magdalene College, Cambridge; three *s* one *d. Educ:* Whitgift Sch., Croydon; Keble Coll., Oxford. Joined Faber & Gwyer Ltd, 1925, Dir 1928; succeeded by Faber & Faber Ltd, 1929, Dir 1929-45, Vice-Chm. 1945-60. *Publications:* essays and addresses on typography. *Recreations:* listening to music, oriental art, gardening. *Address:* Much Hadham Hall, Herts. *T:* Much Hadham 2663. *Club:* Athenæum.
See also Baron Donaldson of Kingsbridge.

DELAMERE, 4th Baron *cr* 1821; **Thomas Pitt Hamilton Cholmondeley;** Captain Welsh Guards; Director, Proved Securities Ltd; *b* 19 Aug. 1900; *e s* of 3rd Baron and Lady Florence Cole (*d* 1914), 4th *d* of 4th Earl of Enniskillen; *S* father, 1931; *m* 1st, 1924, Phyllis Anne (marriage dissolved, 1944), *e d* of late Lord George Scott, OBE; one *s* two *d*; 2nd, 1944, Ruth Mary Clarisse, (marriage dissolved, 1955), *yr d* of 1st Baron Mount Temple; 3rd, 1955, Diana Colvile, *yr d* of late Seymour Caldwell and of Mrs Caldwell, The Red House, Hove, Sussex. *Educ:* Eton. *Heir: s* Hon. Hugh George Cholmondeley [*b* 18 Jan. 1934; *m* 1964, Mrs Ann Willoughby Tinne, *o d* of late Sir Patrick Renison, GCMG; one *s*]. *Address:* Soysambu, Elementeita, Kenya. *Clubs:* White's, Turf.
See also Major Sir Evelyn Delves Broughton.

DELANEY, Shelagh; playwright; *b* Salford, Lancs, 1939; one *d. Educ:* Broughton Secondary Sch. *Plays:* A Taste of Honey, Theatre Royal, Stratford, 1958 and 1959, Wyndhams, 1959, New York, 1960 and 1961 (Charles Henry Foyle New Play Award, Arts Council Bursary, New York Drama Critics' Award); The Lion in Love, Royal Court 1960, New York 1962. *Films:* A Taste of Honey, 1961 (British Film Academy Award, Robert Flaherty Award); Charlie Bubbles, 1968 (Writers Guild Award for best original film writing). *TV series:* The House that Jack Built, BBC TV, 1977. *Publications:* A Taste of Honey, 1959 (London and New York); The Lion in Love, 1961 (London and New York); Sweetly Sings the Donkey, 1963 (New York), 1964 (London). *Address:* c/o CMA, 555 Madison Avenue, New York, NY 10022, USA; c/o Hope Leresche & Steele, 11 Jubilee Place, SW3 3TE.

DELARGEY, His Eminence Reginald John, Cardinal; *see* Wellington (NZ), Archbishop of, (RC).

de la RUE, Sir Eric (Vincent), 3rd Bt, *cr* 1898; *b* 5 Aug. 1906; *s* of Sir Evelyn Andros de la Rue, 2nd Bt, and Mary Violet (*d* 1959), *e d* of John Liell Francklin of Gonalston, Notts; *S* father 1950; *m* 1st, 1945, Cecilia (*d* 1963), *d* of late Lady Clementine Waring; two *s*; 2nd, 1964, Christine Schellin, Greenwich, Conn., USA; one *s. Educ:* Oundle. Served War of 1939-45. Capt. Notts Yeomanry, 1942-45. *Heir: s* Andrew George Ilay de la Rue, *b* 3 Feb. 1946. *Address:* Caldra, Duns, Scotland. *T:* Duns 94.

DE LA WARR, 10th Earl *cr* 1761; **William Herbrand Sackville,** DL; Baron De La Warr, 1299 and 1572; Viscount Cantelupe, 1761; Baron Buckhurst (UK), 1864; *b* 16 Oct. 1921; *e s* of 9th Earl De La Warr, PC, GBE, and Diana (*d* 1966), *d* of late Gerard Leigh; *S* father, 1976; *m* 1946, Anne Rachel, *o d* of Geoffrey Devas, Hunton Court, Maidstone; two *s* one *d. Educ:* Eton. Lieut Royal Sussex Regt, 1941-43; Lieut Parachute Regt, 1943; Capt. 1945-46. Contested (C) NE Bethnal Green, 1945; Chm. London Young Conservatives, 1946, Pres. 1947-49. Man. Dir, Rediffusion Ltd, 1974- (Dir, 1968); Director: British Electric Traction Co. Ltd, 1970-; Wembley Stadium Ltd, 1972-; Portals Hldgs Ltd, 1974-; Redifon, 1974-. Hon. Col Sussex ACF, 1969-; Vice-Chm., South East TAVR Assoc. (and Chm. Co. of

Sussex Cttee), 1968-74; Chairman: Sussex County Playing Fields Assoc., 1956-71; London and SE Resettlement Cttee for Ex-Regulars, 1969-74. DL East Sussex, 1975. *Heir: s* Lord Buckhurst, *qv. Address:* Buckhurst Park, Withyham, East Sussex. *T:* Hartfield 346; 93 Eaton Place, SW1. *T:* 01-235 7990. *Clubs:* White's, Pratt's.

DE LA WARR, Sylvia Countess; Sylvia Margaret Sackville, DBE 1957; *d* of William Reginald Harrison, Liverpool; *m* 1st, 1925, David Patrick Maxwell Fyfe (later Earl of Kilmuir, *cr* 1962, PC, GCVO) (*d* 1967); two *d* (and one *d* decd); 2nd, 1968, 9th Earl De La Warr, PC, GBE (*d* 1976). *Address:* Hardings, Withyham, Sussex.

DELAY, Professeur Jean, Commandeur de la Légion d'Honneur; Grand Officier de l'Ordre national du Mérite; Member of the Académie de Médecine since 1955; Member of the Académie Française, since 1959; *b* Bayonne, Pyrénées Atlantiques, 14 Nov. 1907; *m* 1933, Marie-Madeleine Carrez; two *d. Educ:* Faculté de Médecine and Faculté des Lettres Sorbonne. DèsL Sorbonne. Prof. of Mental Diseases, Faculté de Médecine de Paris, 1946-70; Director, L'Institut de Psychologie, Sorbonne, 1951-70. Mem. French Section Unesco. Hon. Member, Royal Society Med.; Dr hc Univs of Zürich, Montreal and Barcelona. Hon. Mem. numerous Foreign Socs. *Publications:* scientific: Les Dissolutions de la mémoire, 1942; Les Dérèglements de l'humeur, 1946; Les Maladies de la mémoire, 1947; La Psycho-Physiologie humaine, 1945; Aspects de la psychiatrie moderne, 1956; Etudes de psychologie médicale, 1953; Méthodes biologiques, 1950, psychométriques, 1956, chimiothérapiques, 1961, en psychiatrie; Introduction à la médecine psychosomatique, 1961; Abrégé de psychologie, 1962; Les démences tardives, 1962; L'électroencéphalographie clinique, 1966; Le syndrome de Korsakoff, 1969; literary: La Cité grise, 1946; Hommes sans nom, 1948; Les Reposantes, 1947; La Jeunesse d'André Gide (grand prix de la Critique), Vol. 1, 1956, Vol. 2, 1957; Une Amitié (André Gide et Roger Martin du Gard), 1968; La Correspondence de Jacques Copeau et Roger Martin du Gard, 1972. *Address:* 53 avenue Montaigne, 75008 Paris. *T:* 359 77-07.

DELBRIDGE, Rt. Rev. Graham Richard; *see* Gippsland, Bishop of.

DELBRÜCK, Prof. Max; Professor of Biology, California Institute of Technology, since 1947; *b* 4 Sept. 1906; *s* of Hans Delbrück and Lina Thiersch; *m* 1941, Mary Bruce; two *s* two *d. Educ:* Univs of Tübingen, Berlin, Bonn and Göttingen. PhD 1930. Visiting Prof., 1956, and Acting Prof., 1961-63, Cologne Univ. Mem., Nat. Acad. of Sciences; Fellow: Leopoldina Acad., Halle; Royal Danish Acad.; Foreign Mem., Royal Soc. Kimber Gold Medal (Genetics), US Nat. Acad. of Sciences; Nobel Prize for Physiology or Medicine (jtly), 1969. Hon. PhD: Copenhagen; Chicago; Harvard; Heidelberg. *Address:* 1510 Oakdale Street, Pasadena, California 91106, USA.

DELFONT, family name of **Baron Delfont.**

DELFONT, Baron *cr* 1976 (Life Peer), of Stepney; **Bernard Delfont,** Kt 1974; Chairman and Chief Executive, EMI Film and Theatre Corporation, since 1969; Chairman: EMI Cinemas Ltd; EMI Leisure Enterprises Ltd; EMI Elstree Studios; Director: EMI Film Distributors Ltd; Bernard Delfont Organisation; Blackpool Tower Company; Trust Houses Forte Leisure Ltd; EMI Film Distributors; The Grade Organisation; *b* Tokmak, Russia, 5 Sept. 1909; *s* of Isaac and Olga Winogradsky; *m* Carole Lynne; one *s* two *d*. Entered theatrical management, 1941; assumed management of: Wimbledon Theatre, 1942; Whitehall Theatre and St Martin's Theatre, 1943; (with Mala de la Marr) Winter Garden, 1944; Saville Theatre, 1946 (now ABC 1 and 2); lease of Prince of Wales Theatre, 1958; assumed management of Comedy Theatre and Shaftesbury Theatre, 1964; New London Theatre, 1973; converted London Hippodrome into Talk of the Town Restaurant, 1958, and presents entertainment there; controls more than 30 cos (theatre, film, television, music, property interests). Presents many of West End's theatrical shows and pantomimes and summer shows in many cities and towns in Great Britain. Past Chief Barker (Pres.), Variety Club of GB, (1969); Pres., Entertainment Artistes' Benevolent Fund, for which presents annual Royal Variety Performance. Companion, Grand Order of Water Rats. Member, Saints and Sinners. *Address:* 30-31 Golden Square, W1R 4AA. *T:* 01-437 9234.
See also Baron Grade.

DELHI, Archbishop of, (RC), since 1967; **Most Rev. Angelo Fernandes;** Member: Vatican Justice and Peace Commission; Office of Human Development of Federation of Asian Bishops'

Conferences; President, World Conference of Religion for Peace, since 1970; *b* 28 July 1913; *s* of late John Ligorio and Evelyn Sabina Fernandes. *Educ:* St Patrick's, Karachi; St Joseph's Seminary, Mangalore; Papal University, Kandy, Ceylon (STL). Secretary to Archbishop Roberts of Bombay, 1943-47; Administrator of Holy Name Cathedral, Bombay, 1947-59; Coadjutor Archbishop of Delhi, 1959-67; Sec. Gen., Catholic Bishops' Conf. of India, 1960-72. Member: Vatican Secretariat for Non-Believers, 1966-71; Secretariat of Synod of Bishops, 1971-74. Hon. DD Vatican, 1959. *Publications:* Apostolic Endeavour, 1962; Religion, Development and Peace, 1971; Religion and the Quality of Life, 1974; Religion and a New World Order, 1976; articles in Clergy Monthly, Vidyajyoti, World Justice, Religion and Society, Social Action, Reality, etc. *Recreations:* music, especially classical, and wide travel on the occasion of numerous meetings in many countries of the world. *Address:* Archbishop's House, Ashok Place, New Delhi 110001, India. *T:* 343457.

DELHI, Bishop of, since 1970; **Rt. Rev. Eric Samuel Nasir;** Moderator, Church of North India, since 1971; *b* 7 Dec. 1916. *Educ:* St Stephen's College, Delhi (MA); St Xavier's College, Calcutta (BT); Westcott House, Cambridge; Bishop's College, Calcutta. Warden, St Paul's Hostel, Delhi, 1942-45, 1951-52, 1956-62; Principal, Delhi United Christian School, 1956-62. Vicar: St Andrew's Church, Rewari, 1942-47; St Mary's Church, Ajmer, 1947-49; St James' Church, Delhi, 1949-51; St Thomas' Church, New Delhi, 1953-56; Holy Trinity Church, Delhi, 1952. Chaplain, St Stephen's College, Delhi, 1945-47. Member, Central Committee, World Council of Churches, 1968-. *Address:* Bishop's House, 1 Church Lane, New Delhi 1. *T:* 387471.

DE L'ISLE, 1st Viscount, *cr* 1956; **William Philip Sidney,** VC 1944; KG 1968; PC 1951; GCMG 1961; GCVO 1963; Baron De L'Isle and Dudley, 1835; Bt 1806; Bt 1818; Chairman, Phoenix Assurance Co. Ltd, since 1966; Chancellor, Order of St Michael and St George, since 1968; Governor-General of Australia, 1961-65; *b* 23 May 1909; *o s* of 5th Baron De L'Isle and Dudley and Winifred (*d* 1959), *e d* of Roland Yorke Bevan and Hon. Agneta Kinnaird, 4th *d* of 10th Baron Kinnaird; *S* father, 1945; *m* 1st 1940, Hon. Jacqueline Corinne Yvonne Vereker (*d* 1962), *o d* of late Field Marshal Viscount Gort of Hamsterley, VC, GCB, CBE, DSO, MVO, MC; one *s* four *d* ; 2nd 1966, Margaret Lady Glanusk, JP, *widow* of 3rd Baron Glanusk, DSO (whom she *m* 1942). *Educ:* Eton; Magdalene Coll., Cambridge. Commissioned Supplementary Reserve, Grenadier Guards, 1929, and served War of 1939-45 with Regt. MP (C) Chelsea, 1944-45; Parly Sec., Ministry of Pensions, 1945; Sec. of State for Air, Oct. 1951-Dec. 1955. Director: Yorkshire Bank; Diners' Club Inc., NY; Phoenix Assce Co. of NY. Pres., British Heart Foundn; Chm., Nat. Assoc. for Freedom. Trustee: Churchill Memorial Trust; RAF Museum. Hon. Fellow Magdalene Coll., Cambridge, 1955. FCA; Hon. FRIBA. Hon. LLD Sydney, 1963. KStJ 1961. *Heir: s* Major Hon. Philip John Algernon Sidney, MBE, Grenadier Guards, *b* 21 April 1945. *Address:* Penshurst Place, near Tonbridge, Kent; Glanusk Park, Crickhowell, Brecon.
See also Baron Middleton, Sir E. H. T. Wakefield, Bt.

DELL, David Michael; Regional Director for Yorkshire and Humberside, Department of Industry, since 1977; *b* 30 April 1931; *s* of Montague Roger Dell and Aimée Gabrielle Dell; unmarried. *Educ:* Rugby Sch.; Balliol Coll., Oxford (MA). 2nd Lieut Royal Signals, Egypt and Cyprus, 1954-55. Admiralty, 1955-60; MoD, 1960-65; Min. of Technol., 1965-70; DTI, 1970; Under Sec., 1976. *Address:* 21 Mountfields, Clarendon Road, Leeds LS2 9PB; 18 Shouldham Street, W1H 5FG. *Clubs:* Royal Automobile; Leeds (Leeds).

DELL, Rt. Hon. Edmund, PC 1970; MP (Lab) Birkenhead since 1964; Secretary of State for Trade, since 1976; *b* 15 Aug. 1921; *s* of late Reuben and Frances Dell; *m* 1963, Susanne Gottschalk. *Educ:* Elementary schls; Owen's Sch., London; Queen's Coll., Oxford (Open Schol.) 1st Cl. Hons Mod. Hist., BA and MA 1947. War Service, 1941-45, Lieut RA (Anti-tank). Lecturer in Modern History, Queen's Coll., Oxford, 1947-49; Executive in Imperial Chemical Industries Ltd, 1949-63. Mem., Manchester City Council, 1953-60. Contested (Lab) Middleton and Prestwich, 1955. Pres., Manchester and Salford Trades Council, 1958-61. Simon Research Fellow, Manchester Univ., 1963-64. Parly Sec., Min. of Technology, 1966-67; Jt Parly Under-Sec. of State, Dept of Economic Affairs, 1967-68; Minister of State: Board of Trade, 1968-69; Dept of Employment and Productivity, 1969-70; Paymaster General, 1974-76. Chm., Public Accts Cttee, 1973-74 (Acting Chm., 1972-73). Boys' Chess Champion of London, 1936. *Publications:* (ed with J. E. C. Hill) The Good Old Cause, 1949; Brazil: The Dilemma of

Reform (Fabian Pamphlet), 1964; Political Responsibility and Industry, 1973; articles in learned journals. *Recreation:* listening to music. *Address:* 4 Reynolds Close, NW11 7EA.

DELL, Ven. Robert Sydney; Archdeacon of Derby, since 1973; *b* 20 May 1922; *s* of Sydney Edward Dell and Lilian Constance Palmer; *m* 1953, Doreen Molly Layton; one *s* one *d*. *Educ:* Harrow County Sch.; Emmanuel Coll., Cambridge (MA); Ridley Hall. Curate of: Islington, 1948; Holy Trinity, Cambridge, 1950; Asst Chaplain, Wrekin Coll., 1953; Vicar of Mildenhall, Suffolk, 1955; Vice-Principal of Ridley Hall, Cambridge, 1957; Vicar of Chesterton, Cambridge, 1966 (Dir, Cambridge Samaritans, 1966-69). Mem., Archbishops' Commn on Intercommunion, 1965-67; Proctor in Convocation and Mem. Gen. Synod of C of E, 1970-. *Publications:* Atlas of Christian History, 1960; contributor to: Charles Simeon, 1759-1836: essays written in commemoration of his bi-centenary, 1959; Jl of Ecclesiastical History. *Recreations:* reading, walking, travelling. *Address:* 72 Pastures Hill, Littleover, Derby DE3 7BB. *T:* Derby 52700.

DELLAL, Jack; Chairman, Highland Electronics Group Ltd, 1971-76; *b* 2 Oct. 1923; *s* of Sulman and Charlotte Dellal; *m* 1952, Zehava Helmer; one *s* four *d*. *Educ:* Heaton Moor Coll., Manchester. Chm., Dalton, Barton & Co. Ltd, 1962-72; Dep. Chm., Keyser Ullman Ltd, 1972-74. Vice-Pres., Anglo-Polish Conservative Society. Officer, Order of Polonia Restituta, 1970. Freeman Citizen of Glasgow, 1971. *Recreations:* lawn tennis, squash, music, art. *Address:* 23 Ilchester Place, W14 8AA. *T:* 01-603 0981; Manor Farm, Brown Candover, Hants. *Clubs:* Royal Thames Yacht, Queen's, Lansdowne, Hurlingham.

DELLER, Alfred, OBE 1970; singer; *b* Margate, Kent, 31 May 1912; *s* of Thomas William Deller and Mary Cave; *m* 1937, Kathleen Margaret Lowe; two *s* one *d*. *Educ:* secondary sch. Lay-Clerk, Canterbury Cathedral, 1941-47; Vicar-Choral, St Paul's Cathedral, 1947-61. Soloist in BBC Third Programme inaugural concert, 1946; sang role of Oberon in first perf. of A Midsummer Night's Dream (opera by Britten), 1960. Formed Deller vocal ensemble Consort, 1950; Deller Consort tours of Australia, NZ, and USA, 1964, 1967, 1969, 1972. Concert tours of America with Desmond Dupré, 1955, 1957, 1959, 1962, 1973. Founder and Artistic Dir, Stour Music Festival, 1963; Founder, Deller Académie de Musique Anglaise, Abbaye de Sennanque, 1971. Festivals: Edinburgh, Aldeburgh, Three Choirs, Royal Danish, Vienna, Stuttgart, Graz, Lucerne, Hitzacker, etc. Hon. Music Adviser, Univ. of Kent. Pres., Catch Club of America. Hon. RAM, 1976. Hon. DLitt Kent, 1977. *Relevant publication:* Hardwick: Alfred Deller, a Singularity of Voice, 1968. *Recreations:* conversation and country life. *Address:* Barton Cottage, The Street, Kennington, Ashford, Kent. *T:* Ashford 23838.

DEL MAR, Norman Rene, CBE 1975; freelance conductor; Conductor, Royal Academy of Music; Conductor and Professor of Conducting, Royal College of Music; *b* 31 July 1919; *m* 1947, Pauline Mann; two *s*. *Educ:* Marlborough; Royal College of Music. Asst Sir Thomas Beecham, Royal Philharmonic Orchestra, 1947; Principal Conductor, English Opera Group, 1949-54; Conductor and Prof. of Conducting, Guildhall Sch. of Music, 1953-60; Conductor: Yorkshire Symphony Orchestra, 1954; BBC Scottish Orchestra, 1960-65; Principal Conductor, Acad. of BBC, 1974-77. FRCM; FGSM; Hon. RAM. Hon. DMus Glasgow, 1974; Hon. DLitt Sussex, 1977. *Publication:* Richard Strauss, 3 vols, 1962-72. *Recreations:* writing, chamber music. *Address:* Witchings, Hadley Common, Herts. *T:* 01-449 4836.

DELMAS, J. P. M. C.; *see* Chaban-Delmas.

DELMER, (Denis) Sefton, OBE 1946; writer on foreign affairs; *b* 24 May 1904; *s* of late Prof. F. S. Delmer, Hobart, Tasmania, English lecturer at Berlin Univ.; *m* 1935, Isabel (marr. diss., 1946), *d* of late Capt. P. O. Nicholas; *m* 1948, Zoë Ursula Black; one *s* one *d*. *Educ:* St Paul's Sch.; Lincoln Coll., Oxford. Joined Daily Express, 1927; Berlin Correspondent of Daily Express, 1928-33; Paris Correspondent, 1933-36; War Correspondent during Spanish Civil War, July 1936-Sept. 1938; Chief European Reporter of the Daily Express from 1937; War Correspondent, Poland 1939, France, 1939-40, with French Army; Foreign Office, 1941-45; rejoined Daily Express, as Chief Foreign Affairs Reporter, 1945-59. Editorial adviser to Der Spiegel, Hamburg, 1963-64. *Publications:* Trail Sinister, 1961; Black Boomerang, 1962; Die Deutschen und ich, 1962; Weimar Germany, 1972; The Counterfeit Spy, 1973. *Address:* The Valley Farm, Lamarsh, near Bures, Suffolk. *T:* Twinstead 222. *Clubs:* Garrick, Press, Lansdowne.

DELMER, Sefton; see Delmer, D. S.

de los ANGELES, Victoria; Cross of Lazo de Dama of Order of Isabel the Catholic, Spain; Condecoracíon Banda de la Orden Civil de Alfonso X (El Sabio), Spain; Opera and Concert-Artiste (singing in original languages), Lyric-Soprano, since 1944; *b* Barcelona, Spain, 1 Nov. 1923; *m* 1948, Enrique Magriñá; two *s*. *Educ:* Conservatorium of Barcelona; University of Barcelona. Studied until 1944 at Conservatorium, Barcelona; first public concert, in Barcelona, 1944; début at Gran Teatro del Liceo de Barcelona, in Marriage of Figaro, 1945; concert tours in Spain and Portugal, 1945 and 1946; winner of first prize at Concours International of Geneva, 1947; Paris Opera first appearance, and début at the Scala, Milan, also South-American concert-tour, 1949; first tour in Scandinavia, first appearance at Covent Garden, and Carnegie Hall Début, 1950; first United States concert tour, and Metropolitan Opera of New York season, 1951. Since 1951 has appeared at the most important opera theatres and concert halls of Europe, South and Central America and Canada; first tour in S Africa, 1953; first tour in Australia, 1956; first appearance, Vienna State Opera, 1957. Opening Festival, Bayreuth, with Tannhäuser, 1961. Gold Medal, Barcelona, 1958; Silver Medal, province of Barcelona, 1959; Medal Premio Roma, 1969, etc. *Address:* Victoria de los Angeles de Magriñá, c/o E. Magriñá, Paseo de Gracia, 87-7-D, Barcelona, Spain.

de LOTBINIÈRE, Lt-Col Sir Edmond; see Joly de Lotbinière.

de LOTBINIÈRE, Seymour Joly, CVO 1956; OBE 1953; *b* 21 Oct. 1905; *s* of late Brig.-Gen. H. G. Joly de Lotbinière, DSO; *m* 1944, Mona Lewis; one *s*. *Educ:* Eton; Trinity Coll., Cambridge. Called to Bar, Lincoln's Inn. On BBC staff, 1932-67. Governor, Bristol Old Vic Trust, 1963-67. CC West Suffolk, 1970-74. *Address:* Brandon Hall, Brandon, Suffolk. *T:* Thetford 810227.
See also Lt-Col Sir Edmond Joly de Lotbinière.

DELVE, Sir Frederick (William), Kt 1962; CBE 1942; Chief Officer, London Fire Brigade, 1948-62, retired; Director and Vice-Chairman, Securicor Ltd; Director, Sound Diffusion Ltd; *b* 28 Oct. 1902; *s* of Frederick John Delve, Master Tailor, Brighton; *m* 1924, Ethel Lillian Morden; no *c*. *Educ:* Brighton. Royal Navy, 1918-23; Fire Service since 1923; Chief Officer, Croydon Fire Brigade, 1934-41; Dep. Inspector-in-Chief of NFS, 1941-43; Chief Regional Fire Officer, No 5 London Region, National Fire Service, 1943-48. Pres., Institution of Fire Engineers, 1941-42; King's Police and Fire Services Medal, 1940. *Address:* 53 Ashley Court, Grand Avenue, Hove, East Sussex.

DELVIN, Lord; title borne by eldest son of Earl of Westmeath, *qv*; not at present used.

DELYSIA, Alice; *b* March 1889; *d* of M. Lapize and Mme. Mathilde Douce; *m* 1944, Captain Kolb-Bernard, DSC, Agent Consulaire (for France). *Educ:* Convent des Sœurs de Nevers. Began under C. B. Cochran in Odds and Ends, 1914; More Pell Mell, Carminetta, As You Were, Afgar; went to America with Afgar, came back to London in Mayfair and Montmartre; went again to America in the Schubert revue Topics of 1924; came back to London in first straight play; successes: Her Past, Princess Charming, A Pair of Trousers, The Cat and The Fiddle, and Mother of Pearl, etc; first appearance in Australia, 1934; returned to London and made several subsequent tours; entered films, 1934, and appeared in Evensong. Enlisted with ENSA, May 1941, acting for troops in whole Middle East, then Normandy, Belgium, Holland, until end of war. King's Medal for Freedom; Africa Star, 8th Army; French Recognition Medal for War Services; Free French Medal; Order of Merit (Lebanon and Syria). *Recreations:* horse riding, walking, swimming.

de MANIO, Jack, MC 1940; Broadcaster; *b* 26 Jan. 1914; *s* of Jean and Florence de Manio; *m* 1st, 1935, Juliet Gravaeret Kaufmann, New York (marr. diss., 1946); one *s*; 2nd, 1946, Loveday Elizabeth Matthews (*widow, née* Abbott). *Educ:* Aldenham. Served War of 1939-45, Royal Sussex Regt; 7th Bn, BEF, 1939-40; 1st Bn, Middle East Forces, 1940-44; Forces Broadcasting, Middle East, 1944-46. Joined Overseas Service, BBC, 1946; BBC Home Service, 1950; resigned to become freelance, 1964. Presenter BBC programmes: Today, 1958-71; Jack de Manio Precisely, 1971-; With Great Pleasure, 1971-. Dir, Neilson McCarthy Ltd. Radio Personality of Year Award, Variety Club of GB, 1964; Radio Personality Award of Year, British Radio Industries Club, 1971. *Publications:* To Auntie with Love, 1967; Life Begins Too Early, 1970. *Recreation:* fishing. *Address:* 105 Cheyne Walk, SW10. *T:* 01-352 0889. *Clubs:* Brooks's, MCC.

DEMANT, Rev. Vigo Auguste, MA, DLitt Oxford; BSc, Hon. DD Durham; *b* 8 Nov. 1893; *s* of late T. Demant, linguist, of Newcastle on Tyne, and Emily Demant; *m* 1925, Marjorie, *d* of late George Tickner, FZS, Oxford; one *s* two *d*. *Educ:* Newcastle on Tyne; Tournan, France; Armstrong Coll., Durham Univ.; Manchester Coll. and Exeter Coll., Oxford; Ely Theological Coll. Curacies: S Thomas, Oxford, S Nicholas, Plumstead, S Silas, Kentish Town; Dir of Research to Christian Social Council, 1929-33; Vicar of S John-the-Divine, Richmond, Surrey, 1933-42; Canon Residentiary, 1942-49, Treasurer, 1948-49, of St Paul's Cathedral; Canon of Christ Church and Regius Professor of Moral and Pastoral Theology in Oxford University, 1949-71. Ex-Mem. Departmental Cttee on Homosexual Offences and Prostitution. Gifford Lecturer, St Andrews, 1957-58. *Publications:* This Unemployment, 1931; God, Man and Society, 1933; Christian Polity, 1936; The Religious Prospect, 1939; Theology of Society, 1947; Religion and the Decline of Capitalism, 1952; A Two-way Religion, 1957; Christian Sex Ethics, 1963. *Recreation:* carpentry. *Address:* 31 St Andrew's Road, Old Headington, Oxford. *T:* Oxford 64022.

de MARGERIE, Roland, CVO 1938; Ambassador of France; Hon. Conseiller d'Etat; *b* 6 May 1899; *s* of late P. de Margerie, KBE, French Ambassador in Berlin, 1922-31, and Jeanne Rostand, sister of the Playwright Edmond Rostand, Mem. of the French Academy; *m* 1921, Jenny, *d* of Edmond Fabre-Luce, Vice-Chm. of the Crédit Lyonnais; two *s* one *d*. *Educ:* Sorbonne; Ecole des Sciences Politiques, Paris. Joined Foreign Office, 1917; Lieut 17th Bn of Chasseurs Alpins, 1918-21; Attaché to French Embassy, Brussels, 1921; Sec., Berlin, 1923; 1st Sec. to the French Embassy, London, 1933-39; mem. of the mission attached to their Majesties during their State visit to France, 1938; Counsellor, 1939; Captain 152nd Regt of the Line, Sept. 1939-Feb. 1940; ADC to Gen. Gamelin, Feb.-March 1940; Private Sec. to the Minister for Foreign Affairs, March 1940; French Consul-Gen., Shanghai, 1940-44; Chargé with the office of the French Embassy in Peking, 1944-46. Asst deleg. negotiations for Brussels Pact, 1948; Minister plenipotentiary, 1949; Director-Gen. of Political Affairs, France, 1955; French Ambassador to the Holy See, 1956-59; to Spain, 1959-62; to the Federal Republic of Germany, 1962-65; Conseiller d'Etat, 1965-70. Comdr Legion of Honour; holds various foreign orders. *Address:* 14 rue St Guillaume, 75007 Paris, France. *Club:* Jockey (Paris).

de MAULEY, 6th Baron, *cr* 1838; **Gerald John Ponsonby;** *b* 19 Dec. 1921; *er s* of 5th Baron de Mauley and Elgiva Margaret, *d* of late Hon. Cospatrick Dundas and Lady Cordeaux; *S* father, 1962; *m* 1954, Helen Alice, *d* of late Hon. Charles W. S. Douglas and *widow* of Lieut-Col B. L. L. Abdy Collins, OBE, MC, RE. *Educ:* Eton; Christ Church, Oxford (MA). Served War of 1939-45, France; Lieut Leics Yeo., Captain RA. Called to Bar, Middle Temple, 1949. Heir: *b* Major Hon. Thomas Maurice Ponsonby, Royal Glos Hussars [*b* 2 Aug. 1930; *m* 1956, Maxine Henrietta, *d* of W. D. K. Thellusson; two *s*]. *Address:* Langford House, Little Faringdon, Lechlade, Glos.

de MAYO, Prof. Paul, FRS 1975; FRSC 1971; Professor of Chemistry, University of Western Ontario, since 1959; *b* 8 Aug. 1924; *s* of Nissim and Anna de Mayo; *m* 1949, Mary Turnbull; one *s* one *d*. *Educ:* Univ. of London. BSc, MSc, PhD London; DèsS Paris. Asst Lectr, Birkbeck Coll., London, 1954-55; Lectr, Univ. of Glasgow, 1955-57; Lectr, Imperial Coll., London, 1957-59; Dir, Photochemistry Unit, Univ. of Western Ontario, 1969-72. *Publications:* Mono-and sesquiterpenoids, 1959; The Higher Terpenoids, 1959; (ed) Molecular Rearrangements, 1963; numerous papers in learned jls. *Address:* 436 St George Street, London, Ontario, Canada. *T:* (office) 679-2473, (home) 679-9026.

de MILLE, Agnes George (Mrs W. F. Prude); Choreographer and Author; *b* New York City; *d* of William C. and Anna George de Mille; *m* 1943, Walter F. Prude; one *s*. *Educ:* University of Calif. (AB *cum laude*). Dance concerts USA, England, Denmark, France, 1929-40; Choreographed: Black Crook, 1929; Nymph Errant, 1933; Romeo and Juliet 1936; Oklahoma, 1943; One Touch of Venus, 1943; Bloomer Girl, 1944; Carousel, 1945; Brigadoon, 1947; Gentlemen Prefer Blondes, 1949; Paint Your Wagon, 1951; The Girl in Pink Tights, 1954; Oklahoma (film), 1955; Goldilocks, 1958; Juno, 1959; Kwamina, 1961; One Hundred and Ten in the Shade, 1963; Come Summer, 1968. Founded and directed Agnes de Mille Dance Theatre, 1953-54. Directed: Allegro, 1947; The Rape of Lucretia, 1948; Out of This World, 1950; Come Summer, 1968; Ballets composed: Black Ritual, 1940; Three Virgins and a Devil, 1941; Drums Sound in Hackensack, 1941; Rodeo, 1942; Tally-Ho, 1944; Fall River Legend, 1948; The Harvest According, 1952; The Rib of Eve, 1956; The Bitter Wierd, 1963; The Wind in the Mountains,

1965; The Four Marys, 1965; The Golden Age, 1966; A Rose for Miss Emily, 1970; Texas Fourth, 1976; Agnes de Mille Heritage Dance Theater, 1973-74, etc. Television shows, for Omnibus, etc. Mem., Nat. Adv. Council of the Arts, 1965-66; Pres., Soc. for Stage Directors and Choreographers, 1966-67. Hon. Degrees: Mills Coll., 1952; Russell Sage College, 1953; Smith Coll., 1954; Northwestern Univ., 1960; Goucher Coll., 1961; University of Calif., 1962; Clark Univ., 1962; Franklin and Marshall Coll., 1966; Western Michigan Univ., 1967; Nasson Coll., 1971; Dartmouth Coll., 1974; Duke Univ. New York Critics Award, 1943, 1944, 1945; Antoinette Perry Award, 1962; Handel Medallion, 1976; and numerous other awards, 1943-58. *Publications:* Dance to the Piper, 1952; And Promenade Home, 1958; To a Young Dancer, 1962; The Book of the Dance, 1963; Lizzie Borden, Dance of Death, 1968; Dance in America, 1970; Russian Journals, 1970; Speak to me, Dance with me, 1973; articles in Vogue, Atlantic Monthly, Good Housekeeping, New York Times, McCall's, Horizon, Esquire. *Club:* Merriewold Country (NY).

DE MOLEYNS; *see* Eveleigh-de-Moleyns.

de MONTMORENCY, Sir Reginald (D'Alton Lodge), 18th Bt, *cr* 1631; *b* 13 March 1899; *y s* of John Kiddell de Montmorency and Ada Margaret Ligonier Balfour; *S* cousin, 1963; *m* 1928, Dorothy Victoria, 2nd *d* of Gilbert Walter Robinson. *Educ:* privately in England and Bruges for art. Served European War 1914-18: Hon. Artillery Co. and Royal Horse Artillery, 1917-19. P. & O., 1915-17, shore service at home and abroad, 1919-25; Manager: (in Bombay) for Bell, Russ & Co. (East India merchants), 1925-33; A. Besse of Arabia and Manager of the Halal Shipping Co., 1933-35. Joined the staff of The Times, 1936 and retired 1967. Travelled widely in Commonwealth and other countries in connection with his work. *Recreations:* swimming, riding, walking and drawing. *Heir: cousin* Arnold Geoffroy de Montmorency, *b* 27 July 1908. *Address:* Bristol Cottage, Putney Heath, SW15. *T:* 01-788 2102. *Club:* Royal Commonwealth Society.

de MOURGUES, Prof. Odette Marie Hélène Louise, PhD, DLitt; Palmes Académiques 1964; Ordre National du Mérite 1973; Professor of French, University of Cambridge, since 1975; Lecturer, Research Fellow and Fellow, Girton College, Cambridge, since 1946; *b* 14 May 1914; *d* of Dr Pierre de Mourgues and Hélène Terle; *m* 1934 (marr. diss. 1943); one *s* decd. *Educ:* Lycée of Le Puy; Univs of Grenoble and Aix-en-Provence. Licence en droit, diplôme d'études supérieures de droit, LèsL, agrégation d'anglais; PhD, DLitt Cantab. Teaching posts, Valence, Digne and Marseille, 1942-45; Asst Lectr, Univ. of Aix-en-Provence, 1944-46; Lectr in French, 1952-68, Reader, 1968-75, Univ. of Cambridge. *Publications:* Metaphysical, Baroque and Précieux Poetry, 1953; Le Jugement Avant-dernier (fiction), 1954; L'Hortensia Bleu (fiction), 1956; La Fontaine: Fables, 1960; O Muse, fuyante Proie, 1962; An Anthology of French 17C Poetry, 1966; Racine or the Triumph of Relevance, 1967; Autonomie de Racine, 1967; essays, articles and revs. *Recreations:* travel, gardening. *Address:* 1 Marion Close, Cambridge. *T:* Cambridge 56865.

DEMPSEY, Andrew; *see* Dempsey, J. A.

DEMPSEY, James; JP; MP (Lab) Coatbridge and Airdrie since Oct. 1959; *b* 6 Feb. 1917; *s* of late James Dempsey; *m* 1945, Jane, *d* of late John McCann; five *s* one *d*. *Educ:* Holy Family Sch., Mossend; Co-operative Coll., Loughborough; National Council of Labour Colls. Served War of 1939-45: Auxiliary Military Pioneer Corps. Member Hospital Board of Management and Board for Industry and Executive Council, National Health Service, National Assistance Board. JP Lanarkshire, 1954; CC Lanarkshire, 1945-. *Address:* The House of Commons, SW1; 113 Thorndean Avenue, Bellshill, Lanarkshire. *T:* 2712.

DEMPSEY, (James) Andrew; Assistant Director of Exhibitions, Arts Council of Great Britain, since 1975; *b* 17 Nov. 1942; *s* of James Dempsey, Glasgow; *m* 1966, Grace, *d* of Dr Ian MacPhail, Dumbarton; one *s* one *d*. *Educ:* Ampleforth Coll.; Glasgow Univ. Whistler Research Asst, Fine Art Dept, Univ. of Glasgow, 1963-65; exhibn work for art dept of Arts Council, 1966-71; Keeper, Dept of Public Relations, V&A, 1971-75. *Address:* 105 Piccadilly, W1.

DENBIGH, 11th Earl of, *cr* 1622 and **DESMOND,** 10th Earl of, *cr* 1622; **William Rudolph Michael Feilding;** *b* 2 Aug. 1943; *s* of 10th Earl of Denbigh and Verena Barbara, *d* of W. E. Price; *S* father, 1966; *m* 1965, Caroline Judith Vivienne, *o d* of Lt-Col Geoffrey Cooke; one *s* two *d*. *Educ:* Eton. *Heir: s* Viscount Feilding, *qv. Address:* Pailton House, Rugby, Warwicks. *T:* Rugby 832726.

DENBIGH, Kenneth George, FRS 1965; MA Cantab, DSc Leeds; Principal of Queen Elizabeth College, University of London, 1966-77; *b* 30 May 1911; *s* of late G. J. Denbigh, MSc, Harrogate; *m* 1935, Kathleen Enoch; two *s*. *Educ:* Queen Elizabeth Grammar Sch., Wakefield; Leeds University. Imperial Chemical Industries, 1934-38, 1945-48; Lecturer, Southampton Univ., 1938-41; Ministry of Supply (Explosives), 1941-45; Lecturer, Cambridge Univ., Chemical Engineering Dept, 1948-55; Professor: of Chemical Technology, Edinburgh, 1955-60, of Chemical Engineering Science, London Univ., 1960-61; Courtauld's Prof., Imperial Coll., 1961-66. Fellow, Imperial Coll., 1976. Hon. DèsSc Toulouse, 1960; Hon. DUniv. Essex, 1967. *Publications:* The Thermodynamics of the Steady State, 1951; The Principles of Chemical Equilibrium, 1955; Science, Industry and Social Policy, 1963; Chemical Reactor Theory, 1965; An Inventive Universe, 1975; various scientific papers. *Address:* 19 Sheridan Road, Merton Park, SW19 3HW.

DENBY, Patrick Morris Coventry; Assistant Director-General (Treasurer and Financial Comptroller), International Labour Office, Geneva, since 1976; *b* 28 Sept. 1920; *s* of Robert Coventry Denby and Phyllis Denby (née Dacre); *m* 1950, Margaret Joy, *d* of Lt-Col C. L. Boyle; two *d* (and one *d* decd). *Educ:* Bradford Grammar Sch.; Corpus Christi Coll., Oxford (Open Scholar) (Honour Mods, Cl. II, MA). War service with Intelligence Corps, as Temp. Lieut RNVR, and with Foreign Office, 1941-46. Unilever Ltd, UK and Australia: management trainee and product manager, 1946-51; joined International Labour Office, 1951: Professional Officer, 1951; Chief of Budget and Control Div., 1959; Chief of Finance and General Services Dept, Treasurer and Financial Comptroller, 1970; Chm., Investments Cttee; Mem., UN Pension Board, 1971-75. *Recreations:* skiing, mountain walking, squash. *Address:* 29 route de Malagnou, 1208 Geneva, Switzerland. *T:* Geneva 351694. *Clubs:* United Oxford & Cambridge University; Swiss Alpine.

DENBY, Richard Kenneth; President of the Law Society of England and Wales, 1977 (Vice-President, 1976); Senior Partner, A. V. Hammond & Co., Bradford; *b* 20 March 1915; *s* of John Henry and Emily Denby; *m* 1939, Eileen (*d* 1974), *d* of M. H. Pickles, CBE; one *s* two *d*. *Educ:* Ackworth School; Leeds Univ. (LLB). Admitted Solicitor, 1937 (First Cl. Hons and Clifford's Inn Prize). Served War of 1939-45: 2nd Lt, The Green Howards, 1940; AFHQ N Africa, 1942; War Office, DAMS MS1(b), 1944; AMS, Lt-Col Northern Command, 1945 (despatches). Director: Bradford & Bingley Building Soc.; Parkland Textile (Holdings) Ltd; Pennine Radio (Bradford Community Radio Ltd). Pres., Bradford Incorporated Law Soc., 1955; Chm., Mental Health Review Tribunal, NE Region; Dep. Commissioner, St John Ambulance for South and West Yorks. *Recreations:* fishing, fell-walking. *Address:* Chilliswood, South Parade, Ilkley, W Yorks. *T:* Ilkley 609076. *Clubs:* Army and Navy, Junior Carlton; Union (Bradford).

DENCH, Judith Olivia, (Judi Dench), OBE 1970; **(Mrs Michael Williams);** actress (theatre, films and television); *b* 9 Dec. 1934; *d* of Reginald Arthur Dench and Eleanora Olave Dench (née Jones); *m* 1971, Michael Williams; one *d*. *Educ:* The Mount Sch., York; Central Sch. of Speech and Drama. *Theatre:* Old Vic seasons, 1957-61: parts incl.: Ophelia in Hamlet; Katherine in Henry V; Cecily in The Importance of Being Earnest; Juliet in Romeo and Juliet; also 1957-61: two Edinburgh Festivals; Paris-Belgium-Yugoslavia tour; America-Canada tour; Venice (all with Old Vic Co.). Subseq. appearances incl.: Royal Shakespeare Co., 1961-62: Anya in The Cherry Orchard; Titania in A Midsummer Night's Dream; Dorcas Bellboys in A Penny for a Song; Isabella in Measure for Measure; Nottingham Playhouse tour of W Africa, 1963; Oxford Playhouse, 1964-65: Irina in The Three Sisters; Doll Common in The Alchemist; Nottingham Playhouse, 1965: Saint Joan; The Astrakhan Coat (world première); Amanda in Private Lives; Variety London Critics' Best Actress of the Year Award for perf. as Lika in The Promise, Fortune, 1967; Sally Bowles in Cabaret, Palace, 1968; London Assurance, Aldwych, 1970, and New, 1972; Major Barbara, Aldwych, 1970; Associate Mem., Royal Shakespeare Co., Stratford-on-Avon, 1969-: Bianca in Women Beware Women, Viola in Twelfth Night, doubling Hermione and Perdita in The Winter's Tale, Portia in The Merchant of Venice, Viola in Twelfth Night, the Duchess in The Duchess of Malfi, Beatrice in Much Ado About Nothing, Lady Macbeth in Macbeth, Adriana in The Comedy of Errors, Regan in King Lear; The Wolf, Oxford and London, 1973; The Good Companions, Her Majesty's, 1974; The Gay Lord Quex, Albery, 1975; Too True to be Good, Aldwych, 1975, Globe, 1976; Pillars of the Community, Aldwych, 1977. Recital tour of W Africa, 1969; RSC tours: Japan and Australia, 1970; Japan, 1972. *Films:* He Who Rides a Tiger; A Study in Terror; Four in the Morning

(Brit. Film Acad. Award for Most Promising Newcomer, 1965); A Midsummer Night's Dream. TV appearances, 1957- (Best Actress of the Year Award from Guild of Television Dirs for Talking to a Stranger, 1967). Awards incl. British and foreign, for theatre, films and TV. *Recreations:* painting, swimming, picking up odds and ends.

DENHAM, 2nd Baron, *cr* 1937, of Weston Underwood; **Bertram Stanley Mitford Bowyer,** 10th Bt, *cr* 1660, of Denham; 2nd Bt, *cr* 1933 of Weston Underwood; *b* 3 Oct. 1927; *s* of 1st Baron and Hon. Daphne Freeman-Mitford, 4th *d* of 1st Baron Redesdale; *S* father 1948; *m* 1956, Jean, *o d* of Kenneth McCorquodale, Fambridge Hall, White Notley, Essex; three *s* one *d. Educ:* Eton; King's Coll., Cambridge. Joined Grenadier Guards, 1945; commissioned Oxford & Bucks LI, 1946; demobilised, 1948. Mem. Westminster CC, 1959-61. A Lord-in-Waiting to the Queen, 1961-64 and 1970-71; Captain of the Yeomen of the Guard, 1971-74. *Recreations:* field sports. *Heir: s* Hon. Richard Grenville George Bowyer, *b* 8 Feb. 1959. *Address:* The Laundry Cottage, Weston Underwood, Olney, Bucks. *T:* Bedford 711535. *Clubs:* White's, Pratt's.

DENHAM, Ernest William; Records Administration Officer, Public Record Office, since 1973; *b* 16 Sept. 1922; *s* of William and Beatrice Denham; *m* 1957, Penelope Agatha Gregory; one *s* one *d. Educ:* City of London Sch.; Merton Coll., Oxford (Postmaster). MA 1948. Naval Intell., UK and SEAC, 1942-45. Asst Sec., Plant Protection Ltd, 1947-49; Asst Keeper 1949, Principal Asst Keeper 1967, Public Record Office; Lectr in Palaeography and Diplomatic, UCL, 1957-73. *Recreation:* armchair criticism. *Address:* 27 The Drive, Northwood, Mddx. *T:* Northwood 27382.

DENHAM, Captain Henry Mangles, CMG 1945; RN, retired; *b* 9 Sept. 1897; *s* of Henry Mangles Denham and Helen Clara Lowndes; *m* 1924, Estelle Margaret Sibbald Currie; one *s* two *d. Educ:* RN Coll., Dartmouth. Went to sea at beginning of European War, serving at Dardanelles in HMS Agamemnon and destroyer Racoon; occupation of the Rhine in HM Rhine Flotilla; round the world cruise with the Prince of Wales in HMS Renown, 1921; served in Mediterranean for long period largely in HMS Queen Elizabeth and Warspite; at Staff Coll., 1935; Comdr of HMS Penelope, 1936-39. Naval Attaché, Scandinavian Countries, 1940; Naval Attaché, Stockholm, 1940-47; retd list, 1947. *Publications:* The Aegean, 1963; Eastern Mediterranean, 1964; The Adriatic, 1967; The Tyrrhenian Sea, 1969; The Ionian Islands to Rhodes, 1972; Southern Turkey, the Levant and Cyprus, 1973. *Recreation:* yachting. *Clubs:* Royal Automobile, Royal Ocean Racing, Royal Cruising; Royal Yacht Squadron (Cowes).

DENHAM, Maurice; Actor since 1934; *b* 23 Dec. 1909; *s* of Norman Denham and Winifred Lillico; *m* 1936, Margaret Dunn (*d* 1971); two *s* one *d. Educ:* Tonbridge Sch. Hull Repertory Theatre, 1934-36; theatre, radio and television, 1936-39. Served War of 1939-45: Buffs, 1939-43; Royal Artillery, 1943-45; despatches, 1946. Theatre, films, radio and television, 1946-. *Recreations:* painting, conducting gramophone records, golf. *Address:* 3 Middle Furlong, Seaford, East Sussex. *Clubs:* Garrick, Green Room; Stage Golfing.

DENHOLM, Ian; *see* Denholm, J. F.

DENHOLM, Sir John (Carmichael), Kt 1955; CBE 1947; President of J. & J. Denholm Ltd; *b* 24 Dec. 1893; *s* of John Denholm and Jane Miller, Greenock, Scotland; *m* 1926, Mary Laura, *d* of Peter Kerr, Greenock; no *c. Educ:* Greenock Acad. Joined family firm, J. & J. Denholm Ltd, 1910; Dir 1922; RNVR: Midshipman, 1910; Sub-Lieut, 1912; Lieut temp. 1915, perm. list 1917; Lieut-Comdr 1925; resigned 1926; served European War, 1914-18; RN Div. Antwerp and Gallipoli, 1914-15; RN HMS Ladybird, 1916-19 (despatches); Regional Shipping Rep. for West Coast Scotland, Ministry of Shipping and Min. of War Transport, 1940-45. Council of Chamber of Shipping: Mem. 1936; Vice-Pres, 1953; Pres. 1954-55. Chm., David Macbrayne Ltd, 1963-64. *Recreation:* golf. *Address:* 3 Octavia Terrace, Greenock. *T:* Greenock 20940. *Club:* Royal Scottish Automobile (Glasgow).
See also Col Sir William Denholm.

DENHOLM, John Ferguson, (Ian), CBE 1974; Chairman: Denholm Ship Management Ltd, since 1972; Denholm Line Steamers Ltd; J. & J. Denholm Ltd; *b* 8 May 1927; *s* of Sir William Lang Denholm, *qv*; *m* 1952, Elizabeth Murray Stephen; two *s* two *d. Educ:* St Mary's Sch., Melrose; Loretto Sch., Musselburgh. Joined J. & J. Denholm Ltd, 1945. Pres., Chamber of Shipping of the UK, 1973-74; Member: Nat. Ports Council, 1974-; Scottish Transport Gp, 1975-. Hon. Norwegian

Consul in Glasgow, 1975-. *Recreations:* sailing, ski-ing. *Address:* Newton of Belltrees, Lochwinnoch, Renfrewshire PA12 4JL. *T:* Lochwinnoch 406. *Clubs:* Royal Thames Yacht; Western (Glasgow).

DENHOLM, Col Sir William (Lang), Kt 1965; TD; DL; Chairman, J. & J. Denholm Ltd, 1966-74; Chairman, Shipping Federation, 1962-65; Joint Chairman, National Maritime Board, 1962-65; President, International Shipping Federation, 1962-67; *b* 23 Feb. 1901; *s* of John Denholm and Jane Miller, Greenock; *m* 1925, Dorothy Jane, *d* of Robert Ferguson, Greenock; two *s* one *d. Educ:* Greenock Academy; Greenock Collegiate. Joined family firm J. & J. Denholm Ltd, 1918. 2nd Lieut 77th (H) Field Regt, RA (TA), 1921; in command, 1939-40; Hon. Col 1945-60. Mem. Gen. and Scottish Cttees, Lloyd's Register of Shipping, 1935-77. Mem. Council, Shipping Federation, 1936; Vice-Chm., 1950-62. Vice-Chm, Glasgow Royal Infirmary and Assoc. Hospitals, 1949-60; Chm., 1960-64. DL County of Renfrew 1950. Chevalier of the Order of St Olav (Norway). *Recreation:* golf. *Address:* Glenmill, Kilmacolm, Renfrewshire. *T:* Kilmacolm 2535. *Clubs:* Western, Royal Scottish Automobile (Glasgow).
See also Sir John Denholm, J. F. Denholm.

DENING, Maj.-Gen. Roland, CB 1942; MVO 1935; MC 1918; DL; IA; psc; retired; *b* 13 Sept. 1888; *s* of late Lt-Gen. Sir Lewis Dening, KCB, DSO, and late Beatrice Catherine Scott; *m* 1917, Clare de Burgh (Kaisar-i-hind Gold Medal, 1942; DGStJ, 1963), *d* of J. H. Garratt, Greystones, Co. Wicklow; one *s* two *d. Educ:* Wellington Coll., Berks; RMA Woolwich. Entered Royal Field Artillery, 1907; Transferred to 18th Bengal Lancers, Indian Army, 1911; served European War 18th (KGO) Lancers, France 1914-18, Palestine and Syria 1918; DAAG 4th Cavalry Div. EEF 1918; DAAG Northforce EEF 1919; Instructor Cavalry Sch., Saugor, 1920-21; Attended Staff Coll., Quetta, 1922; Brigade Major, 1st Risalpur Cavalry Brigade, 1924-28; Brevet Lt-Col, 1930; Commandant, Equitation Sch., Saugor, 1931-34; Commandant, 19th KGO Lancers, 1934-36; Gen. Staff Officer 1st Grade, Peshawar District, 1936-38; Comm. Jullunder Brig. Area, India, 1938; Comdr 1st Abbotabad Inf. Bde, 1940; Maj.-Gen. 1940; Comdr Peshawar District, 1940-43; retired, 1944, Col 19th King George V's Own Lancers, 1945-49. Chm. Housing Cttee, Ottery St Mary UDC, 1948-51; Chm. British Legion Devon County, 1950-54; County Cadet Officer (Ambulance), St John Ambulance Brigade, Devon, 1951-61; Officer Brother, Order of St John of Jerusalem, 1958. Pres. Honiton and District Agricultural Assoc., 1957. Hon. Sec., Sidmouth and Ottery St Mary Div., SS&AFA, 1948-72. DL Devonshire, 1954. *Recreations:* polo, tennis, rackets. *Address:* Tipton Lodge, Tipton St John, near Sidmouth, East Devon EX10 0AW. *T:* Ottery St Mary 2027.

DENINGTON, Dame Evelyn (Joyce), DBE 1974 (CBE 1966); Chairman, Stevenage Development Corporation, since 1966 (Member, since 1950); Chairman, Greater London Council, 1975-76 (Chairman Transport Committee 1973-75); *b* 9 Aug. 1907; *d* of Phillip Charles Bursill and Edith Rowena Bursill; *m* 1935, Cecil Dallas Denington. *Educ:* Blackheath High Sch.; Bedford Coll., London. Journalism, 1927-31; Teacher, 1933-45; Gen. Sec., Nat. Assoc. of Labour Teachers, 1938-47; Member: St Pancras Borough Council, 1945-59; LCC, 1946-65 (Chm. New and Expanding Towns Cttee, 1960-65); GLC, 1964-77 (Chm. Housing Cttee, 1964-67; Dep. Leader (Lab), Opposition, 1967-73); Central Housing Adv. Cttee, 1955-73 (Chm. Sub-Cttee prod. report Our Older Homes); SE Economic Planning Council, 1966-; Chm., New Towns Assoc., 1973-75. Member: Sutton Dwellings Housing Trust, 1976-; North British Housing Assoc., 1976-; St Pancras Housing Assoc., Camden, 1976-; Shackleton Housing Assoc., 1976-; Thames Riparian Housing Assoc., 1976-. Hon. FRIBA; Hon. MRTPI. *Address:* Weale House, 29 Crescent Grove, Clapham, SW4. *T:* 01-622 1275.

DENISON, family name of **Baron Londesborough.**

DENISON, Dulcie Winifred Catherine, (Dulcie Gray); actress, playwright, authoress; *b* 20 Nov. 1920; *d* of late Arnold Savage Bailey, CBE, and of Kate Edith (*née* Clulow Gray); *m* 1939, Michael Denison, *qv. Educ:* England and Malaya. In Repertory in Aberdeen, 1st part Sorrel in Hay Fever, 1939; Repertory in Edinburgh, Glasgow and Harrogate, 1940; BBC Serial, Front Line Family, 1941; Shakespeare, Regents Park; Alexandra in The Little Foxes, Piccadilly; Midsummer Night's Dream, Westminster, 1942; Brighton Rock, Garrick; Landslide, Westminster, 1943; Lady from Edinburgh, Playhouse, 1945; Dear Ruth, St James's; Wind is 90, Apollo, 1946; on tour in Fools Rush In, 1946; Rain on the Just, Aldwych, 1948; Queen Elizabeth Slept Here, Strand, 1949; The Four-poster, Ambassadors, 1950 (tour of S Africa, 1954-55); See You Later

(Revue), Watergate, 1951; Dragon's Mouth, Winter Garden, 1952; Sweet Peril, St James's, 1952; We Must Kill Toni, Westminster; The Diary of a Nobody, Arts, 1954; Alice Through the Looking Glass, Chelsea Palace, 1955, Ashcroft Theatre, Croydon, 1972; appeared in own play, Love Affair, Lyric Hammersmith, 1956; South Sea Bubble, Cape Town, 1956; Tea and Sympathy, Melbourne and Sydney, 1956; South Sea Bubble, Johannesburg, 1957; Double Cross, Duchess, 1958, Cambridge, 1960; Let Them Eat Cake, Cambridge, 1959; Candida, Piccadilly and Wyndham's, 1960; Heartbreak House, Wyndham's, 1961; A Marriage Has Been Arranged, and A Village Wooing (Hong Kong); Shakespeare Recital (Berlin Festival); Royal Gambit for opening of Ashcroft Theatre, Croydon, 1962; Where Angels Fear to Tread, Arts and St Martin's, 1963; An Ideal Husband, Strand, 1965; On Approval, St Martin's, 1966; Happy Family, St Martin's, 1967; Number 10, Strand, 1967; Out of the Question, St Martin's, 1968; Three, Fortune, 1970; The Wild Duck, Criterion, 1970; Clandestine Marriage (tour), 1971; Ghosts, York; Hay Fever (tour), 1972; Dragon Variation (tour), 1973; At the End of the Day, Savoy, 1973; The Sack Race, Ambassadors, 1974; The Pay Off, Comedy, 1974, Westminster, 1975; Time and the Conways (tour), 1976; Ladies in Retirement (tour), 1976; A Murder is Announced, Vaudeville, 1977. *Films include:* They were Sisters, 1944; Wanted for Murder, 1945; A Man about the House, 1946; Mine Own Executioner, 1947; My Brother Jonathan, 1947; The Glass Mountain, 1948; The Franchise Affair, 1951; Angels One Five, 1952; There was a Young Lady, 1953; A Man Could Get Killed, 1965. Has appeared in television plays and radio serials. *Publications: play:* Love Affair; *books:* Murder on the Stairs; Murder in Melbourne; Baby Face; Epitaph for a Dead Actor; Murder on a Saturday; Murder in Mind; The Devil Wore Scarlet; No Quarter for a Star; The Murder of Love; Died in the Red; The Actor and His World (with Michael Denison); Murder on Honeymoon; For Richer, For Richer; Deadly Lampshade; Understudy to Murder; Dead Give Away; Ride on a Tiger; Stage-Door Fright; Death in Denims. *Recreations:* swimming, butterflies (Vice-Pres., British Butterfly Conservation Soc.). *Address:* Shardeloes, Amersham, Bucks.

DENISON, John Law, CBE 1960 (MBE 1945); FRCM; Hon. RAM; Hon. GSM; Director, South Bank Concert Halls (formerly General Manager, Royal Festival Hall), 1965-76; Chairman, Cultural Programme, London Celebrations Committee, Queen's Silver Jubilee; Vice-Chairman, Arts Educational Schools; Member of Council, RCM; *b* 21 Jan. 1911; *s* of late Rev. H. B. W. and Alice Dorothy Denison; *m* 1st, 1936, Annie Claudia Russell Brown (marriage dissolved, 1946); 2nd, 1947, Evelyn Mary Donald (*née* May) (*d* 1958), *d* of John and Mary Scott Moir, Edinburgh; one *d*; 3rd, 1960, Audrey Grace Burnaby (*née* Bowles) (*d* 1970); 4th, 1972, Françoise Charlotte Henriette Mitchell (*née* Garrigues). *Educ:* Brighton Coll.; Royal Coll. of Music. Played horn in BBC Symphony, London Philharmonic, City of Birmingham, and other orchestras, 1934-39. Served War of 1939-45; gazetted Somerset Light Inf., 1940; DAA and QMG 214 Inf. Bde and various staff appts, 1941-45 (despatches). Asst Dir, Music Dept, British Council, 1946-48; Music Dir, Arts Council of Great Britain, 1948-65. *Publications:* articles for various musical publications. *Address:* 62 Pont Street, SW11. *Club:* Army and Navy.

DENISON, (John) Michael (Terence Wellesley); Actor; *b* 1 Nov. 1915; *s* of Gilbert Dixon Denison and Marie Louise (*née* Bain); *m* 1939, Dulcie Gray (*see* D. W. C. Denison). *Educ:* Harrow; Magdalen Coll., Oxford (BA). Dramatic Sch., 1937-38; Westminster Theatre, 1938; Aberdeen Repertory, 1939. First film, 1940. Served War of 1939-45, Royal Signals and Intelligence Corps, 1940-46. Has appeared in following plays: Ever Since Paradise, 1946; Rain on the Just, 1948; Queen Elizabeth Slept Here, 1949; The Four-poster, 1950; Dragon's Mouth, 1952; Sweet Peril, 1952; The Bad Samaritan, 1953; Alice Through the Looking Glass, 1953, 1955 and 1972; We Must Kill Toni, 1954; tour of S Africa, 1954-55; Memorial Theatre, Stratford-on-Avon, 1955; prod. and acted in Love Affair, 1956; A Village Wooing and Fanny's First Play (Edinburgh and Berlin festivals), 1956; Meet Me By Moonlight, 1957; Let Them Eat Cake, 1959; Candida, 1960; Heartbreak House, 1961; My Fair Lady, (Melbourne); A Village Wooing (Hong Kong); Shakespeare Recital (Berlin Festival), 1962; Where Angels Fear to Tread, 1963; Hostile Witness, 1964; An Ideal Husband, 1965; On Approval, 1966; Happy Family; Number 10, 1967; Out of the Question, 1968; Three, 1970; The Wild Duck, 1970; Clandestine Marriage, 1971; The Tempest, 1972; Twelfth Night, 1972; The Dragon Variation (tour), 1973; At the End of the Day, 1973; The Sack Race, 1974; Peter Pan, 1974; The Black Mikado, 1975; The First Mrs Fraser (tour), 1976; The Earl and the Pussycat (tour), 1976; Robert and Elizabeth (tour), 1976; The Cabinet Minister, 1977. *Films include:* My Brother

Jonathan, 1947; The Glass Mountain, 1948; Landfall, 1949; The Franchise Affair, 1950; Angels One Five, The Importance of Being Earnest, 1951; The Truth About Women, 1957. Many television appearances including title role Boyd, QC, 1957-61 and 1963. Director: Allied Theatre Productions, 1966-75; Play Company of London, 1970-74; New Shakespeare Company, 1971-. On Council British Actors Equity Assoc., 1949-76 (Vice-Pres. 1952, 1961-63, 1973); Mem. Drama Panel, Arts Council, 1975-. *Publications:* (with Dulcie Gray) The Actor and His World, 1964; Overture and Beginners, 1973. *Recreations:* golf, painting, watching cricket, gardening, motoring. *Address:* Shardeloes, Amersham, Bucks. *Clubs:* Richmond Golf (Richmond); MCC, Middlesex County Cricket.

DENISON, Michael; *see* Denison, J. M. T. W.

DENISON-PENDER, family name of **Baron Pender.**

DENMAN, family name of **Baron Denman.**

DENMAN, 5th Baron *cr* 1834; **Charles Spencer Denman,** CBE 1976; MC 1942; TD; Bt 1945; *b* 7 July 1916; *e s* of Hon. Sir Richard Douglas Denman, 1st Bt; *S* father, 1957 and to barony of cousin, 1971; *m* 1943, Sheila Anne, *d* of late Lt-Col Algernon Bingham Anstruther Stewart, DSO, Seaforth Highlanders, of Ornockenoch, Gatehouse of Fleet; three *s* one *d*. *Educ:* Shrewsbury. Served War of 1939-45 with Duke of Cornwall's Light Infantry (TA), India, Middle East, Western Desert and Dodecanese Islands; Major, 1943. Contested (C) Leeds Central, 1945. Chairman: Tennant Guaranty Ltd; Overseas Marketing Corporation Ltd; Tennant Budd Ltd. Chm., Marine and General Mutual Life Assurance Soc. Ltd; Deputy Chairman: C. Tennant Sons & Co. Ltd, 1973-; British Bank of the Middle East, 1977-; Director: Consolidated Gold Fields Ltd; Challenge Corporation Ltd. Chairman, Committee for Middle East Trade, 1971-75 (Mem., 1963-75); Member: Advisory Council of Export Credits Guarantee Department, 1963-68; British National Export Council, 1965; Cttee on Invisible Exports, 1965-67; Lord Kitchener Nat. Meml Fund. Governor, Windlesham House Sch. *Heir: s* Hon. Richard Thomas Stewart Denman, *b* 4 Oct. 1946. *Address:* Highden House, Washington, Pulborough, West Sussex. *T:* Findon 2102. *Club:* Brooks's.

DENMAN, Prof. Donald Robert; Professor of Land Economy, Cambridge University, since 1968; Head of Department of Land Economy, Cambridge, since 1962; Fellow of Pembroke College, Cambridge, since 1962; *b* 7 April 1911; 2nd *s* of Robert Martyn Denman and Letitia Kate Denman, Finchley; *m* 1941, Jessica Hope, 2nd *d* of Richard H. Prior, Chichester; two *s*. *Educ:* Christ's Coll., Finchley; London University. BSc (London) 1938; MSc 1940; PhD 1945; MA Cantab 1948; FRICS 1949. Dep. Exec. Off., Cumberland War Agricultural Exec. Cttee, 1939-46; University Lectr, Cambridge Univ., 1948-68. Land Management Cttee of Agricultural Improvement Coun., 1953-60; Member: Church Assembly, 1957-69; Standing Cttee of Istituto de Diritto Agrario Internazionale e Comparato, Florence, 1960-; Cttee of CNAA, 1966-; Nat. Commn of Unesco, 1972-; Advisor on Academic devt of land economy to University of Science and Technology, Kumasi, Ghana and University of Nigeria, 1963-; Advisor to Min. of Co-operation and Rural Affairs, Iran; Consultant, Internat. Union for Conservation of Nature and Nat. Resources, 1972. Mem. Council, University Coll. at Buckingham, 1973-. Vice-Pres., Conservation Soc. Mem., Commonwealth Human Ecology Council, 1971- (Chm., Finance Cttee); Acad. Adv. to Commonwealth Assoc. of Surveying and Land Economy, 1974-. Governor, Canford Sch. Hon. Fellow, Ghana Instn of Surveyors, 1970; Fellow, Royal Swedish Acad. of Forestry and Agriculture, 1971. Gold Medal, RICS, 1972. Ozo Order of Nobility of Iboland, Nigeria (Eze di Igbo Mma and other titles), 1971; Distinguished Order of Homayoun of the Imperial Court of Persia, 1974. *Publications:* Tenant Right Valuation: In History and Modern Practice, 1942; Tenant Right Valuation and Current Legislation, 1948; Estate Capital: The Contribution of Landownership to Agricultural Finance, 1957; Origins of Ownership: A Brief History of Landownership and Tenure, 1958, 2nd edn 1959; Bibliography of Rural Land Economy and Landownership 1900-1957 (*et al*), 1958; (jtly) Farm Rents: A Comparison of Current and Past Farm Rents in England and Wales, 1959; (Ed and contrib.) Landownership and Resources, 1960; (Ed and contrib.) Contemporary Problems of Landownership, 1963; Land in the Market, 1964; (jtly) Commons and Village Greens: A Study in Land Use, Conservation and Management, 1967; (ed and contrib.) Land and People, 1967; Rural Land Systems: A General Classification of Rural Land Systems in Relation to the Surveyors' Profession and Rural Land Reform, 1968; Land Use and the Constitution of Property, 1969; Land Use: An Introduction to Proprietary

Land Use Analysis, 1971; Human Environment: the surveyor's response, 1972; The King's Vista (Persian Land reform), 1973; Prospects of Co-operative Planning (Warburton Lecture), 1973; Land Economy: an education and a career (British Assoc. lecture), 1975; The Place of Property, 1978; numerous monographs, articles and papers in academic and professional jls and nat. press in Britain and abroad. *Recreation:* travel. *Address:* Pembroke College, Cambridge; 12 Chaucer Road, Cambridge. *T:* Cambridge 57725. *Club:* Carlton.

DENMAN, Sir George Roy; *see* Denman, Sir Roy.

DENMAN, Sir Roy, KCB 1977 (CB 1972); CMG 1968; Director-General for External Affairs, Commission of European Communities, since 1977; *b* 12 June 1924; *s* of Albert Edward and Gertrude Ann Denman; *m* 1966, Moya Lade; one *s* one *d. Educ:* Harrow Gram. Sch.; St John's Coll., Cambridge. War Service 1943-46; Major, Royal Signals. Joined BoT, 1948; Asst Private Sec. to successive Presidents, 1950-52; 1st Sec., British Embassy, Bonn, 1957-60; UK Delegn, Geneva, 1960-61; Counsellor, Geneva, 1965-67; Under-Sec., 1967-70, BoT; Deputy Secretary: DTI, 1970-74; Dept of Trade, 1974-75; Second Permanent Sec., Cabinet Office, 1975-77. Mem. negotiating delegn with European Communities, 1970-72. Mem., British Overseas Trade Bd, 1972-75. *Address:* 200 Rue de la Loi, 1049 Brussels, Belgium. *Club:* United Oxford & Cambridge University.

DENNELL, Prof. Ralph; Emeritus Professor of Zoology, University, Manchester, 1975; Beyer Professor of Zoology, 1963-74; *b* 29 Sept. 1907; *m* 1932, Dorothy Ethel Howard; no *c. Educ:* Leeds Grammar Sch.; University of Leeds. Demonstrator in Zoology, University of Leeds, 1929; Grisedale Research Student, University of Manchester, 1932; Asst Lecturer in Zoology, University of Leeds, 1935; Asst Lecturer in Zoology, and Lecturer in Zoology, Imperial Coll., 1937-46; Reader in Experimental Zoology, 1946-48, Prof. of Experimental Zoology, 1948-63, University of Manchester. *Publications:* papers on crustacea, insect physiology, and arthropod integuments, in various zoological periodicals. *Address:* Department of Zoology, The University, Manchester M13 9PL.

DENNING, Baron (Life Peer) *cr* 1957, of Whitchurch; **Alfred Thompson Denning,** PC 1948; Kt 1944; Master of the Rolls since 1962; Hon. Fellow of Magdalen College, Oxford, 1948; Hon. LLD: Ottawa, 1955; Glasgow, 1959; Southampton, 1959; London, 1960; Cambridge, 1963; Leeds, 1964; McGill, 1967; Dallas, 1969; Dalhousie, 1970; Wales, 1973; Exeter, 1976; Columbia, 1976; Hon. DCL Oxford, 1965; *b* 23 Jan. 1899; *s* of Charles and Clara Denning; *m* 1st, 1932, Mary Harvey (*d* 1941); one *s*; 2nd, 1945, Joan, *d* of J. V. Elliott Taylor, and *widow* of J. M. B. Stuart, CIE. *Educ:* Andover Grammar Sch.; Magdalen Coll., Oxford (Demy). 1st Class Mathematical Moderations; 1st Class Mathematical Final School; 1st Class Final Sch. of Jurisprudence; Eldon Scholar, 1921; Prize Student Inns of Court; called to the Bar, 1923; KC 1938; Judge of the High Court of Justice, 1944; a Lord Justice of Appeal, 1948-57; a Lord of Appeal in Ordinary, 1957-62. Chancellor of Diocese of London, 1942-44; and of Southwark, 1937-44; Recorder of Plymouth, 1944; Bencher of Lincoln's Inn, 1944; Nominated Judge for War Pensions Appeals, 1945-48; Chm. Cttee on Procedure in Matrimonial Causes, 1946-47; Chm., Royal Commission on Historical MSS, 1962-. Held enquiry into circumstances of resignation of Mr J. D. Profumo, Sec. of State for War, 1963. Chairman: Cttee on Legal Education for Students from Africa; British Institute of International and Comparative Law. Pres., Birkbeck Coll.; Treas., Lincoln's Inn, 1964. Hon. Bencher, Middle Temple, 1972. Served in RE 1917-19 (BEF France). *Publications:* Joint Editor of Smith's Leading Cases, 1929; of Bullen and Leake's Precedents, 1935; Freedom under the Law, (Hamlyn Lectures), 1949; The Changing Law, 1953; The Road to Justice, 1955. *Address:* 11 Old Square, Lincoln's Inn, WC2. *T:* Holborn 5896; The Lawn, Whitchurch, Hants. *T:* 2144. *Club:* Athenæum.
See also Vice-Adm. Sir N. E. and Lieut-Gen. Sir R. F. S. Denning.

DENNING, Vice-Adm. Sir Norman (Egbert), KBE 1963 (OBE 1945); CB 1961; *b* 19 Nov. 1904; *y s* of late Charles and Clara Denning, Whitchurch, Hants; *m* 1933, Iris, *d* of late Captain R. and Mrs Curtis, Singapore; one *s* one *d* (and one *s* decd). *Educ:* Andover Grammar Sch., Hampshire. Joined RN, 1922; Naval Intelligence Div., Operational Intelligence Centre, Admiralty, 1937-45; Comdr, 1941; Captain 1951; Dir of Administrative Planning, Admty, 1952; Dir, RN Coll., Greenwich, 1956; Rear-Admiral, 1958; Dep. Chief of Naval Personnel, 1958; Dir-Gen. of Manpower, 1959; DNI, 1960-64; Vice-Adm., 1961; Chief

Naval Supply and Secretariat Officer, 1962-64; Deputy Chief of the Defence Staff (Intelligence), 1964-65; Sec., Defence Press and Broadcasting Cttee, 1967-72. *Address:* Rose Cottage, Micheldever, Hants. *T:* 268. *Club:* Royal Automobile.
See also Baron Denning, Lt-Gen. Sir R. F. S. Denning.

DENNING, Lt-Gen. Sir Reginald (Francis Stewart), KCVO 1975; KBE 1946; CB 1944; Chairman, SSAFA, 1953-74; Vice-President, Liverpool School of Tropical Medicine, since 1967; *b* 12 June 1894; 2nd *s* of Charles and Clara Denning, Whitchurch, Hants; *m* 1927, Eileen Violet (OBE 1969), *d* of late H. W. Currie, 12 Hyde Park Place, W2; two *s* one *d. Educ:* privately. 2nd Lieut Bedfordshire Regt, 1915; European War, 1914-18 (severely wounded, despatches). Adjutant, 1st Bedfs and Herts Regt, 1922-25; Adjutant, 2 Bedfs and Herts Regt, 1926-29; Student Staff Coll., Camberley, 1929-30; Bt Major, 1934; Bt Lt-Col, 1939; Brig., 1941; Subst. Col, 1942; Acting Maj.-Gen., 1943; Maj.-Gen., 1944; Lieut-Gen., 1949; Maj.-Gen. i/c Administration South-Eastern Command, 1943-44; Principal Administrative Officer to the Supreme Allied Commander, South-East Asia, 1944-46; Chief of Staff, Eastern Command, 1947-49; GOC Northern Ireland, 1949-52; retired pay, 1952. Col, Bedfs and Herts Regt, 1948 3rd East Anglian Regt (16th/44th Foot), 1958, Royal Anglian Regt, 1964-66 (formed Regt, 1964). DL, County of Essex, 1959-68. CStJ 1946; Commander Legion of Merit (USA), 1946. *Recreations:* hunting, polo, riding. *Address:* Delmonden Grange, Hawkhurst, Kent. *T:* 2286. *Clubs:* Army and Navy, MCC.
See also Baron Denning, Vice-Adm. Sir N. E. Denning.

DENNINGTON, Dudley, FICE; FIStructE; Partner, Bullen & Partners, since 1972; *b* 21 April 1927; *s* of John Dennington and Beryl Dennington (*née* Hagon); *m* 1951, Margaret Patricia Stewart; two *d. Educ:* Clifton Coll., Bristol; Imperial Coll., London Univ. (BSc). ACGI 1947. National Service, 2nd Lieut, RE, 1947-49; Sandford Fawcett and Partners, Consulting Engineers, 1949-51; D. & C. Wm Press, Contractors, 1951-52; AMICE 1953; Manager, Design Office, George Wimpey & Co., 1952-65; GLC 1965-72: Asst Chief Engineer, Construction, 1965-67; Chief Engineer, Construction, 1967-70; Traffic Comr and Dir of Development, 1970-72. FICE 1966. *Recreations:* sailing, mathematics, painting. *Address:* 25 Corkran Road, Surbiton, Surrey. *T:* 01-399 2977. *Club:* Reform.

DENNIS, Maxwell Lewis, CMG 1971; Chairman, South Australia Totalizator Agency Board, since 1973; *b* 19 April 1909; *s* of Frank Leonard and Ethel Jane Dennis; *m* 1935, Bernice Abell; one *d* (one *s* decd). *Educ:* Gladstone High Sch., South Australia. FASA. Entered South Australian Public Service, 1924, Public Service Commissioner, 1965; Chm., Public Service Bd, 1968-73; Mem. Bd, Royal Soc. for the Blind. *Address:* 7/18 Patawalonga Frontage, Glenelg North, South Australia 5045.

DENNIS, Nigel Forbes; writer; *b* 1912; *s* of Lieut-Col M. F. B. Dennis, DSO, and Louise (*née* Bosanquet); *m* 1st, Mary-Madeleine Massias; 2nd, Beatrice Ann Hewart Matthew; two *d. Educ:* Plumtree Sch., S Rhodesia; Odenwaldschule, Germany. Secretary, Nat. Bd of Review of Motion Pictures, NY, 1935-36; Asst Editor and Book Reviewer, The New Republic, NY, 1937-38; Staff Book Reviewer, Time, NY, 1940-58; Dramatic Critic, Encounter, 1960-63; Staff Book Reviewer, Sunday Telegraph, 1961-; Joint Editor, Encounter, 1967-70. *Publications:* Boys and Girls Come out to Play, 1949; Cards of Identity, 1955; Two Plays and a Preface, 1958; Dramatic Essays, 1962; Jonathan Swift, 1964 (RSL Award, 1966); A House in Order, 1966; Exotics (poems), 1970; An Essay on Malta, 1971. *Plays:* Cards of Identity, Royal Court, 1956; The Making of Moo, Royal Court, 1957; August for the People, Royal Court and Edinburgh Festival, 1962. *Recreation:* gardening. *Address:* c/o A. M. Heath & Co., 40 William IV Street, WC2. *Club:* Casino Maltese (Malta).

DENNIS SMITH, Edgar; *see* Smith.

DENNISON, Mervyn William, CBE 1967; MC 1944; JP; DL; Chief Commissioner, Planning Appeals Commission and Water Appeals Commission of N Ireland, since 1973; *b* 13 July 1914; *er s* of Reverend W. Telford Dennison and Hester Mary (*née* Coulter); *m* 1944, Helen Maud, *d* of Claud George Spiller, Earley, Berks; one *s* one *d. Educ:* Methodist Coll., Belfast; Queen's Univ., Belfast (BA); Middle Temple. Called to Bar of Northern Ireland, 1945; Middle Temple, 1964. Served War of 1939-45, with Royal Ulster Rifles and Parachute Regt (POW Arnhem, 1944). Crown Counsel, N Rhodesia, 1947; Legal Draftsman, 1952; Senior Crown Counsel and Parliamentary Draftsman, Federal Govt of Rhodesia and Nyasaland, 1953; Federal Solicitor-Gen., 1959; QC (N Rhodesia) 1960; also Chm.

Road Service Bd, N Rhodesia, and Mem. Central African Air Authority. High Court Judge, Zambia, 1961-67. Secretary, Fermanagh CC, NI, 1967-73. Hon. Col, The Zambia Regt, 1964-66. JP Co. Fermanagh, 1969-, DL, 1972-. CStJ 1964. *Recreations:* fishing, sailing. *Address:* Creevyloughgare, Saintfield, Ballynahinch, Co. Down BT24 7NB. *T:* Saintfield 510397. *Clubs:* Army and Navy; Salisbury (Rhodesia).

DENNISON, Adm. Robert Lee; DSM (US); Legion of Merit (Gold Star); US Navy; Commander in Chief, Atlantic and US Atlantic Fleet and Supreme Allied Commander Atlantic, 1960-63, retired; *b* 13 April 1901; *s* of Ludovici Waters and Laura Florence Lee Dennison; *m* 1937, Mildred Mooney; one *s* one *d. Educ:* US Naval Acad.; Pa State Coll. (MS); Johns Hopkins Univ. (EngD). Ensign, 1923; advanced through grades to Admiral, 1959. Served with Atlantic, Pacific and Asiatic Fleets; comd Ortolan, 1935-37, Cuttlefish, 1937-38; John D. Ford, 1940-41, Missouri, 1947-48; mem. jt war plans cttee of Jt Chiefs of Staff, 1944-45; Asst Chief of Naval Ops (polit-mil. affairs), 1945-47; naval aide to Pres. of USA, 1948-53; Cdr Cruiser Div. 4 Atlantic Fleet, 1953-54; Dir Strategic Plans Div., Asst Chief of Naval Ops (Plans and Policy), mem. jt strategic plans cttee of Jt Chiefs of Staff, 1954-56; Cdr First Fleet, Pacific Fleet, 1956-58; Dep. Chief Naval Ops (Plans and Policy), 1958-59; C-in-C, US Naval Forces, E Atlantic and Mediterranean, 1959-60. Hon. OBE 1946; Commander: Order of Naval Merit (Brazil); Order of the Crown (Belgium); Legion of Honour (France); Grand Cross, Order of Orange-Nassau (Netherlands), Grand Cross, Military Order of Aviz (Portugal). *Address:* c/o Trust Department Office, The Riggs National Bank, Washington, DC, USA. *Clubs:* Ends of the Earth, American (London); Metropolitan, Army-Navy, Chevy Chase (Washington, DC); New York Yacht.

DENNISON, Stanley Raymond, CBE 1946; Vice-Chancellor, since 1972, and Honorary Professor, since 1974, University of Hull; *b* 15 June 1912; *o s* of late Stanley Dennison and Florence Ann Dennison, North Shields; unmarried. *Educ:* University of Durham; Trinity College, Cambridge. Lecturer in Economics, Manchester University, 1935-39; Professor of Economics, University Coll. of Swansea, 1939-45; Lecturer in Economics, Cambridge Univ., 1945-58; Fellow of Gonville and Caius Coll., 1945-58; Prof. of Economics, Queen's Univ. of Belfast, 1958-61; David Dale Prof. of Economics, Univ. of Newcastle upon Tyne, 1962-72; Pro-Vice-Chancellor, 1966-72. Chief Economic Asst, War Cabinet Secretariat, 1940-46. Member: University Grants Cttee, 1964-68; North Eastern Electricity Board, 1965-72; Review Body on Remuneration of Doctors and Dentists, 1962-70; Verdon Smith Cttee on Marketing and Distribution of Fatstock and Carcase Meat, 1964; Scott Cttee on Land Utilisation in Rural Areas, 1942 (Minority Report); Beaver Cttee on Air Pollution, 1954; Waverley Cttee on Med. Services for the Armed Forces, 1955. Chm. of Wages Councils. Chm. Governors, Royal Grammar Sch., Newcastle upon Tyne, 1969-. *Publications:* The Location of Industry and the Depressed Areas, 1939; (with Sir Dennis Robertson) The Control of Industry, 1960; various articles, etc, on economic questions. *Recreation:* music. *Address:* The University of Hull, Cottingham Road, Hull HU6 7RX. *Club:* Reform.

DENNISS, Gordon Kenneth; Senior Partner, Eastman & Denniss, Chartered Surveyors, London, since 1945; *b* 29 April 1915; *e s* of late Harold W. Denniss; *m* 1939, Violet Fiedler, Montreal; one *s* two *d. Educ:* Dulwich Coll.; Coll. of Estate Management. FRICS; MRSH. Articled to uncle, Hugh F. Thoburn, Chartered Surveyor, Kent, developing building estates, 1935, professional asst 1938; Eastman & Denniss: Junior Partner, 1943; sole principal, 1945. Crown Estate Comr, 1965-71. Governing Dir, London Consultants (Middle East), London, 1977-. Farming 1600 acres in E Sussex and Kent. *Recreations:* farming, cricket, fox-hunting (Mem. OSB Hunt, 1947-). *Address:* 6 Belgrave Place, Belgravia, SW1. *T:* 01-235 4858; Lodgefield Farm, Blackham, East Sussex. *T:* Fordcombe 276. *Clubs:* Savile, Farmers', MCC; Surrey County Cricket.

DENNY, Sir Alistair (Maurice Archibald), 3rd Bt, *cr* 1913; *b* 11 Sept. 1922; *er s* of Sir Maurice Edward Denny, 2nd Bt, KBE and of Lady Denny, Gateside House, Drymen, Stirlingshire; *S* father 1955; *m* 1949, Elizabeth *y d* of Sir Guy Lloyd, Bt, *qv*; two *s* (and one *s* decd). *Educ:* Marlborough. Started engineering training with William Denny & Bros. Served War in Fleet Air Arm, 1944-46. Continued engineering training with Alexander Stephen & Sons, Glasgow, and Sulzer Bros., Winterthur, Switzerland; returned to William Denny & Bros, 1948; left, Sept. 1963, when firm went into liquidation. *Recreations:* golf, ski-ing, gardening, photography. *Heir:* s Charles Alistair Maurice Denny, *b* 7 Oct. 1950. *Address:* Damside of Strathairly, Upper Largo, Fife. *T:* Upper Largo 214. *Clubs:* Naval; Royal and Ancient Golf (St Andrews).

DENNY, Sir Anthony Coningham de Waltham, 8th Bt, *cr* 1782, of Tralee Castle, Co. Kerry, Ireland; Partner in Verity and Beverley, Architects and Design Consultants, since 1959; *b* 22 April 1925; *s* of Rev. Sir Henry Lyttleton Lyster Denny, 7th Bt, and Joan Lucy Dorothy, *er d* of Major William A. C. Denny, OBE; *S* father 1953; *m* 1949, Anne Catherine, *e d* of S. Beverley, FRIBA; two *s* one adopted *d. Educ:* Clayesmore Sch. Served War of 1939-45: Middle East, RAF (Aircrew), 1943-47. Anglo-French Art Centre, 1947-50; Mural Painter and Theatrical Designer, 1950-54. Hereditary Freeman of City of Cork. FRSA; MSIAD. *Recreations:* architecture and painting. *Heir:* s Piers Anthony de Waltham Denny, *b* 14 March 1954. *Address:* Daneway House, Sapperton, Cirencester Glos. *T:* Frampton Mansell 232; 11 Chalcot Square, NW1. *T:* 01-722 3047.

DENNY, James Runciman, MBE 1944; MA, MusB Cantab; West Riding Professor of Music, Leeds University, 1950-71; *b* 9 May 1908; *m* 1934, Agatha Nash; one *s* two *d. Educ:* Gresham's Sch., Holt; Royal College of Music; Christ's Coll., Cambridge. Music Dir, Bedford Sch., 1933-37; Music Asst, BBC, Belfast, 1937-39; Head of Midland Regional Music, BBC, and Conductor BBC Midland Chorus and Singers, 1946-50; Leeds Guild of Singers, 1952-55. Pres., Incorporated Soc. of Musicians, 1964. Hon. RAM. Served War of 1939-45, Royal Warwicks Regt; GSO1, India Command. *Publications:* The Oxford School Harmony Course, 1960; Hymn to Christ the King, 1963. *Address:* High Walls, West Winterslow, Salisbury, Wilts. *T:* Winterslow 862412.

DENNY, Sir J(onathan) Lionel P(ercy), GBE 1966; Kt 1963; MC 1918; Hon. DSc; JP; Lord Mayor of London for 1965-66; *b* 5 Aug. 1897; *s* of J. Percy Denny, Putney; *m* 1920, Doris, *d* of R. George Bare, FSI, Putney; one *s. Educ:* St Paul's Sch. Served European War, 1915-19, Lieut E Surrey Regt; active service in France (wounded thrice, MC); Sqdn Leader RAFVR and RAF Regt, 1940-45. Mem. Court of Common Council, for Billingsgate Ward, 1941, Deputy 1951, Chief Commoner 1954, Alderman 1957-70. One of HM Lieuts for the City of London, 1951-70; JP Co. of London, 1951-; JP City of London, 1957-. Livery Companies: Barber-Surgeons (Master, 1938-39); Vintners' (Master, 1960-61); Company of Watermen and Lightermen (Master, 1967). Chm. London Court of Arbitration, 1958-59. Sheriff, City of London, 1961-62. First Chancellor, The City Univ., London, 1966; Hon. DSc. Jt Hon. Col 254 (City of London) Regt RA (TA), 1965-66. KStJ 1966 (OStJ 1961). Vicary Lecture, RCS, 1972. Chevalier, Légion d'Honneur, 1967 and other orders from Liberia, Ivory Coast, Senegal, Austria and Jordan. *Recreation:* motor-cruising. *Address:* 901 Grenville House, Dolphin Square, SW1. *T:* 01-834 4048. *Clubs:* City Livery (Pres. 1959-60), Eccentric, Royal Thames Yacht.

DENNY, Margaret Bertha Alice, (Mrs E. L. Denny), OBE 1946; DL; Under Secretary, Ministry of Transport and Civil Aviation, 1957-58; *b* 30 Sept. 1907; *o d* of late Edward Albert Churchard and late Margaret Catherine (*née* Arnold) and step-*d* of late William Ray Lenanton, JP; *m* 1957, Edward Leslie Denny, JP, formerly Chm., William Denny Bros, Shipbuilders, Dumbarton. *Educ:* Dover County Sch.; Bedford Coll. for Women, London Univ. (BA Hons PhD). Entered Civil Service as Principal Ministry of Shipping, 1940; Asst Sec., 1946. Gov., Bedford Coll., University of London. Member: Scottish Adv. Coun. for Civil Aviation, 1958-67; Western Regional Hospital Board, Scotland, 1960-74; Scottish Cttee, Council of Industrial Design, 1961-71; Gen. Advisory Council, BBC, 1962-66; Gen. Nursing Council, Scotland, 1962; Board of Management, State Hosp., Carstairs; Vice-Chm., Argyll and Clyde Health Bd, 1974-77. County Comr, Girl Guides, Dunbartonshire, 1958-68. DL Dunbartonshire, 1973. Officer, Order of Orange Nassau, 1947. *Address:* Gartochraggan Cottage, Gartocharn, by Alexandria, Dunbartonshire. *T:* Gartocharn 272. *Club:* Western (Glasgow).

DENNY, William Eric, QC 1975; a Recorder of the Crown Court, since 1974; *b* 2 Nov. 1927; *s* of William John Denny and Elsie Denny; *m* 1960, Daphne Rose Southern-Reddin; one *s* two *d. Educ:* Ormskirk Grammar Sch.; Liverpool Univ. (Pres., Guild of Undergraduates, 1952-53; LLB). Called to the Bar, Gray's Inn, 1953. Lectured at LSE, 1953-58. *Recreations:* music, sailing, gardening. *Address:* Entry Hill, Rotherfield, Sussex. *T:* Rotherfield 2179.

DENNY-BROWN, Derek Ernest, OBE 1942; MD NZ, DPhil Oxon, FRCP; J. J. Putnam Professor of Neurology, Emeritus, Harvard University, since 1972; Hon. Col RAMC; *b* 1901; *s* of Charles Denny-Brown; *m* 1937, Sylvia Marie, *d* of late Dr J. O. Summerhayes, DSO; four *s. Educ:* New Plymouth High Sch., NZ; Otago Univ., NZ; Magdalen Coll., Oxford (Hon. Fellow, 1976). Beit Memorial Research Fellow, 1925-28; Rockefeller Travelling Fellow, 1936; formerly Neurologist to St

Bartholomew's Hosp., London, Asst Physician National Hosp., Queen Square, and sometime Registrar to Dept for Nervous Diseases, Guy's Hosp.; former Dir, Neurol. Unit, Boston City Hosp. Harvard University: Prof. of Neurology, 1941-46, and 1967-72; J. J. Putnam Prof. of Neurology, 1946-67. Fogarty Internat. Scholar, Nat. Insts of Health, Bethesda, Maryland, 1972-73. Hon. Fellow, RSM, 1958. Gran Oficier, Order of Hippolite Unanue (Peru), 1963. Sherrington Medal, Royal Society Medicine London, 1962; Jacoby Award, Amer. Neurol. Assoc., 1968. Hon AM Harvard; Hon. LLD Wayne; Hon. LLD Glasgow, 1971; Dr *hc* Brazil; Hon. DSc Otago; Hon. DLit Jefferson, 1977. *Publications:* Selected Writings of Sir Charles Sherrington, 1939; Diseases of Muscle (part author), 1953; The Basal Ganglia, 1962; Cerebral Control of Movement, 1966; Centennial Vol., Amer. Neurol. Assoc., 1975; papers on neurological subjects in scientific journals. *Address:* 3 Mercer Circle, Cambridge, Mass 02138, USA.

DENNYS, Cyril George, CB 1949; MC 1918; retired as Under-Secretary; *b* 25 March 1897; *s* of Lieut-Col A. H. Dennys, IA, and Lena Mary Isabel (*née* Harrison); *m* 1920, Sylvia Maitland (*née* Waterlow); two *d* (and one *d* decd). *Educ:* Malvern Coll.; Trinity Coll., Oxford. Served European War, 1914-18, as Lieut, RGA, 1917-18. Entered Ministry of Labour as Asst Principal, 1919; Principal Private Sec. to Minister of Labour, 1938; Asst Sec., 1938; Principal Asst Sec., Ministry of Supply, 1942-45; Under-Secretary: Ministry of Labour, 1946; Ministry of National Insurance, 1946; Ministry of Pensions and National Insurance, 1953; retired 1962. *Recreation:* golf. *Address:* 38 Belsize Grove, Hampstead, NW3. *T:* 01-722 3964. *Clubs:* United Oxford & Cambridge University; Hadley Wood Golf (Barnet).

DENNYS, Rodney Onslow, MVO 1969; OBE 1943; FSA; FRSA; Somerset Herald of Arms, since 1967; *b* 16 July 1911; *s* of late Frederick Onslow Brooke Dennys, late Malayan Civil Service; *m* 1944, Elisabeth Katharine, *d* of late Charles Henry Greene; one *s* two *d*. *Educ:* Canford Sch.; LSE. Apptd to FO, 1937; HM Legation, The Hague, 1937-40; FO, 1940-41. Commissioned in Intell. Corps, 1941; Lt-Col 1944; RARO, 1946. Reapptd, FO, 1947; 1st Sec. British Middle East Office, Egypt, 1948-50; 1st Sec. HM Embassy: Turkey, 1950-53; Paris, 1955-57; resigned, 1957. Asst to Garter King of Arms, 1958-61; Rouge Croix Pursuivant of Arms, 1961-67. Served on Earl Marshal's Staff for State Funeral of Sir Winston Churchill, 1965, and for the Prince of Wales' Investiture, 1969. Mem. Court, Sussex Univ. CPRE: Mem., Nat. Exec., 1973-; Chm., 1972-77, Vice-Pres., 1977, Sussex Br. Member: Council Harleian Soc. (Chm. 1977-); Exec. Cttee, Soc. Genealogists; Devon Assoc.; Académicien, Académie Internationale d'Héraldique. Freeman of City of London; Liveryman and Freeman of Scriveners Co. Dir, Arundel Castle Trustees Ltd. *Publications:* Flags and Emblems of the World; (jt) Royal and Princely Heraldry of Wales; The Heraldic Imagination; articles in jls on heraldry and kindred subjects. *Recreations:* heraldry, sailing, ornithology. *Address:* College of Arms, EC4V 4BT. *T:* 01-248 1912; Heaslands, Steep, near Crowborough, Sussex. *T:* Crowborough 61328. *Clubs:* Garrick, Chelsea Arts.
See also Graham, Sir Hugh, and Raymond, Greene.

de NORMANN, Sir Eric, KBE 1946; CB 1941; Chairman, Ancient Monuments Board for England, 1955-64; *b* 26 Dec. 1893; *s* of Albert de Normann and Irene Wood; *m* 1921, Winifred Leigh (*d* 1968); one *s. Educ:* Château du Rosey, Switzerland; University Coll. of South Wales. Served European War, 1915-19 (despatches twice); Office of Works, 1920; Imperial Defence Coll., 1935. Dep. Sec., Ministry of Works, 1943-54. FSA. *Address:* Aylesham, Old Avenue, Weybridge, Surrey. *T:* Weybridge 42682. *Club:* Athenæum.

DENSON, John Boyd, CMG 1972; OBE 1965; HM Diplomatic Service; Ambassador to Nepal, since 1977; *b* 13 Aug. 1926; *o s* of late George Denson and of Mrs Alice Denson (*née* Boyd); *m* 1957, Joyce Myra Symondson; no *c. Educ:* Perse Sch.; St John's Coll., Cambridge. Royal Regt of Artillery, 1944; Intelligence Corps, 1946; Cambridge, 1947-51 (English and Oriental Langs Triposes). Joined HM Foreign (now Diplomatic) Service, 1951. Served in Hong Kong, Tokyo, Peking, London, Helsinki, Washington, Vientiane; Asst Head of Far Eastern Dept, Foreign Office, 1965-68; Chargé d'Affaires, Peking, 1969-71; Royal Coll. of Defence Studies, 1972; Counsellor and Consul-Gen., Athens, 1973-77. *Recreations:* looking at pictures, the theatre, wine. *Address:* c/o Foreign and Commonwealth Office, SW1; 19 Gainsborough Court, College Road, Dulwich, SE21. *T:* 01-693 8361. *Club:* United Oxford & Cambridge University.

DENT, family name of **Furnivall Barony.**

DENT, Alan Holmes, FRSA 1970; author, critic and journalist; *b* Ayrshire, Scotland, 7 Jan. 1905; *s* of John Dent, Westmorland, and Margaret Holmes, Yorks. *Educ:* Carrick Academy; Glasgow Univ. London dramatic critic of The Manchester Guardian, 1935-43; dramatic critic of Punch, 1942-43 and again in 1963. Served War of 1939-45, in RN Hosp., 1943-45. Dramatic Critic of News Chronicle, 1945-60; Film Critic of: the Sunday Telegraph, 1961-63; Illustrated London News, 1947-68. Frequent broadcaster since 1942. Shute Lecturer in the Art of the Theatre, Liverpool Univ., 1956. Pres. The Critics' Circle, 1962. Lectured on The Fine Art of Criticism at Toronto Univ., at Boston, at Vassar, at Princeton, and at Long Island and New York Universities, Nov. and Dec., 1966. Text-ed. of Sir Laurence Olivier's films of Henry V, Hamlet, and Richard III (text-adviser). Ed., Bernard Shaw and· Mrs Patrick Campbell: their Correspondence, 1952. Will spend his old age planning a novel called The Milk of Paradise, and concluding his autobiography. *Publications:* Preludes and Studies, 1942; Nocturnes and Rhapsodies, 1950; My Dear America..., 1954; Mrs Patrick Campbell: a biography, 1961; Robert Burns in his Time, 1966; Vivien Leigh; a bouquet, 1969; World of Shakespeare: vol. 1, Plants, 1971; vol. 2, Animals and Monsters, 1972; vol. 3, Sports and Pastimes, 1973; My Covent Garden, 1973. *Address:* Chilterns Manor, Northern Heights, Bourne End, Bucks. *T:* Bourne End 28676.

DENT, Harold Collett; *b* 14 Nov. 1894; *s* of Rev. F. G. T. and Susan Dent; *m* 1922, Loveday Winifred Martin; one *s* one *d. Educ:* Public elementary schs; Kingswood Sch., Bath; London Univ. (external student). Asst Master in secondary schs, 1911-25 (War Service, 1914-19); Head of Junior Dept, Brighton, Hove and Sussex Grammar Sch., 1925-28; first headmaster, Gateway School, Leicester, 1928-31; freelance journalist, 1931-35; asst ed., Book Dept Odhams Press, 1935-40; Ed., The Times Educational Supplement, 1940-51; Educational Correspondent, The Times, 1952-55; Professor of Education and Dir of the Inst. of Education, University of Sheffield, 1956-60; Senior Research Fellow, Inst. of Education, University of Leeds, 1960-62; Lecturer and Asst Dean, Inst. of Education, University of London, 1962-65; Visiting Prof., University of Dublin, 1966; BA; FRSA; Hon. FCP; Hon. FEIS. *Publications:* A New Order in English Education, 1942; The Education Act, 1944; Education in Transition, 1944; To be a Teacher, 1947; Secondary Modern Schools, 1958; The Educational System of England and Wales, 1961; Universities in Transition, 1961; 1870-1970, Century of Growth in English Education, 1970; The Training of Teachers in England and Wales 1700-1975, 1977. *Recreation:* gardening. *Address:* Riccards Spring, Whatlington, Battle, East Sussex. *Club:* Athenæum.

DENT, John, CBE 1976 (OBE 1968); Director, Dunlop Holdings Ltd, since 1970; *b* 5 Oct. 1923; *s* of Harry F. Dent; *m* 1954, Pamela Ann, *d* of Frederick G. Bailey; one *s. Educ:* King's Coll., London Univ. BSc(Eng), CEng, FRAeS, FIMechE, FIEE. Admty Gunnery Estabs at Teddington and Portland, 1944-45; Chief Engr, Guided Weapons, Short Bros & Harland Ltd, Belfast, 1955-60; Chief Engr, Armaments Div., Armstrong Whitworth Aircraft, Coventry, 1961-63; Dir and Chief Engr, Hawker Siddeley Dynamics Ltd, Coventry, 1963-67; Dir, Engrg Gp, Dunlop Ltd, Coventry, 1968-76. President: Coventry and District Engrg Employers' Assoc., 1971 and 1972; Engrg Employers' Fedn, 1974-76 (1st Dep. Pres., 1972-74). Member: Engineering Industries Council, 1975-76; Review Bd for Government Contracts; Royal Dockyards Policy Bd. *Recreations:* gardening, fishing. *Address:* Dunlop Holdings Ltd, Dunlop House, 25 Ryder Street, St James's, SW1Y 6PX. *T:* 01-930 6700; Hellidon Grange, Hellidon, Daventry, Northants. *T:* Byfield 60589.

DENT, Major Leonard Maurice Edward, DSO 1914; Chairman and Managing Director Abco Products, Ltd, 1936-75; Member: Council, Queen's College, London; Governing Body of Oundle School; Court of University of Reading (Treasurer, 1959-63); Berks Branch, Council for Preservation of Rural England (Chairman 1950-64); *b* 18 June 1888; *s* of Edward and Mabel P. Dent; *m* 1920, Hester Anita (*d* 1976), *d* of Col Gerard Clark, 4 Sussex Gardens, W2; one *s* four *d. Educ:* Eton; Trinity Coll., Cambridge, BA. Served European War, 1914-18 (wounded, despatches thrice, DSO, Chevalier Légion d'Honneur); Major RR of O, retd. Master of the Grocers' Company, 1935-36; Berks CC, 1946-58; High Sheriff of Berks, 1948-49. Member: Executive Cttee, City and Guilds of London Institute, 1937-70; KCH Bd of Governors, 1950-63; Chairman: Belgrave Hosp. for Children, 1947-63; City and Guilds of London Art Sch. Cttee, 1958-70. *Recreations:* photography, music, art collecting (especially Rowlandsons). *Address:* Hillfields, Burghfield Common, near Reading. *T:* Burghfield Common 2495. *Clubs:* United Oxford & Cambridge University, MCC.

DENT, Sir Robert (Annesley Wilkinson), Kt 1960; CB 1951; *b* 27 Jan. 1895; *e s* of late R. W. Dent, JP, Flass, Maulds Meaburn, Penrith, and late Edith Vere, OBE, *d* of Rev. F. H. Annesley Clifford Chambers, Glos; *m* 1927, Elspeth Muriel, *d* of Sir Alfred Tritton, 2nd Bt, Upper Gatton Park, Reigate; one *s*. three *d. Educ:* Eton; Trinity Coll., Cambridge. Served European War, 1914-18, with King's Royal Rifle Corps (Lieutenant) in France and Flanders, (wounded, despatches). Rejoined 1940 and served War of 1939-45, with GHQ Home Forces and at the War Office AQMG (Temporary Lieut-Col), 1943-45. Clerk of Public Bills, House of Commons, retired 1959. High Sheriff, Westmorland, 1960. *Recreations:* shooting, gardening. *Address:* Lyvennet Bank, Maulds Meaburn, Penrith, Cumbria CA10 3HN. *T:* Ravensworth (Penrith) 225. *Club:* Army and Navy.

DENT, (Robert) Stanley (Gorrell), RE 1946 (ARE 1935); ARCA (London) 1933; RWA 1954 (ARWA 1951); Principal, Gloucestershire College of Art and Design, 1950-74; *b* 1 July 1909; *o c* of Robert and Hannah Dent; *m* Doris, *o c* of Clement and Mabel Wenban; two *s. Educ:* The Newport Technical Coll.; The Newport, Mon., Sch. of Art and Crafts; Royal College of Art. Volunteered for service in Royal Engineers, 1942, invalided out, 1944. Runner up in Prix-de-Rome Scholarship, 1935; awarded the British Institution Scholarship in Engraving for the year 1933; Works exhibited at the Royal Academy, The Royal Scottish Academy, The New English Art Club, The Royal Society of British Artists, The Art Institute of Chicago, The International Print Makers Exhibition, Calif., and other leading Art Exhibitions. Ministry of Education Intermediate Assessor, 1957-60. Panel Mem. (Fine Art), National Council for Diplomas in Art and Design, 1962-65; Chief Examiner A Level Art and Design, 1963-76. ASIA (Ed) 1967. *Recreations:* travel, painting, music, gardening, spectator sports. *Address:* Wenbans, Ashley Road, Battledown, Cheltenham. *T:* Cheltenham 24742.

DENT-BROCKLEHURST, Mrs Mary, JP; *b* 6 Feb. 1902; *d* of late Major J. A. Morrison, DSO, and late Hon. Mary Hill-Trevor; *m* 1924, Major John Henry Dent-Brocklehurst, OBE (*d* 1949), Sudeley Castle, Glos; one *s* three *d. Educ:* at home. JP and CC, 1949, CA 1958, Glos; High Sheriff, County of Gloucester, 1967. *Recreations:* gardening, beekeeping, travelling, archæology. *Address:* Hawling Manor, Andoversford, Cheltenham, Glos GL54 5TA. *T:* Guiting Power 362.

DENTON, Prof. Eric James, CBE 1974; FRS 1964; ScD; Director, Laboratory of Marine Biological Association, Plymouth, since 1974; Member, Royal Commission on Environmental Pollution, 1973-76; *b* 30 Sept. 1923; *s* of George Denton and Mary Anne (*née* Ogden); *m* 1946, Nancy Emily, *d* of Charles and Emily Jane Wright; two *s* one *d. Educ:* Doncaster Grammar Sch.; St John's Coll., Cambridge; University Coll., London. Research in Radar, TRE Malvern, 1943-46; Biophysics Research Unit, University Coll., London, 1946-48; Lectr in Physiology, University of Aberdeen, 1948-56; Physiologist, Marine Biological Assoc. Laboratory, Plymouth, 1956-74; Royal Soc. Res. Professor, Univ. of Bristol, 1964-74, Hon. Professor, 1975; Carnegie Fellow at Muséum National d'Histoire Naturelle, Paris, 1954-55. Fellow, University Coll., London, 1965. Hon. Sec., Physiological Soc., 1963-69; Sec., Marine Biological Assoc., 1974-. *Publications:* scientific papers in Jl of Marine Biological Assoc., etc. *Recreation:* gardening. *Address:* Fairfield House, St Germans, Saltash, Cornwall PL12 5LS. *T:* St Germans (Cornwall) 204; The Laboratory, Citadel Hill, Plymouth PL1 2PB. *T:* Plymouth 21761.

DENTON-THOMPSON, Aubrey Gordon, OBE 1958; MC 1942; Senior Agricultural Adviser, United Nations Development Programme, and Food and Agriculture Organisation Country Representative in Turkey, since 1976; *b* 6 June 1920; *s* of late M. A. B. Denton-Thompson; *m* 1944, Ruth Cecily Isaac (*d* 1959); two *s* (one *d* decd); *m* 1961, Barbara Mary Wells. *Educ:* Malvern Coll. Served in RA 1940-44; seconded to Basutoland Administration, 1944; apptd to HM Colonial Service, 1945; transferred to Tanganyika as Asst District Officer, 1947; seconded to Colonial Office, 1948-50, District Officer; seconded to Secretariat, Dar es Salaam, as Asst Sec., 1950; Colonial Sec., Falkland Islands, 1955-60; Dep. Permanent Sec., Ministry of Agriculture, Tanganyika, 1960-62; retired from Tanganyika Civil Service, 1963. Man. Dir, Tanganyika Sisal Marketing Assoc. Ltd, 1966-68 (Sec. 1963); Sen. Agricl Advr, UNDP, 1968-, and FAO Country Rep.: Korea, 1970-73, Indonesia, 1973-76. *Address:* UN Development Programme, PK 407 Ankara, Turkey.

d'ENTRÈVES, Alexander Passerin, FRHistS; Professor of Political Theory, University of Turin, 1958-72, retired; *b* 26 April 1902; 4th *s* of Count Hector Passerin d'Entrèyes et Courmayeur; *m* 1931, Nina Ferrari d'Orsara; one *s* one *d. Educ:* University of Turin, Italy; Balliol Coll., Oxford. Doctor of Law, Turin, 1922; DPhil Oxon, 1932; Lecturer, University of Turin, 1929; Prof. University of Messina, 1934, Pavia, 1935, Turin, 1938; Prefect of Aosta, April-May 1945; Mem. of Council of Val d'Aosta, Dec. 1945. Serena Prof. of Italian Studies, University of Oxford, 1946-57; Fellow Magdalen Coll., Oxford, 1946-57. Vis. Prof., Harvard Univ., 1957; Yale Univ., 1960-64. FRHistS; Fellow, Amer. Acad. Arts and Sciences; Member: Société Académique St Anselme, Aosta; Accademia delle Scienze, Turin; Accademia dei Lincei, Rome; Académie de Savoie, Chambéry. *Publications:* The Medieval Contribution to Political Thought, 1939; Reflections on the History of Italy, 1947; Aquinas, Selected Political Writings, 1948; Alessandro Manzoni, 1949; Natural Law, An Introduction to Legal Philosophy, 1951; Dante as a Political Thinker, 1952; The Notion of the State, An Introduction to Political Theory, 1967; other publications in Italian and French. *Recreation:* rambling in the Alps. *Address:* Strada ai Ronchi 48, Cavoretto, Torino, Italy; Castello di Entrèves, Courmayeur, Val d'Aosta, Italy.

DENZA, Mrs Eileen; Legal Counsellor, Foreign and Commonwealth Office, since 1974; *b* 23 July 1937; *d* of Alexander L. Young and Mrs Young; *m* 1966, John Denza; two *s* one *d. Educ:* Aberdeen Univ. (MA); Somerville Coll., Oxford (MA); Harvard Univ. (LIM). Called to the Bar, Lincoln's Inn, 1963. Asst Lectr in Law, Bristol Univ., 1961-63; Asst Legal Adviser, FCO (formerly FO), 1963-74. *Publications:* Diplomatic Law, 1976; article in British Yearbook of Internat. Law. *Recreations:* music, piano playing. *Address:* c/o Foreign and Commonwealth Office, SW1A 2AH.

de PASS, Col Guy Eliot, DSO 1918; OBE 1945; late 4th Dragoon Guards; *b* 30 Oct. 1898; *yr s* of late John de Pass; *m* 1925, Winifred Dorothy, *d* of late Westcott Featherstonehaugh and late Mrs Featherstonehaugh, Durban, Natal; three *d. Educ:* St Andrews, Eastbourne; Eton; Sandhurst. Served European War, 1914-18 (despatches, DSO), 4th Royal Dragoon Guards; Major 4th Batt. Oxford Bucks Light Infantry (TA), 1938; Military Asst to the Quartermaster-Gen. of the Forces, 1940; 2nd in Command 4th Bn Oxford and Bucks Light Infantry, 1939-40; Asst Commandant, Donnington, Salop, 1941; Sub-Area Comdr, Preston, 1943; Dep. Dir Labour 2nd Army (HQ), May 1943-45, NW Europe Campaign (OBE). *Recreation:* shooting. *Address:* Upper House Farm, near Henley-on-Thames, Oxfordshire. *T:* Rotherfield Greys 378. *Club:* Cavalry and Guards.

de PAULA, (Frederic) Clive, CBE 1970; TD 1950 and Clasp 1951; Managing Director, Agricultural Mortgage Corporation Ltd, since 1971; *b* 17 Nov. 1916; 2nd *s* of late F. R. M. de Paula, CBE, FCA; *m* 1950, Pamela Elizabeth Markham Quick (*née* Dean), *widow of* Joseph Bertram Telford Quick; one step *s. Educ:* Rugby Sch.; Spain and France. FCA, JDipMA, FBIM. 2nd Lieut, TA, 1939; Liaison Officer, Free French Forces in London and French Equatorial Africa, 1940; Specially employed Middle East and E Africa, 1941; SOE Madagascar, 1942; comd special unit with 11th E African Div., Ceylon and Burma, 1943; Finance Div., Control Commn, Germany, 1945; demobilised as Major, 1946; Captain 21st Special Air Service Regt (Artists) TA, 1947-56. Joined Robson, Morrow & Co., management consultants, 1946; Partner, 1951; seconded to DEA then to Min. of Technology as an Industrial Adviser, 1967; Co-ordinator of Industrial Advisers to Govt, 1969; returned as Sen. Partner, Robson, Morrow & Co., 1970; Non-Exec. Director: Greens Economiser Group Ltd, 1972; Tecalemit Ltd, 1972. Mem. Council, BIM, 1971-76; Mem., EDC for Agriculture, 1972. Gen. Comr of Income Tax, Winslow Div., Bucks, 1965. Hon. Treas., Schoolmistresses and Governesses Benevolent Instn, 1947. *Publications:* Accounts for Management, 1954; Management Accounting in Practice, 1959; (with A. W. Willsmore) The Techniques of Business Control, 1973; (with F. A. Attwood) Auditing: principles and practice, 1976. *Address:* Arden Long Crendon, Aylesbury, Bucks. *T:* Long Crendon 208279. *Clubs:* Bath, Farmers'.

de PEYER, Charles Hubert, CMG 1956; retired Under-Secretary, Ministry of Fuel and Power (Served with Foreign Office, with rank of Minister in United Kingdom Delegation to European Coal and Steel Community, 1952-56); *b* 24 Oct. 1905; 2nd *s* of Everard Charles de Peyer and Edith Mabel Starkey; *m* 1st, 1930, Flora Collins, singer, New York; one *s* one *d*; 2nd, 1953, Mary Burgess (*d* 1974); two *s* one *d*; 3rd, 1975, Joan, *widow of* Wilfred Fienburgh, MP. *Educ:* Cheltenham Coll.; Magdalen Coll., Oxford (Hons PPE). Entered Civil Service, Mines Dept, 1930. Mem., DoE Waste Management Advr. Council. *Recreations:* gardening, music. *Address:* 350 Chambersbury Lane, Leverstock Green, Hemel Hempstead, Herts. *Club:* Reform.

de PEYER, Gervase; Solo Clarinettist; Conductor; Founder and Conductor, The Melos Sinfonia; Founder Member, The Melos Ensemble of London; Director, London Symphony Wind Ensemble; Associate Conductor, Haydn Orchestra of London; solo clarinettist, Chamber Music Society of Lincoln Center, New York, since 1969; *b* London, 11 April 1926; *m* 1st, 1950, Sylvia Southcombe (marr. diss. 1971); one *s* two *d* ; 2nd, 1971, Susan Rosalind Daniel. *Educ:* King Alfred's, London; Bedales; Royal College of Music. Served HM Forces, 1945 and 1946. Principal Clarinet, London Symphony Orchestra, 1955-72. ARCM; Hon. ARAM. Gold Medallist, Worshipful Co. of Musicians, 1948; Charles Gros Grand Prix du Disque, 1961, 1962; Plaque of Honour for recording, Acad. of Arts and Sciences of America, 1962. Most recorded solo clarinettist in world. *Recreations:* cooking, kite-flying, sport, theatre. *Address:* 16 Langford Place, St John's Wood, NW8. *T:* 01-624 4098.

de PIRO, Alan C. H., QC 1965; a Recorder, since 1972; *b* 31 Aug. 1919; *e s* of late J. W. de Piro; *m* 1947, Mary Elliot (deceased); two *s*; *m* 1964, Mona Addington; one step *s* one step *d. Educ:* Repton; Trinity Hall, Cambridge (Sen. Scholar). MA 1947 (Nat. Sci. and Law). Royal Artillery, 1940-45 (Capt.); West Africa. Called to Bar, Middle Temple, 1947; Inner Temple, 1962; Bencher, Middle Temple, 1971. Member: Gen. Council of the Bar, 1961-65, 1966-70, 1971-73; Senate of the Inns of Court and the Bar, 1976-; Dep. Chairman: Beds QS, 1966-71; Warwicks QS, 1967-71. Vice-Pres., L'Union Internationale des Avocats, 1968-73 (Co-Pres., 1969). Member: Council Internat. Bar Assoc., 1967-; Editorial Advisory Cttee, Law Guardian, 1965-73; Law Panel British Council, 1967-74. Legal Assessor, Disciplinary Cttee, RCVS, 1970-. *Recreations:* conversation, gardening, inland waterways. *Address:* 4 King's Bench Walk, Temple, EC4; The Toll House, Bascote Locks, near Southam, Warwicks; 4 rue d'Anjou, 75008 Paris. *Club:* Hawks (Cambridge).

de POLNAY, Peter; author; *b* 8 March 1906; *m* 1942, Margaret Mitchell-Banks (*d* 1950); one *s*; *m* 1955, Maria del Carmen Rubio y Caparo. *Educ:* privately in England, Switzerland and Italy. Farmed in Kenya. First began to write in Kenya in 1932; was in Paris when Germans entered, worked with early French Resistance, escaped back to England after imprisonment under Vichy Government. *Publications:* Angry Man's Tale, 1938; Children My Children!, 1939; Boo, 1941; Death and Tomorrow, 1942; Water on the Steps, 1943; Two Mirrors, 1944; The Umbrella Thorn, 1946; A Pin's Fee, 1947; The Moot Point, 1948; Into an Old Room, a Study of Edward Fitzgerald, 1949; Somebody Must, 1949; An Unfinished Journey, 1952; Death of a Legend: The True Story of Bonny Prince Charlie, 1953; Fools of Choice, 1955; Before I Sleep, 1955; The Shorn Shadow, 1956; The Clap of Silent Thunder, 1957; Peninsular Paradox, 1958; The Crack of Dawn, 1960; The Gamesters, 1960; Garibaldi, 1961; No Empty Hands, 1961; The Flames of Art, 1962; A Man of Fortune, 1963; Three Phases of High Summer, 1963; The Plaster Bed, 1965; The World of Maurice Utrillo, 1967; Aspects of Paris, 1968; A Tower of Strength, 1969; The Patriots, 1969; A Tale of Two Husbands, 1970; Napoleon's Police, 1970; The Permanent Farewell, 1970; A T-Shaped World, 1971; A Life of Ease, 1971; The Grey Sheep, 1972; The Loser, 1973; The Price You Pay, 1973; The Crow and the Cat, 1974; Indifference, 1974; A Clump of Trees, 1975; None Shall Know, 1976; The Stuffed Dog, 1976; Driftsand, 1977. *Recreation:* French history. *Address:* c/o A. M. Heath & Co. Ltd, 40-42 William IV Street, WC2N 4DD.

de PUTRON, Air Commodore Owen, CB 1951; CBE 1946; RAF retired; *b* 4 July 1893; *s* of late Captain Beaumont de Putron, Guernsey, CI; *m* 1918, Phyllis Patricia, *d* of late Frederick Bestow, Kent; one *d. Educ:* private school. Dominion Service, 1910; seconded to Army, 1914; commissioned Durham Light Infantry, 1914; permanent commn, RAF, 1919; served European War, 1914-18, in France, 1914-15 (very severely wounded; in hospital, 1915-17); attached to RFC, 1917; SO III, Ireland, 1918-20 (despatches); Sqdn Leader, 1930; Staff Officer, Iraq, 1930-33, ADGB, 1933-35; OC Army Co-op. Sqdn, 1935-36; Wing Comdr, 1937; Group Capt., 1940; Air Cdre, 1943; Air ADC, 1945-47, ADC, 1948-51, to King George VI. Provost Marshal and Chief of the Air Force Police, 1942-51; retired, 1951. As Provost Marshal visited many times all Theatres of War, 1943-45, and introduced RAF Police Dogs for guard duties in 1943; was responsible for arranging for RAF Police to take over investigation into murder of fifty allied aircrew officers from breakout from Stalag Luft III. *Address:* Bluehayes, Beer, Devon. *Club:* Royal Air Force.

DERAMORE, 6th Baron *cr* 1885; **Richard Arthur de Yarburgh-Bateson,** Bt 1818; Chartered Architect; Director of, and Design Consultant to, Rodway Smith Advertising Ltd; *b* 9 April 1911; *s*

of 4th Baron Deramore and of Muriel Katherine (*née* Duncombe); *S* brother, 1964; *m* 1948, Janet Mary, *d* of John Ware, MD, Askham-in-Furness, Lancs; one *d. Educ:* Harrow; St John's Coll., Cambridge. AA Diploma, 1935; MA Cantab 1936; ARIBA 1936. Served as Navigator, RAFVR, 1940-45: 14 Sqdn, RAF, 1942-44 and 1945. County Architect's Dept, Herts, 1949-52. *Publications:* freelance articles and short stories. *Recreations:* walking, cycling, motoring, water-colour painting. *Heir:* none. *Address:* Heslington House, Aislaby, Pickering, North Yorks YO18 8PE. *Clubs:* Royal Air Force, Royal Automobile.

DE RAMSEY, 3rd Baron *cr* 1887; **Ailwyn Edward Fellowes,** KBE 1974; TD; DL; Captain RA; Lord Lieutenant of Huntingdon and Peterborough, 1965-68 (of Hunts, 1947-65); *b* 16 March 1910; *s* of late Hon. Coulson Churchill Fellowes and Gwendolen Dorothy, *d* of H. W. Jefferson; *S* grandfather, 1925; *m* 1937, Lilah, *d* of Frank Labouchere, 15 Draycott Avenue, SW; two *s* two *d*. Served War of 1939-45 (prisoner). Pres. Country Landowners' Assoc., Sept. 1963-65. Awarded KBE 1974 for services to agriculture. DL Hunts and Peterborough, 1973, Cambs 1974. *Heir: s* Hon. John Ailwyn Fellowes [*b* 27 Feb. 1942; *m* 1973, Phyllida Mary, *d* of Dr Philip A. Forsyth, Newmarket, Suffolk]. *Address:* Abbots Ripton Hall, Huntingdon. *T:* Abbots Ripton 234. *Club:* Buck's.
See also Lord Ailwyn, Lord Fairhaven.

DERBY, 18th Earl of *cr* 1485; **Edward John Stanley,** MC 1944; DL; Bt 1627; Baron Stanley 1832; Baron Stanley of Preston, 1886; Major late Grenadier Guards; Constable of Lancaster Castle, since 1972; *b* 21 April 1918; *s* of Lord Stanley, PC, MC (*d* 1938), and Sibyl Louise Beatrix Cadogan (*d* 1969), *e d* of Henry Arthur, late Viscount Chelsea, and Lady Meux; *g s* of 17th Earl of Derby, KG, PC, GCB, GCVO; *S* grandfather, 1948; *m* 1948, Lady Isabel Milles-Lade, *yr d* of late Hon. Henry Milles-Lade, and sister of 4th Earl Sondes. *Educ:* Eton; Oxford Univ. Left Army with rank of Major, 1946. President: Merseyside and District Chamber of Commerce, 1972-; Liverpool Chamber of Commerce, 1948-71; NW Area Conservative Assoc., 1969-72. Pro-Chancellor, Lancaster Univ., 1964-71. Lord Lieut and Custos Rotulorum of Lancaster, 1951-68. Alderman, Lancashire CC, 1968-74. Commanded 5th Bn The King's Regt, TA, 1947-51, Hon. Col, 1951-67; Hon. Captain, Mersey Div. RNR, 1955; Hon. Colonel: 1st Bn The Liverpool Scottish Regt, TA, 1964-67; Lancastrian Volunteers, 1967-75; 5th/8th (V) Bn The King's Regt, 1975-; 4th (V) Bn The Queen's Lancashire Regt, 1975-. DL Lancs 1946. Hon. LLD: Liverpool, 1949; Lancaster, 1972. Hon. Freeman, City of Manchester, 1961. *Heir: b* Captain Hon. Richard Oliver Stanley, *qv. Address:* Knowsley, Prescot, Merseyside L34 4AF. *T:* 051-489 6147; Stanley House, Newmarket, Suffolk. *T:* Newmarket 3011. *Clubs:* White's; Jockey (Newmarket).

DERBY, Bishop of, since 1969; **Rt. Rev. Cyril William Johnston Bowles;** *b* Scotstoun, Glasgow, 9 May 1916; *s* of William Cullen Allen Bowles, West Ham, and Jeanie Edwards Kilgour, Glasgow; *m* 1965, Florence Joan, *d* of late John Eastaugh, Windlesham. *Educ:* Brentwood Sch.; Emmanuel Coll., Jesus Coll. (Lady Kay Scholar) and Ridley Hall, Cambridge. 2nd cl., Moral Sciences Tripos, Pt. I, 1936; 1st cl., Theological Tripos, Pt. I, and BA, 1938; 2nd cl., Theological Tripos, Pt. II, 1939; MA 1941. Deacon 1939, Priest 1940, Chelmsford; Curate of Barking Parish Church, 1939-41; Chaplain of Ridley Hall, Cambridge, 1942-44; Vice-Principal, 1944-51; Principal, 1951-63; Hon. Canon of Ely Cathedral, 1959-63; Archdeacon of Swindon, 1963-69. Select Preacher: Cambridge, 1945, 1953, 1958, 1963; Oxford, 1961; Dublin, 1961. Exam. Chaplain to Bishop of Carlisle, 1950-63; to Bishops of Rochester, Ely and Chelmsford, 1951-63; to Bishop of Bradford, 1956-61; to Bishop of Bristol, 1963-69. Hon. Canon, Bristol Cathedral, 1963-69; Surrogate, 1963-69; Commissary to Bishop of the Argentine, 1963-69. Mem., Archbishops' Liturgical Commn, 1955-75. *Publications:* contributor: The Roads Converge, 1963; A Manual for Holy Week, 1967; The Eucharist Today, 1974. *Address:* The Bishop's House, 6 King Street, Duffield, Derby DE6 4EU. *T:* (office) Derby 46744; (home) Derby 840132. *Club:* English-Speaking Union.

DERBY, Archdeacon of; *see* Dell, Ven. R. S.

DERBYSHIRE, Andrew George, FRIBA, FSIA; Partner in practice of Robert Matthew, Johnson-Marshall & Partners; *b* 7 Oct. 1923; *s* of late Samuel Reginald Derbyshire and late Helen Louise Puleston Derbyshire (*née* Clarke); *m* , Lily Rhodes (*née* Binns), widow of late Norman Rhodes; three *s* one *d. Educ:* Chesterfield Grammar Sch.; Queens' Coll., Cambridge; Architectural Assoc. MA (Cantab), AA Dip. (Hons). Admty Signals Estabt and Bldg Research Station, 1943-46. Farmer &

Dark, 1951-53 (Marchwood and Belvedere power stations); West Riding County Architect's Dept, 1953-55 (bldgs for educn and social welfare). Asst City Architect, Sheffield, 1955-61; responsible for co-ord. of central area redevelt. Mem. Research Team, RIBA Survey of Architects' Offices, 1960-62. Since 1961, as Mem. RM, J-M & Partners, associated with: develt of Univ. of York, Central Lancs New Town, NE Lancs Impact Study, Univ. of Cambridge, West Cambridge Develt and New Cavendish Laboratory, Preston Market and Guildhall, London Docklands Study, Hillingdon Civic Centre, Cabtrack and Minitram feasibility studies, Suez Master Plan Study. Member: RIBA Council, 1950-72, 1975-(Vice-Pres. 1976); NJCC, 1961-65; Bldg Industry Communications Res. Cttee, 1964-66 (Chm. Steering Cttee); MoT Urban Res. and Develt Gp, 1967; Inland Transport Res. and Develt Council, 1968; DoE Planning and Transport Res. Adv. Council, 1971-76. Pt-time Mem., CEGB, 1973-; Mem. Bd, Property Services Agency, 1975-. Hon. DUniv York, 1972. *Publications:* (jointly) The Architect and his Office, 1962; broadcasts and contribs on auditorium acoustics, building economics, the planning and construction of univs and new towns, also new forms of public transport. *Recreation:* his family. *Address:* 4 Sunnyfield, Hatfield, Herts AL9 5DX. *T:* Hatfield 65903; 42 Weymouth Street, W1A 2BG. *T:* 01-486 4222.

DERHAM, Sir David (Plumley), KBE 1977 (MBE 1945); CMG 1968; BA, LLM Melbourne; Vice-Chancellor of the University of Melbourne since 1968; *b* 13 May 1920; *s* of late Dr A. P. Derham, CBE, MC, ED, MD, FRACP; *m* 1944, Rosemary, *d* of late Gen. Sir Brudenell White, KCB, KCMG, KCVO, DSO; one *s* two *d. Educ:* Scotch Coll., Melbourne; Ormond Coll., Melbourne Univ. AIF, 1941-45 (Major). Solicitor, 1948; Barrister, 1948-51; Melbourne University: Tutor in Law, Queen's Coll., and Independent Lectr, Constitutional Law, 1949-51; Prof. of Jurisprudence, 1951-64; Vis. Fellow, Wadham Coll., Oxford, 1953; Carnegie Trav. Fellow, 1953-54; Constitutional Consultant, Indian Law Inst, 1958-59; Sen. Res. Fellow and Vis. Lectr, Chicago Univ. Law Sch., 1961; Vis. Prof. Northwestern Univ. Law Sch., 1961; Dean of Faculty of Law, Monash Univ., 1964-68. Mem. Commonwealth Cttee on Future of Tertiary Educn in Australia, 1962-64; Mem. Australian Univs Commn, 1965-68; Chm., Aust. Vice-Chancellors' Cttee, 1975-76. Hon. LLD Monash, 1968. *Publications:* (Ch. 1) Legal Personality and Political Pluralism, 1958; (Ch. 6) Essays on the Australian Constitution, 2nd edn 1961; Paton, Textbook of Jurisprudence (ed) 3rd edn 1964, 4th edn 1972; (with F. K. H. Maher and Prof. P. L. Waller) Cases and Materials on the Legal Process, 1966, 2nd edn 1971; (with F. K. H. Maher and Prof. P. L. Waller) An Introduction to Law, 1966, 3rd edn 1977; articles in legal jls. *Recreations:* tennis, lawn tennis. *Address:* University of Melbourne, Parkville, Melbourne, Vic 3052, Australia. *T:* 347-2349. *Clubs:* Melbourne, Naval and Military, Melbourne Beefsteak, Royal Melbourne Tennis.

d'ERLANGER, Leo Frederic Alfred; Banker, retired; Director of public companies; *b* 2 July 1898; *s* of Baron François Rodolphe d'Erlanger and Elizabetta Barbiellini-Amidei; *m* 1930, Edwina Louise Pru; one *s* one *d. Educ:* Eton; Royal Military Coll., Sandhurst. War of 1914-18, Active Service First Bn Grenadier Guards. Officier de la Légion d'Honneur. *Address:* 10 Rue Robert de Traz, Geneva, Switzerland.

DERMOTT, William; Under Secretary, Head of Agricultural Science Service, Agricultural Development and Advisory Service, Ministry of Agriculture, Fisheries and Food, since 1976; *b* 27 March 1924; *s* of William and Mary Dermott; *m* 1946, Winifred Joan Tinney; one *s* one *d. Educ:* Univ. of Durham. BSc, MSc. Agricl Chemist, Univ. of Durham and Wye Coll., Univ. of London, 1943-46; Soil Scientist, Min. of Agriculture, at Wye, Bangor and Wolverhampton, 1947-70; Sen. Sci. Specialist, and Dep. Chief Sci. Specialist, MAFF, 1971-76. *Publications:* papers on various aspects of agricultural chemistry in scientific journals. *Recreations:* gardening, the countryside. *Address:* 22 Chequers Park, Wye, Ashford, Kent. *T:* Wye 812694.

de ROS, 27th Baroness (in her own right; Premier Barony of England) *cr* 1264; **Georgiana Angela Maxwell;** *b* 2 May 1933; *er d* of Lieut-Comdr Peter Ross, RN (killed on active service, 1940) and *g d* of 26th Baroness de Ros (*d* 1956); *S* grandmother, 1958 (on termination of abeyance); *m* 1954, Comdr John David Maxwell, RN; one *s* one *d. Educ:* Wycombe Abbey Sch., Bucks; Studley Agricultural Coll., Warwicks. NDD 1955. *Heir: s* Hon. Peter Trevor Maxwell, *b* 23 Dec. 1958. *Address:* Old Court, Strangford, N Ireland.

de ROTHSCHILD; *see* Rothschild.

DERRY, Thomas Kingston, OBE 1976; MA, DPhil Oxon; *b* 5 March 1905; *y s* of late Rev. W. T. Derry, Wesleyan Minister; *m* 1930, Gudny, *e d* of late Hjalmar Wesenberg, Commander of Order of Vasa, Oslo, Norway. *Educ:* Kingswood Sch., Bath; Queen's Coll., Oxford (Bible Clerk and Taberdar). 1st Class, Classical Moderations, 1925; 1st Class, Final Sch. of Modern History, 1927; Senior George Webb Medley Scholar, 1927; Gladstone Prizeman, 1928; Sixth Form Master and Chief History Master, Repton Sch., 1929-37; Headmaster, Mill Hill School, 1938-40; Political Intelligence Dept of Foreign Office, 1941-45 (Chief Intelligence Officer, Scandinavia); Asst Master, St Marylebone Grammar Sch., 1945-65; Visiting Prof., Wheaton Coll., Mass, 1961-62. *Publications:* (with T. L. Jarman) The European World, 1950; The Campaign in Norway (official military history), 1952; A Short History of Norway, 1957; (with T. I. Williams) A Short History of Technology, 1960; The United Kingdom Today, 1961; A Short Economic History of Britain, 1965; (with E. J. Knapton) Europe 1815-1914, 1965; Europe 1914 to the Present, 1966; (with T. L. Jarman and M. G. Blakeway) The Making of Britain, 3 vols, 1956-69; A History of Modern Norway, 1814-1972, 1973. *Address:* Nils Lauritssons vei 27, Oslo 8, Norway.

DERRY, Warren, MA; *b* 19 Oct. 1899; *e s* of late Rev. W. T. Derry, Wesleyan minister; *m* 1930, Lorna Adeline, *yr d* of Reginald H. Ferard; one *s* two *d. Educ:* Kingswood Sch., Bath; Magdalen Coll., Oxford (Demy). 2nd Class Hons Classical Moderations, 1920; 1st Class Hons. Final Sch. of English Language and Literature, 1922; Passmore Edwards Scholar, 1922; Asst Master, the Edinburgh Academy, 1922-28; Headmaster Wolverhampton Grammar Sch., 1929-56. *Publication:* Dr Parr, a Portrait of the Whig Dr Johnson, 1966. *Address:* 11 Abbey Court, Edward Street, Bath.

DERRY AND RAPHOE, Bishop of, since 1975; **Rt. Rev. Robert Henry Alexander Eames;** *b* 27 April 1937; *s* of William Edward and Mary Eleanor Thompson Eames; *m* 1966, Ann Christine Daly; two *s. Educ:* Methodist Coll.; Belfast; Queen's Univ., Belfast (LLB (hons), PhD); Trinity Coll., Dublin. Research Scholar and Tutor, Faculty of Laws, QUB, 1960-63; Curate Assistant, Bangor Parish Church, 1963-66; Rector of St Dorothea's, Belfast, 1966-74; Rector of St Mark's, Dundela, 1974-75. Examining Chaplain to Bishop of Down, 1973. *Publications:* A Form of Worship for Teenagers, 1965; The Quiet Revolution—Irish Disestablishment, 1970; Through Suffering, 1973; contribs to New Divinity, Irish Legal Quarterly, Criminal Law Review, etc. *Address:* The See House, Culmore Road, Londonderry, N Ireland. *T:* 0504-51206.

DERWENT, 4th Baron *cr* 1881; **Patrick Robin Gilbert Vanden-Bempde-Johnstone,** CBE 1974; Bt 1795; *b* 26 Oct 1901; *y s* of late Hon. Edward Henry Vanden-Bempde-Johnstone, 2nd *s* of 1st Baron and Hon. Evelyn Agar-Ellis (*d* 1952), *d* of 5th Viscount Clifden; *S* brother 1949; *m* 1929, Marie-Louise, *d* of late Albert Picard, Paris; one *s. Educ:* Charterhouse; RMC, Sandhurst. Commissioned KRRC, 1921; Major, KRRC. Formerly Director: Yorkshire Insurance Co.; National Safe Deposit and Trustee Co. Ltd; past Chm., Reinsurance Corp.; ex-Mem., Horserace Totalisator Bd, Tote Investors Ltd; Past Chm., British Road Fedn. Junior Opposition Whip in House of Lords, 1950-51; Minister of State, Bd of Trade, 1962-63; Minister of State, Home Office, 1963-64; Deputy Speaker, House of Lords, 1970-. *Recreations:* shooting and fishing. *Heir: s* Hon. Robin Evelyn Leo Vanden-Bempde-Johnstone, MVO 1957 [*b* 30 Oct. 1930; *m* 1957, Sybille de Simard de Pitray, *d* of Vicomte de Simard de Pitray and Madame Jeannine Hennessy; one *s* three *d*]. *Address:* Hackness Hall, Scarborough, North Yorks; 48 Cadogan Place, SW1. *Club:* Beefsteak.
See also Earl of Listowel.

DERX, Donald John, CB 1975; Deputy Secretary, Department of Employment, since 1972; *b* 25 June 1928; *s* of John Derx and Violet Ivy Stroud; *m* 1956, Luisa Donzelli; two *s* two *d. Educ:* Tiffin Boys' Sch., Kingston-on-Thames; St Edmund Hall, Oxford (BA). Asst Principal, BoT, 1951; seconded to Cabinet Office, 1954-55; Principal, Colonial Office, 1957; Asst Sec., Industrial Policy Gp, DEA, 1965; Dir, Treasury Centre for Admin. Studies, 1968; Head of London Centre, Civil Service Coll., 1970; Under Sec., Dept of Employment, 1971-72. Governor, Ashridge Management Coll. *Address:* 40 Raymond Road, Wimbledon, SW19 4AP. *T:* 01-947 0682.

DESAI, Shri Morarji Ranchhodji, BA; Prime Minister of India, since March 1977; *b* 29 Feb. 1896. *Educ:* Wilson Coll., Bombay. Entered Provincial Civil Service of Govt of Bombay, 1918; resigned to join the Civil Disobedience Campaign of Mahatma Gandhi, 1930; convicted for taking part in the Movement during 1930-34; Sec., Gujarat Pradesh Congress Cttee, 1931-37 and

1939-46; Minister for Revenue, Co-operation, Agriculture and Forests, Bombay, 1937-39; convicted, 1940-41, and detained in prison, 1942-45; Minister for Home and Revenue, Bombay, 1946-52; Chief Minister of Bombay, 1952-56; Minister for Commerce and Industry, Government of India, 1956-58. Treasurer, All India Congress Cttee, 1950-58; Minister of Finance, Government of India, 1958-63, resigned from Govt (under plan to strengthen Congress) Aug. 1963; Dep. Prime Minister and Minister of Finance, Government of India, 1967-69; Chm., Parly Gp, Congress Party (Opposition), 1969-77; Founder-Chairman, Janata Party, 1977. Hon. Fellow, College of Physicians and Surgeons, Bombay, 1956; Hon. LLD Karnatak Univ., 1957. *Address:* Prime Minister's House, New Delhi, India.

de STE CROIX, Geoffrey Ernest Maurice, FBA 1972; Emeritus Fellow, New College, Oxford, since 1977; *b* 8 Feb. 1910; *s* of Ernest Henry de Ste Croix and Florence Annie (*née* Macgowan); *m* 1st, 1932, Lucile (marr. diss. 1959); one *d* (decd); 2nd, 1959, Margaret Knight; two *s. Educ:* Clifton Coll. (to 1925); University Coll. London (1946-50). BA 1st cl. Hons History, London, 1949; MA Oxon, 1953. Solicitor, 1931. Served War, RAF, 1940-46. Asst Lectr in Ancient Economic History, London Sch. of Economics, and Part-time Lectr in Ancient History, Birkbeck Coll., London, 1950-53; Fellow and Tutor in Ancient History, New Coll., Oxford, 1953-77. J. H. Gray Lectr, Cambridge Univ., 1972-73. *Publications:* The Origins of the Peloponnesian War, 1972; contributions to: Studies in the History of Accounting, 1956; The Crucible of Christianity, 1969; Studies in Ancient Society, 1974; Debits, Credits, Finance and Profits, 1974; articles and reviews in various learned jls. *Recreations:* listening to music, walking. *Address:* Evenlode, Stonesfield Lane, Charlbury, Oxford OX7 3ER. *T:* Charlbury 453.

DE SAUMAREZ, 6th Baron *cr* 1831; **James Victor Broke Saumarez;** Bt 1801; *b* 28 April 1924; *s* of 5th Baron de Saumarez and Gunhild, *d* of late Maj.-Gen. V. G. Balck, Stockholm; *S* father, 1969; *m* 1953, Julia, *d* of late D. R. Charlton, Gt Holland-on-Sea, Essex; twin *s* one *d. Educ:* Eton Coll.; Millfield; Magdalene Coll., Cambridge (MA). Farmer; Director, Shrubland Health Clinic Ltd. *Recreations:* swimming, gardening, photography. *Heir: s* Hon. Eric Douglas Saumarez, *b* 13 Aug. 1956. *Address:* Shrubland Vista, Coddenham, Ipswich, Suffolk. *T:* Ipswich 830220.

DESBOROUGH, Vincent Robin d'Arba, FBA 1966; FSA 1956; Senior Research Fellow, New College, Oxford, since 1968; *b* 19 July 1914; *s* of Maximilian Julius Praetorius, PhD (killed on active service, European War, 1914-18), and of Violet Mary Francesca (*née* Parker; who changed the surname for herself and dependants from Praetorius to a family name of Desborough, by deed-poll, after the death of her husband and the Russian Revolution); *m* 1950, Mary Hobson Appach; one *d* (one *s* decd). *Educ:* Downside Sch.; New Coll., Oxford. BA 1936; BLitt 1939; Charles Oldham Prize, 1939; MA 1949. Macmillan Student, British Sch. of Archæology at Athens, 1937-39. Served War of 1939-45, Royal Artillery (Temp. Captain, 1944). British Coun. (Sec. Registrar, Brit. Inst., Athens), 1946-47; Asst Dir, Brit. Sch. of Archæology at Athens, 1947-48; University of Manchester, 1948-68. Corresp. Mem., German Archæological Institute. Chm., Man. Cttee, British Sch. at Athens, 1968-72. *Publications:* Protogeometric Pottery, 1952; The Last Mycenaeans and their Successors, 1964; The Greek Dark Ages, 1972; contrib. to revised edn of Cambridge Ancient History; articles and reviews in archæological and classical jls. *Address:* 13 Field House Drive, Woodstock Road, Oxford OX2 7NT. *T:* Oxford 52285.

DESHMUKH, Sir Chintaman Dwarkanath, Kt 1944; CIE 1937; President: India International Centre, New Delhi, since 1959; Council for Social Development, since 1969; *b* Bombay Presidency, 14 Jan. 1896; *s* of D. G. Deshmukh, lawyer; *m* 1st, 1920, Rosina, *d* of Arthur Silcox, London; one *d*; 2nd, 1953, Srimathi Durgabai. *Educ:* Elphinstone High Sch.; Elphinstone Coll., Bombay; Jesus Coll., Cambridge (Hon. Fellow 1962). National Science Tripos, pt 1, Frank Smart Prize in Botany, BA, 1917; first in Indian Civil Service Examination, London (open competitive), 1918; passed UK Bar Examination in 1919 and was called to Bar, Inner Temple, 1963. Asst Commissioner, 1920-24; Under Sec. to CP Government, 1924-25; Deputy Commissioner and Settlement Officer, 1926-30; Joint Sec. to 2nd Round Table Conference, 1931; Revenue Sec. to CP Govt, 1932-33; Financial Sec. to Govt of CP and Berar, India, 1933-39; Joint Sec. to the Government of India; Dept of Education, Health and Lands; Officer on Special Duty, Finance Dept, Govt of India; Custodian of Enemy Property, 1939; Sec. to Central Board of Reserve Bank of India, Bombay, 1939-41; Deputy-Governor, 1941-43; Gov., 1943-49, retired, 1949. Pres., Indian Statistical

Inst., Calcutta, 1945-64. India's delegate to the World Monetary Conference at Bretton Woods, 1944. Governor, World Bank and Fund, for India, Washington, 1946; Financial Rep. in Europe and America of Govt of India, 1949-50; Chm. Joint Board of Governors of World Bank and International Monetary Fund, 1950; Mem. Planning Commn, 1950; Minister of Finance, Govt of India, 1950-56, resigned 1956. Chairman: University Grants Commission, India, 1956-60; Administrative Staff Coll. of India, 1959-73; Indian Institute of Public Administration, 1964; Central Sanskrit Bd, 1967-68; Pres., Institute of Economic Growth, 1962-73; Mem. Bd of Trustees, UN Inst. for Trng and Res., 1965-70. Pres., Population Council of India, 1970-75. Vice-Chancellor, Univ. of Delhi, 1962-67. Holds hon. doctorates from US, UK and Indian Univs. Ramon Magsaysay Award (Philippines), 1959. *Publications:* Economic Developments in India, 1957; In the Portals of Indian Universities, 1959; On the Threshold of India's Citizenhood, 1962; Sanskrit Kāvyā-Mālikā, 1968; Reflections on Finance, Education and Society, 1972; Aspects of Development, 1972; The Course of My Life, 1973; Bhagavatgita, 1976. *Recreation:* gardening. *Address:* India International Centre, 40 Lodi Estate, New Delhi, India; CTI, Hyderabad 500768.

DESIO, Prof. Ardito; Professor of Geology (and Past Director of Geological Institute), at the University of Milan, and of Applied Geology, at the Engineering School of Milan, 1931-72, now Emeritus; *b* 18 April 1897; *m* 1932; one *s* one *d. Educ:* Udine and Florence. Grad. Univ. of Florence in Nat. Sciences. Asst, University of Pavia, 1923, also Engineering Sch., Milan, 1924-25 to 1930-31; Lectr in Phys. Geography, University of Milan, 1929-30 and in Palaeontology there until 1935. Pres., Italian Geological Cttee, 1966-73. Dir., Rivista Italiana di Paleontologia e Stratigrafia, 1942; Past Dir., Geologia Tecnica. Member: Ital. Geolog. Soc.; Ital. Assoc. of Geologists; Ital. Order of Geologists; Ital. Paleont. Soc.; Hon. Member: Gesellschaft für Erdkunde zu Berlin, 1941; Italian Geog. Soc., 1955. Faculty of Sciences University of Chile, 1964; Geological Soc. of London, 1964; Indian Paleont. Soc. Corr. Mem., Soc. Géol. Belgique, 1952; Member: Institut d'Egypte, 1936; Accademia Naz. Lincei, 1948; 1st, Lombardo Accad. Scienze Lettere, 1949. Led expedition to K2 (8611 m, 2nd highest peak in the World; reached on 31 July 1954), and 16 expeditions in Africa and Asia. Gold Medal of the Republic of Pakistan, 1954; Gold Medal of the Sciences, Letters and Arts, of Italy, 1956; Patrons medal of Royal Geog. Soc. of London, 1957; USA Antarctic Service Medal, 1974. Kt Grand Cross, 1955. *Publications:* about 350, among them: La spedizione geografica Italiana al Karakoram 1929, 1936; Le vie delle sete, 1950; Geologia applicata all'ingegneria, 1949, 3rd edn 1973; Ascent of K2, 1956 (11 languages, 15 editions); Geology of the Baltoro Basin, 1970; Results of half-a-century investigation on the glaciers of the Ortler-Cevedale, 1973; La Geologia dell'Italia, 1973; Geology of Central Badakhshan (NE Afghanistan), 1975. *Recreation:* alpinist. *Address:* (Office) Piazzale Gorini 15, 20133-Milano. *T:* 292726; (Residence) Viale Maino 14, 20129-Milano. *T:* 709845. *Clubs:* Internat. Rotary; Panatlon; Himalayan; Alpino Touring (Italy); (Hon. Member) Alpin Français; (Hon. Member) Excursionista Carioca.

DESPRÉS, Robert; President, Université du Québec, since 1973; *b* 27 Sept. 1924; *s* of Adrien Després and Augustine Marmen; *m* 1949, Marguerite Cantin; twos two *d. Educ:* Académie de Québec (BA 1943); Laval Univ. (MCom 1947); (postgrad. studies) Western Univ. Comptroller, Québec Power Co., 1947-63; Reg. Manager, Administration & Trust Co., 1963-65; Dep. Minister, Québec Dept of Revenue, 1965-69; Pres. and Gen. Man., Québec Health Insurance Bd, 1969-73. Public Governor, Montreal Stock Exchange. Member: Accounting Res. Adv. Bd, Canadian Inst. of Chartered Accountants; Royal Commn of Inquiry on financial organization and accountability in Govt of Canada, 1977. Mem. Board of Directors: Norcen Energy Resources Ltd; Campeau Corporation; Sidbec-Dosco Ltd; l'Union Canadienne; Centre Internat. de Recherches et d'Etudes en Management; l'Opéra du Québec Corporation. *Publications:* contrib. Commerce, and Soc. of Industrial Accountants Revue. *Recreations:* golf, skiing, reading. *Address:* 890 Dessane, Québec, Québec G1S 3J8, Canada. *T:* 687-2100 (418). *Clubs:* St-Denis, Cercle Universitaire (Québec); Lorette Golf.

de THIER, Jacques; Grand Officer, Order of Léopold II; Commander, Order of Léopold and Order of the Crown, Belgium; Civic Cross (1914-18); Grand Cross of Royal Victorian Order (Hon. GCVO); Director, Compagnie Financière et de Gestion pour l'Etranger (Cometra), Brussels, 1966-73; Counsellor, Cometra Oil Co.; *b* Heusy, Belgium, 15 Sept. 1900; *m* 1946, Mariette Negroponte (*d* 1973); three step *s. Educ:* University of Liège. Doctor of Laws (University of Liège), 1922; Mem. Bar (Liège and Verviers), 1923-29. Attached to Prime

Minister's Cabinet, Brussels, 1929-32; entered Diplomatic Service, 1930; Attaché, Belgian Legation, Berlin, 1932; Chargé d'Affaires in Athens, 1935, Teheran, 1936; First Sec., Berlin, 1937-38; First Sec., then Counsellor, Washington, 1938-44; Chargé d'Affaires, Madrid, 1944-46; Asst to Dir-Gen., Polit. Dept, Min. of Foreign Affairs, Brussels, 1947, then Asst Head of Belgian Mission in Berlin; Consul-Gen. for Belgium, NY, 1948-55; Pres., Soc. of Foreign Consuls in New York, 1954; Belgian Ambassador: to Mexico, 1955-58; in Ottawa, 1958-61; Mem. Belgian Delegns to Gen. Assemblies of UN, 1956, 1957, 1959 and 1960; Belg. Rep. to Security Council, Sept. 1960; Belgian Ambassador to Court of St James's, 1961-65, and concurrently Belgian Perm. Rep. to Council of WEU, 1961-65. Holds foreign decorations. *Recreation:* golf. *Address:* 38 avenue des Klauwaerts, Brussels 5. *Clubs:* Anglo-Belgian; Cercle Royal Gaulois, Cercle du Parc, Royal Golf de Belgique (Brussels).

de THIEUSIES, Vicomte A.; *see* Obert de Thieusies.

DETHRIDGE, Hon. George Leo, CMG 1972; Chairman, Victorian County Court, Australia, 1970-75; *b* 11 Dec. 1903; *s* of John Stewart Dethridge and Margaret Dethridge; *m* 1940, Ada Rosales Thomas; one *s* one *d*. *Educ:* Haileybury Coll.; Univ. of Melbourne. Appointed Judge of County Court, Victoria, Australia, 1946. *Recreations:* golf, swimming. *Address:* 61 South Road, Brighton, Victoria 3186, Australia. *T:* 925030.

de TRAFFORD, Dermot Humphrey, VRD 1963; Chairman: GHP Group Ltd, since 1965 (Managing Director, 1961); Calor Gas Holding, since 1974; *b* 19 Jan. 1925; *s* and *heir* of Sir Rudolph de Trafford, Bt, *qv,* and June Lady Audley (*née* Chaolin), MBE (*d* 1977); *m* 1st, 1946, Patricia Mary Beeley (marr. diss. 1973); three *s* six *d*; 2nd, 1973, Mrs Xandra Caradini Walter. *Educ:* Harrow Sch.; Christ Church, Oxford (MA). Trained as Management Consultant, Clubley Armstrong & Co. Ltd and Orr & Boss and Partners Ltd, 1949-52; Director: Brentford Transformers Ltd (now Brentford Electric Ltd); Hugh Smith & Co. (Possil) Ltd (now Hugh Smith (Glasgow) Ltd); Counting Instruments Ltd, 1953; Imperial Continental Gas Assoc., 1963- (Dep. Chm., 1972-); Petrofina SA, 1971. *Recreations:* golf, ski-ing. *Address:* 59 Onslow Square, SW7. *T:* 01-589 2826. *Clubs:* White's, Royal Ocean Racing; Royal St George's Golf; Island Sailing.

de TRAFFORD, Sir Rudolph Edgar Francis, 5th Bt *cr* 1841; OBE 1919; *b* 31 Aug. 1894; *s* of Sir Humphrey Francis de Trafford, 3rd Bt and Violet Alice Maud (*d* 1925), *d* of James Franklin; *S* brother, 1971; *m* 1st, 1924, June (who obtained a divorce, 1938), *o d* of late Lieut-Col Reginald Chaplin; one *s*; 2nd, 1939, Katherine, *e d* of W. W. Balke, Cincinnati, USA. *Educ:* Downside Sch.; Trinity Coll., Cambridge, BA. Served European War, 1914-18; Intelligence Corps and Gen. Staff GHQ. *Heir: s* Dermot Humphrey de Trafford, *qv. Address:* 70 Eaton Square, SW1. *T:* 01-235 1823. *Club:* White's.

DEUTSCH, André; Chairman and Managing Director, André Deutsch Ltd, since 1951; *b* 15 Nov. 1917; *s* of late Bruno Deutsch, and of Maria Deutsch (*née* Havas); unmarried. *Educ:* Budapest; Vienna; Zurich. First job in publishing, with Nicholson & Watson, 1942; started publishing independently under imprint of Allan Wingate (Publishers) Ltd, 1945; started André Deutsch Limited, in 1951. Founded: African Universities Press, Lagos, Nigeria, 1962; East Africa Publishing House, Nairobi, Kenya, 1964. *Recreations:* travel, ski-ing, publishing, talking. *Address:* 5 Selwood Terrace, SW7.

de VALOIS, Dame Ninette, DBE 1951 (CBE 1947); Founder and Director of the Royal Ballet, 1931-63 (formerly the Sadler's Wells Ballet, Royal Opera House, Covent Garden, and the Sadler's Wells Theatre Ballet, Sadler's Wells Theatre); Founder of The Royal Ballet School (formerly The Sadler's Wells School of Ballet); *b* Baltiboys, Blessington, Co. Wicklow, 6 June 1898; 2nd *d* of Lieut-Col T. R. A. Stannus, DSO, Carlingford; *m* 1935, Dr A. B. Connell. Prima ballerina the Royal Opera Season Covent Garden (International), May to July 1919 and again in 1928. Première danseuse British National Opera Company, 1918; mem. The Diaghileff Russian Ballet, 1923-26; choreographic dir to the Old Vic, the Festival Theatre, Cambridge, and The Abbey Theatre, Dublin, 1926-30; Founder of The National Sch. of Ballet, Turkey, 1947. Principal choreographic works: Job, The Rake's Progress, Checkmate, and Don Quixote. (Jtly) Erasmus Prize Foundn Award (first woman to receive it), 1974. Hon. MusDoc London, 1947; Hon. DLitt: Reading, 1951; Oxford, 1955; Hon. DMus, Sheffield, 1955; Hon. MusD Trinity Coll., Dublin, 1957; Hon. DFA Smith Coll., Mass, USA, 1957; Hon. LLD: Aberdeen, 1958; Sussex, 1975; FRAD 1963. Chevalier of the Legion of Honour, 1950. Gold Albert Medal, RSA, 1964. *Publications:* Invitation to the

Ballet, 1937; Come Dance with Me, 1957; Step By Step, 1977. *Address:* c/o Royal Ballet School, 153 Talgarth Road, W14.

DEVENPORT, Martyn Herbert, MA; Headmaster, Victoria College, Jersey, CI, since Sept. 1967; *b* 11 Jan. 1931; *s* of Horace Devenport and Marjorie Violet (*née* Fergusson); *m* 1957, Mary Margaret Lord; three *s* one *d*. *Educ:* Maidstone Gram. Sch.; Gonville and Caius Coll., Cambridge. Asst Master at Eton Coll., 1957-67. *Recreations:* photography, squash, sailing. *Address:* Victoria College, Jersey, CI. *T:* Central 37591.

DEVERELL, Sir Colville (Montgomery), GBE 1963 (OBE 1946); KCMG 1957 (CMG 1955); CVO 1953; retired from Government Service, Nov. 1962; Secretary-General, International Planned Parenthood Federation, 1964-69; *b* 21 Feb. 1907; *s* of George Robert Deverell and Maude (*née* Cooke); *m* 1935, Margaret Wynne, *d* of D. A. Wynne Wilson; three *s*. *Educ:* Portora Sch., Enniskillen, Ulster; Trinity Coll., Dublin (LLB); Trinity Coll., Cambridge. District Officer, Kenya, 1931; Clerk to Exec. and Legislative Councils, 1938-39; civil affairs Branch, E Africa Comd, 1941-46, serving Italian Somaliland, British Somaliland, Ethiopia; Mem. Lord de la Warr's Delegation, Ethiopia, 1944; seconded War Office in connection Italian Peace Treaty, 1946. Sec., Development and Reconstruction Authority, Kenya, 1946; acted as Financial Sec. and Chief Native Comr, 1949; Administrative Secretary, Kenya, 1949; Colonial Sec., Jamaica, 1952-55; Governor and Comdr-in-Chief, Windward Islands, 1955-59; Governor and Comdr-in-Chief, Mauritius, 1959-62. Chm. UN(FP) Mission to India, 1965; Mem., UN Mission on Need for World Population Inst., 1970; Chairman: UN Family Planning Evaluation Mission to Ceylon, 1971; UN Family Planning Assoc. Feasability Mission, Al Azhar Univ., Cairo, 1972. Constitutional Adviser: Seychelles, 1966; British Virgin Islands, 1973. LLD *jure dignitatis,* Dublin, 1964. *Recreations:* cricket, tennis, squash, golf and fishing. *Address:* 46 Northfield End, Henley-on-Thames, Oxon. *Clubs:* East India, Devonshire, Sports and Public Schools; MCC; Nairobi (Kenya).

DEVEREUX, family name of **Viscount Hereford.**

DEVERS, Gen. Jacob L.; United States Army (retired); Chairman, American Battle Monuments Commission, 1959-69; *b* 8 Sept. 1887; *s* of Philip Kissinger Devers and Ella Kate Loucks; *m* 1st, 1911, George Hays Lyon (*decd*); one *d*; 2nd, 1975, Dorothy Cardwell Ham. *Educ:* York High Sch., York, Pa; US Military Academy, West Point, NY. Chief of Staff, Panama Canal Dept, 1939-40; Cdg Gen., 9th Infantry Division, 1940-41; Cdg Gen. of the Armored Force, 1941-43; Cdg Gen. European Theatre of Operations, US Army, 1943; Deputy Supreme Allied Comdr, Mediterranean Theatre, and Cdg Gen. North African Theatre of Operations, United States Army, 1944; commanded Sixth Army Group in France, 1944-45; Commanding General, Army Ground Forces, USA, 1945-48; Chief Army Field Forces, USA, 1948-49; retired from US Army, 1949. Managing Dir, AAA Foundation for Traffic Safety, Washington, DC 1950. *Recreations:* polo, baseball, golf. *Address:* 1430 33rd Street, Northwest, Washington, DC 20007, USA. *Clubs:* Cosmos, Army-Navy (Washington, DC).

de VESCI, 6th Viscount, *cr* 1776; **John Eustace Vesey;** *b* 25 Feb. 1919; *s* of Lt-Col Hon. Thomas (Eustace) Vesey (*d* 1946) (*b* of 5th Viscount), and Lady Cecily (Kathleen) Vesey (*d* 1976) (a Lady-in-Waiting to the Duchess of Gloucester, 1947-51, a Woman of the Bedchamber to Queen Mary, 1951-53, and an Extra Lady-in-Waiting to the Duchess of Gloucester from 1953), *d* of 5th Earl of Kenmare; *S* uncle 1958; *m* 1950, Susan Anne, *d* of late Ronald (Owen Lloyd) Armstrong Jones, MBE, QC, DL, and of the Countess of Rosse; one *s* two *d* (and one *d* decd). *Educ:* Eton; Trinity Coll., Cambridge. Served War of 1939-45 with Irish Guards, Narvik (wounded), North Africa and Italy. Followed career of Land Agent; now managing own property. FLAS(O), FRICS. *Heir: s* Hon. Thomas Eustace Vesey, *b* 8 Oct. 1955. *Address:* Abbeyleix, Ireland. *T:* Abbeyleix 31162. *Clubs:* Turf, White's.
See also Earl of Rosse.

de VIGIER, William Alphonse; Chairman (also founder and formerly Managing Director) Acrow (Engineers) Ltd; Chairman: Thos. Storey (Engineers) Ltd, Stockport; Adamson & Hatchett Ltd, Dukinfield; E. H. Bentall & Co. Ltd, Maldon; Crawley Bros Ltd, Saffron Walden; Acrow Automation Ltd, Harefield; Acrow Australia Ltd; Acrow Engineers (Pty) Ltd, South Africa; Coles Cranes Ltd; Priestman Bros Ltd, Hull; Steels Engineering Ltd, Sunderland; Tapevex Ltd, Hull; *b* 22 Jan. 1912; *m* 1939, Betty Kendall; two *d*. *Educ:* La Chataigneraie, Coppet, Switzerland. Director: Vigier Cement SA, Switzerland; Acrow Argentina SA; Acrow Peru SA; Acrow

India Ltd; Richmond Screw & Anchor Co., Canada; Inland Steel Pty, South Africa; Japan Steels, Tokyo; Pres., Acrow Corp. of America. Mem., British Airways Bd, 1973-. Knight of Star of the North (Sweden); Grand Commander, Order of Star of Africa. *Recreations:* tennis, skiing, swimming. *Address:* Sommerhaus, Soleure, Switzerland; Tinkers Lodge, Marsh Lane, Mill Hill, NW7; Acrow (Engineers) Ltd, 8 South Wharf, W2. *T:* (business) 01-262 3456. *Club:* East India, Devonshire, Sports and Public Schools.

DE VILLE, Harold Godfrey, (Oscar); Director, BICC Ltd, since 1971; *b* Derbyshire, 11 April 1925; *s* of Harold De Ville and Anne De Ville (*née* Godfrey); *m* 1947, Pamela Fay Ellis; one *s. Educ:* Burton-on-Trent Grammar Sch.; Trinity Coll., Cambridge (MA). Served RN, 1943-46. With Ford Motor Co. Ltd, 1949-65; Gen. Man., Central Personnel Relations, BICC Ltd, 1965-70. Member: Commn on Industrial Relations, 1971-74; Central Arbitration Cttee, 1976-; Council, Advisory, Conciliation and Arbitration Service, 1976-. *Recreations:* golf, reading. *Address:* Bexton Mews, Knutsford, Cheshire. *T:* Knutsford 2270; 146 Whitehall Court, SW1A 2EL. *T:* 01-930 3160.

de VILLIERS, 3rd Baron, *cr* 1910; **Arthur Percy de Villiers;** *b* 17 Dec. 1911; *s* of 2nd Baron and Adelheid, *d* of H. C. Koch, Pietermaritzburg, Natal; *S* father 1934; *m* 1939, Lovett (marr. diss. 1958), *d* of Dr A. D. MacKinnon, Williams Lake, BC; one *s* two *d. Educ:* Magdalen Coll., Oxford. Barrister, Inner Temple, 1938. Farming in New Zealand. Admitted as a barrister to the Auckland Surpreme Court, 1949. *Heir: s* Hon. Alexander Charles de Villiers, *b* 29 Dec. 1940. *Address:* PO Box 66, Kumeu, Auckland, NZ.

DEVINE, Rt. Rev. Joseph; Titular Bishop of Voli and Auxiliary to the Archbishop of Glasgow, (RC), since 1977; *b* 7 Aug. 1937; *s* of Joseph Devine and Christina Murphy. *Educ:* Blairs Coll., Aberdeen; St Peter's Coll., Dumbarton; Scots Coll., Rome. Ordained priest in Glasgow, 1960; postgraduate work in Rome (PhD), 1960-64; Private Sec. to Archbishop of Glasgow, 1964-65; Assistant Priest in a Glasgow parish, 1965-67; Lecturer in Philosophy, St Peter's Coll., Dumbarton, 1967-74; a Chaplain to Catholic Students in Glasgow Univ., 1974-77. Papal Bene Merenti Medal, 1962. *Recreations:* general reading, music, Association football. *Address:* Archdiocesan Office, 19 Park Circus, Glasgow G3 6BE. *T:* 041-332 1680.

DE VITO, Gioconda; Violinist; Professor of Violin at Accademia Di Santa Cecilia, Rome, 1935; *b* 26 July 1907; *d* of Giacomo and Emilia De Vito (*née* Del Giudice), Martina Franca Puglia, Italy; *m* 1949, James David Bicknell; no *c. Educ:* Conservatorio Di Musica Rossini, Pesaro. Began to play violin at age of 8½; final examinations (distinction), Conservatorio Pesaro, 1921; first concert, 1921; first prize, Internat. Competition, Vienna, 1932. World wide musical activities since debut with London Philharmonic Orchestra, 1948, at concert conducted by Victor de Sabata; Royal Philharmonic Soc., 1950; Edinburgh Festival, 1949, 1951, 1953 (took part, 1953, in Festival of the Violin with Yehudi Menuhin and Isaac Stern), and 1960; played at Bath Fest. and Festival Hall with Yehudi Menuhin, 1955; Jury Tchaikowsky Internat. Violin Competition, Moscow, and recitals Moscow and Leningrad. 1958; Soloist, Adelaide Centenary Fest., and toured Australia, 1960; concerts, Buenos Aires, 1961; retired, 1961. Last concerts, Gt Brit., Swansea Festival, Oct. 1961; Continent, Basle Philharmonic, Nov. 1961. Diploma di Medaglia d'Oro del Ministero della Pubblica Istruzione for services to Art, 1957; Academician, Accademia Nazionale di Santa Cecilia, Rome, 1976. *Recreation:* bird watching. *Address:* Flint Cottage, Loudwater, Rickmansworth, Herts. *T:* 72865; Via Cassia 595, Rome. *T:* 3660937.

DEVITT, Lt-Col Sir Thomas Gordon, 2nd Bt, *cr* 1916; Partner of Devitt & Moore, Shipbrokers; Chairman of the National Service for Seafarers; *b* 27 Dec. 1902; *e s* of Arthur Devitt (*d* 1921) *e s* of 1st Bt and Florence Emmeline (*d* 1951), *e d* of late William Forbes Gordon, Manar, NSW; *S* grandfather, 1923; *m* 1st, 1930, Joan Mary (who obtained a divorce, 1936), 2nd *d* of late Charles Reginald Freemantle, Hayes Barton, Pyrford, Surrey; 2nd, 1937, Lydia Mary (marr. diss. 1953), *o d* of late Edward Milligen Beloe, King's Lynn, Norfolk; two *d* ; 3rd, 1953, Janet Lilian, *o d* of late Col H. S. Ellis, CBE, MC; one *s* one *d. Educ:* Sherborne; Corpus Christi Coll., Cambridge. 1939-45 War as Lt-Col, Seaforth Highlanders and OC Raiding Support Regt. Royal Order of Phœnix of Greece with swords. Chm. Macers Ltd, 1961-70. Chm., Board of Governors, The Devitt and Moore Nautical Coll., Pangbourne, 1948-61; Governor, Sherborne Sch., 1967-75. *Heir: s* James Hugh Thomas Devitt, *b* 18 Sept. 1956. *Recreations:* shooting, fishing. *Address:* 49 Lexden Road, Colchester, Essex. *T:* Colchester 77958; 5 Rembrandt Close, Holbein Place, SW1. *T:* 01-730 2653. *Club:* MCC.

DEVLIN, family name of **Baron Devlin.**

DEVLIN, Baron (Life Peer) *cr* 1961, of West Wick; **Patrick Arthur Devlin,** PC 1960; Kt 1948; FBA 1963; High Steward of Cambridge University, since 1966; *b* 25 Nov. 1905; *e s* of W. J. Devlin; *m* 1932, Madeleine, *yr d* of Sir Bernard Oppenheimer, 1st Bt; four *s* twin *d. Educ:* Stonyhurst Coll.; Christ's Coll., Cambridge. President of Cambridge Union, 1926. Called to Bar, Gray's Inn, 1929; KC 1945; Master of the Bench, Gray's Inn, 1947; Treasurer of Gray's Inn, 1963. Prosecuting Counsel to the Mint, 1931-39. Legal Dept, Min. of Supply, 1940-42; Junior Counsel to the Ministries of War Transport, Food and Supply, 1942-45; Attorney-Gen., Duchy of Cornwall, 1947-48; Justice of the High Court, Queen's Bench Div., 1948-60; Pres. of the Restrictive Practices Court, 1956-60; a Lord Justice of Appeal, 1960-61; a Lord of Appeal in Ordinary, 1961-64, retd; Chm. Wiltshire QS, 1955-71. A Judge of the Administrative Tribunal of the ILO, 1964-; Chm., Commn apptd under constn of ILO to examine complaints concerning observance by Greece of Freedom of Assoc. and similar Conventions, 1969-71. Chairman: Cttee of Inquiry into Dock Labour Scheme, 1955-56; Nyasaland Inquiry Commn, 1959; Cttee of inquiry into the port transport industry, 1964-65; Jt Bd for the Nat. Newspaper Industry, 1965-69; Commn of Inquiry into Industrial Representation, 1971-72; Cttee on Identification in criminal cases, 1974-76. Chm., Press Council, 1964-69. Chm. of Council, Bedford Coll., University of London, 1953-59. Pres., British Maritime Law Assoc., 1962-76; Chm. Assoc. Average Adjusters, 1966-67. Hon. LLD: Glasgow 1962; Toronto 1962; Cambridge 1966; Leicester, 1966; Sussex 1966; Durham, 1968; Liverpool, 1970; Hon. DCL Oxon, 1965. *Publications:* Trial by Jury, 1956 (Hamlyn Lectures); The Criminal Prosecution in England (Sherrill Lectures), 1957; Samples of Lawmaking (Lloyd Roberts and other lectures), 1962; The Enforcement of Morals, (Maccabean and other lectures), 1965; The House of Lords and the Naval Prize Bill, 1911 (Rede Lecture), 1968; Too Proud to Fight: Woodrow Wilson's Neutrality, 1974. *Address:* West Wick House, Pewsey, Wilts; Casa da Colina, Praia da Luz, Algarve.
See also William Devlin, P. J. M. Kennedy.

DEVLIN, (Josephine) Bernadette; *see* McAliskey, J. B.

DEVLIN, Stuart Leslie; goldsmith, silversmith and designer in London since 1965; *b* 9 Oct. 1931; *m* 1962, Kim Hose. *Educ:* Gordon Inst. of Technology, Geelong; Royal Melbourne Inst. of Technology; Royal Coll. of Art. DesRCA (Silversmith). DesRCA (Industrial Design/Engrg). Art Teacher, Vic. Educn Dept, 1950-58; Royal Coll. of Art, 1958-60; Harkness Fellow, NY, 1960-62; Lectr, Prahran Techn. Coll., Melbourne, 1962; one-man shows of sculpture, NY and Sydney, 1961-64; Inspr Art in Techn. Schs, Vic. Educn Dept, 1964-65; exhibns of silver and gold in numerous cities USA, Australia, Bermuda, Middle East and UK, 1965-. Executed many commns in gold and silver; designed coins for Australia, Singapore, Cayman Is, Gibraltar, IoM, Burundi, Botswana; designed and made: cutlery for State Visit to Paris, 1972; Duke of Edinburgh trophy for World Driving Championship, 1973; silver to commemorate opening of Sydney Opera House, 1973; Grand National Trophy, 1975, 1976; Australian Bravery Awards, 1975; Regalia for the Order of Australia, 1975-76. Freeman, City of London, 1966; Liveryman, Goldsmiths' Co., 1972. *Recreations:* work, travel. *Address:* 5 Albemarle Way, EC1V 4JB. *T:* 01-253 5471.

DEVLIN, William; Actor; *b* Aberdeen, 5 Dec. 1911; *y s* of William John Devlin, ARIBA, and Frances Evelyn Crombie; *m* 1936, Mary Casson (marr. diss.); one *d* ; *m* 1948, Meriel Moore. *Educ:* Stonyhurst Coll.; Merton Coll., Oxford (BA). Sec. OUDS, 1932-33; studied at Embassy Theatre Sch., 1933-34. New Theatre with John Gielgud, 1934-35 (Hamlet and Noah); Old Vic Company, 1935-36 (Peer Gynt, Cassius, Richard III, Leontes, Lear, etc); except for war period has appeared for Old Vic in every year, 1935-53 (Shylock, Macbeth, Claudius, Brutus, Dogberry, Fluellen, etc.). Parnell in The Lost Leader, Abbey Theatre, Dublin, 1937; Zola, Clemenceau, Gladstone in biogr. plays about them, 1937-38; Ransom in Ascent of F6 and Seth in Mourning becomes Electra, New Theatre, 1938. Joined HM Forces, Sept. 1939, as a Trooper in Horsed Cavalry; commnd in Royal Wilts Yeom. and served with 8th Army in Africa and Italy for 4½ years; released as Major, Nov. 1945. Leading man with Old Vic at Theatre Royal, Bristol, 1945-48. Memorial Theatre, Stratford-on-Avon, seasons 1954 and 1955. First appeared in New York as Bohun, QC in You Never Can Tell, Martin Beck Theatre, 1948; subseq. at Boston as Lear and Macbeth. Played Clemenceau in The Tiger, the first play to be televised in 1936, and has appeared regularly in this medium and also in Sound Broadcasting. Mem., Equity Council, 1957-65. Mem., Monksilver Parish Council, 1967, Chairman 1971, and

1973-74. *Recreations:* golf and fishing. *Address:* Bird's Hill Cottage, Monksilver, Taunton, Som. *T:* Stogumber 389.
See also Baron Devlin.

DEVON, 17th Earl of, *cr* 1553; **Charles Christopher Courtenay,** Bt 1644; RARO Lieutenant (W/Captain) Coldstream Guards; *b* 13 July 1916; *o surv. s* of 16th Earl and Marguerite (*d* 1950), *d* of late John Silva; *S* father, 1935; *m* 1939, Venetia, Countess of Cottenham, *d* of Captain J. V. Taylor; one *s* one *d. Educ:* Winchester; RMC, Sandhurst. Served war of 1939-45 (despatches). *Recreations:* shooting and fishing. *Heir: s* Lord Courtenay, *qv. Address:* Powderham Castle, Exeter. *T:* Starcross 253.

DEVONPORT, 3rd Viscount *cr* 1917, of Wittington, Bucks; **Terence Kearley;** Bt 1908; Baron 1910; Architect and Rural Consultant with Barnett Winskell, since 1972; *b* 29 Aug. 1944; *s* of 2nd Viscount Devonport and of Sheila Isabel, *e d* of Lt-Col C. Hope Murray; *S* father, 1973; *m* 1968, Elizabeth Rosemary, *d* of late John G. Hopton. *Educ:* Aiglon Coll., Vaud, Switzerland; Selwyn Coll., Cambridge (MA, DipArch). Chartered Architect, RIBA. Nuclear Power Group, Dungeness site office, 1963; Fresco restorer, Massada, Israel, 1964; Cambridge Univ., 1964-67 and 1968-70; Waterside and US Pavilion, Expo '70, design teams, with Davis Brody, New York City, 1967-68; Architect, Rehabilitation Div., London Borough of Lambeth, 1971-72. *Recreations:* naturalist, traveller and gourmet; a Turkophile; interests: archæology, shooting and fishing. *Address:* Peasmarsh Place, Rye, West Sussex. *Clubs:* Royal Automobile, Beefsteak, Boodles; Northern Counties (Newcastle upon Tyne).

DEVONS, Prof. Samuel; FRS 1955; Professor of Physics, Columbia University, New York, since 1960 (Chairman, Dept of Physics, 1963-67); Director, History of Physics Laboratory, Barnard College, Columbia University, since 1970; *b* 1914; *s* of Rev. David I. Devons and E. Edleston; *m* 1938, Celia Ruth Toubkin; four *d. Educ:* Trinity Coll., Cambridge. BA 1935; MA, PhD 1939. Exhibition of 1851 Senior Student, 1939. Scientific Officer, Senior Scientific Officer, Air Ministry, MAP, and Ministry of Supply, 1939-45. Lecturer in Physics, Cambridge Univ., Fellow and Dir of Studies, Trinity Coll., Cambridge, 1946-49; Prof. of Physics, Imperial Coll. of Science, 1950-55; Langworthy Prof. of Physics and Dir of Physical Laboratories, Univ. of Manchester, 1955-60. Royal Soc. Leverhulme Vis. Prof., Andhra Univ., India, 1967-68; Balfour Vis. Prof., History of Science, Weizmann Inst., Rehovot, Israel, 1973; Racah Vis. Prof. of Physics, Hebrew Univ., Jerusalem, 1973-74. Rutherford Medal and Prize, Inst. of Physics, 1970. *Publications:* Excited States of Nuclei, 1949; (ed) Biology and Physical Sciences, 1969; (ed) High Energy Physics and Nuclear Structure, 1970; contributions to Proc. Royal Society, Proc. Phys. Soc., etc. *Recreations:* plastic arts, travel. *Address:* Department of Physics, Columbia University, New York, NY 10027, USA.

DEVONSHIRE, 11th Duke of, *cr* 1694; **Andrew Robert Buxton Cavendish,** PC 1964; MC; Baron Cavendish, 1605; Earl of Devonshire, 1618; Marquess of Hartington, 1694; Earl of Burlington, 1831; Baron Cavendish (UK) 1831; Vice-Lord-Lieutenant of the County of Derby since 1957; Chancellor of Manchester University since 1965; *b* 2 Jan. 1920; *o surv s* of 10th Duke of Devonshire, KG, and Lady Mary Cecil (*see* Dowager Duchess of Devonshire), *d* of 4th Marquess of Salisbury, KG, GCVO; *S* father, 1950; *m* 1941, Hon. Deborah Vivian Freeman-Mitford, *d* of 2nd Baron Redesdale; one *s* two *d. Educ:* Eton; Trinity Coll., Cambridge. Served War of 1939-45, Coldstream Guards (MC). Contested (C) Chesterfield Div. of Derbyshire, 1945 and 1950. Parliamentary Under-Sec. of State for Commonwealth Relations, Oct. 1960-Sept. 1962; Minister of State, Commonwealth Relations Office, Sept. 1962-Oct. 1964 and for Colonial Affairs, 1963-Oct. 1964. Executive Steward of the Jockey Club, 1966-69. Mem., Horserace Totalisator Board, 1977-; a Trustee, Nat. Gallery, 1960-68; President: The Royal Hosp. and Home for Incurables; Derbyshire Boy Scouts Assoc.; Arts Employed; Lawn Tennis Assoc., 1955-61; Vice-Pres., Building Societies Assoc. (Pres., 1954-61); Chm. Grand Council, British Empire Cancer Campaign, 1956. Mayor of Buxton, 1952-54. Hon. LLD: Manchester; Sheffield; Hon. Dr Law, Memorial Univ. of Newfoundland. *Publication:* Park Top: a romance of the Turf, 1976. *Heir: s* Marquess of Hartington, *qv. Address:* 4 Chesterfield Street, W1. *T:* 01-499 5803; Chatsworth, Bakewell, Derbyshire. *T:* Baslow 2204; Lismore Castle, Co. Waterford, Eire. *T:* Lismore 20. *Clubs:* Brooks's, Jockey, White's.
See also Rt Hon. Harold Macmillan.

DEVONSHIRE, Dowager Duchess of, (Mary Alice), GCVO 1955; CBE 1946; Mistress of the Robes to The Queen, 1953-66; Chancellor of the University of Exeter, 1956-70; *b* 29 July 1895;

d of 4th Marquis of Salisbury, KG, PC, GCVO, and Lady Cicely Alice Gore (*d* 1955), 2nd *d* of 5th Earl of Arran; *m* 1917, as Lady Mary Cecil, 10th Duke of Devonshire, KG; one *s* (*see* 11th Duke of Devonshire) two *d* (*er s* killed in action, 1944). *Address:* 107 Eaton Square, SW1W 9AA. *T:* 01-235 8798; Moorview, Edensor, Bakewell, Derbyshire. *T:* Baslow 2204.

DE VRIES, Peter; writer; *b* Chicago, 27 Feb. 1910; *s* of Joost and Henrietta (*née* Eldersveld) de Vries; *m* 1943, Katinka Loeser; two *s* one *d. Educ:* Calvin College, Michigan (AB); Northwestern University. Editor, community newspaper, Chicago, 1931; free lance writer, 1931-; associate editor Poetry Magazine, 1938; co-editor, 1942; joined editorial staff New Yorker Magazine, 1944. Mem., Amer. Acad. and Inst. of Arts and Letters. *Publications:* No But I saw the Movie, 1952; The Tunnel of Love, 1954; Comfort Me with Apples, 1956; The Mackerel Plaza, 1958; The Tents of Wickedness, 1959; Through the Fields of Clover, 1961; The Blood of the Lamb, 1962; Reuben, Reuben, 1964; Let Me Count the Ways, 1965; The Vale of Laughter, 1967; The Cat's Pajamas and Witch's Milk, 1968; Mrs Wallop, 1970; Into Your Tent I'll Creep, 1971; Without a Stitch in Time, 1972; Forever Panting, 1973; The Glory of the Hummingbird, 1975; I Hear America Swinging, 1976. *Address:* c/o New Yorker Magazine, 25 W 43rd Street, NYC; (home) 170 Cross Highway, Westport, Conn, USA.

DEW, Leslie Robert; Chairman since 1971 and Non-Marine Underwriter, Roy J. M. Merrett Syndicates; *b* 11 April 1914; *er s* of Robert Thomas Dew, RHA and Ellen Dora Frampton; *m* 1st, 1939, Vera Doreen Wills (marr. diss. 1956); 2nd, 1956, Patricia Landsberg (*née* Hyde); one *s. Educ:* privately. Underwriting Member of Lloyd's, 1950-; Mem. Cttee of Lloyd's, 1969-72, 1974-77; Dep. Chm. of Lloyd's, 1971, 1975; Mem. Cttee, Lloyd's Non-Marine Assoc., 1957- (Dep. Chm. 1963 and 1965, Chm. 1966); Chm., Lloyd's Common Market Working Gp, 1971-; Dep. Chm., British Insurers' European Cttee, 1972. Binney Meml Award for Civilian Bravery, 1975. *Recreations:* music, reading. *Address:* 44 Campden Hill Gate, Duchess of Bedford's Walk, Kensington, W8. *Clubs:* Pilgrims, Royal Automobile.

DEW, Prof. Ronald Beresford; Professor of Management Control and Finance, University of Manchester Institute of Science and Technology, since 1976; *b* 19 May 1916; *s* of Edwyn Dew-Jones, FCA, and Jean Robertson Dew-Jones, BA, (*née* McInnes); *m* 1940, Sheila Mary Smith, BA; one *s* one *d. Educ:* Sedbergh; Manchester Univ. (LLB); Cambridge Univ. (MA). Barrister-at-Law, Middle Temple, 1965. Lieut, RNVR, 1940-45. Asst Managing Dir, P-E Consulting Gp, 1952-62; Director: Kurt Salmon & Co., 1955-62; S. Dodd & Co., 1957-59. Visiting Prof. of Industrial Administration, Manchester Univ., 1960-63; Head of Dept of Management Sciences, Univ. of Manchester Inst. of Science and Technology, 1963-70 and 1974-77; Prof. of Industrial Administration, Manchester Univ., 1963-67; Prof. of Management Sciences, 1971-76. Mem. Council, Internat. Univ. Contact for Management Educn, 1966-71; Dir, Centre for Business Research, 1965-69; Dir, European Assoc. of Management Training Centres, 1966-71; Dep. Chm., Manchester Polytechnic, 1970-72; External Examiner, Univs of: Liverpool, 1967-70; Loughborough, 1968-73; Bath, 1970-73; Khartoum (Sudan), 1967-70. Co-Chm., Conf. of Univ. Management Schools (CUMS), 1970-73; Governor: Manchester Coll. of Commerce, 1966-70; Manchester Polytechnic, 1970-76; Member: Council of BIM, 1971-76 (Bd of NW Region, 1966-); Council of Manchester Business School, 1967-76; Trustee, European Foundation for Management Develt, 1975-77; Consultant on organisation and control, to various internat. cos. FCA, FBIM, FIWM. *Publications:* (co-author) Management Control and Information, 1973; numerous papers in internat. jls, on management control systems. *Recreations:* archaeology, ornithology, bee-keeping, travel. *Address:* University of Manchester Institute of Science and Technology, Department of Management Sciences, Sackville Street, Manchester M60 1QD. *T:* 061-236 3311. *Clubs:* RNVR; St James's (Manchester).

de WAAL, Constant Henrik, CB 1977; Parliamentary Counsel since 1971; Barrister-at-Law; *b* 1 May 1931; *s* of late Hendrik de Waal and of Elizabeth von Ephrussi; *m* 1964, Julia Jessel; two *s. Educ:* Tonbridge Sch. (scholar); Pembroke Coll., Cambridge (scholar). 1st cl. Law Tripos, 1st cl. LLB. Called to the Bar, Lincoln's Inn, 1953; Buchanan Prize, Cassel Scholar. Fellow of Pembroke Coll., Cambridge, and Univ. Asst Lectr in Law, 1958-60. Entered Parliamentary Counsel Office, 1960; with Law Commission, 1969-71. *Recreation:* remaining (so far as possible) unaware of current events. *Address:* 62 Sussex Street, SW1.
See also Very Rev. V. A. de Waal.

De WAAL, Brig. Pieter, CB 1946; CBE 1944; *b* 31 Dec. 1899; *s* of Paul J. De Waal; *m* 1930, Isobel Peebles McLaggan; two *s.*

Educ: Zeerust, Transvaal; Pretoria; Camberley Staff Coll. (psc); Imperial Defence Coll. (idc). BSc Transvaal University Coll. (University of South Africa), 1920. Commissioned in South African Permanent Force, 1922; OC SA Permanent Garrison Artillery, 1930-31; OC Cape Command, 1932; OC Roberts Heights Command, OC Special Service Battalion and Commandant Military Coll., 1933; Dir of Military Operations and Training, Defence Headquarters, 1934-39; UDF Liaison Officer on staff of GOC East Africa Command, 1940; Dep. Chief of Staff, Defence HQ, Pretoria, 1941-43; attached to SHAEF, 1944-45; Quartermaster-Gen. UDF, 1945-50; Naval and Marine Chief of Staff, UDF, 1951-52; Military and Naval Attaché to Union of South Africa Embassy, Washington, DC, USA, and Military, Air and Naval Adviser to High Commissioner for the Union of South Africa at Ottawa, Canada, 1953-54. Retd from R of O, S African Defence Forces, 1960. *Recreation:* woodwork. *Address:* Intaba, Wisteria Road, Claremont, Cape Province, South Africa. *Club:* Civil Service (Cape Town).

de WAAL, Very Rev. Victor Alexander; Dean of Canterbury, since 1976; *b* 2 Feb. 1929; *s* of late Hendrik de Waal and of Elizabeth von Ephrussi; *m* 1960, Esther Aline Lowndes Moir; four *s*. *Educ:* Tonbridge School; Pembroke Coll., Cambridge (MA); Ely Theological College. With Phs van Ommeren (London) Ltd, 1949-50; Asst Curate, St Mary the Virgin, Isleworth, 1952-56; Chaplain, Ely Theological Coll., 1956-59; Chaplain and Succentor, King's Coll., Cambridge, 1959-63; Chaplain, Univ. of Nottingham, 1963-69; Chancellor of Lincoln Cathedral, 1969-76. *Publications:* What is the Church?, 1969; contrib.: Theology and Modern Education, 1965; Stages of Experience, 1965; The Committed Church, 1966. *Recreations:* pottery, fishing. *Address:* The Deanery, Canterbury, Kent CT1 2EP. *T:* Canterbury 65983.
See also C. H. *de Waal*.

DEWAR, family name of **Baron Forteviot.**

DEWAR, Donald Campbell; *b* 21 Aug. 1937; *s* of Dr Alasdair Dewar, Glasgow; *m* 1964, Alison McNair (marr. diss. 1973); one *s* one *d*. *Educ:* Glasgow Acad.; Glasgow Univ. MP (Lab) South Aberdeen, 1966-70; PPS to Pres. of Bd of Trade, 1967. *Address:* 23 Cleveden Road, Glasgow G12 0PQ.

DEWAR, George Duncan Hamilton; chartered accountant; Partner, Peat, Marwick, Mitchell & Co., Glasgow, since 1949; *b* 11 Sept. 1916; *s* of George Readman Dewar and Elizabeth Garrioch Sinclair Hamilton; *m* 1940, Elizabeth Lawson Potts Lawrie; one *s* one *d*. *Educ:* High Sch. of Glasgow. Mem. Inst. Chartered Accountants of Scotland (admitted, 1940; Mem. Coun., 1960-65; Vice-Pres., 1969-70; Pres., 1970-71). *Recreations:* golf, gardening. *Address:* (office) 135 Buchanan Street, Glasgow G1 2JG. *T:* 041-204 1481; (home) 82 Langside Drive, Glasgow G43 2SX. *T:* 041-637 1734. *Clubs:* Caledonian, Western, Royal Scottish Automobile (Glasgow).

DEWAR, Ian Stewart; Under-Secretary, Welsh Office, since 1973; *b* 29 Jan. 1929; *s* of late William Stewart Dewar and of Eileen Dewar (*née* Godfrey); *m* 1968, Nora Stephanie House; one *s* one *d*. *Educ:* Penarth County Sch.; UC Cardiff; Jesus Coll., Oxford (MA). RAF, 1947-49. Asst Archivist, Glamorgan County Council, 1952-53. Entered Min. of Labour, 1953; Asst Private Sec. to Minister, 1956-58; Principal, Min. of Labour and Civil Service Commn, 1958-65; Asst Sec., Min. of Labour, Dept of Employment and Commn on Industrial Relations, 1965-70; Asst Sec., Welsh Office, 1970-73. *Recreations:* history, music. *Address:* 59 Stanwell Road, Penarth, South Glamorgan. *T:* Cardiff 703255.

DEWAR, Prof. Michael James Steuart, FRS 1960; MA, DPhil Oxon; Robert A. Welch Professor of Chemistry, University of Texas, since 1963; *b* 24 Sept. 1918; *s* of Francis D. Dewar, ICS, and Nan B. Keith; *m* 1944, Mary Williamson; two *s*. *Educ:* Winchester Coll. (First Scholar); Balliol Coll., Oxford (Brackenbury, Frazer and Gibbs Scholar; Hon. Fellow, 1974). ICI Fellow in Chemistry, Oxford, 1945; Courtaulds Ltd, Fundamental Research Laboratory, 1945-51; Reilly Lecturer at Notre Dame Univ., USA, 1951; Prof. of Chemistry and Head of Dept of Chemistry at Queen Mary Coll. University of London, 1951-59; Prof. of Chemistry, University of Chicago, 1959-63. Visiting Prof. at Yale Univ., USA, 1957. Hon. Sec. Chemical Soc., 1957-59. Harrison Howe Award of Amer. Chem. Soc., 1961; (first) G. W. Wheland Meml Medal, Univ. of Chicago, 1976. Lectures: Tilden, Chem. Soc., 1954; Falk-Plaut, Columbia Univ., 1963; Daines Memorial, Univ. of Kansas, 1963; Glidden Company, Western Reserve Univ., 1964; Marchon Visiting, Univ. of Newcastle upon Tyne, 1966; Glidden Company, Kent State Univ., 1967; Gnehm, Eidg. Tech. Hochschule, Zurich, 1968; Barton, Univ. of Oklahoma, 1969; Kahlbaum, Univ. of

Basel, 1970; Benjamin Rush, Univ. of Pennsylvania, 1971; Venable, Univ. of N Carolina, 1971; Foster, State Univ. of NY at Buffalo, 1973; Robinson, Chem. Soc., 1974; Sprague, Univ. of Wisconsin, 1974; Bircher, Vanderbilt Univ., 1976; Visiting Professor: Arthur D. Little, MIT, 1966; Maurice S. Kharasch, Univ. of Chicago, 1971; Firth, Sheffield, 1972; Dist. Bicentennial, Univ. of Utah, 1976; Pahlavi, Iran, 1977. Fellow, Amer. Acad. of Arts and Sciences, 1966. *Publications:* The Electronic Theory of Organic Chemistry, 1949; Hyperconjugation, 1962; Introduction to Modern Chemistry, 1965; The Molecular Orbital Theory of Organic Chemistry, 1969; Computer Compilation of Molecular Weights and Percentage Compositions, 1970; The PMO Theory of Organic Chemistry, 1975; papers in scientific journals. *Address:* Department of Chemistry, University of Texas, Austin, Texas 78712, USA. *T:* (512) 471-5053.

DEWAR, Brig. Michael Preston Douglas, CB 1958; CBE 1956; retired; *b* 1 Oct. 1906; *s* of late Vice-Admiral R. G. D. Dewar, CBE, and Mrs S. E. Dewar (*née* Churchill); *m* 1935, Winifred Elizabeth, *née* Murphy (*d* 1971); one *s* one *d*. *Educ:* Winchester Coll. Commissioned 2nd Lieut, The Buffs, 1926; Captain, 1938; Staff Coll., 1939; Major, 1943; OC Home Counties Bde Trg Centre, 1946-47; GSO 1, 6th Airborne Div., 1947-48; Lt-Col, 1948; Jt Services Staff Coll., 1948-49; Col GS, E Africa, 1949-51; Col, 1951; Col Administrative Plans, GHQ, MELF, 1951-52; Dep. Dir Manpower Planning, War Office, 1952-55; Brig., 1955; UK Nat. Military Rep., SHAPE, 1955-58, retired 1959. *Recreations:* golf, gardening, bridge. *Address:* Great Maytham Hall, Rolvenden, near Cranbrook, Kent. *T:* Rolvenden 375. *Club:* Army and Navy.

DEWAR, Robert James, CMG 1969; CBE 1964; Chief of Agricultural Division, Regional Mission for Eastern Africa of the World Bank, since 1974; *b* 1923; *s* of late Dr Robert Scott Dewar, MA, MB, ChB, Dumbreck, Glasgow, and of Mrs Roubaix Dewar, Aberdovey, N Wales; *m* 1947, Christina Marianne, *d* of late Olof August Ljungberger, Stockholm, Sweden; two *s* one *d*. *Educ:* High Sch. of Glasgow; Edinburgh Univ. (BSc, Forestry); Wadham Coll., Oxford. Asst Conservator of Forests, Colonial Forest Service, Nigeria and Nyasaland, 1944-55; Dep. Chief Conservator of Forests, Nyasaland, 1955-60; Chief Conservator of Forests, Dir of Forestry and Game, Nyasaland (now Malawi), 1960-64; Mem. Nyasaland Legislative Council, 1960. Permanent Secretary, Malawi: Min. of Natural Resources, 1964-67 and 1968-69; Min. of Economic Affairs, 1967-68; Min. of Agriculture, 1969; retd from Malawi CS, 1969; Sen. Agriculturalist, Agricl Projects Dept, IBRD, 1969-74. Mem. Nat. Development Council, Malawi, 1966-69. *Recreations:* golf, angling, shooting. *Address:* c/o World Bank, PO Box 30577, Nairobi, Kenya. *T:* Langata 425. *Club:* Royal Commonwealth Society.

DEWAR, Thomas; His Honour Judge Dewar; a Circuit Judge (formerly Judge of the County Court), since 1962; Governor, Birkbeck College, since 1971; *b* 5 Jan. 1909; *s* of James Stewart Dewar and Katherine Rose Dewar; *m* 1950, Katherine Muriel Johnson; one *s*. *Educ:* Penarth Intermediate School; Cardiff Technical Coll.; Sch. of Pharmacy, University of London; Birkbeck Coll., University of London. Pharmaceutical Chemist, 1931; BPharm 1931, PhD 1934, BSc (Botany, 1st cl. hons) 1936, London. Called to Bar, Middle Temple, 1939; Blackstone Pupillage Prize, 1939. Admin. staff of Pharmaceutical Soc., 1936-40; Sec., Middx Pharmaceutical Cttee, 1940-41; Asst Dir, Min. of Supply, 1943; Sec., Wellcome Foundation, 1943-45. Mem. of Western Circuit, 1945-62; Judge of the County Court (circuit 59, Cornwall and Plymouth), 1962-65, (circuit 38, Edmonton, etc), 1965-66 (circuit 41, Clerkenwell), 1966-71; Circuit Judge, SE circuit, 1972-. Presided over inquiry into X-ray accident at Plymouth Hosp., 1962. Mem. Executive Council, Internat. Law Assoc., 1974-. *Publications:* Textbook of Forensic Pharmacy, 1946 and four subsequent editions; scientific papers in Quarterly Jl of Pharmacy and Pharmacology. *Recreations:* horticulture, travel. *Address:* 1 Garden Court, Temple, EC4. *T:* 01-353 3326; Goldenhurst Cottage, Aldington, Kent. *T:* Aldington 420.

DEWAR, William McLachlan, CBE 1970 (OBE 1955); FRSE 1958; MA; Headmaster, George Heriot's School, Edinburgh, 1947-70; Director, Craigmyle (Scotland) Ltd, since 1971; *b* 19 April 1905; *s* of James McLachlan Dewar and Annie Kempie Cuthbert, Crieff; *m* 1935, Mary Sinclair, *d* of late John Anderson, Lerwick; two *s* one *d*. *Educ:* Morrison's Academy, Crieff; Edinburgh Univ.; Rome. MA 1928 (1st Cl. Classics), Vans Dunlop Scholar (Classics), 1927; John Edward Baxter Scholar, 1928. Asst Master, Aberdeen Grammar Sch., 1929-32; Senior Classics Master, Dumfries Academy, 1933-41; Rector, Greenock Academy, 1941-47. Commissioned RAF (VR), 1941;

Mem. Scottish Air Cadet Council, 1948; Air Cadet Council, 1965-68. President: Scottish Schoolmasters' Assoc., 1944; Scottish Secondary Teachers' Assoc., 1947-49; Headmasters' Assoc. of Scotland, 1958-60; Member: Cttee on Grants to Students, 1958-60; Scottish Certificate of Education Examination Board, 1964-73; Scottish Council for Training of Teachers, 1959-67; Departmental Cttees on Secondary Sch. Curriculum, etc. Dir, Edinburgh Chamber of Commerce, 1964-67; Chm. Governors, Moray House Coll. of Education, 1958-71; Chm., City of Edinburgh Valuation Appeal Cttee, 1974-75; Dep. Chm., Lothian Valuation Appeal Panel, 1975-77. FRSA 1968. Hon. DLitt, Heriot-Watt, 1970. Chevalier des Palmes Académiques, 1961. *Publications:* The Law and The Teacher, 1955; numerous papers on classical and educational subjects. *Recreations:* study of puns; teacher politics; formerly hockey. *Address:* 35 Craiglockhart Grove, Edinburgh EH14 1ET. *T:* 031-443 3287.

de WARDENER, Prof. Hugh Edward, MBE 1946; MD, FRCP; Professor of Medicine, University of London, Charing Cross Hospital, since 1960; Honorary Consultant Physician to the Army, since 1975; *b* 8 Oct. 1915; *s* of Edouard de Wardener and Becky (*née* Pearce); *m* 1st, 1939, Janet Lavinia Bellis Simon (marr. diss, 1947); one *s*; 2nd, 1947, Diana Rosamund Crawshay (marr. diss., 1954); 3rd, 1954, Jill Mary Foxworthy (marr. diss., 1969); one *d*; 4th, 1969, Josephine Margaret Storey, MBE; two *s*. *Educ:* Malvern Coll. St Thomas's Hosp., 1933-39; RAMC, 1939-45; St Thomas's Hosp., 1945-60, Registrar, Senior Lecturer, Reader. MRCP 1946, MD 1949, FRCP 1958. Pres. Internat. Soc. of Nephrology, 1969-72. *Publications:* The Kidney: An Outline of Normal and Abnormal Structure and Function, 1973. Papers in various scientific journals. *Recreations:* normal and scything. *Address:* 9 Dungarvan Avenue, Barnes, SW15. *T:* 01-878 3130.

DEWDNEY, Duncan Alexander Cox, CBE 1968; Deputy Chairman, Manpower Services Commission, 1974-77; *b* 22 Oct. 1911; *o s* of late Claude Felix Dewdney and Annie Ross Cox; *m* 1935, Ann, *d* of Walter Riley and Emily Sterratt; two *d*. *Educ:* Bromgrove Sch., Worcs; University of Birmingham (BSc Hons, Cadman Medallist). Served War of 1939-45; RAF, 1940-45 (Wing Comdr); Air Staff appts, Head RE8 MHS (R&D Dept). British Petroleum Co., 1932-36; International Assoc. (Pet. Ind.) Ltd, 1936-40; Research Man., Esso Development Co., 1945-51; joined Esso Petroleum Co., 1951; Dir, 1957; Man. Dir, 1963-67; Vice-Chm., 1968. Seconded to NBPI as Jt Dep. Chm., 1965-66, part-time Mem. Bd, 1967-69. Exec. Dir, Rio Tinto Zinc Corporation, 1968-72; Chairman: Irish Refining Co. Ltd, 1958-65; Anglesey Aluminium, 1968-71; RTZ Britain, 1969-72; RTZ Development Enterprises, 1970-72; Dir, Esso Chemicals SA, 1964. Chairman: National Economic Develt Cttee for the Mechanical Engrg Industry, 1964-68; Welsh Industrial Develt Bd, 1972-75; Underwater Training Centre, 1977-; Dir, The Coverdale Organization, 1974-. Legion of Merit, 1945. *Address:* Salters, Harestock, Winchester, Hants. *T:* Winchester 2034. *Club:* Travellers'.

DEWES, Sir Herbert (John Salisbury), Kt 1973; CBE 1954; DL; JP; Chairman, Cheshire County Council, 1968-74; *b* 30 June 1897; *s* of John Hunt Dewes, solicitor, Tamworth, Staffordshire; *m* 1923, Kathleen, *d* of W. Matthews, Nuneaton; two *s*. *Educ:* Aldenham. County Alderman for Cheshire, 1950; JP 1951, DL 1966, Cheshire. Presidential Award, RSA, 1973. *Address:* 2 Curzon Park, North Chester. *T:* Chester 319136.

de WET, Dr Carel; South African Ambassador to the Court of St James's, 1964-67 and 1972-77; Director of companies; farmer; *b* Memel, OFS, S Africa, 25 May 1924; *g s* of Gen. Christian de Wet; *m* 1949, Catharina Elizabeth (Rina) Maas, BA; one *s* three *d*. *Educ:* Vrede High Sch., OFS; Pretoria Univ. (BSc); University of Witwatersrand (MB, BCh). Served at Nat. Hosp., Bloemfontein; subseq. practised medicine at Boksburg, Transvaal, at Winburg, OFS, and, from 1948, at Vanderbijlpark, Transvaal. Mayor of Vanderbijlpark, 1950-53; MP (Nat. Party) for Vanderbijlpark, 1953-64, for Johannesburg West, 1967-72; Mem. various Parly and Nat. Party Cttees, 1953-64; Minister of Mines and Health, Govt of S Africa, 1967-72. *Recreations:* beef ranching, golf, rugby, cricket, hunting, deep sea fishing. *Address:* Castrol House, PO Box 6424, Johannesburg 2000, South Africa. *T:* (office) 642-4343; (home) 706-6202. *Clubs:* Royal Automobile, East India, Devonshire, Sports and Public Schools, MCC, South Africa, Curzon House, Les Ambassadeurs, Eccentric, Wentworth; Here XVII (Cape Town); Constantia, Zwartkops Golf (Pretoria); Club RSA, New, Rand Park Golf (Johannesburg); Maccauvlei Country (Vereeniging), Emfuleni Golf (Vanderbijlpark); Brits Golf (Brits, Transvaal).

DEWEY, Sir Anthony Hugh, 3rd Bt, *cr* 1917; JP; *b* 31 July 1921; *s* of late Major Hugh Grahame Dewey, MC (*e s* of 2nd Bt), and of Marjorie Florence Isobell (who *m* 2nd, 1940, Sir Robert Bell, KCSI; he died 1953), *d* of Lieut-Col Alexander Hugh Dobbs; *S* grandfather, 1948; *m* 1949, Sylvia, *d* of late Dr J. R. MacMahon, Branksome Manor, Bournemouth; two *s* three *d*. JP Somerset, 1961. *Heir: s* Rupert Grahame Dewey, *b* 29 March 1953. *Address:* Silton Lodge, Gillingham, Dorset. *T:* Bourton 324. *Club:* Army and Navy.

DEWHURST, Prof. Sir Christopher John, Kt 1977; FRCOG, FRCSE; Professor of Obstetrics and Gynaecology, University of London, at Queen Charlotte's Hospital for Women, since 1967; *b* 2 July 1920; *s* of John and Agnes Dewhurst; *m* 1952, Hazel Mary Atkin; two *s* one *d*. *Educ:* St Joseph's Coll., Dumfries; Manchester Univ. MB, ChB. Surg. Lieut, RNVR, 1943-46. Sen. Registrar, St Mary's Hosp., Manchester, 1948-51; Lectr, Sen. Lectr and Reader, Sheffield Univ., 1951-67. Pres., RCOG, 1975-. Hon. FACOG 1976. *Publications:* A Student's Guide to Obstetrics and Gynaecology, 1960, 2nd edn 1965; The Gynaecological Disorders of Infants and Children, 1963; (jtly) The Intersexual Disorders, 1969; (ed) Integrated Obstetrics and Gynaecology for Postgraduates, 1972, 2nd edn 1976. *Recreations:* cricket, gardening, music. *Address:* 39 Old Slade Lane, Iver, Bucks. *T:* Iver 653395. *Club:* Junior Carlton.

DEWHURST, Keith Ward; His Honour Judge Dewhurst; a Circuit Judge, since 1972; *b* 11 March 1924; *s* of James Dewhurst, solicitor, and Mildred Catherine Dewhurst; *m* 1952, Norah Mary Hodgson (marr. diss. 1970); two *d*. *Educ:* Shrewsbury School; Trinity College, Oxford. Called to the Bar, Inner Temple, 1947. Practised on Northern Circuit. *Recreations:* reading, bridge. *Address:* 277 Garstang Road, Fulwood, Preston, Lancs. *T:* Preston 716850.

DEWHURST, Comdr Ronald Hugh, DSO 1940; RN retired; *b* 10 Oct. 1905; *s* of late Robert Paget Dewhurst, ICS, and late Florence Frances Maud Dewhurst; *m* 1928, Torquilla Macleod Lawrence (*d* 1953); one *s* one *d*; *m* 1954, Marion Isabel Dahm; one *d*. *Educ:* Abberley Hall; Osborne; Dartmouth. Joined Royal Navy, 1919; served in submarines, 1927-53; commanded HM submarines H. 33, Seahorse, and Rorqual (DSO and two Bars); Amphion, Taciturn, and RN Detention Quarters, 1953-55; retired to New Zealand, 1955. *Recreations:* fishing, bridge. *Address:* 6 Wychwood Crescent, Rotorua, New Zealand.

DEWING, Maj.-Gen. Richard Henry, CB 1941; DSO 1917; MC 1915; psc; retired; *b* 15 Jan. 1891; *e surv. s* of Rev. R. S. Dewing and Dora, *d* of R. J. Pettiward, of Finborough Hall, Suffolk; *m* 1920, Helen (*d* 1976), *e d* of Lieut-Col A. J. Wogan-Browne, 33rd Cavalry; one *s* (and *e s* killed in action in Libya, 2nd *s* decd, *o d* decd). *Educ:* Haileybury. Commd in RE, 1911; joined 2nd QVO Sappers and Miners, 1914; Capt., 1917; Bt Major, 1919; Major, 1926; Bt Lieut-Col, 1930; Lieut-Col, 1934; Col, 1936; Maj.-Gen., 1939; served in Mesopotamia and Persia, 1915-19 (DSO, MC); Peace Service India, 1913-14, 1920-21; GSO 2 Royal Military Coll., Kingston, Canada, 1927-29; OC 54th Field Co., Bulford; GSO2 Southern Command, 1931-33; Imperial Defence Coll., 1934; Gen. Staff Officer, 1st Grade, War Office, 1936-37; Army Instructor Imperial Defence Coll., 1937-39; Dir of Military Operations, 1939-40; Chief of Staff, Far East, 1940-41; Military Mission, Washington, 1942; Chief of Army-RAF Liaison Staff, Australia, 1943-44; SHAEF Mission to Denmark, 1945. Grand Cross Order of Dannebrog (Denmark); Officer Legion of Merit (USA). *Address:* Nigg, Tain, Ross-shire.

de WINTER, Carl; Deputy Secretary General, Federation of British Artists, since 1968; *b* 18 June 1934; *s* of Alfred de Winter; *m* 1958, Lyndall Bradshaw; one *s* one *d*. *Educ:* Pangbourne. Purser, Orient Line, 1951-60. Art Exhibitions Bureau: PA to Man. Dir, 1961-66; Director, 1967-; Royal Soc. of Portrait Painters: Asst Sec., 1962-; Royal Soc. of Miniature Painters, Sculptors and Gravers: Asst Sec., 1964-67; Sec., 1968-; Royal Soc. of Marine Artists: Asst Sec., 1964-70; Sec., 1971-; Royal Soc. of British Artists: Asst Keeper, 1969-73; Keeper, 1974-; Royal Inst. of Oil Painters: Sec., 1973-; National Soc. of Painters, Sculptors and Printmakers: Sec., 1973-; New English Art Club: Sec., 1973-; United Soc. of Artists: Sec., 1975-. *Recreations:* tennis, gardening, stamp collecting. *Address:* Dalewood Cottage, Mickleham, Surrey RH5 6EH.

DE WOLF, Vice-Adm. Harry George, CBE 1946; DSO 1944; DSC 1944; *b* 1903; *s* of late Harry George De Wolf, Bedford, NS; *m* 1931, Gwendolen Fowle, *d* of Thomas St George Gilbert, Somerset, Bermuda; one *s* one *d*. Served War of 1939-45. Asst Chief of Naval Staff, Canada, 1944-47; Sen. Canadian Naval Officer Afloat, 1947-48; Flag Officer, Pacific Coast, 1948-50; Vice-Chief of Naval Staff, 1950-52; Chm. of Canadian Joint

Staff, Washington, 1953-55; Chief of Naval Staff, Canada, 1956-60, retired. Hon. DSc (M), Royal Military College of Canada, 1966. *Address:* 119 Minto Place, Rockcliffe Park, Ottawa, Ont., Canada; Old Post Office, Somerset, Bermuda.

de WOLFF, Brig. Charles Esmond, CB 1945; CBE 1919 (OBE 1919); LLB; *b* 25 Nov. 1893; *s* of C. L. de Wolff; *m* 1920, Ada Marjorie, *d* of Henry Arnold, Hatch End. Served: European War, 1914-19 (despatches four times, OBE, CBE, Russian Order of Vladimir); Dardanelles and Salonika, South Russia, 1919; 2nd Lieut Royal Sussex Regiment, 1914; transferred RAOC War of 1939-45 (CB); France and Italy; retd pay, 1946. OStJ 1952. *Clubs:* Army and Navy; Union (Malta).

DEWS, Peter; Theatre and TV Director; Artistic Director, Chichester Festival Theatre, since 1977; *b* 26 Sept. 1929; *er s* of John Dews and Edna (Bloomfield); *m* 1960, Ann Rhodes. *Educ:* Queen Elizabeth Grammar Sch., Wakefield; University Coll., Oxford (MA). Asst Master, Holgate and District Grammar Sch., Barnsley, 1952-53; BBC Midland Region Drama Producer (Radio and TV), 1953-63; Dir, Ravinia Shakespeare Festival, Chicago, 1963-64; Artistic Dir, Birmingham Repertory Theatre, 1966-72. Directed: TV: An Age of Kings, 1960 (SFTA Award 1960); The Spread of the Eagle, 1963; Theatre: As You Like It, Vaudeville, 1967; Hadrian VII, Mermaid, 1968, Haymarket and NY, 1969 (Tony Award 1969); Antony and Cleopatra, Chichester, 1969; Vivat Vivat Regina, Chichester, 1970, Piccadilly and NY, 1972; The Alchemist, Chichester, 1970; Crown Matrimonial, Haymarket, 1972, NY 1973; The Director of the Opera, Chichester, 1973; The Waltz of the Toreadors, Haymarket, 1974; King John, Stratford, Ont, 1974; The Pleasure of His Company, Toronto, 1974; Coriolanus, Tel Aviv, 1975; Othello, Chichester, 1975; Equus, Vancouver, 1975; Number Thirteen Rue de l'Amour, Phœnix, 1976; The Circle, Chichester, transf. to Haymarket, 1976; The Pleasure of His Company, Phœnix, 1976; Man and Superman, Don Juan in Hell, When We Are Married, Ottawa, 1977; Julius Caesar, Chichester, 1977. *Recreations:* acting, music. *Address:* 39 Elm Park Gardens, SW10 9QF. *T:* 01-352 9323.

DEXTER, Harold; Organist; Professor and Head of General Musicianship Department, Guildhall School of Music and Drama; Organist, St Botolph's, Aldgate; *b* 7 Oct. 1920; *s* of F. H. and E. Dexter; *m* 1942, Faith Grainger; one *d. Educ:* Wyggeston Grammar Sch., Leicester; Corpus Christi Coll., Cambridge, 1939-41 and 1946. ARCO 1938; College Organ Scholar; John Stewart of Rannoch Scholar, 1940; FRCO 1940; ARCM 1941. BA, MusB 1942; MA 1946; RCO Choirmaster's Diploma; John Brook Prize, 1946; ADCM, 1948. Royal Navy and RNVR, 1941-46. Organist, Louth Parish Church and Music-Master, King Edward VI Grammar Sch., Louth, 1947-49; Organist, Holy Trinity, Leamington Spa, 1949-56; Music Master, Bablake Sch., Coventry, 1952-56; Master of the Music, Southwark Cathedral, 1956-68. FGSM 1962, FRSCM 1964 (Hon. diplomas). *Address:* 8 Prince Edward Road, Billericay, Essex. *T:* Billericay 52042.

DEXTER, John; Director of Production, Metropolitan Opera, New York, since 1974. Actor in repertory, television and radio, until 1957; Associate Dir, National Theatre, 1963. *Plays directed:* 15 plays, 1957-72, Royal Court, incl. The Old Ones, 1972; Pygmalion, Albery, 1974; *for National Theatre:* Saint Joan, 1963; Hobson's Choice, Othello, Royal Hunt of the Sun, 1964; Armstrong's Last Goodnight, Black Comedy, 1965; A Bond Honoured, The Storm, 1966; A Woman Killed With Kindness, Tyger, The Good Natur'd Man, 1971; The Misanthrope, Equus, The Party, 1973; Phaedra Britannica, 1975; *in New York:* Chips With Everything, 1963; Do I Hear a Waltz?, 1965; Black Comedy and White Lies, The Unknown Soldier and His Wife, 1967; *Film:* The Virgin Soldiers, 1968; *Opera:* Benvenuto Cellini, Covent Garden, 1966; House of the Dead, Boris Godunov, Billy Budd, Ballo in Maschera, I Vespri Siciliani, Hamburg; The Devil, Sadler's Wells; La Forza Del Destino, 1975, Paris; I Vespri Siciliani, Aida, 1976, Le Prophète, 1977, Dialogues of the Carmelites, 1977, Lulu, 1977, Metropolitan, NY. *Recreation:* work. *Address:* c/o Metropolitan Opera, Lincoln Center, New York, NY 10023, USA.

DEXTER, Dr Keith; Director-General, Agricultural Development and Advisory Service (Deputy Secretary), Ministry of Agriculture, Fisheries and Food, since 1975; *b* 3 April 1928; *yr s* of Arthur William Dexter, farmer, and Phyllis Dexter; *m* 1954, Marjorie Billbrough; no *c. Educ:* Dixie Grammar Sch., Market Bosworth; Univs of Nottingham and Illinois. BSc London 1948; MS Illinois 1951; PhD Nottingham 1954; Nat. Diploma in Agric. 1948; FIBiol 1975. Asst Agric. Economist, Nottingham Univ., 1948-50; Booth Fellow, Illinois

Univ., 1950-51; Fulbright Trav. Schol., 1950-51; Res. Schol. and Agric. Economist, Nottingham Univ., 1951-54; Agric. Economist, Min. of Agriculture, 1954-56; Principal Agric. Economist, 1956-62; Grade I Adviser, Nat. Agric. Adv. Service, 1962-64; Admin. Staff Coll., Henley, 1963; Sen. Principal Agric. Economist, 1964-68; Dep. Dir of Econs and Statistics, 1968-70; Head of Fatstock Div., 1970-71; Under-Sec. (Meat and Fatstock), MAFF, 1971-75. Mem., ARC, 1975-; Vice-Chm., Adv. Council for Agric., 1975-. Mem. Duke of Edinburgh's 3rd Commonwealth Study Conf., Australia, 1968. *Publications:* (with Derek Barker) Farming for Profits, 1961, 2nd edn 1967; contribs to Jl Agric. Econs. *Recreations:* gardening, fishing. *Address:* 7 The Uplands, Harpenden, Herts AL5 2PG. *T:* Harpenden 3955. *Club:* Farmers'.

de YARBURGH-BATESON, family name of **Baron Deramore.**

d'EYNCOURT, Sir John Jeremy Eustace T.; *see* Tennyson d'Eyncourt.

DE ZOYSA, Sir Cyril, Kt 1955; Proctor of the Supreme Court, Justice of the Peace and Unofficial Magistrate; *b* 26 Oct. 1897. *Educ:* Royal College, Ceylon. Chm. and Gov. Dir, Associated Motorways Group of Cos; Chairman: Sri Lanka Asbestos Products Ltd; Ceylon Synthetic Textiles Ltd; Usha Industries (Ceylon) Ltd; President: Young Men's Buddhist Assoc.; Ceylon Nat. Assoc. for the Prevention of Tuberculosis; Maha Bodhi Soc. of Ceylon; Managing Trustee, Kalutara Bodhi Trust; Vice-Pres., All Ceylon Buddhist Congress. Dep. Pres. of the Ceylon Senate, 1952-55, Pres., 1955-62. Pres., Incorporated Law Soc. of Ceylon, 1956-62; Mem., Council of Legal Educn, 1956-. *Recreation:* cricket (Royal College, Colombo, etc). *Address:* Park Flats, Park Street, Colombo 2, Sri Lanka. *T:* Colombo 22478. *Clubs:* Sinhalese Sports (Trustee and Vice-Pres), Kalutara Town (Sri Lanka).

de ZULUETA, Sir Philip Francis; *see* Zulueta.

DHAVAN, Shanti Swarup; Member, Law Commission, India, since 1972; *b* 2 July 1905; *m* Shakuntala Kapur, *d* of Malik Basant Lal Kapur; two *s* one *d. Educ:* Punjab Univ.; Emmanuel Coll., Cambridge. BA, 1st Cl. Hons History, Punjab Univ., 1925. Hist. Tripos 1931, Law Tripos 1932, Cambridge Univ.; Pres. Cambridge Union, 1932. Called to the Bar, Middle Temple, 1934; Advocate of High Court, Allahabad, 1937, and Senior Advocate of Supreme Court of India, 1958; Lecturer in Commercial Law, Allahabad Univ., 1940-54; Senior Standing Counsel of Govt of Uttar Pradesh, 1956-58; Judge of Allahabad High Court, 1958-67; High Commissioner in UK, 1968-69; Governor of West Bengal, 1969-72. Founder-mem. and Sec., Bernard Shaw Soc., formed 1949. Pres. Indo-Soviet Cultural Soc., Uttar Pradesh Sect., 1965-67. Leader of cultural delegation to Soviet Union, 1966. Lal Bahadur Sastri Meml Lectr, Kerala Univ., Trivandrum, 1973; Pres., All-India Ramayana Conf., Trivandrum, 1973. *Publications:* The Legal system and theory of the State in Ancient India, 1962; Doctrine of sovereignty and colonialism, 1962; Secularism in Indian Jurisprudence, 1964; also papers on Indian Judicial system, UNO and Kashmir, and the Nehru Tradition. *Recreations:* study of Indian jurisprudence, journalism. *Address:* 28 Tashkent Marg, Allahabad 210001, India.

DHENIN, Air Marshal Sir Geoffrey (Howard), KBE 1975; AFC 1953 and Bar, 1957; GM 1943; QHP 1970; MA, MD, DPH; FFCM 1975; FRAeS 1971; Director-General, Medical Services (RAF), since 1974; *b* 2 April 1918; *s* of Louis Richard Dhenin and Lucy Ellen Dagg; *m* 1946, Claude Andree Evelyn Rabut; two *s* two *d. Educ:* Hereford Cathedral Sch.; St John's Coll., Cambridge; Guy's Hosp., London. Joined RAF; various sqdn and other med. appts, Bomber Comd, 2nd TAF, 1943-45 (despatches 1945); pilot trng, 1945-46; various med. officer pilot appts, 1946-58; Staff Coll., Bracknell, 1958-59; comd Princess Mary's RAF Hosp. Akrotiri, Cyprus, 1960-63; comd RAF Hosp. Ely, 1963-66; PMO Air Support Comd, 1966-68; Dir of Health and Research, RAF, 1968-70; Dep. DGMS, RAF, 1970-71; PMO Strike Comd, 1971-73. CStJ 1974. *Recreations:* golf, ski-ing, sub-aqua. *Address:* Ruxbury Lodge, St Ann's Hill, Chertsey, Surrey. *T:* Chertsey 63624. *Clubs:* Royal Air Force, Wentworth.

DHRANGADHRA, Maharaja Sriraj of Halvad-, His Highness Shri Shaktimant Jhaladhip Mahamandlesvar Maharana Sriraj Meghrajji III, KCIE 1947; 45th Ruler (dynastic salute of 13 guns), Head of Jhala-Makhvana Clan and of Shaktimant Order; MP for Jhalwar (Gujarat State), since 1967; *b* 3 March 1923; *s* of HH Maharaja Sriraj Ghanshyamsinhji Saheb, GCIE, KCSI, late Ruler, and HH Maharani Srirajni Anandkunvarba Saheba, Rajmata Saheba; *S* to the Gaddi, 1942, assumed government

1943 on termination of political minority; *m* 1943, Princess Brijrakunvarba Sahiba, *d* of Air Cdre HH Raj-rajeshvar Sarmd-i-Hind Maharajadhiraj Shri Umaidsinhji, GCSI, GCIE, KCVO, Maharaja Sahib of Marwar (Jodhpur); three *s*. *Educ:* Heath Mount Sch.; Haileybury Coll.; St Joseph's Academy, Dehra Dun. Joined the Shivaji Military Sch., Poona, to train for joining Indian Mil. Acad., Dehra Dun; spent nearly a year acquiring administrative experience at Baroda, then at Dhrangadhra; philosophy course, Christ Church, Oxford, 1952-54; took Diploma in Social Anthropology, 1945; research in Indian Sociology, 1955-58 (BLitt Oxon.). FRAS, FRAI; Associate, Royal Historical Soc. Mem. Standing Cttee of Chamber of Princes, 1945; pursued active policy of social and economic reform; was prime mover in Confederation of States scheme, 1945; first state in Saurashtra to accept participation in Constituent Assembly of India; signed Instrument of Accession to India, 1947; First Mem. of Presidium of United State of Saurashtra, later Vice-Pres. Perm. Pres., Girassia Educ. Trust; Pres., Marwar Regency Council, 1965-68; and of Governing Council, Rajkumar Coll., Rajkot, 1966-; Chm. Board of Rulers, Saurashtra States Conf., 1966-; Promoter and Intendant General, Consultation of Rulers of Indian States in Concord for India, 1967-. Mem. Gujarat Legislative Assembly (from Dhrangadhra), Feb.-March 1967, resigned. *Heir: s* Tikaraj Saheb of Halvad-Dhrangadhra, Namdar Jhalavrit Maharajkumar Shri Sodhsalji, *cr* Tikaraj (Yuvaraj), 1961, *b* 22 March 1944. *Address:* Ajitniwas Palace, Dhrangadhra, Jhalawar, Gujarat State, India; Dhrangadhra House, Poona 16, India; A/6 Rashmi, Carmichael Road, Bombay 26, India; 108 Malcha Marg, New Delhi, 110021, India.

DIAMAND, Peter, Hon. CBE 1972; Director, Edinburgh International Festival, 1965-78; *b* 1913; *m* 1st, 1948, Maria Curcio, pianist (marr. diss., 1971); 2nd, Sylvia Rosenberg, violinist; one *s*. *Educ:* Schiller-Realgymnasium, Berlin; Berlin Univ. Studied Law and Journalism in Berlin. Left Germany, 1933; became Private Sec. to Artur Schnabel, pianist. Personal Asst to Dir of Netherlands Opera, Amsterdam, 1946, subsequently Artistic Adviser until 1965; Gen. Manager of Holland Festival, 1948-65. Mem. Board of Netherlands Chamber Orchestra, 1955-. Hon. LLD Edinburgh, 1972. Knight, Order of Oranje Nassau, Holland, 1959; Grosses Ehrenzeichen fuer Verdienste, Austria, 1964; Medal of Merit, Czechoslovakia, 1966; Commander Italian Republic, 1973; Chevalier de l'Ordre des Arts et des Lettres, France. *Address:* 29 St James's Street, SW1. *T:* 01-839 2611. *Clubs:* Arts, New (Edinburgh).

DIAMOND, family name of **Baron Diamond.**

DIAMOND, Baron *cr* 1970 (Life Peer), of the City of Gloucester; **John Diamond,** PC 1965; FCA; Chairman, Royal Commission on Distribution of Income and Wealth, since 1974; *b* Leeds, 30 April 1907; *s* of Henrietta and Rev. S. Diamond, Leeds; *m* ; two *s* two *d*. *Educ:* Leeds Grammar Sch. Qualified as Chartered Accountant, 1931, and commenced practice as John Diamond & Co. MP (Lab) Blackley Div. of Manchester, 1945-51, Gloucester, 1957-70; Chief Secretary to the Treasury, 1964-70 (in the Cabinet, 1968-70); formerly PPS to Minister of Works; Deputy Chm. of Cttees, House of Lords, 1974. Chm. of Finance Cttee, Gen. Nursing Council, 1947-53; Dir of Sadler's Wells Trust Ltd, 1957-64; Hon. Treas., Fabian Soc., 1950-64. *Publications:* Socialism the British Way (jtly), 1948; Public Expenditure in Practice, 1975. *Recreations:* golf, ski-ing, music. *Address:* Aynhoe, Doggetts Wood Lane, Chalfont St Giles, Bucks.

DIAMOND, Anthony Edward John, QC 1974; *b* 4 Sept. 1929; *m* 1965, Joan Margaret Gee; two *d*. *Educ:* Rugby; Corpus Christi Coll., Cambridge (MA). Called to the Bar, Gray's Inn, 1953. *Recreation:* the visual arts. *Address:* 1 Cannon Place, NW3; 4 Essex Court, Temple, EC4. *T:* 01-353 6771.

DIAMOND, Arthur Sigismund, MM 1918; Master of the Supreme Court, Queen's Bench Division, 1952-69; *b* 23 Dec. 1897; *s* of Rev. S. and Mrs Diamond, Leeds; *m* 1st, 1928, Gladys Elkah (*d* 1946), *d* of Edward Lumbrozo Mocatta: one *s* two *d*; 2nd, 1952, Sybil Grace, *d* of Edward Lumbrozo Mocatta. *Educ:* Leeds Grammar Sch.; Trinity Coll., Cambridge (MA, LLD). Called to the Bar, 1921. *Publications:* The Law of Master and Servant, 1st edn 1932; Primitive Law, 1st edn 1935; The Evolution of Law and Order, 1951; The History and Origin of Language, 1959; Primitive Law, Past and Present, 1971. FRAI. *Recreation:* gardening. *Address:* 9 Bracknell Gardens, NW3. *T:* 01-435 4201; Newhouse, Church Lane, Ripe, near Lewes. *T:* Ripe 449.

DIAMOND, Prof. Aubrey Lionel; Professor of Law and Director, Institute of Advanced Legal Studies, University of London, since 1976; Solicitor; *b* 28 Dec. 1923; *s* of Alfred and Millie Diamond, London; *m* 1955, Dr Eva M. Bobasch; one *s* one *d*. *Educ:* elementary schs; Central Foundation Sch., London; London Sch. of Economics (LLB, LLM). Clerical Officer, LCC, 1941-48. Served RAF, 1943-47. Admitted a solicitor, 1951. Sen. Lectr, Law Society's Sch. of Law, 1955-57; Asst Lectr, Lectr and Reader, Law Dept, LSE, 1957-66; Prof. of Law in the Univ. of London (Queen Mary Coll.), 1966-71; Law Comr, 1971-76. Partner in Lawford & Co., Solicitors, 1959-71. Member: Central London Valuation Court, 1956-73; Consumer Advisory Council, BSI, 1961-63; Council, Consumers' Assoc., 1963-71; Consumer Council, 1963-66, 1967-71; Cttee on the Age of Majority, 1965-67; Estate Agents' Council, 1967-70; Council, Law Society, 1976-. Chairman: Social Sciences and the Law Cttee, SSRC, 1977-; Hamlyn Trust, 1977-. Pres., Nat. Fedn of Consumer Groups, 1977- (Chm., 1963-77); Vice-Pres., Inst. of Trading Standards Administration, 1975-. Visiting Professor: University Coll. Dar es Salaam, Univ. of E Africa, 1966-67; Law Sch., Stanford Univ., 1971; Melbourne Univ., 1977. Councillor, Stoke Newington BC, 1953-56. *Publications:* The Consumer, Society and the Law (with G. J. Borrie), 1963 (3rd edn, 1973); Introduction to Hire-Purchase Law, 1967 (2nd edn. 1971); (ed) Instalment Credit, 1970; (co-ed) Sutton and Shannon on Contracts (7th edn) 1970; articles and notes in legal jls and symposia. *Address:* 17 Russell Square, WC1B 5DR. *T:* 01-637 1731.

DIAMOND, George Clifford, OBE 1955; MA; Head Master, Cardiff High School for Boys, retired 1966; *b* 27 Nov. 1902; *m* ; two *s*. *Educ:* Cardiff High Sch.; The Leys Sch., Cambridge; Queens' Coll., Cambridge (Scholar). English Tripos, Class I, History Tripos, Part II, Class II Div. I. Asst Master, Mill Hill Junior Sch., 1926-27; Senior English Master, The Leys Sch., 1927-34. Pres., Welsh Secondary Schools' Assoc., 1957. *Address:* Flat 9A, The Cathedral Green, Llandaff, Glamorgan.

DIAMOND, Prof. Jack, CBE 1969; Whitworth Scholar, MSc (Cambridge and Manchester); FCGI; FIMechE; Beyer Professor of Mechanical Engineering, Manchester University, since 1953; *b* 22 June 1912; *s* of late Alfred John Diamond and Jessie M. Kitchingham; *m* 1943, Iris Evelyn Purvis; three *d*. *Educ:* Chatham Technical Sch.; Royal Dockyard School, Chatham; City and Guilds Coll., London; St John's Coll., Cambridge. Engineering apprenticeship, HM Dockyard, Chatham, 1928-32; Whitworth Scholar, 1932; BSc, ACGI, Wh. Sch. (sen.), 1935. Research in Heat Transfer, University Eng. labs and St John's, Cambridge, 1935-37; MSc 1937; Univ. Demonstrator in Engineering, Cambridge, 1937-39. RN (temp. Engr Officer), 1939-44. RN Scientific Service on loan to Ministry of Supply in Canada and at AERE, Harwell, 1944-53. Member: Governing Board of Nat. Inst. for Research in Nuclear Science, 1957-60; UGC, 1965-73; NRDC, 1966-71; Council, IMechE, 1958-70 (Vice-Pres. 1967-70); Pres., Section G, British Assoc., 1970. Pro-Vice-Chancellor, Manchester Univ., 1970-77. FCGI 1968. Hon. DSc Heriot-Watt, 1975. *Publications:* various, in engineering publications. *Address:* The University, Manchester M13 9PL. *T:* 061-273 3333. *Clubs:* Athenæum, Naval.

DIBBS, (Arthur Henry) Alexander; Director since 1970, and a Deputy Chairman, since 1977, National Westminster Bank Ltd; *b* 9 Dec. 1918; *s* of H. J. Dibbs and P. L. Dibbs (*née* Baker); *m* 1948, Helen Pearl Mathewson; two *d*. *Educ:* Dover Coll.; Whitgift Middle Sch., Croydon. FIB. AMP, Harvard Univ., 1963. Served with Army, 1939-46. Joined Westminster Bank Ltd, 1935; Manager, Croydon Br., 1960; Asst Gen. Man., 1963; Jt Gen. Man., 1966; National Westminster Bank Ltd: Gen. Man., Domestic Banking Div., 1968; Chief Exec. 1972-77. Mem. Cttees, Inst. Bankers. Mem. Bd of Governors, E-SU, 1976-. *Recreations:* golf; watching all sports. *Address:* The Orchard, Deans Lane, Walton on the Hill, Tadworth, Surrey. *Club:* MCC (Mem. Finance Cttee).

DICK, Air Vice-Marshal Alan David, CBE 1968; AFC 1957; FRAeS 1975; Deputy Controller Aircraft/C, Ministry of Defence (Procurement Executive), since 1975; *b* 7 Jan. 1924; *s* of late Brig. Alan MacDonald Dick, CBE, IMS(Retd), and Muriel Angela Dick; *m* 1951, Ann Napier Jeffcoat, *d* of late Col A. C. Jeffcoat, CB, CMG, DSO; two *s* two *d*. *Educ:* Fettes; Aitchison Coll., Lahore; King's Coll., Cambridge. MA. Joined RAF, 1942; SE Asia Command, 1943-45; Fighter Comd, 1945-46. Central Flying Sch., 1950-53; Empire Test Pilots Sch., 1953; Test Pilot, A&AEE, 1954-57; Fighter Comd, 1957-60; RAF Staff Coll., 1960-63; OC 207 Sqdn, Bomber Comd, 1963-64; Supt of Flying, A&AEE, 1964-68; Strike Comd, 1968-69; IDC 1970; MoD Air Staff, 1971-74; Comdt, A&AEE, 1974-75. *Recreations:*

photography, walking, bird watching. *Address:* 44 St Peter's Avenue, Caversham, Reading, Berks RG4 7DD. *Clubs:* Royal Air Force, Royal Commonwealth Society.

DICK, Alick Sydney; industrial consultant; Purchasing Consultant to: Volkswagenwerk AG, Wolfsburg, Germany, since 1968; Audi NSU Auto Union AG, Ingolstadt, Germany, since 1968; *b* 20 June 1916; *s* of Dr W. Dick, Chichester, Sussex; *m* 1940, Betty Melinda Eileen Hill; three *s. Educ:* Chichester High Sch.; Dean Close, Cheltenham. Managing Dir, Standard Triumph International Ltd, Coventry, 1954-61. Pres. of Soc. of Motor Manufacturers and Traders, 1957. Governor: University of Birmingham, 1959; Coll. of Aeronautics, Cranfield, 1960-63. Benjamin Franklin Medal (RSA), 1961. Governor, Dean Close Sch., Cheltenham, 1964. *Recreation:* boats. *Address:* The Thatched Cottage, Hill Wootton, Warwick CV35 7PP. *T:* Kenilworth 54416.

DICK, Clare L.; *see* Lawson Dick.

DICK, Gavin Colquhoun; Under-Secretary, Department of Trade, since 1975; *b* 6 Sept. 1928; *s* of late John Dick and Catherine MacAuslan Henderson; *m* 1952, Elizabeth Frances, *e d* of late Jonathan Hutchinson; two *d. Educ:* Hamilton Academy; Glasgow Univ. (MA); Balliol Coll., Oxford (Snell Exhibnr, MA). National Service, 3rd RTR (Lieut), 1952-54. Asst Principal, BoT, 1954; Principal, 1958; UK Trade Comr, Wellington, NZ, 1961-64; Asst Sec., 1967; Jt Sec., Review Cttee on Overseas Representation, 1968-69. Governor, Coll. of Air Training (Hamble), 1975. *Recreation:* golf. *Address:* Fell Cottage, Bayley's Hill, Sevenoaks, Kent TN14 6NA. *T:* Sevenoaks 53704. *Club:* United Oxford & Cambridge University.

DICK, Prof. George (Williamson Auchinvole), MD (Edinburgh), DSc (Edinburgh), FRCPE, FRCP, FRCPath, MPH (Johns Hopkins); FIMLT, FIBiol; Assistant Director, British Postgraduate Medical Federation, and Postgraduate Dean, SW Thames Regional Health Authority, since 1973; Professor of Pathology, University of London, and Hon. Lecturer and Hon. Consultant, Institute of Child Health, since 1973; *b* 14 Aug. 1914; *s* of Rev. David Auchinvole Dick and Blanche Hay Spence; *m* 1941, Brenda Marian Cook; two *s* two *d. Educ:* Royal High Sch., Edinburgh; Univ. of Edinburgh; The Johns Hopkins Univ., Baltimore, Md, USA. BSc 1939 (1st Cl. Hons Path.); Vans Dunlop Scholar; Buchanan Medal; MD (Gold Medal) 1949. Asst Pathologist, Royal Infirmary, Edinburgh, 1939-40; Pathologist, RAMC, 1940-46; OC Medical Div. (Lt-Col) (EA Comd), 1946; Pathologist, Colonial Med. Res. Service, 1946-51; Rockefeller Foundn Fellow (Internat. Health Div.), Rockefeller Inst., New York and Johns Hopkins Univ., 1947-48; Res. Fellow, Sch. of Hygiene and Public Health, Johns Hopkins Univ., Baltimore, Md, 1948-49; Scientific Staff, MRC, 1951-54; Prof. of Microbiology, QUB, 1955-65; Dir, Bland-Sutton Inst. and Sch. of Pathology, Middlesex Hosp. Med. Sch., Univ. of London, 1966-73; Bland-Sutton Prof. of Pathology, Univ of London, 1966-73. Pres., Inst. of Med. Laboratory Technology, 1966-76; Member: Council, RSM; BMA; Jt Cttee on vaccination and immunisation; Scottish and Central Health Services Councils; Pres., Rowhook Med. Soc., 1975-. Treasurer, RCPath; Adv., Lab. Services, Libyan Arab Republic; Mem., Internat. Epidemiol. Soc.; Cttee Mem., Path. Soc. GB and Ireland. Singapore Gold Medal, Edinburgh Univ., 1952 and 1958; Laurence Biedl Prize for Rehabilitation, 1958; Sims Woodhead Medal, 1976. *Publications:* papers on yellow fever, Uganda S, Zika and other arbor viruses, Mengovirus, Marburgvirus, etc; encephalitis, poliomyelitis; hepatitis (MHV); multiple sclerosis and EHA (rabies) virus; smallpox, poliomyelitis, whooping cough and combined vaccines; vaccine reactions immunisation policies, subacute sclerosing panencephalitis etc, in: Jl Immunol.; Brit. Jl Exp. Path.; BMJ; Lancet; Jl Path. and Bact.; Jl Hyg. Camb.; Trans Royal Soc. Trop. Med. and Hyg.; Update, etc. *Address:* The British Postgraduate Medical Federation, 14-18 Ulster Place, NW1 5HD. *T:* 01-935 8173; (home) Waterland, Rowhook, Horsham RH12 3PX. *T:* Slinfold 790549.
See also J. A. Dick.

DICK, James Browntree, CB 1977; MA, BSc, FInstP, FCIBS, FIOB; Director, Building Research Establishment (formerly Building Research Station), since 1969; *b* 19 July 1919; *s* of James Brownlee Dick and Matilda Forrest; *m* 1944, Audrey Moira Shinn; two *s. Educ:* Wishaw High Sch.; Glasgow Univ. Royal Naval Scientific Service, 1940. Building Research Station: Physics Div., 1947; Head of User Requirements Div., 1960; Head of Production Div., 1963; Asst Dir, 1964; Dep. Dir, 1969. *Publications:* various papers in professional and scientific jls. *Recreations:* reading, gardening, golf. *Address:* 4 Murray Road, Berkhamsted, Herts. *T:* Berkhamsted 2580.

DICK, John Alexander, MC 1944; QC (Scotland) 1963; Sheriff of the Lothians and Borders at Edinburgh, since 1969; *b* 1 Jan. 1920; *y s* of Rev. David Auchinvole Dick and Blanche Hay Spence; *m* 1951, Rosemary Benzie Sutherland; no *c. Educ:* Waid Academy, Anstruther; University of Edinburgh. Undergraduate, 1937; enlisted in London Scottish, 1940; commissioned Royal Scots, 1942; Italy, 1944; Palestine, 1945-46; released 1946, hon. rank of Major. MA (1st Cl. Hons Economics) 1941, LLB (with distinction) 1949, Univ. of Edinburgh. Called to Scots Bar, 1949; Lecturer in Public Law, Univ. of Edinburgh, 1953-60; Junior Counsel in Scotland to HM Commissioners of Customs and Excise, 1956-63. *Recreation:* hill-walking. *Address:* 66 Northumberland Street, Edinburgh EH3 6JE. *T:* 031-556 6081. *Club:* Royal Scots (Edinburgh).
See also Prof. George Dick.

DICK, John Kenneth, CBE 1972; FCA, FRSA; Managing Director since 1957, and Chairman since 1966, Mitchell Cotts Group Ltd; *b* 5 April 1913; *s* of late John Dick and Beatrice May Dick (*née* Chitty); *m* 1942, Pamela Madge, 3rd *d* of late Maurice Salmon and Katie Salmon (*née* Joseph); two *s* (and one *s* decd). *Educ:* Sedbergh. Qual. with Mann Judd & Co., Chartered Accountants, 1936; Partner, Mann Judd & Co., 1947; Mitchell Cotts Group Ltd: Jt Man. Dir, 1957; Sole Man. Dir, 1959; Dep. Chm., 1964; Chm., 1966. Mem., Commonwealth Develt Corp., 1967-; Gov., City of London Soc.; Member: British Nat. Export Cttee, 1968-71; Covent Gdn Mkt Authority, 1976-; Chm., Cttee for Middle East Trade, 1968-71; Pres., Middle East Assoc., 1976- (a Vice-Pres., 1970-76). *Recreation:* golf. *Address:* Langleys, Queens Drive, Oxshott, Surrey. *T:* (office) 01-283 1234. *Clubs:* Caledonian, City of London; Rand (Johannesburg).

DICK, Commodore John Mathew, CB 1955; CBE 1945; VRD; RNVR, retired; Solicitor to Secretary of State for Scotland, 1946-64 (and in Scotland to Treasury); *b* 2 Aug. 1899; *s* of late Mathew Dick, Campbeltown, Argyll, and Margaret Barr; *m* 1930, Anne Moir (*d* 1959), *d* of late Ralph Hill Stewart, Edinburgh; one *s. Educ:* Campbeltown Grammar Sch.; Edinburgh Academy. Entered Royal Naval Volunteer Reserve, 1917; served in Mediterranean and Grand Fleet, 1917-19 (despatches, Order of Crown of Roumania); Lieut RNVR 1924; Comdr 1935 (commanded Edinburgh RNVR 1927-39); Capt. 1940 (Coastal Forces and Admiralty); Commodore 1943; RNVR ADC to the King, 1943-45; retired list, 1946. *Address:* 35 Dick Place, Edinburgh. *Club:* New (Edinburgh).

DICK, Rear-Adm. Royer Mylius, CB 1951; CBE 1943; DSC 1918; *b* 14 Oct. 1897; *s* of Louis Henry Mylius Dick and Edith Alice Guy; *m* 1928, Agnes Mary Harben; one *d* (one *s* killed on active service); *m* 1955, Vera, *widow* of Col Bertram Pott. *Educ:* RN Colls, Osborne and Dartmouth. Midshipman, 1914; at sea, 1914-18 (DSC); Lieut 1918; Comdr 1933; Capt. 1940; Commodore 1st cl. 1942; Rear-Adm. 1949. Dep. Chief of Staff, Mediterranean Station, 1940-42; British Admty Delegn to Washington, 1942; Chief of Staff, Mediterranean Stn, 1942-44 (despatches twice, CBE); HMS Belfast, 1944-46; Dir Tactical and Staff Duties, Admiralty, 1947-48; Chief of Staff to Flag Officer, Western Europe, 1948-50; Naval ADC to the King, 1949; Flag Officer, Training Sqdn, 1951-52; Standing Group Liaison Officer to North Atlantic Council, 1952-55; Vice-Adm. (Acting), 1953; retired list, 1955. Dep. Comr-in-Chief, 1957-62, Comr-in-Chief, 1962-67, SJAB. Dep. Chm., Horticultural Marketing Council, 1960-63; Chairman: Royal United Service Institution, 1965-67; St John Council for London, 1971-75. KStJ 1961; Bailiff Grand Cross, Order of Hosp. of St John of Jerusalem, 1967. Officer Legion of Merit (US) 1943; Officer Legion of Honour, 1943; Croix de Guerre avec palme, 1946. *Address:* 15 Dorchester Court, Sloane Street, SW1. *Clubs:* Army and Navy, Royal Automobile.

DICK-LAUDER, Sir George; *see* Lauder.

DICKENS, Prof. Arthur Geoffrey, CMG 1974; FBA 1966; Director, Institute of Historical Research and Professor of History in the University of London, 1967-77; *b* 6 July 1910; *s* of Arthur James Dickens and Gertrude Helen Dickens (*née* Grasby), both of Hull, Yorks; *m* 1936, Molly, *er d* of Walter Bygott; two *s. Educ:* Hymers Coll., Hull; Magdalen Coll., Oxford. Demy, 1929-32, Senior Demy, 1932-33, of Magdalen Coll.; BA with 1st Class Hons in Mod. Hist., 1932; MA 1936; DLit London, 1965. Fellow and Tutor of Keble Coll., Oxford, 1933-49, Hon. Fellow, 1971; Oxford Univ. Lecturer in Sixteenth Century English History, 1939-49. Served in RA, 1940-45; demobilised as Staff Capt. G. F. Grant Prof. of History, Univ. of Hull, 1949-62; Dep. Principal and Dean of Faculty of Arts, 1950-53; Pro-Vice-Chancellor, 1959-62; Prof. of History, King's Coll., Univ. of London, 1962-67; FKC, 1977. Mem. Senate and Academic Council, Univ. of London, 1974-77. Pres.,

Ecclesiastical History Soc., 1966-68. Member: Advisory Council on Public Records, 1968-76; Adv. Council on Export of Works of Art, 1968-76; Records Cttee, Essex CC, 1965-71; History of Medicine Adv. Panel, Wellcome Trust, 1974-. Chm., Victoria History of the Counties of England, 1967-68. Sec., 1967-73, Chm. and Gen. Sec., 1973-, British Nat. Cttee of Historical Sciences; Foreign Sec., British Acad., 1969- (Vice-Pres., 1971-72); Vice-Pres., RHistS, 1969-73, Hon. Vice Pres., 1976-; Vice-Pres., Historical Assoc., 1976, Hon. Vice-Pres., 1976-; Sec., Anglo-German Group of Historians, 1969-. Editor, Bulletin of the Inst. of Historical Research, 1967-77. Visiting Prof., Univ. of Rochester, NY, 1953-54; Birkbeck Lectr, Trinity Coll., Cambridge, 1969-70. Fellow, 1954, Vis. Prof., 1972, Folger Library, Washington, DC; James Ford Special Lectr, Univ. of Oxford, 1974. FRHistS 1947; FSA 1962. Hon. DLitt Kent, 1976; Hon. DLitt Hull, 1977; Hon. LittD Liverpool, 1977. *Publications:* Lübeck Diary, 1947; The Register of Butley Priory, 1951; The East Riding of Yorkshire, 1954; Lollards and Protestants, 1959; Thomas Cromwell, 1959; Tudor Treatises, 1960; Clifford Letters, 1962; The English Reformation, 1964; Reformation and Society in 16th Century Europe, 1966; Martin Luther and the Reformation, 1967; (ed jtly) The Reformation in England to the Accession of Elizabeth I, 1967; The Counter-Reformation, 1968; The Age of Humanism and Reformation, 1972, UK edn 1977; The German Nation and Martin Luther, 1974; (ed and contrib.) The Courts of Europe, 1977; about 50 articles in: English Historical Review, Church Quarterly Review, Yorkshire Archæological Jl, Cambridge Antiquarian Jl, Bodleian Library Record, Archiv für Reformationsgeschichte, Britain and the Netherlands, Victoria County History, York, Trans Royal Hist. Soc., Jl of Ecclesiastical History, Archæological Jl, Encycl. Britannica, Chambers's Encycl., etc. *Recreations:* travel, 20th Century British art. *Address:* c/o Institute of Historical Research, Senate House, WC1E 7HU. *Club:* Athenæum.

DICKENS, Frank, FRS 1946; MA Cambridge, DSc, PhD London; DIC; FIBiol; *b* 1899; *s* of late John Dickens and Elizabeth Dickens, Northampton; *m* 1925, Molly, *o d* of late Arthur W. and Norah Jelleyman, Northampton; two *d. Educ:* Northampton Grammar Sch.; Magdalene Coll., Cambridge (Scholar). Res. in Organic Chemistry at Imperial Coll. of Science, 1921-23; Lectr in Biochemistry, Middlesex Hospital Medical Sch., whole-time worker for MRC, 1929; Mem. Scientific Staff, MRC, 1931; Research Dir North of England Council of British Empire Cancer Campaign, 1933-46; Philip Hill Professor of Experimental Biochemistry, Middlesex Hosp. Med. Sch., 1946-67, now Emeritus; Dir, Tobacco Research Council Labs, Harrogate, 1967-69. Research for Royal Naval Personnel Cttee of MRC, Nat. Inst. for Medical Research, 1943-44. An Editor of Biochemical Journal, 1937-47; Chm., Biochemical Soc., 1950, Hon. Mem., 1967. Formerly Mem. Scientific Advisory Cttee of the British Empire Cancer Campaign. Chm., British Nat. Cttee for Biochemistry. Hon. Fellow: King's Coll. (University of Newcastle); Leeds Univ. Hon DSc Newcastle upon Tyne, 1972. *Publications:* Chemical and Physiological Properties of the Internal Secretions (with E. C. Dodds); translation of the Metabolism of Tumours (by O. Warburg); ed, Oxygen in the Animal Organism (with E. Neil); Carbohydrate Metabolism and its Disorders (with P. J. Randle and W. J. Whelan); Essays in Biochemistry (with P. N. Campbell); numerous scientific papers mainly in Biochemical Jl. *Recreations:* fishing, photography. *Address:* 9 Doone End, Ferring, West Sussex BN12 5PT. *T:* Worthing 43627.

DICKENS, James McCulloch York; Assistant Director (Industrial Relations), Manpower Services Division, National Water Council, since 1976; *b* 4 April 1931; *e s* of A. Y. Dickens and I. Dickens (*née* McCulloch); *m* 1st, 1955, M. J. Grieve (marr. diss. 1965); 2nd, 1969, Mrs Carolyn Casey. *Educ:* Shawlands Academy, Glasgow; Newbattle Abbey Coll., Dalkeith, Midlothian; Ruskin Coll. and St Catherine's Coll., Oxford. Administrative Asst, National Coal Board, 1956-58; Industrial Relations Officer, National Coal Board, 1958-65; Management Consultant, 1965-66; MP (Lab) West Lewisham, 1966-70; Asst Dir of Manpower, Nat. Freight Corp., 1970-76. *Recreations:* music, theatre, the countryside. *Address:* 32 Hall Drive, Sydenham, SE26 6XB. *T:* 01-778 8677.

DICKENS, Sir Louis (Walter), Kt 1968; DFC 1940; AFC 1938; DL; *b* 28 Sept. 1903; *s* of C. H. Dickens; *m* 1939, Ena Alice Bastable (*d* 1971); one *s* one *d. Educ:* Clongowes Wood Coll.; Cranwell Cadet Coll. Bomber Sqdn, 1923-27; Flying Trng, 1927; Egypt, 1932; Personnel, Air Min., 1932-35; subseq. Flying Instructor, Cranwell; Bomber Comd, France, 1940; Flying Instructor, Canada, 1941-42; Bomber Comd, 1943-44; SHAEF France, 1944-45; retired, 1947. Member: Berkshire CC, 1952-74 (Chm.), 1965-68, Co. Alderman, 1959-73); Wokingham DC,

1974- (Chm., 1974-76). DL Berks, 1966. *Recreation:* golf. *Address:* Fairway, Devil's Highway, Crowthorne, Berks RG11 6BJ. *T:* Crowthorne 2668. *Club:* Royal Air Force.

DICKENS, Monica Enid, (Mrs R. O. Stratton); writer; Founder, The Samaritans, USA; *b* 10 May 1915; *d* of late Henry Charles Dickens, Barrister-at-law, and Fanny Runge; *m* 1951, Comdr Roy Olin Stratton, US Navy; two *d. Educ:* St Paul's Girls' Sch., Hammersmith. *Publications:* One Pair of Hands, 1939; Mariana, 1940; One Pair of Feet, 1942; The Fancy, 1943; Thursday Afternoons, 1945; The Happy Prisoner, 1946; Joy and Josephine, 1948; Flowers on the Grass, 1949; My Turn to Make the Tea, 1951; No More Meadows, 1953; The Winds of Heaven, 1955; The Angel in the Corner, 1956; Man Overboard, 1958; The Heart of London, 1961; Cobbler's Dream, 1963; Kate and Emma, 1964; The Room Upstairs, 1966; The Landlord's Daughter, 1968; The Listeners, 1970; The House at World's End, 1970; Summer at World's End, 1971; Follyfoot, 1971; World's End in Winter, 1972; Dora at Follyfoot, 1972; Spring Comes to World's End, 1973; Talking of Horses, 1973; Last Year when I was Young, 1974; The Horse of Follyfoot, 1975; Stranger at Follyfoot, 1976; It was Like This, 1978. *Recreations:* riding, gardening. *Address:* North Falmouth, Mass 02556, USA.

DICKENSON, Aubrey Fiennes T.; *see* Trotman-Dickenson.

DICKENSON, Lt-Col Charles Royal, CMG 1965; Postmaster-General of Rhodesia, 1964-68, retired; local company director; *b* 17 June 1907; *e s* of Charles Roland and Gertrude Dickenson; *m* 1950, Hendrika Jacoba Margaretha Schippers; two *d. Educ:* Shaftesbury Grammar Sch., Dorset. Entered British Post Office as Engineering Apprentice, 1923; British Post Office HQ, 1932-39. Served War in Royal Signals, 1939-45, attaining rank of Lieut-Col. BPO NW Regional HQ as Asst Controller of Telecommunications, 1945-47; BPO HQ, London, 1947-50; loaned to S Rhodesia Govt, 1950-54; Controller of Telecommunications. Ministry of Posts, Federation of Rhodesia and Nyasaland, 1954-57; Regional Controller for N Rhodesia, Fedn of Rhodesia and Nyasaland, 1957-61; Dep. Postmaster-Gen., Rhodesia and Nyasaland, 1961-62; Postmaster-Gen., Rhodesia and Nyasaland, 1962-63. Hon. Mem., S Africa Inst. of Electronic and Radio Engineers (Hon. M(SA) IERE), 1966. *Recreations:* growing orchids, photography. *Address:* 8 Shiri Road, Greendale, Salisbury, Rhodesia. *T:* Salisbury (Rhodesia) 46264.

DICKENSON, Joseph Frank, PhD, CEng, FIMechE; Director, North Staffordshire Polytechnic, since 1969; *b* 26 Nov. 1924; *s* of late Frank Brand Dickenson and late Maud Dickenson (*née* Beharrell); *m* 1948, Sheila May Kingston; two *s* one *d. Educ:* College of Technology, Hull. BSc (1st Cl. Hons) Engrg, PhD (both London). Engrg apprenticeship and Jun. Engr's posts, 1939-52; Lectr and Sen. Lectr, Hull Coll. of Technology, 1952-59; Head of Dept of Mechanical Engrg and later Vice-Principal, Lanchester Coll. of Technology, 1960-64; Principal, Leeds Coll. of Technology, 1964-69. *Recreations:* tennis, badminton, gardening. *Address:* Burntwood, Hookgate, Market Drayton, Salop. *T:* Ashley 2610.

DICKIE, Rev. Edgar Primrose, MC; MA, BD (Edinburgh); BA Oxon; Emeritus Professor of Divinity, St Mary's College, University of St Andrews, since 1967 (Professor, 1935-67, retired); Extra Chaplain to the Queen in Scotland since 1967 (Chaplain, 1956-67, retired); *b* 12 Aug. 1897; *y* and *o surv. s* of William Dickie, editor of Dumfries and Galloway Standard, and Jane Paterson; *m* 1927, Ishbel Graham Holmes, *d* of Andrew Frier Johnston and Magdalene Ross Holmes, Edinburgh. *Educ:* Dumfries Academy; Edinburgh University; Christ Church, Oxford; New Coll., Edinburgh; Marburg; Tübingen. Served with rank of Captain, 3rd and 1/5th KOSB, Palestine, Flanders, France (wounded, MC). MA Edinburgh, First Class Hons in Classics; Vans Dunlop Scholar; BA Oxford, First Class in Literae Humaniores; at New Coll., Edinburgh, Hamilton Scholar; Fullarton Scholar in Hebrew; Tutor in Greek, 1925-26; Hons Diploma; Senior Cunningham Fellow, 1926; Asst Minister, New North Church, Edinburgh; Ordained, 1927; Minister of St Cuthbert's Church, Lockerbie, 1927-33; Minister of St Anne's Church, Corstorphine, Edinburgh, 1933-35; External Examiner in Biblical Criticism, Edinburgh Univ., 1931-34 and 1934-35; in New Testament Greek, New Coll., Edinburgh, 1931-34; in History of Doctrine, Univ. of Manchester, 1939-41; in Ethics, Queen's Univ., Belfast, 1941; in Systematic Theology, Univ. of Aberdeen, 1942; in Theology, Univ. of Glasgow, 1948, Belfast, 1953. Kerr Lectr in 1936-39; Murtle Lectr, Univ. of Aberdeen, 1941; Gen. Supt of work of Church of Scotland in BEF, 1940, and with BLA, 1944-45 (despatches). Captain St Andrews Univ. OTC, 1941; Convener, Church of Scotland Youth Cttee, 1945-50. Founder-mem.,

Studiorum Novi Testamenti Societas, 1937. Pres. Scottish Sunday School Union, 1955-57; Vice-Pres. Scottish Universities Athletic Club. Governor, St Leonards Sch. Hon. DD Edinburgh, 1946; Hon. LLD St Andrews, 1969. Hon. Life Mem., Students' Union, St Andrews; Hon. Blue, Athletic Union, St Andrews. Companion of Merit and Canon, Order St Lazarus of Jerusalem. *Publications:* Psammyforshort: Rex. Imp.: A Nonsense Story, 1928; The New Divine Order, 1930; translation of Karl Heim's Die Neue Welt Gottes; The Seven Words from the Cross, 1931; Spirit and Truth, 1935; translation of Heim's Das Wesen des Evangelischen Christentums; God Transcendent; translation of Heim's Glaube und Denken (3rd edn); Revelation and Response, 1938; One Year's Talks to Children, 1940; Scottish Life and Character, 1942; A Second Year's Talks to Children, 1943; The Paper Boat, 1943; The Obedience of a Christian Man, 1944; Normandy to Nijmegen, 1946; The Fellowship of Youth, 1947; Mister Bannock: A Nonsense Story, 1947; I Promise (Girl Guides), 1949; It was New to me (Church of Scotland), 1949; God is Light: Studies in Revelation and Personal Conviction, 1953; Thou art the Christ, 1954; A Safe Stronghold, 1955; introductory essay to McLeod Campbell The Nature of the Atonement, 1959; The Unchanging Gospel, 1960; The Father Everlasting, 1965; Remembrance, 1966; occasional articles in Punch, The Scots Magazine, and other periodicals. *Recreations:* hill-walking, winter sports. *Address:* Surma, Hepburn Gardens, St Andrews, Fife. *T:* St Andrews 3617.

DICKINS, Basil Gordon, CBE 1952 (OBE 1945); BSc, ARCS, DIC, PhD; Deputy Controller of Guided Weapons, Ministry of Technology, 1966-68; *b* 1 July 1908; *s* of late Basil Dickins; *m* 1st, 1935, Molly Aileen (*d* 1969), *d* of late H. Walters Reburn; 2nd, 1971, Edith, *widow* of Warren Parkinson. *Educ:* Royal Coll. of Science, London. Royal Aircraft Establishment, 1932; Air Min., 1936, later Min. of Aircraft Production; Head of Operational Research Section, HQ Bomber Command, 1941; Asst Scientific Adviser, Air Ministry, 1945; Dir of Tech. Personnel Administration, Min. of Supply, 1948; Dep. Scientific Adviser to Air Ministry, 1952; Dir of Guided Weapons Research and Development, Min. of Supply, 1956; Dir-Gen. of Atomic Weapons, Min. of Supply, 1959; Dir-Gen. of Guided Weapons, Ministry of Aviation, 1962. *Publications:* papers in Proc. Royal Society and Reports and Memoranda of Aeronautical Research Council. *Address:* Villa Caprice, La Folie, Millbrook, Jersey.

DICKINS, Bruce, MA Cantab; Hon. LittD Manchester; Hon. DLitt Edinburgh; FBA 1959; Elrington and Bosworth Professor of Anglo-Saxon, Cambridge University, Jan. 1946-Sept. 1957, since when Emeritus Professor; Fellow of Corpus Christi College, since 1946; *b* 26 Oct. 1889; *e s* of Henry Everard and Constance Dickins, Nottingham; *m* Mary Geraldine (*d* 1975), *e d* of late Sir Herbert J. C. Grierson; one *s* one *d*. *Educ:* Nottingham High Sch.; Magdalene College, Cambridge (Scholar). 2nd Class (Div. 1) History Tripos, Pt 1; 1st Class, Mediæval and Modern Languages Tripos; Allen Scholar. Acted for two years as Censor in War Office; served as 2nd Lieut, Hampshire Regt; Capt. on staff of Leeds Group and Sector, Home Guard, 1940-43; Lecturer, 1919-25, and Reader, 1925-31, in English Language, Edinburgh Univ.; Professor of English Language, Leeds Univ., 1931-45; sometime Donaldson Bye-Fellow for Research of Magdalene Coll., Cambridge; Pres. Yorks Soc. for Celtic Studies, 1936-38; Pres. Viking Soc., 1938-39; Pres. John Mason Neale Soc., 1952-57; Pres. Cambridge Antiquarian Soc., 1953-55. Sandars Reader in Bibliography, 1968-69. Sir Israel Gollancz Memorial Prize (British Academy), 1955. *Publications:* Runic and Heroic Poems of the Old Teutonic Peoples, 1916, 1968; Robert Henryson, The Testament of Cresseid, 1925; Scots Poems by Robert Fergusson, 1925; The Runic Inscriptions of Maeshowe, 1930; The Dream of the Rood (with Alan S. C. Ross), 1934; The Conflict of Wit and Will, 1937; John Mitchell Kemble and Old English Scholarship, 1940; (jointly) The Place-names of Cumberland, 1950-52; (with R. M. Wilson) Early Middle English Texts, 1951; Henry, First Duke of Lancaster, 1966; (with Alfred Fairbank) The Italic Hand in Tudor Cambridge, 1962; Two Kembles, 1974; contribs to various linguistic, literary, bibliographical, and archæological jls; Jt Editor, Leeds Studies in English and Kindred Languages, 1932-40; Editor, Yorkshire Celtic Studies, 1938-40; Dir and Gen. Editor, English Place-Name Soc., 1946-51; Pres. Cambridge Bibliographical Soc., 1951-57, and Jt Editor of its Transactions, 1949-68. *Address:* c/o Hilton Hall, Hilton, Huntingdon, Cambs PE18 9NG. *T:* Papworth St Agnes 417.

DICKINSON, family name of **Baron Dickinson.**

DICKINSON, 2nd Baron *cr* 1930, of Painswick; **Richard Clavering Hyett Dickinson;** *b* 2 March 1926; *s* of late Hon.

Richard Sebastian Willoughby Dickinson, DSO (*o s* of 1st Baron) and May Southey, *d* of late Charles Lovemore, Melsetter, Cape Province, S Africa; *S* grandfather, 1943; *m* 1957, Margaret Ann, *e d* of Brig. G. R. McMeekan, *qv*; two *s*. *Heir: s* Hon. Martin Hyett Dickinson, *b* 30 Jan. 1961. *Address:* Painswick House, Painswick, Glos. *T:* Painswick 3207.
See also Dowager Viscountess Davidson.

DICKINSON, Arthur Harold, CMG 1946; OBE 1938; KPM 1928; *b* 5 Oct. 1892; *s* of late Walter Dickinson, formerly of Leighton Hall, Caversham, and of Mary Mechan; *m* 1920, Ethel Constance Kitchen (*d* 1961); one *s* one *d*. *Educ:* Bromsgrove Sch. Cadet, Colonial Police Service, 1912; served in Straits Settlements; Inspector-Gen. of Police, Straits Settlements, 1939, and in addition Civil Security Officer, Malaya; Prisoner of War in Singapore, Feb. 1942-Aug. 1945; retired Nov. 1946. *Address:* Swallows' Corner, Maidenhead Court, Berks.

DICKINSON, Basil Philip Harriman; Under Secretary, Department of the Environment (formerly Ministry of Transport), 1959-74; *b* 10 Sept. 1916; *yr s* of F. H. and I. F. Dickinson; *m* 1941, Beryl Farrow; three *s* one *d*. *Educ:* Cheltenham Coll.; Oriel Coll., Oxford. *Address:* c/o Child & Co., 1 Fleet Street, EC4Y 1BD.

DICKINSON, Sir Harold (Herbert), Kt 1975; Chairman, New South Wales Public Service Board, since 1971; *b* 27 Feb. 1917; *s* of late William James Dickinson and Barwon Venus Clarke; *m* 1946, Elsie May Smith; two *d*. *Educ:* Singleton Public Sch.; Tamworth High Sch.; Univ. of Sydney (LLB, 1st Cl. Hons). Barrister-at-Law. Served War, 2nd AIF HQ 22 Inf. Bde, 1940-45 (despatches); Japanese POW (Sgt). Dept of Lands, NSW, 1933-40; NSW Public Service Bd, 1946-60: Sec. and Sen. Inspector, 1949-60; Chief Exec. Officer, Prince Henry Hosp., 1960-63; NSW Public Service Bd: Mem., 1963-70; Dep. Chm., 1970-71. Hon. Mem., NSW Univs Bd, 1967-71; Hon. Dir, Prince Henry, Prince of Wales, Eastern Suburbs Teaching Hosps, 1965-75, Chm. of Dirs, 1975-; Governor, NSW Coll. of Law, 1972-77. *Publications:* contribs to administration jls. *Recreation:* sailing. *Address:* 649 Old South Head Road, Rose Bay North, NSW 2030, Australia. *T:* 371-7475. *Clubs:* Union (Sydney); Royal Automobile Club of Australia.

DICKINSON, Rt. Rev. John Hubert, MA; Vicar of Chollerton, 1959-71; Hon. Canon in Newcastle Cathedral, 1947-71; *m* 1937, Frances Victoria, *d* of late Rev. C. F. Thorp; two *d*. *Educ:* Jesus Coll., Oxford; Cuddesdon Coll. Deacon, 1925; Priest, 1926; Curate of St John, Middlesbrough, 1925-29; SPG Missionary, South Tokyo, 1929-31; Asst Bishop of Melanesia, 1931-37; Vicar of Felkirk-with-Brierley, 1937-42; Vicar of Warkworth, 1942-59. *Address:* Wingrove, Riding Mill, Northumberland.

DICKINSON, Rear-Adm. (retired) Norman Vincent, CB 1953; DSO 1942, and Bar, 1944; DSC 1920; *b* 29 May 1901; *s* of late Dr Thomas Vincent Dickinson, MD, and Beatrice Frances Evans; *m* 1930, Rosamond Sylvia, *d* of late Vice-Admiral L. W. Braithwaite, CMG; two *s*. *Educ:* RN Colls, Osborne and Dartmouth. Midshipman, HMS Royal Sovereign, 1917-20; Lieut S Africa Station, 1923-25; specialised in Physical Training, 1926; Training Special Entry Cadets, HMS Erebus, 1927; Term Lieut RNC Dartmouth, 1931; 1st Lieut Boys' Training Establishment, HMS Ganges, 1934; Comdr, 1936; Asst Dir Physical Training Admiralty, 1937; served War of 1939-45 (despatches thrice); Atlantic Convoys, 1940; Capt., 1942; North Africa landing, 1942; Sicily landing, 1943; Salerno landing, 1943; Sen. Officer Inshore Sqdn, Corsica, 1943; Senior Naval Officer, Northern Adriatic, 1944; Senior Officer 18 Minesweeping Flotilla operating from Southern Ireland, 1945; Head of Naval Branch, Berlin, 1947; HMS Victorious (Training Squadron), 1948; Capt. of Royal Naval Coll., Dartmouth, 1949-51; Rear-Adm., 1951; Flag Officer (Flotillas) Indian Fleet, 1951-53; retired, 1954. Chevalier Légion d'Honneur, 1944; Croix de Guerre with Palm, 1944; Officer, Legion of Merit, 1944. *Recreation:* gardening. *Address:* Dials Close, Lower Wield, near Alresford, Hants. *T:* Preston Candover 269. *Club:* Special Forces.

DICKINSON, Patric (Thomas); poet, playwright and freelance broadcaster; *b* 26 Dec. 1914; *s* of Major A. T. S. Dickinson, 51 Sikhs, FF, IA, and Eileen Constance Kirwan; *m* 1946, Sheila Dunbar Shannon; one *s* one *d*. *Educ:* St Catharine's Coll., Cambridge (Crabtree Exhibitioner). Asst Schoolmaster, 1936-39. Artists' Rifles, 1939-40. BBC, 1942-48 (Feature and Drama Dept); Acting Poetry Editor, 1945-48. Sometime Gresham Prof. in Rhetoric at the City University. Atlantic Award in Literature, 1948; Cholmondeley Award for Poets, 1973. *Publications:* The Seven Days of Jericho, 1944; Theseus and the Minotaur and Poems, 1946; Stone in the Midst and Poems, 1948; The Sailing

Race (poems), 1952; The Scale of Things (poems), 1955; The World I See (poems), 1960; This Cold Universe (poems), 1964; A Round of Golf Courses, 1951; Aristophanes Against War, 1957; The Aeneid of Vergil, 1960; A Durable Fire (play), 1962. Anthologies: Soldiers' Verse, 1945; Byron (selected), 1949; Poems to Remember, 1958; The Good Minute (autobiog.), 1965; Poet's Choice (jt editor), 1967; Selected Poems, 1968; More Than Time (poems), 1970; Aristophanes (translation), vols I and II, 1970; A Wintering Tree (poems), 1973; The Bearing Beast (poems), 1976; The Return of Odysseus (libretto for Malcolm Arnold), 1977. *Recreation:* golf, (Cambridge Blue, 1935). *Address:* 38 Church Square, Rye, East Sussex. *T:* Rye 2194. *Club:* Savile.

DICKINSON, Reginald Percy, OBE 1964; *b* 13 Feb. 1914; *s* of Percy and Nellie Dickinson; *m* 1943, Marjorie Ellen Lillistone; two *s*. *Educ:* Grammar school. BScEng London Univ., 1943; FRAeS, CEng. Air Min., Martlesham Heath, 1936; RAE, 1937; Aircraft and Armament Exper. Estabt, 1942: Supt of Performance, 1953, Supt Weapon Systems, 1962; Dir, Aircraft Develt (B), Min. of Aviation, 1965; Dir Gen. Mil. Aircraft Projects, 1974-75. *Recreations:* sailing, golf. *Address:* Tall Trees, Sunnyside, Fleet, Hants GU13 8LF. *T:* Fleet 6512. *Clubs:* Civil Service; Highcliffe Sailing.

DICKINSON, Prof. Robert Eric; Professor of Geography, University of Arizona, 1967-75, retired; formerly Professor of Geography, University of Leeds, 1958, and Research Professor, 1963; *b* 9 Feb. 1905; *m* 1941, Mary Winwood; no *c*. *Educ:* Upholland Grammar Sch., near Wigan; Leeds University. BA Hons (1st Cl. Geog.), Leeds, 1925; DipEd, Leeds, 1926; MA (Geog.), Leeds, 1928; PhD London, 1932. Asst Lectr in Geography, University Coll., Exeter, 1926-28; University Coll., London: Asst Lectr, 1928-32, Lectr, 1932-41, Reader in Geog., 1941-47; Prof. of Geog., Syracuse Univ., NY, 1947-58. Visiting Prof. at Univs of: California, 1960-61; Washington, 1963; Nebraska, 1963; Kansas State Univ., 1964; Arizona, 1967; Laval, 1968. Rockefeller Fellow, 1931-32 (USA), 1936-37 (Europe), Guggenheim Fellow, 1957-58. *Publications:* Making of Geography, 1932, repr. 1977; The German Lebensraum, 1943; The Regions of Germany, 1944; City, Region and Regionalism, 1945; The West European City, 1951; Germany: A General and Regional Geography, 1952; The Population Problem of Southern Italy, 1955; City and Region, 1964; City and Region in Western Europe, 1967; Makers of Modern Geography, 1969; Regional Ecology, 1970; Regional Concept, 1975; Environments of America, 1975. *Address:* Department of Geography, University of Arizona, Tucson, Arizona 85721, USA.

DICKINSON, Ronald Arthur, CMG 1964; Chairman, Exim Credit Management and Consultants, since 1971; *b* 7 Nov. 1910; *s* of J. H. Dickinson, JP, Cartmel and Oldham, Lancs; *m* 1939, Helen, *d* of Joseph Severs, Oldham, Lancs. *Educ:* schools and univs. Joined ECGD, Under-Sec., 1965-70. Governor, Sports Foundn, 1976-. Order of Merit, Admiral Class, Brazil, 1971. *Recreation:* any sport. *Address:* 86 Regency Lodge, NW3 5EB. *T:* 01-722 2655. *Club:* Overseas Bankers.

DICKINSON, Ronald Sigismund Shepherd, CMG 1967; Secretary, Air Travel Reserve Fund Agency, since 1975; *b* 30 March 1906; *s* of Walter Sigismund Dickinson and Janet (*née* Shepherd); *m* 1932, Vida Evelyn, 4th *d* of Roger Hall and Maud (*née* Seaton); one *d*. *Educ:* Dulwich Coll.; London Sch. of Economics. AIB 1936. Min. of Aircraft Production, 1941; Principal, 1943; Civil Aviation Dept, Air Min., 1944; Min. of Civil Aviation, 1946; Asst Sec., 1947; Rees-Jeffreys Post-Graduate Research Student, LSE, 1950-51; Civil Air Attaché, British Embassy, Washington, 1952-54; Civil Aviation Adviser to Fedn of W Indies, Trinidad, 1961-62; UK Representative on Council of ICAO, Montreal, 1962-69. 1st Vice-Pres. of Council of ICAO, 1966-67. *Address:* Flat 1, 3 Sandrock Road, Tunbridge Wells, Kent. *Club:* Royal Commonwealth Society.

DICKINSON, Prof. Thorold (Barron), CBE 1973; Professor of Film in the University of London (Slade School of Fine Art), 1967-71, now Emeritus; *b* Bristol, 16 Nov. 1903; *s* of Ven. Charles Henry Dickinson, sometime Archdeacon of Bristol, and Beatrice Vindhya (*née* Thorold); *m* 1929, Irene Joanna Macfadyen, AA Dipl., RIBA. *Educ:* Clifton Coll.; Keble Coll., Oxford. Entered film industry, 1926; film editor, subseq. film director and script writer. Directed (among others): Gaslight, 1940; The Next of Kin, 1941. Organised Army Kinematograph Service Production Group and produced 17 military training films, 1942-43. Directed Men of Two Worlds, 1944-45; collab. scripts of: Mayor of Casterbridge; Then and Now; directed: The Queen of Spades, 1949; Secret People, 1951; Hill 24 Doesn't Answer, 1953-55. Produced Power Among Men, 1958-59, and

many short films for UN. Vice-Pres., Assoc. of Cine-Technicians, 1936-53. Mem. of Cttee, Nat. Film Archive, 1950-56; Chm., Brit. Film Acad., 1952-53; Mem., Cttee administering Brit. Film Inst. Experimental Fund, 1952-56; Chief, Film Services Office of Public Information, UN, NY, 1956-60; Senior Lecturer in Film, Slade School of Fine Art, UCL, 1960-67. Consultant to Amer. Film Inst., 1968; Hon. film consultant, CNAA, 1973-76; Vis. Prof. of Film, Univ. of Surrey, 1975-. Mem. Board, New York Film Council, 1958-60. Pres., International Federation of Film Societies, 1958-66 (Hon. Pres., 1966); Hon. Mem., Assoc. of Ciné and TV Technicians, 1977. PhD Fine Arts/Film, University of London, 1971; DUniv Surrey, 1976. *Publications:* (with Catherine de la Roche) Soviet Cinema, 1948; A Discovery of Cinema, 1971; contribs to periodicals: Sight and Sound, Bianco e Nero, Geog. Mag., Soviet Studies, Screen Digest, Times Higher Educn Supplement, Film Comment (NY). *Recreations:* theatre, film, walking, reading. *Address:* 17 Queensborough Mews, Porchester Terrace, W2. *T:* 01-229 6100; Sheepdrove Cottage, Lambourn, Berks. *T:* Lambourn 71393. *Club:* Athenæum.

DICKINSON, William Michael, MBE 1960; publisher; Managing Director, Africa Research Ltd, since 1966; *b* 13 Jan. 1930; *s* of Comdr W. H. Dickinson, RN, retd, and late Ruth Sandeman Betts; *m* 1971, Enid Joy Bowers; one *s* two *d*. *Educ:* St Edward's Sch., Oxford. Army Service, 1948-51; 2/Lieut, Ox. and Bucks LI, Sept. 1948; seconded Somaliland Scouts; Lieut 1950; Colonial Service Devonshire Course, 1951-52; Somaliland Protectorate: Admin. Officer, 1952; Dist. Officer, 1953-54; Asst Sec. (Political), 1955-56; seconded to British Liaison Org., Ethiopia, as Sen. Asst Liaison Officer, 1957-59; Brit. Liaison Officer in charge, 1959; transf. N Rhodesia as Dist Officer, 1960; Dist Comr, 1961; seconded to Foreign Office as HM Consul-Gen., Hargeisa, 1961-63; Principal, External Affairs Section, Office of Prime Minister, N Rhodesia, during 1964; Senior Principal, Ministry of Foreign Affairs, Government of Zambia. *Address:* c/o Africa Research Ltd, 18 Lower North Street, Exeter. *T:* Exeter 76190.

DICKSON, Alexander Graeme, (Alec), CBE 1967 (MBE 1945); MA Oxon; Hon. Director Community Service Volunteers, since 1962; *b* 23 May 1914; *y s* of late Norman Dickson and Anne Higgins; *m* 1951, Mora Hope Robertson, artist, author of numerous travel books and biographies. *Educ:* Rugby; New Coll., Oxford. Private Sec. to late Sir Alec Paterson, 1935; editorial staff: Yorkshire Post, 1936-37; Daily Telegraph, 1937-38, Germany; refugee relief, Czechoslovakia, winter 1938-39. Served War of 1939-45: Cameron Highlanders; 1st KAR (Abyssinian Campaign); led E Africa Comd mobile educn unit. Displaced Persons Directorate, Berlin, 1946-48; introd Mass Educn, Gold Coast, 1948-49; founded Man O' War Bay Training Centre, Cameroons and Nigeria, 1950-54; Chief Unesco Mission, Iraq, 1955-56; refugee relief, Austro-Hungarian frontier, winter 1956-57. Founder and first Dir, Voluntary Service Overseas, 1958-62; founded Community Service Volunteers, 1962, developing concept of 'A Year Between' for students, linking curriculum to human needs, promoting tutoring in schools, involving disadvantaged and unemployed young people in social service. Shared experience with US Peace Corps, 1961, 1969; India, 1968, 1972; Hong Kong, 1968, 1974; Israel, 1970; Nigeria, 1970, 1975, 1976; Malta, 1971; Nepal, 1972; New Zealand, 1972; Papua New Guinea, 1973; Bahamas, 1975; US Nat. Student Volunteer Program, Washington DC and Alaska, 1975; Ontario, 1975; Sri Lanka, Australia, Japan, 1976. Consultant to Commonwealth Secretariat, 1974-77. Hon. LLD Leeds, 1970. *Publications:* (with Mora Dickson) A Community Service Handbook, 1967; School in the Round, 1969; A Chance to Serve, 1976; articles on community development and youth service. *Recreations:* identical with work- involving young people in community service, at home or overseas. *Address:* 19 Blenheim Road, W4. *T:* 01-994 7437.
See also M. G. Dickson.

DICKSON, Arthur Richard Franklin, CBE 1974; Chairman, Industrial Tribunals (part-time), since 1972; *b* 13 Jan. 1913; *m* 1949, Joanna Maria Margaretha van Baardwyk; four *s*. *Educ:* Rusea's Secondary Sch. and Cornwall Coll., Jamaica. Called to the Bar, Lincoln's Inn, 1938. Judicial Service. HM Overseas Judiciary: Jamaica, 1941; Magistrate, Turks and Caicos Islands, 1944-47; Asst to Attorney-Gen., and Legal Draftsman, Barbados, 1947-49; Magistrate, British Guiana, 1949-52; Nigeria, 1952-62: Magistrate, 1952-54; Chief Magistrate, 1954-56; Chief Registrar, High Court, Lagos, 1956-58; Judge of the High Court, Lagos, 1958-62; retired. Temp. appointment, Solicitors Dept, GPO London, 1962-63; served Northern Rhodesia (latterly Zambia), 1964-67; Judge of the High Court, Uganda, 1967-71; Deputy Chm., Middlesex QS, July-Aug.,

1971; Chief Justice, Belize, 1973-74; Judge of the Supreme Court, Anguilla (part-time), 1972-76. *Publication:* Revised Ordinances (1909-1941) Turks and Caicos Islands, 1944. *Recreations:* gardening, walking, swimming, riding. *Address:* No 1 The Pleasance, Kinsbourne Green, Harpenden, Herts AL5 3NA. *T:* Harpenden 3703. *Club:* Royal Commonwealth Society.

DICKSON, Bertram Thomas, CMG 1960; BA, PhD; *b* Leicester, 20 May 1886; *s* of J. T. Dickson of Leicester; *m* 1910, Florence (decd), *d* of W. Roberts; one *s* one *d. Educ:* Queen's Univ., Kingston, Ontario (BA); Cornell Univ.; McGill Univ., Montreal (PhD). Served European War, 1914-18: Agricultural Officer, 1st British Army, 1917-18; Commandant, 1st British Army Sch. of Agriculture, 1918-19. Professor of Economic Botany, McGill Univ., 1919-26; Prof. of Plant Pathology, McGill Univ., 1926-27; Chief, Division of Plant Industry, CSIRO, Canberra, 1927-51; Delegate, 2nd Session, FAO Conference, Copenhagen, 1946; Mem., UNESCO Arid Zone Advisory Cttee, 1952-57; UN Adviser, Desert Research Institute of Egypt, 1958-59. Pres., Canberra Repertory Soc., 1932-41; Exec. Mem., Australian National Research Council, 1932-47; Pres., Legacy Club, Canberra, 1933; Pres., Australian Institute of Agricultural Science, 1945-46 (Vice-Pres., 1935-39); Chm., Canberra Univ. Coll., 1954-60. *Address:* 75 Ewos Parade, Cronulla, NSW 2230, Australia.

DICKSON, Dr David, CB 1969; Director, W. & R. Chambers Ltd, since 1969; *b* 1 Nov. 1908; *s* of Robert and Elizabeth Dickson, Crieff, Perthshire; *m* 1935, Isabella Sword Grant, *d* of A. P. Grant, Easterhouse, Lanarkshire; one *s. Educ:* Morrison's Acad., Crieff; University of Edinburgh. Asst Classics Teacher, Royal High Sch., Edinburgh, 1931-38; Principal Classics Teacher, Alloa Acad., 1938-40; HM Inspector of Schools, 1940; HM Chief Inspector of Schools, 1955; HM Senior Chief Inspector of Schools, Scottish Educn Dept, 1966-69. Governor, Donaldson's School for the Deaf, 1969-. *Recreations:* golf, gardening. *Address:* 7 Albert Place, Stirling. *T:* Stirling 4760.

DICKSON, Air Vice-Marshal Edward Dalziel, CB 1953; CBE 1946; RAF (Medical Branch), Retired; MD, FRCSE; Hon. Civilian Consultant in Oto-Laryngology to the Royal Air Force since 1955; *b* 10 Feb. 1895; *s* of late Dr E. D. Dickson, Physician, HBM Embassy, Constantinople; *m* 1st, Ethel Sinclair (*d* 1974), *d* of J. E. Grey, Pres. Royal College of Veterinary Surgeons, Edinburgh; one *s*; 2nd, 1975, Doris Muriel McGregor Millar, *d* of G. Millar, MC, FRCSE. *Educ:* privately; Edinburgh Univ.; London; Paris. MD (Edinburgh) 1951; MB, ChB (Edinburgh) 1918; FRCSE 1922; DLO RCPS Eng. 1925. Served European War, 1914-18, Capt. RAMC; ENT Specialist, 1918-22, Salonika, Serbia, Turkey. Hon. Aural Surg. British Hosp. (82nd Gen.), Constantinople, 1922; late Asst OP Dept, Central London Throat, Nose and Ear Hosp. Joined RAF 1923; Sqdn Ldr 1929; Wing Comdr 1935; Group Capt. 1940; Air Commodore, 1947; Air Vice-Marshal, 1951. KHS, 1948-52; QHS 1952-55. Senior Consultant, RAF, 1951-55. Consultant in Oto-Laryngology, RAF, 1938-55. FRSM (Pres. Section of Otology, 1952-53); Life Mem. Scottish Oto-Laryngological Soc.; Mem. Otological Sub-Cttee, Flying Personnel Research Cttee, and Life Member: British Assoc. of Oto-Laryngologists; British Soc. of Audiology; Pres., Royal Nat. Inst. for the Deaf, 1975- (Chm., 1960-71). Pres., IX Internat. Congress in Audiology, London, 1968. Sir William Dalby Prize in Otology, Royal Society of Medicine (jointly); Silver Medal for Distinguished Service (Serbia), 1920; Medal of Merit 1st Class (Czecho-Slovakia), 1946. *Publications:* contrib. to Aviation Oto-Laryngology (jointly), 1947; chapter on intense sound and ultrasound, in Industrial Medicine and Hygiene, Vol. II, 1954; numerous papers and reports on aviation otology and rhinology in learned journals. *Recreations:* gardening, music, conjuring. *Address:* 15 Frogston Road East, Liberton, Edinburgh EH17 8AB. *T:* 031-664 2573. *Clubs:* Royal Air Force, Savage; Magic Circle; University Union (Edinburgh).

DICKSON, Eileen Wadham, (Mrs C. F. Dickson); *d* of John Edward Latton, Librarian to Inner Temple, and Ethel Letitia Baker; *m* 1931, Charles Frederick Dickson, OBE. *Educ:* Convent of the Sacred Heart, Roehampton; Bruges, Belgium. Served War of 1939-45 with WVS and on Executive Council of Stage Door Canteen. Joined Harper's Bazaar, 1949; Fashion Editor, 1951; Editor, 1953-65. *Recreations:* theatre, reading, racing, gardens. *Address:* 4 Stack House, Cundy Street, SW1. *T:* 01-730 7675; Grimsdyke, Aldworth, Berks. *T:* Compton 247.

DICKSON, Prof. Gordon Ross; Professor of Agriculture, University of Newcastle upon Tyne, since 1973; *b* 12 Feb. 1932; *s* of T. W. Dickson, Tynemouth; *m* 1956, Dorothy Stobbs; two *s* one *d. Educ:* Tynemouth High Sch.; Durham Univ. BSc (Agric) 1st cl. hons 1953, PhD (Agric) 1958, Dunelm. Tutorial Research Student, Univ. Sch. of Agric., King's Coll., Newcastle upon

Tyne, 1953-56; Asst Farm Dir, Council of King's Coll., Nafferton, Stocksfield-on-Tyne, 1956-58; Farms Director for the Duke of Norfolk, 1958-71; Principal, Royal Agric. Coll., Cirencester, 1971-73. Dep. Chm., Central Council, Agricl and Horticl Cooperation; Mem., MAFF Agricl and Horticl Adv. Council. *Address:* School of Agriculture, University of Newcastle upon Tyne, Newcastle upon Tyne NE1 7RU; Tyneholme, 44 Moor Crescent, Gosforth, Newcastle upon Tyne NE3 4AQ.

DICKSON, (Horatio Henry) Lovat; writer and publisher; *b* 30 June 1902; *s* of Gordon Fraser Dickson and Josephine Mary Cunningham; *m* 1934, Marguerite Isabella, *d* of A. B. Brodie, Montreal; one *s. Educ:* Berkhamsted Sch.; University of Alberta (MA). Lecturer in English, Univ. of Alberta, 1927-29; Associate Editor, Fortnightly Review, 1929-32; Editor of Review of Reviews, 1930-34; Managing Dir of Lovat Dickson Ltd (Publishers), 1932-38; Director: Macmillan & Co. (publishers), 1941-64; Pan Books Ltd, 1946-64; Reprint Soc., 1939-64. Hon. LLD Alberta, 1968; Hon. DLitt Western Ontario, 1976. *Publications:* The Green Leaf, 1938; Half-Breed, The Story of Grey Owl, 1939; Out of the West Land, 1944; Richard Hillary, 1950; two vols of autobiog.: Vol. I, The Ante-Room, 1959; Vol. II, The House of Words, 1963; H. G. Wells, 1969; Wilderness Man, 1973; Radclyffe Hall at the Well of Loneliness, 1975. *Address:* 21 Dale Avenue, Toronto, Canada. *Clubs:* Garrick; Toronto Hunt.

DICKSON, Ian Anderson, WS; Sheriff of South Strathclyde, Dumfries and Galloway, formerly Lanarkshire, at Hamilton, since Dec. 1961; *b* Edinburgh, 1905; *s* of Robert Anderson Dickson, DDS, and Marie Anne Morris; *m* 1943, Margaret Forbes, *o d* of James John and Annabella Florence Ross, Glenfuir, Falkirk; four *s. Educ:* Edinburgh Academy; Harrow; Edinburgh Univ. (BL). A practising Solicitor, first in Edinburgh and, 1934-61, in Coatbridge; Mem. Coatbridge Town Council, 1937-44; Burgh Prosecutor, Coatbridge, 1944-60; Hon. Sheriff-Substitute of Lanarkshire at Airdrie, 1955-61. *Recreations:* motoring, bridge, pottering, formerly Scouting (for 50 years) and golf. *Address:* 9 Cleveden Gardens, Glasgow G12 0PU. *T:* 041-339 7731; Rockview, Elie, Fife. *T:* 30234. *Clubs:* Western (Glasgow); Royal Burgess Golfing Society (Edinburgh); Golf House (Elie).

DICKSON, Jennifer (Joan), (Mrs R. A. Sweetman), RA 1976 (ARA 1970); RE 1965; freelance graphic artist and designer; *b* 17 Sept. 1936; 2nd *d* of John Liston Dickson and Margaret Joan Turner, S Africa; *m* 1962, Ronald Andrew Sweetman; one *s. Educ:* Goldsmith's College Sch. of Art, Univ. of London; Atelier 17, Paris. Taught at Eastbourne Sch. of Art, 1959-62 (French Govt Schol., to work in Paris under S. W. Hayter). Directed and developed Printmaking Dept, Brighton Coll. of Art, 1962-68; developed and directed Graphics Atelier, Saidye Bronfman Centre, Montreal, 1970-72. Has held appointments of Vis. Artist at following Universities: Ball State Univ., Muncie, Indiana, 1967; Univ. of the West Indies, Kingston, Jamaica, 1968; Univ. of Wisconsin, Madison, 1972; Ohio State Univ., 1973; Western Illinois Univ., 1973; Haystack Mountain Sch. of Crafts, Maine, 1973; Prof., Faculty of Fine Arts, Concordia Univ., Montreal, 1973-77; Vis. Artist, Queen's Univ., Kingston, Ont., 1977. Founder Mem., Brit. Printmakers' Council. Prix des Jeunes Artistes (Gravure), Biennale de Paris, 1963; Major Prize, World Print Competition, San Francisco, 1974. *Publications:* suites of original etchings: Genesis, 1965; Alchemic Images, 1966; Eclipse, 1968; Song of Songs, 1969; Out of Time, 1970; Fragments, 1971; Sweet Death and Other Pleasures, 1972; Homage to Don Juan, 1975; Body Perceptions, 1975; The Secret Garden, 1976. *Address:* 508 Gilmour Street, Ottawa, Ontario K1R 5L4, Canada.

DICKSON, John Abernethy, CB 1970; Director-General and Deputy Chairman, Forestry Commission, 1968-76; *b* 19 Sept. 1915; *yr s* of late John and Williamina Dickson; *m* 1942, Helen Drummond, *o d* of Peter Drummond Jardine; two *d. Educ:* Robert Gordon's Coll., Aberdeen; Aberdeen Univ. MA 1936; BSc (For.) 1938. Joined Forestry Commn, 1938; District Officer, 1940; seconded to Min. of Supply, Home Grown Timber Production Dept, 1940-46; Divisional Officer, 1951; Conservator, 1956; Dir (Scotland), 1963; Comr Harvesting and Marketing, 1965. Dir, Economic Forestry (Scotland), 1977-. Chm., Standing Cttee on Commonwealth Forestry, 1968-; Vice-Pres., Commonwealth Forestry Assoc., 1975- (Chm., 1972-75). Hon. LLD Aberdeen, 1969. FBIM 1975. *Recreation:* golf. *Address:* 56 Oxgangs Road, Edinburgh EH10 7AY. *T:* 031-445 1067. *Club:* Caledonian.

DICKSON, Leonard Elliot, CBE 1972; MC 1945; TD 1951; DL; Solicitor, Dickson, Haddow & Co., since 1947; *b* 17 March 1915;

s of Rev. Robert Marcus Dickson, DD, Lanark, and Cordelia Elliot; *m* 1950, Mary Elisabeth Cuthbertson; one *s* one *d. Educ:* Uppingham, Rutland; Univ. of Cambridge (BA 1936); Univ. of Glasgow (LLB 1947). Served War, with 1st Bn Glasgow Highlanders, HLI, 1939-46. Clerk to Clyde Lighthouses Trust, 1953-65. Chm., Lowland TAVR, 1968-70; Vice-Chm. Glasgow Exec. Council, NHS, 1970-74. DL Glasgow, 1963. *Recreations:* travel, gardening. *Address:* 21 Ralston Road, Bearsden, Glasgow G61 3BA. *T:* 041-942 0317. *Club:* Royal Scottish Automobile (Glasgow).

DICKSON, Lovat; see Dickson, H. H. L.

DICKSON, Murray Graeme, CMG 1961; *b* 19 July 1911; *s* of Norman and Anne Dickson. *Educ:* Rugby; New Coll., Oxford. Prison Service (Borstals), 1935-40. Served War of 1939-45, in Force 136. Entered Colonial Service, 1947; Education Officer, Sarawak, 1947, Deputy Dir of Education, 1952, Dir of Education, 1955-66; retd. Unesco adviser on educl planning to Govt of Lesotho, 1967-68. *Address:* Flat 150, Whitehall Court, SW1.
See also A. G. Dickson.

DICKSON, Dame Violet (Penelope), DBE 1976 (CBE 1964; MBE 1942); *b* Gautby, Lincs, 3 Sept. 1896; *d* of Neville Lucas-Calcraft and Emily Delmar Lindley; *m* 1920, Captain Harold Richard Patrick Dickson, CIE (*d* 1959); one *s* one *d. Educ:* Miss Lunn's High Sch., Woodhall Spa; Les Charmettes, Vevey, Switzerland. Mesopotamia, 1921-22; Quetta, Baluchistan, 1923-23; Bikaner, Rajputana, 1924-28; Bushire, Iran, 1928-29; Kuwait, 1929-. FRZS; Mem.RCAS. *Publications:* Wild Flowers of Kuwait and Bahrain, 1955; Forty Years in Kuwait, 1971. *Recreations:* shooting, riding, tennis, swimming. *Address:* Seef, Kuwait, Arabia. *T:* 432310.

DICKSON, Marshal of the Royal Air Force Sir William (Forster), GCB 1953 (KCB 1952; CB 1942); KBE 1946 (CBE 1945; OBE 1934); DSO 1918; AFC 1922; idc; psa; *b* 24 Sept. 1898; *s* of late C. C. Forster Dickson, Chancery Registrar's Office, Royal Courts of Justice, and of late Agnes Nelson Dickson, Northwood, Mddx; *m* 1932, Patricia Marguerite, *d* of late Sir Walter Allen, KBE; one *d* (and one *d* decd). *Educ:* Bowden House, Seaford; Haileybury Coll. Royal Naval Air Service, 1916-18 (DSO, despatches thrice); transferred to RAF, 1918; Permanent Commn in RAF, 1919; employed on Naval Flying work, 1919-21; Test Pilot, RAE, 1921-22; Air Ministry, 1923-26; No 56 (Fighter) Sqdn, 1926-27; RAF Staff Coll., Andover, 1927-28; posted to India, 1929; served on NW Frontier, 1929-30 and at HQ RAF Delhi (despatches); commanded RAF Station, Hawkinge, and No 25 (Fighter) Squadron, 1935-36; Directing Staff, Staff Coll., 1936-38; Imperial Defence Coll., 1939; Dir of Plans, Air Ministry, 1941-42; commanded Nos 9 and 10 Groups in Fighter Comd, 1942-43; commanded No 83 Group in TAF, 1943-44; commanded Desert Air Force, 1944; Asst Chief of Air Staff (Policy), Air Ministry, 1945-46; Vice-Chief of Air Staff, Air Ministry, 1946-48; C-in-C, MEAF, 1948-50; Mem. for Supply and Organisation, Air Council, 1950-52; Chief of the Air Staff, 1953-56; Chm. of the Chiefs of Staff Cttee, 1956-59; Chief of Defence Staff, 1958-59. President: Royal Central Asian Soc., 1961-65; Ex-Services Mental Welfare Soc., 1960-76; Haileybury Soc., 1962; Forces Help Society and Lord Roberts Workshops, 1974-. Master, The Glass Sellers' Co., 1964. Russian Order of Suvarov, 1944; USA Legion of Merit. *Address:* Foxbriar House, Cold Ash, Newbury, Berks. *Club:* Royal Air Force.

DICKSON MABON, Rt. Hon. Jesse; see Mabon, Rt Hon. J. D.

DIEDERICHS, Hon. Dr Nicolaas, DMS; State President of the Republic of South Africa, since 1975; *b* 17 Nov. 1903; *s* of Adriaan Petrus Johannes Diederichs; *m* 1932, Margaretha Jacoba Potgieter; one *s* two *d. Educ:* Boshof High Sch.; Grey Univ. Coll.; Univs of Munich, Cologne, Berlin and Leiden, MA, DLitt et DPhil. MP: Randfontein, 1948-58; Losberg, 1958-74; Overvaal, 1974-75. Minister of Econ. Affairs, 1958-67, of Mines, 1961-64, of Finance, 1967-75. Former Chm., Economic Inst., Decimal Coinage Commn. Chancellor, Randse Afrikaanse Universiteit, 1968. Hon. DCom, Univ. of OFS, 1971; Hon. DComm: Stellenbosch, 1973; Randse Afrikaanse, 1976; Pretoria, 1976. Hon. Citizen, New Orleans; Freeman of several S African cities and towns. Kt Grand Cross, Order of Merit, Italy; Grand Cross, Order of Merit, Paraguay. *Publications:* Vom Leiden und Dulden; Die Volkebond; Nasionalisme as Lewensbeskouing; Die Kommunisme; numerous articles and brochures. *Recreations:* reading, golf. *Address:* State President's Residence, Pretoria, Republic of South Africa.

DIEFENBAKER, Rt. Hon. John (George), PC 1957; PC (Can.) 1957; CH 1976; QC; MP; LLD, DCL and LittD (Hon.); Doctor of Humanities (Hon.); Doctor of Sacred Letters (Hon.); FRSC; MP for Prince Albert, Sask., since Aug. 1953 (Lake Centre, 1940-53); lawyer; Leader of Canadian Progressive Conservative Party, Dec. 1956-Sept. 1967; Leader of HM Loyal Opposition, Parliament of Canada, during Spring 1957, and again April 1963-Sept. 1967; Prime Minister of Canada, June 1957-April 1963; *b* Grey County, Ont., 18 Sept. 1895; *s* of William Thomas Diefenbaker and Mary Florence (*née* Bannerman); *m* 1st, 1929, Edna Brower (*d* 1950); 2nd, 1953, Olive Evangeline, LLD, DCL (*d* 1976), *d* of Rev. Dr C. B. Freeman; one step *d. Educ:* Univ. of Saskatchewan, Saskatoon. BA 1915, MA 1916, in Political Science; served overseas with 196th Bn, as a Lieut, invalided 1917; LLB 1919, University of Saskatchewan. Called to the Bar of Saskatchewan, 1919; KC 1929; QC (Ont.) 1960. Admitted to Bars of Ontario, Alberta and BC; Hon. Bencher: Gray's Inn; Law Society of Upper Canada; Law Soc. of Saskatchewan; Hon. Mem., Illustre Nacional Colegio de Abogados (Mexico). Private practice or in partnerships (senior partner), Prince Albert, from 1919. Mem. of Council of Canadian Bar Association Saskatchewan (Vice-Pres., 1939-42; became Hon. Life Mem., 1957). Contested (Conservative) Prince Albert, 1925, 1926; elected MP Lake Centre, 1940. Chm. of first British Commonwealth Conf., at which Delegates from Congress of US attended, Ottawa, 1943; attended UN Assembly, as Adviser to Progressive Conservative Representative on Canadian Delegn, San Francisco, 1945; Mem. Canadian Delegn of Empire Parliamentary Assoc. in Bermuda and in Washington, DC, 1946; Mem. Canadian Delegn to Commonwealth Parl. Assoc. in New Zealand and Australia, 1950; Mem. Canadian Delegn to UN, 1952; Mem. Canadian Delegn to NATO Parliamentary Assoc., 1955. Minister in Attendance on the Queen, during her visit to N America, 1957; accompanied her on visit to Chicago, Royal Tour of 1959. Leader of Canadian Delegn to Conf. of Commonwealth Prime Ministers, London, 1957, 1960, 1961, 1962. Made World Tour of Commonwealth and NATO countries, 1958. Hon. Col. North Saskatchewan Regt, Royal Canadian Inf. Corps; Hon. Freeman, City of London, 1963. Hon. Chief: Cree Indians (Chief Great Eagle); Sioux (Chief Walking Buffalo); Kainai Chieftains (Chief Many Spotted Horses). 33°. Scottish Rite Mason. Chancellor, Univ. of Saskatchewan, 1968-. Holds 35 hon. degrees from universities and colleges both in Canada and abroad. Hon. FRSC; FRAIC. *Publication:* One Canada, 1976. *Address:* House of Commons, Ottawa, Canada.

DIESKAU, Dietrich F.; see Fischer-Dieskau.

DIETRICH, Marlene; actress; *b* Berlin, 27 Dec. 1904; *d* of Eduard von Losch and Josephine Felsing; *m* 1924, Rudolph Sieber (*d* 1976); one *d. Educ:* Berlin; Weimar. Max Reinhardt Sch. of Theatre; Stage, Berlin and Vienna; First notable film, The Blue Angel; films in America since 1930, incl. Desire, Destry Rides Again, Foreign Affair, Garden of Allah, Golden Earrings, Rancho Notorious, Scarlet Empress, Shanghai Express, Stage Fright, Witness for the Prosecution; naturalised as an American, 1937; numerous stage appearances in Europe, Great Britain, America and all continents; Special Tony Award, 1967-68. Officier, Légion d'Honneur, 1972; US Medal of Freedom. *Publication:* Marlene Dietrich's ABC, 1962. *Recreation:* tennis.

DIGBY, family name of **Baron Digby.**

DIGBY, 12th Baron (Ire.) *cr* 1620, and 5th Baron (GB) *cr* 1765; **Edward Henry Kenelm Digby,** JP; Vice Lord-Lieutenant (formerly Vice-Lieutenant), Dorset, since 1965; Captain, late Coldstream Guards; *b* 24 July 1924; *o s* of 11th and 4th Baron Digby, KG, DSO, MC, and Hon. Pamela Bruce, OBE, *y d* of 2nd Baron Aberdare; *S* father, 1964; *m* 1952, Dione Marian, *yr d* of Rear-Adm. Robert St Vincent Sherbrooke, VC, CB, DSO; two *s* one *d. Educ:* Eton; Trinity Coll., Oxford; RMC. Served War of 1939-45. Capt., 1947; Malaya, 1948-50; ADC to C-in-C: FARELF, 1950-51; BAOR, 1951-52. Dep. Chm., SW Economic Planning Council, 1972-; Mem. Council, Royal Agricultural Soc. England, 1954; Chm., Royal Agricultural Soc. of Commonwealth, 1966-77. Pres., 1976, Vice Pres., 1977, Royal Bath and West Soc. Dorchester Rural District Councillor, 1962; Dorset County Councillor, 1966 (Vice Chm. CC, 1977); Mem. Dorset Agric. Exec. Cttee. Dir, Brooklyns Westbrick Ltd. DL 1957, JP 1959, Dorset. *Recreations:* ski-ing, shooting, racing, tennis. *Heir:* *s* Hon. Henry Noel Kenelm Digby, *b* 6 Jan. 1954. *Address:* Minterne, Dorchester, Dorset. *T:* Cerne Abbas 370. *Club:* Pratt's.
See also W. A. Harriman.

DIGBY, Adrian, CBE 1964; MA Oxon; FSA; Keeper, Department of Ethnography, British Museum, 1953-69; excavated Maya site of Las Cuevas, British Honduras, 1957; *b* 13 June 1909; *s* of late William Pollard Digby, FInstP, MIME, MIEE; *m* 1939, Sylvia Mary, *d* of late Arnold Inman, OBE, KC; two *d. Educ:* Lancing; Brasenose Coll., Oxford. Entered British Museum as Asst Keeper, 1932. Hon. Asst Sec. of International Congress of Anthropological and Ethnological Sciences, London, 1934; Hon. Sec. of International Congress of Americanists, Cambridge, 1952. Served in Intelligence Division Naval Staff, Admiralty, 1942-44; Hydrographic Dept, Admiralty, 1944-45. Vis. Prof. in Archaeology, Univ. de Los Andes, Bogota, 1970. Pres. Sect. H of The British Association for the Advancement of Science, 1962; Vice-Pres. Royal Anthropological Inst., 1962, 1966. *Publications:* Ancient American Pottery (with G. H. S. Bushnell), 1955; Maya Jades, 1964; articles on anthropological subjects in Man and in Chambers's Encyclopædia. *Address:* The Paddocks, Eastcombe, Stroud, Glos GL6 7DR. *T:* Bisley (Glos) 409.

DIGBY, George F. Wingfield; retired Keeper Emeritus, Victoria and Albert Museum; *b* 2 March 1911; 2nd *s* of late Col F. J. B. Wingfield Digby, DSO; *m* 1935, Cornelia, *d* of Prof. H. Keitler, University of Vienna; one *s* (decd). *Educ:* Harrow; Trinity Coll., Cambridge; Grenoble Univ.; Sorbonne; Vienna. Asst Keeper, Dept of Textiles, Victoria and Albert Museum, 1934; seconded to Education Office, Jamaica (Jamaica Coll.), 1941-45; Asst Keeper (1st class), Victoria and Albert Museum, 1946; Keeper of Dept of Textiles, 1947-72; retired 1973. *Publications:* The Work of the Modern Potter in England, 1952; Meaning and Symbol in Three Modern Artists, 1955; Symbol and Image in William Blake, 1957; (jtly) History of the West Indian Peoples (4 vols for schools); (part author) The Bayeux Tapestry, 1957; (contributor) Brussels Colloque International: La Tapisserie flamande au XVII-XVIII siècle, 1959; (contributor) Colston Research Soc. Papers: Metaphor and Symbol, 1960; Elizabethan Embroidery, 1963; The Devonshire Hunting Tapestries, 1971; Tapestries, Mediaeval and Renaissance, 1977; (trans.) Islamic Carpets and Textiles in the Keir Collection, 1977. *Recreations:* oriental ceramics and contemporary hand-made pottery. *Address:* Raleigh Lodge, Castleton, Sherborne, Dorset. *See also S. W. Digby.*

DIGBY, Very Rev. Richard Shuttleworth Wingfield, MA; Dean of Peterborough since 1966; *b* 19 Aug. 1911; *s* of late Everard George Wingfield Digby and Dorothy (*née* Loughnan); *m* 1936, Rosamond Frances, *d* of late Col W. T. Digby, RE; two *s* one *d. Educ:* Nautical Coll., Pangbourne; Royal Navy; Christ's Coll., Cambridge; Westcott House, Cambridge. BA 1935; MA 1939. Asst Curate of St Andrew's, Rugby, 1936-46. Chaplain to the Forces (4th Cl. Emergency Commn), 1940-45; POW, 1940-45. Vicar of All Saints, Newmarket, 1946-53; Rector of Bury, Lancs, 1953-66; Rural Dean of Bury, 1962-66. Pres. and Chm., Bury Trustee Savings Bank, 1953-66; Dep. Chm., Trustee Savings Bank Assoc., North-West Area, 1965-66. Hon. Canon of Manchester Cath., 1965; Hon. Chaplain to Regt XX, The Lancs Fusiliers, 1965. Chm. CofE Council for Places of Worship, 1976-. *Recreations:* walking, golf. *Address:* The Deanery, Peterborough. *T:* Peterborough 62780. *Club:* Army and Navy.

DIGBY, Simon Wingfield, TD 1946; DL; MA; *b* 1910; *s* of late Col F. J. B. Wingfield Digby, DSO; *m* 1936, Kathleen Elizabeth, *d* of late Hon. Mr Justice Courtney Kingstone, Toronto, Canada; one *s* one *d. Educ:* Harrow Sch.; Trinity Coll., Cambridge. Delegate to International Studies Conference, 1934. Prospective Conservative Candidate for West Dorset, Jan. 1937-June 1941; MP (U) West Dorset, 1941-Feb. 1974; a Conservative Whip, 1948-51. Barrister-at-law, Inner Temple; served in Army (TA), Aug. 1939-June 1945 in UK and NW Europe; Major, 1943. Civil Lord of the Admiralty, 1951-57. Mem. of Empire Parl. Delegn to East Africa, 1948 and Inter-Parliamentary Union Delegation to Chile, 1962. Pres., Wessex Young Conservatives, 1947-50; Chairman: Conservative Forestry Sub-Cttee, 1959-67; Shipping and Shipbuilding Cttee, 1964-74. Member: Coastal Pollution Select Cttee, 1966-68; Select Cttee on Procedure; Public Accounts Cttee. Delegate (C), Council of Europe Assembly and Assembly of WEU, 1968-74 (Leader, 1972-74). Pres., Soc. of Dorset Men. DL Dorset, 1953. Order of Leopold and Order of White Lion. *Recreations:* fishing, bloodstock breeding. *Address:* Sherborne Castle, Sherborne, Dorset. *T:* Gillingham 62650; Coleshill House, Coleshill, near Birmingham. *Club:* Carlton.
See also G. F. W. Digby, Sir Rupert Hardy, Bt.

DIGBY, Ven. Stephen Basil W.; *see* Wingfield-Digby.

DIGGINES, Christopher Ewart, CMG 1974; HM Diplomatic Service, retired; British High Commissioner, Port of Spain, Trinidad and Tobago, 1973-77; British High Commissioner (non-resident), Grenada, 1974-77; *b* 2 July 1920; *s* of late Sir William Diggines; *m* 1946, Mary Walls; one *s* one *d. Educ:* Haileybury Coll.; Trinity Coll., Oxford. Army, 1940-46. Senior History Master, Birkenhead Sch., 1948-49; apptd to CRO, 1949; Office of the UK High Comr in India (Madras), 1952-56; Canadian National Defence Coll., 1958-59; UK Mission to UN (1st Sec.), 1959-62; British Deputy High Commissioner, Kingston, Jamaica, 1962-64; Foreign and Commonwealth Office (formerly Commonwealth Office), 1964-69; Counsellor (Commercial), Lusaka, 1969-73. *Address:* 115 Middle Street, Deal, Kent. *Club:* United Oxford & Cambridge University.

DIGNAN, Maj.-Gen. Albert Patrick, MBE 1952; FRCS, FRCSI; QHS 1974; Director of Army Surgery and Consulting Surgeon to the Army since 1973; Hon. Consultant Surgeon, Royal Hospital, Chelsea; Hon. Consultant in Radiotherapy and Oncology, Westminster Hospital; *b* 25 July 1920; *s* of Joseph Dignan; *m* 1952, Eileen White; two *s* one *d. Educ:* Trinity Coll., Dublin (Med. Schol.). MB, BCh, BAO, BA 1943, MA, MD 1968, FRCSI 1947, FRCS 1976. Prof. of Physiol. Prize, TCD. Posts in Dublin, Belfast and Wigan; subseq. NS Sen. Specialist in Surgery, Major RAMC Malaya; Sen. Registrar in Surgery, Bristol Royal Infirmary and Wanstead Hosp.; Sen. Specialist in Surgery, BAOR Mil. Hosps and Consultant Surg., Brit. Mil. Hosps Singapore and Tidworth, 1953-68; Brig., and Consulting Surg., Farelf, 1969-70; Consultant Surg., Mil. Hosp. Tidworth, 1971-72; Consultant Surgeon, Queen Alexandra Mil. Hosp. Millbank, 1972-73. Fellow, Association of Surgeons of GB and Ireland. *Publications:* papers in Brit. Jl Surgery, BMJ, Jl of RAMC, Postgrad. Med. Jl, Univ. Singapore Med. Soc. Med. Gazette. *Recreations:* gardening, golf. *Address:* 28 Coldstream Gardens, West Hill Road, Putney, SW18.

DIKE, Prof. Kenneth Onwuka, MA, PhD; Andrew W. Mellon Professor of African History, Harvard University, since 1973; *b* 17 Dec. 1917; *s* of late Nzekwe Dike, merchant; *m* 1953, Ona Patricia, *d* of R. R. Olisa, MBE; two *s* three *d* (and one *d* decd). *Educ:* Dennis Memorial Grammar Sch., Onitsha; Achimota Coll., Ghana; Fourah Bay Coll., Sierra Leone; Univ. of Durham (BA); Univ. of Aberdeen (MA); London Univ. (PhD). Appointed Lectr in History, UC, Ibadan, 1950-52; Sen. Res. Fellow, W African Inst. of Social and Economic Res., 1952-54; University Coll., Ibadan: Sen. Lectr, Dept of History, 1954-56; Prof. of History, 1956-60; Vice-Principal, 1958-60; University of Ibadan: Vice-Chancellor, 1960-67; Dir, Inst. of African Studies, 1962-67; Chm., Planning Cttee, Univ. of Port Harcourt, 1967-71; Prof. of History, Harvard Univ., 1971-73. Founder and Dir, Nat. Archives of Nigeria, 1951-64; Chm. Nigerian Antiquities Commn, 1954-67; Pres., Historical Soc. of Nigeria, 1955-67; Chm., Assoc. of Commonwealth Univs, 1965-66. Chm., Commn for Review of Educational System in Eastern Region; Mem., Ashby Commn on Higher Educn in Nigeria; Chm. Organising Cttee, Internat. Congress of Africanists. FRC 1962. FRHistS 1956; Fellow Amer. Acad. of Arts and Scis, 1972. Hon. LLD: Aberdeen, 1961; Northwestern, 1962; Leeds, 1963; London, 1963; Columbia, 1965; Princeton, 1965; Hon. DLitt: Boston, Mass, 1962; Birmingham, 1964; Ahmadu Bello, 1965; Ibadan; Hon. DSc Moscow, 1963. *Publications:* Report on the Preservation and Administration of Historical Records in Nigeria, 1953; Trade and Politics in the Niger Delta 1830-1885, 1956; A Hundred Years of British Rule in Nigeria, 1957; The Origins of the Niger Mission, 1958; also articles in learned journals on Nigerian and West African history. *Address:* 275 Widener Library, Harvard University, Cambridge, Mass 02138, USA. *Clubs:* Royal Commonwealth Society; Metropolitan (Lagos, Nigeria); Odd Volumes (Boston, Mass).

DILHORNE, 1st Viscount *cr* 1964, of Green's Norton; **Reginald Edward Manningham-Buller;** Baron, 1962; Bt, 1886; PC 1954; Kt 1951; DL; a Lord of Appeal in Ordinary since 1969; *b* 1 Aug. 1905; *o s* of Lt-Col Sir Mervyn Manningham-Buller, 3rd Bt; S to father's Baronetcy, 1956; *m* 1930, Lady Mary Lilian Lindsay, 4th *d* of 27th Earl of Crawford, KT, PC; one *s* three *d. Educ:* Eton; Magdalen Coll., Oxford. BA 1926. Called to Bar, Inner Temple, 1927. KC 1946. MP (C) Daventry Div. of Northamptonshire, 1943-50, and for South Northants, 1950-62. Parliamentary Sec. to Min. of Works, May-Aug. 1945; Mem., Rushcliffe Cttee on Legal Aid, 1944-45; Mem., Parliamentary Delegn to USSR, 1945, and Anglo-American Cttee on Palestine, 1946. Solicitor Gen., 1951-54; Attorney-Gen., Oct. 1954-July 1962; Lord High Chancellor of Great Britain, 1962-64. Recorder of Kingston-upon-Thames, Jan.-July 1962. Hon. DCL, South Methodist Univ., Dallas, Texas; Hon. LLD, McGill Univ., Canada. DL, Northants, 1967. *Heir:* *s* Hon. John Mervyn Manningham-Buller, late Coldstream Guards [*b* 28 Feb. 1932; *m* 1955, Gillian Evelyn (marr. diss. 1973), *d* of Col George Stockwell; two *s* one *d*]. *Address:* 6 King's Bench Walk,

Temple, EC4. *T:* 01-583 5836; Horninghold Manor, near Market Harborough, Leicestershire. *T:* Hallaton 641. *Clubs:* Pratt's, Buck's.

DILKE, Sir John Fisher Wentworth, 5th Bt *cr* 1862; *b* 1906; *e s* of Sir Fisher Wentworth Dilke, 4th Bt, and Ethel Clifford (*d* 1959); *S* father, 1944; *m* 1st, 1934, Sheila (marr. diss. 1949), *d* of Sir William Seeds, KCMG; two *s*; 2nd, 1951, Iris Evelyn, *d* of late Ernest Clark. *Educ:* Winchester; New Coll., Oxford. Foreign Office, 1929; Editorial Staff, The Times, 1936 (Moscow corresp., 1939); rejoined Foreign Service, 1939; BBC External Service, 1950; farmer, 1956. *Heir:* s Charles John Wentworth Dilke, *b* 1937. *Address:* Ludpits, Etchingham, East Sussex.

DILKE, Mary Stella F.; *see* Fetherston-Dilke.

DILL, Sir (Nicholas) Bayard, Kt 1955; CBE 1951; Senior Partner, Conyers, Dill & Pearman, Barristers-at-Law, since 1948; *b* 28 Dec. 1905; *s* of Thomas Melville and Ruth Rapalje Dill; *m* 1930, Lucy Clare Dill; two *s*. *Educ:* Saltus Grammar Sch., Bermuda; Trinity Hall, Cambridge. Law Tripos Cantab, 1926. Mem. Colonial Parliament (for Devonshire Parish), 1938-68; Mem. HM Exec. Council, 1944-54; Chairman: Board of Trade, 1935-42, also Bd of Educn, 1940, and Board of Works, 1942-48, Bermuda; St David's Island Cttee, 1940-43; Public Works Planning Commn, 1942-49; Board of Civil Aviation, 1944-63; Bermuda Trade Development Bd, 1957-59; Mem., Legislative Council, Bermuda, 1968-73. Served as Capt., Bermuda Volunteer Engs, 1936-44. Chancellor of Diocese of Bermuda, 1950-. *Recreations:* sailing, golf. *Address:* Newbold Place, Devonshire, Bermuda. *T:* 2-4463. *Clubs:* Anglo-Belgian; Royal Thames Yacht; Royal and Ancient Golf (Scotland); Royal Bermuda Yacht (Commodore, 1936-38), Mid-Ocean, Royal Hamilton Amateur Dinghy (Bermuda); India House, Canadian, Cruising of America (NYC).

DILLISTONE, Rev. Canon Frederick William, DD; Fellow and Chaplain, Oriel College, Oxford, 1964-70, Fellow Emeritus, 1970; Canon Emeritus of Liverpool Cathedral since 1964; *b* 9 May 1903; *s* of late Frederick Dillistone; *m* 1931, Enid Mary, *d* of late Rev. Cecil Francis Ayerst; two *s* one *d*. *Educ:* Brighton Coll.; BNC, Oxford (Scholar). BA 1924; BD 1933; DD 1951. Deacon, 1927; Priest, 1928; Vicar of St Andrew, Oxford, 1934-38; Prof. of Theology, Wycliffe Coll., Toronto, 1938-45; Prof. of Theology, Episcopal Theological Sch., Cambridge, Mass, 1947-52; Canon Residentiary and Chancellor of Liverpool Cathedral, 1952-56; Dean of Liverpool, 1956-63. Hulsean Preacher, Cambridge, 1953; Select Preacher, Oxford, 1953-55; Select Preacher, Cambridge, 1960; Stephenson Lectr, Univ. of Sheffield, 1966; Bampton Lectr, Univ. of Oxford, 1968; Vis. Fellow, Clare Hall, Cambridge, 1970; Zabriskie Lectr, Virginia Theol. Seminary, 1971. Asst Editor, Theology Today, 1951-61. Hon. DD: Knox Coll., Toronto, 1946; Episcopal Theological Sch., Cambridge, Mass, 1967. Chaplain OStJ, 1958. *Publications:* The Significance of the Cross, 1945; The Holy Spirit in the Life of To-day, 1946; Revelation and Evangelism, 1948; The Structure of the Divine Society, 1951; Jesus Christ and His Cross, 1953; Christianity and Symbolism, 1955; Christianity and Communication, 1956; The Novelist and the Passion Story, 1960; The Christian Faith, 1964; Dramas of Salvation, 1967; The Christian Understanding of Atonement, 1968; Modern Answers to Basic Questions, 1972; Traditional Symbols and the Contemporary World, 1972; Charles Raven: a biography, 1975; C. H. Dodd: a biography, 1977; Editor, Scripture and Tradition, 1955; Editor, Myth and Symbol, 1966; contributor to: The Doctrine of Justification by Faith, 1954; A Companion to the Study of St Augustine, 1955; Steps to Christian Understanding, 1958; The Ecumenical Era in Church and Society, 1959; Metaphor and Symbol, 1961; The Theology of the Christian Mission, 1961; Christianity and the Visual Arts, 1964; Mansions of the Spirit, 1966; Christianity in its Social Context, 1967; Studies in Christian History and Interpretation, 1967; Christ for us Today, 1968; Grounds of Hope, 1968; Man, Fallen and Free, 1969; Sociology, Theology and Conflict, 1969; Christ and Spirit in the New Testament, 1973; Religion and Art as Communication, 1974. *Recreation:* gardening. *Address:* 15 Cumnor Rise Road, Oxford. *T:* Cumnor 2071.

DILLON, family name of Viscount Dillon.

DILLON, 20th Viscount *cr* 1622; **Michael Eric Dillon;** Count in France, *cr* 1711; local Lt-Col retired, RHG; *b* 13 Aug. 1911; *o s* of 19th Viscount, and Juanita (*d* 1962), *d* of Brig.-Gen. Charles Edward Beckett, CB; *S* father, 1946; *m* 1939, Irène Marie France, *y d* of René Merandon du Plessis, Whitehall, Mauritius; four *s* three *d* (and one *d* decd). *Educ:* Eton; RMC Sandhurst. 2nd Lieut 15/19th Hussars, 1931; seconded to Transjordan Frontier Force, 1935; Lieut RHG, 1937; Capt., 1939; Major,

1946; retired, 1952. Knight of the Sovereign Order of Malta; Officer of Order of Orange-Nassau (Netherlands). *Heir:* s Hon. Charles Henry Robert Dillon [*b* 18 Jan. 1945; *m* 1972, Jane, *d* of John Young, Birtle, Lancs; one *s*. *Educ:* Downside; RMA Sandhurst; Royal College of Art, Kensington]. *Address:* Rath House, Termonfeckin, Drogheda, Co. Louth, Ireland. *Club:* Kildare Street and University (Dublin).

DILLON, C(larence) Douglas; Chairman, US & Foreign Securities Corporation; Managing Director, Dillon, Read & Co. Inc.; *b* Geneva, Switzerland, 21 Aug. 1909; *s* of Clarence Dillon; *m* 1931, Phyllis Ellsworth; two *d*. *Educ:* Groton Sch.; Harvard Univ. (AB). Mem., NY Stock Exchange, 1931-36; US and Foreign Securities Corporation and US and International Securities Corporation, 1937-53 (Dir, 1938-53; Pres., 1946-53); Dir, Dillon, Read & Co. Inc., 1938-53 (Chm. of Bd, 1946-53); American Ambassador to France, 1953-57; Under-Sec. of State for Economic Affairs, USA, 1957-59, Under-Sec. of State, USA, 1959-61; Sec. of the Treasury, USA, 1961-65. Served US Naval Reserve, 1941-45 (Lieut-Comdr; Air Medal, Legion of Merit). Dir, Council on Foreign Relations, 1965- (Vice-Chm. 1977-); Pres., Board of Overseers, Harvard Coll., 1968-72; Chairman: Rockefeller Foundn, 1971-75; Brookings Instn, 1969-75. Trustee: Metropolitan Museum of Art (President, 1970-). Hon. Dr of Laws: New York Univ., 1956; Lafayette Coll., 1957; Univ. of Hartford, Conn, 1958; Columbia Univ., 1959; Harvard Univ., 1959; Williams Coll., 1960; Rutgers Univ., 1961; Princeton Univ., 1961; University of Pennsylvania, 1962; Bradley Univ., 1964; Middlebury Coll., 1965. *Address:* Far Hills, New Jersey, USA.

DILLON, George Brian Hugh, QC 1965; Barrister-at-Law; *b* 2 Oct. 1925; *s* of late Captain George Crozier Dillon, RN; *m* 1954, Alisoun, *d* of late Hubert Samuel Lane, MC; two *s* two *d*. Called to the Bar, Lincoln's Inn, 1948. *Address:* 13 Old Square, Lincoln's Inn, WC2A 3UA. *T:* 01-405 5441.

DILLON, John Vincent, CMG 1974; Ombudsman for Victoria (Commissioner for Administrative Investigations) since 1973; *b* 6 Aug. 1908; *s* of Roger Dillon and Ellen (*née* Egan); *m* 1935, Sheila Lorraine D'Arcy; three *s* one *d*. *Educ:* Christian Brothers Coll., Melbourne. AASA. Mem. Public Service Bd, 1941-54; Stipendiary Magistrate City Court, 1947-61; Chm., Medical Salaries Cttee, 1959-62; Under-Sec., Chief Sec.'s Dept, Vic, 1961-73; Chm., Racecourses Licences Bd, 1961-73. *Recreations:* racing, bowls, reading. *Address:* 25 Kelvin Grove, Armadale, Vic 3143, Australia. *Clubs:* Athenæum, Green Room, Victoria Racing, Victoria Amateur Turf, Moonee Valley Racing, Melbourne Cricket (Melbourne).

DILLON, Sir Robert William Charlier, 8th Bt *cr* 1801; Baron of the Holy Roman Empire, 1782; *b* 17 Jan. 1914; *s* of Robert Arthur Dillon (*d* 1925) and Laura Maud (*d* 1915), *widow* of J. Lachlin McCliver, New Zealand; *S* kinsman, 1925; *m* 1947, Synolda, *d* of late Cholmondeley Butler Clarke and of Mrs Cholmondeley-Clarke, late of Holywell, Co. Tipperary. *Heir:* none. *Address:* Overdene, Wentworth Place, Co. Wicklow, Ireland.

DILLON, Thomas Michael, QC 1973; a Recorder of the Crown Court since 1972; *b* 29 Nov. 1927; *yr s* of Thomas Bernard Joseph Dillon, Birmingham, and Ada Gladys Dillon (*née* Noyes); *m* 1956, Wendy Elizabeth Marshall Hurrell; two *s* one *d*. *Educ:* King Edward's Sch., Aston, Birmingham; Birmingham Univ. (LLB); Lincoln Coll., Oxford (BCL). Called to Bar, Middle Temple, 1952. 2nd Lieut, RASC, 1953-54. In practice as barrister, 1954-; Part-time Chm. of Industrial Tribunals, 1968-74. *Recreations:* reading, listening to music. *Address:* 1 Fountain Court, Birmingham B4 6DR. *T:* 021-236 5721.

DILLWYN-VENABLES-LLEWELYN, Sir John Michael; *see* Venables-Llewelyn.

DILNOT, Mary, (Mrs Thomas Ruffle); Director, IPC Women's Magazines Group, since 1976; Editor, Woman's Weekly, since 1971; *b* 23 Jan. 1921; 2nd *d* of George Dilnot, author, and Ethel Dilnot; *m* 1974, Thomas Ruffle. *Educ:* St Mary's Coll., Hampton. Joined Woman's Weekly, 1939. *Recreations:* home interests, reading, travel. *Address:* 28 Manor Road South, Hinchley Wood, Surrey.

DIMBLEBY, David; freelance broadcaster and newspaper proprietor; Managing Director, Dimbleby Newspaper Group, since 1966; *b* 28 Oct. 1938; *e s* of (Frederick) Richard and Dilys Dimbleby; *m* 1967, Josceline Rose, *d* of Thomas Gaskell; one *s* two *d*. *Educ:* Glengorse Sch.; Charterhouse; Christ Church, Oxford (MA); Univs of Paris and Perugia. News Reporter, BBC Bristol, 1960-61; Presenter and Interviewer on network programmes on: religion (Quest), science for children (What's New?), politics (In My Opinion), Top of the Form, etc, 1961-63; Reporter, BBC2 (Enquiry), and Dir films, incl.: Ku-Klux-Klan, The Forgotten Million, Cyprus: Thin Blue Line, 1964-65; worked as asst to his father in family newspaper business at Richmond, Surrey, 1965, being apptd Managing Dir on his father's death. Special Correspondent CBS News, New York; documentary film (Texas-England) and film reports for '60 minutes', 1966-; Reporter, BBC1 (Panorama), 1967-69; Commentator, Current Events, incl. President Nixon's visit to Britain, 1969; Presenter, BBC1 (24 Hours), 1969-72; various commentaries and films incl. Yesterday's Men, 1971; Chairman, The Dimbleby Talk-In, 1971-74; Presenter, BBC 1 (Panorama), 1974-. Films for: Reporter at Large, 1973; Presenter, Election Campaign Report, 1974. *Address:* 14 King Street, Richmond, Surrey TW9 1NF.

DIMECHKIE, Nadim; Ambassador of Lebanon to the Court of St James's, since 1966; *b* Lebanon, 5 Dec. 1919; *s* of Badr and Julia Dimechkie; *m* 1946, Margaret Alma Sherlock; two *s. Educ:* American Univ. of Beirut (BA, MA Economics). Deleg., Jt Supply Bd for Syria and Lebanon, 1942-44; Dir Gen., Min. of Nat. Economy, 1943-44; Counsellor, Lebanese Embassy, London, 1944-49; Consul-Gen., Ottawa, 1950; Dir, Economic and Social Dept, Min. of Foreign Affairs, 1951-52; Chargé d'Affaires, Cairo, 1952; Minister, 1953-55; Minister, Switzerland, 1955-57; Ambassador to USA, 1958-62; Dir, Economic Affairs, Min. of Foreign Affairs, 1962-66. Lebanese Order of Cedars, UAR Order of Ismail and Order of Merit; Syrian Order of Merit; Tunisian Order of Merit; Greek Order of Phoenix. *Address:* 21 Kensington Palace Gardens, W8. *T:* 01-229 7265. *Clubs:* Travellers', Hurlingham, Royal Automobile; Metropolitan, Chevy Chase (Washington); Cercle de Beirut, Aero (Beirut).

DIMMOCK, Peter, CVO 1968; OBE 1961; Director, American Broadcasting Company Worldwide Syndication TV Sports, since 1977; *b* 6 Dec. 1920; *e s* of late Frederick Dimmock, OBE, and of Paula Dimmock (*née* Hudd); *m* 1960, Mary Freya (Polly), *e d* of late Sir Richard Elwes, OBE, TD; three *d. Educ:* Dulwich Coll.; France. TA; RAF pilot, instr, and Air Ministry Staff Officer, 1939-45. After demobilisation became Press Association correspondent; joined BBC as Television Outside Broadcasts Producer and commentator, 1946; produced both studio and outside broadcasts, ranging from documentaries to sporting, theatrical and public events; has produced or commentated on more than 500 television relays, including Olympic Games 1948, Boat Race 1949, first international television relay, from Calais, 1950, King George VI's Funeral, Windsor, 1952. Produced and directed television outside broadcast of the Coronation Service from Westminster Abbey, 1953; first TV State Opening of Parliament, 1958; first TV Grand National, 1960; TV for Princess Margaret's Wedding, 1960. Created BBC Sportsview Unit and introduced new television programme Sportsview, 1954, regular compère of this weekly programme, 1954-64; Gen. Manager and Head of Outside Broadcasts, BBC TV, 1954-72; responsible for Liaison between BBC and Royal Family, 1963-77; Gen. Manager, BBC Enterprises, 1972-77. Sports Adviser, European Broadcasting Union, 1959-72. Mem., Greater London and SE Sports Council, 1972-77; Chm., Sports Develt Panel, 1976-77. *Publications:* Sportsview Annuals, 1954-65; Sports in View, 1964. *Recreations:* flying, gliding, winter sports, golf. *Address:* ABC Sports Inc., American Broadcasting Company, 1330 Avenue of the Americas, New York, NY 10019, USA. *Clubs:* Garrick, Carlton, Turf, Hurlingham, Royal Mid-Surrey.

DIMSDALE, Sir John Holdsworth, 3rd Bt *cr* 1902; *b* 31 Dec. 1901; *s* of 2nd Bt and Edith Kate (*d* 1911), *d* of late John Connacher; *S* father, 1923; *m* 1949, Gisela Panova (*d* 1969); *m* 1975, Mrs A. E. G. Cleaton, Ryde, Isle of Wight. *Address:* 16 Willis Road, Swaythling, Southampton SO2 2NT. *T:* Southampton 550151.

DIMSON, Gladys Felicia, (Mrs S. B. Dimson), CBE 1976; Member of GLC for Battersea North, since 1973; Member, Inner London Education Authority, since 1970; *b* 23 July 1917; *o d* of late I. Sieve, BA; *m* 1936, Dr S. B. Dimson, *e s* of late Rev. Z. Dimson; one *d. Educ:* Laurel Bank Sch., Glasgow; Glasgow Univ.; London Sch. of Economics. Voluntary social worker, mainly in E London, 1950-63; Co-opted Mem., Children's Cttee, LCC, 1958-65; Chm., gp of LCC Children's Homes and of a voluntary Hostel for Girls; Educn Counsellor, Marriage Guidance Council. Member: Home Office Advisory Cttee on Juvenile Delinquency, 1963-65 (Chm. Sub-Cttee on Transition from Sch. to Work); a Youth Employment Cttee, 1960-; Hendon Gp Hosp. Management Cttee, 1965-70; Exec., Greater London Labour Party, 1964-74; Toynbee Housing Soc., 1967-; Bd of

Governors, Nat. Hosp. for Nervous Diseases, 1976-; GLC Haringey, 1964-67, Wandsworth, 1970-73; (Vice-Chm.) GLC Ambulance Cttee; GLC Housing Cttee: Mem. (co-opted), 1968-70; Labour Spokesman, 1970-73, and 1977-; Chm., 1973-75. Mem., Bd of Management, Shelter, 1976- (Trustee, Shelter Housing Aid Centre); Chm., Toynbee Housing Assoc., 1976-. Contested (Lab) Hendon South, at Gen. Election, 1970. *Recreations:* ski-ing, walking in the country, lazing in the sun; reading (incl. thrillers); theatre; watching TV. *Address:* 34 Sheldon Avenue, Highgate, N6 4JR. *T:* 01-340 5133.

DINEEN, Ven. Frederick George K.; *see* Kerr-Dineen.

DINESEN, Thomas, VC 1918; French Croix de Guerre; Danish Knight of Danebrog; Civil Engineer; *b* 1892; *e s* of late Capt. W. Dinesen; *m* 1926, Jonna Lindhardt; two *s* two *d. Educ:* Rungsted Sch.; Polytechnical Sch., Copenhagen. Served European War, 1917-19, with Royal Highlanders of Canada; farmer in Kenya Colony, 1920-23. *Publications:* No Man's Land, 1929 (translated from Danish into English under the title Merry Hell); Twilight on the Betzy (Denmark, Norway, Sweden and Finland), 1951, (England and Holland), 1952; The Axe (Denmark), 1959; Boganis (Denmark), 1972; Anne Margrethe, my Great-Grandmother, 1974; Tanne, My Sister Karen Blixen (UK, as My Sister, Isak Dinesen), 1975. *Recreation:* travelling. *Address:* Leerbaek, Vejle, Denmark. *T:* 05 85 30 75.

DINEVOR; *see* Dynevor.

DINGLE, Herbert, DSc, ARCS; Professor Emeritus of History and Philosophy of Science, University College, London, 1955 (Professor, 1946-55); formerly Professor of Natural Philosophy, Imperial College of Science and Technology, South Kensington; *b* 2 Aug. 1890; *s* of James Henry Dingle and Emily Jane Gorddard; *m* 1918, Alice (*d* 1947), *d* of late Frederick Westacott; (one *s* decd). *Educ:* Plymouth Science, Art, and Technical Schs; Imperial Coll. of Science and Technology. Mem. of British Government Eclipse Expeditions, 1927, 1932 and 1940 (cancelled owing to war); Mem. Internat. Astronomical Union, 1928-; Vice-Pres. Internat. Union for the History of Science, 1953-56; Pres. Brit. Soc. for History of Science, 1955-57; Pres., Royal Astronomical Society, 1951-53, Hon. Sec., 1929-32, Vice-Pres., 1938-39, 1942-44, 1948-50, 1953-54; Lowell Lecturer, Boston, USA, 1936; Corresp. Member: Inst. of Coimbra; Inst. of Advanced Studies, Cordoba, Argentina. *Publications:* Relativity for All, 1922; Modern Astrophysics, 1924; Science and Human Experience, 1931; Through Science to Philosophy, 1937; The Special Theory of Relativity, 1940; Mechanical Physics, 1941; Subatomic Physics, 1942; Science and Literary Criticism, 1949; Practical Applications of Spectrum Analysis, 1950; The Scientific Adventure, 1952; The Sources of Eddington's Philosophy, 1954; (with 1st Visc. Samuel) A Threefold Cord, 1961; Science at the Crossroads, 1972; The Mind of Emily Brontë, 1974; scientific papers in Proc. Royal Soc., Monthly Notices of Royal Astronomical Soc., Nature, Brit. Jl for the Philosophy of Science, Encyclopædia Britannica, etc; part author: Splendour of the Heavens, 1923; Life and Work of Sir Norman Lockyer, 1929; The New World Order, 1932; The New Learning, 1933; Science To-Day, 1934; (ed) A Century of Science, 1951; (ed jtly) Chemistry and Beyond: essays by F. A. Paneth, 1965. *Address:* 118 Marlborough Avenue, Hull, North Humberside HU5 3JX. *T:* Hull 443565. *Club:* Athenæum.

DINGLE, Sir Philip (Burrington), Kt 1964; CBE 1954; Town Clerk of Manchester, 1944-66; *b* 19 Sept. 1906; *s* of Frederick Burrington Dingle and Jessie Roberta Elizabeth (*née* Needham); *m* 1938, Kathleen Mary, *d* of late Cecil Hurst, Sheffield; one *s d. Educ:* Cheltenham Coll.; Sheffield Univ. LLM Sheffield, 1928. Articled to late Sir William Hart, Town Clerk of Sheffield, 1924-28; admitted Solicitor, 1928; Asst Solicitor to Sheffield Corporation, 1928-37; Dep. Town Clerk, Manchester, 1938-44; Member: Advisory Council on Child Care, 1948-52; Advisory Council on Clean Air, 1957-67; Council of Cheltenham Coll., 1956-70 (Life Mem., 1965). Pres., Soc. of Town Clerks, 1961-62. Chm., City of Manchester Boy Scouts, 1946-66, Pres., 1968-72. Hon. LLD Manchester, 1960. *Address:* 93 Furniss Avenue, Dore, Sheffield S17 3QN.

DINGLE, Prof. Robert Balson, PhD; FRSE; Professor of Theoretical Physics, University of St Andrews, since 1960; *b* 26 March 1926; *s* of late Edward Douglas Dingle and Nora Gertrude Balson; *m* 1958, Helen Glenronnie Munro; two *d. Educ:* Bournemouth Secondary Sch.; Cambridge University. PhD 1951. Fellow of St John's Coll., Cambridge, 1948-52; Theoretician to Royal Society Mond. Lab., 1951-52; Chief Asst in Theoretical Physics, Technical Univ. of Delft, Holland, 1952-53; Fellow, Nat. Research Council, Ottawa, 1953-54; Reader in Theoretical Physics, Univ. of WA, 1954-60. *Publications:*

Asymptotic Expansions: their derivation and interpretation, 1973; contribs to learned journals. *Recreations:* music, local history, gastronomy. *Address:* 6 Lawhead Road East, St Andrews, Fife, Scotland. *T:* St Andrews 4287.

DINGLEY, Allen Roy, FRCS; Consulting Surgeon, Royal National Throat, Nose and Ear Hospital, London; Consulting Aural Surgeon, Sutton Hospital; *b* 28 Oct. 1892; *s* of Allen Dingley, FRCS. *Educ:* Leys Sch., Cambridge. Brackenbury Surgical Scholar, St Bart's Hospital, 1916. Mesopotamia Exped. Force, 1917-20, Surgical Specialist, 1919-20. Late Chief Asst, Throat Department, St Bart's Hospital. *Publications:* articles in medical journals on otolaryngology. *Recreation:* golf. *Address:* Cantley Cottage, Court Road, Banstead, Surrey. *T:* Burgh Heath 50378. *Club:* Walton Heath Golf.

DINGWALL, Baroness; *see* Lucas of Crudwell and Dingwall.

DINGWALL, Eric John, MA, DSc (London), PhD (London, Faculty of Science); anthropologist; Hon. Assistant Keeper, The British Library (Reference Division), retired; Hon. Vice-President, Magic Circle; *s* of Alexander Harvey Dingwall, Ceylon. *Educ:* privately; Pembroke Coll., Cambridge. Formerly on staff, Cambridge Univ. Library; Dir, Dept of Physical Phenomena, American Soc. for Psychical Research, New York, 1921; Research Officer, Soc. for Psychical Research, 1922-27, investigating many American and European mediums in New York, Boston, Paris, Copenhagen, Warsaw, Munich, Gratz, etc, publishing results in Proc. and Jl of the SPR; toured Spain, 1935; went to the West Indies, 1936, to study special social and religious conditions in Trinidad and Haiti with reference to abnormal mental phenomena; went to Poland, S America, W Indies, and USA, 1937. Attached to Ministry of Information and to a Dept, Foreign Office, 1941-45. *Publications:* Joint Editor, Revelations of a Spirit Medium, 1922; Studies in the Sexual Life of Ancient and Mediæval Peoples, I, Male Infibulation, 1925; How to Go to a Medium, 1927; Ghosts and Spirits in the Ancient World, 1930; The Girdle of Chastity, 1931; Artificial Cranial Deformation, 1931; How to Use a Large Library, 1933; Editor of English edn of Woman (Ploss-Bartels), 1935; Racial Pride and Prejudice, 1946; Some Human Oddities, 1947; Very Peculiar People, 1950; (with K. M. Goldney and T. H. Hall) The Haunting of Borley Rectory, 1956; (with J. Langdon-Davies) The Unknown-is it nearer?, 1956; The American Woman, 1956; (with T. H. Hall) Four Modern Ghosts, 1958; The Critics' Dilemma, 1966; Editor of and contributor to: Abnormal Hypnotic Phenomena, 1967-68; contributions to English and foreign publications. *Recreation:* studying rare and queer customs. *Address:* 171 Marine Court, St Leonards-on-Sea, East Sussex. *Club:* National Liberal.

DINGWALL, John James, OBE 1964; HM Inspector of Constabulary for Scotland, 1966-70; *b* 2 Sept. 1907; *s* of late James Dingwall, Bannockburn, Stirling; *m* 1932, Jane Anne, *d* of late James K. Halliday, Falkirk; two *d*. *Educ:* Bridge of Allan and Stirling. Stirlingshire Constabulary, 1927-49; Stirling and Clackmannan Police Force, 1949-55; seconded to Directing Staff, Scottish Police Coll., 1953-55; Chief Constable of Angus, 1955-66. *Recreations:* angling, shooting, golf. *Address:* 56 Carlogie Road, Carnoustie, Angus.

DINGWALL, Walter Spender, MA; Secretary Chichester Diocesan Fund, 1946-61, retired; *b* 14 Dec. 1900; *s* of late Rev. Walter Molyneux Dingwall and Sophia Spender; *m* 1932, Olive Mary Loasby; no *c*. *Educ:* Marlborough Coll.; Christ Church, Oxford. Sixth Form Master at St Edward's Sch., Oxford, 1923-37; nine years Bursar of the Sch., ten years Housemaster; Headmaster, Hurstpierpoint Coll., Sussex, 1937-45; Hon. Sec. and Treasurer, Public Schools Bursars' Assoc., 1932-38. *Address:* The White House, Woodmancote, near Henfield, West Sussex BN5 9ST.

DINGWALL-SMITH, Ronald Alfred, CB 1977; Under-Secretary (Principal Finance Officer), Scottish Office, since 1970; *b* 24 Feb. 1917; *m* 1946; one *s* one *d*. *Educ:* Alleyn's Sch., Dulwich; London School of Economics (evening classes). Entered Civil Service as Clerical Officer, Ministry of Transport, 1934; Exchequer and Audit Dept, 1935-47; Scottish Educn Dept, 1947-65; Scottish Development Dept, 1965-70. *Recreations:* golf, bowls, gardening. *Address:* 3 Frogston Terrace, Edinburgh EH10 7AD. *T:* 031-445 2727. *Club:* Royal Commonwealth Society.

DINKEL, Ernest Michael, RWS 1957; ARCA; Head of The School of Design, Edinburgh College of Art, 1947-60, retired; *b* 24 Oct. 1894; *s* of Charles and Lucy Dinkel; *m* 1st, 1929, Kathleen Hanks (*d* 1936); 2nd, 1941, Emmy Keet, ARCA; two *s* two *d* (and one *s* decd). *Educ:* Huddersfield Sch. of Art; War

Service abroad, 1916-19, on the Somme (general and war service medals). Royal Coll. of Art, 1921-25, Student. RIBA Owen Jones Scholarship, 1926. Asst to Prof. Robert Anning Bell and Prof. Tristram, at Royal Coll. of Art, 1925-40; Head of Stourbridge Sch. of Art, 1940-47; Exhibitor: Royal Academy, Royal Scottish Academy, Royal Society of Painters in Water Colours, RWEA and private exhbns; designer, Royal Hunt Cup and Topham Trophy; work in Tate Gallery. *Recreations:* glass engraving; pottery, sculpture; wide interest in art subjects. *Address:* The Grange, Bussage, near Stroud, Glos. *T:* Brimscombe 2368.

DINSDALE, Richard Lewis; Chairman, West of England Newspapers Ltd, 1969-72; *b* 23 June 1907; *m* 1930, Irene Laverack; one *d*. *Educ:* Hull Technical Coll. Joined Hull Daily Mail as reporter, 1926; Editorial posts: Newcastle Evening World; Chief Sub-editor, Manchester Evening News; Dep. Chief Sub-editor, Daily Express, Manchester; Evening News, London; Daily Mirror, 1940-42; War Service, 1942-46; Copy-taster, Daily Mirror, 1946, successively Chief Sub-editor, Dep. Night Editor, Night Editor; Dep. Editor, 1955; seconded Daily Herald as Editorial Adviser, 1961; Dep. Editor, Daily Herald, 1962; Dep. Editor, The Sun, 1964, Editor, 1965-69. *Recreations:* sea fishing, golf. *Address:* West Lodge, Horsepool Street, Higher Brixham, Devon. *T:* Brixham 4608.

DINWIDDY, Thomas Lutwyche; Master of the Supreme Court (Chancery Division), 1958-73; *b* 27 Aug. 1905; *o c* of late Harry Lutwyche Dinwiddy, Solicitor, and late Ethel Maude (*née* McArthur); *m* 1935, Ruth, *d* of late Charles Ernest Rowland Abbott, Barrister-at-Law and Bencher of Lincoln's Inn; three *s*. *Educ:* Winchester; New Coll., Oxford (BA). Solicitor, Dec. 1930; Partner in Frere Cholmeley & Co., 28 Lincoln's Inn Fields, WC2, 1933-57. Council of Law Soc., 1953-57. Served RA (TA), 1939-45; Staff Coll., Camberley, 1943; demobilised as Major. *Recreations:* golf, watching cricket, motoring, gardening. *Address:* Northolme, 48 Saxmundham Road, Aldeburgh, Suffolk.

DIONISOTTI-CASALONE, Carlo, FBA 1972; Professor of Italian, Bedford College (formerly Bedford College for Women), University of London, 1949-70; *b* 9 June 1908; *s* of Eugenio Dionisotti-Casalone and Carla Cattaneo; *m* 1942, Maria Luisa Pinna-Pintor; three *d* (and one *d* decd). *Educ:* Turin, Italy. Dottore in lettere, Univ. of Turin, 1929; Libero Docente di Letteratura Italiana, Univ. of Turin, 1937; Asst di Letteratura Italiana, Univ. of Rome, 1943; Italian Lectr, Univ. of Oxford, 1947; MA Oxon, 1947. *Publications:* Indici del giornale storico della letteratura italiana (Turin), 1945; Guidiccioni-orazione ai nobili di Lucca (Rome), 1946; Bembo-Savorgnan, Carteggio d'amore (Florence), 1950; Oxford Book of Italian Verse (revised edn), 1952; Bembo, Prose e Rime (Turin), 1960; Geografia e storia della letter. ital. (Turin), 1967. *Address:* 44 West Heath Drive, NW11.

DIPLOCK, Baron (Life Peer) *cr* 1968, of Wansford; **(William John) Kenneth Diplock**, PC 1961; Kt 1956; a Lord of Appeal in Ordinary since 1968; *b* 8 Dec. 1907; *s* of W. J. Hubert Diplock, Croydon; *m* 1938, Margaret Sarah, *d* of George Atcheson, Londonderry. *Educ:* Whitgift; University Coll., Oxford. Barrister, Middle Temple, 1932, Bencher, 1956, Dep. Treas., 1973, Treas., 1974. Sec. to Master of the Rolls, 1939-48. Served War of 1939-45, RAF, 1941-45. KC 1948; Recorder of Oxford, Dec. 1951-Jan. 1956. Judge of High Court of Justice, Queen's Bench Div., 1956-61; a Lord Justice of Appeal, 1961-68. Judge of Restrictive Practices Court, 1960-61 (Pres., 1961). Mem., Lord Chancellor's Law Reform Cttee, 1952-69. Hon. Fellow of University Coll., Oxford, 1958. Pres., Nat. Assoc. of Parish Councils, 1962-66; Vice-Pres., Brit. Maritime Law Assoc., 1964, Pres., 1975; Chm., Inst. of Advanced Legal Studies, 1973-. Chairman: Permanent Security Commn, 1971-; Advisory Bd (Comparative Law), Brit. Inst. of Internat. and Comparative Law, 1959-67; Council of Legal Education, 1969-70 (Chm., Bd of Studies, 1963-69); Law Advisory Cttee, Brit. Council, 1966; Dep. Chm., Boundary Commn for England, 1958-61. Hon. Pres., Assoc. of Law Teachers, 1971-75; Pres., Inst. of Arbitrators, 1977. Hon. Fellow, American Bar Foundation, 1969. Hon. LLD Alberta, 1972; Hon. DCL Oxon, 1977. *Recreation:* hunting. *Address:* 1 Crown Office Row, Temple, EC4; Wansford in England, Peterborough. *Club:* Athenæum.

DIRAC, Prof. Paul Adrien Maurice, OM 1973; FRS 1930; BSc Bristol, PhD Cantab; Lucasian Professor of Mathematics, Cambridge, 1932-69, now Professor Emeritus; Fellow of St John's College, Cambridge; Professor of Physics, Florida State University, since 1971; *b* 8 Aug. 1902; *m* 1937, Margit Wigner, Budapest. Mem. Pontifical Academy of Sciences, 1961. Nobel Prize in Physics for 1933; Royal Medal of Royal Society, 1939;

Copley Medal of Royal Society, 1952. *Publications:* Principles of Quantum Mechanics, 1930; General Theory of Relativity, 1975; papers on quantum theory. *Address:* Department of Physics, Florida State University, Tallahassee, Florida 32306, USA; St John's College, Cambridge.

DISBREY, Air Vice-Marshal William Daniel, CB 1967; CBE 1945 (OBE 1943); AFC 1939; *b* London, 23 Aug. 1912; *s* of Horace William Disbrey; *m* 1939, Doreen Alice, *d* of William Henry Ivory, Stevenage; two *d. Educ:* Minchenden Sch. Joined RAF as an Apprentice, 1928; gained Cadetship to RAF Coll., Cranwell, 1931; No 3 Fighter Sqdn, 1933-34; Fleet Air Arm, 1934-37; Engr Specialist Course, Henlow, 1937-39; Engr Officer, No 13 Group HQ, 1940-41; Engr Officer, HQ Fighter Comd, 1941-43; Chief Engr Officer, 2nd TAF, 1943-46; Staff Coll. Course, 1946; CO, No 12 Sch. of Technical Training, 1946-48; Sen. Technical Officer, Royal Indian Air Force, 1948-51; Min. of Supply, 1951-54; Chief Engr Officer, Bomber Comd, 1954-57; Imperial Defence Coll., 1957; Dir of Research and Development, Bombers, Min. of Aviation, 1958-61; Comdt, No 1 Radio Sch., Locking, 1961-64; Dir-Gen. of Engineering (RAF), 1964-67; AO Engineering, Bomber Comd, 1967, Strike Comd, 1968-70, retired. Manager, Tech. Trng Inst., Airwork Services, Saudi Arabia, 1970. CEng; FIMechE; FRAeS. *Recreations:* golf, sailing. *Address:* Old Heatherwode, Buxted, East Sussex. *T:* Buxted 2104. *Club:* Royal Air Force.

DISLEY, John Ivor; Member of Countryside Commission; Chairman, Silva Compasses Ltd; *b* Gwynedd, 20 Nov. 1928; *s* of Harold Disley and Marie Hughes; *m* 1958, Sylvia Cheeseman; two *d. Educ:* Oswestry High Sch.; Loughborough Coll. (Hon. DCL). Schoolmaster, Isleworth, 1951; Chief Instructor, CCPR Nat. Mountaineering Centre, 1955; Gen. Inspector of Educn, Surrey, 1958; Dir, Ski Plan, 1971. Member: Adv. Sports Council, 1964-71; Mountain Leadership Trng Bd, 1965; Canal Adv. Bd, 1965-66; Internat. Orienteering Fedn, 1972; Vice-Chm., Sports Council, 1974-76; Chairman: Duke of Edinburgh's Award Expedn Panel, 1965-66; Sports Develt Cttee, Sports Council, 1975; British Orienteering Fedn, 1969-72; Dep. Leader, Sir John Hunt Endeavour Expedn, Tatras, 1967; Dir, World Orienteering Championships, 1976. Mem., Royal Commn on Gambling, 1976-. British athletics team, 1950-59; Brit. record holder steeplechase, 1950-56; world record holder steeplechase, 1952, 1955; Welsh mile record holder, 1952-57; bronze medal, Olympics, Helsinki, 1952; Olympic finalist, Melbourne, 1956; Sportsman of the Year, 1955; Captain, British Team, 1955-56. *Publications:* Tackle Climbing, 1959; Young Athletes Companion, 1961; Orienteering, 1966; Expedition Guide for Duke of Edinburgh's Scheme, 1965; Your Way with Map and Compass, 1971. *Recreations:* orienteering, mountaineering, skiing. *Address:* Hampton House, Upper Sunbury Road, Hampton, Mddx TW12 2DW. *T:* 01-979 1707. *Club:* Climbers'.

DISNEY, Harold Vernon, CBE 1956; Manager, Engineering Division, Reactor Group, UK Atomic Energy Authority, 1969-72, retired; *b* 2 July 1907; *s* of Henry Disney and Julia Vernon; *m* 1936, Lucy Quinton; two *d. Educ:* Hallcroft Higher Standard Sch., Ilkeston; Nottingham Univ. Coll. Internat. Combustion, 1931-35; ICI (Alkali), 1935-46. On loan to Min. of Supply (RFF's), 1941-46. Dept of Atomic Energy, 1946-54; UKAEA: Asst Dir, Defence Projects, Industrial Gp, 1954; Dir of Engineering, Industrial Gp, 1958; Man. Dir, Engineering Gp, Risley, 1962. FIMechE 1947. *Recreation:* gardening. *Address:* Delph House, Delphfields Road, Appleton, Warrington, Cheshire. *T:* Warrington 62984.

DITCHBURN, Robert William, FRS 1962; Professor of Physics, University of Reading, 1946-68, now Emeritus; *b* 14 Jan. 1903; *e s* of William and Martha Kathleen Ditchburn; *m* 1929, Doreen May, *e d* of Arthur Samuel Barrett; one *s* three *d. Educ:* Bootle Secondary Sch.; Liverpool Univ.; Trinity Coll., Cambridge (Entrance and Senior Scholar, Hooper Prizeman, Isaac Newton Student). Fellow of Trinity Coll., Dublin, 1928-46; Prof. of Natural and Experimental Philosophy in Dublin Univ., 1929-46; Temp. Principal Experimental Officer, Admiralty, 1942-45. Mem. of Royal Irish Academy, 1931; Registrar for Social Studies, Trinity Coll., Dublin, 1930-44; Vice-Pres. Physical Soc., 1958; Vice-Pres. Inst. of Physics and Physical Soc., 1960-62. FInstP. *Publications:* Light, 1952; Eye-Movements and Visual Perception, 1973; and scientific papers. *Recreations:* walking, music. *Address:* 9 Summerfield Rise, Goring, Reading RG8 0DS.

DIVER, Hon. Sir Leslie Charles, Kt 1975; President, Legislative Council, Western Australia, 1960-74; Member, Legislative Council (Country Party) for Central Province, Western Australia, 1952-74; *b* Perth, Australia, 4 Nov. 1899; *s* of late J. W. Diver; *m* 1st, 1922, Emma J., *d* of late F. Blakiston; one *s* two *d*; 2nd, 1971, Mrs Thelma May Evans. Farmer and grazier. Chairman: Kellerberrin Road Bd, 1940, 1942-46; Hon. Royal Commn on Retailing of Motor Spirits, 1956. Chm., Sixth Aust. Area Conf., Commonwealth Parly Assoc., 1961; Rep. WA Parlt, Town Planning Adv. Cttee. Warden, State War Meml, 1967-68. *Recreations:* bowls, Australian rules football. *Address:* 48 Sulman Avenue, Salter Point, Como, WA 6152, Australia. *Clubs:* Eastern Districts (Kellerberrin); Manning Memorial Bowling.

DIVERRES, Prof. Armel Hugh; Professor of French and Head of Department of Romance Studies, University College of Swansea, since 1974; *b* Liverpool, 4 Sept. 1914; *o s* of late Paul Diverres and Elizabeth (*née* Jones); *m* 1945, Ann Dilys, *d* of late James and Enid Williams; one *s* two *d. Educ:* Swansea Grammar Sch.; University Coll., Swansea; Univ. of Rennes; Sorbonne, Paris. MA (Wales), LèsL (Rennes), Docteur de l'Université de Paris. Fellow of Univ. of Wales, 1938-40; served in RA and Int. Corps, 1940-46, Captain. Asst Lectr in French, 1946-49, Lectr, 1949-54, Univ. of Manchester; Sen. Lectr in French, 1954-57, Carnegie Prof., 1958-74, Dean, Faculty of Arts, 1967-70, Univ. of Aberdeen. Governor, Aberdeen Coll. of Education, 1971-74. Member: CNAA Lang. Board, 1965-; Welsh Jt Educn Cttee, 1975-. Officier des Palmes Académiques, 1971. *Publications:* Voyage en Béarn by Froissart (ed), 1953; La Chronique métrique attribuée à Geffroy de Paris (ed), 1956; Chatterton by A. de Vigny (ed), 1967; articles and reviews in learned journals. *Recreation:* hill walking. *Address:* 23 Whiteshell Drive, Langland, Swansea, W Glamorgan. *T:* Swansea 60322; University College of Swansea, Singleton Park, Swansea SA2 8PP.

DIVERS, Brig. Sydney Thomas, CB 1955; CBE 1944 (OBE 1940); DSO 1942; TD; company director; *b* 30 Jan. 1896; *s* of William and Alice Divers, Greenwich, Kent; *m*; two *s* two *d. Educ:* Greenwich Central Sch. Served Army, 1914-18, 1939-45 (USA Bronze Star, 1944; despatches 5 times); TA, 1914-19, 1924-51. Royal Observatory, Greenwich, 1910-14; HM Customs and Excise, 1919-34; Assistance Board, 1935-46; Ministry of Pensions and National Insurance, 1946-54 (Controller, Newcastle upon Tyne, 1951-54); Under-Sec.: Min. of Supply, 1956; Admiralty, 1957-59; UN Adviser, Administration: Burma, 1954-55; Nepal, 1959-62; Asia and Far East, 1962-64; UN Adviser, Social Security: Iraq, 1965-66; Trinidad 1967; Saudi Arabia 1971. Inst. of Public Administration; British Inst. of Management. *Recreations:* fishing, gardening, cattle breeding. *Address:* RD 2, Winton, Southland, New Zealand. *Club:* National Liberal.

DIVINE, Arthur Durham, CBE 1976 (OBE 1946); DSM 1940; (David Divine); author and journalist; formerly War Correspondent and Defence Correspondent, Sunday Times (until 1975); *b* 27 July 1904; 2nd *s* of Arthur Henry and Mabel Divine, Cape Town; *m* 1931, Elizabeth Ann, 2nd *d* of Sir Ian MacAlister; two *d. Educ:* Rondebosch High Sch., Cape Town; Kingswood Coll., Grahamstown, S Africa. Cape Times, 1922-26 and 1931-35, where founded daily column of World Comment; has travelled extensively in Europe, Africa, Asia, N and S America, and the Pacific. *Publications:* Sea Loot, 1930; They Blocked the Suez Canal, 1936; The Pub on the Pool, 1938; Tunnel from Calais, 1943, and many other thrillers; The Merchant Navy Fights, The Wake of the Raiders, Behind the Fleets, 1940, in conjunction with Ministry of Information; Destroyer's War, 1942; Road to Tunis, 1944; Navies in Exile, 1944; Dunkirk, 1945, and many boys' books. Under pseudonym of David Rame: Wine of Good Hope, 1939; The Sun Shall Greet Them, 1941. Under name of David Divine: The King of Fassarai, 1950; Atom at Spithead, 1953; The Golden Fool, 1954; Boy on a Dolphin, 1955; The Nine Days of Dunkirk, 1959; These Splendid Ships, 1960; The Iron Ladies, 1961; The Daughter of the Pangaran, 1963; The Blunted Sword, 1964; The Broken Wing, 1966; The Stolen Seasons, 1967; The Key of England, 1968; The North-West Frontier of Rome, 1969; The Three Red Flares, 1970; Mutiny at Invergordon, 1970; Certain Islands, 1972; The Opening of the World, 1973; *Films:* Atom at Spithead; Boy on a Dolphin; Dunkirk. *Address:* 24 Keats Grove, Hampstead, NW3 2RS. *T:* 01-435 6928.

DIX, Alan Michael; Director General, Motor Agents' Association Ltd, since 1976; *b* 29 June 1922; *s* of late Comdr Charles Cabry Dix, CMG, DSO, RN, and Ebba Sievers; *m* 1955, Helen Catherine McLaren; one *s* one *d. Educ:* Stenhus Kostskole, Denmark. Escaped Nazi occupied Denmark to Scotland, 1943; joined RAF, commissioned 1944. President, Capitol Car Distributors Inc., USA, 1958-67; Gp Vice-Pres., Volkswagen of America, USA, 1967-68; Man. Dir, Volkswagen (GB) Ltd, London, 1968-72; Pres., Mid Atlantic Toyota Inc., USA, 1972-73; Dir Marketing, British Leyland International, 1973-74;

Proprietor, Alan M. Dix Associates, 1974-76. Chm., Motor Agents Pensions Administrators Ltd, 1977-; Dir, Hire Purchase Information Ltd, 1977-. FIMI, FInstM, FIMH, MBIM. King Christian X war medal, 1947. *Publications:* contribs to automotive trade jls. *Recreations:* yachting, photography; the study of professional management (internat. speaker on management and organisation). *Address:* 112 Speed House, Barbican, EC2Y 8AB. *T:* 01-638 6571; Drumnacree, St Ninians Road, Alyth, Perthshire PH11 8AP. *T:* Alyth 2101. *Clubs:* Danish, Royal Air Force, Burkes; Royal Air Force Yacht (Hamble).

DIX, Geoffrey Herbert; Secretary-General, The Institute of Bankers, since 1971; *b* 1 March 1922; *o s* of Herbert Walter and late Winifred Ada Dix; *m* 1945, Margaret Sybil Hurlwaite, MA (Cantab); one *s. Educ:* Watford Grammar Sch.; Gonville and Caius Coll., Cambridge. MA (Mod. langs). Served War, 1942-45: commissioned into Royal Devon Yeomanry; later served with HQ 1st Airborne Corps. Inst. of Export, 1946-51; with Inst. of Bankers, 1951-: Asst Sec., 1956; Under-Sec. 1962; Dep. Sec. 1968. Mem., Jt Cttee for National Awards in Business Studies, 1960-76. *Recreations:* Mozart, theatre. *Address:* 102 Harestone Valley Road, Caterham, Surrey. *T:* Caterham 42837. *Clubs:* Overseas Bankers; Caterham Players.

DIX, Victor Wilkinson, MA, MB, BChir Cantab, FRCS, MRCP; retired; Professor Emeritus, University of London. Assistant Surgeon, The London Hospital, 1930-37; Surgeon, The London Hospital, 1937-64. *Address:* 8 Shandon Close, Tunbridge Wells, Kent. *T:* Tunbridge Wells 30839.

DIXEY, Sir Frank, KCMG 1972 (CMG 1949); OBE 1929; DSc; FRS 1958; FGS; Geological Adviser and Director of Colonial Geological Surveys, Colonial Office, 1947-59; British Technical Aid Consultant to Water Development Department, Cyprus, 1967-73; Consultant Hydrologist, 1960-74, including service overseas with UN organisations; *b* 7 April 1892; *m* 1919, Helen Golding (*d* 1961); one *d* (decd); *m* 1962, Cicely Hepworth. *Educ:* Barry Grammar Sch.; University of Wales. Served European War, 1914-18, RGA, 1915-18; Govt Geologist, Sierra Leone, 1918-21; Dir of Geological Survey, Nyasaland, 1921-39; Dir of Water Development, N Rhodesia, 1939-44; Dir of Geological Survey, Nigeria, 1944-47. Geological Soc. Murchison medallist, 1953; Geol. Soc. S Africa Draper medallist, 1945 and Hon. Mem., 1959; Corresponding Mem. Geological Soc., Belgium, 1947, Hon. Mem., 1958. Alexander du Toit Memorial Lecturer, Johannesburg, 1955. Hon. Fellow, Inst. Min. and Met., 1958; Founder Fellow, Fellowship of Engineering, 1976. *Publications:* Practical Handbook of Water Supply, 1931, 2nd edn 1950; official reports and scientific papers on geology, geomorphology, and mineral resources of African States. *Address:* Woodpecker Cottage, Bramber, Steyning, West Sussex BN4 3WE. *T:* Steyning 812313. *Club:* Athenæum.

DIXEY, John, OBE 1976; Employment Affairs Adviser, Institute of Practitioners in Advertising, since 1977; Secretary, Association of Midland Advertising Agencies, since 1977; *b* 29 March 1926; *s* of John Dixey and Muriel Doris Dixey; *m* 1948, Pauline Seaden; one *s* one *d*. *Educ:* Battersea Grammar Sch. Served Royal Marines and Royal Fusiliers, 1944-47. Press Telegraphist, Yorkshire Post and Glasgow Herald, 1948-59; Asst to Gen. Sec., Nat. Union of Press Telegraphists, 1959; Labour Officer, Newspaper Soc., 1959-63; Labour Adviser, Thomson Organisation Ltd, 1963-64; Asst Gen. Man., Liverpool Daily Post & Echo, 1964-67; Executive Dir, Times Newspapers, 1967-74; Special Adviser to Man. Dir, Thomson Org., 1974; Dir, Newspaper Publishers Assoc. Ltd, 1975-76. Former Mem., Printing and Publishing Industry Trng Bd; former Governor, London Coll. of Printing. *Recreations:* cooking, photography. *Address:* 23 West Hill, Sanderstead, Surrey. *T:* 01-657 7940.

DIXEY, Paul (Arthur Groser); Chairman of Lloyd's, 1973, 1974 (Deputy Chairman, 1967, 1969, 1972); *b* 13 April 1915; *e s* of late Neville Dixey, JP (Chairman of Lloyd's, 1931, 1934 and 1936), and Marguerite (*née* Groser); *m* 1939, Mary Margaret Baring, JP, 2nd *d* of late Geoffrey Garrod; four *s* one *d*. *Educ:* Stowe; Trinity Coll., Cambridge. Elected an Underwriting Mem. of Lloyd's, 1938. Served War of 1939-45, Royal Artillery. Member: London Insce market delegn to Indonesia, 1958; Dunmow RDC, 1958-64; Cttee, Lloyd's Underwriters' Assoc., 1962-74; Cttee, Salvage Assoc., 1962-74; Cttee, Lloyd's, 1964-70, 1972-75; Gen. Cttee, Lloyd's Register of Shipping, 1964-; Chm., Salvage Assoc., 1964-65. Chm., Paul Dixey Underwriting Agencies Ltd, 1973-76; Dir, Merrett Dixey Syndicates Ltd, 1976-. Mem. Council, Morley Coll., 1952-62; Chm. Governors, Vinehall Sch., 1966-73. Leader, Barn Boys' Club, 1949-61. *Recreations:* riding, fly-fishing. *Address:* Little Easton Spring, Dunmow, Essex CM6 2JD. *T:* Great Dunmow 2840.

DIXON, family name of Baron Glentoran.

DIXON; see Graham-Dixon.

DIXON, Bernard; Chairman, Dixon Group of Malting and Light Industrial Companies, Pampisford, Cambs, since 1960; chairman and director of a number of brewing and malting companies; *b* Redcar, Yorks, 23 Dec. 1906; 3rd *s* of late Capt. Thomas Robert Dixon and Lily Jane (*née* Barry), Thriplow Place, near Royston, Herts; *m* 1930, Olive Marie, *d* of G. H. Watts, Cambridge; four *d*. *Educ:* Campbell Coll., Belmont, Belfast, NI; British Sch. of Malting and Brewing; University of Birmingham. Chm. and Man. Dir, Flowers Breweries Ltd, 1947-58. Sometime examiner, Institute of Brewing, Mem. Publications Cttee, Journal of Inst. of Brewing, Chm. London Section, Inst. of Brewing, 1939-40. Winner numerous awards at home and abroad for brewery products, including championship, London, 1929 and 1930 and Grand Prix, Brussels, Prague, Pilsen. Patentee of inventions used throughout brewing industry. Formerly Hon. Sec. Bedfordshire Brewers' Assoc. and Mem. Brewers' Soc. Cttee on Replanning. Commissioned, Cambs Regt, 1929; Sports Officer, 1930; commissioned, Home Guard, 1940. Breeder of pure-bred Arabian Horses which have been exported to Government studs in all parts of the world; Governor of the Arab Horse Soc. Past Pres. Old Campbellian Soc. *Publications:* technical papers to various sections of Institute of Brewing and Incorporated Brewers' Guild. *Recreations:* hunting, farming, golf. *Address:* Pampisford Place, Pampisford, Cambs CB2 4EW. *Clubs:* Bath, Royal Automobile; Kildare Street and University (Dublin).

DIXON, Dr Bernard; Editor of New Scientist, 1969-77 (Deputy Editor, 1968-69); *b* Darlington, 17 July 1938; *s* of late Ronald Dixon and Grace Peirson; *m* 1963, Margaret Helena Charlton; two *s* one *d*. *Educ:* Queen Elizabeth Grammar Sch., Darlington; King's Coll., Univ. of Durham; Univ. of Newcastle upon Tyne. BSc, PhD. Luccock Res. Fellow, 1961-64, Frank Schon Fellow, 1964-65, Univ. of Newcastle; Asst Editor, 1965-66, Dep. Editor, 1966-68, World Medicine. Chm., Cttee, Assoc. of British Science Writers, 1971-72; Member: Soc. for General Microbiology, 1962; Gen. Cttee, BAAS, 1976-. MIBiol 1965. *Publications:* (ed) Journeys in Belief, 1968; What is Science For?, 1973; Magnificent Microbes, 1976; Invisible Allies, 1976; Atoms and Humours, 1978; numerous articles in scientific and general press on microbiology, and other scientific topics; research papers in Jl of General Microbiology, etc, mostly on microbial biochemistry. *Recreation:* playing Scottish traditional music, collecting old books. *Address:* 81 Falmouth Road, Chelmsford, Essex. *T:* Chelmsford 58421.

DIXON, Cecil Edith Mary, MBE 1939; formerly Professor of Piano and Accompaniment, RCM, retired; *b* 27 Nov.; *d* of James Dickson and Margaret Emily Dixon. *Educ:* New Zealand and Australia. Was on the original staff of the BBC, remained there until Sept. 1943; toured for CEMA as a free-lance pianist till 1946; studied piano under Herbert Sharpe and the Royal College of Music and later with Tobias Matthay. *Recreations:* dogs and country walks. *Address:* 17 Milner Street, SW3 2QB. *T:* 01-589 0030.

DIXON, Sir (Francis Wilfred) Peter, KBE 1959 (CBE 1952); MB, BS; FRCS; Air Vice-Marshal retired; Consultant in Surgery to the RAF, retired 1966; *b* 4 Oct. 1907; *s* of late Frederick Henry Dixon, New Norfolk, Tas.; *m* 1940, Pamela Ruby, *d* of late Brig. Charles C. Russell, MC, RA (Retd), London; two *s* one *d*. *Educ:* Newman Coll.; Melbourne Univ. MB, BS, Melbourne, 1930; FRCS Ed. 1937; FRCS 1949; DO Oxford, 1936. House Surgeon, St Vincent's Hosp., Melbourne. Joined RAF 1930; Wing-Comdr 1943; served War of 1939-45 (despatches); Aden, Normandy, SW Pacific; Air Cdre 1949; Air Vice-Marshal, 1957. Civilian Consultant in Surgery, RAF, 1966-. Lady Cade Medal, RCS, 1963. *Publications:* contribs to medical journals. *Recreation:* sailing. *Address:* Hill House, Snape Bridge, near Woodbridge, Suffolk. *T:* Snape 404.

DIXON, Guy Holford, JP; Barrister-at-Law; a Deputy Circuit Judge, since 1975, and honorary Recorder of Newark-on-Trent, since 1972; *b* 20 March 1902; *s* of late Dr Montague Dixon, Melton Mowbray; unmarried. *Educ:* Abbotsholme Sch., Derbs; Repton Sch.; University Coll., Oxford. BA (History) Oxon, 1925. Called to the Bar, Inner Temple, 1929. Recorder of Newark-on-Trent, 1965-71; Deputy Chairman: Leics QS, 1960-71; Northampton County QS, 1966-71; a Recorder, 1972-75. Lay Canon, Leicester Cathedral, 1962. JP Leics, 1960. *Recreation:* looking at and collecting pictures. *Address:* The Old Rectory, Brampton Ash, Market Harborough, Leics. *T:* Dingley 200; Burton Overy, Leics. *T:* Great Glen 2274. *Club:* Reform.

DIXON, Jack Shawcross, OBE 1969; HM Diplomatic Service, retired 1976; b 8 March 1918; s of Herbert Dixon and Helen (née Woollacott); m 1941, Ida Hewkin; one d. Educ: Oldham Hulme Grammar Sch.; London Sch. of Economics (BScEcon). Served in Royal Welch Fusiliers and RAOC attached Indian Army, 1940-46. Colonial Office, 1948; entered HM Foreign (subseq. Diplomatic) Service, 1949; FO, 1949; HM Political Agency, Kuwait, 1950; Rep. of Polit. Agent, Mina al Ahmadi, 1951; FO, 1952; 1st Sec., Singapore, 1956; HM Consul, Barcelona, 1959; FO, 1962; 1st Sec., Rome, 1966; FCO, 1971; Head of Treaty and Nationality Dept, FCO, 1973-76. Recreations: observing wildlife, photographing butterflies, philately. Address: 26 Brook Court, Meads Road, Eastbourne, E Sussex BN20 7PY. Club: Royal Commonwealth Society.

DIXON, Sir John George, 3rd Bt cr 1919; b 17 Sept. 1911; s of Sir John Dixon, 2nd Bt and Gwendolen Anne (d 1974), d of Sir Joseph Layton Elmes Spearman, 2nd Bt; S father, 1976; m 1947, Caroline, d of late Charles Theodore Hiltermann; one d. Educ: Cranleigh. Heir: b Nigel Dixon, Captain RN, retd [b 28 Feb. 1920; m 1948, Margaret Josephine, d of late M. J. Collett; one s]. Address: Avenue des Mousquetaires 19, La Tour de Peilz, Vaud, Switzerland.

DIXON, Jon Edmund, CMG 1975; Under Secretary, Ministry of Agriculture, Fisheries and Food, since 1971; b 19 Nov. 1928; e s of Edmund Joseph Claude and Gwendoline Alice Dixon; m 1953, Betty Edith Stone; two s two d. Educ: St Paul's Sch., West Kensington; Peterhouse, Cambridge. Natural Sciences Tripos Part I and Part II (Physiology). Asst Principal, Min. of Agric. and Fisheries, 1952; Private Sec. to successive Parliamentary Secretaries, 1955-58; Principal, 1958; Asst Sec., 1966; Under-Sec., 1971; Minister in UK Delegn, subseq. Office of Permanent Rep., to EEC, 1972-75. Recreations: musical composition, oil painting, carpentry, gardening, walking. Address: Ministry of Agriculture, Fisheries and Food, Whitehall Place, SW1.

DIXON, Prof. Kendal Cartwright, MA, MD, PhD, FRCPath; Professor of Cellular Pathology, University of Cambridge, since 1973; Fellow of King's College, Cambridge, since 1937; b 16 Feb. 1911; s of late Prof. Henry H. Dixon, ScD, FRS, Dublin Univ., and Dorothea, d of late Sir John Franks, CB, Blackrock, Co. Dublin; m 1938, Anne, d of late F. D. Darley, Stillorgan, Co. Dublin; one s one d. Educ: St Stephen's Green Sch., Dublin; Haileybury; Trinity Coll., Dublin; King's Coll., Cambridge (Scholar); Dun's Hosp., Dublin; St Bartholomew's Hosp., London. 1st cl. Pt 1 1932, 1st cl. Pt 2 (Biochem.) 1933, Nat. Scis Tripos Cantab; MB, BChir Cantab 1939. Asst to Prof. of Physiol., Dublin Univ., 1936; RAMC, 1940-45, Specialist in Pathology; Univ. of Cambridge: Official Fellow of King's Coll., 1945; Univ. Demonstrator in Chem. Path., 1946, Lectr 1949; Tutor for Advanced Students, King's Coll., 1951-59; Dir of Studies in Medicine, King's Coll., 1959-73; Reader in Cytopathology, 1962-73. Mem. European Soc. Pathology. Publications: chapters in books and articles in med. jls principally on cellular disorder and death, fatty change, and neuronal metabolism. Recreation: the mountains of Kerry. Address: King's College, Cambridge. Clubs: Kildare Street and University (Dublin); Dooks Golf.

DIXON, Malcolm, FRS 1942; MA, PhD, ScD Cantab; Emeritus Professor of Enzyme Biochemistry, Cambridge University, since 1966; b 18 April 1899; s of Allick Page Dixon and Caroline Dewe Dixon (née Mathews). Educ: Emmanuel Coll., Cambridge. BA 1920; began research in biochemistry under Sir F. G. Hopkins, 1921; 1851 Exhibition Senior Student, 1924-27; Senior Demonstrator in Biochemistry, University of Cambridge, 1923-27; University Lecturer in Biochemistry, 1928-44; Reader in Enzyme Biochemistry, Cambridge University, 1945-65; Prof. of Enzyme Biochemistry, 1966; Dir of Sub-Dept of Enzyme Biochemistry, Cambridge Univ., 1945-66; Fellow of King's Coll., Cambridge, 1950-66, Hon. Fellow, 1968-. Pres. of the Commission on Enzymes of the Internat. Union of Biochemistry, 1956-61. Publications: Manometric Methods, 1934, 3rd edn 1951; Multi-enzyme Systems, 1949; Enzymes (with Prof. E. C. Webb), 1958, 2nd edn 1964 (also Russian, Japanese and Italian edns); numerous papers dealing with the subject of enzymes, with special reference to biological oxidation processes and cell-respiration. Recreation: music. Address: Biochemical Laboratory, Cambridge. T: Cambridge 51781. Club: Athenæum.

DIXON, Margaret Rumer H.; see Haynes Dixon.

DIXON, Michael George, OBE 1964; Chief Passport Officer, Foreign and Commonwealth Office, since 1967; b 10 March 1920; s of Sidney Wilfrid and Elsie Dixon. Educ: Enfield Grammar Sch. Foreign Office, 1937. HM Forces, 1940-46

(POW, Far East). Recreation: gardening. Address: 9 Ridge Crest, Enfield, Mddx. T: 01-363 3408.

DIXON, Sir Peter; see Dixon, Sir (F. W.) P.

DIXON, Peter Vibart; Press Secretary and Head of Information Division, HM Treasury, since 1975; b 16 July 1932; s of Meredith Vibart Dixon and Phyllis Joan (née Hemingway); m 1955, Elizabeth Anne Howie Davison; three s. Educ: Summer Fields; Radley Coll.; King's Coll., Cambridge (BA Classics and Law 1955, MA 1959). Royal Artillery, 1951-52. Asst Principal, HM Treasury, 1955; Office of Lord Privy Seal, 1956; Treasury, 1956-62: Private Sec. to Economic Sec., 1959; Principal, 1960; Colonial Office, 1963; CS Selection Bd, 1964-65; Treasury, 1965-72, Asst Sec., 1969; Counsellor (Economic), HM Embassy, Washington, 1972-75. Mem. Exec. Council, RIPA. Address: 17 Lauriston Road, Wimbledon SW19 4TJ. T: 01-946 8931. Club: National Economists (Washington, DC).

DIXON, Piers; Stockbroker; b 29 Dec. 1928; s of late Sir Pierson Dixon, GCMG, CB (British Ambassador in New York and Paris) and of Lady (Ismene) Dixon; m 1st, 1960, Edwina (marr. diss. 1973), d of Rt Hon. Lord Duncan-Sandys, qv; two s; 2nd, 1976, Janet, d of R. D. Aiyar, FRCS, and widow of 5th Earl Cowley. Educ: Eton (schol.); Magdalene Coll., Cambridge (exhibnr); Harvard Business Sch. Grenadier Guards, 1948. Calvin Bullock, investment bankers, New York and London, 1954; Philip Hill, Higginson, merchant bankers, 1958; S. G. Warburg and Co., merchant bankers, 1961; Sheppards and Chase, stockbrokers, 1964-; Underwriting Mem. of Lloyd's. Sponsor, Centre for Policy Studies, 1976-. Contested (C) Brixton, 1966; MP (C) Truro, 1970-Sept. 1974; Sec., Cons. Backbenchers' Finance Cttee, 1970-71, Vice-Chm., 1972-74; sponsor of Rehabilitation of Offenders Act, 1974. Publications: Double Diploma, 1968; Cornish Names, 1973. Recreations: tennis, squash, modern history. Address: 22 Ponsonby Terrace, SW1. T: 01-828 6166. Clubs: Brooks's, Pratt's, City University.

DIXON, Maj.-Gen. Roy Laurence Cayley, CB 1977; MC 1944; Chief of Staff, Allied Forces, Northern Europe, since 1977; b 19 Sept. 1924; s of late Lt-Col S. F. Dixon, MC and of Mrs S. F. Dixon, Mattingley, Hants. Educ: Haileybury; Edinburgh Univ. Commnd Royal Tank Regt, 1944; served in armd units and on staff; psc 1956; Instructor, Staff Coll., 1961-64; comd 5th Royal Tank Regt, 1966-67; Royal Coll. of Defence Studies, 1971; Comdr Royal Armd Corps, Germany, 1968-70; qual. helicopter pilot, 1973; Dir, Army Air Corps, 1974-76. Publications: articles in mil. jls. Recreations: ski-ing, sailing, theatre, music. Address: c/o Lloyds Bank Ltd, Cox's and King's Branch, 6 Pall Mall, SW1Y 5NH. Club: Army and Navy.

DIXON, Stanley; Chairman, Midland-Yorkshire Tar Distillers Ltd, 1968-71; b 12 Aug. 1900; m 1936, Ella Margaret Hogg; two s. Educ: Leeds Grammar Sch.; Queen's Coll., Oxford. Articled to Leather & Veale, Chartered Accountants in Leeds, 1924-27; Manager, Leather & Veale (later Peat, Marwick, Mitchell & Co.), Leeds, 1927-35; Sec., Midland Tar Distillers Ltd, 1935-66; Dir, Midland Tar Distillers Ltd (later Midland-Yorkshire Holdings Ltd), 1943-71. Pres., Inst. of Chartered Accountants in England and Wales, 1968-69. Hon. DSocSc Birmingham, 1972. Publications: The Case for Marginal Costing, 1967; The Art of Chairing a Meeting, 1975. Recreations: Church affairs, gardening and music. Address: 83 Norton Road, Stourbridge, West Midlands DY8 2TB. T: Stourbridge 5672.

DIXON, Group Captain William Michael, CBE 1972; DSO 1943; DFC 1941; AFC 1958; Director of Aircraft Projects (RAF), Ministry of Defence, 1972-75; b 29 July 1920; s of late William Michael Dixon; m 1944, Mary Margaret (d 1957), d of late William Alexander Spence, MC, MM; three s. Educ: Hartlepool. Served War of 1939-45, Bomber Comd; Air Staff, Rhodesian Air Trng Gp, 1946-49; psa 1949; comd No 2 (Bomber) Sqdn RAAF, 1952-55; comd No 192 Sqdn RAF, 1955-58; jssc 1958; comd RAF Feltwell, 1961-63; Sen. Officer Admin No 1 (Bomber) Gp, 1963-66; Sen. Personnel SO HQ Air Support Comd, 1966-68; DCAS, Royal Malaysian Air Force, 1968-73; ADC to the Queen, 1968-73. Recreation: natural history. Address: Lower Farm, Sutton, Stanton Harcourt, Oxford. T: Oxford 881553. Club: Royal Air Force.

DIXON-NUTTALL, Major William Francis, DSO 1916; TD; late RE (TF); JP; retired as Director United Glass Ltd, 8 Leicester Street, WC2 (1926-54), Dec. 1954; Commissioner for Income Tax; e s of late F. R. Dixon-Nuttall, JP; m 1917, Gladys Lena (d 1975) o d of W. Henry Gregory, Caldecott, Aughton, and Glenorchy Lodge, Dalmally; one s. Address: Esher Place Avenue, Esher, Surrey. Club: Junior Carlton.

DOBB, Erlam Stanley, CB 1963; TD; *b* 16 Aug. 1910; *m* 1937, Margaret Williams; no *c. Educ:* Ruthin; University Coll. of N Wales. Chartered Surveyor and Land Agent, Anglesey, Denbigh and Merioneth, 1930-35; Asst Land Comr, to Dir, Agricultural Land Service, MAFF, 1935-70; a Dep. Dir-Gen., Agricl Develt and Adv. Service, MAFF, 1971-73; Dir-Gen., 1973-75. Mem., ARC, 1973-75; Vice-Chm., Adv. Council for Agriculture and Horticulture in England and Wales, 1974-75. Chm. Trustees, T. P. Price Charity, Markshall Estate, Essex. Governor, Royal Agricultural College, 1960-75. Royal Welch Fusiliers (TA), 1938-46, Major. FRICS; FRAgS. *Publications:* professional contributions to journals of learned societies. *Recreations:* golf, gardening. *Address:* Churchgate, Westerham, Kent. *T:* Westerham 62294. *Clubs:* Farmers'; Crowborough Beacon Golf, Limpsfield Chart Golf.

DOBBIE, Mitchell Macdonald, CB 1951; *b* 2 Oct. 1901; *s* of James Dobbie, Ayr, and Jean Macdonald; *m* 1931, Evelyn Willison (*d* 1967), *e d* of R. W. Grieve, Edinburgh. *Educ:* Ayr Academy; University of Edinburgh (MA, LLB). Called to Bar, Gray's Inn, 1927. Entered Inland Revenue Dept, 1925; Ministry of Labour, 1928; Private Sec. to Parl. Sec., 1934; transferred to Dept of Health for Scotland, 1938; Asst Sec., 1939; Principal Asst Sec., 1945; seconded to Ministry of Home Security as Principal Officer, Scotland Civil Defence Region, 1943-45; Under-Sec., Min. of Housing and Local Govt, 1948; Principal Establishment Officer, 1956-63; retd 1963, and re-employed in Scottish Development Dept, 1963-66; Secretary of Commissions for Scotland, 1966-72. JP City of Edinburgh. *Address:* 13 Eton Terrace, Edinburgh EH4 1QD. *T:* 031-332 3150. *Clubs:* New, Scottish Arts (Edinburgh).

DOBBS, Prof. (Edwin) Roland, PhD, DSc; Hildred Carlile Professor of Physics, University of London, and Head of Department of Physics, Bedford College, since 1973; *b* 2 Dec. 1924; *s* of late A. Edwin Dobbs, AMIMechE, and Harriet Wright; *m* 1947, Dorothy Helena Jeeves, *o d* of Alderman A. F. T. Jeeves, Stamford, Lincs; two *s* one *d. Educ:* Queen Elizabeth's Sch., Barnet; University College London. BSc Hons 1943, PhD 1949; DSc London 1977; FInstP 1964; FIOA 1977. Temp. Exptl Officer, Admiralty Signal Estabt, Witley, 1943-46; DSIR Res. Student, UCL, 1946-49; Lectr in Physics, QMC, Univ. of London, 1949-58; Res. Associate in Applied Maths, 1958-59, Associate Prof. of Physics, 1959-60, Brown Univ., USA; Mem., Gonville and Caius Coll., Cambridge, 1960-; AEI Fellow, Cavendish Lab., Univ. of Cambridge, 1960-64; Prof. and Head of Dept of Physics, Univ. of Lancaster, 1964-73. Mem., Nuclear Physics Bd, SRC, 1974-77. Visiting Professor: Brown Univ., 1966; Wayne State Univ., 1969; Univ. of Tokyo, 1977. Pres., Inst. of Acoustics, 1976-78; Hon. Sec., Inst. of Physics, 1976-. Hon. Fellow, Indian Cryogenics Council, 1977. *Publications:* research papers on metals and superconductors in Procs of Royal Soc., and on solid state physics and acoustics in Jl of Physics, Physical Rev. Letters, Physical Acoustics, etc. *Recreations:* travel, theatre, talking shop. *Address:* 20 North Gate, Prince Albert Road, St John's Wood, NW8 7RE. *T:* 01-722 6650.

DOBBS, Joseph Alfred, CMG 1972; OBE 1957 (MBE 1945); TD 1945; HM Diplomatic Service, retired; *b* Abbeyleix, Ireland, 22 Dec. 1914; *s* of John L. Dobbs and Ruby (*née* Gillespie); *m* 1949, Marie, *d* of Reginald Francis Catton, Sydney; four *s. Educ:* Worksop Coll.; Trinity Hall, Cambridge (Schol). Pres., Cambridge Union Soc., 1936. Served War of 1939-45, Major, Royal Artillery (despatches). Joined Foreign Office, 1946; served Moscow, 1947-51, 1954-57 and 1965-68; FO, 1951-54; Delhi, 1957-61; Warsaw, 1961-64; Rome, 1964-65; Consul-Gen., Zagreb, 1969-70; Minister, Moscow, 1971-74. *Recreations:* riding, gardening. *Address:* The Coach House, Charlton Musgrove, Wincanton, Somerset BA9 8ES. *T:* Wincanton 33356.

DOBBS, Mattiwilda; Order of North Star (Sweden), 1954; opera singer (coloratura soprano); *b* Atlanta, Ga, USA; *d* of John Wesley and Irene Dobbs; *m* 1957, Bengt Janzon, Dir. of Information, Nat. Ministry of Health and Welfare, Sweden; no *c. Educ:* Spelman Coll., USA (BA); Columbia Univ., USA (MA). Studied voice in NY with Lotte Leonard, 1946-50; special coaching Paris with Pierre Bernac, 1950-52. Marian Anderson Schol., 1948; John Hay Whitney Schol., 1950; 1st prize in singing, Internat. Comp., Geneva Conservatory of Music, 1951. Appeared Royal Dutch Opera, Holland Festival, 1952. Recitals, Sweden, Paris, Holland, 1952; appeared in opera at La Scala, Milan, 1953; Concerts, England and Continent, 1953; Glyndebourne Opera, 1953-54, 1956, 1961; Covent Garden Opera, 1953, 1954, 1956, 1958; command performance, Covent Garden, 1954. Annual concert tours: US, 1954-; Australia, New Zealand, 1955, 1959, and 1968; Israel, 1957 and 1959; USSR concerts and opera (Bolshoi Theater), 1959; San Francisco Opera, 1955; début Metropolitan Opera, 1956; there annually, 1956-. Appearances Hamburg State Opera, 1961-63; Royal Swedish Opera, 1957 and subseq. annually; Norwegian and Finnish Operas, 1957-64. Vis. Prof., Univ. of Texas at Austin, 1973-74; Prof., Univ. of Illinois, 1975; Prof., Univ. of Georgia, 1976-77. *Address:* Apartment 802, 130 26th Street NW, Atlanta, Ga 30309, USA.

DOBBS, Captain Richard Arthur Frederick; Lord-Lieutenant of County Antrim, 1975 (HM Lieutenant for County Antrim, 1959-75); *b* 2 April 1919; *s* of Senator Major Arthur F. Dobbs, DL, of Castle Dobbs, and Hylda Louisa Dobbs; *m* 1953, Carola Day, *d* of Christopher Clarkson, Old Lyme, Conn, USA; four *s* one *d. Educ:* Eton; Magdalene Coll., Cambridge (MA). Served War: 2nd Lieut Irish Guards (Supp. Reserve), 1939; Captain 1943. Called to Bar, Lincoln's Inn, 1947; Member, Midland Circuit, 1951-55. *Address:* Castle Dobbs, Carrickfergus, County Antrim, N Ireland. *T:* Whitehead 2238. *Club:* Cavalry and Guards.

DOBBS, Richard Heyworth, MD, FRCP; Consulting Pædiatrician: London Hospital, 1946-71; Queen Elizabeth Hospital for Children, 1939-71; Southend Hospital Group, 1946-71; Professor of Paediatrics, Ahmadu Bello University, Nigeria, since 1972; *b* 10 May 1905; of British parentage; *m* 1930, Phyllis Leon; one *s* one *d. Educ:* Bedales Sch.; Downing Coll., Cambridge; London Hosp. MRCS, LRCP 1930; MB Cantab 1931; MD 1941; MRCP 1936; FRCP 1947. Pres., British Paediatric Assoc., 1970. Paediatrician, Internat. Grenfell Assoc., Newfoundland, Jan.-June 1972. Editor, Archives of Disease in Childhood, 1954-69. *Publications:* (in collab.) Midwifery, 1940, 5th edn 1962; Leigh's Subacute Sclerosing Encephalopathy; Hyperammonaemia, 1969. *Recreations:* gardening and travel. *Address:* 3 Oakhill Way, Hampstead, NW3. *T:* 01-435 4010; Department of Paediatrics, Ahmadu Bello University, Zaria, Nigeria.

DOBBS, Roland; *see* Dobbs, E. R.

DOBINSON, Prof. Charles Henry, CMG 1969; Professor of Education, University of Reading, 1951-68, now Emeritus; *b* 7 Oct. 1903; *s* of late Henry Mark Dobinson, and late Florence Gertrude (*née* Agate); *m* 1929, Dorothy Maude Shooter; one *s* one *d. Educ:* Brockley County Grammar Sch., London; Wadham Coll., Oxford (MA). 2nd Cl. Hons Hon. Mods Maths; 1st Cl. Hons Oxford Hon. Sch. of Nat. Science (Geology); Diploma in Educn, Oxford; BSc London. Biology Master, Mill Hill Sch., 1927-33; Headmaster, King Edward VI Grammar Sch., Five Ways, Birmingham, 1933-45; Reader in Education, Oxford Univ., 1945-51. An adviser to UK first delegation to Unesco, 1946; Chm. Educn Cttee, Nat. Fedn of Community Assocs, 1949-62; a Governor of Unesco Internat. Inst. of Educn, Hamburg, 1950-65; Member: Banjo Commn on Education in Western Region of Nigeria, 1960-61; Advisory Commn on Higher Teacher Training in the Sudan, 1964. Visiting Prof., Summer Schs of Syracuse, New York, 1950, Arkansas, 1950, 1952, 1967, Syracuse, 1955, 1957, Cornell, 1959, Alberta, 1960, Missouri, 1961, 1963, 1964, 1966, 1968, 1970, 1973, Calgary, 1969. FGS. *Publications:* (ed) Education in a Changing World, 1950; Technical Education for Adolescents, 1951; Schooling 1963-1970, 1963; Jean-Jacques Rousseau, 1969; (ed) Comenius, 1970; A Taste of Educational Philosophy, 1976; various school text-books between 1929 and 1966; articles in UK press, 1970-, on technical educn in France and Germany; articles in educational press of UK, USA, France and Sweden. *Recreations:* gardening and reading. *Address:* The Old Barn, Sonning Common, near Reading, Berks. *T:* Kidmore End 2191.

DOBREE, John Hatherley, MS, FRCS; Consultant in Ophthalmology, St Bartholomew's Hospital, London, EC1, since 1956; Senior Ophthalmic Surgeon, North Middlesex Hospital, N18, since 1947; *b* 25 April 1914; *s* of Hatherley Moor Dobree, OBE, and Muriel Dobree (*née* Hope); *m* 1941, Evelyn Maud Smyth; two *s. Educ:* Victoria Coll., Jersey; St Bartholomew's Hosp. MS London 1947; FRCS 1950. House Physician, Metropolitan Hosp., E8, 1938-39; House Surgeon, Western Ophthalm. Hosp., 1940. Served in RAMC, 1940-46, in MEF, as RMO and Ophthalmic Specialist. Chief Asst, Eye Dept, St Bartholomew's Hosp., 1946-51. FRSocMed (Past Sec., Sect. of Ophthalmology); Vice-Pres. and Past Hon. Sec. Ophthalmological Soc. of UK; Dep. Master, Oxford Ophth. Congress, 1976. *Publications:* The Retina, vol. x, in Sir Stewart Duke-Elder's System of Ophthalmology, 1967; (with E. S. Perkins) Differential Diagnosis of Fundus Conditions, 1971. *Recreations:* archaeology, walking. *Address:* 113 Harley Street, W1. *T:* 01-935 9189; 2 Nottingham Terrace, NW1. *T:* 01-486 6227.

DOBROSIELSKI, Marian, PhD Zürich; Banner of Labour, 1st Class 1975 (2nd Class 1973); Knight Cross of the Order of Polonia Restituta, 1964; Director, Polish Institute of International Affairs, since 1971; Ambassador ad personam, since 1973; *b* 25 March 1923; *s* of Stanislaw and Stefania Dobrosielski; *m* 1950; one *d. Educ:* Univ. of Zürich; Univ. of Warsaw. Served in Polish Army in France, War of 1939-45. With Min. of Foreign Affairs, 1948-; Polish Legation, Bern, 1948-50; Head of Section, Min. of Foreign Affairs, 1950-54; Asst Prof., Warsaw Univ. and Polish Acad. of Sciences, 1954-57; Mem. Polish delegn to UN Gen. Assembly, 1952, 1953, 1958, 1966, 1972-76. First Sec., Counsellor, Polish Embassy in Washington, 1958-64; Min. of Foreign Affairs: Counsellor to Minister, 1964-69; Acting Dir, Research Office, 1968-69; Polish Ambassador to London, 1969-71. Univ. of Warsaw: Associate Prof., 1966; Vice-Dean of Faculty of Philosophy, 1966-68; Dir, Inst. of Philosophy, 1971-73 (Chm. Scientific Council, 1969). Chm., Editorial Bd of Studia Filozoficzne, 1968-69; Sec., Polish Philos. Soc., 1955-57 and 1965-69. Mem. Polish United Workers Party (Sec. Party Org., Univ. of Warsaw, 1956-57, 1968-69); Chm., Polish Cttee for European Security and Co-operation, 1973- (Vice-Chm., 1971-73). Hon. Vice-Pres., Scottish-Polish Cultural Assoc., Glasgow, 1969-71; Chm., Polish delegn to 2nd stage Conf. on Security and Co-operation in Europe, 1973-75. *Publications:* A Basic Epistemological Principle of Logical Positivism, 1947; The Philosophical Pragmatism of C. S. Peirce, 1967; On some contemporary problems: Philosophy, Ideology, Politics, 1970; (trans. and introd) Selection of Aphorisms of G. C. Lichtenberg, Oscar Wilde, Karl Kraus, M. von Ebner-Eschenbach, 4 vols, 1970-74; On the Theory and Practice of Peaceful Coexistence, 1976; numerous articles on philosophy and internat. problems in professional jls. *Recreation:* tennis. *Address:* Polish Institute of International Affairs, ul Warecka 1A, Warszawa, Poland.

DOBRY, George Leon Severyn, CBE 1977; QC 1969; a Recorder of the Crown Court, since 1977; *b* 1 Nov. 1918; *m* 1948, Margaret Headley Smith, *e d* of late Joseph Quartus Smith, JP, Woolpits, Saling, Essex; two *d. Educ:* Edinburgh Univ. (MA). Served War of 1939-45: Army, 1939-42; Air Force, 1942-46. Called to Bar, Inner Temple, 1946; Bencher 1977. Mem. Council, Justice, 1956-68. Adviser to Sec. of State for Environment and Sec. of State for Wales on Develt Control, 1973-75; Co-opted Mem., Docklands Jt Cttee, 1974-76. *Publications:* Woodfall's Law of Landlord and Tenant, 25th edition (one of the Editors), 1952; Blundell and Dobry, Town and Country Planning, 1962; Blundell and Dobry Planning Appeals and Inquiries, 1962, 2nd edn, 1970; Hill and Redman, Landlord and Tenant (Cons. Editor), 16th edn, 1976; Review of the Development Control System (Interim Report), 1974 (Final Report), 1975; Control of Demolition, 1974; (ed jtly) Development Gains Tax, 1975; (Gen. Editor) Encyclopedia of Development Law, 1976. *Address:* 2 Paper Buildings, Temple, EC4. *T:* 01-353 5835; (Residential Chambers) 1 Harcourt Buildings, Temple, EC4. *T:* 01-583 6208. *Clubs:* Travellers', Carlton.

DOBSON, Maj.-Gen. Anthony Henry George, CB 1968; OBE 1953; MC 1944; BA Cantab; Inspector, Department of the Environment (Housing and Planning), since 1969; *b* 15 Dec. 1911; *s* of late Col Arthur Curtis Dobson, DSO, Royal Engineers, and late Susanna (*née* Oppenheim); *m* 1945, Nellie Homberger; two *s* two *d. Educ:* Cheltenham Coll.; Royal Military Academy, Woolwich; Clare Coll., Cambridge. Commissioned Royal Engineers, 1931; hons degree (mech. science), Cambridge, 1934; service in UK, 1934-37; seconded to RAF for survey duties, Iraq, 1938-39. Served War of 1939-45: Middle East (Egypt, Turkey, Iraq), 1939-42; Prisoner of War, Italy, 1942-43; interned in Switzerland after escape, 1944; North-West Europe (Holland and Germany), 1945. Germany, 1945-50; Manpower planning Dept, War Office, 1950-53; in comd, Engineer Regt, Hong Kong, 1953-56; Engr branch, War Office, 1956-59; Chief Engr, HQ Eastern Comd, UK, 1959-62; DQMG, HQ BAOR, 1962-64; Chief Engr, HQ North AG/BAOR, 1964-67, retd. Lt-Col 1945; Col 1956; Brig. 1959; Maj.-Gen. 1964. *Recreations:* travel, gardening. *Address:* Ramillies, Compton Way, Moor Park, Farnham, Surrey. *T:* Runfold 2350. *Clubs:* Army and Navy, Ski Club of Great Britain; Kandahar Ski.

DOBSON, Christopher Selby Austin, CBE 1976; FSA; Librarian, House of Lords, 1956-77; *b* 25 Aug. 1916; *s* of late Alban Tabor Austin Dobson, CB, CVO, CBE; *m* 1941, Helen Broughton, *d* of late Capt. E. B. Turner, Holyhead; one *s* one *d. Educ:* Clifton Coll.; Emmanuel Coll., Cambridge (BA). With National Council of Social Service, 1938-39. Served War of 1939-45, Lieut Middx Regt (despatches). Asst Principal (Temp.), Ministry of Education, 1946-47; Asst Librarian, House of Lords, 1947-56.

Publication: (ed) Oxfordshire Protestation Returns 1641-42, 1955. *Recreations:* collecting books, mezzotints, stamps, etc. *Address:* 60 Homefield Road, Bromley, Kent BR1 3AL. *T:* 01-460 2303. *Clubs:* Athenæum; (Hon.) Rowfant (Cleveland).

DOBSON, Cowan; RBA, FRSA; Hon. RP; portrait painter; *s* of late H. J. Dobson, RCA; *m* 1931, Phyllis, *e d* of Lancelot Bowyer. Studied Edinburgh, Paris, London. Exhibited RA for over 50 years, and in leading galleries throughout the world. Commissioned by Govt to paint RAF VCs of War of 1914-18, now in Imperial War Museum. *Works include:* King Haakon; King Olaf; King George of Greece; Adm. Beatty; Amy Johnston; artist's wife Phyllis; Earl Atlee; King and Queen of Iraq; Duke of Argyll, and many civic dignitaries and industrialists. *Recreation:* magic. *Address:* Studio, 62 South Edwardes Square, W8. *T:* 01-602 6361. *Club:* Hurlingham.

DOBSON, Sir Denis (William), KCB 1969 (CB 1959); OBE 1945; QC 1971; Clerk of the Crown in Chancery and Permanent Secretary to the Lord Chancellor, 1968-77; *b* 17 Oct. 1908; *s* of late William Gordon Dobson, Newcastle upon Tyne; *m* 1st, 1934, Thelma (marr. diss. 1947), *d* of Charles Swinburne, Newcastle upon Tyne; one *s* one *d* ; 2nd, 1948, Mary Elizabeth, *d* of J. A. Allen, Haywards Heath; two *s* one *d. Educ:* Charterhouse; Trinity Coll., Cambridge (MA, LLB). Solicitor, 1933. Served in RAF, 1940-45 (Desert Air Force, 1942-45). Called to the Bar, Middle Temple, 1951; Bencher, 1968. Dep. Clerk of the Crown in Chancery and Asst Permanent Sec. to Lord Chancellor, 1954-68. Mem., Adv. Council on Public Records, 1977-. *Address:* 50 Egerton Crescent, SW3. *T:* 01-589 7990. *Club:* Athenæum.

DOBSON, Prof. Eric John, MA, DPhil Oxon; FBA 1973; Professor of English Language, Oxford University, since 1964; *b* 16 Aug. 1913; *o s* of John and Lottie Frances Dobson; *m* 1940, Francis Margaret Stinton; two *s* one *d. Educ:* North Sydney High Sch.; Wesley Coll., Sydney Univ.; Merton Coll., Oxford. BA (1st cl. Hons English) Sydney, 1934; 1st in Final Hon. Sch. of English 1937, DPhil 1951, Oxford. Tutor in English, Sydney Univ., 1934-35; Wentworth Travelling Fellow of Sydney Univ., 1935-38; Harmsworth Sen. Schol. of Merton Coll., 1938-40; Lecturer in English, University of Reading, 1940-48. Served in Intelligence Div., Naval Staff, Admiralty, 1943-45. Lecturer in English, Jesus Coll. and St Edmund Hall, Oxford, 1948-54; Reader in English Lang., Oxford Univ., 1954-64 (title of Prof. from 1960); Professorial Fellow of Jesus Coll., Oxford, 1954-. Hon. Treas., Philological Soc., 1974-. *Publications:* English Pronunciation 1500-1700, 1957, 2nd edn 1968; The Phonetic Writings of Robert Robinson, 1957; Edition of Hymn to the Virgin in Trans. of Cymmrodorion Soc., 1954; The Affiliations of the MSS of Ancrene Wisse, in English and Medieval Studies, 1962; The Date and Composition of Ancrene Wisse (Gollancz Memorial Lecture, Brit. Acad., 1966); The English Text of the Ancrene Riwle (MS Cleopatra C. vi), 1972; Moralities on the Gospels, 1975; The Origins of Ancrene Wisse, 1976; (with F. Ll. Harrison) Medieval English Songs, 1977; articles and reviews in journals. *Address:* 9 Davenant Road, Oxford. *T:* Oxford 56222.

DOBSON, Commodore John Petter, CBE 1961; DSC 1940; RD 1940; RNR (retired); *b* 2 Sept. 1901; *s* of Lieut-Comdr John Dobson, RNR and Alice Martha (*née* Petter); *m* 1942, Edith Agnes Ferguson; one *d. Educ:* Middlesbrough High Sch.; Liverpool Coll.; HMS Conway. Midshipman, RNR, 1917; Cadet, Canadian Pacific, 1919; Submarines, 1924; Navigator, RMS Empress of Australia; with Royal trip to Canada and US; subsequently called up, 1939. Minesweeping, 1939-42; Cdre of Convoys, 1942-44, including Normandy Landings; Admiralty Berthing Officer, Sydney, NSW, 1944-45. In command CPS, 1946-61; Master, Empress of Canada (Flagship of Canadian Pacific Steamships Ltd), 1961-62; retired, 1962. Mem., Hon. Company of Master Mariners. Freeman and Liveryman of City of London. *Address:* Sea View Cottage, Sandsend, Whitby, North Yorks. *T:* Sandsend 222. *Club:* Whitby Conservative.

DOBSON, Sir Patrick John H.; *see* Howard-Dobson.

DOBSON, Raymond Francis Harvey; Director of Industrial Relations Personnel and Services, British Caledonian Airways, since 1970; *b* 26 April 1925; *s* of Tom Noel Dobson; *m* 1947, Vivienne Joyce Martin; three *s* one *d. Educ:* Purbrook Park Sch., Portsmouth. Radio Officer, Merchant Navy, 1940-47; Post Office, 1947-66. Trade Union Official, Postal Workers' Union, 1950-66 (Mem. Nat. Exec., 1960-66). MP (Lab) Bristol North-East, 1966-70; PPS, Min. of Technology, 1967-69; Asst Govt Whip, 1969-70; Member: Select Cttee of Estimates, 1966-67; Select Cttee for Science and Technology, 1969. Member: Board, Gambia Airways, 1974-77; Board, Sierra Leone Airways, 1974-; Board, Air Liberia, 1976-; Air Transport and Travel Ind. Trng

Board, 1973-. *Address:* Tanquards, Reigate Hill, Reigate, Surrey. *T:* Reigate 43914.

DOBSON, Sir Richard (Portway), Kt 1976; President, BAT Ltd, since 1976; Chairman, British Leyland Ltd, since 1976; *b* 11 Feb. 1914; *s* of Prof. J. F. Dobson; *m* 1946, Emily Margaret Carver; one step *d. Educ:* Clifton Coll.; King's Coll., Cambridge. Flt-Lt, RAF, 1941-45 (Pilot). Joined British American Tobacco Co. Ltd, 1935: served in China, 1936-40; China, Rhodesia and London, 1946-76; Dir, 1955; Dep. Chm., 1962; Vice-Chm., 1968; Chm., 1970-76. Director: Molins Ltd, 1970-; Commonwealth Development Finance, 1974-; Exxon Corporation (USA), 1975-; Davy International Ltd, 1975-; Foseco Minsep, 1976-; Lloyds Bank International, 1976-. Chm., British-North American Res. Assoc., 1976-. *Publication:* China Cycle, 1946. *Recreations:* fly fishing, golf. *Address:* 16 Marchmont Road, Richmond upon Thames, Surrey. *T:* 01-940 1504. *Clubs:* United Oxford & Cambridge University; Richmond Golf, Royal Wimbledon Golf.

DOCHERTY, Dr Daniel Joseph, JP; Manpower Services Commissioner since 1974; *b* 24 Oct. 1924; *s* of Michael Joseph Docherty and Ellen Stewart; *m* 1952, Dr Rosemary Catherine Kennedy; eight *s* two *d. Educ:* St Aloysius' Coll.; Anderson Coll. of Medicine; Glasgow Univ. LRCP, LRCS, LRFPS. Glasgow Town Councillor, 1959-75; Sen. Magistrate, City of Glasgow, 1964-65; Chm. of Police Cttee, 1967-68; Chm. of Educn Cttee, 1971-74. Mem. Council, Open Univ., 1972-75. JP Glasgow, 1961. *Recreation:* travel. *Address:* 26 Newlands Road, Glasgow G43 2JE. *T:* 041-632 5031.

DOCKER, Sir Bernard (Dudley Frank), KBE 1939; *b* 1896; *o s* of late Frank Dudley Docker, CB; *m* 1949, Norah, *widow* of Sir William Collins. *Educ:* Harrow. *Recreations:* golf, shooting, yachting. *Clubs:* Royal London Yacht; St Helier Yacht.

DOCKER, Rt. Rev. Ivor Colin; *see* Horsham, Bishop Suffragan of.

DODD, Air Vice-Marshal Frank Leslie, CBE 1968; DSO 1944; DFC 1945; AFC 1944 and Bars, 1955 and 1958; AE 1945; Administrator, MacRobert Trusts, since 1974; *b* 5 March 1919; *s* of Frank H. Dodd and Lillian (*née* Willis); *m* 1942, Joyce L. Banyard; one *s* three *d. Educ:* King Edward VI Sch., Stafford; Reading University. RAFVR, 1938; CFS course and Flying Instructor, 1940-44; No 544 Sqdn (photo-reconnaissance), 1944-46; CO 45 Sqdn (Beaufighters), 1947-48; CFS Staff and HQ Flying Trng Comd, 1948-52; pfc 1952-53; Chief Instructor CFS, 1953-55; psc 1955; CO 230 OCU Waddington (Vulcans), 1955-59; Gp Captain Trng HQ Bomber Comd, 1959-61; CO RAF Coningsby (Vulcans), 1961-63; idc 1964; AOC and Comdt CFS, 1965-68; MoD (Dir Estabs), 1968-70. Dir Gen., Linesman Project, 1970-74, retired. *Recreations:* golf, music. *Address:* The Lodge, Tarland, Aberdeenshire AB3 4TB. *T:* Tarland 304. *Clubs:* Royal Air Force; Royal Northern (Aberdeen).

DODD, Rev. Harold, MB, ChM (Liverpool), FRCS, LRCP; Hon. Curate, All Soul's Church, W1, 1970; Emeritus Surgeon to: St Mary's Hospital Group, Paddington; King George Hospital, Ilford; Royal Hospital, Richmond; Royal London Homoeopathic Hospital; *b* 13 March 1899; *e s* of Alfred Ledward Dodd and Annie Elizabeth Marshall; *m* 1945, Mary, *yr d* of late R. H. Bond; one *s. Educ:* University of Liverpool; Guy's Hosp. RAF (pilot), 1917-19; MB, ChB (Distinction in Surgery) Liverpool, 1922, O. T. Williams Prizeman for 1923; House Surgeon, House Physician, Surgical Tutor and Registrar, Liverpool Royal Infirmary, 1923-26; Asst Medical Superintendent, St Luke's Hosp., Chelsea, 1926-28; Resident Medical Officer, Royal Northern Hosp., N7, 1928-30. Past Pres., Assoc. of Consultants and Specialists of Reg. Bd Hosps. Fellow, Assoc. of Surgeons of Great Britain; FRSM (Ex-Pres. Section of Proctology). *Publications:* (with F. B. Cockett) Pathology and Surgery of the Veins of the Lower Limb, 1956, 2nd edn, 1976; surgical papers in medical journals. *Address:* 22 Campden Hill Gate, Duchess of Bedford's Walk, W8 7QH. *T:* 01-937 9297.

DODD, Prof. James Munro, DSc, PhD; FRS 1975; FRSE. Professor of Zoology, University College of North Wales, since 1968; *b* 26 May 1915; *m* 1951, Margaret Helen Ingram Macaulay (*née* Greig), BSc (Aberdeen), PhD (Harvard); three *s. Educ:* The White House Sch., Brampton, Cumberland; Univ. of Liverpool. BSc hons (Cl. 1) 1937; DipEd 1938. PhD St Andrews, 1953; DSc St Andrews, 1968. Biology Master, Cardigan Grammar Sch., 1938-40. Royal Air Force (Navigator and Staff Navigator), 1940-46. Asst in Zoology, Univ. of Aberdeen, 1946-47; Lectr in Zoology, Univ. of St Andrews, in charge of Gatty Marine Laboratory, 1947-57; Reader in Zoology, Univ. of St Andrews, and Dir of Gatty Marine Laboratory, 1957-60; Prof. of Zoology, Leeds Univ., 1960-68. Chm., British Nat. Cttee for Biology, 1972-. Trustee, BM (Natural History), 1975-. FRSE 1957. Editor-in-Chief, General and Comparative Endocrinology. *Publications:* contributor to Marshall's Physiology of Reproduction, The Thyroid Gland, The Pituitary Gland, and to zoological and endocrinological jls. *Recreations:* fishing, photography, music. *Address:* Weirglodd Wen, Bulkeley Road, Bangor, Gwynedd.

DODD, Kenneth Arthur, (Ken Dodd); professional entertainer, comedian, singer and actor, since 1957; *b* 1931; *s* of Arthur and Sarah Dodd; unmarried. *Educ:* Holt High Sch., Liverpool. Frequently appears at the Palladium, London, etc. Pantomime, Robinson Crusoe, Coventry Theatre, 1969-70; Malvolio in Twelfth Night, Liverpool, 1971; HaHa, Liverpool, 1973. *Recreations:* racing, soccer, reading. *Address:* 76 Thomas Lane, Knotty Ash, Liverpool LI4 5NX.

DODDERIDGE, Morris, CBE 1974 (OBE 1962); British Council Representative, Rome, 1970-75, retired; *b* 17 Oct. 1915; *s* of Reginald William Dodderidge and Amy Andrew; *m* 1941, Esme Williams; two *s* one *d. Educ:* Hertford Grammar Sch.; King's Coll., London; Inst. Educn, London. BA 1st cl. hons English 1937; Brewer Prize for Lit.; Teachers Dip. 1938; DipEd 1952. Asst Master, Hele's Sch., Exeter, 1938-40. War of 1939-45, Royal Signals; served N Africa, Italy, Austria (Captain, despatches). Joined British Council, 1946: Dir of Studies, Milan, 1947-53; Rep., Norway, 1953-57; Teaching of English Liaison Officer, 1957-59; Dir, Recruitment Dept, 1959-64; Controller: Recruitment Div., 1964-66; Overseas Div. A, 1966-67; Home Div. I, 1967-68; Appts Div., 1968-70. *Publications:* Man on the Matterhorn, 1940; (with W. R. Lee) Time for a Song, 1965. *Recreations:* golf, swimming, viticulture. *Address:* 35 St Catharine's Road, Broxbourne, Herts. *T:* Hoddesdon 62339; Il Fossaccio, Canonica 77, Todi, Perugia, Italy.

DODDS, Denis George, CBE 1977; LLB (London); CompIEE; Solicitor; Chairman, Merseyside and North Wales Electricity Board, 1962-78; (Deputy Chairman, 1960-62); *b* 25 May 1913; *s* of Herbert Yeaman Dodds and Violet Katharine Dodds; *m* 1937, Muriel Reynolds Smith; two *s* three *d. Educ:* Rutherford Coll., Newcastle upon Tyne; King's Coll., Durham Univ. Asst Solicitor and Asst Town Clerk, Gateshead, 1936-41. Served Royal Navy (Lieut RNVR), 1941-46. Dep. Town Clerk and Dep. Clerk of the Peace, City of Cardiff, 1946-48; Sec., S Wales Electricity Board, 1948-56; Chief Industrial Relations Officer, CEA and Industrial Relations Adviser, Electricity Council, 1957-59. *Recreations:* music and gardening. *Address:* Arley, 27 Dowhills Road, Blundellsands, Liverpool L23 8SJ. *T:* 051-924 6001.

DODDS, Eric Robertson, MA Oxon; Hon. DLitt (Manchester, Dublin, Edinburgh, Birmingham, and Belfast); FBA; Corresponding Member of Academia Sinica, Bavarian Academy, American Academy of Arts and Sciences; Membre de l'Institut de France; Hon. Fellow, University College, Oxford; Hon. Student of Christ Church, Oxford; Regius Professor of Greek, University of Oxford, 1936-60; *b* 26 July 1893; *o s* of Robert Dodds, Headmaster of Banbridge Academy; *m* 1923, Annie (*d* 1973), *yr d* of late Rev. Canon A. D. Powell. *Educ:* Campbell Coll., Belfast; University Coll., Oxford. Lectr in Classics at University Coll., Reading, 1919-24; Prof. of Greek in the University of Birmingham, 1924-36. *Publications:* Select Passages Illustrative of Neoplatonism, 2 vols, 1923 and 1924; Thirty-two Poems, 1929; Proclus' Elements of Theology, 1933; Journal and Letters of Stephen MacKenna, 1936; Euripides' Bacchae, 1944; The Greeks and the Irrational, 1951 (Kenyon Medal, British Academy, 1971); Plato's Gorgias, 1959; Pagan and Christian in an Age of Anxiety, 1965; The Ancient Concept of Progress and other essays on Greek literature and belief, 1973; Missing Persons (autobiog.), 1977. *Recreation:* psychical research. *Address:* Cromwell's House, Old Marston, Oxford.

DODDS, George Christopher Buchanan, CMG 1977; Assistant Under-Secretary of State, Ministry of Defence, 1964-76; *b* 8 Oct. 1916; *o s* of George Hepple Dodds and Gladys Marion (*née* Ferguson), Newcastle upon Tyne; *m* 1944, Olive Florence Wilmot Ling; no *c. Educ:* Rugby; Gonville and Caius Coll., Cambridge (BA). Entered Secretary's Dept, Admiralty, 1939; Royal Marines, 1940-41; Private Sec. to Sec. of the Admiralty, 1941-43; Asst Private Sec. to Prime Minister, June-Aug. 1944; Asst Sec., 1951; idc, 1959. *Recreations:* bird-watching, walking, golf, bridge. *Address:* 5 Bryanston Square, W1. *T:* 01-262 2852. *Club:* Royal Mid-Surrey Golf.

DODDS, Gladys Helen, MD, FRCS, FRCSE, FRCOG; Hon. Consultant Obstetrician and Gynæcologist, Queen Charlotte's and North East Metropolitan Hospitals, London, retired; *b* Kirkcaldy, Fife, 1898; *d* of James Dodds and Elizabeth Paterson. *Educ:* High Sch., Dunfermline; Univ. of Edinburgh. House Surg., Royal Maternity Hosp. and Royal Hosp. for Sick Children, Edinburgh; 1st Asst, Obstetric Unit, University Coll. Hosp., London. *Publications:* Gynecology for Nurses, 1946; Midwives' Dictionary; contributions to the Encyclopædia of Medical Practice and to medical journals. *Address:* 22 Ravelston Heights, Edinburgh EH4 3XL.

DODDS, Harold Willis; President, Princeton University, 1933-June 1957; *b* Utica, Penna, 28 June 1889; *s* of Samuel Dodds and Alice Dunn; *m* 1917, Margaret Murray. *Educ:* AB Grove City (Pa) Coll., 1909; AM Princeton, 1914; PhD Pennsylvania, 1917. Instructor in Economics, Purdue Univ., 1914-16; Asst Prof. of Political Science, Western Reserve Univ., 1919-20; Sec., National Municipal League, 1920-28; Editor, National Municipal Review, 1920-33; Prof. of Politics, Princeton Univ., 1927-33; Executive Sec., US Food Administration, Pa, 1917-19; Electoral Adviser to Govt of Nicaragua, 1922-24; Technical Adviser to President, Tacna-Arica Plebiscitary Commn, 1925-26; Chief Adviser to President, National Board of Elections of Nicaragua, 1928; Consultant to Cuban Govt in Election Law Procedure, 1935; Chm., American Delegation, Anglo-American Conf. on the Refugee Problem, 1943, Bermuda; Chm., The President's Cttee on Integration of Medical Services in the Armed Forces, 1946; Mem., The President's Advisory Commn on Universal Training, 1947. Pres., Assoc. of American Univs, 1952-54; Chm., Personnel Task Force of Commn on Organization of Exec. Branch of the Govt, 1954-55; Chm., Joint Congressional Commn on James Madison Memorial. *Publications:* Out of This Nettle... Danger, 1943; The Academic President: Educator or Caretaker, 1962; various reports, pamphlets and articles on political and public administration. *Recreations:* golf and gardening. *Address:* 87 College Road W, Princeton, NJ, USA. *Clubs:* Athenæum (London); Century, Princeton (New York); Nassau (Princeton).

DODDS, James Pickering, CB 1954; Under-Secretary, Department of Health and Social Security, 1968-73; *b* 7 Feb. 1913; *s* of James Thompson and Elizabeth Fingland Dodds; *m* 1942, Ethel Mary Gill; two *d. Educ:* Queen Elizabeth's Grammar Sch., Darlington; Jesus Coll., Cambridge. Entered Ministry of Health, 1935; Nuffield Home Civil Service Travelling Fellowship, 1950; Under-Sec., 1951; Dir of Establishments and Orgn, 1965-68. *Address:* 21 Luttrell Avenue, Putney, SW15.

DODDS, Sir Ralph (Jordan), 2nd Bt *cr* 1964; *b* 25 March 1928; *o s* of Sir (Edward) Charles Dodds, 1st Bt, MVO, FRS, and Constance Elizabeth (*d* 1969), *o d* of late J. T. Jordan, Darlington; *S* father, 1973; *m* 1954, Marion, *er d* of late Sir Daniel Thomas Davies, KCVO; two *d. Educ:* Winchester; RMA, Sandhurst. Regular commission, 13/18th Royal Hussars, 1948; served UK and abroad; Malaya, 1953 (despatches); resigned, 1958. Underwriting Member of Lloyd's, 1964. *Address:* Picton House, Thames Ditton, Surrey. *Clubs:* Cavalry and Guards, Hurlingham.

DODDS-PARKER, Sir (Arthur) Douglas, Kt 1973; MA (Oxford); company director since 1946; *b* 5 July 1909; *o s* of A. P. Dodds-Parker, FRCS, Oxford; *m* 1946, Aileen, *d* of late Norman B. Coster and late Mrs Alvin Dodd, Grand Detour, Ill., USA; one *s. Educ:* Winchester; Magdalen Coll., Oxford. BA in Modern History, 1930; MA 1934. Entered Sudan Political Service, 1930; Kordofan Province, 1931-34; Asst Private Sec. to Governor-General, Khartoum, 1934-35; Blue Nile Province, 1935-38; Public Security Dept, Khartoum, 1938-39; resigned 1938; joined Grenadier Guards, 1939; employed on special duties, March 1940; served in London, Cairo, East African campaign, North Africa, Italy and France, 1940-45; Col, 1944 (despatches, French Legion of Honour, Croix de Guerre). MP (C): Banbury Div. of Oxon, 1945-Sept. 1959; Cheltenham, 1964-Sept. 1974; Jt Parly Under-Sec. of State for Foreign Affairs, Nov. 1953-Oct. 1954, Dec. 1955-Jan. 1957; Parly Under-Sec. for Commonwealth Relations, Oct. 1954-Dec. 1955. Chairman: British Empire Producers Organisation; Joint East and Central Africa Board, 1947-50; Conservative Commonwealth Council, 1960-64; Cons. Parly Foreign and Commonwealth Cttee, 1970-73; Delegate to Council of Europe, North Atlantic and W European Assemblies, 1965-72; Mem., British Parly Delegn to European Parlt, Strasbourg, 1973-75. *Address:* 9 North Court, Great Peter Street, SW1; Parsonage Farm, Churchill, Oxon. *Clubs:* Carlton, Special Forces; Leander.

DODGE, John V.; Senior Editorial Consultant, Encyclopædia Britannica, since 1972; *b* 25 Sept. 1909; *s* of George Dannel Dodge and Mary Helen Porter; *m* 1935, Jean Elizabeth Plate;

two *s* two *d. Educ:* Northwestern Univ., Evanston, Ill., USA; Univ. of Bordeaux, Bordeaux, France. Free-lance writer, 1931-32; Editor, Northwestern Alumni News and official publications of Northwestern Univ., 1932-35; Exec. Sec., Northwestern Univ. Alumni Assoc., 1937-38; Asst Editor, Encyclopædia Britannica, and Associate Editor, Britannica Book of the Year, 1938-43. US Army, 1943-46 (Intelligence). Associate Editor, Ten Eventful Years and Asst Editor, Encyclopædia Britannica, 1946-50; Editor, Britannica World Language Dictionary, 1954; Managing Editor, Encyclopædia, 1950-60; Executive Editor, 1960-64; Senior Vice-Pres., Editorial, 1964-65; Senior Editorial Consultant, 1965-70; Vice-Pres., Editorial, 1970-72. Conseiller Editorial, Encyclopædia Universalis (Paris), 1968-; Editorial Advisor: Britannica Internat. Encyclopædia (in Japanese), Tokyo, 1969-; Enciclopedia Mirador (Rio de Janeiro) and Enciclopedia Barsa (Mexico City), 1974-. *Address:* 3851 Mission Hills Road, Northbrook, Ill 60062, USA. *T:* (312) 272-0254.

DODS, Sir Lorimer (Fenton), Kt 1962; MVO 1947; Emeritus Professor of Child Health, University of Sydney, since 1960; Chairman, Children's Medical Research Foundation, Sydney, since 1966 (Hon. Director, 1960-66); *b* 7 March 1900; British; *m* 1927, Margaret Walsh; one *s* one *d. Educ:* Sydney Church of England Gram. Sch., N Sydney; St Paul's Coll., University of Sydney (1918-23). Served 1st AIF, 1918. Gen. Med. Practice, 1926-37; Pædiatric Practice, 1937-39 and 1945-49 (served 2nd AIF, RAAMC, Lt-Col, Middle East and New Guinea, 1939-45). Prof. of Child Health, University of Sydney, and Dir of Commonwealth Inst. of Child Health, 1949-60. *Publications:* various pædiatric contribs. *Address:* 8 Albert Street, Edgecliff, NSW 2027, Australia. *T:* 32 2152. *Clubs:* Union, Royal Sydney Golf (Sydney).

DODSON, family name of **Baron Monk Bretton.**

DODSON, Sir Derek (Sherborne Lindsell), KCMG 1975 (CMG 1963); MC 1945; HM Diplomatic Service; Ambassador to Turkey, since 1977; *b* 20 Jan. 1920; *e* and *o* surv. *s* of Charles Sherborne Dodson, MD, and Irene Frances Lindsell; *m* 1952, Julie Maynard Barnes; one *s* one *d. Educ:* Stowe; RMC Sandhurst. Commissioned as 2nd Lieut in Royal Scots Fusiliers, 1939, and served in Army until Feb. 1948. Served War of 1939-45 (MC): India, UK, Middle East, and with Partisans in Greece and N Italy. Mil. Asst to Brit. Comr, Allied Control Commn for Bulgaria, July 1945-Sept. 1946; GSO 3, War Office, Oct. 1946-Nov. 1947; apptd a Mem. HM Foreign Service, 1948; 2nd Sec., 1948; Acting Vice-Consul at Salonika, Sept. 1948; Acting Consul Gen. there in 1949 and 1950; Second Sec., Madrid, 1951; promoted First Sec., Oct. 1951; transferred to Foreign Office, Sept. 1953; apptd Private Sec. to Minister of State for Foreign Affairs, 1955; First Sec. and Head of Chancery, Prague, Nov. 1958; Chargé d'Affaires there in 1959, 1960, 1961, 1962; promoted and apptd Consul at Elisabethville, 1962; Transf. FO and apptd Head of the Central Dept, 1963; Counsellor, British Embassy, Athens, 1966-69; Ambassador: to Hungary, 1970-73; to Brazil, 1973-77. *Recreations:* shooting, fishing, walking. *Address:* 47 Ovington Street, SW3. *T:* 01-589 5055; Gable House, Leadenham, Lincoln. *T:* Loveden 72212. *Clubs:* Boodle's, Travellers'.

DODSWORTH, Geoffrey Hugh, FCA, JP; MP (C) South West Hertfordshire since Feb. 1974; *b* 7 June 1928; *s* of late Walter J. J. Dodsworth and Doris M. Baxter; *m* 1st, 1949, Isabel Neale (decd) one *d*; 2nd, 1971, Elizabeth Ann Beeston; one *s* one *d. Educ:* St Peter's Sch., York. Mem. York City Council, 1959-65; JP York 1961, now JP Herts. Dir, Grindlays Bank Ltd, 1976-. *Recreation:* riding. *Address:* Woodcote, Frithsden Copse, Berkhamsted, Herts. *T:* Berkhamsted 2323. *Club:* Carlton.

DODSWORTH, Sir John Christopher S.; see Smith-Dodsworth.

DODWELL, Prof. Charles Reginald, MA, PhD, LittD; FBA 1973; FRHistS, FSA; Pilkington Professor of History of Art and Director of Whitworth Gallery, University of Manchester, since 1966; *b* 3 Feb. 1922; *s* of William Henry Walter and Blanche Dodwell; *m* 1942, Sheila Juliet Fletcher; one *s* one *d. Educ:* Gonville and Caius Coll., Cambridge (MA, PhD, LittD). Served War, Navy, 1941-45. Research Fellow, Caius Coll., 1950-51. Sen. Research Fellow, Warburg Inst., 1950-53; Lambeth Librarian, 1953-58; Fellow, Lectr, Librarian, Trinity Coll., Cambridge, 1958-66. Visiting scholar, Inst. of Advanced Studies, Princeton, USA, 1965-66. *Publications:* The Canterbury School of Illumination, 1954; Lambeth Palace, 1958; The Great Lambeth Bible, 1959; The St Albans Psalter (section 2) 1960; Theophilus: De Diversis Artibus, 1961; Reichenau Reconsidered, 1965; Painting in Europe 800-1200, 1971; Early English Manuscripts in Facsimile, vol. xviii (section 2), 1972. Articles in Burlington Magazine, Gazette des Beaux Arts, Atti del 18 Congresso Internazionale di studi sull'alto medioevo (Spoleto), Jumièges, Congrès Scientifique du 13 Centenaire, l'Archéologie, etc. *Recreations:* badminton, table-tennis, opera. *Address:* The Old House, 12 Park Road, Cheadle Hulme, Cheshire SK8 7DA. *T:* 061-485 3923.

DODWELL, David William, CIE 1946; BA (Hons) Oxon, MA, PhD, Columbia; Economic Adviser to Joseph Lucas Ltd, Birmingham, 1948-63, retd; *b* 13 Dec. 1898; *s* of Frederick William Dodwell and Martha Ann Williams Dodwell (*née* Carpenter), Banbury, Oxon; *m* 1924, Marcia Ada Bausor Bradley (later Rev. M. A. B. Dodwell, MA Oxon, of the Christian Community, Birmingham; she *d* 1964), *d* of late W. Harris Bradley, Wolverhampton; two *s* one *d* (and one adopted *d*). *Educ:* Grimsbury Council Sch., Banbury; Banbury Grammar Sch.; Balliol Coll., Oxford (the first pupil of a state secondary sch. to win a Balliol scholarship); Brackenbury Scholar of Balliol in Modern History, 1915. 2nd Lieut, Worcs Regt, served in Egypt, 1917-19. BA Oxon, 2nd class Hons Mod. Hist., 1921. Entered ICS and arrived Madras, 1922; served as Asst Collector, Sub-Collector and Collector in various districts of Madras Province, 1922-25, 1928-32, and 1934-35. Tutor to HH the Maharajah of Travancore, 1925-28. Beit Prize of Oxford Univ. for essay on British Nationality, 1929; granted special leave to hold a Commonwealth Fund Service Fellowship at Graduate Sch. of Economics, Columbia Univ., New York, 1932-34; MA 1933, PhD 1934, Columbia, in economics; attached to Finance Dept of Madras Govt, 1935; Finance Sec. to the Govt of Madras, 1942-48; retd, 1948. Mem. OEEC Mission to USA to study motor industry, 1952. *Publications:* Treasuries and Central Banks, 1934; Ways and Means Procedure, 1936. *Recreations:* gardening, music. *Address:* 2 Blackwell Close, Towcester, Northants.

DOGGART, George Hubert Graham; Headmaster, King's School, Bruton, since 1972; *b* 18 July 1925; *e s* of Alexander Graham Doggart and Grace Carlisle Hannan; *m* 1960, Susan Mary, *d* of R. I. Beattie, Eastbourne; one *s* two *d. Educ:* Winchester; King's Coll., Cambridge. BA History, 1950; MA 1955. Army, 1943-47 (Sword of Honour, 161 OCTU, Mons, 1944); Coldstream Guards. On staff at Winchester, 1950-72 (exchange at Melbourne C of E Grammar Sch., 1963); Housemaster, 1964-72. HMC Schools rep. on Nat. Cricket Assoc., 1964-75; Pres., English Schools Cricket Assoc., 1965-; Member: Cricket Council, 1968-71, 1972; MCC Cttee, 1975-. *Publication:* (ed) The Heart of Cricket: memoir of H. S. Altham, 1967. *Recreations:* literary and sporting (captained Cambridge v Oxford at cricket, Association football, rackets and squash, 1949-50; played in Rugby fives, 1950; played for England v W Indies, two tests, 1950; captained Sussex, 1954). *Address:* Headmaster's House, King's School, Bruton, Somerset. *Clubs:* MCC, Lord's Taverners; Hawks.

DOGGART, James Hamilton, MA, MD, FRCS; Consulting Surgeon, Moorfields, Westminster and Central Eye Hospital and Hospital for Sick Children, Great Ormond Street; Past Chairman, British Orthoptic Board; FRSM; Livery of the Society of Apothecaries of London; Ophthalmological Society, Société belge d'Ophtalmologie, Société française d'Ophtalmologie; Hon. Member: Australian, NZ and Peruvian Ophthalmological Societies; Oto-Neuro-Ophth. Soc. of the Argentine; Canadian Ophthalmological Society; formerly: Lecturer, Institute of Ophthalmology; Examiner for British Orthoptic Board; (in Fellowship of Ophthalmology) RCSI; Faculty of Ophth. representative on Council of RCS; Examiner in Ophthalmology, Royal Coll. of Surgeons and Physicians, University of Belfast, and for FRCS, 1954-60; formerly Pres. and Mem. Council, Faculty of Ophthalmologists and Fellow and Councillor, Hunterian Society; Hon. Secretary, Editorial Committee, British Journal Ophthalmology; surgeon-oculist in London, 1929-72; *b* 22 Jan. 1900; *s* of late Arthur Robert Doggart, Bishop Auckland; *m* 1st, 1928, Doris Hilda Mennell; one *d* ; 2nd, 1938, Leonora Sharpley Gatti; one *s. Educ:* Bishop's Stortford Coll.; King's Coll., Cambridge (Scholar); St Thomas's Hospital. Surg. Sub-Lt, RNVR, 1918; Schol., King's Coll., Cambridge, 1919-22; Mem. Anglo-American Physiological Exped. to Andes, 1921; Ophth. Ho. Surg., St Thomas's Hosp., 1923-24; Ho. Surg., Casualty Officer, Royal Northern Hosp., 1925-26; appts at Royal Westminster Ophthalmic Hosp.; Clinical Asst, Refraction Asst, Chief Clin. Asst and Pathologist, 1926-30; appts at Moorfields Eye Hosp.; Clin. Asst, Refraction Asst, Chief Clin. Asst, 1927-34, Asst Med. Officer to Physico-Therapy Dept, 1930-31, Lang Research Schol., 1930-33; Clin. Asst, London Hosp., 1929-34; Ophth. Surg., East Ham Memorial Hosp., 1930-31; appts at St George's Hosp.: Asst Ophth. Surg., 1931-46, Ophth. Surg., 1946-49; Lectr in Ophthalmology, St George's Hosp. Med. Sch., University of London, 1931-49; Ophth. Surg., Lord Mayor Treloar Hosp.,

1932-37; Asst Surgeon, Central London Ophthalmic Hosp., 1934-38; Ophth. Surg., Hosp. for Sick Children, Great Ormond Street, 1936-63; Lectr in Ophth., Inst. of Child Health, 1936-63; Hon. Secretary: Section of Ophthalmology, RSM, 1935-37; Ophthalmological Soc., 1939-40, 1946-47. Chm., Cttee of Horatian Soc., 1965-69. Sq/Ldr, W/Cdr, RAF, Med. Br., 1940-45. CStJ 1962. *Publications:* Diseases of Children's Eyes, 1947, 2nd edn, 1950; Children's Eye Nursing, 1948; Ocular Signs in Slit-Lamp Microscopy, 1949; Ophthalmic Medicine, 1949; Chapters in: Moncrieff's Nursing of Sick Children, 1948; Garrod Batten and Thursfield's Diseases of Children, 1949; Stallard's Modern Practice in Ophthalmology, 1949; Berens' Diseases of the Eye, 1949; Parsons and Barling's Diseases of Children, 1954; Treves and Rogers' Surgical Applied Anatomy, 1952; Gaisford and Lightwood's Pædiatrics for the Practitioner, 1955; Thérapeutique Médicale Oculaire; articles in British Encyclopædias of Medical and Surgical Practice; papers in Brit. Jl Ophth. etc. *Recreations:* walking, reading. *Address:* Albury Park, Albury, Guildford, Surrey. *T:* Shere 3289. *Clubs:* English-Speaking Union; Hawks (Cambridge).

DOGGETT, Frank John, CB 1965; retired; Deputy Chairman, UKAEA, 1971-76; Director, National Nuclear Corporation, 1973-76; *b* 7 Jan. 1910; *s* of Frank Hewitt and Charlotte Doggett; *m* 1st, 1940, Clare Judge (*d* 1956); one *d* ; 2nd, 1957, Mary Battison. *Educ:* Mathematical Sch., Rochester; University of London (LLB). Inland Revenue, 1929; Air Ministry, 1938; MAP, 1940; MOS, 1946, Under-Sec., 1957-59; Under-Sec., Min. of Aviation, 1959-66, Dep. Sec., 1966-67; Dep. Sec. (A), Min. of Technology, 1967-70; Under-Sec., Dept of Trade and Industry, 1970-71. *Address:* The Jays, Ridgeway Road, Dorking, Surrey. *T:* Dorking 5819.

DOIG, Sir James (Nimmo Crawford), Kt 1970; Chairman, U. E. B. Industries Ltd; *b* 21 Aug. 1913; *s* of David Dickson Doig; *m* 1943, Rita Elizabeth Lowe; two *s* one *d. Educ:* Alan Glen's School and Royal Technical College, Glasgow. Managing Director, U.E.B. Industries Ltd, 1948-; Chairman, 1965-. *Recreations:* yachting, painting. *Address:* 48 Paritai Drive, Auckland, New Zealand. *Clubs:* Northern, Wellesley, Royal NZ Yacht Squadron (all NZ).

DOIG, Peter Muir; MP (Lab) West Dundee since Nov. 1963; *b* 27 Sept. 1911; *m* 1938, Emily Scott; two *s. Educ:* Blackness Sch., Dundee. Served RAF, 1941-46. Sales Supervisor with T. D. Duncan Ltd, Bakers, Dundee, until 1963. Mem., TGWU; joined Labour Party, 1930; Mem. of Dundee Town Council, 1953-63, Hon. Treasurer, 1959-63. Contested (Lab) S Aberdeen, 1959. *Recreation:* chess. *Address:* House of Commons, SW1; 29 Riverside Road, Wormit, Fife.

DOIG, Ralph Herbert, CMG 1974; CVO 1954; Chairman, Executive Committee, Western Australia's 150th Anniversary Celebrations (1979), since 1975; *b* 24 Feb. 1909; *s* of late William and Rose Doig; *m* 1937, Barbara Crock; two *s* four *d. Educ:* Guildford Grammar Sch.; University of Western Australia (BA, DipCom). Entered Public Service of WA, 1926; Private Sec. to various Premiers, 1929-41; Asst Under-Sec., Premier's Dept, 1941; Under-Sec., Premier's Dept, and Clerk of Executive Council, Perth, Western Australia, 1945-65; Public Service Comr, W Australia, 1965-71; Chm., Public Service Board, WA, 1971-74. State Director: visit to Western Australia of the Queen and the Duke of Edinburgh, 1954; visit of the Duke of Edinburgh for British Empire and Commonwealth Games, 1962; visit of the Queen and the Duke of Edinburgh, 1963. *Recreation:* bowls. *Address:* 3 Marapana Road, City Beach, WA 6015, Australia. *T:* 85-9640.

DOISY, Prof. Edward A.; Professor Emeritus of Biochemistry and Director Emeritus of Edward A. Doisy Department of Biochemistry, St Louis University School of Medicine, since 1965; *b* Hume, Ill., 13 Nov. 1893; *s* of Edward Perez and Ada Alley Doisy; *m* 1st, 1918, Alice Ackert (*d* 1964); four *s* ; 2nd, 1965, Margaret McCormick. *Educ:* Univ. of Illinois (AB 1914, MS 1916); Harvard (PhD 1920). Hon. ScD: Yale, 1940; Washington, 1940; Chicago, 1941; Central Coll., 1942; Illinois, 1960; Gustavus Adolphus Coll., 1963; Hon. Dr, Paris, 1945; Hon. LLD, St Louis, 1955. Asst in Biochemistry, Harvard Medical Sch., 1915-17; Army Service, 1917-19; Instructor, Associate and Associate Prof. in Biochemistry, Washington Univ. Sch. of Medicine, 1919-23; Prof. of Biochemistry and Chm. of Dept, St Louis Univ. Sch. of Medicine, 1923-65; Distinguished Service Prof., 1951-65. Member: American Soc. of Biological Chemists (Pres. 1943-45); American Chem. Soc.; Endocrine Soc. (Pres. 1949-50); American Assoc. for the Advancement of Science; Soc. for Experimental Biology and Medicine (Pres. 1949-51); National Academy of Sciences; American Philosophical Soc.; Amer. Acad. Arts and Sci.;

Pontifical Acad. of Sci.; Foundation or Memorial Lectr at New York, Kansas, Pittsburgh, Chicago, Cleveland, Minnesota, Rochester; several medals and awards; shared the Nobel Prize in Physiology and Medicine for 1943 with Dr Henrik Dam. *Publications:* more than 100 papers in medical and scientific journals. *Recreations:* golf, hunting and fishing. *Address:* Apt. 4b, Colonial Village Apts, Webster Groves, Mo 63119, USA; St Louis University School of Medicine, 1402 South Grand Boulevard, St Louis, Missouri 63104. *T:* 664-9800 ext. 121.

DOKE, Dr Clement Martyn, MA, DLitt; Professor Emeritus of Bantu Philology, University of the Witwatersrand; retired; *b* Bristol, 1893; *s* of late Rev. J. J. Doke, Baptist Minister; *m* 1919, Hilda F. Lehman (*d* 1948); one *s* four *d. Educ:* Transvaal Univ. Coll., Pretoria; London Univ. Came to S Africa, 1903; Staff of SA Baptist Mission Soc. in Lambaland, North Rhodesia, 1914-21; completed translation of New Testament into Lamba, 1918; appointed to staff of Univ. of the Witwatersrand, 1923; undertook research trip to NW Kalahari to study Phonetics of Qhung Bushman, 1925; research in NW Rhodesia in Phonetics among the Lamba, 1926; research in NW Rhodesia among the Ila, 1927; seconded by S Rhodesian Govt for linguistic survey of native languages of S Rhodesia, and awarded Carnegie travelling fellowship for the year 1929; Editor of the South African Baptist, 1922-47; Joint-editor of Bantu Studies, 1931-41; Joint-editor of African Studies, 1942-53. Chm. of the Central Orthography Cttee of the Union Government Advisory Cttee on African Studies, 1929; Chm. of the Inter-University Cttee on African Studies, 1935; Pres., Baptist Union of S Africa, 1949-50. Hon. DLitt Rhodes Univ., 1971; Hon. LLD Witwatersrand Univ., 1972. *Publications:* The Grammar of the Lamba Language; Hygiene Reader in Lamba, 1922; Dissertation on the Phonetics of the Zulu Language, 1923; Outline of Phonetics of the Language of the Qhung Bushmen, 1925; The Phonetics of the Zulu Language, Outline of Lamba Phonetics, 1926; Lamba Folklore and Proverbs (American Folklore Soc.), 1927; Text-Book of Zulu Grammar, 1927, 6th edn 1961; (ed) Grammar of the Sesuto Language (Jacottet); An Outline of Ila Phonetics, 1928; (with Rev. B. H. Barnes) The Pronunciation of the Bemba Language; The Problem of Word-division in Bantu, 1929; The Unification of the Shona Dialects (Govt Blue-Book); The Lambas of Northern Rhodesia; A Comparative Study in Shona Phonetics, 1931; (ed) Xhosa Baptist Hymnal, 1932; English-Lamba Vocabulary, 1933, 2nd rev. edn 1963; Bantu Linguistic Terminology, 1935; Text-Book of Lamba Grammar, 1938; Bantu: Modern Grammatical, Phonetical, and Lexicographical Studies since 1860, 1945; (ed) Longmans' Zulu Readers: Imvulamlomo, Ingqaqamazinyo, Ufundukhuphuke, 1946; Unokuhlekisa, Unozizwe, Usokuzula, 1947; Izinkamb'eAfrika, 1949; Ukuhlakaniph'eAfrika, 1950; (with late B. W. Vilakazi) Zulu-English Dictionary, 1948; The Southern Bantu Languages, 1954; Zulu Syntax and Idiom, 1955; (with late S. M. Mofokeng) Text-Book of Southern Sotho Grammar, 1957; (with D. McK. Malcolm and J. M. A. Sikakana) English and Zulu Dictionary, 1958; Lamba Bible Dictionary, 1959; trans. Bible into Lamba, 1959; Graded Lamba Grammar and Exercises, 1963; Trekking in South-Central Africa 1913-1919, 1975. *Address:* Flat 19, Marina Hills, Keam Road, Baysville, East London 5201, South Africa. *T:* East London 20433.

DOLCI, Danilo; Coordinator, Centro Studi e Iniziative, since 1958 (Founder); *b* Sesana, Trieste, 1924; *s* of Enrico Dolci and Mely Kontely. *Educ:* University of Rome; University of Milan. Came to Sicily to work for improvement of social conditions, 1952; arrested and tried for non-violent "reverse strike" to find work for unemployed, 1958. Mem. Internat. Council of War Resisters' International, 1963. Hon. DPhil, Univ. of Berne, 1968; Lenin Peace Prize, 1958; Gold Medal, Accademia Nazionale dei Lincei, 1969; Sonning Prize, 1971; Etna Taormina Poetry Prize, 1975. *Publications:* Banditi a Partinico, 1955; Inchiesta a Palermo, 1956; Spreco, 1960; Conversazioni, 1962; Verso un mondo nuovo, 1964 (trans. A New World in the Making, 1965); Chi Gioca Solo, 1966; Chissá se i pesci piangono (documentazione di un'esperienza educativa), 1973; Poema umano, 1973; Non esiste il silenzio, 1974; Esperienze e riflessioni, 1974; Il Dio delle zecche, 1976. *Address:* Centro Studi, Largo Scalia 5, Partinico (PA), Italy. *T:* 781905; Centro di formazione, Trappeto (PA). *T:* 788 312.

DOLE, John Anthony; Under-Secretary, Freight Directorate, Department of Transport, since 1976; *b* 14 Oct. 1929; *s* of Thomas Stephen Dole and Winifred Muriel (*née* Henderson); *m* 1952, Patricia Ivy Clements; two *s*. *Educ:* Bideford Grammar Sch.; Berkhamsted Sch. Air Ministry: Exec. Officer, 1950; Higher Exec. Officer, 1959; Principal, 1964; Ministry of Transport: Principal, 1965; Asst Sec. (Roads Programme), 1968; Administrator of Sports Council, 1972-75. *Publications:* plays: Cat on the Fiddle, 1964; Shock Tactics, 1966; Lucky for Some,

1968; Once in a Blue Moon, 1972; Top Gear, 1976. *Recreations:* writing, philately. *Address:* 240 Upton Road South, Bexley, Kent DA5 1QS.

DOLIN, Anton, (Patrick Healey-Kay); dancer and choreographer; Artistic Director, Les Grands Ballets, Montreal; Co-Chairman, Ballet Department, Indiana University; *b* Slinfold, Sussex, 27 July 1904; *s* of H. G. Kay and Helen Maude Kay (*née* Healey). Joined Diaghilev's Russian Ballet Company in 1923, creating a number of roles; in 1927 danced with Karsavina at the London Coliseum in Le Spectre de la Rose; and later in the year founded the Nemchinova-Dolin Ballet with Nemchinova; rejoined the Diaghilev Company in 1929 (prominently associated with the Camargo Soc.); principal dancer with the Vic-Wells Ballet Company, 1931-35; with Markova-Dolin Ballet Co., 1935-37; organised (with Julien Braunsweg) London's Festival Ballet, 1950; led Festival Ballet in 19-week tour of United States and Canada, 1954-55, and in tour of Europe, 1958; has danced principal rôle in all classical and many modern works; has worked also for films, and in revue, etc. His choreographic works for the ballet include: Hymn to the Sun, The Nightingale and the Rose, Rhapsody in Blue, Espagnol, The Pas de Quatre, Variations for Four, Ravel's Bolero, The Swan of Tuonela (Sibelius). Guest Dir of Ballet, Rome Opera. Produced Nutcracker, Giselle, Swan Lake in many contries. The Queen Elizabeth Coronation award, 1954. Awarded The Order of The Sun by the Pres. of Peru, 1959. *Publications:* Divertissement, 1930; Ballet Go Round, 1939; Pas de Deux, 1950; Markova, 1953; Autobiography, 1960; The Sleeping Ballerina, 1966. *Recreation:* travel. *Address:* c/o Barclays Bank Ltd, 5 Hanover Square, W1.

DOLL, Sir Richard; *see* Doll, Sir W. R. S.

DOLL, Prof. Sir (William) Richard (Shaboe), Kt 1971; OBE 1956; FRS 1966; DM, MD, FRCP, DSc; Regius Professor of Medicine, University of Oxford, since 1969; *b* Hampton, 28 Oct. 1912; *s* of Henry William Doll and Amy Kathleen Shaboe; *m* 1949, Joan Mary Faulkner, MB, BS, MRCP, DPH; one *s* one *d*. *Educ:* Westminster Sch.; St Thomas's Hosp. Med. Sch., London. MB, BS 1937; MD 1945; FRCP 1957; DSc London 1958. RAMC, 1939-45. Appts with Med. Research Council, 1946-69; Mem. Statistical Research Unit, 1948; Dep. Dir, 1959; Dir, 1961-69. Hon. Associate Physician, Central Middlesex Hosp., 1949-69; Teacher in Medical Statistics and Epidemiology, University Coll. Hosp. Med. Sch., 1963-69; Member: MRC, 1970-74; Royal Commn on Environmental Pollution, 1973-; Scientific Council of Internat. Cancer Research Agency, 1966-70 and 1975-; Council, Royal Society, 1970-71 (a Vice-Pres., 1970-71); Chairman: Adverse Reaction Sub-Cttee, Cttee on Safety of Medicines, 1970-; UK Co-ordinating Cttee on Cancer Research, 1972-. Hon. Lectr London Sch. of Hygiene and Tropical Med., 1956-62; Milroy Lectr, RCP, 1953; Marc Daniels Lectr, RCP, 1969; William Julius Mickle Fellow, Univ. of London, 1955. Hon DSc: Newcastle, 1969; Belfast, 1972; Reading, 1973; Newfoundland, 1973; Hon. DM Tasmania, 1976. David Anderson Berry Prize (jt), RSE 1958; Bisset Hawkins Medal, RCP, 1962; UN award for cancer research, 1962; Gairdner Award, Toronto, 1970; Buchanan Medal, Royal Soc., 1972; Presidential award, NY Acad. Sci., 1974; Prix Griffuel, Paris, 1976; Gold Medal, RIPH&H, 1977. *Publications:* Prevention of Cancer: pointers from epidemiology, 1967; articles in scientific journals on aetiology of lung cancer, leukaemia and other cancers, also aetiology and treatment of peptic ulcer; author (jt) Med. Research Council's Special Report Series, 1951, 1957, 1964. *Recreations:* food and conversation. *Address:* 13 Norham Gardens, Oxford. *T:* Oxford 55207.

DOLLAR, Jean Marguerite, FRCS; Surgeon Royal Eye Hospital; Ophthalmic Surgeon: Elizabeth Garrett Anderson Hospital, Royal Free Hospital, and St Olave's Hospital, Bermondsey. *Educ:* London Sch. of Medicine for Women. MRCS, LRCP 1926; MB, BS 1927; DOMS 1929; MS London 1935; FRCS 1936. Formerly: Surgical Registrar, Royal Eye Hosp.; House Surgeon, Elizabeth Garrett Anderson Hospital, and King Edward VII Hospital, Windsor; Hunterian Professor Royal College of Surgeons of England. *Publications:* contribs to medical press.

DOLLERY, Prof. Colin Terence, FRCP; Professor of Clinical Pharmacology at Royal Postgraduate Medical School, University of London, since 1965; *b* 14 March 1931; *s* of Cyril Robert and Thelma Mary Dollery; *m* 1958, Diana Myra (*née* Stedman); one *s* one *d*. *Educ:* Lincoln Sch.; Birmingham Univ. (BSc, MB,ChB); FRCP 1968. House officer: Queen Elizabeth Hosp., Birmingham; Hammersmith Hosp., and Brompton Hosp., 1956-58; Hammersmith Hospital: Med. Registrar, 1958-60; Sen. Registrar and Tutor in Medicine, 1960-62; Consultant

Physician, 1962-; Lectr in Medicine at Royal Postgrad. Med. Sch., 1962-65. Chevalier de l'Ordre National du Mérite (France), 1976. *Publications:* The Retinal Circulation, 1971 (New York); numerous papers in scientific jls concerned with high blood pressure and drug action. *Recreations:* travel, amateur radio, work. *Address:* 101 Corringham Road, NW11 7DL. *T:* 01-458 2616. *Club:* Athenæum.

DOLLEY, Christopher; Director for Book Development, IPC, since 1973; *b* 11 Oct. 1931; *yr s* of late Dr Leslie George Francis Dolley and of Jessie, Otford, Kent; *m* 1966, Christine Elizabeth Cooper; three *s*. *Educ:* Bancrofts Sch.; Corpus Christi Coll., Cambridge. Joined Unilever, 1954; with Unilever subsidiaries, 1954-62: G. B. Ollivant Ltd, 1954-59; United Africa Co., 1959-62. Joined Penguin Books Ltd as Export Manager, 1962; became Dir, 1964, Man. Dir, 1970-73, Chm., 1971-73; Exec. Vice-Pres., Penguin Books Inc., Baltimore, 1966; Director: Penguin Publishing Co., 1969-73 (Jt Man. Dir, 1969); Pearson Longman Ltd, 1970-73; The Hamlyn Group; Farvise Ltd, since 1976; Mem., Nat. Film Finance Corp., 1971-. Chm., Damis Gp Ltd. *Publication:* (ed) The Penguin Book of English Short Stories, 1967. *Recreations:* golf, gardening, collecting. *Address:* Fulwood House, Bolton Avenue, Windsor, Berks. *T:* Windsor 66961. *Clubs:* Savile; 14 West Hamilton Street (Baltimore, Md).

DOLLEY, Professor Michael, MRIA, FSA; Professor of Historical Numismatics, Queen's University of Belfast, since 1975; *b* 6 July 1925; *s* of late A. H. F. Dolley and Margaret (*née* Horgan); *m* 1950, (Phyllis) Mary Harris; two *s* four *d*. *Educ:* Wimbledon Coll.; King's Coll., Univ. of London (BA). MRIA 1964; FSA 1955; FRHistS 1965. Assistant Keeper: Nat. Maritime Museum, 1948-51; BM, 1951-63; Queen's Univ. of Belfast: Lectr in Med. Hist., 1963-69; Reader, Dept of Mod. Hist., 1969-75. Foreign Corresp. Mem., Royal Swedish Acad. of Letters, Hist. and Antiquities, 1970. *Publications:* Anglo-Saxon Pennies, 1964; Viking Coins of the Danelaw and of Dublin, 1965; The Hiberno-Norse Coins in the British Museum, 1966; The Norman Conquest and the English Coinage, 1966; Anglo-Norman Ireland, 1972; Medieval Anglo-Irish Coins, 1972; vols of jt authorship; papers in jls, mainly numismatic. *Recreations:* conversation and Irish and Manx history. *Address:* Mavis Bank, 33 Higher Brimley Road, Teignmouth, Devon. *T:* Teignmouth 2994.

DOLMETSCH, Carl Frederick, CBE 1954; Director of Haslemere Festival since 1940; specialist and authority on early music and instruments; recording artist in England and America; *b* 23 Aug. 1911; *s* of Arnold Dolmetsch and Mabel Johnston; *m*; one *s* two *d* (and one *s* decd). *Educ:* privately. Began studying music with Arnold Dolmetsch at age of 4; first performed in public at 7, first concert tour at 8, first broadcast on violin and viol, 1925, at 14 years of age; virtuoso recorder-player at 15. Toured and broadcast in America, 1935 and 1936; recorder recitals, Wigmore Hall, Feb. and Nov. 1939, and annually, 1946-; toured and broadcast on radio and TV in Holland, 1946; Italy and Switzerland, 1947; Sweden, 1949; New Zealand, 1953; France, 1956; America, 1957; Switzerland, Austria, Germany, Holland, 1958; Belgium, America, 1959; Sweden, Austria, Germany, 1960; Australia, 1965; Colombia, 1966; France, Sweden, 1967; Alaska and Canada, 1969; Japan, 1974; America (yearly), 1961-. Frequent broadcasts in this country and abroad. Musical Dir of Soc. of Recorder Players, 1937; Mem. Incorporated Soc. of Musicians; Mem. Art Workers' Guild, 1953; Patron Early Music Soc., University of Sydney. Hon. Fellow of Trinity Coll. of Music, 1950. Hon. DLitt University of Exeter, 1960. Hon. Fellow London Coll. of Music, 1963. *Publications:* Recorder Tutors, 1957, 1962 and 1970; edited and arranged numerous publications of 16th-, 17th- and 18th-century music; contrib. to many music jls. *Recreations:* ornithology, natural history. *Address:* Jesses, Haslemere, Surrey GU27 2BS. *T:* Haslemere 3818.

DOLPHIN, Rear-Adm. George Verner Motley, CB 1957; DSO 1944; retd; *b* 1902; *s* of late Capt. George Manaton Dolphin, Royal Navy, and late Anne Clare Savory; *m* 1926, Phyllis Margaret Dickinson; one *s*. *Educ:* RN Colls Osborne and Dartmouth. Entered RN, 1916; served in destroyers, 1924-32; Term Lieut, RNC Dartmouth. Served War of 1939-45: HMS Sheffield, on Northern Patrol, 1939; HMS Hermione, in Malta Convoys, 1940-41 (despatches); HMS Ramillies, E Africa, 1943; Capt. GG3 and Naval Officer in charge Gold Area for Normandy landings (DSO); Capt. of RNAS Rattray, 1945. Admiralty, Bath (DNE), 1946; Capt. of Dockyard, Portsmouth, 1948; Sen. Officer (Afloat), New Zealand Navy and Capt. of HMNZS Bellona and Black Prince, 1950; Cdre, Harwich, 1953; Admiral Superintendent, HM Dockyard, Chatham, 1954-58. *Recreations:* sailing, tennis, golf.

DOLTON, David John William; Chief Executive, Equal Opportunities Commission, since 1976; *b* 15 Sept. 1928; *e s* of Walter William and Marie Frances Duval Dolton; *m* 1959, Patricia Helen Crowe; one *s* one *d*. *Educ:* St Lawrence Coll., Ramsgate. FCIS, MBIM, MIPM, MInstAM. Various appointments in Delta Metal Co. Ltd, 1950-76, incl. Commercial Director, Extrusion Division, and Director of Administration and Personnel, Rod Division, 1967-76. Governor, The Queen's Coll., Birmingham, 1974-. Liveryman, Worshipful Co. of Gold and Silver Wyre Drawers. *Recreations:* music, reading, formerly mountaineering now mountain and hill walking, swimming, travel. *Address:* Goyt Cliff, 63 Strines Road, Marple, Stockport, Cheshire SK6 7DT.

DOMB, Prof. Cyril, PhD; FRS 1977; Professor of Theoretical Physics, King's College, University of London, since 1954; *m* Shirley Galinsky; three *s* three *d*. *Educ:* Hackney Downs Sch.; Pembroke Coll., Cambridge. Major Open Schol., Pembroke Coll., 1938-41; Radar Research, Admiralty, 1941-46; MA Cambridge, 1945; Nahum Schol., Pembroke Coll., 1946; PhD Cambridge, 1949; ICI Fellowship, Clarendon Laboratory, Oxford, 1949-52; MA Oxon, 1952; University Lecturer in Mathematics, Cambridge, 1952-54. *Publications:* (ed) Clerk Maxwell and Modern Science, 1963; (ed) Memories of Kopul Rosen, 1970; (ed with M. S. Green) Phase Transitions and Critical Phenomena, vols 1 and 2, 1972, vol 3, 1974, vols 5a, 5b, 6, 1976; (ed, with A. Carmell) Challenge, 1976; articles in scientific journals. *Recreation:* walking. *Address:* c/o King's College, Strand, WC2R 2LS.

DOMINGO, Placido; tenor singer; *b* Madrid, 21 Jan. 1941; *s* of Placido Domingo and Pepita (*née* Embil), professional singers; *m* Marta Ornelas, lyric soprano; three *s*. *Educ:* Instituto, Mexico City; Nat. Conservatory of Music, Mexico City. Operatic début, Monterrey, as Alfredo in La Traviata, 1961; with opera houses at Dallas, Fort Worth, Israel, to 1965; NY City Opera, 1965-; débuts: at NY Metropolitan Opera, as Maurizio in Adriana Lecouvreur, 1968; at La Scala, title role in Ernani, 1969; at Covent Garden, Cavaradossi in Tosca, 1971; sings, appears on TV, makes recordings, throughout USA and Europe. *Recreations:* piano, swimming. *Address:* Metropolitan Opera Company, Lincoln Center Plaza, New York, NY 10023, USA; 30 Herrick Avenue, Teaneck, NJ 07666.

DOMVILLE, Sir Gerald Guy, 7th Bt *cr* 1814; Lieut-Comdr RNVR; *b* 3 March 1896; 3rd *s* of late Rear-Adm. Sir William Cecil Henry Domville, CB, 4th Bt, and Moselle (*d* 1957), *d* of Henry Metcalf Ames, Linden, Northumberland; *S* brother, 1930; *m* 1920, Beatrice Mary (who obtained a divorce, 1930), *o c* of late Brig.-Gen. R. S. Vandeleur, CB, CMG; no *c*. *Educ:* Wellington Coll. Served European War, 1915-19 and War of 1939-45. *Heir:* none. *Address:* 60 Knightsbridge, SW1. *T:* 01-235 2121. *Clubs:* Royal Thames Yacht, Portland, MCC.

DON, Kaye Ernest; Chairman and Managing Director, US Concessionaires Ltd, retired 1965; *b* 10 April 1891; *s* of Charles Frederick Don; *m* 1932, Eileen (marr. diss.), *d* of Leonard F. Martin, New York; two *s* one *d*; *m* 1954, Valerie Evelyn, *d* of Ronald Farquar Chapman. *Educ:* Wolverhampton Grammar Sch. Commenced career in the rubber industry, with which was associated until 1915, when joined HM Forces; demobilised, 1919; first served in the Army Service Corps and was discharged on medical grounds; rejoined Royal Flying Corps as pilot in 1916; after serving on the Western Front was posted to British Mission; before the War, raced motor cycles, and took up motor car racing in 1920 and high speed motor boat racing in 1931; British Motor Racing Champion, 1928, 1929; World Water Speed Records: Buenos Aires, 103-104 mph, 1931; Italy, 110 mph, 1931; Loch Lomond, 119 mph, 1932; Internat. Motor Yachting Union Medal, 1931; travelled extensively in America, South America, Australia, South Africa and Europe. *Recreation:* golf. *Address:* Marton, Chobham, Surrey. *T:* Chobham 8256.

DON-WAUCHOPE, Sir P. G.; *see* Wauchope.

DONALD, Alan Ewen; HM Diplomatic Service; Political Adviser to the Governor of Hong Kong, 1974-77; *b* 5 May 1931; 2nd *s* of late R. T. Donald and Mrs Louise Donald; *m* 1958, Janet Hilary Therese Blood; four *s*. *Educ:* Aberdeen Grammar Sch.; Fettes Coll., Edinburgh; Trinity Hall, Cambridge. BA, LLB. HM Forces, 1949-50. Joined HM Foreign Service, 1954: Third Sec., Peking, 1955-57; FO, 1958-61: Private Sec. to Parly Under-Sec., FO, 1959-61; Second, later First Sec., UK Delegn to NATO, Paris, 1961-64; First Sec., British Chargé d'Affaires Office, Peking, 1964-66; Personnel Dept, Diplomatic Service Admin. Office, later FCO, 1967-71; Counsellor (Commercial), British Embassy, Athens, 1971-73. *Recreations:* piano, military history,

Chinese studies. *Address:* c/o Foreign and Commonwealth Office, SW1; Applebys, Chiddingstone Causeway, near Penshurst, Kent. *Clubs:* United Oxford & Cambridge University; Aula (London/Cambridge).

DONALD, Craig Reid Cantlie, CMG 1963; OBE 1959; Bursar of Malvern College, since 1964; *b* 8 Sept. 1914; *s* of Rev. Francis Cantlie and Mary Donald, Lumphanan, Aberdeenshire; *m* 1945, Mary Isabel Speid; one *d. Educ:* Fettes; Emmanuel Coll., Cambridge (Scholar). BA 1937, MA 1947. Administrative Officer, Cyprus, 1937. Military Service, 1940-46, Lieut.-Col. Commissioner, Famagusta, 1948. Registrar, Cooperative Societies, 1951; Deputy Financial Sec., Uganda, 1951; Sec. to the Treasury, 1956-63. *Recreation:* country pursuits. *Address:* 55 Geraldine Road, Malvern WR14 3NU. *T:* Malvern 61446. *Club:* Travellers'.

DONALD, Air Marshal Sir (David) G.; *see* Donald, Sir Grahame.

DONALD, David William Alexander, OBE 1946; TD 1950; General Manager and Actuary, The Standard Life Assurance Company, since 1970; *b* 3 Feb. 1915; *s* of David Donald and Wilhelmina Ewan. *Educ:* High Sch. of Dundee. FFA 1936. Commnd TA, 1937; served War of 1939-45, Black Watch (RHR), Britain and India; GSO2, Staff Duties, WO, 1943; GSO1, Staff Duties GHQ India, 1944; DAA&QMG 155 (L) Inf. Bde TA, 1949-56. Joined Standard Life Assce Co., 1932: Sen. Asst Actuary, 1946; Jt Actuary, 1949; Actuary, 1962; Dep. Gen. Man., 1969. Pres. Faculty of Actuaries, 1969-71; Chm. Associated Scottish Life Offices, 1974-76; Chm. Bd of Governors, Red House Home, 1966-74; Mem. Council, Edinburgh Festival Soc. Ltd, 1977-; Dir, Scottish Nat. Orchestra Soc. Ltd, 1977-. *Publications:* Compound Interest and Annuities-Certain, 1953; contrib. actuarial jls. *Recreations:* music, golf, wine and food. *Address:* 15 Hermitage Drive, Edinburgh EH10 6BX. *T:* 031-447 2562. *Clubs:* New, Hon. Company of Edinburgh Golfers (Edinburgh); Royal and Ancient (St Andrews).

DONALD, Prof. Ian, CBE 1973 (MBE 1946); MD; FRCS (Glasgow); FRCOG; FCO&G (SA); Regius Professor of Midwifery, University of Glasgow, 1954-76, now Emeritus Professor; *b* 27 Dec. 1910; British; *m* 1937, Alix Mathilde de Chazal Richards; four *d. Educ:* Warriston Sch., Moffat; Fettes Coll., Edinburgh; Diocesan Coll., Rondebosch, Cape. BA Cape Town, 1930; MB, BS London, 1937; MD London, 1947; MRCOG 1947; FRCOG 1955; FRCS (Glasgow) 1958; FCO&G (South Africa) 1967; Hon. FACOG 1976. Served War of 1939-45 with Royal Air Force (Medical), 1942-46 (despatches). Reader in Obstetrics and Gynæcology, St Thomas's Hosp. Medical Sch., 1951; Reader, University of London, Inst. of Obstetrics and Gynæcology, 1952; Leverhulme Research Scholar, 1953; Blair Bell Memorial Lecturer, RCOG, 1954. Eardley Holland Gold Medal, 1970; Blair Bell Gold Medal, RSM, 1970; Victor Bonney Prize, RCS, 1970-72; MacKenzie Davidson Medal, BIR, 1975. *Publications:* Practical Obstetric Problems, 1955, 5th edn 1977; articles on respiratory disorders in the newborn, in Lancet and Jl of Obst. and Gynæc. Brit. Empire, and on ultrasonics in diagnosis, in Lancet. *Recreations:* sailing, music, painting. *Address:* 9 Hamilton Drive, Glasgow, G12 8DN. *T:* 041-339 5050.

DONALD, Prof. Kenneth William, DSC 1940; MA, MD, DSc, FRCP, FRCPE, FRSE; Professor of Medicine, University of Edinburgh, 1959-76, now Emeritus Professor; Senior Physician, Royal Infirmary, Edinburgh; Physician to the Queen in Scotland, 1967-76; *b* 25 Nov. 1911; *s* of Col William Donald, MC, RA and Julia Jane Donald, Sandgate; *m* 1942, Rêthe Pearl, *d* of D. H. Evans, Regents Park. *Educ:* Cambridge Univ.; St Bartholomew's Hosp. Kitchener Scholar and State Scholar, 1930; Senior Scholar, Emmanuel Coll., Cambridge, 1933. Served with Royal Navy, 1939-45: Senior MO, 1st and 5th Flotilla of Destroyers; Senior MO, Admiralty Experimental Diving Unit. Chief Asst, Med. Prof. Unit and Cattlin Research Fellow, St Bartholomew's Hosp., 1946-48; Rockefeller Travelling Research Fellow, Columbia Univ., 1948-49; Senior Lecturer in Medicine, Inst. Diseases of the Chest, Brompton Hosp., 1949-50; Reader in Medicine, Univ of Birmingham and Physician, Queen Elizabeth Hosp., Birmingham, 1950-59. Scientific Consultant to the Royal Navy. Physician to the Royal Navy in Scotland. Medical Consultant to Scottish Dept of Home and Health; Member: Commonwealth Scholarship Commn; Medical Sub-Cttee, UGC; RN Personnel Research Cttee (Chm.) of MRC; Scottish Adv. Cttee on Med. Research; Council and Scientific Adv. Cttee, British Heart Foundn; Scottish Gen. Nursing Council; Chairman: Under-Water Physiology Sub-Cttee of MRC; Physiology Adv. Cttee, NCB; Adv. Gp on Health Care Aspects of Industrial Developments in North Sea. Governor, Inst. of

Occupational Medicine, Edinburgh. *Publications:* contribs to scientific and medical jls concerning normal and abnormal function of the lungs, the heart and the circulation and high pressure physiology in relation to diving and submarines, drowning, resuscitation. *Recreations:* reading, theatre, fishing. *Address:* Nant-y-Celyn, Cloddiau, Welshpool, Powys SY21 9JE. *T:* Welshpool 2859. *Club:* Athenæum.

DONALD, Prof. Maxwell Bruce, SM (MIT); ARCSc; Hon. MIChemE; FRIC; Emeritus Professor of Chemical Engineering in the University of London; *b* 20 July 1897. *Educ:* Felsted Sch.; Royal Coll. of Science; Massachusetts Inst. of Technology. Served European War, Lieut and ADC, RA, 1915-19. Sir Alfred Yarrow Scholar, 1921; Demonstrator in Physical Chemistry, Royal College of Science, 1923; Chemical Engineer, Chilean Nitrate Producers Assoc., 1925; Adviser on bitumen emulsions, Royal Dutch-Shell Group, 1929; Lecturer in Chemical Engineering, University Coll., London, 1931; Reader, 1947; Ramsay Memorial Prof., 1951-65. Hon. Sec., Institution of Chemical Engineers, 1937-49, Moulton medallist, 1937, Osborne Reynolds medallist, 1940; Vice-Pres. 1950. DSIR Visitor to British Baking Research Assoc., 1949. *Publications:* (with H. P. Stevens) Rubber in Chemical Engineering, 1933 and 1949; Elizabethan Copper, 1955; Elizabethan Monopolies, 1961. *Address:* Rabbit Shaw, 6 Stagbury Avenue, Chipstead, Surrey CR3 3PA. *T:* Downland 53365.

DONALDSON, family name of **Baron Donaldson of Kingsbridge.**

DONALDSON OF KINGSBRIDGE, Baron *cr* 1967 (Life Peer), of Kingsbridge; **John George Stuart Donaldson,** OBE 1943; Minister for the Arts, Department of Education and Science, since 1976; retired farmer; *b* 9 Oct. 1907; *s* of Rev. S. A. Donaldson, Master of Magdalene, Cambridge, and Lady Albinia Donaldson (*née* Hobart-Hampden); *m* 1935, Frances Annesley Lonsdale (*see* F. A. Donaldson); one *s* two *d. Educ:* Eton; Trinity Coll., Cambridge. Pioneer Health Centre, Peckham, 1935-38; Road Transport, 1938-39. Royal Engineers, 1939-45. Farmed in Glos, and later Bucks. Mem., Glos Agric. Exec. Cttee, 1953-60. Parly Under-Sec. of State, NI Office, 1974-76. Hon. Sec. Nat. Assoc. Discharged Prisoners Aid Socs, 1961; Chairman: Nat. Assoc. for the Care and Resettlement of Offenders, 1966-74; Bd of Visitors, HM Prison, Grendon, 1963-69; Consumer Council, 1968-71; EDC for Hotel and Catering Industry, 1972-74; Nat. Cttee Family Service Units, 1968-74; Cttee of Enquiry into conditions of service for young servicemen, 1969; British Fedn of Zoos; Pres., RSPB, 1975-. Member, SE Regional Planning Council, 1966-69. Director: Royal Opera House, Covent Garden, 1958-74; Sadler's Wells, 1963-74; British Sugar Corp., 1966. *Recreations:* music in general, opera in particular. *Address:* 1 Chalcot Crescent, NW1. *Club:* Brooks's.

See also R. H. I. de la Mare.

DONALDSON OF KINGSBRIDGE, Lady; *see* Donaldson, Frances Annesley.

DONALDSON, David Abercrombie, RSA 1962 (ARSA 1951); RP 1964; Painter; Head of Painting School, Glasgow School of Art, since 1967; *b* 29 June 1916; *s* of Robert Abercrombie Donaldson and Margaret Cranston; *m* 1949, Maria Krystyna Mora-Szorc; one *s* two *d. Educ:* Coatbridge Sec. Sch.; Glasgow Sch. of Art. Travelling Scholarship, 1938. Joined Staff of Glasgow Sch. of Art, 1940. Paintings in private collections in America and Europe and public collections in Scotland. Sitters include: The Queen, 1968; Sir Hector Hetherington; Dame Jean Roberts; Sir John Dunbar; Lord Binning; Rev. Lord McLeod; Mrs Winifred Ewing; Miss Joan Dickson; Earl of Haddo; Sir Samuel Curran; Roger Ellis. Hon. LLD Strathclyde, 1971. *Recreation:* painting. *Address:* Endrick Hill, Drymen, by Glasgow, G63 OBG; 19 Redcliffe Square, SW10. *T:* 01-373 1991. *Club:* Art (Glasgow).

DONALDSON, Sir Dawson, KCMG 1967; BSc; CEng, FIEE; Chairman, Commonwealth Telecommunications Board, 1962-69, retired; *b* 29 Dec. 1903; *s* of Dawson Donaldson and Ada M. Gribble; *m* 1928, Nell Penman; two *s* two *d. Educ:* Auckland Grammar Sch.; New Zealand Univ. New Zealand Post and Tels Dept, 1922-62; Executive Engineer, 1928-48; Superintending Engineer, 1948-54; Dep. Dir Gen., 1954-60; Dir Gen., 1960-62. *Recreations:* bowls and garden. *Address:* 2 Ridd Crescent, Karori, Wellington, New Zealand.

DONALDSON, Dorothy Mary, (Lady Donaldson), JP; Alderman, City of London Ward of Coleman Street, since 1975; *b* 29 Aug. 1921; *d* of late Reginald George Gale Warwick and of Dorothy Alice Warwick; *m* 1945, Sir John Francis Donaldson, *qv*; one *s* two *d*. *Educ:* Portsmouth High Sch. for Girls (GPDST); Wingfield Morris Orthopædic Hosp.; Middlesex Hosp., London. SRN 1946. Chm., Women's Nat. Cancer Control Campaign, 1967-69; Vice-Pres., British Cancer Council, 1970; Member: NE Met. Regional Hosp. Bd, 1970-74; NE Thames RHA, 1976-. Governor, London Hosp., 1971-74; Mem., Cities of London and Westminster Disablement Adv. Cttee, 1974-. Mem., Inner London Educn Authority, 1968-71; Mem., City Parochial Foundn, 1969-75; Governor, City of London Sch. for Girls, 1971; Mem., Court of Common Council, City of London, 1966-75; Mem. Guild of Freemen, City of London, 1970; Liveryman, Gardeners' Co., 1975. Freedom City of Winnipeg, 1968. JP Inner London, 1960; Mem., Inner London Juvenile Court Panel, 1960-65. *Recreations:* gardening, sailing, pedestrian ski-ing. *Address:* 54 Gloucester Crescent, NW1. *T:* 01-485 5450. *Clubs:* Royal Cruising, Royal Lymington Yacht, Bar Yacht.

DONALDSON, Air Cdre Edward Mortlock, CB 1960; CBE 1954; DSO 1940; AFC 1941 (and bar 1947); Air Correspondent, The Daily Telegraph, since 1961; *b* 22 Feb. 1912; *s* of C. E. Donaldson, Malay Civil Service; *m* 1st, 1936, Winifred Constant (marr. diss., 1944); two *d*; 2nd, 1944, Estellee Holland (marr. diss., 1956); one *s*; 3rd, 1957, Anne, Sofie Stapleton. *Educ:* King's Sch., Rochester; Christ's Hosp., Horsham; McGill Univ., Canada. Joined RAF, 1931; 3 Sqdn, Upavon, Kenley and Sudan until 1936; Flight Comdr, 1 Sqdn, 1936-38; Flight-Lieut 1936; Sqdn Leader 1938; Comdr, 151 Sqdn, 1938-40; Chief Instructor, 5 Flying Training Sch., 1941; Wing Comdr, 1940; went to US to build four air Gunnery Schs, 1941, and teach USAF combat techniques; Group Capt., 1942; Mem. USAF Board and Directing Staff at US Sch. of Applied Tactics, 1944; Comdr RAF Station, Colerne, RAF first jet station, 1944; in comd RAF Station, Milfield, 1946; in comd RAF High Speed Flight, 1946; holder of World's Speed Record, 1946; SASO, No. 12 Group, 1946-49; in comd Air Cadet Corps and CCF, 1949-51; in comd RAF Station, Fassberg, Germany, 1951-54; Joint Services Staff Coll., 1954; Dir of Operational Training, Air Ministry, 1954-56; Air Cdre, 1954; Dep. Comdr Air Forces, Arabian Peninsular Command, 1956-58; Commandant, Royal Air Force Flying Coll., Manby, 1958-61; retd. Legion of Merit (US), 1948. *Recreations:* shooting, sailing, golf. *Address:* 41 Princes Gate Mews, SW7. *Clubs:* Royal Air Force, Royal Victoria Yacht.

DONALDSON, Frances Annesley, (Lady Donaldson of Kingsbridge); *b* 13 Jan. 1907; *d* of Frederick Lonsdale and Leslie Lonsdale (*née* Hoggan); *m* 1935, John George Stuart Donaldson (*see* Lord Donaldson of Kingsbridge); one *s* two *d*. *Publications:* Approach to Farming, 1941, 6th edn 1946; Four Years' Harvest, 1945; Milk Without Tears, 1955; Freddy Lonsdale, 1957; Child of the Twenties, 1959; The Marconi Scandal, 1962; Evelyn Waugh: portrait of a country neighbour, 1967; Actor Managers, 1970; Edward VIII, 1974 (Wolfson History Award, 1975). *Recreations:* gardening, golf. *Address:* 1 Chalcot Crescent, NW1 8YE. *T:* 01-722 4695.

DONALDSON, Prof. Gordon, FBA 1976; Professor of Scottish History and Palæography, University of Edinburgh, since 1963; *b* 13 April 1913; *s* of Magnus Donaldson and Rachel Hetherington Swan. *Educ:* Royal High Sch., Edinburgh; Universities of Edinburgh and London. Asst in HM Gen. Register House, Edinburgh, 1938; Lecturer in Scottish History, University of Edinburgh, 1947, Reader, 1955. Mem. Royal Commission on the Ancient and Historical Monuments of Scotland, 1964-. Hon. DLitt Aberdeen, 1976. *Publications:* The Making of the Scottish Prayer Book of 1637, 1954; A Source Book of Scottish History, 1952-61; Register of the Privy Seal of Scotland, vols v-viii, 1957-66; Shetland Life under Earl Patrick, 1958; Scotland: Church and Nation through sixteen centuries, 1960, 2nd edn, 1972; The Scottish Reformation, 1960, repr. 1972; Scotland-James V to James VII, 1965, repr. 1971; The Scots Overseas, 1966; Northwards by Sea, 1966; Scottish Kings, 1967; The First Trial of Mary Queen of Scots, 1969; Memoirs of Sir James Melville of Halhill, 1969; (comp.) Scottish Historical Documents, 1970; Mary Queen of Scots, 1974; Who's Who in Scottish History, 1974; Scotland: The Shaping of a Nation, 1974; contribs to Scottish Historical Review, English Historical Review, Transactions of Royal Historical Society, etc. *Address:* Preston Tower Nursery Cottage, Prestonpans, East Lothian EH32 9EN. *T:* Prestonpans 811100.

DONALDSON, John Coote, CIE 1939; MC; Indian Civil Service, retired; *b* 24 May 1895; *s* of late John Donaldson, KC, Dublin; *m* 1933, Barbara Maud, *d* of late Hon. Sir Charles Henry Bayley Kendall; one *s* one *d*. *Educ:* Felsted; Trinity Coll., Dublin (MA). Entered Indian Civil Service, 1920. *Address:* Medlars, Fairy Road, Seaview, IoW. *T:* Seaview 2379.

DONALDSON, Hon. Sir John (Francis), Kt 1966; **Hon. Mr Justice Donaldson;** Judge of the High Court of Justice, Queen's Bench Division, since 1966; *b* 6 Oct. 1920; *er s* of late Malcolm Donaldson, FRCS, FRCOG, and late Evelyn Helen Marguerite Maunsell; *m* 1945, Dorothy Mary (*see* Dorothy Mary Donaldson); one *s* two *d*. *Educ:* Charterhouse; Trinity Coll., Cambridge. Sec. of Debates, Cambridge Union Soc., 1940; Chm. Federation of University Conservative and Unionist Assocs, 1940; BA (Hons) 1941; MA 1959. Commissioned Royal Signals, 1941; served with Guards Armoured Divisional Signals, in UK and NW Europe, 1942-45; and with Military Government, Schleswig-Holstein, 1945-46; Hon. Lieut-Col, 1946. Called to Bar, Middle Temple, 1946; Harmsworth Law Scholar, 1946; QC 1961; Bencher 1966; Mem. Gen. Council of the Bar, 1956-61, 1962-66, Junior Counsel to Registrar of Restrictive Trading Agreements, 1959-61; Dep. Chm., Hants QS, 1961-66; Mem. Council on Tribunals, 1965-66; Pres., Nat. Industrial Relations Court, 1971-74. Mem. Croydon County Borough Council, 1949-53. Vice-Pres., British Maritime Law Assoc., 1969-. FBIM 1974. *Publications:* Jt Ed., Lowndes and Rudolf on General Average and the York-Antwerp Rules (8th edn), 1955, (9th edn), 1964 and (10th edn), 1975; contributor to title Insurance, in Halsbury's Laws of England (3rd edn), 1958. *Recreations:* sailing, do-it-yourself. *Address:* Royal Courts of Justice, Strand, WC2. *T:* 01-405 7641; (home) 01-485 5450. *Clubs:* Royal Cruising, Bar Yacht, Royal Lymington Yacht.

DONALDSON, Timothy Baswell, CBE 1973; Governor, Central Bank of the Bahamas, since 1974; *b* 2 Jan. 1934; *s* of late Rev. Dr T. E. W. Donaldson and of M. B. Donaldson; *m* 1957, Donna Ruth Penn; two *s*. *Educ:* Fisk Univ., Tennessee (BA Hons); Univ. of Minnesota; Columbia Univ. FIB. Lectr in Maths, Fisk Univ., 1957-58; Sen. Master, Clarendon Coll., Jamaica, 1959-61; Headmaster, Prince Williams High Sch., 1961-63; Sen. Inspector, Bahamas Min. of Educn, 1963-64; Asst Sec., 1964-66, Controller of Exchange, 1966-68, Min. of Finance, Bahamas; Manager, 1968-70, Chm., 1970-74, Bahamas Monetary Authority. Founder Mem., Rotary Club of E Nassau (Past Sec. and Vice Pres.). Pres., Gym Tennis Club. Hon. LLD London Inst. for Applied Research, 1972. *Publications:* numerous articles on international finance in periodicals and journals. *Recreations:* tennis, swimming. *Address:* (office) PO Box N-4868, Nassau, Bahamas. *T:* 22193; (home) PO Box ES-5116, Nassau, Bahamas. *T:* 42742.

DONALDSON, Rear-Adm. Vernon D'Arcy; *b* 1 Feb. 1906; *s* of Adm. Leonard Andrew Boyd Donaldson, CB, CMG, and of Mary Mitchell, *d* of Prof. D'Arcy Thompson, Queen's Coll., Galway; *m* 1946, Joan Cranfield Monypenny of Pitmilly, (The Lady Pitmilly), *d* of James Egerton Howard Monypenny. *Educ:* RN Colls, Osborne and Dartmouth. Entered Royal Navy, Sept. 1919; Midshipman, 1923; Sub-Lieut 1927, Lieut 1928; specialised in Torpedoes and served as Torpedo Officer in HMS Vernon, 8th Dest. Flot., China Stn, and HMS Glorious; Comdr Dec. 1939, and served in Plans Div. Admlty, as exec. officer HM Ships Birmingham and Frobisher in Eastern Fleet, and on staff of C-in-C Eastern Fleet; Capt. Dec. 1944. Asst-Dir, TASW Div., Naval Staff, 1945-47; Naval Attaché, China, 1948-49; commanded HMS Gambia, 1950-51; Dir TASW div., Naval Staff, 1952-54; ADC to the Queen, 1953-54; Dep. Chief of Supplies and Transport, Admiralty (acting Rear-Adm.), 1955-57; retired, 1957. *Address:* 36 Tregunter Road, SW10.

DONCASTER, Bishop Suffragan of, since 1976; **Rt. Rev. David Stewart Cross;** *b* 4 April 1928; *s* of Charles Stewart and Constance Muriel Cross; *m* 1954, Mary Margaret Workman Colquhoun; one *s* two *d*. *Educ:* Trinity Coll., Dublin (MA 1956). Deacon 1954, priest 1955; Curate of Hexham, 1954-57; on staff of Cathedral and Abbey Church of St Alban, St Albans, Herts, 1957-63; Precentor, 1960-63; Curate of St Ambrose, Chorlton-on-Medlock and Asst Chaplain to Manchester Univ., 1963-67; BBC Producer in religious broadcasting, 1968-76 (Religious Broadcasting Assistant, BBC North, 1968-71, then Religious Broadcasting Organiser, Manchester Network Production Centre, 1971-76). *Recreations:* photography, making music and exchanging puns. *Address:* Danum House, 344 Grimesthorpe Road, Sheffield S4 7EW. *T:* Sheffield 386555.

DONCASTER, Archdeacon of; *see* Rogers, Ven. E. J. G.

DONCASTER, John Priestman, CBE 1967; MA; formerly Keeper, Department of Entomology, British Museum (Natural History), 1961-68, retired; *b* 20 Nov. 1907; *s* of Charles Doncaster and Hilda Priestman; *m* 1938, Frances Julia Gaynesford Walter; one *d*. *Educ:* St Catharine's Coll., Cambridge. Joined British Museum as Asst Keeper in charge of Exhibition Section, 1937; entered Dept of Entomology, 1951. *Address:* 3 Devonshire Road, Harpenden, Herts AL5 4TJ.

DONEGALL, 7th Marquess of, *cr* 1791; **Dermot Richard Claud Chichester;** Viscount Chichester and Baron of Belfast, 1625; Earl of Donegall, 1647; Earl of Belfast, 1791; Baron Fisherwick (GB), 1790; Baron Templemore, 1831; Hereditary Lord High Admiral of Lough Neagh; late 7th Queen's Own Hussars; one of HM Bodyguard, Honourable Corps of Gentlemen at Arms, since 1966; *b* 18 April 1916; 2nd *s* of 4th Baron Templemore, PC, KCVO, DSO, and Hon. Clare Meriel Wingfield, 2nd *d* of 7th Viscount Powerscourt, PC Ireland (she *d* 1969); *S* father 1953, and to Marquessate of Donegall, 1975; *m* 1946, Lady Josceline Gabrielle Legge, *y d* of 7th Earl of Dartmouth, GCVO, TD; one *s* two *d*. *Educ:* Harrow; RMC, Sandhurst. 2nd Lt 7th Hussars, 1936; Lt 1939; served War of 1939-45 in Middle East and Italy (prisoner); Major, 1944; retired, 1949. *Recreations:* hunting, shooting, fishing. *Heir: s* Earl of Belfast, *qv*. *Address:* Dunbrody Park, Arthurstown, Co. Wexford, Eire. *T:* Duncannon 4. *Clubs:* Cavalry and Guards; Kildare Street and University (Dublin).

DONEGAN, Rt. Rev. Horace W(illiam) B(aden), Hon. CBE 1957; DD; *b* Matlock, Derbyshire, England, 17 May 1900; *s* of Horace George Donegan and Pembroke Capes Hand. *Educ:* St Stephen's, Annandale, NY; Oxford University, England; Harvard Divinity School; Episcopal Theological Seminary, Rector, Christ Church, Baltimore, 1929-33; Rector, St James' Church, NYC, 1933-47; Suffragan Bishop of New York, 1947-49; Bishop Coadjutor of New York, 1949-50. Bishop of New York, 1950-72. Vice-Pres., Pilgrims, USA; President: St Hilda's and St Hugh's Sch., NY; House of Redeemer, NY; Episcopal Actors Guild, NY; Chaplain, Veterans of Foreign Wars; Episcopal Visitor: Sisters of St Helena; Community of the Holy Spirit; Trustee, St Luke's Hosp., NY. Award, Conf. of Christians and Jews; Medal of City of New York; Medal of Merit, St Nicholas Society, NY; Citation, NY Hospital Assoc.; Harlem Arts & Culture Award. Churchill Fellow, Westminster Coll., Fulton, Mo. Hon. degrees: DD: New York Univ., 1940; Univ. of South, 1949; Trinity, 1950; Bard, 1957; King's Univ., Halifax, 1958; Berkley Divinity School, New Haven, Conn., 1969; STD: Hobart, 1948; General Theological Seminary, 1949; Columbia Univ., 1960; DCL Nashotah, 1956; Sub Prelate OStJ, 1956; Grand Cross St Joanikije, 1956; Legion of Honour, France, 1957; Silver Medal of Red Cross of Japan, 1959; Holy Pagania from Armenian Church, 1960; Grand Kt, Order of St Denys of Zante (Greece), 1959. *Publications:* articles in religious publications. *Recreations:* golf, swimming, painting. *Address:* Manhattan House, 200 E 66th Street, New York, NY 10021. *Clubs:* Athenæum, Royal Automobile (London); Union, Union League, Pilgrims, Century Association, Columbia Faculty, Tuxedo Park (all of New York).

DONERAILE, 9th Viscount, *cr* 1785; **Richard St John St Leger;** Baron Doneraile, 1776; *b* 29 Oct. 1923; *o s* of 8th Viscount and of Sylvia St Leger; *S* father 1957; *m* 1945, Melva Jean Clifton; three *s* two *d*. *Educ:* George Washington Sch., USA. In lumber business and real estate. *Heir: s* Hon. Richard Allen St Leger [*b* 17 Aug. 1946; *m* 1969, Kathleen Mary, *e d* of N. Simcox, Co. Cork].

DONIACH, Prof. Israel, MD (London); FRCPath 1963; FRCP 1968; Professor of Morbid Anatomy in University of London, London Hospital, 1960-76, now Emeritus Professor; *b* 9 March 1911; *yr s* of late Aaron Selig and late Rahel Doniach; *m* 1933, Deborah Abileah; one *s* (one *d* decd). *Educ:* University Coll. and Hosp., London. Asst Pathologist, St Mary's Hosp., London, 1935-37; Clinical Pathologist and Cancer Research Asst, Mount Vernon Hosp., Northwood, 1937-43; Senior Lecturer in Morbid Anatomy, Postgraduate Medical Sch. of London, 1943-59, Reader, 1959-60. *Publications:* papers in morbid anatomy and experimental pathology in various journals. *Address:* 25 Alma Square, NW8. *T:* 01-286 1617.

DONKIN, Air Cdre Peter Langloh, CBE 1946; DSO 1944; retired; *b* 19 June 1913; *s* of Frederick Langloh and Phyllis Donkin; *m* 1941, Elizabeth Marjorie Cox; two *d*. *Educ:* Sherborne; RAF Coll., Cranwell. Commissioned RAF, 1933; No. 16 Sqdn, 1933-38; British Mission in Poland, 1939; CO 225 Sqdn, 1940; CO 239 Sqdn, 1941-42; CO 35 Wing, 1943-44; Sch. Land Air Warfare, 1945; HQ, RAF Levant, 1946; RCAF Staff Coll., 1948-49; Exchange USAF, 1950; CO, RAF Chivenor, 1951-53; Air Attaché, Moscow, 1954-57; Asst Chief of Staff, HQ Allied Air Forces, Central Europe, 1957-58; idc, 1959; AOC, RAF, Hong Kong, 1960-62. *Recreations:* shooting, yachting. *Address:* Coombe Cross, Templecombe, Som. *Club:* Carlton.

DONLEAVY, James Patrick; Author; *b* 23 April 1926; *m* Valerie Heron (marr. diss.); one *s* one *d* ; *m* Mary Wilson Price. *Educ:* schs in USA; Trinity Coll., Dublin. *Publications:* The Ginger Man (novel), 1955; Fairy Tales of New York (play), 1960; What They Did In Dublin With The Ginger Man (introd. and play), 1961; A Singular Man (novel), 1963 (play, 1964); Meet My Maker The Mad Molecule (short stories), 1964; The Saddest Summer of Samuel S (novella), 1966 (play, 1967); The Beastly Beatitudes of Balthazar B (novel), 1968; The Onion Eaters (novel), 1971; The Plays of J. P. Donleavy, 1972; A Fairy Tale of New York (novel), 1973; The Unexpurgated Code: A Complete Manual of Survival and Manners, 1975; The Destinies of Darcy Dancer, Gentleman (novel), 1977. *Address:* Levington Park, Mullingar, Co. Westmeath, Ireland.

DONNE, Sir John (Christopher), Kt 1976; Chairman, SE Thames Regional Health Authority, since 1973; *b* 19 Aug. 1921; *s* of late Leslie Victor Donne, solicitor, Hove, and Mabel Laetitia Richards (*née* Pike); *m* 1945, Mary Stuart (*née* Seaton); three *d*. *Educ:* Charterhouse. Royal Artillery, 1940-46 (Captain); served Europe and India. Solicitor, 1949; Notary Public; Partner, Donne Mileham & Haddock; Pres., Sussex Law Soc., 1969-70. Chm., SE (Metropolitan) Regional Hosp. Bd, 1971-74. Governor, Guy's Hosp., 1971-74, Guy's Hosp. Med. Sch., 1974; Chm., RHA Chairmen, 1974-76; Mem., Gen. Council, King Edward's Hosp. Fund for London, 1972-; a Governing Trustee, Nuffield Provincial Hosp. Trust, 1975-; Dir, Nuffield Health and Soc. Services Fund, 1976-. Liveryman, Hon. Company of Broderers. Mem. Editorial Bd, Jl Medical Ethics, 1977-. *Recreations:* genealogy, gardening, photography, music, tennis. *Address:* Copyhold, Partridge Green, Horsham, West Sussex. *T:* Partridge Green 710462. *Clubs:* Junior Carlton, Pilgrims, MCC; Butterflies, Sussex Martlets.

DONNER, Frederic Garrett; Chairman of the Board of Trustees, Alfred P. Sloan Foundation, 1968-75, retired; Director, General Motors Corporation, 1942-74 (Chairman, 1958-67); *s* of Frank Donner and Cornelia (*née* Zimmerman); *m* 1929, Eileen Isaacson; one *d* (and one *s* decd). *Educ:* University of Michigan, Ann Arbor, Michigan, USA. General Motors Corporation, 1926; Dir, Communications Satellite Corporation, 1964-77; Trustee, Sloan-Kettering Inst. for Cancer Research, NY, 1964-75. Holds hon. doctorates and foreign decorations. *Address:* 825 Fifth Avenue, New York, NY 10021, USA. *Clubs:* Links, University (NY City); Creek Country, North Hempstead Country (Long Island, NY).

DONNER, Sir Patrick William, Kt 1953; MA; DL; *b* 1904; *s* of late Ossian Donner and Violet Marion McHutchen, Edinburgh; *m* 1938, Hon. Angela Chatfield (*d* 1943), *er d* of 1st Baron Chatfield, GCB, OM, KCMG, CVO, Admiral of the Fleet; *m* 1947, Pamela *y d* of Rear Adm. Herbert A. Forster, MVO; one *s* two *d*. *Educ:* abroad and Exeter Coll., Oxford. Studied Imperial development and administration, 1928-30; MP (C) West Islington, 1931-35; Basingstoke Div. of Hants, 1935-55; Hon. Sec., India Defence League, 1933-35; Parliamentary Private Sec. to Sir Samuel Hoare, Home Sec., 1939; Mem. Advisory Cttee on Education in the Colonies, 1939-41; Parliamentary Private Sec. to Col Oliver Stanley, Sec. of State for the Colonies, 1944; Dir, National Review Ltd, 1933-47; Mem. Executive Council Joint East and Central African Board, 1937-54. Volunteered RAFVR 1939; served at HQ Fighter Command; Acting Sqdn Leader, 1941. Chm. Executive Cttee of the Men of the Trees, 1959-62. Mem., Art Panel of the Arts Council, 1963-66. High Sheriff of Hants, 1967-68; DL Hants 1971. *Recreations:* music, travel, landscape gardening. *Address:* Hurstbourne Park, Whitchurch, Hants. *T:* Whitchurch 2230.

DONNISON, David Vernon; Chairman, Supplementary Benefits Commission, since 1975 (Deputy Chairman, 1973-75); *b* 19 Jan. 1926; *s* of F. S. V. Donnison, *qv*; *m* 1950, Jean Elizabeth (*née* Kidger); two *s* two *d*. *Educ:* Marlborough Coll., Wiltshire; Magdalen Coll., Oxford. Asst Lecturer and Lecturer, Manchester Univ., 1950-53; Lecturer, Toronto Univ., 1953-55; Reader, London Sch. of Economics, 1956-61; Prof. of Social Administration, 1961-69; Dir, Centre for Environmental Studies, 1969-76. Vis. Prof., LSE, 1976-. Chm., Public Schs Commission, 1968-70. Hon. DLitt Bradford, 1973. *Publications:* The Neglected Child and the Social Services, 1954; Welfare Services in a Canadian Community, 1958; Housing since the Rent Act, 1961; The Government of Housing, 1967; An Approach to Social Policy, 1975; Social Policy and Administration Revisited, 1975. *Address:* 38 Douglas Road, N1 2LD. *T:* 01-226 7956.

DONNISON, Frank Siegfried Vernon, CBE 1943; Indian Civil Service (retired); *b* 3 July 1898; *s* of Frank Samuel and of Edith Donnison; *m* 1923, Ruth Seruya Singer, MBE, JP (*d* 1968); one *s* one *d*. *Educ:* Marlborough Coll.; Corpus Christi Coll., Oxford. Served with Grenadier Guards, 1917-19; ICS (Burma), 1922; Chief Sec. to Govt of Burma, 1946; military service, Burma, 1944-45 (despatches). Historian, Cabinet Office, Historical

Section, 1949-66. *Publications:* Public Administration in Burma, 1953; British Military Administration in the Far East, 1943-46, 1956; Civil Affairs and Military Government, North-West Europe, 1944-46, 1961; Civil Affairs and Military Government, Central Organization and Planning, 1966; Burma, 1970. *Recreation:* music. *Address:* Lower Cross Farmhouse, East Hagbourne, Didcot OX11 9LD. *T:* Didcot 3314. *Club:* Royal Automobile.
See also Professor D. V. Donnison.

DONOUGHMORE, 7th Earl of (*cr* 1800), **John Michael Henry Hely-Hutchinson;** Baron Donoughmore, 1783; Viscount Suirdale, 1800; Viscount Hutchinson (UK), 1821; *b* 12 Nov. 1902; *er s* of 6th Earl of Donoughmore, KP, PC, and Elena (*d* 1944), *d* of late M. P. Grace, New York; *S* father, 1948; *m* 1925, Dorothy Jean (MBE 1947), *d* of late J. B. Hotham; two *s* one *d. Educ:* Winchester; Magdalen Coll., Oxford. MP (C) Peterborough Div. of Northants, 1943-45. Grand Master, Freemasons' Grand Lodge of Ireland, 1964. *Heir: s* Viscount Suirdale, qv. *Address:* Knocklofty, Clonmel, Ireland. *Club:* Kildare Street and University (Dublin).

DONOUGHUE, Bernard; Senior Policy Adviser to the Prime Minister, since 1974; *s* of late Thomas Joseph Donoughue and of Maud Violet Andrews; *m* 1959, Carol Ruth Goodman; two *s* two *d. Educ:* Secondary Modern Sch. and Grammar Sch., Northampton; Lincoln Coll. and Nuffield Coll., Oxford. MA, DPhil (Oxon). Henry Fellow, Harvard, USA. Mem., Editorial Staff: The Economist, Sunday Times, Sunday Telegraph. Sen. Res. Officer, PEP, 1960-63; Lectr, Sen. Lectr, Reader, LSE, 1963-. Member: Sports Council, 1965-71; Commn of Enquiry into Association Football, 1966-68; Ct of Governors, LSE, 1968-74; Civil Service Coll. Adv. Council, 1976-. *Publications:* (ed jtly) Oxford Poetry, 1956; Wage Policies in the Public Sector, 1962; Trade Unions in a Changing Society, 1963; British Politics and the American Revolution, 1964; (with W. T. Rodgers) The People into Parliament, 1966; (with G. W. Jones) Herbert Morrison: portrait of a politician, 1973. *Recreations:* football, politics. *Address:* 7 Brookfield Park, NW5.

DONOVAN, Prof. Desmond Thomas; Yates-Goldsmid Professor of Geology and Head of Department of Geology, University College, London, since 1966; *b* 16 June 1921; *s* of T. B. Donovan; *m* 1959, Shirley Louise Saward; two *s* one *d. Educ:* Epsom Coll.; University of Bristol. BSc 1942; PhD 1951; DSc 1960. Asst Lectr in Geology, University of Bristol, 1947; Lectr in Geology, Bristol, 1950; Prof. of Geology University of Hull, 1962. *Publications:* Stratigraphy: An Introduction to Principles, 1966; (ed) Geology of Shelf Seas, 1968; papers on fossil cephalopods, Jurassic stratigraphy, Pleistocene deposits, marine geology. *Address:* University College, Gower Street, WC1E 6BT. *T:* 01-387 7050. *Club:* Athenæum.

DONOVAN, Hedley (Williams); Editor-in-Chief, Time Inc., since 1964; *b* 24 May 1914; *s* of Percy Williams Donovan and Alice Dougan Donovan; *m* 1941, Dorothy Hannon; two *s* one *d. Educ:* University of Minnesota; Hertford Coll., Oxford (Hon. Fellow, 1977). BA (*magna cum laude*) Minn., 1934; BA Oxon. 1936. Hon. LittD: Pomona Coll., 1966; Mount Holyoke, 1967; Boston, 1968. Hon. DHL: South-western at Memphis, 1967; Rochester, 1968; Hon. LLD: Carnegie-Mellon, 1969; Lehigh, 1976. US Naval Reserve, active duty, 1942-45 (Lieut-Comdr). Reporter, Washington Post, 1937-42; Writer and Editor, 1945-53, Managing Editor, 1953-59, Fortune; Editorial Dir, Time Inc., 1959-64. Trustee: New York Univ.; Mount Holyoke Coll.; Carnegie Endowment for Internat. Peace; Ford Foundn; Dir, Council on Foreign Relations; Fellow, Amer. Acad. of Arts and Sciences. Phi Beta Kappa; Rhodes Scholar. *Address:* Time Inc., Time & Life Building, Rockefeller Center, New York, NY 10020, USA. *T:* Judson 6-1212. *Clubs:* University, Century, (both New York); 1925 F Street (Washington DC); Manhasset Bay Yacht (Long Island); Sands Point Golf.

DOOLITTLE, Lt-Gen. James H.; Hon. KCB 1945; Trustee, 1963-69 (Chairman of Executive Committee and Vice-Chairman, Board of Trustees, 1965-69), Aerospace Corporation; Chairman of Board, Space Technology Laboratories, Inc., 1959-62; Director: Mutual of Omaha Insurance Co.; United Benefit Life Insurance Co.; Companion Life Insurance Co.; Tele-Trip Co., Inc.; *b* 14 Dec. 1896; *s* of Frank H. Doolittle and Rosa C. Shephard; *m* 1917, Josephine E. Daniels; two *s. Educ:* University of California (AB); MIT (MS, ScD). US Army Air Force, 1917-30; Manager, Aviation Dept, Shell Oil Co., 1930-40; USAAF, 1940-45. Dir, Shell Oil Company, 1946-67 (Vice-Pres., 1946-59). *Publications:* various scientific. *Recreations:* shooting, fishing. *Address:* 5225 Wilshire Boulevard, Room 702, Los Angeles, Calif 90036, USA.

DORAN, John Frederick, CEng, FInstGasE, MInstM; Chairman, East Midlands Gas Region, 1974-77; *b* 28 July 1916; *s* of Henry Joseph and Clara Doran; *m* 1940, Eileen Brotherton; two *s. Educ:* Wandsworth Technical Coll.; Wimbledon Technical Coll. Served War, Fleet Air Arm, 1943-46. Various appts Gas Light & Coke Co (subseq. North Thames Gas Bd), 1935-53; Dist Manager, Hornsey Dist, North Thames Gas Bd, 1953; Regional Sales Manager, North Western Div., North Thames Gas Bd, 1955-57. Southern Gas Board: Regional Sales and Service Manager, Southampton Region and Dorset and Bournemouth Regions, 1957-65; Marketing Manager, 1965-67; Commercial Manager, 1968-69; Commercial Dir, 1970-71; Commercial Dir and Bd Mem., 1971-73. Dep. Chm., East Midlands Gas Region, 1973. *Publications:* technical papers to Instn Gas Engrs. *Recreations:* golf, gardening. *Address:* Heronshaw, 43 The Woodlands, Forest Park, Market Harborough, Leicestershire LE16 7BW. *T:* Market Harborough 2113.

DORATI, Antal; composer and conductor; Principal Conductor, Royal Philharmonic Orchestra, since 1974; Music Director, Detroit Symphony Orchestra, since 1977; *b* Budapest, 9 April 1906; *s* of Alexander Dorati and Margit (*née* Kunwald); *m* 1st, 1929, Klara Korody; one *d* ; 2nd, 1971, Ilse von Alpenheim. *Educ:* Royal Academy of Music, Budapest; University of Vienna. Conductor: Royal Opera House, Budapest, 1924-28; Münster State Opera, 1929-32; Musical Director: Ballet Russe de Monte Carlo, 1932-40; Ballet Theatre, NY, 1940-42; New Opera Co., NY, 1942-43; Musical Dir and Conductor: Dallas Symph. Orch., 1944-49; Minneapolis Symph. Orch., 1944-60; Chief Conductor: BBC Symphony Orchestra, 1963-66; Stockholm Philharmonic Orch., 1966-74; Musical Dir, Nat. Symphony Orch., Washington, DC, 1970-77. Guest conductor of major orchestras of the world, Salzburg, Holland, Venice, Lucerne, Berlin Festivals, etc; London Symphony, New Philharmonia, London Philharmonic, Royal Philharmonic, Israel Philharmonic orchestras, etc. Holder of 19 recording awards in America and Europe. DrMus: Macalister Coll., St Paul, 1958; George Washington Univ., 1975; Dr (hc) Humanities Maryland, 1976. Mem., Royal Swedish Academy of the Arts. Comdr, Order of Vasa; Chevalier of Arts and Letters, France; Order of Letters and Arts, Austria. Compositions include: The Way (dramatic cantata); Symphony I; Missa Brevis; The two enchantments of Li-Tai-Pe; String Quartet; Cello Concerto; Nocturne and Capriccio for oboe and strings; Magdalena (ballet); Seven Pictures for Orch.; Madrigal Suite; String Octet; Largo Concertato for String Orch.; 'Chamber-Music', Song Cycle for Sopr. and small orch.; Night Music for flute and small orch.; Variations on a theme of Bartok for piano, Piano Concerto; Threni for String Orch.; American Serenades for String Orch.; The Voices; Ot Enek. *Recreations:* painting sketching, reading, art collecting. *Address:* c/o Ibbs & Tillet, 124 Wigmore Street, W1; c/o ICM, 40 West 57th Street, New York, NY 10019, USA.

DORE, Ronald Philip, FBA 1975; Fellow, Institute of Development Studies, University of Sussex, since 1969; *b* 1 Feb. 1925; *s* of Philip Brine Dore and Elsie Constance Dore; *m* 1957, Nancy Macdonald; one *s* one *d. Educ:* Poole Grammar Sch.; SOAS, Univ. of London (BA). Lectr in Japanese Instns, SOAS, London, 1951; Prof. of Asian Studies, Univ. of BC, 1956; Reader, later Prof. of Sociol., LSE, 1961. *Publications:* City Life in Japan, 1958; Land Reform in Japan, 1959; Education in Tokugawa Japan, 1963; (ed) Aspects of Social Change in Modern Japan, 1967; British Factory, Japanese Factory, 1973; The Diploma Disease, 1976; The Japanese Village, 1978. *Recreation:* daydreaming. *Address:* 157 Surrenden Road, Brighton, East Sussex. *T:* Brighton 501370.

DORKING, Suffragan Bishop of, since 1968; **Rt. Rev. Kenneth Dawson Evans;** *b* 7 Nov. 1915; *s* of late Dr Edward Victor Evans, OBE; *m* 1939, Margaret, *d* of J. J. Burton; one *s. Educ:* Dulwich Coll.; Clare Coll., Cambridge. Ordained, 1938; Curate of: St Mary, Northampton, 1938-41; All Saints', Northampton, 1941-45; Rector of Ockley, 1945-49; Vicar of Dorking, 1949-63. Hon. Canon of Guildford, 1955-63; Ed., Guildford Diocesan Publications, 1947-61; Archdeacon of Dorking and Canon Residentiary of Guildford Cathedral, 1963-68. Mem., Bishop's Finance Commn, 1957. *Address:* 13 Pilgrims Way, Guildford, Surrey. *T:* Guildford 67978.

DORKING, Archdeacon of; see Purcell, Ven. W. H. S.

DORLAND, Arthur Garratt, BA, MA, PhD; FRSC; Professor of History and Head of the History Department, University of Western Ontario, London, Ontario, 1920-56 (appointed Prof. J. B. Smallman Professor of History, 1955), retired 1956, Emeritus Professor, 1971; *b* Wellington, Prince Edward County, Ont,

1887; *s* of John T. Dorland, Jun., of Wellington, and Lavina Hubbs of Bloomfield, Ont; *m* 1912, Ellen Uprichard, *d* of Joseph H. Malone, Dublin; three *s* one *d. Educ:* Ashburton House, London, England; Bloomfield Public Sch.; Pickering Coll.; Queen's Univ.; Yale Univ.; Chicago Univ. Teacher of History and English, and Housemaster, Pickering Coll., 1911-14; Currier Fellow in History, Yale, 1914-15; Lecturer in History, Queen's Univ., Kingston, 1916-20; Clerk of Canada Yearly Meeting of the Religious Soc. of Friends, 1924. Pres. Coll. and Secondary Sch. Dept of Ontario Education Assoc., 1949; Pres. Section II Royal Society of Canada, 1949; Associate Ed., The Loyalist Gazette, 1966. Hon. LLD Univ. of Western Ontario, 1963. Canada Centennial Medal, 1967. *Publications:* The Royal Disallowance in Massachusetts, 1917; British North America since (1713), published in Expansion of the Anglo-Saxon Nations, 1920; A History of the Society of Friends (Quakers) in Canada, 1927; The Origins of the Holy Alliance, 1939; Our Canada, A History textbook, 1949; Former Days and Quaker Ways, 1965, 2nd illus. edn 1972; The Quakers in Canada, 1968. *Recreations:* gardening, boating. *Address:* Fair Acre, Wellington, Ont, Canada.

DORMAN, Lt-Col Sir Charles (Geoffrey), 3rd Bt *cr* 1923; MC 1942; *b* 18 Sept. 1920; *o s* of Sir Bedford Lockwood Dorman, 2nd Bart, CBE and Lady Constance Phelps Dorman (*née* Hay), (*d* 1946); *S* father 1956; *m* 1954, Elizabeth Ann (marr. diss. 1972), *d* of late George Gilmour Gilmour-White, OBE; one *d. Educ:* Rugby Sch.; Brasenose Coll., Oxford (MA). Commissioned, 1941; served with 3rd The King's Own Hussars at Alamein (MC) and in Italian Campaign; Commissioned to 13th/18th Royal Hussars (QMO), 1947; GSO1, 1961-70; retired. *Recreation:* gliding. *Heir: cousin* Philip Henry Keppel Dorman, *b* 19 May 1954. *Address:* Hutton Grange, Great Rollright, Chipping Norton, Oxon OX7 5SQ. *T:* Hook Norton 737535.

DORMAN, Sir Maurice Henry, GCMG 1961 (KCMG 1957; CMG 1955); GCVO 1961; MA; Chief Commander, St John Ambulance, since 1975; Chairman, Wiltshire Area Health Authority, since 1974; Director: MLH Consultants, since 1971; Ramsbury Building Society, since 1972; *b* 7 Aug. 1912; *s* of late John Ehrenfried and late Madeleine Louise Dorman; *m* 1937, Florence Monica Churchward Smith, DStJ 1968; one *s* three *d. Educ:* Sedbergh Sch.; Magdalene Coll., Cambridge. Administrative Officer, Tanganyika Territory, 1935; Clerk of Councils, Tanganyika, 1940-45; Asst to the Lt-Governor, Malta, 1945; Principal Asst Sec., Palestine, 1947; Seconded to Colonial Office as Asst Sec., Social Services Dept, 1948; Dir of Social Welfare and Community Develt, Gold Coast, 1950; Colonial Sec., Trinidad and Tobago, 1952-56; Actg Governor of Trinidad, 1954, 1955; Governor, Comdr-in-Chief and Vice-Adm., Sierra Leone, 1956-61, after independence, Governor-Gen., 1961-62; Governor and Comdr-in-Chief, Malta, 1962-64, after independence, Governor-Gen., 1964-71. Dep. Chm., Pearce Commn on Rhodesian Opinion, 1971-72. Chm., Swindon HMC, 1972-74. Chm. Bd of Governors, Badminton Sch. A Trustee, Imperial War Museum, 1972-; Almoner, Venerable Order of St John, 1972-75. Hon. DCL Durham, 1962; Hon. LLD Royal Univ. Malta, 1964. KStJ 1957. Gran Croce Al Merito Melitense (Soc. Ordine Militaire di Malta), 1966. *Recreations:* once sailing, squash, and sometimes golf. *Address:* The Old Manor, Overton, Marlborough, Wilts. *T:* Lockeridge 600; 42 Lennox Gardens, SW1. *T:* 01-584 8698. *Clubs:* Athenæum; Casino Maltese (Valletta).
See also R. B. Dorman.

DORMAN, Richard Bostock; HM Diplomatic Service; Counsellor, Pretoria, since 1977; *b* 8 Aug. 1925; *s* of late John Ehrenfried and late Madeleine Louise Dorman; *m* 1950, Anna Illingworth; one *s* two *d. Educ:* Sedbergh Sch.; St John's Coll., Cambridge. Army Service (Lieut, S Staffs Regt), 1944-48; Asst Principal, War Office, 1951; Principal, 1955; transferred to Commonwealth Relations Office, 1958; First Sec., British High Commission, Nicosia, 1960-64; Dep. High Commissioner, Freetown, 1964-66; SE Asia Dept, FO, 1967-69; Counsellor, Addis Ababa, 1969-73; Commercial Counsellor, Bucharest, 1974-77. *Address:* 67 Beresford Road, Cheam, Surrey. *T:* 01-642 9627. *Club:* Royal Commonwealth Society.
See also Sir M. H. Dorman.

DORMAND, John Donkin; MP (Lab) Easington since 1970; a Lord Commissioner of HM Treasury, since Oct. 1974; *b* 27 Aug. 1919; *s* of Bernard and Mary Dormand; *m* 1963, Doris Robinson; one step *s* one step *d. Educ:* Bede Coll., Durham; Loughborough Coll.; Univs of Oxford and Harvard. Teacher, 1940-48; Education Adviser, 1948-52 and 1957-63; District Education Officer, Easington RDC, 1963-70. An Asst Govt Whip, 1974. *Recreations:* music, sport. *Address:* Lynton, Stockton Road, Easington, Peterlee, Co. Durham.

DORMER, family name of **Baron Dormer.**

DORMER, 16th Baron *cr* 1615; **Joseph Spencer Philip Dormer;** Bt 1615; landowner and farmer; *b* 4 Sept. 1914; *s* of 14th Baron Dormer, CBE, and Caroline May (*d* 1951), *y d* of Sir Robert Cavendish Spencer Clifford, 3rd Bt; *S* brother, 1975. *Educ:* Ampleforth; Christ Church, Oxford. Formerly Captain, Scots Guards; served War of 1939-45. Consultant, Thomas Comely & Sons Ltd. Member of Council, West Midlands Area Conservative Assoc. *Heir: cousin* Robert Francis Edward Baptist Dormer, *b* 27 June 1904. *Address:* Orchard Hill, Birlingham, Pershore, Worcs; Grove Park, Warwick. *Club:* Cavalry and Guards.

DORMER, Sir Cecil Francis Joseph, KCMG 1937; MVO; *b* 14 Feb. 1883; *y s* of late Hon. Hubert Dormer, and *g s* of 11th Baron Dormer; *m* 1915, Lady Mary A. C. Feilding (*d* 1973), *e d* of 9th Earl of Denbigh. *Educ:* St Augustine's Coll., Ramsgate. Clerk in Foreign Office, 1905; Acting 2nd Sec. in Diplomatic Service, 1911; Asst Private Sec. to Sec. of State for Foreign Affairs (Viscount Grey, KG, and Mr Balfour) 1915-19; Chargé d'Affaires, Caracas, 1919-21; Sec. of British Legation to the Holy See, Rome, 1921-25; Counsellor of Embassy at Tokio, 1926-29; Envoy Extraordinary and Minister Plenipotentiary Bangkok, 1929; Oslo, 1934; Ambassador to Polish Government in London, 1941-43. Grand Cross, Order of St Olav (Norway), 1940; Norwegian War Medal. *Address:* St Anne's Nursing Home, Wokingham, Berks.

DORNHORST, Antony Clifford, CBE 1977; MD, FRCP; Professor of Medicine, St George's Hospital Medical School, since 1959; Civilian Consultant in Aviation Medicine to RAF, since 1973; *b* 2 April 1915; *s* of Ernst Dornhorst and Florence, *née* Partridge; *m* 1946, Helen Mary Innes; three *d. Educ:* St Clement Danes Sch.; St Thomas's Hosp. Medical Sch. MB BS London 1937; MD London 1939; FRCP 1955. Junior Appointments, St Thomas' Hosp., 1937-39. Served with RAMC, mostly in Mediterranean theatre, 1940-46. Reader in Medicine, St Thomas's Hosp. Medical Sch., 1949-59. Member: MRC, 1973-77; SW Thames RHA, 1974-. *Publications:* papers in various journals on normal and abnormal physiology. *Recreation:* music. *Address:* 8 Albert Place, W8. *T:* 01-937 8782.

DORRELL, Ernest John; Secretary, Headmasters' Conference, since 1975; General Secretary, Secondary Heads Association, since 1978 (Secretary, Incorporated Association of Headmasters, 1975-77); *b* 31 March 1915; *s* of John Henry Whiting Dorrell and Amy Dorrell (*née* Roberts); *m* 1940, Alwen Irvona Jones; one *s* one *d. Educ:* Taunton Sch.; Exeter Coll., Oxford (Exhibr). Hon. Mods and Lit. Hum., MA. Served with 71 Field Regt and HQ 46 Div. RA, 1940-46. Asst Master, Dauntsey's Sch., 1937-40 and 1946-47; Admin. Asst, WR Educn Dept, 1947; Dep. Dir of Educn, Oxfordshire CC, 1950; Dir of Educn, Oxfordshire CC, 1970; Report on Educn in Helena, 1974. *Recreations:* walking, travel, golf. *Address:* Crossways, Shillingford, Oxford. *T:* Warborough 8386.

DORSET, Archdeacon of; see Sharp, Ven. R. L.

DORWARD, Ivor Gardiner Menzies Gordon, FRIBA, FRIAS; Architect Principal in private practice, since 1960; Member, Royal Fine Art Commission for Scotland, since 1976; *b* 18 Oct. 1927; *s* of William Gordon Dorward and Jean Lawson Dorward (*née* Skinner); *m* 1954, Priscilla Purves Tindal, DA Edin.; two *d. Educ:* Royal High Sch., Edinburgh; Blackpool Grammar Sch.; Edinburgh Coll. of Art. DA 1953; FRIBA 1969. Served RAF, 1945-48. Various travelling scholarships in Europe and Africa, 1951, 1952 and 1953. Architect in private practice, Dorward, Matheson, Gleave & Partners, 1960-. Principal works include university, hospital, and both local and central government buildings. Royal Scottish Acad. Medal for Architecture, 1971. *Recreations:* drawing, sailing, Bull Terriers. *Address:* 50 Sherbrooke Avenue, Glasgow G41 4SB. *T:* 041-427 1771; Kerryfern, Strone, Argyll PA23 8RR. *T:* Dunoon 84416. *Club:* Glasgow Art (Glasgow).

DORWARD, William, OBE 1977; Deputy Director of Commerce and Industry, Hong Kong Government, since 1974; *b* 25 Sept. 1929; *s* of Alexander and Jessie Dorward; *m* 1960, Rosemary Ann Smith; one *s. Educ:* Morgan Academy, Dundee. Colonial Office, 1951-53; Commerce and Industry Dept, Hong Kong Govt, 1954-74; Counsellor (Hong Kong Affairs) UK Mission, Geneva, 1974-76. *Recreations:* travel, music, cinema, literature. *Address:* 18 Queen's Gardens, Hong Kong. *T:* 5-246292; 38 Bingham Terrace, Dundee, Scotland. *Clubs:* Junior Carlton; Hong Kong, Hong Kong Cricket.

DOS SANTOS, Sir Errol Lionel, Kt 1946; CBE 1939; *b* 1 Sept. 1890; *s* of Solomon and Margaret dos Santos; *m* 1st, 1915; one *s* one *d*; 2nd, 1939, Enid Hilda Jenkin, Bath, England; two *d*. *Educ:* St Mary's Coll., Trinidad. Entered Trinidad Civil Service as a junior clerk in the Treasury; Financial Sec., 1941; Colonial Sec., 1947; retired from Colonial Service, 1948. Dir, Alstons Ltd, 1948, Chm. 1953-61. *Address:* c/o Alstons Ltd, Trinidad. *Clubs:* Royal Commonwealth Society (West Indian); Union, Queen's Park Cricket, Portuguese (Trinidad).

DOSSOR, Rear-Adm. Frederick, CB 1963; CBE 1959; with UBM Hoversystems and Premmit Ltd; *b* 12 March 1913; *s* of John Malcolm Dossor and Edith Kate Brittain; *m* 1951, Pamela Anne Huxley Newton; two *d*. *Educ:* Hymers Coll., Hull; Loughborough Coll. BSc(Eng.) London; FIEE. Post Graduate Apprentice and Junior Engineer, Metropolitan Vickers Electrical Co., Manchester, 1935-39; Dept of Dir of Electrical Engineering, Admiralty, 1939-50; Electrical Specialisation, Royal Navy, 1950-65; Chief Staff Officer (Technical), staff of Comdr-in-Chief, Portsmouth, 1961-63; Polaris Project Officer in the Ministry of Technology, 1963-67; Dir of Hovercraft, DTI (formerly Min. of Technology), 1968-71. Retired from Royal Navy, 1965. *Recreations:* gardening, golf. *Address:* 1a Lynch Road, Farnham, Surrey. *Club:* Royal Commonwealth Society.

DOTRICE, Roy; actor (stage, films and television); *b* 26 May 1925; *m* 1946, Kay Newman, actress; three *d*. *Educ:* Dayton and Intermediate Schs, Guernsey, CI. Served War of 1939-45: Air Gunner, RAF, 1940; PoW, 1942-45. Acted in Repertory, 1945-55; formed and directed Guernsey Theatre Co., 1955; Royal Shakespeare Co., 1957-65 (Caliban, Julius Caesar, Hotspur, Firs, Puntila, Edward IV, etc); World War 2½, New Theatre, London, 1966; Brief Lives, Golden Theatre, New York, 1967; Latent Heterosexual and God Bless, Royal Shakespeare Co., Aldwych, 1968; Brief Lives (one-man play), Criterion, 1969 (over 400 perfs; world record for longest-running solo perf.), toured England, Canada, USA, 1973, Mayfair, 1974 (over 150 perfs); Broadway season, 1974; Australian tour, 1975; Peer Gynt, Chichester Festival, 1970; One At Night, Royal Court, 1971; The Hero, Edinburgh, 1970; Mother Adam, Arts, 1971; Tom Brown's Schooldays, Cambridge, 1972; The Hollow Crown, seasons in USA 1973 and 1975, Sweden 1975; Gomes, Queen's, 1973; The Dragon Variation, Duke of York's, 1977. *Films include:* Heroes of Telemark, Twist of Sand, Lock up Your Daughters, Buttercup Chain, Tomorrow, One of Those Things, Nicholas and Alexandra; *Television:* appearances in: Dear Liar, Brief Lives, The Caretaker (Emmy award), Imperial Palace, Misleading Cases, Clochemerle, Dickens of London, etc. TV Actor of the Year Award, 1968. *Recreations:* fishing, riding. *Address:* Talbot House, St Martin's Lane, WC2. *Club:* Garrick.

DOUGAN, (Alexander) Derek; Chairman, Professional Footballers' Association, since 1970; Chief Executive, Kettering Town Football Club, since 1975; *b* 20 Jan. 1938; *s* of John and Josephine Dougan; *m* 1963, Jutta Maria; two *s*. *Educ:* Mersey Street primary sch., Belfast; Belfast Technical High School. Professional footballer with: Distillery, NI, 1953-57; Portsmouth, 1957-59; Blackburn Rovers, 1959-61; Aston Villa, 1961-63; Peterborough, 1963-65; Leicester, 1965-67; Wolverhampton Wanderers, 1967-75. Represented N Ireland at all levels, from schoolboy to full international, more than 50 times. *Publications:* Attack! (autobiog.), 1969; The Sash He Never Wore (autobiog.), 1972; The Footballer (novel), 1974; On the Spot (football as a profession), 1974. *Recreations:* watching football, playing squash. *Address:* Oakfield, 56 Redhouse Road, Tettenhall, Wolverhampton, West Midlands.

DOUGHERTY, Maj.-Gen. Sir Ivan Noel, Kt 1968; CBE 1946; DSO 1941; ED; *b* Leadville, NSW, 6 April 1907; *m* 1936, Emily Phyllis Lofts; two *s* two *d* (and one *d* decd). *Educ:* Leadville Primary Sch.; Mudgee High Sch.; Sydney Teachers' Coll.; Sydney Univ. (BEc). NSW Education Dept: Asst Teacher, 1928-32; Dep. Headmaster, 1933-39; Headmaster, 1946-47; Dist Inspector of Schs, 1948-53; Staff Inspector 1953-55. Commissioned Sydney Univ. Regt, 1927. Capt. 1931; Unattached List, 1932-34; transf. to 33/41 Bn. 1934; Major, 1938; Command, 33rd Bn, 1938; Lieut-Col 1939. Served War of 1939-45 (DSO and Bar, CBE, despatches thrice); Australian Imperial Force, Second-in-Command, 2/2 Inf. Bn, 1939-40; Commanded 2/4 inf. Bn (Libya, Greece, Crete campaigns), 1940-42; Brig. 1942; commanded 23 Bde, 1942; commanded 21 Bde, South-West Pacific, 1942-45. R of O, 1946-47; commanded 8th Bde, Austr. Mil. Forces, 1948-52; Maj.-Gen., 1952; commanded 2nd Div., 1952-54; Citizen Military Forces Member, Australian Mil. Bd, 1954-57; R of O, 1957-64; Retired List, 1964; Hon. Col, Australian Cadet Corps, Eastern Command, 1964-70; Representative Hon. Col, Australian Cadet Corps, 1967-70. Dir of Civil Defence for NSW, 1955-73. Mem.

Council, Nat. Roads and Motorists' Assoc., 1969-. Mem. Senate, 1954-74, Dep. Chancellor, 1958-66, Hon. LLD, Univ. of Sydney. *Address:* 4 Leumeah Street, Cronulla, NSW 2230, Australia. *T:* 523-5465. *Club:* Imperial Service (Sydney).

DOUGHTY, Dame Adelaide, DBE 1971 (CBE 1964); *b* 2 Dec. 1908; *d* of E. H. Shackell, Melbourne, Australia; *m* 1931, Charles John Addison Doughty, QC (*d* 1973); one *s* one *d*. *Educ:* St Catherine's Sch., Melbourne; St Hilda's Coll., Oxford (BA). Chm., Nat. Women's Advisory Cttee, Conservative Party, 1963-66; Chm., Nat. Union of Conservative and Unionist Party, 1967; Governor: English-Speaking Union, 1958-72 (Dep.-Chm. 1971-72); Skinners' Company's School for Girls, 1951-. Mem. Grand Council, Cancer Res. Campaign, 1974. *Address:* Flat 4, 89 Onslow Square, SW7 3LT. *T:* 01-584 5126.

DOUGHTY, George Henry; General Secretary, Technical and Supervisory Section, Amalgamated Union of Engineering Workers, 1971-74, retired; Member: Royal Commission on Distribution of Income and Wealth Central Arbitration Committee; *b* 17 May 1911; British; *m* 1941, Mildred Dawson; two *s*. *Educ:* Handsworth Tech. Sch.; Aston Technical Coll. Draughtsman; trained at General Electric Co., Birmingham, 1927-32; employed as Design Draughtsman: English Electric, Stafford 1932-33; GEC Birmingham, 1934-46. With Draughtsmen's & Allied Technician's Assoc., 1946-71, General Secretary, 1952-71. Mem., Gen. Council of TUC, 1968-74; Member: Design Council, 1974-; Independent Review Cttee, 1976-; Chm., EDC for Electrical Engrg, 1974-. *Publications:* various technical and Trade Union publications. *Recreation:* photography. *Address:* Short Way, Whitton, Twickenham, Middx. *T:* 01-894 0299.

DOUGLAS, family name of **Viscount Chilston, Baron Douglas of Barloch, Earl of Morton,** and **Marquess of Queensberry.**

DOUGLAS OF BARLOCH, 1st Baron, *cr* 1950, of Maxfield, Sussex; **Francis Campbell Ross Douglas,** KCMG 1947; MA; LLD (hc), Royal University of Malta; Partner in Douglas & Company, Solicitors; *b* Manitoba, 21 Oct. 1889; *s* of late Francis J. B. Douglas; *m* 1st, Minnie Findlay Smith, MA, JP, CStJ (*d* 1969); one *d*; 2nd, Adela Elizabeth, widow of Captain George La Croix Baudains, DSO, MC. *Educ:* Glasgow Univ. Journalist, Accountant, Solicitor; MP (Lab) for North Battersea, 1940-46; Parliamentary Private Sec. to Parliamentary Sec. of Board of Education, 1940-45; Parliamentary Private Sec. to Home Sec., 1945-46; Temp. Chm., House of Commons and Chm. of Standing Cttees, 1945-46; Chm. of Estimates Cttee, 1945-46; Mem. of Railway Assessment Authority, 1938-46; Mem. of Anglo-Scottish Railway Assessment Authority, 1941-46; Mem. of Public Works Loan Board, 1936-46; Chm. of Finance Cttee of LCC, 1940-46; Governor and Comdr-in-Chief of Malta, 1946-49; Vice-Chm. of Corby Development Corp., 1950-62; Deputy Speaker of House of Lords, 1962-; FRAS; KStJ. *Publications:* Land Value Rating, 1961; numerous pamphlets and articles on land tenure, taxation, soil fertility and nutrition. *Heir:* none. *Address:* 8 Cambridge Road, SW11. *T:* 01-228 2247; Maxfield Manor, Three Oaks, Sussex. *T:* Hastings 751074.

DOUGLAS, Dr Alexander Edgar, FRS 1970; FRSC 1954; Principal Research Officer, National Research Council of Canada, since 1973 (Director, Division of Physics, 1969-73); *b* 12 April 1916; *s* of Donald Douglas and Jessie F. Douglas (née Carwardine); *m* 1945, Phyllis H. Wright; two *s* one *d*. *Educ:* Univ. of Saskatchewan; Pennsylvania State University. BA 1939, MA 1940, Saskatchewan; PhD Penn 1948. Nat. Research Council of Canada: Research Scientist, Acoustics Lab., 1942-46; Spectroscopy Lab., 1948; Assoc. Dir, Div. of Pure Physics, 1967. Fellow, American Physical Soc., 1970; Pres., Canadian Assoc. of Physicists, 1975. *Publications:* numerous articles on spectroscopy and molecular structure. *Address:* 150 Blenheim Drive, Ottawa, Ont, Canada. *T:* 746-1453.

DOUGLAS, Prof. Alexander Stuart; Regius Professor of Medicine, University of Aberdeen, since 1970; *b* 2 Oct. 1921; *s* of late Dr R. Douglas, MOH for Moray and Nairn; *m* 1954, Christine McClymont Stewart; one *s* one *d*. *Educ:* Elgin Academy, Morayshire. Mil. Service, RAMC, 1945-48 (despatches 1947). Research Fellow, Radcliffe Infirmary, Oxford, and Postgrad. Med. Sch., London, 1951-53; Lectr, Sen. Lectr and Reader in Medicine, Univ. Dept of Med., Royal Infirmary, Glasgow, 1953-64; Hon. Consultant status, 1957; Prof. of Med., Univ. of Glasgow, 1964-70; secondment to Univ. of East Africa with hon. academic rank of Prof., 1965; Hon. Consultant Physician in Administrative Charge of wards, Royal Infirmary, Glasgow, 1968-70. *Publications:* scientific papers on blood coagulation, etc. *Recreations:* curling, travel. *Address:* Department of Medicine, University Medical Buildings,

Foresterhill, Aberdeen AB9 2ZD. *T:* Aberdeen 23423 (ext. 2454).

DOUGLAS, Lt-Col Archibald Vivian Campbell, MA; JP; DL; *b* 6 Nov. 1902; *s* of late Brig.-Gen. D. C. Douglas, CB, Mains, Milngavie, Dunbartonshire; *m* 1927, Elizabeth Cicely, 2nd *d* of late Sir Maurice de Bunsen, 1st Bt, PC, GCMG, GCVO, CB; two *d. Educ:* Eton; Christ Church, Oxford. 2nd Lieut Scots Guards, 1925; Captain 1931; Lt-Col 1943, DL 1953, Dunbartonshire; Mem. of Royal Company of Archers (Queen's Body Guard for Scotland). Vice-Lieutenant Co. Dunbarton, 1957-68. JP Perthshire, 1962. *Address:* Laraich, Aberfoyle, by Stirling. *T:* Aberfoyle 232. *Club:* New (Edinburgh).

DOUGLAS, Arthur John Alexander, CMG 1965; OBE 1962; Assistant Secretary, Ministry of Overseas Development, since 1975; *b* 31 May 1920; *s* of Alexander and Eileen Douglas; *m* 1948, Christine Scott Dyke; two *d. Educ:* Dumfries Academy; Edinburgh Univ. Royal Navy, 1940-45. District Officer, Basutoland, 1946; Seconded Colonial Office, 1957; Administration Sec., Bechuanaland, 1959; Government Sec. and Chief Sec. 1962-65; Dep. Commissioner for Bechuanaland, 1965-66; Min. of Overseas Develt, 1967-. *Address:* 57 Lucastes Avenue, Haywards Heath, West Sussex. *Club:* Royal Commonwealth Society.

DOUGLAS, Lord Cecil Charles; late Lt KOSB and RFC; *b* 27 Dec. 1898; 2nd *s* of 10th Marquess of Queensberry; *m* 1927, Ruby St B. Kirkley, 2nd *d* of De Vere Fenn; one *d. Educ:* Lancing; RMC, Sandhurst. Served European War, 1914 (wounded). *Address:* 42 Green Street, W1. *T:* 01-499 3343. *Clubs:* White's; Puffins (Edinburgh).

DOUGLAS, Prof. Charles Primrose, FRCOG; Professor of Obstetrics and Gynæcology, University of Cambridge, since 1976; *b* 17 Feb. 1921; *s* of Dr C. Douglas, Ayr, Scotland; *m* 1948, Angela Francis; three *s* one *d. Educ:* Loretto Sch.; Peterhouse; Edinburgh Univ. Surg. Lieut RNVR, 1944-47. Registrar and Sen. Registrar, Victoria Infirmary, Glasgow, 1950-59; William Waldorf Astor Foundn Fellow, 1957; Visiting Fellow, Duke Univ., NC, 1957; Sen. Lectr, Univ. of the West Indies, 1959-65; Prof. of Obst. and Gyn., Royal Free Hosp. Sch. of Medicine, 1965-76. Member: Bd of Governors, Royal Free Hosp., 1972-74; Camden and Islington AHA, 1974-76. *Publications:* contribs to BMJ, Amer. Heart Jl, Jl of Obst. and Gynæc. of Brit. Commonwealth, etc. *Recreations:* tennis, equestrian events, skin diving. *Address:* Old Mill House, Linton Road, Balsham, Cambs. *Club:* Royal Naval Volunteer Reserve (Scotland).

DOUGLAS, David Charles, MA Oxon; Hon. DLitt Wales; Hon. DLitt Exeter; Docteur *hc,* Caen; FBA 1949; Emeritus Professor of History, Bristol University, since 1963; Hon. Fellow, Keble College, Oxford; *b* London, 1898; *o s* of Dr J. J. Douglas and Margaret E. Peake; *m* 1932, Evelyn Helen, *o d* of Dr B. M. Wilson; one *d. Educ:* Sedbergh; Keble Coll., Oxford (Louisa Wakeman Scholar). 1st Class Hons in Modern History, Oxford, 1921; University Research Scholar in Medieval History and Thought, Oxford, 1922-24; Lecturer in History, Glasgow Univ., 1924-34; Prof. of History, University Coll. of the South West, 1934-39; Prof. of Medieval History, Leeds Univ., 1939-45; Prof. of History, Bristol Univ., 1945-63; Dean of the Faculty of Arts, 1958-60; Trustee of London Museum, 1945-70; David Murray Lectr to University of Glasgow, 1946, Sir Walter Raleigh Lectr to Brit. Acad., 1947; Ford's Lectr in English History, Oxford Univ., 1962-63; Lewis Fry Memorial Lectr, Bristol Univ., 1969. Vice-Pres., Royal Historical Soc., 1953-57; Pres., Bristol and Glos Archæological Soc., 1956. *Publications:* The Norman Conquest, 1926; The Social Structure of Medieval East Anglia, 1927; The Age of the Normans, 1928; Feudal Documents from the Abbey of Bury St Edmunds, 1932; The Development of Medieval Europe, 1935; English Scholars, 1939 (James Tait Black Memorial Prize); Domesday Monachorum, 1944; The Rise of Normandy, 1947; William the Conqueror, 1964; The Norman Achievement 1050-1100, 1969; The Norman Fate 1100-1154, 1976; General Editor, English Historical Documents, 1953, etc.; articles in English Historical Review, Times Lit. Supplt, History, Economic History Review, Revue Historique, French Studies, etc. *Recreation:* book-collecting. *Address:* 4 Henleaze Gardens, Bristol. *Club:* United Oxford & Cambridge University.

DOUGLAS, Sir Donald (Macleod), Kt 1972; MBE 1943; ChM St Andrews, MS Minn, FRCSE; FRCS; FRSE 1973; Surgeon to the Queen in Scotland; Professor of Surgery, University of Dundee (formerly Queen's College), 1951-76; Surgeon, Ninewells Hospital, Dundee, 1951-76; *b* 28 June 1911; *s* of William Douglas and Christina Broom; *m* 1945, Margaret Diana Whitley; two *s* two *d. Educ:* Madras Coll.; Universities of

St Andrews and Minnesota. Commonwealth Fellow in Surgery, Mayo Clinic, University of Minnesota, USA, 1937-39; First Asst in Surgery, British Postgraduate Medical Sch., 1939-40; RAMC, 1941-45; Reader in Experimental Surgery, University of Edinburgh, 1945-51; Asst Surgeon, Edinburgh Municipal Hospitals, 1945; formerly Surgeon, Royal Infirmary, Dundee. Assoc. Asst Surgeon, Royal Infirmary, Edinburgh. Dean of Faculty of Medicine, Univ. of Dundee, 1969-70. President: RCSE, 1971-73; Assoc. of Surgeons of GB and Ireland, 1964; Surgical Research Soc. of GB, 1966-69; Harveian Soc., 1974. Hon. FACS, 1972; Hon. FRCSI, 1973. Hon. DSc St Andrews, 1972. *Publications:* Wound Healing, 1965; The Thoughtful Surgeon, 1970; Surgical Departments in Hospitals, 1971. *Address:* The Whitehouse of Nevay, Newtyle, Angus. *T:* Newtyle 315.

DOUGLAS, Donald Wills; President Douglas Aircraft Co. Inc., 1928-57, Chairman, 1957-67, Hon. Chairman since 1967; *b* 6 April 1892; *s* of William Edward Douglas and Dorothy Locker; *m* 1954, Marguerite Tucker; four *s* one *d* (by a previous marr.). *Educ:* United States Naval Acad.; MIT (BSc 1914). Asst Instructor in aero-dynamics, Mass. Inst. of Tech., 1914-15; Chief Engineer, G. L. Martin Co., Los Angeles, 1915-16; Chief Civilian Aero Engineer, US Signal Corps, 1916; Chief Engineer, G. L. Martin Co., Cleveland, 1916-20; Pres., Douglas Co., 1920-28. President's Certificate of Merit, 1947; Guggenheim Medal, 1939; Collier Trophy, 1940; Comdr, Order of Orange-Nassau, 1950; Chevalier, Legion of Honour, 1950. *Recreations:* yachting, fishing, hunting. *Address:* 14948 Camarosa Drive, Pacific Palisades, Calif. 90272, USA. *Club:* Los Angeles Yacht (Wilmington, Calif.).

DOUGLAS, Sir (Edward) Sholto, Kt 1977; Solicitor of the Supreme Court of Queensland, since 1934; *b* 23 Dec. 1909; *s* of Hon. Mr Justice E. A. Douglas and Annette Eileen Power; *m* 1939, Mary Constance Curr. *Educ:* St Ignatius Coll., Riverview, Sydney. Queensland Law Society Incorporated: Mem. Council, 1954-76; Actg Pres., 1960; Pres., 1962-64; Mem., Statutory Cttee, 1976-77; Member: Legal Assistance Cttee, Qld, 1965-77; Solicitors' Bd, 1969-75; Exec. Mem., Law Council of Aust., 1973-75. President: Taxpayers Assoc. of Qld, 1955-58; Federated Taxpayers of Aust., 1957-58; Mem. Adv. Cttee, Terminating and Permanent Building Socs, 1966-77. Pres., Qld Div., Nat. Heart Foundn, 1976-77 (Vice-Pres., 1966-75); Vice-Pres., RSPCA, 1965-77. *Recreations:* racing, gardening. *Address:* 81 Markwell Street, Hamilton, Brisbane, Qld 4007, Australia. *T:* 268.2759. *Clubs:* Queensland, Brisbane (Pres. 1965), Tattersalls, Royal Queensland Golf, Queensland Turf, Tattersalls Racing, Brisbane Amateur Turf (all Brisbane).

DOUGLAS, Gavin Stuart, RD 1970; QC (Scot.) 1971; *b* 12 June 1932; *y s* of late Gilbert Georgeson Douglas and Rosena Campbell Douglas. *Educ:* South Morningside Sch.; George Heriot's Sch.; Edinburgh Univ. MA 1953, LLB 1955. Qual. as Solicitor, 1955; nat. service with RN, 1955-57. Admitted to Faculty of Advocates, 1958; Sub-editor (part-time), The Scotsman, 1957-61; Mem. Lord Advocate's Dept in London (as Parly Draftsman), 1961-64; returned to practice at Scots Bar, 1964; Junior Counsel to BoT, 1965; Counsel to Scottish Law Commn, 1965; Hon. Sheriff in various sheriffdoms, 1965; a Chm. of Industrial Tribunals, 1966; Counsel to Sec. of State for Scotland under Private Legislation Procedure (Scotland) Act 1936, 1969-75, Sen. Counsel, 1975-. *Recreations:* golf, ski-ing. *Address:* 1 India Buildings, Victoria Street, Edinburgh EH1 2EX. *Clubs:* University Staff (Edinburgh); RNVR (Glasgow).

DOUGLAS, Henry Russell, FJI; Legal Manager, News Group Newspapers, since 1976; *b* Bishopbriggs, Lanarkshire, 11 Feb. 1925; 2nd *s* of Russell Douglas and Jeanie Douglas Douglas (*née* Drysdale); *m* 1951, Elizabeth Mary, *d* of late Ralph Nowell, CB; two *s* three *d. Educ:* various Scottish and English Grammar Schools; Lincoln Coll., Oxford (MA Hons). Served RNVR, 1943-46 (Sub-Lt, submarines). Merchant Navy, 1946-47; Oxford Univ., 1947-50; Liverpool Daily Post, 1950-69; The Sun, 1969-76. Inst of Journalists, 1956: Fellow, 1969; Pres., 1972-73; Chm. of Executive, 1973-76; Mem. Press Council, 1972-; Mem. Council, Newspaper Press Fund, 1973; Founder Mem. and Treasurer, Media Society, 1973. *Publications:* ephemeral. *Recreations:* chess, travel, history. *Address:* Austen Croft, 31 Austen Road, Guildford, Surrey. *T:* Guildford 76960. *Clubs:* United Oxford & Cambridge University; Surrey County Cricket, Tyrrell's Wood Golf.

DOUGLAS, Very Rev. Hugh Osborne, CBE 1961; DD, LLD; Dean of the Chapel Royal in Scotland, since 1974; Chaplain to The Queen since 1959; Minister at Dundee Parish Church (St Mary's), 1951-77; Moderator of the General Assembly of the Church of Scotland, May 1970- May 1971; *b* Glasgow, 11 Sept.

1911; s of Rev. Robert Baillie Douglas, DD, missionary in W India, and Mary Isabella Osborne. m 1939, Isabel Crammond, d of William Rutherford, Coldstream, Berwicks; one s two d. Educ: Glasgow Academy; Glasgow Univ.; Trinity Coll., Glasgow. MA 1st Cl. Hons (Classics), 1932. Licensed to preach by Presbytery of Glasgow, 1935; Asst, Govan Old Parish Church, 1935-39; Ordained, Glasgow, 1937; Minister: St John's Leven, 1939; North Leith, Edinburgh, 1942. Member: Legal Aid Central Cttee of Law Soc. of Scotland, 1955-; Scottish Religious Advisory Cttee of BBC, 1956-58; Gen. Advisory Council of BBC, 1966-69; Convener of Gen. Assembly's Special Cttee on Fourth Centenary of the Reformation, 1955-60; Convener of Gen. Assembly's Special Cttee on Religious Education, 1960-64. Centenary Preacher, St Andrew's Church, Brisbane, 1962. Visiting Lectr, Christian Council of Ghana, 1967. Hon. Governor, Glasgow Acad., 1971. Hon. DD St Andrews, 1958; Hon. LLD Dundee, 1971. Publications: Coping with Life, 1964; various pamphlets and articles. Recreation: golf. Address: Broomlea, 7A Windmill Road, St Andrews. T: St Andrews 3232. Club: New (Edinburgh).

DOUGLAS, James Albert Sholto, CMG 1966; Director, IDA/IBRD Education Project Implementation Unit, since 1969; b 23 April 1913; s of Dr James Henry Sholto Douglas and Cécile Anne (née Brotherson); m 1945, Marjorie Lucille (née Reynolds); two s. Educ: Privately in Guyana (Brit. Guiana); Culford Sch., England. Entered Brit. Guyana CS in Commissary's Dept 1932; various posts in Dist Admin, 1933-48; Asst Dist Comr, 1948; Dist Comr, 1953; seconded as a Local Govt Comr, 1957; Dep. Comr of Local Govt, 1960; Permanent Sec., Community Develt and Educn, 1961, Home Affairs 1961-66; Min. of Education, 1966; retired from Guyana Civil Service, 1972. Recreations: swimming, riding. Address: 93 Duke Street, Georgetown, Guyana. T: 61403. Club: Royal Commonwealth Society.

DOUGLAS, James Archibald, MA, DSc; FGS; Professor Emeritus, Geology, in the University of Oxford since 1950; b 1 Dec. 1884; s of James Herbert Douglas, Ilkley, Yorks; m 1914, Hannah Call Weddell (d 1966); two s two d. Educ: Haileybury Coll.; Keble Coll., Oxford. Fellow University Coll., Oxford, 1937. Former Sec. and Vice-Pres. Geological Soc. of London. Served European War, Captain 1st Batt. Gordon Highlanders and 172 Tunnelling Co., RE; Lieut-Col, OC 6th Oxon (Oxford City) Bn HG, 1941. Bolitho Gold Medal, Royal Geol Society, Cornwall, 1939. Foreign Mem., Geol. Soc. of Peru, 1952. Recreation: yachting. Address: Saxonbury, Yarmouth, Isle of Wight. T: Yarmouth 760380.

DOUGLAS, James Murray; Secretary-General, Country Landowners Association, since 1970; b 26 Sept. 1925; s of Herbert and Amy Douglas, Brechin; m 1950, Julie Kemmner; one s one d. Educ: Morrison's Acad., Crieff; Aberdeen Univ. (MA); Balliol Coll., Oxford (BA). Entered Civil Service, 1950; Treasury, 1960-63; Asst Sec., Min. of Housing and Local Govt, 1964; Sec. to Royal Commn on Local Govt, 1966-69; Vice-Pres., Confedn of European Agriculture, 1971; Mem., Econ. Develt Cttee for Agriculture, 1972. Publications: various articles on local govt and landowning. Recreations: tennis, music. Address: 1 Oldfield Close, Bickley, Kent. T: 01-467 3213. Club: United Oxford & Cambridge University.

DOUGLAS, Katharine Greenhill; Matron, St Mary's Hospital, Paddington, W2, 1949-63, retired; b 13 Jan. 1908; yr d of Rev. Daniel Greenhill Douglas and of Catherine Eudora Douglas. Educ: St Andrews Sch., Bexhill-on-Sea. Student Nurse, Nightingale Training Sch., St Thomas's Hospital, 1932-36; SRN 1936; Staff Nurse, St Thomas's Hospital, 1936-37; Pupil Midwife, Gen. Lying-In Hospital, SE1, 1937-38; SCM 1938; Ward Sister, St Thomas's Hospital, 1938-43; Administrative Sister, 1943-45; Dep. Matron, 1945-49. Chm., Standing Nursing Advisory Cttee, 1951-57; Mem. of Central Health Services Council, 1951-57. Recreations: music, needlework, tennis. Address: 33 Digdens Rise, Epsom, Surrey. T: Epsom 22048.

DOUGLAS, Kenneth; Chairman: Kenton Shipping Services, Darlington, since 1968; Douglas (Kilbride) Ltd, since 1972; Chairman and Managing Director, Steel Structures Ltd, since 1974; b 28 Oct. 1920; British; m 1942, Doris Lewer; one s two d. Educ: Sunderland Technical Coll. Dep. Shipyard Manager, Vickers Armstrong Naval Yard, Newcastle-upon-Tyne, 1946-53; Dir and Gen. Manager, Wm Gray & Co. Ltd, West Hartlepool, 1954-58; Managing Director: Austin & Pickersgill Ltd, Sunderland, 1958-69; Upper Clyde Shipbuilders Ltd, 1969-72; Dep. Chm., Govan Shipbuilders, 1971-73. Recreations: fishing, golf. Address: Dentdale, Tower Road, Darlington, Co. Durham; Kirkstile, Romaldkirk, Barnard Castle, Co. Durham. Club: Western (Glasgow).

DOUGLAS, Prof. Mary; Professor of Social Anthropology, University College London, since 1970; b 25 March 1921; d of Gilbert Charles Tew and Phyllis Twomey; m 1951, James A. T. Douglas, OBE; two s one d. Educ: Univ. of Oxford (MA, BSc, PhD). Returned to Oxford, 1946, to train as anthropologist; fieldwork in Belgian Congo, 1949-50 and 1953; Lectr in Anthropology, Univ. of Oxford, 1950; Univ. of London, 1951-. Res. Scholar, Russell Sage Foundn, NY, 1977. Publications: The Lele of the Kasai, 1963; Purity and Danger, 1966; Natural Symbols, 1970; Implicit Meanings, 1976. Address: 22 Hillway, N6 6QA. T: 01-340 6469. Club: United Oxford & Cambridge University.

DOUGLAS, Richard Giles; Director: Berry Wiggins, 1975-77; Ferguson Brothers (Port Glasgow), since 1975; b 4 Jan. 1932; m 1954, Jean Gray, d of Andrew Arnott; two d. Educ: Co-operative College, Stanford Hall, Loughborough; Univ. of Strathclyde. Engineer (Marine); Mem. AEF. Tutor organiser in Adult Educn, Co-operative movement, 1957; Sectional Educn Officer, Scotland, 1958-61; Lectr in Economics, Dundee Coll. of Technol., 1964-70. Contested (Lab): South Angus, 1964, Edinburgh West, 1966, Glasgow Pollok, March 1967; (Lab and Co-op) Clackmannan and E Stirlingshire, Oct. 1974; MP (Lab and Co-op) Clackmannan and E Stirlingshire, 1970-Feb. 1974. Hon. Mem., Univ. of Strathclyde Staff Club. Address: Braehead House, High Street, Auchtermuchty, Fife.

DOUGLAS, Sir Robert (McCallum), Kt 1976; OBE 1956; Chairman, Robert M. Douglas Holdings Limited, since 1952; b 2 Feb. 1899; s of John Douglas and Eugenia McCallum; m 1927, Millicent Irene Tomkys Morgan; one s one d. Educ: Terregles Sch.; Dumfries Academy. Served Army, 1916-19. Served 10 years with civil engineering contracting co., 1920-30; founded Douglas Group of Companies, 1930. Mem., MPBW Midland Regional Jt Adv. Cttee, 1940-46. Federation of Civil Engineering Contractors: Chm., Midland Section, 1942-43 and 1947-48; Chm. Council, 1948-49; Pres., 1958-60; Chm. Council, Burton-on-Trent Graduate Medical Centre. Recreations: shooting, farming. Address: Dunstall Hall, Barton-under-Needwood, Burton-on-Trent, Staffordshire DE13 8BE. T: Barton-under-Needwood 2471. Clubs: Caledonian; Birmingham (Birmingham).

DOUGLAS, Prof. Ronald Walter, DSc, FInstP, FSGT; Professor of Glass Technology, University of Sheffield, 1955-75; b 28 March 1910; s of John H. P. and A. E. Douglas; m 1933, Edna Maud Cadle; two s. Educ: Latymer Upper Sch.; Sir John Cass Coll., London. Mem., Research Staff, research Laboratories of General Electric Company, 1927-55. Pres., Internat. Commn on Glass, 1972-75. Publications: (with S. Frank) A History of Glassmaking, 1972; many papers on the physics of glass and semiconductors. Address: Burford Lea, Eymore, West Hill, Ottery St Mary, Devon.

DOUGLAS, Sir Sholto; see Douglas, Sir E. S.

DOUGLAS, Sir Sholto (Courtenay Mackenzie), 5th Bt, cr 1831; MC 1918; b 27 June 1890; s of Donald Sholto Mackenzie Douglas (d 1928), and Edith Elizabeth Anne (d 1933), y d of George Robinson, Bagatelle, Mauritius; S cousin 1954; m 1929, Lorna Tichborne, d of Captain Hugh Nangle; two d. Served European War, 1914-18 (MC) and War of 1939-45 with Seaforth Highlanders. Heir: none. Address: 192 Cooden Drive, Cooden, Sussex.

DOUGLAS, William Orville; Associate Justice, Supreme Court of United States, Washington, DC, 1939-75, retired; b 16 Oct. 1898; s of William Douglas and Julia Bickford Fiske; m 1st, 1923, Mildred Riddle; one s one d; 2nd, 1954, Mercedes Hester; 3rd, 1963, Joan Martin; 4th, Cathleen Heffernan. Educ: Whitman Coll., Washington; Columbia Univ. Law Sch., New York City. Practised Law in New York City, 1925-27; Mem., Columbia Law Sch., Faculty 1925-28 and Yale Law Sch. Faculty, 1928-34; Dir, Protective Cttee Study, Securities and Exchange Comm., 1934-36; Mem., Securities and Exchange Comm., 1936-39, Chm., 1937-39. Fellow Royal Geographical Soc., London. Publications: Democracy and Finance, 1940; Being an American, 1948; Of Men and Mountains, 1950; Strange Lands and Friendly People, 1951; Beyond the High Himalayas, 1952; North From Malaya, 1953; Almanac of Liberty, 1954; Russian Journey, 1956; We The Judges, 1956; The Right of People, 1958; Exploring the Himalaya, 1958; West of the Indus, 1958; America Challenged, 1960; My Wilderness-The Pacific West, 1960; A Living Bill of Rights, 1961; Muir of the Mountains, 1961; My Wilderness-East to Katahdin, 1961; Democracy's Manifesto, 1962; Mr Lincoln and the Negroes, 1963; Freedom of the Mind, 1963; The Anatomy of Liberty, 1963; A Wilderness Bill of Rights, 1965; The Bible and the

Schools, 1966; Farewell to Texas, 1967; Toward a Global Federalism, 1969; Points of Rebellion, 1970; International Dissent, 1971; Holocaust or Hemispheric Co-operation, 1972; The Three Hundred Year War, 1972; Go East Young Man, 1974; contrib. to various legal periodicals. *Recreations:* horseback riding, hiking. *Address:* Supreme Court of the US, Washington, DC 20543, USA; Goose Prairie, Washington 98929, USA. *Clubs:* University (Washington, DC); Yale, Circumnavigators', Explorers', Overseas Press Club (NY City); Himalayan (Delhi, India).

DOUGLAS, Rt. Hon. Sir William (Randolph), PC 1977; Kt 1969; Chief Justice of Barbados, since 1965; *b* Barbados, 24 Sept. 1921; *e s* of William P. Douglas and Emily Frances Douglas (*née* Nurse); *m* 1951, Thelma Ruth (*née* Gilkes); one *s* one *d. Educ:* Bannatyne Sch. and Verdun High Sch., Verdun, Que., Canada; McGill Univ. (BA, Hons); London Sch. of Economics (LLB). Private Practice at Barbados Bar, 1948-50; Dep. Registrar, Barbados, 1950; Resident Magistrate, Jamaica, 1955; Asst Attorney-Gen., Jamaica, 1959; Solicitor-Gen., Jamaica, 1962; Puisne Judge, Jamaica, 1962. Chm., Commonwealth Caribbean Council of Legal Education, 1971-; Member: Internat. Labour Organisation's Cttee of Experts on the Application of Conventions and Recommendations; Inter-American Juridical Cttee; President: Barbados Assoc. for the Blind and Deaf; UN Assoc. of Barbados; Barbados Boy Scouts Assoc. *Address:* Leland, Pine Gardens, St Michael, Barbados. *T:* 92030. *Club:* Barbados Yacht.

DOUGLAS-HAMILTON, family name of **Duke of Hamilton** and **Earl of Selkirk.**

DOUGLAS-HAMILTON, Lord James Alexander; MP (C) Edinburgh West since Oct. 1974; *b* 31 July 1942; 2nd *s* of 14th Duke of Hamilton, and *b* of 15th Duke of Hamilton, *qv*; *m* 1974, Hon. Priscilla Susan Buchan, *d* of Baron Tweedsmuir, *qv* and Baroness Tweedsmuir of Belhelvie, *qv. Educ:* Eton College, Balliol Coll., Oxford (MA, Mod. History; Oxford Boxing Blue, 1961; Pres., Oxford Univ. Cons. Assoc., 1963; Pres., Oxford Union Soc., 1964); Edinburgh Univ. (LLB, Scots Law). Advocate at Scots Bar, 1968. Town Councillor, Murrayfield-Cramond, Edinburgh, 1972. Captain Cameronian Co., 2 Bn Low Vols (TAVR), 1972. *Publication:* Motive for a Mission: The Story Behind Hess's Flight to Britain, 1971. *Recreations:* golf, forestry. *Address:* 3 Blackie House, Lady Stair's Close, Edinburgh. *T:* 031-225 1482. *Clubs:* New (Edinburgh); Hon. Company of Edinburgh Golfers.

DOUGLAS-HOME, family name of **Baroness Dacre** and **Baron Home of the Hirsel.**

DOUGLAS-HOME, Hon. David Alexander Cospatrick; Director, Morgan Grenfell & Co. Ltd, since 1974; *b* 20 Nov. 1943; *o s* of Baron Home of the Hirsel, *qv*; *heir* to Earldom of Home; *m* 1972, Jane Margaret, *yr d* of Col J. Williams-Wynne, *qv. Educ:* Eton College; Christ Church, Oxford (BA 1966). Director: Gulf Development Co., 1974-; Arab Morgan Grenfell Finance Co. Ltd, 1974- (Dep. Chm., 1975-); Morgan Grenfell Egyptian Finance Co. Ltd, 1975-77; Arab-British Chamber of Commerce, 1975-. Member, Committee for Middle East Trade, 1973-75. Governor, Ditchley Foundn, 1977-. *Recreations:* shooting, fishing, gardening, cricket. *Address:* 11 Moore Street, SW3. *Club:* Turf.

DOUGLAS-HOME, Hon. William; *see* Home.

DOUGLAS-MANN, Bruce Leslie Home; MP (Lab) Merton, Mitcham and Morden, since 1974 (North Kensington, 1970-74); *b* 23 June 1927; *s* of Leslie John Douglas-Mann, MC and Alice Home Douglas-Mann; *m* 1955, Helen Tucker; one *s* one *d. Educ:* Upper Canada Coll., Toronto; Jesus Coll., Oxford. Leading Seaman, RN, 1945-48; Oxford, 1948-51; Solicitor, private legal practice, 1954-. Contested (Lab): St Albans, 1964; Maldon, 1966; Vice-Chm., Parly Lab. Party Environment Gp, 1972-; Chm., Parly Lab. Party Housing and Construction Gp, 1974-. Chm., Soc. of Lab. Lawyers. Pres., Socialist Environment Res. Assoc., 1973-; Mem. Bd, Shelter, 1974-. Mem., Kensington or Kensington and Chelsea Borough Council, 1962-68. *Publications:* pamphlets: (ed) The End of the Private Landlord, 1973; Accidents at Work—Compensation for All, 1974. *Address:* 26 Queensdale Road, W11. *T:* 01-727 6780.

DOUGLAS-PENNANT, family name of **Baron Penrhyn.**

DOUGLAS-SCOTT-MONTAGU, family name of **Baron Montagu of Beaulieu.**

DOUGLAS-WILSON, Ian, MD, FRCPE; Editor of the Lancet, 1965-76; *b* 12 May 1912; *o s* of late Dr H. Douglas-Wilson; *m* 1939, Beatrice May, *e d* of late R. P. Bevan; one *s* two *d. Educ:* Marlborough Coll.; Edinburgh Univ. MB ChB 1936; MD (commended) Edinburgh 1938; FRCP Edinburgh 1945. Served with RAMC, 1940-45 (temp. Major). House-physician, Royal Infirmary, Edinburgh, 1937; joined the Lancet staff, 1946; Asst Ed., 1952-62; Dep. Ed., 1962-64. Dr (*hc*) Edinburgh, 1974. *Publications:* contribs to medical jls. *Address:* 14 St Matthew's Drive, Bickley, Bromley, Kent. *T:* 01-467 1703.

DOUGLAS-WITHERS, Maj.-Gen. John Keppel Ingold, CBE 1969; MC 1943; Assistant Director and Group Personnel Manager, Jardine Matheson & Co. Ltd, Hong Kong, since 1974; *b* 11 Dec. 1919; *s* of late Lt-Col H. H. Douglas-Withers, OBE, MC, FSA, and of Mrs V. G. Douglas-Withers; *m* 1945, Sylvia Beatrice Dean, Croydon, Surrey; one *s* one *d. Educ:* Shrewsbury Sch.; Christ Church, Oxford. Diploma in French, Univ. of Poitiers, 1938; Associate of Inst. of Linguists, in French and German, 1939. Commissioned into RA, 1940; Service in UK, Iraq, Western Desert, N Africa and Italy, 1940-45. Instr in Gunnery, Sch. of Artillery, Larkhill, 1945-47; service in Canal Zone, 1948-49; attended Staff Coll., Camberley, 1950; Staff appt in WO (Mil. Ops), 1951-53; service in The King's Troop, RHA, 1954-55; Instr, Staff Coll., Camberley, 1956-58; Battery Comdr, G Bty, Mercers Troop, RHA, 1959-60; Staff appt in WO (Mil. Sec. Dept), 1961; commanded 49 Field Regt in BAOR and Hong Kong, 1962-64; student at IDC, 1965; Comd 6 Inf. Bde in BAOR, 1966-67; Chief of Staff, 1st Brit. Corps, 1968-69; GOC SW District, 1970-71; Asst Chief of Personnel and Logistics, MoD, 1972-74; retired 1974. Col Comdt RA, 1974-. *Recreations:* golf, history, music. *Address:* c/o Australia and New Zealand Banking Group, 71 Cornhill, EC3. *Clubs:* East India, Devonshire, Sports and Public Schools, MCC; Hong Kong.

DOUGLASS, family name of **Baron Douglass of Cleveland.**

DOUGLASS OF CLEVELAND, Baron *cr* 1967 (Life Peer); **Harry Douglass,** Kt 1964; General Secretary, Iron and Steel Trades Confederation, 1953-67; *b* 1 Jan. 1902; *m* 1926, Edith Amer; one *d. Educ:* Elementary Sch. and WEA. Mem. Brit. Labour Party Exec. 1948-53; Pres., Internat. Metalworkers Federation, 1950-59; Member: Trades Union Congress, 1953-67 (Chm., 1966-67); Council, DSIR, 1954-59; Advisory Council, Export Credits Guarantee Dept, 1954-57, 1965-67; Iron and Steel Board, 1960-67; Export Council for Europe, 1961-67; NEDC, 1962-67; (part-time) Electricity Council, 1966-71; Monopolies Commn, 1967-70; Chairman: TUC Economic Cttee, 1962-67; British Productivity Council, 1962-67. *Address:* 5 The Chase, Stanmore, Mddx. *T:* (home) 01-954 2101.

DOULTON, Alfred John Farre, CBE 1973 (OBE 1946); TD 1954; psc 1943; MA Oxon; Head of Statistical Team and Comptroller, Independent Schools Information Service, since 1974; *b* 9 July 1911; *s* of H. V. Doulton, Housemaster, Dulwich Coll., and Constance Jessie Farre, Dulwich; *m* 1940, Vera Daphne, *d* of A. R. Wheatley, Esher; four *s* one *d. Educ:* Dulwich Coll.; Brasenose Coll., Oxford (Classical Scholar). Asst Master, Uppingham School, 1934-40. Served War, 1940-46 (despatches twice); DAAG 11 Army Group, 1944; active service, Burma, Malaya, Java, 1945-46; DAQMG 4 Corps, AA&QMG 23 Indian Division, 1945-46. Burma Star, Far East and GS Medal with Java Clasp. Head of Classics and Housemaster of The Lodge, Uppingham Sch., 1946; Headmaster, Highgate Sch., 1955-74. Vice-Chm., HMC, 1967 (Hon. Treasurer, 1964-74). Alderman, Haringey, 1968-71 (Vice-Chm. Educn Cttee). Consultant, Polytechnic of Central London, 1975. Trustee: Kelly Coll.; Uppingham Sch. *Publications:* The Fighting Cock, 1951; Highgate School 1938-1944: the story of a wartime evacuation, 1976. *Recreations:* music, cricket, books, dinghy sailing, ornithology. *Address:* 85 Queen Alexandra Mansions, Hastings Street, WC1H 9DP. *T:* 01-837 5738. *Clubs:* Athenæum, MCC.

DOUNE, Lord; John Douglas Stuart; *b* 29 Aug. 1966; *s* and *heir* of 20th Earl of Moray, *qv.*

DOURO, Marquess of; Arthur Charles Valerian Wellesley; Director, Deltec Banking Corporation Ltd, since 1973; Deputy Chairman, Thames Valley Broadcasting, since 1975; *b* 19 Aug. 1945; *s* and *heir* of 8th Duke of Wellington, *qv*; *m* 1977, Antonia von Preussen, *d* of late Prince Frederick of Prussia and of Lady Brigid Ness. *Educ:* Eton; Christ Church, Oxford. Contested (C) Islington N, Oct. 1974. Governor, Archbishop Tenison's Grammar Sch., 1975-. *Address:* 58 Eaton Place, SW1. *T:* 01-235 4258; Stratfield Saye, Reading. *T:* Turgis Green 639.

DOVE, Maj.-Gen. Arthur Julian Hadfield, CB 1948; CBE 1946 (MBE 1937); *b* Marton, New Zealand, 25 Aug. 1902; *s* of late Rev. J. Ll. Dove; *m* 1948, Betty Eyre Godson Bartholomew; one *d. Educ:* Haileybury Coll.; RMA, Woolwich. 2nd Lieut RE, 1922; served Palestine, 1936-38 (MBE, despatches, Bt Major). Served War of 1939-45, France, 1940; Dep. Director HG, 1942; CRE Guards Armoured Div., 1942-43; Chief Engineer, Combined Ops., 1943-44; Dep. Director of Military Ops, 1944-47; WO rep. with Council of Foreign Ministers and at Peace Conference, 1946-47; Dep. Adjutant General, BAOR, 1948-50; Brigadier, General Staff (Staff Duties), GHQ, MELF, 1951-53; Director of Quartering, War Office, 1954-57; Technical Director, FBI, 1957-61; retired 1957. Colonel Comdt RE, 1961-66. *Recreation:* fencing. *Address:* Moors Farm, Reigate Heath, Surrey. *T:* Reigate 45436. *Club:* Royal Commonwealth Society.

DOVE, Sir Clifford (Alfred), Kt 1967; CBE 1960 (MBE 1944); ERD 1963; FCIT; Chairman, British Transport Docks Board, 1970-71; Director-General and Member, Mersey Docks and Harbour Board, Liverpool, 1965-69 (General Manager, 1962); Member: National Ports Council, 1967-71; Council Institute of Transport, 1963-66 (Vice-President, 1964-65); Chairman Merseyside and District Section, Institute of Transport, 1964-65; Council, Dock and Harbour Authorities Assoc., 1970-71 (Executive Committee, 1962-69, Chairman, 1965-67, Vice-President, 1971); *b* 1 Dec. 1904; *e s* of Frederick George Dove and Beatrice Dove (*née* Warren); *m* 1936, Helen Taylor, *d* of James Wilson; no *c. Educ:* Russell Sch.; West Ham Municipal Coll.; London School of Economics. Joined Port of London Authority, 1921; Asst Port Director, Calcutta, 1945-46; Asst to Gen. Manager, Tees Conservancy Comrs, 1947-52; Gen. Manager, Ports, Nigeria and British Cameroons, 1952-54; Chm. and Gen. Manager, Nigeria Ports Authority, 1954-61; Mem. Nigeria Railway Corp., 1955-61; Mem. Nigeria Coal Corp., 1956-61; Comr of St John, Nigeria, 1956-61; Vice-Chm., Nat. Stadium Board of Nigeria, 1959-61; First Chm., Inst. of Transport, Nigeria Sect., 1959-61. Member: NW Economic Planning Council, 1965-69; Economic Develt Cttee for Movement of Exports, 1965-69; Exec. Cttee, Nat. Assoc. of Port Employers, 1968-69. Served War, 1939-46 (despatches, MBE): enlisted RE as 2nd Lieut, 1939; BEF, 1940; Middle East, 1941-44; Military Dock Supt., Alexandria, 1942-44; Dep. Asst Director of Transportation, MEF, 1944; AQMG (Movements) India and Embarkation Comdt, Calcutta, 1946; Demob., as Lt-Col. Joined Suppl. Reserve, 1947; retd, 1956, as Lt-Col. OStJ 1956. FRSA 1967. *Publication:* (with A. H. J. Bown) Port Operation and Administration, 1950. *Recreation:* golf. *Address:* Rubbles Edge Cottage, Burley, Ringwood, Hants. *T:* Burley 2384. *Clubs:* East India, Devonshire, Sports and Public Schools; Royal Lymington Yacht.

DOVENER, John Montague, QC 1972; *b* 7 Dec. 1923; *s* of John Reginald Dovener and Pinky (*née* Wilmott); *m* 1973, Shirley (*née* Donn). *Educ:* Shrewsbury. Pilot, RAF, 1941-47; 5 years Captain RA/TA, 470 Regt RA/TA. Called to Bar, Middle Temple, 1953. *Address:* 2 Pump Court, Temple, EC4Y 7AH.

DOVER, Suffragan Bishop of, since 1964; **Rt. Rev. Anthony Paul Tremlett;** *b* 14 May 1914; *s* of late Laurence and Nyda Tremlett; unmarried. *Educ:* King's Sch., Bruton; King's Coll., Cambridge; Cuddesdon Theological Coll. Ordained, 1938; Curate of St Barnabas, Northolt Park, Middx. Chaplain to the Forces (Emergency Commission), 1941-46 (despatches). Domestic Chaplain to the Bishop of Trinidad, BWI, 1946-49; Chaplain of Trinity Hall, Cambridge, 1949-58; Vicar of St Stephen with St John, Westminster, 1958-64. *Address:* Upway, St Martin's Hill, Canterbury, Kent. *T:* Canterbury 64537.

DOVER, Sir Kenneth James, Kt 1977; DLitt; FRSE 1975; FBA 1966; President of Corpus Christi College, Oxford, since 1976; *b* 11 March 1920; *o s* of P. H. J. Dover, London, Civil Servant; *m* 1947, Audrey Ruth Latimer; one *s* one *d. Educ:* St Paul's Sch. (Scholar); Balliol Coll., Oxford (Domus Scholar); Gaisford Prize, 1939; 1st in Classical Hon. Mods., 1940; DLitt 1974; Hon. Fellow, 1977. Served War of 1939-45; Army (RA), 1940-45; Western Desert, 1941-43, Italy, 1943-45 (despatches). Ireland Scholar, 1946; Cromer Prize (British Academy), 1946; 1st in Litt. Hum., Derby Scholar, Amy Mary Preston Read Scholar, 1947; Harmsworth Sen. Scholar, Merton Coll., 1947; Fellow and Tutor, Balliol Coll., 1948-55; Prof. of Greek, Univ. of St Andrews, 1955-76. Visiting Lecturer, Harvard, 1960. Dean of the Faculty of Arts, St Andrews, 1960-63, 1973-75. Sather Prof. of Classical Literature, University of California, 1967. President: Soc. for Promotion of Hellenic Studies, 1971-74; Classical Assoc., 1975. *Publications:* Greek Word Order, 1960; Commentaries on Thucydides, Books VI and VII, 1965; ed, Aristophanes' Clouds, 1968; Lysias and the Corpus Lysiacum, 1968; (with A. W. Gomme and A. Andrewes) Historical

Commentary on Thucydides, vol. IV, 1970; (ed) Theocritus, select poems, 1971; Aristophanic Comedy, 1972; Greek Popular Morality in the Time of Plato and Aristotle, 1974; articles in learned journals; Co-editor, Classical Quarterly, 1962-68. *Recreations:* historical linguistics, country walking. *Address:* Corpus Christi College, Oxford.

DOW, Christopher; *see* Dow, J. C. R.

DOW, David Rutherford, MB, ChB (with distinction), MD (with commendation), DPH, FRCPE, FRSE; LLD University of St Andrews, 1959; Professor of Anatomy, University of St Andrews (Queen's College, Dundee), 1925-58, now Emeritus; Master of Queen's College, Dundee, 1954-58; *b* Crail, Fifeshire, 1887; *o s* of late Dr Dow, MA, MD, Crail; *m* 1942, Agnes W. Morton, MA, MB, ChB, Hon. LLD Dundee 1968. *Educ:* Waid Academy, Anstruther; University of St Andrews. Lecturer and Senior Demonstrator of Anatomy, University of St Andrews; Life Member of Anatomical Society of Great Britain and Ireland; Dundee Branch BMA (Pres., 1936-37). Hon. President, Crail Golfing Society. Commission RAMC 1st Southern General Hospital, Birmingham. *Publications:* papers in various journals. *Recreations:* golf, shooting, fishing. *Address:* 13 Marketgate, Crail, Fife. *T:* Crail 302. *Club:* Royal and Ancient (St Andrews).

DOW, Harold Peter Bourner; QC 1971; *b* 28 April 1921; *s* of late Col H. P. Dow and P. I. Dow; *m* 1943, Rosemary Merewether, *d* of late Dr E. R. A. Merewether, CB, CBE, FRCP; two *s* one *d. Educ:* Charterhouse; Trinity Hall, Cambridge (MA). Served RAF (Air Crew), 1941-42. Min. of Supply, 1943-45. Barrister, Middle Temple, 1946. *Publications:* Restatement of Town and Country Planning, 1947; National Assistance, 1948; Rights of Way (with Q. Edwards), 1951; ed, Hobsons Local Government, 1951 and 1957 edns. *Recreations:* music, painting. *Address:* 2 Garden Court, Temple, EC4. *T:* 01-353 4741; The Priory, Brandeston, near Woodbridge, Suffolk. *T:* Earl Soham 244.

DOW, Sir Hugh, GCIE, *cr* 1947 (CIE 1932); KCSI, *cr* 1940 (CSI 1937); KStJ; *b* 8 May 1886; *s* of Alfred Dow; *m* 1913, Ann (CBE 1947, CStJ, K-i-H Gold Medal) (*d* 1956), *d* of J. Sheffield; one *s* one *d. Educ:* Aske's Hatcham Sch.; University Coll. London. Entered ICS, 1909; Secretary, Finance Dept, Bombay, 1923; Financial Adviser, Public Works in Sind, 1925; Financial Adviser, Public Works and Development, Bombay, 1926; Revenue Officer, Lloyd (Sukkur) Barrage, 1927; Member of the Sind Conference, 1932; Chairman of Sind Administrative Cttee, 1933-34; Joint Secretary, Commerce Dept; 1934; Secretary to the Govt of India, Commerce Dept, 1936-39; Director-General of Supply, and President of the War Supply Board, India, 1939-41; Governor of Sind, 1941-46; Governor of Bihar, 1946-47; Consul-General, Jerusalem, 1948-51; Chairman, Ordination Funds Commission, 1952; Chairman Royal Commission on East Africa, 1952-54; Chairman of Council, Royal Central Asian Society, 1957-58. *Address:* 16 Pall Mall, SW1. *Club:* Athenæum.

DOW, James Findlay; Consulting Physician, St George's Hospital, SW1; Physician to King Edward VII Hospital for Officers; *b* 13 May 1911; *s* of John Archibald Dow and Jetta Findlay; *m* 1952, Dr Jean Millbank; two *s* two *d. Educ:* Strathallan; St John's Coll., Cambridge; Middlesex Hospital. Resident posts at Middlesex and Brompton Hospitals; St George's Hospital, SW1, from 1947. MB, BChir Cantab., MRCP 1938, FRCP 1948. Major, RAMC, 1947-49. Examiner in Medicine, Cambridge and London Universities, 1950-63. Member Board of Governors, St George's Hospital, 1962; Member Assoc. of Physicians; Member British Society of Gastro-Enterology. *Publications:* Papers in medical journals on gastro-enterology. *Recreations:* golf, fishing. *Address:* 149 Harley Street, W1. *T:* 01-935 4444. *Clubs:* Caledonian, MCC.

DOW, (John) Christopher (Roderick); Executive Director, Bank of England, since 1973; *b* 25 Feb. 1916; *s* of Warrender Begernie and Amy Langdon Dow; *m* 1960, Clare Mary Keegan; one *s* three *d. Educ:* Bootham Sch., York; Brighton, Hove and Sussex Grammar Sch.; University College London, Fellow 1973. Economic Adviser, later Senior Economic Adviser, HM Treasury, 1945-54; on staff, and Dep. Dir, National Inst. for Economic and Social Research, 1954-62; Treasury, 1962-63; Asst Sec.-Gen., OECD, Paris, 1963-73. *Publications:* The Management of the British Economy, 1945-1960, 1964; Fiscal Policy for a Balanced Economy (jointly), 1968. Various articles in learned jls. *Address:* c/o Bank of England, Threadneedle Street, EC2. *Club:* Reform.

DOW, R(onald) Graham; His Honour Judge Dow; a Circuit Judge (formerly County Court Judge), since 1959; *b* 7 Dec. 1909; *s* of John Graham Dow and Bessie Graham Dow; *m* 1937,

Dorothy May Christie; two s. *Educ:* Kelvinside Academy; Uppingham Sch.; University Coll., Oxford. Called to Bar, 1932. Military Service, 1939-45. *Recreations:* golf and gardening. *Address:* 2 Kirkwick Avenue, Harpenden, Herts. *T:* Harpenden 2006.

DOWD, Ronald, AO 1976; tenor; with Australian Opera Company, since 1972; *b* Sydney, Australia, 23 Feb. 1914; *s* of Robert Henry Dowd and Henrietta (*née* Jenkins); *m* 1938, Elsie Burnitt Crute (English born); one *s* one *d. Educ:* Sydney. Prior to Army service in Australia, New Guinea and the Celebes, was a bank officer. Upon discharge, adopted full-time singing and performed for various opera organisations and Australian Broadcasting Commission in the Commonwealth. Came to UK for Sadler's Wells, 1956, and returned to Australia by arrangement with Elizabethan Theatre Trust; then rejoined Sadler's Wells, 1959, remaining for a year. Since then has been fully engaged in concerts and opera singing with leading conductors and organisations, including Royal Opera House. Toured NZ and Australia for Australian Broadcasting Commission, 1964; toured Continent with Sadler's Wells, 1963 and 1965. Chm., opera panel, Australian Council for the Arts, 1973-. *Recreations:* squash and coin collecting. *Address:* 10 Marion Crescent, Lapstone, NSW 2773, Australia. *T:* 047-391024. *Club:* Savage (London).

DOWDEN, Richard George; Editor, Catholic Herald, since 1976; *b* 20 March 1949; *s* of Peter Dowden and Eleanor Dowden; *m* 1976, Penny Mansfield. *Educ:* St George's Coll., Weybridge, Surrey; London Univ. (BA History). Volunteer Teacher, Uganda, 1971-72; Asst Sec., Justice and Peace Commn, 1973-76. *Recreation:* dreams of having time for recreation. *Address:* 47 Highbury Hill, N5. *T:* 01-253 7973.

DOWDING, family name of **Baron Dowding.**

DOWDING, 2nd Baron *cr* 1943, of Bentley Priory; **Derek Hugh Tremenheere Dowding;** Wing Commander, RAF, retired; *b* 9 Jan. 1919; *s* of (Air Chief Marshal) 1st Baron Dowding, GCB, GCVO, CMG, and Clarice Maud (*d* 1920), *d* of Captain John Williams, IA; *S* father, 1970; *m* 1st, 1940, Joan Myrle (marr. diss. 1946), *d* of Donald James Stuart, Nairn; 2nd, 1947, Alison Margaret (marr. diss. 1960), *d* of Dr James Bannerman, Norwich and *widow* of Major R. M. H. Peebles; two *s*; 3rd, 1961, Odette L. M. S. Hughes, *d* of Louis Joseph Houles. *Educ:* Winchester; RAF College, Cranwell. Served War of 1939-45, UK and Middle East; in comd No 49 (B) Sqdn, 1950; Wing Commander, 1951. Gen. Sec., Sea Cadet Assoc. (formerly Navy League), 1977-. *Heir: s* Hon. Piers Hugh Tremenheere Dowding, *b* 18 Feb. 1948. *Address:* c/o Lloyds Bank Ltd, 6 Pall Mall, SW1.

DOWDING, Michael Frederick, CBE 1973; Chairman, Michael Dowding Associates Ltd, consulting engineers; Director: Davy Loewy Ltd; Ashmore Benson Pease Ltd; James Armstrong & Co. Ltd; Rolair (UK) Ltd; *b* 19 Nov. 1918; *s* of late Guy Francis Dowding and of Frances Constance Dowding (*née* Bragger); *m* 1947, Rosemary, *d* of Somerville Hastings, MS, FRCS; one *s* two *d. Educ:* Westminster; Magdalene Coll., Cambridge. MA Cantab. CEng, FIMechE. Served War, 1939-45, Major RA (despatches, 1945). Joined Davy & United Engineering Co., 1946: Man. Dir, 1961-64; Chm., Davy Ashmore International, 1964-70; Dir, Davy Ashmore Ltd, 1962-72. Mem., Finnish British Technological Cttee, 1969. Vice-Pres., Iron and Steel Inst., 1965; Pres. elect, The Metals Soc. Commander, Knights of Finnish Lion, 1st Class, 1969. *Publications:* various technical papers to Iron and Steel Inst. and foreign metallurgical socs. *Recreations:* painting, stalking, fishing. *Address:* Wye House, Ashford-in-the-Water, Bakewell, Derbyshire. *T:* Bakewell 2832; Bod Isaf Farm, Aberdaron, Gwynedd. *Clubs:* Brooks's, MCC.

DOWELL, Anthony James, CBE 1973; Senior Principal, Royal Ballet, Covent Garden, since 1967; *b* 16 Feb., 1943; *s* of late Catherine Ethel and Arthur Henry Dowell; unmarried. *Educ:* Hampshire Sch., St Saviour's Hall, Knightsbridge; Royal Ballet Sch., White Lodge, Richmond, Surrey; Royal Ballet Sch., Barons Court. Joined Opera Ballet, 1960; 1st Company, for Russian Tour, 1961; created The Dream, 1964; Italian Tour, 1965; promoted Principal Dancer, 1966; Eastern Europe Tour, 1966; Japanese Tour, 1975; created Shadow Play, 1967; American Tours and Metropolitan Opera House, New York, 1968, 1969, 1972; created: Pavane, 1973; Manon, 1974. Principal role in: La Fête Etrange, 1963; Napoli, 1965; Romeo and Juliet, 1965; Song of the Earth, 1966; Card Game, Giselle, Swan Lake, 1967; The Nutcracker, Cinderella, Monotones, Symphonic Variations, new version of Sleeping Beauty, Enigma Variations, Lilac Garden, 1968; Raymonda Act III, Daphnis and Chloe, La Fille Mal Gardée, 1969; Dances at a Gathering, 1970; La

Bayadère, Meditation from Thaïs, Afternoon of a Faun, Anastasia, 1971; Triad, Le Spectre de la Rose, Giselle, 1972; Agon, Firebird, 1973; La Bayadère, 1973; Manon, 1974; Four Schumann Pieces, Les Sylphides, 1975; Four Seasons, 1975; Scarlet Pastorale, 1976. Dance Magazine award, NY, 1972. *Recreations:* painting, paper sculpture, theatrical costume design. *Address:* Royal Opera House, Covent Garden, WC2.

DOWER, Col. Alan Vincent Gandar, TD; DL; MFH; *b* 1898; *s* of late J. W. G. Dower and Mrs Dower, 17 Sussex Place, NW1; *m* 1928, Aymée Lavender, Jun. Com. (Temp. Sen. Com.) ATS, *d* of Capt. Sir George James Robert Clerk, 9th Bt, and Hon. Lady Clerk (*sister* of 6th Baron Sherborne, DSO); one *d. Educ:* RMC, Sandhurst; Oxford Univ. 2nd Lieut RW Surrey Regt, 1915; 2nd Lieut 2nd Dragoon Guards, 1916; served in France during European War, 1916-17; attached Royal Air Force, 1918; Capt. 2nd Dragoon Guards; Reserve of Officers, 1928; Major 35th AA Bn, RE, 1937; Lt-Col comdg 36th AA Bn, 1938-40; Comdg 39th (Lancs. Fus.) SL Regt, 1940; Comdg 84th SL Regt, 1951; Hon. Colonel 609 HAA Regt RA, 1947-55; Hon. Col, 4th Middx Bn Mobile Def. Corps, 1956-; Colonel, 1948, retired, 1954; Member Middx TA Association; MP (C), Stockport, 1931-35, Cumberland (Penrith and Cockermouth Div.), 1935-50; Member of Select Cttee on Estimates, 1938-39; Member Select Cttee of Public Accounts, 1945-. Freeman of City of London; Liveryman, Barbers Company; FRGS; FZS. MFH South Oxfordshire Hunt, 1950-53; Joint Master Old Berkeley Hunt, 1953-; County Pres. for Oxfordshire, St John Ambulance Bde and Association, 1953- (Mem., Chapter General, 1971-). Member Executive and Council, Royal Society of St George; Patron, SSAFA Middlesex Appeals Cttee. DL, Middlesex, 1961-65; DL Greater London, 1965-. KStJ. *Recreations:* hunting, big game shooting, polo, tennis, golf. *Address:* 35 Lowndes Street, SW1. *T:* 01-235 1491; Newington House, Warborough, Oxfordshire. *T:* Warborough 205; High Head Castle, Cumbria. *Clubs:* Carlton, Naval and Military, Princes, Hurlingham, Queen's; Muthaiga (Nairobi).

DOWER, E. L. G.; *see* Gandar Dower.

DOWLING, Kenneth; Assistant Director of Public Prosecutions, since 1976; *b* 30 Dec. 1933; *s* of Alfred and Mary Dowling; *m* 1957, Margaret Frances Bingham; two *d . Educ:* King George V Grammar Sch., Southport. Called to the Bar, Gray's Inn, 1960. RAF, 1952-54. Immigration Branch, Home Office, 1954-61; joined DPP Dept: Legal Asst, 1961; Sen. Legal Asst, 1966; Asst Solicitor, 1972. *Recreation:* reading. *Address:* 4-12 Queen Anne's Gate, SW1H 9AZ. *T:* 01-213 5259.

DOWN, Alastair Frederick, OBE 1944 (MBE 1942); MC 1940; TD 1951; Chairman and Chief Executive, The Burmah Oil Co. Ltd, since 1975; *b* 23 July 1914; *e s* of Frederick Edward Down and Margaret Isobel Down (*née* Hutchison); *m* 1947, Maysie Hilda Mellon; two *s* two *d. Educ:* Edinburgh Acad.; Marlborough Coll. Commissioned in 7th/9th Bn, The Royal Scots (TA), 1935. CA 1938. Joined British Petroleum Co. Ltd in Palestine, 1938. Served War of 1939-45 (despatches twice, MC, MBE, OBE, Kt Comdr, Order of Orange Nassau, with swords, 1946): Middle East, N Africa, Italy and Holland, with Eighth Army and 1st Canadian Army as Lt-Col and full Col. Rejoined BP, in Iran, 1945-47; Head Office, 1947-54; Canada, 1954-62 (Chief Rep. of BP in Canada, 1954-57; Pres., BP Group in Canada, 1957-62); Pres. BP Oil Corpn, 1969-70; Man. Dir, 1962-75 and Dep. Chm., 1969-75, BP Co. Ltd. Member: Review Body for pay of doctors and dentists, 1971-74; Television Adv. Cttee, 1971-72. FRSA 1970; JDipMA (Hon.), 1966. *Recreations:* shooting, golf, fishing. *Address:* The Hold, Manningford Bruce, Pewsey, Wilts; 15 Rutland Gate, SW7. *Clubs:* Bath; Mount Royal (Montreal); York, Toronto (Toronto); Ranchmen's (Calgary).

DOWN, Barbara Langdon; *see* Littlewood, Lady (Barbara).

DOWN, Lt-Gen. Sir Ernest Edward, KBE 1953 (CBE 1943); CB 1949; late King's Shropshire Light Infantry; *b* 10 Feb. 1902. 2nd Lieut Dorset Regt, 1923; transferred to King's Shropshire Light Infantry, from Dorset Regt, 1935; Brigade Major, 1937-39; Colonel, 1944; temp. Maj.-Gen., 1944; Maj.-Gen., 1945; Lt-Gen., 1952; GOC British troops in Greece, 1947-48; Commander British Military Mission to Greece, 1948-49. Commander Mid-West District and 53rd (Welsh) Infantry Division (TA), 1950-52; Gen. Officer Commanding-in-Chief, Southern Command, 1952-55; retired, 1955. Colonel KSLI 1955-57. *Address:* Whistlers Mead, Appleshaw, near Andover, Hants.

DOWN, Norman Cecil Sommers, CMG 1955; Senior Principal Inspector of Taxes, Inland Revenue, 1946-Dec. 1956, retired; *b* 9

Sept. 1893; *s* of late James Erskine Down; *m* 1st, 1917, Edith Gertrude (*née* Steddy) (*d* 1961); two *d*; 2nd, 1962, Agnes (*née* Sandham). *Educ:* St Lawrence Coll., Ramsgate. Inland Revenue since 1912; served European War, 1914-19, in 4th Gordon Highlanders, 51st Div. (Captain, despatches, wounded thrice). *Publications:* Temporary Heroes, 1918; Temporary Crusaders, 1919. *Address:* Binnlands, Swan Lane, Edenbridge, Kent TN8 6AJ. *T:* Edenbridge 3129.

DOWN and CONNOR, Bishop of, (RC), since 1962; **Most Rev. William J. Philbin,** DD; *b* 26 Jan. 1907; *s* of late James Philbin and Brigid (*née* O Hora). *Educ:* St Nathy's Coll., Ballaghaderreen; St Patrick's, Maynooth. Priest, 1931; DD Maynooth, 1933. Curate, Eastbourne, 1933; Secondary teacher, Ballaghaderreen, 1934; Prof. of Dogmatic Theology, Maynooth, 1936; Bishop of Clonfert, 1953. *Publications:* Does Conscience Decide?, 1969; To You Simonides, 1973; pamphlets on socio-moral questions; Irish translation of St Patrick's writings. Contributor to The Irish Theological Quarterly, Studies, The Irish Ecclesiastical Record. *Address:* Lisbreen, Somerton Road, Belfast 15. *T:* 776185.

DOWN and DROMORE, Bishop of, since 1970; **Rt. Rev. George Alderson Quin.** *Educ:* Trinity College, Dublin (MA). Deacon, 1937, priest 1938, Down; Curate of St Jude, Ballynafeigh, Belfast, 1937-39; Dean's Vicar of St Anne's Cathedral, Belfast, 1939-41; Holywood, 1941-43; Incumbent of Magheralin, 1943-51; Vicar of Ballymacarrett, 1951-58; Canon of St Anne's Cathedral, Belfast, 1955-56; Archdeacon of Down 1956-70; Exam. Chaplain to Bishop of Down and Dromore, 1957-70; Rector of Bangor, Dio. Down, 1958-70. *Address:* The See House, Knockdene Park, S Belfast.

DOWNE, 11th Viscount, *cr* 1680; **John Christian George Dawnay;** Bt 1642; Baron Dawnay of Danby (UK) *cr* 1897; *b* Wykeham, 18 Jan. 1935; *s* of 10th Viscount Downe, OBE and Margaret Christine (*d* 1967), *d* of Christian Bahnsen, NJ; *S* father, 1965; *m* 1965, Alison Diana, *d* of I. F. H. Sconce, MBE; one *s* one *d. Educ:* Eton Coll.; Christ Church, Oxford. 2nd Lieut, Grenadier Guards, 1954-55. Non-marine broker at Lloyd's, 1957-65. Director: Brookdeal Electronics Ltd, 1962-; Dawnay Faulkner Associates Ltd, 1968-; Feedmobile Ltd, 1972-, etc. *Publications:* contributions to various journals. *Recreation:* linear circuit design. *Heir: s* Hon. Richard Henry Dawnay, *b* 9 April 1967. *Address:* Wykeham Abbey, Scarborough, North Yorks. *T:* Wykeham 2404; 5 Douro Place, W8. *T:* 01-937 9449. *Clubs:* Pratt's, Cavalry and Guards'.

DOWNER, Hon. Sir Alexander (Russell), KBE 1965; MA; High Commissioner for Australia in the United Kingdom, 1964-72; *b* Adelaide, 7 April 1910; *s* of late Hon. Sir John Downer, KCMG, KC, MP, Adelaide, a founder of the Australian Commonwealth and a former Premier of S Australia; *m* 1947, Mary I., *d* of late Sir James Gosse, Adelaide; one *s* three *d. Educ:* Geelong Grammar Sch.; Brasenose Coll., Oxford (MA, Dip. of Economics and Political Science). Called to Bar, Inner Temple, 1934; admitted South Australian Bar, 1935. Served 8th Div. AIF, 1940-45 (Prisoner-of-War, Changi Camp, Singapore, for 3½ years). Member Board Electricity Trust of South Australia, 1946-49; MP (Liberal) Angas, Australia, 1949-64; Australian Minister for Immigration, 1958-63. Member: Australian Parliamentary Foreign Affairs Cttee, 1952-58; Australian Constitution Review Cttee, 1956-59; Commonwealth Parliamentary Delegation to Coronation, 1953; Board of National Gallery, S Australia, 1946-63; Pres. Royal Over-Seas League, S Australia Branch, 1946-62; a Governor, E-SU, 1973. Freeman, City of London, 1965. FRSA 1968. Hon. LLD Birmingham, 1973. *Recreations:* travelling, collecting antiques, reading. *Address:* Martinsell, Williamstown, South Australia 5351; 26-27 Queen's Gate Gardens, SW7. *Clubs:* Brooks's, Junior Carlton, (Hon.) Cavalry and Guards; Adelaide (Adelaide); Union (Sydney).

DOWNES, George Robert, CB 1967; Director, Operations and Overseas, Post Office, 1967-71, Director of Special Studies, June-Dec. 1971, retired; *b* 25 May 1911; *o s* of late Philip George Downes; *m* Edna Katherine Millar; two *d. Educ:* King Edward's Grammar School, Birmingham; Grocers', London. Entered GPO, 1928; Assistant Surveyor, 1937; Asst Principal, 1939. Served War of 1939-45: RNVR, in destroyers, 1942-45. Principal, GPO, 1946; Principal Private Sec. to: Lord President of the Council, 1948-50, Lord Privy Seal, 1951; Assistant Secretary, 1951; Imperial Defence College, 1952; Deputy Regional Director, GPO London, 1955; Dir, London Postal Region, 1960-65; Dir of Postal Services, 1965-67. *Recreations:* music, gardening. *Address:* Muircraig, Gordon Avenue, Stanmore, Mddx.

DOWNES, George Stretton, CBE 1976; Deputy Receiver for the Metropolitan Police District, 1973-76; retired; *b* London, 2 March 1914; *e s* of late George and Rosalind S. Downes; *m* 1939, Sheilah Gavigan; two *s* two *d. Educ:* Cardinal Vaughan Sch., Kensington. Joined Metropolitan Police Office, 1934; Secretary, 1969. *Recreations:* golf, gardening. *Address:* 45 Westbury Road, New Malden, Surrey.

DOWNES, M. P.; *see* Panter-Downes.

DOWNES, Ralph (William), CBE 1969; Organist, Brompton Oratory, 1936-78, now Organist Emeritus; Curator-Organist, Royal Festival Hall, since 1954; *b* 16 Aug. 1904; *s* of James William and Constance Edith Downes; *m* 1929, Agnes Mary (*née* Rix); one *s. Educ:* Derby Municipal Secondary Sch. (Scholar); Royal College of Music, London; Keble Coll., Oxford. ARCM 1925, MA 1931, BMus 1933. Asst Organist, Southwark Cathedral, 1924; Organ Scholar, Keble Coll., 1925-28; Director of Chapel Music and Lecturer, Princeton Univ., USA, 1928-35; Organ Prof., RCM, 1954-75. Organ Curator to LCC, 1949. Consultant to the Corporation of Croydon, 1960; Designer and Supervisor of organs in: Buckfast Abbey, 1952; Royal Festival Hall, 1954; Brompton Oratory, 1954; St John's Cathedral, Valletta, Malta, 1961; Fairfield Halls, 1964; Paisley Abbey, 1968; Trinity Coll., Dublin, 1969; Gloucester Cathedral, 1971, and others. Recitals and performances in: Aldeburgh, 1948-76, Belgium, France, Germany, Holland, Italy, Switzerland, also radio and TV. Jury mem., organ festivals, Amsterdam, Haarlem, Munich, St Albans. Received into the Catholic Church, 1930. Hon. RAM 1965; Hon. FRCO 1966; FRCM 1969. KSG 1970. *Publications:* Miscellaneous articles on the organ, compositions for keyboard and chorus. *Address:* 9 Elm Crescent, Ealing, W5 3JW. *T:* 01-567 6330.

DOWNEY, Gordon Stanley; Deputy Secretary, Treasury, since 1976; *b* 24 April 1928; *s* of Stanley William and Winifred Downey; *m* 1952, Jacqueline Goldsmith; two *d. Educ:* Tiffin's Sch.; London Sch. of Economics (BSc(Econ)). Served RA, 1946-48. Ministry of Works, 1951; entered Treasury, 1952; Asst Private Sec. to successive Chancellors of the Exchequer, 1955-57; on loan to Ministry of Health, 1961-62; Asst Sec., 1965, Under-Sec., 1972, Head of Central Unit, 1975, Treasury. *Recreations:* reading, tennis, visual arts. *Address:* 52 Sandy Lane, Petersham, Richmond, Surrey. *T:* 01-940 3557.

DOWNEY, Air Vice-Marshal John Chegwyn Thomas, CB 1975; DFC 1945, AFC; Deputy Controller of Aircraft (C), Ministry of Defence, 1974-75, retired; *b* 26 Nov. 1920; *s* of Thomas Cecil Downey and Mary Evelyn Downey; *m* Diana, (*née* White); one *s* two *d. Educ:* Whitgift Sch. Entered RAF 1939; served War of 1939-45 in Coastal Command (DFC 1945 for his part in anti-U-boat ops). Captained Lincoln Aries III on global flight of 29,000 miles, during which London-Khartoum record was broken. RAF Farnborough 1956-58; commanded Bomber Comd Develt Unit 1959-60; head of NE Defence Secretariat, Cyprus, 1960-62; Comd RAF Farnborough, 1962-64; a Dir, Op. Requirements (RAF) MoD, 1965-67; IDC, 1968; Comdt, RAF Coll. of Air Warfare, Manby, Jan./Oct. 1969; Comdr Southern Maritime Air Region, 1969-71; Senior RAF Mem., RCDS, 1972-74. *Publication:* Management in the Armed Forces: an anatomy of the military profession, 1977. *Recreation:* sailing. *Address:* Windmill House, Windmill Field, Old Bosham, Chichester, West Sussex. *Club:* Royal Air Force.

DOWNEY, William George, CB 1967; Consultant to Civil Aviation Authority, since 1976; Director, Harland and Wolff, since 1975; *b* 3 Jan. 1912; *s* of late William Percy Downey; *m* 1936, Iris, *e d* of late Ernest Frederick Pickering; three *d. Educ:* Southend Grammar Sch. ACWA 1935, ACA 1937, FCA 1960. Ministry of Aircraft Production, 1940; Ministry of Supply, 1946 (Director of Finance and Administration, Royal Ordnance Factories, 1952-57); Ministry of Aviation, 1959; Under-Secretary, 1961; Chm., Steering Gp, Develt Cost Estimation, 1964-66; Min. of Technology, 1967, Min. of Aviation Supply, 1970; DTI, 1971; Management Consultant to Procurement Exec., MoD, 1972-74; Under Sec., NI Office, 1974-75. *Address:* Starvelarks, Dawes Heath Rd, Rayleigh, Essex. *T:* Rayleigh 4138.

DOWNIE, Prof. Allan Watt, FRS 1955; Professor of Bacteriology, Liverpool University, 1943-66, now Emeritus Professor; *b* 5 Sept. 1901; *s* of William Downie, Rosehearty, Aberdeenshire; *m* 1936, Nancy McHardy; one *s* two *d. Educ:* Fraserburgh Academy, Aberdeen Univ. MB, ChB, Aberdeen Univ., 1923; MD, 1929; DSc, 1937. Lecturer Aberdeen Univ., 1924-26, Manchester Univ. 1927-34; Senior Freedom Research Fellow, London Hospital, 1935-39; Member Scientific Staff, Nat. Institute Medical Research, 1939-43. Voluntary Asst,

Rockefeller Inst. Med. Research, New York City, USA, 1934-35. Vis. Prof., Medical Sch., Univ. of Colorado, Denver, 1966-69, 1971, 1973. Founder Fellow, RCPath. Hon. LLD Aberdeen Univ., 1956. *Publications:* (Jt) Virus and Rickettsial Diseases of Man, 1950; numerous articles in scientific journals. *Recreations:* golf, fishing, ornithology. *Address:* Canna, College Close, Birkdale, Merseyside. *T:* Southport 67269.

DOWNIE, Prof. Robert Silcock; Professor of Moral Philosophy, Glasgow University, since 1969; *b* 19 April 1933; *s* of Robert Mackie Downie and late Margaret Barlas Downie; *m* 1958, Eileen Dorothea Flynn; three *d. Educ:* The High Sch. of Glasgow; Glasgow Univ.; The Queen's Coll., Oxford. MA, first cl. hons, Philosophy and Eng. Lit., Glasgow, 1955; Russian linguist, Intelligence Corps, 1955-57; Ferguson Schol., 1958; BPhil Oxford Univ., 1959; Lectr in Moral Philosophy, Glasgow Univ., 1959; Vis. Prof. of Philosophy, Syracuse Univ., NY, USA, 1963-64; Sen. Lectr in Moral Philosophy, Glasgow Univ., 1968. *Publications:* Government Action and Morality, 1964; Respect for Persons (jt), 1969; Roles and Values, 1971; Education and Personal Relationships (jt), 1974; Values in Social Works (jt), 1976; contribs to: Mind, Philosophy, Analysis, Aristotelian Society, Political Studies. *Recreation:* music. *Address:* Department of Moral Philosophy, University of Glasgow G12 8QQ. *T:* 041-339 8855.

DOWNING, Dr Anthony Leighton; Partner, Binnie & Partners, Consulting Engineers, since 1973; *b* 27 March 1926; *s* of Sydney Arthur Downing and Frances Dorothy Downing; *m* 1952, Kathleen Margaret Frost; one *d. Educ:* Arnold Sch., Blackpool; Cambridge and London Universities. BA Cantab. 1946; BSc Special Degree 2 (1) Hons. London, 1950; DSc London 1967. Joined Water Pollution Research Lab., 1946; seconded to Fisheries Research Lab., Lowestoft, 1947-48; granted transfer to Govt Chemist's Lab., 1948; returned to WPRL as Scientific Officer, 1950; subsequently worked mainly in field of biochemical engrg; Dir, Water Pollution Res. Lab., 1966-73. FIChemE 1975; Fellow Institute Water Pollution Control, 1965; FIBiol 1965; Hon. FIPHE 1965; FIWES 1975. FRSA. *Publications:* papers in scientific and technical journals. *Recreations:* golf, gardening. *Address:* 2 Tewin Close, Tewin Wood, Welwyn, Herts. *T:* Bulls Green 474. *Club:* Knebworth Golf.

DOWNING, Henry Julian; HM Diplomatic Service, retired; *b* 22 March 1919; *o s* of Henry Julian Downing and Kate Avery; *m* 1951, Ruth Marguerite Ambler. *Educ:* Boys' High Sch., Trowbridge; Hertford Coll., Oxford. Indian Civil Service (Madras) 1941-47. Joined HM Foreign Service, 1947; 2nd Secretary, Madras and Dacca, 1947-50; Foreign Office, 1950-52; 1st Secretary (Commercial), Istanbul, 1952-56; Foreign Office, 1956-58; 1st Secretary and Head of Chancery, Kabul, 1958-62; Foreign Office, 1963-65; HM Consul-General, Lourenço Marques, 1965-69; Head of Claims Dept, 1969-71, of Migration and Visa Dept, 1971-73, FCO; Consul-Gen., Cape Town, 1973-77. *Recreations:* swimming, walking, bird watching. *Address:* 8b Greenaway Gardens, Hampstead, NW3. *T:* 01-435 2593. *Club:* United Oxford & Cambridge University.

DOWNMAN, Prof. Charles Beaumont Benoy, PhD; Sophia Jex-Blake Professor of Physiology, University of London, at the Royal Free Hospital School of Medicine, since 1960; *b* 1916; *s* of Rev. Leonard Charles and Sarah Alice Downman; *m* 1947, Thaïs Hélène Barakan; one *s* one *d. Educ:* City of London Sch.; St Thomas's Hospital Medical Sch., MRCSEng, LRCP, 1941; PhD London, 1953. FRSocMed; Member: Physiological Society; EEG Society. *Publications:* papers in medical journals. *Address:* Royal Free Hospital School of Medicine, Hunter Street, Brunswick Square, WC1N 1BP; 4 Wendover Drive, New Malden, Surrey KT3 6RN.

DOWNS, Brian Westerdale, MA Cantab; Fellow (Master, 1950-63) of Christ's College, Cambridge; Professor of Scandinavian Studies, 1950-60; *b* 4 July 1893; *s* of late James Downs, OBE, JP; *m* Evelyn Wrangham (*née* Doubble). *Educ:* Abbotsholme Sch.; Christ's Coll., Cambridge (Entrance Scholar). First Class Honours (with distinction), Medieval and Modern Languages Tripos, 1915; Charles Oldham Shakespeare Scholar, 1914, and Allen Scholar, 1918. Lecturer in Modern Languages and English, Christ's Coll., Cambridge, 1918; Fellow, 1919, Tutor, 1928; Member of Council of Senate, Univ. of Cambridge, 1939-44, and 1954-60; Vice-Chancellor of Univ. of Cambridge, 1955-57; Founder Trustee, Churchill Coll., Cambridge. Representative of the British Council in the Netherlands, 1945-46. DLitt (*hc*), Hull. Commander, Royal Swedish Order of the North Star, 1954; Officier de la Légion d'Honneur, 1957; Chevalier, Royal Danish Order of Dannebrog, 1971. *Publications:* Cambridge Past and Present, 1926; Richardson,

1928; Ibsen, the Intellectual Background, 1946; (with Miss B. M. Mortensen) Strindberg, 1949; A Study of Six Plays by Ibsen, 1950; Norwegian Literature, 1860-1920, 1966; translations from the French, Dutch and German; editions of Shamela and Richardson's Familiar Letters. *Recreation:* walking. *Address:* Christ's College, Cambridge CB2 3BU; 20 Marlborough Court, Grange Road, Cambridge CB3 9BQ. *Club:* Athenæum.

DOWNS, Diarmuid, CEng, FIMechE; Chairman and Managing Director, Ricardo & Co. Engineers (1927) Ltd, since 1976; *b* 23 April 1922; *s* of John Downs and Ellen McMahon; *m* 1951, Mary Carmel Chillman; one *s* three *d. Educ:* Gunnersbury Catholic Grammar Sch.; City Univ., London (BScEng). CEng, FIMechE 1961. Ricardo & Co. Engineers (1927) Ltd, 1942-: Head, Petrol Engine Dept, 1947; Dir, 1957; Man. Dir, 1967. Mem., Adv. Council for Applied R&D, 1976-. Vice-President: IMechE, 1971-; Fédération Internationale des Sociétés d'Ingénieurs des Techniques de l'Automobile, 1975. *Publications:* papers on internal combustion engines in British and internat. engrg jls and conf. proc. *Recreation:* theatre. *Address:* The Downs, 143 New Church Road, Hove, East Sussex BN3 4DB. *T:* Brighton 419357. *Clubs:* St Stephen's; Hove (Hove).

DOWNS, Mrs George Wallingford; see Tureck, Rosalyn.

DOWNS, Leslie Hall, CBE 1942; MA Cantab; FIMechE; Chairman, 1936-71, Rose, Downs & Thompson Ltd, Old Foundry, Hull, retired; former Chairman, Rose Downs (Holdings) Ltd, Hull; Chairman, Barnsley Canister Co. Ltd, Barnsley; formerly Director, Blundell-Permaglaze (Holdings) Ltd; *b* 6 June 1900; *s* of late Charles Downs, Hull and Bridlington; *m* 1930, Kathleen Mary Lewis; three *d. Educ:* Abbotsholme Sch., Derbys; Christ's Coll., Cambridge (Scholar, BA, 1922, MA, 1927). European War, Artists' Rifles; served engineering apprenticeship and subsequently employed in various positions with Rose, Downs & Thompson Ltd; Past President Hull Chamber of Commerce and Shipping; Custodian Trustee, Hull Trustee Savings Bank; Former Treasurer and Member of Council, Hull Univ., retd 1976. Hon. DSc Hull Univ. *Recreations:* fly-fishing, cabinet making, reading. *Address:* King's Mill, Driffield, North Humberside. *T:* Driffield 43204; Rowling End Farm, Newlands, Keswick, Cumbria. *T:* Braithwaite 335.

DOWNSHIRE, 7th Marquess of, *cr* 1789; **Arthur Wills Percy Wellington Blundell Trumbull Sandys Hill;** Viscount Hillsborough, Baron Hill, 1717; Earl of Hillsborough, Viscount Kilwarlin, 1751; Baron Harwich (Great Britain), 1756; Earl of Hillsborough and Viscount Fairford, 1772; Hereditary Constable of Hillsborough Fort; late Lieut Berks Yeomanry; *b* 7 April 1894; *s* of 6th Marquess and Katherine, 2nd *d* of Hon. Hugh Hare, Forest House, Bracknell, Berks, and *g d* of 2nd Earl of Listowel; *S* father, 1918; *m* 1953, Mrs Noreen Gray-Miller, *d* of late William Barraclough. *Heir: nephew* (Arthur) Robin Ian Hill [*b* 10 May 1929; *m* 1957, Hon. Juliet Mary Weld-Forester, *d* of 7th Baron Forester, and of Marie Louise Priscilla, CStJ, *d* of Sir Herbert Perrott, 6th Bt, CH, CB; two *s* one *d*]. *Address:* 21 Wilton Crescent, Belgrave Square, SW1.

DOWNSIDE, Abbot of; see Roberts, Rt Rev. D. J.

DOWNWARD, Maj.-Gen Peter Aldcroft, DSO 1967; DFC 1952; General Officer Commanding West Midlands District, since 1976; *b* 10 April 1924; *s* of late Aldcroft L. Downward and of Mary (*née* Halton); *m* 4 July 1953, Hilda Hinckley Wood (*d* 1976); two *s. Educ:* King William's Coll., Isle of Man. Enlisted 1942; 2nd Lieut, The South Lancashire Regt (Prince of Wales's Volunteers), 1943; served with 13th Bn (Lancs) Parachute Regt, NW Europe, India, Far East, 1944-46, Greece and Palestine, 1947; transf. to Glider Pilot Regt, 1948; Berlin Airlift, 1949, Korea, 1951-53; 1st Bn The South Lancs Regt (PWV) in Egypt and UK, 1953-54; instructor at Light Aircraft Sch., 1955-56; RAF Staff Coll., 1958; War Office, 1959-60; BAOR, 1961-63; Brigade Major 127 Bde, 1964; Comd 4th Bn The East Lancs Regt, 1965-66; Comd 1st Bn The Lancs Regt (PWV), Aden, 1966-67; Allied Forces N Europe, Oslo, 1968-69; instructor, Sch. of Infantry, 1970-71; Comd Berlin Inf. Bde. 1971-74; Comdt, Sch. of Infantry, 1974-76. *Recreations:* sailing, skiing, shooting. *Address:* Wrockwardine Hall, Telford, Salop TF6 5DG. *T:* Telford 42878. *Club:* Army and Navy.

DOWNWARD, Sir William Atkinson, Kt 1977; Lord-Lieutenant of Greater Manchester, since 1974; Councillor, Manchester City Council, 1964-75; Alderman, Manchester, 1971-74; *b* 5 Dec. 1912; *s* of late George Thomas Downward; *m* 1946, Enid, *d* of late Ald. Charles Wood. *Educ:* Manchester Central High Sch.; Manchester Coll. of Technology. Mem., Court of Governors,

Manchester Univ., 1969; Hon. LLD Manchester, 1977. Dir, Royal Exchange Theatre Co., 1976-; Chairman: Manchester Overseas Students Welfare Conf., 1972-; Peterloo Gall., 1974-. Lord Mayor of Manchester, 1970-71. DL Lancs, 1971. KStJ 1974. *Address:* 23 Kenmore Road, Northenden, Manchester M22 4AE. *T:* 061-998 4742.

DOWSE, Maj.-Gen. Sir Maurice Brian, KCVO 1953; CB 1952; CBE 1947 (OBE 1940); retired; *b* 10 Sept. 1899; *s* of late Bishop Charles Dowse, and of Mrs Charles Dowse; unmarried. *Educ:* Wellington Coll.; RMC, Sandhurst. 2nd Lieut 1918; Lieut 1920; Captain, 1927; Major, 1936; Lt-Col, 1941; Brigadier, 1943; Maj.-Gen. 1951. Served Royal Welch Fusiliers and on Staff at home and overseas, 1918-44; on Staff at home and Far East, 1944-53; retired, 1953. *Address:* 39 Hyde Park Gate, SW7. *Club:* Travellers'.

DOWSETT, Prof. Charles James Frank, MA, PhD Cantab; FBA 1977; Calouste Gulbenkian Professor of Armenian Studies, University of Oxford, and Fellow of Pembroke College, Oxford, since 1965; *b* 2 Jan. 1924; *s* of late Charles Aspinall Dowsett and Louise, *née* Stokes; *m* 1949, Friedel, *d* of Friedrich Lapuner, Kornberg, E Prussia. *Educ:* Owen's Sch.; St Catherine's Society, Oxford, 1942-43; Peterhouse, Cambridge (Thomas Parke Scholar), 1947-50 (Mod. and Mediaeval Languages Tripos, Part I, 1st Class Russian, 1st Class German, 1948, Part II, Comparative Philology, 1st Class with distinction, 1949). Treasury Studentship in Foreign Languages and Cultures, 1949-54. Ecole Nationale des Langues Orientales Vivantes, Univ. de Paris, 1950-52 (diplôme d'arménien); Ecole des Langues Orientales Anciennes, Institut Catholique de Paris, 1950-53 (diplôme de géorgien); Lecturer in Armenian, School of Oriental and African Studies, University of London, 1954; Reader in Armenian, 1965. Vis. Prof., Univ. of Chicago, 1976. Member: Council, RAS, 1972-76; Philological Soc., 1973-77. *Publications:* The History of the Caucasian Albanians by Movses Dasxuranci, 1961; The Penitential of David of Ganjak, 1961; (with J. Carswell) Kütahya Armenian Tiles, vol. 1, The Inscribed Tiles, 1972; articles in Bulletin of the School of Oriental and African Studies, Le Muséon, Revue des Etudes Arméniennes, The Geographical Journal, W. B. Henning Memorial Volume, 1970, etc; translations from Flemish (Felix Timmermans' Driekoningentryptiek: "A Christmas Triptych", 1955, Ernest Claes' De Witte: "Whitey", 1970); as Charles Downing (children's books): Russian Tales and Legends, 1956; Tales of the Hodja, 1964; Armenian Folktales and Fables, 1972. *Address:* Pembroke College, Oxford. *Club:* United Oxford & Cambridge University.

DOWSON, Maj.-Gen. Arthur Henley, CB 1964; CBE 1961 (OBE 1945); Director-General, Ordnance Survey, 1961-65, retired; *b* 7 Dec. 1908; *s* of late Kenneth Dowson and Beatrice Mary (*née* Davis); *m* 1933, Mary Evelyn, *d* of Col. A. J. Savage, DSO; one *d. Educ:* Haileybury; RMA; King's Coll., Cambridge (BA). Commissioned in RE, 1928; War Service in NW Europe, N Africa, Italy. Director of Military Survey, War Office and Air Ministry, 1957. ADC to the Queen, 1958-61; Maj-Gen. 1961. Chm., Norfolk Broads Consortium Cttee, 1966-71. FRICS 1949. Bronze Star (USA) 1945. *Address:* 15 Venn's Lane, Hereford. *T:* Hereford 4197.

DOWSON, Prof. Duncan; Professor of Engineering Fluid Mechanics and Tribology, University of Leeds, since 1966, and Director of The Institute of Tribology, Department of Mechanical Engineering, Univ. of Leeds, since Dec. 1967; *b* 31 Aug. 1928; *o s* of Wilfrid and Hannah Dowson, Kirkbymoorside, York; *m* 1951, Mabel, *d* of Mary Jane and Herbert Strickland; one *s* (and one *s* decd). *Educ:* Lady Lumley's Grammar Sch., Pickering, Yorks; Leeds Univ. BSc Mech Eng. Leeds, 1950; PhD Leeds, 1952; DSc Leeds, 1971. Research Engineer, Sir W. G. Armstrong Whitworth Aircraft Co., 1953-54; Univ. of Leeds: Lecturer in Mechanical Engineering, 1954; Sen. Lecturer, 1963; Reader, 1965; Prof. 1966. Chm., Tribology Group Cttee, IMechE, 1967-69. CEng, FIMechE, Fellow ASME. James Clayton Fund Prize (jtly), IMechE, 1963; Thomas Hawksley Gold Medal, IMechE, 1966; Gold Medal, British Soc. of Rheology, 1969; Nat. Award, ASLE, 1974; ASME Lubrication Div. Best Paper Awards (jt), 1975, 1976; ASME Melville Medal (jt), 1976. *Publications:* Elastohydrodynamic Lubrication-the fundamentals of roller and gear lubrication (jointly), 1966, 2nd edn 1977; papers on tribology, published by: Royal Society; Instn of Mech Engineers; Amer. Soc. of Mech. Engineers; Amer. Soc. of Lubrication Engineers. *Recreations:* travel, astronomy, photography. *Address:* 23 Church Lane, Adel, Leeds LS16 8DQ. *T:* Leeds 678933.

DOWSON, Graham Randall: Chairman: Mooloya Investments, since 1975; Erskine House Investments, since 1975; *b* 13 Jan. 1923; *o s* of late Cyril James Dowson and late Dorothy Celia (*née* Foster); *m* 1954, Fay Weston (marr. diss. 1974); two *d* ; *m* 1975, Denise Shurman. *Educ:* Alleyn Court Sch.; City of London Sch.; Ecole Alpina, Switzerland. Served War of 1939-45 (1939-43 and Africa Stars, Atlantic and Defence Medals, etc); RAF, 1941-46 (Pilot, Sqdn-Ldr). Sales, US Steel Corporation (Columbia Steel), Los Angeles, 1946-49; Sales and Senior Commentator, Mid South Network (MBS), radio, US, 1949-52; Dir, Rank Organization Ltd, 1960-75, Chief Exec., 1974-75; Director: A. C. Nielsen Co., Oxford, 1953-58; Michael Peters Ltd, 1975-; Logoptics Ltd, 1975-; Annual Reports Ltd, 1975-; Carron Co. (Holdings) Ltd, 1976-. Chm., European League for Econ. Co-operation (British Section), 1972-. Vice-Pres., NPFA, 1974-. *Recreation:* sailing. *Address:* 193 Cromwell Tower, Barbican, EC2. *T:* 01-588 0396. *Clubs:* Brooks's, Carlton; Royal London Yacht (Vice-Commodore), Royal Cork Yacht, Royal Southern Yacht, Royal Air Force Yacht.

DOWSON, Philip Manning, CBE 1969; Senior Partner, Ove Arup Partnership, since 1969; Partner, Arup Associates, since 1963; *b* 16 Aug. 1924; *s* of Robert Dowson and Ina Cowen Dowson; *m* 1950, Sarah Crewdson; one *s* two *d. Educ:* Gresham's Sch.; University Coll., Oxford; Clare Coll., Cambridge (MA). AA Dip., ARIBA. Oxford, 1942-43; Lieut, RNVR, 1943-47; Cambridge, 1947-50; Architectural Association, 1950-53; joined Ove Arup & Partners, 1953. Member: Royal Fine Art Commn, 1971-; Craft Adv. Cttee, 1972. Governor, St Martin's Sch. of Art, 1975-. *Publications:* articles for technical press. *Recreation:* sailing. *Address:* 7 Soho Square, W1V 6QB. *T:* 01-734 8494; 1 Pembroke Studios, Pembroke Gardens, W8. *Club:* Garrick.

DOYLE, Rear-Adm. Alec Broughton, CBE 1937; Royal Australian Navy; *b* 5 Oct. 1888; *s* of James H. and Rebekah Doyle, Invermien, Scone, NSW; *m* 1917, Charlotte Madge, *d* of Dr Herbert Lillies, Armadale, Victoria, Australia; two *s. Educ:* Scone Grammar Sch., NSW; The King's Sch., Parramatta, NSW; Sydney Univ., NSW. Bachelor of Engineering, 1911; joined Royal Australian Navy, 1912; sea service, 1914-18; Squadron Engineer Officer, 1929-32; Engineer Manager, Royal Australian Naval Dockyard, Garden Island, and General Overseer, Naval Shipbuilding and Repair, Sydney, 1933-42; Engineer Captain, 1934; Director of Engineering (Naval), 1942-43; Engineer Rear-Admiral, 1943; Third Naval Member Australian Commonwealth Naval Board, Navy Office, Melbourne, and Chief of Construction, 1943-48; retired 1948. *Recreations:* pastoral pursuits. *Address:* c/o PO Box 164, Scone, NSW 2337, Australia. *Clubs:* Union, University, Royal Sydney Golf (Sydney).

DOYLE, Brian André; Hon. Mr Justice B. A. Doyle; Director, Law Development Commission, Zambia, since 1975; Member, Botswana Court of Appeal, since 1974; *b* 10 May 1911; *s* of John Patrick Doyle, ICS and Louise Doyle (*née* Renard); *m* 1937, Nora (*née* Slattery); one *s* one *d. Educ:* Douai Sch.; Trinity Coll., Dublin. BA, LLB. Called to Irish Bar, 1932; Magistrate, Trinidad and Tobago, 1937; Resident Magistrate, Uganda, 1942; Solicitor-Gen., Fiji, 1948; Attorney-Gen., Fiji, 1949; KC (Fiji), 1950, later QC; Attorney-Gen., N Rhodesia, 1956; Minister of Legal Affairs and Attorney-Gen., Northern Rhodesia (Zambia, 1964), 1959-65, retired as minister, 1965; Chm., Local Govt Service Commn, Zambia, 1964; Justice of Appeal, 1965; Chief Justice and Pres., Supreme Court of Zambia, 1969-75. *Recreations:* fishing, golf. *Address:* c/o Law Development Commission, PO Box 3670, Cha Cha Cha Road, Lusaka, Zambia. *Clubs:* Fiji, Lusaka, Chainama Hills Golf.

DOYLE, Sir John (Francis Reginald William Hastings), 5th Bt, *cr* 1828; *b* 3 Jan. 1912; *s* of Col Sir Arthur Havelock James Doyle, 4th Bt, and Joyce Ethelreda (*d* 1961), 2nd *d* of Hon. Greville Howard; *S* father, 1948; *m* 1947, Diana, *d* of late Col Steel, Indian Army; one *d. Educ:* Eton; RMC Sandhurst. Served Palestine, 1938 (medal with clasp); War of 1939-45, in France, Italy, Greece; Major, Cameronians and Royal Irish Fusiliers; retired, 1950. *Address:* Glebe House, Camolin, Co. Wexford.

DOYLE, Brig. Richard Stanislaus, CBE 1957 (OBE 1954); MBIM; DL; Chairman, Crafts Advisory Committee, Scottish Development Agency, since 1977; *b* 6 Oct. 1911; *s* of Richard Joseph Doyle, Dublin; *m* 1940, Rae Phyllis, *d* of H. D. Pascoe, Northampton; two *s* one *d. Educ:* O'Connell Sch., Dublin; University Coll., Dublin. Served War of 1939-45 (despatches, 1945): RAOC, Burma, Malaya; Col DDOS, Burma Comd, 1945; Col i/c Admin. Cyprus, 1955-58; Brig., and Dir of Quartering, War Office, 1960-62; retd, 1962. Gen. Manager, Glenrothes Development Corp., 1962-76. Mem., Court of St Andrews

Univ., 1971, Regent St Salvator's Coll., 1976, Mem., 8 Cttees, 1977-. DL Fife, 1976. *Recreations:* golf and work. *Address:* 11 Union Street, St Andrews, Fife. *T:* St Andrews 2519. *Clubs:* Army and Navy; New (Edinburgh).

D'OYLY, Sir John (Rochfort), 13th Bt, *cr* 1663; Commander, RN retired; *b* 19 April 1900; *s* of Sir (Hastings) Hadley D'Oyly, 11th Bt, and Beatrice, *d* of late Francis Bingham Clerk, JP; *S* brother, Sir Charles Hastings D'Oyly, 12th Bt, 1962; *m* 1930, Kathleen, *er d* of late Robert Brown Gillespie, Halgolle, Yatiyantota, Ceylon (marr. diss. 1944); two *d* (one *s* decd). *Educ:* Hill Brow, Eastbourne; Eastmans Royal Naval Academy, Southsea; HMS Conway. Served European War, 1916-18, with Grand Fleet; Baltic Operations, 1919. Gonville and Caius Coll., Cambridge, 1920-21. Specialised in physical and recreational training, 1921-22; Mediterranean, 1923-25; Term Officer at Royal Naval Coll., Dartmouth, 1925-27; East Indies, 1928-30; HMS St Vincent Boys' Training Establishment, 1930-32; Fleet Physical and Recreational Training Officer, Mediterranean, 1932-35; Asst Superintendent, RN Sch. of Physical and Recreational Training, Portsmouth, 1936-38. Served European War, 1939-45; Comdr of the Coll., RNC, Greenwich; Atlantic; East Indies; Pacific; retd, 1946. *Heir: half-brother,* Nigel Hadley Miller D'Oyly [*b* 6 July 1914; *m* 1940, Dolores (*d* 1971), *d* of R. H. Gregory; one *s* two *d*]. *Address:* c/o Lloyds Bank Ltd, 39 Piccadilly, W1. *Club:* Royal Naval and Royal Albert Yacht (Portsmouth).

D'OYLY CARTE, Dame Bridget, DBE 1975; Managing Director, Bridget D'Oyly Carte Ltd, since 1961; Vice-Chairman, Savoy Hotel Ltd, since 1971; *b* 25 March 1908; *d* of late Rupert D'Oyly Carte and Lady Dorothy Milner Gathorne-Hardy; *m* 1926, 4th Earl of Cranbrook (marr. diss. 1931); resumed maiden name by deed poll, 1932. *Educ:* privately in England and abroad, and at Dartington Hall, Totnes (Dance-Drama Group). Savoy Hotel, 1933-39; evacuated nursery schools and child welfare work, 1939-47; Man. Director of D'Oyly Carte Opera Company, Director of Savoy Hotel Ltd and Savoy Theatre Ltd, 1948; Founder and Trustee of D'Oyly Carte Opera Trust Ltd, 1961. *Recreations:* country living and gardening; reading, theatre and music. *Address:* 1 Savoy Hill, WC2R 0BP. *T:* 01-836 4343.

DRABBLE, His Honour John Frederick, QC 1953; retired; a Circuit Judge (formerly County Court Judge) 1965-73; *b* 8 May 1906; *s* of late Joseph and Emily Drabble, Conisbrough, Yorks; *m* 1933, Kathleen Marie Bloor; one *s* three *d. Educ:* Mexborough Grammar Sch.; Downing Coll., Cambridge (MA). Called to Bar, 1931. Served War of 1939-45, RAF, 1940-45, finally as Sqdn Leader. Recorder of Huddersfield, 1955-57; of Kingston-upon-Hull, 1957-58. *Publications:* Death's Second Self, 1971; Scawsby, 1977. *Address:* St Mary's, Martlesham, Woodbridge, Suffolk. *T:* Kesgrave 2615.
See also Margaret Drabble.

DRABBLE, Margaret, (Mrs Swift); author; *b* 5 June 1939; 2nd *d* of His Honour J.F. Drabble, *qv*; *m* 1960, Clive Walter Swift (marr. diss. 1975); two *s* one *d. Educ:* The Mount Sch., York; Newnham Coll., Cambridge. Lives in London. E. M. Forster Award, Amer. Acad. of Arts and Letters, 1973. Hon DLitt Sheffield, 1976. *Publications:* A Summer Birdcage, 1963; The Garrick Year, 1964; The Millstone, 1966 (filmed, as A Touch of Love, 1969); Wordsworth, 1966; Jerusalem the Golden, 1967; The Waterfall, 1969; The Needle's Eye, 1972; (ed with B. S. Johnson) London Consequences, 1972; Arnold Bennett, a biography, 1974; The Realms of Gold, 1975; (ed) The Genius of Thomas Hardy, 1976; (ed jtly) New Stories 1, 1976; The Ice Age, 1977.

DRAIN, Geoffrey Ayrton, JP; General Secretary, National and Local Government Officers Association, since 1973; *b* 26 Nov. 1918; *s* of Charles Henry Herbert Drain, MBE, and Ann Ayrton; *m* 1950, Dredagh Joan Rafferty (marr. diss. 1959); one *s. Educ:* Preston Grammar Sch.; Bournemouth Sch.; Skipton Grammar Sch.; Queen Mary Coll., Univ. of London, BA, LLB. Called to Bar, Inner Temple, 1955. Served War, 1940-46. Asst Sec., Inst. of Hosp. Administrators, 1946-52; Exec., Milton Antiseptic Ltd, 1952-58; Dep. Gen.-Sec., NALGO, 1958-73; Mem. Gen. Council, TUC, 1973-; Pres., Nat. Fedn. of Professional Workers, 1973-75; Staff Side Sec., Health Service Admin. and Clerical Staffs Whitley Council, 1962-72; Member: NW Metropolitan Regional Hosp. Bd and N London Hosp. Management Cttee, 1967-74; Lord Chancellor's Adv. Cttee on Legal Aid, 1974-76; Layfield Cttee of Inquiry into Local Govt Finance, 1974-76; NEDO Sector Working Party for Paper and Board Ind., 1976- (Chm.); Insolvency Law Review Cttee, 1976-; Council, Industrial Soc., 1974-. Trustee, Young Volunteer Force Foundn, 1974-. Hampstead Borough Councillor, 1956-58; contested (Lab), Chippenham, 1950; JP N Westminster, 1966.

Freeman of City of London and Liveryman of Coopers' Company. *Publication:* The Organization and Practice of Local Government, 1966. *Recreations:* cricket, football, walking, studying birds, bridge. *Address:* Flat 3, Centre Heights, Swiss Cottage, NW3 6JG. *T:* 01-722 2081. *Clubs:* Reform, MCC.

DRAKE, Antony Elliot, CBE 1967 (OBE 1945); *b* 15 June 1907; *s* of Francis Courtney Drake and Mabel Grace (*née* Drake); *m* 1935, Moira Helen Arden Wall; one *s* one *d. Educ:* Aldenham Sch.; New Coll., Oxford. Indian Civil Service, 1930; Bihar and Orissa, 1931-37; seconded to Indian Political Service, 1937; served Rajputana, 1937-39; Baluchistan, 1939-43; Mysore (Sec. to Resident), 1943-46; Rajkot (Political Agent, E Kathiawar), 1946-47; appointed to Home Civil Service, HM Treasury, 1947; Asst Sec., 1950; on loan to UK Atomic Energy Authority as Principal Finance Officer, 1957; transferred permanently to UKAEA, 1960; Finance and Programmes Officer, 1964-69; retd, 1969. Member: Hosp. Management Cttee, Royal Western Counties Hosp. Group, 1970-74; Reg. Fisheries Adv. Cttee, SW Water Authority, 1975. *Recreations:* fishing, golf. *Address:* Winneford Farm House, Awliscombe, Honiton, Devon. *T:* Honiton 2502. *Club:* Flyfishers'.

DRAKE, Sir (Arthur) Eric (Courtney), Kt 1970; CBE 1952; Deputy Chairman, P&O, since 1976; Director: Kleinwort Benson Lonsdale Ltd; Toronto-Dominion Bank, Canada; Société Française des Petroles BP; Hudson's Bay Company; Peninsular and Oriental Steam Navigation Company, and other cos; *b* 29 Nov. 1910; *e s* of Dr A. W. Courtney Drake; *m* 1st, 1935, Rosemary Moore; two *d*; 2nd, 1950, Margaret Elizabeth Wilson; two *s. Educ:* Shrewsbury; Pembroke Coll., Cambridge (MA; Hon. Fellow 1976). With The British Petroleum Co. Ltd, 1935-75: Man. Dir, 1958-62; Dep. Chm., 1962-69; Chm., 1969-75. Pres., Chamber of Shipping, 1964; Hon. Mem., General Council of British Shipping, 1975-; Member: Gen. Cttee, Lloyd's Register of Shipping, 1960-; MoT Shipping Adv. Panel, 1962-64; Cttee on Invisible Exports, 1969-75; Bd of Governors, Pangbourne Nautical Coll., 1958-69; Court of Governors, London Sch. of Economics and Political Science, 1963-74; Governing Body of Shrewsbury Sch., 1969-; Cttee of Management, RNLI, 1975-; Life Mem., Court of City Univ., 1969-; Pres., City and Guilds Insignia Award Assoc., 1971-75; Hon. Petroleum Adviser to British Army, 1971-. Hon. Mem., Honourable Co. of Master Mariners, 1972; Hon. Elder Brother of Trinity House, 1975; Freeman of City of London, 1974; one of HM Lieutenants, City of London. Hon. DSc Cranfield, 1971; Hon. Fellow, UMIST, 1974. Hambro British Businessman of the Year award, 1971. Comdr, Ordre de la Couronne, Belgium, 1969; Kt Grand Cross of Order of Merit, Italy, 1970; Officier, Légion d'Honneur, 1972; Order of Homayoun, Iran, 1974; Comdr, Ordre de Leopold, Belgium, 1975. *Address:* The Old Rectory, Cheriton, Alresford, Hants. *T:* Bramdean 334. *Clubs:* London Rowing; Royal Yacht Squadron, Leander, Royal Cruising.

DRAKE, Sir Eric; see Drake, Sir A. E. C.

DRAKE, (Frederick) Maurice, DFC 1944; QC 1968; a Recorder of the Crown Court since 1972; *b* 15 Feb. 1923; *o s* of Walter Charles Drake and late Elizabeth Drake; *m* 1954, Alison May, *d* of late W. D. Waterfall, CB; two *s* three *d. Educ:* St George's Sch., Harpenden; Exeter Coll., Oxford. MA Hons 1948. Served War of 1939-45, RAF 96 and 255 Squadrons. Called to Bar, Lincoln's Inn, 1950, Bencher, 1976. Dep. Chm., Beds QS, 1966-71; Dep. Leader, Midland and Oxford Circuit, 1975-. Standing Senior Counsel to RCP, 1972-. Chm. Governors, Aldwickbury Prep. Sch. (Trust), 1969-; Governor, St George's Sch., Harpenden, 1975-. Hon. Alderman, St Albans DC, 1976-. *Recreations:* music, gardening, countryside. *Address:* The White House, West Common Way, Harpenden, Herts. *T:* Harpenden 2329; 4 Paper Buildings, Temple, EC4.

DRAKE, Jack Thomas Arthur H.; see Howard-Drake.

DRAKE, Sir James, Kt 1973; CBE 1962; Director, Leonard Fairclough Ltd, since 1972; *b* 27 July 1907; *s* of James Drake and Ellen (*née* Hague); *m* 1937, Kathleen Shaw Crossley; two *d. Educ:* Accrington Grammar Sch.; Owens Coll.; Manchester Univ. (BSc). CEng, FICE, FIMunE, PPInstHE. Jun. Engrg Asst, Stockport Co. Borough, 1927-30; Sen. and Chief Engrg Asst, Bootle Co. Borough, 1930-37; Blackpool Co. Borough: Dep. Engr and Surveyor, 1937-38; Borough Engr and Surveyor, 1938-45; County Surveyor and Bridgemaster, Lancs CC, 1945-72 (seconded to Min. of Transport as Dir of NW Road Construction Unit, 1967-68). Hon. Fellow, Manchester Polytechnic, 1972. Hon. DSc Salford, 1973. Mem., Fellowship of Engrg. *Publications:* Road Plan for Lancashire, 1949; Motorways, 1969. *Recreation:* golf. *Address:* 21 Beauclerk

Road, St Annes-on-Sea, Lancs. *T:* St Annes 721635. *Clubs:* Royal Automobile, Royal Over-Seas League; Royal Lytham and St Annes Golf, Blackpool North Shore Golf.

DRAKE, James Mackay Henry M.; *see* Millington-Drake.

DRAKE, Brig. Dame Jean Elizabeth R.; *see* Rivett-Drake.

DRAKE, John Edmund Bernard, CBE 1973; DSC 1945; retired as Special Adviser on Personnel Management to Civil Service (1970-73); *b* 15 Nov. 1917; *s* of late D. H. C. Drake, CIE; *m* 1942, Pauline Marjory Swift; three *s. Educ:* Blundells Sch.; Exeter Coll., Oxford (BA). Served War, RNVR. Executive, Burmah-Shell, India, 1945-57; Gen. Manager, Shell Co of Ceylon, 1955; Overseas Staff Manager, Burmah Shell, 1957-62; Gen. Manager Personnel, Shell Mex and BP, 1962-69. *Recreations:* travel, sailing, reading, music. *Address:* Farm House, Coldharbour Lane, Hildenborough, Kent. *T:* Hildenborough 832102.

DRAKE, Maurice; *see* Drake, F. M.

DRAKELEY, Thomas James, CBE 1952; DSc, PhD; FRIC, FPRI; *b* Barwell, Leicester, 17 Dec. 1890; *o s* of late Thomas Drakeley; *m* Margaret (*d* 1957), *e d* of late Frank T. Hill. *Educ:* Sir Walter St John's Sch.; University Coll., London. Senior Lecturer in Chemistry, at the Wigan and District Mining and Technical Coll., 1912-19; Head of Dept of Chemistry and Rubber Technology at Northern Polytechnic, 1919-31; Principal, Northern Polytechnic, 1932-55 and 1958-61; Dir, National Coll. of Rubber Technology, Holloway, N7, 1948-55 and 1958-61; Deleg. for UK on International Dairy Federation; Ed. Transactions of Instn of the Rubber Industry, 1925-50; Mem. of Council of Chemical Soc., 1930-33; Mem. of Appeals Tribunal (England and Wales) for further Education and Training Scheme, Ministry of Labour and National Service, 1945-52; Pres. Assoc. of Principals of Technical Institutions, 1946-47; Mem. Regional (London and Home Counties) Advisory Council for Higher Technological Education, 1947-55; Vice-Chm. Regional (London and Home Counties) Academic Board. 1947-52, Chm. 1952-55; Mem. Nat. Advisory Council on Education for Industry and Commerce, Min. of Education, 1948-55; Chm. Northern Group Hosp. Management Cttee, 1956-60. Hancock Medal, Instn of the Rubber Industry, 1952, Life Vice-Pres. 1958-, Chm. of Council, 1962-65, Pres., 1966-68; Vice-Pres., Royal Assoc. of British Dairy Farmers, 1972. *Publications:* research publications. *Address:* 101 Barrington Court, Pages Hill, N10 1QH. *T:* 01-883 3667.

DRAPER, Alan Gregory; Chairman, NATO Budget Committees, since 1977; *b* 11 June 1926; *s* of late William Gregory Draper and Ada Gertrude (*née* Davies); *m* 1953, Muriel Sylvia Cuss (marr. diss.); three *s*; *m* 1977, Jacqueline Grubel. *Educ:* Leeds Grammar Sch.; The Queen's Coll., Oxford (2nd Cl. Hons Mods, 2nd Cl. Lit. Hum., MA). RNVR, 1945; Sub-Lt, 1946-47. Admiralty: Asst Principal, 1950; Private Sec. to Civil Lord of the Admiralty, 1953-55; MoD, 1957-60; Head of Polit. Sect., Admiralty 1960-64; First Sec., UK Delegn to NATO, 1964-66; Asst Sec., MoD, 1966-; Counsellor, UK Delegn to NATO, 1974-77. *Recreations:* reading, travel, tennis, indifferent golf. *Address:* c/o Barclays Bank, 16 Whitehall, SW1A 2EA. *T:* 01-930 9323. *Club:* Naval.

DRAPER, Prof. Col Gerald Irving Anthony Dare, CBE 1965; Professor of Law, University of Sussex, since 1976; a Chairman of Industrial Tribunals, since 1966; *b* 30 May 1914; *o s* of late Harold Irving Draper and Florence Muriel Short; *m* 1951, Julia Jean, *e d* of late Captain G. R. Bald, RN. *Educ:* privately, and by late Hubert Brinton; King's Coll., London Univ. (Law Schol. 1933; LLB Hons 1935); LLM London 1938. Admitted Solicitor, 1936; called to the Bar, Inner Temple, 1946. Irish Guards, Ensign and Subaltern, 1941-44; seconded to Judge-Advocate-General's Office, 1945-48; Mil. Prosecutor (War Crimes Trials, Germany), 1945-49; Legal Advr, Directorate of Army Legal Staff, 1950-56; retd as Col, 1956. Lectr in Internat. Law, 1956, Reader, 1964, Univ. of London; Reader, Univ. of Sussex, 1967-76. Vis. Prof., Cairo, 1965; Lionel Cohen Lectr, Hebrew Univ., Jerusalem, 1972; Vis. Lectr at UK Staff Colls, and Defence Acads, Vienna, Hamburg, Newport RI, and Tokyo. UK Deleg., Internat. Red Cross Confs, 1957-73; Legal Advr to UK Delegn, Diplomatic Conf. on Law of War, 1974-77. Fellow of NATO, 1958. *Publications:* Red Cross Conventions, 1958; Hague Academy Lectures, 1965; Civilians and NATO Status of Forces Agreement, 1966; articles in learned journals, incl. British Year Book of Internat. Law, Internat. Affairs, Internat., and Comp. Law Qly. *Recreations:* Egyptology, history of Penitentials; (for leisure) sitting in the sun. *Address:* 16 Southover High Street, Lewes, Sussex. *T:* Lewes 2387; University of Sussex, Falmer,

Brighton. *T:* Brighton 66755. *Clubs:* Cavalry and Guards; Cercle de la Terrasse (Geneva).

DRAPER, (John Haydn) Paul; Senior Planning Inspector, Department of Environment, since 1977; *b* 14 Dec. 1916; *o c* of late Haydn Draper, clarinet player, and Nan Draper; *m* 1941, Nancy Allum, author and journalist; one *s* one *d* (and one *d* decd). *Educ:* LCC primary sch.; Bancroft's Sch.; University Coll. London. Engr in Post Office, 1939-48; Royal Signals, Signalman to Major, Middle East, N Africa, Sicily, NW Europe (despatches), 1940-46; MoT, 1948-64 and 1968-70; Jt Principal Private Sec. to Minister, 1956-58; Asst Sec., 1959; Counsellor (Shipping), British Embassy, Washington, 1964-67; BoT, 1967-68; Under-Sec., 1968; DoE, 1970-74; Senior Planning Inspector, 1973-74; Resident Chm., Civil Service Selection Bd, 1975-76. *Address:* 24 Gordon Mansions, Huntley Street, WC1E 7HF.

DRAPER, Michael William; Under Secretary, and Head of Industries and Exports Division, Department of Health and Social Security, since 1976; *b* 26 Sept. 1928; *s* of John Godfrey Beresford Draper and Aileen Frances Agatha Draper (*née* Masefield); *m* 1952, Theodora Mary Frampton, *o d* of Henry James Frampton, *qv*; one *s* two *d. Educ:* St Edward's Sch., Oxford. FCA. Chartered Accountant, 1953; various posts in England, Ireland, Burma, Nigeria, Unilever Ltd, 1953-64; joined Civil Service, 1964; Principal, Min. of Power, 1964; Asst Sec., DHSS, 1972. Lay Chm., Woking Deanery Synod. *Recreations:* mountain walking, church affairs. *Address:* Pantiles, Ivy Lane, Woking, Surrey. *T:* Woking 60221.

DRAWBELL, James Wedgwood; Managing Editor, and Editorial Consultant, with Geo. Newnes Ltd (1946-64); previously Editor, Sunday Chronicle (1925-46); *b* 15 April 1899. *Educ:* Edinburgh. Worked on newspapers in New York (The World); Montreal (Montreal Star); Edinburgh (Evening Dispatch); served with Royal Scots Fusiliers, European War of 1914-18. *Publications:* Dorothy Thompson's English Journey, 1942; All Change Here, 1943; Night and Day, 1945; Drifts my Boat, 1946; The Long Year, 1958; The Sun Within Us, 1963; Time on My Hands, 1968; A Garden, 1970; Scotland: Bitter-Sweet, 1972. *Address:* c/o Midland Bank, 70 St Martin's Lane, WC2N 4JZ. *Clubs:* Scottish Liberal, Kilspindie Golf.

DRAYCOTT, Douglas Patrick, MA Oxon; QC 1965; a Recorder, since 1972 (Recorder of Shrewsbury, 1966-71); *b* 23 Aug. 1918; *s* of George Draycott and Mary Ann Draycott (*née* Burke); *m* Elizabeth Victoria Hall (marr. diss. 1974); two *s* three *d. Educ:* Wolstanton Grammar Sch.; Oriel Coll., Oxford (MA). War Service: Royal Tank Regiment and General Staff, 1939-46. Barrister-at-Law, Middle Temple, 1950, Master of the Bench, 1972. Joined Oxford Circuit, 1950, and practised from Chambers in Birmingham, 1950-65. *Address:* 1 Essex Court, Temple, EC4Y 9AR. *T:* 01-353 6717, 1974.

DRAYCOTT, Gerald Arthur; a Recorder of the Crown Court, since 1972; *b* 25 Oct. 1911; *s* of Arthur Henry Seely Draycott and Maud Mary Draycott; *m* 1939, Phyllis Moyra Evans; two *s* one *d. Educ:* King Edward's Sch., Stratford-on-Avon. FCII. Called to Bar, Middle Temple, 1938. Served in RAF, 1939-46 (Sqdn Ldr). Practised at Bar, SE Circuit, from 1946. *Recreations:* children, dogs, gardening. *Address:* Nethergate House, Saxlingham Nethergate, Norwich NR15 1PB. *T:* Hempnall 224. *Club:* Norfolk County (Norwich).

DRAYSON, Rear-Adm. Edwin Howard, CB 1945; CBE 1942 (OBE 1937); retired; *b* 1889; *m* 1914, Hilda Jeannie (*d* 1974), *d* of Isaac Harding; two *d* (one *s* killed in action, 1944); *m* 1974, Mrs Barbara Bennett. *Address:* Crail Cottage, Shute, Axminster, Devon.

DRAYSON, George Burnaby; MP (C) Skipton, since 1945; *b* 9 March 1913; *s* of late Walter Drayson, Stevenage, Herts, and Dorothy Dyott, *d* of late Captain Hugo Burnaby, RN; *m* 1939, Winifred Heath (marr. diss., 1958); one *d*; *m* 1962, Barbara Radonska-Chrzanowska, Warsaw. *Educ:* Borlasse Sch. Entered City, 1929; Mem. Stock Exchange, 1935-54; Company Director. Commnd Essex Yeomanry, 1931, Captain, 1938; served RA in Western Desert (TD, despatches, prisoner of war, June 1942-Sept. 1943, escaped twice, finally walked 500 miles to freedom). Member: Inter-Parliamentary Union Delegn to Turkey, 1947; CPA delegns to Caribbean, 1967, Ceylon, 1970, N Zealand, 1974. Mem., Expenditure Cttee, 1970-74. Chairman: Parly All Party East/West Trade Cttee; British-Polish Parly Gp; Vice-Chm., British-Venezuelan Parly Gp. *Recreations:* fishing, walking (completed London to Brighton walk, 1939); foreign travel. *Address:* House of Commons, SW1A 0AA; Linton House, Linton-in-Craven, Skipton, North Yorks. *T:* Grassington 752362. *Club:* Royal Automobile.

DRAYSON, Robert Quested, DSC 1943; MA; Headmaster of Stowe, since 1964; *b* 5 June 1919; *s* of late Frederick Louis Drayson and late Elsie Mabel Drayson; *m* 1943, Rachel, 2nd *d* of Stephen Spencer Jenkyns; one *s* two *d. Educ:* St Lawrence Coll., Ramsgate; Downing Coll., Cambridge. Univ. of Cambridge: 1938-39, 1946-47; History Tripos, BA 1947, MA 1950. Served RNVR, 1939-46; Lieut in command HM Motor Torpedo Boats. Asst Master and Housemaster, St Lawrence Coll., 1947-50; Asst Master, Felsted Sch., 1950-55; Headmaster, Reed's Sch., Cobham, 1955-63. FRSA 1968. *Recreations:* hockey (Cambridge Blue, 1946, 1947; Kent XI (Captain), 1947-56); golf. *Address:* Stowe School, Buckingham. *T:* Buckingham 3165. *Club:* Hawks (Cambridge).

DRENNAN, Alexander Murray, MD Edinburgh 1924; MB, ChB 1906; FRCPE 1914; FRSE 1932; Professor of Pathology, Edinburgh, 1931-54, retired; Professor Emeritus; *b* Jan. 1884; *s* of late Alexr Drennan, Dunalwyn, Helensburgh; *m* 1909; one *s* two *d. Educ:* Larchfield, Helensburgh; Kelvinside Academy Glasgow; Edinburgh Univ. Professor of Pathology, Otago Univ., Dunedin, NZ, 1914-28; Professor of Pathology, Queen's Univ. Belfast, 1928-31; Temporary Acting Lt-Comdr, RNVR (Sp.), 1942-47. *Publications:* various articles on pathological subjects, etc. *Recreations:* fishing, motoring, sailing. *Address:* Lochard Cottage, Kinlochard, Stirling FK8 3TL. *Club:* Royal Scottish Automobile (Glasgow).

DRENNAN, John Cherry, CBE 1959; JP; Senator, Northern Ireland, 1961-72; HM Lieutenant for Co. Londonderry, 1965-74; *b* 1899; *s* of late John Wallace Drennan, Carse Hall, Limavady, Co. Londonderry; *m* 1926, Margaret, *d* of late Charles Macfarlane, West Hartlepool; two *d* (one *s* decd). *Educ:* Foyle Coll., Londonderry. JP 1923, High Sheriff, 1955, DL 1955, Co. Londonderry. *Address:* Deerpark, Limavady, Co. Londonderry, N Ireland. *T:* Limavady 2321.

DRESCHFIELD, Ralph Leonard Emmanuel, CMG 1957; *b* 18 March 1911; *s* of late Henry Theodore and Jessie Mindelle Dreschfield; unmarried. *Educ:* Merchiston Castle Sch.; Trinity Hall, Cambridge (BA). Called to Bar, 1933; entered Colonial Service, 1938, and apptd resident Magistrate, Uganda; served in War of 1939-45, in 4th King's African Rifles; Crown Counsel, Uganda, 1948; Solicitor-Gen., Uganda, 1949; QC 1950; Attorney-Gen., Uganda, 1951-62. Chm. Trustees of Uganda National Parks, 1952-62. Sec., Community Council of Essex, 1963-76. Parly Counsel, Law Reform, Bermuda, 1976-. *Recreation:* yachting. *Address:* c/o Attorney General, Hamilton, Bermuda. *Clubs:* Royal Ocean Racing, Bar Yacht, Little Ship; West Mersea Yacht.

DREVER, James; Principal and Vice-Chancellor, University of Dundee, 1967-78; *b* 29 Jan. 1910; *s* of late Prof. James Drever; *m* 1936, Joan Isabel Mackay Budge; one *s* one *d. Educ:* Royal High Sch., Edinburgh; Universities of Edinburgh (MA Hons Philosophy, 1932) and Cambridge (MA Moral Science Tripos, 1934). FRSE. Asst, Dept of Philosophy, Edinburgh, 1934-38; Lecturer in Philosophy and Psychology, King's Coll., Newcastle, 1938-41; Royal Navy, 1941-45; Prof. of Psychology, Univ. of Edinburgh, 1944-66. Visiting Professor, Princeton Univ., 1954-55. Editor, British Journal of Psychology, 1954-58; President: British Psychological Soc., 1960-61; Internat. Union of Scientific Psychology, 1963-66. Member: Cttee on Higher Education, 1961-63; SSRC, 1965-69; Adv. Council, Civil Service Coll., 1973-; Oil Develt Council for Scotland, 1973-; Perm. Cttee of Conf. of European Rectors, 1975-; Chm., Advisory Council on Social Work, in Scotland, 1970-74. Dir, Grampian Television Ltd, 1973-. *Publications:* papers and reviews. *Address:* Craiglochie House, by Glencarse, Tayside.

DREW, Sir Arthur (Charles Walter), KCB 1964 (CB 1958); JP; retired; Permanent Under-Secretary of State (Administration), Ministry of Defence, and Member, Admiralty, Army (from 1964) and Air Force Boards, 1968-72; *b* 2 Sept. 1912; *er s* of late Arthur Drew, Mexico City, and Louise Schulte-Ummingen; *m* 1943, Rachel, *er d* of G. W. Lambert, *qv*; one *s* three *d. Educ:* Christ's Hospital; King's Coll., Cambridge. Asst Principal, War Office, 1936; Private Sec. to successive Secs of State for War, 1944-49; IDC, 1949; International Staff, NATO, 1951-53; Dep. Under Sec. of State, Home Office, 1961-63; last Permanent Under Sec. of State, War Office, 1963-64; Permanent Under-Sec. of State (Army), MoD, 1964-68. Warden, Drapers' Co., 1970, Master, 1977-78. Trustee: British Museum (Natural History), 1972-; British Museum, 1973-; Imperial War Museum, 1973-; Nat. Army Museum, 1975-; RAF Museum, 1976-; Member: Standing Commn on Museums and Galleries, 1973-; Council, Nat. Trust, 1974-. JP 1963, 1973-; Richmond. Coronation Medal, 1953. *Recreation:* building. *Address:* 2 Branstone Road, Kew, Surrey TW9 3LB. *T:* 01-940 1210. *Club:* Reform.

DREW, Brig. Cecil Francis, DSO 1918; *b* 1890; *o s* of late Albert Francis Drew, JP of Foston, Farnham Royal, Bucks; *m* 1915, Elizabeth Seymour Hawker; one *s* (and one *s* decd). *Educ:* Highgate and Royal Milit. Acad.; Joined The Cameronians, 1910; served European War (despatches twice, DSO); temp. Lt-Col, 1917-19; Brevet Lt-Col, 1932; Lt-Col, 1936; Col, 1938; Brigadier, 1939; GSO 3, War Office, 1919-22; GSO 3, Scottish Command, 1924; DAA and QMG Highland Area, 1925-27; DAQMG South China Command, 1927-28; GSO 51st (Highland) Division, 1929-33; commanded 1st Bn The Cameronians, 1936-38; AAG War Office, 1938-39; Comd East Lancs Area, 1939-40; Comd 183 Inf. Brigade, 1940-42; Brigadier i/c Administration, 1st Corps District, 1942; AAG Southern Command, 1943; Gen. Staff, GHQ Home Forces, 1944-45; retired pay, 1945. JP Bucks, 1949. *Address:* Gatehouse Cottages, Framfield, near Uckfield, East Sussex. *Club:* Army and Navy.

DREW, Charles Edwin, MVO 1952; VRD 1960; FRCS; Surgeon, Westminster Hospital since 1951; Thoracic Surgeon, St George's Hospital, since 1955; Civilian Consultant in Thoracic Surgery to the Royal Navy; Hon. Consultant in Thoracic Surgery to the Army (to Queen Alexandra Hospital, Millbank, since 1960); Hon. Consulting Thoracic Surgeon, King Edward VII Hospital, Midhurst; *b* 1916; *s* of Edwin Frank Drew, Croydon; *m* 1950, Doreen, *d* of Frederick James Pittaway, Stocksfield, Northumberland; one *s* one *d. Educ:* Westminster City Sch.; King's Coll., London. MB, BS London 1941; MRCS, LRCP 1941; FRCS 1946. Served War of 1939-45, RNVR (Surgeon-Comdr 1957). Formerly Chief Asst and Surg. Registrar, Westminster Hosp.; Chief Surgical Asst, Brompton Hosp. Mem. Soc. Thoracic Surgeons: FRSocMed. *Publications:* papers in med. jls. *Address:* 17 Rodway Road, SW15. *T:* 01-788 7030; 97/24 John Islip Street, SW1. *T:* 01-828 4709.

DREW, Sir Ferdinand (Caire), Kt 1960; CMG 1951; FASA; Under-Treasurer, South Australia and Chairman State Grants Committee, 1946-60, retired; *b* Adelaide, S Aust., 1 May 1895; *s* of late Charles H. Drew, Adelaide; *m* 1934, Chrissie A., *d* of George M. McGowan; one *s* two *d. Educ:* Rose Park Public Sch.; Muirden Coll. Asst Auditor-Gen., 1936-39; Asst Under-Treasurer, 1939-46. Chm. Supply and Tender Board, 1943-49; Mem. Industries Development Cttee, 1942-49; Mem. Board of State Bank of South Australia, 1948-73 (Dep. Chm. 1963); Director: Unit Trust of SA; United Insurance Co. Ltd; Chrysler Aust. Ltd, 1963-74; Chm., Board of Electricity Trust, South Australia, 1949-70 (Mem., 1949-74). *Address:* 614 Anzac Highway, Glenelg East, SA 5045, Australia.

DREW, Prof. George Charles, MA; London University Professor of Psychology, University College, since 1958; *b* 10 Dec. 1911; *e s* of George Frederick Drew; *m* 1936, Inez Annie, *d* of F. Hulbert Lewis; one *s* one *d. Educ:* St George's Sch., Bristol; Bristol, Cambridge and Harvard Univs. Viscount Haldane of Cloan studentship, Cambridge, 1935-36; Rockefeller Fellowship, Harvard Univ., 1936-38; Rockefeller Research Fellowship, Cambridge, 1938-42; Psychological Adviser, Air Ministry, 1942-46; Lecturer in Psychology, University of Bristol, 1946-49, Reader, 1949-51, Prof. of Psychology, 1951-58. Mem. Vision Research Council, 1965-67. Vis. Prof., University of Calif, Berkeley, USA, 1967-68. C. S. Myers Lectr, 1973. Founder Mem., Exper. Psych. Soc., 1946 (Pres. 1950-51, 1959-60); Pres., British Psych. Soc., 1962-63; Pres. and Chm., Org. Cttee, 19th Internat. Congress of Psychology, 1969. Dean of Science, UCL, 1973-76. *Publications:* articles on animal behaviour, learning, vision, and other psychological problems, in various British and American journals. *Address:* University College, Gower Street, WC1E 6BT.

DREW, Harry Edward, CB 1970; Chairman, Robert Stuart (London) Ltd, since 1974; Director: EPS (Research & Development) Ltd, since 1972; Quality Audit and Advisory Services, since 1973; *b* 18 Jan. 1909; 2nd *s* of W. H. Drew and F. E. Drew (*née* Brindley), Gillingham, Kent; *m* 1937, Phyllis (*née* Flippance); one *s. Educ:* Wesleyan Sch., Gillingham; RAF Apprentice Sch., Flowerdown, RAF, 1924-37; Air Min. Research Stn, Bawdsey, 1937; Works Man., Radio Prodn Unit, Woolwich, Min. of Supply, 1943; Officer i/c, Research Prototype Unit, W. Howe, Bournemouth, Min. of Aircraft Prodn, 1946; Asst Dir, 1951, Dir, 1959, Electronic Prodn, Min. of Supply, London; Dir of Techn. Costs, Min. of Aviation, London, 1964; Dir-Gen. of Quality Assurance, Min. of Technology, 1966-70; Chief Exec., Defence Quality Assurance Bd, MoD, 1970-72. FIERE (Mem. Charter Council); FIProdE; FIWM (Nat. Chm., 1966-68, Vice-Pres., 1969). Hon. CGIA 1974. Warden, Worshipful Co. of Scientific Instrument Makers. *Publications:* papers on training and quality and reliability. *Recreations:* photography, reading, gardening. *Address:* 25 Celtic Avenue, Shortlands, Kent. *T:* 01-460 3988. *Clubs:* Civil Service, City Livery.

DREW, Jane Beverly, FRIBA; FIArb; architect; Partner in firm of Fry Drew and Partners, since 1946; *b* 24 March 1911; *m* 1st; two *d*; 2nd, 1942, Edwin Maxwell Fry, *qv. Educ:* Croydon. Was in partnership with J. T. Alliston, 1934-39; independent practice, 1939-45; in partnership with Maxwell Fry, 1945-. Asst Town Planning Adviser to Resident Minister, West African Colonies, 1944-45; Senior Architect to Capital project of Chandigarh, Punjab, India, 1951-54; Beamis Prof. Mass Inst. of Techn., Jan.-June, 1961; Vis. Prof. of Architecture, Harvard, Feb-March 1970; Bicentennial Prof., Utah Univ., 1976. Completed work includes housing, hospitals, schools, and colleges in UK, West Africa, including Univs in Nigeria, Middle East and India; a section of Festival of Britain, 1951; town planning, housing and amenity buildings in Iran, W Africa and India. Current work, Education Inst., Mauritius, school work, office conversion, the Open University. Pres., Architectural Association, 1969. Hon LLD Ibadan, 1966; DUniv Open Univ., 1973. *Publications:* (with Maxwell Fry) Architecture for Children, 1944; (with Maxwell Fry and Harry Ford) Village Housing in the Tropics, 1945; (Founder Editor, 1945-) Architects' Year Book; (with Maxwell Fry) Architecture in the Humid Tropics; Tropical Architecture, 1956; (with Maxwell Fry) Architecture and the Environment, 1976. *Recreations:* reading, writing, friends. *Address:* 63 Gloucester Place, W1. *T:* 01-935 3318. *Clubs:* Institute of Contemporary Arts, French.

DREW, John Alexander, CB 1957; *b* 19 July 1907; *s* of Charles Edward Drew, Okehampton, Devon, and Ethel Margaret Drew; *m* 1930, Edith Waud Marriott; two *s* (and one *s* decd). *Educ:* Gram. Sch., Okehampton. Entered CS, 1928; Secretaries' Office, HM Customs and Excise, 1935-40; employed on special duties, 1940-45; Asst Sec., Cabinet Office, 1945-48; Bd of Trade, 1948-50; Asst Under-Sec. of State, Ministry of Defence, 1951-67, retired, 1967. US Medal of Freedom with Bronze Palm, 1946. *Address:* 28 Montague Avenue, Sanderstead, Surrey. *T:* 01-657 3264.

DREW, Lt-Gen. Sir (William) Robert (Macfarlane), KCB 1965 (CB 1962); CBE 1952 (OBE 1940); KStJ 1977 (CStJ 1965); FRCP; *b* 4 Oct. 1907; *s* of late William Hughes Drew and Ethel Macfarlane; *m* 1934, Dorothy, *d* of late Alfred E. Dakingsmith, Bowral, NSW; one *s* one *d. Educ:* Sydney Gram. Sch.; Sydney Univ. MB, BS, BSc Sydney, 1930; DTM&H (Eng.), 1938; MRCP 1938; FRCP 1945; FRCPEd, 1966; FRACP, 1966; FACP 1966; Hon. FRCS 1970. Joined RAMC, 1931; served India, France (Dunkirk), Iraq, MELF; MO, War Cabinet Offices, 1943-46; Consulting Physician to the Army, 1959-61; Commandant, Royal Army Medical Coll., 1960-63; Dir of Medical Services, British Army of the Rhine, 1963-64; Dir-Gen., Army Medical Services, 1965-69. Dep. Dir, British Postgraduate Med. Fedn, 1970-76 (Mem. Governing Body, 1954-56, 1967-69). QHP, 1959-69. Leishman Prize, Royal Army Medical Coll., 1938; Goulstonian Lecturer, RCP, 1946; Mitchener Medallist, RCS, 1955; Lettsomian Lecturer, Medical Soc., London, 1961. Prof. Medicine, Royal Faculty of Med., Baghdad, 1946-52; Lectr Westminster Med. Sch., 1954-59; Pres. Clin. Section, Royal Society of Medicine, 1968-70, Hon. Fellow, 1973. Hon. Sec. and later Councillor: Royal Society of Tropical Medicine and Hygiene (Pres., 1971-73); Med. Soc. of London (Pres., 1967-68); Australia and NZ Med. Assoc. (Chm.); Councillor: Royal Society of Medicine; RCP (Vice-Pres., 1970-71); Hunterian Soc.; Mem. Bd of Governors: Hospital for Sick Children, Gt Ormond Street, London; Moorfields Eye Hosp.; Star and Garter Home for Disabled Sailors, Soldiers and Airmen; Royal Sch. for Daughters of Officers of the Army; Member: Assoc. Physicians Gt Britain and Ireland; Exec. Cttee, Forces Help Soc.; Control Bd, Army Benevolent Fund; Bd, Kennedy Inst. of Rheumatology; Cttee, St John Ophthalmic Hospital of Jerusalem; Cttee of Management, Sir Oswald Stoll Foundn. HM Comr, The Royal Hosp., Chelsea. Hunterian Orator, Hunterian Soc., 1966. FRSA 1965. Hon. Member: Sydney Univ. Med. Soc., 1965; Anglo-German Med. Soc., 1970. Comdr Order of El-Rafidain (Iraq), 1951. *Publications:* in medical journals. *Recreations:* travel, gardening. *Address:* c/o Williams and Glyn's Bank, 22 Whitehall, SW1. *Clubs:* Army and Navy; Australian, Royal Sydney Golf (Sydney).

DREW-SMYTHE, Henry James; *see* Smythe.

DREWE, Geoffrey Grabham, CIE 1947; CBE 1958 (OBE 1942); *b* 3 May 1904; 2nd *s* of late Alfred John Drewe, Bournemouth; *m* 1934, Christine Evelyn Isabel Young; two *d. Educ:* Cheltenham Coll.; Pembroke Coll., Oxford. Entered ICS, 1928; served in various parts of Sind and Bombay Provinces; Collector and Dist. Magistrate, Ahmedabad, 1938-43; Home Sec. to Government of Bombay, 1944-47; retired from Indian Civil Service, 1947. Asst to Hon. Treasurers of Cons. Party, 1948-70; Manager, Cons. Party Bd of Finance, 1965-70. *Recreation:*

gardening. *Address:* Westering, Haven Road, Canford Cliffs, Poole, Dorset. *Club:* East India, Devonshire, Sports and Public Schools.

DREYER, Adm. Sir Desmond (Parry), GCB 1967 (KCB 1963; CB 1960); CBE 1957; DSC; JP; Member, Armed Forces Pay Review Body, since 1971; Gentleman Usher to the Sword of State, since 1973; *b* 6 April 1910; *yr s* of late Adm. Sir Frederic Dreyer, GBE, KCB; *m* 1st, 1934, Elisabeth (*d* 1958), *d* of late Sir Henry Chilton, GCMG; one *s* one *d* (and one *s* decd); 2nd, 1959, Marjorie Gordon, *widow* of Hon. R. G. Whiteley. Served War of 1939-45 (DSC). Cdre First Class, 1955. Chief of Staff, Mediterranean, 1955-57; Asst Chief of Naval Staff, 1958-59; Flag Officer (Flotillas) Mediterranean, 1960-61; Flag Officer Air (Home), 1961-62; Comdr, Far East Fleet, 1962-65; Second Sea Lord, 1965-67; Chief Adviser (Personnel and Logistics) to Sec. of State for Defence, 1967-68. Rear-Adm., 1958; Vice-Adm., 1961; Adm., 1965. Principal Naval ADC to the Queen, 1965-68. Mem. Nat. Bd for Prices and Incomes, 1968-71. Pres., Royal Naval Benevolent Trust, 1970-; Chm., Regular Forces Employment Assoc. JP Hants 1968; High Sheriff for Hampshire, 1977-78. *Address:* 35 Brompton Square, SW3 2AE. *T:* 01-584 1647; Brook Cottage, Cheriton, near Alresford, Hants SO24 0QA. *T:* Bramdean 215.

DREYFUS, Pierre; Grand Officier, Légion d'Honneur; *b* Paris, 18 Nov. 1907; *s* of Emmanuel Dreyfus, Banker, and Madeleine (*née* Bernard); *m* 1936, Laure Ullmo; one *d. Educ:* Lycée Janson-de-Sailly; Faculty of Law, Univ. of Paris (Dip., Dr of Law). Inspector-Gen. of Industry and Commerce, Chief of Gen. Inspectorate, and Dir of Cabinet to Minister of Industry and Commerce, M Robert Lacoste, 1947-49; Pres., Commn of Energy of the Plan, and Dir of the Cabinet to Minister of Industry and Commerce, M Bourgès-Maunoury, 1954. President: Houillères de Lorraine, 1950-55; Charbonnages de France, 1954; Société des Aciers Fins de l'Est, 1955. President Director-General, Régie Nationale des Usines Renault, 1955-75; Pres., Renault-Finance. *Address:* 53 avenue Champs-Elysées, Paris, France.

DRIDAN, Julian Randal, CMG 1955; Chairman, Electricity Trust of South Australia since 1970 (Member since 1953); *b* 24 Nov. 1901; *s* of Sydney John Dridan and Eliza Gundry Dridan; *m* 1925, Ivy Viola Orr; two *d. Educ;* South Australian Sch. of Mines; University of Adelaide (BE). Entered service with Govt of S Australia, 1923; construction of locks and weirs on River Murray, 1923-34; District Engineer, 1934-44; Deputy Engineer-in-Chief, 1946; Engineer-in-Chief, 1949; Dir and Engineer-in-Chief, 1960-66. Mem. River Murray Commission, 1947-66. Coronation Medal, 1953. *Recreations:* bowls, fishing. *Address:* 555 Fullarton Road, Mitcham, South Australia. *Club:* Rotary (Adelaide).

DRINAN, Adam; *see* Macleod, Joseph T. G.

DRING, Lt-Col Sir (Arthur) John, KBE 1952; CIE 1943; JP; DL; *b* 4 Nov. 1902; *s* of late Sir William Dring, KCIE; *m* 1934, Marjorie Wadham (*d* 1943); two *d*; *m* 1946, Alice Deborah, *widow* of Maj.-Gen. J. S. Marshall, CB, DSO, OBE, and *o d* of late Maj.-Gen. Gerald Cree, CB, CMG. *Educ:* Winchester Coll.; RMC, Sandhurst. Joined Guides Cavalry, 1923; Indian Political Service, 1927; Asst Private Sec. to Viceroy, 1930-32; Deputy Commissioner, Dera Ismail Khan, 1935-36; Sec. to Governor, NWFP, 1937-40; Political Agent, South Waziristan, 1940-42 (despatches); Sec. to NWFP Govt Development Depts; Revenue Commissioner, NWFP; Chief Sec. NWFP, 1947; Prime Minister of Bahawalpur, 1948-52; Adviser to Governor of Gold Coast on Togoland Plebiscite, 1955-56. Adviser to Governor-Gen. of Nigeria and the Governor of the Northern Region for the N & S Cameroons Plebiscite, 1959. JP 1954, DL 1973, Hants. *Recreations:* riding and gardening. *Address:* Ava Cottage, Purbrook, Hants. *T:* Waterlooville 3000.

DRING, (Dennis) William, RA 1955 (ARA 1944); RWS; *b* 26 Jan. 1904; *s* of William Henry Dring; *m* 1931, Grace Elizabeth Rothwell; one *s* two *d. Educ:* Slade Sch. of Fine Art. Portrait and landscape painter; during the war official war artist to Ministry of Information, Admiralty, and Air Ministry. *Address:* Windy Ridge, Compton, Winchester, Hants. *T:* Twyford, Hants 712181.

DRING, Lieut-Col Sir John; *see* Dring, Lieut-Col Sir A. J.

DRING, Richard Paddison; Editor of Official Report (Hansard), House of Commons, since 1972; *b* 6 Nov. 1913; *s* of late Fred Dring and late Florence Hasleham Dring, East Sheen; *m* 1939, Joan Wilson, St Albans; one *s. Educ:* St Paul's School. Served Army, 1942-46. Herts Advertiser, 1932; Press Association,

1936; Official Report (Hansard), House of Commons, 1940: Asst Editor, 1954; Dep. Editor, 1970. *Recreations:* golf, riding. *Address:* 24 Vicarage Drive, SW14 8RX. *T:* 01-876 2162. *Clubs:* Press Gallery; Richmond Golf.

DRING, William; see Dring, D. W.

DRINKALL, John Kenneth, CMG 1973; HM Diplomatic Service; High Commissioner in Jamaica, and Ambassador (non-resident) to Haiti, since 1976; *b* 1 Jan. 1922; *s* of J. H. Drinkall; *m* 1961, Patricia Ellis; two *s* two *d. Educ:* Haileybury Coll.; Brasenose Coll., Oxford. Indian Army, 1942-45. Entered HM Foreign Service, 1947; 3rd Sec., Nanking, 1948; Vice-Consul, Tamsui, Formosa, 1949-51; Acting Consul, 1951; Foreign Office, 1951-53; 1st Sec., Cairo, 1953-56; Foreign Office, 1957-60; 1st Sec., Brasilia, 1960-62; Foreign Office, 1962-65. Appointed Counsellor, 1964; Counsellor: Nicosia, Cyprus, 1965-67; British Embassy, Brussels, 1967-70; FCO, 1970-71; Canadian Nat. Defence Coll., 1971-72; Ambassador to Afghanistan, 1972-76. *Recreations:* lawn tennis, golf, racquets and squash. *Address:* c/o Foreign and Commonwealth Office, SW1. *Clubs:* Royal Automobile, All England Lawn Tennis.

DRINKWATER, John Muir, QC 1972; a Recorder of the Crown Court, since 1972; *b* 16 March 1925; *s* of late Comdr John Drinkwater, OBE, RN (retd); *m* Jennifer Marion, *d* of Edward Fitzwalter Wright, Morley Manor, Derbs; one *s* four *d. Educ:* RNC Dartmouth. HM Submarines, 1943-47; Flag Lieut to C-in-C Portsmouth and First Sea Lord, 1947-50; Lt-Comdr 1952; invalided 1953. Called to Bar, Inner Temple, 1957. Mem., Boundary Commn for England, 1977-. Governor, St Mary's Hosp., 1960-64. *Recreations:* swimming, squash, travel. *Address:* Meysey Hampton Manor, Cirencester, Glos GL7 5JS. *T:* Poulton 366; 161 Cranmer Court, SW3 3HF. *T:* 01-584 2176. *Club:* Garrick.

DRIVER, Sir Arthur (John), Kt 1962; JP; *b* 1900; *s* of Percy John Driver, East Sheen, and Mary Amelie Driver; *m* 1937, Margaret, *d* of Hugh Semple McMeekin, Carnmoney, Northern Ireland; one *s* one *d.* Served in Royal Air Force, 1918. Pres. of Law Soc., 1961-62. JP, Supplementary List. *Address:* Frogmore Cottage, East Clandon, Surrey. *Club:* Reform.

DRIVER, His Honour Major Arthur Robert, AMIEA; *b* Albany, W Australia, 25 Nov. 1909; *s* of late Henry and Mary Driver, Western Australia; *m* 1st, 1936; one *s* one *d*; 2nd, 1949, Marjorie Campbell, *d* of George Leighton, Wodonga, Victoria, Australia; one *d. Educ:* Hale Sch., Perth, Western Australia; University of Western Australia. Civil Engineer, PWD of WA, 1928-39. War of 1939-45, AMF; Regimental Officer 2/4 Aust. Pioneer Bn, Bde Major, 23rd Aust. Inf. Bde, GSO II (Ops.), Advanced HQ, AMF, 1940-45. Administrator of the Northern Territory and President of Legislative Council of N Territory, Australia, 1946-51; Australian Chief Migration Officer, Rome, 1951-54; Austria and Germany, 1954-56; Chief of Operations, Inter-Governmental Cttee for European Migration, Geneva, 1956-60. Company Dir, 1960-72, retired. *Recreations:* golf, fishing. *Address:* 35 Amaroo Drive, Buderim, Qld 4556, Australia. *Clubs:* Naval and Military, United Services; Headland Golf (Buderim) (Pres.).

DRIVER, Eric William; Chairman, Mersey Regional Health Authority, since 1973; *b* 19 Jan. 1911; *s* of William Weale Driver and Sarah Ann Driver; *m* 1st, 1938, Winifred Bane; two *d*; 2nd, 1972, Sheila Mary Johnson. *Educ:* Strand Sch., London; King's Coll., London Univ. (BSc). FICE. Civil Engr with ICI Ltd, 1938-73, retd as Chief Civil Engr Mond Div. *Recreations:* dinghy sailing (racing), hill walking, gardening. *Address:* Chapel House, Crowley, Northwich, Cheshire CW9 6NX. *Clubs:* Royal Yachting Association; Budworth Sailing.

DRIVER, Thomas; General Secretary, National Association of Teachers in Further and Higher Education, 1976-77; *b* 9 Sept. 1912; *s* of Joseph and Eliza Driver; *m* 1936, Thora Senior; one *s* one *d. Educ:* Sheffield Univ. (BA, DipEd). Barnsley Central Sch., 1937-42; Keighley Jun. Techn. Sch., 1942-45; Barnsley Techn. Sch., 1945-47; Doncaster Coll. of Technology, 1947-68. Gen. Sec., Assoc. of Teachers in Technical Institutions, 1969-76. *Recreations:* walking, reading. *Address:* Arundel, Plantagenet Road, Barnet, Herts EN5 5JQ.

DROGHEDA, 11th Earl of, *cr* 1661 (Ireland); **Charles Garrett Ponsonby Moore,** KG 1972; KBE 1964 (OBE 1946); Baron Moore of Mellifont, 1616; Viscount Moore, 1621; Baron Moore of Cobham (UK), 1954; Chairman of the Financial Times Ltd, 1971-75 (Managing Director, 1945-70); Director: Pearson Longman Ltd; Economist Newspaper Ltd; Industrial and Trade Fairs Holdings (Chairman, 1958-77); Earls Court & Olympia Ltd; Governor, The Royal Ballet; *b* 23 April 1910; *o s* of 10th Earl of Drogheda, PC, KCMG; *S* father, 1957; *m* 1935, Joan, *o d* of late William Henry Carr; one *s. Educ:* Eton; Trinity Coll., Cambridge. 2nd Lieut Royal Artillery (TA), 1939; Captain 1940. On staff of Ministry of Production, 1942-45. Chairman: Newspaper Publishers' Assoc., 1968-70; Royal Opera House, Covent Garden Ltd, 1958-74. Pres., Contemporary Dance Theatre; Jt Chm., Youth and Music. Pres., Institute of Directors, 1975-76. Trustee, British Museum, 1974-. Chm., London Celebrations Cttee, Queen's Silver Jubilee, 1977. Commander: Legion of Honour (France), 1960; Ordine al Merito (Italy), 1968; Grand Officier de l'Ordre de Léopold II (Belgium), 1974. *Heir:* Viscount Moore, *qv. Address:* Parkside House, Englefield Green, Surrey. *T:* Egham 2800. *Clubs:* White's, Garrick.
See also Sir Richard Latham, Bt.

DROMGOOLE, Jolyon; MA Oxon; Assistant Under-Secretary of State, General Staff, Ministry of Defence, since 1976; *b* 27 March 1926; 2nd *s* of Nicholas and Violet Dromgoole; *m* 1956, Anthea, *e d* of Sir Anthony Bowlby, 2nd Bt, *qv*; five *d* (incl. triplets). *Educ:* Christ's Hospital; Dulwich Coll.; University Coll., Oxford, 1944. 2nd Cl. Hons (History), MA. Served War: entered HM Forces, 1944; commissioned 14/20 King's Hussars, 1946. University Coll., 1948-50. Entered Administrative Cl., Civil Service; assigned to War Office, 1950; Private Sec. to Permanent Under-Sec., 1953; Principal, 1955; Private Sec. to Sec. of State, 1964; Asst Sec., 1965; Command Sec., HQ FARELF, Singapore, 1968-71; Royal Coll. of Defence Studies, 1972; Under-Sec., Broadcasting Dept, Home Office, 1973-76. *Recreations:* polo, literature. *Address:* 42 Upper Montagu Street, W1. *T:* 01-262 4904; Montreal House, Barnsley, Glos. *T:* Bibury 331. *Clubs:* Athenæum; Stourhead Polo (Dorset).

DROMORE, Bishop of, (RC), since 1976; **Most Rev. Francis Gerard Brooks,** DD, DCL; *b* Jan. 1924. Priest, 1949. Formerly President, St Colman's Coll., Violet Hill, Newry. *Address:* Bishop's House, Newry, Co. Down, N Ireland.

DRONFIELD, John, OBE 1971; MA Cambridge; JP; Headmaster of St Peter's School, York, 1937-67; *b* Heather, Leics, 23 Dec. 1898; *er s* of late Matthew H. Dronfield, Heather, Leics; *m* 1939, Sheila Mary Ross, *e d* of F. W. Williams, Greystones, Co. Wicklow; two *s* two *d. Educ:* Ashby-de-la-Zouch; Emmanuel Coll., Cambridge. War Service, 1917-19; 2nd Lieut in 2nd Hampshire Regt 1918; Asst Master and House Tutor at Stanley House Sch., Edgbaston, 1923-26; Asst Master at Worksop Coll., 1926-37; Housemaster of Talbot's House in 1927, and for six years Senior Housemaster and Sixth form Mathematical Master at Worksop; Acting Headmaster of Worksop, Aug.-Dec. 1935. JP City of York, 1942. *Address:* Askham Bryan, York. *T:* York 705757.

DRONFIELD, Ronald; Chief Insurance Officer for National Insurance, Department of Health and Social Security, since 1976; *b* 21 Dec. 1924; *m* 1966, Marie Renie (*née* Price). *Educ:* King Edward VII Sch., Sheffield; Oriel Coll., Oxford. RN, 1943-46. Entered Min. of National Insurance, 1949; Principal Private Sec. to Minister of Pensions and Nat. Insce, 1964-66; Cabinet Office, 1970-71. *Recreation:* reading, history mainly. *Address:* Cumberland House, Cumberland Place, Southampton. *T:* Southampton 34541. *Club:* Royal Commonwealth Society.

DROWLEY, Air Vice-Marshal Thomas Edward, CB 1947; CBE 1943 (OBE 1933); *b* 23 March 1894. Director of Equipment, RAF delegation, Washington, 1941-46; Director-General of Equipment, Air Ministry, 1946-49; retd 1949. Legion of Merit (Commander) USA. *Address:* Cedarwood, Christmas Lane, Farnham Common, Slough, Bucks. *T:* Farnham Common 4151.

DRUCKER, Prof. Peter (Ferdinand); writer and consultant; Clarke Professor of Social Science, Claremont Graduate School, Claremont, Calif, since 1971; *b* 19 Nov. 1909; *s* of Adolph B. Drucker and Caroline (*née* Bond); *m* 1937, Doris Schmitz; one *s* three *d. Educ:* Austria, Germany, England. Investment banker, London, 1933-36; newspapers, 1937-41; Professor of Philosophy and Politics, Bennington Coll., Bennington, Vt, USA, 1942-49; Prof. of Management, NY Univ., 1950-72. Management Consultant (internat. practice among businesses and govts) (as well as Professorships), 1948-. Holds nine hon. doctorates from Univs in Belgium, GB, Japan, Switzerland, USA. Hon. FBIM; FAAAS; Fellow: Amer. Acad. of Management; Internat. Acad. of Management. Order of Sacred Treasure, Japan; Grand Cross, Austria. *Publications:* End of Economic Man, 1939; Future of Industrial Man, 1942; Concept of Corporation, 1946; The New Society, 1950; Practice of Management, 1954; America's Next Twenty Years, 1959; Landmarks of Tomorrow, 1960; Managing for Results, 1964; The Effective Executive, 1967; The Age of

Discontinuity, 1969; Technology, Management and Society, 1970; Men, Ideas and Politics, 1971; The New Markets... and other essays, 1971; Management: tasks, responsibilities, practices, 1974; The Unseen Revolution: how pension fund socialism came to America, 1976. *Recreations:* mountaineering; Japanese history and paintings. *Address:* 636 Wellesley Drive, Claremont, Calif 91711, USA. *T:* (714) 621-1488.

DRUMALBYN, 1st Baron, *cr* 1963; **Niall Malcolm Stewart Macpherson,** PC 1962; KBE 1974; *b* 3 Aug. 1908; 3rd *s* of late Sir T. Stewart Macpherson, CIE, LLD, Newtonmore, Inverness-shire; *m* Margaret Phyllis, *d* of late J. J. Runge and of Mrs N. C. Ross (*see* N. C. Runge); two *d* (and one *d* decd). *Educ:* Edinburgh Academy; Fettes Coll.; Trinity Coll., Oxford (Scholar). First Class Honour Mods. 1929; First Class Litt Hum. 1931; MA; Rugby Football Blue, 1928. Business training with J. & J. Colman Ltd; Manager Turkish branch, 1933-35; Export branch, London, 1936-39. Commissioned Queen's Own Cameron Highlanders, TA June 1939: Staff Coll., 1942; Temp. Major 1942; MP (Nat L) 1945-50 (Nat L and U), 1950-63, Dumfriesshire. Scottish Whip, 1945-55; Chm., Commonwealth Producers' Organisation, 1952-55, Pres., 1967-70. Dep. Pres., Associated British Chambers of Commerce, 1970. Member BBC General Advisory Council, 1950-55. Joint Under-Sec. of State for Scotland, 1955-60; Parly Sec., Board of Trade, 1960-62; Minister of Pensions and National Insurance, 1962-63; Minister of State, BoT, 1963-64; Minister without Portfolio, 1970-74. Chm., Advertising Standards Authority, 1965-70, and 1974-77. *Heir:* none. *Address:* High Larch, Iver Heath, Bucks. *Club:* Royal Automobile.

DRUMLANRIG, Viscount; Sholto Francis Guy Douglas; *b* 1 June 1967; *s* and *heir* of 12th Marquess of Queensberry, *qv*.

DRUMMOND, family name of **Earl of Perth** and of **Baron Strange.**

DRUMMOND, Lieut-Gen. Sir Alexander; *see* Drummond, Lieut-Gen. Sir W. A. D.

DRUMMOND, Maj.-Gen. Anthony John D.; *see* Deane-Drummond.

DRUMMOND, Dame (Edith) Margaret, DBE 1966 (OBE 1960); MA; Director of the Women's Royal Naval Service, 1964-June 1967; *b* 4 Sept. 1917; *d* of Prof. Robert James Drummond and Marion (*née* Street). *Educ:* Park Sch., Glasgow; Aberdeen Univ. Joined WRNS, April 1941 and progressed through various ranks of the Service. *Recreations:* gardening, reading, concerts and friends. *Address:* Somersham Cottage, Saxlingham, Holt, Norfolk. *Club:* University Women's.

DRUMMOND, Lieut-Gen. (Retd) Sir (William) Alexander (Duncan), KBE 1957 (CBE 1951; OBE 1945); CB 1954; SPk 1969; Director-General, Army Medical Services, War Office, 1956-61 (Deputy Director-General, 1954-56); late RAMC; *b* 16 Sept. 1901. *Educ:* Dundee Univ. MRCS, LRCP 1924; DLO Eng. 1932; FRCS 1947. Formerly: Registrar, Throat, Nose and Ear Hospital, Golden Square; Registrar, Throat, Nose and Ear Dept, Charing Cross Hosp. Served War of 1939-45 (despatches five times, OBE). Col Comdt RAMC, 1961-66. Formerly HM Comr, Royal Hospital, Chelsea. KStJ, 1959. Hon. LLD: Birmingham, 1959; Punjab, 1960. *Publications:* contributions to medical journals. *Address:* c/o Grindlay's Bank, 13 St James's Square, SW1; Chase Lodge, 27 Clapham Common North Side, SW4.

DRUMMOND, William Norman; Deputy Secretary, Department of Manpower Services, Northern Ireland, since 1974; *b* 10 July 1927; *s* of Thomas and Martha Drummond, Lurgan; *m* 1958, Pamela Joyce Burnham; two *d*. *Educ:* Lurgan Coll.; Queen's Univ. Belfast (BSc (Hons)). Physicist, Iraq Petroleum Co., Kirkuk, Iraq, 1950-54; Reed's Sch., Cobham, 1954-57; Northern Ireland Civil Service, 1957-. *Recreations:* gardening, reading. *Address:* Magheralave Park East, Lisburn, Northern Ireland. *T:* Lisburn 4104.

DRUMMOND-WOLFF, Henry; *b* 16 July 1899; *s* of late Cecil Drummond-Wolff (*s* of Rt Hon. Sir Henry Drummond-Wolff, PC, GCB, GCMG), and Zaida Drummond-Wolff, Caplanne, Billère, Pau, BP, France; *m* 1933, Margaret, *d* of late Gibson Fahnestock, Newport, Rhode Island, USA; one *d*. *Educ:* Radley (Scholar); RMC Sandhurst (Prize Cadet). Served with Royal Flying Corps, 1917; retired from Royal Air Force, 1919; contested Rotherham Feb. 1933; MP (C) Basingstoke Division of Hants, 1934-35. Life Mem., Commonwealth Parliamentary Assoc. Member of: Grand Council of Primrose League; Migration Council, 1951; Cttee of Empire Economic Union, 1934- (Vice-Chm. 1949; President 1952); Council of Empire Industries Association, 1934-; Council of Empire Industries Association and British Empire League. Has travelled extensively in Europe, USA, and Commonwealth. *Publications:* British Declaration of Independence, 1947; Declaration of Independence and Interdependence, 1948; Commonwealth, 1949; Sovereignty and Fiscal Freedom, 1952; Commonwealth Development and Defence, 1953; Constructive Conservatism, 1953; The Rule of Reciprocity, 1954; Europe and the Commonwealth, 1961; The Commonwealth, 1962; Commonwealth, 1966; The Common Market, 1971; The Five Principles, 1973. *Recreation:* travel. *Address:* Beau Rivage, Lausanne, Switzerland; Newport, Rhode Island, USA. *Clubs:* Carlton, Pratt's, Royal Air Force, 1900; Clambake (Newport, USA).

DRUON, Maurice Samuel Roger Charles; Officier de la Légion d'Honneur; Commandeur des Arts et Lettres; author; Member of the French Academy since 1966; Minister for Cultural Affairs, France, 1973-74; Member, Franco-British Council, since 1972; *b* Paris, 23 April 1918; *s* of René Druon de Reyniac and Léonilla Jenny Samuel-Cros; *m* 1968, Madeleine Marignac. *Educ:* Lycée Michelet and Ecole des Sciences Politiques, Paris. Ecole de Cavalerie de Saumur, aspirant, 1940; joined Free French Forces, London, 1942; Attaché Commissariat à l'Intérieur et Direction de l'Information, 1943; War Correspondent, 1944-45; Lieut de réserve de cavalerie. Journalist, 1946-47; awarded Prix Goncourt, 1948, for novel Les Grandes Familles; Prix de Monaco, 1966. Commandeur de l'Ordre Royal du Phénix de Grèce; Grand Officier du Mérite de l'Ordre de Malte; Commandeur de l'Ordre de la République de Tunisie; Grand Officier du Lion du Sénégal; Grand Croix du Mérite de la République Italienne; Grand Croix de l'Aigle Aztèque du Mexique. *Publications:* Lettres d'un Européen, 1944; La Dernière Brigade (The Last Detachment), 1946 (publ. in England 1957); Les Grandes Familles, La Chute des Corps, Rendez-Vous aux Enfers, 1948-51 (trilogy publ. in England under title The Curtain falls, 1959); La Volupté d'Etre (Film of Memory), 1954 (publ. in England 1955); Les Rois Maudits (The Accursed Kings), 1955-60 (six vols: The Iron King, The Strangled Queen, The Poisoned Crown, The Royal Succession, The She-Wolf of France, The Lily and the Lion, publ. in England 1956-61); Tistou les pouces verts (Tistou of the green fingers), 1957 (publ. in England 1958); Alexandre le Grand (Alexander the God), 1958 (publ. in Eng. 1960); Des Seigneurs de la Plaine- (The Black Prince and other stories), 1962 (publ. in Eng. 1962); Les Mémoires de Zeus I (The Memoirs of Zeus), 1963 (in Eng. 1964); Bernard Buffet, 1964; Paris, de César à Saint Louis (The History of Paris from Caesar to St Louis), 1964 (in Eng. 1969); Le Pouvoir, 1965; Les Tambours de la Mémoire, 1965; Le Bonheur des Uns, 1967; L'Avenir en désarroi, 1968; Vézelay, colline éternelle, 1968; Nouvelles lettres d'un Européen, 1970; Une Eglise qui se trompe de siècle, 1972; La Parole et le Pouvoir, 1974; Oeuvres complètes, 24 vols, 1973-75; Quand un roi perd la France (Les Rois Mandits T), 1977; *plays:* Mégarée, 1942; Un Voyageur, 1953; La Contessa, 1962; *song:* Le Chant des Partisans (with Joseph Kessel and Anna Marly), 1943 (London). *Recreations:* riding, travel. *Address:* 73 rue de Varenne, 75007 Paris, France. *Club:* Savile.

DRURY, Sir Alan (Nigel), Kt 1950; CBE 1944; FRS 1937; MA, MD Cantab; FRCP; MRCS; *b* 3 Nov. 1889; *s* of Henry George and Elizabeth Rose Drury; *m* 1916, Daphne Marguerite Brownsword (*d* 1975); one *s* one *d*. *Educ:* Merchant Taylors' Sch., London; Gonville and Caius Coll., Cambridge; St Thomas' Hospital, London. George Henry Lewes Student in Physiology; War service, Major RAMC, DADMS (Sanitary) 9th Secunderabad Div., India; late Fellow of Trinity Hall, Cambridge; late Huddersfield Lecturer in Special Pathology, University of Cambridge; Mem. of Scientific Staff, Medical Research Council, 1921-43; late Dir Lister Institute; Mem. of Scientific Staff, Agricultural Research Council, 1952-60. Hon. Fellow Trinity Hall. *Publications:* in Heart, Journal of Physiology, Quarterly Journal of Experimental Physiology, etc. *Address:* 36 Gretton Court, High Street, Girton, Cambridge CB3 0QN. *T:* Cambridge 77181.

DRURY, Allen Stuart; Author; *b* Houston, Texas, 2 Sept. 1918; *s* of Alden M. and Flora A. Drury. *Educ:* Stanford Univ. (BA). Served with US Army, 1942-43. Ed., The Tulare (Calif) Bee, 1939-41; county ed., The Bakersfield Californian, Bakersfield, Calif, 1941-42; United Press Senate Staff, Washington, DC, 1943-45; freelance correspondent, 1946; Nation Ed., Pathfinder Magazine, Washington, DC, 1947-53; National Staff, Washington Evening Star, 1953-54; Senate Staff, New York Times, 1954-59. Sigma Delta Chi Award for Editorial Writing, 1942; hon. LitD, Rollins Coll., Winter Park, Fla, 1961. *Publications:* Advise and Consent, 1959 (Pulitzer Prize for Fiction, 1960); A Shade of Difference, 1962; A Senate Journal,

1963; That Summer, 1965; Three Kids in a Cart, 1965; Capable of Honor, 1966; "A Very Strange Society", 1967; Preserve and Protect, 1968; The Throne of Saturn, 1971; Courage and Hesitation: inside the Nixon administration, 1972; Come Nineveh, Come Tyre, 1973; The Promise of Joy, 1975; A God Against the Gods, 1976; Return to Thebes, 1977; Anna Hastings, 1977. *Address:* c/o Doubleday & Co., 245 Park Avenue, New York, NY 10017, USA. *Clubs:* Cosmos, University, National Press (Washington, DC); Bohemian (San Francisco).

DRURY, Charles Mills, CBE 1946 (MBE 1942); DSO 1944; ED 1956; MP for Montreal St Antoine-Westmount, House of Commons of Canada, since 1962; *b* 17 May 1912; *s* of Victor Montague Drury, Montreal, and Pansy Jessie Mills, Ottawa; *m* 1939, Jane Ferrier Counsell (decd); two *s* two *d*. *Educ:* Bishops Coll. Sch., Lennoxville, Quebec; Royal Military Coll. of Canada, Kingston, Ontario; McGill Univ., Montreal (BCL); University of Paris, France. Practised at law, 1936-39; served War of 1939-45, Canadian Army (final rank Brig.). Chief of UNNRA Mission to Poland, 1945-46; Dept of External Affairs, Canada, 1947-48; Dep. Minister of National Defence, Canada, 1949-55; Minister, Dept of Defence Production, and Minister of Industry, 1963-68; Pres., Treasury Bd, 1968-74; Minister of Public Works, Canada, and Minister of State for Science and Technol., 1974-76; responsible for Nat. Res. Council of Canada, 1963-76. Chevalier de la Légion d'Honneur (France), 1946; Order of Polonia Restituta (Poland), 1946. *Address:* House of Commons, Ottawa, Ont. K1A 0A6, Canada. *Clubs:* Rideau (Ottawa); Royal St Lawrence Yacht (Dorval, Que).

DRURY, Rev. Canon John Henry; Residentiary Canon of Norwich Cathedral, since 1973; *b* 23 May 1936; *s* of Henry and Barbara Drury; *m* 1972, (Frances) Clare Nineham; two *d*. *Educ:* Bradfield; Trinity Hall and Westcott House, Cambridge. MA (Hist. Pt 1, Cl. 1; Theol. Pt 2, Cl. 2/1). Curate, St John's Wood Church, 1963; Chaplain of Downing Coll., Cambridge, 1966; Chaplain and Fellow of Exeter Coll., Oxford, 1969; Res. Canon of Norwich Cathedral and Examining Chaplain to Bp of Norwich, 1973. Editor, Theology, 1976-. *Publications:* Angels and Dirt, 1972; Luke, 1973; Tradition and Design in Luke's Gospel, 1976; articles and reviews in Jl of Theol. Studies, Theology, Expository Times. *Recreations:* Mozart, gardening, reading. *Address:* 26 The Close, Norwich. *T:* Norwich 24825. *Club:* Clerical Boat (Norwich).

DRURY, Paul Dalou, PPRE; etcher and painter; Principal, Goldsmiths' College School of Art, 1967-69, retired; *b* London, 14 Oct. 1903; *s* of late Alfred Drury, RA; *m* 1937, Enid Marie, painter, *o c* of late Victor Solomon; one *s*. *Educ:* King's Coll. Sch.; Bristol Grammar Sch.; Westminster Sch.; Goldsmiths' Coll. Sch. of Art (British Institution Scholarship in Engraving, 1924). Served War, 1939-45; Plaster (Orthopædic) Dept, Queen Mary's Hosp., Roehampton. Since 1923 has exhibited etchings, paintings and drawings at the Royal Academy, galleries in England, and prints at representative exhibitions of British Art in Paris, Vienna, Florence, Stockholm, Buenos Aires, Tokyo, etc., and in Canada and the USA; etchings and drawings acquired by the Print Room, British Museum, Ashmolean, Imperial War Museum, Contemporary Art Soc., Boston, USA, and by various museums and galleries in the provinces and abroad. Fellow, Royal Soc. of Painter-Etchers and Engravers, 1926, President, 1970-75. Mem., Faculty of Engraving, British Sch. at Rome, 1948-74. Governor, West Surrey Coll. of Art, 1969-74. *Recreations:* music, walking. *Address:* Rangers Cottage, Nutley, Uckfield, East Sussex. *T:* Nutley 2857. *Club:* Arts.

DRYDEN, Sir John (Stephen Gyles), 8th and 11th Bt *cr* 1795 and 1733; *b* 26 Sept. 1943; *s* of Sir Noel Percy Hugh Dryden, 7th and 10th Bt, and of Rosamund Mary, *e d* of late Stephen Scrope; *S* father, 1970; *m* 1970, Diana Constance, *o d* of Cyril Tomlinson, Highland Park, Wellington, NZ; one *s*. *Educ:* Oratory School. *Heir: s* John Frederick Simon Dryden, *b* 26 May 1976. *Address:* c/o Midland Bank Ltd, Redhill, Surrey.

DRYSDALE, Sir (George) Russell, Kt 1969; Australian artist; Director, Pioneer Sugar Mills Ltd; *b* Bognor Regis, Sussex, 7 Feb. 1912; *s* of late George Russell Drysdale; *m* 1st, 1935, Elizabeth (*d* 1963), *d* of J. Stephen; one *d* (one *s* decd); 2nd, 1965, Maisie Joyce Purves-Smith. *Educ:* Grange Sch., Sussex; Geelong Grammar Sch.; George Bell Art Sch., Melbourne; Grosvenor Sch. of Art, London; La Grande Chaumière, Paris. Mem., Commonwealth Art Adv. Bd, 1962-73. *Exhibitions include:* Leicester Galleries, 1950, 1958, 1965, 1972; NSW Art Gallery, 1960; Queensland Art Gallery, 1961. Represented in permanent collections: Tate Gallery; Metropolitan Museum, NY; National Galleries of Queensland, NSW, W Australia, S

Australia, Victoria. *Publication:* (jt author) Journey among Men, 1962. *Recreations:* natural history, pre-history, travelling about the inland of Australia. *Address:* Bouddi Farm, Kilcare Heights, Hardy's Bay, NSW 2256, Australia. *Clubs:* Union, Australasian Pioneers (Sydney).

D'SOUZA, Most Rev. Albert V.; *b* Mangalore, India, 5 April 1904. Priest, 1928; nominated Auxiliary Bishop of Mysore, 1959; consecrated Bishop, 1959; nominated Archbishop of Calcutta, Aug. 1962; took possession of Archdiocesan See of Calcutta, Dec. 1962; retired, 1969. *Address:* St Anthony's Institutes, Mangalore 2, Karnataka, India.

DUBLIN, Archbishop of, and Primate of Ireland, since 1977; **Most Rev. Henry Robert McAdoo,** PhD, STD, DD; *b* 1916; *s* of James Arthur and Susan McAdoo; *m* 1940, Lesley Dalziel Weir; one *s* two *d*. *Educ:* Cork Grammar School; Mountjoy School, Dublin; Trinity College, Dublin. Deacon, 1939; Priest, 1940; Curate of Holy Trinity Cathedral, Waterford, 1939-43; Incumbent of Castleventry with Ardfield, 1943-48 (with Kilmeen, 1947-48); Rector of Kilmocomogue, Diocese of Cork, 1948-52; Rural Dean of Glansalney West and Bere, 1948-52; Canon of Kilbrittain in Cork Cathedral, and Canon of Donoughmore in Cloyne Cathedral, 1949-52; Dean of Cork, 1952-62; Canon of St Patrick's Cathedral, Dublin, 1960-62; Bishop of Ossory, Ferns and Leighlin, 1962-77. Member, Anglican-Roman Catholic Preparatory Commission, 1967-68; Jt Chm., Anglican-Roman Catholic International Commission, 1969-. *Publications:* The Structure of Caroline Moral Theology, 1949; John Bramhall and Anglicanism, 1964; The Spirit of Anglicanism, 1965. *Address:* The See House, 17 Temple Road, Milltown, Dublin 6. *Club:* Kildare Street and University (Dublin).

DUBLIN, Archbishop of, and Primate of Ireland, (RC), since 1972; **Most Rev. Dermot Ryan;** *b* 27 June 1924; *s* of Dr Andrew Ryan and Theresa (*née* McKenna). *Educ:* Belvedere Coll.; Holy Cross Coll., Clonliffe; UC Dublin; St Patrick's, Maynooth; St John Lateran Univ. and Gregorian Univ., Rome; Pontifical Biblical Inst., Rome. BA Dublin 1945; STL 1952, LSS 1954, Rome; MA NUI 1954. Priest, 1950; Chaplain: Mount Anville Convent, Dublin, 1950; Mater Hosp., Dublin, 1954; Prof. of Fundamental Dogmatic Theology, Clonliffe, and Asst Dean, 1955; Prof. (part-time) of Eastern Languages, UC Dublin, 1957; Prof. of Semitic Languages, UC Dublin, 1969. *Publications:* contrib. to The Furrow, Irish Theol Quarterly, Library of Catholic Knowledge, Catholic Commentary on Holy Scripture, etc. *Recreations:* golf, squash. *Address:* Archbishop's House, Dublin 9, Eire. *T:* Dublin 373732.

DUBLIN, Auxiliary Bishop of, (RC); *see* Dunne, Most Rev. Patrick.

DUBLIN, (Christ Church), Dean of; *see* Salmon, Very Rev. T. N. D. C.

DUBLIN, (St Patrick's), Dean of; *see* Griffin, Very Rev. V. G. B.

DU BOULAY, Prof. Francis Robin Houssemayne; Professor of Mediæval History in the University of London, at Bedford Coll., since 1960; *b* 19 Dec. 1920; *er s* of Philip Houssemayne Du Boulay and Mercy Tyrrell (*née* Friend); *m* 1948, Cecilia Burnell Matthews; two *s* one *d*. *Educ:* Christ's Hospital; Phillip's Academy, Andover, Mass., USA; Balliol Coll., Oxford. Williams Exhibitioner at Balliol Coll., 1939; Friends' Ambulance Unit and subsequently Royal Artillery, 1940-45; MA 1947; Asst lecturer at Bedford Coll., 1947, Lecturer, 1949; Reader in Mediæval History, in University of London, 1955. FRHistS (Hon. Sec., 1961-65). *Publications:* A Handlist of medieval ecclesiastical terms, 1952; The Register of Archbishop Bourgchier, 1953; Medieval Bexley, 1961; Documents Illustrative of Medieval Kentish Society, 1964; The Lordship of Canterbury, 1966; An Age of Ambition, 1970; (ed jtly) The Reign of Richard II, 1972; various essays and papers in specialist journals and general symposia. *Address:* Broadmead, Riverhead, Sevenoaks, Kent. *Club:* Réform.

du BOULAY, Roger William H.; *see* Houssemayne du Boulay.

DuBRIDGE, Lee A(lvin); *b* 21 Sept. 1901; *s* of Frederick A. and Elizabeth Browne DuBridge; *m* 1st, 1925, Doris May Koht (*d* 1973); one *s* one *d*; 2nd, 1974, Arrola B. Cole. *Educ:* Cornell Coll., Mt Vernon, Ia (BA); University of Wisconsin (MA, PhD). Instructor in Physics, University of Wisconsin, 1925-26; Nat. Research Council Fellow at Calif. Inst. Tech., 1926-28; Asst Prof. Physics, Washington Univ. (St Louis, Mo.), 1928-33; Assoc. Prof., Washington Univ., 1933-34; Prof. of Physics and Dep. Chm., University of Rochester (NY), 1934-46; Dean of

Faculty, University of Rochester, 1938-42; on leave from University of Rochester, 1940-45, as Dir of Radiation Lab. of Nat. Def. Research Comm. at MIT, Cambridge; Pres., California Inst. of Techn., Pasadena, 1946-69, Pres. Emeritus, 1969-; Science Adviser to President of USA, 1969-70. Hon. ScD: Cornell Coll.; Mt Vernon, Iowa, 1940; Weslyan Univ., Middletown, Conn., 1946; Polytechnic Inst. of Brooklyn, New York, 1946; University of Brit. Columbia, Can., 1947; Washington Univ., St Louis, Mo, 1948; Occidental Coll., 1952; Maryland, 1955; Columbia, 1957; Indiana, 1957; Wisconsin, 1957; Pennsylvania Mil. Coll., Chester, Pa, 1962; DePauw, Indiana, 1962; Pomona Coll., Claremont, Calif., 1965; Carnegie Inst. of Techn., Pittsburgh, 1965; Hon. LLD: California, 1948; Rochester, 1953; Southern California, 1957; Northwestern, 1958; Loyola, Los Angeles, 1963; Notre Dame, Indiana, 1967; Illinois Inst. Technology, 1968; Hon. LHD: University Judaism, Los Angeles, 1958; Redlands, 1958; Hon. DCL, Union Coll., Schenectady, NY, 1961; Hon. DSc: Rockefeller Institute, NY, 1965; Tufts Univ., 1969; Syracuse Univ., 1969; Rensselaer Polytech. Inst., 1970. King's Medal, 1946; Research Corp. Award, 1947; Medal for Merit of US Govt, 1948, Golden Key Award, 1959; Leif Erikson Award, 1959; Arthur Noble Award, 1961; Golden Plate Award, 1973. *Publications:* Photoelectric Phenomena (with A. L. Hughes), 1932; New Theories of Photoelectric Effect (Paris), 1934; Introduction to Space, 1960; articles in various scientific and other journals. *Address:* 5309 Cantante, Laguna Hills, Calif 92653, USA. *T:* 714-830-7689. *Clubs:* Sunset (Los Angeles); Bohemian (San Francisco).

DUBUFFET, Jean; artist (exclusively since 1942); *b* Le Havre, 31 July 1901; *s* of George S. Dubuffet and Jeanne (*née* Paillettle); *m* 1st, 1927, Paulette Bret (marr. diss., 1935); one *d*; 2nd, 1937, Emilie (Lili) Carlu. *Educ:* art schs, Paris. Settled at Vence, 1955, after travels. *Exhibitions include:* Paris, 1944; Pierre Matisse Gall., NY, 1947; Cercle Volney and Galerie Rive Gauche, Paris, 1954; ICA, London, 1955; Tooth, London, 1958; Daniel Cordier, Paris, 1960, 1962, 1963; Musée des Arts Décoratifs, Paris, 1961; Museum of Modern Art, NY, 1962, 1968; Robert Fraser, London, 1962, 1964, 1966; Tate Gall., London, 1966; NY, 1966-67; Galerie Jeanne Bucher, Paris, 1967, 1969; Basle, 1968; Galerie Moos, Geneva, 1970; Centre national des arts contemporains, Paris, 1970. *Publications:* Prospectus aux amateurs de tout genre, 1946; Prospectus et tous écrits (2 vols), 1967; Asphyxiante culture, 1968; Edifices, 1968; L'homme du commun à l'ouvrage, 1973; La botte à nique, 1973. *Address:* 51 rue de Verneuil, 75007 Paris, France.

DU CANE, Comdr Peter, CBE 1964 (OBE 1942); CEng, FIMechE; FRINA; AFRAeS; FRSA; Royal Navy, retired; Consultant, Vosper Ltd, Shipbuilders, Portsmouth, (Managing Director, 1931-63; Deputy Chairman, 1963-73); *b* 18 March 1901; *s* of C. H. C. Du Cane, DL, Braxted Park, Essex, and Dorothy Blenkinsopp (*née* Coulson), Newbrough Park, Northumberland; *m* 1929, Victoria Geraldine Pole Carew; one *s* two *d*. *Educ:* RNC, Osborne, Dartmouth, Keyham and Greenwich. Served as midshipman afloat, European War, 1917-18; Fleet Air Arm as pilot and technical officer, 1940-41. Specialised design and construction high speed craft including Bluebird II, holder of world's unlimited water speed record at 141.7 mph, for which awarded Segrave Medal for year 1939, also John Cobb's Crusader, first boat to exceed 200 mph, 1952. Designs include many Motor Torpedo Boats used by Royal Navy, Royal Barge, and High Speed Rescue Launches for RAF, also Tramontana, winner of Daily Express Internat. Offshore Power Boat Race, 1962; I and II winners of All British Daily Express Cowes/Torquay, 1964. *Publications:* High Speed Small Craft, 1951, 4th edn, 1974; An Engineer of Sorts, 1972. *Address:* Seamark, Glandore, Co. Cork, Ireland. *T:* Leap 95. *Club:* Royal Yacht Squadron (Cowes).

du CANN, Col Rt. Hon. Edward Dillon Lott, PC 1964; MP (C) Taunton Division of Somerset since Feb. 1956; Chairman, Cannon Assurance Ltd; Director: Lonrho Ltd; James Beattie Ltd; Bow Group Publications Ltd; *b* 28 May 1924; *er s* of C. G. L. du Cann, Barrister-at-Law, and Janet (*née* Murchie); *m* 1962, Sallie Innes, *e d* of late James Henry Murchie, Caldy, Cheshire; one *s* two *d*. *Educ:* Colet Court; Woodbridge Sch.; St John's Coll., Oxford (MA, Law). Served with RNVR, 1943-46. Contested West Walthamstow Div., Gen. Election, 1951; Contested Barrow-in-Furness Div., Gen. Election, 1955. Vice-Pres., Somerset and Wilts Trustee Savings Bank, 1956-75; Founder, Unicorn Group of Unit Trusts, 1957; Chairman: Barclays Unicorn Ltd and associated cos, 1957-72; Keyser Ullman Holdings Ltd, 1970-75. Chm., Association of Unit Trust Managers, 1961. Mem., Lord Chancellor's Adv. Cttee on Public Records, 1960-62; Joint Hon. Sec.: UN Parly Group, 1961-62; Conservative Parly Finance Group, 1961-62; Mem., Select Cttee on House of Lords Reform, 1962; Economic Sec. to the

Treasury, 1962-63; Minister of State, Board of Trade, 1963-64; Founder Chm., Select Cttee on Public Expenditure, 1971-72; Mem., Select Cttee on Privilege, 1972-; Chm., Select Cttee on Public Accounts, 1974-; Chm., 1922 Cttee, 1972-; Chm., Liaison Cttee of Select Cttee Chairmen, 1974-; Chairman: Cons. Party Organisation, 1965-67; Burke Club, 1973-. Pres., Anglo-Polish Cons. Soc., 1972-74. Patron, Assoc. of Insurance Brokers. Visiting Fellow, Univ. of Lancaster Business School, 1970-. Commodore, 1962, Admiral, 1974, House of Commons Yacht Club. Hon. Col, 155 (Wessex) Regt, RCT (Volunteers), 1972-. Lecturer, broadcaster. Elected Freeman of Taunton Deane Borough, 1977. *Publications:* Investing Simplified, 1959; articles on financial and international affairs (incl. The Case for a Bill of Rights, How to Bring Government Expenditure within Parliamentary Control, etc). *Recreations:* travel, gardening, sailing. *Address:* 9 Tufton Court, Tufton Street, SW1. *T:* 01-222 5950; Cothay Barton, Greenham, Wellington, Somerset. *Clubs:* Carlton, Pratt's; Royal Thames Yacht; Somerset County (Taunton).
See also R. D. L. Du Cann.

Du CANN, Richard Dillon Lott, QC 1975; *b* 27 Jan. 1929; *yr s* of C. G. L. du Cann; *m* 1955, Charlotte Mary Sawtell; two *s* two *d*. *Educ:* Steyning Grammar Sch.; Clare Coll., Cambridge. Called to Bar, Gray's Inn, 1953; Treasury Counsel, Inner London QS, 1966-70; Treasury Counsel, Central Criminal Court, 1970-75. *Publications:* (with B. Hayhoe) The Young Marrieds, 1954; The Art of the Advocate, 1964. *Address:* 29 Newton Road, W2 5AF. *T:* 01-229 3859.
See also Col Rt Hon. E. D. L. du Cann.

DUCAT, David; Chairman, The Metal Box Co. Ltd., 1967-70, retired (Managing Director 1949-66; Vice-Chairman 1952-66; Deputy Chairman 1966-67); *b* 1 June 1904; *s* of William John and Amy Ducat; *m* 1933, Hilary Mildred Stokes; three *s* one *d*. *Educ:* Merchant Taylors' Sch.; Gonville and Caius Coll., Cambridge (MA). ACIS 1935. Min. of Production, 1942-45. British Tin Box Manufacturers Fedn: Chm., 1952-61; Vice-Chm., 1961-69. Mem. Court of Assts, Merchant Taylors' Co., 1956- (Master, 1964). Vice-Pres., British Inst. of Management (Council Chm., 1966-68); Mem. Coun., City University, 1966-71. FCIS 1967. *Address:* Morar, 16 Sandy Lodge Road, Moor Park, Rickmansworth, Herts. *T:* Rickmansworth 73562.

DUCAT-AMOS, Air Comdt Barbara Mary, CB 1974; RRC 1971; QHNS 1972; Matron-in-Chief, Princess Mary's Royal Air Force Nursing Service, since 1972, and Director of Royal Air Force Nursing Service, since 1976; *b* 9 Feb. 1921; *d* of late Captain G. W. Ducat-Amos, Master Mariner, and Mrs M. Ducat-Amos. *Educ:* The Abbey Sch., Reading; St Thomas's Hosp., London (The Nightingale Trng Sch.). SRN 1943; CMB Pt 1 1948. PMRAFNS, 1944-47: served in RAF Hosps, UK and Aden; further training; nursing in S Africa and SW Africa, 1948-52; rejoined PMRAFNS, 1952: served in RAF Hosps as General Ward and Theatre Sister, UK, Germany, Cyprus, Aden and Changi (Singapore); Matron 1967; Sen. Matron 1968; Principal Matron 1970. *Recreations:* music, theatre, travel. *Address:* Ministry of Defence DNS (RAF), 1-6 Tavistock Square, WC1H 9NL. *T:* 01-430 8203. *Clubs:* Royal Air Force, United Nursing Services.

DUCCI, Dr Roberto, Grand Cross, Italian Order of Merit; Ambassador of Italy to the Court of St James's, since 1975; *b* 8 Feb. 1914; *s* of Gino Ducci and Virginia Boncinelli; *m* 1951, Wanda Matyjewicz; two *s*. *Educ:* Univ. of Rome (Dr of Law). Entered Foreign Service, 1937; served: Ottawa, 1938; Newark, NJ, 1940; Italian Delegn to Peace Conf., 1946; Warsaw, 1947; Rio de Janeiro, 1949; Italian Delegn to NATO and OEEC, 1950-55; Chm., Drafting Cttee, Rome Treaties, 1956-57; Asst Dir, General Economic Affairs, 1955-57; Ambassador to Finland, 1958-62; Head, Italian Delegn to Brussels, UK-EEC Conf., 1961-63; Dep. Dir-Gen. for Political Affairs, 1963-64; Ambassador to: Yugoslavia, 1964-67; Austria, 1967-70; Director-General for Political Affairs, 1970-75. Mem. Bd, European Investment Bank, 1958-68. *Publications:* Prima Età di Napoleone, 1933; Questa Italia, 1948; L'Europa Incompiuta, 1971; D'Annunzio Vivente, 1973; Contemporaries, 1976; numerous political essays and articles. *Recreations:* riding, collecting frail things. *Address:* Italian Embassy, 4 Grosvenor Square, W1Y 2EH. *Clubs:* Reform, Garrick; Circolo della Caccia (Rome).

DUCHÊNE, Louis-François; Director, Centre for Contemporary European Studies, Sussex University, since 1974; *b* 17 Feb. 1927; *s* of Louis Adrien Duchêne and Marguerite Lucienne Duchêne (*née* Lainé); *m* 1952, Anne Margaret Purves; one *d*. *Educ:* St Paul's Sch.; London Sch. of Economics. Leader writer, Manchester Guardian, 1949-52; Press attaché, High Authority,

European Coal and Steel Community, Luxembourg, 1952-55; Correspondent of The Economist, Paris, 1956-58; Dir, Documentation Centre of Action Cttee for United States of Europe (Chm. Jean Monnet), Paris, 1958-63; Editorial writer, The Economist, London, 1963-67. Dir, Internat. Inst. for Strategic Studies, 1969-74. *Publications:* (ed) The Endless Crisis, 1970; The Case of the Helmeted Airman, a study of W. H. Auden, 1972. *Address:* 3 Powis Villas, Brighton, East Sussex, BN1 3HD. *T:* Brighton 29258.

DUCIE, 6th Earl of *cr* 1837; **Basil Howard Moreton;** Baron Ducie, 1763; Baron Moreton, 1837; *b* 15 Nov. 1917; *s* of Hon. Algernon Howard Moreton (2nd *s* of 4th Earl) (*d* 1951), and Dorothy Edith Annie, *d* of late Robert Bell; *S* uncle 1952; *m* 1950, Alison May, *d* of L. A. Bates, Pialba, Queensland; three *s* one *d. Heir: s* Lord Moreton, *qv. Address:* Tortworth House, Tortworth, Wotton-under-Edge, Glos.

DUCKER, Herbert Charles, BSc London; NDA; Field Officer Groundnut Research, under the Federal Ministry of Agriculture, Rhodesia and Nyasaland, now retired; *b* 13 May 1900; *s* of Charles Richard and Gertrude Louise Ducker; *m* 1925, Marjorie, *y d* of late Charles Tuckfield, AMICE; two *s* one *d. Educ:* Kingston Grammar Sch., Kingston-on-Thames; South-Eastern Agricultural Coll., Wye; Imperial Coll. of Science, South Kensington. British Cotton Industry Research Assoc. Laboratories; Asst Cotton Specialist, Nyasaland, 1922; Cotton Specialist, Empire Cotton Growing Corporation, Nyasaland, 1925-56; Superintendent-Curator of the National Botanic Gardens, Salisbury, Southern Rhodesia, under the Federal Ministry of Agriculture, of Rhodesia and Nyasaland, 1957. *Publications:* Annual Reports on Cotton Research work 1925-55, carried out in Nyasaland; articles on cotton growing. *Recreation:* fishing. *Address:* 6 Sarsden Fife Avenue/5th Street, Salisbury, Rhodesia. *Club:* Royal Over-Seas League.

DUCKHAM, Prof. Alec Narraway, CBE 1950 (OBE 1945); Professor of Agriculture, University of Reading, 1955-69; *b* 23 Aug. 1903; *e s* of Alexander Duckham, FCS, and Violet Ethel Duckham (*née* Narraway); *m* 1932, Audrey Mary Polgreen (*d* 1969), St Germans, Cornwall; one *s* two *d. Educ:* Oundle Sch.; Clare Coll., Cambridge. MA (Hons) Cantab.: Cambridge Dip. Agric. Sci. (dist. in Animal Husbandry), 1926; FIBiol; Silver Research Medallist, Royal Agricultural Society, England, 1926. Research and Advisory work on Animal Husbandry at Cambridge, Aberdeen, Belfast, 1927-39. Chm. Home and Overseas Agric. Supplies Cttees and Dir of Supply Plans Div., Min. of Food, 1941-45. Agric. Attaché, Brit. Embassy, Washington, and Agric. Adviser to UK High Comr, Ottawa, 1945-50. Asst Sec. to Min. of Agriculture and Fisheries, 1950-54. Liaison Officer (SE Region), to the Minister of Agriculture, Fisheries and Food, 1965-70. Vice-Chm., Alex. Duckham and Co. Ltd, 1945-68. *Publications:* Animal Industry in the British Empire, 1932; American Agriculture, 1952 (HMSO); The Fabric of Farming, 1958; Agricultural Synthesis: The Farming Year, 1963; (with G. B. Masefield) Farming Systems of the World, 1970; (ed with J. G. W. Jones and E. H. Roberts) Food Production and Consumption, 1976. *Recreations:* painting and music. *Address:* 5 Woolacombe Drive, Elm Road, Reading RG6 2UA. *Club:* Royal Automobile.

DUCKMANTON, Talbot Sydney, CBE 1971; General Manager, Australian Broadcasting Commission, since 1965 (Deputy General Manager, 1964-65); *b* 26 Oct. 1921; *s* of Sydney James Duckmanton. Joined Australian Broadcasting Commission, 1939. War Service: AIF and RAAF. President: Asian Broadcasting Union, 1973-; Commonwealth Broadcasting Assoc., 1975-. *Address:* c/o Australian Broadcasting Commission, 145 Elizabeth Street, Sydney, NSW 2000, Australia. *T:* 310211. *Clubs:* Legacy, Australian, Tattersalls (Sydney).

DUCKWORTH, Arthur; *see* Duckworth, G. A. V.

DUCKWORTH, Brian Roy; a Recorder of the Crown Court, since 1972; *b* 26 July 1934; *s* of Roy and Kathleen Duckworth; *m* 1964, Nancy Carolyn Holden; three *s* one *d. Educ:* Sedbergh Sch.; Worcester Coll., Oxford (MA). Called to Bar, Lincoln's Inn, 1958; Mem. Northern Circuit. Councillor, Blackburn RDC, 1960-74 (Chm. 1970-72). *Recreations:* golf, gardening, motor sport. *Address:* Close House, Abbey Village, Chorley, Lancs. *T:* Brinscall 830425. *Clubs:* St James's (Manchester); Pleasington Golf.

DUCKWORTH, (George) Arthur (Victor), JP; *b* 3 Jan. 1901; *e s* of Major A. C. Duckworth of Orchardleigh Park, Frome; *m* 1927, Alice, 3rd *d* of John Henry Hammond, New York; three *d*; *m* 1945, Elizabeth, *o d* of Alfred Ehrenfeld, Bridgeham Farm,

Forest Green, Surrey; two *d*; *m* 1968, Mary, *y d* of Archdeacon Edmund Hope, and widow of Captain K. Buxton. *Educ:* Eton; Trinity Coll., Cambridge (BA). MP (C) Shrewsbury Div. of Salop, 1929-45; Parliamentary Private Sec. to G. H. Shakespeare, 1932-39. Served War of 1939-45, 36th (Middlesex) AA Bn RA, 1939-41. CC Somerset, 1949-64; JP Somerset, 1957. *Address:* Orchardleigh Park, Frome, Somerset. *T:* Beckington 306. *Clubs:* Travellers', Garrick.

DUCKWORTH, John Clifford; Chairman, IDJ Investment Services Ltd; Director: Spear & Jackson International Ltd; Bridon Ltd; Ultra Electronic Holdings Ltd; *b* 27 Dec. 1916; *s* of late H. Duckworth, Wimbledon, and of Mrs A. H. Duckworth (*née* Woods); *m* 1942, Dorothy Nancy Wills; three *s. Educ:* KCS, Wimbledon; Wadham Coll., Oxford. Telecommunications Research Establishment, Malvern: Radar Research and Development, 1939-46; National Research Council, Chalk River, Ont., 1946-47; Atomic Energy Research Establishment, Harwell, 1947-50; Ferranti Ltd: Chief Engineer, Wythenshawe Laboratories, 1950-54; Nuclear Power Engineer, Brit. Electricity Authority, 1954-58; Central Electricity Authority, 1957-58; Chief Research and Development Officer, Central Electricity Generating Board, 1958-59; Man. Dir., Nat. Research Develt Corp., 1959-70. Pres., Institute of Fuel, 1963-64; Vice-Pres., Parliamentary and Scientific Cttee, 1964-67. Chm., Science Mus. Adv. Council, 1972-. Vice-Pres., IEE, 1974-. *Recreations:* swimming, colour photography, cartography. *Address:* Wells House, Whitchurch, near Pangbourne, Berks. *Club:* Athenæum.

DUCKWORTH, Captain Ralph Campbell Musbury, CBE 1946 (OBE 1943); CEng; RN, retired; *b* 11 June 1907; 2nd *s* of Major Arthur Campbell Duckworth, DL, JP, Orchardleigh Park, Frome, Som; *m* 1945, Ruby Cortez, 2nd Officer WRNS, *o d* of A. W. Ball, Sydenham, London. *Educ:* Royal Naval Colleges, Osborne and Dartmouth. War of 1939-45: served as Lieut-Comdr and Torpedo Officer of HMS Illustrious, 1940-41; Comdr 1941 and staff of C-in-C Mediterranean and C-in-C Levant, 1941-43; OBE for duties in planning and execution of operations for capture of Sicily; Dep. Chief of Staff (acting Capt.) to Vice-Adm. Administration, British Pacific Fleet, 1944-45 (CBE); Captain 1946; Dep. Dir Underwater Weapons Dept, Admiralty, 1946-48; Naval Attaché, British Embassy, Rio de Janeiro, 1949-51; Imperial Defence Coll., 1952; Capt., 1st Destroyer Sqdn, 1953-54; Staff of C-in-C, Mediterranean, 1954-55. Member: Northern Ireland Development Council, 1956-65; Dollar Exports Council, 1956-59; Manager, Industrial Engineering, Morgan Crucible Co. Ltd, 1956-58; Commercial Manager Elliott Bros (London) Ltd, 1959-61; Dir, British Mechanical Engrg Fedn, 1963-68. *Recreations:* gardening and travelling. *Address:* 9 Cadogan Street, SW3. *T:* 01-589 4991.

DUCKWORTH, Major Sir Richard Dyce, 3rd Bt, *cr* 1909; *b* 30 Sept. 1918; *s* of Sir Edward Dyce Duckworth, 2nd Bt, and Cecil Gertrude, *y d* of Robert E. Leman; *S* father, 1945; *m* 1942, Violet Alison, *d* of Lieut-Col G. B. Wauchope, DSO; two *s. Educ:* Marlborough Coll. Started business in 1937, retired 1969. *Recreations:* sailing, golf, squash, shooting. *Heir: s* Edward Richard Dyce Duckworth, [*b* 13 July 1943; *m* 1976, Patricia, *o d* of Thomas Cahill]. *Address:* Dunwood Cottage, Shootash, Romsey, Hants. *T:* Romsey 513228.

du CROS, Sir Claude Philip Arthur Mallet, 3rd Bt *cr* 1916; *b* 22 Dec. 1922; *s* of Sir (Harvey) Philip du Cros, 2nd Bt, and of Dita, *d* of late Sir Claude Coventry Mallet, CMG; *S* father, 1975; *m* 1st, 1953, Mrs Christine Nancy Tordoff (marr. diss. 1974), *d* of late F. R. Bennett, Spilsby, Lincs; one *s*; 2nd, Mrs Margaret Roy Cutler, *d* of late R. J. Frater, Gosforth, Northumberland. *Heir: s* Julian Claude Arthur Mallet du Cros, *b* 23 April 1955. *Address:* G'lengarry, St Peter, Jersey.

DUDBRIDGE, Bryan James, CMG 1961; retired from HM Overseas Civil Service, Nov. 1961; Deputy Director, formerly Associate Director, British Council of Churches Department of Christian Aid, 1963-72; *b* 2 April 1912; *o s* of late W. Dudbridge, OBE, and of Anne Jane Dudbridge; *m* 1943, Audrey Mary, *o d* of late Dr and Mrs Heywood, Newbury; two *s* one *d. Educ:* King's Coll. Sch., Wimbledon; Selwyn Coll., Cambridge. Appointed to Colonial Administrative Service as Cadet in Tanganyika, 1935; Asst Dist Officer, 1937; Dist Officer, 1947; Sen. Dist Officer, 1953; Actg Provincial Commr, Southern Province; Administrative Officer (Class IIA), 1955, and Actg Provincial Commissioner (Local Government); Provincial Commissioner, Western Province, 1957; Minister for Provincial Affairs, 1959-60, retd. *Publications:* contrib. Journal of African Administration, and Tanganyika Notes and Records. *Recreations:* natural history, and wildfowl. *Address:* Bridge Farm, High Halden, Ashford, Kent. *T:* High Halden 221. *Club:* Royal Commonwealth Society.

DUDDING, Sir John (Scarbrough), Kt 1963; DL; Chairman, Humberside Area Health Authority, since 1974; *b* 28 Nov. 1915; *s* of Col Thomas Scarbrough Dudding, OBE, MRCS, LRCP, RAMC, and Maude Campbell Dudding; *m* 1945, Enid Grace Gardner, The Old Hall, Tacolneston, Norwich; one *s* one *d. Educ:* Cheltenham Coll.; Jesus Coll., Cambridge (BA Hons). Entered Colonial Service, posted to Nigeria, 1938. War service with Nigeria Regt of Royal West African Frontier Force, in Nigeria, India and Burma, 1940-45. Dep. Comr of the Cameroons and Actg Comr, 1956-58; Permanent Sec., Ministries Federal Nigerian Govt with responsibilities for Works, Surveys, Transport, Aviation, and Communications, 1959-63; retd, 1964. Chairman: Scunthorpe HMC, 1967-74; Lincolnshire Cttee VSO, 1966-73; Lincolnshire Regional Arts Assoc., 1970-73; Pres., Winterton Agricl Soc. Lindsey CC, 1967-74; DL Lincoln, 1971-, Humberside 1974. FRSA 1971. *Recreations:* gardening, local history and book-collecting. *Address:* Scarbrough House, Winteringham, Scunthorpe, South Humberside DN15 9ND. *T:* Scunthorpe 732 393. *Club:* Royal Commonwealth Society.

DUDGEON, Air Vice-Marshal Antony Greville, CBE 1955; DFC 1941; MBIM 1968; with McKinsey & Co., management advisers; *b* 6 Feb. 1916; *s* of late Prof. Herbert William Dudgeon, Guy's Hosp. and Egyptian Government Service; *m* 1942, Phyllis Margaret, *d* of late Group Capt. John McFarlane, OBE, MC, AFC, Lowestoft, Suffolk; one *s* one *d. Educ:* Eton; RAF Cranwell; Staff Coll., Flying Coll.; Polytechnic London. RAF Service, 1933-68, in UK, Europe, Near, Middle and Far East, USA; personnel work, training, operations, flight safety, organisation of new formations, liaison with civilian firms and youth organisations; NATO Staff; 6 command appointments; 3,500 hours as pilot. *Publications:* A Flying Command (under pen-name Tom Dagger), 1962; several stories contributed to Blackwood's Magazine. *Recreations:* writing, photography, swimming, golf; (languages, French, Egyptian). *Address:* Manager of Professional Staff Services, McKinsey & Co., 40 Avenue George V, Paris VIII, France; 3 Quick Street, Islington, N1. *Clubs:* Royal Air Force, MCC; Travellers' (Paris).

DUDGEON, Henry Alexander, CMG 1976; HM Diplomatic Service; Minister, Canberra, since 1976; *b* 12 Aug. 1924; *er s* of late John Brown Dudgeon and late Alison Dudgeon (*née* Winton); *m* 1952, Marjorie Patricia, *d* of Joseph Harvey, MD; no *c. Educ:* Knox Academy, Haddington; Magdalene Coll., Cambridge. Served in HM Forces, 1943-47; entered HM Foreign Service, 1949; served at: FO, 1949-52; Sofia, 1952-54; Amman, 1954-58; FO, 1958-61; 1st Sec. and Head of Chancery, Madrid, 1961-66; Counsellor and Head of Chancery, Havana, 1966-69; Civil Service Research Fellow at Glasgow Univ., 1969-70; Head of Marine and Transport Dept, FCO, 1970-74. Dep. Leader, UK Delegn to Third UN Conf. on Law of the Sea, 1974-75. *Recreation:* bridge. *Address:* c/o Foreign and Commonwealth Office, SW1; 295 Fir Tree Road, Epsom Downs, Surrey. *T:* Burgh Heath 52637. *Clubs:* Travellers'; Union (Sydney); Royal Canberra Golf.

DUDGEON, Prof. John Alastair, CBE 1977; MC 1942 and Bar 1943; TD 1947, Bars 1950 and 1956; DL; Consultant Microbiologist, Hospital for Sick Children, Great Ormond Street, since 1960; Professor of Microbiology since 1972, Dean since 1974, Institute of Child Health, University of London; *b* 9 Nov. 1916; *yr s* of late Prof. L. S. Dudgeon; *m* 1st, 1945, Patricia Joan Ashton (*d* 1969); two *s*; 2nd, 1974, Joyce Kathleen Tibbetts. *Educ:* Repton Sch.; Trinity Coll., Cambridge; St Thomas's Hosp., London. MB, BCh 1944; MA, MD Cantab 1947; FRCPath 1967; MRCP 1970; FRCP 1974. Served in London Rifle Bde and 7th Bn Rifle Bde, 1936-43; transf. to RAMC, 1944; Specialist in Pathology RAMC, 1945. Asst Pathologist, St Thomas's Hosp., 1947; Sen. Lectr, St George's Hosp. Med. Sch., 1953; Head of Virus Research, Glaxo Labs, 1958; Hosp. for Sick Children, Great Ormond Street: Asst Pathologist, 1948; Hon. Consultant Virologist, 1953; Mem. Bd of Governors, 1962-69, 1970-; Mem. Cttee of Management, Inst. of Child Health (Univ. of London), 1966-; Hon. Consultant in Pathology to Army, 1977-. Mem. Court of Assts, Soc. of Apothecaries of London, 1974. DL Greater London, 1973. OStJ 1958. *Publications:* contrib. Modern Trends in Paediatrics, Modern Trends in Med. Virology, BMJ, Clinical Virology. *Recreation:* sailing. *Address:* 1 Devonshire Place, W1N 1PA. *T:* 01-935 6703. *Clubs:* Army and Navy; Aldeburgh Yacht.

DUDLEY, 4th Earl of, *cr* 1860; **William Humble David Ward;** Baron Ward, 1644; Viscount Ednam, 1860; *b* 5 Jan. 1920; *e s* of 3rd Earl of Dudley, MC, TD, and Rosemary Millicent, RRC (*d* 1930), *o d* of 4th Duke of Sutherland; *S* father, 1969; *m* 1st, 1946, Stella (marr. diss., 1961), *d* of M. A. Carcano, *qv*; one *s* twin *d*; 2nd, 1961, Maureen Swanson; one *s* five *d. Educ:* Eton; Christ

Church, Oxford. Joined 10th Hussars, 1941, Adjt, 1944-45; ADC to Viceroy of India, 1942-43. Served War of 1939-45 (wounded). Director: Baggeridge Brick Co. Ltd; Tribune Investment Trust Ltd. *Heir: s* Viscount Ednam, *qv. Address:* 6 Cottesmore Gardens, W8; Vention House, Putsborough, N Devon. *Clubs:* White's, Pratt's; Royal Yacht Squadron.

DUDLEY, Baroness (14th in line), *cr* 1439-1440 (called out of abeyance, 1916); **Barbara Amy Felicity Wallace;** *b* 23 April 1907; *o d* of 12th Baron Dudley and Sybil Augusta (*d* 1958), *d* of late Rev. Canon Henry William Coventry; *S* brother, 1972; *m* 1929, Guy Raymond Hill Wallace (*d* 1967), *s* of late Gen. Hill Wallace, CB, RHA; three *s* one *d. Recreations:* floral watercolours (has exhibited Royal Watercolour Society, Conduit St); gardening. *Heir: e s* Hon. Jim Anthony Hill Wallace [*b* 9 Nov. 1930; *m* 1962, Nicola Jane, *d* of Lt-Col Philip William Edward Leslie Dunsterville; two *s*]. *Address:* Hill House, Kempsey, Worcestershire. *T:* Worcester 820253.

DUDLEY, Bishop Suffragan of, since 1977; **Rt. Rev. Anthony Charles Dumper;** *b* 4 Oct. 1923; *s* of Charles Frederick and Edith Mildred Dumper; *m* 1948, Sibylle Anna Emilie Hellwig; two *s* one *d. Educ:* Surbiton Grammar School; Christ's Coll., Cambridge (MA); Westcott House, Cambridge. Relief Worker, Germany, 1946-47; ordained, 1947; Curate, East Greenwich, 1947-49; Vicar of South Perak, Malaya, 1949-57; Archdeacon of North Malaya, 1955-64; Vicar of Penang, Malaya, 1957-64; Dean of St Andrew's Cathedral, Singapore, 1964-70; Vicar of St Peter's, Stockton on Tees, and Rural Dean of Stockton, 1970-77. *Publication:* Vortex of the East, 1963. *Recreations:* walking, gardening. *Address:* Bishop's House, Halesowen Road, Cradley Heath, West Midlands. *T:* 021-550 3407.

DUDLEY, Archdeacon of; *see* Campling, Ven. C. R.

DUDLEY, Prof. Hugh Arnold Freeman, FRCSE, FRCS, FRACS; Professor of Surgery, St Mary's Hospital, London, since 1973; *b* 1 July 1925; *s* of W. L. and Ethel Dudley; *m* 1947, Jean Bruce Lindsay Johnston; two *s* one *d. Educ:* Heath Grammar Sch., Halifax; Edinburgh and Harvard Univs. MB, ChB Edin. 1947; ChM (Gold Medal and Chiene Medal) Edin. 1958; FRCSE 1951; FRACS 1965; FRCS 1974. Lecturer in Surgery, Edinburgh Univ., 1954-58; Sen. Lectr, Aberdeen Univ., 1958-63; Foundation Prof. of Surgery, Monash Univ., Melbourne, 1963-72. *Publications:* Principles of General Surgical Management, 1958; Access and Exposure in Abdominal Surgery, 1963; (ed) Rob and Smiths Operative Surgery, 1976-77; Hamilton Bailey's Emergency Surgery, 1977; Communication in Medicine and Biology, 1977; papers in med. jls. *Recreations:* accidentally and unintentionally annoying others; surgical history. *Address:* 33 Chilworth Mews, W2 3RG. *T:* 01-402 7507; West Broombrae, Glenbuchat, Aberdeenshire. *T:* Glenkindie 341.

DUDLEY, Prof. Norman Alfred, CBE 1977; PhD; Lucas Professor of Engineering Production, University of Birmingham, since 1959; Head of Department of Engineering Production and Director of University Institute for Engineering Production, since 1976; Chartered Engineer; *b* 29 Feb. 1916; *s* of Alfred Dudley; *m* 1940, Hilda Florence, *d* of John Miles; one *s* two *d. Educ:* Kings Norton Grammar Sch.; Birmingham Coll. of Technology. BSc London, PhD Birmingham. FIProdE, MBIM; industrial training and appts: H. W. Ward & Co. Ltd, 1932-39; Imperial Typewriter Co. Ltd, 1940-45; Technical Coll. Lectr, 1945-52; Sen. Lectr, Wolverhampton and Staffs, 1948-52; Lectr in Eng. Prod., 1952, Reader, 1956, University of Birmingham. Chm., Manufacturing Processes Div., Birmingham Univ. Inst. for Advanced Studies in Engineering Sciences, 1965-68. Director: Birmingham Productivity Services Ltd; West Midlands Low Cost Automation Centre. Governor, Dudley and Staffs Tech. Coll.; Member: Council, West Midlands Productivity Assoc.; Council Internat. Univ. Contact for Management Education, 1957; Council, Instn of Prod. Engineers, 1959-61 (Chm., Research Cttee, 1965-66); UK Delegn to UNCSAT Geneva, 1963; W Midlands Economic Planning Council, 1970-; Adv. Panel on Economic Develt, West Midlands Metropolitan CC, 1976-; Council, Nat. Materials Handling Centre. Pres., Midlands Operational Research Soc., 1966-. Editor, International Journal of Production Research, 1961-. J. D. Scaife Medal, 1958. *Publications:* Work Measurement: Some Research Studies, 1968; various papers on Engineering Production. *Address:* 24 White House Green, Solihull, West Midlands. *T:* 021-705 8349.

DUDLEY-SMITH, Ven. Timothy; Archdeacon of Norwich, since 1973; *b* 26 Dec. 1926; *o s* of Arthur and Phyllis Dudley Smith, Buxton, Derbyshire; *m* 1959, June Arlette MacDonald; one *s* two *d. Educ:* Tonbridge Sch.; Pembroke Coll., and Ridley

Hall, Cambridge. BA 1947, MA 1951; Certif. in Educn 1948. Deacon, 1950; priest, 1951; Asst Curate, St Paul, Northumberland Heath, 1950-53; Head of Cambridge Univ. Mission in Bermondsey, 1953-55; Hon. Chaplain to Bp of Rochester, 1953-60; Editor, Crusade, and Editorial Sec. of Evangelical Alliance, 1955-59; Asst Sec. of Church Pastoral-Aid Soc., 1959-65, Sec., 1965-73; Commissary to Archbp of Sydney, 1971-; Exam. Chap. to Bp of Norwich, 1971-. *Publications:* Christian Literature and the Church Bookstall, 1963; What Makes a Man a Christian?, 1966; A Man Named Jesus, 1971; contributor to various hymn books. *Recreations:* reading, verse, woodwork, family and friends. *Address:* Rectory Meadow, Bramerton, Norwich NR14 7DW. *T:* Surlingham 251. *Club:* Norfolk (Norwich).

DUDLEY-WILLIAMS, Sir Rolf (Dudley), 1st Bt, *cr* 1964; *b* 17 June 1908; *s* of Arthur Williams, Plymouth; assumed and adopted surname of Dudley-Williams, by Deed Poll, 1964; *m* 1940, Margaret Helen, *er d* of F. E. Robinson, OBE, AMIMechE; two *s. Educ:* Plymouth Coll.; Royal Air Force Coll., Cranwell. Gazetted, 1928, Flying Officer, 1930; Central Flying Sch., 1933, invalided from service, 1934. Founded Power Jets Ltd, 1936, to develop Whittle system of jet propulsion; Managing Dir, 1941. Mem. Council Soc. of British Aircraft Constructors, 1944; Companion Royal Aeronautical Society, 1944. Contested (C) Brierley Hill, 1950. MP (C) Exeter, 1951-66; PPS to Sec. of State for War, 1958; PPS to Minister of Agriculture, 1960-64. Chm., Western Area of National Union of Conservative Assocs, 1961-64. *Heir: s* Alastair Edgcumbe James Dudley-Williams [*b* 26 Nov. 1943; *m* 1972, Diana Elizabeth Jane, twin *d* of R. H. C. Duncan; two *d*]. *Address:* The Old Manse, South Petherton, Som. *T:* South Petherton 40143. *Club:* Royal Air Force.

DUDMAN, George Edward, CB 1973; Editor, Statutes in Force, since 1977; *b* 2 Dec. 1916; *s* of William James Dudman and Nora Annie (*née* Curtis); *m* 1955, Joan Doris, *d* of late Frederick John Eaton; one *s* one *d. Educ:* Merchant Taylors' Sch., London; St John's Coll., Oxford (MA). Royal Artillery, 1940-46; Control Commn, Germany, 1946-49. Called to Bar, Middle Temple, 1950. Law Officers' Dept, 1951; Legal Sec., Law Officers' Dept, 1958; Legal Advr, DES, 1965-77. *Recreations:* painting, gardening, cooking. *Address:* 10 Viga Road, Grange Park, N21. *T:* 01-360 5129.

DUDMAN, Ven. Robert William; Archdeacon of Lindsey and Fourth Canon Residentiary of Lincoln Cathedral since 1971; *b* 4 Dec. 1925; *s* of late Robert and Jane Dudman, Basingstoke; *m* 1954, Betty Shannon; one *s* two *d. Educ:* King's Coll., Taunton; Lincoln Theol Coll.; Univ. of Hull (BA). Able Seaman, RN, 1944-47. Deacon, 1952; Priest, 1953. Curate: Shiregreen, Sheffield, 1952-53; Wombwell, 1953-55; Frodingham, Scunthorpe, 1955-57; Industrial Chaplain to Bp of Lincoln, 1957-71; Rector of Scotton, 1960-71; Canon and Prebend of Norton Episcopi, Lincoln Cath., 1968. *Address:* The Archdeaconry, Cantilupe Chantry, Lincoln LN2 1PX. *T:* Lincoln 25784.

DUESBURY, Rev. Julian Percy T.; see Thornton-Duesbury.

DUFF, Sir (Arthur) Antony, KCMG 1973 (CMG 1964); CVO 1972; DSO 1944; DSC; HM Diplomatic Service; Deputy Under-Secretary of State, Foreign and Commonwealth Office, since 1975; Deputy to Permanent Under-Secretary of State, Foreign and Commonwealth Office, since 1976; *b* 25 Feb. 1920; *s* of late Adm. Sir Arthur Allen Morison Duff, KCB; *m* 1944, Pauline Marion, *d* of Capt. R. H. Bevan, RN, and *widow* of Flt-Lieut J. A. Sword; one *s* two *d* (and one step *s*). *Educ:* RNC, Dartmouth. Served in RN, 1937-46. Mem., Foreign (subseq. Diplomatic) Service, 1946; 3rd Sec., Athens, Oct. 1946; 2nd Sec., 1948; 2nd Sec., Cairo, 1949; 1st Sec., 1952; transferred Foreign Office, Private Sec. to Minister of State, 1952; 1st Sec., Paris, 1954; Foreign Office, 1957; Bonn, 1960; Counsellor, 1962; British Ambassador to Nepal, 1964-65; Commonwealth Office, 1965-68; FCO, 1968-69; Dep. High Comr, Kuala Lumpur, 1969-72; High Comr, Nairobi, 1972-75. *Address:* c/o Foreign and Commonwealth Office, SW1. *Clubs:* Athenæum, Royal Commonwealth Society.

DUFF, Sir (Charles) Michael (Robert Vivian), 3rd Bt *cr* 1911; Lieutenant of Gwynedd, since 1974 (Lord Lieutenant of Caernarvonshire, 1960-74); *b* 3 May 1907; *s* of 2nd Bt and Lady (Gladys Mary) Juliet Lowther, *o d* of 4th Earl of Lonsdale (Lady Juliet Duff; *d* 1965); *S* father, 1914; *m* 1949, Lady Caroline Paget (*d* 1976), *e d* of 6th Marquess of Anglesey, GCVO; one adopted *s. Educ:* Sandhurst. Flying Officer late RAFVR. DL 1946, Vice-Lieutenant 1957-60, Caernarvonshire; High Sheriff of Anglesey, 1950-51. KStJ. *Recreations:* shooting and hunting. *Address:* Vaynol Park, Bangor, N Wales. *T:* Bangor 42. *Club:* White's.

DUFF, Sir Michael; see Duff, Sir C. M. R. V.

DUFF, Patrick William; Fellow of Trinity College, Cambridge; *b* 21 Feb. 1901; 3rd *s* of J. D. Duff, Fellow of Trinity College, Cambridge, and Laura, *d* of Sir William Lenox-Conyngham, KCB. *Educ:* Winchester; Trinity Coll., Cambridge; Munich Univ.; Harvard Law Sch. 1st Class, Classical Tripos Parts I and II; Craven and Whewell Scholar; Tancred Scholar of Lincoln's Inn; Fellow of Trinity, 1925; Lecturer, 1927; Tutor, 1938; Senior Tutor, 1945; Dean of Coll., 1950; Vice-Master, 1960. Regius Prof. of Civil Law, Cambridge, 1945-68. Barrister-at-Law, 1933. Cambridge Borough Councillor, 1947-51. Fellow of Winchester Coll., 1948-76; Warden, 1959-62. Pres. Soc. of Public Teachers of Law, 1957-58. Hon. Bencher of Lincoln's Inn, 1959. *Publications:* The Charitable Foundations of Byzantium (in Cambridge Legal Essays presented to Doctor Bond, Prof. Buckland and Prof. Kenny), 1926; The Personality of an Idol (in Cambridge Law Journal), 1927; Delegata Potestas Non Potest Delegari (in Cornell Law Quarterly), 1929; Personality in Roman Private Law, 1938; Roman Law Today (in Tulane Law Review), 1947. *Recreation:* scouting. *Address:* Trinity College, Cambridge.

DUFF, Col Thomas Robert G.; see Gordon-Duff.

DUFF GORDON, Sir Andrew (Cosmo Lewis), 8th Bt, *cr* 1813; *b* 17 Oct. 1933; *o s* of Sir Douglas Duff Gordon, 7th Bt and Gladys Rosemary (*d* 1933), *e d* of late Col Vivien Henry, CB; *S* father, 1964; *m* 1st, 1967, Grania Mary (marr. diss. 1975), *d* of Fitzgerald Villiers-Stuart, Ireland; one *s*; 2nd, 1975, Eveline Virginia, BA, *d* of S. Soames, Newbury; one *s. Educ:* Repton. Served with Worcs Regiment and 1st Bn Ches Regt, 1952-54. Mem. of Lloyd's, 1962-. *Recreations:* golf, shooting, skiing. *Heir: s* Cosmo Henry Villiers Duff Gordon, *b* 18 June 1968. *Address:* Downton House, Walton, Presteigne, Powys. *T:* New Radnor 223; 27 Cathcart Road, SW10. *Clubs:* City University; Kington Golf.

DUFFERIN and AVA, 5th Marquess of, *cr* 1888; **Sheridan Frederick Terence Hamilton-Temple-Blackwood;** Baron Dufferin and Clandeboye, Ireland, 1800; Baron Clandeboye, UK, 1850; Earl of Dufferin, Viscount Clandeboye, 1871; Earl of Ava, 1888, and a Bt; *b* 9 July 1938; *o s* of 4th Marquess (killed in action, 1945) and Maureen (she *m* 1948, Major Desmond Buchanan, MC, from whom she obtained a divorce, 1954; *m* 1955, John Cyril Maude, *qv*), 2nd *d* of late Hon. (Arthur) Ernest Guinness; *S* father, 1945; *m* 1964, Serena Belinda Rosemary, *d* of Group Capt. (Thomas) Loel Evelyn Bulkeley Guinness, *qv*. *Educ:* Eton Coll. Trustee, Wallace Collection, 1973-. *Address:* 4 Holland Villas Road, W14. *T:* 01-937 3163; Clandeboye, Co. Down, Northern Ireland.

DUFFUS, Sir Herbert (George Holwell), Kt 1966; *b* 30 Aug. 1908; *e s* of William Alexander Duffus, JP, and Emily Henrietta Mary (*née* Holwell); *m* 1939, Elsie Mary (*née* Hollinsed); no *c. Educ:* Cornwall Coll., Jamaica. Admitted as Solicitor: Jamaica, 1930, England, 1948. Resident Magistrate, Jamaica, 1946-58; Called to the Bar, Lincoln's Inn, 1956; acted as Puisne Judge, Jamaica, 1956-58; Puisne Judge, Jamaica, 1958-62; Judge of Appeal, Jamaica, 1962-64; Pres. Court of Appeal, 1964-67; Chief Justice of Jamaica, 1968-73; Acting Governor General of Jamaica, 1973. Chm., Commn of Enquiry into Prisons of Jamaica, 1954; Chm., Commn of Enquiry into the administration of justice and police brutality in Grenada, WI, 1974. Chm. of The Police Service Commission (Jamaica), 1958-68. Pres., Boy Scouts Assoc., Jamaica, 1967-70. Chancellor of the Church (Anglican) in Jamaica, 1973-76. *Address:* 6 Braywick Road, PO Box 243, Kingston 6, Jamaica. *T:* 92-70171.

DUFFUS, Hon. Sir William (Algernon Holwell), Kt 1971; Justice of the Courts of Appeal for Bahamas, Bermuda, Belize and the Turks and Caicos Islands, since 1975; *b* Jamaica, 13 Aug. 1911; *s* of William Alexander Duffus, JP, and of Emily (*née* Holwell); *m* Helen Hollinsed; two *s* one *d. Educ:* Cornwall Coll. and Titchfield Sch., Jamaica. Solicitor, Supreme Court, Jamaica, 1933. In private practice in Jamaica. Legal Service, Jamaica, 1935; Magistrate, Jamaica, 1943; Magistrate, Nigeria, 1949, Chief Magistrate, 1953. Called to the Bar, Gray's Inn, 1954; Chief Registrar of the Federal Supreme Court, Nigeria, 1955; Judge of High Ct, W Nigeria, 1957; Justice of Ct of Appeal for E Africa, 1964, Vice-Pres., 1969, Pres., 1970-75. *Address:* Cudworth Cottage, Great Wilbraham, Cambridge CB1 5JD. *T:* Cambridge 880530.

DUFFY, (Albert Edward) Patrick, PhD; MP (Lab) Sheffield, Attercliffe, since 1970; Parliamentary Under-Secretary of State for Defence (Navy), Ministry of Defence, since 1976; *b* 17 June 1920. *Educ:* London Sch. of Economics (BSc(Econ.), PhD);

Columbia Univ., Morningside Heights, New York, USA. Served War of 1939-45, Royal Navy, as an Officer (6 years service). Lecturer, University of Leeds, 1950-63, 1967-70. Visiting Prof., Drew Univ., Madison, NJ, 1966-70, Associate Prof., 1970-. Contested (Lab) Tiverton Division of Devon, 1950, 1951, 1955. MP (Lab) Colne Valley Division of Yorks, 1963-66; Chairman: Parly Labour Party Economic and Finance Gp, 1965-66, 1974-76; Trade and Industry Sub-Cttee of Select Cttee on Expenditure; PPS to Sec. of State for Defence, 1974-76. *Publications:* contrib. to Economic History Review, Victorian Studies, Manchester School, etc. *Address:* 169 Bennetthorpe, Doncaster, South Yorks. *Clubs:* Naval; Trades and Labour (Doncaster).

DUFFY, Hugh Herbert White; *b* 24 Aug. 1917; *y s* of late Hugh Duffy and Catherine Duffy (*née* White); *m* 1946, Hylda, *y d* of Stanley Swales, Fleetwood; one *s. Educ:* Stonyhurst Coll.; Durham Univ. (LLB). Commnd 9th Bn, Durham LI (TA), 1937; BEF, 1940; wounded France, 1940; discharged owing to wounds, 1942. Admitted solicitor, 1943. Joined Public Trustee Office (Manchester Br.), 1944, transf. London, 1956; Chief Admin. Officer, 1970-73; Asst Public Trustee, 1973-75; Public Trustee, 1975. *Recreations:* reading, motoring, watching sport on TV. *Address:* c/o Public Trustee Office, Kingsway WC2B 6JX. *T:* 01-405 4300.

DUFFY, Maureen Patricia; author; *b* 1933; *o c* of Grace Rose Wright. *Educ:* Trowbridge High Sch. for Girls; Sarah Bonnell High Sch. for Girls; King's College, London (BA). Co-founder, Writers' Action Group; Dep. Chm., Writers Guild of GB. *Publications:* That's How It Was, 1962; The Single Eye, 1964; The Microcosm, 1966; The Paradox Players, 1967; Lyrics for the Dog Hour (poetry), 1968; Wounds, 1969; Rites (play), 1969; Love Child, 1971; The Venus Touch, 1971; The Erotic World of Faery, 1972; I want to Go to Moscow, 1973; A Nightingale in Bloomsbury Square (play), 1974; Capital, 1975; Evesong (Poetry), 1975; The Passionate Shepherdess, 1977; *visual art:* Prop art exhibn (with Brigid Brophy), 1969. *Address:* 8 Roland Gardens, SW7 3PH.

DUFFY, Patrick; *see* Duffy, A. E. P.

DUFTY, Arthur Richard, CBE 1971; Master of the Armouries in HM Tower of London, 1963-76, full-time, 1973-76; *b* 23 June 1911; *s* of T. E. Dufty, and Beatrice (*née* Holmes); *m* 1937, Kate Brazley (*née* Ainsworth); one *s* two *d. Educ:* Rugby; Liverpool School of Architecture. War service in RN. On staff of Royal Commn on Historical Monuments, 1937-73, Sec. and Gen. Editor 1962-73, with responsibility for Nat. Monuments Record, inc. Nat. Buildings Record, 1964-73. Editor, 1952-56, Vice-Pres., 1960-64, Hon. Vice-Pres., 1976-, Royal Archaeological Inst; Sec., 1954-64, Vice-Pres. 1964-67, and 1975-, Soc. of Antiquaries; Vice-Pres., Council for Brit. Archaeology, 1962-65. Member: Ancient Monuments Bd for England, 1962-73 and 1977-; Guildford Dio. Adv. Cttee, 1947-74; Council for Care of Churches, 1949-60; Council for Places of Worship, 1976-; 2nd Bridges Commn on Redundant Churches, 1961-63; Council of Georgian Gp, 1954-63; Council, Nat. Army Museum, 1963-; Historic Bldgs Adv. Cttee, GLC, 1964-67; Conf. of Dirs of Nat. Museums, 1963-76; Management Cttee of Inst. of Archaeology, Univ. of London, 1965-75; Royal Commn on Historical Monuments, 1975-. Vice-Chm., Cathedrals Advisory Cttee, 1965-. Chairman: (first) Surrey Local History Council (Council of Social Service for Surrey), 1965-73; British Cttee, Corpus Vitrearum Medii Aevi, 1970- (sponsored by British Acad.); London Dio. Adv. Cttee, 1973-; Standing Cttee on Conservation of West Front of Wells Cathedral, 1974-. Directed, for Soc. of Antiquaries, repair and rehabilitation of Kelmscott, William Morris's home in Oxfordshire, 1964-67. Hon. Freeman, Armourers and Brasiers' Co., 1974. Hon. Mem., Art Workers' Guild. ARIBA 1935-74; FSA 1946. *Publications:* Kelmscott: an illustrated guide, 1970; (with F. H. Cripps-Day) *Fragmenta Armamentaria* IV: Supplementary list of armour preserved in English Churches, 1939; ed 5 RCHM Inventories (incl. authorship of accounts of King's College Chapel, Corfe Castle, etc) and 5 occasional publications; Intr. Vol. to Morris's Story of Cupid and Psyche, 1974; articles in learned jls. *Recreations:* viewing sales; taking pleasure in Victorian and Art Nouveau; music. *Address:* 46 Trafalgar Court, Farnham, Surrey. *Clubs:* Athenæum, Arts, Naval.

DUGARD, Arthur Claude, CBE 1969; Chairman, Cooper & Roe Ltd, since 1952 (formerly Joint Managing Director); *b* 1 Dec. 1904; *s* of Arthur Thomas Turner Dugard, Nottingham; *m* 1931, Christine Mary Roe, Nottingham; two *s. Educ:* Oundle Sch., Northants. Joined Cooper & Roe Ltd, Knitwear manufacturers, 1923 (Dir, 1936; Man. Dir, 1947). President: Nottingham Hosiery Manufrs Assoc., 1952-53; Nat. Hosiery Manufrs Fedn,

1959-61; Nottingham Chamber of Commerce, 1961-62. First Chm., CBI North Midland Regional Council, 1965-66; Chm. British Hosiery & Knitwear Export Gp, 1966-68; Mem. East Midlands Economic Planning Council, 1967-72. Liveryman, Worshipful Co. of Framework Knitters, 1949-. *Recreation:* golf. *Address:* 16 Hollies Drive, Edwalton, Nottingham NG12 4BZ. *T:* Nottingham 233217.

DUGDALE, family name of **Baron Crathorne.**

DUGDALE, Amy K.; *see* Browning, A. K.

DUGDALE, John Robert Stratford; Lord-Lieutenant of Salop, since 1975; *b* 10 May 1923; 2nd *s* of Sir William Francis Stratford Dugdale, 1st Bt, and Margaret, 2nd *d* of Sir Robert Gordon Gilmour, 1st Bt; *m* 1956, Kathryn Edith Helen (see K. E. H. Dugdale); two *s* two *d. Educ:* Eton; Christ Church, Oxford. Chm., Telford Develt Corp., 1971-75. Mem., Salop County Council. KStJ 1976. *Recreation:* sleeping. *Address:* Tickwood Hall, Much Wenlock, Salop. *T:* Telford 882644. *Clubs:* Brooks's, White's, MCC. *See also Sir William Dugdale, Bt.*

DUGDALE, Kathryn Edith Helen, CVO 1973; JP; Woman of the Bedchamber to the Queen since 1955 (Temporary Extra, 1961-71); *b* 4 Nov. 1923; *d* of Rt Hon. Oliver Stanley, PC, MC, MP and Lady Maureen Vane-Tempest Stewart; *m* 1956, John Robert Stratford Dugdale, *qv;* two *s* two *d. Educ:* many and varied establishments. Served with WRNS. JP Salop, 1964. Employee of Greater London Fund for the Blind. Comdr, Royal Order of North Star (Sweden), 1956. *Recreations:* gardening, reading, pottering. *Address:* Tickwood Hall, Much Wenlock, Salop. *T:* Telford 882644. *See also M. C. Stanley.*

DUGDALE, Norman, CB 1974; Permanent Secretary, Ministry of Health and Social Services, Northern Ireland, since 1970; *b* 6 Feb. 1921; *yr s* of William and Eva Dugdale, Burnley, Lancs; *m* 1949, Mary Whitehead. *Educ:* Burnley Grammar Sch.; Manchester Univ. (BA). Asst Principal, Bd of Trade, 1941; Min. of Commerce, NI, 1948; Asst Sec., Min. of Health and Local Govt, NI, 1955; Sen. Asst Sec., Min. of Health and Local Govt, NI, 1964; Second Sec., Min. of Health and Social Services, 1968. Governor, Nat. Inst. for Social Work, London, 1965-; Mem. Court, New University of Ulster, 1971. *Publications:* The Disposition of the Weather (poems), 1967; A Prospect of the West (poems), 1970; Night-Ferry (poems), 1974; contribs to various literary periodicals. *Recreations:* prevaricating; next week-end. *Address:* Massey Park, Belfast 4, Northern Ireland. *T:* 63370.

DUGDALE, Sir William (Stratford), 2nd Bt *cr* 1936; MC 1943; JP; DL; *b* 29 March 1922; *er s* of Sir William Francis Stratford Dugdale, 1st Bt, and Margaret, 2nd *d* of Sir Robert Gordon Gilmour, 1st Bt, of Liberton and Craigmillar; *m* 1st, 1952, Lady Belinda Pleydell-Bouverie (*d* 1961), 2nd *d* of 6th Earl of Radnor; one *s* three *d;* 2nd, 1967, Cecilia Mary, *e d* of Sir William Malcolm Mount, 2nd Bt, *qv;* one *s* one *d. Educ:* Eton; Balliol Coll., Oxford. Served War of 1939-45, Grenadier Guards (Captain). Admitted as Solicitor, 1949. Dir, Phoenix Assurance Co., 1968-. Mem., Warwicks County Council, 1964-76; Chm., Severn Trent Water Authority; Governor, Lady Katherine Leveson's Hosp., Temple Balsall. High Steward, Stratford upon Avon, 1977. JP 1951, DL 1955, High Sheriff 1971, Warwicks. *Heir: s* William Matthew Stratford Dugdale, *b* 22 Feb. 1959. *Address:* Blyth Hall, Coleshill, near Birmingham. *T:* Coleshill 62203; Merevale Hall, Atherstone. *T:* Atherstone 3143; 24 Bryanston Mews West, W1. *T:* 01-262 2510. *Clubs:* Brooks's, White's, MCC; Jockey (Newmarket). *See also J. R. S. Dugdale.*

DUGGAN, Rt. Rev. John Coote; *see* Tuam, Killala and Achonry, Bishop of.

DUGMORE, Rev. Prof. Clifford William, DD; Editor of The Journal of Ecclesiastical History since 1950; British Member of Editorial Board of Novum Testamentum since 1956; *b* 9 May 1909; *s* of late Rev. Canon William Ernest Dugmore, MA, RD, and late Frances Ethel Dugmore (*née* Westmore); *m* 1938, Ruth Mabel Archbould Prangley (*d* 1977); one *d. Educ:* King Edward VI Sch., Birmingham (foundation scholar); Exeter Coll., Oxford; Queens' Coll., Cambridge. Oxford: BA (Hons Sch. of Oriental Studies), 1932; MA and James Mew Rabbinical Hebrew Scholar, 1935; BD 1940; DD 1957. Cambridge: BA (by incorporation) 1933; MA 1936; Norrisian Prizeman 1940; Select Preacher 1956; Hulsean Lecturer, 1958-60. Deacon 1935, Priest 1936; Asst Curate of Holy Trinity, Formby, 1935-37; Sub-Warden St Deiniol's Library, Hawarden, 1937-38; Rector of

Ingestre-with-Tixall, 1938-43; Chaplain of Alleyn's Coll. of God's Gift, Dulwich, 1943-44; Rector of Bredfield and Dir of Religious Education, dio. St Edmundsbury and Ipswich, 1945-47; Sen. Lecturer in Ecclesiast. Hist., University of Manchester, 1946-58; Tutor to Faculty of Theology, 1958; Prof. of Ecclesiastical History, King's Coll., Univ. of London, 1958-76, Emeritus Prof., 1976-. Chm. of British Sous-Commission of Commission Internationale d'Histoire Ecclésiastique, 1952-62; Pres. of the Ecclesiastical History Soc., 1963-64; Mem. of the Senate, 1964-71, Proctor in Convocation, 1970-, University of London. FKC 1965; FRHistS 1970. *Publications:* Eucharistic Doctrine in England from Hooker to Waterland, 1942; The Influence of the Synagogue upon the Divine Office, 1944 (2nd edn 1964); (ed) The Interpretation of the Bible 1944 (2nd edn 1946); The Mass and the English Reformers, 1958; Ecclesiastical History No Soft Option, 1959. Contributor to: Chambers's Encyclopædia, 1950 (Advisory Editor, 1960-); Weltkirchenlexikon 1960; Studia Patristica IV, 1961; Neotestamentica et Patristica, 1962; The English Prayer Book, 1963; A Companion to the Bible, 2nd revised edn, 1963; Studies in Church History I, 1964 (also ed); Studies in Church History II, 1965; Eucharistic Theology then and now, 1968; Man and his Gods, 1971; Aspects de l'Anglicanisme, 1974; Gen. Editor, Leaders of Religion, 1964-; articles and reviews in Journal of Theological Studies, Journal of Ecclesiastical History, Theology, History, etc. *Recreations:* motoring and philately. *Address:* 77 The Street, Puttenham, Surrey. *T:* Guildford 810460.

DUGUID, Prof. John Bright, CBE 1966; MD (Aberdeen); Adviser in Histopathology, Institute for Medical Research, Kuala Lumpur, Malaya, Nov. 1960-69, retired; Emeritus Professor of Pathology, University of Durham, Professor, 1948-60; *b* 5 May 1895; *s* of John Duguid, Farmer, Black Dog, Belhelvie, Aberdeenshire; *m* 1925, Agnes Mildred Emslie Benzie, MB, ChB (*d* 1973); one *s* one *d. Educ:* Friends Sch., Wigton, Cumberland; Gordon's Coll., Aberdeen, MB, ChB (Aberdeen) 1920; MD (Aberdeen), 1925. Asst in dept of Pathology, Aberdeen Univ., 1922; Lecturer in Morbid Anatomy and Histology, Victoria Univ., Manchester, 1925; Lecturer in Pathology, Welsh Nat. Sch. of Medicine, Cardiff, 1926; Prof. of Pathology and Bacteriology, University of Wales, 1932. *Publications:* The Dynamics of Atherosclerosis, 1976; articles on arterial diseases and lung pathology. *Recreation:* angling. *Address:* 17 Cairn Road, Bieldside, Aberdeen.

du HEAUME, Sir (Francis) Herbert, Kt 1947; CIE 1943; OBE 1932; KPM 1924; Indian Police Medal; *b* 27 May 1897; *s* of George du Heaume, OBE; *m* 1923, Blanche Helen Learmonth Tainsh; two *s.* Served European War, 1914-18, Captain, 15th London Regt; joined Indian Police, 1920; Principal, Police Training Sch., Punjab, 1934-42; Deputy Inspector-Gen. of Police, 1942-47. *Address:* c/o Grindlay's Bank Ltd, 13 St James's Square, SW1.

DUKE, family name of **Baron Merrivale.**

DUKE, Cecil Howard Armitage; Director of Establishments and Organisation, Ministry of Agriculture, Fisheries and Food, 1965-71; *b* 5 May 1912; *s* of John William Duke and late Gertrude Beatrice (*née* Armitage); *m* 1939, Eleanor Lucy (*née* Harvie); one *s* one *d. Educ:* Selhurst Gram. Sch.; LSE. RNVR, 1942-45 (Corvettes). Entered Civil Service, 1929; Asst Princ., 1940; Princ., 1945; Private Sec. to Lord Presidents of the Council, 1951-53; Asst Sec., Land Drainage Div. and Meat Div., 1953; Under-Sec., 1965. *Recreations:* walking, gardening, watching Sussex cricket. *Address:* 22 Fairways Road, Seaford, East Sussex. *T:* Seaford 894338.

DUKE, Sir Charles (Beresford), KCMG 1956 (CMG 1954); CIE 1947; OBE 1946; Director-General, Middle East Association, 1964-70; *b* 19 Dec. 1905; *o s* of late Arthur Herbert and Ann Victoria Duke, of Bangkok, Siam and Marlow, Bucks; *m* 1938, Morag Craigie, *o d* of Capt. Patrick Grant; two *d. Educ:* Charterhouse; Lincoln Coll., Oxford. Entered Indian Civil Service, 1928; appointed to United Provinces of Agra and Oudh, 1929; transferred to Indian Political Service, 1934; Asst Private Sec. to Viceroy, 1934-38; Sec. to Governor, NWFP, 1940-41; Political Agent, Waziristan, 1941-43; External Affairs Dept, Govt of India, New Delhi, 1943-47; transferred to HM Foreign Service, 1947; served in Pakistan, FO, Persia and Egypt, 1947-54; HM Ambassador to Jordan, 1954-56 and to Morocco, 1957-61; retired, 1961. *Recreation:* reading. *Address:* 15 Westgate Terrace, SW10; Cadenham Grange, Cadnam, near Southampton. *Club:* Athenæum.

DUKE, Maj.-Gen. Sir Gerald (William), KBE 1966 (CBE 1945); CB 1962; DSO 1945; DL; Director, Brixton Estate Ltd, since 1971; *b* 12 Nov. 1910; *e s* of late Lieut-Col A. A. G. Duke,

Indian Army; *m* 1946, Mary Elizabeth, *er d* of late E. M. Burn, Church Stretton; one *s* one *d. Educ:* Dover Coll.; RMA Woolwich; Jesus Coll., Cambridge. Commissioned RE, 1931; served Egypt and Palestine, 1936-39; War of 1939-45, in Western Desert and Italy; BGS Eighth Army, 1944; North West Europe, Brig. Q (Movements), 21st Army Group, 1944; CRE 49th Div., 1945. Chief Engineer, Malaya Comd, 1946; idc 1948; Mil. Attaché, Cairo, 1952-54; Comdt Sch. of Mil. Engineering, 1956-59. Commodore Royal Engineer Yacht Club, 1957-60. DPS, WO, 1959-62; Engineer-in-Chief (Army), 1963-65; retired. Col Comdt, RE, 1966-75. Chm., SS&AFA, Kent, 1973-; Pres., Scout Assoc., Kent, 1974-. Governor of Dover Coll. FICE. DL Kent, 1970. *Recreations:* sailing, golf. *Address:* Little Barnfield, Hawkhurst, Kent. *T:* Hawkhurst 3214. *Clubs:* Royal Ocean Racing; Royal Burnham Yacht.

DUKE, Brig. Jesse Pevensey, DSO 1919; MC; *b* 10 June 1890; *s* of Lieut-Col Olliver Thomas Duke and Blanche Wheeler; *m* 1936, Marion (*d* 1973), widow of Major G. W. H. Massey. *Educ:* Wellington Coll.; Sandhurst. Gazetted to Royal Warwickshire Regt, 1910; served in international occupation of North Albania, 1914, subsequent to Balkan War; various Staff appointments in European War, 1914-18 (DSO, MC, Bt Majority); GSO 3 North Russia, 1920; Staff Coll., Camberley, 1921-22; GSO 3 and 2 Northern Command, 1923-27; Instructor, RMC Sandhurst, 1929-32; Commanded 1st Bn Royal Warwickshire Regt, 1934-36; 1936-47: Col at War Office; AAG, HQ Eastern Command, 153 Inf. Bde; AAG Scottish Command; Army HQ India, Dir of Organisation, Selection of Personnel, India (temp. Brig.); retired, 1947. British Resident, CCG, 1947-50. *Recreations:* golf, painting. *Address:* c/o Lloyds Bank, 6 Pall Mall, SW1.

DUKE, Rt. Rev. Michael Geoffrey H.; *see* Hare Duke.

DUKE, Neville Frederick, DSO 1943; OBE 1953; DFC and Two Bars, 1942, 1943, 1944; AFC 1948; MC (Czech) 1946; Managing Director, Duke Aviation; Manager, Dowty Group Aircraft Operating Unit; Technical Adviser, Consultant, and Chief Test Pilot, Miles Aviation Ltd; *b* 11 Jan. 1922; *s* of Frederick and Jane Duke, Tonbridge, Kent; *m* 1947, Gwendoline Dorothy Fellows. *Educ:* Convent of St Mary and Judds Sch., Tonbridge, Kent. Joined Royal Air Force (cadet), 1940, training period, 1940; 92 Fighter Sqdn, Biggin Hill, 1941; Desert Air Force: 112 Fighter Sqdn, Western Desert, 1941-42, 92 Fighter Sqdn, Western Desert, 1943, Chief Flying Instructor, 73 Operational Training Unit, Egypt, 1943-44, Commanding 145 Sqdn Italy (Fighter), 1944, 28 enemy aircraft destroyed. Hawker Aircraft Ltd test flying, 1945; Empire Test Pilots Sch., 1946; RAF high speed flight, 1946 (world speed record); test flying Aeroplane and Armament Experimental Estab., Boscombe Down, 1947-48; resigned from RAF as Sqdn Leader, 1948; test flying Hawker Aircraft Ltd, 1948; Commanding 615 (County of Surrey) Sqdn, Royal Auxiliary Air Force, Biggin Hill, 1950; Chief Test Pilot, Hawker Aircraft Ltd, 1951-56 (Asst Chief, 1948-51). FRSA 1970; ARAeS 1948. World records: London-Rome, 1949; London-Karachi, 1949; London-Cairo, 1950. World Speed Record, Sept. 1953. Closed Circuit World Speed Record, 1953. Gold Medal Royal Danish Aero Club, 1953; Gold Medal, Royal Aero Club, 1954; two De la Vaux Medals, FAI, 1954; Segrave Trophy, 1954; Queen's Commendation, 1955. Member: RAF Escaping Soc.; United Service & Royal Aero Club (Associate); Royal Aeronautical Soc. *Publications:* Sound Barrier, 1953; Test Pilot, 1953; Book of Flying, 1954; Book of Flight, 1958; The Crowded Sky (anthology), 1959. *Recreations:* sporting flying, yachting. *Address:* St Mary's, Sidlesham, W Sussex. *Clubs:* Royal Air Force, Royal Air Force Yacht; Royal Cruising, Royal Naval Sailing.

DUKE, Robin Antony Hare, CVO 1975; CBE 1970 (OBE 1961); British Council Representative in Japan, 1967-77; *b* 21 March 1916; *s* of late Reginald Franklyn Hare Duke, CBE, and Diana (*née* Woodforde); *m* 1945, Yvonne, *d* of late R. W. O. Le Bas, OBE; four *s* one *d. Educ:* Lancing Coll.; Brasenose Coll., Oxford (MA). Royal Artillery, 1939-46 (staff, ME, Italy, Greece, 1942-45; Political Adviser's Office, Athens, 1945-46). Joined British Council, 1947; Budapest, 1948-50; Dir, British Inst., Salonika, 1950-51; Athens, 1951-52; Dep. Dir, Visitors Dept, 1952-55; Representative, Chile, 1955-61; Dep. Controller, Books, Arts and Science Div., 1961-66; Controller, 1966-67; Rep., Japan, 1967-77, retd. Order of Sacred Treasure (Japan), 3rd Cl., 1975. *Recreations:* gardening, music, theatre. *Address:* c/o Hoare's Bank, 16 Waterloo Place, SW1. *Club:* Travellers'.

DUKE-ELDER, Sir Stewart, GCVO 1958 (KCVO 1946); Kt 1933; GCStJ, FRS 1960; MA (first-class Hons.), BSc (Sp. Distinction), DSc, PhD (London), MD (gold medal), ChB (St Andrews); FRCS, FRCP; Extra Surgeon-Oculist to the Queen, 1965-73, Surgeon-Oculist, 1952-65 (formerly to King Edward

VIII and to King George VI): Counsellor, Order of St John; Hon. Ophthalmic Consultant to the Royal Air Force; Ophthalmic Consultant, London Transport; Director of Research, Institute of Ophthalmology, University of London, 1947-65; President, 1965; Hon. Consulting Ophthalmic Surgeon, St George's Hospital, London and Moorfields Eye Hospital; Fellow University College, London, and Institute of Ophthalmology; surgeon-oculist in London, 1929-76; *m* 1928, Phyllis Mary, MB, BS, *d* of W. Edgar, London. *Educ:* St Andrews and London Univs. St Andrews Univ., 1st Foundation Scholar, 1915; British Assocn medallist, 1915; Demr. of Physiology (St Andrews), 1918; University Coll. Scholar, 1919; Demonstrator of Anatomy, 1920; Pres. Students' Union and Representative Council, 1921; Royal Infirmary, Edinburgh, 1922; St George's Hospital London, 1923; Henry George Plimmer Research Fellow, 1925; Sir Francis Laking Research Scholar, 1926-29; Paul Philip Reitlinger Prizeman, 1926; BMA Scholar, 1927; BMA Middlemore Prizeman, 1928; William Mackenzie Memorial Medallist (Glasgow), 1929; Research Associate, UC, London, 1930; Howe Lecturer in Ophthalmology, Harvard Univ., USA, 1930; Nettleship Medal for Research in Ophthalmology, 1933; Howe Medallist (USA), 1946; Research Medallist, American Medical Association, 1947; Donders Medallist (Holland), 1947; Doyne Medallist, Oxford, 1948; Proctor Lect., USA, 1951; Gullstrand Medallist (Sweden), 1952; Craig Prizeman (Belfast), 1952; Medallist, Strasbourg Univ., 1952, Ghent Univ., 1953; Gonin Medallist (International), 1954; Lister Medal, 1956; Bowman Medal, 1957; Ophthalmiatreion Medal, Athens, 1957; Charles Mickle Fellow, Toronto, 1959; Proctor Medal (USA) 1960; Fothergillian Medal, 1962; Lang Medal (Royal Society of Medicine), 1965. Served in Army during War of 1939-45 (Brigadier, RAMC), 1940-46; Consulting Ophthalmic Surgeon to the Army, 1946-61, now Emeritus; Examiner in Ophthalmology, RCS, 1947-51; Editor, Ophthalmic Literature; Chm. Editorial Board, British Jl Ophthalmology, 1948-73. Hon. Life Pres., International Council of Ophthalmology; Past President: Faculty of Ophthalmologists; Ophthalmological Soc., UK; Hon. Member: American, Canadian, Australian, French, Belgian, Danish, German, Swedish, Dutch, Swiss, Italian, Lombardy, Greek, Pan-American, Mexican, Egyptian, All-Indian and Hyderabad Ophthalmic Socs; National Association for Research in Ophthalmology (USA); Ophthalmic Institute of Australia; Australian Coll. of Ophthalmology; Hon. Life Pres., Greek Ophthalmological Soc.; Hon. Mem. Royal Society Sciences, Uppsala; Fellow, Med. Soc. Sweden; Royal Netherlands Acad. of Sciences; Hon. Fellow, Internat. Soc. of Eye Surgeons; Hon. For. Mem., l'Académie royale de médecine de Belgique; Amer. Acad. Arts and Sciences; Member: Med. Acad., Rome; Royal Acad., Athens; Chm., Med. Advisory Cttee, Royal Commonwealth Soc. for the Blind; Consultant, National Soc., Prevention of Blindness, USA; Canadian Nat. Inst. Blindness; Hon. Fellow American Medical Assoc.; American Acad. Ophthalmology; Pan-American Med. Soc.; Pan-American Surg. Assoc.; Hon. DSc (Northwestern, McGill, Manchester), Hon. MD (Dublin), DM (Utrecht, Strasbourg, Ghent, Athens), LLD (St Andrews); Hon. FRCS Edinburgh; FACS; FRACS; Hon. FRSM; Fellow, UMIST; Hon. Col RAMC; Bronze Star Medal (USA); Star of Jordan (1st class). Kt Comdr, Royal Order of the Phoenix (Greece); Comdr of Orthodox Crusaders, Order of the Holy Sepulchre (Jerusalem). *Publications:* Text-Book of Ophthalmology, Vols I-VII, 1932-54; System of Ophthalmology, Vols I-XV, 1958-76; Century of International Ophthalmology, 1958; British Ophthalmological Monographs, III, 1927; IV 1930; Recent Advances in Ophthalmology, 1927, 4th edn 1951; Diseases of the Eye (16th edn), 1969; The Practice of Refraction, 8th edn, 1968; numerous scientific and clinical papers in the Proceedings of the Royal Society, Board of Research for Industrial Fatigue, and other British, European and American ophthalmic journals, etc. *Address:* 28 Elm Tree Road, NW8. *T:* 01-286 9491. *Club:* Athenæum.

DUKES, Dame Marie; *see* Rambert, Dame Marie.

DULBECCO, Dr Renato; Distinguished Research Professor, The Salk Institute for Biological Studies, since 1977; *b* 22 Feb. 1914; *s* of late Leonardo Dulbecco and late Maria Virdia; *m* 1963, Maureen R. Muir Dulbecco; one *s* two *d. Educ:* Univ. of Turin Medical Sch. (MD). Assistente, Univ. of Turin: Inst. Pathology, 1940-46; Anatomical Inst., 1946-47; Res. Assoc., Indiana Univ., 1947-49; Sen. Res. Fellow, 1949-52, Assoc. Prof., 1952-54, Prof. 1954-63, California Inst. Technology; Vis. Prof., Rockefeller Inst., 1962; Royal Soc. Vis. Prof. at Univ. of Glasgow, 1963-64; Resident Fellow, Salk Inst., Calif, 1963-72; Imperial Cancer Research Fund: Asst Dir of Res., 1972-74; Dep. Dir of Res., 1974-77. MNAS; Foreign Member: Academia dei Lincei, 1969; Royal Society, 1974. (Jtly) Nobel Prize for Medicine, 1975. Hon.

DSc Yale, 1968; Hon. LLD Glasgow, 1970. *Publications:* (jtly) Microbiology, 1967; numerous in sci. jls. *Recreation:* music. *Address:* The Salk Institute, PO Box 1809, San Diego, Calif 92112, USA. *Club:* Athenæum.

DULVERTON, 2nd Baron, *cr* 1929, of Batsford; **Frederick Anthony Hamilton Wills,** CBE 1974; TD; MA Oxon; Bt 1897; *b* 19 Dec. 1915; *s* of 1st Baron Dulverton, OBE, and Victoria May, OBE (*d* 1968), 3rd *d* of Rear-Adm. Sir Edward Chichester, 9th Bt, CB, CMG; *S* father, 1956; *m* 1st, 1939, Judith Betty (marr. diss., 1960), *e d* of late Lieut-Col Hon. Ian Leslie Melville, TD; two *s* two *d* ; 2nd, 1962, Ruth Violet, *o d* of Sir Walter Farquhar, 5th Bt. *Educ:* Eton; Magdalen Coll., Oxford (MA). Commissioned Lovat Scouts (TA), 1935; Major, 1943. President: Timber Growers' Orgn Ltd; Bath and West and Southern Counties Agric. Soc., 1973; British Deer Soc., 1973; Three Counties Agric. Soc., 1975; Member: Red Deer Commn; Scottish Adv. Ctte to Nature Conservancy Council. Joint Master: N Cotswold Foxhounds, 1950-56; Heythrop Foxhounds, 1967-70. Chm., Dulverton Trust. *Heir: s* Hon. Gilbert Michael Hamilton Wills, *b* 2 May 1944. *Address:* Batsford Park, Moreton-in-Marsh, Glos. *T:* 50303; Fassfern, Kinlocheil, Fort William, Inverness-shire. *T:* Kinlocheil 232. *Club:* Boodles's.

DULY, Sidney John, MA; Consultant on the carriage of goods by sea; *b* London, 30 Oct. 1891; *s* of Henry Charles Duly; *m* 1916, Florence, *d* of William George Smith. *Educ:* St Olave's Gram. Sch.; Corpus Christi Coll., Cambridge; Berlin Univ. Till 1941 Head of the Dept for the Scientific Study of Commercial Products, City of London Coll. Visited Pacific Coast of N America for Furness Withy, to find cause of rusting of canned goods on voyage home (a success), 1926; further voyages of investigation in 1927, 1929, 1930, 1932, 1933, 1934, 1935, 1936 and 1937. A Governor, City of London College, 1950-70. Dir, Cargocaire Ltd, 1946-60. *Address:* 34 Sheldon Court, Bath Road, Worthing, West Sussex.

du MAURIER, Dame Daphne, DBE 1969; **(Lady Browning);** writer; *b* 1907; 2nd *d* of late Sir Gerald du Maurier; *m* 1932, Lieut-Gen. Sir Frederick A. M. Browning, GCVO, KBE, CB, DSO (*d* 1965); one *s* two *d. Educ:* privately; in Paris. Began writing short stories and articles in 1928; first novel appeared 1931. *Publications:* The Loving Spirit, 1931; I'll Never Be Young Again, 1932; The Progress of Julius, 1933; Gerald, a Portrait, 1934; Jamaica Inn, 1936; The du Mauriers, 1937; Rebecca, 1938; Frenchman's Creek, 1941; Hungry Hill, 1943; The King's General, 1946; The Parasites, 1949; My Cousin Rachel, 1951; The Apple Tree, 1952; Mary Anne, 1954; The Scapegoat, 1957; The Breaking Point, 1959; The Infernal World of Branwell Brontë, 1960; Castle Dor (continuation of MS left by late Sir Arthur Quiller-Couch (Q)), 1962; The Glassblowers, 1963; The Flight of the Falcon, 1965; Vanishing Cornwall, 1967; The House on the Strand, 1969; Not After Midnight, 1971; Rule Britannia, 1972; Golden Lads: a study of Anthony Bacon, Francis and their Friends, 1975; The Winding Stair: Francis Bacon, his Rise and Fall, 1976; *autobiography:* Growing Pains, 1977; *drama: The Years Between, 1945; September Tide, 1948; edited:* The Young George du Maurier, 1951. *Recreations:* walking and swimming. *Address:* Kilmarth, Par, Cornwall. *See also Viscount Montgomery of Alamein* .

DUMBELL, Dr Keith Rodney; Professor of Virology, University of London at St Mary's Hospital Medical School, since 1964; *b* 2 Oct. 1922; *s* of late Stanley Dumbell and Dorothy Ellen (*née* Hewitt); *m* 1st, 1950, Brenda Margaret (*née* Heathcote) (*d* 1971); two *d* ; 2nd, 1972, Susan (*née* Herd); two *s. Educ:* Wirral Gram. Sch.; University of Liverpool, MB, ChB 1944; MD (Liverpool), 1950. FRCPath 1975. Asst Lecturer, Dept of Bacteriology, University of Liverpool, 1945-47; Mem. of Scientific Staff, MRC, 1947-50; Junior Pathologist, RAF, 1950-52; Asst in Pathology and Microbiology, Rockefeller Inst. for Medical Research (Dr Peyton Rous' laboratory), 1952-53; Lecturer in Bacteriology, University of Liverpool, 1952-58; Senior Lecturer, 1958-64. *Publications:* articles in various medical and scientific journals. *Address:* 19 Hillcroft Crescent, Ealing, W5. *T:* 01-997 5528.

DUMFRIES, Earl of; John Colum Crichton-Stuart; *b* 26 April 1958; *s* and *heir* of 6th Marquess of Bute, *qv. Address:* Mount Stuart, Rothesay, Isle of Bute. *T:* Rothesay 2730.

DUMINY, Jacobus Petrus; Principal and Vice-Chancellor, University of Cape Town, 1958-67; *b* 16 Dec. 1897; *s* of Johan Andreas Duminy and Maria Catherina Zeederberg; *m* 1930, Gwendoline Ellen Finnemore; two *s* one *d. Educ:* Cape Town Univ. (MA); Oxford Univ. (Rhodes Scholar) (MA, BSc); the Sorbonne. Lecturer in Mathematics and Astronomy, Transvaal

Univ. Coll., 1923; Prof. in Mathematics, University of Pretoria, 1930. Principal, Pretoria Technical Coll., 1942. First Vice-Pres., Rotary International, 1969-70. Coronation Medal, 1953. Hon. LLD: Natal, 1962; Rhodes, 1967; Cape Town, 1973. *Publications:* various papers on scientific and educational subjects. *Recreations:* tennis, reading, writing, music, drama. *Address:* 2 Winchcombe, The Cotswolds, Kenilworth, Cape 7700, S Africa. *Clubs:* Vincent's (Oxford); City (Pretoria); Owl; WP Sports; WP Cricket; City and Civil Service (Cape Town).

DUMMETT, George Anthony, CEng, FIChemE; Chairman, Council of Engineering Institutions, 1976-77 (Vice-Chairman, 1975); *b* 13 Oct. 1907; *s* of George Herbert Dummett and Gertrude (*née* Higgins); *m* 1st, 1931, Peggy Schaeffer; 2nd, 1939, Ursula Margarete Schubert; two *s* one *d*. *Educ:* Rugby Sch.; Birmingham Univ.; Pembroke Coll., Cambridge. MA. Research in phys. chem., Cambridge Univ., 1930-32; Research Asst, Thorncliffe Coal Distillation Ltd, 1932-35; APV Co. Ltd (then Aluminium Plant and Vessel Co. Ltd): Technical Res. Asst, 1935; Laboratory Man., 1943; Chem. Engrg Dept Man., 1948; Scientific Man., 1949; Res. Dir, 1956; Dep. Man. Dir, 1965-72; Dir, APV (Holdings) Ltd, 1962-72; Dep. Chm., APV Internat., 1965-72; Director: Diamond Power Specialty Ltd, 1958-; ACE Machinery (Holdings) Ltd, 1972-. Chm., Res. Cttee, FBI, 1958-65; Pres., IChemE, 1968-69. Fellow, Fellowship of Engineering, 1977. Chm., European Fedn Chemical Engrng, 1977-78. Hon. Member: Soc. de Chimie Ind., 1969; Dechema, 1976. *Publications:* numerous papers on chemical and biochemical engrg, metallurgy, etc. *Recreations:* music, mountaineering, gardening, stamp collecting. *Address:* Gowans, Possingworth Close, Cross-in-Hand, Heathfield, Sussex TN21 0TL. *T:* Heathfield 2085. *Clubs:* Alpine, Climbers, Anglo-Belgian.
See also *M . A . E . Dummett , R . B . Dummett* .

DUMMETT, Michael Anthony Eardley, FBA 1968; Fellow, since 1950 and Senior Research Fellow, since 1974, All Souls College, Oxford; *b* 27 June 1925; *s* of George Herbert Dummett and Iris Dummett (*née* Eardley-Wilmot); *m* 1951, Ann, *d* of Arthur and Kitty Chesney; three *s* two *d* (one *s* one *d* decd). *Educ:* Sandroyd Sch.; Winchester Coll. (1st Scholar); Christ Church, Oxford. Major hist. schol. (Ch. Ch.), 1942. Served in Army, 1943-47: in RA and Intell. Corps (India, 1945, Malaya, 1946-47, Sgt). Ch. Ch., Oxford, 1947-50, First Class Hons, PPE, 1950. Asst Lectr in Philosophy, Birmingham Univ., 1950-51; Commonwealth Fund Fellow, Univ. of California, Berkeley, 1955-56; Reader in the Philosophy of Mathematics, Univ. of Oxford, 1962-74; Sub-Warden, All Souls College, 1974-76. Vis. Lectr, Univ. of Ghana, 1958; Vis. Professor: Stanford Univ., several occasions, 1960-66; Univ. of Minnesota, 1968; Princeton Univ., 1970; Rockefeller Univ., 1973; William James Lectr in Philosophy, Harvard Univ., 1976. Founder Mem., Oxford Cttee for Racial Integration, 1965 (Chm., Jan.-May 1966); Member: Exec. Cttee, Campaign Against Racial Discrimination, 1966-67; Legal and Civil Affairs Panel, Nat. Cttee for Commonwealth Immigrants, 1966-68; Chm., Jt Council for the Welfare of Immigrants, 1970-71 (Vice-Chm., 1967-69, 1973-75). *Publications:* Frege: philosophy of language, 1973; The Justification of Deduction, 1973; Elements of Intuitionism, 1977; Truth and other Enigmas, 1977; contrib. entry on Frege, to Encyclopedia of Philosophy (ed P. Edwards), 1967; (with Ann Dummett) chapter on Rôle of the Government, in Justice First (ed L. Donnelly), 1969; articles in: Aristotelian Soc. Proceedings, Philos. Review, Econometrica, Jl of Symbolic Logic, Zeitschrift für mathematische Logik, Dublin Review, New Blackfriars, Clergy Review, Jl of Warburg and Courtauld Insts. *Recreations:* listening to the blues, investigating the history of card games, reading science fiction. *Address:* 54 Park Town, Oxford. *T:* Oxford 58698.

DUMMETT, Robert Bryan, CBE 1973; Chairman, London Board, Commercial Bank of Australia, since 1975 (Member, since 1972); Director, Midland and International Banks Ltd, since 1975; *b* 15 July 1912; 2nd *s* of G. H. Dummett; *m* 1936, Mary, *d* of R. A. Grieve; one *s* one *d*. *Educ:* Rugby Sch.; Göttingen Univ.; Trinity Coll., Cambridge. Joined Anglo-Iranian Oil Co., 1936. HM Legation, Berne, 1941-45. Managing Dir, BP Marketing Interests in Australia, 1953-57; a Man. Dir, BP Ltd, 1957-72; a Dep. Chm., BP Ltd, 1967-72. Grand Officer, Order of Merit (Italy), 1967, Cavaliere di Gran Croce, 1970. *Recreation:* gardening. *Address:* Gulson's, Boxted, Essex. *T:* Boxted 207; 4 Audley Square, W1. *T:* 01-499 2884. *Club:* Australian (Melbourne).

DUMPER, Rt. Rev. Anthony Charles; *see* Dudley, Bishop Suffragan of.

DUNALLEY, 6th Baron *cr* 1800; **Henry Desmond Graham Prittie;** Lt-Col (retired) late The Rifle Brigade; *b* 14 Oct. 1912;

er *s* of 5th Baron Dunalley, DSO, and Beatrix Evelyn (*d* 1967), *e d* of late James N. Graham of Carfin, Lanarkshire; *S* father, 1948; *m* 1947, Philippa, *o d* of late Hon. Philip Cary; two *s* one *d*. *Educ:* Stowe; RMC, Sandhurst. Retd 1953. *Recreation:* fishing. *Heir:* *s* Hon. Henry Francis Cornelius Prittie, *b* 30 May 1948. *Address:* Glendalough Lodge, Recess, Co. Galway. *Club:* Kildare Street and University (Dublin).
See also Hon. *T. C. F. Prittie.*

DUNBAR, Alexander Arbuthnott; Director, Scottish Arts Council, since 1971; *b* 14 March 1929; *yr s* of Sir Edward Dunbar, 9th Bt; *m* 1965, Elizabeth Susannah, *d* of Rev. Denzil Wright; one *s* one *d*. *Educ:* Wellington Coll., Berks; Pembroke Coll., Cambridge (MA). Mil. Service, Lieut QO Cameron Highlanders, 1947-49. Called to the Bar, Inner Temple, 1953. Joined ICI, 1954: Asst Sec., Wilton Works, 1959-63. Joined North Eastern Assoc. for the Arts, 1963, Sec. 1964, Dir 1967; Director: Northern Arts Assoc., 1967-69; UK and British Commonwealth Branch, Calouste Gulbenkian Foundn, 1970-71. Sec., Standing Conf. of Regional Arts Assocs, 1967-69. *Publications:* contribs to various jls. *Recreations:* art, theatre, ski-ing. *Address:* 53 Northumberland Street, Edinburgh EH3 6JQ.

DUNBAR, Alexander Robert, CBE 1964 (OBE 1956); FCIT; transport consultant; *b* 20 Oct. 1904; *s* of Robert MacKay Dunbar and Isabella Dunbar; *m* 1941, Margaret Wilby; one *s* one *d*. *Educ:* Whitehill Sch., Glasgow. Traffic Apprentice, LNER, 1924; various Rly Operating appts. Operating Supt (Eastern) BR, 1948; Asst Gen. Man., N Eastern Region, 1954; Manpower Adviser, British Transport Commission, 1958; Mem., British Railways Board, 1962. Chm., British Express Carriers Ltd, 1969-72. Chm., St Margaret's House Settlement; Member: Ind. Trng Service Bd; London University Appointments Board. Past Pres., Chartered Inst. of Transport; Past Pres. Rly Study Assoc.; Lieut-Col, Engineer and Rly Staff Corps, RE (TA). OStJ. *Publications:* various papers, Inst. of Transport. *Recreations:* walking and fishing. *Address:* Garden Cottage, New Lodge, Windsor Forest, Berks. *T:* Winkfield Row 2696; 29 John Street, WC1. *T:* 01-405 5602.

DUNBAR of Northfield, Sir Archibald (Ranulph), 11th Bt *cr* 1700; *b* 8 Aug. 1927; *er s* of Sir (Archibald) Edward Dunbar, 9th Bt (by some reckonings 10th Bt) and Olivia Douglas Sinclair (*d* 1964), *d* of Maj.-Gen. Sir Edward May, KCB, CMG; *S* father, 1969; *m* 1974, Amelia Millar Sommerville, *d* of Horace Davidson; one *s* two *d*. *Educ:* Wellington Coll.; Pembroke Coll., Cambridge; Imperial Coll. of Tropical Agriculture, Trinidad. Mil. Service, 2nd Lt, Cameron (att. Gordon) Highlanders, 1945-48. Entered Colonial Agricultural Service, Uganda, as Agricultural Officer, 1953; retired, 1970. *Publications:* A History of Bunyoro-Kitara, 1965; Omukama Chwa II Kabarega, 1965; The Annual Crops of Uganda, 1969; various articles in Uganda Jl. *Recreations:* cross-country running, swimming. *Heir:* *s* Edward Horace Dunbar, Younger of Northfield, *b* 18 March 1977. *Address:* The Old Manse, Duffus, Elgin, Scotland. *T:* Hopeman 270. *Club:* New (Edinburgh).

DUNBAR, Charles, CB 1964; Director, Fighting Vehicles Research and Development Establishment, Ministry of Defence, 1960-67; *b* 12 Jan. 1907; *s* of John Dunbar, Barrow-in-Furness, Lancs; *m* 1933, Mary Alice (*née* Clarke), Barnes, SW; two *d*. *Educ:* Grammar Sch., Barrow-in-Furness; Manchester Univ. (MSc). National Physical Laboratory, Dept of Scientific and Industrial Research, 1929-43; Tank Armament Research Establishment, Min. of Supply, 1943-47; Fighting Vehicles Research and Development Establishments, 1947-67, retired. *Publications:* contribs to learned journals. *Recreations:* golf, fishing. *Address:* Edenwood, Chobham Road, Camberley, Surrey. *T:* Camberley 26592.
See also Peter Graham.

DUNBAR, Maj.-Gen. Charles Whish, CBE 1968; *b* 2 June 1919; *s* of late Dr J. Dunbar, FRCS, Auchterarder, Scotland; *m* 1941, Jean Elinor Kerr Morton; two *s* one *d*. *Educ:* Glasgow High Sch.; Glasgow Univ. Commnd 2nd Lieut into Royal Northumberland Fusiliers, 1940; served with Maritime RA, 1940-43; served with Para. Regt 1944-48; transf. to RA 1945; Transf. to Highland Light Inf., 1946; Co. Comdr with a Para. Bn and DAA&QMG and Bde Major, Para. Bde Palestine, 1945-48; Staff Coll., 1949; Co. Comdr with HLI, N Africa, Malta and Egypt, 1951-53; Bde Major, Para. Bde, Cyprus; Suez, 1956; 2 i/c Para. Bn, 1957; Jordan, 1958; comd Depot RHF, 1958-59; comd 1 RHF in Aden, Malta and Libya, 1960-62; comd Inf. Bde Gp, Germany, 1962-65; IDC, 1966; Brig. Gen. Staff, HQ, MELF, Aden, 1967; GOC North West District, 1968-70; Director of Infantry, 1970-73, retired 1973; Col, Royal Highland Fusiliers, 1969-. Vice-Pres., ACF Assoc. (Scotland), 1976-. Dir, British

Red Cross Soc., Perth and Kinross, 1977-. Mem., Royal Company of Archers (Queen's Body Guard for Scotland). *Recreation:* general sport. *Address:* Milton, Auchterarder, Perthshire PH3 1DP. *T:* Auchterarder 2242. *Club:* Army and Navy.

DUNBAR, Sir David H.; *see* Hope-Dunbar.

DUNBAR of Durn, Sir Drummond Cospatrick Ninian, 9th Bt, *cr* 1697; MC 1943; Major Black Watch, retired; *b* 9 May 1917; *o s* of Sir George Alexander Drummond Dunbar, 8th Bt and Sophie Kathleen (*d* 1936), *d* of late J. Benson Kennedy; *S* father, 1949; *m* 1957, Sheila Barbara Mary, *d* of John B. de Fonblanque, London; one *s. Educ:* Radley Coll.; Worcester Coll., Oxford. BA 1938. Served War of 1939-45, Middle East, Sicily, Normandy (wounded twice, MC). Retired pay, 1958. *Heir: s* Robert Drummond Cospatrick Dunbar, *Younger* of Durn, *b* 17 June 1958. *Address:* Beaufield House, St Saviour, Jersey, Channel Islands. *Club:* Naval and Military.

DUNBAR of Mochrum, Sir Jean Ivor, 13th Bt *cr* 1694; *b* 4 April 1918; *s* of Sir Adrian Ivor Dunbar of Mochrum, 12th Bt and Emma Marie (*d* 1925), *d* of Jean Wittevrongel; *S* father, 1977; *m* 1944, Rose Jeanne, *d* of Henry William Hertsch; two *s* one *d*. Formerly Sergeant, Mountain Engineers, US Army. *Heir: s* James Michael Dunbar, *b* 17 Jan. 1950.

DUNBAR, Sir J(ohn) Greig, Kt 1962; DL; company director since 1931; *b* 19 Sept. 1906; *s* of John Gillison Dunbar and Anne Gardner Greig; *m* 1931, Elizabeth Hart Roy; two *s* one *d. Educ:* Royal High Sch., Edinburgh. Banking Apprenticeship, 1923-27; Company Sec., 1930; Bank Dir, 1963; Director: Royal Bank of Scotland, 1963-71; United Biscuits (Holdings) Ltd, 1965-71. Chm. Transport Users Consultative Cttee for Scotland, 1963-; Member: Council, Scottish Special Housing Assoc. Ltd, 1964-69; South of Scotland Electricity Bd, 1969-; Scottish Local Govt Staff Commn, 1973. Lord Provost, City of Edinburgh, 1960-63. DL, City of Edinburgh, 1963. Hon. LLD (Edinburgh), 1962. *Address:* 30 Midmar Gardens, Edinburgh EH10 6DZ. *Club:* New (Edinburgh).

DUNBAR of Hempriggs, Dame Maureen Daisy Helen, (Lady Dunbar of Hempriggs), Btss (8th in line) *cr* 1706 (NS); *b* 19 Aug. 1906; *d* of Courtenay Edward Moore and Janie King Moore (*née* Askins); *m* 1940, Leonard James Blake (assumed the name of Dunbar, in lieu of Blake, on claiming succession to the Hempriggs baronetcy after death of kinsman, Sir George Cospatrick Duff-Sutherland-Dunbar, 7th Bt, in 1963; claim established and title recognised by Lyon Court, 1965); one *s* one *d. Educ:* Headington Sch.; Royal Coll. of Music. LRAM 1928. Music teacher at: Monmouth Sch. for Girls, 1930-33; Oxford High Sch., 1935-40; Malvern Coll., 1957-68. *Heir:* (to mother's Btcy) *s* Richard Francis Dunbar of Hempriggs, younger [*b* 8 Jan. 1945 (assumed the name of Dunbar, 1965); *m* 1969, Elizabeth Margaret Jane Lister]. *Address:* 51 Gloucester Street, Winchcombe, Cheltenham, Glos. *T:* Winchcombe 602 122; Ackergill Tower, Wick, Caithness. *T:* Wick 2812.

DUNBAR-NASMITH, Rear-Adm. David Arthur, CB 1969; DSC 1942; DL; retired 1972; Deputy Chairman, Highlands and Islands Development Board, since 1972; *b* 21 Feb. 1921; *e s* of late Admiral Sir Martin Dunbar-Nasmith, VC, KCB, KCMG, DL, and of late Justina Dunbar-Nasmith, CBE, DStJ; *m* 1951, Elizabeth Bowlby; two *s* two *d. Educ:* Lockers Park; RNC, Dartmouth. To sea as Midshipman, 1939. War Service, Atlantic and Mediterranean, in HM Ships Barham, Rodney, Kelvin and Petard. In comd: HM Ships Haydon 1943, Peacock 1945-46, Moon 1946, Rowena 1946-48, Enard Bay 1951, Alert 1954-56, Berwick, and 5th Frigate Squadron, 1961-63; Commodore, Amphibious Forces, 1966-67. RN and Joint Service Staff Colls, 1948-49; Staff of Flag Officer 1st Cruiser Squadron, 1949-51; NATO HQ, SACLANT, 1952-54 and SACEUR, 1958-60; Dir of Defence Plans, Min. of Defence, 1963-65; Naval Secretary, 1967-70; Flag Officer, Scotland and N Ireland, 1970-72. Comdr 1951; Capt. 1958; Rear-Adm. 1967. Mem., Countryside Commn for Scotland, 1972-76. Mem. Queen's Body Guard for Scotland (Royal Company of Archers), 1974-. DL Moray, 1974. *Recreations:* sailing, ski-ing and shooting. *Address:* Glen of Rothes, Rothes, Moray. *T:* Rothes 216. *Clubs:* New (Edinburgh); Highland (Inverness); Royal Ocean Racing. *See also J. D. Dunbar-Nasmith.*

DUNBAR-NASMITH, James Duncan, CBE 1976; RIBA; PPRIAS; Partner, Law & Dunbar-Nasmith, architects, Edinburgh (founded 1957); *b* 15 March 1927; *y s* of late Adm. Sir Martin Dunbar-Nasmith, VC, KCB, KCMG, DL and of late Justina Dunbar-Nasmith, CBE, DStJ. *Educ:* Lockers Park; Winchester. Trinity Coll., Cambridge (BA); Edinburgh Coll. of

Art (DA). ARIBA 1954. Lieut, Scots Guards, 1945-48. President: Royal Incorporation of Architects in Scotland, 1971-73; Edinburgh Architectural Assoc., 1967-69. Member: Council, RIBA, 1967-73 (a Vice-Pres., 1972-73; Chm., Bd of Educn, 1972-73); Royal Commn on Ancient and Historical Monuments of Scotland, 1972-; Ancient Monuments Bd for Scotland, 1969- (interim Chm., 1972-73); Historic Buildings Council for Scotland, 1966-; Edinburgh Festival Soc., 1966-; Trustee, Scottish Civic Trust, 1971-; Chm., Scottish Exec. Cttee of European Architectural Heritage Year. *Recreations:* music, theatre, ski-ing, sailing. *Address:* 16 Dublin Street, Edinburgh EH1 3RE. *T:* 031-556 8631. *Clubs:* Royal Ocean Racing; New (Edinburgh). *See also D. A. Dunbar-Nasmith.*

DUNBOYNE, 28th Baron by Summons, 18th Baron by Patent; **Patrick Theobald Tower Butler; His Honour Judge The Lord Dunboyne;** a Circuit Judge, since 1972; *b* 27 Jan. 1917; *e s* of 27th Baron Dunboyne and Dora Isolde Butler (*d* 1977), *e d* of Comdr F. F. Tower; *S* father, 1945; *m* 1950, Anne Marie, *d* of late Sir Victor Mallet; one *s* three *d. Educ:* Winchester; Trinity Coll., Cambridge (MA). Pres. of Cambridge Union. Lieut Irish Guards (Suppl. Res.); served European War, 1939-44 (prisoner, then repatriated); Foreign Office, 1945-46. Barrister-at-Law, Middle Temple (Harmsworth Scholar), Inner Temple, South-Eastern Circuit, King's Inns, Dublin. In practice 1949-71. Dep. Chm., Mddx Quarter Sessions, 1963-65. Recorder of Hastings, 1961-71; Dep. Chm., QS: Kent, 1963-71; Inner London 1971-72. Commissary Gen., Diocese of Canterbury, 1959-71. *Publications:* The Trial of J. G. Haigh, 1953; (with others) Cambridge Union, 1815-1939, 1953; Butler Family History, 1966. *Recreations:* rowing, lawn tennis, chess. *Heir: s* Hon. John Fitzwalter Butler [*b* 31 July 1951; *m* 1975, Diana Caroline, *yr d* of Sir Michael Williams, *qv*; one *d*]. *Address:* 36 Ormonde Gate, SW3 4HA. *T:* 01-352 1837. *Clubs:* Irish; International Lawn Tennis Clubs of Great Britain (Pres.) and of USA; All England Lawn Tennis Club (Wimbledon); Pitt, Union (Cambridge).

DUNCAN, Alfred Charles; *b* 1886; *s* of Samuel Duncan and Mary (*née* McDowell); *m* 1st, 1913, Elizabeth Oakley; two *s* ; 2nd 1930, Gwendoline Davies. *Educ:* Dublin and London Univs. Banking and business experience in Winnipeg, Canada, 1906-08; company and private secretarial experience in City of London, 1910-11; articled clerk to Messrs Franklin Wild & Co., Chartered Accountants, City of London, 1912-16. Served European War, 1914-18, with Artists Rifles, 1917-18. Qualified as Chartered Accountant, 1919. Odhams Press Ltd: Chief Accountant, 1920; Sec. and Chief Acct, 1921; Exec. Dir and Sec., 1942; Financial Dir, 1946; Financial and Joint Managing Dir, 1947; Chm., 1949-60. *Recreations:* golf, literature, preferably philosophical. *Address:* 7 Sherbrook Close, Budleigh Salterton, Devon. *T:* Budleigh Salterton 3416. *Club:* Golfers.

DUNCAN, Prof. Archibald Alexander McBeth; Professor of Scottish History and Literature, Glasgow University, since 1962; *b* 17 Oct. 1926; *s* of Charles George Duncan and Christina Helen McBeth; *m* 1954, Ann Hayes Sawyer, *d* of W. E. H. Sawyer, Oxford; two *s* one *d. Educ:* George Heriot's Sch.; Edinburgh Univ.; Balliol Coll., Oxford. Lecturer in History, Queen's Univ., Belfast, 1951-53; Lecturer in History, Edinburgh Univ., 1953-61; Leverhulme Research Fellow, 1961-62. Mem. Royal Commn on the Ancient and Historical Monuments of Scotland, 1969-. *Publication:* Scotland: The Making of the Kingdom, 1975. *Address:* 17 Campbell Drive, Bearsden, Glasgow G61 4NF.

DUNCAN, Prof. Archibald Sutherland, DSC 1943; FRCSE, FRCPE, FRCOG; Executive Dean of the Faculty of Medicine and Professor of Medical Education, Edinburgh University, 1966-76; *b* 17 July 1914; *y s* of late Rev. H. C. Duncan, *k-i-H,* DD and late Rose Elsie Edwards; *m* 1939, Barbara, *d* of late John Gibson Holliday, JP, Penrith, Cumberland. *Educ:* Merchiston Castle Sch.; Universities of Edinburgh, Neuchâtel and Heidelberg. MB, ChB Edinburgh, 1936. Resident hosp. appts in Edinburgh and London, 1936-41. Served RNVR Surg. Lieut-Comdr (surg. specialist), 1941-45 (DSC). Temp. Cons. in Obst. and Gynæc., Inverness, 1946; Lectr in Univ. and part-time Cons. Obstetr and Gynæcol., Aberdeen, 1946-50; Sen. Lectr, University of Edinburgh and Obstetr. and Gynæcol. to Western Gen. Hosp., Edinburgh 1950-53; Prof. of Obstetrics and Gynæcology in the Welsh National Sch. of Medicine, Univ. of Wales, 1953-66; Cons. Obstetrician and Gynæcologist, United Cardiff Hosps, 1953-66; Advisor in Obstetrics and Gynæcology to Welsh Hosp. Board, 1953-66. Member: Clin. Res. Bd of MRC, 1965-69; Council, RCSE, 1968-73; GMC, 1974-; Lothian Health Bd, 1977-. Chm., Scottish Council on Disability, 1977-. Hon. Pres., Brit. Med. Students Assoc., 1965-66. Mem., James IV Assoc. of Surgeons. Associate Editor, British Jl of Medical

Education, 1971-75; Consulting Editor, Jl of Medical Ethics; Jt Editor, Dictionary of Medical Ethics. *Publications:* contribs on scientific and allied subjects in various med. jls. *Recreations:* mountains, photography. *Address:* 1 Walker Street, Edinburgh EH3 7JY. *T:* 031-225 7657. *Clubs:* Naval; New (Edinburgh).

DUNCAN, Sir Arthur (Bryce), Kt 1961; Convener Dumfriesshire County Council, 1961-68, retired; *b* 27 Aug. 1909; 2nd *s* of J. B. Duncan, Newlands, Dumfries; *m* 1936, Isabel Mary Kennedy-Moffat; four *s* one *d. Educ:* Rugby; St John's Coll., Cambridge. Chm., The Nature Conservancy, 1953-61, retd. Chm. of Dirs, Crichton Royal Hospital Bd, 1958-72. DL, Dumfriesshire, 1967-69, Lord Lieutenant 1967-69. *Recreations:* ornithology, entomology and shooting. *Address:* Castlehill, Kirkmahoe, Dumfries DG1 1RD.

DUNCAN, Brian Arthur Cullum, CB 1972; CBE 1963 (MBE 1949); QC 1972; Judge Advocate General of the Forces, 1968-72; *b* 2 Feb. 1908; *yr s* of late Frank Hubert Duncan, LDS, RCS, and late Edith Jane Duncan (*née* Cullum); *m* 1934, Irene Flora Templeman, *o c* of late John Frederick Templeman and late Flora Edith Templeman; two *s* two *d. Educ:* Queens' Coll., Cambridge (MA). Called to the Bar, Lincoln's Inn, 1931. Practised South Eastern Circuit, Central Criminal Court, North London Sessions, and Herts and Essex Sessions. Commissioned RAF, April 1940; relinqd commn, 1950 (Wing Comdr). Joined JAG's Dept, 1945. Dep. Judge Advocate Gen. (Army and RAF): Middle East, 1950-53; Germany, 1954-57; Far East, 1959-62; Vice Judge Advocate Gen., 1967-68. *Recreations:* tennis, swimming. *Address:* Culverlands, Neville Park, Baltonsborough, Glastonbury, Som. *Club:* Naval and Military.

DUNCAN, Colin; *see* Duncan, (P.) C.

DUNCAN, David Francis; HM Diplomatic Service, retired; *b* 22 Feb. 1923; *s* of late Brig. William Edmondstone Duncan, CVO, DSO, MC, and of Mrs Magdalene Emily Duncan (*née* Renny-Tailyour). *Educ:* Eton; Trinity Coll., Cambridge. Served War, RA, 1941-46 (despatches). Entered Foreign (later Diplomatic) Service, 1949; Foreign Office, 1949-52; Bogotá, 1952-54; UK Delegn to ECSC, Luxembourg, 1954-55; FO, 1955-58; Baghdad, 1958; Ankara, 1958-60; FO, 1960-62; Quito, 1962-65; Phnom Penh, 1965 (as Chargé d'Affaires); FO (later Foreign and Commonwealth Office), 1965-70; Islamabad, 1970-71; Counsellor, UK Delegn to Geneva Disarm. Conf., 1971-74; Ambassador to Nicaragua, 1974-76; retired 1976. *Recreations:* skiing, walking, photography, travel. *Address:* 8 Eaton Mews South, SW1. *Clubs:* Travellers', Hurlingham.

DUNCAN, Rev. Denis Macdonald, MA, BD; Director, Highgate Counselling Centre, since 1969; Associate Director and Training Supervisor, Westminster Pastoral Foundation, since 1971; *b* 10 Jan. 1920; *s* of late Rev. Reginald Duncan, BD, BLitt and late Clarice Ethel (*née* Hodgkinson); *m* 1942, Henrietta Watson McKenzie (*née* Houston); one *s* one *d. Educ:* George Watson's Boys' Coll., Edinburgh; Edinburgh Univ.; New Coll., Edinburgh. Minister of: St Margaret's, Juniper Green, Edinburgh, 1943-49; Trinity Duke Street Parish Church, Glasgow, 1949-57; Founder-editor, Rally, 1956-67; Managing Editor, British Weekly, 1957-70 (Man. Dir, 1967-70); Man. Dir, DPS Publicity Services Ltd, 1967-74; broadcaster and scriptwriter, Scottish Television, 1963-68; concert promotion at Edinburgh Festival and elsewhere, 1966-; Concert series "Communication through the Arts" poetry/music anthologies (with Benita Kyle), 1970-. Chm., Internat. Cttee of World Assocs of Pastoral Care and Counselling, 1977-. FIBA (FIICS) 1976. *Publications:* (ed) Through the Year with William Barclay, 1971; (ed) Through the Year with Cardinal Heenan, 1972; (ed) Daily Celebration, vol. 1, 1972, vol. 2, 1974; Marching Orders I, 1973; (ed) Every Day with William Barclay, 1973; (ed) Through the Year with J. B. Phillips, 1974; Marching On, 1974; Here is my Hand, 1977. *Recreations:* cricket, badminton. *Address:* 1 Cranbourne Road, N10 2BT. *T:* 01-883 1831. *Club:* Arts.

DUNCAN, George; Chairman, Lloyds and Scottish Ltd, since 1976 (Deputy Chairman, 1975-76); *b* 9 Nov. 1933; *s* of William Duncan and Catherine Gray Murray; *m* 1965, Frauke; one *d. Educ:* London Sch. of Economics (BSc(Econ)); Wharton Sch.; Univ. of Pennsylvania (MBA). Mem., Inst. of Chartered Accountants (FCA); FBIM. Chief Executive, Truman Hanbury Buxton and Co. Ltd, 1967-71; Chief Executive, Watney Mann Ltd, 1971-72; Vice-Chm., Internat. Distillers and Vintners Ltd, 1972; Chief Exec., Yule Catto & Co. Ltd, 1973-75. *Recreations:* opera, tennis, shooting. *Address:* Fisher's Gate, Withyham, Hartfield, East Sussex. *T:* Hartfield 246.

DUNCAN, George Alexander; Fellow Emeritus of Trinity College, Dublin, since 1967; Pro-Chancellor of the University of Dublin, 1965-72; *b* 15 May 1902; *s* of Alexander Duncan and Elizabeth Linn; *m* 1932, Eileen Stone, MSc, *d* of William Henry Stone and Sarah Copeland; one *d. Educ:* Ballymena Academy; Campbell Coll., Belfast; Trinity Coll., Dublin; University of North Carolina. BA, LLB 1923, MA 1926; Research Fellow on the Laura Spelman Rockefeller Memorial Foundation, 1924-25; Prof. of Political Economy in the University of Dublin, 1934-67; Registrar of TCD, 1951-52, and Bursar, 1952-57. Leverhulme Research Fellow, 1950; Visiting Fellow, Princeton Univ., 1963-64. Mem. of IFS Commissions of Inquiry into Banking, Currency and Credit, 1934-38; Agriculture, 1939; Emigration and Population, 1948. Planning Officer (temp.) in Ministry of Production, London, 1943-45; Economic Adviser to British National Cttee of Internat. Chambers of Commerce, 1941-47. Vice-Pres., Royal Dublin Society; Life Mem., Mont Pelerin Soc. Formerly Member: Irish National Productivity Cttee; Council Irish Management Inst.; Exec. Bd, Dublin Economic Research Inst.; Internat. Inst. of Statistics. *Publications:* numerous papers in the economic periodicals. *Recreations:* travel, walking. *Address:* 7 Braemor Park, Churchtown, Dublin 14. *T:* Dublin 970442. *Club:* Kildare Street and University (Dublin).

DUNCAN, Dr George Douglas; Regional Medical Officer, East Anglian Regional Health Authority, since 1973; *s* of late George Forman Duncan and Mary Duncan (*née* Davidson); *m* 1949, Isobel (*née* Reid); two *s* one *d. Educ:* Robert Gordon's Coll., Aberdeen; Aberdeen Univ. MB, ChB 1948, DPH 1952, FFCM 1972. Various hosp. appts; Asst MOH Stirlingshire, Divisional MO Grangemouth, 1953-57; Asst Sen. MO, Leeds RHB, 1957-60; Dep. Sen. Admin. MO, Newcastle RHB, 1960-68; Sen. Admin. MO, East Anglian RHB, 1968-73. *Address:* Clare House, Witchford, Ely, Cambs. *T:* Ely 2776; East Anglian Regional Health Authority, Union Lane, Chesterton, Cambridge. *T:* Cambridge 61212.

DUNCAN, Prof. James Playford, ME Adelaide, DSc Manchester; Professor of Mechanical Engineering, University of British Columbia, since 1966; *b* 10 Nov. 1919; *s* of late Hugh Sinclair Duncan and of Nellie Gladys Duncan, Dunbar, Goodwood, Adelaide, S Australia; *m* 1942, Jean Marie Booth; three *s* one *d. Educ:* Scotch Coll., Adelaide; University of Adelaide, S Australia. Executive Engineer, Richards Industries Ltd, Keswick, S Australia, 1941-46; Senior Physics Master, Scotch Coll., Adelaide, 1946-47; Lecturer in Mechanical Engineering, University of Adelaide, 1948-49, Senior Lecturer, 1950-51 and 1953-54; Turbine Engineer, Metropolitan Vickers Electrical Co., Trafford Park, Manchester, 1952; Turner and Newall Research Fellow, University of Manchester, 1955; Lecturer in Mechanical Engineering, University of Manchester, 1956; Prof. of Mechanical Engineering, University of Sheffield, 1956-66. *Recreations:* sailing, flautist. *Address:* 25 Oceanview Road, PO Box 137, Lions Bay, BC V0N 2E0, Canada. *T:* (604) 921-7191.

DUNCAN, James Stuart, CMG 1946; Hon. Air Commodore; company director; *b* 1893; *m* 1936, Victoria Martinez Alonso, Cordoba, Spain; one *s* two *d. Educ:* Coll. Rollin, Paris. Joined Massey-Harris Ltd, Berlin, 1909; went to Canada, 1911. Served with UK Forces in 1914-18 War, rising to be Capt. and Adjutant of 180th Brigade 16th Irish Divisional Artillery. Apptd Gen. Manager Massey-Harris Co., 1936; Pres. 1941; Chm. and Pres. 1949 until his resignation in 1956. Apptd Actg Dep. Minister of Defence for Air, 1940, when he took over leadership of Brit. Commonwealth Air Trg Plan; declined invitation of Prime Minister, in summer 1940, to join Federal Cabinet as Minister of Air. Chm., Combined Agricl & Food Cttee of UNRRA, 1941-42; Mem. Nat. Res. Council, Ottawa, during War Years. Past Chm.: Toronto Bd of Trade, Toronto Community Chest, Canadian Council of Internat. Chambers of Commerce, Montreal; Hon. Pres., Toronto section, "Free Fighting French"; Chm. Dollar Sterling Trade Council, 1949-61. First Canadian chosen by Nat. Sales Exec. Organization as "Canadian Businessman of the Year," 1956; Chm., Nat. Conf. on Engrg, Sci. and Tech. Manpower, NB, 1956; organizer and Dep. Chm. Canadian Trade Mission to the UK, 1957. On accepting Chairmanship of Hydro-Electric Power Commn of Ont., Nov. 1956, resigned from bd of many Canadian cos incl. Argus Corp. Ltd, Canada Cement, Ltd, Canadian Bank of Commerce, Internat. Nickel of Canada, Ltd, Page-Hersey Tubes; resigned from Chmship Hydro-Electric Power Commn of Ont., 1961. Upon establishing residence in Bermuda, Aug. 1961, resigned from Gov., University Toronto; Chm., Dollar Sterling Trade Coun.; Chm., Australian-Canadian Assoc.; Dir, Industrial Foundn on Educn; Dir, Atomic Energy of Canada, Ltd; Chm., Royal Conservatory of Music Cttee. Hon. LLD, Dartmouth Coll., NH, USA, 1957. Chevalier, French Legion of Honour;

Croix de Lorraine; King Haakon VII Cross of Liberation. *Publications:* Russia's Bid for World Supremacy, 1955; The Great Leap Forward, 1959; Russia Revisited, 1960; In The Shadow of the Red Star, 1962; A Businessman Looks At Red China, 1965; Not a One-Way Street (autobiography), 1971. *Address:* Somerset House, Paget, Bermuda. *Clubs:* York (Toronto); Mid Ocean, Royal Bermuda Yacht (Bermuda); River (New York); Sotogrande (Spain).

DUNCAN, John Spenser Ritchie, CMG 1967; MBE 1953; HM Diplomatic Service; Ambassador to Morocco, since 1975; *b* 26 July 1921; *s* of late Rev. J. H. Duncan, DD; *m* 1950, Sheila Conacher, MB, ChB, DObstRCOG; one *d. Educ:* George Watson's Boys' Coll.; Glasgow Acad.; Dundee High Sch.; Edinburgh Univ. Entered Sudan Political Service, 1941. Served in HM Forces, 1941-43. Private Sec. to Governor-Gen. of the Sudan, 1954; Dep. Adviser to Governor-Gen. on Constitutional and External Affairs, 1955; appointed to Foreign (subseq. Diplomatic) Service, 1956; seconded to Joint Services Staff Coll., 1957; Political Agent, Doha, 1958; Dep. Dir-Gen., British Information Services, New York, 1959-63; Consul-Gen., Muscat, 1963-65; Head of Personnel Dept, Diplomatic Service, 1966-68; Minister, British High Commn, Canberra, 1969-71; High Comr, Zambia, 1971-74. *Publications:* The Sudan: A Record of Achievement, 1952; The Sudan's Path to Independence, 1957. *Recreation:* golf. *Address:* c/o Foreign and Commonwealth Office, SW1; 7A Blackford Road, Edinburgh EH9 2DT. *Club:* New (Edinburgh).
See also K . P . Duncan .

DUNCAN, Dr Kenneth Playfair, FRCPE; Director of Medical Services, Health and Safety Executive, since 1975; *b* 27 Sept. 1924; *s* of late Dr J. H. Duncan, MA, BPhil, DD, and H. P. Duncan (*née* Ritchie); *m* 1950, Dr Gillian Crow, MB, ChB; four *d. Educ:* Kilmarnock Acad.; Glasgow Acad.; Dundee High Sch.; St Andrews Univ. BSc, MB, ChB; DIH. House Surg., Dundee Royal Infirmary, 1947; RAMC, 1948-50; Gen. Practice, Brighton, 1950-51; Area MO, British Rail, 1951-54; Chief Medical Officer: SW Gas Bd, 1954-58; UKAEA, 1958-69; Head of Health and Safety, BSC, 1969-75. External Examiner in Occupational Health, Univ. of Dundee, 1970-74; Examiner in Occupational Health, Soc. of Apothecaries, 1974-. Vis. Prof., London Sch. of Hygiene and Tropical Medicine, 1977. Mem., MRC, 1975-; Mem., IHAC, 1960-74. Pres., Soc. of Occupational Medicine, 1970. *Publications:* contrib. medical and scientific jls on radiological protection and gen. occupational health topics. *Recreation:* gardening. *Address:* Westfield, Steeple Aston, Oxon OX5 3SD. *T:* Steeple Aston 40277.
See also J . S . R . Duncan .

DUNCAN, Maj.-Gen. Nigel William, CB 1951; CBE 1945; DSO 1945; DL; *b* 27 Nov. 1899; *s* of George William and Edith Duncan, Earlston, Guildford; *m* 1928, Victoria Letitia Troyte, *d* of late Capt. J. E. Acland, Wollaston House, Dorchester, Dorset; three *d. Educ:* Malvern Coll.; RMC Sandhurst. 2nd Bn The Black Watch, 1919; transf. Royal Tank Corps, 1923; Captain, 1931; Major, 1938; Lieut-Col, 1940; Col, 1943; Brig. 30 Armoured Bde, 1943, 2nd Armoured Bde, 1946; Comdr Royal Armoured Corps Centre, 1947; Maj.-Gen., 1949; Dir Royal Armoured Corps, WO, 1949-52; retired pay, 1952. Col Comdt Royal Tank Regt, 1952-58. Lieut-Governor Royal Hospital, Chelsea, 1953-57. DL Dorset, 1959. *Address:* The Old Parsonage, Kimmeridge, Wareham, Dorset. *T:* Corfe Castle 722. *Club:* Army and Navy.

DUNCAN, (Peter) Colin, MC 1918; QC 1963; Barrister-at-Law; *b* 3 Oct. 1895; *s* of late Peter Thomas Duncan, MD and late Emma Gertrude, *er d* of late Rev. E. H. Genge. *Educ:* Rugby Sch.; Trinity Coll., Oxford. Barrister-at-Law, 1928; Master of the Bench, Inner Temple, 1960. Recorder of Bury St Edmunds, 1949-63; Recorder of Norwich 1963-68. Served European War, 1914-18, Queen's Royal Regiment, Capt. (despatches, MC), Gallipoli, Egypt, Palestine, France, Flanders; War of 1939-45, staff appointments, Lieut-Col. *Publication:* (with Anthony Hoolahan) Guide to Defamation Practice, 1953 (revised edn, 1958). *Address:* 5 New Road, Ham Common, Richmond, Surrey. *T:* 01-940 5716; 1 Brick Court, Temple, EC4. *T:* 01-353 8845.

DUNCAN, Ronald; *b* 6 Aug. 1914; *s* of Reginald John and Ethel Duncan; *m* 1941, Rose Marie Hansom; one *s* one *d. Educ:* Switzerland; Cambridge Univ. Editor, Townsman, 1938-46; founded Devon Festival of the Arts, 1953. The English Stage Company, 1955. This way to the Tomb, first produced 1945 at Mercury Theatre, London; The Eagle has Two Heads, London, Sept. 1946; The Rape of Lucretia, Glyndebourne, 1946; Stratton, Theatre Royal, Brighton, 1949; Nothing Up My Sleeve, Watergate, 1950; Our Lady's Tumbler, Salisbury Cathedral,

1951; Don Juan, 1953; The Death of Satan, 1954; The Catalyst, 1956; Abelard and Heloïse, 1960 and 1975; Christopher Sly, 1962, Pforzheim Opera House; The Seven Deadly Virtues, 1968. *Publications:* The Dull Ass's Hoof, 1941; Postcards to Pulcenella, 1942; Journal of a Husbandman, 1944; This Way to the Tomb, 1946; The Rape of Lucretia, 1946; Home Made Home, 1947; Ben Jonson, 1947; Songs and Satires of the Earl of Rochester, 1948; Stratton, a play, 1948; Jan's Journal, 1948; The Typewriter, a play, 1948; Beauty and the Beast, 1948; Pope's Letters, 1948; The Cardinal, 1949; The Mongrel and other Poems, 1950; Tobacco growing in England, 1950; Our Lady's Tumbler, 1951; Selected Writings of Mahatma Gandhi, 1951; The Blue Fox, 1951; Don Juan, 1952; Jan at the Blue Fox, 1952; Where I Live, 1953; Jan's Journal; The Death of Satan, 1954; Judas, 1959; The Solitudes and other poems, 1960; Judas, 1960; St Spiv, 1960; Abelard and Heloïse, 1961; Anthology of Classical Songs, 1962; All Men Are Islands (Vol i, autobiog.), 1964; The Catalyst, 1965; O-B-A-F-G, 1965; How to Make Enemies (Vol. ii, autobiog.), 1968; The Perfect Mistress and other stories, 1969; Unpopular Poems, 1969; Man, Part I of poem, 1970, Part II, 1972, Part III, 1973, Parts IV and V, 1974; Collected Plays, Vol. 1, 1971; A Kettle of Fish and other stories, 1971; Torquemada, 1971; Dante's *De Vulgari Eloquentia,* 1973; Obsessed (Vol. iii, autobiog.), 1976; The Precarious Garden (Vol. iv, autobiog.), 1976; Mr and Mrs Mouse, 1977; For the Few, 1977. *Address:* Welcombe, near Bideford, Devon. *T:* Morwenstow 375. *Club:* Garrick.

DUNCAN, Stanley Frederick St Clare; HM Diplomatic Service; Head of Consular Department, Foreign and Commonwealth Office, since 1977; *b*.13 Nov. 1927; *yr s* of late Stanley Gilbert Scott Duncan and of Louisa Elizabeth Duncan; *m* 1967, Jennifer Jane Bennett; two *d. Educ:* Latymer Upper Sch. FRGS. India Office, 1946; CRO, 1947; Private Sec. to Parly Under-Sec. of State, 1954; Second Sec., Ottawa, 1954-55; Brit. Govt Information Officer, Toronto, 1955-57; Second Sec., Wellington, 1958-60; First Sec., CRO, 1960; seconded to Central African Office, 1962-64; Mem., Brit. Delegn to Victoria Falls Conf. on Dissolution of Fedn of Rhodesia and Nyasaland, 1963; First Sec., Nicosia, 1964-67; FCO, 1967-70; FCO Adviser, Brit. Gp, Inter-Parly Union, 1968-70; Head of Chancery and First Sec., Lisbon, 1970-73; Consul-General and subsequently Chargé d'Affaires in Mozambique, 1973-75; Counsellor (Political), Brasilia, 1976-77. Officer, Military Order of Christ (Portugal), 1973. *Recreations:* countryside pursuits. *Address:* 91 Gloucester Street, SW1. *Club:* Hurlingham.

DUNCAN, William Burr Mckinnon, CBE 1972; FIMechE; Deputy Chairman, Imperial Chemical Industries Ltd, since 1977; *b* 16 Dec. 1922; *m* 1951, Christina Boyd Worth; one *s* two *d. Educ:* Ardrossan Acad.; Glasgow Univ.; Royal Coll. of Science and Technology (1st Cl. Hons Mech Eng). Joined ICI, 1941; engrg duties, Billingham Div., 1950; Chief Engr and Engrg Dir, Agricl Div., 1961; Gp Gen. Manager, Man Services, 1964; Pres., ICI America, 1966; Dir, Can. Ind. Ltd, 1968; Pres. and Chief Exec., ICI North America Ltd, 1970; Dir, Fib. Ind. Inc., 1970; Dir, ICI Ltd, 1971; Chm., ICI Americas Inc., 1974; Dir, NEB, 1975. *Recreations:* golf, tennis, music, bridge. *Address:* Imperial Chemical Industries Ltd, Imperial Chemical House, Millbank, SW1P 3JF. *T:* 01-834 4444. *Club:* Union (New York).

DUNCAN MILLAR, Ian Alastair, MC; CEng, MICE; JP, DL; Convener, Tayside Regional Council, since 1975 (Councillor and Chairman, 1974-75); Director: Macdonald Fraser & Co. Ltd, Perth, since 1961; Hill Farming Research Organisation, since 1966; Member, Royal Company of Archers (Queen's Body Guard for Scotland), since 1956; *b* 22 Nov. 1914; *s* of late Sir James Duncan Millar and Lady Duncan Millar (*née* Forester Paton); *m* 1945, Louise Reid McCosh; two *s* two *d. Educ:* Gresham's Sch., Holt; Trinity Coll., Cambridge (MA). Served with Corps of Royal Engineers, 1940-45 (Major; wounded; despatches): 7th Armoured Div., N Africa and Normandy; 51 (Highland) Div., France and Germany. Contested Parly Elections (L): Banff, 1945; Kinross and W Perthshire, 1949 and 1963. Depute Chm., North of Scotland Hydro-Electric Bd, 1970-72 (Mem., 1957-72). Chm., United Auctions (Scotland) Ltd, 1967-74. Mem. Ct, Dundee Univ., 1975-. Perth CC 1945-75: Chm. Planning Cttee, 1954-75; Convener, 1970-75; Chm. Jt CC of Perth and Kinross, 1970-75. DL 1963, JP 1952, Perthshire. *Recreations:* studying and catching salmon, shooting, meeting people. *Address:* Remony, Aberfeldy, Perthshire. *T:* Kenmore 209. *Clubs:* Royal Automobile; Royal Golfing Society (Perth).

DUNCAN-SANDYS, family name of **Baron Duncan-Sandys.**

DUNCAN-SANDYS, Baron *cr* 1974 (Life Peer); **Duncan Edwin Duncan-Sandys**, PC 1944; CH 1973; Founder, Civic Trust and President, since 1956; President, Europa Nostra, since 1969; Chairman, Lonrho Ltd, since 1972; *b* 24 Jan. 1908; *o s of* Captain George Sandys, formerly MP for Wells, and Mildred, *d* of Duncan Cameron, Ashburton, New Zealand; *m* 1st, 1935, Diana (marr. diss. 1960; she *d* 1963), *d* of late Rt Hon. Sir Winston Churchill; one *s* two *d*; 2nd, 1962, Marie-Claire, *d* of Adrien Schmitt, Paris, and formerly Viscountess Hudson; one *d*. *Educ:* Eton; Magdalen Coll., Oxford (MA). Entered Diplomatic Service, 1930; served in Foreign Office and British Embassy, Berlin; MP (C) Norwood Div. of Lambeth, 1935-45, Streatham, 1950-Feb. 1974; Political Columnist of Sunday Chronicle, 1937-39; Member Nat. Exec. of Conservative Party, 1938-39; Commissioned in Territorial Army (Royal Artillery), 1937; served in Expeditionary Force in Norway, 1940; Lt-Col 1941; disabled on active service, 1941; Financial Sec. to War Office, 1941-43; Parly Sec., Ministry of Supply, responsible for armament production, 1943-44; Chm., War Cabinet Cttee for defence against German flying bombs and rockets, 1943-45; Minister of Works, 1944-45; Minister of Supply, Oct. 1951-Oct. 1954; Minister of Housing and Local Govt, Oct. 1954-Jan. 1957; Minister of Defence, Jan. 1957-Oct. 1959; Minister of Aviation, Oct. 1959-July 1960; Secretary of State for Commonwealth Relations, July 1960-Oct. 1964, and also Secretary of State for the Colonies, July 1962-Oct. 1964. Founded European Movement, 1947, Chm. International Executive until 1950; Chm., Parly Council of European Movement, 1950-51; Mem. Parly Assembly of Council of Europe and of WEU, 1950-51, 1965- (Leader British Delegns, 1970-72); Chm. British Section, Franco British Council, 1972-; Chm. Internat. Organising Cttee, European Architectural Heritage Year, 1975. Mem., Gen. Adv. Council, BBC, 1947-51. Director, Ashanti Goldfields Corporation, 1947-51 and 1966-72. Hon. Vice-Pres., Nat. Chamber of Trade, 1951-. Hon. MRTPI, 1956; Hon. FRIBA, 1968. Freeman of Bridgetown, Barbados, 1962. Grand Cross, Order of Merit, Italy, 1960; Order of Sultanate of Brunei, 1973; Medal of Honour, City of Paris, 1974; Gold Cup of European Movement, 1975; Goethe Gold Medal, Hamburg Foundn, 1975; Grand Cross of Order of Crown, Belgium, 1975. *Recreation:* abstract painting. *Address:* 86 Vincent Square, SW1P 2PG. *T:* 01-834 5886.
See also P. Dixon, D. Walters.

DUNCOMBE, family name of **Baron Feversham**.

DUNCOMBE, Sir Philip (Digby) Pauncefort-, 4th Bt *cr* 1859; DL; *b* 18 May 1927; *o s* of Sir Everard Pauncefort-Duncombe, 3rd Bt, DSO, and of Evelyn Elvira, *d* of Frederick Anthony Denny; *S* father, 1971; *m* 1951, Rachel Moyra, *d* of Major H. G. Aylmer; one *s* two *d*. *Educ:* Stowe. 2nd Lieut, Grenadier Guards, 1946; served in Palestine, 1947-48; Malaya, 1948-49; Cyprus, 1957-59; Hon. Major, retired 1960, Regular Army Reserve. County Comdt, Buckinghamshire Army Cadet Force, 1967-70. DL Bucks 1971. *Heir:* s David Philip Henry Pauncefort-Duncombe, *b* 21 May 1956. *Address:* Great Brickhill Manor, Milton Keynes, Bucks MK17 9BE. *T:* Great Brickhill 205. *Club:* Cavalry and Guards.

DUNCUMB, Dr Peter, FRS 1977; Assistant Director, Tube Investments Research Laboratories, since 1972; *b* 26 Jan. 1931; *s* of late William Duncumb and of Hilda Grace (*née* Coleman); *m* 1955, Anne Leslie Taylor, two *s* one *d*. *Educ:* Oundle Sch.; Clare Coll., Cambridge (BA 1953, MA 1956, PhD 1957). DSIR Res. Fellow, Cambridge Univ., 1957-59; Res. Scientist and Gp Leader, Tube Investments Res. Labs, 1959-67, Head, Physics Dept, 1967-72. Hon. Mem., Microbeam Analysis Soc. of America, 1973. C. V. Boys Prize, Inst. of Physics, 1966. *Publications:* numerous on electron microscopy and analysis in Jl of Inst. of Physics. *Recreations:* hill walking, family genealogy. *Address:* 5 Woollards Lane, Great Shelford, Cambridge. *T:* Shelford 3064.

DUNDAS, family name of **Viscount Melville**, and of **Marquess of Zetland**.

DUNDAS, Lord; Robin Lawrence Dundas; *b* 5 March 1965; *s* and *heir* of Earl of Ronaldshay, *qv*.

DUNDAS, Group Captain Hugh Spencer Lisle, CBE 1977; DSO 1944 and Bar 1945; DFC 1941; RAF retired; DL; Managing Director, British Electric Traction Co. Ltd, since 1973; Chairman: Humphries Holdings Ltd, since 1975; Redifon Ltd, since 1970; Deputy Chairman, Rediffusion Television Ltd, since 1970; Director: Broadcast Relay Service (Overseas) Ltd; Rediffusion Holdings Ltd; Rediffusion Incorp.; Rediffusion Ltd; Redifon Telecommunications Ltd; Thames Television Ltd; United Transport Co. Ltd; *b* 22 July 1920; *s* of late Frederick

James Dundas and Sylvia Mary (*née* March-Phillipps); *m* 1950, Hon. Enid Rosamond Lawrence, 2nd *d* of 1st Baron Oaksey and 3rd Baron Trevethin; one *s* two *d*. *Educ:* Stowe. Joined 616 (S Yorks) Sqdn AAF 1939; served in UK Fighter Comd Sqdn, 1939-43; N Africa, Malta, Sicily, Italy, 1943-44; perm. commn 1944; comd 244 Wing, Italy, 1944-46 (Gp Captain; despatches 1945); retd 1947. Comd 601 (Co. London) Sqdn RAuxAF, 1947-50. Beaverbrook Newspapers, 1948-60: various editorial and managerial posts; joined Exec. Staff, Rediffusion Ltd, 1961: Dir, 1966; Dep. Man. Dir, 1968; Man. Dir 1970-74. Mem. Council, and Finance and General Purposes Cttee, RAF Benevolent Fund, 1976-; Mem. Council, Nat. Soc. for Cancer Relief, 1976-. DL Surrey, 1969. *Address:* 55 Iverna Court, W8 6TU. *T:* 01-937 0773; The Schoolroom, Dockenfield, Farnham, Surrey. *T:* Frensham 2331. *Clubs:* White's, Royal Air Force.

DUNDAS, Robert Giffen, CBE 1961; HM Diplomatic Service, retired 1969; *b* 4 March 1909; *s* of James Dundas and Grace Haxton Giffen; *m* 1938, Pauleen Gosling; three *s* one *d*. *Educ:* Edinburgh Univ. Entered Levant Consular Service, 1931; Vice-Consul: Beirut, 1931; Cairo, 1932; Third Sec., Ankara, 1934; Vice-Consul: Casablanca, 1936; Alexandria, 1938; Suez, 1939; Baghdad, 1941; Consul, Tangier, 1944; assigned to Foreign Office, 1947; Consul, Kermanshah, 1949; Consul-General: Tabriz, 1950; Salonika, 1952; New Orleans, 1955; Stuttgart, 1958; Alexandria, 1961; HM Counsellor and Consul-Gen., Benghazi, 1963-66; Consul-Gen., Amsterdam, 1966-69. *Publications:* contrib. (fiction) to Argosy etc. *Address:* The Old Forge, Marstow, near Ross-on-Wye, Herefordshire.

DUNDAS, Sir Robert (Whyte-Melville), 6th Bt, *cr* 1821; JP; *b* 31 Oct. 1881; *o surv. s* of Sir George Whyte Melville Dundas, 5th Bt, and Matilda Louisa Mary (*d* 1945), *d* of Minden J. Wilson; *S* father 1934; *m* 1926, Dorothea (*d* 1963), *er d* of late A. W. Wiseman, MA, MusBac, Monmouth; no *c*. *Educ:* Trinity Coll., Glenalmond; Keble Coll., Oxford, MA. Administrative Officer, Nigeria, 1911-30. JP Perthshire, 1940. *Recreation:* cricket. *Address:* Comrie House, Comrie, Perthshire. *T:* Comrie 330. *Club:* New (Edinburgh).

DUNDEE, 11th Earl of, *cr* 1660 (Scotland); **Henry James Scrymgeour-Wedderburn**, PC; LLD; JP, DL; Viscount Dudhope and Lord Scrymgeour, *cr* 1641 (Scotland); Lord Inverkeithing, *cr* 1660 (Scotland); Lord Glassary, *cr* 1954 (UK); Hereditary Royal Standard-Bearer for Scotland; *b* 3 May 1902; *s* of Col Henry Scrymgeour-Wedderburn, *de jure* 10th Earl and Edith (*d* 1968), *d* of John Moffat, CE, Ardrossan, and Jessie Fulton Arthur; *S* father 1924 (claim admitted by Cttee for Privileges, House of Lords, as Viscount, 1952, as Earl, 1953); *m* 1946, Patricia Katherine, *widow* of Lieut-Col (Hon.) David Scrymgeour-Wedderburn, and *d* of late Col Lord Herbert Montagu Douglas Scott; one *s* (and two step *d*). *Educ:* Winchester; Balliol Coll., Oxford. Pres. Oxford Union, Oct. 1924; MP (U) Western Renfrew, 1931-45; Parliamentary Under-Sec. of State for Scotland, 1936-39; served with 7th Black Watch, 1939-41; Additional Parl. Under-Sec. of State, Scottish Office 1941-42. Minister without Portfolio, 1958-61; Minister of State for Foreign Affairs, 1961-64; Asst Dep. Leader, 1960-62, Dep. Leader, 1962-64, House of Lords. Hon. LLD St Andrews, 1954. *Heir:* s Lord Scrymgeour, *qv*. *Address:* Birkhill, Cupar, Fife. *TA:* Gauldry. *T:* Gauldry 209. *Clubs:* Carlton, Travellers', White's, Pratt's; New (Edinburgh).
See also Sir Iain Moncreiffe of that Ilk, Bt, Baron Teynham.

DUNDERDALE, Comdr Wilfred Albert, CMG 1942; MBE 1920; RNVR, retired; *b* 24 Dec. 1899; *s* of late Richard Albert Dunderdale, Shipowner, and Sophie Dunderdale; *m* 1952, Dorothy Brayshaw Hyde. Trained as Naval Architect, 1914-17; served with Mediterranean Fleet, 1918-22 (despatches twice); Lieut RNVR, 1920; transferred to British Embassy, Constantinople, 1922-26; Paris, 1926-40; Comdr, 1939. Russian Order of St Anne; Polonia Restituta; French Legion of Honour (Officer); French Croix de Guerre with palm; United States Legion of Merit (Officer). *Recreations:* yachting, tennis. *Address:* Castlefield, Bletchingley, Surrey RH1 4LB. *T:* Godstone 3121. *Clubs:* Boodle's; Royal Harwich Yacht (Harwich).

DUNDONALD, 14th Earl of, *cr* 1669, **Ian Douglas Leonard Cochrane**; Lord Cochrane of Dundonald, 1647; Lord Cochrane of Paisley and Ochiltree, 1669; Chairman, Secure Holdings Ltd, de Jersey & Co. (Finland) Ltd and associated companies; a Representative Peer for Scotland, 1959-63; *b* 6 Dec. 1918; *s* of late Hon. Douglas Robert Hesketh Roger Cochrane (2nd *s* of 12th Earl) and of Hon. Mrs Douglas Cochrane (*d* 1960), Hawkhurst, Kent; *S* uncle 1958; *m* 1960, Aphra Farquhar (*d* 1972), *d* of late Comdr George Fetherstonhaugh; one *s* one *d*. *Educ:* Wellington Coll.; RMC, Sandhurst. Joined 1 Battalion

The Black Watch, 1938; Adjutant, 16 DLI, 1940-41; Staff Capt. 139 Inf. Bde, 1941-42; Staff Coll., Camberley, 1942 (psc); Asst Mil. Landing Officer, 51 (H) Div., 1943; GSO 3 and GSO 2, HQ Eighth Army, 1943; Company Comdr 6 Bn The Black Watch, 1944-45; Bde Major, 180 Inf. Bde, 1946-47; GSO 2, Army Air Transport Development Centre, 1947-49; Company Comdr 1 Bn The Black Watch, 1949-51; DAQMG, SHAPE, 1951; GSO 2, SD3, War Office and GSO 2, Army Council Secretariat, 1952-53; retired 1953. North American Representative, Atlantic Shipbuilding Co., 1953-54. Mem., UK Delegn to NATO Citizens Convention, Paris, 1962. Chm. Anglo-Chilean Soc., 1958-65. Pres., Ayr and Bute Assoc. of Youth Clubs. Vice-Pres., Royal Caledonian Schs. Mem. Council, Anglo-Finnish Soc. *Recreations:* shooting, sailing, ski-ing, golf. *Heir:* s Lord Cochrane, *qv. Address:* Lochnell Castle, Ledaig, Argyll; Beacon Hall, Benenden, Kent. *Club:* Carlton.

DUNEDIN, Bishop of, since 1976; **Rt. Rev. Peter Woodley Mann;** *b* 25 July 1924; *s* of Edgar Allen and Bessie May Mann; *m* 1955, Anne Victoria Norman; three *d*. *Educ:* Prince Alfred Coll., Adelaide; St John's Coll., Auckland (Fellow); Univ. of London (BD). Deacon, Dio. Waiapu, 1953; priest, 1954; Curate: Waiapu Cathedral, 1953-55; Rotorua, 1955-56; Vicar: Porangahau, 1956-61; Dannevirke, 1961-66; Vicar of Blenheim and Archdeacon of Marlborough, 1966-71; Vicar of St Mary's and Archdeacon of Timaru, 1971-75; Vicar of St James' Lower Hutt, 1975-76. *Recreations:* tennis, athletics. *Address:* Bishop's House, 10 Claremont Street, Roslyn, Dunedin, NZ. *T:* 60710.

DUNGEY, Prof. James Wynne, PhD; Professor of Physics, Imperial College, University of London, since 1965; *b* 30 Jan. 1923; *s* of Ernest Dungey and Alice Dungey; *m* 1950, Christine Scotland (*née* Brown); one *s* one *d*. *Educ:* Bradfield; Magdalene Coll., Cambridge (MA, PhD). Res. Fellow, Univ. of Sydney, 1950-53; Vis. Asst Prof., Penn State Coll., 1953-54; ICI Fellow, Cambridge, 1954-57; Lectr, King's Coll., Newcastle upon Tyne, 1957-59; Sen. Principal Scientific Officer, AWRE, Aldermaston, 1959-63; Res. Fellow, Imperial Coll., London, 1963-65. Fellow, Amer. Geophysical Union, 1973. *Publications:* Cosmic Electrodynamics, 1958; papers on related topics. *Recreations:* music, sailing. *Address:* 35 Kensington High Street, W8 5BA. *T:* 01-937 1181.

DUNGLASS, Lord (courtesy title used by heirs to Earldom of Home before title was disclaimed); *see under* Douglas-Home, Hon. D. A. C.

DUNHAM, Cyril John; Director, Nationwide (formerly Co-operative Permanent) Building Society, since 1944; *b* 22 April 1908; *m* 1936, Vera Georgia; one *s* two *d*. *Educ:* Watford Gram. Sch.; Coll. of Estate Management. FRICS 1929. Technical Adviser, War Damage Commn, 1941; Vice-Chm., Peterborough New Town Develt Corp., 1968-73; Vice-President: Building Societies Assoc. (Chm., 1961-63); Internat. Union of Building Socs. Has also served on: Wembley Borough Council; Nat. House-Builders Registration Council; Town and Country Planning Assoc. *Address:* 15 Turner Close, Hampstead, NW11. *T:* 01-455 8348.

DUNHAM, Sir Kingsley (Charles), Kt 1972; FRS 1955; FRSE; PhD Dunelm, 1932; SD Harvard, 1935; FGS; Hon FIMM; Director, Institute of Geological Sciences, 1967-75; *b* Sturminster Newton, Dorset, 2 Jan. 1910; *s* of Ernest Pedder and Edith Agnes Dunham; *m* 1936, Margaret, *d* of William and Margaret Young, Choppington, Northumberland; one *s*. *Educ:* Durham Johnston Sch.; Hatfield Coll., Durham Univ.; Adams House, Harvard Univ. Temporary Geologist, New Mexico Bureau of Mines, 1934; HM Geological Survey of Great Britain; Geologist, 1935-45; Senior Geologist 1946; Chief Petrographer, 1948; Prof. of Geology, Univ. of Durham, 1950-66, Emeritus, 1968-; Sub-Warden of Durham Colls, 1959-61; Miller Prof., University of Ill., 1956; Member: Council, Royal Society, 1965-66 (Foreign Sec., A Vice-Pres., 1971-76; Royal Medal, 1970); Council for Scientific Policy (Min. of Ed. & Sci.), 1965-66. President: Instn Mining and Metallurgy, 1963-64 (Gold Medal, 1968); Yorks Geological Soc., 1958-60 (Sorby Medal, 1964); Internat. Union of Geological Sciences, 1969-72; Geological Soc. of London, 1966-68 (Council 1949-52, 1960-64; Bigsby Medal, 1954; Murchison Medal, 1966; Wollaston Medal, 1976); Brit. Assoc. for Advancement of Science, 1972-73; Mineralogical Soc., 1975-. Trustee, British Museum (Natural History), 1963-66. Member Geology-Geophysics Cttee (NERC) 1965-70; Chairman: Internat. Geol. Correlation Project (IUGS-UNESCO), 1973-76; Council for Environmental Science and Engineering, 1973-75. Pres., Durham Univ. Soc., 1973-75. Founder Fellow, Fellowship of Engineering, 1976. Hon. Member: Royal Geol Soc. Cornwall (Bolitho Medal 1972); Geol. Soc. of India, 1972; Hon. Foreign Fellow, Geol. Soc. of America;

Corr. Foreign Mem., Austrian Acad. of Scis, 1971; Hon. Foreign Member: Société Géologique de Belge, 1974; Bulgarian Geological Soc., 1975. Fellow, Imperial Coll., 1976. Hon. DSc: Dunelm, 1946; Liverpool, 1967; Birmingham, 1970; Illinois, 1971; Leicester, 1972; Michigan, 1973; Canterbury, 1973; Edinburgh, 1974; Exeter, 1975; Hon. ScD Cantab, 1973. Haidinger Medaille der Geologischen Bundesanstalt, 1976. Hon. Citizen of Texas, 1975. *Publications:* Geology of the Organ Mountains, 1935; Geology of the Northern Pennine Orefield, 1948; (as Editor) Symposium on the Geology, Paragenesis and Reserves of the Ores of Lead & Zinc, 2nd edn, 1950; Fluorspar, 1952; Geology of Northern Skye (with F. W. Anderson) 1966; articles in Quarterly Jl of Geological Soc., Mineralogical Magazine, Geological Magazine, American Mineralogist, etc. *Recreations:* music (organ and pianoforte); gardening. *Address:* Charleycroft, Quarryheads Lane, Durham. *T:* Durham 3977. *Clubs:* Athenæum; Smeatonian; Geological Society's.

DUNICAN, Peter Thomas, CBE 1977; FICE, FIStructE, FIEI; Chairman, Ove Arup Incorporated, since 1977; *b* 15 March 1918; *s* of Peter Dunican and Elsie Alice McKenzie; *m* 1942, Irene May Jordan; two *s* one *d* (and one *d* decd). *Educ:* Central Sch., Clapham; Battersea Polytechnic. FICE 1971, FIStructE 1959, FIEI 1970. Asst, S. H. White & Son, Civil Engineers, 1936-43; Structural Engr, Ove Arup & Partners, Consulting Engineers, 1943-49, Sen. Partner 1956-. Instn of Structural Engineers: Mem. Council, 1964-; Vice-Pres., 1971-77; Pres., 1977-78. Part-time Dir, National Bldg Agency, 1964-. Member: LCC Adv. Cttee on London Bldg Act and Byelaws, 1957; Min. of Housing Working Party to revise Model Bldg Byelaws, 1960; Bldg Regulations Adv. Cttee, 1962-65; Council, Architect. Assoc., 1968-69. Univ. Science and Technol. Bd of Science Research Council: Mem., Aeronaut. and Civil Eng Cttee, 1968-71; Mem., National Jt Consultative Cttee, 1974; Chm., Jt Bldg Gp, 1973-76. *Publications:* professional, technical and philosophical papers to jls dealing with construction industry in general and struct. eng in particular. *Recreations:* working in the garden and going to to the opera. *Address:* 60 Ryecroft Road, SW16 3EH. *T:* 01-670 7056. *Club:* Danish.

DUNITZ, Prof. Jack David, FRS 1974; Professor of Chemical Crystallography at the Swiss Federal Institute of Technology (ETH), Zürich, since 1957; *b* 29 March 1923; *s* of William Dunitz and Mildred (*née* Gossmann); *m* 1953, Barbara Steuer; two *d*. *Educ:* Hillhead High Sch., Glasgow; Hutcheson's Grammar Sch., Glasgow; Glasgow Univ. (BSc, PhD). Post-doctoral Fellow, Oxford Univ., 1946-48, 1951-53; California Inst. of Technology, 1948-51, 1953-54; Vis. Scientist, US Nat. Insts of Health, 1954-55; Sen. Res. Fellow, Davy Faraday Res. Lab., Royal Instn, London, 1956-57. Vis. Prof., Iowa State Univ., 1965; British Council Lectr, 1965; Treat B. Johnson Meml Lectr, Yale Univ., 1965; 3M Lectr, Univ. of Minnesota, 1966; Vis. Prof., Tokyo Univ., 1967; Overseas Fellow of Churchill Coll., Cambridge, 1968; Vis. Prof., Technion, Haifa, 1970; Reilly Lectr, Univ. Notre Dame, US, 1971; Kelly Lectr, Purdue Univ., 1971; Gerhard Schmidt Meml Lectr, Weizmann Inst. of Sci., 1973; George Fisher Baker Lectr, Cornell Univ., 1976. Jt Editor, Perspectives in Structural Chemistry, 1967-71; Mem. Editorial Bd: Helvetica Chimica Acta, 1971-; Structure and Bonding, 1971-. *Publications:* papers on various aspects of crystal and molecular structure in Acta Crystallographica, Helvetica Chimica Acta, Jl Chem. Soc., Jl Amer. Chem. Soc., etc. *Recreation:* walking. *Address:* (office) Organic Chemistry Laboratory, ETH, Universitätstrasse 16, CH-8092 Zürich, Switzerland. *T:* CH (01) 326211; (home) Obere Heslibachstrasse 77, 8700 Kusnacht, Switzerland. *T:* CH (01) 9101723.

DUNK, Sir William (Ernest), Kt 1957; CBE 1954; retired as Chairman Commonwealth of Australia Public Service Commission (1947-62); formerly Commissioner, British Phosphates Commission and Christmas Island Phosphates Commission; Director, General Television Corporation and other companies; *b* S Australia, 11 Dec. 1897; *s* of Albert L. Dunk; *m* 1922, Elma K. Evans; one *s* one *d*. *Educ:* Kapunda High Sch., Australia. Australian Public Service from 1914; Auditor-General's Office, 1914-39, Adelaide, New Guinea, London, Sydney; Treasury, 1939-45, as Asst Sec., Special War Services, Dir Reverse Lend Lease, 1943-45; Permanent Sec., Dept of External Affairs, 1945-46. *Address:* 7 Tintern Avenue, Toorak, Victoria 3142, Australia. *Clubs:* Commonwealth (Canberra); Melbourne (Melbourne).

DUNKELD, Bishop of, (RC), since 1955; **Rt. Rev. Mgr William Andrew Hart;** *b* Dumbarton, 9 Sept. 1904; *s* of Daniel Hart and Margaret Gallagher. *Educ:* St Mungo's Academy, Glasgow; St Mary's Coll., Blairs, Aberdeen; Royal Scots Coll. and Pontifical Univ., Valladolid, Spain. Asst Priest, St Mary's, Hamilton, 1929-33; St John's, Glasgow, 1933-39; Army Chaplain, 1939-45;

Asst Priest, St Michael's, Glasgow, 1945-48; Vice-Rector, Royal Scots Coll., Valladolid, 1948-49; Parish Priest, St Nicholas', Glasgow, 1949-51, St Saviour's, Glasgow, 1951-55. *Address:* Bishop's House, 29 Roseangle, Dundee DD1 4LX. *T:* 24327.

DUNKERLEY, Harvey John, CBE 1953; Controller, Midland Region, BBC, 1948-64, retired; now actively engaged in farming; *b* 10 Oct. 1902; *s* of Joseph Braithwaite Dunkerley and Rose Maria (*née* Harvey); *m* 1st, 1928, Kay Hargreaves (*d* 1958); 2nd, 1961, Thelma Couch; one *s* three *d. Educ:* Owen's Sch., London; Magdalen Coll., Oxford (2nd class Hons Mod. Hist.). Announcer, BBC, Savoy Hill, 1924; Asst, BBC Relay Station, Liverpool, 1924; Education Officer, BBC, Manchester, 1928; Programme Dir, BBC Midland Region, 1933; BBC European Service, Sept. 1939, latterly as Dep. to Controller. *Recreation:* country life. *Address:* Gallipot Farm, Broadway, Worcs. *T:* Evesham 830395.

DUNKLEY, Sir Herbert Francis, Kt 1943; *b* 2 July 1886; *s* of Charles Dunkley, JP; *m* 1912, Gwendoline Scott Willows Wilson (*d* 1956); no *c. Educ:* Wellingborough Sch.; St John's Coll., Cambridge. Called to Bar, Lincoln's Inn, 1921; Joined Indian Civil Service and posted to Burma, 1910; became a District Judge, 1918; Divisional Judge, 1921; Puisne Judge, High Court, Rangoon, 1930-46; Acting Chief Justice, 1945-46; retired 1947. *Publications:* Digest of Burma Rulings, 1872-1937 (2 vols). *Address:* 209 Grosvenor Square, Rondebosch, Cape Town, South Africa.

DUNKLEY, Captain James Lewis, CBE 1970 (OBE 1946); RD 1943; Marine Manager, P&O Lines, 1971-72 (Marine Superintendent, 1968-71); *b* 13 Sept. 1908; *s* of William E. Dunkley, Thurlaston Grange, Warwickshire; *m* 1937, Phyllis Mary Cale; one *d. Educ:* Lawrence Sheriff Sch., Rugby; Thames Nautical Training Coll., HMS Worcester. Junior Officer, P&O Line, 1928; Captain, 1954; Cdre, 1964. RNR: Sub-Lt, 1931; Comdr, 1951; Captain, 1956. Master, Honourable Co. of Master Mariners, 1970. *Recreations:* gardening, collecting. *Address:* 4 Lancaster Gardens, Clacton-on-Sea, Essex. *T:* Clacton 23047. *Club:* City Livery.

DUNLAP, Air Marshal Clarence Rupert, CBE 1944; CD; RCAF retired; *b* 1 Jan. 1908; *s* of late Frank Burns Dunlap, Truro, Nova Scotia; *m* 1935, Hester, *d* of late Dr E. A. Cleveland, Vancouver, BC; one *s. Educ:* Acadia Univ.; Nova Scotia Technical Coll. Joined RCAF 1928 as Pilot Officer; trained as pilot and specialised in aerial survey; later specialised in armament; Dir of Armament, RCAF HQ Ottawa on outbreak of War; commanded: RCAF Station, Mountain View, Ont., Jan.-Oct. 1942; RCAF Station, Leeming, Yorks, Dec. 1942-May 1943; 331 Wing BNAF, May-Nov. 1943; 139 Wing TAF, Nov. 1943-Feb. 1945; 64 Base, Middleton St George, Feb.-May 1945; Dep., AMAS, AFHQ, Ottawa, 1945-48; Air Mem. for Air Plans, AFHQ, Ottawa, 1948-49; AOC North-West Air Command, Edmonton, Alberta, 1949-51; Commandant of National Defence Coll., Kingston, Ont., 1951-54; Vice Chief of the Air Staff, AFHQ, Ottawa, 1954-58; Dep. Chief of Staff, Operations, SHAPE, Paris, 1958-62; Chief of Air Staff, AFHQ, Ottawa, 1962-64; Dep. C-in-C, N Amer. Air Def. Comd, 1964-67. Hon. DCL Acadia Univ., 1955; Hon. DEng Nova Scotia Technical Coll., 1967. *Address:* Island Park Towers, 195 Clearview Avenue, Ottawa, Ontario K1Z 6S1, Canada. *T:* 728 3637. *Club:* Royal Ottawa Golf (Ottawa).

DUNLEATH, 4th Baron, *cr* 1892; **Charles Edward Henry John Mulholland**, TD; DL; Member (Alliance) for North Down, Northern Ireland Constitutional Convention, 1975-76; Chairman, Carreras of Northern Ireland, since 1974; *b* 23 June 1933; *s* of 3rd Baron Dunleath, CBE, DSO, and of Henrietta Grace, *d* of late Most Rev. C. F. D'Arcy, Archbishop of Armagh; *S* father, 1956; *m* 1959, Dorinda Margery, *d* of late Lieut-Gen. A. E. Percival, CB, DSO and Bar, OBE, MC. *Educ:* Eton; Cambridge Univ. Served with 11th Hussars, 1952-53, with N Irish Horse, 1954-69, Lt-Col 1967-69; Captain, Ulster Defence Regt, 1971-73; Lt-Col, NIH, RARO, 1973-. Mem. (Alliance), N Down, NI Assembly, 1973-75. Governor of BBC for N Ireland, 1967-73; Mem. Admin. Council, King George's Jubilee Trust, 1974-75; Pres., Royal Ulster Agric. Soc., 1973-76. DL, Co. Down, 1964-. *Recreations:* vintage motoring, mixtures and mutations. *Heir:* cousin Major Sir Michael Mulholland, Bt, *qv. Address:* Ballywalter Park, Co. Down, Northern Ireland. *T:* Ballywalter 203. *Clubs:* Cavalry and Guards; Ulster (Belfast).

DUNLEAVY, Philip, JP; company director since 1975; Leader, Cardiff City Council, 1974-76; *b* 5 Oct. 1915; *s* of Michael and Bridget Dunleavy; *m* 1936, Valerie Partridge; two *s* two *d. Educ:* St Cuthbert's Sch., Cardiff. Served War, TA (Sgt), 1939-46. Post Office, 1930-39 and 1946-75 (Executive Officer, 1960-

75). Mem., Cardiff City Council. JP 1960. *Recreations:* youth, conservation, local historical research, local govt political activity.

DUNLOP, Agnes M. R.; *see* Kyle, Elisabeth.

DUNLOP, Rear-Adm. Colin Charles Harrison, CB 1972; CBE 1963; DL; Director General: Cable Television Association, since 1977; National Television Rental Association, since 1977; *b* 4 March 1918; *s* of late Engr Rear-Adm. S. H. Dunlop, CB; *m* 1941, Moyra Patricia O'Brien Gorges; two *s* (and one *s* decd). *Educ:* Marlborough Coll. Joined RN, 1935; served War of 1939-45 at sea in HM Ships Kent, Valiant, Diadem and Orion; subseq. HMS Sheffield, 1957-59; Sec. to 1st Sea Lord, 1960-63; comd HMS Pembroke, 1964-66; Programme Evaluation Gp, MoD, 1966-68; Director, Defence Policy (A), MoD, 1968-69; Comdr, British Naval Staff, Washington, 1969-71; Chief Naval Supply and Secretariat Officer, 1970-74; Flag Officer, Medway, and Port Adm., Chatham, 1971-74, retd 1974. DL Kent 1976. *Recreations:* cricket, shooting. *Address:* Chanceford Farm, Sand Lane, Frittenden, near Cranbrook, Kent. *T:* Frittenden 242. *Clubs:* Army and Navy; MCC, I Zingari, Free Foresters, Incogniti, RN Cricket, Band of Brothers.

DUNLOP, Cdre David Kennedy B.; *see* Buchanan-Dunlop.

DUNLOP, Maj.-Gen. Dermott, CB 1949; CBE 1944; *b* 3 Nov. 1898; *s* of late Lieut-Col A. S. Dunlop, RA, Knowle, Lustleigh, S Devon; *m* 1935, Ethel Whitson Scott; two *s. Educ:* Sandroyd; Charterhouse; RMA, Woolwich. Commissioned RA 1916; served European War, 1916-19, France and Flanders, RHA (wounded); service at Home and Abroad in various Regtl Staff and Instructional appts, 1919-39; Bde Comdr UK, 1940-41; Middle East and 8th Army, 1942-45; UK, 1946-47; Comdr 2nd Army Group, RA, Tripolitania, 1947-48; GOC, Singapore District, 1948-51, and MEC, Colony of Singapore, 1948-51; Major, 1938; Temp. Lieut-Col 1939; Temp. Brig. 1941; Temp. Maj.-Gen., 1948; Maj.-Gen. 1949; retired, July 1951. Employed Colonial Office, 1951-66. *Address:* c/o Lloyd's Bank Ltd, Cox's and King's Branch, 6 Pall Mall, SW1.

DUNLOP, Sir Derrick (Melville), Kt 1960; BA Oxon; MD; FRCP; Extra Physician to the Queen in Scotland since 1965 (Physician, 1961-65); Professor Emeritus of Therapeutics and Clinical Medicine, University of Edinburgh and Consulting Physician, Royal Infirmary, Edinburgh (Professor, 1936-62); *b* 1902; *s* of late George Harry Melville Dunlop, MD, FRCPE; *m* 1936, Marjorie, *d* of late H. E. Richardson, WS; one *s* one *d. Educ:* Oxford and Edinburgh Univs. Formerly: Chairman: Medicines Commn (1969-71); Ministry of Health's Cttee on Safety of Drugs (1964-69); British Pharmacopœia Commission; Vice-Chm. Regional Hosp. Board, SE of Scotland; Mem. Scottish Sec. of State's Adv. Cttee on Medical Research; Ministry of Health's Cttees on Drug Addiction and on Food Policy; Health Services Council's Cttee on Prescribing; Chm. Ministry of Agriculture's Cttee on Food Additives; Chm. Scottish Post-Graduate Medical Assoc.; Chm., Seager Evans, 1969-71; Sim's Commonwealth Travelling Prof.; Lumleian and Croonian Lectr, RCP London. Ed. Quarterly Jl of Med. Hon. Fellow, Brasenose Coll., Oxford, 1968. Hon. FACP; Hon. FRCPE 1972. Hon. LLD Edinburgh, 1967; Hon. DSc: Birmingham, 1967; Eire, 1968; Bradford, 1970. *Publications:* Clinical Chemistry in Practical Medicine; Textbook of Medical Treatment; numerous med. papers. *Recreation:* reading. *Address:* 28 Saxe-Coburg Place, Edinburgh EH3 5BP. *T:* 031-332 2170. *Club:* New (Edinburgh).

DUNLOP, Prof. Douglas Morton; Professor of History, Columbia University, New York, since 1963; *b* 25 Feb. 1909; *o s* of Rev. H. Morton Dunlop and Helen Oliver, *e d* of W. D. Dunn; *m* 1948, Margaret Sinclair, *y d* of Major A. R. Munro, TD, Hillend, Edinburgh. *Educ:* Glasgow Academy; Glasgow Univ.; University Coll. Oxford. Scholar, 1928-32; Vans Dunlop Scholar in Medicine, Edinburgh Univ., 1933; Trinity Coll., Glasgow, 1934-37; Brown Downie Fellow, 1937; Maclean Scholar, 1937 and 1938; University of Bonn, 1937-39; BA Oxon 1939, MA 1960. Trinity Hall, Cambridge (MA) 1950; DLitt Glasgow, 1955. Travelled in Turkey and Syria, 1938; Syria (Jabal Ansariyah), 1939; Asst to Prof. of Hebrew, Glasgow Univ., 1939-46. NFS 1942-44. Asst to Prof. of Oriental Langs, 1947-48, Lectr in Semitic Langs, 1948-50, St Andrews Univ.; Mem. CCG, 1948; Lectr in Islamic History, Cambridge Univ., 1950-62. Visiting Prof. of History, Columbia Univ., 1962-63. FRAS; FIAL. *Publications:* The History of the Jewish Khazars, 1954; The Fusul al-Madani (Aphorisms of the Statesman) of al-Farabi, 1961; Arabic Science in the West, 1965; Arab Civilization to AD 1500, 1971; original papers and reviews in British and foreign Orientalist publications, and articles in encyclopædias. *Recreations:* hill-walking, Scottish history. *Address:* 423 West 120th Street, New York, NY 10027, USA. *T:* 749-6557; 46 Owlstone Road, Cambridge. *T:* 54147.

DUNLOP, Sir (Ernest) Edward, Kt 1969; CMG 1965; OBE 1947; Consultant Surgeon; Consultant, Royal Melbourne Hospital, since 1967; *b* Wangaratta, Australia, 12 July 1907; *s* of James Henry and Alice Emily Maud Dunlop; *m* 1945, Helen Raeburn Ferguson, *d* of Mephan Ferguson; two *s. Educ:* Benalla High Sch.; Victorian Coll. of Pharmacy, Melbourne; Ormond Coll., Melbourne Univ.; St Bartholomew's, London. Qual. in Pharmacy, Gold Medallist, 1928; MB, BS Melbourne Univ., 1st Cl. Hons and Exhibn 1934; MS Melbourne 1937; FRCS 1938; FRACS 1947; FACS 1964. Membre Titulaire, Internat. Soc. of Surgeons; Mem., James IV Assoc. of Surgeons, 1971. Ho. Surg. and Registrar, Royal Melbourne Hosp., 1935-36; Royal Children's, Melbourne, 1937; Brit. Post-Grad. Med. Sch., Hammersmith, 1938; Specialist Surgeon, EMS London, St Mary's, Paddington, 1939. Served War, 1939-46 (despatches, OBE); RAAMC (Capt. to Col), Europe. Middle East and Far East. Hon. Surg. Royal Melbourne Hosp., 1946, Senior Hon. Surg. 1964-67; Hon. Surg. Victorian Eye and Ear Hosp., 1949, Hon. Life Governor, 1967; Cons. Surg., Peter MacCallum Clinic, Cancer and Repatriation Dept. Colombo Plan Adviser, Thailand and Ceylon 1956, India 1960-64; Team Leader, Australian Surgical Team, South Vietnam, 1969-75; CMO, British Phosphate Commn, 1974. Vice-Pres. Victorian Anti-Cancer Council (Chm. Executive, 1975). Cecil Joll Prize and Lectr, RCS 1960. Pres. Aust.-Asian Assoc., Victoria; Pres. Ex-POW and Relatives Assoc., Victoria; Chm., Prime Minister's POW Relief Fund; President: Australian Ex-POW Assoc., 1971-73; Victorian Foundn on Alcoholism and Drug Dependence; Chm., Adv. Cttee on Drug Educn, Victorian Min. of Health, 1972-; Member: Standing Cttee on Health Problems of Alcohol, Nat. Health and Medical Res. Council, 1973; Council, Ormond Coll.; Cttee, Nurses' Meml Centre, Melbourne; Exec., Vict. Red Cross Soc.; Victorian Cttee, Queen's Jubilee Appeal, 1977; Vice-Pres., 3rd Asian Pacific Congress of Gastroenterology, 1968; Vice-Pres., Melbourne Scots Soc., 1974-75. Australian of the Year Award, 1977. Hon. Mem., Assoc. of Surgeons of India, 1974. Hon. Fellow Pharmaceutical Soc. of Victoria; Hon. Fellow AMA, 1973. Hon. DSc (Punjab), 1966. Freedom of City, Wanganui, NZ, 1962. *Publications:* Carcinoma of the Oesophagus; Reflections upon Surgical Treatment, 1960; Appendix of Into the Smother, 1963; contribs to med. and surg. jls. *Recreations:* farming, travelling, golf; Rugby Union football (Blue, Aust. Caps 1932-34, British Barbarians 1939); formerly boxing (Blue). *Address:* (home) 605 Toorak Road, Toorak, Victoria 3142, Australia. *T:* 20 4749; (professional) 14 Parliament Place, East Melbourne, Victoria 3002, Australia. *T:* 63 1214. *Clubs:* Melbourne; Naval and Military, Peninsula Golf, Melbourne Cricket (Melbourne); Barbarian Football.

DUNLOP, Frank, CBE 1977; Founder, 1969, Director, 1969-77 and Consultant, since 1977, The Young Vic; *b* 15 Feb. 1927; *s* of Charles Norman Dunlop and Mary Aarons. *Educ:* Kibworth Beauchamp Grammar Sch.; University Coll., London. BA Hons, English. Postgrad. Sch. in Shakespeare, at Shakespeare Inst., Stratford-upon-Avon; Old Vic Sch., London. Served with RAF before going to University. Director of: (own young theatre co.) Piccolo Theatre, Manchester, 1954; The Enchanted, for Bristol Old Vic Co., 1955; Arts Council Midland Theatre Co., 1955; Associate Dir, Bristol Old Vic, 1956; Writer and Dir, Les Frères Jacques' presentation, Adelphi, 1960; Director: Théâtre de Poche, Brussels, 1959-60; London première, The Bishop's Bonfire, Mermaid, 1960; Nottingham Playhouse, 1961-63; Schweyk, Mermaid, 1963; New Nottingham Playhouse, 1963-64; The Taming of the Shrew, Univ. Arts Centre, Oklahoma, 1965; Any Wednesday, Apollo, 1965; Too True to be Good, Edinburgh Fest., also Strand and Garrick, 1965; Saturday Night and Sunday Morning, Prince of Wales, 1966; (Founder and Dir) Pop Theatre, 1966; The Winter's Tale and The Trojan Women, Edin. and Venice Festivals, also Cambridge Theatre, London, 1966; The Burglar, Vaudeville, 1967; Getting Married, Strand, 1967; A Midsummer Night's Dream and The Tricks of Scapin, Edin. Fest. and Saville Theatre, London, 1967; Assoc. Dir, 1967-71 and Admin. Dir, 1968-71, The Nat. Theatre; productions: Nat. Theatre: Edward II (Brecht and Marlowe); Home and Beauty; Macrune's Guevara; The White Devil; Captain of Kopenik; Young Vic: (author and Dir) Scapino 1970, NY 1974, LA 1975, Australia 1975, Oslo 1975; The Taming of the Shrew, 1970; The Comedy of Errors, 1971; The Maids, Deathwatch, 1972; The Alchemist, 1972; Bible One, 1972; French Without Tears, 1973; Joseph and the Amazing Technicolor Dreamcoat (Roundhouse and Albery Theatre), 1973, NY 1976; Much Ado About Nothing, 1973; Macbeth, 1975; Antony and Cleopatra, 1976; for Théâtre National de Belgique: Pantagleise, 1970; Antony and Cleopatra, 1971;

Pericles, 1972; for Royal Court: A Sense of Detachment, 1972; RSC: Sherlock Holmes, Aldwych, 1974, NY 1974; Habeas Corpus, NY 1975; The New York Idea, The Three Sisters, NY 1977. Mem., Arts Council Young People's Panel, 1968. Governor, Central School of Arts and Crafts, 1970. Hon. Fellow of Shakespeare Inst. *Recreation:* travel. *Address:* The Young Vic Theatre, The Cut, SE1 8LP.

DUNLOP, John; MP (UUUP) Mid-Ulster since 1974; *b* 20 May 1910; *s* of Martin T. and Agnes Dunlop, Belfast; *m* 1st, 1936, Ruby Hunter; two *s* (and one *s* decd); 2nd, 1970, Joyce Campbell. *Educ:* primary sch. and techn. college. Apprentice multiple grocers, 1926; assumed management, 1934; acquired own business, 1944; still in catering. Mem. (VULC), Mid-Ulster, NI Assembly, 1973-74. Civil Defence Medal and ribbon 1945. *Recreations:* music, choral singing, amateur soccer. *Address:* Manor House, Moneymore, Magherafelt, Co. Londonderry BT4 5BG. *T:* 064-874 206.

DUNLOP, Sir John (Wallace), KBE 1971; Australian Company Director; Chairman: Edwards Dunlop and Co. Ltd; Australian Estates Ltd; Director: Australian Industry Development Corporation; Rothmans of Pall Mall (Australia) Ltd; Lansing Bagnall (Aust.) Pty Ltd; *b* 20 May 1910; *s* of late W. P. Dunlop, Sydney; *m* 1st, 1932, Phyllis Haley; one *s* one *d*; 2nd, 1960, Patricia Lloyd Jones. *Educ:* Tudor House; Geelong Grammar Sch.; Univ. of Sydney. Member (Bd or Cttee): Inst. of Directors in Australia, 1968-; Sydney Advisory Bd, the Salvation Army, 1970. *Address:* 9 Duxford Street, Paddington, NSW 2021, Australia. *T:* 3583217. *Clubs:* Australian, Union, Royal Sydney Golf (all Sydney).

DUNLOP, Norman Gordon Edward; Chief Executive, Commercial Union Assurance Co. Ltd, 1972-77; *b* 16 April 1928; *s* of Ross Munn Dunlop, CA; *m* 1952, Jean Taylor; one *s* one *d. Educ:* Trinity Coll., Glenalmond. CA. Thompson McLintock & Co., Glasgow, 1945-56; De Havilland and Hawker Siddeley Companies, 1956-64; Commercial Union Assce Co. Ltd, 1964. Director: Govett European Trust Ltd, 1972-; Montagu Boston Investment Trust. *Recreations:* gardening, fishing, ski-ing. *Address:* 40 Addisland Court, Holland Villas Road, W14 8DA. *T:* 01-602 3503.

DUNLOP, Richard B.; *see* Buchanan-Dunlop.

DUNLOP, Roy Leslie, CMG 1965; The Clerk of the Parliament, Queensland, 1954-68; *b* 14 April 1899; *s* of E. J. D. Dunlop; *m* 1925, Olive M. F. Black; one *s. Educ:* Rockhampton. Parliamentary service, 1920-68; 2nd Clerk-Asst, 1920-32; Clerk-Asst and Sergeant-at-Arms, 1933-54. Hon. Sec., Commonwealth Parliamentary Assoc., 1954-68. *Address:* 30 Ralston Street, Wilston, Queensland 4051, Australia. *T:* 356-3914.

DUNLOP, Sir Thomas, 3rd Bt, *cr* 1916; Partner, Thomas Dunlop & Sons, Ship & Insurance Brokers, Glasgow, since 1938; *b* 11 April 1912; *s* of Sir Thomas Dunlop, 2nd Bt; *S* father, 1963; *m* 1947, Adda Mary Alison, *d* of T. Arthur Smith, Lindsaylands, Biggar, Lanarks; one *s* two *d. Educ:* Shrewsbury; St John's Coll., Cambridge (BA). Chartered Accountant, 1939. Former Chm., Savings Bank of Glasgow. Member: Cttee of Princess Louise Scottish Hosp., Erskine; Royal Alfred Merchant Seamen's Soc.; Governor, Hutcheson's Educational Trust. OStJ 1965. *Recreations:* shooting, fishing, golf. *Heir:* *s* Thomas Dunlop, *b* 22 April 1951. *Address:* The Corrie, Kilmacolm, Renfrewshire. *T:* Kilmacolm 3239. *Club:* Western (Glasgow).

DUNLOP, Sir William (Norman Gough), Kt 1975; JP; Managing Director, Dunlop Farms Ltd; *b* 9 April 1914; *s* of Norman Matthew Dunlop and Alice Ada Dunlop (*née* Gough); *m* 1940, Ruby Jean (*née* Archie); three *s* three *d. Educ:* Waitaki Boys' High Sch. Farmer in Canterbury, NZ. President: Federated Farmers, NZ, 1973-74; Coopworth Sheep Soc., NZ, 1971-74; Member: Agriculture Adv. Council, NZ, 1970-74; Immigration Adv. Council, NZ, 1971-; Transport Adv. Council, NZ, 1971-; Trustee, Todd Foundn, 1973-; Chm., Neurological Foundn (Canterbury), 1975-; Dep. Chm., NZ Meat and Wool Board Electoral Coll., 1973; Director: Rural Bank & Finance Corp., NZ, 1974-; New Zealand Light Leathers, 1973-. Internat. Visitors Award, US Dept of State, 1971. JP 1972. *Recreations:* music, gardening. *Address:* Brenley, No 5 RD, Christchurch, NZ. *T:* Burnham 757. *Clubs:* Civil Service (Wellington); Canterbury (Christchurch).

DUNLUCE, Viscount; *see under* Antrim, 14th Earl of (who succeeded 1977, but continues to be known as Viscount Dunluce).

DUNMORE, 9th Earl of, *cr* 1686; **John Alexander Murray;** Viscount Fincastle, Lord Murray, 1686; Baron Dunmore (UK),

1831; Public Relations consultant; Director, Charles Barker Scotland Ltd; *b* 3 April 1939; *g s* of 8th Earl of Dunmore, VC, DSO, MVO; *o s* of Viscount Fincastle (killed in action, 1940) and Hon. Pamela Kate Hermon-Hodge (who *m* 2nd, 1944, Capt. Follett Watson Bell, RA), *e d* of 2nd Baron Wyfold, DSO, MVO; *S* grandfather, 1962; *m* 1967, Anne Augusta, *e d* of T. C. Wallace, Dounby, Orkney; two *d. Educ:* Eton. National Service, 1957-59, TA Service, 1959-65, The Queen's Own Cameron Highldrs. PRO, Schweppes (USA) Ltd, New York, 1964-67; MIPR 1968. *Recreation:* hill walking. *Heir: kinsman* Reginald Arthur Murray [*b* 17 July 1911; *m* 1948, Patricia Mary, *d* of Frank Coles; two *d*]. *Address:* 14 Regent Terrace, Edinburgh EH7 5BN. *Club:* Caledonian.

DUNN, Lt-Col Sir (Francis) Vivian, KCVO 1969 (CVO 1954); OBE 1960; FRAM; Royal Marines (retired, 1968) as Principal Director of Music; *b* 1908; *s* of Captain W. J. Dunn, MVO, Royal Horse Guards; *m* 1938, Margery Kathleen Halliday. *Address:* c/o Royal Marines School of Music, Deal, Kent.

DUNN, Col George Willoughby, CBE 1959; DSO 1943 and Bar 1944; MC 1943; TD 1949; DL; Partner, Clark, Oliver Dewar & Webster, Solicitors, Arbroath; Director, Alliance Trust and other companies; Member of Queen's Body Guard for Scotland (Royal Company of Archers); *b* 27 March 1914; *s* of Willoughby Middleton Dunn, coal owner, Lanarkshire; *m* 1944, Louise Wilson, *er d* of Alexander Stephen MacLellan, LLD, ship builder and engr, Glasgow; two *d. Educ:* Trinity Coll., Glenalmond; Glasgow Univ. BL 1937; Solicitor, 1937. Served War of 1939-45 with 51st Highland Div., Middle East, N Africa, Sicily and NW Europe; Col late TA The Black Watch. Chm., Royal British Legion Scotland, 1971-74. DL Angus 1971. *Recreations:* golf, fishing. *Address:* Letham House, St Vigeans, Arbroath, Angus. *T:* Arbroath 72538. *Clubs:* Naval and Military; New (Edinburgh); Eastern (Dundee); Royal and Ancient (St Andrews).

DUNN, James Anthony; MP (Lab) Kirkdale Division of Liverpool since 1964; Parliamentary Under-Secretary of State, Northern Ireland Office, since 1976; *b* 30 Jan. 1926; *s* of James Richard Dunn and Margaret (*née* McDermott); *m* 1954, Dorothy (*née* Larkey); two *s* two *d. Educ:* St Teresa's Sch., Liverpool; London Sch. of Economics and Political Science. Chairman: Newsham Community Council; Lyster Youth Club; St John's Youth Centre, Liverpool. Member: Internat. Playgrounds Assoc.; Episcopal Commn for Justice and Peace; Governors, Kirkdale Community Centre; Liverpool City Council, 1958-66. Mem. Bd, British Inst. for the Achievement of Human Potential; Assoc. Mem., Philadelphia Inst. and World Organisation for the Achievement of Human Potential. Opposition Whip, 1971-74; a Lord Comr, HM Treasury, 1974-76. Member: Estimates Cttee; House of Commons Services Ctte. *Recreation:* youth clubs. *Address:* 45 Lisburn Lane, Liverpool L13 9AF. *T:* 051-226 6054.

DUNN, Brig. Keith Frederick William, CBE 1941; DL; retired; *b* 31 July 1891; *s* of Brig.-Gen. R. H. W. Dunn, DL, Althrey, Wrexham, and Constance, *d* of Maj.-Gen. G. E. Erskine; *m* 1st, 1915, Ava (*d* 1938), *d* of Brig.-Gen. H. F. Kays, CB; one *s* one *d* (and one *s* decd); 2nd, 1946, Joan, *d* of Sir Frank Beauchamp, 1st Bt, CBE and *widow* of Major Claude de Lisle Bush. *Educ:* Wellington Coll.; RMA 2nd Lieut RA 1911. Served European War, 1914-19 (despatches). Equitation Sch., Weedon, 1922-25; Adjt RMA, 1926-29; Lieut-Col 1938; served in North West Europe, 1939; Brig. 1939; CRA, 1st Cavalry Div., 1939-40; comd 5th Cavalry Bde, MEF, 1940-41; retd 1942; re-employed, comd Glos Sub-District, 1942-45. Chief Training Officer, Min. of Agriculture and Fisheries, 1946-47. DL Glos, 1960. *Recreations:* hunting, golf. *Address:* Bencombe House, Uley, Dursley, Glos. *T:* Uley 255. *Club:* Army and Navy.
See also Sir R. H. W. Dunn.

DUNN, Air Marshal Sir Patrick Hunter, KBE 1965 (CBE 1950); CB 1956; DFC 1941; FRAeS; *b* 31 Dec. 1912; *s* of late William Alexander Dunn, Ardentinny, Argyllshire; *m* 1939, Diana Ledward Smith; two *d. Educ:* Glasgow Academy; Loretto; Glasgow Univ. Commissioned, 1933, Pre-war service in flying boats; as flying instructor 500 (County of Kent) Sqdn, AAF; with the Long Range Development Unit and as instructor at the Central Flying Sch. War service included command of 80 and 274 Fighter Squadrons and 71 OTU, all in Middle East (1940-42); at Air Ministry, and in Fighter Command, Sector Commander, 1945-46. Post-war service in Air Ministry, 1947-48; Malaya, 1949-50; NATO Defence Coll., 1950-52; Fighter Command, 1953-56; ADC to the Queen, 1953-58. AOC and Commandant, RAF Flying Coll., 1956-58; Deputy Air Sec., 1959-61; AOC No. 1 Group, Bomber Command, 1961-64; AOC-in-Chief, Flying Training Command, 1964-66; retired

from RAF, 1967. Director i/c Management Services, British Steel Corp., 1967-68; resigned to become Dep. Chm., British Eagle Internat. Airlines Ltd; Chm., Eagle Aircraft Services, 1969; Aviation Consultant, British Steel Corporation, 1969-76. Mem. Council, Air League, 1968-73 and 1975- (Dep. Chm., 1972-73; Chm., Defence Cttee, 1968-73); Mem., British Atlantic Cttee, 1976-. A Trustee and Governor of Loretto, 1959-; Chm., Fettesian-Lorettonian Club, 1972-75. *Recreations:* squash, tennis, sailing, shooting. *Address:* Little Hillbark, Cookham Dean, Berks. *Clubs:* Royal Air Force, Hurlingham.
See also Sir John Denton Marsden, Bt.

DUNN, Sir Robin Horace Walford, Kt 1969; MC 1944; **Hon. Mr Justice Dunn;** Judge of the High Court of Justice Family Division (formerly Probate, Divorce and Admiralty Division), since 1969; Presiding Judge, Western Circuit, since 1974; *b* 16 Jan. 1918; *s* of Brig. K. F. W. Dunn, *qv*, and of Ava, *d* of Brig.-Gen. H. F. Kays, CB; *m* 1941, Judith, *d* of late Sir Gonne Pilcher, MC; one *s* one *d* (and one *d* decd). *Educ:* Wellington; Royal Military Academy, Woolwich (Sword of Honour). First Commissioned, RA, 1938; RHA, 1941; Staff Coll., 1946; retired (hon. Major), 1948. Served War of 1939-45; France and Belgium, 1939-40; Western Desert and Libya, 1941-42; Normandy and NW Europe, 1944-45 (wounded thrice, despatches twice, MC). Called to Bar (Inner Temple), 1948; Master of the Bench, Inner Temple, 1969. Western Circuit, Junior Counsel to Registrar of Restrictive Trading Agreements, 1959-62; QC 1962. Treas., Gen. Council of the Bar, 1967-69 (Mem., 1959-63); Chm. Betting Levy Appeal Tribunal, 1964-69; Dep. Chm., Somerset QS, 1965-71; Mem., Lord Chancellor's Cttee on Legal Educn, 1968-69. *Recreation:* hunting. *Address:* 42 Roland Way, SW7. *T:* 01-373 1319; Lynch, Allerford, Somerset. *T:* Porlock 862509.

DUNN, Prof. Thomas Alexander; Professor of Literature and Head of Department of English Studies, University of Stirling, since 1966; *b* 6 March 1923; *s* of James Symington Dunn and Elizabeth Taylor; *m* 1947, Joyce Mary Armstrong; two *s* one *d . Educ:* Dumfries Academy; Edinburgh Univ. (MA, PhD). Served War, Pilot, Fleet Air Arm, Sub-Lt (A) RNVR, 1942-45. Univ. of Ghana, 1953, Prof., 1960; Prof., Univ. of Lagos, 1964-65; Visiting Prof., Univ. of Western Ontario, 1965-66; University of Stirling: Mem., Academic Council, 1966-, Univ. Court, 1968-72; Chm., Board of Studies for Arts, 1975-; Chm., MacRobert Arts Centre, 1973-. Member: Inter-Univ. Council for Higher Educn Overseas, 1967-75; Scottish Univs Council on Entrance, 1968-74; Consultative Cttee on the Curriculum, 1968-76. Member: Scottish Arts Council, 1969-; Arts Council of Gt Britain, 1971-73; Broadcasting Council for Scotland, 1972-76; Films of Scotland, 1972-; Chairman: Univs Cttee on Scottish Literature, 1970-; Drama Cttee, 1972-; Grants to Publishers Panel, 1975-; Pres., Assoc. for Scottish Literary Studies, 1972-76. *Publications:* Philip Massinger: the man and the playwright, 1957; (with D. E. S. Maxwell) Introducing Poetry, 1966; Massinger and Field: The Fatal Dowry, 1969; (ed) Universitas (Ghana), 1955-63; (ed) Fountainwell Drama Texts. *Recreations:* gardening, theatre and arts generally. *Address:* Coney Park, 121 Henderson Street, Bridge of Allan, Stirling FK9 4RQ. *T:* Stirling 833373. *Club:* Stirling and County (Stirling).

DUNN, Sir Vivian; see Dunn, Sir F. V.

DUNNE, Irene, (Mrs F. D. Griffin), Hon. Doctor of Music, Hon. LLD; *b* Louisville, Kentucky, USA, 20 Dec. 1904; *d* of Joseph A. Dunne and Adelaide A. Henry; *m* 1927, Dr Francis D. Griffin (*d* 1965); one *d. Educ:* Loretta Academy, St Louis, Mo., USA; Chicago Musical Coll., Chicago. Acted in the original Show Boat, 1929. Entered motion pictures, 1931; first film Cimarron. Films include: Back Street, Awful Truth, Roberta, Anna and the King of Siam, Life with Father, I Remember Mama, The Mudlark (as Queen Victoria), Never a Dull Moment. Laetare Medal, University of Notre Dame. Mem. Defence Advisory Cttee, US, to advise on welfare matters in the women's services, 1951; Mem. US Delegation to United Nations 12th Gen. Assembly. *Recreation:* golf. *Address:* 461 North Faring Road, Moment, Los Angeles, Calif 90024, USA. *T:* Crestview 56226.

DUNNE, Most Rev. Patrick, DD; Auxiliary Bishop of Dublin, (RC) and titular Bishop of Nara since 1946; Parish Priest of St Mary's Haddington Road, Dublin; Dean of the Metropolitan Chapter; Vicar-General; *b* Dublin, 3 June 1891. *Educ:* Holy Cross Coll., Clonliffe, Dublin; Irish Coll., Rome. Ordained in Rome, 1913; Sec. to Archbishops of Dublin, 1919-43; Parish Priest, Church of the Holy Family, Aughrim Street, Dublin, 1943-47; Domestic Prelate, 1943. *Address:* St Mary's, Haddington Road, Dublin.

DUNNET, Prof. George Mackenzie, PhD; Regius Professor of Natural History and Head of Department of Zoology, University of Aberdeen, since 1974; *b* 19 April 1928; *s* of John George and Christina I. Dunnet; *m* 1953, Margaret Henderson Thomson; one *s* two *d*. *Educ:* Peterhead Academy; Aberdeen Univ. BSc (1st cl. hons) 1949; PhD 1952. Research Officer, CSIRO, Australia, 1953-58; Lectr in Ecology, Dir Culterty Field Stn, Univ. of Aberdeen, 1958-66, Sen. Lectr 1966-71; Sen. Research Fellow, DSIR, NZ, 1968-69; Prof. of Zoology, Univ. of Aberdeen, 1971-74. FRSE 1970;FInstBiol 1974. *Publications:* contrib. Ibis, Jl Applied Ecol., Aust. Jl Zool., CSIRO Wildl. Res. *Recreations:* hill walking, photography. *Address:* Culterty House, Newburgh, Ellon, Aberdeenshire AB4 0AA. *T:* Newburgh (Aberdeen) 633. *Club:* Royal Commonwealth Society.

DUNNETT, Alastair MacTavish; Chairman, Thomson Scottish Petroleum Ltd, since 1972; Director, Scottish Television, since 1975; Member Executive Board, The Thomson Organisation Ltd, since 1973; *b* 26 Dec. 1908; *s* of David Sinclair Dunnett and Isabella Crawford MacTavish; *m* 1946, Dorothy Halliday; two *s*. *Educ:* Overnewton Sch.; Hillhead High Sch., Glasgow. Commercial Bank of Scotland, Ltd, 1925; Co-founder of The Claymore Press, 1933-34; Glasgow Weekly Herald, 1935-36; The Bulletin, 1936-37; Daily Record, 1937-40; Chief Press Officer, Sec. of State for Scotland, 1940-46; Editor, Daily Record, 1946-55; Editor, The Scotsman, 1956-72; Man. Dir, The Scotsman Publications Ltd, 1962-70, Chm., 1970-74. Smith-Mundt Scholarship to USA, 1951. Governor, Pitlochry Festival Theatre. Member: Scottish Tourist Board, 1956-69; Press Council, 1959-62; Council of Nat. Trust for Scotland, 1962-69; Council of Commonwealth Press Union, 1964-; Edinburgh Univ. Court, 1964-66; Edinburgh Festival Soc. Ltd, 1967-. *Publications:* Treasure at Sonnach, 1935; Heard Tell, 1946; Quest by Canoe, 1950, repr. 1967, as It's Too Late in the Year; Highlands and Islands of Scotland, 1951; (as Alec Tavis) The Duke's Day, 1970; (ed) Alistair Maclean Introduces Scotland, 1972; *plays:* The Original John Mackay, Glasgow Citizens, 1956; Fit to Print, Duke of York's, 1962. *Recreations:* sailing, riding, walking. *Address:* 87 Colinton Road, Edinburgh EH10 5DF. *T:* 031-337 2107. *Clubs:* Caledonian; Scottish Arts, New (Edinburgh).

DUNNETT, Denzil Inglis, CMG 1967; OBE 1962; HM Diplomatic Service; Diplomatic Service Chairman, Civil Service Selection Board, since 1976; *b* 21 Oct. 1917; *s* of late Sir James Dunnett, KCIE and late Annie (*née* Sangster); *m* 1946, Ruth Rawcliffe (*d* 1974); two *s* one *d*. *Educ:* Edinburgh Acad.; Corpus Christi Coll., Oxford. Served with RA, 1939-45. Diplomatic Service: Foreign Office, 1947-48; Sofia, 1948-50; Foreign Office, 1950-53; UK Delegn to OEEC, Paris, 1953-56; Commercial Sec., Buenos Aires, 1956-60; Consul, Elisabethville, 1961-62; Commercial Counsellor, Madrid, 1962-67; seconded to BoT, 1967-70; Counsellor, Mexico City, 1970-73; Ambassador to Senegal, Mauritania, Mali and Guinea, 1973-76, and to Guinea-Bissau, 1975-76. *Recreations:* golf, music. *Address:* 11 Victoria Grove, W8. *T:* 01-584 7523. *Club:* Oxford & Cambridge University.

DUNNETT, Sir George Sangster, KBE 1952; CB 1950; *b* 12 May 1907; *e s* of late Sir James Dunnett, KCIE; *m* 1938, Margaret Rosalind (*d* 1977), *er d* of David Davies, MD, Tunbridge Wells; one *s* three *d*. *Educ:* Edinburgh Academy; Corpus Christi Coll., Oxford. Bd of Educn, 1930; Treasury, 1931; Min. of Civil Aviation, 1946; Dep. Sec., Min. of Agriculture and Fisheries, 1947-56; Chm., Sugar Board, 1956-70. *Recreations:* golf, philosophy. *Address:* Basings Cottage, Cowden, Kent. *T:* Cowden 398. *Club:* Athenæum.

DUNNETT, Jack; MP (Lab) Nottingham East, since 1974 (Central Nottingham, 1964-74); *b* 24 June 1922; *m* 1951; two *s* three *d*. *Educ:* Whitgift Middle Sch., Croydon; Downing Coll., Cambridge (MA, LLB). Served with Cheshire Regt, 1941-46 (Capt.). Admitted Solicitor, 1949. Middlesex CC, 1958-61; Councillor, Enfield Borough Council, 1958-61; Alderman, Enfield Borough Council, 1961-63; Councillor, Greater London Council, 1964-67. Former PPS to: Minister of State, FCO; Minister of Transport. *Recreation:* watching professional football (Chairman, Notts County Football Club). *Address:* Whitehall Court, SW1A 2EP. *T:* 01-839 6962.

DUNNETT, Sir (Ludovic) James, GCB 1969 (KCB 1960; CB 1957); CMG 1948; Permanent Under-Secretary of State, Ministry of Defence, 1966-74; *b* 12 Feb. 1914; *s* of late Sir James Dunnett, KCIE; *m* 1944, Olga Adair; no *c*. *Educ:* Edinburgh Acad.; University Coll., Oxford. Entered Air Ministry, 1936; Private Sec. to Permanent Sec., 1937-44; transferred to Ministry of Civil Aviation, 1945; Under Sec., 1948; Under Sec., Min. of

Supply, 1951, Deputy Sec., 1953; Deputy Sec., Min. of Transport, 1958; Permanent Secretary: Min. of Transport, 1959-62; Min. of Labour, 1962-66. Mem., SSRC, 1977-. Visiting Fellow, Nuffield Coll., Oxford, 1964-72. Chm., Inst. of Manpower Studies, 1977-. *Recreation:* golf. *Address:* 2 Warwick Square, SW1. *T:* 01-834 5144.

DUNNING, John Ernest Patrick, CBE 1973; retired; Director, Rocket Propulsion Establishment, Westcott, 1955-72; *b* 19 Sept. 1912; *s* of late Rev. E. M. Dunning, MA, sometime Rector of Cumberworth and Denby Dale, Yorks; *m* 1939, Mary Meikle Robertson. *Educ:* Wheelwright Gram. Sch., Dewsbury; Downing Coll., Cambridge (Exhibr, MA). 1st cl. hons Mech. Scis Tripos, 1935. Blackstone Ltd, Stamford, 1935-37; Bristol Aeroplane Co. Ltd (Engines), 1937-38; Armstrong Whitworth Securities Ltd (Kadenacy Dept), 1938-40; RAE, 1940-50; Asst Dir, Min. of Supply, 1950-55; Dir, Engine Research, Min. of Supply, 1955. FRAeS, FIMechE; FRSA. *Publications:* scientific and technical papers. *Address:* 24 Coombe Hill Crescent, Thame, Oxon. *T:* Thame 3893. *Club:* North Oxford Golf.

DUNNING, Prof. John Harry, PhD; Professor of International Investment and Business Studies, since 1974 and Head of Department of Economics since 1964, University of Reading; *b* 26 June 1927; *m* 1st, 1948, Ida Teresa Bellamy (marr. diss. 1975); one *s*; 2nd, 1975, Christine Mary Brown. *Educ:* Lower Sch. of John Lyon, Harrow; University Coll. London (BSc (Econ); PhD). Research Asst, University Coll. London, 1951-52; Lectr and Sen. Lectr, Univ. of Southampton, 1952-64; Prof. of Economics, Univ. of Reading, 1964-74. Visiting Prof.: Univ. of Western Ontario, Canada; Univ. of California (Berkeley), 1968-69; Boston Univ., USA, 1976. Consultant to UN and OECD. Member: SE Economic Planning Council, 1966-68; Chemicals EDC, 1968-77; UN Study Gp on Multinational Corps, 1973-74. Dir of Economists: Advisory Gp Ltd; Witton House Ltd. Hon. PhD Uppsala, 1975. *Publications:* American Investment in British Manufacturing Industry, 1958; British Industry (with C. J. Thomas), 1963; Economic Planning and Town Expansion, 1963; Studies in International Investment, 1970; The Multinational Enterprise (ed), 1971; An Economic Study of the City of London (with E. V. Morgan), 1971; (ed) International Investment, 1972; (ed) Economic Analysis and the Multinational Enterprise, 1974; (with R. D. Pearce) Profitability and Performance of World's Largest Industrial Companies, 1975; US Industry in Britain, 1976; (with T. Houston) UK Industry Abroad, 1976; Studies in the Multinational Enterprise, 1978; numerous articles in learned and professional jls. *Address:* University of Reading, Whiteknights Park, Reading, Berks. *T:* Reading 85123.

DUNNING, Sir Simon (William Patrick), 3rd Bt, *cr* 1930; *b* 14 Dec. 1939; *s* of Sir William Leonard Dunning, 2nd Bt, and of Kathleen Lawrie, *d* of J. P. Cuthbert, MC; *S* father, 1961; *m* 1975, Frances Deirdre Morton, *d* of Major Patrick Lancaster; one *d*. *Educ:* Eton. *Recreation:* shooting. *Address:* Low Auchengillan, Blanefield, by Glasgow. *T:* Blanefield 70323. *Clubs:* Turf; Western (Glasgow); Royal Perth Golfing Society.

DUNNINGTON-JEFFERSON, Lt-Col Sir John Alexander, 1st Bt, *cr* 1958; Kt 1944; DSO 1917; LLD (hon.) Leeds; DUniv. York; DL, JP; *b* 10 April 1884; *s* of late Capt. Mervyn Dunnington-Jefferson of Thicket Priory, York; *m* 1938, Isobel, *d* of Col H. A. Cape, DSO; one *s* one *d*. *Educ:* Eton; RMC, Sandhurst. Entered Army (Royal Fusiliers), 1904; retired 1919 with rank of Lieut-Col; served European War, 1914-18 (despatches six times, Bt Major, DSO); St Maurice and St Lazarus (Italy); Couronne and Croix de Guerre (Belgium); Legion of Honour (France). E Riding Yorks CC, 1922-74 (Chm., 1936-68). JP 1921, DL 1936, E Riding Yorks (later N Yorks). *Heir: s* Mervyn Stewart Dunnington-Jefferson [*b* 5 Aug. 1943; *m* 1971, Caroline Anna, *o d* of J. M. Bayley; one *d*]. *Address:* Deighton House, Escrick, York. *Clubs:* Travellers'; Yorkshire (York).

DUNPARK, Hon. Lord; Alastair McPherson Johnston, TD; BA, LLB; FSAScot; a Senator of the College of Justice in Scotland and Lord of Session, since 1971; *b* 15 Dec. 1915; *s* of late Rev. A. M. Johnston, BD, Stirling; *m* 1939, Katharine Margaret (Bunty), *d* of Charles Mitchell, Chislehurst; three *s*. *Educ:* Merchiston Castle Sch.; Jesus Coll., Cambridge; Edinburgh Univ. RA (TA), 1939-46 (despatches); Staff Coll., Haifa, 1943; Major 1943. Mem. of Faculty of Advocates, 1946; QC (Scotland), 1958. Sheriff of Dumfries and Galloway, 1966-68; Mem., Scottish Law Commn, 1968-71. Chairman: The Cockburn Assoc. (Edinburgh Civic Trust), 1969-74; Royal Artillery Assoc., E of Scotland District, 1946-60, Scottish Region, 1962-; Edinburgh Marriage Guidance Council, 1969-72 (Pres., 1973-); Council, St George's Sch. for Girls, Edinburgh,

1973-; Edinburgh Legal Dispensary, 1961-. Hon. Fellow, Edinburgh Univ., 1969. *Publications:* Jt Editor, 3rd edn of Walton's Law of Husband and Wife, 1951; Jt Editor, 7th edn of Gloag and Henderson's Introduction to Law of Scotland, 1968. *Recreations:* fishing, golf. *Address:* 8 Heriot Row, Edinburgh EH3 6HU. *T:* 031-556 4663; Parkend, Stichill, Roxburghshire. *T:* Stichill 256. *Club:* New (Edinburgh).

DUNPHIE, Maj.-Gen. Sir Charles (Anderson Lane), Kt 1959; CB 1948; CBE 1942; DSO 1943; *b* 20 April 1902; *s* of late Sir Alfred Dunphie, KCVO, Rotherfield Greys, Oxon; *m* 1931, Eileen, *d* of late Lieut-Gen. Sir Walter Campbell, KCB, KCMG, DSO; one *s* one *d. Educ:* RN Colls Osborne and Dartmouth; RMA Woolwich. Commissioned into RA, 1921; served War of 1939-45 (wounded, despatches); Brig. RAC, 1941; Comdr 26 Armoured Bde, 1942-43; Dep. Dir RAC, War Office, 1943-45; Temp. Maj.-Gen., Dir Gen. Armoured Fighting Vehicles 1945-48; retired 1948. Joined Vickers Ltd, 1948; Chm., 1962-67. One of HM's Honourable Corps of Gentlemen-at-Arms, 1952-62. US Legion of Merit (Commander); US Silver Star. *Address:* Elliscombe House, Wincanton, Somerset. *Club:* Army and Navy.

DUNPHY, Rev. Thomas Patrick, SJ; Vicar for Religious Sisters in Devon and Dorset, since 1977; *b* Donnybrook, Dublin, 17 Aug. 1913; *o s* of Thomas Joseph Dunphy and Agnes Mary (*née* Rogers), Dublin. *Educ:* Wimbledon Coll. Joined Soc. of Jesus, 1932; Priest, 1946. Headmaster of St John's (preparatory sch. of Beaumont Coll.), 1949-64; Rector, Beaumont Coll., 1964-67; Socius to the Provincial of the Society of Jesus, 1967-71; Rector, Stonyhurst Coll., 1971-77. *Address:* Syon Abbey, South Brent, Devon.

DUNRAVEN and MOUNT-EARL, 7th Earl of, *cr* 1822; **Thady Windham Thomas Wyndham-Quin;** Baron Adare, 1800; Viscount Mountearl, 1816; Viscount Adare, 1822; Bt 1871; *b* 27 Oct. 1939; *s* of 6th Earl of Dunraven and Mount-Earl, CB, CBE, MC, and Nancy, *d* of Thomas B. Yuille, Halifax County, Va; *S* father 1965; *m* 1969, Geraldine, *d* of Air Commodore Gerard W. McAleer, CBE, MB, BCh, DTM&H, Wokingham; one *d. Educ:* Ludgrove; Le Rosey. *Address:* Adare Manor, Adare, Co. Limerick, Ireland. *Clubs:* White's; Kildare Street and University (Dublin).

DUNROSSIL, 2nd Viscount, *cr* 1959; **John William Morrison;** HM Diplomatic Service; Counsellor, British Embassy, Brussels, since 1975; *b* 22 May 1926; *e s* of William Shepherd Morrison, 1st Viscount Dunrossil, PC, GCMG, MC, QC; *S* father, 1961; *m* 1st, 1951, Mavis (marr. diss. 1969), *d* of A. Ll. Spencer-Payne, LRCP, MRCS, LDS; three *s* one *d*; 2nd, 1969, Diana Mary Cunliffe, *d* of C. M. Vise; two *d. Educ:* Fettes; Oxford. Royal Air Force, 1945-48, Flt-Lieut (Pilot). Joined Commonwealth Relations Office, 1951; Asst Private Sec. to Sec. of State, 1952-54; Second Sec., Canberra, 1954-56; CRO, 1956-58; First Sec. and Acting Deputy High Commissioner, Dacca, East Pakistan, 1958-60; First Sec., Pretoria/Capetown, 1961-64; FO, 1964-68; seconded to Intergovernmental Maritime Consultative Org., 1968-70; Counsellor and Head of Chancery, British High Commn, Ottawa, 1970-74. *Heir:* s Hon. Andrew William Reginald Morrison, *b* 15 Dec. 1953. *Address:* c/o Foreign and Commonwealth Office, SW1; 1 Temple Gardens, EC4. *Clubs:* Royal Air Force, Royal Commonwealth Society; Cercle Royal Gaulois (Brussels).

DUNSANY, 19th Baron of, *cr* 1439; **Randal Arthur Henry Plunkett;** Lieut-Col (retd) Indian Cavalry (Guides); *b* 25 Aug. 1906; *o s* of 18th Baron Dunsany, DL, LittD, and Rt Hon. Beatrice, Lady Dunsany (*d* 1970); *S* father, 1957; *m* 1st, 1938, Mrs Vera Bryce (from whom he obtained a divorce, 1947), *d* of Señor G. De Sà Sottomaior, São Paulo, Brazil; one *s*; 2nd, 1947, Sheila Victoria Katrin, widow of Major John Frederick Foley, Baron de Rutzen, DL, JP, CC, Welsh Guards (killed in action, 1944), *o d* of Sir Henry Philipps, 2nd Bt; one *d. Educ:* Eton. Joined the 16th/5th Lancers (SR), 1926; transferred to the Indian Army, 1928, Guides Cavalry, Indian Armoured Corps, retired, 1947. *Heir:* s Hon. Edward John Carlos Plunkett [*b* 10 Sept. 1939. *Educ:* Eton; Slade Sch. of Fine Art]. *Address:* (Seat) Dunsany Castle, Co. Meath, Ireland. *T:* 046-25198. *Clubs:* Beefsteak, Bath, Cavalry and Guards; Kildare Street and University (Dublin).

DUNSHEATH, Percy, CBE 1946; MA Cantab, DSc (Eng) London; Hon. DEng Sheffield; Hon. LLD London; Member of Senate, University of London, 1946-67; *b* 16 Aug. 1886; *s* of late Hugh and Anna Dunsheath, Sheffield; *m* 1st, 1910, Elizabeth Alice, *d* of W. D. F. Vincent, Acton; one *d* decd and one *s* killed on active service; 2nd, 1938, Cissie Providence (*d* 1976), *d* of C. Houchen, Hempnall, Norwich. *Educ:* Sheffield Grammar Sch.;

Universities of Sheffield, London and Cambridge (Mech. Sci. Tripos). GPO Engineer in Chief's office, 1908-19. Served European War, 1914-18; commissioned; France (despatches twice, OBE). Research Dir, W. T. Henley's, 1919; subs. Chief Engineer; retd, 1946. President, Instn of Electrical Engineers, 1945-46, Hon. mem., 1964-; Chm. of Convocation, University of London, 1949-61. Mem. Heyworth Cttee on Univ. appointments Boards, 1964. Pres. Internat. Electrotechnical Commn (1955-58); Pres. British Electrical Development Association (1952-53); Past Chm. Govs Woolwich Polytechnic; Pres. ASLIB (Assoc. Special Libraries Information Bureau), 1949, 1950; Chairman: London Reg. Academic Board Technical Educ., 1947-53; FBI Educ. Cttee, 1951-55; Cttee on Shortage of Science Teachers, 1954. Chm., Cambridge Instrument Co., 1956-63 (Dir 1950-64). Faraday lecturer, 1947; Royal Institution Christmas Lectures, 1949. Hon. Fellow, University Coll., London, 1967. *Publications:* The Graduate in Industry, 1947; (ed) A century of Technology, 1951; The Electric Current, 1951; Industrial Research, 1956; Convocation in the University of London, 1958; Electricity: How it works, 1960; A History of Electrical Engineering, 1961; Giants of Electricity, 1967; Dordogne Days, 1972; Nearly Ninety, 1975; many papers and articles on scientific, technical and educational subjects. *Recreation:* water colour painting. *Address:* Wotton Cottage, Westcott, Dorking RH4 3NG. *T:* Dorking 81552.

DUNSTAN, (Andrew Harold) Bernard, RA 1968 (ARA 1959); painter; *b* 19 Jan. 1920; *s* of late Dr A. E. Dunstan; *m* 1949, Diana Maxwell Armfield; three *s. Educ:* St Paul's; Byam Shaw Sch.; Slade Sch. Has exhibited at RA since 1945. Many one-man exhibitions; now exhibits regularly at Agnews, Bond St. Pictures in public collections include London Museum, Bristol Art Gall., Nat. Gall. of NZ, Arts Council, Nat. Portrait Gall., and many in private collections. Member: New English Art Club; Royal West of England Acad. *Publications:* Learning to Paint, 1970; Painting in Progress, 1976; Painting Methods of the Impressionists, 1976. *Recreations:* music, walking in London. *Address:* 10 High Park Road, Kew, Richmond, Surrey. *T:* 01-876 6633.

DUNSTAN, Hon. Donald Allan; Premier of South Australia, 1967, and since 1970; MP (Labor) since 1953; *b* 21 Sept. 1926; of S Australian parents; *m* 1st, 1949, Grete Ellis (marr. diss.); two *s* one *d*; 2nd, 1976, Adele Koh. *Educ:* St Peter's Coll. and Univ. of Adelaide, S Australia. Attorney-Gen. of S Australia, 1965; Premier, Treasurer, Attorney-Gen. and Minister of Housing, 1967-68; Leader of Opposition, 1968-70. Freeman of City of Georgetown, Penang, 1973. *Address:* 15 Clara Street, Norwood, SA 5067, Australia. *T:* 227-2688. *Club:* Adelaide Democratic.

DUNSTAN, Maj.-Gen. Donald Beaumont, CB 1972; CBE 1969 (MBE 1954); GOC Field Force Command, Sydney, since 1974; *b* 18 Feb. 1923; *s* of late Oscar Reginald Dunstan and of Eileen Dunstan; *m* 1947, Beryl June Dunningham; two *s. Educ:* Prince Alfred Coll., South Australia; RMC, Duntroon. Served War of 1939-45: Regimental and Staff appts in SW Pacific Area, 1942-45. Served in Korea, 1954; Instructor, Staff Coll., Camberley, 1959-60; Vietnam, 1968; Commander Aust. Force, Vietnam, 1971; Chief of Material, 1972-74. *Recreation:* golf. *Address:* Field Force Command, Victoria Barracks, Sydney, NSW 2021, Australia. *Clubs:* Imperial Service (Sydney); Royal Canberra Golf.

DUNSTAN, Rev. Prof. Gordon Reginald; F. D. Maurice Professor of Moral and Social Theology, King's College, London, since 1967; Chaplain to the Queen, since 1976; *b* 25 April 1917; *yr s* of late Frederick John Menhennet and Winifred Amy Dunstan (*née* Orchard); *m* 1949, Ruby Maud (*née* Fitzer); two *s* one *d. Educ:* Plymouth Corp. Gram. Sch.; University of Leeds; College of the Resurrection, Mirfield. BA, 1st cl. Hist., 1938, Rutson Post-Grad. Schol. 1938, MA w dist. 1939, Leeds Univ.; FSA 1957; Hon. DD Exeter 1973; Fellow, King's College London, 1974. Deacon 1941, priest 1942; Curate, King Cross, Halifax, 1941-45; Huddersfield, 1945-46; Sub Warden, St Deiniol's Library, Hawarden, 1945-49; Vicar of Sutton Courtney with Appleford, 1949-55; Lecturer, Wm Temple Coll., 1947-49; Ripon Hall, Oxford, 1953-55; Minor Canon, St George's Chapel, Windsor Castle, 1955-59; Westminster Abbey, 1959-67; Canon Theologian, Leicester Cathedral, 1966-. Sec., C of E Council for Social Work, 1955-63; Sec., Church Assembly Jt Bd of Studies, 1963-66; Editor of Crucible, 1962-66; Editor of Theology, 1965-75; Dep. Priest in Ordinary to the Queen, 1959-64, Priest in Ordinary, 1964-76; Select Preacher: University of Cambridge 1960, 1977; Leeds, 1970; Hulsean Preacher, 1977. Lectures: Prideaux, Univ. of Exeter, 1968; Moorhouse, Melbourne, 1973. Gresham's Prof. in Divinity, City Univ., 1969-71. Mem. Council, Canterbury and York Soc., 1950-. Mem. or Sec. cttees on social and ethical problems; Vice-Pres., 1965-66, and Chm. Brit. Cttee, of Internat. Union of Family Organizations, 1964-66; Member: London Medical Gp and Soc. for Study of Medical Ethics, 1967-; Adv. Gp on Transplant Policy, Dept of Health, 1969; Council of Tavistock Inst. of Human Relations & Inst. of Marital Studies, 1969-; Adv. Gp on Arms Control and Disarmament, FCO, 1970-74; Adv. Cttee on Admin. of Cruelty to Animals Act, Home Office, 1975-. Pres., Open Section, RSM, 1976-78. *Publications:* The Family Is Not Broken, 1962; The Register of Edmund Lacy, Bishop of Exeter 1420-1455: vol. I, 1963; vol. II, 1966; vol. III, 1967; vol. IV, 1971; vol V, 1972; A Digger Still, 1968; Not Yet the Epitaph, 1968; The Sacred Ministry, 1970; The Artifice of Ethics, 1974; A Moralist in the City, 1974; (ed) Duty and Discernment, 1975. *Recreations:* local history, music. *Address:* King's College, Strand, WC2R 2LS. *T:* 01-836 5454; 34 Cranes Park, Surbiton, Surrey. *T:* 01-399 9249.

DUNSTAN, Ivan, PhD; CChem, FRIC; Director Materials Quality Assurance, Ministry of Defence (Procurement Executive), since 1974; *b* 27 Aug. 1930; *s* of Edward Ernest and Sarah Kathleen Dunstan; *m* 1955, Monica Jane (*née* Phillips); two *s* one *d*. *Educ:* Falmouth Grammar Sch.; Bristol Univ. (BSc). Joined Scientific Civil Service, working at Explosives Research and Development Estabt, Waltham Abbey, 1954; became Supt of Gen. Chemistry Div., 1967; Warren Spring Laboratory (Dept of Trade and Industry) as Dep. Dir (Resources), 1972-74. *Publications:* research papers on analytical and synthetic chem.; contribs to Annual Reports on Progress of Applied Chem., and to encyclopaedia, etc. *Recreations:* sailing, tennis, badminton, gardening. *Address:* 5 Aldock, Welwyn Garden City, Herts AL7 4QF. *T:* Welwyn Garden 22272. *Club:* Civil Service.

DUNSTER, (Herbert) John; Deputy Director General, Health and Safety Executive, since 1976; *b* 27 July 1922; *s* of Herbert and Olive Grace Dunster; *m* 1945, Rosemary Elizabeth, *d* of P. J. Gallagher; one *s* three *d*. *Educ:* University Coll. Sch.; Imperial College of Science and Technology (ARCS, BSc). Scientist, UK Atomic Energy Authority, 1946-71; Asst Dir, Nat. Radiological Protection Bd, 1971-76. Mem., Internat. Commn on Radiological Protection, 1977-. *Publications:* numerous papers in technical jls. *Recreations:* music, dinghy sailing, photography. *Address:* Hill Cottage, 65 Castlebar Road, Ealing, W5 1DA. *T:* 01-997 0439. *Club:* Royal Commonwealth Society.

DUNTZE, Sir George (Edwin Douglas), 6th Bt, *cr* 1774; CMG 1960; *b* 1 June 1913; *o s* of Sir George Puxley Duntze, 5th Baronet, and Violet May, *d* of late Henry M. Sanderson; *S* father, 1947; *m* 1st, 1941, Joan, *d* of late Major F. E. Bradstock, DSO, MC (marr. diss. 1966); one *d*; 2nd, 1966, Nesta, *e d* of late Thomas R. P. Herbert, Newport, Mon. *Educ:* Shrewsbury Sch.; Trinity Coll., Oxford. (MA). Entered Colonial Administrative Service, 1936. Provincial Comr, Uganda, 1952-61. *Heir:* *kinsman,* John Alexander Duntze [*b* 13 Nov. 1909; *m* 1935, Emily Ellsworth, *d* of Elmer E. Harlow, USA]. *Address:* 25 Ennismore Gardens, SW7. *Clubs:* Hurlingham; Leander.

DUNWICH, Bishop Suffragan of, since 1977; **Rt. Rev. William Johnston;** *b* 7 July 1914; *s* of late Dr W. Johnston; *m* 1943, Marguerite Pemberton, 2nd *d* of late H. Macpherson, Headingley Hall, Leeds; no *c*. *Educ:* Bromsgrove Sch.; Selwyn Coll., Cambridge; Westcott House, Cambridge. Asst Curate, S Michael, Headingley, Leeds, 1939-43; Asst Curate, Knaresborough, 1943-45; Vicar of Stourton, Yorks, 1945-49; Vicar of Armley, Leeds, 1949-56; Vicar of St Chad, Shrewsbury, 1956-64; Archdeacon of Bradford, 1965-77. *Address:* 52 Church Road, Old Newton, Stowmarket, Suffolk IP14 4ED.

DUNWOODY, Gwyneth (Patricia); MP (Lab) Crewe, since Feb. 1974; *b* 12 Dec. 1930; *d* of late Morgan Phillips and of Baroness Phillips, *qv*; *m* 1954, Dr John Elliott Orr Dunwoody, *qv* (marr. diss. 1975); two *s* one *d*. MP (Lab) Exeter, 1966-70; Parly Sec. to BoT, 1967-70; Mem., European Parlt, 1975-. Dir, Film Production Assoc. of GB, 1970-74. *Address:* 113 Cromwell Tower, Beech Street, EC2Y 6DD.

DUNWOODY, Dr John (Elliott Orr); general practitioner; Medical Officer, Staff Health Service, St George's Hospital, SW17, since 1976; Chairman, Kensington, Chelsea and Westminster Area Health Authority (Teaching), since 1977 (Vice-Chairman, 1974-77); *b* 3 June 1929; *s* of Dr W. O. and Mrs F. J. Dunwoody; *m* 1954, Gwyneth Patricia (*née* Phillips), *qv* (marr. diss. 1975); two *s* one *d*. *Educ:* St Paul's Sch.; King's Coll., London Univ.; Westminster Hosp. Med. Sch. MB, BS London; MRCS, LRCP 1954. House Surgeon, Westminster (Gordon) Hosp., 1954; House Physician, Royal Berks Hosp., 1954-55; Sen. House Physician, Newton Abbot Hosp., 1955-56;

Family Doctor and Medical Officer, Totnes District Hosp, 1956-66. MP (Lab) Falmouth and Camborne, 1966-70; Parly Under-Sec., Dept of Health and Social Security, 1969-70. Member: Exec. Cttee, British Council; Council, Westminster Med. Sch.; (co-opted) Social Services Cttee, Westminster City Council. Hon. Dir, Action on Smoking and Health. Governor, Pimlico Sch. *Publication:* (jtly) A Birth Control Plan for Britain, 1972. *Address:* 214 Ashley Gardens, SW1. *T:* 01-828 9201.

DUNWORTH, John Vernon, CB 1969; CBE 1955; Director, National Physical Laboratory, 1964-76; *b* 24 Feb. 1917; *o c* of late John Dunworth and Susan Ida (*née* Warburton); *m* 1967, Patricia Noel Boston; one *d*. *Educ:* Manchester Grammar Sch.; Clare Coll., Cambridge; Denman Baynes Research Studentship, 1937, Robins Prize, 1937; MA, PhD; Twisden Studentship and Fellowship, Trinity Coll., 1941. War Service: Ministry of Supply on Radar Development, 1939-44; National Research Council of Canada, on Atomic Energy Development, 1944-45. Univ. Demonstrator in Physics, Cambridge, 1945. Joined Atomic Energy Research Establishment, Harwell, 1947. Alternate United Kingdom Member on Organising Cttee of UN Atoms for Peace Confs in Geneva, 1955 and 1958. Pres., Internat. Cttee of Weights and Measures, 1975- (Vice-Pres., 1968-75). Fellow Amer. Nuclear Soc. 1960. Chm., British Nuclear Energy Soc., 1964-70; Vice-President, Institute of Physics: Physical Soc., 1966-70. CEng 1966. Comdr (with Star), Order of Alfonso X el Sabio, Spain, 1960. *Address:* The Warbuck, Kirk Michael, Isle of Man. *T:* Kirk Michael 359. *Club:* Athenæum.

DUPONT-SOMMER, André; Member of the Institut de France (Secrétaire Perpétuel de l'Académie des Inscriptions et Belles-Lettres) since 1961; Hon. Professor: the Collège de France; the Sorbonne; Director of Studies, Ecole des Hautes Etudes, since 1938; *b* 23 Dec. 1900. Gen. Sec., Collège de France, 1934; Pres., Institut d'Etudes Sémitiques, University of Paris, 1952. Member: Accademia dei Lincei, 1972; Osterreichische Akademie der Wissenschaften, 1974. Officier de la Légion d'Honneur; Comdr des Palmes académiques. *Publications:* Le Quatrième Livre des Machabées, 1939; La Doctrine gnostique de la lettre "Wâw", 1946; Les Araméens, 1949; Aperçus préliminaires sur les manuscrits de la mer Morte, 1950 (publ. Eng. The Dead Sea Scrolls. A preliminary Study, 1952); Nouveaux Aperçus sur les manuscrits de la mer Morte, 1953 (publ. Eng. The Jewish sect of Qumran and the Essenes, 1954); Le Livre des Hymnes découvert près de la mer Morte, 1957; Les inscriptions araméennes de Sfiré, 1958; Les écrits esséniens découverts près de la mer Morte, 1959 (Eng. trans., The Essene Writings from Qumran); articles in Revue d'Assyriologie, Revue d'Histoire des Religions, Semitica, Syria, Jl of Semitic Studies, Vetus Testamentum, etc. *Address:* 25 Quai de Conti, 75006 Paris, France. *T:* 326.02.92.

DUPPA-MILLER, John Bryan Peter; see Miller, J. B. P. D.

DUPPLIN, Viscount; Charles William Harley Hay; *b* 20 Dec. 1962; *s* and *heir* of 15th Earl of Kinnoull, *qv*.

du PRÉ, Jacqueline, OBE 1976; British violoncellist; *b* 1945; *m* 1967, Daniel Barenboim, *qv*. *Educ:* studied with William Pleeth both privately and at Guildhall Sch. of Music, with Paul Tortelier in Paris, and with Rostropovich in Moscow. Concert début at Wigmore Hall at age of sixteen, followed by appearances on the continent and with principal English orchestras and conductors. Soloist in London and at Bath and Edinburgh Festivals. N American début, 1965. Continued studies in Moscow with Rostropovitch, 1966, returning later to USSR as soloist with BBC Symphony Orchestra. Toured N America, and appeared New York and at World Fair, Montreal; subseq. concerts, major musical centres, 1967. Awarded Suggia Gift at age of ten; Gold medal, Guildhall Sch. of Music, and Queen's Prize, 1960; City of London Midsummer Prize, 1975; FGSM, 1975; FRCM; Hon. RAM. *Address:* c/o Harold Holt Ltd, 134 Wigmore Street, W1H 0DJ.

DUPREE, Sir Peter, 5th Bt *cr* 1921; *b* 20 Feb. 1924; *s* of Sir Victor Dupree, 4th Bt and of Margaret Cross; *S* father, 1976; *m* 1947, Joan, *d* of late Captain James Desborough Hunt. *Heir:* *cousin* Thomas William James David Dupree, *b* 5 Feb. 1930. *Address:* Great Seabrights, Galley Wood, near Chelmsford, Essex.

DUPUCH, Hon. Sir (Alfred) Etienne (Jerome), Kt 1965; OBE 1949; KCSG, OTL, CHM; Editor-Proprietor, The Tribune, Nassau, Bahamas; *b* Nassau, 16 Feb. 1899; *s* of Leon Edward Hartman Dupuch, Founder of The Tribune; *m* 1928, Marie Plouse, USA; three *s* three *d*. *Educ:* Boys' Central Sch., Nassau; St John's Univ., Collegeville, Minn., USA. Served War, 1914-18, BWI Regt; Rep. for Inagua, House of Assembly, Bahamas, 1925-42; Eastern District, New Providence, 1949-56; MLC,

1960-64; Mem. Senate, 1964-68. Hon. LittD, Hon. LLD. IAPA Award for breaking down racial discrimination in Bahamas, 1956; IAPA Award for successful defence of Freedom of Press, 1969; Citation from Associated Press N American Editors' Assoc. for outstanding coverage of fire on SS Yarmouth Castle, 1965; Paul Harris Award for work in social services (Rotary Club of Lucaya, Freeport). Has RSA medal and several decorations from governments of three nations. *Publication:* The Tribune Story, 1967. *Address:* Camperdown Heights, PO Box N-3207, Nassau, Bahamas. *Clubs:* East India, Devonshire, Sports and Public Schools; East Nassau Rotary, East Hill (Nassau).

DURAND, Rev. Sir (Henry Mortimer) Dickon (Marion St George), 4th Bt *cr* 1892; Curate-in-Charge, St Benedict's, Ashford, Mddx, since 1975; *b* 19 June 1934; *s* of Lt-Comdr Mortimer Henry Marion Durand, RN (*y s* of 1st Bt) (*d* 1969), and Beatrice Garvan-Sheridan, *d* of Judge Sheridan, Sydney, NSW; *S* uncle, 1971; *m* 1971, Stella Evelyn, *d* of Captain C. C. L'Estrange; one *s* one *d*. *Educ:* Wellington College; Sydney University; Salisbury Theological College. Curate: All Saints, Fulham, 1969-72; St Leonard's, Heston, 1972-74. *Recreations:* heraldry, philately, model railways, printing, militaria, painting, poetry, travel. *Heir: s* Edward Alan Christopher Percy Durand, *b* 21 Feb. 1974. *Address:* c/o Barclays Bank, Cobham, Surrey.

DURAND, Victor Albert Charles, QC 1958; *s* of Victor and Blanche Durand; *m* 1935, Betty Joan Kirchner; one *s* one *d*. *Educ:* Howard High Sch. (Kitchener Scholar). LLB, BSc, AMInstCE. Served War 1939-45 with RE. Called to Bar, Inner Temple, 1939. Dep. Chm., Warwicks QS, 1961. *Address:* Queen Elizabeth Building, Temple, EC4Y 9BS.

DURANT, Rear-Adm. Bryan Cecil, CB 1963; DSO 1953; DSC 1945; DL; *b* 17 June 1910; *o s* of Francis Durant and Dulce, *d* of Fraser Baddeley; *m* 1st, 1939, Pamela (*d* 1963), *yr d* of Brig.-Gen. William Walter Seymour; three *d* (and one *s* decd); 2nd, 1967, Rachel, *d* of late Col Hon. David Bruce, and of Hon. Mrs David Bruce. *Educ:* Radley. Entered Royal Navy, 1929; specialised in navigation, 1935. War of 1939-45; actions in HMS Dorsetshire in Atlantic and Indian Oceans including sinking of Bismarck, 1940-42; sunk by Japanese aircraft, 1942 (despatches); actions in HMS Victorious off North Norway, Sabang, Palembang, Okinawa and Japan, 1942-45; suicide Bomber attacks, 1945 (DSC). Comdr 1945; Capt. 1951; Comd 4th Frigate Sqdn in Korean War, 1952-54 (DSO). Dir, Ops Div., Admlty, 1957; Captain of the Fleet, Home Fleet, 1959; Chief of Staff Far East Station, 1961-63; retired list, 1963. Dir-Gen., Navy League, 1964-75. ADC to the Queen, 1960. Liveryman, Fishmongers Co. DL Greater London, 1970. Commendador Henriquina (Portuguese), 1960. *Address:* The Old House, Bighton, near Alresford, Hants. *Club:* Army and Navy.

DURANT, Robert Anthony Bevis, (Tony Durant); MP (C) Reading North, since Feb. 1974; *b* 9 Jan. 1928; *s* of Captain Robert Michael Durant and Mrs Violet Dorothy Durant (*née* Bevis); *m* 1958, Audrey Stoddart; two *s* one *d*. *Educ:* Dane Court Prep. Sch., Pyrford, Woking; Bryanston Sch., Blandford, Dorset. Royal Navy, 1945-47. Coutts Bank, Strand, 1947-52; Cons. Party Organisation, 1952-67 (Young Cons. Organiser, Yorks; Cons. Agent, Clapham; Nat. Organiser, Young Conservatives). Mem. Select Cttee Parly Comr (Ombudsman), 1974-. Parliamentary Consultant: The Film Production Association of Great Britain Ltd; Astoria Holdings Ltd, div. of Delta Metal Co. Ltd. Mem., Inland Waterways Adv. Council, 1975-. Dir, British Industrial Scientific Film Assoc., 1967-70; Company Sec., Talking Pictures Ltd, 1972-. *Recreations:* boating, golf. *Address:* Hill House, Surley Row, Caversham, Reading RG4 8ND. *Club:* St Stephen's.

DURANT, William James, BA, MA, PhD; engaged in writing; *b* North Adams, Mass, 5 Nov. 1885; *s* of Joseph Durant and Mary Allors, of French-Canadian stock; *m* 1913, Ida Kaufman (Ariel Durant); one *s* one *d*. *Educ:* St Peter's Coll., Jersey City, NJ; Columbia Univ., New York. Prof. of Latin and French, Seton Hall Coll., South Orange NJ, 1907-11; Instructor in Philosophy, Columbia Univ., 1917; Dir of Labour Temple Sch., 1914-27. Presidential Medal of Freedom, 1977. *Publications:* Philosophy and the Social Problem, 1917; The Story of Philosophy, 1926; Transition, 1927; The Mansions of Philosophy, 1929; Adventures in Genius, 1931; The Story of Civilization (11 vols): Our Oriental Heritage, 1935; The Life of Greece, 1939; Cæsar and Christ, 1944; The Age of Faith, 1950; The Renaissance, 1953; The Reformation, 1957; (with Ariel Durant) The Age of Reason Begins, 1961; The Age of Louis XIV, 1963; The Age of Voltaire, 1965; Rousseau and Revolution, 1967 (Pulitzer Prize, 1968); The Age of Napoleon, 1975; The Lessons of History, 1968; Interpretations of Life, 1970. *Recreations:* none. *Address:* 5608 Briarcliff Road, Los Angeles, Calif 90028, USA.

DURBIN, Prof. James; Professor of Statistics, University of London (London School of Economics), since 1961; *b* 30 June 1923; *m* 1958, Anne Dearnley Outhwaite; two *s* one *d*. *Educ:* St John's Coll., Cambridge. Army Operational Research Group, 1943-45. Boot and Shoe Trade Research Assoc., 1945-47; Dept of Applied Economics, Cambridge, 1948-49; Asst Lectr, then Lecturer, in Statistics, London Sch. of Economics, 1950-53; Reader in Statistics, 1953-61. *Publications:* Distribution Theory for Tests based on the Sample Distribution Function, 1973; articles in statistical journals, incl. Biometrika, Jl of Royal Statistical Society, etc. *Recreations:* sailing, opera, theatre. *Address:* 31 Southway, NW11. *T:* 01-458 3037.

DURBIN, Leslie, CBE 1976; MVO 1943; silversmith; *b* 21 Feb. 1913; *s* of late Harry Durbin and of Lillian A. Durbin; *m* 1940, Phyllis Ethel Durbin (*see* Phyllis E. Ginger); one *s* one *d*. *Educ:* Central Sch. of Arts and Crafts, London. Apprenticed to late Omar Ramsden, 1929-39; full-time schol., 1938-39, travelling schol., 1939-40, both awarded by Worshipful Co. of Goldsmiths. Started working on own account in workshop of Francis Adam, 1940-41. RAF, Allied Central Interpretation Unit, 1941-45. Commissioned by Jt Cttee of Assay Offices of GB to design Silver Jubilee Hall Mark. Hon. LLD Cambridge, 1963. Council of Industrial Design Awards for Silver for the 70's. *Address:* 298A Kew Road, Richmond TW9 3DU.

DURBRIDGE, Francis (Henry); playwright and author; *b* 25 Nov. 1912; *s* of late Francis and Gertrude Durbridge; *m* 1940, Norah Elizabeth Lawley; two *s*. *Educ:* Bradford Grammar Sch.; Wylde Green Coll.; Birmingham Univ. After period in stockbroker's office, began to write (as always intended); short stories and plays for BBC; many subseq. radio plays, including Promotion, 1933; created character of Paul Temple. Entered Television with The Broken Horseshoe, 1952 (the first adult television serial); other serials followed; Portrait of Alison, 1954; My Friend Charles, 1955; The Other Man, 1956; The Scarf 1960; The World of Tim Frazer (Exec. Prod.), 1960-61; Melissa, 1962; Bat Out of Hell, 1964; Stupid Like a Fox, 1971; The Doll, 1976. The television serials have been presented in many languages, and are continuing; novels, based on them, have been published in USA, Europe, etc. The European Broadcasting Union asked for a radio serial for an internat. market (La Boutique, 1967, being broadcast in various countries); German, French and Italian productions, 1971-72. Films include two for Korda and Romulus, 1954-57. Stage plays: Suddenly at Home, 1971; The Gentle Hook, 1974; Murder With Love, 1976. *Publications:* include contribs to newspapers and magazines, at home and abroad. *Recreations:* family, reading, travel. *Address:* 4 Fairacres, Roehampton Lane, SW15 5LX. *Club:* Royal Automobile.

DURHAM, 6th Earl of, *cr* 1833; Baron Durham, 1828; Viscount Lambton, 1833 [Disclaimed his Peerages for life, 1970]; *see under* Lambton, A. C. F.

DURHAM, Baron; a subsidiary title of Earldom of Durham (disclaimed 1970), used by Hon. Edward Richard Lambton, *b* 19 Oct. 1961, *heir* to disclaimed Earldom.

DURHAM, Bishop of, since 1973; **Rt. Rev. John Stapylton Habgood,** MA, PhD; *b* 23 June 1927; *s* of Arthur Henry Habgood, DSO, MB, BCh, and Vera (*née* Chetwynd-Stapylton); *m* 1961, Rosalie Mary Anne Boston; two *s* two *d*. *Educ:* Eton; King's Coll., Cambridge; Cuddesdon Coll., Oxford. Univ. Demonstrator in Pharmacology, Cambridge, 1950-53; Fellow of King's Coll., Cambridge, 1952-55; Curate of St Mary Abbots, Kensington, 1954-56; Vice-Principal of Westcott House, Cambridge, 1956-62; Rector of St John's Church, Jedburgh, 1962-67; Principal of Queen's College, Birmingham, 1967-73. Hon. DD Durham, 1975. *Publication:* Religion and Science, 1964. *Recreation:* repairing toys. *Address:* Auckland Castle, Bishop Auckland, Co. Durham. *T:* Bishop Auckland 2576. *Club:* Athenæum.

DURHAM, Dean of; *see* Heaton, Very Rev. E. W.

DURHAM, Archdeacon of; *see* Perry, Ven. M. C.

DURIE, Sir Alexander (Charles), Kt 1977; CBE 1973; Director-General, The Automobile Association, 1964-77; *b* 15 July 1915; *er s* of late Charles and Margaret Durie (*née* Gardner), Shepton Mallet, Somerset; *m* 1941, Joyce, *o c* of late Lionel and Helen Hargreaves (*née* Hirst), Leeds and Bridlington, Yorks; one *s* one *d*. *Educ:* Queen's Coll., Taunton. Joined Shell-Mex and BP Ltd, 1933. Served War of 1939-45, Royal Artillery; Gunnery Staff Course (IG), 1941; Lieut-Col 1945. Dir Shell Co. of Australia Ltd, 1954-56; Dir, 1962, Man. Dir, 1963-64, Shell-Mex and BP Ltd; Director: Mercantile Credit Co. Ltd, 1973-; Thomas Cook

Group Ltd, 1974-; Provident Association for Medical Care Ltd, 1977-. Mem. Council, Motor and Cycle Trades Benevolent Fund, 1959-73; Vice-Pres. British Assoc. of Industrial Editors, 1959-71; Gen. Commissioner of Income Tax, 1960-; FBIM, 1959, Council Mem., 1962-73, Chm. Exec. Cttee, 1962-65, Vice-Chm. Council, 1962-67, Chm., Bd of Fellows, 1970-73 (Verulam Medal 1973); Member: Nat. Road Safety Adv. Council, 1965-68; Adv. Council on Road Res., 1965-68; Brit. Road Fedn Ltd, 1962- (Vice-Chm.); Council, Internat. Road Fedn Ltd, London, 1962-64; Marketing Cttee, BTA, 1970-77; Adv. Cttee on Traffic and Safety, TRRL, 1973-77; Vice-Pres., Alliance Internationale de Tourisme, 1965-71, Pres., 1971-77; Chm., Indep. Schs Careers Orgn, 1969-73 (Vice-Pres., 1973-); Governor: Ashridge Coll., 1963-; Queen's Coll., Taunton, 1969-. Mem. Cttee, Surrey CCC, 1970-74, 1975-. Freeman of City of London and Liveryman, Worshipful Co. of Paviors, 1965. FCIT; Hon. FInstHE 1969. Spanish Order of Touristic Merit Silver Medal, 1977. *Recreations:* cricket, curling, golf, racing. *Address:* Redwood House, Windlesham, Surrey GU20 6AD. *T:* Bagshot 72035. *Clubs:* MCC, Junior Carlton; Royal and Ancient; Berkshire Golf.

DURKIN, Air Marshal Sir Herbert, KBE 1976; CB 1973; Controller of Engineering and Supply (RAF), since 1976; *b* 31 March 1922; *s* of Herbert and Helen Durkin, Burnley, Lancs; *m* 1951, Dorothy Hope, *d* of Walter Taylor Johnson, Burnley; one *s* two *d*. *Educ:* Burnley Grammar Sch.; Emmanuel Coll., Cambridge (MA). Commissioned into Tech. Br., RAF, Oct. 1941. Served War, with No 60 Gp, until 1945. India, 1945-47, becoming ADC to AOC-in-C India; Central Bomber Estabt, 1947-50; Sqdn Ldr, 1950; Atomic Weapons Research Estabt, 1950-52; RAF Staff Coll., 1953; Chief Signals Officer, AHQ, Iraq, 1954-56; Wing Comdr, Chief Instr of Signals Div. of RAF Tech. Coll., 1956-58; Air Ministry, 1958-60; jssc, 1961; HQ, 2 ATAF, 1961-63; Gp Capt 1962; Sen. Tech. Staff Officer, HQ Signals Command, 1964-65; Comdt, No 2 Sch. of Tech. Trg, Cosford, 1965-67; Air Cdre, 1967; Director of Eng (Policy), MoD, 1967-69; IDC, 1970; AOC No 90 Group, RAF, 1971-73; Dir-Gen. Engineering and Supply Management, 1973-76. CEng, FIEE, FRAeS; MBIM. *Recreation:* golf. *Address:* c/o Lloyds Bank, Sevenoaks, Kent. *Club:* Royal Air Force.

DURLACHER, Sir Esmond (Otho), Kt 1972; Consultant to Wedd Durlacher Mordaunt & Co. since 1967; *b* 8 Oct. 1901; 2nd *s* of Frederic Henry Keeling Durlacher and Violet Mabel, *d* of Sir Reginald Hanson, 1st Bt, Thorpe Satchville, Leics; *m* 1st, 1930, Lady Sheila Jackson (marr. diss. 1947); two *s* one *d*; 2nd, 1953, Mrs Elizabeth Steele. *Educ:* Repton; Trinity Hall, Cambridge. Member of Stock Exchange, London, 1926-77; Senior Partner, F. & N. Durlacher, Stock-Jobbers, 1936, then Senior Partner, Durlacher Oldham Mordaunt Godson & Co., retd 1966. Mem. Bd of Governors, St George's Hosp., 1944-71; Chm., Bd of Governors, Allhallows Sch., Rousdon, Devon, 1972-77; Chm., Victoria Hosp. for Children, Tite Street, 1957-67. *Address:* Wootton Fitzpaine Manor, Bridport, Dorset. *T:* Charmouth 455. *Clubs:* Buck's, Portland.
See also Sir L. G. Durlacher.

DURLACHER, Adm. Sir Laurence (George), KCB 1961 (CB 1957); OBE 1943; DSC 1945; retired; *b* 24 July 1904; *s* of late Frederick Henry Keeling Durlacher and V. M. Durlacher (*née* Hanson); *m* 1934, Rimma, *d* of late R. V. Sass-Tissovsky; one *s* one *d*. *Educ:* RNC Osborne and Dartmouth. Lieut 1927; Comdr 1939; Capt. 1944; Cdre 1st Class, 1952; Rear-Adm. 1955; Vice-Adm. 1958; Adm. 1961. On Staff of Adm. of the Fleet Viscount Cunningham of Hyndhope during N Africa, Sicily and Italian Campaigns (despatches); commanded HMS Volage, 1944-45; Admiralty, 1945-47; commanded 3rd Destroyer Flotilla, Mediterranean, 1949-50; commanded Admiralty Signals and Radar Establishments, 1950-52; Chief of Staff to C-in-C Far East Station, 1952-54; Dep. Chief of Naval Personnel (Personal Services), at Admiralty, 1955-57; Flag Officer Commanding Fifth Cruiser Squadron and Flag Officer Second-in-Command, Far East Station, 1957-58; Dep. Chief of Naval Staff and Fifth Sea Lord, 1959-62; retired, 1962. US Legion of Merit, 1945. *Address:* Mas Tournamy, 06250 Mougins, A-M, France.
See also Sir E. O. Durlacher.

DURNFORD-SLATER, Adm. Sir Robin (Leonard Francis), KCB 1957 (CB 1955); *b* 9 July 1902, *s* of Captain L. Slater, Royal Sussex Regiment (killed in action, 1914), and Constance Dorothy Durnford-Slater; *m* 1936, Mary Alice Hilleary, *d* of late Col E. H. Gregson, CMG, CIE; one *s* one *d*. *Educ:* Osborne; Dartmouth. Comdr, 1938; Capt., 1944; Rear-Adm., 1953; Vice-Adm., 1956; Adm., 1959. Served War of 1939-45; Executive officer, HMS Hermes, HMS Vernon; Senior Officer, 42nd and subseq. 7th Escort Grp Western Approaches; Trg Capt. Western Approaches; Dir of Underwater Weapons, Admiralty (Bath).

Post War: Senior Officer 1st Escort Flotilla, Far East; Commandant Sch. of Amphibious Warfare; Capt. HMS Gambia; Dep. Controller, Admiralty, 1953-56; Flag Officer, 2nd in Command, Mediterranean Fleet, 1956-58; Commander-in-Chief, The Nore, 1958-61; retd. Flag Officer Naval Brigade, Coronation, 1953. Comdr of the Legion of Honour, 1958. *Recreation:* golf. *Address:* Passfield Place, Liphook, Hants.

DURRANDS, Kenneth James, DGS (Birm), MSc, CEng, FIMechE, MIEE; Rector, The Polytechnic, Queensgate, Huddersfield, since 1970; *b* 24 June 1929; *s* of A. I. Durrands, Croxton Kerrial; *m* 1956 (marr. diss. 1971), one *s*. *Educ:* King's Sch., Grantham; Nottingham Technical Coll.; Birmingham Univ. (DGS). Min. of Supply Engrg Apprentice, ROF, Nottingham, 1947-52; Techn. Engr, UKAEA, Risley, 1954-58; Lecturer in Mechanical and Nuclear Engrg, Univ. of Birmingham, 1958-61; Head of Gen. Engrg Dept, Reactor Engrg Lab., UKAEA, Risley, 1961-67; Mem. Council, IMechE, 1963-66; Visiting Lecturer, Manchester Univ., 1962-68; Technical Dir, Vickers Ltd, Barrow Engrg Works, 1967-70. Member: Ind. Technologies Tribology Cttee, DTI, 1969-74; Educn and Training Cttee, DTI, 1969-74; DoI Cttee for Ind. Technologies, 1975- (Chm., Educn and Trng Cttee); Council and Court, Leeds Univ., 1970-; Court, Bradford Univ., 1973-; Nat. Council for Diplomas in Art and Design, 1970-74; IMechE Tribology Cttee, 1971-; CNAA Cttee for Science and Technol., 1971-75; CNAA Engr Bd, 1971-; CNAA Cttee for Art and Design, 1974-75; Hon. Sec./Treas., Cttee of Dirs of Polytechnics, 1970-. *Publications:* several technical papers. *Recreations:* motor sport, gardening, squash rackets. *Address:* Church Cottage, Croxton Kerrial, Grantham, Lincolnshire. *Club:* Athenæum.

DURRANT, Albert Arthur Molteno, CBE 1945; CEng; FIMechE; FCIT; FRSA; retired from London Transport Board; *b* 11 Sept. 1898; *s* of late Sir Arthur I. Durrant, CBE, MVO; *m* 1922, Kathleen, *d* of Arthur J. Wright; no *c*. *Educ:* Alleyn's Sch., Dulwich. Joined London Gen. Omnibus Co., 1919; Chief Engineer (Buses and Coaches), London Passenger Transport Bd, 1935-40; Director of Tank Design, Ministry of Supply, 1940-45; Chief Mechanical Engineer (Road Services) London Transport, 1945-65. *Address:* 108 Chiltern Court, Baker Street, NW1 5SR.

DURRANT, Maj.-Gen. James Thom, CB 1945; DFC 1941; City Councillor, Johannesburg, since 1968; *b* 1913; *s* of late J. C. Durrant, Hertford and Johannesburg; *m* 1970, Margaret, *d* of late Archie White, Johannesburg. Commanded a group in Air Command, South-East Asia, 1945; Dir-Gen. South African Air Force, 1947-51; retired, 1952. *Address:* 71 First Avenue East, Parktown North, Johannesburg, South Africa.

DURRANT, Sir William Henry Estridge, 7th Bt, *cr* 1784; JP (NSW); *b* 1 April 1901; *s* of Sir William Durrant, 6th Bt; *S* father 1953; *m* 1927, Georgina Beryl Gwendoline, *d* of Alexander Purse, Kircubbin, Co. Down, N Ireland; one *s* one *d*. Served War of 1939-45 (Pacific Area). NSW Registrar, Australian Inst. of Company Dirs, 1959-. *Heir: s* William Alexander Estridge Durrant [*b* 26 Nov. 1929; *m* 1953, Dorothy (BA), *d* of Ronal Croker, Quirindi, NSW; one *s* one *d*]. *Address:* Woodside Gardens, Yardley Avenue, Waitara, NSW 2077, Australia.

DURRELL, Gerald Malcolm; Zoologist and Writer since 1946; regular contributor to BBC Sound and TV Services; *b* Jamshedpur, India, 7 Jan. 1925; *s* of Lawrence Samuel Durrell, Civil Engineer, and Louisa Florence Dixie; *m* 1951, Jacqueline Sonia Rasen; no *c*. *Educ:* by Private Tutors, in France, Italy, Switzerland and Greece. Student Keeper, Whipsnade, 1945-46; 1st Animal Collecting Expedition, British Cameroons, 1947-48; 2nd Cameroon Expedition, 1948-49; Collecting trip to British Guiana, 1949-50; began writing, script writing and broadcasting, 1950-53; trip with wife to Argentine and Paraguay, 1953-54; filming in Cyprus, 1955; 3rd Cameroon Expedition with wife, 1957; Trans-Argentine Expedition, 1958-59; Expedition in conjunction with BBC Natural History Unit, Sierra Leone, 1965; collecting trip to Mexico, 1968; Aust. Expedn, 1969-70. Founder and Hon. Director: Jersey Zoological Park, 1958; Jersey Wildlife Preservation Trust, 1964. Founder Chm. SAFE Internat. USA, 1972. FZS; (Life) FIAL; FRGS; FRSL 1972; MBOU; MIBiol. *Films for TV:* 1st series, 1956; Two in the Bush, 1962; Catch Me a Colobus, 1966; Animal People-Menagerie Manor, 1967; Garden of the Gods, 1967. *Publications:* The Overloaded Ark, 1953; Three Singles to Adventure, 1954; The Bafut Beagles, 1954; The New Noah, 1955; The Drunken Forest, 1956; My Family and Other Animals, 1956; Encounters with Animals, 1958; A Zoo in my Luggage, 1960; The Whispering Land, 1961; Island Zoo, 1961; Look at Zoos, 1961; My Favourite Animal Stories, 1962; Menagerie Manor, 1964; Two in the Bush, 1966; Rosy is My

Relative, 1968; The Donkey Rustlers, 1968; Birds, Beasts and Relatives, 1969; Fillets of Plaice, 1971; Catch Me a Colobus, 1972; Beasts in My Belfry, 1973; The Talking Parcel, 1974; The Stationary Ark, 1976; Garden of the Gods, 1977; contribs to Zoo Life, etc. *Recreations:* reading, riding, filming, photography, drawing, swimming, study of the History and Maintenance of Zoological Gardens. *Address:* Jersey Zoo Park, Les Augres Manor, Trinity, Jersey, Channel Isles. *T:* Central 61949.
See also Lawrence G. Durrell.

DURRELL, Lawrence George, FRSL 1954; lately Director of Public Relations, Government of Cyprus; *b* 27 Feb. 1912; *m* 1937, 1947 and 1960; two *d. Educ:* College of St Joseph, Darjeeling, India; St Edmund's Sch., Canterbury. Formerly: Foreign Service Press Officer, Athens and Cairo; Press Attaché, Alexandria; Dir of Public Relations, Dodecanese Islands; Press Attaché, Belgrade, Yugoslavia; Dir of British Council Institutes of Kalamata, Greece, and Cordoba, Argentina. Mellon Lectr in Humanities, Calif. Inst. of Technology, Pasadena, 1975. *Publications:* (novel, under pseudonym Charles Norden) Panic Spring, 1937; The Black Book, 1938 (France and USA), 1973 (England); Private Country (poetry), 1943; Prospero's Cell, 1945; (trans) Four Greek Poets, 1946; Cities, Plains and People, 1946; Cefalu, 1947 (republished as The Dark Labyrinth, 1958); On Seeming to Presume, 1948; (trans) Pope Joan, 1948; Sappho (verse play), 1950; Reflections on a Marine Venus, 1953; The Tree of Idleness, 1955; Selected Poems, 1956; Bitter Lemons, 1957 (Duff Cooper Memorial Prize); White Eagles Over Serbia (juvenile), 1957; The Alexandria Quartet: Justine, 1957, Balthazar, 1958 (Prix du Meilleur Livre Etranger, Paris), Mountolive, 1958, Clea, 1960; Esprit de Corps, 1957; Stiff Upper Lip, 1958; (ed) The Best of Henry Miller, 1960; Collected Poems, 1960, new edn with additions and revisions, 1968; An Irish Faustus (verse play), 1963; The Ikons, 1966; The Revolt of Aphrodite: Tunc, 1968, Nunquam, 1970; Spirit of Place: letters and essays on travel, 1969; The Red Limbo Lingo: a poetry notebook for 1968-70, 1971; Vega and other poems, 1973; Monsieur, or the Prince of Darkness, 1974 (James Tait Black Memorial Prize); The Best of Antrobus, 1975; Selected Poems, 1976; Sicilian Carousel, 1976; A Treasury of Greek Islands, 1978. *Recreation:* travel. *Address:* c/o Grindlay's Bank, 13 St James's Square, SW1.
See also Gerald M. Durrell.

DÜRRENMATT, Friedrich; Swiss author and playwright; *b* Konolfingen, Switzerland, 5 Jan. 1921; *s* of Reinhold Dürrenmatt, pastor, and Hulda (*née* Zimmermann); *m* 1946, Lotti Geissler; one *s* two *d. Educ:* Gymnasium, Bern; University of Bern; University of Zürich. Prix Italia, 1958; Schillerpreis, 1960; Grillparzer-Preis, 1968; Kunstpreis, Bern, 1969; Hon DLitt, Temple Univ. Philadelphia, 1969. *Publications: plays:* Es steht geschrieben, 1947; Der Blinde, 1948; Romulus der Grosse, 1949; Die Ehe des Herrn Mississippi (The Marriage of Mr Mississippi), 1952 (produced New York, Fools Are Passing Through, 1958; filmed, 1961); Nächtliches Gespräch mit einem verachteten Menschen, 1952; Ein Engel kommt nach Babylon (An Angel Comes to Babylon), 1953; Der Besuch der alten Dame, 1956 (The Visit, produced New York, 1958, London, 1960) (Eng. trans., by Patrick Bowles, publ. 1962); Frank V-Oper einer Privatbank, 1960; Die Physiker, 1962 (prod. Aldwych Theatre, London as The Physicists, 1963); The Meteor (prod. Aldwych Theatre, London, 1966); Die Wiedertäufer, 1967; The Deadly Game (prod. Savoy Theatre, 1967); König Johann, nach Shakespeare, 1968; Play Strindberg, 1969; Titus Andronicus, nach Shakespeare, 1970; Porträt eines Planeten, 1970 (Portrait of a Planet, prod London, 1973); Komödien, I, II, III, 1972; Der Mitmacher, 1973; Die Frist, 1976; *plays for radio:* Der Doppelgänger; Der Prozess um des Esels Schatten; Nächtliches Gespräch; Stranitzki und der Nationalheid; Herkules und der Stall des Augias; Das Unternehmen der Wega; Die Panne; Abendstunde im Spätherbst; *essays and criticism:* Theater-Schriften und Reden I, II (Eng. trans., Writings on Theatre and Drama, 1977); Theater-probleme; Gerechtichkeit und Recht; Friedrich Schiller, Rede; Gespräch mit Heinz Ludwig Arnold, 1976; Zusammenhänge: Essay über Israel, 1976; Der Mitmacher: ein Komplex, 1976; Frankfurter Rede, 1977; *novels:* Pilatus, 1949; Der Nihilist, 1950; Die Stadt (short stories), 1952; Der Richter und sein Henker, 1952 (Eng. trans. by Therese Pol, The Judge and His Hangman, 1955); Der Verdacht, 1953 (Eng. trans. as The Quarry, by Eva H. Morreale), 1962; Griechе sucht Griechin, 1955; Die Panne, 1956 (Eng. trans. by R. and C. Winston, The Dangerous Game, 1960); Das Versprechen, 1958 (Eng. trans. by R. and C. Winston, The Pledge, 1959); Der Sturz, 1971. *Recreations:* painting and astronomy. *Address:* Pertuis du Sault 34, Neuchâtel, Switzerland.

du SAUTOY, Peter Francis, CBE 1971 (OBE 1964); Vice-Chairman, Faber Music Ltd, since 1977 (Chairman, 1971-76); *b* 19 Feb. 1912; *s* of late Col E. F. du Sautoy, OBE, TD, DL; *m* 1937, Phyllis Mary (Mollie), *d* of late Sir Francis Floud, KCB, KCSI, KCMG; two *s. Educ:* Uppingham (Foundn Schol.); Wadham Coll., Oxford (Sen. Class. Schol.). MA, 1st cl. Lit. Hum. Dept of Printed Books, British Museum, 1935-36; Asst Educn Officer, City of Oxford, 1937-40; RAF, 1940-45; joined Faber & Faber Ltd, 1946; Dir, Dec. 1946; Vice-Chm., 1960-71; Chm., 1971-76, editorial consultant, 1977-; Chm., Faber and Faber (Publishers) Ltd, 1971-76; Mem. Bd, Yale Univ. Press Ltd, London, 1977-. Mem. Council, Publishers Assoc., 1957-63, 1965-77 (Pres., 1967-69); Mem. Exec. Cttee, Internat. Publishers Assoc., 1972-76; Pres., Groupe des Editeurs de Livres de la CEE, 1973-75. Mem. Council, Aldeburgh Festival-Snape Maltings Foundn Ltd, 1976-. *Publications:* various articles on publishing. *Recreations:* reading, writing, listening to music. *Address:* 31 Lee Road, Aldeburgh, Suffolk. *T:* Aldeburgh 2838. *Club:* Garrick.

DUTHIE, Prof. Robert Buchan, MA Oxon, MB, ChM; FRCSE, FRCS; Nuffield Professor of Orthopædic Surgery, Oxford University; Professorial Fellow, Worcester College, Oxford; Surgeon, Nuffield Orthopædic Centre, Oxford; Consultant Adviser in Orthopaedics and Accident Surgery to Department of Health and Social Security; *b* 4 May 1925; 2nd *s* of late James Andrew Duthie and late Elizabeth Jean Duthie, Edinburgh; *m* 1956, Alison Ann Macpherson Kittermaster, MA; two *s* two *d. Educ:* Aberdeen Grammar Sch.; King Edward VI Gram. Sch., Chelmsford; Heriot-Watt Coll., Edinburgh; University of Edinburgh Med. Sch. Robert Jones Prize 1947, MB, ChB 1948, ChM (with dist.) (Gold Medal for Thesis) 1956, University of Edinburgh; FRCSE 1953. Ho. Surg. Royal Infirmary, 1948-49; Ho. Phys., Western Gen. Hosp., Edinburgh, 1949. Active service in Malaya, RAMC, 1949-51. Registrar, Royal Infirmary, Edinburgh, 1951-53; David Wilkie Res. Schol. of University of Edinburgh, 1953-; Res. Fellow of Scottish Hosps Endowment Research Trust, Edinburgh, 1953-56; Res. Fellow, Nat. Cancer Inst., Bethesda, USA, 1956-57; Extern. Mem. of MRC in Inst. of Orthopædics, London and Sen. Registrar, 1957-58; Prof. of Orthopædic Surg., University of Rochester Sch. of Medicine and Dentistry and Orthopædic Surg.-in-Chief, University of Rochester Med. Centre, 1958-66. Mem., Royal Commn on Civil Liability and Compensation for Personal Injury, 1973-; Chm. Adv. Cttee of Res. in Artificial Limbs and Appliances, DHSS, 1975. Governor: St Edward's Sch., Oxford; Oxford Sch. for Boys. Fellow Brit. Orthopædic Assoc.; Member: Internat. Soc. for Orthopædic Surgery and Traumatology; Orthopædic Research Soc.; Inter-urban Orthopædic Club: Internat. Orthopædic Club. Amer. Rheumatism Assoc. President's Prize, Soc. Internat. de Chirurgie, 1957. *Publications:* (co-author) Textbook of Orthopædic Surgery, 6th edn, 1973; contribs to med. and surg. jls relating to genetics, histochemistry, transplantation, pathology, neoplasia of musculo-skeletal tissues, and clinical subjects. *Recreations:* family, tennis. *Address:* Nuffield Orthopædic Centre, Headington, Oxford; Barna Brow, Harberton Mead, Headington, Oxford. *T:* 62745.

DUTHIE, Sir William (Smith), Kt 1959; OBE 1943; *b* 22 May 1892; *s* of Lewis Duthie, Portessie, Banffshire; *m* 1921, Elizabeth Tyson (*d* 1977); one *s* one *d. Educ:* Rathven and Buckie Schs. Bank of Scotland, 1908-11; Canadian Bank of Commerce, 1911-20; Canadian Army, 1915-16, Gordon Highlanders, 1916-18 (severely wounded); business in London, 1921 onwards; advised Food Defence Plans Dept Board of Trade on Bread Supplies from Oct. 1938; Chm. London Bread Supplies Cttee, 1939; Area Bread Officer London and SE England, 1940; Dir of Emergency Bread Supplies, Ministry of Food, 1941; Dep. Chief UNRRA Balkans Mission, Jan. 1945. MP (U) Banffshire, 1945-64. Resigned Party Whip, Oct. 1962-May 1964. Chairman: House of Commons Cons. and Unionist Mems. Fisheries Sub-Cttee, 1951-62; House of Commons Scottish Unionist Mems Cttee, 1958; Royal National Mission to Deep Sea Fishermen, 1954-71. FSAScot 1976. Freeman, Burgh of Buckie, Banffshire, 1960. *Publication:* ed with C. L. Foster: Letters from the Front, 1914-18, for Canadian Bank of Commerce, 1919. *Recreations:* golf, sailing, archæology. *Address:* Todearth Croft, Holmsburn Leslie, Insch, Aberdeenshire. *T:* Insch 436. *Club:* Caledonian.

du TOIT, Very Rev. Lionel Meiring Spafford, MA; Dean of Carlisle, 1960-73, Dean Emeritus, 1973; *b* 1903; 3rd *s* of late Justice A. P. N. du Toit, S Africa; *m* 1933, Gladys Evelyn, 2nd *d* of late J. D. Hatt, Elsfield, Oxford; one *s* (decd). *Educ:* Manchester Grammar Sch.; Merton Coll., Oxford. Deacon 1928, Priest 1929; Asst Curate: Rochdale Parish Church, 1928-31; Swinton Parish Church, 1931-35; Rector, Christ Church, Moss Side, Manchester, 1935-43; Chaplain, Manchester Royal Infirmary, 1935-43; Lecturer, Egerton Hall Theological Coll.,

1932-38; Vicar, St Mary's, Windermere, 1943-60. Proctor in Convocation, 1950-70; Dep. Prolocutor, York Convocation, 1967-70. *Recreation:* gardening. *Address:* The White House, Hospital Road, Bury St Edmunds, Suffolk. *T:* Bury St Edmunds 4125.

DUTTON, family name of **Baron Sherborne.**

DUTTON, James Macfarlane; HM Diplomatic Service; Consul-General, Gothenburg, since 1975; *b* 3 June 1922; *s* of late H. St J. Dutton and Mrs E. B. Dutton; *m* 1958, Jean Mary McAvoy; one *s. Educ:* Winchester Coll.; Balliol Coll., Oxford. Dominions Office, 1944-46; Private Sec. to Permanent Under Sec., 1945; Dublin, 1946-48; CRO, 1948-50; Asst Private Sec. to Sec. of State, 1948; 2nd Sec., New Delhi, 1950-53; CRO, 1953-55; 1st Sec., Dacca and Karachi, 1955-58, Canberra, 1958-62; Head of Constitutional and Protocol Dept, CRO, 1963-65; Canadian Nat. Defence Coll., 1965-66; Dep. High Comr and Counsellor (Commercial), Colombo, 1966-70; Head of Rhodesia Econ. Dept, FCO, 1970-72; attached CSD, 1972-73; seconded to: British Electrical & Allied Manufacturers Assoc. (Dir, Overseas Affairs), 1973-74; Wilton Park and European Discussion Centre, 1974-75. *Recreations:* golf, trout-fishing. *Address:* c/o Foreign and Commonwealth Office, SW1. *Club:* Royal Commonwealth Society.

DUTTON, Ralph Stawell, FSA; *b* 25 Aug. 1898; *s* of late Henry John Dutton, Hinton Ampner House, Hants. *Educ:* Eton; Christ Church, Oxford. Employed in the Foreign Office, 1939-45. High Sheriff of Hants, 1944. A Trustee of the Wallace Collection, 1948-69. Member: Cttees of Nat. Trust, 1955-73; Historic Buildings Council, 1963-72. *Publications:* The English Country House, 1935; The English Garden, 1937; The Land of France (with Lord Holden), 1939; The English Interior, 1948; Wessex, 1950; The Age of Wren, 1951; London Homes, 1952; Normandy and Brittany, 1953; The Victorian Home, 1954; The Châteaux of France, 1957; English Court Life, 1963; Hinton Ampner, A Hampshire Manor, 1968; Hampshire, 1970. *Address:* Hinton Ampner House, Alresford, Hants. *T:* Bramdean 222; 95N Eaton Square, SW1. *T:* 01-235 2950. *Club:* Brooks's.

DUTTON, Reginald David Ley; *b* 20 Aug. 1916; *m* 1952, Pamela Jean (*née* Harrison); two *s* one *d. Educ:* Magdalen Coll. Sch., Oxford. Joined OUP; subseq. joined leading British advertising agency, London Press Exchange (now Lopex Ltd), 1937. During War of 1939-45 served in Royal Navy. Returned to agency after his service; there, he worked on many of major accounts; Dir, 1954; Man. Dir and Chief Exec., 1964; Chm., 1971-76; retired 1976. Pres. Inst. Practitioners in Advertising, 1969-71; Chm., Jt Ind. Council for TV Advertising Research, 1973-75; Mem. Council, BIM, 1970-74; FIPA 1960. Councillor, Canterbury CC, 1976-. *Recreation:* deep sea fishing. *Address:* 3 Bournemouth Drive, Herne Bay, Kent. *T:* Herne Bay 5790.

DUVAL, Sir Francis (John), Kt 1977; CBE 1970; Chairman: Arafura Mining Co. Pty Ltd; Duval Pastoral Co. Pty Ltd; Dover Fisheries Pty Ltd; Duval and Co. (Japan); *b* Narrandera, NSW, Australia, 31 Aug. 1909; *s* of late Francis William Duval; *m* 1960, Chieko, *d* of late Isakichi Hanada. *Educ:* Chatswood High, NSW. Served War, 1939-45: Major AIF, ME, Ceylon, New Guinea and Japan. *Recreations:* golf, deep sea game fishing. *Address:* Churinga House, 1 Old Beach Road, Old Beach, Tasmania 7402, Australia. *T:* Hobart 49-1155. *Clubs:* Royal Automobile, Imperial Service, Australian Jockey (Sydney); Commonwealth (Canberra); Tokyo (Tokyo, Japan).

du VIGNEAUD, Prof. Vincent; Professor of Chemistry, Department of Chemistry, Cornell University, New York, 1967-75; Emeritus Professor of Biochemistry, Cornell University Medical College, New York, NY; *b* 18 May 1901; *s* of Alfred Joseph and Mary du Vigneaud; *m* 1924, Zella Zon Ford; one *s* one *d. Educ:* University of Illinois (BS 1923, MS 1924); University of Rochester, NY, USA (PhD 1927). Asst Biochemist, Philadelphia Gen. Hosp. and Graduate School of Medicine, University of Pa, 1924-25; Asst Biochemist, Graduate School of Medicine, University of Rochester, NY, USA, 1925-27; Nat. Research Council Fellow, Johns Hopkins Univ. Medical Sch., 1927-28; Kaiser Wilhelm Inst, Dresden, Germany; University of Edinburgh Medical Sch.; UCH Medical Sch., London, 1928-29; Assoc. Dept of Chemistry, Univ. of Illinois, 1929-30; Asst Prof., 1930-32; Prof. and Head of Dept of Biochemistry, George Washington Univ. Sch. of Medicine, 1932-38. Mem., Bd of Trustees, Rockefeller Univ. Numerous scientific awards, 1936-. Mem. Royal Society of Sciences of Upsala (Sweden), 1950; Chandler Medal, Columbia Univ., 1955; Nobel Laureate in Chemistry, 1955; Willard Gibbs Medal, 1956. Hon. FRSE 1951; Hon. Fellow Chemical Soc. (London), 1955; Hon. FRIC 1959. Hon. ScD: New York Univ., 1955; Yale, 1955;

Univ. of Illinois, 1960; Univ. of Rochester, 1965; St Louis Univ., 1965; George Washington Univ., 1968. *Publications:* A Trail of Research in Sulfur Chemistry and Metabolism and Related Fields, 1952; articles in: Jl of Biological Chemistry; Jl of Amer. Chemical Soc.; Jl of Medicinal Chemistry; Biochemistry. *Address:* 200 White Park Road, Ithaca, New York 14850, USA.

DWORKIN, Prof. Ronald Myles; Professor of Jurisprudence, Oxford University, since 1969; Fellow of University College, Oxford, since 1969; *b* 11 Dec. 1931; *s* of David Dworkin and Madeline Talamo; *m* 1958, Betsy Celia Ross; one *s* one *d. Educ:* Harvard Coll.; Oxford Univ.; Harvard Law Sch. Legal Sec. to Judge Learned Hand, 1957-58; Associate, Sullivan & Cromwell, New York, 1958-62; Yale Law School: Associate Prof. of Law, 1962-65; Prof. of Law, 1965-68; Wesley N. Hohfeld Prof. of Jurisprudence, 1968-69. Rosenthal Lectr, Northwestern Univ., 1975; Academic Freedom Lectr, Univ. of Witwatersrand, 1976. Vis. Prof. of Philosophy, Princeton Univ., 1974-75; Prof. of Law, NY Univ. Law Sch., 1975-; Prof.-at-Large, Cornell Univ., 1976-; Vis. Prof. of Philosophy and Law, Harvard Univ., 1977. Co-Chm., US Democratic Party Abroad, 1972-76. *Publications:* Taking Rights Seriously, 1977; (ed) The Philosophy of Law, 1977; several articles in legal and philosophical jls. *Address:* University College, Oxford. *Clubs:* Garrick; Oxford American Democrats (Oxford).

DWYER, Most Rev. George Patrick; *see* Birmingham, Archbishop of, (RC).

DWYER, Air Vice-Marshal Michael Harington, CB 1961; CBE 1955; retired; *b* 18 Sept. 1912; *s* of late M. H. Dwyer, Royal Garrison Artillery; *m* 1936, Barbara, *d* of late S. B. Freeman, CBE; one *s* one *d. Educ:* Oundle Sch. Entered RAF, 1931; served India, 1933-36; UK and NW Europe, 1939-45; Middle East, 1949-51; Air Officer Commanding No 62 Group, 1954-56; SASO No 3 Group, RAF, 1956-57; Student at Imperial Defence Coll., 1958; No 3 Group, 1959-61; AOA, HQ Bomber Command, 1961-65; Regional Dir of Civil Defence, North-West Region, 1966-68. Chm., Harington Carpets, 1973-74. *Address:* Island House, Rambledown Lane, West Chiltington, Sussex.

DYALL, Valentine; actor; *b* 7 May 1908; *s* of late Franklin Dyall; *m* 1936, Marjorie Stonor (decd), *d* of Hon. Maurice Stonor; *m* 1940, Babette Holder (decd), adopted *d* of N. F. Holder; two *s;* *m* Kay Woodman; one *d. Educ:* Harrow; Christ Church, Oxford. Began acting career at the Old Vic, 1930 and continued regularly on the West End stage until 1938; subsequently mainly in films and broadcasting. First appeared in films, 1941, and has acted in numerous pictures. Took the role of The Man in Black in a radio series. *Publications:* Unsolved Mysteries, 1954; Famous Sea Tragedies, 1955; Flood of Mutiny, 1957. *Recreations:* fishing, golf. *Address:* c/o Essanay Ltd, 75 Hammersmith Road, W14 8UZ.

DYBALL, Maj.-Gen. (Hon.) Antony John, CBE 1970 (OBE 1966); MC 1945; TD; *b* 10 July 1919; *s* of John Francis Dyball; *m* 1941, Elizabeth Margaret Siddle; one *d. Educ:* Downsend; Epsom College. London Irish Rifles (TA); joined Depot RUR, Armagh, 1939; 1st Bn RUR, part of 6th Airborne Div., NW Europe, 1945 (MC); Trng Major, RUR Depot at Ballymena, 1954-56; comd Queen's Univ. OTC, Belfast, 1956-58; Bde Major, 124 Inf. Bde (TA), 1958-60; CO, London Irish Rifles (TA), 1960-62; AAG, Middle East Comd, 1963-65; Bde Comdr, 107 Independent Inf. Bde (TA), 1965-67; Chief of Staff, HQ Northern Ireland, 1967-69, and Dep. Dir Ops, 1969-70 (acting Maj.-Gen.); Dep. Comdr, Northumberland District, 1970-73, retired; Hon. Maj.-Gen., 1973. *Recreations:* golf, racing. *Address:* 49 Palewell Park, East Sheen, SW14. *T:* 01-878 0394.

DYDE, John Horsfall, CBE 1970 (OBE 1957); Chairman, Eastern Gas Board, 1959-69; *b* 4 June 1905; *m* 1930, Ethel May Hewitt; two *s. Educ:* Scarborough High Sch.; University of Leeds (MSc). Engineer and Manager, North Middlesex Gas Co., 1937-42; prior to nationalisation was Engineer and Gen. Manager of Uxbridge, Maidenhead, Wycombe & District Gas Co. and Slough Gas & Coke Co.; also Technical Director of group of undertakings of the South Eastern Gas Corp. Ltd; Dep.-Chm., Eastern Gas Board, 1949. President: Western Junior Gas Assoc., 1935-36; Southern Assoc. of Gas Engineers and Managers, 1949-50; Institution of Gas Engineers, 1951-52; British Road Tar Association. CEng, MIChemE; Hon. FIGasE. *Recreations:* golf, sailing. *Address:* Stable End, Thellusson Lodge, Aldeburgh, Suffolk. *T:* Aldeburgh 3148.

DYE, Maj.-Gen. Jack Bertie, CBE 1968 (OBE 1965); MC; Director, Volunteers, Territorials and Cadets, 1971-74; Major-General late Royal Norfolk Regiment; *b* 1919. Served War of 1939-45 (MC). Brigadier, 1966; psc. Commanded South Arabian

Army, 1966-68; GOC Eastern District, 1969-71. Col Comdt, The Queen's Division, 1970-; Col, Royal Anglian Regt, 1976- (Dep. Col, 1974-76).

DYER, Charles; playwright and novelist; actor-director (as Raymond Dyer); *b* 7 July 1928; *s* of James Sidney Dyer and Florence (*née* Stretton); *m* 1959, Fiona Thomson, actress; three *s*. *Educ:* Queen Elizabeth's Sch., Barnet. *Plays:* Clubs Are Sometimes Trumps, 1948; Who On Earth!, 1951; Turtle in the Soup, 1953; The Jovial Parasite, 1954; Single Ticket Mars, 1955; Time, Murderer, Please, and Poison In Jest, 1956; Wanted— One Body!, 1958; Prelude to Fury, 1959 (also wrote theme music); Rattle of A Simple Man, 1962 (also in Berlin, Paris, NY, Rome); Staircase, 1966 (for RSC; also in NY, Paris, Amsterdam, Berlin, Rome); Mother Adam, Paris, Berlin, 1970, London, 1971, 1973, NY, 1974; The Loving Allelujah, 1974; as R. Kraselchik: Red Cabbage and Kings, 1960 (also wrote theme music); *screenplays:* Rattle, 1964; Insurance Italian Style, 1967; Staircase, 1968; Brother Sun and Sister Moon, 1970. Also directed plays for the stage and television. Acted in: *plays:* Worm's Eye View, 1948; Room For Two, 1955; Dry Rot, 1958; *films:* Cuptie Honeymoon, 1947; Britannia Mews, 1949; Road Sense, 1950; Off The Record, 1952; Pickwick Papers, 1952; Dockland Case, 1953; Strange Case of Blondie, 1953; Naval Patrol, 1959; Loneliness of the Long Distance Runner, 1962; Mouse On The Moon, 1962; Knack, 1964; Rattle of A Simple Man, 1964; How I Won The War, 1967; Staircase, 1968; *television series:* Hugh and I, 1964. *Publications:* (as Charles Dyer): plays: Wanted—One Body!, 1961; Time, Murderer, Please, 1962; Rattle Of A Simple Man, (Fr.) 1963; Staircase, 1966; Mother Adam, 1970; The Loneliness Trilogy, 1972; Hot Godly Wind, 1973; novels: Rattle Of A Simple Man, 1964; Charlie Always Told Harry Almost Everything, 1969 (USA and Europe, 1970); The Rising of our Herbert, 1972. *Recreations:* amateur music and carpentry. *Address:* Old Wob, Gerrards Cross, Bucks.

DYER, Maj.-Gen. Godfrey Maxwell, CBE 1970 (OBE 1941); DSO 1945; psc, psa; Chairman, "Not Forgotten Association", since 1961; Managing Director, Old Palace Wine Co. Ltd, since 1962; *b* 10 Dec. 1898; *s* of A. R. Dyer, Winchester; *m* 1927, Evelyn Mary, *d* of George List, London and S Africa; two *s* (and one *s* decd). *Educ:* Bishops Stortford Coll.; Royal Military Coll., Sandhurst. 2nd Lt, IA, 1917. Served European War, 1914-19 (India and Middle East); War of 1939-45 (India, Middle East and Burma); GSO2, Air HQ India, 1940; GSO1, GHQ India, 1941 (OBE): Lt-Col and Comdt, 13th DCO Lancers, 1941; Iraq, Persia, N Africa; Brig. 1942; Bde Comdr, 1942-45; Burma (despatches twice, DSO); Dep. QMG, GHQ India, 1945; Maj.-Gen., 1945; retd, 1945. Pres., Assoc. of British Officers of the Indian Army, 1975-. *Address:* 28 Bushwood Road, Kew, Richmond, Surrey. *T:* 01-948 2976. *Club:* Cavalry and Guards. *See also Mark Dyer.*

DYER, Sir Henry Peter Francis S.; *see* Swinnerton-Dyer.

DYER, Mark; His Honour Judge Dyer; a Circuit Judge, since 1977; *b* 20 Nov. 1928; *er s* of Maj.-Gen. G. M. Dyer, *qv*; *m* 1953, Diana, *d* of Sir Percy Lancelot Orde, CIE; two *d*. *Educ:* Ampleforth Coll.; Christ Church, Oxford (MA). 2nd Lieut: Royal Scots Greys, 1948-49; The Westminster Dragoons (2nd CLY) TA, 1950. Called to the Bar, Middle Temple, 1953; Mem., Gen. Council of the Bar, 1965-69. Dep. Chm., Isle of Wight QS, 1971. A Recorder of the Crown Court, 1972-77. *Address:* Furbelow House, 17 King Street, The Green, Richmond, Surrey; Watermill Cottage, Wherwell, Andover, Hants. *Club:* Cavalry and Guards.

DYER-SMITH, Rear-Adm. John Edward, CBE 1972; Director-General Aircraft (Naval), Ministry of Defence, 1970-72, retired; *b* 17 Aug. 1918; *s* of Harold E. Dyer-Smith and Emily Sutton; *m* 1940, Kathleen Powell; four *s* one *d*. *Educ:* Devonport High Sch.; RN Engineering Coll.; Imperial Coll. of Science. Served War of 1939-45: Engineer Officer, HMS Prince of Wales, 1940-41; Asst Fleet Engr Officer, Eastern Fleet, 1942-43; HMS Illustrious, 1943. Various MAP and Min. of Aviation appts, 1946-54; Head of Naval Air Dept, RAE, 1957-61; Dir of RN Aircraft/Helicopters, Min. of Aviation, 1961-64; Defence and Naval Attaché, Tokyo, 1965-67; Superintendent, RN Aircraft Yard, Belfast, 1968-70. *Recreations:* painting, golf. *Address:* Casa Gomila, Alcaufar, Menorca. *Club:* Royal Automobile.

DYKE, Sir Derek William H.; *see* Hart Dyke.

DYKES, Hugh John; MP (C) Harrow (East) since 1970; Partner in Simon & Coates, Stockbrokers, London, since 1968; *b* 17 May 1939; *s* of Richard Dykes and Doreen Ismay Maxwell Dykes; *m* 1965, Susan Margaret Dykes (*née* Smith); three *s*. *Educ:* Weston

super Mare Grammar Sch.; Pembroke Coll. Cambridge. Contested (C) Tottenham, Gen. Elec., 1966. PPS: to three Parly Under-Secs of State for Defence, 1970; to Parly Under-Sec. of State in Civil Service Dept attached to Cabinet Office, 1973; Mem., European Parlt, Strasbourg, 1974. Sec., Cons. Parly European Cttee, 1974-. Mem., Wider Share Ownership Council; Research Sec., Bow Gp, 1965; Chm., Coningsby Club, 1969. *Publications:* (ed) Westropp's "Invest £100", 1964, and Westropp's "Start your own Business", 1965; many articles and pamphlets on political and financial subjects. *Recreations:* music, theatre, swimming, travel. *Address:* House of Commons, SW1. *T:* 01-219 3000. *Club:* Beefsteak.

DYKES BOWER, Sir John, Kt 1968; CVO 1953; Hon. DMus Oxon, 1944; MA, MusB Cantab; Hon. RAM; FRCM; Hon. FRCO; Hon. FTCL; FRSCM; Hon. Secretary, Royal College of Organists, since 1968; Organist of St Paul's Cathedral, 1936-67; *b* 13 Aug. 1905; 3rd *s* of late Ernest Dykes Bower, MD, Glos; unmarried. *Educ:* Cheltenham Coll.; Corpus Christi Coll., Cambridge (Organ Scholar). John Stewart of Rannoch Scholar in Sacred Music, 1922-28; Organist and Master of the Choir of Truro Cathedral, 1926-29; Succentor, 1929; Organist of New Coll., Oxford, 1929-33; of Durham Cathedral, 1933-36; Conductor of the Oxford Harmonic Soc., 1930-33; Lecturer in Music at University of Durham, 1934; Fellow of Corpus Christi Coll., Cambridge, 1934-37; Associate Dir of Royal Sch. of Church Music, 1945-52; Pres., Incorporated Association of Organists, 1949-50; Pres. of the Royal College of Organists, 1960-62. Master, Worshipful Co. of Musicians, 1967-68. RAFVR 1940-45, with rank of Squadron Leader. *Address:* Flat 4z, Artillery Mansions, SW1. *Club:* Athenæum.
See also S. E. Dykes Bower.

DYKES BOWER, S(tephen) E(rnest), MA; FRIBA; FSA; Surveyor of the Fabric of Westminster Abbey, 1951-73, now Emeritus; Consulting Architect, Carlisle Cathedral, 1947-75; *b* 18 April 1903; 2nd *s* of Ernest Dykes Bower, MD; unmarried. *Educ:* Cheltenham Coll.; Merton Coll., Oxford (Organ Schol.); Architectural Assoc. Sch. of Architecture. Private practice as architect since 1931, work chiefly domestic and ecclesiastical. Architect for: New High Altar, Baldachino and American Memorial Chapel, St Paul's Cathedral (with W. Godfrey Allen); enlargement of Bury St Edmunds Cathedral; Cathedral Library and Bishop's Palace, Exeter; completion of Lancing Coll. Chapel; re-building of Gt Yarmouth Parish Church; St Vedast, Foster Lane, EC; and other churches in London and country; work in Canterbury, Winchester, Norwich, Ely, Gloucester, Wells, Oxford, Carlisle, Peterborough and other cathedrals, Oxford and Cambridge Colls, Public Schs, Halls of City Livery Cos, etc. *Publications:* papers and addresses on architectural subjects. *Address:* Quendon Court, Quendon, near Saffron Walden, Essex. *T:* Rickling 242. *Clubs:* Athenæum, United Oxford & Cambridge University.
See also Sir J. Dykes Bower.

DYMOKE, Rear-Adm. Lionel Dorian, CB 1974; Deputy Director-General Ships, Ministry of Defence, 1974-76; *b* 18 March 1921; *s* of Henry Lionel Dymoke and Dorothy (*née* Briscoe); *m* 1st, 1952, Patricia Pimlott (*d* 1968); one *s*; 2nd, 1970, Iris Hemsted (*née* Lamplough). *Educ:* Nautical Coll., Pangbourne. Entered Royal Navy, 1938; Comdr 1953; Captain 1961; Rear-Adm. 1971. *Address:* 3 Woodland Place, Bath, Avon. *T:* Bath 64228.

DYMOND, Charles Edward, CBE 1967;HM Diplomatic Service, retired; *b* 15 Oct. 1916; *s* of Charles George Dymond and Dora Kate Dymond (*née* Gillingham); *m* 1945, Dorothy Jean Peaker; two *s* two *d*. *Educ:* Tiverton Grammar Sch.; Exeter Univ. BSc (Econ) London. Royal Artillery, 1939-46; BoT Regional Div., 1946; Trade Commn Service, 1951; Trade Comr, Johannesburg, 1951; Cape Town, 1955; Nairobi, 1957; Sen. Trade Comr, Lagos, 1963-64; Counsellor (Commercial), Lagos, 1965-66; Counsellor i/c, British High Commn, Auckland, 1967-73; Comr for Pitcairn Island, 1970-72; Consul-General, Perth, 1973-76. *Recreations:* music, photography. *Address:* PO Box 15, Sawyers Valley, WA 6074, Australia.

DYNEVOR, 9th Baron *cr* 1780; **Richard Charles Uryan Rhys;** *b* 19 June 1935; *s* of 8th Baron Dynevor, CBE, MC; *S* father, 1962; *m* 1959, Lucy, *d* of Sir John Rothenstein, *qv*; one *s* three *d*. *Educ:* Eton; Magdalene Coll., Cambridge. *Heir: s* Hon. Hugo Griffith Uryan Rhys, *b* 19 Nov. 1966. *Address:* 18 Brook Green, W6. *T:* 01-603 4720.

DYSART, Countess of (11th in line), *cr* 1643; **Rosamund Agnes Greaves;** Baroness Huntingtower, 1643; *b* 15 Feb. 1914; *d* of Major Owain Greaves (*d* 1941), RHG, and Wenefryde Agatha, Countess of Dysart (10th in line); *S* mother, 1975. *Heir: sister*

Lady Katherine Grant of Rothiemurchus [b 1 June 1918; m 1941, Colonel John Peter Grant of Rothiemurchus, MBE; one s one d]. Address: Barham House, Heasley Mill, South Molton, N Devon.

DYSON, Rev. Canon Anthony Oakley, BD, MA, DPhil; a Canon of St George's Chapel, Windsor Castle, since 1974, Custodian, since 1975; b 6 Oct. 1935; s of Henry Oakley Leslie Dyson and Lilian Dyson; m 1960, Edwina Anne Hammett; two s. Educ: William Hulme's Grammar Sch., Manchester; Univs of Cambridge and Oxford. 2nd Lieut, West Yorks Regt, 1954-56; Emmanuel Coll., Cambridge, 1956-59; Exeter Coll., Oxford and Ripon Hall, Oxford, 1959-61; Curate of Putney, Dio. Southwark, 1961-63; Chaplain of Ripon Hall, Oxford, 1963-69; Principal of Ripon Hall, 1969-74. Licensed to Officiate Dio. Oxford, 1965-75. Examng Chaplain to Bishops of Carlisle and Sheffield; Select Preacher, Univ. of Oxford, 1971; Hensley Henson Lectr, Univ. of Oxford, 1972-73. Editor, The Teilhard Review, 1966-72. Publications: Existentialism, 1965; Who is Jesus Christ?, 1969; The Immortality of the Past, 1974; We Believe, 1977; contribs to Evolution Marxism and Christianity, 1967; What Kind of Revolution?, 1968; A Dictionary of Christian Theology, 1969; The Christian Marxist Dialogue, 1969; Teilhard Reassessed, 1970; Oxford Dictionary of the Christian Church, 2nd edn, 1974; Education and Social Action, 1975; Ernst Troeltsch and the Future of Theology, 1976; The Language of the Church in Higher and Further Education, 1977; Theology, The Modern Churchman, Study Encounter, TLS, etc. Recreations: literature, sport. Address: 12 The Cloisters, Windsor Castle, Berks SL4 1NJ. T: Windsor 52979.

DYSON, Edith Mary Beatrice, OBE 1946; RRC 1948, Bar to RRC 1952; b 18 June 1900. Educ: Greenhead, Huddersfield. Student Nurse, Royal Free Hospital, London, 1919-24; joined Army Nursing Service, 1924, Germany (with the Army of Occupation, 1926), also India, Burma; served War of 1939-45, i/c nursing units Hong Kong; Prisoner of War, 1941-45; War Office, 1946-48; Col, Queen Alexandra's Royal Army Nursing Corps and Deputy Dir Army Nursing Services, 1951-52; retired 1952. Address: Vine Cottage, Higher Trevilla, Feock, Cornwall.

DYSON, Fred; General Secretary, National Union of Dyers, Bleachers and Textile Workers, since 1973; b 28 Sept. 1916; s of James Dyson and Jane Anne Dyson (née Ashwood); m 1946, Beatrice Lilian (née Goepel); one d. Educ: Nields Council School. MIWP. Served with RAFVR, 1940-46. Woollen Spinner, 1934-39 and 1946-53; National Union of Dyers, Bleachers and Textile Workers: Organiser, 1953; Work Study Officer, 1958; No 4 District Sec., Manchester Area, 1970; Asst Gen. Sec., 1972. Mem. TUC General Council, 1975. Member: Garment and Allied Industries Requirements Bd, 1976-; Industrial Injuries Adv. Council, 1977-. Recreations: landscape painting, swimming. Address: 11 Hill End Grove, Great Horton, Bradford BD7 4RP. T: Bradford 75466. Clubs: Slaithwaite Working Men's (Slaithwaite); Shipley Trades Hall (Shipley); Lidgett Green Working Men's (Bradford).

DYSON, Prof. Freeman John, FRS 1952; Professor, School of Natural Sciences, Institute for Advanced Study, Princeton, New Jersey, since 1953; b 15 Dec. 1923; s of late Sir George Dyson, KCVO; m 1st, 1950, Verena Esther (née Huber) (marr. diss. 1958); one s one d; 2nd, 1958, Imme (née Jung); four d. Educ: Winchester; Cambridge; Cornell University. Operational research for RAF Bomber Command, 1943-45. Fellow of Trinity Coll., Cambridge, 1946-50; Commonwealth Fund Fellow at Cornell and Princeton, USA, 1947-49; Mem. of Institute for Advanced Study, Princeton, USA, 1949-50; Professor of Physics, Cornell Univ., Ithaca, NY, USA, 1951-53. Mem. of National Academy of Sciences (USA), 1964. Lorentz Medal, Royal Netherlands Acad. of Sciences, 1966; Hughes Medal, Royal Soc., 1968; Max Planck Medal, German Physical Soc., 1969. Publications: contrib. to The Physical Review, Annals of Mathematics, etc. Address: Institute for Advanced Study, Princeton, NJ 08540, USA. Club: Athenæum.

DYSON, Dr James, FRS 1968; Deputy Chief Scientific Officer, National Physical Laboratory, 1975-76; retired 1976; b 10 Dec. 1914; s of George Dyson and Mary Grace (née Bateson); m 1st, Ena Lillian Turner (marr. diss. 1948); one d; 2nd, 1948, Marie Florence Chant (d 1967); 3rd 1975, Rosamund Pearl Greville Shuter. Educ: Queen Elizabeth Sch., Kirkby Lonsdale; Christ's Coll., Cambridge. BA 1936; MA 1960; ScD 1960. Student Apprentice, BT-H Co., Rugby, 1936-39; Research Engr, BT-H Co., Rugby, 1939-46; Consultant (Optics), AEI Research Lab., Aldermaston, 1946-63; Supt, Div. of Mech. and Optical Metrology, NPL, 1963-74. FInstP 1960; Hon. Fellow Royal Microscopical Soc., 1969. Publications: Interferometry, 1969; papers on applied optics in learned jls. Recreations: astronomy,

mechanical occupations, music, people, deploring the motor-car. Address: 19 Hansler Grove, East Molesey, Surrey KT8 9JN. T: 01-979 6403.

DYSON, John Michael; Master of the Supreme Court of Judicature (Chancery Division) since 1973; b 9 Feb. 1929; s of late Eric Dyson, Gainsborough and Hope Patison (née Kirkland). Educ: Bradfield Coll.; Corpus Christi Coll., Oxford. 2nd Lieut, Royal Tank Regt, 1948. Admitted Solicitor, 1956; Partner, Field Roscoe & Co., 1957 (subseq. Field Fisher & Co. and Field Fisher & Martineau). Address: 10 Barnsbury Square, N1 1JL. T: 01-607 4360. Club: United Oxford & Cambridge University.

DYSON, Richard George; Deputy Chairman, Antony Gibbs Holdings Ltd, since 1976; b 17 July 1909; 2nd s of late Charles Dyson and late Ellen Gwendoline Dyson (née Barrington-Ward), Huddersfield, Yorks; m 1940, Lorna Marion, d of late H. H. Elkin, Alexandria, Egypt, and Port Lincoln, Australia; four s (two d decd). Educ: Charterhouse (Sen. Schol.); Christ Church, Oxford (Open Classical Exhibn). MA 1st cl. Hons in Hon. Mods and Greats. Joined Barclays Bank Ltd, 1933; transf. to Barclays Bank DCO, 1936; served overseas in Egypt, Sudan and E Africa until 1945; apptd an Asst Gen. Manager, 1951, a Gen. Manager, 1959, a Vice-Chm., 1967, and the Dep. Chm., 1968-76 (Bank renamed Barclays Bank International Ltd, 1971); Director: Barclays Bank Ltd, 1972; Barclays Bank of Nigeria Ltd; and other cos within Barclays Gp; Chm., Lombard Assoc., 1962-63. Vice-Pres. Council, Inst. of Bankers, 1974- (Mem. 1963-74, Dep. Chm. 1970, Pres. 1972-74); Dir, Commonwealth Develt Finance Co. Ltd, 1968-; Governor: Sutton's Hosp. in Charterhouse; Charterhouse Sch., Godalming. FIB 1960. Recreations: cricket, gardening, golf. Address: Brickfields, Chobham, Surrey. T: Chobham 8150. Clubs: MCC; Free Foresters.

E

EABORN, Prof. Colin, PhD, DSc (Wales); FRS 1970; FRIC; Professor of Chemistry, University of Sussex, since 1962; b 15 March 1923; s of Tom Stanley and Caroline Eaborn; m 1949, Joyce Thomas. Educ: Ruabon Grammar Sch., Denbighshire; Univ. Coll. of N Wales, Bangor. Asst Lecturer, 1947, Lecturer, 1950, and Reader 1954, in Chemistry, Univ. of Leicester. Research Associate, Univ. of California at Los Angeles, 1950-51; Robert A. Welch Visiting Scholar, Rice Univ., Texas, 1961-62; Erskine Fellow, Univ. of Canterbury (NZ), 1965; Pro-Vice Chancellor (Science), Univ. of Sussex, 1968-72; Dist. Prof., New Mexico State Univ., 1973; Canadian Commonwealth Fellow, Univ. of Victoria, BC, 1976. Hon. Sec., Chemical Society, 1964-71, Vice-Pres., Dalton Div., 1971-75; Chm., British Cttee on Chemical Educn, 1967-69; Mem., Italy/UK Mixed Commn, 1972-. F. S. Kipping Award, Amer. Chem. Soc., 1964; Organometallic Award, Chem. Soc., 1975; Ingold Lectureship and Medal, Chem. Soc., 1976. Publications: Organosilicon Compounds, 1960; Organometallic Compounds of the Group IV Elements, Vol. 1, Part 1, 1968; numerous publications, mainly in Jl of Chem. Soc. and Jl of Organometallic Chemistry (Regional Editor). Address: School of Molecular Sciences, University of Sussex, Brighton BN1 9QJ. T: Brighton 66755.

EADEN, Maurice Bryan; HM Diplomatic Service; Consul General, Karachi, since 1975; b 9 Feb. 1923; s of William Eaden and Florence Ada Eaden (née Hudson); m 1947, Nelly Margaretha Dorgelo; three s. Educ: Bemrose Sch., Derby. Served Army, 1942-47. Foreign Office, 1947; Vice-Consul, Leopoldville, 1955; First Secretary (Commercial): Addis Ababa, 1958; Beirut, 1963; FO, 1967; First Sec. (Commercial), Bombay, 1970; Counsellor (Administration), Brussels, 1972-75. Recreations: walking in Derbyshire; languages. Address: c/o Foreign and Commonwealth Office, SW1; British Consulate General, Karachi, Pakistan; New Houses, Cressbrook, Buxton, Derbyshire. T: Tideswell 871404. Clubs: Civil Service, Royal Commonwealth Society, Royal Over-Seas League; Sind, Boat (both Karachi).

EADIE, Alexander, BEM 1960; JP; MP (Lab) Midlothian since 1966; Parliamentary Under-Secretary of State, Department of Energy, since 1974; b 23 June 1920; m 1941; one s. Educ: Buckhaven Senior Secondary Sch. Coal-miner from 1934. Chm., Fife County Housing Cttee, 9 yrs; Chm., Fife County Educn Cttee, 18 mths; Governor, Moray House Teachers' Training Coll., Edinburgh, 5 years; Exec. Committee: Scottish Council of

Labour Party, 9 yrs; NUM Scottish Area, 2 yrs; Mem., Eastern Regional Hosp. Bd (Scotland), 14 yrs. Contested Ayr, 1959 and 1964; Former PPS to Miss M. Herbison, MP, Minister of Social Security, and Mem. of Parly Select Cttee on Scottish Affairs; Opposition Front Bench Spokesman on Energy (incl. N Sea Oil), 1973-74; Chairman: Parly Labour Party Power and Steel Gp; Miners' Parly Gp; Vice-Chm., Parly Trade Union Group. JP Fife, 1951. *Recreations:* bowling, gardening. *Address:* Balkerack, The Haugh, East Wemyss, Fife. *T:* Buckhaven 3636.

EADIE, Mrs Ellice (Aylmer), CBE 1966; Standing Counsel to General Synod of Church of England, since 1972; *b* 30 June 1912; *d* of late Rt Rev. R. T. Hearn, LLD, sometime Bishop of Cork, and of late Dr M. E. T. Hearn, MD, FRCPI; *m* 1946, John Harold Ward Eadie. *Educ:* Cheltenham Ladies' Coll.; St Hugh's Coll., Oxford. Called to Bar, Gray's Inn, 1936. Flt Officer, WAAF, 1941-46. Parliamentary Counsel Office, 1949-72, Parly Counsel, 1968-72. *Address:* 74 Roebuck House, Palace Street, SW1E 5BD. *T:* 01-828 6158.

EADY, family name of **Baron Swinfen.**

EAGERS, Derek; Under-Secretary, Department of Trade, since 1975; *b* 13 Sept. 1924; *s* of late Horace Eagers and Florence (*née* Green); *m* 1953, Hazel Maureen Henson; two *s.* *Educ:* King Edward VII Sch., Sheffield; Brasenose Coll., Oxford. RNVR, 1943-47. Min. of Fuel and Power, 1949; UK Atomic Energy Authority, 1955-57; British Embassy, Washington, 1958-60; Principal Private Sec. to successive Ministers of Power, 1963-65; Petroleum Counsellor, Washington, 1966-68; Min. of Power (subseq. Min. of Technology, Dept of Trade and Industry), 1969; Dept of Industry, 1974. *Recreations:* concealing his true ignorance of cricket; gardening, railway history. *Address:* 12 The Waldrons, Oxted, Surrey RH8 9DY. *T:* Oxted 2808.

EAGGER, Brig. Arthur Austin, CBE 1944 (OBE 1940), TD 1945; Consultant to Slough Industrial Health Service, since 1963; *b* 14 March 1898; *s* of Edward and Elsie Eagger; *m* 1st, 1935, Kate Mortimer Hare (*d* 1946); three *s*; 2nd, 1948, Barbara Noel Hare. *Educ:* Aberdeen Univ. (MB ChB 1922). Lieut 6th Bn Gordon Hldrs. Commissioned RAMC (TA), 1928; late DDMS 1 Airborne Corps. Medical Dir Slough Industrial Health Service, retired 1963. Bronze Star (USA), 1945. *Publications:* Industrial Resettlement (Proc. RSM), 1952; Health in the Factory (Jl Royal Institute of Public Health and Hygiene), 1953; Venture in Industry, 1965. *Address:* 1 Underwood Close, Dawlish, Devon EX7 9RY. *T:* Dawlish 864597.

EAGLESHAM, Eric John Ross, MA, BEd, LLB; Professor of Education, Durham University, 1947-66, retired; Professor Emeritus, 1966; *b* 29 Oct. 1905; 3rd *s* of late Reverend David Eaglesham, Chapelknowe, Canonbie, Dumfriesshire; *m* 1957, Nancy, *yr d* of late J. F. Rintoul; three *s* one *d.* *Educ:* Dumfries Acad.; Edinburgh Univ., 1923-27, 1930-31. Asst Teacher, Gretna Sch., 1927-30; Asst Teacher, Lockerbie Academy, 1931-35; Lecturer, Education Dept, Manchester Univ., 1936-38; Master of Method, Jordanhill Training Centre, Glasgow, 1938-40; RAF, rank Flight Lieut, on planning staff of Air Ministry dealing with questions of International Law, 1941-42; Principal Master of Method, Jordanhill Training Centre, Glasgow, 1942-43; Depute Dir of Studies, Jordanhill Training Centre, 1944-46. *Publications:* From School Board to Local Authority, 1956; Morant on the March (Yearbook of Education), 1957; The Foundations of Twentieth Century Education in England, 1967; articles in various learned journals. *Address:* The Croft, Park Road, Scotby, Cumbria.

EAGLETON, Guy Tryon; *b* 1 July 1894; *s* of late John Eagleton and of Violet Marion Eagleton; *m* 1947, Amy Rubina Gothard; no *c.* *Educ:* Aldenham Sch. Solicitor, 1919; Asst Clerk Haberdashers' Company, 1925; Clerk of the Haberdashers' Company, 1931-50, retired. *Recreations:* golf and gardening. *Address:* 31 Hillydeal Road, Otford, Sevenoaks, Kent TN14 5RT. *T:* Otford 3220. *Club:* Royal Blackheath Golf (Captain General, Sen. Past Captain).

EAKER, Lt-Gen. Ira Clarence, Hon. KCB 1945; Hon. KBE 1943; DSM, US Army (2 Oak Leaf Clusters), US Navy; DFC (Oak Leaf Cluster); Silver Star; Legion of Merit; *b* Field Creek, Texas, 13 April 1896; *s* of Y. Y. Eaker and Dona Lee; *m* Ruth Huff Apperson; no *c.* *Educ:* South Eastern State Teachers' Coll., Durant, Okla; University of Southern California; Columbia Univ., 2nd Lieut of Infantry, Regular Army, 1917; Capt. 1920; Major, 1935; Lieut-Col (temp.) 1937; Lieut-Col 1940; Col (temp.), 1941; Brig.-Gen. (temp.) Jan. 1942; Maj.-Gen. (temp.) Sept. 1942; Lieut-Gen. (temp.) 1943; permanent Brig.-Gen. RA 1944. Served in Philippines, 1919-22; pilot of one of planes of Pan-American Flight round South America, 1926-27 (DFC);

chief pilot of Airplane Question Mark on refuelling endurance flight, 1929, establishing a new world flight endurance record (Oak Leaf Cluster for DFC). In command of VIII Bomber Command in European Theatre of Operations, 1942; commanded Eighth Air Force, 1942-44 and also US Army Air Forces in UK, 1943-44; comd. Mediterranean Allied Air Forces in Italy, 1944; Dep. Comdg Gen. Army Air Forces and Chief of Air Staff, US, 1945-47; retired 1947. Vice-President: Hughes Tool Co., 1947-57; Douglas Aircraft, 1957-61. Author, syndicated weekly column on subjects in nat. security area, 1962-. French Legion of Honour (Grand Officer) and many other foreign decorations. *Publications:* (with Gen. Arnold); Army Flyer, This Flying Game, Winged Warfare. *Address:* c/o Hughes Aircraft Co., 1612 K Street NW, Washington, DC 20006, USA.

EAMES, Eric James, JP; Lord Mayor of Birmingham, 1974-75, Deputy Lord Mayor, 1975-76; *b* Highley, Shropshire, 13 April 1917; *s* of George Eames; *m* (marr. diss.); one *s.* *Educ:* Highley Sch., Highley, Shropshire. Mem., Governing Board, Internat. Center for Information Co-operation and Relationship among World's Major Cities; Governor, Harper Adams Agric. Coll. *Recreations:* gardening, do-it-yourself enthusiast. *Address:* 78 Westley Road, Acocks Green, Birmingham B27 7UH. *T:* 021-706 7629.

EAMES, Rt. Rev. Robert Henry Alexander; *see* Derry and Raphoe, Bishop of.

EARDLEY-WILMOT, Sir John (Assheton), 5th Bt *cr* 1821; MVO 1956; DSC 1943; Staff of Monopolies Commission since 1967; *b* 2 Jan. 1917; *s* of Commander Frederick Neville Eardley-Wilmot (*d* 1956) (*s* of 3rd Bt) and Dorothy Little (*d* 1959), formerly of Brooksby, Double Bay, Sydney; *S* uncle, 1970; *m* 1939, Diana Elizabeth, *d* of Commander Aubrey Moore, RN, and Mrs O. Bassett; one *s* one *d.* *Educ:* Stubbington; RNC, Dartmouth. Motor Torpedo Boats, 1939-43; served HMS Apollo, 1944; HMS Fencer, 1945-46; RN Staff Course, 1950; Commander 1950; HMS Opossum, 1951-53; Cabinet Office, 1954-57; Admiralty, 1958-67; retired 1967, as Deputy Director Naval Administrative Planning. AMBIM 1965; FRSA 1970. Liveryman, Worshipful Co. of Paviours. Freeman, City of London (by Redemption). Norwegian War Medal. *Recreation:* fishing. *Heir:* s Michael John Assheton Eardley-Wilmot [*b* 13 Jan. 1941; *m* 1971, Wendy, *y d* of A. J. Wolstenholme; one *s* one *d*]. *Address:* 4 Margravine Gardens, W6. *T:* 01-748 3723. *Club:* Enton Fishing.

EARL, Christopher Joseph, MD, FRCP; Physician to: Neurological Department, Middlesex Hospital, since 1971; National Hospital, Queen Square, since 1958; Moorfields Eye Hospital, since 1959; Consultant Neurologist, King Edward VII Hospital for Officers, since 1966 and Hospital of St John and St Elizabeth, since 1967; Civilian Consultant in Neurology, Royal Air Force, since 1976; *b* 20 Nov. 1925; *s* of Christopher and Winifred Earl, Ashbourne, Derbyshire; *m* 1951, Alma Patience Hopkins, Reading; two *s* three *d.* *Educ:* Cotton Coll.; Guy's Hosp. House phys. and house surg., Guy's Hosp., and MO, RAF, 1948-50. Lecturer in Chemical Pathology, Guy's Hosp., 1950-52; Research Fellow, Harvard Med. Sch., and Neurological Unit, Boston City Hosp., 1952-54; Resident MO, Nat. Hosp., Queen Square, 1954-56; Chief Asst, Neurological Dept, Guy's Hosp., 1956-58; Physician, Neurological Dept, London Hosp., 1961-71. Hon. Dir of Photography, Royal Society of Medicine, 1967-73. Hon. Sec., Assoc. British Neurologists, 1968-74. Vice-Pres., Med. Defence Union; Chm., Cttee on Neurology, RCP. *Publications:* Papers in learned jls on Biochemistry and Neurology. *Recreation:* reading history. *Address:* 23 Audley Road, Ealing, W5. *T:* 01-997 0380. *Club:* Garrick.

EARL, Eric Stafford; Clerk to the Worshipful Company of Fishmongers, since 1974; *b* 8 July 1928; *s* of late Alfred Henry Earl and Mary Elizabeth Earl; *m* 1951, Clara Alice Alston. *Educ:* SE Essex Technical Coll.; City of London Coll. Served with RA, 1946-48. Joined Fishmongers' Co. 1948: Accountant, 1961-68; Asst Clerk, 1969-73; Actg Clerk, 1973-74; Liveryman, 1977. Clerk to Governors of Gresham's Sch., 1974-; Hon. Sec., Shellfish Assoc. of Great Britain; Secretary: Atlantic Salmon Research Trust Ltd; City and Guilds of London Art School Ltd; Jt Hon. Sec., Central Council for Rivers Protection; Hon. Asst River Keeper of River Thames; Mem., Nat. Anglers' Council; Mem. Council, Anglers' Co-operative Assoc. Director: Hulbert Property Co. Ltd; Hulbert Property Holdings Ltd. *Recreations:* fishing, gardening, tennis, cricket. *Address:* Dolphins, Watling Lane, Thaxted, Essex CM6 2RA. *T:* Thaxted 758. *Club:* Flyfishers'.

EARLE, Air Chief Marshal Sir Alfred, GBE 1966 (KBE 1961; CBE 1946); CB 1956; *b* 1907; *s* of late Henry Henwood Earle, and Mary Winifred Earle, Beaworthy, Devon; *m* 1st, 1934, Phyllis Beatrice (*d* 1960), *o d* of W. J. Rice, Watford; one *s* one *d*; 2nd, 1961, Rosemary, *widow* of Air Vice-Marshal F. J. St G. Braithwaite, and *d* of late G. Grinling Harris, Clifford's Inn. *Educ:* Shebbear Coll., Beaworthy, Devon. Graduated from Royal Air Force Coll., Cranwell, 1929. Served in Bomber Squadrons in United Kingdom and Iraq and as instructor at RAF Sch. of Photography, 1930-38; psa 1939; Training Command, 1940; Air Ministry, in Directorate of Plans, 1941-42; Comd No 428 RCAF Sqdn and stations in Bomber Comd, 1942-43; Offices of War Cabinet and Minister of Defence (attended Cairo and Yalta Confs), 1943-45; AOC No 300 Transport Grp (Austr.) and No 232 Transport Grp (Far East), 1945-46; Directing Staff, RAF Staff Coll., 1946-49; idc 1950; Comd RAAF Staff Coll., 1951-53; Air Ministry, Dir of Policy (Air Staff), 1954; Asst Chief of Air Staff (Policy), 1955-57; AOC No 13 Group, 1957-59; Deputy Chief of Defence Staff, 1960-62; AOC-in-C, Technical Training Command, 1962-64; Vice-Chief of Defence Staff, 1964-66; retd 1966; Dir Gen. of Intelligence, Min. of Defence, 1966-68. Chm., Waveney DC, 1974-76. *Recreation:* gardening. *Address:* 16 Park Lane, Southwold, Suffolk. *Club:* Royal Air Force.

EARLE, Arthur Frederick; President, Boyden Consulting Group Ltd, since 1974; Associate, Boyden Associates, since 1974; *b* Toronto, 13 Sept. 1921; *s* of Frederick C. Earle and Hilda M. Earle (*née* Brown); *m* 1946, Vera Domini Lithgow; two *s* one *d*. *Educ:* Toronto; London Sch. of Economics (BSc (Econ.), PhD). Royal Canadian Navy (Rating to Lieut Comdr), 1939-46. Canada Packers Ltd, 1946-48; Aluminium Ltd cos in British Guiana, West Indies and Canada, 1948-53; Treas., Alumina Jamaica Ltd, 1953-55; Aluminium Union, London, 1955-58; Vice-Pres., Aluminium Ltd Sales Inc., New York, 1958-61; Dir, 1961-74, Dep. Chm., 1961-65, Man. Dir, 1963-65, Hoover Ltd; Pres., Internat. Investment Corp. for Yugoslavia, 1972-74. Principal, The London Graduate School of Business Studies, 1965-72. Member: Commn of Enquiry, Jamaican Match Industry, 1953; Consumer Council, 1963-68; NEDC Cttee on Management Educn, Training and Develt, 1967-69; NEDC for Electrical Engineering Industry. Governor: Ashridge Management Coll., 1962-65; LSE, 1968; NIESR, 1968-74; Governor and Mem. Council, Ditchley Foundn, 1967. Fellow, London Business Sch., 1973. Thomas Hawksley Lecture, IMechE, 1968. *Publications:* numerous, on economics and management. *Recreations:* hill climbing, model ship building. *Address:* Suite 2701 Commerce Court North, PO Box 389, Toronto, Ont. M5L 1G3, Canada. *T:* (416) 869-3848; apt 804 Old Mill Towers, 39 Old Mill Road, Toronto, Ont. M8X 1G6. *T:* (416) 231-4505. *Club:* Travellers'.

EARLE, Lt-Col Charles, DSO 1945; OBE 1943; jssc; psc; *b* 23 Nov. 1913; *s* of late Col Maxwell Earle, CB, CMG, DSO; *m* 1st, 1939, Marguerite (marr. diss., 1956), 2nd *d* of Herbert Carver; one *s* two *d*; 2nd, 1957, Fenella, *o d* of late H. C. Whitehouse. *Educ:* Wellington; RMC. Grenadier Guards, 1933; Lt-Col 1953, Retired 1958. Sec.-Gen., Internat. Cargo Handling Assoc., 1961-72. Served War of 1939-45 in NW Europe, Africa and Italy. Adjt RMA Sandhurst, 1948. Croix de Guerre with palm, France, 1943. *Address:* Blandford House, Sutton Montis, Yeovil, Somerset BA22 7HF. *T:* Corton Denham 258.

EARLE, Ven. E(dward) E(rnest) Maples; Archdeacon of Tonbridge, 1953-76, Archdeacon Emeritus since 1976; Vicar of Shipbourne, Kent, since Nov. 1959; *b* 22 Dec. 1900; 2nd *s* of Ernest William Earle and Lilian Geraldine Earle (*née* Hudson); *m* 1966, Mrs Jocelyn Mary Offer, *widow* of Canon C. J. Offer. *Educ:* London Coll. of Divinity; St John's Coll., Durham University (LTh, MA). Vicar of: St John, Bexley, 1936-39; Rainham (Kent), 1939-44; Secretary Rochester Diocesan Reorganisation Cttee, 1944-52, Great Appeal Cttee, etc., 1944-49; Hon. Canon, Rochester Cathedral, 1949; Rector of Chatham, 1950-52; Proctor in Convocation, 1950-53. Rector of Wrotham 1952-59. *Recreations:* artistic and architectural interests. *Address:* The Vicarage, Shipbourne, Kent. *T:* Plaxtol 478.

EARLE, Rev. George Hughes, SJ; MA; Headmaster of Stonyhurst College, 1963-72; *b* 20 Sept. 1925; *s* of late Lieut-Col F. W. Earle, DSO, JP, Morestead House, Winchester, and late Marie Blanche Lyne-Stivens. *Educ:* Pilgrims' Sch., Winchester; Westminster Sch.; Peter Symonds' Sch., Winchester; Balliol Coll., Oxford. Served with RAF, 1943-47. Joined Soc. of Jesus, 1950. Taught at Beaumont Coll., 1955-57, and Stonyhurst Coll., 1962-63. *Recreations:* none; wasting time. *Address:* Southwell House, 39 Fitzjohn's Avenue, NW3 5JT.

EARLE, Sir Hardman Alexander Mort, 5th Bt, *cr* 1869; TD; *b* 19 Aug. 1902; *s* of Lieut-Col Sir Algernon Earle, 4th Bt, and Edith, *d* of General Disney Leith, CB, of Glenkindie, Aberdeenshire, and *sister* of 7th Lord Burgh; *S* father, 1945; *m* 1931, Maie, *d* of John Drage, The Red House, Chapel Brampton; one *s* one *d*. *Educ:* Eton. *Heir: s* Hardman George Algernon Earle [*b* 4 Feb. 1932; *m* 1967, Diana Gillian Bligh, *y d* of late Col F. F. B. St George, CVO; one *s* one *d*]. *Address:* 14 Kensington Gate, W8. *Club:* Cavalry and Guards.

EARLE, Ion, TD 1946; Assistant to the Directors, Clive Discount Co., since 1973; *b* 12 April 1916; *s* of late Stephen Earle and of E. Beatrice Earle (*née* Blair White); *m* 1946, Elizabeth Stevens, US citizen; one *s* one *d. Educ:* Stowe Sch.; University Coll., Oxford; Université de Grenoble. Federation of British Industries, Birmingham, 1938-51, London, 1952-60; Chief Executive, Export Council for Europe, 1960-64; Dep. Dir-Gen., BNEC, 1965-71 (Dir, 1964-65); Head of Personnel, Kleinwort Benson Ltd, 1972. Royal Artillery, TA, 1939-46 (Major). *Recreations:* golf, tennis, gardening. *Address:* 5 McKay Road, Wimbledon Common, SW20 0HT. *T:* 01-946 5831. *Club:* Royal Wimbledon Golf.

EARLE, Rev. John Nicholas Francis, (Rev. Nick Earle); Headmaster, Bromsgrove School, since 1971; *b* 14 Nov. 1926; *s* of John William Arthur Earle and Vivien Constance Fenton (*née* Davies); *m* 1959, Ann Veronica Lester; one *s* two *d. Educ:* Winchester Coll.; Trinity Coll., Cambridge. 1st cl. Maths Tripos pt 2, 1st cl. Theol. Tripos pt 1; MA. Deacon, 1952; Priest, 1953. Curate, St Matthew, Moorfields, 1952-57; PARS Fellow, Union Theol Seminary, New York, 1957-58; Lectr, St Botolph, Aldgate, 1958-61; Asst Master, Dulwich Coll., 1961-71. *Publications:* What's Wrong With the Church?, 1961; Culture and Creed, 1967; Logic, 1973. *Recreations:* travel, gardening. *Address:* Headmaster's House, Bromsgrove School, Worcs B61 7DU. *T:* Bromsgrove 32774.

EARLES, Prof. Stanley William Edward, PhD, DScEng; CEng; FIMechE; Professor of Mechanical Engineering and Head of Department of Mechanical Engineering, King's College, University of London, since 1976; *b* 18 Jan. 1929; *s* of William Edward Earles and late Winnifred Anne Cook; *m* 1955, Margaret Isabella Brown; two *d . Educ:* King's Coll., Univ. of London (BScEng, PhD, DScEng, AKC). CEng, FIMechE 1976. Nuffield Apprentice, Birmingham, 1944-50; King's Coll., Univ. of London, 1950-53; Scientific Officer, Royal Naval Scientific Service, 1953-55; Queen Mary Coll., Univ. of London: Lectr in Mech. Eng, 1955-69; Reader in Mech. Eng, 1969-75; Prof. of Mech. Eng, 1975-76. James Clayton Fund prize, IMechE, 1967. *Publications:* papers and articles in Proc. IMechE, Jl of Mech. Eng Science, Jl of Sound and Vibration, Wear, Proc. ASME and ASLE, and Eng. *Recreations:* squash rackets, tennis, gardening. *Address:* Woodbury, Church Lane, Wormley, Broxbourne, Herts EN10 7QF. *T:* Hoddesdon 64616.

EASON, Henry, CBE 1967; JP; a Vice-President of the Institute of Bankers, 1969-75, and Consultant with special reference to overseas relationships, 1971-74 (Secretary-General, 1959-71); *b* 12 April 1910; *s* of late H. Eason and F. J. Eason; *m* 1939, Isobel, *d* of Wm Stevenson; one *s* two *d. Educ:* Yarm (Schol.); King's Coll., University of Durham. Graduated with distinction in economics and history. Barrister-at-law, Gray's Inn. Served Lloyds Bank until 1939; Asst Sec., Institute of Bankers, 1939. Served War of 1939-45 and until 1946, with Royal Air Force (Wing Commander, despatches twice); Asst Dir, Military Gov. (Banking), NW Europe, 1944-46; United Nations Adviser (Banking) to Pakistan Govt, 1952; Deputy Sec., Institute of Bankers, 1956; Governor, City of London Coll., 1958-69; Mem., British National Cttee, Internat. Chamber Commerce, 1959-74. Director: Internat. Banking Summer Sch., 1961, 1964, 1970; Cambridge Banking Seminar, 1968 and 1969. Editor, Jl Inst. of Bankers, 1959-71. Hon. FIB 1971. JP Bromley 1967. Gen. Comr of Income Tax, Bromley, 1973-76. *Publications:* contributions to professional journals. *Recreations:* golf, walking, gardening, world travel. *Address:* 12 Redgate Drive, Bromley BR2 7BT. *T:* 01-462 1900. *Clubs:* Gresham; Overseas Bankers; Langley Park Golf.

EASON, His Honour Robert Kinley; HM's First Deemster, Clerk of the Rolls and Deputy Governor of the Isle of Man, since 1974; *b* 12 April 1908; 2nd *s* of Henry Alexander Eason and Eleanor Jane Eason (*née* Kinley); *m* 1937, Nora Muriel, *d* of Robert Raisbeck Coffey, Douglas, IOM. *Educ:* Douglas High Sch.; King William's Coll., IOM; University Coll. London. LLB (Hons). Called to Bar, Gray's Inn, 1929; Advocate, Manx Bar, 1930. High Bailiff and Chief Magistrate, Isle of Man, 1961-69; HM's Second Deemster, IOM, 1969-74. Chairman: Criminal Injuries Compensation Tribunal, IOM, 1969-74; IOM Income

Tax Appeal Comrs, 1974; IOM Unit Trust Tribunal, 1968-74; Tourist (IOM) Appeal Tribunal, 1969-74; Chm. of Trustees: Cunningham House Scout and Guide Headquarters, 1964-; Ellan Vannin Home, 1971-; Trustee, Manx Merchant Navy Help Soc., 1974. President: Ellynyn Ny Gael, 1974; IOM Anti-Cancer Assoc., 1969-; Wireless Telegraphy Appeal Bd for IOM, 1971-; Legion Players, 1971-; SS&AFA, IOM Br., 1973-; Licensing Appeal Court, 1969-74; past Pres., IOM Soc. for Prevention of Cruelty to Animals. *Recreation:* organ music. *Address:* Lynton, Devonshire Road, Douglas, Isle of Man. *T:* Douglas, IOM 5278. *Clubs:* Ellan Vannin, Manx Automobile (Douglas).

EASSON, Rt. Rev. Edward Frederick; *b* 29 July 1905; *s* of Edward Easson and Ada Jessie Easson (*née* Betsworth); *m* 1937, Mary Forbes Macdonald; two *s*. *Educ:* Morgan Academy, Dundee; St Andrews Univ.; Edinburgh Theological College. Maths and Science Master at Lasswade Secondary School, 1929-31; Assistant Curate of St Peter's, Lutton Place, 1933-36, with charge of St Aidan's, Craigmillar, 1936-39; Rector of St Peter's, Peterhead, and Chaplain to HM Prison, 1940-48; Diocesan Inspector of Schools, 1945-55; Canon of St Andrew's Cathedral, Aberdeen, 1946; Rector of St Devenick's, Bieldside, 1948-56; Dean of Aberdeen and Orkney, 1953-56; Bishop of Aberdeen and Orkney, 1956-72. Hon. DD St Andrews, 1962. *Address:* 25 Corbiehill Avenue, Davidsons Mains, Edinburgh EH4 5BX.

EAST, Frederick Henry, CB 1976; MInstP, CEng, FIEE, FRAeS; Deputy Secretary, and Chief Weapon System Engineer (Polaris), Ministry of Defence, since 1976; *b* 15 Sept. 1919; *s* of Frederick Richard East; *m* 1942, Pauline Isabel Veale Horne (*d* 1972). *Educ:* Skinners' Company's Sch., Tunbridge Wells; University Coll., Exeter (Visc. St Cyres Schol., Tucker and Franklin Prize, 1939). BSc London 1940. Joined Research Dept, Min. of Aircraft Production, 1940; various appts in RAE, 1942-57; Asst Dir of Air Armament Research and Develt, Min. of Supply/Aviation, 1957-62; Head of Weapon Project Gp, RAE, 1962-67; Student, IDC, 1968; Asst Chief Scientific Adviser (Projects), MoD, 1969-70; Dir, Royal Armament Res. and Develt Establishment, 1971-75. *Publications:* contrib. to: Application of Critical Path Techniques, 1968; official reports, and articles in jls. *Address:* Ministry of Defence, Main Building, Whitehall, SW1. *Club:* Athenæum.

EAST, Gerald Reginald Ricketts; a Civil Service Commissioner, since 1974; *b* 17 Feb. 1917; *s* of late R. B. East and Dora East (*née* Ricketts); *m* 1944, Anna Elder Smyth; one *s* two *d*. *Educ:* Peter Symonds' Sch.; St Edmund Hall, Oxford. Goldsmiths' Company's Exhibnr; MA 1945. Royal Artillery, 1939-46; Control Commn for Germany, 1946-47; Asst Principal, War Office, Oct. 1947; Private Sec. to Under-Sec. of State for War, 1949; Directing Staff Imperial Defence Coll., 1952-54; Private Sec. to Sec. of State for War, 1954-55; Asst Sec. (Inspector of Establishments), 1958; Comd Sec., BAOR, 1961-64; Asst Sec. (Establishments), MoD, 1965-70; Asst Under-Sec. of State, MoD, 1970-74. *Address:* 43 Manor Road North, Esher, Surrey. *T:* 01-398 2446. *Club:* Royal Commonwealth Society.

EAST, Grahame Richard, CMG 1961; Special Commissioner of Income Tax, 1962-73; *b* 1908; 2nd *s* of William Robert and Eleanor East; *m* 1937, Cynthia Mildred, *d* of Adam Louis Beck, OBE; two *s* two *d*. *Educ:* Bristol Grammar Sch.; Corpus Christi Coll., Oxford. Asst Master, Royal Belfast Academical Institution, Belfast, 1929; Inland Revenue Dept, Secretaries Office, 1930, Asst Sec., 1941. *Address:* 44 Devonshire Road, Sutton, Surrey. *T:* 01-642 0638.

EAST, Kenneth Arthur, CMG 1971; HM Diplomatic Service; Ambassador to Iceland, since 1975; *b* 9 May 1921; *s* of H. F. East; *m* 1946, Katherine Blackley; two *s* three *d*. *Educ:* Taunton's Sch; Southampton Univ. Served HM Forces, 1942-46. India Office/Commonwealth Relations Office, 1946-50; Asst Private Sec. to Sec. of State; First Secretary: Ottawa, 1950-53; Colombo, 1956-60; Head of East and General Africa Dept, CRO, 1961-63; Head of Personnel Dept, CRO, 1963-64; Counsellor, Diplomatic Service Administration, 1965; Counsellor and Head of Chancery, Oslo, 1965-70; Minister, Lagos, 1970-74. *Address:* c/o Foreign and Commonwealth Office, SW1.

EAST, Sir (Lewis) Ronald, Kt 1966; CBE 1951; retired as Chairman, State Rivers and Water Supply Commission, Victoria (1936-65) and as Commissioner, River Murray Commission, Australia (1936-65); *b* 17 June 1899; *s* of Lewis Findlay East, ISO, Evansford, Vic., Australia and Annie Eleanor (*née* Burchett) Brunswick, Vic.; *m* 1927, Constance Lilias Keil, MA, Kilwinning, Ayrshire; three *d*. *Educ:* Scotch Coll., Melbourne; Melbourne Univ. BCE (Melbourne) 1922; MCE (Melbourne)

1924. Mem., Snowy Mountains Coun., until 1965; Pres., Instn of Engrs, Austr., 1952-53; Mem. Coun., Instn of Civil Engrs, 1960-62; Vice-Pres., Internat. Commn on Irrigation and Drainage, 1959-62. Hon. Fellow, Instn of Engineers, Australia, 1969. Kernot Memorial Medal, University of Melbourne, 1949; Peter Nicol Russell Memorial Medal, Instn of Engineers, Australia, 1957. *Publications:* River Improvement, Land Drainage and Flood Protection, 1952; A South Australian Colonist of 1836 and his Descendants, 1972; The Kiel Family and related Scottish Pioneers, 1974; More Australian Pioneers: the Burchetts and related families, 1976; many technical papers on water conservation and associated subjects in Proc. Instn Engs, Austr., Proc. Instn Civil Engrs, Amer. Soc. Civil Engrs and other jls. *Recreation:* handicrafts (model engineering). *Address:* 57 Waimarie Drive, Mt Waverley, Victoria 3149, Australia. *T:* Melbourne 277-4315.

EAST, Sir Ronald; *see* East, Sir L. R.

EAST, Ronald Joseph; Director: Guest, Keen & Nettlefolds (UK) Ltd, since 1974; GKN Forgings Ltd; Corporate Staff Director, Group Supplies, Guest, Keen & Nettlefolds Ltd, since 1976; *b* 17 Dec. 1931; *s* of Joseph William and Marion Elizabeth Emma East; *m* 1955, Iris Joyce Beckwith; two *d*. *Educ:* Clare Coll., Cambridge Univ. (MA). Engineering Apprenticeship, Ford Trade Sch., Ford Motor Co. Ltd, 1945-52. Troop Comdr, RA (Lieut), 1953-55. Managerial posts in economics, product planning, finance, and engineering areas of Ford Motor Co. Ltd, 1959-65; Guest, Keen & Nettlefolds Ltd: Corporation Staff Dir of Planning, 1965-70; Planning Exec., Automotive and Allied Products Sector, 1972-73; Chairman: GKN Castings Ltd, 1974-77; GKN Kent Alloys Ltd, 1974-77; GKN Shotton Ltd, 1974-77. Dir, Programme Analysis and Review (PAR) and Special Advisor to Chief Sec. to the Treasury, 1971-72. *Recreations:* walking, ski-ing, ethnology, dramatic art. *Address:* The Waldrons, Feckenham, Worcs. *T:* Astwood Bank 2486.

EAST, William Gordon; Professor of Geography in the University of London at Birkbeck College, 1947-70, now Emeritus Professor; *b* 10 Nov. 1902; *s* of George Richard East and Jemima (*née* Nicoll); *m* 1934, Dorothea Small; two *s* two *d*. *Educ:* Sloane Sch., Chelsea; Peterhouse, Cambridge. Open scholarship in History, 1921, and research studentship, 1924, at Peterhouse. BA (Hons), Cambridge Univ., with Class I in Historical Tripos, Part II, 1924. MA 1928; Thirlwall Prizeman of Cambridge Univ., 1927. Asst in historical geography, London Sch. of Economics, 1927; temp. administrative officer in Ministry of Economic Warfare and Foreign Office, 1941-45; Reader in Geography in University of London, 1946. Visiting Professor: Univ. of Minnesota, 1952; Univ. of California, Los Angeles, 1959-60; Univ. of Michigan, 1966-67; Univ. of Wisconsin, 1969-70; Univ. of Saskatchewan, 1971. Myres Memorial Lectr, Oxford Univ., 1970-71. Mem., RGS Council, 1956-59; Pres., Inst. of British Geographers, 1959. Murchison Award, RGS, 1972. *Publications:* The Union of Moldavia and Wallachia, 1859, 1929, repr. 1973; An Historical Geography of Europe, 1935; The Geography Behind History, 1938; Mediterranean Problems, 1940; (ed jtly) The Changing Map of Asia, 1950, 1971; (Jt) The Spirit and Purpose of Geography, 1951; (ed jtly) The Changing World, 1956; (ed) The Caxton Atlas, 1960; (ed) Regions of The British Isles, 1960-; The Soviet Union, 1963, 2nd edn 1976; (ed) Batsford historical geography series, 1973-; (jt) Our Fragmented World, 1975; contributions to journals of geography, history and foreign affairs. *Address:* Wildwood, Danes Way, Oxshott, Surrey. *T:* Oxshott 2351.

EAST AFRICA, Archdiocese of; divided into two archdioceses of Kenya and Tanzania.

EAST ANGLIA, Bishop of, (RC), since 1976; **Rt. Rev. Alan Charles Clark;** *b* 9 Aug. 1919; *s* of William Thomas Durham Clark and Ellen Mary Clark (*née* Compton). *Educ:* Westminster Cathedral Choir Sch.; Ven. English Coll., Rome, Italy. Priest, 1945; Curate, St Philip's, Arundel, 1945-46; postgrad. studies, Rome, 1946-48; Doctorate in Theol., Gregorian Univ., Rome, 1948; Tutor in Philosophy, English Coll., Rome, 1948-53, Vice-Rector, 1954-64; Parish Priest, St Mary's, Blackheath, SE3, 1965-69; Auxiliary Bishop of Northampton, 1969-76; Titular Bishop of Elmham, 1969-76. *Peritus* at Vatican Council, 1962-65; Jt Chm., The Anglican/Roman Catholic Internat. Commn, 1969-. Freeman, City of London, 1969. *Recreation:* music. *Address:* The White House, 21 Upgate, Poringland, Norwich NR14 7SH. *T:* Framingham Earl 2202.

EASTAUGH, Rt. Rev. Cyril, MC 1917; MA (Oxon); Principal of the Society of the Faith, since 1972; *b* 22 Dec. 1897; *y s* of late Robert Wilgress Eastaugh; *m* 1948, Lady Laura Mary Palmer, *d* of 3rd Earl of Selborne, PC, CH; one *s* two *d*. *Educ:* Christ

Church, Oxford; Cuddesdon College. Served European War, 1914-18, S Staffs Regt. Chaplain, Cuddesdon Coll., 1930-34; Vice-Principal, 1934-35; Vicar of St John the Divine, Kennington, 1935-49; Suffragan Bishop of Kensington, 1949-61; Bishop of Peterborough, 1961-72. Hon. Canon of Southwark, 1945; Proctor in Convocation, 1943. Chaplain and Sub-Prelate of the Order of St John of Jerusalem, 1961-. *Address:* Blackmoor House, Liss, Hants. *T:* Bordon 3777. *Club:* Athenæum.

EASTAUGH, Rt. Rev. John (Richard Gordon); Hereford, Bishop of.

EASTCOTT, Harry Hubert Grayson, MS; FRCS; Consultant Surgeon, St Mary's Hospital, and Lecturer in Surgery, St Mary's Hospital Medical School since 1955; Consultant in Surgery and Vascular Surgery to the Royal Navy since 1957; Surgeon, Royal Masonic Hospital since 1964; Consultant Surgeon, King Edward VII Hospital for Officers, since 1965; *b* 17 Oct. 1917; *s* of Harry George and Gladys Eastcott; *m* 1941, Doreen Joy, *e d* of Brenchley Ernest and late Muriel Mittell; four *d. Educ:* Latymer Sch.; St Mary's Hosp. Medical School and Middlesex Hospital Medical Sch., University of London; Harvard Med. Sch. War of 1939-45, Junior surgical appts and service as Surgeon Lieut, RNVR up till 1946. Surg. Lieut Comdr RNVR, London Div., until 1957. MRCS; LRCP; MB, BS (Hons), 1941; FRCS 1946; MS (London), 1951. Sen. Registrar, 1950 as Hon. Cons. to St Mary's and Asst Dir Surgical Unit; Research Fellow in Surgery, Harvard Med. Sch., and Peter Bent Brigham Hosp., Boston, Mass, 1949-50; Hunterian Prof., RCS, 1953; recognised teacher, 1953, and Examr, 1959, in surgery, University of London; Hon. Surg., RADA, 1959-; Mem. Court of Examrs, RCS, 1964-70, Mem. Council, 1971-; External Examr in Surgery: Queen's Univ., Belfast, 1964-67; Cambridge Univ., 1968; Univ. of Lagos, Nigeria, 1970-71. Editorial Sec., British Jl of Surgery, 1972-. FRSocMed (Hon. Sec., Section of Surgery, 1963-65, Vice-President, 1966, Pres., 1977); Fellow Medical Soc. of London (Hon. Sec., 1962-64, Vice-Pres. 1964, Pres., 1976). Mem., Soc. Apothecaries, 1967 (Pres., 1976). Fothergill Gold Medal, 1974. Hon. FACS, 1977. *Publications:* Arterial Surgery, 1969, 2nd edn 1973; various articles on gen. and arterial surgery, and on tissue transplantation and preservation, Lancet, Brit. Jl of Surg., etc.; contrib. chap. of peripheral vascular disease, Med. Annual, 1961-73; various chaps in textbooks on these subjects. *Recreations:* music, languages, travel, ski-ing, and a lifelong interest in aeronautics. *Address:* 4 Upper Harley Street, NW1 4PN. *T:* 01-935 2020. *Clubs:* Garrick; Middlesex County Cricket.

EASTER, Bertie Harry, CMG 1944; CBE 1936 (MBE 1927); BA; retired as Resident Tutor, Windward Islands, for University College of the West Indies (Extra-Mural Studies); *b* 4 June 1893; *s* of Samuel and Lucy Elizabeth Easter; *m* 1930, Hazel Marie Swabey; one *s. Educ:* Christ's Coll., Finchley. Head Master, St Mary's Coll., St Lucia and Secondary Sch., Grenada; Dir of Education, Grenada; Acting Colonial Sec. (or Administrator), Grenada, Jamaica; Dir of Education, Jamaica, 1932-48; Information Officer and Officer i/c Broadcasting, 1939; served European War, Royal Naval Div. and Scots Guards (Lieut). Emeritus Pres., St Lucia Archæol and Hist. Soc. *Address:* Castries, St Lucia, West Indies.

EASTERBROOK, Prof. William Thomas James, FRSC 1957; Professor of Economics, University of Toronto, Canada, 1956, now Professor Emeritus; Chairman, Department of Political Economy, University of Toronto, 1961-70; *b* 4 Dec. 1907; *s* of W. J. Easterbrook and Emily McKerr; *m* 1937, Dorothy Mary Walker; two *s* one *d. Educ:* Universities of Manitoba, Toronto, and Harvard. BA (Hon.) Manitoba, 1933; University of Toronto Sch. of Grad. Studies, 1933-36; MA 1935; Harvard Univ., 1936-37; PhD, University of Toronto, 1937. Dept Economics, Univ. of Manitoba, 1938-40 and 1942-47; Guggenheim Fellow, 1940-41; Research Associate, Research Center in Entrepreneurial History, Harvard Univ., 1949 (leave of absence from Toronto). Vice-Pres. Economic History Assoc. (US), 1959-61; Trustee, Business History Inc., 1959-; Mem. Research Cttee on Culture and Communications (Ford Foundation), 1953-55. Pitt Prof. of American History and Institutions, Cambridge Univ., 1955-56; Marshall Lecturer, University of Cambridge, 1956; Professorial Fellow of Jesus Coll. Cambridge, 1955-56; MA Cantab. 1956. Economic Adviser, Ministry of Economic Affairs and Develt Planning, Tanzania, 1966-67. LLD Manitoba, 1963. *Publications:* Agricultural Credit in Canada, 1937; Canadian Economic History (with H. Aitken), 1955; Approaches to Canadian Economic History (with M. H. Watkins), 1968; articles contrib. to Canadian Jl of Economics and Political Science, Jl of Economic History, American Economic Review, etc.; also to Canada (ed George Brown) UN Series, and The Progress of Underdeveloped Countries (ed B. Hoselitz).

Address: 50 Prince Arthur Avenue, Apt 1901, Toronto 5, Canada. *Club:* University Faculty (Toronto).

EASTHAM, (Thomas) Michael, QC 1964; a Recorder, and Honorary Recorder of Cambridge, since 1972; *b* 26 June 1920; *y s* of late His Hon. Sir Tom Eastham, QC; *m* 1942, Mary Pamela, *o d* of Dr H. C. Billings; two *d. Educ:* Harrow; Trinity Hall, Cambridge. Served with Queen's Royal Regiment, 1940-46 (Capt.). Called to the Bar, Lincoln's Inn, 1947, Bencher, 1972. Recorder: of Deal, 1968-71; of Cambridge, 1971. Inspector, Vehicle and General Insurance Company, 1971. *Address:* 7a Porchester Terrace, W2. *T:* 01-723 0770; 5 Essex Court, Temple, EC4. *T:* 01-353 2440.

EASTICK, Brig. Sir Thomas (Charles), Kt 1970; CMG 1953; DSO 1942; ED 1939; JP (for the State of South Australia); Chairman Standing Committee "Call to the People of Australia", 1951-57; President, El Alamein Group (SA), 1946-60; Chairman of Trustees, Poppy Day Fund (Inc.); President of Australia Day Council, S Australian Branch (Federal), 1962-65 and since 1976; Chairman of Trustees Services Cemeteries Trust; Deputy Chairman, World War II Fund; *b* 3 May 1900; *s* of Charles William Lone and Agnes Ann Eastick; *m* 1925, Ruby Sybil Bruce; five *s. Educ:* Goodwood Sch., Australia. Senior Cadets, 1914-18; Citizen Forces, 1918 (Artillery); Lieut 1922, Capt. 1926, Major 1930, Lieut-Col 1939. Served War of 1939-45 (despatches, ED, DSO); raised and commanded 2/7 Aust. Fd Regt 1940-43; Middle East, Alamein; Brig., CRA 7 Aust. Div., 1943; CRA 9 Aust. Div., 1944; Comdr Kuching Force, 1945; took Japanese surrender and relieved Kuching Prisoner Compound; administered comd 9 Aust. Div., Dec. 1945-Feb. 1946, when Div. disbanded. Hon. ADC to Governor-Gen. of Australia, 1950-53; Mem., Betting Control Board, 1954-65; State Pres. Returned Sailors, Soldiers and Airmen's Imperial League of Australia, S Australia, 1950-54-61-72; Comdr HQ Group Central Command, 1950-54. Pres., SA Womens Meml Playing Fields, 1954-. Col Comdt, Royal Australian Artillery, 1955-60. Pres. Engine Reconditioners Assoc. of Austr., 1958-61. FAIM. Comp. Most Excellent Order of the Star of Sarawak, 1946. Rotary Club of Adelaide Service Award, 1969-70. *Recreation:* photography. *Address:* Astana, Cameron Avenue, Kingston Park, S Australia 5049, Australia. *Club:* Naval, Military and Air Force of SA (Adelaide).

EASTMAN, Rev. Canon Derek Ian Tennent, MC 1945; Canon of St George's Chapel, Windsor, since 1977; *b* 22 Jan. 1919; *s* of Archibald Tennent Eastman and Gertrude Towler Eastman (*née* Gambling); *m* 1949, Judith Mary, *e d* of Canon Philip David Bevington Miller; three *s* one *d. Educ:* Winchester; Christ Church, Oxford; Cuddesdon Theol. Coll. BA 1941; MA 1946. Coldstream Guards, 1940-46: Guards Armoured Div., Temp. Major. Cuddesdon Theol. Coll., 1946-48; Deacon 1948; Priest 1949; Asst Curate, Brighouse, 1948-51; Priest-in-Charge, St Andrew's, Caversham, 1951-56; Vicar: Headington, Oxford, 1956-64; Banbury, 1964-70; Archdeacon of Buckingham, and Vicar of Chilton and Dorton, 1970-77. Proctor in Convocation for Dio. of Oxford, 1964-70. Mem., General Synod, 1975-77. *Recreations:* sea fishing, painting. *Address:* 4 The Cloisters, Windsor Castle, Berks SL4 1NJ. *T:* Windsor 64142.

EASTON, Admiral Sir Ian, KCB 1975; DSC 1946; Commandant, Royal College of Defence Studies, 1976-77; retired 1978; *b* 27 Nov. 1917; *s* of Walter Easton and Janet Elizabeth Rickard; *m* 1st, 1943, Shirley Townend White (marr. diss.); one *s* one *d*; 2nd, 1962, Margharetta Elizabeth Martinette Van Duyn de Sparwoude; one *d. Educ:* The Grange, Crowborough; RNC, Dartmouth. Entered Royal Navy, 1931, and, as an actg Sub-Lt, qualified as a pilot, 1939. During War of 1939-45 served as pilot in HM Ships Glorious, Ark Royal and Formidable and as Direction Officer HMS Indefatigable; Comdr, 1952; Naval Staff Coll., 1953; on staff of BJSM, Washington, 1955-57; Staff Direction Officer, on Staff of Flag Officer Aircraft Carriers, 1957-59; JSSC, 1959; Captain, 1960; Asst Dir of Tactical and Weapons Policy Div., 1960-62; two years exchange service with RAN, in command of HMAS Watson, 1962-64; Naval Asst to Naval Member of Templer Cttee, 1965; Dir of Naval Tactical and Weapons Policy Div., 1966-68; Comdg Officer of HMS Triumph, Far East, 1968-69; Asst Chief of the Naval Staff (Policy), 1969-71; Flag Officer, Admiralty Interview Bd, 1971-73; Head of British Defence Staff and Defence Attaché, Washington, 1973-75. *Recreations:* boats, books, gardening. *Address:* Causeway Cottage, Freshwater, Isle of Wight. *T:* Freshwater 2775. *Club:* Royal Solent Yacht (Yarmouth, IoW).

EASTON, Air Cdre Sir James (Alfred), KCMG 1956; CB 1952; CBE 1945; RAF retired; Deputy Chairman, Host Committee for 1974 World Energy Conference, since 1972; *b* 11 Feb. 1908; *s* of late W. C. Easton, Winchester; *m* 1939, Anna Mary (*d* 1977), *d* of Lieut-Col J. A. McKenna, Ottawa; one s one d. *Educ:* Peter Symonds' Sch., Winchester; RAF Coll., Cranwell. Joined RAF 1926; served NWF India, 1929-32, Egypt, 1935-36, and Canada, 1937-39, as Air Armament Adviser to Dept of National Defence; despatches, 1940; Group Capt., 1941; Air Cdre, 1943; Dir in Air Staff Branch, Air Ministry, 1943-45, and then in RAF Delegation, Washington; retired, 1949; attached Foreign Office, 1945-58; HM Consul-Gen., Detroit, 1958-68. Res. Consultant on Trade Develt of Great Lakes Area, USA, 1968-71. Officer Legion of Merit (US). *Publication:* The Transportation of Freight in the Year 2000, 1970. *Recreations:* travel and travel literature, gardening, golf. *Address:* 390 Chalfonte Avenue, Grosse Pointe Farms, Mich 48236, USA; 71 Cornwall Gardens, SW7. *T:* 01-937 0430. *Clubs:* Royal Air Force; Country, Detroit (Detroit).

EASTWOOD, Christopher Gilbert, CMG 1947; Assistant Under-Secretary of State, Colonial Office, 1947-52, and 1954-66; *b* 21 April 1905; *s* of late W. Seymour Eastwood, West Stoke House, Chichester, and Cecil Emma Eastwood; *m* 1934, Catherine Emma, *d* of late John Douglas Peel, Stonesfield Manor, near Oxford; one *s* three *d. Educ:* Eton (Schol.); Trinity Coll., Oxford. Entered Home Civil Service, 1927; appointed to Colonial Office; Private Sec. to High Commissioner for Palestine, 1932-34; Sec. of International Rubber Regulation Cttee, 1934; Private Sec. to Lord Lloyd and Lord Moyne when Secs of State for Colonies, 1940-41. Prin. Asst Sec. Cabinet Office, 1945-47; Commissioner of Crown Lands, 1952-54. *Address:* Stonesfield Manor, near Oxford. *T:* Stonesfield 222.

EASTWOOD, Sir Eric, Kt 1973; CBE 1962; FRS 1968; Consultant, GEC-Marconi Electronics Ltd, since 1975 (Chief Scientist, 1974-75); Director: Marconi-Elliott Computers, since 1969; Marconi Company, since 1963; Marconi Instruments, since 1962; *b* 12 March 1910; *s* of George Eastwood and Eda (*née* Brooks); *m* 1937, Edith (*née* Butterworth); two *s. Educ:* Oldham High Sch.; Manchester Univ.; Christ's Coll., Cambridge. PhD 1935; MSc 1932; FIEE 1951 (Pres., IEE, 1972-73); FInstP 1968. Academic work, 1936-41. Sqdn Ldr, RAF, 1941-46 (despatches). Head of Radiation Laboratory, Nelson Research Lab., English Electric Co., 1946-48; Dep. Dir of Research, Marconi Wireless Telegraph Co., 1948-54; Dir, 1954-62. Dir of Research, English Electric, 1962-68; Dir of Research, General Electric-English Electric Companies, 1968-74. Mem., SRC, 1968-74. Hon. DSc: Exeter, 1969; Cranfield, 1971; Aston, 1975; City, 1976; Hon. DTech Loughborough, 1970; Hon. FUMIST, 1971. Wakefield Medal, RAeS, 1961; Glazebrook Medal, Inst. of Physics and Physical Soc., 1970; Sir James Alfred Ewing Medal, ICE, 1976. *Publications:* Radar Ornithology, 1967; various papers on spectroscopy, radar techniques, radar meteorology, radar ornithology in Proc. Physical Soc., Proc. Royal Society, Nature, etc. *Recreation:* music ('cello, flute). *Address:* Greenlanes, Little Baddow, Danbury, Essex. *T:* Danbury 3240.

EASTWOOD, Major Sir Geoffrey (Hugh), KCVO 1965 (CVO 1956); CBE 1945; *b* 17 May 1895; *s* of late John Edmund Eastwood. Served 1914-19, 3rd King's Own Hussars. Hon. Attaché, Brit. Emb., Paris, 1919-21; Clerk and Prin. Clerk, House of Lords, 1924-58. Comptroller to Gov.-Gen. of Canada, 1941-46; Comptroller to the Princess Royal, 1959-65; Extra Equerry to the Queen, 1965. *Address:* Wilderness House, Hampton Court Palace, Surrey. *T:* 01-977 5550. *Clubs:* Brooks's, MCC.

EASTWOOD, (George) Granville, OBE 1973; General Secretary, Printing and Kindred Trades Federation, 1958-73; *b* 1906; *s* of George and Anne Eastwood; *m* 1st, 1934, Margaret Lambert (*d* 1967); no *c*; 2nd, 1971, Elizabeth Gore Underwood. *Educ:* Burnley Council. Compositor, Burnley, 1927; Asst Sec., Printing and Kindred Trades Fedn, 1943-58. Workpeople's Sec., HMSO Deptl Whitley Council, 1958-73; Jt Secretary: Printing and Allied Trades Jt Industrial Council, 1958-66; Jt Bd for Nat. Newspaper Industry, 1965-67. Member: Council, Printing Industry's Research Assoc., 1958-73; City and Guilds of London Inst., 1958-73; Council, Inst. of Printing, 1961-; ILO Printing Conf., Geneva, 1963; Econ. Develt Cttee for Printing and Publishing, 1966-72; Printing and Publishing Industry Trng Bd, 1968-74; Industrial Arbitration Bd, 1973-76; Editorial Adv. Bd, Ind. Relns Digest, 1973-; DHSS Community Health Council, 1974-76; Advisory, Conciliation and Arbitration Service Panel, 1976-; toured USA and Europe with EDC Jt Mission, 1968. Governor: Chelsea Sch. of Art, 1963-; Nat. Heart Hosp., Brompton Hosp. and London Chest Hosp., 1969-76. *Publications:* George Isaacs, 1952; Harold Laski, 1977. *Recreations:* reading, gardening. *Address:* 16 The Vineries, Enfield, Mddx. *T:* 01-363 2502.

EASTWOOD, Sir John (Bealby), Kt 1975; Chairman since 1963 and Managing Director since 1959, J. B. Eastwood Ltd; *b* 9 Jan. 1909; *s* of William Eastwood and Elizabeth Townroe Eastwood (*née* Bealby); *m* 1929, Constance Mary (*née* Tilley); two *d. Educ:* Queen Elizabeth's Grammar Sch., Mansfield. Civil Engr and Contractor, 1925; founded W. & J. B. Eastwood Ltd, 1945. OStJ 1972. *Recreations:* shooting, horse-racing, golf, cricket. *Address:* Oxton Manor, Oxton, Notts. *Clubs:* Farmers', Carlton.

EASTWOOD, Dr Wilfred; Senior Partner, Eastwood and Partners, Consulting Engineers, since 1972; *b* 15 Aug. 1923; *s* of Wilfred Andrew Eastwood and Annice Gertrude Eastwood; *m* 1947, Dorothy Jean Gover; one *s* one *d.* Road Research Laboratory, 1945-46; University of Manchester, 1946-47; University of Aberdeen, 1947-53; University of Sheffield, 1954-70: Head, Dept of Civil Engrg, 1964-70; Dean, Faculty of Engrg, 1967-70. Pres., IStructE, 1976-77. *Publications:* papers in Proc. ICE and Jl IStructE, etc. *Address:* 242 Abbeydale Road South, Sheffield S17 3LL. *T:* 364645. *Club:* Yorks County Cricket.

EATES, Edward Caston, CMG 1968; MVO 1961; QPM 1961; CPM 1956; Commissioner, The Royal Hong Kong Police, 1967-69, retired; re-employed at Foreign and Commonwealth Office, 1971-76; *b* London, 8 April 1916; *o s* of late Edward Eates and Elizabeth Lavinia Issac Eates (*née* Caston); *m* 1941, Maureen Teresa McGee; no *c. Educ:* Highgate Sch.; King's Coll., London (LLB). Asst Examr, Estate Duty Office, 1935. Army, 1939-46: 22nd (Cheshire) Regt, later Royal Tanks; served with 2nd Derbs Yeomanry, Western Desert and NW Europe, 1941-44; Adjt 1943; Sqdn Ldr 1944; Staff Coll., Quetta (sc), 1945; DAAG Nagpur District. Apptd to Colonial Police Service, Nigeria, 1946; Sen. Supt, Sierra Leone, 1954; Comr, The Gambia, 1957; Asst Comr, 1963, Dep. Comr, 1966, Hong Kong. *Recreations:* cricket and association football (inactive); travel, motoring. *Address:* Banjul, Toadpit Lane, Ottery St Mary, Devon. *T:* Ottery St Mary 2838. *Clubs:* Royal Commonwealth Society, East India, Devonshire, Sports and Public Schools; Surrey County Cricket.

EATHER, Maj.-Gen. Kenneth William, CB 1947; CBE 1943; DSO 1941; Executive Director, Water Research Foundation of Australia, 1958; *b* 1901. Served War of 1939-45; AMF, Middle East and SW Pacific (despatches, DSO, CBE). *Address:* 7, 82/84 Houston Road, Kingsford, NSW 2032, Australia. *T:* 6631176. *Club:* Imperial Service (Sydney).

EATON, Air Vice-Marshal Brian Alexander, CB 1969; CBE 1959; DSO and Bar, DFC, American Silver Star; Air Officer Commanding, Operational Command, RAAF, since 1973; *b* Launceston, Tas, 15 Dec. 1916; *s* of S. A. Eaton; *m* 1952, Josephine Rumbles; one *s* two *d.* Carey Grammar Sch., Melbourne; RAAF Coll., Pt Cook. Served war of 1939-45: Co 3 Sqdn N Africa-Medit., 1943, CO 239 Wing RAF Italy, 1944-45. UK, 1945-46; OC 81 Fighter Wing, Japan, 1948; OC BCAIR, 1948-49; OC 78 Wing Malta, 1952-54; Dir of Ops, RAAF HQ, 1955; OC Williamtown RAAF and Comdt Sch. of Land-Air Warfare, 1957-58; Dir Joint Service Plans, 1959-60; Imp. Defence Coll., 1961; Dir-Gen. of Operational Requirements, 1962; Deputy Chief of Air Staff, 1966-67; AOC HQ 224 Mobile Group (RAF) Far East Air Force, Singapore, 1967-68; Chief of Staff HQFEAF, 1968-69; Air Mem. for Personnel, Dept of Air, Canberra, 1969-73. *Recreations:* shooting, fishing. *Address:* Headquarters Operational Command, RAAF, Penrith, NSW 2750, Australia. *Clubs:* Commonwealth (Canberra); Imperial Service (Sydney).

EATON, Cyrus Stephen; industrialist and banker; Partner, Otis & Co., bankers; Organizer Republic Steel Corp. and United Light & Power Co.; Chairman Board of Directors: Chesapeake & Ohio Railway; Detroit Steel Corporation; Steep Rock Iron Mines Ltd; Director: Cleveland-Cliffs Iron Co.; Cleveland Electric Illuminating Co.; Kansas City Power & Light Co.; Sherwin-Williams Co.; Baltimore & Ohio Railroad Co.; *b* Nova Scotia, 27 Dec. 1883; *s* of Joseph Howe Eaton and Mary Adelle McPherson; *m* 1st, 1907, Margaret House; two *s* five *d*; 2nd, 1957, Anne Kinder Jones, *d* of Judge Walter Tupper Kinder; one step-*d. Educ:* McMaster Univ., Toronto (BA); Acadia Univ. (DCL). Trustee: University of Chicago, Denison Univ., Case Institute of Technology, Harry S. Truman Library, Metropolitan Park Board, Cleveland Museum of Natural History; Mem. of Coll. of Electors, Hall of Fame, Royal Norwegian Academy of Sciences, American Council of Learned Societies; American Historical Assoc., Amer. Philosophical Assoc. FAAS. Initiator Pugwash Intellectual Life Confs (Assoc. of Amer. Colls), 1956; Pugwash Internat. Confs of Nuclear Scientists, 1957; Member: Amer. Shorthorn Breeders' Assoc.; Amer. Acad. of Political and Social Science. Holds several hon. doctorates in Law from American, Canadian and European universities. Received Internat. Lenin Peace Prize, 1960. *Publications:* The Third Term "Tradition," 1940; Financial Democracy, 1941; The Professor Talks to Himself, 1942; Investment Banking-Competition or Decadence, 1944; A New Plan to re-open the US Capital Market, 1945; A Capitalist Looks At Labor, 1947; Is the Globe Big Enough for Capitalism and Communism?, 1958; Canada's Choice, 1959; The Engineer as Philosopher, 1961; and numerous articles and speeches on economics, politics and international affairs. *Recreations:* MFH Summit Hunt, tennis, yachting, ski-ing and skating. *Address:* Acadia Farms, Northfield, Ohio 44067, USA; Terminal Tower, Cleveland, Ohio 44101; Deep Cove Farms, Chester, Nova Scotia, Canada. *Clubs:* Union, Mayfield, Chagrin Valley Hunt, Summit Hunt (Cleveland); Metropolitan (New York); Glenelg Fishing; Royal Nova Scotia Yacht Squadron (NS).

EATON, Vice-Adm. Sir John (Willson Musgrave), KBE 1956; CB 1953; DSO 1941; DSC 1941; RN retired; *b* Nov. 1902; 2nd *s* of Dr Walter Musgrave Eaton and Margaret Emily (*née* Ibbetson); *m* 1945, Cynthia Mary Hurlstone, *widow* of Major Gerald Tatchell, The Royal Lincolnshire Regiment; (two *step-d*). *Educ:* Temple Grove, Eastbourne; RNC Osborne and RNC Dartmouth. HMS Barham, Midshipman, 1919-21; HM Destroyers, 1922-25; HM Submarines, 1925-28; HMS Malaya, 1928-30; HM Destroyers, 1930-38; Student RN Staff Coll., 1939; HM Destroyers, 1939-43; HMS Sheffield, 1945; HMS St Vincent, 1946-48; idc, 1948-49; Dir of RN Staff Coll., Greenwich, 1949-51; Flag Officer Commanding HM Australian Fleet, Oct. 1951-53; Flag Officer Commanding Reserve Fleet, 1954-55; C-in-C America and West Indies Station, 1955-56; Dep. Supreme Allied Comdr Atlantic, Oct. 1955-Dec. 1957. *Recreations:* golf, shooting. *Address:* Dolphins, Church Street, Kelvedon, Essex CO5 9AH. *T:* Kelvedon 283.

EAYRS, Prof. John Thomas, PhD, DSc; Sands Cox Professor of Anatomy, University of Birmingham, 1968-77; *b* 23 Jan. 1913; *s* of late Thomas William Eayrs, AMICE, and Florence May (*née* Clough); *m* 1941, Frances Marjorie Sharp; one *s* two *d*. *Educ:* King Edward's, Birmingham; University of Birmingham. In industry until 1938. War service: Pte Royal Warwicks Regt, 1939-40; 2nd Lieut Manchester Regt, 1940; Lieut 1940; Capt. 1941; Major 1942; Worcester Regt, 1943; sc Staff Coll., Camberley, 1944. University of Birmingham: Peter Thompson Prize, 1947; John Barritt Melson Memorial Gold Medal, 1947; Lectr in Anatomy, 1948; Bertram Windle Prize, 1950; Sen. Lectr 1955; Research Fellow, Calif. Inst. of Technology, 1956-57; Reader in Comparative Neurology, Birmingham, 1958; Henry Head Research Fellow, Royal Society, London, 1957-62; Prof. of Neuroendocrinology, Birmingham, 1961; Fitzmary Prof. of Physiology, London Univ., 1963-68. Governor, King Edward's Foundn, Birmingham, 1968-. *Publications:* Scientific Papers dealing with developmental neuroendocrinology and behaviour in Jl Endocrin., Jl Anat. (London), Anim. Behav., etc. *Recreations:* cricket, foreign travel and languages. *Address:* 51 Old Street, Upton upon Severn, Hereford and Worcester; Penllyn Dyfi, Aberangell, Powys.

EBAN, Abba; a Member of the Knesset, since 1959; Minister of Foreign Affairs, Israel, 1966-74; *b* 2 Feb. 1915, Cape Town, SA; *s* of Avram and Alida Solomon; *m* 1945, Susan Ambache; one *s* one *d*. *Educ:* Cambridge Univ. (MA). Res. Fellow and Tutor for Oriental Languages, Pembroke Coll., Cambridge, 1938. Liaison officer of Allied HQ with Jewish population in Jerusalem, 1942-44; Chief Instructor, Middle East Arab Centre, Jerusalem, 1944-46; Jewish Agency, 1946-47; Liaison Officer with UN Special Commn on Palestine, 1947; UN: Representative of provisional govt of Israel, 1948; Permanent rep., 1949-59; Vice-Pres., General Assembly, 1953; Ambassador to USA, 1950-59; Minister without Portfolio, 1959-60; Minister of Educn and Culture, 1960-63; Dep. Prime Minister, 1963-66. Pres., Weizmann Inst. of Science, 1958-66; Vice-Pres., UN Conf. on Science and Technology in Advancement of New States, 1963; Mem., UN Adv. Cttee on Science and Technology for Develt. Fellow: World Acad. of Arts and Sciences; Amer. Acad. of Arts and Sciences. Hon. Doctorates include: New York; Boston; Maryland; Cincinnati; Temple; Brandeis; Yeshiva. *Publications:* The Modern Literary Movement in Egypt, 1944; Maze of Justice, 1946; Social and Cultural Problems in the Middle East, 1947; The Toynbee Heresy, 1955; Voice of Israel, 1957; Tide of Nationalism, 1959; Chaim Weizmann: a collective biography, 1962; Reality and Vision in the Middle East (Foreign Affairs), 1965; Israel in the World, 1966; My People, 1968; My Country, 1972; articles in English, French, Hebrew and Arabic. *Address:* The Knesset, Jerusalem, Israel.

EBBISHAM, 2nd Baron, *cr* 1928, of Cobham, Surrey; **Rowland Roberts Blades,** Bt, *cr* 1922; TD; MA; *b* 3 Sept. 1912; *o s* of 1st Baron Ebbisham, GBE, and Margaret (MBE 1943, Officer

Legion of Honour, OStJ) (*d* 1965), *d* of Arthur Reiner, Sutton, Surrey; *S* father, 1953; *m* 1949, Flavia Mary, *y d* of Charles Meade, Pen y lan, Meifod, Montgomeryshire; three *d*. *Educ:* Winchester; Christ Church, Oxford (MA). Served War of 1939-45; Lieut 98th (Surrey and Sussex Yeo.) Field Regt, RA. Master, Mercers' Co., 1963; Common Councilman, City of London, 1947-; Chm., City Lands Cttee, and Chief Commoner, Corp. of London, 1967-68; one of HM Lieutenants, City of London, 1966-. Pres., London Chamber of Commerce, 1958-61; Pres., Assoc. of British Chambers of Commerce, 1968-70; Mem., European Trade Cttee, BOTB, 1973-; Hon. Treasurer, BPIF, 1971-; Director: Williams, Lea Group; Bedford General Insurance Co. Ltd; Private Patients Plan Ltd; Chm., Anglo-Dal Ltd. Vice-Pres. The London Record Society. Captain, Surrey II XI, 1946-54; Order of Yugoslav Flag with gold wreath, 1976. *Address:* The Old Rectory, Blechingley, Surrey. *T:* Godstone 3388. *Clubs:* Bath, MCC.

See also Rear-Adm. John E. H. McBeath .

EBERHART, Richard (Ghormley); Professor Emeritus of English and Poet in Residence, Dartmouth College, USA; *b* Austin, Minn, 5 April 1904; *s* of late Alpha La Rue Eberhart and late Lena Eberhart (*née* Lowenstein); *m* 1941, Helen Elizabeth Butcher, Christ Church, Cambridge, Mass; one *s* one *d*. *Educ:* Dartmouth Coll., USA (AB); St John's Coll., Cambridge Univ., England (BA, MA); Harvard Univ. Grad. Sch. of Arts and Sciences. Taught English, 1933-41, also tutor to son of King Prajadhipok of Siam for a year. Served War in USN Reserve finishing as Lieut-Comdr, 1946; subseq. entered Butcher Polish Co., Boston, Mass, as Asst Man., finishing as Vice-Pres. (now Hon. Vice-Pres. and Mem. Bd of Directors). Founder (and first Pres.) Poet's Theatre Inc., Cambridge, Mass, 1950. Called back to teaching, 1952, and has served as Poet in Residence, Prof., or Lecturer at University of Washington, University of Conn., Wheaton Coll., Princeton, and in 1956 was apptd Prof. of English and Poet in Residence at Dartmouth Coll. Class of 1925 Chair, 1968 (being absent as Consultant in Poetry to the Library of Congress, 1959-61). Visiting Professor: Univ. of Washington, 1967, Jan.-June 1972; Columbia Univ., 1975; Distinguished Vis. Prof., Florida Univ., 1974 and 1977 (President's Medallion, 1977); Regents Prof., Univ. of California, Davis, 1975; First Wallace Stevens Fellow, Timothy Dwight Coll., Yale, 1976. Shelley Memorial Prize; Bollingen Prize, 1962; Pulitzer Prize, 1966; Fellow, Acad. of Amer. Poets, 1969 (Nat. Book Award, 1977). Advisory Cttee on the Arts, for the National Cultural Center (later John F. Kennedy Memorial Center), Washington, 1959; Member: Nat. Inst. of Arts and Letters, 1960; Nat. Acad. of Arts and Sciences, 1967; Elliston Lecturer on Poetry University of Cincinnati, 1961. Apptd Hon. Consultant in American Letters, The Library of Congress, 1963-66, reapptd, 1966-69. Hon. Pres., Poetry Soc. of America, 1972. Participant, Poetry International, London, 1973. Hon. LittD: Dartmouth Coll., 1954; Skidmore Coll., 1966; Coll. of Wooster, 1969; Colgate Univ., 1974. Phi Beta Kappa poem, Harvard, 1967; Hon. Mem., Alpha Chapter, Mass, 1967. *Publications:* (concurrently in England and America): A Bravery of Earth, 1930; Reading the Spirit, 1936; Selected Poems, 1951; Undercliff, Poems, 1946-53, also Great Praises, 1957; Collected Poems, 1930-60, 1960; Collected Verse Plays, 1962 (USA); The Quarry, 1964; Selected Poems, 1930-65, New Directions, 1965; Thirty One Sonnets, 1967 (USA); Shifts of Being, 1968; Fields of Grace, 1972 (Nat. Book Award nominee, 1973); Poems to Poets, 1975; Collected Poems 1930-1976, 1976; To Eberhart from Ginsberg: a letter about 'Howl', 1956, 1976; Selected Prose, 1978. Recorded Readings of his Poetry, 1961, 1968. Two documentary films, 1972, 1975. *Recreations:* swimming, cruising, tennis, flying 7-ft kites. *Address:* 5 Webster Terrace, Hanover, New Hampshire 03755, USA. *Clubs:* Century (New York); Buck's Harbor Yacht (S Brooksville, Maine); Signet (Harvard).

EBERLE, Vice-Adm. James Henry Fuller; Chief of Fleet Support, since 1977; *b* 31 May 1927; *s* of late Victor Fuller Eberle and of Joyce Mary Eberle, Bristol; *m* 1950, Ann Patricia Thompson, Hong Kong; one *s* two *d*. *Educ:* Clifton Coll.; RNC Dartmouth and Greenwich. Served War of 1939-45 in MTBs, HMS Renown, HMS Belfast; subseq. in Far East; qual. Gunnery Specialist 1951; Guided Missile Develt and trials in UK and USA, 1953-57; Naval Staff, 1960-62; Exec. Officer, HMS Eagle, 1963-65; comd HMS Intrepid, 1968-70; Asst Chief of Fleet Support, MoD (RN), 1971-74; Flag Officer Sea Training, 1974-75; Flag Officer Carriers and Amphibious Ships, 1975-77. Comdr 1959; Captain 1966; Rear-Adm. 1971; Vice-Adm. 1977. Mem. Council, RUSI, 1972. *Recreations:* defence studies, hunting (Master of Britannia Beagles), tennis (Vice-Pres., RN Lawn Tennis Assoc.), squash (Pres. RN Squash Racquets Assoc.). *Address:* Village Farm, Holne, Devon. *T:* Poundsgate 281. *Clubs:* Farmers', Queen's; Society of Merchant Venturers (Bristol).

EBERT, Prof. Carl (Anton Charles), CBE 1960; Opera Director; naturalized American citizen; *b* Berlin, 20 Feb. 1887; *s* of Maria and Wilhelm Ebert; *m* 1st, 1912, Lucie Splisgarth (marr. diss., 1923); one *s* (and one *d* decd); 2nd, 1924, Gertrude Eck; one *s* two *d*. *Educ:* Berlin, Friedrich Werder'sche Oberrealschule; Max Reinhardt's Sch. of Dramatic Art. Actor; Max Reinhardt's Deutsches Theater, Berlin, 1909-14; Schauspielhaus, Frankfurt, 1915-22; Staatstheater, Berlin, 1922-27; Founder and Dir of Schools of Dramatic Art: Frankfurt 1919, Berlin, Hochschule für Musik (Prof.), 1925; Gen.-Intendant (and Producer), Landestheater, Darmstadt, 1927-31; Intendant, Staedtische Oper, Berlin, 1931-33; A Director: Actors' Union, 1919-27; Deutscher Bühnenverein, 1927-33. Guest Producer since 1933 at Zürich, Basel, Maggio Musicale Florence, Verona, Salzburg Festival, Colon, Buenos Aires, Burgtheater and State Opera, Vienna, Cambridge Theatre, London (New London Opera Company), Scala, Milan, Royal Opera, Copenhagen, Metropolitan, New York; Artistic Dir and Producer, Glyndebourne Festival Opera, 1934-59; Producer Edinburgh Festival, 1947-55. Adviser on Theatrical Affairs to Turkish Min. of Educn, Ankara, 1936-47; Founder of Turkish State Sch. for Opera and Drama and of Turkish National Theatre. Prof. and Head of Opera Dept, University of S Calif, Los Angeles, 1948-54; Gen. Dir Guild Opera Co., Los Angeles, 1950-54, Artistic Dir since 1954; Intendant, Staedtische Oper, Berlin, 1954-61; Pres. German Section of International Theatre Institute, 1956-61. Guest Producer: Glyndebourne, 1962, 1963; Opera House, Zürich, 1963, 1965; Wexford Festival, 1965; Deutsche Oper, Berlin, 1967. Master Classes, BBC TV, 1965, 1967. Awarded Ernst Reuter Plakette, City of Berlin, 1957. Hon. MusDoc, Edinburgh, 1954, Hon Doc. of Fine Arts, University of S California, Los Angeles, 1955. Knight, Dannebrog Order, Denmark; Das Grosse Verdienstkreuz mit Stern, Germany; Das Grosse Ehrenzeichen for services to Mozart, Austria, 1959; Hon. Comdr of the Order of the British Empire, 1960; La Grande Médaille d'Argent de la Ville de Paris, 1961; Commendatore, Order of Merit (Italy), 1966; Hon. Member: Deutsche Oper, Berlin, 1961; Landestheater, Darmstadt, 1963; Hon. Life Mem., Bd of Dirs, Opera Guild of S Calif, LA, 1965. *Address:* 809 Enchanted Way, Pacific Palisades, Calif 90272, USA. *T:* 454-6705. *Club:* PEN (Internat.).

EBERT, Peter; Producer; Intendant, Staatstheater Wiesbaden, since 1975; General Administrator, Scottish Opera Company, since 1977 (Director of Productions, 1965-77); *b* 6 April 1918; *s* of Carl Ebert, *qv*, and Lucie Oppenheim; *m* 1st, 1944, Kathleen Havinden; two *d*; 2nd, 1951, Silvia Ashmole; five *s* three *d*. *Educ:* Salem Sch., Germany; Gordonstoun, Scotland. BBC Producer, 1948-51; 1st opera production, Mefistofele, Glasgow, 1951; Mozart and Rossini guest productions: Rome, Naples, Venice, 1951, 1952, 1954, 1955: Wexford Festival: 12 prods, 1952-65; 1st Glyndebourne Fest. prod., Ariecchino, 1954, followed by Seraglio, Don Giovanni, etc.; 1st Edinburgh Fest. prod., Forza del Destino, 1955; Chief producer: Hannover State Opera, 1954-60; Düsseldorf Opera, 1960-62; directed opera class, Hannover State Conservatory, 1954-60; Head of Opera studio, Düsseldorf, 1960-62. Guest productions in Europe, USA, Canada. TV productions of Glyndebourne operas, 1955-64; 1st TV studio prod., 1963; Opera Adviser to BBC TV, 1964-65. First drama prod., The Devils, Johannesburg, 1966; first musical, Houdini, London, 1966. Dir, Opera Sch., University of Toronto, 1967-68; Intendant: Stadttheater, Augsburg, 1968-73; Stadttheater Bielefeld, 1973-75. *Recreation:* raising a family. *Address:* Staatstheater, Wiesbaden, Germany; Ades House, Chailey, Lewes, Sussex. *T:* Newick 2441.

EBOO PIRBHAI, Count Sir; Kt 1952; OBE 1946; Director of Companies; *b* 25 July 1905; *m* 1925, Kulsambai; two *s* three *d* (and one *s* decd). *Educ:* Duke of Gloucester Sch., Nairobi. Representative of HH The Aga Khan. Member, Nairobi City Council, 1938-43. MLC Kenya, 1952-60; Member of various other official bodies; President Central Muslim Association; President Aga Khan Supreme Council, Africa, Europe, Canada and USA. Given title of Count, created by HH The Aga Khan, 1954. Brilliant Star of Zanzibar, 1956; Order of Crescent Cross of the Comores, 1966. *Address:* PO Box 40898, Nairobi, Kenya. *T:* 65049. *Clubs:* Reform, Lansdowne, Royal Commonwealth Society; Nairobi, Muthaiga (Kenya).

EBRAHIM, Sir (Mahomed) Currimbhoy, 4th Bt, *cr* 1913; BA, LLB, Advocate, Pakistan; Member, Standing Council of the Baronetage, 1961; *b* 24 June, 1935; *o s* of Sir (Huseinali) Currimbhoy Ebrahim, 3rd Bt, and Alhaja Lady Amina Khanum, *d* of Alhaj Cassumali Jairajbhoy; *S* father 1952; *m* 1958, Dur-e-Mariam, *d* of Minuchehir Ahmud Ghulamaly Nana; three *s* one *d*. *Recreations:* tennis (Karachi University No 1, 1957, No 2, 1958), cricket, table-tennis, squash, reading (literary), art, poetry writing, debate, quotation writing. *Heir: s*

Zulfiqar Ali Currimbhoy Ebrahim, *b* 5 Aug. 1960. *Address:* Bait-ul-Aman, 33 Mirza Kalig Beg Road, Jamshed Quarters, Karachi, Pakistan.

EBRINGTON, Viscount; Charles Hugh Richard Fortescue; *b* 10 May 1951; *s* and *heir* of 7th Earl Fortescue, *qv*; *m* 1974, Julia, *er d* of Air Commodore J. A. Sowrey. *Educ:* Eton.

EBSWORTH, Brig. Wilfrid Algernon, CB 1950; CBE 1943; *b* 1 Feb. 1897; *s* of Rev. Algernon Frederic Ebsworth and Mary Frances Harcourt-Vernon; *m* 1st, 1925, Cynthia (*d* 1975), *d* of Edward Charles Bleck, CMG; one *s* one *d*; 2nd, 1976, Mrs Ethel Ridyard Dodd. *Educ:* Tonbridge Sch.; RMC Sandhurst. Served European War, 1914-18, 2nd Lieut The Sherwood Foresters (twice wounded). Regimental and Staff Service, Egypt, Turkey, and India, 1919-27; Staff Coll., 1928-29; Regimental and Staff Service in England, 1930-38; Instructor, Staff Coll., 1938-39; War of 1939-45, commanded 1st Bn The Sherwood Foresters, Palestine, 1939-40; GSO 1, Middle East, 1940-41 (despatches); Comd 22nd and 30th East African Brigades, Brig. Gen. Staff, East African Command and 15 Indian Corps, Burma, 1942-45; Comdr, British Army Staff, France, 1946-47; Dep. Fortress Comdr, Gibraltar, 1947-50; retd pay, 1950. Légion d'Honneur (Officier), Croix de Guerre avec palme, 1947 (France). *Address:* 32 Gretton Court, Girton, Cambridge.

EBURY, 6th Baron, *cr* 1857; **Francis Egerton Grosvenor;** *b* 8 Feb. 1934; *s* of 5th Baron Ebury, DSO and Ann Acland-Troyte; *heir-pres.* to 7th Earl of Wilton, *qv*; *S* father 1957; *m* 1st, 1957, Gillian Elfrida (Elfin) (marr. diss. 1962), *d* of Martin Soames, London; one *s*; 2nd, 1963, Kyra (marr. diss. 1973), *d* of late L. L. Aslin; 3rd, 1974, Suzanne Jean, *d* of Graham Suckling, Christchurch, NZ; one *d*. *Educ:* Eton. *Recreation:* golf. *Heir: s* Hon. Julian Francis Martin Grosvenor, *b* 8 June 1959. *Address:* 5 Landale Road, Toorak, Vic. 3142, Australia. *Club:* Savage (Melbourne).

ECCLES, family name of Viscount Eccles.

ECCLES, 1st Viscount, *cr* 1964; 1st Baron, *cr* 1962; **David McAdam Eccles,** PC 1951; KCVO 1953; MA Oxon; Chairman, British Library Board, since 1973; *b* 18 Sept. 1904; *s* of late W. McAdam Eccles, FRCS and Anna Coralie, *d* of E. B. Anstie, JP; *m* 1928, Sybil (*d* 1977), *e d* of Viscount Dawson of Penn, PC, GCVO, KCB, KCMG; two *s* one *d*. *Educ:* Winchester, New Coll., Oxford. Joined Ministry of Economic Warfare, Sept. 1939; Economic Adviser to HM Ambassadors at Madrid and Lisbon, 1940-42; Ministry of Production, 1942-43. MP (C) Chippenham Div. of Wilts, 1943-62; Minister of Works, 1951-54; Minister of Education, 1954-57; Pres. of the Board of Trade, 1957-59; Minister of Education, Oct. 1959-July 1962; Paymaster-General, with responsibility for the arts, 1970-73. Trustee, British Museum, 1963-, Chm. of Trustees, 1968-70. Dir, Courtaulds, 1962-70. Chm., Anglo-Hellenic League, 1967-70. Pres., World Crafts Council, 1974-. Hon. Fellow, RIBA. *Publications:* Half-Way to Faith, 1966; Life and Politics: A Moral Diagnosis, 1967; On Collecting, 1968. *Heir: s* Hon. John Dawson Eccles, *qv*. *Address:* Dean Farm, Chute, near Andover, Hants; 6 Barton Street, SW1. *T:* Chute Standen 210. *Clubs:* Brooks's, Roxburghe.
See also Marquess of Lansdowne.

ECCLES, Sir John Carew, Kt 1958; FRS 1941; FRSNZ; FAA; *b* 27 Jan. 1903; *s* of William James and Mary Eccles; *m* 1st, 1928, Irene Frances Miller (marr. diss. 1968); four *s* five *d*; 2nd, 1968, Helena Táboříková. *Educ:* Melbourne Univ.; Magdalen Coll., Oxford. Melbourne University: 1st class Hons MB, BS 1925; Victoria Rhodes Scholar, 1925. Univ. of Oxford: Christopher Welch Scholar; 1st class Hons Natural Science (Physiology), 1927; MA 1929; DPhil 1929; Gotch Memorial Prize, 1927; Rolleston Memorial Prize, 1932. Junior Res. Fellow, Exeter Coll., Oxford, 1927-32; Staines Med. Fellow, Exeter Coll., 1932-34; Fellow and Tutor of Magdalen Coll., and Univ. Lectr in Physiology, 1934-37; Dir, Kanematsu Memorial Inst. of Pathology, Sydney, 1937-44; Prof. of Physiology: Univ. of Otago, Dunedin, NZ, 1944-51; ANU, Canberra, 1951-66; Mem., Inst. for Biomedical Res., Chicago, 1966-68; Dist. Prof. and Head of Res. Unit of Neurobiology, Health Sci. Faculty, State Univ. of NY at Buffalo, 1968-75, now Dist. Prof. Emeritus. Lectures: Waynflete, Magdalen Coll., Oxford, 1952; Herter, Johns Hopkins Univ., 1955; Ferrier, Royal Soc., 1959; Sherrington, Liverpool Univ., 1966; Patten, Indiana Univ., 1972; Pahlavi, Iran, 1976. Pres., Australian Acad. of Science, 1957-61. Member: Pontifical Acad. of Science; Deutsche Akademie der Naturforscher Leopoldina. Foreign Hon. Member: Amer. Acad. of Arts and Sciences; Amer. Philosophical Soc.; Amer. Neurological Soc.; Accademia Nazionale dei Lincei. Hon. Life Mem., New York Acad. of

Sciences, 1965; Foreign Associate, Nat. Acad. of Sciences; For. Mem., Max-Planck Soc. Hon. Fellow: Exeter Coll., Oxford, 1961; Magdalen Coll., Oxford, 1964; Amer. Coll. of Physicians, 1967. Hon. ScD Cantab; Hon. DSc: Oxon; Tasmania; British Columbia; Gustavus Adolphus Coll., Minnesota; Marquette Univ., Wisconsin; Loyola, Chicago; Yeshiva, NY; Hon. LLD Melbourne; Hon. MD Charles Univ., Prague. (Jointly) Nobel Prize for Medicine, 1963; Baly Medal, RCP, 1961; Royal Medal, Royal Soc., 1962; Cothenius Medal, Deutsche Akademie der Naturforscher Leopoldina, 1963. *Publications:* (jt author) Reflex Activity of Spinal Cord, 1932; Neuro-physiological Basis of Mind, 1953; Physiology of Nerve Cells, 1957; Physiology of Synapses, 1964; (jt author) The Cerebellum as a Neuronal Machine, 1967; The Inhibitory Pathways of the Central Nervous System, 1969; Facing Reality, 1970; The Understanding of the Brain, 1973; (jt author) The Self and Its Brain, 1977; papers in Proc. Royal Soc., Jl of Physiology, Jl of Neurophysiology, Experimental Brain Research. *Recreations:* walking, European travel. *Address:* Ca' a la Gra', CH 6611 Contra, Ticino, Switzerland. *T:* 093-672931.

ECCLES, Hon. John Dawson; Managing Director, since 1968, Chairman, 1976, Head Wrightson & Co. Ltd; Chairman, Ransome Hoffman Pollard, since 1977; *b* 20 April 1931; *er s* and *heir* of 1st Viscount Eccles, *qv*; *m* 1955, Diana Catherine, *d* of Raymond Sturge, *qv*; one *s* three *d*. *Educ:* Winchester Coll.; Magdalen Coll., Oxford (BA). Director: Glynwed Ltd; British Nuclear Associates Ltd; Davy International Ltd, 1977-; Finance for Industry; Finance Corp. for Industry; Northern Industrial Develt Bd. Mem. (part-time), Monopolies and Mergers Commn, 1976-. *Address:* Moulton Hall, Richmond, N Yorks. *T:* Barton 227.

ECCLESHARE, Colin Forster; formerly London Manager and Director Group Projects, Cambridge University Press; *b* 2 May 1916; *yr s* of Albert and Mary Alice Eccleshare, Derby; *m* 1942, Elizabeth, *e d* of late H. S. Bennett, FBA, and of Joan Bennett, *qv*; one *s* two *d* (and one *d* decd). *Educ:* Bemrose Sch., Derby; St Catharine's Coll., Cambridge (MA). Joined Cambridge Univ. Press, 1939. Served War, 1940-46; commissioned RE; Captain Survey Directorate, War Office, 1944; Major, HQ, ALFSEA, 1945. Rejoined Cambridge Univ. Press, 1946; Asst London Manager, 1948; London Manager, 1963-72; Dir Group Projects, 1972-77. Mem. Council, Publishers Assoc., 1965-71; Treasurer, 1971-73; Pres., 1973-75; Vice Pres., 1975-77. Board Mem., Book Development Council, 1968-70 (Chm., 1975-77); Member: Books Advisory Panel, British Council; Exec. and Internat. Cttees, Internat. Publishers' Assoc.; Groupe des Editeurs du Livre de la CEE; Chairman: Other-Media Cttee of Internat. Scientific, Technical and Medical Publishers Gp; Soc. of Bookmen, 1977-. Missions (for Publishers Assoc., BDC, Brit. Council) to: Hungary, USSR, 1964; Philippines, Japan, 1968; Pakistan, 1971; USSR, Australia, 1974; Saudi Arabia, 1976; Israel, 1977. *Publications:* contributor to The Bookseller, 1950-62. *Address:* 4 Branch Hill, NW3. *T:* 01-794 3496; Tyddyn Pandy, Barmouth. *T:* Barmouth 280315. *Club:* Garrick.

ECCLESTON, Harry Norman, PRE 1975 (RE 1961; ARE 1948); RWS 1975 (ARWS 1964); Artist Designer at the Bank of England Printing Works since 1958; *b* 21 Jan. 1923; *s* of Harry Norman Eccleston and Kate Pritchard, Coseley, Staffs; *m* 1948, Betty Doreen Gripton; two *d*. *Educ:* Sch. of Art, Bilston; Coll. of Art, Birmingham; Royal College of Art. ATD 1947; ARCA (1st Class) 1950. Studied painting until 1942. Served in Royal Navy, 1942-46; Temp. Commn, RNVR, 1943. Engraving Sch., Royal College of Art, 1947-51; engraving, teaching, free-lance graphic design, 1951-58. Pres., Royal Soc. of Painter-Etchers and Engravers, 1975-. *Recreation:* reading. *Address:* 110 Priory Road, Harold Hill, Romford, Essex. *T:* Ingrebourne 40275. *Club:* Arts.

ECHLIN, Sir Norman David Fenton, 10th Bt, *cr* 1721; Captain 14/1st Punjab Regiment, Indian Army; *b* 1 Dec. 1925; *s* of Sir John Frederick Echlin, 9th Bt, and Ellen Patricia (*d* 1971), *d* of David Jones, JP, Dublin; *S* father, 1932; *m* 1953, Mary Christine, *d* of John Arthur, Oswestry, Salop. *Educ:* Masonic Boys' School, Dublin. *Heir:* none. *Address:* Nartopa, 36 Marina Avenue, Appley, Ryde, IoW.

ECKERSLEY, Thomas, OBE 1948; RDI 1963; FSIA; Head of Department of Design, London College of Printing, since 1958; *b* Sept. 1914; *s* of John Eckersley and Eunice Hilton; *m* Daisy Eckersley; three *s*; *m* 1966, Mary Kessell, painter. *Educ:* Salford Sch. of Art. Free-lance Graphic Designer for London Transport, Shell Mex, BBC, GPO, MOI, Unicef, CoID and other leading concerns since 1936. Work exhibited in Sweden, USA, Paris, Hamburg, Lausanne, Milan, Amsterdam; permanent collection of work in V&A Museum and Nat. War Museum. Mem. of

Alliance Graphique Internationale; Hon. Fellow, Manchester Coll. of Art and Design. *Publications:* contribs to Graphis, Gebrauchsgraphik, Form und Technik, Art and Industry, Print Design and Production, Penrose Annual. *Recreation:* cricket. *Address:* 71a Fitzjohn's Avenue, NW3. *T:* 01-794 2250.

EDDEN, Alan John, CMG 1957; HM Diplomatic Service, retired; *b* 2 Dec. 1912; *s* of late Thomas Frederick Edden and Nellie Shipway; *m* 1939, Pauline Klay; one *s*. *Educ:* Latymer Sch., Edmonton; Gonville and Caius Coll., Cambridge (Exhibitioner). Served at HM Legation, Bangkok, 1935; Batavia, 1938; Foreign Office, 1939; HM Legation, Bangkok, 1940; HM Legation, Tehran, 1942; Kermanshah, 1944; with SHAEF, May 1945; Actg Consul-Gen. Amsterdam, June 1945; Foreign Office, Oct. 1945; HM Embassy, Warsaw, 1948; Brit. Information Services, New York, 1951; FO, 1953; Counsellor, Foreign Office, 1954-58; Counsellor, HM Embassy, Beirut, 1958-62; HM Consul-Gen., Durban, 1962-66; HM Ambassador to: Cameroon, Central African Republic, Gabon and Chad, 1966-70; Equatorial Guinea, 1969-70; Lebanon, 1970-71. *Recreation:* music. *Address:* 77 Hosking Road, Pietermaritzburg, South Africa. *Club:* Victoria (Pietermaritzburg).

EDDEN, Vice-Adm. Sir (William) Kaye, KBE 1960 (OBE 1944); CB 1956; DL; *b* 27 Feb. 1905; *s* of late Major H. W. Edden, The Cameronians, and late Mrs H. W. Edden (*née* Neilson); *m* 1936, Isobel Sybil Pitman (*d* 1970), Bath, *g d* of Sir Isaac Pitman; one *s*. *Educ:* Royal Naval Colls, Osborne and Dartmouth. Comdr. 1938; Admiralty, 1938-40; served War of 1939-45: HMS London, 1941-42; Staff C-in-C, Eastern Fleet, 1942-44 (OBE); Capt. 1944, Admty, 1944-47; RNAS Yeovilton, 1947-49; Capt. (D) 6th Destroyer Sqdn, and HMS Battleaxe, 1949-51; Admiralty, 1951-53; Rear-Adm. 1954; Commandant, Jt-Services Staff Coll., Latimer, 1953-56; Flag Officer Commanding Fifth Cruiser Sqdn and Flag Officer Second-in-Command, Far East Station, 1956-57; Vice-Adm. 1957; Admiral Commanding Reserves, 1958-60, retd 1960. DL West Sussex, 1977. *Address:* Littlecroft, Old Bosham, West Sussex PO18 8LR. *T:* Bosham 573119. *Clubs:* Army and Navy; Bosham Sailing.

EDDEY, Prof. Howard Hadfield, CMG 1974; FRCS, FRACS, FACS; Professor of Surgery, University of Melbourne, at Austin Hospital and Repatriation General Hospital, 1967-75, now Emeritus; also Dean of Austin Hospital and Repatriation General Hospital Clinical School, 1971-75; *b* Melbourne, 3 Sept. 1910; *s* of Charles Howard and Rachel Beatrice Eddey; *m* 1940, Alice Paul; two *s* one *d*. *Educ:* Melbourne Univ.; St Bartholomew's Hosp. Med. Sch. BSc, MB BS, 1934; FRCS 1938; FRACS 1941; FACS 1964; Hallet Prize of RCS of Eng., 1938. Served War, 1941-45: AAMC, Major and Surgical Specialist; served in PoW camps: Changi (Singapore); Sandakan and Kuching (Borneo). Hon. Surgeon, Royal Melbourne Hosp., 1947-67; Cons. Surg., 1967, Royal Melbourne and Royal Women's Hosps; Peter MacCallum Clinic. Mem. AMA, 1935; Mem., Faculty of Med., Univ. of Melbourne, 1950-75 (Mem. Convocation, 1965-67); Indep. Lectr in Surgical Anatomy, Univ. of Melb., 1950-65; Dean, Royal Melb. Hosp. Clin. Sch., 1965-67; Colombo Plan Visitor to India, 1960-65; Cons. in Surg., Papuan Med. Coll., 1965-68; Mem. Cancer Inst. Bd, 1958-67; Mem. Med. and Sci. Cttee, Anti-Cancer Council of Vic., 1958-67; (Chm., Melb. Med. Postgrad. Cttee, 1963-71; Vice-Pres., Aust. Postgrad. Fedn in Med., 1965-71. Mem. Council, RACS, 1967-75 (Mem. Bd of Examrs, 1958-75, Chm. Bd, 1968-73; Hon. Librarian, 1968-75). Mem. Med. Bd of Vic., 1968-; Mem. Austin Hosp. Bd of Management, 1971- (Vice-Pres., 1975-). Hunterian Prof., RCS, 1960; Vis. Prof. of Surg., Univ. of Singapore, 1962; Leverhulme Fellow, Univ. of Melb., 1974; Vis. Prof. of Surg., Univ. of Hong Kong, 1974. *Publications:* many, in sci. jls, particularly in relation to diseases of salivary glands and cancer of mouth. *Recreations:* travel, gardening. *Address:* 12 Briony Place, Mona Vale, Sydney, NSW 2103, Australia. *Clubs:* Naval and Military (Melbourne); Melbourne Cricket.

EDDIE, Sir George (Brand), Kt 1966; OBE 1948; JP; retired; *b* 14 Nov. 1893; *s* of William and Jessie Eddie, Banchory, Kincardineshire; *m* 1926, Mary, *d* of George Ferguson, Glasgow; one *s* two *d*. *Educ:* Banchory. Secretary/Agent, Blackburn Trades Council and Labour Party, 1920-60; Vice-Chm. and Chm., NW Regional Council of Labour Party, 1940-; Mem., Blackburn Town Council, 1927- (Leader, 1945-68). Freeman, Blackburn Co. Borough, 1960. JP Blackburn, 1946. DL Lancs, 1968-76. *Recreations:* golf, bowls, motoring. *Address:* 44 Willow Trees Drive, Blackburn, Lancs. *T:* Blackburn 56088.

EDDISON, Rear-Adm. Talbot Leadam, CB 1961; DSC 1945; *b* 10 June 1908; *e s* (*yr twin*) of late Edwin and Mrs Eddison (*née*

Leadam); *m* 1932, Doris (*née* Mavrogordato); one *s* one d. *Educ:* Royal Naval Coll., Dartmouth. Entered Dartmouth 1922. Commodore, Royal Naval Barracks, Devonport, 1958-59; Rear-Adm. 1959; served as Vice-Naval Dep. to Supreme Allied Comdr Europe, 1959-62; retired, 1962. *Address:* 4 Halton Close, Bransgore, Christchurch, Dorset BH23 8HZ. *T:* Bransgore 72593. *Club:* Royal Commonwealth Society.

EDDLEMAN, Gen. Clyde Davis; DSM (US); Silver Star; Legion of Merit; Bronze Star; Philippines Distinguished Service Star; Vice-Chief of Staff, US Army, 1960-62; *b* 17 Jan. 1902; *s* of Rev. W. H. Eddleman and Janie Eddleman (*née* Tureman); *m* 1926, Lorraine Heath; one *s* (and one *s* decd). *Educ:* US Military Academy, West Point, New York. Commissioned 2nd Lieut of Infantry upon graduation from US Military Academy, 1924. Advanced, through the ranks, and reached grade of Gen. 1959. Comdr, Central Army Group (NATO), and C-in-C, US Army, Europe, at Heidelberg, Germany, 1959-60. Knight Commander's Cross, Order of Merit (Germany). *Recreations:* hunting, fishing. *Address:* 4400 33rd Road N, Arlington, Va, USA.

EDDY, Prof. Alfred Alan; Professor of Biochemistry, University of Manchester Institute of Science and Technology since 1959; *b* 4 Nov. 1926; Cornish parentage; *s* of Alfred and Ellen Eddy; *m* 1954, Susan Ruth Slade-Jones; two *s*. *Educ:* Devonport High Sch.; Open scholarship Exeter Coll., Oxford, 1944; BA 1st Class Hons, 1949. ICI Research Fellow, 1950; DPhil 1951. Joined Brewing Industry Research Foundation, Nutfield, 1953. *Publications:* various scientific papers. *Address:* Larchfield, Buxton Road, Disley, Cheshire.

EDE, Jeffery Raymond; Keeper of Public Records since 1970; *b* 10 March 1918; *e s* of late Richard Arthur Ede; *m* 1944, Mercy, *d* of Arthur Radford Sholl; one *s* one d. *Educ:* Plymouth Coll.; King's Coll., Cambridge (MA). Served War of 1939-45, Intell. Corps (despatches); GSO2 HQ 8 Corps District, BAOR, 1945-46. Asst Keeper, Public Record Office, 1947-59; Principal Asst Keeper, 1959-66; Dep. Keeper, 1966-69. Lectr in Archive Admin., Sch. of Librarianship and Archives, University Coll., London, 1956-61; Unesco expert in Tanzania, 1963-64. Chm., British Acad. Cttee on Oriental Documents, 1972; Vice Pres., Internat. Council on Archives, 1976. Pres., Soc. of Archivists, 1974-77. FRHistS 1969. *Publications:* Guide to the Contents of the Public Record Office, Vol. II (major contributor), 1963; articles in archival and other professional jls. *Recreations:* theatre, countryside. *Address:* 36 North Road, Berkhamsted, Herts. *T:* Berkhamsted 4291. *Club:* Royal Commonwealth Society.

EDEL, (Joseph) Leon; Citizens Professor of English, University of Hawaii, since 1970; *b* 9 Sept. 1907; *e s* of Simon Edel and Fanny (*née* Malamud), Pittsburgh, Pa; *m* 1950, Roberta J. Roberts (separated 1974); no *c*. *Educ:* McGill Univ., Montreal (BA 1927, MA 1928); Univ. of Paris (Docteur-ès-Lettres 1932). Served with US Army in France and Germany, 1943-47: Bronze Star Medal (US), 1945; Chief of Information Control, News Agency, US Zone, 1946-47. Asst Prof., Sir George Williams Coll., Montreal, 1932-34; miscellaneous writing and journalism, 1934-43; Christian Gauss Seminar in Criticism, Princeton Univ., 1951-52; New York University: Vis. Prof., 1952-53; Associate Prof., 1953-55; Prof. of English, 1955-66; Henry James Prof. of English and American Letters, 1966-72. Guggenheim Fellow, 1936-38, 1965-66; Alexander Lectures, Toronto, 1956; Vis. Professor: Indiana, 1954; Hawaii, 1955, 1969, 1970; Harvard, 1959-60; Purdue, 1970; Centenary Vis. Prof., Toronto, 1967. Pres., US Center of PEN, 1957-59. Fellow, Amer. Acad. of Arts and Sciences, 1959; Bollingen Fellow, 1959-61. Member: Nat. Inst. of Arts and Letters, 1964- (Sec., 1965-67); Amer. Acad. of Arts and Letters, 1972; Council, Authors' Guild, 1965-68 (Pres., 1969-70). FRSL 1970. Hon. Member: W. A. White Psychiatric Inst., 1966; Amer. Acad. Psychoanalysis, 1975. Hon. DLitt: McGill, 1963; Union Coll., Schenectady, 1963. Nat. Inst. of Arts and Letters Award, 1959; US Nat. Book Award for non-fiction, 1963; Pulitzer Prize for biography, 1963; AAAL Gold Medal for biography, 1976. *Publications:* James Joyce: The Last Journey, 1947; (ed) The Complete Plays of Henry James, 1949; (with E. K. Brown) Willa Cather, 1953; The Life of Henry James: The Untried Years, 1953, The Conquest of London, 1962, The Middle Years, 1963, The Treacherous Years, 1969, The Master, 1972; The Psychological Novel, 1955; (ed) Selected Letters of Henry James, 1956; Literary Biography, 1957; (ed) The Complete Tales of Henry James, 12 vols, 1962-65; (ed) The Diary of Alice James, 1964; (ed) Literary History and Literary Criticism, 1965; Thoreau, 1970; (ed) Henry James: Stories of the Supernatural, 1971; (ed) Harold Goddard Alphabet of the Imagination, 1975; (ed) Henry James Letters: vols I and II, 1843-1875, 1975; (ed) Edmund Wilson: The Twenties, 1975.

Recreations: music, swimming. *Address:* Department of English, University of Hawaii, 1733 Donaghho Road, Honolulu, Hawaii 96822, USA. *T:* 948-8805. *Clubs:* Athenæum; Century, Outrigger Canoe (Honolulu).

EDELL, Stephen Bristow; Law Commissioner since 1975; *b* 1 Dec. 1932; *s* of late Ivan James Edell and late Hilda Pamela Edell; *m* 1958, Shirley Ross Collins; two *s* one d. *Educ:* St Andrew's Sch., Eastbourne; Uppingham. LLB London. Legal Mem., RTPI. Commnd RA, 1951. Articled to father, 1953; qual. Solicitor 1958; Partner, Knapp-Fishers (Westminster), 1959-75. *Publications:* Inside Information on the Family and the Law, 1969; The Family's Guide to the Law, 1974. *Recreations:* family life; music, opera, theatre; early astronomical instruments; avoiding gardening; interested in problems of developing countries. *Address:* The Old Farmhouse, Twineham, Haywards Heath, Sussex. *T:* Hurstpierpoint 832058.

EDELMAN, Prof. Gerald Maurice, MD, PhD; Vincent Astor Distinguished Professor of Biochemistry, The Rockefeller University, New York, since 1974; *b* NYC, 1 July 1929; *s* of Edward Edelman and Anna Freedman; *m* 1950, Maxine Morrison; two *s* one d. *Educ:* Ursinus Coll. (BS); University of Pennsylvania (MD); The Rockefeller University (PhD). Med. Hse Officer, Massachusetts Gen. Hosp., 1954-55; Asst Physician, Hosp. of The Rockefeller Univ., 1957-60; The Rockefeller University: Asst Prof. and Asst Dean of Grad. Studies, 1960-63; Associate Prof. and Associate Dean of Grad. Studies, 1963-66; Prof., 1966-74. Trustee, Rockefeller Brothers Fund, 1972-. Associate, Neurosciences Res. Program, 1965-. Chairman: Adv. Bd, Basel Inst. Immunology, 1970-; Bd Governors, Weizmann Inst. of Science, 1971-; non-resident Fellow and Mem. Bd Trustees, Salk Inst. for Biol. Studies; Member: Bd Overseers, Faculty Arts and Scis, Univ. of Pa; Bd Scientific Overseers, Jackson Lab.; Adv. Cttee, Carnegie Inst. of Washington. Member: Nat. Acad. Scis.; Amer. Acad. Arts Scis; Amer. Philosophical Soc., 1977; Fellow, NY Acad. Scis; Member: Amer. Soc. Biol Chemists; Amer. Assoc. Immunologists; Genetics Soc. of America; Harvey Soc. (Pres., 1975-76); Amer. Chem. Soc.; Amer. Soc. Cell Biol.; Soc. for Developmental Biol.; Sigma XI; Alpha Omega Alpha; Hon. Mem. Japanese Biochem. Soc. Spencer Morris Award, Univ. of Pennsylvania, 1954; Eli Lilly Award in Biol Chem., Amer. Chem. Soc., 1965; Annual Alumni Award, Ursinus College, 1969; (jtly) Nobel Prize in Physiology or Medicine, 1972; Albert Einstein Commemorative Award, Yeshiva Univ., 1974; Buchman Meml Award, Caltech, 1975; Rabbi Shai Shacknai Meml Prize in Immunology and Cancer Res., Hebrew Univ. Hadassah Med. Sch., 1977. Hon. DSc: Pennsylvania, 1973; Gustavus Adolphus Coll., Minn., 1975; Hon. ScD: Ursinus Coll., 1974; Williams Coll., 1976; Hon. MD Univ. Siena, Italy, 1974. *Recreation:* music. *Address:* Department of Biochemistry, The Rockefeller University, 66th Street, New York, NY 10021, USA; 35 East 85th Street, New York, NY 10028, USA.

EDEN, family name of **Earl of Avon** and of **Barons Auckland** and **Henley.**

EDEN, Conrad W., TD; DMus Lambeth 1973; BMus Oxon; Hon. FRCO; retired 1974; *m* 1943, Barbara L., *d* of late Rev. R. L. Jones, Shepton Mallet. *Educ:* Wells Cath. Sch.; Rugby; RCM; St John's Coll., Oxford. Organist, Wells Cathedral, 1933-36; Durham Cathedral, 1936-74. *Address:* The Vale, Highmore Road, Sherborne, Dorset. *T:* Sherborne 3488.

EDEN, Edward Norman; Under Secretary, Metrology, Quality Assurance and Standards Division, Department of Prices and Consumer Protection (formerly Department of Trade and Industry), since 1971; *b* 5 Nov. 1921; *o s* of late Edward Eden and late Eva Eunice Eden; *m* 1st, 1967, Madge Nina Savory (*d* 1969); 2nd, 1974, Norma Veronica Berringer. *Educ:* Bancroft's Sch.; University Coll. London (BSc(Eng), PhD). Served RN, 1941-46. Senior Scientific Officer, Min. of Fuel and Power, 1953, Senior Principal Scientific Officer 1965, DCSO 1967-71; Head, Fuel Policy Planning Unit, Min. of Technology, later DTI, 1969-71. *Publications:* articles in learned jls. *Recreations:* walking, bird watching, odd-jobbing. *Address:* 13 Allison Grove, Dulwich, SE21 7ER. *T:* 01-693 7267.

EDEN, Rt. Hon. Sir John (Benedict), 9th Bt *cr* 1672 and 7th Bt *cr* 1776; PC 1972; MP (C) Bournemouth West since Feb. 1954; Director: Chesham Amalgamations & Investments; Central & Sheerwood Ltd; Associated Book Publishers Ltd; Lady Eden's Schools Ltd; *b* 15 Sept. 1925; *s* of Sir Timothy Calvert Eden, 8th and 6th Bt and Patricia, *d* of Arthur Prendergast; *S* father, 1963; *m* 1st, 1958, Belinda Jane (marr. diss. 1974), *o d* of late Sir John Pascoe; two *s* two d; 2nd, 1977, Margaret Ann, Viscountess Strathallen. Lieut Rifle Bde, seconded to 2nd KEO Goorkha

Rifles and Gilgit Scouts, 1943-47. Contested (C) Paddington North, 1953. Mem. House of Commons Select Cttee on Estimates, 1962-64; Vice-Chm., Conservative Parly Defence Cttee, 1963-66; Chm., Defence Air Sub-Cttee; Hon. Sec., Space Sub-Cttee; Vice-Chm., Aviation Cttee, 1963-64; Additional Opposition Front Bench Spokesman for Defence, 1964-66; Jt Vice-Chm., Cons. Parly Trade and Power Cttee, 1966-68; Opposition Front Bench Spokesman for Power, 1968-70; Minister of State, Min. of Technology, June-Oct. 1970; Minister for Industry, DTI, 1970-72; Minister of Posts and Telecommunications, 1972-74; Mem., Expenditure Cttee, 1974-76; Chm., House of Commons Select Cttee on European legislation etc, 1976-. Vice-Chm., Assoc. of Conservative Clubs Ltd, 1964-67, Vice-Pres., 1970-; Pres., Wessex Area Council, Nat. Union of Conservative and Unionist Assocs, 1974-77. UK Deleg. to Council of Europe and to Western European Union, 1960-62; Mem., NATO Parliamentarians' Conf., 1962-66. Pres., Independent Schs Assoc., 1969-71; a Vice-Pres., Nat. Chamber of Trade, 1974-. *Heir: s* Robert Frederick Calvert Eden, *b* 30 April 1964. *Address:* 29 Eldon Road, W8; Knoyle Place, East Knoyle, Salisbury, Wilts. *Clubs:* Boodle's, Pratt's.

EDEN, Dr Richard John; Reader in Theoretical Physics, since 1964, and Head of Energy Research Group, since 1974, Cavendish Laboratory, University of Cambridge; Fellow of Clare Hall, Cambridge, since 1966; *b* 2 July 1922; *s* of James A. Eden and Dora M. Eden; *m* 1949, Elsie Jane Greaves; one *s* one *d* and one step *d*. *Educ:* Hertford Grammar Sch.; Peterhouse, Cambridge. BA 1943, MA 1948, PhD 1951. War service, 1942-46, Captain REME, Airborne Forces. Cambridge Univ.: Bye-Fellow, Peterhouse, 1949-50; Stokes Student, Pembroke Coll., 1950-51; Clare Coll.: Research Fellow, 1951-55; Official Fellow, 1957-66; Dir of Studies in Maths, 1951-53, 1957-62; Royal Soc. Smithson Res. Fellow, 1952-55; Mem., Princeton Inst. for Advanced Study, 1954, 1959, 1973; Sen. Lectr in Physics, Univ. of Manchester, 1955-57; Lectr in Maths, Univ. of Cambridge, 1957-64 (Stokes Lectr, 1962); Head of High Energy Theoretical Physics Gp, Cavendish Lab., Cambridge, 1964-74; Vis. Scientist: Indiana Univ., 1954-55; Univ. of California, Berkeley, 1960, 1967; Vis. Professor: Univ. of Maryland, 1961, 1965; Columbia Univ., 1962; Scuola Normale Superiore, Pisa, 1964; Univ. of Marseilles, 1968; Univ. of California, 1969. Mem., UK Adv. Council on Energy Conservation, 1974-; Energy Adviser to UK NEDO, 1974-. Smiths Prize, Univ. of Cambridge, 1949; Maxwell Prize and Medal, Inst. of Physics, 1970. *Publications:* (jtly) The Analytic S Matrix, 1966; High Energy Collisions of Elementary Particles, 1967; Energy Conservation in the United Kingdom (NEDO report), 1975; papers and review articles on nuclear physics and theory of elementary particles. *Recreations:* painting, reading, gardening, travel. *Address:* Cavendish Laboratory, Cambridge. *T:* Cambridge 66477; 6 Wootton Way, Cambridge. *T:* Cambridge 55591.

EDES, (John) Michael; HM Diplomatic Service; on sabbatical at the Royal Institute of International Affairs; *b* 19 April 1930; *s* of late Lt-Col N. H. Edes and Mrs Louise Edes, *d* of late B. B. Blakeney, Oklahoma City, USA. *Educ:* Blundell's Sch.; Clare Coll., Cambridge (Scholar; BA); Yale Univ. (MA). HM Forces, 1948-49; Mellon Fellow, Yale Univ., 1952-54; 3rd Sec., FO, 1954; Middle East Centre for Arabic Studies, Lebanon, 1955; 2nd Sec. and Asst Political Agent, Dubai, 1956-57; FO, 1957-59 (Moscow, 1959); 2nd Sec. and Private Sec. to HM Ambassador, Rome, 1959-61, also Hon. Sec. to Governors of British Inst., Florence; FO, 1961-62; 1st Sec., UK Delegn to Conf. on Disarmament, Geneva, 1962-65 (UK Mission to UN, NY, 1963); FO, 1965-68; on secondment to Cabinet Office, 1968-69; Asst Head Arabian Dept, FCO, 1969-71; Counsellor, 1971; Ambassador to the Yemen Arab Republic, 1971-73; Mem., UK Delegn to Conf. on Security and Co-operation in Europe, Geneva, 1973-74; Head, Permanent Under-Secretary's Dept, FCO, 1974-77. Cavaliere Italian Order of Merit, 1961. *Recreations:* listening to music, gardening. *Address:* c/o Foreign and Commonwealth Office, SW1. *Clubs:* Athenæum; Hawks (Cambridge).

EDEY, Prof. Harold Cecil, BCom (London), FCA; Professor of Accounting, London School of Economics, University of London, since 1962; *b* 23 Feb. 1913; *s* of Cecil Edey and Elsie (*née* Walmsley); *m* 1944, Dilys Mary Pakeman Jones; one *s* one *d*. *Educ:* Croydon High Sch. for Boys; LSE. Chartered Accountant, 1935. Commnd in RNVR, 1940-46. Lectr in Accounting and Finance, LSE, 1949-55; Reader in Accounting, Univ. of London, 1955-62; Pro-Dir, LSE, 1967-70. Mem., UK Adv. Coun. on Educn for Management, 1961-65; Mem., Academic Planning Bd for London Grad. Sch. of Business Studies, and Governor, 1965-71; Chm., Arts and Social Studies Cttee, CNAA, 1965-71, and Mem. Council, 1965-73; Chm., Bd of Studies in Econs, 1966-71, Mem. Senate, 1975-, University of

London; Mem. Council, Inst. of Chartered Accountants in England and Wales, 1969-. Hon. LLD CNAA, 1972. *Publications:* (with A. T. Peacock) National Income and Social Accounting, 1954; Business Budgets and Accounts, 1959; Introduction to Accounting, 1963; (with B. S. Yamey and H. Thomson) Accounting in England and Scotland 1543-1800, 1963; (with B. V. Carsberg) Modern Financial Management, 1969; (with B. S. Yamey) Debits, Credits, Finance and Profits, 1974; articles in various jls. *Address:* 9 Thanescroft Gardens, Croydon CRO 5JR.

EDGAR, Gilbert Harold Samuel, CBE 1960; Chairman: H. Samuel Group of Companies, since 1935; Priory Gate Estates Ltd, since 1946; Underwriting Member of Lloyd's; *b* 1 Jan. 1898; *er s* of Edgar Samuel Edgar, Liverpool; *m* 1st, 1923, Eileen Victoria (*d* 1970), *yr d* of Sir Stuart Samuel, 1st Bt, MP for Tower Hamlets Div., 1900-18; one *d* (and one *d* decd); 2nd, 1971, Jessica Estelle Moritz. *Educ:* Charterhouse. Served European War, 1916, Lieut RHA (wounded); War of 1939-45, Sqdn Ldr, RAAF (Actg Wing Comdr). Mem. Coun., Royal Eye Hosp., 1934-60; assisted in foundn of Chair of Ophthalmology, RCS and Royal Eye Hosp., 1943; Governor, King's Coll. Hosp. Gp, 1951-61; on Bldg Cttee, RCOG, 1959-62; Founder, Edgar-Gentilli Memorial Schol. and Prize connected with Cancer Research. Contested (C) Smethwick, Gen. Elec. and By Elec., 1945; Chm. Wycombe Div. Conservative Assoc., 1955-60. CC, 1952-74, CA, 1964, Bucks. Lay Sheriff of City of London, 1963-64. Thames Conservancy, 1965-74. Trustee, Charterhouse Tercentenary Fund, 1948-63; Governor, Thomas Sutton's Hosp. in Charterhouse; Master, Worshipful Co. of Clockmakers, 1967-68. Hon. Fellow, RCOG, 1964. *Recreations:* farming, golf, shooting, fishing. *Address:* E 5, Albany, W1. *T:* 01-734 7836; Burrow Farm, Hambleden, Henley-on-Thames, Oxon RG9 6LT. *T:* Hambleden (Bucks) 256. *Clubs:* Bath, United and Cecil, City Livery; Huntercombe Golf (Oxon).

EDGAR, Lieut-Gen. Hector Geoffrey, CB 1960; CBE 1955; General Officer Commanding Eastern Command, Australian Military Forces, 1960-63; *b* 31 Oct. 1903; *s* of Thomas George Edgar, Wedderburn, Vic., Australia; *m* 1929, Margaret A. (*d* 1972), *d* of Charles Cooper; two *s* one *d*. *Educ:* Albert Park Grammar Sch.; RMC Duntroon, Canberra; idc; psc; pac. Training in India, 1925-26; Military Coll. of Science, Woolwich, 1933-36. Served with Third Australian Div., New Guinea and Bougainville; Chief Instructor, Senior Wing, Australian Staff Coll., 1945; Inspector-Gen., Munitions, 1946-47; Dep. Dir, Staff Duties, Army HQ, 1948-49; IDC, 1950; Comdt, Australian Staff Coll., 1951-53; Dir of Staff Duties, 1954; Dep. Chief of Gen. Staff, and Mem., Military Board, Army Headquarters, 1954-58; GOC Southern Command, 1958-60. First Superintendent, Rocket Range, Woomera, South Australia, 1949. *Address:* 21 Glen Road, Toorak, Victoria 3142, Australia.

EDGCUMBE, family name of **Earl of Mount Edgcumbe.**

EDGE, Geoffrey; MP (Lab) Aldridge-Brownhills since Feb. 1974; *b* 26 May 1943; single. *Educ:* London Sch. of Econs (BA); Birmingham Univ. Asst Lectr in Geography, Univ. of Leicester, 1967-70; Lectr in Geog., Open Univ., 1970-74. Bletchley UDC, 1972-74 (Chm. Planning Sub-cttee 1973-74); Milton Keynes District Councillor, 1973-76 (Vice-Chm. Planning Cttee, 1973-75); Mem. Bucks Water Bd, 1973-74. PPS to Minister of State for Educn, Feb.-Oct. 1974, 1976-, to Minister of State, Privy Council Office, Oct. 1974-76. *Publications:* (ed jtly) Regional Analysis and Development, 1973; Open Univ. booklets on industrial location and urban development. *Recreations:* music, reading, touring. *Address:* 32 Warren Bank, Simpson, Milton Keynes, Bucks; 31 Dudley Road West, Tividale, Warley, Worcs. *T:* 021-557 3858. *Clubs:* Castle, Walsall Wood Labour (Walsall).

EDGE, Sir Knowles, 2nd Bt *cr* 1937; JP; *b* 31 Dec. 1905; *s* of Capt. Sir William Edge, 1st Bt, and Ada (*d* 1973), *d* of I. Ickringill, Keighley; *S* father, 1948; *m* 1932, Dorothea Eunice (*d* 1976) *y d* of Robert Walker, Newhaven, Conn, USA; two *s*. *Educ:* Bolton Sch.; Trinity Hall, Cambridge. Formerly Chm. and Man. Dir William Edge & Sons Ltd and assoc. cos. Contested Hillsborough Div. of Sheffield, 1950. Mem. of Bolton Town Council, 1931-58. Chm., British Federation of Music Festivals, 1951-76. Mem. Cttee of Management, Royal National Lifeboat Institution. JP Lancs 1955. *Recreation:* yacht cruising. *Heir: s* William Edge [*b* 5 Oct. 1936; *m* 1959, Avril Elizabeth Denson; two *s* two *d*]. *Address:* 1 Seafield Road, Lytham, Lancs. *Club:* Athenæum.

EDGE, Maj.-Gen. Raymond Cyril Alexander, CB 1968; MBE 1945; FRICS 1949; Director General, Ordnance Survey, 1965-69, retired; *b* 21 July 1912; *s* of Raymond Clive Edge and Mary (*née* Masters); *m* 1939, Margaret Patricia, *d* of William Wallace

McKee, Tyrone, N Ireland; one *s* one *d*. *Educ:* Cheltenham Coll.; RMA; Caius Coll., Cambridge (BA). Commissioned in RE, 1932. Served in India, Royal Bombay Sappers and Miners and Survey of India, 1936-39. War Service in India, Burma (despatches), and Malaya. Lt-Col 1951; Col 1954; Dir (Brig.) Ordnance Survey, 1961; Maj.-Gen. 1965. Col Comdt, RE, 1970-75 (Representative Col Comdt, 1974). Mem., Sec. of State for the Environment's Panel of Independent Inspectors, 1971-. Chairman: Assoc. British Geodesists, 1963-65; Geodesy Sub-Ctte Royal Soc., 1968-75; Field Survey Assoc., 1968-70. Pres., Section E, British Assoc., 1969. Member: Council, RGS, 1966-69; Council, RICS, 1966-72 (Vice-Pres. 1970-72); Land Surveyors Council (Chm. 1970-72). *Publications:* various papers on geodetic subjects in Bulletin Géodesique and other publications. *Recreations:* sailing, music. *Address:* Greenway House, North Curry, near Taunton, Som. *T:* North Curry 358. *Club:* Army and Navy.

EDGEWORTH-JOHNSTONE, Maj.-Gen. Ralph, CBE 1947; *b* 23 Nov. 1893; *s* of Ralph William Johnstone; *m* 1933, Cecily Margaret Thorp. *Educ:* France and Germany. Enlisted Fort Garry Horse, 1914; served European war, 1914-18 (wounded twice); commissioned Royal North'd Fusiliers, 1915. Retired, 1938, to join Public Relations Directorate War Office; Asst Dir, Lieut-Col, 1940; Dep. Dir, Brig., 1944; Dir, Maj.-Gen., 1946-52. *Address:* c/o Lloyds Bank, 6 Pall Mall, SW1.

EDGEWORTH JOHNSTONE, Prof. Robert; see Johnstone.

EDIE, Thomas Ker; His Honour Judge Edie; a Circuit Judge, South Eastern Circuit, since 1972; *b* 3 Oct. 1916; *s* of H. S. Ker Edie, Kinloss, Morayshire; *m* 1945, Margaret, *d* of Rev. A. E. Shooter, TD; four *s* one *d*. *Educ:* Clifton; London Univ. Called to Bar, Gray's Inn, 1941. Metropolitan Magistrate, 1961-70; Dep. Chm. Middlesex QS, 1970-71. *Address:* Worfield Lodge, Pennington Road, Southborough, Kent.

EDINBURGH, Bishop of, since 1975; **Most Rev. Alastair Iain Macdonald Haggart;** Primus of the Episcopal Church in Scotland, since 1977; *b* 10 Oct. 1915; *s* of Alexander Macdonald Haggart and Jessie Mackay; *m* 1945, Margaret Agnes Trundle; two *d*. *Educ:* Hatfield Coll. (Exhibr); Durham Univ. (Exhibnr); Edinburgh Theol College. LTh 1941; BA 1942; MA 1945. Deacon, 1941, Priest 1942. Curate: St Mary's Cath., Glasgow, 1941-45; St Mary's, Hendon, 1945-48; Precentor, St Ninian's Cath., Perth, 1948-51; Rector, St Oswald's, King's Park, Glasgow, 1951, and Acting Priest-in-Charge, St Martin's, Glasgow, 1953-58; Synod Clerk of Glasgow Dio. and Canon of St Mary's Cath., Glasgow, 1958-59; Provost, St Paul's Cathedral, Dundee, 1959-71; Principal and Pantonian Prof., Episcopal Theological Coll., Edinburgh, 1971-75; Canon, St Mary's Cathedral, Edinburgh, 1971-75. Exam. Chap. to Bp of Brechin, 1964. Hon LLD Dundee, 1970. *Recreations:* walking, reading, listening to music, asking questions. *Address:* 19 Eglinton Crescent, Edinburgh EH12 5BY.

EDINBURGH, Dean of; see Brady, Very Rev. E. W.

EDINBURGH, Provost of (St Mary's Cathedral); see Crosfield, Very Rev. G. P. C.

EDMENSON, Sir Walter Alexander, Kt 1958; CBE 1944; DL; shipowner; *b* 1892; 2nd *s* of late Robert Robson Edmenson; *m* 1918, Doris Davidson (*d* 1975); one *d* (and one *s* killed in action, 1940). Served European War, 1914-18, RFA (despatches). Min. of War Transport Rep., N Ireland, 1939-45. President: The Ulster Steamship Co. Ltd; G. Heyn & Sons Ltd; Director: The Belfast Banking Co. Ltd, 1946-70; The North Continental Shipping Co. Ltd, 1946-70; The Belfast Bank Executor & Trustee Co. Ltd, 1946-70; Commercial Insurance Co. of Ireland Ltd, 1964-72; Member Board: BEA, 1946-63; Gallaher Ltd, 1946-66. Chm., N Ireland Civil Aviation Adv. Council, 1946-61; Member: Bd, Ulster Transport Authority, 1948-64; Council, Chamber of Shipping, 1943-73; Lloyd's Register of Shipping, 1949-74; Belfast Harbour Comr, 1940-61; Irish Lights Comr. DL Belfast, 1951. Amer. Medal of Freedom with Palms, 1945. *Address:* 101 Bryansford Road, Newcastle, Co. Down. *Clubs:* Brooks's; Ulster (Belfast); Kildare Street and University (Dublin).

EDMONDS, Cecil John, CMG 1941; CBE 1930 (OBE 1925); *b* 26 Oct. 1889; *y s* of late Rev. Walter and Laura Edmonds; *m* 1935, Alison, *o c* of late George Hooper, Birmingham; one *s* two *d*; *m* 1947, Phyllis, 2nd *d* of late F. L. Stephenson, Skegness; one *s*. *Educ:* Bedford Sch.; Christ's Hosp.; Pembroke Coll., Cambridge. Student Interpreter in HM Levant Consular Service, 1910; acting Vice-Consul, Bushire, 1913; Asst Political Officer, Mesopotamia, 1915 (Temp. Captain), SW Persia, 1917;

Political Officer, British Forces, NW Persia, 1919 (Temp. Major, Special List); Special Duty in S Kurdistan, 1922; Divisional Adviser and Administrative Inspector in the Kirkuk and Sulaimani provinces under Iraq Govt, 1922; Political Officer with military columns in Kurdistan, 1924; Liaison Officer with League of Nations Commission of Inquiry into frontier between Iraq and Turkey, 1925; Asst Adviser, Min. of Interior, Iraq, 1926; Consul, 1928; British Assessor, League of Nations Commn of Inquiry into the frontier between Iraq and Syria, 1932; Mem. of Demarcation Commn of Iraqi-Syrian Frontier, 1933; Adviser, Min. for Foreign Affairs, Iraq, 1933; Mem. of Iraqi Delegation to League of Nations, annually 1932-38; Adviser to the Ministry of the Interior, Iraq, 1935-45; Consul-Gen., 1937. Order of the Rafidain (Cl. II), 1945; UK Perm. Deleg. to Internat. Refugee Organisation, 1947; Minister in HM Foreign Service, 1948; retired, 1950. Lecturer in Kurdish, Sch. of Oriental and African Studies, University of London, 1951-57. Burton Memorial Medal, 1963; Sykes Memorial Medal, 1966. *Publications:* Kurds, Turks and Arabs, 1957; (jt) A Kurdish-English Dictionary, 1966; A Pilgrimage to Lalish, 1967; contributions on Persian, Arabian and Kurdish subjects. *Recreation:* gardening. *Address:* 5 Longslip, Langton Green, near Tunbridge Wells, Kent TN3 0BT. *T:* Langton 2771. *Club:* Athenæum.

EDMONDS, Charles; see Carrington, C. E.

EDMONDS, Edward Reginald, CMG 1954; *b* 25 Nov. 1901; *y s* of late G. F. Edmonds; *m* 1928, Edna May Dennis (*d* 1955); one *s* one *d*; *m* 1956, Dorothy Edith (*d* 1970) (she *m* 1st, 1923, Ewart G. Sheaves; he *d* 1925), *er d* of late Benjamin George Bishop, Woodford Green, Essex. *Educ:* King's Coll., London Univ. (BA). Entered Colonial Office, 1917; Asst Principal, 1938; Principal, 1941; Asst Sec., 1947; retired, 1961. Served in Uganda, 1926-28. *Address:* Prested Hall, Kelvedon, Essex. *T:* Kelvedon 70156.

EDMONDS, John Christopher, CVO 1971; HM Diplomatic Service; Special Adviser on Disarmament, Foreign and Commonwealth Office, since 1977; *b* 23 June 1921; *s* of late Captain A. C. M. Edmonds, OBE, RN, and late Mrs. Edmonds; *m* 1st, 1948, Elena Tornow (marr. diss., 1965); two *s*; 2nd, 1966, Armine Williams. *Educ:* Kelly College. Entered Royal Navy, 1939; psc, 1946. Staff: of NATO Defence Coll., Paris, 1953-55; of C-in-C Home Fleet, 1956-57 (Comdr, 1957); of Chief of Defence Staff, 1958-59. Entered Diplomatic Service, 1959; Foreign Office, 1959-60; 1st Secretary (Commercial), Tokyo, 1960-62; FO, 1963-67; 1st Secretary and Head of Chancery, Ankara, 1967-68; Counsellor: Ankara, 1968-71; Paris, 1972-74; Head of Arms Control and Disarmament Dept, FCO, 1974-77. *Recreations:* golf, gardening, travel. *Address:* c/o Foreign and Commonwealth Office, SW1; North Lodge, Sonning, Berks. *Club:* Army and Navy.

EDMONDS, Robert Humphrey Gordon, CMG 1969; MBE 1944; HM Diplomatic Service; Visiting Fellow, Woodrow Wilson International Centre for Scholars, Washington, 1977; *b* 5 Oct. 1920; *s* of late Air Vice-Marshal C. H. K. Edmonds, CBE, DSO; *m* 1st, 1951, Georgina Combe (marr. diss. 1975); four *s*; 2nd, 1976, Mrs Enid Balint, widow of Dr Michael Balint. *Educ:* Ampleforth; Brasenose Coll., Oxford. Pres., Oxford Union, 1940. Served Army, 1940-46; Intelligence Officer, Western Desert, N African and Italian Campaigns; attached to Political Div., Allied Commn for Austria, 1945-46. Entered Foreign Service, Dec. 1946; served Cairo, 1947; FO, 1949; Rome, 1953; Warsaw, 1957; FO, 1959 (promoted Counsellor, 1962); Caracas, 1962; Head of American Dept, FO, 1966-67; Head of Mediterranean Dept, CO, 1967-68; Head of Southern European Dept, FCO, 1968-69; Minister, Moscow, 1969-71; High Comr, Nicosia, 1971-72; Vis. Fellow, Glasgow Univ., 1973-74; Asst Under Sec. of State, FCO, 1974-77. *Publication:* Soviet Foreign Policy 1962-1973: the paradox of super-power, 1975. *Recreations:* swimming, travel. *Address:* The Apple House, Cardross Stables, Port of Menteith, Stirling FK8 3JY. *Club:* Turf.

EDMONDS, Sheila May, MA, PhD; Fellow and Vice-Principal of Newnham College, Cambridge (Fellow since 1945, Vice-Principal since 1960); Lecturer in Mathematics, Newnham College, since 1945; *b* 1 April 1916; *d* of Harold Montagu Edmonds and Florence Myra Edmonds. *Educ:* Wimbledon High Sch.; Newnham Coll., Cambridge. Research Student of Westfield Coll., 1939-40, and of Newnham Coll., 1940-41; Research Fellow of Newnham Coll., 1941-43; Asst Lecturer, Newnham Coll., 1943-45. *Publications:* papers in mathematical journals. *Address:* Newnham College, Cambridge. *T:* Cambridge 62273.

EDMONDS, Winston Godward, CBE 1966; ERD 1945; Managing Director, Manchester Ship Canal Co., 1961-70; *b* 27 Nov. 1912; *s* of Wilfred Bell Edmonds and Nina (*née* Godward); *m* 1940, Sheila Mary (*née* Armitage); one *s. Educ:* Merchant Taylors'. Joined LNER, first as traffic apprentice and then in various positions, 1930-46; Manchester Ship Canal Co.: Commercial Manager, 1947-58; Manager, 1959-61. *Recreations:* golf, philately. *Address:* Myrtle Cottage, 1 Clark Lane, West Bollington, Macclesfield, Cheshire SK10 5AH. *T:* Bollington 72345. *Club:* St James's (Manchester).

EDMONDSON, family name of **Baron Sandford.**

EDMONDSON, Anthony Arnold; His Honour Judge Edmondson; a Circuit Judge (formerly County Court Judge and Commissioner, Liverpool and Manchester Crown Courts), since 1971; *b* 6 July 1920; *s* of late Arnold Edmondson; *m* 1947, Dorothy Amelia Wilson, Gateshead-on-Tyne; three *s* one *d. Educ:* Liverpool Univ. (LLB Hons); Lincoln Coll., Oxford (BCL Hons). Served RA (Adjutant), 1940-44; RAF (Pilot), 1944-46; thereafter RA (TA) and TARO. Called to the Bar, Gray's Inn, 1947; William Shaw Schol. 1948; practised on Northern Circuit, 1948-71; Chairman, Liverpool Dock Labour Bd Appeal Tribunal, 1955-66; Mem. Court of Liverpool Univ., 1960-. Dep. Chm., Lancashire QS, 1970-71; JP Lancs, 1970. *Recreations:* walking, fishing. *Address:* County Sessions House, Preston, Lancs.

EDMONDSON, Leonard Firby; Executive Council Member, Amalgamated Union of Engineering Workers, since 1966; Member of General Council, Trades Union Congress, since 1970; *b* 16 Dec. 1912; *s* of Arthur William Edmondson and Elizabeth Edmonson; unmarried. *Educ:* Gateshead Central Sch. Served apprenticeship as engr, Liner Concrete Machinery Co. Ltd, Newcastle upon Tyne, 1929-34; worked in a number of engrg, ship-bldg and ship-repairing firms; shop steward and convener of shop stewards in several firms. AUEW: Mem., Tyne Dist Cttee, 1943-53; Tyne Dist Sec., 1953-66. CSEU: Mem., Exec. Council, 1966; Pres., 1976-77. Member: Shipbldg Industry Trng Bd, 1966-; Adv., Conciliation and Arbitration Service Council, 1976-; Royal Commn on Legal Services, 1976-. Mem., Birtley Canine Soc. *Recreation:* exhibiting Shetland sheep dogs. *Address:* 6 Kenwood Gardens, Low Fell, Gateshead, Tyne and Wear NE9 6PN. *T:* Low Fell 879167. *Clubs:* English Shetland Sheep Dog; Northern Counties Shetland Sheep Dog; Manors Social.

EDMONSTONE, Sir Archibald (Bruce Charles), 7th Bt *cr* 1774; *b* 3 Aug. 1934; *o* surv. *s* of Sir Charles Edmonstone, 6th Bt, and Gwendolyn Mary, *d* of late Marshall Field and Mrs Maldwin Drummond; *S* father, 1954; *m* 1st, 1957, Jane (marr. diss. 1967), *er d* of Maj.-Gen. E. C. Colville, *qv*; two *s* one *d* ; 2nd, 1969, Juliet Elizabeth, *d* of Maj.-Gen. C. M. F. Deakin, *qv*; one *s* one *d. Educ:* St Peter's Court; Stowe Sch. *Heir: s* Archibald Edward Charles Edmonstone, *b* 4 Feb. 1961. *Address:* Duntreath Castle, Blanefield, Stirlingshire.
See also Sir A. R. J. B. Jardine, Captain Sir C. E. McGrigor.

EDMONTON (Alberta), Bishop of, since 1976; **Rt. Rev. John Arthur William Langstone;** *b* 30 Aug. 1913; *s* of Arthur James Langstone and Coullina Cook; *m* 1944, Alice Patricia Whitby; two *s. Educ:* Univ. of Toronto (BA); Trinity Coll., Toronto (LTh); Yale Univ. (MDiv). Asst Curate, St John Baptist, Toronto, 1938; Chaplain, Cdn Army, 1943; Exec. Officer, Dio. Toronto, 1947; Rector: Trinity Church, Port Credit, Toronto, 1950; St George's, Edmonton, 1958; St Faith's, Edmonton, 1969; Canon of All Saints' Cathedral, Edmonton, 1963; Archdeacon of Edmonton, 1965; Exec. Archdeacon, 1971. *Address:* 10033 84 Avenue, Edmonton, Alberta T6E 2G6, Canada. *T:* 439-7344.

EDMONTON, Bishop Suffragan of, since 1975; **Rt. Rev. William John Westwood;** *b* 28 Dec. 1925; *s* of Ernest and Charlotte Westwood; *m* 1954, Shirley Ann, *yr d* of Dr Norman Jennings; one *s* one *d. Educ:* Grove Park Gram. Sch., Wrexham; Emmanuel Coll. and Westcott House, Cambridge. MA Cantab. Soldier, 1944-47. Curate of Hull, 1952-57; Rector of Lowestoft, 1957-65; Vicar of S Peter Mancroft, Norwich, 1965-75; Hon. Canon, Norwich Cathedral, 1969-75; Rural Dean of Norwich, 1966-70, City Dean, 1970-73. Member: General Synod, 1970-75 and 1977-; Archbishop's Commission on Church and State, 1966-70; Press Council, 1975-; Church Commissioner, 1973-; Chm. Governors, Coll. of All Saints, Tottenham, 1976-. Formerly Chm. of three Housing Assocs. *Recreation:* modern poetry. *Address:* 167 Friern Barnet Lane, N20 0NN. *T:* 01-445 3109.

EDMUND-DAVIES, family name of **Baron Edmund-Davies.**

EDMUND-DAVIES, Baron *cr* 1974 (Life Peer), of Aberpennar, Mid Glamorgan; **Herbert Edmund Edmund-Davies,** PC 1966; Kt 1958; a Lord of Appeal in Ordinary, since 1974; Life Governor and Fellow, King's College, London University; Hon. Fellow, Exeter College, Oxford; *b* 15 July 1906; 3rd *s* of Morgan John Davies and Elizabeth Maud Edmunds; *m* 1935, Eurwen Williams-James; three *d. Educ:* Mountain Ash Grammar Sch.; King's Coll., London; Exeter Coll., Oxford. LLB (London) and Postgraduate Research Scholar, 1926; LLD London, 1928; BCL (Oxon) and Vinerian Scholar, 1929; called to Bar, Gray's Inn, 1929; QC 1943; Bencher, 1948; Treasurer, 1965-; Lecturer and Examiner, London School of Economics, 1930-31; Army Officers' Emergency Reserve, 1938; Infantry OCTU; commissioned in Royal Welch Fusiliers, 1940; Lt-Col; later seconded to JAG's Dept; Asst Judge Advocate-General, 1944-45; Recorder of Merthyr Tydfil, 1942-44; of Swansea, 1944-53; of Cardiff, 1953-58; Chm., QS for Denbighshire, 1953-64; Judge of High Court of Justice, Queen's Bench Division, 1958-66; a Lord Justice of Appeal, 1966-74. Foreign Office Observer, Cairo espionage trials, 1957. Chairman: Lord Chancellor's Cttee on Limitation of Actions, 1961; Tribunal of Inquiry into Aberfan Disaster, 1966; Council of Law Reporting 1967-72; Home Secretary's Criminal Law Revision Cttee, 1969-77. President University College of Swansea, 1965-75 (Member Court of Governors, 1948-); Pro-Chancellor, Univ. of Wales, 1974-. Hon. Life Member, Canadian Bar Assoc.; CIBA Foundn Trustee; Hon. Member, Royal Soc. of Medicine. Hon. LLD Wales, 1959. *Publications:* Law of Distress for Rent and Rates, 1931; miscellaneous legal writings. *Address:* House of Lords, SW1; 5 Gray's Inn Square, WC1. *Clubs:* Reform; Cardiff and County (Cardiff); City (Chester); Bristol Channel Yacht.

EDMUNDS, Christopher Montague, MusD; Member Corporation, and Examiner, Trinity College of Music, London, since 1940; *b* 26 Nov. 1899; 2nd *s* of Charles Edmunds; *m* 1923, Kathleen, *d* of Arthur Vaughan-Jones; one *s* one *d. Educ:* King Edward VI Sch., Camp Hill, Birmingham; Birmingham Univ.; Manchester Univ.; Birmingham Sch. of Music. 1st Cl. Hons BMus Birmingham, 1922; MusD, Manchester, 1936. Theory Teacher and Dir of opera class, Birmingham Sch. of Music, 1928-45; Principal, Birmingham Sch. of Music, 1945-56; Fellow Birmingham Sch. of Music; Fellow Trinity Coll. of Music. *Publications:* compositions include: The Blue Harlequin (opera); chamber and orchestral music; vocal and instrumental music; Romance, 1946 (pianoforte and orchestral work, commissioned by BBC). *Recreations:* cruising, gardening. *Address:* 247 Mereside Way North, Solihull, West Midlands B92 7AY. *T:* 021-706 8055.

EDNAM, Viscount; William Humble David Jeremy Ward; *b* 27 March 1947; *s* and *heir* of Earl of Dudley, *qv* and of Stella Viscountess Ednam, *d* of M. A. Carcano, *qv*; *m* 1972, Sarah (marr. diss. 1976), *o d* of Sir Alastair Coats, Bt, *qv*; *m* 1976, Debra Louise Pinney, *d* of George Robert Pinney and Marjorie Elvera Pinney. *Educ:* Eton; Christ Church, Oxford. *Address:* Rowlandson Ground, near Coniston, Cumbria. *T:* Coniston 397.

EDWARD, David Alexander Ogilvy, QC (Scotland) 1974; President, Consultative Committee of the Bars and Law Societies of the European Community; *b* 14 Nov. 1934; *s* of J. O. C. Edward, Perth; *m* 1962, Elizabeth Young McSherry; two *s* two *d. Educ:* Sedbergh Sch.; University Coll., Oxford; Edinburgh Univ. Sub-Lt RNVR (Nat. Service); HMS Hornet, 1956-57. Admitted Advocate, 1962; Clerk of Faculty of Advocates, 1967-70, Treasurer, 1970-77; Trustee, Nat. Library of Scotland, 1966-; Leader, UK Delegn to Consultative Cttee of Bars and Law Societies, 1976-77; Mem. Law Adv. Panel, British Council. *Publications:* The Professional Secret, Confidentiality and Legal Professional Privilege in the EEC; articles in legal jls. *Recreations:* gardening, photography. *Address:* 32 Heriot Row, Edinburgh EH3 6ES; Ardargie Cottage, Forgandenny, Perthshire. *Clubs:* New, Scottish Arts (Edinburgh).

EDWARDES, family name of **Baron Kensington.**

EDWARDES, Michael Owen; Chief Executive, since 1972, and Chairman and Chief Executive since 1974, Chloride Group Ltd; *b* 11 Oct. 1930; *s* of Denys Owen Edwardes and Audrey Noel (*née* Copeland); *m* 1958, Mary Margaret (*née* Finlay); three *d. Educ:* St Andrew's Coll., Grahamstown, S Africa; Rhodes Univ. (BA Law). Man. Dir, Chloride Central Africa, 1963; Dir, Chloride Group Ltd, 1969-. Member: CBI Council, 1974-; Nat. Enterprise Bd, 1975- (and of Organising Cttee, 1975); EDC for Electrical Engrg Industry, 1975-77; Queen's Award Review Cttee, 1975. FBIM 1973 (Mem. Council, 1974; a Vice-Chm., 1976-). Young Businessman of the Year (Guardian), 1975.

Recreations: water ski-ing, sailing, squash, tennis. *Address:* (home) Kromme House, Portland Terrace, The Green, Richmond, Surrey TW9 1QQ; (office) 52 Grosvenor Gardens, SW1W 0AU. *T:* 01-730 0866. *Clubs:* Lansdowne; Rand (Johannesburg).

EDWARDES JONES, Air Marshal (Retd) Sir (John) Humphrey, KCB 1957 (CB 1954); CBE 1943; DFC 1940; AFC 1941; retired 1961; *b* 15 Aug. 1905; *s* of late G. M. Edwardes Jones, KC and G. R. Johnston; *m* 1935, Margaret Rose Graham; one *s* one *d. Educ:* Brighton Coll.; Pembroke Coll., Cambridge. Entered RAF, Sept. 1926; served in Egypt, 4 Flying Training Sch. and 208 Sqdn, 1930-35; Commanded: No 213 Fighter Sqdn, 1937-40; No 56 Op. Trg Unit, 1940; Nos 60 and 58 OTU's, 1941; Exeter Fighter Sector, 1942; No 323 Fighter Wing, Algiers, Nov. 1942; AOC, No 210 Group, Algiers, 1943; idc 1950; Dir of Plans, Air Ministry, 1951. Commandant, Sch. of Land/Air Warfare, RAF, Old Sarum, Wilts, 1955-57; Comdr-in-Chief, 2nd Tactical Air Force, and Comdr, 2nd Allied Tactical Air Force, 1957-61. Legion of Honour (French), 1946. *Recreation:* golf. *Address:* Old Marks, Holtye, Sussex. *T:* Cowden 317. *Club:* Royal Air Force.

EDWARDES-KER, Lt-Col Douglas Rous, OBE; Managing Director, Exe Shellfish Ltd; Principal, Seale Hayne Agricultural College, Newton Abbot, 1919-33; *b* 21 Jan. 1886; *s* of late Dr George Cordy Edwardes-Ker, Woodbridge, Suffolk; *m* 1912, Frances Edith Watts, Rampside, Lancs; two *s. Educ:* Woodbridge Sch.; Brasenose Coll., Oxford (Open Scholar). MA Oxon., 1st Class Hons; BSc London, 1st Class Hons. Coll. Warden and Mem. of Staff of South-Eastern Agricultural Coll., Wye, 1909-14; enlisted in Buffs, Aug. 1914; Commission in Royal Engineers, rising to rank of Lt-Col; Asst Dir of Gas Services, BEF, France (OBE, despatches thrice; two French Croix de Guerre, one avec palme). *Recreations:* lawn tennis, for ten years Mem. of Devon County Team, and Vice-Chm. Devon County LTA; fly-fishing. *Address:* Green Hollow, Exmouth, Devon. *TA:* Exmouth. *T:* 2738. *Club:* Oxford University Alembic.

EDWARDS, family name of **Baron Chelmer.**

EDWARDS, Brig. Arthur Bertie Duncan, CBE 1943; MC; *b* 29 April 1898; *s* of Joseph Arthur Edwards, Portsmouth, and Rosa May Duncan, Isle of Wight; *m* 1925, Clara Elizabeth, 3rd *c* of late Edmund Barkworth, JP, Seaton, Devon; three *s. Educ:* RMA Woolwich. 2nd Lieut RE 1916; Capt. 1926; Major 1935; Lt-Col 1942; Temp. Col 1943, Temp. Brig. 1943; Col 1945; Brig. 1949. Served France, 1917-18 (BWM and VM); India, 1918-19; Iraq, 1919-20 (MC, BGS with Iraq clasp); India, 1920-22; England, 1922-35; Malta, 1935-39; England, 1939-40; France, 1940 (despatches); Greece, 1940-41; Libya, 1941; CRE Eighth Army Troops Engineers, Libya and Egypt, 1941-42 (despatches twice, OBE, North African Star); Dep. Chief Engineer, N Delta Defences, Egypt, 1942; Chief Engineer, Malta, 1942-43 (CBE); Chief Engineer, British Troops in Egypt, 1943; No 13 CE Works (Construction), Middle East, 1943-44; Engineer Adviser, AA Command, England, 1944; Dep. Dir Works 21 Army Group BLA and BAOR, 1944-48 (despatches; Kt Comdr of Orange-Nassau with swords); Chief Engineer, Eastern Command, United Kingdom, 1948-51; retired, 1951. *Address:* c/o Lloyds Bank Ltd, 6 Pall Mall, SW1. *Club:* Royal Commonwealth Society.

EDWARDS, Arthur Frank George; Vice-Chairman, Thames Water Authority, since 1973; *b* 27 March 1920; *o s* of Arthur Edwards and Mabel (Elsie) Edwards; *m* 1946, Joyce May Simmons; one *s* one *d. Educ:* West Ham Grammar Sch.; Garnett Coll., London; West Ham Coll. of Technology. CEng, FIChemE, MSE; Hon. FISWM. Various posts with Ever Ready (GB) Ltd, 1936-50; Prodn Man., J. Burns & Co. Ltd, 1950-53; various lectrg posts, 1954-65; Organiser for science and techn. subjects, London Boroughs of Barking and Redbridge, 1965-. Member: West Ham Co. Borough Council, 1964-65; Newham Council, 1964- (Mayor, 1967-68); GLC, 1964- (Dep. Chm., 1970-71; Chm., Public Services Cttee, 1973-77); Chm. of Governors, NE London Polytechnic, 1972-. Mem., Fabian Soc. *Recreations:* reading, Association football (watching West Ham United). *Address:* 18 Wanstead Park Avenue, E12 5EN. *T:* 01-989 8613; Room 190, County Hall, SE1 7PB. *T:* 01-633 5000. *Clubs:* West Ham Supporters', Newham North West Labour.

EDWARDS, Carl Johannes; stained glass artist; *b* 15 Feb. 1914; *m* 1941, Kathleen Margaret Selina Morgan; two *d. Educ:* studied Art under James Hogan, RDI, and at various London Art Schs. Chief Designer Whitefriars Glass Works, 1948; resigned 1952. Governor Harrow Sch. of Art, 1949; Liveryman, Worshipful Company of Glaziers, 1949. Chief works in: Cairo

Cathedral; Liverpool Cathedral; House of Lords; Lambeth Palace Chapel; Temple Church; Royal Air Force Church, St Clement Dane's; Portsmouth Cathedral; St David's Cathedral, Wales; Auckland Cathedral, NZ; Westminster Sch., and several works in concrete and glass for England and abroad. *Recreations:* golf and music. *Address:* The Glasshouse, 11 Lettice Street, Fulham, SW6 4EH. *T:* 01-736 3113; 36 Denman Drive South, NW11. *Clubs:* Challoner; Highgate Golf.

EDWARDS, Charles Harold, FRCP; Dean of St Mary's Hospital, Paddington, since 1974; *b* 1913; *m* 1959; one *s* two *d. Educ:* Guy's Hosp. Med. Sch. MRCS 1937; LRCP 1937; MRCP 1946; FRCP 1961. Formerly: Resident Medical Appts, Guy's Hosp.; Resident Med. Officer, Nat. Hosp., Queen Square; Neurological Registrar, St Mary's Hosp., Paddington; Consultant Physician, Dept Nervous Diseases, St Mary's Hosp., 1954-; Consultant Neurologist: Royal Nat. Throat, Nose and Ear Hosp., 1955-; King Edward VII Hosp., Windsor, 1952-; Canadian Red Cross Meml Hosp., Taplow, 1952-; Maidenhead Hosp., 1952-. Mem., British Assoc. of Neurologists; FRSocMed. *Publications:* Neurology of Ear, Nose and Throat, 1973; Neurological Section: Synopsis of Otolaryngology, 1967; Scott-Brown, Diseases of Ear, Nose and Throat, 1971; contrib. Qly Jl Medicine, Lancet, etc. *Recreations:* words, gardening. *Address:* St Mary's Hospital, Paddington, W2 1PG. *T:* 01-262 1280; 139 Harley Street, W1. *T:* 01-935 2205. *Club:* Garrick.

EDWARDS, Sir Christopher (John Churchill), 5th Bt *cr* 1866; *b* 16 Aug. 1941; *s* of Sir (Henry) Charles (Serrell Priestley) Edwards, 4th Bt and of Lady (Daphne) Edwards (*née* Birt); *S* father, 1963; *m* 1972, Gladys Irene Vogelgesang; one *s. Educ:* Frensham Heights, Surrey; Loughborough, Leics. *Heir: s* David Charles Priestley Edwards, *b* 23 Feb. 1974. *Address:* 6133 Laurel Grove, North Hollywood, Calif 91606, USA.

EDWARDS, Sir Clive; *see* Edwards, Sir J. C. L.

EDWARDS, Corwin D.; Professor of Economics, University of Oregon, 1963-71, now Professor Emeritus; Associate Editor, Antitrust Bulletin, since 1967; *b* 1 Nov. 1901; *s* of Granville D. Edwards and Ida May Moore; *m* 1st, 1924, Janet Ward; one *s* one *d*; 2nd, 1948, Gertrud Greig. *Educ:* Univ. of Missouri (BA); Oxford Univ. (BLitt); Cornell Univ. (PhD). Asst Prof. of Economics, New York Univ., 1926-33; Economist and Tech. Dir, Consumers' Advisory Bd, National Recovery Administration, 1933-35; co-ordinator, trade practice studies, Nat. Recovery Admin., 1935; Economist, President's Cttee of Industrial Analysis, 1936; Asst Chief Economist, Federal Trade Commn, 1937-39; Chief of Staff, Amer. Tech. Mission to Brazil, 1942-43; Economist, Chm. Policy Bd, Anti-Trust Div., Dept of Justice, 1939-44; Consultant on Cartels, Dept of State, 1943-48; Prof. of Economics, Northwestern Univ., 1944-48; Head of Mission on Japanese Combines, 1946; Dir, Bureau of Economics, Federal Trade Commn, USA, 1948-53; US Rep., ad hoc Cttee on Restrictive Business Practices, 1952-53; Pitt Prof., Cambridge Univ., 1953-54; Prof. of Economics, Univ. of Virginia, 1954-55; Prof. of Business and Government, Graduate Sch. of Business, Univ. of Chicago, 1955-63. Member: Consumers Adv. Council, USA, 1967-69; Cttee on social effects of computer technology, Nat. Sci. Foundn. 1971-72. Chm., section on internat. enterprises, internat. mergers and internat. jt ventures, Conf. on Internat. Economy and Competition Policy, Tokyo, 1973. *Publications:* Maintaining Competition, 1949; Big Business and the Policy of Competition, 1956; The Price Discrimination Law: A Review of Experience, 1959; Trade Regulation Overseas, the National Laws, 1966; Control of Cartels and Monopolies, an International Comparison, 1967; Studies of Foreign Competition Policy and Practice (for Canadian govt), 1976; American Antitrust Policy toward Conduct by Powerful Enterprises, and, American and German Policy toward Conduct by Powerful Enterprises, 1977; Co-author: Economic Behavior, 1931; Economic Problems in a Changing World, 1939; A Cartel Policy for the United Nations, 1945; various govt reports and articles in professional jls. *Recreations:* swimming, sailing. *Address:* 11 New Jersey Avenue, Lewes, Delaware 19958, USA.

EDWARDS, Rev. Canon David Lawrence; Canon of Westminster and Rector of St Margaret's, Westminster, since 1970, Sub-Dean, since 1974; Speaker's Chaplain, since 1972; *b* 20 Jan. 1929; *s* of Lawrence Wright and Phyllis Boardman Edwards; *m* 1960, Hilary Mary (*née* Phillips); one *s* three *d. Educ:* King's Sch., Canterbury; Magdalen Coll., Oxford. Lothian Prize, 1951; 1st cl. hons Mod. Hist., BA 1952; MA 1956. Fellow, All Souls Coll., Oxford, 1952-59. Deacon, 1954; Priest, 1955. On HQ staff of Student Christian Movement of Gt Brit. and Ireland, 1955-66; Editor and Man. Dir, SCM Press Ltd, 1959-66; Gen. Sec. of Movt, 1965-66. Curate of: St John's, Hampstead, 1955-58; St

Martin-in-the-Fields, 1958-66; Fellow and Dean of King's College, Cambridge, 1966-70; Exam. Chaplain: to Bp of Manchester, 1965-73; to Bp of Durham, 1968-72; to Bp of Bradford, 1972; to Bp of London, 1974-; to Archbishop of Canterbury, 1975-; Asst Lectr in Divinity, Univ. of Cambridge, 1967-70. Hulsean Lectr, 1967; Six Preacher, Canterbury Cathedral, 1969. Chairman: Churches' Council on Gambling, 1970-; Christian Aid, 1971-. *Publications:* A History of the King's School, Canterbury, 1957; Not Angels But Anglicans, 1958; This Church of England, 1962; God's Cross in Our World, 1963; Religion and Change, 1969; F. J. Shirley: An Extraordinary Headmaster, 1969; The Last Things Now, 1969; Leaders of the Church of England, 1971; What is Real in Christianity?, 1972; St Margaret's, Westminster, 1972; The British Churches Turn to the Future, 1973; Ian Ramsey, Bishop of Durham, 1973; Good News in Acts, 1974; What Anglicans Believe, 1974; Jesus for Modern Man, 1975; A Key to the Old Testament, 1976; Today's Story of Jesus, 1976; The State of the Nation, 1976; (ed) The Honest to God Debate, 1963. *Address:* 5 Little Cloister, Westminster, SW1P 3PL. *T:* 01-222 6939.

EDWARDS, Donald Isaac, CBE 1965 (OBE 1958); Managing Director, Independent Television News, 1968-71; *b* 27 Sept. 1904; *s* of late Isaac Edwards, Bolton, Lancs; *m* 1930, Enid Bent; two *s. Educ:* Bolton Sch.; Emmanuel Coll., Cambridge (MA). Tillotsons Newspapers, 1926-28; Daily News, 1928-30; Allied Newspapers, 1930-33; Daily Telegraph, 1933-39; BBC: Asst European News Editor, 1940-42; European News Editor, 1942-45; Correspondent in India, 1946; Dir, European News, 1946-48; Head of External Services, News Dept, 1948-58; Editor, News, 1958-60; News and Current Affairs, 1960-67; Gen. Man., Local Radio Development, 1967-68. *Publications:* The Two Worlds of Donald Edwards (autobiography), 1970; contribs to various books on journalism and broadcasting. *Recreations:* music, golf, walking. *Address:* Spindles, Miles Lane, Cobham, Surrey. *T:* Cobham 2257.

EDWARDS, Douglas John; Joint Chairman and Managing Director, Louis C. Edwards & Sons (Manchester) Ltd; *b* 18 March 1916; *s* of Louis Edwards; *m* 1st, 1941, Emmeline H. Haslam (*d* 1964); two *s*; 2nd, 1973, Valerie Barlow-Hitchen. *Educ:* De La Salle Coll., Salford. Member of Lloyd's, 1965-. Joined Manchester Conservative Party, 1947; Mem. Manchester City Council, 1951-74; Alderman, 1967-74; Lord Mayor of City of Manchester, 1971-72; Greater Manchester Metropolitan CC, 1974- (High Sheriff, 1975). Freeman and Liveryman, Co. of Playing Cards Makers, 1974. Polonia Restituta, 1972. *Recreations:* golf, sailing. *Address:* Juniper Hill, Warrington Road, Mere, Knutsford, Cheshire. *T:* Bucklow Hill 830345. *Clubs:* Carlton; Lloyd's Yacht; Antibes Yacht.

EDWARDS, Edward George, PhD, BSc, FRIC; Vice-Chancellor and Principal, University of Bradford, 1966-78; Principal of Bradford Institute of Technology, 1957-66; *b* 18 Feb. 1914; *m* 1940, Kathleen Hewitt; two *s* two *d. Educ:* Cardiff High Sch.; University of South Wales; Cardiff Coll. of Technology. Lecturer in Chemistry, University of Nottingham, 1938-40; Research Chemist (ICI Ltd), 1940-45; Head of Dept of Chemistry and Applied Chemistry, Royal Technical Coll., Salford, 1945-54; Principal, Coll. of Technology, Liverpool, 1954-57. *Publications:* various research papers in chemical jls; articles and papers on higher educn, technological innovation, university planning. *Recreations:* philosophy, music, walking, travel. *Address:* Corner Cottage, Westwood Drive, Ilkley, West Yorks. *T:* Ilkley 2137.

EDWARDS, Geoffrey Francis, CBE 1975 (OBE 1968; MBE 1956); TD; HM Diplomatic Service, retired; *b* 28 Sept. 1917; *s* of late Oliver Edwards, Langley, Bucks, and Frances Margaret Edwards; *m* 1st, 1949, Joyce Black (*d* 1953); one *d*; 2nd, 1961, Johanna Elisabeth Franziska Taeger. *Educ:* Brighton Coll. Joined Pixley & Abell, Bullion Brokers, 1936. Commissioned 117 Fd Regt, RA (TA), June 1939; served with 117 Fd Regt and 59 (Newfoundland) Heavy Regt RA in NW Europe, 1939-45; joined Control Commn for Germany, 1945; joined British Military Govt, Berlin, 1949; First Sec. (Economic), 1956; Economic Adviser, British Mil. Govt, Berlin, 1956; established in Diplomatic Service, 1966; Consul-General, Berlin, 1966-75. *Recreations:* gardening, fishing, golf. *Address:* c/o Midland Bank, 202 Sloane Street, SW1X 9RG.

EDWARDS, George, FFARCS; Consulting Anæsthetist: St George's, General Lying-in (St Thomas'), Samaritan (St Mary's) and Queen Charlotte's Hospitals; *b* 14 Jan. 1901; *m* 1934, Jean Lilian Smith, MD; one *s. Educ:* Royal Grammar Sch., Worcester; St George's Hospital (Johnson Anatomy Prize). MRCS, LRCP 1926; DA, RCP and S 1936; FFARCS 1948. RAMC, 1941-44; Lt-Col. Adviser in Anæsthetics, BNAF and

CMF. Hon. Mem. (Pres. 1945-46), Sect. Anæsthetics, RSocMed. Mem. of Bd of Faculty of Anæsthetists, RCS, 1948-54; first Hewitt Lectr, RCS, 1950; first Snow Memorial Lectr, Assoc. of Anæsthetists, 1958. *Publications:* articles in medical journals. *Address:* 7 Chiltern Hills Road, Beaconsfield, Bucks. *T:* Beaconsfield 3504.

EDWARDS, Sir George (Robert), OM 1971; Kt 1957; CBE 1952 (MBE 1945); FRS 1968; Chairman, British Aircraft Corporation Ltd, 1963-75; Pro-Chancellor, University of Surrey, appointed Dec. 1964; *b* 9 July 1908; *m* 1935, Marjorie Annie (*née* Thurgood); one *d. Educ:* S West Essex Tech. Coll.; London Univ. (BScEng). Gen. engineering, 1928-35; joined Design Staff, Vickers-Aviation Ltd, Weybridge, 1935; Experimental Manager, Vickers-Armstrongs Ltd, Weybridge Works, 1940. Chief Designer, Weybridge Works, 1945; Dir, Vickers Ltd, 1955-67. Pres., Royal Aeronautical Soc., 1957-58; Vice-Pres., Royal Society of Arts, 1958-61. Mem., Royal Instn, 1971-. Vice-Pres., Surrey CCC, 1974. CEng; Hon. Fellow: RAeS 1960; IMechE; Manchester Coll. of Science and Technology; Hon. FAIAA. Hon. DSc: Southampton, 1962; Salford, 1967; Cranfield Inst. of Technology, 1970; City Univ., 1975; Hon. DSc(Eng) London, 1970; Hon. LLD Bristol, 1973. George Taylor Gold Medal, 1948; British Gold Medal for Aeronautics, 1952; Daniel Guggenheim Medal, 1959; Air League Founders Medal, 1969; Albert Gold Medal (RSA), 1972; Royal Medal, Royal Soc., 1974. *Publications:* various papers and lectures in Jl RAeS, Amer. Inst. of Aeronautical Sciences and Amer. Soc. of Automotive Engrs. *Recreations:* golf, sailing, painting. *Address:* Albury Heights, White Lane, Guildford, Surrey. *T:* Guildford 4488. *Clubs:* Athenæum; Royal Air Force Yacht.

EDWARDS, Harold Clifford, CBE 1945; MS, FRCS, FRCOG, FACS (Hon.); Honorary Colonel RAMC; Consulting Surgeon to King's College Hospital; Emeritus Lecturer, and Director, Department of Surgery, King's College Hospital Medical School, 1956-70; Surgeon to Royal Masonic Hospital, 1956-70; Consulting Surgeon to King Edward VII Hospital for Officers, 1956-70; St Saviour's Hospital; Consultant Adviser in Surgery to the Minister of Health, 1956-70; Surgeon Emeritus to the Evelina Hospital for Children; *b* 15 Aug. 1899; *s* of William Evans Edwards and Mary Selina Jones; *m* 1926, Ida Margaret Atkinson Phillips; two *s. Educ:* University Coll., Cardiff; King's College Hospital, London. Served in Royal Engineers, 1917-19; entered University Coll., Cardiff, 1919; MRCS, LRCP, MB, BS 1923; FRCS 1926; MS London Univ., 1928; Hon. Surgeon to King's Coll. Hosp., 1928, and to Evelina Hosp. for Children, 1931; Robert Jones Gold Medal for an Essay upon Injuries to Muscles and Tendons, 1930, and Jacksonian Prize of RCS for a Dissertation on Diverticula of the Intestine, 1932; Hunterian Prof., RCS, 1934; Consulting Surg. Southern Comd, England, 1942-44; Consulting Surg., Central Mediterranean Forces, 1944-46; late Dean of King's College Hosp. Medical Sch. Past Master, Worshipful Soc. of Apothecaries. Mem. Court of Examiners, 1931-60, and Mem. Council, 1955-71, RCS (past Vice-Pres.). Examiner in Surgery, Univs of London, Cambridge, Wales, Birmingham, Dublin and Bristol. Chm., Armed Forces Adv. Cttee on Postgraduate Med. and Dental Officers, 1971-; President: British Soc. of Gastroenterology, 1961; Assoc. of Surgeons of Gt Brit. and Ireland, 1962; FRCOG 1971; Hon. Fellow: American Surgical Assoc.; Assoc. of Surgeons of W Africa; Assoc. of Surgeons of West Indies; Mem. Académie de Chirurgie. Former Editor of GUT the British Jl of Gastroenterology. Hon. Gold Medal, RCS, 1972. *Publications:* Surgical Emergencies in Children, 1935; Diverticula and Diverticulitis of the Intestine, 1939; Recent Advances in Surgery, 1954; papers in BMJ, Lancet, etc. *Recreation:* gardening. *Address:* Nickersons, Barton, Cambridge. *T:* Comberton 2367. *Club:* Athenæum.

EDWARDS, (H. C.) Ralph, CBE 1953; BA; FSA; Adviser on Works of Art to the Historic Buildings Councils of England and Wales, 1954-75; Keeper, Department of Woodwork, Victoria and Albert Museum, 1937-54, retired Oct. 1954; *b* 24 June 1894; *s* of late Rev. W. A. Edwards, formerly Rector of Tredington, Shipston-on-Stour, and of Edith Lilian, *e d* of late C. J. Collins Prichard, Pwyllywrach, near Cowbridge, Glamorgan; *m* 1926, Marjorie Ingham Brooke; three *s. Educ:* privately; Hertford Coll., Oxon. BA (War Degree). War of 1914-18, 2nd Lieut, twice invalided; Middle Temple, Final Bar Exam. 2nd Cl.; Mem. of Editorial staff of Country Life, 1921-26; Asst, Dept of Woodwork, Victoria and Albert Museum, 1926-28; Asst Keeper, 1st Class, 1928; Keeper, 2nd Class, 1937, 1st Class, 1945. Member: The Court of Govs, and Council, Nat. Museum of Wales and of Cttees of Art and Archæology (Chm., 1958-61); Cttee, Slade Sch. of Art. *Publications:* (with late Percy Macquoid) The Dictionary of English Furniture, 3 vols, 1924-27 (2nd edn, rev. and enl., 1953; one volume edn 1963); Georgian Cabinet-makers (with late Margaret Jourdain) (3rd edn 1955);

Early Conversation Pictures, 1954; Introd. to Cat. for RA Exhibn "English Taste in the Eighteenth Century", 1955-56 and for exhibns for Arts Council and GLC; Co-Editor the Connoisseur Period Guides, 1956-58; various official publications and many articles on English pictures and decorative art in Apollo, Burlington Magazine and Connoisseur. *Address:* Suffolk House, Chiswick Mall, W4. *T:* 01-994 3381; Pontesgob Mill Cottage, Fforest, Abergavenny, Gwent. *Club:* Athenæum.

See also R. N. Edwards.

EDWARDS, Air Cdre Sir Hughie (Idwal), VC 1941; KCMG 1974; CB 1959; DSO 1942; OBE 1947; DFC 1941; Governor of Western Australia, 1974-75; *b* W Australia, 1 Aug. 1914; *s* of late Hugh Edwards; *m* 1942, Cherry Kyrle (*d* 1966), widow of Flight Lieut H. R. A. Beresford; one *s* one *d*; *m* 1972, Mrs Dorothy Carew Berrick. *Educ:* Fremantle, W Australia. Joined Regular Australian Army, 1934; transferred to RAAF, 1935, to RAF, 1936. Served War of 1939-45, in European, Middle and Far East theatres (despatches, DFC, VC, DSO). Commandant, Central Fighter Establishment, 1958-60; ADC to the Queen, 1960-63; idc 1961; Dir of Estabts, Air Ministry, 1962-63, retd. Australian Representative, Selection Trust, 1964-74. KStJ 1974. *Recreations:* squash, cricket. *Address:* 42 New Beach Road, Darling Point, NSW 2027, Australia. *Clubs:* White's, Royal Air Force, MCC; Union (Sydney), Imperial Service (Sydney).

EDWARDS, Iorwerth Eiddon Stephen, CMG 1973; CBE 1968; MA, LittD; FBA 1962; Keeper of Egyptian Antiquities, British Museum, 1955-74; *b* 21 July 1909; *s* of late Edward Edwards and Ellen Jane (*née* Higgs); *m* 1938, Elizabeth, *y d* of late Charles Edwards Lisle; one *d* (one *s* decd). *Educ:* Merchant Taylors'; Gonville and Caius Coll., Cambridge (Major Scholar). Merchant Taylors' Sch. Exhibitioner and John Stewart of Rannoch Univ. Scholar, Cambridge, 1928; 1st Cl. Oriental Languages Tripos, Parts I and II, 1930-31; Mason Prize, Tyrwhitt Scholarship and Wright Studentship, 1932. Entered Dept of Egyptian and Assyrian Antiquities, British Museum, 1934; seconded to Foreign Office; attached to British Embassies, Cairo and Baghdad, and to Secretariat, Jerusalem, 1942-45. T. E. Peet Prize, Liverpool Univ., 1947. Visiting Prof., Brown Univ., Providence, RI, USA, 1953-54. Pioneered and chose objects for Tutankhamun Exhibition, London, 1972. Mem., Unesco-Egyptian Min. of Culture Archaeol. Cttee for saving monuments of Philae, 1973-. Vice-Pres. Egypt Exploration Soc.; Mem. of German Archæological Inst.; Associate Mem., Inst. of Egypt; Mem., Cttee of Visitors of Metropolitan Museum of Art, NY; Corres. Mem., Fondation Egyptologique Reine Elisabeth. *Publications:* Hieroglyphic Texts in the British Museum, Vol. VIII, 1939; The Pyramids of Egypt, 1947, 2nd edn 1961; Hieratic Papyri in the British Museum, 4th Series (Oracular Amuletic Decrees of the Late New Kingdom), 1960; The Early Dynastic Period in Egypt, 1964; Joint Editor of The Cambridge Ancient History (3rd edn), 1970; Treasures of Tutankhamun (Catalogue of London exhibn), 1972; Treasures of Tutankhamun (Catalogue of US exhibn), 1976; Tutankhamun's Jewelry, 1976; Tutankhamun: his tomb and its treasures, 1976; articles in Journal of Egyptian Archæology and other scientific periodicals. *Recreations:* golf, gardening. *Address:* Morden Lodge, Morden, Surrey. *T:* 01-648 6023. *Club:* Athenæum.

EDWARDS, James Keith O'Neill; (Jimmy Edwards), DFC 1945; MA (Cantab); MFH; *b* 23 March 1920; *s* of late Prof. R. W. K. Edwards and late Mrs P. K. Edwards; *m* 1958, Valerie Seymour (marr. diss. 1969). *Educ:* St Paul's Cathedral Choir Sch.; King's Coll. Sch., Wimbledon; St John's Coll., Cambridge. Served War of 1939-45, in RAF, 1940-46. Windmill Theatre, London, 1946; Adelphi Theatre, 1950-51, 1952-54, 1954-55 and 1960-61; Take It From Here, BBC, 1948-59; Does The Team Think?, BBC, 1957-77; Whack-O!, BBC Television, 1957-61 and 1971-72; Seven Faces of Jim, 1961-62; Six More Faces of Jim, 1962-63; Bold as Brass, 1964; John Jorrocks, Esq., BBC-2, 1966; Fosset Saga, ATV, 1969. *Films:* Three Men in a Boat, 1957; Bottoms Up, 1960; Nearly a Nasty Accident, 1961. *Stage:* Big Bad Mouse, Shaftesbury, 1966-68; Prince of Wales, 1971; Halfway up the Tree, Queen's, 1968; Maid of the Mountains, Palace, 1972; Hulla Baloo, Criterion, 1972. Lord Rector of Aberdeen Univ., 1951-54. *Publication:* Take It From Me, 1952. *Recreations:* foxhunting, polo, flying, squash, brass bands. *Address:* c/o O'Neill Productions Ltd, Atheralls Farm, Fletching, Uckfield, East Sussex TN22 3TD. *T:* Newick 2258. *Club:* Savile.

EDWARDS, John; Editor, Yorkshire Post, since 1969; *b* 2 Jan. 1932; *s* of late Arthur Leonard Edwards; *m* 1954, Nancy Woodcock; one *s* one *d*. *Educ:* Wolverhampton Municipal Grammar School. Entered journalism, Wolverhampton Chronicle; subseq. worked on newspapers and magazines in

Fleet Street and provinces; from 1961, Yorkshire Post: Dep. Night Editor, Business Editor, Asst Editor and Dep. Editor. Director: Yorkshire Post and Evening Post Ltd; East Yorkshire Printers Ltd. *Address:* 34 Wayside Avenue, Harrogate, N Yorks. *T:* Harrogate 887487. *Club:* Authors'.

EDWARDS, Sir John (Arthur), Kt 1970; CBE 1953; President, London Rent Assessment Panel, 1968-73 (Vice-President, 1965-68); *b* 1 June 1901; *s* of late John Edwards, JP, and Mary Elizabeth Cromar, Rossett; *m* 1932, Dorothy Margaret, *y d* of late Sir Richard Williams, OBE, DL, JP, Bangor, North Wales; two *s*. *Educ:* Grove Park Sch., Wrexham. FRICS. Chartered Surveyor. Articles and various appointments as a Chartered Surveyor and Land Agent, 1919-28; joined Valuation Office, 1929; Dep. Chief Valuer, Valuation Office, Bd of Inland Revenue, 1950-65. *Recreation:* golf. *Address:* 16 Oakridge Avenue, Radlett, Herts. *T:* 6550.

EDWARDS, John Basil, CBE 1972; JP; Chairman, Magistrates Association, since 1976; *b* 15 Jan. 1909; *s* of Charles and Susan Edwards; *m* 1935, Molly Patricia Philips; one *s* two *d*. *Educ:* King's Sch., Worcester; Wadham Coll., Oxford (BA Hons Jurisprudence, MA). Commnd Royal Warwickshire Regt (RE) TA, 1938. Admitted Solicitor, 1933. Worcester CC, 1936; Mayor of Worcester, 1947-49; Alderman, City of Worcester, 1948. Magistrates Association: Mem. Council, 1960; Chm., Worcestershire Br., 1960-66; Hon. Treasurer, 1968-70; Dep. Chm., 1970-76. Mem., James Cttee on Distribution of Criminal Business, 1973-75. Chm., Worcester Three Choirs Festival, 1947-72. Freeman, City of London. Liveryman: Haberdashers Company; Distillers Company. JP Worcs 1940; Chm., Worcester City Justices, 1951-. *Recreation:* gardening. *Address:* Meadow End, Cradley, near Malvern, Worcs. *T:* Ridgway Cross 219. *Club:* Anglo-Belgian.

EDWARDS, John Braham Scott, MA (Oxon); Barrister, since 1954; a Recorder of the Crown Court, since 1972; *b* Bristol, 29 March 1928; *s* of late Lewis Edwards and late Hilda Edwards (*née* Scott); *m* 1963, Veronica Mary, *d* of late Lt-Col Howard Dunbar (killed in action, 1942), and of Mrs Brodie Good; one *s* two *d*. *Educ:* Royal Masonic Schools, Bushey; Merton Coll., Oxford. BA Cl. I, Jurisprudence, 1951. National service, Pte, Gloucestershire Regt, and Lieut, Intell. Corps, 1946-48. Teaching Fellow, Univ. of Chicago Law Sch., 1952-53; Harmsworth, Barstow, Scholar; Secretary-Gen. of Internat. Law Assoc., 1960-. Bencher, Middle Temple, 1973-. Churchwarden, St Anne's, Kew. *Recreations:* golf, gardening. *Address:* Queen Elizabeth Building, Temple EC4Y 9BS. *T:* 01-353 0832; 17 Ennerdale Road, Kew TW9 3PG. *T:* 01-940 8734. *Clubs:* Roehampton; Hampshire (Winchester).

EDWARDS, Sir (John) Clive (Leighton), 2nd Bt *cr* 1921; *b* 1916; *s* of 1st Bt and Kathleen Ermyntrude (*d* 1975) *d* of late John Corfield, JP; *S* father, 1922. *Educ:* Winchester Coll. Volunteered and served in the Army, 1940-46. *Recreations:* motoring, gardening. *Heir:* none. *Address:* Milntown, Lezayre, near Ramsey, Isle of Man.

EDWARDS, John Lionel; Certification Officer for Trade Unions and Employers' Associations, since 1976; *b* 29 Aug. 1915; *s* of Rev. Arthur Edwards and Constance Edwards; *m* 1948, Cecily Miller; one *s* two *d*. *Educ:* Marlborough; Corpus Christi Coll., Oxford. Entered Scottish Office, 1938. Served War, (Army), 1940-45. Min. of Labour, 1945: Principal Private Sec. to Minister of Labour, 1956; Asst Sec., 1956; Sec., NEDC, 1968-71; Under-Sec., Dept of Employment, 1971-75. *Address:* Marchmont, Hollybank Road, West Byfleet, Surrey. *T:* Byfleet 43459. *Club:* United Oxford & Cambridge University.

EDWARDS, Joseph Robert, CBE 1963; JP; Deputy Chairman, Associated Engineering, since 1969; Vice Chairman, Lucas (Industries) Ltd, since 1976; Director, British Printing Corporation; *b* 5 July 1908; *y s* of late Walter Smith Edwards and Annie Edwards, Gt Yarmouth; *m* 1936, Frances Mabel Haddon Bourne (*d* 1975); three *s* one *d*; *m* 1976, Joan Constance Mary Tattersall. *Educ:* High Sch., Great Yarmouth. Joined Austin Motor Co., Birmingham, 1928; Hercules factory, 1939; rejoined Austin Motor Co., 1941; Gen. Works Manager, 1951; Local Dir, 1953; Works Dir, 1954; Dir of Manufacturing, British Motor Corp., 1955; Managing Director: British Motor Corp., 1966-68; Pressed Steel/Fisher Ltd, 1956-67; Dep. Chm., Harland & Wolff Ltd, 1968-70, Chm. 1970. Pres., Motor Industry Research Assoc. Mem., Commn on Industrial Relations to 1974. JP Oxford, 1964. Hon. MA Oxon, 1968. *Recreation:* golf. *Address:* Yatscombe, Boars Hill, Oxford. *T:* Oxford 35261. *Club:* Royal Motor Yacht.

EDWARDS, Julie Andrews; see Andrews, J.

EDWARDS, Prof. Kenneth Charles, CBE 1970; Professor of Geography in the University of Nottingham (first holder of the Chair), 1948-70, now Emeritus Professor; b 2 March 1904; s of C. W. Edwards, Southampton; m 1937, Barbara Joyce West, Southsea; no c. Educ: Itchen Grammar Sch.; University Coll., Southampton. Asst Lectr in Geography and Demonstrator in Geology, University Coll., Nottingham, 1927; Indep. Lecturer in Geography and Head of Dept of Geography, University Coll., Nottingham, 1934; Reader in Geography, 1939; seconded to Ministry of Town and Country Planning, as Regional Research Officer for East Midlands, 1944-46; Temp. appt as Acting-Head of Dept of Geography, University Coll., Auckland, NZ, 1951; Dean of Faculty of Law and Social Sciences, Univ. of Nottingham, 1958-61. Founder, and Chm., Editorial Cttee of the East Midland Geographer, 1954. Pres., Section E British Assoc. for the Advancement of Science, 1959; Pres., Inst. of British Geographers, 1960; Pres., Geographical Assoc., 1963. Visiting Prof., Makerere Univ. Coll., Uganda, 1963; Murchison Grant, RGS, 1964. Mem., East Midlands Economic Planning Council, Dept of Economic Affairs, 1966-72. Order of the Crown of Oak, and Order of Merit, Grand Duchy of Luxembourg; Cross of the Order of the Restitution of Poland. Publications: Sweden; Dalarna Studies, 1940; The Land of Britain; Nottinghamshire, 1944; Luxembourg (NID), 1944; Studies in Regional Planning (ed G. H. J. Daysh); The East Midlands, 1949; (with F. A. Wells) A Survey of the Chesterfield Region, 1950; (with H. H. Swinnerton and R. H. Hall) The Peak District, 1962; Nottingham and its Region (ed), 1966; (co-organiser) Atlas du Luxembourg, 1971; various contribs and research papers to geog. periodicals. Recreations: walking, including field excursions at home and abroad; music. Address: 24 Bramcote Drive, Beeston, Notts. T: 25-7309.

EDWARDS, Rt. Rev. Lewis Mervyn Charles-; see Charles-Edwards.

EDWARDS, Sir Martin Llewellyn, Kt 1974; DL; Solicitor; Consultant with Edwards, Geldard & Shepherd, Cardiff; part-time Chairman of Industrial Tribunals, since 1975; b 21 May 1909; s of Charles Ernest Edwards, Solicitor, and Annie Matilda Edwards (née Llewellyn); m 1936, Dorothy Ward Harrap; one s two d (and one d decd). Educ: Marlborough Coll.; Lincoln Coll., Oxford (MA). Admitted Solicitor, 1934. Commnd in RAuxAF, 1937; served RAF (Gen. Duties Br.), UK and Middle East, 1939-45; Mem. Council and Gen. Purposes and Finance Cttees, Glamorgan T&AFA, 1946-68 (Vice-Chm., Air, 1961-68). Mem. Council, Law Society, 1957 (Vice-Pres. 1972-73, Pres., 1973-74; Chm., Educn and Trng Cttee, 1966-69). Pres., Associated Law Socs of Wales, 1960-62; Pres., Incorporated Law Soc. for Cardiff and District, 1969-70. Mem. Lord Chancellor's Cttee on Legal Educn, 1967-71. Mem. Council, UWIST, 1969-; Mem., Drinking and Driving Cttee, DoE, 1974-76. Governor, Coll. of Law, 1967- (Chm. of Governors, 1969-72). DL Glamorgan, 1961. Recreations: walking, gardening, photography. Address: Pentwyn Farm, Lisvane, Cardiff CF4 5SP. T: Cardiff 751813. Clubs: Army and Navy; Cardiff and County (Cardiff).

EDWARDS, Nicholas; see Edwards, R. N.

EDWARDS, Owen; Controller, BBC Wales, since 1974; b 26 Dec. 1933; m 1958, Shân Emlyn; two d. Educ: Leighton Park, Reading; Lincoln Coll., Oxford (MA). Cataloguer, Nat. Library of Wales, 1958-60; BBC Wales: Compère, TV Programme Heddiw, 1961-66; Programme Organiser, 1967-70; Head of Programmes, 1970-74. Recreations: swimming, walking. Address: Coed-y-Pry, 12 Lady Mary Road, Cardiff, South Glamorgan. T: Cardiff 751469.

EDWARDS, Prof. Philip Walter, PhD; King Alfred Professor of English Literature, University of Liverpool, since 1974; b 7 Feb. 1923; er s of late R. H. Edwards, MC, and late Mrs B. Edwards; m 1st, 1947, Hazel Margaret (d 1950), d of late Prof. C. W. and Mrs E. R. Valentine; 2nd, 1952, Sheila Mary, d of R. S. and Mrs A. M. Wilkes, Bloxwich, Staffs; three s one d. Educ: King Edward's High Sch., Birmingham; Univ. of Birmingham. MA, PhD Birmingham; MA Dublin. Royal Navy, 1942-45 (Sub-Lieut RNVR). Lectr in English, Univ. of Birmingham, 1946-60; Commonwealth Fund Fellow, Harvard Univ., 1954-55; Prof. of English Lit., TCD, 1960-66; Fellow of TCD, 1962-66; Vis. Prof., Univ. of Michigan, 1964-65; Prof. of Lit., Univ. of Essex, 1966-74; Vis. Prof., Williams Coll., Mass, 1969; Vis. Fellow, All Souls Coll., Oxford, 1970-71. Publications: Sir Walter Ralegh, 1953; (ed) Kyd: The Spanish Tragedy, 1959; Shakespeare and the Confines of Art, 1968; (ed) Pericles Prince of Tyre, 1976; (ed with C. Gibson) Massinger, Plays and Poems, 1976; numerous articles on Shakespeare and literature of his time in Shakespeare

Survey, Proc. British Acad., etc. Address: 12 South Bank, Oxton, Birkenhead L43 5UP. T: 051-652 6089.

EDWARDS, Quentin Tytler, QC 1975; a Recorder of the Crown Court since 1974; Chancellor, Diocese of Blackburn, since 1977; b 16 Jan. 1925; s of Herbert Jackson Edwards and Juliet Hester Edwards; m 1948, Barbara Marian Guthrie; two s one d. Educ: Bradfield Coll.; Council of Legal Educn. Royal Navy, 1943-46. Called to Bar, Middle Temple, 1948; Bencher, 1972. Licensed Reader, Dio. of London, 1967; Mem., Legal Adv. Commn of General Synod of Church of England, 1973. Hon. MA (Archbp of Canterbury), 1961. Publications: (with Peter Dow) Public Rights of Way and Access to the Countryside, 1951; (with K. Macmorran, et al) Ecclesiastical Law, 3rd edn, Halsbury's Laws of England, 1955; What is Unlawful?, 1959; (with J. N. D. Anderson, et al) Putting Asunder, 1966. Recreations: the open air; the table; architecture. Address: 13 South Grove, Highgate, N6 6BJ. T: 01-340 4861.

EDWARDS, Ralph; see Edwards, H. C. R.

EDWARDS, Richard Lionel, QC 1952; b 1 Aug. 1907; s of late Lionel T. Edwards, BA, JP, Weston Underwood, Olney, Bucks; m 1944, Eleanor Middleton, d of late Sir Henry Japp, KBE; no c. Educ: Rugby Sch.; Oriel Coll., Oxford. Called to English Bar, 1930; Bencher of Lincoln's Inn, 1957. Recreations: gardening, Italian painting and fishing. Address: Weston Underwood, Olney, Bucks. T: Bedford 711312.

EDWARDS, Robert; MP (Lab and Co-op) Wolverhampton South East, since 1974 (Bilston, 1955-74); National Officer of Transport and General Workers' Union, since 1971; b 1906; m 1933, Edith May Sandham (d 1970); one s. Educ: Council Schs and Technical Coll. Served with Republicans in Spain during Spanish civil war. Mem. delegns to Russia, 1926 and 1934. Mem. Liverpool City Council, 1929-32; Nat. Chm., ILP, 1943-48; Founder Pres., Socialist Movement for United States of Europe. Contested (ILP) Chorley 1935, Stretford 1939 and Newport 1945. Gen. Sec., Chemical Workers' Union, 1947-71; Chm., Chem. Section, ICF, 1971-. Vice-President: British Section European League for Economic Co-operation; Economic Research Council; Council of Europe, 1969-70; Dep. Leader, British Delgn to Council of Europe, and Chm., Defence Cttee, WEU Assembly, 1968-; Leader, British Delegn, N Atlantic Assembly, 1968-69. Chm., Parly Gp for Industrial Common Ownership, 1976-; Mem., European Parlt, 1977-. Editor, The Chemical Worker. Corton Beach (Holdings) Ltd, 1969-, Chm. 1971-. Trustee, Scott Bader Commonwealth, 1969. Publications: Chemicals-Servant or Master; A Study of a Master Spy, etc. Address: House of Commons, SW1.

EDWARDS, Robert John; Editor, Sunday Mirror, since 1972; b 26 Oct. 1925; m 1952, Laura Ellwood (marr. diss. 1972); two s two d; m 1977, Brigid Segrave. Educ: Ranelagh Sch., Bracknell. Editor, Tribune, 1951-54; Dep. Editor, Sunday Express, 1957-59; Man. Editor, Daily Express, 1959-61; Editor: Evening Citizen, Glasgow, 1962-63; Daily Express, 1963-65; The Sunday People, 1966-72; Dir, Mirror Group Newspapers, 1976-. Broadcaster. Address: Sunday Mirror, 33 Holborn, EC1P 1DQ. Clubs: Kennel, Variety Club of Great Britain; Royal Southern Yacht.

EDWARDS, Robert Septimus Friar, CVO 1964; CBE 1963; b 21 Oct. 1910; y s of late Augustus C. Edwards and of Amy Edwards; m 1946, Janet Mabel Wrigley; one s two d. Educ: Hereford Cathedral Sch. Chief Engineering Asst, Hereford, until 1936; Min. of Transport, Highway Engineering, 1936-43; Principal, Min. of War Transport, 1943; Mem. British Merchant Shipping Mission, Washington, DC, 1944-46. Sec. Gen. Internat. Conf. on Safety of Life at Sea, 1948; Principal Private Sec. to Minister of Transport, 1949-51; Shipping Attaché, British Embassy, Washington, DC, 1951-54; Dir of Sea Transport, 1954-57; Gen. Manager, London Airports, 1957-63; Gen. Manager, 1967-69, Dir-Gen., 1969-71, Mersey Docks and Harbour Board. Chm., Morris & David Jones Ltd, 1973-74. Called to the Bar, Middle Temple, 1941. Recreation: golf. Address: Bryn-y-Groes, Nannerch, Clwyd CH7 5QS. T: Hendre 418.

EDWARDS, (Roger) Nicholas; MP (C) Pembroke since 1970; Conservative spokesman on Welsh affairs, since 1975; Director: P. A. International & Sturge Underwriting Agency Ltd; Globtik Tankers Ltd; Globtik Management Ltd; b 25 Feb. 1934; s of (H. C.) Ralph Edwards, qv; m 1963, Ankaret Healing; one s two d. Educ: Westminster Sch.; Trinity Coll., Cambridge, 1954-57; read History: BA 1957, MA, 1968. Member of Lloyds, 1965-. Publications: articles and reviews in The Connoisseur and other jls. Recreations: fishing, gardening, collecting English drawings.

Address: Pontesgob Mill, Fforest Coalpit, near Abergavenny, Gwent; 20 Chester Row, SW1; Peach House, Rhos, Haverfordwest, Dyfed.

EDWARDS, Dr Roger Snowden, CBE 1964; JP; Chairman, Gas Industry Training Board, 1965-74; *b* 19 Dec. 1904; *s* of late Herbert George Edwards and late Margaret Alice Edwards; *m* 1935, Eveline Brunton; two *s* one *d. Educ:* Enfield Grammar Sch.; Imperial Coll. of Science. Junior Staff, Imperial Coll. of Science, 1925-28; Physicist, British Xylonite Co., 1928-29; Physicist, Boot Trade Research Association, 1929-39; Dir, Co-operative Wholesale Soc., 1939-49. Chairman: Council of Industrial Design, 1947-52 (Mem., 1944-47); NE Gas Board, 1949-66; Mem., Gas Council, 1966-70. JP Harrogate, 1960; Surrey, 1966. *Recreation:* golf. *Address:* 23 Manor Way, Letchworth, Herts SG6 3NL.

EDWARDS, Prof. Sir Samuel Frederick, (Sir Sam Edwards), Kt 1975; FRS 1966; John Humphrey Plummer Professor of Physics, Cambridge University, since 1972; Fellow, Caius College, since 1972; *b* 1 Feb. 1928; *s* of Richard and Mary Jane Edwards, Manselton, Swansea; *m* 1953, Merriell E. M. Bland; one *s* three *d. Educ:* Swansea Grammar Sch.; Caius Coll., Cambridge (MA, PhD); Harvard University. Inst. for Advanced Study, Princeton, 1952; Univ. of Birmingham, 1953; Univ. of Manchester, 1958, Prof. of Theoretical Physics, 1963-72. Chm., SRC, 1973-77. UK Deleg. to NATO Science Cttee, 1974-; Mem., Planning Cttee, Max-Planck Gesellschaft, 1974-. Vice-Pres., Institute of Physics, 1970-73 (Mem. Council, 1967-73); Mem. Council, Inst. of Mathematics and its Applications, 1976-. Member: Physics Cttee, SRC, 1968-73 (Chm. 1970-73); Polymer Cttee, SRC, 1968-73; Science Bd, SRC, 1970-73; Council, European Physical Soc., 1969-71 (Chm., Condensed Matter Div., 1969-71); UGC, 1971-73; Defence Scientific Adv. Council, 1973- (Chm., 1977-); Metrology and Standards Req. Bd, Dept of Industry, 1974-; Adv. Council on R&D, Dept of Energy, 1974-. FInstP; FIMA. Hon. DTech Loughborough, 1975; Hon. DSc: Salford, Edinburgh, 1976. Maxwell Medal and Prize, Inst. of Physics, 1974. *Publications:* contribs to learned jls. *Address:* 7 Penarth Place, Cambridge. *T:* Cambridge 66610. *Club:* Athenæum.

EDWARDS, Stewart Leslie, CMG 1967; Under-Secretary, Department of Trade, retired; *b* 6 Nov. 1914; *s* of late Walter James and Lilian Emma Edwards; *m* 1940, Dominica Jeanne Lavie, *d* of Joseph Lavie and Jeanne Jauréguiberry; two *s. Educ:* King's Sch., Canterbury; Corpus Christi Coll., Cambridge (Foundn Scholar). BA 1936; MA 1943. Appointed to War Office, 1937; Asst Private Sec. to Sec. of State, 1939-40; Private Sec. to Civil Mem. of Army Council, 1940-42. Military service, 1942-44. Called to the Bar, Inner Temple, 1947. Seconded from War Office to OEEC, 1948-51; Board of Trade, 1951-65; Minister (Economic), Bonn, 1965-70; Under-Sec., DTI later Dept of Trade, 1970-74. *Recreations:* music, reading, hill-walking, wine. *Address:* Wildshaw House, West Heath, Limpsfield, Surrey. *T:* Oxted 4753.

EDWARDS, Vero C. W.; *see* Wynne-Edwards.

EDWARDS, William (Henry); solicitor; *b* 6 Jan. 1938; *s* of Owen Henry Edwards and S. Edwards; *m* 1961, Ann Eleri Rogers; one *s* three *d. Educ:* Sir Thomas Jones' Comprehensive Sch.; Liverpool Univ. LLB. MP (Lab) Merioneth, 1966-Feb. 1974; contested (Lab) Merioneth, Oct. 1974. Mem., Historic Building Council for Wales, 1971-76. Editor, Solicitors Diary. *Recreations:* golf, Association football (from the terraces). *Address:* Bryniau Golau, Bala, Gwynedd.

EDWARDS, William Philip Neville, CBE 1949; *b* 5 Aug. 1904; *s* of late Neville P. Edwards, Orford, Littlehampton, Sussex; *m* 1st, 1931, Hon. Sheila Cary (*d* 1976), 2nd *d* of 13th Viscount Falkland; two *s*; 2nd, 1976, Joan, *widow* of Norman Mullins. *Educ:* Rugby Sch.; Corpus Christi Coll., Cambridge; Princeton Univ., USA (Davison Scholar). Joined Underground Electric group of companies, 1927; shortly afterwards appointed Sec. to Lord Ashfield, Chm. of Board; First Sec. of Standing Jt Cttee of Main Line Railway Companies and of LPTB, 1933; Officer of Board as Personal Asst to Gen. Manager of Railways, 1937; Outdoor Supt of Railways, 1938; Public Relations Officer of Board, 1939; Asst to Chm. of Supply Council of Min. of Supply, 1941-42; Head of Industrial Information Div. of Min. of Production and Alternate Dir of Information of British Supply Council in N America, 1943-45; Dir of Overseas Information Div. of BoT, 1945-46; Head of British Information Services in USA, 1946-49. A Dir, Confedn of British Industry (previously FBI), 1949-66; Man. Dir, British Overseas Fairs Ltd, 1959-66, Chm., 1966-68. UK Associate Dir, Business International SA, 1968-75; Chm., Public Relations (Industrial) Ltd, 1970-75.

Chevalier (1st class) of Order of Dannebrog (Denmark), 1955; Commander of Order of Vasa (Sweden), 1962. *Recreations:* golf, gardening. *Address:* Dawes Mead, Leigh, Reigate, Surrey. *Club:* Carlton.

EDWARDS-JONES, Ian, QC 1967; *b* 17 April 1923; *o s* of late Col H. V. Edwards-Jones, MC, DL, Swansea, Glam; *m* 1950, Susan Vera Catharine McClintock, *o d* of E. S. McClintock and of Mrs A. MacRossie; three *s. Educ:* Rugby Sch.; Trinity Coll., Cambridge (BA). Capt., RA, N Africa, Italy, Palestine, 1942-47. Called to Bar, Middle Temple, Lincoln's Inn, 1948, Bencher, Lincoln's Inn, 1975. *Recreations:* fishing, shooting, photography. *Address:* 7 Stone Buildings, Lincoln's Inn, WC2A 3SZ. *T:* 01-405 3886/7. *Clubs:* United Oxford & Cambridge University; Bar Yacht.

EDWARDS-MOSS, Sir John (Herbert Theodore), 4th Bt *cr* 1868; *b* 24 June 1913; *s* of late Major John Edwards-Moss and Dorothy Kate Gwyllyam, *e d* of late Ven. Henry William Watkins, DD; *S* uncle, Sir Thomas Edwards-Moss, 3rd Bt, 1960; *m* 1951, Jane Rebie, *d* of Carteret John Kempson; five *s* one *d. Educ:* Downhouse, Rottingdean. *Heir: s* David John Edwards-Moss, *b* 2 Feb. 1955. *Address:* Ruffold Farm, Cranleigh, Surrey.

EELES, Air Cdre Henry, CB 1956; CBE 1943; retired as Director of Administrative Plans, Air Ministry, 1959; *b* 12 May 1910; *yr s* of Henry Eeles, Newcastle upon Tyne; *m* 1st, 1940, Janet (*d* 1960), *d* of Major J. H. Norton; two *s* one *d*; 2nd, 1963, Pamela Clarice, *d* of Comdr G. A. Matthew, Royal Navy. *Educ:* Harrow. Entered RAF Coll., 1929; Commnd Dec. 1930; Sqdn Ldr 1938; Group Capt. 1949; Air Cdre 1955. Comdt RAF Coll. and AOC RAF Cranwell, 1952-56. *Address:* The Cottage, Sutton Veny, Warminster, Wilts.

EFFINGHAM, 6th Earl of, *cr* 1837; **Mowbray Henry Gordon Howard;** 16th Baron Howard, of Effingham, *cr* 1554; *b* 29 Nov. 1905; *er s* of 5th Earl and Rosamond Margaret, *d* of late E. H. Hudson; *S* father, 1946; *m* 1st, 1938, Manci Maria Malvina Gertler (marr. diss. 1946); 2nd, 1952, Gladys Irene Kerry (marr. diss. 1971); 3rd, 1972, (Mabel) Suzanne Mingay Cragg, *d* of late Maurice Jules-Marie Le Pen, Paris, and *widow* of Wing Comdr Francis Talbot Cragg. *Educ:* Lancing. Served War 1939-45, RA and 3rd Maritime Reg. *Recreations:* shooting, fishing, philately. *Heir: n* Lt-Comdr David Peter Mowbray Algernon Howard, RN [*b* 29 April 1939; *m* 1964, Anne Mary Sayer; one *s*]. *Address:* House of Lords, SW1.

EGAN, Dr Harold; Government Chemist since 1970; *b* 23 Dec. 1922; *o s* of late Silas Henry Egan and Jenny Egan (*née* Vanner); *m* 1948, Daphne Marian Downing Cleeland; one *s. Educ:* Chiswick County Sch.; Acton Technical Coll.; Imperial Coll. London. BSc, PhD, DIC. St George's Hosp., London (Biochemical Dept), 1940-43; Dept (later Laboratory) of the Government Chemist, 1943-. Vis. Prof. of Food Science, Queen Elizabeth Coll., Univ. of London, 1973. Member: Food Standards Cttee. British Hallmarking Council. Pres. Applied Chem. Div., Internat. Union of Pure and Applied Chemistry, 1973-77. FRIC, FRSH, FIFST, FRNS. *Publications:* various papers on trace analysis, particularly pesticide residues and other contaminants. *Recreations:* maps, books on Home Counties, London. *Address:* 49 Medway Gardens, Wembley, Mddx HA0 2RJ. *T:* 01-928 7900. *Club:* Athenæum.

EGDELL, Dr John Duncan; Regional Medical Officer, Mersey Regional Health Authority, since 1977; *b* 5 March 1938; *s* of John William Egdell and Nellie (*née* Thompson); *m* 1963, Dr Linda Mary Flint; two *s* one *d. Educ:* Clifton Coll.; Univ. of Bristol. MB, ChB (Bristol) 1961; DipSocMed (Edin.) 1967; MFCM 1973. Ho. Phys. and Ho. Surg., Bristol Gen. Hosp., 1961-62; gen. practice, 1962-65; Med. Administration: with Newcastle Regional Hosp. Bd, 1966-69; with South Western Regional Hosp. Bd, 1969-74; Regional Specialist in Community Med., South Western Regional Health Authority, 1974-76; Regional Medical Postgrad. Co-ordinator, Univ. of Bristol, 1973-76. *Recreations:* delving into the past; investigating the obscure. *Address:* 8 Kingsmead Road North, Oxton, Birkenhead, Merseyside L43 6TB. *T:* 051-653 7810.

EGELAND, Leif; *b* 19 Jan. 1903; *s* of late J. J. Egeland, Consul for Norway in Natal, and Ragnhild Konsmo; *m* 1942, Marguerite Doreen, *d* of late W. J. de Zwann, Waterkloof, Pretoria; one *d. Educ:* Durban High Sch.; Natal University Coll.; Oxford Univ. MA English Lang. and Literature, Natal Univ. Coll.; MA, Hons BA, Jurisprudence, BCL Oxon; Rhodes Scholar (Natal), Trinity Coll., Oxford, 1924-27; official Fellow in Law and Classics, Brasenose Coll., 1927-30; Harmsworth Scholar, Middle Temple, 1927-30; Barrister, Middle Temple, 1930, bencher, 1948; Hon. LLD Cambridge, 1948. Admitted as

Advocate of Supreme Court of S Africa, 1931; Vice-Consul for Norway, Natal, 1931-44; MP (House of Assembly) for Durban (Berea), 1933-38, for Zululand, 1940-43; SA Minister to Sweden, 1943, to Holland and Belgium, 1946. Served War of 1939-45, as AJAG, in UDF, 1940-43; Middle East with 6th Armoured Div. of UDF, 1943. SA Delegate to San Francisco Conf., 1945, to 1st Gen. Assembly of UN, London, 1946, to Final Assembly of League of Nations, 1946; SA delegate and Pres. of Commn on Italian Political and Territorial Questions at Peace Conf., Paris, 1946. High Comr in London for the Union of South Africa, 1948-50; Chm., Standard General Insurance Co. Ltd. Nat. Chm., South Africa Inst. of Internat. Affairs; Chm., Smuts Memorial Trust; Vice Pres. and Exec. Trustee, South Africa Foundn. FRSA 1948. *Recreation:* tennis. *Address:* 11 Fricker Road, Illovo, Johannesburg, S Africa. *Clubs:* Rand, Inanda (S Africa).

EGERTON, family name of **Duke of Sutherland** and **Earl of Wilton.**

EGERTON, Maj.-Gen. David Boswell, CB 1968; OBE 1956; MC 1940; General Secretary, Association of Recognised English Language Schools, since 1971; *b* 24 July 1914; *s* of Vice-Admiral W. de M. Egerton, DSO, and late Anita Adolphine (*née* David); *m* 1946, Margaret Gillian, *d* of Canon C. C. Inge; one *s* two *d. Educ:* Stowe; RMA Woolwich. Commissioned Royal Artillery, Aug. 1934; served in India, 1935-39, including ops in Waziristan, 1937; France and Belgium, 1940 (MC); Egypt 1942, Italy 1944 (wounded). Attended first Technical Staff course, RMCS, 1946; BJSM, Washington, DC, 1950-52; Asst Chief Engineer in charge of ammunition development, Royal Armament R&D Estabt, 1955-58; idc 1959; Army Mem., Defence Research Policy Staff, 1959-62; Comdt, Trials Estabt Guided Weapons, RA, 1962-63; Army Mem., Air Defence Working Party, 1963-64; Dir-Gen. of Artillery, Ministry of Defence, Army Dept, 1964-67; Vice-Pres., Ordnance Board, 1967-69, President, 1969-70; retired 1970. Col Comdt, RA, 1970-74. *Recreations:* swimming, gardening, travel. *Address:* Pendrys, West Clandon, Surrey. *T:* Guildford 222640. *Club:* Army and Navy.

EGERTON, Sir John Alfred Roy, (Jack Egerton), Kt 1976; Chairman: Trade Union Building Society; Labor Enterprise Pty Ltd; Labor Broadcasting Pty Ltd, etc; President, Queensland Trades and Labor Council, since 1957; Member, Federal Executive of ALP, since 1970 (Senior Vice-President, 1972); *b* Rockhampton, 11 March 1918; *s* of J. G. Egerton, Rockhampton; *m* 1940, Moya, *d* of W. Jones; one *s. Educ:* Rockhampton High Sch.; Mt Morgan High Sch.; Australian Admin. Staff Coll. A Union Exec. Officer, 1941-; Federal Officer of Boilermakers' Union, 1951-66 (Vice-Pres. Fed. Council; rep. Union in China, 1956); Official, Metal Trades Fedn, 1951-67. Aust. Rep. ILO Congresses, Geneva: 1960, 1966, 1968, 1974; Qld Rep. to ACTU Congress and ALP Fed. Conf.; Pres., ALP Qld Exec., 1968- (Mem. Qld Central Exec., 1958); Mem., ACTU Interstate Exec., 1969-. Dir, Qantas Airways Ltd, 1973-. Member: Duke of Edinburgh Study Conf. Cttee, 1967-74; Griffith Univ. Council. *Recreations:* reading, Rugby League (Vice-Pres. and Dir, Qld), golf, trotting. *Address:* 1 Hunter Street, Albion, Queensland 4010, Australia. *Clubs:* NSW and Queensland League, Virginia Golf, Albion Park Trotting.

EGERTON, Sir Philip John Caledon G.; *see* Grey Egerton.

EGERTON, Sir Seymour (John Louis), GCVO 1977 (KCVO 1970); Director, Coutts & Co., Bankers, since 1947 (Chairman, 1951-76); *b* 24 Sept. 1915; *s* of late Louis Egerton and Jane, *e d* of Rev. Lord Victor Seymour; unmarried. *Educ:* Eton. Served War of 1939-45, in Grenadier Guards. Dir, Phoenix Assurance Co. Ltd (Dep. Chm.); Local Dir, National Westminster Bank. Governor, St George's Hosp., 1958-73. Treasurer, Boy Scouts' Assoc., 1953-64; Vice-Pres., Corporation of the Church House. Sheriff of Greater London, 1968. *Address:* Flat A, 51 Eaton Square, SW1. *T:* 01-235 2164. *Clubs:* Boodle's, Beefsteak, Pratt's.

EGERTON, Stephen Loftus; HM Diplomatic Service; Consul-General, Rio de Janeiro, since 1977; *b* 21 July 1932; *o s* of late William le Belward Egerton, ICS, and late Angela Doreen Loftus Bland; *m* 1958, Caroline, *er d* of Major and Mrs E. T. E. Cary-Elwes, Thurton Hall, Norwich; one *s* one *d. Educ:* Summer Fields; Eton (King's Scholar 1946, Newcastle Scholar 1951); Trinity Coll., Cambridge (Major Scholar). BA 1956, MA 1960. 2nd Lieut, 60th Rifles (KRRC), 1952-53. Entered Foreign Service, 1956; Middle East Centre for Arab Studies, Lebanon, 1956-57; Political Officer and Court Registrar, Kuwait, 1958-61; Private Sec. to Parliamentary Under-Secretary, FO, 1961-62; Northern Dept, FO, 1962-63; Oriental Sec. and later also Head

of Chancery, Baghdad, 1963-67; First Sec., UK Mission to the UN, New York, 1967-70; Asst Head of Arabian and Near Eastern Depts, FCO, 1970-72; Counsellor and Head of Chancery, Tripoli, 1972-73; Head of Energy Dept, FCO, 1973-77. *Recreations:* conversation, coins and medals. *Address:* 31 Crescent Wood Road, Dulwich, SE26. *Clubs:* Travellers'; Greenjackets.

EGGERS, Henry Howard, CMG 1950; OBE 1945; Director, Cable & Wireless Ltd, 1954-69 (Managing Director, 1955-69); *b* 13 Nov. 1903; *yr s* of late H. A. F. Eggers, London; *m* 1936, Sheila (marr. diss. 1949), *d* of late F. R. Addie, Dunblane; one *s* one *d. Educ:* Dulwich Coll.; Magdalen Coll., Oxford. Central and South American merchant, 1924-39; Ministry of Economic Warfare, 1940-45; HM Treasury, 1945-54. Order of Istiqlal (Jordan), 1965. *Address:* The Barn, Ockenden Lane, Cuckfield, Sussex. *T:* Haywards Heath 54363.

EGGINTON, Anthony Joseph; Director of Engineering and Nuclear Physics, Science Research Council, since 1974; *b* 18 July 1930; *s* of Arthur Reginald Egginton and Margaret Anne (*née* Emslie); *m* 1957, Janet Leta, *d* of late Albert and Florence Herring; two *d. Educ:* Selhurst Grammar Sch., Croydon; University Coll., London. BSc 1951. Res. Assoc., UCL, 1951-56; AERE Harwell (Gen. Physics Div.), 1956-61; Head of Beams Physics Gp, NIRNS Rutherford High Energy Lab., 1961-65; Head of Machine Gp, SRC Daresbury Nuclear Physics Lab., 1965-72; Head of Engrg Div., SRC London Office, 1972-74. *Publications:* papers and articles in jls and conf. proceedings on particle accelerators and beams. *Recreations:* sport, reading, music. *Address:* The Close, Boar's Hill, Oxford. *T:* Oxford 739077.

EGGLESTON, Anthony Francis, OBE 1968; Headmaster, Felsted School, since 1968; *b* 26 Jan. 1928; *s* of late J. F. Eggleston and Mrs J. M. Barnard, Harrow, Middx; *m* 1957, Jane Morison Buxton, JP, *d* of late W. L. Buxton, MBE and late Mrs F. M. M. Buxton, Stanmore, Middx; one *s* two *d. Educ:* Merchant Taylors' Sch., Northwood (Schol.); St John's Coll., Oxford (Sir Thomas White Schol.). BA 1949, MA 1953; 2nd cl. hons Chemistry. National Service, 1950-52; 2nd Lieut, RA, Suez Canal Zone. Asst Master, Cheltenham Coll., 1952-54; Sen. Science Master, English High Sch., Istanbul, 1954-56; Asst Master, Merchant Taylors' Sch., Northwood, 1956-62; Principal, English Sch., Nicosia, 1962-68. Governor: British School of Brussels, 1970-; Orwell Park Sch., 1971-; Quainton Hall Sch., Harrow, 1972; Ingatestone Anglo-European Comprehensive Sch., 1973. *Recreations:* archaeology, architecture. *Address:* School House, Felsted, Dunmow, Essex. *T:* Great Dunmow 820258.

EGGLESTON, Prof. Harold Gordon; Professor of Pure Mathematics in London University and Head of Department of Mathematics, at Royal Holloway College, since 1966; *b* 27 Nov. 1921; 2nd *s* of H. T. and E. M. Eggleston, Bents Green, Sheffield; *m* 1955, Elizabeth, *o d* of F. R. and C. A. W. Daglish, Beamish, County Durham; two *s* one *d. Educ:* High Storrs Grammar Sch., Sheffield; Trinity Coll., Cambridge. Lecturer and Senior Lecturer, University Coll. of Swansea, 1948-53; Lecturer, University of Cambridge, 1953-58; Prof. of Mathematics, University of London at Bedford Coll., 1958-66. *Publications:* Problems in Euclidean Space, 1957; Convexity, 1958; Elementary Real Analysis, 1962. *Address:* Royal Holloway College, Englefield Green, Surrey.

EGGLESTON, Hon. Sir Richard (Moulton), Kt 1971; Chancellor, since 1975, and Consultant, Faculty of Law, since 1974, Monash University; Director, Barclays Australia Ltd, since 1974; *b* Hampton, Vic, Australia, 8 Aug. 1909; *s* of late John Bakewell Eggleston and Elizabeth Bothwell Eggleston (*née* McCutcheon); *m* 1934, Marjorie, *d* of late F. E. Thom; one *s* three *d. Educ:* Wesley Coll., Melbourne; Univ. of Melbourne (LLB). Barrister, 1932-41 and 1945-60. Staff of Defence Dept, 1942-45; Indep. Lectr in Equity, Melbourne Univ., 1940-49; KC 1950. Judge: Supreme Ct of Norfolk Is, 1960-69; Supreme Ct of ACT, 1960-74; Commonwealth Industrial Ct, 1960-74; Pres., Trade Practices Tribunal, 1966-74. Hon. Treas., Victorian Bar Council, 1953-56 (Chm., 1956-58); Mem., Bd of Aust. Elizabethan Theatre Trust, 1961-67; Fellow, Queen's Coll., Univ. of Melbourne, 1964-; Pro-Chancellor, ANU, 1968-72. Chm., Company Law Adv. Cttee, 1967-73. Hon. LLD Melbourne, 1973. *Recreations:* painting, golf, billiards, music. *Address:* 17 Russell Street, Toorak, Victoria 3142, Australia. *T:* 20 5215. *Clubs:* Australian (Melbourne); University (Sydney); Commonwealth (Canberra).

EGGLESTON, Prof. Samuel John, BScEcon, MA, Dlitt; Professor of Education, University of Keele, since 1967;

Chairman, Board of Social Sciences, since 1976; *b* 11 Nov. 1926; *s* of Edmund and Josephine Eggleston, Dorchester; *m* 1957, Greta, *d* of James and Alice Patrick, Hereford; two *s* two *d*. *Educ:* Chippenham Grammar Sch.; LSE (BScEcon 1957); Univ. of London Inst. of Educn (MA 1965). Univ. of Keele, DLitt 1977. Teacher, Suffolk and Worcs, 1950-54; Leverhulme Scholarship, LSE, 1954-57; Teacher, Beds, and Headteacher, Oxfordshire, 1957-60; Lectr, Loughborough Coll. of Educn, 1960-63; Lectr, later Sen. Lectr, Leicester Univ., 1963-67. Vis. Commonwealth Fellow, Canada, 1973-74; Ext. Examnr and Consult., Univ. of Science, Malaysia, 1973-76; Consult. and Rapporteur General, Internat. Conf. on Teacher Policies, OECD, 1974. Chairman: Sociology Sect., Internat. Comparative Educn Soc. Convention, San Francisco, 1975; Cttee on Youth Res., Nat. Youth Bureau, 1975-. Director: DES Res. Project, Structure and Function of Youth Service, 1968-74; Schs Council Project, Design and Craft Educn, 1968-74; Member: Adv. Cttee, Nuffield Foundn enquiry, Prep. of Teachers of Socially Deprived, 1968-72; House of Commons Working Gp, Educn for Eradication of Colour Prejudice, 1969-; Schs Council Working Party, Whole Curriculum, 1970-74; Adv. Cttee, Nuffield Foundn Physics Interface Proj., 1971-76; Council of Europe Working Party, Diversif. of Tertiary Educn, 1972-; Exec. Cttee, Standing Conf. of Studies in Educn, 1972-; Educnl Res. Bd, SSRC, 1973-77; Educn Cttee, CNAA, 1977-; Anglo-Italian Working Party, Educnl Problems, 1975; Coord. Cttee, Assessment of Performance Unit, DES, 1975-; Panel on Public Disorder and Sporting Events, SSRC, 1976-. Adjudicator, Craft and Design, Welsh National Eisteddfod, 1977. Editor, Studies in Design Education and Craft, 1968-; Chm. Editorial Board: Sociological Rev., 1970-; Paedagogica Europaea, Educnl Yearbook of Council of Europe and Europ. Cult. Foundn, 1976- (Editor in Chief, 1968-76); Gen. Editor: The Contemporary Sociology of the School, 1975-; New Developments in the Curriculum, 1975-. Hon. Fellow, Coll. of Craft Educn, 1972. *Publications:* The Social Context of the School, 1967; (with G. N. Brown) Towards an Education for the 21st Century, 1969; (ed with A. R. Pemberton) International Perspectives of Design Education, 1973; (ed) Contemporary Research in the Sociology of Education, 1974; Adolescence and Community, 1976; New Developments in Design Education, 1976; The Sociology of the School Curriculum, 1977; The Ecology of the School, 1977; articles in books and jls, incl. Sociol., Brit. Jl of Sociol., New Soc., Educnl Res., Brit. Jl of In-Service Educn, Brit. Jl of Teacher Educn, Res. Intelligence. *Recreations:* work in design and craft,skiing, riding, travel, gardening, listening and talking. *Address:* Hallaton House, Whitmore Heath, Newcastle under Lyme, Staffs ST5 5JA. *T:* Whitmore 680483.

EGGLETON, Anthony, CVO 1970; Federal Director, Liberal Party of Australia, since 1975; Special Adviser to the Leader of the Opposition, and Director of Communications, Federal Liberal Party, 1974-75; *b* 30 April 1932; *s* of Tom and Winifred Eggleton; *m* 1953, Mary Walker, Melbourne; two *s* one *d*. *Educ:* King Alfred's Sch., Wantage. Journalist, Westminster Press Group, 1948-50; Editorial Staff, Bendigo Advertiser, Vic, 1950-51; Australian Broadcasting Commn, 1951-60 (Dir of ABC-TV News Coverage, 1956-60); Dir of Public Relations, Royal Australian Navy, 1960-65; Press Sec. to Prime Ministers of Australia, 1965-71 (Prime Ministers Menzies, Holt, Gorton, McMahon); Commonwealth Dir of Information, London, 1971-74. Australian Public Relations Inst.'s 1st Award of Honour, 1968. *Address:* c/o Parliament House, Canberra, ACT 2600, Australia. *T:* 732564. *Club:* (Foundn Pres.) National Press (Canberra).

EGLINTON and WINTON, 18th Earl of, *cr* 1507; **Archibald George Montgomerie;** Lord Montgomerie, 1448; Baron Seton and Tranent, 1859; Baron Kilwinning, 1615; Baron Ardrossan (UK), 1806; Earl of Winton (UK), 1859; Hereditary Sheriff of Renfrewshire; *b* 27 Aug. 1939; *s* of 17th Earl of Eglinton and Winton and Ursula, *er d* of Hon. Ronald Watson, Edinburgh; *S* father, 1966; *m* 1964, Marion Carolina, *o d* of John Dunn-Yarker; four *s*. *Educ:* Eton. *Heir: s* Lord Montgomerie, *qv*. *Address:* The Dutch House, West Green, Hartley Wintney, Hants.

EGLINTON, Prof. Geoffrey, PhD, DSc; FRS 1976; Professor of Organic Geochemistry, University of Bristol, since 1973; *b* 1 Nov. 1927; *s* of Alfred Edward Eglinton and Lilian Blackham; *m* 1955, Pamela Joan Coupland; two *s* one *d*. *Educ:* Sale Grammar Sch.; Manchester Univ. (BSc, PhD, DSc). Post-Doctoral Fellow, Ohio State Univ., 1951-52; ICI Fellow, Liverpool Univ., 1952-54; Lectr, subseq. Sen. Lectr and Reader, Glasgow Univ., 1954-67; Sen. Lectr, subseq. Reader, Bristol Univ., 1967-73. Gold Medal for Exceptional Scientific Achievement, NASA, 1973; Hugo Müller Silver Medal, Chemical Soc., 1974. *Publications:* Applications of Spectroscopy to Organic Chemistry, 1965;

Organic Geochemistry: methods and results, 1969; 'Chemsyn', 1972 (2nd edn 1975); contrib. Nature, Geochim. Cosmochim. Acta, Phytochem., Chem. Geol., Sci. American. *Recreations:* gardening, walking, sailing. *Address:* Oldwell, 7 Redhouse Lane, Bristol BS9 3RY. *T:* Bristol 683833. *Club:* Rucksack (Manchester).

EGMONT, 11th Earl of, *cr* 1733; **Frederick George Moore Perceval;** Bt 1661; Baron Perceval, 1715; Viscount Perceval, 1722; Baron Lovell and Holland (Great Britain), 1762; Baron Arden, 1770; Baron Arden (United Kingdom), 1802; *b* 14 April 1914; *o s* of 10th Earl and Cecilia (*d* 1916), *d* of James Burns Moore, Montreal; *S* father, 1932; *m* 1932, Ann Geraldine, *d* of D. G. Moodie; one *s* one *d* (and two *s* decd). *Heir: s* Viscount Perceval, *qv*. *Address:* Two-dot Ranch, Nanton, Alberta, Canada.

EGREMONT, 2nd Baron *cr* 1963, and **LECONFIELD,** 7th Baron *cr* 1859; **John Max Henry Scawen Wyndham;** *b* 21 April 1948; *s* of John Edward Reginald Wyndham, MBE, 1st Baron Egremont and 6th Baron Leconfield, and of Pamela, *d* of Captain the Hon. Valentine Wyndham-Quin, *qv*; *S* father, 1972. *Educ:* Eton; Christ Church, Oxford (BA Modern History). *Publication:* The Cousins, 1977. *Heir: b* Hon. Harry Hugh Patrick Wyndham, *b* 28 Sept 1957. *Address:* Petworth House, Petworth, West Sussex. *T:* Petworth 42447.

EHRMAN, John Patrick William, FBA 1970; historian; *b* 17 March 1920; *o s* of late Albert and Rina Ehrman; *m* 1948, Elizabeth Susan Anne, *d* of late Vice-Adm. Sir Geoffrey Blake, KCB, DSO; four *s*. *Educ:* Charterhouse; Trinity Coll., Cambridge (MA). Served Royal Navy, 1940-45. Fellow of Trinity Coll., Cambridge, 1947-52; Historian, Cabinet Office, 1948-56; Lees Knowles Lectr, Cambridge, 1957-58; James Ford Special Lectr, Oxford, 1976-77. Hon. Treas., Friends of the National Libraries; Trustee of the Nat. Portrait Gall., 1971-; Member: Reviewing Cttee on Export of Works of Art, 1970-76; Royal Commn on Historical Manuscripts, 1973-; Chm., Adv. Cttee to British Library Reference Div., 1975-; Vice-Pres., Navy Records Soc., 1968-70, 1974-76. FSA 1958; FRHistS. *Publications:* The Navy in the War of William III, 1953; Grand Strategy, 1943-5 (2 vols, UK Official Military Histories of the Second World War), 1956; Cabinet Government and War, 1890-1940, 1958; The British Government and Commercial Negotiations with Europe, 1783-1793, 1962; The Younger Pitt: the years of acclaim, 1969. *Address:* Sloane House, 149 Old Church Street, SW3 6EB; Clobb Copse, Buckler's Hard, Beaulieu, Hants. *Clubs:* Beefsteak, Garrick.

EIGEN, Manfred; Director at Max-Planck-Institut für biophysikalische Chemie, Göttingen, since 1964; *b* 9 May 1927; *s* of Ernst and Hedwig Eigen; *m* 1952, Elfriede Müller; one *s* one *d*. *Educ:* Göttingen Univ. Dr rer. nat. (Phys. Chem.) 1951. Research Asst, Inst. für physikal. Chemie, Göttingen Univ., 1951-53; Asst, Max-Planck-Institut für physikal. Chemie, 1953; Research Fellow, Max-Planck-Gesellschaft, 1958; Head of separate dept of biochemical kinetics, Max-Planck-Inst., 1962. Andrew D. White Prof. at Large, Cornell Univ., 1965; Hon. Prof., Technische Hochschule Braunschweig, 1965. For. Hon. Mem., Amer. Acad. of Arts and Sciences, 1964; Mem. Leopoldina, Deutsche Akad. der Naturforscher, Halle, 1964; Mem., Akad. der Wissenschaften, Göttingen, 1965; Hon. Mem., Amer. Assoc. Biol Chemists, 1966; For. Assoc., Nat. Acad. of Scis, Washington, 1966; For. Mem., Royal Soc., 1973. Dr of Science *hc*, Washington, Harvard and Chicago Univs, 1966. Has won prizes, medals and awards including Nobel Prize for Chemistry (jointly), 1967. *Publications:* numerous papers in Z. Elektrochem., Jl Phys. Chem., Trans Faraday Soc., Proc. Royal Soc., Canad. Jl Chem., ICSU Rev., and other learned jls. *Address:* Max-Planck-Institut für biophysikalische Chemie, Karl-Friedrich Bonhoeffer Institut, D3400 Göttingen-Nikolausberg, Germany.

EILON, Prof. Samuel; Professor and Head of Department of Management Science (formerly Management Engineering Section), Imperial College of Science and Technology, University of London, since 1963; Director, Amey Roadstone Corporation, since 1974; *b* 13 Oct. 1923; *s* of Abraham and Rachel Eilon; *m* 1946, Hannah Ruth (*née* Samuel); two *s* two *d*. *Educ:* Reali Sch., Haifa; Technion, Israel Inst. of Technology, Haifa; Imperial Coll., London. PhD 1955, DSc(Eng) 1963, London. FIMechE, FIProdE. Engr, Palestine Electric Co. Ltd, Haifa, 1946-48; Officer, Israel Defence Forces, 1948-52; CO of an Ordnance and workshop base depot (Major); Res. Asst, Imperial Coll., 1952-55; Lectr in Production Engrg, Imperial Coll., 1955-57; Associate Prof. in Industrial Engrg, Technion, Haifa, 1957-59; Reader, and Head of Section, Imperial Coll., 1959-63. Professorial Research Fellow, Case-Western-Reserve

Univ., Cleveland, Ohio, 1967-68. Vis. Fellow, University Coll., Cambridge, 1970-71. Past Mem. of several cttees of IProdE and DES. Member Council: Operational Res. Soc., 1965-67; Inst. of Management Scis, 1970-72. Advisor, P-E Consulting Gp, 1961-71; Principal and Dir, Spencer Stuart and Associates, 1971-74. Chief Editor, OMEGA, Internat. Jl of Management Science, 1972-; Dep. Editor, Management Science, 1969-77. Two Joseph Whitworth Prizes for papers, IMechE, 1960. Founder Fellow, Fellowship of Engineering, 1976. *Publications:* Elements of Production Planning and Control, 1962; Industrial Engineering Tables, 1962; (jtly) Exercises in Industrial Management, 1966; (jtly) Industrial Scheduling Abstracts, 1967; (jtly) Inventory Control Abstracts, 1968; (jtly) Distribution Management, 1971; Management Control, 1971; (jtly) Applications of Management Science in Banking and Finance, 1972; (jtly) Applied Productivity Analysis for Industry, 1976; Aspects of Management, 1977; numerous scientific papers. *Recreations:* theatre, tennis, walking. *Address:* 1 Meadway Close, NW11 7BA; Imperial College, Exhibition Road, SW7 2BX. *T:* 01-589 5111. *Club:* Athenæum.

EISENHOWER, Milton Stover; President, The Johns Hopkins University, 1956-67, 1971-72, now President Emeritus; *b* 15 Sept. 1899; *s* of David Jacob and Ida Stover Eisenhower; *m* 1927, Helen Elsie Eakin (decd); one *s* one *d. Educ:* Kansas State Univ. (BS); Univ. of Edinburgh. City Ed., Abilene (Kan.) Daily Reflector, 1918 and 1920-21; Asst Prof. Journalism, Kansas State Univ., 1924; Amer. Vice-Consul, Edinburgh, 1924-26; Asst to Sec. of Agric., 1926-28; Dir Inf., US Dept of Agric., 1928-41, Land Use Co-ordinator, 1937-42; Dir, War Relocation Authority, 1942; Assoc. Dir, Office of War Inf., 1942-43; Pres., Kansas State Univ., 1943-50; Pres., Pennsylvania State Univ., 1950-56. Mem. Fact-finding Board in Gen. Motors labor-management dispute, 1945; Famine Emergency Relief Ctee, 1946; Exec. Bd Unesco, 1946; President's Cttee on Government Organisation, 1953-60; Nat. Advisory Cttee on Inter-American Affairs, 1960; Special Ambassador and Personal Rep. of US Pres., on Latin Amer. Affairs, 1953, 1957, 1958, 1959, 1960; Chm., US Nat. Commn for Unesco, 1946-48; Deleg., Unesco Confs, 1946-47-48-49. Mem., President's Commn on Higher Educn, 1946; Problems and Policies Cttee, Amer. Council on Educn, 1950-53; Exec. Cttee, Assoc. Land-Grant Colls and Univs, 1944-47, 1950-53, Chm., 1946-47, 1952-53; Pres. Assoc. 1951-52. Chm. Nat. Cttee for The People Act, 1951-53; Director: Fund for Adult Educn, 1953-61; Freedoms Foundn Inc., 1951-; The Geisinger Memorial Hosp., 1952-; Mem., Atlantic-Pacific Interoceanic Canal Study Commn, 1965-70; Chairman, President's Commn on: Causes and Prevention of Violence, 1968-69; Internat. Radio Broadcasting, 1972-73. Also trusteeships, etc both past and present. Holds numerous hon. degrees (including LLD Johns Hopkins), foreign orders, etc. *Publications:* The Wine is Bitter, 1963; The President is Calling, 1974; ed many publications for US Dept of Agric.; articles for Scholar, Sat. Evening Post, Colliers, Country Gentlemen, etc. *Address:* Evergreen House, 4545 North Charles Street, Baltimore, Md 21210, USA. *T:* 338-7670. *Clubs:* Johns Hopkins (Baltimore); Mill Reef (Antigua).

EKIN, Maj.-Gen. Roger Gillies, CIE 1946; IA, retired; *b* 18 Nov. 1895; *yr s* of T. C. Ekin, MInstCE; *m* 1st, 1923, Phyllis Marian (*d* 1967), *er d* of Maj.-Gen. Sir Henry Croker, KCB, CMG; one *s* two *d;* 2nd, 1972, Mona de Hamel, *widow* of Etienne Bruno de Hamel. *Educ:* Westminster; RMC Sandhurst. First Commissioned, 1914; Palestine campaign, 1916-19; on Operations in Waziristan, 1920-21; Operations NWFP, 1930; Brevet Lt-Col 1936; Comdt 5th Bn FF Rifles, 1937-40; Comd Kohat Bde Ahmedzal Ops, 1940; Col 1939; Comdt Tactical Sch., India, 1940-41; Comd 46 Inf. Bde, Burma campaign, 1941-42; Nowshera Bde, 1942-45; Kohat (Independent) Bde, 1945-46. Despatches five times. GOC Bihar and Orissa Area, India, 1946-47; retired, 1947; Sec., Hereford Diocesan Board of Finance, 1947-61. *Address:* Waverley Abbey House, near Farnham, Surrey. *Club:* Naval and Military.

EKING, Maj.-Gen. Harold Cecil William, CB 1959; CBE 1954; DSO 1945; retired Jan. 1960; *b* 17 Nov. 1903; *s* of Harold Turney Eking; *m* 1st 1933, Eileen (*née* Brewer); one *s;* 2nd, 1943, Betty (*née* Stokes); one *d. Educ:* Rugby Sch.; RMA Woolwich. Commissioned Royal Engineers, 1924; Staff Coll., 1940; GSO1, 4 Div., 1941; 46 Div., 1942-43; CRE, 78 Div., 1943-44; CE, 13 Corps, 1944; Comd Engr Gp, Italy and Burma, 1945-46; CRE, Bde Comd and 2 i/c 10 Indian Div., 1946-47; Col GS, SME, 1948-50; Col AQ, Hong Kong, 1950; DDPS, War Office, 1951-54; Comdt, Sch. of Military Engineering, 1954-56; Chief Engineer, HQ Northern Army Group, 1956-60. *Address:* Pugg's Meadow, Kington Magna, Gillingham, Dorset. *Club:* Army and Navy.

EKLUND, Dr (Arne) Sigvard; Director General, International Atomic Energy Agency, Vienna, since Dec. 1961; *b* Kiruna, Sweden, 1911; *m* 1941, Anna-Greta Johansson; one *s* two *d. Educ:* Uppsala Univ., Sweden (DSc). Assoc. Prof. in Nuclear Physics, Royal Inst. of Technology, Stockholm, 1946-56; Dir of Research, later Reactor development Div., AB Atomenergi, 1950-61. Conference Sec.-Gen., 2nd Internat. UN Conf. on Peaceful Uses of Atomic Energy, 1958. Fellow, Amer. Nuclear Soc., 1961; Member: Royal Swedish Acad. of Engineering Sciences, 1953; Royal Swedish Acad. of Sciences, 1972; Hon. Mem., British Nuclear Energy Soc., 1963. Dr *hc* : Univ. of Graz, 1968; Acad. of Mining and Metallurgy, Cracow, 1971; Univ. of Bucarest, 1971; Chalmers Inst. of Technol., Gothenberg, 1974. (Jointly) Atoms for Peace Award, 1968; Golden Medal of Honour, Vienna, 1971; Henry DeWolf Smyth Nuclear Statesman Award, 1976. Hon. Senator, Univ. of Vienna, 1977. Kt Comdr, Order of North Star, Sweden, 1971. *Publications:* Studies in Nuclear Physics, 1946 (Sweden); articles on peaceful uses of nuclear energy. *Address:* International Atomic Energy Agency, Kärntnerring 11, 1010 Vienna I, Austria. *T:* Vienna 52 45 11.

ELAM, His Honour Henry; a Circuit Judge (formerly Deputy Chairman of the Court of Quarter Sessions, Inner London), 1954-76; barrister-at-law; *b* 29 Nov. 1903; *o s* of Thomas Henry Elam, 33 Sackville Street, W1; *m* 1st, 1930, Eunice (*d* 1975), *yr d* of J. G. Matthews, 41 Redington Road, NW3; one *d*; 2nd, 1975, Doris A. Horsford. *Educ:* Charterhouse; Lincoln Coll., Oxford (MA). Called to Bar, Inner Temple, 1927; Western Circuit; Junior Prosecuting Counsel to the Treasury, Central Criminal Court, 1937; late Dep. Judge Advocate, RAF; Recorder of Poole, 1941-46; 2nd Junior Prosecuting Counsel, 1942-45; 1st Junior, 1945-50; 3rd Senior, Jan.-March 1950; 2nd Senior, 1950-53; Recorder of Exeter, 1946-53; Dep. Chm., West Kent QS, 1947-53. Mem. of Tin Plate Workers' Co. *Recreation:* flyfishing. *Address:* Clymshurst, Burwash Common, East Sussex. *T:* West Burwash 335.

ELATH, Eliahu, PhD; President Emeritus, Hebrew University, Jerusalem; Israeli diplomatist; Chairman, Board of Governors, Israel Afro-Asian Institute; *b* 30 July 1903; *s* of Menachem and Rivka Epstein (Elath); *m* 1931, Zehava Zalel, *Educ:* Hebrew Univ., Jerusalem; American Univ., Beirut, Lebanon. Reuter's Corresp. in Syria and Lebanon, 1931-34. Mem. Political Dept of Jewish Agency for Palestine in Jerusalem, 1934-45; Dir Political Office of Jewish Agency for Palestine in Washington, 1945-48; Special Representative of Provisional Govt of Israel in USA, 1948; Ambassador of Israel to USA, 1948-50; Minister of Israel, 1950-52, Ambassador, 1952-59, to the Court of St James's. Pres., Israel Oriental Soc. Vice-Pres., Jewish Colonization Assoc. (ICA). Hon. PhD: Brandeis; Wayn; Hebrew Union Coll.; Dropsie Coll., USA. *Publications:* The Bedouin, Their Customs and Manners, 1933; Trans-Jordan, 1934; Israel and her Neighbours, 1960; The Political Struggle for Inclusion of Elath in the Jewish State, 1967; San Francisco Diary, 1971; British Routes to India, 1971; Zionism and the Arabs, 1974; Zionism and the UN, 1977; contribs to Quarterly of Palestine Exploration Fund, Jl of Royal Central Asian Society, Encyclopædia Britannica. *Address:* 17 Bialik Street, Beth Hakerem, Jerusalem, Israel. *T:* 524615.

ELBORNE, Sydney Lipscomb, MBE 1918; Chairman of Hunts Quarter Sessions, 1947-63; *b* 6 July 1890; *e s* of late William Elborne, MA, Wootton House, Peterborough; *m* 1925, Cavil Grace Mary, *d* of late George E. Monckton, Fineshade Abbey, Northants; one *s* one *d. Educ:* King's Sch., Peterborough; Trinity Coll. Cambridge (MA). Asst Inspector of High Explosives (Technical), The Royal Arsenal, Woolwich, 1914-18; called to Bar, Inner Temple, 1919; Mem. Midland Circuit; Mem. Gen. Council of the Bar, 1940-47; former Asst Recorder of Birmingham; Mem. Hunts CC, 1930-45; JP Hunts, 1932. Pres. Soc. of Chairmen and Dep. Chm. of Quarter Sessions, 1955. Mem. Mr Justice Austen Jones's Cttee on County Court procedure, 1947; a Trustee and Mem. Council, Northants Record Soc.; formerly Trustee of Peterborough Museum Soc. and Maxwell Art Gallery; Mem. Area Cttee (No 11) Legal Aid, 1950-69. Contested (C) Leicester (Bosworth Div.), 1929 and Manchester (Ardwick), by-election, 1931. *Recreation:* FGS, ARIC. *Address:* Water Newton, Peterborough. *T:* Peterborough 233223; 2 Hare Court, Temple, EC4. *Club:* Carlton.

ELDER, Hugh, MA; *b* 1905; *s* of late Rev. Hugh Elder, MA, Edinburgh; *m* 1939, Winifred Mary, *o d* of late Col M. Stagg, OBE, RÉ; one *s* (and one *s* decd). *Educ:* Edinburgh Academy; Edinburgh Univ. (Scholar); Corpus Christi Coll., Oxford. MA Hons Classics, Edinburgh, 1927; BA, Lit. Hum. 1929, MA 1934, Oxford. Asst Master at Sherborne Sch., 1929-35; Asst Master at Fettes Coll., 1935-38; Headmaster of Dean Close Sch.,

Cheltenham, 1938-46; Headmaster of Merchant Taylors' Sch., 1946-65. *Recreations:* music, golf. *Address:* Millbrook, Huish Episcopi, Langport, Somerset.

ELDER, Sir (William) Stewart D.; *see* Duke-Elder.

ELDER-JONES, His Honour Thomas; a Circuit Judge (formerly Judge of County Courts), 1953-76; *b* 4 Oct. 1904; *o s* of late David Jones, JP, Foxcote Grange, Andoversford, shipowner, and late Anne Amelia (Roberts); *m* 1948, Hon. Diana Katherine Taylor (*née* Russell), *o d* of 25th Baron de Clifford; one adopted *d* one step *s*. *Educ:* Shrewsbury; Trinity Coll., Oxford (MA). Barrister-at-law, Inner Temple, 1927. Served 1939-43, 2nd Royal Gloucestershire Hussars, retired, rank of Hon. Major. Sec. National Reference Tribunal for Coal Mining Industry, 1943-53; Judge of County Courts Circuit 34 (Brentford and Uxbridge), 1953-57, Circuit 52 (Bath-Swindon), 1957-76. At Bar practised in Common Law and Coal Mining matters. *Recreation:* fox-hunting. *Address:* The Dower House, Somerford Keynes, Cirencester, Glos. *T:* Ashton Keynes 296. *Club:* Cavalry and Guards.

ELDERFIELD, Maurice; Director of Finance, Ferranti Ltd, since 1977; *b* 10 April 1926; *s* of Henry Elderfield and Kathleen Maud Elderfield; *m* 1953, Audrey June (*née* Knight); one *s* three *d*. *Educ:* Southgate Grammar Sch. FCA. Fleet Air Arm, 1944-47. Thomson, Kingdom & Co., Chartered Accountants (qual. 1949), 1947-49; Personal Asst to Man. Dir, Forrestell, Land, Timber & Railway Co., 1949-57; Group Chief Accountant, Stephens Group, 1957-60; various posts, Segas, culminating in Board Mem. and Dir for Finance, 1960-73; Dir of Finance, Southern Water Authority, 1973-75; PO Board Mem. for Finance and Corporate Planning, 1975-76. *Recreations:* golf, tennis, squash. *Address:* Hadleigh, Cansiron Lane, Ashurst Wood, East Grinstead RH19 3SD. *Club:* Gravetye Manor Country.

ELDON, 5th Earl of, *cr* 1821; **John Joseph Nicholas Scott;** Baron Eldon 1799; Viscount Encombe 1821; *b* 24 April 1937; *s* of 4th Earl of Eldon, GCVO, and Hon. Magdalen Fraser, OBE (*d* 1969), *d* of 16th Baron Lovat; *S* father, 1976; *m* 1961, Comtesse Claudine de Montjoye-Vaufrey et de la Roche, Vienna; one *s* two *d*. *Educ:* Ampleforth; Trinity Coll., Oxford. 2nd Lieut Scots Guards (National Service). Lieut AER. *Heir: s* Viscount Encombe, *qv*. *Address:* 2 Coach House Lane, Wimbledon, SW19.

ELDRIDGE, Eric William, CB 1965; OBE 1948; Consultant with Lee and Pembertons, solicitors, since 1971; *b* 15 April 1906; *o s* of late William Eldridge; *m* 1936, Doris Margaret Kerr; one *s* one *d*. *Educ:* Millfields Central Sch.; City of London Coll. Admitted Solicitor (Hons), 1934. Chief Administrative Officer, Public Trustee Office, 1955-60; Asst Public Trustee, 1960-63; Public Trustee, 1963-71. *Address:* Old Stocks, Gorelands Lane, Chalfont St Giles, Bucks. *T:* Chalfont St Giles 2159.

ELDRIDGE, John Barron; Chairman, Matthews Wrightson Holdings Ltd, since 1971; *b* 28 May 1919; *s* of William John Eldridge and Jessie Winifred (*née* Bowditch); *m* 1940, Marjorie Potier; one *s* two *d*. *Educ:* Lancing Coll. FIA 1950. Dir, Matthews Wrightson Holdings Ltd, 1964. Croix de Guerre 1944. *Address:* Castleton, Warwicks Bench Road, Guildford, Surrey. *T:* Guildford 62687.

ELDRIDGE, Lt-Gen. Sir (William) John, KBE 1954 (CBE 1941); CB 1944; DSO 1919; MC; Chairman, Kearney and Trecker, CVA Ltd, 1957-68; *b* 2 March 1898; *s* of late William Henry Eldridge; *m* 1954, Violet Elizabeth (*d* 1956), *e d* of John Cane, Wrexham. 2nd Lieut RA 1915; served European War, France and Belgium, 1916-18 (wounded, despatches twice, DSO, MC); Iraq Operations, 1919-20; War of 1939-45 (despatches, CBE, Bar to DSO). Dir-Gen. of Artillery, Ministry of Supply, 1945-48; Comdt Mil. Coll. of Science, 1948-51; GOC Aldershot District, 1951-53; Controller of Munitions, Min. of Supply, 1953-57, retired. Col Comdt: RA, 1951-61; Glider Pilot Regt, Glider Pilot and Parachute Corps, 1951-57. *Address:* Fir Acre, Ash Vale, Surrey. *Club:* Royal Air Force.

ELEK, Prof. Stephen Dyonis, MD, DSc; FRCP; Professor of Medical Microbiology in the University of London, 1957-74, now Emeritus; Consultant Bacteriologist, St George's Hospital, SW1, 1948-73; *b* 24 March 1914; *s* of Dezso and Anna Elek; *m* Sarah Joanna Hall; three *d*. *Educ:* Lutheran High Sch., Budapest, Hungary; St George's Hosp. Med. Sch., Univ. of London. MB, BS 1940; MD 1943; PhD 1948; DPH 1943; DSc 1958; MRCP 1960; FRCPath 1964. Clinical Pathologist, Maida Vale Hosp. for Nervous Diseases, 1946-47; Laking-Dakin Fellow, 1942-43; Fulbright Fellow, Harvard Medical Sch., 1956.

Member: Pathological Soc. of Great Britain; American Society for Microbiology; New York Academy of Sciences; Soc. of Gen. Microbiology, etc. Editor, Jl of Medical Microbiology, 1972-74. *Publications:* Staphylococcus pyogenes and its Relation to Disease, 1959; scientific papers relating to diphtheria, leprosy, vaccination against mental retardation etc, in Lancet, BMJ, Jl Path. and Bact., Brit. Jl Exper. Path. *Recreations:* sculpting, walking. *Address:* Avenue de Cour 155, 1007 Lausanne, Switzerland. *T:* 26.58.14. *Club:* Athenæum.

ELEY, Prof. Daniel Douglas, OBE 1961; ScD, PhD Cantab; MSc, PhD Manchester; FRS 1964; Professor of Physical Chemistry, University of Nottingham, since 1954; Dean of Faculty of Pure Science, 1959-62; *b* 1 Oct. 1914; *s* of Daniel Eley and Fanny Allen Eley, *née* Ross; *m* 1942, Brenda May Williams, MA, MB, BChir (Cantab), 2nd *d* of B. T. Williams, Skewen, Glam; one *s*. *Educ:* Christ's Coll., Finchley; Manchester Univ.; St John's Coll., Cambridge. Manchester Univ.: Woodiwiss Schol. 1933, Mercer Schol. 1934, Darbishire Fellow 1936, PhD 1937; PhD, 1940, ScD 1954, Cambridge. Bristol Univ.: Lectr in Colloid Chemistry, 1945; Reader in Biophysical Chemistry, 1961. Lectures: Reilly, Univ. of Notre Dame (USA), 1950; Sir Eric Rideal, Soc. of Chem. Industry, 1975. Medal of Liège Univ., 1950; Mem. Council of Faraday Soc., 1951-54, 1960-63; Vice-Pres., 1963-. Corresp. Mem., Bavarian Acad. of Sciences, 1971. Meetings Sec., British Biophysical Soc., 1961-, Hon. Sec., 1963-65. Scientific Assessor to Sub-Cttee on Coastal Pollutions, House of Commons Select Cttee on Science and Technology, 1967-68. *Publications:* Ed., Adhesion, 1961; papers in Trans Faraday Soc., Proc. Royal Soc., Jl Chem. Soc., Biochem. Jl, etc. *Recreations:* hill walking, lawn tennis, ski-ing. *Address:* Chemistry Department, Nottingham University, University Park, Nottingham.

ELEY, Sir Geoffrey (Cecil Ryves), Kt 1964; CBE 1947; Director: Equity & Law Life Assurance Society, since 1948; Member Committee, Royal United Kingdom Benevolent Association; Vice-President, Middle East Association; *b* 18 July 1904; *s* of late Charles Cuthbert Eley, JP, VMH, East Bergholt Place, Suffolk, and of Ethel Maxwell Eley (*née* Ryves); *m* 1937, Penelope Hughes, *d* of late Adm. Sir Frederick Wake-Walker, KCB, CBE; two *s* two *d*. *Educ:* Eton; Trinity Coll., Cambridge; Harvard Univ. (Davison Scholar). On Editorial Staff of Financial News, 1926-28; banking, finance and brokerage in England, France, Switzerland and the USA, 1928-32; London Manager of Post and Flagg, members of New York Stock Exchange, 1932-39; Naval Intelligence Div., Admiralty, 1939-40; Capital Issues Cttee, 1940-41; Min. of Supply as Dir of Contracts in charge of Capital Assistance to Industry, 1941-46; Min. of Supply as Dir of Overseas Disposals, 1946-47. Mem., London Electricity Bd, 1949-59. Chm., British Drug Houses Ltd, 1948-65; Dep. Chm. and Chm., Brush Group, 1953-58; Chairman: Richard Thomas & Baldwin's Ltd, 1959-64; Richard Crittall Holdings Ltd, 1948-68; Thomas Tilling Ltd, 1965-76 (Dir, 1950-76); Heinemann Group of Publishers Ltd, 1965-76; Dep. Chm., British Bank of the Middle East, 1952-77 (Dir, 1950-77); Vice-Chm., BOC International Ltd, 1964-76 (Dir, 1959-76); Dir, Bank of England, 1949-66. Leader, UK Trade Mission to Egypt, Sudan and Ethiopia, 1955. High Sheriff, Co. of London, 1954-55; High Sheriff of Greater London, 1966. *Recreations:* gardening, the arts, foreign travel. *Address:* 27 Wynnstay Gardens, Allen Street, W8 6UR. *T:* 01-937 0797; The Change House, Great Yeldham, Essex. *T:* Great Yeldham 260. *Clubs:* Brooks's, Beefsteak.

ELEY, John L.; *see* Lloyd-Eley.

ELGIN, 11th Earl of, *cr* 1633, and **KINCARDINE, 15th Earl of,** *cr* 1647; **Andrew Douglas Alexander Thomas Bruce,** DL; JP; Baron Bruce of Kinloss, 1604, Baron Bruce of Torry, 1647; Baron Elgin (UK), 1849; 37th Chief of the Name of Bruce; late Scots Guards; Brigadier of Royal Company of Archers, HM Body Guard for Scotland; Hon. Colonel, Elgin Regiment, Canada; *b* 17 Feb. 1924; *e s* of 10th Earl of Elgin. KT, CMG, TD and Hon. Katherine Elizabeth Cochrane (DBE 1938), *er d* of 1st Baron Cochrane of Cults; *S* father, 1968; *m* 1959, Victoria, *o d* of Dudley Usher, MBE and Mrs Usher of Larach Bhan, Kilchrennan, Argyll; three *s* two *d*. *Educ:* Eton. Balliol College, Oxford (BA Hons, MA Hons). Served War of 1939-45 (wounded). Director: Dominion Ins. Co.; Gurr, Johns & Co.; Royal Highland and Agricultural Soc., 1973-75; Pres., Scottish Amicable Life Assurance Soc., 1975-. Chm., Nat. Savings Cttee for Scotland, 1972-. County Cadet Commandant, Fife, 1952-65. Hon. Col, 153(H) Regt RCT(V), TAVR, 1976-. JP 1951, DL 1955, Fife. Grand Master Mason of Scotland, 1961-65. Brigade Pres. of the Boys' Brigade. Hon. LLD Dundee, 1977. Freeman: City of Bridgetown, Barbados; City of Regina; Port Elgin. *Heir: s* Lord Bruce, *qv*. *Address:* Broomhall, Dunfermline KY11

3DU. *T:* Limekilns 222. *Clubs:* Beefsteak, Caledonian, Pratt's; New (Edinburgh); Royal Scottish Automobile (Pres.) (Glasgow).

ELGOOD, Captain Leonard Alsager, OBE 1919; MC 1915; DL; JP; FRSE; Director, The Distillers Co. Ltd, 1943-60; Chairman, United Glass Ltd, 1951-61; Director, Royal Bank of Scotland, 1946-66, Extraordinary Director, 1966-68; Chairman of Committee on Natural Resources of Scotland (Scottish Council for Development and Industry), 1958-62; *b* 13 Dec. 1892; *s* of late William Alsager Elgood, Dundee, and late Mrs Elgood; *m* 1917, Jenny Coventry Wood, *d* of late R. A. Harper Wood and late Mrs Wood, Perth; two *s. Educ:* Dundee High Sch. Served with the Black Watch (Capt.), 1914-19 (despatches thrice); retd, 1919. Chartered Accountant, 1919; Sec., John Dewar & Sons Ltd, Perth, 1936; Sec., The Distillers Co. Ltd, 1939. DL 1948, JP 1943, County of the City of Edinburgh. *Address:* 16 Cumlodden Avenue, Edinburgh EH12 6DR. *T:* 031-337 6919.

ELIBANK, 14th Lord *cr* 1643 (Scotland); **Alan D'Ardis Erskine-Murray;** Bt (Nova Scotia) 1628; Personnel Manager, Shell International Petroleum Company, since 1955; *b* 31 Dec. 1923; *s* of Robert Alan Erskine-Murray (*d* 1939) and Eileen Mary (*d* 1970), *d* of late John Percy MacManus; *S* cousin, 1973; *m* 1962, Valerie Sylvia, *d* of late Herbert William Dennis; two *s. Educ:* Bedford Sch.; Peterhouse, Cambridge (MA Law). Barrister-at-Law. RE, 1942-47; Cambridge Univ., 1947-49; Practising Barrister, 1949-55; Shell International Petroleum Co., 1955-. *Recreations:* golf, tennis. *Heir:* s Master of Elibank, *qv. Address:* The Coach House, Charters Road, Sunningdale, Ascot, Berks SL5 9QB. *T:* Ascot 22099. *Club:* MCC.

ELIBANK, Master of; Hon. Robert Francis Alan Erskine-Murray; *b* 10 Oct. 1964; *s* and *heir* to 14th Lord Elibank, *qv.*

ELIOT, family name of **Earl of St Germans.**

ELIOT, Lord; Peregrine Nicholas Eliot; *b* 2 Jan. 1941; *o s* of 9th Earl of St Germans, *qv,* and of late Helen Mary, *d* of late Lieut-Col Charles Walter Villiers, CBE, DSO, and Lady Kathleen Villiers; *m* 1964, Hon. Jacquetta Jean Frederika Lampson, *d* of 1st Baron Killearn and Jacqueline Aldine Lesley (*née* Castellani); three *s. Educ:* Eton. *Recreation:* mucking about. *Heir:* s Hon. Jago Nicholas Aldo Eliot, *b* 24 March 1966. *Address:* Port Eliot, St Germans, Cornwall. *Clubs:* Pratt's; Cornish.

ELIOT, Ven. Canon Peter Charles, MBE 1945; TD 1945; Archdeacon of Worcester, 1961-75; now Archdeacon Emeritus; Residentiary Canon, Worcester Cathedral, 1965-75; now Canon Emeritus; *b* 30 Oct. 1910; *s* of late Hon. Edward Granville Eliot and late Mrs Eliot; *m* 1934, Lady Alethea Constance Dorothy Sydney Buxton, *d* of 1st and last Earl Buxton, PC, GCMG, and late Countess Buxton; no *c. Educ:* Wellington Coll.; Magdalene Coll., Cambridge. Commissioned in Kent Yeomanry (Lt-Col Comdg, 1949-52), 1933. Admitted Solicitor, 1934; Partner in City firm until 1953. Studied at Westcott House, Cambridge, 1953-54; made Deacon to serve in Parish of St Martin-in-the-Fields, London, 1954; Priest, 1955; Vicar of Cockermouth, 1957-61; Rural Dean of Cockermouth and Workington, 1960-61; Vicar of Cropthorne with Charlton, 1961-65. *Recreations:* amateur acting (Canterbury Old Stagers); sketching; sight-seeing. *Address:* The Old House, Kingsland, Leominster, Herefordshire HR6 9QS. *T:* Kingsland 285. *Club:* Travellers'.

ELIOTT of Stobs, Sir Arthur Francis Augustus Boswell, 11th Bt *cr* 1666; Chief of the Clan Elliot; *b* 2 Jan. 1915; *s* of Sir Gilbert Alexander Boswell, 10th Bt, and Dora Flournoy Adams, *o d* of late Alexander Stephens Hopkins, Atlanta, Georgia, USA; *S* father, 1958; *m* 1947, Frances Aileen, *e d* of late Sir Francis McClean, AFC; one *d. Educ:* Harrow; King's Coll., Cambridge. BA 1936, MA 1949. 2nd Lieut, King's Own Scottish Borderers (TA), 1939, Major, 1944. Served in East Africa and Burma with King's African Rifles, 1941-45. Member of Queen's Body Guard for Scotland, Royal Company of Archers. *Publication:* The Elliots, the story of a Border Clan, 1974. *Address:* Redheugh, Newcastleton, Roxburghshire. *T:* Liddesdale 213. *Clubs:* New, Puffin's (Edinburgh); Leander.

ELKAN, Prof. Walter; Professor of Economics since 1966 and rotating Head of Department of Economics since 1968, Durham University; *b* Hamburg, 1 March 1923; *s* of Hans Septimus Elkan and Maud Emily (*née* Barden); *m* Susan Dorothea (*née* Jacobs); one *s* two *d. Educ:* Frensham Heights; London Sch. of Economics. BSc (Econ), PhD. Army, 1942-47; Research Asst, LSE, 1950-53; Sen. Res. Fellow, E African Inst. of Social Research, 1954-58; Vis. Res. Assoc., MIT and Lectr, N Western Univ., 1958; Lectr in Econs, Makerere UC, 1958-60; Lectr in

Econs, Durham Univ., 1960. Vis. Res. Prof., Nairobi Univ., 1972-73. Mem. Council, REconS; Associate, Inst. of Development Studies. Former Pres., African Studies Assoc.; Mem., Northern Economic Planning Council. Sometime consultant to Govts of Basutoland, Mauritius, Solomon Is, Fiji, Kenya and others. *Publications:* An African Labour Force, 1956; Migrants and Proletarians, 1960; Economic Development of Uganda, 1961; Introduction to Development Economics, 1973; articles on contemp. African econ. history in econ. and other social science jls; ILO, UNESCO, IBRD and British Govt reports. *Recreation:* music. *Address:* 23-6 Old Elvet, Durham. *T:* Durham 64466.

ELKES, Prof. Joel, MD, ChB; FACP, FAPA; Distinguished Service Professor, The Johns Hopkins University, since 1974; Henry Phipps Professor and Director, Department of Psychiatry and Behavioral Sciences, The Johns Hopkins University School of Medicine, since 1963; Psychiatrist-in-Chief, The Johns Hopkins Hospital, Baltimore, Maryland, 1963-73; *b* 12 Nov. 1913; *s* of Dr Elkanan Elkes and Miriam (*née* Malbin); *m* 1943, Dr Charmian Bourne; one *d*; *m* 1975, Josephine Rhodes, MA. *Educ:* private schools; Lithuania and Switzerland; Univ. of Birmingham Med. Sch. (MB, ChB 1947; MD Hons 1949). MRCS, LRCP 1941. University of Birmingham: Sir Halley Stewart Research Fellow, 1942-45; Lectr, Dept of Pharmacology, 1945-48; Senior Lectr and Actg Head of Dept, 1948-50; Prof. and Chm., Dept of Experimental Psychiatry, 1951-57; Clinical Professor of Psychiatry, George Washington Univ. Med. Sch., Washington, 1957-63; Chief of Clinical Neuropharmacology Research Center, Nat. Inst of Mental Health, Washington, 1957-63; Dir, Behavioral and Clinical Studies Center St Elizabeth's Hosp., Washington, 1957-63; Dir, Foundns Fund for Research in Psychiatry, 1964-68; Consultant, WHO, 1957-. Vis. Fellow, New York Univ. and New England Med. Center, Boston, 1950; Samuel McLaughlin Prof. in residence, McMaster Univ., 1975; Benjamin Franklin Fellow, RSA, 1974. President: (first) Amer. Coll. of Neuropsychopharmacology, 1962; Amer. Psychopathological Assoc., 1968. Formerly Member: Council, Internat. Collegium N Psychopharm; Central Council, Internat. Brain Research Organisation, UNESCO (Chm., Sub-Cttee on Educn). Fellow: Amer. Acad. of Arts and Scis; Amer. Psych. Assoc.; Amer. Coll. of Psychiatry; RCPsych, GB; Amer. Coll. of Neuropsychopharmacol. Member: RSM; Physiological Soc., GB; Pharmacological Soc., GB; British Psychological Soc.; British Electro Encephalographic Soc.; Soc. for Study of Drug Addiction; Amer. Soc. for Pharmacology and Experimental Therapeutics; Soc. of Biological Psychiatry; Acad. of Medicine, Washington; New York Acad. of Science; Sigma Xi; Scientific Assoc.; Acad. of Psychoanalysis. *Publications:* papers to various jls and symposia. *Recreation:* painting. *Address:* 110 West 39th Street, Baltimore, Md 21210, USA. *Clubs:* Cosmos (Washington); West Hamilton Street (Baltimore).

ELKIN, Adolphus Peter, CMG 1966; DLitt; retired as Professor of Anthropology, University of Sydney (1933-56), now Emeritus Professor; *b* 27 March 1891; *s* of Reuben and Ellen Elkin; *m* 1922, Sara Thompson; two *s. Educ:* East Maitland High Sch.; St Paul's Coll., Sydney; University of Sydney (MA); University of London (PhD). C. of E Clergyman (Parishes), 1915-25; Australian Nat. Research Council Fellow, 1927-31; St Paul's College: Fellow, 1935-66; Chm., 1960, 1963-66. Editor (Hon.) of Oceania (Internat. Jl of Anthropology), 1933-; Founder (1966) and Editor (hon.), Jl of Archæology and Physical Anthropology in Oceania; Founder, Jl of Human Biology in Oceania, 1971. Pres., Royal Soc. of New South Wales, 1941; Vice-Chm., Aborigines' Welfare Board of New South Wales, 1941-69; Chm., Aust. Nat. Research Council, 1953-55. Crown Trustee, 1946-72, and Pres. 1961-68, the Australian Museum; Fellow of Senate, Univ. of Sydney, 1959-69; Chm., Council Internat. House (Univ. of Sydney), 1972- (Chm., Finance Cttee, 1966-). Macrossan Memorial Lectr, Univ. of Queensland, 1944; David Lectr (Aust. and NZ Assoc. for the Advancement of Science), 1949; Centenary Oration, Royal Soc. of NSW, 1966. Hon. Life Fellow, Pacific Science Assoc., 1961. DLitt *hc* Sydney, 1970. Medal of Royal Society of NSW, 1949; James Cook Medal, 1955; Mueller Medal, 1957; H. E. Gregory Medal, 1961. *Publications:* The Australian Aborigines: How to Understand Them, 1938 (5th edn 1974); Our Opinions and the National Effort, 1941; Society, the Individual and Change, 1941; Wanted-a Charter for the Peoples of the South-West Pacific, 1943; Citizenship for the Aborigines, 1944; Social Anthropology in Melanesia, 1953; The Diocese of Newcastle: A History, 1955; Aboriginal Men of High Degree, 1946, 2nd edn 1977; Pacific Science Association: Its History and Role in International Cooperation, 1961; contribs to Oceania, American Anthropologist, etc. *Recreations:* music; formerly cricket and tennis. *Address:* 15 Norwood Avenue, Lindfield, NSW 2070, Australia. *T:* Sydney 46.4521.

ELKIN, Alexander, CMG 1976; Special Adviser on European Communities Law, Foreign and Commonwealth Office, since 1970; *b* Leningrad (St Petersburg), 2 Aug. 1909; *o c* of Boris and Anna Elkin; *m* 1937, Muriel Solomons, Dublin. *Educ:* Grunewald Gymnasium and Russian Sch., Berlin; Univs of Berlin, Kiel and London. DrJur Kiel 1932, LLM London 1935. Called to the Bar, Middle Temple, 1937; practised at English Bar, 1937-39; BBC Monitoring Service, 1939-42; war-time govt service, 1942-45; Associate Chief, Legal Service, UN Interim Secretariat, London, 1945-46; Asst Dir, UN European Office, Geneva, 1946-48; Legal Adviser to UNSCOB, Salonica, 1948; Dep. Legal Adviser, later Legal Adviser, OEEC (OECD 1960-), Paris, 1949-61; UNECA Legal Consultant, formation of African Develt Bank and Econ. Council for Africa, 1962-64; Actg Gen. Counsel of ADB, 1964-65; UNDP Legal Consultant, formation of Caribbean Develt Bank, 1967-68. Legal consultancies for: WHO, 1948; CCTA, 1962-63; IBRD, 1966; W Afr. Regional Gp, 1968; OECD, 1975. Lectured: on Europ. payments system and OEEC/OECD activs, Univ. of the Saar, 1957-60, and Univ. Inst. of Europ. Studies, Turin, 1957-65; on drafting of treaties, UNITAR Seminar, The Hague, for legal advisers and diplomats of devel. countries, 1967-, etc. Ford Foundn Leadership Grant, 1960. Temp. Legal Editor, FO, 1967. *Publications:* contrib. European Yearbook, Jl du Droit Internat., Revue Générale de Droit Internat. Public, Survey of Internat. Affairs 1939-1946, Travaux pratiques de L'Institut de Droit Comparé de la Faculté de Droit de Paris, etc. *Recreations:* reading, visiting art collections, travel. *Address:* 140 Hamilton Terrace, NW8; 22 Old Buildings, Lincoln's Inn, WC2. *Club:* Travellers'.

ELKINGTON, Reginald Geoffrey, CB 1962; *b* 24 Dec. 1907; *s* of Harold and Millicent Elkington; *m* 1935, Bertha Phyllis, *d* of William and Bertha Dyason; one adopted *s* one adopted *d. Educ:* Battersea Grammar Sch.; Fitzwilliam Coll., Cambridge. Inland Revenue, 1929-42; Min. of Supply, 1942-57 (Under-Sec., 1954); DSIR, 1957-65; Principal Establishment Officer, Min. of Technology, 1964-67; retired from Civil Service, 1967; Estabt Officer (part-time), Monopolies Commn, 1968-73. Sec., AERE Harwell, 1948-51. *Recreations:* gardening, crossword solving. *Address:* Maranwood, Highfield Road, West Byfleet, Surrey. *T:* Byfleet 43766.

ELKINS, Sir Anthony (Joseph), Kt 1952; CBE 1944; Chairman: British Match Corporation Ltd, 1964-72; Gestetner Ltd, 1964-72; Vice-Chairman, Army & Navy Stores Ltd, 1965-71 (Director, 1954-72); *b* 30 May 1904; *s* of late Dr and Mrs F. A. Elkins, Herts; *m* 1930, Mabel Brenda Barker (decd); three *s* one *d ; m* 1944, Ines Erna Miller (*née* Neele) (marr. diss.); *m* 1969, Nora Christianne Elliot (*née* Rowe). *Educ:* Haileybury Coll. With Gillanders Arbuthnot & Co. Ltd in India, 1924-54 (Chm., 1945-54); Chm., Darjeeling-Himalayan Railway Co. Ltd, 1945-48. Controller of Supplies (Bengal Circle), 1941-45; served on Cttees of India's First Five-Year Plan, 1949-51. President: Bengal Chamber of Commerce, 1949; Associated Chambers of Commerce of India, 1949; UK Citizens' Assoc. of India, 1953; Inst. of Export, 1967-70; Vice-Pres., Imperial Bank of India (Bengal Circle), 1949. Chm. of Bryant & May Ltd, 1955-64; Dir, Phoenix Assce Co., WA, 1973-74. Chairman: London and South-Eastern Resettlement Cttee, Regular Forces Resettlement Service, 1968-69 (Mem., 1961-69); Regional Industrial Cttee, Nat. Savings Movement, 1969-71. *Address:* 23 Clontarf Street, Sorrento, WA 6020, Australia. *Clubs:* Oriental; Western Australian Turf; Bengal, Royal Calcutta Turf (Calcutta), etc.
    See also Sir Robert Elkins.

ELKINS, Vice-Adm. Sir Robert (Francis), KCB 1958 (CB 1954); CVO 1952; OBE 1942; *b* 12 Jan. 1903; *er s* of Dr F. A. Elkins, Leavesden, Kings Langley; *m* 1940, Gwendolen Hurst Flint. *Educ:* RNC, Osborne and Dartmouth. Qualified as Interpreter (German), 1928; specialised in Gunnery, 1929; Commander, 1937; in comd HMS Bideford, 1939-40 (despatches, 1940); Prisoner of War, 1940; Comdr, HMS Renown, 1940; Capt. Dec. 1942; in comd HMS Dido, 1944-45; idc 1949; in comd HMS Ocean, 1949-50; in comd HMS Excellent, 1950-52; ADC to King George VI, 1952; ADC to the Queen until July 1952; Rear-Adm. 1952; Vice-Adm. 1955; Flag Officer, 2nd in Comd, Far East Station, 1955-56; Admiral, British Joint Staff Mission, Washington, 1956-58, retired 1959. *Recreations:* all outdoor sports. *Address:* Branlea, Foreland Road, Bembridge, IoW. *T:* Bembridge 2522. *Club:* Naval and Military.
    See also Sir Anthony Elkins.

ELLACOMBE, Air Cdre John Lawrence Wemyss, CB 1970; DFC 1942 (Bar 1944); MBIM; Director, Scientific Services, St Thomas' Hospital, since 1973; *b* Livingstone, N Rhodesia, 28 Feb. 1920; *s* of Dr Gilbert H. W. Ellacombe; *m* 1951, Wing Officer Mary Hibbert, OBE, WRAF; one *s* two *d. Educ:* Diocesan Coll., Rondebosch, Cape. War of 1939-45: RAF, 1939;

Fighter Command and Two ATA Force, 1940-45 (Pilot, Battle of Britain). Aden, 1946-48; RAF Staff Coll., 1948-49; Fighter Command, 1949-57; BJSM, Washington, 1959. JSSC, 1959-60; Gp Captain, CO RAF Linton on Ouse, to Nov 1962; CFE, to Aug. 1965; Defence Operational Analysis Estabt, West Byfleet, 1965-68; Air Cdre, Commander Air Forces Gulf, 1968-70; Dir of Ops (Air Defence and Overseas), MoD (Air), 1970-73. *Recreations:* photography, golf, cricket. *Address:* 33 The Drive, Northwood, Middlesex HA6 1HW. *Club:* Royal Air Force.

ELLEN, Patricia Mae H.; *see* Hayward Ellen.

ELLENBOROUGH, 8th Baron *cr* 1802; **Richard Edward Cecil Law;** Partner, McAnally, Montgomery & Co. (Stockbrokers); Director, Towry Law & Co.; *b* 14 Jan. 1926; *s* of 7th Baron and Helen Dorothy, *o d* of late H. W. Lovatt; *S* father, 1945; *m* 1953, Rachel Mary, *o d* of late Major Ivor Hedley; three *s. Educ:* Eton Coll.; Magdalene Coll., Cambridge. *Heir: s* Hon. Rupert Edward Henry Law, *b* 28 March 1955. *Address:* Broadfield House, Wadhurst, East Sussex. *T:* Wadhurst 2426. *Clubs:* Gresham, Turf.

ELLERTON, Air Commodore Alban Spenser, CBE 1944 (OBE 1919); RAF; Air ADC to the King, 1944 (ADC, 1949); *b* 3 Oct. 1894; 6th *s* of Alfred Ellerton, Hampstead; *m* 1919, Maureen Gilliland (*d* 1971), *o c* of T. F. Husband, ISO; two *s. Educ:* privately; Germany. Enlisted Coldstream Guards, Aug. 1914, on return from Germany; commission RFC 1916; Major HQ RFC 1917 (despatches twice); permanent commission RAF 1918; retd 1949. *Address:* 1 West Street, Rye, Sussex. *Club:* Royal Air Force.

ELLERTON, Geoffrey James, CMG 1963; MBE 1956; an Executive Director, Ocean Transport & Trading Ltd, since 1972; Member Council, Liverpool University, since 1974; *b* 25 April 1920; *er s* of late Sir Cecil Ellerton; *m* 1946, Peggy Eleanor, *d* of late F. G. Watson; three *s. Educ:* Highgate Sch.; Hertford Coll., Oxford (MA). Military Service, 1940-45. Apptd Colonial Administrative Service as District Officer, Kenya, 1945. Acted as Minister for Defence, 1960 and 1962. Retired as Permanent Sec., Prime Minister's Office and Sec. to the Cabinet, at time of Kenya's Independence, Dec. 1963. Sec. to the Maud and Mallaby Cttees on Management and Staffing in Local Government, 1964. Joined Elder Dempster Lines, 1965, Chm., 1972-74. *Recreations:* music, reading. *Address:* Greygarth, Wood Lane, Parkgate, Merseyside L64 6QZ. *T:* 051-336 3692. *Clubs:* Reform, MCC; Nairobi.

ELLES, family name of **Baroness Elles.**

ELLES, Baroness *cr* 1972 (Life Peer), of the City of Westminster; **Diana Louie Elles;** Opposition Front Bench spokesman, since 1975; *b* 19 July 1921; *d* of Col Stewart Francis Newcombe, DSO and Elisabeth Chaki; *m* 1945, Neil Patrick Moncrieff Elles, *qv*; one *s* one *d. Educ:* private Schs, England, France and Italy; London University (BA Hons). Barrister-at-law. Care Cttee worker in S London, 1956-72. UK Delegn to UN Gen. Assembly, 1972; Mem., UN Sub-Commn on Prevention of Discrimination and Protection of Minorities, 1973-75; UN special rapporteur on Human Rights, 1974-; Mem., British delegn to European Parlt, 1973-75. Mem., Cripps Cttee on legal discrimination against women; Chm., Sub-cttee of Women's Nat. Adv. Cttee (Conservative Party) on one-parent families (report publ. as Unhappy Families); Internat. Chm., 1973-, and Chm., British Section, European Union of Women, 1970-74; Chm., Cons. Party Internat. Office, 1973-. *Publication:* The Housewife and the Common Market (pamphlet), 1971. *Address:* 75 Ashley Gardens, SW1; Villa Fontana, Ponte del Giglio, Lucca, Italy.

ELLES, Neil Patrick Moncrieff; Chairman, Value Added Tax Appeals Tribunal, since 1972; *b* 8 July 1919; *s* of Edmund Hardie Elles, OBE and Ina Katharine Hilda Skene; *m* 1945, Diana Louie Newcombe (*see* Baroness Elles); one *s* one *d . Educ:* Eton; Christ Church, Oxford (MA). War Service, RAF, 1939-45. Called to the Bar, Inner Temple, 1947; Tutor, Company Law and Conveyancing, Council of Legal Educn, 1950-57; Sec., Inns of Court Conservative and Unionist Taxation Cttee, 1957-71; Mem., Special Study Gp, Commn on Law of Competition, Brussels, 1962-67. *Publications:* The Law of Restrictive Trade Practices and Monopolies (with Lord Wilberforce and Alan Campbell), 1966; Community Law through the Cases, 1973. *Recreations:* fishing, listening to music, the cultivation of vines. *Address:* 75 Ashley Gardens, SW1. *T:* 01-828 0175; Villa Fontana, Ponte del Giglio, Lucca, Italy. *Clubs:* Flyfishers', MCC.

ELLES, Robin Jamieson, CBE 1974 (OBE 1945; MBE 1942); JP; County Director, Dunbartonshire British Red Cross Society, since 1968; *b* 4 Jan. 1907; *er s* of late Bertram Walter Elles, Malayan Civil Service, and late Jean Challoner Elles; *m* 1932, Eva Lyon Scott Elliot, *d* of Lt-Col William Scott Elliot; one *s. Educ:* Marlborough Coll.; Trinity Hall, Cambridge. BA 1928, MA 1950. Sudan Political Service, 1929-34; J. & P. Coats Ltd, India and China, 1935-40; Army, 1940-45: OETA Abyssinia, 1941; Sudan Defence Force, 1942-45, Libya and Tripolitania, Temp. Lt-Col Comdg 10 SDF Inf. Bn, 1944-45; J. & P. Coats Ltd, Personnel, 1946-66, retd 1966. Chm. of Governors, Paisley Coll. of Technology, 1966-76 (Governor, 1950-76); Chairman: Scottish Adv. Cttee, Nat. Youth Employment Council, 1962-71; Nat. Youth Employment Council, 1971-74. JP Dunbartonshire, 1952. *Publications:* various papers. *Recreations:* fishing, rowing (Cambridge Blue, 1927 and 1929; rowed for Leander, 1929). *Address:* Rogart, Garelochhead, Dunbartonshire. *T:* Garelochhead 810304. *Club:* Leander (Henley-on-Thames).

ELLINGWORTH, Richard Henry; HM Diplomatic Service; on secondment to Department of Energy, since 1975; *b* 9 March 1926; *s* of Vincent Ellingworth; *m* 1952, Joan Mary Waterfield; one *s* three *d. Educ:* Uppingham; Aberdeen Univ.; Magdalen Coll., Oxford (Demy). Served War of 1939-45: RA, and Intelligence Corps, 1944-47. Oxford, 1947-50 (first Lit. Hum.); HM Embassy, Japan, 1951-55; FO, 1955-59; HM Embassy: Belgrade, 1959-63; Japan, 1963-68 (Olympic Attaché, 1964); Head of Oil Dept., FCO, 1969-71; Research Associate, Internat. Inst. for Strategic Studies, 1971-72; Counsellor, Tehran, 1972-75. *Publications:* (with A. N. Gilkes) An Anthology of Oratory, 1946; Japanese Economic Policy and Security, 1972. *Recreations:* gardening, music. *Address:* The Mount, Sparepenny Lane, Farningham, Kent. *T:* Farningham 863709. *Club:* Travellers'.

ELLIOT; see Scott-Elliot.

ELLIOT, family name of **Baroness Elliot of Harwood** and **Earl of Minto.**

ELLIOT OF HARWOOD, Baroness *cr* 1958 (Life Peer); **Katharine Elliot,** DBE 1958 (CBE 1946); JP; *b* 15 Jan. 1903; *d* of Sir Charles Tennant, 1st Bt, Innerleithen, Peeblesshire, and late Mrs Geoffrey Lubbock; *m* 1934, Rt Hon. Walter Elliot, PC, CH, MC, FRS, LLD, MP (*d* 1958); no *c. Educ:* Abbot's Hill, Hemel Hempstead; Paris. Chairman: Nat. Assoc. of Mixed Clubs and Girls' Clubs, 1939-49; Adv. Cttee on Child Care for Scotland, 1956-65; Women's Nat. Adv. Cttee of Conservative Party, 1954-57; Nat. Union of Conservative and Unionist Assocs, 1956-67; Carnegie UK Trust, 1965- (Trustee, 1937-); Consumer Council, 1963-68; Lawrie & Symington Ltd, Lanark. Member: Women's Consultative Cttee, Dept of Employment and Productivity (formerly Min. of Labour), 1941-51, 1958-70; Home Office Adv. Cttee on Treatment of Offenders, 1946-62; King George V Jubilee Trust, 1936-68; NFU. UK Delegate to Gen. Assembly of UN, New York, 1954, 1956 and 1957. Contested (C) Kelvingrove Div. of Glasgow, March 1958. Roxburghshire: CC 1946-75 (Vice-Convener, 1974); JP Roxburghshire, 1968-. Farms in Roxburghshire. FRSA 1964. Hon. LLD Glasgow, 1959. Grand Silver Cross, Austrian Order of Merit, 1963. *Publication:* Tennants Stalk, 1973. *Recreations:* foxhunting, golf, music. *Address:* Harwood, Bonchester Bridge, Hawick, Roxburghshire; 17 Lord North Street, Westminster, SW1. *T:* 01-222 3230.

ELLIOT, Prof. Harry, CBE 1976; FRS 1973; Professor of Physics at Imperial College, London, since 1960 (Assistant Director of Physics Department, 1963-71); *b* 28 June 1920; *s* of Thomas Elliot and Hannah Elizabeth (*née* Littleton), Weary Hall, Cumberland; *m* 1943, Betty Leyman; one *s* one *d. Educ:* Nelson Sch., Wigton; Manchester Univ. MSc, PhD. Served War, Signals Branch, RAF, incl. liaison duties with USN, 1941-46. Manchester Univ.: Asst Lectr in Physics, 1948-49; Lectr in Physics, 1949-54; Imperial Coll.: Lectr in Physics, 1954-56; Sen. Lectr in Physics, 1956-57; Reader in Physics, 1957-60. Mem., Science Research Council, 1971. Hon. Prof., Universitad Mayor de San Andres, 1957; Mem., Internat. Academy of Astronautics, 1963; Hon. ARCS, 1965. Holweck Prize and Medal, Inst. of Physics and Société Française de Physique, 1976. *Publications:* papers on cosmic rays, solar physics and magnetospheric physics in scientific jls; contrib. scientific reviews and magazine articles. *Recreation:* painting. *Address:* Department of Physics, The Blackett Laboratory, Imperial College, SW7 2BZ. *T:* 01-589 5111 (ext. 2301).

ELLIOT, James Robert McDowell, CMG 1949; OBE 1945; *b* 1 Jan. 1896; *e s* of late Lieut-Col R. H. Elliot, IMS (and Ophthalmic Surgeon), and late Mrs E. C. I. Elliot; *m* 1922, Joan

Helen Caudery, *d* of late Capt. A. S. Littlejohns, CMG, RN, and late Mrs Littlejohns; one *s* one *d. Educ:* Lancing Coll., Sussex. Served European War, 1914-19, in 2/4th Bn Wilts Regt, and Machine Gun Corps, Capt. (Actg Major). Cadet, Uganda, 1920; ADC 1922; District Officer, 1931; Senior District Officer, 1944; Provincial Commissioner, Uganda, 1945. Retired from Colonial Civil Service, Jan. 1950. Compiled labour enquiry reports, 1936 and 1937. *Address:* c/o Grindlay's Bank Ltd, 13 St James's Square, SW1; Flat A, 263 Goldhurst Terrace, NW6 3EP.

ELLIOT, Sir John, Kt 1954; High Sheriff of Greater London, 1970-71; *b* London, 6 May 1898; *m* 1924, Elizabeth, *d* of late Dr A. S. Cobbledick; one *s* one *d. Educ:* Marlborough; Sandhurst. European War in 3rd Hussars; after four years in journalism joined former Southern Rly, 1925, in charge public relations (first in UK). Visited USA, Canada, frequently; Deputy General Manager, Southern Rly, 1937, Gen. Manager, 1947; Chief Regional Officer, Southern Region, British Railways, 1948-49. London Midland Region, Euston, 1950-51; Chairman: Railway Exec., 1951-53; London Transport, 1953-59; Pullman Car Co., 1959-63; Thos. Cook & Son Ltd, 1959-67; Willing & Co. Ltd, 1959-70; London and Provincial Poster Group Ltd, 1965-71. Director: Commonwealth Development Corp., 1959-66; Railway Air Services, Channel Islands Airways, 1933-48; Thomas Tilling Ltd, 1959-70; British Airports Authority, 1965-69; Cie Internationale des Wagons-Lits, 1960-71. Vice-Pres., Internat. Union of Railways (UIC), 1947 and 1951-53. Formerly Col. (Comdg) Engineer and Railway Staff Corps, Royal Engineers, 1956-63. Visited Australia, at invitation of Govt of Victoria, to report on rail and road transport 1949, 1966, 1970, and E Africa, 1969, on transport study (World Bank), 1968. FInstT (Pres., 1953-54). Mem. Société de l'histoire de Paris, 1958-. Officier, Légion d'Honneur; American Medal of Freedom. *Publications:* The Way of the Tumbrils (Paris during the Revolution), 1958; Where our Fathers Died (Western Front 50 years after), 1964; regular newspaper feature, Speaking of That...; book reviews; many papers on transport. *Recreations:* gardening, shooting, fishing, cricket (Vice-Pres. Essex CCC), military history. *Address:* Stonyfield, Great Easton, Dunmow, Essex. *Clubs:* Cavalry and Guards, MCC.

ELLIOT, Captain Walter, DSC 1944; RN Retd; *b* 17 Feb. 1910; *s* of John White Elliot and Frances Hampson; *m* 1936, Thelma Pirie Thomson; four *d. Educ:* HMS Conway; Royal Naval Coll. Joined RN, 1929; specialised in Naval Aviation. Served War of 1939-45 (DSC, despatches); retired, 1958. Took Economics Degree, London Univ., 1958 (BSc Econ). In business, 1958-60. MP (C) Carshalton and Banstead, 1960-Feb. 1974. *Recreations:* fencing, fishing, tennis. *Address:* 6 Ennismore Street, SW7. *Club:* International Sportsmen's.

ELLIOT-SMITH, Alan Guy, CBE 1957; *b* 30 June 1904; *s* of late F. Elliot-Smith; *m* 1939, Ruth Kittermaster; no *c. Educ:* Charterhouse; Oriel Coll., Oxford. Hons Mod. Lang. Sch., 1925; Asst Master, Harrow Sch., 1925-40; Headmaster, Cheltenham Coll., 1940-51; Mem., Harrow UDC, 1933-36; Deleg. to Inst. of Pacific Relations Conf., Calif., 1936; lectured to German teachers on Education, 1947 and 1948; lectured to Service units in the Middle East, 1949; Head-master of Victoria Coll., Cairo, 1952-56; Representative in Nigeria of the West Africa Cttee, 1957-58; Headmaster, Markham Coll., Lima, Peru, 1960-63. *Recreations:* travel, reading. *Address:* Bevois Mount, Rowsley Road, Eastbourne, Sussex.

ELLIOTT, Alan Fraser, MA; Headmaster, Mill Hill School, since Sept. 1974; *b* 12 March 1929; *s* of Rev. Norman and Mrs Winifred Elliott; *m* 1955, Sheila (*née* West); three *d. Educ:* Bristol Grammar Sch.; New College, Oxford (MA). Asst Master and Housemaster, Marlborough Coll., 1954-74; Lectr, Univ. of Toronto, 1961-62. *Publication:* (ed) Euripides, Medea, 1969. *Recreation:* cottaging. *Address:* The Grove, The Ridgeway, Mill Hill, NW7 1QS. *T:* 01-959 1006.

ELLIOTT, David Murray; Counsellor at UK Representation to the European Communities, Brussels, since 1975; *b* 8 Feb. 1930; *s* of Alfred Elliott and Mabel Kathleen Emily Elliott (*née* Murray); *m* 1956, Ruth Marjorie Ingram; one *d* (one *s* decd). *Educ:* Bishopshalt Grammar Sch.; London Sch. of Economics and Political Science (BScEcon). Nation Service, RAF, 1951-54; Gen. Post Office, 1954-57; seconded to Federal Ministry of Communications, Nigeria, 1958-62; GPO, 1962-69; Asst Secretary: Min. of Posts and Telecommunications, 1969-74; Dept of Industry, 1974-75; on loan to HM Diplomatic Service, 1975-. *Recreation:* reading The Times. *Address:* 31 Ailsa Road, St Margaret's, Twickenham, Mddx TW1 1QJ. *T:* 01-892 8961.

ELLIOTT, Denholm Mitchell; actor, stage and films; *b* 31 May 1922; *m* 1954, Virginia McKenna (marr. diss. 1957; she *m* 1957,

Bill Travers); *m* 1962, Susan Darby Robinson; one *s* one *d*. *Educ:* Malvern. *Plays:* The Guinea-Pig, Criterion, 1946; Venus Observed, St James's, 1949; Ring Round the Moon, Martin Beck, New York, 1950; Sleep of Prisoners, St Thomas's, Regent Street, 1950; Third Person, Criterion, 1951; Confidential Clerk, Lyric, 1954; South, Arts, 1955; Who Cares, Fortune, 1956; Camino Real, Phœnix, 1957; Traveller Without Luggage, Arts, 1958; The Ark, Westminster, 1959; Stratford-on-Avon Season, 1960; Write Me a Murder, Belasco Theatre, New York, 1961; The Seagull, The Crucible, Ring Round the Moon, Nat. Repertory Co., New York, 1963-64; Come as You Are, New, 1970; Chez Nous, Globe, 1974; The Return of A. J. Raffles, Aldwych, 1975; Heaven and Hell, Greenwich, 1976. *Films:* Sound Barrier, 1949; The Cruel Sea, 1952; They Who Dare, 1953; Pacific Destiny, 1955; Scent of Mystery, 1959; Station Six Sahara, 1962; Nothing But the Best, 1963; King Rat, 1964; The High Bright Sun, 1964; You Must Be Joking, 1965; Alfie, 1966; Here we go round the Mulberry Bush, 1967; The Seagull, 1968; Too Late the Hero, 1969; Madame Sin, 1972; A Doll's House, 1973; The Apprenticeship of Duddy Kravitz, 1974; Russian Roulette, 1976. Has awards, London and New York. *Recreations:* ski-ing, golf. *Address:* 75 Albert Street, Regent's Park, NW1. *Club:* Garrick.

ELLIOTT, Frank Abercrombie, MD, FRCP; Professor of Neurology, Emeritus, University of Pennsylvania; *b* 18 Dec. 1910; *s* of Arthur Abercrombie Elliott and Kathleen Gosselin; *m* 1st, 1940, Betty Kathleen Elkington; two *d*; 2nd, 1970, Mrs Josiah Marvel (*née* Hopkins). *Educ:* Rondebosch; Univ. of Cape Town. Univ. entrance schol., 1928; Lewis Memorial schol., 1930-34; MB, ChB Cape Town, with Hons and Gold Medal; Hiddingh Travelling Fellowship, 1936-39. House Surg. and House Phys. to professorial units, Cape Town; House Physician, British Postgrad. Sch. of Medicine and Nat. Hosp. for Nervous Diseases, London; Resident MO, Nat. Heart Hosp. RAMC, 1943-48, Lt-Col; Adviser in Neurology, India and War Office. FRCP 1948; FACP 1973. Physician to Charing Cross Hosp., 1947-58; to Moorfields Eye Hospital, 1949-58; Lecturer and Examiner, London Univ. Member: Assoc. of British Neurologists; Assoc. of British Physicians; Internat. Soc. of Internal Medicine; Am. Acad. of Neurology; Philadelphia Neurological Soc. *Publications:* (ed) Clinical Neurology, 1952; Clinical Neurology, 1964 (2nd edn, 1971); papers on neurological subjects in scientific journals. *Address:* Pennsylvania Hospital, Philadelphia, Pa 19107, USA.

ELLIOTT, George, FRICS; Chief Executive, British Urban Development Services Unit, since 1975; Partner, Edmond Shipway and Partners, since 1963; *b* 20 Aug. 1932; *s* of Harry Elliott and Nellie Elizabeth Elliott; *m* 1958, Winifred Joan; one *s* one *d*. *Educ:* Sir George Monoux Grammar Sch.; SW Essex Technical Coll. FRICS 1966. *Recreation:* travel. *Address:* Flat 8.6, Stirling Court, Marshall Street, W1V 1LQ. *T:* 01-437 3133. *Club:* Junior Carlton.

ELLIOTT, Harold William, CBE 1967; *b* 24 Nov. 1905; *s* of late W. J. Elliott and Ellen Elliott; *m* Betty (*d* 1976), *d* of late C. J. Thumling and Mrs V. A. Thumling; two *s* one *d*. *Educ:* Brighton Coll. Apprenticed to Adolf Saurer, AG Arbon, Switz., 1924; joined Pickfords Ltd, 1926. Mem., Road and Rail Central Conf., 1938; Transport Adv. Cttee, Food Defence Plans Dept, BoT, 1939; Asst Divisional Food Officer (Transport), London, 1940; Controller of Road Transport, Min. of Supply, 1941; Mem., Salvage Bd; Dir of Transport, Middle East Supply Centre, Cairo, 1943; Mem., Road Haulage Central Wages Bd and Vice-Chm., Meat Transport Organisation Ltd, 1945; Gen. Man., Hay's Wharf Cartage Co. Ltd, Pickfords Ltd and Carter Paterson & Co. Ltd, 1947; Chief Officer (Freight), Road Transport Exec.; Mem., Coastal Shipping Adv. Cttee, 1948; Mem. Bd of Management, Brit. Road Services, and Dir, Atlantic Steam Navigation Co. Ltd, 1959; Man. Dir, Pickfords Ltd, 1963-70, Chm., 1970; Life Mem., Road Haulage Assoc. Trustee, Sutton Housing Trust, 1971-; Chm., Holmwood Common Management Cttee, 1971; Governor, Brighton Coll., 1955 (Chm. Governors, 1974-). Liveryman, Worshipful Co. of Carmen. FCIT (a Vice-Pres., 1970-71). *Address:* Stumbleholt, near Dorking, Surrey. *T:* Dorking 6514. *Club:* Anglo-Belgian.

ELLIOTT, Sir Hugh (Francis Ivo), 3rd Bt *cr* 1917; OBE 1953; Editor, Technical Publications and Research Consultant, International Union for Conservation of Nature; *b* 10 March 1913; *er s* of Sir Ivo Elliott, 2nd Bt; *S* father, 1961; *m* 1939, Elizabeth Margaret, *er d* of A. G. Phillipson; one *s* two *d*. *Educ:* Dragon Sch.; Eastbourne Coll.; University Coll., Oxford. Tanganyika Administration, 1937; Administrator, Tristan da Cunha, 1950-52; Permanent Sec., Min. of Natural Resources, Tanganyika, 1958; retired, 1961. Commonwealth Liaison Officer for International Union for Conservation of Nature,

1961-66; acting Sec.-Gen., 1962-64, Sec.-Gen., 1964-66, Sec. Ecology Commn, 1966-70. Trustee, British Museum (Natural History), 1971-; Hon. Sec., British Ornithologists' Union, 1962-66, Vice-Pres. 1970-73, Pres., 1975-. Netherlands Order of Golden Ark, 1973. *Publications:* (ed) Proc. 2nd World Conf. on Nat. Parks, Yellowstone, 1972; contributor to Ibis and various ornithological and conservation jls. *Recreations:* ornithology, travel. *Heir: s* Clive Christopher Hugh Elliott, PhD [*b* 12 Aug. 1945; *m* 1975, Marie-Thérèse, *d* of H. Ruttimann]. *Address:* 173 Woodstock Road, Oxford. *T:* Oxford 55469.

ELLIOTT, Hugh Percival, CMG 1959; retired, 1967; *b* 29 May 1911; *s* of late Major P. W. Elliott, IA; *m* 1951, Bridget Rosalie, *d* of late Rev. A. F. Peterson. *Educ:* St Lawrence Coll., Ramsgate; Hertford Coll., Oxford. Joined Colonial Administrative Service, Nigeria, 1934; seconded Colonial Office, 1946; Supervisor, Colonial Service Courses, London, 1948-50; Senior District Officer, 1954; Permanent Sec., 1956; Adviser, Govt of Eastern Nigeria, 1962-67. Many visits to Ethiopia, Kenya, Rhodesia etc, to support the initiatives for Moral Re-Armament of African friends, 1968-78. CON, 1964 (Comdr, Order of the Niger, Nigeria). *Address:* 14 Eldon Avenue, Shirley, Croydon, Surrey.

ELLIOTT, Maj.-Gen. James Gordon, CIE 1947; retd; *b* 6 April 1898; *s* of late Dr William Elliott, Welshpool, Montgomeryshire; *m* 1931, Barbara Eleanor, *y d* of William Douglas, Malvern; one *s* one *d*. *Educ:* Blundell's Sch. Commissioned, Indian Army, 1916; 1st Punjab Regt, 1922; GSO2 Staff Coll., Quetta, 1935-37; Dir Military Training, India, 1942-43; Bde Comdr, 1943-44; Dep. Welfare Gen., India, 1945-46; Dep. Sec. (Mil.), Defence Cttee, India, 1947-48; retired 1948. *Publications:* Administrative Aspect of Tactics and Training, 1938; The Story of the Indian Army, 1939-45, 1965; The Frontier 1839-1947, 1968; Field Sports in India 1800-1947, 1973; India, 1976. *Recreations:* gardening, fishing. *Address:* 13 Barnfield Avenue, Exmouth, Devon. *Club:* Naval and Military.

ELLIOTT, Prof. John Huxtable, FBA 1972; Professor of History, Institute for Advanced Study, Princeton, NJ, since 1973; *b* 23 June 1930; *s* of Thomas Charles Elliott and Janet Mary Payne; *m* 1958, Oonah Sophia Butler. *Educ:* Eton College; Trinity College, Cambridge (MA, PhD). Fellow of Trinity Coll., Cambridge, 1954-67; Asst Lectr in History, Cambridge Univ., 1957-62; Lectr in History, Cambridge Univ., 1962-67; Prof. of History, KCL, 1968-73. Wiles Lectr, Queen's Univ., Belfast, 1969. Corresp. Fellow, Real Academia de la Historia, Madrid, 1965; Fellow, Amer. Acad. Arts and Scis, 1977. Corresponding Member: Hispanic Soc. of America, 1975; Real Academia Sevillana de Buenas Letras, 1976. *Publications:* The Revolt of the Catalans, 1963; Imperial Spain, 1469-1716, 1963; Europe Divided, 1559-1598, 1968; The Old World and the New, 1492-1650, 1970; ed (with H. G. Koenigsberger) The Diversity of History, 1970. *Address:* The Institute for Advanced Study, Princeton, NJ 08540, USA; 73 Long Road, Cambridge CB2 2HE. *T:* Trumpington 3332.

ELLIOTT, Sir Norman (Randall), Kt 1967; CBE 1957 (OBE 1946); MA; Chairman of the Electricity Council, 1968-72; Chairman, Howden Group, since 1973; Director, Newarthill & McAlpine Group, since 1972; *b* 19 July 1903; *s* of William Randall Elliott and Catherine Dunsmore; *m* 1963, Phyllis Clarke. *Educ:* privately; St Catharine's Coll., Cambridge. Called to the Bar, Middle Temple, 1932 (J. J. Powell Prizeman, A. J. Powell Exhibitioner). London Passenger Transport Board; London and Home Counties Joint Electricity Authority; Yorkshire Electric Power Co.; 21 Army Group: first as CRE (Royal Engineers) then, as Col, Deputy Dir of Works, 21 Army Group (OBE); Chief Engineer and Manager, Wimbledon Borough Council; Gen. Manager and Chief Engineer, London and Home Counties Joint Electricity Authority and sometime Chm. and Dir, Isle of Thanet Electric Supply Co., and Dir, James Howden & Co. Ltd; Chairman: S-E Electricity Bd, 1948-62; S of Scotland Electricity Bd, 1962-67; Member: Brit. Electricity Authority, 1950 and 1951; Central Electricity Authority, 1956 and 1957; Electricity Council, 1958-62; N of Scotland Hydro-Electric Bd, 1965-69. *Publication:* Electricity Statutes, Orders and Regulations, 1947, rev. edn 1951. *Recreations:* ball games and the theatre. *Address:* 3 Herbrand Walk, Cooden, East Sussex. *Clubs:* Athenæum; Western (Glasgow); Royal Northern Yacht.

ELLIOTT, Oliver Douglas; British Council Representative in Nigeria, since 1976; *b* 13 Oct. 1925; *y s* of late Walter Elliott and Margherita Elliott, Bedford; *m* 1954, Patience Rosalie Joan Orpen; one *s*. *Educ:* Bedford Modern Sch.; Wadham Coll., Oxford (MA); Fitzwilliam House, Cambridge. Served RNVR (Sub-Lt), 1944-47. Colonial Educn Service, Cyprus, 1953-59;

joined British Council, 1959; served Lebanon, 1960-63; Dep. Rep., Ghana, 1963; Dir, Commonwealth I Dept, 1966; Dir, Service Conditions Dept, 1970; Dep. Educn Advr, India, 1973. *Recreations:* golf, gardening. *Address:* c/o Personnel Records, British Council, 10 Spring Gardens, SW1.

ELLIOTT, Ralph Edward; *b* 7 May 1908; *y s* of late Frederick Worsley Elliott, Ruckinge, Kent; *m* 1934, Phyllis, 2nd *d* of late William Douglas Craig, Kingsnorth, Kent; two *s* one *d*. *Educ:* Ashford Gram. Sch. Entered Westminster Bank Ltd, later National Westminster Bank Ltd, Rochester, 1926; Chief Gen. Man., 1966-68; Jt Chief Exec., 1968-70; Dir, 1969-76; Dep. Chm., 1970-73. Trustee, Leonard Cheshire Foundn, 1972-. FIB. *Address:* Little Hendra, Shire Lane, Chorleywood, Herts. *T:* Chorleywood 2223.

ELLIOTT, Sir Randal (Forbes), KBE 1977 (OBE 1976); President, New Zealand Medical Association, since 1976; *b* 12 Oct. 1922; *s* of Sir James Elliott and Lady (Ann) Elliott (*née* Forbes), MBE; *m* 1949, Pauline June Young; one *s* six *d*. *Educ:* Wanganui Collegiate Sch.; Otago Univ. MB, ChB (NZ), 1947; DO, 1953; FRCS, FRACS. Group Captain, RNZAF. Ophthalmic Surgeon, Wellington Hospital, 1953-. Chm. Council, NZ Med. Assoc. CStJ 1975. *Publications:* various papers in medical jls. *Recreations:* sailing, skiing, mountaineering. *Address:* 88 The Terrace, Wellington, New Zealand. *T:* 721-375. *Club:* Wellington (NZ).

ELLIOTT, Air Vice-Marshal Robert D.; *see* Deacon Elliott.

ELLIOTT, Sir (Robert) William, Kt 1974; MP (C) Newcastle upon Tyne North since March 1957; Vice-Chairman, Conservative Party Organisation, 1970-74; *b* 11 Dec. 1920; *s* of Richard Elliott; *m* 1956, Jane Morpeth; one *s* four *d* (of whom two are twin *d*). *Educ:* Morpeth Grammar Sch. Farmer, 1939-, at Low Heighley, Morpeth, Northumberland. Parliamentary Private Secretary: to joint Parliamentary Secs, Ministry of Transport and Civil Aviation, April 1958-Oct. 1959; to Under-Sec., Home Office, Nov. 1959-60; to Minister of State, Home Office, Nov. 1960-61; to Sec. for Technical Co-operation, 1961-63; Asst Govt Whip (unpaid), 1963-64; Opposition Whip, 1964-70; Comptroller of the Household, June-Sept. 1970. *Address:* Low Heighley, Morpeth, Northumberland. *T:* Morpeth 3247. *Clubs:* Carlton, Farmers'; Northern Counties, Conservative (Newcastle upon Tyne).

ELLIOTT, Prof. Roger James, FRS 1976; Wykeham Professor of Physics, Oxford University, since 1974; Fellow of New College, Oxford, since 1974; *b* Chesterfield, 8 Dec. 1928; *s* of James Elliott and Gladys Elliott (*née* Hill); *m* 1952, Olga Lucy Atkinson; one *s* two *d*. *Educ:* Swanwick Hall Sch., Derbyshire; New Coll., Oxford (MA, DPhil). Research Fellow, Univ. of California, Berkeley, 1952-53; Research Fellow, UKAEA, Harwell, 1953-55; Lectr, Reading Univ., 1955-57. Fellow of St John's College, Oxford, 1957-74; University Reader, Oxford, 1964-74; Senior Proctor, 1969; Delegate, Oxford Univ. Press, 1971-. Visiting Prof., Univ. of California, Berkeley, 1961; Miller Vis. Prof., Univ. of Illinois, Urbana, 1966; Loeb Lectr, Harvard Univ., 1967; Seaver Lectr, USC, 1972. Maxwell Medal, Inst. of Physics, 1968. *Publications:* Magnetic Properties of Rare Earth Metals, 1973; Solid State Physics and its Applications (with A. F. Gibson), 1973; papers in Proc. Royal Soc., Jl Phys., Phys. Rev., etc. *Recreations:* tennis, squash. *Address:* 11 Crick Road, Oxford. *T:* Oxford 58369.

ELLIOTT, Sydney Robert; Editor of the Daily Herald, 1953-57; *b* 31 Aug. 1902; *o surv. s* of Robert Scott Elliott and Helen Golden; *m* 1927, Janet Robb Johnston; two *s* one *d* (one *s* decd). *Educ:* Govan High Sch., Glasgow. Managing Editor, Reynolds News, 1929; Editor, Evening Standard, 1943; Political Adviser, Daily Mirror, 1945; Managing Dir, The Argus and Australian Post, Melbourne, 1949; Gen. Manager, Daily Herald, 1952. Collaborated with author of George Wigg by Lord Wigg, 1972. *Publications:* Life of Sir William Maxwell, 1922; Co-operative Storekeeping; Eighty Years of Constructive Revolution, 1925; England, Cradle of Co-operation, 1937. *Address:* 5 Frognal Close, Hampstead, NW3. *T:* 01-435 4149.

ELLIOTT, Walter Archibald, MC 1943; QC (Scotland) 1963; President, Lands Tribunal for Scotland, since 1971; *b* 6 Sept. 1922; 2nd *s* of late Prof. T. R. Elliott, CBE, DSO, FRS, Broughton Place, Broughton, Peeblesshire; *m* 1954, Susan Isobel Mackenzie Ross, Kaimend, North Berwick; two *s*. *Educ:* Eton; Trinity Coll., Cambridge; Edinburgh Univ. Active service in Italy and North West Europe with 2nd Bn Scots Guards, 1943-45; captured and escaped, Salerno landings (MC); demobilised, Staff Capt., 1947. Barrister-at-law, Inner Temple, 1950; Advocate at Scottish Bar, 1950. Standing Junior Counsel to Accountant of Court and later to Minister of Aviation. Mem., Legal Aid Central Cttee, 1966-70; Mem., Royal Company of Archers (Queen's Body Guard for Scotland). *Publications:* articles in legal periodicals. *Recreations:* gardening, ski-ing, shooting. *Address:* Morton House, Fairmilehead, Edinburgh. *T:* 031-445 2548. *Clubs:* New, Arts (Edinburgh).

ELLIOTT, Sir William; *see* Elliott, Sir R. W.

ELLIOTT, William Rowcliffe, CB 1969; Senior Chief Inspector, Department of Education and Science, 1968-72, retired; *b* 10 April 1910; *s* of Thomas Herbert Elliott and Ada Elliott (*née* Rowcliffe); *m* 1937, Karin Tess, *d* of Ernest and Lilly Classen; one *s*. *Educ:* St Paul's Sch.; The Queen's Coll., Oxford. Schoolmaster, 1933-36; HM Inspector of Schools: in Leeds, 1936-39; in Leicestershire, 1940-44; in Liverpool, 1944-48; Staff Inspector: for Adult Education, 1948-55; for Secondary Modern Education, 1955-57; Chief Inspector for Educational Developments, 1957-59; for Secondary Educn, 1959-66; Dep. Sen. Chief Insp., 1966-67. Pres., Section L, British Assoc., 1969; Mem., Oxfam Governing Council, 1974-. *Publication:* Monemvasia, The Gibraltar of Greece, 1971. *Recreations:* village life; photography; writing, cyclamen-growing. *Address:* Astwick House, Farthinghoe, Brackley, Northants. *T:* Banbury 710388. *Club:* Royal Over-Seas League.

ELLIOTT-BINNS, Edward Ussher Elliott, CB 1977; Under-Secretary, Scottish Home and Health Department, since 1966; *b* 24 Aug. 1918; *e s* of Leonard and Anna Elliott-Binns; *m* 1942, Katharine Mary McLeod, *d* of late Dr J. M. Caie; one *d*. *Educ:* Harrow; King's Coll., Cambridge. Served with Army, 1939-46; Leics Regt and Special Forces (Major). Asst Principal, Scottish Home Dept, 1946; Principal, 1948; Asst Sec., Royal Commn on Capital Punishment, 1949-53; Private Sec. to Minister of State, Scottish Office, 1956-57; Asst Sec., 1957. *Address:* 22 Wilton Road, Edinburgh EH16 5NX. *T:* 031-667 2464. *Club:* Special Forces.
See also P . J . Harrop .

ELLIS; *see* Scott-Ellis.

ELLIS; *see* Williams-Ellis.

ELLIS, Arthur Robert Malcolm, DL; His Honour Judge Ellis; a Circuit Judge (formerly Judge of County Courts), since 1971; *b* 27 June 1912; *s* of David and Anne Amelia Ellis, Nottingham; *m* 1938, Brenda Sewell; one *d*. *Educ:* Nottingham High Sch. Admitted Solicitor, 1934; called to the Bar, Inner Temple, 1953. Chm., Nottingham Council of Social Service, 1950-55; Dep. Chm., E Midland Traffic Area, 1955-; Chm., Ministry of Pensions and National Insurance Tribunal, Sutton-in-Ashfield, Notts, 1961-64, resigned; Chm., Min. of Pensions and Nat. Insce Tribunal, Notts, 1964-. Chm., Notts QS, 1963-71 (Dep.-Chm., 1962-63); Chm., Derbyshire QS, 1966-71 (Dep.-Chm., 1965-66). DL Notts, 1973. *Recreations:* golf, bridge. *Address:* Overfields, 104 Cropwell Road, Radcliffe-on-Trent, Notts. *T:* Radcliffe-on-Trent 664. *Clubs:* Borough (Nottingham); Royal Overseas League (Nottingham Branch).

ELLIS, Sir Charles Drummond, Kt 1946; FRS 1929; BA, PhD; Scientific Adviser to: British American Tobacco Co. Ltd; Gas Council; Battelle Memorial Institute; Tobacco Research Council; Governor, Harrow; *b* 11 Aug. 1895; *s* of A. C. Ellis; *m* 1925, Paula Warzcewska. *Educ:* Harrow; RMA Woolwich; Trinity Coll., Cambridge. Fellow and Lectr of Trinity Coll., Cambridge; Lectr in Dept of Physics in Univ. of Cambridge; Wheatstone Prof. of Physics, King's Coll., London, 1936-46; Scientific Adviser to Army Council, 1943-46; Mem. Advisory Council on Scientific Research and Technical Development to Ministry of Supply, 1943-46; Scientific Mem. of National Coal Board, 1946-55; Pres. British Coal Utilisation Research Association, 1946-55; Mem. Advisory Council to Ministry of Fuel and Power, 1947-55; Mem. of Court of Governors, Administrative Staff Coll.; Senior Scientific Adviser Civil Defence London Region, 1947-65; Mem. Gas Council's Research Advisory Cttee, 1955-. *Publications:* (with Sir Ernest Rutherford and James Chadwick) Radiations from Radioactive Substances, 1930; various papers on radioactivity and connected problems. *Address:* Seawards, Cookham Dean, Berks. *T:* Marlow 3166. *Club:* Athenæum.

ELLIS, Rt. Rev. Edward; *b* 1899; *s* of A. Ellis. *Educ:* Ratcliffe Coll.; Ven. English Coll., Rome; Gregorian Univ., DD and PhD. Formerly Administrator at St Barnabas's Cathedral, Nottingham; Bishop of Nottingham, (RC), 1944-74. *Address:* Nazareth House, Old Lenton, Nottingham.

ELLIS, Rear-Adm. Edward William, CB 1974; CBE 1968; Private Secretary to the Lord Mayor of London, since 1974; *b* 6 Sept. 1918; *s* of Harry L. and Winifred Ellis; *m* 1945, Dilys (*née* Little); two *s*. Joined RN, 1940; War service afloat in HM Ships Broadwater and Eclipse, and liaison duties in USS Wichita and US Navy destroyer sqdn; psc 1952; Staff of Flag Officer Flotillas, Mediterranean, 1954-55; Sec. to 4th Sea Lord, 1956-58; Sec. to C-in-C South Atlantic and South America, 1959-60; HM Ships Bermuda and Belfast, 1960-62; Head of C-in-C Far East Secretariat, 1963-65; Sec. to C-in-C Portsmouth and Allied C-in-C Channel, 1965-66; Sec. to Chief of Naval Staff and 1st Sea Lord, 1966-68; Cdre RN Barracks Portsmouth, 1968-71; Adm. Pres., RNC Greenwich, 1972-74. Cmdr 1953; Captain 1963; Rear-Adm. 1972. Freeman of the City of London, 1974. Commander, Royal Order of Danebrog, 1974. *Recreations:* golf, gardening. *Address:* 14 Bede House, Manor Fields, Putney, SW15. *Club:* Army and Navy.

ELLIS, Prof. Harold, MA, MCh, DM, FRCS; Professor of Surgery, University of London; Hon. Consultant Surgeon, Westminster Hospital, since 1962; *b* 13 Jan. 1926; *s* of Samuel and Ada Ellis; *m* 1958, Wendy Mae Levine; one *s* one *d. Educ:* Queen's Coll. (State Scholar and Open Scholar in Natural Sciences), Oxford; Radcliffe Infirmary, Oxford. BM, BCh, 1948; FRCS, MA, 1951; MCh 1956; DM 1962. House Surgeon, Radcliffe Infirmary, 1948-49; Hallett Prize, RCS, 1949. RAMC, 1949-51. Res. Surgical Officer, Sheffield Royal Infirm., 1952-54; Registrar, Westminster Hosp., 1955; Sen. Registrar and Surgical Tutor, Radcliffe Infirm., Oxford, 1956-61; Sen. Lectr in Surgery, Westminster Hosp., 1961-62. Mem. Council, RCS, 1974-. Member: Association of Surgeons; British Soc. of Gastroenterol.; Surgical Research Soc.; Council, British Assoc. of Surgical Oncology. *Publications:* Clinical Anatomy, 1960; Anatomy for Anaesthetists, 1963; Lecture Notes on General Surgery, 1965; Principles of Resuscitation, 1967; History of the Bladder Stone, 1970; General Surgery for Nurses, 1976; numerous articles on surgical topics in medical journals. *Recreation:* medical history. *Address:* 16 Bancroft Avenue, N2. *T:* 01-348 2720.

ELLIS, Harold Owen, CMG 1958; OBE 1952; CEng; FIEE; *b* 11 April 1906; *s* of Owen Percy Ellis, accountant, and Kate Beatrice Ellis, Plymouth; *m* 1932, Phyllis Margaret Stevenson (decd); *m* 1954, Ella Stewart Mathieson. *Educ:* Sutton Secondary Sch., Plymouth. Apprentice, Devonport Dockyard. Engineering Inspector, Post Office, 1926; Executive Engineer, 1940. Served Army, 1944-47, Col. Asst Controller-Gen., Posts and Telegraphs, Control Commn, Germany, 1947; Postmaster-Gen., Nyasaland, 1949; Dir of Posts and Telegraphs, Federation of Nigeria, 1954; Postmaster-Gen., E Africa, 1958; retd Colonial Service, 1962; Administrative Consultant, 1962-66. Has attended many internat. conferences on telecommunications, sometimes representing Britain. *Publications:* technical articles and papers. *Recreations:* sailing, swimming, photography. *Address:* Turbruad, Banchory, Kincardineshire AB3 4AE.

ELLIS, Herbert; *see* Ellis, W. H. B.

ELLIS, Humphry Francis, MBE 1945; MA; writer; *b* 1907; 2nd *s* of late Dr John Constable Ellis, Metheringham, Lincs and Alice Marion Raven; *m* 1933, Barbara Pauline Hasseldine; one *s* one *d. Educ:* Tonbridge Sch.; Magdalen Coll., Oxford (Demy). 1st cl. Hon. Mods, 1928; 1st cl. Lit. Hum., 1930. Asst Master, Marlborough Coll., 1930-31. Contributor to Punch, 1931-68; Editorial staff, 1933; Literary and Dep. Ed., 1949-53. Privilege Mem., RFU, 1952-. Served War of 1939-45 in RA (AA Command). *Publications:* So This is Science, 1932; The Papers of A. J. Wentworth, 1949; Why the Whistle Went (on the laws of Rugby Football), 1947; Co-Editor, The Royal Artillery Commemoration Book, 1950; Editor, Manual of Rugby Union Football, 1952; Twenty Five Years Hard, 1960; Mediatrics, 1961; A. J. Wentworth, BA (Retd), 1962; The World of A. J. Wentworth, 1964; contribs to Countryman and The New Yorker. *Recreation:* fishing. *Address:* Hill Croft, Kingston St Mary, Taunton, Somerset. *T:* Kingston St Mary 264. *Clubs:* Garrick, MCC.

ELLIS, John; MP (Lab) Brigg and Scunthorpe, since Feb. 1974; *b* Hexthorpe, Doncaster, 22 Oct. 1930; *s* of George and Hilda Ellis; *m* 1953, Rita Butters; two *s* two *d. Educ:* Rastrick Gram. Sch., Brighouse. Laboratory technician, Meteorological Office, 1947-63; Vice-Chm., Staff side, Air Min. Whitley Council, 1961-63; Member Relations Offr, Co-op. Retail Services, Bristol/Bath Region, 1971-74. Mem., Easthampstead RDC, 1962-66; Mem., Bristol City Council, 1971-. Contested (Lab) Wokingham, 1964; MP (Lab) Bristol North-West, 1966-70; PPS to Minister of State for Transport, 1968-70; an Asst Govt Whip, 1974-76. JP, North Riding Yorks, 1960-61. *Recreations:* gardening, cricket. *Address:* 102 Glover Road, Scunthorpe, South Humberside.

ELLIS, John; Deputy Director (Projects and Research), Military Vehicles and Engineering Establishment, Chertsey, since 1974; *b* 9 Jan. 1925; *s* of Frank William and Alice Ellis; *m* 1958, Susan Doris (*née* Puttock). *Educ:* Leeds Univ. BSc, 1st cl. hons. Mech. Eng; CEng, MIMechE. Hydro-Ballistic Research Estabt, Admty, 1945-47; David Brown & Sons Ltd, Huddersfield, 1948; RAE, Min. of Supply (Structures Dept, Armament Dept, Weapons Dept), 1948-68; MVEE (formerly FVRDE), MoD, 1968-. *Recreations:* mountaineering, motoring, golf. *Address:* Well Diggers, 1 and 2 New Cottages, New Pond Road, Compton, Guildford, Surrey. *T:* Godalming 7788.

ELLIS, John Rogers, MBE 1943; MA, MD, FRCP; Physician to the London Hospital since 1951; Dean, London Hospital Medical College, since 1968; Secretary, Association for the Study of Medical Education, since 1957; *b* 15 June 1916; 3rd *s* of late Frederick William Ellis, MD, FRCS; *m* 1942, Joan, *d* of late C. J. C. Davenport; two *s* two *d. Educ:* Oundle Sch.; Trinity Hall, Cambridge; London Hosp. Served RNVR, 1942-46, Mediterranean and Far East, Surg.-Lt Gen. Practice, Plymouth, 1946; Sen. Lectr, Med. Unit, London Hosp., 1948-51; Sub-Dean, London Hosp. Med. Coll., 1948-58; Asst Registrar, RCP, 1957-61; Physician to Prince of Wales Gen. Hosp., 1958-68; PMO (part-time), Min. of Health, 1964-68. Member: UGC's Med. Sub-cttee, 1959-69; WHO Expert Adv. Cttee on Educn and Trng of Med. and ancillary personnel, 1963-; Jt Bd of Clinical Nursing Studies; Council, RCP; formerly Member: Porritt (Med. Services) Cttee; Royal Commn on Med. Educn. Lectures: Goulstonian, RCP, 1956; Wood-Jones, Univ. of Manchester, 1960; Porter, Univ. of Kansas, 1960; Sir Charles Hastings, BMA, 1964; Anders, Coll. of Physicians, Pa, 1965; Adams, RCSI, 1965; Shattuck, Massachusetts Med. Soc., 1969; Vis. Lecturer: Teaching Inst., Assoc. of Amer. Med. Colls, 1957, 1960 and 1963; Ghana Acad. of Sciences, 1967. Corr. Mem., Royal Flemish Acad. of Medicine; Hon. Mem., Royal Swedish Med. Soc.; Hon. Consultant, Nat. Bd of Med. Examiners, USA. Member Bd of Governors: London Hosp., 1968-; Queen Mary Coll., 1968-; Mem. Governing Body, Brit. Post-graduate Med. Fedn; Governor, CARE for the mentally handicapped; formerly Member Bd of Governors: Inst. of Psychiatry; Bethlem Royal and Maudsley Hosps. Editor, British Jl of Medical Education. *Publications:* articles on medical education in medical and scientific journals. *Recreations:* painting, gardening. *Address:* Little Monkhams, Woodford Green, Essex. *T:* 01-504 2292.

ELLIS, Prof. John Romaine; Professor of Automobile Engineering, since 1960, Director, 1960-76, School of Automotive Studies, Cranfield; *b* 30 Sept. 1922; *m* 1947, Madelaine Della Blaker; one *s* one *d. Educ:* Tiffin Sch., Kingston-on-Thames. Royal Aircraft Establishment, 1944-56; Fairey Aviation Company, 1946-48; Royal Military Coll. of Science, Shrivenham, near Swindon, Wilts, 1949-60. *Recreations:* golf, tennis, music. *Address:* School of Automotive Studies, Cranfield Institute of Technology, Cranfield, Bedford. *T:* Bedford 750111.

ELLIS, Joseph Stanley, CMG 1967; OBE 1962; Head of News Department, Commonwealth Office, 1967; retired; *b* 29 Nov. 1907; *m* 1933, Gladys Harcombe; one *s. Educ:* Woodhouse Grove, Bradford; University Coll., University of London. Journalist, Manchester Evening News, 1930-40; Publications Div., Min. of Inf., 1941-45; Seconded to Dominions Office for service in Australia until 1949. Central Office of Information, 1949-51; Regional Information Officer, Karachi, 1952; Dir, British Information Services: Pakistan, 1953-55; Canberra, Australia, 1955-58; Kuala Lumpur, Malaya, 1958-62; Head, Information Services Dept, Commonwealth Office, 1962-66. *Recreation:* cricket. *Address:* Downview Close, Hindhead, Surrey.

ELLIS, Mary; actress; singer; *b* New York City, 15 June 1901; *m* 1st, L. A. Bernheimer (decd); 2nd (marr. diss.); 3rd, Basil Sydney (marr. diss.); 4th, J. Muir Stewart Roberts (decd). *Educ:* New York. Studied art for three years; studied singing with Madame Ashforth. First Stage appearance, Metropolitan Opera House, New York, in Sœur Angelica, 1918; with Metropolitan Opera House, 1918-22; first appearance dramatic stage, as Nerissa in Merchant of Venice, Lyceum, New York, 1922; was the original Rose Marie (in the musical play, Rose Marie), Imperial, 1924; The Dybbuk, New York, 1925-26; Taming of the Shrew, 1927, and many New York leads followed; first appearance on London stage, as Laetitia in Knave and Quean, Ambassadors', 1930; in following years alternated between London and US. From 1932-39: London: Strange Interlude, 1932; Double Harness, 1933; Music in the Air, 1933; Glamorous Night, Drury Lane, 1935; Innocent Party, St James's, 1937; 2 years, Hollywood, 1936-37; Dancing Years, Drury Lane, 1939. From 1939-43: doing hospital welfare work and giving concerts for troops. Re-appeared on stage as Marie Foret in Arc de Triomphe, Phœnix, London, 1943; Old Vic (at Liverpool Playhouse), 1944 (Ella Rentheim in John Gabriel Borkman; Linda Valaine in Point Valaine; Lady Teazle in The School for Scandal); Maria Fitzherbert in The Gay Pavilion, Piccadilly, 1945; Season at Embassy: Mrs Dane's Defence, also tour and première of Ian Hay's Hattie Stowe, 1946-47; post-war successes include: Playbill, Phœnix, 1949; Man in the Raincoat, Edinburgh, 1949; If this be Error, Hammersmith, 1950. Stratford-on-Avon Season, 1952: Volumnia in Coriolanus. London: After the Ball (Oscar Wilde-Noel Coward), Globe, 1954-55; Mourning Becomes Electra, Arts, 1955-56; Dark Halo, Arts, 1959; Look Homeward Angel, Pembroke Theatre, Croydon, 1960; Phœnix, 1962. First appeared in films, in Bella Donna, 1934; films, 1935-38; (Hollywood) Paris in the Spring: The King's Horses; Fatal Lady; Glamorous Night; Gulliver's Travels, 1961; Silver Cord (revival), Yvonne Arnaud, Guildford, 1968; Mrs Warren's Profession, Yvonne Arnaud, Guildford, 1970. Has made several major television appearances; Television plays, 1956-: Shaw's Great Catherine, Van Druten's Distaff Side and numerous others. In 1965 designed small house in hills behind Nice where she paints and studies, when she can get away from London. *Recreations:* painting, travel, writing. *Address:* c/o Chase Manhattan Bank, 1 Mount Street, W1.

ELLIS, Maxwell (Philip), MD, MS, FRCS; Dean of the Institute of Laryngology and Otology, University of London, 1965-71; Consulting Surgeon, Royal National Throat, Nose and Ear Hospital; Consulting Ear, Nose and Throat Surgeon, Central Middlesex Hospital; *b* 28 Feb. 1906; *s* of Louis Ellis; *m* 1935, Barbara Gertrude Chapman (*d* 1977). *Educ:* University Coll., London (Exhibitioner), Fellow 1975; University Coll. Hosp. (Bucknill Exhbnr). Liston and Alexander Bruce Gold Medals, Surgery and Pathology, UCH, 1927-29. MB, BS (London), Hons Medicine, 1930; MD 1931; FRCS 1932; MS 1937; Geoffrey Duveen Trav. Student, Univ. of London, 1934-36; Leslie Pearce Gould Trav. Schol., 1934, Perceval Alleyn Schol. (Surg. research), 1936, UCH; Hunterian Prof., RCS, 1938. RAFVR, 1940-45 (Wing-Comdr). FRSM, also Mem. Council; Past Pres., Section of Otology; Hon. Treasurer and Mem. Council, Med. Soc. London (Hon. Sec. 1961-63; Pres., 1970-71); Hon. Member: Assoc. of Otolaryngologists of India; Salonika Soc. of Otolaryngology; Athens Soc. of Otolaryngology; Corresp. Mem., Société Française d'Oto-Rhino-Laryngologie; Hon. Corresp. Mem., Argentine Soc. of Otolaryngology. Lectr on Diseases of Ear, Nose and Throat, Univ. of London, 1952-. *Publications:* Modern Trends in Diseases of the Ear, Nose and Throat (Ed. and part author), 1954, 2nd edn 1971; Operative Surgery (Rob and Smith), Vol. 8 on Diseases of the Ear, Nose and Throat (Ed. and part author), 1958; 2nd edn 1969; Clinical Surgery (Rob and Smith), Vol. 11, Diseases of the Ear, Nose and Throat (Ed. and part author), 1966; Sections in Diseases of the Ear, Nose and Throat (Ed. Scott-Brown), 1952, new edns 1965, 1971; Sections in Cancer, Vol. 4 (Ed. Raven), 1958; Section in Modern Trends in Surgical Materials (Ed. Gillis), 1958; papers in various medical and scientific jls. *Recreations:* golf, gardening; formerly bridge and squash rackets. *Address:* 149 Harley Street, W1N 2DE. *T:* 01-935 4444; 48 Townshend Road, NW8. *T:* 01-722 2252. *Clubs:* Royal Automobile; Sunningdale Golf.

ELLIS, Osian Gwynn, CBE 1971; harpist; Professor of Harp, Royal Academy of Music, London, since 1959; *b* Ffynnongroew, Flints, 8 Feb. 1928; *s* of Rev. T. G. Ellis, Methodist Minister; *m* 1951, Rene Ellis Jones, Pwllheli; two *s. Educ:* Denbigh Grammar Sch.; Royal Academy of Music. Has broadcast and televised extensively. Has given recitals/concertos all over the world; shared poetry and music recitals with Dame Peggy Ashcroft, Paul Robeson, Burton, C. Day-Lewis, etc. Mem., Melos Ensemble; solo harpist with LSO. Member of Music and Welsh Adv. Cttees, British Council. Works written for him include Harp Concertos by Hoddinott, 1957 and by Mathias, 1970; Jersild, 1972; from 1960 worked with Benjamin Britten who wrote Harp Suite in C (Op. 83) for him. Has made many recordings of recitals, Welsh folk songs, etc. Film, The Harp, won a Paris award; other awards include Grand Prix du Disque and French Radio Critics' Award. FRAM 1960. Hon. DMus Wales, 1970. *Address:* 90 Chandos Avenue, N20. *T:* 01-445 7896; Glanrafon, Aberdaron, Pwllheli, N Wales.

ELLIS, Robert Thomas; MP (Lab) Wrexham since 1970; *b* 15 March 1924; *s* of Robert and Edith Ann Ellis; *m* 1949, Nona Harcourt Williams; three *s* one *d. Educ:* Universities of Wales and Nottingham. Works Chemist, ICI, 1944-47; Coal Miner, 1947-55; Mining Engineer, 1955-70; Manager, Bersham Colliery, N Wales, 1957-70. Mem., European Parlt, 1975-. *Publication:* Mines and Men, 1971. *Recreations:* golf, reading, music. *Address:* Whitehurst House, Whitehurst, Chirk, Wrexham. *T:* Chirk 3462.

ELLIS, Roger Henry, MA; FSA; FRHistS; Secretary, Royal Commission on Historical Manuscripts, 1957-72; *b* 9 June 1910; *e s* of late Francis Henry Ellis, Debdale Hall, Mansfield; *m* 1939, Audrey Honor, *o d* of late H. Arthur Baker, DL; two *d. Educ:* Sedbergh (scholar); King's College, Cambridge (scholar, Augustus Austen Leigh Student). 1st Cl. Class. Tripos, 1933. Asst Keeper, Public Record Office, 1934; Principal Asst Keeper, 1956. Served War of 1939-45: Private, 1939; Major, 5th Fusiliers, 1944; Monuments, Fine Arts and Archives Officer in Italy and Germany, 1944-45. Lectr in Archive Admin, Sch. of Librarianship and Archives, University Coll. London, 1947-57. Mem. London Council, British Inst. in Florence, 1947-55; Hon. Editor, British Records Assoc., and (first) Editor of Archives, 1947-57, Chm. Council, 1967-73, Vice-Pres., 1971-. Vice-Pres., Business Archives Council, 1958-; Member: Adv. Council on Export of Works of Art, 1964-72; Jt Records Cttee of Royal Soc. and Historical MSS Commn, 1968-76; Pres., Soc. of Archivists, 1964-73. A Manager, 1973-76, a Vice-Pres., 1975-76, Royal Instn. Corresp. Mem., Indian Historical Records Commn. *Publications:* Catalogue of Seals in the Public Record Office; opuscula and articles in British and foreign jls on care and use of archives and MSS. *Recreations:* poetry, travel, the arts, gardening (unskilled). *Address:* Cloth Hill, 6 The Mount, Hampstead, NW3; Clappers, West Harting, near Petersfield, Hants. *Club:* Athenæum.

ELLIS, Roger Wykeham; Master of Marlborough College, since 1972; *b* 3 Oct. 1929; *s* of Cecil Ellis, solicitor, and Pamela Unwin; *m* 1964, Margaret Jean Stevenson; one *s* two *d. Educ:* St Peter's Sch., Seaford; Winchester Coll.; Trinity Coll., Oxford (Schol., MA). Royal Navy, 1947-49. Asst Master, Harrow Sch., 1952-67, and Housemaster of the Head Master's House, 1961-67; Headmaster of Rossall Sch., 1967-72. Member: Harrow Borough Educn Cttee, 1956-60; Wilts County Educn Cttee, 1975-. *Recreations:* golf, fishing. *Address:* Marlborough College, Wilts.

ELLIS, Ronald, CEng, FIMechE; Head of Defence Sales, Ministry of Defence, since 1976; *b* 12 Aug. 1925; *s* of William Ellis and Besse Brownbill; *m* 1956, Cherry Hazel Brown; one *s* one *d. Educ:* Preston Grammar Sch.; Manchester Univ. (BScTech Hons 1949). CEng, FIMechE 1949. Man. Dir, Leyland Truck and Bus, 1968; Dir, British Leyland Motor Corp. Ltd, 1970. FRSA, FCIT. *Recreations:* fishing, sailing, swimming. *Address:* The Finches, Knotty Green, Beaconsfield, Bucks. *Club:* Naval and Military.

ELLIS, Sir Thomas Hobart, Kt 1953; *b* 11 Oct. 1894; *s* of late Rev. Herbert Ellis. *Educ:* Manchester Grammar Sch.; Queen's Coll., Oxford. Entered Indian Civil Service, 1919; Additional Judge of High Court, Calcutta, 1944-47; Judge of High Court of East Bengal, 1947-53; Chief Justice, 1953-54. Acting Governor of East Bengal, Sept.-Dec. 1954. Officer on Special Duty, Government of Pakistan, 1955-57. *Recreations:* photography, trekking. *Address:* 1 Gibwood Road, Northenden, Manchester M22 4BR; c/o Grindlay's Bank, 13 St James's Square, SW1.

ELLIS, Vivian; Lt-Comdr RNVR; composer; author; Deputy President, Performing Right Society, since 1975; *s* of Harry Ellis and Maud Isaacson. *Educ:* Cheltenham Coll. (Musical Exhibition). Commenced his career as concert pianist after studying under Myra Hess; studied composition at the Royal Academy of Music; first song published when fifteen; his first work for the theatre was the composition of additional numbers for The Curate's Egg, 1922; contributed to The Little Revue and The Punch Bowl Revue, 1924; to Yoicks, Still Dancing, and Mercenary Mary, and composer of By the Way, 1925; to Just a Kiss, Kid Boots, Cochran's Revue, My Son John, Merely Molly and composer of Palladium Pleasures, 1926; to Blue Skies, The Girl Friend, and Clowns in Clover, 1927; to Charlot, 1928; and composer of Peg o' Mine, Will o' The Whispers, Vogues and Vanities, 1928; to A Yankee at the Court of King Arthur, The House that Jack Built, and (with Richard Myers) composer of Mister Cinders, 1929; part-composer of Cochran's 1930 Revue, and composer of Follow a Star and Little Tommy Tucker, 1930; part-composer of Stand Up and Sing, and Song of the Drum (with Herman Finck), and composer of Folly to be Wise, and Blue Roses, 1931; part-composer of Out of the Bottle, 1932; composer of Cochran's revue Streamline, 1934; Jill Darling, 1935; music and lyrics of Charlot Revue, The Town Talks, 1936; Hide and Seek, 1937; The Fleet's Lit Up, Running Riot, Under Your Hat, 1938; composer (to Sir A. P. Herbert's libretto) Cochran light operas: Big Ben, 1946; Bless the Bride, 1947; Tough at the Top, 1949; Water Gipsies, 1955; music and lyrics of And So To Bed, 1951; music for The Sleeping Prince, 1954; music and lyrics of Listen to the Wind, 1954; Half in Earnest (musical adaptation of The Importance of Being Earnest), 1958; composer of popular songs; many dance items; Coronation Scot;

also music for the films Jack's the Boy, Water Gipsies, 1932; Falling for You, 1933; Public Nuisance No 1, 1935; Piccadilly Incident, 1946, etc. Ivor Novello Award for outstanding services to British music, 1973. *Publications: novels:* Zelma; Faint Harmony; Day Out; Chicanery; *travel:* Ellis in Wonderland; *autobiography:* I'm on a See-Saw; *humour:* How to Make your Fortune on the Stock Exchange; How to Enjoy Your Operation; How to Bury Yourself in the Country; How to be a Man-about-Town; Good-Bye, Dollie; contrib: The Rise and Fall of the Matinée Idol: biography of Jack Buchanan; *for children:* Hilary's Tune; Hilary's Holidays; The Magic Baton. *Recreations:* gardening, painting, operations. *Club:* Garrick.

ELLIS, Wilfred Desmond, OBE 1952; TD; DL; Customer Service and Conversion Manager, Gas Council, 1968-73; Lay Member, Press Council, 1969-76; *b* 7 Nov. 1914; 2nd *s* of late Bertram V. C. W. Ellis and late Winifred Dora Ellis; *m* 1947, Effie Douglas, JP, *d* of late Dr A. Barr, Canonbie, Scotland; one *s* two *d*. *Educ:* Temple Grove; Canford. Commissioned as 2nd Lt, Middlesex Regt, 1937. Served War of 1939-45 at home and NW Europe with Middlesex Regt (despatches, 1944). Rejoined TA, 1947, retiring as Dep. Comdt 47 (L) Inf. Bde, 1962; County Comdt, Mddx Army Cadet Force, 1958-62; ADC to the Queen, 1966-69. Joined Gas Industry, 1932; Uxbridge, Maidenhead, Wycombe & Dist. Gas Co. until War of 1939-45; returned to Company until nationalisation; served with North Thames Gas Bd in various appts until joining Gas Council Research Station, Watson House, 1963, as Asst, and then Dep. Dir; transf. to Gas Council, 1966, as Manager, Conversion Executive. DL (Greater London), 1964. Fellow, Inst. of Marketing. *Recreations:* shooting, local affairs. *Address:* Lea Barn, Winter Hill, Cookham Dean, Berkshire SL6 9TW. *T:* Maidenhead 4230. *Club:* Bath.

ELLIS, Dr (William) Herbert (Baxter), AFC 1954; Underwriting Member of Lloyd's; Member, Employment Medical Advisory Service, since 1973; *b* 2 July 1921; *er s* of William Baxter Ellis and Georgina Isabella Ellis (*née* Waller); *m* 1948, Margaret Mary Limb (marr. diss. 1977); one *s* one *d*. *Educ:* Oundle Sch.; Durham Univ. (MD, BS). Royal Navy, 1945-59: Surg. Comdr, Fleet Air Arm Pilot. Motor industry, 1960-71; research into human aspects of road traffic accidents, 1960-71; Dir-Gen., Dr Barnardo's, 1971-73; dir of various companies. *Publications:* Physiological and Psychological Aspects of Deck Landings, 1954; various on the human factor in industrial management. *Recreations:* walking, sun, water. *Address:* c/o Midland Bank Ltd, 5 Threadneedle Street, EC2. *Clubs:* Army and Navy, Naval and Military.

ELLIS-REES, Hugh Francis; Under Secretary, Department of Transport, since 1976; *b* 5 March 1929; *s* of late Sir Hugh Ellis-Rees, KCMG, CB and Lady (Eileen Frances Anne) Ellis-Rees; *m* 1956, Elisabeth de Mestre Gray; three *s* one *d*. *Educ:* Ampleforth Coll.; Balliol Coll., Oxford. Served Grenadier Guards, 1948-49. Asst Principal, War Office, 1954; Principal 1958; Asst Private Sec. to Sec. of State, 1955-58 and 1961-62; Private Sec. to Minister of Defence (Army), 1965-68; Asst Sec. 1968; DoE, 1970; Cabinet Office, 1972-74; Under Sec., DoE, 1974-76. *Recreations:* squash, canals, collecting books. *Address:* 4 St George's Court, Gloucester Road, SW7 4QZ. *T:* 01-584 7218.

ELLISON, Ven. Charles Ottley; Archdeacon of Leeds, 1950-69, Emeritus since 1969; Honorary Canon of Ripon Cathedral, 1953-62; *b* 8 Feb. 1898; *s* of late S. Ellison, Leeds; *m* 1926, Lavinia (*d* 1970), *d* of late J. E. MacGregor, Flers-Breucq, Nord, France; one *d*. *Educ:* Wrekin Coll.; University of Leeds (BSc); Ripon Hall, Oxford. Curate of St Chad, Far Headingley, Leeds, 1932-37; Vicar of Kippax, 1937-46; Surrogate, 1942-75; Rural Dean of Whitkirk, 1944-46; Vicar of Wetherby, 1946-55; Vicar of St John's, Briggate, Leeds, 1955-65. Pres., Yorks Assoc. of Change-Ringers, 1947-66; Chm., C of E Council for Social Aid, 1967-69; Mem., C of E Pensions Board, 1962-70. *Recreations:* numismatics, Sherlock Holmes. *Address:* 1 Burton Dene, Burton Crescent, Leeds LS6 4DN. *T:* Leeds 752191. *Club:* Leeds (Leeds).

ELLISON, Rt. Rev. and Rt. Hon. Gerald Alexander; *see* London, Bishop of.

ELLISON, John Harold, VRD 1948; His Honour Judge Ellison; a Circuit Judge, since 1972; Chancellor of the Dioceses of Salisbury and Norwich, since 1955; *b* 20 March 1916; *s* of late Harold Thomas Ellison, MIMechE, and late Mrs Frances Amy Swithinbank, both of Woodspeen Grange, Newbury; *m* 1952, Margaret Dorothy Maud, *d* of Maynard D. McFarlane, Pasadena, Calif; three *s* one *d*. *Educ:* Uppingham Sch.; King's Coll., Cambridge (MA). Res. Physicist, then Engr, Thos Firth & John Brown Ltd, Sheffield; Lieut, RE, TA (49th WR) Div.,

1937-39; Officer in RNVR, 1939-51 (retd as Lt-Comdr): Gunnery Specialist, HMS Excellent, 1940; Sqdn Gunnery Officer, 8 Cruiser Sqdn, 1940-42; Naval Staff, Admty, 1942-44; Staff Officer (Ops) to Flag Officer, Western Mediterranean, 1944-45. Called to Bar, Lincoln's Inn, 1948; practised at Common Law Bar, 1948-71. Governor, Forres Sch. Trust, Swanage. FRAS. *Publication:* (ed) titles Allotments and Smallholdings, and Courts, in Halsbury's Law of England, 3rd edn, and Allotments and Smallholdings, 4th edn. *Recreations:* organs and music, sailing, ski-ing, shooting. *Address:* Goose Green House, Egham, Surrey TW20 8PE. *T:* Egham 2392. *Clubs:* Athenæum; Bar Yacht.

ELLISON, Sir Ralph Henry C.; *see* Carr-Ellison, Sir R. H.

ELLISON, Randall Erskine, CMG 1960; ED 1946; *b* 6 March 1904; 2nd *s* of late Rev. Preb. J. H. J. Ellison, CVO, Rector of St Michael's, Cornhill, EC, and Mrs Ellison; unmarried. *Educ:* Repton Sch.; New Coll., Oxford (MA). Superintendent of Education, Northern Provinces, Nigeria, 1928; seconded to British Somaliland as Dir of Education, 1938-43; Military Service with British Somaliland and Nigerian Forces, 1940-43; Asst Dir of Education, Tanganyika, 1945; Deputy Dir, 1946; Deputy Dir of Education, Northern Region, Nigeria, 1955; Dir of Education, 1956; Adviser on Education, 1957. Chm., Public Service Commission, Northern Region, Nigeria, 1958, retired 1961. Asst Sec., Church Assembly, Dean's Yard, SW1, 1962-63. Chm., Africa Cttee of CMS, 1969-73; Mem. Council, Westfield Coll., London Univ., 1964 (Chm., 1967-68; Hon. Treasurer, 1969-76). Hon. Steward, Westminster Abbey, 1964. *Publication:* An English-Kanuri Sentence Book, 1937. *Recreations:* choral singing, chamber music. *Address:* 32 Oppidans Road, Hampstead, NW3 3AG. *Clubs:* United Oxford & Cambridge University, Royal Commonwealth Society.

ELLISON, Prof. William, BSc, PhD (Dunelm); JP; Professor of Agriculture, University College of Wales, Aberystwyth, 1946-Sept 1978; Vice-Principal of the College, 1966-68; *b* 28 June 1911; *o s* of late William Ellison, Eden Hall, Horden, Co. Durham; *m* 1937, Florence Elizabeth, *yr d* of late J. W. Robinson; two *d*. *Educ:* St Cuthbert's Gram. Sch.; King's Coll., Newcastle upon Tyne, Durham Univ. Asst Lectr, Agricultural Botany, UCW Aberystwyth, 1934. Seconded as Chief Technical Adviser to Montgomeryshire WAEC, 1940-46. Hill Farming Research Organization, 1958-66. Member: UGC Agric. Cttee, 1965-75; NERC Land Use Research Cttee. Pres., Section M, Brit. Assoc. for Advancement of Science, 1966. JP County of Cardigan, 1957. *Publications:* Marginal Land in Britain, 1953; numerous contribs to scientific and agric. jls, on land reclamation, land use, grassland and crop production. *Recreations:* tennis, cricket. *Address:* Institute of Rural Science, Penglais, Dyfed. *T:* 3111. *Club:* Farmers'.

ELLMAN-BROWN, Hon. Geoffrey, CMG 1959; OBE 1945; FCA 1950 (ACA 1934); *b* 20 Dec. 1910; *s* of John and Violet Ellman-Brown; *m* 1936, Hilda Rosamond Fairbrother; two *s* one *d*. *Educ:* Plumtree Sch., S Rhodesia. Articled to firm of Chartered Accountants in London, 1929-34; final Chartered Accountant exam. and admitted as Mem. Inst. of Chartered Accountants of England and Wales, 1934. In Rhodesia Air Force (rising to rank of Group Capt.), 1939-46. Resumed practice as Chartered Accountant, 1946-53. Entered S Rhodesia Parliament holding ministerial office (Portfolios of Roads, Irrigation, Local Government and Housing), 1953-58. Re-entered Parliament, 1962, Minister of Finance; re-elected, 1962-65, in Opposition Party. Pres. Rhodesia Cricket Union, 1950-52; Mem. S African Cricket Board of Control, 1951-52. Chairman: Rothmans of Pall Mall (Rhodesia) Ltd; The Rhodesia Sugar Assoc.; Sugar Sales (Private) Ltd; Discount Co. of Rhodesia Ltd; Industrial Promotion Corp. Central Africa Ltd; Salisbury Portland Cement Ltd; C. T. Bowring and Associates Rhodesia (Pvt) Ltd; Bowmakers (CA) (Pvt) Ltd; Director: Barclays Bank in Rhodesia; Rhodesian Acceptances Ltd; Hippo Valley Estates Ltd; Colonial Mutual Life Assurance Soc. Ltd; Freight Services Ltd; Rho-Abercom Investments Ltd. Independence Commemorative Decoration, 1970. *Recreations:* cricket, golf, shooting, fishing. *Address:* PO Box 8426, Salisbury, Rhodesia. *T:* 706381. *Clubs:* Salisbury, Royal Salisbury Golf (Salisbury, Rhodesia); Ruwa Country.

ELLMANN, Richard, MA Oxon; PhD Yale; Goldsmiths' Professor of English Literature, Oxford University, since 1970; *b* Highland Park, Michigan, 15 March 1918; *s* of James Isaac Ellmann and Jeanette (*née* Barsook); *m* 1949, Mary Donahue; one *s* two *d*. *Educ:* Highland Park High Sch.; Yale Univ. (MA, PhD); Trinity Coll., Dublin (LittB). Served War of 1939-45, Office of Strategic Services, USNR, 1943-46. Instructor at Harvard, 1942-43, 1947-48; Briggs-Copeland Asst Prof. of Eng.

Composition, Harvard, 1948-51; Prof. of English, Northwestern Univ., 1951, Franklin Bliss Snyder Prof., 1963-68; Prof. of English, Yale, 1968-70. Rockefeller Fellow, 1946-47; Guggenheim Fellow, 1950, 1957, 1970; Kenyon Review Fellow Criticism, 1955-56; Fellow, Sch. of Letters, Indiana Univ., 1956, 1960; Senior Fellow, 1966-72; Frederick Ives Carpenter Vis. Prof., Univ. of Chicago, 1959, 1968, 1975, 1976, 1977. Mem. Editorial Committee: Publications of the Modern Language Assoc., 1968-73; American Scholar, 1968-74. FRSL; Fellow, Amer. Acad. and Inst. of Arts and Letters. National Book Award, 1960. Hon. DLitt NUI, 1976. *Publications:* Yeats: The Man and the Masks, 1948; The Identity of Yeats, 1954; James Joyce: a biography, 1959; Eminent Domain, 1967; Ulysses on the Liffey, 1972; Golden Codgers, 1973; The Consciousness of Joyce., 1977; Edited: Selected Writings of Henri Michaux (trans.), 1951; My Brother's Keeper, by Stanislaus Joyce, 1958; (with others) Masters of British Literature, 1958; Arthur Symons: The Symbolist Movement in Literature, 1958; (with Ellsworth Mason) The Critical Writings of James Joyce, 1959; Edwardians and late Victorians, 1959; (with Charles Feidelson, Jr) The Modern Tradition, 1965; Letters of James Joyce (Vols II and III), 1966; James Joyce: Giacomo Joyce, 1968; The Artist as Critic: Oscar Wilde, 1970; Oscar Wilde: twentieth century views, 1970; (with Robert O'Clair) Norton Anthology of Modern Poetry, 1973; Selected Letters of James Joyce, 1975; New Oxford Book of American Verse, 1976. *Address:* New College, Oxford. *Clubs:* The Signet (Harvard); Elizabethan (Yale).

ELLSWORTH, Robert; Deputy Secretary of Defense, 1976-77; *b* 11 June 1926; *s* of Willoughby Fred Ellsworth and Lucille Rarig Ellsworth; *m* 1956, Vivian Esther Sies; one *s* one *d. Educ:* Univs of Kansas (BSME) and Michigan (JD). Active service, US Navy, 1944-46, 1950-53 (Lt-Comdr). Mem. United States Congress, 1961-67; Asst to President of US, 1969; Ambassador and Permanent Representative of US on N Atlantic Council, 1969-71; Asst Sec. of Defense (Internat. Security Affairs), 1974-75. Mem. Council, IISS, 1973-. Hon. LLD: Ottawa, 1969; Boston, 1970. *Recreations:* tennis, ski-ing, swimming. *Address:* 2801 New Mexico Avenue NW, Washington, DC 20007, USA.

ELLWOOD, Air Marshal Sir Aubrey (Beauclerk), KCB 1949 (CB 1944); DSC; DL; *b* 3 July 1897; *s* of late Rev. C. E. Ellwood, Rector of Cottesmore, Rutland, 1888-1926; *m* 1920, Lesley Mary Joan Matthews; one *s* one *d* (and one *s* decd). *Educ:* Cheam Sch.; Marlborough Coll. Joined Royal Naval Air Service, 1916; permanent commission RAF 1919. Served India 1919-23 and 1931-36 in RAF; RAF Staff Coll., Air Min., Army Co-operation Comd variously, 1938-42; AOC No. 18 Group RAF, 1943-44; Temp. Air Vice-Marshal, 1943; SASO HQ Coastal Comd RAF, 1944-45; Actg Air Marshal, 1947; a Dir-Gen. of Personnel, Air Ministry, 1945-47. Air Marshal, 1949; AOC-in-C, Bomber Command, 1947-50; AOC-in-C, Transport Command, 1950-52; retired, 1952. Governor and Commandant, The Church Lads' Brigade, 1954-70. DL Somerset, 1960. *Recreations:* riding, fishing, music. *Address:* The Old House, North Perrott, Crewkerne, Somerset.
See also M. O. D. Ellwood.

ELLWOOD, Captain Michael Oliver Dundas, DSO 1940; *b* 13 July 1894; *s* of late Rev. C. E. Ellwood, Cottesmore, Rutland. *Educ:* Cheam Sch., Surrey; RN Colls, Osborne and Dartmouth. Entered Royal Navy, 1907; retired as Comdr, 1934; rejoined as Capt. on retired list, 1939; reverted to retired list, Sept. 1946. *Club:* Army and Navy.
See also Sir Aubrey Ellwood.

ELMHIRST, Air Marshal Sir Thomas (Walker), KBE 1946 (CBE 1943); CB 1945; AFC 1918; RAF retired; Lieutenant-Governor and Commander-in-Chief of Guernsey, 1953-Oct. 1958; *b* 15 Dec. 1895; 4th *s* of late Rev. W. H. Elmhirst, Elmhirst, near Barnsley, Yorks; *m* 1st, 1930, Katharine Gordon (*d* 1965), 4th *d* of William Black, Chapel, Fife; one *s* one *d*; 2nd, 1968, Marian Louisa, *widow* of Col Andrew Ferguson and *d* of late Lt-Col Lord Herbert Montagu-Douglas-Scott. *Educ:* RN Colls, Osborne and Dartmouth. RN, 1908-15, Dardanelles and Dogger Bank in HMS Indomitable; RN Air Service, 1915-18; RAF as Major, Comdg Naval Airship Patrol Station, Anglesey, 1918 (AFC); RAF Staff Coll., 1925; commanded No. 15 Bomber Squadron and Abingdon Wing, 1935-37; 1st British Air Attaché to HM Embassy, Ankara, 1937-39; Dep. Dir Intelligence Air Ministry and Air Cdre HQ Fighter Comd, 1940 (Battle of Britain); RAF mem. of British Mission for Staff conversations with Turkish Gen. Staff, Ankara, 1941; AOC RAF Egypt, 1941 (despatches twice); 2nd in Comd Desert Air Force (Alamein campaigns), 1942 (CBE); Air Officer i/c Administration NW Africa, TAF, 1943 (despatches, CB, Tunis and Sicily campaigns); 2nd in Comd British Air Forces in NW Europe, Normandy-Germany campaign (KBE, despatches), 1944-45;

Asst Chief of Air Staff (Intelligence), 1945-47; Chief of Inter-Service Administration in India, 1947; first C-in-C Indian Air Force, 1947-50; retd, 1950. Hon. Air Marshal in the Indian Air Force, 1950. Fife County Councillor, 1950; Civil Defence Controller Eastern Zone, Scotland, 1952-53. DL, County of Fife, 1960-70. Comdr, US Legion of Merit; Grand Officer, Crown of Belgium and Croix de Guerre; Comdr, Legion of Honour and French Croix de Guerre. KStJ 1954. *Recreations:* grandchildren and fishing. *Address:* The Cottage, Dummer, Basingstoke, Hants. *Club:* Royal Air Force.

ELMSLIE, Maj.-Gen. Alexander Frederic Joseph, CB 1959; CBE 1955; psc; *b* 31 Oct. 1905. Commissioned in Royal Army Service Corps, 29 Jan. 1925, and subsequently served in Shanghai, Ceylon, E. Africa and Singapore; Lieutenant 1927; Captain 1935; served War of 1939-45 (despatches); Major, 1942; Lt-Col 1948; Temp. Brig. 1944; Brig. 1953; Maj.-Gen. 1958. Dep. Dir of Supplies and Transport, War Office, 1953-55; Dir of Supplies and Transport, GHQ Far East Land Forces, 1956-57; Inspector, RASC, War Office, 1957-60, retired. Chairman Traffic Commissioners: NW Traffic Area, 1962-64; SE Traffic Area, 1965-75. Hon. Col 43 (Wessex) Inf. Div. Coln, RASC, TA, 1960-64; Col Comdt, RASC, 1964-65; Col Comdt, Royal Corps of Transport, 1965-69. CEng; FIMechE; FCIT; Fellow, Royal Commonwealth Soc. *Address:* c/o Barclays Bank Ltd, Station Parade, Eastbourne, Sussex.

ELPHIN, Bishop of, (RC), since 1971; **Most Rev. Dominic Joseph Conway;** *b* 1 Jan. 1918; *s* of Dominic Conway and Mary Hoare. *Educ:* Coll. of the Immaculate Conception, Sligo; Pontifical Irish Coll., Pontifical Lateran Univ., Pontifical Angelicum Univ., Gregorian Univ. (all in Rome); National Univ. of Ireland. BPh, STL, DEcclHist, Higher Diploma Educn. Missionary, Calabar Dio., Nigeria, 1943-48; Professor: All Hallows Coll., Dublin, 1948-49; Summerhill Coll., Sligo, 1949-51; Spiritual Dir, 1951-65, Rector, 1965-68, Irish Coll., Rome; Sec.-Gen., Superior Council of the Propagation of the Faith, Rome, 1968-70; Auxiliary Bishop of Elphin, 1970-71. *Address:* St Mary's, Sligo, Ireland. *T:* 2670.

ELPHINSTONE, family name of Lord **Elphinstone.**

ELPHINSTONE, 18th Lord *cr* 1509; **James Alexander Elphinstone;** Baron (UK) 1885; *b* 22 April 1953; *s* of Rev. Hon. Andrew Charles Victor Elphinstone (*d* 1975) (2nd *s* of 16th Lord) and of Hon. Mrs Andrew Elphinstone, *qv. S* uncle, 1975. *Educ:* Eton Coll.; Royal Agricultural Coll., Cirencester. *Address:* Drumkilbo, Meigle, Perthshire. *T:* Meigle 216.

ELPHINSTONE, Hon. Mrs Andrew (Jean Frances), CVO 1953; *b* 22 Feb. 1923; *d* of late Capt. A. V. Hambro; *m* 1st, 1942, Capt. Hon. Vicary Paul Gibbs, Grenadier Guards (killed in action, 1944), *er s* of 4th Baron Aldenham; one *s* (and one *d* decd); 2nd, 1946, Rev. Hon. Andrew Charles Victor Elphinstone (*d* 1975), 2nd *s* of 16th Lord Elphinstone, KT; one *s* (see 18th Lord Elphinstone) one *d*. Lady-in-Waiting to the Queen as Princess Elizabeth, 1945; Extra Woman of the Bedchamber to the Queen, 1952-. *Address:* Maryland, Worplesdon, Surrey. *T:* Worplesdon 2629.

ELPHINSTONE, Sir Douglas; *see* Elphinstone, Sir M. D. W.

ELPHINSTONE of Glack, Sir John, 11th Bt *cr* 1701, of Logie Elphinstone and Nova Scotia; Land Agent with Imperial Chemical Industries Ltd, since 1956; *b* 12 Aug. 1924; *s* of Thomas George Elphinston (*d* 1967), and of Gladys Mary Elphinston, *d* of late Ernest Charles Lambert Congdon; *S* uncle, 1970; *m* 1953, Margaret Doreen, *d* of Edric Tasker; four *s. Educ:* Eagle House, Sandhurst, Berks; Repton; Emmanuel College, Cambridge (BA). Lieut, Royal Marines, 1942-48. Chartered Surveyor. Past Pres., Cheshire Agricultural Valuers' Assoc.; Past Chm., Land Agency and Agric. Div., Lancs, Cheshire and IoM Branch, RICS; Mem., Lancs River Authority, 1970-74. *Recreations:* shooting, ornithology, cricket. *Heir:* s Alexander Elphinston, *b* 6 June 1955. *Address:* Pilgrims, Churchfields, Sandiway, Northwich, Cheshire. *T:* Sandiway 883327.

ELPHINSTONE, Rev. Kenneth John Tristram; Vicar-General of Province of York, since 1972; Dean of the Arches Court of Canterbury and Auditor of the Chancery Court of York, since 1977; Member of York Convocation and General Synod, since 1973; *b* 29 Nov. 1911; 3rd *s* of late Canon M. C. Elphinstone and Mrs C. G. Elphinstone; *m* 1938, Felicity, 4th *d* of late Sir Gerald Hurst, QC; one *d* (one *s* decd). *Educ:* Loretto; Jesus Coll., Cambridge (MA). Served War of 1939-45, Rifle Bde (Temp. Captain; POW). Called to Bar, Inner Temple, 1934; Mem., Lincoln's Inn, 1938, Bencher 1977; Mem. Gen. Council of the Bar, 1956-60. Chancellor: Diocese of Chester, 1950-77;

Hereford, 1953-77; York, 1970-77. Ordained deacon and priest, 1964; Vicar of South Stoke, Somerset, 1966-74. Mem. Governing Body, SPCK, 1972-. *Publications:* (with K. M. Macmorran) Handbook for Churchwardens and Parochial Church Councillors, new edn, 1977; Handbook of Parish Property, 1973. *Recreation:* walking. *Address:* 3 Enterpen Hall, Hutton Rudby, Yarm, Cleveland TS15 0EL. *T:* Hutton Rudby 700047. *Club:* Athenæum.

See also Sir *M . D . W . Elphinstone , Bt .*

ELPHINSTONE, Sir (Maurice) Douglas (Warburton), 5th Bt *cr* 1816; TD 1946; retired, 1973; *b* 13 April 1909; *s* of Rev. Canon Maurice Curteis Elphinstone (4th *s* of 3rd Bt) (*d* 1969), and Christiana Georgiana (*née* Almond); *S* cousin, 1975; *m* 1943, Helen Barbara, *d* of late George Ramsay Main; one *s* one *d*. *Educ:* Loretto School, Musselburgh; Jesus Coll., Cambridge (MA). FFA; FRSE. Actuary engaged in Life Assurance companies until 1956 (with the exception of the war); Manager of Stock Exchange, London, 1957-74. War service with London Scottish and Sierra Leone Regt, RWAFF, mainly in W Africa and India. *Publications:* technical papers mainly in Trans Faculty of Actuaries and Jl Inst. of Actuaries. *Recreation:* gardening. *Heir: s* John Howard Main Elphinstone, *b* 25 Feb. 1949. *Address:* Wetheral Crook, Scotby, Carlisle CA4 8EE. *T:* Scotby 280.

See also Rev . *K . J . T . Elphinstone .*

ELRINGTON, Christopher Robin, FSA, FRHistS; Editor, Victoria History of the Counties of England, since 1977; *b* 20 Jan. 1930; *s* of Brig. Maxwell Elrington, DSO, OBE, and Beryl Joan (*née* Ommanney); *m* 1951, Jean Margaret (*née* Buchanan), ARIBA; one *s* one *d*. *Educ:* Wellington Coll., Berks; University Coll., Oxford (MA); Bedford Coll., London (MA). FSA 1964; FRHistS 1969. Asst to Editor, Victoria County History, 1954; Editor for Glos, 1960; Dep. Editor, 1968. British Acad. Overseas Vis. Fellow, Folger Shakespeare Library, Washington DC, 1976. Hon. Gen. Editor, Wilts Record Soc., 1962-72. *Publications:* Divers Letters of Roger de Martival, Bishop of Salisbury, 2 vols, 1963, 1972; Wiltshire Feet of Fines, Edward III, 1974; articles in Victoria County History and in learned jls. *Address:* 34 Lloyd Baker Street, WC1X 9AB. *T:* 01-837 4971.

EL-SADAT, Mohamed Anwar; President of the Arab Republic of Egypt, since 1970; *b* 25 Dec. 1918; *s* of Mohamed El-Sadat; *m* 1949, Jehan El-Sadat; one *s* three *d*. *Educ:* Military Coll., Cairo (graduated 1938). Signal Officer, 1938; excommunicated from Army for underground work against British Occupation, 1942; efforts to liberate Egypt led him to prison many times; Mem., Free Officers Underground Org., 1951; Editor-in-Chief, Al-Gomhouria newspaper, 1953; Sec., Islamic Conf. and National Union, 1957; Head of Parliament, 1960; Head of Afro-Asian Solidarity Council, 1961; Vice-Pres. of Egypt, 1969. Decorations from: Yugoslavia, 1956; Greece, 1958; German Democratic Republic, 1965; Bulgaria, 1965; Rumania, 1966; Finland, 1967; Iran, 1971; Saudi Arabia, 1974. *Publications:* Unknown Pages, 1955; The Secrets of the Egyptian Revolution, 1957; The Story of Arab Unity, 1957; My Son, This is your Uncle Gamal, 1958; The Complete Story of the Revolution, 1961; For a New Resurrection, 1963. *Recreations:* reading literary works and watching films. *Address:* The Presidential Palace at Abdeen, Cairo, Arab Republic of Egypt.

EL SAWI, Amir; Ambassador of the Democratic Republic of the Sudan to the Court of St James's, since 1976; *b* 1921; *m* 1946, El Sura Mohamed Bella; three *s* six *d*. *Educ:* University Coll., Khartoum; Univ. of Bristol. Min. of Interior, 1944-49; Admin. Officer, Merowi Dist, Northern Province, 1950-51; Asst Dist Comr, Kosti Dist, Blue Nile Prov., 1951-53; Asst Sudan Agent, Cairo, 1953-55; Dist Comr, Gadaraf Dist, Kassala Prov., 1955-56; Asst Permanent Sec., Min. of Foreign Affairs, 1956-58, Min. of Interior, 1958-59; Dep. Governor, Northern Prov., 1959-60; Dep. Perm. Sec., Min. of Interior, 1960-64, Perm. Sec., 1964-70; Perm. Sec., Min. of Civil Service and Admin. Reform, 1971-73; Dep. Minister and Doyen of Sudan Civil Service, 1973-76. *Recreations:* swimming, tennis. *Address:* 3 Cleveland Row, SW1A 1DD. *T:* 01-839 8080.

ELSDEN, Sidney Reuben, BA, PhD (Cambridge); Professor of Biology, University of East Anglia, since 1965; *b* 13 April 1915; *er s* of late Reuben Charles Elsden, Cambridge; *m* 1st, 1942, Frances Scott Wilson (*d* 1943); 2nd, 1948, Erica Barbara Scott, *er d* of late Grahame Scott Gardiner, Wisbech, Cambs; twin *s*. *Educ:* Cambridge and County High Sch. for Boys; Fitzwilliam House, Cambridge. Lecturer, Biochemistry, University of Edinburgh, 1937-42; Mem. Scientific Staff of ARC Unit for Animal Physiology, 1943-48; Sen. Lectr in Microbiology, Univ. of Sheffield, 1948-59; Hon. Dir, ARC Unit for Microbiology, Univ. of Sheffield, 1952-65; Dir, ARC Food Research Inst.,

1965-77. Visiting Prof. of Microbiology, Univ. of Illinois, Urbana, Ill, USA, 1956. Pres., Soc. for General Microbiology, 1969-72, Hon. Mem. 1977. *Publications:* contribs to scientific jls on metabolism of micro-organisms. *Recreations:* gardening, angling. *Address:* 26a The Street, Costessey, Norwich NR8 5DB. *Club:* National Liberal.

ELSTOB, Peter (Frederick Egerton); Secretary-General, International PEN, since 1974 (Hon. Press Officer, 1970-74); Managing Director: Archive Press Ltd, since 1964 (co-founder 1963); Yeast-Pac Co. Ltd, since 1970 (co-founder and Director, 1938-70); writer and entrepreneur; *b* London, 22 Dec. 1915; *e s* of Frederick Charles Elstob, chartered accountant, RFC, and Lillian Page, London; *m* 1st, 1937, Medora Leigh-Smith (marr. diss. 1953); three *s* two *d*; 2nd, 1953, Barbara Zacheisz; one *s* one *d*. *Educ:* private schs, London, Paris, Calcutta; state schs, NY and NJ; Univ. of Michigan. Reporter, salesman, tourist guide, 1931-36; pilot, Spanish Civil War, 1936 (imprisoned and expelled); RTR, 1940-46 (despatches); with A. B. Eiloart: bought Arts Theatre Club, London, 1941; founded Peter Arnold Studios (artists' and writers' colony, Mexico), 1951-52, and Archives Designs Ltd, 1954-62; Director: MEEC Prodns (Theatre), 1946-54; Peter Arnold Properties, 1947-61; City & Suffolk Property Ltd, 1962-70; ABC Expedns, 1957-61; Manager, Small World Trans-Atlantic Balloon Crossing, 1958-59. Chm., Dorking Divl Lab. Party, 1949-50. *Publications:* (autobio.) Spanish Prisoner, 1939; (with A. B. Eiloart) The Flight of the Small World, 1959; novels: Warriors for the Working Day, 1960; The Armed Rehearsal, 1964; military history: Bastogne the Road Block, 1968; The Battle of the Reichswald, 1970; Hitler's Last Offensive, 1971; Condor Legion, 1973; (ed) A Register of the Regiments and Corps of the British Army; (ed series) PEN International Books; PEN Broadsheet. *Recreations:* collecting modern 1st edns and Spanish Civil War material, visiting battlefields, playing the Stock Exchange unsuccessfully, travelling. *Address:* 22 Belsize Park Gardens, NW3 4LH. *T:* 01-722 6263; Coolderry, Massey's Lane, East Boldre, Hants. *T:* Beaulieu 612428. *Clubs:* Savage, PEN, Society of Authors; Authors Guild (New York).

ELSTUB, Sir St John (de Holt), Kt 1970; CBE 1954; BSc, CEng, FIMechE, FInstP; Chairman, Imperial Metal Industries Ltd, 1972-74, Managing Director, 1962-74; Director: Rolls-Royce Ltd, since 1971; British Engine Boiler & Electrical Insurance Co.; Hill Samuel Group Ltd; Tube Investments Ltd; Averys Ltd; Regional Director (West Midlands and Wales), National Westminster Bank Ltd; *b* 16 June 1915; *s* of Ernest Elstub and Mary Gertrude (*née* Whitaker); *m* 1939, Patricia Arnold; two *d*. *Educ:* Rugby Sch.; Manchester Univ. Joined ICI, Billingham, 1936. Served War of 1939-45 as RAF Bomber Pilot; Supt, Rocket Propulsion Dept, Ministry of Supply, 1945. Joined ICI Metals Div., 1947, Prod. Dir, 1950, Man. Dir, 1957, Chm., 1961; Director: Royal Insurance Co., 1970-76; The London & Lancashire Insurance Co., 1970-76; The Liverpool, London & Globe Insurance Co., 1970-76. Past Pres., British Non-Ferrous Metals Federation. Chm., Jt Government/Industry Cttee on Aircraft Industry, 1967-69; Member: Plowden Cttee on Aircraft Industry, 1964-65; Engrg Industry Trng Bd, 1964-72; Midlands Electricity Bd, 1966-75; Review Bd for Govt contracts, 1969-75; Pres., IMechE, 1974-75. A Guardian, Birmingham Assay Office; Governor, Administrative Staff Coll., Henley, 1962-74; Mem. Council, Univ. of Aston in Birmingham, 1966-72 (Vice-Chm. 1968-72); Life Governor, Univ. of Birmingham. FBIM. Hon. DSc Univ. of Aston in Birmingham, 1971. *Recreations:* landscape gardening, travel, motor sport. *Address:* Perry House, Hartlebury, Worcs DY10 4HY. *T:* Hartlebury 327. *Club:* Army and Navy.

ELTON, family name of **Baron Elton.**

ELTON, 2nd Baron *cr* 1934, of Headington; **Rodney Elton,** TD 1970; an Opposition Spokesman, House of Lords, since 1976; Publisher (Yendor Books); Deputy Secretary, Committee on International Affairs, Synod of Church of England, since 1976; *b* 2 March 1930; *s* of 1st Baron Elton and of Dedi (*d* 1977), *d* of Gustav Hartmann, Oslo; *S* father, 1973; *m* 1958, Anne Frances (from whom separated, 1974), *e d* of Brig. R. A. G. Tilney, *qv*; one *s* three *d*. *Educ:* Eton; New Coll., Oxford (MA). Farming, 1957-74. Assistant Master, Loughborough Grammar Sch., 1962-67; Assistant Master, Fairham Comprehensive School for Boys, Nottingham, 1967-69; Lectr, Bishop Lonsdale College of Education, 1969-72. Cons. Whip, House of Lords, Feb. 1974-76. Director: Overseas Exhibition Services Ltd; Building Trades Exhibition Ltd. Late Captain, Queen's Own Warwickshire and Worcs Yeo.; late Major, Leics and Derbys (PAO) Yeo. Lord of the Manor of Adderbury, Oxon. *Heir: s* Hon. Edward Paget Elton, *b* 28 May 1966. *Address:* House of Lords, SW1. *Club:* Cavalry and Guards.

ELTON, Sir Charles (Abraham Grierson), 11th Bt *cr* 1717; *b* 23 May 1953; *s* of Sir Arthur Hallam Rice Elton, 10th Bt, and of Lady Elton; *S* father, 1973. *Address:* Clevedon Court, Somerset BS21 6QU.

ELTON, Charles Sutherland, FRS 1953; Director, Bureau of Animal Population, Department of Zoological Field Studies, 1932-67, and Reader in Animal Ecology, Oxford University, 1936-67; Senior Research Fellow, Corpus Christi College, Oxford, 1936-67, Hon. Fellow since Oct. 1967; *b* 29 March 1900; *s* of late Oliver Elton; *m* 1st, 1928, Rose Montague; no *c*; 2nd, 1937, Edith Joy, *d* of Rev. Canon F. G. Scovell; one *s* one *d*. *Educ:* Liverpool Coll.; New Coll., Oxford. First Class Hons Zoology, Oxford, 1922; served as Ecologist on Oxford Univ. Expedition to Spitsbergen, 1921, Merton Coll. Arctic Expedition, 1923, Oxford Univ. Arctic Expedition, 1924 and Oxford Univ. Lapland Expedition, 1930. Mem. Nature Conservancy, 1949-56. Foreign Hon. Mem., Amer. Acad. of Arts and Sciences, 1968. Linnean Soc. Gold Medal, 1967; Darwin Medal, Royal Soc., 1970; John and Alice Tyler Ecology Award, 1976. *Publications:* Animal Ecology, 1927; Animal Ecology and Evolution, 1930; The Ecology of Animals, 1933; Exploring the Animal World, 1933; Voles, Mice and Lemmings, 1942; The Ecology of Invasions by Animals and Plants, 1958; The Pattern of Animal Communities, 1966. *Recreations:* natural history, reading. *Address:* 61 Park Town, Oxford OX2 6SL. *T:* Oxford 57644.

ELTON, Prof. Geoffrey Rudolph, LittD; PhD; FBA 1967; Professor of English Constitutional History, Cambridge, since 1967; *b* 17 Aug. 1921; changed name to Elton under Army Council Instruction, 1944; *er s* of late Prof. Victor Ehrenberg, PhD; *m* 1952, Sheila Lambert; no *c*. *Educ:* Prague; Rydal Sch. London External BA (1st Cl. Hons) 1943; Derby Student, University Coll. London, 1946-48; PhD 1949. Asst Master, Rydal Sch., 1940-43. Service in E Surrey Regt and Int. Corps (Sgt), 1944-46. Asst in History, Glasgow Univ., 1948-49; Univ. Asst Lectr, Cambridge, 1949-53, Lectr, 1953-63, Reader in Tudor Studies, 1963-67. Visiting Amundson Prof., Univ. of Pittsburgh, Sept.-Dec. 1963; Vis. Hill Prof., Univ. of Minnesota, 1976. Lectures: Ford's, Oxford, 1972; Wiles, Belfast, 1972; Hagey, Waterloo, 1974. Founder and Pres., List & Index Soc., 1965-; Pres., Royal Hist. Soc., 1972-76; FRHistS 1954; Fellow of Clare Coll., Cambridge, 1954-; LittD 1960. For. Mem., Amer. Acad. Arts and Scis, 1975. *Publications:* The Tudor Revolution in Government, 1953; England under the Tudors, 1955; (ed) New Cambridge Modern History, vol. 2, 1958, new edn 1975; Star Chamber Stories, 1958; The Tudor Constitution, 1960; Henry VIII: an essay in revision, 1962; Renaissance and Reformation (Ideas and Institutions in Western Civilization), 1963; Reformation Europe, 1963; The Practice of History, 1967; The Future of the Past, 1968; The Sources of History: England 1200-1640, 1969; Political History: Principles and Practice, 1970; Modern Historians on British History 1485-1945: a critical bibliography 1945-1969, 1970; Policy and Police: the enforcement of the Reformation in the age of Thomas Cromwell, 1972; Reform and Renewal, 1973; Studies in Tudor and Stuart Politics and Government: papers and reviews, 1946-1972, 2 vols, 1974; contribs to English Hist. Review, Econ. Hist. Rev., History, Hist. Jl, Times Lit. Supplement, Listener, etc. *Recreations:* squash rackets, joinery, gardening, and beer. *Address:* Clare College, Cambridge; Faculty of History, West Road, Cambridge. *T:* Cambridge 61661.
See also L . R . B . Elton .

ELTON, George Alfred Hugh; Chief Scientific Adviser (Food), Ministry of Agriculture, Fisheries and Food, since 1971; *b* 25 Feb. 1925; *s* of H. W. Elton and Mrs V. E. Elton (*née* Clowes); *m* 1951, Theodora Rose Edith Kingham; two *d*. *Educ:* Sutton County Sch.; London Univ. (evening student). BSc 1944, PhD 1948, DSc 1956, FRIC 1951; FIBiol 1976. Mem. Faculty of Science, Univ. of London, 1951-58; Reader in applied Phys. Chemistry, Battersea Polytechnic, 1956-58; Dir, British Baking Industries Res. Assoc., 1958-66; Dir, Flour Milling and Baking Res. Assoc., 1967-70; Chief Sci. Adviser (Food), MAFF, 1971; Head of Food Science Div., 1972-73, Dep. Chief Scientist, 1972, Under-Sec. 1974. Chairman: Consultative Cttee of Dirs of Food Res. Orgs, 1971; Working Party on Heavy Metals in Food, 1971-73; Steering Gp on Food Surveillance, 1971-73; Member: Council, British Nutrition Foundn, 1971; Nat. Food Survey Cttee, 1971; Cttee on Medical Aspects of Food Policy, 1971; Fisheries Res. and Develt Bd, 1972; Cttee on Medical Aspects of Chemicals in Food and the Environment, 1974; Council, Chemical Soc., 1972-75. Co-inventor, Chorleywood Bread Process (Queen's Award to Industry 1966); Silver Medallist, Royal Soc. of Arts, 1969. *Publications:* research papers on chemistry, physics and food science in jls of various learned societies. *Recreations:* cricket, golf. *Address:* Green Nook,

Bridle Lane, Loudwater, Rickmansworth, Herts. *Clubs:* Athenæum, Savage, MCC.

ELTON, John; see Elton, P. J.

ELTON, John Bullen; Master of the Supreme Court, Queen's Bench Division, since 1966; *b* 18 Jan. 1916; *s* of Percy Maden Elton, company director; *m* 1939, Sonia; three *d*. *Educ:* Bishop's Stortford Coll.; Brasenose Coll., Oxford. Called to the Bar, Inner Temple, 1938. RNVR, 1943-46. *Recreation:* sailing. *Address:* 3 Ailsa Road, St Margaret's, Twickenham, Middx. *Club:* Royal Victoria Yacht.

ELTON, Air Vice-Marshal John Goodenough, CB 1955; CBE 1945; DFC 1940; AFC 1935; *b* 5 May 1905; *s* of late Rev. George G. Elton, MA Oxon; *m* 1st, 1927, Helen Whitfield (marr. diss.); one *s*; 2nd, 1949, Francesca Cavallero. *Educ:* St John's, Leatherhead. Entered RAF, 1926; service in UK, 1926-31; Singapore, 1932-35 (AFC); Irak, 1939. Served War of 1939-45 (despatches twice, DFC, CBE); CO 47 Sqdn, Sudan, 1940; HQ, ME, Cairo, 1941; comd in succession Nos 242, 238 and 248 Wings, N Africa, 1942; CO RAF Turnberry, Scotland, 1943; CO RAF Silloth, Cumberland, 1944; AOA, HQ Mediterranean Allied Coastal Air Force, 1945-46; idc 1947; Dep. Dir, Air Min., 1948; RAF Mem., UK Delegn, Western Union Military Cttee, 1949-50; Comdt, Sch. of Tech. Training, Halton, 1951; Air Attaché, Paris, 1952; Air Officer i/c Administration, HQ Bomber Comd, 1953-56; Chief of Staff to the Head of British Jt Services Mission, Washington, DC, 1956-59; retired, 1959. *Address:* 64 Lexham Gardens, W8. *Club:* Royal Air Force.

ELTON, Prof. Lewis Richard Benjamin, MA, DSc; FInstP, FIMA, FRSA; Head of Institute for Educational Technology, since 1967, and Professor of Science Education, since 1971, University of Surrey; *b* 25 March 1923; *yr s* of late Prof. Victor Leopold Ehrenberg, PhD, and Eva Dorothea (*née* Sommer); *m* 1950, Mary, *d* of Harold William Foster and Kathleen (*née* Meakin); three *s* one *d*. *Educ:* Stepanska Gymnasium, Prague; Rydal Sch., Colwyn Bay; Christ's Coll., Cambridge (Exhibr); Univ. Correspondence Coll., Cambridge, and Regent Street Polytechnic; University Coll. London (Univ. Research Studentship). BA 1945, Certif.Ed 1945, MA 1948, Cantab; BSc (External) 1st Cl. Hons Maths 1947, PhD 1950, London. Asst Master, St Bees Sch., 1944-46; Asst Lectr, then Lectr, King's Coll., London, 1950-57; Head of Physics Dept: Battersea Coll. of Technology, 1958-66; Univ. of Surrey, 1966-69; Prof. of Physics, Surrey, 1964-71; Research Associate: MIT, 1955; Stanford Univ., 1956; Niels Bohr Inst., Copenhagen, 1962; Vis. Professor: Univ. of Washington, Seattle, 1965; UCL, 1970-; Univ. of Sydney, 1971; Univ. of Sao Paulo, 1975; Member: Governing Body, Battersea Coll. of Technology, 1962-66; Council, Univ. of Surrey, 1966-67; Council for Educational Technology of UK, 1975-; Army Educn Adv. Bd, 1976-; Convener, Standing Conf. of Physics Profs, 1971-74; Chairman: Governing Council, Soc. for Research into Higher Educn, 1976-. *Publications:* Introductory Nuclear Theory, 1959, 2nd edn 1965, Spanish edn 1964; Nuclear Sizes, 1961, Russian edn 1962; Concepts in Classical Mechanics, 1971; contribs to sci. jls on nuclear physics, science educn and educnl technology. *Recreation:* words. *Address:* 107 Farnham Road, Guildford, Surrey GU2 5PF. *T:* Guildford 60285.
See also G . R . Elton .

ELTON, (Peter) John, MC 1944; Director: Hill Samuel Group Ltd, since 1976; Hill Samuel & Co. Ltd, since 1976; Non-executive Chairman, Alcan Aluminium (UK) Ltd, since 1976; *b* 14 March 1924; 2nd *s* of Sydney George Elton; *m* 1948, Patricia Ann Stephens; two *d*. *Educ:* Eastbourne Coll.; Clare Coll., Cambridge. Indian Army: 14th Punjab Regt, 1942-45 (twice wounded). Hons Degree, Econs and Law, Cambridge. Man. Dir, Alcan Aluminium (UK) Ltd, 1967-74, Exec. Chm. 1974-76; Chairman: Alcan Booth Industries Ltd, 1968-76; Alcan (UK) Ltd, 1967-76; Dir, Alcan Aluminium Ltd, 1972-77. *Recreations:* sailing, shooting. *Address:* Salternshill Farm, Buckler's Hard, Beaulieu, Hants. *T:* Buckler's Hard 206. *Clubs:* Bath, Bucks; Royal Southampton Yacht.

ELVEDEN, Viscount; Arthur Edward Rory Guinness; *b* 10 Aug. 1969; *s* and *heir* of Earl of Iveagh, *qv*.

ELVIN, Herbert Lionel; Director of the University of London Institute of Education, 1958-73 (Professor of Education in Tropical Areas, 1956-58); Director, Department of Education, UNESCO, Paris, 1950-56; *b* 7 Aug. 1905; *e s* of late Herbert Henry Elvin; *m* 1934, Mona Bedortha, *d* of Dr C. S. S. Dutton, San Francisco; one *s*. *Educ:* elementary schs; Southend High Sch.; Trinity Hall, Cambridge (1st Class Hons, History and English). Commonwealth Fellow, Yale Univ., USA, Fellow of

Trinity Hall, Cambridge, 1930-44; Temporary Civil Servant (Air Min., 1940-42, MOI, 1943-45); Principal, Ruskin Coll., Oxford, 1944-50. Parliamentary candidate (Lab), Cambridge Univ., 1935; Formerly: Pres., English New Education Fellowship; Pres., Council for Education in World Citizenship; Chm., Commonwealth Educn Liaison Cttee. Member: Cttee on Higher Education; Govt of India Educn Commn; University Grants Cttee, 1946-50; Central Advisory Council for Education (England) and Secondary School Examinations Council. *Publications:* Men of America (Pelican Books), 1941; An Introduction to the Study of Literature (Poetry), 1949; Education and Contemporary Society, 1965. *Recreations:* most games indifferently; formerly athletics (half-mile, Cambridge *v* Oxford, 1927). *Address:* 4 Bulstrode Gardens, Cambridge. *T:* Cambridge 58309.

ELVIN, Violetta, (Violetta Prokhorova), (Signora Fernando Savarese); ballerina; a prima ballerina of Sadler's Wells Ballet, Royal Opera House, London (now The Royal Ballet), 1951-56; *b* Moscow, 3 Nov. 1925; *d* of Vassilie Prokhorov, engineer, and Irena Grimouzinskaya, former actress; *m* 1st, 1944, Harold Elvin (divorced 1952), of British Embassy, Moscow; 2nd, 1953, Siegbert J. Weinberger, New York; 3rd, 1959, Fernando Savarese, lawyer; one *s. Educ:* Bolshoi Theatre Sch., Moscow. Trained for ballet since age of 8 by: E. P. Gerdt, A. Vaganova, M. A. Kojuchova. Grad, 1942, as soloist; made mem. Bolshoi Theatre Ballet; evacuated to Tashkent, 1943; ballerina Tashkent State Theatre; rejoined Bolshoi Theatre at Kuibishev again as soloist, 1944; left for London, 1945. Joined Sadler's Wells Ballet at Covent Garden as guest-soloist, 1946; later became regular mem. Has danced all principal rôles, notably, Le Lac des Cygnes, Sleeping Beauty, Giselle, Cinderella, Sylvia, Ballet Imperial, etc. Danced four-act Le Lac des Cygnes, first time, 1943; guest-artist Stanislavsky Theatre, Moscow, 1944, Sadler's Wells Theatre, 1947; guest-prima ballerina, La Scala, Milan, Nov. 1952-Feb. 1953 (Macbeth, La Gioconda, Swan Lake, Petrouchka); guest artist, Cannes, July 1954; Copenhagen, Dec. 1954; Teatro Municipal, Rio de Janeiro, May 1955 (Giselle, Swan Lake, Les Sylphides, Nutcracker, Don Quixote and The Dying Swan); Festival Ballet, Festival Hall, 1955; guest-prima ballerina in Giselle, Royal Opera House, Stockholm (Anna Pavlova Memorial), 1956; concluded stage career when appeared in Sleeping Beauty, Royal Opera House, Covent Garden, June 1956. *Appeared in films:* The Queen of Spades, Twice Upon a Time, Melba. Television appearances in Russia and England. Has toured with Sadler's Wells Ballet, France, Italy, Portugal, United States and Canada. *Recreations:* chess, tennis, swimming. *Address:* Marina di Equa, 80066 Seiano, Bay of Naples, Italy. *T:* 081-879 8520.

ELWORTHY, family name of **Baron Elworthy.**

ELWORTHY, Baron *cr* 1972 (Life Peer); **Marshal of the Royal Air Force Samuel Charles Elworthy,** KG 1977; GCB 1962 (KCB 1961; CB 1960); CBE 1946; DSO 1941; MVO 1953; DFC 1941; AFC 1941; Constable and Governor of Windsor Castle, since 1971; Lord-Lieutenant of Greater London, since 1973; *b* 23 March 1911; *e s* of late P. A. Elworthy, Gordon's Valley, Timaru, New Zealand; *m* 1936, Audrey, *o d* of late A. J. Hutchinson, OBE; three *s* one *d. Educ:* Marlborough; Trinity Coll., Cambridge. Commissioned in RAFO 1933, transferred to Auxiliary Air Force, 1934; called to Bar, Lincoln's Inn, 1935, Hon. Bencher 1970; permanent commission in RAF, 1936; War Service in Bomber Comd; Acting Air Cdre, 1944; Air Vice-Marshal, 1957; Air Marshal, 1960; Air Chief Marshal, 1962; Marshal of the RAF, 1967. Comdt RAF Staff Coll., Bracknell, 1957-59; Deputy Chief of Air Staff, 1959-60; C-in-C, Middle East, 1960-63; Chief of Air Staff, 1963-67; Chief of the Defence Staff, 1967-71. Director, 1971-: British Petroleum; Plessey; Nat. Bank of NZ. Chairman: Royal Commission for the Exhibition of 1851; King Edward VII Hospital for Officers, 1971-; Royal Over-Seas League, 1971-76. Mem. Council, Bradfield Coll., 1968-; Governor: Wellington Coll., 1970-; Marlborough Coll., 1974-. Hon. Freeman, Skinners' Co., 1968-, Master 1973-74. KStJ 1976. *Address:* Norman Tower, Windsor Castle, Berks. *Clubs:* Bath, Royal Air Force; Leander.

ELWYN-JONES, family name of **Baron Elwyn-Jones.**

ELWYN-JONES, Baron *cr* 1974 (Life Peer), of Llanelli and Newham; **Frederick Elwyn-Jones,** PC 1964; CH 1976; Kt 1964; Lord High Chancellor of Great Britain since 1974; *b* 24 Oct. 1909; *s* of Frederick and Elizabeth Jones, Llanelli, Carmarthenshire; *m* 1937, Pearl Binder; one *s* two *d. Educ:* Llanelli Grammar Sch.; University of Wales, Aberystwyth; Gonville and Caius Coll., Cambridge (Scholar, MA, Pres. Cambridge Union); Hon. Fellow, 1976. Called to Bar, Gray's Inn, 1935, Bencher, 1960; QC 1953; QC (N Ireland) 1958. Major

RA (TA); Dep. Judge Advocate, 1943-45. MP (Lab) Plaistow Div. of West Ham, 1945-50, West Ham South, 1950-74, Newham South 1974; PPS to Attorney-Gen., 1946-51; Attorney General, 1964-70. Recorder: of Merthyr Tydfil, 1949-53; of Swansea, 1953-60; of Cardiff, 1960-64; of Kingston-upon-Thames, 1968-74. Member of British War Crimes Executive, Nuremberg, 1945. UK Observer, Malta Referendum, 1964. Mem., Inter-Departmental Cttee on the Court of Criminal Appeal, 1964. Mem. of Bar Council, 1956-59. Pres., University Coll., Cardiff, 1971-. FKC, 1970. Hon. LLD: University of Wales, 1968; Ottawa Univ., 1975; Columbia Univ., NY, 1976. Hon. Freeman of Llanelli. *Publications:* Hitler's Drive to the East, 1937; The Battle for Peace, 1938; The Attack from Within, 1939. *Recreation:* travelling. *Address:* House of Lords, SW1.

ELY, 8th Marquess of, *cr* 1801; **Charles John Tottenham; Bt** 1780; Baron Loftus, 1785; Viscount Loftus, 1789; Earl of Ely, 1794; Baron Loftus (UK), 1801; Headmaster, Boulden House, Trinity College School, Port Hope, Ontario, since 1941; *b* 30 May 1913; *s* of G. L. Tottenham, BA (Oxon), and Cécile Elizabeth, *d* of J. S. Burra, Bockhanger, Kennington, Kent; *g s* of C. R. W. Tottenham, MA (Oxon), Woodstock, Newtown Mount Kennedy, Co. Wicklow, and Plâs Berwyn, Llangollen, N Wales; *S* cousin, 1969; *m* 1938, Katherine Elizabeth (*d* 1975), *d* of Col W. H. Craig, Kingston, Ont; three *s* one *d. Educ:* Collège de Genève, Internat. Sch., Geneva; Queen's Univ., Kingston, Ont (BA). Career as Schoolmaster. *Recreation:* fishing. Heir: *e s* Viscount Loftus, *qv. Address:* Trinity College School, Port Hope, Ontario, Canada. *T:* 885 5209. *Club:* University (Toronto).

ELY, Bishop of, since 1977; **Rt. Rev. Peter Knight Walker,** MA; *b* 6 Dec. 1919; *s* of late George Walker and of Eva Muriel (*née* Knight); *m* 1973, Mary Jean, JP 1976, *yr d* of Lt-Col J. A. Ferguson, OBE. *Educ:* Leeds Grammar Sch. (Schol.); The Queen's Coll., Oxford (Hastings schol.; Cl. 2 Classical Hon. Mods. 1940, Cl. 1 Lit. Hum. 1947; MA Oxon 1947); Westcott House, Cambridge. MA Cantab by incorporation, 1958. Served in RN (Lieut, RNVR), 1940-45. Asst Master: King's Sch., Peterborough, 1947-50; Merchant Taylors' Sch., 1950-56. Ordained, 1954; Curate of Hemel Hempstead, 1956-58; Fellow, Dean of Chapel and Lectr in Theology, Corpus Christi Coll., Cambridge, 1958-62 (Asst Tutor, 1959-62); Principal of Westcott House, Cambridge, 1962-72; Hon. Canon of Ely Cathedral, 1966-72; Bishop Suffragan of Dorchester, and Canon of Christ Church, Oxford, 1972-77. Select Preacher: Univ. of Cambridge, 1962, 1967 (Hulsean); Univ. of Oxford, 1975; Examining Chaplain to Bishop of Portsmouth, 1962-72. A Governor, St Edward's Sch., Oxford. *Publications:* Contrib. to: Classical Quarterly; Theology. *Address:* The Bishop's House, Ely, Cambs CB7 4DW. *T:* Ely 2749.

ELY, Dean of; *see* Carey, Very Rev. M. S.

ELY, Archdeacon of; *see* Long, Ven. J. S.

ELYAN, Prof. Sir (Isadore) Victor, Kt 1970; Professor of Law, and Dean of the Faculty of Law, Durban-Westville University, since 1973; Chief Justice of Swaziland, 1965-70, retired; *b* 5 Sept. 1909; *s* of Jacob Elyan, PC, JP and Olga Elyan; *m* 1939, Ivy Ethel Mabel Stuart-Weir (*d* 1965); no *c*; *m* 1966, Rosaleen Jeanette O'Shea. *Educ:* St Stephen's Green Sch., Dublin; Trinity Coll., Dublin Univ. BA 1929, LLB 1931, MA 1932, TCD. Admitted a Solicitor of Supreme Court of Judicature, Ireland, 1930; Barrister-at-Law, King's Inns 1949, Middle Temple, 1952. Resident Magistrate, HM Colonial Legal Service, Gold Coast, 1946-54; Senior Magistrate, 1954-55; Judge of Appeal of the Court of Appeal for Basutoland, the Bechuanaland Protectorate and Swaziland, 1955-66; Puisne Judge, High Courts of Basutoland and the Bechuanaland Protectorate, 1955-65; on occasions acted as Judge between 1953 and 1955, Gold Coast; as Justice of Appeal, West African Court of Appeal; and as Chief Justice of Basutoland, the Bechuanaland Protectorate and Swaziland, also Pres. Court of Appeal, during 1956, 1961 and 1964; Judge of Appeal: Court of Appeal for Botswana, 1966-70; Court of Appeal for Swaziland, 1967-70; Court of Appeal, Lesotho, 1968-70. Served War, 1942-46; attached to Indian Army, 1944-46; GSO2 Military Secretary's Branch (DAMS), 1945-46 in rank of Major. Mem., Internat. Adv. Bd, The African Law Reports, 1969. *Publications:* Editor, High Commission Territories Law Reports, 1956, 1957, 1958, 1959, 1960. *Recreation:* sailing. *Address:* PO Box 3052, Durban, Natal, South Africa.

EMANUEL, Aaron, CMG 1957; Consultant to OECD; *b* 11 Feb. 1912; *s* of Jack Emanuel and Jane (*née* Schaverien); *m* 1936, Ursula Pagel; two *s* one *d. Educ:* Henry Thornton Sch., Clapham; London Sch. of Economics (BSc Econ.). Economist at

International Institute of Agriculture, Rome, 1935-38; Board of Trade, 1938; Ministry of Food, 1940; Colonial Office, 1943; Ministry of Health, 1961; Dept. of Economic Affairs, 1965; Min. of Housing and Local Govt, 1969; Under-Sec., Dept of the Environment, 1970-72; Chm., West Midlands Econ. Planning Bd, 1968-72; Vis. Sen. Lectr, Univ. of Aston in Birmingham, 1972-75. *Publication:* Issues of Regional Policies, 1973. *Address:* 119 Salisbury Road, Moseley, Birmingham B13 8LA. *T:* 021-449 5553.

EMANUEL, Richard Wolff, MA, DM Oxon, FRCP; Physician to Department of Cardiology, Middlesex Hospital, since 1963; Lecturer in Cardiology, Middlesex Hospital Medical School since 1963; Physician to National Heart Hospital since 1963; Lecturer to Institute of Cardiology since 1963; *b* 13 Jan. 1923; *s* of Prof. and Mrs J. G. Emanuel, Birmingham; *m* 1950, Lavinia Hoffmann; three *s. Educ:* Bradfield Coll.; Oriel Coll., Oxford; Middlesex Hospital. House Appts at Middx Hospital, 1948 and 1950. Captain RAMC, 1948-50; Med. Registrar, Middx Hosp., 1951-52; Sen. Med. Registrar, Middx Hosp., 1953-55; Sen. Med. Registrar, Nat. Heart Hosp., 1956-58; Fellow in Med., Vanderbilt Univ., 1956-57; Sen. Med. Registrar, Dept of Cardiology, Brompton Hosp., 1958-61; Asst Dir, Inst. of Cardiology and Hon. Asst Physician to Nat. Heart Hosp., 1961-63. Advr in Cardiovascular Disease to Sudan Govt, 1969-. Vis. Lecturer: Univ. of Med. Sciences and Chulalongkorn Univ., Thailand; Univ. of the Philippines; Univ. of Singapore; Univ. of Malaya; Khartoum Univ.; St Cyre's Lectr, London, 1968; Ricardo Molina Lectr, Philippines, 1969. Has addressed numerous Heart Socs in SE Asia. Asst Sec., British Cardiac Soc., 1966-68, Sec., 1968-70. FACC; Hon. Fellow, Philippine Coll. of Cardiology; Hon. Mem., Heart Assoc. of Thailand. Member: Brit. Acad. of Forensic Sciences (Med.); Cardiological Cttee, RCP; Assoc. of Physicians of GB and Ireland. Asst Editor, British Heart Journal. *Publications:* various articles on diseases of the heart in British and American jls. *Recreations:* XVIIIth century glass, fishing, sailing. *Address:* 6 Upper Wimpole Street, W1M 7TD. *T:* 01-935 3243; 6 Lansdowne Walk, W11. *T:* 01-727 6688; Canute Cottage, Old Bosham, near Chichester, West Sussex. *T:* Bosham 3318. *Club:* Bath.

EMBLING, John Francis, CB 1967; Deputy Under-Secretary of State, Department of Education and Science, 1966-71; *b* 16 July 1909; *m* 1940, Margaret Gillespie Anderson; one *s. Educ:* University of Bristol. Teaching: Dean Close, 1930; Frensham Heights, 1931; Lecturer: Leipzig Univ., 1936; SW Essex Technical Coll., 1938 (Head of Dept, 1942); Administrative Asst, Essex LEA, 1944; Ministry of Education: Principal, 1946; Asst Secretary, 1949; Under-Secretary of State for Finance and Accountant-General, Dept of Education and Science, 1960-66. Research Fellow in Higher Educn, LSE, 1972-73, Univ. of Lancaster, 1974-76. Mem. Council, Klagenfurt Univ., 1972-. Grand Cross, Republic of Austria, 1976. *Address:* The Old Rectory, Wixoe, Suffolk. *T:* Ridgewell 241. *Clubs:* Athenæum, English-Speaking Union.

EMBRY, Air Chief Marshal Sir Basil Edward, GCB 1956 (KCB 1953; CB 1945); KBE 1945; DSO 1938; DFC 1945; AFC 1926; retired as Commander, Allied Air Forces, Central Europe, North Atlantic Treaty Organisation, 1956; *b* 28 Feb. 1902; *s* of late James Embry, MA Cantab; *m* 1928, Hope, *d* of late Captain C. S. Elliot, RN; three *s* one *d. Educ:* Bromsgrove Sch. First Commission, 1921; served Iraq, 1922-27 (AFC) (ops in Kurdistan and Southern Desert); served Central Flying Sch. (A1 flying instructor), 1929-32; RAF Staff Coll.; psc 1933; India, 1934-39; Mohmand Operations, 1935 (despatches); Waziristan, 1937-38 (DSO); War of 1939-45 (despatches thrice, three Bars to DSO, CB, DFC, KBE); served in Bomber and Fighter Commands, Western Desert and 2nd TAF; Comd of No 2 Group Ops over Norway, NW Europe, Great Britain, 1939-41; Western Desert, 1941-42; NW Europe, 1943-45. ADC to the King, 1941-43; Asst Chief of Air Staff (Training), Air Ministry, 1945-48; Air Officer Commanding-in-Chief, Fighter Command, 1949-53. Chm., Rural Traders Co-operative of WA; Dep. Chm., Arabian/Australian Marketing Co. Chm., Cancer Res. Foundn of WA. Pres., RAF Escaping Soc. Knight Commander, 1st Class, Order of Dannebrog; Grand Officer Order of Orange Nassau, with swords; Comdr of Legion of Honour; Croix de Guerre. Hon. Freedom of Borough and Cinque Port of Dover; Freeman City of London; Hon. Liveryman, Worshipful Company of Glass-Sellers. Former Gen. Pres., Farmers Union of W Australia. *Publication:* Mission Completed, 1957. *Recreations:* farming, shooting, fishing. *Address:* Ardua, Cape Riche, via Albany, WA 6330, Australia. *T:* Mettler 473026.

EMDEN, Alfred Brotherston, MA; Hon. DLitt; FBA 1959; FSA; Principal of St Edmund Hall, Oxford, 1929-51; Hon. Fellow of Lincoln College and St Edmund Hall; *b* 22 Oct. 1888; *e s* of His

Honour Judge Alfred Emden. *Educ:* King's Sch., Canterbury; Lincoln Coll., Oxford (Scholar); Inner Temple. Head of Edghill House, Sydenham, 1913-15; AB (RNVR), 1915-19, serving in HMS Parker; Tutor and Bursar, St Edmund Hall, 1919; Vice-Principal, 1920; Member of the Hebdomadal Council, 1935-47; Lieut-Commander RNVR (Sp.), 1942-44. Corr. Fellow, Mediaeval Academy of America. Hon. LittD Cambridge. *Publications:* An Oxford Hall in Medieval Times, 1927; Joint Editor (with Prof. Sir F. M. Powicke) of Rashdall's Medieval Universities, 1936; Biographical Register of the University of Oxford to AD 1500, in 3 vols, 1957-59; Biographical Register of the University of Cambridge to 1500, 1963; A Survey of Dominicans in England, 1967; Biographical Register of the University of Oxford 1501-1540, 1974. *Address:* Dunstan Cottage, Old Headington, Oxford.

EMELEUS, Prof. Harry Julius, CBE 1958; FRS 1946; MA, DSc; Professor of Inorganic Chemistry, University of Cambridge, 1945-70; now Professor Emeritus; Fellow of Sidney Sussex College, Cambridge; Fellow of Imperial College, London; *b* 22 June 1903; *s* of Karl Henry Emeleus and Ellen Biggs; *m* 1931, Mary Catherine Horton; two *s* two *d. Educ:* Hastings Grammar Sch.; Imperial Coll., London. 1851 Exhibition Senior Student, Imperial Coll. and Technische Hochschule, Karlsruhe, 1926-29; Commonwealth Fund Fellow, Princeton Univ., 1929-31; Member of Staff of Imperial Coll., 1931-45. President: Chemical Society, 1958; Royal Institute of Chemistry, 1963-65. Trustee, British Museum, 1963-72. Hon. Fellow, Manchester Institute of Science and Technology. Hon. Member: Austrian, Finnish, Indian and French Chemical Societies; Finnish Scientific Academy; Royal Academy of Belgium; Akad. Naturf. Halle; Akad. Wiss. Göttingen; Spanish Royal Society for Physics and Chemistry. Hon. Doctor: Ghent; Kiel; Lille; Paris; Tech. Hoch. Aachen; Marquette; Kent. Lavoisier Medal, French Chem. Society; Stock Medal, Gesellschaft Deutsche Chemiker; Davy Medal, Royal Society, 1962. *Publications:* scientific papers in chemical journals. *Recreation:* fishing. *Address:* 149 Shelford Road, Trumpington, Cambridge CB2 2ND. *T:* Trumpington 2374.

EMELEUS, Karl George, CBE 1965; MA, PhD; MRIA; Professor of Physics, Queen's University, Belfast, 1933-66, now Emeritus; *b* 4 Aug. 1901; *s* of Karl Henry Emeleus and Ellen Biggs; *m* 1928, Florence Mary Chambers; three *s* one *d. Educ:* Hastings Grammar Sch.; St John's Coll., Cambridge. Hon. ScD Dublin; Hon. DSc NUI. *Address:* c/o Queen's University of Belfast, Belfast BT7 1NN.

EMERTON, Audrey C., OStJ; SRN, SCM, RNT; Regional Nursing Officer, South East Thames Regional Health Authority, since 1973. Formerly: Chief Nursing Officer, Tunbridge Wells and Leybourne HMC; Principal Nursing Officer, Education, Bromley HMC; Senior Tutor, Experimental 2 year and 1 year Course, St George's Hosp., SW1. Kent County Nursing Officer, St John Ambulance Brigade. *Address:* SE Thames Regional Health Authority, Randolph House, 46-48 Wellesley Road, Croydon CR9 3QA. *T:* 01-686 8877.

EMERTON, Rev. Prof. John Adney; Regius Professor of Hebrew, Cambridge, since 1968; Fellow of St John's College, since 1970; *b* 5 June 1928; *s* of Adney Spencer Emerton and Helena Mary Emerton; *m* 1954, Norma Elizabeth Bennington; one *s* two *d. Educ:* Minchenden Grammar Sch., Southgate; Corpus Christi Coll., Oxford; Wycliffe Hall, Oxford. BA (1st class hons Theology), 1950; 1st class hons Oriental Studies, 1952; MA 1954. Canon Hall Jun. Greek Testament Prize, 1950; Hall-Houghton Jun. Septuagint Prize, 1951, Senior Prize, 1954; Houghton Syriac Prize, 1953; Liddon Student, 1950; Kennicott Hebrew Fellow, 1952. Corpus Christi Coll., Cambridge, MA (by incorporation), 1955; BD 1960; DD 1973. Deacon, 1952; Priest, 1953. Curate of Birmingham Cathedral, 1952-53; Asst Lecturer in Theology, Birmingham Univ., 1952-53; Lecturer in Hebrew and Aramaic, Durham Univ., 1953-55; Lecturer in Divinity, Cambridge Univ., 1955-62; Reader in Semitic Philology and Fellow of St Peter's Coll., Oxford, 1962-68. Visiting Prof. of Old Testament and Near Eastern Studies, Trinity Coll., Toronto Univ., 1960. Select Preacher before Univ. of Cambridge, 1962, 1971. Sec., Internat. Org. for the study of the Old Testament, 1971-. Hon. DD Edinburgh, 1977. *Publications:* The Peshitta of the Wisdom of Solomon, 1959; The Old Testament in Syriac: Song of Songs, 1966; articles in Journal of Semitic Studies, Journal of Theological Studies, Theology, Vetus Testamentum, Zeitschrift für die Alttestamentliche Wissenschaft. *Address:* 34 Gough Way, Cambridge CB3 9LN.

EMERY, Rt. Rev. Anthony Joseph; *see* Portsmouth, Bishop of, (RC).

EMERY, Eleanor Jean, CMG 1975; HM Diplomatic Service, retired; British High Commissioner to Botswana, 1973-77; *b* 23 Dec. 1918; *d* of Robert Paton Emery and Nellie Nicol Wilson. *Educ:* Western Canada High Sch., Calgary, Alberta; Glasgow Univ. MA Hons in History, 1941. Dominions Office, 1941-45; Asst Private Sec. to Sec. of State, 1942-45; British High Commn, Ottawa, 1945-48; CRO, 1948-52; Principal Private Sec. to Sec. of State, 1950-52; First Sec., British High Commn, New Delhi, 1952-55; CRO, 1955-58; First Sec., British High Commn, Pretoria/Cape Town, 1958-62; Head of South Asia Dept, CRO, 1962-64; Counsellor, British High Commn, Ottawa, 1964-68; Head of Pacific Dependent Territories Dept, FCO, 1969-73. *Address:* 68 College Road, SE21 7LY.
See also J. M. Emery.

EMERY, George Edward; Director General of Defence Accounts, Ministry of Defence, since 1973; *b* 2 March 1920; *s* of late Frederick and Florence Emery; *m* 1946, Margaret (*née* Rice); two *d*. *Educ:* Bemrose Sch., Derby. Admiralty, 1938; Min. of Fuel and Power, 1946; Min. of Supply, 1951; Min. of Aviation, 1959; Min. of Technology, 1967; Principal Exec. Officer, 1967; Asst Sec., Min. of Aviation Supply, 1970; Ministry of Defence: Asst Sec., 1971; Exec. Dir, 1973; Under-Sec., 1973. *Recreations:* amateur dramatics, gardening. *Address:* 3 The Orchard, Freshford, Bath BA3 6EW. *T:* Limpley Stoke 3561.

EMERY, Sir (James) Frederick, Kt 1957; JP; Company Director; *b* 17 Dec. 1886; *s* of William Joseph and Ruth Emery; *m* 1912, Florence Beatrice Gradwell; one *s* one *d*. *Educ:* Manchester Univ. MP (U) West Salford, 1935-45; Member of Salford City Council, 1921-35 (Councillor 1921-33, Alderman, 1933-35); Pres. North Fylde Conservative Association; Mayor of Salford, 1932-33. JP Salford 1927. *Address:* Illawalla, Thornton-le-Fylde, Lancs. *T:* Thornton 2976. *Club:* Constitutional.

EMERY, Joyce Margaret; Secretary of the Post Office, since 1975; *b* 11 Aug. 1932; *d* of Robert Paton Emery and Nellie Nicol (*née* Wilson). *Educ:* Earl Grey Sch., Calgary, Canada; Hillhead High Sch., Glasgow; Glasgow Univ. (MA 1st Cl. Hons French and German, 1956). Post Office: Asst Principal, 1956; Private Sec. to Dir Gen., 1960; Principal, 1961; Asst Sec., 1967; Dir, Chairman's Office, 1970. *Recreation:* getting organised. *Address:* 18 Fairlawns, 21 Putney Hill, SW15 6BD. *T:* 01-789 1137.
See also E. J. Emery

EMERY, Peter; MA; FInstPS; MP (C) Honiton, since 1967 (Reading, 1959-66); *b* 27 Feb. 1926; *s* of late F. G. Emery, Highgate; *m* 1st, 1954 (marr. diss.); one *s* one *d*; 2nd, 1972, Elizabeth, *y d* of late G. J. R. Monnington; one *s* one *d*. *Educ:* Scotch Plains, New Jersey, USA; Oriel Coll., Oxford. Joint Founder and First Secretary of the Bow Group. Parliamentary Private Secretary: to Rt Hon. David Ormsby-Gore, Minister of State for Foreign Affairs, 1960-61; to Rt Hon. Joseph Godber, when Minister of State for Foreign Affairs, 1961-63, when Secretary of State for War, 1963, and when Minister of Labour, 1963-64; Jt Hon. Secretary, 1922 Cttee, 1964-65; Opposition Front Bench Spokesman for Treasury, Economics and Trade, 1964-66; Parliamentary Under-Secretary of State: DTI, 1972-74; Dept of Energy, 1974. Jt Vice-Chm., Conservative Finance Cttee, 1970-72; Chm., Cons. Housing and Construction Cttee, 1974-75. Member, Delegation to CPA Conference, Westminster, 1961; Member CPA Delegation to Canada, 1962; Delegate, Council of Europe and WEU, 1962-64, 1970-72. Chm., Shenley Trust Services Ltd; Director: Property Growth Insurance, 1966-72; Phillips Petroleum-UK Ltd, 1963-72; Institute of Purchasing and Supply, 1961-72; Secretary-General, European Federation of Purchasing, 1962-72; Chairman, Consultative Council of Professional Management Organisations, 1968-72. *Recreations:* sliding down mountains, tennis, cricket and golf. *Address:* Tytherleigh Manor, near Axminster, Devon. *T:* South Chard 309; 15 Tufton Court, Tufton Street, SW1. *T:* 01-222 6666. *Club:* Carlton.

EMERY-WALLIS, Frederick Alfred John; Leader, Hampshire County Council, since 1975 (County Councillor, since 1973; Vice-Chairman, 1975-76); Chairman, Southern Tourist Board, since 1976; *b* 11 May 1927; *o s* of Frederick Henry Wallis and Lillian Grace Emery Coles; *m* 1960, Solange, *o d* of William Victor Randall, London, and Albertine Beaupere, La Guerche-sur-l'Aubois; two *d*. *Educ:* Blake's Academy, Portsmouth. Royal Signals SCU4 (Middle East Radio Security), 1945-48. Portsmouth City Council, 1961-74; Lord Mayor, 1968-69; Alderman, 1969-74. Chairman: Portsmouth Develt and Estates Cttee, 1965-74; Portsmouth Papers Editorial Bd, 1966-; S Hampshire Plan Adv. Cttee, 1969-74; South Portsmouth Conservative Assoc., 1971-. Mem. Economic Planning Council for the South East, 1969-74; Vice-Chm., Portsmouth

Polytechnic, 1967-75; Pres., Hampshire Field Club, 1971-74. Hon. Fellow, Portsmouth Polytechnic, 1972. *Publications:* various publications concerning history and develt of Portsmouth and Hampshire. *Recreations:* reading, music. *Address:* Froddington, Craneswater Park, Portsmouth. *T:* Portsmouth 31409.

EMETT, Rowland; artist and inventor; *b* 1906; *m* 1941, Mary. His humorous mechanical machines, displayed all over the world, include: Far Tottering Railway, Festival of Britain, 1951, and Ontario Science Centre; Forget-Me-Not Computer, Philadelphia, and Ontario Science Centre; Exploratory Moon-Probe Lunacycle (MAUD), Smithsonian National Air and Space Museum; Emett Vintage Car of the Future, Museum of Science and Industry, Chicago; Featherstone Kite Openwork Basket-Weave Mark Two Gentleman's Flying Machine, a Cleveland shopping precinct. Designs for Chitty Chitty Bang Bang (film), 1968. Has designed wall-coverings. Contrib. drawings to Punch and Life. *Address:* Wild Goose Cottage, 113 East End Lane, Ditchling, Hassocks, East Sussex. *T:* Hassocks 2459.

EMLYN, Viscount; Colin Robert Vaughan Campbell; *b* 30 June 1962; *s* and *heir* of Earl Cawdor, *qv*.

EMMERSON, Mrs. C. L.; see Peto, G. E.

EMMERSON, Sir Harold Corti, GCB 1956 (KCB 1947; CB 1942); KCVO 1953; *b* 1896; *m* 1931, Lucy Kathleen Humphreys; two *s* three *d*. *Educ:* Warrington Secondary Sch. Served War of 1914-18 in Royal Marine Artillery. Ministry of Labour, 1920; Secretary Government Mission on Industrial Conditions in Canada and United States, 1926-27; Secretary Royal Commn on Unemployment Insurance, 1930-32; Principal Private Secretary to Ministers of Labour, 1933-35; Secretary Department of Commissioner for Special Areas, 1938-39; Principal Officer, Civil Defence, Northern Region, 1939-40; Under-Secretary Ministry of Home Security, 1940-42; Chief Industrial Commissioner, Ministry of Labour, 1942-44; Deputy-Secretary and Director General of Man Power, 1944-46; Permanent Secretary: Ministry of Works, 1946-56; Ministry of Labour, 1956-59. Member: Security Inquiry Cttee, 1961; Council on Prices, Productivity and Incomes, 1960-62; War Works Commission, 1960-64; Council on Tribunals, 1961-64. Chairman, London Government Staff Commn, 1963-65. Hon. MA Liverpool. *Publication:* The Ministry of Works, 1956. *Address:* 26 Millfield, Berkhamsted, Herts. *Clubs:* Athenæum, Arts.

EMMERSON, Rt. Rev. Ralph; see Knaresborough, Bishop Suffragan of.

EMMERSON, Dr Thomas, MInstP; Consultant, GKN Ltd, since 1971; *b* 28 Aug. 1909; *s* of James Emmerson and Agnes McCartney; *m* 1938, Dorothy, *d* of C. J. R. Tipper; two *s*. *Educ:* Leeds Grammar Sch.; Leeds Univ. (Schol.; BSc, PhD (Physics)). Radio Valve Industry, 1933-36; Adm. Scientific Service, 1936-45; GKN Group, 1945-: Dir of Research, 1949-68; Corporate Staff Dir of Research and Products, 1968-70. Mem., Industrial Grants Cttee, DSIR, 1953-63; Mem. Council: Brit. Welding Res. Assoc., 1963-68; Welding Inst., 1968-74. British Association for the Advancement of Science: Chm., W Midlands Br., 1964-74; Mem. Council, 1962-; Gen. Sec., 1974-. Member: Appts Bd, Univ. of Leeds, 1966-71; Glazebrook Cttee, 1966-68; Bessborough Cttee of Enquiry on Res. Assocs, 1972-73; Mem., latterly Chm., Adv. Council on R & D for Steel Ind. (ACORD), 1968-75. *Recreations:* lawn tennis, music, landscape gardening. *Address:* Highfield, Trysull, near Wolverhampton WV5 7JB. *T:* Wombourne 3387.

EMMET, family name of **Baroness Emmet of Amberley.**

EMMET OF AMBERLEY, Baroness *cr* 1964 (Life Peer); **Evelyn Violet Elizabeth Emmet,** JP; DL; *b* Cairo, 18 March 1899; *er d* of 1st Baron Rennell of Rodd, PC, GCB, GCMG, GCVO (*d* 1941), and Lilias Guthrie (*d* 1951); *m* 1923, T. A. Emmet, late Royal Navy (*d* 1934), Amberley Castle, Sussex; two *s* two *d*. *Educ:* St Margaret's Sch., Bushey, and abroad; Lady Margaret Hall, Oxford (MA). JP Sussex, 1936. Member LCC, 1925-34 (Chairman several cttees); Member W Sussex CC, 1946-67; Alderman, 1952-66 (Chairman numerous cttees). Co. Organiser, WVS, 1938-45. Chairman: Conservative Women's National Advisory Cttee, 1951-54; Nat. Union of Conservatives, 1955-56; Lord Chancellor's Legal Aid Advisory Cttee, 1966-72. Full British Delegate to Assembly of United Nations in New York, 1952, and 1953. MP (C) East Grinstead Division East Sussex, 1955-64. A Dep. Speaker and a Dep. Chm. of Cttees, House of Lords, 1968-77; Mem., Select Cttee of the House of Lords EEC

Cttee, 1974-77. DL West Sussex, 1977. *Recreation:* gardening. *Address:* Amberley Castle, Amberley, West Sussex. *T:* Bury (Sussex) 319; 3 Grosvenor Cottages, Eaton Terrace, SW1. *T:* 01-730 4627.

EMMET, Dorothy Mary, MA Oxon and Manchester; *b* 1904; *d* of late Rev. C. W. Emmet, Fellow of University Coll., Oxford, and late Gertrude Julia Emmet (*née* Weir). *Educ:* St Mary's Hall, Brighton; Lady Margaret Hall, Oxford. Classical Exhibitioner, Lady Margaret Hall, Oxford, 1923; Hon. Mods Class I, 1925; Lit. Hum. Class I, 1927. Tutor, Maesyrhaf Settlement, Rhondda Valley, 1927-28 and 1931-32; Commonwealth Fellow, Radcliffe Coll., Cambridge, Mass, USA, 1928-30; Research Fellow, Somerville Coll., Oxford, 1930-31; lecturer in Philosophy, Armstrong Coll., Newcastle upon Tyne, 1932-38 (now Newcastle Univ.); lecturer in Philosophy of Religion, University of Manchester, 1938-45; Reader in Philosophy, 1945-46; Prof. of Philosophy, University of Manchester, 1946-66; Prof. Emeritus, 1966. Stanton Lecturer in Philosophy of Religion, University of Cambridge, 1950-53. Visiting Professor: Barnard Coll., Columbia Univ., New York, 1960-61; Univ. of Ibadan, Nigeria, 1974. President Aristotelian Society, 1953-54. Dean of the Faculty of Arts, University of Manchester, 1962-64. Hon. Fellow, Lady Margaret Hall, Oxford. Fellow, Lucy Cavendish Coll., Cambridge. Hon. DLitt: Glasgow, 1974; Leicester, 1976. *Publications:* Whitehead's Philosophy of Organism, 1932; Philosophy and Faith, 1936; The Nature of Metaphysical Thinking, 1945; Function, Purpose and Powers, 1958, 2nd edn 1972; Rules, Roles and Relations, 1966; (ed with Alasdair MacIntyre) Sociological Theory and Philosophical Analysis, 1970; contributions to philosophical journals. *Recreations:* gardening, reading. *Address:* 11 Millington Road, Cambridge.
See also Prof. R. C. Wilson.

EMMETT, Harold Leslie; Assistant Under-Secretary of State, Ministry of Defence, since 1972; *b* 20 Sept. 1919; 4th *s* of Alfred and Charlotte Emmett (*née* Frith); *m* 1943, Phyllis Mabel (*née* Tranah); three *s* one *d.* Gillingham Grammar Sch., Kent. Joined Civil Service (Admiralty), 1939; transf. to War Office, 1948; Principal, 1951; Asst Sec., 1960; Command Sec., HQ BAOR, 1964-67; Imperial Defence College, 1968; seconded to Home Office for service with New Scotland Yard, 1969-70. *Recreation:* golf. *Address:* 9 Oakdale Road, Tunbridge Wells, Kent. *T:* Tunbridge Wells 22658.

EMMINGER, Otmar, Dr oec. publ.; Governor, Deutsche Bundesbank (Federal Bank), since 1977; Chairman, Monetary Committee of OECD, since 1969; *b* Augsburg, 2 March 1911; *s* of Erich Emminger, Senatspräsident (Reichsminister der Justiz, 1923-24) and Maria Scharff; *m* 1966, Dr rer. pol. Gisela Boden; two *s. Educ:* in Law and Economics, at Univs of Berlin, Munich, Edinburgh, and London Sch. of Economics. Mem. and Div. Chief, Inst. for Business Research (Institut für Konjunkturforschung), Berlin, 1935-39. Served War of 1939-45. Div. Chief, Bavarian Min. of Economics, 1947-50; Mem. German Delegn to OEEC, Paris, 1949-50; Dir, Research and Statistics Dept, Bank deutscher Länder, 1951-53; Mem. Bd of Governors, Deutsche Bundesbank (Federal Bank), 1953-69, Dep. Governor, 1970-77; Exec. Dir, IMF, Washington, 1953-59; Dep. Chm., Monetary Cttee, EEC, 1958-77; Chm., Deputies of Group of Ten, 1964-67. *Publications:* Die englischen Währungsexperimente der Nachkriegszeit, 1934; Die bayrische Industrie, 1947; Deutschlands Stellung in der Weltwirtschaft, 1953; Währungspolitik im Wandel der Zeit, 1966; The Price of Gold, 1967; Zwanzig Jahre deutsche Geldpolitik, 1968. *Recreations:* ski-ing, hiking. *Address:* Frankfurt am Main, Hasselhorstweg 36, West Germany. *T:* 1582112.

EMMS, David Acfield, MA; Master, Dulwich College, since 1975; *b* 16 Feb. 1925; *s* of Archibald George Emms and Winifred Gladys (*née* Richards); *m* 1950, Pamela Baker Speed; three *s* one *d. Educ:* Tonbridge Sch.; Brasenose Coll., Oxford. BA Hons Mod. Langs Oxford, 1950, Diploma in Education, 1951; MA 1954. Rugby football, Oxford *v* Cambridge, 1949, 1950. Served War of 1939-45, RA, 1943-47. Undergraduate, 1947-51; Asst Master, Uppingham Sch. (Head of Mod. Languages Dept, CO, CCF Contingent), 1951-60; Headmaster of: Cranleigh School, 1960-70; Sherborne School, 1970-74. Vice-Pres., Independent Schs Careers Organisation. *Recreations:* travel, ski-ing. *Address:* Elm Lawn, Dulwich Common, SE21; The Old Post Office, Lodsworth, Sussex. *Club:* East India; Devonshire, Sports and Public Schools.

EMMS, John Frederick George, FIA; Chief General Manager, Commercial Union Assurance Company Ltd, since 1977; *b* 2 Sept. 1920; *s* of late John Stanley Emms and of Alice Maud Emms (*née* Davies); *m* 1942, Margaret Alison Hay; one *s* one *d*

(and one *s* decd). *Educ:* Harrow County Sch.; Latymer Upper Sch. FIA. Served War RA/RCS, 1939-46. Joined Commercial Union Assurance Co. Ltd, 1938; Investment Manager, 1968-70; Chief Investment Manager, 1970-72; Dir, 1972; Exec. Dir, 1974. Member: (and past Chm.) Spastics Soc.; Finance Sub-Cttee, British Red Cross. Mem. Adv. Panel, NCB Superannuation and Pension Schemes. *Recreations:* sport, reading. *Address:* 7 Eastglade, Pinner, Middlesex HA5 3AN. *T:* 01-868 6151.

EMPSON, Sir Charles, KCMG 1956 (CMG 1943); Foreign Service, retired; *b* 24 April 1898; *s* of late Arthur Reginald Empson, Yokefleet, East Yorks; *m* 1931, Monica, *d* of late Canon J. W. S. Tomlin; one *s* one *d. Educ:* Harrow; Magdalene Coll., Cambridge. War Service, 1917-19 (Mesopotamia); joined staff of Civil Commissioner, Bagdad, 1920, and remained on staff of High Commissioner, Bagdad, until 1934 (Consul, 1924-32, Commercial Secretary, 1932-34); Commercial Agent for Palestine, 1934-38; Commercial Secretary HM Embassy, Rome, 1938-39; Commercial Counsellor, HM Embassy, Cairo, 1939-46; Minister (Economic), Special Commission in SE Asia, 1946-47; Minister (Commercial) HM Embassy, Rome, 1947-50; Minister (Commercial) HM Embassy, Washington, 1950-55; Ambassador to Chile, 1955-58. Rural District Councillor, Bridge-Blean, 1960-74. *Address:* Seatonden, Ickham, Canterbury, Kent. *Club:* English-Speaking Union.

EMPSON, Adm. Sir (Leslie) Derek, GBE 1975; KCB 1973 (CB 1969); Consultant, EMI Ltd, since 1976; Commander-in-Chief Naval Home Command and Flag Officer Portsmouth Area, 1974-75; Flag ADC to The Queen, 1974-75; *b* 29 Oct. 1918; *s* of Frank Harold Empson and Madeleine Norah Empson (*née* Burge); *m* 1958, Diana Elizabeth Kelly; one *s* one *d. Educ:* Eastbourne Coll.; Clare Coll., Cambridge (Class. Exhibn). Athletics Blue, 1939; BA 1940. Joined Royal Navy for pilot duties, 1940, commd as Sub-Lieut (A) RNVR, 1940; flew as Fleet Air Arm pilot, 1940-45; perm. commn in RN, 1944; Naval Asst to First Sea Lord, 1957-59; Comd HMS Eagle, 1963-65; Imp. Def. Coll., 1966; Flag Officer, Aircraft Carriers, 1967-68; Asst Chief of Naval Staff (Operations and Air), 1968-69; Comdr, Far East Fleet, 1969-71; Second Sea Lord and Chief of Naval Personnel, 1971-74. Comdr 1952; Captain 1957; Rear-Adm. 1967; Vice-Adm. 1970; Adm. 1972. Chm. of Governors, Eastbourne Coll., 1972-. *Address:* Deepdale, Hambledon, Hants. *T:* Hambledon 451. *Clubs:* MCC; Hawks (Cambridge), Achilles.

EMPSON, William, FBA 1976; Professor of English Literature, Sheffield University, 1953-71, now Emeritus; *b* 27 Sept. 1906; *s* of late A. R. Empson, Yokefleet Hall, Howden, Yorks, and Laura (*née* Micklethwait); *m* 1941, Hester Henrietta Crouse; two *s. Educ:* Winchester; Magdalene Coll., Cambridge. Chair of English Literature, Bunrika Daigaku, Tokyo, 1931-34; Professorship in English Literature, Peking National University, then part of the South-Western Combined Universities, in Hunan and Yunnan, 1937-39; BBC Chinese Editor, 1941-46, after a year in BBC Monitoring Dept; returned to Peking National Univ., 1947, Prof., Western Languages Department. Hon. LittD East Anglia, 1968; Hon. DLitt Bristol, 1971; Hon. LittD: Sheffield, 1974; Cambridge, 1977. *Publications:* Seven Types of Ambiguity, 1930; Poems, 1935; Some Versions of Pastoral, 1935; The Gathering Storm (verse), 1940; The Structure of Complex Words, 1951; Collected Poems, 1955; Milton's God, 1961; (ed with D. Pirie) Selected Poems of Coleridge, 1972. *Address:* Studio House, 1 Hampstead Hill Gardens, NW3.

EMSLIE, Rt. Hon. Lord; George Carlyle Emslie, PC 1972; MBE 1946; Lord Justice-General of Scotland and Lord President of the Court of Session, since 1972; *b* 6 Dec. 1919; *s* of late Alexander and Jessie Blair Emslie; *m* Lilias Ann Mailer Hannington; three *s. Educ:* The High School of Glasgow; The University of Glasgow (MA, LLB). Commissioned A&SH, 1940; served War of 1939-45 (despatches): North Africa, Italy, Greece, Austria, 1942-46; psc Haifa, 1944; Brigade Major (Infantry), 1944-46. Advocate, 1948; Advocate Depute (Sheriff Courts), 1955; QC (Scotland) 1957; Sheriff of Perth and Angus, 1963-66; Dean of Faculty of Advocates, 1965-70; Senator of Coll. of Justice in Scotland and Lord of Session, 1970-72. Chm., Scottish Agricultural Wages Bd, 1969-73; Mem., Council on Tribunals (Scottish Cttee), 1962-70. Hon. Bencher, Inner Temple, 1974. Hon. LLD Glasgow, 1973. *Recreation:* golf. *Address:* 47 Heriot Row, Edinburgh EH5 6EX. *T:* 031-225 3657. *Clubs:* New (Edinburgh); The Honourable Company of Edinburgh Golfers.

EMSLIE, George Carlyle; *see* Emslie, Rt Hon. Lord.

EMSLIE, Prof. Ronald Douglas, FDSRCS; Dean of Dental Studies, Guy's Hospital Medical and Dental Schools, since 1968; Professor of Periodontology and Preventive Dentistry, University of London, since 1970; *b* 9 March 1915; *s* of late Alexander G. H. Emslie and Elizabeth Spence; *m* 1951, Dorothy, *d* of William A. Dennis, Paris, Ill, USA; four *s. Educ:* Felsted Sch.; Guy's Hosp. Dental Sch., London (BDS); Univ. of Illinois, Chicago (MSc). FDSRCS Eng., 1950. Served War: Surg. Lt (D) RNVR, 1943-46; Surg. Lt Comdr (D) RNVR, 1946. Half-time Asst in Dept of Preventive Dentistry, Guy's Hosp., 1946-48, also in private practice with Mr E. B. Dowsett; Research Fellow, Univ. of Illinois, Chicago, 1948-49; Head of Dept of Preventive Dentistry, Guy's Hosp., 1949-55; Reader in Preventive Dentistry, Univ. of London (Guy's Hosp. Dental Sch.), 1956-62; Prof. of Preventive Dentistry, Univ. of London (Guy's Hosp. Dental Sch.), 1963-70. Pres., Brit. Soc. of Periodontology, 1959-60; Chm., Dental Health Cttee of BDA, 1963-69; Member: Internat. Dental Fedn; Amer. Dental Soc. of London; Internat. Assoc. for Dental Research; Bone and Tooth Soc.; Bd of Faculty of Dental Surgery, RCS (Vice-Dean, 1976-77); Fluoridation Soc. (Chm. 1970-). Past Pres., Odontological Section, RSM; Vis. Lectr, Univ. of Illinois, 1956; Nuffield Grant to study dental aspects of facial gangrene, in Nigeria, Sept.-Dec. 1961; Chm., Bd of Studies in Dentistry, Univ. of London. Sci. Advr, Brit. Dental Jl, 1961- (Sci. Asst Ed., 1951-61); WHO expert adv. panel on dental health; Consultant in Periodontology to RN, 1971-. Fellow, BDA. *Publications:* various contribs to dental literature. *Recreations:* tennis, sailing, old motor cars. *Address:* Little Hale, Woodland Way, Kingswood, Surrey. *T:* Mogador 2662.

EMSON, Air Marshal Sir Reginald (Herbert Embleton), KBE 1966 (CBE 1946); CB 1959; AFC 1941; Inspector-General of the Royal Air Force, 1967-69; *b* 11 Jan. 1912; *s* of Francis Reginald Emson, Hitcham, Buckinghamshire; *m* 1934, Doreen Marjory, *d* of Hugh Duke, Holyport, Maidenhead, Berkshire; two *s* two *d. Educ:* Christ's Hospital; RAF Coll., Cranwell. Joined RAF, 1931; served War of 1939-45 in Aeroplane Armament Establishment Gunnery Research Unit, Exeter; Fighter Command Headquarters and Central Fighter Establishment. Director, Armament Research and Development (Air), Ministry of Supply, 1950-59; Commander RAF Staff and Air Attaché, British Defence Staffs, Washington, 1961-63; Asst Chief of Air Staff (Operational Requirements), 1963-66; Dep. Chief Air Staff, 1966-67. Group Captain, 1943; Air Commodore, 1958; Air Vice-Marshal, 1962; Air Marshal (Acting), 1966. *Address:* Vor Cottage, Holyport, Maidenhead, Berks. *T:* Maidenhead 21992. *Club:* Royal Air Force.

ENCOMBE, Viscount; John Francis Thomas Marie Joseph Columba Fidelis Scott; *b* 9 July 1962; *s* and *heir* of 5th Earl of Eldon, *qv*.

ENDERBY, Prof. John Edwin; Professor of Physics, University of Bristol, since 1976; Associate Editor, Philosophical Magazine, since 1975; *b* 16 Jan. 1931; *s* of Thomas Edwin Enderby and Rheita Rebecca Hollinshead (*née* Stather); *m* 1957, Jennifer Mary (*née* Henson); one *s* one *d. Educ:* Chester Grammar Sch.; London Univ. (BSc, PhD). Lecturer in Physics: Coll. of Technology, Huddersfield, 1957-60; Univ. of Sheffield, 1960-67; Reader in Physics, Univ. of Sheffield, 1967-69; Prof. in Physics and Head of the Dept, Univ. of Leicester, 1969-76. Visiting Fellow, Battelle Inst., 1968-69; FInstP 1970-. *Publications:* (jointly): Physics of Simple Liquids, 1968; Amorphous and Liquid Semiconductors, 1974; many publications on the structure and properties of liquids in: Phil. Mag. Adv. Phys, Jl Phys, Proc. Royal Soc., etc. *Recreations:* gardening, watching Association football. *Address:* 174A Stoke Lane, Westbury-on-Trym, Bristol BS9 3RS. *T:* Bristol 685210.

ENDERBY, Col Samuel, CVO 1977; DSO 1943; MC 1939; JP; *b* 15 Sept. 1907; *s* of Col Samuel Enderby and Mary Cuninghame; *m* 1936, Pamela, *e d* of Major Charles Beck Hornby, DSO; two *s* one *d. Educ:* Uppingham Sch.; RMC Sandhurst. Regular soldier, commissioned 5th Fusiliers, 1928. Served War, 1936-46: MEF, CMF, comd 2/4th KOYLI and 2/5 Leicester Regt; Commandant, Sch. of Infantry: ACRE, 1945-46; Netheravon, 1947-48; comd, 7th Bn Royal Northumberland Fusiliers, 1949; retd 1949. JP 1956; High Sheriff of Northumberland, 1968. Mem., Hon. Corps of Gentlemen at Arms, 1954, Standard Bearer, 1976. *Address:* The Riding, Hexham, Northumberland. *T:* Hexham 2250. *Club:* Army and Navy.

ENDERL, Dr Kurt H.; Ambassador of Austria to the Court of St James's, since 1975; *b* 12 April 1913; *s* of Hugo Enderl and Karoline Enderl; *m* 1967, Adele Leigh. *Educ:* Vienna Univ. (Dr of Law). 3rd Sec., Austrian Legation, London, 1946-47; Chargé d'Affaires, Aust. Legation, New Delhi, 1950-53; Austrian

Minister in Israel, 1955-58; Head of Multilateral Economic Dept, Min. of Foreign Affairs, Vienna, 1958-61; Austrian Ambassador: in Poland, 1962-67; in Hungary, 1967-72; Chief of Protocol, Vienna, 1972-74. *Recreations:* tennis, ski-ing. *Address:* Austrian Embassy, 18 Belgrave Square, SW1.

ENDERS, Dr John Franklin; Chief, Virus Unit, Division of Infectious Diseases, Children's Medical Center, Boston, Mass; University Professor Emeritus, Harvard University, USA; *b* 10 Feb. 1897; *s* of John Ostrom Enders and Harriet Goulden Whitmore; *m* 1927, Sarah Frances Bennett (*d* 1943); one *s* one *d*; 1951, Carolyn Bernice Keane; one step *s. Educ:* St Paul's Sch., Concord, NH; Yale Univ. (BA 1919); Harvard Univ. (MA 1922, PhD 1930). USNR Flying Corps, 1917-20. Teaching and research in field of infectious diseases of man, 1927-. Member Faculty Harvard Medical Sch., 1929-; Civ. Cons. to Secretary of War on Epidemic Diseases in Army, 1942-46; Member Commn on Virus Dis, US Army, 1949-68; Member WHO Expert Advisory Panel on Virus Diseases, 1958. Passano Award, 1953; Lasker Award, 1954; Nobel Laureate, 1954, in Physiology and Medicine; Cameron Prize, 1960; Ricketts Award, 1962; Robert Koch Medal, 1963; US Presidential Medal of Freedom, 1963. Commander of the Republic of Upper Volta, 1965. Member: National Academy of Sciences (US); American Philosophical Society; Academie Nat. de Med. (France); Deut. Akad. d. Naturforsch. (Leopoldina); Hon. Member: RSM (England); Acad. Roy. de Med. (Belgium); Foreign Mem., Royal Soc. (England); Associé honoraire étranger, Académie des Sciences, Inscriptions et Belles-Lettres de Toulouse; Associé étranger, Académie des Sciences de l'Institut de France. Fellow American Academy of Arts and Sciences. Hon. FACS. Holds several honorary degrees. *Publications:* (joint) Immunity: Principles and Application in Medicine and Public Health, 1939; papers in scientific journals. *Recreations:* fishing, sailing. *Address:* 64 Colbourne Crescent, Brookline, Mass 02147, USA. *T:* Longwood 6-3539. *Clubs:* Country (Brookline); Harvard, Saturday (Boston, Mass).

ENERGLYN, Baron *cr* 1968 (Life Peer), of Caerphilly; **William David Evans,** MSc, DSc, PhD; DL; Professor of Geology, University of Nottingham, since 1949; formerly Dean of the Faculty of Pure Science; *b* 25 Dec. 1912; *s* of Councillor D. G. Evans; *m* 1941, Jean Thompson Miller; no *c. Educ:* Caerphilly Grammar Sch.; University Coll., Cardiff. Geologist to HM Geological Survey of Great Britain, 1939; Member of Regional Survey Board of Ministry of Fuel and Power for South Wales Coalfield, 1945; Senior Lecturer in Geology, University College of South Wales and Monmouthshire, 1947. FGS 1939; FRGS 1944; FLS 1945; MIME 1952; MIMM 1949. MSc Wales, 1938; PhD London, 1940. DL Notts, 1974. Hon. Fellow, Mark Twain Soc. of America, 1976. *Publications:* Through the Crust of the Earth, 1974; research papers in Trans and Proc. of Geol Society of London, Royal Geog. Society, Institute of Mining and Metallurgy, etc, on geology of older rocks of Wales, and Cornwall, and cause of dust diseases among coalminers and metalliferous miners at home and abroad. *Address:* 14 Village Close, Edwalton, West Bridgford, Nottinghamshire. *Club:* Reform.

ENFIELD, Viscount; Thomas Edmund Byng; *b* 26 Sept. 1936; *s* and *heir* of 7th Earl of Strafford, *qv*; *m* 1963, Jennifer Mary, *er d* of late Rt Hon. W. M. May, PC, FCA, MP, and of Mrs May, Mertoun Hall, Holywood, Co. Down; two *s* two *d. Educ:* Eton; Clare Coll., Cambridge. Lieut, Royal Sussex Regt (National Service). *Recreation:* gardening. *Heir: s* Hon. William Robert Byng, *b* 10 May 1964. *Address:* Abbots Worthy House, Abbots Worthy, Winchester, Hants. *T:* Winchester 881333.

ENGELS, Johan Peter; Chairman, Philips Electronic and Associated Industries Ltd, 1964-73; *b* Rotterdam, Holland, 6 March 1908; *m* 1935, Christina Pieternella van Hoeflaken; three *s* one *d. Educ:* Holland. Joined Philips, in Holland, 1928. Moved to England and appointed Managing Director of Philips Electrical Ltd, 1961; appointed Director of Philips Electronic & Associated Industries Ltd, 1962, and Chairman, 1964. Officer, Order of Orange Nassau (Holland), 1968. *Recreations:* golf, swimming, reading, gardening. *Address:* 11/12 Hanover Square, W1. *T:* 01-499 9555.

ENGHOLM, Sir Basil Charles, KCB 1968 (CB 1964); company director; *b* 2 Aug. 1912; *o s* of late C. F. G. Engholm; *m* 1936, Nancy, *er d* of Lifford Hewitt, St Anthony, Rye; one *d. Educ:* Tonbridge Sch.; Sorbonne, Paris; Sidney Sussex Coll., Cambridge (Law Tripos, MA). Member of Gray's Inn; Metal business, New York, 1933-34; entered Ministry of Agriculture and Fisheries, 1935; War of 1939-45: part-time NFS; Principal Private Secretary to Minister of Agriculture and Fisheries, 1943-45; Asst Secretary, 1945; Under-Secretary, 1954; Fisheries

Secretary, 1960-62; Dep. Secretary, 1964-67; Permanent Sec., MAFF, 1968-72. Governor, Sadler's Wells Theatre. *Recreations:* reading, writing, archaeology and painting. *Address:* Meadway, Meadway, NW11. *T:* 01-455 3975. *Club:* United Oxford & Cambridge University.

ENGINEER, Sir Noshirwan Phirozha, Kt 1945; Lawyer; practising in India; *b* 22 Jan. 1884; *m* 1916, Jerbai Jamsetji Kanga; one *s* two *d. Educ:* Elphinstone Coll., Bombay. Dakshina Fellow, Elphinstone Coll.; a solicitor of Bombay High Court, 1910-21; an Advocate (original side) of Bombay High Court from 1921; Additional Judge Bombay High Court, 1936-38; Advocate-General of Bombay, 1942-45; Advocate-General of India, 1945-50. *Address:* Sakar Apartment, Pochkhanawala Road, Worli, Bombay 18, India. *Clubs:* Willingdon Sports (Bombay); Delhi Gymkhana.

ENGLAND, Frank Raymond Wilton; *b* 24 Aug. 1911; *s* of Joseph and Florence England; *m* 1939, Margaretta Helen Wells; one *d. Educ:* Christ Coll., Finchley. Served War, Pilot, RAF, 1941-45. Apprenticeship with Daimler Co. Ltd, Hendon, 1927-32; Racing Mechanic to: Sir Henry Birkin, Whitney Straight, Era Ltd, Richard Seaman, B. Bira, 1932-38; Service Engr, Service Dept Supt, Alvis Limited, 1938-40. Service Manager, Jaguar Cars Ltd, 1946-56; Service Dir, 1956-61; Asst Man. Dir, 1961-66; Dep. Man. Dir, 1966-67; Jt Man. Dir, 1967; Dep. Chm., 1968; Chm. and Chief Executive, 1972; retd as Chm., Jan. 1974. *Recreation:* motor sport. *Address:* 196 Gmundnerberg, 4813 Altmünster, Austria. *Clubs:* Royal Air Force, British Racing Drivers'.

ENGLAND, Glyn, BSc(Eng); CEng, FIEE, FIMechE, FBIM; Chairman, Central Electricity Generating Board, since 1977 (part-time Member, 1975-77); *b* 19 April 1921; *m* 1942, Tania Reichenbach; two *d. Educ:* Penarth County Sch.; Queen Mary Coll., London Univ. (BSc (Eng)); London School of Economics. Department of Scientific and Industrial Research, 1939. War service, 1942-47. Electricity Supply Industry 1947-; Chief Ops Engr, CEGB, 1966-71; Dir-Gen., SW Region, 1971-73; Chm., SW Electricity Bd, 1973-77. Sometime Labour Mem., Herts CC; Mem. Council, Magistrates' Assoc. Consultant to Internat. Atomic Energy Agency. JP Welwyn, Herts, 1962-71. *Publications:* papers on: Clean Air, Conservation of Water Resources, Economic Growth and the Electricity Supply Industry, Security of Electricity Supplies. *Recreation:* actively enjoying the countryside. *Address:* Woodbridge Farm, Ubley, Bristol BS18 6PX. *T:* Blagdon 62479.

ENGLAND, Rear-Adm. Hugh Turnour, CB 1947; DSO 1943 (Bar 1944); *b* 1884; *s* of late Captain W. G. England, RN; *m* Alice Marian (*d* 1968), *d* of late Rev. Claypon Bellingham, Dunany, Co. Louth, Ireland; one *s* two *d* (and one *s* killed on active service, Fleet Air Arm, War of 1939-45). *Educ:* Eastman's; HMS Britannia. Joined RN 1900. Served S African War; European War, 1914-19, Dardanelles and E Mediterranean (despatches, severely wounded); War of 1939-45, Commodore of Convoy, Principal Sea Transport Officer, Middle East, 1941-43; Commodore-in-Charge, Hamburg, and in command German Minesweeping Administration, 1945-47 (Croix de Guerre, France). ADC to the King, 1934; Rear-Adm. 1935; retired, 1935. *Address:* Dunany, Togher, Drogheda, Co. Louth, Eire. *T:* 041-52147.

ENGLAND, Peter Tiarks Ede; Deputy Under-Secretary of State (Army), Ministry of Defence, since 1976; *b* 4 April 1925; *s* of Benjamin and late Mabel Gwendoline Ranke England; *m* 1st, 1947; one *s* two *d*; 2nd, 1956, Veronica Ella Lydia Everett. *Educ:* Charterhouse; Magdalene Coll., Cambridge (Exhibr; MA). RNVR, 1943-46; Cambridge, 1946-49; joined War Office, 1949; Principal, 1953; Comd Sec., Western Comd, 1961-63; Asst Sec., 1963; Asst Under-Sec. of State, MoD, 1970; Under-Sec., CSD, 1973-74; Dep. Sec., NI Office, 1974-76. *Recreations:* hill walking, model railways. *Address:* 3 Engayne Gardens, Upminster, Essex RM14 1UY. *T:* Upminster 29096. *Club:* United Oxford & Cambridge University.

ENGLE, George Lawrence Jose, CB 1976; one of the Parliamentary Counsel since 1970; *b* 13 Sept. 1926; *o s* of Lawrence Engle; *m* 1956, Irene, *d* of late Heinz Lachmann; three *d. Educ:* Charterhouse (scholar); Christ Church, Oxford (Marjoribanks and Dixon schols, MA). Served RA, 1945-48 (2nd Lt, 1947). Firsts in Mods and Greats; Cholmeley Schol., Lincoln's Inn, 1952; called to Bar, Lincoln's Inn, 1953. Joined parly counsel office, 1957; seconded as First Parly Counsel, Fedn of Nigeria, 1965-67; with Law Commn, 1971-73. *Publications:* Law for Landladies, 1955; contributor to: Ideas, 1954, and O Rare Hoffnung, 1960. *Recreations:* book-hunting, oriental and Islamic pots, bricolage. *Address:* 32 Wood Lane, N6. *T:* 01-340 9750.

ENGLEDOW, Sir Frank Leonard, Kt 1944; CMG 1935; FRS 1946; MA, BSc; Fellow of St John's College, Cambridge; Drapers' Professor of Agriculture, Cambridge University, 1930-57; *b* 1890; *m* Mildred (*d* 1956); four *d. Educ:* St John's Coll., Cambridge. The Queen's Own (Royal West Kent Regt), 1914-18; Adjutant, 5th Batt. Mesopotamian Expeditionary Force; retiring rank Lt-Col; asst Director of Agriculture, Mesopotamia, 1918-19. *Address:* Hadleigh, Huntingdon Road, Girton, Cambridge CB3 0LH.

ENGLISH, Sir Cyril (Rupert), Kt 1972; Educational Consultant; Director-General, City and Guilds of London Institute, 1968-76; *b* 19 April 1913; *s* of William James and Edith English; *m* 1936, Eva Moore; two *s. Educ:* Northgate Sch., Ipswich. BScEng Ext. London, 1934. Technical teacher, 1935-39. Served Royal Navy, 1939-46, Lieut-Commander (E). HM Inspector of Schools, 1946-55; Staff Inspector (Engineering), 1955-58; Chief Inspector of Further Education, in connection with Industry and Commerce, 1958-65; Senior Chief Inspector, Dept of Education and Science, 1965-67. Member, Anglo-American Productivity Team, 1951; attended Commonwealth Education Conferences, Delhi, 1962, Ottawa, 1964. Chairman: British Assoc. for Commercial and Industrial Educn, 1970-71, 1971-72; RAF Educn Adv. Cttee; Member: Services Colleges Cttee, 1965-66; Adv. Bd, RAF Coll., Cranwell; Academic Adv. Council, Royal Defence Acad.; Bd of Dirs, Industrial Training Service; Central Training Council; CTC Gen. Policy Cttee; Nat. Adv. Council for Educn in Industry and Commerce; Council for Tech. Educn and Training for Overseas Countries (Bd Mem., Chm. Educn Cttee); Reg. Adv. Council for Technol. Educn (London and Home Counties); Schools Science and Technology Cttee; Educn Cttee, IMechE; Associated Examining Bd; Cttee of Inquiry into Training of Teachers (James Cttee); Standing Conf. on Schs' Science and Technology; Cttee on Regular Officer training (Army). Vice-Pres., Soc. Electronic and Radio Technicians, 1972-74, Pres., 1975. Governor, Imperial Coll. FIMechE; FIProdE; FIMarE. Hon. Fellow, Inst. of Road Transport Engrs, 1971. Hon. Fellow, Manchester Polytechnic, 1976. Hon. DTech Brunel, 1970; Hon. DSc Loughborough, 1973; DUniv Open, 1974. *Recreations:* music, gardening. *Address:* Coombe Lodge, Blagdon, Bristol BS18 6RG. *Club:* Naval.

ENGLISH, David; Editor, Daily Mail, since 1971; *b* 26 May 1931; *m* 1954, Irene Mainwood; one *s* two *d. Educ:* Bournemouth Sch. Daily Mirror, 1951-53; Feature Editor, Daily Sketch, 1956; Foreign Correspondent: Sunday Dispatch, 1959; Daily Express, 1960; Washington Correspdt, Express, 1961-63; Chief American Correspdt, Express, 1963-65; Foreign Editor, Express, 1965-67; Associate Editor, Express, 1967-69; Editor, Daily Sketch, 1969-71. *Publication:* Divided They Stand (a British view of the 1968 American Presidential Election), 1969. *Recreations:* reading, ski-ing, boating. *Address:* Daily Mail, EC4Y 0JA. *T:* 01-353 6000. *Clubs:* Press; Royal Temple Yacht.

ENGLISH, Gerald; Professor, Royal College of Music, since 1960; *b* 6 Nov. 1925; *m* 1954, Jennifer Ryan; two *s* two *d. Educ:* King's Sch., Rochester. After War service studied at Royal College of Music and then began career as lyric tenor; subsequently travelled in USA and Europe, appeared at Sadler's Wells, Covent Garden and Glyndebourne and recorded for major gramophone companies. *Address:* 63 Springfield Road, NW8. *T:* 01-328 0401.

ENGLISH, Michael; MP (Lab) Nottingham (West) since 1964; *b* 24 Dec. 1930; *s* of late William Agnew English; *m* 1976, Carol Christine Owen. *Educ:* King George V Grammar Sch., Southport; Liverpool Univ. (LLB). Joined Labour Party, 1949; Rochdale County Borough Council, 1953-65 (Chairman Finance Cttee until 1964); contested (Lab) Shipley Div., WR Yorks, 1959. Member, official parliamentary panel NUGMW. Employed until 1964 as Asst Manager of department concerned with organisation and methods in subsidiary of large public company. Parliamentary Private Secretary, Board of Trade, 1966-67; Chairman: Parly Affairs Gp of Parly Lab. Party, 1970-76; Gen. Sub-Cttee of House of Commons Expenditure Cttee, 1974-; Mem., Chairmen's Panel, House of Commons. *Recreation:* reading history. *Address:* House of Commons, SW1. *T:* 01-219 3000.

ENGLISH, Commander Reginald Wastell, DSO 1940; Royal Navy; *b* 12 April 1894; *s* of late Marcus Valentine English, Orton Longueville, Peterborough, and Emmeline Fanny Whytehead, Acomb, York; *m* 1916, Olive Taylor (*d* 1964), Ermington, Devon; one *s* two *d. Educ:* Orleton Sch., Scarborough; Osborne and Dartmouth Colleges. Served RN, 1907-20, 1939-44. A/S Trawlers, home, USA, S Africa (DSO Dover). *Address:* Montgomery House, Long Melford, Suffolk.

ENNALS, Rt. Hon. David Hedley, PC 1970; MP (Lab) Norwich North, since Feb. 1974; Secretary of State for Social Services, since 1976; *b* 19 Aug. 1922; *s* of A. F. Ennals, 8 Victoria Terrace, Walsall, Staffs; *m* 1950, Eleanor Maud Caddick (marr. diss. 1977); three *s* one *d*; *m* 1977. Mrs Katherine Tranoy. *Educ:* Queen Mary's Grammar School, Walsall; Loomis Inst., Windsor, Conn, USA. Served with HM Forces, 1941-46: Captain, RAC. Secretary, Council for Education in World Citizenship, 1947-52; Secretary, United Nations Association, 1952-57; Overseas Sec., Labour Party, 1957-64. MP (Lab) Dover, 1964-70; PPS to: Minister of Overseas Development, 1964; Minister of Transport, 1966; Parly Under-Sec. of State, Army, 1966-67; Parly Under-Sec., Home Office, 1967-68; Minister of State: DHSS, 1968-70; FCO, 1974-76. Campaign Dir, Nat. Assoc. for Mental Health, 1970-73; Chairman: Peter Bedford Housing Associates, 1972-74; Campaign for Homeless and Rootless, 1972-74; Ockenden Venture, 1972-76 (Dep. Chm. 1968-72). Chm., John Bellers Ltd, 1972-74. *Publications:* Strengthening the United Nations, 1957; Middle East Issues, 1958; United Nations Peace Force, 1960; United Nations on Trial, 1962; Out of Mind, 1973. *Recreation:* camping. *Address:* 8 St Anne's Close, N6.
See also *J. A. F. Ennals, M. Ennals.*

ENNALS, John Arthur Ford; Director, United Kingdom Immigrants Advisory Service, since 1970; *b* Walsall, 21 July 1918; *e s* of Arthur Ford Ennals, MC, and Jessie Edith Ennals (*née* Taylor); one *s* one *d*. *Educ:* Queen Mary's Grammar Sch., Walsall; St John's Coll., Cambridge. MA (History and Psychology). Rotary Travelling Schol. to USA, 1935. Pres., British Univs League of Nations Soc., and Mem. Cttee, Cambridge Union, 1938-39. Lectr for British Council, Roumania and Yugoslavia, 1939-40; War Corresp., Greece, Yugoslavia, Albania, 1941; on staff of British Embassy, Madrid, 1941-42, and Foreign Office, 1942-43. Served War: Egypt, Italy and Yugoslavia, 1943-45. Secretary-Gen., World Fedn of UN Assocs, working with UN, UNESCO, ILO and WHO, 1946-56; Gen.-Sec. and Tutor in Internat. Relations, Ruskin Coll., Oxford, 1956-66; Dir-Gen., UN Assoc., 1966-70 (Mem. UNA Exec. Cttee, 1956-70 and 1973-77). Member: Exec. Cttee, World Fedn of UN Assocs, 1966- (Vice-Pres., 1973-77); OXFAM Exec., 1965-75; Exec. Council, Assoc. of Supervisory Staffs, Executives and Technicians, 1960-69. Nat. Trustee, Assoc. of Scientific Technical and Managerial Staffs, 1969-; Chm., Anti-Apartheid Movement, 1968-76; Member: Community Relations Cttee, Baptist Union, 1971-; Community and Race Relations Unit, British Council of Churches, 1971-; Exec. Cttee, British Council for Aid to Refugees, 1977-. *Recreations:* travelling in Europe, Asia, Africa and the Americas; walking in Wales; broadcasting; writing. *Address:* Blue Cottage, Hedgerley, Bucks. *T:* (home) Farnham Common 4302; (office) 01-240 5176. *Club:* India.
See also *Rt Hon. D. H. Ennals, M. Ennals.*

ENNALS, Kenneth Frederick John; Under-Secretary, Department of the Environment, since 1976; *b* 10 Jan. 1932; *s* of Ernest Ennals and Elsie Dorothy Ennals; *m* 1958, Mavis Euphemia; one *s* two *d*. *Educ:* Alleyn's Sch., Dulwich; (part-time) LSE (BScEcon). Joined Export Credits Guarantee Dept, 1952; Principal, DEA, 1965-69; Min. of Housing and Local Govt, later DoE, 1969; Asst Sec., 1970. *Recreations:* reading, architecture, dog-walking. *Address:* St Anthony's, Tuesley Lane, Godalming, Surrey. *T:* Godalming 7239.

ENNALS, Martin; Secretary General, Amnesty International, since 1968; *b* 27 July 1927; *s* of A. Ford Ennals and Jessie E. Ennals (*née* Taylor); *m* 1951, Jacqueline B. Ennals (*née* Morris); one *s* one *d*. *Educ:* Queen Mary's Sch., Walsall; London Sch. of Economics. BScEcon (Internat. Relations). UNESCO, 1951-59; Gen. Sec., National Council for Civil Liberties, 1960-66; Information Officer, Nat. Cttee for Commonwealth Immigrants, 1966-68 (resigned in protest at Govt's Commonwealth Immigration Act, 1968). *Recreations:* escapist television and ski-ing. *Address:* 4 Rochester Terrace, NW1. *T:* 01-485 6015.
See also *Rt Hon. D. H. Ennals, J. A. F. Ennals.*

ENNISKILLEN, 6th Earl of, *cr* 1789; **David Lowry Cole,** MBE 1955; DL, JP; Baron Mountflorence, 1760; Viscount Enniskillen, 1776; Baron Grinstead (UK), 1815; farmer, Kenya and N Ireland; *b* 10 Sept. 1918; *er s* of Hon. Galbraith Lowry Egerton Cole (*d* 1929) (3rd *s* of 4th Earl of Enniskillen) and of Lady Eleanor Cole, *d* of 2nd Earl of Balfour; *S* uncle, 1963; *m* 1st, 1940, Sonia Mary Syers (from whom he obtained a divorce, 1955); one *s* one *d*; 2nd, 1955, Nancy Henderson MacLennan, former American Vice Consul. *Educ:* Eton; Trinity Coll., Cambridge. BA Agric. 1940. Served War of 1939-45, Captain Irish Guards: Kenya Emergency, 1953-55, Provincial Comdt, Kenya Police Reserve (MBE). MLC for North Kenya, 1961-63.

Formerly: Member Kenya Meat Commn; Member Exec., Kenya National Farmers Union; Vice-Chairman Kenya Stockowners Council; Member Exec., Kenya Board of Agriculture; Member Board: Land and Agric. Bank of Kenya; East African Diatomite Syndicate Ltd. Captain, Ulster Defence Regt, 1971-73. Mem., Fermanagh CC, 1963-69; DL 1963, JP 1972, co. Fermanagh. *Recreations:* shooting, golf, fishing. *Heir: s* Viscount Cole, *qv*. *Address:* Florence Court, Enniskillen, N Ireland. *T:* Florencecourt 229; PO Box 47345, Nairobi, Kenya. *Clubs:* Carlton, Turf; Muthaiga Country (Nairobi); Mombasa (Kenya).
See also *Sir J. H. Muir, Bt.*

ENNISMORE, Viscount; Francis Michael Hare; *b* 28 June 1964; *s* and *heir* of 5th Earl of Listowel, *qv*.

ENNOR, Sir Arnold Hughes, (Sir Hugh Ennor), Kt 1965; CBE 1963; Secretary, Commonwealth Department of Science, since 1973; *b* 10 Oct. 1912; *s* of Arnold Martin and Charlotte van de Leur Ennor; *m* 1939, Violet Phyllis Argall; one *s* one *d*. *Educ:* Melbourne Univ. DSc Melbourne, 1943. Research Biochemist, Baker Institute of Medical Research, Melbourne, 1938-42; Research with Ministry of Munitions and Armed Forces, 1942-46; Wellcome Research Fellow, Dept of Biochemistry, Oxford Univ., 1946-48; Professor of Biochemistry, Australian National University, Canberra, 1948-67; Dean of John Curtin School of Medical Research, 1953-67; Deputy Vice-Chancellor, Australian National Univ., 1964-67; Secretary: Commonwealth Dept of Educn and Science, 1967-73; Commonwealth Dept of Science, 1973-. Hon. DSc NSW, 1968; Hon. MD Monash, 1969. *Publications:* numerous contributions to Biochemical Journal, Journal of Biological Chemistry, etc. *Recreation:* tennis. *Address:* 3a Vancouver Street, Red Hill, Canberra, ACT 2603, Australia. *T:* 95 9426. *Clubs:* Commonwealth (Canberra); Athenæum (Melbourne).

ENRICI, Most Rev. Domenico, JCD; Apostolic Nuncio, Delegate for Pontifical Representations, Vatican City, since 1973; *b* 9 April 1909; *s* of late Domenico Enrici and of Maria Dalmasso Enrici. *Educ:* Diocesan Seminary, Cuneo; Pontifical Gregorian Univ. and Pontifical Ecclesiastical Academy, Rome. Ordained, 1933; parochial work in Dio. Cuneo, 1933-35. Served at various Apostolic Nunciatures and Delegations: Ireland, 1938-45; Egypt, 1946-48; Palestine and Jordan, 1948-53; Formosa, Free China, 1953-55; apptd Titular Archbp of Ancusa, 1955; Apostolic Internuncio to Indonesia, 1955-58; Apostolic Nuncio to Haiti and Apostolic Delegate to West Indies, 1958-60; Apostolic Internuncio to Japan, 1960-62; Apostolic Delegate to Australia, New Zealand and Oceania, 1962-69; Apostolic Delegate to GB and Gibraltar, 1969-73. *Address:* Secretariat of State, Vatican City, Italy.

ENRIGHT, Dennis Joseph; freelance writer and teacher; Director, Chatto and Windus, since 1974; *b* 11 March 1920; *s* of late George Enright; *m* 1949, Madeleine Harders; one *d*. *Educ:* Leamington Coll.; Downing Coll., Cambridge. MA Cantab; DLitt Alexandria. Lecturer in English, University of Alexandria, 1947-50; Organising Tutor, University of Birmingham Extra-Mural Dept, 1950-53; Vis. Prof., Kōnan Univ., Japan, 1953-56; Vis. Lecturer, Free University of Berlin, 1956-57; British Council Professor, Chulalongkorn Univ., Bangkok, 1957-59; Prof. of English, Univ. of Singapore, 1960-70; Hon. Prof. in English, Univ. of Warwick, 1975-. Co-Editor, Encounter, 1970-72. FRSL 1961. Cholmondeley Poetry Award, 1974. *Publications: poetry:* The Laughing Hyena, 1953; Bread Rather Than Blossoms, 1956; Some Men Are Brothers, 1960; Addictions, 1962; The Old Adam, 1965; Unlawful Assembly, 1968; Selected Poems, 1969; Daughters of Earth, 1972; The Terrible Shears, 1973; Rhyme Times Rhyme (for children), 1974; Sad Ires, 1975; *novels:* Academic Year, 1955; Heaven Knows Where, 1957; Insufficient Poppy, 1960; Figures of Speech, 1965; The Joke Shop (for children), 1976; Wild Ghost Chase (for children), 1978; *criticism:* The Apothecary's Shop, 1957; English Critical Texts (co-editor), 1962; Conspirators and Poets, 1966; Shakespeare and the Students, 1970; Man is an Onion, 1972; (ed) A Choice of Milton's Verse, 1975; Samuel Johnson: Rasselas, 1976; *travel:* The World of Dew: Japan, 1955; Memoirs of a Mendicant Professor, 1969; *translation:* The Poetry of Living Japan (co-editor), 1957; contributor to: Scrutiny, Encounter, Listener, etc. *Recreations:* reading, writing, television, listening to music. *Address:* c/o Chatto & Windus, 40-42 William IV Street, WC2.

ENSOR, (Alick Charles) David; journalist and author; *b* 27 Nov. 1906; *s* of Charles William Ensor, MRCS, LRCP, and Helen Margaret Creighton Ensor; *m* 1st, 1932, Norah Russell (marr. diss.); one *s* two *d*; 2nd, 1944, Frances Vivienne Mason. *Educ:* Westminster Sch. Solicitor, 1928; Prosecuting Solicitor, Newcastle upon Tyne, 1932; Prosecuting Solicitor, Metropolitan

Police, 1935; Law Lecturer, Police Coll., Hendon, 1935; Deputy Clerk of Peace, Middlesex, 1937; Clerk of Peace, London, 1938. War service with Army in France, Africa, Far East, 1939-44. Practised as Solicitor in Brussels, 1945-47. Retired from Law and farmed in Dorset, 1948. MP (Lab) Bury and Radcliffe, 1964-70; Member Select Cttee on Estimates, 1964-68; Chm., House of Commons Catering Cttee, 1969-70. Has broadcast regularly for radio and television since 1957. Films include: The Trials of Oscar Wilde; The Pot Carriers; Death and the Sky Above. Vice-Pres., Mark Twain Soc. of America, 1977-. *Publications:* Thirty Acres and a Cow, 1955; I was a Public Prosecutor, 1958; Verdict Afterwards, 1960; With Lord Roberts through the Khyber Pass, 1963; contributions to Local Government Law in England and Wales, Journal of Criminal Law. *Recreations:* gardening, travelling. *Address:* 107 avenue Puig del Mas, 66650 Banyuls-sur-Mer, France.

ENSOR, David; see Ensor, A. C. D.

ENSOR WALTERS, P. H. B.; see Walters.

ENTERS, Angna; mime; dancer; painter; sculptor; author; dramatist; composer; choreographer; scene and costume designer for the theatre; *b* NYC, US, 28 April 1907; *o c* of Edward Enters and Henriette Gasseur-Styleau; *m* Louis Kalonyme. *Educ:* privately and self-educated in US; Europe; Egypt; Greece. Theatre début New York, 1924, presenting in solo performance a new theatre form in which she combined for the first time the arts of mime, dance, music, costume, scenic design; originated phrase dance-mime now in Amer. dictionaries; first performer to be presented in a theatrical performance, 1943, by Metropolitan Museum of Art, NYC; presented for her 25th Broadway (NY) season, 1959; a nationwide television broadcast, in US, presented a composite portrait of her work in theatre, painting, writing, 1959. London début, St Martin's Theatre, 1928; many subseq. British seasons including television. Paris début, 1929; Am. Rep. in Internat. Theatre Season presented by C. B. Cochran, Queen's Theatre, 1931. Rep. Am. Nat. Theatre and Acad., at Internat. Arts Festival, Berlin, and tour of W Germany. Guggenheim Foundation Fellowships, 1934 and 1935 (research in Greece, Egypt, Near East). Début exhibn of painting, NY, 1933, many subseq. Début exhibn of paintings in London, Eng., 1934 and subseq. Début exhibn of sculpture, New York, 1945; subseq. one-woman shows of painting and sculpture in US and Canada. Works are in Metropolitan Museum of Art, New York, etc. Painted mural, modern Penthouse Theatre of University of Washington, Seattle, 1950. Rep. in Exhibns, NY Museum of Modern Art, 1953. First work in Ceramics exhibited in New York and Los Angeles, 1953. Lecture tours US, 1954-. Prof. of Acting, Baylor Univ., Waco, Texas, and Director of plays, Dallas Theatre Center, Dallas, Texas, 1961-62. Fellow: Center for Advanced Studies, Wesleyan Univ., Middletown, Conn, 1962-; Pennsylvania State Univ., 1970. Films based on her original stories: Lost Angel, Tenth Avenue Angel, Silly Girl, 1944-47; You Belong to Me, 1950. Created and staged Commedia dell' Arte (play within play seq.) in film Scaramouche, 1951; Dir, also designer of stage settings and costumes, for play, Yerma, by G. Lorca (Broadway, NY, etc.), 1958. Plays produced: Love Possessed Juana, 1946; The Unknown Lover-A Modern Psyche, 1947. *Publications:* First Person Plural (self-illustr.), 1937; Love Possessed Juana (self-scored and illustr. play), 1939; Silly Girl (self-illustr. autobiog.), 1944; A Thing of Beauty (novel), 1948; The Flowering Bud (novel), 1955 (publ. London, 1956, as Among the Daughters); Artist's Life (self-illustrated), 1957; Artist's Life (publ. London, 1959); (trans.) Chantecler, by E. Rostand, 1960; Mime for Actors, 1961; The Loved and the Unloved (novel), 1961; Angna Enters on Mime, 1965; also illustrated Best American Short Stories of 1945; article on Pantomime, Encyclopædia Britannica. *Address:* 35 West 57th Street, NY 10019, USA.

ENTHOVEN, Roderick Eustace, FRIBA; FSA; architect in private practice; *b* 30 May 1900; *o* surv. *s* of late Ernest James Enthoven, Great Ote Hall, Wivelsfield, Sussex, and Rosaline Mary Eustace Smith; *m* 1933, Cecilia Mary Le Mesurier; three *s.* *Educ:* Clifton College. Received architectural education at Architectural Association Sch., 1919-24, qualifying with SADG Medal, Architectural Association Diploma. Partner in Enthoven & Mock; Partner in Pakington & Enthoven until war of 1939-45. Civil Camouflage Officer to Air Ministry, 1940-44; served in Italy as Monuments, Fine Arts and Archives Officer, 1944-45. Pres. Architectural Association, 1948-49; Vice-Pres. RIBA, 1951-53. Master of the Art Workers' Guild, 1976. *Publications:* contributor to various architectural journals. *Recreations:* theatre, foreign travel. *Address:* 3 Berkeley Gardens, Kensington Church Street, W8 4AP. *T:* 01-229 1482; 4 Raymond Buildings, Gray's Inn, WC1R 5BP. *Club:* Athenæum.

ENTWISTLE, Sir (John Nuttall) Maxwell, Kt 1963; Consultant Solicitor and Notary; Director of companies; Under-writing Member of Lloyd's since 1964; *b* 8 Jan. 1910; *s* of Isaac and Hannah Entwistle; *m* 1940, Jean Cunliffe McAlpine, *d* of late Dr John and Amy Margaret Penman; two *s.* *Educ:* Merchant Taylors' Sch., Great Crosby. Solicitor, 1931; Notary Public, 1955. Liverpool City: Councillor, 1938; Alderman, 1960; Leader of Liverpool City Council, when initiated preparation of develt plan for City centre. Chairman: Merseyside Development Cttee; Mersey Tunnel Cttee, 1961-63. Chairman: Abbeyfield Liverpool Soc. Ltd, 1970-75; Council of Management, League of Welldoers, 1972-74. Mem., Liverpool Univ. Court and Council, 1955-64. President: Edge Hill Liverpool Conservative Assoc., 1963-71; Liverpool Clerks Assoc., 1964-. Merchant Taylors' School: Chm., Appeal Cttee, 1969-74; Pres., Old Boys' Assoc., 1969-70; Governor, 1969-75. Chm., Lunesdale Foxhounds, 1977-78. *Recreations:* gardening, shooting. *Address:* Stone Hall, Sedbergh, Cumbria. *T:* Sedbergh 20700. *Clubs:* Old Hall (Liverpool); Royal Thames Yacht.

EPHRAUMS, Maj.-Gen. Roderick Jarvis, CB 1977; OBE 1965; Major-General Royal Marines, Commando Forces, 1976-78, retired; *b* 12 May 1927; *s* of Hugh Cyril Ephraums and Elsie Caroline (*née* Rowden); *m* 1955, Adela Mary (*née* Forster); two *s* one *d.* *Educ:* Tonbridge. Commnd 2nd Lieut, RM, 1945; HMS Mauritius, 1946-48; 3 Commando Bde, RM, 1952-54; Staff Coll., Camberley, 1960; Bde Major, 3 Commando Bde, 1962-64; CO, 45 Commando RM, 1969-71; Royal Coll. of Defence Studies, 1972; Comdr, 3 Commando Bde, 1973-74; NATO Defense Coll., Rome, 1975. *Recreations:* shooting, fishing, sailing. *Address:* Damside, Leysmill, by Arbroath, Angus. *T:* Friockheim 226. *Club:* Army and Navy.

EPSTEIN, Prof. (Michael) Anthony; Professor of Pathology and Head of Department, University of Bristol; also Hon. Consultant Pathologist, Bristol Health District (Teaching), since 1968; *b* 18 May 1921; *yr s* of Mortimer and Olga Epstein; *m* 1950, Lisbeth Knight; two *s* one *d.* *Educ:* St Paul's Sch., London; Trinity Coll., Cambridge (Perry Exhibr, 1940); Middlesex Hosp. Medical Sch. MA, MD, DSc, PhD; FRCPath. Ho. Surg., Middlesex Hosp., London, and Addenbrooke's Hosp., Cambridge, 1944; Lieut and Captain, RAMC, 1945-47; Asst Pathologist, Bland Sutton Inst., Mddx Hosp. Med. Sch., 1948-65, with leave as: Berkeley Travelling Fellow, 1952-53; French Govt Exchange Scholar at Institut Pasteur, Paris, 1952-53; Vis. Investigator, Rockefeller Inst., NY, 1956. Reader in Experimental Pathology, Mddx Hosp. Med. Sch., 1965-68; Hon. Consultant in Experimental Virology, Mddx Hosp., 1965-68. Major lectures: Edgar Allen Meml, Yale Univ., 1960; Kettle Meml, Royal Coll. of Pathologists, 1971; Distinguished Scientist Series, Tulane Univ., 1972; Sydney Watson Smith, RCPE, 1973; Collège de France, Paris, 1975; Long Fox Meml, Bristol, 1976; Chinese Acad. of Medical Scis, Peking, 1977. Member: Cttee, Pathological Soc. of GB and Ire., 1969-72; Council, and Vice-Pres., Pathology Section of RSM, 1966-72; Study Gp on Classification of Herpes Viruses, of Internat. Commn for Nomenclature of Viruses, 1971-; Scientific Adv. Bd, Harvard Med. Sch.'s New England Regional Primate Center, 1972-; MRC and Cancer Research Campaign Jt Cttee, 1973-; Cttee, British Soc. for Cell Biology, 1974-. Discovered in 1964 a new human herpes virus, now known as Epstein-Barr virus, which causes infectious mononucleosis and appears to be implicated in some forms of human cancer (Burkitt's lymphoma and nasopharyngeal carcinoma). Paul Ehrlich and Ludwig Darmstaedter Prize and Medal of W German Paul Ehrlich Foundn, 1973. *Publications:* over 110 scientific papers in internat. jls on tumour cell structure, viruses, tumour viruses, Burkitt's lymphoma, and the EB virus. Jt Founder Editor, The Internat. Review of Experimental Pathology (vols 1-17, 1962-77). *Address:* Department of Pathology, University of Bristol Medical School, University Walk, Bristol BS8 1TD. *T:* Bristol 24161 (ext 606).

ERDELYI, Prof. Arthur, FRS 1975; FRSE; Professor of Mathematics, University of Edinburgh, since 1964; *b* 2 Oct. 1908; *s* of Ignac Diamant and Friderike (*née* Roth); *m* 1942, Eva Neuburg; no *c.* *Educ:* Madách Imre Fögimnázium, Budapest; Deutsche Technische Hochscule, Brno; Universities of Prague and Edinburgh. Cand. Ing. (Brno) 1928; Dr rer. nat. (Prague) 1938; DSc (Edinburgh) 1940. Asst Lectr, then Sen. Lectr, University of Edinburgh, 1941-49; Vis. Prof. of Maths, Calif Inst. of Technology, 1947-48; Prof. of Maths, Calif Inst. of Techn., 1949-64; Vis. Professor: Hebrew Univ., Jerusalem, 1956-57; Univ. of Melbourne, 1970. Scientific Cons. to Admty during War of 1939-45. FRSE 1945; For. Mem., Acad. of Sciences, Turin, 1953. Gunning Victoria Jubilee Prize, RSE, 1977. *Publications:* (jtly) Higher Transcendental Functions, 3 vols, 1953-55; (jtly) Tables of Integral Transforms, 2 vols, 1954;

Asymptotic Expansions, 1956; Operational Calculus and Generalized Functions, 1962; past and present jt editor of several math. periodicals; contrib. research papers and reviews to encycls and math. jls. *Recreations:* music, walking. *Address:* Mathematics Department of the University, James Clerk Maxwell Building, The King's Buildings, Mayfield Road, Edinburgh EH9 3JZ. *T:* 031-667 1081.

EREAUT, Sir (Herbert) Frank (Cobbold), Kt 1976; Bailiff of Jersey, since 1975; Judge of the Court of Appeal in Guernsey, since 1976; *b* 6 May 1919; *s* of Herbert Parker Ereaut and May Julia Cobbold; *m* 1942, Kathleen FitzGibbon; one *d*. *Educ:* Tormore Sch., Upper Deal, Kent; Cranleigh Sch., Surrey; Exeter Coll., Oxford. BA 1946, MA 1966. RASC, 1940-46: N Africa, Italy and NW Europe; 2nd Lieut 1940; Lieut 1941; Captain 1943. Called to Bar, Inner Temple, 1947; Solicitor-General, Jersey, 1958-62, Attorney-General, 1962-69; Dep. Bailiff of Jersey, 1969-74. OStJ 1974. *Recreations:* music, gardening. *Address:* Les Cypres, St John, Jersey, Channel Islands. *T:* Central 22317.

ERICKSON, Prof. John; Professor of Politics, University of Edinburgh, since 1969; *b* 17 April 1929; *s* of Henry Erickson and Jessie (*née* Heys); *m* 1957, Ljubica (*née* Petrović); one *s* one *d*. *Educ:* South Shields High Sch.; St John's Coll., Cambridge (MA). Research Fellow, St Anthony's Coll., Oxford, 1956-58; Lectr, Dept of History, St Andrews Univ., 1958-62; Lectr, Sen. Lectr and Reader, Dept of Government, Univ. of Manchester, 1962-67; Visiting Prof., Russian Research Center, Univ. of Indiana, 1967; Reader, Lectr in Higher Defence Studies, Univ. of Edinburgh, 1967. *Publications:* The Soviet High Command 1918-1941, 1962; Storia dello Stato Maggiore Sovietico, 1963; ed, The Military-Technical Revolution, 1966; ed, The Armed Services and Society, 1970; Soviet Military Power, 1971; The Road to Stalingrad, 1975. *Recreations:* military models and music. *Address:* 13 Ravelston House Road, Edinburgh EH4 3LP. *T:* 031-332 1787.

ERKIN, Feridun Cemal, Hon. GBE; Minister of Foreign Affairs, Turkey, 1962-65; *b* 1899; *m* Madame Mukaddes Feridun Erkin (*d* 1955). *Educ:* Galatasaray Lyceum, Istanbul; Faculty of Law, University of Paris. First Sec., London, 1928-29; Chief of Section, Ankara, 1930-33; Counsellor and Chargé d'Affaires, Berlin, 1934-35; Consul-Gen., Beirut, 1935-37; Dir-Gen., Econ. Dept, Min. of Foreign Affairs, 1937; Dir-Gen., Polit. Dept, 1939; Asst Sec.-Gen., 1942; Deleg, UN Conf. San Francisco, 1945; Sec.-Gen. of Min., 1945; Chm. Turkish Delegn, final session of League of Nations, 1946; Ambassador to Italy, 1947-48; to USA, 1948-55; to Spain, 1955-57; to France, 1957-60; to the Court of St James's, 1960-62. Lately Senator. Turkish Governor to Internat. Banks, 1954; Mem. Internat. Diplomatic Academy, 1949-; Mem. Inst. of France, 1959-. Holds Grand Cross of several foreign Orders, including Grand Cross of the Legion of Honour of France. *Recreation:* classical music. *Address:* Sarayarkasi Sokak, Doğan Apartmani 24/9, Ayaspaşa, Istanbul, Turkey.

ERLANGER, L. F. A.; *see* d'Erlanger.

ERLEIGH, Viscount; Simon Charles Henry Rufus Isaacs; stockbroker; *b* 18 May 1942; *e s* and *heir* of 3rd Marquess of Reading, *qv. Educ:* Eton. Lieut in 1st Queen's Dragoon Guards, 1961-64. Mem. London Stock Exchange. *Address:* 3 Charlwood Place, SW1. *T:* 01-828 7382. *Club:* Cavalry and Guards.

ERNE, 6th Earl of, *cr* 1789; **Henry George Victor John Crichton,** DL, JP; Baron Erne 1768; Viscount Erne (Ireland), 1781; Baron Fermanagh (UK), 1876; *b* 9 July 1937; *s* of 5th Earl and Lady Katharine Cynthia Mary Millicent (Davina) Lytton (who *m* 1945, Hon. C. M. Woodhouse, *qv*), *yr d* of 2nd Earl of Lytton, KG, PC, GCSI, GCIE; *S* father, 1940; *m* 1958, Camilla Marguerite, *er d* of late Wing-Comdr Owen G. E. Roberts, and of Mrs Roberts, 30 Groom Place, Belgrave Square, SW1; one *s* four *d*. *Educ:* Eton. Page of Honour to the Queen, 1952-54 (to King George VI, 1952). Joined RN as Ord. Seaman, 1956; Lieut, North Irish Horse, 1959-66. Member: Royal Ulster Agricultural Society; Royal Forestry Society. DL, JP Co. Fermanagh. *Recreations:* sailing, shooting. *Heir: s* Viscount Crichton, *qv. Address:* Crom Castle, Newtown Butler, Co. Fermanagh. *T:* Newton-butler 208; 16 Chesham Mews, Belgrave Square, SW1. *Clubs:* White's, Turf; Royal Yacht Squadron (Cowes).
See also Duke of Abercorn.

ERRINGTON, Viscount; Evelyn Rowland Esmond Baring; *b* 3 June 1946; *e s* of 3rd Earl of Cromer, *qv; m* 1971, Plern Isarangkun Na Ayudhya, *e d* of Dr Charanphat Isarangkun Na Ayudhya, Thailand. *Educ:* Eton. Director: Exploration Holdings Inc.; Moray Petroleum & Development Co. Ltd; Lai

Tong Trading Co. Ltd; Asiaweek Ltd; Waco Corporation Ltd; Waco Corporation (Overseas) Ltd; Promotion Advisory Services Ltd. Mem. Council, St John Ambulance Assoc., Hong Kong. *Address:* GPO Box 2905, Hong Kong; 7B Bowen Road, Hong Kong. *T:* 5-236426, (office) 5-229179. *Clubs:* Turf, Oriental; Hong Kong, Royal Hong Kong Yacht (Hong Kong).

ERRINGTON, Col Sir Geoffrey (Frederick), 2nd Bt *cr* 1963; Colonel, The King's Regiment, since 1975; *b* 15 Feb. 1926; *er s* of Sir Eric Errington, 1st Bt, JP, and Marjorie (*d* 1973), *d* of A. Grant Bennett; *S* father, 1973; *m* 1955, Diana Kathleen Forbes, *o d* of late E. Barry Davenport, Edgbaston, Birmingham; three *s*. *Educ:* Rugby Sch.; New Coll., Oxford. psc 1958; AMBIM 1969. GSO 3 (Int.), HQ 11 Armd Div., 1950-52; GSO 3, MI3 (b), War Office, 1955-57; Bde Major 146 Inf. Bde, 1959-61; Coy Comdr, RMA Sandhurst, 1963-65; Military Assistant to Adjutant-General, 1965-67; CO 1st Bn, The King's Regt, 1967-69; GSO 1, HQ 1st British Corps, 1969-71; Col. GS, HQ NW District, 1971-74. Chm., The King's and Manchester Regts Assoc., 1971-75; AAG MI (Army) MoD, 1974-75; retired 1975. *Recreations:* sailing, skiing. *Heir: s* Robin Davenport Errington, *b* 1 July 1957. *Address:* Stone Hill Farm, Sellindge, Ashford, Kent TN25 6AJ. *T:* Sellindge 3191; 203A Gloucester Place, NW1 6BU. *Club:* Army and Navy.

ERRINGTON, Sir Lancelot, KCB 1976 (CB 1962); Second Permanent Secretary, Department of Health and Social Security, 1973-76; *b* 14 Jan. 1917; *e s* of late Major L. Errington; *m* 1939, Katharine Reine, *o d* of late T. C. Macaulay; two *s* two *d*. *Educ:* Wellington Coll.; Trinity Coll., Cambridge. Entered Home Office, 1939. Served RNVR, 1939-45. Transferred to Ministry of National Insurance, 1945; Principal Private Sec. to Minister of National Insurance, 1951; Asst Sec., 1953; Under-Sec., 1957-65; Cabinet Office, 1965-68; Min. of Social Security, 1968; Asst Under-Sec. of State, DHSS, 1968-71, Dep. Under-Sec. of State, 1971-73. *Recreation:* sailing. *Address:* St Mary's, Fasnacloich, Appin, Argyll. *T:* Appin 331.

ERRINGTON, Richard Percy, CMG 1955; Chartered Accountant (FCA); *b* 17 May 1904; 2nd *s* of Robert George Errington and Edna Mary Errington (*née* Warr); *m* 1935, Ursula, *d* of Henry Joseph Laws Curtis and Grace Barton Curtis (*née* Macgregor); one *d*. *Educ:* Sidcot Sch. Asst Treasurer, Nigeria Government, 1929-37; Colonial Administrative Service: Nigeria, 1937-46; Nyasaland, 1946-48; Financial Sec. to Govt of Aden Colony (also Mem. Bd of Trustees of Port of Aden), 1948-51; Chm., Aden Port Trust, 1951-60. Mem. Governor's Exec. Council, Aden, 1948-58. Unofficial Mem. Aden Colony Legislative Council, 1951-60 (Official Mem., 1948-51). Chairman: Aden Soc. for the Blind, 1951-60; Aden Lab. Advisory Bd, 1951-57. Area Comr, St John Amb. Bde, 1964-71. SBStJ, 1965. *Recreations:* golf, swimming, walking. *Address:* Whitecliffs, Wodehouse Road, Old Hunstanton, Norfolk. *T:* Hunstanton 2356.

ERROLL, Countess of, 23rd in line, *cr* 1452; **Diana Denyse Hay;** Lady Hay, 1429; Baroness of Slains, 1452; 27th Hereditary Lord High Constable of Scotland, *cr* 1314; Celtic title, Mac Garaidh Mhor; 32nd Chief of the Hays since 1171; Senior Great Officer, Royal Household in Scotland; OStJ 1949; *b* 5 Jan. 1926; *d* of 22nd Earl and Lady Idina Sackville (*d* 1955), *d* of 8th Earl De La Warr; *S* father 1941; *m* 1st, 1946, Sir Ian Moncreiffe of that Ilk, 11th Bt (marr. diss. 1964), *qv*; two *s* one *d*; 2nd, 1964, Major R. A. Carnegie; one *s. Heir: s* Lord Hay, *qv. Address:* Crimonmogate, Lonmay, Aberdeenshire. *T:* Lonmay 202.

ERROLL OF HALE, 1st Baron, *cr* 1964; **Frederick James Erroll,** PC 1960; MA, FIEE; FIMechE; Chairman, Bowater Corporation, since 1973; *b* 27 May 1914; *s* of George Murison Erroll, engineer, and Kathleen Donovan Edington, both of Glasgow and London; *m* 1950, Elizabeth, *o d* of R. Sowton Barrow, Exmouth, Devon. *Educ:* Oundle Sch.; Trinity Coll., Cambridge. Engineering Apprenticeship, 1931-32; Cambridge Univ., 1932-35; Engineer at Metropolitan-Vickers Electrical Co. Ltd, Manchester, 1936-38; Commissioned into 4th County of London Yeomanry (Sharpshooters), TA, 1939; technical appointments in connection with Tank Construction and Testing, 1940-43; service in India and Burma, 1944-45; Col 1945. MP (C) Altrincham and Sale, 1945-64. A Dir of Engineering and Mining Companies until April 1955; Parly Sec., Min. of Supply, April 1955-Nov. 1956; Parly Sec., BoT, 1956-58; Economic Sec. to the Treasury, Oct. 1958-59; Minister of State, BoT, 1959-61; Pres., BoT, 1961-63; Minister of Power, 1963-64. Chairman: ASEA Ltd; Consolidated Gold Fields Ltd; SF Air Treatment Ltd; Whessoe Ltd. Member: Council Inst. Directors, 1949-55, and 1965- (Chm. Council, 1973-76, Pres., 1976-); NEDC, 1962-63. President: London Chamber of Commerce, 1966-69; Hispanic and Luso-Brazilian Councils, 1969-73;

British Export Houses Assoc., 1969-72. Dep. Chm., Decimal Currency Board, 1966-71; Chm., Cttee on Liquor Licensing, 1971-72; Pres., Electrical Research Assoc., 1971-74; Chm., AA, 1974-. FRSA 1971. *Heir:* none. *Address:* 21 Ilchester Place, W14 8AA. *T:* 01-602 2195; Foxholes, Pinkneys Green, Maidenhead. *T:* Marlow 4197. *Club:* Carlton.

ERROLL, Master of; *see under* Hay, Lord.

ERSKINE; *see* St Clair-Erskine.

ERSKINE, family name of **Earls of Buchan** and **Mar and Kellie,** and of **Baron Erskine of Rerrick.**

ERSKINE OF RERRICK, 1st Baron, *cr* 1964; **John Maxwell Erskine,** Bt 1961; GBE 1956 (CBE 1946); Kt 1949; LLD; FRSE; DL, JP; Governor of Northern Ireland, 1964-68; General Manager, 1932-53, and Director, 1951-69, The Commercial Bank of Scotland Ltd, subsequently National Commercial Bank of Scotland, now absorbed in Royal Bank of Scotland; Member Queen's Body Guard for Scotland (Royal Company of Archers), since 1935; formerly Chairman, Securicor (Scotland) Ltd; formerly Director, Caledonian Insurance Co., Guardian Assurance Co., and other companies; President, Scottish Savings Committee, 1958-72 (Chairman, 1945-58); Chairman Scottish Hospital Endowments Research Trust (Hospital Endowments Scotland Act), 1953-71; Vice-President, Trustee Savings Banks Association; Foundn Mem., The Thistle Foundation; *b* 14 Dec. 1893; *s* of late John Erskine, Kirkcudbright; *m* 1922, Henrietta, CStJ, *d* of late William Dunnett, East Canisbay, Caithness; one *s* one *d. Educ:* Kirkcudbright Acad.; Edinburgh Univ. Admitted Solicitor; Pres. Inst. of Bankers in Scotland, 1937-40; Pres. Edinburgh Chamber of Commerce and Manufacturers, 1941-44 (Hon. Life Mem., 1968); First Chm. Central Cttee of Scottish Chambers of Commerce (now the Scottish Chamber of Commerce), 1942-44; Mem. Hetherington Deptl Cttee on Hospital Policy in Scotland, 1942; Chm. King George and Queen Elizabeth Officers' Club, Edinburgh, for Overseas Personnel under Empire Societies War Hosp. Cttee (War 1939-45), latterly Chm. Scottish Cttee (CBE); Mem. Postmaster General's Adv. Coun., 1945-49; Mem. Scottish Cttee on Scottish Financial and Trade Statistics (Catto Cttee), 1950-52; Chm. Transp. Users' Consultative Cttee for Scotland, 1954-57; Mem. Central Transp. Consultative Cttee, 1954-57; Mem. Scottish Transp. Council, 1955-56; Pres. Scottish Council of Social Service, 1949-57 (Chm. 1945-49); Pres. Edinburgh Union of Boys' Clubs, 1945-56; Trustee and Mem. Exec. Cttee Carnegie Trust for Scottish Univs, 1944-57; Mem. Cttee of Management, Royal Victoria Hosp. Tuberculosis Trust, 1944-56; Mem. Nat. Ref. Tribunal for Coal Mining Industry, 1956-59; Member: War Works Commn, 1945-59; N of Scotland Hydro-Electric Bd, 1948-59 (Dep. Chm. 1960, 1961). Hon. Life Mem., N Ireland Chamber of Commerce and Industry, 1968; Hon. Mem., Company of Merchants of City of Edinburgh, 1970. Freeman, Royal Burgh of Kirkcudbright, 1967. JP 1932, DL 1940, Edinburgh. FRSE 1933; Hon. FRCPE 1972. Hon. LLD: Glasgow, 1962; Queen's Univ., Belfast, 1968. KStJ 1965. *Heir: s* Major Hon. Iain Maxwell Erskine, *qv. Address:* The Croft, Westside, Churchfields Avenue, Weybridge, Surrey. *T:* Weybridge 54261. *Clubs:* New, Caledonian (Edinburgh) (Hon. Life Mem.).
See also Sir Robert George Erskine.

ERSKINE, Lord; James Thorne Erskine; Social Worker, Social Work Department, Grampian Regional Council, Elgin, since 1976; *b* 10 March 1949; *s* and *heir* of 13th Earl of Mar and 15th Earl of Kellie, *qv; m* 1974, Mrs Mary Mooney, *yr d* of Dougal McD. Kirk. *Educ:* Eton; Moray House Coll. of Education, 1968-71. Community Service Volunteer, York, 1967-68; Community Worker, Richmond-Craigmillar Parish Church, Edinburgh, 1971-73; Sen. Social Worker, Family and Community Services, Sheffield District Council, 1973-76. *Recreations:* hill walking, railways, gardening. *Address:* Claremont House, Alloa, Clackmannanshire. *T:* Alloa 2020; Birchfield, Nethy Bridge, Inverness-shire. *T:* Nethy Bridge 613. *Club:* Royal Over-Seas League.

ERSKINE, Sir David; *see* Erskine, Sir T. D.

ERSKINE, Sir George; *see* Erskine, Sir R. G.

ERSKINE, Hon. Iain Maxwell; advertising and public relations consultant; professional photographer; Director, Sibley, Thomson & Partners Ltd, Middle East consultants, and other companies; *b* 22 Jan. 1926; *o s* and *heir* of Baron Erskine of Rerrick, *qv; m* 1st, 1955, Marie Elisabeth (now Countess of Caledon) (marr. diss. 1964), *d* of Major Burton Allen, Benvhier House, Ballachulish; no *c* ; 2nd, 1974, Maria Josephine, *d* of late

Dr Joseph Klupt and of Mona Lilias Klupt, Sheen Gate Gardens, SW14; one *d*. *Educ:* Harrow. Served War of 1939-45: 2nd Lieut Grenadier Guards, 1945. ADC, RMA, 1951-52; Comptroller to Governor-Gen. of New Zealand, 1960-61; retd as Major, 1963. PRO to Household Bde, 1964-66. Associate Dir, Saward Baker & Co. Ltd (Advertising), 1967-. Chm., Guards Flying Club. MInstM, MIPR, Mem., Inst. of Dirs. Chevalier, Legion of Honour. OStJ. Chevalier, Chaîne des Rôtisseurs. *Recreations:* fishing, flying, food, photography. *Address:* 10 Chesham Place, SW1. *T:* 01-235 3489. *Club:* Cavalry and Guards.

ERSKINE, Ralph; architect; own practice (in Sweden since 1939, both on land and on a Thames Barge at Drottningholm; also at Byker, Newcastle upon Tyne); *b* 24 Feb. 1914; *s* of late George and Mildred Erskine; *m* 1939, Ruth Monica Francis; one *s* two *d. Educ:* Friends' Sch., Saffron Walden, Essex; Regent Street Polytechnic (architecture). ARIBA 1936; AMTPI 1938; SAR 1965. Won number of prizes in arch. comps in Sweden; one year's study at Academy for Fine Arts, Sweden, 1945. *Work executed:* town plans; workers' houses; co-operative housing and industrial housing; flats; hostels; factories; ski-hotel; shopping centre; school; town hall; hall of residence at Clare Coll., Cambridge; churches; housing estates at Newmarket and Killingworth; clearance scheme, Byker, Newcastle upon Tyne; design of new town, Resolute Bay, Canada; University Library, Stockholm. Lecturing: in America, Canada, Japan and many countries in Europe. Hon. Dr, Lund Univ., Sweden, 1975. For. Mem., Royal Acad. of Arts, Sweden, 1972. Hon Fellow of AIA, 1966; SAR's Kasper Sahlin prize for 1971; Ytong Prize, 1974. *Publications:* for several arch. magazines, on building in northern climates, etc. *Recreations:* ski-ing, skating, swimming, yachting, ice yachting, sailing barge Verona, etc. *Address:* Gustav III's väg, Drottningholm, Sweden. *T:* 7590352.

ERSKINE, Sir (Robert) George, Kt 1948; CBE 1945; Member of Directors' Advisory Committee of Morgan Grenfell & Co. Limited; Director: London & Provincial Trust Ltd (Chairman 1954-71); Alan Paine Ltd; Member of London Advisory Committee, Scottish Council (Development and Industry); Member Council, RAF Benevolent Fund; *b* 5 Nov. 1896; *s* of late John Erskine, Kirkcudbright; unmarried. *Educ:* Kirkcudbright Academy; Edinburgh Univ. (BL). On staff of National Bank of Scotland, 1913-29, when joined Morgan Grenfell; Director, 1945-67. Served European War, 1914-18. Dep. Chm. NAAFI, 1941-52; Pres. Institute of Bankers, 1954-56; Master of Glaziers' Company, 1960-61; Mem. Jenkins Cttee on Company Law, 1959-62. High Sheriff of Surrey, 1963-64. Mem., Law Soc. of Scotland. Freeman, City of London; Past Grand Senior Deacon, United Grand Lodge of England. *Address:* Busbridge Wood, Godalming, Surrey. *T:* Hascombe 378. *Clubs:* Caledonian, City of London.
See also Baron Erskine of Rerrick.

ERSKINE, Sir (Thomas) David, 5th Bt, *cr* 1821; JP; DL; Convener, Fife County Council, 1970-73; *b* 31 July 1912; *o surv. s* of Sir Thomas Wilfred Hargreaves John Erskine, 4th Bt, and late Magdalen Janet, *d* of Sir Ralph Anstruther, 6th Bt of Balcaskie; *S* father, 1944; *m* 1947, Ann, *er d* of late Lt-Col Neil Fraser-Tytler, DSO, MC, and of Christian Helen Fraser-Tytler, CBE, *qv* ; two *s* (and one *d* decd). *Educ:* Eton; Magdalene Coll., Cambridge. Employed by Butterfield & Swire, London and China, in 1934 and served with them in China, 1935-41. Joined HM Forces in India and commissioned into Indian Corps of Engineers. Served with them in Mid-East, India and Malaya, being demobilised in 1945 with rank of Major. JP Fife, 1951; DL Fife, 1955. *Heir: s* Thomas Peter Neil Erskine [*b* 28 March 1950; *m* 1972, Catherine, *d* of Col G. H. K. Hewlett]. *Address:* West Newhall House, Kingsbarns, Fife. *T:* Crail 228. *Club:* New (Edinburgh).

ERSKINE-HILL, Sir Robert, 2nd Bt, *cr* 1945; Member of the Royal Company of Archers, Queen's Body Guard for Scotland; Chartered Accountant; partner in firm of Chiene and Tait, Chartered Accountants, Edinburgh; *b* 6 Feb. 1917; *er s* of Sir Alexander Galloway Erskine-Hill, 1st Bt, KC, DL, and Christian Hendrie, MBE (*d* 1947), *o d* of John Colville, MP, Cleland, Lanarkshire; *S* father, 1947; *m* 1942, Christine Alison, *o d* of late Capt. (A) Henry James Johnstone of Alva, RN; two *s* two *d. Educ:* Eton; Trinity Coll., Cambridge (BA). Served War of 1939-45, in RNVR. *Heir: s* Alexander Roger Erskine-Hill, *b* 15 Aug. 1949. *Address:* Quothquhan Lodge, Biggar, Lanarkshire. *T:* Tinto 332.

ERSKINE-LINDOP, Audrey Beatrice Noël; novelist; *b* London; *d* of late Lt-Col A. H. Erskine-Lindop, MC, and of Ivy Monck-Mason; *m* 1945, Dudley Gordon Leslie, scriptwriter and playwright. *Educ:* Convent of Our Lady of Lourdes, Hatch End,

Middx; Blackdown Sch., Wellington, Somerset. Started career in Worthing Repertory Company; became scriptwriter (England and Hollywood). Books have been published in numerous countries. *Plays:* Beware of Angels (in collaboration with Dudley Leslie), prod Westminster Theatre, 1959; Let's Talk Turkey, prod 1955. Freeman of City of London, 1954. *Publications:* In Me My Enemy, 1948; Soldiers' Daughters Never Cry, 1949; The Tall Headlines, 1950; Out of the Whirlwind, 1951; The Singer Not the Song, 1953 (Book Society choice; filmed, 1961); Details of Jeremy Stretton, 1955; The Judas Figures, 1956; I Thank a Fool, 1958; The Way to the Lantern, 1961; Nicola, 1964; I Start Counting, 1966 (Prix Roman Policier, France, 1968); Sight Unseen, 1969; Journey into Stone, 1973; The Self-Appointed Saint, 1975. *Recreations:* history (particularly collecting relics of favourite historical characters); anything to do with birds and cats; very fond of the wilder type of countryside; favourite music: bag pipes. *Address:* Gray Tiles, Niton Undercliff, IoW PO38 2NA. *T:* Niton 730291; Kestorway, Chagford, South Devon. *T:* Chagford 2157. *Clubs:* Ghost, Pen.

ERSKINE-MURRAY, family name of **Lord Elibank.**

ERTZ, Susan, FRSL; writer; *d* of Charles Edward Ertz and Mary Gertrude Le Viness of New York; *m* 1932, Major J. Ronald McCrindle, CMG, OBE, MC (*d* 1977). *Publications:* Novels: Madam Claire; Nina; Afternoon; Now East, Now West; The Galaxy; Julian Probert, Face to Face (short stories); The Proselyte, 1933; Now We Set Out, 1934; Woman Alive, 1935; No Hearts to Break, 1937; Big Frogs and Little Frogs (short stories), 1938; Black, White, and Caroline (for children), 1938; One Fight More, 1940; Anger in the Sky, 1943; Two Names upon the Shore, 1947; The Prodigal Heart, 1950; The Undefended Gate, 1953; Charmed Circle, 1956; In the Cool of the Day, 1961; Devices and Desires, 1972; The Philosopher's Daughter, 1976; contributions to various periodicals. *Recreations:* painting, gardening, travel. *Address:* 17 Sloane Court West, SW3. *T:* 01-730 6361; Lossenham Manor, Newenden, Hawkhurst, Kent. *T:* Northiam 2196.

ERVINE-ANDREWS, Lieut-Col Harold Marcus, VC 1940; East Lancashire Regiment, retired; *b* 29 July 1911; *s* of late C. C. Ervine-Andrews, New Ross, Wexford, Southern Ireland; *m* 1939, Betty, *er d* of R. I. Torrie; one *s* one *d. Educ:* Stonyhurst Coll.; Royal Military Coll., Sandhurst. 2nd Lieut East Lancs Regt, 1932; Captain 1940; Temp. Major, 1940; War Subst. Major, 1942; Temp. Lieut-Col 1942; served with RAF during North-West Frontier of India Operations, 1936-37 (medal and two clasps, despatches) and NW Frontier, 1938-39; served in France with BEF (VC); attached to RAF in UK, 1940; on loan to Australian Military Forces, 1941; attached RAAF, 1942; GSO 1 Air HQ Allied Land Forces in South-West Pacific Area, 1943; commanding No. 61 Carrier-Borne Army Liaison Section, 1944; SALO in 21st Aircraft Carrier Squadron (East Indies), 1945; Lieut-Col Commanding No. 18 Infantry Holding Bn, 1946; attached to The Army Mobile Information Unit, 1948; Asst Dir of Public Relations to BAOR, 1951, as a Lieut-Col; retired pay, 1952. *Address:* Butterwell, Nanstallon, Bodmin, Cornwall. *T:* Lanivet 515.

ESAKI, Leo; IBM Fellow since 1967; Manager, Device Physics, IBM T. J. Watson Research Center, since 1962; *b* 12 March 1925; *s* of Soichiro Esaki and Niyoko Ito; *m* 1959, Masako Araki; one *s* two *d. Educ:* Univ. of Tokyo. MS 1947, PhD 1959. Sony Corp., Japan, 1956-60; IBM Research, 1960-. Research in tunnelling in semiconductor junctions which led to the discovery of the tunnel diode, now working on man-made semiconductor superlattice in search of predicted quantum mechanical effect. Councillor-at-Large, Amer. Phys. Soc., 1971; Dir, Amer. Vacuum Soc., 1972; Mem., Japan Academy, 1975; For. Associate, Nat. Acad. of Sciences, USA, 1976; For. Associate, Nat. Acad. of Engineering, USA, 1977. Nishina Meml Award, 1959; Asahi Press Award, 1960; Toyo Rayon Foundn Award, 1961; Morris N. Liebmann Meml Prize, 1961; Stuart Ballantine Medal, Franklin Inst., 1961; Japan Academy Award, 1965; Nobel Prize for Physics (jtly), 1973. Order of Culture, Japan, 1974. *Publications:* numerous papers in learned jls. *Address:* IBM Thomas J. Watson Research Center, PO Box 218, Yorktown Heights, New York 10598, USA. *T:* (914) 945-2342.

ESCRITT, Charles Ewart, OBE 1970; MA; Secretary, Oxford University Appointments Committee, 1947-70; Fellow, Keble College, Oxford, 1965-70; *b* 26 Aug. 1905; *s* of late Rev. Charles Escritt; *m* 1939, Ruth Mary, *d* of late T. C. Metcalf; two *s* one *d. Educ:* Christ's Hospital; Keble Coll., Oxford. Asst Master, Bromsgrove Sch., 1928; Staff of Tootal Broadhurst Lee Co. Ltd, 1933-46. Served War of 1939-45: 42 Div. RASC (TA), 1939; 18 Div. RASC, Capt. 1940; POW, Singapore and Thailand, 1942-

45. *Recreation:* Japanese studies. *Address:* 32 Portland Road, Oxford. *T:* Oxford 57072.

ESCRITT, Maj.-Gen. Frederick Knowles, CB 1953; OBE 1943; MRCS; late RAMC, retired Nov. 1953; *b* 29 Nov. 1893; *s* of Harold Teal Escritt; *m* 1931, Elsa Alfrida, *d* of Director Larssen, Stockholm; one *d. Educ:* Dulwich Coll.; Guy's Hosp. MRCS, LRCP, 1918. Joined RAMC, Nov. 1918 (1914-15 Star, British War and Victory Medals). Served War of 1939-45 (Gen. Service Iraq, 1939-45 Star, Burma Star, Defence and War Medals, 1939-45). ADMS Eastern and 14 Armies, 1942-45; DDMS 1 Corps Dist, BAOR, 1945-47; Inspector of Training, AMS, 1950-51; DDMS, Eastern Command, 1951-53. QHS, 1952-53. Order of St John (Officer Brother), 1952. *Address:* 31 Pine Bank, Hindhead, Surrey. *Club:* Royal Automobile.

ESDAILE, Philippa Chichele, DSc, FLS; Reader in Biology, University of London, and Head of Biology Department, King's College of Household and Social Science, 1921-51; *b* 1888; *y d* of late George Esdaile, Manchester and late Georgina, *d* of George Doswell, Somerset. *Educ:* Manchester High Sch. for Girls. Graduated Univ. of Manchester, 1910; Research Fellow of University of Manchester and University Coll., Reading; Acting Head of Zoology Dept, Bedford Coll., University of London, 1915-20; Senior Lecturer in Zoology, Birkbeck Coll., University of London, 1920-21; Vice-Pres. of Linnean Soc. of London, 1932-33; Member: Makerere-Khartoum Education Commission, 1937; Advisory Committee on Education, Colonial Office, 1933-38; Committee on Nutrition in the Colonial Empire, Econ. Adv. Coun., 1933; Federation of Univ. Women; Crosby Hall. Formerly Mem. of Coun. of Girls' Public Day Sch. Trust, Ltd. Mem., Governing Body of Hatfield Sch., Herts. *Publications:* Economic Biology for Students of Social Science, Parts 1 and 2; various scientific papers. *Address:* Mansard Gables, Burnham Green Road, Tewin, Herts.

ESDALE, Mrs G. P. R.; *see* Lindop, Patricia J.

ESHELBY, Prof. John Douglas, FRS 1974; Professor of the Theory of Materials, University of Sheffield, since 1971; *b* 21 Dec. 1916; *s* of Alan Douglas and Doris Mason Eshelby; unmarried. *Educ:* privately; Univ. of Bristol. BSc, MA, PhD. Temp. Exper. Officer, HMS Vernon, 1939-40; RAF, 1940-46; res. worker, Univ. of Bristol, 1946-52; Res. Assoc., Univ. of Illinois, 1952-54; Lectr, Univ. of Birmingham, 1954-64; res. worker, Cavendish Lab., Univ. of Cambridge, 1964-66; Fellow of Churchill Coll., 1965-66; Reader, Univ. of Sheffield, 1966-71. Vis. Prof., Technische Hochschule, Stuttgart, 1963. *Publications:* articles on lattice defects and continuum mechanics in various learned jls. *Address:* 9 Beech Court, Beech Hill Road, Sheffield S10 2SA.

ESHER, 4th Viscount, *cr* 1897; Baron *cr* 1885; **Lionel Gordon Baliol Brett,** CBE 1970; MA; PPRIBA; FILA; Rector and Vice-Provost, Royal College of Art, 1971-Aug. 1978; *b* 18 July 1913; *o s* of 3rd Viscount Esher, GBE; *S* father, 1963; *m* 1935, Christian, *e d* of late Col Ebenezer Pike, CBE, MC; five *s* one *d. Educ:* Eton (Scholar); New Coll., Oxford (Scholar). BA (1st Class), 1935; RIBA Ashpitel Prizeman, 1939. Served War in RA, 1940-45; France and Germany, 1944-45 (despatches); Major. Architect Planner, Hatfield New Town, 1949-59; major housing projects: Hatfield, Stevenage, Basildon, Southampton; consultant architect: Downside Abbey; Maidenhead Town Centre; Abingdon Town Centre; Portsmouth City Centre; York City Centre; Santiago, Chile and Caracas, Venezuela (both for UNDP). Lecture tours: USA 1953; India, 1954; Australia, 1959; S America, 1970. Governor, Museum of London; Member: Royal Fine Art Commn, 1951-69; Adv. Bd for Redundant Churches (Chm., 1977-); Advisory Council, Victoria and Albert Museum, 1967-72; Arts Council of GB, 1972- (Chm., Art Panel); Vice-Pres., RIBA, 1958-59, 1962-63, 1964-65; Pres., 1965-67; Trustee, Soane Museum. Hon. DLitt Strathclyde Univ., 1967; Hon. DUniv York, 1970. Hon. Fellow, Amer. Inst. of Architects. *Publications:* Houses, 1947; The World of Architecture, 1963; Landscape in Distress, 1965; York: a study in conservation, 1969; Parameters and Images, 1970; (with Elisabeth Beazley) Shell Guide to North Wales, 1971. *Recreation:* landscapes. *Heir:* s Hon. Christopher Lionel Baliol Brett [*b* 23 Dec. 1936; *m* 1st, 1962, Camilla Charlotte (marr. diss. 1970), *d* of Sir (Horace) Anthony Rumbold, 10th Bt, *qv*; one *s* two *d*; 2nd, 1971, Valerie Harrington; one *s* twin *d*]. *Address:* Christmas Common Tower, Watlington, Oxford. *Club:* Athenæum.

See also Sir Martyn G. Beckett, Sir Evelyn Shuckburgh.

ESMONDE, Sir Anthony Charles, 15th Bt, *cr* 1629; *b* 18 Jan. 1899; 3rd *s* of Dr John Esmonde, MP; *S* brother (Capt. Sir John Lymbrick Esmonde, Bt) 1958; *m* 1927, Eithne Moira Grattan, *y* *d* of Sir Thomas Grattan Esmonde, 11th Bt; three *s* three *d*. *Educ:* Clongowes Wood Coll.; Germany. Surgeon Lieut, RN, 1921-25; LRCS & P Ireland, 1921. TD Wexford, 1951-73; Consultative Assembly, Council of Europe, 1954 (Cttees of Agriculture and Non-represented nations); Mem. Irish National Health Council, 1956. Mem. Catholic Truth Soc. of Ireland, 1936. Mem. Royal Dublin Soc., 1938. Knight of Honour and Devotion, Order of Malta, 1957. *Recreations:* agriculturist; fishing, shooting, etc. *Heir: e s* John Henry Grattan Esmonde, SC, TD [*b* 27 June 1928; *m* 1957, Pamela Mary, *d* of late Francis Stephen Bourke, FRCPI; three *s* two *d*. SC 1971; TD (Fine Gael) Wexford, 1973-]. *Address:* Ballynastragh, Gorey, Co. Wexford, Eire. *T:* Arklow 7182.

ESPLEN, Sir William Graham, 2nd Bt, *cr* 1921; Shipowner; *b* 29 Dec. 1899; *s* of 1st Bt and Laura Louise (*d* 1936), *d* of late John Dickinson, Sunderland; *S* father, 1930; *m* 1928, Aline Octavia (marr. diss. 1951), *y d* of late A. Octavius Hedley; one *s*. *Educ:* Harrow; Cambridge. Joined Royal Naval College, Keyham, 1918; retired, 1922. *Recreation:* fishing. *Heir: s* John Graham Esplen [*b* 4 Aug. 1932; *m* 1956, Valerie Joan, *yr d* of Maj.-Gen. A. P. Lambooy, CB, OBE, and late Doris Lambooy; one *s* three *d*]. *Address:* Heron Bridge, Newsham, Richmond, Yorks. *Club:* Royal Automobile.

ESPLIN, Air Vice-Marshal Ian (George), CB 1963; OBE 1946; DFC 1943; retired (voluntarily) 1965; *b* 26 Feb. 1914; *s* of late Donald Thomas Esplin and Emily Freame Esplin; *m* 1944, Patricia Kaleen Barlow; one *s* one *d*. *Educ:* Sydney Univ.; Oxford Univ. BEc 1936; MA 1939. Rowing Blue, 1934 and 1935. NSW Rhodes Schol., 1937. Entered RAF from Oxford, 1939. Served War of 1939-45, as Pilot in Night-Fighters; destroyed three enemy aircraft at night; also served at CFS and in HQ, SEAC; Air Min. (Policy), 1945; Comd Desford, 1947; Dep. Senior Personnel Staff Officer, HQ Reserve Comd, 1948; Directing Staff, RAF Staff Coll., 1950-51; Comd first Jet All Weather Wing, Germany (No 148), 1952-54; Flying Coll. Course, 1954; Dep. Dir of Operational Requirements, Air Min., 1955-58; Comd RAF Wartling, 1958-60; Dir of Operational Reqts, 1960-62; Comdr, RAF Staff and Air Attaché, Washington, DC, 1963-65; Dean, Air Attaché Corps, 1964-65. *Recreations:* golf, tennis, swimming, ski-ing. *Address:* c/o National Westminster Bank Ltd, West End Office, 1 St James's Square, SW1. *Clubs:* Vincent's (Oxford); Leander (Henley-on-Thames).

ESSAAFI, M'hamed, Grand Officier, Order of Tunisian Republic, 1963; Secretary-General, Ministry of Foreign Affairs, Tunis, 1969-70 and since 1976; *b* 26 May 1930; *m* 1956, Hedwige Klat; one *s* one *d*. *Educ:* Sadiki Coll., Tunis; Sorbonne, Paris. Secretariat of State for For. Affairs, 1956; 1st Sec., Tunisian Embassy, London, 1956; 1st Sec., Tunisian Embassy, Washington, 1957; Secretariat of State for For. Affairs, Tunis: Dir of Amer. Dept, 1960; America and Internat. Confs Dept, 1962; Ambassador to London, 1964-69; Ambassador to Moscow, 1970-74; Ambassador to Bonn, 1974-76. *Recreation:* shooting. *Address:* Ministry of Foreign Affairs, Tunis, Tunisia.

ESSAME, Enid Mary, MA Cantab; JP; Headmistress of Queenswood School, 1943-71; 2nd *d* of Oliver Essame. *Educ:* Wyggeston Gram. Sch., Leicester; Girls' High Sch., Newark; Newnham Coll., Cambridge (Hist. Tripos, 1928); King's Coll., University of London (Certificate of Education, 1929). Mary Ewart Travelling Scholar, Newnham Coll., 1934-35; AM in Education, American Univ., Washington, DC, USA, 1935. Asst Headmistress Queenswood Sch., 1935-43. British Council lecturer, India and Pakistan, 1953, Nigeria, 1961. Governor, Chorleywood Coll. for Girls with Little or No Sight, 1962. Hon. Sec. Assoc. of Headmistresses of Boarding Schools, Pres. 1962-64. Chm., Assoc. of Ind. and Direct Grant Schools. Governor: St Helen's Sch., Northwood; Channing Sch., Highgate; Trustee, Stormont Sch., Potter's Bar. JP Herts 1952-. *Address:* 4 Elmroyd Avenue, Potters Bar, Herts. *T:* Potters Bar 53255. *Clubs:* Royal Over-Seas League, Arts Theatre.

ESSAYAN, Michael, QC 1976; *b* 7 May 1927; *s* of Kevork Loris Essayan and late Rita Sirvarte (*née* Gulbenkian); *m* 1956, Geraldine St Lawrence Lee Guinness, *d* of K. E. L. Guinness, MBE; one *s* one *d* . *Educ:* France; Harrow; Balliol Coll., Oxford (1st Cl. Class. Hon. Mods 1949, 1st Cl. Lit. Hum. 1951, MA). Served with RA, 1945-48 (Palestine, 1947-48). Iraq Petroleum Co., London and ME, 1951-56. Called to the Bar, Middle Temple 1957, joined Lincoln's Inn *ad eundem* 1958. *Publications:* The New Supreme Court Costs (with M. J. Albery, QC), 1960; (ed with Hon. Mr Justice Walton) Adkin's Landlord and Tenant, 15th, 16th and 17th edns. *Recreations:* wine and wife. *Address:* 6 Chelsea Square, SW3. *T:* 01-352 6786; 9 Old Square, Lincoln's Inn, WC2. *T:* 01-405 0846. *Club:* Brooks's.

ESSEN, Louis, OBE 1959; FRS 1960; DSc, PhD; retired; *b* 6 Sept. 1908; *s* of Fred Essen and Ada (*née* Edson); *m* 1937, Joan Margery Greenhalgh; four *d*. *Educ:* High Pavement Sch., Nottingham; London Univ. (Ext.). BSc 1928, PhD 1941, DSc 1948, London. Joined the National Physical Laboratory, 1929; Senior Principal Scientific Officer, 1956-60; Deputy Chief Scientific Officer, 1960-72. Charles Vernon Boys Prize, Phys. Soc. 1957; Tompion Gold Medal, Clockmakers' Company, 1957; Wolfe Award, 1959; A. S. Popov Gold Medal, USSR Acad. of Sciences, 1959. Hon. FUMIST, 1971. *Publications:* Velocity of Light and Radio Waves, 1969; The Special Theory of Relativity, 1971; scientific papers. *Recreations:* walking, gardening, music. *Address:* High Hallgarth, 41 Durleston Park Drive, Great Bookham, Surrey KT23 4AJ. *T:* Bookham 54103.

ESSENDON, 2nd Baron, *cr* 1932, of Essendon; **Brian Edmund Lewis;** 2nd Bt, *cr* 1918; *b* 7 Dec. 1903; *s* of 1st Baron and Eleanor (*d* 1967), *d* of R. H. Harrison of West Hartlepool; *S* father, 1944; *m* 1938, Mary, *widow* of Albert Duffil and *d* of late G. W. Booker, Los Angeles. *Educ:* Malvern; Pembroke Coll., Cambridge. *Recreation:* golf. *Address:* Avenue Eglantine 5, Lausanne 1006, Switzerland. *T:* 23.58.97. *Club:* Bath.

ESSEX, 9th Earl of, *cr* 1661; **Reginald George de Vere Capell,** TD; Baron Capel, 1641; Viscount Malden, 1661; *b* 9 Oct. 1906; *o s* of 8th Earl of Essex and Mary Eveline (*d* 1955), *d* of late W. R. Stewart Freeman; *S* father, 1966; *m* 1st, 1937, Mrs Mary Reeve Strutt (marr. diss. 1957), *d* of Gibson Ward, Bermuda; 2nd, 1957, Nona Isobel (*née* Miller), Christchurch, NZ (*widow* of Frank Smythe). *Educ:* Eton; Cambridge. Lt-Col, 1947; Commanded 16th Airborne Div., Signals Regt (TA), 1948. Hon. Col 47 Signals Regt, Mddx Yeo., 1957. *Heir: kinsman* Robert Edward de Vere Capell [*b* 13 Jan. 1920; *m* 1942, Doris Margaret, *d* of G. F. Tomlinson; one *s*]. *Address:* Floyds Farm, Wingrave, Aylesbury, Bucks. *T:* Aston Abbotts 220. *Clubs:* Bath, MCC.

ESSEX, Francis William, CMG 1959; retired from HMOCS; *b* 29 June 1916; *s* of Frank Essex; *m* 1947, Marjorie Muriel Joyce Lewis; two *s*. *Educ:* Royal Grammar Sch., High Wycombe; Reading Univ.; Exeter Coll., Oxford. Joined Colonial Administrative Service, Sierra Leone, 1939; Asst District Commissioner, 1942; District Commissioner, 1948; Principal, HM Treasury, 1951; Dep. Financial Sec., Sierra Leone, 1953; Financial Sec., British Guiana, 1956-60; Financial Sec. to High Comr for Basutoland, Bechuanaland and Swaziland, 1960-64; Counsellor, British Embassy, South Africa, 1964-65; Sec. for Finance and Development, later Permanent Sec., Min. of Finance, Commerce and Industry, Swaziland, 1965-68; Principal, ODM, 1968-76. Mem., Pearce Commn on Rhodesian opinion, 1971-72. *Address:* c/o Barclays Bank, High Street, High Wycombe, Bucks.

ESSEX, Mary; *see* Bloom, Ursula.

ESSEX, Rosamund Sibyl, MA; Member of Staff, Christian Aid, British Council of Churches, since 1960; *b* 26 July 1900; *d* of late Rev. Herbert J. Essex and late Rachel Watson; unmarried; one adopted *s*. *Educ:* Bournemouth High Sch. for Girls; St Hilda's Coll., Oxford. Editorial staff of the Church Times, 1929-47; Asst Ed., 1947-50; Editor, 1950-60. Chm. Religious Press Group, 1952-53 and 1957-58. Commissioned and licensed a Reader in the Church of England, dio. St Albans, 12 July 1969. *Publications:* (with Sidney Dark) The War Against God, 1937; Into the Forest, 1963; Woman in a Man's World (autobiog.), 1977. *Recreation:* photography. *Address:* 32 Holywell Hill, St Albans, Herts AL1 1BZ. *T:* St Albans 53424. *Club:* Royal Commonwealth Society.

ESSLEMONT, Mary, CBE 1955; MA, BSc, MB, ChB, DPH, LLD, JP; *d* of late George Birnie Esslemont, MP for South Aberdeen. *Educ:* Aberdeen High Sch. for Girls; Aberdeen Univ. Asst, Botany Dept, University of Aberdeen, 1915-17; Science Lecturer, Stockwell Training Coll., London, 1917-19; Asst MOH, Keighley, Yorks, 1924-29; Gen. Practitioner, Aberdeen, 1929, now retired. Fellow: BMA, 1959; RCGP, 1969. Mem., Aberdeen Univ. Court, 1947-74. Hon. LLD, University of Aberdeen, 1954. JP for County of City of Aberdeen. *Recreation:* travel. *Address:* Mile End House, 30 Beechgrove Terrace, Aberdeen AB2 4ED. *T:* 53601. *Club:* Soroptimist Headquarters.

ESSLIN, Martin Julius, OBE 1972; Professor of Drama, Stanford University, California (for two quarters annually), since 1977; *b* 8 June 1918; *s* of Paul Pereszlenyi and Charlotte Pereszlenyi (*née* Schiffer); *m* 1947, Renate Gerstenberg; one *d*. *Educ:* Gymnasium, Vienna; Vienna Univ.; Reinhardt Seminar of Dramatic Art, Vienna. Naturalized, 1947. Joined BBC, 1940; Producer and Scriptwriter, BBC European Services, 1941-55; Asst Head, BBC European Productions Dept, 1955; Asst Head,

Drama (Sound), BBC, 1961; Head of Drama (Radio), BBC, 1963-77. Awarded title Professor by Pres. of Austria, 1967; Vis. Prof. of Theatre, Florida State Univ., 1969-76. *Publications:* Brecht, A Choice of Evils, 1959; The Theatre of the Absurd, 1962; (ed) Beckett (anthology of critical essays), 1965; Harold Pinter, 1967; The Genius of the German Theatre, 1968; Reflections, Essays on Modern Theatre (NY), 1969 (UK, as Brief Chronicles, 1970); The Peopled Wound: the plays of Harold Pinter, 1970, rev. edn as Pinter: a study of his plays, 1973; (ed) The New Theatre of Europe, 1970; Artaud, 1976; An Anatomy of Drama, 1976. *Recreations:* reading, book collecting. *Address:* 64 Loudoun Road, NW8. *T:* 01-722 4243; Ballader's Plat, Winchelsea, Sussex. *T:* Winchelsea 392; c/o Department of Drama, Stanford University, Stanford, Calif. 94305, USA. *Club:* Garrick.

ESSWOOD, Paul Lawrence Vincent; singer (counter-tenor); Professor, Royal College of Music, since 1973; *b* West Bridgford, Nottingham, 6 June 1942; *s* of Alfred Walter Esswood and Freda Garratt; *m* 1966, Mary Lillian Cantrill, ARCM; two *s. Educ:* West Bridgford Grammar Sch.; Royal Coll. of Music (ARCM). Lay-Vicar, Westminster Abbey, 1964-71. Specialist in baroque performance; has made recordings of Bach, Handel, Purcell, Monteverdi, Cavalli, etc; first broadcast, BBC, 1965; co-founder: Pro Cantione Antiqua; A Cappella Male Voice Ensemble for Performance of Old Music, 1967; operatic debut in Cavalli's L'Erismena, Univ. of California, Berkeley, 1968; performed in major festivals: Edinburgh, Leeds Triennial, English Bach, Vienna, Salzburg, Naples, Israel, Lucerne, Flanders, Wexford, Holland. *Recreations:* philately, sports, aquariology. *Address:* 6 Gowan Avenue, SW6 6RF. *T:* 01-736 3141.

ESTCOURT, Maj.-Gen. Edward Noel Keith, DSO 1944; OBE 1945; psc; *b* 17 Dec. 1905; *s* of E. A. Estcourt, Gloucester and B. M. Carr-Calthorp, Norfolk; *m* 1938, Pamela Wellesley; two *s* one *d. Educ:* Cheltenham Coll.; RMA Woolwich. Commissioned RA, 1925. Served War of 1939-45: N Africa, Italy and Greece. Staff Coll., Camberley, 1940; GSO1 1st Inf. Div., 1944-45; GSO1 4th Inf. Div., 1945-46. Dep. Dir Mil. Ops, War Office, 1951-55; Dep. Comdt, NATO Defence Coll., 1955-57; Commandant, NATO Defence Coll., Paris, 1958. Principal, Ashridge Coll., 1958-62. Bronze Star, USA, 1945. *Recreations:* shooting, fishing, golf. *Address:* Trip The Daisy, Idstone, Swindon, Wilts.

ESTES, Elliott M.; President and Chief Operating Officer, General Motors Corporation, Detroit, USA, since 1974; *b* Mendon, Mich. General Motors Corporation: Chief Engr, Pontiac Motor Div., 1956-61; Gen. Manager and Corp. Vice-Pres., 1961-65; Vice-Pres. and Gen. Manager, Chevrolet, 1965-69; Gp Exec., Car and Truck Gp, 1969-70; Gp Vice-Pres., Overseas Operations, 1970-72; Exec. Vice-Pres., Operations Staff and Dir, 1972-74. *Address:* 3044 West Grand Boulevard, Detroit, Mich 48202, USA.

ESTYN EVANS, Emyr; see Evans, E. E.

ETHERINGTON-SMITH, (Raymond) Gordon (Antony), CMG 1962; HM Diplomatic Service; retired; *b* 1 Feb. 1914; *o s* of late T. B. Etherington-Smith and Henriette de Pitner; *m* 1950, Mary Elizabeth Besly; one *s* three *d. Educ:* Downside; Magdalen Coll., Oxford. Entered FO, 1936. Served at: Berlin, 1939; Copenhagen, 1939-40; Washington, 1940-42; Chungking, 1943-45; Kashgar, 1945-46; Moscow, 1947; Foreign Office, 1947-52; Holy See, 1952-54; Counsellor, Saigon, 1954-57; The Hague, 1958-61; Office of UK Commissioner-Gen. for South-East Asia, Singapore, 1961-63; Ambassador to Vietnam, 1963-66; Minister, and Dep. Commandant, Berlin, 1966-70; Ambassador to Sudan, 1970-74. *Recreations:* fishing, squash rackets, travel. *Address:* The Old Rectory, Melbury Abbas, Shaftesbury, Dorset SP7 0DZ. *T:* Shaftesbury 3105. *Clubs:* Buck's, Oriental.

ETHERTON, Ralph, MA; Barrister-at-Law; *b* 11 Feb. 1904; *o s* of late Louis Etherton and Bertha Mary, *d* of late John Bagge; *m* 1944, Johanne Patricia, *y d* of late Gerald Cloherty, Galway, Ireland; one *s* one *d. Educ:* Charterhouse; Trinity Hall, Cambridge. Called to Bar, Inner Temple, 1926, and joined Northern Circuit, practised at Common Law Bar until 1939; Municipal Reform Candidate LCC election, N Camberwell 1931, and W. Fulham 1937; served in RAFVR (Special Duties), Flt Lt, 1940-42; MP (Nat. C) for Stretford div. of Lancs, 1939-45; contested (Nat. C) Liverpool (Everton div.), 1935, Stretford div. of Lancs, 1945; engaged in commerce, 1945-73. Chm. of Coningsby Club, 1933-34; Mem. of Parliamentary Delegation to Australia and New Zealand, 1944. *Recreations:* travel, riding. *Address:* Greentree Hall, Balcombe, Sussex RH17 6JZ. *T:* Balcombe 319. *Clubs:* Carlton, Pratt's.

ETIANG, Paul Orono, BA London; Minister of State in the President's Office, Uganda, since 1974; *b* 15 Aug. 1938; *s* of late Kezironi Orono and Adacat Ilera Orono; *m* 1967, Zahra Ali Foum; two *s* one *d. Educ:* Makerere Univ. Coll. Uganda Admin. Officer, 1962-64; Asst Sec., Foreign Affairs, 1964-65; 3rd Sec., 1965-66, 2nd Sec., 1966-67, Uganda Embassy, Moscow; 1st Sec., Uganda Mission to UN, New York, 1968; Counsellor, 1968-69, High Commissioner, 1969-71, Uganda High Commission, London; Chief of Protocol and Marshal of the Diplomatic Corps, Uganda, 1971; Permanent Sec., Uganda Min. of Foreign Affairs, 1971-73; Minister of State for Foreign Affairs, 1973. *Recreations:* chess, classical music, billiards. *Address:* Office of the President, Parliamentary Buildings, Kampala, Uganda.

ETON, Robert; see Meynell, L. W.

ETTLINGER, Prof. Leopold David; Professor of History of Art, University of California, Berkeley, since 1970; *b* 20 April 1913; *s* of Dr Emil Ettlinger, University Librarian, and Dora (*née* Beer); *m* 1st, 1939, Amrei (*née* Jacoby); she *d* 1955; 2nd, 1959, Madeline (*née* Noirot); 3rd, 1973, Helen (*née* Shahrokh). *Educ:* Stadtgymnasium Halle; Universities of Halle and Marburg. Social Worker for Refugee Children from Germany, 1938-41; Asst Master, King Edward VI Grammar Sch., Five Ways, Birmingham, 1941-48; Asst Curator, Photographic Collection, Warburg Institute, University of London, 1948-51; Curator of Photographic Collection, 1951-56; Lectr, Warburg Inst., 1956-59; Durning Lawrence Prof. of History of Art, Univ. of London, 1959-70. Fellowship, Inst. for Advanced Study, Princeton, 1956; Vis. Professor: Yale Univ., 1963-64; Univ. of Calif, Berkeley, 1969; Univ. of Bonn, 1975-76. FSA 1962-. British Academy award, 1963. *Publications:* (with R. G. Holloway) Compliments of the Season, 1947; The Art of the Renaissance in Northern Europe, in New Cambridge Modern History, Vol. I, 1957; Kandinsky's "At Rest", 1961; Art History Today, 1961; The Sistine Chapel before Michelangelo: Religious Imagery and Papal Politics, 1965; (with Helen S. Ettlinger) Botticelli, 1976; contribs to Journal of Warburg and Courtauld Insts, Burlington Magazine, Architectural Review, Connoisseur, Italian Studies and other jls. *Address:* Department of Art, University of California, Berkeley, Calif 94720, USA.

ETZDORF, Hasso von; *b* 2 March 1900; *s* of Rüdiger von Etzdorf-Neumark and Agnes Maria Lorentz; *m* Katharina Otto-Margonin. *Educ:* Universities of Berlin, Göttingen, Halle (LLD). German Foreign Office, 1928; served in Berlin, Tokyo, Rome, Genoa (Consul-Gen.); Dep. Head, German Office for Peace Questions, Stuttgart, 1947-50; FO, Bonn, 1950-53; Head of German Delegn at Interim Cttee for Eur. Def. Community in Paris, rank of Minister, 1953; Dep. Sec.-Gen., WEU, London, 1955; Ambassador of German Federal Republic to Canada, 1956-58; Dep. Under-Sec. and Head of Western Dept, FO, Bonn, 1958-61; Ambassador of German Fed. Rep. to Court of St James's, 1961-65. GCVO (Hon.) 1964; Order of Merit with Star, Federal Republic of Germany, 1957. *Address:* 8019 Eichtling, Post Moosach, Obb, Germany. *T:* Glonn (08093) 1402. *Clubs:* Travellers', White's.

EUGSTER, General Sir Basil, KCB 1970 (CB 1966); KCVO 1968; CBE 1962; DSO 1945; MC 1938, and Bar, 1940; DL; C-in-C, United Kingdom Land Forces, 1972-74; *b* 15 Aug. 1914; *er s* of late Oscar Louis Eugster, DSO, Kempston Hoo, near Bedford; *m* 1939, Marcia Elaine, *er d* of late Air Commodore Sir Percy Smyth-Osbourne, CMG, CBE; two *s. Educ:* Beaumont; Christ Church, Oxford (MA). 2nd Lieut Irish Guards, 1935. Served War of 1939-45 in Narvik, Italy and NW Europe; Bde Maj., HQ 140 Inf. Bde, 1943-44; GSO 2 (Ops); HQ 5 Corps CMF, Oct-Nov., 1944; OC 3rd Bn IG, Jan.-Feb., 1945; GSO 1, Guards Div., Dec. 1945-Jan. 1947; OC 2nd Bn, Irish Guards, 1947; JSSC, 1950; OC 1st Bn, Irish Guards, 1951-54; AAG War Office, 1954-56; Comdt, Eaton Hall Officer Cadet Sch., 1956-58; Comdt Mons Officer Cadet Sch., 1958; IDC 1959; Comd, 3rd Inf. Bde Gp, and Dhekelia Area, Cyprus, 1959-62; Comdt Sch. of Infantry, Warminster, 1962-63; GOC 4 Div., BAOR, 1963-65; GOC London Dist, and Maj.-Gen. Comdg Household Bde, 1965-68; Commander, British Forces, Hong Kong, 1968-70; GOC-in-C, Southern Comd, 1971-72. ADC (Gen.), 1973-74; retired 1974; Col, Irish Guards, 1969, Hon. Col 1974-, London Irish Co., N Irish Mil. (V). DL Devon, 1977. *Address:* Holmedown, Exbourne, N Devon. *T:* Exbourne 241. *Clubs:* White's, Pratts'.

EURICH, Richard Ernst, RA 1953 (ARA 1942); Artist (Painter); *b* Bradford, 14 March 1903; *s* of late Professor Frederick Wm Eurich; *m* 1934, Mavis Llewellyn Pope; two *d* (one *s* decd). *Educ:* St George's Sch., Harpenden; Bradford Grammar Sch. Studied art at Bradford Sch. of Arts and Crafts, and Slade Sch., London; held One Man Show of drawings at Goupil Gallery in

1929, and several exhibitions of paintings at Redfern Gallery; exhibited at Royal Academy, New English Art Club and London Group; works purchased by Contemporary Art Soc. and Chantrey Bequest; Painting, Dunkirk Beach 1940, purchased for Canadian Government; Official War Artist, 1941-45; representative works in various public galleries. *Recreations:* music and gardening. *Address:* Appletreewick, Dibden Purlieu, Southampton. *T:* Hythe (Hants) 842291.

EUSTON, Earl of; James Oliver Charles FitzRoy, MA, ACA; *b* 13 Dec. 1947; *s* and *heir* of 11th Duke of Grafton, *qv*; *m* 1972, Lady Clare Kerr, BA, *d* of Marquess of Lothian, *qv*; two *d. Educ:* Eton; Magdalene Coll., Cambridge (MA). *Address:* 6 Vicarage Gardens, W8.

EUWE, Dr Machgielis; Officer, Order of Oranje Nassau, 1936; Ridder van de Nederlandse Leeuw, 1971; President, International Chess Federation, since 1970; *b* 20 May 1901; *m* 1926, Carolina Elizabeth Bergman; three *d. Educ:* Amsterdam Univ. Mathematical: University, 1918; Final proof, 1923; Dissertation (doctor-degree), 1926; Chess: Champion of Holland, 1921, Amateur Champion of the World, 1928, World Champion (Universal) being still amateur, by winning a match against Alekhine (15½-14½), 1935, lost the title in the return match against Alekhine (9½-15½), 1937; several wins in tournaments, especially in British tournaments. Chm. Cttee installed by Euratom which studied process of human thinking with particular relation to chess, 1961-63. Dir Netherlands Automatic Information Processing Research Centre, 1959-64; Prof., Univ. of Tilburg, 1964-71 (Extraordinary Prof. in Automation at Univ. Rotterdam, 1964-71). *Publications:* Dutch: Practische Schaaklessen, 1927; Schaakopeningen, 1937; Eindspelen, 1940; Positiespel en Combinatiespel, 1949; Middenspelen, 1951; English: Strategy and Tactics, 1936; From my Games, 1938; Judgment and Planning, 1953; The Logical Approach to Chess (with U. Blaine and J. F. S. Rumble), 1958; A Guide to Chess Endings (with David Hooper), 1959; Master against Amateur, 1963; Road to Mastery (with Prof. W. Meiden), 1963; The Development of Chess Style, 1966; Fischer and his Predecessors, 1977; Bedrijfsvoering met de Computer, 1969; several other publications on automatic data processing. *Address:* Mensinge 40, Amsterdam-Buitenveldert, Netherlands.

EVAN-COOK, John Edward, JP; *b* 25 Oct. 1902; 2nd *s* of late Evan Cook, JP, of London; *m* 1928, Winifred Elizabeth, *d* of Joseph Samuel Pointon; no *c. Educ:* Westminster City Sch. Served War, 1940-46, Major, RAOC. Adviser on Packaging, War Office, 1940-46. Vice-Chm. London District Rotary, 1950-52; Pres. Rotary Club of Camberwell, 1948. Chairman: Bd of Visitors, HM Prison, Brixton, 1967-73; Evan-Cook Group (retd); Inst. of Packaging (Nat. Chm., 1954, President, 1954-57); Min. of Labour & Nat. Service Local Disablement Cttee, 1959-67. Estates Governor, Dulwich, 1973-. Chief Scouts' Medal of Merit, 1962; Silver Acorn, 1968. Past Master, Worshipful Company of Paviors; Liveryman: Worshipful Co. of Carmen; Worshipful Co. of Farmers. Sheriff of London, 1958-59; Common Councilman, City of London, 1960-66 and 1972-77. JP City of London, 1950. Order of Homayoun, 3rd Class (Iran); Grand Cross of Merit, Order of Merit (Federal Republic of Germany). *Address:* Old Deaks, Cuckfield, Sussex. *T:* Haywards Heath 3220. *Clubs:* City Livery (Pres., 1964-65), United Wards, Royal Automobile.

EVAN-JONES, Cecil Artimus, CBE 1971 (MBE 1944); Secretary, Institute of Chartered Accountants in England and Wales, 1962-71, retired; *b* 1 March 1912; *m* 1941, Eileen Marjorie Yates; two *d. Educ:* St Edward's Sch., Oxford. Industry, 1931-39; served War of 1939-45, Gordon Highlanders; Dep. Sec., Soc. of Incorporated Accountants, 1946-57; with Inst. of Chartered Accountants, 1957-. *Recreations:* shooting, fishing. *Address:* Warehead House, Halnaker, Chichester, West Sussex. *T:* Halnaker 330. *Clubs:* MCC, East India, Devonshire, Sports and Public Schools; Royal London Yacht.

EVANG, Karl; Norwegian physician; Director-General, Norwegian Health Services, 1939-72; *b* 19 Oct. 1902; *s* of Jens Ingolf Evang and Beate, *née* Wexelsen; *m* 1929, Gerda Sophie Landmark Moe; one *s* three *d. Educ:* Oslo Univ. (MD). On Staff, Oslo Municipal Hosp., 1932-34; MO, State Factor, Inspection Office, 1937-38; represented Norway at UNRRA, FAO, and WHO, 1943-. Pres., 2nd World Health Assembly, 1949; Chm., WHO Exec. Bd, 1966; Member: WHO Panel on Public Health Administration; Norwegian Soc. of Hygiene. Vis. Prof. of Social Medicine, Univ. of Tromsø, 1973. Hon. FRSM. Hon. Fellow, Amer. Public Health Assoc. (Bronfman Prize, 1970). Léon Bernard Medal and Prize, WHO, 1966. *Publications:* Birth Control, 1930; Norwegian Medical Dictionary, 1933; Race Policy and Reaction, 1934; Education to Peace, 1947; The

Rehabilitation of Public Health in Norway, 1947; The Public Health Services, 1948; Sexual Education, 1951; Health Service, Society and Medicine, 1958; Health Services in Norway, 1960, 4th edn 1976; Use and Abuse of Drugs, 1966; Current Narcotic Problems, 1967; Health and Society, 1974. *Address:* Måltrostveien 11B, Oslo 13, Norway.

EVANS, family name of **Barons Energlyn, Evans of Hungershall** and **Mountevans.**

EVANS OF HUNGERSHALL, Baron *cr* 1967 (Life Peer), of Borough of Royal Tunbridge Wells; **Benjamin Ifor Evans,** Kt 1955; MA, DLit London; FRSL; *b* London, 19 Aug. 1899; *y s* of Benjamin Evans; *m* 1923, Marjorie Ruth, *d* of late John Measures, Ifield; one *d. Educ:* Stationers' Company's Sch.; University Coll., London. Prof. of English at Southampton, Sheffield and London; Principal, Queen Mary Coll. (University of London), 1944-51; Provost, University Coll., London, 1951-66. Educational Dir of the British Council, 1940-44; Vice-Chm. of Arts Council, 1946-51; Chairman: Educational Advisory Council, Thames Television; Linguaphone Institute. Vice-Pres., RSL, 1974, Chm. 1975-77. Fellow: UCL; Queen Mary Coll. Hon. Dr of Letters, University of Paris; Hon. LLD, University of Manchester. Officer of the Legion of Honour; Chevalier, Order of the Crown of Belgium; Comdr, Order of Orange Nassau; Comdr, Order of Dannebrog. *Publications:* Encounters, 1926; English Poetry in the Later Nineteenth Century, 1933; The Limits of Literary Criticism, 1933; Keats, 1934; edns, with W. W. Greg, of The Commody of Susanna, and Jack Juggler, 1937; Tradition and Romanticism, 1940; A Short History of English Literature, 1940; English Literature (for British Council), 1944; in Search of Stephen Vane, 1946; The Shop on the King's Road, 1947; Literature Between the Wars, 1948; A Short History of English Drama, 1948; The Church in the Markets, 1948; (with Mary Glasgow) The Arts in England, 1948; The Use of English, 1949; (with Marjorie R. Evans) A Victorian Anthology, 1949; The Language of Shakespeare's Plays, 1951; Science and Literature, 1954; English Literature: Values and Traditions, 1962. *Address:* 1317 Minster House, St James Court, Buckingham Gate, SW1. *Club:* Athenæum.

EVANS, A. Briant; Hon. Consulting Gynæcological Surgeon, Westminster Hospital and Chelsea Hospital for Women; Hon. Consulting Obstetric Surgeon, Queen Charlotte's Maternity Hospital; *b* 26 June 1909; *e s* of late Arthur Evans, OBE, MD, MS, FRCS; *m* 1939, Audrey Marie, *er d* of late Roland Eveleigh Holloway; three *s. Educ:* Westminster Sch.; Gonville and Caius Coll., Cambridge; Westminster Hosp. MA, MB, BCh Cantab; FRCS; FRCOG. Sometime Examiner in Obstetrics to Univs of Cambridge and London and to Royal College of Obstetricians and Gynæcologists. Temp. Lieut-Col RAMC, served in Egypt, Italy and Austria; OC No. 9 Field Surgical Unit. *Address:* West Emlett, Black Dog, Crediton, Devon. *T:* Morchard Bishop 217. *Club:* Army and Navy.

EVANS, Albert; *b* 10 June 1903, *s* of Moses Richard Evans; *m* 1929, Beatrice Joan, *d* of F. W. Galton. *Educ:* LCC Sch.; WEA. MP (Lab) West Islington, Sept. 1947-Feb. 1950, South-West Islington, 1950-70; retired; Member: Islington Borough Council, 1937-47; LCC, 1946-49. *Address:* Abbey Lodge, 3 Hooks Hill Road, Sheringham, Norfolk.

EVANS, Alfred Thomas, (Fred Evans); BA; MP (Lab) Caerphilly, since July 1968; *b* 24 Feb. 1914; *s* of Alfred Evans, Miner, and Sarah Jane Evans; *m* 1939, Mary (*née* O'Marah); one *s* two *d. Educ:* Primary and Grammar Schs; University of Wales. Head of Dept, Grammar Sch., Bargoed, Glam, 1937-49; Headmaster, Bedlinog Secondary Sch., Glam, 1949-66; Headmaster, Lewis Boys Grammar Sch., Pengam, Mon, 1966-68. Contested (Lab) Leominster, 1955, Stroud, 1959; Organising Agent, Caerphilly Constituency Labour Party, 1962-66. Chm., Welsh Parly Lab. Party, 1977; a Chm., Private Bills Cttee. *Address:* House of Commons, SW1; Menai, Dilwyn Avenue, Ystradmynach, Hengoed, Mid Glam. *Clubs:* Aneurin Labour (Caerphilly); Labour (Bargoed).

EVANS, Alun S.; *see* Sylvester-Evans.

EVANS, Sir Anthony (Adney), 2nd Bt, *cr* 1920; *b* 5 Aug. 1922; *s* of Sir Walter Harry Evans, 1st Bt, and Margaret Mary, *y d* of late Thomas Adney Dickens; *S* father 1954; married; two *s* one *d. Educ:* Shrewsbury; Merton Coll., Oxford. *Club:* Leander (Henley).

EVANS, Anthony Howell Meurig, RD 1968; QC 1971; a Recorder of the Crown Court, since 1972; *b* 11 June 1934; *s* of David Meurig Evans, *qv*; *m* 1963, Caroline Mary Fyffe Mackie, *d* of Edwin Gordon Mackie, *qv*; one *s* two *d. Educ:* Bassaleg Sec.

Grammar Sch., Mon; Shrewsbury Sch.; St John's Coll., Cambridge. Nat. Service, RNVR, 1952-54 (Lt-Comdr RNR). BA 1957, LLB 1958, Cantab. Called to Bar, Gray's Inn, 1958 (Arden Scholar and Birkenhead Scholar). Fellow, Internat. Acad. of Trial Lawyers, NY, 1975. *Publication:* (Jt Editor) The Law of the Air (Lord McNair), 1964. *Recreations:* sailing, music. *Address:* 4 Essex Court, Temple, EC4. *T:* 01-353 6771; Milan House, Overton, near Swansea, West Glamorgan. *Clubs:* Cardiff & County; Royal Wimbledon Golf, Bosham Sailing.

EVANS, (Arthur) Mostyn; General Secretary, Transport and General Workers Union, since 1978; Member, TUC General Council, since 1977; *b* 13 July 1925; *m* 1947, Laura Bigglestone; three *s* three *d. Educ:* Cefn Coed Primary Sch., S Wales; Church Road Secondary Modern Sch., Birmingham. District Officer, Birmingham, Chem. and Eng. Industries, 1956; Regional Officer, Midlands, 1960; Nat. Officer, Eng., 1966; National Secretary: Chem., Rubber, and Oil Industries, 1969; Engineering Industries, 1969; (Automotive Section), TGWU, 1969-73; Nat. Organiser, TGWU, 1973-78. Part-time Mem., Nat. Bus Co., 1976-. *Recreation:* music. *Address:* 6 Highland Drive, Hemel Hempstead, Herts. *T:* 57503.

EVANS, Sir Arthur Trevor, Kt 1954; Controller of Death Duties, 1951-57; *b* 7 Nov. 1895; *er s* of Benjamin Evans; *m* 1925, Mary Dagmar (*d* 1977), *d* of J. H. Powell, JP, Aberdare, Glam; one *s* one *d. Educ:* Stationers' Company's Sch.; King's Coll., London. LLB. Asst Controller of Death Duties, 1944. Dep. Controller, 1947. *Address:* Flat 1, Cliff Court, Rottingdean, Brighton BN2 7JD.

EVANS, Sir Athol (Donald), KBE 1963 (CBE 1954; MBE 1939); retired as Secretary for Home Affairs, Government of the Federation of Rhodesia and Nyasaland (Sept. 1953-Dec. 1963); *b* 16 Dec. 1904; *s* of Henry Evans; *m* 1931, Catherine Millar Greig; one *s* two *d. Educ:* Graeme Coll. and Rhodes Univ., Grahamstown, S Africa (BA, LLB). Joined S Rhodesia Public Service, 1928: consecutively Law Officer, Legal Adviser, Mem. of Public Services Board, and Sec. for Internal Affairs. Chairman of: Board of Trustees Rhodes National Gallery; Rhodesia National Trust; Nat. Council for Care of Aged. Past District Governor, Rotary International. Gold Cross of St Mark (Greece), 1962. *Recreations:* tennis, shooting. *Address:* 8 Harvey Brown Avenue, Salisbury, Rhodesia. *T:* 82171. *Club:* Salisbury (Rhodesia).

EVANS, Sir Bernard, Kt 1962; DSO 1941; ED 1944; FRAIA; architect; Consultant, Bernard Evans & Partners Pty Ltd, since 1972 (Governing Director, 1946-72, retired); Director, Sun Alliance & London Insurance Group, Victoria; Managing Director, Withalit Pty Ltd; *b* 13 May 1905; *s* of Isaac Evans and Lucy (*née* Tunnicliffe); *m* 1929, Dorothy May Evans (*née* Ellis), *d* of William and Mary Ellis; one *s* two *d. Educ:* private sch.; Melbourne Technical Coll. Raised 2/23rd Bn, AIF, War of 1939-45; 24th Bde 9th Div.; served Tobruk, El Alamein (Brig.), Lae and Finschhaven (despatches thrice, DSO, ED). Architect; notable buildings: London Ct, Perth, WA; CRA and Legal & General Assurance Society Pty Ltd, Melbourne, Vic. Lord Mayor of Melbourne, 1959-61 (Councillor, Gipps Ward, 1949-74). Comr Melb. and Metropolitan Bd of Works; Pres. Royal Melbourne Institute of Technology, 1958-60; Pres. Princes Hill Village, 1958-75; Pres. Royal Commonwealth Society, Victorian Br., 1960-; Past Nat. Pres. Royal Commonwealth Society. Mem. Inst. of Dirs, London. Cavaliere dell' Ordine della Stella della Solidarieta Italiana, 1971. *Recreation:* artist in oils. *Address:* Warrawee, 735 Orrong Road, Toorak, Victoria 3142, Australia. *T:* 24-5591. *Clubs:* Athenæum, Naval and Military (Melbourne); VRC, VATC, RACV, Kelvin, West Brighton (all Melbourne, Australia).

EVANS, Briant; see Evans, A. B.

EVANS, Rt. Rev. Bruce Read; see Port Elizabeth, Bishop of.

EVANS, Carey; see Evans, D. C. R. J.

EVANS, Sir Charles; see Evans, Sir R. C.

EVANS, Vice-Adm. Sir Charles (Leo Glandore), KCB 1962 (CB 1958); CBE 1953; DSO 1941; DSC 1940; Chairman, various British and Australian Companies; *b* 2 Aug. 1908; *o s* of Major S. G. Evans, MC; *g s* of Gen. Leopold Evans and Col John Crosbie; *m* 1942, Kyriakoula, 3rd *d* of Gen. Doulcaris, Athens, Greece. Entered Royal Naval Coll., 1922; specialised as a pilot, 1930; served as fighter pilot in Aircraft Carriers in Norwegian, Dunkirk, Mediterranean and Middle East campaigns and in North Sea, Mediterranean and Pacific theatres in War of 1939-45 (despatches thrice, DSC, DSO); Naval Air Attaché in USA,

1946 and 1947; Dir of Air Warfare Division, Naval Staff, The Admiralty, 1950-51; Commanding HMS Ocean (CBE) in Mediterranean and Korea, 1951 and 1952; student Imperial Defence Coll., 1953; Commodore, RN Barracks, Portsmouth, 1954 and 1955; Flag Officer, Flying Training, 1956-57; Deputy Chief of Naval Personnel and Head of Directorate of Officer Appointments, 1957-59; Flag Officer, Aircraft Carriers, 1959-60; NATO Deputy Supreme Allied Commander, Atlantic, 1960-62, retired. Pres., Fleet Air Arm Officers Assoc. 1963. Dir-Gen., British Film Producers' Assoc., 1964-67; Vice-Pres., Film Production Assoc. of GB, 1967-68; Chm., Central Casting Ltd, 1967-68. *Club:* Army and Navy.

EVANS, Charles Tunstall, CMG 1948; *b* 16 May 1903; *e s* of late Frank Alfred and Beatrice Evans, Birmingham; *m* 1938, Kathleen, *e d* of late Ernest Armstrong, Hankham Place, Pevensey; one *s* one *d* (and one *s* decd). *Educ:* King Edward's Sch., Birmingham; Christ's Coll., Cambridge. Colonial Administrative Service: Administrative Officer, Palestine, 1925; Deputy Dist Comr, 1939; Principal Asst Sec. 1942; Senior Dist Comr (Galilee), 1945; retired on termination of British Mandate, 1948. Seconded to Colonial Office, 1935-37; called to Bar (Middle Temple), 1941. Admitted solicitor, 1949. Asst Sec.-Gen., Order of St John of Jerusalem, 1950-51, Sec.-Gen., 1951-68, Registrar, 1968-75. Councillor, Cuckfield UDC, 1953-68, Chm., 1962-65. A Chm., Gen. Comrs of Income Tax. *Address:* Ash Lodge, 3 Calbourne, Muster Green, Haywards Heath, West Sussex RH16 4AQ. *T:* Haywards Heath 51435. *Club:* East India, Devonshire, Sports and Public Schools.
See also Prof. C. F. Evans, Sir Reginald Payne, Rt Rev. W. A. E. Westall.

EVANS, Rev. Prof. Christopher Francis, MA; Professor of New Testament Studies, King's College, London, 1962-77; *b* 7 Nov. 1909; 2nd *s* of Frank and Beatrice Evans; *m* 1941, Elna Mary, *d* of Walter and Elizabeth Burt; one *s. Educ:* King Edward's Sch., Birmingham; Corpus Christi Coll., Cambridge. Asst Curate, St Barnabas, Southampton, 1934-38; Tutor Schol. Canc. Linc., 1938-44; Chaplain and Divinity Lecturer, Lincoln Training Coll., 1944-48; Chaplain, Fellow and Lecturer in Divinity, Corpus Christi Coll., Oxford, 1948-58, Emeritus Fellow, 1977; Lightfoot Prof. of Divinity in the University of Durham and Canon of Durham Cathedral, 1959-62. Select Preacher, University of Oxford, 1955-57; Proctor in Convocation for University of Oxford, 1955-58; Exam. Chaplain: to Bishop of Bristol, 1948-58; to Bishop of Durham, 1958-62; to Archbishop of Canterbury, 1962-74; to Bishop of Lichfield, 1969-75. FKC, 1970. Hon. DLitt Southampton, 1977. *Publications:* Christology and Theology, 1961; The Lord's Prayer, 1963; The Beginning of the Gospel, 1968; Resurrection and the New Testament, 1970; (ed jtly) The Cambridge History of the Bible: vol. I, From the Beginnings to Jerome, 1970; Is 'Holy Scripture' Christian?, 1971; Theological Explorations, 1977; contribs to Journal of Theological Studies, Theology and Religious Studies, to Studies in the Gospels and to Christian Faith and Communist Faith. *Recreation:* fishing. *Address:* 4 Church Close, Cuddesdon, Oxford. *T:* Wheatley 4406; 5 The Square, Clun, Craven Arms, Salop.
See also C. T. Evans, Rt Rev. W. A. E. Westall.

EVANS, Collis William, CB 1958; CBE 1949; Under Secretary, Ministry of Civil Aviation, 1948-59; *b* 27 May 1895; *s* of late W. J. Evans, Folkestone; *m* 1st, 1938, Annie Urquhart (*d* 1957); 2nd, 1970, Hilda Stewart. Served European War, 1914-18, Yeomanry and RFA, Middle East, Macedonia and France. Exchequer and Audit Dept, 1914; Principal, Air Ministry, 1938; Financial Adviser to HQ RAF, Middle East and North Africa, 1938-43; Adviser on Administration and Finance, Transport Command, 1943; Asst Sec., Dept of Civil Aviation, 1944. *Address:* Ringle Crouch, Nash, near Bletchley, Bucks MK17 0EP. *T:* Whaddon 285.

EVANS, David; Under-Secretary, Ministry of Agriculture, Fisheries and Food, since 1976; *b* 7 Dec. 1935; *yr s* of William Price Evans and Ella Mary Evans; *m* 1960, Susan Carter Connal, *yr d* of late Dr John Connal and Antoinette Connal; one *s* one *d. Educ:* Welwyn Garden City Grammar Sch.; University Coll. London (BScEcon). Joined Min. of Agriculture, Fisheries and Food, 1959; Private Sec. to Parliamentary Sec. (Lords), 1962-64; Principal, 1964; Principal Private Sec. to Ministers, 1970-71; Asst Sec., 1971; seconded to Cabinet Office, 1972-74. *Address:* 18 Fairdale Gardens, SW15 6JW. *T:* 01-789 4449.

EVANS, Prof. David Alan Price, FRCP; Chairman, Department of Medicine, and Director of Nuffield Unit Medical Genetics, University of Liverpool, since 1972; Consultant Physician, Liverpool Royal Infirmary and Broadgreen Hospital, Liverpool, since 1965; *b* 6 March 1927; *s* of Owen Evans and Ellen (*née*

Jones). *Educ:* Univ. of Liverpool (MD, PhD, MSc); Johns Hopkins Univ. House Physician, House Surg. and Med. Registrar, United Liverpool Hosps; Fellow, Dept of Medicine, Johns Hopkins Hosp., 1958-59; Lectr 1960-62, Sen. Lectr 1962-68, Personal Chair, 1968-72, Dept of Medicine, Univ. of Liverpool. Life Mem., Johns Hopkins Soc. of Scholars, 1972. *Publications:* medical and scientific, principally concerned with genetic factors determining responses to drugs. *Recreation:* country pursuits. *Address:* 28 Montclair Drive, Liverpool L18 0HA. *T:* 051-722 3112; Pen-yr-Allt, Paradwys, Llangristiolus, Bodorgan, Gwynedd LL62 5PD. *T:* Bodorgan 346.

EVANS, His Honour David Carey Rees Jones, MA, BCL Oxon; Judge of County Courts, 1946-71; Deputy Chairman, Quarter Sessions, Norfolk, retired; *b* 3 March 1899; *s* of late Sir David W. Evans; *m* 1937, Margaret Willoughby Gale; one *d. Educ:* Sherborne Preparatory Sch.; Sherborne Sch.; Jesus Coll., Oxford (Scholar); Gray's Inn (Holt Scholar). Called to Bar, 1923; S Wales and Chester Circuit, practising at Cardiff; formerly part-time Lecturer in Law at University Coll. of S Wales and Mon, Cardiff. Chm. of Ministry of Labour Tribunals for Breconshire and Merthyr, 1937-46; Recorder of Merthyr Tydfil, 1945-46. 2nd Lieut RGA 1918-19. *Address:* 16 Cross Street, Hoxne, Diss, Norfolk. *Club:* Norfolk (Norwich).

EVANS, Ven. David Eifion; Archdeacon of Cardigan since 1967; *b* 22 Jan, 1911; *e s* of John Morris Evans, Borth, Cards; *m* 1941, Iris Elizabeth Gravelle; one *s. Educ:* Ardwyn, Aberystwyth; UCW, Aberystwyth; St Michael's Coll., Llandaff. BA 1932; MA 1951. Deacon, 1934; Priest, 1935. Curate: Llanfihangel-ar-Arth, 1934-36; Llanbadarn Fawr, 1936-40; Chaplain to the Forces, 1940-45; Vicar, Llandeloy with Llanrheithan, 1945-48; Penrhyncoch, 1948, with Elerch, 1952-57; St Michael, Aberystwyth, 1957-67; Rural Dean, Llanbadarn Fawr, 1957-67; Chaplain, Anglican Students, 1966-67; Canon of St David's Cathedral (Caerfai), 1963-67; Vicar: Llanafan with Llanwnnws, 1967-69; Newcastle Emlyn, 1969-. Mem. Governing Body of Church in Wales, 1956-; Mem. Court of Governors, and Mem. Council, UCW, Aberystwyth, 1958-; Sub-Visitor, St David's Univ. Coll., Lampeter, 1972. *Publications:* contribs to Jl of Hist. Soc. of Church in Wales and other Welsh Church periodicals. *Recreation:* reading. *Address:* The Vicarage, Newcastle Emlyn, Dyfed. *T:* Newcastle Emlyn 710385.

EVANS, His Honour David Eifion (Puleston), QC 1954; Member Foreign Compensation Commission, 1963-75; *b* 8 Dec. 1902; *s* of late John Owain Evans, CBE and Margaret Anne Evans; *m* 1933, Roberta (*d* 1966), *y d* of Sir Robert McAlpine, 1st Bt. *Educ:* Towyn Sch.; University Coll. of Wales, Aberystwyth; Downing Coll., Cambridge (Foundation Schol., MA, LLB). Barrister, Gray's Inn, 1926, practised London, Wales and Chester Circuit; commissioned RASC 1940; Office of Judge Advocate Gen., 1941-45, Major; resumed practice, 1945; Mem. General Council of the Bar, 1955-56; Chm., Radnorshire Quarter Sessions, 1959-62; Deputy Chm., Brecknock Quarter Sessions, 1960-62; County Court Judge, Circuit No. 28 (Mid-Wales and Shropshire), 1956-62. *Club:* Reform.

EVANS, Air Chief Marshal Sir David (George), KCB 1977; CBE 1967 (OBE 1962); Commander-in-Chief, RAF Strike Command, and Commander-in-Chief, UK NATO Air Forces, since 1977; *b* Windsor, Ont, Canada, 14 July 1924; *s* of William Stanley Evans, Clive Vale, Hastings, Sussex; *m* 1949, Denise Marson Williamson-Noble, *d* of late Gordon Till, Hampstead, London; two *d* (and two step *s*). *Educ:* Hodgson Sch., Toronto, Canada; North Toronto Collegiate. Served War, as Pilot, in Italy and NW Europe, 1944-45. Sqdn Pilot, Tactics Officer, Instructor, 1946-52; Sqdn Comdr, Central Flying Sch., 1953-55; RAF Staff Coll. course, 1955; OC No 11 (F) Sqdn, in Germany, 1956-57; Personal Staff Officer to C-in-C, 2nd Allied TAF, 1958-59; OC Flying, RAF, Coltishall, 1959-61; Coll. of Air Warfare course, 1961; Air Plans Staff Officer, Min. of Defence (Air), 1962-63; OC, RAF Station, Gutersloh, Germany, 1964-66; IDC, 1967; AOC, RAF Central Tactics and Trials Organisation, 1968-70; ACAS (Ops), 1970-73; AOC No 1 (Bomber) Group, RAF, 1973-76; Vice-Chief of Air Staff, 1976-77. Queen's Commendation for Valuable Service in the Air (QCVSA), 1955. *Recreations:* rep. RAF at Rugby football and winter sports (Pres. RAF Winter Sports Assoc.); has rep. Gt Brit. at Bobsleigh in World Championships, Commonwealth Games and, in 1964, Olympic Games. *Address:* Royal Bank of Canada, 2 Cockspur Street, SW1. *Club:* Royal Air Force.

EVANS, Prof. Sir David (Gwynne), Kt 1977; CBE 1969; FRS 1960; Demonstrator, Sir William Dunn School of Pathology, University of Oxford, since 1976; *b* 6 Sept. 1909; *s* of Frederick George Evans, Atherton, Manchester; *m* 1937, Mary (*née* Darby); one *s* one *d. Educ:* Leigh Grammar Sch.; University of

Manchester. BSc, 1933; MSc, 1934; PhD, 1938; DSc, 1948. Demonstrator and Asst Lecturer in Chemistry, Dept of Bacteriology, University of Manchester, 1934; Mem. of Scientific Staff, Dept of Biological Standards, Nat. Inst. for Medical Research, London, 1940; Reader in Chemical Bacteriology, Dept of Bacteriology, University of Manchester, 1947; Head of Biological Standards Control Laboratory, Nat. Inst. for Medical Research, London, 1955-58; Dir, Dept of Biological Standards, 1958-61; Prof. of Bacteriology and Immunology, 1961-71, now Emeritus, London Sch. of Hygiene and Tropical Medicine; Dir, Lister Inst. of Preventive Medicine, 1971-72; Dir, Nat. Inst. for Biological Standards and Control, 1972-76. Member: WHO Expert Panel on Biological Standardization, 1956-77; Governing Body, Animal Virus Res. Inst., Pirbright, 1964-75; MRC, 1965-69; Northumberland Cttee on Foot-and-Mouth Disease, 1968-69; Cttee on Safety of Medicines, 1973-77; British Pharmacopœia Commn, 1973-77; Chm., Veterinary Adv. Cttee, Horserace Betting Levy Bd, 1973-. Pres., Soc. for General Microbiology, 1972-75. FRCPath, 1965. BMA Stewart Prize Award, 1968. *Publications:* numerous scientific papers, mainly on bacteriology and immunology. *Recreation:* listening to opera. *Address:* 10 Nourse Close, Woodeaton, Oxford. *T:* Oxford 56632.

EVANS, Sir David (Lewis), Kt 1958; OBE 1947; BA, BLitt, Hon. DLitt Wales; Keeper of Public Records, Jan. 1959-Oct. 1960, retired (Deputy Keeper of the Records, 1954-58); Commissioner, Historical MSS Commission, since 1954; *b* 14 Aug. 1893; *s* of Rev. David Evans and Margaret Lewis; *m* 1923, Marie Christine (*d* 1966), *d* of Edwin Austin, JP; two *d. Educ:* Bridgend County Sch.; University Coll. of Wales, Aberystwyth; Jesus Coll., Oxford. Lieut, Duke of Wellington's Regt, 1915-19, France and Belgium (despatches). Entered Public Record Office, 1921; Principal Asst Keeper, 1947. Lectr, Administrative History and Archive Administration, Sch. of Librarianship and Archives, University Coll. London, 1947-54. FRHistS (Vice-Pres. 1956-60); Council, Hon. Soc. of Cymmrodorion; Member: Advisory Council on Public Records, 1959-65; History and Law Cttee, Bd of Celtic Studies; Exec Committee: Internat. Council on Archives, 1953-68 (Vice-Pres. 1956-60); Pres. 4th Internat. Congress of Archivists, Stockholm, 1960; Governor: British Film Institute, 1961-64; Nat. Library of Wales, 1961- (Council, 1962-); Nat. Museum of Wales, 1965-. *Publications:* Flintshire Ministers' Accounts, 1328-1352, 1929; History of Carmarthenshire: Chapter on Later Middle Ages, 1935; (part author) Notebook of John Smibert, Painter, Mass Hist. Soc., 1969; articles, reviews, in Cymmrodorion Transactions, Eng. Hist. Review, Nat. Lib. of Wales Jl, Virginia Hist. Soc. Trans, etc. *Recreation* . walking in Wales. *Address:* 2 Bay Court, Doctors Commons Road, Berkhamsted, Herts. *T:* Berkhamsted 3636. *Club:* National Liberal.

EVANS, David Meurig; His Honour Judge Meurig Evans; a Circuit Judge (formerly County Court Judge), since 1957; *b* 9 Sept. 1906; *s* of H. T. Evans, Aberayron, Cards; *m* 1933, Joyce Diedericke Sander (decd), St Albans; two *s* two *d* ; *m* 1969, Mrs Anne Blackmore. *Educ:* Cardiff High Sch.; Aberayron County Sch.; Cardiff Technical Coll. Journalist on staff of Western Mail and The Economist, 1925-31. Called to Bar, Gray's Inn, 1931; practised on Wales and Chester Circuit, 1932-57; Chairman, Cardigan QS, Denbigh QS, Dep. Chm., Anglesey and Caenarvon QS, 1958-71. Served 1940-45, Lieut-Comdr RNVR. Chm., Medical Appeal Tribunal for Wales, 1952-57; Pres., Council of HM Circuit Judges, 1975-. *Recreations:* golf and yachting. *Address:* Bryn-Owen, Menai Bridge, Gwynedd. *T:* Menai Bridge 712253. *Clubs:* Royal Welsh, Royal Anglesey, etc. See also A. H. M. Evans.

EVANS, David Milne; Assistant Under-Secretary of State, Ministry of Defence, 1967-77; *b* 8 Aug. 1917; *s* of Walter Herbert Evans, MSc and Florence Mary Evans (*née* Milne); *m* 1946, Gwynneth May (*née* Griffiths), BA. *Educ:* Charterhouse; Gonville and Caius Coll., Cambridge (Schol.; Wrangler, Math. Tripos). Administrative Class, Home Civil Service (War Office), 1939. Served in Army (Major, RA), 1940-45. Asst Sec., 1954; Imp. Def. Coll., 1954; Asst Under-Sec. of State, MoD, 1967-71; Under-Sec., CS Dept, 1972. Coronation Medal, 1953. *Address:* 13 Copse Hill, Purley, Surrey. *T:* 01-660 4372.

EVANS, David Morgan; Barrister, Wales and Chester Circuit; *b* 12 April 1892; *e s* of late Evan Price Evans and Sarah Anne Evans, Glasallt Isaf, Llangadoc, Carmns; *m* 1924, Mary Gwynydd, 2nd *d* of late Thomas Lloyd, Havenholme, Hadley Wood and Mrs J. T. Lewis, 9 Dawson Place, Bayswater, W2; two *s* one *d* (and one *s* decd). *Educ:* Llangadoc Sch.; Llandovery Coll.; Jesus Coll., Oxford (Classical Exhibn). MA Oxon. Barrister-at-law, Gray's Inn (Arden Prize). Legal Chm. Appellate Tribunal (Prescriptions) for South Wales under 1945

National Health Act; retd as Gen. Commissioner and Land Tax Commissioner; Deputy Chm. Cardiganshire Quarter Sessions, 1953-64. Formerly Legal Chm., Cardiff City's Rent Tribunal; Parish Councillor; Chm. Cardiff Mothercraft Clinic; Hon. Treasurer Oxford Soc., E Glam and Mon Br.; former Barr. Mem. Legal Aid Executive Cttee No 5 Area. Served 1915-19; Infantry; Artists' Rifles; Lieut 5th Bn (TF), The Welch Regt; 159 Bde Staff EEF Palestine, Egypt and Syria. *Recreations:* reading, gardening, fishing. *Address:* 33 Park Place, Cardiff; Brynderi, Hollybush Road, Cyncoed, Cardiff. *T:* Cardiff 33313; Cardiff 752148; Llanarth, Dyfed 383.
See also T. M. Evans.

EVANS, David M.; *see* Moule-Evans.

EVANS, David Philip, CBE 1968; MSc, PhD, FRIC; Principal, Glamorgan Polytechnic, Treforest, Pontypridd, Glam, 1970-72; *b* 28 Feb. 1908; *s* of D. C. and J. Evans, Port Talbot, Glam; *m* 1938, Vura Helena (*née* Harcombe); one *s. Educ:* Port Talbot County Grammar Sch.; University Coll., Cardiff. Lectr in Chemistry, Cardiff Technical Coll., 1934-44; Principal: Bridgend Technical Coll., Glam, 1944-52; Glamorgan Coll. of Technology, Treforest, 1952-70. *Publications:* numerous papers in various chemical jls. *Recreations:* fishing, gardening, music. *Address:* Forest Lodge, 117 Pantmawr Road, Whitchurch, Cardiff. *T:* Cardiff 63544; Glennydd, 1 Derlwyn, Capel Dewi, Llandyssul, Dyfed.

EVANS, Eben, OBE 1976; Controller, Books Division, British Council, since 1976; *b* 1 Nov. 1920; *s* of John Evans and Mary Evans; *m* 1946, Joan Margaret Howells; two *s* two *d. Educ:* Llandovery Grammar Sch.; University Coll. of Wales, Aberystwyth (BA 1948). Served War, 1941-46 (Army, Captain). Appointed to British Council, 1948; Cardiff, 1948-55; Thailand, 1955-59; Gambia, 1959-62; Ghana, 1962-64; Personnel Dept, London, 1964-68; Representative: Algeria, 1968-73; Yugoslavia, 1973-76. *Recreations:* walking, music. *Address:* 15 Boulters Court, Maidenhead, Berks. *T:* Maidenhead 28479.

EVANS, Rt. Rev. Edward Lewis, BD, MTh; *b* 11 Dec. 1904; *s* of Edward Foley Evans and Mary (*née* Walker). *Educ:* St Anselm's, Croydon; Tonbridge Sch.; Bishops' Coll., Cheshunt. BD London 1935, MTh 1938. Deacon, 1937; priest 1938; Curate of St Mary's, Prittlewell, Essex, 1937-39; Warden of St Peter's, Theological Coll., Jamaica, 1940-49; Rector, Kingston Parish Church, Jamaica, 1949-52; Rector of Woodford and Craigton, 1952-57; Archdeacon of Surrey, Jamaica, 1950-57; Bishop Suffragan of Kingston, 1957-60; Bishop of Barbados, 1960-71. *Publication:* A History of the Diocese of Jamaica, 1977. *Address:* Bungalow 1, Terry's Cross, Woodmancote, Henfield, Sussex BN5 9SX.

EVANS, Edward Walter, CMG 1931; *b* 1890; 2nd *s* of late Arthur Evans; *m* 1923, Margaret, *d* of late J. K. Young, Barrister-at-Law; two *s* one *d. Educ:* Marlborough Coll.; Corpus Christi Coll., Oxford (Classical Scholar). 1st Class Classical Mods, 1st Class Lit. Hum.; appointed to Colonial service, 1914; served in various dependencies in East Africa and Caribbean area before retiring from post of Colonial Sec., Mauritius, in 1939, after administering the Government of Mauritius on various occasions; during 1939-45 War served in Gibraltar and on Overseas Services of BBC; served on Control Commission for Germany, 1945-46; employed in History Dept Bristol Univ., 1946-55. *Publications:* contrib. Mind, vol LXXX. *Address:* Medway Farm, Askerswell, Dorchester, Dorset.
See also R. M. Evans.

EVANS, Ven. Eifion; *see* Evans, Ven. D. E.

EVANS, Prof. Emyr Estyn, CBE 1970; Emeritus Professor of Geography, and Hon. Fellow, Institute of Irish Studies, Queen's University of Belfast; Leverhulme Emeritus Fellow, 1970-72; *b* 29 May 1905; 4th *s* of Rev. G. O. and Elizabeth Evans, Shrewsbury; *m* 1931, Gwyneth Lyon, *e d* of Prof. Abel Jones, Aberystwyth; four *s. Educ:* Welshpool County Sch.; University Coll. of Wales, Aberystwyth. BA Geography and Anthropology, 1925, MA 1931, DSc 1939. Independent Lecturer in Geography, QUB, 1928-44; Reader, 1944-45; Prof., 1945-68; Dir, Inst. of Irish Studies, 1965-70; Dean of the Faculty of Arts, 1951-54; Mem. of Senate. Tallman Visiting Professor: Bowdoin Coll., Maine, 1948-49; Visiting Professor: Indiana Univ., 1964; Louisiana State Univ., 1969. Chm., Historic Monuments Advisory Council (NI) and Mem. Adv. Council, Republic of Ireland; President: Ulster Folk Life Soc. and Ulster Archæological Soc.; Ulster Architectural Heritage Soc.; former Chm. of Trustees, Ulster Folk and Transport Museum; Trustee, Ulster Museum; Vice-Pres., Montgomeryshire Soc.; Hon. Mem. and former Vice-Pres., Prehistoric Soc. Former Member:

Executive Cttee, NI Council of Social Service; NI Tourist Bd; Pres. Sect. E 1958 and Sect. H 1960, Brit. Assoc. for the Advancement of Science (first Chm. NI Area Cttee); Sir James Frazer Memorial Lectr, 1961; Sir Everard im Thurn Memorial Lectr, 1966; Wiles Lectr, 1971. Chm., Northern Ireland Government Cttee on Itinerants; Vice-Chm., Cttee on Nature Conservation. FSA; MRIA; Hon. MRTPI. Hon. ScD Bowdoin, 1949; Hon. LittD Dublin, 1970; Hon. LLD QUB, 1973; Hon. DLitt NUI, 1975. Victoria Medal, RGS, 1973. *Publications:* France, A Geographical Introduction, 1937; (joint) Preliminary Survey of the Ancient Monuments of Northern Ireland, 1940; Irish Heritage, 1942; A Portrait of Northern Ireland (Festival of Britain) 1951; Mourne Country, 1951, rev. edn 1967; Lyles Hill: A Late Neolithic Site in County Antrim, 1953; Irish Folk Ways, 1957; Prehistoric and Early Christian Ireland, 1966; (ed) Facets from Gweedore, 1971; The Personality of Ireland (Wiles Lectures), 1973; The Personality of Wales (BBC Wales Annual Lecture), 1973; (ed) Harvest Home: the last sheaf, 1975; papers in scientific journals. *Address:* 100 Malone Road, Belfast. *T:* 668510. *Club:* Ulster Arts (Hon. Member) (Belfast).

EVANS, Ven. Eric; *see* Evans, Ven. T. E.

EVANS, Ven. Eric Herbert; Archdeacon of Warrington, 1959-70, Emeritus since 1970; *b* 31 Jan 1902; *s* of late Captain E. B. Evans. *Educ:* Liverpool Institute; Bishop Wilson Theological Coll., Isle of Man. Rector of North Meols, Diocese of Liverpool, 1948-68. *Recreation:* travelling. *Address:* 36 Salford Road, Ainsdale, Southport, Merseyside. *T:* Southport 78715.

EVANS, Evan Stanley, CBE 1951; FRCS; Medical Superintendent, Lord Mayor Treloar Hospital, Alton, 1946-69, retired; Chairman, Queen Elizabeth's Foundation for the Disabled, Leatherhead, since 1942; Chairman, Treloar Trust; *b* 2 July 1904; *e s* of David Evans; *m* 1934, Muriel Gordon, *y d* of Peter Henderson; five *s. Educ:* St Bartholomew's Hospital. MRCS, LRCP, 1927; FRCS 1931; MB, BS London 1932; House Surg. and House Surg. (orthop.), St Bartholomew's Hosp., 1928; Medical Supt, Heatherwood Hosp., Ascot, 1932; Medical Supt, Queen Mary's Hosp., Carshalton, 1942. Hon. Cons. Orthop. Surgeon: Treloar Orthop. Hosp.; Lord Mayor Treloar Trust; Queen Elizabeth's Foundn for Disabled; Farnham Hosp. Fellow Brit. Orthop. Assoc.; Founder Mem. Exec. Cttee of British Council of Rehabilitation; formerly Chm. Exec. Cttee, Central Council for the Disabled; Vice-Pres., Jt Examination Board for orthopædic nursing. *Publications:* articles on non-pulmonary tuberculosis and cerebral palsy, in medical journals and books. *Address:* Highfield, Derby Road, Haslemere, Surrey GU27 1BP. *T:* Haslemere 51934.

EVANS, Sir Francis (Edward), GBE 1957; KCMG 1946 (CMG 1944); DL; Agent for the Government of N Ireland in Great Britain, 1962-66; *b* 4 April 1897; *s* of late Thomas Edward Evans, Belfast; *m* 1920, Mary (*d* 1976), *d* of late Rev. Prof. James Dick, MA, DD, Belfast; no *c. Educ:* Royal Academy, Belfast; London Sch. of Economics. Served European War, Lieut Royal Irish Rifles, 1915-19; Consular Service, 1920; Vice-Consul in New York, 1920-26, Boston, 1926-29, Colon, Panama, 1929-32, and Boston, 1932-34; Consul at Los Angeles, 1934-39; in Foreign Office, 1939-43; Consul at New York, 1943; Consul-Gen., 1944-50; Asst Under-Sec. of State, FO, 1951; British Ambassador to Israel, 1952-54 (Minister, 1951-52); British Ambassador to the Argentine, 1954-57. Dep. Chm. Northern Ireland Development Coun., 1957-65. Pres., Central Council, Ulster 71 Festival. Hon. Col, 6th (T) Bn Royal Ulster Rifles, 1961-67, (T&AVR), 1967-71. Hon. LLD Queen's Univ., Belfast; Hon. DCL Ripon Coll., Wisconsin; Hon. DLitt New University of Ulster. DL Belfast, 1959. KStJ. *Address:* 180 Upper Malone Road, Dunmurry, Belfast. *Clubs:* Travellers'; Ulster (Belfast).

EVANS, Fred; *see* Evans, Alfred T.

EVANS, Frederick Anthony, CVO 1973; General Secretary, The Duke of Edinburgh's Award Scheme, 1959-72; *b* 17 Nov. 1907; *s* of Herbert Anthony Evans, mining engineer, and Pauline (*née* Allen); *m* 1934, Nancy (*née* Meakin); two *s* one *d. Educ:* Charterhouse; Corpus Christi, Cambridge. Manager Doondu Coffee Plantation, Kenya, 1927-31; Colonial Service, 1934; Asst District Officer, Nigeria, 1935-39; Provincial Commissioner and Asst Colonial Sec., Gambia, 1940-47; Colonial Sec., Nassau, Bahamas, 1947-51; Acting Governor, 1950; Permanent Sec., Gold Coast (later Ghana), 1951-57. Dir, Anglo-Gambian Archæological Expedition, 1965-66. *Recreations:* golf, ski-ing. *Address:* Bamber Cottage, Saintbury Hill, Froyle, Hants; 11 Iverna Gardens, Kensington, W8. *Club:* Royal Commonwealth Society.

EVANS, Lt.-Gen. Sir Geoffrey (Charles), KBE 1954 (CBE 1945); CB 1946; DSO 1941 (bars 1942, 1944); retired, 1957; b 13 March 1901; s of late Col C. R. Evans, DSO; m 1928, Ida Louise, d of late H. R. Sidney; no c. Educ: Aldenham Sch.; Royal Military Coll., Sandhurst. 2nd Lieut The Royal Warwickshire Regt, 1920; Adjutant: 1st Bn, 1926-29; 7th Bn (TA), 1934-35; Staff Coll., 1936-37. Served War of 1939-45 (despatches five times): Bde Major, N Africa and Eritrea, 1940-41; OC 1st Bn Royal Sussex Regt, N Africa, 1941-42; Comdt Staff Coll., Quetta, 1942; Brig. Comd., India, 1943; Brig., Gen. Staff 4 Corps, Burma, 1943-44; Bde Commander, Burma, 1944; GOC 5 and 7 Indian Divs, Burma, 1944-45; GOC Allied Land Forces, Siam, 1945-46; GOC 42 (Lancs) Div. and North-West District, 1947-48; Dir of Military Training War Office, 1948-49; GOC 40 Div., Hong Kong, 1949-51; Temp. Comd. (Lt.-Gen.), British Forces, Hong Kong, 1951-52; Asst Chief of Staff (Org. and Trng), Supreme HQ, Allied Powers, Europe, 1952-53; GOC-in-C, Northern Command, 1953-57; retired. Hon. Col 7th Bn The Royal Warwickshire Regt, 1959-64. A Vice-Pres., Nat. Playing Fields Assoc.; Chairman: London and Middlesex Playing Fields Association, 1959-70; Anglo-Thai Soc., 1967-71. Comr, Royal Hosp., Chelsea, 1968-76. DL Greater London, 1970-76. Publications: The Desert and the Jungle, 1959; (with A. Brett-James) Imphal, 1962; The Johnnies, 1964; Slim as Military Commander, 1969; Tannenberg 1410:1914, 1971; Kensington, 1975; contrib. chapters: The Decisive Battles of the 20th Century, 1975; War Lords, 1976; articles and reviews. Recreation: fishing. Address: 11 Wellington Square, SW3. Club: Naval and Military.

EVANS, George Ewart; author, lecturer, and broadcaster, since 1948; b 1 April 1909; s of William and Janet Evans, Abercynon, Glamorgan; m 1938, Florence Ellen Knappett; one s three d. Educ: Abertaf Sch.; Mountain Ash Grammar Sch.; UC Cardiff. BA Hons Classics Wales, 1930; DipEd 1931. Writer of short stories, verse, radio and film scripts; specialized in history and folk life of the village. Univ. of Essex: Major Burrows Lectr, 1972; Vis. Fellow, 1973-75. Mem. Exec. Cttee, Oral History Soc.; Pres., Section H (Anthropology), British Assoc. for Advancement of Science, Swansea, 1971. Publications: The Voices of the Children, 1947; Ask the Fellows who Cut the Hay, 1956; (ed) Welsh Short Stories, 1959; The Horse in the Furrow, 1960; The Pattern Under the Plough, 1966; The Farm and the Village, 1969; Where Beards Wag All, 1970; (with David Thomson) The Leaping Hare, 1972; Acky, 1973; The Days That We Have Seen, 1975; Let Dogs Delight, 1975; From Mouths of Men, 1976. Recreations: walking, gardening, watching Rugby football. Address: 19 The Street, Brooke, Norwich NR15 1JW. T: Brooke 50518.
See also David Gentleman.

EVANS, Rear-Adm. George Hammond, CB 1968; Planning Inspector, Department of the Environment, since 1972; b 15 Jan. 1917; er s of late William and Edith Evans; m 1949, Margaret Ruth, d of late Captain C. C. Bell, DSO, RN, and Mrs Bell; one s. Educ: Bristol Grammar Sch. Commanded: HMS Eggesford, 1943-45; HMS Nepal, 1949-50; Naval Mem., Jt Intelligence Staff, Far East Station, 1951-52; Trng Comdr, RN Barracks, Chatham, 1952-54; Commanded: HMS Modeste, 1954-56; HMS Temeraire, 1957-58; Senior British Naval Officer, Ceylon, 1958-60; Deputy Asst Chief of Staff, SHAPE, 1960-62; Dir of Naval Recruiting, 1962-64; Capt. of Dockyard, Rosyth, 1964-66; Naval Deputy, Allied Forces, Northern Europe, 1966-69. Commander 1951; Capt. 1957; Rear-Adm. 1966; psc 1946; jssc 1957; retired, 1969. Royal Humane Society Medal for Lifesaving, 1942. Recreations: golf, sailing. Address: Long Farthings, West Burton, near Leyburn, North Yorks. T: Aysgarth 213. Club: Army and Navy.

EVANS, Sir Geraint Llewellyn, Kt 1969; CBE 1959; Opera Singer; Principal Baritone, Royal Opera House, Covent Garden; b 16 Feb. 1922; m 1948, Brenda Evans Davies; two s. Educ: Guildhall Sch. of Music. Has sung at: Royal Opera House, Covent Garden (since 1948); Glyndebourne Festival Opera; Vienna State Opera; La Scala, Milan; Metropolitan Opera, New York; San Francisco Opera; Lyric Opera, Chicago; Salzburg Festival Opera; Edinburgh Festival Opera; Paris Opera; Teatro Colon, Buenos Aires; Mexico City Opera; Welsh Nat. Opera; Scottish Opera; Berlin Opera; Teatr Wielki, Warsaw. Dir, Harlech Television Ltd. Governor, London Opera Centre. Pres., Guild for Promotion of Welsh Music. FGSM 1960. Worshipful Company of Musicians Sir Charles Santley Meml Award, 1963; Harriet Cohen Internat. Music Award (Opera Medal), 1967. Hon. DMus: Wales, 1965; Leicester, 1969. Hon. RAM 1969. Address: 34 Birchwood Road, Petts Wood, Kent.

EVANS, Godfrey; see Evans, T. G.

EVANS, Gwyneth, OBE 1975; Member of Development Commission, 1969-75; b 29 Feb. 1912; d of Griffith and Ellen Roberts; m 1936, Daniel Marcus Evans; three s one d. Educ: Grammar Sch. for Girls, Brecon. Did voluntary work with Red Cross and WVS (now WRVS) during War of 1939-45. Member: Merioneth CC, 1949-74 (Alderman, 1969-74 (1st woman Alderman), Chm., Social Services Cttee); Gwynedd CC, 1974-; Member: Children's Regional Planning Cttee for Wales (Chm., 1972-74); North Wales Police Authority; Lord Wolfenden's Cttee on Voluntary Orgns, 1974-. Mem., Court of Univ. of Wales. Recreation: reading. Address: Cartre, Ffestiniog, Gwynedd. T: Ffestiniog 709. Club: Ladies VAD.

EVANS, Gwynfor; MP (Plaid Cymru) Carmarthen, July 1966-1970, and since Oct. 1974; President, Plaid Cymru, since 1945 (Vice-Pres. 1943-45); b 1 Sept. 1912; s of Dan Evans and Catherine Mary Richard; m 1941, Rhiannon Prys Thomas; four s three d. Educ: Gladstone Road Elementary Sch.; County Sch., Barry; University of Wales, Aberystwyth; St John's Coll., Oxford. Qual. Solicitor, 1939. Hon. Sec. Heddychwyr Cymru (Welsh Pacifist movement), 1939-45; Chm. Union of Welsh Independents, 1954. Member: Carmarthen CC, 1949-74; Ct of Govs, University of Wales and UC, Aberystwyth; Council Univ. of Wales, and UC Aberystwyth. Past Mem. Welsh Broadcasting Council. Hon. LLD Wales, 1973. Publications: Plaid Cymru and Wales, 1950; Rhagom i Ryddid, 1964; Aros Mae, 1971; Wales can Win, 1973; Land of My Fathers, 1974. Address: Talar Wen, Llangadog, Sir Gaerfyrddin, Dyfed. T: Llangadog 567.

EVANS, Sir Harold, 1st Bt, cr 1963; CMG 1957; OBE 1945; b 29 April 1911; s of Sidney Evans and Gladys Mary Lythgoe; m 1945, Elizabeth Jaffray; one d (one s decd). Educ: King Edward's Sch., Stourbridge. Editorial staff of newspapers in Worcs and Sheffield, 1930-39; Freelance Journalism, 1939-40; British Volunteers in Finland, 1940; Staff of British Legation, Helsinki, 1940-42; Min. of Information Rep. in W Africa (Staff of Resident Minister), 1942-45; Dep. Public Relations Officer, Colonial Office, 1945-53; Chief Information Officer, Colonial Office, 1953-57; Public Relations Adviser to the Prime Minister, 1957-64; Head of Information and Research, Independent Television Authority, 1964-66; Adviser on Public Relations to Bd, Vickers Ltd, 1966-76; Chm., Health Educn Council, 1973-76. Publications: Men in the Tropics, Anthology, 1949; various contributions. Address: 3 Challoners Close, Rottingdean, East Sussex. T: Brighton 33397.

EVANS, Harold Matthew; Editor, Sunday Times, since 1967; b 28 June 1928; s of Frederick and Mary Evans; m 1953, Enid, d of late John Parker and of Susan Parker; one s two d. Educ: St Mary's Road Central Sch., Manchester; Durham Univ. BA 1952, MA Dunelm 1966. Ashton-under-Lyne, Lancs, Reporter Newspapers, 1944-46 and 1949; RAF, 1946-49; Durham Univ., 1949-52; Manchester Evening News, 1952; Commonwealth Fund Fellow in Journalism, Chicago and Stanford Univs, USA, 1956-57; Asst Ed, Manchester Evening News, 1958-61; Ed., Northern Echo, 1961-66; Editor-in-Chief, North of England Newspaper Co., 1963-66; Chief Asst to Editor, Sunday Times, 1966; Managing Editor, Sunday Times, 1966. Member, Executive Board: Times Newspapers Ltd, 1968-; International Press Inst., 1974-; Dir, The Sunday Times Ltd, 1968-. Publications: The Active Newsroom, 1961; Editing and Design (five volumes): vol. 1, Newsman's English, 1972; vol. 5, Newspaper Design, 1973; vol. 2, Newspaper Text, 1974; vol 3, Newspaper Headlines, 1974; vol. 4, Pictures on a Page, 1977; (jointly) We Learned To Ski, 1974. Recreations: music, table-tennis, chess, ski-ing. Address: The Sunday Times, Thomson House, 200 Gray's Inn Road, WC1. T: 01-837 1234. Clubs: Garrick, Royal Automobile.

EVANS, (Harry) Lindley, CMG 1963; Pianist; Composer; retired as Professor of Pianoforte, NSW State Conservatorium of Music, Sydney, Australia, 1928-66, a Governor, 1966-73; b 18 Nov. 1895; British; m 1926, Marie Florence Stewart. Educ: St George's Grammar Sch., Capetown, South Africa. Pianist with Dame Nellie Melba, 1922-31. Celebrated a 40-year partnership in giving two-piano recitals, 1964. Melody Man in Children's Hour (ABC) since its inception, 1940. Pres., Musical Assoc. of NSW (life Mem.); Past Pres., Fellowship of Australian Composers (Life Mem.). Publications: many musical compositions. Recreations: bowls, yachting. Address: 47/84 St George's Crescent, Drummoyne, NSW, Australia. T: 81-3896. Club: Savage (Sydney) (Life Mem.; Pres. 13 yrs).

EVANS, Sir Haydn T.; see Tudor Evans.

EVANS, Maj.-Gen. Henry Holland, CB 1972; b Harrogate, 18 Nov. 1914; o s of Major H. Evans; m 1939, Norah Mary, d of F. R. Lawson, Wolstanton, Staffs; one s one d. Educ: King James

Grammar Sch., Almondbury, near Huddersfield; Manchester Univ. Commissioned Duke of Wellington's Regt (TA), 1936; Regular Army Commission in AEC, 1939; Officer Instructor, Duke of York's Royal Mil. Sch., 1939-41; Staff Officer: 43 (Wessex) Div., 1942-45; War Office, 1945-48; Chief Educn Officer, Malta and Libya, 1948-51; various RAEC appts, incl. Headmaster DYRMS and Chief Inspector of Army children's schools, to 1963; CEO, Northern Comd, 1963-65; CEO, BAOR, 1965-68; Dir of Army Educn, 1969-72. Sec., Council for Accreditation of Corresp. Colls, 1973-75. Mem., Sevenoaks Town Council, 1973-76. Governor, Sevenoaks Sch., 1974-. *Address:* Quarry Chase, Seal Hollow Road, Sevenoaks, Kent. *T:* Sevenoaks 56603. *Club:* Army and Navy.

EVANS, Hubert John Filmer, CMG 1958; LLD; HM Diplomatic Service, retired; Central Asian Research Centre, 1965-70; *b* 21 Nov. 1904; *y s* of late Harry Evans and late Edith Gwendoline Rees; *m* 1948, Marjory Maureen Filmer (*née* Carrick), *widow* of Col R. A. M. Tweedy. *Educ:* City of London Sch.; Jesus Coll., Oxford (Classical Scholar); Montpellier. Studied oriental languages with Ross, Minorsky, and in the East. Entered Indian Civil Service, 1928; served as Magistrate in various districts of United Provinces, 1929-37; Deputy Commissioner of Delhi, and Pres., Delhi Municipal Council, 1938-42; Sec. Delhi Administration, 1942-45; Collector of Agra, 1945-47; appointed to Foreign Service, 1947; at the Foreign Office, 1948-50; Financial Adviser to Persian Gulf Residency, 1950-51; Consul-Gen. at Meshed, 1951; in Latin America, 1952-54; Consul-Gen., Rotterdam, 1955-56; HM Ambassador to Korea, 1957-61. Hon. Sec., Royal Central Asian Soc. and Chm. Ed. Board 1965-70. Hon. MRAS; Hon. LLD Korea, 1960; Freedom of Seoul, 1960. *Publications:* various in oriental jls. *Recreations:* The Persian Poets, and travel. *Address:* Manoir d'Arlette, Fatouville, Eure, Normandy, France. *Club:* Athenæum.

EVANS, Hywel Eifion, CB 1974; Welsh Secretary, Ministry of Agriculture, Fisheries and Food, 1968-75; *b* 24 Jan. 1910; *s* of late Gruffydd Thomas and Winnifred Evans, Felin Rhydhir, Pwllheli, Caernarvonshire; *m* 1939, Mary Elizabeth, *d* of late Richard and Hannah Jones, Gilfach, Glanywydden, Llandudno; one *s* one *d. Educ:* Pwllheli Grammar Sch.; University Coll. of North Wales, Bangor. BSc (Hons) (Agric.). Research Asst, Dept of Agricultural Economics, UCW, Aberystwyth, 1934-40; Dist and Dep. Exec. Officer, Leicester WAEC, 1940-46; County Advisory Officer: Radnor AEC, 1946-47; Carmarthen AEC, 1947-57; Dep. Regional Dir, Nat. Agricl Advisory Service for Wales, 1957-59, Regional Dir, 1959-66; Dep. Dir, Nat. Agricl Adv. Service (London), 1967-68. FRAgSs, 1972. *Publications:* articles on agricultural, economic and sociological topics in Welsh Jl of Agriculture, Agriculture, and other jls. *Recreations:* idling, fishing, shooting. *Address:* Fflur y Main, Maeshendre, Waunfawr, Aberystwyth, Wales. *T:* Aberystwyth 3828. *Club:* Farmers'.

EVANS, Sir Hywel (Wynn), KCB 1976 (CB 1972); Permanent Secretary, Welsh Office, since 1971; *b* 30 May 1920; *s* of late Dr T. Hopkin Evans, MusDoc and Adelina Evans; *m* 1949, Jessie Margaret Templeton; one *d. Educ:* Liverpool Collegiate Sch.; Liverpool Univ. RA and Intell. Corps, 1940-46 (despatches). Joined Min. of Labour, as Asst Principal, 1947; seconded to FO, 1952-54; Commonwealth Fellow, 1957-58; Private Sec. to Ministers of Labour, 1959-60; Sec., NEDC, 1964-68; Asst Under-Sec. of State, Welsh Office, 1968-71. Mem., Gorsedd of Bards of Wales. US Bronze Star, 1945. *Publication:* Governmental Regulation of Industrial Relations, 1960 (USA). *Recreations:* opera, watching rugby. *Address:* Coed-yr-Iarll, St Fagans, Cardiff, S Wales CF5 6DU. *T:* Cardiff 565214. *Clubs:* Reform; Cardiff and County (Cardiff).

EVANS, Sir Ian William G.; *see* Gwynne-Evans.

EVANS, Ioan (Lyonel); JP; MP (Lab and Co-op) Aberdare, since Feb. 1974; *b* 1927; *m* 1949, Maria Evans, JP (*née* Griffiths); one *s* one *d. Educ:* Llanelly Grammar Sch.; University Coll., Swansea. Has held various Co-op. (incl. Sec. Birm. and Dist Co-op. Party) and Labour Party offices. MP (Lab and Co-op) Birmingham Yardley, 1964-70; Subseq. PPS to Postmaster-Gen.; Asst Govt Whip, 1966-68; Comptroller of HM Household, 1968-70. Formerly Vice-Chm. West Midlands Parly Labour Group of MP's; Chm., Parly Labour Party Trade Gp, 1974-; Vice-Chairman: Parly Labour Party Disabled Gp, 1974-; Parly Labour Party Prices and Consumer Protection Gp, 1974-; Co-op. Parly Gp, 1974-; Hon. Secretary: Welsh Lab. MPs Gp; Welsh Parly Party. Formerly Vice-Chm., UK Parly delegn to Consultative Assembly of Council of Europe; formerly Mem., UK Delegn to Assembly of WEU; Hon. Sec., Parly Assoc. for World Govt, 1974-; Mem. Exec. Cttee, British Branch, IPU. Co-opted Mem., W Bromwich Educn Cttee; Governor, W

Bromwich Grammar Sch.; Lectr for WEA and NCLC; Dir, Internat. Defence and Aid Fund, 1970-74; Member: Exec. Cttee, Wales Council of Labour; Exec. Cttee, Christian Action Council. Chm., Justice for Rhodesia, 1973-. JP: Birmingham, 1960-70; Middlesex, 1970-. *Address:* 169 Eastcote Road, Ruislip, Mddx. *T:* Ruislip 75251.

EVANS, James Donald; Editor and Editor-in-Chief, The Northern Echo, Darlington, since 1966; Director, North of England Newspapers, since 1971; *b* 12 Nov. 1926; *yr s* of Arthur Evans and Isabella McKinnon Evans; *m* 1946, Freda Bristow; two *s* three *d. Educ:* Royal Grammar Sch., High Wycombe. Jun. Reporter, Bucks Free Press, 1943-45; Army, 1945-48; Chief Reporter, Maidenhead Advertiser, 1948-50; Northern Echo: District Chief Reporter, 1950-60; Industrial Corresp., 1961-65; Industrial Editor, 1965-66. *Recreations:* driving, reading. *Address:* 4 Harewood Hill, Darlington, Co. Durham. *T:* Darlington 68710. *Clubs:* National Liberal; New (Darlington).

EVANS, Col J(ames) Ellis, CBE 1973 (OBE 1952); TD 1947; JP; Vice Lord-Lieutenant of Clwyd, since 1977; *b* 6 Aug. 1910; *s* of James William Evans and Eleanor Evans, MBE, JP; unmarried. *Educ:* Epworth Coll., Rhyl. Chartered Accountant (FCA). Joined TA, 1937; served War of 1939-45, RA: France, 1940; N Africa, 1941-44; Italy, 1944-45; comd 384 Light Regt RA (RWF), TA, 1947-52; Dep. CRA, 53 (Welsh) Div., 1953-57; Chm. Denbigh and Flint TA Assoc., 1961-68; Chm., Wales and Mon TA&VRA, 1971-74 (Vice-Chm., 1968-71). Mem., Prestatyn UDC, 1939-74 (Chm. 1947); Mayor, Prestatyn Town Council, 1974-75. Clwyd, formerly Flintshire: JP 1951; DL 1953; High Sheriff, 1970-71; Vice-Lieut, 1970-74. Chm., North Wales Police Authority, 1976-. *Recreations:* lawn tennis (played for Wales and Lancashire, 1936-48), gardening. *Address:* Trafford Mount, Gronant Road, Prestatyn, Clwyd. *T:* Prestatyn 4119. *Clubs:* East India, Devonshire, Sports and Public Schools; City (Chester); Cardiff and County (Cardiff).

EVANS, John; MP (Lab) Newton, since Feb. 1974; *b* 19 Oct. 1930; *s* of late James Evans, miner and Margaret (*née* Robson); *m* 1959, Joan Slater; two *s* one *d. Educ:* Jarrow Central School. Apprentice Marine Fitter, 1946-49 and 1950-52; Nat. Service, Royal Engrs, 1949-50; Engr, Merchant Navy, 1952-55; joined AUEW, 1952; joined Labour Party, 1955; worked in various industries as fitter, ship-building and repairing, steel, engineering, 1955-65. Mem. Hebburn UDC, 1962, Leader 1969, Chm. 1972; Sec./Agent Jarrow CLP, 1965-68, resigned. Mem., European Parlt, 1975-; Chm., Regional Policy, Planning and Transport Cttee, European Parlt, 1976-. Hon. Vice-Pres., Nat. Union of Labour and Socialist Clubs. *Recreations:* watching football, reading, gardening. *Address:* 6 Kirkby Road, Culcheth, Warrington, Cheshire WA3 4BS. *T:* Culcheth 766322. *Clubs:* Labour (Jarrow); Daten (Culcheth).

EVANS, John; *see* Evans, N. J. B.

EVANS, Prof. John Davies, FBA 1973; Director, University of London Institute of Archæology, and Professor of Archæology in the University of London, since 1973; *b* 22 Jan. 1925; *o s* of Harry Evans and Edith Haycocks; *m* 1957, Evelyn Sladdin. *Educ:* Liverpool Institute High Sch. (open schol. in English to Pemb. Coll.); Pembroke Coll., Cambridge. War Service, 1943-47. BA 1948, MA 1950, PhD 1956. Fellow of British Institute of Archæology at Ankara, 1951-52; Research Fellow of Pembroke Coll., Cambridge, 1953-56; Prof. of Prehistoric Archæology, London Univ., 1956-73. Pres., Prehistoric Soc., 1974-; Mem., Permanent Council, Internat. Congress of Prehistoric and Protohistoric Scis, 1975-; Chm., Area Archaeol Adv. Cttee for SE England, 1975-. FSA 1955 (Dir, 1975-); Corr. Mem., German Archæological Inst., 1968. *Publications:* Malta (Ancient Peoples and Places Series), 1959; (with Dr A. C. Renfrew) Excavations at Saliagos, near Antiparos, 1968; The Prehistoric Antiquities of the Maltese Islands, 1971; papers and reports in archæological journals. *Recreations:* walking, listening to music. *Address:* Institute of Archæology, Gordon Square, WC1H 0PY.

EVANS, John Field, QC 1972; a Recorder of the Crown Court, since 1972; *b* 27 Sept. 1928; 2nd *s* of late John David Evans, Llandaff, and Lucy May Evans (*née* Field). *Educ:* Cardiff High Sch.; Exeter Coll., Oxford (MA). Pilot Officer, RAF, 1948-49. Called to Bar, Inner Temple, 1953; in practice as a barrister. Dep. Chm., Worcestershire QS, 1964-71. *Recreation:* golf. *Address:* 1 Fountain Court, Birmingham B4 6DR. *T:* 021-236 5721; 1 Brick Court, Temple, EC4. *T:* 01-353 8845. *Clubs:* Garrick; Vincent's (Oxford).

EVANS, John Isaac Glyn; Director of Weapons Production (Naval) since 1970; *b* 1 April 1919; *s* of William Evans; *m* 1943,

Hilda Garratt Evans (*née* Lee); two *s* one *d. Educ:* Ystalyfera Grammar Sch.; University Coll., Swansea (BSc Physics, BSc Elec. Engineering). Engineer, GEC, 1940-41. Served War, Captain REME, 1941-46. Development Engineer, GEC, 1946-50; Works Group Engineer, Admiralty, 1950-53; main grade, 1953-59; senior grade, 1959-64; superintending grade, 1964-67; Dep. Dir, 1967-70. FIEE. *Recreations:* tennis, badminton, cricket. *Address:* 16 Woodland Grove, Claverton Down, Bath, Avon.

EVANS, John Kerr Q.; *see* Quarren Evans.

EVANS, John Marten Llewellyn, CBE 1956 (MBE 1945); JP; Official Solicitor to the Supreme Court of Judicature, 1950-70; *b* 9 June 1909; *s* of late Marten Llewellyn Evans, Solicitor, and Edith Helena (*née* Lile); *m* 1943, Winifred Emily, *y d* of late Austin Reed; one *s* one *d. Educ:* Rugby Sch.; Trinity Coll., Oxford. Admitted Solicitor, 1935; Legal Asst to the Official Solicitor, 1937. Served War of 1939-45, Major RA. Senior Legal Asst to the Official Solicitor, 1947; Asst Master in Lunacy, 1950. Vice-Chm., Austin Reed Group Ltd, 1969-77. Master of Worshipful Company of Cutlers, 1967-68. JP City of London, 1969. *Recreations:* the theatre, cricket, golf, tennis. *Address:* The Paddock, Waltham St Lawrence, Reading, Berks. *Clubs:* Garrick, MCC.

EVANS, Ven. John Mascal; Archdeacon of Surrey since 1968; *b* 17 May 1915; *s* of Rev. Edward Foley Evans and Mary Evans; *m* 1941, Mary Elizabeth (*née* Rathbone); three *s* two *d. Educ:* St John's Sch., Leatherhead; Brasenose Coll., Oxford; Wells Theological Coll. Asst Curate, St Martin's, Epsom, 1938; Perpetual Curate, Stoneleigh, Epsom, 1942, All Saints, Fleet, 1952; Vicar, St Mary, Walton-on-Thames, 1960-68; Hon. Canon of Guildford, 1963-. *Recreations:* outdoor sports, fishing. *Address:* Bowmans, Coxcombe Lane, Chiddingfold, Surrey.

EVANS, John Robert, MD, DPhil, FRCP (Can.); President, University of Toronto, Canada, since July 1972; *b* 1 Oct. 1929; *s* of William Watson Evans and Mary Thompson; *m* 1954, Gay Glassco; four *s* two *d. Educ:* Univ. of Toronto (MD); Oxford Univ. (Rhodes Schol.) (DPhil). Jr interne, Toronto Gen. Hosp., 1952-53; Hon. Registrar, Nat. Heart Hosp., London, 1955; Asst Res.: Sunnybrook Hosp., Toronto, 1956; Toronto Gen. Hosp., 1957; Ontario Heart Foundn Fellow, Hosp. for Sick Children, Toronto, 1958; Chief Res. Physician, Toronto Gen. Hosp., 1959; Research Fellow, Baker Clinic Research Lab., Harvard Med. Sch., 1960; Markle Schol. in Acad. Med., Univ. of Toronto, 1960-65; Associate, Dept of Med., Faculty of Med., Univ. of Toronto, 1961-65; Asst Prof., 1965-66; Dean, Faculty of Med., McMaster Univ., 1965-72, Vice-Pres., Health Sciences, 1967-72. Director, Dominion Foundries and Steel Ltd. Hon. LLD: McGill, 1972; Dalhousie, 1972; McMaster, 1972; Queen's, 1974; Wilfrid Laurier, 1975; Hon. DSc Meml Univ. of Newfoundland, 1973. *Recreations:* ski-ing, fishing, farming. *Address:* University of Toronto, Toronto, Ontario M5S 1A1, Canada; 93 Highland Avenue, Toronto, Ontario M4W 2A4, Canada.

EVANS, John Roger W.; *see* Warren Evans.

EVANS, John Yorath Gwynne; Deputy Director (Air), Royal Aircraft Establishment, 1972-76; semi-retired; Consultant, Royal Aircraft Establishment, since 1976; *b* 10 Feb. 1922; *s* of Randell and Florence Evans, Carms; *m* 1948, Paula Lewis, *d* of late Roland Ford Lewis; two *s* one *d. Educ:* UCW Aberystwyth. Royal Aircraft Estabt, 1942; attached to RAF, Germany, 1945-46; Supt Wind Tunnels, RAE Bedford, 1958; Head of Aerodynamics Dept, RAE, 1971. *Publications:* contrib. various sci. and techn. jls. *Recreations:* sailing, travel, reading. *Address:* Sanderstead, Dene Close, Lower Bourne, Farnham, Surrey. *T:* Farnham (Surrey) 21380.

EVANS, Rt. Rev. Kenneth Dawson; *see* Dorking, Suffragan Bishop of.

EVANS, Laurence James, CBE 1977; HM Diplomatic Service, retired; HM Consul-General at Barcelona and Andorra, 1973-77; Doyen, Barcelona Consular Corps, 1974-76, Hon. Doyen 1976-77; *b* 16 Dec. 1917; *s* of Albert Victor and Margaret Evans; *m* 1940, Clare Mary (*née* Kolb); one *d. Educ:* Alsop High Sch., Liverpool; Univ. of Liverpool (BA Hons, French); Univ. of Rennes (Diploma). Reader in the Faculté des Lettres, Univ. of Rennes, 1938-39. HM Forces (Intell. Corps), 1939-45. Foreign Office, Asst Principal, 1946-47; Bd of Inland Revenue (HM Inspector of Taxes), 1947-49; rejoined Foreign Service and apptd to Brussels, 1950-51; HM Vice-Consul, Khorramshahr, 1951-52; FO, 1952-54; Second Sec. and Vice-Consul, Ciudad Trujillo, Dominican Republic, 1954-57 (Chargé d'Affaires, 1955 and 1957); FO, 1957-63 (Asst Head of Communications, 1959); HM

Consul, New York, 1963-66; Asst Head of Personnel Dept (Ops), DSAO, 1966-69; HM Consul-Gen., Geneva, 1969-73. *Recreations:* swimming, music. *Address:* 16 Oakhurst Rise, Carshalton Beeches, Surrey SM5 4AG. *T:* 01-643 3023. *Clubs:* Travellers', Royal Commonwealth Society.

EVANS, Lindley; *see* Evans, (Harry) Lindley.

EVANS, Dr Luther Harris; retired librarian and government official; *b* near Sayersville, Bastrop County, Texas, USA, 13 Oct. 1902; *s* of George Washington and Lillie Johnson Evans; *m* 1925, Helen Murphy; one *s. Educ:* University of Texas; Leland Stanford Univ., USA. AB 1923, MA 1924 Texas; PhD Stanford, 1927; Doctor of Humane Letters, Yale, 1946; LLD Pa Mil. Coll., 1948, British Columbia Univ., 1948; DL Loyola Coll, 1950; Denison Univ., 1961; DLitt Brown Univ., 1953; LLD Columbia, 1953; LLD Dartmouth Coll., 1956; Doctor of the Humanities Washington Univ., 1959; Marietta Coll. 1962; Dr of Literature Adelphi Coll., 1960. Instructor in freshman orientation course in problems of citizenship, Stanford Univ., 1924-27; Instructor in Government, New York Univ., 1927-28; Instructor in Political Science, Dartmouth Coll., 1928-30; Asst Prof. of Politics, Princeton Univ., 1930-35; Dir, Historical Records Survey of Work Projects Administration, 1935-39; Dir of Legislative Reference Service, Library of Congress, 1939-40; Chief Asst Librarian, on occasion Acting Librarian of Congress, 1940-45; Librarian of Congress, 1945-53. Member: UNESCO Executive Board, 1949-53; US Nat. Commission for UNESCO 1946-52 (Chm. 1952); (adviser, London Conference on an international educational and cultural organisation, 1945; deleg. or adviser, General Conf., UNESCO, 1947-53); Dir-Gen. United Nations Educational, Scientific and Cultural Organisation, 1953-58; Mem. US National Commission for UNESCO, 1959-63; Senior Staff Mem. Brookings Instn, Washington, DC, 1959-61; Dir Nat. Educn Assoc. Project on Educational Implications of Automation, Washington, DC, 1961-62; Dir, Internat. Collections, Columbia Univ., New York, 1962-71. Vis. Prof. in Library Studies, Univ. of Puerto Rico, 1972. Chm., Washington Area Cttee on Refugees, 1960-62; Chm., US Cttee for Refugees, 1962-71; Member Nat. Board: UNA of USA, 1964-69; Amer. Civil Liberties Union, 1964-69; Chm. Exec. Cttee, Commn to Study Organisation of Peace, 1966-. Pres., World Fedn, USA, 1971-. Hon. Vice-Pres. Library Association (Eng.); Hon. Mem., Association of Special Libraries and Information Bureaux (Eng.); Member: American Library Assoc. (life-mem.); Nat. Education Assoc. (life mem.); American Political Science Assoc.; Soc. for Internat. Development; Manuscript Soc. Decorations awarded by: Brazil, France, Japan, Lebanon and Peru. *Publications:* The Virgin Islands, from naval base to new deal, 1945; (with others) Survey of Federal (US) Departmental Libraries, 1961; The Decade of Development: problems and issues (with others), 1966; The United States and UNESCO, 1971; articles and book reviews in professional journals. *Address:* 209 Harriet Drive, San Antonio, Texas 78216, USA.

EVANS, Maurice; Actor-manager; *s* of Alfred Herbert Evans, JP (Dorset). *Educ:* Grocers' Company Sch. Commenced theatrical career at Festival Theatre, Cambridge; later in a series of plays at Wyndham's, London; made his first successes in John van Druten's Diversion and R. C. Sherriff's Journey's End; following several years of appearances in West End became leading man at the Old Vic, where he was seen as Hamlet, Richard II, Petruchio, Benedick, etc.; went to America, 1936, to play Romeo to Katharine Cornell's Juliet; also appeared as the Dauphin in St Joan, Napoleon in St Helena. Produced and played title role Richard II, New York City, 1937; uncut Hamlet, 1938-39; produced and played Falstaff in Henry IV (Part 1), 1939; appeared as Malvolio in Twelth Night with Helen Hayes, 1940-41; produced and played title role in Macbeth, New York City, 1941-42; in each play toured provinces extensively. Went on a lecture tour in aid of British War Relief, 1941. Captain US Army, 1942; disch. with rank of Major, 1945. Played Hamlet in own GI version, 1945-46, New York; 1946-47, in provinces (acting version published Doubleday & Co., 1947). Produced and starred in Man and Superman, New York, 1947-48, establishing record New York run for play of Bernard Shaw; toured provinces, 1948-49; produced, and co-starred with Edna Best in Terence Rattigan's Browning Version, 1949; starred in Shaw's The Devil's Disciple, New York, and toured provinces, 1950; revived Richard II at NY City Center, 1951; starred in Dial 'M' for Murder, New York, 1952-54, and toured provinces, 1954; starred in Shaw's The Apple Cart, New York and provinces, 1956-57; produced and starred in Shaw's Heartbreak House, New York, 1959-60; starred in Tenderloin (musical), New York, 1960-61; The Aspern Papers, New York, 1961-62; with Helen Hayes in Shakespeare Revisited, A Program For Two Players, at Stratford (USA) and on tour, 1962-63; produced The Teahouse of the August Moon (Pulitzer-Critics' prize),

1953; No Time for Sergeants, 1955; Artistic Supervisor, New York City Center Theatre Company, 1949-51. Made first American picture 1950, co-starring with·Ethel Barrymore in Kind Lady; also made Androcles and the Lion, Warlord, Jack of Diamonds, Planet of the Apes, Rosemary's Baby, Thin Air, Planet of the Apes Revisited, and, in England, Gilbert and Sullivan, 1952 and Macbeth, 1960. Became United States citizen, 1941. *Address:* c/o Charles H. Renthal & Co., 641 Lexington Avenue, New York, NY 10022, USA. *Club:* Players (New York).

EVANS, Meurig; *see* Evans, David Meurig.

EVANS, Michael; *see* Evans, T. M.

EVANS, Michael Nordon, CMG 1964; Permanent Secretary, Ministry of Health and Housing, Kenya, 1960-64, retired; now British Vice-Consul, Cape Town; *b* 27 April 1915; *s* of Christmas and Lilian Margaret Louise Evans, Tunbridge Wells; *m* 1st, 1939, Mary Stockwood; one *d*; 2nd, 1951, Mary Josephine Suzette van Vloten; one *d. Educ:* Eastbourne Coll.; Queens' Coll., Cambridge. Apptd District Officer in Colonial Administrative Service, Kenya, 1939; African Courts Officer, Kenya, 1953; Dep. Commissioner for Local Government, 1954; Permanent Sec., 1958. *Recreations:* judo, tennis, golf, photography. *Address:* Glengariff, Stellenbosch Road, Somerset West, Cape Province, South Africa. *Clubs:* Hawks (Cambridge); Nairobi.

EVANS, Mostyn; *see* Evans, Arthur M.

EVANS, Dr (Noel) John (Bebbington); Deputy Chief Medical Officer (Deputy Secretary), Department of Health and Social Security, since 1977; *b* 26 Dec. 1933; *s* of William John Evans and Gladys Ellen (*née* Bebbington); *m* 1st, 1960, Elizabeth Mary Garbutt (marr. diss.); two *s* one *d*; 2nd, 1974, Eileen Jane McMullan. *Educ:* Hymers Coll., Hull; Christ's Coll., Cambridge (scholar); Westminster Medical Sch., London; London Sch. of Hygiene and Tropical Med. (Newsholme prize, Chadwick Trust medal and prize). MA, MB, BChir; FRCP, DPH (Dist.), FFCM. Called to Bar, Gray's Inn, 1965. House officer posts at: Westminster, Westminster Children's, Hammersmith, Central Middlesex and Brompton Hosps, 1958-60; Medical Registrar and Tutor, Westminster Hosp., 1960-61; Asst MoH, Warwickshire CC, 1961-65; Dept of Health and Social Security (formerly Min. of Health), 1965-, SPMO 1974-77; Sir Wilson Jameson Travelling Fellowship, 1966. *Publications:* The Organisation and Planning of Health Services in Yugoslavia, 1967; contribs to med. jls. *Recreations:* canals, photography. *Address:* 2 Meadow Way, Rickmansworth, Herts. *T:* Rickmansworth 43840.

EVANS, Lady Olwen Elizabeth C.; *see* Carey Evans.

EVANS, Prof. Peter Angus, DMus; FRCO; Professor of Music, University of Southampton, since 1961; *b* 7 Nov. 1929; *y s* of Rev. James Mackie Evans and Elizabeth Mary Fraser; *m* 1953, June Margaret Vickery. *Educ:* West Hartlepool Grammar Sch.; St Cuthbert's Soc., University of Durham. BA (1st cl. hons Music), 1950; BMus, MA 1953; DMus 1958; FRCO 1952. Music Master, Bishop Wordsworth's Sch., Salisbury, 1951-52. Lecturer in Music, University of Durham, 1953-61. Conductor, Palatine Opera Group, 1956-61; Opera Conductor, Hovingham Festival, 1959; Conductor, Southampton Philharmonic Soc., 1965-. *Publications:* Sonata for Oboe and Piano, 1953; Three Preludes for Organ, 1955; Edns of 17th Century Chamber Music, 1956-58; contributor to Die Musik, in Geschichte und Gegenwart, since 1955, to A Concise Encyclopædia of Music, 1958, and to the New Oxford History of Music, 1974; writer and reviewer, especially on 17th century and contemporary music. *Address:* 9 Bassett Close, Southampton. *T:* Southampton 68125.

EVANS, Dr Philip Rainsford, CBE 1968; Physician-Paediatrician to the Queen, 1972-76; Physician, The Hospital for Sick Children, Great Ormond Street, 1946-75; *b* 14 April 1910; 2nd *s* of Charles Irwin Evans, headmaster of Leighton Park Sch., and Katharine Evans; *m* 1935, Dr Barbara Dorothy Fordyce Hay-Cooper; three *s* one *d. Educ:* Sidcot Sch., Winscombe, Som; Leighton Park Sch., Reading; Manchester University. BSc 1930, MSc 1941, MB, ChB 1933, MD 1941, Manchester; MRCP 1935, FRCP 1945, London. Rockefeller Travelling Research Fellow, 1937-38; Asst Pædiatrician, Johns Hopkins Hosp., Baltimore, 1938-39; Asst Physician to Children's Dept, King's Coll. Hosp., London, 1939-46; Dir, Dept of Paediatrics, Guy's Hosp., 1946-71; Dir, British Tay-Sachs Foundn, 1971-74. Served War of 1939-45, RAMC, N Africa and Italy, 1942-46 (despatches); Hon. Col AMS. Editor, Archives of Disease in Childhood, 1947-54. Hon. Mem., British, French and American Pædiatric Socs.

Member, Cttee on Milk Composition, 1957-59, Ministry of Agriculture, Fisheries and Food. FRSM (Pres., Section of Pædiatrics, 1968-69); Hon. Sec. British Pædiatric Assoc., 1954-59; Hon. Consultant to the Army in Pædiatrics, 1962-66; Visiting Prof., Faculty of Medicine, Saigon, 1967-68; late Examr Universities of Bristol, Leeds, Birmingham, Cambridge, and RCP; Mem. Council, RCP, 1962-65; Censor, RCP, 1972-74. (Jointly) Dawson Williams Prize, BMA, 1969. *Publications:* (joint) Infant Feeding and Feeding Difficulties, 1954; Jt Editor, Garrod, Batten and Thursfield's Diseases of Children, 1953; original papers in med. journals. *Address:* 24 Abbey Road, NW8 9AX. *T:* 01-624 1668.

EVANS, Phyllis Mary Carlyon, MA; Education Officer, Winchester Cathedral; Headmistress, St Swithun's School, Winchester, 1952-73; *b* 17 April 1913; *d* of L. L. C. Evans, late Headmaster of Swanbourne House Sch., Bletchley, Bucks, and of Mrs M. Evans (*née* Gore-Browne). *Educ:* Wycombe Abbey Sch., Bucks; St Hugh's Coll., Oxford. Lit Hum, 1935. Classics mistress, St Mary's, Calne, 1935-39; Yates Theology Scholar St Hugh's Coll., Oxford, 1939-40; Degree in Theology, 1940; MA 1940. Senior Classics mistress, The Alice Ottley Sch., Worcester, 1940-45; Head Mistress, Wellington Diocesan Sch. for Girls, Marton, New Zealand, 1946-51. Representative of Winchester Diocese in Church Assembly, 1957-70; Member: Winchester Dio. Bd of Finance; Winchester Dio. Councils for Ministry and Education; Winchester Dio. Bishop's Council; Dio. Pastoral Cttee; Lay Co-Chm., Winchester Deanery Synod. Lay Reader. Fellow of Woodard Corp. Governor: Church Schs Co.; St Michael's Sch., Petworth; Rookesbury Park Sch., Wickham, Hants. *Address:* 10b Edgar Road, Winchester.

EVANS, Very Rev. Raymond Ellis; Dean of Monmouth and Vicar of St Woolos, Newport, Gwent, 1953-75; *m* 1944, Alice Craigie, *d* of John and Alice Logan, Stirling, Scotland; two *c. Educ:* St David's Coll., Lampeter; St John's Coll., Oxford (MA). Deacon, 1934; Priest, 1935; Curate of Penmaen, 1934-36, of St John the Evangelist, Newport, 1936-44; Vicar of St Andrew's, Newport, 1944-47; Examining Chaplain to Bishop of Monmouth, 1946; Vicar of Blackwood, 1947-52; Sec. Monmouth Diocesan Conf., 1951; Vicar of St Mark, Newport, 1952-53. *Address:* 23 Stelvio Park Drive, Newport, Gwent NPT 3EL.

EVANS, Raymond John Morda, MA, PhD; JP; Headmaster, Silcoates School, 1960-July 1978; *b* 1 Oct. 1917; 2nd *s* of late Rev. J. Morda Evans, Congregational Minister; *m* 1942, Catherine Mair Gernos Davies, *er d* of late Rev. J. Gernos Davies, Congregational Minister; one *s* two *d* (and one *s* decd). *Educ:* Silcoates Sch., near Wakefield; (Casberd Scholar) St John's Coll., Oxford. BA Oxon (Mod. Langs), 1939, MA 1942; MA, PhD London (Russian Lang. and Lit.), 1959. Dauntsey's Sch., 1939-40; Intelligence Corps (Captain), 1940-46; Leeds Grammar School, 1946-52; Head of Dept of Modern Languages, Royal Naval Coll., Greenwich, 1952-60. *Publications:* contrib. to Slavonic and Eastern European Review, and to Mariners' Mirror. *Recreation:* swimming. *Address:* (until July 1978) Headmaster's House, Silcoates School, Wrenthorpe, Wakefield WF2 0PD. *T:* Wakefield 76915; (from July 1978) 16 Kepstorn Road, West Park, Leeds 16.

EVANS, Prof. Rhydwyn Harding, CBE 1958; MSc, DSc Manchester, PhD Leeds; FICE, FIMechE, FIStructE, MSocCE France, Hon. MIPlantE; Professor of Civil Engineering and Administrative Head of Engineering Departments, University of Leeds, 1946-68, Emeritus Professor, 1968; *b* 9 Oct. 1900; *s* of late David Evans, Tygwyn, Pontardulais, Glam; *m* 1929, Dilys Elizabeth, *o c* of late George Rees, Welsh Poet and Hymnologist, and Kate Ann Rees, London; one *s. Educ:* Llanelly Grammar Sch.; University of Manchester. Mercantile Marine, 1918-20. BSc top 1st class Graduate Prizeman, 1923; MSc 1928; PhD 1932; DSc 1943. Demonstrator, Asst Lecturer, Lecturer, Senior Lecturer and later Reader in Civil Engineering, University of Leeds, 1926-46; Dean, Faculty of Tech. University of Leeds, 1948-51; Pro-Vice-Chancellor, University of Leeds, 1961-65. Lectures: Unwin Meml ICE, 1960; first George Hondros Meml, WA, 1970. IStructE: Vice-Pres., 1948-49; Chm., Yorks Br., 1940-41, 1955-56 and 1958-59 (Yorkshire Br. Prize, 1946-47 and 1950-51); ICE: Chm. Yorks Assoc., 1942-43 and 1952-53; Mem. Council, 1949-52; Mem., Joint Matriculation Bd, Manchester, 1949-68; Chm., Leeds Univ. Min. of Labour and NS Bd, 1949-60; first Chm., Trng Consultative Cttee, Cement and Concrete Assoc., 1966-73. Hon. Mem., Concrete Soc., 1970. Hon. DèsSc Ghent, 1953; Hon. DTech Bradford, 1971. Rugby Engrg Soc. Student's Prize, 1925; Telford Premiums, 1942-43-44; Medal, Ghent Univ., 1949, 1953; George Stephenson Gold Medal, 1956; Institution of Water Engineers, Instn Premium, 1953; Reinforced Concrete

Assoc. Medal, 1961; Instn of Struct. Engrs: Research Diploma, 1965; Certif. of Commendation, 1970; Henry Adams Award, 1971. *Publications:* Prestressed Concrete (with E. W. Bennett), 1962; Concrete Plain, Reinforced Prestressed, Shell (with C. B. Wilby), 1963; Reinforced and Prestressed Concrete (with F. K. Kong), 1975; papers on elasticity and plasticity of concrete and other building materials; strain and stress distribution in reinforced concrete beams and arches; pre-stressed concrete; extensibility, cracking and tensile stress-strain of concrete; bond stresses; shear stresses; combined bending and shear stresses; torsional stresses; preflexed pre-stressed concrete beams; lightweight aggregate concrete; vibration and pressure moulding of concrete in Journals of Institutions of Civil, Struct. and Water Engineers, Concrete Soc., Philosophical Magazine, Engineer, Engineering, Civil Engineering and Public Works. *Recreations:* motoring, travel, gardening. *Address:* 23 Christopher Drive, Pontlliw, Swansea. *T:* 891961.

EVANS, Richard Mark; HM Diplomatic Service; Minister (Economic), Paris, since 1977; *b* 15 April 1928; *s* of Edward Walter Evans, *qv*; *m* 1973, Rosemary Grania Glen Birkett. *Educ:* Dragon Sch., Oxford; Repton Sch.; Magdalen Coll., Oxford. BA (Oxon) 1949. Joined HM Foreign (now Diplomatic) Service: Third Sec., London, 1952-55; Third Sec., Peking, 1955-57; Second Sec., London, 1957-62; First Sec.: Peking, 1962-64; Berne, 1964-68; London, 1968-70; Counsellor, 1970; Head of Near Eastern Dept, FCO, 1970-72, Head of Far Eastern Dept, 1972-74; Fellow, Centre for Internat. Affairs, Harvard Univ., 1974-75; Commercial Counsellor, Stockholm, 1975-77. *Recreations:* travel, reading, music. *Address:* 16 Trigon Road, SW8. *Club:* United Oxford & Cambridge University.

EVANS, Robert; Chairman, East Midlands Gas Region, since 1977; *b* 28 May 1927; *s* of Gwilym Evans and Florence May Evans; *m* 1950, Lilian May (*née* Ward); one *s* one *d*. *Educ:* Old Swan Coll.; Blackburn Coll.; City of Liverpool Coll. (Tech.); Liverpool Univ. D. Napier & Son Ltd, 1943-49; North Western Gas Bd, 1950-56; Burmah Oil Co. (Pakistan), 1956-67; Dir of Engrg, Southern Gas Bd, 1962-72; Dep. Dir (Ops), Gas Council, 1972; Dir of Operations, British Gas, 1972-75; Dep. Chm., North Thames Gas, 1975-77. *Recreations:* motoring, reading, golf. *Address:* East Midlands Gas, PO Box 145, De Montfort Street, Leicester LE1 9DB.

EVANS, Sir (Robert) Charles, Kt 1969; MA, FRCS; Principal, University College of North Wales, since 1958; Vice-Chancellor, University of Wales, 1965-67, and 1971-73; *b* 19 Oct. 1918; *o s* of late R. C. Evans and of Mrs Charles Evans; *m* 1957, Denise Nea Morin; three *s*. *Educ:* Shrewsbury Sch.; University Coll., Oxford. BM, BCh Oxon 1943; MA Oxon 1947; FRCS 1949. RAMC, 1943-46 (despatches). Surgical Registrar, United Liverpool Hosps, and Liverpool Regional Hosps, 1947-57. Hunterian Prof., Royal College Surg. Eng., 1953. Dep. Leader, Mt Everest Expedition, 1953; Leader, Kangchenjunga Expedition, 1955; Pres., Alpine Club, 1967-70; Mem. Council, Royal Geog. Society, 1960-61. Hon. DSc Wales, 1956. Cullum Medal, American Geog. Soc., 1954; Livingstone Medal, Scottish Geog. Soc., 1955; Founder's Medal, Royal Geog. Society, 1956. *Publications:* Eye on Everest, 1955; On Climbing, 1956; Kangchenjunga-The Untrodden Peak, 1956; articles in Alpine Journal, Geographical Journal, etc. *Address:* Bryn Haul, Bangor, N Wales. *T:* Bangor 2144. *Club:* Alpine.

EVANS, Maj.-Gen. Robert Noel, FFARCS; QHP 1976; Director of Medical Services, Headquarters BAOR, since 1977; *b* 22 Dec. 1922; *s* of William Evans and Norah Moynihan; *m* 1950, Mary Elizabeth O'Brien; four *s* one *d*. *Educ:* Christian Brothers Sch., Tralle, Co. Kerry; National University of Ireland (MB, BCh, BAO 1947). DTM&H 1961; FFARCS 1963. Commnd RAMC 1951; Consultant Anaesthetist, 1963; CO BMH Rinteln, 1969-71; ADMS 4th Div., 1971-73; DDMS HQ BAOR, 1973-75; Comdt, RAMC Trng Centre, 1975-77. *Recreations:* gardening, walking, music. *Address:* 32 Folly Hill, Farnham, Surrey. *T:* Farnham 26938.

EVANS, Roger W.; *see* Warren Evans.

EVANS, Very Rev. Seiriol John Arthur, CBE 1969; Dean of Gloucester, 1953-72; *b* 22 Nov. 1894; *er s* of Rev. John Arthur Evans, DD, Sible Hedingham, Essex, and Amelia Annie Price; *m* 1928, Selina Georgiana, *d* of Rev. Charles Francis Townley, CBE, Fulbourn Manor, Cambridge; no *c*. *Educ:* King's Sch., Worcester; King's Coll., Cambridge; Salisbury Theological Coll. Asst Master at Felsted Sch., 1917-19; Deacon, 1920; Priest, 1921; Curate of St Mary and All Saints, Calverhinster, 1920-22; Minor Canon and Sacrist of Gloucester Cathedral and Assistant Master at King's Sch., Gloucester, 1922-23; Precentor of Ely Cathedral and Headmaster of the Choir Sch., 1923-29; Rector of

Upwell-Christchurch 1929-47; Chaplain RNVR, 1940-45; Proctor in Convocation for Diocese of Ely, 1940-47; Archdeacon of Wisbech, 1945-53; Rector of Upwell-St Peter, 1947-53. Chairman: Council for the Care of Churches, 1954-71; Ely Diocesan Adv. Cttee, 1976-. Mem. of the Royal Commission on Historical Manuscripts, 1957; Church Commissioner, 1958-68; Trustee, National Portrait Gallery, 1963-70. FSA 1935; FRHistS 1940; Fellow, St Michael's Coll., Tenbury, 1958. *Publications:* A Short History of Ely Cathedral, 1925; Ely Chapter Ordinances (Camden Misc.: Vol. XVII), 1940; The Medieval Estate of Ely Cathedral Priory: a preliminary survey, 1973. *Address:* The Old Manor, Fulbourn, near Cambridge. *Club:* Athenæum.

EVANS, Sir Sidney Harold; *see* Evans, Sir Harold.

EVANS, Very Rev. Sydney Hall, CBE 1976; Dean of Salisbury, since 1977; *b* 23 July 1915; *s* of William and Winifred Evans; *m* 1941, Eileen Mary (*née* Evans); two *s* one *d*. *Educ:* Bristol Grammar Sch.; St Chad's Coll., Durham. MA 1940, BD 1945, Durham. Deacon 1939, priest 1940; Curate of Bishop Auckland, Co. Durham, 1939-41; Curate of Ferryhill, Co. Durham, 1941-43. Chaplain RAFVR, 1943-45. Chaplain and Lecturer, King's Coll., London, 1945-48; Warden of King's Coll. post-graduate coll. at Warminster, 1948-56; Dean of King's Coll., London, 1956-77; Hon. Canon of Southwark, 1959-77; Preacher of Gray's Inn, 1960-77; Exam. Chaplain to Bishops of Southwark, Chelmsford, Truro, Durham, London. Public Orator, Univ. of London, 1972-74. FKC 1955. *Recreations:* walking and bird-watching. *Address:* The Deanery, Salisbury, Wilts.

EVANS, Ven. (Thomas) Eric; Archdeacon of Cheltenham, since 1975; Residentiary Canon of Gloucester Cathedral, since 1969; *b* 1928; *s* of Eric John Rhys Evans and late Florence May Evans; *m* 1957, Linda Kathleen Budge; two *d*. *Educ:* St David's Coll., Lampeter (BA); St Catherine's Coll., Oxford (MA); St Stephen's House, Oxford. Ordained, 1954; Curate, Margate Parish Church, 1954-58; Sen. Curate, St Peter's, Bournemouth, 1958-62; Founder and 1st Dir, Bournemouth Samaritans; Diocesan Youth Chaplain, dio. Gloucester, 1962-69; Wing Chaplain, ATC, 1963-69; Hon. Chaplain: Gloucester Coll. of Educn, 1968-75; Gloucestershire Constabulary, 1977-. Chm., Glos Trng Cttee, 1967-69; Vice-Chm., Glos Assoc. for Mental Health, 1965-; Proctor in Convocation and Mem. Gen. Synod of C of E, 1970-; Member: Standing Cttee of House of Clergy; Exec. Cttee, Council for Places of Worship; Canon Missioner, dio. Gloucester, 1969-. *Recreations:* travel, esp. Middle East, biblical archaeology. *Address:* 9 College Green, Gloucester. *T:* Gloucester 20620. *Clubs:* Junior Carlton; Downhill Only (Wengen).

EVANS, (Thomas) Godfrey, CBE 1960; *b* Finchley, 1920; *s* of A. G. L. Evans; *m* 1973, Angela Peart; one *d*. *Educ:* Kent Coll., Canterbury. Joined Kent County Staff at age of 16. First kept wicket for England in Test *v* India, 1946; first overseas Test tour, Australia and New Zealand, 1946-47; has also played in Test matches in W Indies and S Africa. Has played in 91 Test matches (world record 1959); dismissed 218 batsmen in Test cricket from behind the stumps, 88 more than Oldfield, the previous record-holder, and retained the record until 1976; the only wicket-keeper to have dismissed more than 200 victims and scored over 2000 runs in Test cricket; holds world record for not conceding a bye while 1,054 runs were scored in a Test series (Australia, 1946); holds record for longest Test innings without scoring (95 minutes *v* Australia, Adelaide, 1947); holds jointly, with Charles Barnett, record for fastest score before lunch in a Test match (98 *v* India, Lord's, 1952); in making 47 in 29 minutes was three runs off the fastest 50 in Test cricket (*v* Australia, Old Trafford, 1956); first Englishman to tour Australia with MCC four times after War of 1939-45. *Publications:* Behind the Stumps, 1951; Action in Cricket, 1956; The Gloves Are Off, 1960. *Recreations:* real tennis, golf, squash. *Club:* Petworth Real Tennis.

EVANS, Thomas Henry, CBE 1957; DL; LLM; Clerk of the Peace, Clerk of the County Council, and Clerk to Lieutenance for Staffordshire, 1942-72; Clerk of Staffordshire Magistrates Courts Committee, 1952-72; Clerk of Staffordshire County and Stoke-on-Trent Police Authority, 1968-72; *b* 1907; *s* of late Henry Evans, Bootle, Lancs. *Educ:* Merchant Taylors' Sch., Crosby, Lancs; University of Liverpool (LLM). Admitted Solicitor, 1930. Asst Solicitor with Surrey County Council, 1930-35; Asst County Solicitor and later Dep. Clerk of Staffs County Council, 1935-42. Member: Cttee on Consolidation of Highway Law, 1958; Interdepartmental Cttee (Streatfeild) on business of Criminal Courts, 1958; Nat. Advisory Coun. on Training of Magistrates, 1964-73. DL Staffs, 1947. *Publication:* contributor to Macmillan's Local Government Law and Administration. *Address:* 108 Holland Road, Hove, East Sussex.

EVANS, (Thomas) Michael, QC 1973; a Recorder of the Crown Court, since 1972; *b* 7 Sept. 1930; *s* of David Morgan Evans, *qv*; *m* 1956, Margaret Valerie Booker; one *s* four *d. Educ:* Brightlands Prep. Sch., Newnham, Glos; Marlborough Coll., Wilts; Jesus Coll., Oxford (MA (Juris.)). Called to the Bar, Gray's Inn, 1954; Wales and Chester Circuit, 1955; Legal Chm., Mental Health Review Tribunal for Wales, 1970. *Recreations:* golf, sailing. *Address:* 29 Sherborne Avenue, Cyncoed, Cardiff. *T:* 752085. *Club:* Cardiff and County (Cardiff).

EVANS, Sir Trevor (Maldwyn), Kt 1967; CBE 1963; Director, Beaverbrook Newspapers Ltd, 1954-69; Industrial Consultant, Beaverbrook Group, since 1967; *b* 21 Feb. 1902; *s* of late Samuel Evans and late Margaret Evans, Abertridwr, Glam; *m* 1930, Margaret, *d* of late J. B. Gribbin and late S. J. Gribbin, Heaton Moor, Ches; one *s* one *d. Educ:* Pontypridd Gram. Sch. Journalist, Glamorgan Free Press, Pontypridd, 1922-24; South Wales News, 1924-26; Daily Dispatch, 1926-28; Daily Mail, 1928-30; Daily Express, 1930-70 (Industrial Correspondent, 1930-67). Dir, Internat. Press Centre. Mem. Press Council, 1964-75. *Publications:* Strange Fighters, We British, 1943; Ernest Bevin, biography, 1946; The Great Bohunkus, biography of Ian Mackay, 1953. *Recreations:* watching Rugby and cricket; listening to discussion groups. *Address:* 17 Wolsey Close, Kingston Hill, Surrey. *T:* 01-942 6016. *Clubs:* Reform, Press. *See also* D. E. Butler.

EVANS, Ulick Richardson, CBE 1973; FRS 1949; ScD Cambridge 1932; ScD *hc* Dublin 1947; scientific writer and consultant; Emeritus Reader in Science of Metallic Corrosion, Cambridge University (Reader, 1945-54); Hon. Fellow, King's College, Cambridge; *b* 31 March 1889; unmarried. *Educ:* Marlborough Coll.; King's Coll., Cambridge. Served European War, 1914-18, Army (Signal Service), 1914-19. Engaged in research, writing and teaching at Cambridge Univ., 1921-55 (main subjects: Metallic Corrosion and the growth of thin Films on Metals). Hon. Dr of Metallurgy, Sheffield Univ., 1961. Palladium Medallist, Electrochemical Soc., 1955; Hothersall Medallist, 1957; Gold Medallist, Inst. of Metal Finishing, 1961; Cavallaro Medallist, 1971. Hon. Fellow UMIST, 1973. *Publications:* Metals and Metallic Compounds (4 vols), 1923; Corrosion of Metals, 1924 and 1926; Metallic Corrosion, Passivity and Protection, 1937 and 1946; Introduction to Metallic Corrosion, 1948 (and 1963); The Corrosion and Oxidation of Metals, 1960, supplementary vols, 1968 and 1976; papers in Proc. Royal Society, Trans. Faraday Soc., J. Chem. Soc., J. Iron Steel Inst., J. Inst. Met., etc. *Address:* 19 Manor Court, Grange Road, Cambridge. *T:* Cambridge 55005. *Club:* United Oxford & Cambridge University.

EVANS, Sir Vincent; see Evans, Sir W. V. J.

EVANS, William, MD, DSc, FRCP; Consulting Physician: to Cardiac Department, London Hospital; to National Heart Hospital; and to Institute of Cardiology; Consulting Cardiologist to Royal Navy, 1946-67; Hon. Cardiologist to Royal Society of Musicians; *b* 24 Nov. 1895; *s* of late Eben Evans, Tregaron, Cardiganshire; *m* 1936, Christina (*d* 1964), *d* of late John Lessels Downie, Kirkcaldy. *Educ:* University Coll. of Wales, Aberystwyth; London Hospital; London Univ., MB, BS (London) 1925, hons in Surgery; MD (London) 1927; FRCP 1937; DSc (London) 1944; K. E. D. Payne Prize in Pathology, 1927; Hutchinson Triennial Prize in Clinical Surgery, 1929; Liddle Triennial Prize in Pathology, 1931; Sydney Body Gold Medal, 1954; Strickland Goodall Lect., 1942; Finlayson Lect., 1947; St Cyres Lect., 1952; Gerrish Milliken Lect., University of Philadelphia, 1954; First Rufus Stolp Memorial Lect., University of Evanston, Ill., 1954; Carbutt Memorial Lect., 1957; Schorstein Lect., 1961; Wiltshire Lect., 1961. First Leonard Abrahamson Memorial Lecture, Royal College of Surgeons in Ireland, Dublin, 1963; Sir Thomas and Lady Dixon Lecture, Belfast, 1965. Formerly Asst Dir to Medical Unit, Paterson Medical Officer and Chief Asst to Cardiac Dept, London Hosp. Served European War, 1914-18, Combatant Officer, Lancs Fusiliers, and Battalion Education Officer. Hon. DSc (Wales), 1961. Mem. American Heart Assoc.; Hon. Mem. British Cardiac Soc.; Hon. Mem. Soc. of Phys. in Wales; Hon. FRSM. Guest Lecturer at Centenary Meetings of Royal Melbourne Hospital, 1948. High Sheriff of Cardiganshire, 1959. Hon. Mem. Order of Druids, 1960. *Publications:* Student's Handbook of Electrocardiography, 1934; Cardiography (2nd edn, 1954); Cardiology (2nd edn, 1956); Cardioscopy, 1952; Diseases of the Heart and Arteries, 1964; Journey to Harley Street, 1969; Diary of a Welsh Swagman, 1975; various papers on medical and cardiological subjects in Quarterly Jl of Med., Lancet, BMJ and Brit. Heart Jl. *Recreations:* fishing, gardening, farming. *Address:* Bryndomen, Tregaron, Dyfed, West Wales. *T:* Tregaron 404.

EVANS, William Campbell, OBE 1976; General Manager, Redditch Development Corporation, since 1976; *b* 13 Jan. 1916; *s* of Frank Randolph Evans and Elizabeth Evans; *m* 1939, Sarah A. Duckworth; one *s* one *d. Educ:* Calday Grange Grammar Sch., West Kirby, Cheshire; Bury High Sch., Bury, Lancs. IPFA; FCA. Served RASC and RE, 1939-42. Local Govt Finance: Bury, 1932-38; Newton-le-Willows, Lancs, 1938-39 and 1942-44; Wolverhampton, 1944-53; Dep. Borough Treas., Northampton, 1953-58; Borough Treas., West Bromwich, 1958-64; Chief Finance Officer, Redditch Develt Corp., 1965-76. Mem. Council, IMTA/CIPFA, 1969-, Vice-Pres., 1976-77, Pres., 1977-78. *Recreations:* gardening, music, watching sport. *Address:* Helmsley, Church Road, Bradley Green, near Redditch, Worcs. *T:* Hanbury 457.

EVANS, William Edis Webster; *b* London, 26 Aug. 1908; *yr s* of late Rev. William Evans, Rector of Brondesbury; *m* 1956, Jean Hilda, *widow* of Andrew Allan and *d* of late Robert Smith Marshall, Forfar, Angus. *Educ:* Merchant Taylors' Sch., London. Editorial staff, John o' London's Weekly, 1928-39; Dep. Editor, 1951; Editor, 1953-54. Asst Editor, PTO, 1939; Gen. Editor, Country Life Books, 1954-67. Served RAF, 1940-47; Middle East, Italy, Germany; Wing Comdr (despatches). *Publications:* Editor (with Tom Scott) of In Praise of Golf, 1949; The Golfers' Year, 1950 and 1951; Rubs of the Green, 1969; The Encyclopaedia of Golf, 1971. *Recreations:* golf, reading. *Address:* 16 Chatterton Court, Kew Road, Richmond, Surrey TW9 2AR. *T:* 01-940 7789. *Club:* Royal Mid-Surrey Golf.

EVANS, William Ewart; Judge of the High Court of Lesotho, 1967-73 (Acting Chief Justice, 1968); Judge of High Court of Northern Rhodesia and of the Rhodesia and Nyasaland Court of Appeal, 1953-62; *b* 24 May 1899; *s* of late John William Evans and Catherine Evans, Swansea, S Wales; *m* 1919, Agnes May Wilson; one *s* four *d. Educ:* Swansea Grammar Sch. Served European War, 1917-19, in King's Royal Rifle Corps and Royal Army Service Corps. Called to Bar, 1934; practised on South Wales Circuit; Colonial Legal Service, 1938; acted in various judicial capacities; Resident Magistrate, Lusaka, Livingstone, N'Dola, Broken Hill, and Luanshya, 1940; Acting Judge High Court, N Rhodesia, 1951, 1953. *Recreation:* gardening. *Address:* 4 Crowhill Road, Borrodale, Salisbury, Rhodesia.

EVANS, William John; retired as General Secretary of Associated Society of Locomotive Engineers and Firemen (Oct. 1960-July 1963); Civil Representative, National Association for Employment of Regular Sailors, Soldiers and Airmen, 1963-69; *b* 4 Oct. 1899; *m* 1919; one *s. Educ:* Eccles Grammar Sch. Joined LNW Railway, 1916. Royal Navy Service, 1916-21. Great War and Victory Medals; Mine Clearance Service Medal. Served as Executive Cttee Mem. of Trade Union, 1934-39; Pres. of Executive Cttee, 1937-38-39; Organising Sec., 1939-56; Asst Gen. Sec., 1956-60. Mem., Eastern Region Railways Board, 1963-66. Mem., Eccles Town Council, 1932-34. *Recreations:* boxing, bowling, and Association football. *Address:* 15 Mordaunt Drive, Sutton Coldfield, West Midlands B75 5PT.

EVANS, Sir (William) Vincent (John), GCMG 1976 (KCMG 1970; CMG 1959); MBE 1945; QC 1973; Barrister-at-Law; Chairman, Bryant Symons & Co. Ltd, since 1964; *b* 20 Oct. 1915; *s* of Charles Herbert Evans and Elizabeth (*née* Jenkins); *m* 1947, Joan Mary Symons; one *s* two *d. Educ:* Merchant Taylors' Sch.; Wadham Coll., Oxford. 1st Class Hons, Jurisprudence, 1937; BCL, 1938; MA, 1941; elected Cassel Scholar, Lincoln's Inn, 1937; called to Bar, Lincoln's Inn, 1939. Served in HM Forces, 1939-46. Legal Adviser (Lt-Col) to British Military Administration, Cyrenaica, 1945-46; Asst Legal Adviser, Foreign Office, 1947-54; Legal Counsellor, UK Permanent Mission to the United Nations, 1954-59; Legal Counsellor, FO, 1959-60; Dep. Legal Adviser, FO, 1960-68; Legal Adviser, FCO, 1968-75, retired. Chm., European Cttee on Legal Cooperation, Council of Europe, 1969-71; UK Rep. Council of Europe Steering Cttee on Human Rights, 1976-; Mem., Human Rights Cttee set up under Internat. Covenant on Civil and Political Rights, 1977-; Mem., Council of Management, British Inst. of Internat. and Comparative Law. *Recreation:* gardening. *Address:* (home) 4 Bedford Road, Moor Park, Northwood, Mddx. *T:* Northwood 24085; (office) 2 Hare Court, Temple, EC4. *T:* 01-353 0076. *Club:* Athenæum.

EVANS-ANFOM, Emmanuel, FRCSE 1955; Chairman, National Council for Higher Education, Ghana, since 1974; *b* 7 Oct. 1919; *m* 1952, Leonora Francetta Evans; three *s* one *d. Educ:* Achimota School; Edinburgh University (MB; ChB; DTM&H). House Surgeon, Dewsbury Infirmary, 1948-49; Medical Officer, Gold Coast Medical Service, 1950-56; Specialist Surgeon, 1956-67; Senior Lecturer, Ghana Medical School, 1966-67; Vice-Chancellor, Univ. of Science and

Technology, Kumasi, 1967-74. Mem., WHO Expert Panel on Med. and Paramed. Educn, 1972-. Titular Mem., Internat. Assoc. Surgeons; Past President: Ghana Medical Assoc.; Assoc. of Surgeons of W Africa; FICS. Fellow, Ghana Acad. Arts and Sciences, 1971. Chm., Ghana Hockey Assoc. Hon. DSc Salford, 1974. *Publication:* Aetiology and Management of Intestinal Perforations, Ghana Med. Jl, 1963. *Recreations:* hockey, music, art. *Address:* National Council for Higher Education, PO Box M28, Accra, Ghana.

EVANS-BEVAN, Sir Martyn Evan, 2nd Bt *cr* 1958; *b* 1 April 1932; *s* of Sir David Martyn Evans-Bevan, 1st Bt, and of Eira Winifred, *d* of late Sidney Archibald Lloyd Glanley; *S* father, 1973; *m* 1957, Jennifer Jane Marion, *d* of Robert Hugh Stevens; four *s*. *Educ:* Uppingham. Entered family business of Evan Evans Bevan and Evans Bevan Ltd, 1953; Director, Whitbread (Wales) Ltd and local director, Phoenix Assurance Co. High Sheriff of Breconshire, 1967. *Recreations:* shooting and fishing. *Heir: s* David Gawain Evans-Bevan, *b* 16 Sept. 1961. *Address:* Felinnewydd, Llandefalle, Brecon, Powys. *Club:* Carlton.

EVANS-FREKE, family name of **Baron Carbery.**

EVE, family name of **Baron Silsoe.**

EVE, Hon. David Malcolm T.; *see* Trustram Eve.

EVELEIGH, Rt. Hon. Sir Edward Walter, PC 1977; Kt 1968; ERD; MA; **Rt. Hon. Lord Justice Eveleigh;** a Lord Justice of Appeal, since 1977; *b* 8 Oct. 1917; *s* of Walter William and Daisy Emily Eveleigh; *m* 1940, Vilma Bodnar; *m* 1953, Patricia Helen Margaret Bury; two *s* (and one *s* decd). *Educ:* Peter Symonds; Brasenose Coll., Oxford (Hon. Fellow 1977). Commissioned in the Royal Artillery (Supplementary Reserve), 1936; served War of 1939-45 (despatches, 1940). Called to Bar, Lincoln's Inn, 1945, Bencher 1968; QC 1961. Recorder of Burton-on-Trent, 1961-64; of Gloucester, 1964-68; Chm., QS, County of Oxford, 1968-71 (Dep. Chm., 1963-68); a Judge of the High Court of Justice, Queen's Bench Div., 1968-77; Presiding Judge, SE Circuit, 1971-76. Pres., British-German Jurists' Assoc., 1974-. *Address:* Royal Courts of Justice, Strand, WC2. *Club:* Garrick.

EVELEIGH, Air Vice-Marshal Geoffrey Charles, CB 1964; OBE 1945; RAF retired; *b* 25 Oct. 1912; *s* of Ernest Charles Eveleigh, Henley-on-Thames; *m* 1939, Anthea Josephine, *d* of F. H. Fraser, Ceylon; one *s* one *d*. *Educ:* Brighton Coll.; RAF Coll., Cranwell. Joined RAF, 1932; served War of 1939-45 in Bomber Command and No 2 Group; Dep. Chief of Air Staff, Royal New Zealand Air Force, 1955-57; Air Commodore, 1957; Dir-Gen. of Signals, Air Ministry, 1959-61; Air Vice-Marshal, 1961; Air Officer, Administration, Fighter Command, 1961-64; retd 1965. *Address:* Cán Tirana, PO Box 20, Puerto de Pollensa, Mallorca, Spain. *Club:* Royal Air Force.

EVELEIGH-DE-MOLEYNS, family name of **Baron Ventry.**

EVELING, Walter Raphael Taylor, CBE 1960; Chartered Surveyor, retired, 1968; Dep. Chief Valuer, Inland Revenue, 1965-68 (Asst Chief Valuer, 1951); *b* 8 March 1908; *s* of late Raphael Eveling, Hampstead Garden Suburb; *m* 1935, Annie Ferguson Newman, Belfast; one *s*. *Educ:* Paradise House Sch., Stoke Newington. Joined the Valuation Office, Inland Revenue, 1935. FRICS. *Address:* 11 Thornhill Close, Ramsey, Isle of Man.

EVELYN, (John) Michael, CB 1976; Assistant Director of Public Prosecutions, 1969-76 (Under-Secretary, 1972); *b* 2 June 1916; *s* of Edward Ernest Evelyn and Kate Rosa Underwood. *Educ:* Charterhouse; Christ Church, Oxford (MA). Called to Bar, 1939. Army service, 1939-46. Dept of Dir of Public Prosecutions, 1946-. *Publications:* numerous crime novels (written under pseudonym Michael Underwood) from 1954. *Recreations:* writing, reading, opera, cinema, travel. *Address:* Riverbank, Datchet, Slough SL3 9BY. *Club:* Garrick.

EVERALL, John (Harold); Hon. Treasurer, Royal Agricultural Society of the Commonwealth, 1966-75; *b* 12 Oct. 1908; *s* of late William and Annie Heynes Everall, Shrawardine Castle, Shrewsbury; *m* 1935, Breda, *d* of late Gerald J. Sherlock, Ballsbridge, Dublin; one *s* one *d*. *Educ:* Malvern Coll. Chartered Surveyor (Agriculture) and Pedigree Cattle Breeder (retired). War of 1939-45, Intelligence Officer (Captain), 4 Salop Bn, HG. Past President: Hereford Herd Book Soc.; Nat. Cattle Breeders' Assoc.; Shropshire and Montgomeryshire Agric. Valuers' Assoc.; Shropshire Chamber of Agric.; Vice-Pres., Shropshire and W Midland Agric. Soc., 1964-. Vice-Chairman: Hants and Winchester Br. E-SU, 1974-76; Shrewsbury Div. Conservative Assoc., 1946-50; Livestock Cttee of Brit. Agric. Export Council,

1967-70; (rep. BAEC at Santarem, Portugal, Fairs, 1967 and 1969). Former Mem. Exec. Cttee: Farmers' Club; Royal Smithfield Club; former Hon. Sec., Shropshire, Herefordshire and Mid-Wales branch, RICS. Mem. Council, Royal Agric. Soc. of Eng., 1949-70 (resigned). Rep. UK: World Confs of Pedigree Hereford Cattle Breeders, Hereford 1951, Kansas City, USA, 1960 and Dublin 1964; Royal Agric. Soc. of the Commonwealth Confs (as one of three delegs) at Sydney 1963, Toronto 1967, Nairobi 1969, Christchurch (NZ), 1973. Mem., Stapledon Trust Memorial Cttee, 1969-. Internat. Judge of Pedigree Hereford Cattle and owner of Shrine herd (dispersed 1968). Judged: Palermo, Argentina, 1944 and 1963; Sydney, 1963; Nairobi (Borans), 1969; also at Royal of England, Royal Highland, Royal Welsh and Royal Dublin Shows. Director, QMP Ltd, 1958-65. Freeman of Kansas City, USA, and City of London (Liveryman). *Recreations:* shooting, fishing, beagling (Chm., Meon Valley Beagles Hunt Cttee, 1972-); formerly fox-hunting (Mem. S Shropshire Hunt Cttee, 1953-68). *Address:* Courtyards, Crawley, Winchester SO21 2PZ. *T:* Sparsholt 273. *Club:* Travellers'.

EVERARD, Maj.-Gen. Sir Christopher E. W.; *see* Welby-Everard.

EVERARD, Lt-Col Sir Nugent Henry, 3rd Bt, *cr* 1911; late The Duke of Wellington's Regiment (W Riding); *b* 28 Feb. 1905; *er s* of 2nd Bt and Louisa Cole, *d* of R. H. Metge, MP, Athlumney, Navan; *S* father, 1929; *m* 1933, Frances Audrey (*d* 1975), *y d* of J. C. Jesson; one *s* one *d*. Retired with the hon. rank of Lt-Col, 1958. *Heir: s* Robin Charles Everard [*b* 5 Oct. 1939; *m* 1963, Ariel Ingrid, *e d* of Col Peter Cleasby-Thompson, The Manor House, Cley-next-the-Sea; one *s* two *d*].

EVERARD, Timothy John; HM Diplomatic Service; Economic and Commercial Counsellor, Athens, since 1974; *b* 22 Oct. 1929; *s* of late Charles M. Everard and late Monica M. Everard (*née* Barford); *m* 1955, Josiane Romano; two *s* two *d*. *Educ:* Uppingham Sch.; Magdalen Coll., Oxford. BA (Mod. Langs). Banking: Barclays Bank DCO, 1952-62, in Egypt, Sudan, Kenya, Congo (Manager for Congo). Entered Foreign (later Diplomatic) Service: First Sec., FO, 1962-63; First Sec., Commercial, Bangkok, 1964-66; resigned to take up directorship in Ellis & Everard Ltd, 1966-67. Rejoined Foreign and Commonwealth Office, Oct. 1967: First Sec., FO, 1967-68; Bahrain, 1969-72 (First Sec. and Head of Chancery, HM Political Residency); seconded to Northern Ireland Office, FCO, April-Aug. 1972; Consul-Gen., then Chargé d'Affaires, Hanoi, 1972-73. *Recreations:* golf, tennis. *Address:* c/o Foreign and Commonwealth Office, SW1; Leagues, Stonecross, Crowborough, East Sussex. *T:* Crowborough 3278; 15 Carlyle Mansions, Cheyne Walk, SW3. *T:* 01-352 8474. *Club:* Reform.

EVEREST, Arthur Ernest, DSc, PhD, FRIC; Fellow of the Society of Dyers and Colourists; retired; *b* 1888; *m* 1914, Annie Kathleen Broome; two *d*. *Educ:* Wrekin Coll.; University of Birmingham and on the Continent. Formerly Managing Director John W. Leitch & Co. Ltd and associated companies; Vice-Pres. of Royal Institute of Chemistry, 1936-39, Mem. of Council, 1933-36 and 1945-48; Mem. of Council of Assoc. of Brit. Chemical Manufacturers, 1934-54; Mem. of Governing Council Wrekin Coll., 1934-74. *Publications:* two books and various memoirs on Chemical and allied subjects. *Address:* The Mount, 5 Yew Tree Close, Rufforth, York YO2 3RG. *T:* Rufforth 278.

EVERETT, Christopher Harris Doyle, MA; JP; Headmaster, Tonbridge School, since 1975; *b* 20 June 1933; *s* of Alan Doyle Everett, MS, FRCS, and Annabel Dorothy Joan Everett (*née* Harris); *m* 1955, Hilary (Billy) Anne (*née* Robertson); two *s* two *d*. *Educ:* Winchester College; New College, Oxford. MA (Class. Mods and Lit. Hum.). Grenadier Guards, Nat. Service, 1951-53. HM Diplomatic Service, 1957-70; posts included Beirut, Washington and Foreign Office; Headmaster, Worksop Coll., 1970-75. *Recreations:* reading, walking, tennis. *Address:* School House, Tonbridge, Kent. *Club:* Royal Commonwealth Society.

EVERETT, Rear-Adm. Douglas Henry, CB 1950; CBE 1946 (MBE 1919); DSO 1940; *b* 16 June 1900; *s* of Douglas and Blanche Everett, Park House, Broadlands, Romsey; *m* 1932, Margery Annette Yeldham; three *s* one *d*. *Educ:* Oakham Sch.; Cadet HMS Conway, 1913; RN Coll., Dartmouth. Served European War, 1916-18; War of 1939-45 (despatches twice); Flag Officer, Ground Training, 1949-51; Pres. Admiralty Interview Board, 1951-52; retired list, 1952. Chilean Order of Merit, 1939. *Address:* Gillinghams, Milford-on-Sea, Lymington, Hants. *T:* Milford-on-Sea 2368.

EVERETT, Douglas Hugh, MBE 1946; Leverhulme Professor of Physical Chemistry, University of Bristol, since 1954; Dean of Faculty of Science, 1966-68; Pro-Vice-Chancellor, 1973-76; *b* 26 Dec. 1916; *e s* of Charles Everett and Jessie Caroline; *m* 1942, Frances Elizabeth Jessop; two *d. Educ:* Grammar Sch., Hampton-on-Thames; University of Reading; Balliol Coll., Oxford. Wantage Scholar, Reading Univ., 1935-38; Kitchener Scholar, 1936-39; BSc, 1938; Ramsay Fellow, 1939-41; DPhil 1942. Special Scientific Duties, WO, 1942-45. ICI Fellow, Oxford Univ., 1945-47; Chemistry Lecturer, Dundee Univ. Coll., 1947; MA 1947; Fellow, Lecturer and Tutor, Exeter Coll., Oxford, 1947-48; Prof. of Chemistry, Dundee Univ. Coll., University of St Andrews, 1948-54. Chm., Internat. Union of Pure and Applied Chemistry Commn on Colloid and Surface Chemistry, 1969-73. FRSE 1950; DSc 1956. Mem., Building Research Board, DSIR, 1954-61; a Vice-Pres., Faraday Soc., 1958-61, 1963-65, 1968-70, Pres., 1976-78; Mem. Chemical Soc. Council, 1961-64, 1972-74 (Tilden Lectr, 1955; Award in Colloid and Surface Chemistry, 1971). *Publications:* Introduction to Chemical Thermodynamics, 1959, 2nd edn, 1971; papers on Physical Chemistry in scientific jls. *Address:* School of Chemistry, The University, Bristol BS8 1TS.

EVERETT, Richard Marven Hale, QC 1952; JP; **His Honour Judge Everett;** a Circuit Judge (formerly Judge of County Courts), since 1971; *b* 26 June 1909; *s* of B. R. Everett, Solicitor; *m* 1935, Kathleen Lucy Eve; one *s. Educ:* Repton. Called to Bar, Gray's Inn, 1933; Master of the Bench, Gray's Inn, 1959, Treasurer, 1977. Recorder of: Deal, 1959-68; Maidstone, 1968-71; Leader, SE Circuit, 1968-71. Served War of 1939-45, in Army, 1941-43. JP Herts, 1953. *Publications:* Joint Ed. 4 edns of Willis' Workmen's Compensation Acts. *Recreation:* golf. *Address:* 54 Ashley Gardens, SW1. *T:* 01-828 3811. *Clubs:* Royal Automobile; Essex.

EVERINGTON, Geoffrey Devas, QC 1968; Barrister-at-Law; *b* 4 May 1915; *s* of late Herbert Devas Everington, MB and Muriel Frances Everington, Sanderstead; *m* 1951, Laila Nissen Hovind; four *s* three *d. Educ:* Westminster. Called to Bar, Gray's Inn, 1939, Bencher 1976; commenced practice at Bar, 1945. *Recreations:* music, tennis. *Address:* South Gable, Granville Road, Limpsfield, Oxted, Surrey. *T:* Oxted 4000.

EVERS, Claude Ronald; MA; Warden of Pendley Residential Centre of Adult Education, 1967-73; *b* 17 Jan. 1908; *s* of late C. P. Evers (formerly housemaster at Rugby Sch.); *m* 1935, Marjorie Janet Ironside Bruce; four *s. Educ:* Rugby; Trinity Coll., Oxford. Asst Master, Wellington Coll., 1931-35; Asst Master, Rugby Sch., 1936-40; Headmaster of Berkhamsted Sch., 1946-53; Headmaster of Sutton Valence Sch., 1953-67. War service (Royal Warwicks Regt), 1940-45. Chm., Pendley Shakespeare Festival. Old Stager. *Publication:* Rugby (Blackie's Public School Series), 1939. *Address:* 8 Pelham Square, Brighton, East Sussex.

EVERS, H(enry) Harvey, MS, FRCS, FRCOG; Professor of Obstetrics and Gynæcology, University of Durham, 1950-58 (now Emeritus), also Obstetrician and Gynæcologist in charge of the Department at Royal Victoria Infirmary and Princess Mary Maternity Hospital, Newcastle upon Tyne, 1950-58 (now Hon. Obstetrician and Gynæcologist); Pastoral Visitor, Newcastle Regional Hospital Board; *b* 28 May 1893; 2nd *s* of Charles Henry Evers, Medical Practitioner; *m* 1923, Marian Isabel Graham; two *s. Educ:* Royal Grammar Sch., Newcastle upon Tyne; University of Durham. Co. of Northumberland, Sch. and Univ. Schol., 1911; Gibson, Outterson-Wood, etc. Schols, 1914; MB, BS (1st Cl. Hons), Durham, 1916; MS Durham (Hons), 1921; MRCS, LRCP, 1916; FRCS 1921. Surg. Prob. (RNVR), 1914-15; Capt., RAMC, 1916-20. Foundation Mem. Royal College of Obstetrics and Gynæcology, 1933; FRCOG 1937. Pastoral Visitor, Regional Adviser and Assessor, Newcastle upon Tyne, 1948; External Examiner, Univs of London, Liverpool, Manchester, Sheffield, Wales; Examiner Conjoint Bd, RCOG, Central Midwives Bd, etc.; Past Pres. North of England Obst. and Gyn. Soc. Formerly: House Surg. (General, Eye and Throat, Nose and Ear), Royal Victoria Infirmary, Newcastle upon Tyne, 1915; Hon. Asst Surg., Hosp. for Sick Children; Demonstrator in Anatomy and Operative Surgery, 1920; Lectr in Obstetrics and Gynæcology, 1930. *Publications:* various medical. *Recreations:* fishing, golf. *Address:* Oakwood Lodge, Clayton Road, Newcastle upon Tyne NE2 1TL. *T:* Newcastle upon Tyne 81-4441.

EVERSLEY, Prof. David Edward Charles, PhD; teacher and research worker; Centre for Studies in Social Policy, since 1976; Visiting Professor, School of Environmental Studies, University College London, since 1976; *b* 22 Nov. 1921; *s* of Dr Otto Eberstadt and Dela Morel; *m* 1945, Edith Wembridge; one *s* three *d. Educ:* Goethe-Gymnasium, Frankfurt/Main; Leighton Park Sch., Reading; London Sch. of Economics. BSc (Econ) (London), PhD (Birmingham). Asst Lectr, Lectr, then Reader, in Economic (and then Social) Hist., Univ. of Birmingham, 1949-66. Dir, W Midlands Social and Polit. Res. Unit, 1962-65; Reader in Population and Regional Studies, Univ. of Sussex, 1966; Dir, Social Research Unit, Univ. of Sussex, 1967-69; Prof., 1969. Hon. Sec., Midlands New Towns Soc., 1958-62; Chief Planner (Strategy), Greater London Council, 1969-72; Centre for Environmental Studies, 1972-76; Visiting Prof. of Demography, Univ. of California at Berkeley, 1965. Mem., W Midlands Economic Planning Coun., 1965-66; Corr. Mem., German Acad. for Urban and Regional Planning, 1972-; Pres., Commn sur la Démographie Historique, Internat. Congress of Hist. Sciences, 1965-70. Chm., Regional Studies Assoc., 1972-75. Chm., Social Responsibility Council, Society of Friends (Quakers), 1972-75. *Publications:* Rents and Social Policy, 1955; Social Theories of Fertility and the Malthusian Debate, 1959, new US edn 1975; (with D. Keate) The Overspill Problem in the West Midlands, 1958; (ed with D. V. Glass) Population in History, 1965; (with Lomas and Jackson) Population Growth and Planning Policy, 1965; (with F. Sukdeo) The Dependants of the Coloured Commonwealth Population of England and Wales, 1969; (with D. Donnison) London: urban patterns, problems and policies, 1973; The Planner in Society, 1973; A Question of Numbers?, 1973; (ed and contrib. with J. Platts) Public Resources and Private Lives, 1976; numerous chaps in collected vols; contribs to Victoria History of the Counties of England; articles in jls of history, demography and planning. *Recreations:* walking, talking, working. *Address:* Hummerstons, Cottered, Buntingford, Herts. *T:* Cottered 354; 12 Hanger Court, Hanger Green, W5.

EVERSON, Sir Frederick (Charles), KCMG 1968 (CMG 1956); Director, BPB Industries Ltd; economics consultant; *b* 6 Sept. 1910; *s* of Frederick Percival Everson; *m* 1937, Linda Mary Clark; three *s* one *d. Educ:* Tottenham County Sch., Middlesex. BSc (Econ.) London. Entered Civil Service, July 1928; Consular Service, Dec. 1934. Chief Administrative Officer, British Embassy, Bonn, Germany, 1953-56; Ambassador to El Salvador, 1956-60; Commercial Counsellor, British Embassy, Stockholm, 1960-63; Minister (Economic), British Embassy, Paris, 1963-68. *Address:* 8 Gainsborough Court, College Road, Dulwich, SE21 7LT. *T:* 01-693 8125.

EVERY, Sir John (Simon), 12th Bt, *cr* 1641; *b* 24 April 1914; *er s* of Sir Edward Oswald Every, 11th Bt and Lady (Ivy Linton) Every (*d* 1976); *S* father, 1959; *m* 1st, 1938, Annette Constance (marr. diss., 1942), *o c* of late Major F. W. M. Drew, Drewscourt, Co. Cork; 2nd, 1943, Janet Marion, *d* of John Page, Blakeney, Norfolk; one *s* two *d. Educ:* Harrow. Served War of 1939-45. Capt., Sherwood Foresters. Business Co. Dir, 1945-60, Dir of private companies. *Recreations:* cricket, tennis, shooting. *Heir:* *s* Henry John Michael Every [*b* 6 April 1947; *m* 1974, Susan Mary, *er d* of Kenneth Beaton, Hartford, Hunts]. *Address:* Egginton, near Derby. *T:* Etwall 2245. *Club:* MCC.

EVETTS, Lt-Gen. Sir John (Fullerton), Kt 1951; CB 1939; CBE 1937; MC; *b* 30 June 1891; *s* of late Lieut-Col J. M. Evetts, Tackley Park, Oxon; *m* 1916, Helen Phyllis, *d* of late Captain C. A. G. Becher, Burghfields, Bourton on the Water, Glos; one *s. Educ:* Temple Grove; Lancing; Royal Military Coll., Sandhurst; Staff Coll., Camberley. Entered Army, 1911; joined The Cameronians (Scottish Rifles); served European War, 1914-18 (MC, despatches); Lieut 1913; Captain 1915; temp. Major Machine Gun Corps, 1916; Bt-Major 1929; Substantive, 1929; Bt Lt-Col 1931; Substantive Lt-Col Royal Ulster Rifles, 1934; Col 1935; Maj.-Gen. 1941; employed with Iraq Army, 1925-28; DAAG War Office, 1932; Commander British Troops in Palestine, 1935; GSO1 Palestine, 1936; Brig. Comd. 16th Inf. Bde, Palestine and Trans-Jordan, 1936-39 (despatches); BGS, HQ, Northern Command, India, 1939-40; Comdr Western (Indept) Dist, India, 1940-41; Divl Comdr, 1941 (despatches); Asst CIGS, 1942; Senior Military Adviser to Minister of Supply, 1944-46; retired pay, 1946; Head of British Ministry of Supply Staff in Australia, 1946-51, and Chief Executive Officer Joint UK-Australian Long Range Weapons, Board of Administration, 1946-49. Managing Dir, 1951-58, Chm., 1958-60, Rotol Ltd and Brit, Messier. OStJ. Legion of Merit (US), 1943. *Address:* Pepper Cottage, Kemerton, near Tewkesbury, Glos. *Club:* Army and Navy.

EWALD, Paul P., FRS 1958; DrPhil; Professor Emeritus of Physics, Polytechnic Institute of Brooklyn, since 1959; Professor of Physics, 1949-59, and Head of Department, 1949-57, Polytechnic Institute of Brooklyn; *b* Berlin, Germany, 23 Jan. 1888; *s* of Paul Ewald, Historian (Univ. Berlin), and Clara Ewald, Portrait-Painter; *m* 1913, Ella (Elise Berta) (née

Philippson); two *s* two *d. Educ:* Victoria Gymnasium, Potsdam; Univs of Cambridge, Göttingen and Munich (DrPhil 1912). Lecturer in Theoretical Physics, Univ. of Munich, 1918; Prof. of Theoretical Physics, TH Stuttgart, 1921-37; Lecturer, later Prof. of Mathematical Physics, The Queen's Univ., Belfast, 1939-49. Corresp. Mem. Acad. Göttingen, 1937; Fellow Nat. Acad. Arts and Sci., US, 1954; Membre d'honneur Société Française de Minéralogie et de Cristallographie, 1955; Ehrenmitglied, Deutsche Mineralog. Ges., 1958. Mem. Exec. Cttee, Internat. Union of Crystallography, 1948-66, Pres., 1960-1963. Corresp. Mem. Bavarian Acad. Sci., 1962; Fellow, Deut. Akad. d. Naturforscher (Leopoldina), 1966. Hon. Mem., Cambridge Philosophical Soc., 1968. Dr *hc*; TH Stuttgart, 1954; Univ. de Paris, 1958; Adelphi Univ., 1966; Univ. Munich, 1968; Polytechnic Inst., Brooklyn, 1972. *Publications:* Kristalle und Röntgenstrahlen, 1923 (Germany); 50 Years of X-ray Diffraction, 1962 (Oosthoek, Holland). Contrib. Thermodynamics and Physics of Matter, 1955 (USA), etc. Editor: Zeitschrift für Kristallographie, 1923-37; Acta Crystallographica, 1948-59. *Address:* 108 Sheldon Road, Ithaca, NY 14850, USA.

EWANS, Martin Kenneth; HM Diplomatic Service; Head of East African Department, Foreign and Commonwealth Office, since 1973; *b* 14 Nov. 1928; *s* of late John Ewans; *m* 1953, Mary Tooke; one *s* one *d. Educ:* St Paul's; Corpus Christi Coll., Cambridge (major scholar, MA). Royal Artillery, 1947-49, 2nd Lt. Joined Commonwealth Relations Office, 1952; Second Sec., Karachi, 1954-55; First Sec.: Ottawa, 1958-61; Lagos, 1962-64; Kabul, 1967-69. Counsellor, Dar-es-Salaam, 1969-73. *Recreation:* sailing. *Address:* c/o Foreign and Commonwealth Office, SW1. *Club:* Royal Commonwealth Society.

EWART, Sir (William) Ivan (Cecil), 6th Bt, *cr* 1887; DSC 1945; JP; Chairman, William Ewart Investments Ltd, Belfast, since 1977 (Ewart New Northern Ltd, Belfast, 1973-77); *b* 18 July 1919; *s* of late Major William Basil Ewart (*y s* of late Frederick William Ewart, 1st *s* of 1st Bt); *S* kinsman (Sir Talbot Ewart, 5th Bt), 1959; *m* 1948, Pauline Chevallier (*d* 1964), *e d* of late Wing Comdr Raphael Chevallier Preston, OBE, AFC, JP, Abbey Flat, Bellapais, Kyrenia, Cyprus; one *s* two *d. Educ:* Radley. Joined Ulster Div., RNVR, 1938. Served War of 1939-45; Lieut, RNVR; service in Coastal Forces (Motor Torpedo-Boats), 1939-42; POW, Germany, 1942-45 (DSC). Chairman: William Ewart & Son Ltd, Linen Manufacturers, 1968-73. Pres., NI Chamber of Commerce and Industry, 1974. A Northern Ireland Delegate to the Duke of Edinburgh's Study Conf. on the Human Problems of Industrial Communities within the Commonwealth and Empire, Oxford, 1956; Pres., Church of Ireland's Young Men's Soc., 1951-61 and 1975-76; Chm. Flax Spinners Assoc., 1961-66; Pres., Oldpark Unionist Assoc., 1950-68. Belfast Harbour Comr, 1968-. High Sheriff for County Antrim, 1976. *Recreations:* travel, gliding, photography. *Heir: s* William Michael Ewart, *b* 10 June 1953. *Address:* Hill House, Hillborough, Co. Down, Ireland BT26 6AE. *T:* Hillsborough 68300. *Clubs:* Naval; Ulster (Belfast).

EWART EVANS, George; see Evans, G. E.

EWART JAMES, William Henry; His Honour Judge Ewart James; a Circuit Judge, since 1974; *b* 15 Dec. 1910; *e s* of Rev. David Ewart James; *m* 1941, Esmé Vivienne, *y d* of Edward Lloyd, Liverpool and Gresford; two *s* one *d. Educ:* Bishop's Stortford Coll.; Worcester Coll., Oxford. MA (Mod. Hist.). Private Sec. to J. H. Morgan, KC, Counsel to the Indian Princes, 1936; Asst. Sec. European Gp, Bengal Legislature, 1937-38; travelled Far East and America, 1936-39. Served War: in Grenadier Guards, Royal Welch Fusiliers and 1st Airborne Div., Sept. 1939-Dec. 1945. Called to the Bar, 1948; Counsel to the Post Office, Western Circuit, 1957-70; Dep. Chm., Devon QS, 1968-71; a Recorder of the Crown Court, 1972-74. Mem., Hants CC, 1952-74; Alderman, 1965; Chm., Local Govt Cttee, 1963-74. *Recreation:* travel. *Address:* Westfield, Upton Grey, Basingstoke, Hants. *T:* Long Sutton (Hants) 230. *Club:* Special Forces.

EWBANK, Anthony Bruce, QC 1972; a Recorder of the Crown Court, since 1975; *b* 30 July 1925; *s* of late Rev. Harold Ewbank and Gwendolen Ewbank (*née* Bruce); *m* 1958, Moya McGinn; four *s* one *d. Educ:* St John's Sch., Leatherhead; Trinity Coll., Cambridge (MA). RNVR, 1945-47 and 1951-56. Called to Bar, Gray's Inn, 1954. Junior Counsel to Treasury in Probate matters, 1969. *Recreations:* walking, sailing, swimming. *Address:* Dunally House, Walton Lane, Shepperton, Mddx; 1 King's Bench Walk, Temple, EC4. *T:* 01-353 4423.

EWBANK, Prof. Inga-Stina; Hildred Carlile Professor of English at Bedford College, University of London, since 1974; *b* 13 June 1932; *d* of Gustav and Ingeborg Ekeblad; *m* 1959, Roger Ewbank; one *s* two *d. Educ:* Högre Allmämma Läroverket för Flickor, Gothenburg; Univs of Carleton (BA), Gothenburg (Fil.kand.), Sheffield (MA) and Liverpool (PhD). William Noble Fellow, Univ. of Liverpool, 1955-57; Res. Fellow at Shakespeare Inst., Univ. of Birmingham, 1957-60; Univ. of Liverpool: Asst Lectr, 1960-63; Lectr, 1963-70; Sen. Lectr, 1970-72; Reader in English Literature, Bedford Coll., Univ. of London, 1972-74. Vis. Lectr, Univ. of Munich, 1959-60; Vis. Assoc. Prof., Northwestern Univ., 1966; Vis. Prof., Harvard Univ., 1974. *Publications:* Their Proper Sphere: A Study of the Brontë Sisters as Early-Victorian Female Novelists, 1966; Shakespeare, Ibsen and the Unspeakable (Inaugural Lecture), 1975; chapter in, A New Companion to Shakespeare Studies, 1971; (with Peter Hall) Ibsen's John Gabriel Borkman: An English Version, 1975; chapters in other books; contrib. Shakespeare Survey, Ibsen Yearbook, Rev. Eng. Studies, Mod. Lang. Rev., English Studies, etc. *Recreations:* same as work: reading, theatre; children. *Address:* 19 Woodfield Road, Ealing, W5. *T:* 01-997 2895.

EWBANK, Maj.-Gen. Sir Robert Withers, KBE 1964 (CBE 1954); CB 1957; DSO 1945; MA; late Royal Engineers; retired; President Emeritus, Fellowship of National Officers' Christian Unions; *b* 20 July 1907; *s* of late Brig.-Gen. W. Ewbank, CB, CIE, RE and Mrs Ewbank, *d* of late Col Barrow, IMS; *m* 1932, Isobel Joyce Forster; one *s* two *d. Educ:* Weymouth Coll.; Royal Military Academy, Woolwich (King's and Pollock Medals, Armstrong Memorial Prize for Science); Christ's Coll., Cambridge (Scholar; MA 1st Class Hons Mech. Sciences Tripos). Garrison Engineer, Trincomalee, Ceylon, 1934-36; Adjt, Kent Fortress RE TA, 1936-39; GSO2 War Office, 1939-41; Instructor Staff Coll., Camberley, 1941-42; GSO1 War Office, 1942-44; Comdr, Royal Engineers, 50 Northumbrian Division, BLA, 1944-46; Col Q (Movements) War Office, 1946-49; Student Imperial Defence Coll., 1950; Sec. Chiefs of Staff Cttee, Ministry of Defence, 1951-53; Chief of Staff, British Army Staff, Washington, USA, 1954-56; Dir of Movements, War Office, 1956-58; Chief of Staff, HQ Northern Army Group, 1958-60; Commandant, Royal Military Coll. of Science, 1961-64; retd 1964. Pres., Officers' Christian Union of GB, 1965-76. *Recreations:* photography, climbing, travel, ski-ing. *Address:* 5 Petworth Court, Overstrand, Rustington, West Sussex. *T:* Rustington 6345.

EWBANK, Ven. Walter Frederick; Archdeacon of Carlisle and Canon Residentiary of Carlisle Cathedral, since 1977; Administrator of Church House, Carlisle and Chairman, Diocesan Board of Finance and Diocesan Glebe Committee, since 1977; *b* Poona, India, 29 Jan. 1918; *er s* of late Sir Robert Benson Ewbank, CSI, CIE, and Frances Helen, *d* of Rev. W. F. Simpson; *m* 1st, 1941, Ida Margaret, 3rd *d* of late John Haworth Whitworth, DSO, MC, Inner Temple; three *d*; 2nd, 1976, Mrs Josephine Alice Williamson, MD, ChB, FRCOG. *Educ:* Shrewsbury Sch.; Balliol Coll., Oxford. Classical Scholar of Balliol, 1936; 1st, Classical Hon. Mods, 1938; 2nd, Hon. Sch. of Theology, 1946; BA and MA 1946; Bishops' Coll., Cheshunt, 1946; BD 1952. Friends' Ambulance Unit, 1939-42; Deacon, 1946; Priest, 1947; Asst Curate, St Martin's, Windermere, 1946-49; Dio. Youth Chaplain and Vicar of Ings, 1949-52; Chap. to Casterton Sch. and Vicar of Casterton, 1952-62; Domestic Chap. to Bp of Carlisle and Vicar of Raughtonhead, 1962-66; Hon. Canon of Carlisle Cath., 1966; Vicar of St Cuthbert's, Carlisle, and Chap. to Corporation, 1966-71; Rural Dean of Carlisle, 1970-71; Archdeacon of Westmorland and Furness and Vicar of Winster, 1971-77. Proctor in Convocation and Mem. Ch Assembly, 1957-70; Mem., Canon Law Standing Commn, 1968-70; Diocesan Dir: of Ordinands, 1962-70; of Post Ordination Trng, 1962-66; Vice-Chm., Diocesan Synod, 1970-. Chm., Carlisle Tithe Barn Restoration Cttee, 1968-70. Winter War Remembrance Medal (Finland), 1940. *Publications:* Salopian Diaries, 1961; Morality without Law, 1969; articles in Church Quarterly Review. *Recreation:* reading and writing Latin. *Address:* c/o 3 The Abbey, Carlisle CA3 8TZ. *Clubs:* Royal Over-Seas League; County (Carlisle).
See also A. C. Renfrew.

EWEN, Peter; Chartered Accountant; *b* 4 June 1903; *s* of Alexander H. and Elizabeth Ewen, Liverpool; *m* 1932, Janet Howat (*née* Allan); two *d. Educ:* Merchant Taylors, Crosby. Qualified as Chartered Accountant, 1927; after 4 years in India joined Allan Charlesworth & Co., 1931; Partner, 1938; Senior Partner, 1953; retired, 1969. Dir of companies; Chm., Westinghouse Brake and Signal Co. Ltd, 1962-74. *Address:* Kestor, Moretonhampstead, Devon. *T:* Moretonhampstead 307. *Club:* Oriental.

EWENS, John Qualtrough, CMG 1971; CBE 1959; First Parliamentary Counsel, Commonwealth of Australia, 1948-72; *b* 18 Nov. 1907; *er s* of L. J. Ewens, Adelaide; *m* 1935, Gwendoline, *e d* of W. A. Wilson, Adelaide; two *s. Educ:* St Peter's Coll., Adelaide; Univ. of Adelaide. LLB 1929. Barrister and Solicitor, S Australia, 1929. Legal Asst, Attorney-General's Dept, Commonwealth of Australia, 1933; Sen. Legal Officer, 1939; Asst Parly Draftsman, 1945; Principal Asst Parly Draftsman, 1948; First Parly Counsel (formerly called Parly Draftsman), 1948; Actg Solicitor-Gen. and Actg Sec., Commonwealth of Australia Attorney-Gen.'s Dept, numerous occasions, 1953-70. Mem. Council: Canberra UC, 1945-60; Australian Nat. Univ., 1960-75. *Publications:* articles in legal periodicals. *Recreations:* reading, music, bowls, motoring. *Address:* 57 Franklin Street, Forrest, ACT 2603, Australia. *T:* Canberra 95 9283.

EWER, Prof. Tom Keightley, HDA; BVSc; PhD; MRCVS; Professor of Animal Husbandry, Bristol University, 1961-77; retired; *b* 21 Sept. 1911; *s* of William Edward Frederick Ewer and Maria Louisa Wales; *m* 1st, 1937, Iva Rosalind Biddle; three *s*; 2nd, 1959, Margaret June Fischer; three *d* one step *s* two step *d. Educ:* Fowey Grammar Sch.; Sydney Univ. (BVSc); Cambridge Univ. (PhD). Veterinary research with NZ Govt, 1938-45; Senior Lecturer, Univ. of NZ, 1945-47; Wellcome Research Fellow, University of Cambridge, 1947-50; Prof. of Animal Husbandry, University of Queensland, 1950-61. *Publications:* contrib. to scientific publications, on animal nutrition and veterinary education. *Recreation:* music. *Address:* Langford House, Langford, near Bristol. *T:* Churchill 581.

EWIN, Sir David Ernest Thomas F.; *see* Floyd Ewin.

EWING; *see* Orr-Ewing and Orr Ewing.

EWING, Vice-Adm. Sir Alastair; *see* Ewing, Vice-Adm. Sir R. A.

EWING, Sir Alexander (William Gordon), Kt 1959; MA (Edinburgh), PhD (Manchester); Emeritus Professor of Audiology and Education of the Deaf and Director (1944-64) of Audiology and Education of the Deaf in the University of Manchester; *b* 6 Dec. 1896; *s* of late Rev. A. Gordon C. Ewing, MA, formerly Rector of St Vincent's Episcopal Church, Edinburgh; *m* 1st, 1922, Irene R. Goldsack (*d* 1959); no *c*; 2nd, 1961, Ethel Constance Goldsack. *Educ:* St Clare Preparatory Sch., Walmer, Kent; Dean Close Sch., Cheltenham; University of Edinburgh; University of Manchester. Service in HM Forces, 1918-19. Directed private clinic for deaf children and held hon. special lectureship in Dept of Educ. of the Deaf, University of Manchester, 1922-44. Norman Gamble Prize of the Royal Society of Medicine and Actonian Prize of Royal Institution, 1943 (with Dr Irene Ewing); Hon. Mem. Amer. Otological Soc., 1946-; Hon. Fellow Manchester Med. Soc., 1964-; (with Dr Irene Ewing) visited schs for the deaf in Canada, and in Australia and New Zealand at invitation of Govts concerned, to inspect and advise about their provision of education for the deaf, and conducted post-grad. courses during a summer session at North-Western Univ., Ill, 1949. Mem. Med. Research Council's Cttee on the Physiology of Hearing and Cttee on the Educational Treatment of Deafness, 1932-52; Pres. Brit. Association of the Hard of Hearing, 1956-; Vice-Pres., National Coll. of Teachers of the Deaf, 1965-; Vice-Pres., Health Visitors' Assoc., 1966-. Hon. LittD, Ithaca, NY; Hon. LLD Manchester. *Publications:* Aphasia in Children, 1930; The Handicap of Deafness, 1938; (with I. R. Ewing) Opportunity and the Deaf Child, 1947; Speech and the Deaf Child, 1954 (with I. R. Ewing); Educational Guidance and the Deaf Child, 1957 (with others); New Opportunities for Deaf Children, 1961 (with I. R. Ewing); Teaching Deaf Children to Talk, 1964 (with E. C. Ewing); Hearing Aids, Lipreading and Clear Speech, 1967 (with E. C. Ewing); Hearing-Impaired Children under Five: a guide for parents and teachers, 1971 (with E. C. Ewing); articles and papers in the Journal of Laryngology and Otology, Lancet, Practitioner, Proc. Royal Society of Medicine, Teacher of the Deaf. *Recreations:* gardening, travel. *Address:* Horseshoe Cottage, Alderley Edge, Cheshire. *T:* Alderley Edge 583258.

EWING, Harry; MP (Lab) Stirling, Falkirk and Grangemouth, since 1974 (Stirling and Falkirk, Sept. 1971-1974); Parliamentary Under-Secretary of State, Scottish Office, since Oct. 1974; *b* 20 Jan. 1931; *s* of Mr and Mrs William Ewing; *m* 1954, Margaret Greenhill; one *s* one *d. Educ:* Fulford Primary Sch., Cowdenbeath; Beath High Sch., Cowdenbeath. Contested (Lab) East Fife, 1970. Mem., Union of Post Office Workers. *Recreations:* bowls, gardening. *Address:* 16 Robertson Avenue, Leven, Fife. *T:* Leven 2123.

EWING, Vice-Adm. Sir (Robert) Alastair, KBE 1962; CB 1959; DSC 1942; *b* 10 April 1909; *s* of Major Ian Ewing and Muriel Adèle Child; *m* 1940, Diana Smeed, *d* of Major Harry Archer, DSO; one *s. Educ:* Royal Naval Coll., Dartmouth. In command of Destroyers during War of 1939-45; NATO Standing Group Staff, 1950-51; Imperial Defence Coll., 1952; in command of HMS Vanguard, 1953-54; Dir of Naval Staff Coll., Greenwich, 1954-56; Naval Sec. to First Lord of the Admiralty, 1956-58; Flag Officer Flotillas (Mediterranean), 1958-60; Adm. Commanding Reserves and Inspector of Recruiting, 1960-62; retd list, 1962. *Address:* 428 Chilean Avenue, Palm Beach, Florida 33480, USA. *Club:* Naval and Military.

EWING, Air Vice-Marshal Vyvyan Stewart, CB 1954; CBE 1951; RAF Medical Branch, retired; Principal Medical Officer, Home Command, 1953-55. MB, ChB (St Andrews); Diploma in Public Health. Air Vice-Marshal, 1951; retired, 1955. CStJ. *Address:* Sunset Cottage, 10 Staunton Avenue, Hayling Island, Hants. *T:* Hayling Island 3159.

EWING, Mrs Winifred Margaret; MP (SNP) Moray and Nairn, since Feb. 1974; *b* 10 July 1929; *d* of George Woodburn and Christina Bell Anderson; *m* 1956, Stewart Martin Ewing; two *s* one *d. Educ:* Queen's Park Sen. Sec. Sch.; University of Glasgow (MA, LLB). Qual. as Solicitor, 1952. Lectr in Law, Scottish Coll. of Commerce, 1954-56; Solicitor, practising on own account, 1956-. Sec., Glasgow Bar Assoc., 1961-67, Pres., 1970-71. MP (Scottish Nationalist) for Hamilton, Nov. 1967-70. Vice-Pres. and Mem. Nat. Exec., Scottish National Party. Mem., European Parlt, 1975-. Mem., Exec. Cttee, Scottish Council for Develt and Industry, 1972-. Pres., Glasgow Central Soroptimist Club, 1966-67. *Address:* 52 Queen's Drive, Glasgow G42 8BP. *T:* 041-423 1765.

EWUSIE, Joseph Yanney; Vice Chancellor, University of Cape Coast, Ghana, since 1973; *b* 18 April 1927; *s* of Samuel Mainsa Wilson Ewusie and Elizabeth Dickson; *m* 1959, Stella Turkson; four *s. Educ:* Winneba Anglican Sch.; Mfantsipim Sch.; University Coll. of the Gold Coast; Univ. of Cambridge. BSc (London), PhD (Cantab). Lectr in Botany, Univ. of Ghana, 1957-62; Gen. Sec. (Chief Exec.), Ghana Academy of Sciences (highest learned and res. org. in Ghana), 1963-68; Univ. of Cape Coast: Associate Prof. of Botany and Head of Dept, 1969-72; Prof. and Head, Dept of Botany, 1973; Dean, Faculty of Science, 1971-74; Pro-Vice Chancellor, 1971-73. Medal (Govt of Hungary) for internat. understanding between Ghana and Hungary, 1964. *Publications:* School Certificate Biology for Tropical Schools, 1964, 4th edn 1974; Tropical Biological Drawings, 1973. *Address:* University of Cape Coast, Cape Coast, Ghana. *T:* Cape Coast 2378.

EXETER, 6th Marquess of, *cr* 1801, **David George Brownlow Cecil,** KCMG 1943; Baron Burghley, 1571; Earl of Exeter, 1605; DL; Hereditary Grand Almoner; Lord Paramount of the Soke of Peterborough; *b* 9 Feb. 1905; *e s* of 5th Marquess of Exeter, KG, CMG; *S* father, 1956; *m* 1st, 1929, Lady Mary Theresa Montagu-Douglas-Scott (marr. diss. 1946), 4th *d* of 7th Duke of Buccleuch; three *d*; 2nd, 1946, Diana Mary Forbes, *widow* of Col David Forbes and *er d* of late Hon Arnold Henderson; one *d. Educ:* Eton; Magdalene Coll., Cambridge, MA. Lieut Grenadier Guards, retired 1929, re-employed 1939; served War of 1939-45: Staff Captain, 1940; Major, Dep. Asst Dir, 1941, Lt-Col, Asst Dir, Tank Supply, 1942; Controller of Aircraft Repairs and Overseas Supplies, Min. of Aircraft Production, 1942-43; Hon. Colonel: 5th Bn Northants Regt, 1939-48; Bermuda Militia, 1935-46. MP (U) Peterborough Div., Northants, 1931-43; Parly Private Secretary to: late Lord Hailsham for World Economic Conf.; Parly Sec. at Min. of Supply, 1939-41; Chm. Economy Cttee, Raw Materials, 1939-43; Governor and C-in-C of Bermuda, 1943-45. Leader, UK Industrial Mission to Pakistan, 1950, and to Burma, 1954. Rector of St Andrews Univ., 1949-52. Mayor of Stamford, 1961. President: Amateur Athletic Assoc., 1936-76; Internat. Amateur Athletic Fedn, 1946-76; British Olympic Assoc., 1966-77 (Chm., 1936-66); Mem., Internat. Olympic Cttee, 1933-, Vice-Pres., 1952-66, now Doyen. Chairman: Propaganda Cttee, Nat. Fitness Council, 1938; Organising and Exec. Cttee for 1948 Olympic Games in London; Fedn of Chambers of Commerce of British Commonwealth, 1952-54; President: Young Britons Assoc., 1933-37; Junior Imperial League, 1939 (Chm., 1933-37); Council, Radio Industry, 1952; BTA, 1966-69. Director: National Westminster Bank Ltd; Lands Improvement Co.; Firestone Tyre & Rubber Co. Ltd; Trustee, Trust Houses Forte. Mem. Exec. Cttee, King George VI Nat. Memorial Fund. Pres., CUAC, 1926-27; Winner of: Oxford v Cambridge 120 yards hurdles and 220 yards hurdles, 1925, 1926, 1927; eight British Championships, 1928; Olympic 400 metres hurdles, 1928; 5th, 110 metre hurdles, 4th, 400 metre hurdles, and 2nd, 4x400 metres, Olympic Games, 1932; 1st three times, Empire Games, 1930; many other races at home and abroad. Hunted own private pack of foxhounds, 1935-39; Joint-Master: E Sussex, 1939-53; Old Berkshire Hunt, 1953-57; Burghley Hunt, 1957-67; Pres., BHS, 1963. DL Northants, 1937-46, Huntingdon and Peterborough, 1965-. Hon. FRCS. Hon. LLD St Andrews, 1942. KStJ. *Recreations:* hunting, shooting, fishing, athletics. *Heir: b* Lord (William) Martin Alleyne Cecil, *qv. Address:* Burghley House, Stamford, Lincs. *Clubs:* Pratt's, Junior Carlton (Pres., 1956-).

See also Baron Barnard, Lt-Col Hon. *P. E. Brassey, Sir G . H . C . Floyd , Bt , Baron Hotham .*

EXETER, Bishop of, since 1973; **Rt. Rev. Eric Arthur John Mercer;** *b* 6 Dec. 1917; *s* of Ambrose John Mercer, Kent; *m* 1951, Rosemary Wilma, *d* of John William Denby, Lincs; one *s* one *d. Educ:* Dover Gram. Sch.; Kelham Theol. Coll. Enlisted Sherwood Foresters, 1940, commnd 1940; Capt. and Adjt, 14th Foresters, 1943; served Italy (despatches), 1944; Staff Coll., Haifa, 1944; DAA&QMG, 66 Inf. Bde, Palestine, 1945; GSO2 (SD), HQ, MEF, 1945. Returned Kelham Theol. Coll., 1946-47. Ordained, Chester, 1947; Curate, Coppenhall, Crewe, 1947-51; Priest in charge, Heald Green, 1951-53; Rector, St Thomas', Stockport, 1953-59; Chester Diocesan Missioner, 1959-65; Rector, Chester St Bridget, 1959-65; Hon. Canon of Chester Cathedral, 1964; Bishop Suffragan of Birkenhead, 1965-73. Nat. Chm., CEMS, 1974. *Publication:* (contrib.) Worship in a Changing Church, 1965. *Address:* The Palace, Exeter EX1 1HY.

EXETER, Dean of; *see* Chapman, Very Rev. C. T.

EXETER, Archdeacon of; *see* Ward, Ven. A. F.

EXHAM, Maj.-Gen. Robert Kenah, CB 1952; CBE 1949 (OBE 1946); MC 1940; Director Land/Air Warfare, War Office, 1957-60, retired; *b* 25 Jan. 1907; *s* of late Col Frank Simeon Exham, DSO; *m* 1940, Avril Mary, *d* of late Major F. Langley Price; two *s. Educ:* Radley Coll. Served North-West Frontier of India, 1935 (despatches twice, medal with clasp); War of 1939-45 (despatches, MC). Maj.-Gen. late Duke of Wellington's Regt (West Riding). *Address:* Tall Trees, Beech Hill, Mayford, Woking, Surrey GU22 0SB. *T:* Woking 62783.

EXMOUTH, 10th Viscount *cr* 1816; **Paul Edward Pellew; Bt** 1796 (Pellew of Treverry); Baron 1814; *b* 8 Oct. 1940; *s* of 9th Viscount Exmouth and Maria Luisa, Marquesa de Olias (Spain, *cr* 1652; *S* 1940), *d* of late Luis de Urquijo, Marques de Amurrio, Madrid; *S* father, 1970; *m* 1st, 1964 (marr. diss. 1974); one *d* ; 2nd, 1975, Rosemary Countess of Burford. *Educ:* Downside. Mem. Cross benches, House of Lords. Mem., Inst. of Dirs. *Heir: b* Hon. Peter Irving Pellew, *b* 20 Oct. 1942. *Address:* Canonteign, near Exeter, Devon.

EXTON, Clive; scriptwriter and playwright; *b* 11 April 1930; *s* of late J. E. M. Brooks and of Marie Brooks (*née* Rolfe); *m* 1957, Margaret Josephine Reid; one *s* two *d. Educ:* Christ's Hospital. Worked in advertising, 1946-48; served with HM Forces as Private, 1948-50; unsuccessful actor, stage manager and occasional waiter, 1950-59. *TV plays:* No Fixed Abode, 1959; The Silk Purse; Where I Live; Some Talk of Alexander; Hold My Hand, Soldier; I'll Have You to Remember; The Big Eat; The Trial of Doctor Fancy; Land of my Dreams; The Close Prisoner; The Bone Yard; Are You Ready for the Music?; The Rainbirds; Killers (series); The Crezz (series). *Stage play:* Have You Any Dirty Washing, Mother Dear?. *Films:* Night Must Fall; Isadora; Entertaining Mr Sloane; Ten Rillington Place; Running Scared; Doomwatch; The House in Nightmare Park; Hornblower and the Privateer. *Publications:* No Fixed Abode (in Six Granada Plays, anthol.), 1960; Have You Any Dirty Washing, Mother Dear? (in Plays of the Year, vol. 37), 1970. *Address:* c/o A. D. Peters & Co., 10 Buckingham Street, WC2.

EXTON-SMITH, Prof. Arthur Norman, MD; FRCP; Professor of Geriatric Medicine, University College Hospital Medical School, London, since 1973; *b* 7 Jan. 1920; *s* of Arthur and Ethel Exton-Smith; *m* 1951, Jean Barbara Belcher; one *s* one *d . Educ:* Nottingham High Sch.; Pembroke Coll., Cambridge (MA, MD). FRCP 1964. Consultant Physician: Whittington Hosp., London, 1951-65; UCH, 1965-73. *Publications:* Medical Problems of Old Age, 1955; contrib. Lancet, BMJ. *Address:* 20 Grange Avenue, Totteridge, N20 8AD. *T:* 01-445 9833.

EYRE, Hon. Dean Jack; New Zealand High Commissioner to Canada, 1968-73 and since 1976; *b* Westport, NZ, 1914; *m* ; two *s* one *d. Educ:* Hamilton High Sch.; Auckland University Coll. Served War of 1939-45, Lieut in RNVR. Electrical importer and manufacturer. MP (Nat) North Shore, 1949-66; Minister of

Customs, Industries and Commerce, Social Security, Defence, Police, War Pensions, Housing, State Advances, Tourist and Health Resorts, New Zealand, 1954-57; Minister in Charge of Police, 1960-63; Minister of Defence, 1960-66; Minister i/c Tourism, 1961-66. *Recreations:* yachting, fishing. *Address:* New Zealand High Commission, Suite 804, Commonwealth Building, 77 Metcalfe Street, Ottawa, Canada K1P 5L6. *Clubs:* Royal New Zealand Yacht Squadron, Northern, Officers (Auckland); Wellington, United Services (Wellington).

EYRE, Graham Newman, QC 1970; a Recorder of the Crown Court, since 1975; *b* 9 Jan. 1931; *s* of Newman Eyre; *m* 1954, Jean Dalrymple Walker; one *s* three *d. Educ:* Marlborough Coll.; Trinity Coll., Cambridge. BA 1953, LLB 1954, MA 1958. Council Prizewinner, 1954. Called to Bar, Middle Temple, 1954; Harmsworth Law Schol., Middle Temple, 1955, Lincoln's Inn, 1971. *Publications:* Rating Law and Valuation, 1963; contrib. Jl Planning Law. *Address:* Walberton House, Walberton, West Sussex. *T:* Yapton 205. *Club:* Athenæum.

EYRE, Sir Oliver E. C.; *see* Crosthwaite-Eyre.

EYRE, Reginald Edwin; MP (C) Birmingham (Hall Green) since May 1965; a Vice-Chairman, Conservative Party Organisation, since 1975; *b* 28 May 1924; *s* of late Edwin Eyre. *Educ:* King Edward's Camp Hill Sch., Birmingham; Emmanuel Coll., Cambridge (MA). Midshipman and Sub-Lieut, RNVR, War of 1939-45. Admitted a Solicitor, 1950; Senior Partner, Eyre & Co., solicitors, Birmingham. Hon. Consultant, Poor Man's Lawyer, 1948-58. Contested (C) Birmingham (Northfield) 1959; Conservative Political Centre: Chm., W Midlands Area, 1960-63; Chm., National Advisory Cttee, 1964-66; Opposition Whip, 1966-70; a Lord Comr of the Treasury, June-Sept. 1970; Comptroller of HM Household, 1970-72; Parly Under-Sec. of State, DoE, 1972-74. *Address:* Fulbrook House, Upper Fulbrook, Stratford-on-Avon, Warwicks. *T:* Snitterfield 304; Fountain Court, Steelhouse Lane, Birmingham B4 6EB. *T:* 021-236 3002. *Clubs:* Carlton; Conservative (Birmingham).

EYRE, Ven. Richard Montague Stephens; Archdeacon of Chichester since 1975; *b* 1929; *s* of Montague Henry and Ethel Mary Eyre; *m* 1963, Anne Mary Bentley; two *d . Educ:* Charterhouse; Oriel Coll. and St Stephen's House, Oxford. MA Oxon. Deacon 1956, priest 1957; Curate, St Mark's Church, Portsea, 1956-59; Tutor and Chaplain, Chichester Theological Coll., 1959-62; Chaplain, Eastbourne Coll., 1962-65; Vicar of Arundel, 1965-73; Vicar of Good Shepherd, Brighton, 1973-75. *Recreations:* golf, music, wine, travel. *Address:* 4 Canon Lane, Chichester, W Sussex.

EYRES-MONSELL, family name of **Viscount Monsell.**

EYSENCK, Prof. Hans Jurgen, PhD, DSc; Professor of Psychology, University of London, Institute of Psychiatry, since 1955; Director, Psychological Department, Maudsley Hospital, since 1946; *b* 4 March 1916; *s* of Eduard Anton and Ruth Eysenck; *m* 1st, 1938, Margaret Malcolm Davies; one *s* ; 2nd, 1950, Sybil Bianca Giuletta Rostal; three *s* one *d. Educ:* school in Germany, France and England; Univ. of London. BA 1938, PhD 1940, DSc 1964. Senior Research Psychologist, Mill Hill Emergency Hosp., 1942-46; Reader in Psychology, Univ. of London (Inst. of Psychiatry), 1950-54; Visiting Prof., Univ. of Pennsylvania, 1949-50; Visiting Prof., Univ. of California, Berkeley, 1954. *Publications:* Dimensions of Personality, 1947; The Scientific Study of Personality, 1952; The Structure of Human Personality, 1953; Uses and Abuses of Psychology, 1953; The Psychology of Politics, 1954; Sense and Nonsense in Psychology, 1957; Dynamics of Anxiety and Hysteria, 1957; Perceptual Processes and Mental Illness, 1957; (ed) Handbook of Abnormal Psychology, 1960, 2nd edn, 1972; (ed) Behaviour Therapy and the Neuroses, 1960; (ed) Experiments in Personality, 1960; (ed) Experiments with Drugs, 1963; (ed) Experiments in Behaviour Therapy, 1964; (ed) Experiments in Motivation, 1964; Crime and Personality, 1964; Causes and Cures of Neurosis, 1965; Fact and Fiction in Psychology, 1965; Smoking, Health and Personality, 1965; The Biological Basis of Personality, 1968; Personality Structure and Measurement, 1969; Race, Intelligence and Education, 1971; Psychology is about People, 1972; (ed) Readings in Introversion-Extraversion, 3 vols, 1971; (ed) Lexikon der Psychologie, 3 vols, 1972; The Measurement of Intelligence, 1973; The Inequality of Man, 1973; (ed jtly) The Experimental Study of Freudian Theories, 1973; (ed jtly) Encyclopaedia of Psychology, 1973; (with Glenn Wilson) Know Your Own Personality, 1975; (ed) Case Studies in Behaviour Therapy, 1976; Sex and Personality, 1976; (with S. B. G. Eysenck) Psychoticism as a Dimension of Personality 1976; You and Neurosis, 1977; Die Zukunft der Psychologie, 1977; Editor-in-Chief, Behaviour Research and Therapy, 1963-;

(ed) International Monographs of Experimental Psychology; some 500 articles in British, American, German, Spanish and French Jls of Psychology. *Recreations:* walking, tennis, chess, detective stories, squash. *Address:* 10 Dorchester Drive, SE24.

EYSTON, Capt. George Edward Thomas, OBE 1948; MC; MIMechE; MSAE; *b* 28 June 1897; *s* of E. R. J. Eyston; *m* 1924; two *d*. *Educ:* Stonyhurst; Trinity Coll., Cambridge. Served in European War, 1914-18, Lieut 3 Battalion Dorset Regt, and Staff Capt. Royal Artillery (despatches twice, wounded); served 2nd World War, a Regional Controller, Min. of Prodn. Holder of Land Speed Record three times in America and many other World's Records Motoring. Awarded Segrave Trophy, 1937, Gold Medal of AIACR; Chevalier of Legion of Honour. *Publications:* Flat Out; (with Barre Lyndon) Motor Racing and Record Breaking, 1935; (with W. F. Bradley) Speed on Salt, 1936; (ed) Fastest on Earth, 1939; Safety Last, 1976. *Address:* 524 Hillside Terrace, West Orange, New Jersey, USA. *Clubs:* Royal Automobile, Hawks, Leander; Royal Yacht Squadron; Seawanaka Corinthian (NY).

EYTON, Anthony John Plowden, ARA 1976; Part-time Lecturer, Camberwell School of Art, since 1956; Visiting Teacher, Royal Academy Schools, since 1963; *b* 17 May 1923; *s* of Captain John Seymour Eyton, ICS, and Phyllis Annie Tyser; *m* 1960, Frances Mary Capell; three *d*. *Educ:* Twyford Sch.; Canford Sch.; Camberwell Sch. of Art (NDD). Abbey Major Scholarship in Painting, 1950-51. Elected Mem., London Gp, 1958; Head of Painting Dept, St Lawrence Coll., Kingston, Ont, 1969-71. One Man Exhibitions: St George's Gall., 1955; Galerie de Seine, 1957; New Art Centre, 1959, 1961, 1968; New Grafton Gall., 1973; William Darby Gall., 1975. Fellowship awarded by Grocers' Co. (for work and travel in Italy), 1974. Prize, John Moore's Exhibn, Liverpool, 1972; First Prize, Second British Internat. Drawing Biennale, Middlesbrough, 1975. *Recreation:* gardening. *Address:* 34 Hanbury Street, E1. *T:* 01-247 8547.

EYTON, Mrs Selena Frances W.; *see* Wynne-Eyton.

EZARD, Clarence Norbury, CBE 1954 (OBE 1942); Retired as Ambassador to Costa Rica; *b* 6 Oct. 1896; *m* 1936, Olive Lillian Vaneus. *Educ:* Carlisle Grammar Sch.; Emmanuel Coll., Cambridge. Probationer Vice-Consul in General Consular Service, 1924; Acting Vice-Consul, Havana, 1926; Chargé d'Affaires, May-Oct. 1928; Sec. to Special Mission at Inauguration of Pres. of Republic of Cuba, with Temp. rank of 3rd Sec. in Diplomatic Service, 1929; Subst. rank of Vice-Consul, 1929; Vice-Consul at Bogotá, 1930; local rank of 2nd Sec. in Dipl. Service, 1930; in charge of Consulate at Havana, March-June 1931, of Legation April-June 1931. Transferred to New York, 1932, to Piræus, 1934. Acting Consul at Athens, 1935 and 1936; Consul at Beira, 1938; Montevideo, 1945, with rank of Consul and 1st Sec.; Consul-Gen., Gdansk, 1946; Consul-Gen., Haifa, 1949; Minister to Costa Rica, 1953; Ambassador to Costa Rica, 1956; retired, 1957. *Address:* Three Fields, Mayfield, East Sussex. *Club:* Junior Carlton.

EZEILO, Prof. James Okoye Chukuka, PhD; Vice-Chancellor, University of Nigeria, Nsukka, since 1975; *b* 17 Jan. 1930; *s* of Josiah Ezeilo and Janet Ezeilo; *m* 1960, Phoebe Uchechuku; two *s* two *d*. *Educ:* Dennis Memorial Grammar Sch., Onitsha; University Coll., Ibadan (MSc London); Queens' Coll., Cambridge (PhD). University of Ibadan: Lectr in Maths, 1958-62; Sen. Lectr in Maths, 1962-64; Prof. of Maths, 1964-66; Prof. of Maths, Univ. of Nigeria, Nsukka 1966-75. Pres., Nigerian Math. Assoc., 1972-74; Mem., Nigerian Council for Science and Technol., 1970-75; Foundation Mem., Nigerian Acad. of Sciences. *Publications:* over 50 papers on differential equations in math. jls. *Recreation:* gardening. *Address:* Vice-Chancellor's Lodge, University of Nigeria, Nsukka, Anambra State, Nigeria. *T:* Nsukka 48.

EZRA, Sir Derek, Kt 1974; MBE 1945; Chairman: National Coal Board, since 1971 (Deputy Chairman, 1967-71; Member, since 1965); British Institute of Management, since 1976; *b* 23 Feb. 1919; *s* of David and Lillie Ezra; *m* 1950, Julia Elizabeth Wilkins. *Educ:* Monmouth Sch.; Magdalene Coll., Cambridge (MA, Hon. Fellow, 1977). Army, 1939-47. Representative of NCB at Cttees of OEEC and ECE, 1948-52; Mem. of UK Delegation to High Authority of European Coal and Steel Community, 1952-56; Regional Sales Manager, NCB, 1958-60; Dir-Gen. of Marketing, NCB, 1960-65. Director: J. H. Sankey & Son Ltd; Sankey Building Supplies; Associated Heat Services Ltd, British Fuel Co. Chm., CBI Europe Cttee; Pres., W European Coal Producers' Assoc.; Member: British Overseas Trade Bd, 1972- (Chm., European Trade Cttee); Adv. Council for Energy Conservation, 1974-; Energy Commn, 1977-; Ct of Governors, Administrative Staff Coll., 1971-; Governor,

London Business Sch., 1974-. *Address:* c/o Hobart House, Grosvenor Place, SW1. *T:* 01-235 2020.

F

FABER, Julian Tufnell; Chairman, Willis Faber Ltd, 1972-77; *b* 6 April 1917; *s* of late Alfred and Edith Faber; *m* 1944, Ann Caroline, *e d* of Rt Hon. Harold Macmillan, *qv*, and late Lady Dorothy Macmillan; four *s* one *d*. *Educ:* Winchester; Trinity Coll., Cambridge. Joined Willis, Faber & Dumas Ltd, 1938. Served Welsh Guards (Major 2nd Bn), 1939-45. Director: Willis, Faber & Dumas Ltd, 1952; Willis, Faber & Dumas (Agencies) Ltd, 1965; Taisho Marine & Fire Insurance Co. (UK) Ltd, 1972; Willis Faber (Middle East) SAL, 1973; Morgar Grenfell Ltd, 1974-77; Allianz International Insurance Co., 1974. *Address:* 3 Chester Square, SW1W 9HH. *T:* 01-730 6474. *Clubs:* White's, City of London.
See also Rt . Hon . M . V . Macmillan .

FABER, Richard Stanley, CMG 1977; FRSL; HM Diplomatic Service; Assistant Under Secretary of State, Foreign and Commonwealth Office, since 1975; *b* 6 Dec. 1924; *er s* of late Sir Geoffrey Faber and of Enid, *d* of Sir Henry Erle Richards, KCSI, KC; unmarried. *Educ:* Westminster Sch.; Christ Church, Oxford (MA). RNVR, 1943-46. 1st cl. Lit. Hum. Oxon; Pres., Oxford Union Soc., 1949. Joined HM Foreign (subseq. Diplomatic) Service, 1950; service in FO and in Baghdad, Paris, Abidjan, Washington; Head of Rhodesia Political Dept, FCO, 1967-69; Counsellor: The Hague, 1969-73; Cairo, 1973-75. *Publications:* Beaconsfield and Bolingbroke, 1951; The Vision and the Need: Late Victorian Imperialist Aims, 1966; Proper Stations: Class in Victorian Fiction, 1971; French and English, 1975. *Address:* c/o Foreign and Commonwealth Office, SW1. *Club:* Travellers'.

FACK, Robbert; Chevalier, Order of Netherlands Lion 1971; Officer, Order of Orange Nassau 1960; Ambassador of the Netherlands to the Court of St James's, since 1976; also, concurrently, Ambassador to Iceland, since 1976; *b* 1 Jan. 1917; *m* 1943, Patricia H. Hawkins; four *s*. *Educ:* Univ. of Amsterdâm. Military service, 1937-45. Min. of Foreign Affairs, The Hague, 1945-46; New York (UN), 1946-48; Min. of Foreign Affairs, 1948-50; Rome, 1950-54; Canberra, 1954-58; Bonn, 1958-63; Min. of Foreign Affairs, 1963-68; Ambassador-at-large, 1968-70; Perm. Rep. to UN, New York, 1970-74. Holds various foreign decorations. *Address:* 8 Palace Green, W8. *T:* 01-584 5040.

FAGE, Arthur, CBE 1953; FRS 1942; FRAeS, ARCS; formerly Superintendent of the Aerodynamics Division of National Physical Laboratory; *b* 4 March 1890; *s* of William John and Annie Fage; *m* 1920, Winifred Eliza Donnelly (*d* 1951); one *s* one *d*. *Educ:* Portsmouth Royal Dockyard Sch.; Royal College of Science (Royal Exhibitioner). *Publications:* numerous scientific papers, mostly on aero- and hydro-dynamics in Proc. Royal Society, etc. *Address:* 65 High Point, Richmond Hill Road, Edgbaston, Birmingham B15 3RS.
See also J . D . Fage .

FAGE, Prof. John Donnelly, MA, PhD; Director of Centre of West African Studies and Professor of African History, University of Birmingham, since 1963, and Dean of Faculty of Arts since 1975; *b* 3 June 1921; *s* of Arthur Fage, *qv*; *m* 1949, Jean, *d* of late Frederick Banister; one *s* one *d*. *Educ:* Tonbridge Sch.; Magdalene Coll., Cambridge (MA, PhD). Served War, Pilot with RAFVR (Flt Lt), 1941-45. Bye-Fellow, Magdalene Coll., Cambridge, 1947-49; Lectr and Sen. Lectr, Univ. Coll. of the Gold Coast, 1949-55; Prof. of History, 1955-59, and Dep. Principal, 1957-59; Lectr in African History, SOAS, Univ. of London, 1959-63. Visiting Prof., Univ. of Wisconsin, Madison, 1957, and Smith Coll., Northampton, Mass, 1962; Dep. Dean, Faculty of Arts, Univ. of Birmingham, 1973-75; Founding Hon. Sec., African Studies Assoc. of the UK, 1963-66 (Vice-Pres. 1967-68, Pres. 1968-69); Council Mem., Internat. African Inst., 1965-75, and Consultative Dir, 1975-; Mem., UNESCO Scientific Cttee for Gen. History of Africa, 1971-; Mem. Culture Adv. Cttee of UK Nat. Commn for UNESCO (Vice-Chm., 1976-); FRHistS. Hon. Fellow, SOAS, Univ. of London. Editor (with Roland Oliver), The Jl of African History, 1960-73; Gen. Editor (with Roland Oliver), The Cambridge History of Africa, 8 vols, 1975-. *Publications:* An Introduction to the History of West Africa, 1955 (3rd edn 1962); An Atlas of African History,

1958 (2nd edn, 1977); Ghana, a Historical Interpretation, 1959; A Short History of Africa (with Roland Oliver), 1962 (5th edn 1975); A History of West Africa, 1969; (ed) Africa Discovers Her Past, 1970; (ed with Roland Oliver) Papers on African Prehistory, 1970; Africa, a history, 1977; articles in historical and Africanist jls. *Recreations:* doing things to houses and gardens. *Address:* 17 Antringham Gardens, Birmingham B17 3QL. *T:* 021-455 0020. *Club:* Athenæum.

FAGG, Bernard Evelyn Buller, MBE 1962; MA; FSA; FMA; Curator, Pitt Rivers Museum, Oxford, 1963-75; *b* 8 Dec. 1915; *s* of late W. P. Fagg and Mrs L. Fagg; *m* 1942, Mary Catherine, *d* of G. W. Davidson; one *s* two *d* (and two *s* decd). *Educ:* Dulwich Coll.; Downing Coll., Cambridge. Nigerian Admin. Service, 1939-47. War service with West African Engineers, East African Campaign, 1939-43. Dept of Antiquities, Republic of Nigeria, 1947-64 (Dir, 1957-64); Lincoln Coll., Oxford, 1964; Fellow of Linacre Coll., 1965-75, Emeritus Fellow, 1976. *Publications:* Nok Terra Cottas, 1977; contribs to learned jls. *Address:* 45 Woodstock Road, Oxford. *T:* 54875. *Club:* Leander (Henley-on-Thames).

FAGG, William Buller, CMG 1967; ethnologist; tribal art historian and consultant; Keeper, Ethnography Department (from 1972 the Museum of Mankind), British Museum, 1969-74 (Deputy Keeper, 1955-69); *b* 28 April 1914; *s* of late William Percy Fagg and late Lilian Fagg. *Educ:* Dulwich Coll.; Magdalene Coll., Cambridge. Sir Wm Browne's Medal for Latin Epigram; Montagu Butler Prize for Latin Hexameters; BA Classics, 1936; Archaeology and Anthropology, 1937; MA 1939. Asst Keeper Dept of Ethnography, BM, 1938; seconded to Bd of Trade, Industries and Manufactures Dept, 1940-45. Royal Anthropological Institute: Hon. Sec., 1939-56; Mem. Council, 1966-69, 1972-75, 1976-; Vice-Pres., 1969-72; Patron's Medal, 1966; Hon. Editor, Man: A Monthly Record of Anthropological Science, 1947-65, Hon. Librarian, 1976-. Chm., UK Cttee for First World Festival of Negro Arts, Dakar, 1966; Trustee: UK African Festival Trust, 1973-77; Chm., African Fine Art Gallery Trust, 1974-; Consulting Fellow in African Art, Museum of Primitive Art, NY, 1957-. Consultant on Tribal Art to Christies, 1974-. Fieldwork: Nigeria and Congo, 1949-50; Nigeria, 1953, 1958-59, 1971, 1974; Cameroon, 1966; Mali, 1969. Organised and arranged many loan exhibns including: Nigerian Art (Arts Council), London, Manchester, Bristol, 1960, Munich, Basel, 1961; African Art, Berlin Festival, 1964, Musée des Arts Décoratifs, Paris, 1964-65; African Sculpture, Nat. Gall. of Art, Washington, DC, Kansas City Art Gall., and Brooklyn Museum, 1970. FRSA (Silver-Medallist, 1951). Member: Reindeer Council of UK; Royal African Soc.; RIIA; Internat. African Inst.; Museums Assoc.; African Studies Assoc.; ICA; Assoc. of Art Historians. *Publications:* The Webster Plass Collection of African Art, British Museum, 1953; (with E. Elisofon) The Sculpture of Africa, 1958; Afro-Portuguese Ivories, 1959; Nigerian Images, 1963 (awarded P. A. Talbot Prize, 1964, and grand prize for best work on African art at World Festival of Negro Arts, Dakar, 1966); (with Margaret Plass) African Sculpture: An Anthology, 1964; Tribes and Forms in African Art, 1966; African Tribal Sculptures, 2 vols, 1967; Arts of Western Africa, Arts of Central Africa (UNESCO), 1967; African Tribal Images (The Katherine White Reswick Collection of African Art), 1968; African Sculpture (Washington, DC), 1970; Miniature Wood Carvings of Africa, 1970; The Tribal Image: wooden figure sculpture of the world, 1970; African Sculpture from the Tara Collection, 1971; (ed) The Living Arts of Nigeria, 1971; Eskimo Art in the British Museum, 1972; numerous exhibn catalogues, articles in Man, etc. *Recreations:* photography (esp. of art, incl. ancient churches), listening to music, cycling, travel, geopolitics. *Address:* 6 Galata Road, Barnes, SW13 9NQ. *T:* 01-748 6620.

FAGGE, Sir John William Frederick, 11th Bt, *cr* 1660; *b* 28 Sept. 1910; *s* of late William Archibald Theodore Fagge (*b* of 9th Bt) and Nellie (*d* 1924), *d* of H. T. D. Wise; *S* uncle, 1940; *m* 1940, Ivy Gertrude, *d* of William Edward Frier, 15 Church Lane, Newington, Kent; one *s* one *d*. *Heir: s* John Christopher Fagge, *b* 30 April 1942. *Address:* 26 The Mall, Faversham, Kent.

FAIR, Donald Robert Russell, OBE (mil.) 1945; Board Member, Central Electricity Generating Board, 1975-77; *b* 26 Dec. 1916; *s* of Robert Sidney Fair and Mary Louie Fair; *m* 1941, Patricia Laurie Rudland; one *s*. *Educ:* Roan Sch., Blackheath; King's Coll., London Univ. (BSc, AKC). CEng, FInstP, FInstF. Served War of 1939-45, RAF (Wing Comdr; despatches 1944; USAAF Commendation 1944). Lectr, RMA Sandhurst, 1948-50; UK AEA, 1950-62; Energy Consultant, Central Electricity Generating Bd, 1962-77. *Recreations:* sailing, cricket. *Address:* Rozelle, St James' Close, Birdham, Chichester, Sussex PO20 7HE. *T:* Chichester 512711. *Clubs:* Little Ship, Island Sailing.

FAIRBAIRN, Sir Brooke; *see* Fairbairn, Sir J. B.

FAIRBAIRN, David; Metropolitan Stipendiary Magistrate since 1971; Deputy Circuit Judge, since 1972; *b* 9 Aug. 1924; *s* of Ernest Hulford Fairbairn and late Iva May Fairbairn; *m* 1946, Helen Merriel de la Cour Collingwood, *d* of Harold Lewis Collingwood; two *s* two *d*. *Educ:* Haileybury Coll.; Trinity Hall, Cambridge (MA). Served War of 1939-45, Lieut, RNVR, in Mediterranean. Called to Bar, Middle Temple, 1949; Central Criminal Court Bar Mess; South Eastern Circuit; Herts and Essex QS; Dep. Chm., Surrey QS, 1969-71. Liveryman, Gold and Silver Wyre Drawers' Company, 1957-. *Recreations:* golf, tennis, country life. *Address:* Wollards Farm, Mayes Green, Ockley, Dorking, Surrey.

FAIRBAIRN, Hon. Sir David Eric, KBE 1977; DFC 1944; Australian Ambassador to the Netherlands, since 1977; *b* 3 March 1917; *s* of Clive Prell Fairbairn and Marjorie Rose (*née* Jowett); *m* 1945, Ruth Antill (*née* Robertson); three *d*. *Educ:* Geelong Grammar Sch.; Cambridge Univ. (MA). MP (L) Commonwealth of Australia, 1949-75; Minister: for Air, 1962-64; for Nat. Develt, 1964-69; for Educn and Science, March-Aug. 1971; for Defence, 1971-72. *Recreations:* golf, ski-ing, tennis. *Address:* 2/3 Tasmania Circle, Forrest, ACT 2603, Australia. *T:* 950932. *Clubs:* Leander (Henley); Hawks (Cambridge); Melbourne (Melbourne); Commonwealth (Canberra); Albury (Albury).

FAIRBAIRN, Douglas Chisholm, CIE 1945; CBE 1956; MA; retired; formerly Director, Thomas Hamling & Co. Ltd, St Andrew's Dock, Hull; *b* 1904; *s* of late Rev. R. T. and Mrs Fairbairn; *m* 1938, Agnes, *d* of late Rev. William amd Mrs Arnott; two *s*. *Educ:* George Heriot's, Edinburgh; Edinburgh Univ. (MA). Formerly: Secretary Bengal Chamber of Commerce and Industry, Calcutta, 1938-56, also in that capacity Sec. Associated Chambers of Commerce of India; Chm., Hull Fishing Vessel Owners and Hull Fishing Industry Associations, 1957-62. JP, City and County of Kingston-upon-Hull, 1966-71. *Recreations:* golf, gardening. *Address:* Wildwood, Inchmarlo Road, Banchory, Kincardineshire AB3 3RR.

FAIRBAIRN, Douglas Foakes, CBE 1971; Co-ordinator of Operations, Commonwealth Development Corporation, since 1971; *b* 9 Oct. 1919; *s* of William and Florence Fairbairn; *m* 1947, Gertrude Betty Buswell; two *s*. *Educ:* John Lyon Sch., Harrow; Royal School of Mines, Imperial Coll., London Univ. BSc (Hons), ARSM. Served War, RAF (Sqdn Ldr), 1940-46. Commonwealth Development Corp., 1948-; Regional Controller: Central Africa, 1959-66; West Africa, 1966-71. Dir, Bank of Rhodesia and Nyasaland, 1961-63; Chm., Central African Airways, 1964-68; Mem., Central African Power Corp., 1961-. *Recreation:* golf. *Address:* 11 Portland Terrace, The Green, Richmond, Surrey TW9 1QQ. *T:* 01-948 1921. *Clubs:* Oriental; Northwood Golf (Mddx).

FAIRBAIRN, Sir (James) Brooke, 6th Bt *cr* 1869, of Ardwick; *b* 10 Dec. 1930; *s* of Sir William Albert Fairbairn, 5th Bt, and of Christine Renée Cotton, *d* of late Rev. Canon Robert William Croft; *S* father, 1972; *m* 1960, Mary Russell, *d* of William Russell Scott, MB, ChB, FFARCS; two *s* one *d*. *Educ:* Stowe. Proprietor of J. Brooke Fairbairn & Co., textile converters and wholesalers dealing in furnishing fabrics. *Heir: s* Robert William Fairbairn, *b* 10 April 1965. *Address:* 9 The High Street, Barkway, near Royston, Herts. *T:* Barkway 392.

FAIRBAIRN of Fordell, Nicholas Hardwick, QC(Scot.) 1972; MP (C) Kinross and Perthshire West, since Oct. 1974; Baron of Fordell; *b* 24 Dec. 1933; *s* of William Ronald Dodds Fairbairn, DPsych, and Mary Ann More-Gordon of Charleton and Kinnaber; *m* 1962, Hon. Elizabeth Mary Mackay, *e d* of 13th Baron Reay; three *d* (and one *s* one *d* decd). *Educ:* Loretto and Edinburgh Univ., educated in spite of both. MA, LLB. Author, farmer, painter, poet, TV and radio broadcaster, dress-designer, landscape gardener, bon viveur and wit. Called to Scots Bar 1957. Cons. Candidate, Central Edinburgh, 1964, 1966. Mem., Council of World Population Crisis, 1968-70; Vice-Pres., Scottish Minorities Group. Founder and Hon. Pres., Soc. for Preservation of Duddingston Village; Mem., Edinburgh Festival Council, 1971-. Chairman: Traverse Theatre, 1964-72; Edinburgh Brook Adv. Centre, 1968-75; Waverley Broadcasting Co., 1973-74; Dir, Ledlanet Nights, 1960-73. Chm., Scottish Soc. for Defence of Literature and the Arts. Pres., Dysart and Dundonald Pipe Band. Private exhibns Edinburgh, 1960, 1962, 1968-74, and in public exhibns. *Publication:* contrib., Alistair Maclean Introduces Scotland, 1972. *Recreations:* bunking and debunking. *Address:* Fordel Castle, By Dunfermline, Fife. *T:* Dalgety Bay 823311. *Clubs:* Puffins, Beefsteak, Chatham Dining; New (Edinburgh).

FAIRBAIRN, Sir Robert, Kt 1975; JP; Chairman, Clydesdale Bank Ltd, since 1975 (Director, since 1967; General Manager, 1958-71; Vice-Chairman, 1971-75); *b* 25 Sept. 1910; *s* of late Robert Fairbairn and Christina Fairbairn; *m* 1939, Sylvia Lucinda, *d* of late Rev. Henry Coulter; two *s* one *d. Educ:* Perth Academy. Joined service of The Clydesdale Bank at Perth, 1927; Beckett & Whitehead Prizeman, Inst. of Bankers, 1934; Midland Bank, 1934. Lt-Comdr (S) RNVR, 1939-46. Asst Gen. Manager, Clydesdale & North of Scotland Bank, 1951. Director: Commercial Union Assurance Group (Local Board); Scottish Amicable Life Assurance Soc. (Chm., 1976-); Midland Bank Finance Corp. Ltd, 1967-74; Clydesdale Bank Finance Corp. Ltd, 1967-; Clydesdale Bank Insurance Services Ltd, 1970-; Second Great Northern Investment Trust; Scottish Western Investment Co.; Newarthill Ltd; Midland Bank Ltd, 1975-; Chm., Scottish Computer Services Ltd. A Dir, British Nat. Oil Corp., 1976-. Glasgow Chamber of Commerce (Vice-Pres., 1969-76). Pres., Inst. of Bankers in Scotland, 1961-63; Vice-Pres., Scottish Economic Soc. (Pres. 1966-69); Chairman: Scottish Industrial Develt Advisory Bd, 1972; Cttee of Scottish Bank General Managers, 1963-66; Vice-Chm., Inst. of Fiscal Studies (Scotland), 1976-; Vice-Pres., British Bankers Assoc., 1966-68; Member: Scottish Council (Develt and Industry), Vice-Pres., 1967-68; Scottish Council of CBI. FIB, FIB (Scot); FRSA; FBIM. JP Glasgow, 1962. *Recreations:* golf, fishing. *Address:* The Grange, Hazelwood Road, Bridge of Weir, Renfrewshire. *T:* Bridge of Weir 2102. *Clubs:* Caledonian, MCC; Western (Glasgow); Corinthian Casuals; Royal and Ancient (St Andrews).

FAIRBAIRN, Thomas Charles; Hon. RCM; dramatist and producer of opera and pageants; *b* 26 March 1874; *s* of Charles Fairbairn and Emma Bastow; *m* 1904, Antonie Seiter, a singer of opera; two *s. Educ:* New Holland; Maxton, Scotland. Began as Engineer; later, Operatic vocalist and stage manager, Moody Manners Opera Co.; produced in Covent Garden and Drury Lane for Beecham Opera Cos; ran own opera cos in Surrey Theatre; produced opera in India and Burma; produced own dramatic version of Hiawatha, with the Royal Choral Society, Royal Albert Hall, 1924 (an annual event); founded Fairbairn Pageant Choir for Elijah in 1934; same year produced Hiawatha, Open Air Theatre, Scarborough, and other works, including Faust and Tannhäuser, all in Pageant form; Elijah, a Passion Pageant, and Faust with the Fairbairn Pageant Choir, Royal Albert Hall, 1936, 1937, 1938, and 1939. Produced Hiawatha in the Exhibition Building, Melbourne, Australia, 1939; in 1940 began to dramatise in music, drama and pageant form, The Holy Bible, from the fall of Lucifer/Satan, until the second coming of Christ, in 14 separate pageant performances, completed in 1972. *Publications:* Robert Burns, a folk song opera, produced by the Peoples Theatre, Dumbarton, 1939; The Bible Story, edn for schools, 1972. *Recreations:* writing, and endeavouring to restore the past glories of Glastonbury. *Address:* 41 Essex Park, W Finchley, N3.

FAIRBANK, Alfred John, CBE 1951; FRSA; calligrapher; *b* 12 July 1895; *er s* of Alfred John and Emma Fairbank; *m* 1919, Elsie Kneeshaw; one *s* (one *d* decd). Entered Civil Service, 1911; Senior Executive Officer, Admiralty, 1949-55; retired from Civil Service, 1955. Pres. Soc. of Scribes and Illuminators, 1951-63; Vice-Pres. of Soc. for Italic Handwriting; Member: Soc. of Designer Craftsmen; Art Workers Guild; The Double Crown Club. Leverhulme Research Awards, 1956 and 1957. Designer and responsible for production of The Books of Remembrance of the Royal Air Force, Church of St Clement Danes. *Publications:* A Handwriting Manual, 1932, 9th edn 1975; A Book of Scripts, 1949; Editor and calligrapher of Beacon Writing Books I-VI, 1958; (with Berthold Wolpe) Renaissance Handwriting, 1960; (with Dr R. W. Hunt) Humanistic Script of the Fifteenth and Sixteenth Centuries, 1960; A Roman Script for Schools, 1961; (with Prof. Bruce Dickins) The Italic Hand in Tudor Cambridge, 1962; The Story of Handwriting, 1970; Augustino da Siena, 1975. *Relevant publication:* Calligraphy and Palæography: Essays presented to Alfred Fairbank on his seventieth birthday, 1965. *Address:* 27 Granville Road, Hove, East Sussex BN3 1TG. *T:* Brighton 733431.

FAIRBANKS, Maj.-Gen. Cecil Benfield, CB 1950; CBE 1946 (MBE 1940); retired 1958; Administrative Secretary, National Council of Social Service, 1958-65; *b* 12 June 1903; *s* of F. C. Fairbanks, Montreal, Canada; *m* 1936, Rosamonde Beryl Fisher; one *s* one *d. Educ:* Marlborough Coll.; Keble Coll., Oxford. Commissioned with The Sherwood Foresters, Jan. 1924; Adjutant 1st Foresters, 1935-38; Adjutant 5th Foresters TA, 1938-40. Served UK, 1924-35; West Indies, 1935-38; War of 1939-45, France, 1939-40; Middle East, 1941-45 (Irak, 1943, Italy, 1945); France and Germany, 1945-46. OC 14th Foresters, 1943; Comd Inf. Bde, 1944-46; BGS 1947; idc 1948; Dir of Inf.,

1948-49; GOC Nigeria Dist, 1949-52; Chief Army Instructor, Imperial Defence Coll., 1953-54; GOC Rhine District, British Army of the Rhine, 1955-58, retd. Col The Sherwood Foresters, 1958-65. *Address:* Candy Lane House, Fen Street, Nayland, Colchester, Essex. *Club:* Army and Navy.

FAIRBANKS, Douglas (Elton), (Jr), KBE 1949; DSC 1944; Captain, USNR, retired; company director, producer, actor; Chairman: Douglas Fairbanks Ltd; Douglair Corporation; Fairbanks International, Inc.; Fairtel, Inc. (US); Boltons Trading Corp. Inc., etc., and of associated companies, in US and UK, since 1946; Formerly Director or Special Consultant: Scripto Pens Ltd (US and UK), 1952-73; Golden Cycle and subsidiaries, 1965-73; Rambagh Palace Hotel, Ltd (Jaipur, India); Cavalcade Film Co. Ltd (UK), etc; *b* New York City, 9 Dec. 1909; *s* of Douglas Elton Fairbanks, Denver, Colorado, and Anna Beth Sully, Providence, RI; *m* 1939, Mary Lee Epling, Keystone, W Virginia; three *d. Educ:* Bovée Sch., Knickerbocker Greys, Collegiate Mil. Sch., NY; Pasadena Polytechnic, Harvard Mil. Sch., Los Angeles; tutored privately in London and Paris. Began career as film actor, 1923, on stage 1927. Organised own producing company, UK, 1935. Studied painting and sculpture, Paris, 1922-24; began writing, professionally, 1928; articles and essays on public affairs, etc., 1936-. Vice-Pres. Franco-British War Relief and National Vice-Pres. Cttee "Defend America by Aiding the Allies", 1939-40; Presidential Envoy, Special Mission to Latin America, 1940-41; one-time Consultant to Office of the Presidency (Washington, DC); Lieut (jg), USNR, 1941; promoted through grades to Capt., 1954. National Chm., CARE Cttee, 1947-50; Nat. Vice-Pres. Amer. Assoc. for the UN, 1946-60; Pres. Brit.-Amer. Alumni Assoc. 1950; Bd Gov., English-Speaking Union of the US, 1949-60; Nat. Chm., Amer. Relief for Korea, 1950-54; Trustee, Edwina Mountbatten Trust; Mem. Council, American Museum in Brit.; a Governor and Exec. Cllr, Royal Shakespeare Theatre; Governor, Ditchley Foundations; Trustee, Wellington Museum Trust; Co-Chm., US Capitol Bicentenary 1776-1976; Guild of St Bride's Church, Fleet Street, EC; Mem., Council on Foreign Relations (NY); Vis. Fellow, St Cross Coll., Oxford; MA Oxon; Senior Churchill Fellow, Westminster Coll., Fulton, Mo; Hon. DFA Westminster Coll., Fulton, Mo, USA; Hon. LLD Univ. of Denver, Colo; Silver Star Medal (US); Legion of Merit ("Valor" clasp) (US), Special Naval Commendation (US), KJStJ 1950, etc; Officer Legion of Honour (Fr.), Croix de Guerre with Palm (Fr.); Knight Comdr Order of George I (Greece); Knight Grand Officer, Order del Merito (Chile); Grand Officer, Order of Merit (Italy); Comdr Order of Orange Nassau (Neth.); Officer of: Orders of Crown (Belg.), of Star of Italy, Cross of Mil. Valour (Italy), Southern Cross (Brazil), Hon. Citizen and National Medal of Korea, etc. *Films include:* Stella Dallas; Little Caesar; Outward Bound; Morning Glory; Catherine the Great; The Amateur Gentleman; The Prisoner of Zenda; Gunga Din; The Corsican Brothers; Sinbad the Sailor; The Exile; The Fighting O'Flynn; State Secret. *Plays include:* Young Woodley; Romeo and Juliet; The Jest; Man in Possession; Moonlight is Silver; My Fair Lady; The Pleasure of his Company; The Secretary Bird; Present Laughter. *Publications:* short stories, poems, articles, to periodicals. *Relevant publication:* Knight Errant, by Brian Connell. *Recreations:* swimming, tennis, golf, travel. *Address:* The Beekman, 575 Park Avenue, New York, NY 10021, USA; The Vicarage, 448 North Lake Way, Palm Beach, Florida 33480, USA; (offices) 10 Park Place, St James's, SW1; 360 Park Avenue, New York, NY 10017, USA. *Clubs:* White's, Buck's, Naval and Military, Garrick; Puffin's (Edinburgh); Brook, Knickerbocker, Century (NY); Metropolitan (Washington, DC); Raquet (Chicago); Myopia Hunt (Hamilton, Mass); Travellers' (Paris).

FAIRCLOUGH, Anthony John; Director, Central Unit on Environmental Pollution, Department of the Environment, since 1974; *b* 30 Aug. 1924; *m* 1957, Patricia Monks; two *s.* Ministry of Aircraft Production and Ministry of Supply, 1944-48; Colonial Office, 1948; Secretary, Nyasaland Commn of Inquiry, 1959; Private Secretary to Minister of State for Commonwealth Relations and for the Colonies, 1963-64; Assistant Secretary, 1964; Head of Pacific and Indian Ocean Dept, Commonwealth Office (formerly Colonial Office), 1964-68; Head of W Indian Dept, FCO, 1968-70; Head of New Towns 1 Div., DoE, 1970-72; Under-Sec., 1973; Head of Planning, Minerals and Countryside Directorate, 1973, of Planning, Sport and Countryside Directorate, 1973-74. Senior UK Commissioner at Sessions of South Pacific Commn, 1965-67; Chm., Environment Cttee, OECD, 1976-; British Co-Chm., Jt UK/USSR Cttee established under UK/USSR Agreement on cooperation in field of Environmental Protection, 1974-; Mem., Royal Soc.'s British Nat. Cttee on Problems of Environment, 1974-. Observing Mem., Governing Body, Chiswick Sch., 1973-.

Address: 6 Cumberland Road, Kew, Richmond, Surrey. *Club:* Civil Service.

FAIRCLOUGH, Hon. Ellen Louks, PC (Can.) 1957; FCA 1965; Vice-President, Secretary and Director, Hamilton Trust and Savings Corporation; Member of Progressive Conservative Party, Canada; *b* Hamilton, Ont, 28 Jan. 1905; *d* of Norman Ellsworth Cook and Nellie Bell Louks; *m* 1931, David Henry Gordon Fairclough; one *s. Educ:* Hamilton Public and Secondary Schs. Certified Public Accountant, public practice, 1935-57. Hamilton City Council, Alderman, 1946-49; Controller, 1950. Elected to House of Commons as Progressive Conservative mem. for Hamilton West, 1950; re-elected at gen. elections, 1953, 1957, 1958, 1962, defeated in 1963 election. Sec. of State for Canada, 1957-58; Minister of Citizenship and Immigration, 1958-62; Postmaster-Gen., 1962-63. LLD (*hc*), McMaster Univ., 1975. *Recreations:* music, reading and photography. *Address:* 25 Stanley Avenue, Hamilton, Ont, Canada. *T:* Hamilton 522-5248.

FAIRCLOUGH, Wilfred, RE; RWS; ARCA (London); Assistant Director, Kingston Polytechnic, and Head of the Division of Design, 1970-72, retired; Principal of Kingston College of Art, Surrey, 1962-70; *b* 13 June 1907; *s* of Herbert Fairclough and Edith Amy Milton; *m* 1936, Joan Cryer; one *s* one *d. Educ:* Royal College of Art, London, 1931-34 (Diploma 1933); British Sch. at Rome, Italy, 1934-37; Rome Scholar in Engraving, 1934-37. Army and Royal Air Force, 1942-46. Rome Scholarships, Faculty of Engraving, 1951 (Chm., 1964-73); Leverhulme Research Award, 1961. RE 1946 (ARE 1934); RWS 1968 (ARWS 1961). Chairman: Assoc. of Art Instns, 1965-66; Assessors, Vocational Courses of Surrey CC. *Work in public and private collections: paintings:* Min. of Supply; Min. of Works; Surrey CC; Scottish Modern Art Assoc.; Beaumont Coll.; *drawings:* British Museum; V&A Museum; Arts Council; Contemporary Art Soc.; Wye Coll., London Univ.; English Electric Co.; Art Galls at Blackburn, Kingston-upon-Thames, Worthing; Graves Art Gall., Sheffield; Atkinson Art Gall., Southport; *prints:* British Museum, V&A Museum; Ashmolean Museum, Oxford; Contemporary Art Soc.; British Sch. at Rome; South London Art Gall.; Stoke Educn Authority; Wye Coll., London Univ.; Gottenburg Museum; Print Collectors Club. *Publications:* work reproduced: Recording Britain; Londoners' England; Royal Academy Illustrated; Studio; Fine Prints of the Year; Print Collectors Quarterly; illustrated article, Leisure Painter, 1969; paintings, drawings and prints. *Address:* 12 Manorgate Road, Kingston-upon-Thames, Surrey. *Club:* Arts.

FAIREY, Michael John; Regional Administrator, North East Thames Regional Health Authority, since 1973; *b* 20 Sept. 1933; *s* of Ernest John Saunder Fairey and late Lily Emily (*née* Pateman); *m* 1958, Audrey Edwina Kermode; two *s* one *d. Educ:* Queen Elizabeth's Sch., Barnet; Jesus Coll., Cambridge (MA). Deputy House Governor, The London Hosp., 1962, House Governor 1972. *Publications:* various articles in med. and computing jls. *Recreations:* church music, history of medieval exploration, Rugby football. *Address:* 42B Oakleigh Park South, N20 9JN. *Club:* Athenæum.

FAIRFAX, family name of **Baron Fairfax of Cameron.**

FAIRFAX OF CAMERON, 14th Baron, *cr* 1627; **Nicholas John Albert Fairfax;** *b* 4 Jan. 1956; *e s* of 13th Baron and Sonia, *yr d* of late Capt. Cecil Gunston, MC; *S* father, 1964. *Educ:* Eton. *Recreations:* sailing, skiing, tennis. *Heir: b* Hon. Hugh Nigel Thomas Fairfax, *b* 29 March 1958. *Address:* Gays House, Holyport, near Maidenhead, Berks. *T:* Maidenhead 27956; 159 Ebury Street, SW1. *T:* 01-730 2955.

FAIRFAX, Sir Vincent Charles, Kt 1971; CMG 1960; Company Director and Pastoralist, Australia; *b* 26 Dec. 1909; *s* of late J. H. F. Fairfax; *m* 1939, Nancy, *d* late Dr C. B. Heald, CBE, FRCP; two *s* two *d. Educ:* Geelong Church of England Grammar Sch., Australia; Brasenose Coll., Oxford Univ. (BA). Staff, John Fairfax & Sons Pty Ltd, 1933; Advertising Manager, 1937-38. Major, Australian Imperial Forces, 1940-46. Director: John Fairfax & Sons Pty Ltd, 1946-53; John Fairfax Ltd (Publishers, Sydney Morning Herald), 1956; Chm. Australian Sectn, Commonwealth Press Union, 1950-73; Chm. Stanbroke Pastoral Co. Pty Ltd, 1964; Director: Bank of NSW, 1953; Australian Mutual Provident Soc., 1956 (Chm. 1966); Chief Comr Scout Assoc., for NSW, 1958-68, for Australia, 1969-73; Dep. Pres., Royal Agric. Society of Commonwealth, 1966; Mem. C of E Property Trust, 1950-71; Trustee, Walter and Eliza Hall Trust, 1953-; Mem. Council: Art Gall. Soc. of NSW, 1953-69; Royal Flying Doctor Service, 1954-71; Royal Agric. Society of NSW, 1956 (Pres., 1970); Mem., Glebe Administration Bd, 1962-73; Rector's Warden, St Mark's, Darling Point, 1948-71.

Recreations: tennis, golf, trout fishing. *Address:* Elaine, 550 New South Head Road, Double Bay, Sydney, NSW 2000, Australia. *T:* 36 1416. *Clubs:* Bath, Leander; Commonwealth (Canberra); Melbourne (Melbourne); Union, University, Royal Sydney Golf (Sydney); Queensland (Brisbane).

FAIRFAX, Sir Warwick (Oswald), Kt 1967; MA; Director: John Fairfax & Sons Ltd (The Sydney Morning Herald, The Sun Herald, The Sun, The Australian Financial Review, The National Times, and other publications); Director, David Syme & Co. Ltd; Vice President, Australian Elizabethan Theatre Trust; Chairman, Australian Opera Auditions Council; owns Harrington Park; *b* 1901; *o s* of Sir James Oswald Fairfax, a Proprietor and Dir of John Fairfax and Sons, Ltd, and Mabel, *d* of Capt. Francis Hixson, RN; *m* 1928, Marcie Elizabeth, *o d* of David Wilson, Barrister of Sydney; one *s* one *d*; *m* 1948, Hanné Anderson, 2nd *d* of Emil Bendixsen, Copenhagen; one *d*; *m* 1959, Mary, *o d* of Kevin Wein; one *s. Educ:* Geelong Grammar Sch., St Paul's Sch., Sydney Univ.; Balliol Coll., Oxford. 2nd Class Hons in Sch. of Philosophy, Politics and Economics; joined staff of John Fairfax and Sons, Ltd, 1925; Dir, 1927; Managing Dir 1930; Chairman of Dirs, 1956-76. Plays: A Victorian Marriage, Vintage for Heroes, The Bishop's Wife, performed Sydney, 1951, 1952, 1956. *Publications:* Men, Parties, and Policies, 1943; The Triple Abyss: towards a modern synthesis, 1965; ed, A Century of Journalism (The Sydney Morning Herald), 1931. *Recreations:* the arts, philosophy, motoring and vintage cars. *Address:* John Fairfax & Sons Ltd, Box 506, GPO Sydney, Australia; Fairwater, 560 New South Head Road, Double Bay, Sydney, NSW 2028, Australia; Harrington Park, Narellan, NSW 2567. *Clubs:* Carlton, Oriental, Australian, Union, Pioneers, Royal Sydney Yacht Squadron (Sydney).

FAIRFAX-CHOLMELEY, Francis William Alfred, CBE 1960; Director: Barclays Bank Ltd, 1957-73; Barclays Bank SA, France, 1968-75 (Chairman, 1968-70); *b* 20 Sept. 1904; *e s* of Hugh Charles Fairfax-Cholmeley, JP of Brandsby, York, and of Alice Jane (*née* Moverley); *m* 1940, Janet Meta, *e d* of Sir John Ogilvy-Wedderburn, 11th and 5th Bt; two *d* (one *s* decd). *Educ:* Eton; Magdalene Coll., Cambridge (MA). Joined Barclays Bank Ltd, 1926; Local Dir, 54 Lombard Street, 1939-48; Resident Dir in Paris, Barclays Bank (France) Ltd, 1948-64, Chm., 1964-68; Local Dir, Foreign Branches, 1964-66, and Pall Mall East, 1966-68; Hon. Dir, Banque de Bruxelles SA. Served RA, 1939-45 (Major). *Address:* Balendoch, Meigle, Perthshire. *T:* Meigle 318.

FAIRFAX-LUCY, Sir Edmund (John William Hugh Cameron-Ramsay-), 6th Bt *cr* 1836; painter; *b* 4 May 1945; *s* of Sir Brian Fulke Cameron-Ramsay-Fairfax-Lucy, 5th Bt and of Hon. Alice Caroline Helen Buchan, *o d* of 1st Baron Tweedsmuir, PC, GCMG, GCVO, CH; *S* father, 1974; *m* 1974, Sylvia Suzanne, *d* of W. G. Ogden. *Educ:* City and Guilds of London Art Sch.; Royal Academy Schs of Art. *Heir: cousin* Duncan Cameron Cameron-Ramsay-Fairfax-Lucy, FCA [*b* 18 Sept. 1932; *m* 1964, Janet Barclay, *o d* of P. A. B. Niven; one *s* one *d*]. *Address:* Charlecote Park, Warwick.

FAIRFIELD, (Josephine) Letitia Denny, CBE 1919; MD, ChB Edinburgh; DPH London; Barrister-at-Law of the Middle Temple; *b* 1885; *e d* of late C. Fairfield. *Educ:* Richmond High Sch.; Edinburgh Univ.; University Coll., London. Bathgate Memorial Prize of Royal College of Surgeons, Edinburgh, 1904; MB, ChB, Edinburgh, 1907; MD, 1911; Area Medical Controller QMAAC 1917; and transferred to the RAF Medical Service, 1918; RAMC, 1940-42; Lieut-Col (retired) RAMC; Senior Medical Officer, London County Council, 1911-48. Pres., Medico-Legal Soc., 1957 and 1958. Papal Medal, Pro Ecclesia et Pontifice, 1966. *Publications:* Trial of John Henry Straffen, 1954; Epilepsy, 1954. *Address:* 60 Beaufort Mansions, Beaufort Street, SW3. *T:* 01-352 3917.

FAIRFIELD, Sir Ronald (McLeod), Kt 1970; CBE 1966; BScEng, CEng, FIMechE, FIEE, FIEEE; Chairman: Chemring Ltd, since 1963; Automatic Light Controlling Co. Ltd, since 1963; Royal Worcester Ltd, since 1975 (Director, since 1971); Royal Worcester Spode Ltd, since 1976; Deputy Chairman, since 1974, Director, since 1972, Ransome, Hoffmann, Pollard Ltd; *b* Newcastle upon Tyne, 25 May 1911; *er s* of late Geoffrey Fairfield and Inez Helen Thorneycroft McLeod; *m* 1st, 1939, Mary Moore (marr diss. 1952); 2nd, 1971, Margaret Josephine Wiggans. *Educ:* Llandaff Cathedral Sch.; King Edward's Sch., Bath; Erith Tech. Coll.; London Univ. Trainee Apprentice, Callender's Cable & Con. Co. Ltd, 1929; Research Engr, 1932; Mullard Radio Valve Co., 1934; rejoined Callender Co., 1937 as Tech. Man. Leigh Works, and Erith Works, 1942; on amal. of Brit. Ins. Cables Ltd and Callender Co. in 1945 to form BICC, became Chief Engr (Designs and Processes) of new Co.; Director and General Manager: former St Helens Cable & Rubber Co. Ltd, 1948-51; W. T. Glover & Co. Ltd, 1952; BIC (Sub. Cables) Ltd, 1953 (later Dep. Chm.); apptd BICC Bd, 1954 as Dir (Prod. and Engrg); Dir (Home Ops), 1958; Asst Man. Dir, 1960; Jt Man. Dir, 1962; Dep. Chm. and Man. Dir 1963-70, Dep. Chm. 1970-72; Chm., BIC Con. Co. Ltd, 1964-68; Dep. Chm., Submarine Cables Ltd, 1961-66; Chm., European Cables Ltd, 1962-72. Mem., Cablemakers War Emergency Tech. Cttee; Mem. Cttee, Transmission Sect. (later Supply Sect.), IEE, 1943-45; IEE Premium for 1956-57; Mem., NEDC for Elec. Engrg Industry, 1964-71; Member Council, BEAMA (Pres., 1968-69). Gilbreth Gold Medal, Inst. of Work Study Practitioners, 1970. *Publications:* various Tech. papers. *Recreations:* game shooting, forestry. *Address:* Courts Farm, Haslemere, Surrey. *T:* Haslemere 3485.

FAIRGRIEVE, (Thomas) Russell, CBE 1974; TD 1959; JP; MP (C) Aberdeenshire West, since Feb. 1974; *b* 3 May 1924; *s* of Alexander Fairgrieve, OBE, MC, JP, and Myma Margaret Fairgrieve; *m* 1954, Millie Mitchell; one *s* three *d. Educ:* St Mary's Sch., Melrose; Sedbergh School. Major 8th Gurkha Rifles (Indian Army), 1946. Major, KOSB, 1956. Man. Dir, Laidlaw & Fairgrieve Ltd, 1958; Dir, Joseph Dawson (Holdings) Ltd, 1961. Selkirk County and Galashiels Town Councillor, 1949; Pres., Scottish Conservative Assoc., 1965, Vice-Chm., 1971; Chm., Conservative Party in Scotland, 1975. JP Selkirkshire, 1962. *Recreation:* golf. *Address:* Pankalan, Boleside, Galashiels, Selkirk TD1 3NX. *T:* Galashiels 2278. *Clubs:* Carlton; New (Edinburgh); Royal and Ancient (St Andrews).

FAIRHALL, Hon. Sir Allen, KBE 1970; FRSA; Member, House of Representatives, 1949-69; *b* 24 Nov. 1909; *s* of Charles Edward and Maude Fairhall; *m* 1936, Monica Clelland, *d* of James and Ellen Ballantyne; one *s. Educ:* East Maitland Primary and High Sch.; Newcastle Tech. Inst. Founded commercial broadcasting stn 2KO, 1931; Supervising Engr, Radio and Signals Supplies Div., Min. of Munitions, 1942-45; Pres., Austr. Fedn of Commercial Broadcasting Stns, 1942-43. Mem. Australian Delegn to UN Gen. Assembly, 1954; Minister for Interior and Works, 1956-58; Minister for Supply, 1961-66; Minister for Defence, 1966-69. Mem. Newcastle CC, 1941. Hon. DSc Univ. of Newcastle, 1968. *Recreations:* amateur radio; deep sea fishing. *Address:* 7 Parkway Avenue, Newcastle, NSW 2300, Australia. *T:* 2.2295. *Clubs:* Tattersall's, National (Sydney); Newcastle (Newcastle).

FAIRHAVEN, 3rd Baron *cr* 1929 and 1961 (new creation); **Ailwyn Henry George Broughton;** DL; JP; *b* 16 Nov. 1936; *s* of 2nd Baron Fairhaven and Hon. Diana Rosamond (*d* 1937), *o d* of late Captain Hon. Coulson Fellowes; *S* father, 1973; *m* 1960, Kathleen Patricia, *d* of Col James Henry Magill, OBE; three *s* two *d. Educ:* Eton; RMA, Sandhurst. Royal Horse Guards, 1957-71. Mem., Jockey Club, 1977-. DL Cambridgeshire and Isle of Ely, 1973; JP Bottisham 1975. *Recreation:* shooting. *Heir:* *s* Hon. James Henry Ailwyn Broughton, *b* 25 May 1963. *Address:* Anglesey Abbey, Cambridge. *T:* Cambridge 811746. *Club:* Turf.

FAIRHURST, William Albert, CBE 1961; Chairman, Bridge Design Consultants Pty Ltd, Sydney; Consultant to W. A. Fairhurst & Partners, Glasgow (formerly F. A. Macdonald & Partners), Consulting Civil Engineers, since 1971 (Senior Partner, 1940-71); *b* 21 Aug. 1903; *s* of John Robert Fairhurst and Elizabeth Ann Massey, Alderley Edge, Cheshire; *m* 1937, Elizabeth Robertson Jardine; one *s* one *d. Educ:* Cavendish Road Sch., W Didsbury; Manchester Coll. of Technology. FICE; FIStructE; FNZIE; FInstHE: Mem. Assoc. Cons. Engrs; Mem. Soc. Civil Engrs, France. Designer of many bridges, including Queen's Bridge, Perth, Howford Bridge, Ayrshire, Kingston Bridge, Glasgow, and new Tay Road Bridge. Mem. of Royal Fine Art Commission for Scotland, 1963-72. Pres. of Scottish Chess Assoc., 1957-69; British Chess Champion, 1937; eleven times Scottish Chess Champion and seventeen times West of Scotland Chess Champion; awarded title of International Chess Master by Internat. Federation of Chess, 1951. Chess Correspondent, Glasgow Herald, 1959-69. FRSA. Hon. LLD St Andrews, 1968. *Publications:* Arch Design Simplified; (jointly) Design and Construction of Reinforced Concrete Bridges; numerous papers on bridges and structural engineering to engineering institutions. *Recreations:* bridge, art, chess. *Address:* 1 Lynedoch Terrace, Glasgow G3 7XQ. *T:* 041-332 8754; 59 Luton Avenue, Pakuranga, Auckland, New Zealand. *Clubs:* Royal Automobile; Glasgow Art.

FAIRLEY, Alan Brand; Deputy Chairman of Grand Metropolitan Hotels Ltd, 1970-73; First President of Mecca Ltd since 1972; *b* Edinburgh, *s* of James Fairley and Jane Alexander;

m 1942, Roma Josephine Haddow; one *d. Educ:* George Watson's Coll., Edinburgh. Joined family catering business (Fairleys of Edinburgh) from college, 1919; opened Dunedin dance hall where broadcast bands and cabaret artists, 1923; opened Piccadilly Club (first night club in Glasgow), internat. stars and bands, 1926; formed a number of Scottish cos to run dance halls, 1934-37; partnership with Carl Heimann to run dance halls all over UK, 1936 (until his death, 1968). Served War of 1939-45, Army Catering Corps, 1940-45, Major. Acquired lease of Café de Paris, London, 1943, and re-opened it, 1948, presenting Noel Coward, Marlene Dietrich, Maurice Chevalier and many others. Created Mecca Ltd, now notable for its promotion of Miss World, TV Come Dancing and Carl-Alan award for outstanding contributions to ballroom dancing, after the Christian names of its founders; Jt Chm. with Carl Heimann, Mecca Ltd, 1952, Chm. Mecca Ltd 1968: Mecca Ltd merged with Grand Metropolitan Hotels Ltd, 1970. Member: Variety Club of Great Britain and Réunion des Gastronômes (both in London). *Recreations:* swimming, golf. *Address:* The Field House, Cronkbourne Village, Tromode, Isle of Man. *Club:* Saints and Sinners.

FAIRLEY, Prof. Barker, MA Leeds, PhD Jena; Hon. LittD: Leeds; Waterloo (Canada); Toronto; Carleton; York (Canada); Western; Hon. LLD Alberta; FRSC; Emeritus Professor of German in University College, University of Toronto; *b* Barnsley, Yorks, 21 May 1887; *s* of Barker and Charlotte Fairley; *m* 1914, Margaret Adele Keeling (*d* 1968), Bradford, Yorks; one *s* one *d. Educ:* Universities of Leeds and Jena. Lektor in English at University of Jena, 1907-10; Lecturer in German at University of Alberta, 1910; Henry Simon Prof. of German Language and Literature, Manchester Univ., 1932-36. Corresp. Fellow, British Acad., 1972. *Publications:* Charles M. Doughty, 1927; Goethe as revealed in his Poetry, 1932; A Study of Goethe, 1947; Goethe's Faust, 1953; Heinrich Heine, An Interpretation, 1954; Wilhelm Raabe, an Introduction to his Novels, 1961; (trans.) Goethe, Faust, 1970; Poems of 1922, 1972. *Address:* Department of German, The University, Toronto, Ontario M5S 1A1, Canada.

FAIRLIE, Professor Alison (Anna Bowie); Professor of French, University of Cambridge, and Professorial Fellow, Girton College, since 1972; *b* 23 May 1917; *e d* of Rev. Robert Paul Fairlie, MA, Minister of the Church of Scotland, and of Florence A. A. Wilson. *Educ:* Ardrossan Acad.; Dumfries Acad.; Penrhos Coll.; St Hugh's Coll. Oxford; Sorbonne. BA 1st Cl. in Final Hons Sch. of Medieval and Mod. Langs, Oxon; MA, DPhil (Oxon). Doctoral Research: in Paris, 1938-40 (interruptions for voluntary war-work); in Oxford, 1940-42; Temp. Admin. Officer, Foreign Office, 1942-44; Lectr in French, Girton Coll., 1944-67; Staff Fellow and Dir of Studies in Mod. Langs, Girton Coll., 1946-67; Univ. Lectr in French, Cambridge, 1948-67, Reader in French, 1967-72. Vice-Pres., Soc. for French Studies, 1965-66 and 1968-69, Pres., 1966-68; Mem. Council, Assoc. Internationale des Etudes françaises, 1969-; Editorial Bd of French Studies, 1972-. Hon. Fellow, St Hugh's Coll., Oxford, 1972. *Publications:* Leconte de Lisle's Poems on the Barbarian Races, 1947; Baudelaire: Les Fleurs du Mal, 1960 (repr. 1975); Flaubert: Madame Bovary, 1962 (repr. 1976); contrib.: to Acta of colloquia, on Baudelaire, Constant, Flaubert, Nerval, etc.; to presentation vols; to learned jls in France, England, Italy, Australia, etc. *Recreations:* reading, travel. *Address:* 11 Parker Street, Cambridge CB1 1JL. *T:* Cambridge 58465.

FAIRLIE-CUNINGHAME, Sir William Alan; *see* Cuninghame.

FAIRMAN, Prof. Herbert Walter; Emeritus Professor of Egyptology, University of Liverpool (Brunner Professor of Egyptology, 1948-74); Special Lecturer in Egyptology, University of Manchester, 1948-69; *b* 9 March, 1907; *s* of Rev. W. T. Fairman, DD; *m* 1937, Olive Winnifred Nicholls; one *s* one *d. Educ:* Goudhurst Sch. for Boys, Goudhurst, Kent; University of Liverpool. Excavations of the Egypt Exploration Soc. at Armant and Tell el Amarna (Egypt), 1929-36, and Sesebi and Amarah West (Sudan), 1936-48. Field Dir, Egypt Exploration Society's Nubian Expedition, 1937-48. *Publications:* The Triumph of Horus, 1974; chapters on the inscriptions in: Mond and Myers, The Bucheum, 1934; Frankfort and Pendlebury, The City of Akhenaten II, 1933; (also editor) Pendlebury, The City of Akhenaten III, 1950; articles in Journal of Egyptian Archaeology, Annales du Service des Antiquités de l'Egypte and Bulletin de l'Institut français d'archéologie orientale. *Recreations:* swimming, walking. *Address:* 6 Garth Drive, Mossley Hill, Liverpool L18 6HW. *T:* 051-724 2875.

FAIRN, (Richard) Duncan; Assistant Under-Secretary of State, Home Office, 1964-67; *b* 1 June 1906; *s* of Percy Frederick and

Mary Fairn; *m* 1930, Marion Cristina, *d* of James M. Sturrock; one *s*. *Educ:* Elementary Sch.; Battersea County (now Henry Thornton) Sch.; failed Bank of England entrance; London Sch. of Economics, BSc (Econ). Voluntary prison teacher and visitor, 1926-30. Education Officer, Pettit Farm Settlement, Dagenham, 1929-30; Joint Warden, The Settlement, York, 1930-38; Dep. Governor, Manchester Prison, 1938-39; Dep. Governor, Wakefield Prison, 1939-42; Governor, Rochester Borstal, 1942-45; First Principal, Prison Service Staff Coll., Wakefield, 1945-48; Asst Comr of Prisons, 1948-55; a Comr of Prisons, 1955-63, when Prison Commn was dissolved; Dir of Prison Administration, 1952-60; Chief Dir, Prison Dept, Home Office, 1960-64; Training Officer, Lord Chancellor's Office, 1967-72. Visited various parts of the world to advise on prison administration, 1955-69; Chm. Cttee on Detention Camps in Kenya, 1959. Swarthmore Lectr, Society of Friends, 1951; Vis. Lectr, UN Inst. at Fuchū, Tokyo, 1967; visited Nigeria to advise on prison admin, 1973. Pres., Pinner Branch of UNA, 1970-; Vice-Pres., Nat. Assoc. of Prison Visitors, 1970-; Member: Council of National Book League, 1951-77; European Cttee on Crime Problems (Strasbourg), 1964-67; Internat. Penal and Penitentiary Foundn, 1965-67; UK delegn to UN Social Develt Commn, 1967-71; Parole Bd, 1967-71; UN Adv. Cttee of Experts on Prevention of Crime and Treatment of Offenders, 1970-72; Peter Bedford Project, 1974-76. Governor, Leighton Park Sch., 1961-76. Chairman: Management Cttee, E London Family Service Unit, 1958-; Bd of Governors, Bedales Sch., 1963-65; John Bellers Ltd, 1974-; Peter Bedford Trust, 1977-; Civil Service Selection Bds, 1972-76. *Publications:* Quakerism, a faith for ordinary men, 1951; The Disinherited Prisoner (Eleanor Rathbone Memorial Lecture), 1962; contrib.: Changing Concepts of Crime and its Treatment, 1966; various criminological jls; DNB Supplement, 1961-70. *Recreations:* reading, walking, music and people. *Address:* Lavender Cottage, 82 Paines Lane, Pinner, Mddx HA5 3BL. *T:* 01-866 9650. *Clubs:* Authors', Nat. Film Theatre.

FAIRWEATHER, Brig. Claude Cyril, CB 1967; CBE 1965 (OBE 1944); TD 1944; DL, JP; Chairman, North of England TA&VRA, 1968-71; *b* 17 March 1906; *s* of Nicholas Fairweather, Middlesborough; *m* 1930, Alice Mary, *e d* of late Sir William Crosthwaite; one *s* one *d*. *Educ:* St Peter's Sch., York. 2nd Lieut, Royal Corps of Signals, 1928; Lt-Col 1941; Col 1943; Brig. 1945. Chm., North Riding T&AFA, 1950-53 and 1962-68; Member: TA Advisory Cttee and TA Exec. Cttee, 1968-71. Co. Comdr, NR Yorks. St John Amb. Bde; Hon. Col, 34 (N) Signal Regt (V), 1967-75; Chairman: N Riding Co. Cadet Cttee, 1947-52; St Luke's Hosp. Man. Cttee, Middlesborough, 1959-74; Cleveland AHA, 1973-76. Retd Company Dir. DL 1949, JP 1963, NR Yorks. CStJ 1974. *Recreations:* golf, cricket, Rugby football. *Address:* The White Lodge, Hutton Rudby, Yarm, Cleveland. *T:* Hutton Rudby 700598. *Clubs:* Army and Navy; Cleveland (Middlesborough); Royal and Ancient (St Andrews).

FAIRWEATHER, Dr Frank Arthur; Senior Principal Medical Officer, Department of Health and Social Security, since 1972; *b* 2 May 1928; *s* of Frank and Maud Harriet Fairweather; *m* 1953, Christine Winifred Hobbs; two *s*. *Educ:* City of Norwich Sch.; Middlesex Hospital. MB, BS 1954; MRCPath 1963, FRCPath 1975; FIBiol 1972. Clinical house appts, Ipswich Gp of Hosps, 1955-56; Pathologist, Bland Sutton Inst. of Pathology, and Courtauld Inst. of Biochem., Middlesex Hosp., Soho Hosp. for Women, 1956-60; Jt Sen. Registrar in Histopathology, Middlesex and West Middlesex Hosps, 1961-62; Chief Med. Adviser and Cons. Pathologist, Benger Labs, 1962-63; Chief Pathologist, British Industrial Biological Res. Assoc., Carshalton, and Hon. Sen. Lectr, RCS, 1963-65; Associate Res. Dir, Wyeth Labs, Taplow, 1965-69; Sen. Med. Officer, DHSS, and Principal Med. Officer, Cttee on Safety of Medicines, 1969-72; Mem. Expert Panels on Environmental Pollution to WHO and Hon. Lectr in Pathology, Middlesex Hosp., 1972-; Mem., EEC Scientific Cttee for Food, 1976-. *Publications:* various toxicological and medical papers. *Recreations:* angling, gardening, painting. *Address:* 394 London Road, Langley, Slough, Berks SL3 7HX.

FAITHFULL, family name of **Baroness Faithfull**.

FAITHFULL, Baroness *cr* 1975 (Life Peer), of Wolvercote, Oxfordshire; **Lucy Faithfull**, OBE 1972; *b* 26 Dec. 1910; *d* of Lt Sydney Leigh Faithfull, RE (killed 1916) and late Elizabeth Adie Faithfull (*née* Algie); unmarried. *Educ:* Talbot Heath Sch. (formerly Bournemouth High Sch.). Social Science Dipl., Birmingham Univ., 1933; Family case work training (Charity Welfare Organisation, now Family Welfare Assoc.), 1936, and Cert. in Child Care, 1969. Club Leader and Sub-Warden, Birmingham Settlement, 1932-35; Asst Organiser, Child Care,

LCC Education Dept, 1935-40; Regional Welfare Officer (Evacuation Scheme), Min. of Health, 1940-48; Inspector in Children's Br., Home Office, 1948-58; Oxford City Council: Children's Officer, 1958-70; Director of Social Services, 1970-74; retired, 1974. Chm., Adoption Resource Exchange; Mem. Council and Exec. Finance Cttee, Dr Barnardo's; Trustee and Mem. Cttee: Bessel Leigh Sch. for Maladjusted Children; Bridgehead Trust (hostel for adolescent boys). Hon. MA Oxford, 1974. *Recreations:* friends, travel, garden. *Address:* 303 Woodstock Road, Oxford OX2 7NY. *T:* Oxford 55389.

FALCON, Norman Leslie, FRS 1960; *b* 29 May 1904; 2nd *s* of late Thomas Adolphus Falcon, MA, RBA; *m* 1938, Dorothy Muriel, 2nd *d* of late F. G. Freeman, HM Consular Service; two *s* one *d*. *Educ:* Exeter Sch.; Trinity Coll., Cambridge. MA Cantab. Joined Anglo-Persian Oil Company as geologist, 1927; FGS, FRGS, 1927; Geological Exploration in Persia, UK and elsewhere, 1927-40. Served War of 1939-45, Intelligence Corps, 1940-45. Rejoined Anglo-Iranian Oil Company as Geologist on Head Office staff, 1945; Chief Geologist, 1955-65, Geological Adviser, 1965-72, British Petroleum Co Ltd. FInstPet, 1959; Geological Soc. of London: Mem. Council, 1954-58, 1967-71; Foreign Sec. 1967-70; Murchison Medal, 1963; Royal Geographical Society: Mem. Council, 1966-69; Vice-Pres. 1973; Founder's Medal, 1973. Mem., NERC, 1968-71. Hon. Mem., American Assoc. Petroleum Geologists, 1973. Bronze Star Medal (USA), 1945. *Publications:* geological papers. *Recreations:* outdoor pursuits. *Address:* The Downs, Chiddingfold, Surrey. *T:* Wormley 3101.

FALCONER, Prof. Alexander Frederick, VRD; BLitt, MA; FRSL; Professor of English in the University of St Andrews since 1955; *s* of Alexander W. Falconer and Emily Henrietta Carlow Falconer. *Educ:* Universities of Glasgow and St Andrews; Magdalen Coll., Oxford. Lecturer, St Salvator's Coll., St Andrews, 1935-39. Served in Home and Eastern Fleets, rank of Lieut, and Lt-Comdr RNVR, 1940-45. Senior Lecturer in Univ. of St Andrews, 1946. Mem. of group of editors for Boswell's correspondence at Yale, 1952-. Folger Fellow, 1958. Jt Gen. Editor, Percy Letters Series, 1964. Naval Officer i/c, St Andrews Univ. Unit, RNR. Trustee, Nat. Library of Scotland, 1956-. Mem., Royal Inst. of Navigation. *Publications:* A. Spir, Right and Wrong (trans.), 1954; The Percy Letters, Vol. IV, 1954, Vol. VI, 1960; Shakespeare and the Sea, 1964; A Glossary of Shakespeare's Sea and Naval Terms, 1965; articles and reviews. *Address:* 6 Alexandra Place, St Andrews. *T:* St Andrews 3457. *Clubs:* Naval, Mayfair.
See also Peter S. Falconer.

FALCONER, Prof. Douglas Scott, FRS 1973; FRSE 1972; Professor of Genetics, University of Edinburgh, and Director, Agricultural Research Council's Unit of Animal Genetics, since 1968; *b* 10 March 1913; *s* of Gerald Scott Falconer and Lillias Harriet Gordon Douglas; *m* 1942, Margaret Duke; two *s*. *Educ:* Edinburgh Academy; Univ. of St Andrews (BSc); Univ. of Cambridge (PhD. ScD). Scientific Staff of Agricultural Research Council, 1947-68. *Publications:* Introduction to Quantitative Genetics, 1960; papers in scientific jls. *Recreations:* music, walking, sailing. *Address:* Institute of Animal Genetics, West Mains Road, Edinburgh EH9 3JN. *T:* 031-667 1081.

FALCONER, Douglas William, MBE 1946; QC 1967; *b* 20 Sept. 1914; *s* of late William Falconer, S Shields; *m* 1941, Joan Beryl Argent, *d* of late A. S. Bishop, Hagley, Worcs; one *s* one *d*. *Educ:* South Shields; King's Coll., Durham Univ.; BSc (Hons) Physics, 1935. Served War of 1939-45 (Hon. Major): commissioned E Yorks Regt, 1939. Called to Bar, Middle Temple, 1950, Bencher 1972. Apptd 1970 to exercise appellate jurisdiction of BoT under Trade Marks Act; Member: of Departmental Cttee to review British trade mark law and practice, 1972-73; Standing Adv. Cttee on Patents, 1975-; Standing Adv. Cttee on Trade Marks, 1975-; Senate of Four Inns of Court, 1973-74; Senate of Four Inns of Court and the Bar, 1974-77. *Publications:* (Jt Editor) Terrell on the Law of Patents (11th and 12th edns), 1965 and 1971. *Recreations:* music, theatre. *Address:* 6 Pump Court, Temple, EC4. *T:* 01-353 8588; Ridgewell House, West Street, Reigate, Surrey. *T:* Reigate 44374.

FALCONER, Lieut-Col Sir George Arthur, KBE 1947; CIE 1942; DL; *b* 3 June 1894; *s* of late E. J. Falconer; *m* 1925, Esther, *d* of late Major M. Boyd-Bredon; one *s* (decd). Served in Great War, 1914-17, with 4th Hussars; 2nd Lieut 1916; Indian Army, Cavalry, 1917; Capt. 1921; Major, 1935; Lt-Col 1943; Asst Consul-Gen. Meshed, 1919-21; Indian Political Service, 1923; Under Sec. Persian Gulf Residency, 1924-26; Asst Resident, Aden, 1927-29; Kashmir, 1929-31; Sec. to Resident, Kolhapur, 1932-33, Baroda, 1933-35; HM Consul, Kerman (Persia), 1937-42; Pol. Agent, Bhopal, 1942-44; HM Minister in Nepal, 1944-

47; United Kingdom Ambassador to Nepal, 1947-51; retired 1951. CC, W Suffolk, 1955-74 (Vice-Chm., 1965-70; CA, 1966); DL, High Sheriff, Suffolk, 1964. Mem. Church Assembly, 1955-70. OStJ. *Address:* Orchard House, Monks Eleigh, near Ipswich, Suffolk IP7 7AU. *T:* Bildeston 740296. *Club:* Army and Navy.

FALCONER, Sir James Fyfe, Kt 1973; MBE 1944; JP; Town Clerk of Glasgow, 1965-75; *b* 18 Nov. 1911; *m* 1938, Jessie Elizabeth Paterson; two *s* two *d. Educ:* Queen's Park Secondary Sch.; Glasgow University. Law Apprentice, 1926-32; Solicitor, 1932-48; Town Clerk Depute, 1948-59; Senior Town Clerk Depute, 1959-65. JP Glasgow, 1962. *Recreations:* gardening, angling. *Address:* 101 St Andrew's Drive, Glasgow G41 4RA. *T:* 041-423 0681.

FALCONER, Peter Serrell, FRIBA, FRSA; Senior Partner, The Falconer Partnership, Architects and Consultants, since 1959; *b* 7 March 1916; *s* of Thomas Falconer, FRIBA, and Florence Edith Falconer; presumed heir to the Lordship of Falconer of Halkerton, vacant since 1966; *m* 1941, Mary Hodson; three *s* one *d. Educ:* Bloxham Sch., Banbury. Commenced practice in Stroud, as partner in Ellery Anderson Roiser & Falconer, 1944; became Sen. Partner, 1959 (with br. office in Adelaide, SA, 1970). Specialist in materials handling and industrial architecture; Mem., Materials Handling Inst.; Founder Mem., Industrial Inst. of Architects' Internat., HQ in Vienna. *Publications:* Building and Planning for Industrial Storage and Distribution, 1975; contributor to: Architectural Review; Architects' Jl; Material Handling magazines. *Recreations:* restoring historic buildings, garden planning, motor sport. *Address:* St Francis, Lammas Park, Minchinhampton, Stroud, Glos. *T:* Brimscombe 2188.

FALETAU, 'Inoke Fotu; High Commissioner for Tonga in London since Oct. 1972; Ambassador for Tonga to: France, since Dec. 1972; Federal Republic of Germany, since Oct. 1976; Belgium, Luxembourg, Netherlands and European Economic Community, since 1977; *b* 24 June 1937; 2nd *s* of 'Akau'ola Sateki Faletau and Celia Lyden; *m* 'Evelini Ma'ata Hurrell; three *s* three *d. Educ:* St Peter's, Cambridge, NZ; Tonga High Sch.; Auckland Grammar Sch.; UC Swansea; Manchester Univ. Joined Tonga Civil Service, 1958; Asst Sec., Prime Minister's Office, 1965; Sec. to Govt, 1969; seconded to Univ. of South Pacific, 1971; Sec. to Govt, 1972. *Recreations:* Rugby, tennis, reading, bridge, fishing. *Address:* Greenbanks, Lyndale, NW2. *T:* 01-435 0634. *Clubs:* Royal Commonwealth Society, Travellers' (Hon.), Hurlingham (Hon.); Nuku'alofa Yacht and Motor Boat.

FALK, Sir Roger (Salis), Kt 1969; OBE 1945; Member, Monopolies and Mergers Commission, since 1965; Chairman: Sadler's Wells Foundation, since 1976; British European Associated Publishers; London Board, Provincial Insurance Co. Ltd; *b* 22 June 1910; *s* of Lionel David Falk; *m* 1938, Margaret Helen (*née* Stroud) (*d* 1958); one *s* two *d. Educ:* Haileybury (Life Governor, 1971-); Geneva Univ. Gen. Manager's Office, Rhodesia Railways, Bulawayo, 1931; D. J. Keymer & Co: Manager in Bombay and Calcutta, 1932-35; Dir, 1935-49; Managing Dir, 1945-49; Vice-Chm., 1950; formerly Dir, P-E International Ltd (Chm., 1973-76). Shoreditch Borough Council, 1937-45. Dir-Gen. British Export Trade Research Organisation (BETRO) from 1949 until disbandment. Chairman: Furniture Development Council, 1963-; Central Council for Agric. and Hort. Cooperation, 1967-75. Member: Council of Industrial Design, 1958-67; Council, RSA, 1968-74. President: Design and Industries Assoc., 1971-72. Served War of 1939-45, RAFVR; Wing-Comdr, 1942. *Publication:* The Business of Management, 1961, 5th rev. edn 1976. *Recreations:* writing, music, reading, theatre. *Address:* 603 Beatty House, Dolphin Square, SW1. *T:* 01-828 3752. *Clubs:* Garrick, MCC.

FALKENDER, Baroness *cr* 1974 (Life Peer); of West Haddon, Northants; **Marcia Matilda Falkender,** CBE 1970; Personal and Political Secretary to Rt Hon. Sir Harold Wilson, since 1956; *b* March 1932; *d* of Harry Field; *m* 1955, George Edmund Charles Williams (marr. diss. 1960). *Educ:* Northampton High School; Queen Mary Coll., Univ. of London. BA Hons Hist. Secretary, Transport House, 1955-56. Member: Prime Minister's Film Industry Working Party, 1975-76; Interim Cttee on Film Industry, 1977-. *Publication:* Inside Number 10, 1972. *Address:* 3 Wyndham Mews, Upper Montagu Street, W1.

FALKINER, Lt-Col Sir Terence (Edmond Patrick), 8th Bt of Annmount, Cork, *cr* 1778; DL; late Coldstream Guards; retired 1956; *b* 17 March 1903; *s* of 7th Bt and Kathleen (*d* 1948), *e d* of Hon. Henry Robert Orde-Powlett, 2nd *s* of 3rd Baron Bolton; *S* father, 1917; *m* 1925, Mildred, *y d* of Sir John Cotterell, 4th Bt; two *s* three *d. Educ:* St Anthony's, Eastbourne; The Oratory

Sch., Edgbaston. DL, Herefordshire, 1965. KStJ. *Heir:* s Edmond Charles Falkiner [*b* 24 June 1938; *m* 1960, Janet Iris, *d* of Arthur E. B. Darby, Bromyard, Herefordshire; two *s*]. *Address:* Kingsthorne House, Hereford. *T:* Wormelow 343.

FALKINGHAM, Very Rev. John Norman; Rector of St Paul's, Manuka, ACT, since 1975; Canon of St Saviour's Cathedral, Goulburn, since 1976; Warden, Community of the Holy Name, since 1969; *b* 9 Feb. 1917; 2nd *s* of Alfred Richard Falkingham and Amy Grant (*née* Macallister); *m* 1947, Jean Dorothy Thoren; two *d. Educ:* Geelong Gram. Sch., Corio, Vic.; Trinity Coll., University of Melbourne. BA (Hons) Melbourne 1940; ThL (1st Cl. Hons) Australian Coll. of Theol.; prizes for Divinity and Biblical Greek. Deacon, 1941; Priest, 1942. Curate of Holy Trinity, Surrey Hills, Vic., 1941-44; Chaplain, Trinity Coll., Univ. of Melbourne, 1944-50; Incumbent, St Paul's, Caulfield, Vic., 1950-61. Exam. Chaplain to Archbishop of Melbourne, 1947-61; Lectr in Theol. Faculty, Trinity Coll., Melbourne, 1950-60; Canon of St Paul's Cath., Melbourne, 1959-61; Dean of Newcastle, NSW, 1961-75. Sec., Liturgical Commn of Gen. Synod, 1966-; Mem. Bd of Delegates, Aust. Coll. of Theology, 1962-. *Publications:* articles in various jls. *Recreation:* walking. *Address:* St. Paul's Rectory, Canberra Avenue, Manuka, ACT 2603, Australia. *T:* 959009. *Club:* Newcastle.

FALKLAND, 14th Viscount and 14th Lord Cary, *cr* 1620; **Lucius Henry Charles Plantagenet Cary;** *b* 25 Jan. 1905; *e s* of 13th Viscount Falkland and Ella Louise (*d* 1954), *e d* of E. W. Catford; *S* father, 1961; *m* 1st, 1926, Joan Sylvia (who obtained a divorce, 1933), *d* of Capt. Charles Bonham Southey, of Frinton-on-Sea; two *d* ; 2nd, 1933, Constance Mary, *d* of late Capt. Edward Berry; one *s* ; 3rd, 1958, Charlotte Anne (marr. diss. 1974), *e d* of late Bevil Granville, Chadley, Wellesbourne, Warwick. *Educ:* Eton. Flying Officer RAFVR, 1941-45 (invalided). *Heir:* s Master of Falkland, *qv. Address:* 18 Tower Park, Fowey, Cornwall. *T:* Fowey 3211. *Clubs:* Carlton, Royal Commonwealth Society; Royal Fowey Yacht.
See also Sir W. V. H. Nelson, Bt.

FALKLAND, Master of; Hon. Lucius Edward William Plantagenet Cary; Chief Executive, C. T. Bowring Trading (Holdings) Ltd; Director: Bowmaker (Plant) Ltd; Bowring Steamship Co. Ltd; *b* 8 May 1935; *s* and *heir* of 14th Viscount Falkland, *qv* ; *m* 1962, Caroline Anne, *o d* of late Lt-Comdr Gerald Butler, DSC, RN, and Mrs Anne Skimming, Shotters Farm, Newton Valence, Hants; one *s* two *d* (and one *d* decd). *Educ:* Wellington Coll.; Alliance Française, Paris. Late 2nd Lieut 8th Hussars. *Recreations:* birdwatching, motorcycling, cinema. *Address:* Court House, Winchfield, near Basingstoke, Hants. *T:* Hartley Wintney 3273. *Clubs:* Brooks's; Berkshire Golf.

FALKNER, Sir (Donald) Keith, Kt 1967; Hon. DMus Oxon, 1969; FRCM; Hon. RAM; Hon. GSM; Hon. FTCL; Hon. FLCM; Director, Royal College of Music, 1960-74; professional singer; *b* Sawston, Cambs, 1900; *y s* of late John Charles Falkner; *m* 1930, Christabel Margaret, *o d* of Thomas Fletcher Fullard, MA; two *d. Educ:* New Coll. Sch.; Perse Sch.; Royal College of Music; Berlin, Vienna, Paris. Has sung at all principal festivals in England, and many European cities; toured USA eight times, including concerts with Boston Symphony, New York Philharmonic, Cincinnati, St Louis, and Philadelphia Orchestras; toured South Africa, 1935, 1939, 1955, 1962; Canada in 1953; New Zealand in 1956. British Council Music Officer for Italy, 1946-50. Prof. of the Dept of Music at Cornell Univ., USA, 1950-60. Served European War, 1914-18, in RNAS, 1917-19; War of 1939-45, RAFVR, 1940-45. *Recreations:* cricket, golf, lawn tennis, squash rackets, walking. *Address:* Low Cottages, Ilketshall St Margaret, Bungay, Suffolk. *T:* Bungay 2573. *Clubs:* Athenæum, Royal Automobile, MCC.

FALL, Brian James Proetel; HM Diplomatic Service; Counsellor and Head of Chancery, British Embassy, Moscow, since 1977; *b* 13 Dec. 1937; *s* of John William Fall, Hull, Yorkshire, and Edith Juliette (*née* Proetel); *m* 1962, Delmar Alexandra Roos; three *d* . *Educ:* St Paul's Sch.; Magdalen Coll., Oxford; Univ. of Michigan Law Sch. Joined HM Foreign (now Diplomatic) Service, 1962; served in Foreign Office UN Dept, 1963; Moscow, 1965; Geneva, 1968; Civil Service Coll., 1970; FO Eastern European and Soviet Dept and Western Organisations Dept, 1971; New York, 1975; Harvard Univ. Center for Internat. Affairs, 1976. *Address:* c/o Foreign and Commonwealth Office, King Charles Street, SW1A 2AH; 2 St Helena Terrace, Richmond, Surrey. *T:* 01-940 7683. *Club:* Travellers'.

FALLA, Paul Stephen; *b* 25 Oct. 1913; *s* of Norris Stephen Falla and Audrey Frances Stock, Dunedin, New Zealand; *m* 1958,

Elizabeth Shearer; one *d. Educ:* Wellington and Christ's Colls, NZ; Balliol Coll., Oxford (Scholar). Appointed to Foreign Office, 1936; served HM Embassies, Warsaw, 1938-39, Ankara, 1939-43, Tehran, 1943; Foreign Office, 1943-46; UK Delegation to UN, New York, 1946-49; Foreign Office, 1949-67 (Dep. Dir of Research, 1958-67). Member: Exec. Cttee, Translators' Assoc., Soc. of Authors, 1971-73 (Vice-Chm., 1973); Council, Inst. Linguists, 1975-; Cttee, Translators' Guild, 1975-. Scott Moncrieff prize, 1972. *Publications:* about 40 book translations from various languages, 1967-77. *Recreations:* reading, (history, philosophy, poetry); languages and linguistics. *Address:* 63 Freelands Road, Bromley, Kent BR1 3HZ. *T:* 01-460 4995. *Club:* Travellers'.

FALLA, Sir Robert Alexander, KBE 1973; CMG 1959; FRSNZ; Chairman, Nature Conservation Council, New Zealand, since 1962; *b* 21 July 1901; *s* of G. Falla; *m* 1928, Elayne M., *d* of A. Burton, Te Aroha; one *s* two *d. Educ:* Auckland Grammar Sch.; Auckland Univ. (MA, DSc). Lecturer, Auckland Teachers' Training Coll., 1925-30; Asst Zoologist, British, Australian and New Zealand Antarctic Research Expedition, 1929-31; Ornithologist, Auckland War Memorial Museum, 1931-35; Asst Dir, 1936-37; Dir, Cant Museum, 1937-47; Dir, Dominion Museum, Wellington, 1947-66. Served War of 1939-45. Delegate, First Gen. Conference, New Zealand Nat. Commission, UNESCO, 1946; Mem. Ross Sea Cttee, 1955. Polar Medal (bronze). *Publications:* Scientific papers and reports on Antarctic birds of Mawson expedition. *Address:* Kotari Road, Day's Bay, Wellington, New Zealand.

FALLE, Sir Sam, KCVO 1972; CMG 1964; DSC 1945; HM Diplomatic Service; High Commissioner in Nigeria, since 1977; *b* 19 Feb. 1919; *s* of Theodore and Hilda Falle; *m* 1945, Merete Rosen; one *s* three *d. Educ:* Victoria Coll., Jersey, CI. Served Royal Navy, 1937-48; joined Foreign (subseq. Diplomatic) Service, 1948; British Consulate, Shiraz, Iran, 1949-51; British Embassy, Tehran, 1952; British Embassy, Beirut, 1952-55; FO, 1955-57; British Embassy, Baghdad, 1957-61; Consul-Gen., Gothenburg, 1961-63; Head of UN Dept, FO, 1963-67; with Lord Shackleton's mission to Aden 1967; Deputy High Comr, Kuala Lumpur, 1967-69; Ambassador to Kuwait, 1969-70; High Comr, Singapore, 1970-74; Ambassador to Sweden, 1974-77. *Recreation:* swimming. *Address:* c/o Foreign and Commonwealth Office, SW1.

FALLON, Peter, QC 1971; a Recorder of the Crown Court, since 1972; *b* 1 March 1931; *s* of Frederick and Mary Fallon; *m* 1955, Zina Mary (*née* Judd); one *s* two *d. Educ:* Leigh Grammar Sch.; St Joseph's Coll., Blackpool; Bristol Univ. (LLB Hons). Called to Bar, Gray's Inn, 1953. Thereafter commissioned in RAF for three years: Flying Officer; promoted Flt Lt in Reserve. Commenced law practice as pupil, 1956. *Publications:* Crown Court Practice: Sentencing, 1974; contrib. Proc. RSM. *Recreations:* golf, fishing, painting. *Address:* Nutgrove House, Chew Magna, near Bristol. *T:* Chew Magna 2611. *Club:* Mendip Golf.

FALLOWS, Rt. Rev. William Gordon; see Sheffield, Bishop of.

FALMOUTH, 9th Viscount, *cr* 1720; **George Hugh Boscawen;** 26th Baron Le Despencer, 1264; Baron Boscawen-Rose, 1720; Lord-Lieutenant of Cornwall, since 1977; *b* 31 Oct. 1919; 2nd but *e* surv. *s* of 8th Viscount; *S* father, 1962; *m* 1953, Elizabeth Price Browne; four *s. Educ:* Eton Coll.; Trinity Coll., Cambridge. Served War, 1939-46, Italy. Capt., Coldstream Guards. DL Cornwall, 1968. *Heir: s* Hon. Evelyn Arthur Hugh Boscawen [*b* 13 May 1955; *m* 1977, Lucia Vivian-Neal, *e d* of R. W. Vivian-Neal]. *Address:* Tregothnan, Truro, Cornwall; Buston, Hunton, Kent. *Club:* Athenæum.
See also Hon. R. T. Boscawen.

FALSHAW, Sir Donald, Kt 1967; retired; *b* 22 Jan. 1905; *s* of James and Martha Falshaw; *m* 1937, Jessie Louise Taylor; no *c. Educ:* Lancaster Royal Gram. Sch.; Sidney Sussex Coll., Cambridge. Indian Civil Service (Punjab), 1928-66: District and Sessions Judge, 1932-46; Judge, Lahore High Court, 1946-47; Judge, Punjab High Court, India, after partition, 1947-66, Chief Justice, Dec. 1961-May 1966. *Recreations:* cricket, racing. *Address:* 125 Kenilworth Court, Putney, SW15. *T:* 01-788 8058. *Club:* East India, Devonshire, Sports and Public Schools.

FALVEY, Senator Hon. Sir John (Neil), KBE 1976; QC 1970; Attorney-General, Fiji, since 1970; *b* 16 Jan. 1918; *s* of John Falvey and Adela Falvey; *m* 1943, Margaret Katherine, *d* of Stanley Weatherby; three *s* two *d* (and one *d* decd). *Educ:* Eltham and New Plymouth Convent Schs; Whangarei High Sch.; Otago Univ. (BA); Auckland Univ. (LLB). Colonial Admin. Service (incl. mil. service, Fiji and Gilbert and Ellice Is),

1940-48; private legal practice, 1949-70. Mem., Legislative Council, 1953-72; Senator and Leader of Govt Business, 1972-. Hon. Danish Consul, 1950-70. Chevalier (First Cl.), Royal Order of Dannebrog, 1968. *Recreation:* golf. *Address:* Crown Law Office, Government Buildings, Suva, Fiji. *T:* 211580. *Clubs:* Fiji, Defence, Fiji Golf.

FANE, family name of **Earl of Westmorland.**

FANE, Harry Frank Brien, CMG 1967; OBE 1957 (MBE 1945); Department of Employment and Productivity, retired 1968; *b* 21 Aug. 1915; *s* of late Harry Lawson Fane and Edith (*née* Stovold); *m* 1947, Stella, yr *d* of John Hopwood; two *d. Educ:* William Ellis Sch.; Birkbeck Coll., London. Joined Ministry of Labour, 1933. HM Forces, 1940-45: Major, Royal Corps of Signals (despatches); served in N Africa, Italy and Austria. British Embassy, Washington: First Sec. (Labour), 1950-56; Counsellor (Labour), 1960-66. Regional Controller, Dept of Employment and Productivity (formerly Min. of Labour), Birmingham, 1966-68. *Address:* 40 Winterbourne Road, Solihull, West Midlands.

FANE TREFUSIS, family name of **Baron Clinton.**

FANNER, Peter Duncan; Metropolitan Stipendiary Magistrate since 1972; a Deputy Circuit Judge, since 1974; *b* 27 May 1926; *s* of late Robert William Hodges Fanner, solicitor, and Doris Kitty Fanner; *m* 1949, Sheila Eveline England; one *s* one *d. Educ:* Pangbourne Coll. Admitted Solicitor of the Supreme Court, 1951 (holder Justices' Clerks' Society's prize). Served War of 1939-45, Pilot in Fleet Air Arm, Lieut (A) RNVR, 1944-47. Asst Clerk to Bromley Justices, 1947-51; Dep. Clerk to Gore Justices, 1951-56; Clerk to Bath Justices, 1956-72. Mem. Council of Justices' Clerks' Society, 1966-72; Assessor Mem. of Departmental Cttee on Liquor Licensing, 1971-72. Chairman: Bath Round Table, 1963-64; No Fixed Abode, 1973-75. *Publications:* Stone's Justices' Manual; contrib. to Justice of the Peace, The Magisterial Officer, The Lawyer's Remembrancer. *Recreations:* motoring, caravanning, sailing. *Address:* Thames Magistrates Court, Aylward Road, E1. *T:* 01-488 6516.

FANSHAWE, Maj.-Gen. Sir Evelyn Dalrymple, Kt 1961; CB 1946; CBE 1942; DL; *b* 25 May 1895; *e s* of late Gen. Sir Hew Dalrymple Fanshawe, KCB, KCMG; *m* 1920, Marie, *e d* of late Sir Victor Harari, CMG; no *c. Educ:* King's Sch., Canterbury; Royal Military Coll., Sandhurst. 2nd Lieut The Queen's Bays. 1914; served European War, 1914-18, France, Egypt, Palestine, Mesopotamia, Persia, Russia, Syria (1914 star, Allied and Victory medals); ADC, GOC Cavalry Corps, 1915; seconded to RFC 1915-19; returned to Regt and made Adjutant, 1919; Lieut-Col The Queen's Bays, 1935; Col, 1938; Brig. to Comd. 20th Mech. Cav. Bde 1939; Comd. 20 Armd Bde 1940-41; Maj.-Gen. Armd Training and Comdr RAC Training Establishment, 1942-45; retired pay, 1945. UNRRA Dir in British Zone of Germany, 1945-48. Dir of the International Refugee Organisation in British Zone of Germany, 1948-52; Mission to Dominion Countries on behalf of UNO, 1952. Chm., Pre-Services Cttee, Northants TA Assoc., 1953-65; Pres., Northants Spastic Assoc.; Pres. Northants Outward Bound Cttee; Vice-President: Northants County Amateur Athletic Assoc.; Northants County Cricket Club. Hon. Treas. East Midlands Area, Conservative and Unionist Associations, 1952-67; Chm., Kettering Div., Conservative and Unionist Assoc., 1953-65 (Pres. 1965); Chm. of Stallion Cttee, Hunters Improvement Soc. (President 1965, 1975); President: Ponies of Britain Club, 1962; National Pony Soc., 1966, 1975. High Sheriff, Northants, 1960; DL Northants, 1961. King's Coronation Medal, 1937. *Recreations:* hunting, polo, yachting, shooting and fishing, racing, flying. *Address:* Guilsborough House, Northampton. *T:* Guilsborough 258. *Clubs:* Cavalry and Guards; Royal Armoured Corps Yacht; Travellers' (Paris).

FANSHAWE, Maj.-Gen. George Drew, CB 1954; DSO 1944; OBE 1944; *b* 27 Sept. 1901; *s* of Lt-Col Edward Cardwell Fanshawe; *m* 1934, Dorothy Elizabeth Norman-Walker; one *s* one *d. Educ:* Tonbridge. 2nd Lieut, RFA, 1922, Lieut 1924. RHA 1928; Capt. 1935; Adjt Herts Yeomanry, 1935; Brigade-Maj., RA, 1939, CO 1942; CRA, 3 Div., 1945; 5th Anti-Aircraft Bde, 1949; Comdr 1st Anti-Aircraft Group, 1952-55; retired 1955. BRA Southern Comd, 1950. Col. Comdt, Royal Artillery, 1956-66 (Representative Col Comdt, 1961-62). High Sheriff, Wilts, 1961-62; Alderman, Wilts CC. CStJ. Order of Merit (US). *Address:* Farley Farm, Farley, Wilts. *T:* Farley 202. *Club:* Army and Navy.

FANSHAWE, Captain Thomas Evelyn, CBE 1971; DSC 1943; RN retd; Captain of the Sea Cadet Corps and Secretary to the Sea Cadet Council since 1972; Nautical Assessor to House of

Lords; *b* 29 Sept. 1918; *s* of Rev. Richard Evelyn Fanshawe and Mrs Isobel Fanshawe (*née* Prosser Hale); *m* 1944, Joan Margaret Moxon; one *s* two *d*. *Educ:* Dover Coll.; Nautical Coll., Pangbourne. FRHS. Served 1939-45 in destroyers and frigates and comdg HMS Clover (DSC, despatches 1943 and 1944); HM Ships Ocean, Constance and Phoenix, 1945-51; comd HM Ships: Zest and Obedient, 1951-54; Loch Insh, 1955-57; Temeraire, 1957-59; Tyne, 1959-61; NATO Defence Coll. and Liaison Officer with C-in-C Southern Europe, 1961-64; comd HMS Plymouth and Captain (D) 29th Escort Sqdn, 1964-66; Sen. Naval Officer Persian Gulf and Comdr Naval Forces Gulf, 1966-68 (Cdre); SBNO and Naval Attaché, S Africa (Cdre), 1969-71; ADC to the Queen, 1970-71; retd 1971. Cmdr 1955; Captain 1961. *Recreations:* gardening, golf, general interest in sport. *Address:* Freshwater House, Stroud, Petersfield, Hants. *T:* Petersfield 2430. *Clubs:* Naval, MCC; Royal Naval (Portsmouth).

FAREED, Sir Razik, Kt, *cr* 1951; OBE 1948; Member of Ceylonese Parliament, from 1952; Member of Senate, Ceylon, 1947-52; Member, State Council of Ceylon until Ceylon Independence Act, 1947; Founder, only Muslim Ladies' College in Ceylon; Founder and President, Moors' Islamic Cultural Home (Inc.); Life Pres., All Ceylon Moors Assoc. Is a Ceylon Moor by race and a Muslim by religion. Life Mem., Orchid Circle of Sri Lanka; Mem., Sri Lanka Sufi Study Circle. *Address:* Hajara Villa, Fareed Place, Colombo 4, Sri Lanka. *T:* 88357 and 28928. *Clubs:* Ceylon Turf, Ceylon Poultry (Vice-Pres.).

FARGHER, John Adrian, CMG 1957; The South Australian Railways Commissioner, 1953-66; *b* 13 Jan. 1901; *s* of Philip and Matilda Maud Fargher; *m* 1926, Elsie Pearl, *d* of Charles French; one *s* one *d* (and one *d* decd). *Educ:* Melbourne Univ (MCE). *Publications:* has contributed a number of Papers to Journal of The Institution of Engineers, Australia. *Recreation:* golf. *Address:* 8 Cambridge Terrace, Brighton, South Australia 5048, Australia.

FARIDKOT, Col HH Farzand-i-Saadat Nishan Hazrrat-i-Kaisar-i-Hind, Raja Sir Har Indar Singh Brar Bans Bahadur, Ruler of, KCSI 1941; *b* 29 Jan. 1915; *S* father as Raja, 1919; *m* 1933. *Educ:* Aitchison Chiefs Coll., Lahore. Full Ruling Powers, 1934; is one of Ruling Princes of India; Hon. Col Sikh LI; Hon. Col Bengal Engineer Group; MLA Pepsu LA. Salute, 11 guns. Formerly Mem. National Defence Council of India and of Standing Cttee of Chamber of Princes. *Address:* Faridkot, Punjab, India.

FARINGDON, 3rd Baron *cr* 1916; **Charles Michael Henderson;** Bt 1902; *b* 3 July 1937; *s* of Hon. Michael Thomas Henderson (*d* 1953) (2nd *s* of 1st Baron) and Oonagh Evelyn Henderson, *er d* of late Lt-Col Harold Ernest Brassey; *S* uncle, 1977; *m* 1959, Sarah Caroline, *d* of J. M. E. Askew, *qv*; three *s* one *d*. *Educ:* Eton College; Trinity College, Cambridge (BA). *Heir: s* Hon. James Harold Henderson, *b* 14 July 1961. *Address:* Buscot Park, Faringdon, Oxon; Barnsley Park, Cirencester, Glos.

FARLEY, Dr Francis James Macdonald, FRS 1972; Dean, Royal Military College of Science, Shrivenham, since 1967; *b* 13 Oct. 1920; *er s* of late Brig. Edward Lionel Farley, CBE, MC; *m* 1945, Josephine Maisie Hayden; three *s* one *d*. *Educ:* Clifton Coll.; Clare Coll., Cambridge. MA 1945; PhD 1950; ScD Cantab 1967. Air Defence Research and Development Establishment, 1941-45 (first 3cm ground radar, Doppler radar); Chalk River Laboratories, 1945-46; Research Student, Cavendish Lab., Cambridge, 1946-49; Auckland Univ. Coll., NZ, 1950-57; attached AERE, 1955; CERN, Geneva, 1957-67 (muon g-2 experiment). Vis. Lectr, Univ. of Bristol, 1965-66. Rep. NZ at UN Conf. on Atomic Energy for Peaceful Purposes, 1955. FInstP. *Publications:* Elements of Pulse Circuits, 1955; Progress in Nuclear Techniques and Instrumentation, Vol. I, 1966, Vol. II, 1967, Vol. III 1968; scientific papers on nuclear physics, electronics and high energy particle physics. *Recreations:* gliding (FAI gold and diamond); ski-ing, tennis. *Address:* Royal Military College of Science, Shrivenham, Swindon SN6 8LA. *T:* Shrivenham 782551. *Club:* Athenæum.

FARMAR, Hugh William, MVO 1973; Clerk to the Drapers' Company, 1952-73; Member of the Court of the Company since 1974; Governor (Treasurer 1952-73), Queen Mary College, University of London, Hon. Fellow, 1967; Member: Council, Fairbridge Society; Council, King Edward VII Hospital Fund; *b* 6 June 1908; *o s* of late Col H. M. Farmar, CMG, DSO, and Violet, *y d* of late Sir William Dalby and Hyacinthe Wellesley; *m* 1944, Constantia, *o d* of late Rt Hon. Sir Horace Rumbold, 9th Bt, GCB, and late Etheldred, Lady Rumbold, CBE; two *s*. *Educ:* Eton; Balliol Coll., Oxford. 2nd class clerk, Charity Commn, 1937; RAFVR, 1939-46 (on staff, Resident Minister, Accra,

1942-43; Asst Private Sec. to Sec. of State for Air 1945-46). Principal clerk, Charity Commn, 1946. Hon. LLD William and Mary Coll., Virginia, 1968. *Publications:* The Cottage in the Forest, 1949; A Regency Elopement, 1969; articles and broadcasts on travel and country subjects. *Recreations:* country pursuits. *Address:* Wasing Old Rectory, Aldermaston, Reading, Berks. *T:* Tadley 4873. *Clubs:* Brooks's, Pratt's.
See also Sir H. Anthony Rumbold, Bt, Lord Swinfen.

FARMBROUGH, Ven. David John; Archdeacon of St Albans, since 1974; *b* 4 May 1929; 2nd *s* of late Charles Septimus and late Ida Mabel Farmbrough; *m* 1955, Angela Priscilla Hill; one *s* three *d*. *Educ:* Bedford Sch.; Lincoln Coll., Oxford. BA 1951, MA 1953. Westcott House, Cambridge. Deacon, 1953, priest, 1954; Curate of Bishop's Hatfield, 1953-57; Priest-in-charge, St John's, Hatfield, 1957-63; Vicar of Bishop's Stortford, 1963-74; Rural Dean of Bishop's Stortford, 1973-74. Mem., Gen. Synod, 1972-. *Publications:* In Wonder, Love and Praise, 1966; Belonging, Believing, Doing, 1971. *Recreations:* sailing, gardening. *Address:* 6 Sopwell Lane, St Albans, Herts AL1 1RR. *T:* St Albans 57973.

FARMER, Prof. Edward Desmond; Louis Cohen Professor of Dental Surgery, since 1957, Director of Post-Graduate Dental Studies, since 1972, Dean of the Faculty of Medicine, since 1977 and Pro-Vice-Chancellor, 1967-70, University of Liverpool; *b* 15 April 1917; *s* of late S. R. and L. M. Farmer; *m* 1942, Mary Elwood Little; one *s* two *d*. *Educ:* Newcastle-under-Lyme High Sch.; Univ. of Liverpool (1936-41); Queens' Coll., Cambridge (1948-50). MA Cantab, 1955; MDS Liverpool, 1951; FDSRCS 1952; MRCPath 1967, FRCPath 1968. RNVR, Surgeon Lieut (D), 1942-45; Lectr in Parodontal Diseases, Univ. of Liverpool, 1950-57; Nuffield Fellow, 1948-50. Hon. Cons. Dent. Surg. to Bd of Govs of United Liverpool Hosps and Liverpool AHA (Teaching), formerly Liverpool Regional Hosp. Bd. Member Council: Brit. Soc. of Periodontology, 1954-59 (Pres. 1957-58); RSM, Odonto. Sect., 1965-68. Member: Central Cttee and Exec., Hosp. Dental Service, 1964-76; Negotiating Cttee of Central Cttee for Hosp. Medical Services, 1968-76; Bd of Govs, United Liverpool Hosps, 1968-71; UGC Dental Sect., 1968-; Conf. and Exec., Dental Post-Grad. Deans, 1972-77; Cttee of Dental Teachers and Res. Workers Gp, BDA, 1974-; Liverpool AHA(T) (and Chm., Regional Dental Cttee), 1975-77; RHA, 1977; Faculty of Dental Surgery, RCS, 1974-; Dental Cttee of Medical Defence Union; Council, Medical Insurance Agency; Exec., Teaching Hospitals Assoc.; Vice-Chm., Commn of Dental Educn, Fedn Dentaire Internat.; President: NW Br. BDA, 1967-68; Hospitals' Gp, BDA, 1972-73; Assoc. for Dental Educn in Europe, 1976-. *Publications:* (with F. E. Lawton) Stones' Oral and Dental Diseases, 5th edn, 1966; papers in Proceedings Royal Society Med., Jl of Gen. Microbiology, Brit. Med. Jl, Dental Practitioner; Internat. Dental Jl. *Recreations:* golf, gardening, painting and enjoyment of the countryside. *Address:* Heath Moor, Beacon Lane, Heswall, Merseyside L60 0DG. *T:* 051-342 3179.

FARMER, Sir George; *see* Farmer, Sir L. G. T.

FARMER, Rev. Herbert Henry, MA Cantab, Hon. DD Glasgow; Emeritus Professor of Systematic Theology 1935-60, in Westminster College, Cambridge; *b* 27 Nov. 1892; *s* of William Charles Farmer and Mary Ann Buck; *m* 1923, Gladys Sylvie Offord; one *s* two *d*. *Educ:* Owen's Sch., Islington; Peterhouse, Cambridge (1st cl. Moral Sciences Tripos; Burney Studentship in the Philosophy of Religion, University of Cambridge); Westminster Coll., Cambridge. Minister of Presbyterian Church, Stafford, 1919-22; Minister of St Augustine's Presbyterian Church, New Barnet, 1922-31; Carew Lecturer, Hartford Seminary Foundation, USA, 1930; Riley Prof. of Christian Doctrine, Hartford Seminary Foundation, USA, 1931-35; Barbour Prof. of Systematic Theology, Westminster Coll. (Presbyterian), Cambridge, 1935-60; Norris-Hulse Prof. of Divinity, Cambridge University, 1949-60; Fellow of Peterhouse, Cambridge, 1950-60. Stanton Lecturer in the Philosophy of Religion, University of Cambridge, 1937-40; Warrack Lecturer, 1940; Lyman Beecher Lecturer, Yale Univ., 1946; Gifford Lecturer, Glasgow Univ., 1950-51. *Publications:* Things Not Seen, 1927; Experience of God, 1929; The World and God, 1935; The Healing Cross, 1938; The Servant of the Word, 1941; Towards Belief in God, 1942; God and Men, 1948; Revelation and Religion, 1954; The Word of Reconciliation, 1967. *Address:* Norgil, Yewtree Road, Grange-over-Sands, Cumbria.

FARMER, Hugh Robert Macdonald, CB 1967; *b* 3 Dec. 1907; *s* of late Charles Edward Farmer and late Emily (née Randolph); *m* 1st, 1934, Penelope Frances (*d* 1963), *d* of late Capt. Evelyn Boothby, RN; one *s* three *d*; 2nd, 1966, Jean, *widow* of Peter Bluett Winch. *Educ:* Cheam Sch.; Eton Coll.; New Coll.,

Oxford. House of Commons: Asst Clerk, 1931; Sen. Clerk, 1943; Clerk of Private Bills and Taxing Officer, and Examr of Petitions for Private Bills, 1958-60; Clerk of Cttees, 1960-65; Clerk/Administrator, 1965-72, retired 1972. *Recreations:* golf, gardening. *Address:* Grayswood Cottage, Haslemere, Surrey. *T:* Haslemere 3129. *Club:* MCC.

FARMER, Sir (Lovedin) George (Thomas), Kt 1968; LLD, MA, FCA, JDipMA; Coordinator, Rover and Triumph, 1972-73; Chairman: Rover Co. Ltd, 1963-73; Zenith Carburetter Co. Ltd, 1973-77; *b* 13 May 1908; *m* 1938, Editha Mary Fisher; no *c. Educ:* Oxford High Sch. 2nd Vice-Chm. and Mem. Adv. Cttee, Metalurgica de Santa Ana, Madrid, 1963-74; Dep. Chm., British Leyland Motor Corp., 1972-73; Director: Empresa Nacional de Automcamiones, 1968-73; ATV Network Ltd, 1968-75. President: Birmingham Chamber of Commerce, 1960-61; Soc. of Motor Manufrs and Traders, 1962-64 (Dep. Pres., 1964-65; Chm., Exec. Cttee, 1968-72); Past Mem., Advisory Council, ECGD (Board of Trade); Mem., UK Committee of Federation of Commonwealth and British Chambers of Commerce; Past Vice-Pres., West Midlands Engineering Employers' Assoc.; Governor, Chm. Finance Cttee, Dep. Chm. Executive Council (Chm., 1966-75), Royal Shakespeare Theatre; Pres., Loft Theatre, Leamington Spa. Pro-Chancellor, Birmingham Univ., 1966-75; Hon. LLD Birmingham, 1975. Pres., Automobile Golfing Soc. Mem. Court, Worshipful Co. of Coach and Coach Harness Makers. *Recreations:* theatre, golf, fishing. *Address:* Fairford, 8 Hill Park, Ballakillowey, Colby, Isle of Man. *T:* Port St Mary 2573. *Club:* Royal and Ancient (St Andrews).

FARNCOMBE, Charles Frederick, CBE 1977; FRAM; Musical Director: Handel Opera Society, since 1955; Royal Court Theatre, Drottningholm, Sweden, since 1970; *b* 29 July 1919; *o s* of Harold and Eleanor Farncombe, both of London; *m* 1963, Sally Mae (*née* Felps), Riverside, Calif, USA; one *d. Educ:* London Univ., 1936-40 (Archibald Dawnay Scholarship in Civil Engrg, 1936) (BSc Hons (Eng) 1940); Royal Sch. of Church Music, 1947-48; Royal Academy of Music, 1948-51 (RAM, Mann Prize). Civil Engr to John Mowlem & Co, 1940-42. Served War, 1942-47, as Captain in REME, in 21st Army Gp. Free Lance Conductor: formed Handel Opera Soc. (with encouragement of late Prof. Dent), 1955; Chief Conductor, Royal Court Theatre, Drottningholm, Sweden, 1970-. AMICE, 1945 (resigned later); FRAM 1963 (ARAM 1962). Hon DMus Columbus Univ., Ohio, USA, 1959. Gold Medal of the Friends of Drottningholm, 1971; Hon. Fellow Royal Swedish Academy of Music, 1972. *Recreations:* cajoling singers, swimming, cottage on Offa's Dyke. *Address:* c/o 2 Westover Road, SW18.

FARNDALE, Maj.-Gen Martin Baker; Director of Military Operations, MoD (Army), since 1978; *b* Alberta, 6 Jan. 1929; *s* of Alfred Farndale and Margaret Louise Baker; *m* 1955, Margaret Anne Buckingham; one *s. Educ:* Yorebridge Grammar Sch., Yorks. Joined Indian Army, 1946; RMA, Sandhurst, 1947; commnd RA, 1948; Egypt, 1949; 1st RHA, 1950-54 (Germany from 1952); HQ 7 Armoured Div., 1954-57; Staff College, 1959; HQ 17 Gurkha Div., Malaya, 1960-62; MoD, 1962-64; comd Chestnut Troop 1st RHA, Germany and Aden, 1964-66; Instructor, Staff Coll., 1966-69; comd 1st RHA, UK, N Ire., Germany, 1969-71; MoD, 1971-73; comd 7th Armoured Bde, 1973-75. Dir, Public Relations (Army), 1976-78. *Publications:* Story of Royal Artillery 1914-18, 1976; articles for British Army Rev. and Jl RA. *Recreation:* military history. *Address:* c/o Lloyds Bank, Cox's and King's Branch, 6 Pall Mall, SW1. *Club:* East India, Devonshire, Sports and Public Schools.

FARNHAM, 12th Baron, *cr* 1756; **Barry Owen Somerset Maxwell;** Bt (Nova Scotia) 1627; Director, Brown, Shipley & Co. Ltd (Merchant Bankers), since 1959; Chairman, Brown, Shipley Holdings Ltd, since 1976; *b* 7 July 1931; *s* of Hon. Somerset Arthur Maxwell, MP (died of wounds received in action, 1942), and Angela Susan (*d* 1953), *o d* of late Capt. Marshall Owen Roberts; *S* grandfather 1957; *m* 1959, Diana Marion, *er d* of Nigel Gunnis; two adopted d. *Educ:* Eton; Harvard Univ. *Heir: b* Hon. Simon Kenlis Maxwell [*b* 12 Dec. 1933; *m* 1964, Karol Anne, *d* of Maj.-Gen. G. E. Prior-Palmer, CB, DSO, and Katherine Edith Bibby; two *s* one *d* (of whom one *s* one *d* are twins)]. *Address:* 11 Earl's Court Gardens, SW5; Farnham, Co. Cavan. *Clubs:* Boodle's; Kildare Street and University (Dublin).

FARNHILL, Rear-Adm. Kenneth Haydn, CB 1968; OBE 1945; Secretary, Defence, Press and Broadcasting Committee, since 1973; *b* 13 April 1913; *s* of late H. Haydn Farnhill, Bedford; *m* 1938, Helen May, *d* of late W. Houghton, Southsea; one *s* one *d. Educ:* Bedford. Joined RN, 1930. Served 1939-45: Home Fleet, Admty, Eastern Fleet. Sec. to Controller of Navy, 1953-56; Captain, RN Supply Sch., 1958-59; IDC 1960; Dir of

Management and Support of Intelligence, MoD, 1966-69. Comdr 1948; Captain 1957; Rear-Adm. 1966; retd 1969. *Address:* 1 Christchurch Gardens, Widley, Portsmouth, Hants. *T:* Cosham 77187.

FARNSWORTH, John Windsor; Chairman, East Midlands Economic Planning Board, 1965-72; *b* 5 May 1912; *yr s* of late Arthur Claude and Annie Farnsworth, Derby; *m* 1938, Betty Mary Bristow; two *s. Educ:* Hanley High Sch.; Balliol Coll., Oxford; Univ. of Birmingham. Asst Comr, Nat. Savings Cttee, 1935; transf. to Min. of Nat. Insurance, 1948; Regional Controller, N Midland Region, Min. of Pensions and Nat. Insurance, 1961; transf. to Dept of Economic Affairs, 1965; Min. of Housing and Local Govt, later Dept of the Environment, 1969. Pres., Nottingham and E Mids Group, Royal Inst. of Public Administration, 1966-68. *Address:* 143 Melton Road, West Bridgford, Nottingham. *T:* Nottingham 231937.

FARQUHAR, Charles Don Petrie, JP; Lord Provost and Lord Lieutenant of City of Dundee 1975-77; Area Manager, Community Industry, since 1972; engineer; *b* 4 Aug. 1937; *s* of late William Sandeman Farquhar and Annie Preston Young Farquhar; *m* 1960, Marlowe Joan Crawford Farquhar; two *d. Educ:* Liff Road and St Michael's Primary Schs, Dundee; Stobswell Secondary Sch., Dundee. Served with Royal Engineers (Trng NCO); subseq. supervisory staff, plant engrg. Mem., Labour Party Parly Panel; City Councillor, Dundee, 1965-75 (ex-Convener, Museums, Works and Housing Cttees); Mem. Council of Management, Scottish Special Housing Assoc. JP Dundee, 1974. *Recreations:* fresh-water angling, gardening, caravanning, numismatics, do-it-yourself. *Address:* 68 Foggyley Gardens, Dundee DD2 3LU. *T:* Dundee 610707.

FARQUHAR, Lt-Col Sir Peter (Walter), 6th Bt, *cr* 1796; DSO 1943 (and Bar 1944); JP; 16th/5th Lancers; RAC Reserve of Officers, retired; *b* 8 Oct. 1904; *s* of 5th Bt and Violet (*d* 1959), *d* of Col Charles Seymour Corkran, late Grenadier Guards; *S* father, 1918; *m* 1937, Elizabeth Evelyn, *d* of late Francis Cecil Albert Hurt; three *s. Educ:* Eton; RMC, Sandhurst. Served War of 1939-45, France, Middle East and Italy (wounded thrice, DSO and Bar). Pres., Swindon Council of Boys' Clubs; Vice-Pres., Nat. Assoc. of Boys' Clubs. Joint-Master of Portman Hounds, 1947-59. JP Dorset, 1955. *Heir: s* Michael Fitzroy Henry Farquhar [*b* 29 June 1938; *m* 1963, Veronica Geraldine, *e d* of Patrick Hornidge, Newton Ferrers, and of Mrs M. F. L. Beebee, Walton, Radnorshire; two *s*]. *Address:* West Kington House, Chippenham, Wiltshire SN14 7JE. *T:* Castle Combe 782331.
See also Baron Dulverton.

FARQUHARSON of Invercauld, Captain Alwyne Arthur Compton, MC 1944; JP; Head of Clan Farquharson; *b* 1 May 1919; *er s* of late Major Edward Robert Francis Compton, JP, DL, Newby Hall, Ripon, and Isle of Mull, and Sylvia, *y d* of A. H. Farquharson; recognised by Lord Lyon King of Arms as Laird of Invercauld (16th Baron of Invercauld; *S* aunt 1941), also as Chief of name of Farquharson and Head of Clan, since 1949; assumed (surname) Compton as a third fore-name and assumed surname of Farquharson of Invercauld, by warrant granted in Lyon Court, Edinburgh, 1949; *m* 1949, Frances Strickland Lovell, *d* of Robert Pollard Oldham, Seattle, Washington, USA. *Educ:* Eton; Magdalen Coll., Oxford. Joined Royal Scots Greys, 1940. Served War, 1940-45, Palestine, N Africa, Italy, France (wounded); Captain 1943. County Councillor, Aberdeenshire, 1949-75, JP 1951. *Address:* Invercauld, Braemar, Aberdeenshire. *T:* Braemar 213. *Club:* Bath.

FARQUHARSON, Donald Henry, QC 1972; a Recorder of the Crown Court, since 1972; *b* 1928; *yr s* of Charles Anderson Farquharson, Logie Coldstone, Aberdeenshire, and Florence Ellen Fox; *m* 1960, Helen Mary, *er d* of Comdr H. M. Simpson, RN (retd), Abbots Brow, Kirkby Lonsdale, Westmorland; three *s* (one *d* decd). *Educ:* Royal Commercial Travellers Sch.; Keble Coll., Oxford (MA). Called to Bar, 1952. Dep. Chm., Essex QS, 1970. *Recreations:* opera, walking. *Address:* (home) Kumra Lodge, Kelvedon Hatch, Brentwood, Essex. *T:* Coxtie Green 72213; (profl) 2 Harcourt Buildings, Temple, EC4. *T:* 01-353 2622.

FARQUHARSON, Sir James (Robbie), KBE 1960 (CBE 1948; OBE 1944); retired, and is now farming; *b* 1 Nov. 1903; *s* of Frank Farquharson, Cortachy, Angus, Scotland, and Agnes Jane Robbie; *m* 1933, Agnes Binny Graham; two *s. Educ:* Royal Technical College, Glasgow; Glasgow Univ. BSc Glasgow 1923. Asst Engineer, LMS Railway, 1923-25; Asst Engineer, Kenya and Uganda Railway, 1925-33; Senior Asst Engineer, Kenya and Uganda Railway, 1933-37; Asst to Gen. Manager, Tanganyika

Railways, 1937-41; Chief Engineer, Tanganyika Railways, 1941-45; General Manager, Tanganyika Railways, 1945-48; Deputy General Manager, East African Railways, 1948-52; Gen. Manager, Sudan Railways, 1952-57; Gen. Manager, East African Railways and Harbours, 1957-61; Asst Crown Agent and Engineer-in-Chief of Crown Agents for Overseas Governments and Administrations, 1961-65. Chm., Millbank Technical Services Ordnance Ltd, 1973-75; Mem., Exec. Cttee, Scottish Council for Develt and Industry. *Publication:* Tanganyika Transport, 1944. *Recreation:* cricket. *Address:* Kinclune, by Kirriemuir, Angus, Scotland. *T:* Kingoldrum 210. *Club:* Nairobi (Kenya).

FARQUHARSON, Robert Alexander, CMG 1975; HM Diplomatic Service; Ambassador to Yugoslavia, since 1977; *b* 26 May 1925; *s* of late Captain J. P. Farquharson, DSO, OBE, RN, and late Mrs Farquharson (*née* Prescott-Decie); *m* 1955, Joan Elizabeth, *o d* of Sir (William) Ivo Mallet, *qv*; three *s* one *d*. *Educ:* Harrow; King's Coll., Cambridge. Served with RNVR, 1943-46. Joined Foreign (now Diplomatic) Service, 1949; 3rd Sec., Moscow, 1950; FO, 1952; 2nd Sec., Bonn, 1955; 1st Sec., Panama, 1958; Paris, 1960; FO, 1964; Counsellor, Dir of British Trade Develt, S Africa, 1967; Minister, Madrid, 1971; Consul-Gen., San Francisco, 1973. *Address:* c/o Foreign and Commonwealth Office, SW1; The Old Rectory, Tollard Royal, Wilts. *Clubs:* Naval and Military, Flyfishers'.

FARQUHARSON-LANG, William Marshall, CBE 1970; Member, National Health Service (Scotland) Staff Commission, 1972-77; *b* 2 July 1908; *s* of late Very Rev. Marshall B. Lang, DD, sometime Moderator, Gen. Assembly of Church of Scotland, and Mary Eleanor Farquharson Lang; *m* 1937, Sheila Clive Parker; one *d*. *Educ:* Edinburgh Acad.; Edinburgh Univ. (MA); London Univ. Sudan Political Service (Educn), 1931-55; Dep. Dir of Educn (Sudan Govt), 1950-55. Mem., 1959, Chm., 1965-72, NE Regional Hosp. Board; Vice-Chm., Scottish Health Services Council, 1964-66; Chm., Cttee on Admin. Practice of Hosp. Bds in Scotland, 1966; Rector's Assessor and Mem., Aberdeen Univ. Court, 1965-76. Mem., Kincardine CC, 1956-59. Laird of Finzean, Aberdeenshire, 1938-61. Hon. LLD Aberdeen, 1972. Coronation Medal, 1953. Sudan Republic Medal, 1977. *Recreations:* fishing, country activities. *Address:* Balnahard House, Finzean, Aberdeenshire. *T:* Feughside 270. *Clubs:* Royal Northern (Aberdeen); New (Edinburgh).

FARR, Dennis Larry Ashwell; Director, City Museums and Art Gallery, Birmingham, since 1969; *b* 3 April 1929; *s* of late Arthur William Farr and late Helen Eva Farr (*née* Ashwell); *m* 1959, Diana Pullein-Thompson (writer), *d* of Captain H. J. Pullein-Thompson, MC, and Joanna (*née* Cannan); one *s* one *d*. *Educ:* Luton Grammar Sch.; Courtauld Inst. of Art, London Univ. (BA, MA). Asst Witt Librarian, Courtauld Inst. of Art, 1952-54; Asst Keeper, Tate Gallery, 1954-64; Curator, Paul Mellon Collection, Washington, DC, 1965-66; Sen. Lectr in Fine Art, and Dep. Keeper, University Art Collections, Univ. of Glasgow, 1967-69. Fred Cook Meml Lecture, RSA, 1974. Hon. Art Adviser, Calouste Gulbenkian Foundation, 1969-73; British Council Fine Arts Adv. Cttee, 1971-; Member: Wright Cttee on Provincial Museums and Galleries, 1971-73; Museums Assoc. Council, 1971-74; Art Panel, Arts Council, 1972-; ICOM(UK) Exec. Bd, 1976-. FRSA 1970; FMA 1972. *Publications:* William Etty, 1958; Catalogue of the Modern British School Collection, Tate Gallery (with M. Chamot and M. Butlin), 1964; British Sculpture since 1945, 1965; New Painting in Glasgow, 1968; Pittura Inglese 1660-1840, 1975; English Art 1870-1940, 1978; articles in: Apollo, Burlington Magazine, etc. *Recreations:* riding, reading, foreign travel. *Address:* Fernhill, 51 St Bernard's Road, Olton, Solihull, West Midlands B92 7DF. *T:* 021-706 9340; The Cottage, Longborough, Glos. *Clubs:* Athenæum, Institute of Contemporary Arts.
See also Denis Cannan.

FARR, George Theodore, FRICS; Commissioner of Valuation for Northern Ireland, since 1970; *b* 4 Oct. 1920; *e s* of George Theodore Symons Farr and Sylvia Farr; *m* 1942, Muriel, *yr d* of T. J. Dempster; one *s* two *d*. *Educ:* Belfast Technical Coll.; Coll. of Estate Management. Entered NI Civil Service, in Valuation and Ordnance Survey Dept of Min. of Finance, 1937. Served War, in Royal Engineers, 1939-46 (despatches, Central Med.). Valuation Div., 1946-47; Belfast Corp., 1947-48, subseq. Valuation Div. Chm. NI Br., RICS, 1974-75; Mem., Council for NI on Gen. Council, RICS, 1977-. Mem., Belfast County Scout Council. *Recreation:* Boy Scout movement. *Address:* 127 Upper Lisburn Road, Finaghy, Belfast BT10 0LG. *T:* Belfast 614735. *Club:* Civil Service.

FARR, John Arnold; MP (C) Harborough Division of Leicestershire since 1959; Member of Lloyd's; *b* 25 Sept. 1922; *er*

s of late Capt. John Farr, JP, and Mrs M. A. Farr, JP; *m* 1960, Susan Ann, *d* of Sir Leonard Milburn, 3rd Bt, and of Joan Lady Milburn, Guyzance Hall, Acklington, Northumberland; two *s*. *Educ:* Harrow. RN, 1940-46; now in Reserve. Executive Dir, Home Brewery and Apollo Productions Ltd, 1950-55. Pres. Worksop Boys Club, 1951-55. Contested Ilkeston, General Election, 1955. Past Member: East Midlands Land Tribunal and Council of Notts Branch of Country Landowners Association. *Recreations:* cricket and shooting. *Address:* Shortwood House, Lamport, Northants. *T:* Maidwell 260; 11 Vincent Square, Westminster, SW1; Tanrago, Beltra, Co. Sligo. *T:* Beltra 6. *Clubs:* Boodle's, MCC.

FARR, Air Vice-Marshal Peter Gerald Desmond, CB 1968; OBE 1952; DFC 1942; retired; Director, Brain Research Trust, since 1973; *b* 26 Sept. 1917; *s* of late Gerald Farr and Mrs Farr (*née* Miers); *m* 1949, Rosemarie, *d* of late R. S. Haward; two *s* one *d*. *Educ:* Tonbridge Sch. Commnd. in RAF, 1937; flying duties, Middle East, 1938-39; served War of 1939-45, Middle East, India and Burma; OC, No. 358 Sqdn, 1944-45; OC, RAF Pegu, 1945-46; Air Min., 1947-50; OC, 120 Sqdn, 1950-51; Dep. Dir, Jt Anti-Submarine sch., 1952-54; OC, RAF Idris, 1954-55; Air Min., Policy and Plans, 1956-58; Directing Staff, Jt Services Staff Coll., 1959; SASO, Malta, 1960-63; OC, RAF Kinloss, 1963-64; Air Officer Administration, RAF Germany, 1964-68; HQ Strike Command, 1968-69; AO i/c Admin, Strike Comd, 1969-72. *Recreations:* golf, fishing, music. *Address:* c/o Lloyds Bank, Great Missenden, Bucks. *Club:* Royal Air Force.

FARRANT, Maj.-Gen. Ralph Henry, CB 1964; retd; Chairman, Royal National Lifeboat Institution, since 1975; *b* 2 Feb. 1909; *s* of late Henry Farrant, MICE, Rye, Sussex; *m* 1932, Laura Bonella, *d* of late Lieut-Col G. Clifford M. Hall, CMG, DSO; two *d*. *Educ:* Rugby; RMA, Woolwich. 2nd Lieut, RA 1929; Field and Mountain Artillery till 1938. War of 1939-45: Tech. Appts in Min. of Defence (I) and HQ, MEF, 3rd British Inf. Div., 1944. Lieut-Col 1950, Min. of Supply; Col 1954; Brig. 1957; Dir of Munitions, Brit. Jt Services Mission, Washington, 1955-58; Sen. Mil. Officer, Armament R&D Estabt, 1958-61; Maj.-Gen. 1961; Vice-Pres., Ordnance Board, 1961-63; Pres. of Ordnance Bd, War Office, 1963-64. Yachtsman's Award, RYA, 1973. *Recreation:* sailing. *Address:* King's Acre, Grange Road, Wareham, Dorset. *Clubs:* Army and Navy, Royal Yacht Squadron, Royal Ocean Racing, Royal Artillery Yacht.

FARRAR-HOCKLEY, Lt-Gen. Sir Anthony Heritage, KCB 1977; DSO 1953 and bar 1964; MBE 1957; MC 1944; author (Military History); GOC South East District, since 1977; *b* 8 April 1924; *s* of late Arthur Farrar-Hockley; *m* 1945, Margaret Bernadette Wells; two *s* (and one *s* decd). *Educ:* Exeter Sch. War of 1939-45 (despatches, MC): enlisted under-age in ranks of The Gloucestershire Regt and served until Nov. 1942; commissioned into newly forming 1st Airborne Div., campaigning in Greece, Italy, S France, to 1945. Palestine, 1945-46; Korea, 1950-53; despatches, 1954; Cyprus and Port Said, 1956; Jordan, 1958; College Chief Instructor, RMA Sandhurst, 1959-61; commanded parachute bn in Persian Gulf and Radfan campaign, 1962-65; Principal Staff Officer to Dir of Borneo Ops, 1965-66; Comdr, 16 Parachute Bde, 1966-68; Defence Fellowship, Exeter Coll., Oxford, 1968-70 (BLitt); DPR (Army), 1970; Comdr, Land Forces, N Ireland, 1970-71; GOC 4th Div., 1971-73; Dir, Combat Development (Army), 1974-77. Col Comdt, Prince of Wales's Div., 1974-. *Publications:* The Edge of the Sword, 1954; (ed) The Commander, 1957; The Somme, 1964; Death of an Army, 1968; Airborne Carpet, 1969; War in the Desert, 1969; General Student, 1973; Goughie: the Life of General Sir Hubert Gough, GCB, GCMG, KCVO, 1975. *Recreations:* cricket, badminton, walking. *Address:* Wellesley House, Aldershot, Hants; Pye Barn, Moulsford, Oxon. *Club:* Savage.

FARRELL, Arthur Acheson, CB 1962; *b* Portadown, 29 July 1898; *s* of late Arthur T. Farrell, Portadown, solicitor, and of Ellen Moorcroft, *d* of late Hugh Anderson, Belfast; *m* 1st, 1925, Margaret Kerr (*d* 1945), *d* of Archibald Irwin, JP, Belfast; three *s*; 2nd, 1954, Wilhelmina (*d* 1973) (*sister* of 1st wife). *Educ:* Campbell Coll., Belfast; Trinity Coll., Dublin. Royal Artillery, 1917-19. Chartered Accountant, 1922; Registrar of Claims Tribunal, 1923; Civil Service, Northern Ireland: Ministry of: Finance, Asst Principal, 1924; Home Affairs, Dep. Principal, 1928, Principal, 1935, Asst Sec., 1939; Public Security, 1940; Commerce, 1954-58. Comptroller and Auditor-Gen. for Northern Ireland, 1959-63, retired. *Recreations:* photography, bowls, carpentry. *Address:* 19 Donegall Park, Finaghy, Belfast 10, Northern Ireland. *T:* Belfast 615238.

FARRELL, Arthur Denis, CMG 1970; *b* 27 Jan. 1906; *s* of Joseph Jessop Farrell, CBE; *m* 1953, Margaret Madeline (*née* Cox); one

s. *Educ:* St Paul's Sch.; Balliol Coll., Oxford. Sixth Form (Classical) Master, Sedbergh Sch., 1929-30, Bradford Grammar Sch., 1930-36; called to the Bar, Middle Temple, 1937; Sixth Form (Classical) Master, Bedford Sch., 1939-41; served RAF, 1941-46. Squadron-Leader; Crown Counsel, Singapore, 1947-51: Legal Draftsman, Fedn of Malaya, 1951-56; Solicitor-Gen., Fedn of Malaya, 1956-58; QC 1957; Puisne Judge, Kenya, 1958-69 (Acting Chief Justice, 1968). Coronation Medal, 1953. *Recreations:* golf, photography, music. *Address:* 64 East Avenue, Bournemouth, Dorset.

FARRELL, James; Procurator Fiscal, South Strathclyde, Dumfries and Galloway (formerly Lanarkshire) at Airdrie, since 1955; Solicitor; *s* of Thomas Farrell and Margaret Farrell (*née* Quigley); *m* 1952, Margaret Clare O'Brien; one *s* three *d*. *Educ:* Our Lady's High Sch., Motherwell; St Patrick's Coll., Armagh, N Ireland; Glasgow Univ. (BL). In private practice as a solicitor, prior to joining Procurator Fiscal Service of the Crown. In latter (and present) capacity, Prosecutor for the Crown in the Sheriff Court, leading evidence at inquiries, there, into circumstances of death, particularly in suspicious, sudden and unexplained circumstances, fatal accidents, and where the public interest generally is involved; precognition and preparation of cases for High Court of Justiciary, and investigation relating to estates where the Crown may have to intervene as Ultimus Haeres, etc. *Recreations:* golf, bridge, gardening, photography, motoring, walking. *Address:* Clairville, Belleisle Avenue, Uddingston, Glasgow G71 7AP. *T:* (home) Uddingston 3385; (office) Coatbridge 21241. *Club:* St Mungo's Academy FP Centenary (Glasgow).

FARRELL, James Gordon; author; *b* 23 Jan. 1935; *s* of William Farrell and Josephine Farrell (*née* Russell). *Educ:* Rossall Sch.; Brasenose Coll., Oxford (BA). Harkness Fellowship, New York, 1966-68. *Publications:* The Lung, 1964; A Girl in the Head, 1967; Troubles, 1970 (Geoffrey Faber Memorial Prize); The Siege of Krishnapur, 1973 (Booker Prize); The Singapore Grip, 1978. *Address:* c/o Deborah Rogers Ltd, 29 Goodge Street, W1.

FARRELL, James T.; Novelist and Critic; *b* Chicago, Ill, 27 Feb. 1904; *m* Dorothy Butler (divorced); *m* Hortense Alden (divorced, 1955); one *s*; re-married Dorothy Butler (separated). *Educ:* De Paul (now DePaul) Univ., Chicago; Univ. of Chicago; New York Univ., no degrees. Worked for express company, in gasoline filling station, as salesman, etc; received John Simon Guggenheim Memorial Foundation Fellowship in Creative Literature, 1926-37; Nat. Inst. Arts and Letters, NYC. Formerly Adjunct Prof., St Peter's Coll., Jersey City, NJ; in residence, Richmond Coll., Richmond, Va, Sept. 1969-Feb. 1970; Vis. Writer, English Dept, Glasboro Coll., NJ, 1973. Hon. Dr of Letters: Miami Univ., Oxford, Ohio, 1968; Columbia Coll., Chicago, 1974; Glassboro Coll., 1976. Messing Award for Contributions to Literature, St Louis Univ. Library Associates, 1973. *Publications:* Studs Lonigan; A Note on Literary Criticism; Fellow Countrymen (in US as The Collected Short Stories of James T. Farrell); A World Never Made; Gas House McGinty (in US only); No Star is Lost; Tommy Gallagher's Crusade, 1939; Father and Son, 1940 (in England, 1943); Ellen Rogers, 1941 (in England, 1942); $1000 a Week and Other Stories, 1942; My Days of Anger, 1943 (England 1945); To Whom it may Concern, 1944; The League of Frightened Philistines and other Papers; Bernard Clare, 1946 (England 1948); When Boyhood Dreams Come True, 1946; More Fellow-Countrymen, 1946; Literature and Morality, 1947; The Life Adventurous, 1947; A Misunderstanding, 1948; The Road Between, 1949; (under pseudonym of Jonathan Lituleson Fogarty) The Name is Fogarty; An American Dream Girl, 1950; This Man and This Woman, 1951; Yet Other Waters, 1952; The Face of Time (England), 1953; Reflections at Fifty (England), 1954; French Girls are Vicious, 1955; A Baseball Diary, also A Dangerous Woman and Other Stories, 1957; It Has Come to Pass, 1958; Boarding House Blues (novel), 1961; Side Street (stories), 1961; Sound of the City (stories), 1962; The Silence of History (novel), 1963; What Time Collects (novel), 1967; The Collected Poems of James T. Farrell, 1965; Lonely For the Future (novel), 1966; When Time Was Born (prose poem), 1966; New Year's Eve, 1929 (novel), 1967; A Brand New Life (novel), 1968; Childhood Is Not Forever and other Stories, 1969; Judith (novel), 1969; Invisible Swords (novel), 1970; Judith and other stories, 1973; The Dunne Family, 1976. *Address:* c/o Doubleday & Co., 277 Park Avenue, New York, NY 10017, USA.

FARRELL, M. J.; see Keane, Mrs Robert.

FARRELL, Timothy Robert Warwick; Organist, Choirmaster and Composer at HM Chapels Royal, St James's Palace, since 1974; *b* 5 Oct. 1943; *m* 1975, Penelope Walmsley-Clark. *Educ:* Diocesan Coll., Cape Town; Royal Coll. of Music, London, etc.

FRCO, ARCM (piano and organ). Asst Organist, St Paul's, Knightsbridge, 1962-66; Asst Organist, St Paul's Cath., 1966-67; Sub-organist, Westminster Abbey, 1967-74; Organ Tutor at Addington Palace, RSCM, 1966-73. Broadcaster, gramophone records, etc. *Recreations:* golf, walking, sailing. *Address:* St James's Palace, SW1.

FARREN, Most Rev. Neil, DD, DCL; *b* 25 March, 1893; *s* of John Farren and Margaret McLaughlin. *Educ:* St Columb's Coll., Derry; University Coll. (NUI) Dublin; Maynooth Coll., Rome. Prof. St Columb's Coll., Derry, 1920-27 (Maths and Science), Pres., 1927-39; Bishop of Derry, 1939-74. An Asst to Papal Throne. *Publication:* Domicile and Quasidomicile, 1920. *Address:* Mellifont, Grianan Park, Buncrana, Co. Donegal. *T:* Buncrana 66.

FARRER, Brian Ainsworth; a Recorder of the Crown Court (Midland/Oxford Circuit) since 1974; *b* 7 April 1930; *s* of A. E. V. A. Farrer and Gertrude (*née* Hall); *m* 1960, Gwendoline Valerie (*née* Waddoup); two *s* one *d*. *Educ:* King's Coll., Taunton; University Coll., London (LLB). Called to the Bar, Gray's Inn, 1957. *Recreations:* golf, music, chess, bridge. *Address:* Shutt Cross House, Aldridge, Staffs. *T:* Aldridge 52410.

FARRER, Charles Matthew, CVO 1973; Private Solicitor to the Queen, since 1965; Partner in Messrs Farrer & Co, Solicitors, since 1959; *b* 3 Dec. 1929; *s* of Sir (Walter) Leslie Farrer, *qv*, and Hon. Lady Farrer; *m* 1962, Johanna Creszentia Maria Dorothea Bennhold; one *s* one *d*. *Educ:* Bryanston Sch.; Balliol Coll., Oxford (MA). *Recreations:* travel, reading. *Address:* 6 Priory Avenue, Bedford Park, W4. *T:* 01-994 6052. *Club:* United Oxford & Cambridge University.

FARRER, Margaret Irene, OBE 1970; Chairman of Central Midwives Board since 1973; *b* 23 Feb. 1914; *e d* of Alfred and Emblyn Farrer. *Educ:* Poltimore Coll., Exeter; UCH London. SRN, SCM, DN (London), MTD, RST. Midwifery Tutor, General Lying-in Hosp., 1942-49; Matron: St Mary's Hosp., Croydon, 1949-56; Forest Gate Hosp., 1956-71; Chief Nursing Officer, Thames Gp, 1971-74. Member: Central Midwives Bd, 1952-; Central Health Services Council, 1963-74; NE Metropolitan Regional Hosp. Bd, 1969-74; NE Thames Regional Health Authority, 1973-76; Editorial Bd, Midwife and Health Visitor; Hon. Treas., Royal Coll. of Midwives, 1967-76. *Recreations:* gardening, walking. *Address:* Coombe Brook, Dawlish, South Devon. *T:* Dawlish 863323.

FARRER, Sir (Walter) Leslie, KCVO 1948; solicitor (retired); *b* 30 Jan. 1900; 2nd *s* of late Bryan Farrer, Binnegar Hall, Wareham, Dorset; *m* 1926, Hon. Marjorie Laura Pollock, *d* of 1st Viscount Hanworth; one *s* one *d*. *Educ:* Rugby; Balliol. Admitted a Solicitor, 1926; Partner Messrs Farrer & Co., 1927-64; Mem. Council of Law Soc., 1945-52; Mem. Disciplinary Cttee under Solicitors Acts, 1953-63. Private Solicitor to King George VI and to the Queen, 1937-64. Director, London Life Assoc. Ltd (Pres., 1966-73). Pres. Selden Soc., 1955. Prime Warden, Fishmongers' Co., 1968-69. *Recreations:* reading and sight-seeing. *Address:* Charlwood Place Farm, Charlwood, Surrey. *T:* Norwood Hill 862413. *Club:* Travellers'.
See also C. M. Farrer.

FARRER-BROWN, Leslie, CBE 1960; JP; Consultant; Director, Nuffield Foundation, 1944-64; Chairman, Alliance Building Society, since 1975 (Director since 1969); *b* 2 April 1904; *er s* of late Sydney and Annie Brown; *m* 1928, Doris Evelyn, *o d* of late Herbert Jamieson; two *s*. *Educ:* LSE (BSc Econ.), Hon. Fellow 1975; Gray's Inn (Barrister-at-Law, 1932). Asst Registrar, LSE, 1927-28; on Administrative Staff, Univ. of London, 1928-36; Sec., Central Midwives Bd, 1936-45; seconded to Min. of Health, 1941-44. Pres., Surrey and Sussex Rent Assessment Panel, 1965-76. Vice-President, Inst. of Race Relations, 1968-72; Royal Commonwealth Soc., 1969-. Sec., Interdepartmental Cttee on Med. Schs, 1942-44. Chairman: Malta Med. Services Commn, 1956; Highgate Juvenile Court, 1952-61; Highgate Court, 1961-65; Nat. Council of Social Service, 1960-73; Centre for Educational Television Overseas, 1962-70; Overseas Visual Aid Centre, 1958-70; Voluntary Cttee on Overseas Aid and Develt, 1965-76; Centre for Information on Language Teaching, 1966-72; Cttee for Res. and Develt in Modern Languages, 1964-70; Rhodesia Med. Sch. Cttee; Univ. of London Inst. of Child Health, 1966-76. Member: Colonial Adv. Med. Cttee, 1946-61; Colonial Social Science Res. Council, 1954-61; Med. Educn Cttee of UGC, 1945-52; Rating of Charities Cttee, 1958-59; Adv. Council, BBC, 1956-65; Court of Governors, LSE; Chm. Council and Sen. Pro-Chancellor, Univ. of Sussex, 1976-. Trustee, Nuffield Provincial Hospitals Trust, 1955-67; UK Trustee, Commonwealth Foundn, 1966-. JP: Middx, 1947-65;

East Sussex, 1966-. Hon. FDSRCS. Hon. LLD: Birmingham; Witwatersrand; Hon. DSc Keele. *Publication:* (jt) A Short Textbook on Public Health and Social Services. *Recreations:* travel, painting. *Address:* Dale House, Keere Street, Lewes, East Sussex. *Club:* Athenæum.

FARRIMOND, Herbert Leonard, CBE 1977; Chairman, British Transport Hotels, since 1976; Member Council, Advisory, Conciliation and Arbitration Service, since 1974; *b* 4 Oct. 1924; *s* of late George and Jane Farrimond, Newcastle upon Tyne; *m* 1951, Patricia Sara (*née* McGrath); one *s. Educ:* St Cuthbert's Grammar Sch., Newcastle upon Tyne; Durham Univ. BA (Hons) Politics and Economics. Australian Dept of Labour and Nat. Service, 1948-50; Imperial Chemical Industries Ltd, and Imperial Metal Industries Ltd, 1950-68; Upper Clyde Shipbuilders Ltd, 1968-69; Dir of Personnel, Dunlop Ltd, 1969-72; Mem., British Railways Bd, 1972-77. Director: British Rail Engineering Ltd.; British Rail Shipping and Internat. Services Div.; Transmark Ltd (Chm.); Governor, British Transport Staff Coll. Ltd. FCIT; FIPM. *Recreations:* golf, gardening, music. *Address:* Crinan, 26 Box Lane, Boxmoor, Herts. *T:* Hemel Hempstead 52348.

FARRINGTON, Sir Henry Francis Colden, 7th Bt, *cr* 1818; RA retired; *b* 25 April 1914; *s* of Sir Henry Anthony Farrington, 6th Bt, and Dorothy Maria (*d* 1969), *o d* of Frank Farrington; *S* father, 1944; *m* 1947, Anne, *e d* of late Major W. A. Gillam, DSO; one *s* one *d. Educ:* Haileybury. Retired from Army, 1960 (Major). *Heir: s* Henry William Farrington, *b* 27 March 1951. *Address:* Quarry Cleeve, Wiveliscombe, Taunton TA4 2TG. *T:* Wiveliscombe 23219.

FARRIS, Hon. John Lauchlan; Hon. Chief Justice Farris; Chief Justice of British Columbia and Administrator of Province of British Columbia, since 1973; *b* 5 Sept. 1911; *s* of late Senator John Wallace de Beque Farris, QC and late Dr Evlyn Fenwick Farris; *m* 1933, Dorothy Colledge; one *s* two *d. Educ:* Univ. of British Columbia (BA); Harvard Law Sch. (LLB). Lectured on commercial law, Univ. of British Columbia, 1945-55. KC (Canada) 1950. Past Pres., Vancouver Bar Assoc.; Past Chm. of Bd of Governors, Crofton House Sch.; Past Pres., Harvard Club of Vancouver; Pres., Canadian Bar Assoc., 1971-72 (Past Vice-Pres. for BC); Fellow, Amer. Coll. of Trial Lawyers. Hon. Member: Amer. Bar Assoc.; Manitoba Bar Assoc.; Law Soc. of Saskatchewan. Senior Partner, Farris Farris Vaughan Wills & Murphy, until 1973. *Recreations:* boating, woodworking. *Address:* 1403 Angus Drive, Vancouver, BC V6H 1V2, Canada. *T:* (604) 738-1264. *Clubs:* Vancouver (Vancouver); Union (Victoria); Royal Vancouver Yacht, West Vancouver Yacht.

FARROW, Leslie William, CBE 1947; FCA, FID, FRSA; chartered accountant; *b* 7 Oct. 1888; *s* of late Albert Lee Farrow and Elfleda Susan Taylor; *m* 1915, Elsie Beatrice Allman; three *d. Educ:* Alleyn's, Dulwich; London Sch. of Economics. Formerly: dir of public companies, mem. of the Bacon Development Board; Deputy Controller of Paper, 1939-40; Dir for Commercial Relations, 1940-42; Deputy Chm. Rubber Control Board, 1942; Deputy Dir-Gen. (raw materials), Ministry of Supply, 1942; Chm. National Brick Advisory Council, Ministry of Works and Planning, 1942; Chm. Paper Economy Cttee, Ministry of Production, 1942; Mem. of Board of Referees, 1948. Paper Trade Gold Medal Award, 1967. *Address:* Dengie Manor, near Southminster, Essex. *T:* Tillingham 216. *Club:* City of London.

FARROW, Mia (Villiers); actress; *b* 9 Feb. 1945; *d* of John Villiers Farrow and Maureen O'Sullivan; *m* 1970, André Previn, *qv*; three *s* two *d*. TV series: Peyton Place, 1965. Films: Secret Ceremony, 1968; Rosemary's Baby, 1969; John and Mary, 1970; The Public Eye, 1972; The Great Gatsby, 1974. Plays: London stage: Mary Rose, 1973; The Three Sisters, 1974; The House of Bernarda Alba, 1974; Peter Pan, 1975; Royal Shakespeare Company, 1975: The Marrying of Ann Leete, 1975; The Zykovs, Ivanov, 1976; A Midsummer Night's Dream, Leicester, 1976. David Donatello Award, Italy, 1969; Best Actress awards: French Academy, 1969; San Sebastian, 1969; Rio de Janeiro, 1970. *Address:* Surrey, England; Vineyard Haven, Mass, USA.

FARVIS, Prof. William Ewart John, OBE; FIEE; BSc; Member of Science Research Council, since 1976; Professor of Electrical Engineering, University of Edinburgh, since 1976; *b* 12 Dec. 1911. *Educ:* London and Bristol Univs. Student, Instn of Electrical Engineers, 1932; Associate Mem., 1936; Mem., 1943; Fellow, 1956. His Dept in Edinburgh Univ. was awarded Wolfson Foundation Research Grant of £130,700 over 5 yrs for setting up a micro electronics liaison unit. Member, Polytechnics Cttee of SRC, 1977-. *Address:* Department of Electrical Engineering, Edinburgh University, King's Buildings, Mayfield

Road, Edinburgh EH9 3JL. *T:* 031-667 1081, ext. 3260; c/o Institution of Electrical Engineers, Savoy Place, WC2. *T:* 01-240 1871.

FARWELL, Rt. Rev. Gerard Victor; Abbot of Worth, since 1965; Abbot President of English Benedictine Congregation, since 1967; *b* 15 Oct. 1913; 3rd *s* of late Frederick Arthur Farwell and Monica Mary Quin. *Educ:* St Benedict's, Ealing. Entered Downside Abbey, 1932; Housemaster at Downside Sch., 1946-48; Bursar at Worth, 1950-57; Prior of Worth, 1957-65. *Address:* Worth Abbey, Crawley, West Sussex RH10 4SB.

FATEH, A. F. M. Abul; High Commissioner for Bangladesh in the United Kingdom, since 1976; *b* 28 Feb. 1926; *s* of Abdul Gafur and Zohra Khatun; *m* 1956, Mahfuza Banu; two *s. Educ:* Dacca, Bangladesh. MA (English Lit.). Carnegie Fellow in Internat. Peace, 1962-63. Entered Pakistan Foreign Service, 1949; 3rd Secretary: Paris, 1951-53; Calcutta, 1953-56; 2nd Sec., Washington, DC, 1956-60; Dir, Min. of Foreign Affairs, Karachi, 1961-65; 1st Sec., Prague, 1965-66; Counsellor, New Delhi, 1966-67; Dep. High Comr for Pakistan, Calcutta, 1968-70; Ambassador of Pakistan, Baghdad, 1971; Adviser to Actg President of Bangladesh, July, 1971; Foreign Sec., Bangladesh, Jan. 1972; Ambassador of Bangladesh, Paris, 1972-75. *Address:* Bangladesh High Commission, 28 Queen's Gate, SW7 5JA. *T:* 01-584 0081.

FATT, Prof. Paul, FRS 1969; Professor of Biophysics, University College, London, since 1976 (Reader, 1956-76), Fellow 1973. *Publications:* papers in: Jl of Physiology, Proc. Royal Soc., etc. *Address:* Department of Biophysics, University College, Gower Street, WC1.

FAULDS, Andrew Matthew William; MP (Lab) Warley East, since 1974 (Smethwick, 1966-74); *b* 1 March 1923; *s* of late Rev. Matthew Faulds, MA, and of Doris Faulds; *m* 1945, Bunty Whitfield; one *d. Educ:* George Watson's, Edinburgh; King Edward VI Grammar Sch., Louth; Daniel Stewart's, Edinburgh; High Sch., Stirling; Glasgow Univ. Three seasons with Shakespeare Memorial Co., Stratford-upon-Avon; BBC Repertory Co.: Jet Morgan in Journey into Space (BBC). Has appeared in over 35 films and many TV and radio performances. Parliamentary Private Secretary: to Minister of State for Aviation, Min. of Technology, 1967-68; to Postmaster General, 1968-69; Opposition spokesman for the Arts, 1970-73; Chm., British br., Parly Assoc. for Euro-Arab Cooperation, 1974-. *Recreation:* cosseting his constituents. *Address:* 14 Albemarle Street, W1. *T:* 01-499 7589.

FAULKNER, Hon. Arthur James; MP (Labour) for Roskill, NZ, since 1957; President, New Zealand Labour Party, since 1976; *b* Auckland, NZ, 1921; *m* 1945, May Cox; two *s* three *d. Educ:* Otahuhu District High Sch., NZ. Served War of 1939-45 with RAF as Spitfire pilot in UK, N Africa and Europe. Formerly a credit manager. Labour Party organiser for North Island, 1952-57. Contested (Lab) Franklin, 1951; North Shore, 1954. Parliamentary experience on Select Cttees on Defence, Foreign Affairs, Statutes Revision, Local Govt Convener of Labour Caucus Cttees on Defence and Foreign Affairs. Fact-finding missions to South-East Asia, 1963 and 1967; travelled to Europe and UK to discuss EEC matters, 1969. Minister of Defence, Minister i/c War Pensions and Rehabilitation, 1972-74; Minister of Labour and State Services, 1974-75. *Recreations:* fishing, boating, aviation. *Address:* 1 Inverness Avenue, Mt Roskill, Auckland, New Zealand.

FAULKNER, Prof. Douglas, WhSch, BSc, PhD; CEng, FRINA, FIStructE, MSNAME; RCNC; Head of Department of Naval Architecture and Ocean Engineering, University of Glasgow, since 1973; *b* 29 Dec. 1929; *s* of Vincent and Florence Faulkner; *m* 1954, Jenifer Ann Cole-Adams; three *d. Educ:* Sutton High Sch., Plymouth; HM Dockyard Technical Coll., Devonport; RNC, Greenwich. Aircraft Carrier Design, 1955-57; Production Engrg, 1957-59; Structural Research at NCRE, Dunfermline, 1959-63; Asst Prof. of Naval Construction, RNC, Greenwich, 1963-66; Structural Adviser to Ship Dept, Bath, 1966-68; Naval Construction Officer att. to British Embassy, Washington DC, 1968-70, and Mem. Ship Research Cttee, Nat. Acad. of Scis, 1968-71; Res. Associate and Defence Fellow, MIT, 1970-71; Structural Adviser to Ship Dept, Bath, and to the Merrison Box Girder Bridge Cttee, 1971-73. UK Rep., Standing Cttee, Internat. Ship Structures Congress, 1973-. *Publications:* chapters in Ship Structural Design Concepts (Cornell Maritime Press), 1975; papers related to structural design of ships, in Trans RINA, Jl of Ship Res., Internat. Shipbuilding Progress, etc. *Recreations:* hill walking, squash, swimming, music, chess. *Address:* Woodstock, 52 Buchanan Street, Milngavie, Glasgow G62 8AP. *T:* 041-956 4773.

FAULKNER, Sir Eric (Odin), Kt 1974; MBE 1945; Director: Lloyds Bank Ltd (Chairman, 1969-77); Vickers Ltd; *b* 21 April 1914; *s* of late Sir Alfred Faulkner, CB, CBE; *m* 1939, Joan Mary, *d* of Lt-Col F. A. M. Webster; one *s* one *d*. *Educ:* Bradfield; Corpus Christi Coll., Cambridge (Hon. Fellow, 1975). Joined Glyn, Mills & Co., 1936. Served War of 1939-45, Royal Artillery and Leics Yeomanry; Staff Coll.; Bde Major RA, GSO2; commanded 91 Field Regt RA. Rejoined Glyn, Mills & Co., 1946; Local Dir, 1947-50; Exec. Dir, 1950-68; Dep. Chm., 1959-63; Chm., 1963-68. Chm., Cttee of London Clearing Bankers, 1972-74. Pres., British Bankers' Assoc., 1972-73; Chairman: Industrial Soc., 1973-76; City Communications Organisation, 1976-; Jt Dep. Chm., Finance for Industry, 1977-. Warden of Bradfield Coll., 1965. *Recreations:* fishing and walking; formerly cricket and Association football (CUAFC XI 1935). *Address:* Chart Cottage, Seal Chart, Kent. *Club:* Boodle's.

FAULKNER, Capt. George Haines, CB 1947; DSC 1916; Royal Navy; *b* 27 April 1893; *s* of Rev. Thomas George Faulkner and Kate Nicholls; *m* 1st, 1924, Kathleen (*d* 1947), *d* of Dr Henry Wilson, Cheadle, Cheshire; no *c*; 2nd, 1959, Marjorie Lucy Rowland (*d* 1974), Lustleigh, Devon. *Educ:* Lickey Hills Sch., Worcs; RN Colleges, Osborne and Dartmouth. Osborne, 1906; Midshipman, 1910. Served European War, 1914-18, in destroyers (despatches) Battle of Heligoland Bight, special promotion to Lieut; commanded HMS Mystic, Thruster and Patriot, 1918-19; psc 1922-23; served in HMS Hood on Special Service Squadron World Cruise, 1923-24; commanded HMS Voyager, 1926-28; Comdr 1928; Capt. 1935; commanded HMS Bideford, 1937-38; Chief of Staff and Capt. on Staff of C-in-C the Nore, 1939-41; in command of HMS Berwick, 1941-43; Chief of Staff to C-in-C South Atlantic, with rank of Commodore 2nd class and stationed at Capetown, 1943-45; retired list, 1945; re-appointed. First Naval Mem. of New Zealand Naval Board and Chief of Naval Staff, NZ, with rank of Commodore 2nd Class, 1945-47; reverted to retired list, 1947. *Address:* Lynnfield, Lustleigh, Devon. *T:* 215.

FAULKNER, Hugh (Branston); Hon. Director, Help the Aged, since formation in 1962; Managing Director, London Guardian Estate Agency Ltd and director of other companies; *b* Lutterworth, 8 June 1916; *s* of Frank and Ethel Faulkner; *m* 1954, Anne Carlton Milner; one *s* one *d*. *Educ:* Lutterworth Grammar Sch. ACIS. Educn Administration, City of Leicester, 1936-46; Organising Sec., Fellowship of Reconciliation, 1946-54; business career in estate agency from 1954. Christian peace delegate to USSR, 1952, followed by lecture tour in USA, 1953, on internat. relations. Trustee: Phyllis Trust; Lester Trust; Voluntary and Christian Service. *Recreations:* music, gardening. *Address:* 54 Courtenay Gardens, Upminster, Essex. *T:* Upminster 24579. *Club:* National Liberal.

FAULKNER, Dr Hugh Charles; Hon. Adviser to Regional Health Authority, Tuscany; Hon. Lecturer in Social Medicine, Bedford College, University of London, since 1976; Medical Secretary, Medical Practitioners' Union (ASTMS), and Medical Editor of Medical World, 1971-76; *b* 22 Sept. 1912; *s* of Frank Whitehead Faulkner and Emily Maud Knibb; *m*; one *s* two *d*. *Educ:* Oundle Sch.; London Hosp. MRCS, LRCP, MRCGP. Boys' Club Manager, 1932-35; qual. MRCS, LRCP, 1943. Served War, RAMC, 1944-46. Gen. Practitioner, 1948-76. Mem. Council of Medical Practitioners' Union, 1948-76. *Publications:* Medicina di Base in due paesi, Gran Bretagne e l'URSS, 1977; articles in Medical World, Lancet, etc. *Recreation:* attacking the Establishment. *Address:* La Galera, Passo del Sugame, Greve-in-Chianti, Firenze, Italy.

FAULKNER, Most Rev. Leonard Anthony; *see* Townsville, Bishop of, (RC).

FAULKNER, Sir Percy, KBE 1964; CB 1950; Controller of HM Stationery Office and Queen's Printer of Acts of Parliament, 1961-67; *b* 11 May 1907; *s* of late Thomas Faulkner and Margaret A. Hood; *m* 1933, Joyce Rosemary Lois MacDonogh; one *s* one *d*. *Educ:* Royal Academical Institution, Belfast; Trinity Coll., Dublin. Entered Ministry of Transport, 1930; Private Sec. to Permanent Sec., 1935-37; Asst Sec., 1942; Under-Sec., 1947; Dep. Sec. (Inland Transport), 1957; Dep. Sec. (Shipping), 1958-61; Chm. British Cttee on Prevention of Pollution of the Sea by Oil, 1953-57; rep. UK at various international conferences on shipping matters, 1947-60. *Address:* St Columbs, Watford Road, Northwood, Mddx. *T:* Northwood 21700. *Club:* Athenæum.

FAULKS, Hon. Sir Neville (Major Ginner), Kt 1963; MBE 1944; TD 1946; **Hon. Mr Justice Faulks;** Judge of the High Court of Justice, Family Division (formerly Probate, Divorce and Admiralty Division), since 1963; *b* 27 Jan. 1908; *s* of M. J. Faulks, MA and Ada Mabel Faulks; *m* 1st, 1940, Bridget Marigold Bodley (*d* 1963); two *s* one *d*; 2nd, 1967, Elizabeth, widow of Rt Rev. A. G. Parham, MC; one step *s* four step *d*. *Educ:* Uppingham Sch. (scholar); Sidney Sussex Coll., Cambridge (Exhibitioner). Called to the Bar, LLB, 1930; QC 1959. Joined TA; served War of 1939-45 (despatches twice), Alamein. Prosecuting Counsel to Bd of Trade and other ministries at Central Criminal Court, etc., 1946-59. Recorder of Deal, 1957-59; Recorder of Norwich, 1959-63. Chm., Cttee to review Defamation Act, 1952, 1971-74. *Publications:* Fraser on Libel (ed, with late Mr Justice Slade); Investigation into the Affairs of H. Jasper and Company Limited, 1961. *Recreations:* the company of his wife, The Times crossword puzzle. *Address:* 8 Donne Place, SW3 2NG. *T:* 01-581 2611; Wallis's Cottage, Bowden, Dartmouth, South Devon. *T:* Stoke Fleming 597.

See also P. R. Faulks.

FAULKS, Peter Ronald, MC 1943; a Recorder of the Crown Court, since 1972; solicitor in private practice, since 1949; *b* 24 Dec. 1917; *s* of late M. J. Faulks and A. M. Faulks (*née* Ginner); *m* 1949, Pamela Brenda, *d* of Peter Lawless; two *s*. *Educ:* Tonbridge; Sidney Sussex Coll., Cambridge (MA). Served War of 1939-45, Duke of Wellington's Regt, Dunkirk, N Africa, Anzio, etc; Major 1943; wounded 3 times. Admitted a solicitor, 1949. Dep. Chm., Agricultural Land Tribunal (SE England), 1972; Pres., Berks, Bucks and Oxon Law Soc., 1976-77. *Recreation:* country life. *Address:* Downs Cottage, Westbrook, Boxford, Newbury, Berks. *T:* Boxford 382. *Clubs:* MCC, Farmers'.

See also Hon. Sir Neville Faulks.

FAURE, Edgar (Jean); President, National Assembly, France, since 1973; *b* Béziers, 18 Aug. 1908; *s* of Jean-Baptiste Faure and Claire Faure (*née* Lavit); *m* 1931, Lucie Meyer (*d* 1977); two *d*. *Educ:* Ecole de Langues Orientales, Paris. Advocate, Paris Court of Appeal, 1929; Dir of Legislative Services to the Presidency, Council of French Cttee of Nat. Liberation, 1943-44; Asst Deleg. to War Crimes Trials, Nuremberg, 1945; Deputy for the Jura (Radical-Socialist), 1946-58; Mayor of Port-Lesney (Jura), 1947-70; Pres., General Council of the Jura, 1949-67; Secretary of Finance, 1949-50; Minister of Budget, 1950-51; Minister of Justice, 1951-52; Prime Minister, Jan.-Feb. 1952; Pres, Commn of Foreign Affairs of Nat. Assembly, 1952-53; Minister of Finance and Economic Affairs, 1953-54; Minister of Foreign Affairs, Jan.-Feb. 1955; Prime Minister, Feb. 1955-Jan. 1956; Minister of Finance, May-June 1958; Senator for the Jura, 1959-66; Deputy for Doubs, 1966-73; Prof. of Law, Univ. of Dijon, 1962-66; Minister of Agriculture, 1966-68; Minister of Education, 1968-69; Dir of Research, Faculty of Law, Besançon, 1970-72; Pres., Internat. Commn of Develt of Educn, 1971-72; Mayor of Pontarlier, 1971; Minister of State for Social Affairs, 1972-73; Pres., Regional Council, Franche-Comté, 1974-. *Publications:* La politique française du pétrole, 1939; M Langois n'est pas toujours égal à lui-meme (novel), 1950; Le serpent et la tortue (study of China), 1957; La disgrace du Turgot, 1961; Etude sur la capitation de Dioclétian d'après le panégyrique VIII, Prévoir le present, 1966; Philosophie d'une réforme, 1969; L'âme du combat (essay), 1970; Ce que je crois, 1971; Apprendre à être (Rapport de la Commission internationale sur le développement de l'éducation, Unesco), 1972; Pour un nouveau contrat social, 1973. *Address:* 83 avenue Foch, Paris 16e, France; Ermitage de Beaulieu, 77350 France; Hôtel de Lassay, Assemblée nationale, 75007 Paris, France. *Clubs:* Racing, Golf de la Boulie (France).

FAUTEUX, Rt. Hon. (Joseph Honoré) Gérald, PC (Can.) 1970; CC (Canada) 1974; Counsel, O'Brien, Hall, Saunders, since 1974; Chief Justice of Canada, 1970-73; Judge, Supreme Court of Canada, 1949-73; *b* St Hyacinthe, PQ, 22 Oct. 1900; *s* of Homère Fauteux and Héva Mercier; *m* 1929, Yvette Mathieu, Montreal; two *s* three *d*. *Educ:* Collège Sainte-Marie, Montreal; University of Montreal (law degree). Practised law in Montreal; Crown Attorney, 1929; KC Canada 1933; QC Canada 1952; Asst Chief Crown Counsel, 1930-36; Chief Crown Counsel, 1939-44. Life mem. Canadian Bar Assoc., Hon. Sec. of that Assoc. for several years; legal adviser to the Royal Canadian Mounted Police for several years. Prof., 1936-50, Dean, 1949, Law Faculty of McGill Univ.; Univ. of Ottawa: Dean of Law Faculty, 1953-62; Chm. Bd of Govs (of reorganized Univ.) 1965-67; Chancellor, Univ. of Ottawa, 1973. Judge of the Superior Court in Montreal, 1947. Acted as legal adviser to Royal Commission appointed to investigate spying activities in Canada. Hon. LLD: University of Ottawa, 1953; Laval Univ., Quebec, 1957; University of Sudbury, 1958; University of Montreal, 1962; Hon. DCL McGill Univ., Montreal, 1955. *Recreations:* outdoor sports. *Address:* (home) 937 St Clare Road, Town of Mont Royal, PQ, Canada. *T:* 342-5000; (office)

2100 Place du Canada, Montreal, PQ, Canada. *T:* 878-4201. *Club:* Cercle Universitaire (Ottawa).

FAVILLE, Air Vice-Marshal Roy, CBE 1945; *b* Aug. 1908; *s of* late L. W. Faville, Hamilton, New Zealand; *m* 1936, Beatrice Marie Louise, *d* of late Major (retired) J. E. Orr; one *s* one *d. Educ:* Canterbury Coll., University of New Zealand (BEng.). Commissioned, RAF, 1932; OC 42 (TB) Sqdn, 1940-41; OC 140 Wing, 1946-47; Air Force Staff at British Joint Services Mission, USA, 1950-52; Imperial Defence Coll., 1953; OC, RAF, St Eval, 1954. RAF Staff Coll., Bracknell; Asst Comdt, 1955-56; Commandant Aug. 1956; Air Officer Commanding No. 22 Group, RAF, Buntingsdale Hall, Market Drayton, Shropshire, 1957-60, retired 1960. Gen. Manager, Libya, Richard Costain (Middle East) Ltd, 1960-64. Sec., Torch Trophy Trust, 1968-70. *Address:* 103 Collingwood House, Dolphin Square, SW1. *Club:* Royal Air Force.

FAWCETT, Colin, QC 1970; *b* 22 Nov. 1923; *s of* late Frank Fawcett, Penrith; *m* 1952, Elizabeth Anne Dickson; one *s* one *d. Educ:* Sedbergh. Commnd Border Regt, 1943. Called to Bar, Inner Temple, 1952. *Recreations:* fishing, music. *Address:* Fairings, Valley Way, Gerrards Cross, Bucks. *T:* Gerrards Cross 83999.

FAWCETT, James Edmund Sandford, DSC 1942; Professor of International Law, King's College London, since 1976; President, European Commission of Human Rights, since 1972 (Member, since 1962); *b* 16 April 1913; *s of* Rev. Joseph Fawcett and Edith Fawcett; *m* 1937, Frances Beatrice, 2nd *d* of late Dr E. A. Lowe; one *s* four *d. Educ:* Rugby Sch.; New Coll., Oxford. Practised at the Bar, 1937-39 and 1950-55. Fellow of All Souls Coll., Oxford, 1938. Served War of 1939-45, Royal Navy. Asst Legal Adviser to FO, 1945-50 (to UK Delegn to UN and British Embassy, Washington, 1948-50); Gen. Counsel, IMF, 1955-60; Fellow of All Souls Coll., Oxford, 1960-69; Dir of Studies, RIIA, 1969-73. Vis. Fellow, Southampton Univ., 1974. Mem., Inst. of Internat. Law, 1973-; Hon. Mem., Soc. of Public Teachers of Law, 1974-; Mem., Legislative Cttee of Internat. Union for the Conservation of Nature, 1969. *Publications:* British Commonwealth in International Law, 1963; International Law and the Uses of Outer Space, 1968; The Law of Nations (Penguin), 1968; The Application of the European Convention on Human Rights, 1969; numerous articles. *Recreations:* astronomy, piano. *Address:* King's College, Strand, WC2R 2LS.

FAWCETT, John Harold; HM Diplomatic Service; Head of Chancery, Warsaw, since 1975; *b* 4 May 1929; *yr s of* late Comdr Harold William Fawcett, OBE, RN, and of late Una Isobel Dalrymple Fawcett (*née* Gairdner); *m* 1961, Elizabeth Shaw; one *s. Educ:* Radley (Scholar); University Coll., Oxford (Scholar). 1st cl. Hon. Mods 1951, 2nd cl. Lit. Hum. 1953. Nat. Service, RN (Radio Electrician's Mate), 1947-49. British Oxygen Co., 1954-63 (S Africa, 1955-57). Entered Foreign Service, 1963; FO, 1963-66; 1st Sec. (Commercial), Bombay, 1966-69; 1st Sec. and Head of Chancery, Port-of-Spain, 1969-70; Asst, Caribbean Dept, FCO, 1971-72; Head of Icelandic Fisheries Unit, Western European Dept, FCO, 1973; Amb. to Democratic Republic of Vietnam, 1974. *Recreations:* walking, gardening. *Address:* c/o Foreign and Commonwealth Office, SW1. *Clubs:* Brooks's, Savile; Royal Bombay Yacht.

FAWCUS, Sir (Robert) Peter, KBE 1964 (OBE 1957); CMG 1960; Overseas Civil Service, retd; *b* 30 Sept. 1915; *s of* late A. F. Fawcus, OBE; *m* 1943, Isabel Constance (*née* Ethelston); one *s* one *d. Educ:* Charterhouse; Clare Coll., Cambridge. Served RNVR, 1939-46. Joined Colonial Service (District Officer, Basutoland), 1946; Bechuanaland Protectorate: Govt Sec., 1954; Resident Commissioner, 1959; HM Commissioner, 1963-65; retd 1965. *Address:* Dochart House, Killin, Perthshire.

FAWKES, Sir Randol (Francis), Kt 1977; Attorney-at-Law, since 1948; *b* 20 March 1924; *s of* Edward Ronald Fawkes and Mildred Fawkes (*née* McKinney); *m* 1951, Jacqueline Fawkes (*née* Bethel); three *s* one *d. Educ:* public schools in the Bahamas. Called to the Bar, Bahamas, 1948. A founder: Citizen Cttee, 1949; People's Penny Savings Bank, 1951. Elected Mem. (Progressive Liberal Party), House of Assembly, 1956; promoted law establishing Labour Day as Public Holiday, 1961. Founder, and Pres. 1955-, Bahamas Fedn of Labour (led 19 day general strike which resulted in major labour and political reforms, 1958). Represented Labour Party at constitutional confs in London, 1963 and 1968; addressed UN Cttee of 24 on preparation of Bahamas for independence, 1966. *Publications:* You Should Know Your Government, 1949; The Bahamas Government, 1962; The New Bahamas, 1966; The Faith That Moved The Fountain: a memoir of a life and the times, 1977. *Recreations:* simming, music, Bible tract writing. *Address:* PO Box N-7625, John F. Kennedy Drive, Nassau, NP, Bahamas. *T:* (office) 809-32-34053; (home) 809-32-34855.

FAY, Edgar Stewart, QC 1956; **His Honour Judge Fay;** a Circuit Judge (formerly an Official Referee of the Supreme Court of Judicature), since 1971; *b* 8 Oct. 1908; *s of* late Sir Sam Fay; *m* 1st, Kathleen Margaret, *e d* of late C. H. Buell, Montreal, PQ, and Brockville, Ont; three *s* ; 2nd, Jenny Julie Henriette, *yr d* of late Dr Willem Roosegaarde Bisschop, Lincoln's Inn; one *s. Educ:* Courtenay Lodge Sch.; McGill Univ.; Pembroke Coll., Cambridge (MA). Called to Bar, Inner Temple, 1932; Master of the Bench, 1962. Recorder: of Andover, 1954-61; of Bournemouth, 1961-64; of Plymouth, 1964-71; Dep. Chm., Hants QS, 1960-71. Member: Bar Council, 1955-59, 1966-70; Senate of Four Inns of Court, 1970-72. Chm., Inquiry into Crown Agents, 1975-77. *Publications:* Why Piccadilly?, 1935; Londoner's New York, 1936; Discoveries in the Statute Book, 1937; The Life of Mr Justice Swift, 1939. *Address:* Knox End, Ashdon, Saffron Walden, Essex. *T:* Ashdon 275; 13 Egbert Street, NW1. *T:* 01-586 0725.

FAYRER, Sir John (Lang Macpherson), 4th Bt *cr* 1896; caterer; *b* 18 Oct. 1944; *s of* Sir Joseph Herbert Spens Fayrer, 3rd Bt, DSC, and Helen Diana Scott (*d* 1961), *d* of late John Lang; *S* father, 1976. *Educ:* Edinburgh Academy; Scottish Hotel School, Univ. of Strathclyde. Assoc. Mem. Royal Soc. of Health; Mem. Hotel and Catering Inst. *Heir: cousin* Colin Robert Fayrer [*b* 28 Feb. 1907; *m* 1946, Evelyn Elinor May, *d* of late T. A. Carey; two *d*]. *Address:* Overhailes, Haddington, East Lothian.

FAZAN, Sidney Herbert, CMG 1946; CBE 1934 (OBE 1930); *b* 27 June 1888; *s of* Dr C. H. Fazan, Wadhurst, Sussex; *m* 1924, Sylvia (marr. diss., 1946), *d* of Brian Hook, Church, Surrey; one *s* four *d* ; *m* 1949, Phyllis, *d* of John Jeffery; one *s* one *d. Educ:* Epsom Coll.; Christ Church, Oxford. Provincial Commissioner, Kenya, and mem. of Legislative Council, 1936-42; Liaison Officer with East African Forces, 1943-46. *Address:* 110 Dorset Road, Bexhill-on-Sea, East Sussex.

FEA, William Wallace; Director, Guest, Keen & Nettlefolds Ltd, 1958-72 (Deputy Chairman, 1968-72); *b* Cordova, Argentina, 3 Feb. 1907; *s of* Herbert Reginald Fea and Hilda Florence Fea (*née* Norton); *m* 1935, Norah Anne, *d* of Richard Festing; one *s* (and one *s* decd). *Educ:* Cheltenham Coll. (schol.); Brasenose Coll., Oxford (schol.; BA). ACA 1932; FCA. Mem., Council, Inst. of Chartered Accountants, 1953-71; Mem. Council, BIM, 1969-73; Management Cttee, AA, 1971-77. *Recreations:* (mostly geriatric) squash racquets, ski-ing, shooting, lawn tennis, listening to music. *Address:* The Lowe, Worfield, near Bridgnorth, Salop. *T:* Worfield 241. *Clubs:* Lansdowne; Edgbaston Priory (Birmingham).

FEARN, John Martin, CB 1976; Secretary, Scottish Education Department, 1973-76; *b* 24 June 1916; *s of* William Laing Fearn and Margaret Kerr Fearn; *m* 1947, Isobel Mary Begbie, MA, MB, ChB; one *d. Educ:* High Sch. of Dundee; Univ. of St Andrews (MA); Worcester Coll., Oxford. Indian Civil Service, Punjab, 1940-47; District Magistrate, Lahore, 1946; Scottish Home Dept, 1947; Asst Sec., 1956; Under-Sec., 1966; Under-Sec., Scottish Educn Dept, 1968. *Recreation:* golf. *Address:* 31 Midmar Gardens, Edinburgh EH10 6DY. *T:* 031-447 5301. *Club:* New (Edinburgh).

FEARN, Patrick Robin; HM Diplomatic Service; Counsellor, Head of Chancery and Consul General, British Embassy, Islamabad, since 1977; *b* 5 Sept. 1934; *s of* Albert Cyprian Fearn and Hilary (*née* Harrison); *m* 1961, Sorrel Mary Lynne Thomas; three *s* one *d. Educ:* Ratcliffe Coll.; University Coll., Oxford (BA Hons, Mod. Langs). Nat. Service, Intelligence Corps, 1952-54. Overseas marketing, Dunlop Rubber Co. Ltd, 1957-61; entered Foreign service, 1961; FO, 1961-62; Third, later Second Sec., Caracas, 1962-64; Havana, 1965; First Sec., Budapest, 1966-68; FCO, 1969-72; Head of Chancery, Vientiane, 1972-75; Asst Head of Science and Technol. Dept, FCO, 1975-76. *Recreations:* tennis, golf, reading, family life. *Address:* c/o Foreign and Commonwealth Office, SW1; 8 Victoria Grove Mews, Ossington Street, W2. *T:* 01-229 9496; 14 Gastard, Corsham, Wilts. *T:* Corsham 713067.

FEARNLEY, John Thorn; HM Diplomatic Service, retired; *b* 9 Feb. 1921; *o s of* Tom Fearnley and Grace Gertrude (*née* Thorn); *m* 1947, Margaret Ann Davies (marr. diss. 1974); two *s* three *d. Educ:* Manchester Gram. Sch.; Caius Coll., Cambridge (Scholar). Served with RN, 1942-46. Joined Foreign Service, 1947; FO, 1947-48; New York (UN), 1948-50; Tehran, 1950-52; FO, Civil Service Selection Bd, 1953; Tehran, 1953-56; Berlin, 1956-58; FO, 1958-60; Lagos, 1960-62; Paris, 1962-65. Head of Oil Dept, FO, 1965-69; Senior Officers' War Course, RN Coll.,

Greenwich, 1969; Consul-Gen., Frankfurt, 1969-75; Consul-Gen., Sydney, 1975-76. *Recreation:* Monmouth. *Address:* 9 Whitehill Close, Monmouth, Gwent NP5 4FG. *T:* Monmouth 3493. *Club:* United Oxford & Cambridge University.

FEARNLEY SCARR, J. G.; *see* Scarr.

FEATHER, Norman, FRS 1945; FRSE 1946; PhD Cantab; Professor of Natural Philosophy, University of Edinburgh, 1945-75, now Emeritus; *b* Crimsworth, WR Yorks, 16 Nov. 1904; *s* of Samson and Lucy Feather; *m* 1932, Kathleen Grace Burke; one *s* twin *d. Educ:* Bridlington Sch., E Yorks; Trinity Coll., Cambridge (Scholar). BA Cantab, BSc London, 1926; PhD Cantab, 1930. Fellow of Trinity Coll., 1929-33; Associate in Physics, Johns Hopkins Univ., Baltimore, Md, 1929-30; University Demonstrator in Physics, Cambridge, 1933-35; Leverhulme Fellow and Lecturer, University of Liverpool, 1935-36; Fellow and Lecturer in Natural Sciences, Trinity Coll., Cambridge; University Lecturer in Physics, 1936-45. Mem. Ct, Heriot-Watt Univ., 1977-. Gen. Sec., 1956-66, and Pres., 1967-70, RSE. Mackdougall-Brisbane Prize, 1968-70. Hon. LLD Edinburgh, 1975. *Publications:* An Introduction to Nuclear Physics, 1936; Lord Rutherford, 1940; Nuclear Stability Rules, 1952; An Introduction to the Physics of Mass, Length and Time, 1959; An Introduction to the Physics of Vibrations and Waves, 1961; Electricity and Matter: an introductory survey, 1968; Matter and Motion, 1970; numerous papers on radioactivity and nuclear physics in Proc. Royal Society and other jls. *Address:* Department of Physics, James Clerk Maxwell Building, Mayfield Road, Edinburgh EH9 3JZ; 9 Priestfield Road, Edinburgh EH16 5HJ. *T:* 031-667 2631.

FEATHERSTONE, Col William Patrick Davies, MC 1944; TD 1960; Vice Lord-Lieutenant of Staffordshire, since 1976; farmer; *b* 17 Sept. 1919; *s* of late Henry Walter Featherstone, OBE, MD, Hon. LLD, JP, and of Margery Eveline (*née* Harston); *m* Joan Llewellyn, *d* of Lt-Col R. H. Waddy, DSO; two *s* one *d. Educ:* Rugby Sch.; Trinity Coll., Cambridge (BA). Served War, 1939-46: RA, France, Belgium, Holland and Germany. Staffs Yeomanry, 1948-62; Lt-Col Comdg, 1959-62; Hon. Col 1972. Member: W Midlands TAVR Assoc.; Lichfield Diocesan Synod and Bd of Finance, 1976-. DL 1963, JP 1967, Staffs; High Sheriff of Staffs, 1969. *Recreations:* shooting, nature conservation. *Address:* Yoxall Lodge, Newchurch, near Burton-on-Trent, Staffs. *T:* Hoar Cross 237.

FEAVER, Rt. Rev. Douglas Russell; *see* Peterborough, Bishop of.

FEENY, Max Howard; a Recorder of the Crown Court, since 1972; *b* 5 Nov. 1928; *s* of late Howard Raymond John Feeny and of Frances Kate Feeny (*née* Muspratt); *m* 1952, June Elizabeth (*née* Camplin); three *s* four *d. Educ:* Stonyhurst Coll.; Oratory Sch.; Univ. of Birmingham (LLB). Called to Bar, Inner Temple, 1953. *Recreation:* golf. *Address:* 8 Talbot Road, Birkenhead L43 2HH. *Club:* Athenæum (Liverpool).

FEHILY, Rt. Rev. Mgr Thomas Francis; Principal RC Chaplain (Army), 1973-77; *b* 16 Nov. 1917; *s* of late Patrick and Mary Fehily, Ballineen, Co. Cork. *Educ:* Capuchin Franciscan Coll., Rochestown, Co. Cork; St Kieran's Coll., Kilkenny. Ordained, 1942; Motherwell Dio., 1943-53. Commissioned Army Chaplain, 1953; served: Germany, 1953-56; Malaya, 1956-59; Germany and Berlin, 1959-63; RMA, Sandhurst, 1963-66. Senior Chaplain: NI, 1966-67; Singapore, 1967-69; HQ 1 Br. Corps, 1969-71; Western Command, 1971; Northern Command, 1972-73. *Recreations:* fishing, golf. *Address:* St John's, Blackwood, Kirkmuirhill, Lanarkshire ML11 9RZ.

FEHR, Basil Henry Frank; Chairman, Frank Fehr & Co. Ltd London and group of companies, since 1957; Chairman, Fehr Bros Inc. New York and group of companies, since 1970; *b* 11 July 1912; *s* of Frank E. Fehr, CBE and Jane (*née* Poulter); *m* 1st, 1936, Jane Marner (*née* Tallent) (marr. diss. 1951); two *s* one *d*; 2nd, 1951, Greta Constance (*née* Bremner) (marr. diss. 1971); one *d* one step *d*; 3rd, 1974, Anne Norma (*née* Cadman); one *d. Educ:* Rugby Sch.; Neûchatel Ecole de Commerce, Switzerland. Served War, 1939-45: HAC, later Instr, Gunnery Sch. of Anti-Aircraft, RA; retd Major. Joined father in family firm, Frank Fehr & Co., 1934; Partner, 1936; Governing Dir, Frank Fehr & Co. London, 1948; Pres., Fehr Bros (Manufactures) Inc. New York, 1949. Chairman: Cocoa Assoc. of London, 1952; London Commodity Exchange, 1954; London Oil and Tallow Trades Assoc., 1955; Copra Assoc. of London, 1957; Inc. Oilseed Assoc., 1958; United Assocs Ltd, 1959. Elected to Baltic Exchange, 1936; Dir, Baltic Mercantile and Shipping Exchange, 1963-69 and 1970-, Vice Chm. 1973-75, Chm. 1975-77. *Recreations:* sports generally, farming. *Address:* Slodden Farm, Dymchurch, Romney Marsh, Kent. *T:*

Dymchurch 2241; 64 Queen Street, EC4R 1ER. *T:* 01-248 5066. *Clubs:* City Livery, Aldgate Ward, MCC, Royal Automobile; West Kent Cricket; Littlestone Golf.

FEIBUSCH, Hans; painter, mural painter, lithographer, sculptor, writer; *b* 15 Aug. 1898; *s* of Dr Carl Feibusch and Marianne Ickelheimer; *m* 1935, Sidonie (*d* 1963), *e d* of D. Gestetner. *Educ:* Frankfurt a/M and Munich Univs. Studied at the Berlin Academy, at Paris Art Schs, in Florence and Rome; received German State award and grant in 1931; pictures in German Public Galleries; work banned and destroyed by Nazis in 1933; since then in London; large mural paintings in churches: St Wilfred's, Brighton; St Elizabeth's, Eastbourne; St Martin's, Dagenham; St John's, Waterloo Road, SE1; St Ethelburga's, Bishopsgate; St Alban's, Holborn; Town Hall, Dudley; Civic Centre, Newport, Mon; Chichester Cathedral; Chichester Palace; Parish Churches, Egham, Goring, Wellingborough, Welling, Preston, Plumstead, Eltham, Portsmouth, Bexley Heath, Wembley, Merton, Southwark, Harrow, Exeter, Battersea, Rotherhithe, Plymouth, Coventry, Christchurch Priory, Bournemouth, Christ Church, St Laurence, Sydney, Portmeirion, Bath; West London Synagogue. 5 one-man exhibns. Much portrait and figure sculpture, 1975-. German Cross of Merit, 1967. *Publications:* Mural Painting, 1946; The Revelation of Saint John, 1946. *Recreations:* music and poetry. *Address:* 30 Wadham Gardens, NW3. *Club:* Athenæum.

FEILDEN, Bernard Melchior, CBE 1976 (OBE 1969); FRIBA 1968 (ARIBA 1949); Partner, Feilden and Mawson, Chartered Architects, 1956-77; Director International Centre for the Preservation and Reconstruction of Cultural Property, Rome, since 1977; *b* 11 Sept. 1919; *s* of Robert Humphrey Feilden, MC, and Olive Feilden (*née* Binyon); *m* 1949, Ruth Mildred Bainbridge; two *s* two *d. Educ:* Bedford Sch. Exhibr, Bartlett Sch. of Architecture, 1938. Served War of 1939-45: Bengal Sappers and Miners. AA Diploma (Hons), 1949; Bratt Colbran Schol., 1949. Architect, Norwich Cathedral, 1963-77; Surveyor to the Fabric: York Minster, 1965-77; St Paul's Cathedral, 1969-. Hoffman Wood Prof. of Architecture, Leeds Univ., 1973-74. Mem., Ancient Monuments Bd (England), 1964-; Mem. Council, RIBA, 1972-77; President: Ecclesiastical Architects' and Surveyors' Assoc., 1975-77; Guild of Surveyors, 1976-77. FSA 1969; FRSA 1973. Corresp. Mem., Architectes en Chef, France. DUniv York, 1973. *Publication:* The Wonder of York Minster, 1976; articles in Architectural Review, Chartered Surveyor, AA Quarterly. *Recreations:* painting, sailing, fishing, photography. *Address:* 6 The Close, Norwich NR1 4DH. *T:* 26623; 13Via Di San Michele, Rome. *Club:* Athenæum.
See also G. B. R. *Feilden.*

FEILDEN, Geoffrey Bertram Robert, CBE 1966; FRS 1959; MA Cantab, FIMechE; Director-General, British Standards Institution, since 1970 (Deputy Director-General, 1968-70); *b* 20 Feb. 1917; *s* of Major R. H. Feilden, MC, RFA, and Olive (*née* Binyon); *m* 1st, Elizabeth Ann Gorton; one *s* two *d*; 2nd, Elizabeth Diana Angier (*née* Lloyd). *Educ:* Bedford Sch.; King's Coll., Cambridge. Lever Bros. and Unilever Ltd, 1939-40; Power Jets Ltd, 1940-46; Ruston and Hornsby Ltd, 1946-59; Chief Engineer, Turbine Dept, 1949; Engineering Dir, 1954; Man. Dir, Hawker Siddeley Brush Turbines Ltd, and Dir of Hawker Siddeley Industries Ltd, 1959-61; Gp Technical Dir, Davy-Ashmore Ltd, 1961-68. Member: Cttees and Sub-Cttees of Aeronautical Research Council, 1947-62; BTC Res. Adv. Council, 1956-61; Council for Sci. and Indust. Res. of DSIR, 1961-65; Design Council (formerly CoID), 1966- (Dep. Chm., 1977-); Central Adv. Council for Science and Technology, 1970-71; Vis. Cttee to RCA, 1968-. Member, Royal Society Delegation: to USSR, 1965; Latin America, 1968; People's Republic of China, 1975. Technical Adviser to Govt of India, 1968. DSIR Visitor to Prod. Engineering Res. Assoc. of Gt Brit., 1957-65, and to Machine Tool Industry Res. Assoc., 1961-65. Member Council: Royal Society (a Vice-Pres., 1967-69); IMechE, 1955-61, 1969-; Univ. of Surrey, 1977-. Dir, Averys Ltd, 1974-. Hon. DTech Loughborough, 1970; Hon. DSc QUB, 1971; Hon. FIStructE 1976. *Publications:* Gas Turbine Principles and Practice (contributor), 1955; First Bulleid Memorial Lecture (Nottingham Univ.), 1959; Report, Engineering Design, 1963 (Chm. of Cttee); numerous papers and articles on engineering subjects. *Recreations:* sailing, ski-ing, driving kitchen and garden machines. *Address:* Greys End, Rotherfield Greys, Henley-on-Thames, Oxon. *T:* Rotherfield Greys 211; 2 Park Street, W1A 2BS. *T:* 01-629 9000. *Club:* Athenæum.
See also B. M. *Feilden.*

FEILDEN, Sir Henry (Wemyss), 6th Bt *cr* 1846; Civil Service, Clerical, since 1960; *b* 1 Dec. 1916; *s* of Col Wemyss Gawne Cunningham Feilden, CMG (*d* 1943) (3rd *s* of 3rd Bt) and of

Winifred Mary Christian, *d* of Rev. William Cosens, DD; *S* cousin, Sir William Morton Buller Feilden, 5th Bt, 1976; *m* 1943, Ethel May, 2nd *d* of John Atkinson, Annfield Plain, Co. Durham; one *s* two *d*. *Educ:* Canford Sch.; King's Coll., London. Served War, RE, 1940-46. *Recreation:* watching cricket. *Heir: s* Henry Rudyard Feilden, *b* 26 Sept. 1951. *Address:* Little Dene, Heathfield Road, Burwash, Etchingham, East Sussex TN19 7HN. *T:* Burwash 882205. *Club:* MCC.

FEILDEN, Maj.-Gen. Sir Randle Guy, KCVO 1953; CB 1946; CBE 1944 (OBE 1943); DL; *b* 14 June 1904; *e s* of Major P. H. G. Feilden; *m* 1929, Mary Joyce, *d* of Sir John Ramsden, 6th Bt; two *s* (and one *s* decd). *Educ:* Eton; Magdalene Coll., Cambridge. Coldstream Guards, 1925; ADC GOC London Dist, 1933-36; Regimental Adjutant, 1936-39; Staff Capt. 7 Gds Bde 1939-40; DAQMG 3 Div. April-Sept. 1940; AQMG 5 Corps, 1940-41; AA and QMG Guards Armoured Division, 1941-42; DQMG: Home Forces, Feb.-Aug. 1943; 21 Army Group, Aug. 1943-45; Rhine Army, Aug. 1945-March 1946; VQMG, War Office, 1947-49; retired pay, 1949. Oxfordshire: High Sheriff 1971, DL 1975. A Steward of the Jockey Club, 1952, senior Steward, 1954, 1961, 1965-73; Chm., Turf Board, 1965-. *Recreations:* cricket, shooting, racing. *Address:* Old Manor House, Minster Lovell, Oxford. *T:* Asthall Leigh 228; 3 Kingston House South, SW7. *T:* 01-589 7135. *Clubs:* Turf, Pratt's, White's.

FEILDING, family name of **Earl of Denbigh.**

FEILDING, Viscount; Alexander Stephen Rudolph Feilding; *b* 4 Nov. 1970; *s* and *heir* of Earl of Denbigh and Desmond, qv.

FELDBERG, Wilhelm Siegmund, CBE 1963; MD Berlin; MA Cantab; FRS 1947; Professor Emeritus; Personal Grant Holder, National Institute for Medical Research, London, since Nov. 1974; Hon. Lecturer, University of London, since 1950; *b* 19 Nov. 1900; *m* 1925, Katherine (*d* 1976), *d* of late Karl Scheffler; one *d* (and one *s* decd). Reader in Physiology, Cambridge Univ., until 1949; Head of Physiology and Pharmacology Division, National Institute for Medical Research, London, 1949-65 (Hon. Head of Division, 1965-66); Head, Lab. of Neuropharmacology, Nat. Inst. for Med. Res., 1966-74. Dunham Lecturer, Harvard Univ., 1953; Evarts Graham Memorial Lectr., Washington Univ., St Louis, USA, 1961; Aschoff Memorial Lectr, Freiburg Univ., Germany, 1961; Dixon Memorial Lectr, RSM, 1964; William Withering Lectr, 1966; Nat. Research Council of Canada/Nuffield Foundn Lectr, 1970-71; Ferrier Lectr, Royal Soc., 1974. Hon. Member: Br. Pharmacol. Soc.; RSM; Physiol. Soc.; Soc. française d'allergie; Deutsche Phys. Gesell.; Deutsche Pharm. Gesell. Hon. MD: Freiburg, Berlin, Cologne, Liège; Hon. DSc Bradford, 1973; Hon. LLD: Glasgow, 1976; Aberdeen, 1977. Grand Cross, Order of Merit of German Federal Republic, 1961. Baly Medal, 1963; Schmiedeberg Plakette, 1969; Stöhr Medal, 1970. *Publications:* Histamin (with E. Schilf); A Pharmacological Approach to the Brain from its Inner and Outer Surface, 1963; articles in med. and scientific jls. *Address:* National Institute for Medical Research, Mill Hill, NW7 1AA. *T:* 01-959 3666; Lavenham, 74 Marsh Lane, Mill Hill, NW7 4NT. *T:* 01-959 5545.

FELL, Anthony; MP (C) Yarmouth Division of Norfolk, 1951-66 and since 1970; *b* 18 May 1914; *s* of Comdr David Mark Fell, RN; *m* 1938; one *s* one *d*. *Educ:* Bedford Grammar School; New Zealand. Contested (C) Brigg, 1948, South Hammersmith, 1949 and 1950. *Address:* 11 Denny Street, SE11 4UX.

FELL, Charles Percival, LLD; President, Empire Life Assurance Co., Kingston, Ont, 1934-68; Director, Canadian Surety Co., 1947-72; Hon. Director and Member Toronto Advisory Board, Royal Trust Co.; Hon. Governor, McMaster University (Chancellor, 1960-65); *b* Toronto, 1894; *s* of I. C. Fell and Sarah (Branton) Fell, both of Toronto, Ont.; *m* Grace E. Matthews; three *s* one *d*. *Educ:* Winchester Public Sch.; University of Toronto Schs; McMaster Univ. Associated with Dillon, Read & Co., NY, 1921-24; Dominion Securities Corp., Toronto, 1925-29; Chm. Canadian group, Investment Bankers Assoc. of America, 1928. Mem. Bd of Referees (Excess Profits Tax Act, Canada), Ottawa, 1940-45. Pres., Art Gall. of Toronto, 1950-53; Chm., Bd of Trustees, Nat. Gall. of Canada, 1953-59. Coronation Medal, Canada, 1953. Hon. LLD McMaster Univ., 1957. *Address:* 52 Park Lane Circle, Don Mills, Ont. M3C 2N2, Canada. *T:* 447-7523. *Clubs:* York; Toronto.

FELL, Dame Honor Bridget, DBE 1963; FRS 1952; medical research worker, Department of Immunology, University of Cambridge, since 1970; Director, Strangeways Research Laboratory, Cambridge, 1929-70; Foulerton Research Fellow,

Royal Society, 1941-67; Fellow of Girton College, Cambridge, 1955; *b* 22 May 1900; *d* of Col William Edwin Fell and Alice Fell (née Pickersgill-Cunliffe). *Educ:* Wychwood Sch., Oxford; Madras Coll., St Andrews; Edinburgh Univ. BSc (Edinburgh) 1922; PhD (Edinburgh) 1924; DSc (Edinburgh) 1930; MA (Cantab) 1955. Research Student, DSIR, 1922; Research Asst, MRC, 1924; Junior Beit Fellow, 1924; 4th Year Beit Fellow, 1927; Senior Beit Fellow, 1928; Messel Research Fellow, Royal Society, 1931; Royal Society Research Professor, 1963-67. Hon. LLD: Edinburgh, 1959; Glasgow, 1970; Hon. DSc: Oxon, 1964; London, 1967; Hon. ScD: Smith Coll., USA, 1962; Harvard, 1964; Cambridge, 1969; Hon. MD Leiden 1976; Foreign Member: Royal Netherlands Academy, 1964; Serbian Acad. Sci. and Arts, 1975; Hon. Fellow, Somerville Coll., Oxford, 1964; Fellow, King's Coll., London, 1967. Prix Charles-Leopold Mayer, French Academy of Science, 1965. *Publications:* various communications to biological and medical journals. *Recreation:* travel. *Address:* 42b Queen Edith's Way, Cambridge. *T:* Cambridge 47022.

FELL, Robert, CB 1972; CBE 1966; Chief Executive, The Stock Exchange, since 1975; *b* 6 May 1921; *s* of Robert and Mary Ann Fell, Cumberland; *m* 1946, Eileen Wicks; two *s* one *d*. *Educ:* Whitehaven Grammar School. War Office, 1939; military service, 1940-46 (despatches); BoT, 1947; Trade Comr, Qld, 1954-59; Asst Sec., Tariff Div., 1961; Commercial Counsellor, Delhi, 1961-66; Under-Sec. i/c export promotion, 1967-71; Sec., ECGD, 1971-74. Mem., British Overseas Trade Board, 1972-75; Pres., City Branch, BIM, 1976-. FBIM; FRSA. *Recreations:* Rugby football (watching), gardening. *Address:* Dalegarth, Guildown Avenue, Guildford, Surrey. *T:* Guildford 72204. *Club:* Travellers'.

FELL, Sheila Mary, RA 1974 (ARA 1969); artist since 1950; *b* 20 July 1931; *d* of late John and of Anne Fell, Aspatria, Cumberland. *Educ:* Thomlinson Grammar Sch., Wigton, Cumberland; Carlisle Sch. of Art; St Martin's Sch. of Art, London. One Man Exhibitions: Beaux Arts Gallery, London, 1955, 1958, 1960, 1962, 1964; Derwent Centre, Cockermouth, Cumberland, 1961; Middlesbrough Art Gall., 1962; Maryport Educational Settlement, Cumberland, 1964; Abbot Hall Art Gall., Kendal, 1965; Queen Square Gall., Leeds, 1965; Stone Gall., Newcastle upon Tyne, 1967, 1969; Ashgate Gall., Farnham, 1974. Paintings in Public Collections: Arts Council; Contemporary Art Soc.; Tate Gallery; Municipal Galleries of Carlisle, Liverpool, Middlesbrough, Southport, Sunderland, Swindon and Newcastle upon Tyne; Abbot Hall Art Gall., Kendal; work purchased by Eastbourne Art Gallery for permanent collection, 1973. Works in many private Collections. FRSA 1973. 2nd prize, Junior Section, John Moore's Liverpool Competition, 1957; Boise Travelling Scholarship, 1958; awarded £500 (Arts Council purchase award scheme), 1967; Austin Abbey Award for Research into Mural Painting, 1970. *Publication:* chapter in Breakthrough, ed Ronald Goldmann, 1968. *Recreations:* travelling, reading, visiting friends. *Address:* 41 Redcliffe Square, SW10.

FELL, Captain William Richmond, CMG 1957; CBE 1947; DSC 1941; RN retd; Admiralty Marine Salvage Officer, Grade I, 1948-60; *b* 31 Jan. 1897; *s* of Walter Fell, MD Oxon, and Margaret Richmond; *m* 1921, Phyllis (née Munday); two *s*. *Educ:* Wellington Coll., New Zealand. Joined RN 1915; Midshipman HMS Warspite, 1916-17 (Jutland); Dover Patrol, 1917-18. Served in submarines, 1918-39; first comd, 1925. War of 1939-45 (despatches, DSC): "Q" boat ops, 1940; Norway, 1941; Combined ops, 1941-42; rejoined submarines, 1942; Comd Human Torpedo ops, 1942-43. Training officer, midget submarines, 1943; Comd of HMS Bonaventure, in rank of Capt. (midget submarines), 1943-47, home and Pacific waters. Boom Defence and Salvage Officer, 1948 (Malta and Med.); retired with rank of Capt., 1948, and joined Admty Salvage; Ship Target Trials home and abroad, 1949-50; Salvage ops at home, 1951-56; Suez, as Principal Salvage Officer, 1956-57. Legion of Merit, Officers' Class, 1947 (US). *Publications:* short stories contributed to Blackwood's, 1945-49; The Sea Surrenders, 1960; The Sea our Shield, 1966. *Recreations:* yachting, fishing. *Address:* Mahina Bay, Eastbourne, Wellington, NZ.

FELLINI, Federico; film director since 1950; *b* 20 Jan. 1920; *s* of late Urbano Fellini and Ida Barbiani; *m* 1943, Giulietta Masina. *Educ:* Bologna, Italy. Journalist, 1937-39; radio-author, scenario writer, etc, 1939-42. Has gained many prizes and awards in every part of the world including four "Oscars" (1957, 1958, 1964, 1975) for films La Strada, Le Notti di Cabiria, 8½ and Amarcord. Films include: (as Assistant Director and writer) Quarta Pagina, 1942; Roma Città Aperta, 1944-45; Paisà, 1946; Il Delitto di Giovanni Episcopo, 1947; In Nome della Legge, 1948-49; La Città si Defende, 1951; Il Brigante di Tacca di Lupo,

1953; San Francesco Giullare di Dio, 1954; Fortunella, 1956; (as Director) Luci del Varietà, 1950; Lo Sceicco Bianco, 1952; I Vitelloni, 1953; Agenzia Matrimoniale, 1953; La Strada, 1954; Il Bidone, 1955; Cabiria, 1957; La Dolce Vita, 1960; The Temptation of Dr Antonio, 1962; 8½, 1963 (foreign awards); Giulietta Degli Spiriti, 1965; Never Bet the Devil Your Head, 1968; Director's Blocknotes, 1969; Satyricon, 1969; The Clowns, 1970; Fellini's Roma, 1972; Amarcord, 1974; Casanova, 1976. *Publications:* Amarcord (trans. Nina Rootes), 1974; Quattro film, 1975. *Address:* 110 Via Margutta, Rome.

FELLOWES, family name of **Barons Ailwyn** and **De Ramsey.**

FELLOWES, Maj.-Gen. Halford David, CB 1957; DSO 1945; *b* 2 Aug. 1906; *er s* of late Major Halford Le M. Fellowes, 47th Sikhs (retd), Tenterden; *m* 1st, 1932, Angela Mary (marr. diss. 1941), *d* of P. E. Cammiade, ICS (retd); one *d*; 2nd, 1942, Rosemary, *er d* of late Brig.-Gen. Sir Terence Keyes, KCIE, CSI, CMG. *Educ:* St Paul's Sch., London. Royal Marines: 2nd Lieut 1924; Lieut 1927; Capt. 1936; A/Maj. 1940; A/Lt-Col 1940; Bt Major 1941; A/Col 1945; T/Brig. 1945; Major 1946; A/Lieut-Col 1947; Lieut-Col 1948; A/Col 1952; Col 1952; Maj.-Gen. 1954. Served HM Ships Berwick, Resolution, Sheffield, Base Defences Mediterranean, 1935-36; RM Siege Regt, 1940-42; GSO1, Special Service Group, 1943-44; 42 Commando RM (SE Asia), 1944-45 (wounded in Arakan, 1945); HQ 3 Commando Bde, 1945-46; GSO1 (Trg), RM office, 1947-49; Commando Sch., RM, 1949-52; Depot, RM Deal, 1952-54; psc 1943; jssc 1947. Commander Plymouth Group, Royal Marines, 1954-57, retired. *Recreation:* golf. *Address:* Cedar Cottage, Brede, Rye, East Sussex TN31 6EH. *T:* Brede 882743. *Clubs:* Army and Navy; Rye Golf.

FELLOWES, Brig. Reginald William Lyon, CBE 1943; *b* 6 Aug. 1895; *s* of late Frederick William Fellowes and late Mrs Fellowes, The Grange, Hitchin; *m* 1921, Dulcie M. B. H. Peel; two *s*; *m* 1947, M. G. Joan Beard. *Educ:* Wellington Coll.; RMA Woolwich. 2nd Lieut RFA Aug. 1914; served in France, Belgium, and Italy, 1914-19 (MC and Bar, despatches); psc; retired with rank of Major, 1938; mobilised Sept. 1939, France, Iraq and Persia, Sicily and Italy (CBE, despatches, Legion of Honour); released Aug. 1945, hon. rank Brig. *Address:* Cladich, Dalmally, Argyll. *T:* Dalmally 246. *Club:* New (Edinburgh).

FELLOWES, Sir William (Albemarle), KCVO 1964 (CVO 1952); DL; Agent to the Queen, Sandringham Estate, 1936-64, retired; Member of firm, Savills (formerly Alfred Savill, Curtis & Henson, before that Alfred Savill & Sons) (Land Agents and Valuers), 1964-77; *b* 10 Sept. 1899; 2nd *surv. s* of Charles Arthur Fellowes and Mary Fellowes; *m* 1934, Jane Charlotte, *d* of Brig.-Gen. A. F. H. Ferguson; two *s* two *d*. *Educ:* Winchester Coll.; Oriel Coll., Oxford. Agent to: Major W. S. Gosling, Hassobury Estate, Essex, 1925-30; Old Warden Estates, Beds, 1930-36. Became Agent to King George VI, 1936. Served with Scots Guards, 1940-45. DL Norfolk, 1965. FLAS 1927; Associate of the Chartered Surveyors, 1923. FRICS 1964. *Recreations:* shooting and fishing. *Address:* Flitcham House, Flitcham, King's Lynn, Norfolk. *T:* Hillington 346.

FENBY, Eric William, OBE 1962; Professor of Harmony, Royal Academy of Music, since 1964; *b* 22 April 1906; *s* of late Herbert Henry and Ada Fenby; *m* 1944, Rowena Clara Teresa Marshall; one *s* one *d*. *Educ:* Municipal Sch., Scarborough; privately. Amanuensis to Frederick Delius, 1928-34; Mus. Adv. Boosey & Hawkes, 1936-39; début as composer, BBC Promenade Concerts, 1942. Captain, RAEC Sch. of Educn, Cuerdon Hall, 1942-45. Mus. Dir, N Riding Coll. of Educn, 1948-62; Artistic Dir, Delius Centenary Festival, 1962; Pres. Delius Soc., 1964-; Chm., Composers' Guild of Great Britain, 1968, Mem. Council, 1970. Visiting Prof. of Music and Composer in Residence, Jacksonville Univ., Fla, USA, 1968. Mem. Cttee of Management, Royal Philharmonic Soc., 1972. Hon. Mem., RAM, 1965. *Publications:* Delius as I Knew Him, 1936, rev. edn 1966; Menuhin's House of Music, 1969; Delius, 1971. *Recreations:* walking, chess. *Address:* 35 Brookfield, Highgate West Hill, N6. *T:* 01-340 5122. *Club:* Royal Academy of Music.

FENDALL, Prof. Neville Rex Edwards, MD; Professor of Tropical Community Health, School of Tropical Medicine, University of Liverpool, since 1971; *b* 9 July 1917; *s* of Francis Alan Fendall and Ruby Inez Matthews; *m* 1942, Margaret Doreen (*née* Beynon). *Educ:* University College Hosp. (MD, BSc); London Sch. of Hygiene and Tropical Med. (DPH, FFCM). Colonial Medical Service, 1944-64, Dir of Med. Services, Kenya; Staff Mem., Rockefeller Foundn, 1964-66; Regional Dir, Population Council Inc., New York, 1966-71. Mem., Panel of Experts, WHO, 1960-77; Consultant: World Bank; UNFA; ODM; Cento; IDRC; APHA; USAID; Overseas

govts. Visiting Lecturer: Harvard, 1966-77; Inst. of Tropical Medicine, Marseilles; Univ. of Glasgow; Univ. of Bradford; Vis. Counsellor, Univ. of Hawaii; Commonwealth Foundn Travelling Lectr, 1976. *Publication:* Auxiliaries in Health Care, 1972 (English, French, Spanish edns). *Recreation:* gardening. *Address:* Tropical Community Health, School of Tropical Medicine, University of Liverpool, Liverpool L3 5QA. *T:* (official) 051-709 7611. *Clubs:* Royal Commonwealth Society; Athenæum (Liverpool).

FENDER, Percy George Herbert; Chairman and Managing Director, London Wine Exchange; Director (formerly Chairman), Crescens Robinson & Co. Ltd; *b* 22 Aug. 1892; *s* of Percy Robert Fender and Lily Herbert; *m* 1924, Ruth Marion Clapham (*d* 1937); one *s* one *d*; *m* 1962, Susan (Victoria Gordon) (*d* 1967), *er d* of Capt. and Mrs J. T. Kyffin, South Brent. *Educ:* St George's Coll., Weybridge; St Paul's Sch. Cricket for Sussex, 1910-13, for Surrey, 1914-36, toured Australia for MCC, 1920-21; also South Africa, 1922-23; toured Australia for Star as First Special Cricket Correspondent for any newspaper, 1928-29; Capt. Surrey, 1921-32; Special Cricket Correspondent for Evening News, Tests of 1934-38. Contributor to Field, Sporting and Dramatic, Observer, etc; Cricket for England Home and Abroad, 1920-24, etc; Football for Casuals, Corinthians and Fulham. Began in Lancs Paper Mill then same in Belgium, etc; Secretariat Concours Hippique Brussels Cinquantenaire, 1912; created Herbert Fender & Co., 1920, retired as Chm. and Man. Dir., 1977; served Royal Fusiliers, 1914-15, Royal Flying Corps, 1915 and Royal Air Force, 1915-18; rejoined RAF, 1940-46 (despatches, Invasion of Europe). Mem. LCC for Norwood Div. of Lambeth, 1952-55 and 1955-58. DL County of London, 1958; Greater London, 1965-76. Freeman, City of London. Pres., Horsham and District Football Assoc., 1963-. *Publications:* Defending the Ashes, 1921; Turn of the Wheel, 1929; The Tests of 1930, 1930; Kissing the Rod, 1934; Lonsdale Library on Cricket; ABC of Cricket, 1937, BBC and Television Cricket, etc. *Recreations:* cricket, football, billiards, golf, writing, shooting. *Address:* (office) 14 West Street, Horsham, Surrey; (home) Old Strood, Nowhurst Lane, Broadbridge Heath, near Horsham, Sussex RH12 3PJ. *Club:* Royal Air Force.

FENN, Nicholas Maxted; HM Diplomatic Service; Counsellor, British Embassy, Peking, since 1975; *b* 19 Feb. 1936; *s* of Rev. Prof. J. Eric Fenn and Kathleen (*née* Harrison); *m* 1959, Susan Clare (*née* Russell); two *s* one *d*. *Educ:* Kingswood Sch., Bath; Peterhouse, Cambridge (MA). Third Sec., British Embassy, Rangoon, 1959-63; Asst Private Sec. to Sec. of State for Foreign and Commonwealth Affairs, 1963-67; First Secretary: British Interests Sect., Swiss Embassy, Algiers, 1967-69; Public Relations, UK Mission to UN, NY, 1969-72; Dep. Head, Energy Dept, FCO, 1972-75. *Recreation:* sailing. *Address:* Applecroft, Chainhurst, Marden, Tonbridge, Kent TN12 9SS. *T:* Hunton 438. *Club:* United Oxford & Cambridge University.

FENNELL, John Desmond Augustine, QC 1974; a Recorder of the Crown Court since 1972; Barrister-at-Law; *b* 17 Sept. 1933; *s* of Dr A. J. Fennell, Lincoln; *m* 1966, Susan Primrose, *d* of J. M. Trusted, Belgravia, SW1; one *s* two *d*. *Educ:* Ampleforth; Corpus Christi Coll., Cambridge. Served with Grenadier Guards, 1956-58. Called to the Bar, Inner Temple, 1959; Dep. Chm., Bedfordshire QS, 1971; Chm., Buckingham Div. Cons. Assoc., 1976-. *Address:* 2 Crown Office Row, Temple, EC4Y 7HJ. *T:* 01-353 1365; Lawn House, Winslow, Buckingham MK18 3AJ. *T:* Winslow 2464. *Club:* Cavalry and Guards.

FENNELL, Prof. John Lister Illingworth, MA, PhD Cantab; Professor of Russian, Oxford University, since 1967; Fellow of New College, Oxford; *b* 30 May 1918; *s* of Dr C. H. Fennell and Sylvia Mitchell; *m* 1947, Marina Lopukhin; one *s* one *d*. *Educ:* Radley Coll.; Trinity Coll., Cambridge. Served with Army, 1939-45. Asst Lectr, Dept of Slavonic Studies, Cambridge Univ., 1947-52; Reader in Russian and Head of Dept of Slavonic Languages, Nottingham Univ., 1952-56; Lectr in Russian, Oxford Univ., 1956-67, Fellow and Praelector in Russian, University Coll., Oxford, 1964-67. Vis. Lectr, Harvard Univ., 1963-64; Visiting Professor: Univ. of Calif at Berkeley, 1971, 1977; Virginia Univ., 1974. Organiser, 3rd Internat. Conf. of Historians of Muscovy, Oxford, 1975. Joint Editor: Oxford Slavonic Papers; Russia Mediaevalis. *Publications:* The Correspondence between Prince A. M. Kurbsky and Ivan IV, 1955; Ivan the Great of Moscow, 1961; The Penguin Russian Course, 1961; Pushkin, 1964; Kurbsky's History of Ivan IV, 1965; The Emergence of Moscow, 1968; (ed jtly) Historical Russian Reader, 1969; (ed) Nineteenth Century Russian Literature, 1973; (with A. Stokes) Early Russian Literature, 1974; Cambridge Modern History, Vol. II, Chap. 19; articles in Slavonic and East European Review, Jahrbücher für Geschichte

Osteuropas, etc. *Recreation:* music. *Address:* 8 Canterbury Road, Oxford. *T:* Oxford 56149.

FENNER, Mrs Bernard; *see* Fenner, Mrs Peggy.

FENNER, Tan Sri Sir Claude Harry, KBE 1965 (MBE 1946); CMG 1963; Special Representative in Malaysia of the Rubber Growers' Assoc.; *b* 16 Jan. 1916; *s* of late Major C. H. Fenner, MBE, Indian Army; *m* 1941, Joan Margaret, *d* of late J. Fenner, Brisbane, Queensland; one *d. Educ:* Highgate Sch. Probationary Asst Supt, Federated Malay States Police, 1936; Supt, 1950; Asst Commissioner, 1953; Senior Asst Commissioner (Head of Special Branch), 1954; Dep. Sec. (Security and Intelligence), Prime Minister's Dept, March 1958; Commissioner of Police, Sept. 1958; Dir of Police Affairs, 1962; Inspector Gen. of Police, Malaysia, 1963-66. War Service with Special Forces (Force 136), 1942-45, Lieut-Col. Colonial Police Medal, 1950; Queen's Police Medal, 1957. Panglima Mangku Negara, Fedn of Malaya, 1961; National Order of Vietnam, 3rd cl., 1965; Dato Paduka Makhota Brunei, 1966. *Recreations:* all forms of sport. *Address:* 1A Jalan Girdle, Kuala Lumpur, Malaysia. *T:* KL 27354. *Club:* Special Forces.

FENNER, Prof. Frank John, CMG 1976; MBE 1944; FRS 1958; FAA 1954; FRCP 1967; Professor of Environmental Studies and Director, Centre for Resource and Environmental Studies, Australian National University, since 1973; *b* 21 Dec. 1914; *s* of Charles and Emma L. Fenner; *m* 1944, Ellen Margaret Bobbie Roberts; one *d* (and one *d* decd). *Educ:* Thebarton Technical High Sch.; Adelaide High Sch.; Univ. of Adelaide. MB, BS (Adelaide) 1938; MD (Adelaide) 1942; DTM (Sydney) 1940. Served as Medical Officer, Hospital Pathologist, and Malariologist, AIF, 1940-46; Francis Haley Research Fellow, Walter and Eliza Hall Inst. for Medical Research, Melbourne, 1946-48; Rockefeller Foundation Travelling Fellow, 1948-49; Prof. of Microbiology, 1949-73, and Dir, John Curtin Sch. of Med. Research, 1967-73, ANU; Overseas Fellow, Churchill Coll., Cambridge, 1962-63. Fogarty Schol., Nat. Insts of Health, USA, 1973-74; For. Associate, Nat. Acad. of Scis, USA, 1977; David Syme Prize, Univ. of Melbourne, 1949; Harvey Lecture, Harvey Soc. of New York, 1957; Leeuwenhoek Lecture, Royal Society, 1961; Matthew Flinders Lecture, Australian Acad. of Science, 1967; Mueller Medal, Australian and New Zealand Assoc. for the Advancement of Science, 1964. Hon. MD Monash, 1966. Britannica Australia Award for Medicine, 1967. *Publications:* The Production of Antibodies (with F. M. Burnet), 1949; Myxomatosis (with F. N. Ratcliffe), 1965; The Biology of Animal Viruses, 1968, 2nd edn 1974; Medical Virology (with D. O. White), 1970, 2nd edn 1976; Classification and Nomenclature of Viruses, 1976; numerous scientific papers, dealing with virology, epidemiology, bacteriology, and environmental problems. *Recreations:* gardening, tennis, fishing. *Address:* 8 Monaro Crescent, Red Hill, Canberra, ACT 2603, Australia. *T:* 95-9176.

FENNER, Mrs Peggy, (Mrs B. Fenner); *b* 12 Nov. 1922; *m* 1940, Bernard Fenner; one *d. Educ:* LCC School, Brockley; Ide Hill, Sevenoaks. Contested (C) Newcastle-under-Lyme, 1966; MP(C) Rochester and Chatham, 1970-Sept. 1974; Parly Sec., MAFF, 1972-74; Mem., British Delegn to European Parlt, Strasbourg, 1974. Member: West Kent Divisional Exec. Educn Cttee, 1963-72; Sevenoaks Urban District Council, 1957-71 (Chairman, 1962 and 1963); Exec. of Kent Borough and Urban District Councils Assoc., 1967-71; a Vice-Pres, Urban District Councils Assoc., 1971. *Recreations:* reading, travel, theatre, gardening. *Address:* 12 Star Hill, Rochester, Kent. *T:* Medway 42124.

FENNESSY, Sir Edward, Kt 1975; CBE 1957 (OBE 1944); BSc; FIEE, FRIN; Deputy Chairman, Post Office Corporation, 1975-77; Managing Director (Telecommunications), 1969-77; *b* 17 Jan. 1912; *m* 1937, Marion Banks; one *s* one *d. Educ:* Univ. of London. Telecommunications Research, Standard Telephones and Cables, 1934-38; Radar Research, Air Min. Research Station, Bawdsey Manor, 1938. War of 1939-45: commissioned RAFVR, 1940; Group Captain, 1945; staff No 60 Group, RAF, 1940-45; resp. for planning and construction radar systems for defence of UK, and Bomber Ops. Joined Bd of The Decca Navigator Co., 1946; Managing Director: Decca Radar Ltd, 1950-65; The Plessey Electronics Group, 1965-69. Chairman: British Telecommunications Research Ltd, 1966-69; Electronic Engineering Assoc., 1967-68. Pres., Royal Institute of Navigation, 1975-. DUniv Surrey, 1971. *Recreations:* sailing, golf. *Address:* Northbrook, Littleford Lane, Shamley Green, Surrey. *T:* Bramley 2444. *Clubs:* Royal Air Force; Island Sailing.

FENTON, Air Cdre Harold Arthur, CBE 1946; DSO 1943; DFC 1942; BA; AFRAeS; *b* Gallegos, Patagonia, Argentine, 9 Feb. 1909; *s* of Dr E. G. Fenton, FRCSI, DPH, Co. Sligo and J.

Ormsby, Glen Lodge, Ballina, Co. Mayo; *m* 1935, H. de Carteret; no *c. Educ:* Sandford Park Sch.; Trinity Coll., Dublin (BA 1927). Joined RAF 1928. Served India, 1930-33. Flying Instructor at Air Service Training Ltd, Hamble, until outbreak of war. During war commanded: Fighter Sqdn, Battle of Britain; Fighter Wing, and Fighter Group, Western Desert and Libya; Fighter Sector, London Area. Finished war as Senior Staff Officer, Germany (83 Group) (despatches thrice). Managing Dir, Deccan Airways Ltd, Hyderabad, Deccan, until 1947; Gen. Manager of Airways Training Ltd, 1947-48; Operations Manager, BOAC, 1949-52; Managing Dir, Peter Jones, 1952-58. *Recreations:* gardening, sailing. *Address:* Le Vallon, St Brelade, Jersey, Channel Islands. *T:* 41172.

FENTON, Roy Pentelow, CMG 1960; Chief Executive, Keyser Ullmann (Holdings) Ltd, since 1975; *b* 1 July 1918; *s* of late Heber Fenton, Salford; *m* 1941, Daphne, *d* of late E. Cheason; one *s. Educ:* Salford Grammar Sch. Served, 1939-46; commissioned Lancs Fusiliers. United Kingdom Alternate Mem., Management Board of European Payments Union, 1954-57; Governor, Central Bank of Nigeria, 1958-63; Dep. Chief of Central Banking Information Dept, Bank of England, 1963-65; Chief, Overseas Dept, Bank of England, 1965-75. UK Mem., Man. Bd of European Monetary Agreement, 1967-72, Vice-Chm., 1968-72. *Address:* Flat K, 23 Warwick Square, SW1V 2AB. *T:* 01-821 0920; Burnham House, Burnham Market, King's Lynn, Norfolk. *T:* Burnham Market 291. *Clubs:* East India, Devonshire, Sports and Public Schools, Overseas Bankers.

FENTON, Wilfrid David Drysdale, CBE 1963; FRSE; BSc, MIEE; Managing Director, British Electricity International Ltd (Electricity Council's overseas consultancy service), since 1976; *b* 27 March 1908; *s* of late David Fenton, Edinburgh; *m* 1st, 1955, Isobel Stewart (marr. diss. 1974); no *c*; 2nd, 1974, Elaine Herman, *d* of late Louis Surut, New York. *Educ:* George Watson's Coll., Edinburgh; Edinburgh Univ. Called to Bar, Middle Temple, 1937. Kennedy and Donkin, Cons. Engrs, London, 1931-33; Central Electricity Bd, London, 1933-38; Personal Asst to Gen. Manager, Midland Counties Electric Supply Co., 1938-44; Commercial Engr, 1944-48, Sec. and Commercial Engr, 1948-55, N of Scotland Hydro-Electric Bd; Chm., 1955-62, Uganda Electricity Bd; Chm., S Wales Electricity Bd, 1962-68; Chm., London Electricity Bd, 1968-72; Dep. Chm., CEGB, 1972-75; Man. Dir, Overseas Consultancy Services, Electricity Council 1975-76 (Dir, 1970-75). Dir, Uganda Development Corp., 1955-57; Hon. Treas., 1956-57, Vice-Chm., 1957-62, Makerere Univ. Coll.; Chm. Mulago Hosp. (Kampala) Autonomy Cttee, 1961. *Recreation:* golf. *Address:* 31 Cadogan Lane, SW1 9DR. *Clubs:* Caledonian, Royal Commonwealth Society.

FENWICK, Robert George, CBE 1975; QPM 1969; HM Inspector of Constabulary, 1967-77; *b* 1913; *s* of late George R. F. Fenwick, Horton Grange, Northumberland; *m* 1943, Eileen Winifreda, *d* of late James Carstairs Dodds, Buenos Aires. *Educ:* Dame Allan's Sch. Barrister-at-Law, Gray's Inn, 1951. Metropolitan Police, 1934-59; seconded to Foreign Office for duties in São Paulo, Brazil, 1957-58; Directing Staff, Police Coll., 1959-60; Asst Chief Constable, Glos, 1960-62; Chief Constable, Salop, 1962-67. *Address:* Ebor House, Kingsland, Shrewsbury, Salop. *T:* Shrewsbury 4158. *Clubs:* East India, Devonshire, Sports and Public Schools; Salop County (Shrewsbury).

FERENS, Sir Thomas (Robinson), Kt 1957; CBE 1952; *b* 4 Jan. 1903; *e s* of late J. J. T. Ferens, Hull; *m* 1934, Jessie, *d* of P. G. Sanderson, Hull and Scarborough; two *d. Educ:* Rydal; Leeds Univ. (BSc Eng). *Recreation:* fly-fishing. *Address:* Sunderlandwick, Driffield, North Humberside. *T:* Driffield 42323.

FERGUS, Most Rev. James, DD; *b* Louisburgh, Co. Mayo, 23 Dec. 1895. *Educ:* St Jarlath's College, Tuam; and at Maynooth. Ordained priest, 1920; studied Dunboyne; Curate, Glenamaddy, 1921, Tuam, 1924; Archbishop's secretary, 1926; Administrator, Westport, 1943; Parish Priest, Ballinrobe, 1944; Bishop of Achonry, 1947-76. *Address:* Ballaghaderreen, Co. Roscommon, Eire.

FERGUSON, Ernest Alexander; Under-Secretary and Accountant-General, Department of Employment, since 1973; *b* 26 July 1917; *s* of William Henry and Lilian Ferguson; *m* 1940, Mary Josephine Wadsworth; two *s. Educ:* Priory Sch., Shrewsbury; Pembroke Coll., Cambridge. Scholar, Pembroke Coll., 1935-39; MA 1944. Served War, RA (Captain), 1940-45. Entered Ministry of Labour, 1945; Principal, 1948; Asst Sec., 1962. Chm., Central Youth Employment Executive, 1967-69;

Sec. to NEDC, 1971-73. *Recreations:* sport, mountaineering, reading. *Address:* 25 Balcombe Road, Horley, Surrey. *T:* Horley 5254. *Clubs:* Civil Service, Army and Navy.

FERGUSON, Prof. John, FIAL; Dean and Director of Studies in Arts, The Open University, since 1969; *b* 2 March 1921; *s* of Prof. Allan and Dr Nesta Ferguson; *m* 1950, Elnora Dixon; no *c. Educ:* Bishops Stortford Coll.; St John's Coll., Cambridge. BD 1st cl. hons London, 1944; BA 1st cl. hons with double distinction Class. Tripos Cantab, 1947; Henry Carrington and Bentham Dumont Koe Studentship, 1947; Denny Studentship, 1947; Kaye Prize, 1951 (for essay in early Church History). Civil Defence, 1941-45; Master at Bishops Stortford Coll., 1945-46; Lectr in Classics, King's Coll., Newcastle upon Tyne, 1948-53; Sen. Lectr in Classics, Queen Mary Coll., London, 1953-56; Prof. of Classics, Univ. of Ibadan, 1956-66 (Dean, Faculty of Arts, 1958-59, 1960-61); Hill Vis. Prof. 1966-68, Prof. 1968-69, Univ. of Minnesota; Old Dominion Vis. Prof. Humanities, Hampton Inst., Va, 1968-69. Dep. Chm. of Senate, Open Univ., 1969-74. Vis. Prof., Univ. of Florida, 1977; Emily Hobhouse Meml Lectr, 1961; Alex Wood Meml Lectr, 1971; Kinchin Smith Meml Lectr, 1972; Herbert Collins Meml Lectr, 1976; Rodes-Helm Lectr, 1977; Montgomery Lectr, 1977-79. Chm. 1953-56, Vice-Chm. 1969-, Fellowship of Reconciliation; Vice-Chm., UNA; British Council of Churches: Chm., Educn Dept, 1971-74; Community Affairs Div., 1974-; Chm., Classical Assoc. of Nigeria; Chm., Information and Preparation Section, Christians Abroad; Vice-Pres., Orbilian Soc., 1973- (Pres., 1972); Governor: Milton Keynes Coll. of Educn, 1971-73; W London Inst. of Higher Educn; Mill Hill Sch.; Chm., British and Foreign Schools Soc. *Publications:* The Enthronement of Love, 1950; (ed) Studies in Christian Social Commitment, 1954; Pelagius, 1956; (jtly) Letters on Pacifism, 1956; Christian Faith for Today, 1956; The UN and the World's Needs, 1957; (ed) Plato Republic X, 1957; Moral Values in the Ancient World, 1958; (jtly) The Emergent University, 1960; (ed) Studies in Cicero, 1962; Foundations of the Modern World, 1963; (jtly) The Enduring Past, 1965; (jtly) Nigeria under the Cross, 1965; Ibadan Verses, 1966; (ed) Ibadan Versions, 1967; The Wit of the Greeks and Romans, 1968; Christian Byways, 1968; (jtly) Africa in Classical Antiquity, 1969; Socrates: A Source-Book, 1970; Religions of the Roman Empire, 1970; American Verses, 1971; Some Nigerian Church Founders, 1971; Sermons of a Layman, 1972; The Place of Suffering, 1972; A Companion to Greek Tragedy, 1972; Aristotle, 1972; The Heritage of Hellenism, 1973; The Politics of Love, 1973; (ed) War and the Creative Arts, 1973; (rapporteur) Non-violent Action: a Christian appraisal, 1973; Clement of Alexandria, 1974; Utopias of the Classical World, 1975; The Open University from Within, 1975; Danilo Dolci, 1975; An Illustrated Encyclopaedia of Mysticism and the Mystery Religions, 1976; O My People, 1977; War and Peace in the World's Religions, 1977; *Open University Course Units:* (jtly) Humanities and the Study of Civilisation, 1971; Technology, Society, Religion and the Arts: Some Questions, 1971; Which was Socrates?, 1971; What is a Gospel?, 1971; The Yorubas of Nigeria, 1971; The Medieval Inheritance and the Revival of Classical Learning, 1972; Thomas Jefferson, 1972; (jtly) Rousseau and Goethe, 1972; Religious Revival in England, 1972; Huckleberry Finn, 1973; Plato's Theory of Forms, 1973; Thucydides and the Peloponnesian War, 1973; (jtly) World War II and the Arts, 1973; The Peace Movement, 1973; Petronius and Juvenal, 1974; Roman Britain in the Early Empire, 1974; (jtly) Social Life in the Early Empire, 1974; (jtly) Two Oedipus Plays, 1977; The Bacchae, 1977; Alcestis, 1977; *plays:* The Camp, 1956; The Trial, 1957; The Road to Heaven, 1958; Job, 1961; Editor, Nigeria and the Classics, Vols I-IX; Jt Editor, Reconciliation Quarterly; numerous articles on classical subjects, theology, internat. affairs and literature. *Recreations:* cricket, fell-walking, book-hunting, church architecture, drama, opera, conducting madrigals. *Address:* Higham Cross House, Hanslope, Milton Keynes MK19 7HP. *T:* Hanslope 418. *Clubs:* Athenæum; MCC; Union (Cambridge).

FERGUSON, John McIntyre, CBE 1976; CEng, FIEE, FIMechE; engineering consultant, since 1973; *b* 16 May 1915; *s* of Frank Ferguson and Lilian (*née* Bowen); *m* 1941, Margaret Frances Tayler; three *s. Educ:* Armstrong Coll., Durham Univ. BScEng (1st Cl. Hons). English Electric Co., Stafford: Research, 1936; Chief Engr, 1953; Dir Engrg, Heavy Electric Products, 1965; Dir of Engrg, GEC Power Engrg Co., 1969. Member: Metrication Bd, 1969-76; Science Res. Council, 1972-76; UGC, 1977-. *Recreations:* golf, sailing. *Address:* Leacroft, 19 St John's Road, Stafford ST17 9AS. *T:* Stafford 3516. *Club:* Royal Commonwealth Society.

FERGUSON, Sir Neil Edward J.; *see* Johnson-Ferguson.

FERGUSON DAVIE, Rev. Sir (Arthur) Patrick, 5th Bt *cr* 1641 and *re-created* 1847 for General Henry Ferguson, husband of Juliana, *d* of Sir John Davie, 8th Bt of Creedy; TD 1954; Hon. Chaplain to Bishop of Exeter, 1949-73; *b* 17 March 1909; *s* of late Lt-Col Arthur Francis Ferguson Davie, CIE, DSO (3rd *s* of 3rd Bt), and late Eleanor Blanche Daphne, *d* of late C. T. Naylor (she *m* 1918, Major J. H. W. Knight-Bruce, who *d* 1951; she *d* 1964); *S* uncle, 1947; *m* 1949, Iris Dawn Cable-Buller, *o d* of Capt. and Hon. Mrs Buller, Downes, Crediton; one *s. Educ:* Wellington Coll.; Lincoln Coll., Oxford (MA). Ely Theological Coll., 1932-34; Deacon, 1934, Priest, 1935. Asst Curate, Littleham-cum-Exmouth, 1934-37; St Augustine's, Kilburn, NW6, 1938-39; CF (TA), 1937-45; Hon. CF 1945. Served with 4th Bn Devonshire Regt in UK and Gibraltar, 1939-43; CMF, N Africa and Italy, 1943-45; Vicar of St John's Torquay, 1945-48; Rural Dean of Cadbury, 1966-68. *Publication:* The Bishop in Church, 1961. *Recreation:* shooting. *Heir:* *s* Antony Francis Ferguson Davie, *b* 23 March 1952. *Address:* Blackburne House, 1 Culross Street, W1; Skalatos, Klepini, Kyrenia, Cyprus, via Mersin 10, Turkey.

FERGUSON JONES, Hugh; *see* Jones, H. F.

FERGUSSON, family name of **Baron Ballantrae.**

FERGUSSON of Kilkerran, Sir Charles, 9th Bt *cr* 1703; *b* 10 May 1931; *s* of Sir James Fergusson of Kilkerran, 8th Bt, and Frances, *d* of Edgar Dugdale; *S* father, 1973; *m* 1961, Hon. Amanda Mary Noel-Paton, *d* of Lord Ferrier, *qv*; two *s. Educ:* Eton; Edinburgh and East of Scotland Coll. of Agriculture (Scottish Diploma in Agric.). *Heir:* *s* Adam Fergusson, *b* 29 Dec. 1962. *Address:* Kilkerran, Maybole, Ayrshire KA19 7SJ. *T:* Crosshill 207.

FERGUSSON, Ewen Alastair John; HM Diplomatic Service; Private Secretary to the Foreign and Commonwealth Secretary, since 1975; *b* 28 Oct. 1932; *er s* of late Sir Ewen MacGregor Field Fergusson; *m* 1959, Sara Carolyn, *d* of late Brig-Gen. Lord Esmé Gordon-Lennox, KCVO, CMG, DSO and *widow* of Sir William Andrew Montgomery-Cuninghame, 11th Bt; one *s* two *d. Educ:* Rugby; Oriel Coll., Oxford (MA). 2nd Lieut, 60th Rifles (KRRC), 1954-56. Joined Foreign (now Diplomatic) Service, 1956; Asst Private Sec. to Minister of Defence, 1957-59; British Embassy, Addis Ababa, 1960; FO, 1963; British Trade Development Office, New York, 1967; Counsellor, Office of UK Permanent Rep. to European Communities, 1972-75. *Recreations:* listening to music, wine tasting. *Address:* c/o Foreign and Commonwealth Office, SW1. *Club:* Royal Automobile.

FERGUSSON, Ian Victor Lyon; *b* 22 Jan. 1901; *y s* of late Rev. Dr John Moore Fergusson; *m* 1927, Hannah Grace (*née* Gourlay); three *s* one *d. Educ:* Berkhamsted Sch. Joined Evans Medical Ltd. (then Evans Sons Lescher & Webb Ltd), 1919; Dir, 1927; Man. Dir, 1941; Chm. and Man. Dir, Evans Medical Ltd, 1943-62; Dir, Glaxo Group Ltd, 1961-62; Dir, Carless Capel & Leonard Ltd, 1964-72. Pres., Chemists Federation, 1940-41; Chm., Assoc. British Pharmaceutical Industry, 1946-47. Mem., Liverpool Regional Hospital Board, 1958-61. *Recreations:* fishing, gardening. *Address:* Orchard Lodge, Avon Dassett, via Leamington Spa, Warwickshire. *T:* Farnborough 228.

FERGUSSON, Sir James H. H.; *see* Colyer-Fergusson.

FERGUSSON, John Douglas, FRCS; Honorary Consultant; Surgeon, St Peter's, St Paul's and St Philip's Hospitals; Surgeon and Urologist, Central Middlesex Hospital; *b* 5 Dec. 1909; *s* of John Newbery Fraser Fergusson and Mildred Gladys (*née* Mercer); *m* 1st, 1936, Alice Alyne (*d* 1968), *d* of Hon. Mr Justice Maartensz; two *s*; 2nd, 1969, Myrtle, *d* of Maj.-Gen. K. M. Body, CB, CMG, OBE. *Educ:* St Peter's, York; Cambridge Univ.; St Thomas' Hosp. 1st Class Hons Nat. Science Tripos, 1931; Coll. Prizeman and Scholar, St John's Coll., Cambridge; Open Univ. Scholar, St Thos Hosp.; Sutton Sams Prize, 1934, and Cheselden Medal for Surgery, 1936, St Thos Hosp.; MA 1945, MD 1946 Cantab; FRCS 1936; Hunterian Prof., RCS, 1945-46. Formerly Dir of Teaching and Res., Inst. of Urology, Univ. of London. Fellow and late Mem. of Council, Assoc. of Surgeons of Gt Britain and Ireland; Pres., British Assoc. of Urological Surgeons, 1970-72; Member: Internat. Soc. of Urology; Bd of Governors, St Peter's, St Paul's and St Philip's Hospitals; FRSocMed (Pres. of Section of Urology, 1962-63). Hon. Editor, British Journal of Urology, 1966-72. Formerly Associate Examiner in Surgery, Univ. of London. *Publications:* various contribs to surgical and urological journals. *Recreation:* fishing. *Address:* 149 Harley Street, W1. *T:* 01-935 8273.

FERMAN, James Alan; Secretary, British Board of Film Censors, since 1975; *b* New York, 11 April 1930; *m* 1956, Monica Sophie (*née* Robinson); one *s* one *d*. *Educ:* Great Neck High Sch., NY; Cornell Univ. (BA Hons); King's Coll., Cambridge (MA Hons). Actor and univ. lectr until 1957; author/adaptor, Zuleika (musical comedy), Saville Theatre, 1957; Television Director: ABC, 1957-59; ATV, 1959-65; freelance, chiefly at BBC, 1965-75; drama series incl.: The Planemakers, Probation Officer, Emergency Ward 10; plays incl.: The Pistol, Who's A Good Boy Then? I Am, Kafka's Ameria, Death of a Private, Before the Party, Chariot of Fire, When the Bough Breaks, Terrible Jim Fitch; documentaries incl.: Decisions of Our Time, The Four Freedoms, CURE; stage productions incl.: Three Sisters, Mooney and His Caravans, This Space Is Mine; wrote and dir., Drugs and Schoolchildren, film series for teachers and social workers. Lectr in Community Studies, Polytechnic of Central London, 1973-76 (Dir and Chm., Community Mental Health Prog. in assoc. with MIND); Educn Adviser, Standing Conf. on Drug Abuse; Vice-Pres., Assoc. for Prevention of Addiction. *Recreations:* reading and hill-walking. *Address:* The Fairhazel Co-operative, Canfield Gardens, NW6; British Board of Film Censors, 3 Soho Square, W1. *T:* 01-437 2677.

FERMOR, Patrick Michael Leigh, DSO 1944; OBE 1943; author: Hon. Citizen of Herakleion, Crete, 1947, Gytheion, Laconia, 1966, and of Kardamyli, Messenia, 1967; *b* 11 Feb. 1915; *s* of late Sir Lewis Leigh Fermor, OBE, FRS, DSc, and Eileen, *d* of Charles Taaffe Ambler; *m* 1968, Hon. Mrs Joan Rayner, *d* of 1st Viscount Monsell, PC, GBE. *Educ:* King's Sch., Canterbury. After travelling for four years in Central Europe, Balkans and Greece, enlisted in Irish Guards, 1939; 2nd Lieut, "I" Corps, 1940; Lieut, British Mil. Mission, Greece, 1940; Liaison Officer, Greek GHQ, Albania; campaigns of Greece and Crete; 2 years in German occupied Crete with Cretan Resistance, commanded some minor guerilla operations; Major 1943; team-commander in Special Allied Airborne Reconnaissance Force, N Germany, 1945. Dep.-Dir British Institute, Athens, till middle 1946; travelled in Caribbean and Central American republics, 1947-48. *Publications:* The Traveller's Tree (Heinemann Foundation Prize for Literature, 1950, and Kemsley Prize, 1951); trans. Colette, Chance Acquaintances, 1952; A Time to Keep Silence, 1953; The Violins of Saint Jacques, 1953; Mani, 1958 (Duff Cooper Meml Prize; Book Society's Choice); (trans.) The Cretan Runner (George Psychoundakis), 1955; Roumeli, 1966; A Time of Gifts, 1977. *Recreation:* travel. *Address:* c/o Messrs John Murray, 50 Albemarle Street, W1. *Clubs:* Travellers', White's, Pratt's, Special Forces.

FERMOR-HESKETH, family name of Baron Hesketh.

FERMOY, 5th Baron *cr* 1856; Edmund James Burke Roche; Chairman, Eddington Bindery Ltd; Director, Kennetco Estates Co. Ltd; *b* 20 March 1939; *s* of 4th Baron Fermoy and Ruth Sylvia (*see* Dowager Lady Fermoy); *S* father, 1955; *m* 1964, Lavinia Frances Elizabeth, *o d* of late Capt. John Pitman and of Mrs Pitman, Foxley House, Malmesbury, Wilts; two *s* one *d*. *Educ:* Eton; Sandhurst; RAC, Cirencester. Capt., Royal Horse Guards (The Blues), retd 1967. Trustee, Pheasant Trust; Hon. Dir, Hawk Trust, 1975-. District Councillor (Hungerford), Newbury DC, 1976-. *Recreation:* steeplechasing. *Heir:* *s* Hon. Patrick Maurice Burke Roche, *b* 11 Oct. 1967. *Address:* Eddington House, Hungerford, Berks. *T:* Hungerford 2540; 36 Eaton Square, SW1. *T:* 01-235 1514. *Clubs:* White's, Turf, 1,001.

FERMOY, Dowager Lady; Ruth Sylvia; (Rt. Hon. Ruth Lady Fermoy), CVO 1966; OBE 1952; JP; Woman of the Bedchamber to Queen Elizabeth the Queen Mother since 1960 (an extra Woman of the Bedchamber, 1956-60); *b* 2 Oct. 1908; *y d* of late W. S. Gill, CB, Dalhebity, Bieldside, Aberdeenshire; *m* 1931, Edmund Maurice Burke Roche, 4th Baron Fermoy (*d* 1955); one *s* (*see* 5th Baron Fermoy) two *d*. JP Norfolk, 1944. Freedom of King's Lynn, 1963. Hon. RAM 1968; Hon. MusD; DUniv East Anglia 1975. *Address:* 36 Eaton Square, SW1.

FERNALD, John Bailey; *b* 21 Nov. 1905; *s* of C. B. Fernald and Josephine Harker; *m* 1942, Jenny Laird; one *d*. *Educ:* Marlborough Coll.; Trinity Coll., Oxford. Pres., OUDS, 1927; Dramatic Editor, The Pall Mall Magazine, 1929; first professional production, Arts Theatre, 1929; subsequently produced plays continuously in London till 1936, when became Associate Producer for Associated British Pictures Corporation; returned to theatre, 1938; on teaching staff of Royal Academy of Dramatic Art, 1934-40. Joined RNVR, 1940 and served almost continuously at sea until 1945; left service with rank of Lieut-Comdr. Dir of Productions, Reunion Theatre, 1946; Dir of the Liverpool Playhouse, 1946-49; subsequently produced: The Love of Four Colonels, Wyndham's; The White Sheep of the

Family, Piccadilly; The First Born, Winter Garden: Nightmare Abbey and Dial M for Murder, Westminster; Escapade, Strand; The Devil's General, Savoy; Crime and Punishment (Television); Saint Joan, St Martin's; The Remarkable Mr Pennypacker, New; The House by the Lake, Duke of York's; Jubilee Production of Peter Pan; Tea and Sympathy, Comedy; Hedda Gabler, Nye Teater, Oslo; The Love of Four Colonels, Kansanteatteri, Helsinki; Ghosts, Old Vic; The Tchekov Centenary Production of The Seagull, Edinburgh Festival and Old Vic; The Affair, Henry Miller Theatre, New York; The Schoolmistress, Savoy; The Enchanted, Arts Theatre; Ivanov, Uncle Vanya, The Seagull, and various plays at Arts Theatre and elsewhere; 1st production in England of Bertolt Brecht's The Caucasian Chalk Circle, Vanbrugh Theatre, RADA, Anton Tchekov's The Cherry Orchard at the National Theatre, Pretoria and Johannesburg; Private Lives, Bristol Old Vic. Shute Lectr on the Art of the Theatre, Liverpool Univ., 1948. Principal, Royal Academy of Dramatic Art, 1955-65; Dir, John Fernald Co., Meadowbrook Theatre, Rochester, Mich, and Prof. of Dramatic Art, Oakland Univ., Rochester, Mich, 1966-70; Prof., Dept of Theatre, NY State Univ., 1970-71; returned from USA, 1972, now largely concerned with teaching of acting at various drama schs and directing classical revivals at various repertory theatres. Awarded Silver Medal of Royal Soc. of Arts, 1966. *Publications:* The Play Produced: a Manual of Stage Production, 1933; Destroyer from America, 1942; Sense of Direction, 1968; contrib. to Encyclopaedia Britannica, 1972. *Recreations:* music, travelling, looking at cats, and producing the plays of Anton Tchekov. *Address:* 2 Daleham Mews, NW3. *T:* 01-435 2992. *Club:* Garrick.

FERNANDES, Most Rev. Angelo; *see* Delhi, Archbishop of, (RC).

FERNANDO, Most Rev. Nicholas Marcus; *see* Colombo, Archbishop of, (RC).

FERNS, Prof. Henry Stanley, MA, PhD Cantab; Professor of Political Science, University of Birmingham, since 1961; *b* Calgary, Alberta, 16 Dec. 1913; *er s* of Stanley and Janie Ferns; *m* 1940, Helen Maureen, *d* of John and Eleanor Jack; three *s* one *d*. *Educ:* St John's High Sch., Winnipeg; Univ. of Manitoba; Trinity Coll., Cambridge. Research Scholar, Trinity Coll., Cambridge, 1938. Secretarial staff of Prime Minister of Canada, 1940; Asst Prof. of History and Government, Univ. of Manitoba, 1945; Fellow, Canadian Social Science Research Council, 1949; Lectr in Modern History and Government, Univ. of Birmingham, 1950; successively Sen. Lectr, Head of Dept and Prof. of Political Science, Dean, Faculty of Commerce and Social Sci., 1961-65. Pres., Bd of Dirs, Winnipeg Citizens' Cooperative Publishing Co. Ltd, 1946-48; Member of various Conciliation Boards appointed by Minister of Labour of Govt of Manitoba, 1947-49. Vice-Chm., British Assoc. of Canadian Studies. *Publications:* (with B. Ostry) The Age of McKenzie King: The Rise of the Leader, 1955 (Toronto and London), 2nd edn 1976; Britain and Argentina in the Nineteenth Century, 1960 (Oxford); Towards an Independent University, 1969; Argentina, 1969; The Argentine Republic 1516-1971, 1973; articles in learned jls. *Recreations:* journalism, idling and pottering about. *Address:* 1 Kesteven Close, Sir Harry's Road, Birmingham B15 2UT. *T:* 021-440 1016.

FERNYHOUGH, Ven. Bernard; Archdeacon of Oakham, since 1977; Canon Residentiary of Peterborough Cathedral, since 1977; *b* 2 Sept. 1932; *s* of Edward and Edith Fernyhough; *m* 1957, Freda Malkin; one *s* one *d*. *Educ:* Wolstanton Grammar Sch.; Saint David's Coll., Lampeter (BA 1953). Precentor, Trinidad Cathedral, 1955-61; Rector of Stoke Bruerne with Grafton Regis and Alderton, 1961-67; Vicar of Ravensthorpe with East Haddon and Holdenby, 1967-77; Rural Dean: Preston, 1965-67; Haddon, 1968-70; Brixworth, 1971-77; Non-Residentiary Canon, Peterborough Cathedral, 1974-77. *Address:* 18 Minster Precincts, Peterborough. *T:* Peterborough 62762.

FERNYHOUGH, Rt. Hon. Ernest, PC 1970; MP (Lab) Jarrow since May 1947; *b* 24 Dec. 1908; British; *m* 1934, Ethel Edwards; one *s* one *d* (and one *s* decd). *Educ:* Wood Lane Council Sch. Full-time official, Union of Shop, Distributive and Allied Workers, 1936-47. PPS to the Prime Minister, 1964-67; Jt Parly Under-Sec. of State, Dept of Employment and Productivity (formerly Min. of Labour), 1967-69. Freeman, Borough of Jarrow, 1972. *Address:* House of Commons, SW1.

FERNYHOUGH, Brigadier Hugh Edward, CBE 1956; DSO 1945; retired; *b* 15 April 1904; *s* of late Col Hugh Clifford Fernyhough and Mrs Beatrice Fernyhough; *m* 1943, Mary, *d* of late T. D. and Mrs Moore, Mill Down, Clyst St Mary, Exeter;

one s. *Educ:* Wellington Coll., Berks; RMA Woolwich. 2nd Lieut 1924; Lieut 1927; Capt. 1937; grad. Staff Coll., Camberley, 1939; GSO2, 12 Corps, 1940; GSO2, Instr, Staff Coll., Camberley, 1941; Comdt (Col) NZ Staff Coll., 1942-43; OC 53 (London) Medium Regt, 1944-45; Comdt (Col) RA, OCTU, 1945-46; CRA (Col) HQ, E Africa, 1947-48; Col i/c Admin., E Africa, 1948-49; AAG, RA, War Office, 1949-52; CRA 40 Inf. Div. (Hong Kong), 1952-53; Dep. Dir, RA, 1954-56; retd 1956. Col Comdt, Royal Artillery, 1957-62. *Address:* Mill Down, Clyst St Mary, Exeter. *T:* Topsham 4568. *Club:* Army and Navy.

FEROZE, Rustam Moolan, FRCS, FRCOG; Consultant Obstetrician and Gynæcologist; King's College Hospital; Consulting Obstetrician and Gynæcologist: Queen Charlotte's Maternity Hospital; Chelsea Hospital for Women; *b* 4 Aug. 1920; *s* of Dr J. Moolan-Feroze; *m* 1947, Margaret Dowsett. *Educ:* Sutton Valence Sch.; King's Coll. Hospital, London. MRCS, LRCP 1943; MB, BS 1946; MRCOG 1948; MD (Obst. & Dis. Wom.) London 1952; FRCS 1952; FRCOG 1962. Dean, Inst. of Obstetrics and Gynæcology, Univ. of London, 1954-67. Senr Registrar: Chelsea Hosp. for Women, and Queen Charlotte's Maternity Hosp., London, 1953-54; Hosp. for Women, Soho Square, and Middlesex Hosp., 1950-53; Resident Medical Officer, Samaritan Hosp. for Women, 1948. *Publications:* contribs to medical jls and to Integrated Obstetrics and Gynaecology for Postgraduates, 1976. *Address:* 127 Harley Street, W1. *T:* 01-935 8157. *Club:* Naval.

FERRANTI; see de Ferranti.

FERRAR, William Leonard; Principal, Hertford College, Oxford, 1959-64; *b* 21 Oct. 1893; *s* of George William Parsons and Maria Susannah Ferrar; *m* 1923, Edna O'Hara; one *s. Educ:* Queen Elizabeth's Hospital, Bristol; Bristol Grammar Sch.; Queen's Coll., Oxford. Open Mathematical Schol., Queen's, 1912; Univ. Junior Math. Schol., 1914; Sen. Schol., 1922; MA Oxon 1920; DSc Oxon 1947. Served European War, 1914-18, in ranks, Artillery and Intelligence, 1914-19. Lecturer, University Coll. of N Wales, Bangor, 1920-24; Sen. Lecturer, Edinburgh, 1924-25; Fellow, Hertford Coll., Oxford, 1925-59, Bursar, 1937-59. Formerly mem. Hebdomadal Council, Gen. Board and the Chest, Oxford Univ.; Sec., London Math. Soc., 1933-38. *Publications:* Convergence, 1938; Algebra, 1941; Higher Algebra for Schools, 1945, Part II, 1948; Finite Matrices, 1951; Differential Calculus, 1956; Integral Calculus, 1958; Mathematics for Science, 1965; Calculus for Beginners, 1967; Advanced Mathematics for Science, 1969; various research papers, 1924-37. *Recreations:* gardening; a little music. *Address:* 21 Sunderland Avenue, Oxford.

FERRARI, Enzo; President and Managing Director of Ferrari Automobili SpA Sefac, 1940-77; *b* Modena, 20 Feb. 1898; *s* of Alfredo Ferrari and Adalgisa Bisbini; *m* 1923, Laura Garello; one *s* decd. *Educ:* State sch.; Professional Institute of Technology. Started as tester, Turin, 1918; later with CMN, Milan; tester, driver, sales executive, Alfa Romeo, 1920-39; subsequently Dir, Alfa Corse; Pres. and Managing Dir of Scuderia Ferrari, later of Auto Avio Construzione Ferrari, 1940-60. Builder of racing, sports and gran turismo cars in factory built at Maranello in 1943 and reconstructed in 1946. Commendatore, 1928; Cavaliere del Lavoro, 1952. Hon. doctorate in engineering, Bologna, 1960. *Publication:* Le mie giole terribili (autobiog.). *Address:* viale Trento Trieste 31, Modena, Italy. *T:* 24081-24082; (office) Maranello, Modena, Italy. *T:* 91161-91162.

FERRER, José Vicente; actor, director and producer, USA; *b* 8 Jan. 1912; *s* of Rafael Ferrer and Maria Providencia (*née* Cintron); *m* 1st, 1938, Uta Hagen (marr. diss. 1948); one *d* ; 2nd, 1948, Phyllis Hill (marr. diss. 1953); 3rd, 1953, Rosemary Clooney (marr. diss. 1967); three *s* two *d. Educ:* Princeton Univ. AB (architecture), 1933. First appearance, The Periwinkle, Long Island show-boat, 1934; Asst Stage Manager Summer Theatre Stock Co., NY, 1935; first appearance NY stage, 1935; A Slight Case of Murder, 1935; Boy Meets Girl, 1935; Spring Dance, Brother Rat, 1936; In Clover, 1937; Dir Princeton Univ. Triangle Club's Fol-de-Rol, 1937; How To Get Tough About It, Missouri Legend, 1938; Mamba's Daughters, Key Largo, 1939; first star rôle, Lord Fancourt Babberley, Charley's Aunt, 1940; producer and dir, The Admiral Had A Wife, 1941; staged and co-starred, Vickie, 1942; Let's Face It, 1943; played Iago to Paul Robeson's Othello, Theatre Guild, 1943, 1944, 1945; producer and dir Strange Fruit, 1945; Play's The Thing, Richard III, Green Goddess, 1946; producer and star, Cyrano, 1946; Design For Living, Goodbye Again, 1947; Gen. dir to NY Theatre Co., City Centre, 1948; Silver Whistle, Theatre Guild, 1948; produced, directed and appeared in Twentieth Century, 1950; produced, directed, Stalag 17; The Fourposter, 1951; producer,

dir and appeared in The Shrike, 1952; The Chase, 1952; staged My 3 Angels, 1953; dir and co-author, Oh Captain, 1958; producer, dir, and starred in, Edwin Booth, 1959; dir, The Andersonville Trial, 1960; starred in, The Girl Who Came to Supper, 1963-64; Man of La Mancha, 1966; dir, Cyrano de Bergerac, Chichester, 1975; *Films include:* Joan of Arc, 1947; Whirlpool, 1949; Crisis, Cyrano, 1950; Anything Can Happen, 1951; Moulin Rouge, 1952; Miss Sadie Thompson (Rain), Caine Mutiny, 1953; Deep in My Heart, 1955; Cockleshell Heroes, The Great Man, 1957; The High Cost of Loving, I Accuse, The Shrike (Dir, starred), 1958; Return to Peyton Place (Dir), 1962; State Fair (Dir), 1963; Nine Hours to Rama, Lawrence of Arabia, 1963; Cyrano et D'Artagnan, Train 349 From Berlin, The Greatest Story Ever Told, 1964; Ship of Fools, Enter Laughing, 1966. Holds hon. degrees. Various awards for acting, etc, since 1944, include American Academy of Arts and Letters Gold Medal, 1949; Academy Award, 1950 (Best Actor, Cyrano). *Recreation:* tennis. *Address:* MEW Company, 151 North San Vicente Boulevard, Beverly Hills, Calif 90211, USA.

FERRERS, 13th Earl *cr* 1711; **Robert Washington Shirley;** Viscount Tamworth 1711; Bt 1611; Joint Deputy Leader of the Opposition, House of Lords, since 1976; *b* 8 June 1929; *o s* of 12th Earl Ferrers and Hermione Morley (*d* 1969); *S* father, 1954; *m* 1951, Annabel Mary, *d* of Brig. W. G. Carr, *qv* ; two *s* three *d. Educ:* Winchester Coll.; Magdalene Coll., Cambridge. MA (Agric.). Lieut Coldstream Guards, 1949 (as National Service). A Lord-in-Waiting, 1962-64, 1971-74; Parly Sec., MAFF, 1974. Mem., Armitage Cttee on political activities of civil servants, 1976-. Vice-Chm., East Anglian Trustee Savings Bank, 1971-75; Chm., Trustee Savings Bank of Eastern England, 1977-; Director: Norwich Union Life Insurance Soc.; Norwich Union Fire Insurance Soc. Ltd; Scottish Union & National Insurance Co.; Maritime Insurance Co. Mem. of Council, Hurstpierpoint Coll., 1959-68. *Heir: s* Viscount Tamworth, *qv. Address:* Hedenham Hall, Norfolk. *T:* Woodton 250. *Club:* Beefsteak.

FERRIER, Baron *cr* 1958, of Culter (Life Peer); **Victor Ferrier Noel-Paton**, ED; DL; *b* Edinburgh, 1900; *s* of late F. Noel-Paton, Dir-Gen. of Commercial Intelligence to the Govt of India; *m* 1932, Joane Mary, *d* of late Sir Gilbert Wiles, KCIE, CSI; one *s* three *d. Educ:* Cargilfield and The Edinburgh Academy. Commercial and Industrial Management, Bombay, 1920-51; one time Dir and Chm. of a number of Cos in India and UK; Pres., Bombay Chamber of Commerce. MLC (Bombay), and Hon. ADC to Governor of Bombay. Served RE, 1918-19, IAF (Major, ED), 1920-46, and IARO. Mem. of Royal Company of Archers. DL, Lanarks, 1960. *Recreations:* shooting, gardening. *Address:* Bankhead, East Linton, East Lothian. *T:* Whitekirk 234. *Clubs:* Cavalry and Guards; Beefsteak; New (Edinburgh).
See also Sir Charles Fergusson, Bt.

FERRIER, Sir (Harold) Grant, Kt 1969; CMG 1964; Vice Chairman, Weir Group (Australia) Pty Ltd; *b* 26 Aug. 1905; *m* 1949, Margaret James; one *d. Educ:* Sydney Grammar Sch. CEng, MIMarE. President: Metal Trades Employers' Assoc., 1949-51; Australian Metal Industries Assoc., 1951-52; Chamber of Manufactures of NSW, 1963-65; Associated Chambers of Manufactures of Aust., 1963-65; Chairman: The Commonwealth Portland Cement Co. Ltd and subsids, 1952-71; Associated Portland Cement Manufacturers (Australia) Ltd, 1952-71; State Develt Corp. of NSW, 1966-69; Heavy Engineering Industry Adv. Cttee to Commonwealth Govt, 1957-67; Nat. Employers Policy Cttee, 1962-64; Dep. Employer Mem., Gov. Body, ILO. Pres., Internat. Organisation of Employers, Geneva, 1966-67. *Recreations:* yachting and fly-fishing. *Address:* 9 Cliff View Road, Leura, NSW 2781, Australia. *Clubs:* Commonwealth (Canberra); Royal Sydney Yacht Squadron, Royal Sydney Golf, Rugby Union.

FERRIER, Prof. Robert Patton, FRSE 1977; Professor of Natural Philosophy, University of Glasgow, since 1973; *b* 4 Jan. 1934; *s* of William McFarlane Ferrier and Gwendoline Melita Edwards; *m* 1961, Valerie Jane Duncan; two *s* one *d. Educ:* Glebelands Sch. and Morgan Academy, Dundee; Univ. of St Andrews (BSc, PhD). MA Cantab, FInstP. Scientific Officer, AERE Harwell, 1959-61; Res. Assoc., MIT, 1961-62; Sen. Asst in Res., Cavendish Lab., Cambridge, 1962-66; Fellow of Fitzwilliam Coll., Cambridge, 1965-73; Asst Dir of Res., Cavendish Lab. 1966-71; Lectr in Physics, Univ. of Cambridge, 1971-73; Guest Scientist, IBM Res. Labs San José, Calif, 1972-73. *Publications:* numerous papers in Phil. Mag., Jl Appl. Physics, Jl Physics, etc. *Recreations:* do-it-yourself, golf, reading crime novels. *Address:* Glencoe, 31 Thorn Road, Bearsden, Dunbartonshire G61 4BS. *T:* 041-942 0328.

FERRIS, see Grant-Ferris, family name of Baron Harvington.

FERRIS, Paul Frederick; author and journalist; b 15 Feb. 1929; o c of late Frederick Morgan Ferris and of Olga Ferris; m 1953, Gloria Moreton; one s one d. Educ: Swansea Gram. Sch. Staff of South Wales Evening Post, 1949-52; Womans Own, 1953; Observer Foreign News Service, 1953-54. Publications: novels: A Changed Man, 1958; Then We Fall, 1960; A Family Affair, 1963; The Destroyer, 1965; The Dam, 1967; Very Personal Problems, 1973; The Cure, 1974; The Detective, 1976; non-fiction: The City, 1960; The Church of England, 1962; The Doctors, 1965; The Nameless: abortion in Britain today, 1966; Men and Money: financial Europe today, 1968; The House of Northcliffe, 1971; The New Militants, 1972; Dylan Thomas, 1977; contribs to The Observer; radio and TV programmes. Address: c/o Curtis Brown Ltd, 1 Craven Hill, W2. T: 01-262 1011.

FERRYMAN, Col E. E. M.; see Mockler-Ferryman.

FESSEY, Mereth Cecil, CB 1977; Director, Business Statistics Office, 1969-77, retired; b Windsor, Berks, 19 May 1917; s of late Morton Fessey and Ethel Fessey (née Blake), Bristol; m 1945, Grace Lilian, d of late William Bray, Earlsfield, London; one s two d. Educ: Westminster City Sch.; LSE, Univ. of London. London Transport, 1934; Army, 1940; Min. of Transport, 1947; Board of Trade, 1948; Statistician, 1956; Chief Statistician, 1965. Chm. of Council, Inst. of Statisticians, 1970-73; Vice Pres. and Mem., Council, Royal Statistical Soc. Publications: articles and papers in: Economic Trends; Statistical News; The Statistician; Annales de Sciences Economiques Appliquées, Louvain; etc. Recreations: chess, walking. Address: Undy House, Undy, Gwent NP6 3BX. T: Magor 478.

FETHERSTON-DILKE, Mary Stella, CBE 1968; RRC 1966; Organiser, Citizens' Advice Bureau, since 1971; b 21 Sept. 1918; d of late B. A. Fetherston-Dilke, MBE. Educ: Kingsley Sch., Leamington Spa; St George's Hospital, London (SRN). Joined QARNNS, 1942; Matron-in-Chief, QARNNS, 1966-70, retired. OStJ 1966. Recreations: archery, antiques. Address: 12 Clareville Court, Clareville Grove, SW7.

FEUILLÈRE, Edwige; Chevalier de la Légion d'Honneur; Commandeur des Arts et Lettres; French actress; b 29 Oct.; m (divorced). Educ: Dijon; Paris. Plays include: La Dame aux camélias; Sodome et Gomorrhe; L'Aigle a deux têtes; Partage de midi; Pour Lucrèce; La Parisienne; Phèdre; Lucy Crown; Constance; Rodogune; La Folle de Chaillot; Delicate Balance; Sweet Bird of Youth. Films include: L'Idiot; Olivia; Le Blé en herbe; L'Aigle a deux têtes; En cas de malheur; La vie à deux; Les amours célèbres; Le crime ne paye pas; La chair de l'orchidée. Address: 19 Rue Eugène Manuel, Paris XVIe.

FEVERSHAM, 6th Baron cr 1826; Charles Antony Peter Duncombe; free-lance journalist; b 3 Jan. 1945; s of Col Antony John Duncombe-Anderson and G. G. V. McNalty; S (to barony of) kinsman, 3rd Earl of Feversham (the earldom having become extinct), 1963; m 1966, Shannon (d 1976) d of late Sir Thomas Foy, CSI, CIE; two s one d. Educ: Eton; Middle Temple. Chairman: Yorkshire Arts Assoc., 1969; Standing Conf. of Regional Arts Assocs, 1969-76. Governor, Leeds Polytechnic, 1969-76. Pres., Soc. of Yorkshiremen in London, 1974; Co-Pres. (with Ted Hughes) The Arvon Foundn, 1976-. Publications: A Wolf in Tooth (novel), 1967; Great Yachts, 1970. Heir: s Hon. Jasper Orlando Slingsby Duncombe, b 14 March 1968. Address: Beckdale House, Helmsley, York.

FEYNMAN, Prof. Richard (Phillips); Professor of Physics, California Institute of Technology, Pasadena, Calif, since 1951; b 11 May 1918; s of Melville Feynman and Lucille (née Phillips); m 1960, Gweneth Howarth, Ripponden, Yorks; one s one d. Educ: MIT; Princeton Univ. Los Alamos, N Mex. Atomic Bomb Project, 1943-46; Cornell Univ., 1946-51. Nobel Prize for Physics (jointly), 1965. Mem. Brazilian Acad. of Sciences; Fellow (Foreign), Royal Soc., London. Publications: The Feynman Lectures in Physics, 1963; The Character of Physical Law, 1965; Statistical Mechanics, 1972; Photon-Hadron Interactions, 1972; papers in Physical Review on quantum electro-dynamics, liquid helium, theory of beta-decay. Recreations: Mayan Hieroglyphics, opening safes, playing bongo drums, drawing, biology experiments (none done well). Address: 2475 Boulder Road, Altadena, Calif 91001, USA. T: 213-797-1262.

FFOLKES, Sir Robert (Francis Alexander), 7th Bt cr 1774; b 2 Dec. 1943; o s of Capt. Sir (Edward John) Patrick (Boschetti) ffolkes, 6th Bt (s of Sir Francis ffolkes, 5th Bt, MVO), and of Geraldine (d of late William Roffey, Writtle, Essex); S father,

1960. Educ: Stowe Sch.; Christ Church, Oxford. Address: Starlings, Yoxford, Saxmundham, Suffolk. T: Yoxford 387. Club: Turf.

FFORDE, Sir Arthur (Frederic Brownlow), GBE 1964; Kt 1946; MA Oxon; b 23 Aug. 1900; s of late Arthur Brownlow fforde, Indian Civil Service, and Mary Alice Storer Branson; m 1926, Mary Alison, yr d of late James MacLehose, printer to University of Glasgow; two s one d. Educ: Rugby Sch.; Trinity Coll., Oxford. Admitted Solicitor, 1925; Partner in firm of Linklaters & Paines, London, 1928-48; Mem. of Council of Law Soc., London, 1937-48; Deputy Dir-Gen., Ministry of Supply, (Finance) 1940, (Contracts) 1941; Under-Sec., Contracts Finance, Ministry of Supply, 1943; Under-Sec., HM Treasury, 1944-45; Head Master of Rugby Sch., 1948-57; Chm., the British Broadcasting Corporation, 1957-64; Mem., Central Board of Finance of Church of England, 1957-70 (Vice-Chm., 1957-60, Chm., 1960-65); Director, 1957-70: Equity & Law Life Assurance Society Ltd; National Westminster Bank Ltd, and other cos. Hon. LLD University of Wales. Address: Wall's End, Wonersh, near Guildford, Surrey.
See also M. W. McCrum.

FFORDE, John Standish; an Executive Director of the Bank of England, since 1970; b 16 Nov. 1921; 4th s of late Francis Creswell Fforde and late Cicely Creswell; m 1951, Marya, d of late Joseph Retinger; three s one d. Educ: Rossall Sch.; Christ Church, Oxford (1st cl. Hons PPE). Served RAF, 1940-46. Prime Minister's Statistical Branch, 1951-53; Fellow, Nuffield Coll., Oxford, 1953-56; entered Bank of England, 1957; Dep. Chief, Central Banking Information Dept, 1959-64; Adviser to the Governors, 1964-66; Chief Cashier, 1966-70. Publications: The Federal Reserve System, 1945-49, 1953; An International Trade in Managerial Skills, 1957. Recreations: travel, walking. Address: 106 Hawtrey Road, NW3. T: 01-722 8216.

FFOWCS WILLIAMS, Prof. John Eirwyn; Rank Professor of Engineering (Acoustics), University of Cambridge, and Professorial Fellow, Emmanuel College, Cambridge, since 1972; b 25 May 1935; m 1959, Anne Beatrice Mason; one s one d. Educ: Friends Sch., Great Ayton; Derby Techn. Coll.; Univ. of Southampton. BSc, MA Cantab, PhD. CEng, FRAeS, FInstP, FIMA, Fellow Acoustical Soc. of America. Engrg Apprentice, Rolls-Royce Ltd, 1951-55; Spitfire Mitchell Meml Schol. to Southampton Univ., 1955-60; Aerodynamics Div., NPL, 1960-62; Bolt, Beranek & Newman Inc., 1962-64; Reader in Applied Maths, Imperial Coll. of Science and Technology, 1964-69; Rolls Royce Prof. of Theoretical Acoustics, Imperial Coll., 1969-72. Exec. Consultant, Rolls Royce Ltd, 1969-; Chm., Noise Research Cttee, ARC, 1969-76. Publications: articles in Philosophical Trans Royal Soc., Jl of Fluid Mechanics, Jl IMA, Jl of Sound Vibration, Annual Reviews of Fluid Mechanics, Random Vibration, Financial Times; (jtly) film on Aerodynamic Sound. Recreations: friends and cigars. Address: 298 Hills Road, Cambridge CB2 2QG. T: Cambridge 48275.

FFRANGCON-DAVIES, Gwen; Actress; d of David Ffrangcon-Davies, the famous singer, and Annie Frances Rayner. Educ: South Hampstead High Sch.; abroad. First London success The Immortal Hour, 1922; created the part of Eve in Shaw's Back to Methuselah; principal successes, Tess, in Tess of the Durbevilles, Elizabeth Barrett, in The Barretts of Wimpole Street, Anne of Bohemia, in Richard of Bordeaux. Played Lady Macbeth to Macbeth of John Gielgud, Piccadilly, 1942. Appeared, in association with Marda Vanne, in leading parts in various plays in S Africa, 1943-46. Returned to England, 1949; played in Adventure Story, St James's, 1949; Stratford Festival, 1950, as Katherine in King Henry VIII; Portia in Julius Cæsar, Regan in King Lear (again Katherine, Old Vic. 1953); Madame Ranevsky in The Cherry Orchard, Lyric, 1954; Aunt Cleofe in Summertime, Apollo, 1955; Rose Padley in The Mulberry Bush, Royal Court, 1956; Agatha in The Family Reunion, Phoenix, 1956; Miss Madrigal in The Chalk Garden, Haymarket, 1957; Mrs Callifer in The Potting Shed, Globe Theatre, 1958; Mary Tyrone in Long Day's Journey into Night, Edinburgh Fest. and Globe, 1958; Queen Isolde in Ondine, Aldwych, 1961; Queen Mother in Becket, Aldwych, 1961; Hester Bellboys in A Penny for a Song, Aldwych, 1962; Beatrice in Season of Goodwill, Queen's, 1964; Amanda in The Glass Menagerie, Haymarket, 1965; Uncle Vanya, Royal Court, 1970; Films: The Burning, 1967; Leo the Last, 1969. Recreation: gardening. Address: c/o Larry Dalzell, 3 Goodwins Court, WC2.

FFRENCH, family name of Baron ffrench.

FFRENCH, 7th Baron, cr 1798; Peter Martin Joseph Charles John Mary ffrench; b 2 May 1926; s of Capt. Hon. John Martin Valentine ffrench (d 1946), s of 5th Baron, and of Sophia, d of late Signor Giovanni Brambilla, Villa Sucota, Como, Italy; *S* uncle 1955; *m* 1954, Sonia Katherine, *d* of Major Digby Cayley; one *s* two *d. Heir: s* Hon. Robuck John Peter Charles Mario ffrench, *b* 14 March 1956. *Address:* Castle ffrench, Ballinasloe, Co. Galway.

FFRENCH-BEYTAGH, Canon Gonville Aubie; Rector of St Vedast-alias-Foster, London, since 1974; Hon. Canon of Johannesburg, since 1972 and of Canterbury, since 1973; *b* 26 Jan. 1912; *s* of Leo Michael and Edith ffrench-Beytagh; unmarried. *Educ:* Monkton Combe Sch., Bath; Bristol Grammar Sch.; St Paul's Theol Coll., Grahamstown (LTh). Priest 1939. Tramp and casual labourer, New Zealand, 1929-33; clerk in Johannesburg, 1933-36; Parish Priest and Diocesan Missioner, Johannesburg Dio., 1939-54; Dean of Salisbury, Rhodesia, 1955-65; Dean of Johannesburg, 1965-72; detained, tried, convicted and sentenced to 5 yrs imprisonment under SA Terrorism Act, 1971-72; conviction and sentence quashed by Appellate Div. and returned to England, 1972. *Publications:* Encountering Darkness, 1973; Encountering Light, 1975. *Recreations:* drink, companionship and science fiction. *Address:* St Vedast's Rectory, Foster Lane, EC2. *T:* 01-606 3998.

FICKLING, Benjamin William, CBE 1973; FRCS, FDS RCS; Honorary Consultant Dental Surgeon, since 1974; formerly Dental Surgeon: St George's Hospital, SW1, 1936-74; Royal Dental Hospital of London, 1935-74; Mount Vernon Centre for Plastic and Jaw Surgery (formerly Hill End), 1941-74; Civilian Dental Consultant to Royal Navy since 1954; *b* 14 July 1909; *s* of Robert Marshall Fickling, LDS RCS, and Florence (*née* Newson); *m* 1943, Shirley Dona, *er d* of Albert Latimer Walker, FRCS; two *s* one *d. Educ:* Framlingham; St George's Hosp. Royal Dental Hospital. William Brown Senior Exhibition, St George's Hosp., 1929; LDS RCS, 1932; MRCS, LRCP, 1934; FRCS 1938; FDS, RCS 1947. Charles Tomes Lecturer, RCS 1956. Formerly Examiner: in Dental Surgery, RCS; Univ. of London and Univ. of Edinburgh. Dean of Faculty of Dental Surgery, 1968-71, and Mem. Council, Royal College of Surgeons, 1968-71 (Vice-dean, 1965); Fellow Royal Society of Medicine (Pres. Odontological Section, 1964-65); Pres., British Assoc. of Oral Surgeons, 1967-68; Mem GDC, 1971-74. Dir., Med. Sickness Annuity and Life Assurance Soc. Ltd. *Publications:* (joint) Injuries of the Jaws and Face, 1940; (joint) Chapter on Faciomaxillary Injuries and Deformities in British Surgical Practice, 1951. *Address:* 129 Harley Street, W1. *T:* 01-935 1882; Linksview, Linksway, Northwood, Mddx. *T:* Northwood 22035. *Club:* Ski Club of Great Britain.

FIDDES, James Raffan, QC (Scot.) 1965; *b* 1 Feb. 1919; *er s* of late Sir James Raffan Fiddes, CBE; *m* 1954, Edith Margaret, 2nd *d* of late Charles E. Lippe, KC. *Educ:* Aberdeen Gram. Sch.; Glasgow Univ. (MA, 1942; LLB 1948); Balliol Coll., Oxford, (BA 1944). Advocate, 1948. *Address:* 23 South Learmonth Gardens, Edinburgh EH4 1EZ. *T:* 031-332 1431. *Club:* Scottish Arts (Edinburgh).

FIDGE, Sir (Harold) Roy, Kt 1967; JP; Commissioner since 1956, Chairman since 1963, Geelong Harbor Trust; *b* Warracknabeal, Vic., 24 Dec. 1904; *s* of Edward Fidge, Beulah, Vic.; *m* 1st, 1934, Mavis Melba Jane (*d* 1948), *d* of James Robert Burke, Warracknabeal; one *s* one *d*; 2nd, 1949, Nance, *d* of George Davidson, Sydney, NSW. *Educ:* Geelong High Sch.; Geelong Coll.; Ormond Coll., University of Melbourne (LLB). Admitted Barrister and Solicitor, Supreme Court of Victoria, 1929. Royal Australian Navy, 1940-45; Lt-Comdr RANR. Councillor, City of Geelong, 1939-40, and 1946-; Mayor of City of Geelong, 1954-56 and 1964-68. Hon. Nat. Sec.-Treas, Assoc. of Apex Clubs, 1934-40, 1946-47; President: East Geelong Br., Aust. Red Cross Soc., 1961-67; Geelong E Techn. Sch. Council, 1960-65; Geelong Law Assoc., 1959-60 (Hon. Sec.-Treas., 1934-40, 1945-54); Member: Exec. Cttee of Municipal Assoc. of Victoria, 1964-; Council, Assoc. of Port and Marine Authorities of Aust., 1968-. Victorian Employers' Fedn Community Service Award, 1967. *Recreations:* gardening, woodwork. *Address:* 23 Meakin Street, Geelong, Victoria 3219, Australia. *T:* Geelong 95304. *Clubs:* Geelong, RSL, Ex-Navalmen's Assoc., Legacy, Victoria League, Geelong Rotary (Hon.) (all Australia).

FIDLER, Alwyn G. Sheppard, CBE 1963; MA, BArch, DipCD, FRIBA, FRTPI; architect and town planning consultant (A. G. Sheppard Fidler and Associates), since 1964; Director, Building Centre Trust and Building Centre Ltd, since 1974; *b* 8 May 1909; *e s* of late W. E. Sheppard Fidler and Phoebe M. Williams; *m* 1936, Margaret (*d* 1977), *d* of Capt. J. R. Kidner, Newcastle upon Tyne; one *s. Educ:* Holywell Gram. Sch.; University of Liverpool; British Sch. at Rome. Tite Finalist, 1930; studied in USA, 1931; Victory Schol., 1933; Rome Schol. in Architecture, 1933-35. Chief Architect: Land Settlement Assoc., 1937;

Barclays Bank Ltd, 1938; Sen. Tech. Intelligence Officer, Min. of Home Security, 1940-46; Chief Archt, Crawley New Town, 1947-52 (Housing Medals of Min. of Housing and Local Govt in 1951, 1952 and 1954); City Archt of Birmingham, 1952-64 (Distinction in Town Planning, 1955, for work at Crawley and Birmingham Redevelopment Areas); private practice, 1964-74. Council Mem., 1953-62, 1963-75, Vice-Pres., 1958-60, Chm. Practice Cttee, 1958-62, Treasurer, 1974-75, External Examr in Architecture, 1958-, RIBA. Pres. City and Borough Architects Soc., 1956-58; Chm. Exec. Cttee, British Sch. at Rome, 1972- (Chm., Fac. of Architecture, 1958-72). Mem., Royal Commn for the Exhibn of 1851. Chm. ARC of UK, 1960-63; Mem. Jt Consultative Cttee of Architects, Quantity Surveyors and Builders, 1958-61; Mem. Birmingham and Five Counties Architectural Assoc. (Mem. Council, 1956-, Vice-Pres., 1960-62, Pres., 1962-64); Chm. Assoc. of Building Centres, 1964-72; Member Council: Building Centre Gp, 1971-; Royal Albert Hall, 1974-; Gov., Coll. of Estate Management, 1965-72; Mem. SE Regional Adv. Cttee to Land Commn, 1967-70. Mem. or past Mem., of many other councils and cttees. *Publications:* Contrib. to professional jls. *Recreations:* travel and gardening. *Address:* Woodlands, Alma Road, Reigate, Surrey. *T:* Reigate 43849. *Club:* Royal Automobile.

FIDLER, Michael M., JP; President, General Zionist Organisation of Great Britain, since 1973; Founder and Director, Conservative Friends of Israel, since 1974; Chairman, International Organisation Committee, World Jewish Congress, since 1975; business consultant; Managing Director, Wibye Ltd, since 1968; *b* 10 Feb. 1916; *s* of Louis Fidler and Goldie Fidler (*née* Sherr); *m* 1939, Maidie (*née* Davis); one *s* one *d. Educ:* Salford Grammar Sch.; Salford Royal Tech Coll. Cllr, Borough of Prestwich, 1951-63; Mayor, 1957-58; Alderman, 1963-74. Pres., Middleton, Prestwich and Whitfield Div. Cons. Assoc., 1965-69; Chm., Divl Educn Exec. (Prestwich, Whitfield and Radcliffe), Lancs CC, 1967-69. MP (C) Bury and Radcliffe, 1970-Sept. 1974; Sec., Canadian Gp of Cons. Commonwealth Overseas Cttee, 1970-71; Treasurer, Parly Migraine Gp, 1970-74. Lectr, Extra Mural Dept, Manchester Univ., 1966-. Man. Director: H. & L. Fidler Ltd, 1941-70; Michael Lewis Ltd, 1942-70. Member: Grand Council, CBI, 1965-67; Nat. Exec., Nat. Assoc. of British Manufacturers, 1953-65. President: Fedn of Jewish Youth Socs of Gt Britain and Ireland, 1951-; Manchester Union of Jewish Socs, 1964-; Council of Manchester and Salford Jews, 1966-68 (Hon. Sec., 1950-53; Hon. Treasurer, 1953-55; Vice-Pres, 1954-60); Holy Law Congregation, Manchester, 1967-70; Bd of Deputies of British Jews, 1967-73; Vice-President: Children and Youth Aliyah Cttee for Gt Britain, 1968-; Mizrachi, Hapoel-Hamizrachi Fedn of Gt Britain and Ireland, 1968-; Hillel Foundn of Gt Britain, 1968-; Life Vice-President: Manchester Jewish Bd of Guardians, 1967-; Manchester Jewish Social Services, 1967-; Vice-Chairman: World Conf. on Jewish Educn, 1968-; World Conf. of Jewish Organisations, 1967-73; Member Exec. Cttee: Council of Christians and Jews, Manchester Branch, 1966-; World Meml Foundn for Jewish Culture, 1968-; World Conf. on Jewish Material Claims against Germany, 1968-. Patron, All Party Cttee for release of Soviet Jewry, 1971-. Governor: Strand Grammar Schools, 1955-74; Inst. of Contemporary Jewry, Hebrew Univ. of Jerusalem, 1967-; St Peter's RC Grammar Sch., 1968-; Bury Grammar Schools, 1970-74. President: British Parks Lawn Tennis Assoc., 1952-59; SE Lancs Amateur Football League, 1966-67; Prestwich Heys Amateur Football Club, 1965-; Member: House of Commons Motor Club, 1970-74; Parly Flying Club, 1971-74. JP Co. Lancs, 1958. FRGS, FRAS, FREconS, FIAI. *Publications:* One Hundred Years of the Holy Law Congregation, 1964; articles. *Recreations:* politics, travel, reading, filming, foreign affairs, education. *Address:* 51 Tavistock Court, Tavistock Square, WC1. *T:* 01-387 4925; 1 Woodcliffe Lodge, Sedgley Park Road, Prestwich, Manchester M25 8AL. *T:* 061-773 1471. *Clubs:* Embassy; Milverton Lodge (Manchester).

FIELD, Brig. Anne; Director, Women's Royal Army Corps, since 1977; Hon. ADC to the Queen, since 1977; *b* 4 April 1926; *d* of Captain Harold Derwent and Annie Helena Hodgson. *Educ:* Keswick Sch.; St George's, Harpenden; London Sch. of Economics. Joined ATS, 1947; commissioned: ATS, 1948; WRAC, 1949; Lt-Col, 1968; Col, 1971. *Address:* c/o Barclays Bank Ltd, Keswick, Cumbria. *Club:* Lansdowne.

FIELD, Arnold, OBE 1965; Joint Field Commander, National Air Traffic Services, since 1974; *b* 19 May 1917; *m* 1943, Kathleen Dulcie Bennett; one *s* one *d. Educ:* King Edward's Grammar Sch., Birmingham. RAF, 1940-46 (Sqdn Ldr). Civil Air Traffic Control Officer, 1946; Centre Supt, Scottish Air Traffic Control Centre, 1954; Centre Supt, London Air Traffic Control Centre, 1957; Divisional Air Traffic Control Officer,

Southern Div., 1963; Dir, Civil Air Traffic Ops, 1969. Master, Guild of Air Traffic Control Officers, 1958; Pres., Internat. Fedn of Air Traffic Control Officers, 1970. *Publications:* articles in Intervia, Times Supplement, Flight, Controller. *Recreations:* vintage cars, boating. *Address:* Footprints, Stoke Wood, Stoke Poges, Bucks. *T:* Farnham Common 2710. *Club:* Bentley Drivers (Long Crendon).

FIELD, Edward, DSO 1918; Retired; Rag Merchant; President, Dewsbury Chamber of Commerce, 1954-57; *b* 22 May 1898; *s* of late Joseph Field and Louisa Wardell; *m* 1st, 1924, Florrie (*d* 1972), *d* of Alderman F. Greenwood, Dewsbury; one *d*; 2nd, 1973, Jennie Philipson, *widow* of Gordon Philipson, Scarborough. *Educ:* The Wheelwright Grammar Sch., Dewsbury. Artists' Rifles, 1916; 2nd Lieut, MG Corps, 1917 (DSO, despatches); Asst Officer in charge of Salvage Inspectorate, 1918; Managing Dir and Chm., Joseph Field, Ltd; Pres. British Woollen Rag Merchants Association, 1945-48; Technical Officer Wool Control (Salvage Section), 1940-45; Waste (MR) Wages Council; CO 2nd Cadet Battalion KOYLI (Major), 1942-46. Chm. Dewsbury and District Employment Cttee, 1956-68. FInstD, 1955-68. *Publications:* various articles on Social Credit 1930-46. *Recreations:* contract bridge (Yorks Individual Champion, 1960, Yorks Pairs Championship, 1961), motoring. *Address:* Greendale Court, Sea Cliff Crescent, Scarborough YO11 2XY. *T:* Scarborough 66446. *Club:* Dewsbury (Dewsbury).

FIELD, Frank; Director: Child Poverty Action Group, since 1969; Low Pay Unit, since 1974; *b* 16 July 1942; *s* of Walter and Annie Field. *Educ:* St Clement Danes Grammar Sch.; Univ. of Hull (BSc (Econ)). Teacher: at Southwark Coll. for Further Education, 1964-68; at Hammersmith Coll. for Further Education, 1968-69. Mem., Hounslow BC, 1964-68. Contested (Lab) Buckingham S, 1966. *Publications:* (ed, jtly) Twentieth Century State Education, 1971; (ed, jtly) Black Britons, 1971; (ed) Low Pay, 1973; Unequal Britain, 1974; (ed) Are Low Wages Inevitable?, 1976; (ed) Education and the Urban Crisis, 1976; (ed) The Conscript Army: a study of Britain's unemployed, 1976; (jtly) To Him Who Hath: a study of poverty and taxation, 1976. *Recreation:* book collecting. *Address:* Flat 2, 118 Barrowgate Road, W4. *T:* 01-994 3771.

FIELD, Frank Eustace; Chief Justice of the Supreme Court of the Windward Islands and Leeward Islands, 1963-67; retired. *Educ:* Harrison College, Barbados. Puisne Judge, Supreme Court, Barbados, 1957-63; Solicitor-Gen., Barbados, 1954-57. *Address:* Grand Anse, St George's, Grenada, West Indies.

FIELD, John, CBE 1967; ARAD; Artistic Director, Royal Academy of Dancing, since 1975; Director, Royal Academy of Dancing, since 1976; *b* 22 Oct. 1921; *m* 1958, Anne Heaton. *Educ:* Wheatley Boys' Sch., Doncaster. Sadler's Wells Ballet Co., 1939; RAF, 1942-46; Principal, Sadler's Wells Ballet Co., 1947-56; Resident Dir, Sadler's Wells Theatre Ballet, 1956-57; Asst Dir, 1957-70, Co-Dir, July-Dec. 1970, Royal Ballet Co.; Dir of Ballet, La Scala, Milan, 1971-74. *Address:* c/o Yorkshire Bank, 56 Cheapside, EC2. *Club:* Garrick.

FIELD, Sir John (Osbaldiston), KBE 1967; Kt 1962; CMG 1959; first Governor, Gilbert and Ellice Islands Colony, 1972-73 (Resident Commissioner, 1970-71); *b* 30 Oct. 1913; *s* of late Frank Osbaldiston Field; *m* 1951, Irene Margaret, 2nd *d* of late Harold Godfrey Judd, CBE. *Educ:* Stellenbosch Boys' High Sch. S Africa; Magdalene Coll., Cambridge (MA). Colonial Administrative Service, Nigeria, 1936; Senior District Officer, 1951; Resident, 1954; Commissioner of the Cameroons, 1956; UK Special Representative for British Cameroons at UN Trusteeship Council, 1956-61; Commissioner of Southern Cameroons, 1960-61; Governor and C-in-C of St Helena, 1962-68; Staff Liaison Officer, HM Overseas Civil Service, 1968-69; acting Administrator, Montserrat, 1969. *Recreation:* fishing. *Address:* Fairfield, PO Box 35, Himeville 4585, Natal, South Africa. *Club:* United Oxford & Cambridge University.

FIELD, John William, CMG 1951; JMN 1964; MD; DSc; Colonial Medical Service, retired; *b* 5 Aug. 1899; *s* of late Walter Field, Birmingham, England; *m* 1921, Elsie Mary, *d* of late William Dodd, Cardiff; one *s* three *d. Educ:* Oldbury Secondary Sch.; Birmingham Univ. Served European War, 1917-19. MB, ChB (Birmingham), 1924; Medical Officer, Malayan Medical Service, 1925; MD (Birmingham, Hons), 1929; Malaria Research Officer, Inst. for Med. Research, Federation of Malaya, 1931. Chalmers Medal, Royal Society of Tropical Medicine, 1941. Interned by Japanese in Singapore, 1942-45. Dir, Institute for Medical Research, Federation of Malaya, 1949-56. Mem., Expert Adv. Panel on Malaria, WHO, 1956-76. Hon. DSc (Malaya), 1959. *Publications:* various papers on tropical medicine. *Address:* The Knoll, Whitchurch, Ross-on-Wye, Herefordshire.

FIELD, Brig. Leonard Frank, CB 1953; CBE 1945; *b* 6 March 1898; *s* of Major Joseph Thomas Field and Amelia Phillips; *m* 1923, Genevieve Bowyer; one *s. Educ:* Bedford; RMC, Sandhurst. Served European War: commissioned 2nd Lieut, 1916; War of 1939-45: DDMI (Far East), 1941; Dir of Intelligence, SW Pacific Command, 1942; Chief Chinese Liaison Officer, Burma, 1942; Military Attaché: China, 1545-49; Indo-China, 1951-52. Brig. 1952; retired Nov. 1952. Knight Comdr, Order of Orange Nassau (with Swords), 1945. *Address:* c/o Lloyds Bank Ltd (Cox's & King's), 6 Pall Mall, SW1.

FIELD, Stanley Alfred; Chairman: William Baird & Co. Ltd; Winterbottom Trust Ltd; Director: Butterfield Harvey Ltd; Thomas Cook Group Ltd; Dawson International Ltd; Automobile Association Ltd; Merchants Trust Ltd; Expanded Metal Co. Ltd; NA Holdings Ltd; *b* 1913; *m* 1950, Doreen Plunkett; one *s* two *d.* Senior Partner, W. N. Middleton & Co., 1946-53; Man. Dir, Prestige Group Ltd, 1953-58; Dir, Venesta Ltd, 1956- (Chm., 1958-64). Liveryman, Glass Sellers Company. *Address:* (office) City Wall House, 84-90 Chiswell Street, EC1Y 4TP; (home) Glasses, Graffham, Petworth, West Sussex GU28 0PU. *Clubs:* Carlton, City Livery.

FIELD, William James; *b* 22 May 1909; *s* of late Frederick William Field, Solicitor; unmarried. *Educ:* Richmond County Sch.; London Univ.; abroad. Joined Labour Party, 1935; Parliamentary Private Sec. to Sec. of State for War, May-Oct. 1951 (to Under-Sec. for War, 1950-51); Chm. South Hammersmith Divisional Labour Party, 1945-46; contested Hampstead Div., General Election, 1945; MP (Lab) North Paddington, Nov. 1946-Oct. 1953. Mem. Hammersmith Borough Council, 1945-53, and Leader of that Council, 1946-49; a Vice-Pres. of Assoc. of Municipal Corporations, 1952-53; for several years, mem. Metropolitan Boroughs' Standing Joint Cttee and of many local govt bodies. Volunteered for Army, Sept. 1939 and served in ranks and as officer in Intelligence Corps and RASC.

FIELD-FISHER, Thomas Gilbert, QC 1969; TD 1950; a Recorder of the Crown Court, since 1972; *b* 16 May 1915; *s* of Caryl Field-Fisher, Torquay; *m* 1945, Ebba, *d* of Max Larsen, Linwood, USA. *Educ:* King's Sch., Bruton; Peterhouse, Cambridge. BA 1937, MA 1942. Called to Bar, Middle Temple, 1942, Bencher, 1976. Served Queen Victoria's Rifles, KRRC, 1939-47 (despatches). Judge Advocate Gen.'s Dept, 1945-47. Vice-Chm., London Council of Social Service, 1966-; Dep.-Chm., SW Agricultural Land Tribunal, 1967-; Deputy Chairman: Bar Council, 1962-66; Cornwall QS, 1968-71. Chm., Maria Colwell Inquiry, 1973-74. *Publications:* Animals and the Law, 1964; Rent Regulation and Control, 1967; contribs to Halsbury's Laws of England, 3rd and 4th edns, Law Jl, and other legal publications. *Recreations:* tennis, dogs, collecting watercolours, social welfare. *Address:* 38 Hurlingham Court, SW6. *T:* 01-736 4627. *Clubs:* Hurlingham, International Lawn Tennis of Great Britain.

FIELDEN, Frank, MA (Dunelm); Secretary, Royal Fine Art Commission, since 1969; *b* 3 Oct. 1915; *s* of Ernest and Emma Fielden, Greenfield, Yorks; *m* 1939, Margery Keeler; two *d. Educ:* University of Manchester. Graduated, 1938. Served 1939-45 with Royal Engineers (Special Forces), France, N Africa, Italy, Germany. Town Planning Officer to Nigerian Government, 1945-46; Lecturer and Sen. Lectr, University of Durham, 1946-59; Prof. of Architecture, Univ. of Strathclyde, 1959-69. Mem., Royal Fine Art Commn for Scotland, 1965-69. RIBA Athens Bursar, 1950, Bronze Medallist 1960. Chairman: Soc. of Architectural Historians of Great Britain, 1965-67; Richmond Soc., 1971-74. *Publications:* articles in professional journals and national press. *Recreations:* music, gardening, travel, food and wine. *Address:* 84 Cornwall Gardens, SW7. *T:* 01-584 7165. *Clubs:* Athenæum, Arts.

FIELDGATE, Alan Frederic Edmond, CMG 1945; *b* 20 Nov. 1889; *m* 1915, Dorothy Alice Thomas. *Educ:* Worcester Coll., Oxford (BA). Asst District Commissioner, Gold Coast Colony, 1915; District Commissioner, 1922; Provincial Commissioner, 1934-46. *Address:* Olde Court, Higher Lincombe Road, Torquay, Devon.

FIELDHOUSE, Sir Harold, KBE 1949 (OBE 1934); CB 1947; Secretary, National Assistance Board, 1946-59, retired; Member of Letchworth Garden City, Welwyn Garden City and Hatfield Corporations, retired; Vice-President, Age Concern; *b* Leeds, Yorks; *e s* of Frank and Mary Ellen Fieldhouse; *m* 1922, Mabel Elaine Elliott, Conisborough, Yorks; two *s. Educ:* Armley

Higher Grade Sch., Leeds. Asst Clerk, Leeds Board of Guardians, 1909-30; Public Assistance Officer, City of Leeds, 1930-34; Regional Officer, Asst Sec. and Under-Sec. Assistance Board, 1934-46. *Recreations:* golf, bridge, music, reading. *Address:* 5 Gayton Court, Harrow, Mddx. *T:* 01-427 0918. *Clubs:* City Livery; Grim's Dyke Golf, West Hill Golf.
See also J. D. E. Fieldhouse.

FIELDHOUSE, Rear-Adm. John David Elliott; Flag Officer, Submarines, and Commander, Submarine Force, Eastern Atlantic Area, since 1976; *b* 12 Feb. 1928; *s* of Sir Harold Fieldhouse, *qv*; *m* 1953, Margaret Ellen Cull; one *s* two *d. Educ:* RNC Dartmouth. MINucE. Midshipman, E Indies Fleet, 1945-46; entered Submarine Service, 1948; comd HMS Acheron, 1955; CO HMS Dreadnought, 1964-66; Exec. Officer, HMS Hermes, 1967; Captain SM10 (Polaris Sqdn), 1968-70; Captain HMS Diomede, 1971; Comdr, Standing Naval Force Atlantic, 1972-73; Dir, Naval Warfare, 1973-74; Flag Officer, Second Flotilla, 1974-76. *Recreations:* home, family and friends. *Address:* Pippins, 16 Ryde Place, Lee-on-Solent, Hants. *T:* Lee-on-Solent 550892.

FIELDING, Colin Cunningham; Director, Admiralty Surface Weapons Establishment, since 1977; *b* 23 Dec. 1926; *s* of Richard Cunningham and Sadie Fielding; *m* 1953, Gillian Aerona (*née* Thomas); one *d. Educ:* Heaton Grammar Sch., Newcastle upon Tyne; Durham Univ. BSc Hons Physics. British Scientific Instruments Research Assoc., 1948-49; RRE Malvern, 1949-65; Asst Dir of Electronics R&D, Min. of Technology, 1965-68; Head of Electronics Dept, RRE Malvern, 1968-73; RCDS, 1973-74; Dir of Scientific and Technical Intelligence, MoD, 1975-77. *Publications:* papers in Proc. IEE, Proc. IERE, Nature. *Recreations:* yachting, tennis, music. *Address:* 27 Norlands Crescent, Chislehurst, Kent BR7 5RN. *T:* 01-467 2526. *Club:* Athenæum.

FIELDING, Fenella Marion; actress; *b* London, 17 Nov. 1934. *Educ:* North London Collegiate Sch. Cockles and Champagne, and Pay the Piper, Saville, 1954; Luba in Jubilee Girl, Victoria Palace, 1956; Lady Parvula de Panzoust in Valmouth, Lyric, Hammersmith, 1958, and Saville, 1959; Pieces of Eight, Apollo, 1959; Five Plus One, Lyceum, Edinburgh Fest., 1961; Phoebe in As You Like It, also Lydia Languish in The Rivals, Pembroke Th., Croydon, 1961; Twists (Best Revue Performance of the Year in Variety, 1962), Arts; Annie Wood in Doctors of Philosophy, New Arts, 1962; Ellen in Luv, New Arts, 1963; So Much to Remember-The Life Story of a Great Lady, The Establishment, and Vaudeville, 1963; Cyprienne in Let's Get a Divorce, Mermaid, and Comedy, 1966; Mrs Sullen in The Beaux Stratagem, and Baroness de Champigny in The Italian Straw Hat, Chichester Fest. Th., 1967; Mrs Gracedew in The High Bid, Mermaid, 1967; Lysistrata in Lysistrata, Univ. of Oklahoma, 1968; Arkadina in The Seagull, Nottingham Playhouse, 1968; Hedda in Hedda Gabler, Phoenix, Leicester, 1969; Nora in A Doll's House, Univ. of Sussex, 1970; Colette in Colette, Ellen Stewart Th. (first appearance in New York), 1970; Fish out of Water, 1971; Colette, 1971; The Second Mrs Tanqueray, 1972. *Recreation:* reading. *Address:* c/o David White Associates, 34 Berkeley House, Hay Hill, W1.

FIELDING, Frank Stanley, OBE 1966; Deputy Consul-General, Toronto, since 1975; *b* 21 Dec. 1918; *s* of John Edgar Fielding and Anne; *m* 1944, Lela Coombs; one *s. Educ:* St Albans Sch.; UCL; King's Coll., London. Diploma in Journalism. HM Forces, 1940-46. Control Commn for Germany, 1946-48; Third Sec., Brit. Embassy, Vienna, 1948-50; Second Sec., Brit. Embassy, Beirut, 1950-55; Vice Consul, Cleveland, 1955-56; First Secretary: Brit. Embassy, Djakarta, 1956-60; FO, 1960-62; Consul (Commercial), Cape Town, 1962-65; First Sec., Brit. Embassy, Pretoria, 1965-68; Consul, NY, 1968-69; Dep. High Comr, Brisbane, 1969-72; Counsellor (Commercial), Singapore, 1972-75. *Recreations:* golf, fishing. *Address:* 376 Russell Hill Road, Toronto, Ont, Canada. *T:* Toronto 4849119. *Club:* Royal Canadian Military Institute (Toronto).

FIELDING, Gabriel, (Alan Gabriel Barnsley); Professor of English, Washington State University, since 1967; *b* 25 March 1916; *s* of late George Barnsley, Clerk in Holy Orders, and Katherine Mary (*née* Fielding-Smith), a descendant of Henry Fielding, the novelist; *m* 1943, Edwina Eleanora Cook, Storrington, Sussex; three *s* two *d. Educ:* The Grange Sch., Eastbourne; St Edward's Sch., Oxford; Trinity Coll., Dublin; St George's Hospital, London. BA, TCD, 1939. MRCS (Eng.), LRCP (London) 1942. Served with RAMC, 1943-46 (Capt.). Dep. Medical Officer, HM Training Establishment, Maidstone, Kent, 1954-64. Appointed Author in Residence (Prof. of English) to Washington State Univ., USA, 1966-67. Hon. DLitt Gonzaga Univ., Spokane, Washington, 1967. *Publications:*

poetry: The Frog Prince and Other Poems, 1952; Twenty-Eight Poems, 1955; *novels:* Brotherly Love, 1954; In the Time of Greenbloom, 1956; Eight Days, 1958; Through Streets Broad and Narrow, 1960; The Birthday King (W. H. Smith Prize for Literature, 1964), 1963; Gentlemen in Their Season, 1966; *short stories:* New Queens for Old (a novella and nine stories), 1972 (Governor's Literary Award, Washington State, 1972). *Recreations:* televised news; competitions, space; theology; walking. *Address:* 945 Monroe Street, Pullman, Washington, USA.

FIELDING, Ven. Harold Ormandy; Archdeacon of Rochdale, since 1972; Vicar of St Peter, Bolton, since 1965; *b* 13 Nov. 1912; *s* of Harold Wolstencroft and Florence Ann Fielding; *m* 1939, Elsie Whillance; three *s* one *d. Educ:* Farnworth Grammar Sch.; Magdalene Coll., Cambridge (MA); Ripon Hall, Oxford. Curate: St Mary, Leigh, 1936-40; St Paul, Walkden, 1940-44; Vicar of St James, New Bury, 1944-65; Hon. Canon of Manchester, 1965-72; Rural Dean of Bolton, 1965-72. *Address:* The Vicarage, Churchgate, Bolton, Lancs. *T:* Bolton 33847.

FIELDING, Leslie; HM Diplomatic Service; Director, Commission of the European Communities, Brussels, since 1973; *b* 29 July 1932; *o s* of late Percy Archer Fielding and of Margaret (*née* Calder Horry). *Educ:* Queen Elizabeth's Sch., Barnet; Emmanuel Coll., Cambridge (1st Cl. Hons, historical tripos pt II; hon. bac. scholar; MA); School of Oriental and African Studies, London. Served with Royal Regt of Artillery, 1951-53. Entered HM Diplomatic Service, 1956; served in: Tehran, 1957-60; Foreign Office, 1960-64; Phnom Penh (Chargé d'Affaires), 1964-66; Paris, 1967-70; FCO, 1970-73; Counsellor and Dep. Head of Planning Staff, 1973. Seconded for service with Directorate Gen. of External Relations, European Commission, 1973. *Recreation:* life in the country. *Address:* c/o European Commission, 200 rue de la Loi, 1049 Brussels, Belgium. *T:* 735.00.40. *Club:* Travellers'.

FIELDS, Gracie, CBE 1938; MA; actress; *b* Rochdale, 9 Jan. 1898; *d* of Fred Stansfield and late Sarah Jane Bamford; *m* 1st, Archie Pitt (Selinger) from whom she obtained a divorce 1940 (he *d* 1940); 2nd, 1940, Monty Banks (Mario Bianchi) (*d* 1950), Film Director; 3rd, 1952, Boris Alperovici, Capri. *Educ:* Rochdale. Nine Command Performances, 1928, 1931, 1937, 1947, 1950, 1951, 1952, 1957, 1964. Silvania Television Award, 1956, for outstanding performance by an actress, in The Old Lady Shows Her Medals. Received hon. freedom of Rochdale, 1938. Order of St John of Jerusalem. MA (*hc*) Victoria Univ. Manchester, 1940. *Publication:* Sing as We Go, 1960. *Address:* Canzone del Mare, 80073, Capri, Italy.

FIENNES; see Twisleton-Wykeham-Fiennes.

FIENNES, family name of Baron Saye and Sele.

FIENNES, Sir Maurice (Alberic Twisleton-Wykeham-), Kt 1965; CEng; FIMechE; Engineering and Industrial Consultant; Associate Consultant, L. H. Manderstam & Partners Ltd, since 1977; Chairman and Managing Director of Davy-Ashmore Ltd, 1961-69; *b* 1 March 1907; *s* of Alberic Arthur Twisleton-Wykeham-Fiennes and Gertrude Theodosia Pomeroy Colley; *m* 1st, 1932, Sylvia Mabel Joan (marr. diss., 1964), *d* of late Major David Finlay, 7th Dragoon Guards. two *s* three *d*; 2nd, 1967, Erika Hueller von Huellenried, *d* of Dr Herbert Hueller, Vienna. *Educ:* Repton; Armstrong Coll., Newcastle upon Tyne. Apprenticeship with Ransomes and Rapier Ltd, Ipswich; joined Sir W. G. Armstrong, Whitworth & Co Ltd (Engineers), Newcastle-upon-Tyne, 1930; with The United Steel Companies Ltd, 1937, first as Commercial Asst to Managing Dir, then in charge Gun Forgings and Gun Dept at Steel Peech & Tozer; Gen. Works Dir, Brush Electrical Engineering Co. Ltd, 1942; Managing Dir, Davy and United Engineering Go. Ltd, 1945; Managing Dir, Davy-Ashmore Ltd, 1960. Steel Industry Advr for UN Industrial Develt Orgn to Govt of Peru, 1974-75. Mem. Economic Develt Cttee for Mech. Eng, 1964-67; Pres. of Iron and Steel Institute, 1962-63; Chairman: Athlone Fellowships Cttee, 1966-71; Overseas Scholarships Bd, CBI, 1970-76; Mem., Reserve Pension Bd, 1974-75. Governor, Yehudi Menuhin School, 1969. *Recreations:* music, grandchildren. *Address:* Gowers Close, Sibford Gower, Banbury, Oxon OX15 5RW. *T:* Swalcliffe 292. *Club:* Bath.

FIENNES, Very Rev. Hon. Oliver William Twisleton-Wykeham-; Dean of Lincoln, since 1969; *b* 17 May 1926; *yr s* of 20th Baron Saye and Sele, OBE, MC, and Hersey Cecilia Hester, *d* of late Captain Sir Thomas Dacres Butler, KCVO; *m* 1956, Juliet, *d* of late Dr Trevor Braby Heaton, OBE; two *s* two *d. Educ:* Eton; New College, Oxford; Cuddesdon College. Asst Curate, New Milton, Hants, 1954; Chaplain, Clifton College,

Bristol, 1958; Rector of Lambeth, 1963. ChStJ 1971. *Address:* The Deanery, Lincoln.

FIENNES, Sir Ranulph Twisleton-Wykeham-, 3rd Bt, *cr* 1916; *b* 7 March 1944; *s* of Lieut-Col Sir Ranulph Twisleton-Wykeham-Fiennes, DSO, 2nd Bt (died of wounds, 1943) and Audrey Joan, *yr d* of Sir Percy Newson, 1st Bt; *S* father 1944; *m* 1970, Virginia Pepper. *Educ:* Eton. Liveryman, Vintners' Company, 1960. French Parachutist Wings, 1965. Lieut, Royal Scots Greys, 1966, Captain 1968 (retd 1970). Attached 22 SAS Regt, 1966, Sultan of Muscat's Armed Forces, 1968 (Dhofar Campaign Medal, 1969; Sultan's Bravery Medal, 1970). T&AVR 1971, Captain RAC. Leader of British expeditions: White Nile, 1969; Jostedalsbre Glacier, 1970; Headless Valley, BC, 1971. *Publications:* A Talent for Trouble, 1970; Ice Fall in Norway, 1972; The Headless Valley, 1973; Where Soldiers Fear To Tread, 1975. *Recreations:* alpinism, langlauf, photography. *Heir:* none. *Address:* St Peter's Well, Lodsworth, Petworth, West Sussex. *T:* Lodsworth 302.

FIFE, 3rd Duke of, *cr* 1900; **James George Alexander Bannerman Carnegie;** Master of Southesk; *b* 23 Sept. 1929; *o s* of 11th Earl of Southesk, *qv*, and Princess Maud (*d* 1945); *S* aunt, Princess Arthur of Connaught (Dukedom of Fife), 1959; *m* 1956, Hon. Caroline Cicely Dewar (marr. diss. 1966), *er d* of 3rd Baron Forteviot, *qv*; one *s* one *d*. *Educ:* Gordonstoun. Nat. Service, Scots Guards (Malayan Campaign), 1948-50. Royal Agricultural College. Senior Liveryman Cloth-workers' Company, and Freeman City of London. Pres. of ABA, 1959-73, Vice-Patron, 1973; Dep. Pres., West Ham Boys' Club; a Vice-Patron, Braemar Royal Highland Soc.; a Vice-Pres., British Olympic Assoc. *Heir:* s Earl of Macduff, *qv*. *Address:* Elsick House, Stonehaven, Kincardineshire AB3 2NT. *Clubs:* Turf, MCC.

FIFE, Charles Morrison, CB 1950; MA; *s* of Alexander John Fife and Margaret Anne Morrison; *m* 1940, Evelyn Mary Thicthener (*d* 1970); no *c*. *Educ:* King Edward's High Sch., Birmingham; Christ's Coll., Cambridge. Senior Scholar, Christ's Coll., 1922; John Stewart of Rannoch (Univ.) Scholar, 1923; 1st Cl. Classical Trip. Pt I, 1924; Browne (Univ.) Scholar, 1925; 1st Cl. Div. I Classical Trip. Pt II, 1925; 2nd Cl. Hons Economics Trip. Pt II, 1926. Entered Civil Service, War Office, 1926; Private Sec. to Sir Reginald Paterson (Dep. Under Sec. of State), 1934-35; Asst Under-Sec. of State, WO, 1948-64, Ministry of Defence, 1964, retired. Conservator of Wimbledon Common, 1961-68. *Recreation:* golf. *Address:* 4 Cokers Lane, Croxted Road, SE21. *Club:* United Oxford & Cambridge University.

FIFE, Ian Braham, MC 1945; TD (2 bars) 1946; **His Honour Judge Fife;** a Circuit Judge (formerly County Court Judge), since 1965; *b* 10 July 1911; *o s* of late Donald Fulford Fife and Muriel Alice Fife (*née* Pitt); *m* 1947, Pauline, *e d* of late T. R. Parsons and Mrs Winifred Parsons, CBE, Cambridge; two *s* two *d*. *Educ:* Monkton Combe Sch. Served, Royal Fusiliers, 1939-47. Called to Bar, Inner Temple, 1948; Mem. Bar Council, 1960-64. *Publications:* ed (with E. A. Machin): Redgrave's Factories Acts (edns 20-23); Redgrave's Offices and Shops (edns 1 and 2); Redgrave's Health and Safety in Factories; contrib. Halsbury's Laws of England, 3rd and 4th edns. *Address:* 2 Castello Avenue, Putney, SW15. *T:* 01-788 6475.

FIFOOT, Paul Ronald Ninnes; HM Diplomatic Service; Counsellor (Legal Adviser), UK Mission to UN, New York, since 1976; *b* 1 April 1928; *o s* of late Ronald Fifoot, Cardiff; *m* 1952, Erica, *er d* of late Richard Alford, DMD; no *c*. *Educ:* Monkton House Sch., Cardiff; Queens' Coll., Cambridge. BA 1948, MA 1952. Military Service, 1948-50, RASC (2nd Lieut 1949). Called to Bar, Gray's Inn, 1953; Crown Counsel, Tanganyika, 1953; Asst to the Law Officers, 1960; Legal Draftsman (later Chief Parliamentary Draftsman), 1961; retd from Tanzania Govt Service, 1966; Asst Legal Adviser, Commonwealth Office, 1966; Legislative Counsel, Province of British Columbia, 1967; Asst Legal Adviser, Commonwealth (later Foreign and Commonwealth) Office, 1968; Legal Counsellor, 1971; Agent of the UK Govt in cases before the European Commn and Court of Human Rights, 1971-76. *Address:* c/o Foreign and Commonwealth Office, SW1.

FIGG, Leonard Clifford William, CMG 1974; HM Diplomatic Service; Assistant Under Secretary of State, Foreign and Commonwealth Office, since 1977; *b* 17 Aug. 1923; *s* of late Sir Clifford Figg and late Lady (Eileen) Figg (*née* Crabb); *m* 1955, Jane Brown; three *s*. *Educ:* Charterhouse; Trinity Coll., Oxford. RAF, 1942-46 (Flt-Lt). HM Diplomatic Service, 1947; served in: Addis Ababa, 1949-52; FO, 1952-58; Amman, 1958-61; FO, 1961-67; Counsellor, 1965; Deputy Consul-General, Chicago, 1967-69; DTI, 1970-73; Consul General and Minister, Milan,

1973-77. *Recreations:* field sports. *Address:* c/o Foreign and Commonwealth Office, SW1; Court Field House, Little Hampden, Great Missenden, Bucks. *T:* Hampden Row 205. *Club:* Brooks's.

FIGGESS, Sir John (George), KBE 1969 (OBE 1949); CMG 1960; a director of Christie, Manson and Woods Ltd, since 1973; *b* 15 Nov. 1909; *e s* of Percival Watts Figgess and Leonora (*née* McCanlis); *m* 1948, Alette, *d* of Dr P. J. A. Idenburg, The Hague; two *d*. *Educ:* Whitgift Sch. In business in Japan, 1933-38. Commissioned, Intelligence Corps, 1939; Staff Coll., 1941; served with Intelligence Corps, India/Burma Theatre, 1942-45. Attached to UK Liaison Mission, Japan, 1945; Asst Mil. Adviser (Lt-Col), UKLM, Tokyo, 1947-52; GSO1, War Office (MI Directorate), 1953-56; Military Attaché, Tokyo, 1956-61; Information Counsellor, British Embassy, Tokyo, 1961-68; Comr Gen. for Britain, World Exposition, Osaka, Japan, 1968-70. *Publications:* (with Fujio Koyama) Two Thousand Years of Oriental Ceramics, 1960; The Heritage of Japanese Ceramics, 1973; contrib. to Oriental Art, Far Eastern Ceramic Bulletin, etc. *Recreations:* Chinese and Japanese art; sailing. *Address:* The Manor House, Burghfield, Berks. *Club:* Army and Navy.

FIGGIS, Arthur Lenox; His Honour Judge Figgis; a Circuit Judge (formerly Judge of County Courts), since 1971; *b* 12 Sept. 1918; *s* of late Frank Fernesley Figgis and late Frances Annie Figgis; *m* 1953, Alison, *d* of Sidney Bocher Ganthony and late Doris Ganthony; two *s* three *d*. *Educ:* Tonbridge; Peterhouse, Cambridge (MA). Served War, 1939-46, Royal Artillery. Barrister-at-Law, Inner Temple, 1947. *Recreations:* walking (with dog); rifle shooting half-blue, 1939, and shot for Ireland (Elcho Shield), 1935-39. *Address:* Walliswood Farm, Walliswood Ockley, Surrey. *T:* Oakwood Hill 268. *Club:* United Oxford & Cambridge University.

FIGGURES, Sir Frank (Edward), KCB 1970 (CB 1966); CMG 1959; Director, Julius Baer Bank International Ltd, since 1975; *b* 5 March 1910; *s* of Frank and Alice Figgures; *m* 1st, 1941, Aline (*d* 1975), *d* of Prof. Hugo Frey; one *s* one *d*; 2nd, 1975, Ismea, *d* of George Napier Magill and widow of Jack Barker. *Educ:* Rutlish Sch.; New Coll., Oxford. Harmsworth Senior Scholar, Merton Coll., Oxford, 1931; Henry Fellow, Yale Law Sch., 1933; Called to Bar, Lincoln's Inn, 1936; Military Service (RA), 1940-46; Joined HM Treasury, 1946; Dir of Trade and Finance, OEEC, 1948-51; Under-Sec., HM Treasury, 1955-60; Sec.-Gen. to EFTA, 1960-65; Third Secretary, Treasury, 1965-68; Second Permanent Secretary, 1968-71; Dir-Gen., NEDO, 1971-73; Chm., Pay Bd, 1973-74. Chm., Central Wagon Co. Ltd, 1976. Hon. DSc Aston 1975. *Address:* 31 South View, Uppingham, Rutland, Leics. *Club:* Reform.

FILER, Albert Jack, CB 1954; Past President, Brick Development Association Ltd; *b* 14 Aug. 1898; 2nd *s* of Albert James Shephard Filer and Jessie (*née* Marrison); *m* 1923, Violet D., *o d* of late Edward T. Booth, Bexhill, Sussex; one *d*. *Educ:* County Secondary Sch., Holloway, N. Entered Civil Service, 1914, Office of Works. Served European War of 1914-18 in Civil Service Rifles. Principal, 1940, Min. of Works, Asst Sec., 1943, Under Sec., 1948; Gen. Manager, Directorate Gen. of Works, 1958-60, retired from Civil Service, 1960. *Recreation:* golf. *Address:* 1 Heatherwood, Midhurst, West Sussex. *T:* Midhurst 2816.

FILLEUL, Peter Amy, MA; Head Master, William Hulme's Grammar School, Manchester, since Sept. 1974; *b* 7 Aug. 1929; *s* of J. C. Filleul and L. A. Mundy; *m* 1963, Elizabeth Ann Talbot; one *s* one *d*. *Educ:* Victoria Coll., Jersey; Bedford Sch.; (Exhibnr) Exeter Coll., Oxford (MA, DipEd). Royal Air Force, 1952-55. Portsmouth GS, 1955-65; Stationers' Company's Sch., 1965-68; Cardiff High Sch. (Head Master), 1969-74. *Recreations:* rifle shooting, fishing. *Address:* 254 Wilbraham Road, Manchester M16 8PR. *T:* 061-226 2058.

FILON, Sidney Philip Lawrence, TD; Librarian and Secretary to the Trustees, National Central Library, 1958-71, retired; *b* 20 Sept. 1905; *s* of late Prof. L. N. G. Filon, FRS and late Anne Godet; *m* 1st, 1939, Doris Schelling; one *d*; 2nd, 1959, Liselotte Florstedt; one *d*. *Educ:* Whitgift Sch.; University Coll., London (BSc). Sch. of Librarianship, University Coll., London, 1929-30; FLA 1931. National Central Library, 1930-39. Military service, 1939-45. Dep. Librarian, National Central Library, 1946-58. Mem., Library Advisory Council (England), 1966-71. *Address:* 107 Littleheath Road, Selsdon, Surrey.

FILSON, Alexander Warnock; consultant in film industry; *b* 23 Aug. 1913; *s* of late J. T. W. Filson, Indian Police; *m* 1941, Judith Henrietta, *d* of late Major R. H. Greig, DSO, and late Mrs Rokeling; one *s* two *d*. *Educ:* Clifton Coll., (Schol.); The

Queen's Coll., Oxford (Schol.) (MA). Served War of 1939-45 in Army; Asst Sec., Parliamentary Labour Party, 1945-47; Sec. Fabian Soc., 1947-49; Mem. of Kensington Borough Council, 1937-49. Contested (Lab) Brentford and Chiswick, 1955. Director: Fedn of British Film Makers, 1957-66; Film Production Assoc. of GB, 1967-70; Israel Film Industry, London Office, 1971-76. *Publications:* (asst to Prof. G. D. H. Cole) British Trade Unionism Today, 1939; ed (with Prof. G. D. H. Cole) British Working Class Movements, 1789-1875: Select Documents, 1951. *Recreations:* reading and sightseeing. *Address:* 6 Grosvenor Road, Richmond, Surrey. *T:* 01-940 2072.

FINCH; *see* Finch-Knightley.

FINCH, Ven. Geoffrey Grenville; Archdeacon of Basingstoke since 1971; *b* 7 Oct. 1923; *yr s* of late R. A. Finch and of Mrs E. M. Finch; *m* 1951, Margaret Ann Denniston; one *s* three *d*. *Educ:* Quarry Bank High Sch., Liverpool; St Peter's Hall, Oxford; Wycliffe Hall; Wells Theological Coll. Hon. Sch. of Nat. Sci. and Theology (2nd cl), Oxford, 1942-43; MA 1947. Foreign Office and Allied Commission for Austria, 1944-46; Oxford and Wells, 1947-50; ordained, 1950; Curate, Wigan Parish Church, 1950-54; Vicar, S Peter's, Westleigh, Lancs, 1954-59; Rector, Milton Parish Church, Hants, 1960-71; Vicar of Preston Candover and Bradley, Hants, 1971-76. Proctor in Convocation, 1965-70; Rural Dean of Christchurch, Hants, 1966-71. Member: Gen. Synod, 1973-; Central Bd of Finance, CofE, 1975-. *Recreations:* sailing, photography. *Address:* 3 Crossborough Hill, Basingstoke, Hants. *T:* Basingstoke 28572.

FINCH, Sir Harold (Josiah), Kt 1976; Compensation Secretary, South Wales Area, National Union of Mineworkers, since 1939; *b* 2 May 1898; *s* of late Josiah Coleman Finch and Emmie Keedwell; *m* ; one *s* one *d*. *Educ:* Barry Elementary Sch.; Cardiff Evening Schs. Left Sch. at 14; Railway Clerk with Barry Rly Co. (now no longer existent); Sec. Tredegar Valley District of Miners' at Blackwood (Mon.), 1919; Mem. of Mynyddislwyn UDC, 1922-33, Chm., 1932; Asst Compensation Sec., then Sec. South Wales Miners Federation at Cardiff 1934-39. MP (Lab) Bedwellty, 1950-70; Parly Under-Sec. of State, Welsh Office, 1964-66; former Mem., Council of Europe; former Sec., Miners' Parly Gp. Pres., Islwyn Meml Soc. *Publications:* Guide to Workmen's Compensation Acts, 1944; Industrial Injuries Act Explained, 1948; Memoirs of a Bedwellty MP, 1972. *Recreation:* gardening. *Address:* 34 Elim Way, Pontllanfraith, Gwent; 56 Kenwyn Road, Clapham, SW4. *T:* 01-622 6806.

FINCH, Col John Charles W.; *see* Wynne Finch.

FINCH, Maj.-Gen. Lionel Hugh Knightley, CB 1941; DSO 1916, Bar 1917; OBE; FLS; *b* 18 July 1888; *o s* of late Capt. E. H. Franklyn Finch, 30th Regt; *m* 1919, Hildegard, *d* of Mrs J. C. A. Sepp-Clésius, Nijmegen, Holland; one *d*. *Educ:* Cheltenham Coll.; Birmingham Univ.; London Univ. Served European War, 1914-18 (DSO and bar, OBE, despatches, Bt Major); Staff Coll., Camberley, 1924-25; GSO3 at HQ, Northern Command, 1926-27; DAA and QMG at HQ Northumbrian Area, 1928-29; Bt Lt-Col, 1929; commanded Depot, Cheshire Regt, 1930-33; Comdr, Landi Kotal Bde, 1934; DAQMG at Army HQ India, 1934; comd 1st Bn Lancs Fusiliers, 1934-36; Asst Adjutant-Gen., War Office, 1936-39; Dep. Dir of Recruiting and Organisation, War Office, 1939; Dir of Recruiting and Organisation, War Office, 1939-40; Dep. Adjutant-Gen., War Office, 1940; Divisional Comdr, 1940; Chm., War Office Committees, 1940-41; District Comdr, Home Forces, 1941-42; retired, 1943; late The Lancs Fusiliers, The Cheshire Regt, and The Royal Sussex Regt. *Address:* National Westminster Bank, Petworth, West Sussex.

FINCH HATTON, family name of Earl of Winchilsea and Nottingham.

FINCH-KNIGHTLEY, family name of Earl of Aylesford.

FINCHAM, Prof. John Robert Stanley, FRS 1969; Buchanan Professor of Genetics, University of Edinburgh, since 1976; *b* 11 Aug. 1926; *s* of Robert Fincham and Winifred Emily Fincham (*née* Western); *m* 1950, Ann Katherine Emerson; one *s* three *d*. *Educ:* Hertford Grammar Sch.; Peterhouse, Cambridge. BA 1946, PhD 1950, ScD 1964. Bye-Fellow of Peterhouse, 1949-50; Lectr in Botany, University Coll., Leicester, 1950-54; Reader in Genetics, Univ. of Leicester, 1954-60; Head of Dept of Genetics, John Innes Inst., 1960-66; Prof. of Genetics, Leeds Univ., 1966-76; Vis. Associate Prof. of Genetics, Massachusetts Inst. of Technology, 1960-61. Editor, Heredity, 1971-. *Publications:* Fungal Genetics (with P. R. Day), 1963; Microbial and Molecular Genetics, 1965; Genetic Complementation, 1966; papers in Biochemical Jl, Jl Gen. Microbiol., Jl Biol. Chem., Heredity, Jl Molecular Biol., Genet. Res. *Recreation:* listening to music. *Address:* 93A Mayfield Road, Edinburgh.

FINDLATER, Richard, (Kenneth Bruce Findlater Bain); Assistant Editor, The Observer, since 1963; Editor, The Author, since 1961; *b* 23 Dec. 1921; *s* of Thomas Bain and Elizabeth Bruce; *m* 1948, Romany Evens (marr. diss. 1961); three *s* one *d*. *Educ:* Archbishop Tenison's Grammar School. Theatre Critic, Tribune, 1948-57; Literary Editor, Tribune, 1950-57; Editor, Books and Art, 1957-58; Literary Editor and Theatre Critic, Sunday Dispatch, 1958-59; Theatre Critic, Time and Tide, 1960-62; Editor, Twentieth Century, 1961-65. Member: BBC Critics, 1953-69; Arts Council Drama Panel, 1953-62 and 1970-74; Housing the Arts Cttee of Inquiry, 1956-61; Theatre Inquiry, 1967-70. *Publications:* The Unholy Trade, 1952; Grimaldi, 1955; Michael Redgrave: Actor, 1956; Emlyn Williams, 1957; Six Great Actors, 1957; Banned, 1967; (ed) Memoirs of Grimaldi, 1968; (ed) Comic Cuts, 1970; The Player Kings, 1971; (ed) Public Lending Right, 1971; Lilian Baylis, 1975; The Player Queens, 1976; *pamphlets:* The Future of the Theatre, 1959; What are Writers Worth?, 1963; The Book Writers: Who are They?, 1966. *Address:* Fuchsia Cottage, High Street, Milton-under-Wychwood, Oxon. *Club:* Garrick.

FINDLAY, Alexander John, CMG 1937; *b* 1886; *s* of late James Smith Findlay, Aberdeen; *m* 1913, Primrose Alice, *d* of Arthur Aiken, Aberdeen. *Educ:* Aberdeen Grammar Sch.; Aberdeen Univ.; North of Scotland Coll of Agriculture; MA, BSc (Agric.), NDA, NDD. Entered Colonial Agricultural Service 1912; served in Dept of Agriculture, Nigeria, 1912-31; Dir of Agriculture, Zanzibar, 1931-37; retired 1937; Commissioner for the Colonial Exhibit, World's Fair, New York, 1939 and 1940; served Cameroons, 1915, with West African Frontier Force. *Address:* 24 Carden Place, Aberdeen.

FINDLAY, Ian Herbert Fyfe; Chairman, Sedgwick Forbes Holdings Ltd, since 1974; Deputy Chairman, Lloyd's, 1977; *b* 5 Feb. 1918; *s* of Prof. Alexander Findlay and Alice Mary (*née* de Rougemont); *m* 1950, Alison Mary Ashby; two *s* one *d*. *Educ:* Fettes Coll., Edinburgh. Served War, Royal Artillery, 1939-46. Chm., Price Forbes (Holdings) Ltd, 1967; Dep. Chm., Sedgwick Forbes Holdings Ltd, 1972. Mem. Cttee, Lloyd's Insurance Brokers Assoc., 1961-75 and 1966-69; Chm., Non-Marine Cttee, 1967-68; Chm. of Assoc., 1969-70. Fellow of Corporation of Insurance Brokers (Vice-Pres. 1966). Mem., Cttee of Lloyd's, 1971-74, 1976-. *Recreation:* golf. *Address:* 24 Forest Ridge, Keston Park, Kent BR2 6EQ. *T:* Farnborough (Kent) 52993. *Clubs:* City of London; Royal and Ancient Golf (St Andrews); Royal St George's (Sandwich); Addington (Surrey).

FINDLAY, Comdr James Buchanan, CBE 1957; RN (Retd); Director, Bank of Scotland, 1933-71; *b* 7 Jan. 1895; *m* 1923, Mary Sancroft Findlay-Hamilton; three *s* one *d*. *Educ:* Royal Naval Colls, Osborne and Dartmouth. Retired from RN after European War of 1914-18; served in War of 1939-45. *Recreations:* shooting, golf, gardening. *Address:* The Garden House, Carnell, Kilmarnock, Ayrshire. *Club:* Lansdowne.

FINDLAY, Prof. John Niemeyer, FBA 1956; University Professor of Philosophy, Boston University, since 1972; *b* 25 Nov. 1903; 2nd *s* of J. H. L. Findlay, Pretoria, South Africa; *m* 1941, Aileen May, *d* of G. S. Davidson, Wellington, NZ; one *s* one *d* (and one *d* decd). *Educ:* Boys' High Sch., Pretoria; Transvaal Univ. Coll.; Balliol Coll., Oxford (Rhodes Scholar, 1st Lit. hum.); University of Graz. Lecturer in Philosophy, Transvaal University Coll., 1927-33; Prof. of Philosophy, University of Otago, NZ, 1934-44; Prof. of Philosophy, Rhodes University Coll., Grahamstown, S Africa, 1945; Prof. of Philosophy, Natal University Coll., 1946-48; Prof. of Philosophy, King's Coll., Newcastle upon Tyne, Univ. of Durham, 1948-51; University Prof. of Philosophy, King's Coll., Univ. of London, 1951-66. Gifford Lecturer, Univ. of St Andrews, 1964-66. Prof. of Philosophy, Univ. of Texas, 1966-67; Clark Prof. of Moral Philosophy and Metaphysics, Yale Univ., 1967-72. Fellow, Amer. Acad. of Arts and Scis, 1972. FKC 1970. *Publications:* Meinong's Theory of Objects and Values, 1933, new edn, 1963; Hegel: A Re-Examination, 1958; Values and Intentions, 1961; Language, Mind and Value, 1963; The Discipline of the Cave, 1965; The Transcendence of The Cave, 1967; trans. Husserl, Logische Untersuchungen, 1969; Axiological Ethics, 1970; Ascent to the Absolute: metaphysical papers and lectures, 1970; Plato's Written and Unwritten Doctrines, 1974; articles in Mind, Philosophy, Philosophy and Phenomenological Research, Proc. of the Aristotelian Soc., etc. *Address:* 14 Lambolle Road, NW3; 96 Bay State Road, Boston, Mass 02215, USA. *Club:* Royal Commonwealth Society.

FINDLAY, Lt-Col Sir Roland Lewis, 3rd Bt *cr* 1925; Lieutenant-Colonel (retired) 2nd Dragoons (Royal Scots Greys); *b* 14 July 1903; 2nd *s* of Sir John Ritchie Findlay, 1st Bt, KBE, DL, JP; *S* brother, Sir (John) Edmund Ritchie Findlay, 1962; *m* 1st 1927,

Barbara Joan, JP, Northants, *d* of late Major H. S. Garrard, Welton Place, Daventry, Northants; one *d*; 2nd, 1964, Mrs M. M. Cripps. *Educ:* Harrow; Royal Military Coll., Sandhurst. Lieut Royal Scots Greys, 1924, Capt., 1934. Served War of 1939-45, with Royal Scots Greys, 1939-43, Lieut-Col 21st Army Group, 1944; Col, ALFSEA, 1945-46. High Sheriff of Northants, 1956-57; DL Northants 1958-60. *Address:* Toll Bar House, Burley, Rutland, Leics. *Club:* Cavalry and Guards.
See also Sir Hugh Munro-Lucas-Tooth, Bt, Earl of Westmorland.

FINER, Prof. Samuel Edward; Gladstone Professor of Government and Public Administration, University of Oxford, since 1974; *b* 22 Sept. 1915; *y s* of Max and Fanny Finer, 210a Green Lanes, N4; *m* 1st, 1949, Margaret Ann (marr. diss. 1975), 2nd *d* of Sir Andrew McFadyean; two *s* one *d*; 2nd, 1977, Dr Catherine J. Jones, 2nd *d* of T. P. Jones, Prestatyn. *Educ:* Holloway Sch., London; Trinity Coll., Oxford. BA (Oxon) 1st Class Hons Mod. Greats, 1937; 1st Cl. Hons Mod. Hist., 1938; MA (Oxon) 1946; Sen. George Webb-Medley Schol., 1938-40. Served War, 1940-46; Capt. Royal Signals, 1945. Lecturer in Politics, Balliol Coll., Oxford, 1946-49; Junior Research Fellow, Balliol Coll., Oxford, 1949-50; Prof. of Political Institutions, University of Keele, 1950-66; Prof. of Government, Univ. of Manchester, 1966-74; Dep. Vice-Chancellor, University of Keele, 1962-64. Visiting Prof. and Faculty Mem., Institute of Social Studies, The Hague, Netherlands, 1957-59. Visiting Prof. in Government: Cornell Univ., 1962; Hebrew Univ., Jerusalem, 1969; Simon Fraser Univ., BC, 1976; Europ. Univ. Inst., Florence, 1977. Chm. Political Studies Assoc. of UK, 1965-69; Vice-Pres. Internat. Political Science Assoc. FRHistSoc. *Publications:* A Primer of Public Administration, 1950; The Life and Times of Sir Edwin Chadwick, 1952; (with Sir John Maud) Local Government in England and Wales, 1953; Anonymous Empire—a Study of the Lobby in Britain, 1958, 2nd edn 1966; Private Industry and Political Power, 1958; (with D. J. Bartholomew and H. B. Berrington) Backbench Opinion in the House of Commons, 1955-59, 1961; The Man on Horseback: The Rôle of The Military in Politics, 1962, 2nd edn 1976; Comparative Government, 1970; Great Britain, in Modern Political Systems: Europe, ed Macridis and Ward, 1963, 1968, 1972; (ed) Siéyès: What is the Third Estate?, 1963; Pareto: Sociological Writings, 1966; Adversary Government and Electoral Reform, 1975. *Recreation:* oil-painting. *Address:* All Souls College, Oxford.

FINESTEIN, Israel, MA; QC 1970; **His Honour Judge Finestein;** a Circuit Judge, since 1972; *b* 29 April 1921; *y c* of late Jeremiah Finestein, Hull; *m* 1946, Marion Phyllis, *er d* of Simon Oster, Hendon, Mddx. *Educ:* Kingston High School, Hull; Trinity Coll., Cambridge (Major Scholar and Prizeman). MA 1946. Called to the Bar, Lincoln's Inn, 1953. Pres., Jewish Hist. Soc. of England. *Publications:* Short History of the Jews of England, 1956; Sir George Jessel, 1959, etc. *Recreation:* reading history. *Address:* 18 Buttermere Court, Boundary Road, NW8.

FINGALL, 12th Earl of *cr* 1628; **Oliver James Horace Plunkett,** MC; Baron Killeen, 1436; Baron Fingall (UK) 1831; Major, late 17th/21st Lancers; *b* 17 June 1896; *er s* of 11th Earl and Elizabeth Mary Margaret (*d* 1944), *e d* of George Burke, JP, Danesfield, Co. Galway; *S* father, 1929; *m* 1926, Jessica (*d* 1965), *yr d* of late Allan Hughes, Lynch, Allerford, Somerset; *m* 1966, Mrs Clair Richardson, *widow* of Frank Richardson, Geelong, Vic., Aust. *Educ:* Downside. Served European War (MC); retired pay, 1931; in army again, 1939-45. Roman Catholic. *Recreations:* racing and travelling. *Heir:* (to barony of Killeen only) *kinsman,* Baron Dunsany, *qv. Address:* The Commons, Dunsany, Co. Meath. *TA:* Fingall, Dunsany. *T:* Navan 25193. *Clubs:* Cavalry and Guards; Kildare Street and University (Dublin).

FINGERHUT, John Hyman; Consultant, Merck Sharp & Dohme Ltd and Merck Sharp & Dohme International, since 1975 (Chairman, 1967-72); Associate, Bracken Kelner and Associates Ltd (BKA), since 1976; *b* 2 Nov. 1910; *s* of late Abraham Fingerhut and Emily (*née* Rowe); *m* 1950, Beatrice Leigh, FCA; two *s* two *d. Educ:* Manchester Grammar Sch.; Manchester Univ. FBOA 1931; FPS 1971. Pharmaceutical Chemist, 1932. Served with RAC and Infantry, France, Mauritius and E Africa, 1942-46; commnd Royal Pioneer Corps, transf. to Queen's Royal Regt (seconded King's African Rifles); demobilised as Captain. Merck Sharp & Dohme Ltd: medical rep., 1937-42; Sales Man., 1946; Dep. Man. Dir, 1957; Man. Dir, 1963; Regional Dir, Merck Sharp & Dohme International, 1967; Chm., Thomas Morson & Son Ltd, 1967-72. Admin. Staff Coll., Henley, 1960. Mem., New Southgate Group Hosp. Management Cttee, 1972-74. Associate Mem., Faculty of Homœopathy, 1974. *Recreations:* music, reading, gardening,

washing up. *Address:* 76 Green Lane, Edgware, Mddx. *T:* 01-958 6163.

FINGLAND, Stanley James Gunn, CMG 1966; HM Diplomatic Service; High Commissioner to Kenya, since 1975; *b* 19 Dec. 1919; *s* of late Samuel Gunn Fingland and of Agnes Christina (*née* Watson); *m* 1946, Nellie (*née* Lister); one *s* one *d. Educ:* Royal High Sch., Edinburgh. TA 1938. War service, 1939-46 as Major, Royal Signals; served N Africa, Sicily, Italy, Egypt. Commonwealth Relations Office, 1948-; British High Commission, India, 1948-51; Australia, 1953-56; Adviser on Commonwealth and External Affairs to Governor-Gen., Nigeria, 1958-60; British High Commission, Nigeria, 1960; Adviser on Commonwealth and External Affairs to Governor-Gen., Fedn of The W Indies, 1960-61, and to the Governor of Trinidad and Tobago, 1962; British Dep. High Commissioner: Trinidad and Tobago, 1962-63; Rhodesia, 1964-66; High Comr, Sierra Leone, 1966-69; Asst Under-Sec. of State, FCO, 1969-72; Ambassador to Cuba, 1972-75. *Recreations:* tennis, fishing, golf. *Address:* c/o Foreign and Commonwealth Office, SW1. *Club:* Royal Over-Seas League.

FINKELSTEIN, Prof. Ludwik, MSc, CEng, MIEE, MInstP, FInstMC; Professor of Instrument and Control Engineering, since 1970, and Head of Department of Systems Science, since 1974, The City University, London; *b* 6 Dec. 1929; *s* of Adolf and Amalia Finkelstein; *m* 1957, Mirjam Emma, *d* of Dr Alfred and Dr Margarethe Wiener; two *s* one *d. Educ:* Univ. of London (MSc). Physicist, Technical Staff, Electronic Tubes Ltd, 1951-52; Scientist, Instrument Br., NCB Mining Res. Estabt, 1952-59; Northampton Coll., London, and City University, London: Lectr, 1959-61; Sen. Lectr, 1961-63; Principal Lectr, 1963-67; Reader, 1967-70. Visiting Prof., Delft Univ. of Technology, 1973-74. Vice-Pres., Inst. of Measurement and Control. *Publications:* papers in learned jls and conference proc. *Recreations:* books, conversation, Jewish studies. *Address:* The City University, St John Street, EC1V 4PB. *T:* 01-253 4399; 9 Cheyne Walk, Hendon NW4 3QP. *T:* 01-202 6966.

FINLAISON, Brig. (retd) Alexander Montagu, CBE 1957; DSO 1944; *b* 14 March 1904; *s* of Maj.-Gen. J. B. Finlaison, CMG, late Royal Marines, Dedham, Essex; *m* 1935, Monica Mary Louisa, *d* of T. W. Donald, Grendon, Stirling; two *d. Educ:* RN Colls Osborne and Dartmouth; RMC Sandhurst. Commissioned Cameronians (Scottish Rifles), 1924; seconded Sudan Defence Force, 1932-38; served War of 1939-45; Greece, Crete, Sicily, Italy; commanded 2nd Wiltshires, 2nd Cameronians, 17 Infantry Brigade, Italy, 1943-44; BGS, HQ Scottish Command, 1954-57; ADC to the Queen, 1955-57; retired, 1957; Commandant, Queen Victoria Sch., Dunblane, 1957-64. *Address:* Gledenholm, Ae, Dumfries DG1 1RF. *T:* Parkgate 242. *Club:* Naval and Military.

FINLAY, Alexander William; Planning Director, British Airways, since 1974; *b* 28 Nov. 1921; *s* of late Robert Gaskin Finlay and late Alice Finlay; *m* 1949, Ona Margaret Lewis; no *c. Educ:* Tottenham County School. Flt-Lt RAF, 1941-47; various posts, BOAC, 1947-: Gen. Man., Fleet Planning, 1967-71; Planning Dir, 1971-74. FCIT. Vice-Chm., Soc. for Long Range Planning, 1975-. *Recreations:* gardening, photography. *Address:* 7 Alleyn Park, Norwood Green, Mddx. *T:* 01-574 6583.

FINLAY, Bernard, QC 1967; **His Honour Judge Finlay;** a Circuit Judge (formerly County Court Judge), since 1970; *b* 4 July 1913. LLB (Hons I); Bar final (Hons I) (certificate of honour); L. J. Holker Scholar. Called to the Bar, Gray's Inn, 1945, Middle Temple, 1966; practised on South-Eastern Circuit. *Address:* Denbigh Lodge, Denbigh Road, Haslemere, Surrey.

FINLAY, Maj.-Gen. Charles Hector, CB 1966; CBE 1958 (OBE 1942); retired; Hon. National Treasurer, Returned Services League of Australia, since 1969; *b* 6 Oct. 1910; 3rd *s* of Frank J. Finlay and Margaret A. Stephenson; *m* 1935, Helen M., *d* of Arthur P. and Edith M. Adams; two *s. Educ:* Sydney; RMC Duntroon, Australia. Graduated RMC, 1931; Light Horse and Cavalry service, 1931-39; ADC to Gov.-Gen., 1932-35; with 14th/20th Hussars, India, 1935-36. Served War of 1939-45; Western Desert, Syria, New Guinea, Borneo; Comd 2/24 Inf. Bn, 1942-43. Exchange duty, Canada, 1946-49; DMI, 1950-53; Comd Aust. Component BCFK, 1953-54; attended Imperial Def. Coll., 1955; Aust. Army Rep., London, 1956-57; Quartermaster Gen. AMF, 1957-62; Commandant Royal Military Coll., Duntroon, Australia, 1962-67. Hon. Col, Australian Intelligence Corps, 1973. *Recreation:* cricket. *Address:* Amungula, via Queanbeyan, NSW 2620, Australia. *Club:* Naval and Military (Melbourne).

FINLAY, Frank; actor; *b* Farnworth, Lancs, 6 Aug. 1926; *s* of Josiah Finlay; *m* 1954, Doreen Shepherd; two *s* one *d. Educ:* RADA. *Stage:* repertory, 1950-52 and 1954-57; Belgrade, Coventry, 1958; Epitaph for George Dillon, NY, 1958; Royal Court, 1958, 1959-62: Sugar in the Morning; Sergeant Musgrave's Dance; Chicken Soup with Barley, Roots, I'm Talking About Jerusalem; The Happy Haven; Platonov; Chips with Everything; Vaudeville Theatre, 1962; Chichester Festival, 1963: St Joan; The Workhouse Donkey; with National Theatre Co. 1963-70: St Joan, 1963; Willie Mossop in Hobson's Choice, and Iago in Othello (both also Chichester Fest., 1964, Berlin and Moscow, 1965), The Dutch Courtesan (also Chichester Fest.), 1964; Giles Corey in The Crucible, Dogberry in Much Ado About Nothing, Mother Courage, 1965; Joxer Daly in Juno and the Paycock, Dikoy in The Storm, 1966; Bernard in After Haggerty, Aldwych, Criterion, Jesus Christ in Son of Man, Leicester Theatre and Round House (first actor ever to play Jesus Christ on stage in English theatre), 1970; with National Theatre Co.: Peppino in Saturday, Sunday, Monday, 1973, Queen's, 1974; Sloman in The Party, 1973; Freddy Malone in Plunder, Ben Prosser in Watch It Come Down, Josef Frank in Weapons of Happiness, 1976; *films include* , 1962-: The Longest Day, Private Potter, The Informers, A Life for Ruth, Loneliness of the Long Distance Runner, Hot Enough for June, The Comedy Man, The Sandwich Man, A Study in Terror, Othello (nominated for Amer. Acad. award; best actor award, San Sebastian, 1966), The Jokers, I'll Never Forget What's 'Is Name, The Shoes of the Fisherman, Deadly Bees, Robbery, Inspector Clouseau, Twisted Nerve, Cromwell, The Molly Maguires (in Hollywood), Assault, Victory for Danny Jones, Gumshoe, Shaft in Africa, Van Der Valk and the Girl, Van Der Valk and the Rich; Van Der Valk and the Dead; The Three Musketeers; *TV appearances include:* Julius Caesar, Les Misérables, This Happy Breed, The Lie, Casanova (series), Hitler, Don Quixote (best actor award), Voltaire, Merchant of Venice, Bouquet of Barbed Wire (series), 84 Charing Cross Road. *Address:* Granstar Ltd, Al Parker House, 50 Mount Street, W1.

FINLAY, Sir Graeme Bell, 1st Bt, *cr* 1964; ERD; Barrister-at-Law; Sous Juge d'Instruction and Assistant Judge of Petty Debts Court for Jersey, 1972-77; *b* 29 Oct. 1917; *yr s* of late James Bell Pettigrew Finlay and late Margaret Helena, *d* of John Euston Davies, JP, Portskewett House, nr Chepstow, Mon.; *m* 1953, June Evangeline, *y d* of Col Francis Collingwood Drake, OBE, MC, DL, late 10th Royal Hussars, Harlow, Essex; one *s* two *d. Educ:* Marlborough; University College, London. Served War of 1939-45, 2nd Lieut S Wales Borderers (suppl. res.), 1939; 7th (Croix de Guerre) Bn, 24th Regt (Beach Divs), 1940-41; seconded to 5th Royal Gurkha Rifles (Frontier Force), 1942-45; Martial Law Officer, Upper Sind Force (Hur Rebellion), 1943; Acting Major and DAAG, HQ, NW Army, 1945. Hon. Captain, The Royal Regt of Wales. Called to Bar, Gray's Inn, 1946 (Lord Justice Holker Sen. Exhibr); pupil of Lord Hailsham of St Marylebone; President of Hardwicke Society, 1950-51. Presided over first televised joint debate between Oxford and Cambridge Union Societies, 1950. Contested (C) Ebbw Vale, General Election, 1950; MP (C) Epping Division of Essex, 1951-64; Parliamentary Private Secretary to Rt Hon. Iain Macleod, Minister of Health, 1952-55; Asst Whip, 1957-59; Lord Commissioner of the Treasury, 1959-60; Vice-Chamberlain of the Household, 1960-64; Mem., Parly Delegn to Russia, 1960; a Deputy Judge of County Courts, later Circuit Judge, 1967-72; a Dep. Chm., Agricultural Land Tribunal (SE Region), 1971-72. *Publications:* (jt author) Proposals for an Administrative Court, 1970; frequent contributor to Justice of the Peace and Local Government Review. *Recreations:* reading history and painting. *Heir:* s David Ronald James Bell Finlay, *b* 16 Nov. 1963. *Address:* 4 Paper Buildings, Temple, EC4. *T:* 01-353 3366; La Campagne, Rozel, Jersey, CI. *T:* Central 51194. *Clubs:* Travellers'; United (Jersey).
See also J. E. B. Finlay.

FINLAY, Ian; see Finlay, W. I. R.

FINLAY, Jane Little, (Sheena), JP; Co-Chairman, Women's National Commission, since 1975; President, British Federation of University Women, since 1975 (Vice-President 1971-74); *b* 29 Sept. 1917; *e d* of James Whyte Hepburn and Jean Brown, Langside, Glasgow; *m* 1941, John A. R. Finlay, *qv* ; one *s* two *d* (and one *d* decd). *Educ:* Spier's Sch., Beith; Hutcheson's Girls' Grammar Sch., Glasgow; Glasgow Univ. (MA Hons English and Philosophy, 1940); Jordanhill Coll., Glasgow (Teacher's Trng Cert., 1941). Asst Principal, Bd of Inland Revenue, 1941-45 (Private Office, 1943-45). Teaching: Mayfield County Sch., Putney, 1946; Cooper's Sch., Chislehurst (part-time), 1962-73. JP 1966- (Juvenile Panel, 1967-); part-time Mem. Value Added Tax Tribunals, 1973-; Mem (Vice-Chm.), Bromley Community Health Council, 1974-76, Chm., 1976-. UK Deleg., Unesco

Conf., Bonn, 1975. *Recreations:* cooking, reading, gardening, sailing. *Address:* Thornhill, Golf Road, Bickley, Bromley, Kent BR1 2JA. *T:* 01-467 3637. *Club:* Medway Yacht.

FINLAY, John Alexander Robertson, QC 1973; **His Honour Judge John Finlay;** a Circuit Judge, since 1976; *b* 9 Nov. 1917; *o s* of Rev. John Adamson Finlay, MA and Mary Hain Miller; *m* 1941, Jane Little Hepburn (Sheena) (*see* J. L. Finlay); *d* of James Whyte Hepburn; one *s* two *d* (and one *d* decd). *Educ:* High Sch. of Glasgow; Glasgow Univ. (Foulis Schol., John Clerk Schol.); Queen's Coll., Oxford (Schol.). Caird Medal, Melville Medal, MA 1st cl. Philosophy Glasgow, 1939; BA 2nd cl. Jurisprudence 1946, MA 1959, Oxon. Served in RN, 1940-46: Seaman 1940; commnd 1941; Lieut RNVR 1942. Called to Bar, Middle Temple, 1946 (Harmsworth Schol.); Bencher, Middle Temple, 1971; Mem. Bar Council, 1970-74. Recorder of the Crown Court, 1975-76. Acting Deemster, IoM Court of Appeal, 1975. Vice-Chm. Crosby Hall, 1970-75, Chm., 1975-76. Member: Law Guardian Editorial Adv. Cttee, 1971-72; Renton Cttee on Preparation of Legislation, 1973-75. *Publications:* The Trustees Handbook, 1951; The Landlord and Tenant Act, 1954, 1954. *Recreations:* music, sailing. *Address:* Thornhill, Golf Road, Bickley, Bromley, Kent. *T:* 01-467 3637; 16 Old Buildings, Lincoln's Inn, WC2. *T:* 01-405 1325. *Club:* Medway Yacht.

FINLAY, John Euston Bell, CB 1959; OBE 1946; TD 1947; consultant on indirect taxation, since 1968; *b* 11 Sept. 1908; *e s* of late James Bell Pettigrew Finlay and late Margaret Helena Finlay, Douro Court, Cheltenham; *m* 1942, Zoë Josephine, *d* of late Brigadier Edward Lees, DSO, Whyte Cottage, Selsey, Sussex; one *s* one *d. Educ:* Marlborough; Geneva Univ. Junior Legal Asst, Board of Customs, 1933; Senior Legal Asst, 1945. Principal, 1948, Asst Secretary, 1949; Under-Sec., 1954-68; Commissioner and Director of Estab. and Org., 1954-65; Comr i/c Internat. and Tariff Divs, Bd of Customs and Excise, 1965-68; retired, 1968. Chairman, Finance Cttee, Customs Co-operation Council, Brussels, 1967-68. Governor St Dunstan's Educational Foundation, 1964-73. Member Management Cttee, CS Benevolent Fund, 1958-68; Trustee, CS Retirement Fellowship, 1968-. Mem., Chichester DC, 1976-. Commnd from Trooper Inns of Court Regt to 1st (Rifle) Bn The Mon. Regt TA, 1934. Served, 1939-42, with 38 Div., 53 Div. and at Western Command (ADC to GOC-in-C and GSO2) (ops); psc Staff Coll., Camberley, 1942; seconded 1943-45, AIF; served New Guinea, Moluccas, Philippines and Borneo as GSO2 and GSO1, Anglo-Australian Special Airborne Forces (OBE). Hon. Lieut-Colonel. FRGS. *Recreations:* gardening, racing. *Address:* Bernards Gate House, 22 Lavant Road, Chichester, Sussex. *T:* Chichester 527369; 38 Sloane Court West, SW3. *T:* 01-730 5955. *Clubs:* Travellers', Special Forces.

FINLAY, Thomas Victor William, CMG 1948; *b* 14 Nov. 1899; *e s* of Thomas Finlay, Armagh, N Ireland; *m* 1927, Eileen, *d* of John O'Connor, Solicitor, Crossmaglen, Co. Armagh; two *s. Educ:* King's Hospital, Dublin. Army (Inns of Court OTC), 1918-19; Royal Irish and Royal Ulster Special Constabulary, 1920-25; Nigeria Police, 1925; Commissioner of Police, Nigeria, 1946-50, retired. King's Police Medal, Colonial Police Medal, Coronation Medal, 1939-45 War Medal. *Recreations:* golf and bridge. *Address:* Arigideen, 6 Victoria Square, Rostrevor, Co. Down BT34 3EU. *T:* Rostrevor 451.

FINLAY, (William) Ian (Robertson), CBE 1965; MA; HRSA; Director of the Royal Scottish Museum, 1961-71 (Keeper of the Department of Art and Ethnography, 1955-61); Professor of Antiquities to the Royal Scottish Academy, since 1971; *b* Auckland, New Zealand, 2 Dec. 1906; *s* of William R. Finlay and Annie M. Somerville; *m* 1933, Mary Scott, *d* of late W. Henderson Pringle, barrister-at-law; two *s* one *d. Educ:* Edinburgh Academy; Edinburgh Univ. Joined staff of Royal Scottish Museum, 1932; Deputy Regional Officer for Scotland, Ministry of Information, 1942-44; Vice-Chairman, Scottish Arts Council, 1967; Secretary, Royal Fine Art Commission for Scotland, 1953-61. Guest of State Department in US, 1960. Freeman of City of London; Member of Livery, Worshipful Company of Goldsmiths, London; Member: Holyrood (Amenity) Trust; Edinburgh Festival Council, 1968-71. FRSA 1971. Mem., Conseil de Direction, Gazette des Beaux Arts. *Publications:* Scotland, World To-Day Series, 1945; Scottish Art (for British Council), 1945; Art in Scotland, 1948; Scottish Crafts, 1948; The Scottish Tradition in Silver (Saltire booklet), 1948; Scottish Architecture (for schools), 1951; Treasures in Edinburgh, 1951; Scotland, Young Traveller Series, 1953; A History of Scottish Gold and Silver Work, 1956; Scotland, 1957; The Lothians, 1960; The Highlands, 1963; The Young Robert Louis Stevenson, 1965; The Lowlands, 1967; Celtic Art: an introduction, 1973; The Central Highlands, 1976; Priceless Heritage: the future of museums, 1977; articles, reviews and broadcast talks on art and general subjects. *Address:* Currie Riggs, Balerno, Midlothian. *T:* Balerno 3249. *Club:* Scottish Arts (Edinburgh).

FINLAYSON; *see* Gordon-Finlayson.

FINLAYSON, George Ferguson; HM Diplomatic Service; Counsellor (Commercial), Paris, since 1973; *b* 28 Nov. 1924; *s* of late G. B. Finlayson; *m* 1951, Rosslyn Evelyn (*d* 1972), *d* of late E. N. James; one *d. Educ:* North Berwick High Sch. Royal Air Force, 1943-47. Apptd HM Foreign (later Diplomatic) Service, 1949; 2nd Sec. (Inf.), HM Embassy, Rangoon, 1952-54; FO, 1955-59; First Sec., 1959; HM Consul, Algiers, 1959-61; First Sec., HM Embassy, Bamako, 1961-63; HM Consul (Commercial), New York, 1964-68; Counsellor, 1968; Counsellor (Commercial), British High Commn, Singapore, 1969-72; Head of Trade Relations and Exports Dept, FCO, 1972-73. *Recreations:* travel, walking, tennis, swimming. *Address:* c/o Foreign and Commonwealth Office, SW1; 141b Ashley Gardens, SW1. *T:* 01-834 6227; 49 Westgate, North Berwick, East Lothian. *T:* North Berwick 2522. *Club:* Oriental.

FINLAYSON, Maj.-Gen. (William) Forbes, OBE 1955; Director, Army Dental Service, 1966-70; *b* 12 Oct. 1911; *s* of late Lieut-Colonel W. T. Finlayson, OBE, Army Dental Corps, Edinburgh; *m* Anne McEwen, *d* of Walter Stables Smith, Peebles; one *s* one *d. Educ:* George Heriot's Sch., Edinburgh; Royal College of Surgeons, Edinburgh; FDSRCSE 1970. LDS 1933. Lieut, Army Dental Corps, 1935; Captain 1936; Major 1945; Lieut-Colonel 1952; Colonel 1959; Maj.-General 1966. Served in: UK, 1935-39, 1945-50, 1955-59, 1963-; Far East, 1939-45 (POW); BAOR, 1950-52, 1959-63; MELF, 1952-55. QHDS, 1966-70. *Recreations:* Rugby football, golf, tennis, walking. *Address:* Dogwood, Braes, Ullapool, Ross-shire IV26 2SZ.

FINLETTER, Hon. Thomas Knight; *b* 11 Nov. 1893; *m* 1920, Margaret Blaine Damrosch (*d* 1966); two *d*; *m* 1973, Eileen Wechster Geist. *Educ:* Episcopal Academy, Philadelphia, Pa.; University of Pennsylvania, Philadelphia, Pa. Special Assistant to US Secretary of State, Washington, DC, 1941-44; Consultant to US Delegation to UNO Conference at San Francisco, 1945; Chairman President's Air Policy Commission, Washington, DC, 1947. Partner, Coudert Brothers (lawyers), New York, 1926-41, 1944-48; returned to firm, 1965; retired, 1970. Minister in charge of ECA Mission to the United Kingdom, 1948-49; Secretary of the Air Force, United States, 1950-53; Ambassador to NATO, Paris, 1961-65. Hon. LLD: Univ. of Pennsylvania, 1950; Univ. of Rochester, 1950; Syracuse Univ., 1950; College of St Joseph, SJ, 1951; Rutgers Univ., 1959. *Publications:* Principles of Corporate Reorganization, 1937; Cases of Corporate Reorganization, 1938; Law of Bankruptcy Reorganization, 1939; Can Representative Government Do The Job?, 1945; Power and Policy, 1954; Foreign Policy: The Next Phase, 1958; Interim Report on the American Search for a Substitute for Isolation, 1968. *Recreations:* tennis and gardening. *Address:* 151 East 79 Street, New York, NY 10021, USA. *Clubs:* Athenæum (London); Knickerbocker, Century Association, (New York); Metropolitan (Washington).

FINLEY, Michael John; Editorial Director, Kent Messenger Group, since 1972; *b* 22 Sept. 1932; *s* of late Walter Finley and of Grace Marie Butler; *m* 1955, Sheila Elizabeth Cole; four *s. Educ:* King Edward VII Sch., Sheffield. Reporter and Sub-Editor, 1951-56, News Editor, 1960-63, Asst Editor, 1963-64, Editor, 1964-69, Sheffield Morning Telegraph (formerly Sheffield Telegraph); Daily Herald, Manchester, 1956-59; Chief Editorial Exec., Kent Messenger Gp, 1969-72. Chm., Parly and Legal Cttee, Guild of British Newspaper Editors. Member: BBC Region Adv. Council, 1967-69; BBC Gen. Adv. Council, 1971-. Broadcasts on radio and TV, 1972-. *Publication:* contrib. Advertising and the Community, 1968. *Recreations:* golf, sailing, squash, watching rugby and soccer. *Address:* Golford Place, Cranbrook, Kent. *Clubs:* Wig and Pen; Maidstone (Maidstone).

FINLEY, Dr Moses I., FBA 1971; Professor of Ancient History, Cambridge University, since 1970; Master of Darwin College, Cambridge, since 1976; *b* 20 May 1912; became British subject, 1962; *m* 1932, Mary F. Thiers; no *c. Educ:* Syracuse Univ., USA; Columbia Univ., USA. BA Syracuse 1927 (*magna cum laude*) (Phi Beta Kappa); MA Columbia, 1929 and PhD 1950. Held various teaching, research, editorial and consulting posts with: Encyclopaedia of the Social Sciences, 1930-33; Inst. of Social Research (then affiliated with Columbia Univ.), 1937-39; City Coll. of New York, 1934-42; Columbia Univ., 1933-34, 1948-54; exec. posts with war relief agencies, 1942-47. Fellow in History, Columbia Univ., 1934-35; Fellow, Amer. Council of Learned Socs, 1948; Lectr, then Asst Prof. of History, Newark Colls of

Rutgers Univ., 1948-52; Faculty Fellow, Fund for the Advancement of Educn, 1951-52. Lectr in Classics, Cambridge Univ., 1955-64; Fellow, Jesus Coll., 1957-76, Hon. Fellow, 1977; Reader in Ancient Social and Economic History, Cambridge University, 1964-70; Librarian, Jesus Coll., 1960-64; Chm., Faculty Bd of Classics, Cambridge Univ. 1967-69; Chm., Social and Political Sciences Cttee, Cambridge Univ., 1973-74. Sather Prof. of Classical Literature, Univ. of California, Berkeley, 1972; Lectures: First Mason Welch Gross, Rutgers Univ., 1972; Jane Harrison Meml, Newnham Coll., Cambridge, 1972; Mortimer Wheeler Archaeol, British Acad., 1974. Sec., Cambridge Philological Soc., 1959-65, Pres., 1974-76; Convener of Ancient Hist. section, Internat. Economic Hist. Conf., Aix-en-Provence, 1962, Munich, 1965; Chm., sub-cttee on Ancient Hist., Jt Assoc. of Classical Teachers, 1964-71; Pres., Classical Assoc., 1973-74. A Trustee, British Museum, 1977-. Editor: Views and Controversies in Classical Antiquity, 1960-73; Ancient Culture and Society, 1969-. FRHistS, 1970; FRSA, 1971. For. Mem., Royal Danish Acad. of Scis and Letters, 1975. Hon. DLitt Leicester, 1972. Wolfson Literary Award in History, 1974. *Publications:* Studies in Land and Credit in Ancient Athens, 1952; The World of Odysseus, 1954, 2nd edn 1977; (ed) The Greek Historians, 1958; (ed) Slavery in Classical Antiquity, 1960; The Ancient Greeks, 1963; (ed) Josephus, 1965; Aspects of Antiquity, 1968; Ancient Sicily, 1968; Early Greece: the Bronze and Archaic Ages, 1970; The Ancestral Constitution (inaugural lecture), 1971; (ed) Thucydides, 1972; Knowledge for what? (Encyclopaedia Britannica Lecture), 1973; Democracy Ancient and Modern, 1973; (ed) Problèmes de la terre en Grèce ancienne, 1973; The Ancient Economy, 1973; (ed) Studies in Ancient Society, 1974; The Use and Abuse of History, 1975; (with H. W. Pleket) The Olympic Games: the first thousand years, 1976; (ed) Studies in Roman Property, 1976; (ed) Atlas of Classical Archaeology, 1977; articles and reviews in classical, historical and legal jls, and in literary weeklies and monthlies in Britain and the US. *Recreations:* conversation, listening to music, travel. *Address:* Darwin College, Cambridge. *T:* Cambridge 51761; 12 Adams Road, Cambridge CB3 9AD. *T:* Cambridge 57784.

FINN, Donovan Bartley, CMG 1946; FRSC, FCIC; Director of Fisheries, Food and Agriculture Organization of the United Nations, 1946-64, retired; *b* Hendon, 1 March 1900; *s* of Edwin Bartley Finn and Eleanor Penton; *m* 1946, Florence Stewart Daly. *Educ:* University of Manitoba (BSc, MSc); Cambridge Univ. (PhD). Director Fisheries Expt. Station, Prince Rupert, BC, of the Fisheries Research Board of Canada, 1925; Director Fisheries Expt. Station, Halifax, NS, of Fisheries Research Board of Canada, 1934; Chairman Salt Fish Board of Canada, 1939; Deputy Minister of Fisheries, Dominion of Canada, 1940-46; Member Economic Advisory Cttee, Dominion of Canada, 1941; Chairman Food Requirements Cttee, 1943-46. Represented Canada as delegate and adviser at various international bodies and conferences during war with respect to fisheries and food matters. *Publications:* scientific journals, on physics and chemistry of food proteins. *Recreations:* mountaineering, music. *Address:* Castello di Sterpeto, Sterpeto d'Assisi, Perugia, Italy. *Clubs:* Rideau, University (Ottawa).

FINNEY, Albert; actor, stage and film; film director; Associate Artistic Director, English Stage Company, since 1972; *m* 1957, Jane Wenham, actress (marr. diss.); one *s*; *m* 1970, Anouk Aimée. First London appearance in The Party, New, 1958; Cassio in Othello, and Lysander, Stratford-on-Avon, 1959; subsequently in: The Lily White Boys, Royal Court, 1960; Billy Liar, Cambridge Theatre, 1960; Luther, in Luther: Royal Court Theatre and Phoenix Theatre, 1961-62; New York, 1963; Armstrong in Armstrong's Last Goodnight, Miss Julie and Black Comedy, Chichester, 1965, Old Vic, 1966; Love for Love, National Theatre, 1965; Much Ado About Nothing, National Theatre, 1965; A Flea in Her Ear, National Theatre, 1966; A Day in the Death of Joe Egg, NY, 1968; Alpha Beta, Royal Court and Apollo, 1972; Krapp's Last Tape, Royal Court, 1973; Cromwell, Royal Court, 1973; Chez Nous, Globe, 1974; Hamlet, Nat. Theatre, 1975; Tamburlaine, Nat. Theatre, 1976; Uncle Vanya, and Present Laughter, Royal Exchange, Manchester, 1977. Dir., The Freedom of the City, Royal Court, 1973. Films include: Saturday Night and Sunday Morning; Tom Jones; Night Must Fall; Two for the Road; Charlie Bubbles (also Director); Scrooge; Gumshoe; Alpha Beta; Murder on the Orient Express; directed Loot, Royal Court, 1975. Hon. LittD Sussex, 1965. Holds stage and film awards. *Address:* Memorial Films, Aspen House, 25 Dover Street, W1.

FINNEY, Prof. David John, FRS 1955; FRSE; MA, ScD (Cantab); Professor of Statistics, University of Edinburgh, since 1966; Director Agricultural Research Council Unit of Statistics; *b* Latchford, Warrington, 3 Jan. 1917; *e s* of late Robert G. S. Finney and of Bessie E. Whitlow; *m* 1950, Mary Elizabeth

Connolly; one *s* two *d. Educ:* Lymm and Manchester Grammar Schools; Clare Coll., Cambridge. Asst Statistician, Rothamsted Experimental Station, 1939-45; Lecturer in the Design and Analysis of Scientific Experiment, University of Oxford, 1945-54; Reader in Statistics, University of Aberdeen, 1954-63, Professor, 1963-66. United Nations FAO expert attached to Indian Council of Agricultural Research, 1952-73. Scientific Consultant, Cotton Research Corporation, 1959-75. Chm., Computer Bd for Univs and Research Councils, 1970-74 (Mem., 1966-74); Member: Adverse Reactions Sub-Cttee, Cttee on Safety of Medicines, 1963-; BBC General Adv. Council, 1969-76; Visiting Prof. of Biomathematics, Harvard Univ., 1962-63; President of Biometric Society, 1964-65 (Vice-President, 1963, 1966); Fellow: Royal Statistical Soc. (Pres., 1973-74); American Statistical Assoc.; Member: International Statistical Institute; FAO Statistics Advisory Cttee, 1967- (Chm., 1975-); Hon. Fellow Eugenics Society; Hon. Mem., Société Adolphe Quetelet. Weldon Memorial Prize, 1956. Dr *hc,* Faculté des Sciences Agronomiques de l'Etat à Gembloux, Belgium; Hon. DSc City. *Publications:* Probit Analysis, 1947 (3rd edn 1971); Biological Standardization (with J. H. Burn, L. G. Goodwin), 1950; Statistical Method in Biological Assay, 1952 (2nd edn 1964); An Introduction to Statistical Science in Agriculture, 1953 (4th edn 1972); Experimental Design and its Statistical Basis, 1955; Tecnica y Teoria en el diseño de Experimentos, 1957; An Introduction to the Theory of Experimental Design, 1960; Statistics for Mathematicians: An Introduction, 1968. Numerous papers in statistical and biological journals. *Recreations:* travel (active), music (passive), and the 3 R's. *Address:* Statistics Department, University of Edinburgh, James Clerk Maxwell Building, The King's Buildings, Mayfield Road, Edinburgh EH9 3JZ. *T:* 031-667 1081; 43 Cluny Drive, Edinburgh EH10 6DU. *T:* 031-447 2332.

FINNEY, James; Permanent Secretary, Department of Manpower Services for Northern Ireland, since 1976; *b* 21 Jan. 1920; *s* of James and Ellen Finney, Co. Armagh; *m* 1956, Barbara Ann Bennett, Wargrave, Berks; one *s* three *d. Educ:* Royal Belfast Academical Instn; Trinity Coll., Dublin Univ. BA 1st cl. Mods 1942. Royal Engrs, 1943-46. Min. of Educn for N Ireland, 1946-76. *Recreation:* gardening. *Address:* Honeypots, Ballyhanwood Road, Dundonald, Belfast, N Ireland. *T:* Dundonald 3428.

FINNISTON, Sir (Harold) Montague, Kt 1975; BSc, PhD; FRS 1969; Director, Sears Holdings Ltd, since 1976; Chairman: Sears Engineering Ltd; International Combustion (Holdings) Ltd, since 1977; Director: Cluff Oil Ltd; GKN Ltd; Chairman of Council, Scottish Business School, since 1976; President, Institute of Practitioners in Work Study, Organisation and Method, since 1977; *b* 15 Aug. 1912; *s* of late Robert and Esther Finniston; *m* 1936, Miriam Singer; one *s* one *d. Educ:* Allan Glen's Sch., Glasgow; Glasgow Univ.; Royal College of Science and Technology, Glasgow. Lecturer in Metallurgy, Royal College of Science and Technology, 1933-35; Metallurgist, Stewart & Lloyds, 1935-37; Chief Research Officer, Scottish Coke Research Cttee, 1937-40; Metallurgist, RN Scientific Service, 1940-46; seconded to Ministry of Supply, Chalk River, Canada, 1946-47; Chief Metallurgist, UKAEA, Harwell, 1948-58; Man. Director, International Research and Development Co. (Chm. 1968-77), and Technical Director, C. A. Parsons & Co. Ltd, 1959-67; Chairman: Cryosystems Ltd; System Computors Ltd; Electronics Association of the North-East; Director, C. A. Parsons & Co. Ltd; Mem. Board of Thorn-Parsons Co. Ltd and Northern Economic Planning Council, 1963-67; Dep. Chm. (Technical), BSC, 1967-71; Dep. Chm. and Chief Executive, BSC, 1971-73; Chm., BSC, 1973-76. Member: Council British Non-Ferrous Metals Research Assoc., 1965-72 (Vice-Chm. 1969-72; Chm. Research Board, 1965-70); NRDC, 1963-73; NEDC, 1973-76; Advisory Council, R&D (Fuel and Power), Dept of Trade and Industry (formerly Ministry of Power), 1965-74; Ministry of Technology SRC, University Science and Technology Board, 1965-67; NPL Steering Cttee, 1966-68; Exec. Cttee, PEP, 1968-74 (Chm., 1975-); Iron and Steel Adv. Cttee, 1969-73; Academic Adv. Cttee, Cranfield Inst. of Technology, 1970-75; BBC Science Consultative Group, 1971-74. Pres., Ironbridge Gorge Mus. Develt Trust, 1977-. President: Inst. of Metals, 1967-68; Metals Soc., 1974-75; Inst. Metallurgists, 1975-76; ASLIB, 1976- (Vice-Pres., 1974-76); Vice-Pres., Iron and Steel Inst., 1968-73; Gen. Sec., BAAS, 1970-73 (Life Mem.); Mem., Soc. of Chem. Industry, 1974. A Vice- Pres., Royal Soc., 1971-72. Mem., Court of Assts, Worshipful Co. of Tinplate Workers, 1974-. Lectures: Dunn Meml, 1968; 19th Hatfield Meml, 1968; 18th Coal Science, BCURA, 1969; Edward Williams, 1970; Andrew Laing, 1970; Cockcroft, UMIST, 1975; Thomas Graham, Harold Moore, R. W. Mann, Marlew (Scotland), Colquhoun, 1976; Edwards Meml, 1977. Governor, Carmel Coll., 1973-. Vis. Fellow, Univ.

of Lancaster, 1970-. ARTC; FIM; FInstP; FIChemE; FBIM; life FRSA. Hon. Member: American Iron and Steel Inst., 1974; Japan Iron and Steel Inst., 1975 (Tawara Gold Medal, 1975); Indian Inst. of Metals, 1976. Hon. Fellow, UMIST, 1973. Hon. DSc: Strathclyde, 1968; Aston, 1971; City, 1974; Cranfield, 1976; Bath, 1977; DUniv Surrey, 1969; Hon. DCL Newcastle, 1976. Bessemer Medal, Metals Soc., 1974; Silver Medal, Inst. Sheet Metal Engrg; Eichneu Medal, Soc. Française de Metallurgie; A. A. Griffiths Silver Medal, Material Sci. Club; Glazebrook Medal, Inst. of Physics. *Publications:* Editor: Metallurgy of the Rare Metals; Progress in Nuclear Energy; Structural Characteristics of Materials; various scientific papers. *Recreations:* reading, writing and spectator interest in sport. *Address:* Sears Holdings Ltd, 40 Duke Street, W1M 6AN. *T:* 01-408 1180. *Club:* Athenæum.

FINSBERG, Geoffrey, MBE 1959; JP; MP (C) Hampstead, since 1970; Controller of Personnel, and Chief Industrial Relations Adviser, Great Universal Stores, since 1968; Deputy Chairman, GUS Transport Ltd; *b* 13 June 1926; *o s* of late Monte Finsberg, MC, and May Finsberg (*née* Grossman); *m* 1969, Pamela Benbow Hill. *Educ:* City of London Sch. National Chm., Young Conservatives, 1954-57; Mem., Exec. Cttee, Nat. Union of Cons. and Unionist Assocs (Mem. Exec. Cttee, Greater London Area, 1949-); a Vice-Chm., Conservative Party Organisation, 1975-. Borough Councillor: Hampstead, 1949-65; Camden, 1964-74 (Leader, 1968-70). Chairman: Gtr London Area Cons. Local Govt Cttee, 1972-75. Opposition spokesman on Greater London, 1974-; Mem. Exec., 1922 Cttee, 1974-75; Vice-Chm., All Party Retail Cttee; Member: Select Cttee on Expenditure; Trustee Savings Bank Parly Cttee; Hon. Sec., Anglo-Austrian Parly Gp. Director, London & South Eastern Trustee Savings Bank, 1963-75. Vice-Pres., Assoc. of Municipal Corporations, 1971-74 (Dep. Chm., 1969-71); Parly Adviser: London Boroughs Assoc.; Assoc. of Metropolitan Authorities; Member: Post Office Users Nat. Council, 1970-; Council, CBI (Chm., Post Office Panel); Vice-Pres., Nat. Assoc. of Retail Furnishers. Patron, Maccabi Assoc. of GB. Governor, Univ. Coll. Sch. JP Inner London, 1962. *Recreations:* bridge, reading. *Address:* 80 Westbere Road, NW2 3RU. *T:* 01-435 5320.

FINTRIE, Lord; James Alexander Norman Graham; *b* 16 Aug. 1973; *s* and *heir* of Marquis of Graham, *qv.*

FIRBANK, Maj.-Gen. Cecil Llewellyn, CB 1953; CBE 1951; DSO 1944 and Bar 1945; DL; *b* 18 March 1910; *m* 1st, 1934, Audrey Hobhouse (marr. diss. 1952); one *s*; 2nd, 1952, Marye Brenda Fleetwood-Wilson. *Educ:* Cheltenham Coll.; RMC Sandhurst. Gazetted to 1st Somerset LI, 1924; served Egypt, 1926-29; seconded to Royal West African Frontier Force, 1929-34; served with Somerset LI, 1934-42; on active service, North West Europe, 1944-45; Comd 71 Infantry Bde, 1945-46; Staff Coll., 1947-48; Commandant School of Infantry, Warminster, 1948-51; GOC SW District and 43rd Wessex Division (TA), 1951-54; Director of Infantry, War Office, 1955-58; retired pay, 1959. Colonel Commandant, Aden Protectorate Levies, 1958-62; Colonel, Somerset and Cornwall Light Infantry, 1963-68; Dep. Colonel, The Light Infantry (Somerset and Cornwall), 1968-70. Hon. Colonel: 4/5th Somerset LI (TA), 1955-60; North Somerset Yeomanry (44th Royal Tank Regt), 1959-64. Dir, Civil Defence for Wales, 1960-65. DL Somerset, 1959. *Recreations:* cricket, field sports. *Address:* The Owls, Charlton Horethorne, near Sherborne, Dorset. *T:* Corton Denham 279. *Club:* Army and Navy.

FIRNBERG, David; Director, National Computing Centre Ltd, since 1974; *b* 1 May 1930; *s* of L. B. Firnberg and K. L. E. Firnberg; *m* 1957, Sylvia Elizabeth Firnberg (*née* du Cros); one *s* three *d. Educ:* Merchant Taylors' Sch., Northwood. FBCS. Went West, 1953-56; Television Audience Measurement Ltd, 1956-59; ICT/ICL, 1959-72; David Firnberg Associates Ltd, 1972-74. *Publications:* Computers Management and Information, 1973; Cassell's New Spelling Dictionary, 1976. *Address:* The Great House, Buckland Common, Tring, Herts HP23 6NX. *T:* Cholesbury 448. *Clubs:* English-Speaking Union, Wig and Pen, Australian Society.

FIRTH, Maj.-Gen. Charles Edward Anson, CB 1951; CBE 1945; DSO 1943; *b* 9 Oct. 1902; *s* of late Major E. W. A. Firth, Indian Army; *m* 1933, Mary Kathleen (*d* 1977), *d* of late Commander W. St J. Fraser, RN; two *s. Educ:* Wellington Coll., Berks; RMC Sandhurst. 2nd Lieut The Gloucestershire Regt, 1923; Lieut, 1925; Captain, 1935; Staff Coll., 1936-37; War Office, 1938-40; Major, 1940; Middle East: Temp. Lieut-Colonel; AA and QMG 50 Div., 1941-42; OC 1st Royal Sussex Regt in Middle East, 1942-43; Temp. Brigadier, 7th Indian Infantry Bde, 1943; Comd 167 Infantry Bde, 1943-44 (Italy); Comd 21 Tank Bde, 1944 (N. Africa); Comd 2 Infantry Bde, 1944 (Italy); Comdr and Dep.

Comdr British Military Mission to Greece, 1944-45. Colonel 1946; War Office, 1946-48; Comd Area Troops, Berlin (British Sector), 1948-50; Maj.-General, 1950; Comd East Anglian Dist, 1950; GOC Salisbury Plain Dist, 1951-53; Director of Personal Services, War Office, 1953-56. Colonel The Gloucestershire Regt, 1954-64; first Colonel Comdt, Military Provost Staff Corps, 1956-61. Governor, Dauntsey's Sch., 1961- (Vice-Chairman, 1965-). Grand Commander Order of the Phoenix (Greek), 1946. *Recreations:* gardening, writing, fishing. *Address:* Crofton Lodge, Crofton, Marlborough, Wilts SN8 3DW. *T:* Great Bedwyn 270. *Club:* Army and Navy.

FIRTH, David Colin; Headmaster, Cheadle Hulme School, since 1977; *b* 29 Jan. 1930; *s* of Jack and Muriel Firth; *m* 1954, Edith Scanlan; three *s* one *d*. *Educ:* Rothwell Grammar Sch.; Sheffield Univ. (BSc, DipEd). Royal Signals, 1952-54; Stand Grammar Sch., 1954-57; East Barnet Grammar Sch., 1957-61; Bristol Grammar Sch., 1961-73; The Gilberd Sch., 1973-77. *Publications:* A Practical Organic Chemistry, 1966; Elementary Thermodynamics, 1969; (jtly) Introductory Physical Science, 1971. *Recreations:* cricket, fell walking, talking about gardening. *Address:* Cheadle Hulme School, Claremont Road, Cheadle Hulme, Cheadle, Cheshire SK8 6EF.

FIRTH, Edward Michael Tyndall, CB 1951; *b* 17 Feb. 1903; *s* of Edward H. Firth, Sheffield; *m* 1929, Eileen Marie, *d* of Edward Newman, Hove; two *s*. *Educ:* King Edward VII Sch., Sheffield; University College, Oxford. Classical Scholar, 1922-26. Inland Revenue, 1926; Ministry of Health, 1945; Under Secretary, 1947-58; Registrar General, 1958-63. *Address:* 65 Middle Way, Oxford.

FIRTH, Prof. Sir Raymond (William), Kt 1973; MA; PhD; FBA 1949; Professor of Anthropology, University of London, 1944-68, now Emeritus; *b* 25 March 1901; *s* of late Wesley Hugh Bourne Firth and Marie Elizabeth Jane Cartmill; *m* 1936, Rosemary, *d* of late Sir Gilbert Upcott, KCB; one *s*. *Educ:* Auckland Grammar Sch.; Auckland University College; London School of Economics (Hon. Fellow, 1970). Anthropological research in British Solomon Islands, including one year on Tikopia, 1928-29; Lecturer in Anthropology, University of Sydney, 1930-31; Acting Professor of Anthropology, University of Sydney, 1931-32; Lecturer in Anthropology, London School of Economics, 1932-35; Reader, 1935-44; Hon. Secretary Royal Anthropological Institute, 1936-39 (President 1953-55); Research in peasant economics and anthropology in Malaya, as Leverhulme Research Fellow, 1939-40; served with Naval Intelligence Division, Admiralty, 1941-44; Secretary of Colonial Social Science Research Council, Colonial Office, 1944-45; Fellow, Center for Advanced Study in the Behavioral Sciences, Stanford, 1958-59; Prof. of Pacific Anthropology, Univ. of Hawaii, 1968-69. Visiting Professor: British Columbia, 1969; Cornell, 1970; Chicago, 1971; Graduate Center, City Univ. of New York, 1971; Univ. of California, Davis 1974, Berkeley 1977. Life Pres., Assoc. of Social Anthropologists, 1975. Foreign Hon. Member American Academy of Arts and Sciences, 1963; Hon. Member Royal Society, NZ, 1964; Foreign Member: American Philosophical Society, 1965; Royal Soc., NSW; Royal Danish Academy of Sciences and Letters, 1966. Social research surveys: W Africa, 1945; Malaya, 1947; New Guinea, 1951; Tikopia, 1952, 1966; Malaya, 1963. Hon. degrees: DPh Oslo, 1965; LLD Michigan, 1967; LittD East Anglia, 1968; Dr Letters ANU, 1969; DHumLett Chicago, 1968; DSc British Columbia, 1970; DLitt Exeter, 1972. *Publications:* The Kauri Gum Industry, 1924; Primitive Economics of the New Zealand Maori, 1929 (new edn, 1959); Art and Life In New Guinea, 1936; We, The Tikopia: A Sociological Study of Kinship in Primitive Polynesia, 1936; Human Types, 1938 (new edn, 1975); Primitive Polynesian Economy, 1939 (new edn, 1964); The Work of the Gods in Tikopia, 1940 (new edn, 1967); Malay Fishermen: Their Peasant Economy, 1946 (enlarged edn, 1966); Elements of Social Organization, 1951 (new edn 1971); Two Studies of Kinship in London (ed.), 1956; Man and Culture: An Evaluation of the Work of Malinowski (ed.), 1957; Social Change in Tikopia, 1959; History and Traditions of Tikopia, 1961; Essays on Social Organization and Values, 1964; (with B. S. Yamey) Capital Saving and Credit in Peasant Societies, 1964; Tikopia Ritual and Belief, 1967; Rank and Religion in Tikopia, 1970; (with J. Hubert and A. Forge) Families and Their Relatives, 1970; Symbols Public and Private, 1973. *Recreation:* viewing Romanesque art. *Address:* 33 Southwood Avenue, N6 5SA. *Club:* Athenæum.

FISCHER, Annie; Hungarian Pianist; *b* Budapest, 1914. *Educ:* Franz Liszt Landemusikhochschule, Budapest. Studied under Arnold Szekule and Ernst von Dohnanyi. Concert Début, Budapest, at age of eight (performed Beethoven's C Major

Concerto), 1922; began international career as a concert pianist, Zurich, 1926; toured and played in most European Music centres, 1926-39. Concert pianist, Sweden, during War of 1939-45. Returned to Hungary after War and has made concert tours to all parts of the world. Hon. Prof., Acad. of Music, Budapest, 1965. Awarded 1st prize, Internat. Liszt Competition, Budapest, 1933; Kossuth Prizes 1949, 1955, 1965. *Address:* Szent Istvan Park, 14, Budapest XIII, Hungary.

FISCHER, Prof. Ernst Otto; Professor of Inorganic Chemistry, Munich University (Techn); *b* Munich, 10 Nov. 1918; *s* of Prof. Karl T. Fischer and Valentine (*née* Danzer); unmarried. *Educ:* Tech. Univ., Munich. Dip. Chem., 1949; Dr rer. nat., 1952, Habilitation 1954. Associate Prof. of Inorganic Chem., Univ. of Munich, 1957, Prof. 1959, Prof. and Dir, Inorganic Chem. Inst., Tech. Univ., Munich, 1964. Member: Bavarian Acad. of Sciences; Akad. deutscher Naturforscher Leopoldina, 1969; Austrian Acad. of Scis, 1976; Accad. dei Lincei, Italy, 1976; Göttingen Akad. der Wissenschaften, 1977; Soc. of German Chemists, etc; Centennial For. Fellow, Amer. Chem. Soc., 1976. Hon. Dr rer. nat. Munich, 1972; Hon. DSc Strathclyde, 1975. Has received many prizes and awards including the Nobel Prize for Chemistry, 1973 (jointly with Prof. Geoffrey Wilkinson) for their pioneering work, performed independently, on the chem. of organometallic "sandwich compounds". *Publications:* (with H. Werner) Metall-pi-Komplexe mit di- und oligoolefischen Liganden, 1963 (trans. as Metal pi-Complexes Vol. 1, Complexes with di- and oligo-olefinic Ligands, 1966-); numerous contribs to learned jls on organometallic chem., etc. *Recreations:* art, history, travel. *Address:* 16 Sohnckestrasse, 8 Munich-Solln, West Germany.

FISCHER, John; Contributing Editor, Harper's Magazine, since 1967 (Editor-in-Chief, 1953-67); *b* 21 April 1910; *s* of John Simpson and Georgie Caperton Fischer; *m* 1936, Elizabeth Wilson; two *d*. *Educ:* Oklahoma Univ.; Oxford, England (Rhodes Scholar, 1933 and 1934-35). Reporter, Daily Oklahoman, 1932-33; US Dept of Agriculture, 1936; Washington Correspondent for Associated Press, 1937; Board of Economic Warfare, Intelligence Division, 1939; in India as Chief of Economic Intelligence, and Lend-lease, for Foreign Econ. Admin., 1943; Assoc. Editor, Harper's Magazine, 1944-47; Editor-in-Chief, General Book Dept of Harper & Row, Publishers, Inc.; leave of absence from Harper's to join Relief and Rehabilitation mission to the Ukraine, 1946. Member, National Advisory Commn on Rural Poverty. Trustee, Brookings Institution. Regents Prof., Univ. of Calif, 1969; Vis. Fellow, Yale Univ. Hon. Doctor: Kenyon Coll., 1953; Bucknell Univ., 1954; University of Massachusetts, 1956. *Publications:* Why They Behave Like Russians, 1947 (English title: Scared Men in the Kremlin); Master Plan USA, 1951; The Stupidity Problem, 1964; Vital Signs, 1975; articles in Harper's, Life, New Yorker, Reader's Digest. *Recreations:* gardening, music, carpentry, travel. *Address:* Shell Beach Road, Guilford, Conn 06437, USA. *Clubs:* Century Association, American Association of Rhodes Scholars (New York City).

FISCHER-DIESKAU, Dietrich; First Baritone of the Städtische Oper, Berlin, since 1948; Member of Vienna State Opera since 1957; *b* Berlin, 28 May 1925; *s* of Dr Albert Fischer-Dieskau; *m* 1949, Irmgard Poppen (*d* 1963); three *s*. *Educ:* High Sch., Berlin; Music Academy, Berlin. Extensive Concert Tours of Europe and USA; soloist in Festivals at Edinburgh, Salzburg, Bayreuth, Vienna, Berlin, Munich, Holland, Luzern, Prades, etc. Opera roles include: Wolfram, Jochanaan, Almaviva, Marquis Posa, Don Giovanni, Falstaff, Mandryka, Wozzeck, Danton, Macbeth, Hans Sachs. Many recordings. Member of Academy of Arts, Berlin; Hon. RAM, 1972; Honorary Member: Wiener Konzerthausgesellschaft, 1962; Königlich-Schwedische Akad., 1972. Kunstpreis der Stadt Berlin, 1950; Internationaler Schallplattenpreis, since 1955 nearly every year; Orfeo d'oro, 1955 and 1966; Bayerischer Kammersänger, 1959; Edison Prize, 1961, 1964, 1966, 1970; Naras Award, USA, 1962; Mozart-Medaille, Wien, 1962; Berliner Klammersänger, 1963; Electrola Award, 1970; Léonie Sonning Music Prize, Copenhagen, 1975; Golden Gramophone Award, Germany, 1975. Bundesverdienstkreuz (1st class), 1958; Grosses Verdienstkreuz, 1974. *Publications:* Texte Deutscher Lieder, 1968 (The Fischer-Dieskau Book of Lieder, 1976); Auf den Spuren der Schubert-Lieder, 1971; Wagner und Nietzsche, 1974.

FISH, John; Under-Secretary, Head of Establishment General Services Division, Department of Industry, since 1973; *b* 16 July 1920; *s* of late George Fish and of Gertrude Fish; *m* 1948, Frances; two *s*. *Educ:* Lincoln School. Entered Customs and Excise, 1937; Exchequer and Audit Dept, 1939; War service, Pilot in RAF, 1940-46; returned Exchequer and Audit Dept, 1946; transf. BoT, 1949; Principal, 1950; Min. of Materials,

1951; Volta River Preparatory Commn, Accra, 1953; BoT, 1956; Asst Sec., 1960; Min. of Health, 1962; BoT, 1965; DTI, 1970; Under-Sec., 1973; Dept of Industry, 1974. *Recreations:* walking, amateur operatics, carpentry. *Address:* 39 Mundania Road, SE22 0HN. *Club:* Civil Service.

FISHENDEN, Margaret White, DSc, FInstP; Formerly Reader in Applied Heat at Imperial College (University of London), (Mechanical Engineering Department); *y d* of late R. W. White; one *s*. *Educ:* University of Manchester, 1st class Honours in Physics, 1909; Higginbottom Scholar, 1907, Graduate Scholar, 1909; Beyer Fellow, 1910-11; Lecturer, University of Manchester, 1910-15; in charge of research work for Air Pollution Advisory Board of the Manchester Corporation, 1916-22; research work on Atmospheric Conditions, Humidity and Ventilation in Spinning Mills and Weaving Sheds, Domestic Heating, Heat Transfer, etc. *Publications:* House Heating, 1925; The Calculation of Heat Transmission, 1932; An Introduction to Heat Transfer, 1950; scientific and technical papers. *Address:* c/o 8 Severn Road, Chilton, Didcot, Oxon.

FISHER, family name of **Barons Fisher** and **Fisher of Camden** and **Baroness Fisher of Rednal.**

FISHER, 3rd Baron, *cr* 1909, of Kilverstone; **John Vavasseur Fisher,** DSC 1944; JP; DL; Director, Kilverstone Latin-American Zoo and Wild Life Park, since 1973; *b* 24 July 1921; *s* of 2nd Baron and Jane (*d* 1955), *d* of Randal Morgan, Philadelphia, USA; *S* father, 1955; *m* 1st, 1949, Elizabeth Ann Penelope (marr. diss. 1969), *yr d* of late Herbert P. Holt, MC; two *s* two *d*; 2nd, 1970, Hon. Mrs Rosamund Anne Fairbairn. *Educ:* Stowe; Trinity Coll., Cambridge. Member: Eastern Gas Bd, 1962-71; East Anglia Economic Planning Council, 1971-. DL Norfolk, 1968, JP Norfolk, 1970. *Heir: s* Hon. Patrick Vavasseur Fisher, *b* 14 June 1953. *Address:* Kilverstone Hall, Thetford, Norfolk. *T:* Thetford 2222. *Club:* Naval.
See also Baron Clifford of Chudleigh.

FISHER OF CAMDEN, Baron *cr* 1974 (Life Peer), of Camden in Greater London; **Samuel Fisher,** Kt 1967; FCIS; JP; Alderman, London Borough of Camden, since 1971; Vice-President, London Diamond Bourse; President, Board of Deputies of British Jews, since 1973 (Senior Vice-Pres., 1967-73); *b* 20 Jan. 1905; *m* 1930, Millie Gluckstein; one *d* (and one *d* decd). *Educ:* London. Mayor of Stoke Newington, 1953-54; first Mayor of London Borough of Camden, 1965-66. Chairman: London Labour Mayors' Assoc., 1953-; West Central Div. Justices. Chm., European Div., World Jewish Congress. Governor: University Coll. Hosp.; University Coll. Sch. JP Inner London, 1951. *Recreations:* reviewing historical and biographical books. *Address:* 48 Viceroy Court, Prince Albert Road, NW8 7PR. *T:* 01-586 2824.

FISHER OF REDNAL, Baroness *cr* 1974 (Life Peer), of Rednal, Birmingham; **Doris Mary Gertrude Fisher,** JP; Member of the European Parliament, since 1975; Member: Warrington New Town Development Corporation, since 1974; New Towns Staff Commission, since 1976; *b* 13 Sept. 1919; *d* of late Frederick J. Satchwell, BEM; *m* 1939, Joseph Fisher; two *d*. *Educ:* Tinker's Farm Girls Sch.; Fircroft Coll.; Bournville Day Continuation Coll. Member: Birmingham City Council, 1952-74; Labour Party, 1945-; UNESCO study group; Nat. Pres. Co-operative Women's Guild, 1961-62. Contested Ladywood, Birmingham, 1969 by-election; MP (Lab) Birmingham, Ladywood, 1970-Feb. 1974. Mem., GMC; Vice-Pres., Assoc. of Municipal Authorities. JP Birmingham 1961. Hon. Alderman, 1974, Birmingham District Council. *Recreations:* swimming, walking. *Address:* 36 Irwin Avenue, Rednal, Birmingham. *T:* 021-453 3365.

FISHER, Alan Wainwright; General Secretary, National Union of Public Employees, since 1968; Member: TUC General Council, since 1968; London Electricity Board, since 1970; British Airways Board, since 1972; *b* 20 June 1922; *s* of Thomas Wainwright Fisher and Ethel Agnes Fisher; *m* 1958, Joyce Tinniswood; two *s* one *d*. *Educ:* Primary and Secondary Schools in Birmingham. National Union of Public Employees: Junior Clerk, 1939; Midlands Divisional Officer, 1953; Asst General Secretary, 1962. Member: Nat. Jt Council for Local Authorities, Services, 1956- (Chm., 1971-72); Ancillary Staffs Council (Sec. 1965-) and Gen. Council (Chm. 1966-69) of Whitley Councils for Health Services; Potato Marketing Bd, 1969-70; Bd, Centre for Educnl Develt Overseas (Governor 1970-); Nat. Radiological Protection Bd, 1971; Bd, BOAC, 1970-72. *Recreation:* seismography. *Address:* 30 South Row, Blackheath, SE3. *T:* 01-852 2753.

FISHER, Anne; *see* Fisher, Phyllis Anne.

FISHER, Prof. Charles Alfred, MA Cantab; Professor of Geography, School of Oriental and African Studies, University of London, since 1964; *b* 23 April 1916; *er s* of Rev. Charles and Bertha Fisher (*née* Anderson); *m* 1945, Irene Mary Clarke (*d* 1972), ARCM; GRSM; one *s* one *d*. *Educ:* Strand Sch., London; St Catharine's Coll., Cambridge (Exhibr 1935, Scholar 1938, Junior Librarian 1938-40). Geog. Tripos, Parts I and II (First Class Hons), 1937, 1938; University Bartle Frere Exhibr, 1938, 1939; MA 1942; DLitt Komazawa, Tokyo, 1976. Served War of 1939-45 with RE Malaya Comd HQ. Asst Lecturer in Geography, University College of Leicester, 1946; Lecturer in Geography, University College of Wales, Aberystwyth, 1946-49; Senior Research Officer, Institute of Colonial Studies, Oxford, 1950-51; Lecturer in Geography, University (Coll.) of Leicester, 1951-58, Reader, 1958-59; Professor and Head of the Department of Geography, 1959-64, and Director of Centre of Japanese Studies, 1962-64, University of Sheffield. RGS Travelling Fellowship, 1947; Visiting Lecturer in Geography and Visiting Fellow of Trumbull Coll., Yale Univ., 1953-54. Chairman Assoc. of British Orientalists, 1962-63. Editor, Modern Asian Studies, 1967-70. Victoria Medal, RGS, 1974. *Publications:* Geographical Essays on British Tropical Lands, 1956 (Joint Editor); South-east Asia: a Social Economic and Political Geography, 1964; Essays in Political Geography, 1968 (Editor); articles, mostly on political geography of Asia, in Geog. Journal, Econ. Geog., International Affairs, Politique Etrangère, etc. *Recreations:* music and foreign travel. *Address:* School of Oriental and African Studies, University of London, WC1. *Club:* Athenæum.

FISHER, Hon. Charles Douglas; Headmaster, Geelong Church of England Grammar School, since 1974; *b* 8 Oct. 1921; 3rd *s* of late Most Rev. and Rt Hon. Lord Fisher of Lambeth, GCVO, and of Lady Fisher of Lambeth; *m* 1952, Anne Gilmour (*née* Hammond); four *s* two *d*. *Educ:* Marlborough Coll.; Keble Coll., Oxford (MA). Mem. Australian Coll. of Educn. War Service, 1940-45; Oxford Univ., 1945-48; Asst Master, Harrow Sch., 1948-55; Sen. Master, Peterhouse Sch., Rhodesia, 1955-60; Headmaster: Scotch Coll., Adelaide, 1961-69; C of E Grammar Sch., Brisbane, 1970-73. *Address:* Geelong Church of England Grammar School, Corio, Victoria, Australia. *T:* Geelong 75-1452. *Club:* Melbourne (Melbourne).
See also Hon. F. F. Fisher, Hon. Sir H. A. P. Fisher.

FISHER, Major (Hon.) Charles Howard Kerridge, MC 1918; JP; DL; Director of property companies, since 1960; *b* 21 Dec. 1895; *s* of late Charles Henry Fisher, Westbury, Wilts.; *m* 1923, Ethel Mary (*d* 1958), *d* of Sidney Redcliffe Chope, JP, Bideford, Devon; one *s* one *d*; *m* 1967, Gertrude Elizabeth, JP, widow of William Walter Symper, Harrow. *Educ:* Trowbridge High Sch., Wiltshire. Served European War, 1914-18 (MC); with Hon. Artillery Company and RA in Belgium and France; War of 1939-45: Home Guard and Army Welfare Officer; Hon. Major 1958. Manufacturer ladies' clothing, 1923-59, when retired (Company Dir). Member Acton Borough Council, 1940-45 (Educn Cttee, 1945-65). JP 1947, DL 1961, Middlesex (now London). First High Sheriff of Greater London, 1965. Lord Lieutenant's Representative for Acton, 1958-70 (now London Borough of Ealing, 1965-71); Dep. Chairman, Willesden Petty Sessional Division, 1962-69. General Comr of Income Tax, 1965-69. Freeman, City of London, 1947; Liveryman, Haberdashers' Company, 1948; Trustee, Acton Methodist Church, etc; Patron, Local Cadets; President: Boy Scouts Assoc.; Harlesden Branch, British Legion, Vice-President: Acton Branch, British Legion; NW County Met. Area British Legion. Member, War Pension Cttee, Ealing, 1940 (Vice-Chairman 1960). *Recreations:* local social activities. *Address:* 36 Baronsmede, Ealing, W5 4LT. *T:* 01-567 8281. *Clubs:* City Livery, Royal Automobile.

FISHER, Desmond (Michael); Director of Broadcasting Developments, Radio Telefis Eireann, Dublin, since 1975; *b* 9 Sept. 1920; *e s* of Michael Louis Fisher and Evelyn Kate Shier; *m* 1948, Margaret Elizabeth Smyth; three *s* one *d*. *Educ:* St Columb's Coll., Derry; Good Counsel Coll., New Ross, Co. Wexford; University Coll., Dublin (BA (NUI)). Asst Editor, Nationalist and Leinster Times, Carlow, 1945-48; Foreign Editor, Irish Press, Dublin, 1948-51; Economic Correspondent, Irish News Agency, Dublin, 1951-54; London Editor, Irish Press, 1954-62; Editor, Catholic Herald, 1962-66; Dep. Head of News, 1967-73, Head of Current Affairs, 1973-75, Radio Telefis Eireann. *Publications:* The Church in Transition, 1967; contributor to The Economist, The Furrow, Irish Digest and to various Irish, US and foreign magazines. *Address:* Louvain 22, Dublin. *T:* 981434.

FISHER, Doris G.; *b* 1907; *d* of Gathorne John Fisher, Pontypool. *Educ:* Farringtons, Chislehurst; Royal Holloway

Coll., University of London (BA Hons (English) 1929, (French) 1931); Sorbonne. Senior English Mistress, Maidenhead County Gram. Sch. 1934-39; Second Mistress, Dover County Grammar Sch., 1945; Headmistress of Farringtons, Chislehurst, Kent, 1946-57, retired. Lecturer at Westminster Training Coll., 1957-59; Lecturer at Avery Hill Training Coll., 1959-62. *Address:* 245 Latymer Court, W6.

FISHER, Dudley Henry, IPFA; Chairman, Wales Region, British Gas Corporation, since Sept. 1974; *b* 22 Aug. 1922; *s* of Arthur and Mary Fisher; *m* 1946, Barbara Lilian Sexton; one *s* two *d*. *Educ:* City of Norwich Sch. Various accountancy positions in Local Govt and Eastern Electricity Bd, 1938-53. War service, RAF, 1942-46 (Flt Lt). Norther Gas Bd, 1953; Wales Gas Board: Asst Chief Accountant, Dep. Chief Accountant, Chief Accountant, Dir of Finance, 1956-69; Dep. Chm., 1970. *Recreations:* golf, gardening, reading. *Address:* Norwood Edge, 8 Cyncoed Avenue, Cardiff CF2 6SU. *Club:* Cardiff and County (Cardiff).

FISHER, Rt. Rev. and Ven. Edward George; *see* Knapp-Fisher.

FISHER, Hon. Francis Forman, MC 1944; Master of Wellington College, since 1966; *b* 25 Sept. 1919; 2nd *s* of late Most Rev. and Rt Hon. Lord Fisher of Lambeth, GCVO; unmarried. *Educ:* Repton; Clare Coll., Cambridge (MA). Commissioned, The Sherwood Foresters, 1940; served War of 1939-45, Middle East, and Western Desert (POW Tobruk, 1942); escaped and returned to England, 1943; demobilised, rank of Capt., 1946 (MC); returned to Cambridge, 1946; Asst Master, Repton Sch., 1947-54; Housemaster, 1948-54; Warden of St Edward's Sch., Oxford, 1954-66. Incorporated MA Oxford Univ. through Christ Church, 1955. Chm., Headmaster's Conf., 1973. *Recreations:* cricket, hockey (rep. CUHC *v* Oxford, 1947), and other games. *Address:* Wellington College, Berks. *T:* Crowthorne 2261. *Clubs:* East India, Devonshire, Sports and Public Schools; Hawks (Cambridge).
See also Hon. Sir Henry A. P. Fisher, Hon. C. D. Fisher.

FISHER, Francis George Robson, MA Oxon; Chief Master, King Edward's School, Birmingham, since 1974; *b* 9 April 1921; *s* of late John Henry Fisher and Hannah Clayton Fisher; *m* 1965, Sheila Vernon, *o d* of late D. Dunsire and Mrs H. E. Butt; one *s*. *Educ:* Liverpool Coll. (Schol.); Worcester Coll., Oxford (Classical Exhibitioner). Served War of 1939-45; Capt. in Ayrshire Yeomanry, North Africa and Italy, 1942-45. Housemaster and Senior English Master, Kingswood Sch., Bath, 1950-59; Headmaster, Bryanston Sch., 1959-74. *Recreations:* music, lawn tennis, sailing. *Address:* King Edward's School, Birmingham B15 2UA. *T:* 021-472 1672, 021-472 0652.

FISHER, Prof. Frederick Jack, MA; Professor of Economic History, London School of Economics, University of London, 1954-75; *b* 22 July 1908; *s* of A. H. Fisher, Southend-on-Sea; *m* 1943, Barbara Vivienne, *d* of J. E. Whisstock, Southend-on-Sea; one *s* one *d*. *Educ:* Southend High Sch.; London Sch. of Economics. MA. Served RAF, 1941-46. Asst Lecturer and Lecturer in Economic History, London Sch. of Economics, 1935-47; Reader in Economic History, 1947-54. FRHistS. Wiles' Lectr, QUB, 1973. *Publications:* (ed) Essays in the Economic and Social History of Tudor and Stuart England, 1961; (ed) Calendar of Manuscripts of Lord Sackville of Knole, vol II, 1966; contrib. Economica, Economic History Review. *Address:* 22 Lyndale Avenue, NW2.

FISHER, Sir George Read, Kt 1967; CMG 1961; Mining Engineer; President, MIM Holdings Ltd, 1970-75; *b* 23 March 1903; *s* of George Alexander and Ellen Harriett Fisher; *m* 1st, 1927, Eileen Elaine Triggs (*d* 1966); one *s* three *d*; 2nd, 1973, Marie C. Gilbey. *Educ:* Prince Alfred Coll., Adelaide; Adelaide Univ. (BE). Formerly Gen. Manager of Operations for Zinc Corporation Ltd, Broken Hill, NSW; Chm., Mount Isa Mines Ltd, 1953-70. *Recreations:* shooting and bowling. *Address:* 160 Ann Street, Brisbane, Qld 4000, Australia. *Clubs:* Athenæum (Melbourne); Brisbane (Brisbane).

FISHER, Harold Wallace; Director, 1959-69, and Vice-President, 1962-69, Exxon Corporation, formerly Standard Oil Company (New Jersey) New York, retired; *b* 27 Oct. 1904; *s* of Dean Wallace Fisher and Grace Cheney Fisher; *m* 1930, Hope Elisabeth Case; one *s*. *Educ:* Massachusetts Institute of Technology (BSc). Joined Standard Oil Company (NJ), 1927; Dir Esso Standard Oil Co. and Pres. Enjay Co. Inc., 1945. Resided in London, 1954-59. UK Rep. for Standard Oil Co. (NJ) and Chm. of its Coordination Cttee for Europe, 1954-57; Joint Managing Dir, Iraq Petroleum Co. Ltd and Associated Companies, 1957-59. Mem., Marine Bd, Nat. Acad. of Engineering, 1971-74; Vice-Chm., Sloan-Kettering Inst. for

Cancer Research, 1974-75 (Chm., 1970-74); Mem., MIT Corp. Develt Cttee, 1975-; Vice-Chm., and Chm. Exec. Cttee, Community Blood Council of Greater New York, 1969-71. Hon. DSc 1960, Clarkson Coll. of Technology, Nat. Acad. of Engrg. *Publications:* various patents and technical articles relating to the Petroleum Industry. *Recreations:* golf, photography, horology. *Address:* 68 Goose Point Lane, Duxbury, Mass 02332, USA. *Clubs:* Pilgrims, American; University (New York).

FISHER, Hon. Sir Henry (Arthur Pears), Kt 1968; President, Wolfson College, Oxford, since March 1975; *b* 20 Jan. 1918; *e s* of late Lord Fisher of Lambeth, PC, GCVO; *m* 1948, Felicity, *d* of late Eric Sutton; one *s* three *d*. *Educ:* Marlborough; Christ Church, Oxford (Schol.); Gaisford Greek Prose Prize, 1937; 1st Cl. Hon. Mods 1938; BA 1942; MA 1943. Served Leics Regt, 1940-46; Staff Coll., Quetta, 1943; GSO2, 1943-44. GSO1 HQ 14th Army, 1945. Hon. Lieut-Col 1946 (despatches). Fellow of All Souls Coll., 1946-73, Emeritus, 1976-, Estates Bursar, 1961-66, Sub-Warden, 1965-67. Barrister, Inner Temple, 1947, Bencher, 1966; QC 1960; Recorder of Canterbury, 1962-68; a Judge of the High Court of Justice, Queen's Bench Div., 1968-70; Director: J. Henry Schroder Wagg & Co. Ltd, 1970-75; Schroder International Ltd, 1973-75; Thomas Tilling Ltd, 1970-; Equity and Law Life Assurance Soc. Ltd, 1975-. Mem., Gen. Council of the Bar, 1959-63, 1964-68, Vice-Chm., 1965-66, Chm., 1966-68; Vice-Pres., Senate of the Four Inns of Court, 1966-68; Vice-Pres., Bar Assoc. for Commerce, Finance and Industry, 1973-. Chairman: Cttee of Inquiry into Abuse of the Social Security System, 1971; City Cttee on Company Law, 1974-76; conducted inquiry into Confait case, 1976-77. Member: Private Internat. Law Cttee, 1961-63; Coun. on Tribunals, 1962-65; Law Reform Cttee, 1963-66; Council, Marlborough Coll. (Chm., 1977); BBC Programmes Complaints Commn, 1972-; Arthritis and Rheumatism Council; a Governor, Bedales Sch., 1971-75; Member: Governing Body, Imperial Coll., 1973- (Chm., 1975-); Council, RCA; Trustee, Pilgrim Trust, 1965-. *Recreation:* music. *Address:* Wolfson College, Oxford OX2 6UD. *T:* Oxford 56711; 10 Chadlington Road, Oxford OX2 6SY. *T:* Oxford 54340. *Club:* Travellers'.
See also Hon. F. F. Fisher, Hon. C. D. Fisher.

FISHER, Rev. Canon James Atherton; Canon of St George's, Windsor, since 1958, Treasurer, since 1962, Steward, 1972-75; *b* 1 May, 1909; *s* of Rev. Legh Atherton Fisher and Beatrice Edith Fisher; *m* 1938, Joan Gardiner Budden; two *s* one *d*. *Educ:* Haileybury; Sidney Sussex Coll., Cambridge (Scholar); 1st cl. Theological Tripos Pts I and II (Senior Scofield Prize); Cuddesdon Theological Coll; BA 1932, MA 1945; Deacon 1933; Priest, 1934; Asst Curate: St Matthew's, Oxhey, 1933-36; The Priory Church, Dunstable, 1936-39; Chaplain of Bedford Sch., 1939-43; Vicar of St Paul's, Peterborough, 1943-53; Religious Broadcasting Asst, BBC, 1953-58; Chaplain of St Christopher's Coll., Blackheath, 1954-58; Chaplain of Heathfield Sch., Ascot, 1959-64. Founder Mem., Council of St George's House, Windsor Castle (resp. for mid-service Clergy trng), 1966-74. *Address:* 6 The Cloisters, Windsor Castle. *T:* Windsor 66313.
See also P. A. Fisher.

FISHER, Sir John, Kt 1942; *b* 1892; *yr s* of James Fisher, Barrow-in-Furness; *m* 1947, Maria Elsner, *d* of Richard Elsner, Vienna, Austria. *Educ:* Sedbergh; Malvern. President, James Fisher and Sons Limited (Chairman, 1915-76); Chairman: Fisher Line Ltd; Seaway Coasters Ltd; Barrow Housing Company Ltd; Fisher Olsen Shipping Services Ltd; Anchorage Ferrying Services Ltd; International Nuclear Transport Ltd; Sidney Cater & Co. Ltd. Mem. Council, Chamber of Shipping of UK, 1935-74; Chm., Coasting & Home Trade Tramp Section, Chamber of Shipping of UK, 1935-39; Mem., Transport Adv. Council, 1934-39; Chm., Coastal Shipping Adv. Cttee, 1957-62; Dir Coasting and Short Sea Shipping, Min. of War Transport, 1939-46; Chm. United Maritime Authority, European Area, 1945-46; Pres. Baltic and International Maritime Conf., 1951-53. FICS. Served European War, 1914-18, with King's Own Royal Lancaster Regt (Staff Capt. 154 Inf. Brigade, 51st Div., 1915-16). Comdr, Order of Orange Nassau (Netherlands); Officer, Order of Merite Maritime (France); Kt Comdr, Order of Isabel la Católica (Spain). *Address:* Blakeholme Wray, Newby Bridge, Cumbria. *T:* 345. *Clubs:* City of London; Windermere Royal Yacht (Windermere).

FISHER, John Mortimer, CMG 1962; HM Diplomatic Service, retired; Course Director (European Training), Civil Service College, since 1971; *b* 20 May 1915; *yr s* of late Capt. Mortimer Fisher (W Yorks Regt) and Mrs M. S. Fisher (*née* Bailey); *m* 1949, Helen Bridget Emily Caillard; two *s*. *Educ:* Wellington; Trinity Coll., Cambridge. Entered Consular (subseq. Diplomatic) Service, 1937; Probationer Vice-Consul, Bangkok, 1938. Served at Casablanca, 1942, Naples, 1943; 1st Sec. in

Foreign Office, 1946, Mexico City, 1949; Detroit, Mich., USA, 1952; Counsellor in charge of British Information Services, Bonn, 1955; an Inspector in HM Foreign Service, 1959; Counsellor and Consul-Gen. at Bangkok, 1962; Consul-General, Düsseldorf, 1966-70. *Address:* The North Garden, Treyford, Midhurst, West Sussex. *T:* Harting 448.

FISHER, Ven. Leslie Gravatt; Archdeacon of Chester and Canon Residentiary of Chester Cathedral, 1965-75; Vice-Dean, 1973-75; Archdeacon Emeritus since 1975; *b* 18 Aug. 1906; *m* 1935, Dorothy Minnie, (*née* Nash); two *d. Educ:* Hertford Grammar Sch.; London Coll. of Divinity. ALCD 1933. Deacon, 1933; Priest 1934. Curate of Emmanuel, Northwood, 1933-36; Vicar of St Michael and All Angels, Blackheath Park, 1936-39; Rector of Bermondsey, 1939-47; Curate-in-charge, Christ Church, Bermondsey, 1942-47; Chap., Bermondsey Med. Mission Hosp., 1946-47; Home Sec., CMS, and Licensed Preacher, Diocese of Southwark, 1947-; License to Officiate, Bromley, Dio. of Rochester, 1948-. Chm., Church Information Cttee, 1966-75. *Recreations:* music and photography. *Address:* 14 Lamb Park, Chagford, Newton Abbot, Devon. *T:* Chagford 3308.

FISHER, Mrs Margery Lilian Edith; free-lance writer, editor of review journal; *b* 21 March 1913; *d* of Sir Henry Turner, *qv*; *m* 1936, James Maxwell McConnell Fisher (*d* 1970); three *s* three *d. Educ:* Rangi Ruru Sch., Christchurch, NZ; Amberley House Sch., NZ; Somerville Coll., Oxford (MA, BLitt). 1st Cl. Hons English, Oxford. Taught English at Queen Anne's Sch., Caversham, and Oundle Sch., 1939-45; coach for university scholarships and entrance exams; some broadcasting (BBC) of book reviews, free-lance lectr; Editor and proprietor of Growing Point (private jl reviewing children's books); Children's Books Editor, Sunday Times. Eleanor Farjeon Award, 1966; May Arbuthnot Award, USA, 1970. *Publications:* (with James Fisher) Shackleton, a biography, 1957; Intent upon Reading (criticism), 1961, rev. edn 1964; Field Day (novel), 1951; Matters of Fact, 1972; Who's Who in Children's Books, 1975; articles in Review of English Studies. *Recreations:* music, especially choral singing; gardening. *Address:* Ashton Manor, Northampton NN7 2JL. *T:* Roade 862277.

FISHER, Max Henry; Editor, Financial Times, since 1973; *b* 30 May 1922; *s* of Fritz and Sophia Fischer; *m* 1952, Rosemary Margaret Maxwell; two *s* one *d. Educ:* Fichte-Gymnasium, Berlin; Rendcomb Coll.; Lincoln Coll., Oxford. FO Library, working on German War Documents project, 1949-56; Vis. Lectr, Melbourne Univ., 1956; Financial Times, 1957-. *Publication:* (ed with N. R. Rich) The Holstein Papers. *Recreations:* reading, listening to music. *Address:* 16 Somerset Square, Addison Road, W14 8EE. *T:* 01-603 9841. *Club:* Reform.

FISHER, Prof. Michael Ellis, FRS 1971; Horace White Professor of Chemistry, Physics and Mathematics, since 1973; Chairman, Department of Chemistry, since 1975, Cornell University; *b* 3 Sept. 1931; *s* of Harold Wolf Fisher and Jeanne Marie Fisher (*née* Halter); *m* 1954, Sorrel Castillejo; three *s* one *d. Educ:* King's Coll., London. BSc 1951, PhD 1957. Flying Officer (Educn), RAF, 1951-53; London Univ. Postgraduate Studentship, 1953-56; DSIR Sen. Research Fellow, 1956-58. King's Coll., London: Lectr in Theoretical Physics, 1958-62; Reader in Physics, 1962-64; Prof. of Physics, 1965-66; Prof. of Chemistry and Maths, Cornell Univ., 1966-73. Guest Investigator, Rockefeller Inst., New York, 1963-64; Visiting Prof. in Applied Physics, Stanford Univ., 1970-71; 32nd Richtmyer Meml Lectr, 1973; 17th Fritz London Meml Lectr, 1975. John Simon Guggenheim Memorial Fellow, 1970-71; awarded Irving Langmuir Prize in Chemical Physics, 1970. *Publications:* Analogue Computing at Ultra-High Speed (with D. M. MacKay), 1962; The Nature of Critical Points, (Univ. of Colorado) 1964, (Moscow) 1968; Theory of Correlations in the Critical Region (with D. M. Jasnow), 1977; contribs to Proc. Roy. Soc., Phys. Rev., Jl Sci. Insts, Jl Math. Phys., Arch. Rational Mech. Anal., Jl Chem. Phys., Rept Prog. Phys., Rev. Mod. Phys., etc. *Recreations:* Flamenco guitar, travel. *Address:* Baker Laboratory, Cornell University, Ithaca, New York 14853, USA. *T:* (607) 256-4174.

FISHER, Nancy Kathleen; *see under* Trenaman, N. K.

FISHER, Sir Nigel (Thomas Loveridge), Kt 1974; MC 1945; MA (Cambridge); MP (C) Kingston-upon-Thames, Surbiton, since 1974 (Herts, Hitchin, 1950-55, Surbiton, 1955-74); *b* 14 July 1913; *s* of late Comdr Sir Thomas Fisher, KBE, Royal Navy and of late Lady Shakespeare; step *s* of Rt Hon. Sir Geoffrey Shakespeare, Bt, *qv*; *m* 1935, Lady Gloria Vaughan (marr. diss. 1952), *e d* of 7th Earl of Lisburne; one *s* one *d*; *m* 1956, Patricia, *o d* of late Lieut-Col Sir Walter Smiles, CIE, DSO, DL, MP (*see*

Lady Fisher). *Educ:* Eton; Trinity Coll., Cambridge. Hons Degree, Law, Cambridge, 1934. Served War of 1939-45; volunteered Welsh Guards and commissioned as 2nd Lieut 1939; Hook of Holland, Boulogne, 1940 (despatches); Capt., 1940; Major, 1944; N West Europe, 1945 (wounded, MC). Mem., National Executive Cttee of Conservative Party, 1945-47 and 1973-; contested Chislehurst (N Kent), Gen. Election, 1945. Mem. British Parl. Deleg. to Sweden, 1950, W Indies 1955, Malta 1966, Canada 1966, Uganda 1967, St Kitts, Anguilla, 1967. Parly Private Sec. to Minister of Food, 1951-54, to Home Sec., 1954-57; Parly Under-Sec. of State for the Colonies, July 1962-Oct. 1963; Parly Under-Sec. of State for Commonwealth Relations and for the Colonies, 1963-64; Opposition Spokesman for Commonwealth Affairs, 1964-66. Treasurer, CPA, 1966-68, Vice-Chm., UK Br., 1975-76. Mem. Exec., 1922 Cttee, 1960-62, 1969-. Vice-Pres., Building Socs Assoc. Pres., British Caribbean Assoc. Member Executive Committee and Council; Save the Children Fund; Churchill Meml Trust. *Publications:* Iain Macleod, 1973; The Tory Leaders, 1977. *Recreations:* tennis, riding, walking. *Address:* 16 North Court, Great Peter Street, Westminster, SW1. *T:* 01-222 3532; Portavo Point, Donaghadee, Co. Down, N Ireland. *T:* 2596; St George's Court, St George's Bay, Malta, GC. *Club:* MCC.

FISHER, Mrs O. H.; *see* Anderson, Marian.

FISHER, Patricia, (Lady Fisher); Founder and Co-Chairman, Women Caring Trust; *b* 5 April 1921; *d* of late Lieut-Col Sir W. D. Smiles, CIE, DSO, DL, MP for N Down; *m* 1st, 1941, Capt. Neville M. Ford (marr. diss., 1956), 2nd *s* of late Dr Lionel Ford, Headmaster of Harrow and Dean of York; two *d*; 2nd, 1956, Sir Nigel Fisher, *qv. Educ:* privately and abroad. MP (UU) North Down (unopposed return), April 1953-55 (as Mrs Patricia Ford). *Recreations:* sailing, travel. *Address:* 16 North Court, Great Peter Street, SW1; Portavo Point, Donaghadee, Co. Down, N Ireland. *T:* 2596.
See also W. M. J. Grylls.

FISHER, (Phyllis) Anne; Headmistress, Wycombe Abbey School, 1962-74; *b* 8 March 1913; *d* of Rev. L. A. Fisher, Rector of Higham on the Hill, Nuneaton, and Beatrice Fisher (*née* Eustace). *Educ:* Sch. of St Mary and St Anne, Abbots Bromley; Bristol Univ. BA History Hons, 1938. Senior History Mistress: St Helen's, Northwood, 1938-41; St Anne's Coll., Natal, SA, 1941-44; Headmistress, St Winifred's Sch., George, SA, 1944-45; Joint Headmistress, St George's, Ascot, 1946-49; Headmistress, Limuru Girls' Sch., Limuru, Kenya, 1949-57; Headmistress, Arundel Sch., Salisbury, Rhodesia, 1957-61. *Recreations:* study of old churches, the history of painting. *Address:* The Lancastrian Cottage, 22 High Street, Thame, Oxon. *Clubs:* Royal Commonwealth Society, Lansdowne.
See also J . A . Fisher.

FISHER, Rear-Adm. Ralph Lindsay, CB 1957; DSO 1940; OBE 1941; DSC 1943; *b* 18 June 1903; *s* of F. Lindsay Fisher, CBE, one-time Pres. Inst. of Chartered Accountants, and Ethel Owen Pugh, Caernarvon; *m* 1934, Ursula Carver, Torquay; five *d. Educ:* Osborne and Dartmouth. First went to sea, 1920; Commanded: HMS Wakeful, 1940 (Dunkirk, DSO); Musketeer, 1943-45 (sinking of Scharnhorst, DSC); Solebay, 1947-48; Indefatigable, 1952-54. Naval Staff Course, 1934; Jt Services Staff Coll., 1949; Flag Officer Ground Trng (Home Air Comd), 1954-57. Retd, 1957. *Recreation:* sailing. *Address:* Crossaig, by Tarbert, Argyll. *T:* Skipness 234. *Clubs:* Naval and Military, Royal Cruising.

FISHER, Prof. Reginald Brettauer, CBE 1966; Professor of Biochemistry, University of Edinburgh, 1959-76, Dean of Faculty of Medicine, 1972-75; engaged in research, Medical Research Council, since 1976; *b* 13 Feb. 1907; *s* of late Joseph Sudbury and Louie Fisher; *m* 1929, Mary, *d* of late C. W. Saleeby; one *s* three *d. Educ:* King Edward VII Sch., Sheffield; St John's Coll., Oxford. MA, DPhil (Oxon), 1933. University Demonstrator in Biochemistry, Oxford, 1933-59; Rockefeller Travelling Fellow, 1939; Research Officer (on secondment), Min. of Home Security, 1942; Air Ministry, 1943-45; Consultant, US War Dept, 1945. Member: Biochemical Soc.; Physiological Soc.; Royal Society of Medicine. *Publications:* Protein Metabolism, 1954; contributions to Biochem. Jl; Jl Physiol.; Jl Biol. Chem.; Am. Jl Physiol., etc. *Address:* University Laboratory of Physiology, Parks Road, Oxford.

FISHER, Richard Colomb; HM Diplomatic Service; Commercial Counsellor, British Embassy, Rome, since 1976; *b* Hankow, 11 Nov. 1923; *s* of Comdr Richard Fisher, RN and late Phillipa (*née* Colomb), Lee-on-Solent; *m* 1946, Edwine Kempers; two *s. Educ:* RNC Dartmouth. Joined Navy, 1937; to sea as Midshipman, 1941; War Service in submarines, 1943-45; Far

East; flying trng, 1946-47; specialised in navigation/direction, 1948; Comdr 1958; retd from RN and joined Diplomatic Service, 1969; 1st Sec., Bonn, 1970-73; Commercial Counsellor, Warsaw, 1973-76. *Recreations:* history, languages. *Address:* c/o Natwest Bank, Osborne Road, Southsea, Hants. *Club:* Army and Navy.

FISHER, Sydney Humbert, CVO 1948; *b* 9 Feb. 1887; *s* of late Edward Fisher, Aspley Guise, Beds; *m* 1915, Doris Mary (*d* 1974), *d* of late Dr Adam Oakley; two *d* (one *s* missing presumed killed in action). *Educ:* Repton. Joined London North Western Railway, 1904; Chief Operating Manager: LMS Rly, 1944, London Midland Region, Br. Rlys, 1948; late Dep. Chief Regional Officer, London Midland Region, Railway Executive. Medal of Freedom with Bronze Palm (USA). *Address:* 6 The Mead, Cirencester, Glos.

FISHER, Sylvia Gwendoline Victoria; (Signora U. Gardini); Principal Soprano, Royal Opera House, London; *d* of John Fisher and Margaret Fisher (*née* Frawley); *m* 1954, Ubaldo Gardini. *Educ:* St Joseph's Coll., Kilmore, Australia; Conservatorium of Music, Melbourne. Won "Sun" Aria Competition, Melbourne, 1936; International Celebrity Concert in Australia, 1947; tour of Australia, 1955. Operatic Debut in Cadmus and Hermione, 1932; Covent Garden Debut in Fidelio (Leonora), 1948. Appeared in: Rome (Sieglinde), 1952; Cagliari (Isolde), 1954; Bologna (Gutrune), 1955; Covent Garden (Brunnhilde), 1956; Frankfurt Opera House (in Der Rosenkavalier), 1957, etc. *Recreations:* gardening and rare books on singing. *Address:* 24 Dawson Place, W2. *T:* 01-229 0175.

FISHER, Thomas Gilbert F.; *see* Field-Fisher.

FISHER, Prof. William Bayne, DUP; Professor of Geography, University of Durham, since 1956; first Principal of the Graduate Society, Durham University, since 1965; *b* 24 Sept. 1916; unmarried. *Educ:* Darwen Gram. Sch.; Universities of Manchester, Louvain, Paris. Research Scholar, University of Manchester, 1937; RAF 1940; Liaison Officer to French in Syria and Lebanon, 1944; Asst Lectr, University of Manchester, 1946; Lectr University of Aberdeen, 1947; Carnegie Fellow, 1951; Reader, University of Durham, 1954; Dir, Centre of Middle Eastern and Islamic Studies, Durham Univ., 1963-65. Murchison Award, RGS, 1973. *Publications:* Les Mouvements de population en Normandie, 1940; The Middle East, a Physical Social and Regional Geography, 1951; (with H. Bowen-Jones) Spain, a geographical background; (with H. Bowen-Jones and J. C. Dewdney) Malta, 1961; (Ed) The Cambridge History of Iran, Vol. I (The Land of Iran), 1968; (with J. I. Clarke) Populations of the Middle East and North Africa, 1972; various articles in periodicals and works of reference. *Recreations:* music, travel, geographical gastronomy. *Address:* 34 Old Elvet, Durham; Abbey View, 42 South Street, Durham. *T:* Durham 64350 and 64291. *Club:* Athenæum.

FISK, James B(rown); Retired; President, Bell Telephone Laboratories, Inc., NJ, USA, 1973-74; *b* 30 Aug. 1910; *s* of Henry James and Bertha Brown Fisk; *m* 1938, Cynthia Hoar; three *s*. *Educ:* Mass. Inst Technology (BS, PhD); Trinity Coll., Cambridge (Proctor Travelling Fellow). Soc. of Fellows, Harvard Univ., 1936-38; Associate Prof. of Physics, University of North Carolina, 1938-39; Gordon McKay Prof. and Senior Fellow, Harvard Univ., 1948-49; Dir of Research, US Atomic Energy Commn, 1947-48; Bell Telephone Laboratories: 1939-47 and 1949-; Vice-Pres. Research, 1954-55; Executive Vice-Pres., 1955-59; Pres., 1959-73. President's Science Advisory Cttee, 1952-60; Consultant, 1960-73; Gen. Advisory Cttee, Atomic Energy Commission, 1952-58; Chm. Geneva Technical Discussions on Nuclear Tests, 1958. Presidential Certificate of Merit, 1946. Industrial Research Inst. Medal, 1963; Fellow: Amer. Acad. of Arts and Sciences; Amer. Phys. Soc.; IEEE; Member: Nat. Acad. of Sciences; Amer. Philosoph. Soc.; Nat. Acad. of Engrg. Washington Award, Western Soc. of Engineers, 1968; Midwest Res. Inst. Citation, 1968; Founder's Medal, Nat. Acad. of Engrg, 1975; Herbert Hoover Medal, 1976. Holds several Hon. Degrees. *Publications:* various scientific and technical articles in: Proceedings Royal Society, Bell System Technical Journal, Physical Review. *Recreations:* gardening, mountain climbing, golf. *Address:* Bell Telephone Laboratories, Murray Hill, New Jersey 07974, USA. *T:* 201-582-4471 (Murray Hill, NJ). *Clubs:* Harvard (NY City); Ausable (NY); Somerset Hills (NJ).

FISKE, Dudley Astley; Chief Education Officer, Manchester, since 1968; *b* 16 June 1929; *s* of Tom Fiske and late Barbara Fiske; *m* 1958, Patricia Elizabeth, *d* of late Donald MacIver and of Helen MacIver, Weybridge; two *s* one *d*. *Educ:* Berkhamsted Sch.; Merton Coll., Oxford (MA). Asst Master, Barnard Castle Sch., 1953-56; Asst Tutor, Oxford Univ. Dept of Educn, 1956-58; Admin. Asst, East Sussex, 1959-60; Asst Educn Officer, Berkshire, 1961-65; Dep. Educn Officer, Leeds, 1965-68. Mem. Adv. Council on Penal System, 1970-73; Mem., Clothing and Allied Products, ITB, 1969-72; Pres., Educnl Develt Assoc., 1969-74; Mem., Business Educn Council, 1974-; Mem., Adv. Cttee on Supply and Trng of Teachers, 1974-; President: British Educnl Equipment Assoc., 1973-74; Soc. of Educn Officers, 1978; Commonwealth Educn Fellow in Australia, 1974. *Publications:* articles and reviews in educnl jls. *Recreations:* foreign travel, theatre and cinema-going, reading. *Address:* 33 Carlton Road, Hale, Cheshire WA15 8RH. *T:* 061-980 4334. *Club:* Royal Commonwealth Society.

FISON, Sir (Frank Guy) Clavering, Kt 1957; JP; DL; Chairman, Fisons Ltd, 1929-62; *b* 1892; *er* surv. *s* of late J. O. Fison, of Stutton Hall, Ipswich; *m* 1922, Evelyn Alice (OBE 1964), *er d* of late F. L. Bland Rookwood, Copdock, Ipswich; two *d*. *Educ:* Charterhouse; Christ Church, Oxford. Joined Fisons, 1919; retired 1962. MP (U) Woodbridge Div. of Suffolk, 1929-31. Hon. Life Pres., Fisons Ltd. JP East Suffolk, 1942; High Sheriff 1942, DL 1958, Suffolk. *Address:* Crepping Hall, Stutton, Ipswich, Suffolk IP9 2SZ.

FISON, Sir Guy; *see* Fison, Sir R. G.

FISON, Sir (Richard) Guy, 4th Bt *cr* 1905; DSC 1944; Director: Saccone & Speed Ltd since 1952; Charles Kinloch & Co. Ltd, since 1962; *b* 9 Jan. 1917; *er s* of Sir William Guy Fison, 3rd Bt; *S* father, 1964; *m* 1952, Elyn Hartmann; one *s* one *d*. *Educ:* Eton; New Coll., Oxford. Served RNVR, 1939-45. Entered Wine Trade, 1948. Master of Wine, 1954; Freedom (*hc*) of Vintners Co., 1976. *Recreations:* fishing, gardening, swimming in the Mediterranean. *Heir: s* Charles William Fison, *b* 6 Feb. 1954. *Address:* The Gate House, Shrubbs Hill, Chobham, Surrey. *T:* Chobham 8337.

FISTOULARI, Anatole; Principal Conductor of London Philharmonic Orchestra, 1943, now guest conductor; *b* Kiev, Russia, 20 Aug. 1907; obtained British nationality, 1948; *s* of Gregor and late Sophie Fistoulari; *m* 1942, Anna Mahler (marr. diss., 1956); one *d*; 1957, Mary Elizabeth, *y d* of late James Lockhart, Edinburgh. *Educ:* Kiev, Berlin, and Paris. Conducted first concert at age of 7 at Opera House in Kiev and later all over Russia; at 13 gave concerts in Germany and Holland; at 24 conducted Grand Opera Russe in Paris at the Châtelet Theatre with Colonne Orchestra and Chaliapine with whom he then toured France and Spain; then conducted the Ballet de Monte-Carlo with Massine in Drury Lane and Covent Garden before the War; toured with same company all over America, France, and Italy; in England in 1941 started opera production of Sorotchinsky Fair by Moussorgsky; March 1942 gave first Symphony Concert with London Symphony Orchestra and later conducted it regularly at Cambridge Theatre; first concert with London Philharmonic Orchestra in Bristol, Jan. 1943; concert engagements in numerous countries, from 1949. Founder, 1946, and Principal Conductor, London Internat. Orch. Guest conductor for Sadler's Wells Ballet, Royal Opera House, Covent Garden and NY Metropolitan Opera House, 1955; on tour with London Philharmonic Orchestra, to Moscow, Leningrad, Paris, 1956. Has made recordings for several firms. *Recreation:* listening to good concerts. *Address:* 65 Redington Road, NW3. *Club:* Savage.

FITCH, (Ernest) Alan, JP; MP (Lab) Wigan Division, since June 1958; *b* 10 March 1915; *e s* of late Rev. and of Mrs E. W. Fitch; *m* 1950, Nancy Maude, *y d* of late R. Kennard Davis; one *s* one *d*. *Educ:* Kingswood Sch., Bath. Was formerly Mineworker. Asst Whip (paid), 1964-66; a Lord Comr of the Treasury, 1966-69; Vice-Chamberlain, HM Household, Oct. 1969-June 1970; Opposition Whip, 1970-71. Mem., Chairmen's Panel, 1971-. Chm., North West Regional Council of the Labour Party. JP Lancs, 1958. Hon. Freeman, Co. Borough of Wigan, 1974. *Recreations:* reading, walking. *Address:* 117 The Avenue, Leigh, Lancs. *T:* Leigh 673992.

FITT, Gerard; MP (SDLP formerly Repub Lab) Belfast West, since 1966; Member (SDLP), for North Belfast, Northern Ireland Constitutional Convention, 1975-76; Leader, Social Democratic and Labour Party, since 1970; *b* 9 April 1926; *s* of George Patrick and Mary Ann Fitt; *m* 1947, Susan Gertrude Doherty; five *d* (and one *d* decd). *Educ:* Christian Brothers' Sch., Belfast. Merchant Seaman, 1941-53; various positions, 1953-. Councillor for Dock Ward, Belfast Corp., 1958; MP (Eire Lab), Parlt of N Ireland, Dock Div. of Belfast, 1962-72; Mem. (SDLP), N Belfast, NI Assembly, 1973-75; Dep. Chief Exec., NI Exec., 1974. *Recreation:* full-time politics. *Address:* 85 Antrim Road, Belfast, N Ireland BT15 2BJ. *T:* 743226.

FITT, Robert Louis, CMG 1975; Senior Consultant, Sir Alexander Gibb & Partners, since 1974; *b* 9 Aug. 1905; *s* of late R. F. Fitt; *m* 1936, Elsie Ockleshaw, *d* of late William Ockleshaw, Liverpool; one *s*. *Educ:* Launceston and Barnstaple Grammar Schs; City and Guilds Coll., London. BSc; FCGI. Engineer with Sudan Govt, 1927-31; with Mott Hay & Anderson, on Mersey Tunnel and London Underground Extensions, 1931-39. Joined Sir Alexander Gibb & Partners, 1939; Partner, 1946; responsible for industrial develts, irrigation works, water supplies, thermal and hydro-electric power projects, airports, and economic develt surveys, in countries incl. UK, Iran, Iraq, Sudan, Argentina, Kenya, Tanzania, Swaziland, Rhodesia, Australia and Jamaica. Chm., Assoc. of Consulting Engineers, 1961-62; Vice-Pres., Middle East Assoc., 1972, Pres., Internat. Fedn of Consulting Engrs (FIDIC), 1972-74. FICE, FIStructE, FASCE. Order of Homayoun, Iran, Third Class, 1955. *Recreations:* gardening, golf. *Address:* 27 Longdown Lane North, Ewell, Surrey KT17 3HY. *T:* 01-393 1727. *Clubs:* East India, Devonshire, Sports and Public Schools, Royal Commonwealth Society.

FITTER, Richard Sidney Richmond; author and naturalist; Hon. Secretary, Fauna Preservation Society, since 1964; *b* 1 March 1913; *o s* of Sidney and Dorothy Fitter; *m* 1938, Alice Mary (Maisie) Stewart, *e d* of Dr R. S. Park, Huddersfield; two *s* one *d*. *Educ:* Eastbourne Coll.; LSE. BSc(Econ). Research staff: PEP, 1936-40; Mass-Observation, 1940-42; Operational Research Section, Coastal Command, 1942-45; Sec., Wild Life Cons. Special Cttee of Hobhouse Cttee on Nat. Parks, 1945-46; Asst Editor, The Countryman, 1946-59; Open Air Corresp., The Observer, 1958-66; Dir, Intelligence Unit, Council for Nature, 1959-63; Editor, Kingfisher, 1965-72. Member: Survival Service Commn, Internat. Union for Cons. of Nature, 1963- (Chm., Steering Cttee, 1975-); Scientific Authority for Animals, DoE; Trustee, British Nat. Appeal, World Wildlife Fund, 1977-; Hon. Treasurer, Council for Nature; Past Pres., Berks, Bucks and Oxfordshire Naturalists' Trust; formerly Hon. Treasurer and Hon. Sec., British Trust for Ornithology; Chm., Gen. Purposes Cttee, Royal Soc. for Protection of Birds; Editor, The London Naturalist; and council or cttee mem. of numerous nat. history and conservation bodies. Scientific FZS. *Publications:* London's Natural History, 1945; London's Birds, 1949; Pocket Guide to British Birds, 1952; Pocket Guide to Nests and Eggs, 1954; (with David McClintock) Pocket Guide to Wild Flowers, 1956; The Ark in Our Midst, 1959; Six Great Naturalists, 1959; Guide to Bird Watching, 1963; Wildlife in Britain, 1963; Britain's Wildlife: rarities and introductions, 1966; (with Maisie Fitter) Penguin Dictionary of Natural History, 1967; Vanishing Wild Animals of the World, 1968; Finding Wild Flowers, 1972; Birds of Britain and Europe, with North Africa and the Middle East, 1972; (with A. Fitter and M. Blamey) Flowers of Britain and Northern Europe, 1974. *Recreations:* botanising, observing wild and human life, exploring new habitats, reading. *Address:* Drifts, Chinnor Hill, Oxford. *T:* Kingston Blount 51223. *Club:* Athenæum.

FITTON, James, RA 1954 (ARA 1944); FSIA; painter; *b* Oldham, Lancs; *s* of James Fitton and Janet Chadwick; *m* 1928, Margaret Cook; one *s* one *d*. First one man show, Arthur Tooth, New Bond Street, 1933. Member, London Group, 1932-52. Works represented in exhibns: British Art since Whistler, 1939; London Group Jubilee Exhibn, Tate Gallery, 1964. Works in collections of: Contemporary Art Soc.; Chantry Bequest (Tate Gall.); V&A; British Museum; Imperial War Museum; National Gallery of Wales; Manchester, Nottingham, Aberdeen and numerous public and private collections. Chief Assessor to Min. of Educn Nat. Diploma of Design (Pictorial, Painting and Industrial Design), 1940-65. Served on: Arts Council (Art Panel); Colstream Cttee; Summerson Cttee; RCA Council; Chelsea Coll. of Art; Central Coll. of Art and Design; Camberwell Sch. of Art. Mem., latterly Chm., Stamp Adv. Cttee, from 1945 until completion of Definitive Stamp. Drawings and Posters for Min. of Food, 1939-45; London Transport (Underground Posters); Murals for Festival of Britain (Seaside Section). Illustrations for a variety of magazines. Trustee: British Museum, 1968-75; Royal Academy of Arts; Hon. Surveyor, Dulwich Picture Gall.; Governor: Dulwich Coll.; Dulwich Coll. Prep. Sch. Trust. *Publication:* The First Six Months Are the Worst, 1939. *Address:* 10 Pond Cottages, College Road, Dulwich Village, SE21 7LE. *T:* 01-693 1158.

FITTS, Sir Clive (Hamilton), Kt 1963; MD Melbourne, FRCP, FRACP, DTM Sydney; Consulting Physician to: Royal Melbourne Hospital; Royal Women's Hospital; Austin Hospital for Chronic Diseases; Victorian Tuberculosis Service; *b* 14 July 1900; *s* of Hamilton Fitts and Katherine Fitts (*née* Pardey); *m* 1939, Yrsa E., *d* of Prof. W. A. Osborne; two *s* three *d*. *Educ:* Scotch Coll. and Melbourne Church of England Gram. Sch.,

Melbourne; Trinity Coll., University of Melbourne. Post-Graduate: England, Switzerland, USA; Carnegie Scholarship, 1948. Tudor Edwards Meml Lecture, RCP, 1967. Member: Brit. Cardiac Soc.; Brit. Thoracic Soc.; Med. Soc., London; Pres. Cardiac Soc. of Aust. and NZ, 1960; Vice-Pres. RACP, 1958; formerly Mem. Council: University of Melbourne; Melbourne C of E Gram. Sch.; Nat. Heart Foundn, Vice-Pres. and Mem., Exec. Cttee, 1960-65, Hon. Life Mem., 1971; Chm. Felton Bequest Cttee; First Pres., Nat. Gall. Soc. Formerly Mem. Commonwealth Drug Evaluation Cttee. Major AAMC Reserve. *Publications:* various papers on diseases of heart and lungs in medical journals. *Recreations:* mountaineering, tennis (represented University of Melbourne, and Victoria), fly fishing. *Address:* Shoreham, Victoria 3916, Australia; 14 Parliament Place, Melbourne, Victoria 3002, Australia. *T:* 63.1225. *Clubs:* Beefsteak; Melbourne, Beefsteak (Melbourne).

FITZALAN-HOWARD, family name of **Lady Herries** and of **Duke of Norfolk.**

FITZALAN-HOWARD, Maj.-Gen. Lord Michael, KCVO 1971 (MVO 1952); CB 1968; CBE 1962; MC 1944; DL; Her Majesty's Marshal of the Diplomatic Corps, since 1972; *b* 22 Oct. 1916; 2nd *s* of 3rd Baron Howard of Glossop, MBE, and Baroness Beaumont (11th in line), OBE; *b* of 17th Duke of Norfolk, *qv*; granted title and precedence of a Duke's son, 1975; *m* 1st, 1946, Jean (*d* 1947), *d* of Sir Hew Hamilton-Dalrymple, 9th Bt; one *d*; 2nd, 1950, Margaret, *d* of Capt. W. P. Meade-Newman; four *s* one *d*. *Educ:* Ampleforth Coll.; Trinity Coll., Cambridge. Joined Scots Guards, 1938. Served in: North West Europe, 1944-45; Palestine, 1945-46; Malaya, 1948-49; Egypt, 1952-53; Germany, 1956-57 and 1961-66; Commander Allied Command Europe Mobile Forces (Land), 1964-66; Chief of Staff, Southern Command, 1967-68; GOC London Dist, and Maj.-Gen. comdg The Household Division, 1968-71. Col: The Lancs Regt (Prince of Wales's Volunteers), 1966-70; The Queen's Lancashire Regiment, 1970-. Joint Hon. Col, Cambridge Univ. OTC, 1968-71. Chm. Council, TAVR Assocs, 1973-. DL Wilts, 1974. *Address:* St James's Palace, SW1; Fovant House, Fovant, Salisbury, Wilts. *T:* Fovant 617. *Club:* Turf.

FITZCLARENCE, family name of **Earl of Munster.**

FitzCLARENCE, Viscount; Anthony Charles FitzClarence; innkeeper, since 1976; *b* 21 March 1926; *s* and *heir* of 6th Earl of Munster, *qv*; *m* 1st, 1949, Diane Delvigne (marr. diss. 1966); two *d*; 2nd, 1966, Pamela Hyde; one *d*. *Educ:* St Edward's School, Oxford. Served RN, 1942-46, Mediterranean, Far East, Pacific. Graphic Designer, 1946-76. *Recreations:* field sports and bibulous activities. *Address:* The White Lion Inn, Haslemere, Surrey. *T:* Haslemere 3600.

FITZER, Herbert Clyde, CB 1971; OBE 1958; Head of Royal Naval Engineering Service, 1970-71, Director of Engineering (Ships), Navy Department, Ministry of Defence, 1968-71, retired; *b* 3 Nov. 1910; *s* of Herbert John Fitzer; *m* 1938, Queenie Stent; one *d*. *Educ:* Portsmouth Royal Dockyard Sch.; RNC Greenwich; London Univ. 1st cl. hons BSc (Eng) London, 1932; Greenwich Professional Certif. in Electrical Engrg, 1933. CEng, FIEE 1959. Asst Elec. Engr, Admty, 1936; Sheerness Dockyard, 1938; Elec. Engr, Submarine Design, Admty, 1939; Shore Estabs, 1945; Suptg Elec. Engr, Submarine Design, 1950; Asst Dir of Elec. Engrg, Ships Power Systems, 1961; Polaris Project, 1963; Dep. Dir of Elec. Engrg, 1966. Licensed Lay Reader, Dio. Bath and Wells. *Publication:* Christian Flarepath, 1956. *Address:* Meadowcroft, 54 High Street, Saltford, Bristol. *T:* Saltford 2262.

FitzGEORGE-BALFOUR, Gen. Sir (Robert George) Victor, KCB 1968 (CB 1965); CBE 1945; DSO 1950; MC 1939; DL; Chairman, National Fund for Research into Crippling Diseases, since 1975; *b* 15 Sept. 1913; *s* of Robert S. Balfour and Iris (*née* FitzGeorge), 47 Wilton Crescent, SW1; *m* 1943, Mary (Diana), *er d* of Rear-Adm. Arthur Christian, 3 Sloane Gardens, SW3; one *s* one *d*. *Educ:* Eton; King's Coll., Cambridge (BA). Commissioned 2nd Lieut Coldstream Guards, 1934; Palestine, 1936; Middle East, 1937-43; France and NW Germany, 1944-46; commanded 2nd Bn Coldstream Guards, Malaya, 1948-52; idc 1955; Chief of Staff to Governor of Cyprus, 1956; Commanded 1st Guards Brigade, 1957; Chief of Staff, HQ Southern Comd, 1962-63; Dir of Military Operations, Ministry of Defence, 1964-66; Senior Army Instructor, IDC, 1966-68; Vice-Chief of the General Staff, 1968-70; UK Mil. Representative, NATO, 1971-73. ADC (Gen.), 1972-73. Col Comdt, HAC, 1976-. DL West Sussex, 1977. Knight Commander of the Order of Orange Nassau with swords (Netherlands), 1946. *Address:* The Old Rectory, West Chiltington, West Sussex. *T:* West Chiltington 2255. *Club:* Army and Navy.

FITZGERALD, family name of **Duke of Leinster.**

FitzGERALD, Brian S. V.; *see* Vesey FitzGerald.

FITZGERALD, Charles Patrick; Professor of Far Eastern History, Australian National University, 1953-67, now Emeritus; Visiting Fellow, Department International Relations, Australian National University, 1968-69; *b* 5 March 1902; *s* of Dr H. Sauer; *m* 1941, Pamela Knollys; three *d. Educ:* Clifton. China, 1923-27, 1930-32, 1936-38, 1946-50. Leverhulme Fellowship for Anthropological Research in South-West China. DLitt ANU 1968. *Publications:* Son of Heaven, 1932; China, a Cultural History, 1935; The Tower of Five Glories, 1941; (with George Yeh) Introducing China, 1948; Revolution in China, 1951 (revised version (Penguin) as The Birth of Communist China, 1965); The Empress Wu, 1955; Flood Tide in China, 1958; Barbarian Beds: the origin of the chair in China, 1965; A Concise History of Eastern Asia, 1965; The Third China, Chinese Communities in SE Asia, 1965; Des Mantchous à Mao Tse-tong, 1968; History of China, 1969; Communism Takes China, 1970; The Southern Expansion of the Chinese People: Southern Fields and Southern Ocean, 1972; Mao Tsetung and China, 1976. *Address:* 82 Gloucester Terrace, W2; Odalengo Piccolo, 15020, Alessandria, Italy. *Club:* Savile.

FITZ-GERALD, Desmond John Villiers, (29th Knight of Glin); Irish Agent, Christie, Manson & Woods Ltd, since 1975; *b* 13 July 1937; *s* of Desmond Windham Otho Fitz-Gerald, 28th Knight of Glin (*d* 1949), and Veronica (who *m* 2nd, 1954, Ray Milner, CC (Canada), QC, Edmonton, Alta, and Qualicum Beach, Vancouver Island, BC), 2nd *d* of late Ernest Amherst Villiers, MP, and of Hon. Elaine Augusta Guest, *d* of 1st Baron Wimborne; *m* 1st, 1966, Louise Vava Lucia Henriette (marr. diss. 1970), *d* of the Marquis de la Falaise, Paris; 2nd, 1970, Olda Ann, *o d* of T. V. W. Willes, 39 Brompton Sq., SW3; three *d*. *Educ:* Stowe Sch.; University of British Columbia (BA 1959); Harvard Univ. (MA 1961). FSA 1970. Asst Keeper, 1965-72, Dep. Keeper, 1972-75, Dept of Furniture and Woodwork, V&A. Director: National Trust Archive (Dublin), 1976; Historic Irish Tourist Houses Assoc., 1977. Vice-Pres., Irish Georgian Soc. Mem. Council, Walpole Soc. *Publications:* (ed) Georgian Furniture, 1969; (with Maurice Craig) Ireland Observed, a handbook to the buildings and antiquities, 1970; The Music Room from Norfolk House, 1972; (with Edward Malins) Lost Demesnes: Irish Landscape Gardening 1660-1845, 1976; (with Anne Crookshank) The Painters of Ireland, 1978; Catalogues: Irish Houses and Landscapes (jointly), 1963; Irish Architectural Drawings (jointly), 1965; Irish Portraits 1660-1860 (jointly), 1969; articles and reviews on architecture and the decorative arts in many Art periodicals. *Recreations:* architecture, collecting. *Address:* Glin Castle, Glin, Co. Limerick, Ireland. *TA:* Knight Glin. *T:* Glin 3, and 44; 49 Pembroke Road, Dublin 2. *T:* Dublin 689281. *Clubs:* Beefsteak, White's; Kildare Street and University (Dublin).

FITZGERALD, Rev. (Sir) Edward Thomas, 3rd Bt *cr* 1903: a Roman Catholic priest; *b* 7 March 1912; *S* father, Sir John Joseph Fitzgerald, 2nd Bt, 1957, but does not use title. *Heir: b* Rev. Daniel Patrick Fitzgerald, *b* 28 June 1916.

FITZGERALD, Garret, PhD; Member of the Dáil (TD) (Fine Gael Party) for Dublin South East, since 1969; Leader, Fine Gael Party, since 1977; Barrister-at-Law; *b* Dublin, 9 Feb. 1926; *s* of late Desmond FitzGerald (Minister for External Affairs, Irish Free State, 1922-27, and Minister for Defence, 1927-32) and Mabel FitzGerald (*née* McConnell); *m* 1947, Joan, *d* of late Charles O'Farrell; two *s* one *d. Educ:* St Brigid's Sch., Bray; Coláiste na Rinne, Waterford; Belvedere Coll., University Coll., and King's Inns, Dublin. Aer Lingus (Irish Air Lines), 1947-58; Rockefeller Research Asst, Trinity Coll., Dublin, 1958-59; College Lectr, Dept of Political Economy, University Coll., Dublin, 1959-73 (currently on secondment, 1973-). Minister for Foreign Affairs, Ireland, 1973-77. Member: Governing Body of University Coll., Dublin; Senate of National Univ. of Ireland; Seanad Éireann (Irish Senate), 1965-69; Oireachtas Library Cttee, 1965-69; Dáil Cttee on Public Accounts, 1969-73; Internat. Exec. Cttee of European Movement, 1972-73. Vice-President: Fine Gael Party; Electoral Reform Soc., London; (also Past Chm.) Irish Council of European Movement, 1970-73. Governor, Atlantic Inst. of Internat. Relations, Paris, 1972-73; Mem. Exec. Cttee and Council, Inst. of Public Administration; Mem. Council, Statistical and Social Inquiry Soc. of Ireland. Formerly: Irish Correspondent of BBC, Financial Times, Economist and other overseas papers; Economic Correspondent, Irish Times; also Past Managing Dir, Economist Intelligence Unit of Ireland; Economic Consultant to Fedn of Irish Industries and Construction Industry Fedn, and Rep. Body for Guards; Past Member: Senate Electoral Law Commn;

Workmen's Compensation Commn; Transport Advisory Cttee for Second Programme; Cttee on Industrial Organisation; Gen. Purposes Cttee of Nat. Industrial Economic Council. AMInstT. Hon. LLD: New York, 1974; St Louis, 1974. *Publications:* State-sponsored Bodies, 1959; Planning in Ireland, 1968; Towards a New Ireland, 1972, etc. *Address:* Leinster House, Kildare Street, Dublin 2, Ireland. *Clubs:* Stephen's Green (Dublin); Royal Irish Yacht (Dun Laoghaire).

FitzGERALD, Sir George (Peter Maurice), 5th Bt *cr* 1880; 23rd Knight of Kerry; MC 1944; Major, Army, retired; *b* 27 Feb. 1917; *s* of Sir Arthur Henry Brinsley FitzGerald, 4th Bt, and Mary Eleanor (*d* 1967), *d* of late Capt. Francis Forester; *S* father 1967; *m* 1939, Angela Dora Mitchell; one *s* one *d. Educ:* Harrow; RMC, Sandhurst. Commnd into Irish Guards, 1937; 2nd in comd, 1st Bn, 1944; 2nd in comd, 2nd Bn, 1946; retired, 1948. *Heir: s* Adrian James Andrew Denis FitzGerald, *b* 24 June 1940. *Address:* Cedar Court, Alderton, near Woodbridge, Suffolk. *T:* Shottisham 331. *Clubs:* Army and Navy, Pratt's.

FITZGERALD, Brig. (retd) Gerald Loftus, CBE 1956; DSO 1945; *b* 5 May 1907; *s* of late Col D. C. V. FitzGerald, MC, Nairobi Kenya; *m* 1937, Mary Stuart, *d* of late Charles E. Mills, Holbrook, Suffolk; one *s* one *d. Educ:* Wellington Coll.; Royal Military Academy, Woolwich. Commissioned 2nd Lieut RA, 1926; Regimental duty UK and overseas, 1926-39; staff and regimental duty in UK and NW Europe during War of 1939-45. Brit. Mil. Mission to Greece, 1946-48; Chief Instructor, Officer Cadet Sch., 1949-50; Brit. Joint Services Mission, Washington, USA, 1951-52; Comdr Trg Bde, RA, 1953-55; Dep. Dir, War Office, 1956-58; retired pay, 1959. Order of Leopold (with Palm), Belgium, 1945; Croix de Guerre (with Palm), 1945. *Recreations:* field sports, travel. *Club:* Army and Navy.

FITZ-GERALD, Sir Patrick (Herbert), Kt 1955; OBE 1944; retired; *b* 1899; *s* of Gerald and Florence Fitz-Gerald; *m* 1947, Dorothy Preece (marr. diss., 1957; she died 1960). *Educ:* Tonbridge Sch. Served European War, 1914-18 in Irish Guards, and War of 1939-45 as Lieut-Col Sherwood Foresters; despatches twice. *Recreations:* polo and cricket.

FITZGERALD, Prof. Patrick John; Professor of Law, Carleton University, Ottawa, since 1971; *b* 30 Sept. 1928; *s* of Dr Thomas Walter and Norah Josephine Fitzgerald; *m* 1959, Brigid Aileen Judge; two *s* one *d. Educ:* Queen Mary's Grammar Sch., Walsall; University Coll., Oxford. Called to the Bar, Lincoln's Inn, 1951; Fellow, Trinity Coll., Oxford, 1956-60. Professor of Law: Leeds Univ., 1960-66; Univ. of Kent at Canterbury, 1966-71. Visiting Prof., University of Louisville, 1962-63. Special Consultant, Law Reform Commn of Canada, 1973-74. *Publications:* Criminal Law and Punishment, 1962; Salmond on Jurisprudence (12th edn), 1966; This Law of Ours, 1977; *Recreations:* music, golf, bridge. *Address:* 315 Clemow Avenue, Ottawa, Canada.

FITZGERALD, Terence; Chief Charity Commissioner, since 1975; *b* 20 March 1919. *Educ:* Allhallows Sch.; Exeter Coll., Oxford; Middle Temple. Served with Royal Artillery, 1940-46; attached Royal Indian Artillery, 1941-45. Joined Home Office, 1948; Imperial Defence Coll., 1962; HM Treasury, 1963-64; Asst Under-Sec. of State, Home Office, 1964-75. *Address:* Charity Commission, 14 Ryder Street, St James's, SW1Y 6AH.

FitzGERALD, Sir William James, Kt 1944; MC; QC 1936; *b* Cappawhite, Co. Tipperary, May 1894; *s* of late Joseph FitzGerald, MB, Cappawhite; *m* 1st, 1933, Erica (marr. diss., 1946), *d* of F. J. Clarke, Chikupi Ranch, Northern Rhodesia; one *s* ; 2nd, Cynthia Mary, *d* of late W. Foster, Jerusalem. *Educ:* Blackrock Coll.; Trinity Coll., Dublin. Served European War, Durham Light Infantry and XV Corps Mounted Troops (MC and Croix de Guerre); BA 1919; Barrister-at-Law, King's Inns, Dublin, 1922, and Middle Temple; Nigerian Administrative Service, 1920; Police Magistrate, Lagos, 1921; Crown Counsel, Nigeria, 1924; Solicitor-Gen., N Rhodesia, 1932; Attorney-Gen., N Rhodesia, 1933; Palestine, 1937-43; Chief of Justice of Palestine, 1944-48. Pres. Lands Tribunal, 1950-65. Hon. LLD 1960. *Address:* 47 Sussex Square, Brighton, Sussex. *Club:* Athenæum.

FITZGERALD, William Knight, JP; DL; Lord Provost of Dundee, and Lord Lieutenant of the County of the City of Dundee, 1970-73; *b* 19 March 1909; *e s* of John Alexander Fitzgerald and Janet Fitzgerald; *m* 1938, Elizabeth, *d* of Alexander Grant; three *s. Educ:* Robertson Grammar Sch., S Africa. Assessor, Dundee Repertory Theatre, 1967-77; Member: Tayside Economic Consultative Group, 1970-77; Dundee Harbour Trust, 1970-73; University Court, Dundee, 1970-; Dundee Town Council, 1956; City Treasurer, 1967-70;

Chairman: Tay Road Bridge Joint Board, 1970-73 and 1975-; Dundee High Sch. Directors, 1970-73; Vice-Chairman: Dundee Coll. of Art and Technology, 1970-75; Scottish Council on Alcoholism, 1972-; E Scotland Water Bd, 1973-75. Pres., Dundee Bn, Boys' Brigade. Dundee: JP 1948; DL 1974; Vice-Convener, Tayside Regional Council. *Recreations:* gardening, reading. *Address:* Morven, Roxburgh Terrace, Dundee DD2 1NZ. *T:* 68475. *Club:* University (Dundee).

FitzGIBBON, Constantine; see FitzGibbon, R. L. C. L.-D.

FitzGIBBON, Louis Theobald Dillon; *b* 6 Jan. 1925; *s* of Comdr Francis Lee-Dillon FitzGibbon, RN, and Kathleen Clare (*née* Atchison), *widow* of Hon. Harry Lee-Dillon; *m* 1962, Madeleine (*née* Hayward-Surry); one *s* two *d*. *Educ:* St Augustine's Abbey Sch.; Royal Naval Coll., Dartmouth. Royal Navy, 1942-54 (incl. War of 1939-45); Polish interpreter course, 1950-52. Dir, De Leon Properties Ltd, 1954-72. Solicitor's articled clerk, 1960-63. Personal Asst to the then Rt Hon. Duncan Sandys, MP (later Lord Duncan-Sandys), 1967-68; Gen. Sec., British Council for Aid to Refugees, 1968-72; United Nations (UNHCR) Mission to South Sudan, 1972-73; Dir, British Epilepsy Assoc., 1974-76. Hon. Sec., Katyn Memorial Fund, 1971-77; Area Pres., St John Amb. (Hants East), 1974-76. Holds: Sov. Mil. Order of Malta (Kt of Honour and Devotion); Polish Gold Cross of Merit, 1969; Order of Polonia Restituta (Officer, 1971; Comdr, 1972; Kt Comdr, 1977). *Publications:* Katyn—A Crime without Parallel, 1971; The Katyn Cover-up, 1972; Unpitied and Unknown, 1975. *Recreations:* travelling, writing, reading, history. *Address:* 9 Orchard Road, Havant, Hants PO9 1AT. *T:* Havant 4096. *Club:* Carlton.

See also R . L . C . FitzGibbon.

FitzGIBBON, (Robert Louis) Constantine (Lee-Dillon); writer; *b* 8 June 1919; *s* of Comdr Francis Lee-Dillon FitzGibbon, RN, and Georgette Folsom, Lenox, Mass, USA; *m* 1967, Marjorie (*née* Steele); one *d*; (by a previous marr. to Marion (*née* Gutmann) one *s*, *b* 1961). *Educ:* Munich Univ.; Sorbonne; Exeter Coll., Oxford. Served War of 1939-45, British Army (Oxford and Bucks Light Infantry), 1939-42; US Army, 1942-46. Schoolmaster, Saltus Gram. Sch., Bermuda, 1946-47; now independent writer. Mem. Irish Acad. of Letters. FRSL; Fellow, Guggenheim Memorial Foundn, 1966. *Publications:* The Arabian Bird, 1949; The Iron Hoop, 1950; Dear Emily 1952: Miss Finnigan's Fault, Norman Douglas, The Holiday, 1953; The Little Tour, 1954; The Shirt of Nessus, 1955; In Love and War, 1956; The Blitz, 1957; Paradise Lost and More, 1959; When the Kissing had to Stop, 1960; Going to the River, 1963; Random Thoughts of a Fascist Hyena, 1963; The Life of Dylan Thomas, 1965; (ed) Selected Letters of Dylan Thomas, 1966; Through the Minefield, 1967; Denazification, 1969; High Heroic, 1969; Out of the Lion's Paw, 1969; Red Hand: The Ulster Colony, 1971; The Devil at Work (play), 1971; A Concise History of Germany, 1972; In the Bunker, 1973; The Life and Times of Eamon de Valera, 1973; The Golden Age, 1976; Secret Intelligence, 1976; Man in Aspic, 1977; Teddy in the Tree, 1977; and trans from French, German and Italian. Contributor to several newspapers and periodicals in Britain, America and elsewhere. *Address:* St Anne's, Killiney Hill Road, Co. Dublin. *Club:* Beefsteak.

See also L . T . D . FitzGibbon.

FitzHARRIS, Viscount; James Carleton Harris; *b* 19 June 1946; *o s* and *heir* of 6th Earl of Malmesbury, *qv*; *m* 1969, Sally Ann, *yr d* of Sir Richard Newton Rycroft, *qv*; three *s*. *Educ:* Eton; Queen's Coll., St Andrews (MA). *Heir:* s Hon. James Hugh Carleton Harris, *b* 29 April 1970. *Address:* Heather Row Farm House, Nately Scures, Basingstoke, Hants RG27 9JP. *T:* Hook 3138. *Club:* Royal Yacht Squadron.

FITZHERBERT, family name of **Baron Stafford.**

FITZHERBERT, Cuthbert; *b* 24 May 1899; British; 4th *s* of William Joseph Fitzherbert-Brockholes, CBE, and Blanche Winifred Mary, 2nd *d* of late Maj.-Gen. Hon. Sir Henry Hugh Clifford, VC, KCMG, CB; *m* 1930, Barbara (*d* 1975), *e d* of Henry Scrope, Danby; three *s* three *d* (and one *s* decd). *Educ:* Oratory Sch.; New Coll., Oxford (BA). Commissioned Coldstream Guards, 1917; served European War, 1914-18, in 1st Bn Coldstream Guards (wounded). Joined Barclays Bank Ltd, 1922; Union Bank of Manchester, 1923-26; Local Dir, Barclays Bank Ltd, Darlington, 1926; Local Dir, Barclays Bank Ltd, Birmingham, 1939. Served War of 1939-45, with Coldstream Guards, 1940-44. Returned as Gen. Man. (Staff), Barclays Bank Ltd, 1944; a Director: Barclays Bank Ltd (Vice-Chm., 1948-64), 1948-72; Barclays Bank DCO, retd 1971; formerly Dir, London Montrose Investment Trust, retd 1972. *Publication:* (ed) Henry Clifford VC, his letters and sketches from the Crimea, 1953.

Recreations: shooting, stalking. *Address:* 1 Lochmore House, Ebury Street, SW1W 9JX. *T:* 01-730 8710. *Club:* Cavalry and Guards.

See also S. P. E. C. W. Towneley.

FITZHERBERT, Maj.-Gen. Edward Herbert, CBE 1943; DSO 1918; MC; *b* 3 Dec. 1885; *s* of late Col E. H. Fitzherbert, King's Own Royal Lancaster Regt. *Educ:* Rossall Sch.; RMC Camberley. 2nd Lieut, ASC, 1905; Lieut, 1907; Capt., 1914; T/Major, 1914; a/Lieut-Col, 1917; Major, 1924; Lieut-Col, 1931; Col, 1935; Brigadier, 1939; Maj.-Gen., 1941; DAQMG, 1915-17; Asst Dir of Supplies and Transport, War Office, 1937-39; Asst Inspector, RASC, 1939; Inspector, RASC, 1940-43; retired pay, 1943; served European War, 1914-18 (despatches thrice, DSO, MC); served War of 1939-45, 1939-43. Col Commandant RASC, 1947-50. *Recreations:* golf and shooting. *Address:* c/o Lloyds Bank, Ltd, Cox & King's Branch, 6 Pall Mall, SW1. *Clubs:* Naval and Military, MCC.

FitzHERBERT, Giles Eden; HM Diplomatic Service; Counsellor, Kuwait, since 1975; *b* Dublin, 8 March 1935; *e s* of late Captain H. C. FitzHerbert, Irish Guards, and Sheelah, *d* of J. X. Murphy; *m* 1962, Margaret Waugh; two *s* three *d*. *Educ:* Ampleforth Coll.; Christ Church Oxford; Harvard Business Sch. 2nd Lieut, King's Royal Irish Hussars, 1957-58. Vickers da Costa & Co., 1962-66. First Secretary: Foreign Office, 1966; Rome, 1968-71; FO, 1972-75. Contested (L) Fermanagh and South Tyrone, Gen. Elect., 1964. *Address:* 48 Stokenchurch Street, SW6; Cove House, Cove, Tiverton, Devon. *Clubs:* Beefsteak, Le Petit Club Français.

FitzHERBERT, Sir John (Richard Frederick), 8th Bt, *cr* 1784; TD; *b* 15 Sept. 1913; *s* of Ven. Henry E. FitzHerbert, sometime Archdeacon of Derby, and Hon. Margaret Elinor (*d* 1957), *d* of 3rd Baron Heytesbury; *S* uncle, Sir William FitzHerbert, 7th Bt, 1963; *m* 1957, Kathleen Anna Rees; no *c*. *Educ:* Charterhouse; Royal Agricultural Coll., Cirencester. Served War of 1939-45, Sherwood Foresters (TA). FLAS 1950; FRICS 1970. *Recreation:* shooting. *Heir:* nephew Richard Ranulph FitzHerbert, *b* 2 Nov. 1963. *Address:* Tissington Hall, Ashbourne, Derbyshire. *T:* Parwich 246. *Club:* Derby County (Derby).

FITZHERBERT-BROCKHOLES, Michael John, JP; Vice Lord-Lieutenant of Lancashire, since 1977; *b* 12 June 1920; *s* of John William Fitzherbert-Brockholes and Eileen Agnes; *m* 1950, Mary Edith Moore; four *s*. *Educ:* The Oratory Sch.; New Coll., Oxford. Scots Guards, 1940-46. Mem., Lancs CC, 1968-; Chm., Educn Cttee, 1977-. JP 1960, DL 1975, Lancs. *Recreation:* gardening. *Address:* Claughton Hall, Garstang, near Preston, Lancs. *T:* Brock 40286.

FitzHUGH, James, QC 1973; His Honour Judge FitzHugh; a Circuit Judge, since 1976; *b* 2 April 1917; *s* of T. J. FitzHugh and S. FitzHugh (formerly Jocelyn); *m* 1955, Shelagh (*née* Bury), *d* of R. W. and B. Bury, Lytham St Annes. *Educ:* St Bede's Coll., Manchester; Manchester Univ. (BA (Admin)); London Univ. (LLB). Commissioned in Supplementary Reserve of Officers, RA, 1938; War of 1939-45: Captain, GSO. Called to Bar, Gray's Inn, and became a Member of Northern Circuit, 1948. *Recreations:* travel, golf. *Address:* 186 St Leonard's Road East, St Annes on the Sea, Lytham St Annes, Lancs. *T:* St Annes 723068. *Clubs:* St James's (Manchester); Royal Lytham and St Annes Golf.

FITZ-MAURICE, family name of **Earl of Orkney.**

FITZMAURICE; see Petty-Fitzmaurice.

FITZMAURICE, Lt-Col Sir Desmond FitzJohn, Kt 1946; CIE 1941; late RE; *b* 17 Aug. 1893; *s* of John Day Stokes Fitzmaurice, ICS, Tralee, Co. Kerry; *m* 1926, Nancy (*d* 1975), *d* of Rev. John Sherlock Leake, Grayswood, Surrey; one *s* three *d*. *Educ:* Bradfield; RMA, Woolwich; Cambridge Univ. Joined RE, 1914. Served in France, Belgium and Italy, European War, 1914-18 (despatches); Instructor, RMA Woolwich, 1918-20; Cambridge Univ., 1920-22; Instructor, Sch. of Military Engineering, Chatham, 1923, 1924; hp list, 1925; Deputy Mint Master, Bombay, 1929-30; Calcutta, 1931-32; Deputy Master, Security Printing, India, 1932; Master Security Printing and Controller of Stamps, India, 1934; retired. *Address:* Mount Rivers, Killorglin, Co. Kerry.

FITZMAURICE, Sir Gerald (Gray), GCMG 1960; QC 1957; International Law Consultant; Judge of the European Court of Human Rights, since 1974; Judge of the International Court of Justice, 1960-73; *b* 24 Oct. 1901; *s* of late Vice-Admiral Sir Maurice Fitzmaurice, KCVO, CB, CMG, and Mabel Gertrude, *y d* of late S. W. Gray; *m* 1933, Alice Evelina Alexandra Sandberg; two *s. Educ:* Malvern; Gonville and Caius Coll., Cambridge (BA, LLB 1924). Called to Bar, Gray's Inn, 1925; Bencher, 1961; practised, 1925-29; 3rd Legal Adviser to Foreign Office, 1929; seconded as Legal Adviser to Ministry of Economic Warfare, 1939-43; 2nd Legal Adviser, FO, 1945-53 (CMG 1946); Legal Adviser, FO, 1953-60 (KCMG 1954). Legal Adviser to UK Delegations, San Francisco UN Charter Conference, 1945; Paris Peace Conference, 1946. UN Assembly, 1946, 1948-59, Japanese Peace Conference, San Francisco, 1951, and Berlin and Manila Confs, 1954; Counsel for HM Govt in several cases before the International Court of Justice at The Hague; Member: Permanent Court of Arbitration, 1964-; UN Internat. Law Commission, 1955-60 (Pres. 1959); Mem. Inst. International Law (Pres., 1967-69); Pres. Grotius Soc., 1956-60. Hon. Fellow, Gonville and Caius Coll., Cambridge, 1961. Hon. LLD: Edinburgh, 1970; Cantab, 1972; Hon. DJur Utrecht, 1976. *Publications:* articles in British Year Book of International Law, 1931-58, Hague Recueil, 1948 and 1957 and in other legal journals. *Address:* (home) 3 Gray's Inn Square, WC1R 5AH; (professional) 2 Hare Court, Temple, EC4. *Clubs:* Athenæum, United Oxford & Cambridge University.

FitzPATRICK, Air Cdre David Beatty, CB 1970; OBE 1953; AFC 1949 and Bar, 1958; *b* 31 Jan. 1920; *s* of late Comdr D. T. FitzPatrick, RN and Beatrice Anne Ward; *m* 1941, Kathleen Mary Miles; one *d. Educ:* Kenilworth Coll., Exeter; Midhurst. Commnd RAF, 1938; served War of 1939-45, Atlantic, Mediterranean and Far East theatres; comd No 209 Sqdn (Far East), 1944; (GD Pilot) Sqdn flying duty, 1945-52; cfs, pfc and GW Specialist, RAF Henlow, 1952-57; GW (Trials) Project Officer, Min. of Supply, 1957-59; Base Comdr Christmas Island, 1959-60 (British Nuclear Trials); NATO Def. Coll., and jssc, 1960-61; Dep. Dir (Ops) Air Staff, 1961-64; comd RAF Akrotiri and Nicosia, 1964-66; Dir of (Q) RAF, MoD, 1966-69; attached NBPI for special duty, 1969; Dir, Guided Weapons (Trials and Ranges), Min. of Technology, 1969-72; Dir, Guided Weapons Trials, MoD (PE), 1972-74. Retired 1975. MBIM 1970; AFRAeS 1971. *Recreations:* swimming (Pres. Royal Air Force Swimming Assoc.), deep-sea fishing, cricket. *Address:* Whistledown, 38 Courts Mount Road, Haslemere, Surrey. *T:* Haslemere 4589. *Clubs:* Royal Air Force; Naval, Military and Air Force (Adelaide).

FITZPATRICK, Gen. Sir (Geoffrey Richard) Desmond, GCB 1971 (KCB 1965; CB 1961); DSO 1945; MBE 1943; MC 1939; Lieutenant-Governor and Commander-in-Chief, Jersey, since 1974; *b* 14 Dec. 1912; *o s* of late Brig.-Gen. Sir Richard Fitzpatrick, CBE, DSO, and Lady (G. E.) Fitzpatrick; *m* 1944, Mary Sara, *o d* of Sir Charles Campbell, 12th Bt; one *s* one *d. Educ:* Eton; RMC Sandhurst. Commissioned The Royal Dragoons, 1932. Served in Palestine, 1938-39 (MC); War of 1939-45 (despatches, MBE, DSO); in Middle East, Italy, NW Europe. Bt. Lieut-Col 1951; Col 1953; ADC to the Queen, 1959; Maj.-Gen. 1959; Asst Chief of Defence Staff, Ministry of Defence, 1959-61; Dir Mil. Ops, War Office, 1962-64; Chief of Staff, BAOR, 1964-65; Lt-Gen. 1965; GOC-in-C, N Ire., 1965-66; Vice-Chief of Gen. Staff, 1966-68; Gen. 1968; C-in-C, BAOR, and Commander N Army Gp 1968-70; Dep. Supreme Allied Comdr, Europe, 1970-73; ADC (General) to the Queen, 1970-73; Col, The Royal Dragoons, 1964-69; Dep. Col, The Blues and Royals, 1969-74; Col Comdt, RAC, 1971-74. KStJ 1975. *Address:* Government House, Jersey, Channel Islands. *Clubs:* Cavalry and Guards; Royal Yacht Sqdn; Bembridge Sailing.

FITZPATRICK, John Ronald; Solicitor and Parliamentary Officer, Greater London Council, since 1977; *b* 22 Sept. 1923; *s* of Henry Fitzpatrick and Mary Lister; *m* 1952, Beryl Mary Newton; two *s* one *d. Educ:* St Bede's Coll., Manchester; Univ. of Manchester (LLB). Admitted Solicitor, 1947; LMRTPI 1951. Asst Solicitor: Burnley, 1947; Stockport, 1948-51; Asst/Principal Asst Solicitor, Mddx CC, 1951-65; Asst Clerk/Asst Dir-Gen., GLC, 1965-69; Asst Dir, 1969-72, Dir, 1972-77, Planning and Transportation, GLC. *Recreations:* golf, bridge. *Address:* Courtlands, 2 Langley Grove, New Malden, Surrey. *T:* 01-942 8652.

FITZROY, family name of **Viscount Daventry.**

FitzROY, family name of **Duke of Grafton** and of **Southampton Barony.**

FitzROY, Charles; late 2nd Lieutenant Royal Horse Guards and Pioneer Corps; *b* 3 Jan. 1904; *o s* of 4th Baron Southampton, OBE, and late Lady Hilda Mary Dundas, *d* of 1st Marquess of Zetland; *S* father, 1958, as 5th Baron Southampton, but disclaimed his title for life, 16 March 1964; *m* 1st, 1927,

Margaret (*d* 1931), *d* of Prebendary H. Mackworth Drake, Vicar of Paignton; one *s*; 2nd, 1940, Mrs Joan Leslie (marr. diss., 1944); 3rd, 1951, Rachel Christine, *d* of Charles Zaman, Lille, France. *Educ:* Harrow. Served Royal Horse Guards, 1923-25; re-employed, 1940, with RA, Pioneer Corps, 1941. Joint-master, Grove Fox-hounds, 1930-32. *Heir:* (*to disclaimed barony*): *s* Hon. Charles James FitzRoy [*b* 12 Aug. 1928; *m* 1951, Pamela Anne, *d* of E. Henniker, Maidenhead, Berks; one *s* one *d* (and one *s* decd)]. *Address:* Preluna Hotel, Sliema, Malta.

FitzROY NEWDEGATE, Francis Humphrey Maurice, DL; *b* 17 Dec. 1921; *s* of late Comdr Hon. John Maurice FitzRoy Newdegate and *nephew* of Viscount Daventry, *qv; m* 1959, Hon. Rosemary, *e d* of 1st Baron Norrie, GCMG, GCVO, CB, DSO, MC; two *s* one *d. Educ:* Eton. Served War of 1939-45 with Coldstream Guards, N Africa and Italy; Captain 1943. ADC to Viceroy of India, 1946-48. JP 1960, DL 1970, Warwickshire; Vice-Lieut 1974. *Address:* Temple House, Arbury, Nuneaton, Warwickshire. *T:* Nuneaton 383514. *Club:* Boodle's.

FITZSIMMONS, Rt. Hon. William Kennedy, PC (N Ireland) 1965; JP; *b* 31 Jan. 1909; *m* 1935, May Elizabeth Lynd; two *d. Educ:* Skegoniell National Sch.; Belfast Jun. Techn. Sch. Mem., Belfast City and Dist Water Comrs, 1948-57 (Chm. 1954-55); Pres., Duncairn Unionist Assoc.; N Ireland Parliament: MP, Duncairn Div. of Belfast, 1956-72; Dep. Govt Whip, 1961-63; Parl. Secretary: Min. of Commerce, 1961-65; Min. of Home Affairs, 1963-64; Min. of Develt, 1964-65; Min. of Education, 1965-66 and 1968-69; Minister of Development, 1966-68; Minister of Health and Social Services, 1969-72. MRSH; JP Belfast, 1951. *Address:* 4 Tudor Oaks, Holywood, Co. Down, Northern Ireland BT18 0PA.

FITZSIMONS, Robert Allen, FRCS; Hon. Consulting Surgeon to Charing Cross Hospital and to The Metropolitan Hospital; *b* 16 March 1892; *s* of James Fitzsimons and Mary L. McDonald, Sligo; *m* 1927, Mary Patricia, *d* of Thomas McKelvey, Cardiff; one *s* one *d. Educ:* Summerhill Coll., Sligo; Birkbeck Coll., King's Coll., and Charing Cross Hospital Medical Sch., University of London. BSc London 1920; MB, BS London 1930; MRCS, LRCP, 1926; FRCS 1932. Formerly: Analyst to HM Govt Laboratory; House Surgeon and Surgical Registrar to Charing Cross Hosp.; Registrar to Royal National Orthopædic Hospital. Fellow of the Assoc. of Surgeons, Great Britain and Ireland. *Address:* 16 Lansdowne Road, W11. *T:* 01-727 5759.

FITZWALTER, 21st Baron, *cr* 1295; **(Fitzwalter) Brook Plumptre,** JP; Hon. Captain, The Buffs; *b* 15 Jan. 1914; *s* of late George Beresford Plumptre, Goodnestone, Canterbury, Kent; *S* uncle, 1943 (FitzWalter Barony called out of abeyance in his favour, 1953); *m* 1951, Margaret Melesina, *yr d* of (Herbert) William Deedes, JP, Galt, Hythe, Kent; five *s. Educ:* Diocesan Coll., Rondebosch, Cape; Jesus Coll., Cambridge. Served War of 1939-45, with the Buffs (Royal East Kent Regt) in France, Belgium, UK and India; attached RIASC, as Capt. JP Kent, 1949. Landowner and farmer; succeeded to family estate, 1943. *Heir: s* Hon. Julian Brook Plumptre, *b* 18 Oct. 1952. *Address:* Goodnestone Park, Canterbury, Kent. *T:* Nonington 840218.

FITZWILLIAM, WENTWORTH-, family name of **Earl Fitzwilliam.**

FITZWILLIAM, 10th Earl *cr* 1716; **William Thomas George Wentworth-Fitzwilliam,** TD; JP; DL; Baron Fitzwilliam, 1620; Earl Fitzwilliam and Viscount Milton, 1716 (Irish honours); Baron Milton (Great Britain), 1742; Earl Fitzwilliam and Viscount Milton, 1746; Chairman, Milton (Peterborough) Estates Co.; Director: Modport Group Ltd; Neanco Holdings Ltd; Fitzwilliam (Peterborough) Properties Ltd; *b* 28 May 1904; *s* of late George Charles Wentworth-Fitzwilliam (*g g s* of 5th Earl) and Evelyn, *o d* of Charles Stephen Lyster; *S* cousin, 1952; *m* 1956, Joyce (who *m* 1922, Hon. Henry Fitzalan-Howard, later 2nd Visc. FitzAlan of Derwent (marr. diss., 1955; he *d* 1962); two *d*), *e d* of Col Philip Langdale, OBE, Houghton Hall, Yorks. *Educ:* Eton; Magdalene Coll., Cambridge. Joint Master Fitzwilliam Hunt, 1935-; Chm., Peterborough Royal Foxhound Show Soc., 1946-; Pres., Nat. Coursing Club, 1972-. Chm., Peterborough Divisional Cons. Assoc., 1947-75, Pres., 1975-. Patron, Fitzwilliam Coll., Cambridge. JP Peterborough, 1928; DL Huntingdon and Peterborough, 1965. Served War of 1939-45; American Bronze Star Medal. *Recreation:* shooting. *Heir:* none. *Address:* Milton, Peterborough. *T:* Castor 202; Wentworth Woodhouse, Rotherham. *Clubs:* Boodle's, Pratt's, White's.

FLACK, Bertram Anthony; HM Diplomatic Service; Deputy High Commissioner, Ottawa, since 1976; *b* 3 Feb. 1924; *y s* of Dr F. H. Flack and Alice Cockshut, Nelson, Lancs; *m* 1948, Jean

W. Mellor; two *s* two *d. Educ:* Epsom Coll.; Liverpool Univ. (LLB Hons). Enlisted Gren. Gds, 1942; commissioned E Lancashire Regt, 1943; served in NW Europe (Captain). Joined Foreign Service, 1948; served Karachi, 1948-50; Alexandria, 1950-52; Stockholm, 1955-58; Accra, 1958-61; Johannesburg, 1964-67; Dep. High Comr, E Pakistan, 1967-68; Inspector, Diplomatic Service, 1968-70; Head of Communications Dept, FCO, 1971-73; Commercial Counsellor, Stockholm, 1973-75; Canadian Nat. Defence Coll., 1975-76. *Recreations:* cricket, golf. *Address:* c/o National Westminster Bank Ltd, Lord Street, Southport, Merseyside. *Club:* Travellers'.

FLAHIFF, His Eminence Cardinal George Bernard; *see* Winnipeg, Archbishop of, (RC).

FLANDERS, Dennis, RWS 1976 (ARWS 1970); RBA 1970; artist: townscapes and landscapes in pencil and water-colour; *b* 2 July 1915; *s* of late Bernard C. Flanders, ARAM (pianist), and Jessie Marguarite Flanders, ARMS (artist); *m* 1952, Dalma J. Darnley, *o d* of late J. Darnley Taylor and of Mrs Joan Darnley Taylor; one *s* one *d. Educ:* Merchant Taylors' Sch.; Regent Street Polytechnic; St Martin's Art Sch.; Central Sch. of Arts and Crafts, Princess Louise Gold Medal at age of 7. Mem. of St Paul's Watch, 1940-42; Royal Engineers, 1942-46. Occasional drawings for Daily Telegraph and other journals; series of drawings for Yorkshire Post, 1949; Birmingham Post, 1950-51; "Famous Streets," Sunday Times, 1952-53; Special artist to the Illustrated London News, 1956-64. Water-colours (reproduced as prints) of: RMA Sandhurst; Police Coll., Bramshill; St Edward's Sch., Oxford. Drawings in private collections and Nat. War Collection (1939-45), Guildhall Library and Museums at Exeter, York, Lincoln, Kensington, St Marylebone, Walthamstow, Wolverhampton, and Bury, Lancs; also Bank of England. Exhibitor: RA and in provinces: one-man shows: London, 1947, 1951, 1953, 1955, 1964, 1967; Bedford, 1965, 1966; Boston (Lincs), 1966; Southport, 1969; Buxton-Lammas, Norfolk, 1972; Worthing, 1972. Member: Art Workers Guild (Master 1975); The Sette of Odd Volumes; Cttee, Soc. for Protection of Ancient Buildings. Freeman: City of London, 1970; Painter Stainers' Co., 1970. Lord Mayor's Art Award, 1966. *Publications: illustrations:* Bolton Abbey, 1947; Chelsea by Richard Edmonds, 1956; Soho for East Anglia by Michael Brander, 1963; A Westminster Childhood by John Raynor, 1973; The Twelve Great Livery Companies of London, 1973. *Recreations:* walking, riding, reading Who's Who. *Address:* 51 Great Ormond Street, WC1. *T:* 01-405 9317; Baker's Cross House, Cranbrook, Kent. *T:* 2018.

FLANNERY, Martin Henry; MP (Lab) Hillsborough, Sheffield, since Feb. 1974; *b* 2 March 1918; *m* 1949; one *s* two *d. Educ:* Sheffield Grammar Sch.; Sheffield Teachers' Trng College. Served with Royal Scots, 1940-46. Teacher, 1946-74 (Head Teacher, 1969-74). *Recreations:* music, rambling. *Address:* 53 Linaker Road, Sheffield S6 5DS.

FLATLEY, Derek Comedy, FJI; Public Affairs Correspondent, Southend Evening Echo, since 1970; *b* 16 Oct. 1920; *m* 1959, Valerie Eve Stevens; one *d. Educ:* Grammar sch. Trained West Essex Gazette, 1936. Served War of 1939-45: Household Cavalry, 1945. Army newspaper unit, Southend Standard, 1947; Chief Reporter, 1949. Mem., Press Council, 1968-72; Mem. Council (rep. Essex), Inst. of Journalists, 1957- (Pres. 1966-67); also Chairman: Salaries and Conditions Bd of the Inst., 1958-67; Estabt Cttee, 1963-65; Exec., 1967-70. Fellow, Inst. of Journalists, 1962-. *Recreations:* football, cricket, tennis. *Address:* Windyridge House, 22 Earls Hall Avenue, Southend-on-Sea, Essex. *T:* Southend-on-Sea 43485.

FLAVELL, Geoffrey, FRCS; FRCP; Senior Surgeon, Department of Cardiovascular and Thoracic Surgery, The London Hospital, since 1950; Consultant Thoracic Surgeon, Royal Masonic Hospital, since 1957; Senior Thoracic Surgeon, Broomfield Hospital, since 1947; Consultant in Thoracic Surgery to Whipps Cross, Wanstead, Hart, Oldchurch, St Margaret's and Harold Wood Hospitals; *b* 23 Feb. 1913; *o* surviving *s* of late W. A. Flavell, JP, of Wellington, NZ; *m* 1943, Joan Margaret, *o d* of S. Ewart Adams, Hawkwell, Essex; no *c. Educ:* Waitaki; Otago; University of New Zealand; St Bartholomew's Hospital, London. Qualified in medicine, 1937; House appts, St Bartholomew's Hosp., 1937-39; Resident Surgical Officer, Brompton Hosp., 1940-41. Surgeon Specialist, RAF, 1942, O/C Surgical Divs RAF Gen. Hosps, Carthage and Algiers, 1943; RAF Gen. Hosp., Cairo; Adviser in Surgery RAF Med. and Middle East Command, 1944; retired rank of Wing Comdr, 1958. Consultant Thoracic Surgeon, British Legion Hosp., and to LCC, 1946. Senior Registrar to London Hosp., 1947. *Publications:* Introduction to Chest Surgery, 1957; Basic Surgery (Thoracic section), 1958; The Oesophagus, 1963; many

contribs to surgical textbooks and med. jls; various articles on travel, wine and food, in lay periodicals. *Recreations:* history; architecture; literature and art; indulging the senses. *Address:* 22 Downshire Hill, NW3. *T:* 01-435 7099. *Club:* Royal Air Force.

FLAVELLE, Sir (Joseph) Ellsworth, 2nd Bt, *cr* 1917; *b* 25 May 1892; *s* of Sir Joseph Wesley Flavelle, 1st Bt, and Clara, *d* of Rev. Oren Ellsworth; *S* father 1939; *m* 1917, Muriel McEachren; two *s* one *d. Educ:* St Andrew's Coll., University of Toronto. Trustee, Toronto General Hosp.; Mem. of Board, Community Welfare Council of Ontario; Mem. Advisory Council Knights of the Round Table. *Recreations:* yachting, photography. *Heir: s* Joseph David Ellsworth Flavelle [*b* 9 Nov. 1921; *m* 1942, Muriel Barbara, *d* of Reginald Morton; three *d*]. *Address:* Kingswold, RR2, King, Ontario, Canada; 780 Eglington Avenue, Toronto, Ont., Canada. *Clubs:* York, Royal Canadian Yacht (Toronto).

FLEET, Kenneth George; Editor, Business News, The Sunday Times, since 1977; *b* 12 Sept. 1929; *s* of Fred Major Fleet and late Elizabeth Doris Fleet; *m* 1953, (Alice) Brenda, *d* of late Captain H. R. Wilkinson, RD, RNR and Mrs Kathleen Mary Wilkinson; three *s* one *d. Educ:* Calday Grange Grammar Sch., Cheshire; LSE (BScEcons). Jl of Commerce, Liverpool, 1950-52; Sunday Times, 1955-56; Dep. City Editor, Birmingham Post, 1956-58; Dep. Financial Editor, Guardian, 1958-63; Dep. City Editor, Daily Telegraph, 1963; City Editor, Sunday Telegraph, 1963-66; City Editor, Daily Telegraph, 1966-77. Dir, Young Vic, 1976-. Wincott Award, 1974. *Recreations:* theatre, books, music, sport. *Address:* Meadowside, 22 Alderton Hill, Loughton, Essex. *T:* 01-508 2034. *Clubs:* MCC; Chigwell Golf.

FLEETWOOD-HESKETH, Charles Peter F.; *see* Hesketh.

FLEMING, Amy M., MD, DSc, FRCOG; Hon. Consulting Obstetrician and Gynæcologist: St Mary's Hospital, Harrow Road; St Mary Abbot's Hospital, Kensington; Teacher in Queen Charlotte's Hospital, and Institute of Obstetrics and Gynæcology, University of London; *d* of Charles Friskin Fleming and Margaret Burns Elphinstone Waddell. *Educ:* Universities of Glasgow, Vienna, Tübingen. Formerly Prof. of Obstetrics and Gynæcology, University of London; Senior Asst Surgeon Royal Samaritan Hospital for Women, Glasgow, and Royal Maternity and Women's Hospital, Glasgow. *Publications:* papers in Transactions of the Royal Society of Edinburgh, and other medical monographs. *Recreation:* gardening. *Address:* Glentress, Innerleithen Road, Peebles, Scotland EH45 8BE. *T:* Peebles 20518.

FLEMING, Sir Charles (Alexander), KBE 1977 (OBE 1964); FRS 1967; Honorary Lecturer in Geology, Victoria University of Wellington; Chief Palæontologist, New Zealand Geological Survey, Department of Scientific and Industrial Research, 1953-77; *b* 9 Sept. 1916; *s* of Geo. H. Fleming, Auckland, NZ; *m* 1941, Margaret Alison, *d* of S. G. Chambers, Auckland; three *d. Educ:* King's Coll., Auckland; University of Auckland. Boyhood interest in birds and shell-collecting led to participation in Auckland Mus. expedns, 1933-35; student fieldwork on birds of NZ and Chatham Is (basis of papers publ. 1939); Asst Geologist, NZ Geol Survey, 1940; subseq. Palæontologist and Sen. Palæontologist. Overseas service as coastwatcher, Auckland Is, 1942-43. Pres., Ornithol. Soc. NZ, 1948-49; NZ Delegate: Internat. Geol Congresses, 1948, 1960; British Commonwealth Conf. on Geology and Mineral Resources, 1948; Mem. Bd of Trustees: Nat. Art Gall. and National (formerly Dominion) Mus., 1954-76 (Chm., Mus. Council, 1972-75); Nat. Library, 1971-72; NZ Fauna Protection Adv. Council; NZ Nat. Commn for Unesco, 1966-70; Nat. Parks Authority, 1970-; Environmental Council, 1970-73. President: Internat. Paleont. Union (Oceania Filial), 1964-68; Aust. and NZ Assoc. for Advancement of Science, 1968-70. FRSNZ 1952 (Pres. 1962-66); Fellow, Art Galls and Museums Assoc. of NZ, 1956; Corresp. Fellow, American Ornithologists' Union, 1962; Commonwealth and Foreign Fellow, Geol. Soc. London, 1967; For. Mem., Amer. Philosophical Soc., 1973. Several scientific prizes and awards. *Publications:* (ed) Checklist of New Zealand Birds, 1953; trans. Hochstetter's Geology of New Zealand, 1959; Marwick's Illustrations of New Zealand Shells, 1966; geol and palæontol bulletins; about 300 research papers on mollusca, cicadas, birds, geology, palæontology, biogeography. *Recreations:* recorded music, natural history. *Address:* Balivean, 42 Wadestown Road, Wellington, NZ. *T:* Wellington 737-288.

FLEMING, Prof. Charles Mann, CBE 1964; Emeritus Professor of Administrative Medicine, since 1971 (Professor 1960-71), Dean of the Faculty of Medicine, 1959-70, and Dean of Postgraduate Medicine, 1970-72, in University of Glasgow; *b* 1 March 1904; *y s* of John Somerville Fleming and Christina Taylor Gerard, Glasgow; *m* 1930, Margaret Hamilton Barrie, *er* *d* of George Simpson, Newfoundland; one *d. Educ:* Hillhead High Sch; Glasgow Univ. MA 1924, MB, ChB 1929, MD 1933 (Glasgow); MRCPEd 1945, FRCPEd 1952, FRFPS (G.) 1959, FRCP (Glasgow) 1962. Hon. FRCGP 1964. Regional MO, 1937-39, Hospital Officer (Eastern Dist, Scotland), 1939-46, Principal MO, 1946-59, Dept of Health for Scotland. Convener Post-Grad. Med. Board, University of Glasgow, 1959-72; Chm., Western Regional Cttee for Postgrad. Medical Educn, 1970-72; Member: General Medical Council, 1961-73; WHO Expert Advisory Panel on Organisation of Medical Care, 1959-76; Royal Commission on Med. Educn, 1966-68; Central Cttee on Postgraduate Med. Educn (GB), 1967-71; Scottish Council for Postgraduate Med. Educn, 1970-72. Addtl Mem. Gen. Dental Council, 1965-73. *Publications:* contributions to medical journals. *Recreation:* golf. *Address:* 8 Thorn Road, Bearsden, Glasgow. *T:* Bearsden 2810.

FLEMING, Hon. Donald Methuen, PC (Canada) 1957; QC (Ontario) 1944; *b* Exeter, Ont., 23 May 1905; *s* of Louis Charles and Maud Margaret Wright Fleming; *m* 1933, Alice Mildred Watson, Toronto; two *s* one *d. Educ:* public schools and Collegiate Inst., Galt; Univ. of Toronto (BA, LLB); Osgoode Hall Law Sch. Called to Bar, Ontario, 1928; subsequently practised in Toronto, 1928-57; Counsel to Blake, Cassels and Graydon, Barristers and Solicitors, Toronto, 1963-67. MP for Toronto-Eglinton, 1945-63; Minister of Finance and Receiver-General, 1957-62; Minister of Justice and Attorney-General of Canada, 1962-63. A Governor, Internat. Bank and IMF, 1957-63; Chairman: Commonwealth Finance Ministers' Conf., Mont Tremblant, Province of Quebec, 1957; Commonwealth Trade and Economic Conf., Montreal, 1958; OECD, 1961, 1962; Leader: delegn of Canadian Ministers to meetings of US-Canada Jt Trade and Economic Cttee, Washington, 1957, 1960, 1961 (Chm. Ottawa meeting, 1959, 1962), and meeting of Canada-Japan Jt Cttee of Ministers, Tokyo, 1963; Canadian delegn to OEEC Confs, Paris, 1960; Canadian delegate: NATO Conf. of Heads of Govt, Paris, 1957; NATO Ministerial Confs, 1958, 1959, 1961; Commonwealth Parly Confs, London, 1948, Ottawa, 1952, Nairobi, 1954. Has taken part in numerous parly, political, municipal and civic welfare activities and in church affairs. Man. Dir, Bank of Nova Scotia Trust Cos; General Counsel to Bank of Nova Scotia in Bahamas, etc; Chm., M&G (Cayman) Ltd; Director: Gore Mutual Insurance Co.; Empresas Consolidadas Sudamericanos SA; Sceptre Trust Ltd, and numerous other companies. Past Pres., Toronto YMCA. Hon. Mem., Canadian Legion; Hon. Life Mem., Canadian Bar Assoc. DCL hc Bishop's Univ., 1960; LLD hc Waterloo Lutheran Univ., 1967. *Publications:* numerous works and articles on legal subjects; contribs to legal periodicals including Canadian Encyclopedic Digest, Canadian Bar Review, Canadian Abridgement, etc. *Recreations:* all branches of sport. *Address:* Bayview, PO Box N 3016, Nassau, Bahamas. *Clubs:* Canadian (Pres., 1964), Empire, Granite, National, Queen's, Rosedale Golf, Toronto Cricket (Toronto); Rideau, Country (Ottawa); Lyford Cay, Nassau East Hill (Bahamas).

FLEMING, Ian, RSA 1956 (ARSA 1947); RSW 1947; RWA 1975; Head, Gray's School of Art, Aberdeen, 1954-71, retired; *b* 19 Nov. 1906; *s* of John and Catherine Fleming; *m* 1943, Catherine Margaret Weetch; one *s* two *d. Educ:* Hyndland Sch., Glasgow; Glasgow Sch. of Art. Lectr, Glasgow Sch. of Art, 1931-48; Warden, Patrick Allen-Fraser Art Coll., Hospitalfield, Arbroath, 1948-54. Chm., Peacock Printmakers Workshop (Aberdeen), 1973-. *Recreation:* anything Scottish. *Address:* 15 Fonthill Road, Aberdeen. *T:* 20680. *Club:* Rotary (Aberdeen).

FLEMING, Rev. James George Grant, DSO 1917; MC 1917; TD 1939; retired; *b* 2 April 1895; *s* of late James Fleming, Glenfarg, Craigleith, Edinburgh; *m* 1st, 1919, Daisy (*d* 1924), *s* of late Maj. W. J. Trotter, RAMC, Readstown, Co. Meath, Ireland; one *d*; 2nd, 1930, Saidie Caroline, *d* of late W. J. Stewart, MP, Crawfordsburn, Co. Down, Ireland; one *s. Educ:* Stewart's Coll., Edinburgh; Edinburgh Univ. (MA 1928). Army 1914-23. Served European War, 1914-18 (wounded; despatches; DSO; MC); Waziristan FF, 1919-21. Ordained 1930; Minister: Lasswade Old Parish Church, 1930-35; East Church of St Nicholas, Aberdeen, 1935-41; Banchory-St Ternan East Church. Banchory, Kincardineshire, 1952-65. Served 1939-47: SCF 9th (Highland) Div., 1939; SCF 51st (Highland) Div., 1940-42; DACG 1942; Senior Staff Chaplain, India, 1942-44; Asst Chaplain-Gen., L of C and Burma, 1944-46 (despatches twice); Hon. CF (1st class), 1947; C of S Chaplain, CCG and UK High Commission, Germany, 1948-52. Hon. Life Mem., Royal British Legion (Scotland), 1965. *Publications:* various. *Address:* Dunard, Banchory, Kincardineshire. *T:* Banchory 2828. *Club:* Royal Northern (Aberdeen).

FLEMING, Instructor Rear-Adm. Sir John, KBE 1960; DSC 1944; Director of the Naval Education Service, 1956-60; *b* 2 May 1904; *s* of late James Fleming; *m* 1930, Jean Law, *d* of late James Stuart Gillitt, South Shields; no *c. Educ:* Jarrow Grammar Sch.; St John's Coll., Cambridge. BA 1925, MA 1957. Entered RN as Instructor Lieut, 1925; Instr Lieut-Comdr, 1931; Instr Comdr, 1939; Instr Capt., 1950; Instr Rear-Adm., 1956. Asst Dir Naval Weather Service, 1945, Dep. Dir, 1947; Fleet Instructor Officer and Fleet Meteorological Officer, Home Fleet, 1950; Command Instructor Officer, The Nore, 1951; Education Dept, Admiralty, 1952. *Recreation:* gardening. *Address:* Blackdown Cottage, Denbigh Road, Haslemere, Surrey. *T:* Haslemere 2412.

FLEMING, John Bryden; Under-Secretary, Scottish Development Department, since 1974; *b* 23 June 1918; *s* of W. A. Fleming, advocate, and Maria MacLeod Bryden; *m* 1942, Janet Louise Guthrie; one *s* three *d. Educ:* Edinburgh Academy; Univs of Edinburgh and London. MA 1st Cl. Hons Geog. Edinburgh, BScEcon London. Army, 1940-46, RASC and REME (Major). Planning Officer, Dept of Health for Scotland, 1946; Principal, 1956; Asst Sec., Scottish Develt Dept, 1963. *Recreation:* gardening. *Address:* 28 Mortonhall Road, Edinburgh EH9 2HN. *T:* 031-667 0453. *Club:* Royal Commonwealth Society.

FLEMING, Rt. Rev. Launcelot; *see* Fleming, Rt Rev. W. L. S.

FLEMING, Prof. Marston Greig, BSc; PhD; CEng; FIMM; Professor of Mineral Technology, since 1961, and Pro-Rector, since 1974, Imperial College, London University; *b* 1913; *s* of late Alexander Greig Fleming, Montreal; *m* 1951, E. Box, painter; two *s* one *d* (by a previous marriage). *Educ:* Westmount High Sch.; Queen's Univ., Canada. Metallurgist with Canadian goldmining companies, 1936-41. RCAF navigator, 1941-46; Flight Lieut, 1943. Imperial Coll., Royal Sch. of Mines: Lecturer, 1946-51, Senior Lecturer, 1951-58, Reader, 1958-61; Head of Dept of Mining and Mineral Technology, 1967-74; Dean, 1968-71. Mineral processing consultant to governments, mining companies, to DSIR and to HM Govt, at various times, 1946-. Chm., Mineral Processing Cttee, DSIR and Min. of Technology, 1959-66; Mem., Steering Cttee, Warren Spring Lab., 1966-68. Chm. Advisory Panel, BCURA, 1961-66; IMM Council, 1962-, Vice-Pres., 1968-71, Pres., 1971-72; Member: Cttee on Mineral Planning Control, DoE, 1972-75; Chemicals and Minerals Requirements Bd, Dept of Industry, 1972-. British rep., Scientific Cttee, Internat. Mineral Processing Congress, France, 1963, USA, 1964, USSR, 1968, Czechoslovakia, 1970, London 1973 (Chm., 1973-), Italy 1975; Canadian Rep., Council of Commonwealth Mining and Metall. Instns, 1969- (Vice-Chm., 1971-76; Chm., 1976-). Dir, UNESCO Regional Course, Benares, 1964; Chm., Brighton Conf. on the Technologist in the Mineral Ind. of the Future, 1969. Member: Governing Body, Imperial Coll., 1968-; Ct of Governors, Camborne Sch. of Mines, 1971-. Hon. ARSM, 1966. *Publications:* Identification of Mineral Grains (with M. P. Jones), 1965; papers in a number of scientific and technical journals, etc. *Address:* Zoffany House, 65 Strand-on-the-Green, W4. *Club:* Garrick.

FLEMING, Patrick Lyons; Director: United Newspapers Ltd; Bradbury, Agnew & Co. Ltd; *b* Aberdeen, 3 April 1905; *er s* of late Col Frank Fleming, DSO; *m* 1929, Eleanor (*d* 1970), *d* of late H. G. Tapper; two *d. Educ:* Shrewsbury; Lincoln Coll., Oxford (Schol., MA). Dir of numerous companies, mainly connected with what is now the Drayton Gp, 1934-68; Council Member: Inst. of Directors, 1948-75 (Treasurer 1974-75); Aims of Industry, 1952-75; Chm. of Epsom Division Conservative Assoc., 1949-50. *Publications:* sundry contribs to financial jls. *Recreations:* reading, formerly rowing and field sports. *Address:* Baltic House, The Common, Cranleigh, Surrey. *T:* Cranleigh 3676.

FLEMING, Mrs Peter; *see* Johnson, Celia.

FLEMING, Raylton Arthur; Controller (Overseas), Central Office of Information, since 1976; *b* 1925; *s* of Arthur and Evelyn Fleming; *m* 1967, Leila el Doweini; one *s. Educ:* Worksop Coll. Associate Producer, World Wide Pictures Ltd, 1952; Head of Overseas Television Production, Central Office of Information, 1957; Dep. Dir, Films/Television Div., COI, 1961; Asst Controller (Overseas) COI, 1968; Actg Controller (Overseas), 1969; Dir, Exhibns Div. COI, 1971; Controller (Home), COI, 1972-76. *Recreations:* music, opera. *Address:* 18 Aubrey House, Maida Avenue, Little Venice, W2. *T:* 01-723 9071. *Club:* Royal Automobile.

FLEMING, Rt. Rev. William Launcelot Scott, KCVO 1976; DD (Lambeth); MA (Cambridge), MS (Yale); FRSE; *b* 7 Aug. 1906; *y s* of late Robert Alexander Fleming, MD, LLD; *m* 1965, Jane, *widow* of Anthony Agutter. *Educ:* Rugby Sch.; Trinity Hall and Westcott House, Cambridge; Yale Univ. Commonwealth Fund Fellow, Yale Univ., 1929-31; Deacon, 1933; Priest, 1934; Expeditions to Iceland and Spitzbergen, 1932 and 1933; Chaplain and Geologist, British Graham Land Expedition to the Antarctic, 1934-37; Examining Chaplain to Bishop of Southwark, 1937-49, to Bishop of St Albans, 1940-43, to Bishop of Hereford, 1942-49; Fellow and Chaplain, Trinity Hall, Cambridge, 1933-49, Dean, 1937-49; Director of Scott Polar Research Institute, Cambridge, 1947-49; Bishop of Portsmouth, 1949-59; Bishop of Norwich, 1959-71; Dean of Windsor, 1971-76; Register, Order of the Garter, 1971-76; Domestic Chaplain to the Queen, 1971-76. Chaplain RNVR, HMS King Alfred, 1940; HMS Queen Elizabeth, 1940-43; HMS Ganges, 1943-44; Director of Service Ordination Candidates, 1944-46. Chairman: Church of England Youth Council, 1950-61; Archbishops' Advisers for Needs and Resources, 1963. Parly Gp for World Govt: Vice-Chm., 1969-71; Chm., Associate Members, 1971-76. Member: Council, Univ. of E Anglia, 1964-71; Royal Commn on Environmental Pollution, 1970-73; Chairman of Governors, Portsmouth Grammar Sch., 1950-59; Canford Sch., 1954-60; Pres., Young Explorers Trust, 1976. Hon. Chaplain, RNR (RNVR 1950). Hon. Fellow, Trinity Hall, Cambridge, 1956; Hon. Vice-President, Royal Geographical Society, 1961. Hon. DCL Univ. of East Anglia, 1976. *Address:* Tithe Barn, Poyntington, near Sherborne, Dorset DT9 4LF. *T:* Corton Denham 479.

FLEMINGTON, Rev. William Frederick, MA Oxon, BD Cantab; Principal of Wesley House, Cambridge, 1955-67; held Greenhalgh Chair of New Testament Language and Literature, Wesley House, Cambridge, 1937-67, retired; *b* 24 May 1901; *er s* of Rev. William Frederick Flemington and Annie Mary Geden Bate; *m* 1930, Ethel Phyllis Goodenough, *er d* of Rev. John Henry Doddrell; one *s* one *d. Educ:* Liverpool Coll.; Jesus Coll., Oxford (Exhibitioner, 2nd Cl. Classical Hon. Mods, 2nd Cl. Lit. Hum.); Jesus Coll., Fitzwilliam Coll. and Wesley House, Cambridge (Carus Greek Testament Prize; 1st Cl. Theological Tripos, Pt II, Sect. 2, New Testament). Entered Wesleyan Methodist Ministry, 1925; Asst Tutor, Handsworth Coll., Birmingham, 1926-30; Minister in Stourbridge Circuit (Cradley), 1930-33; West Bromwich Circuit, 1933-37; Tutor, Wesley House, 1937-55. Select Preacher, Cambridge Univ., 1944, 1950, 1954. Pres. of Cambridge Theological Soc., 1963-65. *Publications:* The New Testament Doctrine of Baptism, 1948; contributor to Prayer and Worship, 1945; articles and reviews in Expository Times and Jl of Theological Studies. *Recreations:* walking, reading. *Address:* 204 Chesterton Road, Cambridge.

FLEMMING, Cecil Wood, CBE 1964 (OBE 1944); FRCS, MCh; Consultant Orthopædic Surgeon, University College Hospital, London, 1933-65; retired; *b* 20 Aug. 1902; *s* of Percy and Elizabeth Flemming; *m* 1931, Elizabeth, *d* of W. Nelson Haden, JP; two *s* one *d. Educ:* Rugby; Trinity Coll., Oxford. FRCS, 1928; MCh Oxford, 1929. Served War of 1939-45, in RAF (Volunteer Reserve), Air Commodore (OBE). *Publications:* contrib. to learned journals on surgical subjects. *Address:* 34 Hanover Gate Mansions, Park Road, NW1 4SL. *T:* 01-724 1694. *Club:* Reform.

FLEMMING, Sir Gilbert Nicolson, KCB 1953 (CB 1948); *b* 13 Oct. 1897; *s* of Percy Flemming, FRCS, and E. E. Flemming, MD; *m* 1935, Virginia Coit; two *s* two *d. Educ:* Rugby; Trinity Coll., Oxford. Ministry of Education (Board of Education), 1921-59; Permanent Sec. to the Ministry of Education, 1952-59. Mem., Restrictive Practices Court, 1960-64. *Address:* G3 Burton Lodge, Portinscale Road, SW15.
See also J. S. Flemming.

FLEMMING, John Stanton; Official Fellow in Economics, 1965, and Bursar, 1970, Nuffield College, Oxford; Editor, Economic Journal, since 1976; *b* 6 Feb. 1941; *s* of Sir Gilbert Nicolson Flemming, *qv*; *m* 1963, Jean Elizabeth (*née* Briggs); three *s* one *d. Educ:* Rugby Sch.; Trinity and Nuffield Colls, Oxon. BA Oxon 1962, MA 1966. Lecturer and Fellow, Oriel Coll., Oxon, 1963-65; Fellow of Nuffield Coll., Oxon, 1965. Associate Editor: Oxford Economic Papers, 1970-73; Review of Economic Studies, 1973-76. *Publications:* Inflation, 1976; contrib. economic jls. *Address:* 52 Lonsdale Road, Oxford OX2 7EP. *T:* Oxford 57151.

FLETCHER, family name of **Baron Fletcher**.

FLETCHER, Baron *cr* 1970 (Life Peer), of Islington; **Eric George Molyneux Fletcher**, PC 1967; Kt 1964; LLD London; Solicitor; Senior partner of Denton, Hall & Burgin, Gray's Inn and Paris; *b* 26 March 1903; *s* of late Clarence George Eugene Fletcher, Town Clerk of Islington; *m* 1929, Bessie Winifred, *d* of late James Butt, Enfield; two *s* one *d. Educ:* Radley; University of London, LLB London, 1923; Admitted Solicitor, 1924; BA London, 1926; LLD London, 1932; FSA 1954; FRHistS. MP (Lab) East Islington, 1945-70; Minister without Portfolio, 1964-66; Chairman of Ways and Means and Deputy Speaker, House of Commons, 1966-68. Mem. LCC for South Islington, 1934-49 (Chm. Finance Cttee); formerly Mem. Exec. Cttee Fabian Soc.; Dep. Chm., Associated British Picture Corp., 1946-64; Commissioner for Public Works Loans, 1946-55; Senator of London Univ., 1946-50 and 1956-74; Mem. Exec. Cttee Grotius Soc.; Pres. of Seldon Soc., 1967-70; Chm., Management Cttee, Inst. of Archaeology, 1968-73; Governor: Birkbeck Coll., 1934-62; London Sch. of Economics; Member: Evershed Cttee on Practice and Procedure of Supreme Court; Church Assembly, 1962; Commission on Church and State, 1951; Advisory Council on Public Records, 1959-64; Royal Commission on Historical Manuscripts, 1966-; Statute Law Cttee, 1951-76. A Trustee of the British Museum, 1968-77. Chm., Advisory Bd for Redundant Churches, 1969-74. Pres. British Archæological Assoc., 1960-63. *Publications:* The Students' Conflict of Laws, 1928 (with late E. Leslie Burgin); The Carrier's Liability, 1932; miscellaneous articles on legal historical, and archæological subjects. *Recreations:* golf, swimming. *Address:* 3 Gray's Inn Place, WC1. *T:* 01-242 7485; The Barn, The Green, Sarratt, Rickmansworth, Herts WD3 6BP. *T:* King's Langley 65385. *Club:* Athenæum.

FLETCHER, Hon. Sir Alan (Roy), Kt 1972; Minister for Education and Cultural Activities, Queensland, 1968-74; MLA (Country Party) for Cunningham, Queensland, since 1953; *b* Pittsworth, 26 Jan. 1907; *s* of Alexander Roy Fletcher, Pittsworth, and Rosina Wilhemina (*née* McIntyre); *m* 1934, Enid Phair, *d* of James Thompson, Ashburton, NZ; two *s* two *d. Educ:* Pittsworth State Sch.; Scots Coll., Warwick, Qld. Pittsworth Shire: Councillor, 1945-57, Chm., 1949-57. Speaker, Legislative Assembly, Qld, 1957-60; Minister for Lands, 1960-68. Dir, Queensland Co-op. Milling Assoc., 1951-65. Mem., Presbyterian Schs Council, Warwick, 1951-, Chm. 1958-61. Pres., Old Boys' Assoc., Scots Coll., Warwick, 1948-. *Recreations:* cricket, tennis, rifle shooting. *Address:* Te Mata, Mount Tyson, Queensland 4356, Australia. *T:* Mount Tyson 84. *Clubs:* Tattersall's Racing (Brisbane); Brisbane Cricket.

FLETCHER, Alexander MacPherson; MP (C) Edinburgh North since Nov. 1973; *b* 26 Aug. 1929; *s* of Alexander Fletcher and Margaret Muirhead; *m* 1950, Christine Ann Buchanan; two *s* one *d. Educ:* Greenock High School. Chartered Accountant, 1956. Marketing Exec., internat. co., 1956-64; Man. Dir, 1964-71; private practice as Chartered Accountant, 1971-. Mem. East Kilbride Develt Corp., 1971-73. Opposition front bench spokesman on Scottish Affairs, 1977-. Mem., European Parlt, 1976-77. Contested (C) West Renfrewshire, 1970. Elder, Cramond Kirk. *Recreations:* golf, music. *Address:* 14 Cammo Walk, Edinburgh EH4 8AN. *T:* 031-336 3509. *Clubs:* Caledonian; Royal Burgess Golfing Society, Sports (Edinburgh).

FLETCHER, Prof. Basil Alais, MA, BSc; Emeritus Professor, University of Leeds; Research Fellow, Bristol University, 1971; *b* 10 April 1900; *s* of Walter Henry and Julia Fletcher; *m* 1928, Gerrardine Mary, *d* of William Daly; one *s* one *d. Educ:* Ilford Sch., Essex; University Coll., London. Physics Master, Gresham's Sch., Holt, Norfolk, 1922-26; Fellow Commoner, Sidney Sussex Coll., Cambridge, 1926-27; Senior Science Master, Gresham's Sch., Holt, 1927-30; Albert Kahn Fellow for Great Britain, 1930-31; Headmaster, Chippenham Sch., Wilts, 1932-35; Prof. of Education, Dalhousie Univ., Halifax, Canada, 1935-39; Prof. of Education, University Coll., Southampton, 1939-41; Prof. of Education, Bristol Univ., 1941-55; Vice-Principal of the University Coll. of Rhodesia and Nyasaland, Salisbury, 1956-60. *Publications:* Laboratory Physics (with H. W. Heckstall-Smith), 1926; Youth Looks at the World, 1932; Education and Colonial Policy, 1936; Child Psychology for Parents, 1938; The Next Step in Canadian Education, 1939; Education and Crisis, 1946; A Philosophy for the Teacher, 1961; Universities in the Modern World, 1968; The Challenge of Outward Bound, 1971. *Address:* Camerton Lodge, Camerton, Bath.

FLETCHER, Charles Montague, CBE 1952; MD, FRCP; Physician to Hammersmith Hospital, 1952-76; Professor of Clinical Epidemiology, University of London at Royal Postgraduate Medical School, 1973-76 (Reader, 1952-73), now Professor Emeritus; *b* 5 June 1911; *s* of late Sir Walter Morley Fletcher, FRS and Mary Frances Fletcher (*née* Cropper); *m* Louisa Mary Sylvia Seely, *d* of 1st Baron Mottistone; one *s* two *d. Educ:* Eton Coll.; Trinity Coll., Cambridge (Sen. Schol.; rowed in Univ. Boat, 1933); St Bartholomew's Hospital. MA 1936, MD 1945, Cantab; MRCP 1942; FRCP 1947; FFCM

1974. Michael Foster Research Student, Trinity Coll., 1934-36; Nuffield Res. Student, Oxford, 1940-42. Asst Phys., EMS, 1943-44; Dir, MRC Pneumoconiosis Res. Unit, 1945-52. Sec., MRC Cttee on Bronchitis Res., 1954-76; Sec., RCP Cttee on Smoking and Health, 1961-71; WHO Consultant: Pulmonary Heart Disease, 1960; Chronic Bronchitis, 1962; Smoking and Health, 1970. Mem., Central Health Services Cttee and Standing Med. Adv. Cttee, 1966-76; Vice-Chm., Health Educn Council, 1967; Chairman, Action on Smoking and Health (ASH), 1971-. Introd. many TV med. programmes incl. Hurt Mind, 1955, Your Life in Their Hands, 1958-65, Television Doctor, 1969-70. Goulstonian Lectr, RCP, 1947; Mem. Council, RCP, 1959-62; Bissett Hawkins Gold Medal, RCP, 1969. *Publications:* Communication in Medicine, 1973; Natural History of Chronic Bronchitis and Emphysema, 1976; many papers on: first use of penicillin, 1941; dust disease of lungs, 1946-55; bronchitis and emphysema, 1952-76. *Recreations:* music, gardening, beekeeping. *Address:* 20 Drayton Gardens, SW10 9SA. *T:* 01-373 2827; 2 Coastguard Cottages, Newtown, IoW PO30 4PA. *Club:* Brooks's.

FLETCHER, Edward Joseph; MP (Lab) Darlington since 1964; *b* 25 Feb. 1911; *m* Constance Murial, *d* of George Lee, Whickham, Hants; two *d. Educ:* St Mary's Sch., Handsworth; Fircroft Coll., Bourneville, Birmingham. Joined Labour Party, 1926; has held many offices. Member: AEU, 1932 (Mem. Birmingham Dist Cttee); Clerical and Admin. Workers' Union, 1950 (Northern Area Sec., 1949-64); Newcastle City Council, 1952-64 (Chm. Finance Cttee, Dep. Ldr Labour Gp). Chm. N Eastern Assoc. for the Arts, 1961-65. *Address:* House of Commons, SW1.

FLETCHER, Geoffrey Bernard Abbott, MA Cantab; *b* Hampstead, 28 Nov. 1903; *s* of J. Alexander Fletcher and Ursula Constance, *d* of William Richard Rickett and *cousin* of Rt Honourable Sir Joseph Compton-Rickett, MP. *Educ:* Rugby Sch.; King's Coll., Cambridge (Senior Scholar), First Class, Classical Tripos, Part I, 1924; First Class Classical Tripos, Part 2, 1926; Prendergast Student, 1926; Asst Lectr in Classics, University of Leeds, 1927-28; Lectr in Greek, University of Liverpool, 1928-36; Prof. of Classics in the University of Durham, King's Coll., Newcastle upon Tyne, 1937-46, Prof. of Latin, 1946-63; Prof. of Latin, University of Newcastle upon Tyne, 1963-69, now Emeritus Prof. Examiner in Greek, University of Leeds, 1940-42; Examiner in Latin, Queen's Univ., Belfast, 1949-51, University of Wales, 1954-56, Bristol, 1961-63; Dean of Faculty of Arts, University of Durham, 1945-47; Public Orator, University of Durham, 1956-58. *Publications:* an appendix on Housman's Poetry in Housman, 1897-1936, by Grant Richards, 1941; Annotations on Tacitus, 1964; many contributions to classical and other periodicals, British and foreign, and to co-operative works. *Recreations:* music, reading, art-galleries, walking, travel. *Address:* Thirlmere Lodge, Elmfield Road, Gosforth, Newcastle upon Tyne NE3 4BB. *T:* Gosforth 852873. *Club:* Athenæum.

FLETCHER, Geoffrey Scowcroft; artist and author; *b* 3 April 1923; *o s* of Herbert Fletcher and Annie Talence Fletcher; *m* 1953, Mary Jean Timothy. *Educ:* University Coll., London Univ. (Dip. in Fine Art). Abbey Major Schol., British Sch. at Rome, 1948. Drawings appeared in Manchester Guardian, 1950; London drawings and articles featured in The Daily Telegraph, 1958-. Author of television features on unusual aspects of London; has been instrumental in saving a number of metropolitan buildings from demolition. Drawings and paintings in various public and private collections in England and abroad, incl. exhibn of paintings and drawings in possession of Islington Council, 1972; Geoffrey Fletcher Room, decorated with the artist's drawings, opened Selfridge Hotel, London, 1973. Designed enamel box for St Paul's Cathedral Appeal, 1972. *Publications:* The London Nobody Knows (filmed, 1968), 1962; Down Among the Meths Men, 1966; Geoffrey Fletcher's London, 1968; City Sights, 1963; Pearly Kingdom, 1965; London's River, 1966; Elements of Sketching, 1966 (Amer. edn, 1968); London's Pavement Pounders, 1967; London After Dark, 1969; Changing London (Drawings from The Daily Telegraph), 1969; The London Dickens Knew, 1970; London Souvenirs, 1973; Paint It In Water Colour, 1974; Italian Impressions, 1974; Sketch It In Black and White, 1975; Daily Telegraph London Prints, 1975. *Address:* c/o The Daily Telegraph, Fleet Street, EC4.

FLETCHER, Harold Roy, PhD, DSc, FRSE, VMH; Regius Keeper of the Royal Botanic Garden, Edinburgh, 1958-70; Her Majesty's Botanist in Scotland since 1967; Hon. Professor of Botany, University of Edinburgh, since 1968; *b* 14 April 1907; *s* of James Fletcher, Glossop, Derbs; *m* 1941, Evelyn Betty Veronica, *d* of Rev. Dr Andrew David Sloan, St Andrews; one *s* one *d. Educ:* Grammar Sch., Glossop; Victoria Univ.,

Manchester, Asst Lecturer in Botany, University of Aberdeen, 1929-34; Botanist, Royal Botanic Garden, Edinburgh, 1934-51; Dir, Royal Horticultural Society's Gardens, Wisley, Ripley. Woking, Surrey, 1951-54. Asst Regius Keeper, Royal Botanic Garden, Edinburgh, 1954-56. Sec., Internat. Commn for: Horticultural Nomenclature and Registration, 1956-66; Nomenclature of Cultivated Plants, 1956-66; Vice-Pres., Royal Society, Edinburgh, 1961-65; Pres., Botanical Soc., Edinburgh, 1959-60; Pres., Internat. Assoc. of Botanic Gardens, 1964-69; Gen. Sec., 10th Internat. Botanical Congress, 1964. Hon. DSc: Edinburgh 1971; St Andrews, 1972. *Publications:* The Story of the Royal Horticultural Society, 1969; The Royal Botanic Garden, Edinburgh, 1670-1970, 1970; A Quest of Flowers, the Plant Explorations of Ludlow and Sherriff, 1975; numerous scientific papers chiefly on flora of Asia in Trans. Royal Society, Edinburgh, Trans. Botanical Soc., Edinburgh, Kew Bulletin; also numerous articles in horticultural and gardening journals. *Recreations:* music, art appreciation. *Address:* 29 Howard Place, Edinburgh EH3 5JY.

FLETCHER, James Thomas, CBE 1967; Chairman, North Yorkshire County Council, 1973-77 (formerly North Riding of Yorkshire County Council, 1957-73); *b* 3 Dec. 1898; *s* of Thomas Fletcher; *m* 1933, A. Walburn; two *s* one *d. Educ:* St John's Sch., Whitby. Mayor of Borough of Redcar, 1944; Chm., S Tees-side Hosp. Man. Cttee, 1958-; Mem., N Riding Yorks. CC, 1934. *Address:* Fordbridge, 12 Whin Green, Sleights, Whitby, N Yorks. *T:* Sleights 620.

FLETCHER, Sir John Henry Lancelot A.; *see* Aubrey-Fletcher.

FLETCHER, (Leopold) Raymond; MP (Lab) Ilkeston since 1964; Journalist; *b* 3 Dec. 1921; *s* of Leopold Raymond Fletcher, Ruddington, Notts; *m* 1947, Johanna Klara Elisabeth (*d* 1973), *d* of Karl Ising, Berlin; *m* 1977, Dr Catherine Elliott. *Educ:* University Coll., Nottingham. Served 1941-48 with Indian Army Ordnance Corps. Columnist on The Times and contributor to other journals at home and abroad. Vice-Pres., Assembly of Council of Europe, 1974-76; Leader, UK Delegn to Council of Europe and WEU, 1974-76; Leader, Socialist Gp in Council of Europe, 1974-76. Mem., T&GWU. Founder and Council Mem., Airship Assoc. *Publication:* Sixty Pounds a Second on Defence, 1963. *Recreation:* theatre. *Address:* 304 Frobisher House, Dolphin Square, SW1V 3LX.

FLETCHER, Leslie; General Manager (Chief Executive Officer) Williams Deacon's Bank Ltd, 1964-70, Director, 1966-70, retired; *b* 30 Jan. 1906; *s* of late Edward Henry and Edith Howard Fletcher; *m* 1934, Helen, *d* of Frank Turton; one *s* one *d. Educ:* City Gram. Sch., Chester; Manchester Univ. (BA Com). Entered Williams Deacon's Bank Ltd 1922; Asst Gen. Man., 1957; Dep. Gen. Man., 1961. Fellow and Mem. Council, Inst. of Bankers. *Recreations:* lawn tennis, golf. *Address:* Mote Cottage, Burley, near Ringwood, Hants. *T:* Burley 2291.

FLETCHER, Sir Norman Seymour, Kt 1977; agriculturalist and pastoralist, Western Australia. Established the Dirk Brook Stud at Keysbrook in 1948 and pioneered the introduction to WA of the Hereford cattle breed. AASA. Past Pres., Western Australia Royal Agricultural Soc.; has given outstanding service to the agricultural and pastoral industries in WA for 30 years; worked hard for advancement and development of cattle and meat industry, both in the southern areas of WA and in the Kimberleys. *Address:* 6 The Esplanade, Perth, Western Australia. *Clubs:* Weld, Western Australian (Perth).

FLETCHER, Hon. Sir Patrick Bisset, KBE 1958; CMG 1953; sometime MP for Matopo (SR); *b* 1901; 3rd *s* of late Hon. R. A. Fletcher, CBE, JP, Bulawayo, S Rhodesia; *m* 1929, Dorothy Maud, *d* of late Col W. Napier, CMG, Bulawayo, S Rhodesia; one *s* two *d. Educ:* Rondebosch Boys' High Sch.; Rhodes Univ., Grahamstown. Civil Service, 1923-30; Gold Mine Owner and Farmer; elected to S African Parliament, 1936; Mem., War Supplies and Price Advisory Bds, 1940-44. Minister of Agriculture and Lands, 1945-51 (Southern Rhodesia); Minister of Native Affairs, 1951-58; Minister of Lands, 1956-58; Minister of Irrigation and Surveys, 1957-58. Represented S Rhodesia, Coronation, 1953. President: Rhodesia Assoc. for prevention of Tuberculosis; Central African Trade Fair, 1959-. *Recreation:* golf. *Address:* Fletcher Estates, PO Box 37, Sinoia, Rhodesia. *Club:* Bulawayo (Rhodesia).

FLETCHER, Paul Thomas, CBE 1959; Deputy Chairman, Atomic Power Constructions Ltd (Managing Director, 1971); Director, Nuclear Power Co. Ltd; *b* 30 Sept. 1912; *s* of Stephen Baldwin Fletcher and Jessie Carrie; *m* 1941, Mary Elizabeth King; three *s. Educ:* Stornaway Inst., Isle of Lewis; Maidstone Grammar Sch.; Medway Techn. Coll. BSc(Eng); CEng, FICE,

FIMechE, FIEE. Served 3-year apprenticeship with E. A. Gardner & Sons Ltd, Maidstone, remaining for 7 years; joined Min. of Works, 1939, initially in Test Br. of Engrg Div., later with responsibility for variety of engrg services in public bldgs and Govt factories and for plant and equipment for Govt civilian and service res. estabts; Chief Mech. and Elec. Engr, 1951. On formation of UKAEA in 1954, became Dep. Dir of Engrg in Industrial Gp, later Engrg Dir and Dep. Man. Dir; Dir, United Power Co., 1961; Man. Dir, GEC (Process Engrg) Ltd, 1965. Mem. Exec. Council, BSI, 1977. Pres., IMechE, 1975-76. *Publications:* papers to IMechE. *Recreations:* photography, motoring. *Address:* 26 Foxgrove Avenue, Beckenham, Kent BR3 2BA. *T:* 01-650 5563.

FLETCHER, Air Chief Marshal Sir Peter Carteret, KCB 1968 (CB 1965); OBE 1945; DFC 1943; AFC 1952; Director, British Aerospace, since 1977; *b* 7 Oct. 1916; *s* of F. T. W. Fletcher, Oxford (sometime tobacco farmer, Southern Rhodesia), and Dora Clulee, New Zealand; *m* 1940, Marjorie Isobel Kotze; two *d. Educ:* St George's Coll., Southern Rhodesia; Rhodes Univ., S Africa. SR Law Dept, 1937. Served War of 1939-45: SR Air Force, 1939; trans. to RAF, 1941; commanded 135 and 258 Fighter Sqdns and RAF Station Belvedere. Directing Staffs at: RAF Staff Coll., 1945-46; Jt Services Staff Coll., 1946-48; Imp. Defence Coll., 1956-58; Mem. Jt Planning Staff, 1951-53; comdg RAF Abingdon, 1958-60; Dep. Dir Jt Planning Staff, 1960-61; Dir of Opl Requirements (B), Air Min., 1961-63; Asst Chief of Air Staff (Policy and Plans), 1964-66; AOC, No 38 Group, Transport Command, 1966-67; VCAS, 1967-70; Controller of Aircraft, Min. of Aviation Supply (formerly Min. of Technology), 1970-71; Air Systems Controller, Defence Procurement Executive, MoD, 1971-73; Dir, Hawker Siddeley Aviation Ltd, 1974-77. *Recreations:* books, travel. *Address:* Woodlands, Sandy Lane, Tilford, Surrey GU10 2ET. *T:* Frensham 2897.

FLETCHER, Raymond; see Fletcher, L. R.

FLETCHER, Richard Cawthorne, MA; JP; Headmaster, Worcester College for the Blind, since Sept. 1959; *b* 30 Aug. 1916; *s* of late Philip C. Fletcher, MC, and of Edith Maud (née Okell); *m* 1946, Joan Fairlie Woodcock; one *s* one *d. Educ:* Marlborough; University Coll., Oxford. Served Army (Emergency Commn), 1939-46. Asst Master, Charterhouse, 1946-Aug. 1959. *Publication:* (ed) The Teaching of Science and Mathematics to the Blind, 1973. *Recreation:* music. *Address:* The Gables, Whittington Road, Worcester.

FLETCHER-COOKE, Charles Fletcher, QC 1958; MP (C) Darwen Division of Lancashire since 1951; Member, European Parliament, since 1977; *b* 5 May 1914; *yr s* of late Capt. C. A. and Gwendolen May Fletcher-Cooke; *m* 1959, Diana Lady Avebury (whom he divorced, 1967), *d* of late Capt. Edward King and of Mrs J. St Vincent Hand; no surv. *c. Educ:* Malvern Coll. (Scholar); Peterhouse, Cambridge (Schol., MA 1940). Pres., Cambridge Union, 1936; Editor, The Granta, 1936. Called to Bar through Lincoln's Inn, 1938 (1st Class Hons, Bar Final Examination; Studentship and Certificate of Honour), Bencher 1969. Mem. Senate, Four Inns of Court, 1970-74. Served War of 1939-45, in Naval Intelligence Div. and on Joint Intelligence Staff, with rank of Lieut-Comdr, RNVR. Contested (Lab) East Dorset Div., 1945, re-adopted, 1946, but resigned from Labour Party shortly afterwards. Legal Adviser to British Delegation, Danube Conf., Belgrade, 1948; Deleg. to Consultative Assembly of Council of Europe, 1954-55. Mem. of Statute Law Cttee, 1955-61, 1970-; Chm., Select Cttee on Parliamentary Commissioner for Administration, 1974-77. Joint Parliamentary Under-Sec. of State, Home Office, 1961-63. *Publications:* (with others) The Rule of Law; (with M. J. Albery) Monopolies and Restrictive Trade Practices. *Recreations:* tennis, ski-ing, fishing. *Address:* 4 North Court, Great Peter Street, SW1. *T:* 01-799 5859; 2 Paper Buildings, Temple, EC4. *T:* 01-353 1853. *Clubs:* Garrick, Pratt's.
See also Sir John Fletcher-Cooke.

FLETCHER-COOKE, Sir John, Kt 1962; CMG 1952; MA Oxon; *b* 8 Aug. 1911; *er s* of late Charles Arthur and Gwendolen May Fletcher-Cooke; *m* 1949 (marr. diss. 1971); two *s* one *d; m* Marie-Louise, widow of Louis Vicomte Fournier de la Barre. *Educ:* Malvern Coll. (Barham Schol.); University of Paris (Diplomé, degré supérieur); Oxford Univ. (Kitchener Scholar, Senior Exhibitioner, St Edmund Hall). First Cl. Hons Politics, Philosophy and Economics; economic research, Oxford Univ., 1933; Asst Principal, Colonial Office, 1934; Private Sec. to successive Permanent Under-Secs of State for the Colonies, 1937; Officer Malayan CS, 1937; Asst Sec., FMS, 1938; special duty, FMS, 1939; Magistrate, Singapore, 1939; Sec., Foreign Exchange Control, Malaya, 1939; Dist Officer, FMS, 1940.

Served with RAF as intelligence officer, FO, 1942-46; Prisoner of War in Japan, 1942-45. Attached to Colonial Office for special duty and accompanied Constitutional Comr to Malta, 1946; Under-Sec. to Govt of Palestine, 1946-48; Mem. Exec. Council, Palestine, 1947; Special Rep. for Palestine at UN discussions on Palestine, 1948; UK rep. on Special Cttee and later on Trusteeship Council UN, Geneva and Lake Success, 1948-50; Counsellor (Colonial Affairs), Perm. UK Deleg. to UN, New York, 1949-51; Colonial Adviser to UK Deleg. to UN Gen. Assembly, 1948-50 and alternate UK deleg. to UN Gen. Assembly 1949; Colonial Sec., Cyprus, 1951-55. Acted as Governor of Cyprus for various periods, 1951-55. Attached Colonial Office for Special Duty (temp.), 1956; Minister for Constitutional Affairs, Tanganyika, 1956-59; Chief Sec. to the Govt of Tanganyika, 1959-60. Special Rep. of Tanganyika at Ghana Independence Celebrations, 1957, at Economic Commission for Africa, Addis Ababa, 1959, and at Trusteeship Council, UN, New York, 1957, 1958, 1959, 1960 and 1961. Acted as Governor of Tanganyika for various periods, 1959-61; Dep. Governor, Tanganyika, 1960-61. Visiting Prof. (African Affairs) University of Colorado, Boulder, USA, 1961-62, 1966, and 1973-74; Fellow, African Studies Assoc., NY, 1961-. Mem. Constituencies Delimitation Commn for Kenya, 1962; Mem. Exec. Cttee, Overseas Employers' Federation, 1963-67. Contested (C) Luton, Nov. 1963. MP (C) Test Div. of Southampton, 1964-66. Mem. Councils of Royal Commonwealth Society and of United Society for Propagation of the Gospel, 1964-67. Vice-Chm., Internat. Team to review structure and organisation of FAO, Rome, 1967. Dir, Programmes in Diplomacy, Carnegie Endowment for International Peace, New York, 1967-69. Mission for British Govt to Anglo-French Condominium of New Hebrides, 1969. *Publications:* The Emperor's Guest, 1942-45, 1971; contrib. to Parliament as an Export, 1966, and to many periodicals. *Address:* c/o Lloyds Bank, Finsbury Circus Branch, 3 Broad Street Place, EC2. *Club:* Travellers'.
See also Charles Fletcher-Cooke.

FLETCHER-VANE, family name of **Baron Inglewood.**

FLETT, Sir Martin Teall, KCB 1965 (CB 1953); Director: Decca Ltd, since 1972; Siebe Gorman Holdings Ltd, since 1972; *b* 30 July 1911; *s* of late Sir John Smith Flett, KBE, FRS, and of Lady (Mary Jane) Flett (née Meason); *m* 1936, Mary, *er d* of Sir Alec Martin; two *s* one *d. Educ:* George Watson's Coll.; St Paul's Sch.; St John's Coll., Oxford. 1st Class Modern History, 1933; Home Civil Service, Dominions Office, 1933; HM Treasury, 1934; War Cabinet Office, Ministry of Reconstruction and Lord President's Office, 1944-46; Under-Sec., HM Treasury, 1949-56; Alternate UK Dir, International Bank and Financial Counsellor, British Embassy, Washington, 1953-56; Dep. Sec., Ministry of Power, 1956-61; Dep. Under-Sec. of State, Air Ministry, 1961-63; Permanent Under-Sec. of State: Air Min., 1963-64; (RAF), 1964-68, (Equipment), 1968-71, MoD. Pres., Old Pauline Club, 1976. *Address:* 45 Campden Hill Road, W8. *T:* 01-937 9498. *Clubs:* Athenæum, Royal Air Force; Royal Wimbledon Golf.

FLEW, Prof. Antony Garrard Newton; Professor of Philosophy, University of Reading, since 1973; *b* 11 Feb. 1923; *o s* of Rev. Dr R. N. Flew; *m* 1952, Annis Ruth Harty; two *d. Educ:* St Faiths Sch., Cambridge; Kingswood Sch., Bath; Sch. of Oriental and African Studies, London; St John's Coll., Oxford (John Locke Schol., MA); DLitt Keele, 1974. Lectr: Christ Church, Oxford, 1949-50; Univ. of Aberdeen, 1950-54; Prof. of Philosophy: Univ. of Keele, 1954-71; Univ. of Calgary, 1972-73. Many temp. vis. appts. Gavin David Young Lectr, Adelaide, 1963. A Vice-Pres., Rationalist Press Assoc., 1973-. *Publications:* A New Approach to Psychical Research, 1953; Hume's Philosophy of Belief, 1961; God and Philosophy, 1966; Evolutionary Ethics, 1967; An Introduction to Western Philosophy, 1971; Crime or Disease?, 1973; Thinking About Thinking, 1975; The Presumption of Atheism, 1976; Sociology, Equality and Education, 1976; articles in philosophical and other jls. *Recreations:* walking, climbing, house maintenance. *Address:* 26 Alexandra Road, Reading, Berks RG1 5PD. *T:* Reading 61848. *Clubs:* Climber's; Union Society (Oxford).

FLINT, Prof. David, TD, MA, BL, CA; Professor of Accountancy, University of Glasgow, since 1964 (Johnstone Smith Chair, 1964-75); *b* 24 Feb. 1919; *s* of David Flint, JP, and Agnes Strang Lambie; *m* 1953, Dorothy Mary Maclachlan Jardine; two *s* one *d. Educ:* Glasgow High Sch.; University of Glasgow. Served with Royal Signals, 1939-46, Major (despatches). Awarded distinction final examination of Institute of Chartered Accountants of Scotland, 1948. Lecturer, University of Glasgow, 1950-60; Dean of Faculty of Law, 1971-73. Partner, Mann Judd Gordon & Co. Chartered Accountants,

Glasgow, 1951-71. Hon. Pres. Glasgow Chartered Accountants Students Soc., 1959-60. Mem. Council, Scottish Business Sch. Vice-Pres., Scottish Economic Soc.; Vice-Pres., Inst. of Chartered Accountants of Scotland, 1973-75, Pres., 1975-76. *Recreation:* golf. *Address:* 3 Merrylee Road, Newlands, Glasgow G43 2SH. *T:* 041-637 3060.

FLORENCE, Philip Sargant, Hon. CBE 1952; MA (Cantab), PhD (Columbia); Hon. LittD (Hum) (Columbia); Hon. DSocSc (Birmingham); Professor of Commerce, 1929-55, Dean of the Faculty of Commerce and Social Science, 1947-50, University of Birmingham; *b* 25 June 1890; *s* of late Henry Smythe Florence and late Mary Sargant-Florence; *m* 1917, Lella Faye Secor (*d* 1966); two *s*. *Educ:* Rugby Sch.; Caius Coll., Cambridge (History Scholar); 1st Class Economics, 1914, Columbia Univ., New York (Garth Fellow). Organising Sec., British Assoc. Cttee on Fatigue from the Economic Standpoint, 1913-15; Investigator to the Health of Munition Workers' Cttee, 1915-16; Investigator (Associate Sanitarian), US Public Health Service, 1917-21; Lecturer, Bureau of Industrial Research and Bureau of Personnel Administration, New York, 1919-21; University Lecturer in Economics, Cambridge Univ., 1921-29; Staff Lecturer in Economics, Magdalene Coll., Cambridge, 1924-29; Chm., Social Study Cttee, Birmingham Univ., 1930-46; Mem. Council, Royal Economic Society, 1930-61, Vice-Pres., 1972-; Pres. Section F (Economics) British Assoc. for the Advancement of Science, 1937; Visiting Prof. University of Cairo, 1940; Consultant US National Resources Planning Board, 1940-41; Retail Trade Cttee, Board of Trade, 1941; Chm., Greater Birmingham Employment Cttee, 1957-63. Visiting Prof., Johns Hopkins Univ., 1959; Consultant, Jordan Development Bd, 1960-61; Leverhulme Lecturer, University of Malta, 1962; Visiting Prof., University of Rhode Island, 1967-68. *Publications:* Use of Factory Statistics in the Investigation of Industrial Fatigue, 1918; US Public Health Bulletin No. 106, Comparison of an Eight-Hour Plant and a Ten-Hour Plant (in collaboration), 1920; Economics of Fatigue and Unrest, 1924; Over-Population, Theory and Statistics, 1926; Economics and Human Behaviour, 1927; The Statistical Method in Economics and Political Science, 1929; Uplift in Economics, 1930; The Logic of Industrial Organisation, 1933; (joint) Consumers Cooperation in Great Britain, 1938; (joint) County Town, 1946; Investment Location and Size of Plant, 1947; Labour, 1948; The Logic of British and American Industry, 1953, rev. edn 1971; Industry and the State, 1957; Ownership, Control and Success of Large Companies, 1961; Post-War Investment, Location and Size of Plant, 1962; Economics and Sociology of Industry, 1964, rev. edn 1969; Atlas of Economic Structure and Policies, 1970; (jtly) The Roots of Inflation, 1975; articles, etc. in Economic, Sociological, Statistical and Psychological Journals. *Address:* Highfield, 128 Selly Park Road, Birmingham B29 7LH. *T:* 021-472 0498.

FLORY, Prof. Paul John; J. G. Jackson—C. J. Wood Professor in Chemistry, Stanford University, 1965-76, now Emeritus; *b* 19 June 1910; *s* of Ezra Flory and Martha Brumbaugh Flory; *m* 1936, Emily Catherine Tabor; one *s* two *d*. *Educ:* Manchester Coll., Ind; Ohio State Univ. BSc Manchester Coll. 1931; PhD (Phys Chem.) Ohio 1934. Research Chemist, E. I. DuPont de Nemours & Co., 1934-38; Res. Associate, Cincinnati Univ., 1938-40; Res. Chemist, Esso Lab., Standard Oil Co., 1940-43; Section Head, Res. Lab., Goodyear Tire & Rubber Co., 1943-48; Prof., Cornell Univ., 1948-56; Exec. Dir of Res., Mellon Inst., 1956-61; Prof., Stanford Univ., 1961-; Chm., Dept of Chem., Stanford Univ., 1969-71. FAAAS; Fellow, Amer. Phys. Soc.; Member: Amer. Chem. Soc.; Amer. Acad. Arts and Scis; Nat. Acad. Scis; Amer. Philos. Soc.; Nat. Res. Council: Chm., Cttee on Macromolecular Chemistry, 1955-59; Chm., Div. of Chem. and Chem. Technology, 1966-68. Holds numerous medals and awards, including: Priestley Medal (Amer. Chem. Soc.) 1974; Nobel Prize for Chemistry, 1974; US Nat. Medal of Science, 1974; Perkin Medal, Soc. of Chem. Industry, 1977. Hon. ScD: Manchester Coll., 1950; Ohio State, 1970; Hon. DSc Manchester, 1969; Hon. PhD Weizmann Inst. of Sci., Israel, 1976. *Publications:* Principles of Polymer Chemistry, 1953 (trans. Japanese, 1955); Statistical Mechanics of Chain Molecules, 1969 (trans. Japanese, 1971, Russian, 1971); numerous papers on phys. chem. of polymers and macromolecules. *Recreations:* swimming, cycling, hiking. *Address:* Department of Chemistry, Stanford University, Stanford, Calif 94305, USA. *T:* 415-497-4574. *Club:* Chemists' (New York).

FLOUD, Mrs Jean Esther, CBE 1976; MA, BSc(Econ); Principal, Newnham College, Cambridge, since 1972; *b* 3 Nov. 1915; *d* of Annie Louisa and Ernest Walter McDonald; *m* 1938, Peter Castle Floud, CBE (*d* 1960; formerly Keeper of Circulation, Victoria and Albert Museum); one *s* two *d*. *Educ:*

public elementary and selective secondary schools; London School of Economics (BScEcon), Hon. Fellow, 1972. Asst Dir of Educn, City of Oxford, 1940-46; Teacher of Sociology in the University of London (London School of Economics and Inst. of Educn), 1947-62; Official Fellow of Nuffield College, Oxford, 1963-72. Member: Franks Commission of Inquiry into the University of Oxford, 1964-66; University Grants Cttee, 1969-74; Social Science Research Council, 1970-73; Exec. Cttee, PEP, 1975-; Adv. Bd for the Res. Councils, 1976-. Hon. LittD Leeds, 1973. *Publications:* Social Class and Educational Opportunity (with A. H. Halsey and F. M. Martin), 1956; papers and reviews in sociological jls. *Recreations:* books, music. *Address:* Newnham College, Cambridge. *T:* Cambridge 62273.

FLOWER, family name of **Viscount Ashbrook.**

FLOWER, Group Capt. Arthur Hyde, CBE 1939; *b* Bemboka, NSW, 13 Dec. 1892; *s* of late Thomas Flower; *m* 1924, Nina Joan Castleden (*d* 1976), Whitby; no *c*; *m* 1977, Margaret June Wickens. *Educ:* Tilba, NSW. Served with AIF, Egypt and France, 1915-16; Transferred to Royal Flying Corps, 1917; served in No. 42 Squadron, France and Italy, 1917-1918 (French Croix de Guerre with palm); Egypt and Turkey, 1920-23; Egypt, 1926-31 and 1934-36; Palestine, 1937-38 (CBE, despatches); France, Sept. 1939-May 1940; England, 1940-42; SWP Area, Aug. 1942-Nov. 1944; retired May 1945. Comdr Order of Leopold (Belgium). *Recreations:* shooting, golf. *Address:* Garden Cottage, Longwood Road, Heathfield, SA 5153, Australia.

FLOWER, Desmond John Newman, MC 1944; Editorial Consultant, Sheldon Press, since 1973; Chairman, Cassell & Co. Ltd, 1958-71; President, Cassell Australia Ltd, 1965-71; *b* London, 25 Aug. 1907; *o s* of late Sir Newman Flower; *m* 1st, 1931, Margaret Cameron Coss (marr. diss., 1952); one *s*; 2nd, 1952, Anne Elizabeth Smith (marr. diss. 1972); one *s* two *d*. *Educ:* Lancing; King's Coll., Cambridge. Entered Cassell & Co. 1930; Dir, 1931; Literary Dir, 1938; Dep.-Chm., 1952; Chm. Cassell & Co. (Holdings) Ltd, 1958-70. Served War of 1939-45 (despatches, MC); commissioned 1941, 5 Bn Argyll and Sutherland Highlanders later 91 (A&SH) A/T-Regt. Chm., the Folio Society, 1960-71; President des Comités d'Alliance Française en Grande Bretagne, 1963-72. Officier de la légion d'honneur, 1972 (Chevalier 1950). DLitt (*hc*) University of Caen, 1957. *Publications:* founder and editor (with A. J. A. Symons) Book Collector's quarterly, 1930-34; ed, Complete Poetical Works of Ernest Christopher Dowson, 1934; compiled (with Francis Meynell and A. J. A. Symons) The Nonesuch Century, 1936; The Pursuit of Poetry, 1939; (with A. N. L. Munby) English Poetical Autographs, 1938; Voltaire's England, 1950; History of 5 Bn Argyll and Sutherland Highlanders, 1950; (with James Reeves) The War, 1939-1945, 1960. *Recreations:* golf, book collecting. *Address:* 187 Clarence Gate Gardens, NW1 6AR. *T:* 01-262 4690. *Clubs:* Brooks's; Royal and Ancient (St Andrews).

FLOWERS, Sir Brian Hilton, Kt 1969; FRS 1961; Rector of The Imperial College of Science and Technology, since 1973; *b* 13 Sept. 1924; *o s* of late Rev. Harold J. Flowers, Swansea; *m* 1951, Mary Frances, *er d* of Sir Leonard Behrens, *qv*; two step *s*. *Educ:* Bishop Gore Grammar Sch., Swansea; Gonville and Caius Coll. (Exhibitioner), Cambridge (MA); Hon. Fellow, 1974; University of Birmingham (DSc). Anglo-Canadian Atomic Energy Project (Tube Alloys), Montreal and Chalk River, Ont., Canada, 1944-46; Research work in nuclear physics and atomic energy at Atomic Energy Research Establishment, Harwell, 1946-50; Dept of Mathematical Physics, University of Birmingham, 1950-52; Visiting Prof., Mass. Institute of Technology and University of Calif., 1955. Head of Theoretical Physics Div., AERE, Harwell, 1952-58, and Chief Research Scientist, 1958; Prof. of Theoretical Physics, 1958-61; Langworthy Prof. of Physics, 1961-72, Univ. of Manchester. Chairman: Science Research Council, 1967-73; Royal Commn on Environmental Pollution, 1973-76. Member of Council of the Physical Society, 1956-60; Mem. of Council of Inst of Physics and Physical Soc., 1960, and Vice-Pres. 1962-66; Mem., Cttee of Managers, Royal Institution, 1976-; President: Inst. of Physics, 1972-74; European Science Foundn, 1974-; Nat. Soc. for Clean Air, 1977-. Nuffield Vis. Professorship at Universities of British Columbia and Alberta, July-Aug., 1960; Visiting Prof., Cairo Univ., Jan., 1963. Member: Advisory Council on Scientific Policy, 1962-64; Council for Scientific Policy, 1965-67; Adv. Bd for the Res. Council, 1972-73; Computer Agency Council, 1973-75; Adv. Council, Science Policy Foundn, 1975-; Governing Board, National Institute for Research in Nuclear Science, 1962-65; Bd of Governors, Weizmann Inst. of Science, Israel, 1969-; UKAEA, 1971-; Energy Commn, 1977-. Chairman: joint working group on computers for research, 1965; Computer Bd for Univs and Research Councils, 1966-70; Member: Bd of Directors, Fulmer Research Inst., 1972-75; Senatsausschusses für Forschungspolitik und Forschungsplanung der Max-Planck-Gesellschaft, 1973-75. The Queen's Lecture, Berlin, 1973. Editor: Advances in Physics, 1959-63; Cambridge Monographs, 1962-66. Rutherford Medal and Prize, IPPS, 1968. FInstP 1961. Hon. FCGI, 1975; Hon. MRIA (Science Section), 1976; Hon. FIEE, 1975. MA Oxon, 1956; Hon. DSc: Sussex, 1968; Wales 1972; Manchester, 1973; Leicester, 1973; Liverpool, 1974. Chevalier de la Légion d'Honneur, 1975. Publications: (with E. Mendoza) Properties of Matter, 1970; various contribs to scientific periodicals, on the structure of the atomic nucleus, on nuclear reactions, and on science policy. Recreations: music, walking, painting. Address: Imperial College, SW7 2AZ. T: 01-589 5111. Club: Athenæum.

FLOYD, Sir Giles (Henry Charles), 7th Bt cr 1816; Director, Burghley Estate Farms, since 1958; b 27 Feb. 1932; s of Sir John Duckett Floyd, 6th Bt, TD, and of Jocelin Evadne (d 1976), d of late Sir Edmund Wyldbore Smith; S father, 1975; m 1954, Lady Gillian Moyra Katherine Cecil, 2nd d of 6th Marquess of Exeter, qv; two s. Educ: Eton College. High Sheriff of Rutland, 1968. Heir: er s David Henry Cecil Floyd, b 2 April 1956. Address: Tinwell Manor, Stamford, Lincs. T: Stamford 2676. Clubs: Turf, Farmers'.

FLOYD, John Anthony; Chairman: Christie Manson & Woods Ltd, since 1974; Christies International Ltd, since 1976; b 12 May 1923; s of Lt-Col Arthur Bowen Floyd, DSO, OBE; m 1948, Margaret Louise Rosselli; two d. Educ: Eton. Served King's Royal Rifle Corps, 1941-46. Address: 26 Park Village East, NW1 7PZ. T: 01-387 6311. Clubs: Boodle's, White's, MCC.

FLOYD EWIN, Sir David Ernest Thomas, Kt 1974; MVO (4th class) 1954; OBE 1960; MA; Registrar and Receiver of St Paul's Cathedral since 1944; b 17 Feb. 1911; 7th s of late Frederick P. Ewin and Ellen Floyd; m 1948, Marion Irene, d of William R. Lewis; one d. Educ: Eltham. MA (Lambeth) 1962; Notary Public. Past Master, Scriveners Company; Liveryman, Wax Chandlers Company; Past Master, Guild of Freemen of the City of London; Member of Court of Common Council for Ward of Castle Baynard (Dep., 1972-); Vice-Pres., Castle Baynard Ward Club (Chm. 1962); Chm., Corp. of London Gresham Cttee, 1975-76; Surrogate for Province of Canterbury; Trustee, City Parochial Foundn, 1967-; Hon. Dir, British Humane Assoc.; Governor and Member of Court: Sons of the Clergy Corp.; St Gabriel's Coll., Camberwell, 1946-72. Gold Staff Officer at Coronation of HM Queen Elizabeth, 1953. KStJ 1970 (OStJ 1965). Freeman, City of London, 1948. Publications: A Pictorial History of St Paul's Cathedral, 1970; The Splendour of St Paul's, 1973; numerous papers and articles. Recreations: tennis, gardening, fishing. Address: The Chapter House, St Paul's Churchyard, EC4M 8AD. T: 01-236 4128; 8 Amen Court, EC4M 7BU. T: 01-248 6151; Silver Springs, Stoke Gabriel, South Devon. T: Stoke Gabriel 264. Clubs: City Livery, Guildhall.

FLOYER-ACLAND, Lt-Gen. Arthur Nugent, CB 1940; DSO; MC; DL; b 1885; s of late Capt. J. E. Acland and N. L. N. Bankes, Wollaston House, Dorchester, Dorset; m 1913, Evelyn Stafford (d 1973), d of Stafford Still, Lincoln's Inn; one s. Educ: Blundell's Sch., Tiverton. Gazetted to the Duke of Cornwall's Light Infantry, 1907; served European War, France and Italy (DSO, MC, French Croix de Guerre (2 awards), Bt Major, 1917; despatches six times); graduated at Staff Coll., Camberley, 1921; Bt Lieut-Col 1927; Lieut-Col 1931; commanded 1st Bn The Duke of Cornwall's Light Infantry, 1931-34; Col 1934; AAG War Office, 1934-36; Comdr 3rd (Jhelum) Infantry Bde, India, 1936-38; served operations Waziristan NWFP, India, 1937-38 (despatches); Comdr 43rd (Wessex) Div. TA, 1938-39; Military Sec. to Sec. of State for War, 1940-42; Lt-Gen. 1941. High Sheriff, Dorset, 1953; DL Dorset, 1957. Assumed name of Floyer in addition to own name on succeeding to the estate of George Floyer of Stafford House, near Dorchester, 1927. Address: The Paddock, West Stafford, Dorchester, Dorset. Club: Army and Navy.

FLYNN, Most Rev. Thomas; see Achonry, Bishop of, (RC).

FOAD, Roland Walter, CBE 1968; b 7 April 1908; er s of late Walter James Foad and late Frances Mary Foad (née Inge); m 1st, 1934, Isabel Sarah Stewart McKeen (d 1962); one s one d; 2nd, 1966, Maria-Isabel, Marquesa de Piedrabuena. Educ: Manwood's Sch., Sandwich. ACA 1929; FCA 1953 (Mem. Council, 1964-71). Dep. Controller, Raw Materials Accountancy, 1941-45; Chief Accountant, Industrial and Commercial Finance Corporation, 1946-48; Partner,

McClelland Ker & Co., Chartered Accountants, 1949-53; Dir of Finance, Iron and Steel Board, 1954-62, Exec. Mem., 1962-67; UK Chm., Steel Cttee, Council of Assoc., ECSC, 1962-67. Liveryman, Co. of Wheelwrights. Address: 24 Clarendon Avenue, Leamington Spa, Warwicks.

FOAKES, Prof. Reginald Anthony; Professor of English Literature, University of Kent at Canterbury, since 1964; Dean of the Faculty of Humanities, since 1974; b 18 Oct. 1923; 2nd s of William Warren Foakes and Frances (née Poate); m 1951, Barbara, d of Harry Garratt, OBE; two s two d. Educ: West Bromwich Grammar Sch.; Birmingham Univ. (MA, PhD). Fellow of the Shakespeare Inst., 1951-54; Lectr in English, Durham Univ., 1954-62; Sen. Lectr, 1963-64; Commonwealth Fund (Harkness) Fellow, Yale Univ., 1955-56; Visiting Professor: University Coll., Toronto, 1960-62; Univ. of California, Santa Barbara, 1968-69. Publications: (ed) Shakespeare's King Henry VIII, 1957; The Romantic Assertion, 1958; (ed with R. T. Rickert) Henslowe's Diary, 1961; (ed) The Comedy of Errors, 1962; (ed) The Revenger's Tragedy, 1966; (ed) Macbeth and Much Ado About Nothing, 1968; Romantic Criticism, 1968; Coleridge on Shakespeare, 1971; Shakespeare, the Dark Comedies to the Last Plays, 1971. Address: Pinetree House, 16 St Lawrence Forstal, Canterbury, Kent. T: Canterbury 61157.

FODEN, Air Vice-Marshal Arthur, CB 1964; CBE 1960; BSc; CEng; FIEE; Director, Racal Datacom, since 1975; b 19 April 1914; s of Henry Foden, Macclesfield, Cheshire; m 1938, Constance Muriel Foden (née Corkill); one s one d. Educ: Manchester Univ. Electronic Engineer, 1935-37; Education Officer, Royal Air Force, 1937-39; Signals Officer, Royal Air Force, 1939; Dep. Dir, Signals Staff, Min. of Def., 1964-67; Asst Chief of Defence Staff (Signals), 1967-69, retired; Dir (C), Govt Communications HQ, 1969-75. Recreations: gardening, music. Address: Ravenglass, Wargrave, Berks. T: Wargrave 2589.

FODEN, William Bertram, CB 1945; formerly Assistant Under-Secretary of State, Air Ministry; retired; b 19 Sept. 1892; s of late W. G. Foden, Newcastle, Staffs; m 1920, Zélie, d of late G. K. Lemmy, Lewisham; one s one d. Educ: High Sch., Newcastle, Staffs; St John's Coll., Cambridge (scholar). BA 1914; RGA and RE, 1916-18; Research Dept., Woolwich Arsenal, 1918; Air Ministry, 1919-53. Address: 2 Westwood Close, Threshers, Crediton, Devon EX17 3NJ. T: Crediton 2709.

FODEN-PATTINSON, Peter Lawrence; a Deputy Chairman of Lloyd's, 1976; b 14 June 1925; s of late Hubert Foden-Pattinson; m 1956, Joana Foyer (née Henderson); one s. Educ: Downside. Irish Guards, 1943-47. Lloyd's, 1942-: Underwriting Mem., 1956; Mem., Cttee of Lloyd's, 1973-76; Mem., Cttee of Lloyd's Non-Marine Assoc., 1965, Chm. 1971, Dep. Chm. 1970 and 1972. Recreations: boating, music. Address: 24A Shawfield Street, SW3 4BD. T: 01-352 3843.

FOGARTY, Christopher Winthrop, CB 1973; Deputy Secretary, Ministry of Overseas Development, since 1976; b 18 Sept. 1921; s of late Philip Christopher Fogarty, ICS, and late Hilda Spenser Fogarty; m 1961, Elizabeth Margaret Ince (d 1972). Educ: Ampleforth Coll.; Christ Church, Oxford. War Service (Lieut RA), 1942-45. Asst Principal, 1946, Principal, 1949, HM Treasury; Permanent Sec., Min. of Finance of Eastern Nigeria, 1956; Asst Sec., HM Treasury, 1959, Under-Sec., 1966; Treasury Rep., S Asia and FE, 1967-72; Dep. Sec., HM Treasury, and Dir, European Investment Bank, 1972-76. Address: 7 Hurlingham Court, Ranelagh Gardens, SW6 3SH. Clubs: Royal Commonwealth Society, Travellers'; Royal Selangor Golf.
See also M. P. Fogarty, S. W. Fogarty.

FOGARTY, Michael Patrick; Deputy Director, Centre for Studies in Social Policy, London, since 1977 (Senior Fellow, 1973); Professor Associate, Brunel University and Administrative Staff College, Henley; b 3 Oct. 1916; s of late Philip Christopher Fogarty, ICS, and Mary Belle Pye, Galway; m 1939, Phyllis Clark; two s two d. Educ: Ampleforth Coll.; Christ Church, Oxford. Lieut RA, 1940 (wounded, Dunkirk). Nuffield Coll., 1941-51 (Fellow, 1944); Montague Burton Prof. of Industrial Relations, University Coll. of S Wales and Mon, 1951-66; Dir and Prof., Econ. and Social Res. Inst., Dublin, 1968-72. Also held posts in Oxford Institute of Statistics, Nat. Institute of Economic and Social Research, Ministry of Town and Country Planning, and as Asst Editor, The Economist. Chairman: Cttee on Industrial Relations in the Electricity Supply Bd (Ireland), 1968-69; Banks Inquiry, 1970-71; Member: Commn on the Status of Women (Ireland), 1970-72; Commn on Insurance Industry (Ireland), 1970-72; Cttee on Aid to Political Parties, 1975-76. Pres., Newman Assoc., 1957-59; Chm.,

Catholic Social Guild, 1959-63; Mem., Social Welfare Commn, RC Bishops' Conf. (E&W); Vice-Pres. Assoc. of University Teachers, 1964-66. Prospective Parly candidate (Lab) Tamworth, 1938-44; Parliamentary Candidate (L): Devizes, 1964 and 1966; Abingdon, Feb. and Oct. 1974. Vice-Pres. of the Liberal Party, 1964-66. District Councillor, Vale of White Horse, 1973-. Hon. Dr of Political and Social Science, Louvain, 1963. *Publications:* Prospects of the Industrial Areas of Great Britain, 1945; Plan Your Own Industries, 1947; (ed) Further Studies in Industrial Organisation, 1948; Town and Country Planning, 1948; Economic Control, 1955; Personality and Group Relations in Industry, 1956; Christian Democracy in Western Europe, 1820-1953, 1957; The Just Wage, 1961; Under-Governed and Over-Governed, 1962; The Rules of Work, 1963; Company and Corporation—One Law?, 1965; Companies Beyond Jenkins, 1965; Wider Business Objectives, 1966; A Companies Act 1970?, 1967; (with Allen, Allen and Walters) Women in Top Jobs, 1971; Sex, Career and Family, 1971; Women and Top Jobs: the next move, 1972; Irish Entrepreneurs Speak For Themselves, 1974; Forty to Sixty, 1975; Company Responsibility and Participation—A New Agenda, 1975; Pensions—where next?, 1976. *Recreations:* swimming, walking. *Address:* Red Copse, Boars Hill, Oxford. *Club:* National Liberal.
    See also C. W. Fogarty, S. W. Fogarty.

FOGARTY, Susan Winthrop; Under-Secretary and Regional Director, West Midlands, Departments of Transport and the Environment, since 1975; *b* 16 April 1930; *d* of late Philip Christopher Fogarty and late Hilda Spenser Fogarty. *Educ:* Badminton Sch., Bristol; King's Coll., Newcastle. BA Dunelm. Joined Min. of Defence, 1951; joined Scottish Educn Dept, 1955; Private Sec. to Jt Parly Under-Sec. for Scotland, 1957-59; Principal, Scottish Educn Dept, 1959; Min. of Transport, 1960; Asst Sec. 1966; Cabinet Office, 1968; Dept of Environment, 1970; Under Sec., DoE, 1973. *Recreations:* reading history and thrillers, swimming, walking. *Address:* 401 Howard House, Dolphin Square, SW1V 3PF. *T:* 01-821 0666; 1 Edencroft, Wheeleys Road, Edgbaston, Birmingham. *T:* 021-440 2249. *Club:* Royal 2249. *Club:* Royal Commonwealth Society.
    See also C. W. Fogarty, M. P. Fogarty.

FOGEL, Prof. Robert W.; Harold Hitchings Burbank Professor of Economics and Professor of History, Harvard University, since 1975; *b* 1 July 1926; *s* of Harry G. Fogel and Elizabeth (*née* Mitnik); two *s. Educ:* Cornell, Columbia and Johns Hopkins Univs. AB Cornell 1948; AM Columbia 1960; PhD Johns Hopkins 1963. Instructor, Johns Hopkins Univ., 1958-59; Asst Prof., Univ. of Rochester, 1960-64; Assoc. Prof., Univ. of Chicago, 1964-65; Prof., Econs and History, Univ. of Chicago, 1965-75, Univ. of Rochester, 1968-75. Taussig Research Prof., Harvard Univ., 1973-74; Pitt Prof. of Amer. History and Instns, Cambridge Univ., 1975-76. Phi Beta Kappa, 1963; Arthur H. Cole Prize, 1968; Schumpeter Prize, 1971; Bancroft Prize, 1975; Fellow Econometric Soc., 1971; Fellow Amer. Acad. of Arts and Sciences, 1972; Nat. Acad. of Sciences, 1973; Fellow, RHistS, 1974. *Publications:* The Union Pacific Railroad: a case in premature enterprise, 1960; Railroads and American Economic Growth: essays in econometric history, 1964 (Spanish edn 1972); (jtly) The Reinterpretation of American Economic History, 1971 (Italian edn 1975); (jtly) The Dimension of Quantitative Research in History, 1972; (jtly) Time on the Cross: The Economics of American Negro Slavery, 1974; numerous papers in learned jls. *Address:* 50 Garden Street, Cambridge, Mass 02138, USA.

FOGG, Alan; Director, PA International Management Consultants, since 1971; *b* 19 Sept. 1921; *o s* of John Fogg, Dulwich; *m* 1948, Mary Marsh; two *s* one *d. Educ:* Repton; Exeter Coll., Oxford (MA, BSc). Served with RN, 1944-47. Special Advr, CSD, 1970. Chm., Reigate and Banstead Cons. Assoc., 1973-. *Publications:* (with Barnes, Stephens and Titman) Company Organisation: theory and practice, 1970; various papers on management subjects. *Recreations:* travel, gardening. *Address:* Albury Edge, Merstham, Surrey. *T:* Merstham 2023. *Club:* United Oxford & Cambridge University.

FOGG, Albert, CBE 1972; DSc, CEng, FIMechE; *b* 25 Feb. 1909; *o s* of late James Fogg, Bolton. *Educ:* Manchester Univ. Scientific staff, National Physical Laboratory, 1930; Director: Leyland Motor Corporation, 1964-68; British Leyland Motor Corporation Ltd, 1968-74; ENASA (Spain), 1965-74; retired. First Dir, Motor Industry Research Assoc., 1946. Inst. of Mechanical Engineers: T. Bernard Hall Prize, 1945 and 1955; Starley Premium, 1956; James Clayton Prize, 1962. Viva Shield and Gold Medal, Worshipful Company of Carmen, 1962. *Publications:* numerous papers in jls of scientific socs and professional instns. *Recreations:* sport and travel. *Address:* 5

Carisbrooke, Canford Cliffs Road, Poole, Dorset. *T:* Canford Cliffs 709862. *Club:* Royal Automobile.

FOGG, Cyril Percival, CB 1973; Director, Admiralty Surface Weapons Establishment, Ministry of Defence (Procurement Executive), 1973-75, retired; *b* 28 Nov. 1914; *s* of Henry Fogg and Mabel Mary (*née* Orton); *m* 1939, Margaret Amie Millican; two *d. Educ:* Herbert Strutt Sch., Belper; Gonville and Caius Coll., Cambridge (MA, 1st cl. Mechanical Sciences Tripos). Research Staff, General Electric Co., 1936-37; various positions in Scientific Civil Service from 1937 with Air Ministry, Ministries of Aircraft Production, Supply, Aviation and Technology. Head of Ground Radar Dept, RRE Malvern, 1956-58; Dir Electronics R&D (Ground), 1959-63; Imperial Defence Coll., 1961; Dir of Guided Weapons Research, 1963-64; Dir-Gen. of Electronics R&D, Min. of Aviation, 1964-67; Dep. Controller of Electronics, Min. of Technology, later MoD (Procurement Executive), 1967-72. *Address:* 1 Fairfield Close, Old Bosham, Chichester, West Sussex PO18 8JQ.

FOGG, Prof. Gordon Elliott, FRS 1965; Professor and Head of the Department of Marine Biology, University College of North Wales, Bangor, since 1971; *b* 26 April 1919; *s* of Rev. L. C. Fogg; *m* 1945, Elizabeth Beryl Llechid-Jones; one *s* one *d. Educ:* Dulwich Coll.; Queen Mary Coll., London; St John's Coll., Cambridge. BSc (London), 1939; PhD (Cambridge), 1943; ScD (Cambridge), 1966. Sea-weed Survey of British Isles, 1942; Plant Physiologist, Pest Control Ltd, 1943-45; successively Asst Lectr, Lectr and Reader in Botany, University Coll., London, 1945-60; Rockefeller Fellow, 1954; Prof. of Botany, Westfield Coll., Univ. of London, 1960-71. Trustee, BM (Natural Hist.), 1976-. Royal Soc. Leverhulme Vis. Prof., Kerala, 1969-70. Botanical Sec., Soc. for Experimental Biology, 1957-60; President: British Phycological Soc., 1961-62; International Phycological Soc., 1964; Inst. of Biology, 1976-; Chm. Council, Freshwater Biol Assoc., 1974-; Joint Organizing Sec., X International Botanical Congress. Visiting research worker, British Antarctic Survey, 1966, 1974; Biological Gen. Sec., British Assoc., 1967-72, Pres., Section K, 1973. Fellow, QMC, 1976. Hon. LLD Dundee, 1974. *Publications:* The Metabolism of Algae, 1953; The Growth of Plants, 1963; Algal Cultures and Phytoplankton Ecology, 1965; Photosynthesis, 1968; (jointly) The Blue-green Algae, 1973; papers in learned jls. *Recreations:* water colour painting, walking. *Address:* Marine Science Laboratories, Menai Bridge, Gwynedd; Bodolben, Llandegfan, Menai Bridge, Gwynedd. *T:* Menai Bridge 712 641. *Club:* Athenæum.

FOGGIN, (Wilhelm) Myers, CBE 1974; Principal, Trinity College of Music, London, since 1965; *b* 23 Dec. 1908; *m* 1952, Lotte Breitmeyer; one *s* one *d. Educ:* Dr Erlich's Sch., Newcastle upon Tyne; Royal Academy of Music. Concert Pianist; Prof. of Piano, RAM, 1936; Conductor, People's Palace Choral and Orchestral Soc., 1936-49. Intelligence Officer, RAF, 1940-45. Guest Conductor, Carl Rosa Opera, Sadler's Wells Opera and BBC; Dir of Opera, RAM, 1948-65; Conductor, Croydon Philharmonic Soc., 1957-73; Warden, RAM, 1949-65. Dir of Music, Queenswood Sch., 1966-; Pres., Nat. Fedn of Music Socs, 1967-72; Chm., Royal Philharmonic Soc., 1968-. Hon. FTCL, FRAM, FRCM, Hon. GSM. *Address:* 43 Northway, NW11. *T:* 01-455 7527. *Club:* Athenæum.

FOGGON, George, CMG 1961; OBE 1949 (MBE 1945); Director, London Office, International Labour Organisation, since 1976; *b* 13 Sept. 1913; *s* of Thomas Foggon, Newcastle upon Tyne; *m* 1st, 1938, Agnes McIntosh (*d* 1968); one *s*; 2nd, 1969, Audrey Blanch. Joined Min. of Labour, 1930. Served War of 1939-45 (MBE), Wing-Comdr, RAFVR, 1941-46. Seconded to FO, 1946; on staff of Mil. Gov., Berlin, 1946-49; Principal, CO, 1949; Asst Sec., W African Inter-Territorial Secretariat, Gold Coast (now Ghana), 1951-53; Comr of Labour, Nigeria, 1954-58; Labour Adviser: to Sec. of State for Colonies, 1958-61; to Sec. for Techn. Co-op., 1962-64; to Min. of Overseas Development, 1965-66; Overseas Labour Advr, FO later FCO, 1966-76. *Recreations:* walking, photography. *Address:* 8 Churton Place, SW1. *T:* 01-828 1492. *Club:* Oriental.

FOLDES, Andor; international concert pianist since 1933; Head of Piano Master Class, Conservatory, Saarbrücken, 1957-65; *b* Budapest, Hungary, 21 Dec. 1913; *s* of Emil Foldes and Valerie Foldes (*née* Ipolyi); *m* 1940, Lili Rendy (writer); no *c. Educ:* Franz Liszt Academy of Music, Budapest. Started piano playing at 5; first appeared with Budapest Philh. Orch. at 8; studied with Ernest von Dohnanyi, received Master Diploma (Fr. Liszt Acad. of Music, Budapest), 1932. Concerts all over Europe, 1933-39; US debut (NBC Orch.), 1940; toured US extensively, 1940-48. US citizen since 1948. Concerts, since, all over the world. Grand Prix du Disque, Paris, for Bartok Complete Works (piano solo), 1957. Beethoven concerts, Bonn Festival and throughout Europe. Recordings of all Beethoven Sonatas, and works of Mozart and Schubert. Order of Merit, First Class, 1956, Gr. Cross, 1964 (Germany); Commandeur, Mérite Culturel et Artistique (City of Paris), 1968; Medaille d'Argent de la Ville de Paris, 1971. *Publications:* Keys to the Keyboard, 1950; Cadenzas to Mozart Piano Concertos (W Germany); Is there a Contemporary Style of Beethoven-playing?, 1963; various piano compositions. *Relevant publication:* Wolf-Eberhard von Lewinski, Andor Foldes, 1970. *Recreations:* collecting art, reading, writing on musical subjects; swimming, hiking. *Address:* Herrliberg, near Zürich, Switzerland.

FOLEY, family name of **Baron Foley.**

FOLEY, 8th Baron *cr* 1776; **Adrian Gerald Foley;** *b* 9 Aug. 1923; *s* of 7th Baron and Minoru (*d* 1968), *d* of late H. Greenstone, South Africa; *S* father, 1927; *m* 1st, 1958, Patricia Meek (marr. diss. 1971); one *s* one *d*; 2nd, 1972, Ghislaine Lady Ashcombe. *Heir: s* Hon. Thomas Henry Foley, *b* 1 April 1961. *Address: c/o* Marbella Club, Marbella, Malaga, Spain. *Clubs:* White's, Turf.

FOLEY, Rt. Rev. Brian C.; *see* Lancaster, Bishop of, (RC).

FOLEY, Maurice (Anthony); Deputy Director General, Directorate General for Development, Commission of the European Communities, since 1973; *b* 9 Oct. 1925; *s* of Jeremiah and Agnes Foley; *m* 1952, Catherine, *d* of Patrick and Nora O'Riordan; three *s* one *d. Educ:* St Mary's Coll., Middlesbrough. Formerly: electrical fitter, youth organiser, social worker. Member: ETU, 1941-46; Transport and General Workers Union, 1948-; Royal Arsenal Co-operative Soc. MP (Lab), West Bromwich, 1963-73; Joint Parliamentary Under-Sec. of State, Dept of Economic Affairs, 1964-66; Parly Under-Secretary: Home Office, 1966-67; Royal Navy, MoD, 1967-68; FCO, 1968-70. *Address:* Commission of the European Communities, 200 rue de la Loi, 1049 Brussels, Belgium.

FOLEY-BERKELEY, family name of **Baroness Berkeley.**

FOLJAMBE, family name of **Earl of Liverpool.**

FOLKESTONE, Viscount; William Pleydell-Bouverie; *b* 5 Jan. 1955; *s* and *heir* of 8th Earl of Radnor, *qv. Address:* Longford Castle, Salisbury, Wilts. *T:* Salisbury 29732.

FOLL, Hon. Hattil Spencer; retired; *b* 31 May 1890; *s* of John Hattil and Kate Elizabeth Foll; *m* 1915; four *d* (one *s* decd). *Educ:* Clapham Collegiate Sch. Served AIF, European War, 1914-15; Home Forces, 1942-43; Minister for Repatriation and War Service Homes, Australia, 1937-39, and Minister for Health, 1938-39; Minister for the Interior, Commonwealth of Australia, 1939-41, and Minister of Information, 1940-41; Senator for Queensland, 1917-47; has served on numerous select cttees especially relating to returned soldier problems. Formerly pastoralist. *Recreations:* bowls, swimming. *Address:* 6 Arncliffe Avenue, Port Macquarie, NSW 2444, Australia. *T:* 83-1356. *Club:* Port Macquarie Bowling.

FOLLETT, Sir David (Henry), Kt 1967; MA Oxon, PhD London; FInstP; FMA; Director, Science Museum, 1960-73; *b* 5 Sept. 1907; *er s* of Septimus and Rose Annie Follett; *m* 1932, Helen Alison Wilson; three *s* decd. *Educ:* Rutlish Sch.; Brasenose Coll. (Hulme Exhibitioner); Birkbeck Coll. (post-graduate). Joined Adam Hilger Ltd, optical instrument manufacturers, 1929. Asst Keeper, Dept of Physics, Science Museum, 1937. Meteorological Branch, RAFVR, 1939. Returned to Science Museum, 1945; Deputy Keeper, Dept of Physics, 1949; Keeper of Dept of Electrical Engineering and Communications, 1957-60. Governor Imperial Coll. of Science and Technology, 1960-73; Trustee Imperial War Museum, 1960-73; Vice-Pres., Institute of Physics and Physical Soc., 1965-69; Mem., Ancient Monuments Board for England, 1966-77. *Publications:* papers in scientific jls. *Recreations:* gardening, sailing. *Address:* 3 Elm Bank Gardens, Barnes, SW13. *T:* 01-876 8302. *Club:* Athenæum.

FOLLETT, Samuel Frank, CMG 1959; BSc, CEng, FIEE, FRAeS; *b* 21 March 1904; *o s* of Samuel Charles Follett and Kate Bell; *m* 1932, Kathleen Matilda Tupper. *Educ:* Farnham Gram. Sch.; Univ. of London. Electrical Research Assoc., 1924-27; Electrical Engineering Dept, RAE Farnborough, 1927-45; Asst Dir of Instrument R&D (Electrics), Min. of Supply, 1946-50; Dir of Instrument R&D, 1950-54; Dep. Dir-Gen. Aircraft, Equipment, R&D, 1954-56; Dir.-Gen., Min. of Supply Staff, Brit. Jt Services Mission, Washington, DC, 1956-59; Dep. Dir, RAE Farnborough, 1959-63; Dep. Controller of Guided Weapons, Min. of Aviation, 1963-66; Scientific Adviser to BoT, 1966-69. *Address:* Darby Cottage, St Johns Road, Farnham, Surrey. *T:* Farnham 6610.

WW—27

FOLLOWS, Sir (Charles) Geoffry (Shield), Kt, *cr* 1951; CMG 1945; Northern Rhodesia representative on Federal Interim Public Service Commission, 1953-59; *b* 4 July 1896; *m* 1922, Claire Camille, *d* of late Julien Lemarchand. *Educ:* Wellington Sch., Som. 2nd Lieut The King's (Liverpool) Regt 1914; served in France, 1915-18, and in various Staff appts until 1920; Colonial Service, Seychelles, 1920-24; attached Colonial Office, 1925; Gibraltar, 1925-36; N Rhodesia, 1936-45; Chief Financial Adviser to Mil. Admin, Hong Kong, 1945-46; Fin. Sec., Hong Kong, 1946-52; Chm. N Rhodesia Salaries Commn, 1952; Mem. Preparatory Commn on Federation of Rhodesias and Nyasaland, 1952. *Address:* 12 Lanark Road, Salisbury, Rhodesia.

FOLLOWS, Denis, CBE 1967 (MBE 1950); Chairman, British Olympic Association, since 1977; *b* 13 April 1908; *s* of Amos Follows; *m* 1938, Mary Elizabeth Milner; two *d. Educ:* City Sch., Lincoln; Nottingham Univ. (BA). Pres., National Union of Students, 1930-32; Pres., Internat. Confedn of Students, 1932-34; Vice-Pres., 1933, Chm., 1948, Pres., 1972, Universities Athletic Union. Asst Master, Chiswick Grammar Sch. for Boys, 1932-40. Royal Air Force, Flight Lieut, 1940-46. Sec., British Airline Pilots Assoc., 1946-62. Chm., Nat. Jt Council for Civil Air Transport, 1951-52; Secretary of the FA, 1962-73. Hon. Treasurer, CCPR, 1977; Chairman: Major Spectator Sports Div. CCPR, 1973-; Sports Adv. Cttee, Nat. Assoc. of Youth Clubs, 1975-. Dir, Charlton Athletic FC, 1974-. *Recreation:* cricket. *Address:* 70 Barrowgate Road, Chiswick, W4. *T:* 01-994 5782.

FONDA, Henry; actor, USA; *b* Grand Island, Nebraska, USA, 16 May 1905; *s* of William Brace Fonda and Herberta Jaynes; *m* 1965, Shirlee Adams; one *s* two *d* of previous *m. Educ:* University of Minnesota, Minneapolis, Minn. Began acting at Omaha Community Playhouse, Nebraska; subseq. played many parts with touring companies. Made first appearance on New York stage, Guild Theatre, 1929; *stage appearances include:* The Farmer Takes a Wife, 46th Street, 1934; Mister Roberts, Alvin, 1948; Point of No Return, Alvin, 1951; Caine Mutiny Court Martial, Plymouth, 1954; Two for the Seesaw, 1958; Critics' Choice; Silent Night, Lonely Night; A Gift of Time, 1962; Generation, 1965; Our Town; The Time of Your Life; Clarence Darrow (USA and London, 1975). Entered films, 1935; *films include:* Jesse James, Grapes of Wrath, Mister Roberts, The Wrong Man, 12 Angry Men (also produced), Warlock, The Best Man, A Big Hand for the Little Lady, Trail of the Lonesome Pine, You Only Live Once, Young Mr Lincoln, The Lady Eve, The Ox Bow Incident, The Male Animal, My Darling Clementine, The Rounders, Madigan, Yours, Mine and Ours, The Boston Strangler, Once upon a Time... in the West, Too Late the Hero, There Was a Crooked Man, The Cheyenne Social Club, Sometimes a Great Notion, The Serpent, The Red Pony, Ash Wednesday, My Name is Nobody, Mussolini—The Last Days, Midway, Rollercoaster, Last of the Cowboys, Fedora. Served USN, 1942-45. Hon. DHL, Ursinus Coll., 1966. *Address:* c/o John Springer, 667 Madison Avenue, NYC, USA.

FONTAINE, André Lucien Georges; Chief Editor, le Monde, Paris, since 1969; *b* 30 March 1921; *s* of Georges Fontaine and Blanche Rochon Duvigneaud; *m* 1943, Belita Cavaillé; two *s* one *d. Educ:* Paris Univ. (diplomes études supérieures droit public et économie politique, lic.lettres). Joined Temps Present, 1946; with le Monde from 1947; Foreign Editor, 1951. Comdr, Italian Merit; Officer, Orders of Vasa (Sweden) and Lion (Finland); Kt, Danebrog (Denmark) and Crown of Belgium; Order of Tudor Vladimirescu (Romania). *Publications:* L'Alliance atlantique à l'heure du dégel, 1960; Histoire de la guerre froide, vol. 1 1965, vol. 2 1966 (English trans., History of the Cold War, 1966 and 1967); La Guerre civile froide, 1969; Le dernier quart du siècle, 1976; contrib. Foreign Affairs, Affari Esteri, Europa Archiv, etc. *Address:* 6 rue Gounod, 75017 Paris, France. *T:* 246-72-23.

FONTANNE, Lynn; actress; *m* Alfred Lunt (*d* 1977), actor. Began as child in pantomime in Drury Lane; walked on in various London companies with Lewis Waller, Beerbohm Tree, Lena Ashwell; played in touring company with Weedon Grossmith for few seasons, playing name part in Young Lady of 17 and other small parts in various curtain raisers; on tour in Milestones, then revival in London; small parts in My Lady's Dress; then America; many plays with Laurette Taylor; name part in Dulcy, followed by many leads including Goat Song, Strange Interlude, Second Man, Caprice, At Mrs Beams, Pygmalion, The Guardsman, Meteor, Design for Living, Point Valaine, Taming of the Shrew, Idiot's Delight; Amphytrion 38 (NY and London), 1938; There Shall Be No Night (NY and London), 1943; Love in Idleness (O Mistress Mine, in New York); Quadrille (London), 1952; The Great Sebastians (NY), 1956; The Visit (London), 1960; The Sea Gull. Presidential Medal of Freedom, 1964; Antoinette Perry Award; Emmy Award. Holds hon. degrees from 12 universities and colleges.

FONTEYN, Dame Margot; *see* Arias, Dame Margot Fonteyn de.

FOOKES, Janet Evelyn; MP (C) Plymouth, Drake, since 1974 (Merton and Morden, 1970-74); *b* 21 Feb. 1936; *d* of Lewis Aylmer Fookes and Evelyn Margery Fookes (*née* Holmes). *Educ:* Hastings and St Leonards Ladies' Coll.; High Sch. for Girls, Hastings; Royal Holloway Coll., Univ. of London (BA Hons). Teacher, 1958-70. Councillor for County Borough of Hastings, 1960-61 and 1963-70 (Chm. Educn Cttee, 1967-70). Mem., Speaker's Panel of Chairmen, 1976-. Secretary: Cons. Parly Educn Cttee, 1971-75; Parly Animal Welfare Gp., 1974-; Chm. Educn, Arts and Home Affairs Sub-Cttee of the Expenditure Cttee, 1975-; Member: Unopposed Bills Cttee, 1973-75; Services Cttee, 1974-76; Chm., Cons. West Country Mems Cttee, 1976-77, Vice-Chm., 1977. Mem., Nat. Art Collections Fund. *Recreations:* riding, dancing. *Address:* House of Commons, SW1A 0AA; Delphia, 11 Branksome Road, St Leonards-on-Sea TN38 0UA. *T:* Hastings 424108. *Club:* Royal Over-Seas League.

FOOKS, Sir Raymond (Hatherell), Kt 1954; CBE 1949; KPM 1945; Chief Constable of Lincolnshire, 1934-54; *b* 23 June 1888; *s* of late W. H. Fooks, Cerne Abbas, Dorset, and Leigh-on-Sea, Essex; *m* 1st, 1922, Mary Gwendoline (*d* 1926), *d* of late Francis William Baily, Bishopstoke, Hants; one *s* one *d*; 2nd, 1935, Madeline Player (*d* 1953), *widow* of Lieut-Col R. D. Crosby, OBE, MC, The Royal Lincolnshire Regt; 3rd, 1954, Hon. Mrs Mary Josephine Bruce, *widow* of E. H. Bruce, Indian Police Service, and *e d* of 1st Baron Riverdale, GBE, LLD, JP. *Educ:* King Edward VI Sch., and University Coll., Southampton; Exeter Coll., Oxford. BA (London), 1908; MA (Oxford), 1933. Joined Indian Police Service, 1908; Supt, Punjab, 1919-31; served on NW Frontier of India in European War, 1914-19 (despatches); Deputy Inspector-Gen., 1931-33; retired, 1933. Barrister, Inner Temple, 1933. Deputy Pres. of the North Lincs Branch, British Red Cross Soc., 1959-60 (County Dir, 1954-58); DL County of Lincoln, 1956-59. *Recreations:* gardening and study. *Address:* Broom Hill Copse, Boar's Hill, Oxford. *T:* 35401. *Clubs:* Athenæum, Lansdowne.

FOOT, family name of **Baron Caradon** and **Baron Foot.**

FOOT, Baron *cr* 1967 (Life Peer), of Buckland Monachorum; **John Mackintosh Foot;** Senior Partner, Foot & Bowden, Solicitors, Plymouth; Chairman, United Kingdom Immigrants Advisory Service, since 1970; *b* 17 Feb. 1909; 3rd *s* of late Rt Hon. Isaac Foot, PC and Eva Mackintosh; *m* 1936, Anne, *d* of Dr Clifford Bailey Farr, Bryn Mawr, Pa; one *s* one *d*. *Educ:* Forres Sch., Swanage; Bembridge Sch., IoW; Balliol Coll., Oxford. Pres., Oxford Union, 1931; Pres., OU Liberal Club, 1931; BA Oxon (2nd cl. hons Jurisprudence), 1931. Admitted Solicitor, 1934. Served in Army, 1939-45 (Hon. Major); jsc 1944. Contested (L); Basingstoke, 1934 and 1935; Bodmin, 1945 and 1950. Member: Dartmoor National Park Cttee, 1963-74; Commn on the Constitution, 1969-73. *Recreations:* chess, crosswords, defending Dartmoor. *Address:* Yew Tree, Crapstone, Yelverton, Devon. *T:* Yelverton 3417. *Club:* Royal Western Yacht.
See also Baron Caradon, Rt Hon. Sir Dingle Foot, Rt Hon. Michael Foot.

FOOT, Rt. Hon. Sir Dingle (Mackintosh), PC 1967; Kt 1964; QC 1954; *e s* of late Rt. Hon. Isaac Foot; *b* Plymouth, 1905; *m* 1933, Dorothy Mary, *er d* of late William Rowley Elliston, TD, LLB and Ethel Mary Walton, *niece* of Sir Frederick Wilson, Felixstowe (DL Suffolk, MP for Mid Norfolk, 1895). *Educ:* Bembridge Sch., Isle of Wight; Balliol Coll., Oxford. MA Oxon 1960. Pres., Oxford Univ. Liberal Club, 1927; Pres., Oxford Union Soc., 1928; contested Tiverton Div. of Devon, 1929; Dundee, 1945; North Cornwall, 1950 and 1951; MP (L) Dundee, 1931-45; Parliamentary Sec., Min. of Economic Warfare, 1940-45; joined the Labour Party, July 1956; MP (Lab) Ipswich, Oct. 1957-70; Solicitor-Gen., 1964-67. Led British Economic Warfare Delegn to Switzerland, 1945; Mem. of British Delegn to San Francisco Conf., 1945. Called to Bar, Gray's Inn, 1930; Bencher, 1952; Treasurer, 1968; Vice-Treasurer, 1969. Western Circuit. Admitted to Gold Coast Roll of Legal Practitioners, 1948; to Ceylon Roll of Advocates, 1951; to Nigerian Bar, 1955; to Northern Rhodesian Bar, 1956; to Sierra Leone Bar, 1959; to Supreme Court of India (as a Senior Advocate), 1960; to Bahrain Roll of Legal Practitioners, 1962; to Malaya Roll of Legal Practitioners, 1964; to S Rhodesia Roll of Legal Practitioners, 1964, to Northern Ireland Bar, 1970. Has also appeared in courts of Kenya, Uganda, Tanganyika, Nyasaland, Pakistan, Hong Kong, and before Commn of Human Rights at Strasbourg. Chm., Observer Trust, 1953-55. Chm., Soc. of Labour Lawyers, 1960-64. Commander, Order of the Cedars, Lebanon, 1969. Hon. LLD Dundee, 1974.

Publication: British Political Crises, 1976. *Recreation:* football fan. *Address:* 2 Paper Buildings, Temple, EC4. *T:* 01-353 9119. *Clubs:* Garrick, Beefsteak.
See also Baron Caradon, Baron Foot, Rt Hon. Michael Foot.

FOOT, Rt. Hon. Michael, PC 1974; MP (Lab) Ebbw Vale Division of Monmouthshire since Nov. 1960; Lord President of the Council and Leader of the House of Commons, since 1976; Deputy Leader of the Labour Party, since 1976; *b* 23 July 1913; *s* of late Rt Hon. Isaac Foot, PC; *m* 1949, Jill Craigie. *Educ:* Forres Sch., Swanage; Leighton Park Sch., Reading; Wadham Coll., Oxford (Exhibitioner). Pres. Oxford Union, 1933; contested (Lab) Mon, 1935; MP (Lab) Devonport Div. of Plymouth, 1945-55. Sec. of State for Employment, 1974-76. Mem., Labour Party Nat. Exec. Cttee, 1971-. Asst Editor, Tribune, 1937-38; Acting Editor, Evening Standard, 1942; Man. Dir, Tribune, 1945-74, Editor, 1948-52, 1955-60; political columnist on the Daily Herald, 1944-64; former Book Critic, Evening Standard. Hon. Fellow, Wadham Coll. 1969. *Publications:* Guilty Men (with Frank Owen and Peter Howard), 1938; Armistice 1918-39, 1940; Trial of Mussolini, 1943; Brendan and Beverley, 1944; Still at Large, 1950; Full Speed Ahead, 1950; Guilty Men (with Mervyn Jones), 1957; The Pen and the Sword, 1957; Parliament in Danger, 1959; Aneurin Bevan: Vol. I, 1897-1945, 1962; Vol. II, 1945-60, 1973. *Recreations:* Plymouth Argyle supporter, chess, reading, walking. *Address:* House of Commons, SW1.
See also Baron Caradon, Baron Foot, Rt Hon. Sir Dingle Foot.

FOOT, Michael Richard Daniell; historian; *b* 14 Dec. 1919; *s* of late R. C. Foot and Nina (*née* Raymond); *m* twice; one *s* one *d*; 3rd, 1972, Mirjam Michaela, *y d* of Prof. C. P. M. Romme, Leiden. *Educ:* Winchester (scholar); New Coll., Oxford (scholar). Served in Army, 1939-45 (Major RA, parachutist, wounded). Taught at Oxford, 1947-59; research, 1959-67; Prof of Modern Hist., Manchester, 1967-73; Dir of Studies, European Discussion Centre, 1973-74. French Croix de Guerre, 1945. *Publications:* Gladstone and Liberalism (with J. L. Hammond), 1952; British Foreign Policy since 1898, 1956; Men in Uniform, 1961; SOE in France, 1966; (ed) The Gladstone Diaries: vols I and II, 1825-1839, 1968; (ed) War and Society, 1973; (ed with Dr H. C. G. Matthew) The Gladstone Diaries: vols III and IV, 1840-1854, 1975; Resistance, 1976. *Recreations:* reading, talking. *Address:* 88 Heath View, N2 0QB. *Clubs:* Savile, Special Forces.

FOOT, Paul Mackintosh; writer; journalist; with The Socialist Worker, since 1972 (Editor, 1974-75); *b* 8 Nov. 1937; *m*; two *s*. Editor of Isis, 1961; President of the Oxford Union, 1961. TUC delegate from Nat. Union of Journalists, 1967 and 1971. Contested (Socialist Workers Party) Birmingham, Stechford, March 1977. *Publications:* Immigration and Race in British Politics, 1965; The Politics of Harold Wilson, 1968; The Rise of Enoch Powell, 1969; Who Killed Hanratty?, 1971; Why You Should Be a Socialist, 1977. *Address:* c/o The Socialist Worker, Corbridge Crescent, Corbridge Works, E2.

FOOT, Mrs Philippa Ruth, FBA 1976; Senior Research Fellow, Somerville College, Oxford, since 1970; Professor in Residence, University of California at Los Angeles, since 1974; *b* 3 Oct. 1920; *d* of William Sydney Bence Bosanquet, DSO, and Esther Cleveland Bosanquet, *d* of Grover Cleveland, Pres. of USA; *m* 1945, M. R. D. Foot (marr. diss. 1960), *qv*; no *c*. *Educ:* St George's Sch., Ascot; privately; Somerville Coll., Oxford (BA 1942, MA 1946). Somerville Coll., Oxford: Lectr in philosophy, 1947; Fellow and Tutor, 1950-69; Vice-Principal, 1967-69. Formerly Vis. Prof., Cornell Univ., MIT, Berkeley and Princeton. *Publications:* Theories of Ethics (ed), 1967; articles in Mind, Aristotelian Soc. Proc., Philos. Rev., New York Rev. *Address:* 15 Walton Street, Oxford. *T:* Oxford 57130.

FOOTE, Maj.-Gen. Henry Robert Bowreman, VC 1944; CB 1952; DSO 1942; *b* 5 Dec. 1904; *s* of Lieut-Col H. B. Foote, late RA; *m* 1944, Anita Flint Howard (*d* 1970). *Educ:* Bedford Sch. Royal Tank Corps; 2nd Lieut, 1925; Lieut, 1927; Capt., 1936; Staff Coll., 1939; GSO3, WO, 1939; GSO2, WO, 1940; GSO2, Staff Coll., 1940-41; GSO1, 10th Armd Div., 1941-42; OC 7th Royal Tank Regt, 1942; Subst. Major, 1942; GSO1, AFHQ, Italy, 1944; 2i/c, 9th Armd Bde, 1945; Brig. RAC, MELF, 1945-47; Subst. Lieut-Col, 1946; Subst. Col, 1948; OC 2nd Royal Tank Regt, 1947-48; OC Automotive Wing, Fighting Vehicles Proving Establishment, Ministry of Supply, 1948-49; Comd 7th Armd Bde, 1949-50; Maj.-Gen. 1951; Comd 11th Armoured Div., 1950-53; Dir-Gen. of Fighting Vehicles, Min. of Supply, 1953-55; Dir, Royal Armoured Corps, at the War Office, 1955-58; retd. *Address:* Furzfield, West Chiltington Common, Pulborough, West Sussex. *Club:* Army and Navy.

FOOTE, Rev. John Weir, VC 1946; DD, LLD University of Western Ontario, 1947; Minister of Reform Institutions, Government of Ontario, 1950-57; *b* 5 May 1904; *s* of Gordon Foote, Madoc, Ontario; *m* 1929. *Educ:* University of Western Ontario, London, Ont; Presbyterian Coll. (McGill). Served War of 1939-45; Regimental Chaplain with Royal Hamilton Light Infantry (VC). Minister St Paul's Presbyterian Church, Port Hope, Ont. Canadian Army from 1939, Asst Principal Chaplain (P). *Recreations:* golf, fishing. *Address:* Front Road East, Coburg, Ontario, Canada.

FOOTE, Prof. Peter Godfrey; Professor of Scandinavian Studies, University College, London, since 1963; *b* 26 May 1924; 4th *s* of late T. Foote and Ellen Foote, Swanage, Dorset; *m* 1951, Eleanor Jessie McCaig, *d* of late J. M. McCaig and of Margaret H. McCaig; one *s* two *d. Educ:* Grammar Sch., Swanage; University Coll., Exeter; Univ. of Oslo; University Coll., London. BA London 1948; MA London 1951; Fil. dr *hc* Uppsala, 1972. Served with RNVR, 1943-46. Asst Lectr, Lectr and Reader in Old Scandinavian, University Coll., London, 1950-63. Jt Sec., Viking Soc., 1956-, Pres., 1974-76. Member: Royal Gustav Adolfs Academy, Uppsala, 1967; Kungl. Humanistiska Vetenskapssamfundet, Uppsala, 1968; Vísindafélag Islands, 1969; Vetenskapssocieteten, Lund, 1973; Hon. Mem., Isl. Bókmenntafélag, 1965; Pjodvinafélag Isl. í Vesturheimi, 1975; Corresp. Mem., Kungl. Vitterhets Hist. och Antikvitets Akad., Stockholm, 1971. Crabtree Orator, 1968. Commander, Icelandic Order of the Falcon, 1973; Comdr, Royal Order of North Star (Sweden), 1977. *Publications:* Gunnlaugs saga ormstungu, 1957; Pseudo-Turpin Chronicle in Iceland, 1959; Laing's Heimskringla, 1961; Lives of Saints: Icelandic manuscripts in fascimile IV, 1962; (with G. Johnston) The Saga of Gisli, 1963; (with D. M. Wilson) The Viking Achievement, 1970; Jt Editor, Saga Book of Viking Society and Mediæval Scandinavia; Mem. of Ed. Board, Scandinavica; papers in Saga-Book, Arv, Studia Islandica, Islenzk Tunga, etc. *Recreations:* bell-ringing, walking. *Address:* 18 Talbot Road, N6. *T:* 01-340 1860. *Club:* Athenæum.

FOOTMAN, Charles Worthington Fowden, CMG 1952; *b* 3 Sept. 1905; *s* of Rev. William Llewellyn and Mary Elizabeth Footman; *m* 1947, Joyce Marcelle Law; one *s* two *d. Educ:* Rossall Sch.; Keble Coll., Oxford. Colonial Administrative Service, Zanzibar, 1930; seconded to East African Governors' Conference, 1942; seconded to Colonial Office, 1943-46; Financial Sec., Nyasaland, 1947; Chief Sec., Nyasaland, 1951-60. Retired from HM Overseas Civil Service, 1960. Chm., Public Service Commissions, Tanganyika and Zanzibar, 1960-61; Commonwealth Relations Office, 1962-64; Min. of Overseas Development, 1964-70. *Recreations:* golf and tennis. *Address:* c/o National Westminster Bank, Worthing, West Sussex.

FOOTMAN, David John, CMG 1950; MC 1916; MA 1953; *b* 17 Sept. 1895; *s* of Rev. John Footman and Ella Mary (*née* Kennard); *m* 1927, Joan Isabel (marr. diss. 1936; she *d* 1960), *d* of Edmund Footman; no *c. Educ:* Marlborough; New Coll., Oxford. European War, 1914-19, Royal Berks Regt. Levant Consular Service, 1919-29; Foreign Office, 1935-53; Fellow of St Antony's Coll., Oxford, 1953-63, Emeritus Fellow, 1963-. *Publications:* Half-way East, 1935; Pig and Pepper, 1936; Pemberton, 1943; Red Prelude, 1944; The Primrose Path, 1946; Civil War in Russia, 1961; The Russian Revolutions, 1962; Dead Yesterday, 1974. *Address:* 11a Collingham Gardens, SW5. *Club:* Naval and Military.

FOOTS, Sir James (William), Kt 1975; mining engineer; Chairman, MIM Holdings Ltd and Mount Isa Mines Ltd, Queensland, since 1970; Director: Bank of New South Wales; Thiess Holdings Ltd; *b* 1916; *m* 1939, Thora H. Thomas; one *s* two *d. Educ:* Melbourne Univ. (BME). Mem., Federal Govt's Economic Consultative Gp. Pres., Austr. Inst. Mining and Metallurgy, 1974; Pres., Austr. Mining Industry Council, 1974 and 1975. Fellow, Australian Acad. of Technol Scis. Mem. Senate, Univ. of Queensland, 1970. *Address:* GPO Box 1433, Brisbane, Qld 4001, Australia.

FORBES, family name of **Baron Forbes** and of **Earl of Granard.**

FORBES, 22nd Baron *cr* 1442 or before; **Nigel Ivan Forbes,** KBE 1960; JP; DL; Premier Baron of Scotland; Representative Peer of Scotland, 1955-63; Major (retired) Grenadier Guards; Director: Grampian Television Ltd; Sibbald Travel Agency Ltd; Chairman: Scottish Branch, National Playing Fields Association; Rolawn (Turf Growers) Ltd; *b* 19 Feb. 1918; *o s* of 21st Baron and Lady Mabel Anson (*d* 1972), *d* of 3rd Earl of Lichfield; *S* father, 1953; *m* 1942, Hon. Rosemary Katharine Hamilton-Russell, *o d* of 9th Viscount Boyne; two *s* one *d. Educ:* Harrow; RMC Sandhurst. Served War of 1939-45 (wounded);

Adjt, Grenadier Guards, Staff Coll. Military Asst to High Comr for Palestine, 1947-48. Minister of State, Scottish Office, 1958-59. Member: Inter-Parly Union Delegn to Denmark, 1956; Commonwealth Parly Assoc. Delegn to Canada, 1961; Parly Delegn to Pakistan, 1962; Inter-Parly Union Delegn to Hungary, 1965; Inter-Parly Union Delegn to Ethiopia, 1971. Mem., Aberdeen and District Milk Marketing Bd, 1962-72; Mem. Alford District Council, 1955-58; Chm., River Don District Bd, 1962-73. Pres. Royal Highland and Agricultural Society of Scotland, 1958-59; Scottish Council, Scout Assoc., 1970-; Member: Sports Council for Scotland, 1966-71; Scottish Cttee, Nature Conservancy, 1961-67; Institute of Directors. Dep. Chm., Tennant Caledonian Breweries Ltd, 1964-74. DL Aberdeenshire, 1958. *Heir: s* Master of Forbes, *qv. Address:* Balforbes, Alford, Aberdeenshire. *T:* Whitehouse 216. *Club:* Army and Navy.

FORBES, Master of; Hon. Malcolm Nigel Forbes; Financial Director; *b* 6 May 1946; *s* and *heir* of 22nd Baron Forbes, *qv*; *m* 1969, Carole Jennifer Andrée, *d* of N. S. Whitehead, Aberdeen; one *s* one *d. Educ:* Eton; Aberdeen Univ. Director, Instock Disposables Ltd, 1974-. *Address:* Finzeauch, Whitehouse, Alford, Aberdeenshire. *T:* Whitehouse 209. *Club:* Royal Northern (Aberdeen).

FORBES, Hon. Sir Alastair (Granville), Kt 1960; President, Pensions Appeal Tribunals for England and Wales, since 1973 (a Chairman, 1965-73); President, Courts of Appeal for St Helena, Falkland Islands and British Antarctic Territories, since 1965, and Gibraltar, since 1970; *b* 3 Jan. 1908; *s* of Granville Forbes and Constance Margaret (*née* Davis); *m* 1936, Constance Irene Mary Hughes-White; two *d. Educ:* Blundell's Sch.; Clare Coll., Cambridge. Called to the Bar, Gray's Inn, 1932; Magistrate and Govt Officer, Dominica, BWI, 1936; Crown Attorney, Dominica, 1939; Resident Magistrate, Fiji, 1940; Crown Counsel, Fiji, 1942; Solicitor-Gen., Fiji, and Asst Legal Adviser, Western Pacific High Commission, 1945; Legal Draftsman, Federation of Malaya, 1947; Solicitor-Gen., Northern Rhodesia, 1950; Permanent Sec., Ministry of Justice, and Solicitor-Gen., Gold Coast, 1951; Puisne Judge, Kenya, 1956; Justice of Appeal, Court of Appeal for Eastern Africa, 1957; Vice-Pres., Court of Appeal for Eastern Africa, 1958; Federal Justice, Federal Supreme Court of Rhodesia and Nyasaland, 1963-64; Pres., Ct of Appeal for Seychelles, 1965-76. Mem., Panel of Chairmen of Industrial Tribunals (England and Wales), 1965-73; Chairman: Constituencies Delimitation Commissions, N Rhodesia, 1962 and 1963, and Bechuanaland, 1964; Gibraltar Riot Inquiry, 1968. *Publications:* Index of the Laws, Dominica, 1940; Revised Edition of Laws of Fiji, 1944. *Recreations:* fishing, shooting. *Address:* Beeches, Marnhull, Sturminster Newton, Dorset. *T:* Marnhull 458. *Club:* Royal Commonwealth Society.

FORBES, Sir Archibald (Finlayson), GBE 1957; Kt 1943; Chartered Accountant; President: Midland Bank Ltd, since 1975 (Chairman, 1964-75); Spillers Ltd, since 1969 (Chairman, 1965-68); Chairman, The Debenture Corporation Ltd, since 1949; Director of other companies; *b* 6 March 1903; *s* of late Charles Forbes, Johnstone, Renfrewshire; *m* 1943, Angela Gertrude (*d* 1969), *o d* of late Horace Ely, Arlington House, SW1; one *s* two *d. Educ:* Paisley; Glasgow Univ. Formerly Mem. of firm of Thomson McLintock & Co., Chartered Accountants. Joined Spillers Ltd as Executive Dir, 1935. Mem. of various Reorganisation Commns and Cttees appointed by Minister of Agriculture, 1932-39; Dir of Capital Finance, Air Min., 1940; Deputy Sec., Min. of Aircraft Production, 1940-43; Controller of Repair, Equipment and Overseas Supplies, 1943-45 (incl. Operational Control, no 41 and 43 Gps, RAF); Mem. of Aircraft Supply Council, 1943-45; Chairman: First Iron and Steel Board from its formation, 1946, to dissolution 1949; Iron and Steel Board from its inception under the Iron and Steel Act, 1953, until 1959; British Millers' Mutual Pool Ltd, 1952-62 (Dep. Chm. 1940-52); Central Mining and Investment Corp., 1959-64; Midland and International Banks Ltd, 1964-76. Pres., FBI, 1951-53; Chm., Cttee of London Clearing Bankers, 1970-72 (Dep. Chm., 1968-70); Pres., British Bankers' Assoc., 1970-71, 1971-72 (Vice-Pres. 1969-70). Member: Cttee to enquire into Financial Structure of Colonial Develt Corp., 1959; Review Body on Doctors' and Dentists' Remuneration, 1962-65. Hon. JDipMA. *Recreations:* golf and fishing. *Address:* 40 Orchard Court, Portman Square, W1. *T:* 01-935 9304; Mattingley Green Cottage, Mattingley, Hants. *T:* Heckfield 247. *Clubs:* Brooks's, Pratt's, Beefsteak.

FORBES, Bryan; *b* 22 July 1926; *m* 1955, Nanette Newman, actress; two *d. Educ:* West Ham Secondary Sch. Studied at RADA, 1941; entered acting profession, 1942, and (apart from war service) was on West End stage, then in films here and in Hollywood, 1948-60. Formed Beaver Films with Richard

Attenborough, 1959; wrote and co-produced The Angry Silence, 1960. Subseq. wrote, dir. and prod. numerous films; *films include:* The League of Gentlemen, Only Two Can Play, Whistle Down the Wind, 1961; The L-Shaped Room, 1962; Séance on a Wet Afternoon, 1963; King Rat (in Hollywood), 1964; The Wrong Box, 1965; The Whisperers, 1966; Deadfall, 1967; The Madwoman of Chaillot, 1968; The Raging Moon, 1970; The Tales of Beatrix Potter; The Stepford Wives, 1974 (USA); The Slipper and the Rose, 1975 (Royal Film Perf., 1976); (narrator) I am a Dancer. Produced and directed: Edith Evans, I Caught Acting Like the Measles, Yorkshire TV, 1973; Elton John, Goodbye Norma Jean and Other Things, ATV 1973. Man. Dir and Head of Production, ABPC Studios, 1969-71; Man. Dir and Chief Exec., EMI-MGM, Elstree Studios, 1970-71; Dir, Capital Radio Ltd, 1973-. Won British Academy Award, 1960; Writers' Guild Award (twice); numerous internat. awards. Member: BBC Gen. Adv. Council, 1966-69; BBC Schs Council, 1971-73; Trustee, Writers' Guild of GB. *Publications:* Truth Lies Sleeping, 1950 (paperback, 1961); The Distant Laughter, 1972 (paperback, 1973); Notes for a Life, 1974 (paperback, 1977); The Slipper and the Rose, 1976; Ned's Girl: biography of Dame Edith Evans, 1977; contribs to: The Spectator, New Statesman, Queen, and other periodicals. *Recreations:* running a bookshop, reading, landscape gardening, photography. *Address:* The Bookshop, Virginia Water, Surrey.

FORBES of Pitsligo, Sir Charles Edward Stuart-, 12th Bt *cr* 1626; Building contractor, retired; *b* 6 Aug. 1903; *s* of Sir Charles Hay Hepburn Stuart-Forbes, 10th Bt, and Ellen, *d* of Capt. Huntley; *S* brother, 1937; *m* 1966, Ijah Leah MacCabe (*d* 1974), Wellington, NZ. *Educ:* Ocean Bay Coll. *Recreations:* motoring, football, cricket, hockey, swimming, deep sea fishing, hunting, rowing, launching, tennis. *Heir: n* William Daniel Stuart-Forbes [*b* 21 Aug. 1935; *m* 1956, Jannette MacDonald; three *s* two *d*]. *Address:* 33 Dillons Point Road, Blenheim, South Island, NZ.

FORBES, Charles Harington Gordon, CBE 1965 (OBE 1941); Registrar, Principal Probate Registry, Somerset House, 1946-64; *b* 20 Feb. 1896; *s* of Harington G. Forbes, OBE; *m* 1927, Jean J. Beith; one *d. Educ:* Malvern Coll. Entered service of Principal Probate Registry, 1914. Served European War, 1914-18, with The Honourable Artillery Company. *Address:* Chetwynd, Watermill Lane, Bexhill-on-Sea, East Sussex.

FORBES, Colin, RDI 1974; Partner, Pentagram Design, since 1972; *b* 6 March 1928; *s* of Kathleen and John Forbes; *m* 1961, Wendy Schneider; one *s* two *d. Educ:* Sir Anthony Browne's, Brentwood; LCC Central Sch. of Arts and Crafts. Design Asst, Herbert Spencer, 1952; freelance practice and Lectr, LCC Central Sch. of Arts and Crafts, 1953-57; Art Dir, Stuart Advertising, London, 1957-58; Head of Graphic Design Dept, LCC Central Sch. of Arts and Crafts, 1958-61; freelance practice, London, 1961-62; Partner: Fletcher/Forbes/Gill, 1962-65; Crosby/Fletcher/Forbes, 1965-72. Mem., Alliance Graphique Internationale, 1965 (Internat. Pres. 1976). *Publications:* Graphic Design: visual comparisons, 1963; A Sign Systems Manual, 1970; Creativity and Communication, 1971; New Alphabets A to Z, 1973. *Address:* Stockwell Hall, Little Burstead, Billericay, Essex. *T:* Billericay 53917.

FORBES, Donald James, MA; Headmaster, Merchiston Castle School, since 1969; *b* 6 Feb. 1921; *s* of Andrew Forbes; *m* 1945, Patricia Muriel Yeo; two *s* one *d. Educ:* Oundle; Clare Coll., Cambridge (Mod. Lang. Tripos). Capt. Scots Guards, 1941-46; 1st Bn Scots Guards, 1942-46, N Africa, Italy. Asst Master, Dulwich Coll., 1946-55; Master i/c cricket, 1951-55; Headmaster, Dauntsey's Sch., 1956-69. Diploma in Spanish, Univ. of Santander, 1954; Lectr in Spanish, West Norwood Tech. Coll., 1954-55. *Recreations:* cricket, Rugby football, tennis, Rugby fives; history, literature; instrumental and choral music. *Address:* Merchiston Castle School, Colinton, Edinburgh EH13 0PU; Breachacha Castle, Isle of Coll. *Clubs:* Hawks (Cambridge); New (Edinburgh); HCEG (Muirfield).

FORBES of Brux, Hon. Sir Ewan, 11th Bt *cr* 1630, of Craigievar; JP; landowner and farmer; *b* 6 Sept. 1912; 2nd *s* of Sir John Forbes-Sempill, 9th Bt (Forbes) of Craigievar, 18th Lord Sempill; *S* (to Btcy) brother, 1965; *m* 1952, Isabella, *d* of A. Mitchell, Glenrinnes, Banffshire. *Educ:* Dresden; Univ. of Munich; Univ. of Aberdeen. MB, ChB 1944. Senior Casualty Officer, Aberdeen Royal Infirmary, 1944-45; Medical Practitioner, Alford, Aberdeenshire, 1945-55. JP Aberdeenshire, 1969. *Recreations:* shooting, fishing, ski-ing and skating. *Heir: kinsman* John Alexander Cumnock Forbes-Sempill [*b* 29 Aug. 1927; *m* 1st, 1958, Penelope Margaret Ann (marr. diss. 1964), *d* of A. G. Grey-Pennington; 2nd, 1966, Jane Carolyn, *o d* of C. Gordon Evans]. *Address:* Brux Lodge, Alford, Aberdeenshire.

T: Kildrummy 223.
See also Lady Sempill.

FORBES, Dr Gilbert; Regius Professor of Forensic Medicine, University of Glasgow, 1964-74; *b* 5 Aug. 1908; *s* of late George and Jane Gilbert Forbes; *m* 1938, Marian Margaret Macrae Guthrie, Springfield, Fife; one *d. Educ:* Hillhead High Sch., Glasgow; Glasgow Univ. (BSc). MB, ChB Glasgow, 1933; Brunton Memorial Prize, 1933; FRFPSG 1935; FRCSE 1935; MD 1945. House posts at Western Infirmary, Glasgow, 1933-34; Demonstrator in Anatomy, University of Glasgow, 1934-36; Lecturer in Anatomy, University of Aberdeen, 1936-37; Police Surgeon to City of Sheffield and Lecturer in Forensic Medicine, University of Sheffield, 1937-48; Senior Lectr in Forensic Medicine, Univ. of Sheffield, 1948-56; Reader in Forensic Medicine, Univ. of Sheffield, 1956-64. Asst Deputy Coroner to City of Sheffield, 1945-59. At various times external examiner in forensic medicine in Univs of Manchester, Birmingham, Leeds, Glasgow, Aberdeen and Edinburgh. *Publications:* original papers on medico-legal subjects in medical and scientific journals. *Recreation:* motoring. *Address:* Tuctaway, School Lane, Canwick, Lincoln. *T:* Lincoln 31017.

FORBES, Hon. Sir Hugh (Harry Valentine), Kt 1970; **Hon. Mr Justice Forbes;** a Judge of the High Court, Queen's Bench Division, since 1970; an Additional Judge of the Employment Appeal Tribunal, since 1976; *b* 14 Feb. 1917; *e s* of late Rev. H. N. Forbes, sometime Rector of Castle Bromwich; *m* 1st, 1940, Julia Margaret (marr. diss. 1970), *yr d* of Frank Gilbert Weller; one *s* two *d*; 2nd, 1970, Janet Moir, *o d* of Campbell Andrews, MD, Harrow. *Educ:* Rossall; Trinity Hall, Cambridge (1st cl. Law). Served War of 1939-45: Major, Gordon Highlanders; GSO2 War Office and GHQ India. Called to Bar, Middle Temple, 1946; QC 1966; Bencher, 1970. Chm., Lincs (Kesteven) QS, 1967-71 (Dep. Chm., 1961-67); Dep. Chm., Hunts and Peterborough QS, 1965-70. Chancellor: Dio. of Ely, 1965-69; Dio. of Chelmsford, 1969. Chm. Council, Royal Yachting Assoc., 1971-76. *Publication:* Real Property Law, 1950. *Recreations:* sailing, listening to music. *Address:* Royal Courts of Justice, WC2. *Club:* Royal Thames Yacht.

FORBES, Ian, QPM 1966; Deputy Assistant Commissioner, Metropolitan Police and National Co-ordinator, Regional Crime Squads (England and Wales), 1970-72; *b* 30 March 1914; *y s* of John and Betsy Forbes, Auchlossan, Lumphanan, Aberdeenshire; *m* 1941, Lilian Edith Miller, Edgware, Mddx; two *s. Educ:* Lumphanan School, Aberdeenshire. Joined Metropolitan Police, 1939; served in East End, Central London Flying Squad, New Scotland Yard; Detective Superintendent, 1964; served on New Scotland Yard Murder Squad, 1966-69; Commander, No 9 Regional Crime Squad (London area), 1969. *Publication:* Squadman (autobiog.), 1973. *Recreations:* gardening, motoring, reading. *Address:* 13 Richmond Avenue, Compton, Wolverhampton WV3 9JB.

FORBES, Vice-Adm. John Morrison; Flag Officer, Plymouth, Port Admiral Devonport, Commander Central Sub Area, Eastern Atlantic, and Commander Plymouth Sub Area, Channel, since 1977; *b* 16 Aug. 1925; *s* of late Lt-Col R. H. Forbes, OBE, and late Gladys M. Forbes (*née* Pollock); *m* 1950, Joyce Newenham Hadden; two *s* two *d. Educ:* RNC, Dartmouth. Served War: HMS Mauritius, Verulam and Nelson, 1943-46. HMS Aisne, 1946-49; Gunnery course and staff of HMS Excellent, 1950-51; served in RAN, 1952-54; Staff of HMS Excellent, 1954-56; HMS Ceylon, 1956-58; Staff of Dir of Naval Ordnance, 1958-60; Comdr (G) HMS Excellent, 1960-61; Staff of Dir of Seaman Officers' Appts, 1962-64; Exec. Officer, Britannia RN Coll., 1964-66; Operational Comdr and 2nd in Comd, Royal Malaysian Navy, 1966-68; Asst Dir, Naval Plans, 1969-70; comd HMS Triumph, 1971-72; comd Britannia RN Coll., Dartmouth, 1972-74; Naval Secretary, 1974-76. Naval ADC to the Queen, 1974. Kesatria Manku Negara (Malaysia), 1968. *Recreations:* sailing, fishing. *Address:* Admiralty House, Mount Wise, Plymouth PL1 4JH; Thorn Cottage, Station Road, Droxford, Southampton, Hants SO3 1QU. *T:* Droxford 322. *Clubs:* Army and Navy, Royal Cruising, RN Sailing Association; Royal Yacht Squadron (Cowes).

FORBES, Col Sir John Stewart, 6th Bt of Newe *cr* 1823; DSO; JP; Vice-Lieutenant of Aberdeen, since 1973; *b* 8 Jan. 1901; *o surv. s* of 5th Bt and late Emma Theodora, *d* of Robert Maxwell; *S* father, 1927; *m* 1933, Agnes Jessie, *er d* of late Lt-Col D. L. Wilson-Farquharson, DSO; five *d. Educ:* Wellington Coll.; RMA, Woolwich. 2nd Lieut RE, 1920; Temp. Brig. 1948; Col 1949; served Norway Campaign, 1940 (DSO, despatches); Burma, 1944-45 (despatches); retired 1953. Hon. Col 51st (H) Div. Engineers, TA, 1960-67. DL 1953, JP 1955, Aberdeenshire. *Heir: cousin* Major Hamish Stewart Forbes, MBE, MC [*b* 15

Feb. 1916; *m* 1945, Jacynthe Elizabeth Mary, *o d* of late Eric Gordon Underwood; one *s* three *d*]. *Address:* Allargue, Corgarff, Aberdeenshire AB3 8YP. *Clubs:* Brooks's; Royal Northern (Aberdeen).

FORBES, John Stuart; Sheriff of Lothian and Borders, since 1976; *b* 31 Jan. 1936; *s* of John Forbes and Mrs A. R. S. Forbes; *m* 1963, Marion Alcock; one *s* two *d*. *Educ:* Glasgow High Sch.; Glasgow Univ. (MA, LLB). Solicitor, 1959-61; Advocate, Scottish Bar, 1962-76. *Recreations:* squash, tennis, golf. *Address:* 18 Braid Mount, Edinburgh EH10 6JJ. *T:* 031-447 4125. *Club:* Edinburgh Sports.

FORBES, Mrs Muriel Rose, CBE 1963; JP; Alderman, London Borough of Brent, 1972-74; *b* 20 April 1894; *yr d* of John Henry Cheeseright; *m* 1923, Charles Gilbert Forbes (*d* 1957); two *d*. *Educ:* Gateshead Grammar Sch.; Southlands Teacher Training Coll. Member: Willesden Borough Council, 1936-47; Middlesex CC, 1934-65 (Chm., 1960-61); GLC, 1964-67 (Vice-Chm., 1964-66). Chairman: St Charles's Gp Hosp. Management Cttee, 1968-69; Paddington Gp Hosp. Management Cttee, 1963-68; Mem., Central Middx Hosp. Management Cttee, 1948-63 (Vice-Chm., 1952-63). JP County of Middx, 1946. Hon. DTech Brunel Univ., 1966. *Address:* 7 Hamilton Road, Willesden, NW10. *T:* 01-452 7761.

FORBES, Robert Brown; Director of Education, Edinburgh, 1972-75; *b* 14 Oct. 1912; *s* of Robert James Forbes and Elizabeth Jane Brown; *m* 1939, Nellie Shepley; one *s* one *d*. *Educ:* Edinburgh Univ. (MA, MEd). Asst Dir of Educn, Edinburgh, 1946, Depute Dir, 1952. Chm., Scottish Council for Research in Educn, 1972. *Address:* 7 Wilton Road, Edinburgh EH16 5NX. *T:* 031-667 1323.

FORBES, William Alfred Beaumont, QC 1972; a Recorder of the Crown Court, since 1974; a Law Commissioner, since 1977; *b* 29 June 1927; *er s* of William Forbes, MA, FEIS, Aberdeen; *m* 1952, Helen Elizabeth, *er d* of R. A. Harting, FCA, Hillingdon; one *s* two *d*. *Educ:* Aberdeen Grammar Sch.; Galashiels Acad.; George Watson's Boys' Coll., Edinburgh; Univ. of St Andrews (MA, 1st cl. Hons Mod. Hist./Economics); Magdalen Coll., Oxford (BA, 1st cl. Hons Jurisprudence). Jun. Lectr in Law, Magdalen Coll., Oxford, 1953-54, Brasenose Coll., 1954-58. Called to Bar, Gray's Inn, 1953. Junior Prosecuting Counsel, BoT, 1968-72. *Recreation:* golf. *Address:* (home) 5 Queen Anne's Gardens, Bedford Park, W4. *T:* 01-994 4810; (office) Law Commission, Conquest House, 37/38 John Street, Theobalds Road, WC1N 2BQ. *T:* 01-242 0861. *Clubs:* Caledonian; Denham Golf.

FORBES-LEITH of Fyvie, Sir Andrew (George), 3rd Bt *cr* 1923; landed proprietor; *b* 20 Oct. 1929; *s* of Sir R. Ian A. Forbes-Leith of Fyvie, 2nd Bt, KT, MBE, and Ruth Avis (*d* 1973), *d* of Edward George Barnett; *S* father, 1973; *m* 1962, Jane Kate (*d* 1969), *d* of late David McCall-McCowan; two *s* two *d*. *Heir: s* George Ian David Forbes-Leith, *b* 26 May 1967. *Address:* Fyvie Castle, Aberdeenshire. *T:* Fyvie 208; Dunachton, Kingussie, Inverness-shire. *T:* Kincraig 226. *Clubs:* Royal Northern (Aberdeen); Highland (Inverness).

FORBES-SEMPILL; *see* Sempill.

FORD; *see* St Clair-Ford.

FORD, Benjamin Thomas; MP (Lab) Bradford North since 1964; *b* 1 April 1925; *s* of Benjamin Charles Ford and May Ethel (*née* Moorton); *m* 1950, Vera Ada (*née* Fawcett-Fancet); two *s* one *d*. *Educ:* Rowan Road Central Sch., Surrey. Apprenticed as compositor, 1941. War Service, 1943-47, Fleet Air Arm (Petty Officer). Electronic Fitter/Wireman, 1951-64; Convener of Shop Stewards, 1955-64. Pres., Harwich Constituency Labour Party, 1955-63; Clacton UDC, 1959-62; Alderman Essex CC, 1959-65; JP Essex, 1962-67. Chairman: Anglo-Portuguese Gp; Anglo-Malaysian Gp; British-Latin-American Jt Parly Gp; Anglo-Brazilian Gp; IPU British Gp, 1977-; Vice-Chm., PLP Defence Gp; Treasurer, PLP Benevolent Fund, 1975-; Secretary: Anglo-Argentine Gp; Anglo-Venezuelan Gp; Mem., House of Commons Services Cttee; Chm., Jt Select Cttee on Sound Broadcasting, 1976-. *Publication:* Piecework, 1960. *Recreations:* music, shooting, family. *Address:* House of Commons, SW1. *Clubs:* Royal Automobile; Idle Working Men's.

FORD, Prof. Boris, MA; Professor of Education, School of Education, since 1973, Dean of Faculty of Education, since 1977, University of Bristol; *b* 1 July 1917; *s* of late Brig. G. N. Ford, CB, DSO; *m* 1950, Noreen Auty (*née* Collins); one *s* three *d*; *m* 1977, Enid Inglis. *Educ:* Gresham's Sch., Holt, Norfolk; Downing Coll., Cambridge. Army Education, finally OC

Middle East School of Artistic Studies, 1940-46. Chief Ed. and finally Dir, Bureau of Current Affairs, 1946-51; Information Officer, Technical Assistance Bd, UN (NY and Geneva), 1951-53; Sec., Nat. Enquiry into Liberalising Technical Educn, 1953-55; Editor, Journal of Education, 1955-58; first Head of Sch. Broadcasting, Associated-Rediffusion, 1957-58; Educn Sec., Cambridge Univ. Press, 1958-60; Prof. of Education and Dir of the Inst. of Education, Univ. of Sheffield, 1960-63; Prof. of Education, Univ. of Sussex, 1963-73, Dean, Sch. of Cultural and Community Studies (Educnl Studies), 1963-71, Chm., Educn Area, and Dir, Sch. of Educn, 1971-73. Chairman: Nat. Assoc. for the Teaching of English, 1963-65; Educational Dir, Pictorial Knowledge, 1968-71. Gen. Editor, Pelican Guide to English Literature, 1954-61; Editor, Universities Qly, subseq. New Universities Qly, 1955-. *Publications:* Discussion Method, 1949; Teachers' Handbook to Human Rights, 1950; Liberal Education in a Technical Age, 1955; Young Readers: Young Writers, 1960. *Recreation:* music. *Address:* University of Bristol, School of Education, 35 Berkeley Square, Bristol BS8 1JA.

FORD, Brinsley, FSA; Chairman, National Art-Collections Fund, since 1975; Chairman of Trustees, Watts Gallery, Compton (Trustee, since 1955); Secretary, Society of Dilettanti, since 1972; *b* 10 June 1908; *e s* of late Capt. Richard Ford, Rifle Brigade, and Rosamund, *d* of Sir John Ramsden, 5th Bt; *m* 1937, Joan, *d* of late Capt. Geoffrey Vyvyan; two *s* one *d*. *Educ:* Eton; Trinity Coll., Oxford. Joined TA 1939; served for one year as Troop Sergeant Major, RA; commissioned 1941, and transferred to Intelligence Corps (Major 1945). Selected works for Arts Council Festival of Britain and Coronation Exhibitions; a Trustee of the National Gallery, 1954-61; great-grandson of Richard Ford (1796-1858) who wrote the Handbook for Spain; owner of the Ford Collection of Richard Wilsons. Dir, Burlington Magazine, 1952-. Member: Council, Byam Shaw Sch., 1957-73; Exec. Cttee, City and Guilds of London Art Sch., 1976-. Pres., St Marylebone Soc., 1974-77. Officer, Belgian Order of Leopold II; US Bronze Star; Médaille d'Argent de la Reconnaissance Française. *Publications:* The Drawings of Richard Wilson, 1951; contributor to the Burlington Magazine and Apollo. *Address:* 14 Wyndham Place, Bryanston Square, W1. *T:* 01-723 0826. *Club:* Brooks's.

FORD, Charles Edmund, FRS 1965; DSc London, FLS, FZS, FIBiol; Member of Medical Research Council's External Staff, Sir William Dunn School of Pathology, Oxford, since 1971; *b* 24 Oct. 1912; *s* of late Charles Ford and late Ethel Eubornia Ford (*née* Fawcett); *m* 1940, Jean Ella Dowling; four *s*. *Educ:* Slough Grammar Sch.; King's Coll., University of London. Demonstrator, Dept of Botany, King's Coll., University of London, 1936-38; Geneticist, Rubber Research Scheme, Ceylon, 1938-41 and 1944-45. Lieut Royal Artillery, 1942-43. PSO Dept of Atomic Energy, Min. of Supply, at Chalk River Laboratories, Ont, Canada, 1946-49. Head of Cytogenetics Section, MRC, Radiobiology Unit, Harwell, 1949-71. *Publications:* papers on cytogenetics in scientific journals. *Recreations:* travel, friends. *Address:* 156 Oxford Road, Abingdon, Oxon. *T:* Abingdon 20001.

FORD, Colin John; Assistant Keeper, and Keeper of Film and Photography, National Portrait Gallery, since 1972; lecturer, writer and broadcaster on films, theatre and photography; exhibition organiser; *b* 13 May 1934; *s* of John William and Hélène Martha Ford; *m* 1961, Margaret Elizabeth Cordwell; one *s* one *d*. *Educ:* Enfield Grammar Sch.; University Coll., Oxford (MA). Manager and Producer, Kidderminster Playhouse, 1958-60; Gen. Man., Western Theatre Ballet, 1960-62; Vis. Lectr in English and Drama, California State Univ. at Long Beach and UCLA (Univ. Extension), 1962-64; Dep. Curator, Nat. Film Archive, 1965-72. Organiser, 30th Anniv. Congress of Internat. Fedn of Film Archives, London, 1968; Dir, Cinema City Exhibn, 1970; Programme Dir, London Shakespeare Film Festival, 1972. *Film:* Masks and Faces, 1966 (BBC TV version, Omnibus, 1968). *Publications:* (with Roy Strong) An Early Victorian Album, 1974, 2nd edn 1977; The Cameron Collection, 1975; (ed) Happy and Glorious: Six Reigns of Royal Photography, 1977; (principal contrib.) Oxford Companion to Film; articles in many jls. *Recreations:* travel, music, small boats. *Address:* 28 Batchelor Street, Islington, N1 0EG. *T:* 01-278 5898.

FORD, Rt. Rev. Douglas Albert; *see* Saskatoon, Bishop of.

FORD, Rev. Preb. Douglas William C. *see* Cleverley-Ford.

FORD, Edmund Brisco, FRS 1946; MA, DSc Oxon, Hon. DSc Liverpool; Senior Dean, since 1958, Fellow, 1958-71, Fellow Emeritus, since 1976, All Souls College, Oxford; Professor of Ecological Genetics, 1963-69, and Director of Genetics

Laboratory, Zoology Department, 1952-69, Oxford; Emeritus Professor, since 1969; *b* 23 April 1901; unmarried; *s* of Harold Dodsworth Ford and Gertrude Emma Bennett. *Educ:* Wadham Coll., Oxford (Hon. Fellow, 1974). Research worker, Univ. Lectr and Demonstrator in Zoology and Comparative Anatomy, Univ. Reader in Genetics, Oxford; Pres., Genetical Soc. of Great Britain, 1946-49; Mem. of Nature Conservancy, 1949-59; Mem. various scientific (chiefly zoological) societies. Wild Life Conservation Cttee of Ministry of Town and Country Planning, 1945-47 (Cmd Rept 7122). Formerly represented British Empire on Permanent Internat. Cttee of Genetics. Has travelled in USA, NZ, Australia, Near and Far East. Initiated Science of Ecological Genetics. Darwin Medallist, Royal Society, 1954. Delivered Galton Lecture of London Univ., 1939; Woodhall Lectr of the Royal Institution, 1957; Woodward Lectr, Yale Univ., 1959 and 1973. Hon. FRCP 1974. Weldon Memorial Prize, Oxford Univ., 1959. Medallist of Helsinki Univ., 1967. Foreign Mem., Finnish Acad. Pres. Somerset Archæological Soc., 1960-61. *Publications:* Mendelism and Evolution, 1931, 8th edn 1965; (with G. D. Hale Carpenter) Mimicry, 1933; The Study of Heredity (Home University Library), 1938, 2nd edn 1950; Genetics for Medical Students, 1942, 7th edn 1973; Butterflies (Vol. I of New Naturalist Series), 1945, 2nd repr. of 4th edn, 1972, rev. edn 1975; British Butterflies (King Penguin Series), 1951; Moths (New Naturalist Series), 1955, 3rd edn 1972; Ecological Genetics, 1964, 4th edn 1975 (trans: Polish 1967, French 1972, Italian 1977); Genetic Polymorphism (All Souls Monographs), 1965; Evolution Studied by Observation and Experiment, 1973; Genetics and Adaptation, 1976; numerous contribs to scientific jls, on genetical and zoological subjects. Festschrift: Ecological Genetics and Evolution, ed E. R. Creed, 1971. *Recreations:* archæology, literature, travel. *Address:* 5 Apsley Road, Oxford; Zoology Department, South Parks Road, Oxford; All Souls College, Oxford. *TA:* and *T:* Oxford 58147. *Club:* Travellers'.

FORD, Sir Edward, Kt 1960; OBE 1945; Professor of Preventive Medicine and Director of the School of Public Health and Tropical Medicine, University of Sydney, 1947-68, now Emeritus; *b* 15 April 1902; *s* of Edward John and Mary Ford, South Yarra, Victoria. *Educ:* Univ. of Melbourne, Sydney and London. RMO, Melbourne Hosp., 1930; Lectr in Anatomy, Melbourne Univ., 1933; Sen. Lectr in Anatomy and Histology, Melbourne Univ., 1934-36; Lectr, Sch. of Public Health and Tropical Medicine, Sydney, 1937-39. Served War of 1939-45: in Australian Army Middle East, New Guinea, Burma; Senior Malariologist, AIF, and late Dir of Hygiene and Pathology, Aust. Army; Col AAMC, 1940-45. Rockefeller Fellow, 1946; Dean of Faculty of Medicine and Fellow of Senate, Sydney Univ., 1953-57. Vice-Pres., RACP, 1970-73. *Publication:* Bibliography of Australian Medicine 1790-1900, 1976. *Address:* Cahors, Macleay Street, Potts Point, NSW 2011, Australia. *Club:* Australian (Sydney).

FORD, Sir Edward (William Spencer), KCB 1967 (CB 1952); KCVO 1957 (MVO 1949); OStJ 1976; MA; FRSA; DL; Secretary and Registrar of the Order of Merit, since 1975; Secretary to the Pilgrim Trust, 1967-75; *b* 24 July 1910; 4th (twin) *s* of late Very Rev. Lionel G. B. J. Ford, Headmaster of Repton and Harrow and Dean of York, and of Mary Catherine, *d* of Rt Rev. E. S. Talbot, Bishop of Winchester and Hon. Mrs Talbot; *m* 1949, Virginia, *er d* of 1st and last Baron Brand, CMG, and *widow* of John Metcalfe Polk, NY; two *s. Educ:* Eton (King's Schol.); New Coll., Oxford (Open Scholar). 1st Class Hon. Mods; 2nd Class Lit. Hum. (Greats). Law Student (Harmsworth Scholar) Middle Temple, 1934-35. Called to Bar, Middle Temple, 1937 and practised 1937-39; 2nd Lieut (Supplementary Reserve of Officers) Grenadier Guards, 1936; Lieut 1939; served in France and Belgium, 1939-40 (despatches), and in Tunisia and Italy, 1943-44 (despatches), Brigade Major 10th Infantry and 24th Guards Brigades; Instructor at Staff Coll., Haifa, 1944-45. psc†. Asst Private Secretary to King George VI, 1946-52, and to the Queen, 1952-67; Extra Equerry to the Queen, 1955. Dir, London Life Assoc. Member: Central Appeals Adv. Cttee, BBC and IBA, 1969-72, 1976-; Historic Churches Preservation Trust, 1974-; Chm., UK/USA Bicentennial Fellowships Cttee, 1975-. Mem. Ct of Assts, Goldsmiths' Co., 1970-. High Sheriff 1970, DL 1972, Northants. *Address:* 18 Hale House, 34 De Vere Gardens, W8 5AQ. *T:* 01-937 2818; Eydon Hall, Eydon, near Daventry, Northants NN11 6QE. *T:* Byfield 60282. *Clubs:* White's, Beefsteak, MCC.

FORD, Elbur; see Hibbert, Eleanor.

FORD, Air Vice-Marshal Geoffrey Harold, CB 1974; Director-General Engineering and Supply Management, RAF, since 1976; *b* 6 Aug. 1923; *s* of late Harold Alfred Ford, Lewes, Sussex; *m* 1951, Valerie, *d* of late Douglas Hart Finn, Salisbury;

two *s. Educ:* Lewes Grammar Sch.; Bristol Univ. (BSc). Served War of 1939-45: commissioned, 1942; 60 Gp, 1943; Italy and Middle East, 1944-46. 90 (Signals) Gp, 1946-49; Bomber Development, 1954-57; Air Ministry, 1958-61; RAF Technical Coll., 1961-62; Min. of Aviation, 1963-64; Gp Captain, 1963; Chief Signals Officer, RAF Germany, 1965-68; MoD, 1968-72; Air Cdre, 1969; RCDS, 1972; Air Vice-Marshal, 1973; AO Engineering, Strike Command, 1973-76. CEng. FIEE. *Address:* 12 Manor House, Old Church Lane, Stanmore, Middlesex. *Club:* Royal Air Force.

FORD, Gerald Rudolph; President of the United States of America, Aug. 1974-Jan. 1977; lawyer; *b* Omaha, Nebraska, 14 July 1913; (adopted) *s* of Gerald R. Ford and Dorothy Gardner; *m* 1948, Elizabeth (*née* Bloomer); three *s* one *d. Educ:* South High Sch., Grand Rapids; Univ. of Michigan (BA); Law Sch., Yale Univ. (LLB). Served War: US Navy (Carriers), 1942-46. Partner in law firm of Ford and Buchen, 1941-42; Member, law firm of Butterfield, Keeney and Amberg, 1947-49; subseq. with Amberg, Law and Buchen. Member US House of Representatives for Michigan 5th District, 1948-73; Member: Appropriations Cttee, 1951; Dept of Defense Sub-Cttee, etc; House Minority Leader, Republican Party, 1965-73; Vice President of the United States, Dec. 1973-Aug. 1974. Attended Interparly Union meetings in Europe; Mem. US-Canadian Interparly Gp. Holds Amer. Pol. Sci. Assoc.'s Distinguished Congressional Service Award, 1961; several hon. degrees. Delta Kappa Epsilon, Phi Delta Phi. *Publication:* (with John R. Stiles) Portrait of an Assassin, 1965. *Recreations:* outdoor sports (formerly football), ski-ing, tennis, golf. *Address:* PO Box 927, Rancho Mirage, Calif 92270, USA.

FORD, Dr Gillian Rachel; Deputy Chief Medical Officer (Deputy Secretary), Department of Health and Social Security, since 1977; *b* 18 March 1934; *d* of Cecil Ford and Grace Ford. *Educ:* Clarendon Sch., Abergele; St Hugh's Coll., Oxford; St Thomas' Hosp., London. MA, BM, BCh; FFCM. Junior hospital posts, St Thomas', Oxford, Reading, 1959-64; Medical Officer, Min. of Health, 1965, Sen. Med. Officer, 1968; Sen. Principal Med. Officer, DHSS, 1974-77. FRSocMed. *Publications:* papers on health services research and other health subjects in Portfolio for Health, Vol. 1 (Nuffield Provincial Hospitals Trust) and other med. jls. *Recreations:* music, ski-ing, tennis, children's literature. *Address:* 95 Great Brownings, College Road, SE21. *T:* 01-670 7984.

FORD, Harold Frank; Sheriff of Tayside, Central and Fife (formerly Perth and Angus) at Perth, since 1971; *b* 17 May 1915; *s* of Sir Patrick Ford, 1st Bt, and *b* of Sir Henry Ford, *qv*; *m* 1948, Lucy Mary, *d* of late Sheriff J. R. Wardlaw Burnet, KC; one *s* three *d. Educ:* Winchester Coll.; University Coll., Oxford; Edinburgh Univ. War service with Lothians and Border Yeomanry (Prisoner of War, 1940-45): Hon. Capt. Scottish Bar, 1945; Legal Adviser to UNRRA and IRO in British Zone of Germany, 1947. Sheriff Substitute of Perth and Angus at Forfar and Arbroath, 1951-71. *Recreations:* golf, gardening, shooting. *Address:* Broomhill, by Stanley, Perth, Scotland. *T:* Meikleour 288. *Clubs:* New (Edinburgh); Honourable Company of Edinburgh Golfers, Royal Perth Golfing Society.

FORD, Henry, II; Chairman and Chief Executive Officer, Ford Motor Company, Dearborn, Michigan; *b* Detroit, 4 Sept. 1917; *s* of Edsel B. and Eleanor (Clay) Ford; *m* 1st, 1940, Anne McDonnell (marr. diss.); one *s* two *d*; 2nd, 1965, Maria Cristina Vettore Austin. *Educ:* Hotchkiss Sch., Lakeville, Conn.; Yale Univ. With Ford Motor Co. from 1940: Dir, 1938; Vice-Pres., 1943; Executive Vice-Pres., 1944; Pres., 1945; Chm., 1960. Trustee, The Ford Foundation, 1943-76; Mem., Business Council. *Address:* (home) Grosse Pointe Farms, Michigan, USA; (office) 4 Grafton Street, W1.

FORD, Sir Henry Russell, 2nd Bt *cr* 1929; TD; JP; *b* 30 April 1911; *s* of Sir Patrick Ford, 1st Bt, and Jessie Hamilton (*d* 1962), *d* of Henry Field, WS, Moreland, Kinross-shire, and Middlebluf, Manitoba; *S* father, 1945; *m* 1936, Mary Elizabeth, *y d* of late Godfrey F. Wright, Whiddon, Bovey Tracy; one *s* three *d. Educ:* Winchester; New Coll., Oxford. War of 1939-45 served in UK, North Africa and Italy (despatches). Chm., Berwick and E Lothian Unionist Assoc., 1948-50, 1958-60. JP 1951. TD 1960. *Recreations:* golf, gardening. Heir: *s* Andrew Russell Ford [*b* 29 June 1943; *m* 1968, Penelope Anne, *d* of Harry Relph; one *s* one *d*]. *Address:* Seaforth, Gullane, East Lothian. *T:* Gullane 842214. *Club:* Hon. Company of Edinburgh Golfers (Muirfield). *See also Harold Frank Ford.*

FORD, Air Vice-Marshal Howard, CB 1959; CBE 1954; AFC 1944; RAF (retd); *b* 18 Dec. 1905; *s* of late Lewis Ford and Beatrice Leal; *m* 1936, Marie (*d* 1974), *d* of late Daniel O'Reilly,

Cork, and Agnes Mayne, New York. *Educ:* Blundell's Sch.; Pembroke Coll., Cambridge (BA). Represented Cambridge at ski-ing and athletics, also England and Great Britain at athletics; British Olympic Athletic Team, 1928. Joined Royal Air Force, 1930; served War of 1939-45 (AFC). Transferred to Technical Branch, 1951; Dir, Air Armament R&D, Min. of Supply, 1952-55; Senior Technical Staff Officer, Flying Training Command, 1956-59; Vice-Pres. Ordnance Board, 1960-61, Pres., 1962; retired from RAF, 1963. Group Capt., 1947; Air Cdre, 1953; Air Vice-Marshal, 1960. *Club:* Royal Automobile.

FORD, Prof. Sir Hugh, Kt 1975; FRS 1967; Professor of Mechanical Engineering, University of London (Imperial College of Science and Technology), since 1969; Head of the Dept of Mechanical Engineering, since 1965; Director: Scholfields (Holdings) Ltd; Herbert Ltd; Ford and Dain Partners Ltd; André Silentbloc Ltd; *b* 16 July 1913; *s* of Arthur and Constance Ford; *m* 1942, Wynyard, *d* of Major F. B. Scholfield; two *d. Educ:* Northampton Sch.; City and Guilds Coll., Univ. of London. DSc (Eng); PhD. Practical trng at GWR Locomotive Works, 1931-36; researches into heat transfer, 1936-39; R and Eng, Imperial Chemical Industries, Northwich, 1939-42; Chief Engr, Technical Dept, British Iron and Steel Fedn, 1942-45, then Head of Mechanical Working Div., British Iron and Steel Research Assoc., 1945-47; Reader in Applied Mechanics, Univ. of London, 1948-51, Prof., 1951-69. Technical Dir, Davy-Ashmore Group, 1968-71. John Player Lectr, IMechE, 1973. President: Inst. of Metals, 1963; Section 6, British Assoc., 1975-76; Member: Council, IMechE (Vice-Pres., 1972, 1975, Sen. Vice-Pres., 1976, Pres., 1977-78); SRC, 1968-72 (Chm. Engineering Bd); Council, Royal Soc., 1973-74; ARC, 1976-. FIMechE; FICE; Whitworth Schol.; FCGI. Hon. DSc: Salford, 1976; QUB, 1977. Thomas Hawksley Gold Medallist, IMechE, 1948, for researches into rolling of metals; Robertson Medal, Inst. of Metals. *Publications:* Advanced Mechanics of Materials, 1963; papers to Royal Soc., IMechE, Iron and Steel Inst., Inst. of Metals, foreign societies, etc. *Recreations:* gardening, music. *Address:* 18 Shrewsbury House, Cheyne Walk, SW3. *T:* 01-352 3804; Shamley Cottage, Stroud Lane, Shamley Green, Surrey. *T:* Bramley 2366. *Club:* Athenæum.

FORD, James Allan, MC 1946; Principal Establishment Officer (formerly Director of Establishments), Scottish Office, since 1969; *b* 10 June 1920; 2nd *s* of Douglas Ford and Margaret Duncan (*née* Allan); *m* 1948, Isobel Dunnett; one *s* one *d. Educ:* Royal High School, Edinburgh; University of Edinburgh. Served 1940-46, Capt. Royal Scots. Entered Civil Service, 1938; Asst Sec., Dept of Agriculture and Fisheries for Scotland, 1958; Registrar Gen. for Scotland, 1966-69. *Publications:* The Brave White Flag, 1961; Season of Escape, 1963; A Statue for a Public Place, 1965; A Judge of Men, 1968; The Mouth of Truth, 1972. *Address:* 29 Lady Road, Edinburgh EH16 5PA. *T:* 031-667 4489. *Clubs:* Royal Commonwealth Society; Royal Scots, Scottish Arts (Edinburgh).

FORD, Sir John Archibald, KCMG 1977 (CMG 1967); MC 1945; HM Diplomatic Service; Ambassador to Indonesia, since 1975; *b* 19 Feb. 1922; *s* of Ronald Mylne Ford and Margaret Jesse Coghill, Newcastle-under-Lyme, Staffs; *m* 1956, Emaline Burnett, Leesville, Virginia; two *d. Educ:* St Michael's Coll., Tenbury; Sedbergh Sch., Yorks; Oriel Coll., Oxford. Served in Royal Artillery, 1942-46 (temp. Major); demobilised, 1947. Joined Foreign (subseq. Diplomatic) Service, 1947. Third Sec., British Legation, Budapest, 1947-49; Third Sec. and a Resident Clerk, FO, 1949-52; Private Sec. to Permanent Under-Sec. of State, FO, 1952-54; HM Consul, San Francisco, 1954-56; seconded to HM Treasury, 1956-59; attended Course at Administrative Staff Coll., 1959; First Sec. and Head of Chancery, British Residency, Bahrain, 1959-61; Asst, FO Personnel Dept, 1961-63; Asst, FO Establishment and Organisation Dept, 1963; Head of Diplomatic Service Establishment and Organisation Dept, 1964-66; Counsellor (Commercial), Rome, 1966-70; Asst Under-Sec., FCO, 1970-71; Consul-Gen., USA, and Dir-Gen., British Trade Develt in USA, 1971-75. *Recreations:* walking, gardening, sailing. *Address:* c/o Foreign and Commonwealth Office, SW1A 2AL. *Clubs:* Travellers', Farmers'; Yvonne Arnaud Theatre (Guildford).

FORD, (John) Peter, CBE 1969; Chairman and Managing Director, International Joint Ventures Ltd; *b* 20 Feb. 1912; *s* of Ernest and Muriel Ford; *m* 1939, Phoebe Seys, *d* of Herbert McGregor Wood, FRIBA; one *s* two *d. Educ:* Wrekin Coll.; Gonville and Caius Coll., Cambridge. BA (Hons Nat. Sci. Tripos) 1934; MA Cantab 1937. Cambridge Univ. Air Sqdn, 1932-35 (Pilot's A Licence, 1933-). Air Ministry (subsequently FO, RAFVR), 1939-40; Coventry Gauge and Tool Co. Ltd (Asst to Chm.), 1941-45; Gen. Man., Brit. Engineers Small Tools and Equipment Co. Ltd, and Gen. Man. Scientific Exports

(Gt Brit.) Ltd, 1945-48; Man. Dir, Brush Export Ltd, Associated British Oil Engines (Export) Ltd and National Oil Engines (Export) Ltd, and Dir of other associated cos of The Brush Group, 1949-55; Dir, Associated British Engineering Ltd and subsidiaries, 1957-58; Man. Dir, Coventry Climax International Ltd, 1958-63; Director: Plessey Overseas Ltd, 1963-70; Bryant & May (Latin America) Ltd, 1970-73. Chm. Institute of Export, 1954-56, 1965-67; President: Soc. of Commercial Accountants, 1970-74 (Vice-Pres., 1956-70); Soc. of Company and Commercial Accountants, 1974-75; Member: Council, London Chamber of Commerce, 1951-72 (Dep. Chm., 1970-72; Vice-Pres., 1972-); London Ct of Arbitration, 1970-73; FBI, Overseas Trade Policy Cttee, 1952-63; Council British Internal Combustion Engine Manufacturers Assoc., 1953-55; BNEC Cttee for Exports to Latin America, 1964-71 (Chm. 1968-71); NEDO Cttee for Movement of Exports, 1972-75; British Overseas Trade Adv. Council, 1975-. Chm., British Shippers' Council, 1972-75 (Dep. Chm., 1971-72). Chm., British Mexican Soc., 1973-. Freeman of City of London, 1945; Mem. Ct of Assistants, Worshipful Company of Ironmongers; Governor: Wrekin Coll., 1953-57; Oversea Service Coll., 1966-. CEng, CIMechE, CIMarE, MIEE, FIPE. Order of Rio Branco (Brazil), 1977. *Publications:* contributor to technical press and broadcaster on international trade subjects. *Recreations:* Athletics (Cambridge Univ. and Internat. Teams, 1932-35; held various county championships, 1932-37; Hon. Treas. Achilles Club, 1947-58; Pres., London Athletic Club, 1964-66). *Address:* 40 Fairacres, Roehampton Lane, SW15. *T:* 01-876 2146. *Clubs:* United Oxford & Cambridge University, City Livery, MCC; Hawks (Cambridge); Royal Wimbledon Golf.

FORD, Joseph Francis, CMG 1960; OBE 1949; HM Diplomatic Service, retired 1970; Director, Great Britain-China Centre, London, since 1974; *b* 11 Oct. 1912; *s* of J. W. Ford, Chesterfield, Derbs; *m* 1938, Mary Margaret Ford (*née* Taylor); two *s. Educ:* Chesterfield Grammar Sch.; Emmanuel Coll., Cambridge (BA). Appointed probationer Vice-Consul to Peking, Nov. 1935; served at Shanghai, Chungking, Washington, Peking, Hanoi, New Orleans and Saigon; Dir, Res. Dept, FCO (formerly Jt Res. Dept, FO/CO), 1967-70; Dir, Univs Service Centre, Hong Kong, 1970-72. *Address:* 10 Raymond Road, Wimbledon, SW19; Great Britain-China Centre, 22a Queen Anne's Gate, SW1.

FORD, Sir Leslie (Ewart), Kt 1956; OBE 1945; General Manager, Port of London Authority, 1948-64; *b* 27 July 1897; *e s* of late Elias Ford, OBE; *m* 1925, Mary Mabel, *e d* of late Walter Powles, Acocks Green, Warwicks; one *d. Educ:* Cardiff High Sch. Joined GW Railway Co., 1912. Served European War, 1914-18, with Welch Regt and 2nd Bn Monmouthshire Regt. Stationed various South Wales Ports, 1923-39; Chief Docks Manager, 1944. Major, Home Guard, 1941-45. Col Engineer and Railway Staff Corps RE (TA), 1957. CStJ. Commander: Royal Order of North Star (Sweden); Military Order of Christ (Portugal); Order of Dannebrog (Denmark). *Recreation:* golf. *Address:* 26 Bedford Gardens, Campden Hill, W8 7EH. *T:* 01-727 5595.

FORD, Percy; Professor Emeritus, The University of Southampton; *b* 19 Feb. 1894; 4th *s* of George Horace Ford, Brighton; *m* 1921, Grace Lister, Long Eaton; one *s* one *d. Educ:* Varndean Sch.; London Sch. of Economics, University of London (Gerstenberg Scholar). Resident Lecturer, Ruskin Coll.; Lecturer, Amherst Coll., Mass, USA; Lecturer in Dept of Economics, and Sec. of University Extension Board and Tutorial Classes Joint Cttee, King's Coll., Univ. of Durham, 1923-26; Head of Dept and Prof. of Economics, University of Southampton, 1926-59; Sen. Research Fellow, 1959-61. National Service, Ministry of Supply, 1939-46. Hon. LLD Southampton, 1974 (Hon. degrees of LLD conferred on Prof. P. and Mrs G. Ford at the same time). *Publications:* Economics and Modern Industry, 1930; Work and Wealth in a Modern Port, 1934; Incomes, Means Tests and Personal Responsibility, 1939; Economics of Collective Bargaining, 1958; Social Theory and Social Practice, 1969; Parliamentary Papers Series, 1951-62 (with G. Ford): Breviate of Parliamentary Papers, Vol. I, 1900-16; Vol. II, 1917-39, Vol. III, 1940-54; Select List of British Parliamentary Papers, 1833-1899; Hansard's and Catalogue and Breviate of Parliamentary Papers, 1696-1834; editorial work connected with, and selection of, nineteenth century British Parliamentary Papers for 1,000 vol. reprint (complete set presented to Parliament); Select List of Reports of Irish Dail and Senate, 1922-72; Select List of Reports and Other Papers in House of Commons's Journals, 1688-1800; Guide to Parliamentary Papers; Luke Graves Hansard's Diary, 1814-41; (with J. Bound) Coastwise Shipping and the Small Ports, 1951; (with G. Ford and D. Marshallsay) Select List of Parliamentary Papers 1955-64, 1970; (with C. J. Thomas) Industrial Prospects of Southampton, 1951, Shops and Planning, 1953, Housing, 1953, Problem Families, 1955; Ed., Southampton Civic Survey, 1931; Contributor, Britain in Depression, 1935; articles in journals of economics. *Address:* Lane End, Sandgate Lane, Storrington, Pulborough, West Sussex RH20 3HJ; 34 Orchards Way, Southampton.

FORD, Peter; *see* Ford, J. P.

FORD, Raymond Eustace, CBE 1963; MD, MRCP; retired as Principal Medical Officer i/c Regional Medical Service, Ministry of Health (1946-63); *b* 24 April 1898; *s* of Rev. George Ford; *m* 1924, Elsie (*née* Tipping); two *s* one *d*. *Educ:* Sheffield Univ. *Recreations:* golf, gardening. *Address:* St John's Road, Hythe, Kent.

FORD, Lt.-Gen. Sir Robert (Cyril), KCB 1977 (CB 1973); CBE 1971 (MBE 1958); Military Secretary, since 1976; *b* 29 Dec. 1923; *s* of late John Stranger Ford and Gladys Gertrude Ford, Yeampton, Devon; *m* 1949, Jean Claudia Pendlebury, MA (Oxon), *d* of late Gp-Capt. Claude Luther Pendlebury, MC, TD, and late Muriel Pendlebury, Yelverton, Devon; one *s*. *Educ:* Musgrave's. War of 1939-45: commissioned into 4th/7th Royal Dragoon Guards, 1943; served with Regt throughout NW European campaign, 1944-45 (despatches) and in Egypt and Palestine, 1947-48 (despatches). Instructor, Mons OCS, 1949-50; Training Officer, Scottish Horse (TA), 1952-54; Staff Coll., Camberley, 1955; GSO 2 Mil. Ops, War Office, 1956-57; Sqdn Ldr 4/7 RDG, 1958-59; Bde Major, 20th Armoured Bde, 1960-61; Brevet Lt-Col, 1962; Sqdn Ldr, 4/7 RDG, 1962-63; GSO1 to Chief of Defence Staff, 1964-65; commanded 4/7 RDG in S Arabia and N Ireland, 1966-67; Comdr, 7th Armd Bde, 1968-69; Principal Staff Officer to Chief of Defence Staff, 1970-71; Cmdr Land Forces, N Ireland, 1971-73; Comdt, RMA Sandhurst, 1973-76. MBIM 1972. *Recreations:* cricket, tennis, war studies. *Address:* c/o National Westminster Bank, Camberley Town Centre Branch, 45 Park Street, Camberley, Surrey GU15 3PA. *Clubs:* Cavalry and Guards, MCC.

FORD, Robert Webster; HM Diplomatic Service; Consul-General, Bordeaux since 1974; *b* 27 March 1923; *s* of Robert Ford; *m* 1956, Monica Florence Tebbett; two *s*. *Educ:* Alleyne's Sch. Served RAF, 1939-45. Served with British Mission, Lhasa, Tibet and Political Agency in Sikkim and Bhutan, 1945-47; joined Tibetan Govt Service, 1947; advised on and installed Tibet's first radio communication system and broadcasting stn; travelled extensively in Northern and Eastern Tibet, 1947-50; taken prisoner during Chinese Occupation of Tibet, 1950; imprisoned in China, 1950-55; free-lance writer and broadcaster on Chinese and Tibetan affairs, 1955; entered Foreign Service, 1956; 2nd Sec., Saigon, 1957-58; 1st Sec. (Information), Djakarta, 1959; Washington, 1960-62; FO, 1962-67; Consul-Gen., Tangier, 1967-70; Counsellor, 1970; Consul-Gen., Luanda, 1970-74. *Publication:* Captured in Tibet, 1956. *Recreations:* ski-ing on snow and water, gardening, travelling. *Address:* c/o Foreign and Commonwealth Office, SW1; HM Consulate-General, 15 Cours de Verdun, 33081 Bordeaux, Cedex, France. *Clubs:* Royal Commonwealth Society, Royal Geographical Society.

FORD, Sir Sidney (William George), Kt 1967; MBE 1944; President, National Union of Mineworkers, 1960-71; *b* 29 Aug. 1909; *s* of George and Harriet Ford; *m* 1st, 1936, Ivy Elizabeth Lewis (*d* 1964); one *s* two *d*; 2nd, 1965, Sheila Simon. *Educ:* Silver Street Elementary Sch. Joined Staff of Miners' Federation of Great Britain (later NUM), 1925. Mem., Central Transport Consultative Cttee for GB, 1970-. *Address:* 18 Woodland Way, Winchmore Hill, N21. *T:* 01-886 8837.

FORD, Rev. Wilfred Franklin, CMG 1974; *b* 9 Jan. 1920; *s* of Harold Franklin Ford and Sarah Elizabeth Ford; *m* 1942, Joan Mary Holland; three *d*. *Educ:* Auckland Univ., NZ (BA); Trinity Theological Coll., NZ. Served War, NZ Army, 1942-44. Entered Methodist Ministry, 1945; Dir, Christian Educn, Methodist Church of NZ, 1956-68; Pres., Methodist Church of NZ, 1971. Mem., Australian Inst. of Human Relations, 1965; Life Mem., Wellington Marriage Guidance Council. *Publications:* contribs to NZ and internat. jls, on Christian educn. *Recreations:* gardening, reading. *Address:* 8 Ingestre Street, Wanganui, New Zealand.

FORD ROBERTSON, Francis Calder, OBE 1959; *b* 19 March 1901; 3rd *s* of Dr W. Ford Robertson, MD, and Marion Elam; *m* 1928, Cynthia Mary de Courcy Ireland (*d* 1977); two *s*. *Educ:* Edinburgh Academy; Edinburgh Univ. Appointed to Indian Forest Service as probationer, 1923; IFS, 1924-47; Director: Commonwealth Forestry Bureau, Oxford, 1947-64; Dir-Editor, Multilingual Forestry Terminology Project, at Commonwealth

Forestry Inst., Oxford and Washington, DC, USA, 1964-70. Hon. Mem., Soc. of American Foresters, 1970. Hon. MA Oxford, 1952. *Publications:* Our Forests, 1934; (ed) The Terminology of Forest Science, Technology, Practice and Products (English lang. version), 1971; also sundry scientific, mainly bibliographical, articles. *Recreations:* choral singing, gardening, local history and archaeology. *Address:* 54 Staunton Road, Headington, Oxford. *T:* Oxford 62073.

FORDE, Rt. Hon. Francis Michael, PC 1944; Australian High Commissioner in Canada, 1946-53; Dean of the Diplomatic Corps, Ottawa, Canada, 1952-53; *m* 1925, Veronica Catherine O'Reilly; three *d* (one *s* decd). *Educ:* Christian Brothers Coll., Toowoomba, Qld, Aust. School teacher; electrical engineer; Mem. of Qld State Parliament, 1917-22; elected to House of Representatives for Capricornia, Qld Gen. Elections, 1922, 1925, 1928, 1929, 1931, 1934, 1937, 1940, 1943; Mem. Jt Select Cttee on Motion Picture Industry in Australia, 1927, and of Royal Commission on same, 1927-28; Mem. of Joint Cttee on Public Accounts, 1929; Acting Minister for Trade and Customs, Australia, 1929-30; Acting Minister for Markets and Transport, 1930-31; Minister for Trade and Customs, 1930-31, 1932; Dep. Leader Federal Parliamentary Labour Party, 1932-46, and Dep. Leader of the Opposition, 1932-41; Dep. Prime Minister, Minister for Army, Mem. and Vice-Chm. of War Cabinet, Australia, 1941-46; Minister for Defence, 1946; Acting Prime Minister, April-July 1944 and Oct. 1944-Jan. 1945; Prime Minister for short period, 1945; Actg Prime Minister (about two months), 1946. Leader of Australian Delegn to UN Conf., San Francisco, April 25 1945. Mem. for Flinders, Qld Parliament, By-Election, March 1955; re-elected, Gen. Election, May 1956. Represented Australia at Gen. Douglas MacArthur's funeral in USA, 1964. LLD (Hon.): Ottawa Univ., 1950; Montreal Univ., 1952; Laval Univ., 1952; Univ. of Qld, Brisbane, 1972. *Recreations:* tennis, golf, bowls. *Address:* 44 Highland Terrace, St Lucia, Brisbane, Queensland 4067, Australia. *T:* Brisbane 370 9447.

FORDER, Ven. Charles Robert; Archdeacon Emeritus, Diocese of York, since 1974; *b* 6 Jan. 1907; *s* of late Henry Forder, Worstead, Norfolk; *m* 1933, Myra, *d* of late Harry Peat, Leeds; no *c*. *Educ:* Paston Sch., North Walsham; Christ's Coll. and Ridley Hall, Cambridge. Exhibitioner of Christ's Coll. and Prizeman, 1926; 1st Cl. Math. Trip. Part I, 1926, BA (Sen. Opt. Part II) 1928, MA 1932; Ridley Hall, 1928. Curate: St Peter's, Hunslet Moor, 1930-33; Burley, 1933-34; Vicar: Holy Trinity, Wibsey, 1934-40; St Clement's, Bradford, 1940-47; Organising Sec., Bradford Church Forward Movement Appeal, 1945-47; Vicar of Drypool, 1947-55; Rector of Routh and Vicar of Wawne, 1955-57; Canon, and Prebendary of Fenton, York Minster, 1957-76; Rector of Sutton-on-Derwent, 1957-63; Rector of Holy Trinity, Micklegate, York, 1963-66; Archdeacon of York, 1957-72. Chaplain to HM Prison, Hull, 1950-53; Proctor in Convocation, 1954-72; Organising Sec., Diocesan Appeal, 1955-76; Church Comr, 1958-73. *Publications:* A History of the Paston Grammar School, 1934, 2nd edn 1975; The Parish Priest at Work, 1947; Synods in Action, 1970; Churchwardens in Church and Parish, 1976; contrib. to Encyclopædia Britannica. *Recreations:* reading and writing. *Address:* 175A Norwich Road, Wroxham, Norfolk NR12 8RZ. *T:* Wroxham 3186.
See also Prof. H. G. Forder.

FORDER, Prof. Henry George; Professor of Mathematics, Auckland University, 1934-55; Professor Emeritus since 1955; *b* 27 Sept. 1889; *s* of Henry Forder, Worstead, Norwich; *m* 1921, Dorothy (*d* 1970), *d* of William Whincup, Bingham, Notts; no *c*. *Educ:* Paston Grammar Sch., N Walsham; Sidney Sussex Coll., Cambridge. Wrangler, 1910. Mathematical Master at Hulme Grammar Sch., Oldham; High Sch., Cardiff; St Olave's Sch.; Hymers Coll. Hector Medal, Royal Society NZ, 1946. Hon. DSc 1959. *Publications:* Foundations of Euclidean Geometry, 1927 (Dover Reprint, 1958, Rumanian trans., 1970); School Geometry, 1930; Higher Course Geometry, 1931; The Calculus of Extension, 1941 (Chelsea Reprint, 1960); Geometry (Hutchinson's University Library), 1950, Turkish translation, 1965; various articles. *Recreations:* walking and talking. *Address:* Lichfield, Selwyn Village, Port Chevalier, Auckland, NZ.
See also Ven. C. R. Forder.

FORDHAM, Sir (Alfred) Stanley, KBE 1964; CMG 1951; JP; *b* 2 Sept. 1907; HM Lieutenant for Cambridgeshire, since 1975; *e s* of late Alfred Russell Fordham, JP, Melbourn Bury, Cambs, and Caroline Augusta Stanley; *m* 1934, Isabel, *y d* of Juan Ward, Lima, Peru; one *s* one *d*. *Educ:* Eton; Trinity Coll., Cambridge. Vice-Consul, San Francisco, 1930-33; Lima, 1933-36; Guatemala, 1936-43; Los Angeles, 1943-44; Consul and Chargé d'Affaires, San Salvador, 1944-45; Consul, St Louis, 1945-48; transferred to Foreign Office, 1948, and promoted Counsellor (Head of American Dept), 1949; Warsaw, 1951-52; Stockholm, 1952-54; Minister, HM Embassy, Buenos Aires, 1954-56; HM Ambassador to Cuba, 1956-60; HM Ambassador to Colombia, 1960-64; Mem., UK Delegn to UN General Assembly, 1961. Retired from Foreign Service, 1964. JP 1966, High Sheriff 1973-74, Cambs and Isle of Ely. Grand Cross of San Carlos (Colombia). *Recreations:* gardening, shooting. *Address:* Melbourn Bury, Royston, Herts. *T:* Royston 60206. *Clubs:* MCC; Cambridge County.

FORDHAM, Sir Stanley; *see* Fordham, Sir A. S.

FORDHAM, Wilfrid Gurney, QC 1967; *b* 9 Dec. 1902; *s* of Edward Wilfrid Fordham and Sybil Harriet (*née* Langdon-Davies); *m* 1930, Peta Marshall Freeman; one *s. Educ:* St George's, Harpenden; Magdalene Coll., Cambridge. Called to Bar, Inner Temple, 1929; Dep. Circuit Judge, 1972-74; a Recorder of the Crown Court, 1974-76. Contested: (L) Bromley, Kent, 1929, 1930; (Lab) Wycombe, Bucks, 1959. *Publications:* various legal books. *Recreations:* travel, country life. *Address:* 4 Paper Buildings, Temple, EC4. *T:* 01-353 2739; The Summer House, East Hill, Otford, Kent. *Club:* Garrick.

FORDYCE, Catherine Mary, MA (London and Oxford); *b* Wareham, Dorset, 18 Dec. 1898; *d* of Ernest Chilcott, MA, Vicar of Elberton, Glos; *m* 1929, Prof. Christian James Fordyce (*d* 1974). *Educ:* St Mary's Hall, Brighton; Bedford Coll. for Women. London BA Classical Hons Cl. I, 1920; Gilchrist Studentship, 1921; MA (with distinction), 1922; Fellow and Classical Tutor of Lady Margaret Hall, Oxford, 1922-29. *Publications:* articles in Classical Quarterly, 1923; Essay, Myth and Reality, in Adventure, 1927. *Address:* 1 Beaumont Gate, Glasgow G12 9EE.

FORECAST, Kenneth George; Director of Statistics (Under-Secretary), Department of Education and Science, since 1970; *b* 21 Aug. 1925; *s* of George Albert Forecast and Alice Matilda Forecast (*née* Davies); unmarried. *Educ:* William Morris Sch.; SW Essex Techn. Coll. and Sch. of Art, Walthamstow. BSc (Econ) London. Statistical Officer, Min. of Aircraft Production/Min. of Supply, 1945-48; Economist/Statistician with de Zoete & Gorton, Stock Exchange, London, 1948-51; Statistician: Central Statistics Office, Dublin, 1951-58; BoT, London, 1958-66; Chief Statistician, MoT, 1966-70. *Publications:* contribs to Review of Internat. Statistical Inst. and to Jl of Statistical and Social Inquiry Soc. of Ireland. *Address:* 51 Richmond Avenue, Highams Park, E4 9RR. *T:* 01-527 3023. *Club:* Civil Service.

FOREMAN, Carl, CBE (Hon.) 1970; FRSA; screen writer; producer; director; former Managing Director and Executive Producer of Open Road Films Ltd; *b* Chicago, USA. *Educ:* Crane Coll.; Univ. of Illinois; Northwestern Univ., USA. *Film scripts:* So This is New York; Champion; Home of the Brave; The Men; Cyrano de Bergerac; (writer-prod.) High Noon; The Bridge on the River Kwai; (writer-prod.) The Key; (writer-prod.) The Guns of Navarone; (writer-prod.-dir) The Victors; (writer-prod.) Mackenna's Gold; (writer-prod.) Young Winston (Variety Club of GB Show-business Writer Award, 1972; Best Screenplay Award, Writers' Guild of GB, 1972); Executive Producer, films: The Mouse that Roared; Born Free; Otley; The Virgin Soldiers; Living Free. Mem. Bd of Governors: British Film Inst., 1966-71; National Film Sch., 1971-75; Mem. Exec. Council, Film Production Assoc., 1967-75; Pres., Writers' Guild of GB, 1968-75 (Dist. Service Award, 1968); Writers' Guild of Amer. Laurel Award, 1969; Valentine Davies Award, 1977. Comdr, Order of the Phoenix (Greece), 1962. *Publications:* A Cast of Lions, 1966; Young Winston, 1972. *Address:* 1370 Avenue of the Americas, New York, NY 10019, USA. *Clubs:* Savile, Garrick.

FOREMAN, Philip Frank, CBE 1972; DLC; CEng, FRAeS, FIMechE, FIProdE, FBIM; DL; Managing Director, Short Bros Ltd, since 1967; *b* 16 March 1923; *s* of late Frank and Mary Foreman; *m* 1971, Margaret Cooke; one *s. Educ:* Soham Grammar Sch., Cambs; Loughborough Coll., Leics. Royal Naval Scientific Service, 1943-58. Short Bros Ltd, 1958-. Hon. DSc QUB, 1976. *Publications:* papers to: Royal Aeronautical Soc.; Instn of Mechanical Engineers. *Recreation:* golf.

FORESTER; *see* Weld Forester, family name of **Baron Forester.**

FORESTER, 8th Baron *cr* 1821; **George Cecil Brooke Weld Forester;** *b* 20 Feb. 1938; *s* of 7th Baron Forester and of Marie Louise Priscilla, *d* of Col Sir Herbert Perrott, 6th Bt, CH, CB; *S* father, 1977; *m* 1967, Hon. Elizabeth Catherine Lyttelton, 2nd *d*

of 10th Viscount Cobham, KG, PC, GCMG, GCVO, TD; one *s* three *d. Educ:* Eton; Royal Agricultural College, Cirencester (MRAC). *Heir: s* Hon. Charles Richard George Weld Forester, *b* 8 July 1975. *Address:* Willey Park, Broseley, Salop TF12 5JJ. *T:* Telford 882146. *Club:* Farmers'.

FORESTIER-WALKER, Sir Clive Radzivill F.; *see* Walker.

FORFAR, Prof. John Oldroyd, MC; Professor of Child Life and Health, University of Edinburgh, since 1964; *b* 16 Nov. 1916; *s* of Rev. David Forfar, MA and Elizabeth Edith Campbell; *m* 1942, Isobel Mary Langlands Fernback, MB, ChB, DPH; two *s* one *d. Educ:* Perth Acad.; St Andrews Univ. BSc 1938, MB, ChB 1941, St Andrews; MRCP 1947; MRCPE 1948; DCH (London) 1948; FRCPE 1953; MD (Commendation) St Andrews, 1958; FRCP 1964; FRSE 1975. House Officer, Perth Royal Infirmary, 1941; RAMC, 1942-46: Med. Off., 47 Royal Marine Commando, 1943-45 (MC 1944; despatches, 1945); Registrar and Sen. Registrar, Dundee Royal Infirmary, 1946-48; Sen. Lectr in Child Health, St Andrews Univ., 1948-50; Sen. Paediatric Phys., Edinburgh Northern Gp of Hosps, and Sen. Lectr in Child Life and Health, Edinburgh Univ., 1950-64. Pres., Scottish Paediatric Soc., 1972-74; Chm., Medical Gp of Assoc. of British Adoption Agencies, 1966-76. *Publications:* (ed) Textbook of Paediatrics, 1973; contribs to general medical and to paediatric jls and books. *Recreations:* walking, travelling, gardening. *Address:* 110 Ravelston Dykes, Edinburgh EH12 6HB. *T:* 031-337 7081.

FORGE, Andrew Murray; artist, writer; Dean of School of Art, University of Yale, Conn, USA; *b* Hastingleigh, Kent, 10 Nov. 1923; *s* of Sidney Wallace Forge and Joanna Ruth Forge (*née* Bliss); *m* 1950, Sheila Deane (marr. diss.); three *d*; *m* 1974, Ruth Miller. *Educ:* Downs Sch.; Leighton Park; Camberwell Sch. of Art (NDD). Sen. Lectr, Slade Sch., UCL, 1950-64; Head of Dept of Fine Art, Goldsmith's Coll., 1964-70. Trustee: Tate Gallery, 1964-71 and 1972-74; National Gallery, 1966-72; Member: Nat. Council for Diplomas in Art and Design, 1964-72; Jt NCDAD/NACEA Cttee, 1968-70; Calouste Gulbenkian Foundn Cttee to report on future of conservation studies in UK, 1970-72; Pres., London Group, 1964-71. *Publications:* Klee, 1953; Vermeer, 1954; Soutine, 1965; Rauschenberg, 1972; (with C. Joyes) Monet at Giverny, 1975; (ed) The Townsend Journals, 1976. *Recreation:* travel. *Address:* Malthouse, Elmsted, near Ashford, Kent.

FORMAN, Rev. Adam, CBE 1919; *b* 25 Nov. 1876; *s* of J. T. Forman, Las Palmas; *m* 1908, Flora (*d* 1961), *d* of James Smith, Craigielands, Beattock; four *s* one *d* (and one *d* decd). *Educ:* Loretto; Pembroke Coll., Cambridge (MA). Cambridge Rugby XV, 1904-05 and 1905-06. Chaplain, Loretto Sch., Musselburgh, 1907-11; Curate of St Andrew's, Bishop Auckland, 1913-14; Sec. for Sphagnum Moss, Scotland, Red Cross, 1915-18. District Comr, Boy Scouts Assoc., 1936-. Silver Wolf Medal, 1961. Inspector Dumfriesshire Special Constabulary Moffat and Beattock District, 1939-45. *Recreations:* scouting, reading, music. *Address:* Dumcrieff, Moffat, Scotland DG10 9QW. *T:* Moffat 20060. *Club:* New (Edinburgh).
See also Sir D. Forman, M. B. Forman.

FORMAN, Sir Denis, Kt 1976; OBE 1956; Chairman since 1974 and Joint Managing Director since 1965, Granada Television Ltd; Chairman, Novello & Co., since 1971; *b* 13 Oct. 1917; *s* of Adam Forman, *qv*; *m* 1948, Helen de Moulpied; two *s. Educ:* at home; Loretto; Pembroke Coll., Cambridge. Served War, 1940-45: Argyll and Sutherland Highlanders; Commandant, Orkney and Shetland Defences Battle Sch., 1942 (wounded, Cassino, 1944). Chief Production Officer, Central Office of Information Films, 1947; Dir, British Film Inst., 1948-55; Chm., Bd of Governors, British Film Inst., 1971-73. Fellow, British Acad. of Film and Television Arts, 1976. Ufficiale dell'ordine Al Merito della Repubblica Italiana. *Publication:* Mozart's Piano Concertos, 1971. *Recreations:* fishing, music, shooting. *Address:* The Mill House, Howe Street, Great Waltham, Essex. *Club:* Savile.
See also M. B. Forman.

FORMAN, (Francis) Nigel, MP (C) Sutton, Carshalton, since March 1976; *b* 25 March 1943; *s* of late Brig. J. F. R. Forman and of Mrs P. J. M. Forman; *m. Educ:* Dragon Sch., Oxford; Shrewsbury Sch.; New Coll., Oxford; College of Europe, Bruges; Kennedy Sch. of Govt, Harvard; Sussex Univ. Information Officer, CBI, 1970-71; successively European Desk Officer, Head of Foreign Affairs Section and Asst Dir at Conservative Research Dept, 1971-76. *Address:* House of Commons, SW1.

FORMAN, Sir John Denis; *see* Forman, Sir Denis.

FORMAN, Louis, MD London; FRCP; Consultant Dermatologist Emeritus, Guy's Hospital and St John's Hospital for Diseases of the Skin; Hon. Consultant, London Jewish Hospital. *Educ:* Guy's Hosp., Univ. of London. MRCS, LRCP 1923; MB, BS 1924; MRCP 1925; FRCP 1939. Formerly Dermatologist SE Group, London CC; Medical Registrar, Guy's Hosp. Past President: British Assoc. Dermatology; Section of Dermatology, RSM. *Publications:* various articles in med. jls. *Address:* 22 Harley House, Regent's Park, NW1 5HE. *T:* 01-580 3262.

FORMAN, Michael Bertram, TD 1945; Director of Personnel and Organisation, Tube Investments Ltd, since 1973; *b* 28 March 1921; *s* of Rev. A. Forman, *qv*; *m* 1947, Mary Railston-Brown, *d* of Rev. W. R. Railston-Brown; four *d. Educ:* Loretto Sch., Musselburgh; Manchester Coll. of Technology. TA commn, 7th KOSB, 1939. War Service in Inf. and Airborne Forces, 1939-46: UK, Holland, Germany (POW), India. Labour Management, Courtaulds Ltd, 1946-53; Dir, Inst. of Personnel Management, 1953-56; Head of Staff Planning, NCB, 1956-59; Chief Staff Officer, SW Div., NCB, 1959-62; Personnel Relations Adviser and Dep. Dir of Personnel, Tube Investments Ltd, 1962-68, Personnel Dir, Steel Tube Div., 1968-73. Mem. NBPI, 1968-70. FIPM, 1963. *Publications:* contribs IPM Jl and Brit. Jl of Industrial Relations. *Recreations:* reading, gardening, fishing, shooting. *Address:* The Priory, Stoke Prior, Bromsgrove, Worcs. *T:* Bromsgrove 32196. *Club:* Savile.
See also Sir D. Forman.

FORMAN, Miloš; film director; *b* Čáslav, 18 Feb. 1932. *Educ:* Acad. of Music and Dramatic Art, Prague. Director: Film Presentations, Czechoslovak Television, 1954-56; Laterna Magika, Prague, 1958-62. Films directed include: Talent Competition; Peter and Pavla, 1963 (Czech. Film Critics' Award; Grand Prix, Locarno, 1964; Prize, Venice Festival, 1965); A Blonde in Love (Grand Prix, French Film Acad., 1966); The Fireman's Ball, 1967; Taking Off, 1971; (co-dir) Visions of Eight, 1973; One Flew Over the Cuckoo's Nest, 1975 (Academy Award, 1976; BAFTA Award, 1977). *Address:* c/o Robert Lantz, The Lantz Office Inc., 114 East 55th Street, New York, NY 10022, USA.

FORMAN, Nigel; *see* Forman, F. N.

FORMBY, Myles Landseer, CBE 1962; TD 1946; Consulting Otolaryngologist, retired: Consultant Emeritus to the Army, since 1971; University College Hospital, 1933-66, now Hon. Consulting Surgeon; Royal Masonic Hospital, 1948-66; *b* 13 March 1901; *s* of Arthur Formby, South Australia; *m* 1st, 1931, Dorothy Hussey Essex (marr. diss. 1952); one *s* one *d*; 2nd, 1974, Phyllis Mary Helps, *d* of late Engr-Comdr G. S. Holgate, RN. *Educ:* St Peter's Coll., Adelaide, South Australia; Univ. of Adelaide; Magdalen Coll., Oxford. Elder Scholarship, Univ. of Adelaide, 1920 and 1921, Everard Scholarship, 1924; MB, BS, Adelaide, 1924; Rhodes Scholar for S Australia, 1925; BA Oxford, 1927; BSc Oxford, 1928; FRCS 1930; MA Oxford, 1953. Hon. Asst Surg., Ear, Nose and Throat Hosp., Golden Square, 1931; Hon. Surg., Ear, Nose and Throat, Miller Gen. Hosp., 1932; Hon. Asst Surg., Ear, Nose and Throat Dept, University Coll. Hosp., 1933; Hon. Surg., 1940; Hon. Surg., Ear, Nose and Throat Dept, Royal Masonic Hosp., 1948. RAMC TA, Lieut, 1932; Capt., 1933; Major, 1939; Lieut-Col, 1941; Brig. Consulting Oto-Rhino-Laryngologist to the Army, 1943; served in the Middle East, Italy, North West Europe and India, in War of 1939-45. Hon. Civilian Consultant to War Office, 1946. Mem. Court of Examiners, Royal College of Surgeons, 1947-53, Mem. Council, 1952-57; Royal Society of Medicine: Hon. Dir of Photography, 1958-61; Pres., Section of Laryngology, 1959-60; Hon. Treas., 1962-68; Hon. Fellow, 1970; Hon. Laryngologist to Royal Academy of Music; Pres., British Assoc. of Otolaryngologists. Bronze Star, USA, 1945. *Publications:* Dental Infection in the Aetiology of Maxillary Sinusitis, 1934; Treatment of Otitis Media, 1938; Nasal Allergy, 1943; chapters in Diseases of the Ear, Nose and Throat, 1952; The Maxillary Sinus, 1960; Ultrasonic Destruction of the Labyrinth, 1963. *Recreations:* rowing, lacrosse, golf. *Address:* Thorndene, Kithurst Lane, Storrington, West Sussex RH20 4LP. *T:* Storrington 2564. *Clubs:* Royal Automobile; Leander.

FORMSTON, Prof. Clifford; Professor of Veterinary Surgery in the University of London, 1943-74, now Emeritus; former Vice-Principal, Royal Veterinary College (1963); *b* 15 Jan. 1907; *s* of Alfred and Annie Formston; *m* 1934, Irene Pembleton (*d* 1973), *d* of Capt. Roland Wood; one *s* one *d. Educ:* Chester City Grammar Sch.; Royal Veterinary College, London. MRCVS 1928; FRCVS 1944. Mem. of Royal Veterinary Coll. staff, 1928-74, Fellow, 1974. Mem. of Council, RCVS, 1954-62; John Jeyes' Travel Scholarship, 1937; Visiting Professor: Univ. of Cairo,

1960; Univ. of Thessaloniki, 1966; Sir Frederick Hobday Meml Lectr, 1971. Examiner in Veterinary Surgery, Nairobi Univ. Past President: Royal Counties Veterinary Assoc.; Central Veterinary Soc.; British Equine Veterinary Assoc. Examiner in veterinary surgery to Univs of Bristol, Cambridge, Dublin, Glasgow, Liverpool, London, Edinburgh and Khartoum; Hon. Res. Fellow, Inst. of Ophthalmology; Hon. Cons. Veterinary Surg. to Childe-Beale Trust; Vis. Prof., Pahlari Univ., Iran, 1975. Blaine Award, 1971; John Henry Steel Meml Medallist, 1973; Simon Award, 1974; Victory Medal, Central Vet. Soc., 1975. *Publications:* contrib. scientific jls on general surgery and ophthalmology. *Recreations:* golf, gardening, reading. *Address:* 4 Marlow Court, Chase Side, Southgate, N14 5HR.

FORRES, 3rd Baron *cr* 1922, of Glenogil; **John Archibald Harford Williamson;** Bt, 1909; *b* 30 Oct. 1922; *s* of 2nd Baron and Jessie (*d* 1972), *er d* of late William Alfred Harford, JP, Petty France, Badminton, Glos; *S* father, 1954; *m* 1st, 1945, Gillian Ann Maclean (marr. diss. 1967), *d* of Major J. Maclean Grant, RA retd; one *s* two *d*; 2nd, 1969, Cecily Josephine (marr. diss. 1974), *e d* of Sir Alexander Gordon Cumming, 5th Bt, and of Countess Cawdor, and *widow* of 2nd Earl of Woolton. *Educ:* Eton; Trinity Coll., Cambridge. Served War of 1939-45: with Black Watch 51st (Highland) Div., North Africa, Sicily, Normandy (despatches) (Captain, Black Watch (RHR)), with 6th (British) Armoured Div., Italy, Austria, as ADC to Comdr, 1944-45. Director: Balfour Williamson & Co., 1954-67; Lobitos Oilfields Ltd, 1954-65; Bank of London and South America Ltd, 1961-68. UK Rep., Pacific Internat. Trade Fair in Peru, 1961. Pres., Royal Forest Agric. Assoc., Windsor, 1963-64. Founder Mem., British Charollais Cattle Soc., 1961. *Heir: s* Hon. Alastair Stephen Grant Williamson [*b* 16 May 1946; *m* 1969, Margaret, *d* of late G. J. Mallam, New South Wales; two *s*]. *Address:* Glenogil, By Forfar, Angus. *T:* Fern 226. *Clubs:* Brooks's, Pratt's.

FORREST, Prof. Andrew Patrick McEwen; Regius Professor of Clinical Surgery, University of Edinburgh, since 1970; *b* 25 March 1923; *s* of Rev. Andrew James Forrest, BD, and Isabella Pearson; *m* 1955, Margaret Beryl Hall (*d* 1961); one *s* one *d*; *m* 1964, Margaret Anne Steward; one *d. Educ:* Dundee High Sch.; Univ. of St Andrews. BSc 1942; MB, ChB 1945; ChM hons, University Gold Medal, 1954; MD hons, Rutherford Gold Medal, 1958; FRCSE 1950; FRCS 1952; FRCSGlas 1962. Surg.-Lt RNVR, 1946-48. Mayo Foundation Fellow, 1952-53; Lectr and Sen. Lectr, Univ. of Glasgow, 1955-62; Prof. of Surgery, Welsh Nat. Sch. of Medicine, 1962-70. McIlrath Vis. Prof., Royal Prince Alfred Hosp., Sydney, 1969; Nimmo Vis. Prof., Royal Adelaide Hosp., 1973; McLauchlin-Gallie Prof., RCP of Canada, 1974; Lectures: Lister Meml, Canadian Med. Assoc., 1970; Inaugural Bruce, Wellesley Hosp., Toronto, 1970; Michael Williams', RSM, 1970; T. McW. Millar, Edinburgh, 1973; A. B. Mitchell, QUB, 1975; Walker, RCPGlas, 1975; Glyn Evans, RCR, 1976; J. Arthur Smith, Liverpool, 1977; Wade, Stoke, 1977. Member: Medical sub-cttee, UGC, 1967-76; MRC, 1975-; Scientific Adv. Cttee, Cancer Res. Campaign, 1974-. Asst Editor and Editor, Scottish Med. Jl, 1957-61; Hon. Secretary: Scottish Soc. for Experimental Medicine, 1959-62; Surgical Research Soc., 1963-66, Pres., 1974-76; Chm., British Breast Gp, 1974-77. Mem. Council, Assoc. of Surgeons of GB and Ireland, 1971-74; Member: Internat. Surgical Gp, 1963; British Soc. of Gastroenterology, 1960; British Assoc. for Cancer Research, 1961; British Assoc. of Surgical Oncology, 1974; Corresp. Mem., Amer. Surgical Assoc., 1973. *Publications:* (ed jtly) Prognostic Factors in Breast Cancer, 1968; various papers in surgical jls, mainly on gastro-intestinal disease and breast cancer. *Address:* Department of Clinical Surgery, University of Edinburgh. *T:* 031-667 1011. *Club:* RNVR (Glasgow).

FORREST, Geoffrey; Consultant Chartered Surveyor; Chairman, Executive Committee, Association for the Preservation of Rural Scotland, since 1973; *b* 31 Oct. 1909; *er s* of late George Forrest, CA, Rossie Lodge, Inverness; *m* 1st, 1951, Marjorie Ridehalgh; two *s*; 2nd, 1974, Joyce Grey. *Educ:* Marlborough Coll. Chartered Surveyor. Served War of 1939-45, in Lovat Scouts. Joined Forestry Commn, 1946; Chief Land Agent for Forestry Commn in Wales, 1958-64; Chief Land Agent for Forestry Commn in Scotland, 1964-65; Sen. Officer of Forestry Commn in Scotland, 1965-69. Scottish Partner, Knight, Frank & Rutley, 1973-76. *Publications:* papers on land use and estate management in professional jls. *Recreations:* fishing, shooting, lawn tennis. *Address:* Leadervale House, Earlston, Berwickshire TD4 6AJ. *Club:* New (Edinburgh).

FORREST, Cdre (Retd) Geoffrey Cornish; Master of P & O vessel Arcadia from her completion in Jan. 1954 until Oct. 1956; Commodore P & O Fleet, 1955-56; *b* 1898. *Educ:* Thames Nautical Training Coll. (the Worcester). *Recreations:*

photography, chess, bridge. *Address:* 35 Adeline Street, Faulconbridge, NSW 2776, Australia.

FORREST, Sir James (Alexander), Kt 1967; FAA; Chairman: Australian Consolidated Industries Ltd, 1953-77; National Bank of Australasia Ltd, since 1959; Chase NBA Group Ltd, since 1969; Alcoa of Australia Ltd, since 1970; Director: Australian Mutual Provident Society, since 1961 (Chairman, Victoria Branch Board, since 1957); Western Mining Corporation Ltd, since 1970; Partner, Hedderwick Fookes & Alston, Solicitors, 1933-70, Consultant, 1970-73; *b* 10 March 1905; *s* of John and Mary Gray Forrest; *m* 1939, Mary Christina Forrest (*née* Armit); three *s. Educ:* Caulfield Grammar Sch.; Melbourne Univ. RAAF and Dept Aircraft Production, 1942-45. Member: Victoria Law Foundn, 1969-75; Council, Royal Children's Hosp. Research Foundn; Scotch Coll. Council, 1959-71; Council, Monash Univ., 1961-71. Mem. Council, Boy Scouts Assoc. of Aust., 1949-73. FAA 1977. *Recreations:* golf, fishing. *Address:* (business) 19th Floor, AMP Tower, 535 Bourke Street, Melbourne, Victoria 3000, Australia. *T:* 62-6192; (home) 11 Russell Street, Toorak, Victoria 3142, Australia. *T:* 20-5227. *Clubs:* Melbourne, Australian, Naval and Military (Melbourne); Union (Sydney).

FORREST, John Samuel, MA, DSc; FRS 1966; FInstP, CEng; Visiting Professor of Electrical Engineering, University of Strathclyde, since 1964; *b* 20 Aug. 1907; *m* 1940, Ivy May Olding (*d* 1976); one *s. Educ:* Hamilton Acad.; Glasgow Univ. Physicist, Central Electricity Board: Glasgow, 1930; London, 1931; i/c of CEB Research Lab., 1934-40; Founder, 1940, Central Electricity Research Labs, Leatherhead, Dir, 1940-73; Sec., Electricity Supply Research Council, 1949-72. Hunter Memorial Lectr, 1961; Baird Memorial Lectr, 1963; Faraday Lectures, 1963-64; Kelvin Lecture, Royal Philosophical Soc. of Glasgow, 1971; Maurice Lubbock Meml Lecture, 1975. Mem. Bd, Inst. of Physics, 1945-49; Chm., London Br. Inst. of Physics, 1954-58; Chm., Supply Sect. of IEE, 1961-62; Chm., British Nat. Cttee, Conference Internationale des Grands Réseaux Electriques, 1972-76; Pres., Sect. A, Brit. Assoc., 1963; Member Council: IEE; Royal Meteorological Society, 1945-47; Research Associations; Vice-Pres., Royal Soc., 1972-75. Hon. FIEE. Hon. DSc: Strathclyde, 1969; Heriot-Watt, 1972. Coopers Hill War Memorial Prize and Medal, 1941; Willans Medal, 1958. *Publications:* papers on electrical power transmission and insulation. *Address:* Arbores, Portsmouth Road, Thames Ditton, Surrey KT7 0EG. *T:* 01-398 4389. *Club:* Royal Automobile.

FORREST, Richard Haddow, QC 1953; **His Honour Judge Haddow Forrest;** a Circuit Judge, since 1972; Lieutenant Bailiff of Jersey since 1970; *b* 13 Sept. 1908; *o s* of John Duggan and Marie Josephine Forrest; *m* 1936, Monica Constance Neville; two *s* two *d. Educ:* Merchant Taylors' Sch., Crosby; Pembroke Coll., Oxford (MA). Called to the Bar, Gray's Inn, 1932; Bencher, 1960. Recorder of Salford, 1956-64; Presiding Judge, Liverpool Court of Passage, 1964-71; Judge of Courts of Appeal, Jersey and Guernsey, 1965-71. Leader, Northern Circuit, 1968-71. King's Regiment, 1930-45 (SR, 1930-39). *Address:* High Wood, Firle Road, Seaford, Sussex.

FORREST, Rear-Adm. Sir Ronald (Stephen), KCVO 1975; County Commissioner, Devon, St John Ambulance Brigade, since 1976; *b* 11 Jan. 1923; *s* of late Stephen Forrest, MD, and Maud M. McKinstry; *m* 1st, 1947, Patricia (*d* 1966), *e d* of Dr and Mrs E. N. Russell; two *s* one *d*; 2nd, 1967, June (*née* Weaver), *widow* of late Lieut G. Perks, RN; one step *s* one step *d. Educ:* Belhaven Hill; RNC, Dartmouth. War Service at Sea, Lieut 1943 (despatches 1944); Comdr 1955; CO HMS Teazer, 1956; on loan to Pakistan Navy, 1958-60; Captain 1963; jssc 1963; Chief Staff Officer to Adm. Comdg Reserves, 1964; comd Dartmouth Trng Sqdn, 1966; Dir, Seaman Officers Appointments, 1968; CO, HMS London, 1970; Rear-Adm. 1972; Defence Services Secretary, 1972-75. Naval Gen. Service Medal, 1949. *Recreations:* gardening, golf. *Address:* Higher Seavington, Millhayes, Stockland, near Honiton, Devon. *Clubs:* Naval, Army and Navy.

FORREST, Prof. William George Grieve; Wykeham Professor of Ancient History, Oxford University, since 1977; Fellow of New College, Oxford, since 1977; *b* 24 Sept. 1925; *s* of William and Ina Forrest; *m* 1956, Margaret Elizabeth Mary Hall; two *d. Educ:* University College Sch., Hampstead; New Coll., Oxford (MA). Served RAF, 1943-47; New Coll., Oxford, 1947-51; Fellow, Wadham Coll., Oxford, 1951-76. Visiting Professor: Trinity and University Colls, Toronto, 1961; Yale, 1968. *Publications:* Emergence of Greek Democracy, 1966; History of Sparta, 1968; articles in classical and archaeological periodicals. *Address:* 9 Fyfield Road, Oxford. *T:* Oxford 56187; New College, Oxford. *T:* Oxford 48451.

FORREST, Surgeon Rear-Adm. (D) William Ivon Norman, CB 1970; Director of Naval Dental Services, Ministry of Defence, 1968-71; *b* 8 June 1914; *m* 1942, Mary Margaret McMordie Black; three *s. Educ:* Christ's Hospital. Guy's Hospital, 1931-36. LDS, RCS. Dental House Surgeon, Guy's Hosp., 1936-37. Royal Navy: Surg. Lieut (D), 1937; Surg. Lt-Comdr (D), 1943; Surg. Comdr (D), 1950; Surg. Capt. (D), 1960; Surg. Rear-Adm. (D), 1968. Consultant in Dental Surgery, 1963. *Recreations:* golf, gardening, photography. *Address:* 16 Queen's Road, Waterlooville, Hants. *T:* Waterlooville 3139.

FORRESTER, Charles, K-i-H 1944; BSc, FHWC; FRIC, PhD (Edinburgh), MIChemE, SFInstF, FRSE; scientific consultant; *y s* of Wm Fordie Forrester, HM Sasines Office, Edinburgh; *m* Joyce Annie, *o d* of Horace Purver Gripton; one *s* one *d. Educ:* Heriot-Watt Coll., Edinburgh. Prof. of Chemistry, Indian Sch. of Mines, Government of India, 1926, Vice-Principal, 1932, Principal, 1936-48; Chief Scientist's Div., Min. of Power, 1949-60, Dep. Chief Fuel Engr, later Senior Principal Scientific Officer; Brit. Coal Utilisation Res. Assoc., 1960-63; Royal Inst. of Chemistry, Council, 1948-52, 1960-63, Chm. Indian Sect., 1945-48; Institute of Fuel Council, 1932; Mem. of Mining, Geological and Metallurgical Inst. of India (Council, 1932-35 and 1942-48, Vice-Pres., 1938-39); Mem., Basic Chemicals Cttee (Supply Development Council, India), 1942-43; Mem., Fuel Research Cttee, CSIR, Govt of India. Founded, 1938, Blood Bank, Dhanbad, Bihar; social service at Leprosy Hospital, Sijua; advised CID Bihar on forensic laboratory, 1938; Kaisar-i-Hind Medal for public service in India, 1944. Editor, the Plant Engineer, 1953-55. Hon. Fellow, Heriot-Watt Coll. *Publications:* Trans Min. Geol. and Met. Inst. India (bronze, silver, and gold medals and twice Govt of India Prize, Rs 500); Journal of the Institute of Fuel, Proc. Indian Science Cong., Proc. Nat. Inst. Sciences, India; Fuel Research Report No. 1, CSIR (India); Editor and part-contributor, The Efficient Use of Fuel (HMSO), 1958. *Recreations:* gardening, Scottish country dancing, organ and classical music. *Address:* 1 Hampton Grove, Ewell, Epsom, Surrey KT17 1LA. *T:* 01-393 1004.

FORRESTER, John Stuart; MP (Lab) Stoke-on-Trent, North, since 1966; *b* 17 June 1924; *s* of Harry and Nellie Forrester; *m* 1945, Gertrude H. Weaver. *Educ:* Eastwood Council Sch.; City Sch. of Commerce, Stoke-on-Trent; Alsager Teachers' Training Coll. Teacher, 1946-66. Sec., Constituency Labour Party, 1961; Mem., Executive Cttee, Stoke-on-Trent City Labour Party, 1958. Councillor, Stoke-on-Trent, 1970-. *Recreations:* sport, gardening, do-it-yourself. *Address:* House of Commons, SW1.

FORRESTER, Maj.-Gen. Michael, CB 1969; CBE 1963 (OBE 1960); DSO 1943 and Bar, 1944; MC 1939 and Bar, 1941; retired 1970; *b* 31 Aug. 1917; 2nd *s* of late James Forrester, Chilworth, Hants, and Elsie (*née* Mathwin); *m* 1947, Pauline Margaret Clara (marr. diss. 1960), *d* of late James Fisher, Crossmichael; two *s. Educ:* Haileybury. 2nd Lieut, Queen's Royal Regt, 1938; served in Palestine (Arab Rebellion), 1938-39; served War of 1939-45 in Palestine, Egypt, Greece, Crete, Western Desert, Syria, N Africa, Italy and France; GSO3 (Ops), HQ Western Desert Force and HQ 13 Corps, 1941-42; Staff Coll., Haifa, 1942; Bde Major, 132 Inf. Bde, 1942 (despatches); GSO2 (Ops), HQ 13 Corps and HQ 18 Army Gp, 1943; Comdr, 1st/6th Bn, Queen's Royal Regt, 1943-44; wounded, Normandy; GSO1 (Ops), HQ 13 Corps, 1945-46; Mil. Asst to Supreme Allied Comdr Mediterranean, 1947; Mil. Asst to Comdr Brit. Army Staff and Army Mem., Brit. Jt Services Mission, Washington, DC, 1947-50; Co. Comdr, 2nd Bn Parachute Regt, Cyprus and Canal Zone, 1951-52; Dirg Staff, Staff Coll., Camberley, 1953-55; GSO1 (Ops), GHQ East Africa, 1955-57; transf. to Parachute Regt, 1957; Comdr, 3rd Bn Parachute Regt, 1957-60; Col., Military Operations (4), War Office, 1960-61; Comdr, 16 Parachute Bde Gp, 1961-63; Imp. Def. Coll., 1964; GOC 4th Div., BAOR, 1965-67; Dir of Infantry, MoD, 1968-70. Col Comdt, The Queen's Division, 1968-70. *Address:* Pullens, West Worldham, near Alton, Hants. *T:* Alton 84470.

FORRESTER, Prof. Peter Garnett; Director, Cranfield School of Management, since 1967, Dean of Faculty, 1972; Pro-Vice-Chancellor, Cranfield Institute of Technology, since 1976; *b* 7 June 1917; *s* of Arthur Forrester and Emma (*née* Garnett); *m* 1942, Marjorie Hewitt, Berks; two *d. Educ:* Manchester Grammar Sch.; Manchester Univ. (BSc, MSc). FIM, FRSA. Metallurgist, Thomas Bolton & Son Ltd, 1938-40; Research Officer, later Chief Metallurgist, Tin Research Inst., 1940-48; Chief Metallurgist and Research Man., Glacier Metal Co. Ltd, 1948-63; Dep. Principal, Glacier Inst. of Management, 1963-64; Consultant, John Tyzack & Partners, 1964-66; Prof. of Industrial Management, Coll. of Aeronautics, Cranfield, 1966. Chm., Conf. of Univ. Management Schs, 1976-77. *Publications:* numerous scientific and technological papers on metallurgy, bearing materials, tribology. *Recreations:* sailing, walking. *Address:* 5 West Road, Cranfield, Bedford. *T:* Bedford 750111. *Clubs:* Upper Thames Sailing, Helford River Sailing.

FORRESTER, Rev. William Roxburgh; Professor of Practical Theology and Christian Ethics, St Mary's College, St Andrews University, 1934-58; Emeritus Professor; *b* 19 Feb. 1892; *s* of Rev. David Marshall Forrester, DD, and Annie Roxburgh; *m* 1922, Isobel Margaret Stewart McColl (*d* 1976); five *c. Educ:* Glasgow Acad.; Glasgow and Edinburgh Univs. MA (Hons) Edinburgh, 1914; European War: France, Mesopotamia, Persia and India in RFA, 1914-19; Studies at New Coll., Edinburgh; France and Germany, 1919-22; BD, 1924; Minister at Roslin, 1922-28; Minister at Cairns Memorial Church, Edinburgh, 1928-34; Interim Gen. Sec. Scottish National YMCA, 1940-44; DD (Edinburgh) 1939. Cunningham Lecturer, New Coll., Edinburgh, 1947-48-49; LLD St Andrews, 1959. Associate Minister, St Andrew's Presbyterian Church, Nairobi, Nov. 1961-Nov. 1962. *Publications:* Christian Vocation, Studies in Faith and its Relation to Work, 1951; Conversion, 1937, Concern, 1963; The Pen and the Panga, two Addresses on Education and Religion (East Africa), 1965; Your Life and Mine, 1967. *Recreations:* fishing, gardening. *Address:* 7 Newbattle Terrace, Edinburgh EH10 4RU. *T:* 031-447 2870.

FORRESTER-PATON, Douglas Shaw, QC 1965; **His Honour Judge Forrester-Paton;** a Circuit Judge (formerly a Judge of County Courts), since 1970; *b* 1921; 3rd *s* of late Alexander Forrester-Paton, JP; *m* 1948, Agnete, *d* of Holger Tuxen; one *s* two *d. Educ:* Gresham's Sch., Holt; Queen's Coll., Oxford (BA). Called to Bar, Middle Temple, 1947; North East Circuit. Served RAF, 1941-45. Recorder: Middlesbrough, 1963-68; Teesside, 1968-70. *Address:* 24 Kirkby Lane, Great Broughton, Middlesbrough, Cleveland TS9 7HG. *T:* Wainstones 301; 5 King's Bench Walk, Temple, EC4.

FORSBERG, (Charles) Gerald, OBE 1955; Comdr RN (Retd); author; Assistant Director of Marine Services, Ministry of Defence (Navy Department), 1972-75 (Deputy Director, 1958-72); *b* Vancouver, 18 June 1912; *s* of Charles G. Forsberg and Nellie (*née* Wallman); *m* 1952, Joyce Whewell Hogarth, *d* of Dr F. W. Hogarth; one *s* one *d. Educ:* Polytechnic School; Training Ship Mercury; Sir John Cass Coll. Merchant Navy: Cadet to Chief Officer, 1928-38; qual. Master Mariner; transf. RN, 1938. Norwegian campaign, 1940; Malta Convoys, Matapan, Tobruk, Crete, etc, 1940-42; comd HMS Vega as Convoy Escort Comdr, 1943-45 (despatches). Comd HMS Mameluke and HMS Chaplet, 1945-49; comd Salvage Sqdn off Elba in recovery of crashed Comet aircraft in 100 fathoms, 1954. Swam Channel (England-France) in record time, 1957; first person to swim Lough Neagh and Loch Lomond, 1959; British long-distance champion, 1957-58-59; swam Bristol Channel in record time, 1964; many long-distance championships and records, 1951-. Younger Brother of Trinity House, 1958; Civil Service, 1962. Pres. Channel Swimming Assoc., 1963; Master of Navy Lodge, 1966; Liveryman, Hon. Co. of Master Mariners. Freeman, City of London, 1968. *Publications:* Long Distance Swimming, 1957; First Strokes in Swimming, 1961; Modern Long Distance Swimming, 1963; Salvage from the Sea, 1977; many short stories, articles, papers, and book reviews for general periodicals, technical jls and encyclopædia; regular monthly contribs to Swimming Times. *Recreations:* motoring, Association football refereeing, reading. *Address:* c/o Barclays Bank International, Goodenough House, 33 Old Broad Street, EC2. *Clubs:* Royal Automobile; Otter Swimming.

FORSDYKE, Sir (Edgar) John, KCB 1937; MA; Hon. ARIBA; Director and Principal Librarian of British Museum, 1936-50; 2nd *s* of F. P. Forsdyke, Hasketon, Suffolk; *b* 12 Sept. 1883; *m* 1942, Dea Gombrich, violinist, *e d* of Dr Karl Gombrich of Vienna; two *d. Educ:* Christ's Hospital; Keble Coll., Oxford (Scholar and Hon. Fellow). Entered British Museum, 1907; Keeper of Greek and Roman Antiquities in the British Museum, 1932-36. Military service, 1914-19, France, Macedonia, Egypt, Palestine; Capt., RFA. Editor Journal of Hellenic Studies, 1912-23; Hon. Sec. Hellenic Soc.; Hon. Member: Archæological Soc. of Athens; Archæological Inst. of America. *Publication:* Greece before Homer, 1956. *Address:* 13 Sandringham Road, NW11.

FORSTER, Charles Ian Kennerley, CBE 1964; Consultant; *b* 18 July 1911; *s* of Douglas Wakefield Forster; *m* 1942, Thelma Primrose Horton (marr. diss. 1974); one *s* one *d*; *m* 1975, Mrs Loraine Huxtable. *Educ:* Rossall Sch. FIA 1936. Served RA, 1939-45. Statistics Branch, Admty, 1946-54; Ministry of Power, 1954 (Chief Statistician, 1955-65, Dir of Statistics, 1965-69); Min. of Technology, 1969; Under-Sec., Dept of Trade and Industry, 1970-72, retd. *Publications:* contribs to Jls of Inst. of Actuaries and Inst. of Actuaries Students Soc., Trans VII World

Power Conf., Trans Manchester Statistical Soc., Statistical News. *Recreations:* gardening, stamps. *Address:* 140 Watchfield Court, Chiswick, W4. *T:* 01-994 3128.

FORSTER, Brig. Eric Brown, MBE 1952; General Manager, Potato Marketing Board, since 1970; *b* 19 May 1917; *s* of late Frank and Agnes Forster; *m* 1943, Margaret Bessie Letitia, *d* of late Lt-Col Arthur Wood, MBE and late Edith Wood; one *s* two *d. Educ:* Queen Elizabeth Grammar Sch., Hexham. Commnd from RASC ranks into RAPC, 1941. Dir of Cost and Management Accounting (Army Dept), 1967-68. *Recreations:* golf, gardening. *Address:* Littledene, Guildown Avenue, Guildford, Surrey GU2 5HB. *T:* Guildford 62313. *Clubs:* Farmers', MCC; Worplesdon Golf.

FORSTER, Prof. Leonard Wilson, FBA 1976; Schröder Professor of German, University of Cambridge, since 1961; *b* 30 March 1913; *o s* of Edward James Forster, merchant, and Linda Charlotte (*née* Rogers), St John's Wood, NW8; *m* 1939, Jeanne Marie Louise, *e d* of Dr Charles Otto Billeter, Basel; one *s* two *d. Educ:* Marlborough Coll.; Trinity Hall, Cambridge. LittD Cantab, 1976. Thomas Carlyle Student, 1934-35; English Lektor: Univ. of Leipzig, 1934; Univ. of Königsberg, 1935-36; Univ. of Basel, 1936-38; study at Univ. of Bonn, 1935. Fellow and Lectr, Selwyn Coll., Cambridge, 1937; Faculty Asst Lectr, Univ. of Cambridge, 1937; Dr phil., Basel, 1938. Naval Staff Admiralty, 1939-41; Foreign Office, 1941-45; Lt-Comdr RNVR (Sp.), 1945-46. Univ. Lectr in German, Cambridge, 1947-50; Dean and Asst Tutor, Selwyn Coll., 1946-50; Prof. of German, UCL, 1950-61. Pres., Internat. Assoc. for Germanic Studies (IVG), 1970-75. Corresponding Member: Deutsche Akademie für Sprache und Dichtung, 1957; Royal Belgian Academy of Dutch Language and Literature, 1973; Member: Maatschappij der Nederlandse Letterkunde, Leiden, 1966; Royal Netherlands Acad. of Sciences and Letters, 1968. Visiting Professor: Univ. of Toronto, 1957; Univ. of Heidelberg, 1964; McGill Univ., 1967-68; Univ. of Otago, 1968; Utrecht Univ., 1976. Sen. Consultant, Folger Shakespeare Library, Washington, 1975. Gold Medal, Goethe-Institut, Munich, 1966. Hon. DLitt Leiden, 1975. Grosses Verdienstkreuz (Germany), 1976. *Publications:* G. R. Weckherlin, zur Kenntnis seines Lebens in England, 1944; Conrad Celtis, 1948; German Poetry, 1944-48, 1949; The Temper of Seventeenth Century German Literature, 1952; Penguin Book of German Verse, 1957; Poetry of Significant Nonsense, 1962; Lipsius, Von der Bestencigkeit, 1965; Die Niederlande und die Anfänge der deutschen Barocklyrik, 1967; Janus Gruter's English Years, 1967; The Icy Fire, 1969; The Poet's Tongues: multilingualism in Literature, 1971. German Life and Letters (co-ed); articles in British and foreign jls. *Recreation:* foreign travel. *Address:* 49 Maids Causeway, Cambridge. *T:* 57513; Selwyn College, Cambridge. *Club:* Athenæum.

FORSTER, Margaret; author; Chief non-fiction Reviewer, Evening Standard, since 1977; *b* 25 May 1938; *d* of Arthur Gordon Forster and Lilian (*née* Hind); *m* 1960, Edward Hunter Davies, *qv*; one *s* two *d. Educ:* Carlisle and County High Sch. for Girls; Somerville Coll., Oxford (BA). FRSL. Teacher, Barnsbury Girls' Sch., Islington, 1961-63. Mem., BBC Adv. Cttee on Social Effects of Television, 1975-. *Publications: biography:* The Rash Adventurer: the rise and fall of Charles Edward Stuart, 1973; *novels:* Dame's Delight, 1964; Georgy Girl, 1965 (filmscript with Peter Nichols, 1966); The Bogeyman, 1965; The Travels of Maudie Tipstaff, 1967; The Park, 1968; Miss Owen-Owen is At Home, 1969; Fenella Phizacherley, 1970; Mr Bone's Retreat, 1971; The Seduction of Mrs Pendlebury, 1974. *Recreations:* walking on Hampstead Heath, reading contemporary fiction. *Address:* 11 Boscastle Road, NW5. *T:* 01-485 3785.

FORSTER, Oliver Grantham, CMG 1976; MVO 1961; HM Diplomatic Service; Deputy Chief Clerk, Foreign and Commonwealth Office, since 1975; *b* 2 Sept. 1925; 2nd *s* of Norman Milward Forster and Olive Christina Forster (*née* Cockrell); *m* 1953, Beryl Myfanwy Evans; two *d. Educ:* Hurstpierpoint; King's Coll., Cambridge. Served in RAF, 1944-48. Joined Commonwealth Relations Office, 1951. Private Sec. to Parly Under-Sec., 1953-54; Second Sec., Karachi, 1954-56; Principal, CRO, 1956-59; First Sec., Madras, 1959-62; First Sec., Washington, 1962-65; Private Sec. to Sec. of State for Commonwealth Relations, 1965-67; Counsellor, Manila, 1967-70; Counsellor, New Delhi, 1970-75, Minister, 1975. *Address:* c/o Foreign and Commonwealth Office, SW1. *Clubs:* United Oxford & Cambridge University, Royal Commonwealth Society.

FORSTER, Walter Leslie, CBE 1942; Legion of Merit (USA), 1944; BSc; FInstPet; Director, Petrofina Canada Ltd, and other cos; *b* 30 June 1903; *s* of John Mark Forster, Leeds; *m* 1936, Lorna, *d* of T. L. Bonstow, Coulsdon, Surrey; one *s*. *Educ:* Leeds Univ. *Address:* 61 Summit Crescent, Westmount, Montreal, Canada. *Clubs:* University, St James's, Mount Royal (Montreal).

FORSYTH, Jennifer Mary; Under-Secretary, HM Treasury, since 1975; *b* 7 Oct. 1924; *o d* of late Matthew Forsyth, theatrical director, and of Marjorie Forsyth. *Educ:* Frensham Heights; London Sch. of Economics and Political Science (Pres. of Students' Union, 1944-45) (BScEcon). Joined Home Finance Div., Treasury, 1945; Economic Asst, UN Economic Commn for Europe, 1949-51; Information Div., Treasury, 1951-53; Principal, Estabts, Overseas Finance and Planning Divs, 1954-62; UK Treasury Delegn, Washington, 1962-64; Assistant Secretary: DEA, 1965-69; Social Services (Educn), Treasury, 1969-75. Governor, Frensham Heights, 1965-76. *Recreations:* going to the theatre and to the Mediterranean. *Address:* 51 Abingdon Road, W8 6AN.

FORSYTH, William Douglass, OBE 1955; Australian Ambassador, retired 1969; *b* Casterton, Australia, 5 Jan. 1909; of Australian parents; *m* 1935, Thelma Joyce (*née* Sherry); one *s* two *d*. *Educ:* Ballarat High Sch.; Melbourne Univ. (MA, DipEd); Balliol Coll., Oxford (BLitt). Teacher of History, 1931-35; Rockefeller Fellow, Social Studies, Europe, 1936-37 and 1939; Research Fellow, Melbourne Univ., 1940; Editor Austral-Asiatic Bulletin, Melbourne, 1940; Research Sec., Aust. Inst. International Affairs, 1940-41; Australian Dept of Information, 1941-42; Australian Dept of External Affairs, 1942-69: First Sec., 1946; Counsellor, Aust. Embassy, Washington, 1947-48; Aust. rep. Trusteeship Council, 1948 and 1952-55; Sec.-Gen., South Pacific Commission, 1948-51. Australian Member UN Population Commission, 1946-47; Mem., Australian Delegns to UN General Assembly, 1946-48 and 1951-58; San Francisco UN Confs, 1945 and 1955; Minister, Australian Mission to UN, 1951-55; Asst-Sec., Dept of External Affairs, Canberra, 1956-59, 1961-63; Australian Minister to Laos, 1959-60; Australian Ambassador to Viet-Nam, 1959-61; Sec.-Gen., South Pacific Commn, Nouméa, 1963-66; Australian Ambassador to Lebanon, 1967-68. *Publications:* Governor Arthur's Convict System, 1935, reprinted 1970; The Myth of Open Spaces, 1942; Captain Cook's Australian Landfalls, 1970; articles in Economic Record, etc. *Address:* 88 Banks Street, Yarralumla, Canberra, ACT 2600, Australia.

FORSYTHE, Air Cdre James Roy, CBE 1966; DFC; Director of Development, Look Ahead Housing Association Ltd; *b* 10 July 1920; *s* of W. R. and A. M. Forsythe; *m* 1946, Barbara Mary Churchman; two *s* two *d*. *Educ:* Methodist Coll., Belfast; Queen's Univ., Belfast. Bomber Comd, 1944-45; OC, Aberdeen Univ. Air Sqdn, 1952-54; pfc 1955; Principal Staff Officer to Dir-Gen. Orgn (RAF), 1956-58; OC, 16 Sqdn, 1958-60; Dirg Staff, Coll. of Air Warfare, Manby, 1960-62; Head of RAF Aid Mission to India, 1963; Stn Comdr, RAF Acklington, 1963-65; Dep. Dir Air Staff Policy, MoD, 1965-68; Dir Public Relations, Far East, 1968-70; Dir Recruiting, RAF, 1971-73; Dir, Public Relations, RAF, 1973-75. Mem., Inst. of Public Relations. *Recreations:* Rugby, golf. *Address:* 51C Ossington Street, W2 4LY. *T:* 01-229 5119. *Club:* Royal Air Force.

FORT, Mrs Jean; Headmistress of Roedean School, Brighton, 1961-70; *b* 1915; *d* of G. B. Rae; *m* 1943, Richard Fort (*d* 1959), MP Clitheroe Division of Lancs; four *s* one *d*. *Educ:* Benenden Sch.; Lady Margaret Hall, Oxford (MA, DipEd). Asst Mistress, Dartford County Sch. for Girls, 1937-39; WVS Headquarters staff, 1939-40; Junior Civil Asst, War Office, 1940-41; Personal Asst to Sir Ernest Gowers, Sen. Regional Comr for Civil Def., London, 1941-44. Mem., Advertising Standards Authority, 1965-. *Address:* Ruscombe House, Twyford, near Reading, Berks.

FORTE, Sir Charles, Kt 1970; FRSA; Deputy Chairman, Trust Houses Forte Ltd, since 1970, and Chief Executive, since 1971; *b* 26 Nov. 1908; *m* 1943, Irene Mary Chierico; one *s* five *d*. *Educ:* Alloa Academy; Dumfries Coll.; Mamiani, Rome. Fellow and Mem. Exec. Cttee, Catering Inst., 1949; Mem. Small Consultative Advisory Cttee to Min. of Food, 1946; Pres. Italian Chamber of Commerce for Great Britain and Ireland, 1952; Mem. Council: BTA; London Tourist Board. Hon. Consul Gen. for Republic of San Marino. FBIM 1971. Mem. AA, RAC. Grand Officier, Ordine al Merito della Repubblica Italiana; Cavaliere di Gran Croce della Repubblica Italiana. *Publications:* articles for catering trade papers. *Recreations:* golf, fishing, shooting, fencing, music. *Address:* 86 Park Lane, W1. *Clubs:* Caledonian, Arts, Royal Thames Yacht; National Sporting (President).

FORTES, Prof. Meyer, MA, PhD; FBA 1967; William Wyse Professor of Social Anthropology, University of Cambridge, 1950-73; Fellow of King's College, Cambridge; *b* Britstown, Cape, 25 April 1906; *e s* of late Nathan and late Mrs Bertha Fortes, Cape Town, S Africa; *m* 1928, Sonia (*d* 1956), *d* of late N. Donen, Worcester, Cape, SA; one *d*; *m* 1960, Doris Y. Mayer, MD, *d* of late D. S. Yankauer, NY. *Educ:* South African Coll. High Sch., Cape Town; University of Cape Town; University of London. Univ. of Cape Town: Roderick Noble Schol., 1926, Willem Hiddingh Schol., 1927-30; London Sch. of Economics: Ratan Tata Student, 1930-31, Rockefeller Fellow, 1933-34; Fellow, International African Institute, 1934-38; Lectr, LSE, 1938-39; Research Lectr, University of Oxford, 1939-41; National Service, West Africa, 1942-44; Head of Sociological Dept, West African Insitute, Accra, Gold Coast, 1944-46; Reader in Social Anthropology, Oxford, 1946-50. President: Section H, Brit. Assoc. for the Advancement of Science, 1953; Section 25, ANZAAS, 1975. Lectures: Josiah Mason, Univ. of Birmingham, 1949; Frazer, Glasgow, 1956; Henry Myers, Royal Anthrop. Inst., 1960; Lewis Henry Morgan, Univ. of Rochester, USA, 1963; Munro, Univ. of Edinburgh, 1964, 1973; Emanuel Miller Meml, Assoc. Child Psychol. and Psychiatry, 1972; Ernest Jones Meml, Brit. Psychoanalytical Soc., 1973; Marett, Oxford, 1974; Huxley Meml, Royal Anthrop. Inst., 1977. Chm., Assoc. Social Anthropologists, 1970-73. For. Mem., American Philosophical Soc., 1972; Foreign Hon. Mem. Amer. Acad. of Arts and Sciences, 1964. Field Research: Northern Territories, Gold Coast, 1934-37; Nigeria, 1941-42; Ashanti Gold Coast, 1945-46; Bechuanaland, 1948. Pres., Royal Anthropological Institute; Hon. Editor, Jl Royal Anthropological Inst., 1947-53; Mem. Exec. Council, International African Institute; Mem. Exec. Cttee, British Sociological Assoc., 1952-55. Visiting Professor: Chicago Univ., 1954, 1973; Australian Nat. Univ., 1975; Univ. of California, Santa Cruz, 1977; Leverhulme Vis. Prof., Univ. of Ghana, 1971. Fellow: Center for Advanced Study in Behavioral Science, Stanford, 1958-59, and 1967-68; University Coll., London, 1975. Rivers Medal, Royal Anthropological Inst., 1946. Hon. DHL Chicago, 1973; Hon. DLitt Belfast, 1975. *Publications:* The Dynamics of Clanship among the Tallensi, 1945; The Web of Kinship among the Tallensi, 1949; Social Anthropology at Cambridge since 1900, 1953; Oedipus and Job in West African Religion, 1959; Kinship and the Social Order, 1969; Time and Social Structure, 1970; (ed) Marriage in Tribal Societies, 1972; (ed with S. Patterson) Studies in African Social Anthropology, 1975; various papers in psychological and anthropological journals. *Address:* 113 Grantchester Meadows, Cambridge CB3 9JN; King's College, Cambridge.

FORTESCUE, family name of **Earl Fortescue.**

FORTESCUE, 7th Earl *cr* 1789; **Richard Archibald Fortescue,** JP; Baron Fortescue 1746; Viscount Ebrington 1789; *b* 14 April 1922; *s* of 6th Earl Fortescue, MC, TD, and Marjorie (*d* 1964), OBE, *d* of late Col C. W. Trotter, CB, TD; *S* father, 1977; *m* 1st, 1949, Penelope Jane (*d* 1959), *d* of late Robert Evelyn Henderson; one *s* one *d*; 2nd, 1961, Margaret Anne, *d* of Michael Stratton; two *d*. *Educ:* Eton; Christ Church, Oxford. Captain Coldstream Guards (Reserve). JP Oxon, 1964. *Heir: s* Viscount Ebrington, *qv*. *Address:* The Old Farm, Swinbrook, Burford, Oxon. *T:* Burford 3135. *Club:* White's.

FORTESCUE, Trevor Victor Norman; Secretary-General, Food and Drink Industries Council, since 1973; *b* 28 Aug. 1916; *s* of Frank Fortescue; *m* 1st, 1939, Margery Stratford (marr. diss. 1975), *d* of Dr G. H. Hunt; two *s* one *d*; 2nd, 1975, Anthea Maureen, *d* of Robert M. Higgins. *Educ:* Uppingham Sch.; King's Coll., Cambridge. BA 1938; MA 1945. Colonial Administrative Service, Hong Kong, 1939-47 and Kenya, 1949-51 (interned, 1941-45); FAO, UN, Washington, DC, 1947-49 and Rome, 1951-54; Chief Marketing Officer, Milk Marketing Bd of England and Wales, 1954-59; Manager, Nestlé Gp of Cos, Vevey, Switz., 1959-63 and London, 1963-66. MP (C) Liverpool, Garston, 1966-Feb. 1974; an Asst Govt Whip, 1970-71; a Lord Comr of HM Treasury, 1971-73. Chm., British Exec. Cttee, Internat. Grenfell Assoc., 1975-. *Recreations:* marriage to Anthea; Napoleon. *Address:* 34 Stanford Road, W8 5PZ. *T:* 01-937 9214.

FORTEVIOT, 3rd Baron *cr* 1916; **Henry Evelyn Alexander Dewar,** Bt, *cr* 1907; MBE 1943; DL; Chairman, John Dewar & Sons Ltd, 1954-76; former Director, Distillers Co. Ltd; *b* 23 Feb. 1906; 2nd *s* of 1st Baron Forteviot and Margaret Elizabeth, *d* of late Henry Holland; *S* half-brother 1947; *m* 1933, Cynthia Monica, *e d* of late Cecil Starkie, Hethe Place, Cowden, Kent; two *s* two *d*. *Educ:* Eton; St John's Coll., Oxford (BA). Served War of 1939-45, with Black Watch (RHR) (MBE). DL Perth, 1961. *Heir: s* Hon. John James Evelyn Dewar [*b* 5 April 1938; *m*

1963, Lady Elisabeth Waldegrave, 3rd *d* of 12th Earl Waldegrave, *qv* ; one *s* three *d*]. *Address:* Dupplin Castle, Perth, Perthshire. *Club:* Brooks's; Royal (Perth).
See also Duke of Fife.

FORTIER, Most Rev. Jean-Marie; *see* Sherbrooke, Archbishop of, (RC).

FORTY, Francis John, OBE 1952; BSc, FICE, FSA, FRSH, FIMunE; City Engineer, Corporation of London, 1938-64; *b* Hull, Yorks, 11 Feb. 1900; *s* of J. E. Forty, MA Oxon, headmaster, Hull Grammar Sch., and Maud C. Forty; *m* 1st, 1926, Doris Marcon Francis (*d* 1958), *d* of Dr A. G. Francis, BA Cantab, FRCS; one *s* two *d* ; 2nd, 1965, Elizabeth Joyce Tofield. *Educ:* Hymers Coll., Hull; Glasgow Univ. (BSc 1923). RNAS, RAF, 1918-19 (Commnd Pilot). Engineering Asst, Hull; Engineering Asst, York; Chief Engineering Asst, Willesden. Deputy Borough Surveyor, Ealing; Borough Engineer and Surveyor, Ealing, 1934-38. War duties, 1939-45, included i/c City of London Heavy Rescue Service (Civil Defence Long Service Medal). Works include: (with Sir Albert Richardson) St Paul's Garden, 1951; (in consultation with Prof. W. F. Grimes) exposure and preservation of section of Town Wall of London, 1951-53; London Wall new route between Moorgate and Aldersgate Street, with car park underneath, 1959; Blackfriars Bridgehead Improvement with underpass, 1962-; multi-storey car park, Upper Thames Street, 1962; (with Sir Hugh Casson) Walbrook Wharf Public Cleansing Depot and Wharf 1963. Formerly Member: London Regional Bldg Cttee; Nat. Soc. for Clean Air; Roman and Mediaeval London Excavation Council; Festival of Britain Council for Architecture, Town Planning and Bldg Research; Minister of Transport's Parking Survey Cttee for Inner London; Minister of Housing and Local Govt's Thames Flooding Technical Panel; Sussex Archaeological Trust. Liveryman of the Worshipful Company of Painter-Stainers, of the City of London. *Publications:* Bituminous Emulsions for Use in Road Works (with F. Wilkinson), 1932; Swimming Bath Water Purification from a Public Health Point of View (with F. W. Wilkinson), various contribs technical and other jls; notably contrib. on exposure and preservation of Roman and Mediæval work in the Town Wall of London. *Recreations:* gardening, photography, reading. *Address:* Little Oakley, Wilmington, near Polegate, East Sussex. *T:* Alfriston 870268. *Club:* Athenæum.

FORWELL, Dr George Dick, PhD; FRCPE, FRCPGlas; Chief Administrative Officer, Greater Glasgow Health Board, and Hon. Lecturer, Department of Administrative Medicine, Glasgow University, since 1973; *b* 6 July 1928; *s* of Harold C. Forwell and Isabella L. Christie; *m* 1957, Catherine F. C. Cousland; two *d* . *Educ:* George Watson's Coll., Edinburgh; Edinburgh Univ. (MB, ChB 1950; PhD 1955). MRCPE 1957, DIH 1957, DPH 1959, FRCPE 1967, FFCM 1972, FRCPGlas 1974. House Officer and Univ. Clin. Asst, Edinburgh Royal Infirm., 1950-52; RAF Inst. of Aviation Med., 1952-54; MRC and RCPE grants, 1954-56; pneumoconiosis field res., 1956-57; Grad. Res. Fellow and Lectr, Edinburgh Univ. Dept of Public Health and Social Med., 1957-60; Asst Dean, Faculty of Med., Edinburgh Univ., 1960-63; Dep. Sen. and Sen. Admin. MO, Eastern Reg. Hosp. Bd, Dundee, 1963-67; PMO, Scottish Home and Health Dept, 1967-73. *Publications:* papers on clin. res. and on health planning and services, in med. and other jls. *Address:* 60 Whittingehame Drive, Glasgow G12 0YQ. *T:* 041-334 7122.

FORWOOD, Sir Dudley (Richard), 3rd Bt *cr* 1895; Member of Lloyd's; Official Verderer of the New Forest, since 1974; *b* 6 June 1912; *s* of Sir Dudley Baines Forwood, 2nd Bt, CMG, and Norah Isabella (*née* Lockett) (*d* 1962); *S* father, 1961; *m* 1952, Mary Gwendoline (who *m* 1st, Viscount Ratendone, now Marquis of Willingdon; 2nd, Robert Cullingford), *d* of Basil S. Foster. *Educ:* Stowe Sch. Attaché, British Legation, Vienna, 1934-37; Equerry to the Duke of Windsor, 1937-39. Served War of 1939-45, Scots Guards (Major). Master, New Forest Buckhounds, 1956-65; Chairman: New Forest Consultative Panel, 1970-; Crufts, 1973-. Hon. Dir, RASE, 1973. *Recreation:* hunting. *Heir: cousin* Peter Noel Forwood [*b* 1925; *m* 1950, Roy Murphy; six *d*]. *Address:* 43 Addison Road, W14. *T:* 01-603 3620; The Old House, Burley, near Ringwood, Hants. *T:* Burley 2345.

FOSKETT, Douglas John, FLA; Librarian, University of London Institute of Education, since 1957; *b* 27 June 1918; *s* of John Henry Foskett and Amy Florence Foskett; *m* 1948, Joy Ada (*née* McCann); one *s* two *d* . *Educ:* Bancroft's Sch.; Queen Mary Coll., Univ. of London (BA 1939); Birkbeck Coll., Univ. of London (MA 1954). Ilford Municipal Libraries, 1940-48; RAMC and Intell. Corps, 1940-46; Metal Box Co. Ltd, 1948-57. Chairman of Council, Library Assoc., 1962-63, Vice-Pres., 1966-73, Pres., 1976; Hon. Library Adviser, RNID, 1965-; Mem.,

Adv. Cttee on Sci. and Techn. Information, 1969-73; Mem. and Rapporteur, Internat. Adv. Cttee on Documentation, Libraries and Archives, UNESCO, 1968-73; Cons. on Documentation to ILO and to European Packaging Fedn; Cttee Mem., UNISIST/UNESCO and EUDISED/Council of Europe Projects; Member: Army Educn Adv. Bd, 1968-73; Library Adv. Council, 1975-. Visiting Professor: Univ. of Michigan, 1964; Univ. of Ghana, 1967; Univ. of Ibadan, 1967; Brazilian Inst. for Bibliography and Documentation, 1971; Univ. of Iceland, 1974. FLA 1949, Hon. FLA, 1975. *Publications:* Assistance to Readers in Lending Libraries, 1952; (with E. A. Baker) Bibliography of Food, 1958; Information Service in Libraries, 1958, 2nd edn 1967; Classification and Indexing in the Social Sciences, 1963, 2nd edn 1974; Science, Humanism and Libraries, 1964; Reader in Comparative Librarianship, 1977; contrib. to many professional jls. *Recreations:* books, travel, writing, cricket. *Address:* 1 Daleside, Gerrard's Cross, Bucks SL9 7JF. *T:* Gerrard's Cross 82835. *Clubs:* MCC; Sussex CCC.

FOSTER; *see* Hylton-Foster.

FOSTER, Prof. Allan (Bentham); Professor of Chemistry, University of London, since 1966; Head of Division of Chemistry, Chester Beatty Research Institute, Institute of Cancer Research: Royal Cancer Hospital, since 1966; *b* 21 July 1926; *s* of late Herbert and Martha Alice Foster; *m* 1949, Monica Binns; two *s*. *Educ:* Nelson Grammar Sch., Lancs; University of Birmingham. Frankland Medal and Prize, 1947; PhD, 1950; DSc, 1957. University Res. Fellow, University of Birmingham, 1950-53; Fellow of Rockefeller Foundn, Ohio State Univ., 1953-54; University of Birmingham: ICI Res. Fellow, 1954-55; Lectr, 1955-62; Sen. Lectr, 1962-64; Reader in Organic Chemistry, 1964-66. FChemSoc (Mem. Coun., 1962-65, 1967-70); FRIC; MACS. Corresp. Mem., Argentinian Chem. Soc. Regional Editor, Carbohydrate Research. *Publications:* numerous scientific papers mainly in Jl Chem. Soc. and Carbohydrate Research. *Recreations:* golf, gardening, foreign travel. *Address:* Chester Beatty Research Institute, Institute of Cancer Research: Royal Cancer Hospital, Fulham Road, SW3. *T:* 01-352 8133. *Clubs:* Athenæum; Banstead Downs.

FOSTER, Prof. Christopher David, MA; Professor of Urban Studies and Economics, London School of Economics, since 1976; Director, Centre for Environmental Studies, since 1976; *b* 30 Oct. 1930; *s* of George Cecil Foster; *m* 1958, Kay Sheridan Bullock; two *s* three *d*. *Educ:* Merchant Taylors' Sch.; King's Coll., Cambridge (Scholar). Economics Tripos 1954; MA 1959. Hallsworth Research Fellow, Manchester Univ., 1957-59; Senior Research Fellow, Jesus Coll., Oxford, 1959-64; Official Fellow and Tutor, Jesus Coll., 1964-66; Dir-Gen. of Economic Planning, MoT, 1966-70; Head of Unit for Res. in Urban Economics, LSE, 1970-76. Governor, Centre for Environmental Studies, 1967-70. Vis. Prof. of Economics, MIT, 1970. Special Economic Advisor (part time) DoE, 1974; Mem. (part time), PO Bd, 1975. *Publications:* The Transport Problem, 1963; Politics, Finance and the Role of Economics: an essay on the control of public enterprise, 1972; papers in various economic and other journals. *Address:* 6 Holland Park Avenue, W11. *T:* 01-727 4757. *Club:* Reform.

FOSTER, George Arthur C.; *see* Carey-Foster.

FOSTER, Sir Idris (Llewelyn), Kt 1977; MA Wales and Oxon; FSA; Jesus Professor of Celtic in the University of Oxford, 1947-Sept. 1978, and Fellow of Jesus College since 1947; Member Royal Commission on Ancient Monuments in Wales and Monmouthshire; Treasurer, National Library of Wales, since 1964; Member Standing Commission on Museums and Galleries, since 1964; *b* 23 July 1911; *e s* of Harold L. Foster and Ann J. (Roberts), Carneddi, Bethesda, Bangor, Caerns; unmarried. *Educ:* County Sch., Bethesda; University Coll. of North Wales, Bangor; National Univ. of Ireland, Dublin. BA (Wales) with First Class Hons, 1932; University Research Student, 1933-35; MA (Wales) with distinction, 1935; Fellow of University of Wales, 1935; Head of Dept of Celtic, University of Liverpool, 1936-47; Warden of Derby Hall, University of Liverpool, 1946-47; served in Intelligence Div., Naval Staff, Admiralty, 1942-45; Sir John Rhys Memorial Lectr, Br. Acad., 1950; O'Donnell Lectr, Univ. of Edinburgh, 1960, Univ. of Wales, 1971-72; G. J. Williams Lectr, University Coll., Cardiff, 1973; Select Preacher, Univ. of Oxford, 1973-74; President: Soc. for Study of Mediæval Languages and Literature, 1953-58; Cambrian Archaeological Assoc., 1968-69; Court of Nat. Eisteddfod of Wales, 1973-77 (Chm. Council, 1970-73); Irish Texts Soc., 1973-; Chm., Gwynedd Archaeol Trust; Mem., Nat. Cttee for Rescue Archaeol., Wales; formerly Chm., Modern Langs Bd, and Anthropol. and Geography Bd, Oxford; Mem., Council for Welsh Language, 1973-; Hon. Editor, Trans. and publications, Cymmrodorion Soc. *Publications:* (ed with L. Alcock) Culture and Environment, 1963; (ed with Glyn Daniel) Prehistoric and Early Wales, 1965; papers and reviews. *Recreation:* music. *Address:* Jesus College, Oxford; Cae'ronnen, Carneddi, Bangor, Gwynedd. *Club:* Athenæum.

FOSTER, Sir John (Galway), KBE 1964; QC 1950; Barrister-at-Law; *s* of late General Hubert John Foster. *Educ:* Eton; New Coll., Oxford. Fellow of All Souls, 1924; Lectr in Private International Law, Oxford, 1934-39; First Sec., British Embassy, Washington, 1939; Brigadier, General Service, 1944. Recorder of Dudley, 1936-38; Recorder of Oxford, 1938-51 and 1956-64. MP (C) Northwich, Cheshire, 1945-Feb. 1974; Parly Under-Sec. of State, CRO, 1951-Oct. 1954. Mem. Council, Aims of Industry, 1974-; Chairman: Task Force; Facts about Business. Legion of Honour; American Legion of Merit; Croix de Guerre. *Publications:* lectures and articles on constitutional and private international law. *Address:* Parsonage House, Stanton Harcourt, Oxon. *T:* Standlake 231. *Clubs:* Carlton, Pratt's.

FOSTER, Sir John (Gregory), 3rd Bt *cr* 1930; Consultant Physician, George, Cape Province; *b* 26 Feb. 1927; *s* of Sir Thomas Saxby Gregory Foster, 2nd Bt, and Beryl, *d* of late Dr Alfred Ireland; *S* father, 1957; *m* 1956, Jean Millicent Watts; one *s* three *d. Educ:* Michaelhouse Coll., Natal. South African Artillery, 1944-46; Witwatersrand Univ., 1946-51; MB, BCh 1951; Post-graduate course, MRCPE 1955; Medical Registrar, 1955-56; Medical Officer, Cape Town, 1957. DIH London, 1962. *Recreation:* outdoor sport. *Heir: s* Saxby Gregory Foster, *b* 3 Sept. 1957. *Address:* 122 York Street, PO Box 325, George, Cape Province, South Africa. *T:* George 3251. *Club:* Johannesburg Country (S Africa).

FOSTER, Maj.-Gen. John Hulbert; Director Volunteers, Territorials and Cadets, Ministry of Defence, since 1978; *b* 17 May 1925; *yr s* of late Lt-Col Thomas Hyland and Ethel Beatrice Foster; *m* 1947, Monica Davis; one *s* five *d. Educ:* Charterhouse. Commissioned RE, 1945; served: India, Burma, Nigeria, 1945-47; Kenya, 1948-50; Cyprus and Egypt, 1951-53. Instructor: RMA Sandhurst, 1953-56; Staff Coll., 1957; HQ Northern Command, 1958-60; OC, 23 Indep. Field Sqdn, 1961-63; JSSC, 1964; Min. of Defence, 1964-67; CO, 38 Engineer Regt, 1967-69, GSO1, CICC(West), 1969-70; CCRE, 1st British Corps, 1971-72; RCDS, 1973; Engineer-in-Chief (Army), 1975-77. *Recreations:* hunting, shooting, swimming. *Address:* Westow Lodge, Westow, York YO6 7LQ. *T:* Whitwell on the Hill 204. *Club:* Army and Navy.

FOSTER, John Peter; Surveyor of the Fabric of Westminster Abbey since 1973; *b* 2 May 1919; *s* of Francis Edward Foster and Evelyn Marjorie, *e d* of Sir Charles Stewart Forbes, 5th Bt of Newe; *m* 1944, Margaret Elizabeth Skipper; one *s* one *d . Educ:* Eton; Trinity Hall, Cambridge. BA 1940, MA 1946; ARIBA 1949. Commnd RE 1941; served Norfolk Div.; joined Guards Armd Div. 1943, served France and Germany; Captain SORE(2) 30 Corps 1945; discharged 1946. Marshall Sisson, Architect: Asst 1948, later Partner; Sole Principal 1971. Surveyor of Royal Academy of Arts, 1965; Partner with John Peters of Vine Press, Hemingford Grey, 1957-63. Art Workers' Guild, 1971. FSA 1973. *Recreations:* painting, books, travel, shooting. *Address:* Harcourt, Hemingford Grey, Huntingdon, Cambs PE18 9BJ. *T:* St Ives 62200; 2a Little Cloister, Westminster Abbey, SW1P 3PA. *Club:* Athenæum.

FOSTER, Rev. Canon John William, BEM 1946; Vicar of Lythe, diocese of York, since 1973; *b* 5 Aug. 1921; *m* 1943, Nancy Margaret Allen; one *s. Educ:* St Aidan's Coll., Birkenhead. Served Leicestershire Yeomanry, 1939-46; Chaplain, Hong Kong Defence Force, 1958-. Reserve of Officers, Hong Kong Defence Force, 1967-73. Priest 1955; Curate of Loughborough, 1954-57; Chaplain, St John's Cathedral, Hong Kong, 1957-60, Precentor, 1960-63; Dean of Hong Kong, 1963-73; Hon. Canon, St John's Cathedral, Hong Kong, 1973. *Address:* Lythe Vicarage, Whitby, N Yorks.

FOSTER, Lawrence; conductor; Music Director and Chief Conductor, Houston Symphony Orchestra, since 1971; Chief Guest Conductor, Royal Philharmonic Orchestra, since 1969; *b* Los Angeles, 23 Oct. 1941; *s* of Thomas Foster and Martha Wurmbrandt. *Educ:* Univ. of California, LA; studied under Fritz Zweig, Bruno Walter and Karl Böhm. Asst Conductor, Los Angeles Philharmonic, 1965-68; British début, Royal Festival Hall, 1968; Covent Garden début, Troilus and Cressida, 1976. *Recreations:* water skiing, table tennis. *Address:* c/o Harrison/Parrott Ltd, 22 Hillgate Street, W8 7SR.

FOSTER, Leslie Thomas, CB 1966; *b* 24 Sept. 1905; *e s* of Thomas Henry and Elizabeth Foster; *m* 1933, Winifred Marie, *d*

of Henry Stinchcombe. *Educ:* Reading Sch. Entered Office of Comr of Police of the Metropolis, 1930; Private Sec. to Comr (Air Vice-Marshal Sir Philip Game), 1940-41; transferred to Min. of Works, 1942; Principal, 1946; Asst Sec., 1952. Under-Sec., 1958; Dir of Establishments, Min. of Public Building and Works, 1964-67. *Address:* 11 Waldens Park Road, Horsell, Woking, Surrey. *T:* Woking 72777. *Club:* East India, Devonshire, Sports and Public Schools.

FOSTER, Maj.-Gen. Norman Leslie, CB 1961; DSO 1945; Security Adviser, Civil Service Department, since 1974; *b* 26 Aug. 1909; *s* of late Col A. L. Foster, Wimbledon; *m* 1937, Joan Constance, *d* of late Canon T. W. E. Drury; two *s. Educ:* Westminster; RMA Woolwich. 2nd Lieut, RA, 1929; Served War of 1939-45 in Egypt and Italy; CRA 11th Armoured Division, 1955-56; Deputy Military Sec., War Office, 1958-59; Maj.-Gen., 1959; GOC Royal Nigerian Army, 1959-62; Pres., Regular Commissions Board, 1962-65; retired, 1965. Dir of Security (Army), MoD, 1965-73. Col Comdt, Royal Regt of Artillery, 1966-74. *Address:* Besborough, Heath End, Farnham, Surrey. *Club:* Army and Navy.

FOSTER, Maj.-Gen. Peter Beaufoy, MC 1944; Major-General Royal Artillery, British Army of the Rhine, 1973-76; *b* 1 Sept. 1921; *s* of F. K. Foster, OBE, JP, Allt Dinas, Cheltenham; *m* 1947, Margaret Geraldine, *d* of W. F. Henn, sometime Chief Constable of Glos; two *s* one *d* (and one *s* decd). *Educ:* Uppingham School. Commnd RA, 1941; psc 1950; jssc 1958; OC Para. Light Battery, 1958-60; DAMS MS5, WO, 1960-63; Mil. Assistant to C-in-C BAOR, 1963-64; CO 34 Light Air Defence Regt RA, 1964-66; GSO1, ASD5, MoD, 1966-68; BRA Northern Comd, 1968-71; Comdt Royal Sch. of Artillery, 1971-73. Col Comdt, RA, 1977-. *Recreations:* fishing, golf, shooting, gardening. *Address:* Russell Cottage, West Lavington, Devizes, Wilts. *Club:* Naval and Military.

FOSTER, Hon. Sir Peter Harry Batson Woodroffe, Kt 1969; MBE 1943; TD 1946; **Hon. Mr Justice Foster;** a Judge of the Chancery Division of the High Court of Justice since 1969; *b* 5 Dec. 1912; *s* of late Frank Foster; *m* 1937, Jane Hillcoat Easdale, *d* of late James Easdale, Troon, Ayrshire; one *s* three *d. Educ:* Rugby Sch.; Corpus Christi Coll., Cambridge (BA, LLB). Called to the Bar, Inner Temple, 1936; Bencher, Lincoln's Inn, 1963. Fife and Forfar Yeomanry, 1939; War of 1939-45: Dunkirk, 8th Armd Div., Alamein, 18 Army Gp, Tripoli, Col, 21 Army Group, North Western Europe (despatches twice, MBE). Resumed practice, 1945; QC 1957. Mem., Gen. Council of the Bar, 1956-60; Mem., Senate, 1966-69, 1976-. Chm., Chancery Bar Assoc., 1963-68; formerly Member Council: Officers' Assoc.; Royal Albert Hall; Steward British Boxing Board of Control. Church Commissioner for England, 1965-69. Reserve Chm., Conscientious Objectors Tribunal, 1965-69; Chm., Performing Right Tribunal, 1969. *Recreations:* golf, travelling. *Address:* 70 Elizabeth Street, SW1. *T:* 01-730 1984. *Clubs:* White's; Royal and Ancient Golf (St Andrews); Hawks (Cambridge).

FOSTER, Peter Martin, CMG 1975; HM Diplomatic Service; Ambassador and UK Permanent Representative to Council of Europe, since 1974; *b* 25 May 1924; *s* of Frederick Arthur Peace Foster and Marjorie Kathleen Sandford; *m* 1947, Angela Hope Cross; one *s* one *d. Educ:* Sherborne; Corpus Christi Coll., Cambridge. Army (Horse Guards), 1943-47; joined Foreign (now Diplomatic) Service, 1948; served in Vienna, Warsaw, Pretoria/Cape Town, Bonn, Kampala, Tel Aviv; Head of Central and Southern Africa Dept, FCO, 1972-74. *Address:* c/o Foreign and Commonwealth Office, SW1; New Cottage, Abinger Lane, Abinger Common, Surrey. *T:* Dorking 730114.

FOSTER, Robert, CBE 1963 (OBE 1955; MBE 1949); FCIS; President, Savings Banks Institute, 1970-75; *b* 4 March 1898; *s* of Robert Foster; *m* 1927, Edith Kathleen (*née* Blackburn); two *d. Educ:* Rutherford Coll., Newcastle upon Tyne. RNVR, 1915-19. Newcastle-on-Tyne Savings Bank, 1919-24; London Trustee Savings Banks, 1924-63 (Gen. Manager, 1943-63), retired. Mem. Nat. Savings Cttee, 1957-62. Dir, City & Metropolitan Building Soc. Mem. Court, Worshipful Company of Plumbers, 1959-(Master, 1965). *Recreations:* golf, gardening. *Address:* Larchfield, Highercombe Road, Haslemere, Surrey. *T:* Haslemere 4353. *Club:* City Livery.

FOSTER, Sir Robert (Sidney), GCMG 1970 (KCMG 1964; CMG 1961); KCVO 1970; Governor-General and Commander-in-Chief of Fiji, 1970-73 (Governor and C-in-C, 1968-70); retired 1973; *b* 11 Aug. 1913; *s* of late Sidney Charles Foster and late Jessie Edith (*née* Fry); *m* 1947, Margaret (*née* Walker); no *c. Educ:* Eastbourne Coll.; Peterhouse, Cambridge. Appointed Cadet, Administrative Service, Northern Rhodesia, 1936;

District Officer, N Rhodesia, 1938. War Service, 2nd Bn Northern Rhodesia Regt, 1940-43, Major. Provincial Commissioner, N Rhodesia, 1957; Sec., Ministry of Native Affairs, N Rhodesia, 1960; Chief Sec., Nyasaland, 1961-63; Dep. Governor, Nyasaland, 1963-64; High Comr for W Pacific, 1964-68. KStJ 1969. Officer of the Legion of Honour, 1966. *Recreation:* self-help. *Address:* Kenwood, 16 Ardnave Crescent, Southampton SO1 7FJ. *Club:* Leander (Henley).

FOSTER, Air Vice-Marshal William Foster MacNeece, CB 1933; CBE 1922; DSO 1917; DFC 1918; MA Oxon (hon.), 1941; Deputy Lord Mayor of Oxford, 1967 (Lord Mayor, 1966); *b* 21 Aug. 1889; *e s* of Col T. F. MacNeece, Castle Cary, Co. Donegal; *m* 1928, Jean, *d* of Ralph W. Bruce, Langtons, South Weald, Essex: two *d*. *Educ:* Cheltenham Coll.; Sandhurst. Served European War, 1914-18, promoted Lieut-Col RFC, Dec. 1916 (wounded, despatches, DSO, DFC); Chief Staff Officer Royal Air Force in Iraq, March 1921-Oct. 1922 (CBE, Gen. Service Medal and clasp); British Air Representative to Council of League of Nations, 1926-29; commanded No. 1 Air Defence Group Headquarters, 1929-34; retired list, 1937; British Commission for Exchange of Prisoners in Spain, 1938-39; Air Officer Commanding No. 6 Group RAF, 1939; Dep. Head of RAF Delegation, Washington, April 1942-Sept. 1943; Mem. of Combined Chiefs of Staff Cttee, Dec. 1942-May 1943; Head of Inter-Service Liaison Cttee, Washington, Oct. 1943-March 1944; Head of RAF Training Mission to China, Sept. 1944-April 1946; reverted to retired list Oct. 1946. Mem. Oxford City Council, 1950-. Sheriff of Oxford, 1963-64. Comdr of Legion of Merit (USA), Orders Cloud and Banner, and Loshu decoration (China). Assumed surname of Foster by Royal Licence, Aug. 1927. *Publications:* occasional verses in The Times, Spectator, etc, of which An Airman's Te Deum was printed in 1936 to music by Sir Walford Davies and in 1937 to music by Dr Martin Shaw. *Address:* 26 Northmoor Road, Oxford. *T:* 55588; The Corner House, Aldeburgh, Suffolk. *T:* 2568. *Clubs:* Army and Navy, Royal Air Force.

FOSTER-BROWN, Rear-Adm. Roy Stephenson, CB 1958; RN Retired; *b* 16 Jan. 1904; *s* of Robert Allen Brown and Agnes Wilfreda Stephenson; *m* 1933, Joan Wentworth Foster; two *s*. *Educ:* RNC, Osborne and Dartmouth. Specialised in Submarines, 1924-28; specialised in Signals, 1930. Fleet Signal Officer, Home Fleet, 1939-40; Staff Signal Officer, Western Approaches, 1940-44; Comdr HMS Ajax, 1944-46; Capt., 1946; Capt. Sixth Frigate Sqdn, 1951; Dir Signal Div., Admiralty, 1952-53; Capt. HMS Ceylon, 1954; Rear-Adm. 1955; Flag Officer, Gibraltar, 1956-59; retd 1959. Hon. Comdt, Girls Nautical Trng Corps, 1961-. Master, Armourers and Braziers Co., 1964-65, 1974-75. *Recreations:* sailing, shooting, golf, tennis. *Address:* Lee Farm House, Hurley, Berks. *Club:* Army and Navy.

FOSTER-SUTTON, Sir Stafford William Powell, KBE 1957 (OBE (mil.) 1945); Kt 1951; CMG 1948; QC (Jamaica, 1938, Fedn Malaya, 1948); *b* 24 Dec. 1898; *s* of late G. Foster Sutton and Mrs Foster Sutton; *m* 1919, Linda Dorothy, *d* of late John Humber Allwood, OBE, and of Mrs Allwood, Enfield, St Ann, Jamaica; one *d* (one *s* decd). *Educ:* St Mary Magdalen Sch.; private tutor. HM Army, 1914-26; served European War, 1914-18, Infantry, RFC and RAF, active service. Called to the Bar, Gray's Inn, 1926; private practice, 1926-36; Solicitor Gen., Jamaica, 1936; Attorney-Gen., Cyprus, 1940; Col Comdg Cyprus Volunteer Force and Inspector Cyprus Forces, 1941-44; Mem. for Law and Order and Attorney-Gen., Kenya, 1944-48; actg Governor, Aug. and Sept. 1947; Attorney-Gen., Malaya, 1948-50; Officer Administering Govt, Malaya, Sept., Dec. 1950; Chief Justice, Fedn of Malaya, 1950-51; Dir of Man-Power, Kenya, 1944-45; Chm. Labour Advisory Board, Kenya, and Kenya European Service Advisory Board, 1944-48; Pres. of the West African Court of Appeal, 1951-55; Chief Justice, Fedn of Nigeria, 1955-58; Actg Governor-Gen., Nigeria, May-June 1957. Pres., Pensions Appeal Tribunals for England and Wales, 1958-73. Chairman: Zanzibar Commn of Inquiry, 1961; Kenya Regional and Electorial Commns, 1962-; Referendum Observers, Malta, 1964; Council, Britain-Nigeria Assoc. *Address:* 7 London Road, Saffron Walden, Essex.

FOTHERGILL, Dorothy Joan; Director, Postal Pay and Grading, since 1974; *b* 31 Dec. 1923; *d* of Samuel John Rimington Fothergill and Dorothy May Patterson. *Educ:* Haberdashers' Aske's Sch., Acton; University Coll. London. BA (Hons) History. Entered Civil Service as Asst Principal, 1948; Principal, Overseas Mails branch, GPO, 1953; UPU Congress, Ottawa, 1957; Establishments work, 1958-62; HM Treasury, 1963-65; Asst Sec., Pay and Organisation, GPO, 1965; Director: Postal Personnel, 1970; London Postal Region, 1971. *Recreations:* gardening, walking, theatre. *Address:* 38 Andrewes House, Barbican, EC2Y 8AX.

FOU TS'ONG; concert pianist; *b* 10 March 1934; *m* 1960, Zamira Menuhin (marr. diss. 1970); one *s*; *m* 1973, Hijong Hyun. *Educ:* Shanghai and Warsaw. Debut, Shanghai, 1953. Concerts all over Eastern Europe including USSR up to 1958. Arrived in Great Britain, Dec. 1958; London debut, Feb. 1959, followed by concerts in England, Scotland and Ireland; subsequently has toured all five Continents. *Recreations:* many different ones. *Address:* 28 Rosecroft Avenue, NW3.

FOUCHÉ, Jacobus Johannes, DMS (South Africa) 1971; State President of the Republic of South Africa, 1968-75; *b* Wepener, OFS, 6 June 1898; *s* of late J. J. Fouché; *m* 1920, Letta Rhoda, *d* of late T. P. McDonald, Zastron, OFS; one *s*. *Educ:* Victoria Coll., Stellenbosch. MP for Smithfield, 1941-50 and for Bloemfontein West, 1960-68; Administrator of the OFS, 1951-59; Minister of Defence, 1959-66, of Agricultural Technical Services and of Water Affairs, 1966-68. DPhil (*hc*) Univ. of Stellenbosch, 1966. Hon. Col, Regt President Steyn, Bloemfontein. Freeman of several cities and towns in Republic of S Africa. Paraguayan Nat. Order of Merit, 1974. *Recreation:* farming. *Address:* 9 De Jongh Street, Strand, 7140, Republic of South Africa.

FOULDS, Hugh Jon; Director, since 1975, and Group General Manager, since 1977 (General Manager, 1975-77), Finance for Industry Ltd; *b* 2 May 1932; *s* of Dr Edward James Foulds and Helen Shirley (*née* Smith); *m* 1st, 1960, Berry Cusack-Smith (marr. diss. 1970); two *s*; 2nd, 1977, Hélène Senn. *Educ:* Bootham Sch., York. Joined Industrial & Commercial Finance Corporation, 1959: Asst Gen. Manager, 1972; Dep. Gen. Man., 1974; Director, 1974. *Recreations:* tennis, ski-ing, looking at pictures, gardening. *Address:* 72 Loudoun Road, St John's Wood, NW8 0NA. *T:* 01-722 4464.

FOULIS, Sir Ian P. L.; see Liston-Foulis.

FOULKES, Nigel Gordon; Chairman, Civil Aviation Authority, since 1977; Director: Charterhouse Group Ltd, since 1972; Imagic (Holdings), since 1971; Bekaert Group, since 1973; Stone-Platt Industries, since 1975; *b* 29 Aug. 1919; *s* of Louis Augustine and Winifred Foulkes; *m* 1st, 1940, Ann Davison (marr. diss. 1947); one *s* one *d*; 2nd, 1948, Elisabeth Walker. *Educ:* Gresham's Sch., Holt; Balliol Coll., Oxford (Schol., MA). FBIM (Council, 1973-). RAF, 1940-45. Subsequently executive, consulting and boardroom posts with: H. P. Bulmer Ltd; Production-Engineering Ltd; Birfield Ltd; Greaves & Thomas Ltd; International Nickel Ltd; Rank Xerox Ltd (Asst Man. Dir 1964-67, Man. Dir 1967-70); Chm., British Airports Authority, 1972-77. *Address:* Civil Aviation Authority, Space House, 43-59 Kingsway, WC2B 6TE.

FOULKES, Maj.-Gen. Thomas Herbert Fischer, CB 1962; OBE 1945; *b* 29 May 1908; *e s* of late Maj.-Gen. C. H. Foulkes, CB, CMG, DSO; *m* 1947, Delphine Elizabeth Smith; two *s*. *Educ:* Clifton Coll., Bristol (Pres., Old Cliftonian Soc., 1963-65); RMA Woolwich; St Catharine's Coll., Cambridge. BA 1930, MA Cantab 1954. Commissioned into RE, 1928; served in India and Burma, 1931-46 (CRE 39 Indian Div., also CRE 17 Indian Div. during Burma campaign); Comdr Corps RE (Brig.) 1 Br. Corps in BAOR, 1956-57; Chief Engr (Brig.) Middle East, 1957-58; Chief Engr (Brig.) Southern Command, UK, 1958-60; Engineer-in-Chief, War Office, 1960-63. Col Comdt, Royal Engineers, 1963-73. Hon. Col, RE Resources Units, AER, 1964-67; Hon. Col, RE Volunteers (Sponsored Units), T&AVR, 1967-72. Governor: Clifton Coll., 1964; Newells and Desmoor Sch., 1968-. Liveryman, Worshipful Co. of Plumbers of City of London, 1960, Renter Warden, 1971, Upper Warden, 1972, Master, 1973. Pres., Instn of Royal Engrs, 1965-70; CEng, FICE. *Recreations:* shooting, travel, fishing, photography. *Address:* The Warren, Fitzroy Road, Fleet, Hants GU13 8JW. *T:* Fleet (Hants) 6650. *Club:* Army and Navy.

FOURCADE, Jean-Pierre; Officier de l'ordre national du Mérite; Senator, French Republic, from Hauts-de-Seine, since 1977; *b* 18 Oct. 1929; *s* of Raymond Fourcade (Médecin) and Mme Fourcade (*née* Germaine Raynal); *m* 1958, Odile Mion; one *s* two *d*. *Educ:* Collège de Sorèze; Faculté de droit de Bordeaux; Institut d'études politiques de Bordeaux (Dip.); Ecole nationale d'administration; higher studies in Law (Dip.). Inspecteur des Finances, 1954. Cabinet of M. Valéry Giscard d'Estaing: Chargé de Mission, 1959-61; Conseiller technique, 1962, then Dir Adjoint to chef de service, Inspection gén. des Finances, 1962; Chef de service du commerce, at Direction-Gén. du Commerce intérieur et des Prix, 1968-70; Dir-gén. adjoint du Crédit industriel et commercial, 1970; Dir-gén., 1972, and Administrateur Dir-gén., 1973; Ministre de l'Economie et des Finances, 1974-76; Ministre de l'Equipement et de l'Aménagement du Territoire, 1976-77. Mayor of Saint-Cloud,

1971-; Conseiller général of canton of Saint-Cloud, 1973-. Pres., Clubs Perspective et Realités, 1975-. *Address:* 8 Parc de Béarn, 92210 Saint-Cloud, France.

FOURNIER, Jean, CD 1972; Agent General for the Province of Quebec in London since 1971; *b* Montreal, 18 July 1914; *s* of Arthur Fournier and Emilie Roy; *m* 1942, May Coote; five *s*. *Educ:* High Sch. of Québec; Laval Univ. (BA 1935, LLB 1938). Admitted to Bar of Province of Quebec, 1939. Royal Canadian Artillery (NPAM) (Lieut), 1935; Canadian Active Service Force Sept. 1939; served in Canada and overseas, 1939-44; Junior War Staff Coll. (psc), 1941; discharged 1944, Actg Lt-Col. Hon. Mem., Royal 22nd Regt Officers' Mess, The Citadel, Québec. Third Sec., Canadian Dept of External Affairs, 1944; Legal Div., 1944-45, American Div. 1945; Second Sec., Canadian Embassy, Buenos Aires, 1945; Nat. Defence Coll., Kingston, 1948 (ndc); Seconded: to Privy Council Office, 1948-50; to Prime Minister's Office, Oct. 1950-Feb. 1951; First Sec., Canadian Embassy, Paris, 1951; Counsellor, 1953; Consul Gen., Boston, 1954; Privy Council Office (Asst Sec. to Cabinet), 1957-61; Head of European Division (Political Affairs), Dept of External Affairs, 1961-64; Chm., Quebec Civil Service Commn, 1964-71. Pres., Inst. of Public Administration of Canada, 1966-67; Vice-President: Public Personnel Assoc. Canadian Chapter, 1970-71; Conf. of Canadian Civil Service Commn, 1970, 1971. Freedom, City of London, 1976. Pres., Canadian Veterans Assoc. of the UK, 1976-77. Hon. Col, 6th Canadian Field Regt. *Address:* 12 Upper Grosvenor Street, W1. *T:* 01-629 4155; 6 Ilchester Place, W14. *T:* 01-602 2213. *Clubs:* Oriental, Wig and Pen, Canada; Quebec Garrison, Five Lakes Fishing.

FOURNIER, Pierre; 'cellist; Officier Légion d'Honneur; *b* 24 June 1906; *m* 1936, Lydia Antik; one *s*. *Educ:* University and Conservatoire, Paris. Formerly teacher at the National Conservatoire, Paris. Concert soloist every season in the European Capitals as well as in USA, South America and Far East; also soloist playing with chief orchestras. Commander: Ordre national du Mérite (France); Ordre Léopold II (Belgium); Officer, Arts and Letters (Paris); Chevalier with Crown (Luxembourg). *Address:* 14 Parc Château Banquet, Geneva, Switzerland.

FOWDEN, Leslie, FRS 1964; Director, Rothamsted Experimental Station, since 1973; *b* Rochdale, Lancs, 13 Oct. 1925; *s* of Herbert and Amy D. Fowden; *m* 1949, Margaret Oakes; one *s* one *d*. *Educ:* University Coll., London. PhD Univ. of London, 1948. Scientific Staff of Human Nutrition Research Unit of the MRC, 1947-50; Lecturer in Plant Chemistry, University Coll. London, 1950-55, Reader, 1956-64, Prof. of Plant Chemistry, 1964-73; Dean of Faculty of Science, UCL, 1970-73. Rockefeller Fellow at Cornell Univ., 1955; Visiting Prof. at Univ. of California, 1963; Royal Society Visiting Prof., Univ. of Hong Kong, 1967. Member: Advisory Board, Tropical Product Inst., 1966-70; Council, Royal Society, 1970-72. Consultant Dir, Commonwealth Bureau of Soils, 1973; Mem., Scientific Adv. Panel, Royal Botanic Gardens, 1977. For. Mem., Deutsche Akademie der Naturforscher Leopoldina, 1971. *Publications:* contribs to scientific journals on topics in plant biochemistry. *Address:* 7 Ferncroft, 15 Basire Street, N1. *T:* 01-226 7043; 1 West Common, Harpenden, Herts AL5 2JQ. *T:* Harpenden 64628.

FOWELLS, Joseph Dunthorne Briggs, CMG 1975; DSC 1940; Deputy Director General, British Council, 1976-77; *b* 17 Feb. 1916; *s* of late Joseph Fowells and Maud Dunthorne, Middlesbrough; *m* 1st, 1940, Edith Agnes McKerracher (marr. diss. 1966); two *s* one *d*; 2nd, 1969, Thelma Howes (*d* 1974). *Educ:* Sedbergh Sch.; Clare Coll., Cambridge (MA). School teaching, 1938; service with Royal Navy (Lt-Comdr), 1939-46; Blackie & Son Ltd, Educnl Publishers, 1946; British Council, 1947: Argentina, 1954; Representative Sierra Leone, 1956; Scotland, 1957; Dir Latin America and Africa (Foreign) Dept, 1958; Controller Overseas B Division (foreign countries excluding Europe), 1966; Controller Planning, 1968; Controller European Div., 1970; Asst Dir Gen. (Functional), 1972; Asst Dir Gen. (Regional), 1973-76. *Recreations:* golf, sailing. *Address:* 51 Sillwood Street, Brighton, E Sussex BN1 2PS. *T:* Brighton 70349.

FOWKE, Sir Frederick (Woollaston Rawdon), 4th Bt *cr* 1814; *b* 14 Dec. 1910; *e s* of Sir Frederick Ferrers Conant Fowke, 3rd Bt, and Edith Frances Daubeney (*d* 1958), *d* of late Canon J. H. Rawdon; *S* father, 1948; *m* 1948, Barbara, *d* of late E. Townsend; two *d*. *Educ:* Uppingham. Served War of 1939-45, in Derbs Yeomanry, 1939-43 (wounded). *Recreation:* shooting. *Heir: n* David Frederick Gustavus Fowke, *b* 28 Aug. 1950. *Address:* Lower Woolstone Farm, Bishops Tawton, Barnstaple, N Devon.

FOWLE, Brig. John Le Clerc, CB 1946; CIE 1943; *b* 13 Sept. 1893; *e s* of late Col Sir (Henry) Walter Hamilton Fowle, KBE; *m* 1932, Kathleen Sylvestre Le Clerc Fowle, Kaisar-i-Hind Medal (Silver), 1946, ROI 1968, FRSA, Silver and Gold Medallist, Paris Salon, *d* of late Gerald Sichel, FRCS. *Educ:* RN Coll. Osborne, and Sandhurst. Indian Army, 1912-46; joined 15th Lancers (CM), 1913; last appt Comdr Jubbulpore Area, India. Served European War, 1914-19, Mesopotamia, S Persia (despatches); Waziristan, 1920-21 (despatches); War of 1939-45; Eastern Army and Fourteenth Army (despatches). *Recreations:* polo, racing, golf. *Address:* 65 Cheyne Court, Royal Hospital Road, SW3. *T:* 01-351 3878. *Club:* Cavalry and Guards.

FOWLER, Prof. Alastair David Shaw, FBA 1974; Regius Professor of Rhetoric and English Literature, University of Edinburgh, since 1972; *b* 17 Aug. 1930; *s* of David Fowler and Maggie Shaw; *m* 1950, Jenny Catherine Simpson; one *s* one *d*. *Educ:* Queen's Park Sch., Glasgow; Univ. of Glasgow; Univ. of Edinburgh; Pembroke Coll., Oxford. MA Edin. 1952 and Oxon 1955; DPhil Oxon 1957; DLitt Oxon 1972. Junior Res. Fellow, Queen's Coll., Oxford, 1955-59; Instructor, Indiana Univ., 1957; Lectr, UC Swansea, 1959; Fellow and Tutor in English Lit., Brasenose Coll., Oxford, 1962-71; Vis. Prof., Columbia Univ., 1964; Mem. Inst. for Advanced Study, Princeton, 1966; Vis. Prof., Univ. of Virginia, 1969; Vis. Fellow, Council of the Humanities, Princeton Univ., 1974. Mem., Scottish Arts Council, 1976. Gen. Editor, Longman Annotated Anthologies of English Verse, 1977-. *Publications:* (trans. and ed) Richard Wills, De re poetica, 1958; Spenser and the Numbers of Time, 1964; (ed) C. S. Lewis, Spenser's Images of Life, 1967; (ed with John Carey) The Poems of John Milton, 1968; Triumphal Forms, 1970; (ed) Silent Poetry, 1970; (ed with Christopher Butler) Topics in Criticism, 1971; Seventeen, 1971; Conceitful Thought, 1975; Catacomb Suburb, 1976; contribs to jls and books. *Address:* Department of English, David Hume Tower, George Square, Edinburgh EH8 9JX.

FOWLER, Christopher B.; *see* Brocklebank-Fowler.

FOWLER, Derek; Finance Member, British Railways Board, since 1975; *b* 26 Feb. 1929; *s* of late George Edward Fowler and of Kathleen Fowler; *m* 1953, Ruth Fox; one *d*. *Educ:* Grantham, Lincs. Financial appointments with: Grantham Borough Council, 1944-50; Spalding UDC, 1950-52; Nairobi City Council, 1952-62; Southend-on-Sea CBC, 1962-64. British Railways Board: Internal Audit Manager, 1964-67, and Management Acct, 1967-69, W Region; Sen. Finance Officer, 1969-71; Corporate Budgets Manager, 1971-73; Controller of Corporate Finance, 1973-75. Mem. Council, Chartered Inst. of Public Finance and Accountancy (CIPFA), 1974-; FCIT. *Recreation:* cartophily. *Address:* Orchard House, Appletree Lane, Slough, Berks SL3 7HQ. *T:* Slough 20595.

FOWLER, Frank James, CBE 1974 (OBE 1945); TD; Senior Medical Officer, Department of Health and Social Security, 1977; *b* 1 Oct. 1911; *s* of James Edward Fowler and Sarah Anne Fowler; *m* 1949, Josephine Kennedy; two *s* one *d*. *Educ:* King Edward's Sch., Birmingham; Univ. of Birmingham. MB, ChB; FRCP, FFCM. Univ. of Birmingham: Union Sec., 1931-32; Sec., Guild of Undergrads, 1933-34; Mem. Ct of Governors, 1934-36. House appts: Gen. Hosp., Birmingham, 1936; Hallam Hosp., W Bromwich, 1937 and 1946-48; Asst MO, City Hosp., Derby, 1938; commnd RAMC (TA), 1938; Unit MO, UK and France, 1939-41; DADMS 9 Corps, UK and N Africa, 1941-43; ADMS 2 Dist Italy, 1943-44; ADMS Ops Allied Forces HQ, 1944-45; ADMS (Adm.) CMF, 1945. Asst Sen. MO, Oxford RHB, 1948-51; Dep. SAMO, NE Met. RHB, 1951-58; SAMO NW Met. RHB, 1958-73; Reg. MO, Yorks RHA, 1973-76. Mem. Bd and Treas., Faculty of Community Medicine, 1972-77. *Recreations:* pianoforte and organ playing; gardening, walking. *Address:* 146 Copse Hill, SW20 0NP. *T:* 01-946 7912.

FOWLER, Gerald Teasdale; MP (Lab) The Wrekin, 1966-70 and since Feb. 1974; *b* 1 Jan. 1935; *s* of James A. Fowler, Long Buckby, Northants, and Alfreda (*née* Teasdale); *m* 1968, Julie Marguerite, *d* of Wilfrid Brining, Slough. *Educ:* Northampton Grammar Sch.; Lincoln Coll., Oxford; University of Frankfurt-am-Main. Craven Fellowship, Oxford Univ., 1957-59; part-time Lectr, Pembroke Coll., Oxford, 1958-59; Lectr, Hertford and Lincoln Colls, Oxford, 1959-65; Lectr, Univ. of Lancaster, 1965-66; Asst Dir, The Polytechnic, Huddersfield, 1970-72; Prof. of Educnl Studies, Open Univ., 1972-74; Prof. Associate, Dept of Government, Brunel Univ., 1977-. Vis. Prof., Dept of Admin, Strathclyde Univ., 1970-74. Oxford City Councillor, 1960-64; Councillor, The Wrekin DC, 1973-76, Leader, 1973-74. Contested (Lab) Banbury, 1964. Jt Parly Sec., Min. of Technology, 1967-69; Minister of State: Dept of Educn and Science, Oct. 1969-June 1970, March-Oct. 1974 and Jan.-Sept.

1976; Privy Council Office, 1974-76. President: President: Assoc. for Teaching of Social Science, 1976-; Assoc. for Recurrent Educn, 1976-77; Assoc. for Liberal Educn, 1977-; Chm., Youthaid, 1977-. *Address:* 1 St Chad's Close, Wellington, Salop; Flat 18, 36 Buckingham Gate, SW1E 6PB.

FOWLER, Henry Hamill; investment banker; Partner, Goldman, Sachs & Co., New York, since 1969; *b* 5 Sept. 1908; *s* of Mack Johnson Fowler and Bertha Browning Fowler; *m* 1938, Trudye Pamela Hathcote; two *d* (one *s* decd). *Educ:* Roanoke Coll., Salem, Va; Yale Law Sch. Counsel, Tennessee Valley Authority, 1934-38, Asst Gen. Counsel, 1939; Special Asst to Attorney-Gen. as Chief Counsel to Sub-Cttee, Senate Cttee, Educn and Labor, 1939-40; Special Counsel, Fed. Power Commn, 1941; Asst Gen. Counsel, Office of Production Management, 1941; War Production Board, 1942-44; Econ. Adviser, US Mission Econ. Affairs, London, 1944; Special Asst to Administrator, For. Econ. Administration, 1945; Dep. Administrator, National Production Authority, 1951, Administrator, 1952; Administrator, Defense Prodn Administration, 1952-53; Dir Office of Defense Mobilization, Mem. Nat. Security Coun., 1952-53; Under-Sec. of the Treasury, 1961-64; Secretary of the US Treasury, 1965-68. Sen. Mem. of Fowler, Leva, Hawes & Symington, Washington, 1946-51, 1953-61, 1964-65. Chairman: Atlantic Council of US; Inst. of Internat. Educn; US Adv. Cttee on Reform of Internat. Monetary System, 1973-; Director: Corning Glass Works; US Industries Inc.; US and Foreign Securities Corp.; Norfolk & Western Railway Co. Trustee: Roanoke Coll.; Alfred P. Sloan Foundn; Carnegie Endowment for Peace. Hon. Degrees: Roanoke Coll., 1961; Wesleyan Univ., 1966; Univ. of William and Mary, 1966. *Recreation:* tennis. *Address:* 55 Broad Street, New York, NY, USA. *Clubs:* Links, Recess (NYC); Metropolitan (Washington).

FOWLER, John Francis, DSc, PhD; FInstP; Director of Cancer Research Campaign's Gray Laboratory, at Mount Vernon Hospital, Northwood, since 1970; *b* 3 Feb. 1925; *er s* of Norman V. Fowler, Bridport, Dorset; *m* 1953, Kathleen Hardcastle Sutton, MB, BS; two *s* five *d. Educ:* Bridport Grammar Sch.; University Coll. of the South-West, Exeter. BSc 1st class Hons (London) 1944; MSc (London) 1946; PhD (London) 1955; DSc (London) 1974; FInstP 1957. Research Physicist: Newalls Insulation Co. Ltd, 1944; Metropolitan Vickers Electrical Co. Ltd, 1947; Newcastle upon Tyne Regional Hosp. Board (Radiotherapy service), 1950; Principal Physicist at King's Coll. Hosp., SE5, 1956; Head of Physics Section in Medical Research Council Radiotherapeutic Res. Unit, Hammersmith Hosp., 1959 (later the Cyclotron Unit); Reader in Physics, London Univ. at Med. Coll. of St Bartholomew's Hosp., 1962; Prof. of Med. Physics, Royal Postgraduate Med. Sch., London Univ., Hammersmith Hosp., 1963-70, Vice-Dean, 1967-70. Vis. Prof. in Oncology, Mddx Hosp. Med. Sch. President: Hosp. Physicists Assoc., 1966-67; Europ. Soc. Radiat. Biol., 1974-76; Vice-Pres., British Inst. Radiol. Roentgen Award of the British Inst. of Radiology, 1965. *Publications:* contributor: Current Topics in Radiation Research, 1966; Vol. II Radiation Dosimetry, 1967; Cancer: a comprehensive treatise, 1977; papers on radiation dosimetry, radio-biology, radioisotopes, in Brit. Jl Radiology, Brit. Jl Cancer, Physics in Medicine and Biology, Radiology, etc. *Recreations:* theatre; getting into the countryside. *Address:* Gray Laboratory, Mount Vernon Hospital, Northwood, Mddx. *T:* Northwood 28611.

FOWLER, Norman; *see* Fowler, P. N.

FOWLER, Peter Howard, FRS 1964; DSc; Royal Society Research Professor, Physics Department, University of Bristol, since 1964; *b* 27 Feb. 1923; *s* of Sir Ralph Howard Fowler, FRS, and Eileen, *o c* of 1st and last Baron Rutherford; *m* 1949, Rosemary Hempson (*née* Brown); three *d. Educ:* Winchester Coll.; Bristol Univ. BSc 1948, DSc 1958. Flying Officer in RAF, 1942-46 as a Radar Technical Officer. Asst Lectr in Physics, 1948, Lectr, 1951, Reader, 1961, Bristol Univ. Visiting Prof., Univ. of Minnesota, 1956-57. Hughes Medal, Royal Soc., 1974. *Publication:* (with Prof. C. F. Powell and Dr D. H. Perkins) The Study of Elementary Particles by the Photographic Method, 1959. *Recreations:* gardening, meteorology. *Address:* 320 Canford Lane, Westbury on Trym, Bristol.

FOWLER, (Peter) Norman; MP (C) Sutton Coldfield, since Feb. 1974 (Nottingham South, 1970-74); *b* 2 Feb. 1938; *s* of late N. F. Fowler and Katherine Fowler; *m* 1968, Linda Christmas. *Educ:* King Edward VI Sch., Chelmsford; Trinity Hall, Cambridge (MA). Nat. Service commn, Essex Regt, 1956-58; Cambridge, 1958-61; Chm., Cambridge Univ. Conservative Assoc., 1960. Joined staff of The Times, 1961; Special Corresp., 1962-66; Home Affairs Corresp., 1966-70; reported Middle East War, 1967. Mem. Council, Bow Group, 1967-69; Editorial Board,

Crossbow, 1962-69; Vice-Chm., North Kensington Cons. Assoc., 1967-68; Chm., E Midlands Area, Cons. Political Centre, 1970-73. Mem., Parly Select Cttee on Race Relations and Immigration, 1970-; Jt Sec., Cons. Parly Home Affairs Cttee, 1971-72, 1974 (Vice-Chm., 1974); Chief Opposition spokesman, Social Services, 1975-76; Opposition spokesman: Home Affairs, 1974-75; Transport, 1976-. PPS, NI Office, 1972-74. *Publications:* political pamphlets on Home Office subjects including the police. *Recreation:* travel. *Address:* Grounds Cottage, Ox Leys Road, Wishaw, Sutton Coldfield. *T:* 021-351 1478; Flat 34, 24 John Islip Street, SW1.

FOWLER, Robert MacLaren, OC 1967; BA, LLD; Hon. Chairman, BP Canada Ltd, since 1977 (Chairman, 1969-77); President, C. D. Howe Research Institute; *b* 7 Dec. 1906; *s* of late Edward Bruce Fowler and Genevieve Amey Fowler, Peterborough, Ont.; *m* 1934, Sheila Gordon Ramsay, *d* of A. Gordon Ramsay, Toronto, Ont.; three *s* two *d. Educ:* University of Toronto; Osgoode Hall Law Sch., Toronto, Ont. Practised Law, Toronto, Ont., with McMaster, Montgomery, Fleury and Co., 1931-37; Legal Sec. to Chm., Rowell-Sirois Commn on Dominion-Provincial Relations, 1937-39; practised law, Toronto, Ont., with McCarthy and McCarthy, 1939-45; Sec. and Gen. Counsel, of War-time Prices and Trade Board, Ottawa, 1942-45; Pres., Canadian Pulp & Paper Assoc., 1945-72; associated in practice of law with Gowling, Mactavish, Osborne and Henderson, later Gowling and Henderson, 1945-72. Director: Itek Corpn, 1972-; Quaker Oats Co. of Canada Ltd, 1972-; Celanese Canada Ltd; Canadian Enterprise Develt Corp.; Hilton Canada Ltd; Templeton Growth Fund Ltd; Westmount Life Insce Co. Pres., Canadian Institute of International Affairs, 1945-50; Chm. Exec. Council, Canadian Chamber of Commerce, 1953-54; Mem., Economic Council of Canada, 1963-70; Chm.: Royal Commission on Broadcasting, 1956-57; Cttee on Broadcasting, 1964-65. Hon. LLD: Montreal, 1960; McGill, 1974. *Address:* 36 Summit Circle, Westmount, PQ, Canada. *T:* Wellington 5-4500. *Clubs:* Mount Royal (Montreal); University (Toronto).

FOWLER, Sir Robert (William Doughty), KCMG 1966 (CMG 1962); HM Diplomatic Service, retired; Member, Panel of Chairmen, Civil Service Selection Board, since 1972; *b* 6 March 1914; *s* of William and Martha Louise Fowler; *m* Margaret MacFarquhar (*née* MacLeod); one *s* one *d* (twins). *Educ:* Queen Elizabeth's Grammar Sch., Mansfield; Emmanuel Coll., Cambridge. Burma CS, 1937-48; Burma Army (Military Administration), 1944-46; Additional Sec. to Governor of Burma, 1947; Commonwealth Relations Office from 1948; seconded to Foreign Service for UK Delegn to UN, 1950-53; Fedn of Rhodesia and Nyasaland and High Commn Territories Dept, CRO, 1954-56; Brit. Dep. High Comr: Pakistan, 1956-58; Canada, 1960-62; Nigeria, 1963-64. Attended IDC, 1959. British High Comr to Tanzania, Aug. 1964, until diplomatic relations broken off in Dec. 1965; Ambassador to Sudan from 1966 until break in relations in 1967; reappointed Ambassador, 1968-70 (during the break, Administrator of Gibraltar Referendum and Under-Sec. of State, Commonwealth Office). *Recreations:* gardening, painting, photography. *Address:* 7 Leicester Close, Henley-on-Thames, Oxon. *T:* Henley 2404. *Clubs:* Royal Commonwealth Society; Leander (Henley).

FOWLER, Ronald Frederick, CBE 1950; *b* 21 April 1910; *e s* of late Charles Frederick Fowler; *m* 1937, Brenda Kathleen Smith. *Educ:* Bancroft's Sch.; LSE, University of London; Universities of Lille and Brussels. BCom (hons) London, 1931. Sir Ernest Cassel Travelling Scholar, 1929-30; Asst, later Lectr in Commerce, LSE, 1932-40; Central Statistical Office, 1940-50; Dir of Statistics, Min. of Labour, 1950-68; Dir of Statistical Res., Dept of Employment, 1968-72. *Publications:* The Depreciation of Capital, 1934; The Duration of Unemployment, 1968; Some Problems of Index Number Construction, 1970; Further Problems of Index Number Construction, 1973; articles in British and US economic jls. *Address:* 10 Silverdale Road, Petts Wood, Kent. *T:* Orpington 23895. *Club:* Reform.

FOWLER, Prof. William Alfred, PhD; Medal for Merit, USA, 1948; Institute Professor of Physics, California Institute of Technology, since 1970; *b* Pittsburgh, Pa, 9 Aug. 1911; *s* of John McLeod Fowler and Jennie Summers (*née* Watson); *m* 1940, Ardiane Foy Olmsted, Pasadena, Calif.; two *d. Educ:* Ohio State Univ. (B.Eng. Phys); California Inst. of Technology (PhD Phys). Member: Tau Kappa Epsilon; Tau Beta Pi; Sigma Xi. California Inst. of Technology: Research Fellow in Nuclear Physics, 1936-39; Asst Prof. of Physics, 1939-42; Associate Prof. of Physics, 1942-46; Prof. of Physics, 1946-70. Defense record: Research and develt proximity fuses, rocket ordnance, and atomic weapons; Research staff mem.: Sect. T, NDRC, and Div. 4, NDRC, 1941; Asst Dir of Research, Sect. L, Div. 3, NDRC,

1941-45; Techn. Observer, Office of Field Services and New Develts Div., War Dept, in South and Southwestern Pacific Theatres, 1944; Actg Supervisor, Ord. Div., R&D, NOTS, 1945; Sci. Dir, Project VISTA, Dept Defense, 1951-52. Guggenheim Fellow and Fulbright Lectr, Cavendish Laboratory, Univ. of Cambridge, Eng., 1954-55; Guggenheim Fellow, St John's Coll., and Dept Applied Math. and Theor. Phys., Univ. of Cambridge, Eng., 1961-62; Walker-Ames Prof. of Physics, Univ. of Washington, 1963; Visitor, The Observatories, Univ. of Cambridge, Summer 1964; Vis. Prof. of Physics, Mass. Inst. of Technology, 1966; Vis. Fellow, Inst. of Theoretical Astronomy, Univ. of Cambridge, Summers 1967-72. Numerous lectureships in USA, 1957-; those given abroad include: Lectr, Internat. Sch. of Physics "Enrico Fermi", Varenna, 1965. Lectr, Advanced Sch. on Cosmic Physics, Erice, Italy, 1969, in addition to past lectures at Cavendish Laboratory, Cambridge; also Lectr at Research Sch. of Physical Sciences, Australian National Univ., Canberra, 1965; Jubilee Lectr, 50th Aniversary, Niels Bohr Inst., Copenhagen, 1970; Scott Lectr, Cavendish Laboratory, Cambridge Univ., Eng., 1971; George Darwin Lectr, RAS, 1973. Member: Nat. Science Bd, Nat. Science Foundation, USA, 1968-74; Space Science Bd, Nat. Academy of Sciences, 1970-73; Space Program Adv. Council, NASA, 1971. Bd of Directors, American Friends of Cambridge Univ., 1970-, etc. Has attended numerous conferences, congresses and assemblies. Various awards and medals for science etc, both at home and abroad, including Vetlesen Prize, 1973, Nat. Medal of Sci., 1974. Member: Internat. Astro. Union; Amer. Assoc. for Advancement of Science; Amer. Assoc. of Univ. Professors; Nat. Acad. of Sciences; Mem. corres., Soc. Royale des Sciences de Liège; Fellow: Amer. Physical Soc. (Pres., 1976); Amer. Acad. of Arts and Sciences; British Assoc. for Advancement of Science; Benjamin Franklin Fellow, RSA; ARAS. *Publications:* contributor to: Physical Review, Astrophysical Jl, Proc. Nat. Acad. of Sciences, Amer. Jl of Physics, Geophysical Jl, Nature, Royal Astronomical Soc., etc. *Address:* Kellogg Radiation Laboratory 106-38, California Institute of Technology, Pasadena, California 91125, USA. *Clubs:* Cosmos (Washington, DC); Athenæum (Pasadena, Calif); Cambridge and District Model Engineering Society.

FOWLER-HOWITT, William; *see* Howitt, W. F.

FOWLES, John; writer; *b* 31 March 1926; *s* of Robert John Fowles and Gladys May Richards; *m* 1956, Elizabeth Whitton. *Educ:* Bedford Sch.; New Coll., Oxford. English Centre PEN Silver Pen Award, 1969; W. H. Smith Award, 1970. *Publications:* The Collector, 1963; The Aristos, 1965; The Magus, 1966, rev. edn 1977; The French Lieutenant's Woman, 1969; Poems, 1973; The Ebony Tower, 1974; Shipwreck, 1975; Daniel Martin, 1977. *Recreations:* mainly Sabine. *Address:* c/o Anthony Sheil Associates, 52 Floral Street, WC2.

FOWWEATHER, Frank Scott, MSc, MD (Liverpool) 1925; FRCP 1943; FRIC, DPH 1924; Professor of Chemical Pathology, Leeds University, 1946-56, Professor Emeritus, 1956; late Chemical Pathologist, Leeds General Infirmary; *b* 13 Aug. 1892; *e s* of W. T. Fowweather, engineer, late of Bolton, Lancs; *m* 1922, Nellie, *d* of A. N. Godwin Chester, and *g d* of late J. P. Birch, surgeon, Cotton Hall, Denbigh; no *c*. *Educ:* Municipal Secondary Sch., Bolton; Liverpool Univ. BSc, First Class Hons in Chemistry, and awarded Willox Exhibition and Isaac Roberts Scholarship, 1914, and MSc, 1915. Chemist with Evans, Sons, Lescher & Webb Ltd, Runcorn, 1915-16; chemist with British Dyes Ltd, Huddersfield, 1916-17; practised as analytical and consulting chemist at 62 Dale Street, Liverpool, 1917-22; MB, ChB, 1922; in general medical practice at Wallasey and at Ellesmere Port, 1922-24; Lecturer in Chemical Pathology, University of Leeds, 1924-30; Reader, 1930-46. *Publications:* A Handbook of Clinical Chemical Pathology; contributions to scientific journals. *Recreations:* gardening, bookbinding. *Address:* 40 Queensbury, West Kirby, Wirral, Merseyside L48 6EP. *T:* 051-625 8535.

FOX, Ven. (Benjamin) George (Burton), MC 1944; TD 1950; Archdeacon of Wisbech since 1965; Hon. Canon, Ely Cathedral, since 1968; *b* 28 July 1913; *s* of J. B. Fox, Manor Farm, Erpingham, Norfolk; *m* 1943, Hon. Margaret Joan Davidson, *d* of 1st Viscount Davidson, PC, GCVO, CH, CB; one *s* four *d*. *Educ:* Norwich Sch.; University of London. Curate: Emmanuel, Guildford, 1936-38; St Andrew's, Bath, 1938-39. Chaplain, HM Forces, 1939-45. Vicar, Potten End, 1945-46, St Andrew's, Bedford, 1946-50, Dio. St Albans; Rector, Montego Bay, Jamaica, 1950-55; Archdeacon of Cornwall, Jamaica, 1950-55; Vicar, St Etheldreda's, Fulham, 1956-65; Vicar of Haddenham, Dio. Ely, 1965-. *Recreations:* cricket, boxing. *Address:* The Vicarage, Haddenham, Ely, Cambs. *T:* Haddenham 309.
See also A. R. Mellows.

FOX, Bernard Joshua, CBE 1964; QC 1939; Recorder of Belfast, 1944-60, retired; *b* 3 Feb. 1885; *s* of Herman and Dora Fox; *m* 1908, Elizabeth Myers; two *s*. *Educ:* Belfast Royal Academy; Royal University of Ireland. Called to Irish Bar, 1914. Auditor, Law Students Soc. of Ireland, 1913-14. Called to Inner Bar of Northern Ireland, 1939; Legal Adviser to Govt of Northern Ireland, 1939-44; Chairman: Price Regulation Cttee for Northern Ireland, 1940-44; Northern Ireland Teachers' Salaries Cttee, 1957; Northern Ireland Coal Inquiry Cttee, 1961. Hon. LLD Queen's Univ. of Belfast. *Recreations:* golf, bridge. *Address:* No 5 Flat, 693 Antrim Road, Belfast. *T:* Belfast 76058. *Club:* Ulster Reform (Belfast).

FOX, Sir David S.; *see* Scott Fox.

FOX, Douglas Gerard Arthur, OBE 1958; MA, BMus Oxon; FRCO, FRCM; Hon. ARCM; Hon. RAM; MusD Edinburgh 1938; Organist Emeritus, Great St Mary's Church, Cambridge (Organist, 1957-63); *b* 12 July 1893; *s* of Gerard Elsey Fox and Edith Makinson Fox, Clifton, Bristol. *Educ:* Clifton Coll. (Music Scholar); Royal College of Music (Organ Scholar; Challen Gold Medal for pianoforte playing, 1912); Keble Coll., Oxford (Organ Scholar). FRCO 1911 (La Fontaine Prize); ARCM 1912. Lieut 4th Gloucester Regt; lost right arm, France, Aug. 1917; Pres., Oxford Univ. Musical Club, 1918; Dir of Music, Bradfield Coll., 1918-30; composed music for Bradfield Greek Play (Agamemnon), 1925, and Antigone, 1931; Conductor, Newbury Amateur Orchestral Union, 1923-30; Dir of Music, Clifton Coll., 1931-57. Has given several performances of Ravel Piano Concerto for the left hand, with BBC SO, LSO, LPO (some broadcast). Examnr, Associated Bd of Royal Schs of Music. Mem. Council, RCO, 1935-72; President: Incorporated Soc. of Musicians, 1958-59; Cambridge Philharmonic Soc., 1960-68; Co-Pres., Bristol Music Club, 1964. Governor, Clifton Coll., 1958-. Hon. DMus Bristol, 1966. *Publication:* Joseph Haydn: an introduction, 1929. *Address:* Cowlin House, 26 Pembroke Road, Clifton, Bristol BS8 3BB. *T:* Bristol 32848. *Club:* Savile.

FOX, Francis Gordon Ward L.; *see* F. G. W. Lane Fox.

FOX, Ven. George; *see* Fox, Ven. B. G. B.

FOX, Sir (Henry) Murray, GBE 1974; MA, FRICS; Chartered Surveyor, Consultant to Chestertons; Chairman, Trehaven Trust Group; *b* 7 June 1912; *s* of late S. J. Fox and Molly Button; *m* 1941, Helen Isabella Margaret, *d* of late J. B. Crichton; one *s* two *d*. *Educ:* Malvern; Emmanuel Coll., Cambridge. Governor: Christ's Hosp., 1966; Bridewell Royal Hosp., 1966 (Vice-Pres. 1976-); Trustee, Morden Coll., 1976-. Court of Common Council, 1963; Past Master: Wheelwrights' Co.; Coopers' Co.; Alderman, Ward of Bread Street, 1966-; Sheriff, City of London, 1971-72; Lord Mayor of London, 1974-75; one of HM Lieutenants, City of London, 1976-. Order of Rising Sun and Sacred Treasure (Japan), 1971; Order of Stor (Afghanistan), 1971; Order of Orange Nassau (Netherlands), 1972. *Recreations:* golf, reading. *Address:* Flat 2, 45 Beech Street, EC2. *T:* 01-606 3631; (office) Compter House, 4/9 Wood Street, EC2. *T:* 01-606 3055. *Clubs:* City of London, City Livery (Pres. 1966-67).

FOX, (John) Marcus, MBE 1963; MP (C) Shipley, since 1970; a Vice-Chairman, Conservative Party Organisation, since 1976; *b* 11 June 1927; *s* of late Alfred Hirst Fox; *m* 1954, Ann, *d* of F. W. J. Tindall; one *s* one *d*. *Educ:* Wheelright Grammar Sch., Dewsbury. Mem. Dewsbury County Borough Council, 1957-65; contested (C): Dewsbury, 1959; Huddersfield West, 1966. An Asst Govt Whip, 1972-73; a Lord Comr, HM Treasury, 1973-74; Opposition Spokesman on Transport, 1975-76; Mem., Parly Select Cttee on Race Relations and Immigration, 1970-; Sec., Cons. Party's Transport Industries Cttee, 1970-72. *Recreations:* reading, tennis, squash. *Address:* House of Commons, SW1.

FOX, Rt. Rev. Langton Douglas; *see* Menevia, Bishop of, (RC).

FOX, Leslie, DSc Oxon; Professor of Numerical Analysis, Oxford University, and Professorial Fellow, Balliol College, since 1963; Director, Oxford University Computing Laboratory, since 1957; *b* 30 Sept. 1918; *m* 1st, 1943, Paulene Dennis; 2nd, 1973, Mrs Clemency Clements, *er d* of Thomas Fox. *Educ:* Wheelright Grammar Sch., Dewsbury; Christ Church, Oxford. Admiralty Computing Service, 1943-45; Mathematics Div., Nat. Physical Laboratory, 1945-56; Associate Prof., Univ. of California, Berkeley, 1956-57; Research Prof., Univ. of Illinois, 1961-62; Vis. Prof., Open Univ., 1970-71. Pres., Math./Phys. Section, BAAS, 1975. *Publications:* Numerical Solution of Boundary-value Problems in Ordinary Differential Equations, 1957; (ed) Numerical Solution of Ordinary and Partial Differential

Equations, 1962; An Introduction to Numerical Linear Algebra, 1964; (ed) Advances in Programming and Non-Numerical Computation, 1966; Chebyshev Polynomials in Numerical Analysis (with I. J. Parker), 1968; Computing Methods for Scientists and Engineers (with D. F. Mayers), 1968; numerous papers in learned journals. *Recreations:* sport, music, literature. *Address:* 2 Elsfield Road, Marston, Oxford. *T:* Oxford 722668; University Computing Laboratory, 19 Parks Road, Oxford. *T:* Oxford 54409.

FOX, Marcus, see Fox, J. M.

FOX, Hon. Sir Michael John, Kt 1975; **Hon. Mr Justice Fox;** Judge of the High Court of Justice, Chancery Division, since 1975; *b* 8 Oct. 1921; *s* of late Michael Fox; *m* 1954, Hazel Mary Stuart; three *s* one *d. Educ:* Drayton Manor Sch.; Magdalen Coll., Oxford (BCL, MA). Admiralty, 1942-45. Called to the Bar, Lincoln's Inn, 1949, Bencher, 1975; QC 1968. *Address:* Royal Courts of Justice, Strand, WC2. *T:* 01-405 7641.

FOX, Sir Murray; see Fox, Sir H. M.

FOX, Patrick Loftus B.; see Bushe-Fox.

FOX, Paul Leonard; Managing Director and Director of Programmes, Yorkshire Television; Director, Independent Television News, since 1977; *b* 27 Oct. 1925; *o s* of late Dr Walter Fox and Mrs Hilda Fox; *m* 1948, Betty Ruth (*née* Nathan); two *s. Educ:* Bournemouth Grammar Sch.; abroad. Parachute Regt, 1943. Reporter: Kentish Times, 1946; The People, 1947; Scriptwriter, Pathé News, 1947; BBC Television: Scriptwriter, 1950; Editor, Sportsview, 1953, Panorama, 1961; Head, Public Affairs Dept, 1963; Head, Current Affairs Group, 1965. Controller, BBC1, 1967-73. Dir, Trident Television Ltd, 1973-. *Recreations:* television, attending race meetings. *Address:* Trident House, Brooks Mews, W1. *T:* 01-493 1237.

FOX, Sir (Robert) David (John) S.; see Scott Fox.

FOX, Roy, OBE 1967; HM Diplomatic Service; Consul-General, Houston, since 1974; *b* 1 Sept. 1920; *s* of J. S. and A. Fox; *m* 1st, 1943, Sybil Verity; two *s* one *d*; 2nd, 1975, Susan Rogers Turner. *Educ:* Wheelwright Grammar Sch., Dewsbury; Bradford Technical Coll. Served in RNVR, 1940-46. Bd of Trade, 1947-58; British Trade Commissioner: Nairobi, 1958-60; Montreal, 1960-62; Winnipeg, 1962-64; Dep. Controller, Bd of Trade Office for Scotland, 1964-65. First Sec. Commercial, Karachi, 1965-68; Deputy High Comr, E Pakistan, 1968-70; Consul-Gen. and Comm. Counsellor, Helsinki, 1970-74; promoted to Minister, 1977. *Recreations:* golf, reading, tennis. *Address:* c/o Foreign and Commonwealth Office, SW1. *Clubs:* Oriental; Briar (Houston).

FOX, Sir Theodore, Kt 1962; MA, MD Cambridge, LLD Glasgow, DLitt Birmingham; FRCP; *b* 1899; 3rd *s* of late R. Fortescue Fox; *m* Margaret (*d* 1970), *e d* of late W. S. McDougall, Wallington, Surrey; four *s. Educ:* Leighton Park Sch.; Pembroke Coll., Cambridge (scholar); London Hosp. (house physician). Mem. of Friends' Ambulance Unit, BEF, 1918; Ship Surg., 1925; joined staff of The Lancet, 1925; served in RAMC, 1939-42 (late temp. Major); Ed., The Lancet, 1944-64. Dir, Family Planning Assoc., 1965-67. Croonian Lectr, RCP, 1951; Heath Clark Lectr, Univ. of London, 1963; Harveian Orator, RCP, 1965; Maurice Bloch Lectr, Univ. of Glasgow, 1966. Hon. Fellow, Royal Australian Coll. of Gen. Practitioners. *Publication:* Crisis in Communication, 1965. *Address:* Green House, Rotherfield, East Sussex. *T:* Rotherfield 2870. *Club:* Athenæum.

FOX, Wallace, CMG 1973; MD, FRCP, FFCM; Director, Medical Research Council Tuberculosis and Chest Diseases Unit, since 1965; Senior Lecturer, Cardiothoracic Institute; Hon. Consultant Physician, Brompton Hospital, since 1969; WHO Consultant, since 1961; Member of WHO Expert Advisory Panel on Tuberculosis, since 1965; *b* 7 Nov. 1920; *s* of Samuel and Esther Fox; *m* 1956, Gaye Judith Akker; three *s. Educ:* Cotham Grammar Sch., Bristol; Guy's Hosp. MB, BS (London) 1943; MRCS, LRCP, 1943; MRCP 1950; MD (Dist.) (London) 1951; FRCP 1962; FFCM 1976. Ho. Phys., Guy's USA Hosp., 1945-46; Resident Phys., Preston Hall Sanatorium, 1946-50; Registrar, Guy's Hosp., 1950-51; Asst Chest Physician, Hammersmith Chest Clinic, 1951-52; Mem. Scientific Staff of MRC Tuberculosis and Chest Diseases Unit, 1952-56, 1961-65; seconded to WHO, to establish and direct Tuberculosis Chemotherapy Centre, Madras, 1956-61. Marc Daniels Lectr, RCP, London, 1962; First John Barnwell Meml Lectr, US Veterans Admin, 1968; Philip Ellman Lectr, RSocMed, 1976; Martyrs Meml Lectr, Bangladesh Med. Assoc., 1977; Waring

Vis. Prof. in Medicine, Univ. of Colorado and Stanford Univ., 1974. Mem. Tropical Med. Research Bd, 1968-72; Mem., several MRC Cttees; Member: (and then Chm.) Cttee of Therapy of Internat. Union Against Tuberculosis, 1964-71; BCG Vaccination Sub-Cttee, Min. of Health, 1968; Associate Mem., Scientific Cttees and Chm., Exec. Cttee, Internat. Union Against Tuberculosis, 1973; Chm., Acid Fast Club, 1971-72. Co-Editor, Advances in Tuberculosis Research. Elected Corresp. Mem., Amer. Thoracic Soc., 1962; Mem., Mexican Acad. of Medicine, 1976; Hon. Life Mem., Canadian Thoracic Soc., 1976. Sir Robert Philip Medal, Chest and Heart Assoc., 1969; Weber Parkes Prize, RCP, 1973; Carlo Forlanini Gold Medal, Fedn Ital. contra la Tuberculosi e le Malattie Polmonari Sociali, 1976. *Publications:* Reports to Hong Kong Government: Heaf/Fox, 1962; Scadding/Fox, 1975; Reports on tuberculosis services in Hong Kong; numerous contribs to med. jls: on methodology of controlled clinical trials, on epidemiology and on chemotherapy, particularly in tuberculosis, asthma and carcinoma of the bronchus and other respiratory diseases. *Address:* 2 The Orchard, Bedford Park, W4 1JX. *T:* 01-994 0974.

FOX, Winifred Marjorie, (Mrs E. Gray Debros); Under-Secretary, Department of the Environment, 1970-76; *d* of Frederick Charles Fox and Charlotte Marion Ogborn; *m* 1953, Eustachy Gray Debros (*d* 1954); one *d. Educ:* Streatham County Sch.; St Hugh's Coll., Oxford. Unemployment Assistance Board, 1937; Cabinet Office, 1942; Ministry of Town and Country Planning, 1944; Ministry of Housing and Local Govt, 1952 (Under-Sec., 1963); Dept of the Environment, 1970; seconded to CSD as Chm., CS Selection Bd, 1971-72. *Address:* The Coach House, Hinton in the Hedges, S Northants. *T:* Brackley 702100.

FOX-ANDREWS, James Roland Blake, QC 1968; a Recorder, and Honorary Recorder of Winchester, since 1972; *b* 24 March 1922; step *s* of late Norman Roy Fox-Andrews, QC; *m* 1950, Angela Bridget Swift; two *s. Educ:* Stowe; Pembroke Coll., Cambridge. Called to the Bar, Gray's Inn, 1949, Bencher, 1974. Dep. Chm., Devon QS, 1970-71; Recorder of Winchester, 1971. Member: Gen. Council of the Bar, 1968-72; Senate of Inns of Court and the Bar, 1976-. *Publications:* (jtly) Leasehold Property (Temporary Provisions) Act, 1951; contrib. Halsbury's Laws of England, 3rd edn, building contracts, architects and engineers; (jtly) Landlord and Tenant Act, 1954; Business Tenancies, 1970, 2nd edn, 1974. *Address:* 20 Cheyne Gardens, SW3. *T:* 01-352 9484; Lepe House, Exbury, Hants. *Club:* Hampshire (Winchester).

FOX-PITT, Maj.-Gen. William Augustus Fitzgerald Lane, CVO 1966 (MVO 1936); DSO 1940; MC 1916; retired; DL; Member of HM Bodyguard of Hon. Corps of Gentlemen-at-Arms, 1947-66; Lieutenant, 1963-66; (Standard Bearer, 1961-63); *b* 28 Jan. 1896; *s* of late Lieut-Col W. A. Fox-Pitt, Presaddfed, Anglesey; *m* 1931, Mary Stewart, *d* of A. H. H. Sinclair, MD, FRCSE; two *s* one *d. Educ:* Charterhouse. ADC to the King, 1945-47; joined Cheshire Regt 1914; served with Welsh Gds, 1915-39; Comd, 1st Bn, 1934-37; OC Welsh Guards Regt, 1937-40; Comd Gds Bde BEF, 1940, Armd Bde, 1941-43; Comdr, East Kent Dist as Maj.-Gen., 1943; retired with hon. rank of Maj.-Gen. 1947. Mem. Dorset CC 1952; DL Dorset, 1957. *Recreations:* hunting, shooting, golf. *Address:* Marsh Court, Sherborne, Dorset. *T:* Bishops Caundle 230. *Club:* Turf.

FOX-STRANGWAYS, family name of **Earl of Ilchester.**

FOXELL, Rev. Maurice Frederic, KCVO 1965 (CVO 1953; MVO 1942); MA; Extra Chaplain to the Queen since 1965; Honorary Minor Canon St Paul's Cathedral; *b* 15 Aug. 1888; 4th *s* of late Rev. W. J. Foxell, PhD, and Annie Harte; *m* 1914, Mariana (*d* 1975), 2nd *d* of late John Morton Fountain, Hillingdon, Middx; two *s* two *d. Educ:* Christ's Hospital; Queen's Coll., Oxford. Asst Curate St Paul's, Hammersmith, 1911-15; Friern Barnet, 1915-17; Minor Canon St George's Chapel, Windsor Castle, 1917-21; Minor Canon and Succentor, St Paul's Cathedral, 1921-39; Rector of St James's, Garlickhythe, EC4, 1939-64. Sub-Dean of HM Chapels Royal, Sub-Almoner, Deputy Clerk of the Closet, and Domestic Chaplain to the Queen, 1952-65 (to King George VI, 1948-52). *Publication:* Wren's Craftsmen at St Paul's, 1934. *Recreations:* water-colour, wood-engraving, piano. *Address:* The Homes of St Barnabas, Lingfield, Surrey. *T:* Dormans Park 508. *Club:* Athenæum.

FOXLEE, James Brazier; Under Secretary, Ministry of Agriculture, Fisheries and Food, since 1971; *b* 20 Nov. 1921; *s* of late Arthur Brazier Foxlee and late Mary Foxlee (*née* Fisher); *m* 1952, Vera June (*née* Guiver); one *s* two *d. Educ:* Brentwood Sch. Clerical Officer, MAF, 1938. Served War, RNVR,

Ordinary Seaman, 1941; commissioned, 1942; Lieut, in comd Light Coastal Forces craft and mine-sweepers. MAFF: Exec. Officer, 1946; HEO, 1948; SEO, 1950; Principal, 1955 (Welsh Dept, 1955-57; Treas., 1961-62); Asst Sec., 1965 (Regional Controller, Leeds, 1965-69). *Recreations:* cricket, travel, bridge. *Address:* Arran, 43 Foxley Lane, Purley, Surrey CR2 3EH. *T:* 01-660 1085.

FOXLEY-NORRIS, Air Chief Marshal Sir Christopher (Neil), GCB 1973 (KCB 1969; CB 1966); DSO 1945; OBE 1956; FBIM; FRSA; Chairman, Cheshire Foundation, since 1974 (Vice-Chairman, 1972-74); Director, Brookdale Hutton & Associates; Chairman, General Portfolio Life Assurance; *b* 16 March 1917; *s* of Major J. P. Foxley-Norris and Dorothy Brabant Smith; *m* 1948, Joan Lovell Hughes; no *c. Educ:* Winchester; Trinity Coll., Oxford (Hon. Fellow, 1973); Middle Temple. Commissioned RAFO, 1936; France, 1940; Battle of Britain, 1940; various operational tours of duty in wartime. MA 1946. Directing Staff, RAF Staff Coll., 1951-53; idc 1961; Dir of Organization and Admin. Plans, Air Min., 1962; ACDS, 1963; AOC No 224 Gp, FEAF, 1964-67; Dir-Gen., RAF Organization, MoD, 1967-68; C-in-C, RAF Germany and Comdr, NATO 2nd Tactical Air Force, 1968-70; Chief of Personnel and Logistics, MoD, 1971-74; retd. FBIM 1973. *Publications:* various in RUSI and other service jls. *Recreations:* golf, sailing. *Address:* Tumble Wood, Northend Common, Henley-on-Thames. *T:* Turville Heath 457. *Clubs:* Royal Air Force; Huntercombe (Oxon).

FOXON, David Fairweather; Reader in Textual Criticism and Fellow of Wadham College, Oxford, since 1968; *b* 9 Jan. 1923; *s* of late Rev. Walter Foxon and Susan Mary (*née* Fairweather); *m* 1947, Dorothy June (marr. diss. 1963), *d* of late Sir Arthur Jarratt, KCVO; one *d. Educ:* Kingswood Sch., Bath; Magdalen Coll., Oxford. BA 1948, MA 1953. Foreign Office, 1942-45; Asst Keeper, Dept of Printed Books, British Museum, 1950-65; Harkness Fellow, 1959-61; Professor of English, Queen's Univ., Kingston, Ontario, 1965-67; Guggenheim Fellow, 1967-68. Lyell Reader in Bibliography, Oxford, 1975-76; Sandars Reader in Bibliography, Cambridge, 1977-78. Vice-Pres., Bibliographical Soc., 1970-. *Publications:* T. J. Wise and the Pre-Restoration Drama, 1959; Libertine Literature in England, 1660-1745, 1964; (ed) English Bibliographical Sources, 1964-67; English Verse 1701-1750: a catalogue, 1975; contribs to bibliographical jls. *Recreation:* music. *Address:* 7 Fane Road, Marston, Oxford OX3 0RZ. *T:* Oxford 48350.

FOXON, Prof. George Eric Howard, MA, MSc; Professor of Biology, University of London, 1955-72, now Emeritus Professor; Head of Biology Department, Guy's Hospital Medical School, 1948-72; *b* 1908; *s* of George Thomas Foxon, OBE, and Edith Maud (*née* Lewis); *m* 1932, Joan Burlinson; one *s* one *d* (and one *s* decd). *Educ:* King's Coll. Sch., Wimbledon; Queens' Coll., Cambridge. BA 1930, 1st Cl. Hons Nat. Sci. Tripos Pt II, 1931; MA 1934; MSc (Wales) 1943. Asst in Zoology, University of Glasgow, 1932-37; Asst Lectr and Lectr in Zoology, University Coll., Cardiff, 1937-48; Reader in Biology, University of London, 1948-55. Chm. of the British Univs Film Council, 1959-63, 1967-69. Fellow Cambridge Philosophical Soc., FLS; FIBiol; FZS. *Publications:* various scientific papers, mainly dealing with the comparative study of the heart and blood system of vertebrate animals. *Address:* Thorpe Cloud, Woodfield Lane, Ashtead, Surrey. *T:* Ashtead 72306.

FOXTON, Maj.-Gen. Edwin Frederick, CB 1969; OBE 1959; MA; Fellow and Domestic Bursar, Emmanuel College, Cambridge, since 1969; *b* 28 Feb. 1914; *y s* of F. Foxton and T. Wilson; unmarried. *Educ:* Worksop Coll.; St Edmund Hall, Oxford. Commissioned from General List TA, 1937; served: India, 1939-42; Middle East, 1942-45; India, 1945-47 (Chief Educn Officer, Southern Comd, India); War Office, 1948-52; Chief Instructor, Army Sch. of Educn, 1952-55; Dist Educn Officer, HQ Northumbrian District, 1955-57; War Office, 1957-60; Commandant, Army Sch. of Educn, 1961-63; War Office, 1963-65; Chief Educn Officer, FARELF, 1965; Dir of Army Educn, 1965-69. *Address:* Emmanuel College, Cambridge. *Club:* United Oxford & Cambridge University.

FOYLE, Christina Agnes Lilian, (Mrs Ronald Batty); Managing Director, W. & G. Foyle Ltd; *d* of late William Alfred Foyle; *m* 1938, Ronald Batty. *Educ:* Aux Villas Unspunnen, Wilderswil, Switzerland. Began Foyle's Literary Luncheons, 1930, where book lovers have been able to see and hear great personalities. Member: Ct, Univ. of Essex; Council, RSA, 1963-69. DUniv Essex, 1975. *Recreations:* bird-watching, gardening, playing the piano. *Address:* Beeleigh Abbey, Maldon, Essex.

FRAENKEL, Heinrich; freelance author; *b* 28 Sept. 1897; *s* of Benno Fraenkel and Alwina (*née* Taendler); *m* 1936, Gretel Levy-Ries; two *s. Educ:* German schools and universities. Began career in film trade journalism, Berlin; as screen-writer, went to Hollywood for two years but returned to Germany; continued to write screen plays but increasingly interested in politics; emigrated to avoid arrest in night of Reichstag fire, 1933; went to Paris, then London; still made living writing screen-plays but wrote political books, lectured on German history, the roots of Nazism, etc. At war's end, determined to return to Germany; disillusioned by many long trips made for the New Statesman; sought British nationality, 1949. Has written chess column in New Statesman (as Assiac), 1949-76. Order of Merit (1st class) of Fed. Rep. of Germany, 1967. *Publications:* The German People Versus Hitler, 1940; Help Us Germans to Beat the Nazis, 1941; The Winning of the Peace, 1942; The Other Germany, 1943; A Nation Divided, 1949; The Boy Between, 1956; Farewell to Germany, 1958; with Roger Manvell: Dr Goebbels, 1959; Hermann Goering, 1962; The July Plot, 1964; Heinrich Himmler, 1965; The Incomparable Crime, 1967; The Canaris Conspiracy, 1969; History of the German Cinema, 1971; Rudolf Hess, 1971; Inside Hitler, 1973; Seizure of Power, 1974; Adolf Hitler: the man and the myth, 1977. As Assiac: Adventure in Chess, 1950; Delights of Chess, 1960, US, French, Dutch, Spanish and German edns substantially enlgd and revised. *Address:* Christopher Cottage, Thaxted (Dunmow), Essex. *T:* Thaxted 830293. *Club:* Authors'.

FRAGA-IRIBARNE, Manuel; Founder-Member, Popular Alliance, Spain, 1976; elected to the Cortes, 1977; *b* 23 Nov. 1922; *m* 1948, María del Carmen Estévez; two *s* three *d. Educ:* Insts of Coruña, Villalba and Lugo; Univs of Santiago de Compostela and Madrid. Prof. of Polit. Law, Univ. of Valencia, 1945; Prof. of Polit. Sci. and Constit. Law, Univ. of Madrid, 1953; Legal Adviser to the Cortes, 1945; entered Diplomatic Service, 1945; Sec.-Gen., Instituto de Cultura Hispánica, 1951; Sec.-Gen. in Min. of Educn, 1953; Head, Inst. of Polit. Studies, 1961; Minister of Information and Tourism, 1961-69; Ambassador to UK, 1973-75; Interior Minister, Spain, 1975-76. Holds numerous foreign orders. *Publications:* various books on law, polit. sci., history and sociology, incl. one on British Parlt. *Recreations:* shooting, fishing. *Address:* Joaquín María López 72, Madrid (15), Spain. *T:* 244 4980. *Clubs:* Athenæum, Travellers'.

FRAME, Alistair Gilchrist, CEng, FIMechE; Deputy Chief Executive, Rio Tinto-Zinc Corporation Ltd, since 1977; part-time Member, Central Electricity Generating Board; *b* Dalmuir, Dunbartonshire, 3 April 1929; *s* of Alexander Frame and Mary (*née* Fraser); *m* 1953, Sheila (*née* Mathieson); one *d. Educ:* Glasgow and Cambridge Univs. BSc, MA. Director, Reactor and Research Groups, UK Atomic Energy Authority, 1964-68; joined Rio Tinto-Zinc Corp., 1968; appointed to main Board, 1973. *Recreations:* tennis, gardening, walking. *Address:* 13 Montpelier Place, SW7. *T:* 01-581 1796; Birdlands, Holmbury St Mary, Dorking, Surrey. *Club:* Boodle's.

FRAME, Rt. Rev. John Timothy; *see* Yukon, Bishop of.

FRAMPTON, Henry James, CSI 1947; CIE 1941; MC; MA; *b* 14 Aug. 1897; *s* of Henry Manwell Frampton; *m* 1st, Alys Ann Mary, *d* of C. H. Holmes; 2nd, Hilda Mary, *d* of Rev. Alex. Brown; three *s* one *d. Educ:* Christ's Hospital; St John's Coll., Oxford. Joined Indian Civil Service, 1921; retired 1947. *Address:* Frenchay House, Beckspool Road, Frenchay Common, Bristol BS16 1NE.

FRAMPTON, Meredith, RA 1942 (ARA 1934); Honorary Retired Academician; *b* 1894; *s* of Sir George Frampton, RA; *m* 1951, Hilda Norman, *d* of late James B. Dunn, RSA, FRIBA, and of Mrs Dunn, Edinburgh. *Educ:* Westminster. *Address:* Hill Barn, Monkton Deverill, Warminster, Wilts. *Club:* Athenæum.

FRAMPTON, Walter Bennett, OBE 1945; Metropolitan Magistrate, Marylebone Magistrates' Court, 1952-67, retired; *b* 1 Oct. 1903; *er s* of late Walter Frampton, Recorder of Chichester, and Catherine Bennett; *m* 1928, Gwyneth Davies; one *s* one *d. Educ:* Westminster Sch.; London Univ. Called to Bar, Middle Temple, 1925; joined ROC 1939; RAFVR, 1940-45; Wing-Commander, 1941; Senior Administrative Officer, Nos 16 and 19 Groups, RAF (despatches, OBE). Metropolitan Magistrate, 1947. *Recreation:* cricket. *Address:* Cranford, Peppard Common, Henley-on-Thames, Oxon RG9 5JU. *T:* Rotherfield Greys 328.

FRANCE, Sir Arnold William, GCB 1972 (KCB 1965; CB 1957); Chairman, Central Board of Finance, Church of England, since 1973; Director: Rank Organisation; Tube Investments;

Pilkington Bros; *b* 20 April 1911; *s* of late W. E. France; *m* 1940, Frances Margaret Linton, *d* of late Dr C. J. L. Palmer; four *d*. *Educ:* Bishop's Stortford Coll. District Bank, Ltd, 1929-40. Served War of 1939-45, Army, 1940-43; Deputy Economic and Financial Adviser to Minister of State in Middle East, 1943; HM Treasury, 1945; Asst Sec., 1948; Under Sec., 1952; Third Sec., 1960; Ministry of Health: Dep. Sec., 1963-64; Permanent Sec., 1964-68; Chm., Bd of Inland Revenue, 1968-73. Mem., Economic Planning Board, 1960. Chm., Bd of Management, Lingfield Hosp. Sch. *Address:* Thornton Cottage, Lingfield, Surrey. *T:* Lingfield 832278. *Club:* Reform.
   See also J. N. B. Penny.

FRANCIS, (Alan) David, CBE 1959; MVO 1957; *b* 2 Dec. 1900; *m* 1932, Norah Turpin; two *s. Educ:* Winchester; Magdalen Coll., Oxford (MA); Corpus Christi Coll., Cambridge (BA). Passed into General Consular Service, 1923; after course in Economics at Cambridge, appointed Vice-Consul, Antwerp, 1925; served as Vice-Consul at Rotterdam, Panama, Bogota and Prague; was also Lloyds Agent at Prague; served in FO, 1936, appointed Vice-Consul, Brussels, and Consul there, 1937. Attached to Costarican Delegation to Coronation of King George VI. Seconded as Principal in Aliens Dept, Home Office, 1940; Consul at Lisbon, 1941; Barcelona, 1942; First Sec. and Consul, Caracas, 1944; Chargé d'Affaires there, 1946; served in FO, 1947; Consul-Gen. at Danzig, 1949, New Orleans, 1951; Consul-Gen., Oporto, 1955-58; retired, 1958. Mem., Lord Chancellor's Advisory Council on Public Records, 1962-67. FRHistS. *Publications:* The Methuens and Portugal, 1966; The Wine Trade, 1972; The First Peninsular War, 1975; articles in learned periodicals. *Recreation:* walking. *Address:* 21 Cadogan Street, SW3. *Club:* Travellers'.

FRANCIS, Alfred Edwin, OBE 1952; Consultant to major theatre companies in London, Cardiff and Bristol; *b* 27 March 1909; *er s* of Reginald Thomas Francis and Ellen Sophia Francis, Liverpool; *m* 1941, Joan Quayle Stocker, Cheshire; one *s. Educ:* Liverpool Coll.; Liverpool Sch. of Architecture. Song writer and stage designer, 1932-39; Hon. Organising Secretary: Liverpool Ballet Club; ENSA, W Command, 1941-45. Overture commnd by Liverpool Philharmonic Soc., 1943. Dir of Liverpool 1951 Festival, 1950; Admin. Dir (later Chm.), London Old Vic, 1952; Man. Dir (later Vice-Chm.), Television Wales and West, 1959; Exec. Chm. Welsh National Opera (and later Drama) Co., 1968-75. Board Member: London Festival Ballet; D'Oyly Carte Trust; Cardiff New Theatre Trust; former member: Nat. Theatre Bd; Bristol Old Vic Trust; various Arts Council and Welsh Arts Council cttees; Member: British Council Adv. Panel for Drama (former Chm.); Grand Council, Royal Acad. of Dancing. Pres., Vic-Wells Assoc.; Hon. Vice-Pres., UK Cttee for UNICEF (former Chm.). *Recreation:* making a fourth at bridge. *Address:* Durley, Pensford Avenue, Kew, Richmond, Surrey TW9 4HW. *T:* 01-876 1448. *Clubs:* Garrick, Saints and Sinners, Green Room, Arts Theatre; Cardiff and County (Cardiff); Artists (Liverpool) (Hon. Member and former Pres.).

FRANCIS, David; *see* Francis, A. D.

FRANCIS, Dick; author; Racing Correspondent, Sunday Express, 1957-73; *b* 31 Oct. 1920; *s* of George Vincent Francis and Catherine Mary Francis; *m* 1947, Mary Margaret Brenchley; two *s. Educ:* Maidenhead County Boys' School. Pilot, RAF, 1940-45 (Flying Officer). Amateur National Hunt jockey, 1946-48, Professional, 1948-57; Champion Jockey, season 1953-54. Edgar Allan Poe Award, 1970, Mystery Writers of America, for Forfeit. *Publications:* Sport of Queens (autobiog.), 1957; Dead Cert, 1962; Nerve, 1964; For Kicks, 1965; Odds Against, 1965; Flying Finish, 1966; Blood Sport, 1967; Forfeit, 1968; Enquiry, 1969; Rat Race, 1970; Bonecrack, 1971; Smoke Screen, 1972; Slay-Ride, 1973; Knock Down, 1974; High Stakes, 1975; In the Frame, 1976; Risk, 1977. *Recreations:* boating, tennis. *Address:* Penny Chase, Blewbury, Oxon. *T:* Blewbury 850369. *Clubs:* Detection, Crime Writers Association, Sportsman's.

FRANCIS, Sir Frank (Chalton), KCB 1960 (CB 1958); FSA; FMA; Director and Principal Librarian, British Museum, 1959-68; *b* Liverpool, 5 Oct. 1901; *o s* of late F. W. Francis and Elizabeth Chalton; *m* 1927, Katrina McClennon, Liverpool; two *s* one *d. Educ:* Liverpool Inst.; Liverpool Univ.; Emmanuel Coll., Cambridge. Asst Master, Holyhead Co. Sch., 1925-26; British Museum: entered Library, 1926; Sec., 1946-47; Keeper, Dept of Printed Books, 1948-59. Lectr in Bibliography, Sch. of Librarianship and Archives, University Coll., London, 1945-59. David Murray Lectr, Univ. of Glasgow, 1957. Editor, The Library, 1936-53; Jt Editor, Jl of Documentation, 1947-68. Museums Association: Mem. Council, 1960-; Vice-Pres., 1964-65; Pres., 1965-66. Bibliographical Society: Jt Hon. Sec. (with

late R. B. McKerrow), 1938-40; Hon. Sec. 1940-64; Pres., 1964-66. Library Association: Council, 1948-59; Chm. Exec. Cttee, 1954-57; Pres., 1965. President: ASLIB, 1957-58; Internat. Fedn of Library Assocs, 1963-69; Chm. Trustees, Nat. Central Library. Vice-Pres., Unesco Internat. Adv. Cttee on Bibliography, 1954-60. Chairman: Circle of State Librarians, 1947-50; Internat. Cttee of Library Experts, UN, 1948; Council, British Nat. Bibliography, 1949-59; Unesco Provisional Internat. Cttee on Bibliography, 1952; Academic Libraries Section, Internat. Fedn of Library Assocs; Anglo-Swedish Soc., 1964-68. Consultant, Council on Library Resources, Washington, DC, 1959-. Trustee, Imp. War Museum; Governor, Birkbeck Coll. Correspondant, Institut de France; Mem., Bibliographical Soc. of America, and other bibliographical socs; Corresp. Mem., Massachusetts Historical Soc.; Hon. Mem., Kungl. Gustav Adolfs Akademien; Foreign Hon. Mem., Amer. Acad. of Arts and Sciences. Master, Clockmakers' Co., 1974-. Hon. Fellow: Emmanuel Coll., Cambridge; Pierpont Morgan Library, NY; Hon. FLA. Hon. LittD: Liverpool; TCD; Cambridge; Hon. DLitt: British Columbia; Exeter; Leeds; Oxford; New Brunswick; Wales. *Publications:* Historical Bibliography in Year's Work in Librarianship, 1929-38; (ed) The Bibliographical Society, 1892-1942: Studies in Retrospect, 1945; (ed) Facsimile of The Compleat Catalogue 1630, 1956; Robert Copland: Sixteenth Century Printer and Translator, 1961; (ed) Treasures of the British Museum, 1971; translations from German, including W. Cohn, Chinese Art, 1930; articles and reviews in The Library, TLS, etc. *Recreations:* golf, walking, bibliography. *Address:* The Vine, Nether Winchendon, Aylesbury, Bucks. *Clubs:* Athenæum, Royal Commonwealth Society; Grolier (New York).

FRANCIS, Hugh Elvet, QC 1960; practising at Chancery Bar, 1932-39, and since 1945; *b* 28 March 1907; *s* of Maurice Evan Francis, JP, Cemmes, Montgomeryshire and Ellen Francis (née Jones); *m* 1932, Emma Frances Wienholt, *d* of J. G. W. Bowen, Tyddyn, Llanidloes; three *s* one *d* (and one *s* decd). *Educ:* Machynlleth County Sch.; UCW Aberystwyth; St John's Coll., Cambridge. LLB Wales 1st Cl. Hons, 1929; Schol. St John's Coll., Cambridge, 1930; LLB Cantab 1st Cl. Hons, Macmahon Law studentshp, 1931; Arden Schol. and Lord Justice Holker Sen. Schol., Gray's Inn, Certificate of Honour, Bar Final Exams, 1931; Barrister, Gray's Inn, 1932, Bencher, 1956, Treas., 1974; Chancellor of the County Palatine of Durham, 1969-71. Served War of 1939-45 in RA and JAG Dept (despatches). Pres., Iron and Steel Arbitration Tribunal, 1967-74; Chairman: Performing Right Tribunal; Cttee on Rent Acts, 1969-71; Chancery Bar Assoc. Hon. Treas., Bar Council, 1961-64. *Publication:* Jt Ed. Lindley on Partnership, 1950. *Recreations:* fishing, gardening and country pursuits. *Address:* 2 Gray's Inn Square, Gray's Inn, WC1R 5AA. *T:* 01-242 4181. Tyddyn, Llandinam, Powys. *T:* Llanidloes 2448. *Club:* Athenæum.

FRANCIS, Lt-Col John Clement Wolstan, MBE; Vice-Lieutenant of Cambridgeshire, 1958-65; *b* 2 Aug. 1888; *s* of late Major Wolstan Francis, Cambridgeshire; *m* 1918, Evelyn Maud (*d* 1973); JP, *d* of Augustus William Benyon, Windsor; one *s. Educ:* Wellington; Pembroke Coll., Cambridge. Served European War, 1914-18. Major 1920, Lt-Col 1930; retired 1935. DL 1945, High Sheriff, 1954, Cambridgeshire. *Recreations:* horses and shooting. *Address:* Quy Hall, Cambridgeshire. *T:* Bottisham 205. *Clubs:* Cavalry and Guards; Royal Automobile.

FRANCIS, Norman; *see* Francis, W. N.

FRANCIS, Owen, CB 1960; Chairman, London Electricity Board, 1972-76; *b* 4 Oct. 1912; *yr s* of Sidney and Margaret Francis, The White House, Austwick, Yorks; *m* 1938, Joan St Leger (*née* Norman); two *d. Educ:* Giggleswick Sch., Yorks. Entered Civil Service as Asst Auditor, Exchequer and Audit Dept, 1931; Asst Principal, Mines Dept, 1937; Principal, 1940; Asst Sec., Ministry of Fuel and Power, 1943; Under-Sec., Ministry of Power, 1954-61; Mem., 1962-64, Dep. Chm., 1965-72, CEGB. *Recreations:* golf and sailing. *Address:* Low Felling, Clare Hill, Esher, Surrey. *T:* Esher 65126. *Clubs:* St George's Hill Golf (Weybridge); Seaview Yacht.

FRANCIS, Richard Trevor Langford; Director, News and Current Affairs, BBC, since 1977; *b* 10 March 1934; *s* of Eric Roland Francis and Esther Joy (*née* Todd); *m* 1st, 1958, Beate Ohlhagen (marr. diss.); two *s*; 2nd, 1974, Elizabeth Penelope Anne Fairfax Crone. *Educ:* Uppingham Sch.; University Coll., Oxford. BA 1956, MA 1960. Commissioned in RA, 1957. BBC Trainee, 1958-60; TV: Prodn Asst, 1960-62; Producer: Afternoon Programmes, 1962-63; Panorama, 1963-65; Asst Editor: Panorama, 1965-66; 24 Hours, 1966-67; Projects Editor, Current Affairs, TV, 1967-70; Head, EBU Operations for US Elections and Apollo, 1968-69; Head of Special Projects,

Current Affairs, TV, 1970-71; Asst Head, Current Affairs Group, TV 1971-73; Head, EBU Operations for US Elections, 1972; Controller, BBC NI, 1973-77. *Recreations:* offshore sailing, photography, bridge. *Address:* BBC, Broadcasting House, W1A 1AA.

FRANCIS, William Lancelot, CBE 1961; Consultant, Civil Service Department, 1972-75; *b* 16 Sept. 1906; *s* of G. J. Francis and Ethel, *d* of L. G. Reed, Durham; *m* 1st, 1937, Ursula Mary Matthew (*d* 1966); two *s* three *d* ; 2nd, 1968, Margaret Morris. *Educ:* Latymer Upper Sch., Hammersmith; King's Coll., Cambridge. MA, PhD. DSIR Sen. Research Award, Cambridge, 1931-33; Rockefeller Foundn Fellowship in Experimental Zoology, Rockefeller Institute, New York, 1933-34; Science Master, Repton Sch., 1935-40; Radar research and administration in Ministries of Supply and Aircraft Production (TRE Malvern), 1940-45; DSIR Headquarters, 1945-65; Secretary, Science Research Council, 1965-72. Member: Nat. Electronics Council, 1965-72; CERN, 1966-70; Advisory Councils: R&D, Fuel and Power, 1966-72; Iron and Steel, 1966-72; *Publications:* papers on physical chemistry and experimental zoology in scientific jls, 1931-37. *Recreations:* gardening, travel. *Address:* 269 Sheen Lane, SW14. *T:* 01-876 3029. *Club:* Athenæum.

FRANCIS, (William) Norman; His Honour Judge Francis; a Circuit Judge (formerly Judge of County Courts), since 1969; *b* 19 March 1921; *s* of Llewellyn Francis; *m* 1951, Anthea Constance (*née* Kerry); one *s* one *d. Educ:* Bradfield; Lincoln Coll., Oxford (BCL, MA). Served War of 1939-45, RA. Called to Bar, Gray's Inn, 1946. Dep. Chm., Brecknock QS, 1962-71. Trustee, Cardiff Athletic Club. Mem. Representative Body, Church in Wales. *Recreations:* hockey, walking, golf. *Address:* 2 The Woodlands, Lisvane, near Cardiff. *T:* Cardiff 753070.

FRANCKENSTEIN, Baroness Joseph von; see Boyle, Kay.

FRANCKLIN, Comdr (Mavourn Baldwin) Philip, DSC 1940; RN; JP; Lord-Lieutenant of Nottinghamshire, since 1972 (Vice-Lieutenant, 1968-72); *b* 15 Jan. 1913; *s* of Capt. Philip Francklin, MVO, RN (killed in action, 1914); *m* 1949, Xenia Alexandra, *d* of Alex. Davidson, Co. Wicklow; two *s* one *d. Educ:* RNC Dartmouth. Joined RN, 1926. Served War of 1939-45: Norway, N and S Atlantic, Indian Ocean (despatches twice); Asst to 5th Sea Lord, 1947-49; Comdr 1950; Asst Naval Attaché, Paris, 1952-53. DL, 1963, JP 1958, Notts; High Sheriff of Notts, 1965. KStJ 1973. Croix de Guerre (France). *Address:* Gonalston Hall, Nottingham. *T:* Lowdham 3635. *Club:* Boodle's.

FRANÇOIS-PONCET, André, de l'Académie Française, 1952 et de l'Académie des Sciences morales et politiques; LLD; Grand Croix de la Légion d'Honneur; politician, diplomat and writer; Chancellor of the French Institute, 1961-64; *b* Provins, France, 13 June 1887. Served European War, 1914-16, Lieut 304 Infantry Regt (Croix de Guerre). Mem. International Economic Mission, US, 1919; Govt delegate Conference of Genoa and in Ruhr. Founder and Dir, Bulletin de la Société d'Etudes et d'Informations économiques, 1920-24; Mem. Cttee Republican Party; Deputy, 1924-31; Under-Sec. of State, 1928-31; Ambassador to Germany, 1931-38; Ambassador to Italy, 1938-40; Mem. National Council, 1941; arrested by the Gestapo, 1943; liberated by the Allies, May 1945. President of the French Red Cross. Pres. Permanent Commission of International Red Cross, 1949-; French High Commissioner, Allied High Commission, Germany, 1949-55; French Ambassador to Western Germany, May-Sept. 1955. *Publications:* Les Affinités électives de Goethe, 1910; Ce que pense la jeunesse allemande, 1913; La France et le problème des réparations; Discours français; Réflexions d'un républicain moderne; Souvenir d'une Ambassade à Berlin, 1946; De Versailles à Potsdam, 1948; Carnets d'un Captif, 1952; Discours de Réception à l'Académie Française, Au Palais Farnese, 1961. *Address:* 92 rue du Ranelagh, Paris 16e.

FRANK, Mrs Alan; see Tate, Phyllis M. D.

FRANK, Air Vice-Marshal Alan Donald, CB 1967; CBE 1962; DSO 1943; DFC 1941; Bursar, St Antony's College, Oxford, 1970-74; *b* 1917; *s* of late Major N. G. Frank and late M. H. Frank (*née* Donald); *m* 1941, Jessica Ann Tyrrell; two *s* two *d. Educ:* Eton; Magdalen Coll., Oxford. Commanded 51 Squadron Bomber Command, 1943; RAF Staff Coll., 1944; OC 83 Sqdn, 1957; OC RAF Honington, 1958-60; Group Captain Ops, Bomber Comd, 1960-62; Dir Operational Requirements, MoD, 1962-65; Air Attaché and OC, RAF Staff, Washington, 1965-68; SASO, RAF Air Support Command, 1968-70. *Recreations:* skiing, squash, tennis. *Address:* Roundway House, Devizes, Wilts.

FRANK, Sir Charles; see Frank, Sir F. C.

FRANK, Sir Douglas (George Horace), Kt 1976; QC 1964; President of the Lands Tribunal, since 1974; Deputy Judge of the High Court, since 1975; *b* 16 April 1916; *s* of late George Maurice Frank and late Agnes Winifred Frank; *m* 1963, Sheila Frances (*née* Beauchamp); three *d* (and one *s* two *d* by a former marr.; two *step s*). *Educ:* City of London Sch. and privately. War service in Royal Artillery. Called to the Bar, Gray's Inn, 1946 (Master of the Bench, 1970). Asst Commissioner, Boundary Commission for England. Mem., Cttee Public Participation in Planning (Min. Housing and Local Govt), 1968; Chm., Gen. Council of the Bar's Cttee on Administrative Law, 1967-73. *Publications:* various legal. *Recreations:* theatre, skiing. *Address:* 5 Marston Ferry Road, Oxford. *T:* Oxford 58244; 1 Gray's Inn Square, WC1. *T:* 01-242 5949.

FRANK, Sir (Frederick) Charles, Kt 1977; OBE 1946; FRS 1954; DPhil; Henry Overton Wills Professor of Physics and Director of the H. H. Wills Physics Laboratory, University of Bristol, 1969-76 (Professor in Physics, 1954-69); now Emeritus Professor; *b* 6 March 1911; *e s* of Frederick and Medora Frank; *m* 1940, Maia Maita Asché, *y d* of late Prof. B. M. Asché; no *c. Educ:* Thetford Grammar Sch.; Ipswich Sch.; Lincoln Coll., Oxford. BA, BSc, Oxon. 1933; DPhil Oxon. 1937; Hon. Fellow, Lincoln Coll., 1968. Research: Dyson Perrins Laboratory and Engineering Laboratory, Oxford, 1933-36; Kaiser Wilhelm Institut für Physik, Berlin, 1936-38; Colloid Science Laboratory, Cambridge, 1939-40; Scientific Civil Service (temp.), 1940-46; Chemical Defence Research Establishment, 1940, Air Ministry, 1940-46; Research, H. H. Wills Physical Laboratory, Bristol Univ., 1946-; Research Fellow in Theoretical Physics, 1948; Reader in Physics, 1951-54; a Vice-Pres., Royal Society, 1967-69. Hon. DSc: Ghent, 1955; Bath, 1974. *Publications:* articles in various learned journals, mostly dealing either with dielectrics or the physics of solids, in particular crystal dislocations, crystal growth, mechanical properties of polymers and mechanics of the earth's crust. *Address:* Orchard Cottage, Grove Road, Coombe Dingle, Bristol BS9 2RL. *T:* Bristol 68-1708. *Club:* Athenæum.

FRANK, Ilya Mikhailovich; Professor, Moscow University, since 1944; Director of a Laboratory, Joint Nuclear Research Institute, Dubna, since 1957; *b* Leningrad, 23 Oct. 1908; *yr s* of Mikhail Lyudvigovich Frank, Prof. of Mathematics, and Dr Yelizaveta Mikhailovna Gratsianova; *m* 1937, Ella Abramovna Beilikhis, historian; one *s. Educ:* Moscow University (under S. I. Vavilov's guidance). Engaged by State Optical Inst. in Leningrad after graduation and worked at Prof. A. H. Terenin's laboratory, 1931-34 (DSc 1935); Head of nuclear physics lab., Lebedev Inst. Physics, USSR Acad. of Sciences, 1934-57. Subsequently taught at Moscow Univ. Elected Corr. Mem. USSR Acad. of Sciences, 1946. Has participated from beginning in investigations dealing with Vavilov-Cerenkov radiation; carried out many theoretical investigations into Vavilov-Cerenkov effects and in related problems (The Doppler effect in a refractive medium, transition, radiation, etc.) and continues this research. Awarded Nobel Prize for Physics (jointly with P. A. Cerenkov and I. E. Tamm) for discovery and interpretation of Cerenkov effect, 1958; USSR State Prize, 1971. *Address:* Joint Nuclear Research Institute, Dubna, near Moscow, USSR.

FRANK, Sir Robert John, 3rd Bt, *cr* 1920; FRICS, FAI; late Flying Officer, RAFVR; Director, Ashdale Land and Property Co. Ltd, since 1963; *b* 16 March 1925; *s* of Sir Howard Frank, 1st Bt, GBE, KCB, and Nancy Muriel (she *m* 2nd, 1932, Air-Marshal Sir Arthur Coningham, KCB, KBE, DSO), *e d* of John Brooks; *S* brother, killed in action, 1944; *m* 1st, 1950, Angela Elizabeth (marr. diss. 1959), *e d* of Sir Kenelm Cayley, 10th Bt; two *d* ; 2nd, 1960, Margaret Joyce Truesdale; one *s. Heir: s* Robert Andrew Frank, *b* 16 May 1964. *Address:* Ruscombe End, Waltham St Lawrence, near Reading, Berks.

FRANKEL, Dan; *b* 18 Aug. 1900; *s* of Harris Frankel, Mile End; *m* 1921, Lily, *d* of Joseph Marks, Stepney; one *s.* Mem. LCC for Mile End Division of Stepney, 1931-46; MP (Lab) Mile End Division of Stepney, 1935-45. *Address:* 670a Finchley Road, NW11.

FRANKEL, Prof. Joseph; Professor, since 1963, and Head of Department of Politics, 1963-73, University of Southampton; *b* 30 May 1913; *s* of Dr I. and Mrs R. Frankel; *m* 1944, Elizabeth A. Kyle; one *d. Educ:* Univ. of Lwow, Poland (Master of Laws, 1935); Univ. of Western Australia (LLM 1948); Univ. of London (PhD Econ (Internat. Rel.) 1950). Legal Practice, Solicitor, in Poland, 1935-38. Farming in Western Australia, 1938-47; Temp. Asst Lectr, University Coll. London, 1950-51; Lectr and Sen. Lectr, Univ. of Aberdeen, 1951-62. Dean, Faculty of Social Sciences, Univ. of Southampton, 1964-67. Res.

Associate, RIAA, 1972-73. Vis. Prof., International Christian Univ., Tokyo, 1977. *Publications:* The Making of Foreign Policy, 1962, 2nd edn 1967; International Relations, 1963, 2nd edn 1969; International Politics: conflict and harmony, 1969; National Interest, 1970; Contemporary International Theory and the Behaviour of States, 1973; British Foreign Policy 1945-1973, 1975; contribs to International Affairs, etc. *Recreations:* gardening, travel, contemporary theatre and literature, classical and contemporary art and music. *Address:* The Old Rectory, Avington, Winchester, Hants SO21 1DD. *T:* Itchen Abbas 275.

FRANKEL, Sir Otto (Herzberg), Kt 1966; FRS 1953; DSc; DAgr; FRSNZ; FAA; Senior Research Fellow, Division of Plant Industry, CSIRO, Canberra, Australia, since 1966; *b* 4 Nov. 1900; *m* 1939, Margaret Anderson. *Educ:* Vienna; Berlin; Cambridge. Plant Geneticist, 1929-42, and Chief Executive Officer, 1942-49, Wheat Research Institute, NZ; Dir, Crop Research Division, Dept of Scientific and Industrial Research, New Zealand, 1949-51; Chief, Division of Plant Industry, CSIRO, Australia, 1951-62; Member of Executive, Commonwealth Scientific and Industrial Research Organization, Melbourne, Aust, 1962-66. *Publications:* (ed jtly) Genetic Resources in Plants: their exploration and conservation, 1970; (ed jtly) Crop Genetic Resources for Today and Tomorrow, 1975; numerous articles in British, NZ and Australian scientific journals. *Recreations:* ski-ing, gardening, angling. *Address:* 4 Cobby Street, Campbell, Canberra, ACT 2601, Australia. *T:* 479460.

FRANKEL, Prof. Sally Herbert, MA Rand, PhD London, DScEcon London, MA Oxon; Emeritus Professor in the Economics of Underdeveloped Countries, University of Oxford, and Emeritus Fellow, Nuffield College, Oxford (Professor, and Professorial Fellow, 1946-71); *b* 22 Nov. 1903; *e s* of Jacob Frankel; *m* 1928, Ilse Jeanette Frankel; one *s* one *d. Educ:* St John's Coll., Johannesburg; University of the Witwatersrand; London Sch. of Economics. Prof. of Economics, University of Witwatersrand, Johannesburg, 1931-46; responsible for calculations of National Income of S Africa for the Treasury, 1941-48; Jt Editor of South African Journal of Economics from its inception to 1946; Mem. of Union of South Africa Treasury Advisory Council on Economic and Financial Policy, 1941-45; Mem. of Union of South Africa Miners' Phthisis Commission, 1941-42; Commissioner appointed by Govts of Southern and Northern Rhodesia and the Bechuanaland Protectorate to report upon Rhodesia Railways Ltd, 1942-43; Chm. Commission of Enquiry into Mining Industry of Southern Rhodesia, 1945; Mem. East Africa Royal Commission, 1953-55; Consultant Adviser, Urban African Affairs Commn, Govt of S Rhodesia, 1957-58. Vis. Prof. of Econs, Univ. of Virginia, until 1974. *Publications:* Co-operation and Competition in the Marketing of Maize in South Africa, 1926; The Railway Policy of South Africa, 1928; Coming of Age: Studies in South African Citizenship and Politics (with Mr J. H. Hofmeyr and others), 1930; Capital Investment in Africa: Its Course and Effects, 1938; The Economic Impact on Underdeveloped Societies: Essays on International Investment and Social Change, 1953; Investment and the Return to Equity Capital in the South African Gold Mining Industry 1887-1965: An International Comparison, 1967; Gold and International Equity Investment (Hobart Paper 45), 1969; Money: two philosophies, the conflict of trust and authority, 1977. *Recreation:* gardening. *Address:* The Knoll House, Hinksey Hill, Oxford. *T:* Oxford 35345. *Club:* Reform.

FRANKEL, William, CBE 1970; Editor, Jewish Chronicle, 1958-77; *b* 3 Feb. 1917; *s* of Isaac and Anna Frankel, London; *m* 1st, 1939, Gertrude Freda Reed (marr. diss.); one *s* one *d*; 2nd, 1973, Mrs Claire Neuman. *Educ:* elementary and secondary schs in London; London Univ. (LLB Hons). Called to Bar, Middle Temple, 1944; practised on South-Eastern circuit, 1944-55. General Manager, Jewish Chronicle, 1955-58. Director: Jewish Chronicle Ltd; Jewish Gazette Ltd. Vis. Prof., Jewish Theological Seminary of America, 1968-69. JP Co. of London, 1963-69. *Publication:* (ed) Friday Nights, 1973. *Address:* 5 Pump Court, Temple, EC4. *T:* 01-353 2628. *Clubs:* Athenæum, MCC.

FRANKEN, Rose, (Mrs W. B. Meloney); Novelist; Playwright; *b* Texas, 28 Dec. 1895; *m* 1914, Dr S. W. A. Franken (*d* 1932); three *s*; *m* 1937, William Brown Meloney (*d* 1970). *Educ:* Ethical Culture Sch., NYC. *Publications: novels:* Pattern, 1925; Twice Born, 1935, new edn 1970; Call Back Love, 1937; Of Great Riches, 1937 (as Gold Pennies, UK, 1938); Strange Victory, 1939; Claudia: the story of a marriage, 1939; Claudia and David, 1940; American Bred, 1941; Another Claudia, 1943; Women in White, 1945; Young Claudia, 1946; The Marriage of Claudia, 1948; From Claudia to David, 1949; The Fragile Years, The Antic Years (as The Return of Claudia, UK), 1952;

Rendezvous (as The Quiet Heart, UK), 1954; (autobiography) When All is Said and Done, 1963; You're Well Out of Hospital, 1966; Swan Song, 1976; *plays:* Another Language, 1932; (with J. Lewin) Mr Dooley, Jr: a comedy for children, 1932; Claudia, 1941; Outrageous Fortune, 1944; When Doctors Disagree, 1944; Soldier's Wife, 1945; Hallams, 1948; The Wing, 1971; also short stories in Colliers, Liberty, Cosmopolitan, Harper's Bazaar and anthologies.

FRANKENBURG, John Beeching; Legal Adviser, British Council, since 1964; *b* 19 April 1921; *s* of Sidney Frankenburg, JP, and Charis Frankenburg, MA Oxon, SCM, JP; *m* 1952, Pamela Holmes; two *s. Educ:* Stowe; Balliol Coll., Oxford (MA Hons Jurisp.). Called to the Bar, Inner Temple, 1947. Army, 1940; commnd 1941; POW N Africa, 1942; invalided out, 1945. Treas., World Assembly of Youth, 1949-52; Asst Legal Adviser: Dir of Public Prosecutions, 1958-60; British Council, 1960-63. Member Liberal Party: Council, 1947-55; Nat. Exec., 1947-54; Liberal Party Candidate: S Kensington, 1950; Berwick-on-Tweed, 1951; Nuneaton, 1955. Governor, St Andrews Sch., Pangbourne, 1971-. *Publication:* The Young Lawyer (with J. L. Clay and J. A. Baker), 1955. *Recreations:* watching and playing games, reading, mental autolycism. *Address:* Beechings, Pangbourne, Berks. *T:* Pangbourne 3248. *Club:* Englefield Social (Englefield, Berks).

FRANKHAM, Very Rev. Harold Edward; Provost of Southwark since 1970; *b* 6 April 1911; *s* of Edward and Minnie Frankham; *m* 1942, Margaret Jean Annear; one *s* two *d* (and one *s* decd). *Educ:* London Coll. of Divinity (LCD). Ordained, 1941; Curate: Luton, 1941-44; Holy Trinity, Brompton, 1944-46; Vicar of Addiscombe, 1946-52; Rector of Middleton, Lancs, 1952-61; Vicar of Luton, 1961-70. Hon. Canon of St Albans, 1967-70. Exec. Sec., Archbishops' Council on Evangelism, 1965-73. *Recreations:* music, painting, sailing, travel. *Address:* Provost's Lodging, 51 Bankside, SE1. *T:* 01-928 6414; 5 The Maltings, Beccles, Suffolk.

FRANKLAND, family name of **Baron Zouche.**

FRANKLAND, (Anthony) Noble, CBE 1976; DFC 1944; MA, DPhil; FSA; Director of Imperial War Museum since 1960; Biographer of His late Royal Highness The Duke of Gloucester, since 1976; *b* 4 July 1922; *s* of late Edward Frankland, Ravenstonedale, Westmorland; *m* 1944, Diana Madeline Fovargue, *d* of late G. V. Tavernor, of Madras and Southern Mahratta Rly, India; one *s* one *d. Educ:* Sedbergh; Trinity Coll., Oxford. Served Royal Air Force, 1941-45 (Bomber Command, 1943-45). Air Historical Branch Air Ministry, 1948-51; Official Military Historian, Cabinet Office, 1951-58. Rockefeller Fellow, 1953. Deputy Dir of Studies, Royal Institute of International Affairs, 1956-60. Lees Knowles Lecturer, Trinity Coll., Cambridge, 1963. Historical advisor, Thames Television series, The World At War, 1971-74. Vice-Chm., British Nat. Cttee, Internat. Cttee for Study of Second World War, 1976-. Mem., Council, Morley Coll., 1962-66; Trustee: Military Archives Centre, KCL, 1963-; HMS Belfast Trust, 1971- (Vice-Chm., 1972-). *Publications:* Documents on International Affairs: for 1955, 1958; for 1956, 1959; for 1957, 1960; Crown of Tragedy, Nicholas II, 1960; The Strategic Air Offensive Against Germany, 1939-1945 (4 vols) jointly with Sir Charles Webster, 1961; The Bombing Offensive against Germany, Outlines and Perspectives, 1965; Bomber Offensive: the Devastation of Europe, 1970; (ed jtly) The Politics and Strategy of the Second World War (series), 1974-; (ed jtly) Decisive Battles of the Twentieth Century: Land, Sea, Air, 1976. Historical Chapter in Manual of Air Force Law, 1956; other articles and reviews; broadcasts on radio and TV. *Address:* Thames House, Eynsham, Oxford. *T:* Oxford 881327.

FRANKLAND, Noble; *see* Frankland, A. N.

FRANKLIN, Albert Andrew Ernst, CVO 1965; CBE 1961 (OBE 1950); HM Diplomatic Service, retired; *b* 28 Nov. 1914; *s* of Albert John Henry Franklin; *m* 1944, Henrietta Irene Barry; two *d. Educ:* Merchant Taylors' Sch.; St John's Coll., Oxford. Joined HM Consular Service, 1937; served in Peking, Kunming, Chungking, Calcutta, Algiers, Marseilles, Kabul, Basle, Tientsin, Formosa, Düsseldorf and in the FO; HM Consul-General, Los Angeles, USA, 1966-74. Member of Kitchener Association. FRSA 1971. *Recreation:* chinese ceramics and paintings. *Address:* 5 Dulwich Wood Avenue, SE19. *T:* 01-670 2769.

FRANKLIN, Alfred White, FRCP; Hon. Consulting Physician, Department of Child Health, Saint Bartholomew's Hospital; Hon. Consulting Pædiatrician, Queen Charlotte's Maternity Hospital; *b* 1905; *yr s* of Philip Franklin, FRCS; *m* 1943, Ann

Grizel, *er d* of late Rev. Francis Dent Vaisey; two *s* two *d. Educ:* Epsom Coll.; Clare Coll., Cambridge (scholar); St Bartholomew's Hospital. MB, BCh, 1933, FRCP, 1942. Lawrence Scholarship and Gold Medal, 1933 and 1934, St Bartholomew's Hosp.; Temple Cross Research Fellow, Johns Hopkins Hosp., 1934-35. Pædiatrician to Sector III, EMS. Dep. Chm., Attendance Allowance Bd, DHSS, 1970-; Formerly Chm., Invalid Children's Aid Assoc.; Co-founder and Treasurer, The Osler Club, London. Past Pres., British Pædiatric Assoc.; Pres., British Soc. for Medical History, 1974-76. *Publications:* ed, Selected Writings of Sir D'Arcy Power, 1931, and of Sir William Osler, 1951; ed, The Care of Invalid and Crippled Children, 1960; ed, Concerning Child Abuse, 1975; Pastoral Paediatrics, 1976; Widening Horizons of Child Health, 1976; (ed) The Challenge of Child Abuse, 1977; contrib. to books and jls on medical, historical and bibliographical subjects. *Address:* 149 Harley Street, W1N 2DE. *T:* 01-935 4444; The Cottage, Northaw, Herts. *T:* Potters Bar 52184. *Club:* Athenæum.

FRANKLIN, Sir Eric (Alexander), Kt 1954; CBE 1952; *b* 3 July 1910; *s* of late William John Franklin; *m* 1936, Joy Stella, *d* of late George Oakes Lucas, Cambridge. *Educ:* The English Sch., Maymyo; Emmanuel Coll., Cambridge. Appointed to ICS in 1935 and posted to Burma; Subdivisional Officer, 1936-39. Deputy Registrar, High Court of Judicature at Rangoon, 1939-40; District and Sessions Judge, Arakan, 1941-42; Deputy Sec. to Government of Burma at Simla, 1942-45; Registrar, High Court of Judicature at Rangoon, 1946-47; retired prematurely from ICS, 1948. Appointed on contract as Deputy Sec. to Government of Pakistan; Cabinet Secretariat, 1949; Joint Sec., Cabinet Secretariat, 1952; Establishment Officer and Head of Central Organisation and Methods Office, 1953; Establishment Sec. to Government of Pakistan, 1956-58; Chm. Sudan Government Commission on terms of service, 1958-59; Civil Service Adviser to Government of Hashemite Kingdom of Jordan, 1960-63; acting Resident Representative, UN Technical Assistance Board, Jordan, 1961; Senior UN Administrative Adviser to Government of Nepal, 1964-66. Chm., Cambridgeshire Soc. for the Blind, 1969-74, Vice-Pres., 1974. FRSA 1971. El Kawkab el Urdoni (Star of Jordan), 1963. *Recreations:* walking, hill-climbing, music, and caring for dogs. *Address:* The Birches, 16 Cavendish Avenue, Cambridge.

FRANKLIN, George Frederic; formerly Headmaster, Lincoln School, retired Dec. 1957; *b* Greenwich, 28 Dec. 1897; *s* of John and Alice Franklin; *m* 1926, Edith Kate Young; one *s* one *d. Educ:* Roan Sch.; King's Coll., Cambridge. Asst Master, Merchant Taylors' Sch., Crosby; Senior Mod. Langs Master, Christ's Hosp. *Publications:* French and German school texts. *Address:* 30 Station Road, Condover, Shrewsbury, Salop SY5 7BQ.

FRANKLIN, George Henry, RIBA, FRTPI; Physical (Land Use) Planning Adviser, Ministry of Overseas Development, since 1966; *b* 15 June 1923; *s* of late George Edward Franklin, RN, and Annie Franklin; *m* 1950, Sylvia D. Franklin; three *s* one *d. Educ:* Hastings Grammar Sch.; Hastings Sch. of Art; Architectural Assoc. Sch. of Arch. (AADipl); Sch. of Planning and Research for Regional Develt, London (SPDip). Served War of 1939-45: Parachute Sqdn; RE, Europe; Bengal Sappers and Miners, SE Asia. Finchley Boro. Council, 1952-54; Architect, Christian Med. Coll., Ludhiana, Punjab, India, 1954-57; Physical Planning Adviser (Colombo Plan) to Republic of Indonesia, 1958-62, and Govt of Malaysia, 1963-64; Physical Planning Adviser, ODM, 1966- (Overseas Div., Building Research Station, 1966-73, ODM, 1973-). Activities in Commonwealth Assoc. of Planners, Commonwealth Human Ecology Council, United Bibles Socs. *Publications:* papers to internat. confs and professional jls concerning planning, building and housing in the Third World. *Recreations:* work, promotion of physical planning in countries of the Third World; fishing. *Address:* 24 Oakleigh Park North, N20 9AR. *T:* 01-445 0336. *Club:* Royal Commonwealth Society.

FRANKLIN, Henry William Fernehough; Headmaster Epsom College, 1940-1962; *b* 30 June 1901; *s* of Henry Franklin, Schoolmaster; *m* 1931, Phyllis Denham; one *d. Educ:* Christ's Hosp.; Christ Church, Oxford. Asst Master, Radley Coll., 1924-27; Asst Master, Rugby Sch., 1927-39. Chm. of Home Office Departmental Cttee on Punishments in Prisons, Borstals, etc., 1948. Mem., Advertising Standards Authority, 1962-67. *Publications:* Fifty Latin Lyrics, 1955; (with J. A. G. Bruce) Latin Prose Composition, 1937; Latin Reader, 1939. *Recreations:* formerly various games: cricket (OU XI 1924; Essex County XI); Rugby football (OU XV 1923; Barbarian FC), hockey, fives, etc.; also music and change-ringing; nowadays mostly teaching and change-ringing. *Address:* The Cottage, Westward Lane, West Chiltington, Pulborough, West Sussex. *T:* W Chiltington 2282.

FRANKLIN, Michael David Milroy, CMG 1972; Deputy Secretary, Head of the European Secretariat, Cabinet Office, since 1977; *b* 24 Aug. 1927; *o s* of late Milroy Franklin; *m* 1951, Dorothy Joan Fraser; two *s* one *d. Educ:* Taunton Sch.; Peterhouse, Cambridge. Asst Principal, Min. of Agric. and Fisheries, 1950; Economic Section, Cabinet Office (subseq. Treasury), 1952-55; Principal, Min. of Agric., Fisheries and Food, 1956; UK Delegn to OEEC (subseq. OECD), 1959-61; Private Sec. to Minister of Agric., Fisheries and Food, 1961-64; Asst Sec., Head of Sugar and Tropical Foodstuffs Div., 1965-68; Under-Sec. (EEC Gp), MAFF, 1968-73; a Dep. Dir Gen., Directorate Gen. for Agric., EEC, 1973-77. *Address:* 55 Galley Lane, Barnet, Herts. *Club:* United Oxford & Cambridge University.

FRANKLIN, Norman Laurence, CBE 1975 (OBE 1963); MSc, PhD, DSc; Chairman and Managing Director, Nuclear Power Company Ltd, since 1975; Part-time Member, UKAEA, since 1971; *b* 1 Sept. 1924; *s* of William Alexander and Beatrice Franklin; *m* 1949, Bessie Coupland; one *s* one *d. Educ:* Batley Grammar School; University of Leeds. British Coke Res. Assoc., 1945-48; Lecturer in Chemical Engineering, Univ. of Leeds, 1948-55; joined UKAEA, 1955; Mem. for Production, 1969-71. Man. Dir, Chief Executive and Dir, British Nuclear Fuels Ltd, 1971-75; Dir, National Nuclear Corporation Ltd. *Publications:* Statistical Analysis in Chemistry and the Chemical Industry, 1954; The Transport Properties of Fluids, Vol. 4, Chemical Engineering Practice, 1957; Heat Transfer by Conduction, Vol. 7, Chemical Engineering Practice, 1963; papers in Trans Instn of Chemical Engineers, 1953-66. *Recreation:* walking. *Address:* The Evergreens, Greenacre Close, Knutsford, Cheshire WA16 8NL. *T:* Knutsford 3045. *Club:* East India, Devonshire, Sports and Public Schools.

FRANKLIN, Olga Heather, CBE 1950 (MBE 1919); RRC 1946 (ARRC 1942); *b* 20 Sept. 1895; *e c* of late Robert Francis Franklin, OBE. *Educ:* St Michael's Lodge, Stoke, Devonport, VAD, 1915-17; WRNS, 1917-19; King's Coll. Hosp., 1923; Queen Alexandra's Royal Naval Nursing Service, 1927-50; Matron-in-Chief, 1947-50; King's Hon. Nursing Sister (the first appointed), 1947-50; retired, 1950. Prisoner of war, Hongkong, 1941-45. *Address:* Hillcroft, Rottingdean, Brighton BN2 7DL. *T:* Brighton 32202.

FRANKLIN, Richard Harrington, CBE 1973; Consulting Surgeon to the Royal Navy, since 1961; Hon. Consulting Surgeon, Star and Garter Home, Richmond, since 1957, Governor, since 1969; Hon. Visiting Surgeon, Royal Postgraduate Medical School (Surgeon, 1945-71); Emeritus Consultant Surgeon to Kingston and Long Grove Group of Hospitals (Surgeon, Kingston, 1946-71); *b* 3 April 1906; *s* of late P. C. Franklin; *m* 1933, Helen Margaret Kimber, *d* of Sir Henry D. Kimber, Bt; two *s. Educ:* Merchant Taylors' Sch.; St Thomas's Hosp., London Univ. MRCS, LRCP 1930; MB, BS 1930; FRCS 1934. First Asst, Brit. Postgrad. Med. Sch., 1936; Surgeon EMS, 1940-45; Hunterian Prof., RCS, 1947; Bradshaw Lectr, 1973; Grey-Turner Lectr, Internat. Soc. Surg., 1973; Hunterian Orator, RCS, 1977. Vis. Prof., Univ. of California, 1972. Fellow, Med. Soc. of London. Mem. Ct of Examrs, RCS, 1956-66; Examr in Surgery, Cambridge Univ., 1958-69. Vice-Pres. 1960, Pres. 1969-70, Sect. of Surgery, RSM; Mem. Coun., RCS, 1965-77, Vice-Pres., 1974-76; Mem. Coun., Imperial Cancer Research Fund, 1967, Vice-Pres., 1975-. *Publications:* Surgery of the Oesophagus, 1952; articles in various med. jls and text books. *Recreation:* sailing. *Address:* Wolsey House, 4 Montpelier Row, Twickenham, Mddx TW1 2NQ. *T:* 01-892 3592. *Clubs:* Ranelagh Sailing, Aldeburgh Yacht.

FRANKLYN, Charles Aubrey Hamilton, MD Lausanne, MB, BS London, MA *hc* Malaya 1951; MRCS, LRCP 1923; FLS; FSA(Scot.); Physician and Genealogical-historian; *b* Brentwood, Co. Essex, 25 Aug. 1896; *er s* of late Aubrey Hamilton Franklyn and Ethel Mary, *d* of late Walter Gray. *Educ:* Tonbridge Sch.; St Thomas's Hosp.; Universities of London, Lausanne, Oxford (Exeter Coll.), France, 1916-19. Lieut RA (SR), 1915-20; in practice as physician from 1925; temp. MO, P & O Line, 1933; MO (part-time) HM Prison, Lincoln, 1934-37; in EMS (Grade III) from 1939. Mem. of Standing Cttee, University of London, 1927-61 (Senior mem., 1954-61); Bedell of Convocation, University of London, from 1932; a Provincial Supervisor in Charge of Final Degree Examns (June) 1941-56. Mem. BMA, 1923-48; Life Mem. Oxford Soc.; Fellow Philosophical Soc. of England; Mem. Amer. Institute for Philosophical Studies. Hon. Asst to Editor Burke's Landed Gentry, Centenary (15th) edn, 1937, and to Editor Armorial Families, 7th edn, 1929-30 (2 vols). Authority on Academical Dress, University Degrees and Ceremonies, Modern Heraldry and Genealogy, etc. Designer of Official Robes and Academical

Dress for Universities: Malaya, Australian National, Southampton, Hull, and New Univ. of Ulster, Coleraine, Co. Londonderry; designed: armorial ensigns and 3 badges, British Transport Commn, 1956; Arms of Borough of Bridgnorth, 1959; Arms of St Peter's Hall (now College), Oxford. Hon. DLitt: Geneva Theolog. Coll, Vincennes, Ind, 1972; Central Sch. of Religion, Ind. and Redhill, Surrey, 1972. *Publications:* The Bearing of Coat-Armour by Ladies, 1923, repr. with supp. 1973; English and Scottish Heraldry compared and contrasted (Scots. Mag. Jan. 1925); University Hoods and Robes (25 cards), 1926; The Genealogy of the Chavasse Family, 1929; A Genealogical History of The Family of Tiarks of Foxbury, 1929, 2nd edition, rev. and enlarged 1969 (priv. printed); A Genealogical and Heraldic History of Four Families (privately printed), 1932; A Genealogical History of the families of Paulet (or Pawlett), Berewe (or Barrow), Lawrence, and Parker (privately printed), 1964, Supplement, incl. Morgan of Llanfabon, Turner of Oldland in Keymer, Vavasour of Hazlewood, Walwyn of Longford, etc, 1969; A Genealogical History of the Families of Montgomerie of Garboldisham, Hunter of Knap, and Montgomerie of Fittleworth (privately printed), 1967; Academical Dress from the Middle Ages to the Present Day, including Lambeth Degrees (privately printed), 1970; (ed jtly) Haycraft's Degrees and Hoods of the World's Universities and Colleges, 5th edn, 1972; The Genealogy of Anne the Quene (Anne Bullen), 1977; Cuckfield Rural Dist, Official Local Guide (new edn), 1947; A Dedication Service for the Parish Church of St John the Baptist, Mexborough, 1967; contribs to: Enc. Brit.; 5th edn of Grove's Dic. of Music and Musicians; Pears Cyclopædia; Chambers's Enc.; Internat. Enc. of Higher Educn, etc. *Recreations:* music, cats, motoring, travelling, lecturing, and writing, etc. *Address:* Wickham Hill House, Hassocks, West Sussex BN6 9NP. *T:* Hurstpierpoint 832100; c/o National Westminster Bank Ltd, 1 Lee Road, Blackheath, SE3 9RQ; Exeter College, Oxford.

FRANKS, family name of **Baron Franks.**

FRANKS, Baron *cr* 1962, of Headington (Life Peer); **Oliver Shewell Franks,** PC 1949; GCMG 1952; KCB 1946; CBE 1942; FBA 1960; Provost of Worcester College, Oxford, 1962-76; Chancellor of East Anglia University since 1965; *b* 16 Feb. 1905; *s* of late Rev. R. S. Franks; *m* 1931, Barbara Mary Tanner; two *d. Educ:* Bristol Grammar Sch.; Queen's Coll., Oxford (MA). Fellow and Praelector in Philosophy, Queen's College, Oxford, 1927-37; University Lecturer in Philosophy, 1935-37; Visiting Prof., Univ. of Chicago, 1935; Prof. of Moral Philosophy, University of Glasgow, 1937-45; temp. Civil Servant, Ministry of Supply, 1939-46; Permanent Sec. Ministry of Supply, 1945-46; Provost of Queen's Coll., Oxford, 1946-48; British Ambassador at Washington, 1948-52; Director: Lloyds Bank Ltd, 1953-75 (Chm., 1954-62); Schroders; Chm., Friends' Provident & Century Life Office, 1955-62; Cttee of London Clearing Bankers, 1960-62. Mem. of Rhodes Trust 1957-73; Chairman: Bd of Governors, United Oxford Hosps, 1958-64; Wellcome Trust, 1965- (Trustee, 1963-65); Commission of Inquiry into Oxford Univ., 1964-66; Cttee on Official Secrets Act, Section 2, 1971-72; Cttee on Ministerial Memoirs, 1976; Political Honours Scrutiny Cttee, 1976. Mem., National Economic Development Council, 1962-64. Mem. Council, Duchy of Cornwall, 1966-. Pres., Kennedy Memorial Cttee, 1963; Trustee: Pilgrim Trust, 1947-; Rockefeller Foundn, 1961-70. Hon. Fellow: Queen's Coll., Oxford, 1948; St Catharine's Coll., Cambridge, 1966; Wolfson Coll., Oxford, 1967; Worcester Coll., Oxford, 1976; Visiting Fellow, Nuffield Coll., 1959. Hon. DCL, Oxford, and other Honorary Doctorates. *Address:* Blackhall Farm, Charlbury Road, Oxford OX2 6UU. *T:* Oxford 511286. *Club:* Athenæum.

FRANKS, Arthur Temple, CMG 1967; HM Diplomatic Service; Foreign and Commonwealth Office, since 1966; *b* 13 July 1920; *s* of late Arthur Franks, Hove; *m* 1945, Rachel Marianne, *d* of late Rev. A. E. S. Ward, Thame, Oxon; one *s* two *d. Educ:* Rugby; Queen's Coll., Oxford. HM Forces, 1940-46 (despatches). Entered Foreign Service, 1949; British Middle East Office, 1952; Tehran, 1953; Bonn, 1962. *Address:* South Corner, Pachesham Park, Leatherhead, Surrey. *T:* Oxshott 2038. *Clubs:* Travellers'; Sunningdale Golf.

FRANKS, Mrs David; *see* Glauert, Audrey Marion.

FRANKS, Desmond Gerald Fergus; His Honour Judge Franks; a Circuit Judge, since 1972; *b* 24 Jan. 1928; *s* of F. Franks, MC, late Lancs Fus., and E. R. Franks; *m* 1952, Margaret Leigh (*née* Daniel); one *d. Educ:* Cathedral Choir Sch., Canterbury; Manchester Grammar Sch.; University Coll., London (LLB). Called to Bar, Middle Temple, 1952; Northern Circuit; Asst Recorder, Salford, 1966; Deputy Recorder, Salford, 1971; a

Recorder of the Crown Court, 1972. *Recreations:* gardening, photography. *Address:* 4 Beathwaite Drive, Bramhall, Cheshire. *T:* 061-485 6065.

FRANKS, Air Vice-Marshal John Gerald, CB 1954; CBE 1949; RAF retired, 1960; *b* 23 May 1905; *e s* of late James Gordon Franks, and of Margaret, *y d* of Lord Chief Justice Fitz-Gibbon, Dublin; *m* 1936, Jessica Rae West; two *d. Educ:* Cheltenham Coll.; RAF Coll., Cranwell. RAF; commissioned from Cranwell, 1924; Mediterranean, 1928-29; India, 1930-35; Middle East, 1936; RAF Staff Coll., 1939; Air Armament Sch., Manby, 1941; Experimental Establishment, Boscombe Down, 1944; Dir Armament Research and Development, 1945-48; idc 1951; Comdt RAF Technical Coll., Henlow, 1952; Air Officer Commanding No 24 Group, Royal Air Force, 1952-55; Pres. of Ordnance Board, 1959-60. Comdr American Legion of Merit, 1948. *Recreations:* golf, fishing, shooting. *Address:* c/o The Bank of Ireland, National Branch, Cork, Irish Republic.

FRASER, family name of **Barons Fraser of Kilmorack, Fraser of North Cape, Fraser of Tullybelton,** also of **Barons Lovat, Saltoun** and **Strathalmond.**

FRASER OF ALLANDER; Barony of (*cr* 1964); title disclaimed by 2nd Baron; *see under* Fraser, Sir Hugh, 2nd Bt.

FRASER OF KILMORACK, Baron *cr* 1974 (Life Peer), of Rubislaw, Aberdeen; **Richard Michael Fraser,** Kt 1962; CBE 1955 (MBE 1945); Director, Glaxo Holdings Ltd, since 1975; *b* 28 Oct. 1915; *yr s* of late Dr Thomas Fraser, CBE, DSO, TD, DL, LLD, Aberdeen; *m* 1944, Elizabeth Chloë, *er d* of Brig. C. A. F. Drummond, OBE; one *s* (and one *s* decd). *Educ:* Fettes; King's Coll., Cambridge. Begg Exhibition, 1934; James Essay Prize, 1935; BA Hons History, 1937; MA 1945. Served War of 1939-45 (RA); 2nd Lieut 1939; War Gunnery Staff Course, 1940; Capt. Feb. 1941; Major, June 1941; Lieut-Col (GSO1) 1945. Joined Conservative Research Dept, 1946; Head of Home Affairs Sect., 1950-51, Jt Dir, 1951-59, Dir, 1959-64, Chm., 1970-74; Dep. Chm., Cons. Party Orgn, 1964-75; Dep. Chm., Conservative Party's Adv. Cttee on Policy, 1970-75 (Sec., Aug. 1951-Oct. 1964); Sec. to the Conservative Leader's Consultative Cttee (Shadow Cabinet), Oct. 1964-June 1970 and March 1974-75. Smith-Mundt Fellowship, USA, 1952. *Recreations:* reading, music, opera, ballet, travel; collecting and recollecting. *Address:* 18 Drayton Court, Drayton Gardens, SW10. *T:* 01-370 1543. *Clubs:* Brooks's, Carlton, St Stephen's (hon. mem.).
See also T. C. Fraser.

FRASER OF NORTH CAPE, 1st Baron, *cr* 1946, of Molesey; **Admiral of the Fleet Bruce Austin Fraser,** GCB 1944 (KCB 1943; CB 1939); KBE 1941 (OBE 1919); Hon. DCL Oxon; *b* 1888; *s* of late Gen. Alex. Fraser, RE, CB. *Educ:* Bradfield. Was Flag Captain, East Indies; commanded Glorious; Chief of Staff, Mediterranean Fleet; Third Sea Lord and Controller, 1939-42; 2nd-in-Command, Home Fleet, 1942; C-in-C Home Fleet, 1943-44; Adm. 1944; C-in-C Eastern Fleet, 1944; C-in-C British Pacific Fleet, 1945-46; C-in-C Portsmouth, 1947-48; Adm. of the Fleet, 1948; First Sea Lord and Chief of Naval Staff, 1948-51. Hon. Degrees Oxford, Edinburgh and Wales Univs. *Heir:* none. *Address:* 18 Wolsey Road, E Molesey, Surrey. *T:* 01-979 1136.

FRASER OF TULLYBELTON, Baron *cr* 1974 (Life Peer), of Bankfoot; **Walter Ian Reid Fraser,** PC 1974; a Lord of Appeal in Ordinary, since 1975; Member of the Queen's Body Guard for Scotland (Royal Company of Archers); *b* 3 Feb. 1911; *o s* of late Alexander Reid Fraser, stockbroker, Glasgow; *m* 1943, (Mary Ursula) Cynthia (Gwendolen), *o d* of Col I. H. Macdonell, DSO (late HLI); one *s. Educ:* Repton; Balliol Coll., Oxford (scholar). BA Oxon 1932; LLB Glasgow 1935; Advocate, 1936; QC Scotland 1953. Lecturer in Constitutional Law, Glasgow Univ., 1936; and at Edinburgh Univ., 1948. Served Army (RA and staff), 1939-45; UK; Burma. Contested (U) East Edinburgh constituency, Gen. Election, 1955. Mem. Royal Commission on Police, 1960. Dean of the Faculty of Advocates, 1959-64; a Senator of HM Coll. of Justice in Scotland, 1964-74. Hon LLD Glasgow, 1970. Hon. Master of the Bench, Gray's Inn, 1975. *Publication:* Outline of Constitutional Law, 1938 (2nd edn, 1948). *Recreations:* shooting, walking. *Address:* 35 Cleaver Square, SE11. *T:* 01-735 3668; Tullybelton House, Bankfoot, Perthshire. *T:* Bankfoot 312. *Club:* New (Edinburgh).

FRASER, Angus McKay, TD 1965; a Commissioner of Customs and Excise, since 1976; *b* 10 March 1928; *s* of late Thomas Douglas Fraser; *m* 1955, Margaret Neilson (marr. diss. 1968); one *s* one *d. Educ:* Falkirk High Sch.; Glasgow Univ.; Bordeaux Univ. Nat. Service in RA, 1950-52; 44 Parachute Bde (TA), 1953-66. Asst Principal, HM Customs and Excise, 1952; Principal, 1956; HM Treasury, 1961-64; Asst Sec., HM Customs and Excise, 1965; Under-Sec. and Comr of Customs and Excise, 1972; Under-Sec., CSD, 1973. Member: Bd, SITPRO; EDC for Internat. Freight Movement. *Address:* 84 Ennerdale Road, Kew, Richmond, Surrey TW9 2DL. *T:* 01-940 9913. *Club:* Reform.

FRASER, Lady Antonia; writer; *b* 27 Aug. 1932; *d* of 7th Earl of Longford, *qv,* and of Countess of Longford, *qv; m* 1956, Rt Hon. Hugh Charles Patrick Joseph Fraser, *qv* (marr. diss. 1977); three *s* three *d. Educ:* Dragon School, Oxford; St Mary's Convent, Ascot; Lady Margaret Hall, Oxford. Has lectured, broadcast and appeared on television. General Editor, Kings and Queens of England series. Member, Arts Council, 1970-72; Chm., Soc. of Authors, 1974-75. *Publications:* King Arthur and the Knights of the Round Table, 1954 (reissued, 1970); Robin Hood, 1955 (reissued, 1971); Dolls, 1963; A History of Toys, 1966; Mary Queen of Scots (James Tait Black Memorial Prize, 1969), 1969; Cromwell Our Chief of Men, 1973; King James: VI of Scotland, I of England, 1974; (ed) Scottish Love Poems, a personal anthology, 1975; (ed) Love Letters: an anthology, 1976; Quiet as a Nun (novel), 1977; *TV and radio plays:* On the Battlements, 1975; The Heroine, 1976; Penelope, 1976; Charades, 1977. *Recreation:* life. *Address:* c/o Curtis Brown, 1 Craven Hill, W2.

FRASER, Sir Basil (Malcolm), 2nd Bt, *cr* 1921; *b* 2 Jan. 1920; *s* of Sir (John) Malcolm Fraser, 1st Bt, GBE, and of Irene, *d* of C. E. Brightman of South Kensington; *S* father, 1949. *Educ:* Northaw, Pluckley, Kent; Eton Coll.; Queen's Coll., Cambridge. Served War of 1939-45, RE, 1940-42; Madras Sappers and Miners, 1942-46 (despatches). Mem. AA and RAC. *Recreations:* motoring, music, electronic reproduction of sound. *Heir:* none. *Address:* 175 Beach Street, Deal, Kent CT14 6LE. *Clubs:* Bath, Roadfarers'.

FRASER, Sir Bruce (Donald), KCB 1961 (CB 1956); *b* 18 Nov. 1910; *s* of late Maj.-Gen. Sir Theodore Fraser, KCB and late Constance Ruth Fraser (*née* Stevenson); *m* 1939, Audrey, *d* of late Lieut-Col E. L. Croslegh; one *s* one *d* decd. *Educ:* Bedford Sch.; Trinity Coll., Cambridge (Scholar); First Class in Classical Tripos Part I, 1930 and in English Tripos Part II, 1932; BA 1932, MA 1964. Ed. the Granta, 1932. Entered Civil Service as Asst Principal, Scottish Office, 1933; transf. to HM Treasury, 1936; Private Sec. to Financial Sec., 1937, and to Permanent Sec., 1941; Asst Sec., 1945; Under Sec., 1951; Third Sec., 1956-60; Dep. Sec., Ministry of Aviation, Jan.-April 1960; Permanent Sec., Ministry of Health, 1960-64; Joint Permanent Under-Sec. of State, Dept of Education and Science, 1964-65; Permanent Sec., Ministry of Land and Natural Resources, 1965-66; Comptroller and Auditor-General, Exchequer and Audit Dept, 1966-71. *Publication:* Sir Ernest Gowers' The Complete Plain Words, rev. edn 1973. *Address:* Jonathan, St Dogmael's, Cardigan SA43 3LF. *T:* Cardigan 2387. *Club:* Athenæum.

FRASER, Campbell; *see* Fraser, J. C.

FRASER, Maj.-Gen. Colin Angus Ewen, CB 1971; CBE 1968; General Officer Commanding, Southern Command, Australia, 1971-74; *b* Nairobi, Kenya, 25 Sept. 1918; *s* of A. E. Fraser, Rutherglen, Vic.; *m* 1942, Dorothy, *d* of A. Champion; two *s* one *d. Educ:* Johannesburg; Adelaide High Sch.; RMC, Duntroon (grad. 1938); Melbourne Univ. (BA). Served War of 1939-45: UK, Middle East, Pacific. Staff Coll., Camberley, 1946; Dep. Comdr, Commonwealth Div., Korea, 1955-56; Dir, Military Trng, 1957-58; Services Attaché, Burma, 1960-62; Chief of Staff, Northern Command, Brisbane, 1964-68; Commandant, Royal Military Coll., Duntroon, 1968-69; Commander, Australian Force, Vietnam, 1970-71. *Address:* 364 Orana Road, Ocean Shores, Brunswick Heads, NSW 2483, Australia. *Clubs:* Tasmanian (Hobart); United Services (Qld).

FRASER, Colin Neil, QC Scotland 1958; Counsel to Secretary of State under Private Legislation (Scotland) Procedure 1958-71; *b* 21 Sept. 1905; *s* of late Robert Dick Fraser, CA; *m* 1937, Alix Leslie, *d* of late Alexander Stephen, shipbuilder, Glasgow; one *s* two *d. Educ:* Glenalmond; Glasgow Univ. (MA, LLB). Advocate, 1931; RA (Capt.), 1939-46; Pres., Pensions Appeal Tribunal (Scotland), 1946-58. *Recreations:* ski-ing, golf. *Address:* The East House, Birsley Brae, Tranent EH33 1NQ. *T:* 610451. *Club:* New (Edinburgh).

FRASER, Gen. Sir David (William), KCB 1973; OBE 1962; Commandant, Royal College of Defence Studies, since 1978; ADC General to the Queen, since 1977; *b* 30 Dec. 1920; *s* of Brig. Hon. William Fraser, DSO, MC, *y s* of 18th Lord Saltoun and Pamela, *d* of Cyril Maude and *widow* of Major W. La T. Congreve, VC, DSO, MC; *m* 1st, 1947, Anne Balfour; one *d*; 2nd, 1957, Julia de la Hey; two *s* two *d. Educ:* Eton; Christ

Church, Oxford. Commnd into Grenadier Guards, 1941; served NW Europe; comd 1st Bn Grenadier Guards, 1960-62; comd 19th Inf. Bde, 1963-65; Dir, Defence Policy, MoD, 1966-69; GOC 4 Div., 1969-71; Asst Chief of Defence Staff (Policy), MoD, 1971-73; Vice-Chief of the General Staff, 1973-75; UK Mil. Rep. to NATO, 1975-77. *Recreation:* shooting. *Address:* Vallenders, Isington, Alton, Hants. *T:* Bentley 3166. *Clubs:* Turf, Pratt's.

FRASER, Donald Blake, FRCS; FRCOG; Gynæcologist and Obstetrician, St Bartholomew's Hospital, 1946-75; *b* 9 June 1910; *o s* of Dr Thomas B. Fraser, Hatfield Point, NB, Canada; *m* 1939, Betsy, *d* of late Sir James Henderson, KBE; one *s* one *d. Educ:* University of New Brunswick; Christ Church, Oxford. Rhodes Scholar, 1930; BA 1st Cl. Hons, 1932, BM, BCh Oxon 1936; MRCS, LRCP, LMCC, 1936; FRCS, 1939; MRCOG, 1940, FRCOG, 1952. Examiner: Central Midwives Bd; Universities of Oxford and London; Conjoint Bd; Royal College of Obstetricians and Gynæcologists. *Publications:* (joint) Midwifery (textbook), 1956. Articles in medical journals. *Recreation:* philately. *Address:* 73 Harley Street, W1N 1DE. *T:* 01-935 6042.

FRASER, Donald Hamilton, ARA 1975; artist; Tutor, Royal College of Art, since 1958 (Fellow 1970); *b* 30 July 1929; *s* of Donald Fraser and Dorothy Christiana (*née* Lang); *m* 1954, Judith Wentworth-Sheilds; one *d. Educ:* Maidenhead Grammar Sch.; St Martin's Sch. of Art, London; Paris (French Govt Scholarship). One-man Exhibitions: London (Gimpels): 1953, 1957, 1959, 1961, 1963, 1965, 1968, 1969, 1971; New York (Rosenberg): 1958, 1960, 1963, 1964, 1966, 1968, 1970, 1973, 1975; Paris (Craven), 1957; Zürich (Gimpel-Hanover), 1967; Osaka, Japan (Kasahara), 1976; also work in many rep. exhibns of British painting in Europe and N America. Work in public collections includes: Museum of Fine Arts, Boston; Albright-Knox Gall., Buffalo; Carnegie Inst., Pittsburgh; City Art Museum, St Louis; Wadsworth Athenaeum, Hartford, Conn.; Hirshhorn Museum, Washington, DC; Yale Univ. Art Museum; Nat. Gall. of Canada, Ottawa; Nat. Gall. of NSW, Melbourne; Nottingham City Art Gall.; Hull City Art Gall.; Southampton City Art Gall.; Reading City Art Gall.; Rutherstone Loan Coll., Manchester; Arts Council and CAS Collections. Hon. Sec., Artists Gen. Benevolent Inst., 1975-. *Publication:* Gauguin's 'Vision after the Sermon', 1969. *Address:* Bramham Cottage, Remenham Lane, Henley-on-Thames, Oxon. *T:* Henley-on-Thames 4253.

FRASER, Sir Douglas (Were), Kt 1966; ISO 1962; President, Queensland Ambulance Transport Brigade Council; Chairman, Council, Queensland Conservatorium of Music; *b* 24 Oct. 1899; *s* of late Robert John Fraser and Edith Harriet (*née* Shepherd); *m* 1927, Violet Pryke (*d* 1968); three *s. Educ:* State High Sch., Gympie, Qld. Entered Qld State Public Service, 1916; Public Service Board and Public Service Comr's Dept; Sec. to Public Service Comr, 1939; Sen. Public Service Inspector, 1947; Dep. Public Service Comr, 1952; Public Service Comr, 1956; retired 1965; War-time Asst Dir of Civil Defence, Sec., Public Safety Adv. Cttee. *Recreations:* gardening, fishing, music, reading. *Address:* 76 Prince Edward Parade, Redcliffe, Qld 4020, Australia. *T:* 84 5538.

FRASER, Edward; *see* Fraser, J. E.

FRASER, Francis Charles, CBE 1962; FRS 1966; DSc; FIBiol; Deputy Chief Scientific Officer, British Museum (Natural History), 1960-65; re-employed, Principal Scientific Officer, 1965-69, retired 1969; *b* 16 June 1903; *y s* of James and Barbara Anne Fraser, Dingwall, Ross & Cromarty; *m* 1938, Anne Nuttall. *Educ:* Dingwall; Glasgow Univ. Demonstrator, Dept of Geology, University of Glasgow, 1924-25. "Discovery" investigations, 1925-33, with service in Discovery, William Scoresby, Discovery II and at shore station, S Georgia. Danish Atlantide Expedition, W Africa, 1945-46. British Museum (Natural History): Asst Keeper, Mammalian Osteology, 1933-48; Dep. Keeper of Zoology, 1948-57; Keeper of Zoology, 1957-64. Pres., Antarctic Club, 1973-74. Polar Medal, 1942. *Publications:* (with late J. R. Norman) Giant Fishes, Whales and Dolphins, 1937. Technical papers mainly on subjects relating to whales and dolphins. Reports on Cetaceans stranded on the British Coast, 1926-32, 1933-37, 1938-47, 1948-66. *Recreation:* gardening. *Address:* 78 Hayes Road, Bromley, Kent BR2 9AB. *T:* 01-460 3668. *Club:* Athenæum.

FRASER, George MacDonald; author and journalist; *b* 2 April 1925; *s* of late William Fraser, MB, ChB and Anne Struth Donaldson; *m* 1949, Kathleen Margarette, *d* of late George Hetherington, Carlisle; two *s* one *d. Educ:* Carlisle Grammar Sch.; Glasgow Academy. Served in British Army, 1943-47:

Infantryman XIVth Army, Lieut Gordon Highlanders. Newspaperman in England, Canada and Scotland from 1947; Dep. Editor, Glasgow Herald, 1964-69. *Publications:* Flashman, 1969; Royal Flash, 1970; The General Danced at Dawn, 1970; The Steel Bonnets, 1971; Flash for Freedom!, 1971; Flashman at the Charge, 1973; McAuslan in the Rough, 1974; Flashman in the Great Game, 1975; Flashman's Lady, 1977; (film screenplays): The Three Musketeers, 1974; The Four Musketeers, 1975; Royal Flash, 1975; The Prince and the Pauper, 1977. *Recreations:* snooker, picquet, talking to wife, history, singing. *Address:* Baldrine, Isle of Man. *T:* Laxey 384.

FRASER, Air Marshal Sir (Henry) Paterson, KBE 1961 (CBE 1945); CB 1953; AFC 1937; RAF, retired; Concrete Consultant; Chairman: Barclays Unicorn International (Isle of Man) Ltd; Buchan Educational Trust Ltd; *b* 15 July 1907; *s* of late Harry Fraser, Johannesburg, South Africa; *m* 1933, Avis Gertrude Haswell; two *s. Educ:* St Andrews Coll., Grahamstown, South Africa; Pembroke Coll., Cambridge (MA), RAFO, and Pres. University Air Sqdn, Cambridge; joined RAF, 1929; served in India; RAF Engineering Course, Henlow, 1933-34; Aerodynamic Flight, RAE, Farnborough, 1934-38; RAF Staff Coll., 1938; Directorate of War Organization, Air Ministry, 1939-40; commanded Experimental Flying Section, RAE, Farnborough, 1941; Mem. RAF Element, Combined Chiefs of Staff, Washington DC, 1942; Dep. Dir of War Organization, Air Ministry, 1943; Senior Administrative Planner, 2nd Tactical Air Force, 1943-44, and Dep. Air Officer in Charge of Administration, 2nd TAF, 1944-45; commanded Aircraft and Armament Experimental Establishment, Boscombe Down, 1945-46; Dep. Dir (Air Staff) Policy, Air Ministry, 1947-48; Defence Research Policy Staff, Ministry of Defence, 1948-51; idc 1951; Senior Air Staff Officer, Headquarters Fighter Command, 1952-53; Chief of Staff, Headquarters Allied Air Forces, Central Europe, 1954-56; AOC No. 12 Group, Fighter Command, 1956-58; Dir, RAF Exercise Planning, 1959; UK Representative on Permanent Military Deputies Group of Cento, 1959-62; Inspector-Gen., RAF, 1962-64. Taylor Gold Medal of RAeS, 1937; FRAeS. *Address:* Denizli, Ballajora, Maughold, Isle of Man. *Club:* Royal Automobile.

FRASER, Sir Hugh, 2nd Bt *cr* 1961, of Dineiddwg; Chairman, House of Fraser Ltd, since 1966 (Deputy Chairman, 1965; Director, 1958); Director, Harrods Ltd, since 1966 (Chairman 1966-76; Managing Director, 1970-76); Director: John Barker & Co. Ltd, since 1966 (Chairman and Managing Director, 1966-76); Binns Ltd, since 1966 (Chairman and Managing Director 1966-76); Deputy Chairman, Scottish and Universal Investments Ltd (Chairman 1966-76); Chairman: George Outram & Co. Ltd, since 1966; Whyte & Mackay Ltd, since 1973; Director, Highland Tourist (Cairngorm Development) Ltd; *b* 18 Dec. 1936; *s* of 1st Baron Fraser of Allander, DL, LLD, JP (Bt 1961) and of Kate Hutcheon, *d* of late Sir Andrew Lewis, LLD, JP; *S* to father's Btcy, and disclaimed Barony, 1966; *m* 1st, 1962, Patricia Mary (marr. diss. 1971), *e d* of John Bowie; three *d*; 2nd, 1973, Aileen Ross. *Educ:* St Mary's, Melrose; Kelvinside Academy. *Recreations:* farming, show jumping, sailing. *Address:* Cattermuir Lodge, Croftamie, Glasgow G63 0HG. *T:* Drymen 421.

FRASER, Rt. Hon. Hugh Charles Patrick Joseph, PC 1962; MBE; MP (C) Stone Div. of Staffs, 1945-50, Stafford and Stone Division of Staffs, since 1950; *b* 23 Jan. 1918; *s* of 16th Baron Lovat; *m* 1956, Lady Antonia Pakenham (*see* Lady Antonia Fraser) (marr. diss. 1977); three *s* three *d. Educ:* Ampleforth Coll.; Balliol Coll., Oxford; The Sorbonne, Paris. Roman Catholic. Ex-Pres. Oxford Union; war service with Lovat Scouts, Phantom and Special Air Service. PPS to Sec. of State for the Colonies, 1951-54; Parly Under-Sec. of State and Financial Sec., War Office 1958-60; Parly Under-Sec. of State for the Colonies, 1960-62; Sec. of State for Air, 1962-64. Pres., West Midlands Conservative and Unionist Assoc., 1967. Director: Sun Alliance; Ionian Bank; industrial cos. Order of Orange Nassau, Order of Leopold with palm, Belgian Croix de guerre. *Address:* Eilean Aigas, Beauly, Inverness, Scotland; House of Commons, SW1. *Clubs:* Beefsteak, White's.

FRASER, Col Hugh Vincent, CMG 1957; OBE 1946; TD 1947; retired 1960; *b* 20 Sept. 1908; *yr s* of William Neilson and Maude Fraser; *m* 1941, Noreen, *d* of Col M. O'C. Tandy; one *s* one *d. Educ:* Sherborne Sch. Commissioned into Royal Tank Regt; served War of 1939-45, India and Burma, with 14th Army. Military Attaché, Cairo, 1954-56; NATO, Washington DC, 1957-60. *Recreations:* hunting, shooting; Master Aldershot Command Beagles, 1939. *Address:* Cheyney Holt, Steeple Morden, Cambs. *Club:* Army and Navy.

FRASER, Sir Ian, Kt 1963; DSO 1943; OBE 1940; DL; FRSE, FRCS, FRCSI, FACS; Consulting Surgeon, Belfast; Senior Surgeon: Royal Victoria Hospital, Belfast, 1955-66; Royal Belfast Hospital for Sick Children, 1955-66; Director: Provincial Bank of Ireland; Allied Irish Bank; *b* 9 Feb. 1901; *s* of Robert Moore Fraser, BA, MD, Belfast; *m* 1931, Eleanor Margaret Mitchell; one *s* one *d. Educ:* Royal Academical Institution, Belfast; Queen's Univ., Belfast. MB, BCh 1st Cl. Hons 1923; MD 1932; MCh 1927; FRCSI 1926; FRCS 1927; FRSE 1938; FACS 1945. Coulter Schol.; McQuitty Schol.; 1st place in Ire. as FRCSI. Resident Surgical Officer, St Helen's, Lancs; Surgeon: Royal Belfast Hosp. for Sick Children; Royal Victoria Hosp., Belfast, and former Asst Prof. of Surgery. Served War: (overseas) 1940-45: in W Africa, N. Africa, Sicily, Italy (OBE, DSO, Salerno); invasion of France, India; Officer in charge of Penicillin in Research Team, N Africa; Brig, 1945. Hon. Col (TA): No 204 Gen. Hosp., 1961-71; No 4 Field Amb., 1948-71; Surgeon in Ordinary to the Governor of Northern Ireland; Hon. Cons. Surg. to the Army in NI; Chm., Police Authority, Royal Ulster Constabulary, 1970-76; Mem. Adv. Council, Ulster Defence Regt. Past President: RCSI (1956-57); Assoc. of Surgeons GB and Ireland (1957); BMA (1962-63); Irish Med. Graduates Assoc., London, Queen's Univ. Assoc., London; Services Club, QUB; Ulster Med. Soc. President: Ulster Surgical Club; Queen's Univ. Assoc., Belfast; Chm of Convocation and Mem. Senate QUB. Visiting Lecturer: Leicester, Birmingham, Edinburgh, Bradford, London, Sheffield, Dublin, Cheltenham, Rochester, New York, Copenhagen, Glasgow, Manchester, Middlesex Hosp., Bristol, Barnsley, etc; Delegate to various assocs abroad. John Snow Oration, 1967; Downpatrick Hosp. Bi-Centenary Oration, 1967; Bishop Jeremy Taylor Lecture, 1970; Maj.-Gen. Philip Mitchiner Lecture, 1971; Robert Campbell Orator, 1973. Visiting Examiner in Surgery: Liverpool, Cambridge, and Manchester Univs; NUI; Apothecaries' Hall, Dublin; TCD; RCS in Ire.; RCS of Glasgow, Councillor, RCSI; Mem. and Trustee, James IV Assoc. of Surgeons; Mem., Health Educn Cttee, Min. of Health, London; Fellow: BMA; Roy. Soc. Med. Lond.; Roy. Irish Acad. of Med.; Hon. FRCPGlas 1972; Hon. FRCSE; Hon. Fellow, Brit. Assoc. of Paediatric Surgeons; Foreign Mem., L'Académie de Chirurgie, Paris; Hon. Mem., Danish Assoc. of Surgery, Copenhagen; Mem., Internat. Soc. of Surgeons. Hon. Life Governor, Royal Victoria Hosp., Belfast; Governor for GB, Amer. Coll. Surgeons. Hon. DSc Oxon, 1963. GCStJ 1974 (KStJ 1940); Mem., Chapter General, London, and Lieutenant of Commandery of Ards, Ulster, Order of St John. DL Belfast, 1955. Gold Medal: Ulster Hosp. for Women and Children; Royal Belfast Hosp. for Sick Children. Commander: Ordre de la Couronne (Belgium) 1963; Order of Orange Nassau, 1969; Ordre des Palmes Académiques. *Publications:* various monographs on surgical subjects. *Recreations:* golf, formerly hockey and rugby. *Address:* (residence) 19 Upper Malone Road, Belfast. *T:* Belfast 668235; (consulting rooms) 35 Wellington Park, Belfast BTQ 6DN. *T:* Belfast 665543. *Clubs:* Ulster, Malone Golf (Belfast).

FRASER, Lt. Comdr Ian Edward, VC 1945; DSC 1943; RD and Bar; JP; Managing Director, North Sea Diving Services Ltd, since 1965, and Director, Star Offshore Services Ltd; Chairman and Managing Director: Nordive (West Africa) Ltd; North Sea Diving Services Nederland BV; Chairman, Universal Divers Ltd, since 1965 (Managing Director, 1947-65); *b* 18 Dec., 1920; *s* of S. Fraser, Bourne End, Bucks; *m* 1943, Melba Estelle Hughes; four *s* two *d. Educ:* Royal Grammar Sch., High Wycombe; HMS Conway. Merchant Navy, 1937-39; Royal Navy, 1939-47; Lt-Comdr, RNR, 1951-65. JP Wallasey, 1957. Officer, American Legion of Merit. *Publication:* Frogman VC, 1957. *Address:* Clarecourt, 39 Warren Drive, Wallasey, Merseyside. *T:* 051-639 3355.

FRASER, Ian George Inglis, OBE 1975; Representative, British Council, Japan, since 1977; *b* 5 March 1923; *s* of late Rev. George Fraser and Mrs Mary Fraser (*née* Inglis); *m* 1949, Eve Uwins; three *s. Educ:* Bathgate Acad.; Edinburgh Acad.; Edinburgh Univ. (MA 1944). Temp. Asst Principal: Min. of Supply, 1944-46; BoT, 1946-48; British Council, 1948-: Asst, Visitors Dept, 1948-53; Asst Rep., Israel, 1953-56; Asst, Commonwealth Dept, 1956-60; Reg. Dir, Mbale, Uganda, 1960-62; Dep. Rep., Nigeria, 1962-67; Asst Controller, Books, Arts and Science Div., 1967-69; Dep. Controller, Overseas Div. A, 1969-72; Rep., Greece, 1972-76. *Recreations:* books, theatre, travel, talk. *Address:* c/o British Council, 10 Spring Gardens, SW1A 2BN. *T:* 01-930 8466; 16 Kensington Place, W8. *T:* 01-727 2940.

FRASER, Ian James, CBE 1972; MC 1945; Chairman: Rolls-Royce Motors, since 1971; Datastream Ltd, 1977; Deputy Chairman, Lazard Brothers; *b* 7 Aug. 1923; 2nd *s* of late Hon.

Alastair Thomas Joseph Fraser and Lady Sibyl Fraser (*née* Grimston); *m* 1958, Evelyn Elizabeth Anne Grant; two *s* two *d*. *Educ*: Ampleforth Coll.; Magdalen Coll., Oxford. Served War of 1939-45: Lieut, Scots Guards, 1942-45 (despatches, MC). Reuter Correspondent, 1946-56; S. G. Warburg & Co. Ltd, 1956-69; Dir.-Gen., Panel on Take-overs and Mergers, 1969-72; Part-time Mem., CAA, 1972-74. Chm., City Capital Markets Cttee, 1974-; Member: Exec. Cttee, City Communications Centre, 1976-; Cttee on Finance for Industry, NEDC, 1976-. Director: BOC International Ltd, 1972-; Davy International Ltd, 1972-; Chloride Gp Ltd, 1976-; S. Pearson & Son Ltd, 1977. Governor, More House Sch., 1970-75. FRSA 1970; FBIM 1974. Kt of Honour and Devotion, SMO of Malta, 1971. *Recreations*: fishing, gardening, Scottish history. *Address*: 29 Eaton Square, SW1. *T*: 01-235 5503; South Haddon Farm, Skilgate, Taunton, Somerset. *T*: Bampton (Devon) 247. *Clubs*: White's, Beefsteak.

FRASER, Ian Montagu, MC 1945; Deputy Secretary, The Buttle Trust, since 1971; *b* 14 Oct. 1916; *e s* of Col Herbert Cecil Fraser, DSO, OBE, TD, and Sybil Mary Statter; *m* 1st, 1945, Mary Stanley (*d* 1964); one *s* one *d*; 2nd, 1967, Angela Meston, two *s*. *Educ*: Shrewsbury Sch.; Christ Church, Oxford. 1st Cl. Class. Hon. Mods, 1937; 1st Cl. Lit Hum 1939. Regular Commn in Frontier Force Rifles, IA, 1939, and served War of 1939-45, NW Frontier, Iraq, Syria and Western Desert (MC, despatches twice, POW); retired 1948. Executive, Guthrie and Co. Ltd, 1948; Gen. Sec., The John Lewis Partnership, 1956-59, Consultant, 1959-64. RARO, Rifle Bde, 1948-. MP (C) Sutton Div. of Plymouth, 1959-66; PPS to Sec. of State for the Colonies, 1962; Asst Govt Whip, 1962-64; Opposition Whip, 1964-66; Conservative Research Dept, 1966-67. Exec. Dir, GUS Export Corp., 1967-70. *Recreations*: flyfishing, sailing. *Address*: How Hatch, Chipstead, Surrey. *T*: Downland 51944. *Clubs*: Carlton; Royal Western Yacht (Plymouth).

FRASER, Very Rev. Dr Ian Watson, CMG 1973; Chairman, New Zealand Refugee Homes Board, since 1962; retired as Minister of St Stephen's Presbyterian Church, Lower Hutt, Wellington, NZ (1961-73); *b* 23 Oct. 1907; *s* of Malcolm Fraser (*b* Inverness; 1st NZ Govt Statistician) and Caroline (*née* Watson; *b* Napier, NZ); *m* 1932, Alexa Church Stewart; one *s* two *d*. *Educ*: Scots Coll., Wellington, NZ; Victoria Univ. of Wellington (MA (Hons)); Theol Hall, Dunedin; BD (Melb.); Univ. of Edinburgh; Univ. of Bonn, Germany; Union Theol Seminary, NY (STM, ThD). Minister: St Andrew's Presbyterian Church, Levin, 1933-39; Presbyterian Ch., Wyndham, 1939-42; Chaplain, St Andrew's Coll., Christchurch, 1942-48; Minister, St John's Pres. Ch., Papatoetoe, Auckland, 1948-61. Moderator, Presbyterian Church of NZ, 1968-69. Agency Escort for Bank of NSW. Refugee Award of Nat. Council of Churches, 1969. *Publications*: Understandest Thou? (Introd. to NT), 1946; Understanding the OT, 1958; various booklets. *Recreations*: beekeeping, music; until recently, tennis, Rugby refereeing. *Address*: 17 Hinau Street, Linden, Wellington, NZ. *T*: 6204 Tawa.
See also T. R. C. Fraser.

FRASER, (James) Campbell; Chairman and Manging Director, Dunlop Ltd; *b* 2 May 1923; *s* of Alexander Ross Fraser and Annie McGregor Fraser; *m* 1950, Maria Harvey (*née* McLaren); two *d*. *Educ*: Glasgow Univ.; McMaster Univ.; Dundee Sch. of Economics. BCom. Served RAF, 1941-45. Raw Cotton Commn, Liverpool, 1950-52; Economist Intelligence Unit, 1952-57; Dunlop Rubber Co. Ltd, 1957-: Public Relations Officer, 1958; Group Marketing Controller, 1962; Man. Dir, Dunlop New Zealand Ltd, 1967; Exec. Dir, 1969; Jt Man. Dir, 1971; Man. Dir, 1972; Chm., Scottish Television Ltd, 1975-; Dir, Morgan Crucible Co. Ltd. Founder Mem., Past Chm. and Pres., Soc. of Business Economists; Member: NEDC; Econ. Policy Cttee, CBI; President's Cttee, CBI; London Exec. Cttee, Scottish Council, 1972; Cttee, Royal Scottish Corp.; Exec. Cttee, SMMT. FBIM 1971. *Publications*: many articles and broadcasts. *Recreations*: athletics, reading, theatre, cinema, gardening, walking. *Address*: Silver Birches, 4 Silver Lane, Purley, Surrey. *T*: 01-660 1703. *Club*: Caledonian.

FRASER, Prof. Sir James (David), 2nd Bt, *cr* 1943; Professor of Surgery, University of Southampton, since 1970, and Hon. Consultant Surgeon, Southampton University Hospital Group; *b* 19 July 1924; *o s* of Sir John Fraser, 1st Bt, KCVO, MC, and Agnes Govane Herald, The Manse, Duns, Berwickshire; *S* father 1947; *m* 1950, Maureen, *d* of Rev. John Reay, MC, Bingham Rectory, Nottingham; two *s*. *Educ*: Edinburgh Academy; Magdalen Coll., Oxford (BA); Edinburgh Univ. (MB, ChB); ChM 1961; FRCSE 1953; FRCS 1973. RAMC (Major), 1948-51; Senior Lectr in Clinical Surgery, Univ. of Edinburgh and Hon. Cons. Surgeon, Royal Infirmary, Edinburgh, 1951-70. *Recreations*: golf, swimming. *Heir*: *s* Iain Michael Fraser, *b* 27

June 1951. *Address*: Rothiemurchus, St Cross Hill, Winchester, Hants.

FRASER, Col James Douglas, CBE 1976; TD 1950 (1st clasp 1951, 2nd clasp 1958); DL; retired Insurance Broker and Consultant; Chairman, Strathclyde Valuation Appeal Panel, since 1975; *b* 12 July 1914; *s* of John Fraser and Jessie Victoria McCallum or Fraser; *m* 1st, 1944, Esme Latta (*d* 1964); one *s* one *d*; 2nd, 1966, Nancy McGregor or Stewart; one step *d*. *Educ*: Glasgow Acad. ACII 1933. Insurance Broker with Stenhouse Holdings Ltd, 1947-69 (Dir, 1954-69); Insurance Consultant, 1969-74. Commnd TA, 1938; War Service, Highland Light Infantry, 1939-46; Comd 5/6th Bn HLI, 1953-56; Dep. Comdr (Colonel), 154 (Highland) Bde, 1956-58; Chm., Lowland TAVRA, 1973-76. DL Dunbartonshire, 1975. *Recreations*: golf, reading, music. *Address*: Newfield, 6 Gartconnell Drive, Bearsden, Glasgow G61 3BL. *T*: 041-942 3020. *Clubs*: Caledonian; Western, Buchanan Castle Golf (Glasgow).

FRASER, (James) Edward; Under Secretary, Scottish Office Finance Division, since 1976; *b* 16 Dec. 1931; *s* of Dr James F. Fraser, TD, Aberdeen, and late Dr Kathleen Blomfield; *m* 1959, Patricia Louise Stewart; two *s*. *Educ*: Aberdeen Grammar Sch.; Univ. of Aberdeen (MA); Christ's Coll., Cambridge (BA). RA, 1953: Staff Captain 'Q', Tel-el-Kebir, 1954-55. Asst Principal, Scottish Home Dept, 1957-60; Private Sec. to Permanent Under Sec. of State, 1960-62, and to Parly Under-Sec. of State, 1962; Principal: SHHD, 1962-64; Cabinet Office, 1964-66; HM Treasury, 1966-68; SHHD, 1968-69; Asst Secretary: SHHD, 1970-76; Scottish Office Finance Div., 1976. *Recreations*: reading, music, hill walking. *Address*: 59 Murrayfield Gardens, Edinburgh EH12 6DH. *T*: 031-337 2274. *Club*: Royal Commonwealth Society.

FRASER, Very Rev. John Annand, MBE 1940; TD 1945; DD; Moderator of the General Assembly of the Church of Scotland, May 1958-May 1959; Extra Chaplain to The Queen, in Scotland, since 1964 (Chaplain, 1952-64); *b* 21 June 1894; *er s* of Rev. Charles Fraser, BD, Minister of Croy, Inverness-shire, and Elizabeth Annand; *m* 1925, Leila, *d* of Col Ewen Campbell; one *s* one *d*. *Educ*: Robert Gordon's Coll., Aberdeen; Inverness Royal Academy; Universities of Aberdeen and Edinburgh. MA Aberdeen 1919. Served European War, 1914-18: in ranks 4th Bn Gordon Highlanders, 1915, Commd 7th Bn 1917. CF (TA) 1935; SCF, 52nd (Lowland) Div., 1940; Dep. Asst Chaplain Gen., West Scotland Dist, 1942. Asst Minister, St Matthew's, Edinburgh, 1921; Minister of Humbie, East Lothian, 1923; Minister of Hamilton, Second Charge, 1931, First Charge, 1949; Minister, Aberdalgie and Dupplin, Perth, 1960-70. Convener of Maintenance of Ministry Cttee of Church of Scotland, 1950-54; Convener of Business Cttee, 1962-67; Convener of Gen. Administration Cttee, 1962-66; Chm. of Judicial Commn, 1962-66; Chm. of Church of Scotland Trust, 1962-66; Mem. Broadcasting Council for Scotland, 1963-67. Hon. DD Aberdeen, 1951. *Recreations*: fishing, gardening. *Address*: 133 Glasgow Road, Perth. *T*: Perth 21462. *Club*: Caledonian (Edinburgh).

FRASER, John Denis; MP (Lab) Lambeth, Norwood, since 1974 (Norwood, 1966-74); Minister of State, Department of Prices and Consumer Protection, since 1976; *b* 30 June 1934; *s* of Archibald and Frances Fraser; *m* 1960, Ann Hathaway; two *s* one *d*. *Educ*: Sloane Grammar Sch., Chelsea; Co-operative Coll., Loughborough; Law Soc. Sch. of Law (John Mackrell Prize). Entered Australia & New Zealand Bank Ltd, 1950; Army service, 1952-54, as Sergt, RAEC (educnl and resettlement work). Solicitor, 1960; practised with Lewis Silkin and Partners. Mem. Lambeth Borough Coun., 1962-68 (Chm. Town Planning Cttee; Chm. Labour Gp). PPS to Rt Hon. Barbara Castle, 1968-70; Opposition front bench spokesman on Home Affairs, 1972-74; Parly Under-Sec. of State, Dept of Employment, 1974-76. *Recreations*: athletics, walking. *Address*: 44 Pymers Mead, Croxted Road, SE21 8NH. *Club*: York (West Norwood).

FRASER, Rt. Hon. (John) Malcolm, PC 1976; CH 1977; MA Oxon; MP; MHR (L) for Wannon, Victoria, since 1955; Prime Minister of Australia, since 1975; *b* 21 May 1930; *s* of late J. Neville Fraser, Nareen, Vic, Australia; *m* 1956, Tamara, *d* of S. R. Beggs; two *s* two *d*. *Educ*: Melbourne C of E Grammar Sch.; Magdalen Coll., Oxford. Mem. Jt Party Cttee on Foreign Affairs, 1962-66; Minister: for the Army, 1966-68; for Educn and Science, 1968-69, 1971-72; for Defence, 1969-71; Leader of Parly Liberal Party and Leader of the Opposition, 1975. Mem. Council, Aust. Nat. Univ., 1964-66. *Recreations*: fishing, photography. *Address*: Parliament House, Canberra, ACT 2600, Australia. *Clubs*: Melbourne; Commonwealth (Canberra).

FRASER, Sir Keith Charles Adolphus, 6th Bt, *cr* 1806; *b* 14 Sept. 1911; *s* of Major Sir Keith Fraser, 5th Bt, and Lady Dorothy Coventry (*d* 1965), 2nd *d* of 9th Earl of Coventry; *S* father 1935; *m* 1934, Blanca de Undurraga y Sandiford (from whom he obtained a divorce, 1946), *d* of Julio de Undurraga; *m* 1947, Mrs Sybil Craven, *d* of George Savage. *Educ:* Eton; Cambridge. *Heir:* none. *Address:* c/o Brown Shipley & Co. Ltd, Founders Court, EC2.

FRASER, Kenneth Wharton, CMG 1962; OBE 1945; Advertising and Public Relations executive (retired); formerly Dominion President, New Zealand Returned Services' Association; *b* 1 Nov. 1905; *s* of late William Fraser, Edinburgh, Scotland; *m* 1926, Ione May (*d* 1975), *d* of late William James Moor, Auckland, NZ; two *s* three *d*. *Educ:* Auckland, NZ. War service: 1940-45, 2nd NZEF, Lt-Col; Cmdg Officer, 5 Field Regt, NZ Artillery, 1940-41 (then POW to 1945). Dominion Executive, New Zealand Returned Services' Assoc., 1946-48; Dominion Vice-Pres. (NZRSA), 1949-54; Dominion Pres., 1955-62, retired. *Address:* 11 Karu Crescent, Waikanae, New Zealand. *T:* 5784. *Club:* United Services Officers' (Wellington).

FRASER, Kerr; *see* Fraser, W. K.

FRASER, Louis Nathaniel B.; *see* Blache-Fraser.

FRASER, Air Marshal Sir Paterson; *see* Fraser, Air Marshal Sir H. P.

FRASER, Peter Marshall, MC 1944; MA; FBA 1960; Fellow of All Souls College, Oxford, since 1954; Lecturer in Hellenistic History, 1948-64, Reader since 1964; *b* 6 April 1918; *y s* of late Archibald Fraser; *m* 1st, 1940, Catharine, *d* of late Prebendary Heaton-Renshaw (marr. diss.); one *s* three *d*; 2nd, 1955, Ruth Elsbeth, *d* of late F. Renfer, Bern, Switzerland; two *s*; 3rd, 1973, Barbara Ann Stewart, *d* of late L. E. C. Norbury, FRCS. *Educ:* City of London Sch.; Brasenose Coll., Oxford (Hon. Fellow 1977). Seaforth Highlanders, 1941-45; Military Mission to Greece, 1943-45. Sen. Scholar, Christ Church, Oxford, 1946-47; Junior Proctor, Oxford Univ., 1960-61; Domestic Bursar, All Souls Coll., 1962-65. Dir, British Sch. of Archaeol. at Athens, 1968-71. Vis. Prof. of Classical Studies, Indiana Univ., 1973-74. Chm., Managing Cttee, Soc. of Afghan Studies, 1972-. *Publications:* (with G. E. Bean) The Rhodian Peraea and Islands, 1954; (with T. Rönne) Boeotian and West Greek Tombstones, 1957; Rostovtzeff, Social and Economic History of the Roman Empire, 2nd edn, revised, 1957; Samothrace, The Inscriptions, (Vol. ii, Excavations of Samothrace), 1960; E. Löfstedt, Roman Literary Portraits, trans. from the Swedish (Romare), 1958; The Wares of Autolycus; Selected Literary Essays of Alice Meynell (ed.), 1965; E. Kjellberg and G. Säflund, Greek and Roman Art, trans. from the Swedish (Grekisk och romersk konst), 1968; Ptolemaic Alexandria, 1972; Rhodian Funerary Monuments, 1977; articles in learned journals. *Address:* All Souls College, Oxford. *Club:* Athenæum.

FRASER, Sir Robert; *see* Fraser, Sir W. R.

FRASER, Sir Robert Brown, Kt 1949; OBE 1944; Chairman, Independent Television News, 1971-74; *b* 26 Sept. 1904; *s* of Reginald and Thusnelda Fraser, Adelaide, South Australia; *m* 1931, Betty Harris; one *d*. *Educ:* St Peter's Sch., Adelaide; Trinity Coll., Univ. of Melbourne (BA); Univ. of London (BSc Econ.). Leader Writer Daily Herald, 1930-39; Empire Div., Ministry of Information, 1939-41; Dir, Publications Div., Ministry of Information, 1941-45; Controller of Production, Ministry of Information, 1945-46; Dir-Gen., Central Office of Information, 1946-54; Dir-General, ITA, 1954-70. Hon. Fellow, LSE, 1965. Hon. Life Mem., Royal Inst. of Public Administration, 1975; Editor, New Whitehall Series, for Royal Inst. of Public Administration, 1951-70. Gold Medal, Royal Television Soc., 1970. *Address:* Flat 5M, Portman Mansions, Chiltern Street, W1. *Club:* Athenæum.

FRASER, Ronald Petrie, CB 1972; Secretary, Scottish Home and Health Department, 1972-77; *b* 2 June 1917; *yr s* of late T. Petrie Fraser, Elgin; *m* 1962, Ruth Wright Anderson, Edinburgh; one *d*. *Educ:* Daniel Stewart's Coll., Edinburgh; University of Edinburgh; The Queen's Coll., Oxford. Joined Dept of Health for Scotland for work on emergency hosp. service, 1940; Asst Private Sec. to Sec. of State for Scotland, 1944; Cabinet Office, 1947; Sec., Scottish Hosp. Endowments Commn, 1950; Asst Sec., Dept of Health for Scotland, 1954; Asst Sec., Scottish Education Dept, 1961; Under-Sec., 1963; Under-Sec., 1968-71, Dep. Sec., 1971, Min. of Agriculture, Fisheries and Food. *Recreations:* walking, music. *Address:* 40A Lygon Road, Edinburgh EH16 5QA. *T:* 031-667 8298. *Clubs:* New, Scottish Arts (Edinburgh).

FRASER, Rt. Hon. Thomas, PC 1964; Chairman, Commission for Local Authority Accounts in Scotland, since 1974; *b* 18 Feb. 1911; *s* of Thomas and Mary Fraser, Kirkmuirhill, Lanarks; *m* 1935, Janet M. Scanlon, Lesmahagow, Lanarks; one *s* one *d*. *Educ:* Lesmahagow Higher Grade Sch. Left school 1925 and started work in a coal-mine (underground); worked underground, 1925-43; Miners' Union Branch Official, 1938-43; Sec., Lanark Constituency Labour Party, 1939-43; MP (Lab) Hamilton Div. of Lanarks, 1943-67; Joint Parliamentary Under-Sec. of State, Scottish Office, 1945-51; Minister of Transport, 1964-65. Member: Royal Commn on Local Govt in Scotland, 1966-69; Highlands and Islands Develt Bd, 1967-70; Chm., N of Scotland Hydro-Electric Bd, 1967-73; Mem., S of Scotland Electricity Bd, 1967-73; Chairman: Scottish Local Govt Staff Commn, 1973-77; Scottish Local Govt Property Commn, 1976-77. Freeman of Hamilton, 1964. *Address:* 15 Broompark Drive, Lesmahagow, Lanarks.

FRASER, Thomas Cameron, CB 1966; MBE 1945; TD 1951; Principal, Advice Centre on the Organisation of Industrial and Commercial Representation, since 1974; *b* 21 Jan. 1909; *er s* of late Dr Thomas Fraser, CBE, DSO, TD, DL, LLD, Aberdeen; *m* 1934, Dorothy Graham (*d* 1966), *y d* of late Graham Partridge, East Grinstead; two *s* two *d*. *Educ:* Fettes; University Coll., Oxford. Lloyds Bank Ltd, 1931-39. Served RA (TA), 1939-45; Major (GSO2) War Office, 1942; Lt-Col (GSO1) HQ, AA Command, 1943-45. Board of Trade (Central Price Regulation Cttee), 1946. Sec. Wool Textile Delegation, and Wool (and Allied) Textile Employers' Council, Bradford, 1947; appointment changed to Dir, 1958; Industrial Dir, NEDC, 1962-70; Chm., EDC for Wool Textile Industry, 1970-77; Dir, Commn of Inquiry into Industrial Representation, 1970-72; Dir-Gen. (temp.), NEDO, 1973. Mem. British Delegation to International Labour Conferences, Geneva, 1953, 1954, 1956, 1957, 1959, and European Regional Conf., ILO, 1955. Mem., BBC North Regional Advisory Council, 1960-62. *Recreations:* golf, walking. *Address:* 25 Bedford Gardens, W8. *T:* 01-727 0674. *Clubs:* United Oxford & Cambridge University, Royal Automobile.
See also Baron Fraser of Kilmorack.

FRASER, Prof. Thomas Russell Cumming, MD, FRCP; Deputy Director, Medical Research Council, New Zealand; *s* of Malcolm Fraser and Caroline (née Watson); *Educ:* Otago Univ. Medical School. MB, ChB (distinction) 1932; MRCP 1936; DPM (Eng.) 1937; MD (NZ) 1945; FRCP 1948. Hallett Prize, 1935; NZ University Travel Fellowship, 1935; Rockefeller Travel Fellowship, 1938. Formerly Asst Med. Officer, Maudsley Hosp.; Research Fellow in Medicine, Harvard Univ.; Reader in Medicine, Postgrad. Med. Sch., London; Prof. of Clinical Endocrinology in Univ. of London, RPMS, 1957-74. Member: Assoc. Physicians of Gt Brit.; Med. Research Soc. Hon. DSc, NZ. *Publications:* contribs to medical journals. *Address:* c/o Medical Research Council of New Zealand, Department of Surgery, Medical School, Auckland 3, New Zealand.
See also Very Rev. Dr I. W. Fraser.

FRASER, Veronica Mary; Headmistress, Godolphin School, Salisbury, since 1968; *b* 19 April 1933; *o d* of late Archibald Fraser. *Educ:* Richmond County Sch. for Girls; St Hugh's Coll., Oxford. Head of English Department: The Alice Ottley Sch., Worcester, 1962-65; Guildford County Sch. for Girls, 1965-67 (also Librarian). *Address:* Godolphin School, Salisbury, Wilts. *T:* 3059.

FRASER, William, CBE 1969; CEng, FIEE; Chairman, BICC Ltd, 1973-76; *b* 15 July 1911; *e s* of late Alexander Fraser and Elizabeth Williamson Fraser; *m* 1938, Kathleen Mary Moore (*d* 1971), 3rd *d* of late Alderman and Mrs J. W. Moore; two *s* two *d*. *Educ:* Glasgow High Sch.; University Coll. London (BSc Hons). Production Engr, Joseph Lucas Ltd, 1935-37; joined Scottish Cables Ltd, 1937; Dir, 1938; Managing Dir, 1948-62; Chm., 1958-76; Chm., Scottish Cables (S Africa) Ltd, 1950-76; Dir, British Insulated Callender's Cables Ltd, 1959, on entry of Scottish Cables into BICC Group; Exec. Dir (Overseas Cos), 1962-64; Managing Dir (Overseas), 1964-68; Managing Dir (Overseas & Construction Gp), 1968-70; Dep. Chm. and Chief Exec., 1971-73. Vice-Chm., Phillips Cables Ltd (of Canada), 1961-70; Dir and Dep. Chm., Metal Manufactures Ltd (of Australia) and Subsidiaries, 1962-70; Chm., Balfour, Beatty & Co. Ltd, 1969-70; Director: Anglesey Aluminium Ltd, 1971-75; Clydesdale Bank Ltd, 1974-. Chm., Scottish Council of FBI, 1959-61. Pres., Electrical and Electronics Industries Benevolent Assoc., 1974-75. *Recreations:* fishing, shooting, golf. *Address:* Fenwick Lodge, Ewenfield Road, Ayr. *T:* Ayr 65547; 87 Whitehall Court, SW1. *T:* 01-930 3160. *Clubs:* Royal Automobile; Royal Scottish Automobile (Glasgow).

FRASER, William James; JP; Lord Provost of Aberdeen, since 1977; *b* 31 Dec. 1921; *s* of late William and Jessie Fraser; *m* 1961, Mary Ann; three *s* one *d*. *Educ:* York Street Sch., Aberdeen. Mem., Scottish Exec., Labour Party, 1949-74 (Chm., 1962-63). Pres., Aberdeen Trades Council, 1952. JP Aberdeen. *Address:* 79 Salisbury Place, Aberdeen. *T:* Aberdeen 51040.

FRASER, (William) Kerr; Deputy Secretary, Scottish Office, since 1975; *b* 18 March 1929; *s* of A. M. Fraser and Rachel Kerr; *m* 1956, Marion Anne Forbes; three *s* one *d*. *Educ:* Eastwood Sch., Clarkston; Glasgow Univ. (MA, LLB). Joined Scottish Home Dept, 1955; Private Sec. to Parliamentary Under-Sec., 1959, and to Secretary of State for Scotland, 1966-67; Civil Service Fellow, Univ. of Glasgow, 1963-64; Asst Sec., Regional Development Div., 1967-71; Under Sec., Scottish Home and Health Dept, 1971-75. *Address:* 14 Braid Avenue, Edinburgh EH10 6EE. *T:* 031-447 3751.

FRASER, Sir (William) Robert, KCB 1952 (CB 1939); KBE 1944; MA; *b* Hemingford Grey, St Ives, Hunts, 9 Oct. 1891; *es* of Garden William Fraser (W. F. Garden) and Ethel Mary Syson; *g g s* of Francis Fraser, Findrack, Aberdeenshire; *m* 1915, Phyllis (*d* 1970), *d* of William Smith, London; three *s* one *d*. *Educ:* Christ's Hosp.; University Coll., Oxford (MA). First Mods 1912; First Lit. Hum. 1914; entered Treasury, 1914; Principal, 1919; Asst Sec., 1932; Princ. Asst Sec., 1934-39; Sec., Dept of Health for Scotland, 1939-43; Sec. War Damage Commn, 1943, and Central Land Bd, 1947; Dep. Chm. and Permanent Sec., 1949-59; Chm. (part-time), 1959-62. Vice-Pres., Lawn Tennis Assoc. (Chm., 1958, Hon. Treasurer, 1962-70); Vice-Pres. Civil Service Sports Council; Pres., Civil Service Lawn Tennis Assoc. *Recreations:* gardening, crosswords, radio, chess, large print books. *Address:* 33 Hollycroft Avenue, NW3. *T:* 01-435 3566. *Clubs:* United Oxford & Cambridge University, All-England Lawn Tennis.

FRASER DARLING, Sir Frank, Kt 1970; DSc, PhD, LLD; FIBiol, FRSE; *b* 23 June 1903; *m* 1st, 1925, Marian Fraser; one *s*; 2nd, 1948, Averil Morley (*d* 1957); two *s* one *d*; 3rd, 1960, Christina Macinnes Brotchie. *Educ:* University of Edinburgh. On Agricultural Staff, Bucks County Council, 1924-27; Research Student, Inst. of Animal Genetics, Univ. of Edinburgh, 1928-30; Chief Officer, Imperial Bureau of Animal Genetics, 1930-34; Leverhulme Research Fellow, 1933-36; Carnegie Research Fellow, 1936-39; Dir, West Highland Survey, 1944-50; Rockefeller Special Research Fellow, 1950. Senior Lectr in Ecology and Conservation, Univ. of Edinburgh, 1953-58; Vice-Pres., Conservation Foundn, Washington, DC, 1959-72. Member: Royal Commn on Environmental Pollution, 1970-73; Nature Conservancy, 1969-73. Reith Lectr, 1969. Mungo Park Medallist, Royal Scottish Geographical Society, 1947; Centenary Medallist, US Nat. Park Service, 1972. Hon. LLD Glasgow; Hon. DSc: Heriot-Watt; New Univ. of Ulster; Williams Coll., Mass. Commandeur, Order of Golden Ark (Netherlands), 1973. *Publications:* Biology of the Fleece of the Scottish Mountain Blackface Breed of Sheep, 1932; Animal Breeding in the British Empire, 1934; Wild Life Conservation, 1934; A Herd of Red Deer, 1937; Bird Flocks and the Breeding Cycle, 1938; Wild Country, 1938; A Naturalist on Rona, 1939; The Seasons and the Farmer, 1939; Island Years, 1940; The Seasons and the Fisherman, 1941; The Story of Scotland, 1942; Wild Life of Britain, 1943; Island Farm, 1943; The Care of Farm Animals, 1943; Crofting Agriculture, 1945; Natural History in the Highlands and Islands, 1947; Report of the West Highland Survey, 1952; (with A. S. Leopold) Alaska: an Ecological Reconnaissance, 1953; West Highland Survey, 1955; Pelican in the Wilderness; Odyssey of a Naturalist, 1956; Wild Life in an African Territory, 1960; An Ecological Rennaissance of the Mara Plains in Kenya Colony, 1960; The Unity of Ecology, 1963; The Nature of a National Park, 1968; Impacts of Man on the Biosphere, 1969; Wilderness and Plenty (Reith Lectures), 1970; scientific papers. *Recreations:* watching animals, English literature. *Address:* Lochyhill, Forres, Moray. *T:* Forres 2664. *Clubs:* Athenæum; New (Edinburgh).

FRASER McLUSKEY, Rev. James; see McLuskey.

FRASER ROBERTS, John Alexander; see Roberts.

FRASER-TYTLER, Christian Helen, CBE (mil.) 1941; TD; JP; Senior Controller ATS, retired; *b* 23 Aug. 1897; *d* of John Campbell Shairp, Houstoun; *m* 1919, Col Neil Fraser-Tytler, DSO, Croix de Guerre (*d* 1937); two *s d*. *Educ:* Home. Foreign Office, 1917-19; War Office, 1939-43; AA Command until 1945 (TD). JP Inverness-shire, 1958. *Recreation:* fishing. *Address:* Old Clune House, Aldourie, Inverness. *T:* Dores 216; 43 Sussex Square, W2. *T:* 01-723 2565.
See also Sir Thomas David Erskine, Bt, Sir Patrick Morgan.

FRAYN, Michael; writer; *b* 8 Sept. 1933; *s* of late Thomas Allen Frayn and Violet Alice Lawson; *m* 1960, Gillian Palmer; three *d*. *Educ:* Kingston Gram. Sch.; Emmanuel Coll., Cambridge. Reporter, Guardian, 1957-59; Columnist, Guardian, 1959-62; Columnist, Observer, 1962-68. TV: Jamie (play), 1968; Birthday (play) 1969; Imagine a City Called Berlin (documentary), 1975; Vienna—The Mask of Gold (documentary), 1977; stage plays: The Two of Us, 1970; The Sandboy, 1971; Alphabetical Order, 1975; Donkeys' Years, 1976; Clouds, 1976. Somerset Maugham Award, 1966; Hawthornden Prize, 1967; Nat. Press Award, 1970; Evening Standard Drama Award (Best Comedy), 1975; Soc. of West End Theatre (Best Comedy). *Publications:* collections of columns: The Day of the Dog, 1962; The Book of Fub, 1963; On the Outskirts, 1964; At Bay in Gear Street, 1967; *non-fiction:* Constructions, 1974; *novels:* The Tin Men, 1965; The Russian Interpreter, 1966; Towards the End of the Morning, 1967; A Very Private Life, 1968; Sweet Dreams, 1973. *Address:* c/o Elaine Greene Ltd, 31 Newington Green, N16.

FREARS, John Newton, CBE 1955; MA; JP; Pro-Chancellor, Leicester University, since 1962; *b* 29 June 1906; *s* of John Russell Frears and Minnie Keighley Frears (*née* Cape); *m* 1931, Elaine Pochin; one *s* one *d*. *Educ:* Gresham's Sch., Holt; Trinity Coll., Cambridge. Frears & Blacks Ltd, 1928-70 (Chm., 1937-70); Dir, Nabisco-Frears Biscuits Ltd, 1964-71. Dir of Bakeries for UK, Min. of Food, 1941-45. Hon. LLD Leicester, 1967. *Address:* The Gatehouse, Causeway Lane, Cropston, Leics. *T:* Anstey 2581.

FREDERICK, Sir Charles Boscawen, 10th Bt *cr* 1723; *b* 11 April 1919; *s* of Sir Edward Boscawen Frederick, 9th Bt, CVO and Edith Katherine (Kathleen) Cortlandt (*d* 1970), *d* of late Col W. H. Mulloy, RE; *S* father, 1956; *m* 1949, Rosemary, *er d* of late Lt-Col R. J. H. Baddeley, MC; two *s* two *d*. *Educ:* Eton. 2nd Lieut Grenadier Guards, 1942; served N Africa and Italy, 1943-45 (despatches); Capt. 1945; Palestine, 1946-47 (despatches); Malaya, 1948-49; Egypt, 1952-53; Major, 1953. Member: London Stock Exchange, 1954-62; Provincial Brokers Stock Exchange, 1962 (Mem. Council, 1966; Dep. Chm. 1972); Stock Exchange Council, and Chm., Provincial Unit, 1973-75. JP 1960. General Commissioner of Income Tax, 1966. *Recreations:* sailing, fishing. *Heir: s* Christopher St John Frederick, *b* 28 June 1950. *Address:* The Granary, Lerryn, Lostwithiel, Cornwall. *Club:* Royal Fowey Yacht.

FREDERICTON, Bishop of, since 1971; **Rt. Rev. Harold Lee Nutter,** DD; *b* 29 Dec. 1923; *s* of William L. Nutter and Lillian A. Joyce; *m* 1946, Edith M. Carew; one *s* one *d*. *Educ:* Mount Allison Univ. (BA 1944); Dalhousie Univ. (MA 1947); Univ. of King's College (MSLitt 1947). Rector: Simonds and Upham, 1947-51; Woodstock, 1951-57; St Mark, Saint John, NB, 1957-60; Dean of Fredericton, 1960-71. Co-Chairman, NB Task Force on Social Development, 1970-71; Mem., Adv. Cttee to Sec. of State for Canada on Multi-culturalism, 1973. Hon. DD, Univ. of King's College, 1960; Hon. LLD, Mount Allison Univ., 1972. *Publication:* (jointly) New Brunswick Task Force Report on Social Development, 1971. *Address:* 791 Brunswick Street, Fredericton, NB, Canada. *T:* 4558667.

FREEBODY, Air Vice-Marshal Wilfred Leslie, CB 1951; CBE 1943; AFC; RAF Technical Branch; Director of Work Study, at Air Ministry. Squadron Leader, 1937; Acting Air Commodore commanding 226 Group, Air Cdre, 1949; Actg Air Vice-Marshal, 1956; Air Vice-Marshal, 1957. Has Order of Polonia Restituta 3rd class, of Poland.

FREEDMAN, Charles; Commissioner, Customs and Excise, since 1972; *b* 15 Oct. 1925; *s* of late Solomon Freedman, OBE, and of Lilian Freedman; *m* 1949, Sarah Sadie King; one *s* two *d*. *Educ:* Westcliff High Sch.; Cheltenham Grammar Sch.; Trinity Coll., Cambridge (Sen. Schol., BA). Entered HM Customs and Excise, 1947; Asst Sec., 1963. *Address:* Alexander House, 21 Victoria Avenue, Southend-on-Sea, Essex SS99 1AA. *T:* Southend-on-Sea 48944. *Clubs:* Civil Service; Essex Yacht.

FREEDMAN, Louis; Chairman, Ravenseft Properties Ltd; Director, Land Securities Investment Trust Ltd, since 1958; Proprietor, Cliveden Stud; *b* 5 Feb. 1917; 4th *s* of Sampson and Leah Freedman; *m* 1st, 1944, Cara Kathlyn Abrahamson (marr. diss.); one *s* one *d*; 2nd, 1960, Valerie Clarke; one *s*. *Educ:* University College School. FSVA. TA, RE, 1938; commnd RA, 1943; Devonshire Regt, 1944. Mem., Race Relations Bd, 1968-77. Chm., Nat. Assoc. Property Owners, 1971-72; Pres., Racehorse Owners Assoc., 1972-74. Vice-Chm., NE Thames RHA, 1975-. Governor, Royal Hosp. of St Bartholomew the Great, 1971-74; Special Trustee, St Bartholomew's Hosp., 1974-. *Recreations:* horseracing, gardening. *Address:* 51/53 Brick Street, Piccadilly, W1Y 7DU; Cliveden Stud House, Taplow, Maidenhead, Berks. *Clubs:* Garrick; Jockey (Newmarket).

FREEDMAN, Hon. Samuel; Hon. Chief Justice Freedman; Chief Justice of Manitoba, since 1971; *b* Russia, 1908; *s* of Nathan Freedman and Ada (*née* Foxman); came to Canada, 1911; *m* 1934, Claris Brownie Udow; one *s* two *d. Educ:* Winnipeg schs; Univ. of Manitoba. BA 1929, LLB 1933. Called to Manitoba Bar, 1933; KC (Canada) 1944; Judge, Court of Queen's Bench, Manitoba, 1952, Court of Appeal 1960. Chancellor, Univ. of Manitoba, 1959-68; Pres., Manitoba Bar Assoc., 1951-52; Mem. Bd of Governors, Hebrew Univ., Jerusalem, 1955-; Chm., Rhodes Scholarship Selection Cttee, Manitoba, 1956-66; Pres., Medico-Legal Soc. of Manitoba, 1954-55; Mem. Adv. Bd, Centre of Criminology, Univ. of Toronto; Mem. Bd of Dirs, Confedn Centre of the Arts in Charlottetown; one-man Industrial Inquiry Commn, CNR run-throughs, 1964-65. Holds numerous hon. degrees. *Publications:* Report of Industrial Inquiry Commission on Canadian National Railways Run-Throughs, 1965; (chapter) Admissions and Confessions, in, Studies in Canadian Criminal Evidence, ed Salhany and Carter, 1972; contrib. Canadian Bar Review. *Recreations:* walking, golf, reading. *Address:* 425 Cordova Street, Winnipeg, Manitoba R3N 1A5, Canada. *T:* 489-2922. *Club:* Glendale Country (Winnipeg).

FREELAND, Lt-Gen. Sir Ian (Henry), GBE 1971; KCB 1968 (CB 1964); DSO 1944; DL; *b* 14 Sept. 1912; *s* of late Maj.-Gen. Sir H. F. E. Freeland, KCIE, CB, DSO, MVO, RE; *m* 1940, Mary, *d* of late Gen. Sir C. C. Armitage, KCB, CMG, DSO; two *s* one *d. Educ:* Wellington Coll.; RMC, Sandhurst. Commissioned into the Norfolk Regt, 1932; Adjt, 1940; Bde Major 7 Inf. Bde, 1942; GSO2 War Office (MT2), 1943; OC 7 Royal Norfolk, 1944; OC 1/5 Queen's, 1944-45; Col GS, HQ 8 Corps Dist, 1945-46; 2nd i/c 4th Armoured Brigade, 1946; GSO1 (SD), HQ BAOR, 1946-47; GSO1, BAOR Trg Centre, 1947-48; Comdt All Arms Training Centre, 1948-49; GSO1, War Office (Western Union), 1949-50; GSO1, Staff Coll., Camberley, 1951-53; OC 2 R Inniskilling Fusiliers, 1954-56; Comdr, 12 Inf. Bde, 1956-57; Imperial Defence Coll., 1958; Brigadier Q (Ops) War Office, 1959-61; GOC 54 (E Anglian) Div./Dist, 1961-63; GOC, E Africa Comd, 1963; British Land Forces, Kenya, and Kenya Army, 1963-64; Vice Adjt-Gen., MoD, 1965-68; Deputy CGS, 1968; GOC and Director of Operations, N Ireland, 1969-71; retired June 1971. Col, Royal Anglian Regt, 1971-76 (Dep. Col 1966-71). DL Norfolk, 1972. Croix de Guerre, 1940, with Palm (Belgium); Chevalier, Order of Crown, with Palm (Belgium). *Recreations:* shooting, cricket, golf, tennis. *Address:* Foxley Lodge, near Dereham, Norfolk. *Clubs:* Army and Navy; MCC; I Zingari; Free Foresters.

FREELAND, John Redvers, CMG 1973; HM Diplomatic Service; Second Legal Adviser, Foreign and Commonwealth Office, since 1976; *b* 16 July 1927; *o s* of C. Redvers Freeland and Freda Freeland (*née* Walker); *m* 1952, Sarah Mary, *er d* of late S. Pascoe Hayward, QC; one *s* one *d. Educ:* Stowe; Corpus Christi Coll., Cambridge. Royal Navy, 1945 and 1948-51. Called to Bar, Lincoln's Inn, 1952; Mem. *ad eundem,* Middle Temple. Asst Legal Adviser, FO, 1954-63, and 1965-67; Legal Adviser, HM Embassy, Bonn, 1963-65; Legal Counsellor, FCO (formerly FO), 1967-70; Counsellor (Legal Advr), UK Mission to UN, NY, 1970-73; Legal Counsellor, FCO, 1973-76. *Address:* c/o Foreign and Commonwealth Office, SW1. *Club:* Travellers'.

FREELING, Nicolas; writer since 1960; *b* 1927, of English parents; *m* 1954, Cornelia Termes; four *s* one *d. Educ:* primary and secondary schs. Hotel-restaurant cook, throughout Europe, 1945-60; novelist, 1960-. *Publications:* (numerous trans.) Love in Amsterdam, 1961; Because of the Cats, 1962; Gun before Butter, 1962; Valparaiso, 1963; Double Barrel, 1963; Criminal Conversation, 1964; King of the Rainy Country, 1965; Dresden Green, 1966; Strike Out Where Not Applicable, 1967; This is the Castle, 1968; Tsing-Boum, 1969; Kitchen Book, 1970; Over the High Side, 1971; Cook Book, 1971; A Long Silence, 1972; Dressing of Diamond, 1974; What Are the Bugles Blowing For?, 1975; Lake Isle, 1976. *Address:* c/o William Heinemann Ltd, Queen Street, W1X 8BE.

FREEMAN, Sir Bernard; *see* Freeman, Sir N. B.

FREEMAN, David John; Senior Partner, D. J. Freeman & Co., Solicitors; *b* 25 Feb. 1928; *s* of Meyer and Rebecca Freeman; *m* 1950, Iris Margaret Alberge; two *s* one *d. Educ:* Christ's Coll., Finchley. Lieut, Army, 1946-48. Admitted Solicitor, 1952. Dept of Trade Inspector into the affairs of AEG Telefunken (UK) Ltd, and Credit Collections Ltd, 1977. *Recreations:* reading, gardening. *Address:* Flat 10, 6 Hyde Park Gardens, W2. *T:* 01-262 0895; Upper Neatham Mill, Holybourne, Hants. *Club:* Reform.

FREEMAN, Dr Ernest Allan, FIEE, FIMA; Rector, Sunderland Polytechnic, since 1976; *b* 16 Jan. 1932; *s* of William Freeman and Margaret Sinclair; *m* 1957, Mary Jane Peterson; two *d*. *Educ:* Sunderland Technical Coll.; Univ. of Durham. BSc, PhD, Durham; DSc Newcastle upon Tyne; MA (Oxon) 1972. Sunderland Forge & Engineering Co. Ltd. 1949-55; English Electric Co., 1957-58; Ferranti Ltd (Edinburgh), 1958-59; Sunderland Polytechnic, 1959-72; Oxford Univ., 1972-76. *Publications:* contribs in field of control theory and engineering to Wireless Engr, Proc. IEE, Jl of Electronics and Control, Trans AIEE, Electronic Technol., Control, Jl of Optimisation Theory and Application, Trans Soc. of Instrument Technol., Proc. Internat. Fedn for Analogue Computation, Internat. Jl of Control. *Recreations:* swimming, browsing around antique shops. *Address:* Westfield Hall, Mowbray Road, Sunderland SR2 8HX. *T:* Sunderland 79529.

FREEMAN, George Vincent; Under-Secretary (Legal), Treasury Solicitor's Department, 1973-76, retired; *b* 30 April 1911; *s* of Harold Vincent Freeman and Alice Freeman; *m* 1945, Margaret Nightingale; one *d. Educ:* Denstone Coll., Rocester. Admitted Solicitor, 1934; in private practice Birmingham until 1940. Served RN, 1940-46, Lieut RNVR. Legal Asst, Treasury Solicitor's Dept, 1946; Sen. Legal Asst 1950; Asst Treasury Solicitor 1964. *Recreations:* gardening, photography. *Address:* 8 Shelley Close, Ashley Heath, Ringwood, Hants. *T:* Forest Edge 7102. *Club:* Naval.

FREEMAN, Harold Webber; Author; *b* 1899; *s* of Charles Albert Freeman and Emma Mary Ann Mills; *m* Elizabeth Boedecker. *Educ:* City of London Sch.; Christ Church, Oxford (classical scholar). 1st class Hon. Mods, 2nd class Lit. Hum. Main background was work on the land, mostly organic gardening; travelled in Europe (foot and bicycle); casual work as linguist (translation, monitoring, travel trade). Has lived mostly in Suffolk, but also, for long periods, in Italy. *Publications:* Joseph and His Brethren, 1928; Down in the Valley, 1930; Fathers of Their People, 1932; Pond Hall's Progress, 1933; Hester and Her Family, 1936; Andrew to the Lions, 1938; Chaffinch's, 1941; Blenheim Orange, 1949; The Poor Scholar's Tale, 1954; Round the Island: Sardinia Re-explored, 1956. *Address:* c/o National Westminster Bank Ltd, Princes Street, Ipswich.

FREEMAN, Ifan Charles Harold, CMG 1964; TD 1961; Registrar, University of Malawi, 1965-72, retired; *b* 11 Sept. 1910; *s* of late C. E. D. W. Freeman; *m* 1937, Enid, *d* of late Edward Hallum; two *d. Educ:* Friars Sch., Bangor; Univ. of Wales (MA). Served with Royal Artillery, 1939-46 (Major; despatches). Colonial Service: Kenya, 1946-58; Nyasaland, 1958-65. *Recreation:* gardening. *Address:* Swn y Wylan, Marianglas, Gwynedd. *Clubs:* Royal Commonwealth; Mombasa (Kenya).

FREEMAN, His Eminence Cardinal James Darcy; *see* Sydney, Archbishop of, (RC).

FREEMAN, Rt. Hon. John, PC 1966; MBE 1943; Chairman: London Weekend Television, since 1971; Independent Television News, since 1976; LWT (Holdings) Ltd, since 1976; *b* 19 Feb. 1915; *e s* of Horace Freeman, barrister-at-law, New Square, Lincoln's Inn; *m* 1st, 1938, Elizabeth Allen Johnston (marr. diss., 1948); 2nd, 1948, Margaret Ista Mabel Kerr (*d* 1957); one adopted *d*; 3rd, 1962, Catherine Dove (marr. diss. 1976); two *s* one *d*; 4th, 1976, Judith Mitchell; one *d. Educ:* Westminster Sch.; Brasenose Coll., Oxford (Hon. Fellow, 1968). Advertising Consultant, 1937-40. Active Service, 1940-45. MP (Lab) Watford Div. of Herts, 1945-50, Borough of Watford, 1950-55; PPS to Sec. of State for War, 1945-46; Financial Sec., War Office, 1946; Parliamentary Under Sec. of State for War, April 1947; Leader, UK Defence Mission to Burma, 1947; Parliamentary Sec., Ministry of Supply, 1947-51, resigned. Asst Editor, New Statesman, 1951-58; Deputy Editor, 1958-60; Editor, 1961-65. British High Commissioner in India, 1965-68; British Ambassador in Washington, 1969-71. Vice-Pres., Royal Television Soc., 1975-. *Address:* c/o LWT (Holdings) Ltd, South Bank Television Centre, Kent House, SE1.

FREEMAN, Sir (John) Keith (Noel), 2nd Bt *cr* 1945; Director; Associated Leisure Ltd; *b* 28 July 1923; *o s* of Air Chief Marshal Sir Wilfrid Rhodes Freeman, 1st Bt, GCB, DSO, MC, and Gladys, *d* of J. Mews; *S* father 1953; *m* 1946, Patricia Denison, *yr d* of late C. W. Thomas, Sandown, IoW; one *s* one *d. Educ:* Rugby; Christ Church, Oxford. Served War of 1939-45: Flight-Lieut RAF, Europe and Middle East. Joined Courtaulds Ltd, 1946; work study engr, then Asst Manager, Weaving Mill, 1946-53; Glanzstoff-Courtaulds GmbH, Cologne, Germany, 1953-57; Commercial Dir, Courtelle Div., 1957-62; Dir, Viyella International Ltd, 1962; Commercial Dir, then Man. Dir,

Monsanto Textiles SA, 1963-67; Regional Dir, International Wool Secretariat, 1967; Dir, LRC International Ltd, 1968-69; Man. Dir, LR Industries Ltd, 1968-69; Chm., Aristoc Ltd, 1971-73; Dir, Associated Leisure Ltd, 1973-75. *Heir: s* James Robin Freeman, *b* 21 July 1955. *Address:* c/o Midland Bank Ltd, 151 Hoe Street, Walthamstow, E17. *Club:* Hurlingham.

FREEMAN, Joseph William, OBE 1968; Director of Social Service, Leeds, since 1970; *b* 8 April 1914; *s* of Thomas and Emma Freeman; *m* 1939, Louise King; one *s* one *d*. *Educ:* Liverpool Univ.; Toynbee Hall. CQSW. Qual. social worker; Probation Service, Birmingham, 1938; served War of 1939-45: Army, 1940, commnd RA, 1941; Probation Service, Liverpool, 1946; Children's Officer: Warrington, 1948; Bolton, 1951; Sheffield, 1955. *Publications:* papers in social work jls. *Recreation:* music. *Address:* 41 Tredgold Avenue, Leeds LS16 9BS. *T:* Leeds 672315.

FREEMAN, Sir (Nathaniel) Bernard, Kt 1967; CBE 1956; Chairman, Metro-Goldwyn-Mayer Pty Ltd, 1967, retired; *b* 1 Sept. 1896; *s* of Adolph and Malvina Freeman; *m* 1926, Marjorie Arabel (*née* Bloom); one *s* one *d*. *Educ:* Public Sch. and Xavier Coll., Melbourne. Served European War, 1914-18: 38th Bn, 3rd Div., First AIF, and Austr. Flying Corps; inaugurated free films to Austr. Troops, 1939-45. Founded Metro-Goldwyn-Mayer Austr., NZ and S Pacific, 1925; Man. Dir, Metro-Goldwyn-Mayer, 1925-66. First Mem. Chm., Motion Picture Distributors' Assoc. of Austr., 1939-41, also 1963. Chm. various cttees, appeals and trusts, 1945-; National Chm., UNICEF, 1952; Chm., World Refugee Year, NSW, 1960; Chm. of Trustees and Internat. Houses Appeal, Univs of Sydney and NSW; Chm., NSW and Canberra, ANZAC Memorial and Forest in Israel; Mem. Exec., Sydney Opera House Trust, 1962-69; mem. of many other cttees; Life Mem., RSL State Br., 1945-; Life Governor: Royal NSW Instn for Deaf and Blind Children; Vic. Ear and Eye Hosp.; Vic. Sch. for Deaf Children. *Recreations:* swimming, bowls. *Address:* The Penthouse, Santina, 85 Yarranabbe Road, Darling Point, NSW 2027, Australia. *Clubs:* American National (Sydney), City Bowling (Sydney).

FREEMAN, Patrick, MC 1943; QC 1970; *b* 8 June 1919; *s* of late Sir Ralph Freeman. *Educ:* Uppingham Sch.; Worcester Coll., Oxford (MA). Royal Artillery, 1939-45 (despatches 1944); Major. Called to Bar, Inner Temple, 1947. *Address:* Gray's Inn Chambers, Gray's Inn, WC1.

FREEMAN, Paul, ARCS, DSc (London), FRES; Keeper of Entomology, British Museum (Natural History), since 1968; *b* 26 May 1916; *s* of Samuel Mellor Freeman and Kate Burgis; *m* 1942, Audrey Margaret Long; two *d*. *Educ:* Brentwood Sch., Essex; Imperial Coll., London. Demonstrator in Entomology, Imperial Coll., 1938. Captain, RA and Army Operational Research Group, 1940-45. Lecturer in Entomology, Imperial Coll., 1945-47. Asst Keeper, Dept of Entomology, British Museum (Nat. Hist.), 1947-64, Dep. Keeper, 1964-68, Keeper, 1968. Hon. Sec., Royal Entomological Soc. of London, 1958-62 (Vice-Pres., 1956, 1957); Sec., XIIth Internat. Congress of Entomology, London, 1964. *Publications:* Diptera of Patagonia and South Chile, Pt III-Mycetophilidae, 1951; Simuliidae of the Ethiopian Region (with Botha de Meillon), 1953; numerous papers in learned jls, on taxonomy of Hemiptera and Diptera. *Recreations:* gardening, natural history. *Address:* Briardene, 75 Towncourt Crescent, Petts Wood, Orpington, Kent BR5 1PH. *T:* Orpington 27296.

FREEMAN, Sir Ralph, Kt 1970; CVO 1964; CBE 1952 (MBE (mil.) 1945); FICE, FCIT, FASCE; Senior Partner, Freeman, Fox & Partners, Consulting Engineers, since 1962 (Partner since 1947); *b* 3 Feb. 1911; *s* of late Sir Ralph Freeman and late Mary (*née* Lines); *m* 1939, Joan Elizabeth, *er d* of late Col J. G. Rose, DSO, VD, FRIC, Wynberg, Cape, S Africa; two *s* one *d*. *Educ:* Uppingham Sch.; Worcester Coll., Oxford (MA). Construction Engineer: Dorman Long & Co., S Africa, Rhodesia and Denmark, 1932-36 and 1937-39; Braithwaite & Co., 1936-37; on staff of Freeman, Fox & Partners, 1939-46, Admty and other war work; served RE, 1943-45 (Temp. Major) at Exp. Bridging Estab. and later seconded as bridging adviser to CE 21 Army Gp HQ, NW Europe campaign. Consulting Engr to the Queen for Sandringham Estate, 1949-76. Past Pres., Instn of Civil Engrs (Mem. Council, 1951-55 and 1957-61, Vice-Pres., 1962-66; Pres., 1966-67); Member: Governing Body, SE London Techn. Coll., 1952-58; Nat. Cons. Council to Min. of Works, 1952-56; Bd of Governors, Westminster Hosp., 1963-69; Council, Worcester Coll. Soc., 1964-; Adv. Council on Scientific Res. and Develt (MoD), 1966-69; Defence Scientific Adv. Council, 1969-72; Royal Fine Art Commn, 1968-; Council, Assoc. of Consulting Engrs, 1969-72, 1973-77, Chm., 1975-76; Governing Body, Imp. Coll. of Science and Technology, 1975-; Chm.,

Limpsfield Common Local Management Cttee, Nat. Trust, 1972-; Pres., Welding Inst., 1975-77. Col, Engr and Rly Staff Corps RE (T&AVR), 1963-76, Col comdg 1970-74. Hon. Mem., Instn Royal Engrs, 1971; Hon. FIMechE, 1971; Hon. Fellow, Rhodesian Instn of Engrs, 1969; FRSA. Kt, Order of Orange Nassau (Netherlands), 1945. *Publications:* several papers in Proc. ICE. *Recreations:* golf, carpentry, sailing. *Address:* c/o Freeman, Fox & Partners, 25 Victoria Street (South block), SW1H 0EX. *T:* 01-222 8050. *Clubs:* Athenæum, Army and Navy; Leander (Henley-on-Thames).
See also Patrick Freeman, D. L. Pearson.

FREEMAN, Richard Gavin; His Honour Judge Freeman; a Circuit Judge (formerly County Court Judge), since 1968; *b* 18 Oct. 1910; *s* of John Freeman, MD, and Violet Alice Leslie Hadden; *m* 1937, Marjorie Pear; one *s* two *d*; *m* 1961, Winifred Ann Bell. *Educ:* Charterhouse; Hertford Coll., Oxford. Called to Bar, Gray's Inn, 1947. Deputy Chairman, Warwicks Quarter Sessions, 1963-71. Hon. Major, RA. *Recreations:* cricket, gardening. *Address:* 10 Rees Street, N1. *Club:* Streatley Cricket.

FREEMAN, Captain Spencer, CBE 1942; Director, Hospitals Trust (1940) Ltd, Dublin; *b* Swansea, S Wales, 10 Dec. 1892; *s* of late A. Freeman; *m* 1924, Hilda Kathleen, *d* of Charles Simpkin Toler; one *s*. *Educ:* Johannesburg Coll., S Africa; Technical Institute, York, Pa, USA. Up to 1914, Automotive Industry USA; organised entire Mechanical Transport Salvage in France, War of 1914-18; subsequently Consulting Business Engineer; Emergency Services Organisation War of 1939-45, for restoration of production in all munitions factories, Min. of Aircraft Production, Min. of Supply and Admiralty; Min. of Aircraft Production: Dir, 1940-41; Prin. Dir of Regional and Emergency Services Organisation, 1941-44; Business Mem. Industrial and Export Council, Board of Trade, 1944-45. Member: Radio Board (a Cttee of British War Cabinet); Radio Planning and Production Cttee; Radio Production Executive, 1944-45. Served European War, 1914-19, non-commissioned ranks to Capt. (despatches, Mons Medal). MSAE. *Publications:* Production under Fire, 1967; You Can Get to the Top, 1972; Take your Measure, 1972. *Recreations:* all sports. *Address:* Knocklyon House, Templeogue, Dublin 14, Eire. *T:* Dublin 900234. *Clubs:* Naval and Military; Kildare Street and University (Dublin).

FREEMAN-GRENVILLE, family name of **Lady Kinloss.**

FREEMAN-THOMAS, family name of **Marquess of Willingdon.**

FREER, Charles Edward Jesse, DL; *b* 4 March 1901; *s* of late Canon S. Thorold Winckley, FSA and Elizabeth (*née* Freer); changed name to Freer by Deed Poll, 1922; *m* 1st, 1927, Violet Muriel (*d* 1944), *d* of H. P. Gee, CBE, Leicester; two *s* two *d*; 2nd, 1945, Cynthia Lilian, *d* of Leonard R. Braithwaite, FRCS, Leeds; two *d*. *Educ:* Radley Coll. Solicitor, 1924; served RA (TA) in France, 1940; DJAG in Iceland, 1941-42; at SHAEF, 1943-44, Lt-Col. Chm., Leicestershire QS, 1949-71. Chm. Leicester Diocesan Board of Finance, 1946-56; Chm. Mental Health Tribunal, Sheffield Regional Board, 1961-73. A Chm. of Industrial Tribunals, 1966-73. DL 1946, JP 1946-71, Leics. *Recreation:* sailing. *Address:* Shoal House, 48 Pearce Avenue, Parkstone, Dorset. *T:* Parkstone 748393. *Clubs:* East India, Devonshire, Sports and Public Schools; Parkstone Yacht.

FREER, Air Marshal Sir Robert William George, KCB 1977; CBE 1966; Air Officer Commanding No 18 Group, RAF, since Sept. 1975; *b* Darjeeling, 1 Sept. 1923; *s* of William Freer, Fair View, Stretton, Cirencester, Glos; *m* 1950, Margaret, 2nd *d* of late J. W. Elkington and of Mrs M. Elkington, Ruskington Manor, near Sleaford, Lincs; one *s* one *d*. *Educ:* Gosport Grammar Sch. Flying Instructor, S Africa and UK, 1944-47; RAF Coll., Cranwell, 1947-50; served 54 and 614 Fighter Sqdns, 1950-52; Central Fighter Estabt, 1952-54; commanded 92 Fighter Sqdn, 1955-57 (Queen's Commendation, 1955); Directing Staff, USAF Acad., 1958-60; Staff of Chief of Defence Staff, 1961-63; Station Comdr, RAF Seletar, 1963-66; DD Defence Plans (Air), MoD, 1966-67. Air ADC to the Queen, 1969-71; Dep. Comdt, RAF Staff Coll., 1969-71; SASO, HQ Near East Air Force, 1971-72; AOC 11 Group, 1972-75; Dir-Gen., Organisation (RAF), April-Sept. 1975; psa, 1957; pfc, 1960; IDC, 1968. Mem., RUSI. *Recreations:* golf, tennis. *Address:* RAF Northwood, Middlesex; c/o Lloyds Bank, 6 Pall Mall, SW1. *Club:* Royal Air Force.

FREESON, Rt. Hon. Reginald, PC 1976; MP (Lab) Brent East, since 1974 (Willesden East, 1964-74); Minister for Housing and Construction, Department of the Environment, since 1974; *b* 24 Feb. 1926. *Educ:* Jewish Orphanage, West Norwood. Served in Army, 1944-47. Middle East magazines and newspapers, 1946-

48. Joined Labour Party on return to United Kingdom, 1948, and Co-operative Party, 1958. Journalist, 1948-64. Magazines: John Bull, Illustrated, Today, Education. Free-lance for Everybody's Weekly, Tribune, News Chronicle, Daily Mirror, Reader's Digest, Associated Rediffusion TV. Asst Press Officer with Min. of Works, British Railways Board. Has written also for various publications and ghosted books and pamphlets. British rep. of Internat. News Service, HQ Geneva, 1960-62; Editor of Searchlight, against fascism and racialism, 1964-67. Radio and television: housing, urban planning, race relations and foreign affairs. Elected Willesden Borough Council, 1952; Alderman, 1955; Leader of Council, 1958-65; Chm. of new London Borough of Brent, 1964-65 (Alderman, 1964-68). PPS to Minister of Transport, 1964-67; Parly Secretary: Min. of Power, 1967-69; Min. of Housing and Local Govt, 1969-70; Labour Front-Bench Spokesman on Housing, 1970-74. Mem., Internat. Voluntary Service and UNA International Service. Sponsor, Willesden Housing Assocs. Founder-Chairman: Willesden (now Brent) Coun. of Social Service, 1960-62; Willesden Social Action, 1961-63; Willesden and Brent Friendship Council, 1959-63 (Vice-Pres., 1967); Chm., Warsaw Memorial Cttee, 1964-71; Mem., NCCL; Vice-Pres., Campaign for Democracy in Ulster; Mem., Jewish Welfare Bd, 1971 (Mem. Exec., 1973); Mem., Poale Zion, 1964-. *Address:* 159 Chevening Road, NW6.

FREETH, Andrew; see Freeth, H. A.

FREETH, Denzil Kingson; Member of Stock Exchange; *b* 10 July 1924; *s* of late Walter Kingson and late Vera Freeth. *Educ:* Highfield Sch., Liphook, Hants; Sherborne Sch. (Scholar); Trinity Hall, Cambridge (Scholar). Served War, 1943-46: RAF (Flying Officer). Pres. Union Soc., Cambridge, 1949; Chm. Cambridge Univ. Conservative Assoc. 1949; debating tour of America, 1949, also debated in Ireland; Mem. Exec. Cttee Nat. Union, 1955. MP (C) Basingstoke Division of Hants, 1955-64. PPS to Minister of State, Bd of Trade, 1956, to Pres. of the Bd of Trade, 1957-59, to Minister of Educn, 1959-60; Parly Sec. for Science, 1961-63. Mem. Parliamentary Cttee of Trustee Savings Bank Assoc., 1956-61. Mem. Select Cttee on Procedure, 1958-59. Employed by and Partner in stockbroking firms, 1950-61 and 1964-; Mem. of Stock Exchange, 1959-61, 1965-. Churchwarden, All Saints' Church, Margaret St, W1, 1977-. *Recreations:* good food, wine and conversation. *Address:* 66a Warwick Way, SW1V 1RZ. *T:* 01-834 8656. *Clubs:* Carlton; Pitt (Cambridge).

FREETH, Hon. Gordon; High Commissioner for Australia in the United Kingdom, since 1977; *b* 6 Aug. 1914; *s* of Rt Rev. Robert Evelyn Freeth, *qv*; *m* 1939, Joan Celia Carew Baker; one *s* two *d*. *Educ:* Sydney Church of England Grammar Sch.; Guildford Grammar Sch.; Univ. of Western Australia. Rowed for Australia in British Empire Games, Sydney, 1938. Admitted as Barrister and Solicitor, WA; practised Law at Katanning, WA, 1939-49. Served as Pilot, RAAF, 1942-45. Elected to House of Representatives as Member for Forrest, 1949; MP 1949-69; Minister: for Interior and Works, 1958-63; for Shipping and Transport, 1963-68; Assisting Attorney-Gen., 1962-64; for Air, and Minister Assisting the Treasurer, 1968; for External Affairs, 1969; Ambassador to Japan, 1970-73; practised law in Perth, WA, 1973-77. *Recreations:* squash, golf. *Address:* Australian High Commission, Australia House, Strand, WC2. *Club:* Weld (Perth).

FREETH, H. Andrew, RA 1965 (ARA 1955); RE 1946; PPRWS (RWS 1955); RBA 1949; RP 1966; Portrait Painter and Etcher; on staff of St Martin's School of Art, London and Sir John Cass College, Whitechapel; *b* Birmingham, 29 Dec. 1912; *s* of John Stewart Freeth and Charlotte Eleanor Stace, Hastings; *m* 1940, Roseen Marguerite Preston, Beaconsfield; three *s* one *d*. *Educ:* College of Art, Birmingham; British School at Rome, 1936-39 (Rome Scholarship in Engraving). ARE 1938. Served in Intelligence Corps (Major), 1940-46, in Mediterranean theatre; loaned to RAF Middle East as Official War Artist, 1943. Drawings and etchings have been purchased by Contemporary Art Society for British Museum, by Fitzwilliam Museum, by British Council, Bristol, Birmingham and Sunderland Art Galleries, by numerous Oxford and Cambridge Colls, etc; by Nat. Portrait Gall., Ashmolean Museum, Imperial War Museum, and Victoria and Albert Museum; reproduced in various publications. Best known works: (Portraits): Sir Alec Douglas-Home, J. Enoch Powell, W. Somerset Maugham, G. E. Moore, Walter de la Mare, Lord Avon, Sir Bernard Lovell, Lord MacDermott, Lord Chief Justice of N Ireland, also of Bishops (some past) of Dover, London, Peterborough, Derby, Gloucester, St Albans. Pres., RWS, 1974-76. *Address:* 37 Eastbury Road, Northwood, Mddx. *T:* Northwood 21350. *Club:* Athenæum.

FREETH, Rt. Rev. Robert Evelyn, MA Cantab, ThD ACT; *b* 7 April 1886; *s* of Sir Evelyn Freeth and Florence Oakes; *m* 1913, Gladys Mary Snashall; two *s* one *d*. *Educ:* King's Coll. Sch., Wimbledon; Selwyn Coll., Cambridge (scholar), 1905; BA 2nd Cl. Classical Tripos, 1908. Ridley Hall, Cambridge, 1908; MA 1912; Derbyshire Prize, 1915. Deacon, 1909; Priest, 1910; Melanesian Mission, 1909-13; Curate, Christ Church, North Adelaide, South Australia, 1913-14; priest in charge, Angaston, 1914-15; Asst Chaplain, King's Sch., Parramatta, NSW, 1915-16; Precentor, St Andrews Cathedral, Sydney, and Principal of Choir Sch., 1916-18; Chaplain and House Master, King's Sch., Parramatta, 1918-20; Sydney Church of England Grammar Sch., 1920-27; Headmaster, Guildford Grammar Sch., Western Australia, 1928, resigned Dec. 1949. Canon of St George's Cathedral, Perth, WA, 1941-50. Archdeacon of Perth, WA, 1953-61; Asst Bishop of Perth, WA, 1957-62; retd, 1963. *Recreation:* gardening. *Address:* 142 Victoria Avenue, Dalkeith, Western Australia 6009, Australia.
See also G. Freeth.

FREMANTLE, family name of **Baron Cottesloe.**

FRENCH, family name of **Baron De Freyne** and **Earl of Ypres.**

FRENCH, Christopher James Saunders, QC 1966; a Recorder, and Honorary Recorder of Coventry, since 1972; *b* 14 Oct. 1925; 2nd *s* of late Rev. Reginald French, MC, MA, Hon. Chaplain to the Queen, and Gertrude Emily Mary (*née* Haworth); *m* 1957, Philippa, *d* of Philip Godfrey Price, Abergavenny; one *s* one *d*. *Educ:* Denstone Coll.; Brasenose Coll., Oxford. Coldstream Guards, 1943-48 (Capt.). Called to the Bar, Inner Temple, 1950; Master of the Bench, 1975. Dep. Chm., Bucks QS, 1966-71. Recorder of Coventry, 1971-72. *Recreations:* walking, hunting, music, painting. *Address:* 1 Crown Office Row, Temple, EC4. *T:* 01-353 9292. *Club:* Garrick.

FRENCH, Henry William, CBE 1971; BSc (London); CEng, FIEE, FInstP; Senior Chief Inspector, Department of Education and Science, 1972-74; *b* 14 Feb. 1910; *s* of Henry Moxey French and Alice French (*née* Applegate); *m* 1936, Hazel Anne Mary Ainley; two *s*. *Educ:* Varndean School, Brighton; Woolwich Polytechnic. Engineering Technician, 1925-27; Armed Forces (Royal Corps of Signals, Army Educational Corps), 1927-38; Lecturer, Radar Engineering, Mil. Coll. of Science, 1938-46; Dep. Dir, Educn and Training, Electric and Musical Industries, 1946-48; HM Inspector of Schools (Further Education), 1948-56; Regional Staff Inspector (NW), 1956-59; Staff Inspector (Engineering), 1956-65; Chief Inspector for Further Educn for Industry and Commerce, Dept of Educn and Science, 1965-72. FCP 1974. Hon. DSc Loughborough Univ. of Technology, 1966. *Recreations:* polyphonic music, opera, physics of music, travel. *Address:* 26 Crossways, Sutton, Surrey. *T:* 01-642 5277.

FRENCH, Maj.-Gen. John, CB 1960; retired 1961; Chief of Industrial Section, Armament Control Agency, Western European Union, 1962-71; *b* 16 May 1906; *s* of Frederick Featherstonhaugh French and Edith l'Anson (*née* Watson). *m* 1935, Ursula Daphne (*née* Hutton); two *s* one *d*. *Educ:* Oundle; Corpus Christi, Cambridge (BA). Commissioned RTC, 1929; pac Military Coll. of Science, 1938; Instructor of Ballistics, Military Coll. of Science, 1939; Admiralty Research Laboratory, 1941; WTSFF 21 Army Gp, 1945; Dept of Artillery, Min. of Supply, 1946; Mem. of the Ordnance Board, 1949; British Joint Services Mission, Washington, 1952; Department of Artillery, Min. of Supply, 1955; Vice-Pres., Ordnance Board, 1958-60, Pres., 1960-61. *Recreation:* ocean racing. *Address:* c/o Banco Rural y Mediterraneo, Fuengirola (Malaga), Spain. *Clubs:* Royal Ocean Racing, RA Yacht (hon.); RAC Yacht.

FRENCH, Leslie Richard; Actor; *b* Kent, 23 April 1904; *s* of Robert Gilbert French and Jetty Sands Leahy; unmarried. *Educ:* London Coll. of Choristers. Began stage work 1914; early Shakespearean training with Sir Philip Ben Greet; recent parts include Hansel in Hansel and Gretel, Bert in Derby Day; Shakespearean parts include Puck, Ariel, Feste, Costard, etc; The Spirit in Comus; played Feste in the ballet Twelfth Night with the International Ballet at His Majesty's Theatre. Joined the Royal Corps of Signals, 1942; Lord Fancourt Babberly in Charley's Aunt, Christmas 1943. Produced Much Ado About Nothing and The Tempest for OUDS; Everyman as a ballet for the International Ballet Co., Lyric Theatre, 1943; Comus for the International Ballet, London Coliseum, 1946. Recent productions include: Charles and Mary, Cheltenham Festival, 1948; The Servant of Two Masters; Aladdin (Widow Twanky); Mother Goose (Mother Goose); She Stoops to Conquer for Edinburgh Festival (Tony Lumpkin), 1949; pantomime, Cinderella, 1950; The Dish Ran Away, Whitehall, 1950; Midsummer Night's Dream (Puck), Open Air Theatre during

Cheltenham Festival; Open Air Theatre, Regent's Park, 1951; pantomime, Nottingham, 1951-52; The Ghost Train, Huddersfield, 1952; Pisanio in Cymbeline, Attendant Spirit in Comus, Open Air Theatre, 1952; Dyrkin in Out of the Whirlwind, Westminster Abbey, 1953; Open Air Theatre, Cape Town: The Taming of the Shrew, 1956; Midsummer Night's Dream, 1957; As You Like It (Touchstone), 1958; Johannesburg: The Tempest, 1956; Hamlet, 1957; Shakespearean seasons in Cape Town, 1959, 1960, 1961, 1962, 1963, 1966, 1969; Tempest, E. Oppenheimer Theatre, OFS, 1968; The Tell Tale Heart, 1969; An Evening with Shakespeare (tour), 1969; Twelfth Night, Port Elizabeth, 1970; The Way of the World, S Africa, 1970; Co-dir, Open Air Theatre, Regent's Park, 1958. Prod., Twelfth Night (in Great Hall of Hampton Ct Palace), 1965; Le Streghe (for Visconti), 1966; toured USA, 1969-70 and 1970-71: One Man Shakespearean Recitals, and Shylock in Merchant of Venice; The Chaplain in The Lady's not for Burning, Chichester Festival, 1972; toured USA 1973; recitals and prod Twelfth Night; The Tempest, Cape Town, 1973; As You Like It, Port Elizabeth, 1973; Caroline, Yvonne Arnaud Theatre, Dir, Saturday Sunday Monday, Nat. Arts Council, S Africa, 1976; numerous appearances on TV. *Films:* Orders to Kill (M Lafitte), 1957; The Scapegoat (M Lacoste), 1958; The Singer not the Song (Father Gomez); The Leopard (Chevalley), 1963; The Witches, 1966; Happy Ever After, 1966; Joseph of Coppertino, 1966; Death in Venice (Visconti), 1970. Several TV appearances incl. Villette (serial), 1970. First Exhibition of Paintings-oil and water colour, Parsons Gall. Presented with Key to City of Cape Town, Jan. 1963. *Recreations:* gardening and painting. *Address:* 39 Lennox Gardens, SW1. *T:* 01-584 4797; La Stalla, Dosso, Levanto, La Spezia, Italy. *T:* Levanto 807-403. *Club:* Garrick.

FRENCH, Neville Arthur Irwin, CMG 1976; MVO 1968; HM Diplomatic Service; Deputy High Commissioner, Madras, since 1977; *b* 28 April 1920; *s* of late Ernest French and Alice Irwin Powell; *m* 1945, Joyce Ethel, *d* of late Henry Robert Greene, Buenos Aires and Montevideo; one *s* two *d. Educ:* London Sch. of Economics (BSc (Econ)). Fleet Auxiliary and Special Duties, Min. of War Transport, 1939-45. Colonial Admin. Service, Tanganyika, 1948, later HMOCS; District Comr, 1949-61; Principal Asst Sec., (External Affairs), Prime Minister's Office, Dar es Salaam, 1961; retd from HMOCS, 1962; Central African Office, 1963-64; 1st Sec., British High Commn, Salisbury, 1964-66; Head of Chancery, British Embassy, Rio de Janeiro, 1966-69; Asst Head of Western Organisations Dept, FCO, 1970-72; Counsellor, and Chargé d'Affaires, Havana, 1972-75; Governor and C-in-C, Falkland Islands, and High Comr, British Antarctic Territory, 1975-77. Comdr, Order of Rio Branco (Brazil), 1968. *Recreations:* sailing, swimming, books. *Address:* c/o Foreign and Commonwealth Office, SW1; c/o Barclays Bank, 84 High Street, Bideford, Devon.

FREND, Prof. William Hugh Clifford, TD 1959 (Clasp, 1966); DD, FSA; Professor of Ecclesiastical History, since 1969, and Dean of Divinity Faculty, 1972-75, Glasgow University; *b* 11 Jan. 1916; 2nd *s* of late E. G. C. Frend, Shottermill, Surrey and late Edith (*née* Bacon); *m* 1951, Mary Grace, *d* of E. A. Crook, *qv*; one *s* one *d. Educ:* Fernden Sch.; Haileybury Coll. (Schol.); Keble Coll., Oxford (Schol.). 1st cl. hons Mod. Hist., 1937; Craven Fellow, 1937; DPhil 1940; BD Cantab 1964; DD Oxon 1966. Asst Princ., War Office, 1940; seconded Cabinet Office, 1941; FO, 1942; service in N Africa, Italy and Austria, 1943-46; Ed. Bd, German Foreign Min. Documents, 1947-51; Res. Fellow, Nottingham Univ., 1951; S. A. Cook Bye-Fellow, 1952, Fellow, 1956-69, Dir Studies, Archaeology, 1961-69, Gonville and Caius Coll.; University Asst Lectr, 1953, Lectr in Divinity, 1958-69; Birkbeck Lectr in Ecclesiastical History, 1967-68. Chm., AUT (Scotland), 1976-78. Assoc. Dir, Egypt Exploration Soc. excavations at Q'asr Ibrim, Nubia, 1963-64; Guest Scholar at Rhodes Univ., 1964 and Peter Ainslie Mem. Lecturer; Guest Prof., Univ. of S Africa, 1976. Licensed Lay Reader, 1956; Ed., Modern Churchman, 1963. Commission Queen's Royal Regt (TA), 1947-67. FSA 1952; FRHistS 1954. Hon. DD Edinburgh, 1974. *Publications:* The Donatist Church, 1952; Martyrdom and Persecution in the Early Church, 1965; The Early Church, 1965; (contrib.) Religion in the Middle East, 1968; The Rise of the Monophysite Movement, 1972; Religion Popular and Unpopular in the Early Christian Centuries, 1976; articles in Jl Theol Studies, Jl Roman Studies, Jl Eccles. History, etc. *Recreations:* archæology, occasional golf and tennis, writing, collecting old coins and stamps. *Address:* Marbrae, Balmaha, Stirlingshire. *T:* Balmaha 227. *Club:* Authors'.

FRERE, Alexander Stewart, CBE 1946; MA Cantab; *b* 23 Nov. 1896; *m* 1933, Patricia Marion Caldecott, *d* of late Edgar Wallace; two *s* one *d. Educ:* Christ's Coll., Cambridge. Served Royal East Kent Yeomanry, seconded Royal Flying Corps.

European War, 1914-18; edited the Granta, Cambridge, 1920-21; on staff of London Evening News, 1922-23; joined William Heinemann Ltd, Publishers, 1923; Dir, 1926; Man. Dir, 1932-40; Chm., 1945-61; Pres., 1961-62; Mem. of council Publishers Assoc., 1938-39. Assisted organise National Service Campaign, Ministry of Labour and National Service, Jan.-June 1939; Dir of Public Relations, Min. of Labour and National Service, 1940-44. Adviser to HM Govt Delegn to ILO Conf., Columbia Univ., New York, 1941. Chevalier de la Légion d'Honneur, 1953. *Address:* Knoll Hill House, Aldington, Kent. *Clubs:* White's, Garrick, Royal Thames Yacht; Century (NY); Travellers' (Paris).

FRERE, James Arnold, FSA, FRGS; *b* 20 April 1920; *e s* of late John Geoffrey Frere; one adopted *s. Educ:* Eton Coll.; Trinity Coll., Cambridge. Lieut Intelligence Corps, 1944-47. Regular Army R of O, 1949-67. Bluemantle Pursuivant of Arms, 1948-56; Chester Herald of Arms, 1956-60; an Officer of Supreme Court of Judicature, 1966-70. Member: Surrey Archæological Soc. (Council, 1949-53, 1954-58 and 1959-63); American Soc. of Authors; Soc. for the Protection of Ancient Buildings; Council of the Harleian Soc., 1951-66; Hon. Mem. Heraldry Soc. of Southern Africa, 1953-; a Vice-Pres. of Museum of Costume, 1952-60. Press Sec., New Gallery Clinic, 1967-70. Liveryman, Worshipful Co. of Scriveners. *Publications:* The British Monarchy at Home, 1963; (jointly with the Duchess of Bedford) Now... The Duchesses, 1964. *Recreations:* walking, painting, archæology. *Address:* c/o Society of Antiquaries, Burlington House, Piccadilly, W1.

FRERE, Prof. Sheppard Sunderland, CBE 1976; FSA 1944; FBA 1971; Professor of the Archæology of the Roman Empire, Oxford University, since 1966; *b* 23 Aug. 1916; *e s* of late N. G. Frere, CMG; *m* 1961, Janet Cecily Hoare; one *s* one *d. Educ:* Lancing Coll.; Magdalene Coll., Cambridge. BA 1938, MA 1944, LittD 1976, DLitt 1977. Master, Epsom Coll., 1938-40. National Fire Service, 1940-45. Master, Lancing Coll., 1945-54; Lecturer in Archæology, Manchester Univ., 1954-55; Reader in Archæology of Roman Provinces, London Univ. Inst. of Archæology, 1955-62; Prof. of the Archæology of the Roman Provinces, London Univ., 1963-66. Dir, Canterbury Excavations, 1946-60; Dir, Verulamium Excavations, 1955-61. Vice-Pres., Soc. of Antiquaries, 1962-66; Hon. Corr. Mem. German Archæological Inst., 1964, Fellow, 1967; Member: Royal Commn on Hist. Monuments (England), 1966-; Ancient Monuments Board (England), 1966-. Hon. DLitt Leeds, 1977. Editor, Britannia, 1969-. *Publications:* (ed) Problems of the Iron Age in Southern Britain, 1961; Britannia, a history of Roman Britain, 1967 (rev. edn 1974); Verulamium Excavations, vol. I, 1972; papers in learned jls. *Recreation:* gardening. *Address:* All Souls College, Oxford.

FRESHWATER, Prof. Donald Cole; Head of Department of Chemical Engineering, University of Technology, Loughborough, since 1957; *b* 21 April 1924; *s* of Thomas and Ethel May Freshwater; *m* 1948, Margaret D. Worrall; one *s* three *d. Educ:* Brewood Grammar Sch.; Birmingham Univ. (BSc, PhD); Sheffield Univ.; Loughborough Coll. (DLC). Fuel Engineer, Min. of Fuel and Power, 1944; Chemical Engr: APV Co. Ltd, 1948; Midland Tar Distillers Co. Ltd, 1950; Lectr, Dept of Chem. Engrg, Univ. of Birmingham, 1952. Visiting Prof., Univ. of Delaware, USA, 1962; Chm., Chem. Engrg Gp, Soc. of Chemical Industry, 1973-75. *Publications:* Chemical Engineering Data Book, 1959; numerous papers on mass transfer and particle technology in chem. engrg jls. *Recreations:* sailing, collecting watercolours. *Address:* Head of Department of Chemical Engineering, Loughborough University of Technology, Ashby Road, Loughborough, Leics LE11 3TU. *T:* Loughborough 63171. *Club:* Athenæum.

FRETWELL, Elizabeth, OBE 1977; operatic and dramatic soprano; *b* Melbourne, Australia; *m* Robert Simmons; one *s* one *d. Educ:* privately. Joined National Theatre, Melbourne, 1950; came to Britain, 1955; joined Sadler's Wells, 1956; Australia, Elizabethan Opera Co., 1963; tour of W Germany, 1963; USA, Canada and Covent Garden, 1964; tour of Europe, 1965; guest soprano with Cape Town and Durban Opera Cos, South Africa, 1970; joined Australian Opera, 1970. Rôles include Violetta in La Traviata, Leonora in Fidelio, Ariadne in Ariadne auf Naxos, Senta in The Flying Dutchman, Minnie in The Girl of the Golden West, Leonora in Il Trovatore, Aida, Ellen Orford in Peter Grimes, Leonora in Forza del Destino, Alice Ford in Falstaff, Amelia in Masked Ball, Georgetta in Il Tabarro, opening season of Sydney Opera Hse, 1973. Has sung in BBC Promenade Concerts and on TV. *Recreation:* rose-growing. *Address:* c/o Australian Opera, 569 George Street, Sydney, NSW 2000, Australia.

FRETWELL, Sir George (Herbert), KBE 1953; CB 1950; Director General of Works, Air Ministry, 1947-59, retired; *b* 21 March 1900; *s* of late Herbert Fretwell, Ripley, Derbyshire; *m* 1930, Constance Mabel, *d* of late George Ratcliffe, Woodford Green, Essex; no *c. Educ:* Heanor Grammar Sch., Derbs. Entered Air Ministry as Asst Civil Engineer, 1928; Civil Engineer, 1934; Superintending Engineer, 1937; Chief Engineer, 1940; Dep. Dir of Works, 1945, Dir, 1946. *Address:* North Lodge, 2 North Street, Sheringham, Norfolk. *T:* Sheringham 822336.

FRETWELL, Major John Emsley, CMG 1975; HM Diplomatic Service; Assistant Under-Secretary of State, Foreign and Commonwealth Office, since 1976; *b* 15 June 1930; *s* of F. T. Fretwell; *m* 1959, Mary Ellen Eugenie Dubois; one *s* one *d. Educ:* Chesterfield Grammar Sch.; Lausanne Univ.; King's Coll., Cambridge (MA). Served in Army, 1948-50. Joined HM Diplomatic Service, 1953; 3rd Sec., Hong Kong, 1954-55; 2nd Sec., Peking, 1955-57; FO, 1957-59; 1st Sec., Moscow, 1959-62; FO, 1962-67; 1st Sec. (Commercial), Washington, 1967-70; Commercial Counsellor, Warsaw, 1971-73; Head of European Integration Dept (Internal), FCO, 1973. *Recreations:* skiing, walking. *Address:* 20 Seymour Road, SW18.

FREUD, Anna, CBE 1967; Psycho-Analyst; Director of Hampstead Child Therapy Course and Clinic, since 1952; *b* 3 Dec. 1895; *d* of Professor Sigmund Freud and Martha Freud (*née* Bernays). *Educ:* Cottage Lyceum, Vienna. Chm., Vienna Inst. of Psycho-Analysis until 1938; Mem., London Inst. of Psycho-Analysis since then. Hon. degrees: LLD: Clark Univ., USA, 1950; Univ. of Sheffield, 1966; ScD: Jefferson Med. Coll., USA, 1964; Univ. of Chicago, 1966; Yale 1968; MD Univ. of Vienna. Grand Decoration of Honour in Gold, Austria, 1975. *Publications:* Introduction to the Technic of Child Analysis, trans. L. P. Clark (USA), 1928; Psychoanalysis for Parents and Teachers, trans. Barbara Low, 1931; The Ego and Mechanisms of Defence, trans. Cecil Baines, 1937, 3rd edn 1969; (with D. T. Burlingham) Young Children in Wartime, 1942; (with D. T. Burlingham) War and Children, 1944; (with D. T. Burlingham) Infants without Families, 1944; Psychoanalytical Treatment of Children, trans. Nancy Proctor-Gregg, 1946, 2nd edn 1951; (ed jtly) Psychoanalytic Study of the Child, 30 vols, 1945-; (ed with J. Strachey and others) The Standard Edition of the Complete Psychological Works of Sigmund Freud, 24 vols, 1953-56; (with W. D. Wall) The Enrichment of Childhood, 1962; (with T. Bergmann) Children in Hospital (USA), 1966; Normality and Pathology in Childhood, 1966; Indications of Child Analysis, and other papers, 1969; Difficulties in the Path of Psychoanalysis (USA), 1969; Research at the Hampstead Child Therapy Clinic, and other papers 1956-65, 1970; Problems of Psychoanalytic Technique and Therapy, 1973; (with Albert J. Solnit and J. Goldstein) Beyond the Best Interests of the Child, 1973; The Writings of Anna Freud (UK and USA), 1975-, Vols I-VII, 1975; contribs to Internat. Jl of Psycho-Analysis. *Address:* 20 Maresfield Gardens, NW3. *T:* 01-435 2002.

FREUD, Clement Raphael; MP (L) Isle of Ely, since July 1973; writer, broadcaster, caterer; Director, Genevieve Restaurants, London; Director and Trustee: Playboy Club of London Ltd; Berkeley Hotel, Southampton; Consultant, New Mauritius Hotels Ltd, Curepipe; Rector of the University of Dundee, since 1974; *b* 24 April 1924; *s* of late Ernst and Lucie Freud; *m* 1950, Jill, 2nd *d* of H. W. Flewett, MA; three *s* two *d.* Apprenticed, Dorchester Hotel, London. Served War, Royal Ulster Rifles; Liaison Officer, Nuremberg, 1946. Trained, Martinez Hotel, Cannes. Proprietor, Royal Court Theatre Club, 1952-62. Sports writer, Observer, 1956-64; Cookery Editor: Time and Tide, 1961-63; Observer Magazine, 1964-68; Daily Telegraph Magazine, 1968-. Sports Columnist, Sun, 1964-69; Columnist: Sunday Telegraph, 1963-65; News of the World, 1965; Financial Times, 1964-; Daily Express, 1973-75. Liberal spokesman on: educn and science, 1973-74; educn and the arts, 1974-77; NI, broadcasting and the arts, 1977-. Member: Services Cttee of the House, 1973-; Broadcasting Sub Cttee; Security Sub Cttee; Catering Sub Cttee. £5,000 class winner, Daily Mail London-NY air race, 1969. Writer and performer Sweet and Sour (Southern), 1962-64; Freud on Food (Tyne Tees), 1968-71; BBC: Frost Shows; Braden Shows; Jackanory; ITV: (talk shows): Eamon Andrews, Simon Dee; David Jacobs, Late Late Show (Telefis Eireann); Carson Show (NBC, USA), etc. Award winning petfood commercial: San Francisco, Tokyo, Berlin, 1967. BBC (sound) Just a Minute, 1968-. *Publications:* Grimble, 1968; Grimble at Christmas, 1973; contributor to: Punch, Queen, Town, Which, New Yorker, etc. *Recreations:* racing, cricket, backgammon, golf. *Address:* 7 Boundary Road, NW8. *T:* 01-722 1877. *Clubs:* Savile, MCC, Lord's Taverners'. *See also Lucian Freud.*

FREUD, Lucian; painter; *b* 8 Dec. 1922; *s* of late Ernst and Lucie Freud; *m* 1st, 1948, Kathleen Garman (marr. diss. 1952); two *d* ; 2nd, 1953, Lady Caroline Maureen Blackwood (marr. diss. 1957), *d* of 4th Marquess of Dufferin and Ava. *Educ:* Central Sch. of Art; East Anglian Sch. of Painting and Drawing. Worked on merchant ship, 1941. Teacher, Slade Sch. of Art, 1948-58; Vis. Asst, Norwich Sch. of Art, 1964-65. Held his first one-man exhibn, 1944; other one-man shows, 1946, 1950, 1952, 1958, 1963, 1968, 1972; first retrospective exhibn, Hayward Gall., 1974, subseq. Bristol, Birmingham and Leeds. Painted mostly in France and Greece, 1946-48. Rep. GB, Venice Biennale, 1954 (with Francis Bacon, Ben Nicholson). Works included in public collections: Tate Gall.; Museum of Modern Art, NY; Nat. Gall., Melbourne, NSW; Arts Council of GB; British Council; Fitzwilliam Mus., Cambridge; Walker Art Gall., Liverpool; Liverpool Univ.; Hartlepool Art Gall.; Southampton Art Gall.; Beaverbrook Foundn, Fredericton, New Brunswick; V&A Museum; Harris Museum and Art Gallery, Preston, etc; also represented in mixed exhibns, incl. Arts Council Festival of Britain, Sixty Paintings for '51, his picture Interior near Paddington was one of five bought by the Council on recommendation of a selection jury; Cyclamen Mural, Thornhill Bathroom, Chatsworth House, 1962. Prizewinner, Daily Express Young Painters Exhibn, 1954. *Address:* c/o Anthony d'Offay, 9 Dering Street, W1. *See also C. R. Freud.*

FREUND, Sir Otto K.; see Kahn-Freund.

FREYBERG, family name of **Baron Freyberg.**

FREYBERG, 2nd Baron, *cr* 1951, of Wellington, New Zealand, and of Munstead in the Co. of Surrey; **Paul Richard Freyberg,** OBE 1965; MC 1945; Colonel General Staff, late Grenadier Guards; *b* 27 May 1923; *s* of 1st Baron Freyberg, VC, GCMG, KCB, KBE, DSO (and 3 bars), and Barbara, GBE (*d* 1973), *d* of Sir Herbert Jekyll, KCMG, and Lady Jekyll, DBE; *S* father, 1963; *m* 1960, Ivry Perronelle Katharine Guild, Aspall Hall, Debenham, Suffolk; one *s* three *d. Educ:* Eton Coll. Joined NZ Army, 1940; served with 2nd NZEF: Greece, 1941; Western Desert, 1941-42; transferred to British Army, 1942; North Africa, 1943; Italy, 1943-45 (MC); Palestine, 1947-48; Cyprus, 1956-58; British Cameroons, 1961; Comd HAC Infantry Battalion, 1965-68; Defence Policy Staff, MoD, 1968-71; Dir Volunteers, Territorials and Cadets, 1971-75. Staff Coll., 1952; jssc 1958; sowc 1971. *Heir: s* Hon. Valerian Bernard Freyberg, *b* 15 Dec. 1970. *Address:* Munstead House, Godalming, Surrey. *T:* Godalming 6004. *Clubs:* Boodle's, Royal Automobile.

FRICKER, (Anthony) Nigel, QC 1977; Recorder of the Crown Court, Wales and Chester Circuit, since 1975; *b* 7 July 1937; *s* of late Dr William Shapland Fricker and of Margaret Fricker (*née* Skinner); *m* 1960, Marilyn Ann, *d* of A. Martin, Pa, USA; one *s* two *d. Educ:* King's School, Chester; Liverpool Univ. (LLB 1958). President of Guild of Undergraduates, Liverpool Univ., 1958-59. Called to Bar, Gray's Inn, 1960; Member: Gen. Council of the Bar, 1966-70; Senate of the Inns of Court and the Bar and of Gen. Council of the Bar, 1975-78. Prosecuting Counsel to DHSS, Wales and Chester Circuit, 1975-77. *Recreations:* theatre-going, listening to music, gardening. *Address:* Farrar's Building, Temple, EC4Y 7BD. *T:* 01-583 9241. *Club:* Bristol Channel Yacht (Mumbles).

FRICKER, Prof. Peter Racine, FRCO, ARCM; Professor of Music, Music Department, University of California, Santa Barbara, since 1964; Director of Music, Morley College, 1952-64; *b* 5 Sept. 1920; *s* of late Edward Racine Fricker; *m* 1943, Audrey Helen Clench. *Educ:* St Paul's Sch. Royal College of Music, 1937-40. Served War, 1940-46, in Royal Air Force, working in Signals and Intelligence. Has worked as Composer, Conductor, and Music Administrator since 1946. Hon Professorial Fellow, Univ. of Wales, Cardiff, 1971. Hon. RAM, 1966. Hon. DMus (Leeds), 1958. Order of Merit, West Germany, 1965. *Publications:* Four Fughettas for Two Pianos, 1946; Wind Quintet, 1947; Three Sonnets of Cecco Angiolieri da Siena, for Tenor and Seven Instruments, 1947; String Quartet in One Movement, 1948; Symphony No 1, 1948-49; Prelude, Elegy and Finale for String Orchestra, 1949; Concerto for Violin and Orchestra, 1949-50; Sonata for Violin and Piano, 1950; Concertante for Cor Anglais and String Orchestra, 1950; Symphony No 2, 1950; Concertante for Three Pianos, Strings and Timpani, 1951; Four Impromptus for Piano; Concerto for Viola and Orchestra, 1951-53; Concerto for Piano and Orchestra, 1952-54; String Quartet No 2, 1952-53; Rapsodia Concertante for Violin and Orchestra, 1953-54; Dance Scene for Orchestra, 1954; Musick's Empire for Chorus and Small Orchestra, 1955; Litany for Double String Orchestra, 1955; 'Cello Sonata, 1956; Oratorio, The Vision of Judgement, 1956-

58; Octet, 1958; Toccata for Piano and Orchestra, 1958-59; Serenade No 1, 1959; Serenade No 2, 1959; Symphony No 3, 1960; Studies for Piano, 1961; Cantata for Tenor and Chamber Ensemble, 1962; O Longs Désirs: Song-cycle for Soprano and Orchestra, 1963; Ricercare for Organ, 1965; Four Dialogues for Oboe and Piano, 1965; Four Songs for High Voice and Orchestra, 1965; Fourth Symphony, 1966; Fantasy for Viola and Piano, 1966; Three Scenes for Orchestra, 1966; The Day and the Spirits for Soprano and Harp, 1967; Seven Counterpoints for Orchestra, 1967; Magnificat, 1968; Episodes for Piano, 1968; Concertante No 4, 1968; Toccata for Organ, 1968; Saxophone Quartet, 1969; Praeludium for Organ, 1969; Paseo for Guitar, 1970; The Roofs for coloratura soprano and percussion, 1970; Sarabande In Memoriam Igor Stravinsky, 1971; Nocturne for chamber orchestra, 1971; Intrada for organ, 1971; A Bourrée for Sir Arthur Bliss for cello, 1971; Concertante no 5 for piano and string quartet, 1971; Introitus for orchestra, 1972; Come Sleep for contralto, alto flute and bass clarinet, 1972; Fanfare for Europe for trumpet, 1972; Ballade for flute and piano, 1972; Seven Little Songs for chorus, 1972; Gigue for cello, 1973; The Groves of Dodona for six flutes, 1973; Spirit Puck, for clarinet and percussion, 1974; Two Petrarch Madrigals, 1974; Trio-Sonata for Organ, 1974; Third String Quartet, 1975; Fifth Symphony, 1975; Seachant for flute and double bass, 1976; Sinfonia for 17 wind instruments, 1976; also music for film, stage and radio. *Recreation:* travel. *Address:* Department of Music, University of California, Santa Barbara, Calif 93106, USA.

FRIEDMAN, Prof. Milton, PhD; Economist, USA; Senior Research Fellow, Hoover Institution, Stanford University, since 1976; Professor of Economics, University of Chicago, since 1948, on leave; now Professor Emeritus; Member of Research Staff, National Bureau of Economic Research, since 1948; Economic Columnist, Newsweek, since 1967; *b* New York, 31 July 1912; *s* of Jeno Saul and Sarah E. Friedman; *m* 1938, Rose Director; one *s* one *d*. *Educ:* Rutgers (AB), Chicago (AM), and Columbia (PhD) Univs. Associate Economist, Natural Resources Cttee, Washington, 1935-37; Nat. Bureau of Economic Research, New York, 1937-46 (on leave 1940-45). During 1941-45: Principal Economist, Tax Research Div., US Treasury Dept, 1941-43; Associate Dir, Statistical Research Gp, Div. of War Research, Columbia Univ., 1943-45. Fulbright Lecturer, Cambridge Univ., 1953-54; Vis. Prof., Econs, Columbia Univ., 1964-65, etc. Member: President's Commn on an All-Volunteer Armed Force, 1969-70; Commn on White House Fellows, 1971-73. Mem. Bd of Editors, Econometrica, 1957-65; Pres., Amer. Economic Assoc., 1967; Pres., Mont Pelerin Soc., 1970-72. John Bates Clark Medal, Amer. Econ. Assoc., 1951; Fellowships and awards, in USA. Nobel Memorial Prize for Economics, 1976. Member various societies, etc., incl. Royal Economic Soc. (GB). Holds several Hon. doctorates. *Publications:* Income from Independent Professional Practice (with Simon Kuznets), 1946; Sampling Inspection (with others), 1948; Essays in Positive Economics, 1953; A Theory of the Consumption Function, 1957; A Program for Monetary Stability, 1959; Capitalism and Freedom, 1962; Price Theory: a Provisional Text, 1962; A Monetary History of the United States 1867-1960 (with Anna J. Schwartz), 1963; Inflation: Causes and Consequences, 1963; The Balance of Payments: Free versus Flexible Exchange Rates (with Robert V. Roosa), 1967; Dollars and Deficits, 1968; Optimum Quantity of Money and Other Essays, 1969; Monetary vs Fiscal Policy (with Walter W. Heller), 1969; Monetary Statistics of the United States (with Anna J. Schwartz), 1970; A Theoretical Framework for Monetary Analysis, 1971; Social Security: Universal or Selective? (with Wilbur J. Cohen), 1972; An Economist's Protest, 1972; Money and Economic Development, 1973; There's No Such Thing as a Free Lunch, 1975; Price Theory, 1976. *Recreations:* tennis, carpentry. *Address:* Hoover Institution, Stanford, Calif 94305, USA. *Club:* Quadrangle (Chicago).

FRIEL, Brian; writer; *b* 9 Jan. 1929; *s* of Patrick Friel and Christina Friel (*née* MacLoone); *m* 1954, Anne Morrison; one *s* four *d*. *Educ:* St Columb's Coll., Derry; St Patrick's Coll., Maynooth; St Joseph's Trng Coll., Belfast. Taught in various schools, 1950-60; writing full-time from 1960. Lived in Minnesota during first season of Tyrone Guthrie Theater, Minneapolis. *Publications: collected stories:* The Saucer of Larks, 1962; The Gold in the Sea, 1966; *plays:* Philadelphia, Here I Come!, 1965; The Loves of Cass McGuire, 1967; Lovers, 1968; The Mundy Scheme, 1969; Crystal and Fox, 1970; The Gentle Island, 1971; The Freedom of the City, 1973; Volunteers, 1975; Living Quarters, 1976. *Recreations:* reading, trout-fishing, slow tennis. *Address:* Ardmore, Muff, Lifford, Co. Donegal, Ireland. *T:* Muff 30.

FRIEND, Archibald Gordon; His Honour Judge Friend; a Circuit Judge (formerly Deputy Chairman, Inner London, later Middlesex, Quarter Sessions), since 1965; *b* 6 July 1912; *m* 1940, Patricia Margaret Smith; no *c*. Called to Bar, Inner Temple, 1933. Dep. Chm., Herts Quarter Sessions, 1963-71. *Recreation:* gardening. *Address:* The Crown Court, 1 Hans Crescent, SW1X 0LQ. *T:* 01-589 5400.

FRIEND, Bernard Ernest; Member of British Aerospace, and Director of Finance, since 1977; *b* 18 May 1924; *s* of Richard Friend and Ada Florence Friend; *m* 1951, Pamela Florence Amor; one *s* two *d*. *Educ:* Dover Grammar Sch. Chartered Accountant. Flying Officer, RAF, 1943-47. Arthur Young & Co., Chartered Accountants, 1948-55; Comptroller, Esso Petroleum Co. Ltd, 1961-66; Dep. Controller, Esso Europe, 1967-68; Man. Dir, Essoheat, 1968-69; Vice-Pres., Esso Chemicals, Brussels, 1970-73; Chm. and Man. Dir, Esso Chemicals Ltd, 1974-76. *Recreation:* cricket. *Address:* Pharos IV, Barton Common Road, New Milton, Hants. *T:* New Milton 616831. *Club:* Royal Air Force.

FRIEND, Phyllis Muriel, CBE 1972; Chief Nursing Officer, Department of Health and Social Security, since 1972; *b* 28 Sept. 1922; *d* of Richard Edward Friend. *Educ:* Herts and Essex High Sch., Bishop's Stortford; The London Hospital (SRN); Royal College of Nursing (RNT). Dep. Matron, St George's Hospital, 1956-59; Dep. Matron, 1959-61, Matron, 1961-68, Chief Nursing Officer 1969-72, The London Hospital. *Address:* Barnmead, Start Hill, Bishop's Stortford, Herts. *T:* Bishop's Stortford 54873.

FRINK, Elisabeth, CBE 1969; ARA 1972; *b* 14 Nov. 1930; British; *m* 1st, 1955, Michel Jammet (marr. diss. 1963); one *s*; 2nd, Edward Pool, MC (marr. diss. 1974); 3rd, Alexander Csáky. *Educ:* Convent of The Holy Family, Exmouth. Guildford Sch. of Art, 1947-49; Chelsea Sch. of Art, 1949-53. Exhibitions: Beaux Arts Gallery, 1952; St George's Gallery, 1955; exhibits regularly at Waddington and Tooth (formerly Waddington) Gallery, London. Represented in collections in USA, Australia, Holland, Sweden, Germany and Tate Gallery, London. Member: Bd Trustees, British Museum, 1975-; Royal Fine Art Commn, 1976-. *Address:* c/o Waddington and Tooth Gallery, 2 Cork Street, W1.

FRIPP, Alfred Thomas, BM; FRCS; *b* 3 July 1899; *s* of late Sir Alfred Fripp, KCVO, and late Lady M. S. Fripp, *d* of late T. B. Haywood; *m* 1931, Kathleen Kimpton; one *s* two *d*. *Educ:* Winchester; Christ Church, Oxford. 2nd Lieut 1st Life Guards, 1917-18. Christ Church, Oxford, 1919-21; Guy's Hospital, 1921; Surg., Royal National Orthopædic Hospital, 1934-64. Mem., Pensions Appeal Tribunal, 1966-74. FRCS 1927. Pres. Orthopædic Section, RSocMed, 1950-51. *Recreations:* gardening, rowing. *Address:* Mascalls, London Road, Ardingly, East Sussex RH17 6TG. *T:* Ardingly 892351. *Clubs:* Bath; Leander (Henley-on-Thames).

FRISBY, Audrey Mary; Metropolitan Stipendiary Magistrate, since 1972; *b* 22 June 1928; *d* of Hugh and late Olive Jennings, Ashbrook Range, Sunderland; *m* 1961, Roger Harry Kilbourne Frisby, *qv*; two *s* one *d*. *Educ:* Durham High Sch.; Durham Univ. (BA); Oxford Univ. (DPA). Children's Officer, City and County of Cambridge, 1952-56. Called to Bar, Middle Temple, 1956 (Harmsworth Schol.); practised at Criminal Bar, London, 1956-61 and 1967-72 (as Miss A. M. Jennings). *Address:* 20 Newton Road, W2 4SF. *T:* 01-229 1798. *Club:* Hurlingham.

FRISBY, Maj.-Gen. Richard George Fellowes, CB 1963; CBE 1958; DSO 1944; MC 1939; *b* 17 Dec. 1911; *er s* of late Col H. G. F. Frisby, Royal Hants Regt, and late Mrs R. M. Frisby, Bacton Grange, Herefordshire; *m* 1938, Elizabeth Mary, 2nd *d* of late Col W. G. Murray, 3rd King's Own Hussars, Twyford House, Winchester, and late Mrs M. Murray, Pretoria, South Africa; two *s*. *Educ:* Haileybury Coll.; Royal Military College, Sandhurst. Commissioned Hants Regt, 1931; Mohmand Campaign, 1935; British Army Staff, Washington, 1941-42. Commanded: 4 Bn Welch Regt, 1944-45; 1 Bn Hants Regt, 1945-46; 14 Bn Parachute Regt, 1949-51; 1 Bn R Hants Regt, 1951-53; Tactical Wing Sch. of Infantry, 1953-54; 1 Commonwealth Div., Korea, 1955-56; 24 Independent Brigade, 1957-58; Gen. Staff, HQ Eastern Command, 1959-60; GOC 53 Infantry Div. (TA), 1961-63; Maj.-Gen., 1961; Chief of Staff to the C-in-C, Allied Forces, Northern Europe, Dec. 1963-65; retd. *Address:* Woodlands St Mary House, Newbury, Berks RG16 7SL. *T:* Lambourn 71510. *Club:* Army and Navy.

FRISBY, Roger Harry Kilbourne, QC 1969; a Recorder of the Crown Court, since 1972; *b* 11 Dec. 1921; 2nd *s* of late Herbert Frisby and Hylda Mary Frisby; *m* 1961, Audrey Mary (*née*

Jennings), *qv*; two *s* one *d* (and one *s* one *d* by previous marriage). *Educ:* Bablake Sch.; Christ Church, Oxford; King's Coll., Univ. of London. Called to the Bar, Lincoln's Inn, 1950. *Address:* 3 King's Bench Walk, Temple, EC4. *T:* 01-353 0431. *Clubs:* United Oxford & Cambridge University; Hurlingham.

FRISBY, Terence; playright and actor; *b* 28 Nov. 1932; *s* of William and Kathleen Frisby; *m* 1963, Christine Vecchione (marr. diss.); one *s*. *Educ:* Dobwalls Village Sch.; Dartford Grammar Sch.; Central Sch. of Speech Training and Dramatic Art. Substantial repertory acting experience, also TV, films and musicals, 1957-63; appeared in A Sense of Detachment, Royal Court, 1972-73 and X, Royal Court, 1974. Has written many TV scripts, incl. series Lucky Feller, 1976; film, There's A Girl in My Soup, 1970 (Writers Guild Award, Best British Comedy Screenplay). *Publications:* plays: The Subtopians, 1964; There's a Girl in My Soup, 1966; The Bandwagon, 1970; It's All Right if I Do It, 1977. *Recreations:* golf, chess, scuba diving. *Address:* c/o Harvey Unna Ltd, 14 Beaumont Mews, W1. *T:* 01-935 8589. *Clubs:* Wentworth Golf, Brokenhurst Manor Golf.

FRISCH, Otto Robert, OBE 1946; DSc; FRS 1948; Jacksonian Professor of Natural Philosophy, University of Cambridge, 1947-72, now Professor Emeritus; *b* Vienna, Austria, 1 Oct. 1904; *o s* of late Dr Justinian Frisch and Auguste Meitner; *m* 1951, Ursula, *o d* of Karl Blau; one *s* one *d*. *Educ:* Vienna Univ. (Dr phil 1926). Scientific research in Berlin, Hamburg, London, Copenhagen, Birmingham, Liverpool, Oxford, Los Alamos, Harwell, Cambridge. *Publications:* Meet the Atoms, 1947 (London); Atomic Physics Today, 1961 (New York); Working with Atoms, 1965 (Leicester); The Nature of Matter, 1972 (London); numerous papers on various topics in atomic and nuclear physics, in scientific periodicals. *Recreations:* piano, table tennis. *Address:* Trinity College, Cambridge.

FRITH, Anthony Ian Donald; Chairman, South Western Region, British Gas Corporation, since 1973; *b* 11 March 1929; *s* of Ernest and Elizabeth Frith; *m* 1952, Joyce Marcelle Boyce; one *s* one *d*. *Educ:* various grammar schs and techn. colls. CEng, FIGasE, MInstM. Various appts in North Thames Gas Bd and Gas Light & Coke Co., 1945-65; Sales Man. 1965-67, Dep. Commercial Man. 1967-68, North Thames Gas Bd; Marketing Man., Domestic and Commercial Gas, Gas Council, 1968-72; Sales Dir, British Gas Corp., 1972-73. *Publications:* various techn. and prof. in Gas Engineering and other jls. *Recreations:* fishing, boating. *Address:* St David's, 182 Old Frome Road, Combe Down, Bath, Avon.

FRITH, Donald Alfred, MA; Headmaster, Archbishop Holgate's Grammar School, York, since 1959; *b* 13 May 1918; *yr s* of late Charles Henry Frith and Mabel (*née* Whiting); *m* 1941, Mary Webster Tyler, *yr d* of late Raymond Tyler and Rosina Mary (*née* Wiles); four *s* one *d*. *Educ:* Whitgift Sch. (schol.); Christ's Coll., Cambridge (schol.). MA Cantab 1944. Served War, 1940-46; commnd RASC; served in Middle East, Italy and at WO. Deme Warden, University College Sch., 1946-52; Headmaster, Richmond Sch., Yorks, 1953-59. Jt Hon. Sec., Incorporated Assoc. of Headmasters, 1977. *Recreations:* music, gardening, walking. *Address:* Headmaster's House, Archbishop Holgate's Grammar School, York YO1 5HA. *T:* York 23207.

FRITH, Air Vice-Marshal Edward Leslie, CB 1973; *b* 18 March 1919; *s* of late Charles Edward Frith, ISO. *Educ:* Haberdashers' Askes School. Gp Captain, 1961; Air Cdre, 1968; Dir of Personal Services (2) RAF, MoD, 1969-71; Air Vice-Marshal, 1971; Air Officer Administration, Maintenance Comd, later Support Comd, 1971-74. Senior Administrator, Univ. of London. *Recreations:* lawn tennis, bridge. *Address:* 27 Chartwell, 80 Parkside, Wimbledon, SW19 5LN. *T:* 01-789 2979. *Clubs:* All England Lawn Tennis and Croquet, International Lawn Tennis of GB.

FRITH, Brig. Sir Eric (Herbert Cokayne), Kt 1973; CBE 1945 (MBE 1926); DL; JP; Chairman, Official Side, Police Council for UK, 1966-74; *b* 10 Sept. 1897; *s* of late Brig.-Gen. Herbert Cokayne Frith, CB, Taunton; *m* 1925, Joan Margaret, *yr d* of late Major R. B. Graves-Knyfton; one *s*. *Educ:* Marlborough Coll.; RMC Sandhurst. 2nd Lieut Somerset LI, 1915; served European War, 1914-18 (wounded); psc; served War of 1939-45; retd Dec. 1948. Somerset County Council: Mem. 1949 (Chm. 1959-64, Vice-Chm. 1956-59); Alderman 1957. DL 1953, JP 1953, Somerset. Order of Polonia Restituta (Poland), 1945; Medal of Freedom with Silver Palm (US), 1945. *Recreations:* cricket, Rugby football, hunting, shooting, hockey (in the past). *Address:* The Cottage, Mount Street, Taunton TA1 3QE. *T:* Taunton 84180. *Clubs:* Naval and Military; Somerset Stragglers Cricket.

FRODSHAM, Anthony Freer; Director-General, Engineering Employers' Federation, since 1975; Chairman, Machine Tools Economic Development Committee, since 1973; *b* Peking, China, 8 Sept. 1919; *er s* of George William Frodsham and Constance Violet Frodsham (*née* Neild); *m* 1953, Patricia Myfanwy, *o c* of late Cmdr A. H. Wynne-Edwards, DSC, RN; two *s*. *Educ:* Ecole Lacordaire, Paris; Faraday House Engineering Coll., London. DFH, CEng, FIMechE, FIMC, FBIM. Served War, 1940-46: Engineer Officer, RN, Asst Fleet Engr Officer on staff of C-in-C Mediterranean, 1944-46 (despatches, 1945). P-E Consulting Group Ltd, 1947-73: Dir in charge of Midlands Area and Continent of Europe, 1956-63; Man. Dir and Gp Chief Exec., 1963-72; Group Specialist Adviser, United Dominions Trust Ltd, 1973-74; Director: Arthur Young Management Services, 1973-; TACE Ltd, 1974-75. Mem., BNEC Canada Cttee, 1970-71 (Chm., Machinery Sub-gp). Mem. Council: Management Consultants Assoc., 1960-72 (Chm., 1968-70); Fédération Européenne des Associations de Conseils en Organisation, 1960-72; Inst. of Management Consultants, 1962-74 (Pres., 1967-68); CBI, 1975-; Member: Engineering Industry Training Bd, 1975-; W European Metal Working Employers' Assoc., 1975-; Indep. Chm., Internat. Compressed Air and Allied Machinery Cttee, 1976-; a General Commissioner of Tax, 1975-. Mem., Editorial Bd, Handbook for Managers, 1971-74. *Publications:* contrib. to technical jls; lectures and broadcasts on management subjects. *Recreations:* swimming, boating, modern languages. *Address:* (home) 1 The Grange, Wimbledon Common, SW19. *T:* 01-946 3413; (office) Broadway House, Tothill Street, SW1. *T:* 01-930 6314. *Clubs:* Carlton, Royal Automobile, Naval.

FROGGATT, Peter, MD, FRCPI; President and Vice-Chancellor, Queen's University of Belfast, since 1976. MB BCh, BAO 1952; DPH Belfast 1956; MD Dublin 1958; PhD Belfast 1967; FFCM 1972; FRCPI 1973; MRCP 1974; FFOM 1976; FFCMI 1977. Formerly Consultant, Eastern Area, Health and Social Services Board; Dean of Faculty of Medicine (Social and Preventive Medicine), and Prof. of Epidemiology, Queen's Univ., Belfast. Mem. Soc. Social Med.; FSS. *Publications:* (jtly) Causation of Bus-driver Accidents: Epidemiological Study, 1963; contribs to jls. *Address:* Queen's University of Belfast, Belfast, Northern Ireland BT7 1NN; 71 Osborne Park, Belfast BT9 6JP.

FRÖHLICH, Prof. Albrecht, PhD; FRS 1976; Professor of Pure Mathematics, King's College, University of London, since 1962; Head, Department of Mathematics, since 1971; *b* 22 May 1916; *s* of Julius Frölich and Frida Frölich; *m* 1950, Dr Evelyn Ruth Brooks; one *s* one *d*. *Educ:* Realgymnasium, Munich; Bristol Univ. (BSc 1950, PhD 1953). Asst Lectr in Maths, University Coll., Leicester, 1950-52; Lectr in Maths, University Coll. of N Staffs, 1952-55; Reader in Pure Maths, King's Coll., Univ. of London, 1955-62. FKC 1977. *Publications:* Formal Groups, 1968; papers in math. jls. *Recreations:* cooking, eating, walking, music. *Address:* 63 Drax Avenue, Wimbledon, SW20. *T:* 01-946 6550.

FRÖHLICH, Herbert, FRS 1951; DPhil; Professor of Theoretical Physics, The University of Liverpool, 1948-73, Professor Emeritus, since 1973; *b* 9 Dec. 1905; *m* 1950, Fanchon Aungst. *Educ:* Munich. Studied Theoretical Physics at University of Munich; DPhil 1930; Subsequently Privatdozent at Freiburg Univ. Left Germany in 1933. Research Physicist, Lecturer, and Reader in Theoretical Physics, University of Bristol, 1935-48; Prof. of Solid State Electronics, Univ. of Salford, 1973-76, Vis. Fellow, 1976-. Hon. Dr of Science, Rennes, 1955; Hon. LLD Alberta, 1968; Hon. ScD Dublin, 1969. Max Planck Medal, 1972. *Publications:* various scientific papers and books. *Address:* Department of Physics, Oliver Lodge Laboratory, The University, Oxford Street, PO Box 147, Liverpool L69 3BX.

FROME, Sir Norman (Frederick), Kt 1947; CIE 1945; DFC 1918; MSc, FIEE; late Consultant, Messrs Preece, Cardew & Rider, Consulting Engineers; formerly Indian Posts and Telegraphs Department; *b* 23 Sept. 1899; *s* of late John Frome, Bristol; *m* 1928, Edith S. Guyan. *Educ:* Fairfield Grammar Sch.; University of Bristol. Served European War, 1914-18, in RFC and RAF, 1917-18. Joined Indian Posts and Telegraphs Dept, 1923; Dir of Telegraphs, 1937; Postmaster-Gen., 1941; Chief Engineer, 1946. *Publications:* articles on telecommunications, 1928-60. *Recreations:* astronomy, ornithology. *Address:* Elmwood, Gussage All Saints, near Wimborne, Dorset BH21 5ET. *Club:* Royal Commonwealth Society.

FROOD, Alan Campbell; Director of Financial Services, Crown Agents for Oversea Governments and Administrations, since 1976; *b* 15 May 1926; *s* of James Campbell Frood and Margaret

Helena Frood; *m* 1960, Patricia Ann Cotterell; two *s* two *d*. *Educ:* Cranleigh Sch.; Peterhouse, Cambridge (BA Hons). Royal Navy, 1944-47 (Sub-Lt RNVR). Bank of England, 1949; Colonial Admin. Service, 1952; Bankers Trust Co., 1962; Dir, Bankers Trust Internat. Ltd, 1967; Gen. Man., Banking Dept, Crown Agents, 1975. *Recreations:* sailing, gardening. *Address:* West Orchard, Holmbush Lane, Henfield, West Sussex. *T:* Poynings 257.

FROST, Abraham Edward Hardy, CBE 1972; Counsellor, Foreign and Commonwealth Office, since 1972; *b* 4 July 1918; *s* of Abraham William Frost and Margaret Anna Frost; *m* 1972, Gillian (*née* Crossley); two *d*. *Educ:* Royal Grammar Sch., Colchester; King's Coll., Cambridge (MA); London Univ. (BScEcon). FCIS. RNVR, 1940-46 (Lieut). ILO, Geneva, 1947-48; HM Treasury, 1948-49; Manchester Guardian, City Staff, 1949-51; FO (later FCO), 1951-. *Publication:* In Dorset Of Course (poems), 1976. *Address:* 9 Crescent Road, Beckenham, Kent BR3 2NF. *T:* 01-650 4957; Hill View, Buckland Newton, Dorset. *T:* Buckland Newton 415.

FROST, Albert Edward; Director: British Airways Corporation, since 1976; Marks & Spencer Ltd, since 1976; S. G. Warburg & Co. Ltd, since 1976; *b* 7 March 1914; *s* of Charles Albert Frost and Minnie Frost; *m* 1942, Eugénie Maud Barlow. *Educ:* Oulton Sch., Liverpool; London Univ. Called to the Bar, Middle Temple (1st Cl. Hons). HM Inspector of Taxes, Inland Revenue, 1937; Imperial Chemical Industries Ltd: Dep. Head, Taxation Dept, 1949; Dep. Treasurer, 1957; Treasurer, 1960; Finance Dir, 1968; retd 1976. Member: NEDC Cttee on Finance for Industry; Panel on Take-overs and Mergers; Council and Finance Cttee, St Thomas's Med. Sch., London; Council and Finance Cttee, Morley Coll., London; Adv. Council, Assoc. for Business Sponsorship of the Arts; Org. Cttee, Carl Flesch Internat. Violin Competition, London. *Publications:* (contrib.) Simon's Income Tax, 1952; (contrib.) Gunns Australian Income Tax Law and Practice, 1960; articles on financial matters affecting industry and on arts sponsorship. *Recreations:* violinist (chamber music); swimming (silver medallist, Royal Life Saving Assoc.); athletics (county colours, track and cross country); walking; arts generally. *Address:* Michael House, Baker Street, W1A 1DN. *T:* 01-935 4422. *Club:* Royal Automobile.

FROST, David (Paradine), OBE 1970; author, producer, columnist; star of "The Frost Report", "The Frost Programme", "Frost on Friday", "The David Frost Show", "The Frost Interview", etc; Joint Founder, London Weekend Television; Chairman and Chief Executive, David Paradine Ltd, since 1966; *b* 7 April 1939; *s* of late Rev. W. J. Paradine Frost, Beccles, Suffolk. *Educ:* Gillingham Grammar Sch.; Wellingborough Grammar Sch.; Gonville and Caius Coll., Cambridge (MA). Sec., The Footlights; Editor, Granta. LLD, Emerson Coll., USA. BBC Television series: That Was the Week That Was, 1962-63 (in USA, 1963-64); A Degree of Frost, 1963, 1973; Not So Much a Programme, More a Way of Life, 1964-65; The Frost Report, 1966-67; Frost Over England, 1967; Frost Over America, 1970; Frost's Weekly, 1973; The Frost Interview, 1974; We British, 1975-76; Forty Years of Television, 1976; The Frost Programme, 1977. David Frost at the Phonograph (BBC Sound), 1966, 1972. Frost on Thursday (LBC), 1974. ITV series: The Frost Programme, 1966-67, 1967-68; Frost on Friday, 1968-69, 1969-70; The Frost Programme, 1972, 1973; The Sir Harold Wilson Interviews, 1976; A Prime Minister on Prime Ministers, 1977. Other programmes include: David Frost's Night Out in London, (USA), 1966-67; The Next President, (USA), 1968; Robert Kennedy the Man, (USA), 1968; The David Frost Show, (USA), 1969-70, 1970-71, 1971-72; The David Frost Revue (USA), 1971-72, 1972-73; That Was the Year That Was, (USA), 1973; David Frost Presents the Guinness Book of Records (USA), 1973, 1974, 1975, 1976; Frost over Australia, 1972, 1973, 1974, 1977; Frost over New Zealand, 1973, 1974; The Unspeakable Crime (USA), 1975; Abortion—Merciful or Murder? (USA), 1975; The Beatles—Once Upon a Time (USA), 1975; David Frost Presents the Best (USA), 1975; The Nixon Interviews with David Frost, 1976-77; The Crossroads of Civilization, 1977-78. Produced films: The Rise and Rise of Michael Rimmer, 1970; Charley One-Eye, 1972; Leadbelly, 1974; The Slipper and the Rose, 1975; James A. Michener's Dynasty, 1975. Mem., British/USA Bicentennial Liaison Cttee, 1973-. Golden Rose, Montreux, for Frost Over England, 1967; Royal Television Society's Silver Medal, 1967; Richard Dimbleby Award, 1967; Emmy Award (USA), 1970, 1971; Religious Heritage of America Award, 1970; Albert Einstein Award, Communication Arts, 1971. *Stage:* An Evening with David Frost (Edinburgh Fest.), 1966. *Publications:* That Was the Week That Was, 1963; How to Live under Labour, 1964; Talking with Frost, 1967; To England With Love, 1967; The Presidential Debate 1968, 1968; The Americans, 1970; Whitlam

and Frost, 1974; *relevant publication:* David Frost, by Willi Frischauer, 1972. *Address:* 46 Egerton Crescent, SW3.

FROST, Jeffrey Michael Torbet; Executive Director, Committee on Invisible Exports, since 1976; *b* 11 June 1938; *s* of Basil Frost and late Dorothy Frost. *Educ:* Diocesan Coll., Cape, South Africa; Radley Coll.; Oriel Coll., Oxford; Harvard Univ. *Address:* 34 Paradise Walk, SW3. *T:* 01-352 8642.

FROST, Maj.-Gen. John Dutton, CB 1964; DSO 1943 and Bar, 1945; MC 1942; *b* 31 Dec. 1912; *s* of late Brig.-Gen. F. D. Frost, CBE, MC; *m* 1947, Jean MacGregor Lyle; one *s* one *d*. *Educ:* Wellington Coll.; RMC Sandhurst. Commissioned The Cameronians, Sept. 1932; Capt., Iraq Levies, 1938-41; Major and Lt-Col, Parachute Regt, 1941-45; Staff Coll., Camberley, 1946; GSO2, HQ Lowland Dist, 1948-49; GSO2, Senior Officers' Sch., 1949-52; AA and QMG, 17 Gurkha Div., 1952-53; GSO1, 17 Gurkha Div., 1953-55; Comd, Netheravon, 1955-57; Comd, 44 Parachute Bde, 1958-61; Comdr 52nd Lowland Div./District, 1961-64; GOC Troops in Malta and Libya, 1964-66; Comdr Malta Land Force, 1965; retired, 1967. Cross of Grand Officer, SMO, Malta, 1966. *Recreations:* field sports, polo, golf. *Address:* Northend Farm, Milland, Liphook, Hants. *Club:* Army and Navy.

FROST, Norman, CBE 1959; KPM 1950; *b* 18 March 1899; *s* of William Frost and Maud Frost (*née* Strickland); *m* 1927, Ivy Edna (*née* Bush); two *s*. *Educ:* March, Cambs. Royal Engineers (Signals), 1917-20. Peterborough Police, 1926-44; Boston Police, 1944-47; seconded Home Office; Commandant Police Training Sch., 1945-47; Eastbourne Police, 1947-54; Chief Constable of Bristol, 1954-64. OStJ. *Recreation:* collecting antiques. *Address:* Westovers, Wedmore, Somerset. *T:* Wedmore 712568. *Club:* St John House.

FROST, Dame Phyllis Irene, DBE 1974 (CBE 1963); JP; Chairman, Keep Australia Beautiful Council, since 1971; Member: Victorian Prison Advisory Council, Australia, and State Flood Relief Committee, since 1974; State Relief Committee, since 1964; National Fitness Council, since 1957; Past Chairman and Member many community service organisations; *b* 14 Sept. 1917; *née* Turner; *m* 1941, Glenn Neville Frost, LDS, BDSc, JP; three *d*. *Educ:* Croydon Coll., Vic.; St Duthus Coll.; Presbyterian Ladies' Coll.; Univ. of Melbourne. Dip. of Physiotherapy, 1938; studied Criminology, 1955. Past Member: Adult Parole Bd (Female), 1957-74; Youth Advisory Council, 1957-72 (Vice-Chm.). Past Nat. and State appts also include: Past-Pres., Australian Freedom from Hunger Campaign, and many Exec. memberships and positions. Has attended several internat. confs as accredited Aust. delegate or rep. Internat. Council of Women; notably Chairman: Freedom from Hunger Campaign Conf. (4th Session in Rome), 1969; 3rd Regional Congress of FFHC for Asia and the Far East, at Canberra, 1970, and Rome, 1971. Convenor, Public Questions Cttee, Congregational Union of Victoria (Exec. Council Mem. of Union, 1970-). JP Croydon, Vic., 1957-. *Address:* 296 Dorset Road, Croydon, Victoria 3136, Australia. *Clubs:* Royal Commonwealth Society; Royal Automobile (Vic.).

FROST, Hon. Sir Sydney; *see* Frost, Hon. Sir T. S.

FROST, Terence, (Terry Frost); artist; Professor of Painting, University of Reading, since 1977 (formerly Reader in Fine Art); *b* Oct. 1915; *m* 1945; five *s* one *d*. *Educ:* Leamington Spa Central Sch. Exhibitions: Leicester Galls, 1952-58; Waddington Galls, 1958-; B. Schaeffer Gallery, New York, 1960-62; Plymouth 1976; Bristol 1976; Serpentine Gall., 1977. Oil paintings acquired by Tate Gallery, National Gallery of Canada, National Gallery of NSW; also drawing acquired by Victoria and Albert Museum. Other work in public collections; Canada, USA, Germany, Australia, and in Edinburgh, Dublin, Leeds, Hull, Manchester, Birmingham, Liverpool, Bristol, etc. Gregory Fellow in Painting, Univ. of Leeds, 1954-56. *Address:* Gernick Field Studio, Tredavoe Lane, Newlyn, Penzance. *T:* Penzance 5902.

FROST, Hon. Sir (Thomas) Sydney, Kt 1975; Chief Justice of Papua New Guinea, 1975-78; *b* 13 Feb. 1916; *s* of late Thomas and Mary Andree Frost; *m* 1943, Dorothy Gertrude (*née* Kelly); two *s* one *d*. *Educ:* Univ. of Melbourne (LLM). Served 2nd AIF, 1941-45. Barrister, Victoria, 1945; QC (Vic.), 1961; Judge of the County Court of Victoria, 1964; Judge of the Supreme Court of Papua New Guinea, 1964-75. *Recreation:* golf. *Address:* Park Tower, 201 Spring Street, Melbourne, Victoria, Australia. *T:* 662 3239. *Club:* Australian (Melbourne).

FROWEN, Brig. John Harold, DSO 1941; OBE 1941; RA; retired; *b* 14 Sept. 1898; *s* of Fraser Frowen and Elizabeth Mary, *d* of late Sir John Heffernan, KCB, RN. *Educ:* privately; RMA Woolwich. 2nd Lieut RA, 1916; Capt. 1929; Major 1938; Temp. Lieut-Col 1940; Col, 1946; Brig., 1949; served in France and Flanders, 1917-19; India, 1919-26; Home, 1926-29; employed in mission to Egyptian Army, 1939-40; served Western Desert campaigns, Greece, Crete, etc (prisoner); repatriated UK 1943; BRA Southern Army, India Command, 1943-44; Comdt Artillery Sch., India, 1944-47; Comdr AA Bde, UK, 1947-51; loaned Pakistan Army, 1951-52; retd 1952. Sec. RA Institution, 1952-58; Sec. RA Printing Press, 1958-64. *Recreation:* played in Wimbledon lawn tennis tournament, 1929, 1930, 1931. *Address:* 29 Morden Road, SE3. *T:* 01-852 5308. *Club:* Army and Navy.

FROY, Prof. Martin; Professor of Fine Art, University of Reading, since 1972; *s* of late William Alan Froy and Helen Elizabeth Spencer. *Educ:* St Paul's Sch.; Magdalene Coll., Cambridge (one year); Slade Sch. of Fine Art. Dipl. in Fine Art (London). Visiting Teacher of Engraving, Slade Sch. of Fine Art, 1952-55; taught at Bath Acad. of Art, latterly as Head of Fine Art, 1954-65; Head of Painting Sch., Chelsea Sch. of Art, 1965-72. Gregory Fellow in Painting, Univ. of Leeds, 1951-54; Leverhulme Research Award, six months study in Italy, 1963; Sabbatical Award, Arts Council, 1965. Mem., Fine Art Panel, 1962-71, Mem. Council, 1969-71, Nat. Council for Diplomas in Art and Design; Trustee: National Gall., 1972-; Tate Gall. 1975-. *One-Man Exhibitions:* Hanover Gall., London, 1952, 1969; Wakefield City Art Gall., 1953; Leicester Galls, London, 1961; Royal West of England Acad., Bristol, 1964; Park Square Gall., Leeds, 1970; Arnolfini Gall., Bristol, 1970; City Art Gall., Bristol (seven paintings), 1972. *Other Exhibitions:* Internat. Abstract Artists, Riverside Mus., NY, 1950; ICA, London, 1950; Ten English Painters, Brit. Council touring exhibn in Scandinavia, 1952; Figures in their Setting, Contemp. Art Soc. Exhibn, Tate Gall., 1953; Le Congrès pour la Liberté de la Culture Exhibn, Rome, Paris, Brussels, 1955; Pittsburgh Internat., 1955; City Art Gall., Bristol, 1960; Three Painters, Bath Fest. Exhibn, 1970. *Commissions, etc:* Artist Consultant for Arts Council to City Architect, Coventry, 1953-58; mosaic decoration, Belgrade Th., Coventry, 1957-58; two mural panels, Concert Hall, Morley Coll., London, 1958-59. *Works in Public Collections:* Tate Gall.; Mus. of Mod. Art, NY; Chicago Art Inst.; Arts Council; Contemp. Art Soc.; Royal W of England Acad.; Leeds Univ.; City Art Galls of Bristol, Carlisle, Leeds, Southampton and Wakefield. *Address:* Department of Fine Art, University of Reading, London Road, Reading, Berks RG1 5AQ.

FRY, Christopher; dramatist; *b* 18 Dec. 1907; *s* of Charles John Harris and Emma Marguerite Hammond, *d* of Emma Louisa Fry; *m* 1936, Phyllis Marjorie Hart; one *s*. *Educ:* Bedford Modern Sch. Actor at Citizen House, Bath, 1927; Schoolmaster at Hazlewood Preparatory Sch., Limpsfield, Surrey, 1928-31; Dir of Tunbridge Wells Repertory Players, 1932-35; life too complicated for tabulation, 1935-39; The Tower, a pageant-play produced at Tewkesbury Fest., 1939; Dir of Oxford Repertory Players, 1940 and 1944-46, directing at Arts Theatre, London, 1945; Staff dramatist, Arts, 1947. FRSL. Queen's Gold Medal (for Poetry), 1962. *Plays:* A Phoenix Too Frequent, Mercury, 1946; The Lady's Not for Burning, Arts, 1948, Globe, 1949, Chichester, 1972; The Firstborn, Edinburgh Festival, 1948; Thor, with Angels, Canterbury Festival, 1949; Venus Observed, St James's, 1950; The Boy with a Cart, Lyric, Hammersmith, 1950; Ring Round the Moon (translated from French of Jean Anouilh), Globe, 1950; A Sleep of Prisoners, produced St Thomas' Church, Regent Street, W1, 1951; The Dark is Light Enough, Aldwych, 1954; The Lark (trans. from French of Jean Anouilh), Lyric, Hammersmith, 1955; Tiger at the Gates (trans. from French of Jean Giraudoux), Apollo, 1955; Duel of Angels (trans. from Pour Lucrèce, of Jean Giraudoux), Apollo, 1958; Curtmantle, Edinburgh Festival, 1962; Judith (trans. from Giraudoux), Her Majesty's, 1962; A Yard of Sun, National, 1970; Peer Gynt (trans.), Chichester, 1970; Cyrano de Bergerac (trans.), Chichester, 1975. *TV:* The Brontës of Haworth, four plays, 1973; Sister Dora, 1977; The Best of Enemies, 1977. *Film Commentary* for The Queen is Crowned (Coronation film, 1953); *Film scripts:* (participation) Ben Hur; Barabbas; The Bible; The Beggar's Opera. *Publications:* The Boy with a Cart, 1939; The Firstborn, 1946; A Phoenix Too Frequent, 1946; The Lady's Not for Burning, 1949; Thor, with Angels, 1949; Venus Observed, 1950; (trans.) Ring Round the Moon, 1950; A Sleep of Prisoners, 1951; The Dark is Light Enough, 1954; (trans.) The Lark, 1955; (trans.) Tiger at The Gates, 1955; (trans.) Duel of Angels, 1958; Curtmantle, 1961 (Heinemann Award of RSL); (trans.) Judith, 1962; A Yard of Sun, 1970; (trans.) Peer Gynt, 1970; (trans., with J. Kirkup) The Oxford Ibsen, vol. III, Brand and Peer Gynt, 1972; Four television plays: The Brontës at Haworth, 1954; (trans.) Cyrano de Bergerac, 1975. *Address:* The Toft, East Dean, Chichester, West Sussex.

FRY, Prof. Dennis Butler; Emeritus Professor of Experimental Phonetics, University College, London, Professor 1958-75; Hon. Research Fellow, University College London; *b* 3 Nov. 1907; *s* of late F. C. B. Fry and Jane Ann (*née* Butler), Stockbridge, Hants; *m* 1937, Chrystabel, *er d* of late Charles Smith, JP, Brighton; one *s* two *d*. *Educ:* Gosport Grammar Sch.; University of London. Asst Master, Tewkesbury Grammar Sch., 1929-31; Asst Master, Kilburn Grammar Sch., 1931-34; Asst Lecturer in Phonetics, University Coll., London, 1934-37; Lecturer and Superintendent of Phonetics Laboratory, 1937-49. Served as Squadron Leader, RAFVR, 1940-45; in charge of Acoustics Laboratory, Central Medical Establishment, RAF, 1941-45. Reader in Experimental Phonetics, University of London, 1948; Head of Dept of Phonetics, UCL, 1949-71. Editor of Language and Speech. Pres., Permanent Internat. Council for Phonetic Sciences, 1961; Hon. Fellow, College of Speech Therapists, 1964; Fellow, Acoustical Soc. of America, 1966; Governor: Sadler's Wells Foundation, 1966. Trustee, Inst. for Cultural Research. FRSA 1970. *Publications:* The Deaf Child (with E. M. Whetnall), 1963; Learning to Hear, 1970; Homo Loquens, 1977; papers on speech and hearing in scientific and linguistic journals. *Recreation:* music, especially singing. *Address:* 18 Lauriston Road, SW19. *T:* 01-946 3046.

FRY, Donald William, CBE 1970; Director, Atomic Energy Establishment, Winfrith, 1959-73; *b* 30 Nov. 1910; *m* 1934, Jessie Florence (*née* Wright); three *s*. *Educ:* Weymouth Gram. Sch.; King's Coll., London. Research Physicist, GEC Laboratories, 1932; RAE Farnborough (Radio Dept), 1936; Air Min. Research Establishment (later the Telecommunications Research Establishment, TRE) Swanage, 1940; moved with the Estab. to Malvern, 1942; joined staff of AERE (still at Malvern), 1946; demonstrated with other mems of group a new Principle for accelerating particles: the travelling wave linear accelerator, 1947. Awarded Duddell Medal of Physical Soc., 1950; Head of Gen. Physics Div. at AERE Harwell, 1950; Chief Physicist, 1954, Dep. Dir, 1958, AERE Harwell. CEng, FIEE 1946; FIEEE 1960; FInstP 1970; Hon. Freeman of Weymouth, 1958. FKC London, 1959. *Publications:* papers in learned journals. *Address:* Coveway Lodge, Overcombe, near Weymouth, Dorset. *T:* Preston (Weymouth) 833276. *Club:* Royal Dorset Yacht.

FRY, E. Maxwell, CBE 1953; RA 1972 (ARA 1966); BArch, FRIBA, FRTPI; Dist Town Planning; consultant architect and town planner in retirement; active painter; *b* 2 Aug. 1899; *s* of Ambrose Fry and Lydia Thompson; *m* 1927, Ethel Speakman (marr. diss.); one *d*; *m* 1942, Jane B. Drew, *qv*. *Educ:* Liverpool Inst.; Liverpool Univ. Sch. of Architecture. Practised with Walter Gropius as Gropius and Fry, 1934-36; as Maxwell Fry and Jane Drew, 1945-50, as Fry, Drew, Drake, & Lasdun, 1951-58; now as Fry, Drew, Knight & Creamer. Work includes schools, hospitals, working-class and other flats, houses in England and educational buildings in Ghana and Nigeria. Served with Royal Engineers, 1939-44. Town Planning Adviser to Resident Minister for West Africa, 1943-45; Senior Architect to New Capital Chandigarh, Punjab, 1951-54. One-man show, Drian Gall., 1974. Ex-Mem. Royal Fine Art Commission; Corr. Mem. Académie Flamande, 1956; Hon. FAIA 1963; Council Mem. RIBA (Vice-Pres. 1961-62) and RSA; Royal Gold Medal for Architecture, 1964. Hon. LLD Ibadan Univ., 1966. *Publications:* Fine Building, 1944; (jointly with Jane B. Drew) Architecture for Children, 1944; Tropical Architecture, 1964; Art in a Machine Age, 1969; Maxwell Fry: autobiographical sketches, 1975; contribs to architectural and other papers. *Address:* 63 Gloucester Place, W1H 4DJ. *T:* 01-935 3318; The Lake House, Rowfant, Sussex. *T:* Pound Hill 2182.

FRY, Sir John (Nicholas Pease), 4th Bt *cr* 1894; *b* 23 Oct. 1897; *s* of Sir John Pease Fry, 2nd Bt and Margaret Theodora (*d* 1941), *d* of Francis Edward Fox, JP; *S* brother, 1971; *m* 1927, Helen Murray, *d* of late William Gibson Bott, MRCS, JP; one *d* (and one *d* decd). *Educ:* Clifton: Trinity College, Cambridge (BA). Served European War, 1914-18 with Friends Ambulance Unit; War of 1939-45, with Special Constabulary. *Heir:* *b* Francis Wilfrid Fry, OBE [*b* 2 May 1904; *m* 1943, Anne Pease, *e d* of late Kenneth Henry Wilson, OBE, JP]. *Address:* c/o National Westminster Bank Ltd, Molesworth Street, Wadebridge, Cornwall.

FRY, Maxwell; *see* Fry, E. Maxwell.

FRY, Peter Derek; MP (C) Wellingborough since Dec. 1969; Insurance Broker since 1963; *b* 26 May 1931; *s* of Harry Walter Fry and late Edith Fry; *m* 1958, Edna Roberts; one *s* one *d*. *Educ:* Royal Grammar School, High Wycombe; Worcester College, Oxford (MA). Tillotsons (Liverpool) Ltd, 1954-56; Northern Assurance Co., 1956-61; Political Education Officer, Conservative Central Office, 1961-63. Member Bucks County

Council, 1961-67. Contested (C) North Nottingham, 1964, East Willesden, 1966. Secretary: British Yugoslav Parly Gp; Conservative Transport Industry Cttee; Jt Chm., All Party Roads Study Gp; Treasurer, All Party Group on responsible family planning; Vice-Chm., Cons. Transport Ind. Cttee. Played Rugby for Bucks County, 1956-58, Hon. Secretary, 1958-61. *Recreations:* watching Rugby football; reading history and biographies. *Address:* Chiltern Lodge, 27 Poplars Farm Road, Barton Seagrave, Kettering, Northants. *Club:* Royal Automobile.

FRY, Richard Henry, CBE 1965; Financial Editor of The Guardian, 1939-65; *b* 23 Sept. 1900; *m* 1929, Katherine (*née* Maritz); no *c*. *Educ:* Berlin and Heidelberg Univs. *Address:* 8 Montagu Mews West, W1. *T:* 01-262 0817. *Club:* Reform.

FRY, Ronald Ernest, FSS; Director of Economics and Statistics, Departments of the Environment and Transport, since 1975; *b* 21 May 1925; *s* of Ernest Fry and Lilian (*née* Eveling); *m* 1954, Jeanne Ivy Dawson; one *s* one *d*. *Educ:* Wilson's Grammar Sch., Camberwell; Birkbeck Coll., Univ. of London (BSc (Special)). MIS. Telecommunications Technician, Royal Signals, 1944-47; Scientific Asst, CEGB (London Region), 1948-52; Statistician: Glacier Metal Co., London, 1952-54; CEGB HQ, London, 1954-64; Gen. Register Office, 1965-66; Asst Dir of Research and Intelligence, GLC, 1966-69; Chief Statistician: (Social Statistics) Cabinet Office, 1969-74; (Manpower Statistics) Dept of Employment, 1974-75. *Publications:* various technical publns in statistical and other professional jls. *Recreations:* photography, reading, motoring. *Address:* 39 Claremont Road, Hadley Wood, Barnet, Herts EN4 0HR. *T:* 01-440 1393.

FRY, William Norman Hillier-; *see* Hillier-Fry.

FRYARS, Sir Robert (Furness), Kt 1952; *b* 1887; *s* of William Fryars and Mary Emma (*née* Wilsdon); *m* 1915, Doris, *yr d* of William Magall, Newcastle on Tyne; one *s* two *d*. *Educ:* various schools and colls overseas. Served Wars of 1914-19, and 1939-45. Freeman City of London; Hon. Mem. Court Worshipful Company of Blacksmiths. Freeman, City of Fort William (Canada). Formerly Chm., Man. Dir or Dir various public companies, 1930-55; Mem. Nat. Adv. Council for Motor Manfg Industry, 1946-52; Mem. of Council Soc. Motor Mfrs & Traders, 1945; Chm. British Transport Vehicle Mfrs Assoc., 1946-52; Hon. Pres. Asturian Omnibus Co. ALSA (Spain), 1962. FCIS, FREconS. Cross and Kt Comdr, Order of Civil Merit (Spain), 1965. *Recreations:* travel, reading, music, gardening, conversation. *Address:* 18 The Close, Selsey, Chichester, West Sussex PO20 0ET. *T:* Selsey 4407.

FRYBERG, Sir Abraham, Kt 1968; MBE 1941; retired; *b* 26 May 1901; *s* of Henry and Rose Fryberg; *m* 1939, Vivian Greensil Barnard; one *s*. *Educ:* Wesley Coll., Melbourne; Queen's Coll., University of Melbourne. MB, BS (Melbourne) 1928; DPH, DTM (Sydney) 1936; Hon. MD (Qld); Hon. FACMA. Served with 9 Australian Div. (Tobruk, Alamein), 1940-45. Resident Med. Officer, then Registrar, Brisbane Hosp. and Brisbane Children's Hosp., 1929-33; GP, Hughenden, 1934; Health Officer, Qld Health Dept, 1936-46 (except for war service); Dep. Dir-Gen., 1946, Dir-Gen. of Health and Medical Services, Qld, 1947-67, retired. Hon. Col, RAAMC Northern Comd, 1962-67. SBStJ 1958. *Recreations:* racing, bowls. *Address:* 19 Dublin Street, Clayfield, Qld 4011, Australia. *T:* Brisbane 62-2549. *Club:* United Service (Brisbane).

FRYER, Dr Geoffrey, FRS 1972; Senior Principal Scientific Officer, Windermere Laboratory, Freshwater Biological Association, since 1973; *b* 6 Aug. 1927; *s* of W. and M. Fryer; *m* 1953, Vivien Griffiths Hodgson; one *s* one *d*. *Educ:* Huddersfield College. DSc, PhD London. Royal Navy, 1946-48. Colonial Research Student, 1952-53; HM Overseas Research Service, 1953-60: Malawi, 1953-55; Zambia, 1955-57; Uganda, 1957-60; Sen., then Principal Scientific Officer, Freshwater Biological Assoc., 1960-73. *Publications:* (with T. D. Iles) The Cichlid Fishes of the Great Lakes of Africa: their biology and evolution, 1972; numerous articles in scientific jls. *Recreations:* natural history, walking, books, photography. *Address:* Elleray Cottage, Windermere, Cumbria LA23 1AW.

FRYER, Maj.-Gen. (retd) Wilfred George, CB 1956; CBE 1951 (OBE 1941); *b* 1 May 1900; *s* of James and Marion Fryer, Kington, Herefordshire; *m* 1931, Jean Eleanore Graham, *d* of Graham Binny, RSW, Edinburgh; three *s*. *Educ:* Christ Coll., Brecon; RMA Woolwich. Commissioned 2nd Lieut RE, 1919, Regular Army; served in India, Royal Bombay Sappers and Miners, 1933-38; Major RE, Instructor, Sch. of Mil. Engineering, Chatham, 1938. Served War of 1939-45: Lt-Col RE, ADWE & M, GHQ, Middle East, 1941; SO1 to Chief

Engineer, Eighth Army, Western Desert Campaign (OBE), 1941; Col DDWE & M, GHQ, Middle East, 1942; GSO1 to Scientific Adviser to Army Council, 1944; ADWE & M, GHQ and Dep. Chief Engineer, 8 Corps, NW Europe Campaign (despatches), 1944-45; Brig.-Chief Engr, Brit. Army Staff, Washington, DC, 1945; Col E (Equipment), War Office, 1946-48; Brig.-Chief Engr, Singapore Dist, 1948-51; Brig.-Chief Engr, Southern Comd, UK, 1951-53; Maj.-Gen. 1954; Chief Engineer, Middle East Land Forces, 1954-57. "A" Licence air pilot, 1942. MIEE 1952. Chm., Warminster Press Ltd. Nat. Champion, Wayfarer Dinghy, 1960. *Recreations:* ocean racing (Transatlantic Race, 1931), ski-ing, tennis. *Address:* Critchells Green Farmhouse, Lockerley, Romsey, Hants SO5 0JD. *Clubs:* Army and Navy, Royal Ocean Racing, Hurlingham.

FUCHS, Sir Vivian (Ernest), Kt 1958; MA, PhD; FRS 1974; Director of the British Antarctic Survey, 1958-73; Leader Commonwealth Trans-Antarctic Expedition, 1955-58; *b* 11 Feb. 1908; *s* of late E. Fuchs, Farnham, Surrey, and late Violet Anne Fuchs (*née* Watson); *m* 1933, Joyce, 2nd *d* of late John Connell; one *s* one *d* (and one *d* decd). *Educ:* Brighton Coll.; St John's Coll., Cambridge. Geologist with: Cambridge East Greenland Expedn, 1929; Cambridge Expdn to E African Lakes, 1930-31; E African Archæological Expdn, 1931-32; Leader Lake Rudolf Rift Valley Expedn, 1933-34; Royal Geog. Society Cuthbert Peek Grant, 1936; Leader Lake Rukwa Expedn, 1937-38. 2nd Lieut Cambs Regt, TA, 1939; served in W Africa, 1942-43; Staff Coll., Camberley, 1943; served NW Europe (despatches), 1944-46; demobilized (Major), 1946. Leader Falkland Islands Dependencies Survey (Antarctica), 1947-50; Dir FIDSc Bureau, 1950-55. Pres., British Assoc. for Advancement of Science, 1972. Founder's Gold Medal, Royal Geog. Soc., 1951; Silver Medal RSA, 1952; Polar Medal, 1953, and Clasp, 1958; Special Gold Medal, Royal Geog. Soc., 1958; Gold Medal Royal Scottish Geog. Society 1958; Gold Medal Geog. Society (Paris), 1958; Richthofen Medal (Berlin), 1958; Kirchenpauer Medal (Hamburg), 1958; Plancius Medal (Amsterdam), 1959; Egede Medal (Copenhagen), 1959; Hubbard Medal, Nat. Geog. Soc. (Washington), 1959; Explorers Club Medal (New York), 1959; Geog. Soc. (Chicago) Gold Medal, 1959; Geol. Soc. of London Prestwich Medal, 1960. Hon. Fellow, Wolfson (formerly University Coll.), Cambridge, 1970. Hon. LLD Edinburgh 1958; Hon. DSc: Durham 1958; Cantab 1959; Leicester 1972; Hon. ScD Swansea, 1971; Hon. LLD Birmingham, 1974. *Publications:* The Crossing of Antarctica (Fuchs and Hillary), 1958; (ed) Forces of Nature, 1977; geographical and geological reports and papers in scientific jls. *Recreations:* squash racquets, swimming. *Address:* 78 Barton Road, Cambridge. *T:* Cambridge 59238. *Club:* Athenæum.

FUGARD, Athol; playwright, director, actor; *b* 11 June 1932; *s* of Harold David Fugard and Elizabeth Magdalene Potgieter; *m* 1956, Sheila Meiring; one *d*. *Educ:* Univ. of Cape Town. Directed earliest plays, Nongogo, No Good Friday, Johannesburg, 1960; acted in The Blood Knot, touring S Africa, 1961; Hello and Goodbye, 1965; directed and acted in The Blood Knot, London, 1966; Boesman and Lena, S Africa, 1969; directed Boesman and Lena, London, 1971; directed Serpent Players in various prodns, Port Elizabeth, from 1963, directed co-authors John Kani and Winston Ntshona in Sizwe Bansi is Dead, SA, 1972, The Island, 1973, and London, 1973-74; acted in film, Boesman and Lena, 1972; directed and acted in Statements after an Arrest under the Immorality Act, in SA, 1972, directed in London, 1973; wrote Dimetos for Edinburgh Fest., 1975. *Films:* Boesman and Lena; The Guest, 1977. *Publications:* The Blood Knot, 1962; People Are Living There, Hello and Goodbye, 1973; Boesman and Lena, 1973; (jtly) Three Port Elizabeth Plays: Sizwe Bansi is Dead, The Island, Statements after an Arrest under the Immorality Act, 1974. *Recreations:* angling, skin-diving, bird-watching. *Address:* PO Box 5090, Walmer, Port Elizabeth, South Africa.

FULBRIGHT, J. William, Hon. KBE 1975; US Senator (Democrat) for Arkansas, 1945-74; *b* Sumner, Mo, 9 April 1905; *s* of Jay Fulbright and Roberta (*née* Waugh); *m* 1932, Elizabeth Kremer Williams; two *d*. *Educ:* public schools of Fayetteville, Arkansas; University of Arkansas (AB); (Rhodes Scholar) Pembroke Coll., Oxford Univ. (BA, MA); George Washington Univ. Sch. of Law (LLB). Special Attorney, Dept. of Justice, 1934-35; Lectr in Law, George Washington Univ., 1935-36; Mem. Law Sch. Faculty, University of Arkansas, 1936-39, and Pres. of University, 1939-41. Elected to Congress for 3rd Dist of Arkansas, 1942; Mem. Foreign Affairs Cttee. Elected to Senate, 1945, and subsequently; Mem. US Delegn to Gen. Assembly, UN, 1954; Chm. Banking and Currency Cttee of Senate, 1955-59, resigning to become Chm. Senate Cttee on Foreign Relations, also Mem. Finance Cttee and Jt Economic Cttee. First McCallum Meml Lectr, Oxford, 1975. Hon. Fellow,

Pembroke Coll., Oxford, 1949; Fellow, Amer. Acad. of Arts and Sciences (Boston), 1950; Award by Nat. Inst. of Arts and Letters, 1954. Holds several hon. degrees, including DCL Oxford, 1953, and LLD Cantab, 1971. *Publications:* Old Myths and New Realities, 1964; Prospects for the West, 1965; The Arrogance of Power, 1967. *Address:* Fayetteville, Arkansas, USA; 2527 Belmont Road NW, Washington, DC, USA.

FULCHER, Derick Harold, DSC 1944; Chairman, Supplementary Benefit Appeal Tribunals, 1971-75; Interviewer for Civil Service Commission; *b* 4 Nov. 1917; *s* of late Percy Frederick Fulcher and Gertrude Lilian Fulcher; *m* 1943, Florence Ellen May Anderson; one *s* one *d. Educ:* St Olave's Grammar School. Served in Royal Navy, 1940-46 (Lieut, RNVR). Entered Civil Service (War Office), 1936; Asst Principal, Ministry of National Insurance, 1947; Principal, 1950; Admin. Staff Coll., Henley, 1952; Asst Sec. 1959. Seconded to HM Treasury, 1957-59; served on an ILO mission in Trinidad and Tobago, 1967-69; Asst Under-Sec. of State, Dept of Health and Social Security, 1969-70. UK Delegate to and Chairman: NATO Management Survey Cttee, 1970-71; Council of Europe Management Survey Cttee, 1971-72. Head of UK res. project in W Europe into social security provision for disablement, 1971-72; Res. Consultant, Office of Manpower Econs, 1972-73; Served on technical aid mission to Indonesia, 1973; ILO Res. Consultant on Social Security, 1973-77; Consultant to EEC Statistical Office, 1974. Fellow, Inst. for European Health Services Research, Leuven Univ., Belgium, 1974-. *Publication:* Medical Care Systems, 1974. *Recreations:* walking, motoring, travel. *Address:* 100 Downs Road, Coulsdon, Surrey CR3 1AF. *T:* Downland 54231. *Club:* Civil Service.

FULFORD, Robert John; Keeper, Department of Printed Books, British Library (formerly British Museum), since 1967; *b* 16 Aug. 1923; *s* of John Fulford, Southampton; *m* 1950, Alison Margaret Rees; one *s* one *d. Educ:* King Edward VI Sch., Southampton; King's Coll., Cambridge; Charles Univ., Prague. Asst Keeper, Dept of Printed Books, British Museum, 1945-65; Dep. Keeper, 1965-67 (Head of Slavonic Div., 1961-67); Keeper, 1967-. *Address:* 5 Fosse Bank Close, Tonbridge, Kent. *T:* Tonbridge 359310.

FULFORD, Roger Thomas Baldwin, CVO 1970; *b* 24 Nov. 1902; *o* surv. *s* of late Canon Fulford; *m* 1937, Sibell, *widow* of Rev. Hon. C. F. Lyttelton and *d* of late Charles Adeane, CB. *Educ:* St Ronans; Lancing; Worcester Coll., Oxford. Pres. of Union, 1927; called to Bar, 1931; Liberal Candidate for Woodbridge Div. of Suffolk, 1929; for Holderness Div. of Yorks, 1945; for Rochdale, 1950; joined editorial staff of The Times, 1933; Part-time Lecturer in English, King's Coll., London, 1937-48; Asst Censor, 1939-40; Civil Asst War Office, 1940-42; Asst Private Sec. to Sec. of State for Air, 1942-45. Pres., Liberal Party, 1964-65. *Publications:* Royal Dukes, 1933; George IV, 1935; The Right Honourable Gentleman, 1945; The Prince Consort, 1949; Queen Victoria, 1951; History of Glyn's, 1953; Votes for Women, 1957; The Liberal Case, 1959; Hanover to Windsor, 1960; ed (with late Lytton Strachey) The Greville Memoirs, 1937; (ed) The Autobiography of Miss Knight, 1960; (ed) Letters Between Queen Victoria and the Princess Royal: Dearest Child, 1964; Dearest Mama, 1968; Your Dear Letter, 1971; Darling Child, 1976; C. H. Wilkinson, 1965; Samuel Whitbread, 1967; The Trial of Queen Caroline, 1967. *Address:* Barbon Manor, Carnforth, Lancs. *Club:* Boodle's.

FULHAM, Bishop Suffragan of; *see* Gibraltar, Bishop of.

FULLER, Buckminster; *see* Fuller, R. B.

FULLER, Hon. Sir John (Bryan Munro), Kt 1974; MLC, New South Wales, since 1961; NSW Minister for Planning and Environment, 1973-76; Vice-President of Executive Council, 1968-76; Leader of Government in Legislative Council, 1968-76; *b* 22 Sept. 1917; *s* of late Bryan Fuller, QC; *m* 1940, Eileen, *d* of O. S. Webb; one *s* one *d. Educ:* Knox Grammar Sch., Wahroonga. Chm., Australian Country Party (NSW), 1959-64; Minister for Decentralisation and Development, 1965-73. Vice-Pres., Graziers Assoc. of NSW, 1965; Mem. Council, Univ. of NSW, 1967-; Leader of various NSW Govt trade missions to various parts of the world. Fellow Australian Inst. of Export 1969. *Recreations:* tennis, bowls. *Address:* Kallateenee, Coolah, NSW 2853, Australia; Parliament House, Sydney, NSW. *Clubs:* Australian, American National, Associated Schools (Sydney); Coolah Bowling.

FULLER, Major Sir (John) Gerard (Henry Fleetwood), 2nd Bt, *cr* 1910; late Life Guards; *b* 8 July 1906; *s* of 1st Bt and Norah Jacintha (who married secondly Col R. Forestier Walker, DSO, and died 1935), *d* of late C. Nicholas Paul Phipps of Charlcot,

Westbury, Wilts; *S* father, 1915; *m* 1st, 1931, Lady Fiona Pratt (marriage dissolved, 1944), *yr d* of 4th Marquess Camden, GCVO; two *s*; 2nd, 1945, Kathleen Elizabeth, MBE, DStJ (*d* 1964), 5th *d* of late Sir George Farrar, Bt, Chichely Hall, Newport Pagnell, Bucks; 3rd, 1966, Mrs Mary Leventon. *Educ:* Uppingham. 2nd Lieut Life Guards, 1927; Captain 1938; Major, 1941; retired, 1946; served War of 1939-45 (despatches). JP Wilts, 1946; Mem. Wilts CC 1947-71; County Alderman, 1961; Joint Master Avon Vale Fox Hounds, 1947-61, and 1962-64. *Heir: s* John William Fleetwood Fuller [*b* 18 Dec. 1936; *m* 1968, Lorna Marian, *o d* of F. R. Kemp-Potter, Findon, Sussex; two *s*. Major, The Life Guards, 1968]. *Address:* Neston Park, Corsham, Wilts. *T:* Hawthorn 810211; Balmore, Cannich, Inverness-shire. *T:* Cannich 262.

FULLER, Richard Buckminster; American geometer, educator and architect-designer; University Professor Emeritus, Southern Illinois University and University of Pennsylvania; *b* Milton, Mass, 12 July 1895; *s* of Richard Buckminster Fuller and Caroline Wolcott Fuller (*née* Andrews); *m* 1917, Anne Hewlett; one *d* (and one *d* decd). *Educ:* Milton Acad.; Harvard Univ., US Naval Acad. Apprentice machine fitter, Richards, Atkinson & Haserick, 1914; Ensign to Lieut, US Navy, 1917-19; Asst Export Man., Armour & Co., 1919-21; Nat. Accounts Sales Man., Kelly-Springfield Truck Co., 1922; Pres. Stockade Building System, 1922-27; Founder, Pres., 4-D Co., Chicago, 1927-32; Editor and Publisher, Shelter Magazine, Philadelphia, 1930-32; Asst to Dir of Housing Res., Pierce Foundn, NY, and American Radiator & Standard Sanitary Manftg Co., Buffalo, 1930-31; Founder, Dir and Chief Engr, Dymaxion Corp., Bridgeport, 1932-36; Asst to Dir, Res. and Develt, Phelps Dodge Corp., 1936-38; Tech. Consultant, Fortune Mag., 1938-40; Vice-Pres. and Chief Engr, Dymaxion Co. Inc., Delaware, 1940-50; Chief Mech. Engr, US Bd of Econ. Warfare, 1942-44; Special Asst to Dep. Dir, US Foreign Econ. Administration, 1944; Chm. Bd and Chief Engr, Dymaxion Dwelling Machines, 1944-46; Chm. Bd of Trustees, Fuller Research Foundn, Wichita, Kansas, 1946-54; Pres. Geodesics Inc., Forest Hills, 1949-; Pres., Synergetics Inc., Raleigh, NC, 1954-59; Pres. Plydomes Inc., Des Moines, 1957-; Chm. Bd, Tetrahelix Corp., Hamilton, 1959-; Pres., Triton Foundn, Cambridge, Mass, 1967-; Editor-at-large, World Magazine, NY, 1972-75; Internat. Pres., MENSA, Paris, 1975-; Internat. Pres., World Soc. for Ekistics, Athens, 1975-; contrib. Editor, Saturday Review, 1976-; Consultant, Design Science Inst., Philadelphia, 1972-. Charles Eliot Norton Prof. of Poetry, Harvard Univ., 1961-62; Harvey Cushing Orator, Amer. Assoc. of Neuro-Surgeons, 1967; Jahawarlal Nehru Lectr, New Delhi, 1969; Hoyt Fellow, Yale Univ., 1969; World Fellow in Residence, Consortium of Univ. of Pennsylvania, Haverford Coll., Swarthmore Coll., Bryn Mawr Coll., and Univ. City Science Center, 1972-. Holds 26 patents in architecture, transport, cartography (first and only cartography patent awarded in USA) and other fields; *inventions include:* the World Game, Dymaxion house, car, bathroom, map; discovered energetic/synergetic geometry, 1917; geodesic structures, 1947 (over 100,000 geodesic domes erected in 100 countries). *Architect of:* US pavilion for Montreal World Fair, 1967; Samuel Beckett Theatre, St Peter's Coll., Oxford, 1969-; geodesic auditorium, Kfar Menachem Kibutzin, Israel, 1969; Tri-centennial Pavilion of S Carolina, Greenfield, 1970; Religious Center, Southern Illinois Univ., 1971; Chief Architect, internat. airports at New Delhi, Bombay and Madras, 1973; consultant to Architects Team 3, Penang Urban Center, 1974-. Mem. many professional instns; Hon. Fellow, St Peter's Coll., Oxford, 1970; Hon. FRIBA 1968; FAIA 1975; holds hon. degrees from 39 univs/colleges; awards include Industrial Designers Soc. of Amer. (first) Award of Excellence, 1966; Gold Medal, Architecture, Nat. Inst. of Arts and Letters, 1968; Royal Gold Medal for Architecture, RIBA, 1968; Humanist of the Year Award, Amer. Assoc. of Humanists, 1969; Master Designer Award, McGraw Hill, 1969; Gold Medal, Amer. Inst. Architects, 1970. *Publications:* 4D Timelock, 1927; Nine Chains to the Moon, 1938 (UK 1973); The Dymaxion World of Buckminster Fuller (with Robert Marks), 1960 (rev. edn 1973); No More Second Hand God, 1962; Education Automation, 1963 (UK 1973); Ideas and Integrities (ed Robert Marks), 1963; untitled epic poem on history of industrialization, 1963; World Resources Inventory (6 documents) (with John McHale), 1963-67; Operating Manual for Spaceship Earth, 1969; Utopia or Oblivion, 1969; The Buckminster Fuller Reader (ed James Meller), 1970; I Seem to be a Verb (with Jerome Agel and Quentin Fiore), 1970; Intuition, 1972; Earth Inc., 1973; Synergetics: Explorations in the Geometry of Thinking (with E. J. Applethwaite), 1975; many contribs to jls etc. *Address:* 3500 Market Street, Philadelphia, Pa 19104, USA. *T:* (215) 387-2255.

FULLER, Roy Broadbent, CBE 1970; MA Oxon (by Decree); FRSL; poet and author; solicitor; Professor of Poetry,

University of Oxford, 1968-73; b 11 Feb. 1912; e s of late Leopold Charles Fuller, Oldham; m 1936, Kathleen Smith; one s. *Educ:* Blackpool High Sch. Admitted a solicitor, 1934; served Royal Navy, 1941-46; Lieut, RNVR, 1944; Asst Solicitor to Woolwich Equitable Building Soc., 1938-58, Solicitor, 1958-69, Director, 1969-. Vice-Pres., Bldg Socs Assoc., 1969- (Chm. Legal Adv. Panel, 1958-69). A Governor of the BBC, 1972-; Mem., Arts Council, 1976-77 (Chm., Literature Panel, 1976-77). Queen's Gold Medal for Poetry, 1970. *Publications:* Poems, 1939; The Middle of a War, 1942; A Lost Season, 1944; Savage Gold, 1946; With My Little Eye; Byron for Today, 1948; Questions and Answers in Building Soc. Law and Practice; Epitaphs and Occasions, 1949; The Second Curtain, 1953; Counterparts; Fantasy and Fugue, 1954; Image of a Society, 1956; Brutus's Orchard, 1957; The Ruined Boys, 1959; The Father's Comedy, 1961; Collected Poems, 1962; The Perfect Fool, 1963; Buff, 1965; My Child, My Sister, 1965; Catspaw, 1966; New Poems, 1968 (Duff Cooper Memorial Prize 1968); Off Course, 1969; The Carnal Island, 1970; Owls and Artificers: Oxford lectures on poetry, 1971; Seen Grandpa Lately?, 1972; Tiny Tears, 1973; Professors and Gods: last Oxford lectures on poetry, 1973; From the Joke Shop, 1975; An Ill-Governed Coast, 1976; Poor Roy, 1977; (ed) The Building Societies Acts. *Address:* 37 Langton Way, Blackheath, SE3. *T:* 01-858 2334.

FULLER-ACLAND-HOOD, Sir (Alexander) William; see Hood, Sir William Acland.

FULLER-GOOD, Air Vice-Marshal James Laurence Fuller, CB 1957; CVO 1953; CBE 1951; RAF retired; Air Officer Commanding, Air Headquarters, Malaya, 1951-52 (CBE); Director of Personal Services (Air), Air Ministry, 1952-53; Air Officer Commanding No 22 Group, Technical Training Command, 1953-57; Commandant-Gen. of the Royal Air Force Regt and Inspector of Ground Combat Trng, 1957-59, retd. Air Vice-Marshal, 1954. *Address:* PO Box 445, White River, 1240 Eastern Transvaal, S Africa. *Club:* Royal Air Force.

FULLERTON, Peter George Patrick Downing; HM Diplomatic Service; seconded to Department of Energy as Assistant Secretary in Oct. 1977; b 17 Jan. 1930; s of late Major R. A. D. Fullerton and Janet Mary Fullerton (*née* Baird); m 1962, Elizabeth Evelyn Newman Stevens, d of late George Stevens; two s two d. *Educ:* Radley Coll.; Magdalen Coll., Oxford (MA). HMOCS, Kenya, 1953-63, retd as Dist Comr; joined CRO (later FCO), 1963; Private Sec. to Minister of State, 1963-64; Dar-es-Salaam, 1964-65; Lusaka, 1966-69; seconded to British Leyland Motor Corp., 1970; FCO, 1971; Northern Ireland Office, 1972; FCO 1973; Economic and Commercial Counsellor, British High Commn, Canberra, 1974-77. *Address:* c/o Foreign and Commonwealth Office, SW1; Hydon Heath Corner, Godalming, Surrey GU8 4BB. *T:* Hascombe 326. *Clubs:* United Oxford & Cambridge University; Leander.

FULTHORPE, Henry Joseph, FRINA; General Manager, HM Dockyard, Portsmouth (Deputy Director of Naval Construction), 1967-75; b Portsmouth, 2 July 1916; s of Joseph Henry and Clarissa Fulthorpe; m 1939, Bette May Forshew; two s one d. *Educ:* Royal Naval Coll., Greenwich. Principal (Ship) Overseer, Vickers, Barrow-in-Furness, 1943-46; Dep. Manager, HM Dockyard, Malta, 1946-49; Sec., Radiological Defence Panel, 1949-52; Staff Constr, first British atom bomb, Montebello Is, 1952-53; Constr i/c Minesweeper Design, Admty, Bath, 1953-54; Chief Constr, Maintenance, Bath, 1954-56; Dep. Manager, HM Dockyard, Portsmouth, 1956-58; Chief Constructor: HM Dockyard, Singapore, 1958-61; Dockyard Dept, Bath, 1961-63; Asst Dir of Naval Construction, Bath, 1963-64; Production Manager, HM Dockyard, Chatham, 1964-67; Manager, Constructive Dept, HM Dockyard, Portsmouth, 1967. *Recreations:* walking, winemaking, cooking. *Address:* Gerard House, 60 Granada Road, Southsea. *T:* Portsmouth 34876. *Club:* Royal Naval and Royal Albert Yacht (Portsmouth).

FULTON, family name of Baron Fulton.

FULTON, Baron, cr 1966, of Falmer (Life Peer); **John Scott Fulton,** Kt 1964; Chairman of the British Council, 1968-71 (Member Executive Committee, 1964-71); b 27 May 1902; y s of the late Principal A. R. Fulton, Dundee; m 1939, Jacqueline, d of K. E. T. Wilkinson, York; three s one d. *Educ:* Dundee High Sch.; St Andrews Univ; Balliol Coll., Oxford (Exhibitioner). Asst in Logic and Scientific Method, London Sch. of Economics, 1926-28; Fellow, 1928-47, Balliol Coll. Oxford; Tutor in Philosophy, 1928-35; Tutor in Politics, 1935-47; Jowett Lecturer, 1935-38; Jowett Fellow, 1945-47; Rockefeller Fellow, 1936-37; Faculty Fellow, Nuffield Coll., 1939-47; Principal, University Coll. of Swansea, 1947-59; Vice-Chancellor:

University of Wales, 1952-54 and 1958-59; University of Sussex, 1959-67. Principal and Asst Sec., Mines Dept, 1940-42; Principal Asst Sec. Min. of Fuel and Power, 1942-44. Dir Wales and Mon Industrial Estates Ltd, 1948-54. Chairman: Board for Mining Qualifications, 1950-62; Universities Council for Adult Educ., 1952-55; Council of Nat. Inst. of Adult Educ., 1952-55; Commn on educational requirements of Sierra Leone, 1954; Selection Cttee for Miners' Welfare Nat. Scholarships, 1949-59; Nat. Adv. Coun. on the Training and Supply of Teachers, 1959-63; Univs Central Coun. on Admissions, 1961-64; Commn on establishment of a second University in Hong Kong, 1962; Inter Univ. Coun. for Higher Educn Overseas, 1964-68 (Vice-Chm., 1968-); BBC Liaison Advisory Cttee on Adult Education Programmes, 1962-65; a Governor of the BBC, 1965-70 (Vice-Chm. 1965-67 and again 1968-70); BBC Further Education Adv. Coun. for the UK, 1965; Institute of Development Studies, 1966-67; Cttee on the Civil Service, 1966-68; ITA Adult Educn Adv. Cttee, 1962-65; Coun. of Inst. of Educn, University of London, 1967-; Coun. of Tavistock Inst. of Human Relations, 1968-; Manpower Soc., 1973-. Member: Commn. on Royal University of Malta, 1957 (Chm. 1962-72); National Reference Tribunal for Coal Industry of Great Britain, 1957-65; Cttee on University Teaching Methods, 1961-64. Pres., Soc. for Research into Higher Education, 1964-67; Pres., Morley College, 1969. Hon. Fellow, Balliol Coll., Oxford Univ., 1969. Hon. LLD: Chinese Univ. of Hong Kong, 1964; California, 1966; Yale, 1967; Sussex, 1967; Wales, 1968; Dundee, 1968; Hon. DLitt; Ife, 1967; Royal Univ. of Malta, 1967; Carleton, 1970; DUniv Keel, 1971. *Publications:* (with C. R. Morris) In Defence of Democracy, 1935; various articles and named lectures. *Recreation:* golf. *Address:* Brook House, Thornton-le-Dale, Pickering, N Yorks. *T:* Thornton-le-Dale 221. *Club:* Athenæum.

FULTON, Hon. Edmund Davie, PC (Canada) 1957; **Hon. Mr Justice Fulton;** Puisne Judge, Supreme Court of British Columbia, since 1973; b 10 March 1916; s of Frederick John Fulton, KC, and Winifred M. Davie; m 1946, Patricia Mary, d of J. M. Macrae and Christine Macrae (*née* Carmichael), Winnipeg; three d. *Educ:* St Michael's Sch., Victoria, BC; Kamloops High Sch.; University of British Columbia; St John's Coll., Oxford. BA (BC), BA Oxon (Rhodes Scholar, elected 1936). Admitted to Bar of British Columbia, 1940. Served in Canadian Army Overseas as Company Comdr with Seaforth Highlanders of Canada and as DAAG 1st Canadian Inf. Div., 1940-45, including both Italian and Northwest Europe campaigns (despatches); transferred to R of O with rank of Major, 1945. Practised law with Fulton, Verchere & Rogers, Kamloops, BC, 1945-68, and with Fulton, Cumming, Richards & Co., Vancouver, 1968-73. QC (BC) 1957. Elected to House of Commons of Canada, 1945; re-elected in 1949, 1953, 1957, 1958, 1962, 1965. Mem. Senate, University of British Columbia, 1948-57, 1969-75. Acting Minister of Citizenship and Immigration, June 1957-May 1958; Minister of Justice and Attorney Gen., Canada, June 1957-Aug. 1962; Minister of Public Works, Aug. 1962-April, 1963. Hon. Col, Rocky Mountain Rangers, 1959. Mem. Bar of Ontario. Hon LLD: Ottawa, 1960; Queen's, 1963. *Address:* (business) Court House, 800 West Georgia Street, Vancouver 1, BC, Canada; (home) 1632 West 40th Avenue, Vancouver 13, BC. *Clubs:* Vancouver, Shaughnessy Golf and Country (Vancouver); Rideau (Ottawa).

FUNG, Hon. Sir Kenneth Ping-Fan, Kt 1971; CBE 1965 (OBE 1958); JP; Chairman, Fung Ping Fan & Co. Ltd, and Chairman or Director of other companies; Director (and Chief Manager, retd), of The Bank of East Asia Ltd, Hong Kong; b 28 May 1911; yr s of late Fung Ping Shan, JP; m 1933, Ivy (*née* Kan) Shiu-Han, OBE, JP, d of late Kan Tong-Po, JP; four s one d. *Educ:* Government Vernacular Sch.; Sch. of Chinese Studies, Univ. of Hong Kong. Unofficial Mem., Urban Council, 1951-60; Unofficial MLC, 1959-65, MEC, 1962-72; Life Mem., Court of Univ. of Hong Kong; Council of Chinese Univ. of Hong Kong; Fourth Pan-Pacific Rehabilitation Conf.; Pres., Chm., etc. of numerous social organisations, both present and past. Member: Program for Harvard and East Asia (Mem. Internat. Org. Cttee); Rotary Internat. (Paul Harris Fellow). Comr St John Ambulance Bde (first Chinese to serve), 1953-58; first Chinese Hon. ADC to 4 successive Governors and Officers Admin. Govt (rep. StJAB). JP Hong Kong, 1952; KStJ 1958. Hon. degrees: LLD, Chinese Univ. of Hong Kong, 1968; DSocSc, Univ. of Hong Kong, 1969. Founder Mem., Royal Asiatic Soc.; Mem. other Socs and Assocs. Order of the Sacred Treasure (Japan), 1969. *Recreations:* racing, golf, swimming. *Address:* (home) 14 South Bay Road, Hong Kong. *T:* 92514; (office) Fung Ping Fan & Co. Ltd, 2705-2715 Connaught Centre, Hong Kong. *T:* 220311. *Clubs:* Royal Hongkong Jockey (Steward), Royal Hongkong Golf, Royal Hongkong Yacht, Hongkong Polo Assoc., Sports, Hongkong Country, Hongkong, Shek O Country, Hongkong Squash (Life Mem.), Chinese Recreation

(Hon. Pres.), American, Japanese (Pres.), CASAM, Hongkong Automobile Assoc., Rotary, Clear Water Bay Golf and Country (Chm. Organizing Cttee) (all in Hong Kong); Bankers' Club of America, Knickerbocker, Sky, Explorers', Amer. Photographic Soc., Bohemian (all in New York, USA); Hakone Country, Toride Internat. Golf, Hodogaya (Japan).

FUNSTON, G(eorge) Keith; *b* Waterloo, Iowa, USA, 12 Oct. 1910; *s* of George Edwin and Genevieve (Keith) Funston; *m* 1939, Elizabeth Kennedy; one *s* two *d. Educ:* Trinity Coll., Hartford, Conn; Harvard. AB, Trinity Coll., 1932; MBA (*cum laude*), Harvard, 1934. Mem. Research Staff, Harvard Business Sch., 1934-35; Asst to VP Sales, then Asst to Treas., American Radiator & Standard Sanitary, 1935-40; Dir, Purchases & Supplies, Sylvania Electronics, 1940-44; Special Asst to Chm., War Production Bd, 1941-44; Lt-Comdr, US Navy, 1944-46; Pres., Trinity Coll., Hartford, 1944-51; Pres. and Governor, New York Stock Exchange, 1951-67. Chm., Olin Corp., 1967-72; Director: IBM; Metropolitan Life; Republic Steel; AVCO Corp.; Illinois Central Industries; Chemical Bank; Putnam Trust; Hartford Steam Boiler & Insurance Co.; National Aviation; Winn-Dixie Stores; Paul Revere Investors. Holds numerous hon. doctorates. *Recreations:* riding, reading, ski-ing, tennis. *Address:* (home) 74 Vineyard Lane, Greenwich, Conn 06830, USA. *T:* Townsend 9-5524. *Clubs:* Round Hill (Greenwich, Conn.); University, The Century Assoc., The Links, (New York).

FÜRER-HAIMENDORF, Prof. Christoph von, DPhil Vienna; Emeritus Professor and Senior Research Fellow, School of Oriental and African Studies, University of London, since 1976; *b* 27 July 1909; *s* of Rudolf Fürer von Haimendorf und Wolkersdorf; *m* 1938, Elizabeth Barnardo; one *s. Educ:* Theresianische Akademie, Vienna; Vienna Univ. Asst Lecturer, Vienna Univ., 1931-34; Rockefeller Foundation Fellowship, 1935-37; Lecturer, Vienna University, 1938; Anthropological Fieldwork in Hyderabad and Orissa, 1939-43; Special Officer Subansiri, External Affairs Dept, Govt of India, 1944-45; Adviser to HEH the Nizam's Govt and Prof. of Anthropology in the Osmania Univ., 1945-49; Reader in Anthropology with special reference to India, University of London, 1949-51; Prof. of Asian Anthropology, School of Oriental and African Studies, 1951-76 (Dean of Sch., 1969-74, acting Director, 1974-75). Anthropological Research: in India and Nepal, 1953; in Nepal, 1957-; in the Philippines, 1968; in India, 1970, 1976-77. Munro Lectr, Edinburgh Univ., 1959; Visiting Prof., Colegio de Mexico, 1964, 1966. Pres., Royal Anthropological Inst., 1975-77. Corresponding Member: Austrian Academy of Science, 1964; Anthropological Soc. of Vienna, 1970. Rivers Memorial Medal of Royal Anthropological Institute, 1949; S. C. Roy Gold Medal, Asiatic Soc., Calcutta, 1964; Sir Percy Sykes Memorial Medal, Royal Central Asian Soc., 1965; King Birendra Prize, Royal Nepal Acad., 1976. *Publications:* The Naked Nagas, 1939; The Chenchus, 1943; The Reddis of the Bison Hills, 1945; The Raj Gonds of Adilabad, 1948; Himalayan Barbary, 1955; The Apa Tanis, 1962; (joint author) Mount Everest, 1963; The Sherpas of Nepal, 1964; (ed and jt author) Caste and Kin in Nepal, India and Ceylon, 1966; Morals and Merit, 1967; The Konyak Nagas, 1969; (ed and jt author) Peoples of the Earth, vol. 12: The Indian Sub-continent, 1973; (ed and jt author) Contributions to the Anthropology of Nepal, 1974; Himalayan Traders, 1975; Return to the Naked Nagas, 1976; articles in Journal of Royal Anthropological Inst., Man, Anthropos, Geographical Jl, Man in India. *Recreation:* music. *Address:* 32 Clarendon Road, W11. *T:* 01-727 4520, 01-637 2388.

FURLONG, Hon. Robert Stafford, MBE (mil.) 1945; Chief Justice of Newfoundland since 1959; *b* 9 Dec. 1904; *o s* of Martin Williams Furlong, KC, and Mary Furlong (*née* McGrath). *Educ:* St Bonaventure's Coll., St John's, Newfoundland. Called to the Bar, 1926, appointed KC 1944. Temp. Actg Lt-Comdr (S) RNVR. OStJ 1937; Knight of St Gregory 1958. *Recreations:* golf and motoring. *Address:* Judges' Chambers, Court of Appeal, St John's, Newfoundland; (home) 8 Winter Avenue, St John's, Newfoundland. *T:* 2310. *Clubs:* Naval (London); Bally Haly Golf and Country, Crow's Nest (all in St John's).

FURLONG, Ronald (John), FRCS; Orthopædic Surgeon to St Thomas's Hospital since 1946; Hon. Consulting Orthopædic Surgeon to the Army since 1951; *b* 3 March 1909; *s* of Frank Owen Furlong and Elsie Muriel Taffs, Woolwich; *m* 1st, 1936, Elva Mary Ruth Lefeaux (marr. diss., 1947); one *s* three *d*; 2nd, 1948, Nora Christine Pattinson (marr. diss. 1970); one *d*; 3rd, 1970, Eileen Mary Watford. *Educ:* Eltham Coll.; St Thomas's Hosp. MB, BS London 1931; MRCS, LRCP, 1931; FRCS 1934. Served with Royal Army Medical Corps, 1941-46. Home Commands, North Africa and Italy; Brigadier, Consulting Orthopædic Surgeon to the Army, 1946. *Publication:* Injuries of

the Hand, 1957. *Recreations:* reading, history and archæology. *Address:* 149 Harley Street, W1. *T:* 01-935 4444. *Club:* Athenæum.

FURLONGE, Sir Geoffrey (Warren), KBE 1960 (OBE 1942); CMG 1951; *b* 16 Oct. 1903; *s* of Robert Shekleton Furlonge and Agnes Mary (*née* Hatch); *m* 1952, Anne (*d* 1975), *d* of late E. A. Goldsack; *m* 1975, Vera Kathleen, *widow* of late Major Guy Farquhar. *Educ:* St Paul's Sch.; Emmanuel Coll., Cambridge. Entered Levant Consular Service, 1926; served at Casablanca, 1928-31; Jedda, 1931-34; Beirut, 1934-46; Political Officer with HM Forces in the Levant States, 1941-46. At Imperial Defence Coll., 1947; served in FO, 1948 (Head of Commonwealth Liaison Dept, 1948-50, Head of Eastern Dept, 1950-51); Minister (later Ambassador) to Jordan, 1952-54; Minister to Bulgaria, 1954-56; Ambassador to Ethiopia, 1956-59. *Publications:* The Lands of Barbary, 1966; Palestine is my Country, 1969. *Recreation:* chess. *Address:* 57 Princes Gate, SW7.

FURNEAUX, Robin; *see* Birkenhead, 3rd Earl of.

FURNER, Air Vice-Marshal Derek Jack, CBE 1973 (OBE 1963); DFC 1943; AFC 1954; General Manager, Harlequin Wallcoverings Ltd, Benfleet, since 1976; *b* 14 Nov. 1921; *s* of Vivian J. Furner; *m* 1948, Patricia Donnelly; three *s. Educ:* Westcliff High Sch., Essex. Joined RAF, 1941; commnd as navigator, 1942; Bomber Comd (2 tours), 1942-44; Transport Comd, Far East, 1945-47; Navigation Instructor, 1948-50; trials flying, Boscombe Down, 1951-53 and Wright-Patterson, Ohio, 1953-56; Air Min., 1957; OC Ops Wing, RAF Waddington, 1958-60; Planning Staff, HQ Bomber Comd, 1961-63 and SHAPE, Paris, 1964-65; Dep. Dir Manning, MoD (Air), 1966-67; OC RAF Scampton, 1968; AOC Central Reconnaissance Estab., 1969-70; Sec., Internat. Mil. Staff, NATO, Brussels, 1970-73; Asst Air Secretary, 1973-75. FIPM 1975; MBIM 1975. *Recreations:* swimming, mathematical problems, music. *Address:* 2 High Trees, Stock, Essex. *T:* Stock 840753. *Club:* Royal Air Force.

FURNESS, family name of **Viscount Furness.**

FURNESS, 2nd Viscount, *cr* 1918; **William Anthony Furness;** Baron Furness, *cr* 1910, of Grantley; Chairman and Managing Director, United & General Trust Ltd; Vale Trust Ltd; Director other private companies; Theatrical, Film and Record Producer; *b* 31 March 1929; *s* of 1st Viscount and Thelma (*d* 1970), *d* of late Harry Hays Morgan, American Consul-Gen. at Buenos Aires; *S* father, 1940. *Educ:* Downside; USA. Served as Guardsman, Welsh Guards (invalided, 1947). Delegate to Inter-Parliamentary Union Conferences, Washington, 1953, Vienna, 1954, Helsinki, 1955, Warsaw, 1959, Brussels, 1961, Belgrade, 1963. Vice-Chm. University of London Catholic Chaplaincy Assoc., 1953-75; Mem. Council, Hansard Soc. for Parliamentary Govt, 1955-67. President: Aged Poor Soc.; Founder Chm., Anglo-Mongolian Soc., 1963; Chm. Council, Soc. of St Augustine of Canterbury, 1965-73; Governor, Westminster Cathedral Choir Sch. SMO of Malta (joined 1954; Sec., Assoc. of Brit. Members, 1956-65, Sec.-Gen. 1965; Mem. Sovereign Council, 1960-62; Grand Officer of Merit, 1965; Kt of Justice, 1977); Grand Officer, Order of Merit, Italy, 1961; KStJ 1971 (CStJ 1964); KCSG 1966. *Heir:* none. *Address:* 60 St James's Street, SW1. *T:* 01-629 8953. *Clubs:* Boodle's, Carlton; Travellers' (Paris).

FURNESS, Robin; *see* Furness, Sir S. R.

FURNESS, Sir Stephen (Roberts), 3rd Bt *cr* 1913; farmer and sporting/landscape artist (as Robin Furness); *b* 10 Oct. 1933; *e s* of Sir Christopher Furness, 2nd Bt, and of Flower, Lady Furness, OBE, *d* of late Col G. C. Roberts; *S* father, 1974; *m* 1961, Mary, *e d* of J. F. Cann, Cullompton, Devon; one *s* one *d. Educ:* Charterhouse. Entered RN, 1952; Observer, Fleet Air Arm, 1957; retired list, 1962. NCA, Newton Rigg Farm Inst., 1964. Member: Armed Forces Art Soc.; Darlington Art Soc. *Recreations:* looking at paintings, foxhunting, shooting. *Heir:* s Michael Fitzroy Roberts Furness, *b* 12 Oct. 1962. *Address:* Stanhow Farm, Great Langton, near Northallerton, Yorks DL7 0TJ. *T:* Kirkby Fleetham 614.

FURNIVAL JONES, Sir (Edward) Martin, Kt 1967; CBE 1957; Consultant to ICI Ltd, since 1972, to Imperial Group Ltd, since 1976; *b* 7 May 1912; *s* of Edward Furnival Jones, FCA; *m* 1955, Elizabeth Margaret, *d* of Bartholomew Snowball, BSc, AMIEE; one *d. Educ:* Highgate Sch.; Gonville and Caius Coll., Cambridge. BA 1934, MA 1938. Admitted a Solicitor, 1937. Served War of 1939-45: General Staff Officer at Supreme Headquarters, Allied Expeditionary Force, and War Office (despatches, American Bronze Star Medal). Chm. of Bd, Frensham Heights, 1973- (Pres. 1977). *Recreation:* birdwatching. *Address:* The Little House, Oakley, Bedford. *T:* Oakley 2181. *Club:* United Oxford & Cambridge University.

FURNIVALL, Barony *cr* 1295; in abeyance. *Co-heiresses:* Hon. Rosamond Mary Dent (Sister Ancilla, OSB); *b* 3 June 1933; Hon. Patricia Mary Dent [*b* 4 April 1935; *m* 1st, 1956, Captain Thomas Hornsby (marr. diss., 1963; he *d* 1967); one *s* one *d*; 2nd, 1970, Roger Thomas John Bence; one *d*].

FURNIVALL, Maj.-Gen. Lewis Trevor, CB 1964; DSO 1943; Dir of Medical Services, Far East Land Forces, 1965-66; retired 1967; *b* 6 Sept. 1907; *er s* of late Lt-Col C. H. Furnivall, CMG, and late Mrs D. Furnivall (*née* Macbean); *m* 1941, Audrey Elizabeth Furnivall (*née* Gibbins); three *s* one *d. Educ:* Blundell's Sch.; St Mary's Hosp., London. MRCS, LRCP 1931; House Surg., Worcester Gen. Infirmary, 1931; Lieut, RAMC 1931; NW Frontier of India (Mohmand), 1933 (medal and clasp); Capt. 1934; Major 1941; Lieut-Col 1947; Col 1953; Brig. 1960; Maj.-Gen. 1961. Service in India, 1932-38; DADMS, 1939-. War Service, 1939-45 (UK, MELF, Italy, France, Germany); ADMS, 1944-48 (despatches, 1946); DDMS, HQ, BAOR, 1949-52; ADMS, HQ, Land Forces, Hong Kong, 1953-54; ADMS, HQ, Northumbrian Dist, 1955-57; Dep. Chief Med. Officer, SHAPE, 1957-60; Inspector of Training, Army Med. Services, 1960; Deputy Dir Medical Services, Eastern Command, 1961-65. QHS 1961-67. La Médaille d'Honneur du Service de Santé, 1960. *Recreations:* Rugby football, golf, tennis, cricket, swimming, ski-ing. *Address:* Woodside, 80 Lynch Road, Farnham, Surrey. *T:* Farnham 5771. *Clubs:* Farnham Conservative, Hankley Common Golf.

FURSE, Rear-Adm. (John) Paul (Wellington), CB 1958; OBE 1946; CEng; FIMechE; FLS; retired; *b* 13 Oct. 1904; *s* of late Charles Furse, artist, and late Dame Katharine, GBE, RRC, Dir, WRNS; *m* 1929, Cicely Rathbone; one *s. Educ:* Osborne; Dartmouth; RN Engineering Coll., Keyham. Service in Submarines, etc, 1927-39; Asst Naval Attaché, Europe and the Americas, 1940-43; 5th and 4th Submarine Flotillas, 1943-46; Admiralty, 1947, Dir of Aircraft Maintenance and Repair, Admiralty, 1955-58; Dir-Gen. of the Aircraft Dept, Admiralty, 1958-59; retired, 1959. Botanical expeditions in Turkey and Iran, 1960, 1962; Afghanistan, 1964, 1966. VMH 1965. *Publications:* articles on flora of the Middle East in RHS Jl and Year Book, British Iris Soc. Year Book, Alpine Garden Soc. Bulletins. *Recreations:* mountains, ski-ing, botany, painting. *Address:* Hegg Hill, Smarden, Kent. *T:* Smarden 229. *Club:* Army and Navy.

FURTADO, Robert Audley, CB 1970; Special Commissioner, 1946-77, Presiding Commissioner, 1963-77; *b* 20 August 1912; *yr s* of Montague C. Furtado; *m* 1945, Marcelle Elizabeth, *d* of W. Randall Whitteridge; one *s* one *d. Educ:* Whitgift Sch.; University Coll., London. LLB London Univ., 1933; called to Bar, Gray's Inn, 1934. Served War of 1939-45, in Army in India and Burma (Despatches); demobilised rank of Lieut-Col, 1945. *Recreation:* bricolage. *Address:* Aysgarth, Saxonwood Road, Battle, East Sussex. *T:* Battle 3713; 39 Strand Court, Topsham, Devon.
See also J. E. Pater, Prof. David Whitteridge and Sir Gordon Whitteridge.

FUSSELL, Edward Coldham, CMG 1954; Governor, Reserve Bank of New Zealand, 1948-62; *b* Auckland, 16 July 1901; *s* of Rev. James Coldham Fussell; *m* 1935, Eileen, *d* of C. S. Plank; three *s* two *d. Educ:* King's Coll., Auckland; Victoria University Coll. (BA). With National Bank of NZ, 1919-34; Head Office, 1930. Rep. Associated Banks at Monetary Commn, 1934. With Reserve Bank of NZ, 1934-62; Asst to Governors, 1939; Dep.-Gov., 1941-48; rep. Reserve Bank on Royal Commn, 1955. Has attended financial confs in UK and USA, including Bretton Woods Conf., 1944. Served HG, War of 1939-45. Mem., Senate and Grants Cttee, University of NZ, 1951-60; Hon. Treas. University of NZ, 1954-60. *Recreation:* golf. *Address:* 5 Taumaru Avenue, Lowry Bay, Wellington, New Zealand. *T:* 684-686. *Clubs:* Wellington, Rotary International; Heretaunga Golf, Wellington Racing.

FYERS, FitzRoy Hubert; *b* 13 March 1899; *s* of late Major Hubert Alcock Nepean Fyers, MVO, and Evangeline Blanche, *e d* of late Captain Hon. Francis A. J. Chichester and Lady Emily Chichester; *m* 1949, Bryda Hope Collison (*d* 1976), *d* of late Octavius Weir. *Educ:* Eton; RMC, Sandhurst. Entered Rifle Brigade, 1917; served in European War, France, 1918; seconded to Machine Gun Corps, 1920; ADC to Gen. Sir Alex. Godley, British Army of the Rhine, 1922-24, and to Gen. Sir John Du Cane, 1924-25; retired from Army, 1926; Sec. to Sir H. Hesketh

Bell, on special mission to Yugoslavia, 1929; Extra-Equerry to the Duke of Connaught, 1929-30; Equerry to The Duke of Connaught, 1930-39, and Comptroller, 1938-41. Rejoined Rifle Brigade on outbreak of War, Sept. 1939; transferred to King's Own Scottish Borderers, Nov. 1939; on Staff of Lt-Gen. Sir Wm Dobbie, Malta, as Military Asst, 1940 (despatches); Major, 1940; Military Liaison Officer to Rear-Adm., Alexandria, 1942-43; Asst Sergeant-at-Arms, House of Commons, 1945-48. OStJ. *Address:* Cromartie House, Strathpeffer, Ross-shire. *T:* Strathpeffer 468. *Clubs:* Travellers'; New (Edinburgh); Royal Scottish Automobile (Glasgow).

FYFE, Prof. William Sefton, FRS 1969; Chairman, Department of Geology, and Professor of Geology, University of Western Ontario, since 1972; *b* 4 June 1927; *s* of Colin and Isabella Fyfe; *m* 1st, 1968; two *s* one *d*; 2nd, 1972, Marie-Louise Dedouvre. *Educ:* Otago Univ., New Zealand. BSc 1948, MSc 1949, PhD 1952. Univ. of California, Berkeley, Calif: Lecturer in Chemistry, 1952, Reader, 1958; Prof. of Geology, 1959; Royal Soc. Res. Prof. (Geochemistry), Univ. of Manchester, 1967-72. Hon. Fellow, Geological Soc. Amer.; Corresp. Mem., Brazilian Acad. of Science. Mineralogical Soc. of Amer. Award, 1964. *Publications:* Metamorphic Reactions and Metamorphic Facies, 1958; The Geochemistry of Solids, 1964; also numerous scientific papers. *Address:* Department of Geology, University of Western Ontario, London 72, Ontario, Canada.

FYJIS-WALKER, Richard Alwyne, CVO 1976; HM Diplomatic Service; Counsellor (Information), Washington, since 1974; *b* 19 June 1927; *s* of Harold and Marion Fyjis-Walker; *m* 1st, 1951, Barbara Graham-Watson (marr. diss.); one *s*; 2nd, 1972, Gabrielle Josefi. *Educ:* Bradfield Coll.; Magdalene Coll., Cambridge (BA). Army (KRRC), 1945-48. Joined Foreign (subseq. Diplomatic) Service, 1955; served: Amman, 1956; FO, 1957-61; Paris, 1961-63; Cairo, 1963-65; FCO, 1966-71; Counsellor, 1970; Ankara, 1971-74. *Address:* c/o Foreign and Commonwealth Office, SW1.

FYLER, Maj.-Gen. Arthur Roderic, CB 1964; OBE 1954; *b* 28 June 1911; *s* of late Adm. H. A. S. Fyler, CB, DSO, and late Mrs H. A. S. Fyler; *m* 1940, Anthea Mary de Fontaine Stratton, *d* of late Lt-Col F. C. G. Stratton, TD, Nairobi, Kenya; two *s* two *d. Educ:* Charterhouse. 2/Lieut (Sup. Res.) The Buffs, 1931-34; 2/Lieut Queen's Own Royal West Kent Regt, 1934. Served War of 1939-45: E Africa, British Somaliland, Abyssinia (King's African Rifles), NW Europe; despatches 1940 and 1954. AQMG, HQ Land Forces, Hong Kong, 1950-52; OC 1st Bn Queen's Own Royal West Kent Regt, 1953-55; Comd 130 (West Country) Infantry Bde (TA), 1955-58; Dep. Adjt Gen., GHQ, FARELF, 1958-61; Dir of Army Personnel Administration, 1961-64, War Office and MoD (A); retired 1964; reemployed as a Civil Servant by MoD(A), retired 1976. Vice-Chm., Soc. for Protection of Animals in N Africa, 1972, Chm. 1973-; Advisory Dir, Internat. Soc. for Protection of Animals, 1975-; mem. Council, World Fedn for the Protection of Animals, 1976-. Pres., Squash Rackets Assoc., 1975-; Vice-Pres., Kent Squash Rackets Assoc., 1976-. *Recreations:* watching games and sports, appreciation of fine arts, the turf. *Address:* Starlings, Beechwood Road, Beaconsfield, Bucks. *T:* Beaconsfield 3321. *Clubs:* Naval and Military; Devon Dumplings Cricket; Escorts Squash Rackets.

FYNES-CLINTON, David Osbert; *b* 25 Jan. 1909; *s* of late Prof. O. H. Fynes-Clinton, University Coll. of North Wales, Bangor; *m* 1st, 1947, Betty Lawrence; one *s*; 2nd, 1958, Herta Sernetz. *Educ:* Clifton; St John's Coll., Oxford. Entered Consular Service, 1931; Genoa, 1931; Cairo, 1933; Colon, Panama, 1935; La Paz, Bolivia, 1938; Rio de Janeiro, 1940; Luanda, Angola, 1947; Basle, 1949; Consul-Gen. at Tananarive, Madagascar, 1952; Zagreb 1956; retired 1957. Joined Staff of UN, 1958, retired 1970. *Address:* c/o United Nations, Geneva, Switzerland.

G

GABB, (William) Harry, CVO 1974 (MVO 1961); DMus (Lambeth), 1974; Organist, Choirmaster and Composer at HM Chapels Royal, 1953-Easter 1974; Sub-Organist, St Paul's Cathedral, London, 1946-Easter 1974; Professor and Examiner of Organ Playing at The Trinity College of Music, London; Special Commissioner for Royal School of Church Music; Member, Council of the Royal College of Organists; Adjudicator and Recitalist; *b* 5 April 1909; *m* 1936, Helen Burnaford Mutton; one *s*. *Educ:* Scholarship at Royal Coll. of Music for Organ and Composition, ARCO 1928; FRCO 1930; ARCM Solo Organ, 1931; Organist, St Jude's, West Norwood, 1925; Organist and Choirmaster, Christ Church, Gypsy Hill, 1928; Sub-Organist, Exeter Cathedral, also Organist, Church of St Leonard's, Exeter and Heavitree Parish Church, 1929-37; Organist and Master of the Choristers, Llandaff Cathedral, 1937; Lectr, St Michael's Theological Coll., Llandaff; Royal Armoured Corps, War of 1939-45. Returned from Army to Llandaff, Jan. 1946. Played organ at the Coronation of Elizabeth II and at many Royal Weddings and Baptisms. Hon. FTCL, 1954. *Address:* St Lawrence Cottage, Bagshot Road, Chobham, Woking, Surrey. *T:* Chobham 7879.

GABOR, Prof. Dennis, CBE 1970; FRS 1956; DSc London 1964; DrIng Berlin, FInstP, FIEE; Professor Emeritus of Applied Electron Physics in the University of London, at Imperial College of Science and Technology (Reader in Electronics, 1949-58; Professor, 1958-67; Senior Research Fellow, 1967-76); Staff Scientist, CBS Laboratories, Stamford, Connecticut, USA, since 1967; *b* 5 June 1900; *s* of Bertalan Gabor and Ady (*née* Kálmán); *m* 1936, Marjorie Louise Butler, Rugby, *d* of J. T. Kennard Butler. *Educ:* Technical Univ., Budapest; Technische Hochschule, Berlin-Charlottenburg. Asst, TH, Berlin, 1924-26; Research associate, German Res. Assoc. for High Voltage Plants, 1926-27; Research engineer, Siemens & Halske AG, Berlin-Siemensstadt, 1927-33; Research engineer, British Thomson-Houston Co., Rugby, 1934-48. Inventor of holography. Hon. Member Hungarian Academy of Sciences, 1964; Foreign Associate, Nat. Acad. of Sciences, USA, 1973. Thomas Young Medal and Prize, RPS, 1967; Cristoforo Colombo Prize, Genoa, 1967; Rumford Medal, Royal Soc., 1968; Michelson Medal, Franklin Inst., 1968; Medal of Honor, IEEE, 1970; Semmelweiss Medal, American Hungarian Med. Assoc., 1970; Holweck Prize, French Physical Soc., 1971; Nobel Prize for Physics, 1971; George Washington Award, Amer.-Hungarian Studies Foundn, 1973. Hon. FCGI, 1977. Hon. DSc: Southampton, 1970; Delft Univ. of Technology, 1971; Surrey, 1972; Engineering Coll., Bridgeport, 1972; City, 1972; Columbia, NY, 1975; Hon. LLD London, 1973. *Publications:* The Electron Microscope, 1946; Electronic Inventions and their Impact on Civilisation. 1959; Inventing the Future, 1963; Innovations, Scientific, Technological and Social, 1970; The Mature Society, 1972. About 100 scientific papers on electrical transients, gas discharges, electron dynamics, communication theory and physical optics. *Recreations:* swimming, writing on social problems. *Address:* (summer) La Margioretta, Viale dei Gigli 21, 00040 Lavinio Lido (Roma), Italy; (winter) Department of Electrical Engineering, Imperial College, SW7 2BT. *Club:* Athenæum.

GADD, Maj.-Gen. Alfred Lockwood, CBE 1962 (OBE 1955); Linguistic Director, Languages Section, London Chamber of Commerce, since 1972; *b* 10 July 1912; *s* of late Charles A. Gadd; *m* 1st, 1936, Gwenrudd Eluned (*d* 1965), *d* of late Morgan Edwards; one *s* one *d*; 2nd, 1965, Anna Louisa Margaret (*d* 1977), *d* of late Carl-August Koehler. *Educ:* Harvey Grammar Sch., Folkestone; Peterhouse, Cambridge (Open Scholar, MA). Asst Master: Bedford Sch., 1934-35; King's Sch., Rochester, 1935-39; Marlborough Coll., 1939-40. Commissioned Intelligence Corps, 1941; GSO3 War Office, 1942; Major, 1942; Lt-Col 1944; Chief Instructor 5 Formation Coll., 1945; Comdt No 1 Army Coll., 1946; Chief Education Officer, Far ELF, 1947; various Education Staff appts, 1950-62; Dir of Army Education, WO, 1962-65. *Publications:* (as David Gadd): Georgian Summer: the story of 18th century Bath, 1971; The Loving Friends: a portrait of Bloomsbury, 1974. *Recreations:* travel, archæology. *Address:* Greenleaze, Long Sutton, Somerset. *T:* Long Sutton 343.

GADD, John; Chairman, North Thames Gas, since 1977; *b* 9 June 1925; *s* of late George Gadd and of Winifred Gadd, Dunstable, Bedfordshire; *m* 1959, Nancy Jean, *d* of late Pryce Davies, Henley-on-Thames. *Educ:* Cedars Sch., Leighton Buzzard; Cambridgeshire Technical Coll. Joined Gas Industry, 1941. Served War, RNVR, 1943-46. Numerous engineering appts with Southern Gas Bd; attended Administrative Staff Coll., Henley-on-Thames, 1961; Personnel Manager, Southern Gas Bd, 1962; Dep. Chm., Southern Gas Bd, 1969; Chm., Eastern Region, British Gas Corp., 1973. *Recreation:* gardening. *Address:* The Old Vicarage, Willian, Letchworth, Herts. *T:* Letchworth 5283.

GADSBY, Gordon Neville, CB 1972; Department Staff, The Mitre Corporation, McLean, Virginia, USA, since 1976; *b* 29 Jan. 1914; *s* of William George and Margaret Sarah Gadsby; *m* 1938, Jeanne (*née* Harris); two *s* one *d*. *Educ:* King Edward VI Sch., Stratford-upon-Avon; University of Birmingham. BSc

1935, DipEd 1937, Cadbury Prizeman 1937, Birmingham; FRIC 1967. Sen. Chemistry Master, Waverley Gram. Sch., Birmingham, 1937-40; Captain Royal Warwicks Regt, and Sen. Instructor, Applied Chem., RMCS, 1941-46; Princ. Lectr, RMCS, 1946-51; Supt, Special Weapons and Logistics Divs, Army Operational Research Gp, 1951-55; Dep. Sci. Adviser to Army Coun., 1955-59; idc 1960; Dir of Army Operational Science and Research, 1961; Dir, Army Operational Res. Estab., 1961-64; Dir of Biol. and Chem. Defence, Army Dept, MoD, 1965-67; Dep. Chief Scientist (Army), MoD, 1967-68; Dir, Chemical Defence Estabt, Porton, Wilts, 1968-72; Minister, Defence R&D, British Embassy, Washington, 1972-75, retired. *Publications:* Lubrication, 1949; An Introduction to Plastics, 1950. *Recreations:* oil painting, photography. *Address:* 1453 Laburnum Street, Chesterbrook Woods, McLean, Va 22101, USA. *T:* (703) 536-3737; Beech Gate, Hurdle Way, Compton Down, Winchester, Hants. *T:* Twyford (Hants) 2231. *Club:* Cosmos (Washington).

GADSDEN, Peter Drury Haggerston, MA; JP; Company Director; Underwriting Member of Lloyd's; Mineral Marketing Consultant since 1969; *b* Canada, 28 June 1929; *er s* of late Basil Claude Gadsden, ACT, ThL, and late Mabel Florence Gadsden (*née* Drury); *m* 1955, Belinda Ann, *e d* of late Captain Sir (Hugh) Carnaby de Marie Haggerston, 11th Bt; four *d*. *Educ:* Rockport, Belfast; The Elms, Colwall; Wrekin Coll., Wellington; Jesus Coll., Cambridge (MA). 2nd Lieut King's Shropshire LI, attached Oxf. and Bucks LI and Durham LI, Germany, 1948-49; Man. Dir, London subsid. of Australian Mineral Sands Producer, 1964-70; Marketing Economist (Mineral Sands) to UN Industrial Development Organisation, 1969; Director: J. H. Little & Co. Ltd, 1970-; Thomas Hill-Jones Ltd, 1964-; City of London (Arizona) Corp. 1970-; Tehidy Mineral Ltd, 1974-; Guthrie Corp. Ltd, 1974-; Guthrie & Co. (UK) Ltd, 1970-74; Tanjong Tin Dredging Ltd (Alt.), 1975-; Ellingham Estate Ltd, 1974-; Basset Smith & Co. Ltd, 1976-. Mem. London Metal Exchange. President: Nat. Assoc. of Charcoal Manufacturers, 1970-; Embankment Rifle Club, 1975-; Leukaemia Res. Fund, City of London Br., 1975-. Sheriff London, 1970-71; Common Councilman (Cripplegate Within and Without), 1969-71; Alderman, City of London (Ward of Farringdon Without), 1971; Liveryman: Clothworkers' Co., 1965-; Plaisterers' Co. (Hon.), 1975-; Guild of Marketors (Hon.), 1975-; Member: Guild of Freemen (Court); Royal Soc. of St George (City of London Br.); Council, Metropolitan Soc. for the Blind. Governor, Lady Eleanor Holles Sch., 1968-. JP, City of London, 1971 (Inner London Area of Greater London, 1969-71). Hon. FInstM, 1976; Hon. Fellow, Guild of Master Craftsmen, 1977; Regtl Mem. and Hon. Mem. Court, HAC, OStJ 1977. Officier de L'Etoile Equatoriale du République Gabonaise, 1970. *Publications:* The Marketing of Minerals, InstMM transactions, 1971; articles on titanium, zirconium, and hafnium in Mining Jl Annual Reviews. *Recreations:* ski-ing, sailing, walking, photography, farming, forestry. *Address:* Wandylaw House, Chathill, Northumberland NE67 5HG. *T:* Chathill 217. *Clubs:* City of London (Mem. Cttee), City Livery (Mem. Council); United Wards, Farringdon Ward (patron), Fleet Street (Hon.), Presscala (Hon.), Australia, Canada.

GADSDON, Sir Laurence Percival, Kt 1960; formerly Managing Director, Wilson Gray & Co. Pty, Ltd, Perth, WA; Mayor of Cottesloe, WA, 1945-61; *b* Ongar, Essex, 24 March 1897; *s* of Frank Benjamin and Mary Gertrude Gadsdon; *m* 1929, Hilda Mary, *d* of John and Eily Hedges; one *d*. *Educ:* Haberdashers' Aske's Hatcham Boys' Sch., London. Migrated to W Australia, 1913. Served AIF 1914-18 (Gallipoli Star, Gen. Service Medal). Sec., later Vice-Pres., Perth Branch Returned Soldiers Assoc., 1916-20; joined Wilson Gray & Co., 1919. Sec., Treas, Pres., N Cottesloe Surf Life Saving Club, 1918-35, now Life Member; Treas., 1925, Sec. and Pres., Surf Life Saving Assoc. of Australia (WA State Centre), now Life Mem. Councillor of Cottesloe, 1922. Pres. Local Government Assoc. of WA, 1950-60. Hon. Dir of Communications, Civil Defence, and mem. Civil Defence Council, 1939-45. *Recreations:* tennis, surfing and golf. *Address:* 14 Dean Street, Cottesloe, WA 6011, Australia. *T:* 3,2807.

GAEKWAD, Lt-Col Fatesinghrao P.; MP (Independent), Parliament of Gujarat, since 1971; *b* 2 April 1930; *s* of HH Sir Pratapsingh Gaekwar, GCIE, Maharaja of Baroda; *S* father, 1968; title abolished, 1971. *Educ:* privately. MP, Lok Sabha, 1957-67; Parly Sec. to Defence Minister, 1957-62; Mem. Exec. Cttee, Congress Party in Parliament, 1962-67; Mem. Public Accounts Cttee, 1963-64. MP (Congress), Gujarat, 1967-71; Minister for Health and Family Planning, Fisheries, Jails and Sports, State of Gujarat, 1967-71. Chancellor, Univ. of Baroda, 1951-. Chm., Baroda Rayon Corp., 1956-66; Dir, Bank of Baroda Ltd, 1954-66. Chm., Bd of Governors, Nat. Inst. of Sports, 1962-63; Pres., Bd of Control for Cricket in India, 1963-

66 (Mem. CCI and MCC); Summariser for BBC, 1974 Indo-UK Test Series. Former Trustee, World Wildlife Fund (Pres., Indian Nat. Appeal); Member: IUCN; Fauna Preservation Soc.; RSPB; Indian Bd for Wildlife, etc. FZS. Does social work in the former Baroda State (which merged with Bombay in 1949). *Recreations:* photography, cooking, reading, poetry. *Address:* Laxmi Vilas Palace, Baroda 390 001, (Gujarat), India.

GAFFNEY; *see* Burke-Gaffney.

GAGE, family name of **Viscount Gage.**

GAGE, 6th Viscount, *cr* 1720; **Henry Rainald Gage,** KCVO 1939; Bt 1622; Baron Gage (Ireland), 1720; Baron Gage (Great Britain), 1790; DL; *b* 30 Dec. 1895; *o s* of 5th Viscount and Leila (*d* 1916), 2nd *d* of Rev. Frederick Peel, MA, and Hon. Adelaide, *d* of 3rd Baron Sudeley; *S* father, 1912; *m* 1st, 1931, Hon. Alexandra Imogen Clare Grenfell (*d* 1969), *yr d* of 1st Baron Desborough, KG, GCVO; two *s* one *d*; 2nd, 1971, Hon. Mrs Campbell-Gray. *Educ:* Eton; Christchurch, Oxford. Served European War, 1914-18 (wounded); War of 1939-45, Coldstream Guards and Staff; Lord-in-Waiting, 1925-29 and 1931-39; PPS to Sec. of State for India, 1925-29. Vice-Pres., National Federation of Housing Societies and various Sussex County Organisations. DL 1927, Vice Lieutenant, 1957-70, Sussex. *Heir: s* Hon. George John St Clere Gage [*b* 8 July 1932; *m* 1971, Valerie Ann (marr. diss. 1975), *yr d* of J. E. Dutch, Horam, Sussex]. *Address:* Firle, Lewes, Sussex. *T:* Glynde 256. *Clubs:* Brooks's, White's.

GAGE, Sir Berkeley (Everard Foley), KCMG 1955 (CMG 1949); Retired; *b* 27 Feb. 1904; *s* of late Brig.-Gen. M. F. Gage, DSO; *m* 1931, Maria von Chapuis (marr. diss. 1954), Liegnitz, Silesia; two *s*; *m* 1954, Mrs Lillian Riggs Miller. *Educ:* Eton Coll.; Trinity Coll., Cambridge. 3rd Sec. Foreign Office or Diplomatic Service, 1928; appointed to Rome, 1928; transferred to Foreign Office, 1931; 2nd Sec., 1933; Private Sec. to Parl. Under-Sec. of State, 1934; served Peking, 1935; FO 1938; China, 1941; FO 1944; UK Deleg. Dumbarton Oaks Conf., 1944; UK Deleg., San Francisco Conf., April-June 1945; Foreign Service Officer, Grade 5, 1950; Counsellor, British Embassy, The Hague, 1947-50; Chargé d'Affaires, The Hague, in 1947 and 1948; Consul-Gen., Chicago, 1950-54; Ambassador to Thailand, 1954-57; Ambassador to Peru, 1958-63. Chairman: Latin America Cttee, BNEC, 1964-66; Anglo-Peruvian Soc., 1969-71; Member: Council for Volunteers Overseas, 1964-66; Council of Fauna Preservation Soc., 1969-73. Grand Cross, Order of the Sun (Peru), 1964. *Recreations:* walking, photography. *Address:* 24 Ovington Gardens, SW3. *T:* 01-589 0361. *Clubs:* Beefsteak, Buck's, Saints and Sinners; Tavern (Chicago).

GAGE, Conolly Hugh; His Honour Judge Gage; a Circuit Judge (formerly Judge of County Courts), since 1958; Barrister-at-law; Fellow Commoner, Sidney Sussex College, Cambridge, 1962; *b* 10 Nov. 1905; *s* of William Charles Gage and May Guernsey Holmes, *d* of Rt Hon. Lord Justice Holmes; *m* 1932, Elinor Nancy Martyn; one *s* one *d*. *Educ:* Repton; Sidney Sussex Coll., Cambridge. Called to Bar, Inner Temple, 1930; enlisted as Gunner in RA, TA, April 1939; served with First Canadian Army as ADJAG (Br.) (despatches). MP (UU) S Belfast, 1945-52; Recorder of Maldon and Saffron Walden, 1950-52; Chm., Huntingdonshire and Peterborough QS, 1963-71; Dep. Chm., Essex QS, 1955-71. Chm., County Court Rules Cttee, 1974-. Chancellor, dio. of Coventry, 1948-76, of Lichfield, 1954-76. Member, British Delegns to: Commonwealth Relations Conf., Canada, 1949; Consultative Assembly, Council of Europe, 1949-52. *Recreations:* fishing, shooting, gardening. *Address:* Fruit Hill, Widdington, Saffron Walden, Essex. *T:* Saffron Walden 40401. *Clubs:* Carlton, Ulster (Belfast).

GAGGERO, Sir George, Kt 1941; OBE 1934; JP; *b* 5 April 1897; *e s* of late Joseph Gaggero and Mary Dassoy; *m* 1925, Mabel, *o d* of late James Andrews-Speed, CBE, JP, and Mrs Speed; two *s* two *d*. *Educ:* in Gibraltar, Germany and England. Chairman, M. H. Bland & Co. Ltd, 1914-70 (now Hon. President), and Bland Group of cos incl. Rock Hotel Ltd, Bland Cable Cars Ltd, Bland Line, Thomas Mosley & Co. Ltd, and M. H. Bland & Co. (UK) Ltd. Chairman: Gibraltar Stevedoring Co. Ltd, 1948-59; Stevedoring & Cargo Handling Co. Ltd, 1959-65; Gibraltar Shipping Assoc., 1956-60. President: Gibraltar Airways Ltd. (Chm. 1947-66); Gibraltar Employers Fedn, 1928-40. Director: Gibraltar Transporters Ltd, 1930-66; Mackintosh & Co. (Gibraltar) Ltd, 1943-67; Gibraltar Chamber of Comm., 1918-22; Rock Fire Assurance Co. Ltd, 1927-52. City Councillor, 1921-24; Unofficial Mem. Exec. Council, 1924-30 and 1936-43; Chief ARP Warden, Gibraltar, 1938-40; Chairman: Bench of Justices, 1949-59; Bd Dist Comrs, 1940-43; Merchant Navy Welfare Cttee, 1942-47; Member: Public Service Commn, 1956-

58; Merchant Navy Club Cttee, 1922-70; served on many local cttees apptd by the Governor in connection with public matters. Swedish Consul, 1939, Swedish Consul-Gen., 1954-66. FRSA; Coronation Medals, 1937 and 1953; Chevalier (1st Class), Royal Swedish Order of Vasa, 1947. *Address:* 75 Prince Edward's Road, Gibraltar. *Clubs:* Royal Automobile, Royal Thames Yacht; Royal Gibraltar Yacht.

GAILEY, Thomas William Hamilton, CBE 1968; Member, Economic and Social Committee, EEC, since 1973; *b* 7 Oct. 1906; *s* of late Thomas Andrew Gailey, ISO, and late Mabel Gailey; *m* 1st, 1937, Beryl (*d* 1972), *er d* of late Harold Kirkconnel; one *d*; 2nd, 1973, Mary Diana, *y d* of late Frederick Priddle. *Educ:* King's Sch., Rochester; University Coll., Oxford (MA). Served with companies in Tilling Bus Group, 1932-59. Served War of 1939-45, with RAF: Wing Comdr, RAF Transp. Comd and psc, 1943. Vice-Chm., Bristol Wing, Air Trng Corps, 1945-56. Mem., Tilling Gp Management Bd, 1960-64; Chm., Tilling Bus Gp, 1965-68; Dir, Passenger Planning, Transp. Holding Co., 1967-68; Mem., Nat. Bus Company, 1968-74, Chief Executive, 1968-71; Mem., Nat. Council for Omnibus Industry, 1960-69; Dir, Bristol Commercial Vehicles and Eastern Coach Works, 1962-71; Director: Leyland National Co. Ltd; Park Royal Vehicles Ltd, 1969-71. Mem., Scottish Transport Gp, 1968-71. Chm., Public Transp. Assoc., 1967-69. Vice-Chm., Road Operators' Safety Council, 1964-68. Transport Advr, English Tourist Bd, 1972-74. FCIT (Vice-Pres., 1966-68); FRSA. Freeman of City of London; Liveryman, Worshipful Co. of Carmen; Governor, British Transp. Staff Coll. *Publications:* various papers for professional institutes and societies. *Address:* Wheatsheaf Pond Cottage, Liphook, Hants. *T:* Liphook 723467. *Clubs:* Travellers'; Bristol Savages (Bristol).

GAINFORD, 3rd Baron *cr* 1917; **Joseph Edward Pease;** Local Government Officer, Greater London Council Staff; *b* 25 Dec. 1921; *s* of 2nd Baron Gainford, TD, and of Veronica Margaret, *d* of Sir George Noble, 2nd Bt; *S* father, 1971; *m* 1953, Margaret Theophila Radcliffe, *d* of late Henry Edmund Guise Tyndale; two *d*. *Educ:* Eton and Gordonstoun. FRGS; Member, Society of Surveying Technicians. RAFVR, 1941-46. Hunting Aerosurveys Ltd, 1947-49; Directorate of Colonial Surveys, 1951-53; Soil Mechanics Ltd, 1953-58; London County Council, 1958-65; Greater London Council, 1965-. UK Delegate to UN, 1973. Mem., Plaisterers' Co., 1976. *Recreations:* cricket, golf, deer stalking, rough shooting, music, veteran and vintage aviation. *Heir: b* Hon. George Pease [*b* 20 April 1926; *m* 1958, Flora Daphne, *d* of late Dr N. A. Dyce Sharp; two *s* two *d*]. *Address:* 60 Lansdowne Road, W11 2LR. *T:* 01-229 6279. *Clubs:* Athenæum, MCC, Pathfinder.

GAINHAM, Sarah Rachel, (Mrs Kenneth Ames); Author; *b* 1 Oct. 1922; *d* of Tom Stainer and May Genevieve Gainham; *m* 1964, Kenneth Ames (*d* 1975). *Educ:* Newbury High Sch. for Girls; afterwards largely self educated. From 1947 onwards, travelled extensively in Central and E Europe; Central Europe Correspondent of The Spectator, 1956-66. Mem. PEN, England. *Publications:* Time Right Deadly, 1956; Cold Dark Night, 1957; The Mythmaker, 1957; Stone Roses, 1959; Silent Hostage, 1960; Night Falls on the City, 1967 (Book Soc. Choice and US Book of Month Club); A Place in the Country, 1968; Takeover Bid, 1970; Private Worlds, 1971; Maculan's Daughter, 1973; To the Opera Ball, 1975; contrib. to Encounter, Atlantic Monthly, BBC, etc. *Recreations:* theatre, opera, European history. *Address:* c/o Macmillan London Ltd, 4 Little Essex Street, WC2R 3LF.

GAINSBOROUGH, 5th Earl of, (2nd) *cr* 1841; **Anthony Gerard Edward Noel,** Bt 1781; Baron Barham, 1805; Viscount Campden, Baron Noel, 1841; JP; *b* 24 Oct. 1923; *s* of 4th Earl and Alice Mary (*d* 1970), *e d* of Edward Eyre, Gloucester House, Park Lane, W1; *S* father 1927; *m* 1947, Mary, *er d* of Hon. J. J. Stourton (and of Mrs Kathleen Stourton, Withington, Glos), *qv*; four *s* three *d*. *Educ:* Georgetown, Garrett Park, Maryland, USA. Chairman: Oakham RDC, 1952-67; Executive Council RDC's Association of England and Wales, 1963 (Vice-Chairman 1962, Pres., 1965); Pres., Assoc. of District Councils, 1974-; Vice-Chm. Rutland CC, 1958-70, Chm., 1970-73; Chm., Rutland Dist Council, 1973-76. Chm., Bd of Management, Hosp. of St John and St Elizabeth, NW8. Mem. Court of Assistants, Worshipful Co. of Gardeners of London, 1960 (Upper Warden, 1966; Master, 1967). Hon. FIMunE 1969. JP Rutland, 1957, Leics 1974. Knight of Malta, 1948; Bailiff Grand Cross Order of Malta, 1958; Pres. Br. Assoc., SMO, Malta, 1968-74. KStJ 1970. *Recreations:* shooting, sailing. *Heir: s* Viscount Campden, *qv*. *Address:* Exton Park, Oakham, Rutland, Leics. *T:* Oakham 812209. *Clubs:* Boodle's; Bembridge Sailing, Royal Yacht Squadron.

See also Earl of Liverpool, Hon. G. E. W. Noel.

GAINSBOROUGH, George Fotheringham, CBE 1973; PhD, FIEE; Barrister-at-law; Secretary, Institution of Electrical Engineers, since 1962; *b* 28 May 1915; *o s* of late Rev. William Anthony Gainsborough and of Alice Edith (*née* Fennell); *m* 1937, Gwendoline (*d* 1976), *e d* of John and Anne Berry; two *s*. *Educ:* Christ's Hospital; King's Coll., London; Gray's Inn. Scientific Staff, Nat. Physical Laboratory, 1938-46; Radio Physicist, British Commonwealth Scientific Office, Washington, DC, USA, 1944-45; Administrative Civil Service (Ministries of Supply and Aviation), 1946-62. Imperial Defence College, 1960. Secretary, Commonwealth Engineering Conf., 1962-69; Sec.-General, World Fedn of Engineering Organizations, 1968-76. *Publications:* papers in Proc. Instn of Electrical Engineers. *Address:* 19 Glenmore House, Richmond Hill, Richmond, Surrey. *T:* 01-940 8515. *Club:* Athenæum.

GAINSBOROUGH, Hugh, MD, FRCP; Consulting Physician to St George's Hospital, since 1959. *Educ:* Cambridge Univ.; St George's Hosp. Medical Sch. MA Cambridge 1919; MB, ChB, 1921, MD 1928; MRCS 1917; FRCP 1929. Late Examiner in Medicine, Conjoint Board and University of London. Formerly: Physician St George's Hosp., and London Jewish Hospital; Dir of Medical Unit, St George's Hosp. Medical Sch. Fellow Royal Soc. Med.; Member: Biochemical Soc.; Association of Physicians. *Publications:* Principles of Hospital Design (with John Gainsborough), 1964; articles in Quar. Jl Med., Lancet, BM Jl, Biochem. Jl, The Architects' Jl. *Address:* 22 Court Lane Gardens, SE21.

GAIRDNER, Gen. Sir Charles Henry, GBE 1969 (KBE 1960; CBE 1941); KCMG 1948; KCVO 1954; CB 1946; Governor of Tasmania, 1963-68; *b* 20 March 1898; *e surv s* of late C. A. Gairdner, Lisbeg House, County Galway; *m* 1925, Hon. Evelyn Constance Handcock, CStJ, *o d* of 5th Baron Castlemaine, Moydrum Castle, Co. Westmeath; no *c*. *Educ:* Repton; RMA, Woolwich. Entered Army in 1916, served in France and Flanders (wounded); Staff Coll., Camberley, 1933-35; commanded 10th Royal Hussars, 1937-40; GSO 1st grade 7 Armoured Division, 1940-41; Deputy Dir of Plans, Middle East, 1941; GOC 6th Armoured Division, 1942; Commandant, Higher Commanders Sch., 1943. GOC 8th Armoured Division, 1943; CGS North Africa, 1943; Maj.-Gen. Armoured Fighting Vehicles, India, 1944; Maj.-Gen., 1941; Lt-Gen., 1944; Head, UK Liaison Mission, Japan, 1945-46. Prime Minister's Special Representative in Far East, 1945-48. Gov., State of W Australia, 1951-63. Col 10th Royal Hussars, 1949-52; Hon. Col 10th Light Horse, 1952-68; Hon. Col Royal Tasmanian Regt, 1964-68. Hon. Air Commodore, RAAF. KStJ 1951; Hon. DLitt W Australia, 1956; Hon. LLD, University of Tasmania, 1967. American Medal of Freedom with Silver Palm, 1948. *Recreations:* hunting, polo, golf, yachting. *Address:* 24 The Esplanade, Peppermint Grove, W Australia. *Clubs:* Cavalry and Guards; Weld, West Australian (Perth), Royal Perth Yacht, Royal Freshwater Bay Yacht.

GAIRY, Rt. Hon. Sir Eric Matthew, PC 1977; Kt 1977; MP; Prime Minister of Grenada, since 1974; also Minister of External Affairs, Planning and Development Lands and Tourism, Information Service, Public Relations and Natural Resources, since 1974 (date of Independence); *b* 18 Feb. 1922; *m* Cynthia Gairy; two *d*. Member of Legislative Council, 1951-52 and 1954-55; Minister of Trade and Production, 1956-57; Chief Minister and Minister of Finance until 1962; Premier, 1967-74. *Address:* Office of the Prime Minister, St George's, Grenada.

GAISFORD, Prof. Wilfrid Fletcher, MD London, MSc Manchester, FRCP; Czechoslovak Military Medal of Merit, 1st class, 1945; First Professor of Child Health and Pædiatrics and Director of the Department of Child Health, University of Manchester, 1947-67, now Emeritus; *b* 6 April 1902; *s* of Captain Harold Gaisford, RN, and Annie, *d* of Captain Wm Fletcher, RIN; *m* 1933, Mary, *d* of Captain Wm Guppy; one *s* four *d*. *Educ:* Bristol Grammar Sch.; St Bartholomew's Hosp., London, MB London, 1925; MD London, 1928; Post-graduate study in St Louis Children's Hosp., University of Washington, USA, 1928-29; FRCP, 1940; MSc Manchester, 1951. Hon. Asst Physician, East London Children's Hosp., 1932; Member: British Pædiatric Assoc., 1933; Assoc. of Physicians of Gt Britain and Ireland, 1940; Physn, Dudley Road Hosp., Birmingham, 1935-42; Cons. Pædiatrician, Warwicks CC, 1942-47; Leonard Parsons Memorial Lecturer, University of Birmingham, 1954-55; Catherine Chisholm Memorial Lecturer, 1965. Hon. Physician, Royal Manchester Children's Hosp. and St Mary's Hosp., Manchester; Hon. Cons. Pædiatrician, United Manchester Hosp., 1967. Regional Adviser in Child Health, 1948. Hon. Member: Canadian Pædiatric Association, 1949; Swedish Pædiatric Association, 1960; Finnish Pædiatric Association, 1965; Hon. Fellow, American Acad. of Pediatrics,

1962; Pres., British Paediatric Assoc., 1964-65. Extraord. Mem., Swiss Paediatric Soc., 1965; Pres., Paediatric Section, Manchester Med. Soc., 1966-67. *Publications:* contrib. to the Encyclopædia of British Medical Practice, Lancet, BMJ, Practitioner, Archives of Disease in Childhood, Jl Pediatrics, etc. Joint Editor, Pædiatrics for the Practitioner (Gaisford and Lightwood). *Recreation:* gardening. *Address:* Treloyhan, Restronguet Point, Feock, Truro TR3 6RB. *T:* Devoran 862620.

GAITSKELL, Baroness, *cr* 1963, of Egremont (Life Peer); **Anna Dora Gaitskell;** *d* of Leon Creditor; *m* 1937, Rt Hon. Hugh Todd Naylor Gaitskell, PC, CBE, MP (*d* 1963), *s* of late Arthur Gaitskell, Indian Civil Service; two *d* (and one *s* by a former marriage). *Address:* 18 Frognal Gardens, NW3.
See also Sir Arthur Gaitskell.

GAITSKELL, Sir Arthur, Kt 1970; CMG 1949; Member, Commonwealth (formerly Colonial) Development Corporation, 1954-73, retired; *b* Oct. 1900; *s* of late Arthur Gaitskell, ICS; *m* 1939, Jeanne Stephanie, *d* of Col E. C. Townsend, ICS; one *s* two *d*. *Educ:* Winchester Coll.; New Coll., Oxford. Manager, Sudan Plantations Syndicate, 1945-50; Chm. and Managing Dir, Sudan Gezira Board, 1950-52. Consultant, 1952-53; Member: Royal Commission on East Africa, 1953-54; Tanganyika Agricultural Corp., 1955. Research Fellow, Nuffield Coll., Oxford, 1955-58; Nominee of International Bank on Food and Agriculture Commn, Pakistan, 1959-60; Consultant: to Mitchell Cotts, Ethiopia, to Kenya African National Union, Kenya, and to Ford Foundation, Nigeria, 1961-62. Lecturer at Economic Development Institute, International Bank, Washington, 1963. Consultant to: Euphrates Project Authority, 1965; Sir Alex Gibb and Partners on Indus Basin Survey, 1965-66; World Food Program, Mexico, 1966; FAO for Philippines, 1967, for Thailand, 1968. Member: Coun., Overseas Develt Inst., 1965; Adv. Bd, Mekong River, 1968; ILO Mission to Colombia, 1970; Mission to Jamaica for Agric. Sector, Jamaican Govt, 1973. *Publication:* Gezira, 1959. *Address:* Bicknoller, Taunton, Somerset.
See also Baroness Gaitskell.

GAJDUSEK, Daniel Carleton, MD; Laboratory Chief, Study of Child Growth, Development and Behavior and Disease Patterns in Primitive Cultures and Laboratories of Slow Latent and Temperate Virus Infections, National Institutes of Neurological and Communicative Disorders and Stroke, National Institutes of Health, Bethesda, Md, since 1958; *b* Yonkers, NY, 9 Sept. 1923; ten adopted *s* (all from New Guinea and Micronesia). *Educ:* Marine Biological Lab., Woods Hole, Mass; Univ. of Rochester; Harvard Medical Sch.; California Inst. of Technology. Served Medical Corps; appts in various children's hosps; Sen. Fellow, Nat. Research Council, Calif Inst. of Tech., 1948-49; Children's Hosp., Boston, Mass, 1949-51; Research Fellow, Harvard Univ. and Sen. Fellow, Nat. Foundn for Infantile Paralysis, 1949-52; Walter Reed Army Medical Center, 1952-53; Institut Pasteur, Tehran, Iran and Univ. of Maryland, 1954-55; Vis. Investigator, Nat. Foundn for Infantile Paralysis and Walter and Eliza Hall Inst., Australia, 1955-57. Member: Amer. Acad. of Sciences; Soc. for Paediatric Research; Amer. Paediatric Soc.; Amer. Epidemiological Soc. Studied unique forms of virus and brain diseases; shared with Dr Baruch Blumberg Nobel Prize in Physiology or Medicine, for discoveries concerning new mechanisms for the origin and dissemination of infectious diseases, 1976. *Address:* Laboratory of Central Nervous System Studies, NINCDS, National Institutes of Health, Bethesda, Md 20014, USA.

GAJE GHALE, VC 1943; Subedar 2/5 Royal Gurkha Rifles FF; *b* 1 July 1922; *s* of Bikram Ghale; *m* 1939, Dhansuba; no *c*. *Educ:* IA 2nd class certificate of education. Enlisted as a Recruit Boy 2nd Bn 5th Royal Gurkha Rifles FF, Feb. 1935; transferred to the ranks, Aug. 1935; Naik, 1941; Acting Havildar, May 1942; War Subst. Havildar, Nov. 1942; Bn Havildar Major June 1943; Jemadar, Aug. 1943. Waziristan operations, 1936-37 (medal with clasp); Burma, 1942-43 (1939-45 Star, VC). *Recreations:* football, basketball, badminton and draughts.

GALANTE, Mme P. P.; *see* de Havilland, Olivia M.

GALBRAITH, family name of **Baron Strathclyde.**

GALBRAITH, James Hunter; Under Secretary, Department of Employment, since 1975; *b* 16 July 1925; *o s* of late Prof. V. H. Galbraith, FBA, and of Dr G. R. Galbraith; *m* 1954, Isobel Gibson Graham; two *s*. *Educ:* Edinburgh Academy; Balliol Coll., Oxford. Fleet Air Arm, 1944-46. Entered Ministry of Labour, 1950; Private Sec. to Permanent Sec., 1953-55; Jun. Civilian Instructor, IDC, 1958-61; Private Sec. to Minister of Labour, 1962-64; Chm. Central Youth Employment Exec.,

1964-67; Sen. Simon Research Fellow, Manchester Univ., 1967-68; Asst Under-Sec. of State, Dept of Employment and Productivity (Research and Planning Div.), 1968-71; Dir, Office of Manpower Economics, 1971-73; Under-Sec., Manpower Gen. Div., Dept of Employment, 1973-74; Sec., Manpower Services Commn, 1974-75. *Recreations:* golf, fishing. *Address:* 27 Sandy Lodge Lane, Moor Park, Mddx. *T:* Northwood 22458.

GALBRAITH, Prof. John Kenneth; Paul M. Warburg Professor of Economics, Harvard University, 1949-75, now Emeritus Professor; *b* Ontario, Canada, 15 Oct. 1908; *s* of William Archibald and Catherine Galbraith; *m* 1937, Catherine M. Atwater; three *s*. *Educ:* Univ. of Guelph; California Univ. BS, MS, PhD. Tutor, Harvard Univ., 1934-39; Social Science Research Fellow, Cambridge Univ., 1937; Asst Prof. of Economics, Princeton Univ., 1939; Asst Administrator, Office of Price Administration, 1941; Deputy Administrator, 1942-43; Dir, State Dept Office of Economic Security Policy, 1945; Mem. Bd of Editors, Fortune Magazine, 1943-48. United States Ambassador to India, 1961-63 (on leave from Professorship). Reith Lecturer, 1966; Vis. Fellow, Trinity Coll., Cambridge, 1970-71. Chm., Americans for Democratic Action, 1967-69; Pres., Amer. Econ. Assoc., 1972. LLD Bard, 1958; Miami Univ., 1959; University of Toronto, 1961; Brandeis Univ., 1963; University of Mass, 1963; University of Saskatchewan, 1965; Rhode Island Coll., 1966; Boston Coll., 1967; Hobart and William Smith Colls, 1967; Univ. of Paris, 1975; and others. TV series, The Age of Uncertainty, 1977. President's Certificate of Merit; Medal of Freedom. *Publications:* American Capitalism, the Concept of Countervailing Power, 1952; The Great Crash, 1929, 1955; The Affluent Society, 1958, new edn 1970; Journey to Poland and Yugoslavia, 1958; The Liberal Hour, 1960; Made to Last, 1964; The New Industrial State, 1967 (rev. edn, 1972); Indian Painting, 1968; Ambassador's Journal, 1969; Economics, Peace and Laughter, 1971; A China Passage, 1973; Economics and the Public Purpose, 1974; Money: whence it came, where it went, 1975; contribs to learned jls. *Address:* 207 Littaver Center, Harvard University, Cambridge, Mass 02138, USA; 30 Francis Avenue, Cambridge, Mass 02138, USA. *Clubs:* Century (NY); Federal City (Washington).

GALBRAITH, Neil, CBE 1975; QPM 1959; DL; HM Inspector of Constabulary, 1964-76, retired; *b* 25 May 1911; *s* of late Peter and Isabella Galbraith; *m* 1942, Catherine Margaret Thornton; one *s* one *d*. *Educ:* Kilmarnock Academy. Constable to Inspector, Lancs Constabulary, 1931-46. Chief Supt, Herts Constabulary, 1946-51; Asst Chief Constable, Monmouthshire Constabulary, 1951-55; Chief Constable, Leicester City Police, 1956; Chief Constable, Monmouthshire Constabulary, 1957-64. DL Gwent (formerly Monmouth), 1973. *Recreation:* reading. *Address:* Neath House, Trostrey, Usk, Gwent. *T:* Usk 2779.

GALBRAITH, Hon. Thomas Galloway Dunlop; MP (U) for Hillhead Division of Glasgow since 1948; Member of Queen's Body Guard for Scotland (Royal Company of Archers); a Governor of Wellington College; *b* 10 March 1917; *e s* and *heir* of 1st Baron Strathclyde, *qv*; *m* 1956, Simone (marr. diss. 1974), *e d* of late Jean du Roy de Blicquy, Bois d'Hautmont, Brabant; two *s* one *d*. *Educ:* Aytoun House, Glasgow; Wellington Coll.; Christ Church, Oxford (MA); Glasgow Univ. (LLB). Served War of 1939-45, in RNVR (Lieut). 1939-46. Contested (U) Paisley, July 1945; East Edinburgh, Oct. 1945; Asst Conservative Whip, 1950; Scottish Unionist Whip, 1950-57; a Lord Commissioner of the Treasury, 1951-54; Comptroller of HM Household, 1954-55; Treasurer of HM Household, 1955-57; Civil Lord of the Admiralty, 1957-59; Joint Parliamentary Under-Sec. of State, Scottish Office, 1959-62; Joint Parliamentary Sec., Ministry of Transport, 1963-64. Chm., Cttee on Nuclear propulsion for Merchant Ships, 1957-59. Pres. Scottish Georgian Soc., 1970. *Address:* Barskimming, Mauchline, Ayrshire. *T:* Mauchline 334. *Clubs:* Carlton; Conservative (Glasgow); New (Edinburgh).

GALE, Arthur James Victor, MA; *b* 10 Feb. 1895; *s* of James Webb and Emma Gale; *m* 1929, Gwendoline Veysey; one *s* one *d*. *Educ:* Latymer Upper Sch.; Selwyn Coll., Cambridge (Scholar). Special Brigade, RE, 1915-18; Asst Editor of Nature, 1920-38; Joint Editor, 1939-61. Pres., Selwyn Coll. Assoc., 1967-68. *Address:* 12 Hamilton House, Upperton Road, Eastbourne, East Sussex BN21 1LE.

GALE, Prof. Ernest Frederick, FRS 1953; BSc London; BA, PhD, ScD Cantab; Professor of Chemical Microbiology, University of Cambridge, since 1960; Fellow of St John's College, Cambridge; *b* 15 July 1914; *s* of Nellie Annie and Ernest Francis Edward Gale; *m* 1937, Eiry Mair Jones; one *s*. *Educ:* St John's Coll. Cambridge (Scholar). Research in biochemistry, Cambridge, from 1936; Senior Student, Royal Commn for

Exhibition of 1851, 1939; Beit Memorial Fellow, 1941; Scientific Staff of Med. Research Council, 1943; Reader in Chemical Microbiology, University of Cambridge, 1948-60; Dir, Medical Research Council Unit for Chemical Microbiology, 1948-62. Herter Lecturer, Johns Hopkins Hosp., Baltimore, USA, 1948; Commonwealth Travelling Fellow, Hanna Lecturer, Western Reserve Univ., 1951; Harvey Lectr, New York, 1955; Leeuwenhoek Lectr, Royal Society, London, 1956; Malcolm Lectr, Syracuse Univ., 1967; M. Stephenson Meml Lectr, 1971; Linacre Lectr, St John's Coll., Cambridge, 1973. Visiting Fellow, ANU, 1964-65. Meetings Sec., Society for General Microbiology, 1954-58, International Representative, 1963-67 (Pres., 1967-69); Mem. Food Investigation Board, 1954-58; Mem. International Union of Biochemistry Commission on Enzymes, 1957-61. *Publications:* Chemical Activities of Bacteria, 1947; The Molecular Basis of Antibiotic Action, 1972; scientific papers in Biochem. Journal, Journal of General Microbiology, Biochimica et Biophysica Acta, etc. *Recreation:* photography. *Address:* Department of Biochemistry, University of Cambridge. *T:* Cambridge 51781; 25 Luard Road, Cambridge. *T:* Cambridge 47585.

GALE, Hon. George Alexander; Chief Justice of Ontario 1967-76; Vice-Chairman, Ontario Law Reform Commission, since 1977; *b* 24 June 1906; *s* of late Robert Henry and Elma Gertrude Gale; *m* 1934, Hilda Georgina Daly; three *s*. *Educ:* Prince of Wales High Sch., Vancouver; Toronto Univ. (BA); Osgoode Hall Law Sch., Toronto. Called to Ontario Bar, 1932; Partner, Mason, Foulds, Davidson & Gale, 1944; KC (Can.) 1945; Justice, Supreme Court of Ontario, 1946; Justice, Court of Appeal, Ontario, 1963; Chief Justice of High Court of Justice for Ontario, 1964. Formerly Chm. Judicial Council for Provincial Judges; Chm., Cttee on Rules of Practice for Ontario (Mem. 1941-); Mem. Canadian Bar Assoc. (formerly Mem. Council); Hon. Mem., Georgia Bar Assoc.; Hon. Lectr, Osgoode Law Sch.; formerly Mem. Exec. Cttee, Canadian Judicial Council; Mem. Bd of Governors: Wycliffe Coll., Toronto Univ.; formerly, Upper Canada Coll., Toronto; Mem. Delta Kappa Epsilon, Phi Delta Phi (Hon.). Anglican; Warden, St John's, York Mills, for 5 years. Hon. LLD: McMaster, 1968; York (Toronto), 1969. *Publication:* (ed with Holmsted) Practice and Procedure in Ontario, 6th edn. *Recreation:* golf. *Address:* 2 Brookfield Road, Willowdale, Ontario, Canada. *Clubs:* University, Lawyers, (Hon. Mem.) York (Toronto); Toronto Curling, Chippewa Golf.

GALE, George Stafford; journalist, author, broadcaster; *b* 22 Oct. 1927; *e s* of George Pyatt Gale and Anne Watson Gale (*née* Wood); *m* 1951, Patricia Marina Holley; four *s*. *Educ:* Royal Grammar Sch., Newcastle upon Tyne; Peterhouse, Cambridge; Göttingen University. 1st cl. hons Historical Tripos, Cantab, 1948 and 1949. Leader writer, reporter, Labour Corresp., Manchester Guardian, 1951-55; Special and Foreign Corresp., Daily Express, 1955-67; Columnist, Daily Mirror, 1967-69; freelance journalist, 1969-70; Editor, The Spectator, 1970-73; columnist, Daily Express, 1976-. Presenter, phone-in programmes, London Broadcasting, 1973-77. *Publications:* No Flies in China, 1955; (with P. Johnson) The Highland Jaunt, 1973; countless articles. *Recreations:* looking, brooding, disputing, writing poetry, and roasting beef. *Address:* 133 Defoe House, Barbican, EC1. *T:* 01-628 8751; Tattingstone Place, Tattingstone, Suffolk. *T:* Holbrook 797. *Clubs:* Garrick, Press, Wig and Pen; Wivenhoe Arts (Wivenhoe).

GALE, Malcolm, CBE 1964 (MBE 1948); HM Diplomatic Service, retired; *b* 31 Aug. 1909; *s* of late George Alfred Gale and late Agnes Logan Gale (*née* Ruthven); *m* 1st, 1932, Doris Frances Wells; 2nd, 1936, Ilse Strauss; one *s* one *d*. *Educ:* Sedbergh; Madrid Univ. Market Officer, Santiago, 1945; Third Sec., Dec. 1947; Second Sec. (Commercial), Caracas, 1948; First Sec. (Commercial), 1952; First Sec. (Commercial), Ankara, 1953; Actg Counsellor (Commercial), 1954; First Sec. (Commercial), Bahrein, 1955; Consul (Commercial), Milan, 1958; Acting Consul-Gen., Milan, 1958 and 1959; Counsellor, 1959; Counsellor (Commercial): Washington, 1960-64; Lisbon, 1964-67; Minister (Commercial) Buenos Aires, 1967-69. *Recreations:* golf, photography. *Address:* Apartado 32, Sintra, Portugal.

GALE, Michael; Barrister-at-Law; a Recorder of the Crown Court, since 1977; *b* 12 Aug. 1932; *s* of Joseph Gale and Blossom Gale; *m* 1963, Joanna Stephanie Bloom; one *s* two *d*. *Educ:* Cheltenham Grammar Sch.; Grocers' Sch.; King's Coll., Cambridge (Exhibnr; BA History and Law, 1954, MA 1958). National Service, Royal Fusiliers and Jt Services Sch. for Linguists, 1956-58. Called to the Bar, Middle Temple, 1957; Harmsworth Law Scholar, 1958. *Recreations:* the arts and country pursuits. *Address:* 6 Pump Court, Temple, EC4Y 7AR. *T:* 01-353 7242. *Club:* Travellers'.

GALE, Michael Sadler, MC 1945; Assistant Under-Secretary of State, Prison Department, Home Office, since 1972; *b* 5 Feb. 1919; *s* of Rev. John Sadler and Ethel Gale; *m* 1950, Philippa, *d* of Terence and Betty Ennion; three *s* one *d*. *Educ:* Tonbridge Sch.; Oriel Coll., Oxford (Scholar, MA). Served War of 1939-45: enlisted 1939, Royal Fusiliers; commnd 1940, Queen's Own Royal W Kent Regt, Major 1944; served N Africa and NW Europe. Housemaster, HM Borstal, Rochester, 1946-48; Dep. Governor, HM Prison, Durham, 1948-49; Staff Course Tutor, Imperial Trng Sch., Wakefield, 1949-50; Principal, 1950-52; Governor, HM Prison: The Verne, 1952-57; Camp Hill, 1957-62; Wandsworth, 1962-66; Asst Dir, Prison Dept, Home Office, 1966-69; Controller, Planning and Develt, 1969-75; Controller, Operational Administration, 1975-; Mem. Prisons Board, 1969-. *Recreations:* walking, reading, gardening. *Address:* 42 St Cross Road, Winchester, Hants. *T:* Winchester 3836.

GALE, General Sir Richard Nelson, GCB 1954 (KCB 1953; CB 1945); KBE 1950 (OBE 1940); DSO 1944; MC 1918; *b* 25 July 1896; *s* of late Wilfred Gale and Helen Webber Ann, *d* of Joseph Nelson, Townsville, Qld, Australia; *m* 1st, 1924, Ethel Maude Larnack (*d* 1952), *d* of Mrs Jessie Keene, Hove; no *c* ; 2nd, 1953, Daphne Mabelle Eveline, *d* of late Francis Blick, Stroud, Glos. *Educ:* Merchant Taylors' Sch.; Aldenham; RMC, Sandhurst. 2nd Lieut Worcestershire Regt, 1915; Captain DCLI 1930; Major, Royal Inniskilling Fusiliers, 1938; Lt-Col Sept. 1939; Brig. 1941; Maj.-Gen. 1946; act. Lt-Gen. 1945; Lt-Gen. 1947; Gen. 1952; raised and commanded the 1st Parachute Brigade; commanded 6th British Airborne Div.; Deputy Commander 1st Allied Airborne Army, 1945; Commander 1st British Airborne Corps, 1945; 1st Inf. Div. 1946-47; GOC British Troops, Egypt and Mediterranean Command, 1948-49; Dir-Gen. of Military Training, War Office, 1949-52; Commander-in-Chief, Northern Army Group, Allied Land Forces Europe and British Army of the Rhine, 1952-57; retired 1957; re-employed NATO 1958: Dep. Supreme Allied Comdr, Europe, 1958-60. ADC (General) to the Queen, 1954-57; Col, The Worcestershire Regt, 1950-61; Col Comdt, The Parachute Regt, 1956-61. Comdr Legion of Merit (US); Comdr Legion of Honour, Croix de Guerre with palm (France); Grand Officier de La Couronne (Belgium). *Publications:* With the 6th Airborne Division in Normandy, 1948; Call to Arms, 1968; Great Battles of Biblical History, 1969; The Worcestershire Regiment, 1970; Kings at Arms, 1971. *Recreation:* principal interest Eastern and Central Asian affairs. *Address:* Hampton Court Palace, East Molesey, Surrey. *Club:* Army and Navy.

GALES, Kathleen Emily, (Mrs Heinz Spitz); Senior Lecturer in Statistics, London School of Economics, since 1966; *b* 1927; *d* of Albert Henry and Sarah Thomson Gales; *m* 1970, Heinz Spitz. *Educ:* Gateshead Grammar Sch.; Newnham Coll., Cambridge (Exhibr); Ohio Univ. (Schol.). BA Cantab 1950, MA Ohio, 1951. Asst Statistician, Foster Wheeler Ltd, 1951-53; Statistician, Municipal Statistical Office, Birmingham, 1953-55; Res. Asst and part-time Lectr, LSE, 1955-58; Asst Lectr in Statistics, LSE, 1958-60, Lectr, 1960-66. Vis. Assoc. Prof. in Statistics, Univ. of California, 1964-65. Statistical Consultant: Royal Commn on Doctors' and Dentists' Remuneration, 1959; WHO, 1960; Turkish Min. of Health, 1963. Mem. Performing Rights Tribunal, 1974-. *Publications:* (with C. A. Moser and P. Morpurgo) Dental Health and the Dental Services, 1962; (with B. Abel-Smith) British Doctors at Home and Abroad, 1964; (with T. Blackstone et al.) Students in Conflict: LSE in 1967, 1970; articles in Jl RSS. *Recreations:* singing, ski-ing, reading. *Address:* 39 High View Road, E18 2HL. *T:* 01-989 6311.

GALLAGHER, Francis George Kenna, CMG 1963; HM Diplomatic Service, retired; *b* 25 May 1917; *er s* of George and Johanna Gallagher. *Educ:* St Joseph's Coll.; King's Coll., University of London (LLB (Hons)). Clerical officer, Min. of Agric., 1935-38; Asst Examr, Estate Duty Office, 1938-44; served in HM Forces, 1941-45; Examr, Estate Duty Office, 1944-45; apptd a Mem., HM Foreign (subseq. Diplomatic) Service, 1945; Vice-Consul Marseilles, 1946-48; Acting Consul-Gen., there, in 1947; HM Embassy, Paris, 1948-50; FO, 1950-53; First Sec., HM Embassy, Damascus, 1953-55; acted as Chargé d'Affaires, 1953, 1954 and 1955; FO, 1955; appointed Counsellor and Head of European Economic Organisations Dept, 1960; Counsellor (Commercial), HM Embassy, Berne, 1963-65; acted as Chargé d'Affaires (Berne) in 1963 and 1964; Head of Western Economic Dept, CO, 1965-67, of Common Market Dept, 1967-68; Asst Under-Sec. of State, FCO, 1968-71; Ambassador and Head of UK Delegn to OECD, 1971-77. *Recreations:* music, chess. *Address:* 16 Friday Street, Henley-on-Thames, Oxon. *T:* Henley-on-Thames 77142; The Old Courthouse, Kirkwhelpington, Northumberland.

GALLAGHER, Francis Heath, CMG 1957; Hon. Mr Justice Gallagher; Coal Industry Tribunal (Australia), since 1947; *b* 10 Feb. 1905; *s* of James Gallagher; *m* 1938, Heather Elizabeth Clark; no *c*. *Educ:* Sydney Grammar Sch.; University of Sydney. BA 1929, LLB 1933, University of Sydney. Admitted as solicitor, Supreme Court of NSW, 1933. Mem. of Industrial Commn of NSW, 1955-57; Presidential Mem., Commonwealth Arbitration Commn, 1957-71. *Recreations:* reading, gardening, sailing, surfing. *Address:* 2 Foam Crest Avenue, Newport Beach, NSW 2106, Australia. *T:* 99-1724. *Clubs:* Australian Jockey, Turf (Sydney).

GALLAGHER, John Andrew; Vere Harmsworth Professor of Imperial and Naval History, Cambridge University, since 1971; Vice-Master, Trinity College, Cambridge; *b* 1 April 1919; *o c* of Joseph and Mary Adeline Gallagher; unmarried. *Educ:* Birkenhead Institute; Trinity Coll., Cambridge (MA). Major Schol., Trinity Coll., Cambridge, 1937. Royal Tank Regt, 1939-45. Fellow of Trinity Coll., Cambridge, 1948-63 (Dean of Coll., 1960-63, Sen. Research Fellow, 1971-72); University Lectr in History, Cambridge, 1953-63; Beit Prof. of History of British Commonwealth, Oxford, and Fellow of Balliol Coll., 1963-70; Rockefeller Foundn Fellow, 1967; Ford Lectr in English History, Oxford Univ., 1973-74. *Publications:* Africa and the Victorians (with R. E. Robinson), 1961; Locality, Province and Nation (with G. Johnson and A. Seal); chapters in New Cambridge Modern History, volumes VII and XI; articles in learned jls. *Address:* Trinity College, Cambridge.

GALLAGHER, Dame Monica (Josephine), DBE 1976; State President, Catholic Women's League, New South Wales; Councillor, Catholic Women's League, Sydney, since 1958 (National President, 1972-74); *m* 1946, Dr John Paul Gallagher, KCSG; two *s* two *d*. Has been and remains actively associated with: Festival of Light; NSW Div. of Australian Church Women; Catholic Family Life Centre (Board Member); NSW Council on the Aging; Nat. Council of Women, NSW; United Nations Assoc.; Good Neighbour Council; Austcare. *Address:* c/o Catholic Women's League of NSW, State Secretariat Headquarters, 161 Castlereagh Street, Sydney, NSW 2000, Australia; (home) 1 Robert Street, Willoughby, NSW 2068, Australia.

GALLAGHER, Patrick Joseph, DFC 1943; Managing Director, London Broadcasting Co. Ltd, and Independent Radio News Ltd, since 1975; *b* 15 April 1921; *s* of Patrick Gallagher and Mary Bernadine Donnellan; *m* 1950, Veronica Frances Bateman; one *s* . *Educ:* Prior Park, Bath. Served War, 1941-46: Flt Lieut; Pilot, RAFVR. Principal, HM Treasury, 1948-58: ASC, 1956; Adviser, Raisman Commn, Nigeria, 1957-58; Consultant, Urwick, Orr & Partners Ltd, 1958-60; Dir, Ogilvy, Benson & Mather, 1960-65; Man. Dir, Glendinning Internat. Ltd, 1965-69; Pres., Glendinning Cos Inc., 1970-74. *Publications:* contribs to business, advertising and marketing pubns in UK and USA. *Recreations:* music, travel. *Address:* Flat 5, 30 Hans Road, SW3 1RW. *T:* 01-584 3865.

GALLAHER, Patrick Edmund, CBE 1975; Chairman, North West Gas, since 1974; Part-time Member, British Gas Corporation, since 1973; *b* 17 June 1917; *s* of late Cormac and Agnes Gallaher; *m* 1947, Louise Hatfield (*d* 1965); one *s* two *d*. *Educ:* St Philip's Grammar School and College of Technology, Birmingham. Chemist and Engineer, City of Birmingham Gas Dept, 1934-46; Asst Engineer, Redditch Gas Co., 1946-49. With West Midlands Gas Board: Engineer and Manager, Redditch, 1949-53; Divisional Engineer, 1953-62; Regional Distribution Engineer, 1962-64; Distribution Controller, 1964-66; Area Construction Engineer, 1966-67; Area Distribution Engineer, 1967-68. Wales Gas Board (later Wales Gas Region): Dep Chm., 1968-70; Chm., 1970-74. Pres., IGasE, 1977-78. *Recreations:* sailing, gardening, travel. *Address:* March, Warrington Road, Mere, Knutsford, Cheshire.

GALLEY, Robert Albert Ernest, PhD; FRIC; Director, Shell Research Ltd, Woodstock Agricultural Research Centre, Sittingbourne, Kent, 1960-69; *b* 23 Oct. 1909; *s* of John and Jane A. Galley; *m* 1933, Elsie Marjorie Walton; one *s* two *d*. *Educ:* Colfe's Gram. Sch.; Imperial Coll., London. BSc 1930, PhD 1932, FRIC 1944. Research Chemist, Wool Industries Research Assoc., 1932-34; Chemist, Dept of War Department Chemist, 1934-37; Lectr, Sir John Cass Coll., 1937-39; Prin. Exper. Officer, Min. of Supply, Chemical Inspectorate, 1939-45, Flax Establishment, 1945-46; Sen. Prin. Scientific Officer, Agric. Research Council (Sec. Interdepartmental Insecticides Cttees), 1946-50; seconded to Scientific Secretariat, Office of Lord Pres. of Council, 1950-52; Dir, Tropical Products Institute, Dept of Scientific and Industrial Research (formerly Colonial Products Laboratory), 1953-60. *Publications:* papers in Journal of Chem.

Soc., Chemistry and Industry, World Crops, etc. *Recreations:* tennis, gardening, sailing. *Address:* Swanton Old House, Bredgar, near Sittingbourne, Kent. *Club:* Farmers'.

GALLIE, Prof. Walter Bryce; Professor of Political Science, and Fellow of Peterhouse, Cambridge University, since 1967; *b* 5 Oct. 1912; 3rd *s* of Walter S. Gallie, structural engineer; *m* 1940, Menna Humphreys; one *s* one *d. Educ:* Sedbergh Sch.; Balliol Coll., Oxford (Classical Exhibitioner). BA (1st Cl. PPE), 1934, BLitt 1937, MA Oxon, 1947. University Coll. of Swansea: Asst Lectr, Philosophy, 1935; Lectr, 1938; Sen. Lectr, 1948; Prof. of Philosophy, University Coll. of North Staffordshire 1950; Prof. of Logic and Metaphysics, Queen's Univ., Belfast, 1954-67. Visiting Prof., New York Univ., 1962-63; Lectures: Lewis Fry Meml, Bristol Univ., 1964; Wiles, QUB, 1976. Pres., Aristotelian Soc., 1970-71. Served War, 1940-45, ending with rank of Major, Croix de Guerre, 1945. *Publications:* An English School, 1949; Peirce and Pragmatism, 1952; Free Will and Determinism Yet Again (Inaugural Lecture), 1957; A New University: A. D. Lindsay and the Keele Experiment, 1960; Philosophy and the Historical Understanding, 1964; Philosophers of Peace and War, 1978; articles in Mind, Aristotelian Soc. Proc., Philosophy, French Studies, etc. *Recreations:* travelling and reading. *Address:* Peterhouse, Cambridge.

GALLIFORD, Rt. Rev. David George; *see* Hulme, Bishop Suffragan of.

GALLINER, Peter; Director, International Press Institute, since 1975; Chairman, Peter Galliner Associates, since 1970; *b* 19 Sept. 1920; *s* of Dr Moritz and Hedwig Galliner; *m* 1948, Edith Marguerite Goldschmidt; one *d. Educ:* Berlin and London. Reuters, 1944-47; Foreign Manager, Financial Times, 1947-60; Chm. and Man. Dir, Ullstein Publishing Co., Berlin, 1960-64; Vice-Chm. and Man. Dir, British Printing corporation Publishing Gp, 1965-70. Order of Merit, 1st cl. (German Federal Republic). *Recreations:* reading, music. *Address:* 27 Queen's Grove, NW8 6HL. *T:* 01-722 0361; Längenstrasse 110, 8964 Rudolfstetten, Switzerland. *Club:* Reform.

GALLOWAY, 12th Earl of, *cr* 1623; **Randolph Algernon Ronald Stewart;** Lord Garlies, 1607; Bt 1627; Baron Stewart of Garlies (Great Britain), 1796; Lord Lieutenant of Kircudbrightshire, 1932-75; *b* 21 Nov. 1892; *s* of 11th Earl and Amy Mary Pauline (*d* 1942), *d* of Anthony John Cliffe of Bellevue, Co. Wexford; *S* father, 1920; *m* 1924, Philippa Fendall (*d* 1974), *d* of late J. Wendell, New York; one *s* one *d. Educ:* Harrow; RMC, Sandhurst. Gazetted Scots Guards, 1913; served European War, 1914-15 (prisoner); Hon. Attaché, HM Legation at Berne, 1918; ADC to Military Governor at Cologne, 1919; Lt-Col commanding 7th (Galloway) Bn KOSB, 1939-40, now Hon. Col; JP Kirkudbrightshire. Grand Master Mason of Scotland, 1945-49. *Heir: s* Lord Garlies, *qv. Address:* Cumloden, Newton-Stewart, Kirkcudbrightshire. *Clubs:* Carlton; New (Edinburgh).

GALLOWAY, Bishop of, (RC), since 1952; **Rt. Rev. Joseph McGee;** *b* 13 Dec. 1904; *s* of Denis McGee and Sarah McGlinchey. *Educ:* St Dominic's Sch. and Morrison's Academy, Crieff; Blair's Coll., Aberdeen; Royal Scots Coll., Valladolid. Formerly Vicar-General and Canon (Penitentiary) of Dunkeld. *Address:* Candida Casa, 8 Corsehill Road, Ayr. *T:* Ayr 66750.

GALLOWAY, Rev. Prof. Allan Douglas; Professor of Divinity, University of Glasgow, since 1968 and Principal of Trinity College, Glasgow, since 1972; *b* 30 July 1920; *s* of late William Galloway and Mary Wallace Galloway (*née* Junor); *m* 1948, Sara Louise Phillipp; two *s. Educ:* Stirling High Sch.; Univ. of Glasgow; Christ's Coll., Cambridge; Union Theol Seminary, New York. MA, BD, STM, PhD. Ordained, Asst Minister, Clune Park Parish, Port Glasgow, 1948-50; Minister of Auchterhouse, 1950-54; Prof. of Religious Studies, Univ. of Ibadan, Nigeria, 1954-60; Sen. Lectr, Univ. of Glasgow, 1960-66, Reader in Divinity, 1966-68. Hensley Henson Lectr in Theology, Oxford Univ., 1977-78. *Publications:* The Cosmic Christ, 1951; Basic Readings in Theology, 1964; Faith in a Changing Culture, 1966; Wolfhart Pannenberg, 1973. *Recreation:* sailing. *Address:* 11 St Thomas's Place, Cambusbarron, Stirling.

GALLOWAY, Lt-Col Arnold Crawshaw, CIE 1946; OBE 1941; *b* 1901; *o s* of late Percy Christopher Galloway; *m* 1946, Mary, *d* of Arthur William Odgers, Oxford; three *s. Educ:* City of London Sch.; RMC. Member, Middle Temple. Entered Indian Political Service, 1928; Under-Sec. Rajputana, 1929-30; Vice-Consul, Ahwaz, Persia, 1930-31; Vice-Consul, Zahidan, Persia, 1932-33; Under-Sec. to Resident, Persian Gulf, 1934; Sec.,

British Legation, Kabul, Afghanistan, 1935-36; Sec. to Polit. Resident, Persian Gulf, 1937-38; Polit. Agent, Kuwait, Persian Gulf, 1939-41; Polit. Advr to British Forces in Iraq and Persia, 1941-43 (despatches); Consul-Gen., Ahwaz, 1943-44; Polit. Agent, Muscat, 1944-45; Polit. Resident, Persian Gulf, 1945; Polit. Agent, Bahrein, 1945-47; Consul-Gen., Bushire, 1947; Polit. Agent, Kuwait, 1948-49; UK Repres. of Bahrain Petroleum Company Ltd, 1950-68; Chm., Middle East Navigation Aids Service, 1958-68. *Address:* Yeo House, Long Load, near Langport, Somerset. *T:* Long Sutton 329. *Clubs:* Flyfishers', Royal Thames Yacht.

GALLOWAY, Maj.-Gen. Kenneth Gardiner, OBE 1960; QHDS 1971; Director Army Dental Service, 1974-June 1978; *b* 3 Nov. 1917; *s* of David and Helen Galloway, Dundee and Oban; *m* 1949, Sheila Frances (*née* Dunsmor); two *d* (one *s* decd). *Educ:* Oban High Sch.; St Andrews Univ. LDS 1939, BDS 1940. Lieut Army Dental Corps, 1940; Captain 1941; Major 1948; Lt-Col 1955; Col 1963; Brig. 1972; Maj.-Gen. 1974. Served in Egypt, Palestine, Syria and Iraq, 1942-46; Chief Instructor and 2nd in comd, Depot and Training Establishment, RADC, 1956-60; Asst Dir Dental Service, MoD, 1967-71; Dep. Dir Dental Service: Southern Comd, 1971-72; BAOR, 1972-74. OStJ 1960. *Recreations:* tennis, golf, gardening. *Address:* Berwyn Court, Avenue Road, Farnborough, Hants. *T:* Farnborough 44948. *Club:* Lansdowne.

GALLWEY, Sir Philip (Frankland) Payne-, 6th Bt, *cr* 1812; *b* 15 March 1935; *s* of late Lt-Col Lowry Philip Payne-Gallwey, OBE, MC and of Janet, *d* of late Albert Philip Payne-Gallwey; *S* cousin, 1964. *Educ:* Eton; Royal Military Academy, Sandhurst. Lieut, 11th Hussars, 1957. *Recreations:* hunting, shooting, golf. *Heir:* none. *Address:* The Little House, Boxford, Newbury, Berks. *T:* Boxford 315. *Club:* Cavalry and Guards.

GALPERN, Sir Myer, Kt 1960; DL; JP; MP (Lab) Shettleston Division of Glasgow since Oct. 1959; First Deputy Chairman of Ways and Means, since 1976 (Second Deputy Chairman, 1974-76); house furnisher; *b* 1903. *Educ:* Glasgow Univ. Lord Provost of Glasgow and Lord Lieut for the County of the City of Glasgow, 1958-60. Mem. of the Court of Glasgow Univ.; Mem., Advisory Cttee on Education in Scotland. Hon. LLD Glasgow, 1961; Hon. FEIS, 1960. DL, Co. of City of Glasgow, 1962; JP Glasgow. *Address:* House of Commons, SW1; 42 Kelvin Court, Glasgow.

GALPIN, Sir Albert James, KCVO 1968 (MVO, 4th class 1958; 5th class 1945); CBE 1963 (OBE 1953); Secretary, Lord Chamberlain's Office, 1955-68; Serjeant-at-Arms to the Queen, 1955-68; *b* 1903; *s* of C. A. Galpin; *m* 1930, Vera, *d* of J. Tiller; one *s* one *d.* Entered Lord Chamberlain's Office, 1936; Asst Sec., 1941. *Recreation:* scouting. *Address:* Alderman's Cottage, Knowl Hill, Reading, Berks. *T:* Littlewick Green 2637.

GALPIN, Brian John Francis; a Recorder of the Crown Court, since 1972; *b* 21 March 1921; *s* of Christopher John Galpin, DSO and Gladys Elizabeth Galpin (*née* Souhami); *m* 1st, 1947, Ailsa McConnel (*d* 1959); one *d* decd; 2nd, 1961, Nancy Cecilia Nichols; two adopted *s. Educ:* Merchant Taylors' Sch.; Hertford Coll., Oxford. MA 1947. RAF Officer, 1941-45. Editor, Isis, 1946. Called to Bar, 1948. Councillor, Metropolitan Borough of Fulham, 1950-59; Chm., Galpin Soc. for Study of Musical Instruments, 1954-72, Vice-Pres., 1974-; Mem. Cttee, Bach Choir, 1954-61. *Publications:* A Manual of International Law, 1950; Maxwell's Interpretation of Statutes, 10th edn 1953 and 11th edn 1962; contrib. Halsbury's Laws of England, 3rd and 4th edns, Encycl. of Forms and Precedents, Galpin Soc. Jl. *Recreations:* cricket (retired), music, chess. *Address:* St Bruno House, Charters Road, Sunningdale, Berks. *T:* Ascot 20284. *Clubs:* Travellers', Pratt's; Hampshire (Winchester).

GALSWORTHY, Sir Arthur (Norman), KCMG 1967 (CMG 1953); HM Diplomatic Service; retired; *b* 1 July 1916; *s* of late Captain Arthur Galsworthy and late Violet Gertrude Harrison; *m* 1st, 1940, Margaret Agnes Hiscocks (*d* 1973); two *s*; 2nd, 1976, Aylmer Jean Martin. *Educ:* Emanuel Sch.; Corpus Christi Coll., Cambridge. Entered Colonial Office as Asst Principal, Administrative Grade, Oct. 1938. On active service, Dec. 1939-Dec. 1945: enlisted Royal Fusiliers, Sept. 1939; commnd in DCLI, 1940; attached Intelligence Corps, 1941; N Africa (First Army), 1942-43; Captain 1942; Sicily and Italy (Eighth Army), 1943-44; Major 1943; GSO1 with HQ, 21 Army Gp, 1944-45. Returned to Colonial Office, Dec. 1945; Asst Sec. in charge of International Relations Dept of Colonial Office, 1947-51; Chief Sec., West African Inter-Territorial Secretariat, Accra, 1951-54; in charge of Colonial Office Finance Dept, 1954-56; Asst Under-Sec. of State, 1956-65; Dep. Under-Sec. of State, Colonial Office, 1965-66, Commonwealth Office, 1966-68, FCO, 1968-69; British

High Comr in NZ, 1969-72, in Tonga and W Samoa (non-resident), 1970-73; Governor of Pitcairn, 1970-73; Ambassador to Republic of Ireland, 1973-76. *Recreations:* fishing, bird-watching. *Address:* c/o Foreign and Commonwealth Office, SW1; Woodbine Cottage, The Street, Kersey, near Ipswich, Suffolk. *Club:* United Oxford & Cambridge University.
See also Sir J . E . Galsworthy .

GALSWORTHY, Sir John (Edgar), KCVO 1975; CMG 1968; HM Diplomatic Service, retired; *b* 19 June 1919; *s* of Arthur Galsworthy; *m* 1942, Jennifer Ruth Johnstone; one *s* three *d*. *Educ:* Emanuel Sch.; Corpus Christi Coll., Cambridge. HM Forces 1939-41; Foreign Office, 1941-46; Third Sec., Madrid, 1946; Second Sec., Vienna, 1949; First Sec., Athens, 1951; Foreign Office, 1954; Bangkok, 1958; Counsellor, Brussels (UK Delegation to EEC) 1962; Counsellor (Economic), Bonn, 1964-67; Counsellor and subsequently Minister (European Econ. Affairs), Paris, 1967-71; Ambassador to Mexico, 1972-77. *Recreation:* fishing. *Address:* 15 Wallgrave Road, SW5. *T:* 01-373 7217. *Club:* United Oxford & Cambridge University.
See also Sir Arthur Galsworthy.

GALTON, Raymond Percy; author and scriptwriter since 1951 (in collaboration with Alan Simpson, *qv*); *b* 17 July 1930; *s* of Herbert and Christina Galton; *m* 1956, Tonia Phillips; one *s* two *d*. *Educ:* Garth Sch., Morden. *Television:* Hancock's Half Hour, 1954-61 (adaptation and translation, Fleksnes, Norwegian TV); Comedy Playhouse, 1962-63; Steptoe and Son, 1962- (adaptations and translations: Sanford and Son, US TV; Stiefbeen and Zoon, Dutch TV; Albert and Herbert, Swedish TV); Galton-Simpson Comedy, 1969; Clochemerle, 1971; Dawson's Weekly, 1975; The Galton and Simpson Playhouse, 1977; *films:* The Rebel, 1960; The Bargee, 1963; The Wrong Arm of the Law, 1963; The Spy with a Cold Nose, 1966; Loot, 1969; Steptoe and Son, 1971; Steptoe and Son Ride Again, 1973; The Last Fleksnes (Norway and Sweden), 1974; Die Skraphandlerne, 1975; *theatre:* Way Out in Piccadilly, 1966; The Wind in the Sassafras Trees, 1968. Awards: Scriptwriters of the Year, 1959 (Guild of TV Producers and Directors); Best TV Comedy Series, Steptoe and Son, 1962/3/4/5 (Screenwriters Guild); John Logie Baird Award (for outstanding contribution to Television), 1964; Best Comedy Series (Steptoe and Son, Dutch TV), 1966; Best comedy screenplay, Steptoe and Son, 1972 (Screenwriters Guild). *Publications:* (jointly with Alan Simpson, *qv*): Hancock, 1961; Steptoe and Son, 1963; The Reunion and Other Plays, 1966; Hancock's Half Hour, 1974. *Recreations:* reading, worrying. *Address:* The Ivy House, Hampton Court, Mddx. *T:* 01-977 1236.

GALWAY, 11th Viscount, *cr* 1727; **Edmund Savile Monckton-Arundell**; Baron Killard, 1727; *b* 11 Sept. 1900; *s* of William Henry Monckton (*g s* of 5th Viscount) (*d* 1900) and Rose Ethel (*d* 1939), *d* of Henry Vatcher, Rosemount, Jersey; *S* brother, 1977; *m* 1927, Kathleen Joyce (*d* 1975), *yr d* of late James Musgrave, MICE; one *d*. *Educ:* Charterhouse; Clare College, Cambridge (BA 1922, MA 1944). Solicitor, 1930-73. Civil Defence, 1937-58. *Heir: cousin* George Rupert Monckton, Lieut Comdr RCN retd [*b* 13 Oct. 1922; *m* 1944, Fiona Margaret, *d* of Captain W. de P. Taylor; one *s* three *d*]. *Address:* 5 Cranhill Road, Bath, Avon.

GALWAY, James, OBE 1977; fluteplayer; *b* 8 Dec. 1939; *s* of James Galway and Ethel Stewart Clarke; *m* 1972, Anna Christine Renggli; one *s* twin *d* (and one *s* by former *m*). *Educ:* St Paul's Sch., and Mountcollyer Secondary Modern Sch., Belfast; RCM, and Guildhall Sch. of Music, London; Conservatoire National Superieur de Musique, Paris. First post in Wind Band of Royal Shakespeare Theatre, Stratford-on-Avon, followed by periods with Sadler's Wells Orchestra, Royal Opera House Orch., and BBC Symphony Orch.; Principal Flute, London Symphony Orch., and Royal Philharmonic Orch.; Principal Solo Flute, Berlin Philharmonic Orch., 1969-75; now pursuing solo career. Recordings of works by C. P. E. Bach, J. S. Bach, Beethoven, Franck, Mozart, Prokoviev, Reicha, Telemann, and Vivaldi. *Recreations:* music, walking, swimming, films, theatre, TV, chess, backgammon, talking to people. *Address:* c/o London Artists, 124 Wigmore Street, W1H 0AX.

GALWAY and KILMACDUAGH, Bishop of, (RC), since 1976; **Most Rev. Eamonn Casey**, DD; *b* Firies, Co. Kerry, 23 April 1927; *s* of John Casey and late Helena (*née* Shanahan). *Educ:* St Munchin's Coll., Limerick; St Patrick's Coll., Maynooth. LPh 1946; BA 1947. Priest, 1951. Curate, St John's Cath., Limerick, 1951-60; Chaplain to Irish in Slough; set up social framework to re-establish people into new environment; started social welfare scheme; set up lodgings bureau; savings scheme, 1960-63; invited by Cardinal Heenan to place Catholic Housing Aid Soc. on national basis; founded Family Housing Assoc.; Dir, British

Council of Churches; Trustee, Housing the Homeless Central Fund; Founder-Trustee of Shelter (Chm. 1968); Mem. Council, Nat. Fedn of Housing Socs; Mem., Commn for Social Welfare; Founder Mem., Marian Employment Agency; Founder Trustee, Shelter Housing Aid Soc., 1963-69; Bishop of Kerry, 1969-76. *Publication:* (with Adam Ferguson) A Home of Your Own. *Recreations:* music, theatre, concerts, films when time, conversation, motoring. *Address:* Mount St Mary's, Galway; (office) The Diocesan Office, The Cathedral, Galway. *T:* Galway 63566.

GAMBLE, Sir David Arthur Josias, 4th Bt *cr* 1897; *b* 9 Dec. 1907; *e s* of Sir David Gamble, 3rd Bt and Eveline Frances Josephine (*d* 1952), 2nd *d* of late Rev. Arthur R. Cole; *S* father, 1943; *m* 1st, 1932, Elinor Mary (Molly) (*d* 1961), *o d* of Henry E. Cole, Summers, Long Sutton, Hants; one *s*; 2nd, 1965, Evelyn Gamble. *Educ:* Shrewsbury; Wadham Coll., Oxford. BA 1930, MA 1945. Colonial Service, 1930-32; Farmer, 1932-49. Chm. Cirencester RDC, 1958-59. *Heir: s* David Gamble [*b* 5 June 1933; *m* 1956, Dawn Adrienne Stuart; one *s* two *d*]. *Address:* Wood End, Tregony, near Truro, Cornwall.

GAMBLE, Sir (Frederick) Herbert, KBE 1964; CMG 1955; HM Diplomatic Service, retired; *b* 21 May 1907; *s* of Frederick West Gamble and Edith (*née* Moore); *m* 1942, Janine Corbisier de Cobreville; two *d*. *Educ:* Portora Royal School, Enniskillen; Trinity Coll., Dublin. Entered Levant Consular Service, Nov. 1930; HM Consul, Suez, 1945-46; Commercial Counsellor, Bagdad, 1948-52; Commercial Counsellor, Athens, 1952-55; Ambassador to Ecuador, 1955-59; HM Consul-Gen., Los Angeles, 1959-64; HM Ambassador to Bolivia, 1964-67. *Recreations:* tennis, golf. *Address:* Santana, Delgany, Co. Wicklow, Ireland.

GAMES, Abram, OBE 1958; RDI 1959; graphic designer; *b* 29 July 1914; *s* of Joseph and Sarah Games; *m* 1945, Marianne Salfeld; one *s* two *d*. *Educ:* Grocers' Company Sch., Hackney Downs. Studio, 1932-36; freelance designer, 1936-40. Infantry, 1940-41; War Office Poster Designer, 1941-46. Freelance, 1946-; Lecturer Royal College of Art, 1947-53. Postage Stamps for Great Britain and Israel, Festival of Britain, BBC Television, Queen's Award to Industry Emblems. One-man shows of graphic design: London, New York, Chicago, Brussels, Stockholm, Jerusalem, Tel Aviv, São Paulo. Rep. Gt Brit. at Museum of Modern Art, New York; first prizes, Poster Competitions: Helsinki, 1957; Lisbon, 1959; New York, 1960; Stockholm, 1962, Barcelona, 1964; Design Medal, Soc. of Industrial Artists, 1960. Silver Medal, Royal Society of Arts, 1962. Inventor of Imagic Copying Processes. *Publication:* Over my Shoulder, 1960. *Recreations:* painting, travel, carpentry. *Address:* 41 The Vale, NW11. *T:* 01-458 2811.

GAMINARA, Albert William, CMG 1963; HMOCS (retired); *b* 1 Dec. 1913; *s* of late Albert Sidney Gaminara and late Katherine Helen Copeman; *m* 1947, Monica (*née* Watson); one *s* three *d*. *Educ:* City of London Sch.; St John's Coll., Cambridge; Oriel Coll., Oxford. MA Cantab 1943. Appointed to Sierra Leone as Administrative Cadet, 1936; seconded to Colonial Office as Principal, 1947-50; Transferred as Administrative Officer to N Rhodesia, 1950; Mem. of Legislative Council, 1963; Admin. Sec. to Govt of Northern Rhodesia (now Zambia), 1961-63; Sec. to the Cabinet, 1964, Adviser, Cabinet Office, Zambia, 1965. *Recreations:* riding, sailing. *Address:* Stratton House, Over Stratton, South Petherton, Somerset. *Club:* Hawks.

GAMMANS, Lady, (Ann Muriel); FRSA; *d* of late Frank Paul, Warblington, Hants; *m* 1917, David Gammans, 1st and last Bt, *cr* 1955, MP (*d* 1957). *Educ:* Portsmouth High Sch. Travelled widely in the Far East, Europe and North America. Spent many years of her married life in Malaya and Japan. MP (C) Hornsey, 1957-66. Retired March 1966. Order of the Sacred Treasure, 2nd class (Japan), 1971. *Recreation:* travel. *Address:* 34 Ashley Gardens, Ambrosden Avenue, SW1. *T:* 01-834 4558. *Clubs:* Royal Commonwealth Society, (Assoc. Lady Member) Naval and Military.

GAMMELL, James Gilbert Sydney, MBE 1944; CA; Chairman, Ivory & Sime Ltd, since 1975; Director: Bank of Scotland, since 1969; Standard Life Assurance Company, since 1954; *b* 4 March 1920; *e s* of Lt-Gen. Sir James A. H. Gammell, KCB, DSO, MC; *m* 1944, Susan Patricia Bowring Toms, *d* of late Edward Bowring Toms; five *s* one *d*. *Educ:* Winchester Coll. Chartered Accountant, 1949. Served War, Major Grenadier Guards, 1939-46: France, 1940 and 1944, Russia, 1945. *Recreation:* farming. *Address:* Foxhall, Kirkliston, West Lothian EH29 9ER. *T:* Kirkliston 3275. *Club:* New (Edinburgh).
See also J. F. Gammell.

GAMMELL, John Frederick, MC 1943; MA; Headmaster of Repton School since 1968; *b* 31 Dec. 1921; 2nd *s* of Lieut-Gen. Sir James A. H. Gammell, KCB, DSO, MC; *m* 1947, Margaret Anne, *d* of Ralph Juckes, Fiddington Manor, Tewkesbury; two *s* one *d*. *Educ:* Winchester Coll.; Trinity Coll., Cambridge. MA 1953. Asst Master, Horris Hill, Newbury, 1940-41. War Service with KRRC, 1941-44; wounded, 1943; invalided out, 1944. Trinity Coll., Cambridge, 1946-47 (BA); Asst Master, Winchester Coll., 1944-45 and 1947-68; Exchange with Sen. Classics Master, Geelong Grammar Sch., Australia, 1949-50; Housemaster of Turner's, Winchester Coll., 1958-68. *Recreation:* friends. *Address:* The Hall, Repton, Derby DE6 6FH. *T:* (office) Repton 2375, (private) Repton 2187.
See also *J. G. S. Gammell*.

GAMMIE, Gordon Edward; Deputy Secretary, Treasury Solicitor's Department, since 1977; *b* 9 Feb. 1922; *e s* of Dr Alexander Edward Gammie and Ethel Mary Gammie (*née* Miller); *m* 1949, Joyce Rust; two *s*. *Educ:* St Paul's Sch.; The Queen's Coll., Oxford (MA). War service, 1941-45; Captain, 1st Bn Argyll and Sutherland Highlanders. Called to Bar, Middle Temple, 1948. Entered Govt Legal Service, 1949; Asst Solicitor, Mins of Health and of Housing and Local Govt, 1967; Under-Sec. (Principal Asst Solicitor), Min. of Housing and Local Govt, later DoE, 1969-74; Under-Sec., Cabinet Office, 1975-77. Chm., Civil Service Legal Soc., 1970-72. *Recreations:* tennis, listening to music. *Address:* Ty Gwyn, 52 Sutton Lane, Banstead, Surrey. *T:* Burgh Heath 55287.

GANDAR DOWER, Eric Leslie, MA (Law); founder of Aberdeen Airport, Allied Airways (Gandar Dower) Ltd, Aberdeen Flying School Ltd, Aberdeen Flying Club Ltd, and Aberdeen Aerodrome Fuel Supplies Ltd; 3rd *s* of late Joseph Wilson Gandar-Dower and late Amelia Frances Germaine. *Educ:* Brighton Coll.; Jesus Coll., Cambridge. Trained for stage at RADA. Toured with Alan Stevenson, Cecil Barth and Harold V. Neilson's Companies in Kick In, Betty at Bay, The Witness for the Defence, and The Marriage of Kitty. Played wide range of parts on tour with Sir Philip Ben Greet's Shakespeare Company, including Horatio in Hamlet, Antonio in Merchant of Venice, Sicinius Velutus in Coriolanus, Don Pedro in Much Ado About Nothing and Oliver in As You Like It, also in London Shakespeare for Schools LCC Educational Scheme. Wrote and produced The Silent Husband. Toured under own management as Lord Stevenage in Young Person in Pink. Competed King's Cup Air Race 5 years. Holder of FAI Aviators Certificate. Built Dyce (Aberdeen) Airport. Founded Allied Airways (Gandar Dower) Ltd, 1934; Mem. Exec. Council Aerodrome Owners Assoc., 1934-45; Founder Mem. Air Registration Bd; Pioneered Scottish Air Lines Aberdeen/Edinburgh, Aberdeen/Glasgow, Aberdeen/Wick/Thurso/Kirkwall/Stromness and Shetland, which operated throughout 1939-45 War. Pioneered first British/Norwegian Air Line, 1937, Newcastle to Stavanger. Founded, May 1939, 102nd Aberdeen Airport Air Training Corps. Served as Flight Lieut RAFVR, 1940-43. First Chm. and Founder, Assoc. of Brit. Aircraft Operators, 1944. MP (C) Caithness and Sutherland, 1945-50. Attached Mau Mau Campaign, Kenya, 1952-53. *Recreations:* ski-ing, squash, tennis, lawn tennis, swimming, poetry, flying, motoring. *Address:* Westerings, Clos des Fosses, St Martin, Guernsey, Channel Islands. *T:* Guernsey 38637. *Clubs:* Royal Automobile; Hawks, Amateur Dramatic, Footlights (Cambridge); Automobile de France (Paris).

GANDEE, John Stephen, CMG 1967; OBE 1958; HM Diplomatic Service, retired; British High Commissioner in Botswana, 1966-69; *b* 8 Dec. 1909; *s* of John Stephen and Constance Garfield Gandee; *m* 1st, May Degenhardt (*d* 1954); one *s* two *d*; 2nd, Junia Henman (*née* Devine); two *d* (and one step *s* one step *d*). *Educ:* Dorking High Sch. Post Office, Dorking, 1923-30; India Office, 1930-47; Private Sec. to Parly Under-Sec. of State, 1946-47; and 1947-49; Asst Private Sec. to Sec. of State, 1947; First Sec., Ottawa, 1952-54; seconded to Bechuanaland Protectorate, 1958-60 and 1961; seconded to Office of High Comr for Basutoland, Bechuanaland Protectorate and Swaziland, 1960-61; Head of Administration Dept, CRO, 1961-64; Head of Office Services and Supply Dept, Diplomatic Service Administration, 1965-66. *Recreations:* walking, gardening, badminton. *Address:* South View, Holmwood, Dorking, Surrey RH5 4LT. *T:* Dorking 6513.

GANDELL, Captain Wilfrid Pearse, CBE 1940; Royal Navy; *b* 1 Nov. 1886; *s* of T. Pearse Gandell, 16 Earl's Court Square, SW5; *m* 1923, Lilian A. M., BEM 1970, *d* of Maj.-Gen. Maxwell Campbell, RE; one *d* (one *s* decd). *Educ:* Stoke House; HMS Britannia. Went to sea as Midshipman in 1902; specialised in torpedo; present at battle of Jutland in HMS St Vincent; ns 1922; retired in 1929; recalled Sept. 1939; served as Principal Sea

Transport Officer, French Ports, from declaration of war till fall of France (despatches, CBE), then as PSTO Clyde till 1941, both with rank of Commodore; Chief Staff Officer, Plymouth, 1941-44 (US Legion of Merit); Senior Officer Reserve Fleet, Forth Area, 1944-46; reverted to retired list, April 1946. Member: West Sussex CC, 1958-64; Horsham RDC, 1952-64; Asst Chief Warden CD, Horsham Area, 1952-65. RHS medal, 1918. *Address:* Hayes Warren, Slinfold, Horsham, West Sussex RH13 7RF. *T:* Slinfold 790246. *Club:* Naval and Military.

GANDER, L(eonard) Marsland; journalist, war correspondent, author; Television and Radio Correspondent and Critic of The Daily Telegraph 1946-70; *b* London, 27 June 1902; *s* of James Gander and Ellen Marsland; *m* 1931, Hilda Mabel Ellen Rowley; two *s*. *Educ:* Higher Elementary Sch., Stratford; City of London Coll. Reporter, Stratford Express, West Ham, 1919-24; Chief Reporter, Times of India, Bombay, 1924-26; Acting Editor, Illustrated Weekly of India, 1925; Radio Correspondent of the Daily Telegraph, 1926, Television Critic and Correspondent, 1935; War Correspondent of The Daily Telegraph, 1941-45; covered campaigns in Dodecanese, Italy, Southern France, Greece, 1943-44; with 6th Airborne Div. and 1st Canadian Army, Europe, 1945. Chm., Press Club, 1959; Fellow of the Television Soc., 1961 (Mem. Council, 1965). Toured United States for Ford Fund for Advancement of Education, 1963. Special Governor, Crossways Trust Old People's Homes, 1972-75. *Publications:* Atlantic Battle, 1941; Long Road to Leros, 1945; After These Many Quests, autobiography, 1950; Television for All, 1950. *Recreations:* desultory chess, swimming, gardening, washing-up. *Address:* 8 Paddock Green, Rustington, Sussex BN16 3AU. *T:* Rustington 2966. *Clubs:* Press, Savage, Roehampton, Lord's Taverners'.

GANDHI, Mrs Indira (Nehru); Prime Minister of India 1966-77; also Minister for Atomic Energy, 1967-77; *b* 19 Nov. 1917; *d* of late Pandit Jawaharlal Nehru and Kamala Kaul; *m* 1942, Feroze Gandhi (*d* 1960); two *s*. *Educ:* Visva-Bharati. Founded Vanar Sena (Congress children's organisation), 1929; joined Indian National Congress, 1938; Mem., Working Cttee, 1955; Pres., Congress Party, 1959-60; Chm., Citizens' Central Council, 1962; Minister of Information and Broadcasting, 1964-66; Minister for Home Affairs, 1970-73. Dep. Chm., Internat. Union of Child Welfare; Vice-Pres., Indian Coun. of Child Welfare. Hon. DCL Oxon, 1971. *Publication:* India: speeches and reminiscences, 1975. *Address:* 12 Willingdon Crescent, New Delhi, India.

GANDHI, Manmohan Purushottam, MA, FREconS, FSS; Editor, Major Industries of India Annual and Textile Industry Annual; Member, National FAO Committee Advisory Council on Trade; Director: Indian Link Chain Manufacturers Ltd; Zenith Steel Pipes and Industries Ltd; Bombay Oils & Oilseeds Exchange Ltd; Hon. Metropolitan Magistrate, Bombay; *b* 5 Nov. 1901; *s* of late Purushottam Kahanji Gandhi, of Limbdi (Kathiawad); *m* 1926, Rambhagauri, BA (Indian Women's Univ.), *d* of Sukhlal Chhaganlal Shah of Wadhwan. *Educ:* Bahauddin Coll., Junagad; Gujerat Coll., Ahmedabad; Hindu Univ., Benares. BA (History and Econs), Bombay Univ., 1923; MA (Political Econ. and Political Philosophy), Benares Hindu Univ., 1925; Ashburner Prize of Bombay Univ., 1925. Statistical Asst, Govt of Bombay, Labour Office, 1926; Asst Sec., Indian Currency League, Bombay, 1926; Sec., Indian Chamber of Commerce, Calcutta, 1926-36; Sec., Indian Sugar Mills Assoc., 1932-36; Officer-in-Charge, Credit Dept, National City Bank of New York, Calcutta, 1936-37; Chief Commercial Manager, Rohtas Industries Ltd; Dalmia Cement Ltd, 1937-39; Dir, Indian Sugar Syndicate Ltd, 1937-39; Controller of Supplies, Bengal and Bombay, 1941-43; Sec., Indian Nat. Cttee, Internat. Chamber of Commerce, Calcutta, 1929-31; Sec., Fedn of Indian Chambers of Commerce and Industry, 1928-29. Member: East Indian Railway Adv. Cttee, 1939-40; Bihar Labour Enquiry Cttee, 1937-39; UP and Bihar Power Alcohol Cttee, 1938; UP and Bihar Sugar Control Board, 1938; Western Railway Adv. Cttee, Bombay, 1950-52; Small Scale Industries Export Prom. Adv. Cttee; Technical Adviser, Indian Tariff Board, 1947. Hon. Prof., Sydenham Coll. of Commerce, 1943-49. Member: All India Council of Tech. Educn, 1948-73; Governing Body, Seksaria Tech. Inst., Indore, 1962-68; All India Bd of Studies in Commerce, 1948-70; Senate and Syndicate, Bombay Univ., 1957-69; Dir, E. India Cotton Assoc., 1953-73. *Publications:* How to Compete with Foreign Cloth, 1931; The Indian Sugar Industry: Its Past, Present and Future, 1934; The Indian Cotton Textile Industry-Its Past, Present and Future, 1937; The Indian Sugar Industry (annually, 1935-64); The Indian Cotton Textile Industry, (annually, 1937-); Centenary Volume of the Indian Cotton Textile Industry, 1851-1950; Major Industries of India (Annually, 1951-); Problems of Sugar Industry in India, 1946; Monograph on Handloom Weaving in India, 1953; Some Impressions of Japan, 1955. *Recreations:* tennis, badminton, billiards, bridge, swimming. *Address:* Nanabhay Mansions, Pherozeshah Mehta Road, Fort, Bombay 400001, India. *T:* (home) 358805, (office) 261047 and 264839. *TA:* Gandhi care Keen, Bombay. *Clubs:* Radio, National Sports, Rotary (Bombay).

GANDY, Christopher Thomas; HM Diplomatic Service, retired; *b* 21 April 1917; *s* of late Dr Thomas H. Gandy and Mrs Ida Gandy (authoress of A Wiltshire Childhood, Around the Little Steeple, etc); unmarried. *Educ:* Marlborough; King's Coll., Cambridge. On active service with Army and RAF, 1939-45. Entered Foreign Office, Nov. 1945; Tehran, 1948-51; Cairo, 1951-52; FO, 1952-54; Lisbon, 1954-56; Libya, 1956-59; FO, 1960-62; apptd HM Minister to The Yemen, 1962, subsequently Counsellor, Kuwait; Minister (Commercial) Rio de Janeiro, 1966-68. *Publications:* articles in Asian Affairs, Middle East International and The New Middle East. *Recreations:* music, photography, gardening. *Address:* 60 Ambleside Drive, Headington, Oxford. *Club:* Travellers'.

GANDY, Ronald Herbert; Treasurer to the Greater London Council, 1972-77, retired; *b* 22 Nov. 1917; *s* of Frederick C. H. Gandy and Olive (*née* Wilson); *m* 1942, Patricia M. Turney; two *s* one *d*. *Educ:* Banister Court Sch. and Taunton's Sch. (now Richard Taunton Coll.), Southampton. Town Clerk's Dept, Civic Centre, Southampton County Borough Council, 1936; LCC: Admin. Officer, Comptroller's (i.e. Treasurer's) Dept, 1937; Asst Comptroller, 1957; Dep. Comptroller, 1964; Dep. Treasurer, GLC, 1965; Dep. Chief Financial Officer, Inner London Educn Authority, 1967. Mem. CIPFA. *Address:* Braemar, 4 Roughwood Close, Watford, Herts. *T:* Watford 24215.

GANE, Richard Howard; Chairman of the Board of Directors, George Wimpey & Co. Ltd, 1973-76; *b* 5 Nov. 1912; *s* of Richard Howard Gane and Ada (*née* Alford); *m* 1939, Betty Rosemary Franklin (*d* 1976); two *s* one *d*. *Educ:* Kingston Grammar School. Joined George Wimpey & Co. Ltd, 1934; also Chm. of George Wimpey Canada Ltd, and Dir, Markborough Properties Ltd, Toronto, 1965-73. *Recreations:* golf, shooting. *Address:* Waldron, Silverdale Avenue, Walton-on-Thames, Surrey. *T:* Walton-on-Thames 21110.

GANGULY, Most Rev. Theotonius A.; *see* Dacca, Archbishop of, (RC).

GANILAU, Ratu Sir Penaia Kanatabatu, KBE 1974 (OBE 1960); CMG 1968; CVO 1970; DSO 1956; ED 1974; Deputy Prime Minister of Fiji since 1973, and Minister for Home Affairs (conjointly), since 1975; Minister for Fijian Affairs and Rural Development, since 1977; Member of House of Representatives, Fiji; *b* 28 July 1918; Fijian; *m* 1949, Adi Laisa Delaisomosomo Yavaca (decd); five *s* two *d*; *m* 1975, Adi Lady Davila Ganilau. *Educ:* Provincial Sch. Northern, Queen Victoria Meml Sch., Fiji. Devonshire Course for Admin. Officers, Wadham Coll., Oxford Univ., 1947. Served with FIR, 1940; demobilised, retained rank of Captain, 1946. Colonial Admin. Service, 1947; District Officer, 1948-53; Mem. Commn on Fijian Post Primary Educn in the Colony, 1953. Service with Fiji Mil. Forces, 1953-56; demobilised, retained rank of Temp. Lt-Col, 1956; Hon. Col, 2nd Bn (Territorial), FIR, 1973. Seconded to post of Fijian Econ. Develt Officer and Roko Tui Cakaudrove conjoint, 1956; Tour Manager and Govt Rep., Fiji Rugby football tour of NZ, 1957; Dep. Sec. for Fijian Affairs, 1961; Minister for Fijian Affairs and Local Govt, 1965; Leader of Govt Business and Minister for Home Affairs, Lands and Mineral Resources, 1970; Minister for Communications, Works and Tourism, 1972. Mem., Council of Ministers; Official Mem., Legislative Council; Chairman: Fijian Affairs Bd; Fijian Develt Fund Bd; Native Land Trust Bd; Great Council of Chiefs. *Recreation:* Rugby football (rep. Fiji against Maori All Black, 1938 and during Rugby tour of NZ, 1939). *Address:* Ministry of Home Affairs, Government Buildings, Suva, Fiji. *T:* 211401. *Clubs:* United Oxford & Cambridge University; Fiji Defence (Suva, Fiji).

GANNON, Brig. Jack Rose Compton, CBE 1945 (OBE 1942); MVO 1922; *b* 1882; *s* of John Gannon, St John's Coll., Cambridge; *m* 1910, Dorothy (*d* 1971) *d* of George Robertson, Melbourne; one *d*. *Educ:* Sutton Valence; RMC Sandhurst. South Staffords, 1902-06; 23rd and PAVO Cavalry, 1906-26; Commanded Sam Browne's Cavalry, 1927-32; ADC to Lord Willingdon when Governor of Bombay; Personal Military Sec. to Gen. Lord Rawlinson, C-in-C India, 1920-25; served European War, 1914-18; Afghan War, 1919; Mahsud and Waziristan Expeditions, 1919-20 (despatches twice); Asst Military Sec., GHQ Home Forces, 1939-43; Dep. Military Sec., 21 Army Group, 1943-45; Dep. Mil. Sec., BAOR, 1945-46 (despatches twice); retd, 1946. Manager, Hurlingham Club,

1934-39; Hon. Sec., Hurlingham Polo Assoc., 1934-; Pres., Arab Horse Soc., 1951; Pres., Nat. Pony Soc., 1954-. British Horse Society's Medal of Honour, 1970. Comdr of Legion of Merit (US), Knight Comdr of Order of Orange Nassau, Chevalier of Legion of Honour (France), Croix de Guerre (France). *Publication:* Before the Colours Fade, 1976. *Recreations:* formerly: polo, cricket, shooting. *Address:* King Edward VII Hospital, Midhurst, Sussex. *Clubs:* Cavalry and Guards, MCC.

GANZ, Prof. Peter Felix; Professor of German Language and Literature, University of Oxford, since 1972; Fellow of St Edmund Hall, Oxford, since 1972; *b* 3 Nov. 1920; *s* of Dr Hermann and Dr Charlotte Ganz; *m* 1949, Rosemary (*née* Allen); two *s* two *d*. *Educ:* Realgymnasium, Mainz; King's Coll., London. MA 1950; PhD 1954; MA Oxon 1960. Asst Lectr, Royal Holloway Coll., London Univ., 1948-49; Lectr, Westfield Coll., London Univ., 1949-60; Reader in German, Oxford Univ., 1960-72; Fellow of Hertford Coll., Oxford, 1963-72 (Hon. Fellow, 1977). Vis. Professor: Erlangen-Nürnberg Univ., 1964-65 and 1971; Munich Univ., 1970 and 1974. Comdr, Order of Merit, Germany, 1973. Jt Editor: German Life and Letters, 1971-; Beiträge zur Geschichte der deutschen Sprache und Literatur, 1976-. *Publications:* Der Einfluss des Englischen auf den deutschen Wortschatz 1740-1815, 1957; Geistliche Dichtung des 12. Jahrhunderts, 1960; Graf Rudolf, 1964; (with F. Norman and W. Schwarz) Dukus Horant, 1964; (with W. Schröder) Probleme mittelalterlicher Überlieferung und Textkritik, 1967; Jacob Grimm's Conception of German Studies, 1973; Gottfried von Strassburgs 'Tristan', 1977; articles on German medieval literature and language in jls. *Recreations:* music, walking, travel. *Address:* 516 Banbury Road, Oxford OX2 8LG. *T:* Oxford 59342.

GANZONI, family name of **Baron Belstead.**

GARBO, Greta, (Greta Lovisa Gustafsson); film actress; *b* Stockholm, 18 Sept. 1905; *d* of Sven and Louvisa Gustafsson. *Educ:* Dramatic Sch. attached to Royal Theatre, Stockholm. Began stage career as dancer in Sweden. First film appearance in The Atonement of Gosta Berling, 1924; went to US, 1925; became an American Citizen, 1951. Films include: The Torrent, 1926; The Temptress, 1926; Flesh and the Devil, 1927; Love, 1927; The Divine Woman, 1928; The Mysterious Lady, 1928; A Woman of Affairs, 1929; Wild Orchids, 1929; The Single Standard, 1929; The Kiss, 1929; Anna Christie, 1930 (first talking rôle); Susan Lenox, Her Fall and Rise, 1931; Mata Hari, 1931; Grand Hotel, 1932; As You Desire Me, 1932; Queen Christina, 1933; Anna Karenina, 1935; Camille, 1936; Conquest, 1937; Ninotchka, 1939; Two-Faced Woman, 1941.

GARDAM, David Hill, QC 1968; *b* 14 Aug. 1922; *s* of late Harry H. Gardam, Hove, Sussex; *m* 1954, Jane Mary, *d* of William Pearson, Redcar, Yorks; two *s* one *d*. *Educ:* Oundle Sch.; Christ Church, Oxford. MA 1948. War Service, RNVR, 1941-46 (Temp. Lieut). Called to the Bar, Inner Temple, 1949; Bencher 1977. *Recreations:* painting, bee-keeping. *Address:* 22 Old Buildings, Lincoln's Inn, WC2. *T:* 01-405 2072; 53 Ridgway Place, SW19.

GARDENER, Sir (Alfred) John, KCMG 1954 (CMG 1949); CBE 1944; JP; *b* 6 Feb. 1897; *s* of late G. Northcote Gardener, Exeter; *m* 1st, 1929, Dorothy Caroline (*d* 1967), *d* of late Emile Purgold, Liverpool; no *c*; 2nd, 1968, Marion May, *d* of Linden E. W. Huish, Exeter. *Educ:* Heles Sch., Exeter; Trinity Hall, Cambridge. Served in Army in France and Belgium, 1916-18. Joined Consular Service, 1920, and served in various posts in S Persia, Morocco, Syria and USA. In June 1941 served as Political Officer during Syrian Campaign with rank of Lieut-Col (subsequently Col). Served in Foreign Office, 1946-49; British Ambassador to Afghanistan, 1949-51, and to Syria, 1953-56; retired, 1957. JP Devon, 1959. *Address:* c/o Barclay's Bank, Exeter, Devon.

GARDHAM, Arthur John, MS, FRCS; formerly Senior Surgeon to University College Hospital and Examiner in Surgery to University of London; *b* Leytonstone, Essex, Nov. 1899; 2nd *s* of Arthur and Elizabeth Gardham; *m* 1936, Audrey Glenton, 3rd *d* of late Francis Carr, CBE; one *s* two *d*. *Educ:* Bancroft's Sch.; University College and University College Hospital, London. MRCS, LRCP 1921; MB, BS (London), 1923; FRCS 1924; MS (London), 1926. Served RNVR, 1917-18. Qualified 1921; House appts at UCH; Pearce Gould Scholar, 1925; Asst to Prof. Clairmont at Kantonsspital, Zürich, 1925; Surgical Registrar and later Asst Dir of Surgical Unit, UCH. Surgeon to Hampstead Gen. Hosp. (Royal Free Hosp. Group). Served RAMC, 1940-45; Consulting Surgeon to 14th Army and Eastern Comd, India (despatches). Mem. Court of Examiners of RCS, 1945-51; Examiner in Surgery: to Univ. of Cambridge, 1951-57;

to Univ. of Edinburgh, 1957-60; to Univ. of London, 1958-62; associated with Emergency Bed Service of King Edward's Hosp. Fund for London since its foundation in 1938; Hunterian Prof., RCS; Fellow: Royal Society of Medicine (Pres. of Surgical Sect., 1963-64); University Coll., London; Assoc. of Surgeons (Mem. Council, 1957-60). Jt Hon. Sec., Devon and Somerset Staghounds, 1967-70. *Publications*: (with Davies) The Operations of Surgery, 1963, Vol. 2, 1969; Sections of Grey Turner's Modern Operative Surgery; various papers on surgical subjects. *Recreations*: field sports. *Address*: Castle Green, Oare, Brendon, near Lynton, Devon. *T*: Brendon 205.

GARDHAM, Air Vice-Marshal Marcus Maxwell, CB 1972; CBE 1965; Registrar, Ashridge Management College, Berkhamsted, since 1972; *b* 5 Nov. 1916; *s* of late Arthur Gardham, High Wycombe; *m* 1954, Rosemary Hilda (*née* Wilkins); one *s*. *Educ*: Royal Grammar Sch., High Wycombe. Commissioned RAF (Accountant Br), 1939; RAF Ferry Command, 1941; HQ AEAF, 1944. BJSM, Washington, 1946 (SOA); RAPO, 1949; psc 1952; No 16 MU, 1953; 2nd TAF (Org. Staff), 1955; Air Ministry (Personnel Staff), 1957; jssc 1957; Technical Trng Command (Org. Staff), 1959; FEAF (Command Accountant), 1965; Dir of Personal Services, MoD (Air), 1966; Head of RAF Secretarial Br., 1971-72; AOA, RAF Trng Comd, 1969-72. MBIM. *Recreations*: gardening, golf. *Address*: Almond Cottage, Millfield, Berkhamsted. *T*: Berkhamsted 3988. *Club*: Royal Air Force.

GARDINER, family name of Baron Gardiner.

GARDINER, Baron *cr* 1963, of Kittisford (Life Peer); Gerald Austin Gardiner, PC 1964; CH 1975; Chancellor, The Open University, since 1973; *b* 30 May 1900; *s* of late Sir Robert Gardiner; *m* 1st, 1925, Lesly (*d* 1966), *o d* of Edwin Trounson, JP; one *d*; 2nd, 1970, Mrs Muriel Box. *Educ*: Harrow Sch.; Magdalen Coll., Oxford (MA). 2nd Lieut Coldstream Guards, 1918; Pres. Oxford Union and OUDS, 1924; called to the Bar, 1925; KC 1948. Friends Ambulance Unit, 1943-45. Mem. Cttee on Supreme Court Practice and Procedure, 1947-53; Mem. of Lord Chancellor's Law Reform Cttee, 1952-63. A Master of the Bench of the Inner Temple, 1955; Chm. Gen. Council of the Bar, 1958 and 1959; former Chm., Council of Justice; Mem., Internat. Cttee of Jurists, 1971-. Chm (Jt), National Campaign for Abolition of Capital Punishment. Alderman, London County Council, 1961-63. Lord High Chancellor of Great Britain, 1964-70. BA Open Univ., 1977. Hon. LLD: Southampton, 1965; London, 1969; Manitoba, 1969; Law Soc. of Upper Canada, 1969; Birmingham, 1971; Melbourne, 1973; DUniv York, 1966. *Publications*: Capital Punishment as a Deterrent, 1956; (Jt Ed.) Law Reform Now, 1963. *Recreations*: law reform and the theatre. *Address*: 1 Harcourt Buildings, Temple, EC4Y 9DA. *Club*: Garrick.

GARDINER, Lt-Col Christopher John, DSO 1940; OBE 1945; TD 1942; FRSA 1973; DL; RE; late Chairman of Gardiner, Sons and Co. Ltd, Bristol, merchants; *b* 2 June 1907; *s* of Edward John Lucas Gardiner, Clifton, Bristol; *m* 1938, Bridget Mary Taplin; three *s* one *d*. *Educ*: Clifton Coll., Bristol. Commissioned in South Midland RE, TA, in 1926; CRE 48 Div., 59 Div., and 12 Corps Tps RE (despatches thrice). Past Pres., Soc. of Builders Merchants. Governor: Clifton Coll.; Avonhurst Sch. DL Glos 1953; DL Avon 1974. *Recreations*: Rugby (played for Clifton Coll), fishing. *Address*: 3 Norland Road, Clifton, Bristol BS8 3LP. *T*: 35187. *Club*: Constitutional.

GARDINER, Ernest David, CMG 1968; CBE 1967; Head of Science Department, Melbourne Grammar School, 1948-74; Chairman, Commonwealth Government's Advisory Committee on Standards for Science Facilities in Independent Secondary Schools, 1964-76; *b* 14 July 1909; 2nd *s* of Ernest Edward Gardiner and Isabella Gardiner (*née* Notman), Gisborne, Vic.; *m* 1940, Minnie Amanda Neill; one *s* one *d*. *Educ*: Kyneton High Sch.; Melbourne Univ. BSc 1931, BEd 1936, Melbourne; FACE 1968. Secondary Teacher with Educn Dept of Vic., 1932-45; Melbourne Grammar Sch., 1946-. *Publications*: Practical Physics (2 vols), 1948; Practical Problems in Physics, 1959; Problems in Physics, 1969; Practical Physics, 1972. *Recreations*: music, theatre, swimming. *Address*: 122 Ferguson Street, Williamstown, Vic 3016, Australia. *T*: 397 6132.

GARDINER, Frederick Keith, JP; Past President, Neepsend Steel and Tool Corporation, Ltd; *b* Plumstead, Kent; *s* of Frederick Gardiner and Edith Mann; *m* 1929, Ruth Dixon; two *s*. Various editorial positions with newspaper companies in the South of England and at Darlington, York, Oxford and Sheffield; formerly Ed. and Dir, The Sheffield Telegraph; President: Inst. of Journalists, 1950; Hallam Cons. Assoc. FJI. JP Sheffield. *Recreation*: golf. *Address*: 5 Chorley Road,

Fulwood, Sheffield S10 3RJ. *Club*: Hallamshire Golf (Pres.) (Sheffield).

GARDINER, George Arthur; MP (C) Reigate and Banstead since Feb. 1974; *b* 3 March 1935; *s* of Stanley and Emma Gardiner; *m* 1961, Juliet Wells; two *s* one *d*. *Educ*: Harvey Grammar Sch., Folkestone; Balliol Coll., Oxford. 1st cl. hons PPE. Sec., Oxford Univ. Conservative Assoc., 1957. Chief Political Corresp., Thomson Regional Newspapers, 1964-74. Mem. Exec. Cttee, British Council of European Movt, 1971; Mem. Cttee, Conservative Gp for Europe, 1971; Sec., Cons. European Affairs Cttee, 1976-. Contested (C) Coventry South, 1970. *Publications*: Europe for the Regions, 1971; The Changing Life of London, 1973; Margaret Thatcher: from childhood to leadership, 1975. *Address*: House of Commons, SW1.

GARDINER, Dame Helen (Louisa), DBE 1961 (CBE 1952); MVO 1937; *b* 24 April 1901; *y d* of late Henry Gardiner, Bristol. *Educ*: Clifton High School. Formerly in Private Secretary's Office, Buckingham Palace; Chief Clerk, 1946-61. *Recreations*: reading, gardening. *Address*: Higher Courlands, Lostwithiel, Cornwall.

GARDINER, John Eliot; conductor; *b* 20 April 1943; *s* of Rolf Gardiner and Marabel Gardiner; *m* 1971, Cherryl Anne ffoulkes. *Educ*: Bryanston Sch.; King's Coll., Cambridge (MA History, 2nd Cl. Hons); King's Coll., London (Certif. of Advanced Studies in Music, 1966). Founded Monteverdi Choir following performance of Monteverdi's Vespers of 1610, King's Coll., Cambridge, 1964; French Govt Scholarship to study in Paris and Fontainebleau with Nadia Boulanger, 1966-68; youngest conductor of Henry Wood Promenade Concert, Royal Albert Hall, 1968; Début with: Sadler's Wells Opera, Coliseum, conducting The Magic Flute, 1969; Royal Opera House, Covent Garden, conducting Iphigénie en Tauride, 1973; concert revivals in London of major dramatic works of Rameau, culminating in world première of Les Boréades, 1975. *Publications*: (ed) Claude le Jeune Hélas! Mon Dieu, 1971; (ed) Les Boréades: tragic opera by Jean-Philippe Rameau, 1978. *Recreations*: pedigree sheepbreeding, organic corn-growing (in Dorset); ecological rehabilitation in Central Africa. *Address*: Gore Farm, Ashmore, Salisbury, Wilts. *T*: Fontmell Magna 295. *Club*: Le Petit Club Français.

GARDINER, Peter Dod Robin; Headmaster of St Peter's School, York, since Sept. 1967; *b* 23 Dec. 1927; *s* of Brig. R. Gardiner, *qv*; *m* 1959, Juliet Wright; one *s* one *d*. *Educ*: Radley College; Trinity Coll., Cambridge. Asst Master, Charterhouse, 1952-67, and Housemaster, Charterhouse, 1965-67. *Publications*: (ed) Twentieth-Century Travel, 1963; (with B. W. M. Young) Intelligent Reading, 1964; (with W. A. Gibson) The Design of Prose, 1971. *Recreations*: reading, writing, walking, acting. *Address*: St Peter's School, York YO3 6AB.

GARDINER, Brig. Richard, CB 1954; CBE 1946 (OBE 1944); *b* 28 Oct. 1900; *s* of Major Alec Gardiner, RE; *m* 1924, Catherine Dod (*née* Oliver); two *s*. *Educ*: Uppingham Sch.; Royal Military Academy. Commissioned into RFA, 1920; transferred to RE, 1924; Asst Executive Engineer, E Indian Rly, 1927; Sec. to Agent, E Indian Rly, 1930; Exec. Engineer, 1934; Govt Inspector of Rlys, Burma, 1938; reverted to military duty, 1940; Dir of Transportation, India, 1942; reverted to Home Establishment, 1945; Dir of Transportation, War Office, 1948; Dir of Engineer Stores, War Office, 1950; retired Dec. 1953; Man. Dir, Peruvian Corp., Lima, 1954-63. ADC to King George VI, 1951-52, to the Queen, 1952-53. FCIT. *Recreations*: music, gardening. *Address*: Bridgham Farmhouse, Shamley Green, Surrey.
See also *P . D . R . Gardiner*.

GARDINER, Robert (Kweku Atta); Minister of Economic Planning, Ghana, since 1975; *b* Kumasi, Ghana, 29 Sept. 1914; *s* of Philip H. D. Gardiner and Nancy Torraine Ferguson; *m* 1943, Linda Charlotte Edwards; one *s* two *d*. *Educ*: Adisadel Coll., Cape Coast; Ghana; Fourah Bay Coll., Sierra Leone; Selwyn Coll., Cambridge (BA); New Coll., Oxford. Lectr in Economics at Fourah Bay Coll., 1943-46; UN Trusteeship Dept, 1947-49; Dir, Extra-Mural Studies, University Coll., Ibadan, 1949-53; Dir, Dept of Social Welfare and Community Development, Gold Coast, 1953-55; Perm. Sec., Min. of Housing, 1955-57; Head of Ghana Civil Service, 1957-59; Dep. Exec. Sec., Economic Commn for Africa, 1959-60; Mem. Mission to the Congo, 1961; Dir Public Admin. Div., UN Dept of Economic and Social Affairs, 1961-62; Officer-in-Charge, UN Operation in the Congo, 1962-63; Exec. Sec., UN Economic Commn for Africa, Addis Ababa, 1962-75. Chm., Commonwealth Foundation, 1970-73. Reith Lectures, 1965; David Livingstone Vis. Prof. of Economics, Strathclyde, 1970-75; Lectures: Gilbert

Murray Meml, 1969; J. B. Danquah Meml, 1970; Aggrey-Fraser-Guggisberg Meml, 1972. Mem Professional Socs, and activities in internat. affairs. Hon. Fellow: Univ. of Ibadan; Selwyn Coll., Cambridge. Hon. DCL: East Anglia, 1966; Sierra Leone, 1969; Tuskegee Inst., 1969; Liberia, 1972; Hon. LLD: Bristol, 1966; Ibadan, 1967; E Africa, 1968; Haile Sellassie I Univ., 1972; Strathclyde, 1973; Hon. PhD Uppsala, 1966; Hon. DSc: Kumasi, 1968; Bradford, 1969. *Publications:* (with Helen Judd) The Development of Social Administration, 1951, 2nd edn 1959; A World of Peoples (BBC Reith Lectures), 1965. *Recreations:* golf, music, reading, walking. *Address:* Ministry of Economic Planning, Accra, Ghana.

GARDINER, Victor Alec, OBE 1977; Director and General Manager, London Weekend Television, since 1971; Director: London Weekend Television (Holdings) Ltd, since 1976; London Weekend Services Ltd, since 1976; Chairman: Dynamic Technology Ltd, since 1972; Standard Music Ltd, since 1972; *b* 9 Aug. 1929; *m*; one *s* two *d. Educ:* Whitgift Middle Sch., Croydon; City and Guilds (radio and telecommunications). Techn. Asst, GPO Engrg, 1947-49; RAF Nat. Service, 1949-51; BBC Sound Radio Engr, 1951-53; BBC TV Cameraman, 1953-55; Rediffusion TV Sen. Cameraman, 1955-61; Malta TV Trng Man., 1961-62; Head of Studio Prodn, Rediffusion TV, 1962-67; Man. Dir, GPA Productions, 1967-69; Production Controller, London Weekend Television, 1969-71. Mem., Royal Television Soc., 1970- (Vice-Chm. Council, 1974-75; Chm. Papers Cttee, 1975; Chm. Council, 1976-). *Recreations:* music, building, gardening. *Address:* The Gables, Sulhampstead, Reading, Berks RG7 4BS.

GARDINER-HILL, Harold, MBE, MA, MD (Cantab) FRCP; Consultant Physician, St Thomas' Hospital; Fellow Royal Society Medicine; President Section of Endocrinology, 1949-50; Member Association of Physicians, Great Britain; *b* London, 14 Feb. 1891; *e s* of late Hugh Gardiner-Hill, MD; *m* Margaret Helen, *e d* of Sir E. Farquhar Buzzard, 1st Bt, KCVO; three *s. Educ:* Westminster Sch.; Pembroke Coll., Cambridge; St Thomas's Hosp. Mem. Cambridge Univ. Golf Team, 1911-12; Medical Registrar, St Thomas' Hospital, 1920; Royal Army Medical Corps, 1915-18; Royal Air Force Medical Service, 1918-19 (despatches); CO RAF Central Hosp., Finchley, 1919; Asst Medical Unit, St Thomas' Hosp., 1925-28; Asst Physician, Royal Free Hosp., 1928-30; Oliver Sharpe Lectr RCP, 1937. *Publications:* Modern Trends in Endocrinology, 1957; Clinical Involvements, 1958; articles in the Quarterly Jl of Medicine, British Jl of Obstetrics and Gynaecology, Lancet, BMJ, Proc. Royal Soc. Medicine, Practitioner and Jl of Mental Science chiefly on endocrine diseases. *Recreations:* golf (Chm. of Rules of Golf Cttee, Royal and Ancient, 1949-52; Captain, Royal and Ancient, 1956), and other games. *Address:* 149 Harley Street, W1. *T:* 01-935 4444; 30 Stanhope Gardens, SW7. *T:* 01-373 2272. *Clubs:* Carlton; Royal and Ancient (St Andrews).

GARDINER-SCOTT, Rev. William, OBE 1974; MA; Emeritus Minister of Scots Memorial Church and Hospice, Jerusalem (Minister, 1966-73); *b* 23 February 1906; *o s* of late William Gardiner Scott, Portsoy, Banffshire; *m* 1953, Darinka Milo, *d* of late Milo Glogovac, Oakland, Calif; one *d. Educ:* Grange School, Bo'ness, West Lothian; Edinburgh University and New College, Edinburgh. In catering business, 1926-30; graduated in Arts, Edin., 1934; Theological Travel Scholarship to Palestine, 1936; travelled as ship's steward to America and India, 1936; ordained to Ministry of Church of Scotland, 1939; Sub-Warden 1939, Deputy Warden 1940, New College Settlement, Edinburgh; enlisted as Army Chaplain, 1941; served·in Egypt, 1942-44 and developed community centre at RA Depot, Cairo and initiated publication of weekly Scots newspaper, The Clachan Crack; founded Montgomery House, Alexandria, as community centre for all ranks of allied troops, 1943; served in Palestine as Church of Scotland Chaplain for Galilee and district, 1944-46; Senior Chaplain at Scottish Command, 1946-47; Warden of Student Movement House, London, 1947-49; Chaplain at Victoria Univ. Coll., Wellington, NZ, 1950-54; locum tenens St John's West Church, Leith, 1955; Minister of Church of Scotland, Jerusalem, 1955-60; Parish of Abernethy, 1960-66. ChStJ. Distinguished Citizen of Jerusalem. *Recreations:* travel, gardening, cooking, walking. *Address:* St John's Bungalow, PO Box 19901, Jerusalem, Israel.

GARDINI, Signora U.; *see* Fisher, Sylvia.

GARDNER, Antony John; Principal Information Officer, Central Council for Education and Training in Social Work, since 1970; *b* 27 Dec. 1927; *s* of David Gardner, head gardener, and Lillian Gardner; *m* 1956, Eveline A. Burden. *Educ:* Elem. school; Co-operative Coll.; Southampton Univ. Pres. Union, Southampton, 1958-59; BSc (Econ) 1959. Apprentice toolmaker, 1941-45;

National Service, RASC, 1946-48; building trade, 1948-53. Tutor Organiser, Co-operative Union, 1959-60; Member Education Officer, Co-operative Union, 1961-66. Contested (Lab): SW Wolverhampton, 1964; Beeston, Feb. and Oct. 1974; MP (Lab) Rushcliffe, 1966-70. *Recreations:* angling, gardening and the countryside generally. *Address:* 30 Brookside Avenue, East Leake, Loughborough, Leics. *T:* East Leake 2454. *Club:* Parkstone Trades and Labour (Poole).

GARDNER, Arthur Duncan, MA, DM, FRCS, FRCP; Hon. Fellow of University College, Oxford, 1950; Professor Emeritus, Oxford, 1954; *b* 28 March 1884; *s* of late James William Gardner, The Stone House, Rugeley, Staffs; *m* Violet Mary, *d* of late John Fowler Newsam, The Hollies, Broxbourne, Herts; one *s* (and one *s* one *d* decd). *Educ:* Rugby; University Coll., Oxford. Member of Oxford hockey eleven, 1906; St Thomas's Hospital, 1908-15; Beaney Prize, House Surgeon, Casualty Officer, Lectr in Pathology, Research Asst. Radcliffe Travelling Fellowship, Oxford, 1914, Radcliffe Prize, 1923. Served in BEF as British Red Cross Surgeon, 1914; Dir of Standards Lab. (MRC) at Oxford, 1915-36; Reader in Bacteriology with title of Professor, 1936; Rede Lectr, Cambridge, 1953; Litchfield Lectr, Oxford, 1954; late Fellow of University Coll., Oxford; Regius Prof. of Medicine, Univ. of Oxford, 1948-54; Student of Christ Church, 1948-54; Hon. Consultant, Oxford United Hospitals, 1954. *Publications:* Microbes and Ultramicrobes, 1931; Bacteriology for Medical Students and Practitioners, 1933 (4th edn 1953); Penicillin as a chemotherapeutic agent (with Sir Ernst Chain, Lord Florey and others), 1940; numerous contribs to medical scientific jls from 1914. *Address:* South Priory, Ipplepen, South Devon. *T:* Ipplepen 812619.

GARDNER, Sir Douglas Bruce B.; *see* Bruce-Gardner.

GARDNER, Edward Lucas, QC 1960; MP (C) South Fylde, since 1970; a Recorder of the Crown Court, since 1972; *b* 10 May 1912; *s* of late Edward Walker Gardner, Fulwood, Preston, Lancs; *m* 1st, 1950, Noreen Margaret (marr. diss. 1962), *d* of late John Collins, Moseley, Birmingham; one *s* one *d*; 2nd, 1963, Joan Elizabeth, *d* of late B. B. Belcher, Bedford; one *s*. one *d. Educ:* Hutton Grammar Sch. Served War of 1939-45: joined RNVR as ordinary seaman, 1940; served in cruisers, Mediterranean; commnd RNVR; Chief of Naval Information, E Indies, 1945. Journalist (free-lance; Lancashire Daily Post, then Daily Mail) prior to 1940; broadcasting and free-lance journalism, 1946-49; called to Bar, Gray's Inn, 1947; Master of the Bench of Gray's Inn, 1968; admitted to Nigerian and British Guianan Bars, 1962; has also appeared in Courts of Goa, High Court of Singapore, and Supreme Court of India. Deputy Chairman of Quarter Sessions: East Kent, 1961-71; County of Kent, 1962-71; Essex, 1968-71. Contested (C) Erith and Crayford, April 1955; MP (C) Billericay Div. of Essex, 1959-66; PPS to Attorney-General, 1962-63; Chairman: Justice Working Party on Bail and Remands in Custody, 1966; Bar Council Cttee on Parly Privilege, 1967; Chm., Soc. of Cons. Lawyers, 1975 (Chm. Exec. Cttee, 1969-; Chm., Cttee responsible for pamphlets, Rough Justice, on future of the Law, 1968, Crisis in Crime and Punishment, 1971); Exec. Cttee, Justice, 1968. Member: Departmental Cttee on Jury Service, 1963; Cttee on Appeals in Criminal Cases, 1964; Commonwealth War Graves Commn, 1971-. A Governor: Thomas Coram Foundn for Children, 1962-; Queenswood Sch., 1975. Steward, British Boxing Bd of Control, 1975-. *Publication:* (part author) A Case for Trial (pamphlet recommending procedural reforms for committal proceedings implemented by Criminal Justice Act, 1967). *Recreation:* walking. *Address:* 4 Raymond Buildings, Gray's Inn, WC1. *T:* 01-242 4719; Sparrows, Hatfield Broad Oak, Essex; Outlane Head Cottage, Chipping, Lancs. *Clubs:* Garrick, United and Cecil (Chm. 1970).

GARDNER, Dame Frances, DBE 1975; FRCP; Physician, Royal Free Hospital, London, since 1946; Consulting Physician, Hospital for Women, Soho Square, London; Physician, The Mothers' Hospital, London; *b* 28 Feb. 1913; *d* of late Sir Ernest and Lady Gardner; *m* 1958, George Qvist, *qv. Educ:* Headington Sch., Oxford; Westfield Coll., Univ. of London; Royal Free Hospital School of Medicine. BSc London, 1935; MB, BS London, 1940; MD London, 1943; MRCP 1943, FRCP 1952. Medical Registrar, Royal Free Hosp., 1943; Clinical Asst, Nuffield Dept of Medicine, Oxford, 1945; Fellow in Medicine, Harvard Univ., USA, 1946; Chief Asst, National Hosp. for Diseases of the Heart, 1947; late Physician, Royal National Throat, Nose and Ear Hosp., London; former Dean, Royal Free Hosp. Sch. of Medicine. Commonwealth Travelling Fellow, 1962; late Examnr, MB, BS, Univ. of London; Rep. Gen. Med. Schools on Senate of Univ. of London, 1967; Mem., Gen. Med. Council, 1971. Chm., London/Riyadh Univs Med. Faculty Cttee. *Publications:* papers on cardiovascular and other medical subjects in BMJ, Lancet, and British Heart Jl. *Address:* 72 Harley Street, W1. *T:* 01-935 6053.

GARDNER, Frank Matthias, CBE 1967; Borough Librarian, Luton, 1938-72; *b* 13 Jan. 1908; *s* of Ernest Frank Gardner and Lily Gardner, Sheffield; *m* 1936, Lysobel Margaret Watt Smith (*d* 1966); one *s* one *d. Educ:* Firth Park Grammar Sch., Sheffield. FLA 1932. Unesco Consultant, India, 1950-51; Leader, Seminar on Public Libraries in Asia, Delhi, 1954; Pres., Library Assoc., 1964; Mem., Library Adv. Council, 1965-71; Chm., Books and Libraries Panel, British Council, 1966-72; Chm., Public Libraries Section, Internat. Fedn of Library Assocs, 1969-73. CStJ 1962. *Publications:* (ed) Sequels, 1947, 1955, 1967, 1974; Letters to a Younger Librarian, 1948; Delhi Public Library, Evaluation Report (Unesco), 1955; (with M. J. Lewis) Reading Round the World, 1969; Public Library Legislation: a comparative study (Unesco), 1971; (with L. G. Persson) Junior Sequels, 1977. *Recreations:* reading, travel, enjoying church architecture and pictures, contract bridge. *Address:* 1 Ryecroft Way, Luton, Beds. *T:* Luton 22795.

GARDNER, Dame Helen (Louise), DBE 1967 (CBE 1962); FBA 1958; FRSL 1962; DLitt; Emeritus Professor of English Literature, University of Oxford and Hon. Fellow, Lady Margaret Hall and St Hilda's College; *b* 13 Feb. 1908; *d* of late C. H. Gardner and Helen M. R. Gardner. *Educ:* North London Collegiate Sch.; St Hilda's Coll., Oxford. BA Oxford (1st class Hons Sch. of English Lang. and Lit.), 1929; MA 1935; DLitt 1963. Asst Lectr, Royal Holloway Coll., Univ. of London, 1931-34; Lectr, Univ. of Birmingham, 1934-41; Tutor in English Literature, St Hilda's Coll., 1941-54, and Fellow, 1942-66; Reader in Renaissance English Literature, Univ. of Oxford, 1954-66; Merton Prof. of English Literature, Univ. of Oxford and Fellow of Lady Margaret Hall, 1966-75; Vis. Prof., Univ. of California, Los Angeles, 1954; Lectures: Riddell Meml, Univ. of Durham, 1956; Alexander, Univ. of Toronto, 1962; Messenger, Cornell Univ., 1967; T. S. Eliot Meml, Univ. of Kent, 1968. Delegate, Oxford University Press, 1959-75. Mem., Robbins Cttee on Higher Education, 1961-63; Mem., Council for National Academic Awards, 1964-67; Trustee, National Portrait Gallery, 1967-. Hon. DLitt: Durham, 1960; East Anglia, 1967; London, 1969; Birmingham, 1970; Harvard, 1971; Yale, 1973; Warwick, 1976; Hon. LLD Aberdeen, 1967. *Publications:* The Art of T. S. Eliot, 1949; The Divine Poems of John Donne, 1952; The Metaphysical Poets (Penguin), 1957; (ed with G. M. Story) The Sonnets of William Alabaster, 1960; The Business of Criticism, 1960; The Elegies and Songs and Sonnets of John Donne, 1965; A Reading of Paradise Lost, 1965; John Donne: Selected Prose (co-ed with T. Healey), 1967; (ed) Shakespearian and Other Studies by F. P. Wilson, 1969; Religion and Literature, 1971; (rev. and ed) F. P. Wilson, Shakespeare and the New Bibliography, 1971; (ed) The Faber Book of Religious Verse, 1972; (ed) The New Oxford Book of English Verse 1250-1950, 1972; The Composition of Four Quartets, 1977. *Recreations:* gardening, foreign travel. *Address:* Myrtle House, Eynsham, Oxford. *T:* Oxford 881497.

GARDNER, Rear-Adm. Herbert, CB 1976; Chartered Engineer; *b* 23 Oct. 1921; *s* of Herbert and Constance Gladys Gardner; *m* 1946, Catherine Mary Roe, Perth, WA. *Educ:* Taunton Sch.; Weymouth Coll. War of 1939-45; joined Dartmouth, 1940; RN Engineering Coll., Keyham, 1940; HMS Nigeria, Cumberland, Adamant, and 4th Submarine Sqdn, 1944; HM S/M Totem, 1945. Dept of Engr-in-Chief, 1947; HM S/M Telemachus, 1949; Admty Develt Establishment, Barrow-in-Furness, 1952; HMS Eagle, 1954; Comdr, 1956; HMS Caledonia, 1956; HMS Blackpool, 1958; Asst to Manager Engrg Dept, Rosyth Dockyard, 1960; HMS Maidstone, 1963; Capt., 1963; Dep. Manager, Engrg Dept, Devonport Dockyard, 1964; Chief Engr and Production Manager, Singapore Dockyard, 1967; Chief Staff Officer (Technical) to Comdr Far East Fleet, 1968; course at Imperial Defence Coll., 1970; Chief of Staff to C-in-C Naval Home Comd, 1971-73; Vice Pres., Ordnance Bd, 1974-76, Pres., 1976-77. *Recreations:* sailing, golf. *Address:* c/o Lloyds Bank Ltd, Weymouth, Dorset.

GARDNER, Hugh, CB 1966; CBE 1953; *b* 28 March 1910; *yr s* of C. H. Gardner; *m* 1934, Margaret Evelyn Carvalho; one *s* two *d. Educ:* University College Sch.; Merton Coll., Oxford. Served Min. of Agriculture, Fisheries and Food (formerly Min. of Agriculture and Fisheries), 1933-70; Under-Sec., 1953-70, retired; Chm., Assoc. of First Div. Civil Servants, 1945-48. *Publication:* Tales from the Marble Mountain, 1967. *Recreations:* golf, gardening, writing. *Address:* The Cobb, North Road, Berkhamsted, Herts. *T:* Berkhamsted 5677. *Club:* United Oxford & Cambridge University.

GARDNER, James, CBE 1959; RDI 1947; Major RE; industrial designer and consultant; *b* 29 Dec. 1907; *s* of Frederic James Gardner; *m* 1935, Mary Williams; two *s. Educ:* Chiswick and Westminster Schools of Art. Jewellery Designer, Cartier Ltd, 1924-31. Served War of 1939-45, Chief Development Officer, Army Camouflage, 1941-46. Designer, Britain Can Make It Exhibition, 1946; Chief Designer, Festival Gardens, Battersea, 1950; British Pavilion, Brussels, 1958; British Pavilion, Expo '67, Montreal; currently designer to Evoluon Museum, Eindhoven, Netherlands, and St Helens Glass Museum, Lancs; responsible for main display Geological Museum, London, 1972; responsible for visual design of QE2 and a sternwheeler Riverboat for the Mississippi Heritage Centre, York (Architectural Heritage Year, 1975). *Address:* The Studio, 144 Haverstock Hill, Hampstead, NW3.

GARDNER, James Jesse, DL; Chief Executive, Tyne and Wear County Council, since 1973; *b* 7 April 1932; *s* of James and Elizabeth Rubina Gardner; *m* 1955, Diana Sotheran; three *s* one *d. Educ:* Kirkham Grammar Sch.; Victoria Univ., Manchester (LLB). Nat. Service, 1955-57. Articled to Town Clerk, Preston, 1952-55; Legal Asst, Preston Co. Borough Council, 1955; Crosby Borough Council: Asst Solicitor, 1957-59; Chief Asst Solicitor, 1959-61; Chief Asst Solicitor, Warrington Co. Borough Council, 1961-65; Stockton-on-Tees Borough Council: Dep. Town Clerk, 1966; Town Clerk, 1966-68; Asst Town Clerk, Teesside Co. Borough Council, 1968; Associate Town Clerk and Solicitor, London Borough of Greenwich, 1968-69; Town Clerk and Chief Exec. Officer, Co. Borough of Sunderland, 1970-73. DL Tyne and Wear, 1976. FRSA 1976. *Recreations:* golf, music, theatre, food and drink. *Address:* Wayside, 121 Queen Alexandra Road, Sunderland, Tyne and Wear. *T:* Sunderland 282525.

GARDNER, John Linton, CBE 1976; composer; *b* 2 March 1917; *s* of late Dr Alfred Gardner, Ilfracombe, and Muriel (*née* Pullein-Thompson); *m* 1955, Jane, *d* of N. J. Abercrombie, *qv*; one *s* two *d. Educ:* Eagle House, Sandhurst; Wellington Coll.; Exeter Coll., Oxford (BMus). Served War of 1939-45: RAF, 1940-46. Chief Music Master, Repton Sch., 1939-40. Staff, Covent Garden Opera, 1946-52; Tutor: Morley Coll., 1952-76 (Dir of Music, 1965-69); Bagot Stack Coll., 1955-62; London Univ. (extra-mural) 1959-60; Dir of Music, St Paul's Girls' Sch., 1962-75; Prof. of Harmony and Composition, Royal Acad. of Music, 1956-. Conductor: Haslemere Musical Soc., 1953-62; Dorian Singers, 1961-62; European Summer Sch. for Young Musicians, 1966-; Bromley YSO, 1970-. Brit. Council Lecturer: Levant, 1954; Belgium, 1960; Iberia, 1963; Yugoslavia, 1967. Adjudicator, Canadian Festivals, 1974. Member: Arts Council Music Panel, 1958-62; Council, Composers' Guild, 1961- (Chm., 1963; Delegate to USSR, 1963); Cttee of Management, Royal Philharmonic Soc., 1965-72; Brit. Council Music Cttee, 1968. Dir, Performing Right Soc., 1965-. Worshipful Co. of Musicians: Collard Fellow, 1962-64; elected to Freedom and Livery, 1965. Hon. RAM 1959. Bax Society's Prize, 1958. *Works include: orchestral:* Symphony no 1, 1947; Variations on a Waltz of Carl Nielsen, 1952; Piano Concerto no 1, 1957; Sinfonia Piccola (strings), 1960; Occasional Suite, Aldeburgh Festival, 1968; An English Ballad, 1969; Three Ridings, 1970; Sonatina for Strings, 1974; *chamber:* Concerto da Camera (4 insts), 1968; Partita (solo 'cello), 1968; Chamber Concerto (organ and 11 insts), 1969; English Suite (harpsichord), 1971; Sonata Secolare for organ and brass, 1973; Sonata da Chiesa for two trumpets and organ; *ballet:* Reflection, 1952; *opera:* A Nativity Opera, 1950; The Moon and Sixpence, 1957; The Visitors, 1972; Bel and the Dragon, 1973; The Entertainment of the Senses, 1974; Tobermory, 1976; *musical:* Vile Bodies, 1961; *choral:* Cantiones Sacrae 1973; (sop., chor. and orch.), 1952; Jubilate Deo (unacc. chor.), 1957; The Ballad of the White Horse (bar., chor. and orch.), 1959; Herrick Cantata (ten. solo, chor. and orch.), 1961; A Latter-Day Athenian Speaks, 1962; The Noble Heart (sop., bass, chor, and orch.), Shakespeare Quatercentenary Festival, 1964; Cantor popularis vocis, 18th Schütz Festival Berlin, 1964; Mass in C (unacc. chor.), 1965; Cantata for Christmas (chor. and chamb. orch.), 1966; Proverbs of Hell (unacc. chor.), 1967; Cantata for Easter (soli, chor., organ and percussion), 1970; Open Air (chor. and brass band), 1976. Many smaller pieces and music for films, Old Vic and Royal Shakespeare Theatres, BBC. Contributor to: Dublin Review, Musical Times, Tempo, Composer, Listener, Music in Education. *Recreation:* bore-watching. *Address:* 10 Lynton Road, New Malden, Surrey. *T:* 01-942 7322.

GARDNER, John William; writer; Chairman, Common Cause, 1970-77; *b* 8 Oct. 1912; *s* of William Frederick and Marie (Flora) Gardner; *m* 1934, Aida Marroquin; two *d. Educ:* Stanford Univ. (AB 1935, AM 1936); Univ. of Calif. (PhD 1938). 1st Lt-Captain, US Marine Corps, 1943-46. Teaching Asst in

Psychology, Univ. of Calif., 1936-38; Instructor in Psychology, Connecticut Coll., 1938-40; Asst Prof. in Psychology, Mt Holyoke Coll., 1940-42; Head of Latin Amer. Section, Federal Communications Commn, 1942-43. Carnegie Corporation of New York: Staff Mem., 1946-47; Exec. Associate, 1947-49; Vice-Pres., 1949-55; Pres., 1955-67; Pres., Carnegie Foundn for Advancement of Teaching, 1955-67; Sec. of Health, Education and Welfare, 1965-68; Chm., Urban Coalition, 1968-70. Chairman: US Adv. Commn on Internat. Educational and Cultural Affairs, 1962-64; Pres. Johnson's Task Force on Educn, 1964; White House Conf. on Educn, 1965. Dir, Amer. Assoc. for Advancement of Science, 1963-65. Director: New York Telephone Co., 1962-65; Shell Oil Co., 1962-65; Time Inc., 1968-71; American Airlines, 1968-71; Rockefeller Brothers Fund, 1968-; New York Foundn, 1970-. Trustee: Metropolitan Museum of Art, 1957-65; Stanford Univ., 1968-. Benjamin Franklin Fellow, RSA, 1964. Holds hon. degrees from various colleges and univs. USAF Exceptional Service Award, 1956; Presidential Medal of Freedom, 1964; Public Welfare Medal, Nat. Acad. of Science, 1967. *Publications:* Excellence, 1961; (ed) Pres. John F. Kennedy's book, To Turn the Tide, 1961; Self-Renewal, 1964; No Easy Victories, 1968; The Recovery of Confidence, 1970; In Common Cause, 1972; Know or Listen to Those who Know, 1975. *Address:* 2030 M Street NW, Washington, DC 20036, USA.

GARDNER, Kenneth Burslam; Deputy Keeper of Oriental MSS and Printed Books, The British Library, since 1974; *b* 5 June 1924; *s* of D. V. Gardner; *m* 1949, Cleone Winifred Adams; two *s* two *d*. *Educ:* Alleyne's Grammar Sch., Stevenage; University College, London; School of Oriental and African Studies, Univ. of London (BA Hons Japanese). War service, Intelligence Corps (Captain), 1943-47. Assistant Librarian, School of Oriental and African Studies, 1949-54; Assistant Keeper, Department of Oriental Printed Books and MSS, British Museum, 1955-57, Keeper, 1957-70; Principal Keeper of Printed Books, British Museum (later The British Library), 1970-74. *Publications:* contrib. to jls of oriental studies, art and librarianship. *Address:* 1 Duncombe Road, Bengeo, Hertford.

GARDNER, Ralph Bennett, MM 1944; Under Secretary (Legal), Treasury Solicitor's Department, since 1976; *b* 7 May 1919; *s* of Ralph Wilson Gardner and late Elizabeth Emma (*née* Nevitt-Bennett); *m* 1950, Patricia Joan Ward (*née* Bartlett); one *s* one *d*. *Educ:* Worksop Coll. Served War, 1939-46, RA. Admitted a solicitor, 1947; Solicitor, private practice, Chester, 1947-48; Legal Asst, Treasury Solicitor's Dept, 1948; Sen. Legal Asst, 1957; Asst Treas. Solicitor, 1972. Lord of the Manor of Shotwick, County of Chester (by inheritance, 1964). *Recreations:* gardening and local history. *Address:* Wychen, St Mary's Road, Leatherhead, Surrey. *T:* Leatherhead 73161.

GARDNER, W(alter) Frank, CBE 1953; Director, The Prudential Assurance Co. Ltd, 1961-71 (Deputy Chairman, 1965-69); *b* 6 Nov. 1900; *s* of late Walter Gardner and late Emma Mabel Gardner, Streatham Hill, SW2; *m* 1st, 1925, Constance Gladys (*d* 1945), *d* of late Ellen Haydon and late Frederick William Haydon, Norwich; one *d*; 2nd, 1949, Kathleen Lilian, *y d* of late Florence Charlotte and late George William Smith, Hampton Hill, and widow of Dr Frederick Lishman, Bexhill. *Educ:* Dulwich College; Institute of Actuaries. Chief Actuary, Prudential Assurance Co. Ltd, 1945-50; Chief General Manager, 1950-60. Fellow (FIA), 1924; President, 1952-54. FSS 1952. *Publications:* contributions to Journal of Institute of Actuaries. *Recreations:* bowls, cine-photography. *Address:* 8c South Cliff Tower, Eastbourne, East Sussex BN20 7JN. *Clubs:* Junior Carlton; Devonshire (Eastbourne); Eastbourne Bowling.

GARDNER, William Henry, CMG 1948; *b* 20 April 1895; *s* of William John Gardner, Walthamstow, Essex; *m* 1st, 1920, Dorothy Margaret (*d* 1950), *e d* of John William Freeman; one *s*; 2nd, 1964, Elsie Stephenson (*d* 1967), Edinburgh, *d* of Henry Stephenson, Co. Durham. *Educ:* Maynard Road Elementary Sch. and Sir George Monoux Grammar Sch., Walthamstow; King's Coll., London. Entered Civil Service as boy clerk, 1910; second div. clerk, 1913; Staff Clerk, 1929; Principal, WO, 1940; Asst Sec., WO, 1942; Asst Under-Sec. of State, 1952-55; retd from WO, 1955. Served European War, 1914-18, in Queen's Westminster Rifles, 1915-19; Lieut WO Home Guard, 1940-45. Lay Reader: dio. of Chelmsford 1922-; dio. of Edinburgh, 1965; Hon. Sec., Chelmsford Diocesan Union, CEMS, 1925-32, 1958-62; Vice-Chm., 1962-66, Vice-Pres., 1966-72. Dep. Leader, UK delegn to Geneva Conf. on Protection of War Victims, 1949. Hon. Mem., Florence Nightingale Internat. Nurses' Assoc., 1967. *Recreations:* walking, reading. *Address:* 3 Lonsdale Terrace, Edinburgh EH3 9HN. *T:* 031-229 7443. *Clubs:* Royal Commonwealth Society; Essex County Cricket.

GARDNER, William Maving; designer and craftsman in private practice; *b* 25 May 1914; *s* of Robert Haswell Gardner, MIMarE and Lucy (*née* Maving); *m* 1940, Joan Margaret Pollard; two *s* one *d*. Trained at Royal College of Art, 1935-39 (ARCA 1938, Design Sch. Trav. Schol., Scandinavia, 1939). Mem., Royal Mint Panel of Artists, 1938-. Vis. lectr, Central Sch. of Arts and Crafts, 1959-62, Cambridgeshire Coll. of Art and Technology, 1959-62, Hampstead Garden Suburb Inst., 1959-73; Examr in craft subjects AEB City and Guilds of London Inst., 1957-60; served Typography Jury of RSA, Ind. Design Bursary Scheme. FRSA 1955, FSIA 1964, ARHistS, 1969, Leverhulme Res. Fellow, 1969-70. Vis. Prof. and Fine Art Program Lectr, Colorado State Univ., 1963; Churchill Meml Trav. Fellow, 1966-67 (USA, Polynesia, NZ, Australia, Nepal); Hon. Mem., RNS, NZ, 1966. Work exhib. Fort Collins and Denver, Colo, 1963, Monotype House, London, 1965, Portsmouth Coll. of Art, 1965, Hammond Mus., NY, 1970; (with family) Rye Art Gall., 1977. The Queen's Silver Jubilee Medal, 1977. *works include:* HM Privy Council Seal 1955, HM Greater and Lesser Royal Signets 1955, Seal of HM Dependencies, 1955; seals for BMA, 1957, RSA, 1966, Univ. of Aston, Birmingham, 1966; *coinage models:* for Jordan 1950, GB 1953, Cyprus 1955 and 1963, Algeria 1964, Guyana 1967, Dominican Republic 1969, UNFAO (Ceylon 1968, Cyprus 1970, Guyana 1970), Falkland Islands 1974; *medallic work:* includes Britannia Commemorative Soc. Shakespeare Medal 1967, Churchill Meml Trust's Foundn Medal 1969, Nat. Commemorative Soc. Audubon Medal 1970, Internat. Iron and Steel Inst. Medal 1971, Inst. of Metals Kroll medal 1972, and thirty six medallic engravings depicting the history of the Royal Arms, completed 1974; Sri Lanka Medallion for UN FAO, 1976; participant in series of Commonwealth Silver Jubilee crown pieces for Royal Mint, 1977; *calligraphy:* includes Rolls of Honour for House of Commons 1949, LTE 1954, Household Cavalry and the five regiments of Foot Guards, completed 1956, Corps of Royal Marines, MSS for Canterbury Cath. and elsewhere; *work in other media* for Postmaster Gen. (Jersey definitive stamp 1958), Royal Soc. (Tercentenary stained glass window, 1960), King's College, London, 1971, City of London, 1972—and for Univs, schools, presses, libraries, banks, industrial and other authorities, also privately. *Address:* Chequertree, Wittersham, Tenterden, Kent.

GARDNER, Air Commodore William Steven, CB 1958; OBE 1945; DFC 1940 and bar 1941; AFC 1943; *b* 16 Dec. 1909; *s* of late Campbell Gardner, JP, Groomsport, Co. Down, Northern Ireland; *m* 1937, Theodora, *d* of W. G. Bradley, Castlerock, Co. Derry; one *s* one *d* (and one *d* decd). *Educ:* Campbell Coll., Belfast. Joined RAF 1935; served in 106, 44 and 144 Squadrons, Bomber Command, 1939-45. Group Capt. 1951; Air Commodore, 1956; Head of Plans and Operations, CENTO, 1957-59; Acting Air Vice-Marshal, 1963; Provost Marshal, 1960-63; Director-General of Personal Services, 1963. *Recreation:* sailing. *Address:* Corner Cottage, Shipton Green, Itchenor, Sussex. *Club:* Royal Ulster Yacht.

GARDNER-BROWN, Anthony Geoffrey Hopwood, CMG 1958; *b* 1 Oct. 1913; *yr s* of late Rev. F. S. G. Gardner-Brown; *m* 1939, Margaret, *yr d* of H. Sparrow; three *d*. *Educ:* Marlborough; Pembroke Coll., Cambridge. Cadet, Colonial Administrative Service, Northern Rhodesia, 1936; District Officer, 1938; served 1st Bn Northern Rhodesia Regt, East Africa and Ceylon, 1940-43; Supervisor Colonial Service Courses, Cambridge Univ., 1949-51; Asst Sec. (Native Affairs), Northern Rhodesia, 1952; Colonial Sec., Bahamas, 1952-56; Federation of Nigeria: Dep. Chief Sec., 1956-58; Sec. for Defence and External Affairs, 1958-59; Dep. Governor-General, Nov. 1959-Oct. 1960; retired, 1961. Organiser, Community Council of Devon, 1961-63; Chm., Salaries Commn, Windward and Leeward Islands, 1965; Comr on Anomalies, Western Pacific High Commn, 1965; Salaries Comr, Barbados, Mauritius, 1966, Swaziland, 1967, Bermuda, 1969, Hong Kong, 1971. Chm., Somerset County Scout Council, 1967-70. *Recreation:* fishing. *Address:* The Old Rectory, Stawley, Wellington, Somerset. *T:* Greenham 672205.

GARDNER-MEDWIN, Robert Joseph, RIBA, FRTPI; architect and town planning consultant; Professor Emeritus, Liverpool University, since 1973; *b* 10 April 1907; *s* of late Dr and Mrs F. M. Gardner-Medwin; *m* 1935, Margaret, *d* of late Mr Justice and Mrs Kilgour, Winnipeg; four *s*. *Educ:* Rossall Sch., Lancashire; School of Architecture, Liverpool Univ. (BArch, Dipl Civ Des). Commonwealth Fund Fellowship in City Planning and Landscape Design, Harvard Univ., 1933-35; private practice, and architectural teaching at Architectural Association and Regent Street Polytechnic, 1936-40. Served War of 1939-45, with Royal Engineers (Major, RE), 1940-43. Adviser in Town Planning and Housing to Comptroller of Development and Welfare in the British West Indies, 1944-47,

Chief Architect and Planning Officer to Department of Health for Scotland, 1947-52; Roscoe Prof. of Architecture, Liverpool Univ., 1952-73. President, Liverpool Architectural Society, 1966; Chm., Merseyside Civic Soc., 1972-76. FRSA. Golden Order of Merit, Poland, 1976. *Publications:* (with H. Myles Wright, MA, FRIBA) Design of Nursery and Elementary Schools, 1938; contributions to Town Planning Review, Architects' Journal, Journals of the RIBA and the RTPI, etc. *Address:* 6 Kirby Mount, West Kirby, Wirral, Merseyside.

GARDNER-THORPE, Col and Alderman Ronald Laurence, TD 1948 (3 bars); JP; company director; *b* 13 May 1917; *s* of Joseph Gardner and Hannah Coulthurst Thorpe; *m* 1938, Hazel Mary (*née* Dees); one *s*. *Educ:* De la Salle Coll. Commnd Hants Heavy Regt, 1938; served War, 1939-45: France, Germany, Italy, British Army Staff Washington; 1945-47: AA&QMG 56 London Div., and XIII Corps; Grade 1 SO XIII Corps; GSO 1 GHQ CMF; comd 5th Bn The Buffs, 1956-60; Col 1960. Vice-President: David Isaacs Fund, 1973-; City of London Red Cross, 1977-. Member: Kent Territorial Assoc., 1954-62 (Mem. Finance Cttee, 1954); City of London T&AVR Assoc., 1977-; Lord Lieuts Cttee, 1955-; Council, Magistrates' Assoc., 1972-; London Court of Arbitration, 1975-; Public Sch. Governing Body, 1963-; Governor: St John's Coll., Southsea, 1963 (Vice-Chm. Governors, 1976); St Joseph's, Beulah Hill, 1966; Christ's Hosp., 1972; United Westminster Schs, 1974. JP Inner London, 1965 (Dep. Chm. 1968); JP City of London, 1969 (Dep. Chm. 1970); Hon. Treas., Inner London Magistrates, 1972- (Vice Chm., 1977). Freeman, City of London, 1971; Alderman, Ward of Bishopsgate, City of London, 1972; Pres., Bishopsgate Ward Club, 1975. Liveryman, Worshipful Co. of Painter Stainers, 1972 (also Mem. Court, 1972); Member: Court, Hon. Artillery Co., 1972; Guild of Marketors, 1975 (also Mem. Court, 1975). Kt Comdr, Royal Order of the Dannebrog, 1960. *Recreations:* interest in Fine Arts and in City of London tradition. *Address:* 8 Cadogan Square, SW1X 0JU. *Clubs:* Belfry, City Livery, United Wards, Bishopsgate Ward.

GARDYNE, John B.; *see* Bruce-Gardyne.

GARFIELD, Leon; author; *b* 14 July 1921; *s* of David Garfield and Rose Garfield; *m* 1949, Vivien Dolores Alcock; one *d*. *Educ:* Brighton Grammar Sch. Served War, RAMC, 1941-46: attained and held rank of Private. Worked in NHS (biochemistry), until 1969; full-time author, 1969-. *Publications:* Jack Holborn, 1964; Devil-in-the-Fog, 1966; Smith, 1967; Black Jack, 1968; Mister Corbett's Ghost and Other Stories, 1969; The Boy and the Monkey, 1969; The Drummer Boy, 1970; The Strange Affair of Adelaide Harris, 1971; The Ghost Downstairs, 1972; The Captain's Watch, 1972; Lucifer Wilkins, 1973; Baker's Dozen, 1973; The Sound of Coaches, 1974; The Prisoners of September, 1975; The Pleasure Garden, 1976; The Booklovers, 1976; The House of Hanover, 1976; The Lamplighter's Funeral, 1976; Mirror, Mirror, 1976; Moss and Blister, 1976; The Cloak, 1976; The Valentine, 1977; Labour in Vain, 1977; with Edward Blishen: The God Beneath the Sea, 1970; The Golden Shadow, 1973; with David Proctor: Child O'War, 1972. *Recreations:* snooker, collecting pictures and china; also wine, women and song. *Address:* 59 Wood Lane, Highgate, N6. *T:* 01-340 5785. *Clubs:* PEN, Puffin.

GARING, Air Commodore William Henry, CBE 1943; DFC 1940; Director, Bryn Mawr Chianina Stud Cattle Company, since 1975; *b* Corryong, Victoria, 26 July 1910; *s* of late George Garing, retired grazier, and late Amy Evelyn Garing; *m* 1st, 1940 (marr. diss. 1951); one *s* one *d*; 2nd, 1954, Marjorie Irene Smith, Preston, England; two *d*. *Educ:* Corryong Higher Elementary School; Melbourne Technical Coll.; Royal Military Coll., Duntroon, ACT. Began career as Electrical and Mechanical Engineer, 1928; entered RMC, Duntroon, 1929, as specially selected RAAF Cadet; Flying Training in Australia, 1931-32, in UK 1934-35; Seaplane Flying Instructor and Chief Navigation Instructor, Point Cook, Victoria, 1936; commanded Seaplane Squadron, Point Cook; conducted first Specialist Air Navigation Course in Australia, 1938; posted to United Kingdom in 1939; served with No 10 Squadron, RAAF, as Flt Commander in Coastal Command, RAF, 1939; operations in N Atlantic, France and Mediterranean (DFC); flew Lord Lloyd to France for discussions with Pétain Government prior to collapse of France, 1940, and subsequently was pilot to the late Duke of Kent and to Mr Eden (later Viscount Avon), and others (despatches). Arrived Australia, 1941; Senior Air Staff Officer, HQ Northern Area (extended from Neth. Indies through New Guinea, British Solomons to New Caledonia), 1941; commanded No 9 (Ops) Group RAAF, New Guinea, 1942; Milne Bay Campaign, 1942; Buna Campaign, 1942-43 (American DSC); 1943 (CBE); commanded No 1 Operational Training Unit, 1943 (1939-43 star); Director Operational

Requirements, 1944; SASO to RAAF Rep., Washington, 1945-46; OC Western Area, 1947; Joint Services Staff Coll., 1948; Commandant School Land/Air Warfare, NSW, 1950; OC Amberley, Qld, 1951; Imperial Defence Coll., London, 1952. AOC Overseas HQ, London, 1953; AOC RAAF, Richmond, NSW, 1953-55; AOC RAAF and Commandant RAAF Staff Coll., Point Cook, Victoria, 1955-60; Air Officer, South Australia, and OC, RAAF, Edinburgh Field, Salisbury, SA, 1960-64, retired. Exec. Dir, Rothmans Nat. Sport Foundn, Sydney, Australia, 1964; Commercial Relations Manager, Alfred Dunhill Ltd, 1971-75. Holds No 1 Air Navigators' Certificate (Australia); Air Master Navigator (RAF); Freeman, GAPAN. FAIM 1964. *Recreations:* Alpine ski-ing, water ski-ing, yachting, golf, shooting, flying (holds commercial pilot's licence). *Address:* Bryn Mawr, 25 Bangalla Street, Warrawee, NSW 2074, Australia. *Clubs:* Imperial Service, Royal Commonwealth (Sydney).

GARLAKE, Maj.-Gen. Storr, CBE 1949; *b* 11 April 1904; *yr s* of John Storr Inglesby and Dorothy Eleanor Garlake, Cradock, CP; *m* 1932, Catherine Ellen, *er d* of James Wightman, Cape Town; one *s* one *d*. *Educ:* St Andrew's Prep. Sch., Grahamstown; RN Colleges, Osborne and Dartmouth. Joined BSAP, 1925; commissioned 1929; transferred to S Rhodesia Staff Corps, 1933; Maj.-Gen. 1953. Served War of 1939-45, ME and India, 1942-45; Commander Military Forces, S Rhodesia, 1947-53; Imp. Defence Coll., 1949; Chief of General Staff, Federation of Rhodesia and Nyasaland, 1953-59. Additional ADC to the Queen, 1952-54; retired 1959. *Address:* Froghill, PO Box HG 47, Highlands, Salisbury, Rhodesia. *Club:* Salisbury (Salisbury, Rhodesia).

GARLAND, Ailsa Mary, (Mrs John Rollit Mason); broadcaster on TV and radio; *d* of James Francis Garland and Elsie Elizabeth Langley; *m* 1948, John Rollit Mason; one *s*. *Educ:* La Retraite, Clapham Park; St Mary's, Woodford Green, Essex. Fashion Editor, Vogue Export Book, 1947-50; Editor, Shopping Magazine, 1952-53; Woman's Editor, Daily Mirror, 1953-59, Assistant Editor, 1959-60; Editor of Vogue, 1960-63; Director, Condé Nast Publications Ltd, 1961-63; Editor in Chief, Woman's Jl, 1963-68; Editor of Fashion, 1963-68; Dir, Fleetway Publications Ltd, 1963-68; Fashion Coordinator, IPC Magazines Ltd, 1970-72. Governor, London College of Fashion, 1961-68. Mem. Consultative Cttee, Coll. of Fashion and Clothing Technology. *Publication:* Lion's Share (autobiog.), 1970. *Recreations:* gardening, reading, theatre. *Address:* Christmas House, Edwardstone, Suffolk.

GARLAND, Basil; Registrar, Family Division of High Court of Justice; *b* 30 May 1920; *o c* of late Herbert George Garland and Grace Alice Mary Martha Garland; *m* 1942, Dora Mary Sudell Hope; one *s*. *Educ:* Dulwich Coll.; Pembroke Coll., Oxford (MA). Served in Royal Artillery, 1940-46: commnd 1941; Staff Officer, HQ RA, Gibraltar, 1943-45; Hon. Major 1946. Called to Bar, Middle Temple, 1948; Treasury Junior Counsel (Probate), 1965; Registrar, Principal Probate Registry, 1969. *Publications:* articles in Law Jl. *Recreations:* sailing, drama. *Address:* Dalethorpe End, Dedham, Essex. *T:* Colchester 322263. *Clubs:* Cruising Association, Bar Yacht, Royal Harwich Yacht.

GARLAND, (Frederick) Peter (Collison), CVO 1969; QPM 1965; *b* 4 Sept. 1912; *s* of late Percy Frederick Garland, Southsea, Hants; *m* 1945, Gwendolen Mary, *d* of late Henry James Powell, Putney; three *d*. *Educ:* Bradfield Coll. Joined Metropolitan Police, 1934. Served in RAF (Air Crew), 1941-45. Asst Chief Constable of Norfolk, 1952-56, Chief Constable, 1956-75. CStJ 1961. *Address:* 2 Eaton Road, Norwich. *T:* Norwich 53043. *Clubs:* Royal Air Force; Norfolk County (Norwich).

GARLAND, Prof. Henry Burnard, JP; MA, PhD, LittD; Professor of German in the University of Exeter, 1948-72, now Emeritus Professor; *b* 30 Aug. 1907; *s* of late William Garland, Dover, and Alice Mary (*née* Jarry); *m* 1949, Hertha Marie Louise (*née* Wiesener); two *d*. *Educ:* Dover County Sch.; Emmanuel Coll., Cambridge. BA, Mod. & Med. Langs. Tripos, 1st Class with Distinction, 1930; Patterson Prizeman, 1930; Tiarks German Scholar, 1931; Faculty Assistant Lecturer, Cambridge, 1934; MA 1934, PhD 1935, LittD 1970, Cambridge; University Lecturer, Cambridge, 1937. Served War of 1939-45; Cambridge STC, 1940-43; RA, 1943-46, UK, Belgium, Germany (Colonel). Controller and Chief Editor, Die Welt, Hamburg, 1946; Head German Department, University College, Exeter, 1947; Chairman Arts Faculty, 1947-53; Vice-Principal, 1953-55; Acting Principal, 1953-54; Elector, Schröder Chair of German, Cambridge Univ., 1954-74; Deputy Vice-Chancellor, Exeter Univ., 1955-57; Public Orator, 1956-65. JP Exeter, 1961; Member, State Studentship Selection Cttee, Department of Education and Science, 1965-68, Panel Chairman, 1966-68.

Governor, Blundell's Sch., 1969-75. Hon. DLitt Exeter, 1976. Bronze Medal, Univ. of Rennes, 1970; Goethe-Medaille, Goethe-Institut, 1975. *Publications:* Lessing: The Founder of Modern German Literature, 1937, revd edn 1962; Schiller, 1949; Storm and Stress, 1952; Schiller Revisited, 1959; Schiller the Dramatic Writer, 1969; A Concise Survey of German Literature, 1970, expanded edn, 1976; (with Mary Garland) The Oxford Companion to German Literature, 1976; Editions of works by Schiller (3), Lessing, Fontane and H. v. Kleist; Essays on Schiller, Fontane, Schnitzler and the Prussian Army; contributions to Cassell's Encyclopædia of Literature, Collier's Encyclopædia. *Recreations:* music, gardening, bird-watching. *Address:* 5 Rosebarn Avenue, Exeter EX4 6DY. *T:* Exeter 55009.

GARLAND, Patrick Neville, QC 1972; a Recorder of the Crown Court, since 1972; *b* 22 July 1929; *s* of Frank Neville Garland and Marjorie Garland; *m* 1955, Jane Elizabeth Bird; two *s* one *d. Educ:* Uppingham Sch.; Sidney Sussex Coll., Cambridge (MA, LLB). Called to Bar, Middle Temple, 1953; Asst Recorder, Norwich, 1971. *Publications:* articles in legal and technical jls. *Recreations:* shooting, sailing, gardening, industrial archaeology. *Address:* 218 Finchley Road, NW3 6DH. *T:* 01-435 5877; 11 King's Bench Walk, Temple, EC4Y 7EQ. *Clubs:* Norfolk (Norwich); Cumberland Lawn Tennis, Grafham Water Sailing.

GARLAND, Peter; see Garland, F. P. C.

GARLICK, Prof. George Frederick John, BSc, PhD, DSc, FInstP; Professor of Physics, University of Hull, since 1956; *b* 21 Feb. 1919; *s* of George Robert Henry Garlick and Martha Elizabeth (*née* Davies); *m* 1943, Dorothy Mabel Bowsher; one *d. Educ:* Wednesbury High Sch.; Univ. of Birmingham (BSc 1940, PhD 1943, DSc 1955). War service: Scientific Officer (Radar Research). In Charge Luminescence Laboratory, Birmingham Univ., 1946-56 (Research Physicist, 1946-49, Lecturer in Physics, 1949-56). FInstP, 1949. *Publications:* Luminescent Materials, 1949; numerous papers in learned scientific journals. *Recreation:* music (organ). *Address:* 1 Skelton Crescent, Market Weighton, York YO4 3EB. *T:* Market Weighton 2584.

GARLICK, Sir John, KCB 1976 (CB 1973); Second Permanent Secretary, Cabinet Office, since Oct. 1974; *b* 17 May 1921; *m* 1945, Frances Esther Munday; three *d. Educ:* Westcliff High Sch., Essex; University of London. Entered Post Office Engineering Dept, 1937; Ministry of Transport, 1948; Private Secretary to Rt Hon. Ernest Marples, 1959-60; Assistant Secretary, 1960; National Economic Development Office, 1962-64; Under-Sec., Min. of Transport, 1966, later DoE; Dep. Sec., DoE, 1972-73; Dir-Gen., Highways, DoE, 1973-74. *Address:* 16 Astons Road, Moor Park, Northwood, Mddx. *T:* Northwood 24628.

GARLICK, Kenneth John; Keeper of Western Art, Ashmolean Museum, Oxford, since 1968; Fellow of Balliol College, Oxford, since 1968; *b* 1 Oct. 1916; *s* of late D. E. Garlick and Annie Hallifax. *Educ:* Elmhurst Sch., Street; Balliol Coll., Oxford; Courtauld Inst. of Art, London. MA Oxon, PhD Birmingham; FSA, FMA. RAF Signals, 1939-46. Lectr in Art History, Bath Academy of Art, 1946-48; Asst Keeper, Dept of Art, City of Birmingham Museum and Art Gallery, 1948-50; Lectr (Sen. Lectr 1960), Barber Inst. of Fine Arts, Univ. of Birmingham, 1951-68. *Publications:* Sir Thomas Lawrence, 1954; Walpole Society Vol. XXXIX (Lawrence Catalogue Raisonné), 1964; Walpole Society Vol. XLV (Catalogue of Pictures at Althorp), 1976; numerous articles and reviews. *Recreations:* travel, music. *Address:* c/o Ashmolean Museum, Oxford. *T:* Oxford 57522. *Club:* Reform.

GARLICK, Rev. Canon Wilfrid; Rector of Alderley, since 1975; Hon. Canon of Chester since 1958; Hon. Chaplain to the Queen since 1964; *b* 12 Oct. 1910; *s* of late Arthur and Clemence Garlick; *m* 1936, Edith, *d* of late H. Goddard; one *s. Educ:* Oldham Hulme Grammar Sch.; Manchester Univ. (MA *hc* 1968); Egerton Hall Theological Coll. BSc 1931, Manchester. Curate St Andrew, Ancoats, Manchester, 1933-35; Curate St Clement, Chorlton-cum-Hardy, 1935-38; Rector St Nicholas, Burnage, Manchester, 1938-44; Officiating Chaplain to Forces, 1938-44; Vicar of St George, Sheffield, 1944-48; Vicar of St George, Stockport, 1948-75. *Recreations:* golf, travel. *Address:* Alderley Rectory, Nether Alderley, Macclesfield. *T:* Alderley Edge 3134. *Club:* Royal Commonwealth Society.

GARLIES, Lord; Randolph Keith Reginald Stewart; *b* 14 Oct. 1928; *s* and *heir* of 12th Earl of Galloway, *qv; m* 1975, Mrs Lily Budge, *y d* of late Andrew Miller, Duns, Berwickshire. *Educ:* Harrow. *Address:* 4 Bernard Terrace, Edinburgh EH8 9NX.

GARMOYLE, Viscount; Simon Dallas Cairns; *b* 27 May 1939; *er s* and *heir* of 5th Earl Cairns, *qv; m* 1964, Amanda Mary, *d* of late Major E. F. Heathcoat Amory, and of Mrs Roderick Heathcoat Amory, Oswaldkirk Hall, York; three *s. Educ:* Eton; Trinity Coll., Cambridge. *Heir: s* Hon. Hugh Sebastian Cairns, *b* 26 March 1965. *Address:* Queen Hoo Hall, Tewin, Herts. *T:* Tewin 7361. *Club:* Turf.

GARNER, family name of **Baron Garner.**

GARNER, Baron *cr* 1969 (Life Peer), of Chiddingly; **(Joseph John) Saville Garner,** GCMG 1965 (KCMG 1954; CMG 1948); Chairman: Commonwealth Scholarship Commission in the UK, since 1968; Board of Management, Royal Postgraduate Medical School, since 1971; Committee of Management, Institute of Commonwealth Studies, since 1971; Highgate School, since 1976 (Governor since 1962; Treasurer since 1976); London Board, Bank of Adelaide, since 1971 (Director since 1969); *b* 14 Feb. 1908; *s* of Joseph and Helena Maria Garner, Highgate, N; *m* 1938, Margaret Beckman, Cedar Lake, Ind, USA; two *s* one *d. Educ:* Highgate Sch.; Jesus Coll., Cambridge. Appointed Dominions Office, 1930; Private Sec. to successive Secretaries of State, 1940-43; Senior Sec., office of UK High Comr Ottawa, 1943-46; Dep. High Comr for the UK, Ottawa, Canada, 1946-48; Asst Under-Sec., Commonwealth Relations Office, 1948-51; Deputy High Commissioner for the UK in India, 1951-53; Deputy Under-Secretary, Commonwealth Relations Office, 1952-56; British High Commissioner in Canada, 1956-61; Permanent Under-Secretary of State, Commonwealth Relations Office, 1962-65, Commonwealth Office, 1965-68; Head of HM Diplomatic Service, 1965-68. Secretary, Order of St Michael and St George, 1966-68 (Registrar, 1962-66). Chm., Bd of Governors, Commonwealth Inst., 1968-74. Member: Council, Voluntary Service Overseas, 1969-; Security Commission, 1968-73. Bd of Govs, SOAS, Univ. of London, 1968-73. Hon. LLD: Univ. of Brit. Columbia, 1958; Univ. of Toronto, 1959; Hon. Fellow, Jesus College, Cambridge, 1967. President, Old Cholmeleian Society, 1964. *Publications:* The Books of the Emperor Wu Ti (transl. from German), 1930. *Recreations:* gardening, travel. *Address:* 1 Courtenay Square, SE11 5PG. *T:* 01-735 7408; Highdown Farmhouse, Horam, Sussex. *T:* Chiddingly 432. *Club:* Royal Automobile.

GARNER, Alan; author; *b* 17 Oct. 1934; *s* of Colin and Marjorie Garner; *m* 1st, 1956, Ann Cook; one *s* two *d;* 2nd, 1972, Griselda Greaves; one *s* one *d . Educ:* Alderley Edge Council Sch.; Manchester Grammar Sch.; Magdalen Coll., Oxford. *Publications:* The Weirdstone of Brisingamen, 1960; The Moon of Gomrath, 1963; Elidor, 1965; Holly from the Bongs, 1966; The Old Man of Mow, 1967; The Owl Service, 1967 (Library Assoc. Carnegie Medal 1967, Guardian Award 1968); The Hamish Hamilton Book of Goblins, 1969; Red Shift, 1973; (with Albin Trowski) The Breadhorse, 1975; The Guizer, 1975; The Stone Book, 1976; Tom Fobble's Day, 1977; Granny Reardun, 1977; The Aimer Gate, 1978; *play:* Point Omega, 1978; *dance drama:* The Green Mist, 1970; *libretti:* The Bellybag, 1971 (music by Richard Morris); Potter Thompson, 1972 (music by Gordon Crosse). *Recreation:* work. *Address:* Blackden, Cheshire CW4 8BY.

GARNER, Anthony Stuart; Director of Organisation, Conservative Central Office, since 1976; *b* 28 Jan. 1927; *s* of Edward Henry Garner, MC, FIAS, and Dorothy May Garner; *m* 1967, Shirley Doris Taylor; two *s . Educ:* Liverpool Coll. Young Conservative Organiser, 1948-51; Conservative Agent, Halifax, 1951-56; Nat. Organising Sec., Young Conservative Org., 1956-61; Conservative Central Office Agent for: London Area, 1961-64; Western Area, 1964-66; North West Area, 1966-76. *Recreations:* sailing, theatre. *Address:* 1 Blomfield Road, W9. *Clubs:* Junior Carlton, Constitutional; St Stephen's.

GARNER, Frank Harold; farmer since 1971; *b* 4 Dec. 1904; *m* 1929, Hilda May Sheppard; one *d. Educ:* Swindon Technical Sch.; Universities of Cambridge, Oxford, Reading and Minnesota, USA. MA (Cantab), MA (Oxon), MSc (Minnesota, USA); FRAgSs. Assistant to Director of Cambridge University Farm, 1924; University Demonstrator in Agriculture at Cambridge, 1927; University Lecturer (Animal Husbandry) at Cambridge, 1929; Assistant to Executive Officer, Cambridgeshire War Agriculture Executive Cttee, 1939; County Agricultural Organiser, East Suffolk, 1940; General Manager of Frederick Hiam Ltd, 1944-58; Principal, RAC, Cirencester, Glos, 1958-71. Liveryman, Farmers' Livery Co., Master, 1971-72. *Publications:* Cattle of Britain, 1943; The Farmers Animals, 1943; British Dairy Farming, 1946; (with E. T. Halnan and A. Eden) Principles and Practice of Feeding Farm Animals, 1940, 5th edn 1966; (ed) Modern British Farming Systems, 1975. *Recreation:* swimming. *Address:* Collins Farm House, Looseley Row, Princes Risborough, Bucks. *Club:* Farmers'.

GARNER, Frederic Francis, CMG 1959; Ambassador to Costa Rica, 1961-67; retired; *b* 9 July 1910; *m* 1946, Muriel (*née* Merrick). *Educ:* Rugby Sch.; Worcester Coll., Oxford. Joined HM Consular Service in China, 1932; served at Peking, Canton, Shanghai, POW in Japan, 1942-45. Consul, Tangier, 1947-50; First Secretary, Bogota, 1950-54; Consul-General, Shanghai, 1954-56; Head of Consular Department, Foreign Office, 1956-58; Ambassador at Phnom Penh, 1958-61. *Address:* 44 Belgrave Mews South, SW1X 8BT. *T:* 01-235 7507.

GARNER, Frederick Leonard; Chairman, Pearl Assurance Company Ltd, since 1977; *b* 7 April 1920; *s* of Leonard Frank Garner and Florence Emily Garner; *m* 1953, Giovanna Maria Anzani, Italy. *Educ:* Sutton County Sch., Surrey. Served War, RA, 1940-46. Joined Pearl Assurance Co., 1936; rejoined, 1946; sole employment, 1946-. Dir of cos. *Address:* 98 Tudor Avenue, Worcester Park, Surrey. *T:* 01-337 3313, (office) 01-405 8441. *Club:* Royal Automobile.

GARNER, Maurice Richard; post-graduate student of structures of British industrial institutions, University of Kent, since 1974; *b* 31 May 1915; *o s* of Jesse H. Garner; *m* 1943, Joyce W. Chapman; one *s* one *d*. *Educ:* Glendale County Sch.; London Sch. of Economics and Political Science. Royal Armoured Corps, 1942-45 (despatches). Inland Revenue (Tax Inspectorate), 1938-46; BoT, Asst Principal and Principal, 1947; Commercial Sec. and UK Trade Comr in Ottawa, 1948-55; transf. to Min. of Power, 1957; Asst Sec. 1960; Under-Sec., Electricity Div., Min. of Technology, 1969, later DTI, retired 1973. *Recreations:* sailing, reading, oenology. *Address:* Albany Lodge, Staple, Kent CT3 1JX. *T:* Ash 812011.

GARNER, Ronald Arthur; Deputy Chief Valuer (Under-Secretary), Valuation Office, Inland Revenue, since 1974; *b* 25 Feb. 1920; *s* of John Henry Garner, Lieut, RN, and Eliza Kate Garner; *m* 1946, Patricia Mary O'Brien. *Educ:* Devonport High Sch., Plymouth. FRICS. Served with Royal Signals, 1940-46 (despatches 1945). Joined Valuation Office, Inland Revenue, Plymouth, 1936; Suptg Valuer, 1966; Asst Chief Valuer, 1972. *Address:* 8 Oakley Gardens, Chelsea SW3 5QG.

GARNETT, David, CBE 1952; author; *b* 1892; *s* of late Edward and Constance Garnett; *m* 1st, Rachel Alice (*d* 1940), *d* of W. C. Marshall, architect; two *s*; 2nd, 1942, Angelica Vanessa, *o d* of late Clive Bell; four *d*. *Educ:* Royal College of Science, South Kensington. Fellow, Imperial College of Science and Technology, 1956; Hon. DLitt Birmingham, 1977. *Publications:* The Kitchen Garden and its Management; Lady into Fox (Hawthornden and Tait-Black Prizes for 1923); A Man in the Zoo; The Sailor's Return; Go She Must!; The Old Dovecote, 1928; No Love, 1929; The Grasshoppers Come, 1931; A Rabbit in the Air, 1932; Pocahontas, 1933, repr. 1972; Beany-Eye, 1935; War in the Air, 1941; The Golden Echo, 1953; Flowers of the Forest, 1955; Aspects of Love, 1955; A Shot in the Dark, 1958; A Net for Venus, 1959; The Familiar Faces, 1962; Two by Two, 1963; Ulterior Motives, 1966; A Clean Slate, 1971; The Sons of the Falcon, 1972; Purl and Plain, 1973; Plough Over the Bones, 1973; The Master Cat, 1974; Up She Rises, 1977; edited: The Letters of T. E. Lawrence, 1938; The Novels of Thomas Love Peacock, 1948; The Essential T. E. Lawrence, 1951; The White-Garnett Letters, 1968; Carrington: Letters and extracts from her diaries, 1970. *Recreation:* travel. *Address:* Le Verger de Charry, 46 Montcuq, France.

GARNETT, John; see Garnett, W. J. P. M.

GARNETT, Thomas Ronald, MA; Headmaster of Geelong Church of England Grammar School, Australia, 1961-73; *b* 1 Jan. 1915; *s* of E. N. Garnett; *m* 1946, Penelope, *d* of Philip Frere; three *s* two *d*. *Educ:* Charterhouse (Scholar); Magdalene Coll., Cambridge (Scholar). BA 1936, MA 1946. Assistant master: Westminster School, 1936-38; Charterhouse, 1938-52; Master of Marlborough College, 1952-61. Served War of 1939-45, RAF, India and Burma, 1941-46, Squadron Leader (despatches). Cricket for Somerset, 1939. *Recreations:* gardening, ornithology. *Address:* Simmons Reef, Blackwood, via Trentham, Victoria, Australia.

GARNETT, (William) John (Poulton Maxwell), CBE 1970; MA; Director, Industrial Society, since 1962; *b* 6 Aug. 1921; *s* of Dr Maxwell Garnett, CBE, and Margaret Lucy Poulton; *m* 1943, Barbara Rutherford-Smith; two *s* two *d*. *Educ:* Rugby Sch.; Kent Sch., USA; Trinity Coll., Cambridge. Royal Navy, 1941-46 (commnd, 1942). ICI Ltd, 1947-62. Dep. Chm. UNA, 1954-56. Mem., Ct of inquiry into miners' strike, 1972. Mem., Royal Dockyard Policy Bd. *Publications:* The Manager's Responsibility for Communication, 1964; The Work Challenge, 1973, 1977. *Recreations:* sailing, timber construction. *Address:*

31 Charlwood Road, Putney, SW15. *T:* 01-788 5248. *Clubs:* Athenæum; Leander (Henley).
See also P. J. Bottomley.

GARNETT-ORME, Ion; Director, Brown Shipley Holdings Limited (Chairman, 1963-75); Chairman, United States Debenture Corporation Ltd, since 1958; *b* 23 Jan. 1910; *er s* of George Hunter Garnett-Orme and Alice Richmond (*née* Brown); *m* 1946, Katharine Clifton, *d* of Brig.-Gen. Howard Clifton Brown. *Educ:* Eton; Magdalene Coll., Cambridge. Served War, Welsh Guards, 1939-45. Joined: Brown, Shipley & Co, Merchant Bankers, 1945; Bd of London Scottish American Trust Ltd and United States Debenture Corp. Ltd, 1951; Bd of Avon Rubber Co Ltd, 1956-66; Dir, Ellerman Lines Ltd, 1971-75. Chm., St Dunstan's, 1975 (Mem. Council, 1958). *Address:* Founders Court, Lothbury, EC2R 7HE. *Club:* Bath.

GARNHAM, Prof. Percy Cyril Claude, CMG 1964; FRS 1964; MD; Professor of Medical Protozoology (now Emeritus Professor), London University, and Head of Department of Parasitology, London School of Hygiene and Tropical Medicine, 1952-68; Senior Research Fellow, Imperial College Field Station, Ashurst Lodge, Ascot, Berks, since 1968; Visiting Professor, Department of Biology, University of Strathclyde, since 1970; *b* 15 Jan. 1901; *s* of late Lieut P. C. Garnham, RN Division, and late Edith Masham; *m* 1924, Esther Long Price, Talley, Carms; two *s* four *d*. *Educ:* privately; St Bartholomew's Hospital. MRCS, LRCP, 1923, MB, BS London, 1923, DPH Eng. 1924, MD London, 1928 (University Gold Medal); Dipl. de Méd. Malariol., University of Paris, 1931. Colonial Medical Service, 1925-47; on staff of London School of Hygiene and Tropical Medicine, first as Reader, then as Professor, 1947-68, Hon. Fellow, 1976. Heath Clark Lectr, Univ. of London, 1968; Fogarty Internat. Scholar, Nat. Insts of Health, Maryland, 1970, 1972; Manson Orator, 1969, Theobald Smith Orator, 1970. Member, Expert Panel of Parasitic Diseases, of WHO; Hon. Pres., European Fedn of Parasitologists; Past President: British Soc. of Parasitologists; Royal Society of Tropical Medicine and Hygiene; Vice-President: World Federation of Parasitologists; International Association against Filariasis; Corresponding Member: Académies Royales des Sciences d'Outre Mer, et de Médecine, Belgium; Accad. Lancisiana, Rome; Soc. de Geografia da Lisboa; Hon. Member: Amer. Soc. Tropical Medicine: SE Asian Soc. of Parasitology and Tropical Medicine; Société Belge de Médecine Tropicale; Brazilian Soc. Tropical Medicine; Soc. of Protozoologists; Société de Pathologie Exotique (Médaille d'Or, 1971); Acad. Nationale de Médecine, France (Médaille en Vermeil, 1972); Amer. Soc. of Parasitology; Mexican Soc. of Parasitologists; Polish Soc. of Parasitologists; British Soc. of Parasitologists; Groupement des Protistologues de la Langue Française; For. Mem., Danish Royal Acad. of Sciences and Letters, 1976. Hon. FRCP Edinburgh, 1966; FRCP 1967; FIBiol, 1962. Freedom, City of London in Farriers Co., 1964. DSc London, 1952; Hon. Dr, Univ. of Bordeaux, 1965; Academician of Pontifical Acad. of Sciences, 1970. Darling Medal and Prize, 1951; Bernhard Nocht Medal, 1957; Gaspar Vianna Medal, 1962; Manson Medal, 1965; Emile Brumpt Prize, 1970; Mary Kingsley Medal, 1973; Rudolf Leuckart Medal, 1974. *Publications:* Malaria Parasites, 1966; Progress in Parasitology, 1970; numerous papers on parasitology in medical journals. *Recreations:* chamber music and European travel. *Address:* Southernwood, Farnham Common, Bucks. *T:* 3863. *Club:* Nairobi (Kenya).

GARNOCK, Viscount; David Lindesay-Bethune; *b* 9 Feb. 1926; *er s* of 14th Earl of Lindsay, *qv*; *m* 1st, 1953, Hon. Mary Clare Douglas-Scott-Montagu (marr. diss., 1968), *y d* of 2nd Baron Montagu of Beaulieu; one *s* one *d*; 2nd, 1969, Penelope, *er d* of late Anthony Crossley, MP. *Educ:* Eton; Magdalene Coll., Cambridge. Scots Guards, 1943-45. US and Canadian Railroads, 1948-50; Director: John Crossley, Carpet Trades Holdings Ltd, Halifax; Crossley-Karastan Carpet Mills Ltd, Canada; Severn Valley Railway (Holdings) Ltd (Chm.); Festiniog Railway Co. Ltd; Chairman: Romney, Hythe and Dymchurch Light Rly Co., 1976-, Holdings Co., 1976-; Sallingbury Holdings, 1977-; Sallingbury Ltd, 1977-; Director: John Howson Ltd; Abbey Life Insurance Co. of Canada; Bank of Montreal, 1975; Internat. Harvester Co. of GB Ltd, 1977-; Vice-Chm., N American Adv. Gp, BOTB, 1973; Vice-Pres., Transport Trust, 1973; Mem., BTA, 1976-. Chm., British Carpets Export Council, 1976-. Mem., Queen's Body Guard for Scotland (Royal Company of Archers), 1960. *Recreation:* catching up. *Heir:* *s* Master of Garnock, *qv*. *Address:* Combermere Abbey, Whitchurch, Salop. *T:* Burley Dam 287; Kilconquhar House, Fife. *T:* Colinsburgh 291. *Club:* Bath.

GARNOCK, Master of; Hon. James Randolph Lindesay-Bethune; *b* 19 Nov. 1955; *s* and *heir* of Viscount Garnock, *qv*.

Educ: Eton; Univ. of Edinburgh. *Address:* Combermere Abbey, Whitchurch, Salop.

GARNONS WILLIAMS, Basil Hugh; Headmaster of Berkhamsted School, 1953-72; *b* 1 July 1906; 5th *s* of Rev. A. Garnons Williams, Rector of New Radnor; *m* 1943, Margaret Olive Shearme; one *s* two *d. Educ:* Winchester Coll. (Scholar); Hertford Coll., Oxford (Scholar). 1st Hon. Classical Moderations 1927; 2nd Lit Hum 1929; BA 1929; BLitt 1933; MA 1938; Classical VI Form Master, Sedbergh Sch., 1930-35; Marlborough Coll., 1935-45; Headmaster of Plymouth Coll., 1945-53. *Publications:* articles in Classical Quarterly and Greece and Rome; contributor to History of the World (ed by W. N. Weech), 1944. *Address:* 84 High Street, Lavenham, Sudbury, Suffolk CO10 9PT. *T:* Lavenham 247654.

GARNONS WILLIAMS, Captain Nevill Glennie, MBE 1919; Royal Navy (Retired); *b* 1899; *s* of late Rev. Arthur Garnons Williams, Abercamlais, Brecon; *m* 1928, Violet, *d* of late B. G. Tours, CMG; one *d. Educ:* RN Colls, Osborne and Dartmouth; Caius Coll., Cambridge. Joined Royal Navy, 1912; served European War, 1914-18, Jutland (despatches); and War of 1939-45; retired as Captain, 1946. DL 1948, JP 1956, Brecknockshire; Vice-Lieutenant, 1959-64, Lord Lieutenant, 1964-74, Brecknockshire. Mem., Liturgical Commn of Church in Wales; Pres., Brecknock Soc.; Governor, Christ Coll., Brecon. Croix de Guerre (avec Palmes), 1916. KStJ 1973. *Recreations:* forestry, fishing, cricket, scouting. *Address:* Abercamlais, Brecon, Powys. *T:* Sennybridge 206. *Clubs:* Army and Navy, MCC.

GARNSEY, Rt. Rev. David Arthur; *b* 31 July 1909; *s* of Canon Arthur Henry Garnsey and Bertha Edith Frances Garnsey (*née* Benn); *m* 1934, Evangeline Eleanor Wood; two *s* two *d. Educ:* Trinity and Sydney Grammar Schs; St Paul's Coll., University of Sydney; New Coll., Oxford. University of Sydney, BA (1st cl. Latin and Greek) 1930; Travelling Sec. Australian SCM, 1930-31; NSW Rhodes Scholar, 1931, New Coll. Oxford, BA (2nd cl. Lit. Hum.) 1933, 2nd cl. Theol. 1934, MA 1937; Ripon Hall, Oxford, 1933. Deacon, 1934; Priest, 1935; Curate, St Mary the Virgin (University Church), and Inter-Collegiate Sec. of SCM, Oxford, 1934-38; St Saviour's Cathedral, Goulburn, NSW, 1938-41; Rector of Young, NSW, 1941-45; Gen. Sec. Australian SCM, 1945-48; Exam. Chap. to Bp of Goulburn, 1939-45, 1948-58; Head Master Canberra Grammar Sch., 1948-58; Canon of St Saviour's Cathedral, Goulburn, 1949-58; Bishop of Gippsland, 1959-74. Pres., Australian Council of Churches, 1970-73. Chm., Bd of Delegates, Aust. Coll. of Theology, 1971-77; Hon. ThD, Australian Coll. of Theology, 1955. Coronation Medal, 1953. *Publications:* booklets for study. *Recreation:* tennis. *Address:* 33 Dutton Street, Dickson, Canberra 2602, Australia.

GARNSWORTHY, Rt. Rev. Lewis Samuel; *see* Toronto, Bishop of.

GARRAN, Sir (Isham) Peter, KCMG 1961 (CMG 1954); HM Diplomatic Service, retired; Chairman: Quality Assurance Council, British Standards Institution, since 1971; Securicor (Nederland) BV, since 1976; Director, UK Branch, Australian Mutual Provident Society, since 1970; *b* 15 Jan. 1910; *s* of late Sir Robert Randolph Garran, GCMG, QC; *m* 1935, Mary Elisabeth, *d* of late Sir Richard Rawdon Stawell, KBE, MD; two *s* one *d. Educ:* Melbourne Grammar Sch.; Trinity Coll., Melbourne Univ. (BA). Joined Foreign Office, 1934; Foreign posts: Belgrade, 1937-41; Lisbon, 1941-44; Berlin (seconded to CCG as Chief of Political Div.), 1947-50; The Hague, 1950-52; Inspector in HM Foreign Service, 1952-54; Minister (Commercial), Washington, 1955-60; Ambassador to Mexico, 1960-64; Ambassador to the Netherlands, 1964-70. Dir, Lend-Lease Corp., NSW, 1970-78. *Recreation:* gardening. *Address:* Roanoke, Bosham Hoe, Sussex. *T:* Bosham 572347. *Club:* Boodle's.

GARRARD, Henry John; His Honour Judge Garrard; a Circuit Judge (formerly a County Court Judge), since 1965; *b* 15 Jan. 1912; *s* of late C. G. Garrard; *m* 1945, Muriel, *d* of late A. H. S. Draycott, Stratford-on-Avon; one *s* one *d. Educ:* Framlingham Coll., Suffolk. Called to the Bar, Middle Temple, Nov. 1937; Mem. of Oxford Circuit. Served 1939-45, Staffs Yeomanry (QORR) and Worcestershire Regt, East and North Africa, rank of Lieut; prisoner-of-war, 1942-45. Mem. of Mental Health Review Tribunal for Birmingham Area, 1963-65; Recorder of Burton-on-Trent, 1964-65. *Recreations:* family, dogs, country life. *Address:* The General's Farmhouse, Chartley, Stafford. *T:* Dapple Heath 268.

GARRARD, Rev. Lancelot Austin, LLD; BD, MA; Professor of Philosophy and Religion, Emerson College, Boston, USA, 1965-71, now Emeritus; *b* 31 May 1904; *s* of late Rev. W. A. Garrard;

m 1932, Muriel Walsh; two *s. Educ:* Felsted (Scholar); Wadham Coll., Oxford (exhibitioner); Manchester Coll., Oxford; Marburg (Hibbert scholar). 2nd Class, Classical Mods; 2nd Class Lit Hum; Abbot Scholar; BD, MA (Oxon). Asst Master: Edinburgh Acad., 1927; St Paul's Sch., 1928; Unitarian Minister, Dover, 1932-33; Tutor and Bursar, Manchester Coll., Oxford, 1933-43; Minister, Lewins Mead Meeting, Bristol, 1941-43; Liverpool, Ancient Chapel of Toxteth, 1943-52; Tutor, Unitarian Coll., Manchester, 1945-51; Manchester Coll., Oxford, 1952-56; Principal of Manchester Coll., Oxford, 1956-65; Editor of The Hibbert Journal, 1951-62. Hon. Chief, Chickasaw Nation. Hon. LLD (Emerson Coll, Boston). *Publications:* Duty and the Will of God, 1935; The Interpreted Bible, 1946; The Gospels To-day, 1953; The Historical Jesus: Schweitzer's Quest and Ours, 1956; Athens or Jerusalem?, 1965. *Recreation:* cycling. *Address:* 13 Holmlea Road, Goring, Reading, Berks. *Club:* Athenæum.

GARRATT, Gerald Reginald Mansel, MA, CEng, FIEE; FRAeS; retired; Keeper, Department of Aeronautics and Marine Transport, Science Museum, South Kensington, 1966-71; *b* 10 Dec. 1906; *s* of Reginald R. and Florence Garratt; *m* 1931, Ellen Georgina Brooks, Antwerp, Belgium; two *d. Educ:* Marlborough Coll.; Caius Coll., Cambridge. International Telephone & Telegraph Laboratories, 1929-30; RAE, Farnborough, 1930-34; Asst Keeper: Dept of Textiles and Printing, Science Museum, 1934; Dept of Telecommunications, 1936; Dep. Keeper 1949. Served RAF 1939-46 (Wing Comdr). Founder Mem., Cambridge Univ. Air Squadron, 1926. Commissioned RAF Reserve of Officers, 1928; retired 1966 (Wing Comdr). *Publications:* One Hundred Years of Submarine Cables, 1950; The Origins of Maritime Radio, 1972; numerous articles on history of telecommunications. *Recreations:* sailing, amateur radio. *Address:* Littlefield, Parkwood Avenue, Esher, Surrey. *T:* 01-398 1582. *Club:* Royal Automobile.

GARRELS, John Carlyle; retired; Chairman: Monsanto Chemicals Ltd, 1965-71; Monsanto Textiles Ltd, 1970-71; formerly Director: Forth Chemicals Ltd; Monsanto Australia Ltd; Monsanto Oil Co. of UK, Inc.; British Saccharin Sales Ltd; *b* 5 March 1914; *s* of John C. and Margaret Ann Garrels; *m* 1938, Valerie Smith; one *s* two *d. Educ:* Univ. of Michigan (BS (Chem. Eng.); Harvard (Advanced Management Programme). Pennsylvania Salt Mfg Co., Production Supervisor, 1936-42; Monsanto Co.: various appts, 1942-54; Asst Gen. Manager, 1955; Monsanto Chemicals Ltd: Dep. Man. Dir, 1960; Man. Dir, 1961; Chm. and Man. Dir, 1965. Pres., British Plastics Fedn, 1970, 1971. Member: National Economic Development Cttee for Chemical Industry, 1971; Council, Chemical Industries Assoc. *Recreations:* golf, shooting, fishing. *Address:* 3111 SE Fairway West, Stuart, Fla 33494, USA. *T:* 305-283-6132. *Clubs:* American; Sunningdale Golf; Yacht and Country (Stuart, Fla).

GARRETT, Alexander Adnett, MBE 1934; *b* London, 1886; *e s* of late Adnett William Garrett and Marion Walker Bruce; *m* 1928, Mildred (*d* 1975), *g d* of L. S. Starrett, Athol, Mass. *Educ:* Owen's Sch., London; London Sch. of Economics (BSc); King's Coll., London (Gilbart Prizeman); Christ's Coll., Cambridge (Economics Tripos). FCIS; attended the 20th Convention of the American Institute of Accountants, St Louis, USA, 1924; Internat. Congresses on Accounting, Amsterdam, 1926, New York, 1929, and Berlin, 1938; Asst Sec., 4th Internat. Congress on Accounting, London, 1933; sometime Hon. Mem., former Soc. of Incorporated Accountants (Sec. 1919-49, retired 1949; Asst Sec., 1913); visited Accountancy Bodies in Canada, USA, Australia, New Zealand, South Africa, 1947-50. Dept of Applied Economics, Cambridge, 1950-59. Hon. Mem., Australian Soc. of Accountants, 1956. Served Royal Naval Reserve, 1915-31; Comdr (S), RNR (retired). *Publication:* History of the Society of Incorporated Accountants, 1885-1957, 1961. *Address:* 7 King's Bench Walk, Temple, EC4. *T:* 01-353 7880. *Clubs:* Athenæum, Reform.

GARRETT, Lt-Gen. Sir (Alwyn) Ragnar, KBE 1959 (CBE 1944); CB 1957; formerly Chief of the General Staff, Australian Military Forces (1958-60); *b* 12 Feb. 1900; *o s* of Alwyn and Marie Garrett; *m* 1925, Shirley Lorraine Hunter; one *s* one *d. Educ:* Guildford Gram. Sch.; Royal Military Coll., Duntroon. Attached Queen's Bays, India, 1922-23; served with Austr. Mil. Forces, 1923-37; Staff Coll., Camberley, 1938-39; AIF, 1939-46; Comdt, Austr. Staff Coll., 1946; Principal Administrative Officer and Comdt Austr. Component, BCOF, Japan, 1947-49; Comdt Austr. Staff Coll., 1950-51; GOC, Western Command, 1951-52; DCGS Australia, 1953; Adjutant-Gen., 1954; GOC Southern Command, 1954-58; Principal of the Australian Administrative Staff Coll., 1960-65. Chm., Australian Shipping Service, 1966-70. *Recreations:* golf, tennis. *Address:* 16 Blake

Court, Mount Eliza, Victoria, Australia. *Club:* Naval and Military (Melbourne).

GARRETT, Maj.-Gen. Henry Edmund Melvill Lennox, CBE 1975; Vice Adjutant General, Ministry of Defence, since 1976; *b* 31 Jan. 1924; *s* of John Edmund Garrett and Mary Garrett; *m* 1973, Rachel Ann Beadon; one step *s* one step *d*. *Educ:* Wellington Coll.; Clare Coll., Cambridge (MA). Commnd RE, 1944; psc 1956; DAAG, HQ BAOR, 1957-60; US Armed Forces Staff Coll., 1960; OC 7 Field Sqdn RE, 1961-63; GSO2 WO, 1963-65; CO 35 Engr Regt, 1965-68; Col GS MoD, 1968-69; Comdr 12 Engr Bde, 1969-71; RCDS, 1972; Chief of Staff HQ N Ireland, 1972-75; Maj.-Gen. i/c Administration, HQ UKLF, 1975-76. *Recreations:* riding, walking. *Address:* c/o National Westminster Bank Ltd, 24 Kirkgate, Bradford, Yorkshire BD1 1QJ. *Club:* Naval and Military.

GARRETT, John Laurence; MP (Lab) Norwich South since Feb. 1974; *b* 8 Sept. 1931; *s* of Laurence and Rosina Garrett; *m* 1959, Wendy Ady; two *d*. *Educ:* Selwyn Avenue Primary Sch., London; Sir George Monoux Grammar Sch., London; University Coll., Oxford (MA, BLitt); Grad. Business Sch. of Univ. of California at Los Angeles (King George VI Fellow). Labour Officer, chemical industry, 1958-59; Head of Market Research, motor industry, 1959-63; Management Consultant, Dir of Public Services, management consultancy gp, 1963-74. PPS to Minister for Civil Service, 1974, to Minister for Social Security, 1977-. *Publications:* Visual Economics, 1966; (with S. D. Walker) Management by Objectives in the Civil Service, 1969; The Management of Government, 1972; Administrative Reform, 1973; Policies Towards People, 1973 (Sir Frederic Hooper Award); articles and papers on industry, management and govt. *Recreations:* theatre, walking in Norfolk, family life. *Address:* c/o House of Commons, SW1A 0AA.

GARRETT, Sir (Joseph) Hugh, KCIE 1939; CSI 1931; ICS (retired); BA (Cantab); Captain, 10th Devon Bn Home Guard; *b* 22 June 1882; *s* of J. P. Garrett, Highgate; *m* Dilys M. Silvanus; one *d*; *m* 1967, Mrs F. M. Lipson-Ward. *Educ:* Highgate Sch.; Gonville and Caius Coll., Cambridge. Served in various districts of the Bombay Presidency as District Officer in later years chiefly in Gujarat; officiated on several occasions as Chief Sec. to Government of Bombay; Acting Governor of Sind, 1938. *Address:* South Devon Hotel, St Margaret's Road, St Mary Church, Torquay, Devon TQ1 4NP. *Club:* East India, Devonshire, Sports and Public Schools.

GARRETT, Philip Leslie; Editor of The Ironmonger, 1934-53; *b* 11 Nov. 1888; *s* of late Joseph Payne Garrett, Highgate and Eleanor Adelaide Hope; *m* 1914, Phyllis Kathleen (*d* 1972), *d* of late Lewis Medland; two *s* one *d*. *Educ:* Highgate Sch. Admitted a solicitor, 1911; practised in partnership with father; joined editorial staff of The Ironmonger, 1914; Asst Ed., 1926; Mem. of Law Soc. and for many years of Board of Management of Royal Metal Trades Pension and Benevolent Soc.; Hon. Mem. Nat. Federation of Ironmongers and first Hon. Mem. and Governor, Nat. Inst. of Hardware. *Publications:* Literary contributions to various newspapers and periodicals. *Recreations:* ornithology, reading. *Address:* Hilltop, Ballinger, Great Missenden, Bucks. *T:* The Lee 253.

GARRETT, Lieut.-Gen. Sir Ragnar; *see* Garrett, Lieut.-Gen. Sir A. R.

GARRETT, Hon. Sir Raymond (William), Kt 1973; AFC, AEA; JP; President, Legislative Council of Victoria, Australia, 1968-76 (Chairman of Committees, 1964-68); Chairman, Parliamentary Library Committee and Vice-Chairman, House Committee, 1968-76; *b* 19 Oct. 1900; *s* of J. J. P. Garrett, Kew, Australia; *m* 1934, Vera H., *d* of C. E. Lugton; one *s* two *d*. *Educ:* Royal Melbourne Technical Coll.; Univ. of Melbourne. Grad. RAAF Flying Sch., Point Cook, 1926; Citizen Air Force, 1927-37; Commercial Air Pilot, 1927-46. Founded Gliding Club of Vic., and Vic. Gliding Assoc., 1928; British Empire Glider Duration Record, 1931. Served War of 1939-45, RAAF; retd as Gp Captain, 1945 (AFC, AEA). Pres., No 2 Squadron RAAF Asoc. Councillor, Shire of Doncaster and Templestowe, 1954-60; Pres. and Chief Magistrate, 1955-56. Member Legislative Council: for Southern Province, Vic., 1958-70; for Templestowe Province, 1970-76. Member, Statute Law Revision Cttee, 1963-64; Govt Rep. on Council of Monash Univ., 1967-71. Knighted for services in politics, civic affairs and defence, Victoria; Life Governor, Lady Nell Seeing Eye Dog School. Chairman of Directors: Ilford (Aust.) Pty Ltd, 1965-75; Cine Service Pty Ltd. Formerly Pres., Victorian Parly Members' Assoc; Pres., Baden Powell Guild, Victoria. FInstD. *Recreations:* photography, sports cars. *Address:* Flat 4, 24 Tintern Avenue, Toorak, Victoria 3142, Australia. *Clubs:* Royal Automobile, No 10 (London); Air Force (Vic.).

GARRETT, Prof. Stephen Denis, FRS 1967; Professor of Mycology, 1971-73, now Professor Emeritus (Reader 1961-71), and Director of Sub-department of Mycology, 1952-73, University of Cambridge; Fellow of Magdalene College, Cambridge, since 1963; *b* 1 Nov. 1906; *s* of Stephen and Mary Garrett, Leiston, Suffolk; *m* 1934, Ruth Jane Perkins; three *d*. *Educ:* Eastbourne Coll.; Cambridge Univ.; Imperial Coll., London. Asst Plant Pathologist, Waite Agric. Res. Inst., Univ. of Adelaide, 1929-33; Research Student, Imperial Coll., 1934-35; Mycologist, Rothamsted Experimental Stn, 1936-48; Lectr, later Reader, Botany Sch., University of Cambridge, 1949-71. Hon. Mem., British Mycological Soc., 1975. Hon. Fellow, Indian Acad. of Sciences, 1973. *Publications:* Root Disease Fungi, 1944; Biology of Root-infecting Fungi, 1956; Soil Fungi and Soil Fertility, 1963; Pathogenic Root-infecting Fungi, 1970; numerous papers. *Address:* 179 Hills Road, Cambridge CB2 2RN. *T:* Cambridge 47865.

GARRETT, William Edward; MP (Lab) Wallsend since 1964; *b* 21 March 1920; *s* of John Garrett, coal miner, and Frances (*née* Barwise); *m* 1946, Beatrice Kelly; one *s*. *Educ:* Prudhoe Elementary Sch.; London Sch. of Economics. Commenced work in coal mines, 1934; served engineering apprenticeship, 1936-40; employed by ICI, 1946-64; Union Organiser at ICI, 1946-64; Mem. of AEU. Member: Prudhoe UDC, 1946-64; Northumberland County Council, 1955-64. Mem. of Labour Party, 1939-; Labour Candidate for Hexham 1953-55, Doncaster 1957-64. Member: Select Cttee on Agriculture, 1966-69; Expenditure Cttee, 1971-. Parly Adviser, Machine Tools Trades Assoc. *Recreations:* gardening, walking, reading. *Address:* 84 Broomhill Road, Prudhoe-on-Tyne, Tyne and Wear. *T:* Prudhoe 32580. *Club:* Prudhoe Working Men's.

GARRINGTON, Mrs J. L. St C.; *see* Chamberlain, Rev. Elsie D.

GARROD, Prof. Lawrence Paul, MD (Cambridge); FRCP; Vice-President, British Medical Association; Emeritus Professor of Bacteriology, University of London; *b* 7 Dec. 1895; *s* of late Cubitt Garrod and Gertrude Dwelley Davey; *m* 1922, Marjorie, *d* of late Bedford Pierce, MD, FRCP; three *s* one *d*. *Educ:* Sidcot Sch.; King's Coll., Cambridge; St Bartholomew's Hosp. Surg.-Sub-Lieut RNVR 1917-18; Brackenbury Scholar in Medicine, St Bartholomew's Hosp., 1919; Gillson Scholar, Society of Apothecaries, 1923-25; Studied clinical medicine for five years after qualification; from 1925-61 held appointments on staff of Dept of Pathology, St Bartholomew's Hosp.; late Bacteriologist to St Bartholomew's Hosp. and to City of London; Editor, British Jl of Experimental Pathology, 1951-57; late Consultant in Antibiotics to the Army; late Hon. Consultant in Chemotherapy, Royal Postgraduate Med. Sch.; late Examiner in Pathology, Universities of London, Oxford and Cambridge; formerly Pres. Institute of Medical Laboratory Technology. FRSocMed (former Pres. Sect. Pathology). Hon. LLD (Glasgow), 1965. Hon. Alumnus Medical Faculty, University of Louvain. *Publications:* Hospital Infection, 1960-66; Antibiotic and Chemotherapy (jointly), 1963, 4th edn 1973; various papers, mainly on bacteriology and chemotherapy. *Recreations:* music, gardening, golf. *Address:* Stradbroke, Gypsy Lane, Wokingham, Berks.

GARROW, Sir Nicholas, Kt 1965; OBE 1956; JP; retired, 1960; *b* 21 May 1895; *m* 1919; two *s* one *d*. Chm., Northumberland CC, 1952-67 (CC 1925; CA 1937); JP Northumberland, 1936-; Vice-Pres., Royal National Institute for Blind, 1974- (Mem., 1936-); Foundation and Life Mem., Royal Commonwealth Society for the Blind, 1974; Vice-President: North Regional Assoc. for the Deaf, 1975-; Northumberland Playing Fields Assoc., 1975-; Mem., Church of Christ, 1917-, Senior Elder, 1950-. Hon. Alderman, Northumberland CC, 1974. *Address:* 21 Russell Terrace, Bedlington, Northumberland. *T:* Bedlington 823221.

GARRY, Robert Campbell, OBE 1976; Regius Professor of Physiology, University of Glasgow, 1947-70, retired; *b* April 1900; *s* of Robert Garry and Mary Campbell; *m* 1928, Flora Macdonald, *d* of Archibald and Helen Campbell; one *s*. *Educ:* Glasgow Univ. MB, ChB with Hons, Glasgow Univ., 1922; Brunton Memorial Prize; DSc, Glasgow Univ., 1933; continued studies in Freiburg im B, Germany; University Coll., London; Medical Sch., Leeds; Asst and then Lectr, Institute of Physiology, Glasgow Univ.; Head of Physiology Dept, Rowett Research Institute, Aberdeen, 1933-35; Lectr on the Physiology of Nutrition, University of Aberdeen, 1933-35; Prof. of Physiology, University Coll., Dundee, The University of St Andrews, 1935-47; Member: MRC, 1955-59; Sci. Adv. Cttee on Med. Res. in Scotland, 1948-52, 1955-59; Physiol. Sub-Cttee of Flying Personnel Res. Cttee, 1951-75 (Chm., 1967-75); Bd of Management, Hill Farming Res. Orgn, 1963-72. Mem. Physiol. Soc., 1925; foundn Mem., Nutrition Soc., 1941, Pres., 1950-53.

FRSE 1937; FRCPGlas 1948. *Publications:* Papers in scientific periodicals, dealing especially with gastrointestinal physiology and nutrition. *Recreations:* gardening, reading. *Address:* Laich Dyke, Dalginross, Comrie, Perthshire PH6 2HB. *T:* Comrie 474.

GARSIDE, Kenneth; Director of Central Library Services and Goldsmiths' Librarian, University of London, since 1974; *b* 30 March 1913; *s* of Arthur Garside and Ada (*née* Speight); *m* 1951, Anne Sheila Chapman; one *s*. *Educ:* Bradford Grammar Sch.; Univ. of Leeds. BA Mod. Langs 1935, DipEd 1936, MA Spanish 1937. War Service, 1941-46: commnd into Intell. Corps; campaign in NW Europe, 1944-45; GSO2 (Intell.) BAOR, 1946. CO, Univ. of London OTC, 1958-63. Asst Librarian, Univ. of Leeds, 1937-45; Dep. Librarian, UCL, 1945-58; Librarian, King's Coll., London, 1958-74. Mem., Enemy Wartime Publications (Requirements) Cttee, 1946-48; Jt Hon. Sec., Univ. and Res. Section of Library Assoc., 1948-51; Chm., Assoc. of British Theol and Philos. Libraries, 1961-66; Hon. Sec., Council of Mil. Educn Cttees of Univs of UK, 1966-; Sec., Nat. and Univ. Libraries Sect., Internat. Fedn of Library Assocs, 1967-68, Univ. Libraries Sub-Sect., 1967-73; Mem., Univ. of London Cttee on Library Resources, 1968-71; Mem., CNAA Librarianship Bd, 1971-; Mem., British Library Adv. Cttee for Reference Division (Bloomsbury), 1975-. Vice-Chm., British Theatre Museum Assoc., 1971-77. *Publications:* contrib. to literature of librarianship. *Recreations:* travel, wine and food, bird watching. *Address:* Pavilion Cottage, New Road, Esher, Surrey KT10 9NU. *T:* Esher 65157. *Clubs:* Arts, Authors' (Chm. 1969-72).

GARSIDE, Air Vice-Marshal Kenneth Vernon, CB 1962; DFC 1942; Managing Director, Saga Petrochemicals (UK) Ltd; *b* 13 Aug. 1913; *s* of late Dyson Garside, Maidenhead, Berks; *m* 1940, Margery June, *d* of late William Henry Miller, Tanworth-in-Arden; one *s* one *d*. *Educ:* Bradfield Coll.; St John's Coll., Oxford (MA). First commissioned RAF, 1937. Served War of 1939-45 (despatches twice, DFC); Sqdn and War Service in Far East, Mediterranean and Indian Ocean theatres, 1938-44; European theatre, 1944-45. Command and staff appts in UK and USA, 1945-57; Air Cdre 1957; AOC No 16 Group, 1957; Dep. COS, Logistics and Admin., Allied Forces Central Europe, 1958; Dir of Quartering, Air Min., 1959; Air Vice-Marshal 1960; Senior Air Staff Officer, HQ Coastal Command, RAF, 1961-63; AOC No 18 Group, Coastal Command, and Air Officer, Scotland and Northern Ireland, 1963-65. Liveryman, Worshipful Co. of Horners; Freeman of City of London. *Recreations:* rowing (Blue 1936), swimming (Blue 1935). *Address:* Beltons, Cookham Dean, Berks. *Clubs:* Royal Air Force; Vincent's (Oxford); Leander (Henley).

GARSON, Greer; Actress; *b* Northern Ireland, 29 Sept. 1908; *d* of George Garson and Nina Sophia Greer; *m* 1st, Edward A. Shelson (marr. diss.); 2nd, 1943, Richard Ney (marr. diss.); 3rd, 1949, Col E. E. Fogelson, Texas. *Educ:* London and Grenoble Univs. BA Hons London. Birmingham Repertory Theatre, 1932 and 1933; London Theatre debut, Whitehall, 1935; lead roles in 13 London plays; entered films in 1939; *films include:* Goodbye Mr Chips, Pride and Prejudice, When Ladies Meet, Blossoms in the Dust, Mrs Miniver (Academy Award), Random Harvest, Madame Curie, Mrs Parkington, Valley of Decision, That Forsyte Woman, Julius Caesar, The Law and the Lady, Her Twelve Men, Sunrise at Campobello (Golden Globe award), Strange Lady in Town, The Singing Nun, The Happiest Millionaire; *stage appearances include:* Auntie Mame, Tonight at 8.30, Captain Brassbound's Conversion. Appeared in pioneer British TV, on American TV. Hon. DHum, Rollins Coll., Florida, 1950; Hon. Dr in Communication Arts, Coll. of Santa Fe, 1970; Hon. DLitt Ulster, 1977; winner of many awards and medals; current interests include The Greer Garson Theater and Fogelson Library Center, Coll. of Santa Fe; Mem. Bd, Dallas Theater Center; adjunct prof. in drama, S.M.U. Univ., Dallas; Mem., State Commn on the arts in Texas and New Mexico; Mem. Nat. Cttee, St John's Coll., Santa Fe. With husband operates Forked Lightning Ranch, Pecos, New Mexico, also breeding and racing thoroughbred horses (stable includes Ack Ack, horse of the year, 1971). *Recreations:* nature study, music, golf, primitive art. *Address:* Republic Bank Building, Dallas, Texas 75201, USA.

GARSTANG, Cecil, CBE 1969; Director, Thos Cook & Son Ltd, Thos Cook & Son (Continental and Overseas) Ltd and Thos Cook & Son SA Belge, 1964-73 (General Manager, 1960-69, Managing Director, 1969-71); Director and Chairman, 1966-71 of Hernu, Peron & Stockwell Ltd, and England's & Perrott's Ltd; Chairman, Sir Henry Lunn Ltd, and subsidiary companies, 1968-71; *b* 1 Dec. 1904; *s* of Arthur Harold Garstang and Lilian Emma (*née* Meacock); *m* 1930, Winifred Eva Purkiss; two *s*. *Educ:* Salisbury Cath. Sch.; Merchant Taylors' Sch. Joined Thos Cook & Son Ltd, 1924. Served War of 1939-45, Econ. Adv. Br.

of FO and at Supreme HQ of AEF (Lt-Col). Vice-Chm. 1958-59, Chm. 1960-62, Assoc. of British Travel Agents. MTAI. Cavaliere Ufficiale, Order of Merit, Republic of Italy; Commander, Order of the Falcon, Iceland, 1975; Hon. Citizen of New Orleans. *Publications:* various papers on travel and tourism. *Recreations:* travel, reading, gardening. *Address:* 66 Chiltern Avenue, Bushey, Herts. *T:* 01-950 2014. *Clubs:* Travel Luncheon, Skal.

GARSTANG, Walter Lucian, BSc, MA; Headmaster of the Roan School, Greenwich, 1959-68, retired 1968; *b* 2 Sept. 1908; *o s* of late Walter Garstang, MA, DSc; *m* 1933, Barbara Mary, *d* of late Dr S. E. Denyer, CMG, MD; one *s* two *d*. (and one *s* decd). *Educ:* Oundle Sch.; Oxford. Scholar of Trinity Coll., Oxford, 1927-31. Research chemist, The Gas Light and Coke Co., 1931-37; asst master, Oundle Sch., 1937-44; asst master, Merchant Taylors' Sch., 1944-46; senior science master, Maidstone Grammar Sch., 1946-48; Headmaster, Owen's Sch., 1949-54; Headmaster, Loughborough Grammar Sch., 1955-58. *Address:* 6 Clayton Avenue, Hassocks, West Sussex.

GARTHWAITE, Brig. Clive Charlton, CBE 1961; *b* 22 Oct. 1909; *er s* of late Major Alan Garthwaite, DSO, MC, The West Garth, Guisborough, Yorks; *m* 1945, Hon. Elisabeth Clegg-Hill (*née* Smyth-Osbourne) (*d* 1967); one *d*. *Educ:* Wellington Coll., Berks; Royal Military Academy, Woolwich. 2/Lieut Royal Artillery, 1929; Hong Kong 1932-37; Major, 1939. Served in Western Desert, 1941-42 (despatches); GSO1, 1949; Col 1955; Brig. 1959; Comdr 5 Army Group RA, 1956-58; Comdt Sch. of Artillery, Manorbier, 1958-60; Comdr Woolwich Garrison, 1960-63. Retired 1963. ADC 1960-63. *Recreations:* cricket, golf, ski-ing, shooting. *Address:* Larkfield, Bacombe Lane, Wendover, Bucks. *T:* Wendover 622206.

GARTHWAITE, Sir William, 2nd Bt, *cr* 1919; DSC 1941 and Bar, 1942; former Chairman, Sir William Garthwaite (Holdings) Ltd; *b* 3 Jan. 1906; *o s* of Sir William Garthwaite, 1st Bt and Francesca Margherita, *d* of James Parfett; *S* father 1956; *m* 1st, 1931, Hon. Dorothy Duveen (marr. diss., 1937), *d* of 1st Baron Duveen; 2nd, 1945, Patricia Leonard (marr. diss., 1952); one *s*; 3rd, 1957, Patricia Merriel, *d* of Sir Philip d'Ambrumenil; three *s* (one *d* decd). *Educ:* Bradfield Coll., Berks; Hertford Coll., Oxford. Lloyd's Underwriter and Insur. Broker at Lloyd's, 1927-. Contested (C): Hemsworth Div. of W Riding of Yorks, 1931; Isle of Ely, 1935; E Div. of Wolverhampton, 1945. Served War of 1939-45 as pilot, Fleet Air Arm (DSC and bar, despatches thrice, Air Crew Europe Star, Atlantic Star, Africa Star, 1939-45 Star, Defence Medal). Coronation Medal, 1953. *Recreations:* flying, ski-ing, golf and sailing. *Heir:* *s* William Mark Charles Garthwaite, *b* 4 Nov. 1946. *Address:* Garthwaite House, 39 Bell Lane, E1 7LX; Matfield House, Matfield, Kent. *T:* Brenchley 2454. *Clubs:* Bath, Portland, Naval, Royal Automobile, Royal Thames.

GARTON, John Leslie, CBE 1974 (MBE (mil.) 1946); President, Amateur Rowing Association, since 1969 (Committee, 1949); Chairman, Henley Royal Regatta, since 1966 (Steward, 1960); Representative of Amateur Rowing Association, British Olympics Committee, since 1977; *b* 1 April 1916; *er s* of late C. Leslie Garton and Madeline Laurence; *m* 1939, Elizabeth Frances, *d* of late Sir Walter Erskine Crum, OBE; two *s* (and one *s* decd). *Educ:* Eton; Magdalen Coll., Oxford (MA). Commissioned TA, Royal Berkshire Regt, 1938. Served War, in France, 1940; psc 1943; Gen. Staff Ops Br., First Canadian Army HQ, in Europe, 1944-46; transf. to RARO, Scots Guards, 1951. Chm., Coca-Cola Bottling Co. (Oxford) Ltd, 1951-65, Coca-Cola Western Bottlers Ltd, 1966-71. Hon. Sec. and Treas., OUBC Trust Fund, 1959-69; Mem., Finance and Gen. Purposes Cttee, British Olympic Assoc., 1969-77; Thames Conservator, 1970-74; Chm., World Rowing Championships, 1975. Liveryman, Grocers' Company, 1947-. High Sheriff, Bucks, 1977. *Recreations:* supporting the sport of rowing (rowed in Eton VIII, 1934, 1935 (Capt of the Boats, 1935); rowed in the Boat Race for Oxford, 1938, 1939 (Pres. OUBC, 1939), shooting (particularly deer-stalking), fishing. *Address:* Fingest Manor, Henley-on-Thames, Oxfordshire. *T:* Turville Heath 332. *Club:* Leander (elected 1936, Life Mem., 1953, cttee, 1956, Chm. Executive, 1958-59).

GARTON, Prof. William Reginald Stephen, FRS 1969; Professor of Spectroscopy, University of London, Imperial College, since 1964; Associate Head, Department of Physics, Imperial College, since 1970; *b* Chelsea, SW3, 7 March 1912; *s* of William and Gertrude Emma Caroline Garton; *m* 1st, 1940, Margarita Fraser Callingham (marr. diss. 1976); four *d*; 2nd, 1976, Barbara Lloyd (*née* Jones). *Educ:* Sloane Sch., SW10; Chelsea Polytechnic, SW3; Imperial Coll., SW7. BSc, ARCS 1936; DSc 1958. Demonstrator in Physics, Imperial Coll., 1936-39. Served in RAF, 1939-45. Imperial Coll.: Lectr in Physics, 1946-54; Sen. Lectr, 1954-57; Reader, 1957-64. Associate, Harvard Coll. Observatory, 1963-. W. F. Meggers Award, Optical Soc. of America, 1976. Hon DSc, York Univ., Toronto, 1972. *Publications:* contrib. on Spectroscopy in Advances in Atomic and Molecular Physics (ed D. R. Bates), 1966 (New York); numerous papers on Spectroscopy and Atomic Physics. *Recreations:* speliology, Oriental history. *Address:* Department of Physics, Imperial College, SW7. *T:* 01-589 5111; 1 Broomhouse Road, SW6. *T:* 01-736 3454; 7 callé Tico Medina, Mojacar (Almeria), Spain.

GARTRELL, Rt. Rev. Frederick Roy; *see* Columbia, British, Bishop of.

GARVAGH, 5th Baron *cr* 1818; **Alexander Leopold Ivor George Canning;** President, Disaster Relief Association; *b* 6 Oct. 1920; *s* of 4th Baron and Gladys Dora May, *d* of William Bayley Parker; *S* father 1956; *m* 1st, 1947, Christine Edith (marr. diss. 1974), *d* of Jack Cooper; one *s* two *d*; 2nd, 1974, Cynthia Valerie Mary, *d* of Eric E. F. Pretty, CMG, Kingswood, Surrey. *Educ:* Eton; Christ Church, Oxford. Commissioned Corps of Guides Cavalry, Indian Army, 1940; served Burma (despatches). Chairman: Lord Garvagh & Partners Ltd; Stonehaven Tankers Ltd; Independent Chartering Ltd; Director: A.O.D.C. (UK) Ltd; Craftroad Ltd; Consultant Partner, Stummel Towning Co. Member: Baltic Exchange; Court, Painter Stainers Co. MBIM; MIEX; FInstD. *Publications:* contrib. to The Manufacturing Optician, 1949. *Recreations:* travel, motoring, and motor sport; squash; writing articles, short stories, etc. *Heir: s* Hon. Spencer George Stratford de Redcliffe Canning, *b* 12 Feb. 1953. *Address:* 12 South End Row, W8; Lyzzick Gate, Millbeck, Keswick, Cumbria. *Clubs:* Bath, Steering Wheel, No 10 (Inst. of Directors).

GARVEY, Sir Ronald Herbert, KCMG 1950 (CMG 1947); KCVO 1953; MBE 1941; *b* 4 July 1903; *s* of Rev. H. R. Garvey, MA, and Alice M. Lofthouse; *m* 1934, Patricia Dorothy Edge, *d* of Dr V. W. T. McGusty, *qv*; one *s* three *d*. *Educ:* Trent Coll.; Emmanuel Coll., Cambridge. MA 1930; appointed to Colonial Service, 1926, and attached to Western Pacific High Commission, Suva, Fiji; District Officer British Solomon Islands, 1927-32; Asst Sec. Western Pacific High Commission, 1932-40; acted on various occasions as Res. Comr, Gilbert and Ellice Islands Colony; Asst to Res. Comr New Hebrides Condominium, 1940-41; acted as British Res. Comr, New Hebrides, on various occasions; Nyasaland Protectorate, District Officer, 1942-44; Administrator, St Vincent, Windward Islands, BWI, 1944-48; acted as Governor of Windward Is, 1946, 1948; Governor and C-in-C, British Honduras, 1948-52; Governor and C-in-C, Fiji, Governor, Pitcairn Is, Consul-Gen. for Western Pacific, and Senior Commissioner for UK on South Pacific Commission, 1952-58; Lieutenant-Governor of the Isle of Man, 1959-66; Sec., Soil Assoc., 1967-71. Dir, Garvey (London) SA Ltd, 1966. Mem., E Anglia Tourist Bd. KStJ. *Recreations:* golf, deep-sea fishing, gardening. *Address:* The Priory, Wrentham, Beccles, Suffolk.

GARVEY, Sir Terence Willcocks, KCMG 1969 (CMG 1955); HM Diplomatic Service, retired; *b* Dublin, 7 Dec. 1915; *s* of Francis Willcocks Garvey and Ethel Margaret Ray; *m* 1st, 1941, Barbara Hales Tomlinson (marr. diss.); two *s* one *d*; 2nd, 1957, Rosemary, *d* of late Dr Harold Pritchard. *Educ:* Felsted; University Coll., Oxford (Scholar). BA Oxon (1st Class Philosophy, Politics and Economics), 1938; Laming Fellow of The Queen's Coll., Oxford, 1938. Entered Foreign (subsequently Diplomatic) Service, 1938; has served in USA, Chile, Germany, Egypt and at Foreign Office; Counsellor, HM Embassy, Belgrade, 1958-62; HM Chargé d'Affaires, Peking, 1962-65 and Ambassador to Mongolia, 1963-65; Asst Under-Sec. of State, Foreign Office, 1965-68; Ambassador to Yugoslavia, 1968-71; High Comr in India, 1971-73; Ambassador to the USSR, 1973-75. *Recreation:* fishing. *Address:* 11A Stonefield Street, N1 0HW. *Club:* Travellers'.

GARVIN, Clifton Canter, Jr; Chairman of the Board, Exxon Corporation, since 1975; *b* 22 Dec. 1921; *s* of Clifton C. Garvin, Sr, and Esther Ames; *m* 1943, Thelma Volland; one *s* three *d*. *Educ:* Virginia Polytechnic Inst. BSE (ChemEng). Exxon: Process Engr, subseq. Refining Operating Supt, Baton Rouge, Louisiana Refinery, 1947-61; Manager, Supply and Distribution Dept, Exxon Co., USA, Houston, 1961-62; subseq. Vice-Pres., 1962-64; Exec. Asst to Chm., Exxon Corp., NY, 1964-65; Dir, subseq. Exec. Vice-Pres. and Mem. Exec. Cttee, subseq. Pres., Exxon Corp., 1968-75; Chm. of the Bd, Chief Exec. Officer, Chm. of Management Cttee, 1975-. Dir, Treas. and Mem. Exec. Cttee, American Petroleum Inst.; Director: Citicorp and Citibank, PepsiCo, Inc.; NY Urban Coalition; Chm. of Bd and Mem. Exec. Cttee, Council for Financial Aid to Educn. Member: ACS, Amer. Inst. of Chem. Engrs, Business Cttee for the Arts, Inc., Business Council, Business Roundtable, Council on Foreign Relns, Nat. Adv. Council on Minority Engrg, Nat. Petroleum Council, Sloan-Kettering Inst. for Cancer Res., Soc. of Chem. Ind. (Amer. Section), United Way of Amer., Virginia Polytechnic Inst. and State Univ. *Recreations:* golf, bird watching. *Address:* 1251 Avenue of the Americas, New York, NY 10020, USA. *T:* (212) 974-5701. *Clubs:* Blind Brook (Port Chester); The Economic Club of New York; Harvard Business School Club of New York; International (Wash., DC); Links (New York); Stanwich (Greenwich); Twenty-Five Year Club of the Petroleum Industry (Chicago); Augusta National Golf (Augusta).

GARY, Romain, Officier de la Légion d'Honneur; Compagnon de la Libération; Croix de Guerre; author; *b* Tiflis, Georgia, 8 May 1914; *s* of parents named Kacewgary (Kassevgari being the spelling later used); *m* 1st, Lesley Blanch (marr. diss. 1963), *qv*; 2nd, 1963, Jean Seberg (marr. diss.); one *s. Educ:* Lycée de Nice; Aix-en-Provence; Universities of Paris and Warsaw. Served with French Air Force, 1937-40; RAF and Free French Air Force in Africa, Palestine and Russia, 1940-45. Joined French Foreign Service, serving at embassies in UK, Bulgaria and Switzerland; 1st Sec., French Delegation to United Nations; Consul-Gen. for France at Los Angeles, USA, 1956-60. Directed films: Les Oiseaux vont mourir au Pérou, 1968; Kill, 1971. *Publications:* Education Européenne, 1943 (Eng. trans. Forest of Anger; revised as Nothing Important Ever Dies, 1961); Tulipe, 1946; Le Grand Vestiaire, 1949 (Eng. trans. The Company of Men, 1950); Les Couleurs du Jour, 1952 (Eng. trans. Colours of the Day, 1953); Les Racines du Ciel, 1956 (Prix Goncourt, Eng. trans. The Roots of Heaven, 1958); La Promesse de l'Aube, 1959 (Eng. trans. Promise at Dawn, 1962, filmed 1971); Lady L., 1959 (filmed 1965); Frère Océan, 1965; Pour Sganarelle, 1965; La Danse de Gengis Cohn, 1967; La Tête coupable, 1968; Le Mangeur d'étoiles, Adieu Gary Cooper, 1969; Chien Blanc, 1970 (Eng. trans. The White Dog, 1971); Europa, 1972; Les Enchanteurs, 1973; The Gasp, 1973; (as René Deville) Direct Flight to Allah, 1975; Au-delà de cette limite votre ticket n'est plus valable, 1976; The Way Out, 1977. *Address:* c/o Editions Gallimard, 5 rue Sebastien-Bottin, 75007 Paris, France.

GASCH, Mrs Fritz Otto; *see* Baynes, Pauline D.

GASCOIGNE, Bamber, FRSL; author; *b* 24 Jan. 1935; *s* of Derrick Gascoigne and Midi O'Neill; *m* 1965, Christina Ditchburn. *Educ:* Eton (Scholar); Magdalene Coll., Cambridge (Scholar). Commonwealth Fund Fellow, Yale, 1958-59. Theatre Critic, Spectator, 1961-63, and Observer, 1963-64; Co-editor, Theatre Notebook, 1968-74. Theatre: Share My Lettuce, London, 1957-58; Leda Had a Little Swan, New York, 1968; The Feydeau Farce Festival of Nineteen Nine, Greenwich, 1972. Television: presenter of: University Challenge, (weekly) 1962-; Cinema, 1964; (also author) The Christians, 1977; author of: The Four Freedoms, 1962; Dig This Rhubarb, 1963; The Auction Game, 1968. FRSL 1976. *Publications:* Twentieth Century Drama, 1962; World Theatre, 1968; Murgatreud's Empire, 1972; The Heyday, 1973; Ticker Khan, 1974; with photographs by Christina Gascoigne: The Great Moghuls, 1971; The Treasures and Dynasties of China, 1973; The Christians, 1977. *Address:* c/o Curtis Brown, 1 Craven Hill, W2 3EP. *T:* 01-262 1011.

GASCOIGNE, Maj.-Gen. Sir Julian (Alvery), KCMG 1962; KCVO 1953; CB 1949; DSO 1943; DL; *b* 25 Oct. 1903; *e s* of late Brig.-Gen. Sir Frederick Gascoigne, KCVO, CMG, DSO, and Lady Gascoigne, Ashtead Lodge, Ashtead, Surrey; *m* 1928, Joyce Alfreda, *d* of late Robert Lydston Newman and of Mrs Newman; one *s* one *d. Educ:* Eton; Sandhurst. 2nd Lieut Grenadier Guards, 1923; Staff Coll., Camberley, 1938-39; served War of 1939-45, commanding 1st Bn Grenadier Guards, 1941-42; commanding 201 Guards Brigade, 1942-43; North Africa and Italy, 1943 (wounded). Imperial Defence Coll., 1946; Dep. Comdr British Jt Services Mission (Army Staff), Washington, 1947-49. GOC London District and Maj.-Gen. commanding Household Brigade, 1950-53; retired pay, 1953; Mem. of Stock Exchange and Partner in Grievson Grant & Co., 1955-59; Governor and C-in-C Bermuda, 1959-64; Col Commandant, Hon. Artillery Co., 1954-59. Patron, Union Jack Services Clubs, 1977 (Vice-Pres., 1955-64; Pres., 1964-76); a Commr of the Royal Hospital, Chelsea, 1958-59; Chm. Devon and Cornwall Cttee, The National Trust, 1965-75. JP 1966, DL Devon, 1966. KStJ, 1959. *Address:* Sanders, Stoke Fleming, Dartmouth, S Devon. *Clubs:* Cavalry and Guards; Royal Bermuda Yacht.

GASCOIGNE, Hon. Stanley, CMG 1976; OBE 1972; Secretary to the Cabinet, Bermuda, 1972-76; Member, Legislative Council, since 1976; *b* 11 Dec. 1914; *s* of George William Gascoigne and Hilda Elizabeth Gascoigne; *m* 1941, Sybil Wellspring Outerbridge. *Educ:* Mt Allison Univ., Canada (BA 1937): London Univ., England (DipEd 1938): Boston Univ., USA (MEd 1951). Teacher, 1939-51; Inspector of Schools, 1951-59; Director, Marine and Ports Authority, 1959-69; Permanent Sec., Education, 1969-72. *Recreation:* ornithology. *Address:* Alcyone, Shelly Bay, Hamilton Parish, Bermuda. *T:* 3-1304. *Clubs:* Royal Bermuda Yacht, Royal Hamilton Amateur Dinghy (Bermuda).

GASH, Prof. Norman, FBA 1963; FRSL 1973; FRSE 1977; FRHistS; Professor of History, St Salvator's College, University of St Andrews, since 1955; *b* 16 Jan. 1912; *s* of Frederick and Kate Gash; *m* 1935, Dorothy Whitehorn; two *d. Educ:* Reading Sch.; St John's Coll., Oxford. Scholar, St John's Coll.; 1st cl. Hons Mod. Hist., 1933; BLitt, 1934; MA 1938. Temp. Lectr in Modern European History, Edinburgh, 1935-36; Asst Lectr in Modern History, University Coll., London, 1936-40. Served War, 1940-46: Intelligence Corps; Capt. 1942; Major (Gen. Staff), 1945. Lectr in Modern British and American History, St Salvator's Coll., University of St Andrews, 1946-53; Prof. of Modern History, University of Leeds, 1953-55. Fellow Royal Historical Society, 1953; Hinkley Prof. of English History, Johns Hopkins Univ., 1962; Ford's Lectr in English History, Oxford Univ., 1963-64. Vice-Principal, St Andrews Univ., 1967-71. Vice-Pres., Hist. Assoc. of Scotland 1963-64. *Publications:* Politics in the Age of Peel, 1953; Mr Secretary Peel, 1961; The Age of Peel, 1968; Reaction and Reconstruction in English Politics, 1832-1852, 1966; Sir Robert Peel, 1972; Peel, 1976; articles and reviews in Eng. Hist. Review, Trans. Royal Historical Society, and other learned jls. *Recreations:* gardening, swimming. *Address:* Gowrie Cottage, Hepburn Gardens, St Andrews.

GASH, Robert Walker; Chief Executive, Royal County of Berkshire, since 1974; *b* 8 Jan. 1926; *s* of William Edward Gash and Elsie Hutton (*née* Armstrong); *m* 1951, Rosamond Elizabeth Brown; two *s . Educ:* Carlisle Grammar Sch.; Christ Church, Oxford (MA). Solicitor. Asst Solicitor, Cumberland CC, 1955-58; Asst Clerk of Council, Dep. Clerk of Peace, E Suffolk, 1958-68; Dep. Clerk of Council, Dep. Clerk of Peace, Northamptonshire, 1968-72; Clerk of Council, Royal Co. of Berkshire, 1972-74. *Recreations:* Gilbert and Sullivan, crosswords. *Address:* 9 Brocks Way, Shiplake, Henley-on-Thames, Oxon. *T:* Wargrave 3746. *Club:* Berkshire Athenæum (Reading).

GASKILL, William; freelance stage director; Director, Joint Stock Theatre Group, since 1973; *b* 24 June 1930; *s* of Joseph Linnaeus Gaskill and Maggie Simpson. *Educ:* Salt High Sch., Shipley; Hertford Coll., Oxford. Asst Artistic Dir, English Stage Co., 1957-59; freelance Dir with Royal Shakespeare Co., 1961-62; Assoc. Dir, National Theatre, 1963-65; Artistic Director, English Stage Company, 1965-72. *Address:* 124A Leighton Road, NW5.

GASKIN, Catherine; author; *b* Co. Louth, Eire, 2 April 1929; *m* 1955, Sol Cornberg. *Educ:* Holy Cross Coll., Sydney, Australia. Brought up in Australia; lived in London, 1948-55, New York, 1955-67. *Publications:* This Other Eden, 1946; With Every Year, 1947; Dust In Sunlight, 1950; All Else Is Folly, 1951, repr. 1973; Daughter of the House, 1952; Sara Dane, 1955; Blake's Reach, 1958; Corporation Wife, 1960, repr. 1973; I Know My Love, 1962; The Tilsit Inheritance, 1963; The File on Devlin, 1965; Edge of Glass, 1967; Fiona, 1970; A Falcon for a Queen, 1972; The Property of a Gentleman, 1974; The Lynmara Legacy, 1975; The Summer of the Spanish Women, 1977. *Recreations:* music, cinema. *Address:* Ballymacahara, Wicklow, Co. Wicklow, Ireland.

GASKIN, Prof. Maxwell, DFC 1944 (and Bar 1945); Jaffrey Professor of Political Economy, Aberdeen University, since 1965; *b* 18 Nov. 1921; *s* of late Albert and Beatrice Gaskin; *m* 1952, Brenda Patricia, *yr d* of late Rev. William D. Stewart; one *s* three *d . Educ:* Quarry Bank Sch., Liverpool; Liverpool Univ. (MA). Office staff, Lever Bros Ltd, 1939-41. Served War, RAF Bomber Comd, 1941-46. Economist, Raw Cotton Commn, 1949-50; Asst Lectr, Liverpool Univ., 1950-51; Lectr and Sen. Lectr, Glasgow Univ., 1951-65; Visiting Sen. Lectr, Nairobi Univ., 1964-65. Member, Committee of Inquiry: into Bank Interest Rates (N Ire.), 1965-66; into Trawler Safety, 1967-68; Mem. and Chm., Bd of Management for Foresterhill and Associated Hosps, 1971-74; Independent Mem., Scottish Agricl Wages Bd, 1972-; Chm., Industry Strategy Cttee for Scotland (Building and Civil Engrg EDCs), 1974-76. *Publications:* The Scottish Banks, 1965; (co-author and ed) North East Scotland: a survey of its development potential, 1969; articles in economic and banking jls. *Recreations:* music and country life. *Address:* 6

Westfield Terrace, Aberdeen AB2 4RU. *T:* Aberdeen 51614. *Club:* Royal Commonwealth Society.

GASS, Sir Michael David Irving, KCMG 1969 (CMG 1960); HM Overseas Civil Service, retired; *b* 24 April 1916; *e s* of late George Irving Gass and late Norah Elizabeth Mustard; *m* 1975, Elizabeth Periam, *e d* of late Hon. John Acland-Hood, Wootton House, near Glastonbury. *Educ:* King's Sch., Bruton; Christ Church, Oxford (MA); Queens' Coll., Cambridge (BA). Appointed Colonial Administrative Service, Gold Coast, 1939. Served War of 1939-45 (despatches twice) with The Gold Coast Regt, RWAFF; East Africa, Burma; Major. District Commissioner, Gold Coast, 1945; Asst Regional Officer, Ashanti, 1953-56; Permanent Sec., Ministry of the Interior, Ghana, 1956-58; Chief Sec. to the Western Pacific High Commission, 1958-65; Acting High Commissioner for the Western Pacific for periods in 1959, 1961, 1963 and 1964; Colonial Secretary, Hong Kong, 1965-69; Actg Governor, Hong Kong, for periods in 1966, 1967, and 1968; High Comr for W Pacific and British High Comr for New Hebrides, 1969-73. Mem., Somerset CC, 1977-. *Recreation:* ornithology. *Address:* Broadway, Butleigh Wootton, Glastonbury, Somerset. *T:* Street 42856; Fairfield, Stogursey, Bridgwater, Som. *T:* Nether Stowey 251. *Clubs:* East India, Devonshire, Sports and Public Schools; Hong Kong (Hong Kong).

GASSMAN, Lewis, JP; a Recorder of the Crown Court, since 1972; 2nd *s* of late Isaac Gassman and Dora Gassman; *m* 1940, Betty Henrietta, *o c* of late H. Jerrold and Mrs A. F. Annenberg; one *d. Educ:* Sloane Sch.; Law Society's Sch. of Law. Admitted Solicitor, 1933. Borough of Barnes: Councillor and Chm. of Cttees, 1933-41. War of 1939-45: Army service, Capt. RAOC. JP Surrey, 1948, also SW London; Chm., Mortlake Magistrates, 1953-56 and 1961-71. Consultant in law firm of Kershaw, Gassman & Matthews. Mem., Law Society's Standing Cttee on Criminal Law, 1968; a Dep. Chm. of Surrey Quarter Sessions, 1968-71; Chm. of Magistrates, Richmond-upon-Thames, 1971-74. *Recreations:* music, painting, walking. *Address:* 21 Castelnau, Barnes, SW13 9RP. *T:* 01-748 7172. *Club:* Reform.

GATACRE, Rear-Adm. Galfry George Ormond, CBE 1960; DSO 1952; DSC 1941 (and Bar 1942); Company Director; *b* Wooroolin, Australia, 11 June 1907; *s* of R. H. W. Gatacre, Bath, Somerset, and Wooroolin, and of C. E. Gordon, Banchory, Scotland; *m* 1933, Wendy May, *d* of E. A. Palmer, Sydney, Australia; one *s* one *d. Educ:* Brisbane Boys' Coll.; Royal Australian Naval Coll. Service at sea has been in HM and HMA ships around the world. Lieut 1930; Lieut-Comdr 1938; Comdr 1942; Capt. 1948; Rear-Adm. 1958. Australian Naval Attaché in USA, 1953-55; Command of HMAS Melbourne, 1955-56; Dep. Chief of Naval Staff, 1957-58; Flag Officer Comdg HM Australian Fleet, 1959; Head, Australian Joint Services Staff in USA, 1960-61; Flag Officer East Australian Area, 1962-64. *Recreations:* golf, tennis. *Address:* 76 Newcastle Street, Rose Bay, Sydney, Australia. *Club:* Royal Sydney Golf.

GATEHOUSE, Robert Alexander, QC 1969; *b* 30 Jan. 1924; *s* of late Major-Gen. A. H. Gatehouse, DSO, MC; *m* 1st, 1951, Henrietta Swann; 2nd, 1966, Pamela Fawcett. *Educ:* Wellington Coll.; Trinity Hall, Cambridge. Served War of 1939-45: commissioned into Royal Dragoons; NW Europe. Called to the Bar, Lincoln's Inn, 1950. Governor, Wellington Coll., 1970-. *Recreation:* golf. *Address:* 1 Brick Court, Temple, EC4. *T:* 01-353 0777.

GATES, Ernest Everard, MA; formerly Company Director, now retired; *b* 29 May 1903; *o c* of Ernest Henry Gates, Old Buckenham Hall, Norfolk, and Eva, *y d* of George Siggs, JP, Streatham; *m* 1931, Stella, *y d* of Henry Knox Simms. *Educ:* Repton; Corpus Christi Coll., Cambridge. Formerly a director, Manchester Chamber of Commerce (1945-51), and various other companies. Gazetted Lieut RA Sept. 1939; Major, 1941. MP (C) Middleton and Prestwich Div. of Lancs, May 1940-Oct. 1951. PPS to Rt Hon. W. S. Morrison, Min. of Town and Country Planning, 1943-45. *Recreations:* shooting, fishing, stalking, ski-ing, golf, travel. *Address:* Pride's Crossing, Ascot, Berks. *T:* Ascot 22330. *Club:* Portland.

GATES, Thomas S(overeign), Jr; *b* Philadelphia, 10 April 1906; *s* of Thomas Sovereign Gates and Marie (*née* Rogers); *m* 1928, Millicent Anne Brengle; three *d* (one *s* decd). *Educ:* Chestnut Hill Acad.; University of Pennsylvania (AB). Joined Drexel & Co., Philadelphia, 1928; Partner, 1940-. War Service, 1942-45 (Bronze Star, Gold Star): US Naval Reserve (Capt.). Under-Sec. of Navy, 1953-57; Sec. of the Navy, 1957-59; Dep. Sec. of Defense, 1959; Sec. of Defense, USA, Dec. 1959-Jan. 1961. Director: Morgan Guaranty Trust Co., 1971- (Chm., Exec. Cttee, 1961-62, 1965-68, 1969-71; Pres., 1962-65); Bethlehem

Steel Corp.; General Electric Co.; Campbell Soup Co.; Insurance Co. of N America; Philadelphia Contributionship for Insce of Houses from Loss by Fire; Scott Paper Co. Chief of US Liaison Office, Peking, 1976-77. Life Trustee, University of Pennsylvania. Hon. LLD: University of Pa, 1956; Yale Univ. 1961; Columbia Univ. 1961. *Address:* Mill Race Farm, Devon, Pennsylvania, USA; 1 East 66 Street, NYC, USA. *Clubs:* Philadelphia, Racquet (Philadelphia); The Links (NYC); Metropolitan (Washington, DC); Gulph Mills Golf.

GATES, William Thomas George, CBE 1967; Chairman, West Africa Committee, London, 1961-76; *b* 21 Jan. 1908; *s* of Thomas George and Katherine Gates; *m* 1938, Rhoda (*née* Sellars), *d* of Mrs W. E. Loveless; two *s. Educ:* Ilford County High Sch., National Bank of New Zealand, London, 1925-30; John Holt & Co. (Liverpool) Ltd, resident Nigeria, 1930-46; Gen. Manager: Nigeria, 1940; Gold Coast, 1947; Liverpool, 1947; Man. Dir, 1956; Dep. Chm., 1964; retired, 1967. MLC, Nigeria, 1940-46; Director: W African Airways Corp, 1941-46; Edward Bates & Sons (Holdings) Ltd, 1964-70; Edinburgh & Overseas Investment Trust Ltd, Edinburgh, 1964-71. Dist Scout Comr, Northern Nigeria 1940-42; Mem. Liverpool Dist Cttee, Royal National Life-Boat Instn, 1956-73; Mem. Bd of Govs, United Liverpool Hosps, 1958-70; Gen. Comr of Income Tax, 1967-73; Chm., Liverpool Porterage Rates Panel, 1969-74. Chm., Royal African Soc., 1975-77. *Recreations:* golf, fishing, cricket, gardening. *Address:* Stonelands, Bramley, Surrey GU5 0LU. *T:* Hascombe 292. *Clubs:* Travellers', Royal Liverpool Golf (Hoylake).

GATHORNE-HARDY, family name of **Earl of Cranbrook.**

GATTIE, Maj.-Gen. Kenneth Francis Drake, DSO 1917; MC; DL; *b* 22 April 1890; *s* of late Walter Montagu Gattie and Catherine Anne, *d* of late Rev. T. R. Drake. *Educ:* Tonbridge Sch. Commissioned 3rd Monmouthshire Regt, 1910; served on Western front, 1915-Armistice; Adjutant, 3rd Monmouthshire Regt, 1915; Brigade Major, 75th Infantry Brigade, 1916; Capt., South Wales Borderers, 1917; Gen. Staff, GHQ, 1918 (MC, DSO, despatches five times); Brigade Major, Rhine Army, 1919; served in India, 1919-22 and in 1924; psc, Camberley, 1923; Gen. Staff Officer, War Office, 1924; Brevet Major, 1926; Brigade Major, Rhine Army, 1927; Instructor in Tactics, Sch. of Artillery, 1929; DAA and QMG, Highland Area, 1931; Brevet Lieut-Col, 1931; Major, 1934; GSOII, 43rd (Wessex) Division, 1935-37; Lieut-Col 1937; Commanded 1st Bn Queen's Royal Regt (West Surrey) 1937-38; Col, 1938; Commander 2nd (Rawalpindi) Infantry Brigade, India, 1938; acting Maj.-Gen., 1941; temp. Maj.-Gen.; District Commander, India, 1941; retired pay, 1945. DL Brecknock, 1954. *Address:* Tymawr, Llyswen, Brecon, Powys.

GAUDRY, Roger, CC (Canada) 1968; DSc, FRSC; President, International Association of Universities, since 1975; *b* 15 Dec. 1913; *m* 1941, Madeleine Vallée; two *s* three *d. Educ:* Laval Univ. (BA 1933; BSc 1937; DSc 1940); Rhodes Scholar, Oxford Univ., 1937-39. Organic Chemistry, Laval Univ.: Lectr, 1940; Prof., 1945; Full Prof., 1950. Ayerst Laboratories: Asst Dir of Research, 1954; Dir of Research, 1957; Vice-Pres. and Dir of Research, 1963-65. Chm., Science Council of Canada, 1972-75; Rector, Univ. of Montreal, 1965-75. Chm. Bd, UN Univ., 1974-. Parizeau Medal from Assoc. Canadienne Française pour l'Avancement des Sciences, 1958. Hon. doctorates: (Laws) Univ. of Toronto, 1966; (Science) RMC of Kingston, 1966; (Science) Univ. of BC, 1967; (Laws) McGill Univ., 1967; Univ. of Clermont-Ferrand, France, 1967; (Laws) St Thomas Univ., 1968; (Laws) Brock Univ., 1969; (Civil Laws) Bishop's Univ., 1969; (Science) Univ. of Saskatchewan, 1970; (Science) Univ. of Western Ontario, 1976; Hon. Fellow, RCPS (Can.) 1971. *Publications:* author and co-author of numerous scientific papers in organic and biological chemistry. *Address:* 445 Beverley Avenue, Town of Mount Royal, Montreal, PQ H3P 1L4, Canada. *Club:* St Denis (Montreal).

GAULD, William Wallace; Under-Secretary, Department of Agriculture and Fisheries for Scotland, since 1972; *b* 12 Oct. 1919; *e s* of late Rev. W. W. Gauld, DD, of Aberdeen, and Charlotte Jane Gauld (*née* Reid); *m* 1943, Jean Inglis Gray; three *d. Educ:* Fettes; Aberdeen Univ. MA (1st Cl. Hons Classics). Served Pioneer Corps, 1940-46 (Major 1945). Entered Dept of Agriculture for Scotland, 1947; Private Sec. to Secretary of State for Scotland, 1955-57; Asst Sec., 1958; Scottish Development Dept, 1968-72; Mem. Agricultural Research Council, 1972-. *Recreations:* natural history, hill walking. *Address:* c/o Gauld, 27 Raeden Avenue, Aberdeen AB2 4LP. *Club:* Royal Commonwealth Society.

GAULT, Charles Alexander, CBE 1959 (OBE 1947); retired from HM Foreign Service, 1959; *b* 15 June 1908; *o s* of late Robert Gault, Belfast, and late Sophia Ranken Clark; *m* 1947, Madge, *d* of late William Walter Adams, Blundellsands; no *c. Educ:* Harrow; Magdalene Coll., Cambridge. Entered Levant Consular Service, 1931; served in Egypt, Persia, Saudi Arabia, at Foreign Office, India (on secondment to Commonwealth Relations Office), Libya, Israel, Bahrain (HM Political Agent, 1954-59). *Recreation:* walking. *Address:* 103 Old Bath Road, Cheltenham, Glos. *Club:* Oriental.

GAULT, David Hamilton; Executive Chairman, Gallic Management Co. Ltd, since 1974; *b* 9 April 1928; *s* of Leslie Hamilton Gault and Iris Hilda Gordon Young; *m* 1950, Felicity Jane Gribble; three *s* two *d. Educ:* Fettes Coll., Edinburgh. Nat. Service, commnd in RA, 1946-48; Clerk, C. H. Rugg & Co. Ltd, Shipbrokers, 1948-52; H. Clarkson & Co. Ltd, Shipbrokers: Man. 1952-56; Dir 1956-62; Jt Man. Dir 1962-72; Gp Man. Dir, Shipping Industrial Holdings Ltd, 1972-74; Chm., Jebsen (UK) Ltd, 1962-; Chm., Seabridge Shipping Ltd, 1965-73. *Recreations:* gardening, walking. *Address:* Telegraph House, North Marden, Chichester, West Sussex. *T:* Harting 206. *Clubs:* Boodle's, City; India House (New York).

GAUNT, Rev. Canon Howard Charles Adie; Precentor, Winchester Cathedral, 1967-73; Sacrist, 1963 and Hon. Canon, 1966, Canon Emeritus, since 1974; *b* 13 Nov. 1902; *s* of C. F. Gaunt, Edgbaston; *m* 1927, Mabel Valery, *d* of A. E. Bond, Wannerton, near Kidderminster; two *s. Educ:* Tonbridge Sch.; King's Coll., Cambridge. Asst Master: King Edward's Sch., Birmingham, 1928-29; Rugby Sch., 1929-37; Headmaster, Malvern Coll., 1937-53; Chaplain, Winchester Coll., 1953-63. Select Preacher, Universities of Oxford and Cambridge. *Publications:* Two Exiles: A School in Wartime, 1946; School: A Book for Parents, 1950. *Address:* 57 Canon Street, Winchester.

GAUNT, William; Author and Painter; *b* Hull, 1900; *s* of William and Harriet Gaunt; *m* 1935, Mary Catherine O'Reilly (*née* Connolly). *Educ:* Hull Gram. Sch.; Worcester Coll., Oxford. BA Oxon 1922; MA 1926; AICA; Editor of numerous illustrated works, mainly on the Fine Arts. Exhibitions of paintings and drawings at Redfern Gallery, 1930; Leger Gallery, 1932; Reid and Lefevre Galls, 1936; Walker Galls., 1947; retrospective exhbn, Colchester, Hull and London, 1975. Art critic, Evening Standard, 1946; Special Correspondent to The Times on Art Subjects, 1957-. *Publications:* Bandits in a Landscape, 1937; The Pre-Raphaelite Tragedy, 1942; (with F. G. Roe) Etty and the Nude, 1943; British Painting, 1945; (ed) Hogarth, 1947; (ed) William Morris: selections, 1948; The March of the Moderns, 1949; Victorian Olympus, 1952; (with J. Riddell) London in Colour, 1955; Renoir, 1952, 2nd edn, 1971; Chelsea, 1954; The Lady in the Castle (novel), 1956; Arrows of Desire, 1956; Teach Yourself to Study Sculpture, 1957; Kensington, 1958; The Observer's Book of Painting and Graphic Art, 1958; London, 1961; Everyman's Dictionary of Pictorial Art, 1962; ed, G. Vasari, Lives of the Painters, Sculptors and Architects, 1963; A Concise History of English Painting, 1964; The Observer's Book of Modern Art, 1964; Oxford, 1965; The Observer's Book of Sculpture, 1966; A Companion to Painting, 1968; Flemish Cities, 1970; The Impressionists, 1970; The Great Century of English Painting, 1971; Turner, 1971; William de Morgan, 1971; The Restless Century, 1972; The Surrealists, 1972; Painters of Fantasy, 1974; Marine Painting, 1975. *Address:* 35b Lansdowne Road, W11. *T:* 01-727 6762.

GAUNT SUDDARDS, H.; *see* Suddards.

GAUSDEN, Ronald; Chief Inspector, Nuclear Installations Inspectorate, since 1976; *b* 15 June 1921; *s* of Jesse Charles William Gausden and Annie Gausden (*née* Durrant); *m* 1943, Florence May (*née* Ayres); two *s* two *d. Educ:* Varndean Grammar Sch., Brighton; Brighton Techn. Coll. and Borough Polytechnic. CEng, FIEE. RN Sci. Service, 1943-47; AERE, Harwell, 1947-50; UKAEA Windscale Works, Cumbria: Instrument Engr, 1950-53; Asst Gp Man., 1953-55; Gp Man., 1955-60; Nuclear Installations Inspectorate: Principal Inspector, 1960-63; Asst Chief Inspector, 1963-73; Dep. Chief Inspector, 1973-75. *Publications:* contrib. Brit. Nuclear Energy Soc. and Inst. Nuclear Engrs. *Recreations:* golf, shooting, fishing. *Address:* Granary Cottage, Itchingfield, near Horsham, Sussex. *T:* Slinfold 790646.

GAUTIER-SMITH, Peter Claudius, FRCP; Physician, National Hospitals for Nervous Diseases, Queen Square and Maida Vale, since 1962; Dean, Institute of Neurology, since 1975; *b* 1 March 1929; *s* of late Claudius Gautier-Smith and Madeleine (*née* Ferguson); *m* 1960, Nesta Mary Wroth; two *d. Educ:* Cheltenham Coll. (Exhibnr); King's Coll., Cambridge; St

Thomas's Hosp. Med. Sch. MA, MD. Casualty Officer, House Physician, St Thomas' Hosp., 1955-56; Medical Registrar, University Coll. Hosp., 1958; Registrar, National Hosp., Queen Suare, 1960-62; Consultant Neurologist, St George's Hosp., 1962-75. Mem., Bd of Governors, Nat. Hosps for Nervous Diseases, 1975-. *Publications:* Parasagittal and Falx Meningiomas, 1970; papers in learned jls on neurology. *Recreations:* literary (eight novels published under a pseudonym); squash (played for Cambridge v Oxford, 1951; Captain, London Univ., 1954); tennis. *Address:* Institute of Neurology, Queen Square, WC1N 3BG. *T:* 01-837 3611. *Clubs:* MCC, Hawks, Jesters.

GAUTREY, Peter, CMG 1972; CVO 1961; DK (Brunei) 1972; HM Diplomatic Service; High Commissioner in Guyana, since 1975; *b* 17 Sept. 1918; *s* of late Robert Harry Gautrey, Hindhead, Surrey, and Hilda Morris; *m* 1947, Marguerite Etta Uncles; one *s* one *d. Educ:* Abbotsholme Sch., Derbys. Joined Home Office, 1936. Served in Royal Artillery, (Capt.), Sept. 1939-March 1946. Re-joined Home Office; Commonwealth Relations Office, 1948; served in British Embassy, Dublin, 1950-53; UK High Commission, New Delhi, 1955-57 and 1960-63; British Deputy High Commissioner, Bombay, 1963-65; Corps of Diplomatic Service Inspectors, 1965-68; High Comr, Swaziland, 1968-71, Brunei, 1972-75. FRSA 1972. *Recreations:* golf, music, art. *Address:* 24 Fort Road, Guildford, Surrey. *Clubs:* Royal Commonwealth Society, Royal Automobile.

GAUVAIN, (Catherine Joan) Suzette, (Mrs R. O. Murray); Deputy Director of Medical Services, since 1975, and Consultant Advisor on Medical Training, since 1977, Health and Safety Executive; *d* of late Sir Henry Gauvain, MD, MCh, FRCS, and Laura Louise (*née* Butler); *m* 1940, Ronald Ormiston Murray, *qv*; one *s* two *d. Educ:* St James', West Malvern; Grovely Manor, Boscombe; Somerville Coll., Oxford (MA); Radcliffe Infirmary, Oxford. MRCP, FFCM, DPH, DIH. MO, Lord Mayor Treloar Orthop. Hosp., 1943-54; London Sch. of Hygiene and Trop. Med., 1958-73: Dept of Occupational Health, later TUC Centenary Inst. of Occupational Health: Research Asst, 1960-62; Lectr, 1962-69; Sen. Lectr, 1969-73; Employment Med. Adv. Service, Dept of Employment, 1973-: Dep. Chief Employment Med. Adviser, 1973-74; Actg Ch. Employment Med. Adviser, 1974-76. Mem. Permanent Commn, Internat. Assoc. of Occupational Health; Past Chm., London Assoc. of Soc. of Occupational Medicine; Past Pres., London Gp Med. Women's Fedn; Pres., Occupational Med. Sect., RSocMed, 1975-76. Chadwick Lectr, 1975. *Publications:* Occupational Health, a guide to sources of information, 1968, ed 2nd edn 1974; (chapters) Occupational Health Practice, ed Schilling, 1973; papers in BMJ, Lancet, Brit. Jl Occupational Med., Jl Soc. of Occupational Med., etc. *Recreations:* gardening, travelling. *Address:* Pond House, Well, Long Sutton, Basingstoke, Hants. *T:* Long Sutton (Hants) 297. *Club:* Lansdowne.

GAVEY, Clarence John, MD, FRCP; Consulting Physician (Cardiologist) to Westminster Hospital London, Moorfields Eye Hospital and Edenbridge and District War Memorial Hospital; *b* 20 June 1911; 2nd *s* of late Walter John Gavey, Jurat of Royal Court, Guernsey; *m* 1937, Marjorie, *d* of late John Guille, Guernsey; three *d. Educ:* Elizabeth College, Guernsey; London Hospital Medical Sch., Buxton Prize in Anat. and Phys.; MRCS LRCP 1934; MB, BS, London 1934. Formerly Emergency Officer, Ho. Phys., Ho. Phys. to Cardiac Dept, Paterson Schol. and Chief Asst, Cardiac Dept, London Hosp.; Chief Med. Asst, Westminster Hosp. MD London 1936, MRCP 1936, FRCP 1948. Past Examnr in Medicine for London Univ., RCP, University Coll. of West Indies. Goulstonian Lecturer, Royal College of Physicians London, 1949; Buckston Brown Medal, Harveian Soc. London 1950; FRSM (Past Mem. Council and Vice-Pres., Section of Medicine); Mem. Assoc. of Physicians of Gt Britain and Ireland; Mem. Internat. Soc. of Internal Medicine; Mem. British Cardiac Soc.; Mem. London Cardiological Club; Mem. Harveian Soc. of London; Mem. Ophthalmic Soc. of UK. Hon. Lieut-Col RAMC; served MEF, 1942-46. *Publications:* The Management of the "Hopeless" Case, 1952; cardiac articles in French's Differential Diagnosis of Main Symptoms, 1967; various papers in Lancet, Brit. Med. Jl, Brit. Heart Jl, etc. *Address:* Tissington House, 37 Castlemaine Avenue, S Croydon CR2 7HU. *T:* 01-688 4051.

GAVIN, Maj.-Gen. James Merricks Lewis, CB 1967; CBE 1963 (OBE 1953); Director, British Standards Institution, 1967-76; *b* Antofagasta, Chile, 28 July 1911; *s* of Joseph Merricks Gavin; *m* 1942, Barbara Anne Elizabeth, *d* of Group Capt. C. G. Murray, CBE; one *s* two *d. Educ:* Uppingham Sch.; Royal Military Academy; Trinity Coll., Cambridge. 2nd Lieut Royal Engineers, 1931. Mem. Mt Everest Expedn, 1936. Instructor, Royal

Military Academy, 1938; Capt. 1939; served War of 1939-45 in Far East, Middle East, Italy, France, including special operations; Brit. Jt Services Mission, Washington, 1948-51; Commanding Officer, 1951-53; Col Staff Coll., Camberley, 1953-55; BAOR, 1956-58; Comdt (Brig.) Intelligence Centre, Maresfield, 1958-61; Maj.-Gen. 1964; Asst Chief of Staff (Intelligence), SHAPE, 1964-67. Col Comdt, RE, 1968-73. FRSA 1968. *Recreations:* mountaineering, sailing, ski-ing. *Address:* Littlewick Meadow, Knaphill, Surrey. *Clubs:* Naval and Military, Royal Ocean Racing, Alpine.

GAVIN, Malcolm Ross, CBE 1966 (MBE 1945); MA, DSc, CEng, FIEE, FInstP; Chairman of Council, Royal Dental Hospital School of Dental Surgery, University of London, since 1974; *b* 27 April 1908; 3rd *s* of James Gavin; *m* 1935, Jessie Isobel Hutchinson; one *s* one *d. Educ:* Hamilton Acad.; Glasgow Univ. Mathematics Teacher, Dalziel High Sch., Motherwell, 1931-36; Physicist, GEC Res. Labs, Wembley, 1936-47; HMI, Scottish Education Dept, 1947-50; Head of Dept of Physics and Mathematics and Vice-Principal, College of Technology, Birmingham, 1950-55; Prof. of Electronic Engrg and Head of Sch. of Engrg Sci, University Coll. of N Wales, 1955-65; Principal, Chelsea Coll., Univ. of London, 1966-73; Dir, Fulmer Res. Inst., 1968-73. Member: Electronics Res. Coun., Min. of Aviation, 1960-64; Res. Grants Cttee of DSIR (Chm., Electrical and Systems Sub-Cttee, 1964-65); SRC (Mem. Univ. Sci. and Tech. Bd and Chm. Electrical Sub-Cttee, 1965-69, Chm. Control Engineering Cttee, 1969-73; Mem. Engineering Bd, 1969-73); Inter-Univ. Council for Higher Education Overseas, 1967-74; UGC, Hong Kong, 1966-76; Council, European Physical Soc., 1968-70; Murray Cttee, Univ. of London, 1970-72; Council, N Wales Naturalist Trust, 1973-; Council, University Coll. of North Wales, 1974-; Visitor, Nat. Inst. Industrial Psychology, 1970-74; Pres. Inst. of Physics and Physical Soc., 1968-70 (Vice-Pres., 1964-67). Hon. ACT, Birmingham, 1956; Hon. DSc (Ife), 1970. Hon. Fellow, Chelsea Coll. *Publications:* Principles of Electronics (with Dr J. E. Houldin), 1959. Numerous in Jl of IEE, Brit. Jl of Applied Physics, Wireless Engineer, Jl of Electronics, etc. *Recreations:* gardening, walking. *Address:* Swn-y-don, Penmon, Beaumaris, Gwynedd. *T:* Llangoed 234. *Clubs:* Athenæum; Royal Anglesey Yacht.

GAVITO, Vicente S.; *see* Sanchez-Gavito.

GAWNE, Ewan Moore, CSI 1945; CIE 1942; *b* 26 March 1889; *s* of Col J. M. Gawne; *m* 1946, Muriel Henderson (*d* 1947), Camberley. *Educ:* Wellington; Brasenose Coll., Oxford. Entered ICS, 1913; Mem., Board of Revenue, Madras, 1940; retd 1946. *Address:* Vine Cottage, South Warnborough, Basingstoke, Hants.

GAWTHORPE, Brig. John Bernard, CBE 1939; TD; Major (Hon. Brig.) (retired pay), late The West Yorkshire Regiment (Prince of Wales' Own); *b* Ossett, Yorks, 12 Nov. 1891; *e s* of late John H. Gawthorpe, Roundhay, Leeds; *m* 1915, Clarice Turner (*d* 1956), Roundhay; one *d. Educ:* Wakefield; Leeds. Territorial Army: 2nd Lieut 1911; Lieut 1913; Capt. 1915; Regular Army: Capt. (West Yorks Regt) 1917; Temp. Major (Machine Gun Corps), 1917-21; Bt Major, 1919; retd, 1931; Territorial Army: Lieut-Col Comdg 7th (Leeds Rifles) Bn West Yorks Regt 1934; Bt. Col 1938; Col 1938; served European War, France and Belgium, 1915, 1917, 1918 (wounded); North Russia, 1919; Instructor: Machine Gun Sch., 1916 and 1919-21; Technical Officer, 1921-24; Infantry Brigade Commander (temp. Brig.), 1939-40; Active Service France and Belgium 1940, including evacuation of Dunkirk (despatches); Commander, Cambridge Sub-Dist, 1943-44; Hon. Col 12th (Yorks) Bn Parachute Regt (TA), 1949-56. Pres., 1940 Dunkirk Veterans' Assoc., 1975-76. *Recreation:* oil-painting. *Address:* 4 Bramhope Manor, Bramhope, Leeds LS16 9HI. *T:* Arthington 842384.

GAY, Geoffrey Charles Lytton; Consultant, Knight, Frank & Rutley, since 1973; World President, International Real Estate Federation (FIABCI), 1973-75; a General Commissioner for Inland Revenue since 1953; *b* 14 March 1914; *s* of Charles Gay and Ida (*née* Lytton); *m* 1947, Dorothy Ann, *d* of Major Eric Rickman; one *s* two *d. Educ:* St Paul's School. FRICS. Joined Knight, Frank & Rutley, 1929. Served War of 1939-45: Durham LI, BEF, 1940; psc; Lt-Col; Chief of Staff, Sind District, India, 1943. Mem. Westminster City Council, 1962-71. Governor, Benenden Sch.; Mem. Council of St John, London; Liveryman, Broderers' Co. Chevalier de l'Ordre de l'Economie Nationale, 1960. OStJ 1961. *Recreations:* photography, fishing, music, theatre. *Address:* The Down Wood, Blandford Forum, Dorset. *T:* Blandford 4228. *Clubs:* Carlton, Oriental, MCC.

GAY, Rear-Adm. George Wilsmore, CB 1969; MBE 1946; DSC 1943; JP; Director-General of Naval Training, 1967-69; retired;

b 1913; *s* of late Engr Comdr G. M. Gay and Mrs O. T. Gay (*née* Allen); *m* 1941, Nancy Agnes Clark; two *s* one *d. Educ:* Eastman's Sch., Southsea; Nautical Coll., Pangbourne. Entered RN, 1930; Cadet Trng, 1930-32; RNEC, Keyham, 1932-35; HMS Glorious, 1935-37; Engr. Off., HMS Porpoise, 1939-41, HMS Clyde, 1941-43; HMS Dolphin, 1938 and 1943-46; HM Dockyard, Portsmouth, 1946-47; HMS Euryalus, 1947-49; Sqdn Engr Off., 1st Submarine Sqdn, HMS Forth, 1949-50; Trng Comdr, HMS Raleigh, 1951-53; Admiralty Engr Overseer, Vickers Armstrong Ltd, 1953-55; HMS Dolphin, 1956-58; Senior Officer, War Course, Royal Naval Coll., Greenwich, 1958; HM Dockyard, Malta, 1959-60; CO, HMS Sultan, Gosport 1960-63; Chief Staff Off. Material to Flag Off. Submarines, 1963-66; Admty Interview Bd, 1966. Comdr 1947; Capt. 1958; Rear-Adm. 1967. FIMechE (MIMechE 1958). JP Plymouth 1970. *Recreations:* fishing, sailing, gardening. *Address:* 29 Whiteford Road, Mannamead, Plymouth, Devon. *T:* Plymouth 64486. *Club:* Army and Navy.

GAYDON, Prof. Alfred Gordon, FRS 1953; Warren Research Fellow of Royal Society, 1945-74; Professor of Molecular Spectroscopy, Imperial College of Science and Technology, London, 1961-73, now Emeritus; *b* 26 Sept. 1911; *s* of Alfred Bert Gaydon and Rosetta Juliet Gordon; *m* 1940, Phyllis Maude Gaze; one *s* one *d. Educ:* Kingston Grammar Sch., Kingston-on-Thames; Imperial Coll., London. BSc (Physics) Imperial Coll., 1932; worked on molecular spectra, and on measurement of high temperatures, on spectra and structure of flames, and shock waves, 1939-; DSc (London) 1942; Hon. Dr (University of Dijon), 1957. Rumford Medal, Royal Society, 1960; Bernard Lewis Gold Medal, Combustion Inst., 1960. *Publications:* Identification of Molecular Spectra (with Dr R. W. B. Pearse), 1941, 1950, 1963, 1965, 1976; Spectroscopy and Combustion Theory, 1942, 1948; Dissociation Energies and Spectra of Diatomic Molecules, 1947, 1953, 1968; Flames, their Structure, Radiation and Temperature (with Dr H. G. Wolfhard), 1953, 1960, 1970; The Spectroscopy of Flames, 1957, new edn, 1974; The Shock Tube in High-temperature Chemical Physics (with Dr I. Hurle), 1963. *Recreations:* wild-life photography; formerly rowing. *Address:* Dale Cottage, Shellbridge Road, Slindon Common, Sussex. *T:* Slindon 277; Imperial College, SW7. *T:* 01-589 5111.

GAYRE of Gayre and Nigg, Robert, ERD; Lieutenant-Colonel (late Reserve of Officers); ethnologist and armorist; Editor of The Armorial since 1959, The Mankind Quarterly since 1960, etc; Director of several companies; *s* of Robert Gayre of Gayre and Nigg, and Clara Hull; *m* 1933, Nina Mary, *d* of Rev. Louis Thomas Terry and Margaret Nina Hill; one *s. Educ:* University of Edinburgh (MA); Exeter Coll., Oxford. BEF France, 1939; Staff Officer Airborne HQ, 1942; Educnl Adviser, Allied Mil. Govt, Italy, 1943-44; Dir of Educn, Allied Control Commn for Italy, 1944; Chief of Educn and Religious Affairs, German Planning Unit, SHAEF, 1944; Prof. of Anthropology and head of Dept of Anthropo-geography, University of Saugor, India, 1954-56; Falkland Pursuivant Extraord., 1958; Consultore pro lingua Anglica, Coll. of Heralds, Rome, 1954-; Chamberlain to the Prince of Lippe, 1958-; Grand Bailiff and Comr-Gen. of the English Tongue, Order of St Lazarus of Jerusalem, 1961-69; Grand Referendary, 1969-73; Comdr and grand Almoner, 1973-; Sec.-Gen., VIth Internat. Congress of Genealogy, Edinburgh, 1962. Chm., The Seventeen Forty-Five Association. President: Scottish Rhodesia Soc., to 1968; Aberdeenshire and Banffshire Friends of Rhodesia Assoc., 1969-; St Andrew Soc. of Malta, 1968; Ethnological Soc. of Malta; Life Pres., Heraldic Soc. of Malta, 1970-; Hon. Pres., Sicilian Anthropological Soc. Sec.-Gen., Internat. Orders' Commn; Mem. Coun. Internat. Inst. of Ethnology and Eugenics, New York. Mem. Cttee of Honour: Inst. Politicos, Madrid; Cercle Internat. Généalogique, Paris, Mem. Nat. Acad. Sci. of India; Fellow: Collegio Araldico, Rome; Nat. Soc., Naples; Peloritana Acad., Messina; Pontaniana Acad., Naples; Royal Academy, Palermo; F Ist Ital di Geneal. e Arald., Rome; FInstD; FRSH; MInstBE. Hon. or corr. mem. of heraldic and other socs of many countries. Grand Cross of Merit, SMO Malta, 1963 (Kt Comdr, 1957). Holds knighthoods in international and foreign orders, hon. Doctorates from Italian Univs, and heraldic societies' medals, etc. Hon. Lt-Col, ADC to Governor, Georgia, USA, 1969-; Hon. Lt-Col, ADC, State Militia, Alabama. *Publications:* Teuton and Slav on the Polish Frontier, 1944; Italy in Transition, 1946; Wassail! In Mazers of Mead, 1948; The Heraldry of the Knights of St John, 1956; Heraldic Standards and other Ensigns, 1959; The Nature of Arms, 1961; Heraldic Cadency, 1961, Gayre's Booke, 4 vols 1948-59; Who is Who in Clan Gayre, 1962; A Case for Monarchy, 1962; The Armorial Who is Who, 1961-62, 1963-65, 1966-68, 1969-75; Roll of Scottish Arms (Pt I Vol. I, 1964, Pt I Vol. II, 1969); Ethnological Elements of Africa, 1966; More

Ethnological Elements of Africa, 1972; The Zimbabwean Culture of Rhodesia, 1972; Miscellaneous Racial Studies, 2 vols, 1972; The Knightly Twilight, 1974; Aspects of British and Continental Heraldry, 1974; The Lost Clan, 1974; Syro-Mesopotamian Ethnology, 1974; The Mackay of the Rhinns of Islay, 1978; Minard Castle, 1978; contribs Mankind Quarterly, contrib. Encyc. Brit., etc. *Recreations:* yachting, ocean cruising. *Address:* c/o 1 Darnaway Street, Edinburgh EH3 6DW. *T:* 031-225 1896; Lezayre Mount, Ramsey, Isle of Man. *T:* 813854; (owns as feudal baron of Lochoreshyre) Lochore Castle, Fife. *Clubs:* Army and Navy, Royal Thames Yacht; Caledonian (Edinburgh); Pretoria (Pretoria, SA); Casino Maltese (Valletta); Royal Forth Yacht, Royal Highland Yacht, Royal Malta Yacht, etc.

GAZE, Dr Raymond Michael, FRS 1972; FRSE 1964; Head, Division of Developmental Biology, since 1970, and Deputy Director, since 1977, National Institute for Medical Research; *b* 22 June 1927; *s* of late William Mercer Gaze and Kathleen Grace Gaze (*née* Bowhill); *m* 1957, Robinetta Mary Armfelt; one *s* two *d. Educ:* at home; Sch. of Medicine, Royal Colleges, Edinburgh. LRCPE, LRCSE, LRFPSG; MA, DPhil. House Physician, Chelmsford and Essex Hosp., 1949; National Service, RAMC, 1953-55; Lectr, later Reader, Dept of Physiology, Edinburgh Univ., 1955-70. Alan Johnston, Lawrence and Moseley Research Fellow, Royal Soc., 1962-66; Visiting Professor: of Theoretical Biology, Univ. of Chicago, 1972; of Biology, Middlesex Hosp. Med. Sch., 1972-74. Mem. Physiological Soc. *Publications:* The Formation of Nerve Connections, 1970; various papers on neurobiology in Jl Physiology, Quarterly Jl Exper. Physiology, Proc. Royal Soc., etc. *Recreations:* drawing, hill-walking, music. *Address:* 65 Talbot Road, N6 4QX. *T:* 01-340 3870.

GEACH, Gertrude Elizabeth Margaret; see Anscombe, G. E. M.

GEACH, Prof. Peter Thomas, FBA 1965; Professor of Logic, University of Leeds, since Oct. 1966; *b* 29 March 1916; *o s* of Prof. George Hender Geach, IES, and Eleonora Frederyka Adolfina Sgonina; *m* 1941, Gertrude Elizabeth Margaret Anscombe, *qv*; three *s* four *d. Educ:* Balliol Coll., Oxford (Domus Schol.). 2nd cl. Class, Hon. Mods, 1936; 1st cl. Lit. Hum., 1938. Gladstone Research Student, St Deiniol's Library, Hawarden, 1938-39; philosophical research, Cambridge, 1945-51; University of Birmingham: Asst Lectr in Philosophy, 1951; Lectr, 1952; Sen. Lectr, 1959; Reader in Logic, 1961. Stanton Lectr in the Philosophy of Religion, Cambridge, 1971-74; Hägerström Lectr, Univ. of Uppsala, 1975. *Publications:* Mental Acts, 1957; Reference and Generality, 1962; (with G. E. M. Anscombe) Three Philosophers, 1961; God and the Soul, 1969; Logic Matters, 1972; Reason and Argument, 1976; Providence and Evil, 1977; The Virtues, 1977; articles in Mind, Philosophical Review, Analysis, Ratio, etc. *Recreation:* reading stories of detection, mystery and horror. *Address:* Department of Philosophy, The University, Leeds; 3 Richmond Road, Cambridge. *T:* 53950. *Club:* Union Society (Oxford).

GEAKE, Maj.-Gen. Clifford Henry, CB 1945; CBE 1944; Hon. Maj.-Gen. (retired) RAOC; *b* 3 June 1894; *s* of Thomas Henry Geake; *m* 1915, Brenda Mary, *d* of Dr A. W. F. Sayres; two *s.* Served European War, 1914-18, France and Belgium (wounded, despatches); War of 1939-45, Middle East and Italy (despatches, CBE, CB); retired pay, 1946. Officer, Legion of Merit, USA. *Address:* c/o Barclays Bank Ltd, Friary Branch, Guildford, Surrey.

GEAR, William, DA (Edinburgh) 1936; RBSA 1966; Painter; Head of Department of Fine Art, Birmingham Polytechnic (formerly Birmingham College of Art and Design), 1964-75; Member London Group, 1953; *b* Methil, Fife, 2 Aug. 1915; *s* of Porteous Gordon Gear; *m* 1949, Charlotte Chertok; two *s. Educ:* Buckhaven High Sch.; Edinburgh Coll. of Art; Edinburgh Univ.; Moray House Training Coll.; Edinburgh Coll. of Art: Post-grad. schol., 1936-37; Travelling schol., 1937-38; Académie Fernand Leger, Paris, 1937; study in France, Italy, Balkans; Moray House Trg Coll., 1938-39. War Service with Royal Corps of Signals, 1940-46, in Middle East, Italy and Germany. Staff Officer, Monuments, Fine Arts and Archives Br., CCG, 1946-47; worked in Paris, 1947-50; Curator, Towner Art Gallery, Eastbourne, 1958-64. Guest lecturer, Nat. Gall. of Victoria, Melbourne, and University of Western Australia, 1966. Chairman: Fine Art Panel, Nat. Council for Diplomas in Art and Design, 1972; Fine Art Bd, CNAA, 1974. One-man exhibitions since 1944 in various European cities, N and S America, Japan, etc.; London; Gimpel Fils Gall., 1948-; S London Art Gall. (retrospective), 1954; Edinburgh Fest., 1966; (retrospective) Arts Council, N Ireland, 1969; (retrospective) Scottish Arts Council 1969; Univ. of Sussex, 1964-75; RBSA

Birmingham, 1976 (retrospective). Works shown in many exhibitions of contemporary art, also at Royal Acad., 1960, 1961, 1967, 1968. Awarded £500 Purchase prize, Fest. of Britain, 1951; David Cargill Award, Royal Glasgow Inst., 1967; Lorne Fellowship, 1976. FIAL, 1960; FRSA 1971. *Works in permanent collections:* Tate Gall.; Arts Council; Brit. Council; Contemp. Art Soc.; Scottish National Gall. of Modern Art; Scottish Arts Council; Victoria & Albert Museum; Laing Art Gall., Newcastle; Nat. Gall. of Canada; Bishop Suter Art Gall., NZ; Art Gall., Toronto; City Art Gall., Toledo, Ohio; Museum of Art, Tel Aviv; New Coll., Oxford; Cincinnati Art Gall., Ohio; Nat. Gall. of NSW; Bishop Otter Coll., Chichester; City Art Gall., Manchester; Albright Art Gall., Buffalo, NY; Musée des Beaux Arts, Liège; Inst. of Contemp. Art, Lima, Peru; Towner Art Gall., Eastbourne; Brighton Art Gall.; Pembroke Coll., Cambridge; Chelsea Coll. of Physical Educn; Southampton Art Gall.; Univ. of Glasgow; Arts Council of Northern Ireland, Whitworth Art Gall., Manchester; Univ. of Birmingham; City Museum and Art Gall., Birmingham; Aberdeen, Dundee and Glasgow Art Galleries, and in numerous private collections in Gt Britain, USA, Canada, Italy, France, etc. Furnishing textiles designed for various firms. *Recreations:* cricket, music, gardening. *Address:* 46 George Road, Edgbaston, Birmingham B15 1PL.

GEDDES, family name of **Baron Geddes** and of **Baron Geddes of Epsom.**

GEDDES, 3rd Baron *cr* 1942; **Euan Michael Ross Geddes;** Company Director since 1964; *b* 3 Sept. 1937; *s* of 2nd Baron Geddes, KBE, and of Enid Mary, Lady Geddes, *d* of late Clarance H. Butler; *S* father, 1975; *m* 1966, Gillian, *d* of William Arthur Butler; one *s* one *d*. *Educ:* Rugby; Gonville and Caius Coll., Cambridge (MA 1964); Harvard Business School. *Recreations:* golf, bridge, music, gardening. *Heir: s* Hon. James George Neil Geddes, *b* 10 Sept. 1969. *Address:* 15 Bluff Path, The Peak, Hong Kong. *T:* 5-97638; Briar House, Odiham, Basingstoke, Hants. *T:* Odiham 2411. *Club:* Brooks's.

GEDDES OF EPSOM, Baron *cr* 1958, of Epsom (Life Peer); **Charles John Geddes,** Kt 1957; CBE 1950; Chairman, Polyglass Ltd and associated Companies; *b* 1 March 1897; *s* of Thomas Varney Geddes and Florence Louisa Mills. *m* 1920, Julia Burke; one *d*. *Educ:* Blackheath Central Sch. Post Office: boy messenger, telegraph learner, telegraphist. Served European War, 1914-18. RFC. Lieut, 1916-19, Pilot, 1918-19. Formerly: General Sec. of the Union of Post Office Workers; Member of the General Council of the Trades Union Congress (Pres. of the TUC, 1954-55); Retired, 1957. *Recreations:* television, reading, gardening. *Address:* 28 Parkhill Court, Addiscombe Road, Croydon, Surrey CR0 5PJ. *T:* 01-681 1188.

GEDDES, Air Cdre Andrew James Wray, CBE 1946 (OBE 1941); DSO 1943; *b* 31 July 1906; *s* of late Major Malcolm Henry Burdett Geddes, Indian Army, and late Mrs Geddes, Seaford, Sussex; *m* 1929, Anstice Wynter, *d* of late Rev. A. W. Leach, Rector of Leasingham, Lincs; one *s* one *d*. *Educ:* Oakley Hall, Cirencester, Glos; Wellington Coll., Berks; Royal Military Academy Woolwich. 2nd Lt Royal Artillery, 1926; seconded Flying Officer RAF 1928-32; Lieut RA 1929; seconded Flight Lieut RAF 1935-38; Capt. RA 1939; served War of 1939-45 (despatches twice, OBE, DSO, CBE, Commander Legion of Merit, USA); seconded Squadron Leader RAF 1939; Acting Wing Commander RAF 1940; Acting Group Capt., 1942; Acting Air Commodore, 1943; War Subst. Group Capt., 1943; Major RA 1943; Air Commodore Operations and Plans, HQ 2nd TAF for the Invasion. Transferred from RA to RAF, 1945; Air Cdre Dir of Organisation (Establishments), Air Ministry, 1945-47; Group Capt. (subst.), 1947; graduated Imperial Defence Coll., London, 1948; Commanding No. 4 Flying Training Sch. and RAF Station, Heany, S Rhodesia, 1949-51; Dep. Dir of Organisation, Plans, Air Ministry, 1951-54, retd with rank of Air Cdre, 1954; Asst County Civil Defence Officer (Plans), East Sussex County Council, 1957-65; Deputy Civil Defence Officer, Brighton County Borough, 1965-66. Flying Mem., British Hang-gliding Assoc., 1975 (believed to be oldest living hang-glider pilot; first solo when aged 68 years 9 months); qualified instructor/examiner, Nat. Cycling Proficiency Scheme, RoSPA, 1977. *Address:* c/o Midland Bank Ltd, Farnham, Surrey.

GEDDES, Sir (Anthony) Reay (Mackay), KBE 1968 (OBE 1943); Chairman, Dunlop Holdings, since 1968; Director, Pirelli s.p.a., since 1971; *b* 7 May 1912; *s* of late Rt Hon. Sir Eric Geddes, PC, GCB, GBE; *m* 1938, Imogen, *d* of late Captain Hay Matthey, Brixham; two *s* three *d*. *Educ:* Rugby; Cambridge. Bank of England, 1932; Dunlop Rubber Company Ltd, 1935. Served RAFVR, 1939-45. Pres., Soc. of Motor Manufacturers

and Traders, 1958-59; Part-time Mem., UK AEA, 1960-65; Mem. Nat. Economic Devel. Council, 1962-65; Chm., Shipbuilding Inquiry Cttee, 1965-66. Director: Midland Bank Ltd, 1967-; Shell Transport and Trading Co. Ltd, 1968-; Rank Organisation Ltd, 1975-; Adela Investments SA, 1976-. Hon. DSc, Aston, 1967; Hon. LLD Leicester, 1969; Hon. DTech Loughborough, 1970. *Address:* 13 Wilton Crescent, SW1; (office) Dunlop House, Ryder Street, St James's, SW1Y 6PX.

GEDDES, Ford Irvine, MBE 1943; *b* 17 Jan. 1913; *e s* of Irvine Campbell Geddes and Dorothy Jefford Geddes (*née* Fowler); *m* 1945, Barbara Gertrude Vere Parry-Okeden; one *s* four *d*. *Educ:* Loretto Sch.; Gonville and Caius Coll., Cambridge (BA). Joined Anderson Green & Co. Ltd, London, 1934. Served War RE, 1939-45 (Major). Director: Bank of NSW (London Adv. Bd) 1950; Equitable Life Assce Soc., 1955-76 (Pres. 1963-71); Chairman: P&O Steam Navigation Co., 1971-72 (a Dep. Chm., 1968-71; Dir, 1960-72); British United Turkeys Ltd, 1976-; British Shipping Federation, 1965-68; Pres., Internat. Shipping Fedn, 1967-69. *Address:* The Manor, Berwick St John, Shaftesbury, Dorset SP7 0EX. *T:* Donhead 363. *Clubs:* City of London; Union (Sydney).

GEDDES, Sir Reay; *see* Geddes, Sir A. R. M.

GEDLING, Raymond, CB 1969; Deputy Secretary, Department of Health and Social Security, since 1971; *b* 3 Sept. 1917; *s* of late John and late Mary Gedling; *m* 1956, Joan Evelyn Chapple; one *s*. *Educ:* Grangefield Grammar Sch., Stockton-on-Tees. Entered Civil Service as Executive Officer, Min. of Health, 1936; Asst Principal, 1942, Principal, 1947. Cabinet Office, 1951-52; Principal Private Sec. to Minister of Health, 1952-55; Asst Sec., 1955; Under-Sec., 1961; Asst Under-Sec. of State, Dept of Educn and Science, 1966-68; Dep. Sec., Treasury, 1968-71. *Recreations:* walking, chess. *Address:* 27 Wallace Fields, Epsom, Surrey. *T:* 01-393 9060.

GEE, Prof. Geoffrey, CBE 1958; FRS 1951; Sir Samuel Hall Professor of Chemistry, University of Manchester, 1955-76, now Emeritus Professor; *b* 6 June 1910; *s* of Thomas and Mary Ann Gee; *m* 1934, Marion (*née* Bowden); one *s* two *d*. *Educ:* New Mills Grammar Sch.; Universities of Manchester and Cambridge, BSc 1931, MSc 1932, Manchester; PhD 1936, ScD 1947, Cambridge. ICI (Dyestuffs Group) Research Chemist, 1933-38; British Rubber Producers' Research Association: Research Chemist, 1938-47; Dir, 1947-53. Prof. of Physical Chemistry, 1953-55, and Pro-Vice Chancellor, 1966-68, 1972-77, Univ. of Manchester. Pres., Faraday Soc., 1969 and 1970. *Publications:* numerous scientific papers in Transactions of the Faraday Soc., and other journals. *Recreation:* gardening. *Address:* 8 Holmfield Drive, Cheadle Hulme, Cheshire. *T:* 061-485 3713.

GEFFEN, Dr Terence John; Senior Principal Medical Officer, Department of Health and Social Security, since 1972; *b* 17 Sept. 1921; *s* of Maximilian W. Geffen and Maia Geffen (later Reid); *m* 1965, Judith Ann Steward; two *s*. *Educ:* St Paul's Sch.; University Coll., London; UCH. MD, FRCP. House Phys., UCH, 1943; RAMC, 1944-47; hosp. posts, Edgware Gen. Hosp., Hampstead Gen. Hosp., UCH, 1947-55; Min. of Health (later DHSS), 1956-. *Publications:* various in BMJ, Lancet, Clinical Science, etc. *Recreations:* music, reading, bridge. *Address:* 2 Stonehill Close, SW14 8RP. *T:* 01-878 0516.

GELDER, Prof. Michael Graham; W. A. Handley Professor of Psychiatry, University of Oxford, since 1969; Fellow of Merton College, Oxford; *b* 2 July 1929; *s* of Philip Graham Gelder and Margaret Gelder (*née* Graham); *m* 1954, Margaret (*née* Anderson); one *s* two *d*. *Educ:* Bradford Grammar Sch.; Queen's Coll., Oxford. Scholar and first class Hons, Physiology finals, 1950; MA, DM Oxon, FRCP, FRCPsych. Goldsmit Schol., UCH London, 1951; MRC Fellow in Clinical Research, 1962-63; Gold Medallist, Royal Medico-Psychological Assoc., 1962; Sen. Lectr, Inst. of Psychiatry, 1965-67 (Vice-Dean, 1967-68); Physician, Bethlem Royal and Maudsley Hosps, 1967-68. *Publications:* articles in medical jls. *Recreations:* theatre, gardening. *Address:* St Mary's, Jack Straw's Lane, Oxford OX3 0DN.

GELL, Prof. Philip George Houtham, FRS 1969; Professor and Head of Department of Experimental Pathology, Birmingham University, 1968-78; *b* 20 Oct. 1914; *s* of late Major P. F. Gell, DSO, and Mrs E. Lewis Hall; *m* 1941, Albinia Susan Roope Gordon; one *s* one *d*. *Educ:* Stowe Sch.; Trinity Coll., Cambridge; University Coll. Hosp. MRCS, LRCP, 1939; MB, BCh, 1940; FRCPath, 1969. Ho. Phys. to Med. Unit, UCH, 1939; Emergency Public Health Laboratory Service, 1940-43. On staff of Nat. Inst. for Med. Research, 1943-48; Reader in

Dept of Exptl Pathology, Birmingham Univ., 1948-60; Prof. (Personal) of Immunological Pathology, Dept of Exptl Pathology, 1960-68. *Publications:* (ed with R. R. A. Coombs and P. J. Lachmann) Clinical Aspects of Immunology, 3rd edn, 1974; contribs to Jl of Experimental Med., Immunology, etc. *Recreations:* gardening, painting, philosophy of science. *Address:* Wychwood, Cranes Lane, Kingston, Cambridge. *T:* Comberton 2714.

GELL-MANN, Murray; Robert Andrews Millikan Professor of Theoretical Physics at the California Institute of Technology since 1967; *b* 15 Sept. 1929; *s* of Arthur and Pauline Gell-Mann; *m* 1955, J. Margaret Dow; one *s* one *d. Educ:* Yale Univ.; Massachusetts Inst. of Technology. Mem., Inst. for Advanced Study, Princeton, 1951; Instructor, Asst Prof., and Assoc. Prof., Univ. of Chicago, 1952-55; Assoc. Prof. 1955-56, Prof. 1956-66, California Inst. of Technology. Vis. Prof., Collège de France and Univ. of Paris, 1959-60. Overseas Fellow, Churchill Coll., Cambridge, 1966. Mem., President's Science Adv. Commn, 1969-72. Regent, Smithsonian Inst., 1975-; Chm. of Bd, Aspen Center for Physics, 1970-; Vice-Pres. and Chm. of Western Center, Amer. Acad. of Arts and Sciences, 1970-; Mem., Nat. Acad. of Sciences, 1960-. Dannie Heineman Prize (Amer. Phys. Soc.), 1959; Ernest O. Lawrence Award, 1966; Franklin Medal (Franklin Inst., Philadelphia), 1967; John J. Carty Medal (Nat. Acad. Scis), 1968; Research Corp. Award, 1969; Nobel Prize in Physics, 1969. Hon. ScD: Yale, 1959; Chicago, 1967; Illinois, 1968; Wesleyan, 1968; Utah, 1970; Columbia, 1977; Hon. Dr, Turin, 1969. *Publications:* (with Yuval Ne'eman) The Eightfold Way, 1964; various articles in learned jls on topics referring to classification and description of elementary particles of physics and their interactions. *Recreations:* walking in wild country, study of natural history, languages. *Address:* 1024 Armada Drive, Pasadena, Calif 91103, USA. *T:* 213-792-4740. *Clubs:* Cosmos (Washington); Athenæum (Pasadena).

GELLERT, Leon; journalist; *b* Adelaide, 17 May 1892; *s* of J. W. Gellert; *m* 1918, Kathleen Patricia (decd), *y d* of late William Saunders; (one *d* decd). *Educ:* Adelaide High Sch. and Adelaide Univ. (Bundey Prize for English Verse). Served with the original 10th Bn which landed on Gallipoli, 25 April 1915. Co-Editor (with late Sydney Ure Smith), Art in Australia Publications, 1921; later Dir, Art in Australia; Literary Editor and Feature Writer, Sydney Morning Herald, 1942-61. *Publications:* Songs of a Campaign, 1917, illustrd by Norman Lindsay; Isle of San, illstrd by Norman Lindsay, 1919; Desperate Measures, 1929; These Beastly Australians, illustrd by Bernard Hesling, 1944; Week after Week, 1953; Year after Year, 1956. *Address:* 21 Lerwick Avenue, Hazelwood Park, SA 5066, Australia.

GELLHORN, Peter; Conductor, Elizabethan Singers, since 1976; Conductor and Chorus Master, Glyndebourne Festival Opera, 1954-61, rejoined Glyndebourne Music Staff, 1974 and 1975; *b* 24 Oct. 1912; *s* of late Dr Alfred Gellhorn, and late Mrs Else Gellhorn; *m* 1943, Olive Shirley (*née* Layton), 3rd *d* of 1st Baron Layton, CH, CBE; two *s* two *d. Educ:* Schiller Realgymnasium, Charlottenburg; University of Berlin; Berlin Music Acad. After passing final exams (with dist.) as pianist and conductor, left Germany 1935. Musical Dir, Toynbee Hall, London, E1, 1935-39; Asst Conductor, Sadler's Wells Opera, 1941-43. On industrial war service, 1943-45. Conductor, Royal Carl Rosa Opera (115 perfs), 1945-46. Conductor and Head of Music Staff, Royal Opera House, Covent Garden (over 260 perfs), 1946-53; Dir, BBC Chorus, 1961-72. Has also been working at National Sch. of Opera, annually at Summer Sch. of Music at Dartington Hall; broadcasting frequently as conductor or pianist; composes; writes or arranges music for silhouette and puppet films of Lotte Reiniger (at intervals, 1933-). Mem., Music Staff, London Opera Centre; Conductor: Morley Coll. Opera Gp; Barnes Music Club Choir; Mem. of Artistic Dirs, Opera Players Ltd. Lectures on Courses arranged by Oxford Univ. Extra-Mural Delegacy, the WEA, and various County Councils. Musical Dir, Opera Barga, Italy, from foundn, 1967-69. *Recreations:* reading, walking and going to plays. *Address:* 33 Leinster Avenue, East Sheen, SW14 7JW. *T:* 01-876 3949. *Club:* BBC.

GELLNER, Prof. Ernest André, FBA 1974; Professor of Philosophy, London School of Economics, since 1962; *b* Paris, 9 Dec. 1925; *s* of Rudolf Gellner and Anna (*née* Fantl), Prague; *m* 1954, Susan Ryan; two *s* two *d. Educ:* Prague English Grammar Sch.; St Albans County Sch.; Balliol Coll., Oxford. MA (Oxon), PhD (Lond). On staff of London School of Economics, 1949-. *Publications:* Words and Things, 1959; Thought and Change, 1964; Saints of the Atlas, 1969; Cause and Meaning in the Social Sciences, 1973; Contemporary Thought and Politics, 1974; The Devil in Modern Philosophy, 1974; Legitimation of Belief, 1975; numerous contributions to learned jls. *Recreation:* sailing. *Address:* Old Litten Cottage, Froxfield, Petersfield, Hants. *T:* Hawkley 311. *Clubs:* Reform; Chichester Yacht.

GEMMELL, Prof. Alan Robertson; Professor of Biology, University of Keele, 1950-77; *b* 10 May 1913; *s* of Alexander Nicol Gemmell and Mary Robertson; *m* 1942, Janet Ada Boyd Duncanson; two *s. Educ:* Ayr Academy; University of Glasgow. BSc (Hons) Glasgow. Commonwealth Fund Fellow, University of Minnesota, 1935-37 (MS); Agricultural Research at West of Scotland Agricultural Coll., 1937-41; PhD Glasgow, 1939. Lecturer in Botany, Glasgow Univ., 1942-44; Biologist at West Midland Forensic Science Laboratory, 1944-45; Lecturer in Botany, Manchester Univ., 1945-50. Regular broadcaster since 1950. President: Staffs Assoc. of Village Produce Guilds; Nantwich Liberal Assoc.; Cheshire Family Planning Assoc. *Publications:* Science in the Garden, 1963; Gardeners Question Time Books, 1965, 1967; Developmental Plant Anatomy, 1969; The Sunday Gardener, 1974; The Penguin Book of Basic Gardening, 1975; (Associate Editor) Chronica Botanica, Vol. I, 1935; many contributions to scientific journals. *Recreations:* golf, gardening, popular science, reading. *Address:* Highfield House, Aston, Nantwich, Cheshire. *T:* Aston (Nantwich) 408. *Club:* Farmers'.

GENDERS, Rt. Rev. Roger Alban Marson, (Anselm); *see* Bermuda, Bishop of.

GENEVOIX, Maurice (Charles Louis); Grand Croix de la Légion d'Honneur; man of letters; Member of the French Academy since 1946 and Permanent Secretary, 1958-74; *b* 29 Nov. 1890; *m* Suzanne Neyrolles; two *d. Educ:* Lycées d'Orléans, Lakanal; Ecole normale supérieure. Served European War, 1914-18 (Croix de Guerre). Prix Goncourt, 1925. *Publications:* Sous Verdun, 1914; Nuits de guerre, 1917; Au seuil des guitounes, 1918; Jeanne Robelin, 1920; La Boue, 1921; Rémi des Rauches, 1922; Les Eparges, 1923; La Joie, 1924; Euthymos, vainqueur olympique, 1924; Raboliot, 1925; La Boite à pêche, 1926; Les Mains vides, 1928; Cyrille, 1928; L'Assassin, 1930; Rrou, 1931; HOE, 1931; Gai l'amour, 1932; Forêt voisine, 1933; Marcheloup, 1934; Tête baissée, 1935; Bernard, 1937; La Dernière Harde, 1938; Les Compagnons de l'Aubépin, 1938; L'Hirondelle qui fit le printemps, 1941; Laframboise et Bellehumeur, 1942; Eva Charlebois, 1944; Canada, 1945; Sanglar, 1946; L'Ecureuil du bois bourru, 1947; Afrique blanche, Afrique noire, 1949; Ceux de 14, 1950; L'Aventure est en nous, 1952; Fatou Cissé, 1954; Images pour un Jardin sans murs, 1955; Vlaminck, 1956; le Roman de Renard, 1958; Routes de l'Aventure, 1959; Au cadran de mon clocher, 1960; Vaincre à Olympie, 1960; Jeux de Glaces, 1961; La Loire, Agnès et les Garçons, 1962; Derrière les Collines, 1963; Christian Caillard, 1965; Beau-François, 1965. La Forêt perdue, 1967; Jardins sans murs, 1968; Tendre bestiaire, 1968; Bestiaire enchanté, 1969; Bestiaire sans oubli, 1971; La Grèce de Caramanlis, 1972; La Mort de Près, 1972; La Perpétuité, 1974; Un Jour, 1976. *Address:* 17 rue Davioud, 75016 Paris, France. *T:* 520-78-17; Les Vernelles, 45550 St Denis de l'Hôtel, France.

GENGE, Rt. Rev. Mark; *see* Newfoundland, Central, Bishop of.

GENN, Leo John; Actor and Barrister-at-Law; *b* 9 Aug. 1905; *s* of William Genn and Rachel (*née* Asserson); *m* 1933, Marguerite, *d* of Edward van Praag and Catherine (*née* Bonnar); no *c. Educ:* City of London Sch.; St Catharine's Coll., Cambridge (MA). Called to Bar, Middle Temple, 1928. Actor as well as Barrister-at-Law since 1930. First appearance on professional stage, 1930, in A Marriage Has Been Disarranged, Nov., at Eastbourne, Dec. at Royalty, London; various parts at Royalty, 1931-32; Garrick, Gaiety, Wyndham's, 1932-33-34; joined Old Vic Company, appearing in numerous parts in Shakespeare, Shaw, Ibsen, Sheridan, Sept. 1934-March 1936; St Helena, Daly's, 1936; Old Vic: Feb.-April 1937 (in June, Horatio, at Elsinore); The Flashing Stream, The Lyric, 1938. First appearance in New York, April 1939, in same play. Joined Officers' Emergency Reserve, 1938; 2nd Lieut RA 1940; Capt. 1941; Maj. 1942; Lieut-Col 1943; comd No. 1 War Crimes Investigation Team, responsible for Belsen Concentration Camp Investigation; Asst Prosecutor Belsen Trial, 1945. Croix de Guerre, 1945. Resumed career in the theatre. Another Part of the Forest, New York, 1946; Jonathan, Aldwych, 1948; The Seventh Veil, Prince's, 1951; Henry VIII, Old Vic, 1953; The Bombshell, Westminster, 1954; Small War on Murray Hill, New York, 1957; The Hidden River, Cambridge, 1959; The Devil's Advocate, NY, 1961; Fair Game for Lovers, NY, 1964; 12 Angry Men, Queen's, 1964; The Sacred Flame, Duke of York's, 1967; The Only Game in Town, New York, 1968; Caesar and Cleopatra, US, 1968; Dr Faustus, US, 1969. First film, Jump for Glory, 1937. *Films include:* The Drum, Ten Days in Paris, Henry V, Desert Victory (Commentary), Theirs was the Glory (Commentary), Green for Danger, Mourning Becomes Electra, The Snake Pit, The Velvet Touch, The Wooden Horse, Quo Vadis, Plymouth Adventure, Red Beret, Personal Affair, The Green Scarf, Moby Dick,

L'Amant de Lady Chatterley (in French), Beyond Mombasa, The Steel Bayonet, I Accuse, No Time To Die; Too Hot To Handle; It Was Night in Rome; The Longest Day; 55 Days at Peking; Ten Little Indians; Circus of Fear; Connecting Rooms; The Bloody Judge; Rebound; Lizard in a Woman's Skin; Le Silencieux. TV since 1951; broadcasts since 1933; narrator: Coronation Programme, 1937, 1953. King George VI Memorial Programme, 1952; UN opening (from USA), 1947, etc. Distinguished Vis. Prof. of Theatre Arts, Pennsylvania State Univ., 1968, Univ. of Utah, 1969. Governor, Mermaid Theatre; Assessor, Yvonne Arnaud Theatre, Guildford; Councillor, Arts Educational Schools. *Publications:* magazine and newspaper articles. *Recreations:* ball games, books and The Bar. *Address:* Elmhurst Cottages, Itchingfield, Sussex. *T:* Slinfold 344. *Clubs:* Garrick; Stage Golfing; West Sussex Golf (Pulborough); Travellers' (Paris).

GENSCHER, Hans-Dietrich; Federal Minister for Foreign Affairs and Deputy Chancellor, Federal Republic of Germany, since May 1974; Chairman of the Free Democratic Party, since Oct. 1974; *b* Reideburg/Saalkreis, 21 March 1927; *m* Barbara; one *d*. *Educ:* Higher Sch. Certif. (Abitur); studied law and economics in Halle/Saale and Leipzig Univs, 1946-49. Served War, 1943-45. Mem., state-level org. of LDP, 1946. Re-settled in W Germany, 1952: practical legal training in Bremen and Mem. Free Democratic Party (FDP); FDP Asst in Parly Party, 1956; Gen. Sec.: FDP Parly Party, 1959-65; FDP at nat. level, 1962-64. Elected Mem., Bundestag, 1965; a Parly Sec., FDP Parly Party, 1965-69; Dep. Chm., FDP, 1968-74; Federal Minister of the Interior, Oct. 1969 (Brandt-Scheel Cabinet); re-apptd Federal Minister of the Interior, Dec. 1972. He was instrumental in maintaining pure air and water; gave a modern structure to the Federal Police Authority; Federal Border Guard Act passed; revised weapons laws, etc. Mem. Delegn of FDP politicians who met Premier Kosygin in the Kremlin, 1969; campaigned for exchange of declarations of renunciation of force, with all Warsaw Pact countries. *Publications:* Umweltschutz: Das Umweltschutzprogram der Bundesregierung, 1972; Bundestagsreden, 1972. *Recreations:* reading, walking, swimming. *Address:* Auswärtiges Amt, Bonn, Federal Republic of Germany.

GENTLEMAN, David, RDI 1970; graphic designer and painter; *b* 11 March 1930; *s* of Tom Gentleman; *m*; one *d*; 2nd, 1968, Susan, *d* of George Ewart Evans, *qv*; two *d*. *Educ:* Hertford Grammar Sch.; Royal College of Art, 1950-53. Tutor, RCA, 1953-55; since then has worked entirely as designer, illustrator and painter. Work includes: edns of lithographs of architecture and landscape, published 1967, 1970, 1972, 1973, 1975 and 1976; and of screen prints; mural designs and posters (graphic and photographic) for London Transport and National Trust; many British postage stamps (incl. Shakespeare, Churchill, Battle of Britain, Battle of Hastings, British Trees, Prince of Wales Investiture, Ships, Fire Engines, Christmas 1977, etc); illustrations include drawings and engravings for many books and jackets. Exhibitions of watercolours of India, 1970, Covent Garden, 1972, South Carolina, 1973, Bath, 1975, East Africa, 1976; stamp designs, Nat. Postal Mus, 1970; group exhibns of graphics in Amsterdam, 1973, Milan, 1974, Tokyo, 1975. Member: Design Council, 1974-; College Court of RCA; Alliance Graphique Internationale. Phillips Gold Medal for Stamp Design, 1969; Design Council Poster Award, 1973, 1976 and 1977. *Publications:* Fenella in Ireland, in Greece, in Spain, in the South of France, 1967; Design in Miniature, 1972; Everyday Architecture in Towns, in Countryside, at the Seaside, Industrial, 1975 (RIBA wall-charts); illustrations for many books including: Plats du Jour, 1957; Bridges on the Backs, 1961; Swiss Family Robinson, 1963; The Shepherd's Calendar, 1964; Poems of John Keats, 1966; Pattern under the Plough, 1966; The Jungle Book, 1968; covers for New Penguin Shakespeare, 1968-75; Where Beards Wag All, 1970; The Golden Vanity, 1972; St George and the Dragon, 1973; Tales from the Punjab, 1973; Robin Hood, 1977. *Address:* 25 Gloucester Crescent, NW1 7DL. *T:* 01-485 8824.

GENTNER, Dr Wolfgang; Managing Director of the Max-Planck-Institute for Nuclear Physics, Heidelberg, 1958-74; Professor of Physics, University of Heidelberg, 1958-75; *b* Frankfurt-am-Main, 23 July 1906; *s* of Carl G. Gentner, manufacturer; *m* 1931, Alice Pfaehler; one *s* one *d*. *Educ:* Universities of Erlangen and Frankfurt (PhD). Fellowship at Institut du Radium, Lab. Curie, Paris Univ. (Mme P. Curie), 1933-35; Scientific Asst at Inst. of Physics of Kaiser-Wilhelm-Institut for Med. Research, 1936-46; Lectr in Physics, Univ. of Frankfurt, 1937-41; Fellow, Radiation Lab., Univ. of California (Berkeley), 1938-39; Lectr in Physics, Univ. of Heidelberg, 1941-45, Prof. 1945; Prof. of Physics, Freiburg Univ., 1946-58; Dir of CERN, Geneva, 1955-59. Member: Comité des directives

scientifiques, CERN, 1959-; Heidelberger Akad. der Wissenschaften (Pres. 1964-); Bayerische Akad. der Wissenschaften; Akad. Leopoldina; Pontifical Acad. of Science, 1970; Hon. Fellow, Weizmann Inst., Israel, 1965. Officier, Légion d'Honneur, 1965. *Publications:* on biophysics, radioactivity, nuclear physics; (co-author) Atlas of typical expansion chamber photographs, 1954. *Address:* Im Bäckerfeld 6, Heidelberg, Germany. *T:* 42467.

GENTRY, Jack Sydney Bates, CIE 1946; CBE 1965 (OBE 1942); ERD 1964; JP; General Manager Tees Conservancy Commission, 1946-66; retired; *b* 4 Oct. 1899; *s* of Frederick and Emma Gentry; *m* 1931, Beatrice Colleen Cundy Wren. *Educ:* Christ's Hosp. Port of London Authority, 1916, Commercial Superintendent, 1945; commission, Hants Regt, 1918; RE, 1938; served War of 1939-45 (despatches twice); Major, 1939; Lieut-Col, Asst Dir of Docks, 1940; Col, Dep. Dir of Movements, 1942. Dep. Regional Port Dir, Calcutta, 1944-45. JP Co. Durham, 1949. MIT, 1947. *Recreations:* cricket (played for Hants, Surrey, Essex, 1919-26); golf, tennis. *Address:* Pancake Cottage, Loxwood, near Billingshurst, West Sussex RH14 0SJ. *T:* Loxwood 752289. *Clubs:* MCC; Christ's Hospital.

GENTRY, Maj.-Gen. (retd) Sir William George, KBE 1958 (CBE 1950); CB 1954; DSO 1942, and Bar 1945; *b* 20 Feb. 1899; *e s* of late Major F. C. Gentry, MBE and late Mrs F. C. Gentry; *m* 1926, Alexandra Nina Caverhill; one *s* one *d*. *Educ:* Wellington Coll., NZ; RMC of Australia. Commissioned NZ Army, Dec. 1919; attached Indian Army and served in Waziristan, 1921, and Malabar, 1921. Served War of 1939-45 with 2nd NZ Div. (Middle East and Italy): GSO 2 and AA and QMG, 1940; GSO 1, 1941-42; Comd 6 NZ Inf. Bde, 1942-43; DCGS, Army HQ, NZ, 1943-44; Comd 9 NZ Inf. Bde (Italy), 1945. Adjutant Gen., NZ Army, 1949-52; Chief of the Gen. Staff, NZ Army, 1952; retired, 1955. Mem. Licensing Control Commn, 1957-67. Hon. Pres. NZ Boy Scouts Assoc., 1957-67. Greek Military Cross, 1941; United States Bronze Star, 1945. *Address:* 52 Kings Crescent, Lower Hutt, New Zealand. *T:* 660208. *Clubs:* Wellington, United Services (Wellington, NZ).

GEOFFREY-LLOYD, family name of **Baron Geoffrey-Lloyd.**

GEOFFREY-LLOYD, Baron *cr* 1974 (Life Peer), of Broomfield, Kent; **Geoffrey William Geoffrey-Lloyd,** PC 1943; *b* 17 Jan. 1902; *e s* of late G. W. A. Lloyd, Andover House, Newbury. *Educ:* Harrow Sch.; Trinity Coll., Cambridge (MA); Pres. of the Cambridge Union, 1924. Contested (C) SE Southwark, 1924, Ladywood, 1929; Private Sec. to Rt Hon. Sir Samuel Hoare (Sec. of State for Air), 1926-29; Private Sec. to Rt Hon. Stanley Baldwin, 1929-31; MP (U) Ladywood Div. of Birmingham, 1931-45; PPS to Rt Hon. Stanley Baldwin (Lord Pres. of the Council), 1931-35, (Prime Minister), 1935; Parly Under-Sec., Home Office, 1935-39; Sec. for Mines, 1939-40; Sec. for Petroleum, 1940-42; Chm. Oil Control Board, 1939-45; Minister in charge of Petroleum Warfare Dept 1940-45, and Parly Sec. (Petroleum), Min. of Fuel and Power, 1942-45; Minister of Information, 1945; a Governor of BBC, 1946-49; MP (C) King's Norton, Birmingham, 1950-55; Minister of Fuel and Power, 1951-55; MP (C) Sutton Coldfield, 1955-Feb. 1974; Minister of Education, 1957-Oct. 1959; President Birmingham Conservative and Unionist Assoc., 1946-76. *Address:* 77 Chester Square, SW1W 9DY. *T:* 01-730 0014. *Clubs:* Carlton, Pratt's; Conservative (Birmingham).

GEORGE; *see* Lloyd George.

GEORGE, Bishop of, since 1966; **Rt. Rev. Patrick Harold Falkiner Barron;** *b* 13 Nov. 1911; *s* of Albert Harold and Mary Isabel Barron; *m* 1942, Kathleen May Larter; two *s* one *d*. *Educ:* King Edward VII Sch., Johannesburg; Leeds Univ. (BA); College of the Resurrection, Mirfield. Curate: Holy Redeemer, Clerkenwell, London, 1938-40; Boksburg, S Africa, 1940-41; CF (S African), 1941-46; Rector: Zeerust, S Africa, 1946-50; Potchefstroom, 1950-51; Blyvooruitzicht, 1951-55. St Cyprian's Mission, Johannesburg, 1956-59; Archdeacon of Germiston, 1957-58; Dean of Johannesburg, 1959-64; Bishop Suffragan of Cape Town, 1965-66. *Recreation:* gardening. *Address:* Bishop's Lea, George, CP, South Africa. *T:* 2267.

GEORGE, Rev. (Alfred) Raymond, MA, BD; Tutor, Wesley College, Bristol, since 1972; *b* 26 Nov. 1912; *s* of A. H. and G. M. George. *Educ:* Crypt Sch., Gloucester; Balliol Coll., Oxford (1st cl. Hon. Classical Mods, 1st cl. Lit. Hum., BA 1935, MA 1938, BD 1955); Wesley House, Cambridge (1st cl. Theol Tripos, Pt I Sect. B, BA 1937, MA 1962); Marburg Univ. Asst Tutor, Handsworth Coll., Birmingham, 1938-40; ordained as Methodist minister, 1940;Asst Tutor, Hartley-Victoria Coll., Manchester, 1940-42; Circuit Minister, Manchester, 1942-46;

Tutor, Wesley Coll., Headingley, Leeds, 1946-67, Principal, 1961-67; Associate Lectr, Leeds Univ., 1946-67; Actg Head, Theol. Dept, 1967-68; Principal, Richmond Coll., London Univ., 1968-72. Select Preacher, Cambridge, 1963; Member, World Council of Churches Commn on Faith and Order, 1961-75; Pres. of Methodist Conf., 1975-76. *Publications:* Communion with God in the New Testament, 1953; chapter (on The Means of Grace) in A History of the Methodist Church in Great Britain, vol. I (ed R. Davies and G. Rupp), 1965; jt Editor of series: Ecumenical Studies in Worship; also articles in jls. *Address:* 15 Northover Road, Bristol BS9 3LN. *T:* Bristol 503698.

GEORGE, Sir Arthur (Thomas), Kt 1972; solicitor and company director; Chairman: Phillips Australia Holding Ltd; Kooralbyn Ltd, since 1973; Australia Solenoid Holdings Ltd, since 1967; Director, Anderson Meat Industries Ltd, since 1969; Thomas Nationwide Transport Ltd, since 1973; *b* 17 Jan. 1915; *s* of late Thomas George; *m* 1939, Renee, *d* of Anthony Freeleagus; one *d*. *Educ:* Sydney High Sch., NSW. Chairman: Assoc. for Classical Archæology, of Sydney Univ., 1966-; Australian Soccer Fedn., 1969-. Chm. and Founder, The Arthur T. George Foundation Ltd. Grand Commander (Keeper of the Laws), Cross of St Marks, and Gold Cross of Mount Athos, Greek Orthodox Church; Order of Phoenix (Greece). *Recreations:* interested in sport, especially Association football, etc. *Address:* 1 Little Queen's Lane, Vaucluse, NSW 2030, Australia.

GEORGE, Bruce Thomas; MP (Lab) Walsall South since Feb. 1974; *b* 1 June 1942. *Educ:* Mountain Ash Grammar Sch.; UCW Swansea; Univ. of Warwick. BA Politics Wales 1964, MA Warwick 1968. Asst Lectr in Social Studies, Glamorgan Polytechnic, 1964-66; Lectr in Politics, Manchester Polytechnic, 1968-70; Senior Lectr, Birmingham Polytechnic, 1970-74. Patron, Nat. Assoc. of Widows; Co-founder, Sec., House of Commons FC; Hon. Consultant, Confed. of Long Distance Pigeon Racing Assocs; Vice-Pres., Psoriasis Assoc. *Recreations:* Association football, snooker. *Address:* 42 Wood End Road, Walsall, West Midlands WS5 3BG. *T:* Walsall 27898; 35 Vandon Court, SW1H 9HE. *Clubs:* Bentley Labour, Darlaston Labour, Caldmore Liberal; North Walsall, Pleck and Station Street Working Men's Clubs.

GEORGE, Prof. Donald William; Vice-Chancellor and Principal, University of Newcastle, New South Wales, since 1975; Chairman, Australian Atomic Energy Commission, since 1976; *b* 22 Nov. 1926; *s* of late H. W. George, Sydney; *m* 1950, Lorna M. Davey, Parkes, NSW; one *s* one *d*. *Educ:* Univ. of Sydney. BSc, BE, PhD, FIEE, FIMechE, FIEAust, FAIP. Lectr, Elec. Engrg, NSW Univ. of Technology, 1949-53; Exper. Officer, UKAEA, Harwell, 1954-55; Res. Officer, Sen. Res. Officer, AAEC, Harwell and Lucas Heights, 1956-59; Sen. Lectr, Elec. Engrg, Univ. of Sydney, 1960-66; Associate Prof., Elec. Engrg, Univ. of Sydney, 1967-68; P. N. Russell Prof. of Mech. Engrg, Univ. of Sydney, 1969-74. *Publications:* numerous sci. papers and techn. reports. *Address:* University of Newcastle, New South Wales 2308, Australia. *T:* 68-0401.

GEORGE, Griffith Owen, TD; DL; a Recorder of the Crown Court, 1972-74; *b* 5 Dec. 1902; *s* of late John and Emiah Owen George, Hirwaun, Glam; *m* 1937, Anne Elinor, *e d* of late Charles and Anne Edwards, Llandaff; one *s*. *Educ:* Westminster Sch.; Christ Church, Oxford (MA). Beit Prize Essay, 1923; Barrister, Gray's Inn, 1927, Wales and Chester Circuit. Served War of 1939-45, 2nd Lieut RA, 1939; Capt. 1941; Major 1943; on JAG's staff, N Africa, Italy, Middle East, 1943-45. Contested Llanelly (Nat. Con.), 1945. Commissioner in Wales under the National Insurance Acts, 1950-67. Dep. Chm., Glamorgan Quarter Sessions, 1956-66, Chm., 1966-71. JP Glamorgan, 1952-72; DL Glamorgan, 1970. *Address:* The Mount, Peterston super Ely, Glamorgan. *T:* Peterston 358.

GEORGE, Herbert Horace, CB 1944; MC; *b* 1890; *s* of John George, Clapham; *m* 1913, Emily Rose (*d* 1952), *d* of Thomas Eaton, Clapham; no *c*. *Educ:* Westminster City Sch.; Trinity Coll., Cambridge. Entered Civil Service, 1913. Served in RA in European War, 1914-19. Under-Sec. for Finance and Accountant-Gen., Ministry of Health, 1946-50; retired, 1950. *Address:* Fouryews, Telham, Battle, East Sussex. *T:* Battle 2927.

GEORGE, Hywel, CMG 1968; OBE 1963; Bursar, Churchill College, Cambridge, since 1972; *b* 10 May 1924; *s* of Rev. W. M. George and Catherine M. George; *m* 1955, Edith Pirchl; three *d*. *Educ:* Llanelli Gram. Sch.; UCW Aberystwyth; Pembroke Coll., Cambridge. RAF, 1943-46. Cadet, Colonial Admin. Service, N Borneo, 1949-52; District Officer, 1952-58; Secretariat, 1959-62; Resident, Sabah, Malaysia, 1963-66; Administrator, 1967-69, Governor, 1969-70, St Vincent. Panglima Darjah Kinabalu

(with title of Dato), Sabah, 1964; JMN, Malaysia, 1966. CStJ 1969. *Recreations:* tennis, walking. *Address:* 70 Storey's Way, Cambridge. *T:* Cambridge 61200.

GEORGE, Peter John, OBE 1974; HM Diplomatic Service; Counsellor and Consul General, British Embassy, Manila, since 1976; *b* 12 Dec. 1919; *s* of late Cecil John George and Mabel George; *m* 1946, Andrée Louise Pernon; one *d*. *Educ:* Sutton Grammar Sch., Plymouth. Served War, 1939-46: Captain. Home Civil Service, 1936; HM Diplomatic Service, 1966; First Secretary, Commercial: Colombo, 1967-70; Seoul, 1971-73 (Chargé d'Affaires *ai*, 1971 and 1972); Prague, 1973-76. *Recreations:* golf, tennis, ski-ing, bridge. *Address:* c/o Foreign and Commonwealth Office, SW1A 2AH. *Club:* Royal Commonwealth Society.

GEORGE, Rev. Raymond; *see* George, Rev. A. R.

GEORGE, Thomas Neville, FRS 1963; FRSE, FGS, DSc Wales, PhD, ScD Cantab; Professor of Geology in the University of Glasgow, 1947-74, now Emeritus; *b* 13 May 1904; *s* of T. Rupert George, Swansea; *m* 1932, Dr Sarah Davies; no *c*. *Educ:* Dynevor Sch.; Swansea Grammar Sch.; Universities of Wales (Swansea Coll., Sen. Scholar, Univ. Res. Scholar), Cambridge (St John's Coll., Bonney Award) and London (Birkbeck Coll.). Fellow of the University of Wales, 1926. Geologist on HM Geological Survey, 1930; Prof. of Geology and Head of the Dept of Geology and Geography, University Coll. of Swansea, 1933; Woodward Lectr, Yale Univ., 1956; Sen. Foreign Fellow (Nat. Sci. Foundation), Northwestern Univ., 1964; Vis. Prof., Universities of the Witwatersrand, Cape Town, and Natal, 1967; Distinguished Vis. Lectr, Univ. of Saskatchewan, 1974; Leverhulme Emeritus Fellow, 1977. Pres. Geology Section of British Assoc. (Liverpool), 1953. Chairman: Newbattle Abbey Coll. Exec. Cttee; Brit. Assoc. Glasgow Cttee; Mineral Resources Panel (Scottish Council); Geological Conservation Council; Scot. Field Studies Assoc. Vice-Pres., RSE, 1959-61. President: Geol. Soc. London, 1968-70; Assoc. University Teachers, 1959-60; Palæontological Assoc., 1962-64; Assoc. Teachers Geol., 1970-71. Member: Nature Conservancy; Mineral Resources Consultative Cttee (Dept of Education and Science); Geology and Geophysics Cttee (NERC); Oceanography and Fisheries Cttee (NERC); Unit of Coastal Sedimentation (NERC); National Broadcasting Council (Scotland); Ct of Governors, Coleg Harlech. Corr. Mem., Geol. Soc. Belgium. Hon. LLD Wales 1970; Hon. D-ès-Sc (Rennes) 1956. Lyell Medal, Geological Soc. London, 1963; Clough Medal, Geol Soc. Edinburgh, 1973; Kelvin Prize, Roy. Philos. Soc., 1975. Associate Editor, Royal Society. *Publications:* Evolution in Outline, 1951; British Regional Geology: North Wales, 1961; South Wales, 1969; Aspects of the Variscan Fold Belt (in part), 1962; The British Caledonides (in part), 1963; The Geology of Scotland (in part), 1964; University Instruction in Geology, 1965; (contrib.) The Upper Palaeozoic Rocks of Wales, 1974; contributions on geology and palæontology to technical journals. *Address:* c/o Department of Geology, University of Glasgow, Glasgow W2. *T:* 041-339 8855; 1 Princes Terrace, Glasgow G12 9JW.

GEORGE-BROWN, family name of **Baron George-Brown.**

GEORGE-BROWN, Baron *cr* 1970 (Life Peer), of Jevington, Sussex; **George Alfred George-Brown,** PC 1951; Director, First Fortune Holdings, since 1974; *b* 2 Sept. 1914; *s* of George Brown; name changed to George-Brown by deed poll, 1970; *m* 1937, Sophie Levene; two *d*. MP (Lab) Belper Div. of Derbyshire, 1945-70; Parliamentary Private Secretary to Minister of Labour and National Service, 1945-47, to Chancellor of the Exchequer, 1947; Joint Parliamentary Secretary, Ministry of Agriculture and Fisheries, 1947-51; Min. of Works, April-Oct. 1951; First Secretary of State and Secretary of State for Economic Affairs, Oct. 1964-Aug. 1966; Secretary of State for Foreign Affairs, 1966-68. Dep. Leader, Labour Party, 1960-70. Productivity Counsellor, Courtaulds Ltd, 1968-73; Chm., Stewart Title (UK) Ltd, 1974-75; Dep. Chm., G. C. Turner & Co. Ltd, 1977-; Chm., G. B. S. Title (UK) Ltd, 1976-. Order of Cedar of Lebanon, 1971. Biancamano Prize (Italy), 1972. *Publication:* In My Way (memoirs), 1971. *Address:* c/o House of Lords, SW1.
See also R. W. Brown.

GEORGES-PICOT, Jacques Marie Charles, KBE (Hon.) 1963; Commandeur, Légion d'Honneur; Hon. Chairman of the Board, Suez Finance Company (Chairman, 1957-70); *b* 16 Dec. 1900; *s* of Charles Georges-Picot and Marthe Fouquet; *m* 1925, Angéline Pelle; five *s*. *Educ:* Lycée Janson de Sailly, Paris. Inspector of Finance, 1925; Chef de Cabinet, Minister of Budget, 1931; Dir Min. of Finance, 1934; Agent Supérieur in Egypt, of

Suez Canal Co., 1937; Asst Dir-Gen. of Suez Canal Co., 1946; Dir-Gen., 1953; Pres., 1957. Dir, Fondation des Sciences Politiques, Paris. *Publication:* La véritable crise de Suez, 1975. *Recreation:* tennis. *Address:* 2 Square Mignot, 75016 Paris, France. *T:* 727-7968. *Club:* Circle Interallié (Paris).

GERAHTY, Sir Charles Cyril, Kt 1939; QC, Trinidad, 1931; *b* 1888; *s* of Charles Echlin Gerahty; *m* 1st, 1915, Ethel Marian (*d* 1942), *d* of late Dr James Murray, MB, ChB; one *s* (younger killed in action April 1945); 2nd, 1948, Arminell Morshead (*d* 1966); 3rd, 1967, Mary Violet, *widow* of Gerald Watson, late of Pyrford, Woking. *Educ:* Trent Coll. Called to Bar, Middle Temple, 1909; Maj. (retd). 3rd Bn East Lancs Regt; Asst Resident, Nigeria, 1911; on active service, European War, 1914-18; Legal Asst, War Office, 1919; Pres., District Court, Cyprus, 1920; Attorney-Gen., Cyprus, 1926; Attorney-Gen., Trinidad, 1929; Puisne Judge, Straits Settlements (Singapore), 1932; Legal Adviser to Governor of Malta, 1935; Legal Sec. to Government of Malta, 1936; Chief Justice of Trinidad and Tobago and Pres. West Indian Court of Appeal, 1937-43; retired, 1943. Chm. of a Pensions Appeal Tribunal, England, April 1944. Dir-Gen. MGC Branch, Legal Div., CCG, Dec. 1944-July 1946; Acting Attorney-Gen. in Gibraltar, May-Aug. 1949; JP, 1951-55; Dep. Chm. Essex Court of Quarter Sessions, 1951-55. *Address:* Pendean Convalescent Home, Midhurst, Sussex.

GERARD, family name of **Baron Gerard.**

GERARD, 4th Baron, *cr* 1876, Bt 1611; **Robert William Frederick Alwyn Gerard;** *b* 23 May 1918; *o s* of 3rd Baron Gerard, MC, and late Mary Frances Emma, *d* of Sir Martin Le Marchant Hadsley Gosselin, GCVO, KCMG, CB; *S* father, 1953. *Heir: cousin* Rupert Charles Frederick Gerard, MBE [*b* 6 Oct. 1916; *m* 1948, Huguette Reiss-Brian (marr. diss. 1969); two *s*]. *Address:* Blakesware, Ware, Herts. *T:* 3665.

GERARD, Geoffrey; see Gerard, W. G.

GERARD, Rt. Rev. George Vincent, CBE 1944; Assistant Bishop of Sheffield, 1947-71; Residentiary Canon of Sheffield Cathedral, 1960-69; Chairman, House of Clergy, Church Assembly, 1965-70; *b* 24 Nov. 1898; *e s* of late George and late Frederikke Marie Gerard, Snowdon, Canterbury, New Zealand; *m* 1920, Elizabeth Mary Buckley; one *s* one *d.* *Educ:* Waihi Sch., Winchester, NZ; Christ's Coll., Christchurch, NZ; Brasenose Coll., Oxford. Inns of Court, OTC 1917; 2nd Lieut The Buffs, 1918, Lieut 1918 (MC); demobilised, 1919; BA (Oxon), 1921; MA 1925; deacon, 1922; priest, 1923; Vicar of Pahiatua, 1929-32; Petone, 1932-36; St Matthew, Auckland, 1936-38; Bishop of Waiapu, 1938-44; served as Senior Chaplain to the NZ Forces, 1940-41 (prisoner, but repatriated to England, 1943). Senior NZ Chaplain South Pacific, 1944; Hospital Ship, 1945. Vicar and Rural Dean of Rotherham, 1945-60; Hon. Canon of Sheffield, 1947-60. Proctor in Convocation of York, 1950 and 1952-70. *Address:* 18 Barton Court Avenue, New Milton, Hants BH25 7HD.

GERARD, (William) Geoffrey, CMG 1963; Chairman of Directors, Gerard Industries Pty Ltd, S Australia, since 1950 (Managing Director, 1930-76); *b* 16 June 1907; *s* of late A. E. Gerard; *m* 1932, Elsie Lesetta, *d* of late A. Lowe; one *s* one *d.* *Educ:* Adelaide Technical High Sch. Pres., SA Chamber of Manufactures, 1953-54; Pres., Associated Chambers of Manufactures of Aust., 1955; Pres., SA Metal Industries Assoc., 1952 and 1957; Pres., Aust. Metal Industries Assoc., 1962-64; Vice-Chm., Standards Assoc. of Aust., 1956-; Pres., Aust.-Amer. Assoc. in SA Incorp., 1961-63; Chm., Nat. Employers' Assoc., 1964-66; Pres., Liberal and Country League (SA Div. of Liberal Party of Aust.), 1961-64; Mem. Commonwealth Immigration Planning Council, 1956-74; Mem. Commonwealth Manufg Industries Advisory Coun., 1958-62. Past Pres., Electrical Devel. Assoc. of SA and Electrical Manufrs' Assoc. of SA. Captain, Kooyonga Golf Club, SA, 1953-55. *Recreations:* golf, tennis. *Address:* 9 Robe Terrace, Medindie, SA 5081, Australia. *T:* 44 2560. *Clubs:* Adelaide, Commonwealth (Adelaide).

GERARD-PEARSE, Rear-Adm. John Roger Southey; Assistant Chief of Naval Staff (Operations), since 1977; *b* 10 May 1924; *s* of Dr Gerard-Pearse; *m* 1955, Barbara Jean Mercer; two *s* two *d.* *Educ:* Clifton College. Joined RN, 1943; comd HM Ships Tumult, Grafton, Defender, Fearless and Ark Royal; Flag Officer, Sea Training, 1975-76. *Recreations:* sailing, carpentry. *Address:* Ministry of Defence, Main Building, Whitehall, SW1A 2HB.

GERE, John Arthur Giles; Keeper, Department of Prints and Drawings, British Museum, since 1973; *b* 7 Oct. 1921; *o s* of

Arnold Gere and Carol Giles; *m* 1958, Charlotte Douie; one *s* one *d.* *Educ:* Winchester; Balliol College, Oxford. Assistant Keeper, British Museum, 1946; Deputy Keeper, 1966. *Publications:* (with Robin Ironside) Pre-Raphaelite Painters, 1948; (with Philip Pouncey) Catalogue of Drawings by Raphael and his Circle in the British Museum, 1962; Taddeo Zuccaro: his development studied in his drawings, 1969; I disegni dei maestri: il manierismo a Roma, 1971; various exhibition catalogues; contribs to Burlington Magazine, Master Drawings, etc. *Recreation:* ecclesiastical biography. *Address:* 21 Lamont Road, SW10.

GÉRIN, Winifred, (Mrs John Lock), OBE 1975; MA Cantab; FRSL; author; 2nd *d* of F. C. Bourne and Katharine (*née* Hill); *m* 1st, Eugene Gérin (*d* 1945), of Brussels; 2nd, 1954, John Lock; no *c.* *Educ:* Sydenham High Sch. for Girls; Newnham Coll., Cambridge. War of 1939-45 in Political Intelligence Dept of Foreign Office. James Tait Black Mem. Prize, 1968; RSL Heinemann Prize, 1968; Rose Mary Crawshay Prize, 1968. FRSL 1968; Mem. Council, RSL. *Plays:* My Dear Master, Arts Theatre, Leeds, 1955; Juniper Hall, BBC TV, 1956. *Publications:* Anne Brontë, 1959; Branwell Brontë, 1961; The Young Fanny Burney, 1961; Charlotte Brontë, 1967; Horatia Nelson, 1970; (ed) Charlotte Brontë, Five Novelettes (from MSS), 1971; Emily Brontë, 1971; Writers and their Work: the Brontës (2 vols), British Council, 1973; Elizabeth Gaskell: a biography, 1976 (Whitbread award); editorial work. *Recreations:* music, country life, travelling. *Address:* 2 Marlborough Court, Pembroke Road, W8; 3 The Green, Stanford-in-the-Vale, Berks.

GERMAN, Sir Ronald (Ernest), KCB 1965; Kt 1959; CMG 1953; Director: Securicor Ltd since 1967; National Counties Building Society since 1966; *b* 19 Oct. 1905; *m* 1931, Dorothy Sparks; no *c.* *Educ:* HM Dockyard Sch., Devonport. Entered GPO 1925; Asst Dir Posts & Telegraphs Dept, Sudan, 1942; British Post Office, 1945; Postmaster-Gen., East Africa, 1950-58; Dep. Dir Gen. of the Post Office, UK, 1959-60, Dir Gen., 1960-66. Chm. Makerere Coll. Council, 1957-58 (Vice-Chm. 1954). CStJ, 1963. *Address:* Chelwood, 8A Grassington Road, Eastbourne, East Sussex.

GERNSHEIM, Helmut Erich Robert; photo-historian and author; *b* Munich, 1 March 1913; 3rd *s* of Karl Gernsheim, historian of literature at Munich Univ., and Hermine Gernsheim (*née* Scholz); *m* 1942, Alison Eames, London (*d* 1969); no *c*; *m* 1971, Irène Guénin, Geneva. *Educ:* St Anne's Coll., Augsburg; State Sch. of Photography, Munich. Settled in England as free-lance photographer, 1937; became British subject, 1946; during War of 1939-45 made photogr. surveys of historic bldgs and monuments for Warburg Inst. (London Univ.); exhibns of these at Churchill Club and Courtauld Inst., 1945 and 1946, Nat. Gall., 1944; one-man show at Royal Photogr. Society 1948; since 1945 has built up Gernsheim photo-historical collection, now 1964 at University of Texas, Austin; selections were shown at art museums, Europe and America. Re-discovered world's first photograph (taken in 1826), 1952. Co-ed. Photography Yearbook, 1953-55; British Representative World Exhibition of Photography, Lucerne, 1952, Biennale and Unesco Conference on Photography, Paris, 1955, etc. Photographic adviser to Granada TV on first British action still films, 1958-62. Editorial Adviser, Encyclopædia Britannica and several Museums and Universities. Dir, Photo-Graphic Editions. Trustee, Swiss Foundn for Photography. First German cultural prize for photography, 1959. Order of Merit, Germany, 1970. *Publications include:* New Photo Vision, 1942; Julia Margaret Cameron, 1948, revd and enlarged edn, 1975; Lewis Carroll-Photographer, 1949; Beautiful London, 1950; Masterpieces of Victorian Photography, 1951; Those Impossible English, 1952; Churchill, His Life in Photographs, 1955; Creative Photography, 1962; (with Alison Gernsheim): Roger Fenton, 1954; The History of Photography, 1955, new and enlarged edn, 1969; L. J. M. Daguerre, 1956; Queen Victoria, a Biography in Word and Picture, 1959; Historic Events, 1960; Edward VII and Queen Alexandra, 1962; Concise History of Photography, 1965; contrib. Oxford History of Technology, 19th and 20th century; numerous articles in art and photographic journals in many countries. *Recreations:* travelling, classic music, opera, collecting African art. *Address:* Residenza Tamporiva, Via Tamporiva 28, 6976 Castagnola, Ticino, Switzerland. *T:* Lugano 091 515904.

GEROSA, Peter Norman; Under-Secretary, Road Safety, Department of Transport, since 1977; *b* 1 Nov. 1928; *s* of late Enrico Cecil and Olive Doris Gerosa; *m* 1955, Dorothy Eleanor Griffin; two *d.* *Educ:* Whitgift Sch.; London Univ. (Birkbeck). BA (Hons) 1st Cl., Classics. Clerk, Foreign Office, 1945. Exec. Officer, Home Office, 1949. HM Customs and Excise: Asst

Principal, 1953; Principal, 1956; Customs Expert, EFTA, 1961-63. Asst Sec., Min. of Transport, 1966; Dept of the Environment: Asst Sec., 1970; Under-Sec., 1972. *Recreations:* singing, gardening, walking. *Address:* 1 Wray Mill House, Reigate, Surrey. *T:* Redhill 64470.

GERRARD, Prof. Alfred Horace; Professor of Sculpture in University of London at University College Slade School of Fine Art, 1948-68, now Emeritus; *b* 7 May 1899; *m* 1933, Katherine Leigh-Pemberton (*d* 1970); *m* 1972, Nancy Sinclair. *Educ:* Hartford County Council Sch.; Manchester Sch. of Art; Slade Sch. of Fine Art, University Coll., London. Head of Dept of Sculpture, Slade Sch., UCL, 1925-48. Served European War, 1914-18, Cameron Highlanders, 1916-17; RFC, 1917-19; War of 1939-45, Staff Captain, War Office, attached Royal Engineers, 1939-43; war artist, 1944-45; temp. Head, Slade Sch. of Fine Art, 1948-49. RBS Silver Medal, 1960. Fellow, University Coll. London, 1969. *Recreation:* gardening. *Address:* Dairy House, Leyswood, Groombridge, Tunbridge Wells, Kent. *T:* Groombridge 268.

GERRARD, Basil Harding; His Honour Judge Gerrard; a Circuit Judge (formerly a Judge of County Courts), since 1970; *b* 10 July 1919; *s* of late Lawrence Allen Gerrard and Mary (*née* Harding); *m* Sheila Mary Patricia (*née* Coggins), widow of Walter Dring, DSO, DFC (killed in action, 1945); one *s* two *d* and one step *d*. *Educ:* Bryanston Sch.; Caius Coll., Cambridge (BA). Royal Navy, 1940-46. Called to Bar, Gray's Inn, 1947; Recorder of Barrow-in-Furness, 1969-70. Mem., Parole Bd for England and Wales, 1974-76. *Recreations:* golf, gardening. *Address:* Diamond Farm, Plumley, near Knutsford, Cheshire. *T:* Knutsford 2061. *Club:* Knutsford Golf.

GERRARD, Ronald Tilbrook, FICE, FIWE; Senior Partner, Binnie & Partners, Consulting Engineers, since 1974; *b* 23 April 1918; *s* of Henry Thomas Gerrard and Edith Elizabeth Tilbrook; *m* 1950, Cecilia Margaret Bremner; three *s* one *d*. *Educ:* Imperial Coll. of Science and Technology, Univ. of London BSc(Eng). FCGI. FICE 1957; FIWE 1965; MEIC. Served War, RE, 1939-45. Resident Engr, sea defence and hydro-electric works, 1947-50; Asst Engr, design of hydro-power schemes in Scotland and Canada, 1951-54; Binnie & Partners: Sen. Engr, 1954; Partner, 1959; resp. for hydro-power, water supply, river engrg, coast protection and indust. works in UK and overseas. Chm., Assoc. of Cons. Engrs, 1969-70; Mem. Council, ICE, 1974-77. Telford Silver Medal, ICE, 1968. *Publications:* (jtly) 3 papers to ICE. *Address:* 6 Ashdown Road, Epsom, Surrey. *T:* Epsom 24834. *Club:* Athenæum.

GERRARD-WRIGHT, Brig. Richard Eustace John, CBE 1977 (OBE 1971; MBE 1965); on exchange at National Defence College of Canada, 1977-78; *b* 9 May 1930; *s* of Rev. R. L. Gerrard-Wright and Mrs Gerrard-Wright; *m* 1960, Susan Kathleen Young; two *s* two *d*. *Educ:* Christ's Hosp., Horsham, Sussex; RMA, Sandhurst; Staff Coll. (psc) Jt Services Staff Coll. (jssc). Commnd 1949; 1950-70: Platoon Comdr, Egypt; Adjt; Co.Comdr, Germany; ADC to C-in-C, York; Adjt, Co. Comdr, Malaya; Instr, RMA Sandhurst; Co. Comdr, Germany; Staff Coll., India; Bde Major, Kenya; Co. Comdr, Aden and Malta; Bde Major, Malaysia; Bn Comdr, England, NI, and Germany, 1970-73; SO Germany, 1973-75; Bde Comdr, Belfast, 1975-77. *Recreations:* most sports, military history. *Address:* Hillgarth, Woodlands Road, Camberley, Surrey. *T:* Camberley 64717. *Clubs:* Army and Navy, MCC; Free Foresters.

GERSHEVITCH, Dr Ilya, FBA 1967; Reader in Iranian Studies, University of Cambridge, since 1965; *b* Zürich, 24 Oct. 1914; *o s* of Arkadi and Mila Gershevitch, Smolensk, Russia; *m* 1951, Lisbeth, *d* of Josef Syfrig, Lucerne; one *d*. *Educ:* Swiss schools at Locarno and Lugano; Univ. of Rome (classics); Univ. of London (Oriental studies). Dottore in Lettere, Univ. of Rome, 1937; PhD, Univ. of London, 1943. Monitored foreign broadcasts, London, 1942-47; Lecturer in Iranian Studies, Univ. of Cambridge, 1948; MA Cambridge, 1948. First European to penetrate into certain areas of Western Makran (dialect fieldwork), 1956; Vis. Prof. at Columbia Univ., New York, 1960-61 and 1965-66; Fellow of Jesus Coll., Cambridge, 1962; Univ. Exchange Visitor, USSR, 1965; Ratanbai Katrak Lecturer, Univ. of Oxford, 1968. Hon. PhD Berne, 1971. *Publications:* A Grammar of Manichean Sogdian, 1954; The Avestan Hymn to Mithra, 1959; articles in specialist jls, encyclopaedias and collective books. *Recreation:* music. *Address:* 54 Owlstone Road, Cambridge CB3 9JH. *T:* Cambridge 57996.

GERSTENBERG, Richard Charles; *b* Little Falls, NY, 24 Nov. 1909; *s* of Richard Paul Gerstenberg and Mary Julia Booth; *m* 1934, Evelyn Josephine Hitchingham; one *s* one *d*. *Educ:* Univ. of Michigan (AB). General Motors Corporation: Asst

Comptroller, 1949-55; Treasurer, 1956-60; Vice-Pres., in charge of financial staff, 1960-67; in charge of Finance, 1967-70; Vice-Chm. Bd and Chm. Finance Cttee, 1970-72; Chm., 1972-74; a Director, 1967-. Member of Board: National Detroit Corp.; National Bank of Detroit; Detroit Edison Co.; Marsh McLennan Corp.; Miles Laboratories Inc.; Chm., Alfred Sloan Foundn. *Address:* 80 Cranbrook Road, Bloomfield Hills, Michigan, USA. *Clubs:* University, Links (New York City); Recess, Detroit Athletic (Detroit); Bloomfield Hills Country; Paradise Valley Country (Scottsdale, Arizona).

GERVIS-MEYRICK, Sir George David Eliott Tapps-; *see* Meyrick.

GERY, Robert Lucian W.; *see* Wade-Gery.

GETHIN, Lt-Col (Retd) Sir Richard Patrick St Lawrence, 9th Bt, *cr* 1665; late REME; *b* 15 May 1911; *s* of Col Sir Richard Walter St Lawrence Gethin, 8th Bt, and Helen (*d* 1957), *d* of W. B. Thornhill; *S* father 1946; *m* 1946, Fara, *y d* of late J. H. Bartlett; one *s* four *d*. *Educ:* Oundle Sch. Lieut RAOC, 1935; Lieut-Col REME, 1943; Officer Commanding No 11 Vehicle Depot Workshops, until 1957, retired. Restorer of antique furniture. *Publication:* Restoring Antique Furniture, 1974. *Heir:* *s* Richard Joseph St Lawrence Gethin, *b* 29 Sept. 1949. *Address:* Easter Cottage, Bredon, near Tewkesbury, Glos. *T:* Bredon 354.

GETHING, Air Commodore Richard Templeton, CB 1960; OBE 1945; AFC 1939; *b* 11 Aug. 1911; *s* of George A. Gething, Wilmslow, Cheshire; *m* 1940, Margaret Helen, *d* of late Sir Herbert Gepp, Melbourne, Australia; one *s* one *d*. *Educ:* Malvern; Sydney Sussex Coll., Cambridge. Joined RAF, 1933. Served War of 1939-45: Canada; UK; India; Burma. Actg Group Capt., 1943; Group Capt., 1950; Actg Air Commodore, 1956; Dir Operations, Maritime Navigation and Air Traffic, Air Ministry, 1956-60, retired. FIN 1956. *Recreation:* gliding. *Address:* Garden Hill, Kangaroo Ground, Victoria 3097, Australia. *Club:* Royal Air Force.

GHALE, Jemadar Gaje; *see* Gaje Ghale.

GIAEVER, Dr Ivar; Staff Member, General Electric Research and Development Center, since 1958; *b* 5 April 1929; *s* of John A. Giaever and Gudrun (*née* Skaarud); *m* 1952, Inger Skramstad; one *s* three *d*. *Educ:* Norwegian Inst. of Tech.; Rensselaer Polytechnical Inst. ME 1952; PhD 1964. Norwegian Army, 1952-53; Norwegian Patent Office, 1953-54; Canadian General Electric, 1954-56; General Electric, 1956-58. Fellow, Amer. Phys. Soc.; Member: Nat. Acad. of Sciences; Nat. Acad. of Engineering; Amer. Acad. of Arts and Scis; Norwegian Acad. of Scis; Norwegian Acad. of Technology; Norwegian Profl Engrs. Oliver E. Buckley Prize, 1964; Nobel Prize for Physics, 1973; Zworykin Award, 1974. Hon. DSc: RPI, 1974; Union Coll., 1974; Hon. DEng, Michigan Tech. Univ., 1976; Hon. DPhys, Oslo, 1976. *Publications:* contrib. Physical Review, Jl Immunology. *Recreations:* ski-ing, tennis, camping, hiking. *Address:* General Electric Research and Development Center, PO Box 8, Schenectady, New York 12301, USA. *T:* 518-346-8771.

GIAUQUE, William (Francis); Professor of Chemistry, University of California, Berkeley, 1934-62, Emeritus 1962; recalled to active service, 1962-77; continuing research, since 1977; *b* (as US citizen) Niagara Falls, Ont., Canada, 12 May 1895; *s* of William T. S. Giauque and Isabella Jane (*née* Duncan); *m* 1932, Muriel Frances Ashley, BS, PhD; two *s*. *Educ:* High Sch., Niagara Falls; University of Calif. BS 1920, PhD 1922. Faculty of Chemistry, University of Calif.: Instructor, 1922-27; Asst Prof., 1927-30; Assoc. Prof., 1930-34. Government work during War of 1939-45. Member: National Academy of Sciences; Amer. Philosophical Soc.; Amer. Acad. of Arts and Sciences. Hon. DSc Columbia; Hon. LLD Univ. Calif. Nobel prize for Chemistry, 1949; and other awards. *Publications:* about 200 papers in scientific journals. *Address:* 2643 Benvenue Avenue, Berkeley, Calif 94704, USA; University of California, Berkeley, Calif, USA.

GIBB, Andrew (McArthur); a Recorder of the Crown Court since 1977; *b* 8 Sept. 1927; *s* of William and Ruth Gibb; *m* 1956, Olga Mary (*née* Morris); three *d*. *Educ:* Sedbergh; Queens' Coll., Cambridge (MA). Called to the Bar, Middle Temple, 1952. Chm., Cttee of Public Inquiry into fire at Wensley Lodge, Hessle, Humberside, 1977. *Recreations:* golf, reading, music. *Address:* The Firs, Bowdon, Cheshire. *T:* 061-928 4727.

GIBB, George Dutton; Chief Dental Officer, Department of Health and Social Security and Department of Education and Science, since 1971; *b* 9 March 1920; *s* of late Dr William

Forsyth Gibb and Margaret Jane Gibb (*née* Dutton); *m* 1948, Mary Dupree; two *d. Educ:* St Helen's Coll., Southsea; University Tutorial Coll., London; Guy's Hospital. LDS RCS 1950. Enlisted RNVR, 1940; commnd (Exec. Br.) 1941. Gen. Dental Practitioner, High Wycombe, 1950-71. Mem., Bucks Exec. Council, 1957-65; Hon. Sec., Bucks Local Dental Cttee, 1957-65; Mem., Standing Dental Adv. Cttee, 1964-71; Mem., Central Health Services Council, 1967-71; Chm. of Council, British Dental Assoc., 1967-71; Mem., Odontological Section, RSocMed, 1972. *Recreations:* gardening, motoring. *Address:* Yenda, Haw Lane, Bledlow Ridge, High Wycombe, Bucks. *T:* Bledlow Ridge 300.

GIBB, Ian Pashley; Keeper, British Library Reference Division, since 1977; *b* 17 April 1926; *s* of John Pashley Gibb and Mary (*née* Owen); *m* 1953, Patricia Mary Butler; two *s. Educ:* Latymer Upper Sch.; UCL (BA). ALA. Sen. Library Asst, Univ. of London, 1951-52; Asst Librarian, UCL, 1952-58; Dep. Librarian, National Central Library, 1958-73; British Library: Dep. Dir, Science Reference Library, 1973-75; Head of Divl Office, Reference Div., 1975-77. Part-time Lectr, UCL, 1967-77. *Publications:* various articles. *Recreations:* music, watching cricket, bridge. *Address:* 42 On The Hill, Carpenders Park, Watford, Herts. *T:* 01-428 3032.

GIBB, Thomas George, CBE 1975; retired; *b* 21 Feb. 1915; 2nd *s* of late Paul and Phyllis Gibb, Aldeburgh, Suffolk; *m* 1944, Angela, *d* of late Canon and Mrs G. E. H. Theophilus; three *s* one *d. Educ:* St Edward's Sch., Oxford. Joined LNER as Traffic Apprentice, 1933. Commissioned LNER Co. (Supp. Reserve) RE, 1938; Capt. 1939; seconded Min. of Supply, 1941-45. Joined Currie and Co. (Newcastle) Ltd 1945, Dir and Gen. Man., 1947; British Road Services, 1949, appointments including Divisional Manager, NE Div., 1956; Chairman, British Road Services, 1959; Vice-Chm. and Man. Dir, BRS Federation Ltd, 1963-67; Dir, Transport Holding Co., 1967-68; Man. Dir, Freightliners Ltd, 1969-72 (Chm. 1975); Exec. Dir, Nat. Freight Corp., 1972-75. Mem., Road Transport Industry Training Board, 1966-69. *Recreations:* sailing, cricket, golf. *Address:* Carrick House, Tayvallich, Lochgilphead, Argyll. *Club:* Clyde Cruising (Glasgow).

GIBB, Walter Frame, DSO 1945; DFC 1943; JP; Product Support Manager, British Aircraft Corporation Limited; *b* 26 March 1919; British; *m* 1944, Pauline Sylvia Reed; three *d. Educ:* Clifton Coll. Apprentice, Bristol Aero Engines, 1937. RAF, 1940-46. Test Pilot, Bristol Aircraft Ltd, 1946; Asst Chief Test Pilot, 1953; Chief Test Pilot, Bristol Aeroplane Co. Ltd, 1956-60. World Altitude Height Record 63,668 feet in Olympus-Canberra, 1953, and second record 65,890 ft in same machine, 1955. MRAeS. JP Bristol, 1974. *Recreation:* sailing. *Address:* Greystones, Olveston, near Bristol. *T:* Almondsbury 613279. *Club:* Royal Air Force.

GIBB, William Eric, MA, DM Oxon; FRCP; Physician: St Bartholomew's Hospital since 1947; The Metropolitan Hospital since 1952; *b* 30 April 1911; *s* of late James Glenny Gibb, MD, FRCS, and Georgina Henman; *m* 1952, Mary Edith Gertrude Feetham; three *s. Educ:* Rugby Sch.; Oriel Coll., Oxford; St Bartholomew's Hosp. BA Oxon 1st Cl. Hons Final Sch. of Nat. Science; Prox. Access. Theodore Williams Scholarship (Anatomy); BM, BCh Oxon 1936; MRCP 1940; DM Oxon 1947; FRCP 1949; George Herbert Hunt Travelling Schol. (University of Oxford), 1938. Res. House appts, St Bart's Hosp. and Brompton Chest Hosp.; Cattlin Research Scholar, 1947. War service with RAFVR Medical Branch, 1941-46; Actg Wing Comdr i/c a Medical Div. Examiner in Medicine, University of Oxford, 1952-59 and Examiner in Medicine, Examg Bd of England. Fellow, Royal Soc. Med. and Med. Soc. London. *Publications:* various articles in medical journals. *Recreation:* gardening. *Address:* 95 Harley Street, W1. *T:* 01-935 6267.

GIBBENS, (Edward) Brian, MA Oxon; QC 1962; **His Honour Judge Brian Gibbens;** a Circuit Judge, since 1973; *b* 26 Sept. 1912; *s* of Rev. George Percy Gibbens and Dr Fanny Gibbens; *m* 1939, Kathleen Joan Rosier; two *s* one *d. Educ:* Newcastle-under-Lyme High Sch.; St Catherine's Society, Oxford. Called to the Bar, Gray's Inn, 1934; Bencher of Gray's Inn, 1967; practised on Oxford Circuit from 1934. Served in RA and as staff officer, Nov. 1939-45. Major in Army Officers Emergency Reserve, 1946-. Mem. Gen. Council of the Bar, 1947-52, 1964-68, 1969-73; a Recorder of Crown Courts, 1972-73 (Recorder of West Bromwich, 1959-65, of Oxford, 1965-71); Hon. Recorder, City of Oxford, 1972-. Dep. Chm. QS, Oxon., 1964-71; Comr of Assize, Bristol, 1970, Oxford, 1971, Birmingham, 1971; Leader of the Oxford Circuit, 1966-71; Jt Leader, Midland and Oxford Circuit, 1972. Conducted Home Office inquiry into corporal punishments at Court Lees approved sch., 1967; conducted

public inquiry into automatic level crossings after railway accident at Hixon, Staffs, 1968; leading counsel for the Army in Widgery Tribunal of Inquiry into shooting of civilians in Londonderry, 1972. Hon. Mem., Midland Inst. of Forensic Medicine.

GIBBENS, Frank Edward Hilary George; His Honour Judge Frank Gibbens; a Circuit Judge, since 1973; *b* 23 April 1913; *s* of Frank Edward George and Geraldine Edel Gibbens; *m* 1940, Margaret Gertrude Wren; three *d. Educ:* Malvern; Peterhouse, Cambridge (BA). Called to Bar, Inner Temple, 1938. Served War, commission in RAF, 1940-46. Sqdn Leader, rank on demobilisation. On appt as Judge, retired from Bar, 1973. *Recreation:* golf. *Address:* Warren Close, Coombe Hill Road, Kingston-upon-Thames.

GIBBENS, Prof. Trevor Charles Noel, CBE 1977 (MBE 1945); MA, MD; FRCP, FRCPsych; Professor of Forensic Psychiatry, Institute of Psychiatry, London University, since 1967; Hon. Consultant, Bethlem Royal and Maudsley Hospitals, since 1951; Consultant to London Remand Home for Girls, since 1951; *b* 28 Dec. 1912; *s* of George Gibbens and Sarah Jane Hartley; *m* 1950, Patricia Margaret, *d* of A. E. and E. Mullis; two *s* one *d. Educ:* Westminster Sch.; Emmanuel Coll., Cambridge; St Thomas's Hosp., London. RAMC, 1939; POW, 1940-45. Sen. Lectr, Forensic Psychiatry, 1950-67. Member: Cttee on Business of the Criminal Courts (Streatfield Cttee), 1958; Royal Commn on Penal Reform, 1964-66. President: British Acad. of Forensic Sciences, 1967-68; Internat. Soc. of Criminology, 1967-74. Chm., Inst. for Study and Treatment of Delinquency, 1974-; Vice-Chm., Howard League, 1975-; Mem., Parole Board, 1972-75. Member: Adv. Gp on Law of Rape (Heilbron Cttee), 1975; Policy Adv. Cttee to Criminal Law Revision Cttee, 1976-. *Publications:* Shoplifting, 1962; Psychiatric Studies of Borstal Lads, 1963; Cultural Factors in Delinquency, 1966; articles in scientific jls. *Address:* Institute of Psychiatry, de Crespigny Park, SE5 8AF. *T:* 01-703 5411.

GIBBERD, Sir Frederick, Kt 1967; CBE 1954; RA 1969 (ARA 1961); FRIBA, FRTPI, FILA; FSIA; practising as an Architect, Town Planning Consultant and Landscape Architect; *b* 7 Jan. 1908; *e s* of late Frederick Gibberd, Kenilworth, Warwicks; *m* 1st, 1938, Dorothy (*d* 1970), *d* of late J. H. Phillips, Hampstead; one *s* two *d*; 2nd, 1972, Patricia Fox Edwards. *Educ:* King Henry VIII Sch., Coventry. Private practice in London since 1930. Principal buildings include: Pullman Court, Streatham; London Airport, Terminal Buildings and Chapel; Bath Technical College; St Neots Bridge; Hinkley Point and Didcot Power Stations; Metropolitan Cathedral, Liverpool (won in open competition); New Monastery, Douai Abbey; Longmans Green Offices, Harlow; Doncaster Law Courts (with L. J. Tucker); Designs for: Central London Mosque (won in open competition); Duke of Norfolk's Strand Estate; Coutts Bank, Strand and Hotel, Hyde Park Corner. Principal Town Designs: Harlow New Town, Architect-Planner, Memorial Univ., Newfoundland, Master Plan. Civic Centres for: Doncaster; Harlow; Leamington Spa; Nuneaton and St Albans. Shopping Centres: Lansbury Market; Redcar and Stratford-upon-Avon. Principal Landscape and Garden Designs: Harlow, overall landscape design and Water Gardens; Queen's Gardens, Hull; Llyn Celyn and Derwent Reservoirs and Potash Mine at Boulby. Member: Royal Fine Art Commission, 1950-70; Council RIBA, 1959-; President, Building Centre; Past Principal, Architectural Association School of Architecture. Hon. LLD, Liverpool, 1969. RIBA Bronze Medal; Two Festival of Britain Awards; Four Housing Medals; Five Civic Trust Awards. *Publications:* The Architecture of England, 1938; Town Design, 1953; Metropolitan Cathedral of Christ the King, Liverpool, 1968. *Recreation:* gardening. *Address:* 8 Percy Street, W1; The House, Marsh Lane, Harlow, Essex.

GIBBERD, George Frederick, CBE 1962; Consulting Obstetric Surgeon Emeritus: Guy's Hospital; Queen Charlotte's Maternity Hospital; Honorary Consulting Gynæcologist, Samaritan Hospital for Women; *s* of George William Gibberd and Jessie Waters; *m* 1930, Margaret Erica (*d* 1976), *y d* of Leslie Hugh Taffs, Langley, Bucks; two *s* one *d. Educ:* Aske's Haberdashers'; Guy's Hosp. MB, MS London; FRCS; FRCOG; Sometime Examiner in Obstetrics and Gynæcology for Universities of Cambridge, London, Wales, Manchester and Leeds, for Conjoint Examining Board of RCS and RCP, and for RCOG; Vice-Pres. RCOG, 1958-61 (hon. Sec., 1938-47; Mem. Council, 1936-61); Sims-Black Travelling Prof., RCOG, 1952; Mem. of Gynæcological Visiting Society of Great Britain. Temp. Lieut-Col, RAMC. Served War of 1939-45, in North Africa and Italy. Consulting Gynæcological Surg., St John's Hosp., Lewisham. Member: Medical Adv. Cttee, UGC, 1947-59; Maternity Services (Cranbrook) Cttee, 1956-59; Bd of Govs, Guy's Hosp.

Med. Sch., 1956-67, and Guy's Hosp., 1957-69. Hon. MD Melbourne, 1975. *Publications:* A Short Text-Book of Midwifery; (in collaboration) Queen Charlotte's Text-Book of Midwifery; contributions to medical literature. *Address:* 5 Tollgate Drive, College Road, Dulwich, SE21. *Club:* Athenæum.

GIBBINGS, Peter Walter; Chairman, Guardian and Manchester Evening News Ltd, since 1973; *b* 25 March 1929; *s* of late Walter White Gibbings and Margaret Russell Gibbings (*née* Torrance); *m* 1st, Elspeth Felicia Macintosh; two *d*; 2nd, Hon. Louise Barbara, *d* of Viscount Lambert, *qv*; one *s*. *Educ:* Rugby; Wadham Coll., Oxford (Scholar). Called to Bar, Middle Temple, 1953 (Garraway Rice Pupillage Prize; Harmsworth Schol.). Served in 9th Queen's Royal Lancers, 1951-52; Dep. Legal Adviser, Trinidad Oil Co. Ltd, 1955-56; Associated Newspapers Ltd, 1956-60; The Observer, 1960-67 (Deputy Manager and Dir, 1965-67); Man. Dir, Guardian Newspapers Ltd, 1967-73; Dir, Manchester Guardian and Evening News Ltd, 1967-73. Mem., Press Council, 1970-74. *Recreations:* lawn mowing, riding, tennis. *Address:* c/o Guardian and Manchester Evening News Ltd, 164 Deansgate, Manchester M60 2RR.

GIBBINS, Elizabeth Mary, BA; Headmistress, St Mary's School, Calne, Wilts, 1946-72; *b* 2 May 1911; *d* of late Kenneth Mayoh Gibbins, MB, BS. *Educ:* Sandecotes Sch., Parkstone; Westfield Coll., University of London; Cambridge Univ. Training Coll. for Women (Postgraduate). History Mistress, St Brandons Clergy Daughters' Sch., Bristol, 1935-38; Headmistress, Diocesan Girls' Sch., Hongkong, 1939-45, Acting Headmistress, Oct. 1972-May 1973. Hon. Sec., Hong Kong Diocesan Assoc., 1974-. *Address:* 8 Moreton Road, Old Bosham, Chichester, West Sussex. *T:* Bosham 573038.

GIBBON, Gen. Sir John (Houghton), GCB 1977 (KCB 1972; CB 1970); OBE 1945 (MBE 1944); Master-General of the Ordnance, 1974-77; ADC (General) to the Queen, 1976-77; *b* 21 Sept. 1917; *er s* of Brigadier J. H. Gibbon, The Manor House, Little Stretton, Salop; *m* 1951, Brigid Rosamund, *d* of Dr D. A. Bannerman, *qv*; one *s*. *Educ:* Eton; Trinity Coll., Cambridge. Commissioned into Royal Artillery, 1939. Served with 2nd Regt RHA: France, 1939-40; Western Desert, 1940-41; Greece, 1941; on staff of HQ 30 Corps; Western Desert, 1941-43; Sicily, 1943; GSO 1, RA, HQ 21 Army Gp, 1944-45; 6 Airborne Div., Palestine, 1946-47; Instructor and Chief Instructor, RMA Sandhurst, 1947-51; GSO 2, War Office, 1951-53; Battery Comdr, 1953-54; AQMG, War Office, 1955-58; CO Field Regt, BAOR, 1959-60; Bde Comdr, Cyprus, 1962; Dir of Defence Plans, Min. of Def., 1962-64; Sec., Chiefs of Staff Cttee, and Dir, Defence Operations Staff, 1966-69; Dir, Army Staff Duties, MoD, 1969-71; Vice-Chief of the Defence Staff, 1972-74. Col Comdt, RA, 1972-. *Recreations:* rowing, shooting, fishing. *Address:* Moth House, Brown Candover, Alresford, Hants. *T:* Preston Candover 260. *Clubs:* Naval and Military;

GIBBON, Michael, QC 1974; a Recorder of the Crown Court, since 1972; *b* 15 Sept. 1930; 2nd *s* of late F. O. Gibbon; *m* 1956, Malveen Elliot Seager; two *s* one *d*. *Educ:* Brightlands; Charterhouse; Pembroke Coll., Oxford (MA). Commnd in Royal Artillery, 1949. Called to Bar, Lincoln's Inn, 1954. Chm., Electoral Adv. Cttee to Home Sec., 1972. Deputy Chm., Local Govt Boundary Commn for Wales, 1974-. *Recreations:* music, golf. *Address:* Gellihirion, 3 Cefn-Coed Road, Cardiff CF2 6AN. *T:* Cardiff 751852. *Clubs:* Cardiff and County (Cardiff); Royal Porthcawl Golf, Cardiff Golf.

GIBBON, Monk; see Gibbon, W. M.

GIBBON, (William) Monk, PhD (Dublin); FRSL; poet and writer; *b* Dublin, 15 Dec. 1896; *o s* of late Canon William Monk Gibbon, MA, Rural Dean, Taney, Dundrum, Co. Dublin, and Isabel Agnes Pollock (*née* Meredith); *m* 1928, Mabel Winifred, *d* of Rev. Walter Molyneux Dingwall, MA, and Mabel Sophia Spender; two *s* four *d*. *Educ:* St Columba's Coll., Rathfarnham; Keble Coll., Oxford (Open History Exhibn). Served European War, 1914-18, as Officer, RASC; France, 1916-17; Invalided out, 1918. Taught in Switzerland; master at Oldfeld Sch., Swanage (12 yrs). Silver Medal for Poetry, Tailteann Games, 1928. Tredegar Memorial Lecture, Royal Society of Literature, 1952; Tagore Centenary Lecture, Abbey Theatre, Dublin, 1961. Mem. Irish Acad. of Letters, 1960 (Vice-Pres., 1967). *Publications: poetry:* The Tremulous String, 1926; The Branch of Hawthorn Tree, 1927; For Daws to Peck At, 1929; Seventeen Sonnets, 1932; This Insubstantial Pageant (collected poems), 1951; The Velvet Bow and other poems, 1972; *autobiography:* The Seals, 1935; Mount Ida, 1948; Inglorious Soldier, 1968; The Brahms Waltz, 1970; *biography:* Netta (Hon. Mrs Franklin), 1960; *novel:* The Climate of Love, 1961; *ballet and film criticism:*

The Red Shoes Ballet, 1948; The Tales of Hoffmann, 1951; An Intruder at The Ballet, 1952; *travel:* Swiss Enchantment, 1950; Austria, 1953; In Search of Winter Sport, 1953; Western Germany, 1955; The Rhine and its Castles, 1957; Great Houses of Europe, 1962; Great Palaces of Europe, 1964; *literary criticism:* The Masterpiece and the Man, 1959. The Living Torch (an Æ anthology), 1937. *Recreations:* watching ballet and good films. *Address:* 24 Sandycove Road, Sandycove, Co. Dublin, Eire. *T:* 805120.

GIBBONS, Brig. Edward John, CMG 1956; CBE 1947 (MBE 1939); *b* 30 *b* 30 Aug. 1906; *s* of Edward Gibbons, Coventry; *m* 1946, Gabrielle Maria, *widow* of Capt. P. A. Strakosh; one step *d*. *Educ:* King Henry VIII Sch., Coventry; Gonville and Caius Coll., Cambridge. Nigerian Administrative Service, 1929. Army Service, 1941-46: Dir of Civil Affairs, South East Asia Command; Brig. Sec. Eastern Provinces, Nigeria, 1948; Commissioner of the Cameroons (under UK Trusteeship), 1949-56; Dept of Technical Cooperation, 1962-64; Min. of Overseas Develt, 1964-68. *Recreation:* wood engraving. *Address:* 6 Grove House, The Grove, Epsom, Surrey. *T:* Epsom 26657. *Club:* Royal Automobile.

GIBBONS, Sir John Edward, 8th Bt *cr* 1752; Captain (Dorset Regiment); independent; *b* 14 Nov. 1914; *s* of Sir Alexander Doran Gibbons, 7th Bt and Gladys Constance (*d* 1945), *d* of late Rev. Charles Watkins; *S* father 1956; *m* 1937, Mersa Wentworth Foster (marr. diss. 1951), Warmwell House, near Dorchester; one *s* two *d*. *Educ:* Charterhouse. Asst Regional Dir (Nottingham) of Arts Council of Great Britain, 1946-50. Dorset Regt, 1939-45; Staff Officer, 1942-43, Iran and Syria. *Heir: s* William Edward Doran Gibbons [*b* 13 Jan. 1948; *m* 1972, Patricia Geraldine Archer, *d* of Ronald Archer Howse]. *Address:* 2 Malt Cottages, Preston, Weymouth, Dorset. *Club:* MCC.

GIBBONS, Stella Dorothea, FRSL; Poet and Novelist; *b* London, 5 Jan. 1902; *d* of C. J. P. T. Gibbons, MD; *m* 1933, Allan Bourne Webb (*d* 1959), actor and singer; one *d*. *Educ:* N London Collegiate Sch.; University Coll., London. Journalist, 1923-33; BUP, Evening Standard, The Lady. *Publications:* The Mountain Beast (Poems), 1930; Cold Comfort Farm, 1932 (Femina Vie Heureuse Prize, 1933); Bassett, 1934; The Priestess (Poems), 1934; Enbury Heath, 1935; The Untidy Gnome, 1935; Miss Linsey and Pa, 1936; Roaring Tower (Short Stories), 1937; Nightingale Wood, 1938; The Lowland Venus (Poems), 1938; My American, 1939; Christmas at Cold Comfort Farm (Short Stories), 1940; The Rich House, 1941; Ticky, 1943; The Bachelor, 1944; Westwood, 1946; The Matchmaker, 1949; Conference at Cold Comfort Farm, 1949; Collected Poems, 1950; The Swiss Summer, 1951; Fort of the Bear, 1953; Beside the Pearly Water (short stories), 1954; The Shadow of a Sorcerer, 1955; Here Be Dragons, 1956; White Sand and Grey Sand, 1958; A Pink Front Door, 1959; The Weather at Tregulla, 1962; The Wolves were in the Sledge, 1964; The Charmers, 1965; Starlight, 1967; The Snow Woman, 1969; The Woods in Winter, 1970. *Recreations:* reading, listening to music. *Address:* 19 Oakeshott Avenue, Highgate, N6. *T:* 01-340 2566.

GIBBS, family name of **Barons Aldenham** and **Wraxall**.

GIBBS, Dame Anstice (Rosa), DCVO 1967; CBE 1960; retired as Chief Commissioner and Chairman Girl Guides' Association (British Commonwealth) (1956-66); *b* 2 Jan. 1905; *d* of late Archdeacon The Hon. Kenneth Gibbs and late Mrs Gibbs. *Educ:* privately in England and France. Worked with Girl Guides from 1922; Dep. Chief Commissioner, 1954. Mem. Cttee of World Association of Girl Guides and Girl Scouts, 1952-60, Vice-Chm., 1954-60. *Address:* Blacknest Lodge, Brimpton Common, near Reading, Berks. *T:* Tadley 4365.

GIBBS, Air Vice-Marshal Charles Melvin, CB 1976; CBE 1966; DFC 1943; RAF retd; Director General of Personal Services, RAF, 1974-76; *b* 11 June 1921; American father, New Zealand mother; *m* 1947, Emma Pamela Pollard; one *d*. *Educ:* Taumarunui, New Zealand. Joined RNZAF, 1941; service in Western Desert and Mediterranean, 1942-44; Coastal Comd, 1945; India, 1946-47; commanded Tropical Experimental Unit, 1950-52; RAF Staff Coll., 1953; commanded No 118 Squadron, 1954-55; Directing Staff, RAF Staff Coll., 1956-58; Pakistan, 1958-61; Chief Instructor, RAF Chivenor, 1961-63; CO, Wattisham, 1963-66; idc 1967; Defence Policy Staff, 1968-69; Dir of Quartering, 1970-72; AOA, Germany, 1972-74. *Recreations:* fishing, golf. *Address:* Walnut Cottage, Ipswich Road, Ardleigh, Essex. *T:* Colchester 42770. *Clubs:* Royal Air Force; Nayland Golf (Nayland).

GIBBS, Dennis Raleigh, CMG 1962; CVO 1966; DSO 1944; company director; *b* 3 March 1922; *e s* of late Gerard Yardley Gibbs, Epping, and of Carol Gibbs (*née* Francis), London, W2; *m* 1952, Barbara Erica Batty, MB, ChB; two *s* one *d. Educ:* Bradfield Coll. RAF, 1940-46; CO 82 Sqdn, 1942-44; Wing Comdr Air Staff, Air HQ, Burma, 1945. Seconded FO, 1946; Colonial Admin. Service, 1946-56, then E Nigerian Public Service, 1956-64 (Perm. Sec., Min. of Works, 1958, Adv. to Min. of Economic Planning, 1962-64); Administrator of Montserrat, WI, 1964-71. *Recreations:* fishing, shooting, sailing. *Address:* Box 265, Vieux Fort, St Lucia, WI.

GIBBS, Hon. Eustace Hubert Beilby; HM Diplomatic Service; Consul-General, Paris, since 1977; *b* 3 July 1929; 2nd surv. *s* of 1st Baron Wraxall, PC; *b* and *heir-pres.* of 2nd Baron Wraxall, *qv; m* 1957, Evelyn Veronica Scott; three *s* two *d. Educ:* Eton College; Christ Church, Oxford (MA). ARCM 1953. Entered HM Diplomatic Service, 1954; served in Bangkok, Rio de Janeiro, Berlin and Vienna; Counsellor, Caracas, 1971-73; Royal College of Defence Studies, 1974; Inspector, 1975-77. *Recreations:* music, golf. *Address:* British Embassy, 35 rue du Faubourg St Honoré, Paris, France. *Clubs:* Brooks's, Pratt's.

GIBBS, Sir Frank Stannard, KBE, *cr* 1954 (OBE 1939); CMG 1949; *b* 3 July 1895; *m* 1944, Sylvia Madeleine Knight; one *s* one *d.* Probationer Vice-Consul, Genoa, 1920; served Madrid, Rio de Janeiro, Paris, Marseilles, Beira, Milan; Vice-Consul, 1923; transferred to China Consular Service with Consular rank, 1935; Actg Consul-Gen., Canton, 1937, Addis Ababa, 1939; served Rosario and Tunis: Consul-Gen., 1946; Foreign Service Officer, Grade 5, 1947; Consul-Gen., Saigon, 1947-51, with personal rank of Minister, 1950-51; Ambassador to the Republic of the Philippines, 1954-55 (Minister, 1951-54), retired 1955. *Address:* El Rincón, Maitland Close, West Byfleet, Surrey. *T:* Byfleet 46414.

GIBBS, Air Marshal Sir Gerald Ernest, KBE 1954 (CBE 1945); CIE 1946; MC; *b* 3 Sept. 1896; *s* of Ernest William Cecil and Fanny Wilmina Gibbs; *m* 1938, Margaret Jean Bradshaw; one *s* one *d.* Served European War, 1914-18; transferred from Army to RFC 1916, and RAF 1918 (MC and 2 bars, Légion d'Honneur, Croix de Guerre). Served various overseas periods with RAF in Iraq, Palestine, Sudan and Kenya between the two wars. Senior Air Staff Officer of No 11 Group, Fighter Command, 1940-41 during Battle of Britain; Dir of Overseas Operations, Air Ministry, 1942-43; Senior Air Staff Officer, HQ 3rd Tactical Air Force, South-East Asia, 1943-44; Chief Air Staff Officer, Supreme HQ, SEAC, 1945-46; Senior Air Staff Officer, HQ, RAF Transport Command, 1946-48; Head of Service Advisers to UK Delegation and Chm. UK Members of Military Staff Cttee, UN, 1948-51; Chief of Air Staff and Commander-in-Chief, Indian Air Force, 1951-54, retired 1954. *Publication:* Survivor's Story, 1956. *Recreations:* golf, ski-ing, sailing. *Address:* Lone Oak, 170 Coombe Lane West, Kingston-upon-Thames, Surrey. *Clubs:* Royal Air Force; Royal Wimbledon Golf (Wimbledon); Seaford Golf (East Blatchington); Trevose Golf (Cornwall).

GIBBS, Rt. Hon. Sir Harry (Talbot), PC 1972; KBE 1970; **Rt. Hon. Mr Justice Gibbs;** Justice of High Court of Australia since 1970; *b* 7 Feb. 1917; *s* of late H. V. Gibbs, formerly of Ipswich, Qld; *m* 1944, Muriel Ruth (*née* Dunn); one *s* three *d. Educ:* Ipswich Grammar Sch., Qld; Univ. of Queensland (BA, LLM). Admitted as Barrister, Qld, 1939; QC 1957; Judge of Supreme Court of Qld, 1961; Judge of Federal Court of Bankruptcy and of Supreme Court of Australian Capital Territory, 1967. *Address:* 27 Stanhope Road, Killara, NSW 2071, Australia. *T:* 498-6924. *Clubs:* Australian (Sydney); Queensland (Brisbane).

GIBBS, Rt. Hon. Sir Humphrey Vicary, PC 1969; GCVO 1969 (KCVO 1965); KCMG 1960; OBE 1959; Governor of Rhodesia (lately S Rhodesia), 1959-69; *b* 22 Nov. 1902; 3rd *s* of 1st Baron Hunsdon; *m* 1934, Molly Peel Nelson (see Molly Peel Gibbs); five *s. Educ:* Eton; Trinity Coll., Cambridge. Started farming near Bulawayo, 1928. Hon. LLD Birmingham, 1969; Hon. DCL East Anglia, 1969. *Address:* Bonisa Farm, Private Bag 5583W, Bulawayo, Rhodesia. *Clubs:* Athenæum; Bulawayo (Bulawayo, Rhodesia); Salisbury (Salisbury, Rhodesia).

GIBBS, Rt. Rev. John; see Coventry, Bishop of.

GIBBS, Martin St John Valentine, CB 1958; DSO 1942; TD; JP; DL; *b* 14 Feb. 1917; *er s* of late Major G. M. Gibbs, Parkleaze, Ewen, Cirencester; *m* 1947, Mary Margaret (*widow* of late Captain M. D. H. Wills, MC), *er d* of late Col Philip Mitford; two *d. Educ:* Eton. 2nd Lieut, Royal Wilts Yeomanry, 1937; served War of 1939-45 with Royal Wilts Yeo., Major 1942, Lieut-Col 1951, Brevet-Col 1955, Col 1958; Hon. Col: Royal

Wilts Yeomanry Sqdn, T&AVR, 1972-; The Royal Yeomanry, RAC, T&AVR, 1975-; Col Comdt Yeomanry, RAC, 1975-. Gloucestershire: JP 1965; High Sheriff, 1958; DL Wilts 1972. *Recreations:* country pursuits. *Address:* Ewen Manor, Ewen, Cirencester, Glos. *T:* Kemble 206. *Club:* Cavalry and Guards. *See also* Sir R. C. Gibbs.

GIBBS, Dame Molly (Peel), DBE 1969; (Hon. Lady Gibbs); *b* 13 July 1912; 2nd *d* of John Peel Nelson; *m* 1934, Rt Hon. Sir Humphrey Vicary Gibbs, *qv*; five *s. Educ:* Girls' High School, Barnato Park, Johannesburg. *Address:* Bonisa, Private Bag 5583W, Bulawayo, Rhodesia. *T:* Bulawayo 69002.

GIBBS, Prof. Norman Henry, MA, DPhil; Emeritus Fellow, All Souls College, Oxford, since 1977; Chichele Professor of the History of War in the University of Oxford, 1953-77; *b* 17 April 1910; *m* 1941, Joan Frances Leslie-Melville; two *d; m* 1955, Kathleen Phebe Emmett. Open Exhibitioner, Magdalen Coll., Oxford, 1928; Senior Demy, 1931; Asst Lecturer, University Coll., London, 1934-36; Fellow and Tutor in Modern History, Merton Coll., Oxford, 1936. 1st King's Dragoon Guards, 1939; Historical Section, War Cabinet Office, 1943. Chm., Naval Education Advisory Cttee; former Member: Internat. Council of Institute for Strategic Studies; Council, Royal United Service Institution; Research Associate, Center for Internat. Studies, Princeton, 1965-66. Visiting Professor: Univ. of New Brunswick, 1975-76; US Military Academy, West Point, 1978-79. *Publications:* 2nd edition, Keith, British Cabinet System, 1952; The Origins of the Committee of Imperial Defence, 1955; contribs to: Cambridge Modern History (new edn); L'Europe du XIXme et du XXme siècles, (Milan) 1966; (ed) The Soviet System and Democratic Society, 1967; History of the Second World War, Grand Strategy, Vol. 1, 1976. *Address:* All Souls College, Oxford; Flexneys House, Stanton Harcourt, Oxon.

GIBBS, Oswald Moxley, CMG 1976; High Commissioner for Grenada in London, since 1974; *b* 15 Oct. 1927; *s* of Michael Gibbs and Emelda Mary Cobb; *m* 1955, Dearest Agatha Mitchell; two *s* two *d. Educ:* Grenada Boys' Secondary Sch.; City of London Coll. Started as Clerk to a Solicitor, 1948-51; Operator at a Refinery in Curaçao, 1951-55; Civil Servant, 1955-57; Welfare Officer, Eastern Caribbean Commission, London, 1965-67; Trade Secretary, 1967-72; Deputy Commissioner, 1972-73; Actg Commissioner, 1973. *Address:* High Commission for Grenada, King's House, 10 Haymarket, SW1Y 4DA.

GIBBS, Gen. Sir Roland (Christopher), GCB 1976 (KCB 1972); CBE 1968; DSO 1945; MC 1943; Chief of the General Staff, since 1976; ADC General to the Queen, since 1976; *b* 22 June 1921; *yr s* of late Maj. G. M. Gibbs, Parkleaze, Ewen, Cirencester; *m* 1955, Davina Jean Merry; two *s* one *d. Educ:* Eton Coll.; RMC Sandhurst. Commnd into 60th Rifles, 1940; served War of 1939-45 in N Africa, Italy and NW Europe. Comd 3rd Bn Parachute Regt, 1960-62; GSO1, Brit. Army Staff, Washington, 1962-63; Comdr 16 Para. Bde, 1963-66; Chief of Staff, HQ Middle East, 1966-67; IDC 1968; Commander, British Forces, Gulf, 1969-71; GOC 1 (British) Corps, 1972-74; C-in-C, UKLF, 1974-76. Colonel Commandant: 2nd Bn The Royal Green Jackets, 1971-; Parachute Regt, 1972-. *Recreation:* out-of-door sports. *Address:* Shalden Lodge, Alton, Hants. *T:* Alton 82391. *Club:* Turf. *See also* M. St J. V. Gibbs.

GIBBS-SMITH, Charles Harvard; Keeper Emeritus, Victoria and Albert Museum, since 1971; Research Fellow, Science Museum, since 1976; first Lindbergh Professor of Aerospace History, Smithsonian Institution, USA, 1978; aeronautical historian; *b* 22 March 1909; *y s* of late Dr E. G. Gibbs-Smith; *m* 1975, Lavinia Snelling. *Educ:* Westminster; Harvard Univ., USA (Research Fellow and MA). Asst-Keeper, Victoria and Albert Museum, 1932-39, Keeper of Public Relations and Educn Dept, 1947-71; loaned to Ministry of Information, 1939 (Asst-Dir of Photograph Div., 1943, Dir, 1945). Organised photograph libraries of Ministry of Information; Press Censorship; Admiralty Press Div.; USA Office of War Information, London; Radio Times-Hulton Picture Library. Served in ROC 1941-44 (Hon. Mem., 1945). Hon. Companion, and Cttee Mem. History Group, Royal Aeronautical Society; Fellow, Coll. of Psychic Studies; Mem. Soc. for Psychical Res.; Hon. Mem., RPS, 1973. FRSA 1948; FMA 1952; Mem. Bd of Governors, ESU 1956-59. Mem. Bd of Electors, Internat. Aerospace Hall of Fame, 1975. Hon. Fellow, RCA, 1969. Chevalier, Danish Order of the Dannebrog. *Publications:* V. & A. Museum Costume Bibliography, 1936; Basic Aircraft Recognition, 1942; German Aircraft, 1943; Aircraft Recognition Manual, 1944 (new edn 1945); Ballooning, 1948; The Great Exhibition of 1851, 1950; Air League Recognition Manual, 1952; A History of Flying, 1953; Balloons, 1956; The

Fashionable Lady in the 19th Century, 1960; The Invention of the Aeroplane, 1966; The Bayeux Tapestry, 1973; The Art of Observation, 1973; Pioneers of the Aeroplane, 1975; Early Flying Machines, 1975; Science Museum *monographs:* The Aeroplane: an historical Survey, 1960 (2nd edn as Aviation, etc 1970); Sir George Cayley's Aeronautics, 1962; The Wright Brothers, 1963; The World's First Flights, 1965; A Directory and Nomenclature of the First Aeroplanes, 1966; Leonardo da Vinci's Aeronautics, 1967; Clément Ader, his Flight Claims, 1967; A Brief History of Flying, 1968; The Rebirth of European Aviation, 1974. *Novels:* Operation Caroline, 1953; Yankee Poodle, 1955; Escape and be Secret, 1957; articles and broadcasts on art, crime, aeronautical history, etc. *Recreations:* fencing, classification, travel, parapsychology. *Address:* 30 Scarsdale Villas, W8. *T:* 01-937 0497. *Clubs:* Naval and Military, Royal Aero; Harvard (USA).

GIBRALTAR, Bishop of, since 1971, and **Bishop Suffragan of Fulham,** since 1970; **Rt. Rev. John Richard Satterthwaite;** Guild Vicar, St Dunstan-in-the-West, City of London, since 1959; *b* 17 Nov. 1925; *s* of William and Clara Elisabeth Satterthwaite. *Educ:* Millom Grammar Sch.; Leeds Univ. (BA); Coll. of the Resurrection, Mirfield. History Master, St Luke's Sch., Haifa, 1946-48; Curate: St Barnabas, Carlisle, 1950-53; St Aidan, Carlisle, 1953-54; St Michael Paternoster Royal, London, 1955-59, Curate-in-Charge, 1959-65. Gen. Sec., Church of England Council on Foreign Relations, 1959-70 (Asst Gen. Sec., 1955-59); Gen. Sec., Archbp's Commn on Roman Catholic Relations, 1965-70; Hon. Canon of Canterbury, 1963-; ChStJ 1972 (Asst ChStJ 1963); Hon. Canon of Utrecht, Old Catholic Church of the Netherlands, 1969. Holds decoration from various foreign churches. *Recreations:* fell walking, music. *Address:* 19 Brunswick Gardens, W8 4AS. *T:* 01-727 0329. *Club:* Athenæum.

GIBRALTAR, Bishop of, (RC), since 1973; **Rt. Rev. Edward Rapallo,** DCnL; *b* 19 March 1914; *s* of Edward and Anne Rapallo. *Educ:* Pontifical Univ. of Salamanca, Spain; Lateran Univ., Rome (DCnL). Priest, 1937; Port Chaplain, Gibraltar, 1939-45; Cathedral Choir Master, 1945-54; Diocesan Chancellor, 1955-67; Cathedral Administrator, 1956-72; Vicar General, 1967-72; Vicar Capitular 1973. Chaplain of HH The Pope, 1960; Hon. Prelate of HH The Pope, 1967. *Recreations:* reading, music. *Address:* Bishop's House, 4A Engineer Road, Gibraltar. *T:* 3120 and 4688.

GIBRALTAR (Diocese), Auxiliary Bishop of; *see* Isherwood, Rt Rev. H.

GIBRALTAR (Diocese), Assistant Bishops of; *see* Capper, Rt Rev. E. M. H., Weekes, Rt Rev. A. W. M.

GIBRALTAR, Dean of; *see* Pope, Very Rev. R. W.

GIBSON, family name of **Barons Ashbourne** and **Gibson.**

GIBSON, Baron *cr* 1975 (Life Peer), of Penn's Rocks; **Richard Patrick Tallentyre Gibson;** Chairman: Pearson Longman Ltd, since 1967; Financial Times Ltd, since 1975; National Trust, since 1977; *b* 5 Feb. 1916; *s* of Thornely Carbutt Gibson and Elizabeth Anne Augusta Gibson; *m* 1945, Elisabeth Dione Pearson; four *s*. *Educ:* Eton Coll.; Magdalen Coll., Oxford. London Stock Exchange, 1937. Served with Mddx Yeo, 1939-46; N Africa, 1940-41; POW, 1941-43; Special Ops Exec., 1943-45; Political Intell. Dept, FO, 1945-46. Westminster Press Ltd, 1947 (Dir, 1948); Director: Whitehall Securities Corp. Ltd, 1948-60, 1973-; Financial Times and Economist, 1957; S. Pearson & Son Ltd, 1960 (Dep. Chm., 1969; Exec. Dep. Chm., 1975); Royal Exchange Assce, 1961-69. Hon. Treas. Commonwealth Press Union, 1957-67. Chm., Arts Council, 1972-77. Trustee, Historic Churches Preservation Trust, 1958; Member: Exec. Cttee, National Trust, 1963-72; Council, Nat. Trust, 1966; Adv. Council, V&A Museum, 1968-75 (Chm., 1970); UK Arts Adv. Commn, Calouste Gulbenkian Foundn, 1969-72; Redundant Churches Fund, 1970-71; Exec. Cttee, Nat. Art Collections Fund, 1970; Bd, Royal Opera House, 1977-; Trustee, Glyndebourne Fest. Opera, 1965-72 and 1977-. *Recreations:* music, gardening, architecture. *Address:* Penn's Rocks, Groombridge, Sussex. *T:* Groombridge 244. *Clubs:* Garrick, Brooks's.

GIBSON, Sir Alexander (Drummond), Kt 1977; CBE 1967; Principal Conductor and Musical Director, Scottish National Orchestra, since 1959; Founder and Artistic Director, Scottish Opera Company, since 1962; *b* 11 Feb. 1926; *m* 1959, Ann Veronica Waggett; three *s* one *d*. *Educ:* Dalziel; Glasgow Univ.; Royal College of Music; Mozarteum, Salzburg, Austria; Accademia Chigiano, Siena, Italy. Served with Royal Signals,

1944-48. Repetiteur and Asst Conductor, Sadler's Wells Opera, 1951-52; Asst Conductor, BBC Scottish Orchestra, Glasgow, 1952-54; Staff Conductor, Sadler's Wells Opera, 1954-57; Musical Dir, Sadler's Wells Opera, 1957-59. Hon. RAM 1969. Hon. LLD Aberdeen, 1968; Hon. DMus Glasgow, 1972; DUniv Stirling, 1972; Hon. FRCM, 1973; Hon. FRSAM, 1973; Hon. RSA, 1975. St Mungo Prize, 1970; Musician of the Year award, ISM, 1976. *Recreations:* motoring, tennis, reading. *Address:* 15 Cleveden Gardens, Glasgow G12 0PU. *T:* 041-339 6668. *Clubs:* Garrick, Oriental.

GIBSON, Charles William, JP County of London; *b* Fulham, 1889; *m* 1915, Jessie Alice Davison; two *s* one *d*. *Educ:* Elementary Schools; WEA; Morley Working Men's Coll. Lambeth Borough Cllr, 1919-22; Mem. LCC for Kennington, 1928-49; Vice-Chm. LCC, 1941-42; Lambeth-Vauxhall, 1949-56; Chm. LCC Housing Cttee, 1943-50; Alderman, LCC, 1960; Mem. Central Housing Advisory Cttee, 1945-51. MP (Lab.) Kennington Div. of Lambeth, 1945-50, Clapham Div. of Wandsworth, 1950-Sept. 1959. On staff of Transport and General Workers Union. Retired. Hon. Fellow, Institute of Housing. *Address:* 25 Dalmore Road, West Dulwich, SE21. *T:* 01-670 1068.

GIBSON, Sir Christopher (Herbert), 3rd Bt *cr* 1931; Manager and part owner, Granja Avicola Lakanto (Egg Farm), Alta Gracia, Cordoba, since 1968; *b* 2 Feb. 1921; *s* of Sir Christopher H. Gibson, 2nd Bt, and Lady Dorothy E. O. Gibson (*née* Bruce); *S* father, 1962; *m* 1941, Lilian Lake Young, *d* of Dr George Byron Young, Colchester; one *s* three *d*. *Educ:* St Cyprian's, Eastbourne; St George's Coll., Argentina. Served, 1941-45 (5 war medals and stars): 28th Canadian Armd Regt (BCR), Lieut. Plantation Manager, Leach's Argentine Estates, 1946-51; Manager, Encyclopædia Britannica, 1952-55; Design Draughtsman, Babcock & Wilcox, 1956-57; Plantation Manager, Liebig's, 1958-60; Ranch Manager, Liebig's Extract of Meat Co., 1961-64; with Industrias Kaiser, Argentina, 1964-68. *Recreations:* shooting, fishing, tennis, cricket, architecture. *Heir: s* Christopher Herbert Gibson, *b* Argentina, 17 July 1948. *Address:* Calle Urquiza 46, DPTO no 3, Ciudad de Cordoba, Provincia de Cordoba, Argentina, South America.

GIBSON, Rev. Father David, PP; (4th Bt *cr* 1926, but does not use the title); *b* 18 July 1922; *s* of Sir Ackroyd Herbert Gibson, 3rd Bt; (*S* father, 1975). *Address:* Our Lady and St Neot, West Street, Liskeard, Cornwall.

GIBSON, Vice-Adm. Sir Donald Cameron Ernest Forbes, KCB 1968 (CB 1965); DSC 1941; JP; *b* 17 March 1916; *s* of late Capt. W. L. D. Gibson, Queen's Own Cameron Highlanders, and of Elizabeth Gibson; *m* 1939, Marjorie Alice, *d* of H. C. Harding, Horley, Surrey; one *s*. *Educ:* Woodbridge Sch., Suffolk. Cadet, Brit. India SN Co. and Midshipman, Royal Naval Reserve, 1933-37; transf. to Royal Navy, 1937; specialised as Pilot, 1938. Served War of 1939-45: HMS Glorious, Ark Royal, Formidable, Audacity; trng Pilots in USA; Empire Central Flying Sch., 1942; Chief Flying Instr, Advanced Flying Sch., 1946-47; HMS Illustrious, 1947-48; Air Gp Comdr, HMS Theseus, 1948-49; Comdr (Air), RNAS Culdrose, 1950-52; RN Staff Course, 1952-53; Comdr (Air) HMS Indomitable and Glory, 1953-54; Capt. RNAS Brawdy, 1954-56, HMS Dainty, 1956-58; Dep. Dir Air Warfare, 1958-60; Canadian Nat. Defence Coll., 1960-61; Capt., HMS Ark Royal, 1961-63; Rear-Adm. 1963; Flag Officer: Aircraft Carriers, 1963-64; Naval Flying Trg, 1964-65; Naval Air Comd, 1965-68; Vice-Adm. 1967. Dir, HMS Belfast Trust, 1971-72; President: St John's Ambulance, N Devon, 1974; NSPCC, Exeter and E Devon, 1974. JP Barnstaple 1973. *Recreations:* fishing, painting. *Address:* Lower Bealy Court, Chulmleigh, North Devon. *T:* Chulmleigh 264.

GIBSON, Sir Donald (Evelyn Edward), Kt 1962; CBE 1951; DCL; MA, FRIBA (Distinction Town Planning), FRTPI; Controller General, Ministry of Public Building and Works, 1967-69, now Consultant; *b* 11 Oct. 1908; *s* of late Prof. Arnold Hartley Gibson; *m* 1936, Winifred Mary (*née* McGowan); three *s* one *d*. *Educ:* Manchester Gram. Sch.; Manchester Univ. BA Hons Architecture; MA. Work in USA, 1931; private practice, 1933; professional Civil Service (Building Research), 1935; Dep. County Architect, Isle of Ely, 1937; City Architect and Town Planning Officer, County and City of Coventry, 1939; County Architect, Notts, 1955; Dir-Gen. of Works, War Office, 1958-62; Dir-Gen., R&D, MPBW, 1962-67; Hoffmann Wood Prof. of Architecture, University of Leeds, 1967-68. Mem. Central Housing Advisory Cttee, 1951, 1953 and 1954. President: RIBA, 1964-65; Dist Heating Assoc., 1971-. *Publications:* various publications dealing with housing, planning and architecture in RIBA and RTPI Journals. *Recreation:* goat keeping. *Address:* Bryn Castell, Llanddona, Beaumaris, Gwynedd LL58 8TR. *T:* Beaumaris 810399.

GIBSON, Prof. Frank William Ernest, FRS 1976; FAA; Howard Florey Professor of Medical Research and Director of the John Curtin School of Medical Research, Australian National University, since 1977; *b* 22 July 1923; *s* of John William and Alice Ruby Gibson; *m* 1949, Margaret Isabel Nancy; two *d*. *Educ:* Queensland, Melbourne, and Oxford Univs. BSc, DSc (Melb.), DPhil (Oxon). Research Asst, Melbourne and Queensland Univs, 1938-47; Sen. Demonstrator, Melbourne Univ., 1948-49; ANU Scholar, Oxford, 1950-52. Melbourne University: Sen. Lectr, 1953-58; Reader in Chem. Microbiology, 1959-65; Prof. of Chem. Microbiology, 1965-66; Prof. of Biochem. and Head of Biochem. Dept, John Curtin Sch. of Medical Res., ANU, 1967-76. David Syme Research Prize, Univ. of Melb., 1963. FAA 1971. *Publications:* scientific papers on the biochemistry of bacteria, particularly the biosynthesis of aromatic compounds, energy metabolism. *Recreations:* squash, skiing. *Address:* 7 Waller Crescent, Campbell, ACT 2601, Australia. *T:* 49 8463.

GIBSON, Sir John (Hinshelwood), Kt 1969; CB 1962; TD 1944; QC (Scotland) 1961; *b* 20 May 1907; *y s* of late William John Gibson, Solicitor, Falkirk; *m* 1948, Jane, *o d* of late Captain James Watt; one *s* one *d*. *Educ:* Fettes Coll. (Scholar); University of Edinburgh. MA 1928; LLB 1931. Admitted to Faculty of Advocates, and called to Bar (Scot.), 1932. Entered Lord Advocate's Dept, 1945; Legal Sec. and First Parly Draftsman for Scotland, 1961-69; Counsel to Scottish Law Commn, 1969-77. Member: Editorial Bd, Statutes in Force, 1968-77; Cttee on Preparation of Legislation, 1973-75. TA (Royal Artillery), 1931-45 (War service, 1939-45); hon. Major. *Address:* 9 Belgrave Crescent, Edinburgh EH4 3AH. *T:* 031-332 2027. *Club:* New (Edinburgh).

GIBSON, John Peter; engineering consultant; *b* 21 Aug. 1929; *s* of John Leighton Gibson and Norah Gibson; *m* 1954, Patricia Anne Thomas; two *s* three *d*. *Educ:* Caterham Sch.; Imperial Coll., London (BSc (Hons Mech. Engrg), ACGI). Post-grad. apprenticeship Rolls Royce Derby, 1953-55; ICI (Billingham and Petrochemicals Div.), 1955-69; Man. Dir, Lummus Co., 1969-73; Dir Gen. Offshore Supplies Office, Dept of Energy, 1973-76. *Recreations:* work, gardening, handyman. *Address:* Batworthy-on-the-Moor, Kestor, Chagford, Devon TQ13 8EU. *T:* Chagford 3433. *Club:* Royal Scottish Automobile (Glasgow).

GIBSON, John Sibbald; Under-Secretary, Scottish Office, since 1973; *b* 1 May 1923; *s* of John McDonald Frame Gibson and Marion Watson Sibbald; *m* 1948, Moira Helen Gillespie; one *s* one *d*. *Educ:* Paisley Grammar Sch.; Glasgow Univ. Army, 1942-46, Lieut in No 1 Commando from 1943; Far East. Joined Admin. Grade Home Civil Service, 1947; Asst Principal, Scottish Home Dept, 1947-50; Private Sec. to Parly Under-Sec., 1950-51; Private Sec. to Perm. Under-Sec. of State, Scottish Office, 1952; Principal, Scottish Home Dept, 1953; Asst Sec., Dept of Agriculture and Fisheries for Scotland, 1962. *Publications:* Ships of the '45: the rescue of the Young Pretender, 1967; Deacon Brodie: Father to Jekyll and Hyde, 1976. *Recreation:* writing. *Address:* 28 Cramond Gardens, Edinburgh EH4 6PU. *T:* 031-336 2931. *Club:* Scottish Arts (Edinburgh).

GIBSON, John Walter; Under Secretary, Ministry of Defence, since 1977; *b* 15 Jan. 1922; *s* of late Thomas John Gibson and Catherine Gibson (*née* Gregory), Bamburgh, Northumberland; *m* 1951, Julia, *d* of George Leslie Butler, Buxton, Derbyshire; two *s* one *d*. *Educ:* A. J. Dawson Sch., Durham; Sheffield Univ.; University Coll., London. RNVR, 1942-46. Sheffield Univ., 1940-42, 1946-47 (BSc); University Coll., London, 1947-48; Safety-in-Mines Research Estabt, 1948-53; BJSM, Washington, DC, 1953-56; Royal Armament Research and Develt Estabt, 1957-60; Head of Statistics Div., Ordnance Bd, 1961-64; Supt, Assessment Br., Royal Armament Research and Develt Estabt, 1964-66, Prin. Supt, Systems Div., 1966-69; Asst Chief Scientific Adviser (Studies), MoD, 1969-74; Under-Sec., Cabinet Office, 1974-76. FSS 1953. *Address:* 17 Lyndhurst Drive, Sevenoaks, Kent. *T:* Sevenoaks 54589.

GIBSON, Joseph David; High Commissioner for Fiji, since 1976; *b* 26 Jan. 1928; *s* of late Charles Ivan Gibson and Mamao Lavenia Gibson; *m* Emily Susan Bentley; three *s* two *d*. *Educ:* Auckland Univ., NZ (BA); Auckland Teachers' Coll. (Teachers' Cert.). Asst Teacher, Suva Boys' Grammar Sch., 1952-57; Principal: Suva Educnl Inst., 1957; Queen Victoria School, Fiji, 1961-63 (Asst Teacher, 1958-59; Sen. Master, 1960); Educn Officer, Fiji, 1964-66; Asst Dir of Educn, 1967-69; Dep. Dir of Educn, 1970; Permanent Sec. for Educn, 1971-74; Dep. High Comr, London, 1974-76. *Recreations:* golf, fishing. *Address:* 97 Platts Lane, NW3 7NH. *T:* 01-794 1806. *Clubs:* Hurlingham, Travellers', Royal Commonwealth Society, Roehampton; Fiji Defence, Fiji Golf.

GIBSON, Col Leonard Young, CBE 1961 (MBE 1940); TD 1947; DL; company director since 1930; Master of Newcastle and District Beagles since 1946; *b* 4 Dec. 1911; *s* of late William McLure Gibson and Wilhelmina Mitchell, Gosforth; *m* 1949, Pauline Mary Anthony; one *s* one *d*. *Educ:* Royal Grammar Sch., Newcastle upon Tyne; France and Germany. Service in TA, 1933-61: 72nd (N) Fd Regt RA TA, 1933-39; Bde Major RA: 50th (N) Div., rearguard Dunkirk, 1939-40 (MBE, despatches); 43rd (W) Div., 1941-42; GSO2, SE Army, 1942; GSO2 (Dirg Staff), Staff Coll., Camberley, 1942-43; GSO1 Ops Eastern Comd, 1943-44; 2nd in Comd 307 Med. Regt S Notts Hussars, RHA TA, France, Belgium, Holland, Germany, 1944-45 (despatches); GSO1 Mil. Govt Germany, 1945-46; OC 272 (N) Field Regt RA TA, 1956-58; Dep. Comdr RA 50th Inf. Div. TA, 1959-61; Colonel TA, retd. Mem., Northumberland T&AFA, 1958-68. Pres., Masters of Harriers and Beagles Assoc., 1968-69. DL Northumberland, 1971. Croix de Guerre (with Gold Star), France, 1944. *Recreations:* hunting, shooting, fishing, breeding horses and hounds. *Address:* Simonburn Cottage, Humshaugh, Northumberland. *T:* Humshaugh 402. *Clubs:* Army and Navy; Northern Counties (Newcastle upon Tyne).

GIBSON, Hon. Sir Marcus (George), Kt 1970; *b* 11 Jan. 1898; *e s* of late Clyde Gibson, Oatlands, Tasmania, and Lucy Isabel (*née* Stanfield); *m* 1929, Iris Lavinia, *d* of A. E. Shone, East Risdon, Tas; one *s* one *d*. *Educ:* Leslie House Sch., Hobart; Univ. of Tasmania. LLB (Tas) 1921; LLM (Tas) 1924. Served European War: Gunner, AIF, 1917-19. Admitted to bar of Supreme Court, Tasmania, 1921; private practice, 1921-29; Solicitor to the Public Trust Office, 1929-38; Police Magistrate, 1939-42; Asst Solicitor-General, 1942-46; KC 1946; Solicitor-General, 1946-51; Puisne Judge, Supreme Court of Tasmania, 1951-68; on several occasions Actg Chief Justice, Dep. Governor of Tasmania and Administrator, Govt of Tasmania. *Recreations:* theatre, bushwalking. *Address:* 296 Sandy Bay Road, Hobart, Tas. 7005, Australia. *T:* Hobart 235624. *Club:* Tasmanian (Hobart).

GIBSON, Rt. Hon. Sir Maurice White, PC 1975; Kt 1975; **Rt. Hon. Lord Justice Gibson;** Lord Justice of Appeal, Supreme Court of Judicature, Northern Ireland, since 1975; Member, Restrictive Practices Court, since 1971; *b* 1 May 1913; 2nd *s* of late William James Gibson, Montpelier House, Belfast, and of Edith Mary Gibson; *m* 1945, Cecily Winifred, *e d* of late Mr and Mrs Dudley Roy Johnson, Cordova, Bexhill-on-Sea, Sussex; one *s* one *d*. *Educ:* Royal Belfast Academical Institution; Queen's Univ., Belfast (LLB, BA). English Bar Final Exam. First Cl. and Certif. of Honour, 1937; Called to Bar of NI with Special Prize awarded by Inn of Court of NI, 1938; called to Inner Bar, NI, 1956. Puisne Judge, NI High Court of Justice, 1968-75. Apptd Mem. several Govt Cttees on Law Reform in NI; Dep. Chm., Boundary Commn for NI, 1971-75; Mem. Incorp. Council of Law Reporting for NI; Chm., NI Legal Quarterly. Chm., NI Scout Council. *Address:* 13 Broomhill Park, Belfast BT9 5JB. *T:* Belfast 666239. *Clubs:* Ulster (Belfast); Royal Belfast Golf.

GIBSON, Captain Michael Bradford; Official Referee to Lawn Tennis Association and All England Lawn Tennis Club, 1961-75; Managing Director of Racquet Sports International Ltd; Director, Supersports Travel Ltd, since 1977; *b* 20 March 1929; *s* of Lt-Col B. T. Gibson; *m* 1953, Mary Helen Elizabeth Legg; two *s*. *Educ:* Taunton Sch.; RMA Sandhurst; Sidney Sussex Coll., Cambridge (BA). Commnd into RE, 1948, retd 1961. Mem., Inst. of Directors. *Recreations:* hunting, boating. *Address:* Olde Denne, Warnham, Horsham, Sussex. *T:* Horsham 65589. *Clubs:* All England Lawn Tennis and Croquet; Cottesmore Golf.

GIBSON, Rear-Adm. Peter Cecil, CB 1968; *b* 31 May 1913; 2nd *s* of Alexander Horace Cecil Gibson and Phyllis Zeline Cecil Gibson (*née* Baume); *m* 1938, Phyllis Anna Mary Hume, *d* of late Major N. H. Hume, IMS, Brecon; two *s* one *d*. *Educ:* Ealing Priory; RN Engrg Coll., Keyham. RN, 1931; HMS Norfolk, Ef, 1936-38; maintenance test pilot, RN Aircraft Yard, Donibristle, 1940-41; Air Engr Officer, RNAS, St Merryn, 1941-42; Staff of RANAS, Indian Ocean, E Africa, 1942-43, Ceylon, 1943-44; Staff Air Engr. Off., British Pacific Fleet, 1945-46; Aircraft Maintenance and Repair Dept, 1946-49; loan service RAN, 1950-52; Trng Off., RNAS, Arbroath, 1952-54; Engr Off., HMS Gambia, 1954-56 and as Fleet Engr. Off, E Indies, 1955-56; Staff Engr. Off., Flag Off. Flying Trng, 1957-60; Dep. Dir Service Conditions, 1960-61; Dir Engr Officers' Appts, 1961-63; Supt RN Aircraft Yard, Fleetlands, 1963-65; Dep. Controller Aircraft (RN), Min. of Aviation, 1966-67, Min. of Technology, 1967-69, retired, 1969. ADC, 1965-66. Comdr 1946; Capt. 1957; Rear-Adm. 1966. Chm. United Services Catholic Assoc., 1966-69. *Recreations:* vintage cars, bridge. *Address:* 15 Melton Court, SW7. *T:* 01-589 2414. *Clubs:* Army and Navy, Hurlingham.

GIBSON, Prof. Quentin Howieson, FRS 1969; Professor of Biochemistry and Molecular Biology, Cornell University, Ithaca, NY, since 1966; *b* 9 Dec. 1918; *s* of William Howieson Gibson, OBE, DSc; *m* 1951, Audrey Jane, *yr d* of G. H. S. Pinsent, CB, CMG, and Katharine Kentisbeare, *d* of Sir George Radford, MP; one *s* three *d*. *Educ:* Repton. MB, ChB, BAO, Belfast, 1941, MD 1944, PhD 1946, DSc 1951. Demonstrator in Physiology, Belfast, 1941-44; Lecturer in Physiology: Belfast, 1944-46; Sheffield Univ., 1946-55; Professor of Biochem., Sheffield Univ., 1955-63; Prof. of Biophys. Chem., Johnson Research Foundn, University of Pennsylvania, 1963-66. Fellow, Amer. Acad. of Arts and Sciences, 1971. *Recreation:* sailing. *Address:* 98 Dodge Road, Ithaca, NY 14850, USA.

GIBSON, Hon. Sir Ralph (Brian), Kt 1977; Hon. Mr Justice Gibson; a Judge of the High Court, Queen's Bench Division, since 1977; *b* 17 Oct. 1922; 2nd *s* of Roy and Emily Gibson; *m* 1949, Ann Chapman Ruether, Chicago; one *s* two *d*. *Educ:* Charterhouse; Brasenose Coll., Oxford. MA Oxon 1948. Army Service, 1941-45: Lieut, 1st KDG; Captain, TJFF. Called to Bar, Middle Temple, 1948, Bencher 1974; QC 1968. A Recorder of the Crown Court, 1972-77. Bigelow Teaching Fellow, University of Chicago, 1948-49. Mem., Council of Legal Educn, 1971. *Recreation:* sailing. *Address:* 8 Ashley Gardens, SW1. *T:* 01-828 9670. *Clubs:* Athenæum; Emsworth Sailing.

GIBSON, Prof. Robert Donald Davidson, PhD; Professor of French, University of Kent at Canterbury since 1965; *b* Hackney, London, 21 Aug. 1927; *o s* of Nicol and Ann Gibson, Leyton, London; *m* 1953, Sheila Elaine, *o d* of Bertie and Ada Goldsworthy, Exeter, Devon; three *s*. *Educ:* Leyton County High Sch. for Boys; King's Coll., London; Magdalene Coll., Cambridge; Ecole Normale Supérieure, Paris. BA (First Class Hons. French) London, 1948; PhD Cantab. 1953. Asst Lecturer, St Salvator's Coll., University of St Andrews, 1954-55; Lecturer, Queen's Coll., Dundee, 1955-58; Lecturer, Aberdeen Univ., 1958-61; Prof., Queen's Univ. of Belfast, 1961-65. *Publications:* The Quest of Alain-Fournier, 1953; Modern French Poets on Poetry, 1961; (ed) Le Bestiaire Inattendu, 1961; Roger Martin du Gard, 1961; La Mésentente Cordiale, 1963; (ed) Brouart et le Désordre, 1964; (ed) Provinciales, 1965; (ed) Le Grand Meaulnes, 1968; The Land Without a Name, 1975; reviews and articles in: French Studies, The London Magazine, Times Literary Supplement, Encyclopædia Britannica, Collier's Encyclopædia. *Recreations:* reading, writing, talking. *Address:* 97a St Stephen's Road, Canterbury, Kent CT2 7JT.

GIBSON, Sir Ronald (George), Kt 1975; CBE 1970 (OBE 1961); MA Cantab; FRCS, FRCGP; Chairman of Council, British Medical Association, 1966-71; *b* 28 Nov. 1909; *s* of George Edward Gibson and Gladys Muriel, *d* of William George Prince, JP, CC, Romsey, Hants; *m* 1934, Dorothy Elisabeth Alberta, *d* of Thomas Alfred Rainey, Southampton; two *d*. *Educ:* Mill Hill Sch., St John's Coll., Cambridge; St Bartholomew's Hosp., London. Gen. Practitioner; MO, Winchester Coll. and St Swithun's Sch., Winchester. Lieut-Col RAMC (Emergency Reserve), PMO Italian Somaliland, 1944-45. Mem. Council: BMA, 1950-72 (Chm., Representative Body, 1963-66; Chm. Council, 1966-71); RCS, 1962-67 (FRCS 1968); Mem., GMC, 1974-. First Provost, SE Eng. Faculty, Royal College of General Practitioners, 1954 (James Mackenzie Lectr, 1967; FRCGP 1967). Member: Central Health Services Council, 1966-76 (Vice-Chm., 1972-76); (past) Personal Social Services Council, DHSS; Standing Med. Adv. Cttee, 1966-76 (Chm., 1972-76); Adv. Council on Misuse of Drugs; Council, Med. Insurance Agency (Chm.); VAT Tribunals (part time). Mem., Ct of Assts, Worshipful Soc. of Apothecaries of London, 1971 (Liveryman, 1964). Gold Medallist, BMA, 1970. Hon. LLD Wales, 1965. *Publications:* Care of the Elderly in General Practice (Butterworth Gold Medal), 1956; The Satchel and the Shining Morning Face, 1971; The One with the Elephant, 1976; contrib. Lancet, BMJ, etc. *Recreations:* medicine, music, cricket, gardening. *Address:* 21 St Thomas' Street, Winchester, Hants. *T:* Winchester 4582. *Clubs:* Athenæum, MCC.

GIBSON, Major William David; Chairman, W. J. Tatem Ltd, since 1974 (Director, since 1957); *b* 26 Feb. 1925; *s* of G. C. Gibson, Landwade Hall, Exning, Newmarket, Suffolk; *m* 1st, 1959, Charlotte Henrietta (*d* of 1973), *d* of N. S. Pryor, *qv*; three *s* one *d*; 2nd, 1975, Jane Marion, *d* of late Col L. L. Hassell, DSO, MC. *Educ:* St Peter's Court; Harrow; Trinity Coll., Cambridge. Commissioned into Welsh Guards, July 1945; retired as Major, 1957. Dir, West of England Ship Owners Mutual Protection & Indemnity Assoc., 1959-. National Hunt Cttee, Oct. 1959- (Sen. Steward, 1966); Jockey Club, 1966- (Dep. Sen. Steward, 1969-71); Tattersalls Cttee, 1963-69 (Chm., 1967-69). Dir, Racecourse Technical Services Ltd. Upper Warden, Worshipful Co. of Farriers. *Recreations:* racing (won 4 Grand Military Gold Cups,

1950-52 and 1956); shooting, sailing. *Address:* Edradynate, Aberfeldy, Perthshire PH15 2JX. *T:* Strathtay 215. *Clubs:* Bath, Royal Thames Yacht, Pratt's; Royal Yacht Squadron, Royal Perth Golfing Society (Perth).

GIBSON, Air Vice-Marshal William Norman, CBE 1956; DFC; Royal Australian Air Force, retired; Senior Air Staff Officer, Operational Comd, RAAF, 1963-64 and 1966; *b* 28 April 1915; *s* of late Hamilton Ross Gibson; *m* 1938, Grace Doreen, *d* of John Walter Downton, Sydney; one *d*. *Educ:* NZ; Parramatta High Sch.; Point Cook. RAN, 1936-39; RAAF: CO, Port Moresby, 1942; SASO, RAAF Command, 1943-44; SASO, 1st Tactical Air Force, 1947-48; CO, RAAF East Sale, 1953-54; Dir of Training, 1955-56; Air Cdre, Plans, 1957; CO, RAAF Amberley, 1959-62; SASO, HQ Far East Air Force, 1964-66. ADC to HM the Queen, 1955-58. Legion of Merit (USA). *Address:* 26 Hillcrest Avenue, Mona Vale, NSW 2103, Australia. *Club:* Imperial Service (Sydney).

GIBSON-CRAIG-CARMICHAEL, Sir David Peter William, 15th Bt *cr* 1702 (Gibson Carmichael) and 8th Bt *cr* 1831; *b* 21 July 1946; *s* of Sir Archibald Henry William Gibson-Craig-Carmichael, 14th Bt and of Rosemary Anita, *d* of George Duncan Crew, Santiago, Chile; *S* father, 1969; *m* 1973, Patricia, *d* of Marcos Skarnic, Santiago, Chile. *Heir: b* Alasdair John Gibson-Craig-Carmichael, *b* 28 Feb. 1948; *m* 1973, Irene, *d* of Bruno Haverbeck, Santiago, Chile. *Address:* Casilla 2461, Santiago, Chile.

GIBSON-WATT, Rt. Hon. (James) David, PC 1974; MC 1943 and 2 Bars; DL; a Forestry Commissioner, since 1976; *b* 11 Sept. 1918; *er s* of late Major James Miller Gibson-Watt, DL, JP; *m* 1942, Diana, *d* of Sir Charles Hambro; two *s* two *d* (and one *s* decd). *Educ:* Eton; Trinity Coll (BA). Welsh Guards, 1939-46; N African and Italian campaigns. Contested (C) Brecon and Radnor constituency, 1950 and 1951; MP (C) Hereford, Feb. 1956-Sept. 1974; a Lord Commissioner of the Treasury, 1959-61; Minister of State, Welsh Office, 1970-74. FRAgS; Pres., Royal Welsh Agric. Soc., 1976 (Chm. Council, 1976-). Mem., Historic Buildings Council, Wales, 1975-. DL Powys (formerly Radnorshire), 1968. *Address:* Doldowlod, Llandrindod Wells, Powys. *T:* Newbridge-on-Wye 208. *Club:* Boodle's.

GICK, Rear-Adm. Philip David, CB 1963; OBE 1946; DSC and Bar, 1942; Chairman: Emsworth Shipyard Ltd; Emsworth Yacht Harbour Ltd; A. R. Savage, Ltd; Emsworth Marine Engineering Ltd; P.O.Y. (Jersey) Ltd; Vernon's Shipyard Ltd; *b* 22 Feb. 1913; *s* of late Sir William John Gick, CB, CBE; *m* 1938, Aylmer Rowntree; one *s* three *d*. *Educ:* St Lawrence Coll., Ramsgate. Joined RN, 1931; qualified as Pilot, 1936. Capt. 1952; Comd HMS Daring, RNAS, Lossiemouth, HMS Bulwark, 1952-58; Pres., Second Admiralty Interview Board; Rear-Adm. 1961; Flag Officer, Naval Flying Training, 1961-64, retd. *Recreation:* sailing. *Address:* Furzefield, Bosham Hoe, Sussex. *T:* Bosham 572219. *Clubs:* Royal Yacht Squadron, Royal Ocean Racing; Royal Naval Sailing Association; Bosham Sailing.

GIDDEN, Barry Owen Barton, CMG 1962; *b* Southampton, 4 July 1915; *s* of late Harry William Gidden, MA, PhD. *Educ:* King Edward VI Sch., Southampton; Jesus Coll., Cambridge (Scholar; Class. Tripos Pts 1 and 2; BA). Apptd Asst Principal, HM Office of Works, 1939. Served War of 1939-45: BEF, 1939-40, Major 1943. Principal, Min. of Works, 1946; Private Sec. to Minister of Works, 1946-48; Principal, Colonial Office, 1949, Asst Sec 1951; Counsellor, UK Mission to UN, New York, 1954-58; Establishment Officer, Colonial Office, 1958-65; Asst Sec., DHSS, 1965-75. *Recreation:* golf. *Address:* 15 Chesham Street, SW1. *T:* 01-235 4185. *Club:* Walton Heath.

GIDDINGS, Air Marshal Sir (Kenneth Charles) Michael, KCB 1975; OBE 1953; DFC 1945; AFC 1950 and Bar 1955; retired; *b* 27 Aug. 1920; *s* of Charles Giddings and Grace Giddings (*née* Gregory); *m* 1946, Elizabeth McConnell; two *s* two *d*. *Educ:* Ealing Grammar Sch. Conscripted, RAF, 1940; Comd, 129 Sqdn, 1944; Empire Test Pilots Sch., 1946; Test pilot, RAE, 1947-50; HQ Fighter Command, 1950-52; RAF Staff Coll., 1953; OC, Flying Wing, Waterbeach, 1954-56; CFE, 1956-58; OC, 57 Sqdn, 1958-60; Group Captain Ops, Bomber Command, 1960-62; Supt of Flying, A&AEE, 1962-64; Dir Aircraft Projects, MoD, 1964-66; AOC, Central Reconnaissance Estabt, 1967-68; ACAS (Operational Requirements), 1968-71; Chief of Staff No 18 (M) Group, Strike Command, RAF, 1971-73; Dep. Chief of Defence Staff, Op. Requirements, 1973-76. *Recreations:* golf, gardening, music. *Address:* 159 Long Lane, Tilehurst, Reading, Berks. *T:* Reading 23012. *Club:* Royal Air Force.

GIELGUD, Sir (Arthur) John, CH 1977; Kt 1953; Hon. LLD St Andrews 1950; Hon. DLitt Oxon 1953; Actor; *b* 14 April 1904; *s*

of late Frank Gielgud and Kate Terry Lewis; unmarried. *Educ:* Westminster. First appearance on stage at Old Vic, 1921; among parts played are Lewis Dodd in Constant Nymph, Inigo Jollifant in The Good Companions, Richard II in Richard of Bordeaux, Hamlet, and Romeo; Valentine in Love for Love, Ernest Worthing in The Importance of Being Earnest, Macbeth and King Lear. Directed Macbeth, Piccadilly, 1942. Raskolnikoff in Crime and Punishment, Jason in The Medea, New York, 1947. Eustace in The Return of the Prodigal, Globe, 1948; directed The Heiress, Haymarket, 1949; directed and played Thomas Mendip, The Lady's not for Burning, Globe, 1949; Shakespeare Festival, Stratford-on-Avon, 1950; Angelo in Measure for Measure, Cassius in Julius Caesar, Benedick in Much Ado About Nothing, the name part in King Lear; directed Much Ado About Nothing and King Lear; Shakespeare season at Phoenix, 1951-52; Leontes in The Winter's Tale, Phoenix, 1951, directed Much Ado About Nothing and played Benedick, 1952. Season at Lyric, Hammersmith, 1953; directed Richard II and The Way of the World (played Mirabel); played Jaffeir in Venice Preserved; directed A Day by the Sea, and played Julian Anson, Haymarket, Nov. 1953-54; also directed Charley's Aunt, New Theatre, Dec. 1953, and directed The Cherry Orchard, Lyric, May, 1954, and Twelfth Night, Stratford, 1955; played in King Lear and Much Ado About Nothing (also produced Much Ado), for Shakespeare Memorial Theatre Company (London, provinces and continental tour), 1955; directed The Chalk Garden, Haymarket, 1956; produced (with Noel Coward) Nude with Violin, and played Sebastien, Globe, 1956-57; produced The Trojans, Covent Garden, 1957; played Prospero, Stratford, and Drury Lane, 1957; played James Callifer in The Potting Shed, Globe, 1958 and Wolsey in Henry VIII, Old Vic, 1958; directed Variation on A Theme, 1958; produced The Complaisant Lover, Globe, 1959; (Shakespeare's) Ages of Man, Queen's, 1959 (recital, based on Shakespeare anthology of G. Rylands); previous recitals at Edinburgh Fest. and in US, also subseq. in US, at Haymarket, 1960 and tour of Australia and NZ, 1963-64; Gothenburg, Copenhagen, Warsaw, Helsinki, Leningrad, Moscow and Dublin, 1964; produced Much Ado About Nothing, at Cambridge, Mass, Festival, and subseq. in New York, 1959; prod. Five Finger Exercise, Comedy, 1958, NY, 1959; acted in The Last Joke, Phoenix, 1960; prod. Britten's A Midsummer Night's Dream, Royal Opera House, 1961; prod Big Fish Little Fish, New York, 1961; prod Dazzling Prospect, Globe, 1961. Stratford-on-Avon Season, 1961: took part of Othello, also of Gaieff in The Cherry Orchard, Aldwych, 1962; produced The School for Scandal, Haymarket, 1962; prod The School for Scandal, and played Joseph Surface, USA tour, and New York, 1962-63; dir. The Ides of March, and played Julius Caesar, Haymarket, 1963; dir. Hamlet, Canada and USA, 1964; Julian in Tiny Alice, New York, 1965; played Ivanov and directed Ivanov, Phoenix, 1965, United States and Canada, 1966; played Orgon in Tartuffe, Nat. Theatre, 1967; directed Halfway up the Tree, Queen's, 1967; played Oedipus in Oedipus, Nat. Theatre, 1968; produced Don Giovanni, Coliseum, 1968; played Headmaster in 40 Years On, Apollo, 1968; played Sir Gideon in The Battle of Shrivings, Lyric, 1970; Home, Royal Court, 1970, NY 1971 (Evening Standard Best Actor award and Tony award, NY, 1971); dir, All Over, NY, 1971; Caesar and Cleopatra, Chichester Festival, 1971; Veterans, Royal Ct, 1972; dir, Private Lives, Queen's, 1972; dir, The Constant Wife, Albery, 1973; played Prospero, Nat. Theatre, 1974; Bingo, Royal Court, 1974; No Man's Land, Nat. Theatre, 1975, NY 1976; Julius Caesar, Volpone, Nat. Theatre, 1977; dir, The Gay Lord Quex, Albery, 1975; *films include:* (GB and US) The Good Companions, 1932; The Secret Agent, 1937; The Prime Minister (Disraeli), 1940; Julius Caesar (Cassius), 1952; Richard III (Duke of Clarence), 1955; The Barretts of Wimpole Street (Mr Moulton Barrett), 1957; St Joan (Warwick), 1957; Becket (Louis VII), 1964; The Loved One, 1965; Chimes at Midnight, 1966; Mister Sebastian, 1967; The Charge of the Light Brigade, 1968; Shoes of the Fisherman, 1968; Oh What a Lovely War!, 1968; Julius Caesar, 1970; Eagle in a Cage, Lost Horizon, 1973; 11 Harrowhouse, 1974; Gold, 1974; Murder on the Orient Express, 1974; Aces High, 1976; Providence, Joseph Andrews, Portrait of a Young Man, Caligula, 1977. President: Shakespeare Reading Soc., 1958-; RADA, 1977-. Has appeared on Television, including Great Acting, 1967. Hon. degree Brandeis Univ. Companion, Legion of Honour, 1960. *Publications:* Early Stages, 1938; Stage Directions, 1963; Distinguished Company, 1972. *Recreations:* music, painting. *Address:* South Pavilion, Wotton Underwood, Aylesbury, Bucks.

GIELGUD, Val Henry, CBE 1958 (OBE 1942); retired as Head of Sound Drama, BBC, after 35 years; *b* 28 Apr 1900; *s* of late Frank and Kate Terry Gielgud; *m* 1921, Natalie Mamontoff (marr. diss., 1925); *m* 1928, Barbara Druce (marr. diss.); one *s* ; *m* 1946, Rita Vale (marr. diss.); *m* 1955, Monica Grey (marr. diss.); *m* 1960, Vivienne June Bailey. *Educ:* Rugby Sch.; Trinity

Coll., Oxford. Had a somewhat variegated early career, including some time as sec. to an MP, as sub-editor of a comic paper, and as an actor; joined the Radio Times, 1928, and was appointed BBC Dramatic Dir, 1929; since then has written novels, stage plays, broadcast plays, and collaborated in several film scenarios, Death at Broadcasting House, Royal Cavalcade, Café Colette, Talleyrand, and Marlborough. *Publications:* Black Gallantry, 1928; Gathering of Eagles, 1929; Imperial Treasure, 1930; The Broken Men, 1931; Gravelhanger, 1932; Outrage in Manchukuo, 1937; The Red Account, 1939; Beyond Dover, 1940; Confident Morning, 1943; Years of the Locust, autobiog., 1946; How to Write Broadcast Plays; Radio Theatre 1946; Fall of a Sparrow, 1948; Special Delivery, 1949; One Year of Grace, 1950; The High Jump, 1953; Cat, 1956; British Radio Drama, 1922-1956, A Survey, 1957; Gallows' Foot, 1958; To Bed at Noon, 1960; And Died So?, 1961; The Goggle-Box Affair, 1963; Years in a Mirror, 1965; Cats: a personal Anthology, 1966; Conduct of a Member, 1967; A Necessary End, 1969; The Candle-Holders, 1970; The Black Sambo Affair, 1972; My Cats and Myself, 1972; In Such a Night, 1974; A Fearful Thing, 1975; *plays:* Away from it All; Chinese White; Party Manners; Iron Curtain; The Bombshell; Mediterranean Blue; Not Enough Tragedy; Gorgeous George; (with Holt Marvell) Under London; Death at Broadcasting House; Death as an Extra; Death in Budapest; The Television Murder (with Eric Maschwitz). *Recreations:* reading, especially Milit. History, enjoying the society of Siamese cats, talking and travel. *Address:* Wychwood, Barcombe, near Lewes, East Sussex. *Club:* Savile.

GIFFARD, family name of **Earl of Halsbury.**

GIFFARD, (Charles) Sydney (Rycroft), CMG 1976; HM Diplomatic Service; Minister in Tokyo, since 1975; *b* 30 Oct. 1926; *m* 1951, Wendy Patricia Vidal (marr. diss. 1976); one *s* one *d.* Served in Japan, 1952; Foreign Office, 1957; Berne, 1961 and Tokyo, 1964-67; Counsellor, FCO, 1968; Royal Coll. of Defence Studies, 1971; Counsellor, Tel Aviv, 1972. *Address:* c/o Foreign and Commonwealth Office, SW1.

GIFFORD, family name of **Baron Gifford.**

GIFFORD, Earl of; Edward Douglas John Hay; estate agent; *b* 6 Aug. 1947; *s* and *heir* of 12th Marquis of Tweeddale, *qv* , and of Sonia Mary Peake. *Educ:* Milton Abbey, Blandford, Dorset; Trinity Coll., Oxford (BA Hons PPE). *Recreations:* motorcycle, old music, literature, languages. *Address:* 70 Campden Hill Towers, Notting Hill Gate, W11 3QP. *T:* 01-229 8270.

GIFFORD, 6th Baron, *cr* 1824; **Anthony Maurice Gifford;** Barrister at Law, practising since 1966; *b* 1 May 1940; *s* of 5th Baron Gifford and Lady Gifford (*née* Margaret Allen), Sydney, NSW; *S* father 1961; *m* 1965, Katherine Ann, *o d* of Dr Mundy; one *s* one *d. Educ:* Winchester Coll. (scholar); King's Coll., Cambridge (scholar). Student at Middle Temple, 1959-62, called to the Bar, 1962. BA Cantab, 1961. Chm., Cttee for Freedom in Mozambique, Angola and Guiné, 1968-75; Chm., N Kensington Neighbourhood Law Centre, 1974- (Hon. Sec., 1970-74). *Heir: s* Hon. Thomas Adam Gifford, *b* 1 Dec. 1967. *Address:* 1 Gledhow Gardens, SW5. *T:* 01-373 2237.

GIFFORD, Prof. Charles Henry; Winterstoke Professor of English, University of Bristol, 1967-75, Professor of English and Comparative Literature, Jan.-July 1976, retired; *b* 17 June 1913; *s* of Walter Stanley Gifford and Constance Lena Gifford (*née* Henry); *m* 1938, Mary Rosamond van Ingen; one *s* one *d. Educ:* Harrow Sch.; Christ Church, Oxford. BA 1936, MA 1946. War Service, 1940-46, Royal Armoured Corps; Univ. of Bristol: Asst Lectr, 1946; Sen. Lectr, 1955; Prof. of Modern English Literature, 1963. *Publications:* The Hero of his Time, 1950; (with Charles Tomlinson) Castilian Ilexes: versions from Antonio Machado, 1963; The Novel in Russia, 1964; Comparative Literature, 1969; Tolstoy: a critical anthology, 1971; Boris Pasternak: a critical study, 1977; articles and reviews on English and comparative literature. *Address:* 10 Hyland Grove, Bristol BS9 3NR. *T:* Bristol 502504.

GIFFORD, (James) Morris, CBE 1973; FCIT; Director-General, National Ports Council, since 1963 (Member of Council since 1964); *b* 25 March 1922; *y s* of Frederick W. Gifford, Dunfermline; *m* 1943, Margaret Lowe Shaw, MA, Dunfermline; two *s* one *d. Educ:* Dunfermline High Sch.; Edinburgh Univ. MA Hons Classics, 1946. Lieut RA, 1942-45. Called to Bar, Middle Temple, 1951. Shipping Fedn, 1946-55: Asst Sec., Mersey, 1948-50 and Thames, 1950-53; Sec., Clyde, 1954-55; Gen. Man., Nat. Assoc. of Port Employers, and Mem. Nat. Dock Labour Bd, 1955-63. Vice-Pres., CIT, 1975, Pres., 1976. *Recreations:* crosswords, reading, gardening. *Address:* 15 Bourne Avenue, Southgate, N14 6PB. *T:* 01-886 1757. *Club:* Oriental.

GIGGALL, Rt. Rev. George Kenneth; see St Helena, Bishop of.

GILBERT, Carl Joyce; Special Representative for Trade Negotiations, Washington, DC, in the Executive Office of the President, with rank of Ambassador, 1969-71; b 3 April 1906; s of Seymour Parker Gilbert and Carrie Jennings Gilbert (née Cooper); m 1936, Helen Amory Homans; one s. Educ: University of Virginia; Harvard. AB University of Virginia, 1928; LLB Harvard, 1931. Admitted to Mass bar, 1931; Associate Ropes, Gray, Boyden & Perkins, 1931-38; member firm (name changed to Ropes, Gray, Best, Coolidge & Rugg), 1938-48; Treasurer-Vice-Pres., The Gillette Company (formerly Gillette Safety Razor Company), Boston, 1948-56; Pres., 1956-57; Chm. of Board and Chief Exec. Officer, 1957-66; Chm. Exec. Cttee, 1966-68. Hon. LLD Boston Coll., Mass, 1958. Address: Strawberry Hill Street, Dover, Mass. T: State 5-0311. Clubs: Metropolitan (Washington); Somerset, Dedham Country and Polo (Boston).

GILBERT, Frederick; Retired as Special Commissioner of Income Tax; b North Cornwall, 15 Nov. 1899; s of William Gilbert, farmer, and Jessie Cleave; m 1st, Ethel (decd), d of William Baily, Launceston; three d; 2nd, Blanche, d of William Banyard, Cambridge. Recreations: bowls, painting. Address: 5 Pinewoods Court, Collington Rise, Bexhill on Sea, East Sussex. T: Cooden 4967.

GILBERT, Prof. Geoffrey Alan, FRS 1973; Professor of Biochemistry, University of Birmingham, since 1969; b 3 Dec. 1917; s of A. C. Gilbert and M. M. Gilbert (née Cull); m 1948, Lilo M. Gilbert (née Czigler de Egerszalok); two s. Educ: Kingsbury County Sch., Mddx; Emmanuel Coll., Cambridge; Dept of Colloid Science, Cambridge. MA, PhD, ScD (Cantab). Lectr, Chemistry Dept, Univ. of Birmingham, 1943-46. Research Fellow, Medical Sch., Harvard Univ., 1946-47. Univ. of Birmingham: Sen. Lectr, Chemistry Dept, 1947-61, Reader, 1961-69. Chm., British Biophysical Soc., 1974. Publications: articles and papers in scientific jls. Recreations: travel, listening to classical music, photography. Address: 194 Selly Park Road, Birmingham B29 7HY. T: 021-472 0755.

GILBERT, Maj.-Gen. Glyn Charles Anglim, CB 1974; MC 1944; Director, British Deer Society, since 1975; b 15 Aug. 1920; s of C. G. G. Gilbert, OBE, MC, and H. M. Gilbert, MBE; m 1943, Heather Mary Jackson; three s one d. Educ: Eastbourne Coll.; RMC Sandhurst. Commnd 1939; served with 2nd Lincolns, 1940-47, NW Europe and Palestine; Instructor, Sch. of Infantry, 1948-50; 3rd Bn Para. Regt, 1951; psc 1952; staff and regimental appts in MoD, Airborne Forces, Royal Lincolns and Para. Regt, 1952-66, Cyprus, Egypt and Malaya; idc 1966; comd Sch. of Infantry, 1967-70; GOC 3rd Div., 1970-72; Comdt, Joint Welfare Estab., 1972-74, retired. Hon. Col, 1st Bn, The Wessex Regt, TAVR, 1975-. Recreations: golf, gardening. Address: c/o Lloyds Bank Ltd, Warminster, Wilts. Club: Army and Navy.

GILBERT, Prof. John Cannon; Professor of Economics in the University of Sheffield, 1957-73, now Emeritus; Dean of Faculty of Economic and Social Studies, 1959-62; b 28 Sept. 1908; s of James and Elizabeth Louisa Gilbert; m 1938, Elizabeth Hadley Crook; two s. Educ: Bancroft's Sch.; The London Sch. of Economics and Political Science, University of London. Student of the Handels-Hochschule, Berlin (Sir Ernest Cassel Travelling Schol.), 1927-28; BCom Hons London, 1929. Asst on teaching staff, LSE, 1929-31; Lecturer in Economics, Sch. of Economics, Dundee, 1931-41. Ministry of Supply, 1941-45. Lecturer in Economics, University of Manchester, 1945-48; Senior Lecturer in Economics, University of Sheffield, 1948-56, Reader, 1956-57. Mem. Editorial Bd Bulletin of Economic Research, 1949-73. Publications: A History of Investment Trusts in Dundee, 1873-1938, 1939; articles in Economica, Review of Economic Studies, etc. Recreations: walking, hill climbing. Address: 81 High Storrs Drive, Ecclesall, Sheffield S11 7LN. T: Sheffield 663544.

GILBERT, John Orman, CMG 1958; retired; b London, 21 Oct. 1907; s of Rev. T. H. Gilbert, late of Chedgrave Manor, Norfolk; m 1935, Winifred Mary Harris, Dublin; two s. Educ: Felsted Sch., Essex; Pembroke Coll., Oxford. Joined Sarawak Civil Service, 1928; various posts, from Cadet, to District Officer in 1940. During War of 1939-45 served in Bengal Sappers and Miners stationed in India and attained rank of Major. Came back to Sarawak with BM Administration, 1946; Resident, 4th Div., Sarawak, 1946-53; British Resident, Brunei, 1953-58; retd 1959. Coronation Medal, 1953. Recreations: sailing, shooting and fishing. Address: Moonrising, PO Box 100, Somerset West, Cape, South Africa.

GILBERT, Dr John William; MP (Lab) Dudley East, since 1974 (Dudley, 1970-74); Minister of State, Ministry of Defence, since 1976; b April 1927; m 1963, Jean Olive Ross Skinner; two d of previous marriage. Educ: Merchant Taylors' Sch.; St John's Coll., Oxford; New York Univ. (PhD in Internat. Economics, Graduate Sch. of Business Administration). Chartered Accountant, Canada. Contested (Lab): Ludlow, 1966; Dudley, March 1968. Opposition front-bench spokesman on Treasury affairs, 1972-74; Financial Secretary to the Treasury, 1974-75; Minister for Transport, DoE, 1975-76. Member: Fabian Soc.; Royal Inst. of Internat. Affairs; Nat. Council for Civil Liberties; Cooperative Members' Assoc., 1967-73 (Secretary); Labour Economic Finance and Taxation Assoc., 1970-74 (Secretary); NUGMW. Address: House of Commons, SW1. Club: Reform.

GILBERT, Air Vice-Marshal Joseph Alfred, CBE 1974; Air Officer Commanding 38 Group, RAF, since 1977; b 15 June 1931; s of Ernest and Mildred Gilbert; m 1955, Betty, yr d of late William Lishman and of Mrs Eva Lishman; two d. Educ: William Hulme's Sch., Manchester; Univ. of Leeds (BA, Hons Econ. and Pol Science). Commnd into RAF, 1952; Fighter Sqdns, 1953-61; Air Secretary's Dept, 1961-63; RAF Staff Coll., 1964; CO 92 (Lightning) Sqdn, 1965-67; jssc 1968; Sec., Defence Policy Staff, and Asst Dir of Defence Policy, 1968-71; CO, RAF Coltishall, 1971-73; RCDS, 1974; Dir of Forward Policy (RAF), 1975; ACAS (Policy), MoD, 1975-77. Publications: articles in defence jls. Recreations: hockey, tennis, South of France, strategic affairs. Address: HQ 38 Group, RAF, Upavon, Pewsey, Wilts SN9 6BE. Club: Royal Air Force.

GILBERT, Martin (John), MA; FRSL; historian; Fellow of Merton College, Oxford, since 1962; Official Biographer of Sir Winston Churchill since 1968; b 25 Oct. 1936; s of Peter and Miriam Gilbert; m 1st, 1963, Helen Constance, yr d of late Joseph Robinson, CBE; one d; 2nd, Susan, d of Michael Sacher, qv. Educ: Highgate Sch.; Magdalen Coll., Oxford. Nat. Service (Army), 1955-57; Sen. Research Scholar, St Antony's Coll., Oxford, 1960-62; Vis. Lectr, Budapest Univ., 1961; Res. Asst (sometime Sen. Res. Asst) to Hon. Randolph S. Churchill, 1962-67; Vis. Prof., Univ. of S Carolina, 1965; Recent Hist. Correspt for Sunday Times, 1967; Res. Asst (Brit. Empire) for BBC, 1968; Vis. Lectr, Hebrew Univ. of Jerusalem, 1975; Historical Adviser (Palestine) for Thames Television, 1977-78; has lectured on historical subjects at Univs throughout Europe and USA. Governor, Hebrew Univ. of Jerusalem, 1977-. Publications: The Appeasers, 1963 (with Richard Gott) (trans. German, Polish, Rumanian); Britain and Germany Between the Wars, 1964; The European Powers, 1900-1945, 1965 (trans. Italian, Spanish); Plough My Own Furrow: The Life of Lord Allen of Hurtwood, 1965; Servant of India: A Study of Imperial Rule 1905-1910, 1966; The Roots of Appeasement, 1966; Recent History Atlas 1860-1960, 1966; Winston Churchill (Clarendon Biogs for young people), 1966; British History Atlas, 1968; American History Atlas, 1968; Jewish History Atlas, 1969, rev. edn 1976; First World War Atlas, 1970; Winston S. Churchill, vol iii, 1914-1916, 1971, companion volume (in two parts) 1973; Russian History Atlas, 1972; Sir Horace Rumbold: portrait of a diplomat, 1973; Churchill: a photographic portrait, 1974; The Arab-Israeli Conflict: its history in maps, 1974, 2nd edn 1976; Churchill and Zionism (pamphlet), 1974; Winston S. Churchill, vol. iv, 1917-1922, 1975, companion volume (in three parts), 1977; The Jews in Arab Lands: their history in maps, 1975, illustr. edn, 1976 (trans. Hebrew, Arabic, French, German); Winston S. Churchill, vol. v, 1922-1939, 1976, companion volume (in three parts), 1978; The Jews of Russia: Illustrated History Atlas, 1976; Jerusalem Illustrated History Atlas, 1977 (trans. Spanish); Editor: A Century of Conflict: Essays Presented to A. J. P. Taylor, 1966; Churchill, 1967, and Lloyd George, 1968 (Spectrum Books); compiled Jackdaws: Winston Churchill, 1970; The Coming of War in 1939, 1973; contribs historical articles and reviews to jls (incl. Purnell's History of the Twentieth Century). Recreation: drawing maps. Address: Merton College, Oxford. T: Oxford 49651. Club: Athenæum.

GILBERT, Michael Francis, TD 1950; Partner, Trower Still & Keeling, Solicitors; crime writer; b 17 July 1912; s of Bernard Samuel Gilbert and Berwyn Minna Cuthbert; m 1947, Roberta Mary, d of Col R. M. W. Marsden; two s five d. Educ: Blundell's Sch.; London University. LLB 1937. Served War of 1939-45, Hon. Artillery Co., 12th Regt RHA, N Africa and Italy (despatches 1943). Joined Trower Still & Keeling, 1947. Legal Adviser to Govt of Bahrain, 1960. Member: Arts Council Cttee on Public Lending Right, 1968; Royal Literary Fund, 1969; Council of Soc. of Authors, 1975; (Founder) Crime Writers' Assoc.; Mystery Writers of America. Publications: novels: Close Quarters, 1947; They Never Looked Inside, 1948; The Doors Open, 1949; Smallbone Deceased, 1950; Death has Deep Roots, 1951; Death in Captivity, 1952; Fear to Tread, 1953; Sky High, 1955; Be Shot for Sixpence, 1956; The Tichborne Claimant, 1957; Blood and Judgement, 1958; After the Fine Weather,

1963; The Crack in the Tea Cup, 1965; The Dust and the Heat, 1967; The Etruscan Net, 1969; The Body of a Girl, 1972; The Ninety Second Tiger, 1973; Flash Point, 1974; The Night of the Twelfth, 1976; *short stories:* Game Without Rules; Stay of Execution; Petrella at Q, 1977; *plays:* A Clean Kill; The Bargain; Windfall; The Shot in Question; *edited:* Crime in Good Company, 1959; has also written radio and TV scripts. *Recreations:* walking, archery, contract bridge. *Address:* Luddesdown Old Rectory, Cobham, Kent. *T:* Meopham 814272. *Club:* Garrick.

GILBERT, Patrick Nigel Geoffrey; General Secretary of the Society for Promoting Christian Knowledge, since 1971; *b* 12 May 1934; adopted *s* of late Geoffrey Gilbert and Evelyn (*née* Miller), Devon. *Educ:* Cranleigh Sch.; Merton Coll., Oxford. Oxford University Press, 1964-69; Man. Director in Linguaphone Group (Westinghouse), 1970 (with Group, 1969-70). Member: Bd for Mission and Unity of Gen. Synod, 1971-78; Archbishops' Cttee on RC Relations, 1971-; Council of Conf. of British Missionary Socs, 1971-78; Council of Christians Abroad, 1974-; Trustee, World Assoc. for Christian Communication, 1975- (European Vice-Chm., 1975); rep.: to Conf. of European Churches, 1976-; to EEC, 1975-; to Council of Europe, 1976-; Trustee: Harold Buxton Trust; Religious Book Foundation; Overseas Bishoprics Fund, 1973-; Hon. Brother, Art Workers' Guild, 1971 (Trustee, 1975-, Chm. Trustees, 1976-); Chm., Standing Conf. of London Arts Councils, 1975- (Vice-Chm., 1973-75); Founder Chm., Nat. Assoc. Local Arts Councils, 1977-; Chm., Embroiderers' Guild, 1977- (Hon. Treas., 1974-77); Steward, Artists' Gen. Benevolent Instn, 1971-; Vice-Pres., Camden Arts Council, 1974- (Chm., 1970-74); Mem. Gen. Council and Executive, Greater London Arts Assoc., 1968- (Initiator 1972 Festivals of London); Governor: All Saints Coll., Tottenham, 1971-; St Martin's Sch. for Girls, 1971-; Fellow of Corp. of SS Mary and Nicholas (Woodard Schs), 1972- (Chm. S Div. Research Cttee). Lord of the Manor of Cantley Nethehall, Norfolk; Freeman of City of London and Mem. Woolmen's Livery. Order of St Vladimir. *Recreations:* walking, reading, travel (over 100 countries), enjoying the Arts, golf. *Address:* 3 The Mount Square, NW3 6SU. *T:* 01-794 8807. *Clubs:* Athenæum; Walton Heath Golf.

GILBERT, Stuart William; Under-Secretary, Department of the Environment, since 1970; *b* 2 Aug. 1926; *s* of Rodney Stuart Gilbert and Ella Edith (*née* Esgate); *m* 1955, Marjorie Laws Vallance; one *s* one *d*. *Educ:* Maidstone Grammar Sch.; Emmanuel Coll., Cambridge (Open Exhibnr and State Scholar; BA). Served RAF, 1944-47. Asst Principal, Min. of Health, 1949; Asst Private Sec.: to Minister of Housing and Local Govt, 1952; to Parly Sec., 1954; Principal, 1955; Sec., Parker Morris Cttee on Housing Standards, 1958-61, Rapporteur to ECE Housing Cttee, 1959-61; Reporter to ILO Conf. on Workers' Housing, 1960; Asst Sec., Local Govt Finance Div., 1964; Under-Sec. for New Towns, 1970, Business Rents, 1973, Housing, 1974, Planning Land Use, 1977. *Recreations:* pottering about in a dinghy, audio. *Address:* 3 Westmoat Close, Beckenham, Kent. *T:* 01-650 7213. *Club:* United Oxford & Cambridge University.

GILBERT, Brig. Sir William (Herbert Ellery), KBE 1976 (OBE 1945); DSO 1944; Director, New Zealand Security Intelligence Service, 1956-76, retired; *b* 20 July 1916; *s* of Ellery George Gilbert and Nellie (*née* Hall); *m* 1944, Patricia Caroline Anson Farrer; two *s* one *d*. *Educ:* Wanganui Collegiate Sch., NZ; RMC, Duntroon, Australia. NZ Regular Army, 1937-56; War Service with 2NZEF, ME and Italy, 1940-45; retd, Brig. Bronze Star, USA, 1945. *Recreations:* golf, fishing, gardening. *Address:* 38 Chatsworth Road, Silverstream, New Zealand. *T:* UH 86-570. *Club:* Wellington, Wellington Golf (NZ).

GILBEY, family name of **Baron Vaux of Harrowden.**

GILBEY, Sir (Walter) Derek, 3rd Bt, *cr* 1893; Lieut 2nd Bn Black Watch; *b* 11 March 1913; *s* of Walter Ewart Gilbey and Dorothy Coysgarne Sim; *S* grandfather, 1945; *m* 1948, Elizabeth Mary, *d* of Col Keith Campbell and Marjorie Syfret; one *s* one *d*. *Educ:* Eton. Served War of 1939-45 (prisoner). *Heir: s* Walter Gavin Gilbey, *b* 14 April 1949. *Address:* Culross, Faygate, near Horsham, West Sussex. *T:* Faygate 331. *Club:* Portland.

GILCHRIST, Sir Andrew (Graham), KCMG 1964 (CMG 1956); retired as Ambassador and administrator; now fruit farmer; *b* 19 April 1910; *e s* of late James Graham Gilchrist, Kerse, Lesmahagow; *m* 1946, Freda Grace, *d* of late Alfred Slack; two *s* one *d*. *Educ:* Edinburgh Acad.; Exeter Coll., Oxford. Diplomatic career, 1933, included junior posts in Bangkok, Paris, Marseilles, Rabat, Stuttgart, Singapore, Chicago, also in FO; subseq. Ambassador at Reykjavik, Djakarta and Dublin,

retired. Chm., Highlands and Islands Develt Bd, 1970-76. War Service as Major, Force 136 in SE Asia (despatches). *Publication:* Bangkok Top Secret, 1970. *Address:* Arthur's Crag, Hazelbank, by Lanark. *T:* Crossford 263. *Clubs:* Special Forces; New (Edinburgh).

GILCHRIST, (Andrew) Rae, CBE 1961; MD Edinburgh, FRCPE, FRCP, Hon. FRACP, Hon. FRFPS Glasgow; Consulting Physician Royal Infirmary, Edinburgh; *b* 7 July 1899; *o s* of late Rev. Andrew Gilchrist, BA, Edinburgh; *m* 1st, 1931, Emily Faulds (*d* 1967), *yr d* of late W. Work Slater, Edinburgh and Innerleithen, Peeblesshire; one *s* one *d*; 2nd, 1975, Elspeth, widow of Dr Arthur Wightman. *Educ:* Belfast, Edinburgh, New York. RFA 1917-18; MB, ChB Edinburgh, 1921; Lauder-Brunton Prizeman, Milner-Fothergill Medallist, McCunn Medical Res. Scholar, Edinburgh Univ., 1924; MD (gold medal) 1933; resident hospital appointments at Addenbrooke's Hosp., Cambridge, Princess Elizabeth Hosp. for Children, London, E1, and at Royal Infirmary, Edinburgh, 1922-24; Resident Asst Physician Rockefeller Hosp. for Medical Research, New York, USA, 1926-27; Asst Physician, 1930; Physician, Royal Infirmary, Edinburgh, 1939-64; Gibson Lecturer RCP Edinburgh, 1944; Lecturer: Canadian Heart Assoc., 1955; Litchfield Lecture, Oxford Univ., 1956; Californian Heart Assoc., 1957; St Cyres Lecturer, National Heart Hosp., London, 1957; Hall Overseas Lecturer, Australia and NZ, 1959; Carey Coombs Memorial Lecture, Bristol Univ., 1960; Gwladys and Olwen Williams Lecture in Medicine, Liverpool Univ., 1961; Orford Lectr, College of Physicians of S Africa, 1962. William Cullen Prize, 1962 (shared). Pres. of the Royal College of Physicians of Edinburgh, 1957-60. Examr in Med. in Univs of Edinburgh, Glasgow, Aberdeen, St Andrews, East Africa (Makerere Coll.), and Baghdad. Mem. Assoc. of Physicians of Gt Brit., of Brit. Cardiac Soc. Hon. Mem. Cardiac Soc. of Australia and NZ. *Publications:* numerous contributions on disorders of heart and circulation, in British and American medical journals. *Recreation:* fishing. *Address:* Grovedale, 16 Winton Terrace, Edinburgh EH10 7AP. *T:* 031-445 1119. *Clubs:* Flyfishers'; New (Edinburgh).

GILCHRIST, Archibald; Managing Director, Govan Shipbuilders Ltd, since 1971; *b* 17 Dec. 1929; *m* 1958, Elizabeth Jean Greenlees; two *s* one *d*. *Educ:* Loretto; Pembroke Coll., Cambridge (MA). Barclay Curle & Co. Ltd, Glasgow, 1954-64, various managerial posts; ultimately Dir, Swan Hunter Group; Brown Bros & Co. Ltd, Edinburgh, 1964-72: Dep. Man. Dir, 1964; Man. Dir, 1969. *Recreations:* golf, shooting, fishing, music. *Address:* Inchmaholm, Barnton Avenue, Edinburgh. *T:* 031-336 4288. *Clubs:* Western (Glasgow); Hon. Company of Edinburgh Golfers.

GILCHRIST, James Finlay Elder, OBE 1946; Director, Harrisons & Crosfield Ltd (Chairman, 1962-77); *b* 13 Aug. 1903; *s* of late Thomas Dunlop Gilchrist and Agnes Crawford Elder; *m* 1933, Dorothy Joan Narizzano; two *s* one *d*. *Educ:* Glasgow Academy. *Address:* South Cottage, Hapstead Farm, Ardingly, Sussex. *T:* Ardingly 892368. *Club:* East India, Devonshire, Sports and Public Schools.

GILCHRIST, Rae; see Gilchrist, A. R.

'GILES'; see Giles, Carl Ronald.

GILES, Sir Alexander (Falconer), KBE 1965 (MBE 1946); CMG 1960; HM Colonial Service retired; *b* 1915; *o s* of late A. F. Giles, MA, LLD; *m* 1953, Mrs M. E. Watson, *d* of late Lieut-Col R. F. D. Burnett, MC, and widow of Lieut-Col J. L. Watson; two *step s* one *step d*. *Educ:* The Edinburgh Academy; Edinburgh Univ.; Balliol Coll., Oxford (BA). Pres. Oxford Union Soc., 1939. 2nd Lieut the Royal Scots, 1940; attached RWAFF, 1941; 81 (WA) Div., 1943; Lieut-Col comdg 5 GCR, 1945 (MBE, despatches). Cadet Colonial Service, Tanganyika, 1947; Administrator, St Vincent, 1955-62; Resident Commissioner, Basutoland, 1962-65; British Govt Representative, Basutoland, 1965-66. Chairman: Victoria League in Scotland, 1968-70; Scottish Council, Royal Over-Seas League, 1969-70, Central Council, 1972-75. Dir, Toc H, 1968-74. Gen. Sec., Scotland, Royal Over-Seas League, 1976. *Publications:* articles in service jls. *Recreation:* the printed word. *Address:* 14 Belgrave Place, Edinburgh EH4 3AW.

GILES, Carl Ronald, OBE 1959; Cartoonist, Daily and Sunday Express, since 1943; *b* 29 Sept. 1916; *m* 1942, Sylvia Joan Clarke. *Educ:* various schools. Trained as animated cartoonist; Animator for Alexander Korda, 1935; Cartoonist, Reynolds News, 1937-43. Cartoons extensively reproduced in US and syndicated throughout world. Produced and animated Documentary Films for Min. of Information, also War

Correspondent-cartoonist in France, Belgium, Holland and Germany, War of 1939-45. *Publications:* "Giles" Annual, 1945-; various overseas collections. *Recreations:* yachting, engineering, farming. *Address:* Hillbrow Farm, Witnesham, Suffolk. *T:* Witnesham 239. *Clubs:* Savage, British Racing Drivers', Royal Harwich Yacht, Press.

GILES, Sir (Henry) Norman, Kt 1969; OBE 1966; Chairman: Elder Smith Goldsbrough Mort Ltd, Australia, 1967-75; Commonwealth Development Bank Executive Committee, since 1959; P&O Australia Ltd, 1959-75; Director: Commonwealth Banking Corporation, since 1959 (Deputy Chairman, 1959-62 and 1967-75); Reyrolle Pty Ltd; Babock Australian Holdings Ltd; Gove Alumina Ltd, 1969-73; *b* Northam, WA, 3 May 1905; *s* of late J. O. Giles, Claremont, WA; *m* 1929, Eleanor, *d* of late S. J. Barker; one *s* one *d*. *Educ:* Christ Church Grammar Sch., WA. Served War of 1939-45: RAAF, 1941-44; Flt-Lt (Aust. and New Guinea). Mem. Export Develt Council, 1965-70 (Mem. Exec. Cttee, 1966-70; Dep. Chm. 1966-70); Member: Council Aust. Admin. Staff Coll., 1956-75; SA Industrial Develt Adv. Council, 1968-70; Australia Inst., Rotterdam, 1965-75; SA State Cttee, CSIRO, 1962-71; Aust. Japan Business Co-op. Cttee, 1966-75; Pacific Basin Economic Co-op. Cttee, 1968-75; Council, Duke of Edinburgh's Third Commonwealth Study Conf., Aust., 1966-68; Industry Forum, Aust. Acad. of Science, 1967-70. Aust. Wool Industry Adv. Cttee, 1970-72. Joined Elder Smith & Co. Ltd, 1922; Asst Manager for WA, 1944-47; Manager for WA, 1948-52; Gen. Manager, 1952-55; Man. Dir, 1955-62; Gen. Manager, 1962-64, Man. Dir, 1964-67, Chm., 1967-76, Elder Smith Goldsbrough Ltd. Director: Reyrolle Parsons of Australia Ltd, 1969-76 (Chm., 1969-74); Newcastle Engineering Co. Pty Ltd, 1969-76; Newcastle Steel Co. Pty Ltd, 1969-76. Mem. Exec., Nat. Council of Wool Selling Brokers of Australia, WA, 1947-53, SA, 1953-62; Vice-Pres. and Member, WA Chamber of Commerce, 1947-50; Mem. Council for C of E Schools, WA, 1933-53. *Recreations:* bowls, gardening. *Address:* 31/16 King's Park Avenue, Crawley, WA 6009, Australia. *Clubs:* Weld (WA); Union (NSW); Adelaide, Naval, Military and Air Force, Adelaide Oval Bowling (all in SA).

GILES, Rear-Adm. Morgan Charles M.; *see* Morgan-Giles.

GILES, Sir Norman; *see* Giles, Sir H. N.

GILES, Air Commandant Dame Pauline, DBE 1967; RRC; Matron-in-Chief, Princess Mary's Royal Air Force Nursing Service, 1966-70, retired; *b* 17 Sept. 1912. *Educ:* Sheffield. Joined PMRAFNS, Nov. 1937; later appointments included Principal Matron for Royal Air Force Command in Britain and Western Europe; became Matron-in-Chief, PMRAFNS, Sept. 1966. *Address:* 7 Hever Crescent, Bexhill-on-Sea, East Sussex TN39 4HQ. *Club:* Royal Air Force.

GILES, Robert Frederick; Under-Secretary, Ministry of Agriculture, Fisheries and Food, since 1975; *b* 27 Dec. 1918; *s* of Robert and Edith Giles; *m* 1948, Mabel Florence Gentry; two *d*. *Educ:* Drayton Manor Sch., Hanwell. Min. of Agriculture, 1936-39. Royal Navy, 1939-45: CO, HMS Tango, 1942-44. Various assignments, MAF, from 1945; Regional Controller, Northern Region MAFF, 1963-68; Head, Food Standards/Food Science Div., 1968-74; Food Standards and Food Subsidies Gp, 1975. *Recreations:* walking, theatre, wine. *Address:* 20 Arkwright Road, Sanderstead, Surrey CR2 0LD. *T:* 01-657 4118. *Club:* Civil Service.

GILES, Roy Curtis, MA; Head Master, Highgate School, since 1974; *b* 6 Dec. 1932; *s* of Herbert Henry Giles and Dorothy Alexandra Potter; *m* 1963, Christine von Alten; one *s* one *d*. *Educ:* Queen Elizabeth's Sch., Barnet; Jesus Coll., Cambridge (Open Scholar). Asst Master, Dean Close Sch., 1956-60; Lektor, Hamburg Univ., 1960-63; Asst Master, Eton Coll., 1963-74, Head of Modern Languages, 1970-74. Mem., Council of Management, Davies's Educn Services, 1975-; Governor, The Hall, Hampstead, 1976-. *Recreations:* music, theatre. *Address:* Head Master's House, 12 Bishopswood Road, N6 4PR. *T:* 01-340 7626.

GILHAM, Harold Sidney, CB 1956; Asst Comptroller of the Patent Office, Board of Trade, 1955-59, retired. Formerly a Superintending Examiner at the Patent Office. *Address:* 49 Stanley Road, Northwood, Middlesex.

GILL, Austin, CBE 1955; MA, Licencié-ès-lettres; Marshall Professor of French, University of Glasgow, 1966-71, retired; *b* 3 Sept. 1906; *m* 1939, Madeleine Monier. *Educ:* Bury Municipal Secondary Sch.; Universities of Manchester, Grenoble, Paris. Research Fellow, 1929-30, Faulkner Fellow, 1930-31, and Langton Fellow, 1931-33, Manchester Univ. Asst Lecturer in

French, Edinburgh Univ., 1933-34; Lecturer in French, Edinburgh Univ., 1934-43; British Council Representative in French North Africa, 1943-44; British Council Actg Rep. in France, 1944-45; Official Fellow, Tutor in Modern Langs, Magdalen Coll., Oxford, 1945-50 and 1954-66. Dir of Brit. Inst. in Paris, 1950-54. *Publications:* (ed) Les Ramonneurs, 1957; (ed) Life and Letters in France, 1970; articles and reviews in literary and philological journals. *Address:* 15 Beaumont Gate, Glasgow G12 9ED.

GILL, Cecil G. H.; *see* Hope Gill.

GILL, Cyril James, CB 1965; Senior Lecturer in Education, University of Keele, 1968-71, retired (Gulbenkian Lecturer in Education, 1965-68); *b* 29 March 1904; *s* of William Gill, Carnforth, Lancs; *m* 1939, Phyllis Mary, *d* of Joseph Windsor, Ramsey, Isle of Man. *Educ:* Ulverston Grammar Sch.; Liverpool Univ. Sch. Master, Ramsey, IOM and Archbishop Tenison's, London, 1926-42; Head Master, Salford Grammar Sch., 1942-45. HM Inspectorate of Schools, 1945-65; Midland Divisional Inspector, 1954-61; Chief Inspector (Teacher Training), 1961-65. *Publications:* articles on counselling and guidance. *Recreations:* gardening, walking, photography, theatre. *Address:* 3 Vicarage Close, Grange over Sands, Cumbria. *T:* Grange over Sands 2143. *Club:* Royal Over-Seas League.

GILL, Cyril James; Telecommunications Management Consultant, since 1972; *b* 24 Dec. 1907; *s* of William and Alice Gill; *m* 1931, Dae M. (*née* Bingley); one *s* one *d*. *Educ:* Mundella Gram. Sch., Nottingham. Engrg Dept, GPO, 1929-48; Telephone Man., Sheffield, 1949; Princ., Post Office HQ, 1950; Princ. Private Sec. to PMG, 1957; Dep. Dir, External Telecommunications Exec., 1958; Controller of Supplies, 1959; Vice-Dir, ETE, 1964; Dir, External Telecomm. Exec., GPO, 1967-69; Dir, Cable and Wireless Ltd, 1967-69; Chm. Commonwealth Telecomm. Council, 1968-69; Chm. Grading Commn, Nigerian Min. of Communications, 1970-71. *Recreations:* gardening, golf, travel. *Address:* 65 Longton Avenue, Upper Sydenham, SE26 6RF. *T:* 01-699 2745.

GILL, Evan W. T.; Canadian Ambassador to Ireland, 1965-68; *b* 2 Nov. 1902; *s* of Robert Gill; *m* 1930, Dorothy Laurie; two *s* one *d*. *Educ:* RMC, Kingston, Ont.; McGill Univ., Montreal, PQ. Began career with industrial and commercial organs; served Canadian Army, 1940-46; Cabinet Secretariat, 1946-50; External Affairs, 1950; Canada House, 1950-51; High Comr for Canada to Union of S Africa, 1954-57; High Comr for Canada to Ghana, 1957-59; Asst Under-Sec. of State for External Affairs, 1959-62; High Commissioner for Canada in Australia, 1962-64. *Recreations:* golf and fishing. *Address:* St Andrews, New Brunswick, Canada. *Clubs:* Rideau, Country (Ottawa).

GILL, Frank Maxey; Chairman, Gill & Duffus Group Ltd, since 1976; *b* 25 Sept. 1919; fifth *s* of Frederick Gordon Hill, DSO, and Mary Gill; *m* 1st, 1942, Sheila Rosemary Gordon (decd); three *d*; 2nd, 1971, Erica Margaret Fulcher; one *s*. *Educ:* Kingsmead Prep. Sch., Seaford; Marlborough Coll.; De Havilland Aeronautical Technical Sch. Joined Gill & Duffus Ltd, 1940; served RAF (Flt/Lt), 1940-46; rejoined Gill & Duffus Ltd, 1946; Director, 1957; Joint Managing Director, 1959. Pres., Confectioners' Benevolent Fund, 1970. *Recreations:* ocean cruising, golf. *Address:* Tile House, Reigate Heath, Reigate, Surrey. *Clubs:* Royal Cruising; Walton Heath Golf (Surrey).

GILL, Air Vice-Marshal Harry, OBE 1968; Director-General of Engineering and Supply Policy, Royal Air Force, since 1976; *b* 30 Oct. 1922; *s* of John William Gill and Lucy Gill, Newark, Notts; *m* 1951, Diana Patricia, *d* of Colin Wood, Glossop; one *d*. *Educ:* Barnby Road Sch.; Newark Technical Coll. Entered RAF, 1941; pilot trng, 1942; commnd 1943; flying duties, 1943-49; transf. to Equipment Br., 1949; Officer Commanding: Supply Sqdns, RAF Spitalgate and RAF North Coates, 1949-52; HQ Staff No 93 Maintenance Unit Explosives and Fuels Supply Ops, 1952-55; Explosives and Fuels Sch., 1955-58; Staff Officer Logistics Div., HQ Allied Forces Northern Europe, 1958-61; Head of Provision Br., Air Min., 1961-64; Chief Equipment Officer, No 25 Maintenance Unit, RAF Hartlebury, 1964-66; Equipment Staff Officer, HQ Air Forces Middle East, 1966-67; Dep. Dir Supply Systems, MoD Air, 1968-70; RCDS, 1971; Comdt, RAF Supply Control Centre, 1972-73; Dir, Supply Management, MoD Air, 1973-76. *Recreations:* shooting, fishing, squash, tennis, cricket. *Address:* Briar Cottage, Hawley, Surrey. *T:* Camberley 31587. *Club:* Royal Air Force.

GILL, Maj.-Gen. Ian Gordon, CB 1972; OBE 1959 (MBE 1949); MC 1940, Bar 1945; idc, psc; Colonel, 4/7 Royal Dragoon Guards, since 1973; *b* Rochester, 9 Nov. 1919; *s* of late Brig.

Gordon Harry Gill, CMG, DSO and Mrs Doris Gill, Rochester, Kent; *m* 1963, Elizabeth Vivian Rohr, MD, MRCP, *o d* of late A. R. Rohr; no *c. Educ:* Edinburgh House, Hants; Repton School. Commnd from SRO into 4th/7th Roy. Dragoon Guards, 1938; served with Regt in: BEF, France, 1939-40; BLA, NW Europe, 1944-45 (despatches, 1945); Palestine, 1946-48; Tripolitania, 1951-52; Instructor, Armoured Sch., 1948-50; Staff Coll., Camberley, 1952; Bde Maj., HQ Inf. Bde, 1953-55; comdg 4th/7th RDG, 1957-59; Asst Mil. Sec., HQ, BAOR, 1959-61; Coll. Comdt RMA Sandhurst, 1961-62; Imp. Def. Coll., 1963; Comdr, 7th Armoured Bde, 1964-66; Dep. Mil. Sec. 1, MoD (Army), 1966-68; Head, British Defence Liaison Staff, Dept of Defence, Canberra, 1968-70; Asst Chief of Gen. Staff (Op. Requirements), 1970-72, retired. *Recreations:* equitation, skiing, cricket, squash rackets. *Address:* Cheriton House, Thorney, Peterborough PE3 6QD. *Clubs:* Cavalry and Guards, MCC.

GILL, Jack; Under-Secretary, Export Credits Guarantee Department, since 1975; *b* 20 Feb. 1930; *s* of Jack and Elizabeth Gill; *m* 1954, Alma Dorothy; three *d. Educ:* Bolton Sch. Export Credits Guarantee Department: Clerical Officer, 1946; Principal, 1962; Asst Sec., 1970; Asst Sec., Dept of Trade and Industry, 1972-75. National Service, REME, 1948-50. *Recreations:* music, chess. *Address:* 197 Hillbury Road, Warlingham, Surrey CR3 9TJ. *T:* Upper Warlingham 2688.

GILL, Maj.-Gen. John Galbraith, CBE 1943 (OBE 1919); DSO 1918; MC; late RAMC (retired); *b* 6 April 1889; *s* of late R. P. Gill, of Guntur, India; *m* 1915, Madge, *d* of late Rev. George Davidson, BSc, of Edinburgh; no *c. Educ:* Brentwood School, Essex; Edinburgh University. MB, ChB, 1912; DPH (Scot. Conjoint), 1923; DTM&H (Cantab), 1924. Retired pay, 1946. *Address:* Forest Oaks, The Rise, Brockenhurst, Hants S04 7SJ.

GILL, Kenneth; General Secretary, Amalgamated Union of Engineering Workers (Technical, Administrative and Supervisory Section) and Member of General Council of TUC, since 1974; *b* 30 Aug. 1927; *s* of Ernest Frank Gill and Mary Ethel Gill; *m* 1967, Sara Teresa Paterson; two *s* one *d. Educ:* Chippenham Secondary School. Engrg apprentice, 1943-48; Draughtsman Designer, Project Engr, Sales Engr in various cos, 1948-62; District Organiser, Liverpool and Ireland TASS, 1962-68; Editor, TASS Union Jl, 1968-72; Dep. Gen. Sec., 1972-74. *Recreations:* sketching, political caricaturing, kids. *Address:* 164 Ramsden Road, Balham SW12. *T:* 01-675 1489.

GILL, Air Vice-Marshal Leonard William George, DSO 1945; Consultant in personnel planning, since 1973; Manpower and Planning Adviser, P&O Steam Navigation Co., since 1973; *b* 31 March 1918; *s* of L. W. Gill, Hornchurch, Essex, and Marguerite Gill; *m* 1943, Joan Favill Appleyard; two *s* two *d. Educ:* University Coll. Sch., London. Joined RAF, 1937; served in Far East until 1942; then UK as night fighter pilot; comd No 68 Sqdn for last 6 months of war; subseq. served in various appts incl. comd of Nos 85 and 87 night fighter Sqdns and tour on directing staff at RAF Staff Coll.; Stn Comdr No 1 Flying Trng Sch., Linton-on-Ouse, 1957-60; Dir of Overseas Ops, 1960-62; Nat. Def. Coll. of Canada, 1962-63; Dir of Organisation (Estabs), 1963-66; SASO, RAF Germany, 1966-68; Dir-Gen., Manning (RAF), MoD, 1968-73, retired. Vice-Pres., RAF Assoc., 1973- (Pres. E Area, 1974). FIPM; MBIM. *Recreations:* shooting, cricket, boats, amateur woodwork. *Address:* Broomway, 4 Barnfield, Common Lane, Hemingford Abbots, Cambs. *T:* St Ives 66935. *Club:* Royal Air Force.

GILL, Stanley Sanderson; His Honour Judge Gill; a Circuit Judge, since 1972; *b* Wakefield, 3 Dec. 1923; *s* of Sanderson Henry Briggs Gill, OBE and Dorothy Margaret Gill (*née* Bennett); *m* 1954, Margaret Mary Patricia Grady; one *s* two *d. Educ:* Queen Elizabeth Grammar Sch., Wakefield; Magdalene Coll., Cambridge (MA). Served in RAF, 1942-46: tour of operations with 514 and 7 (Pathfinder) Sqdn, 1944-45; Flt Lt 1945. Called to Bar, Middle Temple, 1950; Asst Recorder of Bradford, 1966; Dep. Chm., WR Yorks QS, 1968; County Court Judge, 1971. Chm., Rent Assessment Cttee, 1966. *Recreations:* music, mountaineering, reading. *Address:* Downe, Baldersby, Thirsk, North Yorks. *T:* Melmerby 283.

GILL-CAREY, Chapple, FRCS; former Consulting Surgeon, Royal National Throat, Nose and Ear Hospital; former Consulting Ear, Nose and Throat Surgeon: Hospital of St John and St Elizabeth; Surbiton Hospital; Former Member, Council, Royal College of Surgeons; MRCS Eng, LRCP London 1918; FRCS Ed. 1923; FRCS Eng 1948. Formerly: Surgeon, Ear, Nose and Throat Department, Hospital of St John and St Elizabeth; Chief Clinical Assistant, Ear, Nose and Throat Department, Guy's Hospital; Assistant Surgeon, Central London Throat, Nose and Ear Hospital; Dean of the Institute of Laryngology

and Otology. Fellow Royal Society of Medicine. Ex-President British Association of Otolaryngologists. *Publications:* contributions to medical journals, etc. *Address:* 5 Holly Lodge Gardens, N6 6AA.

GILLAM, Group Captain Denys Edgar, DSO (and 2 bars); DFC (and bar), 1940; AFC 1938; DL; Chairman, Homfray & Co. Ltd; *b* 18 Nov. 1915; *s* of Maj. T. H. J. and D. Gillam; *m* 1945, Nancye Joan Short; one *s* two *d. Educ:* Bramcote, Scarborough; Wrekin Coll., Salop. Joined RAF, 1935; trained No 1 FTS Netheravon; served 29 Fighter Sqdn, Middle East, 1937-39, Meteorological Flight Aldergrove. Award Air Force Cross, 1938. 616 Sqdn (Fighter), 1939-40 (DFC, after Battle of Britain); 312 Sqdn (F), 1940-41; HQ 9 Group till March 1941, rank Sqdn Ldr; commanded 306 Sqdn (Polish), then 615 Sqdn (F) (bar DFC and DSO for shipping attacks in Channel); RAF Staff Coll.; then commanded first Typhoon Wing (despatches); graduated US Command and Gen. Staff Coll.; commanded Tangmere Wing (Typhoons), Jan.-March 1944 (bar, DSO for attacks on V-weapon sites); promoted Group Capt., commanded 20 Sector 2nd TAF, then 146 Wing 2 TAF (Typhoon) till March 1945 (2nd bar DSO); then Group Capt. Ops 84 Group (Main) 2nd TAF. DL for West Riding of Yorks and the City and County of York, 1959. *Recreations:* fishing, shooting, sailing. *Address:* The Glebe, Brawby, Malton, North Yorks. *T:* Kirbymoorside 31530. *Club:* Royal Ocean Racing.

GILLAM, Stanley George, BLitt; MA; Librarian, The London Library, since 1956; *b* 11 Aug. 1915; *s* of Harry Cosier Gillam, Oxford; *m* 1950, Pauline, *d* of Henry G. Bennett, Oxford; one *s. Educ:* Southfield Sch.; Saint Catherine's Coll., Oxford. Bodleian Library, Oxford, 1931-40 and 1946-54. Oxfordshire and Bucks Light Infantry (1st Bucks Bn), 1940-46. Asst Sec. and Sub-Librarian, The London Library, 1954-56. *Publications:* The Building Accounts of the Radcliffe Camera, 1958; articles in The Bodleian Library Record and other periodicals. *Address:* 47 Woodland Way, West Wickham, Kent. *T:* 01-777 1054. *Club:* United Oxford & Cambridge University.

GILLAN, Sir (James) Angus, KBE 1939; CMG 1935; *b* 11 Oct. 1885; *s* of late Rev. James Gillan, DD, and Margaret, *d* of John Wilson; *m* 1917, Margaret Douglas (*d* 1973), *d* of late M. A. Ord-Mackenzie; one *s. Educ:* Edinburgh Acad.; Magdalen Coll., Oxford. Rowed for Oxford 1907, 1909; won Stewards and Olympic IVs (Magdalen) 1908; Grand (Magdalen) 1911; Olympic VIIIs (Leander) 1912; Entered Sudan Political Service, 1909; Asst Political and Intelligence Officer, Sudan Western Frontier Force, 1916 (despatches twice, Order of Nile, 4th Class); Governor Kordofan Province, 1928; Asst Civil Sec., 1932; Civil Sec., 1934, retired 1939; Principal Officer, North Midland Civil Defence Region, Nottingham, 1940-41; Controller, Commonwealth and Empire Div., British Council, 1941-49; British Council Representative in Australia, 1949-51. Fellow, King's Coll., University of London (Treasurer, 1955-70). Pres., Royal Over-Seas League; Past Chairman: Conservative Commonwealth Council; Royal Over-Seas League; Sudan Govt British Pensioners' Assoc.; Anglo-Sudanese Assoc., etc. Order of Nile, 2nd Class, 1935. *Publications:* articles in various journals on the Sudan, Commonwealth affairs and cultural relations. *Recreations:* shooting, unskilled gardening and carpentering. *Address:* Sheep Cote Cottage, Leigh, Surrey. *T:* Norwood Hill 862432. *Clubs:* Athenæum, Leander, Royal Over-Seas League.

GILLARD, Francis George, CBE 1961 (OBE 1946); Consultant to: EMI since 1970; Corporation for Public Broadcasting, Washington, since 1970 (Distinguished Fellow, 1970-73); Public Broadcasting Service, Washington, since 1972; Ford Foundation, since 1970; *b* 1 Dec. 1908; *s* of late Francis Henry Gillard and of late Emily Jane Gillard, Stockleigh Lodge, Exford; unmarried. *Educ:* Wellington Sch., Som.; St Luke's Coll., Exeter (BSc London). Schoolmaster, 1932-41; Freelance broadcaster, 1936-; joined BBC as Talks Producer, 1941; BBC War Correspondent, 1941. BBC Head of West Regional Programmes, 1945-55; Chief Asst to Dir of Sound Broadcasting with Controller rank, 1955-56; Controller, West Region, BBC, 1956-63; Dir of Sound Broadcasting, 1963-68; Man. Dir, Radio, BBC, 1969-70, retired. Chm. of Governors, Wellington Sch., 1974-. FRSA 1971. *Address:* Trevor House, Poole, Wellington, Somerset. *T:* Wellington 2890.

GILLARD, Sir Oliver James, Kt 1975; **Hon. Mr Justice Gillard;** Judge of the Supreme Court of Victoria, since 1962; *b* 2 June 1906; *s* of late E. T. V. Gillard, Stawell, Victoria; *m* 1934, Jean Gillon; three *s. Educ:* Stawell High; Melbourne Univ. BA, LLB. 2nd AIF, 1941-43, Captain. Teacher, Essendon High, 1923-26; Managing Clerk with Vincent Nolan, Solicitor, 1926-31; Barrister, 1930; Legal Office, Commonwealth Dept of

Transport, 1943-44; QC 1950; Mem., Victoria Bar Council, 1957-62 (Chm., 1958-61). Chm., Chief Justice's Law Reform Cttee, 1973-. Director: Murray Valley Coaches Ltd, 1947-50; Barristers' Chambers Ltd, 1959-62; Vary Bros Pty Ltd, 1954-62. Chairman: Churchill Trust (Victoria), 1966-; Youth Adv. Council, 1967-72; State Youth Council, 1973-. Pres., Bayside Area Victoria Boy Scouts Assoc., 1963-71. *Recreations:* reading, golf. *Address:* Judges' Chambers, Supreme Court, Melbourne, Victoria 3000, Australia. *Clubs:* Athenæum, Royal Automobile (Victoria).

GILLEN, Stanley (James); Chairman and Chief Executive Officer, Ford of Europe Inc., 1969-71; Vice-President, Ford Motor Co. USA, 1967-71; Director, Ford of Britain, 1965-71; *b* 10 Aug. 1911; *s* of Bernard J. Gillen, Ohio, and Johanna P. Spillane, Wayne Co., USA; *m* 1935, Mary Elizabeth Marks; three *d. Educ:* St Frederick's High Sch., Pontiac, Mich.; University of Detroit. Fisher Body Div., Gen. Motors Corp., 1933-47; Ford Motor Co., USA: Contract Administrator, Defence Products, 1947-48; Controller, Steel Div., 1948-55; Controller, Tractor and Implement Div., 1955-56; Asst Gen. Man., Steel Div., 1956-60; Gen. Man., Steel Div., 1960-61; Gen. Man., Gen. Parts Div., 1961-65; Man. Dir and Chief Exec. Officer, Ford of Britain, 1965-67; Vice-Pres., Manufacturing Ford of Europe Inc., 1967-69. Chm., Autolite Motor Products Ltd, 1962-65; Director: Ford Credit Co. Ltd, 1965-67; Henry Ford & Son Ltd, Cork, 1965-67; Ford Werke, Germany, 1970-71; Sangamo Weston Ltd, 1972-; Sangamo Electric Co., 1973-75; AMBAC, USA, 1976-; FEMSA, Spain, 1976; Brown Bros Ltd, 1976; Casttenedolo Mfg Co. Spa, Brescia, Italy; Ambac BV Terheijdenseweg, Breda, Holland. Dir, Amer. Chamber of Commerce (UK), 1967; Member: British Manufacturers' Exec. Cttee, SMMT, 1965-67; National Advisory Council for Motor Manufacturing Industry (NACMMI), 1966-67. Design Council Awards Judge, 1976-77, 1977-78. Lord Wakefield Gold Medal, 1971. *Recreations:* golf, ski-ing, shooting, horology. *Address:* Flat 58, Campden Hill Court, Campden Hill Road, W8. *T:* 01-937 3479.

GILLES, Prof. Dennis Cyril; Professor of Computing Science, University of Glasgow, since 1966; *b* 7 April 1925; *s* of George Cyril Gilles and Gladys Alice Gilles (*née* Batchelor); *m* 1955, Valerie Mary Gilles; two *s* two *d. Educ:* Sidcup Gram. Sch.; Imperial Coll., University of London. Demonstrator, Asst Lectr, Imperial Coll., 1945-47; Asst Lectr, University of Liverpool, 1947-49; Mathematician, Scientific Computing Service, 1949-55; Research Asst, University of Manchester, 1955-57; Dir of Computing Lab., University of Glasgow, 1957-66. *Publications:* contribs to Proc. Royal Society and other scientific jls. *Address:* 7 The University, Glasgow G12 8QG. *T:* 041-334 4154.

GILLES, Prof. Chevalier Herbert Michael Joseph, MD; FRCP, FFCM; Alfred Jones and Warrington Yorke Professor of Tropical Medicine, University of Liverpool, since 1972; *b* 10 Sept. 1921; *s* of Joseph and Clementine Gilles; *m* 1955, Wilhelmina Caruana (*d* 1972); three *s* one *d. Educ:* St Edward's Coll., Malta; Royal Univ. of Malta (MD). Rhodes Schol. 1942. BSc Oxon; FMCPH (Nig.), DTM&H. Served War of 1939-45 (1939-45 Star, Africa Star, VM). Mem., Scientific Staff, MRC Lab., Gambia, 1954-58; University of Ibadan: Lectr, Tropical Med., 1958-63; Prof. of Preventive and Social Med., 1963-65; Visiting Prof., Tropical Med., Univ. of Lagos, 1965-68; Sen. Lectr, Tropical Med., Univ. of Liverpool, 1965-70; Prof. of Tropical Med. (Personal Chair), Univ. of Liverpool, 1970; Royal Society Overseas Vis. Prof., Univ. of Khartoum, Sudan, 1979-80. Consultant Physician in Tropical Medicine, Liverpool AHA(T) and Mersey RHA, 1965-; Consultant in Malariology to the Army, 1974; Consultant in Tropical Medicine to the RAF. KStJ 1972. *Publications:* Tropical Medicine for Nurses, 1955, 4th edn 1975; Pathology in the Tropics, 1969, 2nd edn 1976; Management and Treatment of Tropical Diseases, 1971; A Short Textbook of Preventive Medicine for the Tropics, 1973; Atlas of Parasitology and Tropical Medicine, 1976. *Recreations:* tennis, swimming, music. *Address:* 3 Conyers Avenue, Birkdale, Southport PR8 4SZ. *T:* Southport 66664.

GILLESPIE, Prof. Iain Erskine, MD, MSc, FRCS; Professor of Surgery, University of Manchester, since 1970; *b* 4 Sept. 1931; *s* of John Gillespie and Flora McQuarie; *m* 1957, Mary Muriel McIntyre; one *s* one *d. Educ:* Hillhead High Sch., Glasgow; Univ. of Glasgow. MB, ChB, 1953; MD (Hons) 1963; MSc Manchester 1974; FRCSE 1959; FRCS 1963; FRCSGlas 1970. Series of progressive surgical appts in Univs of Glasgow, Sheffield, Glasgow (again), 1953-70. Nat. service, RAMC, 1954-56; MRC grantee, 1956-58; US Postdoctoral Research Fellow, Los Angeles, 1961-; Titular Prof. of Surgery, Univ. of Glasgow, 1969. Vis. Prof. in USA, Canada, S America, Kenya, S Africa, Australia and New Zealand. Member: Cttee of Surgical Res.

Soc. of GB and Ireland, 1975-; Univ. Grants Cttee, Medical Sub-Cttee, 1975-. *Publications:* jt editor and contributor to several surgical and gastroenterological books; numerous articles in various med. jls of GB, USA, Europe. *Recreations:* none. *Address:* 27 Athol Road, Bramhall, Cheshire. *T:* 061-439 2811.

GILLESPIE, Robert, CBE 1951; FCIT; *b* 24 Nov. 1897; *s* of late James Gillespie and Ann Wilson Gillespie; *m* 1928, Isabella Brown, *d* of late Dr Donald Murray, MP; one *s* one *d. Educ:* Queen's Park Sch., Glasgow. Joined Brit. Tanker Co. Ltd, 1922; Asst Manager, 1936; Gen. Manager, 1944; Dir and Gen. Manager, 1946; Managing Dir, 1950-56; a Dir, 1956-67; a Managing Dir of The British Petroleum Co. Ltd, 1956-58, retired; Mem., Council, Chamber of Shipping of UK, 1943-70. Served European War in Army, 1914-19; in ranks with Cameronians (Scottish Rifles) TF in UK; commnd KOSB, served UK, Palestine and France. War of 1939-45, served as Asst Dir, Tanker Div. of Ministry of War Transport, 1942-43. *Recreations:* golf, ornithology, shooting. *Address:* Craigrathan, Kippford, Dalbeattie, Kirkcudbrightshire. *T:* Kippford 653.

GILLESPIE, Prof. Ronald James, PhD, DSc; FRS 1977; FRSC; FRIC; FCIC; Professor of Chemistry, McMaster University, Hamilton, Ont, since 1960; *b* London, England, 21 Aug. 1924; Canadian citizen; *s* of James A. Gillespie and Miriam G. (*née* Kirk); *m* 1950, Madge Ena Garner; two *d. Educ:* London Univ. (BSc 1945, PhD 1949, DSc 1957). FRSC 1965; FCIC 1960; FRIC; Mem., Amer. Chem. Soc. Asst Lectr, Dept of Chemistry, 1948-50, Lectr, 1950-58, UCL; Commonwealth Fund Fellow, Brown Univ., RI, USA, 1953-54; McMaster University: Associate Prof., Dept of Chem., 1958-60; Prof., 1960-62; Chm., Dept of Chem., 1962-65. Professeur Associé, l'Univ. des Sciences et Techniques de Languedoc, Montpellier, 1972-73; Vis. Prof., Univ. of Geneva, 1976. Member: Chem. Soc.; Faraday Soc. Medals: Ramsay, UCL, 1949; Harrison Meml, Chem. Soc., 1954; Canadian Centennial, 1967; Chem. Inst. of Canada, 1977. Awards: Noranda, Chem. Inst. of Canada, 1966 (for inorganic chem.); Amer. Chem. Soc. N-Eastern Reg., 1971 (in phys. chem.); Manufg Chemists Assoc. Coll. Chem. Teacher, 1972; Amer. Chem. Soc., 1973 (for distinguished service in advancement of inorganic chem.); Chem. Inst. of Canada/Union Carbide, 1976 (for chemical educn). *Publications:* Molecular Geometry, 1972 (London; German and Russian trans, 1975); papers in Jl Amer. Chem. Soc., Canadian Jl of Chem., and Inorganic Chem. *Recreations:* skiing, sailing, hiking, camping, Scottish country dancing. *Address:* Department of Chemistry, McMaster University, Hamilton, Ont L8S 4MI, Canada. *T:* (416) 525-9140, ext. 4715.

GILLESPIE, William Hewitt, MD, FRCP; FRCPsych; Emeritus Physician, Maudsley Hospital (Physician, 1936-70); *b* 6 Aug. 1905; *s* of Rev. W. H. Gillespie, Manchuria and Co. Down, and of Isabella B. Gillespie (*née* Grills), Co. Down, N Ireland; *m* 1st, 1932, Dr Helen Turover (*d* 1975); one *s* one *d*; 2nd, 1975, Sadie Mervis. *Educ:* George Watson's Coll.; Universities of Edinburgh and Vienna. University Edinburgh: 1st pl. Open Bursary Exam., 1924, MB, ChB (hons), 1929, Dip. in Psychiatry, 1931, MD 1934; MRCP 1936; FRCP 1962; McCosh Travelling Scholarship, in Vienna, 1930-31. LCC Mental Hosps Service, 1931-36; Lecturer, Inst. of Psychiatry, 1944-70; Dir, London Clinic of Psychoanalysis, 1944-47. Freud Meml Vis. Prof. of Psychoanalysis, Univ. Coll. London, 1976-77. Trng Sec., Inst. of Psychoanalysis, 1947-50; Chm., Inst of Psychoanalysis, 1954-56; President: British Psychoanalytical Soc., 1950-53 and 1971-72; Internat. Psychoanalytic Assoc., 1957-61. FRSocMed. *Publications:* contrib to: Recent Advances in Psychiatry, 1944; Psychiatrie sociale de l'enfant, 1951; Psychoanalysis and the Occult, 1953; The Sexual Perversions, 1956; The Pathology and Treatment of Sexual Deviation, 1964; Foundations of Child Psychiatry, 1968. Various articles in medical, psychiatric and psychoanalytic jls. *Recreations:* music, reading, walking. *Address:* 24 Redington Road, NW3 7RB. *T:* 01-435 0043.

GILLETT, Sir Edward (Bailey), Kt, *cr* 1948; Chartered Surveyor; *b* 2 Aug. 1888; 4th and *y s* of William Edward and Florence Gillett; *m* 1916, Bertha Helen (*d* 1957), *d* of William Henry Moss; two *d. Educ:* Marlborough Coll. Served European War, 1914-18, Capt. East Surrey Regt in Belgium, France and Italy. Pres. of Royal Institution of Chartered Surveyors, 1945-46. Crown Estate Commissioner, 1957-65. *Address:* Stables Cottage, Lydwicke, Slinfold, Horsham, West Sussex.

GILLETT, Eric; Secretary, Scottish Development Department, since 1976; *b* 22 July 1920; *m* 1945, Dorothy; one *s. Educ:* public primary and secondary schs; Downing Coll., Cambridge. Royal Artillery, 1942; Dept of Health for Scotland, 1946; Under-Sec., Scottish Home and Health Dept, 1969-71; Fisheries Sec., Dept of Agric. and Fisheries for Scotland, 1971-76. *Recreations:*

amateur chamber and orchestral music, hill walking. *Address:* 66 Caiystane Terrace, Edinburgh EH10 6SW. *T:* 031-445 1184. *Club:* Royal Commonwealth Society.

GILLETT, Eric Walkey, MA; FRSL; Hon. RCM; *b* Bowdon, 24 Aug. 1893; *s* of Samuel Walkey Gillett and Edith Suzette Barlow; *m* 1st, 1926, Joan Edwards (decd); one *s* (one *d* decd); 2nd, 1962, Nancy Miller (decd). *Educ:* Radley; Lincoln Coll., Oxford. Lectr to the Oxford Univ. Extension Delegacy, 1921; Lectr to the Extension Delegacies of the Universities of Cambridge and London, 1935; Warden of Chancellor's Hall and Lecturer in English Literature, University of Birmingham, 1922-27; Johore Prof. of English Language and Literature, Raffles Coll., Singapore, 1927-32; literary editing, publishing and broadcasting work, 1932-58; Gen. Editor, Royal National Institute for the Blind, 1958-61; RCM staff, 1961-71. London Dramatic Critic, Yorks Post, 1960-65. 2nd Lieut, 7th Batt. Lancs Fusiliers (TF), 1914; wounded 3rd battle of Ypres, Aug. 1917; invalided out with rank of Capt., 1919. *Publications:* Hush (in collaboration), 1920; Books and Writers, 1930; An Anthology of Verse for Children, 1930; Poets of Our Time, 1932; Maria Jane Jewsbury, 1932; Normal English Prose (with late T. Earle Welby), 1934; The Literature of England; AD 500 to 1942 (with W. J. Entwistle), 1943; revised edn, The Literature of England, AD 500 to 1946, 1947; The Literature of England, AD 500-1950, 1952; The Literature of England, AD 500 to 1960, 1961; Elizabeth Ham: By Herself (ed), 1945; J. B. Priestley's All About Ourselves (ed), 1956; Junior Film Annual, 1946-47 (ed), 1946; Eric Gillett's Film Book, 1947; Film Fairyland, 1948; Collins' Film Books, 1948, 1949, 1950, 1951; pamphlets, contributions to various periodicals. *Recreations:* reading, travelling, theatre and broadcasting. *Address:* Flat 4, 29 Brunswick Square, Hove, East Sussex BN3 1EJ. *T:* Brighton 731820. *Clubs:* United Oxford & Cambridge University, Royal Automobile, MCC; Vincent's (Oxford); Hove (Hove).

GILLETT, Maj.-Gen. Peter Bernard, CB 1966; CVO 1973; OBE 1955; Secretary of the Central Chancery of the Orders of Knighthood, since 1968; *b* 8 Dec. 1913; *s* of Bernard George Gillett, OBE, Milford on Sea, Hants; *m* 1952, Pamela Graham, widow of Col R. J. Lloyd Price and *d* of Col Spencer Graham Walker, Winsley, Wilts. *Educ:* Marlborough Coll.; RMA, Woolwich. Commissioned RA, 1934; apptd to RHA, 1945; service in UK and India to 1944; War Office, 1944; BAOR, 1944-45; Staff Coll., 1946; staff appts in UK and E Africa to 1955; Comd 5 RHA, 1955; SHAPE, 1958; CRA 3 Inf. Div., 1959; IDC, 1962; Chief of Staff, HQ Eastern Comd, 1962-65; GOC, 48th Div. TA, W Midland District, 1965-68. Col 1957, Brig. 1961, Maj.-Gen. 1962. Col Comdt, Royal Regt of Artillery, 1968-. *Recreations:* sailing, shooting and travel. *Address:* c/o Lloyds Bank Ltd, 6 Pall Mall, SW1. *T:* (office) 01-834 2837. *Clubs:* Army and Navy, Royal Ocean Racing.

GILLETT, Sir Robin (Danvers Penrose), 2nd Bt *cr* 1959; GBE 1976; RD 1965; Director, Wigham Poland Properties Ltd; Underwriting Member of Lloyd's; Lord Mayor of London for 1976-77; *b* 9 Nov. 1925; *o s* of Sir (Sydney) Harold Gillett, 1st Bt, MC, and Audrey Isabel Penrose Wardlaw (*d* 1962); *S* father, 1976; *m* 1950, Elizabeth Marion Grace, *e d* of late John Findlay, JP, Busby, Lanarks; two *s. Educ:* Nautical Coll., Pangbourne. Served Canadian Pacific Steamships, 1943-60; Master Mariner 1951; Staff Comdr 1957; Hon. Comdr RNR 1971. Younger Brother of Trinity House; Founder Mem., Nautical Inst. City of London (Ward of Bassishaw): Common Councilman 1965-69; Alderman 1969; Sheriff 1973; one of HM Lieuts for City of London, 1975; Chm. Civil Defence Cttee, 1967-68; Pres., City of London Civil Defence Instructors Assoc.; Hon. Treas. City of London Centre, St John Ambulance Assoc.; Liveryman and Warden, Hon. Co. of Master Mariners. Governor: Pangbourne Coll.; King Edward's Sch., Witley. Chancellor, City Univ., 1976-77. Vice-Pres. and Fellow, Inst. Administrative Management. Hon. DSc City, 1976. KStJ 1977 (OstJ 1974). Officer, Order of Leopard, Zaire, 1973; Comdr, Order of Dannebrog, 1974; Order of Johan Sedia Mahkota (Malaysia), 1974; Grand Cross of Municipal Merit (Lima), 1977. *Recreations:* sailing, photography. *Heir: s* Nicholas Danvers Penrose Gillett, *b* 24 Sept. 1955. *Address:* 4 Fairholt Street, Knightsbridge, SW7 1EQ. *T:* 01-589 9860; Bevington House, 24/26 Minories, EC3N 1BY. *T:* 01-709 0505. *Clubs:* City Livery, City Livery Yacht, Guildhall, Royal London Yacht.

GILLIAT, Lt-Col Sir Martin (John), KCVO 1962 (CVO 1954); MBE 1946; Vice-Lieutenant of Hertfordshire, since 1971; Private Secretary to Queen Elizabeth the Queen Mother since 1956; *b* 8 Feb. 1913; *s* of late Lieut-Col John Babington Gilliat and Muriel Helen Lycette Gilliat; unmarried. *Educ:* Eton; RMC, Sandhurst. Joined KRRC, 1933. Served War of 1939-45 (despatches, Prisoner of War). Dep. Military Sec. to Viceroy and

Governor-Gen. of India, 1947-48; Comptroller to Commissioner-Gen. for UK in South-East Asia, 1948-51; Mil. Sec. to Governor-Gen. of Australia, 1953-55. DL Herts, 1963. *Address:* Appletrees, Welwyn, Herts. *T:* Welwyn 4675. *Clubs:* Travellers', Buck's, Brooks's.

GILLIATT, Prof. Roger William, MC; DM; FRCP; Professor of Clinical Neurology, University of London, since 1962; Physician, National Hospital, Queen Square, and Middlesex Hospital; only *s* of late Sir William Gilliatt, KCVO; *m* 1963, Mary Elizabeth, *er d* of A. J. W. Green; one *s* two *d. Educ:* Rugby; Magdalen Coll., Oxford (BA 1st Cl. Hons Nat. Sci. (MA), BM, BCh Oxon 1949); MRCP 1951, FRCP 1961; DM 1955. Served in KRRC, 1942-45 (MC, despatches). Member: Association of British Neurologists; Physiological Soc.; Corr. Mem., Amer. Neurological Assoc.; Hon. Member: Amer. Acad. of Neurology; Société Française de Neurologie; Australian Assoc. of Neurologists. *Publications:* contribs on neurological topics to medical and scientific jls. *Address:* Institute of Neurology, Queen Square, WC1N 3BG. *T:* 01-837 3611.

GILLICK, Rev. John, SJ, MA Oxon; Director, Fons Vitae (Pastoral Institute for Religious), Johannesburg, since 1970; *b* Wallasey, 27 March 1916; 2nd *s* of Laurence Gillick and Catherine Devine. *Educ:* St Francis Xavier's Coll., Liverpool; Heythrop and Campion Hall, Oxford (1st Cl. Hons Mod. History). Asst Master at Mount St Mary's and Beaumont. Two years writing and photography in Italy and Africa. Headmaster, Beaumont Coll., 1964-67; studied psychology at Loyola Univ., Chicago, 1967-68 (MA); Dir, Laboratories for the Training of Religious Superiors in S Africa, 1969. *Publications:* Teaching the Mass, 1961; Baptism, 1962; followed by Teaching the Mass: African, 1963; Teaching the Sacraments: African, 1964; Teaching Confirmation: African, 1964, etc; *illustrations for:* The Breaking of Bread, 1950; The Pilgrim Years, 1956; Our Faith, 1956; The Holy Mass, 1958; Christ Our Life, 1960. *Address:* Holy Trinity Church, 16 Stiemens Street, Braamfontein, Johannesburg 2001, South Africa; c/o 114 Mount Street, W1Y 6AH.

GILLIE, Dame Annis Calder, (Dame Annis Smith), DBE 1968 (OBE 1961); MB, BS London, FRCP; formerly in general medical practice (1925-63); *b* 3 Aug. 1900; *d* of late Rev. Dr Robert Calder Gillie and Emily Japp; *m* 1930, Peter Chandler Smith, MA, FRIBA; one *s* one *d. Educ:* Wycombe Abbey Sch.; University Coll. and University Coll. Hosp., London. Member: BMA Council, 1950-64; Council of Medical Protection Soc., 1946-; Medical Practices Cttee, 1948-60; Med. Women's Federation (Pres. London Assoc., 1942-45, Pres. 1954); Foundn Mem., Royal College of General Practitioners (Chm., 1959-62, Pres., 1964-67); Mem., Central Health Services Advisory Council, 1956-70; North West Regional Hosp. Bd, 1958-63; Mem., Oxford Regional Hosp. Bd, 1964-74. Fellow, UCL, 1969. Hon. MD Edinburgh. *Publications:* contributions to medical jls. *Recreations:* reading, listening. *Address:* Bledington, Kingham, Oxford. *T:* Kingham 360.

GILLIE, (Francis) Blaise, CB 1958; Consultant in Town and Regional Planning; *b* 29 Feb. 1908; *s* of Rev. R. C. Gillie, Presbyterian Minister, and Emily Japp; *m* 1939, Mary Besly; three *s* one *d. Educ:* Gresham's Sch., Holt; Trinity Hall, Cambridge. Entered Ministry of Health, 1930. Asst Gen. Inspector, 1936, Principal, 1937; transf. to Min. of Works and Planning, 1942; Asst Sec., 1943; transf. to Min. of Town and Country Planning, 1943; Imperial Defence Coll., 1948; transf. to Min. of Local Govt and Planning, 1951 (now Dept of Environment); Under-Sec., 1954; Welsh Sec., 1957-63. OECD Consultant on Regional Planning, Turkish Govt, 1963-65; UN appointment, Afghanistan, 1965-67; UN Adviser to Nat. Inst. for Physical Planning and Construction Research, Ireland (An Foras Forbartha), 1967-70; Consultant to Irish Ind. Develt Authy, 1970; Research Associate, Inst. of Social Studies, The Hague, 1971; Sen. Lectr in Town and Regional Planning, American Univ. of Beirut, Lebanon, 1972-76. *Publications:* (pt-author with P. L. Hughes) Some Principles of Land Planning, 1950; Basic Thinking in Regional Planning, 1967; An Approach to Town Planning, 1971. *Recreations:* history, landscape. *Address:* Kennet House, Ramsbury, Wilts.

GILLIES, Sir Alexander, Kt 1959; FRCSEd, FRACS; MChOrth; Consulting Orthopædic Surgeon, Wellington, Nelson and Dannevirke Hospitals, New Zealand; *b* 1891; *s* of Gilbert Gillies; *m* 1920, Effie Lovica, *d* of James Pearson Shaw, Kamloops, BC; one *d* (and one *d* decd). *Educ:* Otago Boys' High Sch.; Edinburgh Univ. MB, ChB. Ed 1923; DMRE Liverpool 1925; FRCSEd 1926; FRACS 1931; MChOrth Liverpool 1936. Fellow, Mayo Clinic, Rochester, Minnesota, 1928. Sen. Orthop. Surg., Wellington Hosp., NZ, 1929-50. President: NZ Red Cross

Soc., 1953-61, now Pres. Emeritus (Counsellor of Honour, 1961); NZ Crippled Children Soc., 1968. Emeritus Fellow, Brit. Orthopædic Assoc., 1966. *Publications:* contrib. med. jls. *Recreation:* golf. *Address:* 35 Pitt Street, Wellington 1, New Zealand.

GILLIES, Prof. Alexander; Professor of German Language and Literature, University of Leeds, 1945-72, Emeritus Professor, since 1972; *b* Sheffield, 26 May 1907; *s* of late A. Gillies and M. Gillies; *m* 1944, Camilla Hill Hay, MA, D de l'Univ. *Educ:* King Edward VII Sch., Sheffield; Universities of Sheffield and Göttingen. 1st cl. Hons Mod. Langs 1927, MA 1928 (Sheffield), DPhil 1933 (Göttingen). Asst Lecturer in German, University of Manchester, 1930-34, Head of Dept of German, University Coll., Hull, 1934-45; Visiting Lecturer on German Lit., Harvard Univ., USA, 1946-47, on leave of absence from Leeds; Dean of the Faculty of Arts, University of Leeds, 1951-53; Chm., Joint Matriculation Board, 1958-61 (Vice-Chm., 1955-58); Chm., Conference of University Teachers of German in Gt Britain and Ireland, 1966-67; Editor, Mod. Language Review, 1943-, and General Editor, 1956-60; co-editor, Year's Work in Modern Language Studies, 1937-40; Hon. Life Mem. Modern Humanities Research Assoc.; Hon. Mem., Modern Language Assoc. of America; sometime External Examiner to the Univs of Belfast, Dublin, Glasgow, Hull, Liverpool, Nottingham, Oxford, St Andrews, Sheffield, Southampton, Reading. General Editor, Blackwell's German Texts. Medal of the Univ. of Tübingen, 1973. *Publications:* Herder and Ossian (Berlin), 1933; Herder, 1945; (ed) J. G. Herder, Journal meiner Reise im Jahre 1769, 1947, 2nd rev. edn 1969; (ed) Herzensergiessungen eines Kunstliebenden Klosterbruders, by W. H. Wackenroder and L. Tieck, 1948, 2nd rev. edn, 1966; Herder, der Mensch und sein Werk, (Hamburg) 1949; Goethe's Faust: an Interpretation, 1957; A Hebridean in Goethe's Weimar: The Reverend James Macdonald and the Cultural Relations between Scotland and Germany, 1969; (ed) J. G. Herder, Uber die neuere deutsche Literatur, 1969; numerous contributions to Encyclopædia Britannica, etc; articles and reviews on German and comparative literature in various European and N American periodicals. *Recreations:* foreign travel, gardening, golf. *Address:* Gates House, Ripley Road, Knaresborough, North Yorks. *T:* Harrogate 862374.

GILLIES, Gordon; see Gillies, Maurice G.

GILLIES, Hugh, CBE 1967; JP; PhD; Convener of County Council of Dunbarton since 1961; Chairman, Dunbarton County Licensing Board, since 1967; *b* 16 Nov. 1903; *s* of Dugald Gillies and Hannah (*née* Greenhalgh); *m* 1933, Marion Rose (*née* Oswald); two *s* one *d. Educ:* Glasgow. Provost, Burgh of Kirkintilloch, 1952-58 (2 terms); Vice-Convener, Dunbarton CC, 1958-61. Mem., Cumbernauld New Town Develt Bd; Mem., Police Council for Gt Britain; Chm., Hosps Bd, Kirkintilloch and Council Hosps. Professional Linguist (knowledge 23 langs). JP 1952, Co. of Dunbarton. Freeman of City of London and Mem. Guild of Freemen. *Recreations:* local government, gardening; speaker on foreign affairs, Robert Burns, and literature in general. *Address:* Craighill, Elm Avenue, Lenzie, Co. of Dunbarton. *T:* 041-776 3293; (business) 041-221 0201. *Clubs:* Edinburgh Liberal; Glasgow Rotary.

GILLIES, (Maurice) Gordon, TD and Bar 1948; QC (Scotland) 1958; Sheriff of South Strathclyde, Dumfries and Galloway (formerly Lanarkshire), at Lanark, since 1958; *b* 17 Oct. 1916; *s* of James Brown Gillies, Advocate in Aberdeen, and Rhoda Ledingham; *m* 1954, Anne Bethea McCall-Smith. *Educ:* Aberdeen Grammar Sch.; Merchiston Castle; Edinburgh Univ. Advocate, 1946; Advocate Depute, 1953-58. *Recreation:* golf. *Address:* Redwalls, Biggar, Lanarkshire. *T:* Biggar 20281. *Clubs:* New (Edinburgh); Hon. Company of Edinburgh Golfers.

GILLILAND, David Jervois Thetford; practising solicitor and farmer; *b* 14 July 1932; *s* of late Major W. H. Gilliland and of Mrs N. H. Gilliland; *m* 1st, 1958, Patricia, *o d* of late J. S. Wilson and late Mrs Wilson (marr. diss. 1976); two *s* three *d* ; 2nd, 1976, Jennifer Johnston, *d* of Denis Johnston. *Educ:* Rockport Prep. Sch.; Wrekin Coll.; Trinity Coll., Dublin. BA 1954, LLB 1955. Qualified as solicitor, 1957, own practice. Mem. ITA, 1965-70; Chm., N Ireland Adv. Cttee of ITA, 1965-70. Mem. Council, Internat. Dendrology Soc., 1966-75; etc. *Recreations:* gardening, sailing, fishing. *Address:* Brook Hall, Londonderry, Northern Ireland. *T:* Londonderry 51297. *Clubs:* Royal Over-Seas League, Naval; Northern Counties (Londonderry).

GILLINGHAM, Francis John, MBE 1944; FRSE 1970; Professor of Neurological Surgery, University of Edinburgh, since 1963; at Royal Infirmary of Edinburgh and Western

General Hospital, Edinburgh, since 1963; Consultant Neuro-Surgeon to the Army in Scotland since 1966; *b* 15 March 1916; *s* of John H. Gillingham, Upwey, Dorset; *m* 1945, Irene Judy Jude; four *s. Educ:* Hardye's Sch., Dorset; St Bartholomew's Hosp. Medical Coll., London. Matthews Duncan Gold Medal, 1939, MRCS, LRCP Oct. 1939; MB, BS (London) Nov. 1939; FRCS 1947; FRCSE 1955; FRCPE 1967. Hon. MD Thessaloniki, 1973. Hunterian Prof., RCS, 1957; Morison Lectr, RCP of Edinburgh, 1960; Colles Lectr, College of Surgeons of Ireland, 1962; Elsberg Lectr, College of Physicians and Surgeons, NY, 1967; Penfield Lectr, Middle East Med. Assembly, 1970. Hon. Mem., Soc. de Neurochirurgie de Langue Française, 1964; Hon. Mem., Soc. of Neurol. Surgeons (USA), 1965; Hon. Mem., Royal Academy of Medicine of Valencia, 1967; Hon. and Corresp. Mem. of a number of foreign neuro-surgical societies. President: Medico-Chirurgical Soc. of Edinburgh, 1965-67; European Soc. of Stereostatic and Functional Neurosurgery, 1972-76; Vice-Pres., RCSE, 1974. *Publications:* Clinical Surgery: Neurological Surgery, 1969; papers on surgical management of cerebral vascular disease, head and spinal injuries, Parkinsonism and the dyskinesias, epilepsy and other neurosurgical subjects. *Recreations:* sailing, travel, photography. *Address:* Easter Park House, Barnton Avenue, Edinburgh EH4 6JR. *T:* 031-336 3528. *Clubs:* English-Speaking Union; New (Edinburgh).

GILLINGHAM, Rev. Canon Peter Llewellyn, MVO 1955; MA 1940; QHC since 1952; Assistant Chaplain, Sherborne Girls' School, since 1977; Hon. Canon of Chichester Cathedral (Wisborough Prebendary), 1969-77, Canon Emeritus since 1977; *b* 3 May 1914; *s* of late Rev. Canon Frank Hay Gillingham; *m* 1947, Diana, *d* of Lieut-Gen. Sir Alexander Hood; two *s* two *d. Educ:* Cheam; Marlborough; Oriel Coll., Oxford. Curate, Tonbridge Parish Church, 1937-40; Curate-in-Charge, St George's Church, Oakdale, Poole, 1940-43. Served War of 1939-45, Chaplain, RNVR, 1943-46; Chaplain, Blundell's Sch., Tiverton, 1946-49; Hon. Chaplain to King George VI, 1949-52; Chaplain to Royal Chapel of All Saints, Windsor Great Park, 1949-55; Vicar of St Mildred's, Addiscombe, 1955; Vicar of St Mary the Virgin, Horsham, 1960-77; Rural Dean of Horsham, 1974-77. *Recreations:* golf, sailing. *Address:* Sherborne Girls' School, Bradford Road, Sherborne, Dorset DT9 3QN.

GILLIS, Bernard (Benjamin), QC 1954; MA Cantab; **His Honour Judge Gillis;** a Circuit Judge (Additional Judge, Central Criminal Court), since 1964; *m* ; one *s. Educ:* Downing Coll., Cambridge, Hon. Fellow, 1976. Squadron Leader, RAF, 1940-45. Called to the Bar, Lincoln's Inn, 1927, Bencher 1960, Treasurer 1976; North Eastern Circuit and Central Criminal Court. Commr, Central Criminal Court, 1959; Commissioner of Assize: Lancaster, 1960; Chelmsford, 1961; Bodmin, 1963. Recorder of Bradford, 1958-64. *Address:* Central Criminal Court, EC4. *Club:* Royal Air Force.

GILLMAN, Bernard Arthur, (Gerry Gillman); General Secretary, Society of Civil and Public Servants, since 1973; *b* 14 April 1927; *s* of Elias Gillman and Gladys Gillman; *m* 1951, Catherine Mary Antonia Harvey. *Educ:* Archbishop Tenison's Grammar Sch. Civil Service, 1946-53; Society of Civil Servants, 1953-. *Recreations:* watching London Welsh Rugby, theatre, music. *Address:* 2 Burnham Street, Kingston-upon-Thames, Surrey KT2 6QR. *T:* 01-546 6905; Society of Civil and Public Servants, 124/126 Southwark Street, SE1 0TU. *Club:* MCC.

GILLMORE, Air Vice-Marshal Alan David, CB 1955; CBE 1944; RAF (retired); *b* 17 Oct. 1905; *s* of late Rev. David Sandeman Gillmore and Allis Emily Widmer; *m* 1931, Kathleen Victoria Morris; three *s. Educ:* St Dunstan's Sch., Burnham-on-Sea; King's Sch., Ely. RAF Cadet Coll., Cranwell, Lincs, 1923-25; Commission in RAF, 1925. Commandant RAF Staff Coll., Bracknell, 1951-53; Senior Air Staff Officer, Far East Air Force, 1953-56; Senior Air Staff Officer, Home Command, 1956-59; retired 1959. *Address:* Southpen, 17 Naish Road, Burnham-on-Sea, Som. *Club:* Royal Air Force.
  See also D . H . Gillmore .

GILLMORE, David Howe; HM Diplomatic Service; Counsellor, UK Delegation, Vienna, since 1975; *b* 16 Aug. 1934; *s* of Air Vice-Marshal A. D. Gillmore, *qv*; *m* 1964, Lucile Morin; two *s . Educ:* Trent Coll.; King's Coll., Cambridge (MA). Reuters Ltd, 1958-60; Asst to Dir-Gen., Polypapier, SA, Paris, 1960-65; Teacher, ILEA, 1965-69; HM Diplomatic Service, 1970; Foreign and Commonwealth Office, 1970-72; First Sec., Moscow, 1972-75. *Publication:* novel A Way From Exile, 1967. *Recreations:* books, music, exercise. *Address:* Foreign and Commonwealth Office, Downing Street, SW1; 19 Ashlone Road, SW15 1LS. *T:* 01-788 0860.

GILLSON, Thomas Huntington, OBE 1973; HM Diplomatic Service, retired; *b* 2 July 1917; *s* of Robert and Ellen Gillson; *m* 1st, Margaret Dorothy Mumford (marr. diss.); two *d*; 2nd, 1969, Elizabeth Anne Fothergill. *Educ:* Emanuel Sch., London. Bd of Educn, 1935; FO, 1937; served with Royal Corps of Signals, 1940-46; Budapest, 1946; FO, 1947; Milan, 1948; Buenos Aires, 1949; Warsaw, 1952; Vice-Consul, Kirkuk, 1953; FO, 1957; 1st Sec. (Information), The Hague, 1959; and Pretoria, 1962; FO, 1966; Head of Chancery and Consul, Kabul, 1970; (Chargé d'Affaires 1970, 1971, 1972); Counsellor, Ankara, 1973, first as Dep. Sec.-Gen. (Econ.) to Central Treaty Organization, and later as Special Asst to Sec.-Gen. *Recreation:* painting. *Address:* Spring Cottage, Queen Street, Yetminster, Dorset DT9 6LL. *T:* Yetminster 872580. *Club:* Royal Commonwealth Society.

GILMOUR, Alexander Clement; Director, Joseph Sebag & Co., since 1972; *b* 23 Aug. 1931; *s* of Sir John Little Gilmour, 2nd Bt, and of Lady Mary Gilmour; *m* 1954, Barbara M. L. Constance Berry; two *s* one *d*. *Educ:* Eton. National Service, commn in Black Watch, 1950-52. With Joseph Sebag & Co., 1954-. Governor, LSE, 1969-; Chairman: Jersey External Trust, 1972-; Nat. Playing Fields Assoc., 1976- (Past-Chm. Appeals Cttee, 10 yrs); Dir, Safeguard Industrial Investments, 1974-. *Recreations:* tennis, skiing, fishing, gardening, golf. *Address:* Denchworth Manor, Wantage, Oxon ODX OX12. *Clubs:* White's; Hon. Company of Edinburgh Golfers.
See also Rt Hon. Sir Ian Gilmour, Bt.

GILMOUR, Colonel Allan Macdonald, OBE 1961; MC 1942, and Bar 1943; Lord-Lieutenant of Sutherland, since 1972; Member: Highland Health Board, since 1973; Sutherland District Council, since 1975; Highland Regional Council, since 1977; *b* 23 Nov. 1916; *o s* of late Captain Allan Gilmour, of Rosehall, Sutherland, and late Mary H. M. Macdonald, of Viewfield, Portree, Skye; *m* 1941, Jean Wood; three *s* one *d*. *Educ:* Winchester Coll. Gazetted, The Seaforth Highlanders, Jan. 1939. Served War, in Middle East, France and Germany (despatches, 1945); DSC (USA) 1945. Staff Coll., 1946; Regimental and Staff Service in: Germany, Middle East, UK, Pakistan and Africa, 1946-67, incl. Instructor, Staff Coll., Quetta, on loan to Pakistan Army, 1952-54. Chief of Gen. Staff, Ghana Armed Forces, 1959-62; service in Congo, 1961-62; retired from Army, 1967. Chairman: Sutherland Council of Social Service, 1973-77; Sutherland District Council, 1975-77. Mem., Sutherland CC, 1970. DL Sutherland, 1971. *Recreations:* fishing, local government. *Address:* Invernauld, Rosehall, Lairg, Sutherland. *T:* Rosehall 204.

GILMOUR, Andrew, CMG 1949; Malayan Civil Service, retired; *b* 18 July 1898; *s* of late James Parlane Gilmour, Solicitor, Burntisland, and late Mima Simpson; *m* Nelle Twigg; two *s* three *d* (and one *s* killed in action). *Educ:* Royal High Sch., Edinburgh; Edinburgh Univ. (MA Hons Classics, 1920). Served European War, 1914-18, Argyll and Sutherland Highlanders, 1915-17. Appointed to Malayan Civil Service, 1921; Asst Controller of Labour, 1923-26; Head of Preventive Service, Singapore, 1927; Resident, Labuan, 1928-29; District Officer, Jasin, 1929-30, Ulu Kelantan, 1930-36; Asst Colonial Sec., SS, 1936-38; Registrar-Gen. of Statistics, SS and FMS, 1938-39; Shipping Controller, Singapore, 1939-41; Defence Intelligence Officer, Hong Kong, Dec. 1941; interned Hong Kong 1942-45; Sec. for Economic Affairs, Singapore, 1946-52; Staff Grade, MCS, 1947; Chm. N Borneo Rubber Commn, 1949; MEC and MLC Singapore (nominated official); acted as Colonial Sec., Singapore, June-Aug. 1948 and March-April 1952; ret. from Colonial Service, 1953; Planning Economist, UN Technical Assistance Mission, Cambodia, 1953-55; Economic Survey Commissioner, British Honduras, 1956. Secretary: British European Assoc., Singapore, 1956-75; Tanglin Trust Ltd, 1961-75; Raeburn Park School Ltd, 1961-75; Editor, BEAM, 1959-75. *Publications:* My Role in the Rehabilitation of Singapore 1946-53, 1973; An Eastern Cadet's Anecdotage, 1974. *Recreations:* cricket (Hon. Life Pres., Singapore Cricket Club); philately (Patron, Singapore Stamp Club). *Address:* Garden Cottage, Gifford, East Lothian EH41 4JE. *T:* Gifford 305. *Clubs:* Royal Over-Seas League; Singapore Cricket (Hon. Life Pres.).

GILMOUR, Rt. Hon. Sir Ian (Hedworth John Little), 3rd Bt *cr* 1926, of Liberton and Craigmillar; PC 1973; MP (C) Chesham and Amersham, since 1974 (Norfolk Central, Nov. 1962-1974); *b* 8 July 1926; *er s* of Lt-Col Sir John Little Gilmour, 2nd Bt, and of Hon. Victoria Laura, OBE, TD, *d* of late Viscount Chelsea (*e s* of 5th Earl Cadogan); *S* father, 1977; *m* 1951, Lady Caroline Margaret Montagu-Douglas-Scott, *yr d* of 8th Duke of Buccleuch and Queensberry, KT, GCVO, PC; four *s* one *d*. *Educ:* Eton; Balliol Coll., Oxford. Served with Grenadier Guards, 1944-47; 2nd Lieut 1945. Called to the Bar, Inner Temple, 1952. Editor, The Spectator, 1954-59. Parly Under-Sec. of State, MoD, 1970-71; Minister of State: for Defence Procurement, MoD, 1971-72; for Defence, 1972-74; Sec. of State for Defence, 1974. *Publications:* The Body Politic, 1969; Inside Right: a study of Conservatism, 1977. *Heir: s* David Robert Gilmour [*b* 14 Nov. 1952; *m* 1975, Sarah Anne, *d* of M. H. G. Bradstock]. *Address:* The Ferry House, Old Isleworth, Mddx. *T:* 01-560 6769. *Club:* White's.
See also A. C. Gilmour.

GILMOUR, Col Sir John (Edward), 3rd Bt, *cr* 1897; DSO 1945; TD; DL; JP; MP (C) East Fife since 1961; *b* 24 Oct. 1912; *o s* of Col Rt Hon. Sir John Gilmour, 2nd Bt, GCVO, DSO, MP, and Mary Louise (*d* 1919), *e d* of late E. T. Lambert, Telham Court, Battle, Sussex; *S* father, 1940; *m* 1941, Ursula Mabyn, *yr d* of late F. O. Wills; two *s*. *Educ:* Eton; Trinity Hall, Cambridge. Served War of 1939-45 (DSO). Bt Col 1950; Lieut, Royal Company of Archers (Queen's Body Guard for Scotland); Hon. Col, The Highland Yeomanry, RAC, T&AVR, 1971-75. Chm., Cons. and Unionist Party in Scotland, 1965-67. DL Fife, 1953. *Heir: s* John Gilmour [*b* 15 July 1944; *m* 1967, Valerie, *yr d* of late G. W. Russell, and of Mrs William Wilson; one *s* two *d*]. *Address:* Montrave, Leven, Fife. *TA:* Leven. *T:* Leven 2159. *Clubs:* Cavalry and Guards; Leander.
See also Dame Anne Bryans, Viscount Younger.

GILMOUR, John Scott Lennox, MA, FLS; Director, University Botanic Garden, Cambridge, 1951-73, retired; Fellow of Clare College, Cambridge, since 1951; *b* London, 28 Sept. 1906; *s* of late T. L. Gilmour, CBE, and Elizabeth, *o d* of late Sir John S. Keltie; *m* 1935, Molly, *y d* of late Rev. M. Berkley; three *d*. *Educ:* Uppingham Sch.; Clare Coll., Cambridge. Curator of the Herbarium and Botanical Museum, Cambridge, 1930-31; Asst Dir of Royal Botanic Gardens, Kew, 1931-46; seconded to Petroleum Div., Min. of Fuel and Power, as Principal Officer, 1940-45. Dir, Royal Horticultural Society's Garden, Wisley, Surrey, 1946-51. Sec., Systematics Assoc., 1937-46. Chm., 1952-55; Pres., Botanical Soc. of the British Isles, 1947-51; Chm. Internat. Commn on Horticultural Nomenclature, 1952-66, and International Cttee on Nomenclatural Stabilization, 1954; Rapporteur, Internat. Commission on the Nomenclature of Cultivated Plants, 1956-65, Chm., 1965-74; Brit. Rep., Council of Internat. Soc. Hort. Sci., 1960-73. Royal Horticultural Society: Victoria Medal of Honour in Horticulture, 1957; Mem. Council, 1957-61, 1962-66, 1968-73; Chm., Orchid Cttee, 1964-73; Veitch Gold Medal, 1966. Cons., new Botanic Garden at Ramat Hanadiv, Israel, 1964-68; Sec.-Treas. the Classification Society, 1964-68, Vice-Pres., 1968-; Mem. Adv. Cttee Hunt Bot. Library, Pittsburgh, 1961-; Mem. Council, Bibliogr. Soc., 1963-68. Sandars Reader, Cambridge, 1971. First Chm., Cambridge Humanists, 1955-57, Pres., 1974-; Dir, Rationalist Press Assoc., 1961-74, Hon. Associate, 1976. *Publications:* British Botanists, 1944; Wild Flowers of the Chalk, 1947; Wild Flowers (in New Naturalist Series with S. M. Walters), 1954, pbk edn 1972; (ed) Thomas Johnson: Botanical Journeys in Kent and Hampstead, 1972; contributions to botanical, bibliographical, and rationalist jls, Jt Editor the New Naturalist, since 1943. *Recreations:* music, book-collecting. *Address:* 5 St Eligius Street, Cambridge. *T:* Cambridge 55776.

GILMOUR, Michael Hugh Barrie; solicitor, retired; Chief Legal Adviser and Solicitor to British Railway Board, 1963-Jan. 1970 (Secretary to Board, Oct. 1965-Jan. 1968); *b* 1 Dec. 1904; *e* surv. *s* of late Thomas Lennox Gilmour, CBE, Barrister, and Elizabeth Hervey, *o c* of late Sir John Scott Keltie, LLD; *m* 1937, Elisabeth, *o d* of late Francis Edward Cuming; one *d*. *Educ:* Leighton Park; abroad. Solicitors Office, Great Western Railway Company, 1929; Solicitor to Company, 1945-47; Solicitor to Railway Executive in Western Region, 1948-49; Chief Solicitor (1949) and Chief Legal Adviser (1951), British Transport Commission, until 1962. Served War of 1939-45, RAFVR, July 1940-Sept. 1941 (Squadron Leader). *Recreations:* walking, reading. *Address:* 55 Strand-on-the-Green, Chiswick, W4 3PD. *Club:* Garrick.

GILPIN, John; Artistic Director, Pittsburgh Ballet Company, Pennsylvania, USA; *b* 10 Feb. 1930; twin *s* of J. and L. M. Gilpin; *m* 1960, Sally Judd. *Educ:* Cone-Ripman Coll. Michael, in Peter Pan, 1942, 1943; and other rôles (stage, films, and broadcasting) until 1945, when he decided to devote himself exclusively to dancing. Awarded Adeline Genée Gold Medal, 1943. With Ballet Rambert, 1945-48; Roland Petit's Ballets de Paris, 1948-49; Grand Ballet du Marquis de Cuevas, 1949-50; Leading dancer, Festival Ballet, 1950-60; formerly guest dancer, Covent Garden. Produced Firebird, Tokyo, 1971. Prix Vaslav Nijinsky, of French Academy of Music and Dance, 1957; Paris International Dance Festival Gold Medal, 1964. *Relevant publication:* John Gilpin by Cyril Swinson. *Recreation:* music. *Address:* 3 Orme Court, W2.

GILPIN, Rt. Rev. William Percy; *b* 26 July 1902; *e s* of late Percy William and Ethel Annie Gilpin. *Educ:* King Edward's, Birmingham; Keble Coll., Oxford. BA 1st class, Theology, 1925; MA 1928. Curate of Solihull, Warwicks, 1925-28; Vice-Principal of St Paul's Coll., Burgh, 1928-30; Chaplain of Chichester Theological Coll., 1930-33; Vicar of Manaccan with St Anthony, 1933-36; Vicar of St Mary, Penzance, 1936-44; Dir of Religious Education, Gloucester, 1944-51; Canon Missioner of Gloucester, 1946-52; Archdeacon of Southwark, 1952-55; Bishop Suffragan of Kingston-upon-Thames, 1952-70. Examining Chaplain to: Bishop of Truro, 1934-44, Bishop of Gloucester, 1945-52. *Recreation:* general railway matters. *Address:* 50 Lower Broad Street, Ludlow, Salop. *T:* Ludlow 3376.

GILROY, John T. Y., ARCA, FRSA; artist; portrait and landscape painter; *b* 30 May 1898; *s* of John William Gilroy, artist; *m* 1924, Gwendoline Peri-Short; one *s*; *m* 1950, Elizabeth Outram Thwaite. *Educ:* King's Coll., Newcastle on Tyne; Royal College of Art, London. Served European War, 1916-18, RFA. British Institute Scholar, 1921; RCA Travelling Scholar, 1922. Exhibition, Upper Grosvenor Galls, 1970. Creator of Guinness posters, 1925-60, also of Royle's publications of humour. Painted many famous portraits throughout Canada and America; also portraits of the Duke of Windsor when King Edward VIII; Queen Elizabeth the Queen Mother; Princess Margaret; Prince Charles; Princess Anne; Field Marshal Earl Alexander of Tunis (Nat. Portrait Gall.); Rt Hon. Edward Heath; Lord Hailsham of Saint Marylebone; Sir Winston Churchill, 1942; Pope John; Sir Aubrey Smith; Sir John Clements; Sir John Gielgud; Sir Malcolm Sargent. Hon. MA Newcastle upon Tyne, 1975. *Publications:* (illustrated) McGill, The Story of a University, 1960; Rough Island Story (News Reel of Depression), 1931-35. *Recreations:* travelling, conversation. *Address:* 10 Holland Park Road, Kensington, W14. *T:* 01-602 3437. *Clubs:* Garrick (Chm.), Works of Art Cttee), Green Room.

GILROY, His Eminence Sir Norman (Thomas), Cardinal, KBE 1969; DD; *b* Sydney, NSW, 22 Jan. 1896; *s* of William James Gilroy and Catherine Slattery. *Educ:* Convent Schools of Sisters of the Good Samaritan and Sisters of Charity; Marist Brothers' School. Entered Postal Department, 1909; Wireless Operator on Commonwealth Transport Steamer Bulla carrying Australian troops to Egypt and Indian troops to the Dardanelles, 1915; present at landing of Troops on Gallipoli, 25 April 1915; entered St Columba's College, Springwood, 1917; Urban College of Propaganda, Rome, 1919; Priest for the Diocese of Lismore, NSW, 1923; Doctor of Theology, 1924; Secretary to the Apostolic Delegate, 1924-31; Secretary to Bishop and Chancellor of the Diocese of Lismore, 1931-34; Bishop of Port Augusta, South Australia, 1935-37; Titular Archbishop of Cypsela and Coadjutor to RC Archbishop of Sydney, 1937-40; Archbishop of Sydney, 1940-71; Cardinal, 1946. *Address:* St John Vianney Villa, Clovelly Road, Randwick, NSW, Australia.

GILSON, Etienne Henry, DLitt, PhD, LLD; Philosopher and Historian; *b* 13 June 1884; *m* 1908, Thérèse Ravisé; one *s* two *d*. *Educ:* Sorbonne. Prof. University of Lille, 1913; University of Strasbourg, 1919; Prof. of Medieval Philosophy, Sorbonne, 1921-32; Dir of Medieval Studies, University of Toronto, 1929; Prof. Coll. de France, 1932-51, retired, Hon. Prof., 1957. Corresp. Mem. British Acad.; Fellow French Acad., 1946. Holds numerous hon. degrees. Commandeur de la Légion d'Honneur; Croix de Guerre; Orden Pour le Mérite. *Publications:* Le Thomisme, 1922; La Philosophie de St Bonaventure, 1924; Introduction à l'étude de St Augustin, 1929; L'esprit de la philosophie médiévale, 1932; La théologie mystique de St Bernard, 1934 (Eng. trans. 1955); Le réalisme méthodique, 1935; Christianisme et philosophie, 1936; The Unity of Philosophical Experience, 1937; Héloïse et Abélard (Eng. trans. 1953); Reason and Revelation in the Middle Ages, 1938; Dante et la Philosophie, 1939; God and Philosophy, 1940; La philosophie au moyen âge, 1945; Being and Some Philosophers, 1949; L'école des muses, 1950 (Eng. trans., Choir of Muses, 1954); Jean Duns Scot, 1952; History of Christian Philosophy in the Middle Ages, 1954; Painting and Reality, 1957; Elements of Christian Philosophy, 1959; The Philosopher and Theology, 1962; Modern Philosophy, 1963; Introduction aux arts du beau, 1963; Matières et formes, 1964; The Spirit of Thomism, 1964; Recent Philosophy, 1966; D'Aristote à Darwin et retour, 1971; La Philosophie au Moyen Age, 2 vols, 1976. *Address:* 9 rue Saint-Romain, 75006 Paris, France.

GILSON, John Cary, CBE 1967 (OBE 1945); Director, Medical Research Council's Pneumoconiosis Research Unit, 1952-76; *b* 9 Aug. 1912; 2nd *s* of late Robert Cary Gilson, MA and late Marianne C. Gilson, MA (*née* Dunstall); *m* 1945, Margaret Evelyn Worthington, MA, *d* of late Robert A. Worthington,

OBE, FRCS; two *s* one *d*. *Educ:* Haileybury Sch.; Gonville and Caius Coll., Cambridge. MB, BChir Cantab 1937; MRCP 1940; FRCP 1956. 1st Asst, London Hosp.; Staff of RAF Inst. of Aviation Medicine, 1940-46; Mem. Scientific Staff of MRC, 1946-, at Pneumoconiosis Research Unit, Asst Ed., Brit. Jl Industr. Med., 1955-64, and on Ed. Bd of various other jls; Pres., British Occupational Hygiene Soc., 1960-61; Pres., Occupational Medicine Section, RSM, 1968-69; Hon. Life Mem., NY Acad. of Sciences, 1966. *Publications:* papers on pulmonary physiology and industrial medicine in scientific jls. *Recreations:* domestic engineering; clouds. *Address:* Hembury Hill Farm, Honiton, Devon. *T:* Broadhembury 203.

GIMSON, Arthur Clive Stanford, MBE 1944; MC 1945; Head Master, Blundell's School, since Sept. 1971; *b* 28 June 1919; *s* of Harold Gimson, Leicester and Janet Marjorie Stanford, Aldringham, Suffolk; *m* 1957, Fiona Margaret Walton; three *s*. *Educ:* Uppingham Sch.; Clare Coll., Cambridge (Exhibr, MA). Royal Artillery, 1939-46; Sub-Warden, Mary Ward Settlement, 1947-48; Asst Master: Bradfield Coll., 1948-55; Melbourne Grammar Sch., 1956; Housemaster, Bradfield Coll., 1957-63; Head Master, Sebright Sch., 1963-70. *Recreations:* mountains and monasteries. *Address:* Blundell House, Blundell's Avenue, Tiverton, Devon. *T:* Tiverton 2543.

GIMSON, George Stanley, QC (Scotland) 1961; Sheriff Principal of Grampian, Highland and Islands, since 1975; Chairman, Pensions Appeals Tribunals, Scotland, since 1975 (President, 1971-75); *b* 1915. *Educ:* High School of Glasgow; Glasgow Univ. Advocate, 1949; Standing Junior Counsel, Department of Agriculture for Scotland and Forestry Commission, 1956-61; Sheriff Principal of Aberdeen, Kincardine and Banff, 1972-74. Mem., Board of Management: Edinburgh Central Hosps, 1960-70 (Chm., 1964-70); Edinburgh Royal Victoria Hosps, 1970-74 (Vice-Chm.); Dir, Scottish Nat. Orchestra Soc. Ltd, 1962-; Trustee, Nat. Library of Scotland, 1963-76; Chm., RSSPCC, Edinburgh, 1972-76. *Address:* The Castle, Inverness. *T:* Inverness 30782; 11 Royal Circus, Edinburgh. *T:* 031-225 8055. *Clubs:* University Staff (Edinburgh); Royal Northern (Aberdeen); Highland (Inverness).

GIMSON, Col Thomas William; *b* 9 July 1904; 2nd *s* of late Thomas Wallis Gimson and Rosina Skerratt Forsyth; *m* 1958, Heather Mary, *d* of late Capt. P. D. C. Eliot, 14th Lancers, Indian Army, and of the Countess of Powis. *Educ:* Brighton Coll.; St John's Coll., Oxford. Commissioned North Staffs Regt; transferred Irish Guards, 1933; Internat. Force HQ, Saar Plebiscite, 1934; Palestine, 1938; Dunkirk, 1940; Combined Ops, 1943; NW Europe, 1944; Military Mission, Moscow, 1945; Military Attaché, Warsaw, 1946-48; Regtl Lt-Col comd Irish Guards, 1948-50; retd pay, 1950. *Address:* Les Pierrugues, 83240 Cavalaire, France. *Club:* Turf.

GINGELL, Air Marshal John, CBE 1973 (MBE 1962); Air Member for Personnel designate (1978); *b* 3 Feb. 1925; *e s* of E. J. Gingell; *m* 1949, Prudence, *d* of Brig. R. F. Johnson; two *s* one *d*. *Educ:* St Boniface Coll., Plymouth. Entered RAF, 1943; Fleet Air Arm, 1945-46 as Sub-Lt (A) RNVR; returned to RAF, 1951; served with Nos 58 and 542 Sqdns; CFS 1954; psc 1959; jssc 1965; comd No 27 Sqdn, 1963-65; Staff of Chief of Defence Staff, 1966; Dep. Dir Defence Ops Staff (Central Staff), 1966-67; Mil. Asst to Chm. NATO Mil. Cttee, Brussels, 1968-70; AOA, RAF Germany, 1971-72; AOC 23 Group, RAF Trng Comd, 1973-75; Asst Chief of Defence Staff (Policy), 1975-78. *Recreations:* ornithology, walking, music. *Address:* c/o Lloyds Bank Ltd, Cox's & King's Branch, 6 Pall Mall, SW1Y 5NH. *Club:* Royal Air Force.

GINGELL, Maj.-Gen. Laurie William Albert, OBE 1966; Major-General Administration, HQ United Kingdom Land Forces, since Oct. 1976; *b* 29 Oct. 1925; *s* of late William George Gingell and of Elsie Grace Gingell; *m* 1949, Nancy Margaret Wadsworth; one *s* one *d*. *Educ:* Farnborough Grammar Sch.; Oriel Coll., Oxford. Commissioned into Royal Gloucestershire Hussars, 1945; transf. Royal Tank Regt, 1947; sc 1956; jssc 1961; Commanded: 1st Royal Tank Regt, 1966-67; 7th Armoured Bde, 1970-71; DQMG, HQ BAOR, 1973-76. ADC to the Queen, 1974-76. *Recreations:* golf, tennis, swimming, reading. *Address:* Kelsey House, Kelsey Road, Salisbury, Wilts. *T:* Salisbury 4816. *Club:* Army and Navy.

GINGER, Phyllis Ethel, (Mrs Leslie Durbin), RWS 1958 (ARWS 1952); Free Lance artist since 1940; *b* 19 Oct. 1907; *m* 1940, Leslie Durbin, *qv*; one *s* one *d*. *Educ:* Tiffin's Girls' Sch., Kingston on Thames. LCC three years' scholarship at Central School of Arts and Crafts, 1937-39. Water colours for Pilgrim Trust Recording Britain Scheme, 1941-42; Royal Academy Exhibitor; Drawings and Lithographs purchased by:

Washington State Library, 1941; Victoria and Albert Museum, 1952; London Museum, 1954; South London Art Gallery, 1960. *Publications:* Alexander the Circus Pony, 1941; book jacket designs; book illustrations include: London by Mrs Robert Henrey, 1948; The Virgin of Aldemanbury, by Mrs Robert Henrey, 1960. *Address:* 298 Kew Road, Kew, Richmond, Surrey. *T:* 01-940 2221.

GINGOLD, Hermione Ferdinanda; Actress; *b* 9 Dec.; *d* of James and Kate Gingold; *m* 1st, Michael Joseph (marr. diss.); one *s* (and one *s* decd); 2nd, Eric Maschwitz (marr. diss.). *Educ:* privately. Started as child actress at His Majesty's Theatre with Sir Herbert Tree in Pinkie and the Fairies. Played in Shakespeare at Old Vic and Stratford on Avon. Five years in intimate revue. O Dad, Poor Dad, Piccadilly, 1965; Highly Confidential, Cambridge, 1965; A Little Night Music, Majestic, New York, 1973, Adelphi, London, 1975. *Films:* Bell, Book and Candle, 1958; Gigi, 1959; Jules Verne's Rocket to the Moon, 1967. Many US television appearances. Has recorded Façade and Lysistrata. *Publications:* The World is Square: my own unaided work, 1945; Sirens should be Seen and Not Heard, 1963; articles and short stories. *Address:* 405 East 54th Street, New York, NY 10022, USA.

GINSBURG, David; MP (Lab) Dewsbury since 1959; *b* 18 March 1921; *o s* of late N. Ginsburg; *m* 1954, Louise, *er d* of late S. P. Cassy. *Educ:* University Coll. Sch.; Balliol Coll., Oxford. Chm. OU Democratic Socialist Club, 1941; 2nd Cl, Hons Sch. of Politics, Philosophy and Economics, 1941. Commissioned Oxford and Bucks LI, 1942; Capt. Intelligence duties, 1944-45. Senior Research Officer, Govt Social Survey, 1946-52; Sec. of Research Dept of Labour Party and Sec. of Home Policy Sub-Cttee of National Executive Cttee, 1952-59; Market Research Consultant; Chm., Parly. and Scientific Cttee, 1968-71. Broadcaster. *Publications:* miscellaneous articles and book reviews in contemporary publications. *Recreations:* walking, swimming, opera. *Address:* 3 Bell Moor, East Heath Road, NW3.

GINSBURY, Norman; playwright; *b* Nov. 1902; *s* of late J. S. and Rachel Cecily Ginsbury; *m* 1945, Dorothy Jennings. *Educ:* London University. Plays produced: Viceroy Sarah, Arts Theatre, 1934, Whitehall Theatre, 1935; Walk in the Sun, "Q", and Embassy, 1939; Take Back Your Freedom (with late Winifred Holtby), Neighbourhood, 1940; The Firstcomers, Bradford Civic Playhouse, 1944; The First Gentleman (written, 1935), New and Savoy, 1945; Belasco, New York, 1956; The Gambler (from the story of Dostoievsky), Embassy, 1946; The Happy Man, New, 1948; Portrait by Lawrence (with M. Moiseiwitsch), Theatre Royal, Stratford, 1949; School for Rivals, Bath Assembly and Old Vic, Bristol, 1949. Also following adaptations of plays by Henrik Ibsen: Ghosts, Vaudeville, 1937; Enemy of the People, Old Vic, 1939; Peer Gynt, Old Vic Season at New Theatre, 1944; A Doll's House, Winter Garden, 1946; John Gabriel Borkman, Mermaid, 1961. A new version of Strindberg's Dance of Death at Tyrone Guthrie Theatre, Minneapolis; and at Yvonne Arnaud Theatre, Guildford, 1966; for the Mayflower 350th anniv., The Forefathers, Athenaeum Theatre, Plymouth, 1970; The Wisest Fool, Yvonne Arnaud, 1974. *Publications:* Viceroy Sarah, 1934; Take Back Your Freedom (collab.), 1939; The First Gentleman, 1946; The Fabulous Moneymaker (prod TV 1959); and the following versions of plays by Ibsen: Ghosts, 1938; Enemy of the People, 1939; Peer Gynt, 1945; A Doll's House, 1950; John Gabriel Borkman, 1960; Rosmersholm, 1961; Pillars of Society, 1962. The Old Lags' League (from a story by W. Pett Ridge, in The Best One-Act Plays of 1960-61; The Shoemaker And The Devil (from a story by Tchehov), in The Best Short Plays of 1968 (NY); The Safety Match (from a story by Tchehov), in Best Short Plays of the World Theatre 1968-73 (NY). *Address:* 10 Bramber House, Michel Grove, Eastbourne, East Sussex. *T:* Eastbourne 29603.

GIOLITTI, Dr Antonio; Member, Commission of the European Communities, since 1977; *b* 12 Feb. 1915; *s* of Giuseppe and Maria Giolitti; *m* 1939, Elena d'Amico; one *s* two *d*. *Educ:* Rome Univ. (Dr Law); Oxford; München. Mem. Italian Parlt, 1946-77; Minister of Budget and Economic Planning, 1964, 1970-72, 1973-74. Member: Italian Communist Party, 1943-57; Italian Socialist Party, 1958-; Exec., Italian Socialist Party, 1958-. *Publications:* Riforme e rivoluzione, 1957; Il comunismo in Europa, 1960; Un socialismo possibile, 1967. *Recreations:* music, walking. *Address:* 200 rue de la Loi, 1049 Brussels, Belgium.

GIPPSLAND, Bishop of, since 1974; **Rt. Rev. Graham Richard Delbridge;** *b* 22 May 1917; *s* of Richard and Evelyn Delbridge; *m* 1943, Audrey Doris Traversi; one *s* three *d*. *Educ:* Moore Theological College, NSW. Scholar in Theology, Australian College of Theology, 1955; Mem., Australian Coll. of Educn, 1970. Director of Youth Work, Sydney, 1943-52; Rector, Holy Trinity, Adelaide, 1952-57; Rector, St Matthew's, Manly, 1957-60; Archdeacon and Senior Chaplain to the Primate of Australia, 1963-68; Asst Bishop of Sydney and Bishop in Wollongong, 1969-74. *Recreation:* bush walking. *Address:* Bishopscourt, PO Box 383, Sale, Victoria 3850, Australia. *Clubs:* Royal Automobile, Sale Men's (Sale, Victoria).

GIRDWOOD, John Graham, CBE 1946; CA; *b* 1890; 2nd *s* of late David Girdwood, Glasgow; *m* 1924, Janet Ellis Kerr (*d* 1976), *d* of late John Hood, Port Glasgow; no *c*. Controller of Canteens, Ministry of Supply, 1941-46; Controller of Admiralty Canteens, 1943-46; Chm. Min. of Health House Building Costs Cttee for England and Wales, 1947-53; Chm. of Aerated Bread Co. Ltd, 1948-58; Chm. of Wm Beardmore & Co. Ltd, 1954-57. Mem. of Council of Inst. of Chartered Accountants of Scotland, 1952-55. *Recreation:* golf. *Address:* 3 Johnston Court, North Street, St Andrews, Fife KY16 9PY. *Clubs:* Junior Carlton; Royal and Ancient (St Andrews).

GIRDWOOD, Ronald Haxton, MD, PhD, FRCP, FRCPE, FRCPath; Professor of Therapeutics, since 1962, Dean of the Faculty of Medicine, since 1975, University of Edinburgh; Physician to Royal Infirmary of Edinburgh since 1951; *b* 19 March 1917; *s* of late Thomas Girdwood; *m* 1945, Mary Elizabeth, *d* of late Reginald Williams, Calstock, Cornwall; one *s* one *d*. *Educ:* Daniel Stewart's Coll., Edinburgh; University of Edinburgh; University of Michigan. MB, ChB (Hons) Edinburgh 1939; Ettles Schol., Leslie Gold Medallist, Royal Victoria Hosp.; Tuberculosis Trust Gold Medallist, Wightman, Beaney and Keith Memorial Prize Winner, 1939; MD (Gold Medal for thesis), 1954. Pres. Edinburgh Univ. Church of Scotland Soc., 1938-39. Served RAMC, 1942-46 (despatches); Nutrition Research Officer and Officer i/c Med. Div. in India and Burma. Lectr in Medicine, University of Edinburgh, 1946; Rockefeller Research Fellow, University of Michigan, 1948-49; Cons. Phys., Chalmers Hosp., Edinburgh, 1950-51; Sen. Lectr in Med. and Cons. Phys., Royal Infirmary, 1951; Vis. Lectr, Dept of Pharmacology, Yale Univ., 1956; Reader in Med., University of Edinburgh, 1958; Examiner for RCPE; sometime External Examiner for Universities of London, Sheffield, St Andrews, Dundee, Dublin and Glasgow; Chm., SE Scotland Regional Blood Transfusion Assoc.; Member: Council, RCPE, 1966-70; South-Eastern Reg. Hosp. Board (Scotland), 1965-69; Board of Management, Royal Infirmary, Edinburgh, 1958-64; Cttee on Safety of Medicines; Adverse Drug Reactions Sub cttee; Exec., Medico-Pharmaceutical Forum, 1972-74; Chairman: Scottish Group of Hæmophilia Soc., 1954-60; Non-Professorial Medical Teachers and Research Workers Gp Cttee (Scot.) of BMA, 1956-62; Scottish Gp of Nutrition Soc., 1961-62; Consultative Council, Edinburgh Medical Gp; Pres. Brit. Soc. for Hæmatology, 1963-64; Member: Coun. Brit. Soc. of Gastroenterology, 1964-68; Council of Nutrition Soc., 1957-60 and 1961-64; numerous Med. Socs; Lay Mem., Scottish Soc. of Artists; Chm., Bd of Management, Scottish Med. Jl and formerly Mem. of Editorial Bds of Blood and of Brit. Jl of Haematology; Mem. Editorial Bd, Brit. Jl of Nutrition, 1960-65; British Council visitor to W African Hosps, 1963, to Middle East, 1977 (Mem. Univ. Projects Gp); Visiting Prof. and WHO Consultant, India, 1965. Cullen Prize, RCPE, 1970. *Publications:* about 200, particularly in relation to nutrition, hæmatology and gastroenterology; (ed with A. N. Smith) Malabsorption, 1969; (ed) Blood Disorders due to Drugs and Other Agents, 1973; contrib. Davidson's Principles and Practice of Medicine, 1974; (ed with S. Alstead) Textbook of Medical Treatment, 1974; (ed) Clinical Pharmacology, 1975. *Recreations:* photography, painting. *Address:* 2 Hermitage Drive, Edinburgh EH10 6DD. *T:* (home) 031-447 5137, (hospital) 031-229 2477. *Clubs:* East India, Devonshire, Sports and Public Schools; University Staff (Edinburgh).

GIRI, Varahagiri Venkata; President of India, 1969-74; *b* Berhampore, 10 Aug. 1894. *Educ:* Nat. Univ. of Ireland. Barrister-at-law. Trade Union leader appointments include: Gen. Sec. and Pres., All India Railwaymen's Fedn; Pres., (twice) All India TUC; Indian workers' deleg. to Internat. Labour Conf., Geneva; workers' rep., Second Round Table Conf., London, 1931. Member, Central Legislative Assembly; Minister of Labour, Industries, Cooperation and Commerce, Madras Ministry, 1937-39; Minister in Madras Govt, 1946; High Commissioner for India in Ceylon, 1947-51; Minister of Labour, Govt of India, 1952-54. Governor: Uttar Pradesh, 1957-60; Kerala, 1960-65; Mysore, 1965-67. Vice-Pres. of India, 1967-69. *Publications:* Industrial Relations; Labour Problems in Indian Industry; Jobs for our Millions; The President Speaks: a compilation of speeches from May 1969-March 1970. *Address:* Girija, 1 Third Block, Jayanagar, Bangalore 11, India.

GIRLING, Maj.-Gen. Peter Howard, CB 1972; OBE 1961; CEng, FIMechE, FIEE, FIERE; Director of Operations, Open University, since 1972; *b* 18 May 1915; *m* 1942, Stella Muriel (*née* Hope); two *d.* Commissioned, RAOC, 1939; transferred to REME, 1942; served War of 1939-45; India, 1945-47; Staff Coll., Camberley, 1948; Egypt, 1949-52; JSSC, Latimer, 1953; BAOR, 1953-55; Col, 1961; WO, 1961-65; HQ FARELF 1965-67; Brig., 1965; Comd Berkshire Sub-District, 1967-68; Comdt, REME Training Centre, 1967-69; Maj.-Gen., 1969; Dir of Electrical and Mechanical Engineering (Army), 1969-72; Col Comdt, REME, 1972-77. *Address:* The Folly, Wicken, Northants. *T:* Wicken 204. *Club:* Army and Navy.

GIROUARD, Mark, PhD; writer and architectural historian; Slade Professor of Fine Art, University of Oxford, 1975-76; *b* 7 Oct. 1931; *s* of Richard D. Girouard and Lady Blanche Girouard; *m* 1970, Dorothy N. Dorf; one *d.* Educ: Ampleforth; Christ Church, Oxford (MA); Courtauld Inst. of Art (PhD); Bartlett Sch., UCL (BSc, Dip. Arc). Staff of Country Life, 1958-66; studied architecture, Bartlett Sch., UCL, 1966-71; staff of Architectural Review, 1971-75. Member: Cttee, Victorian Soc., 1958-66 (Founder Mem. 1958); Royal Fine Art Commn, 1972-; Royal Commn on Historical Monuments (England), 1976-. *Publications:* Robert Smythson and the Architecture of the Elizabethan Era, 1966; The Victorian Country House, 1971; Victorian Pubs, 1975; (jtly) Spirit of the Age, 1975 (based on BBC TV series); Sweetness and Light: the 'Queen Anne' movement 1860-1900, 1977; articles in Country Life, Architect. Rev., Listener. *Address:* 35 Colville Road, W11.

GISBOROUGH, 3rd Baron, *cr* 1917; **Thomas Richard John Long Chaloner;** DL; *b* 1 July 1927; *s* of 2nd Baron and Esther Isabella Madeleine (*d* 1970), *yr d* of late Charles O. Hall, Eddlethorpe; *S* father 1951; *m* 1960, Shane, *e d* of Sidney Newton, London, W8 and *g d* of Sir Louis Newton, 1st Bt; two *s.* *Educ:* Eton. 16th/5th Lancers, 1948-52; Captain Northumberland Hussars, 1955-61; Lt-Col Green Howards (Territorials), 1967-69. CC NR Yorks, 1964-74, Cleveland, 1974-77. DL Cleveland, 1973-. *Recreations:* most sports. *Heir: s* Hon. Thomas Peregrine Long Chaloner, *b* 17 Jan. 1961. *Address:* Gisborough House, Guisborough, Cleveland. *T:* Guisborough 2002. *Club:* Northern Counties (Newcastle upon Tyne).

GISCARD d'ESTAING, Valéry; Grand Croix de la Légion d'Honneur; Croix de Guerre (1939-45); President of the French Republic, since 1974; *b* Coblence, 2 Feb. 1926; *s* of Edmond Giscard d'Estaing and May Bardoux; *m* 1952, Anne-Aymone de Brantes; two *s* two *d.* *Educ:* Lycée Janson-de-Sailly, Paris; Ecole Polytechnique; Ecole Nationale d'Administration. Inspection of Finances: Deputy, 1952; Inspector, 1954; Dep. Dir, Cabinet of Président du Conseil, June-Dec. 1954. Elected Deputy for Puy-de-Dôme, 1956; re-elected for Clermont N and SW, Nov. 1958, for Puy-de Dôme, Nov-Dec. 1962, for Clermont N and SW, March 1967 and June 1968; Sec. of State for Finance, 1959; Minister of Finance, Jan.-April 1962; Minister of Finance and Economic Affairs, April-Nov. 1962 and Dec. 1962-Jan. 1966; Minister of Economy and Finance, 1969-74. Pres., Nat. Fedn of Indep. Republicans, 1966-73 (also a Founder); Pres., comm. des finances de l'économie générale et du plan de l'Assemblée nationale, 1967-68. Mayor of Chamalières, 1967-74. Deleg. to Assembly of UN, 1956, 1957, 1958. *Publication:* Démocratie Française, 1976 (Towards a New Democracy, 1977). *Address:* Palais de l'Elysée, Paris 8e, France; (private) 11 rue Bénouville, Paris 16e, France. *Club:* Polo (Paris).

GISH, Lillian Diana; Actress; *b* 14 Oct. 1899. *Educ:* privately. Began acting in theatre at five years of age and at twelve entered motion pictures. Katrina in Crime and Punishment (with John Gielgud), 1948, The Curious Savage, 1950, Miss Mabel, 1951 (USA). Acting mainly on television, 1952; in play, The Trip to Bountiful (for the Theatre Guild), 1953-54; The Chalk Garden, 1957; The Family Reunion, 1958; directed, The Beggar's Opera, 1958; All the Way House, 1960-61 (won Drama Critics and Pulitzer prize as best play); A Passage to India, play (Chicago), 1962-63; Too True to be Good (G. B. Shaw's play) (New York), 1963; Romeo and Juliet (Stratford Festival Theatre), 1965; Anya (musical), 1967; I Never Sang for my Father, 1968; Uncle Vanya, NY, 1973; A Musical Jubilee (musical), NY, 1975. Lillian Gish and the Movies: the art of film, 1900-28 (concert programmes), Moscow, Paris, London and USA, 1969-73; QE2 World tour, 1975; lecturing and performing for The Theatre Guild at Sea on the Rotterdam, 1975. *Early films include:* Birth of a Nation; Intolerance; Souls Triumphant; Hearts of the World; The Great Love; Broken Blossoms; Way Down East; The Orphans of the Storm; The White Sister; Romola; *later films include:* The Night of the Hunter, 1954; The Cobweb, 1955; Orders to Kill, 1957; The Unforgiven, 1959; Follow Me Boys,

1966; Warning Shot, 1966; The Comedians, 1967. Frequent appearances on television; three TV plays, 1962; TV plays, 1963; Arsenic and Old Lace, TV, 1969. Hon. AFD, Rollins Coll., Fla; Hon. HHD, Holyoke Coll.; Hon. Dr of Performing Arts, Bowling Green State Univ., Ohio, 1976. Hon. Oscar, Acad. Motion Picture Arts and Scis, 1971. Handel Medallion, NYC, 1973. *Publications:* Lillian Gish: an autobiography, 1968; Lillian Gish, The Movies, Mr Griffith and Me, 1969; Dorothy and Lillian Gish, 1973. *Recreation:* travel. *Address:* 430 East 57th Street, New York, NY 10022, USA.

GITTINGS, Robert (William Victor), CBE 1970; LittD Cantab, 1970; poet; biographer; playwright; *b* 1 Feb. 1911; *s* of late Surg.-Capt. Fred Claude Bromley Gittings, RN (retd) and late Dora Mary Brayshaw; *m* 1st, 1934, Katherine Edith Cambell (marr. diss.); two *s* ; 2nd, 1949, Joan Grenville Manton; one *d.* *Educ:* St Edward's Sch., Oxford; Jesus Coll., Cambridge (Scholar). 1st Cl. Historical Tripos, 1933. Research Student, and Research Fellow, Jesus Coll., 1933-38. Supervisor in History, 1938-40; writer and producer for broadcasting, 1940-63; Professor: Vanderbilt University, Tennessee, 1966; Boston Univ., 1970; Univ. of Washington, 1972, 1974 and 1977 (Danz Lectr). *Publications: poetry and verse -plays:* The Roman Road, 1932; The Story of Psyche, 1936; Wentworth Place, 1950; The Makers of Violence (Canterbury Festival), 1951; Through a Glass Lightly, 1952; Famous Meeting, 1953; Out of This Wood (sequence of plays), 1955; This Tower My Prison, 1961; Matters of Love and Death, 1968; Conflict at Canterbury, 1970; American Journey, 1972; Collected Poems, 1976; *biography and criticism:* John Keats: The Living Year, 1954; The Mask of Keats, 1956; Shakespeare's Rival, 1960; (ed) The Living Shakespeare, 1960; (ed with E. Hardy) Some Recollections by Emma Hardy, 1961; (with Jo Manton) The Story of John Keats, 1962; The Keats Inheritance, 1964; (ed) Selected Poems and Letters of John Keats, 1966; John Keats, 1968 (W. H. Smith Literary Award, 1969); John Keats: Selected Letters, 1970; The Odes of Keats, 1970; Young Thomas Hardy, 1975 (Christian Gauss Award, Phi Beta Kappa, 1975); The Older Hardy, 1978; contrib. to Keats-Shelley Memorial Bulletin, Keats-Shelley Journal, Harvard Library Bulletin, etc. *Recreations:* most outdoor pursuits except blood-sports. *Address:* The Stables, East Dean, Chichester, West Sussex. *T:* Singleton 328.

GIULINI, Carlo Maria; conductor; Music Director, Los Angeles Philharmonic Orchestra, since 1978; *b* 9 May 1914; *m* ; three *s.* *Educ:* Accademia Santa Cecilia, Rome; played viola in Santa Cecilia orchestra, and under Bruno Walter and Klemperer. Début as conductor, Rome, 1944; formed Orchestra of Milan Radio, 1951; Principal Conductor, La Scala, Milan, 1953-55; début in Great Britain, conducting Verdi's Falstaff, Edinburgh Festival, 1955. Has conducted notable revivals of Don Carlos and Il Barbiere di Siviglia, Covent Garden. Closely associated with Philharmonia Orchestra, with whom he frequently appears: London, Edinburgh, Lucerne, Vienna and Leeds Festivals. Has also conducted in Holland, Israel and USA. *Recreation:* sailing.

GIVEN, Edward Ferguson, CMG 1968; HM Diplomatic Service; Ambassador to Bahrain, since 1975; *b* 13 April 1919; *o s* of James K. Given, West Kilbride, Ayrshire; *m* 1st, 1946, Philida Naomi Bullwinkle; one *s* ; 2nd, 1954, Kathleen Margaret Helena Kelly. *Educ:* Sutton County Sch.; University Coll., London. Served RA, 1939-46. Entered HM Foreign Service, 1946; 2nd Sec., Paris, 1949; 1st Sec., Rangoon, 1951; FO, 1953; Bahrain, 1957; HM Consul, Bordeaux, 1960; 1st Sec., FO, 1961; Counsellor, Office of Political Adviser to C-in-C Far East, Singapore, 1963; Counsellor: Moscow, 1967; Beirut, 1969; Ambassador, United Republic of Cameroon and Republic of Equatorial Guinea, 1972-75. *Recreation:* sailing. *Address:* c/o Foreign and Commonwealth Office, SW1.

GIVEN, Rear-Adm. John Garnett Cranston, CB 1955; CBE 1945 (OBE 1943); MIMechE, MIMarE; retired from Royal Navy, June 1955; *b* 21 Sept. 1902; *s* of late J. C. M. Given, MD, FRCP, and Mrs May Given, Liverpool; *m* 1931, Elizabeth Joyce (*née* Payne), Brenchley, Kent, and Durban, Natal; one *s* two *d.* *Educ:* King William's Coll., IOM; Charterhouse, Godalming. RNEC Keyham, 1922-25; HMS Hood, 1926; RNC Greenwich, 1928; Admiralty, 1930; HMS Berwick, China Station, 1933; HMS Neptune, 1940; Admiralty, 1942; HMS Howe, East Indies, 1944; Fleet Train, British Pacific Fleet, 1945; Asst Engineer-in-Chief, Admiralty, 1947; Commanding Officer Royal Naval Engineering Coll., Plymouth, 1948-51; idc 1952; Staff of Comdr-in-Chief, The Nore, 1953-55; Managing Dir, Parsons Marine Turbine Co., Wallsend, 1955-62. *Recreations:* fishing and walking. *Address:* c/o National Westminster Bank, 26 The Haymarket, SW1. *Club:* Army and Navy.

GLADSTONE, David Arthur Steuart; HM Diplomatic Service; Counsellor, Head of Chancery, and Political Adviser, British Military Government, Berlin, since 1976; *b* 1 April 1935; *s* of Thomas Steuart Gladstone and Muriel Irene Heron Gladstone; *m* 1961, April (*née* Brunner); one *s* one *d*. *Educ:* Eton; Christ Church, Oxford (BA History). National Service, 1954-56; Oxford Univ., 1956-59. Annan, Dexter & Co. (Chartered Accountants), 1959-60; FO, 1960; MECAS, Lebanon, 1960-62; Bahrain, 1962-63; FO, 1963-65; Bonn, 1965-69; FCO, 1969-72; Cairo, 1972-75. *Recreations:* squash, tennis, music, theatre, cinema, dreaming, carpentry, gardening. *Address:* 2 Mountfort Terrace, N1 1TT. *T:* 01-607 8200.

GLADSTONE, Sir (Erskine) William, 7th Bt *cr* 1846; DL; Chief Scout of United Kingdom and Overseas Branches, since 1972; *b* 29 Oct. 1925; *s* of Charles Andrew Gladstone, (6th Bt), and Isla Margaret, *d* of late Sir Walter Erskine Crum; *S* father, 1968; *m* 1962, Rosamund Anne, *yr d* of late Major A. Hambro; two *s* one *d*. *Educ:* Eton; Christ Church, Oxford. Served RNVR, 1943-46. Asst Master at Shrewsbury, 1949-50, and at Eton, 1951-61; Head Master of Lancing Coll., 1961-69. DL Flintshire, 1969, Clwyd, 1974; Alderman, Flintshire CC, 1970-74. Chm., Rep. Body of Church in Wales, 1977. *Publications:* various school textbooks. *Recreations:* reading history, shooting, gardening. *Heir: s* Charles Angus Gladstone, *b* 11 April 1964. *Address:* Hawarden Castle, Deeside, Clwyd. *T:* Hawarden 532210; Fasque, Laurencekirk, Kincardineshire. *T:* Fettercairn 341.

GLADSTONE, Adm. Sir Gerald Vaughan, GBE 1960; KCB 1957 (CB 1954); *b* 3 Oct. 1901; *yr s* of J. E. Gladstone, Llandaff and Braunton; *m* 1925, Marjorie (Justine), (*d* 1964), *e d* of J. Goring Johnston, NZ; two *s* one *d*; *m* 1966, Mrs Dora Brown (*née* Stewart), *widow* of Capt. (E) W. D. Brown, DSC, RN. *Educ:* RN Colls Osborne and Dartmouth. Midshipman, HMS Tiger, 1917; Rear-Adm. 1952; Vice-Controller of the Navy, 1952-53; Flag Officer Second in Command Far Eastern Station and Flag Officer Comdg 5th Cruiser Sqdn, 1953-55; Vice-Adm. 1955; Comdr, Allied Naval Forces, Northern Europe, 1955-57; Admiral, 1958; Comdr-in-Chief, Far East Station, 1957-60, retired 1960. *Address:* Forsters, Bradpole, Bridport, Dorset.

GLADSTONE, Sir William; *see* Gladstone, Sir E. W.

GLADWIN, Derek Oliver, OBE 1977; JP; Regional Secretary (Southern Region), since 1970, and Vice Chairman, General and Municipal Workers' Union; Member: Post Office Corporation, since 1972; British Aerospace, since 1977; *b* 6 June 1930; *s* of Albert Victor Gladwin and Ethel Gladwin (*née* Oliver); *m* 1956, Ruth Ann Pinion; one *s*. *Educ:* Carr Lane Junior Sch., Grimsby; Wintringham Grammar Sch.; Ruskin Coll., Oxford; London Sch. of Economics. British Railways, Grimsby, 1946-52; fishing industry, Grimsby, 1952-56; Regional Officer 1956-63, Nat. Industrial Officer 1963-70, Gen. and Municipal Workers' Union. Member: Adv. Council on the Penal System; English Tourist Bd; Exec. Cttee, Industrial Soc.; Fabian Soc.; Labour Party's Conf. Arrangements Cttee (Chm.); Duke of Edinburgh's 2nd Commonwealth Conf., Canada, 1962; Trustee, Duke of Edinburgh's Commonwealth Study Conf. (UK Fund). JP Surrey, 1969. *Address:* 2 Friars Rise, Ashwood Road, Woking, Surrey; (office) Cooper House, 205 Hook Road, Chessington, Surrey KT9 1EP *T:* 01-397 8881.

GLADWYN, 1st Baron *cr* 1960; **Hubert Miles Gladwyn Jebb,** GCMG 1954 (KCMG 1949; CMG 1942); GCVO 1957; CB 1947; Grand Croix de la Légion d'Honneur, 1957; Member, Parliament of Europe, 1973-76 (Vice President, Political Committee); *b* 25 April 1900; *s* of late Sydney Jebb, Firbeck Hall, Yorks; *m* 1929, Cynthia, *d* of Sir Saxton Noble, 3rd Bart; one *s* two *d*. *Educ:* Eton; Magdalen Coll., Oxon. 1st in History, Oxford, 1922. Entered Diplomatic Service, 1924; served in Tehran, Rome, and Foreign Office; Private Sec. to Parliamentary Under-Sec. of State, 1929-31; Private Sec. to Permanent Under-Sec. of State, 1937-40; appointed to Ministry of Economic Warfare with temp. rank of Asst Under-Sec., Aug. 1940; Acting Counsellor in Foreign Office, 1941; Head of Reconstruction Dept, 1942; Counsellor, 1943, in that capacity attended the Conferences of Quebec, Cairo, Tehran, Dunbarton Oaks, Yalta, San Francisco and Potsdam. Executive Sec. of Preparatory Commission of the United Nations (Aug. 1945) with temp. rank of Minister; Acting Sec.-Gen. of UN, Feb. 1946; Deputy to Foreign Sec. on Conference of Foreign Ministers, March 1946; Assistant Under-Sec. of State and United Nations Adviser, 1946-47; UK rep. on Brussels Treaty Permanent Commission with personal rank of Ambassador, April 1948; Dep. Under-Sec., 1949-50; Permanent Representative of the UK to the United Nations, 1950-54; British Ambassador to France, 1954-60, retired. Dep. Leader of Liberal Party in House of Lords, and Liberal Spokesman on Foreign Affairs and Defence,

1965-. Vice-Chm., European Movement; former Pres., Atlantic Treaty Assoc.; Chm., Campaign for European Political Community; Mem., Parly Delegns to Council of Europe and WEU Assemblies, 1966-73. Hon. DCL: Oxford; Syracuse, NY 1954; Essex 1974; Hon. Fellow Magdalen Coll. *Publications:* Is Tension Necessary?, 1959; Peaceful Co-existence, 1962; The European Idea, 1966; Half-way to 1984, 1967; De Gaulle's Europe, or, Why the General says No, 1969; Europe after de Gaulle, 1970; The Memoirs of Lord Gladwyn, 1972. *Recreations:* gardening, broadcasting, cooking, shooting and most other forms of sport. *Heir: s* Hon. Miles Alvery Gladwyn Jebb [*b* 3 March 1930. *Educ:* Eton and Oxford]. *Address:* Bramfield Hall, Halesworth, Suffolk. *T:* Bramfield 241; 62 Whitehall Court, SW1. *T:* 01-930 3160. *Club:* Garrick. *See also* H. S. Thomas.

GLAMIS, Lord; Michael Fergus Bowes Lyon; *b* 7 June 1957; *s* and *heir* of 17th Earl of Strathmore and Kinghorne, *qv*. Page of Honour to HM Queen Elizabeth The Queen Mother, 1971-73. *Address:* Glamis Castle, Forfar, Angus.

GLANCY, Dr James Edward McAlinney; Senior Principal Medical Officer, Department of Health and Social Security, 1972-76; *b* 9 Feb. 1914; *s* of Dr Michael James Glancy and Anne Teresa McAlinney; *m* 1945, Margaret Mary Redgrove; one *s* one *d*. *Educ:* Blackrock Coll., Dublin; National Univ. of Ireland (MD). FRCP, FRCPsych. Consultant Psychiatrist: Goodmayes Hosp., 1948-; King George Hosp., Ilford, and Barking Hosp., 1970-; Whipps Cross Hosp., 1948-72; Consultant in Clinical Neurophysiology, Oldchurch Hosp., Romford, 1950-60; Physician Supt, Goodmayes Hosp., 1960-72. *Recreations:* painting, photography, gardening. *Address:* 107 Barley Lane, Ilford, Essex IG3 8XQ.

GLANDINE, Viscount; Richard James Graham-Toler; *b* 5 March 1967; *s* and *heir* of 6th Earl of Norbury, *qv*.

GLANUSK, 4th Baron, *cr* 1899; **David Russell Bailey;** Bt, *cr* 1852; Lieutenant-Commander RN (retired); *b* 19 Nov. 1917; *o s* of late Hon. Herbert Crawshay Bailey, 4th *s* of 1st Baron Glanusk and late Kathleen Mary, *d* of Sir Shirley Harris Salt, 3rd Bt; *S* cousin 1948; *m* 1941, Lorna Dorothy, *o d* of late Capt. E. C. H. N. Andrews, MBE, RA; one *s* one *d*. *Educ:* Orley Farm Sch., Harrow; Eton. RN, 1935-51. Managing Dir, Wandel & Goltermann (UK) Ltd, 1966-; Chm., Hatfield Instruments Ltd. *Heir: s* Hon. Christopher Russell Bailey [*b* 18 March 1942; *m* 1974, Frances, *d* of Air Chief Marshal Sir Douglas Lowe, *qv*]. *Address:* Sawmill House, Park Farm Road, High Wycombe, Bucks.

GLANVILLE, Alec William; Assistant Under-Secretary of State, Probation and After-care Department, Home Office, since 1975; *b* 20 Jan. 1921; *y s* of Frank Foster and Alice Glanville; *m* 1941, Lilian Kathleen Hetherton; one *s* one *d*. *Educ:* Portsmouth Northern Secondary Sch.; Portsmouth Municipal Coll. War service, RAMC, 1939-46. Exchequer and Audit Dept, 1939-47; General, Criminal, Police and Probation and After-care Depts, Home Office, 1947- (seconded to Cabinet Office, 1956-58); Private Sec. to Permanent Under Sec. of State, 1949-50; Principal Private Sec. to Sec. of State, 1960-63; Sec., Interdepartmental Cttee on Mentally Abnormal Offenders, 1972-75. *Address:* Greenham Cottage, Perry Hill, Worplesdon, Guildford, Surrey. *Club:* Royal Commonwealth Society.

GLANVILLE, Brian Lester; author and journalist since 1949; *b* 24 Sept. 1931; *s* of James Arthur Glanville and Florence Glanville (*née* Manches); *m* 1959, Elizabeth Pamela de Boer (*née* Manasse), *d* of Fritz Manasse and Grace Manasse (*née* Howden); two *s* two *d*. *Educ:* Newlands Sch.; Charterhouse. Joined Sunday Times (football correspondent), 1958. *Publications:* The Reluctant Dictator, 1952; Henry Sows the Wind, 1954; Along the Arno, 1956; The Bankrupts, 1958; After Rome, Africa, 1959; A Bad Streak, 1961; Diamond, 1962; The Director's Wife, 1963; The King of Hackney Marshes, 1965; A Second Home, 1965; A Roman Marriage, 1966; The Artist Type, 1967; The Olympian, 1969; A Cry of Crickets, 1970; The Financiers, 1972; The Thing He Loves, 1973; The Comic, 1974; The Dying of the Light, 1976. *Recreation:* playing football. *Address:* 160 Holland Park Avenue, W11. *T:* 01-603 6908. *Club:* Chelsea Casuals.

GLANVILLE BROWN, W(illiam); *see* Brown, W. G.

GLASER, Prof. Donald Arthur; Professor of Physics and Molecular Biology, University of California, since 1960; *b* 21 Sept. 1926; *s* of William Joseph and Lena Glaser. *Educ:* Case Institute of Technology; California Inst. of Technology. Prof., University of Michigan, 1949-59. Henry Russel Award, 1955;

Charles Vernon Boys Prize, 1958; Hon. ScD (Case Inst.), 1959; Amer. Phys. Soc. Prize, 1959; Nobel Prize, 1960. National Science Foundation Fellow, 1961; Guggenheim Fellow, 1961-62; Research Biophysicist (Miller Research Professorship, University of Calif, 1962-64); Mem. National Academy of Sciences (USA), 1962; Fellow Amer. Physical Soc.; Fellow Amer. Assoc. for Advancement of Science; Mem. NY Acad. of Science. *Publications*: articles in Physical Review, Bulletin of Amer. Phys. Soc., Nuovo Cimento, Proc. 5th and 7th Annual Rochester Confs, Proc. CERN, Proc. NY Acad. Sci., Symposium on High Energy Accelerators and Pion Physics, 1956, Proc. 2nd UN Geneva Conf., 1958, Handbuch der Physik, Proc. Kiev Conf., 1959, Jl Molecular Biol., etc. Contributor to Yearbook of the Physical Society, London, 1958. *Address*: 229 Molecular Biology-Virus Laboratory, University of California, Berkeley, Calif 94720, USA.

GLASGOW, 9th Earl of, *cr* 1703; **David William Maurice Boyle**, CB 1963; DSC 1941; Baron Boyle, 1699; Viscount of Kelburn, 1703; Baron Fairlie (UK), 1897; Rear-Admiral, retired; *b* 24 July 1910; *e s* of 8th Earl of Glasgow, DSO; *S* father, 1963; *m* 1st, 1937, Dorothea (marriage dissolved, 1962), *o d* of Sir Archibald Lyle, 2nd Bart; one *s* two *d*; 2nd, 1962, Vanda, the Hon. Lady Wrixon-Becher, 2nd *d* of 4th Baron Vivian. *Educ*: Eton. Served War of 1939-45 in Atlantic, Channel, Arctic and Far East (despatches, DSC). Comdr, 1945; Capt., 1952; Capt. of the Fleet, Home Fleet, 1957-59; Commodore, RN Barracks, Portsmouth, 1959-61; Rear-Adm., 1961; Flag Officer, Malta, 1961-63; retd Sept. 1963. Mem. of the Royal Co. of Archers (Queen's Body Guard for Scotland). *Recreations*: shooting, golf, travel. *Heir*: *s* Viscount of Kelburn, *qv*. *Address*: Kelburn Castle, Fairlie, Ayrshire. *T*: Fairlie 204.
See also Viscount Caldecote, Earl of Cranbrook.

GLASGOW, Archbishop of, (RC), since 1974; **Most Rev. Thomas J. Winning**, DCL, STL. Formerly parish priest, St Luke, Braidhurst, Motherwell; Auxiliary Bishop of Glasgow, 1971-74; parish priest, Our Holy Redeemer's, Clydebank, 1972-74. *Address*: 40 Newlands Road, Glasgow G43 2JD.

GLASGOW, Auxiliary Bishops of, (RC); *see* Devine, Rt Rev. J., Renfrew, Rt Rev. C.McD.

GLASGOW and GALLOWAY, Bishop of, since 1974; **Rt. Rev. Frederick Goldie**, MA, BD; *b* 1 Sept. 1914; *s* of John and Maria Goldie, Glasgow; *m* 1940, Margaret Baker McCrae, MA; one *s* one *d*. *Educ*: Strathbungo Academy, Glasgow; Hatfield Coll., Durham; New Coll. and Coates Hall, Edinburgh. Open Exhibnr, Hatfield Schol., LTh, BA 1938, Durham; BD Edinburgh, 1939; MA Durham, 1946. Curate at Govan, 1938; Rector at Hillington, Glasgow, 1939-49; Lecturer at Theological Coll., Edinburgh, 1940-63; Rector at Dumbarton, 1949-63; Canon of St Mary's Cathedral, Glasgow, 1956; Dean of Glasgow and Galloway, 1963-74; Rector of St Margaret's, Glasgow, 1963-74. *Publication*: A History of the Episcopal Church in Scotland, 1950, rev. edn 1976. *Recreations*: reading, walking. *Address*: Bishop's House, 14 Clevedon Crescent, Glasgow G12 0PB. *T*: 041-339 0554.

GLASGOW and GALLOWAY, Dean of; *see* Singer, Very Rev. S. S.

GLASGOW, Provost of (St Mary's Cathedral); *see* Mansbridge, Very Rev. H. C.

GLASGOW, Mary Cecilia, CBE 1949 (MBE 1942); BA; Director (formerly Chairman), Mary Glasgow Holdings Ltd, Educational Publishers (firm founded 1957); *b* 24 May 1905; *d* of late Edwin Glasgow. *Educ*: Lady Margaret Hall, Oxford (Hons Sch. of French Language and Literature). Inspector of Schs, Bd of Education, 1933-39; Sec.-Gen., The Arts Council of Great Britain (formerly CEMA), 1939-51. Chm., The Opera Players. Chm., Institute of Linguists, 1975- (Diamond Jubilee Medal, 1971). Officier, l'Ordre National du Mérite, 1977 (Chevalier, 1968). *Address*: 5 Justice Walk, Chelsea, SW3 5DE. *T*: 01-352 7457; Entrechaux (Vaucluse), France.

GLASS, Prof. David V., FRS 1971; FBA 1964; Professor of Sociology, University of London, at London School of Economics, since 1948; *b* 2 Jan. 1911; *m* 1942, Ruth Durant (*see* Mrs Ruth Glass); one *s* one *d*. *Educ*: Elementary Sch.; Raine's Grammar Sch.; London Sch. of Economics, London Univ. Chairman, Population Investigation Cttee; Past Pres., British Soc. for Population Studies; Hon. Pres., International Union for Scientific Study of Population; Mem., International Statistical Institute. For. Hon. Mem., Amer. Acad. Arts and Sciences, 1971; For. Associate, Nat. Acad. of Sciences (USA), 1973. Hon. DSc University of Michigan, 1967; Hon. DSocSci Edinburgh,

1973; Hon. DScEcon Queen's Univ. Belfast, 1974. *Publications*: The Town in a Changing World, 1935; The Struggle for Population, 1936; Population Policies and Movements in Europe, 1940; (ed) Introduction to Malthus, 1953; (ed) Social Mobility in Britain, 1954; (with E. Grebenik) The Trend and Pattern of Fertility in Great Britain, 1954; (ed) The University Teaching of Social Sciences: Demography, 1957; Latin American Seminar on Population: Report, 1958; Society: Approaches and Problems for Study, 1962 (co-ed); Differential Fertility, Ability and Educational Objectives, 1962; (ed jtly), Population in History, 1965; (ed jtly) Population and Social Change, 1972; Numbering the People, 1973; papers in Population Studies (Jt Editor), British Journal of Sociology (Jt Editor), Proc. Royal Soc., Phil. Trans. Royal Soc. *Address*: 10 Palace Gardens Terrace, W8.

GLASS, Ven. Edward Brown; Archdeacon of Man, since 1964; Rector of Kirk Andreas, Isle of Man, since 1964; *b* 1 July 1913; *s* of William and Phoebe Harriet Glass; *m* 1940, Frances Katharine Calvert; one *s* two *d*. *Educ*: King William's Coll., IoM; Durham Univ. (MA). Deacon 1937, priest 1938, dio. Manchester; Curate: St Mary's, Wardleworth, Rochdale, 1937; Gorton Parish Church, Manchester, 1937-42; Vicar: St John's, Hopwood, Heywood, Manchester, 1942-51; St Olave's, Ramsey, IoM, 1951-55; Castletown, IoM 1955-64. Sec., Diocesan Convocation, 1958-64; Proctor for Clergy, Convocation of York, 1959-64; Member, Church Assembly and General Synod, 1959-; Warden of Diocesan Readers, 1969-. *Recreations*: gardening, ornithology, touring in Norway. *Address*: Kirk Andreas Rectory, Isle of Man. *T*: Kirk Andreas 289.

GLASS, Sir Leslie (Charles), KCMG 1967 (CMG 1958); HM Diplomatic Service, retired; Chairman, Anglo-Romanian Bank, since 1973; *b* 28 May 1911; *s* of Ernest Leslie and Kate Glass; *m* 1st, 1942, Pamela Mary Gage; two *s* one *d*; 2nd, 1957, Betty Lindsay Hoyer-Millar (*née* Macpherson); two step *d*. *Educ*: Bradfield Coll.; Trinity Coll., Oxford; Sch. of Oriental Studies, London Univ. Indian Civil Service, 1934; Asst Warden, Burma Oilfields, 1937; Settlement Officer, Mandalay, 1939; Far Eastern Bureau Min. of Inf., 1942; Lt-Col Head of Burma Section, Psychological Warfare Div., SEAC; Head of Information Div., Burma Mil. Admin, 1943; Sec. Information Dept, Govt of Burma, 1945; Comr of Settlements and Land Records, Govt of Burma, 1946; joined Foreign Office as 1st Sec. (Oriental Sec.), HM Embassy, Rangoon, 1947; Foreign Office, 1949-50; Head of Chancery, HM Legation Budapest (Chargé d'Affaires, 1951-52), 1950-53; Head of Information Div., British Middle East Office, 1953; seconded to Staff of Governor of Cyprus, 1955-56; Counsellor and Consul-Gen., British Embassy, Washington, 1957-58; Dir-Gen. of British Information Services in the US and Information Minister, British Embassy, Washington 1959-61; Minister employed in the Foreign Office, 1961; Asst Under-Sec. of State, Foreign Office, 1962-65; Ambassador to Romania, 1965-67; Ambassador and Dep. Permanent UK Representative to UN, 1967-69; High Comr in Nigeria, 1969-71, retired; re-employed FCO, 1971-72. Civil Service Selection Board's Panel of Chairmen, 1973-; Governing Council, Bradfield Coll., 1973-. Trustee, Thomson Foundn, 1974-. *Recreation*: fishing. *Address*: Stone House, Ivington, Leominster, Herefordshire. *T*: Ivington 204. *Club*: East India, Devonshire, Sports and Public Schools.

GLASS, Ruth, MA; Director, Centre for Urban Studies, University College London, since 1958; *d* of Eli and Lilly Lazarus; *m* 1st, 1935, Henry Durant (marr. diss. 1941); 2nd, 1942, David V. Glass, *qv*; one *s* one *d*. *Educ*: Geneva and Berlin Univs; London Sch. of Economics; Columbia Univ., NY. Sen. Research Officer, Bureau of Applied Social Research, Columbia Univ., 1940-42; Res. Off., Min. of Town and Country Planning, 1948-50; Hon. Res. Associate, UC London, 1951-71, Vis. Prof., 1972-; Dir, Social Research Unit, Dept of Town Planning, UC London, 1951-58. Hon. FRIBA, 1972. *Publications*: Watling, A Social Survey, 1939; (ed) The Social Background of a Plan, 1948; Urban Sociology in Great Britain, 1955; Newcomers, The West Indians in London, 1960; London's Housing Needs, 1965; Housing in Camden, 1969; contributor to: Town Planning Review; Architectural Review; Population Studies; Internat. Social Science Jl; Monthly Review; Trans. World Congresses of Sociology, etc. *Address*: 10 Palace Gardens Terrace, W8; Eastway Cottage, Walberswick, Suffolk.

GLASSE, Alfred Onslow, CMG 1969; OBE 1952; MC 1917; CEng, FIEE, FNZIE; electrical engineer, New Zealand, retired; *b* 1889; *s* of William Stacey Glasse; *m* 1920, Ellen Emma Griffiths (*d* 1966); two *d*. *Educ*: Otago High Sch. Auckland Electric Power Bd, 1922-57 (Chief Engr, 1925-54, Cons. Engr 1954-57); Cons. Engr other Bds, etc, 1956-66. Member: Auckland City Council, 1956- (Dep. Mayor, 1962-70); Nat. Roads Bd, 1960-63; Auck. Harbour Bridge Authority, 1963-76;

Auck. Metrop. Drainage Bd, 1957-64; Auck. Regional Planning Authority; Auck. War Memorial Mus. Council; Auck. Techn. Inst. Bd; St John Assoc. Past Pres., NZ Instn of Engrs. Also, as Pres. or on Council, numerous other Bds and Cttees. *Publications:* technical papers to various engineering jls. *Address:* 9 Eastbourne Road, Auckland 5, New Zealand. *Club:* Officers' (Auckland).

GLASSE, Thomas Henry, CMG 1961; MVO 1955; MBE 1946; retired as Counsellor in HM Diplomatic Service, and Head of Protocol Department, Foreign Office (1957-61); *b* 14 July 1898; *s* of late Thomas and Harriette Glasse; *m* 1935, Elsie May Dyter (*d* 1965); no *c*; *m* 1966, Ethel Alice Needham. *Educ:* Latymer Foundation Upper Sch., Hammersmith. Entered Civil Service as a Boy Clerk, 1914. Army Service, 1/10th Bn Mx Regt, 1917-19. Joined the Foreign Office, 1921. Delegate of United Kingdom to Vienna Conference on Diplomatic Relations, 1961. *Recreations:* books, music, garden, travel. *Address:* 72 Lynch Road, Farnham, Surrey. *T:* Farnham 6662. *Club:* Travellers'.

GLASSPOLE, Florizel Augustus; Governor-General of Jamaica, since 1974; *b* Kingston, Jamaica, 25 Sept. 1909; *s* of late Rev. Theophilus A. Glasspole (Methodist Minister) and Florence (*née* Baxter); *m* 1934, Ina Josephine Kinlocke; *Educ:* Central British Elementary Sch.; Wolmer's Sch.; Ruskin Coll., Oxford. British TUC Schol., 1946-47. Accountant (practising), 1932-44. Gen. Sec: Jamaica United Clerks Assoc., 1937-48; Jamaica TUC, 1939-52, resigned; Pres. Jamaica Printers & Allied Workers Union, 1942-48; etc. Workers rep. on Govt Bds, etc, 1942-. Mem. Bd of Governors Inst. of Jamaica, 1944-57; Mem., Kingston Sch. Bd, 1944-. MHR (PNP) for Kingston Eastern and Port Royal, 1944; Vice-Pres., People's National Party; Minister of Labour, Jamaica, 1955-57; Leader of the House, 1955-62; Minister of Educn, 1957-62; A Rep. for Jamaica, on Standing Fedn Cttee, West Indies Federation, 1953-; Mem. House of Reps Cttee which prepared Independence of Jamaica Constitution; Mem. Delegn to London which completed Constitution document, 1962. *Recreations:* gardening, agriculture, cricket. *Address:* The Residence of the Governor-General, Kingston, Jamaica.

GLAUERT, Audrey Marion, (Mrs David Franks); JP; Head of Electron Microscopy Department, Strangeways Research Laboratory, Cambridge, since 1956; Fellow of Clare Hall, Cambridge, since 1966; *b* 21 Dec. 1925; *d* of late Hermann Glauert, FRS and Muriel Glauert (*née* Barker); *m* 1959, David Franks, PhD; no *c*. *Educ:* Perse Sch. for Girls, Cambridge; Bedford Coll., Univ. of London. BSc 1946, MSc 1947, London; MA Cantab 1967, ScD Cantab 1970. Asst Lectr in Physics, Royal Holloway Coll., Univ. of London, 1947-50; Mem. Scientific Staff, Strangeways Res. Lab., Cambridge, Sir Halley Stewart Research Fellow, 1950-. Chairman: British Joint Cttee for Electron Microscopy, 1968-72; Fifth European Congress on Electron Microscopy, 1972; Pres., Royal Microscopical Soc., 1970-72, Hon. Fellow, 1973. JP Cambridge, 1975. *Publications:* Fixation Dehydration and Embedding of Biological Specimens, 1974; papers on cell and molecular biology in scientific jls. *Recreation:* sailing. *Address:* 29 Cow Lane, Fulbourn, Cambridge. *T:* Cambridge 880463; Strangeways Research Laboratory, Wort's Causeway, Cambridge. *T:* Cambridge 43231.

GLAVES-SMITH, Frank William, CB 1975; Deputy Director-General of Fair Trading, since 1973; *b* 27 Sept. 1919; *m* 1941, Audrey Glaves; one *s* one *d*. *Educ:* Malet Lambert High Sch., Hull. Inland Revenue, 1938; served with Army, 1940-46. Called to Bar, Middle Temple, 1947. Board of Trade, 1947; Princ. Private Sec. to Pres. of Bd of Trade, 1952-57; Asst Secretary: HM Treasury, 1957-60; Cabinet Office, 1960-62; Bd of Trade, 1962-65; Under-Sec., BoT, 1965-69, Dept of Employment and Productivity, 1969-70, DTI, 1970-73. Mem., Export Guarantees Adv. Council, 1971-73, Dep. Sec., 1975-. *Recreations:* croquet, gardening, sailing. *Address:* Leckhampstead West, Reigate Road, Reigate, Surrey. *T:* Reigate 44070. *Club:* Reform.

GLAVIN, William Francis; Managing Director and Chief Operations Executive, Rank Xerox Ltd, since 1974; *b* 29 March 1932; *m* 1955, Cecily McClatchy; three *s* four *d*. *Educ:* College of the Holy Cross, Worcester, Mass (BS); Wharton Graduate Sch. (MBA). Vice-Pres., Operations, Service Bureau Corp. (subsid. of IBM), 1968-70; Exec. Vice-Pres., Xerox Data Services, 1970; Pres., Xerox Data Systems, 1970-72; Gp Vice-Pres., Xerox Corp., and Pres., Business Development Gp, 1972-74. *Recreations:* golf, music, tennis. *Address:* 56 Cumberland Terrace, NW1 4HJ.

GLAZEBROOK, His Honour Francis Kirkland; a Circuit Judge (formerly a Judge of County Courts), 1950-72; *b* 18 Feb. 1903;

3rd *s* of late William Rimington Glazebrook; *m* 1930, Winifred Mary Elizabeth Davison; one *s* two *d*. *Educ:* Marlborough Coll.; Trinity Coll., Cambridge; Harvard Univ., USA. Called to the Bar, Inner Temple, 1928; Practised in the Common Law. Served War in Army, 1939-45. Croix de Guerre (France); Bronze Star (USA). *Recreations:* fishing, gardening, golf. *Address:* Rectory Park, Horsmonden, Kent.

GLAZEBROOK, Mark; *see* Glazebrook, R. M.

GLAZEBROOK, Reginald Field; formerly Director: Liverpool & London & Globe Insurance Co. Ltd; Liverpool Warehousing Co. Ltd; Liverpool Grain Storage & Transit Co. Ltd; Gandy Belt Ltd; *b* 23 April 1899; *s* of late William Rimington Glazebrook; *m* 1928, Daisy Isabel Broad; four *s*. *Educ:* Marlborough. Served European War, Lieut RFC, 1916-18. Cotton Merchant; Past Pres. Liverpool Cotton Assoc. *Recreations:* fishing, shooting, gardening. *Address:* Brynbella, Tremeirchion, St Asaph, Clwyd LL17 0UE.
See also R . M . Glazebrook .

GLAZEBROOK, (Reginald) Mark; Gallery Director, San José State University, since 1977; writer on art and arranger of exhibitions; *b* 25 June 1936; *s* of Reginald Field Glazebrook, *qv*; *m* 1st, 1965, Elizabeth Lea Claridge (marr. diss., 1969); one *d*; 2nd, 1974, Wanda Barbara O'Neill (*née* Osińska); one *d*. *Educ:* Eton; Pembroke Coll., Cambridge (MA); Slade School of Fine Art. Worked at Arts Council, 1961-64; Lectr at Maidstone Coll. of Art, 1965-67; Art Critic, London Magazine, 1967-68; Dir, Whitechapel Art Gall., 1969-71; Head of Modern English Paintings and Drawings, P. and D. Colnaghi & Co. Ltd, 1973-75. FRSA 1971. *Publications:* (comp.) Artists and Architecture of Bedford Park 1875-1900 (catalogue), 1967; (comp.) David Hockney: paintings, prints and drawings 1960-1970 (catalogue), 1970; Edward Wadsworth 1889-1949: paintings, prints and drawings (catalogue), 1974; (introduction) John Armstrong 1893-1973 (catalogue), 1975; (introduction) John Tunnard (catalogue), 1976; articles in: Studio International, London Magazine. *Recreations:* travelling, theatre, tennis, swimming. *Address:* The Gallery Director, Department of Art, San José State University, San Jose, Calif 95192, USA. *Clubs:* Lansdowne, Chelsea Arts.

GLEADELL, Maj.-Gen. Paul, CB 1959; CBE 1951; DSO 1945; *b* 23 Feb. 1910; *s* of late Captain William Henry and Katherine Gleadell; *m* 1937, Mary Montgomerie Lind, *d* of late Col Alexander Gordon Lind, DSO, and Mrs Lind; two *s* two *d*. *Educ:* Downside Sch.; Sandhurst. Commissioned in The Devonshire Regt, 1930 (Adjutant 1936-39); DAAG, Rawalpindi Dist, 1940; Staff Coll. (Quetta), 1941; Brigade Major 80th Indian Bde, 1942; Commanded 12th Bn The Devonshire Regt (6th Airborne Div.), 1944-45; Secretariat, Offices of the Cabinet and Ministry of Defence, 1945-48; Joint Services Staff Coll., 1948; Col (G S Intelligence), GHQ Far East Land Forces, 1949-51; comd 1st Bn The Devonshire Regt (3rd Inf. Div.), 1951-53; Senior Army Instructor, Joint Services Staff Coll., 1953-55; Brigade Comdr, 24th Independent Infantry Brigade, 1955-56; Imperial Defence Coll., 1957; Chief of Staff to Dir of Operations, Cyprus, 1958-59; in command 44th Div. (TA) and Home Counties District, and Dep. Constable of Dover Castle, 1959-62; Dir of Infantry, 1962-65; Clerk to Governors, Rookesbury Park School, 1966-72, Governor, 1973-. French Croix de Guerre with Palm, 1944. *Address:* Botley House, Botley, Hants SO3 2EA. *Clubs:* Naval and Military, Challoner.

GLEAVE, Ruth Marjory; Headmistress, Bradford Girls' Grammar School, since 1976; *b* 29 May 1926; *d* of Harold Gleave and Alice Lillian Dean. *Educ:* Birkenhead High Sch., GPDST; Univ. of Liverpool (BA Hons Geography, DipEd). Head of Geography Dept, Wade Deacon Girls' Grammar Sch., Widnes, 1947-54; Head of Geography Dept and Deputy Head, Withington Girls' Sch., Manchester, 1954-60; Head, Fairfield High Sch., Droylsden, Manchester, 1960-75. *Recreations:* travel, natural history, outdoor activities, the arts—literature and art. *Address:* Bradford Girls' Grammar School, Squire Lane, Bradford BD9 6RB.

GLEDHILL, Alan, MA Cantab, LLD London; Professor Emeritus of Oriental Laws, University of London, Hon. Fellow, School of Oriental and African Studies; *b* 28 Oct. 1895; *s* of late O. Gledhill, Redroofs, Wells Road, Wolverhampton; *m* 1st, 1922, Mercy (*d* 1963), *d* of Victor Harvey, Calcutta; two *s* one *d*; 2nd, 1967, Marion Glover, *d* of late C. W. Watson, Santa Cruz, Argentine. *Educ:* Fishguard Grammar Sch.; Rugby; Corpus Christi Coll., Cambridge; Gray's Inn. Served European War, 1914-18, Lieut Monmouthshire Regt 1915-16; joined ICS 1920; District and Sessions Judge, 1927; Special Judge, Tharrawaddy, 1930-33; Capt. Army in India R of O 1931-34; War of 1939-45:

Burma Campaign, 1942; Dep. Comr, Cachar, Assam, 1942-43; Actg Lieut-Col, Army in Burma R of O, Dep. Chief Judicial Officer, British Military Administration, Burma, 1944-45 (despatches); Actg Judge High Court Rangoon, Oct. 1945; Puisne Judge, 1946-48; Lecturer in Indian and Burmese Law, Sch. of Oriental and African Studies, 1948-54; Reader in Oriental Laws, 1954-55; Prof. of Oriental Laws, University of London, 1955-63; Lectr in Hindu Law, Inns of Court Sch. of Law, 1955-67. *Publications:* The British Commonwealth: The Development of its Laws and Constitutions, Vol 6, The Republic of India, 1951 (2nd edn, 1964). Vol. 8, The Islamic Republic of Pakistan, 1957 (2nd edn, 1967); Fundamental Rights in India, 1955; The Penal Codes of Northern Nigeria and the Sudan, 1963. *Recreations:* swimming, walking. *Address:* 24 Chichester Court, Church Farm Garden Estate, Rustington, Sussex. *Club:* Royal Commonwealth Society.

GLEDHILL, Anthony John, GC 1967; Detective Sergeant, Metropolitan Police, since 1976; *b* 10 March 1938; *s* of Harold Victor and Marjorie Edith Gledhill; *m* 1958, Marie Lilian Hughes; one *s* one *d. Educ:* Doncaster Technical High Sch., Yorks. Accounts Clerk, Officers' Mess, RAF Bruggen, Germany, 1953-56. Metropolitan Police Cadet, 1956-57; Police Constable, Metropolitan Police, 1957-75. *Recreations:* football, carpentry. *Address:* 98 Pickhurst Lane, Hayes, Bromley, Kent. *T:* 01-462 4033. *Club:* No 4 District Metropolitan Police (Hayes, Kent).

GLEDSTANES, Elsie, RBA 1929 (ARBA 1923); portrait, figure and landscape painter; *d* of late Francis Garner Gledstanes, late mem. Stock Exchange Cttee. *Educ:* Eastbourne; Paris. Studied art at Paris, Slade Sch. and Byam Shaw, and Vicat Cole Sch. of Art; served in WRNS, 1917-18; London Auxiliary Ambulance Driver, 1939-45; WVS Transport, 1941-42; Driver Women's Legion, 1942-45; exhibited works in RA, RBA, RPS, NPS, International Soc. and in the Provinces; works in Imperial War Museum, etc. Mem. of Pastel Soc. FRSA. *Address:* 61 Campden Street, W8 7EL. *T:* 01-727 8663; Glan-y-Gors, Prenteg, Portmadoc. *T:* Portmadoc 2510.

GLEESON, Most Rev. James William; *see* Adelaide, Archbishop of, (RC).

GLEN, Sir Alexander (Richard), KBE 1967 (CBE 1964); DSC 1942 (and Bar, 1945); Chairman, British Tourist Authority, 1969-77; Director, British Transport Hotels, since 1977; Group Chairman, Anglo World Travel, since 1977; *b* 18 April 1912; *s* of late R. Bartlett Glen, Glasgow; *m* 1947, Baroness Zora de Collaert. *Educ:* Fettes Coll.; Balliol Coll., Oxford. BA, Hons Geography. Travelled on Arctic Expeditions, 1932-39; Leader, Oxford Univ. Arctic Expedition, 1935-36; Banking, New York and London, 1936-39. RNVR, 1939-59, Capt. 1955. Export Council for Europe; Dep. Chm., 1960-64; Chm., 1964-66. Member: BNEC, 1966-72; Board of BEA, 1964-70; Nat. Ports Council, 1966-70; Horserace Totalisator Bd, 1976-. Dir, BICC, 1964-70. Member: Adv. Council, V&A Museum, 1976-; Historic Buildings Council, 1976-. Awarded Cuthbert Peek Grant by RGS, 1933; Bruce Medal by RSE, 1938; Andrée Plaque by Royal Swedish Soc. for Anthropology and Geography, 1939; Patron's Gold Medal by RGS, 1940. Polar Medal (clasp Arctic 1935-36), 1942; Norwegian War Cross, 1943; Chevalier (1st Class), Order of St Olav, 1944; Czechoslovak War Cross, 1946. *Publications:* Young Men in the Arctic, 1935; Under the Pole Star, 1937; Footholds Against a Whirlwind (autobiog.), 1975. *Recreations:* travel, ski-ing, sailing. *Address:* Stanton Court, Stanton, Glos. *Clubs:* Travellers', City of London; Explorers (NY).

GLEN, Archibald; Solicitor; *b* 3 July 1909; *m* 1938, Phyllis Mary; one *s* two *d. Educ:* Melville Coll., Edinburgh. Admitted Solicitor, 1932. Town Clerk: Burnley, Lancs, 1940-45; Southend-on-Sea, 1945-71. President: Soc. of City and Borough Clerks of the Peace, 1960; Soc. of Town Clerks, 1963-64; Assoc. of Town Clerks of British Commonwealth, 1963-64, etc. Lay Member, Press Council, 1969-75; Mem., Local Govt Staff Commn for England, 1972-76. Hon. Freeman, Southend-on-Sea, 1971. *Recreations:* golf, swimming. *Address:* Harbour House, 2 Drummochy, Lower Largo, Fife. *T:* Lundin Links 320724.

GLEN HAIG, Mrs Mary Alison, CBE 1977 (MBE 1971); Assistant District Administrator, South Hammersmith District, since 1974; *b* 12 July 1918; *d* of late Captain William James and Mary James; *m* 1943, Andrew Glen Haig (decd). *Educ:* Dame Alice Owen's Girls' School. Mem., Sports Council, 1966-; Chm., Central Council Physical Recreation, 1975-. Hon. Sec., Amateur Fencing Assoc., 1956-64, Pres., 1974-; Pres., Ladies' Amateur Fencing Union, 1964-74. British Ladies' Foil Champion, 1948-50. Olympic Games, 1948, 1952, 1956, 1960; British

Commonwealth Games Gold Medal, 1950-54, Bronze Medal, 1958; Captain, Ladies' Foil Team, 1950-57. *Recreations:* fencing, gardening. *Address:* 66 North End House, W14 0RX. *T:* 01-602 2504; 2 Old Cottages, Holyport Street, Holyport, near Maidenhead, Berks. *T:* Maidenhead 33421. *Club:* Lansdowne.

GLENAMARA, Baron *cr* 1977 (Life Peer), of Glenridding, Cumbria; **Edward Watson Short,** PC 1964; CH 1976; Chairman, Cable and Wireless Ltd, since 1976; *b* 17 Dec. 1912; *s* of Charles and Mary Short, Warcop, Westmorland; *m* 1941, Jennie, *d* of Thomas Sewell, Newcastle upon Tyne; one *s* one *d. Educ:* Bede College, Durham (LLB). Served War of 1939-45 and became Capt. in DLI. Headmaster of Princess Louise County Secondary School, Blyth, Northumberland, 1947; Leader of Labour Group on Newcastle City Council, 1950; MP (Lab) Newcastle upon Tyne Central, 1951-76; Opposition Whip (Northern Area), 1955-62; Dep. Chief Opposition Whip, 1962-64; Parly Sec. to the Treasury and Govt Chief Whip, 1964-66; Postmaster General, 1966-68; Sec. of State for Educn and Science, 1968-70; Lord Pres. of the Council and Leader, House of Commons, 1974-76. Dep. Leader, Labour Party, 1972-76. Hon. FCP, 1965. *Publications:* The Story of The Durham Light Infantry, 1944; The Infantry Instructor, 1946; Education in a Changing World, 1971; Birth to Five, 1974. *Recreation:* painting. *Address:* 4 Patterdale Gardens, Newcastle upon Tyne 7. *T:* Newcastle 661991; Glenridding, Cumbria.

GLENAPP, Viscount; (Kenneth) Peter (Lyle) Mackay, AIB; *b* 23 Jan. 1943; *er s and heir* of 3rd Earl of Inchcape, *qv*; *m* 1966, Georgina, *d* of S. C. Nisbet and of Mrs G. R. Sutton; two *d. Educ:* Eton. Late 2nd Lieut 9/12th Royal Lancers; business career. *Address:* c/o National Westminster Bank Ltd, 56 South Audley Street, W1.

GLENARTHUR, 4th Baron *cr* 1918; **Simon Mark Arthur;** Bt 1903; British Airways Helicopters Pilot, since 1976; *b* 7 Oct. 1944; *s* of 3rd Baron Glenarthur, OBE, and of Margaret, *d* of late Captain H. J. J. Howie; *S* father, 1976; *m* 1969, Susan, *yr d* of Comdr Hubert Wyndham Barry, RN; one *s* one *d. Educ:* Eton. Commissioned 10th Royal Hussars (PWO), 1963; Captain 1970; Major 1973; retired 1975. British Airways Helicopters Ltd, 1976. *Recreations:* shooting, hunting, flying. *Heir:* s Hon. Edward Alexander Arthur, *b* 9 April 1973. *Address:* Birch Hill, Torphins, Banchory, Kincardineshire. *T:* Torphins 287. *Club:* Cavalry and Guards.

GLENAVY, 3rd Baron, *cr* 1921; **Patrick Gordon Campbell,** Bt 1916; Author (as Patrick Campbell); Columnist, Sunday Times, since 1961; *b* 6 June 1913; *s* of 2nd Baron and Beatrice (née Elvery); *S* father, 1963; *m* 1st, 1941, Sylvia Willoughby Lee (marr. diss. 1947); 2nd, 1947, Cherry Lowson Munro (marr. diss. 1966); one *d*; 3rd, 1966, Mrs Vivienne Orme. *Educ:* Rossall; Pembroke, Oxford. Irish Marine Service, 1941-44. Columnist: Irish Times, 1944-47; Sunday Dispatch, 1947-59; Asst Editor, Lilliput Mag., 1947-53. Writes for TV and Screen. *Publications:* A Long Drink of Cold Water, 1950; A Short Trot with a Cultured Mind, 1952; Life in Thin Slices, 1954; Patrick Campbell's Omnibus, 1956; Come Here Till I Tell You, 1960; Constantly in Pursuit, 1962; How to become a Scratch Golfer, 1963; Brewing Up in the Basement, 1963; Rough Husbandry, 1965; My Life and Easy Times, 1967; A Bunch of New Roses, 1967; The Coarse of Events, 1968; The High Speed Gasworks, 1970; Fat Tuesday Tails, 1972; 35 Years on the Job, 1973. *Recreations:* golf and pleasure. *Heir:* b Hon. Michael Mussen Campbell, *b* 25 Oct. 1924. *Address:* La Tranche, Le Rouet 06, France.

GLENCONNER, 2nd Baron, *cr* 1911; **Christopher Grey Tennant;** Bt *cr* 1885; *b* 14 June 1899; *s* of 1st Baron and Pamela (*d* 1928), *d* of late Hon. Percy Scawen Wyndham (she *m* 2nd, 1922, 1st Viscount Grey); *S* father, 1920; *m* 1st, 1925, Pamela (who obtained a divorce, 1935), 2nd *d* of Sir Richard Paget, 2nd Bt; two *s*; 2nd, 1935, Elizabeth Mary, *er d* of late Lieut-Col E. G. H. Powell; one *s* two *d. Heir:* s Hon. Colin Christopher Paget Tennant, *qv. Address:* Rovinia, Liapades, Corfu, Greece. *Club:* White's.

GLENDAY, Dorothea Nonita; MA Oxon; Headmistress, Clifton High School for Girls, 1933-62; President, Association of Headmistresses, 1958-60. *Educ:* Girls' Grammar Sch., Bury, Lancs; St Hugh's Coll., Oxford. Hons Degree in English Language and Literature. Senior English Mistress at Francis Holland Church of England Sch., Graham Street, London, 1921-26. International hockey player. Headmistress of Rugby High Sch., 1926-33. Pres. West of England Branch of Assoc. of Headmistresses, 1946-48; Chm. of Assoc. of Independent and Direct-Grant Schs, 1949-51. *Publication:* Reluctant Revolutionaries, 1974. *Address:* 1 Hayward Road, Oxford. *Club:* University Women's.

GLENDEVON, 1st Baron, *cr* 1964; **John Adrian Hope**; PC 1959; Director and Deputy Chairman, Ciba-Geigy (UK) Ltd; Director: Standard Telephones & Cables; Colonial Mutual Life Assurance Society Ltd; British Electric Traction Omnibus Services Ltd; *b* 7 April 1912; *yr twin s* of 2nd Marquess of Linlithgow, KG, KT, PC; *m* 1948, Elizabeth Mary, *d* of late (William) Somerset Maugham, CH; two *s*. *Educ:* Eton; Christ Church, Oxford (MA 1936). psc†; served War of 1939-45 (Scots Guards) at Narvik, Salerno and Anzio (despatches twice). MP (C) Northern Midlothian and Peebles, 1945-50, Pentlands Div. of Edinburgh, 1950-64; (Joint) Parliamentary Under-Sec. of State for Foreign Affairs, Oct. 1954-Nov. 1956; Parliamentary Under-Sec. of State for Commonwealth Relations, Nov. 1956-Jan. 1957; Jt Parly Under-Sec. of State for Scotland, 1957-Oct. 1959; Minister of Works, Oct. 1959-July 1962. Mem., Departmental Cttee to examine operation of Section 2 of Official Secrets Act, 1971. Chairman: Royal Commonwealth Society, 1963-66; Historic Buildings Council for England, 1973-75. Fellow of Eton, 1956-67. FRSA 1962. *Publication:* The Viceroy at Bay, 1971. *Heir: s* Hon. Julian John Somerset Hope, *b* 6 March 1950. *Address:* Durham House, Durham Place, SW3.

GLENDINING, Rev. Canon Alan; Rector of the Sandringham Group of Parishes, and Domestic Chaplain to the Queen, since 1970; Hon. Canon of Norwich Cathedral, since 1977; *b* 17 March 1924; *s* of late Vincent Glendining, MS, FRCS and Freda Alice; *m* 1948, Margaret Locke, *d* of Lt-Col C. M. Hawes, DSO and Frances Cooper Richmond; one *s* two *d*. *Educ:* Radley; Westcott House, Cambridge. Newspaper publishing, 1945-58. Deacon, 1960; Priest, 1961. Asst Curate, South Ormsby Group of Parishes, 1960-63; Rector of Raveningham Group of Parishes, 1963-70; Rural Dean of Heacham and Rising, 1972-76. *Recreation:* shooting. *Address:* Sandringham Rectory, Norfolk PE35 6EH. *T:* Dersingham 40587.

GLENDINNING, Edward Green; Chief Executive, City of Edinburgh District Council, since 1975; *b* 3 Dec. 1922; *yr s* of late George M. Glendinning and Isabella Green; *m* 1944, Jane Rollo Dodds Greig; one *s* one *d*. *Educ:* Boroughmuir Sch., Edinburgh; Edinburgh Univ. (BL). Lieut RNVR (Air Br., Pilot), 1941-46; Edinburgh Univ., 1940-41 and 1946-48; admitted Solicitor, 1948; Edinburgh Corporation, 1949; Depute Town Clerk, 1959; Town Clerk, City and Royal Burgh of Edinburgh, 1972-75. Comdr, Order of Pole Star (Sweden), 1976. *Recreations:* friends, talking, listening to music, walking (but not too far). *Address:* City Chambers, Edinburgh EH1 1YJ. *T:* 031-225 2424.
See also J. G. Glendinning.

GLENDINNING, James Garland, OBE 1973; Member, London Transport Executive, since 1972; Chairman: London Transport Pension Fund Trustees Ltd, since 1974; North American Property Unit Trust, since 1975; Director, Fine Art Society Ltd, since 1972; *b* 27 April 1919; *er s* of late George M. Glendinning and Isabella Green; *m* 1943, Margaret Donald; one *d*. *Educ:* Boroughmuir Sch., Edinburgh; Military Coll. of Science. Mil. Service, 1939-46: 2nd Bn London Scottish and REME in UK and NW Europe. HM Inspector of Taxes, 1946-49; various appts with Shell Petroleum Co. Ltd, 1950-58; Dir Anglo Egyptian Oilfields Ltd and Dep. Chief Representative Shell-BP companies in Egypt, 1959-61; Gen. Rep. (Kalimantan) for PT Shell Indonesia, 1961-64; Head of Industrial Studies (Diversification) in Shell Internat. Petroleum Co. Ltd, 1964-67; various appts in Japan, 1967-72, incl.: Vice-Pres. Shell Oil Ltd and Shell Enterprises Ltd; Exec. Man. Dir, Japan Shell Technology Ltd; Director: Showa Oil Ltd and Showa Yokkaichi Oil Ltd; Nippon LNG Ltd; West Japan Oil Exploration Ltd; Chm., British Chamber of Commerce in Japan; Mem. Council, Japan Soc., London, 1974-. FCIT. *Recreations:* painting, golf. *Address:* 20 Albion Street, W2 2AS. *Clubs:* Army and Navy, Caledonian; Wyke Green Golf.
See also E. G. Glendinning.

GLENDYNE, 3rd Baron, *cr* 1922; **Robert Nivison**, Bt 1914; Senior Partner in the firm of R. Nivison & Co., Stockbrokers; *b* 27 Oct. 1926; *o s* of 2nd Baron and late Ivy May Rose; *S* father, 1967; *m* 1953, Elizabeth, *y d* of late Sir Cecil Armitage, CBE; one *s* two *d*. *Educ:* Harrow. Grenadier Guards, 1944-47. *Recreations:* shooting, cricket, water-skiing. *Heir: s* Hon. John Nivison, *b* 18 Aug. 1960. *Address:* Hurdcott, Barford St Martin, near Salisbury, Wilts. *Club:* City of London.
See also Maj.-Gen. P. R. Leuchars.

GLENISTER, Prof. Tony William, TD 1963 and Clasp 1969; Professor of Anatomy, University of London, at Charing Cross Hospital Medical School, since 1970; Dean, Charing Cross Hospital Medical School, since 1976; *b* 12 Dec. 1923; *o s* of Dudley Stuart Glenister and Maria (*née* Leytens); *m* 1948,

Monique Marguerite, *o d* of Emile and Marguerite de Wilde; four *s*. *Educ:* Eastbourne Coll.; St Bartholomew's Hosp. Med. Coll. MRCS, LRCP 1947; MB, BS 1948, PhD 1955, DSc 1963, London. House appts, 1947-48; RAMC, 1948-50; Lectr and Reader in Anatomy, Charing Cross Hosp. Med. Sch., 1950-57; Internat. Project Embryological Res., Hubrecht Lab., Utrecht, 1954; Prof. of Embryology, Univ. of London, 1967-70; Vice-Dean, Charing Cross Hosp. Med. Sch., 1966-69 and 1971-76; Hon. Cons. in Clin. Genetics to Charing Cross Gp of Hosps, 1972-; Brig. RAMC, TAVR; Adviser to Dir-Gen. Army Medical Services, 1976-. Apothecaries' Soc. Lectr in History of Medicine, 1971-; Arnott Demonstrator, RCS, 1972; Sec., Anatomical Soc. GB and Ireland, 1974-76. ADMS 44 (Home Counties) Div. TA., 1964-67; CO 217 (London) Gen. Hosp. RAMC(V), 1968-72; QHP 1971-73; Hon. Col 220 (1st Home Counties) Field Amb. RAMC(V), 1973-. Mem., Ealing, Hammersmith and Hounslow AHA, 1976-; sometime examiner: Univs of Cambridge, Liverpool, London, Singapore; NUI; RCS. FLS, FZS. OStJ 1967. *Publications:* (with J. R. W. Ross) Anatomy and Physiology for Nurses, 1965, 2nd edn 1974; (contrib.) A Companion to Medical Studies, ed Passmore, 1963, 2nd edn 1976; (contrib.) Methods in Mammalian Embryology, ed Daniel, 1971; (contrib.) Textbook of Human Anatomy, ed Hamilton, 1976; numerous papers and articles mainly on prenatal development. *Recreations:* the countryside, history. *Address:* The Keep, 42 Marlborough Crescent, Riverhead, Sevenoaks, Kent. *T:* Sevenoaks 51775. *Club:* Army and Navy.

GLENKINGLAS, Baron *cr* 1974 (Life Peer), of Cairndow, Argyll; **Michael Antony Cristobal Noble**, PC 1962; *b* 19 March 1913; 3rd *s* of Sir John Henry Brunel Noble, 1st Bt, of Ardkinglas; *m* 1940, Anne, *d* of Sir Neville Pearson, 2nd Bt, *qv*; four *d*. *Educ:* Eton Coll.; Magdalen Coll., Oxford. Served RAFVR, 1941-45. Argyll County Council, 1949-51. MP (C) Argyllshire, June 1958-Feb. 1974; PPS to Sec. of State for Scotland, 1959; Asst Govt Whip (unpaid), 1960 (Scottish Whip, Nov. 1960); a Lord Comr of the Treasury, 1961-62; Sec. of State for Scotland, 1962-64; President of the Board of Trade, June-Oct. 1970; Minister for Trade, DTI, Oct. 1970-Nov. 1972. Chm., Unionist Party in Scotland, 1962-63. Chairman: Associated Fisheries, 1966-70; Glendevon Farms (Winchburgh), 1969-70; British Agricultural Export Council, 1973-77; Director: John Brown Engineering Ltd, 1973-; Monteith Holdings Ltd, 1974-. *Recreations:* gardening, fishing, shooting. *Address:* Strone, Cairndow, Argyll. *T:* Cairndow 284. *Clubs:* Boodle's; New (Edinburgh); Royal Scottish Automobile (Glasgow).

GLENN, Sir Archibald; *see* Glenn, Sir J. R. A.

GLENN, Senator John H(erschel), Jr; US Senator from Ohio (Democrat), since 1975; *b* Cambridge, Ohio, 18 July 1921; *s* of John H. and Clara Glenn; *m* 1943, Anna Castor; one *s* one *d*. *Educ:* Muskingum Coll., New Concord, Ohio. Joined US Marine Corps, 1943; Served War (2DFC's, 10 Air Medals); Pacific Theater, 1944; home-based, Capt., 1945-46; Far East, 1947-49; Major, 1952; served Korea (5 DFC's, Air Medal with 18 clusters), 1953. First non-stop supersonic flight, Los Angeles-New York (DFC), 1957; Lieut-Col, 1959. In Jan. 1964, declared candidacy for US Senate from Ohio, but withdrew owing to an injury; recovered and promoted Col USMC, Oct. 1964; retired from USMC, Dec. 1964. Became one of 7 volunteer Astronauts, man-in-space program, 1959; made 3-orbit flight in Mercury capsule, Friendship 7, 20 Feb. 1962 (boosted by rocket; time 4 hrs 56 mins; distance 81,000 miles; altitude 160 miles; recovered by destroyer off Puerto Rico in Atlantic). Vice-Pres. (corporate devel't) and Dir, Royal Crown Cola Co., 1962-74. Holds hon. doctorates, US and foreign. Awarded DSM (Nat. Aeronautics and Space Admin.), Astronaut Wings (Navy), Astronaut Medal (Marine Corps), etc, 1962; Galabert Internat. Astronautical Prize (jointly with Lieut-Col Yuri Gagarin), 1963; also many other awards and citations from various countries and organizations. *Address:* 204 Rayburn Senate Office Building, Washington, DC 20515, USA; (home) 3996 Old Poste Road, Columbus, Ohio 43220, USA.

GLENN, Sir (Joseph Robert) Archibald, Kt 1966; OBE 1965; BCE; FIChemE, FIE (Aust.); Chairman: IMI Australia Ltd, since 1973; Collins Wales Pty Ltd, since 1973; I.C. Insurance Australia Ltd, since 1973; Tioxede Australia Ltd, since 1977; Director: Bank of New South Wales, since 1967; Hill Samuel Australia Ltd, since 1973; Alcoa of Australia Ltd, since 1973; *b* 24 May 1911; *s* of late J. R. Glenn, Sale, Vic., Aust.; *m* 1939, Elizabeth M. M., *d* of late J. S. Balderstone; one *s* three *d*. *Educ:* Scotch Coll. (Melbourne); University of Melbourne; Harvard (USA). Joined ICI Australia Ltd, 1935; Design and Construction Engr, 1935-44; Explosives Dept, ICI(UK), 1945-46; Chief Engineer, ICI Australia Ltd, 1947-48; Controller, Nobel Group, 1948-50; General Manager, 1950-52; Managing

Director, 1953-73; Chm., 1963-73; Dir, ICI, London, 1970-75; Chairman: Fibremakers Ltd, 1963-73. Chancellor, La Trobe Univ., 1967-72; Chairman: Council of Scotch Coll.; Ormond Coll. Council, 1976-; Member: Manufacturing Industry Advisory Council, 1960-77; Industrial Design Council, 1958-70; Australia/Japan Business Co-operation Cttee, 1965-75; Royal Melbourne Hospital Bd of Management, 1960-70; Melbourne Univ. Appointments Bd; Council, Inst. of Pacific Affairs, 1976-; Governor, Atlantic Inst. of Internat. Affairs. *Recreations:* golf, tennis, collecting rare books. *Address:* 3 Heyington Place, Toorak, Melbourne, Vic. 3142, Australia. *T:* 20 4453. *Clubs:* Australian, Melbourne, Royal Melbourne Golf, Frankston Golf, Victoria Racing, Melbourne Univ. Boat (all in Melbourne); Australian (Sydney).

GLENN, William James, CB 1968; BA, BAI, FICE; Director-General, Water Engineering, Department of the Environment, 1971-72, retired; *b* 26 June 1911; *s* of late John Glenn, Londonderry; *m* 1937, Wilhelmina Jane Gibson, MA, *d* of late John Gibson, Dublin; two *s. Educ:* Trinity Coll., Dublin Univ. Entered Air Min. as Asst Civil Engr, Directorate Gen. of Works, 1937; Sen. Civil Engr, Air HQ, W Africa, 1944-45; service in Airfield Construction Br, RAF, BAFO Germany, 1948-50; Chief Engr Flying Trng Comd, RAF, 1952-54; Dep. Dir of Works, 1956-57; Chief Engr, Far East Air Force, 1957-59; Dir of Works, 1962-65; Chief Civil Engr, MPBW, 1965-68; Chief Engineer, Min. of Housing and Local Govt, 1968-71. Mem. Bd, Maplin Develt Authy, 1973-74. *Recreation:* golf. *Address:* Bucklers, Hungerford Lane, Shurlock Row, near Reading RG10 0NY. *T:* Shurlock Row 445. *Clubs:* Royal Air Force; East Berkshire Golf.

GLENNIE, Alan Forbes Bourne, CMG 1956; *b* 11 April 1903; *s* of late Vice-Adm. R. W. Glennie, CMG; *m* 1931, Dorothy Sybil, *d* of late J. A. H. Johnston, DSc; one *s* one *d. Educ:* RN Colls Osborne and Dartmouth; Trinity Coll., Cambridge (MA). Joined Provincial Administration, N Rhodesia, 1924; Provincial Commissioner, 1945; Resident Commissioner, Barotseland Protectorate, Northern Rhodesia, 1953-57, retired; Government Sec., St Helena, 1963-65, retired. *Address:* 85 Gibson Road, Kenilworth 7700, Cape Province, RSA. *Club:* Royal Over-Seas League.

GLENNIE, Brig. Edward Aubrey, CIE 1942; DSO 1917; FRAS, FRES, FRGS (Gold Medallist), FGS, FZS; FZS Scientific; Foundation FNI; Fellow, Conchological Society; late RE; *b* 18 July 1889; *s* of late Col E. Glennie; *m* 1923, Agnes Christina, *d* of W. Whigham, late Indian State Railways (one *s* killed on active service, 1944). *Educ:* Haileybury. Entered Army, 1910; Capt. 1916; Major, 1926; Lieut Col, 1934; Col, 1937; late Dir Survey of India; retired 1948; served Mesopotamia, 1916-18 (despatches twice, DSO). *Address:* 15 Shrublands Road, Berkhamsted, Herts.

GLENNIE, Adm. Sir Irvine Gordon, KCB, *cr* 1945 (CB 1943); *b* 22 July 1892; *o surv s* of Capt. Gordon Glennie RN, and Edith, *d* of late Gen. J. Mitchell, RMLI; *m* 1928, Gwen, *d* of Edmund Evans; two *s. Educ:* RN Colls, Osborne and Dartmouth. Comdr 1928; Capt. 1933; Rear-Adm. 1941; Vice-Adm. 1944; served Home Fleet and China, 1910-14; in Destroyers, Grand Fleet, 1915-18; RNC, Dartmouth, 1922-24; commanding Destroyers, 1925-27 and 1932-34; Staff Coll., 1929; Admiralty, 1930-32; Imperial Defence Coll., 1935; commanding HMS Achilles, New Zealand Sqdn, 1936-39; commanding HMS Hood, 1939-41; Rear-Adm. Destroyers, Mediterranean, 1941-42; commanded Home Fleet Destroyers, 1943-44; Comdr-in-Chief, America and West Indies, 1945-46; retired list, 1947. *Address:* Wychwood, Fairfield Close, Lymington, Hants SO4 9NP. *T:* Lymington 2554.

GLENTORAN, 2nd Baron, *cr* 1939, of Ballyalloly; **Daniel Stewart Thomas Bingham Dixon,** 4th Bt, *cr* 1903; PC (Northern Ireland) 1953; KBE 1973; Lord-Lieutenant, City of Belfast, since 1976 (HM Lieutenant, 1950-76); *b* 19 Jan. 1912; *s* of 1st Baron, PC, OBE and Hon. Emily Ina Florence Bingham (*d* 1957), *d* of 5th Baron Clanmorris; *S* father 1950; *m* 1933, Lady Diana Mary Wellesley, *d* of 3rd Earl Cowley; two *s* one *d. Educ:* Eton; RMC Sandhurst. Reg. Army, Grenadier Guards; served War of 1939-45 (despatches); retired 1946 (with hon. rank of Lieut-Col); psc. MP (U) Bloomfield Division of Belfast, NI Parliament, Oct. 1950-Feb. 1961; Parliamentary Sec., Ministry of Commerce, NI, 1952-53; Minister of Commerce, 1953-61; Minister in Senate, NI, 1961-72, Speaker of Senate, 1964-72. Hon. Col 6th Battalion Royal Ulster Rifles, 1956-61, retd rank of Hon. Col. *Heir: s* Hon. Thomas Robin Valerian Dixon, MBE; [*b* 21 April 1935; *m* 1959, Rona, *d* of Capt. G. C. Colville, Mill House, Bishop's Waltham, Hants; three *s*]. *Address:* Drumadarragh House, Doagh, Co. Antrim, Northern Ireland. *T:* Doagh 222. *Club:* Ulster (Belfast).

GLENTWORTH, Viscount; Edmund Christopher Pery; *b* 10 Feb. 1963; *s* and *heir* of 6th Earl of Limerick, *qv.*

GLERAWLY, Viscount; Patrick Annesley; *b* 12 August 1924; *e s* and *heir* of 9th Earl Annesley, *qv* ; *m* 1947, Catherine, *d* of John Burgess, Edinburgh; four *d. Educ:* Strode's Grammar Sch., Egham. *Address:* 35 Spring Rise, Egham, Surrey.

GLIDEWELL, Iain Derek Laing, QC 1969; Barrister-at-law; a Recorder of the Crown Court, since 1976; *b* 8 June 1924; *s* of late Charles Norman and Nora Glidewell; *m* 1950, Hilary, *d* of Clinton D. Winant; one *s* two *d. Educ:* Bromsgrove Sch.; Worcester Coll., Oxford. RAFVR, 1942-46. Called to the Bar, Gray's Inn, 1949, Bencher 1978. Chm., Panels for Examination of Structure Plans: Worcestershire, 1974; W Midlands, 1975. *Recreations:* beagling, walking, spasmodic interest in the Arts. *Address:* Oldfield, Knutsford, Cheshire. *T:* Knutsford 3073. *Clubs:* Garrick; Manchester (Manchester).

GLIN, Knight of; *see* Fitz-Gerald, D. J. V.

GLOAG, John (Edwards); author; *b* 10 Aug. 1896; *s* of Robert McCowan Gloag and Lillian Morgan; *m* 1922, Gertrude Mary, *d* of late Ven. G. H. Ward; one *s* one *d. Educ:* Battersea Grammar Sch.; largely self-educated. Studied architecture at Regent Street Polytechnic, 1911-13; with studio Thornton-Smith Ltd, 1913-16; served in Essex Regt, 1916; Household Brigade Cadet Battalion, 1917; 2nd Lieut Welsh Guards, 1918; served with 1st Bn BEF, May-Aug. 1918, and invalided home; Technical and Art Ed. of the Cabinet Maker, 1922; Ed., 1927; Dir, Pritchard, Wood & Partners Ltd, 1928-61; Public Rel. Dir, Timber Development Assoc., 1936-38. FSA; Hon. FRIBA; Hon. FSIA; RSA Silver Medal, 1943, Bicentenary Gold Medal, 1958. Member: Utility Furniture Advisory Cttee (Board of Trade), 1943-47; Council of Industrial Design, 1949-55; Council of Royal Society of Arts, 1948-56, 1958-63 (Vice-Pres., 1952-54); Bd of Trustees, Sir John Soane's Mus., 1960-70; Chairman: Internat. Conf. on Industrial Design, 1951; Council of Building Centre, 1950-64; Pres. of the Soc. of Architectural Historians of Great Britain, 1960-64. Broadcast talks and short stories, 1933 onwards; Mem. team in: Men Talking; Design in Modern Life; Brains Trust (occasionally Question Master); a few appearances on TV, before and after 1939-45 war. *Publications: fiction:* To-Morrow's Yesterday, 1932; The New Pleasure, 1933; Winter's Youth, 1934; Sweet Racket, 1936; Ripe for Development, 1936; Sacred Edifice, 1937 (new edn, with foreword by Sir Basil Spence, 1954); It Makes a Nice Change, 1938; Documents Marked Secret, 1938; Manna, 1940; Unwilling Adventurer, 1940; I Want an Audience, 1941; Mr Buckby is Not at Home, 1942; Ninety-nine per cent, 1944; In Camera, 1945; First One and Twenty (omnibus), 1946; Kind Uncle Buckby, 1947; All England at Home, 1949; Take One a Week, 1950; Not in the Newspapers, 1953; Slow, 1954; Unlawful Justice, 1962; Rising Suns, 1964; Ceasar of the Narrow Seas, 1969; The Eagles Depart, 1973; Artorius Rex, 1977; *verse:* Board Room Ballads, 1933; *architecture and design:* Colour and Comfort, 1924; Men and Buildings, 1931 (illustr. edn, 1950); Artifex or the Future of Craftsmanship, 1926; English Furniture (Library of English Art), 1934 (6th edn, 1973); Design in Modern Life (ed.), 1934; Industrial Art Explained, 1934; The Place of Glass in Building (ed.), 1942; The Missing Technician in Industrial Production, 1944; The Englishman's Castle, 1944; Plastics and Industrial Design, 1945; House out of Factory (with Grey Wornum, FRIBA), 1945; British Furniture Makers, 1945; Self-training for Industrial Designers, 1947; The English Tradition in Design, 1947 (revised and enlarged edn, 1959); A History of Cast Iron in Architecture (with D. L. Bridgewater, FRIBA), 1948; How to write Technical Books, 1951; A Short Dictionary of Furniture, 1952 (rev. edn, 1965, abridged edn, 1966, enl. rev. edn, 1969); Georgian Grace, 1956, rev. edn 1967; Guide to Western Architecture, 1958, rev. edn 1969; Introduction to Catalogue of Irwin Untermyer Coll. of Eng. Furniture for Metropolitan Museum of Art, NY, 1958; Victorian Comfort, 1961, rev. edn, 1973; Victorian Taste, 1962, rev. edn, 1972; The English Tradition in Architecture, 1963; Architecture (Arts of Man), 1963; The Englishman's Chair, 1964; Enjoying Architecture, 1965; Introduction to Early English Decorative Detail, 1965; (with Maureen Stafford) Guide to Furniture Styles, English and French, 1972; The Architectural Interpretation of History, 1975; *social history:* Home Life in History, 1927, with C. Thompson Walker; Time, Taste and Furniture, 1925; Word Warfare, 1939; The American Nation, 1942 (revised, enlarged edn, with Julian Gloag, 1954); What About Business?, 1943 (enlarged edn entitled What About Enterprise?, 1948); 2000 Years of England, 1952; Advertising in Modern Life, 1959; A Social History of Furniture Design, 1966; *biography:* Mr Loudon's England, 1970. *Recreation:* reading. *Address:* 3 The Mall, East Sheen, SW14 7EN. *T:* 01-876 4530. *Clubs:* Arts, Garrick.

GLOAK, Graeme Frank; Principal Assistant Solicitor, Customs and Excise, since 1971; *b* 9 Nov. 1921; *s* of Frank and Lilian Gloak; *m* 1944, Mary, *d* of Stanley and Jane Thorne; one *s* one *d* (and one *s* decd). *Educ:* Brentwood School. Royal Navy, 1941-46; Solicitor, 1947; Customs and Excise: Legal Asst, 1947; Sen. Legal Asst, 1953; Asst Solicitor, 1967. Sec., Civil Service Legal Soc., 1954-62. *Publication:* (with G. Krikorian and R. K. F. Hutchings) Customs and Excise, in Halsbury's Laws of England, 4th edn, 1973. *Recreations:* badminton, walking, watching cricket. *Address:* Northwold, 123 Priests Lane, Shenfield, Essex. *T:* Brentwood 212748. *Club:* Essex County Cricket (Chelmsford).

GLOCK, Sir William (Frederick), Kt 1970; CBE 1964; Chairman, London Orchestral Concerts Board, since 1975; Artistic Director, Bath Festival, since 1975; *b* London, 3 May 1908. *Educ:* Christ's Hospital; Caius Coll., Cambridge. Studied pianoforte under Artur Schnabel. Joined The Observer, 1934; chief music critic, 1939-45. Served in RAF, 1941-46. Dir, Summer Sch. of Music, Bryanston, 1948, since 1953 at Dartington Hall. Editor of music magazine The Score, 1949-61; adjudicated at Canadian music festivals, 1951; has lectured on music throughout England and Canada. Music Critic, New Statesman, 1958-59; Controller of Music, BBC, 1959-72. Editor, Eulenburg books on music, 1973-. Member: Bd of Dirs, Royal Opera House, 1968-73; Arts Council, 1972-75. Hon. Mem., Royal Philharmonic Soc., 1971. Hon. DMus Nottingham Univ., 1968; DUniv York, 1972. Albert Medal, RSA, 1971. *Address:* Sudbury House, Faringdon, Oxfordshire. *T:* Faringdon 20381.

GLOSSOP, Peter; Principal Baritone, Royal Opera House, Covent Garden, until 1967, now Guest Artist; *b* 6 July 1928; *s* of Cyril and Violet Elizabeth Glossop; *m* 1955, Joyce Elizabeth Blackham (marr. diss. 1977); no *c*; *m* 1977, Michèle Yvonne Amos. *Educ:* High Storrs Grammar Sch., Sheffield. Began singing professionally in chorus of Sadler's Wells Opera, 1952, previously a bank clerk; promoted to principal after one season; Covent Garden Opera, 1962-67. Début in Italy, 1964; La Scala, Milan, début, Rigoletto, 1965. Sang Otello and Rigoletto with Metropolitan Opera Company at Newport USA Festival, Aug. 1967; Rigoletto and Nabucco with Mexican National Opera Company, Sept. 1967. Guest Artist (Falstaff, Rigoletto, Tosca) with American National Opera Company, Oct. 1967. Has sung in opera houses of Bologna, Parma Catania, Vienna, 1967-68, and Berlin and Buenos Aires. Is a recording artist. Hon. DMus, Sheffield, 1970. Winner of 1st Prize and Gold Medal in First International Competition for Young Opera Singers, Sofia, Bulgaria, 1961; Gold Medal for finest performance (in Macbeth) of 1968-69 season, Barcelona. *Films:* Pagliacci, Otello. *Recreations:* New Orleans jazz music, squash rackets. *Address:* Elmcroft, 91 Cambridge Road, Teddington, Mddx. *Club:* Green Room.

GLOSTER, John, MD; Dean of the Institute of Ophthalmology, since 1975; Hon. Consultant, Moorfields Eye Hospital; *b* 23 March 1922; *m* 1947, Margery (*née* Williams); two *s*. *Educ:* Jesus Coll., Cambridge; St Bartholomew's Hosp. MB, BChir 1946; MRCS, LRCP 1946; DOMS 1950; MD Cantab 1953; PhD London 1959. Registrar, Research Dept, Birmingham and Midland Eye Hosp., 1950-54; Mem. Staff, Ophth. Research Unit, MRC, 1954-63; Prof. of Experimental Ophthalmology, Inst. of Ophth., Univ. of London, 1963. FRSocMed; Mem. Ophth. Soc. UK. *Publications:* Tonometry and Tonography, 1966; (jtly) Physiology of the Eye, System of Ophthalmology IV, ed Duke-Elder, 1968; contribs to jls. *Address:* Institute of Ophthalmology, Judd Street, WC1H 9QS; Swakeleys Cottage, 2 The Avenue, Ickenham, Uxbridge, Mddx.

GLOUCESTER, Bishop of, since 1975; **Rt. Rev. John Yates;** *b* 17 April 1925; *s* of late Frank and late Edith Ethel Yates; *m* 1954, Jean Kathleen Dover; one *s* two *d*. *Educ:* Battersea Grammar School; Blackpool Grammar School; Jesus College, Cambridge (MA). RAFVR (Aircrew), 1943-47; University of Cambridge, 1947-49; Lincoln Theological College, 1949-51. Curate, Christ Church, Southgate, 1951-54; Tutor and Chaplain, Lincoln Theological College, 1954-59; Vicar, Bottesford-with-Ashby, 1959-65; Principal, Lichfield Theological College, 1966-72; Bishop Suffragan of Whitby, 1972-75. *Address:* Bishopscourt, Pitt Street, Gloucester GL1 2BQ.

GLOUCESTER, Dean of; *see* Thurlow, Very Rev. A. G. G.

GLOUCESTER, Archdeacon of; *see* Wardle, Ven. W. T.

GLOVER, Anthony Richard Haysom; Deputy Controller, HM Stationery Office, since 1976; *b* 29 May 1934; 2nd *s* of late Arthur Herbert Glover and Marjorie Florence Glover; *m* 1960, Ann Penelope Scupham, *d* of John Scupham, *qv*; two *s* one *d*.

Educ: Culford Sch., Bury St Edmunds; Emmanuel Coll., Cambridge (BA). HM Customs and Excise: Asst Principal, 1957; Principal, 1961; on secondment to HM Treasury, 1965-68; Asst Sec., 1969; Asst Sec., HM Treasury, 1972-76. *Recreations:* music, reading, writing, alpine gardening. *Address:* 7 Hillside Road, Thorpe St Andrew, Norwich. *T:* Norwich 33508.

GLOVER, Derek Harding, CBE 1967; Special Duties Director, British Airways Board, 1975-76 (Member and Group Financial Director, 1971-74); *b* 17 April 1916; *s* of Harold Harding Glover and Dora McRae; *m* 1947, Joan Marjorie Piper; two *s*. *Educ:* Hillcrest Prep. Sch., Frinton-on-Sea; Leys Sch., Cambridge. ACA 1937. Services, 1939-46; BOAC, 1946-71. Chm., International Aeradio Ltd, 1971-76 (Dir, 1963-76); Chm., Airways Pension Scheme, 1971-. *Recreations:* golf, gardening, good food. *Address:* Cockers, Burwash, Etchingham, Sussex.

GLOVER, Sir Douglas, Kt 1960; TD 1945; *b* 13 Feb. 1908; *s* of S. Barnish Glover, Rochdale; *m* 1st, 1934, Agnes May (*d* 1976), *d* of William Brown, JP, Netherlaw, Kirkcudbright, and Longfield, Heaton Mersey; no *c*; 2nd, 1976, Eleanor Hurlimann, *widow* of Erwin Hurlimann, Schloss Frendenberg, Rotkreuz, Kanton Zug, Switzerland. *Educ:* Giggleswick. TA 1939; 7th Manchester Rgt, 52 Div., NW Europe; Lieut-Col comdg Princess Louise Kensington Regt, 49 Div., 1945; despatches, 1946; comdg 9th Manchester Regt TA 1947-50; Bt-Col 1950; TARO 1950. Contested (C) Blackburn, 1945, Stalybridge and Hyde, 1950 and 1951; MP (C) Ormskirk, 1953-70; Mem. Public Accounts Cttee, 1965-70. Chairman Young Conservatives, North-West Area, 1946; Treasurer, North-West, 1951-54; Mem., Nat. Exec. of Conservative Party, 1951-69; Chm. N Western Area, 1956-60; Chm., Nat. Union of Conservative Assocs, 1961-62. Pres., Cheadle Cons. Assoc., 1974-77. Delegate 10th Commonwealth Parl. Conf., Canberra, 1959. Mem. Mr Speaker's Panel of Chm., 1961; Chm. United and Cecil Club, 1962-65; Deleg. 17th Gen. Assembly of the UN, New York, 1962; Vice-Chm., Lancs and Ches Mems Cttee, 1966; Pres., Lancashire Assoc., 1966; Chm., Anti-Slavery Soc., 1965-73; Mem. Coun., Nat. Fedn of Housing Assocs, 1966-72; Chm., Pierhead Housing Soc., 1965-76. Governor, Giggleswick School, 1970 (Chm., 1975-77). Knight Officer, Order of Orange Nassau, 1946. *Address:* Schloss Frendenberg, 6343 Rotkreuz, Kanton Zug, Switzerland. *T:* Rotkrenz (042) 641126; 94 Avenue d'Iena, Paris 16. *T:* 720 0481. *Clubs:* Carlton, Turf.

GLOVER, Sir Gerald (Alfred), Kt 1971; Senior Partner, Glover & Co.; Chairman, Edger Investments Ltd, since 1959; *b* 5 June 1908; *m* 1933, Susan Drage; two *d*. *Educ:* City of London School. Solicitor, 1932. King's Messenger, 1938-40; served War of 1939-45, Mil. Intell., at home and abroad; Major. Conservative Party: Mem. 1935-; Chm. local area, 1945-; Treas. Kettering Div., 1953-67; President: Kettering Cons. Club, 1970; Kettering Cons. Assoc., 1971. Patron, County of London Red Cross; Treas. and Trustee, National Adoption Soc. for England; Founder, East Kent Arts Centre and Gallery; Pres., Kettering and District Scouts; Pres., Northants Agricultural Soc., 1970. Mem., E Midland Area Exec., 1960- (Chm., 1963-71, Vice-Pres., 1972-). CC Northants (Vice-Chm., 1972-74). Freeman and Liveryman, City of London. *Recreations:* bloodstock breeding and racing (bred, raced and owns Privy Councillor, winner of 2000 Guineas, 1962), hunting, landscape gardening, visual art. *Address:* Pytchley House, Northants. *T:* Broughton 258. *Clubs:* White's, Boodle's, Carlton, Law Society.

GLOVER, Harold, CB 1977; Controller of Her Majesty's Stationery Office and Queen's Printer of Acts of Parliament, 1974-77; *b* 29 Jan. 1917; 4th *s* of late George Glover, Wallasey, Ches; *m* 1949, Olive, *d* of late E. B. Robotham, Sawbridgeworth, Herts; two *s*. *Educ:* Wallasey Gram. Sch. Joined Customs and Excise, 1933; joined Min. of Works, 1949 (now DoE); Controller of Supplies, 1957; Under-Secretary, 1967-70; Dep. Master, Royal Mint, 1970-74. Served RAF, 1940-46 (Flt Lieut Signals). FRSA 1963 (Mem Council, 1974-; Bicentenary Medal, 1967); FSIA 1975. *Recreation:* music. *Address:* 23 Walnut Tree Crescent, Sawbridgeworth, Herts. *T:* Bishops Stortford 723256. *Clubs:* Reform, Royal Air Force.

GLOVER, John Neville, CMG 1963; *b* 12 July 1913; *s* of John Robert Glover and Sybil Glover (*née* Cureton); *m* 1st, 1940, Margot Burdick; one *s*; 2nd, 1956, June Patricia Bruce Gaskell. *Educ:* Tonbridge Sch. Commissioned 6th Bn Devonshire Regt (TA), 1933; RAF (Gen. Duties Branch), 1934. Served RAF, 1934-46; RAFRO, 1946-59 (retained rank of Group Capt.). Called to Bar, Gray's Inn, 1949. Appointed to Colonial Legal Service, 1951; served: Ghana (Crown Counsel and Senior Crown Counsel), 1951-57; Western Pacific High Commission (Legal Adviser and Attorney-General, British Solomon Islands Protectorate), 1957-63. QC (Western Pacific), 1962. Retired from HM Overseas Civil Service, 1963. Comr to examine Human Rights Laws in the Bahamas, 1964-65. Legal Draftsman in the Bahamas, 1965-66. Law Revision Comr for certain overseas territories, 1967-. *Recreation:* fishing. *Address:* Clam End, Trebullett, near Launceston, Cornwall. *T:* Coad's Green 347. *Club:* Royal Air Force.

GLOVER, Kenneth Frank; Assistant Under-Secretary of State (Statistics), Ministry of Defence, since 1974; *b* 16 Dec. 1920; *s* of Frank Glover and Mabel Glover; *m* 1951, Iris Clare Holmes. *Educ:* Bideford Grammar Sch.; UC of South West, Exeter; LSE (MScEcon). Joined Statistics Div., MoT, 1946; Statistician, 1950; Statistical Adviser to Cttee of Inquiry on Major Ports (Rochdale Cttee), 1961-62; Dir of Econs and Statistics at Nat. Ports Council, 1964-68; Chief Statistician, MoT and DoE, 1968-74. *Publications:* various papers; articles in JRSS, Dock and Harbour Authority. *Recreations:* boating, idleness. *Address:* Woodhanger, Hale House Lane, Churt, Farnham, Surrey GU10 2LX. *T:* Hindhead 4179; West Wing, Ringmore Lodge, Salty Lane, Shaldon, South Devon TQ14 0AP.

GLOVER, Myles Howard; Clerk of the Skinners' Company since 1959; Hon. Secretary, Governing Bodies' Association since 1967; *b* 18 Dec. 1928; *yr s* of Cedric Howard Glover and Winifred Mary (*née* Crewdson); *m* 1969, Wendy Gillian, *er d* of C. M. Coleman; one *s* two *d. Educ:* Rugby; Balliol Coll., Oxford (MA). Called to the Bar, Lincoln's Inn, 1954. Chm., Cttee of Clerks to Twelve Chief Livery Cos of City of London, 1975-; Member: City & Guilds Art Sch. Cttee, 1960-71; City Univ. Adv. Cttee on the Arts, 1975-. *Recreation:* music. *Address:* Chart House, Great Chart, Ashford, Kent.

GLOVER, Maj.-Gen. Peter James, CB 1966; OBE 1948; *b* 16 Jan. 1913; *s* of late G. H, Glover, CBE, Sheephatch House, Tilford, Surrey, and late Mrs G. H. Glover; *m* 1946, Wendy Archer; one *s* two *d. Educ:* Uppingham; Cambridge (MA). 2nd Lieut RA, 1934; served War of 1939-45, BEF France and Far East; Lieut-Col 1956; Brig. 1961; Comdt, Sch. of Artillery, Larkhill, 1960-62; Maj.-Gen. 1962; GOC 49 Infantry Division TA and North Midland District, 1962-63; Head of British Defence Supplies Liaison Staff, Delhi, 1963-66; Director, Royal Artillery, 1966-69, retd. *Address:* Lukesland, Diptford, Totnes, Devon. *Club:* Army and Navy.

GLOVER, Robert Finlay, TD 1954; Deputy Secretary, Headmasters' Conference and Association, since 1977; *b* 28 June 1917; *yr s* of T. R. Glover, Public Orator in University of Cambridge, and Alice, *d* of H. G. Few; *m* 1941, Jean, *d* of late N. G. Muir, Lincoln; one *s* two *d. Educ:* The Leys Sch.; Corpus Christi Coll., Oxford. Served in Royal Artillery (TA), 1939-46; Staff Coll., Camberley, 1944; Major, 1944. Asst Master, Ampleforth Coll., 1946-50; Head of Classics Dept, King's Sch., Canterbury, 1950-53; Headmaster, Adams' Grammar Sch., Newport, Salop, 1953-59; Headmaster, Monmouth Sch., 1959-76. *Publications:* Notes on Latin, 1954; (with R. W. Harris) Latin for Historians, 1954. *Recreations:* normal. *Address:* Brockhill Lodge, West Malvern Road, The Wyche, Malvern, Worcs WR14 4EJ. *T:* Malvern 64247. *Club:* East India, Devonshire, Sports and Public Schools.

GLOVER, William James, QC 1969; a Recorder of the Crown Court, since 1975; *b* 8 May 1924; *s* of late H. P. Glover, KC and Martha Glover; *m* 1956, Rosemary D. Long; two *s. Educ:* Harrow; Pembroke Coll., Cambridge. Served with Royal West African Frontier Force in West Africa and Burma, 1944-47. Called to Bar, Inner Temple, 1950. Second Junior Counsel to Inland Revenue (Rating Valuation), 1963-69. *Recreation:* golf. *Address:* Little Court, The Bury, Odiham, Hants.

GLUBB, Lt-Gen. Sir John Bagot, KCB 1956; CMG 1946; DSO 1941; OBE 1925; MC; Chief of General Staff, the Arab Legion, Amman, Jordan, 1939-56; *b* 16 April 1897; *s* of late Maj.-Gen. Sir F. M. Glubb, KCMG, CB, DSO; *m* 1938, Muriel Rosemary, *d* of Dr J. G. Forbes; two *s* two *d. Educ:* Cheltenham; Royal Military Academy, Woolwich, Aug. 1914; 2nd Lieut RE, 1915; served in France (wounded thrice, MC); to Iraq as Lieut RE, 1920; resigned commission, 1926, and became Administrative Inspector, Iraq Govt; transferred Transjordan, 1930; Officer Commanding Desert Area, 1932; Officer Commanding Arab Legion, Transjordan, 1939. *Publications:* Story of the Arab Legion, 1948; A Soldier with the Arabs, 1957; Britain and the Arabs, 1959; War in the Desert, 1960; The Great Arab Conquests, 1963; The Empire of the Arabs, 1963; The Course of Empire, 1965; The Lost Centuries, 1967; The Middle East Crisis-A Personal Interpretation, 1967; Syria, Lebanon, Jordan, 1967; A Short History of The Arab Peoples, 1969; The Life and Times of Muhammad, 1970; Peace in the Holy Land, 1971; Soldiers of Fortune, 1973; The Way of Love, 1974; Haroon al

Rasheed, 1976; Into Battle: a soldier's diary of the Great War, 1977. *Address:* West Wood, Mayfield, Sussex.

GLUCKSTEIN, Sir Louis Halle, GBE 1969 (CBE 1964); Kt 1953; TD 1950; QC 1945; Colonel 5th Suffolk Regiment TA; Director, British Transport Hotels Ltd, since 1963; *b* London, 23 Feb. 1897; *s* of late Joseph Gluckstein, OBE, and Francesca (*née* Halle), MBE, JP; *m* 1925, Doreen, *d* of Alexander Klean, London; two *s* one *d. Educ:* St Paul's Sch. (Schol.); Lincoln Coll., Oxford (Schol., MA; Hon. Fellow, 1968). Served European War, 1915-18, Lieut Suffolk Regt (wounded, despatches); served War of 1939-45: France, 1940 (despatches); Italy, 1944. Called to Bar, Lincoln's Inn, 1922, Bencher, 1952, Treasurer, 1970. MP (U) East Nottingham, 1931-45; contested East Nottingham, 1929, 1945 and 1950; contested Holborn and St Pancras South, 1951; DL County of London, 1952-77, retired; Mem., LCC for St Marylebone, 1955-64; Mem., GLC for City of Westminster, 1964-67; Alderman, 1967-73; Chm., Finance and Supplies Commn, 1967-68; Chm., GLC, 1968-69. Chairman: Board of Army Kinema Corp., 1956-68; Services Kinema Corp., 1969-. Pres., Royal Albert Hall, 1965 (Vice-Pres., 1961-65); Vice-Pres., Old Pauline Club, 1958, Pres., 1966-69. Pres., St Marylebone Conservative Assoc., 1967-. A Governor of St Paul's Schools, London, 1968. Mem., Bd of Trustees, London Festival Ballet, 1969-; Pres., St John's Wood Protection Soc., 1973-; Mem. Council, Imp. Soc. of Knights Bachelor, 1973-; Chm., Queen Alexandra's House, 1974-. Commendatore, Italian Order of Merit, 1969. *Recreations:* golf, shooting. *Address:* 39 Elm Tree Road, NW8 9JR. *T:* 01-286 7169. *Clubs:* Carlton, Savage; Leander.

GLUE, George Thomas; Director-General of Supplies and Transport (Naval), Ministry of Defence, 1973-77; *b* 3 May 1917; *s* of Percy Albert Glue and Alice Harriet Glue (*née* Stoner); *m* 1947, Eileen Marion Hitchcock; one *d. Educ:* Portsmouth Southern Secondary School. FInstPS; MBIM. Admiralty: Asst Naval Store Officer, 1937; Dep. Naval Store Officer, Mediterranean, 1940; Naval Store Officer, Mediterranean, 1943; Asst Dir of Stores, 1955; Suptg Naval Store Officer, Devonport, 1960; Dep. Dir of Stores, 1963; Dir of Stores, 1970; Dir, Supplies and Transport (Naval), 1971. *Recreations:* tennis, bridge. *Address:* 102 Cotelands, Croydon, Surrey. *T:* 01-681 6550.

GLUECKAUF, Eugen, DrIng, DSc, FRS 1969; Consultant, Atomic Energy Research Establishment, 1971-78; Editor, Radio-chimica Acta; *b* 9 April 1906; *m* 1934, Irma E. A. Glueckauf (*née* Tepper); one *d. Educ:* Technische Hochschule, Berlin. Research Asst to Prof. F. A. Paneth, Imperial Coll., London, 1934-39; Res. Associate, Durham Colls, 1939-47; Mackinnon Res. Student of Royal Society, 1942-44. Group-leader and later Branch-head in Chem. Div., AERE, Harwell, 1947-71. *Publications:* Atomic Energy Waste, 1961; contribs in fields of: microgasanalysis of atmospheric gases, theory of ion exchange and chromatography, radio chemistry, electrolyte solution chemistry. *Recreations:* gardening, music. *Address:* Bankside, Chilton, Oxon OX11 0RZ. *T:* Rowstock 296.

GLYN, family name of **Baron Wolverton.**

GLYN, Dr Alan, ERD; MP (C) Windsor and Maidenhead, since 1974 (Windsor, 1970-74); *b* 26 Sept. 1918; *s* of John Paul Glyn, late Lieut Royal Horse Guards, Barrister-at-Law, Middle Temple, and late Margaret Johnston, Edinburgh; *m* 1962, Lady Rosula Caroline Windsor Clive, *y d* of 2nd Earl of Plymouth, PC, GCStJ (*d* 1943), St Fagan's, Cardiff, S Wales; two *d. Educ:* Westminster; Caius Coll., Cambridge; St Bartholomew's and St George's Hosps. BA (Hons) Cantab 1939. Qualified medical practitioner, 1948. Served War of 1939-45; Far East, 1942-46; psc 1945; Bde Major, 1946; re-employed Captain (Hon. Major) Royal Horse Guards (ER) until 1967; att. French Foreign Legion, 1960. Called to Bar, Middle Temple, 1955. Co-opted Mem. LCC Education Cttee, 1956-58. MP (C) Clapham Div. of Wandsworth, 1959-64. Member: Chelsea Borough Council, 1959-62; No 1 Divisional Health Cttee (London), 1959-61; Inner London Local Med. Cttee, 1967-; Governing Body, Brit. Postgrad. Med. Fedn; Greater London Cent. Valuation Panel. Former Governor, Henry Thornton and Aristotle Schs; Manager, Macaulay C. of E. Sch., Richard Atkins, Henry Cavendish, Telfescot, Glenbrook and Boneville Primary Schs in Clapham. One of Earl Marshal's Green Staff Officers at Investiture of HRH Prince of Wales, Caernarvon, 1969. Freeman, Worshipful Soc. of the Art and Mystery of Apothecaries of the City of London, 1961. Pro-Hungaria Medal of SMO Malta, 1959. *Publication:* Witness to Viet Nam (the containment of communism in South East Asia), 1968. *Address:* 17 Cadogan Place, Belgrave Square, SW1. *T:* 01-235 2957. *Club:* Carlton.

GLYN, Sir Anthony (Geoffrey Leo Simon), 2nd Bt, *cr* 1927; author; *b* 13 March 1922; *s* of Sir Edward Davson, 1st Bt, and Margot, OBE (*d* 1966), *er d* of late Clayton Glyn and late Mrs Elinor Glyn; *S* father, Sir Edward Rae Davson, KCMG, 1937; assumed by deed poll, 1957, the surname of Glyn in lieu of his patronymic, and the additional forename of Anthony; *m* 1946, Susan Eleanor, barrister-at-law, 1950, *er d* of Sir Rhys Rhys-Williams, 1st Bt, DSO, QC, and Dame Juliet Rhys-Williams, DBE; two *d*. *Educ:* Eton. Jnd Welsh Guards, 1941; served Guards Armoured Div., 1942-45; Staff Capt, 1945. *Publications:* Romanza, 1953; The Jungle of Eden, 1954; Elinor Glyn, a biography, 1955 (Book Society Non-Fiction Choice); The Ram in the Thicket, 1957 (Dollar Book Club Choice); I Can Take it All, 1959 (Book Society Choice); Kick Turn, 1963; The Terminal, 1965; The Seine, 1966; The Dragon Variation, 1969; The Blood of a Britishman, 1970 (US edn, The British; trans. French, Spanish, Japanese). *Recreations:* ski-ing, chess. *Heir: b* Christopher Michael Edward Davson, ACA, late Capt. Welsh Guards [*b* 26 May 1927; *m* 1962, Evelyn Mary (marr. diss. 1971), *o d* of late James Wardrop; one *s* ; 2nd, 1975, Kate, *d* of Ludovic Foster, Greatham Manor, Pulborough]. *Address:* 13 Rue le Regrattier, Ile Saint-Louis, 75004 Paris, France. *T:* 633:3475; Friedegg, Westendorf, Tyrol, Austria. *Clubs:* Savile, Pratt's.

GLYN, Hilary B.; *b* 12 Jan. 1916; *s* of Maurice Glyn and Hon. Maud Grosvenor; *m* 1938, Caroline Bull; one *s* two *d*. *Educ:* Eton; New Coll., Oxford. DipEconPolSc. Joined Gallaher Ltd, 1937. Served, RASC Supp. Reserve, 1939-46 (A/Major). Director, Gallaher Ltd, 1962; Asst. Man. Dir, 1975; retd, 1976. *Recreations:* shooting, horse trials. *Address:* Oakum House, Albury, Ware, Herts SG11 2LW. *T:* Albury 328.
See also J . P . R . Glyn .

GLYN, John Patrick Riversdale, CBE 1974; Chairman: Agricultural Mortgage Corporation Ltd, since 1964; Alexanders Discount Co. Ltd, since 1961; Yorkshire Bank Ltd, since 1970; Dorland (City), since 1972; First National Finance Corporation Ltd, since 1975 (Deputy Chairman, 1974-75); Deputy Chairman, Exchange Telegraph (Holdings) Co., since 1972; Director, Stockholders Investment Trust Ltd, since 1969; a Development Commissioner since 1965; *b* 17 April 1913; *s* of Maurice G. C. Glyn and Hon. Maud Grosvenor; *m* 1937, Audrey Margaret Stubbs; two *s* two *d*. *Educ:* Eton; New Coll., Oxford. Major, Grenadier Guards. A Man. Dir, Glyn, Mills & Co., 1950-70; Chairman: John Govett & Co Ltd, 1970-75; Govett European Trust Ltd, 1972-75. *Recreations:* fishing, shooting. *Address:* The Dower House, Chute Standen, near Andover, Hants. *T:* Chute Standen 228. *Clubs:* Boodle's, Pratt's, City of London.
See also H . B . Glyn .

GLYN, Col Sir Richard Hamilton, 5th Bt *cr* 1800, and 9th Bt *cr* 1759; OBE 1955; TD 1941; DL; *b* 12 Oct. 1907; *e s* of Sir Richard Fitzgerald Glyn, 4th and 8th Bt, DSO; *S* father, 1960; *m* 1st, 1939, Lyndsay Mary Baker (marr. diss. 1969; she *d* 1971); two *s* one *d* ; 2nd, 1970, Mrs Barbara Henwood. *Educ:* Worcester Coll., Oxford. 2nd Lieut QO Dorset Yeo. Fd Regt, RA, TA, 1930; comd 141 Dorset Yeo. Fd Regt, RA, TA, 1944-45; comd 294 QO Dorset Yeo. Fd Regt, RA, TA, 1952-55; Hon. Col 1959; ADC, 1958-62. Called to Bar, Lincoln's Inn, 1935. Dep. Chm., Dorset QS, 1952-57. MP (C) North Dorset, 1957-70. Mem., Chelsea Borough Council, 1948-50 (Vice-Chm., Housing Cttee); Mem., Shaftesbury RDC, 1957. PPS to Sir D. Eccles (Pres. Board of Trade), June-Oct. 1958. Vice-Chm., Cons. Agric. Cttee, 1959-65, Chm., Cons. Army Cttee, Vice-Chm., Cons. Defence Cttee, 1961-68; Mem., Select Cttee on Estimates (Defence and Overseas), 1964-70; Comr, Commonwealth War Graves Commn, 1965-70. Chairman: Kennel Club, 1973-; Canine Consultative Council, 1974-; United and Cecil Club, 1960-64; President: Soc. of Dorset Men, 1963-70; Cruft's Dog Show, 1976- (Chm., 1963-73). DL Dorset 1960. *Publications:* Bull Terriers and How to Breed Them, 1937 (6th edn 1953); A Short Account of the Queen's Own Dorset Yeomanry, 1943; Champion Dogs of the World, 1967; (ed) The World's Finest Horses and Ponies, 1971. *Recreations:* sport, travel and pedigree livestock. *Heir: s* Richard Lindsay Glyn [*b* 3 Aug. 1943; *m* 1970, Carolyn Ann, *d* of R. F. Williams, Pasadena, Calif; one *s* one *d*. *Educ:* Eton]. *Address:* 53 Belgravia Court, Ebury Street, SW1W 0NY. *Clubs:* Pratt's, Kennel.

GLYN-JONES, Sir Hildreth, Kt 1953; TD 1950; FPS 1975; Judge of the High Court of Justice, Queen's Bench Division, 1953-68; *b* 19 March 1895; *s* of late Sir William Samuel Glyn-Jones and Mary Evans; *m* 1921, Kathleen, *d* of Thomas Melville; three *d. Educ:* City of London Sch. Military service, 1914-19 and 1939-44 (Middx Regt, Machine Gun Corps and Judge Advocate-General's Office). Qualified pharmacist, 1920; called

to Bar, Middle Temple, 1921, Bencher, 1951; QC 1943; Wales and Chester circuit; Recorder of Merthyr Tydfil, 1944-45; Recorder of Cardiff, 1945-53. Deputy Chm., Berks Quarter Sessions, 1951-62. JP Berks, 1951. *Address:* Pythouse, near Tisbury, Wilts. *T:* Tisbury 232.

GLYNN, Prof. Ian Michael, MD, PhD, FRS 1970; Professor of Membrane Physiology, University of Cambridge, since 1975; Fellow, Trinity College, since 1955; *b* 3 June 1928; 2nd *s* of Hyman and Charlotte Glynn; *m* 1959, Jenifer Muriel, 2nd *d* of Ellis and Muriel Franklin; one *s* two *d*. *Educ:* City of London Sch.; Trinity Coll., Cambridge; University Coll. Hosp. 1st cl. in Pts I and II of Nat. Sci. Tripos; BA (Cantab) 1949; MB, BChir, 1952; MD 1970. House Phys., Central Mddx Hosp., 1952-53; MRC Scholar at Physiol. Lab., Cambridge; PhD 1956. Nat. Service in RAF Med. Br., 1956-57; Trin. Coll. Res. Fellow, 1955-59, Staff Fellow and Dir of Med. Studies, 1961-73; Cambridge Univ. Demonstrator in Physiology, 1958-63, Lecturer, 1963-70, Reader, 1970-75. Vis. Prof., Yale Univ., 1969. Mem., MRC, 1976-. Chm., Editorial Bd, Jl of Physiology, 1968-70. *Publications:* scientific papers dealing with transport of ions across living membranes, mostly in Jl of Physiology. *Address:* Physiological Laboratory, Cambridge; Daylesford, Conduit Head Road, Cambridge. *T:* Cambridge 53079.

GLYNN, Prudence Loveday, (Lady Windlesham); Fashion Editor of The Times, since 1966; *b* 22 Jan. 1935; *d* of Lt-Col Rupert Trevor Wallace Glynn, MC, and Evelyn Margaret Vernet Glynn; *m* 1965, 3rd Baron Windlesham, *qv* ; one *s* one *d*. *Educ:* The Downs, Seaford, Sussex. Member: Design Council, 1973-; selection panel, Duke of Edinburgh's Design prize, 1971-73; Cttee for Art and Design, CNAA, 1972-; Chm., Fashion and Textile Bd, CNAA, 1976-; Mem. Council, Royal College of Art, 1969-. Consultant to fashion dept, Leicester Polytechnic. Governor, English-Speaking Union, 1972-. FRSA 1974. Cavaliere al merito della Repubblica Italiana, 1975. *Address:* The Times, New Printing House Square, 200 Gray's Inn Road, WC1. *T:* 01-837 1234.

GLYNN GRYLLS, Rosalie; *see* Mander, Lady (Rosalie).

GOAD, Sir (Edward) Colin (Viner), KCMG 1974; Secretary-General, Inter-Governmental Maritime Consultative Organization, 1968-73 (Deputy Secretary-General, 1963-68); Member: Advisory Board, International Bank, Washington DC; Joint Maritime Commission, International Labour Office, Geneva; *b* 21 Dec. 1914; *s* of Maurice George Viner Goad and Caroline (*née* Masters); *m* 1939, Joan Olive Bradley; one *s*. *Educ:* Cirencester Grammar Sch.; Gonville and Caius Coll., Cambridge (Scholar, BA, First Class Hons). Ministry of Transport: Asst Principal, 1937; Principal, 1942; Asst Sec., 1948; Imperial Defence Coll., 1953; Under-Sec., 1963. *Recreations:* gardening, reading, eighteenth-century furniture. *Address:* The Paddock, Ampney Crucis, Glos. *T:* Poulton 353. *Club:* Anglo-Belgian.

GOADBY, Hector Kenneth, FRCP; retired; Hon. Consulting Physician, St Thomas' Hospital, London; *b* 16 May 1902; *s* of late Sir Kenneth Goadby, KBE; *m* 1937, Margaret Evelyn (*née* Boggon); one *s* two *d. Educ:* Winchester; Trinity Coll., Cambridge (MA, MD). MRCS, LRCP 1926; FRCP 1936. Physician, St Thomas's Hosp., 1934-67; Cons. Physician, Southern Army and Eastern Comd, India, 1945; Physician, St Peter's Hosp., Chertsey, 1948. *Publications:* contribs to Jl of Physiology, Lancet, Acta Medica Scandinavica. *Recreations:* sailing, golf. *Address:* Four Oaks Cottage, Beckley, Rye, East Sussex. *T:* Beckley 335. *Clubs:* Royal Cruising; Rye Golf.

GOBBI, Tito; opera singer, baritone; *b* 24 Oct. 1915; *s* of Giovanni and Enrica Weiss; *m* 1937, Tilde de Rensis; one *d. Educ:* Padua Univ. Scholarship, Scala Opera House, 1936-37. Appeared Rome Opera House, 1939. Repertoire of 99 operas. Has sung in all the major opera houses and concert halls throughout the world. Notably Salzburg Festival: Don Giovanni (under Fürtwangler), 1950; Falstaff (under von Karajan), 1957. Has recorded 22 Complete Operas and made numerous other records; has made many films and appeared on television in England, USA and Italy. Started as Stage Director, Lyric Opera of Chicago, Oct. 1965; then Royal Opera House, Covent Garden, Master classes in Italy, USA and England. London. Mem., The Friends of Covent Garden; Hon. Mem., Univ. of Chicago; Hon. RAM. Disco d'Oro (Golden Record), 1959; Leopardo d'Oro, 1962. Hon. Officer, NY Police, 1969. Commendatore al Merito della Repubblica Italiana, 1958; Officer of San Jago, Portugal, 1970; Grand Officer, Order of Merit, Italy, 1976. *Recreations:* painting, driving, shooting, moulding. *Address:* via Valle Della Moletta 47, 00123 La Storta, Rome, Italy. *T:* 6990996. *Clubs:* Arts (London) (Hon. Mem.);

Societa Dante Alighieri; (Patron) Verdi Soc. (Liverpool); Roma Libera (Rome); Lyons (Hon. Mem.).

GOBLE, John Frederick; Solicitor, partner in Herbert Smith & Co., since 1953; Deputy Chairman of the Board of Crown Agents, since 1975; *b* 1 April 1925; *o s* of late John and Evileen Goble; *m* 1953, Moira Murphy O'Connor; one *s* three *d*. *Educ:* Highgate Sch.; Brasenose Coll., Oxford (MA). Served War, 1943-46, Sub-Lieut, RNVR. Admitted solicitor, 1951. A Crown Agent for Oversea Govts and Admins, 1974-. Governor, Highgate Sch., 1976. *Recreations:* music, golf. *Address:* 63 Dovehouse Street, SW3. *T:* 01-352 6169; 62 London Wall, EC2R 7JP. *T:* 01-628 9622. *Clubs:* City University; New Zealand Golf (West Byfleet).

GODBER, Geoffrey Chapham, CBE 1961; DL; Chief Executive, West Sussex County Council, 1974-75, retired (Clerk of the Peace and Clerk to the Council, 1966-74); Clerk to the Lieutenancy of West Sussex, 1974-76 (Sussex, 1968-74); *b* 22 Sept. 1912; *s* of late Isaac Godber, Willington Manor, near Bedford; *m* 1937, Norah Enid (*née* Finney); three *s*. *Educ:* Bedford Sch. LLB (London) 1935; Solicitor, 1936. Deputy Clerk of the Peace, Northants, 1938-44; Clerk of the Peace, Clerk of the County Council and Clerk of the Lieutenancy, Salop, 1944-66; Hon. Sec., Soc. of Clerks of the Peace of Counties, 1953-61 (Chm., 1961-64); Chm., Assoc. of County Chief Executives, 1974-75. Member: Probation Adv. and Trg Bd, 1949-55; Child Care Adv. Council, 1953-56; Cttee of Inquiry into Inland Waterways, 1956-58; Redevelopment Adv. Cttee, Inland Waterways, 1959-62; Waterways Sub-Commn, Brit. Transport, 1959-62; Central Adv. Water Cttee, 1961-70; Minister of Health's Long Term Study Group, 1965-69; S-E Economic Planning Council, 1969-75; CS Adv. Council, 1971-; British Waterways Bd, 1975-; Chichester Harbour Conservancy, 1975-; Shoreham Port Authority, 1976-; Chm., Open Air Museum, Weald and Downland, 1975-. DL W Sussex 1975. *Recreations:* sailing, shooting. *Address:* Pricklows, Singleton, Chichester, West Sussex. *T:* Singleton 238. *Club:* Naval and Military.
See also Sir G . E . Godber , Rt Hon . J . B . Godber .

GODBER, Sir George (Edward), GCB 1971 (KCB 1962; CB 1958); Chairman, Health Education Council, since 1977 (Member, since 1976); *b* 4 Aug. 1908; *s* of late I. Godber, Willington Manor, Bedford; *m* 1935, Norma Hathorne Rainey; two *s* one *d* (and two *s* two *d* decd). *Educ:* Bedford Sch.; New Coll., Oxford (Hon. Fellow, 1973); London Hospital; London Sch. of Hygiene. BA Oxon 1930; DM Oxon 1939; FRCP 1947; DPH London 1936. Medical Officer, Min. of Health, 1939; Dep. Chief Medical Officer, Min. of Health, 1950-60; Chief Medical Officer, DHSS, DES and Home Office, 1960-73. QHP, 1953-56. Scholar in Residence, NIH Bethesda, 1975. Vice-Pres., RCN, 1973. Mem., Argentine Med. Assoc., 1974; Corresp. Mem., Argentine Social Med. Soc., 1974. Fellow: American Hospital Assoc., and American Public Health Assoc., 1961; British Orthopaedic Assoc.; Mem. Dietetic Assoc., 1961; Hon. Member: Faculty of Radiologists, 1958; British Pædiatric Assoc.; Pharmacol. Soc., 1973. FRCOG *ad eundem*, 1966; FRCPsych 1973; FFCM 1974; Hon. FRCS, 1973; Hon. FRSM, 1973. Hon. LLD: Manchester, 1964; Hull, 1970; Nottingham, 1973; Hon. DCL: Newcastle 1972; Oxford 1973. Hon. Fellow, London Sch. of Hygiene and Tropical Medicine, 1976. Bisset Hawkins Medal, RCP, 1965; 150th Anniversary Medal, Swedish Med. Soc., 1966; Leon Bernard Foundn Medal, 1972; Ciba Foundn Gold Medal, 1970; Therapeutics Gold Medal, Soc. of Apothecaries, 1973. Lectures: Thomas and Edith Dixon Belfast, 1962; Bartholomew, Rotunda, Dublin, 1963; Woolmer, Bio-Engineering Soc., 1964; Monkton Copeman, Soc. of Apothecaries, 1968; Michael M. Davis, Chicago, 1969; Harold Diehl, Amer. Public Health Assoc., 1969; Rhys Williams, 1969; W. M. Fletcher Shaw, RCOG, 1970; Henry Floyd, Inst. of Orthopaedics, 1970; First Elizabeth Casson Meml, Assoc. of Occ. Therapists, 1973; Cavendish, W London Med.-Chir. Soc., 1973; Heath Clark, London Univ., 1973; Rock Carling, NPHT, 1975; Thom Bequest, RCSE, 1975; Maurice Bloch, Glasgow, 1975; Ira Hiscock, Yale, 1975; John Sullivan, St Louis, 1975; Fordham, Sheffield, 1976; Lloyd Hughes, Liverpool, 1977. *Publications:* (with Sir L. Parsons and Clayton Fryers) Survey of Hospitals in the Sheffield Region, 1944; The Health Service: past, present and future (Heath Clark Lectures), 1974; Change in Medicine (Rock Carling monograph), 1975; British National Health Service: Conversations, 1977. papers in Lancet, BMJ, Public Health. *Recreation:* golf. *Address:* 21 Almoners' Avenue, Cambridge CB1 4NZ. *T:* Cambridge 47491.
See also G . C . Godber , Rt Hon . J . B . Godber .

GODBER, Rt. Hon. Joseph Bradshaw, PC 1963; MP (C) Grantham Division of Lincs since 1951; Chairman, Retail Consortium, since 1976; *b* 17 March 1914; 5th *s* of late Isaac Godber and B. M. Godber (*née* Chapman), Willington Manor; *m* 1936, Miriam Sanders; two *s*. *Educ:* Bedford Sch. Entered family business, 1932. County Councillor, Beds, 1946-52. Asst Govt Whip, 1955-57; Joint Parliamentary Sec., Min. of Agriculture, Fisheries and Food, 1957-60; Parliamentary Under-Sec. of State, Foreign Office, 1960-61; Minister of State, 1961-63; Sec. of State for War, June-Oct. 1963; Minister of Labour, 1963-64; Leader, British Delegn to: United Nations General Assembly, 1961-62; 18-Power Disarmament Conference, 1962-63; Commonwealth Parly Assoc., 1970; Chief Opposition Spokesman on Agriculture, 1965-70; Minister of State, FCO, 1970-72; Minister of Agriculture, Fisheries and Food, 1972-74. Chairman: Sidney Banks Ltd, 1974-; Tricentrol Ltd, 1976-; Director: Booker McConnell Ltd, 1974-; British Home Stores Ltd, 1977-; Consultant, Beecham's Foods, 1974-. *Recreations:* gardening, shooting. *Address:* Willington Manor, near Bedford. *T:* Cardington 284. *Club:* Carlton.
See also G. C. Godber, Sir G . E . Godber .

GODDARD, Lt.-Gen. Eric Norman, CB 1947; CIE 1944; CBE 1942 (OBE 1919); MVO 1936; MC; IA, retired; *b* 6 July 1897; 3rd *s* of late Arthur Goddard, Chartered Acct, London; *m* 1939, Elizabeth Lynch, *d* of late Major Lynch Hamilton, and late Frances Prioleau; one *s*. *Educ:* Dulwich Coll. Commissioned Indian Army, 1915; service in Mesopotamia, Persia and Kurdistan, 1916-19 (despatches twice, OBE, MC); GSO3 AHQ India, 1923-25; Staff Coll., Quetta, 1928-29; Bde Major, Nowshera Bde, 1932-34; Chitral Relief, 1932 (despatches, bar to MC); Mohmand operations, 1933 (despatches); Bt Major, 1933; GSO2 Eastern Comd, 1934-36; Officer i/c King's Indian Orderly Officers, 1936 (MVO 4th class); Comdt 4th Bn 15 Punjab Regt, 1936; Bt Col 1939 and Col i/c Administration, Burma Army; Brigade Commander, Oct. 1940; Maj.-Gen. i/c Administration Army in Burma, Dec. 1941; served in Burma and on Eastern front, Dec. 1941-Dec. 1944, including Maj.-Gen. i/c Admin 11th Army Group and Allied Land Forces SE Asia, 1943-44 (despatches four times, CIE, CBE); GOC-in-C Southern Comd, India, 1947-48; Subst. Maj.-Gen. 1944; Actg Lieut-Gen. 1947; retired Nov. 1948 with hon. rank of Lieut-Gen. Special appointment CC Germany, 1949-53; Dir of Civil Defence, North-Western Region (Manchester), 1955-63; Pres., East Lancs Br., British Red Cross, 1964-66. *Address:* Muddles Cottage, Sparrows Green, Wadhurst, East Sussex. *T:* Wadhurst 2364. *Clubs:* Army and Navy, Naval and Military.

GODDARD, Maj.-Gen. John Desmond, MC 1944; Staff Director, Government Relations, British Leyland International, since 1972; *b* 13 Jan. 1919; *s* of late Major J. Goddard, HAC, Bombay and Gerrards Cross, Bucks; *m* 1948, Sheila Noel Vera, *d* of late C. W. H. P. Waud, Bombay and St John, Jersey; three *s* one *d*. *Educ:* Sherborne; RMA Woolwich. 2 Lieut, RA, 1939. Served War of 1939-45: France, 1939-40; N Africa, 1943; Italy, 1943-45. Brevet Lt-Col 1957; JSSC 1957; CO, 2 Fd Regt, RA, 1960-62; IDC 1964; CRA, 3 Div., 1965-66; BGS, Directorate Mil. Ops, MoD, 1966-69; Dir, Mil. Assistance Office, MoD, 1969-72, retired. *Recreations:* yachting, riding, shooting, golf, carpentry, gardening. *Address:* Cranford, Pinewood Hill, Fleet, Hants. *T:* Fleet 4825. *Clubs:* Army and Navy; Royal Lymington Yacht.

GODDARD, Air Marshal (retired) Sir (Robert) Victor, KCB 1947 (CB 1943); CBE 1940; MA Cantab; *b* 1897; *s* of late Charles Ernest Goddard, OBE, TD, MD; *m* 1924, Mildred Catherine Jane, *d* of Alfred Markham Inglis; two *s* one *d*. *Educ:* RN Colls Osborne and Dartmouth; Jesus Coll., Cambridge; Imperial Coll. of Science, London. Served European War, 1914-19, with RN, RNAS, RFC and RAF; War of 1939-45 (despatches, CBE, CB, American DSM); Dep. Dir of Intelligence, Air Min., 1938-39; AOA, GHQ, BEF, France, 1939, SASO 1940; Dir of Military Co-operation, Air Ministy, 1940-41; Chief of the Air Staff, New Zealand, and Commander Royal NZ Air Forces, South Pacific, 1941-43; Air Officer i/c Administration, Air Command, South-East Asia, 1943-46; RAF Representative at Washington, USA, 1946-48; Mem. of Air Council for Technical Services, 1948-51; retd 1951. Principal of the Coll. of Aeronautics, 1951-54. Governor (Chm. 1948-57), St George's Sch., Harpenden, 1948-64; Governor, Bryanston Sch., 1957-. Occasional broadcaster, 1934-. *Publications:* The Enigma of Menace, 1959; Flight towards Reality, 1975. *Address:* Meadowgate, Brasted, near Westerham, Kent TN16 1LN.

GODDEN, Ven. Max Leon; Archdeacon of Lewes and Hastings, since 1975 (of Lewes, 1972-75); Vicar of Glynde, Firle and Beddingham, since 1962; *b* 25 Nov. 1923; *s* of Richard George Nobel and Lucy Godden; *m* 1945, Anne, *d* of Kenneth and Edith Hucklebridge; four *d*. *Educ:* Sir Andrew Judd Sch., Tonbridge; Worcester Coll., Oxford (MA 1950). Served RAFVR, 1940-47 (despatches). Deacon, 1952; priest, 1953; Brighton, 1953-57; Hangleton, 1957-62. *Recreations:* life in a country parish, the garden. *Address:* Glynde Vicarage, Lewes, East Sussex. *T:* Glynde 234.

GODDEN, Rumer; *see* Haynes Dixon, Margaret Rumer.

GODDEN, Tony Richard Hillier, CB 1975; Secretary, Scottish Economic Planning Department, since 1973; *b* 13 Nov. 1927; *o s* of late Richard Godden and of Gladys Eleanor Godden; *m* 1953, Marjorie Florence Snell; one *s* two *d. Educ:* Barnstaple Grammar Sch.; London Sch. of Economics. Commissioned, RAF Education Branch, 1950. Entered Colonial Office as Asst Principal, 1951; Private Sec. to Parly Under-Sec. of State, 1954-55; Principal, 1956; Cabinet Office, 1957-59; transferred to Scottish Home Dept, 1961; Asst Sec., Scottish Development Dept, 1964; Under-Sec., 1969. *Recreations:* philately, photography, music. *Address:* 9 Ross Road, Edinburgh EH16 5QN. *T:* 031-667 6556. *Club:* New (Edinburgh).

GÖDEL, Prof. Kurt; Professor, School of Mathematics, Institute for Advanced Study, Princeton, NJ, since 1953; *b* 28 April 1906; *s* of Rudolf and Marianne Gödel; *m* 1938, Adele Porkert; no *c. Educ:* Univ. of Vienna, Austria. Dozent, Univ. of Vienna, 1933-38; Mem., Inst. for Advanced Study, 1933, 1935, 1938-52. Einstein Award (jt), 1951; Nat. Medal of Science, 1974; holds hon. doctorates from Univs in USA, 1951-. Member: Nat. Acad. Sci. (USA); Amer. Phil. Soc.; Amer. Acad. Arts and Sci.; Hon. Mem., London Math. Soc., 1967; For. Mem., Royal Soc., London, 1968; Corresp. Mem., Inst. de France, 1972; Corresp. Fellow, British Academy, 1972. *Publications:* The Consistency of the Continuum Hypothesis, 1940; Contribs to: Monatsh. for Math. und Phys.; Proc. Nat. Acad. Sci.; Reviews of Mod. Phys.; Internat. Cong. Math., 1950; Dialectica, etc. *Address:* Institute for Advanced Study, Princeton, NJ, USA. *T:* WA4-4400.

GODFREY, Derrick Edward Reid, MSc, PhD; Director, Thames Polytechnic, since 1970; *b* 3 May 1918; *s* of Edward Godfrey; *m* 1944, Jessie Mary Richards; three *s* one *d. Educ:* Shooters Hill Grammar Sch.; King's Coll., London. Design and development of aero-engines, with D. Napier & Sons, 1940-45; Lectr and Reader in Applied Mathematics, Battersea Polytechnic, 1945-58; Head of Dept of Mathematics and later Principal, Woolwich Polytechnic, 1958-70. Mem. Council for Nat. Academic Awards, 1964-67. *Publications:* Elasticity and Plasticity for Engineers, 1959; contribs to learned jls, etc, on mathematics and on educational matters. *Recreations:* music, gardening. *Address:* Whitehill, Wrotham, Kent. *T:* Borough Green 882871.

GODFREY, Gerald Michael, QC 1971; *b* 30 July 1933; *s* of late Sidney Godfrey and late Esther (*née* Lewin); *m* 1960, Anne Sheila, *er d* of David Goldstein; three *s* two *d. Educ:* Lower Sch. of John Lyon, Harrow; King's Coll., London Univ. LLB 1952, LLM 1954. Called to the Bar: Lincoln's Inn, 1954; Bahamas, 1972; Hong Kong, 1974. National Service as 2nd Lt, RASC, 1955; Temp. Captain, 1956. In practice at the Chancery Bar, 1957-. Chm., Justice Cttee on Parental Rights and Duties and Custody Suits (Report, 1975); Member: Senate of Inns of Court and the Bar, 1974-; Council of Justice, 1976. *Publication:* Editor, Business Law Review, 1958. *Recreations:* cricket (watching), claret (drinking), children (raising), music (listening). *Address:* 10 Brampton Grove, NW4; 9 Old Square, Lincoln's Inn, WC2A 3SR. *Club:* MCC.

GODFREY, Air Commodore Kenneth Walter, CB 1955; CBE 1954; retired; *b* 23 Jan. 1907; *s* of late Walter Godfrey; *m* 1932, Norah Josephine, *d* of J. Fleeman; one *s.* Granted commission in RAFVR, 1939; Gen. Duties Br., 1940; 22 (Torpedo) Bomber Sqdn; joined RAF Regt on formation, 1942. Served War, 1939-45 (Croix de Guerre with Palm; despatches twice). Comd RAF Regt Wing, Germany, 1945; Directorate of Comd and Staff Training, Air Min., 1946-48; comd RAF Station, Dumfries, 1951; apptd Senior Ground Defence Staff Officer, Technical Training Comd, 1952; Group Capt. 1952; comd Aden Protectorate Levies, 1953-55; Dep. Dir of Ground Defence, Air Ministry, 1955-59; ADC to the Queen, 1958-61; Air Cdre 1959; Dir of Ground Defence, Air Ministry, 1959-62; Actg Air Vice-Marshal, June 1962; Comdt-Gen. RAF Regt, and Inspector of Ground Defence, Air Min., 1962-63. *Recreations:* gardening, golf. *Club:* Royal Air Force.

GODFREY, Dr Malcolm Paul Weston, JP; Dean of Royal Postgraduate Medical School, since 1974; *b* 11 Aug. 1926; *s* of late Harry Godfrey and of Rose Godfrey; *m* 1955, Barbara Goldstein; one *s* two *d. Educ:* Hertford Grammar Sch.; King's Coll., London Univ.; KCH Med. Sch. MB, BS (Hons and Univ. Medal) 1950; MRCP 1955, FRCP 1972. Hosp. posts at KCH, Nat. Heart and Brompton Hosps; RAF Med. Br., 1952-54; Fellow in Med. and Asst Physician (Out-patients Dept) Johns Hopkins Hosp., USA, 1957-58; MRC Headquarters Staff, 1960-

74; MO, 1960; Sen. MO, 1964; Principal MO, 1970; Sen. Principal MO, 1974. Member: Sci. Adv. Panel CIBA Foundn, 1974-; Ealing, Hammersmith and Hounslow Area Health Authority (Teaching), 1975-; Council, Charing Cross Hosp. Med. Sch., 1975-. JP Wimbledon, 1972. *Publications:* contrib. med. jls on cardiac and respiratory disorders. *Recreations:* theatre, planning holidays (sometimes taking them), walking. *Address:* 7 Lancaster Gardens, Wimbledon, SW19 5DG. *T:* 01-946 6192; Royal Postgraduate Medical School, Hammersmith Hospital, Du Cane Road, W12 0HS. *T:* 01-743 2030.

GODFREY, Peter, FCA; Partner in Whinney Murray & Co., Chartered Accountants, since 1959; *b* 23 March 1924; *m* 1951, Heather Taplin; two *s* one *d. Educ:* West Kensington Central Sch.; City of London Coll. Served War, Army, 1942, until released, rank Captain, 1947. Qual. as an Incorporated Accountant, 1949; joined Whinney Smith & Whinney, 1949; admitted to partnership, 1959. Appointed: BoT Inspector into Affairs of Pinnock Finance Co. (GB) Ltd, Aug. 1967; DTI Inspector into Affairs of Rolls-Royce Ltd, April 1971; Mem., ODM Cttee of Inquiry on Crown Agents, April 1975. *Recreations:* family, militaria. *Address:* Oak Tree Cottage, Heathside Park Road, Woking, Surrey. *T:* Woking 60318.

GODLEY, family name of **Baron Kilbracken.**

GODLEY, Hon. Wynne Alexander Hugh; Director of Department of Applied Economics, University of Cambridge, since 1970, and an economic consultant to HM Treasury, since 1975; Fellow, King's College, Cambridge; *b* 2 Sept. 1926; *yr s* of Hugh John, 2nd Baron Kilbracken, CB, KC and Elizabeth Helen Monteith, *d* of Vereker Monteith Hamilton; *m* 1955, Kathleen Eleonora, *d* of Sir Jacob Epstein, KBE; one *d. Educ:* Rugby; New Coll., Oxford; Conservatoire de Musique, Paris. Professional oboist, 1950. Joined Economic Section, HM Treasury, 1956; Dep. Dir, Economic Sect., HM Treasury, 1967-70. Dir, Investing in Success Equities Ltd, 1970-; a Dir, Royal Opera House, Covent Garden, 1976-. Official Advr, Select Cttee on Public Expenditure. *Publications:* articles, in National Institute Review, Economic Jl, London and Cambridge Economic Bulletin, Cambridge Economic Policy Review. *Address:* Eversden House, Great Eversden, Cambs.

GODMAN, Col John, CBE 1957; DL; *b* 9 May 1886; *s* of E. T. Godman, DL; unmarried. *Educ:* Eton. 15/19 Hussars, 1905-30; commanded, 1926-30. Glos County Council, 1931 (Chm., 1946-56). Mem., Severn River Board (Chm., 1950-67). JP 1938, DL 1946, High Sheriff 1942, Gloucestershire. *Recreations:* shooting and fishing. *Address:* Banks Fee, Moreton-in-Marsh, Glos. *T:* Stow-on-the-Wold 5. *Club:* Cavalry and Guards.

GODWIN, Dame (Beatrice) Anne, DBE 1962 (OBE 1952); a Governor of the BBC, 1962-68; a full-time Member of the Industrial Court, 1963-69; *b* 1897. Gen. Sec., Clerical and Administrative Workers' Union, 1956-62. Chm. of the TUC, 1961-62. *Recreations:* talking, gardening, reading. *Address:* 25 Fullbrooks Avenue, Worcester Park, Surrey KT4 7PE. *Club:* English-Speaking Union.

GODWIN, Prof. Sir Harry, Kt 1970; FRS 1945; FGS; FLS; MA, ScD; Professor of Botany, University of Cambridge, 1960-68, Emeritus 1968; Fellow of Clare College, Cambridge, since 1925; *b* 9 May 1901; *m* 1927, Margaret Elizabeth Daniels; one *s* decd. University Reader in Quaternary Research, Cambridge, Oct. 1948-60. Croonian Lectr, Royal Soc., London, 1960. Pres., Xth International Botanical Congress, 1964. Foreign Member: Royal Danish Acad. of Science and Letters; Royal Scientific Soc. of Uppsala; German Acad. of Science Leopoldina; Amer. Acad. Arts and Scis; Hon. Mem., Royal Soc. of New Zealand; MRIA. Hon. ScD, Trinity Coll., Dublin, 1960. Hon. DSc: Lancaster, 1968; Durham, 1974. Prestwick Medal, Geol. Soc., London, 1951; Gold Medal, Linnean Soc., London, 1966. *Publications:* Plant Biology, 1930; History of the British Flora, 1956, new edn, 1975; Fenland: its ancient past and uncertain future, 1978. *Address:* 30 Barton Road, Cambridge CB3 9LF; Clare College, Cambridge. *T:* Cambridge 50883.

GOEHR, Prof. Alexander; composer; Professor of Music, and Fellow of Trinity Hall, University of Cambridge, since 1976; Artistic Director, Leeds Festival, since 1975; *b* 10 Aug. 1932; *s* of Walter and Laelia Goehr; *m* 1st, 1954, Audrey Baker (marr. diss. 1971); three *d*; 2nd, 1972, Anthea Staunton; one *s. Educ:* Berkhamstead; Royal Manchester Coll. of Music; Paris Conservatoire. Lectr, Morley Coll., 1955-57; Music Asst, BBC, 1960-67; Winston Churchill Trust Fellowship, 1968; Composer-in-residence, New England Conservatory, Boston, Mass, 1968-69; Associate Professor of Music, Yale University, 1969-70; West Riding Prof. of Music, Leeds Univ., 1971-76. Hon.

FRMCM; Hon. FRAM 1975. Hon. DMus Southampton, 1973. *Publications:* Fantasia Op. 4; Violin Concerto; Little Symphony; Pastorals; Romanza for 'cello; Symphony in one Movement, Op. 29; Piano Concerto, 1970; Concerto for Eleven, 1972; Metamorphosis/Dance, 1973; Lyric Pieces, 1974; Konzertstück; chamber music; *opera:* Arden must die; *cantatas:* Sutter's Gold; The Deluge; Triptych (Naboth's Vineyard; Shadowplay; Sonata about Jerusalem). *Address:* Trinity Hall, Cambridge; University Music School, Downing Place, Cambridge; c/o Schott & Co Ltd, 48 Great Marlborough Street, W1.

GOFF, E(ric) N(oel) Porter; *b* 24 Dec. 1902; *s* of John Richards Goff, Canon of Kildare and Rector of Portarlington, Ireland, and Alice Weir; *m* 1926, Barbara Denman Hodgson (*d* 1975); two *s*. *Educ:* Trinity Coll., Dublin (Scholar). BA (Senior Moderatorship and Gold Medal), 1924; MA 1929; Deacon 1926; Priest 1927; Curate of Immanuel, Streatham, 1926-29; Christ Church, Westminster, 1929-31; St Michael's, Chester Square, 1931-33; Vicar of Immanuel, Streatham, 1933-39; Provost of Portsmouth, 1939-72. Proctor in Convocation, 1939-72; Church Comr., 1948-72. Select Preacher: Univ. of Oxford, 1952-54; Dublin, 1956, 1959. *Address:* c/o Williams & Glyn's Bank Ltd, Holt's Branch, Kirkland House, Whitehall, SW1A 2DL. *Club:* National Liberal.

GOFF, Sir Ernest (William) Davis-, 3rd Bt *cr* 1905; *b* 11 June 1904; *s* of 2nd Bt and Margaret Aimée, *d* of late Rt Hon. Sir C. S. Scott, GCB; *S* father, 1923; *m* 1941, Alice Cynthia Sainthill Woodhouse (marr. diss. 1960); one *s* three *d*. *Heir: s* Robert William Davis-Goff, *b* 12 Sept. 1915. *Address:* Ardbrack Cottage, Kinsale, Co. Cork, Eire. *Club:* Kildare Street and University (Dublin).

GOFF, Martyn, OBE 1977; Director of the National Book League since 1970; *b* 7 June 1923; *s* of Jacob and Janey Goff. *Educ:* Clifton College. Served in Royal Air Force, 1941-46. Film business, 1946-48; Bookseller, 1948-70. Has lectured on: music; English fiction; teenager morality; the book trade, 1946-70; Fiction reviewer, Daily Telegraph, 1975-. Founder and Chm., Bedford Square Bookbang, 1971. Arts Council Literature Panel, 1970-; Arts Council Trng Cttee, 1973-; Greater London Arts Assoc. Literature Panel, 1973-; British Library Adv. Council, 1977-; Chm., Paternosters '73 Library Adv. Council, 1972-74. FIAL 1958. *Publications:* The Plaster Fabric, 1957; A Short Guide to Long Play, 1957; A Season with Mammon, 1958; A Further Guide to Long Play, 1958; A Sort of Peace, 1960; LP Collecting, 1960; The Youngest Director, 1961; Red on the Door, 1962; The Flint Inheritance, 1965; Indecent Assault, 1967; Why Conform?, 1968; Victorian and Edwardian Surrey, 1972; Record Choice, 1974; Royal Pavilion, 1976. *Recreations:* travel, collecting paintings and sculptures, music. *Address:* The Studio, 11 Cheyne Gardens, Chelsea, SW3 5QU. *T:* 01-352 3164. *Clubs:* Athenæum, Savile.

GOFF, Rt. Hon. Sir Reginald (William), PC 1975; Kt 1966; **Rt. Hon. Lord Justice Goff;** a Lord Justice of Appeal, since 1975; *b* 22 March 1907; *s* of late William Kingsley Goff, East India and China Tea Merchant, and late Louisa Goff; *m* 1944, Marjorie Morwenna Curnow, *d* of late Rev. A. Garfield Curnow, Wallington; two *d*. *Educ:* Sutton County Grammar Sch.; King's Coll. and University Coll., London. LLB (London) First Class Hons, 1928, and Certificate of Honour in the Bar examination, 1928. Called to the Bar, Lincoln's Inn, 1929; Bencher, 1959, Treasurer, 1974. War of 1939-45: Auxiliary Fire Service, 1939-42; RAF, 1942-46 (AJAG, 1945-46). Elected to Gen. Council of Bar, 1958. A Judge of the High Court of Justice, Chancery Div., 1965-75. Fellow, UCL, 1968-; FKC, 1970. *Address:* Kingsley Croft, Downs Way, Tadworth, Surrey. *T:* Tadworth 3636. *Club:* Royal Over-Seas League.

GOFF, Hon. Sir Robert (Lionel Archibald), Kt 1975; DCL; **Hon. Mr Justice Goff;** a Judge of the High Court, Queen's Bench Division, since 1975; *b* 12 Nov. 1926; *s* of Lt-Col L. T. Goff and Mrs Goff (*née* Denroche-Smith); *m* 1953, Sarah, *er d* of Capt. G. R. Cousins, DSC, RN; one *s* two *d* (and one *s* decd). *Educ:* Eton Coll.; New Coll., Oxford (MA 1953, DCL 1972). Served in Scots Guards, 1945-48 (commnd 1945). 1st cl hons Jurisprudence, Oxon, 1950. Called to the Bar, Inner Temple, 1951; Bencher, 1975; QC 1967. Fellow and Tutor, Lincoln Coll., Oxford, 1951-55; in practice at the Bar, 1956-75; a Recorder, 1974-75. Chairman: Council of Legal Educn, 1976-78 (Vice-Chm., 1972-76; Chm., Bd of Studies, 1970-76); Common Professional Examination Bd, 1976-; Member: Gen. Council of the Bar, 1971-74; Senate of Inns of Court and Bar, 1974- (Chm., Law Reform and Procedure Cttee, 1974-76). *Publications:* (with Prof. Gareth Jones) The Law of Restitution, 1966; articles in Modern Law Review. *Address:* Royal Courts of Justice, Strand, WC2.

GOHEEN, Robert Francis; United States Ambassador to India, since 1977; President Emeritus, Princeton University; *b* Venguria, India, 15 Aug. 1919; *s* of Dr Robert H. H. Goheen and Anne Ewing; *m* 1941, Margaret M. Skelly; two *s* four *d*. *Educ:* Princeton Univ. AB 1940; PhD 1948. Instructor, Dept of Classics, Princeton, 1948-50; Asst Prof., 1950-57; Prof., 1957-72. Sen. Fellow in Classics, Amer. Academy in Rome, 1952-53; Dir Nat. Woodrow Wilson Fellowship Program, 1953-56; Pres., Princeton Univ., 1957-72; Chm., Council on Foundns, 1972-77. Member: Bd, Carnegie Foundn for Advancement of Teaching; Bd, Rockefeller Foundation; Bd., Amer. Acad. in Rome; Bd, Equitable Life Assurance Soc.; Bd, Dreyfus Third Century Fund; Bd, Reza Shah Kabir Univ., Iran; American Philological Soc.; American Academy of Arts and Sciences; Phi Beta Kappa. Hon. degrees: Harvard, Rutgers, Yale, Temple, Brown, Columbia, New York, Madras, Pennsylvania, Hamilton, Middlebury, Saint Mary's (Calif), State of New York, Denver, Notre Dame, N Carolina, Hofstra, Nebraska, Dropsie, Princeton; Tusculum Coll.; Trinity Coll., USA; Coll. of Wooster; Jewish Theological Seminary of America; Ripon Coll.; Rider Coll. *Publications:* The imagery of Sophocles' Antigone, 1951; The Human Nature of a University, 1969; articles. *Recreations:* tennis and golf. *Address:* 1 Orchard Circle, Princeton, NJ 08540, USA; Princeton University, Princeton, New Jersey 08540, USA. *T:* 452-3000. *Clubs:* Princeton, (Hon.) University Century Association (New York); (Hon.) University, Cosmos (Washington); (Hon.) Nassau.

GOLD, Arthur Abraham, CBE 1974; President, European Athletic Association, since 1976 (Life Vice President, 1977); Honorary Secretary, British Amateur Athletic Board, 1965-77; *b* 10 Jan. 1917; *s* of late Mark and Leah Gold; *m* 1942, Marion Godfrey, *d* of late N. Godfrey; one *s*. *Educ:* Grocers' Company's Sch. Inst. of Motor Industry Wakefield Gold Medallist, 1945. Internat. high jumper, 1937; Past President: London AC; Middlesex County AAA; Athletics Team Leader Olympic Games: Mexico, 1968; Munich, 1972; Montreal, 1976. Council Mem., European Athletic Assoc., 1966-76; Mem. Council and F&GP Cttee, British Olympic Assoc. *Publications:* Ballet Training Exercises for Athletes, 1960; various contribs to technical books on athletics. *Recreations:* walking, talking, reading, weeding. *Address:* 49 Friern Mount Drive, Whetstone, N20 9DJ. *T:* 01-445 2848. *Club:* London Athletic.

GOLD, Jack; film director; *b* 28 June 1930; British; *m* 1957, Denyse (*née* Macpherson); two *s* one *d*. *Educ:* London Univ. (BSc (Econs), LLB). Asst Studio Manager, BBC radio, 1954-55; Editor, Film Dept, BBC, 1955-60; Dir, TV and film documentaries and fiction, 1960-. Three times winner of SSFTA award, Grand Prix (Monte Carlo); Desmond Davies Award, BAFTA, 1976; Critics Award; International Emmy. *TV films:* Tonight; Death in the Morning; Modern Millionairess; Famine; Dispute; 90 Days; Dowager in Hot Pants; Mad Jack; Stocker's Copper; Arturo Ui; The Lump; Catholics; World of Coppard; The Naked Civil Servant (Italia Prize); *cinema:* The Bofors Gun; The Reckoning; The National Health; Who?; Man Friday; Aces High; The Medusa Touch; *stage play:* The Devil's Disciple, Aldwych, 1976. *Recreations:* music, reading. *Address:* 18 Avenue Road, N6 5DW.

GOLD, John (Joseph Manson); Manager of Public Relations, Hong Kong Mass Transit Railway, since 1975; *b* 2 Aug. 1925; *m* 1953, Berta Cordeiro; one *d*. *Educ:* Clayesmore Sch., Dorset. Yorkshire Evening News, 1944-47; London Evening News, 1947-52; Australian Associated Press (New York), 1952-55; New York Corresp., London Evening News, 1955-66; Editor, London Evening News, 1967-72; Dir, Harmsworth Publications Ltd, 1967-73. Free-lance writer and lectr, Far East, 1973-75. *Address:* Mass Transit Railway Corporation, Hutchison House, Hong Kong.

GOLD, Stephen Charles, MA, MD, FRCP; Physician to: the Skin Department, St George's Hospital; St John's Hospital for Diseases of the Skin; King Edward VII Hospital for Officers; Hon. Consultant in Dermatology: to the Army; to Royal Hospital, Chelsea; *b* Bishops Stortford, Herts, 10 Aug. 1915; *yr s* of late Philip Gold, Stansted, Essex, and late Amy Frances, *er d* of James and Mary Perry; *m* 1941, Betty Margaret, *o d* of late Dr T. P. Sheedy, OBE; three *s* one *d*. *Educ:* Radley Coll.; Gonville and Caius Coll., Cambridge; St George's Hosp. (Entrance Exhibnr); Zürich and Philadelphia. BA 1937; MRCS, LRCP 1940; MA, MB, BChir 1941; MRCP 1947; MD 1952; FRCP 1958. Served RAMC, 1941-46. Late Med. First Asst to Out-Patients, St George's Hosp.; Senior Registrar, Skin Dept, St George's Hosp., Sen. Registrar, St John's Hosp. for Diseases of the Skin; Lectr in Dermatology, Royal Postgraduate Med. Sch., 1949-69. Sec., Brit. Assoc. of Dermatology, 1965-70. FRSM (late Sec. Dermatological Section, Pres., 1972-73); Fellow St

John's Hosp. Dermatological Soc. (Pres., 1965-66). *Address:* 149 Harley Street, W1N 2DE. *T:* 01-935 4444.

GOLD, Prof. Thomas, FRS 1964; Director, Center for Radio-Physics and Space Research, since 1959, and John L. Wetherill Professor, since 1971, Cornell University; *b* 22 May 1920; *s* of Max and Josefine Gold; *m* 1st, 1947, Merle E. Gold (*née* Tuberg); three *d*; 2nd, 1972, Carvel B. Gold (*née* Beyer); one *d*. *Educ:* Zuoz Coll., Switzerland; Trinity Coll., Cambridge. BA Mechanical Sciences (Cambridge), 1942; MA Mechanical Sciences, Cambridge, 1946; ScD, Cambridge, 1969. Fellow Trinity Coll., Cambridge, 1947. British Admiralty, 1942-46; Cavendish Laboratory, Cambridge, 1946-47 and 1949-52; Med. Research Council, Zoological Lab., Cambridge, 1947-49; Sen. Principal Scientific Officer (Chief Asst), Royal Greenwich Observatory, 1952-56; Prof. of Astronomy, 1957-58, Robert Wheeler Willson Prof. of Applied Astronomy, 1958-59, Harvard Univ. Hon. MA (Harvard), 1957. Member: Amer. Philosophical Soc.; Nat. Acad. of Sciences; Fellow, Amer. Acad. of Arts and Sciences. *Publications:* contribs to learned journals on astronomy, physics, biophysics. *Recreations:* ski-ing, travelling. *Address:* Center for Radiophysics and Space Research, Space Sciences Building, Cornell University, Ithaca, NY 14853, USA.

GOLD, Prof. Victor, FRS 1972; Professor of Chemistry, since 1964 and Head of Department of Chemistry since 1971, King's College, University of London; *b* 29 June 1922; *yr s* of late Dr Oscar and Mrs Emmy Gold; *m* 1954, Jean (*née* Sandiford); one *s* one *d*. *Educ:* King's Coll. and University Coll., London, Fellow UCL, 1973, FKC, 1975. BSc 1942, PhD 1945, DSc 1958; FRIC. Tuffnell Scholar 1942-44, Ramsay Meml Medal 1944, UCL; King's Coll., London: Demonstrator, 1944-46; Asst Lectr, 1946-47; Lectr in Chemistry, 1947-56; Reader in Physical Organic Chemistry, 1956-64. Res. Fellow and Resident Dr, Cornell Univ., 1951-52; Vis. Professor: Cornell Univ., 1962, 1963, 1965; Univ. of California, Irvine, 1970; Case Western Reserve Univ., 1975; Vis. Sen. Scientist, Brookhaven Nat. Lab., NY, 1962, 1966. Chm., British Cttee on Chemical Educn, 1977-. Mem. Council: Faraday Soc., 1963-66; Chem. Soc., 1971-74. Editor, Advances in Physical Organic Chemistry, 1963-. *Publications:* pH Measurements: their theory and practice, 1956; (with D. Bethell) Carbonium Ions: an introduction, 1967; (ed, with E. F. Caldin) Proton-Transfer Reactions, 1975; scientific papers, chiefly in Jl Chem. Soc. and Trans Faraday Soc. *Recreations:* music, computing. *Address:* Department of Chemistry, King's College, Strand, WC2R 2LS. *T:* 01-836 5454. *Club:* Athenæum.

GOLDBERG, Prof. Abraham; Regius Professor of Materia Medica, University of Glasgow; Consultant Physician, Stobhill General Hospital, Glasgow; *b* 7 Dec. 1923; *s* of late Julius Goldberg and Rachel Goldberg (*née* Varinofsky); *m* 1957, Clarice Cussin; two *s* one *d*. *Educ:* George Heriot's Sch., Edinburgh; Edinburgh University. MB, ChB 1946, MD (Gold Medal for thesis) 1956, Edinburgh; DSc Glasgow 1966; FRCP, FRCPE, FRCPGlas, FRSE. Nuffield Research Fellow, UCH Med. Sch., London, 1952-54; Eli Lilly Trav. Fellow in Medicine (MRC) in Dept of Medicine, Univ. of Utah; Lectr in Medicine 1956, Titular Prof. 1967, Univ. of Glasgow. Mem., Grants Cttee, Clinical Res. Bd, MRC, 1971-; Chm., Grants Cttee I, Clinical Res. Bd, MRC, 1973-; Mem., Editorial Bd, Jt Formulary Cttee, British Nat. Formulary, 1972-. Editor, Scottish Medical Jl, 1962-63. Lectures: Sydney Watson Smith, RCPE, 1964; Henry Cohen, Hebrew Univ., Jerusalem, 1973. Watson Prize, RCPGlas, 1959; Alexander Fleck Award, Univ. of Glasgow, 1967. *Publications:* (jtly) Diseases of Porphyrin Metabolism, 1962; (ed jtly) Recent Advances in Haematology, 1971; papers on clinical and investigative medicine. *Recreations:* swimming, writing. *Address:* 16 Birnam Crescent, Bearsden, Glasgow. *T:* 041-942 7770.

GOLDBERG, Arthur J(oseph), DJur; lawyer, USA; private practice, Washington DC, since 1971; *b* Chicago, Ill, 8 Aug. 1908; *s* of Joseph Goldberg and Rebecca (*née* Perlstein); *m* 1931, Dorothy Kurgans; one *s* one *d*. *Educ:* City Coll., Chicago; North-western Univ. (JD). Admitted to Bar of Ill., 1929, US Supreme Ct Bar, 1937. Private practice, 1929-48. Gen. Counsel: Congress of Industrial Workers, 1948-55; United Steel workers, 1948-61; Industrial Union Dept, AFL-CIO, 1955-61; Special Counsel, AFL-CIO, 1955-61. Member firm: Goldberg, Devoe, Shadur & Mikva, Chicago, 1945-61; Goldberg, Feller & Bredhoff, Washington, 1952-61; Paul, Weiss, Goldberg, Rifkind, Wharton & Garrison, NY, 1968-71. Sec. of Labor, 1961-62. Associate Judge, US Supreme Court, Washington, 1962-65; US Ambassador to UN, 1965-68; Chm., UNA of USA, 1968-70, Hon. Chm., 1970-. Is a Democrat. Charles Evans Hughes Prof., Woodrow Wilson Sch. of Diplomacy, Princeton Univ., 1968-69; Distinguished Prof., Sch. of Internat. Relations, Columbia Univ., 1969-70; Univ. Prof. of Law and Diplomacy, Amer.

Univ., 1971-73; Vis. Distinguished Prof., Univ. of Calif., SF, 1974-. Assoc. Fellow, Morse Coll., Yale Univ. Member: Chicago Bar Assoc.; Ill. Bar Assoc.; Amer. Bar Assoc.; DC Bar Assoc.; Assoc. Bar City of NY; Amer. Acad. Arts and Scis. Holds numerous awards and Hon. degrees. *Publications:* Civil Rights in Labor-Management Relations: a Labor Viewpoint, 1951; AFL-CIO-Labor United, 1956; Unions and the Anti-Trust Laws, 1956; Management's Reserved Rights, 1956; Ethical Practices, 1958; A Trade Union Point of View, 1959; Suggestions for a New Labor Policy, 1960; The Role of the Labor Union in an Age of Bigness, 1960; The Defenses of Freedom: The Public Papers of Arthur J. Goldberg, 1966; Equal Justice: the Warren era of the Supreme Court, 1972. *Address:* (office) 1101 17 Street NW, Washington, DC 20036, USA; (home) 2801 New Mexico Avenue NW, Washington DC 20007, USA.

GOLDBLATT, Simon, QC 1972. Called to the Bar, Gray's Inn, 1953. *Address:* 2 Garden Court, Temple, EC4Y 9BL.

GOLDBY, Prof. Frank; Professor of Anatomy, London University, St Mary's Hospital Medical School, 1945-70, retired; *b* Enfield, Middlesex, 25 May 1903; *s* of Frank and Ellen Maud Goldby; *m* 1932, Helen Rosa Tomlin; five *s* one *d*. *Educ:* Mercers' School, Holborn; Gonville and Caius College, Cambridge; King's College Hospital; MRCS, LRCP 1926; MRCP 1928; MD (Cambridge), 1936; FRCP, 1963; Resident appointments King's Coll. Hospital, 1926-28; Asst Clinical Pathologist, King's College Hospital, 1929-30; Senior Demonstrator in Anatomy, University College, London, 1931; Lecturer in charge of Anatomy Dept, Hong Kong, 1932-33; Lecturer in Anatomy, University of Cambridge and Fellow of Queens' College, 1934-37; Prof. of Anatomy, Univ. of Adelaide, 1937-45. *Publications:* papers on Embryology and on the Pathology and Comparative Anatomy of the Nervous System. *Address:* 1 St Mark's Court, Barton Road, Cambridge CB3 9LE.

GOLDEN, Grace Lydia, ARCA (London); *d* of H. F. Golden. *Educ:* City of London Sch. for Girls. Art Training at Chelsea Art Sch. and Royal College of Art; further studies at Regent Street Polytechnic; Black and White Illustrator, Posters, Panoramas, watercolour artist and wood-engraver; Exhibitor at Royal Academy, 1936, 1937, 1938 and 1940; watercolour, Summer Evening, Embankment Gardens, and oil-painting, Free Speech, purchased by Chantry Trustees. *Publication:* Old Bankside, 1951. *Recreation:* singing. *Address:* 37 Laurier Road, NW5 1SH.

GOLDFINGER, Ernő, RA 1975; FRIBA 1963; private architect; *b* Budapest, 11 Sept. 1902; *s* of Dr Oscar Goldfinger and Regine (*née* Haiman); *m* 1931, Ursula Ruth Blackwell; two *s* one *d*. *Educ:* Gymnasium, Budapest and Vienna; Le Rosay Rolle, Gstad, Switzerland; Ecole des Beaux Arts, Paris; Inst. d'Urbanisme, Sorbonne, 1927-28. DPLG 1932; RIBA 1946. Main Buildings: Shop, Helena Rubinstein, London, 1926; Monument, Algiers, 1928; House, Broxted, Essex, 1935; Terraced Houses, Willow Road, Hampstead, 1937 (scheduled as bldg of Architect. Interest, 1974); Houses, Bruxelles, 1951; (competition winner) Alex. Fleming House, Min. of Health, 1960 (Civic Trust Award, 1964); French govt's Tourist Offices, London and Paris; houses, flats, schs, neighbourhood units, newspaper bldg offices, warehouse, factories, farm, shops, old people's home, cinema; also Sunlight Studies, 1931 (designed Heliometer Machine). Exhibitions: Sect. of British Pavilion, Internat. Exhibn, Paris, 1937; ICI, Olympia BIF, 1938; MARS Gp, 1938; Grille CIAM, Aix en Provence, 1955; This is Tomorrow, London, 1956. Lecture tours: English and Amer. univs; France, Spain, Hungary. Hon. Sec., Brit. Sect., Internat. Reunion of Architects, parent body of Internat. Union of Archs (UIA), 1936; 1st Org. Sec., UIA, 1946 (drafted Statutes); RIBA Deleg., UIA Council, Cuba and Mexico, 1963; Deleg., UIA Sports Bldgs Commission: Oslo, 1964; Krakow, 1967; Mexico City, 1968. Member: French Sect., CIAM, 1928 (deleg. Congress, Athens, 1933); MARS Gp, 1934; Architect. Assoc., 1935 (Mem. Council, 1960-63, 1965-68); For. Relns Cttee, RIBA, 1937-45; Council, ARCUK, 1941-59; Bldg Req. Sub-cttee, Sci. Adv. Cttee to MPBW, 1943-45; Council of Industrial Design, 1961-65; Cercle d'Etudes Architecturels, Paris, 1975. Hon. Member: AASTA (now ABT), 1937; Assoc. of Hungarian Architects, 1963. FRSA. British Corresp., Architecture d'Aujourd'hui, 1934-74. *Publications:* County of London Plan Explained (jtly), 1945; British Furniture Today, 1951; contrib. Arch. Rev., RIBA Jl, Jl Inst. Amer. Architects, Architect. Year Book; *relevant Publications:* Goldfinger Ernő, by Prof. M. Major, 1973 (Budapest); articles in Architect. Design, Architect. Rev., Archs Jl, Architecture d'Aujourd'hui, Arch. & Urbanism, Tokyo, New Yorker 1957. *Recreations:* travel, architecture. *Address:* 2 Willow Road, Hampstead, NW3 1TH. *T:* 01-435 6166. *Club:* Savile.

GOLDIE, Rt. Rev. Frederick; *see* Glasgow and Galloway, Bishop of.

GOLDING, Dame (Cecilie) Monica, DBE 1958; RRC 1950 (ARRC 1940); *b* 6 Aug. 1902; *o d* of Ben Johnson and Clara (*née* Beames); *m* 1961, Brig. the Rev. Harry Golding, CBE (*d* 1969). *Educ:* Croydon Secondary Sch. Professional training: Royal Surrey County Hospital, Guildford, 1922-25; Louise Margaret Hosp., Aldershot and Queen Victoria's Institute of District Nursing. Joined Army Nursing Services, 1925; India, 1929-34; France, 1939-40; Middle East, 1940-43 and 1948-49; Southern Comd, 1943-44 and 1950-52; WO, 1945-46; India and SE Asia, 1946-48; Far East, 1952-55; Eastern Comd, 1955-56; Matron-in-Chief and Dir of Army Nursing Services, 1956-60, retired (with rank of Brig.), 1960. QHNS 1956-60; Col Commandant, Queen Alexandra's Royal Army Nursing Corps, 1961-66. OStJ 1955. *Recreations:* motoring; amateur bird watching and nature study. *Address:* 9 Sandford Court, 32 Belle Vue Road, Southbourne, Bournemouth, Dorset. *T:* 424122. *Club:* United Nursing Services.

GOLDING, F(rederick) Campbell, MB, ChM, FRCP, DMRE, FFR; retired; Director, X-Ray Diagnostic Department, Middlesex Hospital, 1956-67; Lecturer in Radiology, Middlesex Hospital Medical School; Hon. Consultant Radiologist, Royal National Orthopædic Hospital; Civilian Consultant in Radiology, RN and RAF; Consultant Radiologist, Arthur Stanley Institute for Rheumatic Diseases; Consultant Radiologist, Chelsea Hospital for Women; *b* 4 June 1901; *o s* of late Frederick Golding, Sydney, Australia, and Nell Campbell, Castlemaine, Victoria; *m* 1942, Barbara Hubbard, *d* of late Charles Hubbard, Nassau and of Mrs Hubbard, 15 Grosvenor Square, W1; two *s. Educ:* Scots Coll., Melbourne; St Andrews Coll., University of Sydney. Late Dir, X-Ray Diagnostic Dept, Royal Marsden Hosp.; Examiner in Radiology, Royal College of Physicians, 1954-57. Watson-Jones Lecturer, Royal College of Surgeons, 1964; Mackenzie Davidson Lecturer, British Institute of Radiology, 1961. *Publications:* (contrib.) Textbook of X-Ray Diagnosis by British Authors: (contrib.) Textbook of Rheumatic Diseases; (Jt) Survey of Radiology of the Chest, British Encyclopædia of Medical Practice, 1956; various other medical publications. *Recreation:* fishing in north of Scotland. *Address:* Fisherton de la Mere House, Wylye, Wilts. *T:* Wylye 232.

GOLDING, John; MP (Lab) Newcastle-under-Lyme since Oct. 1969; Parliamentary Under-Secretary of State, Department of Employment, since 1976; *b* Birmingham, 9 March 1931; *m* 1958, Thelma Gwillym; two *s. Educ:* Chester Grammar Sch.; London Univ.; Keele Univ. BA History, Politics, Economics, 1956. Asst Res. Officer, 1960-64, Education Officer, 1964-69, Political and Parly Officer, 1969-, Post Office Engineering Union. PPS to Minister of State, Min. of Technology, Feb.-June 1970; Opposition Whip, July 1970-74; a Lord Comr, HM Treasury, Feb.-Oct. 1974; Mem. Select Cttee on Nationalised Industries. Governor: University Coll. Hosp., 1970-74; Ruskin Coll., 1970-. *Publications:* co-author Fabian Pamphlets: Productivity Bargaining; Trade Unions—on to 1980. *Address:* House of Commons, SW1.

GOLDING, John, PhD; painter; Lecturer in the History of Art, Courtauld Institute, University of London, since 1962; *b* 10 Sept. 1929; *s* of Harold S. Golding and Dorothy Hamer. *Educ:* Ridley Coll. (St Catherine's, Ontario); Univ. of Toronto; Univ. of London. BA; MA; PhD. Tutor in Sch. of Painting, RCA, 1973-. Slade Prof. of Fine Art, Cambridge Univ., 1976-77. *Publications:* Cubism 1907-14, 1959, rev. edn, 1968; (with Christopher Green) Leger & Purist Paris, 1970; Duchamp: The Bride Stripped Bare by her Bachelors, Even, 1972; (ed with Roland Penrose) Picasso, 1881-1973, 1973. *Address:* 24 Ashchurch Park Villas, W12. *T:* 01-749 5221.

GOLDING, John Anthony, CVO 1966; Queen's Messenger, since 1967; *b* 25 July 1920; *s* of George Golding, Plaxtol, Kent; *m* 1950, Patricia May, *d* of Thomas Archibald Bickel; two *s. Educ:* Bedford Sch.; King's Coll., Auckland. Served with King's African Rifles and Military Administration, Somalia, 1939-46 (Captain). Entered Colonial Service, 1946; Dep. Provincial Comr, Tanganyika, 1961; Administrator, Turks and Caicos Is, 1965-67. *Recreations:* gardening, fishing, shooting. *Address:* Elmore House, Sway, Hants.

GOLDING, Dame Monica; *see* Golding, Dame C. M.

GOLDING, William (Gerald), CBE 1966; author; *b* 19 Sept. 1911; *s* of Alec A. and Mildred A. Golding; *m* 1939, Ann, *e d* of late E. W. Brookfield, The Homestead, Bedford Place, Maidstone; one *s* one *d. Educ:* Marlborough Grammar Sch.; Brasenose Coll., Oxford. MA Oxon 1961. FRSL 1955. Hon.

Fellow, Brasenose Coll., Oxford, 1966. Hon. DLitt, Sussex, 1970. *Publications:* Lord of the Flies, 1954 (filmed 1963); The Inheritors, 1955; Pincher Martin, 1956; Brass Butterfly (play), 1958; Free Fall, 1959; The Spire, 1964; The Hot Gates, 1965; The Pyramid, 1967; The Scorpion God, 1971. *Recreations:* music, sailing; Greek. *Address:* Ebble Thatch, Bowerchalke, Wilts. *T:* Broad Chalke 275. *Clubs:* Athenæum, Savile.

GOLDMAN, Peter, CBE 1959; Director of Consumers' Association, since 1964; Patron of International Organisation of Consumers Unions (President, 1970-75); *b* 4 Jan. 1925; *o s* of late Captain Samuel Goldman and Jessie Goldman (*née* Englander); *m* 1st, 1961, Cicely Ann Magnay (marr. diss. 1969); 2nd, 1970, Stella Maris Joyce. *Educ:* Pembroke Coll., Cambridge; London Univ. BA 1st cl. hons History 1946, MA 1950, Cantab; Pres., Cambridge Union; Hadley Prize, Pembroke Coll., 1946; BA 1st cl. hons History, London, 1948. Smith-Mundt Fellowship, USA, 1955-56. Joined Conservative Research Dept, 1946; Head of Home Affairs Section, 1951-55; Dir of Conservative Political Centre, 1955-64; Mem., LCC Educn Cttee, 1958-59; contested (C) West Ham South, 1959, Orpington, 1962; Chm., Coningsby Club, 1958-59, Treas., 1953-58, 1963-; Sec., Research Inst. for Consumer Affairs, 1964-; Sec., Good Food Club, 1965-; Member: Post Office Users' Nat. Council, 1970-72; Community Relations Commn, 1973-75; Wine Standards Bd, 1973-; Cttee of Inquiry into the Future of Broadcasting, 1974-77; Royal Commn on Lega Services, 1976-; Council on Internat. Develt, 1977-. FRSA 1970 (Silver Medal, 1969). *Publications:* County and Borough, 1952; Some Principles of Conservatism, 1956; The Welfare State, 1964; Consumerism: art or science?, 1969; Multinationals and the Consumer Interest, 1974. *Address:* 34 Campbell Court, Queen's Gate Gardens, SW7. *T:* 01-589 9464. *Club:* Carlton.

GOLDMAN, Sir Samuel, KCB 1969 (CB 1964); Chairman: Fraser Ansbacher Ltd, since 1976; Henry Ansbacher Ltd, since 1976; Chairman, Covent Garden Market Authority, since 1976; *b* 10 March 1912; *y s* of late Philip and late Sarah Goldman; *m* 1st, 1933, Pearl Marre (*d* 1941); one *s*; 2nd, 1943, Patricia Rosemary Hodges. *Educ:* Davenant Foundation Sch.; Raine's Sch.; London Sch. of Economics, London Univ. Inter-Collegiate Scholar. BSc (Econ.), First Class Hons in Economics and Gladstone Memorial Prize, 1931; MSc (Econ.), 1933. Hutchinson Silver Medallist. Moody's Economist Services, 1934-38; Joseph Sebag & Co., 1938-39; Bank of England, 1940-47. Entered Civil Service, 1947, as Statistician in Central Statistical Office; transferred to Treasury, Sept. 1947; Chief Statistician, 1948; Asst Sec., 1952; Under-Sec., 1960-62; Third Sec., 1962-68; Second Perm. Sec., 1968-72. UK Alternate Executive Dir, International Bank, 1961-62. Exec. Dir, 1972-74, Man. Dir, 1974-76, Orion Bank Ltd. Member: Council, Royal Economic Soc.; Council, Inst. of Fiscal Studies. Hon. Fellow LSE. *Publication:* Public Expenditure Management and Control, 1973. *Recreation:* gardening. *Address:* The Old Orchard, Danes Hill, Oxshott, Surrey. *T:* Oxshott 2052. *Club:* Reform.

GOLDMANN, Dr Nahum; President of the World Jewish Congress since 1951; *b* 10 July 1895; *s* of Solomon and Rebecca Goldmann; *m* 1934, Alice (*née* Gottschalk); two *s. Educ:* Berlin, Marburg, Heidelberg, Germany. Editor of Encyclopædia Judaica in Berlin, 1922-34; Rep. of Jewish Agency for Palestine with League of Nations, Geneva, 1934-40; Pres., Cttee of Jewish Delegations, 1936-; Mem. Exec. Cttee, Jewish Agency for Palestine, 1934-; Chm. Exec. Cttee, World Jewish Congress, 1936-; Rep., Jewish Agency in USA, 1940-; Chm. Admin. Cttee, World Jewish Congress, 1945-51; Chm., Jewish Agency, 1951 (Pres., 1956-68); Pres., Conf. on Jewish Material Claims against Germany, 1950-; Pres., Memorial Foundation for Jewish Culture, 1965. *Publications:* Memories, 1970; Où va Israel?, 1975; Le Paradoxe Juif, 1977. *Address:* 12 Avenue Montaigne, Paris, France. *T:* 256.22.99; 18 Ahad Haam, Jerusalem. *T:* 38195.

GOLDNEY, Maj.-Gen. Claude Le Bas, CB 1943; CBE 1940; MC; *b* 4 Dec. 1887; *s* of late Col W. H. Goldney, RE; *m* 1938, Nora (*d* 1968), *yr d* of late Surg. Maj.-Gen. Sir Gerald Bomford, KCIE; no *c. Educ:* Dover Coll.; Portsmouth Grammar Sch.; RMA Woolwich. Commnd in Glos Regt 1906; Transf. ASC 1910; served European War, France, 1914-18 (despatches, MC); Col 1937; ADS & T, Egypt, 1938; ADS & T, Aldershot, 1939; served War of 1939-45; DDS & T, 1st Corps, with BEF, to France, 1939; DDS & T, 3rd Corps, until evacuation Dunkirk, 1940 (CBE, CB, despatches thrice); Acting Maj.-Gen. 1941; Dir of Supplies and Transport, GHQ, Middle East Force, 1941-44; ADC to HM the King, 1942-44, retired 1944. *Recreation:* fishing. *Address:* 38 Mount Hermon Road, Woking, Surrey.

GOLDS, Anthony Arthur, CMG 1971; MVO 1961; HM Diplomatic Service, retired; Director, British National Committee, International Chamber of Commerce, since 1977; *b* 31 Oct. 1919; *s* of late Arthur Oswald Golds and Florence Golds (*née* Massey); *m* 1944, Suzanne Macdonald Young; one *s* one *d*. *Educ:* King's Sch., Macclesfield; New Coll., Oxford (Scholar). HM Forces (Royal Armoured Corps), 1939-46; CRO, 1948; 1st Sec., Calcutta and Delhi, 1951-53; Commonwealth Office, 1953-56; Head of Chancery, British Embassy, Ankara, 1957-59; Karachi, 1959-61; Counsellor in Commonwealth Office and Foreign Office, 1962-65; Head of Joint Malaysia/Indonesia Dept, 1964-65; Counsellor, HM Embassy, Rome, 1965-70; Ambassador to the Republic of Cameroon, the Republic of Gabon and the Republic of Equatorial Guinea, 1970-72; High Comr to Bangladesh, 1972-74; Senior Civilian Instructor, RCDS, 1975-76. *Recreations:* music, cricket, golf, literature. *Address:* International Chamber of Commerce, 6/14 Dean Farrar Street, SW1H 0DT. *Club:* United Oxford & Cambridge University.

GOLDSMID, Sir James Arthur d'A.; *see* d'Avigdor-Goldsmid.

GOLDSMITH, Sir James (Michael), Kt 1976; Chairman: Cavenham Ltd; Anglo-Continental Investment & Finance Co. Ltd; Generale Occidentale SA Paris; Director: Société des Hotels Réunis; Banque Rothschild; *b* 26 Feb. 1933; *s* of Frank Goldsmith, OBE and Marcelle Mouiller; *m* 1st, 1953, Maria Isabel Patino (*d* 1954); one *d*; 2nd, 1963, Ginette Lery; one *s* one *d*. *Educ:* Eton College. *Address:* 65/68 Leadenhall Street, EC3A 2BA. *Clubs:* Buck's, Brooks's; Travellers' (Paris).

GOLDSMITH, John Stuart; Assistant Under-Secretary of State, Ministry of Defence, since 1973; *b* 2 Nov. 1924; *o s* of R. W. and S. E. Goldsmith; *m* 1948, Brenda; two *s* one *d*. *Educ:* Whitgift Middle Sch.; St Catharine's Coll., Cambridge. Royal Signals, 1943-47 (Captain). War Office, 1948; Principal, 1952; Treasury, 1961-64; Asst Sec., MoD, 1964; RCDS 1971; Chm. Civil Service Selection Bd, 1973. *Recreations:* gardening, jazz, travel. *Address:* Jonsplat, Orchard Close, East Horsley, Surrey KT24 5EZ. *T:* East Horsley 4525. *Club:* Civil Service.

GOLDSMITH, John Thorburn, CBE 1959; a Manager of the Royal Institution, 1964-67 and 1968-71; Part-time Member, NW Area Gas Board, 1955-64; *b* 30 May 1903; *m* 1932, Monica, *d* of late Capt. Harry Simon; one *d*. *Educ:* Marlborough; Magdalen Coll., Oxford. War of 1939-45, Fire Staff Officer, Grade I, National Fire Service. Dep. Chm., Civil Service Selection Bd, 1945; Chm., Civil Service Selection Board, and a Civil Service Commissioner, 1951-63. Haakon Cross, Norway, 1945; Order of Orange Nassau, Netherlands, 1945. *Publications:* Hildebrand (Children's Stories), 1931, 1949; Three's Company, 1932. *Recreation:* fly-fishing. *Address:* 31 Marsham Court, Marsham Street, SW1P 4JY. *T:* 01-828 1958. *Club:* Flyfishers'.

GOLDSMITH, Mac; retired; *b* 3 July 1902; *s* of David and Klara Goldschmidt; *m* 1936, Ruth (*née* Baum); one *s* one *d*. *Educ:* Oberealschule, Marburg; Technical Coll., Mannheim. Founded Mecano GmbH Frankfurt/M, 1925; Metallgummi GmbH Frankfurt/M, 1933; Metalastik Ltd, Leicester, 1937; British Bundy Tubing Co., Welwyn Garden City, 1937; acquired Precision Rubbers Ltd for Metalastik Ltd, 1955, and merged Metalastik Ltd with John Bull Gp of Cos (Dep. Chm. and Man. Dir); merged with Dunlop Ltd, 1958; retd from Dunlop Gp, 1970. Farmer, Normanton House and Manor Farms, Thurlaston, Leics. Trustee, Leicester Theatre Trust; Life Mem., Ct and Mem., Council, Leicester Univ.; Member: Leicester and District Disablement Adv. Cttee of Dept of Employment; Leicester Museums, Libraries and Publicity Cttee; various cttees, Royal Leicester, Rutland and Wycliffe Soc. for the Blind; Adv. Cttee, Leicester Clinic; Bd of Governors, Jerusalem Coll. of Technology Sch. of Applied Sciences; Life Governor, Hillel House, London; Trustee, Leicester Hebrew Congregation; President: Leicester Maccabi Assoc.; Friends of Leicester City Schools Orchestra; Leicester Symphony Orchestra; Friends of Groby Road Hosp.; Vice-Pres., City of Leicester Competitive Festival of Music. Hon. LLD Leicester, 1971. Freeman, City of Leicester, 1971. *Recreations:* formerly golf, riding, ski-ing. *Address:* 3 Birkdale Avenue, Knighton Road, Leicester LE2 3HA. *T:* Leicester 708127.

GOLDSMITH, Robert, CMG 1974; Minister and Deputy Head, Office of UK Permanent Representative to the European Communities, since 1972; *b* 28 Nov. 1924; *s* of late Stanley Thomas Goldsmith and Ida Goldsmith (*née* Rawlinson); *m* 1957, Eileen Bernadette McCormack (*d* 1974); one *d*. *Educ:* King James Grammar Sch., Almondbury; Manchester Univ.; St Catherine's Society, Oxford. War Service, 1943-45. Hons Sch. of Philosophy, Politics and Economics (1st Class Hons, 1947),

Oxford. Entered Bd of Trade, 1948; UK Treasury and Supply Delegn, Washington (First Sec.), 1953-57; Asst Sec., 1964; Under Sec., 1968; Dep. Sec., 1974. *Recreation:* cricket (Pres. Byfleet Cricket Club). *Address:* c/o Foreign and Commonwealth Office, SW1. *Club:* United Oxford & Cambridge University.

GOLDSMITH, Maj.-Gen. (Retd) Robert Frederick Kinglake, CB 1955; CBE 1952; *b* 21 June 1907; *s* of late Col Harry Dundas Goldsmith, CBE, DSO; *m* 1935, Brenda, *d* of Frank Bartlett, late Ceylon Civil Service; one *s*. *Educ:* Wellington Coll., Berks. Commnd Duke of Cornwall's LI, 1927; served War of 1939-45, in N Africa, Italy, NW Europe; Dep. Chief of Staff, First Allied Airborne Army, 1944-45; comd 131 Inf. Bde (TA), 1950-51; Chief of Staff, British Troops in Egypt, 1951-54, and of HQ Western Command, 1956-59; GOC Yorks District, 1959-62; Col, Duke of Cornwall's LI, 1958-59; Col Somerset and Cornwall LI, 1960-63. Editor, The Army Quarterly, 1966-73. Comdr, Legion of Merit (US) 1945. *Address:* 40 Christchurch Road, Winchester, Hants. *Clubs:* Army and Navy, MCC.

GOLDSTEIN, Alfred, CBE 1977; Senior Partner, R. Travers Morgan & Partners, Consulting Engineers, since 1971; *b* 9 Oct. 1926; *s* of late Sigmund and Regina Goldstein; *m* 1959, Anne Milford, *d* of late Col R. A. M. Tweedy and of Maureen Evans, and step *d* of Hubert Evans; two *s*. *Educ:* Rotherham Grammar Sch.; Imperial Coll., Univ. of London. BSc (Eng); ACGI 1946; DIC. FICE 1959; FIStructE 1959; FIHE 1959; MConsE 1959. Partner, R. Travers Morgan & Partners, 1951; responsible for planning, design and supervision of construction of major road and bridge projects and for planning and transport studies, incl. M23, Belfast Transportation Plan, Clifton Bridge, Nottingham, Elizabeth Bridge, Cambridge, Itchen Bridge, Southampton. Transport Consultant to Govt SE Jt Planning Team for SE Regional Plan; in charge London Docklands Redevelopment Study; Cost Benefit Study for 2nd Sydney Airport for Govt of Australia. Member: Building Research Bd, subseq. Adv. Cttee on Building Research, 1963-66; Civil Engrg EDC on Contracting in Civil Engrg since Banwell, 1965-67; Baroness Sharp's Adv. Cttee on Urban Transport Manpower Study, 1967-69; Commn of Inquiry on Third London Airport, 1968-70; Urban Motorways Cttee, 1969-72; Genesys Bd, 1969-74; Chm., DoE Planning and Tnspt Res. Adv. Council; Mem., TRRL Adv. Cttee on Transport; DoE Environmental Bd. *Publications:* papers and lectures (inc. Criteria for the Siting of Major Airports, 4th World Airports Conf., 1973; Highways and Community Response, 9th Rees Jeffreys Triennial Lecture, RTPI, 1975). *Recreations:* carpentry, music, bridge. *Address:* Wellington House, Strand, WC2R 0AR. *T:* 01-836 5474; Kent Edge, Crockham Hill, Edenbridge, Kent TN8 6TA. *T:* Crockham Hill 227. *Club:* Athenæum.

GOLDSTEIN, Sydney, FRS 1937; MA; PhD; Gordon McKay Professor of Applied Mathematics, Harvard University, Emeritus; *b* 3 Dec. 1903; *o s* of Joseph and Hilda Goldstein, Hull; *m* 1926, Rosa R. Sass, Johannesburg; one *s* one *d*. *Educ:* Bede Collegiate Sch., Sunderland; University of Leeds; St John's Coll., Cambridge. Mathematical Tripos, 1925; Smith's Prize, 1927; PhD, 1928; Rockefeller Research Fellow, University of Göttingen, 1928-29; Lectr in Mathematics, Manchester Univ., 1929-31; Lectr in Mathematics in the Univ. of Cambridge, 1931-45; Fellow of St John's Coll., Cambridge, 1929-32, 1933-45; Leverhulme Research Fellow, Calif. Inst. of Technology, 1938-39; Beyer Prof. of Applied Mathematics, Manchester Univ., 1945-50; Prof. of Applied Mathematics, 1950-55; and Chm. Aeronautical Engineering Dept, 1950-54, Institute of Technology, Haifa, Israel, and Vice-Pres. of the Institute, 1951-54. Worked at Aerodynamics Div., National Physical Laboratory, 1939-45; Adams Prize, 1935. Chm., Aeronautical Research Council, 1946-49. Foreign Mem. of Royal Netherlands Acad. of Sciences and Letters (Section for Sciences), 1950. Hon. Fellow: St John's Coll., Cambridge, 1965; Weizmann Inst. of Science, 1971; Hon. FRAeS, 1971; Hon. FIMA, 1972. Hon. DEng Purdue Univ., 1967; Hon. DSc: Case Inst. of Technology, 1967; The Technion, Israel Inst. of Technology, Haifa, Israel, 1969; Leeds Univ., 1973. Timoshenko Medal of Amer. Soc. of Mech. Engrs (for distinguished contribs to Applied Mechanics), 1965. *Publications:* (ed) Modern Developments in Fluid Dynamics, 1938; Lectures on Fluid Mechanics, 1960; papers on mathematics and mathematical physics, especially hydrodynamics and aerodynamics. *Address:* 28 Elizabeth Road, Belmont, Mass 02178, USA.

GOLDSTONE, David Israel, CBE 1971; JP; Chairman, Sterling McGregor Ltd Group of Companies; *b* Aug. 1908; *s* of Philip and Bessie Goldstone; *m* 1931, Belle Franks; one *s* two *d*. Pres., Manchester Chamber of Commerce and Industry, 1970-72; Chm., NW Regions Chambers of Commerce Council, 1970-73;

Exec. Mem., Association British Chambers of Commerce Nat. Council, 1970-73; Exec. Mem., British Nat. Council, Internat. Chambers of Commerce; Mem., NW Telecommunications Bd; Vice-Pres., Manchester Youth Clubs Assoc.; Mem. local tribunals, charitable organisations, etc. JP Manchester, 1958. *Address:* Dellstar, Elm Road, Didsbury, Manchester, M20 0XD. *T:* 061-445 1868.

GOLDSTONE, Prof. Jeffrey, PhD; FRS 1977; Professor of Physics, Massachusetts Institute of Technology, since 1977; *b* 3 Sept. 1933; *s* of Hyman Goldstone and Sophia Goldstone. *Educ:* Manchester Grammar Sch.; Trinity Coll., Cambridge (MA 1956, PhD 1958). Trinity Coll., Cambridge: Entrance Scholar, 1951; Res. Fellow, 1956; Staff Fellow, 1962; Cambridge University: Lectr, 1961; Reader in Math. Physics, 1976. Vis. appointments: Institut for Teoretisk Fysik, Copenhagen; CERN, Geneva; Harvard Univ.; MIT. *Publications:* articles in learned jls. *Address:* Department of Physics, Massachusetts Institute of Technology, Cambridge, Mass 02139, USA. *T:* (office) 253-6263, (home) 547-3387.

GOLDSTONE, Peter Walter; Metropolitan Stipendiary Magistrate since 1971; a Recorder of the Crown Court, since 1972; *b* 1 Nov. 1926; *y s* of late Adolph Lionel Goldstone and Ivy Gwendoline Goldstone; *m* 1955, Patricia (*née* Alexander), JP; one *s* two *d. Educ:* Manchester Grammar Sch.; Manchester Univ. Solicitor, 1951. Fleet Air Arm, 1944-47. Partner in private practice with brother Julian S. Goldstone, 1951-71. Manchester City Councillor (L), 1963-66; Chm., Manchester Rent Assessment Panel, 1967-71; Reserve Chm., Manchester Rent Tribunal, 1969-71; Dep. Chm., Inner London QS, Nov. 1971. *Recreations:* walking, gardening, reading. *Address:* 2 Old Forge Close, Stanmore, Mddx. *T:* 01-954 1901.

GOLDSWORTHY, Rt. Rev. Arthur Stanley; *see* Bunbury, Bishop of.

GOLDWATER, Barry M(orris); US Senator from Arizona, 1953-64, and since 1969; *b* Phoenix, Arizona, 1 Jan. 1909; *s* of late Baron Goldwater and Josephine Williams; *m* 1934, Margaret Johnson; two *s* two *d. Educ:* Staunton Mil. Acad., Virginia; University of Arizona. 2nd Lieut, Army Reserve, 1930; transferred to USAAF, 1941; served as ferry-command and fighter pilot instructor, Asia, 1941-45 (Lieut-Col); Chief of Staff, Arizona Nat. Guard, 1945-52 (Col); Maj.-Gen., USAF Reserves. Joined Goldwater's Inc., 1929 (Pres., 1937-53). City Councilman, Phoenix, 1949-52; Republican Candidate for the Presidency of the USA, 1964. Member: Advisory Cttee on Indian Affairs, Dept of Interior, 1948-50; Armed Services Cttee; Commerce, Science and Transportation Cttee; Select Cttee on Intelligence; Heard Museum; Museum of Northern Arizona; St Joseph's Hosp.; Vive-Chairman: Amer. Graduate Sch. of Internat. Management; Bd of Regents, Smithsonian Institution; Member: Veterans of Foreign Wars; American Legion; Royal Photographic Society, etc. US Junior Chamber of Commerce Award, 1937; Man of the Year, Phoenix, 1949. 33° Mason. *Publications:* Arizona Portraits (2 vols), 1940; Journey Down the River of Canyons, 1940; Speeches of Henry Ashurst: The Conscience of a Conservative, 1960; Why Not Victory?, 1962; Where I Stand, 1964; The Face of Arizona, 1964; People and Places, 1967; The Conscience of the Majority, 1970; Delightful Journey, 1970; The Coming Breakpoint, 1976. *Address:* PO Box 1601, Scottsdale, Arizona 85252, USA.

GOLIGHER, Prof. John Cedric, ChM, FRCS; Professor of Surgery, Leeds University, 1954-77, and Surgeon, Leeds General Infirmary, 1954-77; *b* Londonderry, N Ireland, 13 March 1912; *s* of John Hunter Goligher, Londonderry; *m* 1952, Gwenllian Nancy, *d* of Norman R. Williams, Melbourne, Aust.; one *s* two *d. Educ:* Foyle Coll., Londonderry; Edinburgh Univ. MB, CHB 1934; ChM 1938, Edinburgh; FRCS, FRCSE 1938. Demonstrator of Anatomy, Edinburgh Univ., 1935-36; House Surg., Edinburgh Royal Infirmary; Res. Surg. Officer, St Mark's Hosp., London; served War 1940-46, RAMC, as Surgical Specialist; then Surgical Registrar, St Mary's Hosp., London; Hon. Asst Surg. (subsequently Surg.), St Mary's Hosp., and St Mark's Hosp. for Diseases of the Rectum and Colon, 1947. Mem. Council, RCS, 1968-. FRSocMed; Fellow, Assoc. Surgeons of Gt Brit. and Ire. (Past Pres.); Mem. Surg. Research Soc.; Mem. Brit. Soc. of Gastroenterology (Past Pres.). Hon. FACS, 1974; Hon. FRCSI, 1977. Hon. MD Göteborg, 1976. *Publications:* Surgery of the Anus, Rectum and Colon, 1961, 3rd edn 1975; (jointly) Ulcerative Colitis, 1968; contribs to books and med. journals, dealing mainly with gastric, colonic and rectal surgery. *Recreations:* reading and travel. *Address:* (professional) 5 Shaw Lane, Leeds 6; Ladywood, Linton, Wetherby, West Yorks.

GOLLIN, Prof. Alfred M., DLitt; Professor of History, University of California, Santa Barbara, since 1967 (Chairman, Department of History, 1976-77); *b* 6 Feb. 1926; 2nd *s* of Max and Sue Gollin; *m* 1st, 1951, Gurli Sørensen (marr. diss.); two *d*; 2nd, 1975, Valerie Watkins (*née* Kilner). *Educ:* New York City Public Schs; City College of New York; Harvard Univ.; New Coll., Oxford (BA); St Antony's Coll., Oxford (MA); DPhil Oxon 1957; DLitt Oxon 1968. Served US Army, 1943-46; taught history at New Coll., Oxford, 1951-54; official historian for The Observer, 1952-59; Lectr, City Coll. of New York, 1959; Univ. of California, Los Angeles: Acting Asst Prof., 1959-60; Research Associate, 1960-61; Associate Prof., Univ. of California, Santa Barbara, 1966-67. Dir, Study Center of Univ. of California, UK and Ire., 1971-73; Mem., US-UK Educnl Commn, 1971-72. Fellow, J. S. Guggenheim Foundn, 1962, 1964, 1971; Fellow, Amer. Council of Learned Socs, 1963, 1975. FRHistS 1976. *Publications:* The Observer and J. L. Garvin, 1960; Proconsul in Politics: a study of Lord Milner, 1964; From Omdurman to V. E. Day: the Life Span of Sir Winston Churchill, 1964; Balfour's Burden, 1965; Asquith, a New View, in A Century of Conflict, Essays for A. J. P. Taylor, 1966; Balfour, in The Conservative Leadership (ed D. Southgate), 1974; articles and reviews in various jls. *Recreation:* swimming. *Address:* Department of History, University of California, Santa Barbara, Calif 93106, USA. *Club:* Reform.

GOLOMBEK, Harry, OBE 1966; Chess Correspondent, The Times, since 1945, and Chess Correspondent, The Observer, since 1955; writer on chess; *b* London, 1 March 1911; *s* of Barnet and Emma Golombek; unmarried. *Educ:* Wilson's Gram. Sch.; London Univ. Ed. British Chess Magazine, 1938, 1939, 1940. Served in RA, 1940-42, Foreign Office, 1942-45. Joint Ed., British Chess Magazine, 1949-; British Chess Champion, 1947, 1949, and 1955 (prize-winner 14 times); 1st prize in 4 international chess tournaments. Recognized as international master by Federation Internationale des Echecs, 1948. Represented Great Britain in 9 Chess Olympiads and capt. Brit. team, Helsinki, 1952, Amsterdam, 1954, Munich, 1958, Leipzig, 1960, Varna, 1962. Pres., Zone 1 World Chess Fedn, 1974-. *Publications:* 50 Great Games of Modern Chess, 1942; Capablanca's 100 Best Games of Chess, 1947; World Chess Championship, 1948, 1949; Pocket Guide to Chess Openings, 1949; Hastings Tournament, 1948-49, 1949; Southsea Tournament, 1949, 1949; Prague, 1946, 1950, Budapest, 1952, 1952; Reti's Best Games of Chess, 1954; World Chess Championship, 1954, 1954; The Game of Chess (Penguin), 1954; 22nd USSR Chess Championship, 1956; World Chess Championship, 1957, 1957; Modern Opening Chess Strategy, 1959; Fischer *v* Spassky 1972, 1973; A History of Chess, 1976; (with W. Hartston) The Best Games of C. H. O'D. Alexander, 1976; Encyclopedia of Chess, 1977. *Recreations:* music, the Stock Exchange and the theatre. *Address:* Albury, 35 Albion Crescent, Chalfont St Giles, Bucks HP8 4ET. *T:* Chalfont 2808. *Clubs:* Athenæum; Surrey County Cricket.

GOLT, Sidney, CB 1964; Consultant; Chairman, Linked Life Assurance Group, since 1972; Adviser on Government Affairs, EMI, since 1971; UK Member, Commonwealth Group of Experts on International Economic Policy, since 1975; *b* West Hartlepool, 31 March 1910; *s* of late Wolf and Fanny Golt; *m* 1947, Jean, *d* of Ralph Oliver; two *d. Educ:* Portsmouth Grammar Sch.; Christ Church, Oxford. PPE 1931; James Mew Scholar, Oxford, 1934; Statistician, Tin Producers' Assoc., 1936-40; joined Central Price Regulation Cttee, 1941; Asst Sec., Bd of Trade, 1945-60; Sec., Central Price Regulation Cttee, 1945-46; Under-Sec., Bd of Trade, 1960-68, Adviser on Commercial Policy, 1964-68, Deputy Secretary, 1968-70. UK Mem., Preparatory Cttee for European Free Trade Assoc., Geneva, 1960; Leader, UK Delegns to UN Conf. on Trade and Development, New Delhi, 1968, and to Trade and Development Bd, 1965-68. *Publications:* Ed., Tin, and Tin World Statistics, 1936-40; (jtly) Towards an Open World Economy, 1972; The GATT Negotiations, 1974; The New Mercantilism, 1974. *Recreations:* travel, reading, bridge. *Address:* The Gore Cottage, Burnham, Bucks. *T:* 4948; 37 Rowan Road, W6. *T:* 01-602 1410. *Club:* Reform.

GOMBRICH, Sir Ernst (Hans Josef), Kt 1972; CBE 1966; FBA 1960; FSA 1961; PhD (Vienna); MA Oxon and Cantab; Director of the Warburg Institute and Professor of the History of the Classical Tradition in the University of London, 1959-76; *b* Vienna, 30 March 1909; *s* of Dr Karl B. Gombrich, Vice-Pres. of Disciplinary Council of Lawyer's Chamber, Vienna, and Prof. Leonie Gombrich (*née* Hock), pianist; *m* 1936, Ilse Heller; one *s. Educ:* Theresianum, Vienna; Vienna Univ. Research Asst, Warburg Inst., 1936-39. Served War of 1939-45 with BBC Monitoring Service. Senior Research Fellow, 1946-48, Lectr, 1948-54, Reader, 1954-56, Special Lectr, 1956-59, Warburg

Inst., Univ. of London; Durning-Lawrence Prof. of the History of Art, London Univ., at University Coll., 1956-59; Slade Prof. of Fine Art in the University of Oxford, 1950-53; Visiting Prof. of Fine Art, Harvard Univ., 1959; Slade Prof. of Fine Art, Cambridge Univ., 1961-63; Lethaby Prof., RCA, 1967-68; Andrew D. White Prof.-at-Large, Cornell, 1970. A Trustee of the British Museum, 1974-; Mem., Standing Commn on Museums and Galleries, 1976-. Hon. Fellow, Jesus Coll., Cambridge, 1963; FRSL 1969; Foreign Hon. Mem., American Academy of Arts and Sciences, 1964; For. Mem., Amer. Philosophical Soc., 1968. Corresponding Member: Accademia delle Scienze di Torino, 1962; Royal Acad. of Arts and Sciences, Uppsala, 1970; Koninklijke Nederlandse Akademie van Wetenschapen, 1973. Hon. FRIBA, 1971. Hon. DLit: Belfast, 1963; London, 1976; Hon. LLD St Andrews, 1965; Hon. LittD: Leeds, 1965; Cambridge, 1967; Manchester, 1974; Hon. DLitt: Oxford, 1969; Harvard, 1976; Hon. Dr Lit. Hum.: Chicago, 1975; Pennsylvania, 1977; DU Essex, 1977. W. H. Smith Literary Award, 1964; Erasmus Prize, 1975; Hegel Prize, 1976. Medal of New York Univ. for Distinguished Visitors, 1970; Ehrenkreuz für Wissenschaft und Kunst, 1st cl., Austria, 1975; Medal of Collège de France, 1977. *Publications:* Weltgeschichte für Kinder, 1936; (with E. Kris) Caricature, 1940; The Story of Art, 1950, 12th edn 1972; Art and Illusion (The A. W. Mellon Lectures in the Fine Arts, 1956), 1960; Meditations on a Hobby Horse, 1963; Norm and Form, 1966; Aby Warburg, an intellectual biography, 1970; Symbolic Images, 1972; In Search of Cultural History, 1972; (jtly) Art, Perception and Reality, 1973; (ed jtly) Illusion in Nature and Art, 1973; Art History and the Social Sciences, 1975; The Heritage of Apelles, 1976; Means and Ends (W. Neurath Lecture), 1976; contributions to learned journals. *Address:* 19 Briardale Gardens, NW3 7PN. *T:* 01-435 6639.
See also R . F . Gombrich .

GOMBRICH, Prof. Richard Francis, DPhil; Boden Professor of Sanskrit, Oxford University, since 1976; Fellow of Wolfson College, Oxford, since 1976; Emeritus Fellow of Balliol, 1977; *b* 17 July 1937; *s* of Sir Ernst Gombrich, *qv*; *m* 1964, Dorothea Amanda Friedrich; one *s* one *d* . *Educ:* Magdalen Coll., Oxford (MA, DPhil); Harvard Univ. (AM). Univ. Lectr in Sanskrit and Pali, Oxford Univ., 1965-76; Fellow of Balliol Coll., 1966-76. *Publications:* Precept and Practice: traditional Buddhism in the rural highlands of Ceylon, 1971; (with Margaret Cone) The Perfect Generosity of Prince Vessantara, 1977; contribs to oriental and anthropological journals. *Recreations:* singing, walking, photography. *Address:* 6 Portland Road, Oxford OX2 7EY.

GOMES, Sir Stanley Eugene, Kt 1959; Retired Chief Justice, West Indies Federation; *b* Georgetown, British Guiana, 24 March 1901; *s* of late Mr and Mrs M. Gomes; *m* 1936, Elaine Vera (*née* Wight). *Educ:* St Joseph's Coll., Dumfries, Scotland; Jesus Coll., Cambridge. BA Cantab, 1923; called to Bar, Gray's Inn, 1924. British Guiana: Magistrate, 1929; Asst Attorney-Gen., 1933; Attorney-Gen., Leeward Islands, 1944; QC 1946; Puisne Judge, Trinidad, 1948. Chief Justice: Barbados, 1957-58; Trinidad, 1958; WI Fedn, 1961. Pres., Brit. Caribbean Court of Appeal, 1962. Retd Dec. 1962. *Recreations:* fishing, golf. *Address:* Wycherley 2, Balmoral Road, Hastings, Barbados.

GOMEZ, Jill; singer; *b* Trinidad, of Spanish and English parents. *Educ:* Royal Academy of Music and Guildhall School of Music, London. Operatic début with Glyndebourne Festival Opera, 1969, where she won the John Christie Award and has subseq. sung leading roles, incl. Mélisande, Calisto, and Anne Truelove in The Rake's Progress; has appeared with The Royal Opera, English Opera Gp and Scottish Opera in roles including Pamina, Ilia, Fiordiligi, The Countess in Figaro, Elizabeth in Elegy for Young Lovers, Tytania, Lauretta in Gianni Schicchi, and the Governess in The Turn of the Screw; she created the role of Flora in Tippett's The Knot Garden, at Covent Garden, and of the Countess in Thea Musgrave's Voice of Ariadne, Aldeburgh, 1974; she sang title role in Massenet's Thaïs at Wexford, 1974, and Jenifer in The Midsummer Marriage with Welsh Nat. Opera, 1976; created title role in William Alwyn's Miss Julie for radio, 1977; Tatiana in Eugene Onegin with Kent Opera, 1977. Concert repertoire includes Rameau, Bach, Handel (Messiah and cantatas), Haydn's Creation and Seasons, Mozart's Requiem and concert arias, Beethoven's Ninth, Berlioz's Nuits d'Eté, Brahms's Requiem, Fauré's Requiem, Ravel's Shéhérazade, Mahler's Second and Fourth Symphonies, Strauss's Four Last Songs, Britten's Les Illuminations and Spring Symphony, and Tippet's A Child of Our Time. Regular engagements in France, Belgium, Holland, Germany, Scandinavia, Switzerland, Italy, Spain and America; festival appearances include Aix-en-Provence, Spoleto, Bergen, Versailles, Flanders and Holland. Recent recordings include

three solo recitals (French, Spanish, and songs by Mozart), Ravel's Poèmes de Mallarmé with Boulez, Handel's Admeto with Alan Curtis, and Mahler's Fourth with André Previn. *Address:* c/o Lies Askonas, 19a Air Street, Regent Street, W1R 6LQ.

GONZÁLEZ, Marco Tulio; Condecoración de la Cruz de Boyacá, 1950; President, Inter-American Bar Association, 1971-72; Ambassador of Ecuador to the Court of St James's, 1967-69; *b* July 1917; *s* of Dr Raúl González and Rosa C. de González; *m* 1946, Mariana Tobar; two *s* one *d.* *Educ:* Central Univ., Quito, Ecuador. Lawyer, 1942. Sec. of Central Univ., 1944-45; Gen. Sec. of Public Administration, 1945-46; Minister of Educn, 1946-47; Consul-Gen. of Ecuador in New Orleans, 1947-48; MP, Ecuador, 1950-52; Pres., Chamber of Agriculture, 1957-62; Senator, 1959-63; Nat. Economics Coun., 1962-63; Minister of Industries, 1966; Dir of Monetary Bd, 1966. Pres. of Ecuadorean Airline, 1957-67. Hon. Citizen of New Orleans, 1947. *Recreations:* tennis, riding. *Address:* Edificio González, Calle Guayaquil 1228, Quito, Ecuador. *Clubs:* Hurlingham; Lawyers' (Quito); Quito Tennis and Golf.

GONZI, Most Rev. Michael, KBE 1946; DD, ICD, BLit; *b* Vittoriosa, Malta, 13 May 1885; *s* of Joseph Gonzi and Margaret Tonna. *Educ:* Malta Seminary; Malta Univ.; Beda Coll., Rome. Priest, 1908; Prof. of Holy Scripture and Hebrew at the Malta Univ., 1915; Sec. to the Archbishop of Malta, 1921; Mem. of the Senate of the Maltese Parliament, 1921; Canon Theologian of the Malta Cathedral, 1923; Bishop of Gozo, 1924; Coadjutor to Bishop of Malta, 1943; Archbishop of Malta, 1943-76; Assistant at the Pontifical Throne, 1949. Bailiff Grand Cross of the Order of Malta, St John of Jerusalem, 1949. *Address:* Archbishop's Palace, Valletta, Malta GC.

GOOCH, Sir Robert Douglas, 4th Bt *cr* 1866; *b* 19 Sept. 1905; *m* ; one *d.* Heir: kinsman, Trevor Sherlock Gooch.

GOOCH, Col Sir Robert Eric Sherlock, 11th Bt, *cr* 1746; KCVO 1973; DSO 1941; DL, JP; Member of HM Body Guard of the Honourable Corps of Gentlemen-at-Arms, 1950-73, Lieutenant, 1968-73 (Clerk of the Cheque and Adjutant, 1963-67, Standard Bearer, 1967-68); *b* 6 May 1903; *e s* of Sir T. V. S. Gooch, 10th Bt, and Florence Meta (*d* 1932), *y d* of late James Draper, St Heliers; *S* father, 1946; *m* 1926, Katharine C. (*d* 1974), *er d* of late Maj.-Gen. Sir E. W. C. Chaytor, KCMG, KCVO, CB; two *s* one *d.* *Educ:* Eton. Served War of 1939-45 (despatches twice, DSO); OC The Life Guards, 1943-46; commanded 1st Household Cavalry Regt, 1942-44. Col commanding The Household Cavalry, 1944-46; retd pay, 1946. Mem. of East Suffolk County Council, 1946-74 (Chm., 1957-67); County Alderman, 1951; High Sheriff of Suffolk, 1950. Mem. of House of Laity of Church Assembly, 1948-55. Mem. Council, Royal Agricultural Soc. of England, 1950 (Dep. Pres., 1960; Pres., 1961; Vice-Pres., 1961; Chm., 1963-67; Trustee, 1964); Liaison Officer to the Minister of Agriculture, 1952-62. Chm. Suffolk Agricultural Exec. Cttee, 1954-62; Pres., The Royal Smithfield Club, 1966. Hon. Col 4th Bn The Suffolk Regt (TA), 1953-61; Hon. Col Suffolk and Cambs Regt (TA), 1961-67. Heir: *s* Richard John Sherlock Gooch, *b* 22 March 1930. *Address:* Benacre Hall, Wrentham, Beccles, Suffolk. *Club:* Turf.

GOOD, Tan Sri Donal Bernard Waters, CMG 1962; JMN (Malaysia), 1965; PSM (Malaysia), 1970; Commissioner of Law Revision, Malaysia, since 1963; *b* 13 April 1907; *er s* of William John and Kathleen Mary Good, Dublin; *m* 1930, Kathryn, *er d* of Frank Lucas Stanley and Helena Kathleen Stanley, Dublin; one *s* one *d.* *Educ:* The High Sch., and Trinity Coll., Dublin. Scholar and Moderator in Classics, TCD, 1927-29; MA 1932; LLB 1933; Barrister, King's Inns, Dublin (Benchers' Prizeman), 1935; Barrister, Gray's Inn, 1948. Resident Magistrate, Kenya, 1940-45; Malayan Planning Unit, 1945; Crown Counsel, Malayan Union, 1946-48; Legal Adviser: Negri Sembilan and Malacca, 1948-49; Johore, 1949-50; Legal Draftsman, Sierra Leone, 1951-52; Legal Adviser, Selangor, 1952; Senior Federal Counsel, Federation of Malaya, 1952-55; Actg Solicitor-Gen., 1953 and 1955; Actg Judge of Supreme Court, 1953; Judge of Supreme Court, 1955-59; Judge of the Court of Appeal, Federation of Malaya, 1959-62. Chm. Detainees Review Commn, 1955-60; Pres. Industrial Court, 1956-57; Chm. Detained Persons Advisory Board, 1960-. Coronation Medal, 1953. *Recreations:* orchid-growing, bridge. *Address:* Attorney-General's Chambers, Kuala Lumpur, Malaysia. *T:* 83551. *Clubs:* Kildare Street and University (Dublin); Selangor, Lake and Ipoh (Malaysia).

GOOD, Air Vice-Marshal J. L. F. F.; *see* Fuller-Good.

GOOD, Prof. Ronald D'Oyley, ScD; Head of Department of Botany, University of Hull, 1928-59, Professor Emeritus, 1959; *b* 5 March 1896; 2nd *s* of William Ernest and Mary Gray Good; *m* 1927, Patty Gwynneth Griffith (*d* 1975); one *d*. *Educ:* Weymouth Coll.; Downing Coll., Cambridge (Senior Scholar). MA, ScD Cantab. Served European War, 1914-18, 4th Bn Dorset Regt, and 2/5th Bn Lincolnshire Regt (France); Staff of Botany Department, British Museum (Nat. Hist.), 1922-28. Trustee, Dorset County Museum. *Publications:* Plants and Human Economics, 1933; The Old Roads of Dorset, 1940, 1966; Weyland, 1945; The Geography of the Flowering Plants, 1947, revd new edn, 1974; A Geographical Handbook of the Dorset Flora, 1948; Features of Evolution in the Flowering Plants, 1956, new edn USA, 1974; contribs to scientific journals. *Address:* 8 Durlston Road, Parkstone, Poole, Dorset. *T:* Parkstone 745132.

GOODACRE, Kenneth, TD 1952; DL; Practising as K. Goodacre & Co., Solicitors; Deputy Clerk to GLC, 1964-68; Clerk and Solicitor of Middlesex CC, 1955-65; Clerk of the Peace for Middlesex, 1959-65; *b* 29 Oct. 1910; *s* of Clifford and Florence Goodacre; *m* 1936, Dorothy, *d* of Harold Kendall, Solicitor, Leeds; one *s*. *Educ:* Doncaster Grammar Sch. Admitted Solicitor, 1934; Asst Solicitor: Doncaster Corp., 1934-35; Barrow-in-Furness Corp., 1935-36; Sen. Solicitor, Blackburn Corp., 1936-39; served War of 1939-45, TA with E Lancs Regt and Staff 53 Div. (Major), and 2nd Army (Lieut-Col); released from Army Service, 1945, and granted hon. rank of Major; Dep. Town Clerk: Blackburn, 1945-49, Leicester, 1949-52; Town Clerk, Leicester, 1952-55. DL, Greater London (DL Middlesex, 1960-65), 1965. *Address:* 4 Chartfield Avenue, Putney, SW15. *T:* 01-789 0794. *Club:* Army and Navy.

GOODALE, Cecil Paul; Under Secretary, Department of Health and Social Security, since 1976; *b* 29 Dec. 1918; *s* of Cecil Charles Wemyss Goodale and Annie Goodale; *m* 1946, Ethel Margaret (*née* Studer). *Educ:* East Sheen County Sch. War Office, 1936; Min. of Supply, 1939; Min. of Health, later DHSS, 1947-: Sen. Exec. Officer, 1950; Principal, 1953; Principal Regional Officer, 1962; Asst Sec., 1967. *Recreations:* music, photography, bowls. *Address:* 17 Parkfield Avenue, East Sheen, SW14. *T:* 01-876 3570.

GOODALE, Sir Ernest (William), Kt 1952; CBE 1946; MC 1917; Director, 1928, Managing Director, 1930-61, Chairman, 1949-71, and Chairman Emeritus since 1971, Warner & Sons Ltd, textile manufacturers: *b* 6 Dec. 1896; *s* of Wm Thos Goodale, Charter Town Clerk of Barnes, Surrey, and Frances Mary Wheatley; *m* 1st, 1924, Gwendolen Branscombe (*d* 1972), *yr d* of late Sir Frank Warner, KBE; one *s* one *d*; 2nd, 1973; Pamela June, *d* of Stanley A. Bone, Betchworth, Surrey. *Educ:* St Catherine's Coll., Richmond, Surrey; Surrey County Sch., Richmond; King's Coll., London Univ. London Univ. OTC, 1914-15; served European War, 2nd Lieut and Lieut Royal Warwicks Regt, 1916-19, Mesopotamia, Persia, Caucasus, etc. Admitted Solicitor, 1920; Partner, Minet, Pering, Smith & Co., London, retired 1928. Member of: Council for Art and Industry, 1934-39; Council of Industrial Design, 1945-49; Ramsden Cttee on Exhibitions and Fairs, 1945; Bd of Trade Advisory Cttees on Exhibitions and Fairs, 1948-65; Chm. Sub-Cttee on BIF ("Goodale Report"), 1953; Chm. BIF Ltd, 1954-56; Inst. of Export (Vice-Pres., 1956-66); Douglas Cttee on Purchase Tax, 1951; Council, Royal College of Art, 1950-53; Hon. Fellow, Society of Industrial Artists and Designers, 1960; Textile Inst., 1937- (Pres. 1939-40 and 1957-59); Silk and Rayon Controller (Min. of Supply), 1939; Pres., Silk and Man-Made Fibres (formerly Rayon) Users' Assoc. (Inc.), 1945-70; Vice-President: International Silk Assoc., 1949-68; British Man-Made (formerly Rayon and Synthetic) Fibres Federation, 1943-74; Chairman: Furnishing Fabric Fedn, 1945-68; Furnishing Fabrics Export Group, 1940-68; Hon. Pres., Furnishing Fabric Manufacturers' Assoc.; a Vice-Pres. and Mem. Grand Council and Cttees, FBI (Chm. Industrial Art Cttee, 1949-62); Mem. Council, CBI, 1965-74; Mem. Council Royal Society Arts, 1935- (Chm., 1949-52, now a Vice-Pres.); Pres. British Colour Council, 1953-70; Mem. Bd of National Film Finance Corp., 1957-69; Mem. Min. of Educn Adv. Council on Art Educn, 1959-66; Mem. for Dorking (North), Surrey CC, 1961-70, Alderman, 1970-74. Liveryman, Worshipful Co. of Weavers, 1929- (Court of Assistants, 1946-. Renter Bailiff, 1956-57, Upper Bailiff, 1957-58); Mem. of Law Soc. *Publications:* Weaving and the Warners, 1971; contributions to trade literature. *Address:* Branscombe, Nutcombe Lane, Dorking, Surrey. *Club:* English-Speaking Union.

See also J.-P. F. E. Warner.

GOODALL, Anthony Charles, MC 1942; **His Honour Judge Goodall;** a Circuit Judge (formerly a Judge of County Courts), since 1968; *b* 23 July 1916; *er s* of late Charles Henry and Mary Helen Goodall, The Manor House, Sutton Veny, Wilts; *m* 1947, Anne Valerie, *yr d* of late John Reginald Chichester and of Audrey Geraldine Chichester, Lurley Manor, Tiverton, Devon; one *s* two *d*. *Educ:* Eton; King's Coll., Cambridge. Called to Bar, Inner Temple, 1939 (Certif. of Hon.). Served War of 1939-45, 1st Royal Dragoons; taken prisoner (twice), 1944. Practised at Bar, 1946-67. *Publications:* (ed jtly) Faraday on Rating; contrib. to Encycl. Court Forms and Precedents. *Address:* Mardon, Moretonhampstead, Devon. *T:* Moretonhampstead 239.

GOODALL, Arthur David Saunders; HM Diplomatic Service; Head of Western European Department, Foreign and Commonwealth Office, since 1975; *b* 9 Oct. 1931; *o c* of late Arthur William Goodall, Whaley Bridge, Derbys, and Maisie Josephine, *y d* of Robert Emmet Byers, Derwent House, West Derby, Lancs; *m* 1962, Morwenna, *y d* of late Percival George Beck Peecock; two *s* one *d*. *Educ:* Ampleforth; Trinity Coll., Oxford. 1st Cl. Hons Lit. Hum., 1954; MA. Served 1st Bn KOYLI (2nd Lieut), 1955-56. Entered HM Foreign (now Diplomatic) Service, 1956; served at: Nicosia, 1956; FO, 1957-58; Djakarta, 1958-60; Private Sec. to HM Ambassador, Bonn, 1961-63; FO, 1963-68; Head of Chancery, Nairobi, 1968-70; FCO, 1970; Counsellor and Dep. Head, Permanent Under-Secretary's Dept, FCO, 1971-73; UK Delegn, MBFR, Vienna, 1973-75. *Publications:* contribs to: Ampleforth Jl; Tablet; Irish Genealogist. *Address:* c/o Foreign and Commonwealth Office, SW1. *Club:* United Oxford & Cambridge University.

GOODALL, David William, PhD (London); DSc (Melbourne); ARCS, DIC, FLS, FIBiol; Senior Principal Research Scientist, CSIRO Division of Land Resources Management, since 1974; *b* 4 April 1914; *s* of Henry William Goodall; *m* 1st, 1940, Audrey Veronica Kirwin (marr. diss. 1949); one *s*; 2nd, 1949, Muriel Grace King (marr. diss. 1974); two *s* one *d*; 3rd, 1976, Ivy Nelms (*née* Palmer). *Educ:* St Paul's Sch.; Imperial Coll. of Science and Technology (BSc). Research under Research Inst. of Plant Physiology, on secondment to Cheshunt and East Malling Research Stns, 1935-46; Plant Physiologist, W African Cacao Research Inst., 1946-48; Sen. Lectr in Botany, University of Melbourne, 1948-52; Reader in Botany, University Coll. of the Gold Coast, 1952-54; Prof. of Agricultural Botany, University of Reading, 1954-56; Dir, CSIRO Tobacco Research Institute, Mareeba, Qld, 1956-61; Senior Principal Research Officer, CSIRO Div. of Mathematical Statistics, Perth, Australia, 1961-67; Hon. Reader in Botany, Univ. of Western Australia, 1965-67; Prof. of Biological Science, Univ. of California Irvine, 1966-68; Dir, US/IBP Desert Biome, 1968-73; Prof. of Systems Ecology, Utah State Univ., 1969-74. *Publications:* Chemical Composition of Plants as an Index of their Nutritional Status (with F. G. Gregory), 1947; ed, Evolution of Desert Biota, 1976; editor-in-chief, Ecosystems of the World (series), 1977-; co-editor: Simulation Modelling of Environmental Problems, 1977; Aridlands: structure and utilization, 1977; numerous papers in scientific journals. *Recreations:* acting, reading, walking. *Address:* CSIRO Division of Land Resources Management, Private Bag, PO Wembley, WA 6014, Australia.

GOODBODY, Gen. Sir Richard (Wakefield), GCB 1963 (CB 1953); KBE 1958; DSO 1943; Bath King at Arms, 1965-76; *b* 12 April 1903; *s* of Gerald E. Goodbody, Woodsdown, Co. Limerick; *m* 1929, Mary Eveline Talbot, Provost's House, Edgmond, Newport, Salop; three *s* one *d*. *Educ:* Rugby; RMA Woolwich. Commissioned RA, 1923; apptd to RHA, 1927; Adjt, HAC, 1936; Bde Major 1st Support Group, 1940; CO 11 RHA, 1942; Comdr 2 Armd Bde, 1943; CRA 7th Armd Div., 1946; Comd 15 Inf. Bde, 1947; Dep. DMT War Office, 1948; Comdt Sch. of Artillery, 1949; GOC 56 (London) Armoured Div., TA, 1951; Dir of Royal Artillery, War Office, 1954; GOC-in-C Northern Comd, 1957-60; Adjt-Gen. to the Forces, 1960-63. Col Commandant: Royal Artillery, 1957-68; Hon. Artillery Co., 1959-66; Royal Horse Artillery, 1960-68; ADC Gen. to the Queen, 1961-63. Retd from the Army, 1963. Governor, The Royal Sch., Bath; Mem., Council of St Dunstan's. *Recreations:* shooting, fishing, gardening. *Address:* Broadlea Farm, Sutton Waldron, Blandford, Dorset. *Club:* Naval and Military.

GOODCHILD, David Hicks, CBE 1973; Partner of Clifford-Turner, Solicitors, since 1962 (resident in Paris); *b* 3 Sept. 1926; *s* of Harold Hicks Goodchild and Agnes Joyce Wharton Goodchild (*née* Mowbray); *m* 1954, Nicole Marie Jeanne (*née* Bentolila); one *s* one *d*. *Educ:* Felsted School. Lieut, Royal Artillery, 1944-48; articled clerk, Longmores, Hertford; qual. Solicitor, 1952; HAC, 1952-56. *Recreations:* golf, cricket. *Address:* 53 Avenue Montaigne, Paris 8, France. *T:* 225-49-27. *Clubs:* MCC, HAC; Polo (Paris).

GOODCHILD, Rt. Rev. Ronald Cedric Osbourne; *see* Kensington, Suffragan Bishop of.

GOODCHILD, Lt-Col Sidney, MVO 1969; DL; retired; Vice-Lieutenant of Caernarvonshire, 1969-74; *b* 4 Jan. 1903; *s* of late Charles Goodchild; *m* 1934, Elizabeth G. P. Everett; two *s* one *d. Educ:* Friars Sch.; Staff Coll., Quetta. Commnd Royal Welch Fusiliers, 1923; 14th Punjab Regt, Indian Army, 1930; Staff Captain, 4th Inf. Bde, 1937; DAQMG (Movements), Army HQ India, 1939; AQMG (Movts), Iraq, 1940; comd 7/14 Punjab Regt, 1942; AQMG, Army HQ India, 1945; comd 1st Sikh LI and 5th Bde, 4th Indian Div., 1946; despatches thrice, 1940-44. Chm., NW Wales War Pensioners' Cttee. Alderman, Caernarvonshire CC, 1972-74. DL Caernarvonshire, 1964; DL Gwynedd, 1974. *Address:* Plas Oerddwr, Beddgelert, Gwynedd, N Wales. *T:* Beddgelert 237.

GOODDEN, Abington, CBE 1956; retired, as a Consul-General, from HM Diplomatic Service, 1960; *b* 7 Dec. 1901; *s* of late Dr Wyndham C. Goodden and Clara Joan (*née* Smith); *m* 1930, Johanna Arnolda Jordaan (*d* 1962), South Africa; one *s. Educ:* Eton (King's Scholar, 1915); King's Coll., Cambridge. Vice-Consul: Hamburg, 1926-27; Lourenço Marques, 1928-30; Naples, 1931-33; Vice-Consul and Third Sec. of Embassy, Santiago (Chile), 1933-37; attached to Special Representative of Cuba at Coronation of HM King George VI, 1937; Vice-Consul, New York, 1937-38; Consul: Valencia, 1939; Madrid, 1939-41; Chargé d'Affaires *ad interim,* Managua (Nicaragua), 1941-42; Consul, Ponta Delgada (Azores), 1943-45; rep. of CCG (British Element) at Frankfurt, 1945-46; Consul and First Sec. of Embassy, Madrid, 1946-47; Dep. Consul-Gen., Batavia (now Djakarta), 1947-49; Commercial Counsellor, HM Embassy, Oslo, 1950-53; Consul-Gen., Seville, 1953-60. Coronation Medal, 1937; Portuguese Life-Saving Society's Medal, 1946. *Address:* 62 Westbourne Terrace, W2.

GOODDEN, Robert Yorke, CBE 1956; RDI 1947; Architect and Designer; Professor, School of Silversmithing and Jewellery, 1948-74, and Pro-Rector, 1967-74, Royal College of Art; *b* 7 May 1909; 2nd *s* of late Lieut-Col R. B. Goodden, OBE and Gwendolen Goodden; *m* 1st, 1936, Kathleen Teresa Burrow; 2nd, 1946, Lesley Macbeth Mitchell; two *s* two *d. Educ:* Harrow Sch. Trained AA Sch. of Architecture, 1926-31; AA Diploma 1932; ARIBA 1933; private practice as architect and designer, 1932-39; served RAFVR, 1940-41; RNVR, 1941-45; resumed private practice, 1946. Joint architect and designer: Lion and Unicorn Pavilion, South Bank Exhibition, 1951; Western Sculpture Rooms, Print Room Gall. and Gall. of Oriental Art, British Museum, 1969-71; designer of: domestic pressed glassware for Chance Brothers, 1934-48; Asterisk Wallpapers, 1934; sports section, Britain Can Make It Exhbn, 1946; Coronation hangings for Westminster Abbey, 1953; gold and silver plate for Corp. of London, Worshipful Co. of Goldsmiths, Royal Society of Arts, Royal Pavilion, South Bank Exhibition, Downing Coll., Cambridge, The Steel Co. of Wales, British American Tobacco Co., SS Canberra, Royal Coll. of Art, and others; of glass for King's Coll., Cambridge, Grosvenor House, Min. of Works, and others; of china for Grosvenor House, SS Oriana and Josiah Wedgwood & Sons; of metal foil mural decorations in SS Canberra, 1961. Consulting Architect to Board of Trade for BIF, Olympia, 1947, Earls Ct, 1949, Olympia, 1950 and 1951. Member: Council of Industrial Design, 1955; National Council for Diplomas in Art and Design, 1961; Adv. Council, V&A Museum, 1977-. Chm., Crafts Adv. Cttee, 1977-. Mem. Council, Essex Univ., 1973. FSIA, 1947; Hon. Fellow, Sheffield Polytechnic, 1971. Hon. Des. RCA, 1952; Hon. Dr RCA, 1974. SIAD Design Medal, 1972. Master of Faculty, RDI, 1959-61. Liveryman, Worshipful Co. of Goldsmiths, Prime Warden 1976. *Publication:* (with P. Popham) Silversmithing, 1972. *Recreation:* daydreaming. *Address:* Prospect, Higham, Colchester, Essex. *T:* Higham 278.

GOODE, Prof. Royston Miles, OBE 1972; Crowther Professor of Credit and Commercial Law, since 1973, Head of Department and Dean of the Faculty of Laws, since 1976, Queen Mary College, University of London; *b* 6 April 1933; *s* of Samuel and Bloom Goode; *m* 1964, Catherine Anne Rueff; one *d. Educ:* Highgate School. LLB London, 1954; LLD London, 1976. Admitted Solicitor, 1955. Partner, Victor Mishcon & Co., solicitors, 1966-71; Consultant 1971-; Mem. Cttee on Consumer Credit, 1968-71; Prof. of Law, Queen Mary Coll., London, 1971-73. Vis. Prof., Melbourne, 1975; Aust. Commonwealth Vis. Fellow, 1975. Chm., Advertising Adv. Cttee, IBA, 1976-. Mem. Council, Justice. *Publications:* Hire-Purchase Law and Practice, 1962, 2nd edn 1970, with Supplement 1975; The Hire-Purchase Act 1964, 1964; (with J. S. Ziegel) Hire-Purchase and Conditional Sale: a Comparative Survey of Commonwealth and American Law, 1965; Introduction to the Consumer Credit Act, 1974; Consumer Credit Legislation; contrib. Halsbury's Laws of England, 4th edn, Encycl. of Forms and Precedents, 4th edn, and other works; articles and notes in legal jls. *Recreations:* chess, reading, walking, browsing in bookshops. *Address:* 7 The Lincolns, Marsh Lane, Mill Hill, NW7 4PD. *T:* 01-959 2896. *Club:* Hendon Chess.

GOODE, Sir William (Allmond Codrington), GCMG 1963 (KCMG 1957; CMG 1952); DL; Chairman, Water Resources Board, 1964-74; *b* 8 June 1907; *e s* of late Sir Richard Goode, CMG, CBE; *m* 1st, 1938, Mary Armstrong Harding (*d* 1947); 2nd, 1950, Ena Mary McLaren; one *d. Educ:* Oakham Sch.; Worcester Coll., Oxford (Classical exhibitioner). Barrister-at-Law, Gray's Inn, 1936. Joined Malayan Civil Service, 1931; District Officer, Raub, 1936-39; Asst Commissioner for Civil Defence, Singapore, 1940. Mobilised in 1st Bn Singapore Volunteer Corps as Lance-Corporal, 1941 (prisoner of war, Singapore, 1942; moved to Thailand for work on the Burma Railway; released 1945). Dep. Economic Sec., Federation of Malaya, 1948; Chief Sec., Aden, 1949-53; Acting Governor, Aden, 1950-51; Chief Sec., Singapore, 1953-57; Governor of Singapore, Dec. 1957-2nd June 1959; Yang di-Pertuan Negara of the State of Singapore and UK Commissioner, Singapore, 1959; Governor and C-in-C, North Borneo, 1960-63. DL Berks 1975. KStJ 1958. *Address:* East Streatley House, Streatley-on-Thames, Berks. *Club:* East India, Devonshire, Sports and Public Schools.

GOODENOUGH, Cecilia Phyllis, MA; STh; DD; Lecturer in Christian Doctrine to Southwark Ordination Course, 1972-76; *b* 9 Sept. 1905; *d* of late Adm. Sir William Goodenough, GCB, MVO. *Educ:* Rochester Grammar Sch.; Liverpool Coll., Huyton; St Hugh's Coll., Oxford, LCC Care Cttee Sec., 1927-30; Sunday Sch. and Evangelistic work, Diocese of Caledonia, Fort St John, BC, Canada, 1931-36; Head of Talbot Settlement, 14 Bromley Hill, Bromley, Kent, 1937-45; Asst to Diocesan Missioner, Diocese of Southwark, 1954-72. Examining Chaplain to the Bishop of Southwark, 1973-. *Address:* 115 Camberwell Grove, Camberwell, SE5 8JH. *T:* 01-701 0093.

GOODENOUGH, Prof. John Bannister; Professor of Inorganic Chemistry, University of Oxford, since 1976; *b* 25 July 1922; *s* of Erwin Ramsdell Goodenough and Helen Lewis Goodenough; *m* 1951, Irene Johnston Wiseman. *Educ:* Yale Univ. (AB, Maths); Univ. of Chicago (MS, PhD, Physics). Meteorologist, US Army Air Force, 1942-48; Research Engr, Westinghouse Corp., 1951-52; Research Physicist (Leader, Electronic Materials Gp), Lincoln Laboratory, MIT, 1952-76. Associate Editor: Materials Research Bulletin, 1966-; Jl Solid State Chemistry, 1969-. Mem., Nat. Acad. of Engrg, 1976-. Dr *hc*, Bordeaux, 1967. *Publications:* Magnetism and the Chemical Bond, 1963; Les oxydes des elements de transition, 1973; numerous research papers in learned jls. *Recreations:* walking, travel, developing countries. *Address:* Inorganic Chemistry Laboratory, Oxford University, South Parks Road, Oxford OX1 3QR. *Club:* Cosmos (Washington, DC).

GOODENOUGH, Kenneth Mackenzie, CMG 1949; MC 1918; *b* Bristol, 30 Oct. 1891; 3rd *s* of late W. T. Goodenough, Bristol; *m* 1916, Florence Alda Bolwell (*d* 1971); two *s. Educ:* Fairfield Sch., Bristol. Entered surveying profession and qualified as a Professional Associate of the Surveyors' Institution. Served European War, 1914-18 in Royal Artillery, commissioned 1917 (MC). Took up business appointment in S Rhodesia, 1928. Pres. Bulawayo Chamber of Commerce, 1942 and 1943; Dep. Mayor of Bulawayo, 1944. High Comr for S Rhodesia, 1946-Jan. 1953. Freeman of City of London; Liveryman of Worshipful Co. of Needlemakers. *Address:* 30 North Shore Road, Hayling Island, Hants. *Club:* Bulawayo (Bulawayo).

GOODENOUGH, Sir Richard (Edmund), 2nd Bt *cr* 1943; *b* 9 June 1925; *e s* of Sir William (Macnamara) Goodenough, 1st Bt, and of Dorothea (Louisa), *er d* of late Ven. and Hon. K. F. Gibbs, DD; *S* father 1951; *m* 1951, Jane, *d* of late H. S. P. McLernon and of Mrs McLernon, Gisborne, NZ; one *s* two *d. Educ:* Eton Coll.; Christ Church, Oxford. Military service, 1943-45, invalided. Christ Church, Oxford, 1945-47. *Heir: s* William McLernon Goodenough, *b* 5 Aug. 1954.

GOODERHAM, Very Rev. Hector Bransby, MA; retired; Hon. Canon, St Mary's Cathedral, Edinburgh, 1971; *b* 11 Oct. 1901; *o s* of Edward Bransby Gooderham and Louisa Elizabeth Gooderham, Richmond, Surrey; *m* 1928, Esther Beatrice, *d* of William Orr, JP, Edinburgh; one *s* one *d. Educ:* George Heriot's Sch.; Edinburgh Univ.; Westcott House, Cambridge. MA 1st Cl. Hons, Edinburgh, 1923 (Vans Dunlop Scholar in Logic and Metaphysics). Curate: St Mary's Cathedral, Glasgow, 1924; St John's, Edinburgh, 1925; Rector: St John's, Selkirk, 1929-37; St

Baldred's, North Berwick, 1937-49; Provost of the Cathedral Church of St Mary, Edinburgh, 1949-56; Vicar of St Peter's, Cranley Gardens, South Kensington, London, 1957-63. Formerly also: Lecturer, Edinburgh Theological Coll., 1934-43; Canon of St Mary's Cathedral, Edinburgh, 1948. *Recreations:* walking, motoring.

GOODERSON, Richard Norman; a Recorder of the Crown Court, since 1972; Reader in English Law, University of Cambridge, since 1967; Fellow, St Catharine's College, Cambridge, since 1948; *b* 3 March 1915; *o s* of late Arthur Gooderson and Clarice Gooderson (*née* Judge); *m* 1939, Marjorie, *yr d* of William Nash; two *s* one *d. Educ:* Northampton Grammar Sch.; St John's Coll., Cambridge (Scholar). BA 1st cl. with distinction Pts I and II Law Tripos; George Long Prizes for Roman Law and for Jurisprudence, Bhaonagar Medal; MA 1948. Called to Bar, Inner Temple, 1946 (certif. of honour). Indian Civil Service, 1938-46; Cambridge Univ.: Lectr, 1949-67; Chm. Faculty of Law, 1970-73; St Catharine's College: Tutor, 1951-65; Senior Tutor, 1965-67; President, 1962-65, 1972-75. Chm., Luton Rent Tribunal, 1960-72; Dep. Chm., Hunts and Peterborough QS, 1970-71. *Publications:* Alibi, 1977; articles in legal jls. *Address:* 1 Newnham Terrace, Cambridge. *T:* Cambridge 58523.

GOODEVE, Sir Charles Frederick, Kt 1946; OBE 1941; FRS 1940; FRIC; FIM; FCIT; MSc Manitoba; DSc London; Comdr RNVR (retired); Consultant, British Steel Corporation, since 1969; Director, London & Scandinavian Metallurgical Co. Ltd, since 1971; *b* 21 Feb. 1904; *s* of Canon F. W. Goodeve, Winnipeg, Canada; *m* 1932, Janet I. Wallace, PhD; two *s. Educ:* Univ. of Manitoba; University Coll., London. Asst Lectr, Univ. of Manitoba; 1851 Exhibition Scholar, 1927; Lectr and later Reader in Physical Chemistry, University Coll., London, Fellow, UCL, 1946; Dep. Dir, Dept of Miscellaneous Weapon Development, Admiralty, 1940-42; Asst and later Dep. Controller for R&D, Admiralty, 1942-45; Dir, BISRA, The Inter-Group Laboratories of the British Steel Corp., formerly British Iron and Steel Research Assoc., 1945-69. Director: ICFC, 1965-74; Technical Develt Capital Ltd, 1964-74; Nat. Indust. Fuel Efficiency Service, 1968-72. Pres., Faraday Soc., 1950-52; Chm., Operational Research Club, 1947-51; Vice-Pres., Parliamentary and Scientific Cttee, 1950-62; Mem., Lord President's Advisory Council on Scientific Policy, 1953-56; Pres. Chemical Section, British Assoc., 1956; Master, Worshipful Co. of Salters, 1958-59; Pres., Iron and Steel Inst., 1961-62; a Vice-Pres., Royal Soc., 1968-70. Scientific Adviser, British Transport Commn, 1948-58. Governor, Imperial Coll., London, 1961-73; Fellow, 1967-. Mem., Council of Tavistock Inst. of Human Relations; Vice-Chm., Orgn for Promoting the Understanding of Society, 1975-. Fellow, Metallurgical Soc. AIME, 1967. Hon. DSc: Manitoba, 1946; Sheffield, 1956; Birmingham, 1962; Newcastle-upon-Tyne, 1970; Salford, 1974. US Medal of Freedom with Silver Palm; Bessemer Gold Medallist, 1962; Carl Lueg Gold Medallist, 1962; Silver Medal, Operational Research Soc., 1964. *Publications:* (part author) Iron and Steel Productivity Report; numerous in scientific journals. *Address:* 38 Middleway, NW11 6SG. *T:* 01-455 7308. *Club:* Athenæum.

GOODFELLOW, Maj.-Gen. Howard Courtney, CB 1952; CBE 1946 (OBE 1943); retired 1954; *b* 28 July 1898; *yr s* of late Thomas Goodfellow, Plymouth; *m* 1928, Vera St John, *yr d* of late H. St J. Hewitt, Salisbury. *Educ:* Plymouth Coll.; RMC Sandhurst. Commissioned into ASC, 1916; served European War, 1914-18, in France and Italy; seconded to Iraq Army, 1928-32; War of 1939-45, served in Italy and NW Europe, rank of Brig. Order of Rafidain, Class IV (Iraq), 1931. *Address:* Chapel Lodge, Greywell, Hants. *T:* Odiham 2076.

GOODHART, Arthur Lehman, (Hon.) KBE 1948; QC 1943; FBA 1952; MA, LLM, LLD, DCL; Master of University College, Oxford, 1951-63, retired; Professor of Jurisprudence, Oxford, 1931-51; Professor Emeritus since 1951; Editor, Law Quarterly Review; *b* NY City, 1 March 1891; *s* of late Philip J. Goodhart and Harriet Lehman; *m* 1924, Cecily, *d* of Eric M. Carter, Beaulieu, Hants; three *s. Educ:* Hotchkiss Sch.; Yale Univ.; Trinity Coll., Cambridge. Asst Corp. Council for NY City, 1915-17; Capt., Ord. USA, 1917-19. University Lectr in Law, Cambridge, 1919-31; Counsel to Amer. Mission to Poland, 1919; Officier d'Académie de France, 1920; Sec. to Vice-Chancellor of Cambridge Univ., 1921-23; Ed., Cambridge Law Journal, 1921-25. Hon. Bencher, Lincoln's Inn, 1938; Hon. Fellow of Trinity Coll., Corpus Christi Coll., Trinity Hall, Cambridge; Hon. Fellow of Nuffield Coll., University Coll., Oxford; Associate Fellow of Jonathan Edwards Coll., Yale Univ.; Chm. Southern Price Regulation Cttee, 1940-51; Member: Royal Commission on the Police; Monopolies Commission; Law Revision Cttee; Supreme Court Procedure

Cttee; Company Law Revision Cttee; Alternative Remedies Cttee; Law Reports Cttee; Amer. Law Inst.; Chm. Internat. Law Assoc.; Curator, Bodleian Library; Deleg., OUP; Pres., Selden Soc., 1964; Pres., Public Teachers of Law, 1950; Vice-Pres., British Academy, 1962; Vice-Pres., Pilgrims, 1963; Pres., American Soc., 1951; Pres., International Assoc. of University Professors, 1948; Pres., Pedestrians' Assoc. for Road Safety, 1951-63; Vice-Président de l'Institut International de Philosophie du Droit; Hon. Mem. American Academy of Arts and Sciences; Visiting Professor: Yale Univ., 1928-29; Harvard Law Sch., 1964; University of Virginia Law School, 1965; McGill Univ. Law Sch., 1966; Tulane Univ. of Louisiana, 1967; Univ. of Arizona, 1967; Scholar-in-Residence, NYC Bar Assoc., 1966. Hon. LLD: Edinburgh; Queen's Univ., Belfast; Yale; Wesleyan Univ.; California; Columbia; London; New York; Williams Coll.; Princeton; Harvard; Dartmouth Coll.; Pennsylvania; Dalhousie; Melbourne; Tulane Univ. of Louisiana; Cincinnati; Hon. DLitt, Cambridge. *Publications:* Poland and the Minority Races, 1920; Essays in Jurisprudence and the Common Law, 1931; Precedent in English and Continental Law, 1934; The Government of Great Britain, 1946; English Contributions to the Philosophy of Law, 1949; Five Jewish Lawyers of the Common Law, 1950; Ed. Pollock's Jurisprudence and Essays, 1961; English Law and the Moral Law, 1953; Law of the Land, 1966; and legal articles and essays. *Address:* University College, Oxford; Whitebarn, Boars Hill, Oxford. *T:* Oxford 35294. *Clubs:* Athenæum, Oxford and Cambridge University, Savile, Pilgrims'; Century, Yale, Alpha Delta Phi, University.
See also P. C. Goodhart.

GOODHART, Rear-Adm. Hilary Charles Nicholas, CB 1972; aerospace consultant; *b* 28 Sept. 1919; *s* of G. C. Goodhart; *m* 1975, Molly Copsey. *Educ:* RNC Dartmouth; RNEC Keyham. Joined RN, 1933; served in Mediterranean in HM Ships Formidable and Dido, 1941-43; trained as pilot, 1944; served as fighter pilot in Burma Campaign, 1945; trained as test pilot, 1946; served on British Naval Staff, Washington, 1953-55; idc 1965; Rear-Adm. 1970; Mil. Dep. to Head of Defence Sales, MoD, 1970-73, retired. British Gliding Champion, 1962, 1967 and 1971. Holder of UK gliding distance record, 360 miles. Freedom of London, 1945; Mem. Ct of Grocers' Co., 1975. US Legion of Merit, 1958. *Recreation:* design of man-powered aircraft. *Address:* Lower Farm, Inkpen Common, Newbury, Berks. *T:* Inkpen 297.

GOODHART, Sir John (Gordon), 3rd Bt *cr* 1911; MA, MB, BChir; General Practitioner since 1947; *b* 14 Dec. 1916; *s* of Gordon Wilkinson Goodhart, MD, FRCP; *S* uncle, 1961; *m* 1944, Margaret Mary Eileen, *d* of late Morgan Morgan, Cray, Brecon; one *s* one *d. Educ:* Rugby; Trinity Hall, Cambridge; Guy's Hospital Med. Sch. MRCS, LRCP, 1941. Served as Surg-Lieut, RNVR, 1942-46. *Recreation:* golf. *Heir:* s Robert Anthony Gordon Goodhart, [*b* 15 Dec. 1948; *m* 1972, Kathleen Ellen, *er d* of Rev. A. D. MacRae, Inverness; one *s* one *d*]. *Address:* Holtye, 17 Mavelstone Close, Bromley, Kent. *T:* 01-460 6700.

GOODHART, Philip Carter; MP (C) Bromley, Beckenham, since March 1957; *b* 3 Nov. 1925; *s* of Prof. Arthur Goodhart, *qv*; *m* 1950, Valerie Winant; three *s* four *d. Educ:* Hotchkiss Sch., USA; Trinity Coll., Cambridge. Served KRRC and Parachute Regt, 1943-47. Editorial staff, Daily Telegraph, 1950-55; Editorial staff, Sunday Times, 1955-57. Contested (C) Consett, Co. Durham, Gen. Election, 1950; Mem. LCC Educn Cttee, 1956-57; PPS to Julian Amery at War Office and Colonial Office, 1958-60; Member: British Delegn to Council of Europe and WEU, 1961-63; British Delegation to UN Gen. Assembly, 1963; NATO Parly Assembly, 1964- (Chm. Arms Standardization Sub-Cttee, 1966-69). Joint Hon. Sec., 1922 Cttee, 1960-. Chm. of Cons. Parly Cttee on Military Matters, 1964-65; Sec., Cons. Parly Defence Cttee, 1967-72, Chm., 1972-74, Vice-Chm., 1974-; Chm., Parly NI Cttee, 1976-; Member: Council, Consumers' Assoc., 1959-68, 1970-; Adv. Council on Public Records, 1970-; Exec. Cttee, British Council, 1974-; Council, RUSI, 1973-76. Mem., FCO Adv. Panel on Arms Control and Disarmament Questions, 1973. *Publications:* The Hunt for Kimathi (with Ian Henderson, GM), 1958; In the Shadow of the Sword, 1964; Fifty Ships that Saved the World, 1965; (with Christopher Chataway) War without Weapons, 1968; Referendum, 1970; (with Ursula Branston) The 1922: the history of the 1922 Committee, 1973; Full-Hearted Consent: the story of the referendum campaign—and the campaign for the referendum, 1975; various pamphlets. *Recreation:* skiing (Chm., Develt Cttee, Nat. Ski Fedn of GB, 1970; Chm., Lords and Commons Ski Club, 1971-73). *Address:* 27 Phillimore Gardens, W8. *T:* 01-937 0822; Whitebarn, Boars Hill, Oxford. *T:* Oxford 735294. *Clubs:* Athenæum, Beefsteak, Carlton, Garrick.

GOODHEW, Victor Henry; MP (C) St Albans Division of Herts since Oct. 1959; *b* 30 Nov. 1919; *s* of late Rudolph Goodhew, Mannings Heath, Sussex; *m* 1st, 1940, Sylvia Johnson (marr. diss.); one *s* one *d*; 2nd, 1951, Suzanne Gordon-Burge (marr. diss. 1972); 3rd, 1972, Eva, *d* of Eduard Wilhelm Rittinghausen. *Educ:* King's Coll. Sch. Served War of 1939-45: RAF, 1939-46; comd Airborne Radar Unit, attached 6th Airborne Div.; Sqdn Ldr 1945. Mem. Westminster City Council, 1953-59. Contested (C) Paddington North, 1955. Mem. LCC, 1958-61. PPS to Mr C. I. Orr-Ewing, OBE, MP (when Civil Lord of the Admiralty), May 1962-63; PPS to Hon. Thomas Galbraith, MP (Jt Parly Sec., Min. of Transport), 1963-64; Asst Govt Whip, June-Oct. 1970; a Lord Comr, HM Treasury, 1970-73. *Recreations:* gardening, sailing, ski-ing. *Address:* 100 Eaton Place, SW1. *T:* 01-235 4911.

GOODING, Air Vice-Marshal Keith Horace, CB 1966; OBE 1951; *b* 2 Sept. 1913; *s* of Horace Milford Gooding, Romsey, Hants; *m* 1st, 1943, Peggy Eileen (*d* 1962), *d* of Albert William Gatfield, Guildford, Surrey; one *s*; 2nd, 1968, Jean, *d* of Maurice Stanley Underwood, Andover, Hants; two *s* one *d* (of whom one *s* one *d* are twins). *Educ:* King Edward VI Sch., Southampton. Joined RAF 1938; served Aden, Fighter Comd, 1939-45; Germany, 1945-47; NATO Defence Coll., 1953-54; NATO, Oslo, 1954-55; Bomber Comd, 1958-61; AOA Maintenance Comd, 1965-68; Dir-Gen. of Equipment, later Supply (RAF), 1968-71, retired. *Recreations:* tennis, bridge. *Address:* c/o Lloyds Bank Ltd, Surbiton, Surrey. *Club:* Royal Air Force.

GOODINGS, Alfred Cecil, MBE 1946; MSc, PhD; Director of Textile Research, Ontario Research Foundation, 1930-67; *b* Leith, Scotland, 10 Sept. 1902; *yr s* of late William George Goodings; *m* 1931, *yr d* of late Rev. F. W. Ambery Smith; two *s*. *Educ:* Leeds Univ. PhD for research in textiles. *Publications:* papers in scientific periodicals relating to textile fibres and technology. *Address:* 101 Collegeview Avenue, Toronto M5P 1K2, Canada.

GOODINGS, Rt. Rev. Allen; see Quebec, Bishop of.

GOODISON, Alan Clowes, CMG 1975; HM Diplomatic Service; Minister, Rome, since 1976; *b* 20 Nov. 1926; *o s* of Harold Clowes Goodison and Winifred Goodison (*née* Ludlam); *m* 1956, Anne Rosemary Fitton; one *s* two *d*. *Educ:* Colfe's Grammar Sch.; Trinity Coll., Cambridge. Scholar, Mod. and Medieval Langs Tripos, first cl.; MA 1951. Army, Lt, Intell. Corps, 1947-49. Foreign Office, Third Sec., 1949; Middle East Centre for Arab Studies, 1950; Cairo, 1950-51; Tripoli, 1951-53; Khartoum, 1953; FO, 1953-56; Second Sec., later First Sec. (Commercial), Lisbon, 1956-59; Amman, 1960-62; FO, 1962-66; Bonn, 1966-68; Counsellor, Kuwait, 1969-71; Head of Trg Dept and Dir, Diplomatic Service Lang. Centre, FCO, 1971-72; Head of S European Dept, FCO, 1973-76. Pres., Beckenham Chorale, 1972-73. Licensed Lay Reader of Anglican Church, 1959-62 and 1966-. Mem. Council, Anglican Centre, Rome, 1977-. *Publications:* trans. numerous articles for Encyclopaedia of Islam. *Recreations:* looking at pictures, reading. *Address:* c/o Foreign and Commonwealth Office, SW1; 32 Kingswood Road, Bromley, Kent BR2 0NF. *Club:* Travellers'.

GOODISON, Nicholas Proctor; stockbroker; Senior Partner, Quilter Hilton Goodison & Co., since 1975; Chairman of The Stock Exchange, since 1976; *b* 16 May 1934; *s* of Edmund Harold Goodison and Eileen Mary Carrington Proctor; *m* 1960, Judith Abel Smith; one *s* two *d*. *Educ:* Marlborough Coll.; King's Coll., Cambridge (Scholar, BA Classics 1958, MA). H. E. Goodison & Co. (now Quilter Hilton Goodison & Co.), Members of the Stock Exchange, 1958; Partner, 1962; elected to Council of Stock Exchange, 1968 (Chm. various standing cttees, 1971-76). Hon. Treas., Furniture History Soc.; Hon. Keeper of Furniture, Fitzwilliam Museum, Cambridge; Mem. Exec. Cttee, Nat. Art-Collections Fund. Director: English Nat. Opera; City Arts Trust; Editorial Dir, Burlington Magazine. FSA, FRSA. *Publications:* English Barometers 1680-1860, 1968, 2nd edn 1977; Ormolu: The Work of Matthew Boulton, 1974; many papers and articles on history of furniture, clocks and barometers. *Recreations:* history of furniture and decorative arts, opera, walking, fishing. *Address:* Garrard House, Gresham Street, EC2; Stock Exchange, EC2. *Club:* Beefsteak.

GOODISON, Robin Reynolds, CB 1964; Consultant to Civil Aviation Authority, since 1977 (Deputy Chairman, 1972-77, Acting Chairman, Jan.-March 1972); *b* 13 Aug. 1912; *s* of Arthur Leathley Goodison; *m* 1936, Betty Lydia, *d* of Comdr L. Robinson, OBE, Royal Navy (retired); three *d*. *Educ:* Finchley Grammar Sch.; University Coll., London Univ. (MA). Joined Ministry of Labour, 1935, transferred to Ministry of Transport,

1936; Principal, 1940; Asst Sec., 1946; Imperial Defence Coll., 1950; Under-Sec., Ministry of Transport and Civil Aviation, 1957, Ministry of Aviation, 1959, Board of Trade, 1966; Second Sec., BoT, 1969-70; Dep. Sec., DTI, 1970-72. *Recreation:* sailing. *Address:* Clansthal, Coldharbour Lane, Bushey, Herts. *T:* Bushey Heath 1911.

GOODLAD, Alastair Robertson; MP (C) Northwich since Feb. 1974; *b* 4 July 1943; *y s* of late Dr John Goodlad and late Isabel (*née* Sinclair); *m* 1968, Cecilia Barbara, 2nd *d* of late Col Richard Hurst and Lady Barbara Hurst; two *s*. *Educ:* Marlborough Coll.; King's Coll., Cambridge (MA, LLB). Contested (C) Crewe Div., 1970. Dir, Bowater Overseas Holdings Ltd. *Address:* 70 Drayton Gardens, SW10 9SB. *T:* 01-373 3858. *Club:* Brooks's.

GOODMAN, family name of **Baron Goodman.**

GOODMAN, Baron, *cr* 1965, of the City of Westminster (Life Peer); **Arnold Abraham Goodman,** CH 1972; MA, LLM; Master of University College, Oxford, since 1976; Senior Partner, Goodman Derrick and Co., Solicitors; Chairman, National Building Agency, since 1973; First President, Theatres Advisory Council, since 1972; *b* 21 Aug. 1913; *s* of Joseph and Bertha Goodman; unmarried. *Educ:* University Coll., London; Downing Coll., Cambridge (Hon. Fellow, 1968). Enlisted Gunner, RA, TA, Sept. 1939, retd as Major, Nov. 1945. Mem., Royal Commn on Working of Tribunals of Enquiry (Evidence) Act, 1921, 1966-; Chm., Cttee of Inquiry on Charity Law, 1974. Chm., Housing Corporation, 1973-77. Chairman: Cttee (on behalf of Arts Council) on London orchestras, 1964, reporting 1965; Arts Council of GB, 1965-72; Theatres' Trust, 1976-; Member: British Council, 1967- (Vice-Chm., 1974-); South Bank Theatre Board, 1968-; Life Mem., Royal Phil. Orch., 1976; Director: Royal Opera House, Covent Garden, 1972-; English National Opera Ltd (formerly Sadler's Wells Trust, Coliseum, Ltd), 1973- (Chm., 1977-); The Observer Ltd, 1976-; Governor, Royal Shakespeare Theatre, 1972-; Pres., Nat. Book League, 1972-. Chairman: Observer Trust, 1967-76; Newspaper Publishers' Assoc., 1970-75; IRC, 1969-71; British Lion Films Ltd, 1965-72; Charter Film Productions, 1973-; Dir of various companies. Mem., British/USA Bicentennial Liaison Cttee, 1973. Governor, College of Law, 1975-. Fellow UCL; Hon. LLD London and other Univs; Hon. DLitt City, 1975. *Address:* Goodman Derrick & Co., 4 Little Essex Street, WC2.

GOODMAN, Geoffrey George; Assistant Editor, since 1976, and Industrial Editor, since 1969, The Daily Mirror; *b* 2 July 1921; *s* of Michael Goodman and Edythe (*née* Bowman); *m* 1947, Margit (*née* Freudenbergova); one *s* one *d*. *Educ:* elementary schs, Stockport and Manchester; grammar schs, London; LSE (BScEcon). RAF, 1940-46. Manchester Guardian, 1946-47; Daily Mirror, 1947-48; News Chronicle, 1949-59; Daily Herald, 1959-64; The Sun (IPC), 1964-69; Daily Mirror, 1969-. Fellow, Nuffield Coll., Oxford, 1974-76. Head of Govt's Counter-inflation Publicity Unit, 1975-76; Member: Labour Party Cttee on Industrial Democracy, 1966-67; Royal Commn on the Press, 1974-77; TGWU; NUJ. Hon. MA Oxon. *Publications:* General Strike of 1926, 1951; "Brother Frank", 1969; contrib. London Inst. of World Affairs, 1948. *Recreations:* pottering, poetry, supporting Tottenham Hotspur FC, and climbing—but not social. *Address:* 64 Flower Lane, Mill Hill, NW7. *Club:* Savile.

GOODMAN, Howard; see Goodman, R. H.

GOODMAN, Prof. John Francis Bradshaw, PhD; FIPM; Frank Thomas Professor of Industrial Relations, University of Manchester Institute of Science and Technology, since 1975; *b* 2 Aug. 1940; *s* of Edwin and Amy Goodman; *m* 1967, Elizabeth Mary Towns; one *s* one *d*. *Educ:* Chesterfield Grammar Sch.; London Sch. of Economics. BSc Econ; PhD. FIPM. Personnel Officer, Ford Motor Co. Ltd, 1962-64; Lectr in Industrial Econs, Univ. of Nottingham, 1964-69; Industrial Relations Adviser, NBPI, 1969-70; Sen. Lectr in Industrial Relations, Univ. of Manchester, 1970-74. *Publications:* Shop Stewards in British Industry, 1969; Shop Stewards, 1973; Rulemaking and Industrial Peace, 1977; contribs to British Jl of Industrial Relations, ILR, Industrial Relations Jl, Monthly Labor Rev., Personnel Management, etc. *Recreations:* fell walking, ornithology, squash, football. *Address:* 24 Regent Close, Bramhall, Stockport, Cheshire. *T:* 061-439 7136.

GOODMAN, M(ichael) Bradley; a Recorder of the Crown Court, since 1972; Vicar-General of the Province of Canterbury, since 1977; *b* 3 May 1930; *s* of Marcus Gordon Goodman and Eunice Irene May Goodman (*née* Bradley); *m* 1967, Patricia Mary Gorringe; two *d* (one *s* decd). *Educ:* Aldenham; Sidney Sussex Coll., Cambridge (MA). Called to Bar, Middle Temple, 1953;

Western Circuit. Chm., William Temple Assoc., 1963-66; Prosecuting Counsel to DHSS, 1975-; Pres., Wireless Telegraphy Appeals Tribunal, 1977; Member: Commn on Deployment and Payment of the Clergy, 1965-67; C of E Legal Adv. Commn, 1973-; General Synod, Church of England, 1977-; Chancellor: Dio. Guildford, 1968-; Dio. Lincoln, 1970-; Dio. Rochester, 1971-; Lay Chm., Dulwich Deanery Synod, 1970-73. Governor: Liddon Hse, London, 1964-; Pusey Hse, Oxford, 1965-. *Address:* Francis Taylor Building, Temple, EC4. *T:* 01-353 7768. *Club:* Hurlingham.

GOODMAN, Rt. Rev. Morse Lamb; *see* Calgary, Bishop of.

GOODMAN, Neville Marriott, CB 1961; MA, MD Cantab; PhD London; DPH London; FRCP; retired as Deputy Chief MO, Ministry of Health (1960-April 1963); *b* 22 April 1898; *o c* of Roger Neville Goodman, MD, and Louisa Harvey Marriott; *m* 1st, 1928, Beatrix Warr Edwards (*d* 1970); 2nd, 1971, Phyllis Mary Bucknell. *Educ:* Mill Hill Sch.; RMC Sandhurst; Pembroke Coll., Cambridge; London Hospital. House physician, surgeon, Receiving Room Officer, Ear, Nose and Throat Dept, London Hosp. Served European War, 1914-18, with 4th Bn The Worcs Regt, 1917-19; retd with rank of Capt. General practice, Lymington, Hants, 1925-32; Asst County MOH, Surrey CC, 1933-34; Min. of Health, 1934-63. Mem., Health Cttee, League of Nations, 1938-45; Br. Delegate Office Internat. d'Hygiène publique, Paris, 1938-45; Dir of Health, European Regional Office, UNRRA, 1945-47; Dir of Field Services, WHO, 1946-49. OStJ 1936; Méd. de la Reconnaissance française. *Publications:* International Health Organisations and their Work, 1952, new edn 1971; Wilson Jameson: Architect of National Health, 1970; articles on medicine and public health. *Recreation:* gardening. *Address:* Mill Wall House, Sandwich, Kent CT13 9BQ. *T:* Sandwich 2344. *Club:* Athenæum.

GOODMAN, Perry; Research Group, Department of Industry, since 1974; *b* 26 Nov. 1932; *s* of Cyril Goodman and Anne (*née* Rosen); *m* 1958, Marcia Ann (*née* Morris); one *s* one *d. Educ:* Haberdashers' Aske's Hampstead Sch.; University Coll., London. BSc, AICeram. Royal Corps of Signals, 1955-57; Jt Head, Chemistry Res. Lab., then Project Leader, Morgan Crucible Co. Ltd, 1957-64; Sen. Scientific Officer, DSIR, 1964-65; Principal Scientific Officer, Process Plant Br., Min. of Technology, 1965-67; 1st Sec. (Scientific), 1968-70, Counsellor (Scientific), 1970-74, British Embassy, Paris. *Recreations:* travel, walking, conversation. *Address:* 118 Westbourne Terrace Mews, W2 6QG. *T:* 01-262 0925.

GOODMAN, (Robert) Howard, ARIBA; DipArch (Hons); Chief Architect, Department of Health and Social Security, since 1971; *b* 29 March 1928; *s* of Robert Barnard Goodman and Phyllis Goodman; *m* 1955, Doris Richardson; two *s. Educ:* St George Grammar Sch., Bristol; Northern Polytechnic, London. Articled pupil, 1944-47; Arch. Asst to City of Bristol, 1947-49; Asst Architect to SW Regional Hosp. Bd, 1949-54. Design of various hosp. projects in SW England; with various private architects, 1954-60; design of several hosps in UK, Africa and India. MOH (now DHSS): Main Grade Arch., 1960; Sen. Grade, 1961; Principal Arch., 1963; Asst Chief Arch., 1966; Chief Arch., 1971. Member: Constr. and Housing Res. Adv. Council; Bldg Res. Estab. Adv. Council. Research and develt into health planning, systems building and computer aided design. *Publications:* contribs to: Hospitals Handbook, 1960; Hospital Design, 1963; Hospital Traffic and Supply Problems, 1968; Portfolio for Health, 1971; Technology of the Eighties, 1972; Industrialised Hospital Building, 1972; CAD Systems, 1976; various articles in architectural, medical and general press. *Recreations:* eating, drinking, talking. *Address:* Cicelyford, Trelech, Gwent. *T:* Trelech 565.

GOODPASTER, Gen. Andrew Jackson; United States Army; DSC (US); DSM (Def.); DSM (Army) (3 Oak Leaf Clusters); DSM (Navy); DSM (Air Force); Silver Star; Legion of Merit (Oak Leaf Cluster); Purple Heart (Oak Leaf Cluster); Superintendent, United States Military Academy, West Point, New York (in grade of Lt-Gen.), since 1977; *b* 12 Feb. 1915; *s* of Andrew Jackson Goodpaster and Teresa Mary Goodpaster (*née* Mrovka); *m* 1939, Dorothy Anderson Goodpaster (*née* Anderson); two *d. Educ:* McKendree Coll., Lebanon, Ill; US Mil. Academy, 1935-39 (BS); Princeton Univ., 1947-50 (MSE, MA, PhD). 11th Eng. Panama, 1939-42; Ex O, 390th Eng. Gen. Svc Regt, Camp Claiborne, La, 1942-43; Comd and Gen. Staff Sch., Ft Leavenworth, Kansas, Feb.-April 1943; CO, 48th Eng. Combat Bn, II Corps, Fifth Army, 1943-44; Ops Div., Gen. Staff, War Dept (incl. Jt War Plans Cttee, JCS, 1945-46), 1944-47; Student, Civil Eng. Course and Polit. Sc. Grad. Sch., Princeton Univ., 1947-50; Army Mem., Jt Advanced Study Cttee, JCS, 1950-51; Special Asst to Chief of Staff, SHAPE,

1951-54; Dist Eng., San Francisco Dist, Calif, July-Oct. 1954; Def. Liaison Officer and Staff Sec. to President of US, 1954-61; Asst Div. Comdr, 3rd Inf. Div., April-Oct. 1961, and CG, 8th Inf. Div., Oct. 1961-Oct. 1962, USAREUR; Sp. Asst (Policy) to Chm., JCS, Washington, DC, Nov. 1962-Jan. 1964; Asst to Chm., JCS, Washington, DC, Jan. 1964-July 1966; Dir Joint Staff, JCS, Washington, DC, Aug. 1966-Mar. 1967; Dir of Sp. Studies, Office Chief of Staff, USA, Washington, DC, April 1967-July 1967; Senior US Army Mem., Mil. Staff UN, May 1967-July 1968; Comdt, Nat. War Coll., Washington, DC, Aug. 1967-July 1968; Mem. US Delegn for Negotiations with N Vietnam, Paris (addl duty), April 1968-July 1968; Dep. Comdr, US Mil. Assistance Comd, Vietnam, July 1968-April 1969; Supreme Allied Commander Europe, 1969-74; C-in-C, US European Command, 1969-74. Sen. Fellow, Woodrow Wilson Internat. Center for Scholars, Washington DC, 1975-76; Prof. of Govt and Internat. Studies, The Citadel, Charleston, SC, 1976-77. *Recreations:* golf, fishing, ski-ing, music. *Address:* United States Military Academy, West Point, NY 10996, USA.

GOODRICH, Rt. Rev. Philip Harold Ernest; *see* Tonbridge, Bishop Suffragan of.

GOODSELL, Sir John William, Kt 1968; CMG 1954; FASA; Company Director, since 1971; Member: State Cancer Council since 1962; Council, University of New South Wales, since 1948; Convocation, Macquarie University, since 1965; Chairman: Unisearch Ltd; Winston Churchill Fellowship Trust; *b* 6 July 1906; *s* of late Major S. P. Goodsell, VD, Croix de Guerre (avec Palme), and of late Mrs L. A. Goodsell; *m* 1932, Myrtle Thelma, *d* of late R. H. Austin; three *d. Educ:* Canterbury High Sch., NSW. Member: Public Library Bd, 1948-55; Public Accountants Registration Bd, 1948-55; Under-Sec. and Comptroller of Accounts, New South Wales Treasury, 1948-55; Pres. Metropolitan Water Sewerage and Drainage Board, Sydney, April 1955-Sept. 1960; Chm., NSW Public Service Bd, 1960-71; Member: Council, Australian Soc. of Accountants, 1959-61; Sydney Harbour Transport Board, 1951-55; Appointments Bd, Univ. of Sydney, 1963-71; Prince Henry Hospital Bd, 1960-76 (Chm., 1960-61); Prince of Wales Hospital Bd, 1961-76; Eastern Suburbs Hospital Bd, 1968-76; Chm., Tax Agents Board, 1948-55; Custodian Trustee, Legislative Assembly Members Superannuation Fund, 1948-55; Trustee, Kuring-gai Chase Trust, 1962-64. Hon. DSc Univ. of NSW. Coronation Medal, 1953. *Recreations:* tennis and fishing. *Address:* 22 King Street, Ashbury, NSW 2193, Australia. *T:* 798 4826.

GOODSON, Lt-Col Sir Alfred Lassam, 2nd Bt *cr* 1922; *b* 1893; *er s* of 1st Bt; *S* father, 1940; *m* 1920, Joan (*d* 1939), *d* of C. J. Leyland, Haggerston Castle, Beal, Northumberland; *m* 1941, Enid Clayton Leyland, *d* of late Robert Clayton Swan, Barrowby Grange, Grantham. *Educ:* Radley. Served European War, 1914-19, Captain City of London Yeomanry, TF, 1916; commanded No 1 Bn Northumberland Home Guard, 1940-45. Master, College Valley Foxhounds, 1924-. *Heir: n* Mark Weston Lassam Goodson [*b* 12 Dec. 1925; *m* 1949, Barbara Mary Constantine, *d* of Surg.-Capt. R. J. McAuliffe Andrews, RN; one *s* three *d*]. *Address:* Corbet Tower, Kelso, Roxburghshire. *T:* Morebattle 203.

GOODSTEIN, Prof. Reuben Louis, PhD, DLit (London); ScD (Cantab); Professor of Mathematics, University of Leicester, since 1948; *b* 15 Dec. 1912; 2nd *s* of late Alexander and Sophia Goodstein; *m* 1938, Louba, *d* of late Samuel Atkin; one *s* one *d. Educ:* St Paul's Sch.; Magdalene Coll., Cambridge (BA, MSc). Scholar and Research Scholar, Magdalene Coll., 1931-35; Lectr in Mathematics, Univ. of Reading, 1935-47; Dean of the Faculty of Science, 1954-57; Pro-Vice-Chancellor, 1966-69, Univ. of Leicester. Hon. Librarian, Mathematical Assoc., 1955-77, Pres., 1975-76; Editor, Mathematical Gazette, 1956-62. Mem. Council, Assoc. for Symbolic Logic, 1965-69. *Publications:* Mathematical Analysis, 1948; Constructive Formalism, 1951, 2nd edn, 1965; The Foundations of Mathematics, 1952; Axiomatic Projective Geometry, 1953, 2nd edn 1962; Mathematical Logic, 1957, 2nd edn 1962; Recursive Number Theory, 1957; Recursive Analysis, 1961; Fundamental Concepts of Mathematics, 1962; Boolean Algebra, 1963; Essays in the Philosophy of Mathematics, 1965; Complex Functions, 1965; Development of Mathematical Logic, 1971; articles in British, continental and American jls. *Address:* University of Leicester, Leicester LE1 7RH.

GOODWIN, Prof. Albert, MA; Professor of Modern History in the University of Manchester, 1953-69 (Dean of the Faculty of Arts, 1966-68), now Emeritus Professor; *b* 2 Aug. 1906; 3rd *s* of Albert and Edith Ellen Goodwin; *m* 1935, Mary Ethelwyn, *e d* of late Capt. W. Millner, Tettenhall, Staffs; two *s* one *d. Educ:*

King Edward VII School, Sheffield; Jesus Coll., Oxford; Sorbonne. Scholar; Gladstone Memorial Prizeman (Oxford), 1926; 1st Cl. Mod. Hist., 1928; Laming Travelling Fellow, The Queen's Coll., Oxford, 1928-29. Asst Lectr in European History, Univ. of Liverpool, 1929-31; Lectr in Mod. Hist. and Economics, 1931, Fellow and Tutor, Jesus Coll., Oxford, 1933; Junior Dean, Librarian and Dean of Degrees, 1931-39; Univ. Lectr in Mod. French Hist., 1938. Staff Officer (Sqdn Ldr) in RAFVR in Air Ministry War Room, 1940-43; Historical Branch, Air Ministry, 1944-45. Senior Tutor, 1947-48, and Vice-Principal of Jesus Coll., Oxford, 1949-51. Examiner in Final Hon. Sch. of Mod. Hist. (Oxford) 1948-49, Chm., 1950; Senior Univ. Lectr in Revolutionary and Napoleonic Period, 1948-53; Vis. Fellow, All Souls Coll., Oxford, 1969-70. Member: Council of Royal Historical Soc. (Vice-Pres.); Royal Commn on Historical MSS; Governor of John Rylands Library, Manchester. *Publications:* The Abbey of St Edmundsbury, 1931; The Battle of Britain (Air Ministry Pamphlet 156), 1943; The French Revolution, 1953; The European Nobility in the Eighteenth Century (contrib. and ed), 1953; A select list of works on Europe and Europe Overseas, 1715-1815 (co-editor contributor), 1956; The Friends of Liberty: the English democratic movement in the eighteenth century, 1978; (ed and contrib.) Vol. VIII New Cambridge Modern History; articles in Eng. Hist. Review, History, Encyclopædia Britannica, etc. *Recreations:* golf, antiques. *Address:* 12 Hound Street, Sherborne, Dorset DT9 3AA. *T:* Sherborne 2280.

GOODWIN, Air Vice-Marshal Edwin Spencer, CB 1944; CBE 1941; AFC. Served European War, 1914-19; Flt Sub-Lieut RNAS, 1916; War of 1939-45 (CBE, CB). Group Capt. 1939; Air Commodore, 1941; Air Vice-Marshal, 1948. Air Officer i/c Administration, HQ Bomber Command, 1945; retired, 1948.

GOODWIN, Dr Eric Thomson, CBE 1975; retired; *b* 30 July 1913; *s* of John Edward Goodwin and Florence Goodwin; *m* 1st, 1940, Isobel Philip (*d* 1976); two *s*; 2nd, 1977, Avis Mary (*née* Thomson). *Educ:* King Edward VI Sch., Stafford; Harrow County Sch.; Peterhouse, Cambridge. BA 1934, Rayleigh Prize 1936, MA 1937, PhD 1938. Asst Lectr, Sheffield Univ., 1937-39; war service: Mathematical Lab., Cambridge, 1939-43; Admty Signal Estabt, Witley, 1943-44; Admty Computing Service, Bath, 1945; Maths Div., Nat. Physical Lab., 1945-71 (Supt 1951-71); Dep. Dir, Nat. Phys. Lab., 1971-74, retd. *Publications:* papers in learned jls on theoretical physics and numerical analysis. *Recreations:* music, reading, the countryside, philately. *Address:* 32 Castle Mount Crescent, Bakewell, Derbyshire DE4 1AT. *T:* Bakewell 3647.

GOODWIN, Prof. Geoffrey Lawrence, BSc (Econ.); Montague Burton Professor of International Relations in the University of London (tenable at London School of Economics) since 1962; *b* 14 June 1916; *s* of Rev. J. H. Goodwin and Mrs E. M. Goodwin; *m* 1951, Janet Audrey (*née* Sewell); one *s* two *d*. *Educ:* Marlborough Coll.; RMC, Sandhurst; London Sch. of Economics. Regular Army Officer, 1936-43 (The Suffolk Regt; Army Physical Training Staff; Combined Ops; Major, comdg Indep. Company, Gibraltar). Foreign Office, 1945-48; London Sch. of Economics, 1948-. Principal, St Catharine's, Windsor Great Park, 1971-72. Comr on Internat. Affairs, World Council of Churches, 1968-76. Mem. Council, RIIA, 1974-. FRSA 1975. *Publications:* (ed.) The University Teaching of International Relations, 1951; Britain and the United Nations, 1958; (ed) New Dimensions of World Politics, 1975; articles in International Affairs, International Organization, Political Studies, etc. *Recreations:* painting, sketching, singing. *Address:* Webbs Farm, Church Lane, Headley, Surrey. *T:* Leatherhead 77354.

GOODWIN, Prof. John Forrest, MD, FRCP; Professor of Clinical Cardiology, Royal Postgraduate Medical School, London, since 1963; Consulting Physician, Hammersmith Hospital, since 1949; *b* 1 Dec. 1918; *s* of late Col William Richard Power Goodwin, DSO, RAMC, and late Myrtle Dale Goodwin (*née* Forrest); *m* 1943, Barbara Cameron Robertson; one *s* one *d*. *Educ:* Cheltenham Coll.; St Mary's Hosp. Medical Sch. (Univ. of London). FRSocMed 1943; MD London 1946; FRCP 1957. Med. Registrar, St Mary's Hosp., 1943-44; Physician, Anglo-Iranian Oil Co., Abadan, 1944-45; Med. 1st Asst, Royal Infirmary, Sheffield, 1946-49; Lectr in Medicine and Cons. Physician, Postgraduate Med. Sch., London, 1949-59; Sen. Lecturer, 1959-63. Visiting Professor: Univ. of California at Los Angeles, 1966; Georgetown Univ. Sch. of Med., Washington, 1973. Member: Brit. Cardiac Soc., 1950 (Pres., 1972-76); Pres., Internat Soc. and Fedn of Cardiology, 1977; Med. Res. Soc., 1952; Assoc. of Physicians of Great Britain and Ireland, 1953; Council, Brit. Heart Foundation, 1964. Member: Società Italiana di Cardiologia, 1964; Thoracic Soc., 1967; Assoc. of European Pædiatric Cardiologists, 1967; Cardiac Soc.

of Australia and NZ; Venezuelan Soc. of Cardiology, 1969; Hon. Member: Swiss Cardiol. Soc.; Cardiac Soc., Ecuador; Hellenic Cardiac Soc., 1974; Fellow Amer. Coll. of Cardiology, 1967; Fellow, Council on Clinical Cardiology, Amer. Heart Assoc., 1970. SPk 1968. Commander, Order of Icelandic Falcon, 1972. *Publications:* (jt ed. with R. Daley and R. E. Steiner) Clinical Disorders of the Pulmonary Circulation, 1960; (with W. Cleland, L. McDonald, D. Ross) Medical and Surgical Cardiology, 1969; (ed with B. Yu) Progress in Cardiology, 1973; papers on diagnosis and treatment of congenital and acquired heart disease in British and foreign cardiac and other journals. *Recreations:* photography, history, travel. *Address:* 18 Augustus Road, Wimbledon Park, SW19. *T:* 01-788 1497. *Clubs:* Athenæum, Royal Society of Medicine.

GOODWIN, Leonard George, CMG 1977; FRCP; FRS 1976; Director, Nuffield Laboratories of Comparative Medicine, Institute of Zoology, The Zoological Society of London, since 1964; Director of Science, Zoological Society of London, since 1966; *b* 11 July 1915; *s* of Harry George and Lois Goodwin; *m* 1940, Marie Evelyn Coates; no *c*. *Educ:* William Ellis Sch., London; University Coll., London; School of Pharmacy, London; University Coll. Hospital. BPharm 1935, BSc 1937, MB, BS 1950, (London). MRCP 1966, FRCP 1972. Demonstrator, Sch. of Pharmacy, London, 1935-39; Head of Wellcome Labs of Tropical Medicine, 1958-63 (Protozoologist, 1939-63). Jt Hon. Sec., Royal Soc. of Tropical Medicine and Hygiene, 1968-74. Chm., Trypanosomiasis Panel, ODM, 1974-. Soc. of Apothecaries Gold Medal, 1975. *Publications:* (pt author) Biological Standardization, 1950; (contrib.) Biochemistry and Physiology of Protozoa, 1955; (jointly) A New Tropical Hygiene, 1960, 2nd edn 1972; (contrib.) Recent Advances in Pharmacology, 1962; many contribs to scientific jls, mainly on pharmacology and chemotherapy of tropical diseases, especially malaria, trypanosomiasis and helminth infections. *Recreations:* Dabbling in arts and crafts especially pottery (slipware), gardening and passive participation in music and opera. *Address:* Shepperlands Farm, Park Lane, Finchampstead, Berks. *T:* Eversley 732153.

GOODWIN, Michael Felix James; Administrative Director, Institute for the Study of Conflict; *b* 31 Jan. 1916; *e s* of late F. W. Goodwin; *m* 1944, Alison, *y d* of Capt. Lionel Trower and Ethel Matheson of Achany; one *s* one *d*. *Educ:* privately. Joined BBC, 1935; North Reg. Drama Dir, 1938; West Reg. Drama Dir, 1939. Served War of 1939-45, in Royal Artillery, 1939-43. Returned to BBC in Features Dept and Overseas News Service, 1943-47. Dramatic critic, The Weekly Review, 1945-46; succeeded Helen Waddell as Asst Editor, The Nineteenth Century and After, 1945-47; Editor, The Twentieth Century (formerly The Nineteenth Century and After), 1947-52; toured US at invitation of State Dept, 1952; Editor, Bellman Books, 1952-55; Dir, Contact Publications, 1955-60; Dir, Newman Neame Ltd, 1960-65. Financial Advr, Internat. Assoc. for Cultural Freedom, Paris, 1967-71. *Publications:* Nineteenth Century Opinion, 1949 (Penguin); Artist and Colourman, 1966; Concise Dictionary of Antique Terms, 1967. *Address:* 16 Cope Place, W8. *T:* 01-937 3802. *Club:* Travellers'.

GOODWIN, Sir Reginald (Eustace), Kt 1968; CBE 1960; DL; Leader of the Labour Party, Greater London Council, since 1964, Leader of the Council, 1973-77, Leader of the Opposition, since 1977; Deputy Chairman, Basildon Development Corporation, since 1970; *b* 3 July 1908; *s* of late Thomas William Goodwin, Streatham, London; *m* 1943, Penelope Mary, *d* of late Capt. R. T. Thornton, MBE, MC, Chepstow, Mon; two *s* one *d*. *Educ:* Strand Sch., London. Tea Buyer in City of London, 1928-34; Asst Gen. Sec., Nat. Assoc. of Boys' Clubs, 1934-45. Served War of 1939-45. Mem., Bermondsey Borough Council, 1937-65 (Leader of Council, 1947-65); Hon. Freeman of the Borough, 1963; Mem. LCC, 1946-65; Alderman, 1961 (Chm. Gen. Purposes Cttee, 1954-58; Establishment Cttee, 1958-60; Housing Cttee, 1960-61; Finance Cttee, 1961-65); Mem., GLC, 1964- (Chm. Finance Cttee, 1964-67; Chm. ILEA Finance Sub-Cttee, 1964-67, 1970-73). Gen. Sec., Nat. Assoc. of Boys' Clubs, 1945-73. Mem. Ct, Univ. of London, 1968-. DL County of London, 1958-. *Recreations:* local government; gardening. *Address:* Twitten Cottage, Marehill, Pulborough, West Sussex. *T:* Pulborough 2202.

GOODWIN, Lt-Gen. Sir Richard (Elton), KCB 1963 (CB 1959); CBE 1954; DSO 1944; DL; *b* 17 Aug. 1908; *s* of late Col W. R. P. Goodwin, DSO, and Mrs Goodwin; *m* 1940, Anthea Mary Sampson; three *s*. *Educ:* Cheltenham Coll.; Royal Military Coll., Sandhurst. Commissioned into Suffolk Regt, 1928; served in India, 1930-38; ADC to Governor of Madras, 1935; Adjutant 2nd Suffolk, 1935-38; 2nd i/c 9th Royal Warwickshire, 1941-42; CO 1st Suffolk, 1943-45; College Comdr, RMA Sandhurst,

1947-49; Comdt, Sch. of Infantry, 1951-54; Comdr, 6th Infty Bde, 1954-57; GOC 49th Infty Div. (TA) and N Midland Dist, 1957-60; GOC, E Africa Comd, 1960-63; Comdr 1st (British) Corps, 1963-66; Military Secretary, MoD (Army), 1966-69. Lieutenant, HM Tower of London, 1969-72. Col 1st E Anglian Regt (Royal Norfolk and Suffolk), 1962-64; Dep. Col The Royal Anglian Regt, 1964-66, Col, 1966-71. DL Suffolk 1973. *Recreations:* hunting and other field sports. *Address:* Barrow House, Barrow, Bury St Edmunds, Suffolk. *Club:* Army and Navy.

GOODWIN, Dr Richard Murphey; Reader in Economics, University of Cambridge, since 1969; *b* 24 Feb. 1913; *s* of William Murphey Goodwin and Mary Florea Goodwin; *m* 1937, Jacqueline Wynmalen; no *c*. *Educ:* Harvard Univ. (AB, PhD); Oxford Univ. (BA, BLitt). Harvard Univ.: Instructor in Econs, 1939-42; Instructor in Physics, 1942-45; Asst Prof. of Econs, 1945-51; Lectr in Econs, Univ. of Cambridge, 1951-69. *Publications:* Elementary Economics from the Higher Standpoint; contrib. Econ. Jl, Econometrica, Review of Econs and Statistics. *Recreations:* painting, walking. *Address:* 1 Belvoir Terrace, Cambridge. *T:* Cambridge 52515; Peterhouse, Cambridge.

GOODWIN, Prof. Trevor Walworth, CBE 1975; FRS 1968; Johnston Professor of Biochemistry, University of Liverpool, since 1966; *b* 22 June 1916; British; *m* 1944, Kathleen Sarah Hill; three *d*. *Educ:* Birkenhead Inst.; Univ. of Liverpool. Lectr 1944, Sen. Lectr 1949, in Biochemistry, University of Liverpool; Prof. of Biochemistry and Agricultural Biochemistry, UCW, Aberystwyth, 1959. Member: Council, Royal Society, 1972, 1974; UGC, 1974-; SRC Science Bd, 1975-; Chm., Brit. Nat. Cttee for Biochem., 1976-. Member: Wirral Educn Cttee, 1974-; Lawes Agricl Trust Cttee, 1977-. Ciba Medallist, Biochemical Soc., 1970. *Publications:* Comparative Biochemistry of Carotenoids, 1952; Recent Advances in Biochemistry, 1960; Biosynthesis of Vitamins, 1964; (with E. I. Mercer) Introduction to Plant Biochemistry, 1972; (ed) Chemistry and Biochemistry of Plant Pigments, 2 vols, 1976; numerous articles in Biochem. Jl, Phytochemistry, etc. *Recreation:* gardening. *Address:* The Beeches, Storeton Road, Birkenhead, Merseyside. *T:* 051-608 2021.

GOODWIN HUDSON, Rt. Rev. Arthur William; *see* Hudson.

GOODY, Prof. John Rankine, FBA 1976; William Wyse Professor of Social Anthropology, University of Cambridge, since 1973; *b* 27 July 1919; *m* 1956, Esther Robinson Newcomb; one *s* four *d*. *Educ:* St Albans Sch.; St John's Coll., Cambridge; Balliol Coll., Oxford. BA 1946, Dip. Anthrop. 1947, PhD 1954, ScD 1969, Cantab; BLitt Oxon 1952. HM Forces, 1939-46. Educnl admin, 1947-49; Cambridge Univ.: Asst Lectr, 1954-59; Fellow, St John's Coll., 1960; Lectr, 1959-71; Dir, African Studies Centre, 1966-73; Smuts Reader in Commonwealth Studies, 1972. *Publications:* The Social Organisation of the LoWiili, 1956; (ed) The Developmental Cycle in Domestic Groups, 1958; Death, Property and the Ancestors, 1962; (ed) Succession to High Office, 1966; (with J. A. Braimah) Salaga: the struggle for power, 1967; (ed) Literacy in Traditional Societies, 1968; Comparative Studies in Kinship, 1969; Technology, Tradition and the State in Africa, 1971; The Myth of the Bagre, 1972; (with S. J. Tambiah) Bridewealth and Dowry, 1973; (ed) The Character of Kinship, 1973; (ed) Changing Social Structure in Ghana, 1975; Production and Reproduction, 1977; contrib. learned jls. *Address:* St John's College, Cambridge. *T:* Cambridge 61621.

GOODY, Most Rev. Launcelot John; *see* Perth (Aust.), Archbishop of, (RC).

GOODYEAR, Prof. Francis Richard David; Hildred Carlile Professor of Latin, University of London, since 1966; Professor and Head of Department, Bedford College, London, since 1966; *b* 2 Feb. 1936; *s* of Francis Goodyear and Gladys Ivy Goodman; *m* 1967, Cynthia Rosalie Attwood; one *s*. *Educ:* Luton Grammar Sch.; St John's Coll., Cambridge. MA, PhD (Cantab). Open schol., St John's Coll., Cambridge, 1953; Craven schol., Hallam Prize, 1956; Classical Tripos, Pts 1 and 2, cl. 1, 1956-57; Chancellor's Medal, H. A. Thomas Studentship, 1957. Research Fellow, St John's Coll., 1959-60; Official Fellow, Queens' Coll., 1960-66; Librarian, Queens' Coll., 1960-64. Dean of Faculty of Arts, Bedford Coll., London, 1971-73; Mem., Adv., Editorial Bd, Cambridge Classical Texts and Commentaries, 1974-; Chm., Bd of Studies in Classics, London Univ., 1977-. Mem., Virgilian Academy of Mantua, 1975. *Publications:* Incerti auctoris Aetna, 1965; Appendix Vergiliana (jt editor), 1966; Corippi Iohannidos libri viii (jt editor), 1970; Tacitus, a survey, 1970; The Annals of Tacitus, vol. i, 1972; papers and reviews in learned jls, contribs

to works of reference. *Recreations:* light reading, wine. *Address:* 56 The Avenue, Hatch End, Mddx HA5 4HA. *T:* 01-428 2644.

GOOLD, Sir George (Leonard), 7th Bt *cr* 1801; *b* 26 Aug. 1923; *s* of Sir George Ignatius Goold, 6th Bt, and Rhoda Goold; *S* father, 1967; *m* 1945, Joy Cecelia, *d* of William Cutler, Melbourne; one *s* four *d*. *Educ:* Port Pirie, S Australia. *Heir: s* George William Goold [*b* 25 March 1950; *m* 1973, Julie Ann, *d* of Leonard Crack]. *Address:* 5 Afford Road, Port Pirie South, SA 5540, Australia. *T:* Pirie 323617.

GOOLD-ADAMS, Richard John Moreton, CBE 1974; MA; Chairman, SS Great Britain Project, since 1968; *b* Brisbane, Australia, 24 Jan. 1916; *s* of Sir Hamilton Goold-Adams, Governor of Qld, and Elsie Riordon, Montreal; *m* 1939, Deenagh Blennerhassett. *Educ:* Winchester; New Coll., Oxford. Served 1939-46 in Army, Major, in Middle East and Italy. The Economist, latterly as an Asst Editor, 1947-55. Councillor: Internat. Inst. for Strategic Studies, 1958-76 (a Founder and Vice-Chm., 1958-62; Chm., 1963-73); National Inst. of Industrial Psychology, 1956-70; Royal Inst. of Internat. Affairs, 1957-; Soc. for Nautical Research, 1970-73, 1975-; Chm., British Atlantic Cttee, 1959-62, Vice-Pres., 1963-. Governor: Atlantic Inst. in Paris, 1962-71; Academic Council, Wilton Park, 1963-. Dep. Chm., Guthrie Estates Agency Ltd, 1962-63, resigned; re-elected to board, 1964; merged into The Guthrie Corp., 1965; Dir, 1965-69. Formerly broadcasting and television on current affairs, and lecturing. *Publications:* South Africa To-day and Tomorrow, 1936; Middle East Journey, 1947; The Time of Power: a reappraisal of John Foster Dulles, 1962; The Return of the Great Britain, 1976. *Recreations:* travelling, photography. *Address:* 11 Richmond Road, Bath, Avon. *Club:* Travellers'.

GOOLDEN, Barbara; novelist; *b* 5 June 1900; *d* of Charles and Isabel Goolden (*née* Armit); one adopted *s*. *Educ:* Community of the Holy Family; two private schools. Has appeared on TV and spoken on radio. *Publications:* The Knot of Reluctance, 1926; The Sleeping Sword, 1928; Children of Peace, 1928; The Conquering Star, 1929; The Waking Bird, 1929; The Ancient Wheel, 1930; Toils of Law, 1931; Thin Ice, 1931; Sugared Grief, 1932; Eros, 1933; Separate Paths, 1933; Slings and Arrows, 1934; Victory to the Vanquished, 1935; Wise Generations, 1936; The Primrose Path, 1936; Morning Tells the Day, 1937; The Wind My Posthorse, 1937; Within a Dream, 1938; Young Ambition, 1938; Call the Tune, 1939; The Asses Bridge, 1940; The Best Laid Schemes, 1941; Crown of Life, 1941; Men as Trees, 1942; Swings and Roundabouts, 1943; Community Singing, 1944; Ichabod, 1945; Daughters of Earth, 1947; Jig Saw, 1948; From the Sublime to the Ridiculous, 1949; Strange Strife, 1952; Venetia, 1952; The China Pig, 1953; Truth is Fallen in the Street, 1953; Return Journey, 1954; Who is my Neighbour?, 1954; Bread to the Wise, 1955; The World His Oyster, 1955; At the Foot of the Hills, 1956; To Have and to Hold, 1956; The Singing and the Gold, 1956; The Nettle and the Flower, 1957; Through the Sword Gates, 1957; The Linnet in the Cage, 1958; The Ships of Youth, 1958; Sweet Fields, 1958; A Pilgrim and his Pack, 1959; For Richer, For Poorer, 1959; Falling in Love, 1960; New Wine, 1960; Where Love is, 1960; To Love and to Cherish, 1961; One Autumn Face, 1961; Against the Grain, 1961; The Little City, 1962; The Pebble in the Pond, 1962; Marriages are Made in Heaven, 1963; Love-in-a-Mist, 1963; Battledore and Shuttlecock, 1963; Fools' Paradise, 1964; The Gentle Heart, 1964; The Gift, 1964; Blight on the Blossom, 1965; A Finger in the Pie, 1965; The Lesser Love, 1965; Anvil of Youth, 1966; Nobody's Business, 1966; A Time to Love, 1966; Second Fiddle, 1967; A Time to Build, 1967; All to Love, 1968; The Eleventh Hour, 1968; The Reluctant Wife, 1968; A Marriage of Convenience, 1969; Today Belongs to Us, 1969; The Snare, 1970; A Question of Conscience, 1970; Fortune's Favourite, 1971; No Meeting Place, 1971; Before the Flame is Lit, 1971; A Leap in the Dark, 1972; A Law for Lovers, 1973; Time to Turn Back, 1973; The Broken Arc, 1974; Mirage, 1974; The Crystal and the Dew, 1975; Goodbye to Yesterday, 1976; *for children:* Minty, 1959; Five Pairs of Hands, 1961; Minty and the Missing Picture, 1963; Minty and the Secret Room, 1964; Trouble for the Tabors, 1966; Top Secret, 1969. *Recreation:* reading. *Address:* Top End, Felcourt, East Grinstead, West Sussex.

GOOLDEN, Richard Percy Herbert; Actor and Broadcaster since 1923; *b* 23 Feb. 1895; *s* of Percy Pugh Goolden Goolden, MA, Barrister-at-Law, and Margarida da Costa Ricci. *Educ:* Charterhouse; New Coll., Oxford. BA 1923, Honour Sch. of Modern Languages (French). Secretary, 1923, OUDS with whom he visited Scandinavia in Loyalties and Mr Pim Passes By, also appeared as Dolon in Doctor Cyril Bailey's production (in Greek) of The Rhesus of Euripides. First professional appearance in 1923 with late J. B. Fagan's newly formed

Repertory Company at The (old) Oxford Playhouse, as Mazzini Dunn in Heartbreak House; Shakespearean Season at The (old) Memorial Theatre, Stratford-on-Avon, 1925; from 1926 worked for some time at The Lyric, Hammersmith, under late Sir Nigel Playfair. Varied career in London and Provinces (also Malta and Canada), in diversity of parts ranging from traditional classical repertoire to Farce, Opera Bouffe, Revue, Single Act Variety and Seaside Piers; among several hundred parts played Mole in Toad of Toad Hall (annually for five years 1930-34, Lyric, Savoy, and Royalty Theatres); Prince Paul in Offenbach's The Grand Duchess, Daly's, 1937; Lord Fancourt Babberley in Charley's Aunt, Haymarket, 1938; Professor Cunninghame in Grouse in June, Criterion, 1939; The Fool in King Lear (with Donald Wolfit), St James's, 1943; in Captain Carvallo, St James's, 1950; in Sir Laurence Olivier's Festival Productions of Caesar and Cleopatra, and Antony and Cleopatra, St James's, 1951; Lord Hector in Anouilh's Leocadia (Time Remembered), Lyric Hammersmith and New, 1954-55; Platina in Montherlant's Malatesta, Lyric, Hammersmith, 1957; Nagg in End Game, Royal Court, 1958; The Mayor in Look After Lulu, Royal Court and New, 1959; The White Rabbit in Alice in Wonderland, Winter Garden, 1959-60; Mr Jones in The Cupboard, Arts Theatre Club, 1961; Politic in Lock Up Your Daughters, Mermaid, 1962 and Her Majesty's, 1962-63; has played Mole in Toad of Toad Hall: Westminster, 1960-61; Saville, 1961-62; Comedy (also directed), 1963-64; Queen's, 1964-65; Comedy, 1965-66, 1966-67; Fortune, 1967-68; Duke of York's, 1968-69, 1970-71 and 1971-72; Strand, 1969-70; Jeanetta Cochrane, 1972-73, 1973-74; Haymarket, 1974-75; Duke of York's, 1975-76; Her Majesty's, 1976-77; in Regent's Park Open Air Theatre: Shallow in Merry Wives of Windsor, 1968; Old Gobbo in Merchant of Venice, 1969; Verges in Much Ado About Nothing, 1970; The Pedant in Taming of the Shrew, 1975; Sir Nathaniel in Love's Labour's Lost, 1976; King of France in Henry V, 1977; Oxford Playhouse: Old Gobbo in Merchant of Venice, Lob in Dear Brutus, 1973; Bernard in Dirty Linen, Arts Theatre Club, 1976. Created popular Radio Characters, Mr Chips (the first presentation of this famous character in any medium), Mr Pim, Mr Penny, Old Ebenezer, and The Little Man in Dr L. du Garde Peach's Children's Hour Historical Playlets; has also appeared in films and television plays. Served European War, 1914-18, in France as a private in RAMC; performed continuously throughout War of 1939-45 at Troop Concerts and in shelters and refugee centres (in French), etc. Favourite parts: Mr Pim, Mole, and The Fool in King Lear. Variety Club Award, 1977. *Recreations:* household repairs and decoration; arguing; and singing Edwardian music-hall songs. *Address:* 15 Oakley Street, SW3 5NT. *T:* 01-352 7123. *Club:* United Oxford & Cambridge University.

GOONERATNE, Tilak Eranga; Ambassador of Sri Lanka to the Commission of the European Communities, and concurrently to Belgium, since 1975; *b* 27 March 1919; *m* 1948, Pamela J. Rodrigo; two *d. Educ:* BA (London Univ.); Ceylon Law Coll. Advocate, Supreme Ct of Ceylon. Joined Ceylon Civil Service, 1943; Asst Sec., Min. of External Affairs, 1947-51; Govt Agent: Trincomalee, 1951-54; Matra, 1954-56; Registrar Gen., Marriages, Births and Deaths, 1956-58; Dir-Gen. of Broadcasting and Dir of Information, Ceylon, 1958-60; Comr Co-operative Develt, 1960-63; Acting Permanent Sec., Min. of Commerce and Trade, 1963; Dir of Economic Affairs, 1963; Dep. Sec. to Treasury, 1963-65; Pres., Colombo Plan Council for Technical Co-operation in S and SE Asia, 1964-65; Ceylon deleg. to UN Gen. Assembly, 1964-65; Dep. Sec.-Gen., Commonwealth Secretariat, London, 1965-70; High Comr in UK, 1970-75. Commonwealth Fund for Technical Co-operation: Chm., Bd of Representatives, 1975-76; Chm., Review Gp of Experts. *Publications:* An Historical Outline of the Development of the Marriage and Divorce Laws of Ceylon; An Historical Outline of the Development of the Marriage and Divorce Laws Applicable to Muslims in Ceylon; Fifty Years of Co-operative Development in Ceylon. *Address:* Embassy of Sri Lanka, 21-22 Avenue des Arts, 1040 Brussels, Belgium.

GOONETILLEKE, Sir Oliver Ernest, GCMG 1954 (KCMG 1948; CMG 1941); KCVO 1954; KBE 1944; BA London; LLD Ceylon; FRSA; FRES; Underwriting Member of Lloyd's, London, since 1964; *b* 1892; *s* of A. E. Goonetilleke; *m* 1920, Esther Jayawardena (*d* 1931); one *s* two *d* ; *m* 1968, Phyllis Millar. Asst Auditor for Railways, Ceylon, 1921; Asst Colonial Auditor, 1924; Colonial Auditor June 1931; Auditor-Gen., July 1931; Civil Defence and Food Commissioner, Ceylon, 1942; Mem., Ceylon War Council, 1942; Financial Sec., 1945-47; Min. of Home Affairs and Rural Development, Ceylon, 1947-48; Ceylon High Comr in London, 1948-51; Min. of Home Affairs and Rural Development, Ceylon, 1951-52; of Agriculture and Food, 1952-53, also Leader of the Senate; Min. of Finance, Ceylon, Oct. 1953-54; Governor-Gen. of Ceylon, 1954-62.

Ceylon Government Deleg. to Internat. Railway Congress, Cairo, 1933; Chm. Retrenchment Commn, 1945. Chairman: Namuwakula Tea Estate Co. Ltd; Rangalla Consolidated Ltd; Kepitigalla Rubber Estates Ltd; Bentota Holdings Ltd; The Rubber Estates of Bentota Ltd; Panagula Rubber Co. Ltd; Elpitiya Rubber Estates Ltd; Colombo Gas Co. Ltd; Director: Plantation & Mining Agencies Ltd; Veeraswamy's Restaurant. *Address:* 14 Albion Gate, Hyde Park Place, W2. *T:* 01-723 5814. *Club:* National Liberal.

GOOSSENS, Leon Jean, CBE 1950; FRCM; Hon. RAM; Solo Oboist; *b* Liverpool, 12 June 1897; *s* of late Eugène Goossens, musician and conductor; *m* 1st, 1926, one *d* ; 2nd, 1933, Leslie, *d* of Brig. A. Burrowes; two *d. Educ:* Christian Brothers Catholic Institute, Liverpool; Liverpool Coll. of Music. Started oboe studies at 10yrs of age with Charles Reynolds; at 14 studied at RCM, London, and at 16 joined (temp.) London Symphony Orchestra on tour with Nikisch; same year toured Wales with Sir Henry Wood and Queen's Hall Orchestra as temp. principal oboist, the following year accepting post as permanency. Served in European War, 1915-18 (wounded). Principal oboe, Royal Philharmonic Orchestra, also at Covent Garden Opera House, Prof. at RCM and RAM. First Recital tour in USA, 1927. Rep. British Music in most European capitals, also at NY World Fair, with Sir Adrian Boult; and Washington with Dr Clarence Raybould; also lecture recitals for BBC, TV, schools, colleges, music clubs. Has produced in England a new school of oboe-playing and has promoted the oboe to the ranks of solo instruments for which leading composers of the day have written and dedicated music, such as concertos, sonatas and chamber works. Cobbett Medal for services to Chamber Music, 1954. Toured Australia and New Zealand, also played in Singapore, 1954. Visited Persia and Turkey, also Austria, 1955. Toured Jugoslavia, 1954. Toured USSR with Music Delegation headed by Master of The Queen's Musick, 1956; Coast to Coast Tour Canada, 1957; toured Scandinavia and Portugal, 1959, USA 1965, Munich 1972, St Moritz and Aberdeen (with Internat. Youth Orch.), 1971-73. Prom. concert, 1972. Recitals in Malta, 1969, 1973. *Relevant publication:* Music in the Wind, by Barry Wynne, 1967. *Recreations:* agriculture and sailing. *Address:* Park Cottage, 7a Ravenscourt Square, W6. *Clubs:* Chelsea Arts, London Corinthian Sailing; Royal Malta Yacht, Malta Union.

GOPAL, Dr Sarvepalli; Professor of Contemporary History, Jawaharlal Nehru University, New Delhi, since 1972; Fellow of St Antony's College, Oxford, since 1966; *b* 23 April 1923; *y c* and *o s* of Sir Sarvepalli Radhakrishnan, Hon. OM, Hon. FBA. *Educ:* Mill Hill School; Madras Univ.; Oxford Univ. MA (Madras and Oxon), BL (Madras), DPhil (Oxon), DLitt (Oxon). Lecturer and Reader in History, Andhra Univ., Waltair, 1948-52; Asst Dir, Nat. Archives of India, 1952-54; Dir, Historical Div., Min. of Extl Affairs, New Delhi, 1954-66 (now Hon. Historical Adviser); Commonwealth Fellow, Trin. Coll., Cambridge, 1963-64; Reader in S Asian History, Oxford Univ., 1966-71. Chm. Nat. Book Trust, India, 1973-76; Member: Indian UGC; UNESCO Exec. Bd, 1976; Vis. Prof., Leeds, 1977. FRHistS. Hon. Prof., Tirupati; Hon. DLitt Andhra Univ. Sahitye Akademi award 1976. *Publications:* The Permanent Settlement in Bengal, 1949; The Viceroyalty of Lord Ripon, 1953; The Viceroyalty of Lord Irwin, 1957; British Policy in India, 1965; Modern India, 1967; Jawaharlal Nehru, vol 1, 1975; general editor, Selected Works of Jawaharlal Nehru; contribs articles to historical jls. *Recreations:* good food and travel. *Address:* St Antony's College, Oxford; 30 Edward Elliot Road, Mylapore, Madras 4, India. *Club:* United Oxford & Cambridge University.

GOPALLAWA, William; President of Sri Lanka, since 1972; Chancellor: University of Sri Lanka, Peradeniya; Vidyodaya University of Sri Lanka, Nugegoda; Vidyalankara University of Sri Lanka, Kelaniya; *b* Dullewe, Matale, 17 Sept. 1897; *s* of Tikiri Banda Gopallawa, and Dullewa Gopallawa Tikiri Kumarihamy; *m* 1928, Seila Rambukwella (*d* 1977); two *s* two *d. Educ:* Dharmaraja Coll. and St Anthony's Coll., Kandy, Ceylon; Law Coll., Colombo. Teacher, 1918-20; enrolled as Proctor of Supreme Court of Ceylon, 1924; practised in Matale, 1924-39; Mem., Urban Council, Matale, 1927-39 (Chm., 1928-34); Municipal Comr, Kandy, 1939; Municipal Comr, Colombo, 1952; retired, 1957. Ambassador for Ceylon: in China, 1958; in USA, 1961 (concurrently Ambassador to Cuba and Mexico with residence in Washington); Governor-General of Ceylon, 1962-72. Chm., Arts Council's Panel for folk-songs and folk-dancing, 1954-56; A Founder, Dodandeniya Buddhist Schs, Matale; Founder Member: Vidyartha Coll., Kandy; Social Service League, Matale; Chief Scout for Sri Lanka. Past Pres., Kandy Rotary Club; Hon. Mem., Rotary Club of Colombo. Hon. LLD: University of Ceylon (Peradeniya), 1962; Vidyalankara University, 1962; Hon. DLitt, Vidyodaya Univ., 1962. Religion:

Buddhist. *Recreations:* cricket, tennis, golf. *Address:* President's House, Colombo, Sri Lanka. *T:* 27821.

GORARD, Anthony John; Managing Director, HTV Ltd, since 1967; Chief Executive, HTV Group, since 1976; *b* 15 July 1927; *s* of William James and Rose Mary Gorard; *m* 1954, Barbara Kathleen Hampton; one *s* three *d. Educ:* Ealing Grammar School. Chartered Accountant, 1951; Manufacturing Industry, 1952-58; Anglia Television Ltd, 1959-67, Executive Director and Member of Management Cttee; Director: Independent Television Publications Ltd, 1968-; Independent Television News Ltd, 1973-; Chairman, British Regional Television Association, 1970-71. *Recreations:* tennis, rambling. *Address:* The Beeches, Chew Magna, Somerset. *T:* Chew Magna 2593.

GORAY, Narayan Ganesh; High Commissioner for India in London, since 1977; *b* 15 June 1907; *s* of Ganesh Govind Gore and Saraswati; *m* 1935, Sumati Kirtani (decd); one *d. Educ:* Fergusson Coll., Poona. BA, LLB. Mem. Congress, Socialist Party, 1934 (Mem. Nat. Exec., 1934); Jt Sec., Socialist Party, 1948; Gen. Sec., Praja Socialist Party, 1953-65, Chm., 1965-69; Member: Lok Sabha, 1957-62; Rajya Sabha, 1970-76. Mayor of Poona, 1968. Editor, Janata Weekly, 1971. *Publications include:* History of the United States of America. *Recreations:* music, painting, writing. *Address:* India House, Aldwych, WC2.

GORDIMER, Nadine; Author; *b* 20 Nov. 1923; *d* of Isidore Gordimer; *m* Reinhold Cassirer; one *s* one *d. Educ:* Convent Sch.; Witwatersrand Univ. *Publications:* The Soft Voice of the Serpent (stories), 1953; The Lying Days (novel), 1953; Six Feet of the Country (stories), 1956; A World of Strangers (novel), 1958; Friday's Footprint (stories), 1960 (W. H. Smith Lit. Award, 1961); Occasion for Loving (novel), 1963; Not for Publication (stories), 1965; The Late Bourgeois World (novel), 1966; South African Writing Today (jt editor), 1967; A Guest of Honour (novel), 1971 (James Tait Black Meml Prize, 1971); Livingstone's Companions (stories), 1972; The Conservationist (novel), 1974 (jtly, Booker Prize 1974; Grand Aigle d'Or, France, 1975); Selected Stories, 1975; Some Monday for Sure (stories), 1976. *Address:* 7 Frere Road, Parktown West, Johannesburg, South Africa.

GORDINE, Dora, (Hon. Mrs Richard Hare); FRBS; FRSA; sculptor and painter; *b* 1906; *d* of late Mark Gordin, St Petersburg, Russia; *m* 1936, Hon. Richard Hare (*d* 1966). Studied sculpture, Paris. First exhibited in the Salon des Tuileries, Paris, 1932. One-man exhibitions: Leicester Galleries, London, 1928, 1933, 1938, 1945, 1949; Flechtheim Gallery, Berlin, 1929. Commissioned to decorate with bronzes new Town Hall in Singapore, 1930-35; built studio and sculpture gallery in London according to her own designs (1936). Spent a year in America, executing commissions in Hollywood and delivering lectures on art (1947). Also represented by Sculpture in American, Asiatic, African and Australian collections. In England 3 works are in Tate Gallery; other bronzes in: Senate House, London Univ.; RIBA; Westminster Infant Welfare Centre; Maternity Ward in Holloway Prison; Esso Petroleum Refinery, Milford Haven; Royal Marsden Hospital, Surrey; Herron Museum of Art, Indianapolis; schs, institutions and many private collections. *Publications:* articles in Journal of Royal Asiatic Society. *Address:* Dorich House, Kingston Vale, SW15.

GORDON, family name of **Marquess of Aberdeen and Temair** and **Marquess of Huntly.**

GORDON, Lord Adam (Granville), KCVO 1970 (CVO 1961); MBE 1945; Comptroller to Queen Elizabeth the Queen Mother, 1953-73; Extra Equerry to Queen Elizabeth the Queen Mother, since 1974; *b* 1 March 1909; *s* of late Lt-Col Douglas Gordon, CVO, DSO, and *brother of* 12th Marquess of Huntly, *qv*; *m* 1947, Pamela, *d* of Col A. H. Bowhill, CBE, Inchmarlo, Banchory, Kincardineshire; two *s. Educ:* Eton. Asst Sec., Hurlingham Club, 1936-39. Served War of 1939-45 (despatches, MBE); Hants Yeomanry in GB, N Africa and Italy; retired 1945, with rank of Major. Sec., Brooks's Club, 1946-53. Mem. Queen's Body Guard for Scotland (Royal Co. of Archers). *Address:* Hethersett, Littleworth Cross, Seale, Surrey. *Clubs:* Brooks's, Pratt's, MCC.

GORDON, (Alexander) Esmé, RSA, FRIBA, FRIAS; *b* 12 Sept. 1910; *s* of Alexander Shand Gordon, WS and Elizabeth Catherine (*née* Logan); *m* 1937, Betsy, *d* of James and Bessie McCurry, Belfast; two *s* one *d. Educ:* Edinburgh Acad.; School of Arch., Edinburgh Coll. of Art. RIBA. Owen Jones Schol., 1934. War Service with RE in Europe. RSA 1967 (ARSA 1956); Sec., RSA, 1973-; Pres., Edinburgh AA, 1955-57; Mem. Scottish

Cttee, Arts Council of Gt Brit., 1959-65. *Work includes:* Third Extension and other work for Heriot-Watt Coll.; Head Office for Scottish Life Assce Co. Ltd; Head Office and Showroom for S of Scotland Elec. Bd; for the High Kirk of St Giles: East End treatment for National Service in Coronation year, War Memorial Chapel, and (in Chapel of Order of Thistle) Memorial to HM King George VI, and other work. *Publications:* A Short History of St Giles Cathedral, 1954; The Principles of Church Building, Furnishing, Equipment and Decoration, 1963; The Royal Scottish Academy 1826-1976, 1976. *Address:* 10a Greenhill Park, Edinburgh EH10 4DW. *T:* 031-447 7530.

GORDON, Alexander John, CBE 1974 (OBE 1967); RIBA; architect; Senior Partner, Alex Gordon and Partners, since 1960; *b* 25 Feb. 1917; *s* of John Tullis Gordon and Euphemia Baxter Simpson Gordon. *Educ:* Swansea Grammar Sch.; Welsh Sch. of Architecture (Diploma with Special Distinction). ARIBA 1949; FRIBA 1962; FSIAD 1975. Served RE, 1940-46. Partnership with T. Alwyn Lloyd, 1948-60. Member: Welsh Arts Council, 1959-73 (Vice-Chm. 1969-73); Central Housing Adv. Cttee, 1959-71; MPBW (now DoE) Cttee for Computer Applications in Construction Industry, 1966-71; Exec. Bd, BSI, 1971-74 (Chm., Codes of Practice Cttee for Building, 1965-77); UGC Planning, Architecture and Building Studies Sub-Cttee, 1971-74; UGC Technology Sub-Cttee, 1974-; Construction and Housing Res. Adv. Council, 1971-; ARCUK, 1968-71; Design Council, 1973-; Council, Architectural Heritage Year (and Welsh Cttee), 1973-76; Royal Fine Art Commn, 1973-; RCA Visiting Cttee, 1973-; Council for Sci. and Soc., 1973-; Bldg Res. Estab. Adv. Council (Chm., 1975-); Adv. Cttee, York Centre for Continuing Educn, 1975; Standing Cttee on Structural Safety, 1976; British Council, Wales Cttee, 1976-; Pres., Comité de Liaison des Architectes du Marché Commun, 1974-75. Trustee, Civic Trust Board for Wales, 1965-. Pres., Building Centre Trust, 1976. Life Mem., Court, UWIST; Vis. Prof., Sch. of Environmental Studies, UCL, 1969, Mem. Bd of Studies, 1970-, Governor, Centre for Environmental Studies, 1974-77. RIBA: Chm., Bd of Educn, 1968-70; Pres., 1971-73; Chm., European Affairs Bd, 1973-. Reg. Dir, Nationwide Bldg Soc., 1972-; Dir, ABS Insurance Agency Ltd, 1975. Hon. Mem., Soc. Mexican Architects; Hon. Corresp. Mem., Fedn of Danish Architects, 1976; Hon. FRAIC; Hon. FAIA, 1974; Hon. FCIBS 1975. Hon. LLD Univ. of Wales, 1972. *Publications:* periodic contribs to professional jls. *Recreations:* skiing, the visual arts. *Address:* 6 Cathedral Road, Cardiff CF1 9XW. *T:* Cardiff 372121; 32 Grosvenor Street, W1. *T:* 01-629 7910.

GORDON, Sir Andrew C. L. D.; *see* Duff Gordon.

GORDON, Rt. Rev. Archibald Ronald McDonald; *see* Portsmouth, Bishop of.

GORDON, Brig. Barbara (Masson), CB 1971; RRC 1964; Matron-in-Chief and Director Army Nursing Service, 1968-73; *b* 28 Jan. 1913 (Scottish); *d* of Major R. G. Gordon, DSO, MC, MB, ChB, RGA (killed on active service, 1918) and late Mrs B. M. Gordon. *Educ:* St Leonards Sch., St Andrews, Scotland. Trained Edinburgh Royal Infirmary, 1933-37, Oxford Radcliffe Infirmary, 1937. Joined QAIMNS, 1939. Served BEF, MELF and in Germany, 1939-45; in UK, Malta, Egypt and Far East, 1945-68. QHNS 1968-73. CStJ 1971. *Recreations:* golf, walking. *Address:* Lettoch, St Andrews, Fife. *T:* St Andrews 3214. *Club:* St Rule (St Andrews).

GORDON, Brian William, OBE 1974; HM Diplomatic Service; Deputy Consul-General, Los Angeles, since 1977; *b* 24 Oct. 1926; *s* of William and Doris Margaret Gordon; *m* 1951, Sheila Graham Young; two *s* one *d. Educ:* Tynemouth Grammar School. HM Forces (Lieut in IA), 1944-47; HM Foreign Service (now Diplomatic Service), 1949-. Served in: Saigon; Libya; Second Sec. in Ethiopia, 1954-58 and in Peru, 1959-61; HM Consul: Leopoldville, Congo, 1962-64; New York, 1965-67; Puerto Rico, 1967-69; Consul-General, Bilbao, 1969-73; Asst Head, Trade Relations and Export Dept, FCO, 1974-77. *Recreations:* golf, walking. *Address:* c/o Foreign and Commonwealth Office, SW1.

GORDON, Mrs Charles; *see* Nerina, Nadia.

GORDON, Charles Addison Somerville Snowden, CB 1970; Clerk Assistant, House of Commons, since 1976; *b* 25 July 1918; *s* of late C. G. S. Gordon, TD, Liverpool, and of Mrs E. A. Gordon, Emberton, Bucks; *m* 1943, Janet Margaret Beattie; one *s* one *d. Educ:* Winchester; Balliol Coll., Oxford. Served in Fleet Air Arm throughout War of 1939-45. Apptd Asst Clerk in House of Commons, 1946; Senior Clerk, 1947; Fourth Clerk at the Table, 1962; Principal Clerk of the Table Office, 1967; Second Clerk Assistant, 1974. Sec., Soc. of Clerks-at-the-Table in Commonwealth Parliaments, and co-Editor of its journal, The Table, 1952-62. *Publications:* Parliament as an Export (jointly), 1966; contribs to: The Table; The Parliamentarian. *Address:* 279 Lonsdale Road, Barnes, SW13 9QB. *T:* 01-748 6735.

GORDON, Dr Christie Wilson, TD 1952; Regional Medical Officer, West Midlands Regional Health Authority, 1973-76; *b* 13 Dec. 1911; *s* of John Wilson Gordon and Mary Gordon; *m* 1942, Robina Alice Munro; one *s*. *Educ:* Academy, Buckie; Univs of Aberdeen, London and Johns Hopkins. MB, ChB 1938; DPH 1946; DrPH Johns Hopkins 1947. FRCP 1971; FFCM 1972; MIBS 1932. House Phys. and House Surg., Aberdeen Royal Infirmary, 1938-39; served War of 1939-45, RAMC; Hon. Lt-Col RAMC (TARO) (Hon. Mem. RAMC Mess 1961); Rockefeller Scholar, 1946-48; part-time Lectr, Hosp. Admin, London Sch. of Hygiene and Trop. Med., 1949-52; part-time Sen. Clinical Lectr, Dept of Social Medicine, Univ. of Birmingham, 1952-. Birmingham Regional Hosp. Board: Admin. MO, Asst, subseq. Dep. Admin. MO, 1948-57; Sen. Admin. MO, 1957-73. QHP, 1974-77. Member: Central Midwives Bd, 1967-73; DHSS Management Study Steering Cttee on Management arrangements for the reorganised NHS, 1971-72; Council, Univ. of Birmingham, 1976-. Sec., Midland Medical Benevolent Soc., 1976-. Fellow, WHO, 1965. Hon LLD Birmingham, 1975. *Publications:* papers on public health and hospital services in Lancet, BMJ, etc. *Recreation:* golf. *Address:* 9 Fountain Road, Edgbaston, Birmingham B17 8NJ. *T:* 021-429 2710. *Clubs:* (Chm.) Aberdeen University (Midlands); Edgbaston Golf.

GORDON, Christopher Martin P.; *see* Pirie-Gordon.

GORDON, Prof. Cyrus H.; Gottesman Professor of Hebrew, New York University, since 1973; *b* 29 June 1908; *s* of Dr Benj. L. and Dorothy Cohen Gordon; *m* 1946, Joan Elizabeth Kendall; two *s* three *d*. *Educ:* University of Pa (AB, MA, PhD). Harrison Schol., University of Pa, 1928-29, and Harrison Fellow, 1929-30; US Army Officer on active duty, 1942-46 (Col, US Air Force Reserve, retired). Instructor of Hebrew and Assyrian, University of Penn., 1930-31; Fellow and Epigrapher, American Schs of Oriental Research in Jerusalem and Baghdad, 1931-35; Fellow, Amer. Coun. of Learned Socs, 1932-33; Teaching Fellow, Oriental Seminary, Johns Hopkins Univ., 1935-38; Lecturer in Hebrew and Ancient History, Smith Coll., 1938-39 and 1940-41; Fellow, Amer.-Scandinavian Foundn, 1939; Mem., Institute for Advanced Study, Princeton, NJ, 1939-40 and 1941-42; Professor of Assyriology and Egyptology, Dropsie Coll., 1946-56; Joseph Foster Prof. of Near Eastern Studies, and Chm., Dept of Mediterranean Studies, Brandeis Univ., 1956-73 (Dean of Graduate Sch. and Associate Dean of Faculty, 1957-58). Mem. Managing Cttee, Amer. Sch. of Classical Studies, Athens, 1958-; Vis. Fellow in Humanities, Univ. of Colorado, March 1967; Vis. Prof., New York Univ., 1970-73; Vis. Prof. in History and Archaeology, Univ. of New Mexico, 1976; Distinguished Vis. Prof. in Humanities, SW Missouri State Univ., 1977; Gay Lectr, Simmons Coll., 1970; Visitor's Fellowship, Japan Foundn, 1974. Fellow: Amer. Acad. of Arts and Sciences, 1968-; Explorers Club, 1968-; Hon. Fellow, Royal Asiatic Soc., 1975. Member: Amer. Oriental Soc.; Soc. of Biblical Literature; Archæological Inst. of America; Amer. Historical Assoc.; Amer. Philological Assoc.; Amer. Assoc. of Univ. Professors. Corresp. Mem., Inst. for Antiquity and Christianity, Claremont Graduate Sch. and University Center, 1967-. Trustee: Boston Hebrew Coll., 1965-; Internat. Council for Etruscan Studies, Jerusalem, 1970-; Fenster Gallery of Jewish Art, Tulsa, Oklahoma, 1977-. Directory of Educational Specialists Award, 1970. *Publications:* Nouns in the Nuzi Tablets, 1936; Lands of the Cross and Crescent, 1948; Ugaritic Literature, 1949; Smith College Tablets, 1952; Ugaritic Manual, 1955; Adventures in the Nearest East, 1957; Hammurapi's Code, 1957; World of the Old Testament, 1958 (rev. edn: The Ancient Near East, 1965); Before the Bible, 1962 (rev. edn: The Common Background of Greek and Hebrew Civilizations, 1965); Ugaritic Textbook, 1965, rev. edn 1967; Ugarit and Minoan Crete, 1966; Evidence for the Minoan Language, 1966; Forgotten Scripts: How they were deciphered and their Impact on Contemporary Culture, 1968, rev. edn 1971; Before Columbus: Links Between the Old World and Ancient America, 1971; Riddles in History, 1974; some works translated other languages; numerous articles in learned jls dealing with Near East, Mediterranean, and pre-Columbian contacts between the Old and New Worlds. *Address:* (home) 130 Dean Road, Brookline, Mass 02146, USA. *T:* 617-734-3046.

GORDON, Maj.-Gen. Desmond Spencer, CB 1961; CBE 1952; DSO 1943; JP; Commissioner-in-Chief, St John Ambulance Brigade, since 1973; *b* 25 Dec. 1911; *s* of late Harold Eastly Gordon and Gwendoline (*née* Blackett); *m* 1940, Sybil Mary Thompson; one *s* one *d*. *Educ:* Haileybury Coll.; RMC Sandhurst. Commissioned into Green Howards, 1932; India, 1933-38: Adjutant, Regimental Depot, 1938-40; War of 1939-45 (despatches 1944): Norway with Green Howards, 1940; Bde Major, 69 Inf. Bde, 1941-42; Student Staff Coll., Quetta, 1942; Comd 1/7 Queens, 1943; Comd 151 (Durham) Inf. Bde, 146 Inf. Bde, 131 Lorried Inf Bde, 1944-46; Col. GSHQ BAOR, 1946-49; Student Joint Service Staff Coll., 1949; GSO1 Inf. Directorate, War Office, 1950; Dep. Dir Inf., War Office, 1951-52; Comd 16 Indep. Para. Bde Gp, 1952-55; Asst Comd RMA Sandhurst, 1956-57; Student, Imperial Defence Coll., 1958; DA & QMG HQ I (BR) Corps, 1959; GOC 4th Division, 1959-61; Chief Army Instructor, Imperial Defence Coll., 1962-64; Asst Chief of Defence Staff (G), 1964-66: Col The Green Howards, 1965-74. JP Hants, 1966. KStJ 1973 (CStJ 1972). Knight Commander, Order of Orange Nassau with swords (Holland), 1947. *Recreations:* fishing, gardening. *Address:* Southfield, Greywell, Basingstoke, Hants. *Club:* Army and Navy.

GORDON, Prof. Donald James, MA Edinburgh, PhD Cantab; FRHistSoc; Professor of English in the University of Reading, 1949-76, now Emeritus; *b* 19 July 1915; *s* of Thomas and Sarah Gordon. *Educ:* Dumfries Academy; University of Edinburgh; Trinity Coll., Cambridge. Lecturer in English: Univ. of Liverpool, 1942-46; Univ. of Reading, 1946-49. Corresp. Mem., Accademia Olimpico of Vicenza, Italy. *Publications:* (with Jean Robertson) A Calendar of Dramatic Records in the Books of the Livery Companies of London, 1485-1640, 1955; (ed) Fritz Saxl: Memorial Essays, 1957; Images of a Poet: W. B. Yeats, 1961; Renaissance Imagination, 1975; papers on problems connected with Renaissance Imagery, and on connexions between literature and visual arts in late nineteenth century. *Address:* 8 Alexandra Road, Reading.

GORDON, Donald McDonald, CMG 1970; HM Diplomatic Service; British High Commissioner, Nicosia, since 1975; *b* 14 Aug. 1921; *s* of late Donald McDonald Gordon and late Anabella Gordon (*née* Wesley); *m* 1948, Molly Denise, *o d* of Maurice Norman, Paris; three *s*. *Educ:* Robert Gordon's Coll., Aberdeen; Aberdeen Univ. Served in RA, 1941-47 (despatches). Entered Foreign (later Diplomatic) Service, 1947; FO, 1947; 2nd Sec. (Commercial), Lima, 1950; 2nd, later 1st Sec. (Commercial), Vienna, 1952; FO, 1956; 1st Sec. and Head of Chancery, Rangoon, 1960; 1st Sec., later Counsellor and Head of Chancery, Pretoria/Cape Town, 1962; Imp. Def. Coll., 1966; Counsellor and Consul-Gen., Saigon, 1967-69; Head of SE Asia Dept, FCO, 1969-72; Dep. High Comr, Kuala Lumpur, 1972-75. *Address:* c/o Foreign and Commonwealth Office, SW1.

GORDON, Rt. Rev. Eric; *see* Gordon, Rt Rev. G. E.

GORDON, Esmé; *see* Gordon, A. E.

GORDON, Rt. Rev. (George) Eric; *b* 29 July 1905; *s* of George Gordon, Dulwich; *m* 1938, Elizabeth St Charaine (*d* 1970), *d* of Lt-Comdr A. J. Parkes, OBE, RN, Squeen, Ballaugh, Isle of Man; one *d*; *m* 1971, Rose Gwynneth Huxley-Jones, FRBS, *d* of Benjamin Holt, Wednesbury, and widow of Thomas Bayliss Huxley-Jones, FRBS, Broomfield, Essex. *Educ:* St Olave's Sch., London; St Catharine's Coll., Cambridge (MA); Wycliffe Hall, Oxford. Deacon, Leicester, 1929; Priest, Peterborough for Leicester, 1930; Vice-Principal, Bishop Wilson Coll., Isle of Man, 1931, Principal, and Domestic Chaplain to Bishop of Sodor and Man, 1935; Rector of Kersal, and Examining Chaplain to Bishop of Manchester, 1942; Rector and Rural Dean of Middleton, Manchester, 1945; Proctor in Convocation, 1948; Provost of Chelmsford Cathedral and Rector of Chelmsford, 1951-66; Bishop of Sodor and Man, 1966-74. *Recreation:* local history. *Address:* Cobden, Queen Street, Eynsham, Oxon. *T:* Oxford 881378.

GORDON, Gerald Henry, QC (Scot.) 1972; LLD; Sheriff of South Strathclyde, Dumfries and Galloway at Hamilton, since 1976; *b* 17 June 1929; *er s* of Simon Gordon and Rebecca Gordon (*née* Bulbin), Glasgow; *m* 1957, Marjorie Joseph, *yr d* of Isaac and Aimée Joseph (*née* Strump), Glasgow; one *s* two *d*. *Educ:* Queen's Park Senior Secondary Sch., Glasgow; Univ. of Glasgow (MA (1st cl. Hons Philosophy with English Literature) 1950; LLB (Distinction) 1953; PhD 1960); LLD Edinburgh 1968. National Service, RASC, 1953-55 (Staff-Sgt, Army Legal Aid, BAOR, 1955). Admitted Scots Bar 1953; practice at Scottish Bar, 1953, 1956-59; Faulds Fellow, Univ. of Glasgow, 1956-59. Procurator Fiscal Depute, Edinburgh, 1960-65. University of Edinburgh: Sen. Lectr, 1965; Personal Prof. of Criminal Law, 1969-72; Head of Dept of Criminal Law and Criminology, 1965-72; Prof. of Scots Law, 1972-76; Dean of Faculty of Law, 1970-73. Commonwealth Vis. Fellow and Vis. Res. Fellow, Centre of Criminology, Univ. of Toronto, 1974-75.

Temporary Sheriff, 1973-76. Mem., Interdepartmental Cttee on Scottish Criminal Procedure, 1970-. *Publications:* The Criminal Law of Scotland, 1967; ed, Renton and Brown's Criminal Procedure (4th edn), 1972; various articles. *Recreations:* Jewish studies, coffee conversation, swimming. *Address:* 52 Eastwoodmains Road, Giffnock, Glasgow G46 6QD. *T:* 041-638 8614.

GORDON, Dr Hugh Walker, MC 1917; MA; MB; FRCP; Consulting Physician to Department of Skin Diseases, St George's Hospital; Consulting Dermatologist to Royal Marsden Hospital and West London Hospital; Fellow Royal Society Medicine (Past President of Section of Dermatology); Member (Past President) British Association of Dermatology; Member of St John's Dermatological Society; *b* Maxwellton, Kirkcudbright, 5 Aug. 1897; *er s* of late H. Sharpe Gordon, OBE, JP, Dumfries, Scotland and of late John Ann, *d* of Hugh Gilmour, London; *m* 1929, Jean Helen, *d* of late H. W. Robertson, Butterfield and Swire, London; one *s* one *d*. *Educ:* Marlborough Coll.; Pembroke Coll., Cambridge (History Exhibitioner); St George's Hospital (entrance scholar); Paris; Vienna, MB, BCh Cambridge, 1926; MRCS 1925; FRCP 1940. Late Vice-Dean, St George's Hosp. Med. Sch., 1946-51, Actg Dean, 1944-46; Dermatologist EMS Sector VII, 1939-46; Med. Officer i/c St George's Hosp., EMS, 1939-45; late Dermatologist to St John's Hosp., Lewisham, Shadwell Children's Hosp. and East Ham Memorial Hosp. Late Resident Med. Officer, St George's Hosp., and House Surg. and House Physician. Served European War, 1914-18, RFA, 1916-18, invalided out of Army. *Publications:* chapters in Modern Practice of Dermatology, 1950; articles on dermatology in med. journals. *Recreations:* country pursuits. *Address:* 3 High Street, Kirkcudbright, SW Scotland. *T:* Kirkcudbright 30740. *Club:* Oriental.

GORDON, Prof. Ian Alistair, CBE 1971; MA; PhD; Professor of English Language and Literature, University of Wellington, NZ, 1936-74, now Emeritus; *b* Edinburgh, 1908; *e s* of Alexander and Ann Gordon; *m* 1936, Mary Ann McLean Fullarton, Ayr; one *s* three *d*. *Educ:* Royal High Sch., Edinburgh; University of Edinburgh. Bruce of Grangehill Bursar, Sloan Prizeman, Gray Prizeman, Scott Travelling Scholar (Italy), Dickson Travelling Scholar (Germany), Elliot Prizeman in English Literature, Pitt Scholar in Classical and English Literature; MA (Hons Classics) 1930, (Hons English) 1932; PhD 1936. Asst Lecturer in English language and lit., University of Edinburgh, 1932; Sub-Ed., Scot. Nat. Dictionary, 1930-36; Dean: Faculty of Arts, Victoria Univ. Coll., Wellington, 1944-47, 1952, 1957-61; Faculty of Languages, 1965-68; Vice-Chancellor Univ. of New Zealand, 1947-52; Chm., Academic Bd, 1954-61. Visiting Professor: KCL 1954; Univ. of Edinburgh, 1962; Univ. of South Pacific, Fiji, 1972; Research Associate, UCL, 1969; Vis. Fellow, Edinburgh Univ., 1974-75; Vis. Fellow in Commonwealth Literature, Univ. of Leeds, 1975; Vis. Prof., France and Belgium, 1976. Member: Copyright Cttee and Tribunal, 1958; UGC, 1960-70; Chairman: English Language Institute,, 1961-72; NZ Literary Fund, 1951-73; Exec. Council, Assoc. of Univs of Br. Commonwealth, 1949-50. NZ representative at internat. confs: Utrecht, 1948; Bangkok, 1960; Kampala, 1961; Karachi, 1961. Army Educ. Service, 2 NZEF, Hon. Major. Hon. LLD Bristol, 1948; Hon. DLitt NZ, 1961; DUniv Stirling, 1975. *Publications:* John Skelton, Poet Laureate, 1943; New Zealand New Writing, 1943-45; The Teaching of English, a study in secondary education, 1947; English Prose Technique 1948; Shenstone's Miscellany, 1759-1763, 1952; Katherine Mansfield, 1954; The Movement of English Prose, 1966; John Galt (biog.), 1972; Word (festschrift), 1974; Undiscovered Country, 1974; Katherine Mansfield's Urewera Notebook, 1977; edited the following works of John Galt: The Entail, 1970; The Provost, 1973; The Member, 1975; The Last of the Lairds, 1976; Short Stories, 1978; part-author: Edinburgh Essays in Scottish Literature, 1933; Essays in Literature, 1934; The University and the Community, 1946; articles in Research journals and other periodicals. *Address:* 91 Messines Road, Wellington, NZ. *Club:* Aorangi Ski, New Zealand (former Pres.).

GORDON, Maj.-Gen. James Leslie, OBE 1944; Deputy Medical Officer of Health, City of Canterbury, 1965-74, retired; *b* 10 Sept. 1909; *s* of Dr James Leslie Gordon and Annie Laycock; *m* 1939, Dorothy Roberson. *Educ:* Epsom Coll.; Middlesex Hosp. MRCS LRCP 1935, DPH London 1948. Commandant, Army Sch. of Health, 1956. Prof. of Army Health, Royal Army Medical Coll., 1958; Dir of Army Health, War Office, 1962-64 (Ministry of Defence, April-May 1964). Mem., Faculty of Community Medicine, RCP, 1972. *Address:* 28 St Stephen's Hill, Canterbury, Kent. *Club:* Naval and Military.

GORDON, Sir John Charles, 9th Bt, *cr* 1706; *b* 4 Jan. 1901; *s* of 8th Bt and Elizabeth, *d* of Rev. John Maitland Ware; *S* father,

1939; *m* 1928, Marion, 3rd *d* of James Wright, Springfield, Sydney; one *s* one *d*. *Heir: s* Robert James Gordon [*b* 17 Aug. 1932; *m* 1976, Helen, *d* of Margery Perry, Cammeray, Sydney]. *Address:* 61 Farrer-Brown Court, Nuffield Village, Castle Hill, NSW 2154, Australia.

GORDON, Brig. John Evison, CIE 1947; OBE 1943; psc†;; retired; *b* 21 June 1901; *s* of Webster Boyle Gordon, CIE, Monkstown, Co. Cork, Eire; *m* 1936, Frances Elizabeth, *d* of Lt-Gen. Sir Joseph Talbot Hobbs, KCB, KCMG; one *d*. *Educ:* Wellington Coll.; RMC, Sandhurst. Commissioned 1920; joined Probyn's Horse (5th King Edward VII's Own Lancers), 1922. Staff Coll., 1935-36. Served NWF of India, 1930-31 and 1937-39; War of 1939-45: DAQMG, 4 Ind. Div., 1940; GSO 1. Staff Coll., Quetta, 1942; AQMG 4 Corps, 1943; temp. Col 1944; temp. Brig. 1945; retired, 1948. *Address:* Manor Farm, Wootton, Boars Hill, Oxford OX1 5JL. *T:* Oxford 735186. *Club:* Army and Navy.

GORDON, John Gunn Drummond, CBE 1964; Director: Grindlays Bank Ltd, since 1969; Steel Brothers Holdings Ltd, since 1974; a Crown Agent, since 1974; *b* 27 April 1909; *s* of late Rev. J. Drummond Gordon, MA, BD, BSc; *m* 1947, Mary Livingstone Paterson; two *s* one *d*. *Educ:* Edinburgh Academy. Served War, King's African Rifles, 1940-45. Career: spent 30 years out of 45, overseas, mainly in Eastern Africa, but also in India, with Grindlays Bank Ltd, finishing up as Group Managing Director; retired 1974. *Address:* Ashdown, 17 Kippington Road, Sevenoaks, Kent TN13 2LJ. *T:* Sevenoaks 54188. *Clubs:* Oriental; Wilderness Golf (Sevenoaks); Nairobi (Nairobi).

GORDON, Kathleen Olivia, CBE 1966; Director, The Royal Academy of Dancing, 1948-68, Hon. Fellow, 1976; *b* 15 Jan. 1898; *d* of George R. Gordon, OBE, MD and Alice Maude Gordon. *Educ:* Manchester High Sch. for Girls; King's Coll., London Univ. With Royal Academy of Dancing, 1924-68; Coronation Award, 1964. *Recreations:* reading, theatre, and ballet. *Address:* 23 Addisland Court, W14. *T:* 01-602 0430.

GORDON, Keith Lyndell, CMG 1971; Justice of Appeal, West Indies Associated States Supreme Court, 1967-72, retired; *b* 8 April 1906; 3rd *s* of late George S. E. Gordon, Journalist, and Nancy Gordon; *m* 1947, Ethel King; one *d*. *Educ:* St Mary's Coll., St Lucia, WI; Middle Temple, London. Magistrate, Grenada, 1938; Crown Attorney, Dominica, 1942; Trinidad and Tobago: Magistrate, 1943-46 and 1949-53; Exec. Off., Black Market Board, 1946-48; Puisne Judge, Windward Islands and Leeward Islands, 1954-59; Puisne Judge, British Guiana, 1959-62; Chief Justice, West Cameroon, 1963-67. *Recreations:* tennis, gardening. *Address:* Vigie, Castries, St Lucia.

GORDON, Sir Lionel Eldred Peter S.; see Smith-Gordon.

GORDON, Patrick W.; see Wolrige-Gordon.

GORDON, Peter Macie, CMG 1964; *b* 4 June 1919; *o s* of late Herbert and Gladys Gordon (*née* Simpson); *m* 1945, Marianne, *er d* of Dr Paul Meerwein, Basle; two *d*. *Educ:* Cotham Sch., Bristol; University Coll., Exeter; Merton Coll., Oxford. Served War, 1940-46; commissioned Argyll and Sutherland Highlanders, 1941; Campaign in North-West Europe, 1944-45 (despatches). Entered Colonial Administrative Service as District Officer, 1946; Senior District Commissioner, 1957; Asst Sec., Ministry of Agriculture, 1958; Under-Sec., 1960; Permanent Sec., Ministry of Agriculture and Animal Husbandry, Kenya, 1961; retired, 1964; Asst Sec., Univ. of Exeter, 1964-70. *Address:* The Manor House, Willersey, Broadway, Worcs.

GORDON, Richard, (Dr Gordon Ostlere); MA, MB, BChir Cambridge, FFARCS, DA; Author; *b* 15 Sept. 1921; *m* 1951, Mary Patten, MRCPE, FFARCS; two *s* two *d*. *Educ:* privately; Selwyn Coll., Cambridge; St Bartholomew's Hosp. Senior Resident Anaesthetist, St Bartholomew's (Hill End) Hosp., 1945-48; Asst Ed., BMJ, 1949-50; Ship Surg., 1950-51; Research Asst and Dep. First Asst, Nuffield Dept of Anaesthetics, Oxford Univ., 1951-52; left medical practice, 1952. *Publications:* Doctor in the House, 1952 (film, 1954, play 1956, radio series 1968, TV series 1969, 1970); Doctor at Sea, 1953 (film 1955, play 1961, TV series 1974); The Captain's Table, 1954 (film 1959); Doctor at Large, 1955 (film 1957, radio series 1969, TV series 1971); Doctor in Love, 1957 (film 1960); Doctor and Son, 1959 (filmed as Doctor in Distress, 1963); Doctor in Clover, 1960 (film 1966, TV series as Doctor in Charge, 1972, 1973, as Doctor on the Go, 1975, 1976, 1977); Doctor on Toast, 1961 (filmed as Doctor in Trouble, 1970); Doctor in the Swim, 1962; Nuts in May, 1964; The Summer of Sir Lancelot, 1965; Love and Sir Lancelot, 1966;

(with wife) A Baby in the House: a guide to practical parenthood, 1966; Doctor in Love (play), 1966; The Facemaker, 1967; Surgeon at Arms, 1968; The Facts of Life, 1969; Doctor on the Boil, 1970; The Medical Witness, 1971; Doctor on the Brain, 1972; Doctor in the Nude, 1973; The Sleep of Life, 1975; Doctor on the Job, 1976; Good Neighbours: Suburbia Observed, 1976 (John Rowan Wilson Award); The Invisible Victory, 1977; Happy Families, 1977; text books and papers on anaesthesia. Contributions to Punch. *Recreations:* watching cricket, fishing, walking, gardening. *Address:* c/o Curtis Brown Ltd, 1 Craven Hill, W2 3EP. *Clubs:* Beefsteak, Garrick, MCC.

GORDON, Robert Wilson, MC 1944; Deputy Chairman of the Stock Exchange, London, 1965-68; Partner, Pidgeon de Smitt (Stockbrokers); *b* 3 March 1915; *s* of late Malcolm Gordon and late Blanche Fayerweather Gordon; *m* 1st, 1946, Joan Alison (*d* 1965), *d* of late Brig. A. G. Kenchington, CBE, MC; one *d*; 2nd, 1967, Mrs Dianna E. V. Ansell (*née* Tyrwhitt-Drake). *Educ:* Harrow. Served War of 1939-45 (despatches); Royal Ulster Rifles, and Parachute Regt; Instructor, Staff Coll., 1943-44. Elected to the Council, Stock Exchange, London, 1956. Chm., Airborne Forces Security Fund, 1974-. *Recreation:* golf. *Address:* 41 Cadogan Square, SW1. *T:* 01-235 4496. *Club:* City of London.

GORDON, Sir Sidney, Kt 1972; CBE 1968 (OBE 1965); CA; JP; MEC; Chairman: Sir Elly Kadoorie Continuation Ltd, since 1971; Rediffusion (Hong Kong) Ltd; Rediffusion Television Ltd; The Hong Kong Building & Loan Agency Ltd; Deputy Chairman: China Light & Power Co. Ltd; Hongkong & Shanghai Hotels Ltd; *b* 20 Aug. 1917; *s* of late P. S. Gordon and of Angusina Gordon; *m* 1950, Olive W. F. Eldon, *d* of late T. A. Eldon and of Hannah Eldon; two *d*. *Educ:* Hyndland Sch., Glasgow; Glasgow Univ. Sen. Partner, Lowe Bingham & Matthews, Chartered Accountants, Hong Kong, 1956-70. MLC, 1962-66, MEC, Hong Kong, 1965-. Chm., Univ. and Polytechnic Grants Cttee, 1974-76. JP Hong Kong, 1961. Hon. LLD The Chinese University of Hong Kong, 1970. *Recreation:* golf. *Address:* 7 Headland Road, Hong Kong. *T:* 5-92577. *Clubs:* Royal Commonwealth Society, Oriental; Hong Kong, Royal Hong Kong Jockey, Royal Hong Kong Golf, Hong Kong Country, Hong Kong Cricket, Shek O Country, etc.

GORDON, Strathearn, CBE 1967 (OBE 1953); Librarian of the House of Commons, 1950-67; *b* 3 Sept., 1902; 2nd *s* of Hon. Huntly D. Gordon, Sheriff-Substitute of Ross and Cromarty, and Violet, *d* of John Gaspard Fanshawe, Parsloes; *m* 1934, Elizabeth, *d* of Lovelace Serjeantson; two *s* one *d*. *Educ:* Edinburgh Academy; RMC Sandhurst. Joined 2nd Bn Highland Light Infantry, 1923; invalided 1927. Clerk in the House of Commons, 1930. *Publications:* Our Parliament, 1945; (with T. G. B. Cocks) A People's Conscience, 1952. *Address:* Avoch House, Avoch, Ross-shire IV9 8RF. *T:* Fortrose 2432. *Club:* Army and Navy.

GORDON, Lt-Col William Howat Leslie, CBE 1957 (MBE 1941); MC 1944; Adviser on overseas business to firms and to Ministry of Overseas Development, 1971-75; *b* 8 April 1914; *o s* of late Frank Leslie Gordon, ISE (retd), FICE and of Madelaine Page (*née* Ker), Broughty Ferry; *m* 1944, Margot Lumb; one *s* three *d*. *Educ:* Rugby; RMA Woolwich. Commnd Royal Signals, 1934; Palestine, Africa, Italy, NW Europe; 1 Armoured, 1 Airborne Divs, 1937-45 (despatches); Instructor, Staff Coll., Camberley, 1947-49. Chief Executive, The Uganda Co. Ltd, 1949-60; John Holt & Co. (Liverpool) Ltd and Lonrho Exports Ltd, 1960-71; MLC Uganda, 1952-57; Director: Gordon Automations Ltd; Rickmansworth & Uxbridge Water Co.; Celling Ltd. *Recreations:* golf, tennis, shooting. *Address:* Shenstone House, Chalfont St Giles, Bucks. *T:* Little Chalfont 2047. *Clubs:* White's, Royal Commonwealth Society, MCC.

GORDON-BROWN, Alexander Douglas; Under-Secretary, Cabinet Office, since 1975; *b* 5 Dec. 1927; *s* of Captain D. S. Gordon-Brown; *m* 1959, Mary Hilton; three *s*. *Educ:* Bryanston Sch.; New Coll., Oxford. BA 1st cl. hons PPE. Entered Home Office, 1951; Asst Private Sec. to Home Sec., 1956; Sec., Franks Cttee on section 2 of Official Secrets Act 1911, 1971; Asst Under-Sec. of State, Home Office, 1972-75. *Recreation:* music. *Address:* 155 Worlds End Lane, Green Street Green, Orpington, Kent.

GORDON-CUMMING, Alexander Roualeyn, CVO 1969; Counsellor (Aviation and Shipping), British Embassy, Washington, DC, USA; *b* 10 Sept. 1924; *s* of late Lt-Comdr R. G. Gordon-Cumming and of Mrs M. V. K. Wilkinson; *m* 1st, 1965, Beryl Joyce Macnaughton Dunn (*d* 1973); one *d*; 2nd, 1974, Elizabeth Patricia Blackley; one *d*. *Educ:* Eton Coll. RAF, 1943; retd with rank of Gp Captain, 1969. Board of Trade,

1969; Asst Sec., Air Div., Dept of Trade and Industry, 1973; seconded HM Diplomatic Service, 1974. *Recreations:* gardening, skiing, fell walking, ballet. *Address:* c/o Foreign and Commonwealth Office, SW1; 2 Wallgrave Road, SW5 0RL. *T:* 01-373 7358; Farinay Cottage, Walderton, Chichester, Sussex. *T:* Compton 393. *Club:* Royal Air Force.

GORDON CUMMING, Sir William Gordon, 6th Bt, *cr* 1804; Royal Scots Greys; *b* 19 June 1928; *s* of Major Sir Alexander Penrose Gordon-Cumming, 5th Bt, and Elizabeth Topham, *d* of J. Topham Richardson, Harps Oak, Merstham; *S* father, 1939; *m* 1953, Elisabeth (marr. diss. 1972), *d* of Maj.-Gen. Sir William Hinde, *qv*; one *s* three *d*. *Educ:* Eton; RMC, Sandhurst. Late Royal Scots Greys; retired 1952. *Heir:* *s* Alexander Penrose Gordon Cumming, *b* 15 April 1954. *Address:* Altyre, Forres, Morayshire.

GORDON DAVIES, Rev. John; *see* Davies, Rev. John G.

GORDON-DUFF, Col Thomas Robert, MC 1945; JP; Lord-Lieutenant of Banffshire since 1964; Convener of County Council, 1962-70; *b* 1911; *er s* of Lachlan Gordon-Duff (killed in action, 1914); *m* 1946, Jean, *d* of late Leslie G. Moir, Bicester; one *s*. *Educ:* Eton; RMC, Sandhurst. Entered Army, 2nd Lieut, Rifle Brigade, 1932; served War of 1939-45 (MC); retired, 1947. Lt-Col 5/6 Bn Gordon Highlanders (TA), 1947, retiring as Col. DL 1948, JP 1959. Vice-Lieut 1961, Banffshire. *Address:* Drummuir, Keith, Banffshire. *T:* Drummuir 224. *Clubs:* Army and Navy; Royal Northern (Aberdeen).

GORDON-FINLAYSON, Air Vice-Marshal James Richmond, DSO 1941; DFC 1940; *b* 19 Aug. 1914; *s* of late Gen. Sir Robert Gordon-Finlayson, KCB, CMG, DSO, and late Lady (Mary) Gordon-Finlayson, OBE; *m* 1953, Margaret Ann (*d* 1965), *d* of Col G. C. Richardson, DSO, MC; one *s* one *d* by a former marriage. *Educ:* Winchester; Pembroke Coll., Cambridge (MA). Mem. Inner Temple, 1935; joined RAF, 1936; ADC to Gov. of Kenya, 1938-39; served in Libya, 1940 and 1941-42, Greece, 1940-41 (despatches), Syria, 1941; Sqdn Ldr 1940; OC 211 Sqdn, 1940-41; RAF Staff Coll., 1942; Air Staff, Air Min., 1942-45; RAF Liaison Offr to HQ, US Army Strategic Air Force, Guam, 1945; Air Staff, Air Comd, SEA, 1945-46; SASO, AHQ, Burma, 1946; OC 48 Sqdn, 1946-47; on directing staff, JSSC, Group Captain 1951; Air Staff, Air Min., 1951-54, OC, RAF Deversoir, 1954; OC, RAF Khormaksar, 1954-56; on staff of HQ Bomber Command, 1956, Asst Comdt, RAF Staff Coll., Bracknell; Air Cdre, 1958; Air Vice-Marshal, 1961; Dir-Gen. of Personal Services, Air Ministry, 1960-63; retired, June 1963. Greek DFC, 1941; Sheikh el Bilharith. *Publications:* Epitaph for a Squadron, 1965; Their Finest Hour, 1976; articles on strategic and air and military affairs in various jls; verse. *Recreations:* fishing, sailing, travel and literary interests. *Address:* Quizas Quizas, Guadarranque, San Roque, Cadiz, Spain. *Clubs:* MCC; RAF Yacht.

See also Maj.-Gen. R. Gordon-Finlayson.

GORDON-FINLAYSON, Maj.-Gen. Robert, OBE 1957 (MBE 1945); JP; DL; *b* 28 Oct. 1916; *yr s* of late Gen. Sir Robert Gordon-Finlayson, KCB, CMG, DSO, DL; *m* 1945, Alexandra, *d* of late John Bartholomew, Rowde Court, Rowde, Wilts; two *s*. *Educ:* Winchester Coll.; RMA, Woolwich. 2 Lt RA, 1936; Major, BEF, 1940; Staff Coll., 1941; Middle East, 1942-43; NW Europe, 1944-45; India and Burma, 1945-47; GSO 1 1945; RHA, 1952-53; JSSC, 1953; Bt Lieut-Col, 1955; AA and QMG, 3 Inf. Div., 1955-57; Near East (Suez Ops), 1956; Middle East, 1958; Lieut-Col 1958; Comdr, 26 Field Regt RA, 1958-59; Col 1959; GSO 1, Staff Coll., 1960-62; Brig. CRA, 49 Div. TA, 1962-64; Brig. DQMG, HQ, BAOR, 1964-66. GOC 49 Inf. Div., TA/N Midland Dist, 1966-67; GOC E Midland District, 1967-70; retd, 1970. Hon. Col, 3rd (Volunteer) Bn The Worcestershire and Sherwood Foresters Regt, TAVR, 1971-; Chm., Notts Co. Army Benevolent Fund, 1970-; Mem., Notts Co. and E Midlands TAVR Assocs, 1971-. Pres., Notts Co. Royal British Legion, 1971-; Vice-President: Notts Co. SSAFA and PDSA, 1970-; Central Notts Scout Assoc., 1971-. JP 1972, High Sheriff 1974, DL 1974, Notts. *Recreations:* shooting, fishing, ski-ing, gardening, walking. *Address:* South Collingham Manor, near Newark, Notts. *T:* Newark 892204; c/o Lloyds Bank Ltd, Cox's & King's Branch, 6 Pall Mall, SW1.

See also Air Vice-Marshal J. R. Gordon-Finlayson.

GORDON-HALL, Maj.-Gen. Frederick William, CB 1958; CBE 1945; *b* 28 Dec. 1902; *s* of Col Frederick William George Gordon-Hall and Clare Frances (*née* Taylor); *m* 1930, Phyllis Dorothy Miller; one *s* one *d*. *Educ:* Winchester Coll.; RMC Sandhurst. Gazetted Royal Tank Corps, 1923; Staff Capt., War Office, 1935-39; Ministry of Supply, 1939-43; HQ Allied Armies in Italy, 1943-45; Military Dir of Studies, Mil. Coll. of Science,

1946-49; Dir of Technical Services (Land), British Joint Staff Mission, Washington, 1950-52; Dir of Inspection of Fighting Vehicles, Ministry of Supply, Dec. 1952-June 1955. Dir-Gen. of Fighting Vehicles, Min. of Supply, 1955-58, retd. *Recreations:* model engineering, foreign travel, cabinet making. *Address:* Whitegates, Salisbury Road, Horsham, West Sussex. *T:* Horsham 3304.

GORDON JONES, Air Marshal Sir Edward, KCB 1967 (CB 1960); CBE 1956 (OBE 1945); DSO 1941; DFC 1941; idc; jssc; qs; Air Officer Commanding-in-Chief, Near East Air Force, and Administrator, Sovereign Base Areas, 1966-69; Commander, British Forces Near East, 1967-69; retired 1969; *b* 31 Aug. 1914; *s* of late Lt-Col Dr A. Jones, DSO, MC, MD, DPh; *m* 1938, Margery Thurston Hatfield; two *s*. Served War of 1939-45 (despatches, DFC, DSO, OBE, Greek DFC). ACOS (Intelligence), Allied Air Forces Central Europe, 1960-61; Air Officer Commanding RAF Germany, 1961-63; Senior RAF Directing Staff, Imperial Defence Coll., 1963-65; AOC, RAF, Malta, and Dep. C-in-C (Air), Allied Forces, Mediterranean, 1965-66. MBIM. Comdr Order of Orange Nassau. *Recreations:* sport, photography, travel, music. *Address:* 14 Chaucer Road, Cambridge. *Club:* Royal Air Force.

GORDON-LENNOX, family name of **Duke of Richmond.**

GORDON LENNOX, Rear-Adm. Sir Alexander (Henry Charles), KCVO 1972; CB 1962; DSO 1942; Serjeant at Arms, House of Commons, 1962-76; *b* 9 April 1911; *s* of Lord Bernard Charles Gordon Lennox and Evelyn (*née* Loch); *m* 1936, Barbara, *d* of Maj.-Gen. Julian Steele; two *s*. *Educ:* Hetherdown, Ascot; RNC Dartmouth. Served as young officer in small ships in Far East and Home Fleet; communication specialist. Served War of 1939-45 (despatches 1943); in ME, East Coast Convoys, Russian Convoys; subsequently commanded HMS Surprise, HMS Mermaid and 2nd Frigate Sqdn, HMS Mercury and HMS Newcastle. Dep. Chief of Supplies and Transport, 1959-62; President, RNC Greenwich, 1961-62. Liberty Medal (Norway). *Recreations:* shooting, fishing and gardening. *Address:* Quags Corner, Minstead, Midhurst, West Sussex. *T:* Midhurst 3623. *Club:* Naval (Portsmouth).

GORDON LENNOX, Lieut-Gen. Sir George (Charles), KBE 1964; CB 1959; CVO 1952; DSO 1943; King of Arms, Order of British Empire, since 1968; *b* 29 May 1908; *s* of late Lord Bernard Charles Gordon Lennox, 3rd *s* of 7th Duke of Richmond and Gordon and late Evelyn Loch, *d* of 1st Baron Loch; *m* 1931, Nancy Brenda Darell; two *s*. *Educ:* Eton; Sandhurst. Served Grenadier Guards, 1928-52; served with Regt and on Staff, war of 1939-45, in Europe, Africa and Far East; Lieut-Col Commanding Grenadier Guards, Jan. 1951-July 1952; Comdr 1st Guards Brigade, 1952-54; Imperial Defence Coll., 1955; BGS (SD and Trg), HQ, BAOR, 1956-57; Gen. Officer Commanding 3rd Div., 1957-59; Commandant Royal Military Acad. Sandhurst, 1960-63; Dir-Gen. of Military Training, 1963-64; GOC-in-C Scottish Comd and Governor of Edinburgh Castle, 1964-66. Col, Gordon Highlanders, 1965. *Recreations:* field sports. *Address:* Gordon Castle, Fochabers, Morayshire. *T:* Fochabers 275. *Club:* Cavalry and Guards.

GORDON LENNOX, Lord Nicholas Charles, MVO 1957; HM Diplomatic Service; Counsellor and Head of Chancery, Paris, since 1975; *b* 31 Jan. 1931; *yr s* of Duke of Richmond and Gordon, *qv*; *m* 1958, Mary, *d* of late Brig. H. N. H. Williamson, DSO, MC; one *s* three *d*. *Educ:* Eton; Worcester Coll., Oxford (Scholar). 2nd Lieut KRRC, 1950-51. Entered HM Foreign Service, 1954; FO, 1954-57; Private Sec. to HM Ambassador to USA, 1957-61; 2nd, later 1st Sec., HM Embassy, Santiago, 1961-63; Private Sec. to Perm. Under-Sec., FO, 1963-66; 1st Sec. and Head of Chancery, HM Embassy, Madrid, 1966-71; seconded to Cabinet Office, 1971-73; Head of News Dept, FCO, 1973-74; Head of N America Dept, 1974-75. *Address:* 26 Chelsea Park Gardens, SW3 6AA. *T:* 01-352 4510. *Clubs:* Travellers', Brooks's, Beefsteak.
See also Earl of March and Kinrara.

GORDON-SMITH, David Gerard; CMG 1971; Director-General in Legal Service, Council of Ministers, European Communities, since 1976; *b* 6 Oct. 1925; *s* of late Frederic Gordon-Smith, QC, and of Elsie Gordon-Smith (*née* Foster); *m* 1952, Angela Kirkpatrick Pile; one *s* one *d*. *Educ:* Rugby Sch.; Trinity Coll., Oxford. Served in RNVR, 1944-46. BA (Oxford) 1948; called to Bar, Inner Temple, 1949; Legal Asst, Colonial Office, 1950; Sen. Legal Asst, 1954; CRO, 1963-65; Asst Legal Adviser, CO, 1965-66; Legal Counsellor, CO, later FCO, 1966-72; Dep. Legal Advr, FCO, 1973-76. *Address:* Kingscote, Westcott, Surrey. *T:* Dorking 5702; 14 Avenue Ptolémée, 1180 Brussels, Belgium.

GORDON-SMITH, Ralph; President, since 1973 (Chairman, 1951-73), Smiths Industries Ltd (formerly Smith and Sons (England) Ltd); *b* 22 May 1905; *s* of late Sir Allan Gordon-Smith, KBE, DL and Hilda Beatrice Cave; *m* 1932, Beryl Mavis Cundy; no *c*. *Educ:* Bradfield Coll. Joined Smiths Industries, 1927; Dir, 1933. Dir of EMI Ltd, 1951-75. FBHI 1961. *Recreations:* shooting, fishing. *Address:* Brook House, Bosham, West Sussex. *T:* Bosham 573475; 23 Kingston House East, Princes Gate, SW7. *T:* 01-584 9428. *Club:* Bosham Sailing.

GORDON WALKER, family name of **Baron Gordon-Walker.**

GORDON-WALKER, Baron *cr* 1974 (Life Peer), of Leyton; **Patrick Chrestien Gordon Walker,** PC 1950; CH 1968; Member, European Parliament, 1975-76; *b* 7 April 1907; *s* of Alan Lachlan Gordon Walker and Dora Marguerite Chrestien; *m* 1934, Audrey Muriel Rudolf; twin *s* three *d*. *Educ:* Wellington Coll; Christ Church, Oxford, MA, BLitt. Student and History Tutor, Christ Church, 1931-40; BBC European Service (German workers), 1940-44; Asst German Service Dir, BBC, 1945. Chm. British Film Institute, 1946; Vice-Chm. British Council, 1947. MP (Lab) Smethwick, 1945-64; contested (Lab) Leyton, Jan. 1965; MP (Lab) Leyton, 1966-Feb. 1974. PPS to Mr Herbert Morrison, MP, 1946; Parliamentary Under-Sec. of State, Commonwealth Relations Office, 1947-50; Sec. of State for Commonwealth Relations, 1950-51; Sec. of State for Foreign Affairs, Oct. 1964-Jan. 1965; Leader, UK Delegn to Council of Europe, 1966; Chm., Book Development Council, 1965-67; Minister without Portfolio during 1967; Sec. of State for Educn and Science, 1967-68. *Publications:* The Sixteenth and Seventeenth Centuries, 1935; Outline of Man's History, 1939; The Lid Lifts, 1945; Restatement of Liberty, 1951; The Commonwealth, 1962; The Cabinet, 1970. *Recreations:* reading and writing. *Address:* 105 Frobisher House, Dolphin Square, SW1V 3LL.
See also Graham C. Greene.

GORDON WATSON, Hugh; *see* Watson.

GORE, family name of **Earl of Arran.**

GORE; *see* Ormsby Gore.

GORE, Frederick John Pym, RA 1972 (ARA 1964); Painter; Head of Painting Department, St Martin's School of Art, WC2, since 1951 and Vice-Principal since 1961; *b* 8 Nov. 1913; *s* of Spencer Frederick Gore and Mary Johanna Kerr. *Educ:* Lancing Coll.; Trinity Coll., Oxford; studied art at Ruskin, Westminster and Slade Schs. Taught at: Westminster Sch. of Art, 1937; Chelsea and Epsom, 1947; St Martin's, 1946-. *One-man exhibitions:* Gall. Borghèse, Paris, 1938; Redfern Gall., 1937, 1949, 1950, 1953, 1956, 1962; Mayor Gall., 1958, 1960; Juster Gall., NY, 1963. *Paintings in public collections include:* Contemporary Art Soc., Leicester County Council, GLC, Southampton, Plymouth, Rutherston Collection and New Brunswick. Served War of 1939-45: Mx Regt and RA (SO Camouflage). *Publications:* Abstract Art, 1956; Painting, Some Principles, 1965. *Recreation:* Russian folk dancing. *Address:* Flat 3, 35 Elm Park Gardens, SW10. *T:* 01-352 4940.

GORE, John Francis, CVO 1941; TD; journalist and author; *b* 15 May 1885; *y s* of late Sir Francis Gore, KCB; *m* 1926, Lady Janet Helena Campbell, *er d* of 4th Earl Cawdor; one *s* two *d*. *Educ:* Radley Coll.; Trinity Coll., Oxford (MA). Barrister-at-Law, Inner Temple, 1909; served European War, 1914-19 (despatches); Captain Bedfordshire Yeomanry; Sec. Training Grants Cttee, Ministry of Labour, 1920; took up journalism, 1923; pen-name The Old Stager, of the Sphere's Newsletter, 1928-64. JP Sussex, 1932-59, Chm. Midhurst Bench, 1944-58. *Publications:* The Trial Stone, 1919; A Londoner's Calendar, 1925; The Way In, 1927; The Ghosts of Fleet Street, 1929; Charles Gore, father and son, 1932; Creevey's life and times, 1934; Nelson's Hardy and his wife, 1935; Sydney Holland, Lord Knutsford, 1936; Geoffrey Colman; Mary, Duchess of Bedford (privately printed), 1938; King George V, 1941 (awarded J. T. Black Memorial Prize, 1941); Creevey, 1948; Edwardian Scrapbook, 1951; Three Howard Sisters (with another), 1955. *Address:* Littlehay, Burley, Ringwood, Hants. *T:* Burley 3306. *Club:* I Zingari.
See also Sir Charles Cave.

GORE, John Kearns; a Recorder of the Crown Court, since 1974; *b* 3 Aug. 1924; *s* of late John Gore, Lathom, Lancs and Mary Evelyn Gore; *m* 1961, June Stananought Pritchard; one *s* one *d*. *Educ:* Worcester Coll., Oxford. BA Hons Jurisprudence 1948. Served with RAFVR, 1943-45, wounded NW Europe 1944. Called to Bar, Gray's Inn, 1949, practised Northern Circuit from 1950. Chm., Nat. Insce Tribunal, 1972-; Chm., Brockhall

Hosp. Enquiry, 1973. Mem. No 7 (NW) Legal Area Cttee, Law Soc., 1970-. *Recreations:* music-making, model railways. *Address:* Fruit Exchange Building, Victoria Street, Liverpool; 2 Pump Court, Temple, EC4; (home) 4 Harrod Drive, Birkdale, Southport, Merseyside. *Club:* Athenæum (Liverpool).

GORE, Paul Annesley, CMG 1964; CVO 1961; JP; *b* 28 Feb. 1921; *o s* of late Charles Henry Gore, OBE and late Hon. Violet Kathleen (*née* Annesley); *m* 1946, Gillian Mary, *d* of T. E. Allen-Stevens; three *s. Educ:* Winchester Coll.; Christ Church, Oxford. Military Service, 1941-46: 16/5 Lancers. Colonial Service, 1948-65; Dep. Governor, The Gambia, 1962-65. JP City of Oxford, 1973-74; JP Suffolk, 1977. *Address:* 1 Burkitt Road, Woodbridge, Suffolk.

GORE, Sir Richard (Ralph St George), 13th Bt *cr* 1621; *b* 19 Nov. 1954; *s* of Sir (St George) Ralph Gore, 12th Bt, and of Shirley, *d* of Clement Tabor; *S* father, 1973. *Educ:* The King's Sch., Parramatta; Univ. of New England. *Heir:* uncle Nigel Hugh St George Gore [*b* 23 Dec. 1922; *m* 1952, Beth Allison (*d* 1976), *d* of R. W. Hooper; one *d*]. *Address:* Wycanna, Talwood, Queensland 4322, Australia.

GORE-BOOTH, family name of **Baron Gore-Booth.**

GORE-BOOTH, Baron *cr* 1969 (Life Peer), of Maltby; **Paul Henry Gore-Booth,** GCMG 1965 (KCMG 1957; CMG 1949); KCVO 1961; HM Diplomatic Service, retired; Director: Grindlays Bank, since 1969; United Kingdom Provident Institution, since 1969; Registrar, Order of St Michael and St George, since 1966; *b* 3 Feb. 1909; *m* 1940, Patricia Mary Ellerton; twin *s* two *d. Educ:* Eton; Balliol Coll., Oxford. Joined Foreign Service, 1933; FO 1933-36; Vienna, 1936-37; Tokyo, 1938-42; Washington, 1942-45; FO, 1945-49; Head of UN (Economic and Social) and Refugees Depts, 1947-48; Head of European Recovery Dept, Foreign Office, 1948-49; Dir British Information Services in United States, 1949-53; Ambassador to Burma, 1953-56; Dep. Under-Sec. (Economic Affairs), Foreign Office, 1956-60; British High Commissioner in India, 1960-65; Permanent Under-Sec. of State, FO, 1965-69; Head of HM Diplomatic Service, 1968-69. Hot Springs Food Conference, 1943; UNRRA Conference, 1943; Chicago Civil Aviation Conference, 1944; San Francisco Conf., 1945; UN Assembly, 1946 (Sec. of UK Deleg.) Jan. and Oct. and 1947. Chm., Disasters Emergency Cttee, 1974-. Chm. Bd of Governors, Sch. of Oriental and African Studies, Univ. of London, 1975-. Chm., Save the Children Fund, 1970-76. Pres. Sherlock Holmes Soc. of London, 1967; Chm., Windsor Music Festival, 1971-73. *Publication:* With Great Truth and Respect (autobiog.), 1974. *Address:* 70 Ashley Gardens, SW1P 1QG. *Clubs:* Athenæum, Baker Street Irregulars.

GORE-BOOTH, Sir Michael; see Booth.

GORE BROWNE, Thomas Anthony; Senior Government Broker since 1973; *b* 20 June 1918; 2nd *s* of Sir Eric Gore Browne, DSO; *m* 1946, Lavinia, *d* of Gen. Sir (Henry) Charles Loyd, GCVO, KCB, DSO, MC; three *s* one *d. Educ:* Eton Coll.; Trinity Coll., Cambridge. Served Grenadier Guards, 1938-48, France, N Africa, Italy. Joined Mullens & Co., 1948, Partner 1949. *Address:* The Old Rectory, Lydlinch, Sturminster Newton, Dorset DT10 2JA. *T:* Sturminster Newton 72074. *Clubs:* Brooks's, White's.

GORE-LANGTON; see Temple-Gore-Langton, family name of Earl Temple of Stowe.

GORELL, 4th Baron *cr* 1909; **Timothy John Radcliffe Barnes;** *b* 2 Aug. 1927; *e s* of 3rd Baron Gorell and Elizabeth Gorell, *d* of Alexander Nelson Radcliffe; *S* father, 1963; *m* 1954, Joan Marion, *y d* of late John Edmund Collins, MC, Sway, Hants; two adopted *d. Educ:* Eton Coll.; New Coll., Oxford. Lieut, Rifle Brigade, 1946-48. Barrister, Inner Temple, 1951. Joined Royal Dutch/Shell Group, 1959. *Heir: b* Hon. Ronald Alexander Henry Barnes [*b* 28 June 1931; *m* 1957, Gillian Picton Hughes-Jones; one *s* one *d*]. *Address:* 4 Roehampton Gate, SW15. *T:* 01-876 6042. *Club:* Roehampton Golf.

GORELL BARNES, Sir William (Lethbridge), KCMG 1961 (CMG 1949); CB 1956; Deputy Chairman: Doulton & Co, since 1969 (Director, since 1966); Royal Group of Insurance Companies, since 1972 (Director, since 1963); Director: Tricentrol Ltd, since 1969; Tarmac Ltd, since 1971; Donald Macpherson Group Ltd, since 1972; *b* 23 Aug. 1909; *y s* of late Sir Frederic Gorell Barnes and Caroline Anne Roper Lethbridge; *m* 1935, Barbara Mary Louise, *e d* of late Brig. A. F. B. Cottrell, DSO, OBE; one *s* three *d. Educ:* Marlborough Coll.; Pembroke Coll., Cambridge, 1st Cl. Classical Tripos Pt I, 1st Cl.

Mod. Langs Tripos Pt 2. Served in HM Diplomatic Service, 1932-39; Offices of War Cabinet, 1939-45, and HM Treasury, 1945-46; Personal Asst to Prime Minister, Oct. 1946-Feb. 1948; Seconded to Colonial Office, 1948; Asst Under-Sec. of State, 1948-59; Dep. Under-Sec. of State, 1959-63. Mem. UK delegn for negotiations with European Economic Community, 1962, retired 1963. Mem. Council, Westfield Coll., London Univ. *Publication:* Europe and the Developing World, 1967. *Recreations:* gardening, walking, reading. *Address:* Mattishall Hall, Dereham, Norfolk. *T:* Mattishall 8181; 25 Bryanston Mews East, W1. *T:* 01-262 7479. *Club:* Reform.

GORING, Marius; Actor; *b* Newport, IOW, 23 May 1912; *s* of Dr Charles Buckman Goring, MD, BSc, and Katie Winifred Macdonald; *m* 1931, Mary Westwood Steel (marr. diss.); one *d*; *m* 1941, Lucie Mannheim (*d* 1976); *m* 1977, Prudence FitzGerald. *Educ:* Perse Sch., Cambridge; Universities of Frankfurt, Munich, Vienna, and Paris. Studied for stage under Harcourt Williams and at Old Vic dramatic school. First stage appearance in London in one of Jean Sterling Mackinlay's matinées, 1927; toured in France and Germany with English Classical Players, 1931; played two seasons at Old Vic and Sadler's Wells, 1932-34. First West End appearance as Hugh Voysey in The Voysey Inheritance, Shaftesbury, 1934; toured France, Belgium, and Holland with Compagnie des Quinze (acting in French), 1934-35; appeared London, 1935-39, in: Hamlet, Noah, The Hangman, Sowers of the Hills, Mary Tudor, The Happy Hypocrite, Girl Unknown, The Wild Duck, The Witch of Edmonton, Twelfth Night, Henry V, Hamlet, The Last Straw, Surprise Item, The White Guard; Satyr. In management at Duke of York's, 1939; produced Nora (A Doll's House); played Ariel in, and partly produced, The Tempest, Old Vic, 1940. Served War of 1939-45, Army, 1940-41; Foreign Office, 1941-45; supervisor of productions of BBC broadcasting to Germany, 1941. Toured British zone of Germany, 1947 (playing in German), 1948; Rosmersholm, Too True to be Good, Cherry Orchard, Marriage, The Third Man, at Arts Theatre; Daphne Laureola, Berlin (playing in German), 1949; The Madwoman of Chaillot, St James's, 1951; Richard III, Antony and Cleopatra, Taming of the Shrew, King Lear, Sratford-upon-Avon, 1953; Antony and Cleopatra, Princes, 1953; Marriage, Wuppertal, 1954; has toured France, Holland, Finland, 1957, and India, 1958, with own company of English comedians; Tonight at 8.30 (in German), Berlin Fest., 1960; Measure for Measure, Stratford-upon-Avon, 1962; A Penny for a Song, Aldwych, 1962; Ménage à Trois, Lyric, 1963; The Poker Session, Globe, 1964; The Apple Cart, Cambridge, 1965; The Bells, Vaudeville, 1968; The Demonstration, Nottingham, 1969; Sleuth, 1970-73. Was one of the founders of London Theatre Studio. Has appeared in a number of films since 1936, including: The Case of the Frightened Lady, A Matter of Life and Death, Take my Life, The Red Shoes, Mr Perrin and Mr Traill, Odette, Circle of Danger, Highly Dangerous, So Little Time, Nachts auf den Strassen (Germany), The Man Who Watched the Trains Go By, Rough Shoot, The Barefoot Contessa, Family Doctor, Ill Met by Moonlight, The Inspector, The Crooked Road, Up from the Beach, 25th Hour. Has broadcast over a number of years and written several radio scripts. Co-prod. and played lead in television series, The Scarlet Pimpernel, 1955; The Expert, 1968-70. Has appeared on TV in England, Germany and France. Vice-Pres. British Actors' Equity Assoc., 1963-65 and 1975-. *Recreations:* skating and riding. *Address:* Middle Court, The Green, Hampton Court, Surrey. *T:* 01-977 4030. *Club:* Garrick.

GORING, Sir William (Burton Nigel), 13th Bt, *cr* 1627; Member of London Stock Exchange since 1963; *b* 21 June 1933; *s* of Major Frederick Yelverton Goring (*d* 1938) (6th *s* of 11th Bt) and Freda Margaret, *o d* of N. V. Ainsworth, 2 Closewalks, Midhurst, Sussex; *S* uncle, Sir Forster Gurney Goring, 12th Bt, 1956; *m* 1960, Hon. Caroline Thellusson, *d* of 8th Baron Rendlesham, *qv,* and of Mrs Patrick Barthropp. *Educ:* Wellington; RMA Sandhurst, Lieut, The Royal Sussex Regt. *Recreation:* bridge. *Heir: b* Edward Yelverton Combe Goring [*b* 20 June 1936; *m* 1969, Daphne Christine Sellar; two *d*]. *Address:* 89 Cornwall Gardens, SW7. *T:* 01-584 3421. *Club:* Hurlingham.

GORLEY PUTT, Samuel; see Putt, S. G.

GORMAN, John Peter, QC 1974; a Recorder of the Crown Court, since 1972; *b* 29 June 1927; *er s* of James S. Gorman, Edinburgh; *m* 1955, Avril Mary (*née* Penfold); one *s* three *d. Educ:* Stonyhurst Coll.; Balliol Coll., Oxford (MA). Called to Bar, Inner Temple, 1953; Midland and Oxford Circuit. Part-time Chm., Industrial Tribunal, 1968-73; Dep. Chm. 1969, Chm. 1972, Agricultural Lands Tribunal (E Midlands); Dep. Chm., Northants QS, 1970-71. *Recreations:* fresh air and doing something. *Address:* 2 Dr Johnson's Buildings, Temple, EC4;

Colbourne House, Ufton, Leamington Spa, Warwicks CV33 9PE. *T:* Harbury 612595. *Club:* United Oxford & Cambridge University; Coventry Golf, Gullane Golf.

GORMAN, John Reginald, CVO 1961; CBE 1974 (MBE 1959); MC 1944; Regional Manager, India, Bangladesh, Sri Lanka, British Airways, since 1975; *b* 1 Feb. 1923; *s* of Major J. K. Gorman, MC; *m* 1948, Heather, *d* of George Caruth, solicitor, Ballymena; two *s* two *d*. *Educ:* Rockport, Haileybury and ISC Portora; Glasgow Univ.; Harvard Business Sch. FCIT, FIPM. Irish Guards, 1941-46, Normandy, France, Belgium, Holland, Germany. Royal Ulster Constabulary, 1946-60; Chief of Security, BOAC, 1960-63 (incl. Royal Tour of India, 1961); Personnel Dir and Mem. Bd of Management, BOAC, 1964-69; Regional Man., Canada, 1969-75. Pres., British Canadian Trade Assoc., 1972-74; Vice-Chm., Federated Appeal of Montreal, 1973-74. Mem. N Amer. Gp, British Overseas Trade Bd. *Recreations:* gardening, country pursuits, backgammon. *Address:* 13 Aurangzeb Road, New Delhi, India. *Clubs:* Cavalry and Guards; St James (Montreal).

GORMAN, Prof. William Moore; Professor of Economics, University of London, since 1967; *b* 17 June 1923; *s* of late Richard Gorman, Lusaka, Northern Rhodesia, and Sarah Crawford Moore, Kesh, Northern Ireland; *m* 1950, Dorinda Scott. *Educ:* Foyle Coll., Derry; Trinity Coll., Dublin. Asst Lectr, 1949, Lectr, 1951, and Sen. Lectr, 1957, in Econometrics and Social Statistics, University of Birmingham; Prof. of Economics, University of Oxford, and Fellow of Nuffield Coll., Oxford, 1962-67. Vice-Pres. 1970-71, Pres. 1972, Econometric Soc. Hon. DSocSc Birmingham, 1973; Hon. DSc(SocSc) Southampton, 1974. *Publications:* articles in various economic journals. *Address:* London School of Economics, Houghton Street, WC2. *T:* 01-405 7686.

GORMANSTON, 17th Viscount *cr* 1478; **Jenico Nicholas Dudley Preston;** Baron Gormanston (UK), 1868; Premier Viscount of Ireland; *b* 19 Nov. 1939; *s* of 16th Viscount and Pamela (who *m* 2nd, 1943, M. B. O'Connor, Irish Guards; he *d* 1961, she *d* 1975), *o d* of late Capt. Dudley Hanly, and of Lady Marjorie Heath (by her 1st marriage); *S* father, who was officially presumed killed in action, France, 9 June 1940; *m* 1974, Eva Antoine Landzianowska; two *s*. *Educ:* Downside. *Heir:* s Hon. Jenico Francis Tara Preston, *b* 30 April, 1974. *Address:* 70 Waterloo Road, Ballsbridge, Dublin 4, Ireland.

GORMLEY, Joseph, OBE 1969; President, National Union of Mineworkers, since 1971; *b* 5 July 1917; *m* 1937, Sarah Ellen Mather; one *s* one *d*. *Educ:* St Oswald's Roman Catholic Sch., Ashton-in-Makerfield. Entered Mining Industry at age of 14 and was employed in practically every underground job in mining. Served as Councillor in Ashton-in-Makerfield. Elected to Nat. Exec. Cttee of Nat. Union of Mineworkers, 1958; Gen. Sec. of North Western Area, 1961, when he relinquished his appt as a JP, owing to other commitments. Mem., Nat. Exec. Cttee, Labour Party, 1963-; former Chm., Internat. Cttee, Labour Party. Member: TUC Gen. Council, 1973-; NRDC, 1977-; Energy Commn, 1977-. *Address:* 1 Springfield Grove, Sunbury-on-Thames, Middlesex.

GORONWY-ROBERTS, family name of **Baron Goronwy-Roberts.**

GORONWY-ROBERTS, Baron *cr* 1974 (Life Peer), of Caernarvon and of Ogwen in the county of Caernarvon; **Goronwy Owen Goronwy-Roberts,** PC 1968; MA; Minister of State, Foreign and Commonwealth Office, and Deputy Leader of House of Lords, since 1975; Fellow, University of Wales, since 1938; *b* 20 Sept. 1913; *yr s* of E. E. and Amelia Roberts, Bethesda, Caernarvonshire; *m* 1942, Marian Ann, *yr d* of David and Elizabeth Evans, Tresalem, Aberdare; one *s* one *d*. *Educ:* Universities of Wales and London; on Continent. Exhibitioner, BA; MA; Univ. of Wales; Research at King's College, London, and on the Continent, 1937-39. Served in Infantry, 1941; Army Reserve, 1941-. Youth Education Officer to Caernarvonshire Education Authority, 1941-44. MP (Lab) Caernarvonshire, 1945-50, Caernarvon, 1950-Feb. 1974; Mem., House of Commons Panel of Chairmen, 1963-64; Minister of State, Welsh Office, 1964-66; Dept of Education and Science, 1966-67; Minister of State, FCO, 1967-69, Bd of Trade, 1969-70; Parly Under-Sec. of State, FCO, 1974-75. Writes and broadcasts on literary and political matters. Member: Court of Governors of University Coll. of Wales and National Museum of Wales; Fabian Society; Trustee, Oppenheimer Trust for Ex-Servicemen. Chm., Regional Economic Council for Wales, 1965-. Formerly: Chm. Hughes and Son Ltd, Publishers, Wrexham; Lectr in Educn, Univ. Coll., Swansea. FRSA 1968. Hon. Freeman, Royal Borough of Caernarvon, 1972. *Recreations:* walking, music, collecting Year Books. *Address:* House of Lords, SW1.

GORST, John Michael; MP (C) Barnet, Hendon North, since 1974 (Hendon North, 1970-74); *b* 28 June 1928; *s* of Derek Charles Gorst and Tatiana (*née* Kolotinsky); *m* 1954, Noël Harington Walker; five *s*. *Educ:* Ardingly Coll.; Corpus Christi Coll., Cambridge (MA). Advertising and Public Relations Manager, Pye Ltd, 1953-63; and Public Relations Consultant, John Gorst & Associates, 1964-. Public relations adviser to: British Lion Films, 1964-65; Fedn of British Film Makers, 1964-67; Film Production Assoc. of GB, 1967-68; BALPA, 1967-69; Guy's Hosp., 1968-74. Dir, Cassius Film Productions Ltd, 1969-. Founder: Telephone Users' Assoc., 1964- (Sec. 1964-70); Local Radio Assoc. 1964 (Sec., 1964-71). Contested (C) Chester-le-Street, 1964; Bodmin, 1966. Sec., Cons. Consumer Protection Cttee, 1973-74. *Recreation:* chess. *Address:* House of Commons, SW1A 0AA. *Club:* Garrick.

GORT, 8th Viscount (Ire.), *cr* 1816; **Colin Leopold Prendergast Vereker,** JP; Baron Kiltarton 1810; company director; *b* 21 June 1916; *s* of Commander Leopold George Prendergast Vereker, RD, RNR (*d* 1937) (*g s* of 4th Viscount) and Helen Marjorie Campbell (*d* 1958); *S* kinsman, 1975; *m* 1946, Bettine Mary Mackenzie, *d* of late Godfrey Greene; two *s* one *d*. *Educ:* Sevenoaks. Trained at Air Service Training, Hamble, in Aeronautical Engineering, etc., 1937-39; served Fleet Air Arm, 1939-45 (despatches). Member of House of Keys, IOM, 1966-71. JP IOM 1962. *Recreations:* golf, gardening. *Heir:* er s Hon. Foley Robert Standish Prendergast Vereker, *b* 24 Oct. 1951. *Address:* Westwood, The Crofts, Castletown, Isle of Man. *T:* Castletown 2545. *Club:* Carlton.

GORTON, Rt. Hon. Sir John (Grey), PC 1968; GCMG 1977; CH 1971; MA; *b* 1911; *m* 1935, Bettina, *d* of G. Brown, Bangor, Me, USA; two *s* one *d*. *Educ:* Geelong Gram. Sch.; Brasenose Coll., Oxford (MA, Hon. Fellow, 1968). Orchardist. Enlisted RAAF, Nov. 1940; served in UK, Singapore, Darwin, Milne Bay; severely wounded in air ops; discharged with rank of Flt-Lt, Dec. 1944. Councillor, Kerang Shire, 1947-52 (Pres. of Shire); Mem., Lodden Valley Regional Cttee. Senator for State of Victoria, Parlt of Commonwealth of Australia, 1949-68 (Govt Leader in Senate, 1967-68); Minister for Navy, 1958-63; Minister Assisting the Minister for External Affairs, 1960-63 (Actg Minister during periods of absence overseas of Minister); Minister in Charge of CSIRO, 1962-68; Minister for Works and, under Prime Minister, Minister in Charge of Commonwealth Activities in Educn and Research, 1963-66; Minister for Interior, 1964-66; Minister for Works, 1966-67; Minister for Educn and Science, 1966-68; MHR (L) for Higgins, Vic, 1968-75; Prime Minister of Australia, 1968-71; Minister for Defence, and Dep. Leader of Liberal Party, March-Aug. 1971; Mem. Parly Liberal Party Exec., and Liberal Party Spokesman on Environment and Conservation and Urban and Regional Develt, 1973-75; Dep. Chm., Jt Parly Cttee on Prices, 1973-75. Contested Senate election (Ind.), ACT, Dec. 1975. *Address:* 8 Hamelin Crescent, Narrabundah, ACT 2604, Australia.

GOSCHEN, family name of **Viscount Goschen.**

GOSCHEN, 4th Viscount *cr* 1900; **Giles John Harry Goschen;** *b* 16 Nov. 1965; *s* of 3rd Viscount Goschen, KBE, and of Alvin Moyanna Lesley, *yr d* of late Harry England, Durban, Natal; *S* father, 1977. *Address:* Hilton House, Crowthorne, Berks.

GOSCHEN, Sir Edward (Christian), 3rd Bt, *cr* 1916; DSO 1944; Rifle Brigade; *b* 2 Sept. 1913; *er s* of Sir Edward Henry Goschen, 2nd Bt, and Countess Mary, 7th *d* of Count Danneskiold, Samsoe, Denmark; *S* father, 1933; *m* 1946, Cynthia, *d* of late Rt Hon. Sir Alexander Cadogan, PC, OM, GCMG, KCB; one *s* one *d*. *Educ:* Eton; Trinity Coll., Oxford. Mem., Stock Exchange Council (Dep. Chm., 1968-71). Commonwealth War Graves Comr, 1977-. *Heir:* s Edward Alexander Goschen, *b* 13 March 1949. *Address:* Lower Farm House, Hampstead Norreys, Newbury, Berks RG16 0SG. *T:* Hermitage 201270.

GOSFORD, 7th Earl of, *cr* 1806; **Charles David Nicholas Alexander John Sparrow Acheson;** Bt (NS) 1628; Baron Gosford 1776; Viscount Gosford 1785; Baron Worlingham (UK) 1835; Baron Acheson (UK) 1847; *b* 13 July 1942; *o s* of 6th Earl of Gosford, OBE, and Francesca Augusta, *er d* of Francesco Cagiati, New York; *S* father, 1966. *Educ:* Harrow; Byam Shaw Sch. of drawing and painting; Royal Academy Schs. *Heir:* u Hon. Patrick Bernard Victor Montagu Acheson [*b* 4 Feb. 1915; *m* 1946, Judith, *d* of Mrs F. B. Bate, Virginia, USA; three *s* two *d*].

GOSLING, Sir Arthur Hulin, KBE 1955; CB 1950; BSc; FRSE; FRICS; Director-General, Forestry Commission, 1948-62, retired; *b* 26 July 1901; 5th *s* of late C. F. Gosling; *m* 1931, Jane Alexander (*d* 1969), *o d* of late Dr M. Bryson. *Educ:* Bell's

Gram. Sch., Coleford, Glos; Edinburgh Univ. District Officer, Forestry Commission, 1928; Divisional Officer, Glasgow, 1938; Asst Comr, Scotland, 1940; Dep. Dir Gen., 1947. Chm. Commonwealth Forestry Assoc., 1963-72. *Address:* The Old Manse, Cerne Abbas, Dorset. *Club:* Athenæum.

GOSLING, Sir Donald, Kt 1976; Joint Chairman, National Car Parks Ltd, since 1950; Chairman, Palmer & Harvey Ltd, since 1967; Director, Lovell Holdings Ltd, since 1975; *b* 2 March 1929; *m* 1959, Elizabeth Shauna, *d* of Dr Peter Ingram and Lecky Ingram; three *s*. Joined RN, 1944; served Mediterranean, HMS Leander. Member: Council of Management, White Ensign Assoc. Ltd, 1970-; Council, World of Property Housing Trust, 1976-; Queen's Silver Jubilee Appeal, Camden, 1977; Chm., Selective Employment Scheme, 1976-; Trustee, Fleet Air Arm Museum, Yeovilton, 1974-. *Recreations:* swimming, sailing, shooting. *Address:* 60 Charlotte Street, W1P 2BB. *T:* 01-637 9191. *Clubs:* Royal Thames Yacht, Royal London Yacht, Royal Naval Sailing Association, Thames Sailing; Saints and Sinners.

GOSLING, Col Richard Bennett, OBE 1957; TD 1947; DL; Chairman, Hearne & Co., since 1971; *b* 4 Oct. 1914; 2nd *s* of late T. S. Gosling, Dynes Hall, Halstead; *m* 1950, Marie Terese Ronayne (*d* 1976), Castle Redmond, Co. Cork; one adopted *s* one adopted *d* (one *s* decd). *Educ:* Eton; Magdalene Coll., Cambridge (MA). CEng, FIMechE, MIMC. Served with Essex Yeomanry, RHA, 1939-45; CO, 1953-56; Dep. CRA, East Anglian Div., 1956-58. Dir-Gen., British Agricl Export Council, 1971-73. Chm., Constructors, 1965-68; Director: P-E International, 1956-76; Doulton & Co., 1962-72; Revertex Chemicals, 1974-. DL Essex, 1954. French Croix de Guerre, 1944. *Recreations:* country pursuits, overseas travel. *Address:* Canterburys, Margaretting, Essex. *T:* Ingatestone 3073. *Clubs:* Bath, MCC; Beefsteak (Chelmsford).

GOSNAY, Maxwell; His Honour Judge Gosnay; a Circuit Judge, since 1973; *b* 31 July 1923; *o s* of William and Milly Gertrude Gosnay; *m* 1959, Constance Ann, *d* of Ben and Constance Mary Hardy; one *s* one *d. Educ:* Leeds Grammar Sch.; Christ Church, Oxford (MA). Called to Bar, Inner Temple, 1945. Asst Recorder, Leeds, 1965-71; Deputy Licensing Authority, Yorks Traffic Comrs, 1965-72; Dep. Chm., WR Yorks QS, 1967-71; a Recorder, 1972-73. *Recreations:* golf, reading. *Address:* 25 Park Lane, Leeds LS8 2EX. *T:* Leeds 663066.

GOSS, Brig. Leonard George, CB 1946; *b* 30 May 1895; *s* of Alfred Herbert Goss, Wellington, NZ; *m* 1920, Ella May, *d* of John Airth Mace, New Plymouth, NZ; one *d. Educ:* New Plymouth Boys' High Sch. (NZ); RMC of Australia. Commissioned in NZ Staff Corps, Lieut 1916; Captain 1919; Major, 1935; Lt-Col 1939; Temp. Brig. 1942. *Recreations:* Rugby, cricket, swimming, boxing. *Address:* 17 Waitui Crescent, Lower Hutt, NZ. *Club:* United Service (Wellington, NZ).

GOSS, Richard Oliver; Under-Secretary, Department of Industry, since 1974; *b* 4 Oct. 1929; *s* of late Leonard Arthur Goss and Hilda Nellie Goss (*née* Casson); *m* Lesley Elizabeth Thurbon; two *s* one *d. Educ:* Christ's Coll., Finchley; HMS Worcester; King's Coll., Cambridge. Master Mariner 1956; BA 1958; MA 1961; FCIT 1970; MNI (Founder) 1972; FNI 1977. Merchant Navy (apprentice and executive officer), 1947-55; NZ Shipping Co. Ltd, 1958-63; Economic Consultant (Shipping, Shipbuilding and Ports), MoT, 1963-64; Econ. Adviser, BoT (Shipping), 1964-67; Sen. Econ. Adviser (Shipping, Civil Aviation, etc), 1967-74; Econ. Adviser to Cttee of Inquiry into Shipping (Rochdale Cttee), 1967-70. Nuffield/Leverhulme Travelling Fellow, 1977-78. Governor, Plymouth Polytechnic, 1973-; Mem. Council: RINA, 1969-; Nautical Inst. (from foundn until 1976); Member: CNAA Nautical Studies Bd, 1971-; CNAA Transport Bd, 1976-. *Publications:* Studies in Maritime Economics, 1968; (with C. D. Jones) The Economies of Size in Dry Bulk Carriers, 1971; (with M. C. Mann, et al) The Cost of Ships' Time, 1974; Advances in Maritime Economics, 1977; papers in various jls, transactions and to conferences. *Recreations:* sailing, gliding, photography, bar billiards. *Address:* 1 Broadfields, Harpenden, Herts AL5 2HJ. *T:* Harpenden 5983. *Club:* Fishers' Green Sailing.

GOSS, Very Rev. Thomas Ashworth; Dean of Jersey, since 1971; *b* 27 July 1912; *s* of George Woolnough Goss and Maud M. (*née* Savage); *m* 1946, Frances Violet Patience Frampton; one *s* one *d. Educ:* Shardlow Hall; Aldenham Sch.; St Andrews Univ. (MA). Deacon, 1937; Priest, 1938; Curate of Frodingham, 1937-41. Chaplain, RAFVR, 1941-47 (PoW Japan, 1942-45). Vicar of Sutton-le-Marsh, 1947-51; Chaplain, RAF, 1951-67; QHC, 1966-67. Rector of St Saviour, Jersey, 1967-71. *Recreations:* gardening, theatricals. *Address:* The Deanery, Jersey, CI. *T:*

Jersey Central 20001. *Clubs:* Royal Air Force; Victoria, Royal Commonwealth, Commonwealth Parliamentary, Société Jersiaise (Jersey).

GOSTLING, Maj.-Gen. Philip le M. S. S.; *see* Stonhouse-Gostling.

GOTHARD, Sir Clifford (Frederic), Kt 1959; OBE 1956; JP; Chartered Accountant in practice, Coxon, Bannister & Gothard, Burton-on-Trent, since 1925; Chairman: Marston, Thompson & Evershed, Ltd; Burton Daily Mail Ltd; The Portland Motor Group Ltd and Subsidiaries, etc; has estate at Drakelowe, Derbyshire; *b* 9 June 1893; *s* of Frederic Gothard and Mary Gothard (*née* Startin); *m* 1961, Margaret Vera Hall, *Educ:* Burton-on-Trent Grammar Sch.; Birmingham Univ. BScEng 1915. Served European War, 1914-18, Royal Artillery (Captain). Institute of Chartered Accountants: Associate, 1924; Fellow 1929. His interests include religious, educational, agricultural bodies. District Staff Officer, Midland Command, with rank of Squadron-Leader; supervised Air Training Corps Units, 1939/45. Mem. of certain special cttees of Assoc. of British Chambers of Commerce, etc; Pres., Burton Div. Conservative Assoc., 1973- (Chm., 1945-73); Vice-Pres., West Midlands Union of Conservative and Unionist Assocs; Mem., Conservative Commonwealth and Overseas Council. JP for County Borough, Burton-on-Trent, 1940-. Life Member: Royal Agricultural Society of England, 1921-; Canadian Chamber of Commerce in Great Britain (Inc.). Court of Governors: Birmingham Univ. (Life Gov.); Keele Univ. *Recreations:* travel, shooting, fishing, sailing, gardening, reading. *Address:* Bearwood House, Burton-on-Trent, Staffs. *T:* 63112, (office) 64866. *Club:* Abbey (Burton-on-Trent).

GOTLEY, Roger Alwyn H.; *see* Henniker-Gotley.

GOTTLIEB, Bernard, CB 1970; Secretariat, Royal Commission on the Distribution of Wealth and Incomes, since 1974; *b* 1913; *s* of late James Gottlieb and Pauline (*née* Littaur); *m* 1955, Sybil N. Epstein; one *s* one *d. Educ:* Haberdashers' Hampstead Sch.; Queen Mary Coll., London Univ. BSc First Class Maths, 1932. Entered Civil Service as an Executive Officer in Customs and Excise, 1932. Air Ministry, 1938; Asst Private Sec., 1941, and Private Sec., 1944, to Permanent Under-Sec. of State (late Sir Arthur Street), Control Office for Germany and Austria, 1945; Asst Sec., 1946. Seconded to National Coal Board, 1946; Min. of Power, 1950; Under-Sec., 1961, Dir of Establishments, 1965-69; Under-Sec., Min. of Posts and Telecommunications, 1969-73; Pay Board Secretariat, 1973-74. Gwilym Gibbon Research Fellow, Nuffield Coll., Oxford, 1952-53. *Address:* 49 Gresham Gardens, NW11. *T:* 01-455 5482. *Club:* Reform.

GOTTMANN, Prof. Jean, FRGS; FBA 1977; Professor of Geography, University of Oxford, since 1968; Fellow of Hertford College, Oxford, 1968; *b* 10 Oct. 1915; *s* of Elie Gottmann and Sonia-Fanny Ettinger Gottmann; *m* 1957, Bernice Adelson. *Educ:* Lycée Montaigne; Lycée St Louis; Sorbonne. Research Asst Human Geography, Sorbonne, 1937-40; Mem., Inst. for Advanced Study, Princeton, NJ, several times, 1942-65; Lectr, then Associate Prof. in Geography, Johns Hopkins Univ., Baltimore, 1943-48; Dir of Studies and Research, UN Secretariat, NY, 1946-47; Chargé de Recherches, CNRS, Paris, 1948-51; Lectr, then Prof., Institut d'Etudes Politiques, University of Paris, 1948-56; Research Dir, Twentieth Century Fund, NY, 1956-61; Prof. Ecole des Hautes Etudes, Sorbonne, 1960-. Pres., World Soc. for Ekistics, 1971-73. Governor, Univ. of Haifa, 1972-. Hon. Mem., Royal Netherlands Geog. Soc., 1963; For. Hon. Mem., Amer. Acad. of Arts and Sciences, 1972. Hon. LLD Wisconsin, 1968; Hon. DSc S Illinois, 1969. Charles Daly Medal of Amer. Geograph. Soc., 1964; Prix Bonaparte-Wyse, 1962; Palmes Académiques, 1968, etc. Chevalier, Légion d'Honneur, 1974. *Publications:* Relations Commerciales de la France, 1942; L'Amérique, 1949 (3rd edn 1960); A Geography of Europe, 1950 (4th edn 1969); La politique des Etats et leur géographie, 1952; Virginia at Mid-century, 1955; Megalopolis, 1961; Essais sur l'Aménagement de l'Espace habité, 1966; The Significance of Territory, 1973. *Address:* 19 Belsyre Court, Woodstock Road, Oxford. *T:* Oxford 57076.

GOUDGE, Elizabeth de Beauchamp; FRSL 1945; *b* 24 April 1900; *d* of late Henry Leighton Goudge, Regius Professor of Divinity in the University of Oxford, and late Ida de Beauchamp Collenette; unmarried. *Educ:* Grassendale, Southbourne; Reading Univ. Writer of novels, children's books, short stories and plays. *Publications: novels:* Island Magic, 1932; The Middle Window, 1933; A City of Bells, 1934; Towers in the Mist, 1936; The Bird in the Tree, 1939; The Castle on the Hill, 1942; Green Dolphin Country, 1944; The Herb of Grace, 1948; Gentian Hill,

1950; The Heart of the Family, 1953; The Rosemary Tree, 1956; The White Witch, 1958; The Dean's Watch, 1960; The Scent of Water, 1963; The Child from the Sea, 1970; *collections of short stories:* Make-Believe, 1949; The Reward of Faith, 1950; White Wings, 1952; The Lost Angel, 1971; *plays:* Three Plays, 1937; *Children's books:* Smokey House, 1938; Henrietta's House (in America: The Blue Hills), 1942; The Little White Horse, 1946 (awarded Carnegie Medal for 1947); The Valley of Song, 1951; Linnets and Valerians, 1964; *biography:* God so Loved the World (Life of Christ), 1951; St Francis of Assisi, 1959; *autobiography:* The Joy of the Snow, 1974; Anthology of Verse and Prose: A Book of Comfort, 1964; 2nd Anthology of Verse and Prose: A Book of Peace, 1967; 3rd Anthology of Verse and Prose: A Book of Faith, 1976. *Recreations:* reading and gardening. *Address:* Rose Cottage, Peppard Common, Henley-on-Thames, Oxon.

GOUDIE, Rev. John Carrick, CBE 1972; on staff of St Columba's, Church of Scotland, Pont Street, since 1973; Principal Chaplain, Church of Scotland and Free Churches (Naval), 1970-73; *b* 25 Dec. 1919; *s* of late Rev. John Goudie, MA and late Mrs Janet Goudie, step *s* of late Mrs Evelyn Goudie; unmarried. *Educ:* Glasgow Academy; Glasgow Univ. (MA); Trinity Coll., Glasgow. Served in RN: Hostilities Only Ordinary Seaman and later Lieut RNVR, 1941-45; returned to Trinity Coll., Glasgow to complete studies for the Ministry, 1945; Asst Minister at Crown Court Church of Scotland, London and ordained, 1947-50; Minister, The Union Church, Greenock, 1950-53; entered RN as Chaplain, 1953. QHC 1970-73. *Recreations:* tennis, the theatre. *Address:* 304 Hawkins House, Dolphin Square, SW1V 3NT. *T:* 01-828 2806. *Club:* Army and Navy.

GOUDIE, Hon. William Henry, MC 1944; Executive Director and Deputy Chairman, Law Reform Commission of Tasmania, since 1974; *b* 21 Aug. 1916; *s* of Henry and Florence Goudie; *m* 1948, Mourilyan Isobel Munro; two *s.* *Educ:* Bristol Grammar School. Solicitor (England), 1938; called to Bar, Gray's Inn, 1952. War service, 1939-45, London Scottish Regt and Som LI; JAG's Dept, 1945-48; Prosecutor, Dep. JA, Officer i/c branches Italy, Greece, Austria; Officer i/c Legal Section War Crimes Gp, SE Europe; Sen. Resident Magistrate, Acting Judge, Kenya, 1948-63; Puisne Judge, Aden, 1963-66; Puisne Judge, Uganda (Contract), 1967-71; Puisne Judge, Fiji (Contract), 1971-73. Editor, Kenya and Aden Law Reports. *Recreations:* golf, swimming. *Address:* 24 Nimala Street, Rosny, Hobart, Tasmania 7018, Australia. *Club:* Royal Commonwealth Society.

GOUGH, family name of Viscount Gough.

GOUGH, 5th Viscount (of Goojerat, of the Punjaub, and Limerick), *cr* 1849; **Shane Hugh Maryon Gough;** Irish Guards, 1961-67; *b* 26 Aug. 1941; *o s* of 4th Viscount Gough and Margaretta Elizabeth (*d* 1977), *o d* of Sir Spencer Maryon-Wilson, 11th Bt; *S* father 1951. *Educ:* Abberley Hall, Worcs; Winchester Coll. Mem. Queen's Bodyguard for Scotland, Royal Company of Archers. *Heir:* none. *Address:* Keppoch Estate Office, Strathpeffer, Ross-shire, IV14 9AD. *T:* Strathpeffer 224; 17 Stanhope Gardens, SW7 5RQ. *T:* 01-370 3569. *Clubs:* Pratt's, White's; MCC.

GOUGH, Cecil Ernest Freeman, CMG 1956; Director and Secretary, British Property Federation, since 1974; Secretary, Associated Owners of City Properties, since 1975; *b* 29 Oct. 1911; *s* of Ernest John Gough; *m* 1938, Gwendolen Lily Miriam Longman; one *s* one *d.* *Educ:* Southend High Sch.; London Sch. of Economics (evening student) (School of Economics Scholar in Law, 1932). LLB 1934. Asst Examiner Estate Duty Office, Board of Inland Revenue, 1930; Air Ministry, 1938; Principal, 1944; Ministry of Defence, 1947; Asst Sec., 1949; on loan to Foreign Office, as Counsellor, United Kingdom Delegation to NATO, Paris, 1952-56; Chairman: NATO Infrastructure Cttee, 1952-53; Standing Armaments Cttee Western European Union, 1956; returned Ministry of Defence, 1956; Under-Sec., 1958; Under-Sec. at the Admiralty, 1962-64; Asst Under-Sec. of State, Min. of Defence, 1964-68. Man. Dir, Airwork (Overseas) Ltd, 1968-71; Dir, Airwork Services Ltd and Air Holdings Ltd, 1968-73. Medal of Freedom (USA), 1947; Coronation Medal, 1953. *Recreations:* cookery, gardening, reading, travel. *Address:* 13 Canonbury Park South, N1. *T:* 01-226 6378. *Club:* Naval and Military.

GOUGH, Brig. Guy Francis, DSO; MC; late Royal Irish Fusiliers; *b* 9 Aug. 1893; *e s* of late Hugh George Gough, Hyderabad, Deccan; *m* 1st, 1914, Dorothy (*d* 1953), *d* of late Edwin Paget Palmer, Castham House, Sussex; one *s* one *d*; *m* 2nd, 1954, Elizabeth Treharn, *d* of Lewis David Thomas, Newton, near Porthcawl. *Educ:* The Oratory Sch.; RMC

Sandhurst. 2nd Lieut, Royal Irish Fusiliers, Aug. 1914; European War, 1914-18. France and Belgium with 1st Royal Irish Fusiliers, and on the Staff (wounded, despatches, MC, 1915 Star); Staff Course, 1916. Commanded 1st Bn Nigeria Regt, 1936-37; War of 1939-45: Commanded ITC Royal Irish Fusiliers, 1st Battalion Royal Irish Fusiliers (in France and Belgium, May 1940), 202nd and 11th Infantry Brigades, Advanced Base I Army (N Africa), North Aldershot Sub-District. DSO, 1939-45 Star, Africa Star (with 1st Army clasp); retd pay, 1946. Control Commission, Germany as a Senior Control Officer, 1947-48. Coronation Medal, 1937. *Recreation:* fly-fishing. *Address:* Glyn Deri, Talybont-on-Usk, near Brecon, Powys LD3 7YP.

GOUGH, Rt. Rev. Hugh Rowlands, CMG 1965; OBE (mil.) 1945; TD 1950; DD Lambeth; *b* 19 Sept. 1905; *o s* of late Rev. Charles Massey Gough, Rector of St Ebbe's, Oxford; *m* 1929, Hon. Madeline Elizabeth, *d* of 12th Baron Kinnaird, KT, KBE; one *d.* *Educ:* Weymouth Coll.; Trinity Coll., Cambridge; London Coll. Divinity. BA 1927, MA Cantab 1931. Deacon, 1928; Priest, 1929; Curate of St Mary, Islington, 1928-31; Perpetual Curate of St Paul, Walcot, Bath, 1931-34; Vicar of St James, Carlisle, 1934-39; Chaplain to High Sheriff of Cumberland, 1937; CF (TA), 1937-45; Chaplain to 4th Bn The Border Regt, 1937-39; Vicar of St Matthew, Bayswater 1939-46; Chaplain to 1st Bn London Rifle Bde, 1939-43; served Western Desert and Tunisia (wounded); Senior Chap. to 1st Armd Div., Tunisia, 1943; DACG 10 Corps, Italy, 1943-45 (despatches); DACG, North Midland Dist, 1945. Hon. Chaplain to the Forces (2nd cl.) 1945. Vicar of Islington, Rural Dean of Islington, 1946-48. Preb. St Paul's Cathedral, 1948; Suffragan Bishop of Barking, 1948-59; Archdeacon of West Ham, 1948-58; Archbishop of Sydney and Primate of Australia, also Metropolitan of New South Wales, 1959-66, retired, 1966. Rector of Freshford, dio. of Bath and Wells, 1967-72; Vicar of Limpley Stoke, 1970-72. Chaplain and Sub-Prelate, Order of St John of Jerusalem, 1959-72. Formerly Member Council: London Coll. of Divinity, Clifton Theol. Coll. (Chm.), Haileybury Coll., Monkton Combe Sch., St Lawrence Coll. (Ramsgate), Chigwell Sch., Stowe Sch., Kingham Hill Trust. Pres. Conference, Haberdashers' Co., 1953 and 1955. Pres. Conference, Educational Assoc., 1956. Mem., Essex County Education Cttee, 1949-59; DL Essex, 1952-59. Hon. DD Wycliffe Coll., Toronto; Hon. ThD, Aust. *Recreations:* shooting, tennis. *Address:* 20 Sion Hill, Bath, Avon BA1 2UJ. *T:* Bath 313660. *Club:* National.

GOUGH, Prof. Jethro; Professor of Pathology, Welsh National School of Medicine, Cardiff, 1948-69, retired; *b* 29 Dec. 1903; *s* of Jabez and Ellen Gough; *m* 1933, Anne (*née* Thomas); two *s.* *Educ:* Mountain Ash County Sch.; Welsh National Sch. of Medicine, Cardiff. BSc, 1924; MRCS, LRCP, 1926; MB, BCh, 1927; MD, 1930; FRCP 1967; Founder FRCPath (Vice-Pres. 1966-68). Demonstrator in Pathology, Cardiff, 1927, Manchester Univ., 1928; Lecturer in Pathology, Cardiff, 1929; Senior Lecturer, Cardiff, 1933. *Publications:* on several subjects relating to Pathology, but especially silicosis and allied conditions. *Address:* 22 Park Road, Whitchurch, Cardiff CF4 7BQ. *T:* Cardiff 65011.

GOUGH, John, CBE 1972; Director of Administration, and Secretary, Confederation of British Industry, 1965-74; *b* 18 June 1910; *o s* of H. E. and M. Gough; *m* 1939, Joan Renee Cooper; one *s* one *d.* *Educ:* Repton Sch.; Keble Coll., Oxford. BA 1st cl. hons History. Senior History Tutor, Stowe Sch., 1933; Fedn of British Industries: Personal Asst to Dir, 1934; Asst Sec., 1940; Sec., 1959; Dir of Administration and Sec., CBI, 1965. *Recreations:* walking, reading, music. *Address:* West Yard, North Bovey, Newton Abbot, Devon. *T:* Moretonhampstead 395. *Club:* Reform.

GOUGH-CALTHORPE, family name of Baron Calthorpe.

GOULBURN; *see* Canberra-Goulburn.

GOULBURN, Maj.-Gen. Edward Henry, DSO and Bar 1944; DL; *b* 27 May 1903; *s* of late Brig.-Gen. C. E. Goulburn, DSO, and of Grace Ethel, *d* of late W. H. Foster, Apley Park, Bridgnorth, Salop. *Educ:* Eton and Sandhurst. Grenadier Guards, 1924; Adjutant, 1st Bn, 1931-34; Adjutant, RMC, Sandhurst, 1938-40; OC 1st Bn Gren. Guards in France, Belgium and Holland, 1942-44; Brigadier Cmdg 8th British Infantry Bde Holland and Germany, 1944-45; 1st Guards Bde, Palestine, 1945-46; Maj.-Gen. Cmdg Allied Military Mission to Italian Army, 1946-47; Lt-Col Comdg Gren. Guards, 1948-50. DL Surrey, 1962. Comdr Order of Orange Nassau. *Recreations:* farming, sport, travel. *Address:* Betchworth House, Betchworth, Surrey. *T:* Betchworth 3315. *Clubs:* Turf, Pratt's. Pratt's.

GOULD, Bryan Charles; MP (Lab) Southampton Test, since Oct. 1974; *b* 11 Feb. 1939; *s* of Charles Terence Gould and Elsie May Driller; *m* 1967, Gillian Anne Harrigan; one *s* one *d*. *Educ:* Auckland Univ. (BA, LLM); Balliol Coll., Oxford (MA, BCL). HM Diplomatic Service: FO, 1964-66; HM Embassy, Brussels, 1966-68; Fellow and Tutor in Law, Worcester Coll., Oxford, 1968-74. *Recreations:* gardening, food, wine. *Address:* 10 Furzedown Road, Southampton SO2 1PN. *T:* Southampton 552427.

GOULD, Cecil Hilton Monk; Keeper and Deputy Director of the National Gallery since 1973; *b* 24 May 1918; *s* of late Lieut Commander R. T. Gould and of Muriel Hilda Estall. *Educ:* Westminster Sch. Served in Royal Air Force: France, 1940; Middle East, 1941-43; Italy, 1943-44; Normandy, Belgium and Germany, 1944-46. National Gallery: Asst Keeper, 1946; Dep. Keeper, 1962. FRSA, 1968. *Publications:* An Introduction to Italian Renaissance Painting, 1957; Trophy of Conquest, 1965; Leonardo da Vinci, 1975; The Paintings of Correggio, 1976; various publications for the National Gallery, including 16th century Italian Schools catalogue; articles in Encyclopædia Britannica, Chambers's Encyclopedia, Dizionario Biografico degli Italiani, and specialist art journals of Europe and USA. *Recreations:* music, ski-ing. *Address:* 6 Palace Gate, W8. *T:* 01-584 9151. *Club:* Reform.

GOULD, Donald (William), BSc (Physiol.), MRCS, DTM&H; writer and broadcaster on medical and scientific affairs; Medical Correspondent, New Statesman, since 1966; *b* 26 Jan. 1919; *s* of late Rev. Frank J. Gould; *m* 1st, 1940, Edna Forsyth; three *s* four *d*; 2nd, 1969, Jennifer Goodfellow; one *s* one *d*. *Educ:* Mill Hill Sch.; St Thomas's Hosp. Med. Sch., London. Orthopædic House Surg., Botley's Park Hosp., 1942; Surg. Lieut, RNVR, 1942-46; Med. Off., Hong Kong Govt Med. Dept, 1946-48; Lectr in Physiol., University of Hong Kong, 1948-51, Sen. Lectr, 1951-57; King Edward VII Prof. of Physiol., University of Malaya (Singapore), 1957-60; Lectr in Physiol., St Bartholomew's Hosp. Med. Coll., London, 1960-61, Sen. Lectr, 1961-63; External Examr in Physiol., University of Durham (Newcastle), 1961-63; Dep. Ed., Medical News, 1963-65; Editor: World Medicine, 1965-66; New Scientist, 1966-69. Chm., Med. Journalists' Assoc., 1967-71; Vice-Chm., Assoc. of British Science Writers, 1970-71. *Publications:* contributions to: Experimentation with Human Subjects, 1972; Ecology, the Shaping Enquiry, 1972; Better Social Services, 1973; scientific papers in physiological jls; numerous articles on medical politics, ethics and science in lay and professional press. *Recreations:* writing poems nobody will publish, listening, talking, and occasionally walking. *Address:* 15 Waterbeach Road, Landbeach, Cambs CB4 4EA. *T:* Cambridge 861243.

GOULD, Maj.-Gen. John Charles, CB 1975; Paymaster-in-Chief and Inspector of Army Pay Services, 1972-75, retired; *b* 27 April 1915; *s* of late Alfred George Webb and Hilda Gould; *m* 1941, Mollie Bannister; one *s* one *d*. *Educ:* Brighton, Hove and Sussex Grammar School. Surrey and Sussex Yeomanry (TA), 1937; Royal Army Pay Corps, 1941; served: N Africa, Sicily, Italy (despatches), Austria, 1941-46; Egypt, Jordan, Eritrea, 1948-51; Singapore, 1957-59; Dep. Paymaster-in-Chief, 1967-72. *Recreations:* golf, sailing. *Address:* Squirrels Wood, Ringles Cross, near Uckfield, East Sussex. *T:* Uckfield 4592. *Clubs:* Lansdowne, MCC.

GOULD, Patricia, RRC 1972; QHNS 1976; Matron-in-Chief, Queen Alexandra's Royal Naval Nursing Service, since 1976; *b* 27 May 1924; *d* of Arthur Wellesley Gould. *Educ:* Marist Convent, Paignton. Lewisham Gen. Hosp., SRN, 1945; Hackney Hosp., CMB Pt I, 1946; entered QARNNS, as Nursing Sister, 1948; accepted for permanent service, 1954; Matron, 1966; Principal Matron, 1970; Principal Matron Naval Hosps, 1975. OStJ (Officer Sister), 1973. *Recreations:* gardening, photography. *Address:* 18 Park Road, Denmead, Portsmouth PO7 6NE. *T:* Waterlooville 55499; Ministry of Defence (Naval), Empress State Building, SW6. *T:* 01-385 1244, extension 2091.

GOULD, R(alph) Blair, MB, ChB Sheffield; DA (England); FFARCS; physician, anæsthetist; Fellow Royal Society of Medicine (Member Section of Anæsthetists); Fellow, Internat. College of Anæsthetists, USA; Fellow, Association of Anæsthetists of Great Britain; Hon. Consultant Anæsthetist: St George's Hospital; Royal Throat Nose and Ear Hospital; *b* Edinburgh, 15 May 1904; *o s* of late Maurice Gould, Bournemouth. *Educ:* King Edward VII Sch., Sheffield; Sheffield Univ. Held Senior Resident appointments at Jessop Hospital for Women, Sheffield; Sheffield Royal Hosp., and West London Hosp., Hammersmith; Surg., Canadian Pacific Steamship Co.; lately: Hon. Asst in the Out-patient Dept., Central London Throat, Nose and Ear Hosp.; Clinical Asst, Central London Ophthalmic Hosp.; Clinical Asst, Aural and Children's Depts, West London Hosp.; Specialist in Anæsthetics: Metropolitan Reg. Hosp. Bds, etc; EMS for London; Senior Consultant Anæsthetist: German Hosp.; Brentwood Dist Hosp.; Royal Nat. Throat Hosp.; Sch. of Dental Surgery, Royal Dental Hosp. (also Lectr); Anæsthetist to LCC and Royal Eye Hosp.; Hon. Anæsthetist: St John's Hosp., Lewisham; Romford Victoria Hosp.; Queen Mary's Hosp., Sidcup; Editor, Anæsthesia; *Publications:* various communications to the medical journals. *Recreations:* music, photography. *Address:* 25 Briardale Gardens, NW3. *T:* 01-435 2646.

GOULD, Sir Ronald, Kt 1955; General Secretary, National Union of Teachers, 1947-70; (First) President of World Confederation of Organizations of the Teaching Profession, 1952-70; Member, Community Relations Commission, 1968-73; *b* 9 Oct. 1904; *s* of late Fred Gould, OBE; *m* 1928, Nellie Denning Fish; two *s*. *Educ:* Shepton Mallet Grammar Sch.; Westminster Training Coll. Asst Master Radstock Council Sch., 1924-41; Headmaster Welton County Sch., 1941-46. Dep. Chm., ITA, 1967-72. Chm. Norton Radstock UDC, 1936-46; Pres. NUT, 1943-44; Hon. Fellow; Educational Inst. of Scotland; College of Preceptors, 1965. Hon. MA Bristol, 1943; Hon. LLD: British Columbia, 1963; McGill, 1964; St Francis Xavier, NS, 1969; Leeds 1971; DUniv. York 1972. Officier, Ordre des Palmes Académiques, 1969. *Publications:* The Changing Pattern of Education, 1965; Chalk Up the Memory (autobiog.), 1976. *Address:* Grasmere, 21 Lakenheath, Southgate, N14.

GOULD, Thomas William, VC 1942; late Lieutenant RNVR; *b* 28 Dec. 1914; *s* of late Mrs C. E. Cheeseman and late Reuben Gould (killed in action, 1916); *m* 1941, Phyllis Eileen Eldridge; one *s*. *Educ:* St James, Dover, Kent. Royal Navy, 1933-37; Submarines, 1937-45 (despatches); invalided Oct. 1945. Business Consultant, 1965-; company director. *Address:* 47 Meadowcroft, St Albans, Herts.

GOULD, Sir Trevor (Jack), Kt 1961; Justice of Appeal, Fiji Court of Appeal, since 1965; *b* 24 June 1906; *s* of Percy Clendon and Elizabeth Margaret Gould; *m* 1934, May Milne; one *s* two *d*. *Educ:* Auckland Gram. Sch.; Auckland Univ. Coll., NZ. Barrister and Solicitor, Supreme Court of New Zealand, 1928; Supreme Court of Fiji, 1934; Crown Counsel, Hong Kong, 1938; served War, 1941-45 (prisoner of war). Actg Puisne Judge, Hong Kong, 1946, Puisne Judge, 1948; Acting Chief Justice, Hong Kong, 1953-55; Senior Puisne Judge, Hong Kong, 1953-58; Justice of Appeal, Court of Appeal for Eastern Africa, 1958-63; Vice-Pres. Court of Appeal for Eastern Africa, 1963-65. *Recreation:* sports. *Address:* 21 Mount St John Avenue, Auckland 3, New Zealand. *Club:* The Northern (Auckland).

GOULDEN, Gontran Iceton, OBE 1963; TD 1946 (and 3 Clasps); FRIBA; Consultant in construction industry; *b* 5 April 1912; *s* of late H. G. R. Goulden, Canterbury, and Alice Mildred Iceton; *m* 1937, Phyllis Nancye, *d* of J. W. F. Crawfurd, Dublin; two *s* one *d*. *Educ:* St Edmund's Sch., Canterbury; Paris; London Univ. (Dipl.). Commissioned RA (TA) 1931, Capt. 1936, Major 1939; served UK, Ceylon (GSO2 to C-in-C), India and SEAC (CO 6 Indian HAA Regt I Artillery; Comd 13 AA Bde), 1939-45; T/Lieut-Col 1943; A/Brig. 1945 (despatches twice); Lieut-Col 1947, Bt Col 1953. Col 1954; Deputy Commander, an AA Brigade, 1954-58; TARO 1960; Hon. Col 452 HAA Rgt RA (TA), 1960-61; Hon. Col 254 Fd Regt RA (TA) 1964-65; Mem. Mddx TA&AFA, 1947-53. Surveyor to Wellcome Archæol. Exped. to Near East, 1934-35; Asst to Graham Dawbarn, 1935-39. Teaching staff of Architectural Association Sch. of Architecture, 1945-46. Chief Tech. Officer and Dep. Dir, the Building Centre, 1947-61, Dir, 1962-68, Dir-Gen., 1968-74, Dep. Chm., 1974-77; Governor, Building Centre Trust, 1974-. Mem. of Council AA, 1949-58 (Pres., 1956-57). Hon. Sec. Modern Architectural Research (MARS) group, 1950-53. Member: Architects Registration Council of the UK, 1954-56, 1963-64, 1971-72; RIBA Council, 1956-57, 1962-65; ARCUK/RIBA Observer Liaison Cttee of Architects of the Common Market, 1963-72; Dir, VIth Congress Intern Union of Architects, 1961; Chm. UIA and Foreign Relations Cttee, RIBA, 1962-65. Treasurer UIA, 1965-75; Mem., Franco-British Union of Architects; Honorary Corresponding Mem. Danish Architectural Assoc., 1965; Pres. International Union of Building Centres, 1962-63, Sec.-Gen. 1969-; Mem. Council, Modular Soc., 1955-59. Sec., The Architecture Club, 1958-64; Member: Min. of Transport Advisory Cttee on landscaping of trunk roads, 1963-64; Ministry of Public Building and Works Cttee on the Agrément System, 1964-65; General Council of BSI, 1964-67. Governor: St Edmund's Sch., Canterbury; St Margaret's Sch., Bushey, 1949-59. Lecturer and broadcaster on architectural subjects. Hereditary Freeman of City of Canterbury. *Publications:* Bathrooms, 1966; regular contrib. to architectural papers. *Recreations:* travel, sailing. *Address:* 28 St Peter's Square, Hammersmith, W6 9NW. *T:* 01-748 6621.

GOULDEN, Mark; Chairman, W. H. Allen & Co. Ltd, Publishers, 1939-76; Director, Howard and Wyndham Ltd, 1971-76; *b* Clifton, Bristol; 2nd *s* of late Morris and Eve Goulden; *m*; two *s* one *d.* Began journalism with Cambridge Daily News; served Royal Engineers, Managing Editor and Dir, Eastern Morning News and Hull Evening News, 1923-30; Managing Editor, Yorkshire Evening News, Leeds, 1930-32; Managing Editor Sunday Referee, 1932-36; Editor-in-Chief, Argus Press Ltd; Managing Editor, Cavalcade and other publications: Director: Illustrated Publications Ltd, Bicycle Publishing Co. Ltd; Macfadden's Magazines Ltd, 1937-40; written and lectured extensively on newspapers, advertising and publishing. British Delegate World Advertising Convention, Philadelphia, 1927; former member Nat. Council Advertising Clubs: Council Newspaper Proprietors Assoc., etc.; inventor, Gouldris Matrix Machine; a pioneer of civil aviation in England. *Recreations:* flying, motoring, golf. *Address:* 48 Lowndes Square, SW1. *Clubs:* Press, Paternosters, Savage; Players' (New York).

GOULDING, Sir Basil; *see* Goulding, Sir W. B.

GOULDING, Hon. Sir (Ernest) Irvine, Kt 1971; **Hon. Mr Justice Goulding;** Judge of the High Court of Justice, Chancery Division, since 1971; *b* 1 May 1910; *s* of late Dr Ernest Goulding; *m* 1935, Gladys, *d* of late Engineer Rear-Adm. Marrack Sennett; one *s* one *d. Educ:* Merchant Taylors' Sch., London; St Catharine's Coll., Cambridge, Hon. Fellow, 1971. Served as Instructor Officer, Royal Navy, 1931-36 and 1939-45. Called to Bar, Inner Temple, 1936; QC 1961; Bencher, Lincoln's Inn, 1966. Pres., Internat. Law Assoc., British branch. *Address:* 9 Constitution Hill, Woking, Surrey. *T:* Woking 61012. *Club:* Travellers'.

GOULDING, Lt-Col Terence Leslie Crawford P.; *see* Pierce-Goulding.

GOULDING, Sir (William) Basil, 3rd Bt *cr* 1904; Director: Fitzwilton Ltd; Bank of Ireland Ltd; Rio-Tinto Zinc Corp. Ltd; Irish Pensions Trust; *b* 4 Nov. 1909; *s* of Sir Lingard Goulding, 2nd Bt, and Nesta Violet (*d* 1968) (she *m* 2nd, 1938, Stanley Adams, who *d* 1965), *d* of late Hon. Mr Justice Wright, and *g d* of Sir Croker Barrington, 4th Bt; *S* father, 1935; *m* 1939, Valerie Hamilton, LLD (Chairman and Managing Director, Central Remedial Clinic, Dublin), *o d* of 1st Viscount Monckton of Brenchley, PC, GCVO, KCMG, MC, QC, and *g d* of Sir Thomas Colyer-Fergusson, 3rd Bt; three *s. Educ:* Winchester Coll.; Christ Church, Oxford. War of 1939-45, Wing Comdr RAFVR. *Heir: s* William Lingard Walter Goulding [*b* 11 July 1940. *Educ:* Winchester Coll.; Trinity Coll., Dublin. Headmaster of Headfort School, Kells]. *Address:* Dargle Cottage, Enniskerry, Co. Wicklow, Eire.

GOURLAY, Gen. Sir (Basil) Ian (Spencer), KCB 1973; OBE 1956 (MBE 1948); MC 1944; Chairman, International Executive Committee, United World Colleges, since 1975; *b* 13 Nov. 1920; *er s* of late Brig. K. I. Gourlay, DSO, OBE, MC; *m* 1948, Natasha Zinovieff; one *s* one *d. Educ:* Eastbourne Coll. Commissioned, RM, 1940; HMS Formidable, 1941-44; 43 Commando, 1944-45; 45 Commando, 1946-48; Instructor, RNC Greenwich, 1948-50; Adjt RMFVR, City of London, 1950-52; Instructor, RM Officers' Sch., 1952-54; psc 1954; Bde Major, 3rd Commando Bde, 1955-57 (despatches); OC RM Officers' Trng Wing, Infantry Training Centre RM, 1957-59; 2nd in Comd, 42 Commando, 1959-61; GSO1, HQ Plymouth Gp, 1961-63; CO 42 Commando, 1963-65; Col GS, Dept of CGRM, Min. of Defence, 1965-66; Col 1965; Comdr, 3rd Commando Bde, 1966-68; Maj.-Gen. Royal Marines, Portsmouth, 1968-71; Commandant-General, Royal Marines, 1971-75; Lt-Gen., 1971; Gen., 1973. Admiral, Texas Navy. Vice Patron, RM Museum. *Recreations:* do-it-yourself, watching cricket, playing at golf. *Address:* c/o Lloyds Bank Ltd, 15 Blackheath Village, SE3. *Clubs:* Army and Navy, MCC.

GOURLAY, Harry Philp Heggie, JP; MP (Lab) Kirkcaldy, since 1974 (Kirkcaldy Burghs, Oct. 1959-1974); *b* 10 July 1916; *s* of William Gourlay; *m* 1942, Margaret McFarlane Ingram; no *c. Educ:* Kirkcaldy High Sch. Coachbuilder, 1932; Vehicle Examiner, 1947. Mem. Kirkcaldy Town Council, 1946, Hon. Treasurer, 1953-57; Magistrate, 1957-59; Vice-Chm. Fife Education Cttee, 1958; Mem. Hospital Management Cttee; Sec. Kirkcaldy Burghs Constituency Labour Party, 1945-59; Mem. Estimates Cttee, 1959-64; Chm. Scottish Parly Labour Group, 1963-64 and 1976-; Government Whip, 1964-66; a Lord Comr of the Treasury, 1966-68; Dep. Speaker and Dep. Chm. of Ways

and Means, 1968-70. *Recreations:* chess, golf. *Address:* 34 Rosemount Avenue, Kirkcaldy, Fife. *T:* Kirkcaldy 61919.

GOURLAY, Gen. Sir Ian; *see* Gourlay, Gen. Sir B. I. S.

GOURLAY, Dame Janet; *see* Vaughan, Dame Janet.

GOW, Andrew Sydenham Farrar, MA; FBA 1943; Hon. DLitt (Durham); Hon LLD (Edinburgh); Fellow of Trinity College, Cambridge; on committee of National Art-Collections Fund; *b* 27 Aug. 1886; *e s* of Rev. James Gow, LittD, sometime Headmaster of Westminster, and Gertrude Sydenham, *d* of G. P. Everett-Green. *Educ:* Rugby Sch.; Trinity Coll., Cambridge. Porson Prizeman, 1906, 1907; Browne Medallist, 1907, 1908; Charles Oldham Scholar, 1909, 1910; Fellow of Trinity Coll., 1911; Asst Master at Eton Coll., 1914-25; Trinity Coll., Cambridge: Lectr, 1925-46; Tutor, 1929-42; Praelector, 1946-51; University Lectr, 1925-51; Brereton Reader in Classics, 1947-51; a Trustee of the National Gallery, 1947-53. Kenyon Medal, British Acad., 1972. *Publications:* A. E. Housman: A Sketch and List of his Writings, 1936; Letters from Cambridge (1939-1944), 1945; Theocritus (text, translation, and commentary), 2 vols, 1950, 2nd edn 1953, repr. 1965, 1974; Bucolici Graeci (Oxford Classical Texts), 1952, 2nd impression 1958; The Greek Bucolic Poets (introd. and trans.), 1953, repr. (USA), 1972; The Greek Anthology: sources and ascriptions, 1958; Machon (introd., text, and commentary), 1965; (with A. F. Scholfield) Nicander (text, trans., and notes), 1953; (with Prof. D. L. Page) The Greek Anthology: Hellenistic Epigrams (text and commentary), 2 vols, 1965; The Garland of Philip (text, translation and commentary) 2 vols, 1968; contribs to Jl of Hellenic Studies, Jl of Philology, Classical Quarterly, Classical Review, etc; editor of A. E. Housman's Manilius (edn 2), 1937, and with Prof. D. S. Robertson, of W. Ridgeway's The Early Age of Greece, vol. II, 1931. *Address:* Trinity College, Cambridge. *T:* Cambridge 58201.

GOW, Ian, TD 1970; MP (C) Eastbourne since Feb. 1974; *b* 11 Feb. 1937; *yr s* of late Dr A. E. Gow and Mrs Helen Gordon Gow; *m* 1966, Jane Elizabeth Packe; two *s. Educ:* Winchester. Solicitor 1962; Partner, Joynson-Hicks & Co., Solicitors. Contested (C): Coventry East, 1964; Clapham, 1966. *Recreations:* tennis, cricket, gardening. *Address:* The Dog House, Hankham, Pevensey, East Sussex. *T:* Eastbourne 763316; 120 Pavilion Road, SW1. *T:* 01-235 8293. *Clubs:* Cavalry and Guards, MCC.

GOW, Maj.-Gen. James Michael; Director of Army Training, Ministry of Defence, since 1975; *b* 3 June 1924; *s* of late J. C. Gow and Mrs Alastair Sanderson; *m* 1946, Jane Emily Scott; one *s* four *d. Educ:* Winchester College. Commnd Scots Guards, 1943; served NW Europe, 1944-45; Malayan Emergency, 1949; Equerry to Duke of Gloucester, 1952-53; psc 1954; Bde Major 1955-57; Regimental Adjt Scots Guards, 1957-60; Instructor Army Staff Coll., 1962-64; comd 2nd Bn Scots Guards, Kenya and England, 1964-66; GSO1, HQ London District, 1966-67; comd 4th Guards Bde, 1968-70; idc 1970; BGS (Int) HQ BAOR and ACOS G2 HQ Northag, 1971-73; GOC 4th Div. BAOR, 1973-75. Col Comdt Intelligence Corps, 1973-. Mem. Royal Company of Archers (QBGS). *Publications:* articles in mil. and hist. jls. *Recreations:* sailing, squash, shooting, music, travel, reading. *Address:* Long Vere House, Loxhill, Hascombe, Surrey. *T:* Hascombe 230. *Clubs:* Pratt's, Cavalry and Guards.

GOW, Brig. John Wesley Harper, CBE 1958 (OBE 1945); DL; JP; retired Shipowner; *b* 8 April 1898; *s* of late Leonard Gow, DL, LLD, Glasgow, and Mabel A. Harper, *d* of John W. Harper, publisher, Cedar Knoll, Long Island, NY; *m* 1925, Frances Jean, JP (*d* 1975), *d* of James Begg, Westlands, Paisley; three *s. Educ:* Cargilfield; Sedbergh; RMC Sandhurst; Trinity Coll., Oxford. Entered Scots Guards, 1917; severely wounded, France. Late partner, Gow Harrison & Co. Mem. Queen's Body Guard for Scotland (Royal Company of Archers), 1941. MFH, Lanarkshire and Renfrewshire, 1949-54; Pres. Royal Caledonian Curling Club, 1958-60; Chm. West Renfrewshire Unionist Assoc., 1947-60, Pres. 1960-68; Vice-Pres. of RNLI and Chm. Glasgow Branch, 1937-73; Mem. Council and Pres. West of Scotland Br. SS&AFA, 1955-; Vice-Chm., Erskine Hosp.; Earl Haig Fund Officers Assoc. (Scotland), 1947-75; Mem. Glasgow TA & AFA, 1947-56. Served War of 1939-45: Scots Guards, RARO; Lt-Col attached RA (LAA), NW Europe; commanded 77 AA Bde, RA (TA), 1947-48; Brig. 1948. Hon. Col 483 HAA (Blythswood) Regt RA, TA, 1951-56; Hon. Col 445 LAA Regt RA (Cameronians) TA, 1959-67, later 445 (Lowland) Regt RA (TA). DL Renfrewshire (formerly City of Glasgow), 1948; JP Renfrewshire, 1952. Lord Dean of Guild, Glasgow, 1965-67. OStJ 1969. Chevalier Order of Crown of Belgium and Croix de Guerre (Belgian), 1945. *Recreations:* curling, hunting, shooting.

Address: The Old School House, Beith Road, Howwood, Renfrewshire PA9 1AW. *T:* Kilbarchan 2503. *Clubs:* Army and Navy; Western (Glasgow); Prestwick Golf.

GOW, Neil, QC (Scot.) 1970; Sheriff of South Strathclyde, at Ayr, since 1976; *b* 24 April 1932; *s* of Donald Gow, oil merchant, Glasgow; *m* 1959, Joanna, *d* of Comdr S. D. Sutherland, Edinburgh; one *s*. *Educ:* Merchiston Castle Sch., Edinburgh; Glasgow and Edinburgh Univs. MA, LLB. Formerly Captain, Intelligence Corps (BAOR). Carnegie Scholar in History of Scots Law, 1956. Advocate, 1957-76. Standing Counsel to Min. of Social Security (Scot.), 1964-70. Contested (C): Kirkcaldy Burghs, Gen. Elections of 1964 and 1966; Edinburgh East, 1970; Mem. Regional Council, Scottish Conservative Assoc. An Hon. Sheriff of Lanarkshire, 1971. FSA (Scot.). *Publications:* A History of Scottish Statutes, 1959; Jt Editor, An Outline of Estate Duty in Scotland, 1970; numerous articles and broadcasts on legal topics and Scottish affairs. *Recreations:* golf, books, antiquities. *Address:* Old Auchenfail Hall, by Mauchline, Ayrshire. *T:* Mauchline 50822; Easter Saltoun Hall, by Pencaitland, East Lothian EH34 5OS. *Club:* Hon. Company of Edinburgh Golfers (Muirfield).

GOW, Dame Wendy; *see* Hiller, Dame Wendy.

GOW, Very Rev. William Connell; Dean of Moray, Ross and Caithness, 1960-77; Canon of St Andrew's Cathedral, Inverness, 1953-77, Hon. Canon, since 1977; Rector of St James', Dingwall, 1940-77; *b* 6 Jan. 1909; *s* of Alexander Gow, Errol, Perthshire; *m* 1938, Edith Mary, *d* of John William Jarvis, Scarborough; two *s*. *Educ:* Edinburgh Theological Coll.; Durham Univ. (LTh). Deacon, 1936; Priest, 1937; Curate St Mary Magdalene's, Dundee, 1936-39. Awarded Frihetsmedalje (by King Haakon), Norway, 1947. *Recreations:* fishing, bridge. *Address:* 14 Mackenzie Place, Maryburgh, Ross-shire.

GOWANS, Sir Gregory; *see* Gowans, Sir U. G.

GOWANS, James Learmonth, CBE 1971; FRCP 1975; FRS 1963; Secretary of the Medical Research Council, since 1977; *b* 7 May 1924; *s* of John Gowans and Selma Josefina Ljung; *m* 1956, Moyra Leatham; one *s* two *d*. *Educ:* Trinity Sch., Croydon; King's Coll. Hosp.; Lincoln Coll., Oxford. MB, BS (London) 1947; MA, DPhil (Oxford) 1953. Medical Research Council Exchange Scholar, Pasteur Institute, Paris, 1953; Staines Medical Research Fellow, Exeter Coll., Oxford, 1955-60. Fellow, St Catherine's Coll., Oxford, 1961-; Henry Dale Res. Prof. of Royal Society, 1962-77; Hon. Dir, MRC Cellular Immunology Unit, 1963-77; Member: MRC, 1965-69; Adv. Bd for Res. Councils, 1977-; Chm. Biological Research Bd, 1967-69. Hon. ScD Yale, 1966; Hon. DSc Chicago, 1971. Gairdner Foundn Award, 1968; (with J. F. A. P. Miller) Paul Ehrlich Award, 1974; Royal Medal, Royal Society, 1976. *Publications:* articles in scientific journals. *Address:* Medical Research Council, 20 Park Crescent, W1.

GOWANS, Hon. Sir (Urban) Gregory, Kt 1974; Judge of Supreme Court of Victoria, Australia, 1961-76; *b* 9 Sept. 1904; *s* of late James and Hannah Theresa Gowans; *m* 1937, Mona Ann Freeman; one *s* four *d*. *Educ:* Christian Brothers Coll., Kalgoorlie, WA; Univs of Western Australia and Melbourne. BA (WA) 1924; LLB (Melb.) 1926. Admitted Victorian Bar, 1928; QC 1949; Mem., Overseas Telecommunications Commn (Aust.), 1947-61; Lectr in Industrial Law, Melb. Univ., 1948-56. *Recreation:* bush walking. *Address:* 68 Studley Park Road, Kew, Melbourne, Australia. *T:* 86-8714. *Club:* Melbourne (Melbourne).

GOWDA, Prof. Deve Javare, (De-Ja-Gou); Vice-Chancellor, University of Mysore, 1969-76; *b* Chakkare, Bangalore, 6 July 1918; *s* of Deve Gowda; *m* 1943, Savithramma Javare Gowda; one *s* one *d*. *Educ:* Univ. of Mysore. MA Kannada, 1943. Mysore University: Lectr in Kannada, 1946; Asst Prof. of Kannada and Sec., Univ. Publications, 1955; Controller of Examinations, 1957; Principal, Sahyadri Coll., Shimoga, Mysore Univ., 1960; Prof. of Kannada Studies, 1966. Soviet Land Award, 1967. *Publications:* (as De-Ja-Gou) numerous books in Kannada; has also edited many works. *Recreations:* writing, gardening. *Address:* c/o University of Mysore, Mysore 5, India. *T:* (office) 23555, (home) 20150.

GOWENLOCK, Prof. Brian Glover, PhD, DSc; FRSE; FRIC; Professor of Chemistry, Heriot-Watt University, since 1966; *b* 9 Feb. 1926; *s* of Harry Hadfield Gowenlock and Hilda (*née* Glover); *m* 1953, Margaret L. Davies; one *s* two *d*. *Educ:* Hulme Grammar Sch., Oldham; Univ. of Manchester (BSc, MSc, PhD). DSc Birmingham. FRIC 1966; FRSE 1969. Asst Lectr in Chemistry 1948, Lectr 1951, University Coll. of Swansea; Lectr

1955, Sen. Lectr 1964, Univ. of Birmingham; Dean, Faculty of Science, Heriot-Watt Univ., 1969-72. Vis. Scientist, National Res. Council, Ottawa, 1963; Erskine Vis. Fellow, Univ. of Canterbury, NZ, 1976. Mem., UGC, 1976-. *Publications:* Experimental Methods in Gas Reactions (with Sir Harry Melville), 1964; First Year at the University (with James C. Blackie), 1964; contribs to scientific jls. *Recreations:* genealogy, foreign travel. *Address:* 49 Lygon Road, Edinburgh EH16 5QA. *T:* 031-667 8506.

GOWER; *see* Leveson Gower.

GOWER, Most Rev. Godfrey Philip, DD; *b* 5 Dec. 1899; *s* of William and Sarah Ann Gower; *m* 1932, Margaret Ethel Tanton; two *s* one *d*. *Educ:* Imperial College, University of London; St John's College, Winnipeg, University of Manitoba. Served RAF, 1918-19. Deacon 1930; Priest 1931; Rector and Rural Dean of Camrose, Alta, 1932-35; Rector of Christ Church, Edmonton, Alta, 1935-41; Exam. Chaplain to Bishop of Edmonton, 1938-41; Canon of All Saints' Cathedral, 1940-44. Chaplain, RCAF, 1941-44. Rector of St Paul's, Vancouver, 1944-51; Bishop of New Westminster, 1951-71; Archbishop of New Westminster, and Metropolitan of British Columbia, 1968-71. Holds Hon. doctorates in Divinity. *Address:* 1522 Everall Street, White Rock, BC V4B 3S8, Canada. *T:* 531-7254.

GOWER, Sir (Herbert) Raymond, Kt 1974; MP (C) Barry Division of Glamorganshire since 1951; Director: Welsh Dragon Securities Ltd, 1961-67; Broughton & Co. (Bristol) Ltd since 1961; Deane-Spence Ltd, Cranleigh and London, SW1, 1963-71; Welsh Industrial Investment Trust Ltd; journalist and broadcaster; *b* 15 Aug. 1916; *s* of late Lawford R. Gower, FRIBA, County Architect for Glamorgan, and Mrs Gower; *m* 1973, Cynthia, *d* of Mr and Mrs James Hobbs. *Educ:* Cardiff High Sch.; Univ. of Wales; Cardiff Sch. of Law. Solicitor, admitted 1944; practised Cardiff, 1948-63; Partner, S. R. Freed & Co., Harewood Place, W1, 1964-. Contested (C) Ogmore Division of Glamorgan, general election, 1950. Political Columnist for Western Mail for Cardiff, 1951-64. Parliamentary Private Secretary: to Mr Gurney Braithwaite, 1951-54, to Mr R. Maudling, 1951-52, to Mr J. Profumo, 1952-57, to Mr Hugh Molson, 1954-57, Min. of Transport and Civil Aviation, and to Minister of Works, 1957-60. Member: Speaker's Conf. on Electoral Law, 1967-69, 1971-74; Select Cttee on Expenditure, 1970-73; Treasurer, Welsh Parly Party, 1966-; Vice Chm., Welsh Cons. Members, 1975- (Chm., 1970-74); Dir, Assoc. of Cons. Clubs Ltd, 1962-65. Governor, University Coll., Cardiff, 1951-; Member Court of Governors: National Museum of Wales, 1952-; National Library of . Wales, 1951-; University Coll., Aberystwyth, 1953-; Vice-President: National Chamber of Trade, 1956-; Young Conservatives of Wales, 1952-; Cardiff Business Club, 1952; South Wales Ramblers, 1958-; Sec., Friends of Wales Soc. (Cultural); Mem., Welsh Advisory Council for Civil Aviation, 1959-62; President: Wales Area Conservative Teachers' Assoc., 1962-; Glamorgan (London) Soc., 1967-69; Chm., Penray Press Ltd and Barry Herald Newspaper, 1955-64; Director: Nicholson Construction Ltd, 1957-66; Welsh Dragon Unit Trust (Management Co.), 1962-67 (Jt Founder); Building and Construction Co. Ltd, Cardiff, 1962-64; Welsh Industrial Securities Ltd, 1965-68. FInstD 1958. *Recreations:* cricket, tennis, squash rackets, and travelling in Italy. *Address:* House of Commons, SW1; 1 Dorchester Avenue, Cardiff. *T:* Cardiff 44280; 45 Winsford Road, Sully, South Glam. *Clubs:* Carlton, Royal Over-Seas League.

GOWER, John Hugh, QC 1967; **His Honour Judge Gower;** a Circuit Judge, since 1972; *b* 6 Nov. 1925; *s* of Henry John Gower, JP and Edith (*née* Brooks); *m* 1960, Shirley Mameena Darbourne; one *s* one *d*. *Educ:* Skinners' Sch., Tunbridge Wells. RASC, 1945-48 (Staff Sgt). Called to Bar, Inner Temple, 1948. Dep. Chm., Kent QS, 1968-71. Pres., Tunbridge Wells Council of Voluntary Service, 1974-. Hon. Vice-Pres., Kent Council of Voluntary Service, 1971-. Governor: Skinners' Sch., Tunbridge Wells, 1957-76; Sacred Heart Sch., Tunbridge Wells, 1972-. Freeman, City of London (by purchase), 1960. *Recreations:* fishing, foxhunting, gardening. *Address:* The Coppice, Lye Green, Crowborough, East Sussex. *T:* Crowborough 4395.

GOWER, Laurence Cecil Bartlett, FBA 1965; Solicitor; Vice-Chancellor, University of Southampton, since 1971, Hon. Professor of Law, since 1972; *b* 29 Dec. 1913; *s* of Henry Lawrence Gower; *m* 1939, Helen Margaret Shepperson, *d* of George Francis Birch; two *s* one *d*. *Educ:* Lindisfarne Coll.; University Coll., London. LLB 1933; LLM 1934. Admitted Solicitor, 1937. Served War of 1939-45, with RA and RAOC. Sir Ernest Cassel Prof. of Commercial Law in University of London, 1948-62, Visiting Prof., Law Sch. of Harvard Univ., 1954-55; Adviser on Legal Educn in Africa to Brit. Inst. of

Internat. and Comparative Law and Adviser to Nigerian Council of Legal Educn, 1962-65; Prof. and Dean of Faculty of Law of Univ. of Lagos, 1962-65; Law Comr, 1965-71; Holmes Lectr, Harvard Univ., 1966. Fellow of University Coll., London; Comr on Company Law Amendment in Ghana, 1958; Member: Jenkins Cttee on Company Law Amendment, 1959-62; Denning Cttee on Legal Education for Students from Africa, 1960; Ormrod Cttee on Legal Education, 1967-71; Royal Commn on the Press, 1975-77. Trustee, British Museum, 1968-. Hon. Fellow, LSE, 1970; Hon. LLD: York Univ., Ont; Edinburgh Univ.; Dalhousie Univ. *Publications:* 15th edn Pollock's Law of Partnership; Principles of Modern Company Law, 1954, 3rd edn 1969; Independent Africa: The Challenge to the Legal Profession, 1967; numerous articles in legal periodicals. *Recreation:* travel. *Address:* The University, Southampton SO9 5NH. *Club:* Athenæum.

GOWER, Sir Raymond; *see* Gower, Sir H. R.

GOWER ISAAC, Anthony John; *see* Isaac, A. J. G.

GOWER-JONES, Ven. Geoffrey; Archdeacon of Lancaster since 1966; Vicar of St Stephen-on-the-Cliffs, Blackpool, since 1950; *b* 30 April 1910; *s* of late Rev. William Gower-Jones; *m* 1938, Margaret, *d* of late John Alexander; one *s* one *d. Educ:* Brasenose Coll., Oxford; Wells Theological Coll. Ordained 1934; Curate: St Paul, Royton, 1934-39; Prestwich, 1939-43; Vicar, Belfield, 1943-50. Canon of Blackburn, 1962-66; Rural Dean of Fylde, 1962; Rural Dean of Blackpool, 1963-66. *Address:* St Stephen's Vicarage, Blackpool, Lancs FY2 9RB. *T:* Blackpool 51484.

GOWING, Rt. Rev. Eric Austin; *see* Auckland, (NZ), Bishop of.

GOWING, Prof. Lawrence Burnett, CBE 1952; MA Dunelm 1952; painter and writer on painting; Slade Professor of Fine Art at University College London, since 1975; *b* 21 April 1918; *s* of late Horace Burnett and Louise Gowing; *m* Jennifer Akam Wallis; three *d. Educ:* Leighton Park Sch., and as a pupil of William Coldstream. Exhibitions: 1942, 1946, 1948, 1955, 1965; works in collections of Contemp. Art Soc., Tate Gallery, National Gallery of Canada, National Gallery of South Australia, British Council, Arts Council, Ashmolean Museum and galleries of Brighton, Bristol, Manchester, Middlesbrough, Newcastle, Nottingham, etc. Prof. of Fine Art, Univ. of Durham, and Principal of King Edward VII Sch. of Art, Newcastle upon Tyne, 1948-58; Principal, Chelsea Sch. of Art, 1958-65; Keeper of the British Collection, and Dep. Dir of the Tate Gallery, 1965-67; Prof. of Fine Art, Leeds Univ., 1967-75. Adjunct Prof. of History of Art, Univ. of Pa, 1977-. Mem. Arts Council, 1970-72, and 1977-, Art Panel, 1953-58, 1959-65, 1969-72, 1976-, Dep. Chm., 1970-72, Chm. Art Films Cttee, 1970-72; a Trustee of Tate Gallery, 1953-60 and 1961-64; a Trustee of National Portrait Gallery, 1960-; Trustee, British Museum, 1976-; a Member of National Council for Diplomas in Art and Design, 1961-65; Chairman: Adv. Cttee on Painting, Gulbenkian Foundation, 1958-64. *Publications:* Renoir, 1947; Vermeer, 1952; Cézanne (catalogue of Edinburgh and London exhibns), 1954; Constable, 1960; Vermeer, 1961; Goya, 1965; Turner: Imagination and Reality, 1966; Matisse (Museum of Modern Art, New York), 1966, (London), 1968; Hogarth (Tate Gallery exhibition), 1971; Watercolours by Cézanne (Newcastle and London exhibn), 1973; many exhibition catalogues and writings in periodicals. *Address:* 49 Walham Grove, SW6. *T:* 01-385 5941.

GOWING, Prof. Margaret Mary, FBA 1975; FRHistS; Professor of the History of Science, University of Oxford, and Fellow of Linacre College, since 1973; *b* 26 April 1921; *d* of Ronald and Mabel Elliott; *m* 1944, Donald J. G. Gowing (*d* 1969); two *s. Educ:* Christ's Hospital; London Sch. of Economics (BSc(Econ)). Bd of Trade, 1941-45; Historical Section, Cabinet Office, 1945-59; Historian and Archivist, UK Atomic Energy Authority, 1959-66; Reader in Contemporary History, Univ. of Kent, 1966-72. Member: Cttee on Deptl Records (Grigg Cttee), 1952-54; Adv. Council on Public Records, 1974-; BBC Archives Adv. Cttee, 1976-. Dir, Contemporary Scientific Archives Centre. Royal Society Wilkins Lectr, 1976. Hon. DLitt Leeds, 1976. *Publications:* (with Sir K. Hancock) British War Economy, 1949; (with E. L. Hargreaves) Civil Industry and Trade, 1952; Britain and Atomic Energy, 1964; Dossier Secret des Relations Atomiques, 1965; Independence and Deterrence: vol. I, Policy Making, vol. II, Policy Execution, 1974; various articles and reviews. *Address:* Linacre College, Oxford.

GOWING, Prof. Noel Frank Collett; Consultant Pathologist and Director of the Department of Histopathology, The Royal Marsden Hospital, SW3, since 1957; Professor of Tumour

Pathology (formerly Senior Lecturer), Institute of Cancer Research: The Royal Cancer Hospital; *b* 3 Jan. 1917; *s* of Edward Charles Gowing and Annie Elizabeth Gowing; *m* 1942, Rela Griffel; one *d. Educ:* Ardingly Coll., Sussex; London Univ. MRCS, LRCP 1941; MB, BS, London, 1947; MD London, 1948. Served RAMC (Capt.), 1942-46, 52nd (Lowland) Div. Lectr in Pathology, St George's Hosp. Med. Sch., 1947-52; Sen. Lectr in Pathology and Hon. Cons. Pathologist, St George's Hosp., 1952-57. FRCPath (Founder Fellow, Coll. of Pathologists, 1964). *Publications:* articles on pathology in medical journals. *Recreations:* gardening, astronomy. *Address:* 9 Top Park, Beckenham, Kent. *T:* 01-650 8556.

GOWON, Gen. Yakubu Danjuma; jssc, psc; enrolled as a student, University of Warwick, Oct. 1975; Head of the Federal Military Government and C-in-C of Armed Forces of the Federal Republic of Nigeria 1966-75; *b* Pankshin Div., Benue-Plateau State, Nigeria, 19 Oct. 1934; *s* of Yohanna Gowon (of Angas tribe, a Christian evangelist of CMS) and Saraya Gowon; *m* 1969, Victoria Hansatu Zakari; one *s* one *d. Educ:* St Bartholomew's Sch. (CMS), Wusasa, and Govt Coll., Zaria, Nigeria; Regular Officer, Special Trng Sch., Teshie, Ghana; Eaton Hall Officer Cadet Trng Sch., Chester, RMA, Sandhurst, Staff Coll., Camberley and Joint Services Staff Coll., Latimer (all in England). Enlisted, 1954; Adjt, 4th Bn Nigerian Army, 1960 (Independence Oct. 1960); UN Peace-Keeping Forces, Congo, Nov. 1960-June 1961 and Jan.-June 1963 (Bde Major). Lt-Col and Adjt-Gen., Nigerian Army, 1963; Comd, 2nd Bn, Nigerian Army, Ikeja, 1966; Chief of Staff, 1966; Head of State and C-in-C after July 1966 coup; Maj.-Gen. 1967. Maintained territorial integrity of his country by fighting, 1966-70, to preserve unity of Nigeria (after failure of peaceful measures) following on Ojukwu rebellion, and declared secession of the Eastern region of Nigeria, July 1967; created 12 equal and autonomous states in Nigeria, 1967; Biafran surrender, 1970. Promoted Gen., 1971. Is a Christian; works for internat. peace and security within the framework of OAU and UNO. Hon. LLD Cambridge, 1975. Holds Grand Cross, etc, of several foreign orders. *Publication:* Faith in Unity, 1970. *Recreations:* squash, lawn tennis, pen-drawing, photography, cinephotography. *Address:* c/o Nigerian High Commission, 9 Northumberland Avenue, WC2; Warwick University, Coventry CV4 7AL.

GOWRIE, 2nd Earl of, *cr* 1945; **Alexander Patric Greysteil Ruthven;** Baron Ruthven of Gowrie, 1919; Baron Gowrie, 1935; Viscount Ruthven of Canberra and Dirleton, 1945; *b* 26 Nov. 1939; *er s* of late Capt. Hon. Alexander Hardinge Patrick Hore-Ruthven, Rifle Bde, and Pamela Margaret (as Viscountess Ruthven of Canberra, she *m* 1952, Major Derek Cooper, MC, The Life Guards), 2nd *d* of late Rev. A. H. Fletcher; *S* grandfather, 1955; *m* 1st, 1962, Xandra (marr. diss. 1973), *yr d* of Col R. A. G. Bingley, CVO, DSO, OBE; one *s*; 2nd, 1974, Adelheid Gräfin von der Schulenburg, *y d* of late Fritz-Dietlof, Graf von der Schulenburg. *Educ:* Eton; Balliol Coll., Oxford. Visiting Lectr, State Univ. of New York at Buffalo, 1963-64; Tutor, Harvard Univ., 1965-68; Lectr in English and American Literature, UCL, 1969-72. A Conservative Whip, 1971-72; Parly Rep. to UN, 1971; a Lord in Waiting (Govt Whip), 1972-74; Opposition Spokesman on Economic Affairs, 1974-. *Publications:* A Postcard from Don Giovanni, 1972; (jt) The Genius of British Painting, 1975; (jt) The Conservative Opportunity, 1976. *Recreation:* wine. *Heir: s* Viscount Ruthven of Canberra and Dirleton, *qv. Address:* 34 King Street, Covent Garden, WC2. *T:* 01-240 2371.

GOYDER, George Armin, CBE 1976; Managing Director, British International Paper Ltd, 1935-71; *b* 22 June 1908; *s* of late William Goyder and Lili Julia Kellersberger, Baden, Switzerland; *m* 1937, Rosemary, 4th *d* of Prof. R. C. Bosanquet, Rock, Northumberland; five *s* three *d. Educ:* Mill Hill Sch.; London Sch. of Economics; abroad. Gen. Man., Newsprint Supply Co., 1940-47 (responsible for procurement supply and rationing of newsprint to British Press); The Geographical Magazine, 1935-58. Mem., Gen. Synod of C of E (formerly Church Assembly), 1948-75; Chm., Liberal Party Standing Cttee on Industrial Partnership, 1966. Chm., Centre for Internat. Briefing, Farnham Castle. Founder Trustee, William Blake Trust; Governor: Mill Hill Sch., 1943-69; Monkton Combe Sch.; Trustee and Hon. Fellow, St Peter's Coll., Oxford; Mem. Council, Wycliffe Hall; Founder Mem. and Sec., British-North American Cttee, 1969. *Publications:* The Future of Private Enterprise, 1951, 1954; The Responsible Company, 1961; The People's Church, 1966; The Responsible Worker, 1975. *Recreations:* music, old books, theology. *Address:* Pindars, Rotherfield Greys, Henley-on-Thames, Oxon RG9 4PJ. *Club:* Reform.

GRAAFF, Sir de Villiers, 2nd Bt *cr* 1911; MBE 1946; BA Cape, MA, BCL Oxon; Barrister-at-Law, Inner Temple; Advocate of the Supreme Court of S Africa; MP for Hottentots Holland in Union Parliament 1948-58, for Rondebosch, Cape Town, 1958-77; *b* 8 Dec. 1913; *s* of 1st Bt and Eileen (*d* 1950), *d* of Rev. Dr J. P. Van Heerden, Cape Town; *S* father, 1931; *m* 1939, Helena Le Roux, *d* of F. C. M. Voigt, Provincial Sec. of Cape Province; two *s* one *d*. Served War of 1939-45 (prisoner, MBE). Leader, United Party, S Africa, 1956-77; formerly Leader of Official Opposition. Hon. LLD, Rhodes. *Heir: s* David de Villiers Graaff [*b* 3 May 1940; *m* Sally Williams; one *s* one *d*]. *Address:* De Grendel, Tijgerberg, Cape, South Africa. *Club:* Civil Service (Cape Town).

GRACE, Sir John (Te Herekiekie), KBE 1968; MVO 1953; AEA (RNZAF) 1950; New Zealand High Commissioner in Fiji, 1970-73; sheep and cattle station owner since 1958; *b* 28 July 1905; *s* of John Edward Grace, JP and Rangiamohia Herekiekie; *m* 1st, 1940, Marion Linton McGregor (*d* 1962); no *c*; 2nd, 1968, Dorothy Kirkcaldie. *Educ:* Wanganui Boys' Coll.; Te Aute Coll., Hawkes Bay. Served War of 1939-45, Royal NZ Air Force (Sqdn-Ldr). NZ Public Service, 1926-58: Private Sec. to Ministers of the Crown incl. three Prime Ministers, 1947-58; Member: NZ Historic Places Trust, 1952-68; NZ Geographic Bd, 1952-68; Maori Purposes Fund Bd, 1961-68; Maori Educn Foundn, 1962-68; Nature Conservation Coun., 1963-68; Nat. Coun. of Adult Educn, 1964-68; Lake Taupo Forest Trust, 1968-; Fiji Leper Trust Bd, 1972; Rotoaira Forest Trust, 1974-; Tuwharetoa Trust Bd, 1974-; Lake Taupo Reserves Bd, 1975-; Vice-Pres. and Dominion Councillor, NZ Nat. Party, 1959-67. JP 1947. *Publication:* Tuwharetoa, a History of the Maori People of the Taupo District, NZ. *Recreations:* golf, trout fishing, gardening. *Address:* Te Waka Station, Parapara Road, RD3 Wanganui, New Zealand. *T:* Wanganui 28-501. *Clubs:* Wellesley (Wellington); Wanganui (Wanganui).

GRACE, Dr Michael Anthony, FRS 1967; Reader in Nuclear Physics, Oxford University, since 1972; Student and Tutor in Physics, Christ Church, since 1959; *b* 13 May 1920; *er s* of late Claude Saville Grace, Haslemere, Surrey, and Evelyn Doris (*née* Adams); *m* 1948, Philippa Agnes Lois, *o d* of Sir (Vincent) Zachary Cope, MD, MS, FRCS; one *s* three *d*. *Educ:* St Paul's; Christ Church, Oxford. MA 1948; DPhil 1950. Mine Design Dept, HMS Vernon, 1940-45. ICI Research Fellowship, Clarendon Laboratory, Oxford, 1951; University Sen. Res. Officer, Dept of Nuclear Physics, 1955-72; Lectr in Physics, Christ Church, 1958, Censor, 1964-69; Dr Lee's Reader in Physics, 1972. Governor: St Paul's Schools, 1959; Harrow School, 1969. *Publications:* papers in various jls including Phil. Mag., Proc. Royal Soc., Proc. Phys. Soc., Nuclear Physics. *Recreations:* lawn tennis, swimming. *Address:* 13 Blandford Avenue, Oxford, *T:* Oxford 58464. *Club:* Athenæum.

GRACEY, John Halliday; Commissioner of Inland Revenue since 1973; *b* 20 May 1925; *s* of Halliday Gracey and Florence Jane (*née* Cudlipp); *m* 1950, Margaret Procter; three *s*. *Educ:* City of London Sch.; Brasenose Coll., Oxford. Army, 1943-47. Entered Inland Revenue, 1950; HM Treasury, 1970-73. *Address:* 3 Woodberry Down, Epping, Essex. *T:* Epping 72167. *Club:* Reform.
See also T . A . Lloyd Davies .

GRACIAS, His Eminence Cardinal; see Bombay, Cardinal-Archbishop of.

GRACIE, George H. H.; see Heath-Gracie.

GRACIE, Instructor Capt. Henry Stewart, CB 1956; MA; FSA; RN retired; *b* 6 Aug. 1901; *s* of late Capt. G. S. Gracie, Leonard Stanley, Glos; *m* 1932, Dorothy Constance (*d* 1960), *d* of Rev. Edward Senior, Sheffield. *Educ:* Pocklington Sch.; St John's Coll., Cambridge (BA). Joined RN as Instr Lt, 1923; Instr Comdr 1937; Instr Capt. 1949. Command Instructor Officer Portsmouth (actg Capt.), 1946-49; Fleet Instructor Officer, Mediterranean, 1949-52; Dir of Studies, RN Coll., Greenwich, 1953-56. Naval ADC to the Queen, 1955-56. Retired 1956. Hon. Editor, Trans Bristol and Glos Archæological Soc., 1956-73. *Publications:* papers in various archæological jls. *Recreations:* prehistoric archæology. *Address:* Thrupp House, Stroud, Glos GL5 2DD. *T:* Stroud 4572.

GRADE, family name of Baron Grade.

GRADE, Baron *cr* 1976 (Life Peer), of Elstree, Herts; **Lew Grade,** Kt 1969; Chairman and Chief Executive, Associated Television Corporation Ltd; President (former Chairman and Managing Director), ATV Network Ltd, since 1977; Managing Director, Incorporated Television Company Ltd; *b* 25 Dec. 1906; *s* of late Isaac Winogradsky and of Olga Winogradsky; *m* 1942, Kathleen Sheila Moody; one *s*. *Educ:* Rochelle Street Sch. Joint Managing Dir of Lew and Leslie Grade Ltd, until Sept. 1955; Dep. Managing Dir of Associated Television Ltd, 1958-; Chairman: Stoll Theatres Corp., 1973-; Moss Empires, 1973-. Director: Bermans (Holdings) Ltd; Bentray Investments Ltd; Associated Television Corp. (International) Ltd (Switzerland); Ambassador Bowling Ltd; Independent Television Corp. (USA); Planned Holdings Ltd; Pye Records Ltd; ATV Merchandising Ltd. *Address:* ATV House, Great Cumberland Place, W1A 1AG.
See also Baron Delfont.

GRADE, Michael Ian; Director of Programmes, London Weekend Television Ltd, since 1977; *b* 8 March 1943; *s* of Leslie Grade and *g s* of Olga Winogradski; *m* 1967, Penelope Jane (*née* Levinson); one *s* one *d* . *Educ:* St Dunstan's Coll., London. Daily Mirror: Trainee Journalist, 1960; Sports Columnist, 1964-66; Theatrical Agent, Grade Organisation, 1966; formed London Management and Representation, 1969, Jt Man. Dir until 1973; London Weekend Television: Dep. Controller of Programmes (Entertainment), 1973; Mem. Bd, 1977-. *Recreation:* entertainment. *Address:* 37a Alleyn Park, Dulwich Village, SE21 8AT. *T:* 01-761 0919. *Club:* Coombe Hill Golf (Surrey).

GRADY, John William; Consultant, Samuel Montagu & Co. Ltd, since 1975 (Executive Director, 1969-75); Financial Controller, Newlon Housing Trust, since 1975; *b* London, 6 April 1915; *s* of late John William Grady and Teresa (*née* Moore); *m* 1939, Edith Mary Green; one *s* one *d*. *Educ:* St Olave's Sch. Entered Post Office as Exec. Off., 1935; Higher Exec. Off., 1946; Sen. Exec. Off. in Organisation and Methods Br., 1950; Asst Accountant Gen., 1955; Financial Adviser, External Telecommunications, 1962; Dep. Dir of Finance, 1964; Dir of Giro and Remittance Services, PO, 1965-69. *Recreations:* music, walking. *Address:* 20 Highsett, Cambridge CB2 1NX. *T:* Cambridge 60119.

GRAEME, Bruce, (Pseudonym of **Graham Montague Jeffries**); Novelist; *s* of late William Henry Jeffries; *m* 1925, Lorna Hélène, *d* of Capt. Hay T. Louch; one *s* one *d*. *Educ:* Privately. Finish of education interrupted by Great War; volunteered for Queen's Westminster Rifles; after demobilization became free-lance journalist; travelled several times to USA and France on various commissions, published short stories, 1921-25; interested in film work; financed, produced and sold one reel comedy, 1919-20; resumed this lifelong interest in films as script writer, and producer, 1942; entered Gray's Inn, 1930. *Publications:* The Story of Buckingham Palace, 1928; The Story of St James's Palace, 1929; A Century of Buckingham Palace, 1937; The Story of Windsor Castle, 1937; Blackshirt, 1925; The Trail of the White Knight, 1926; The Return of Blackshirt, 1927; Hate Ship, 1928; Trouble, 1929; Blackshirt Again, 1929; Through the Eyes of the Judge, 1930; The Penance of Brother Alaric, 1930; A Murder of Some Importance, 1931; Unsolved, 1931; Gigins Court, 1932; Alias Blackshirt, 1932; The Imperfect Crime, 1932; Impeached, 1933; Epilogue, 1933; An International Affair, 1934; Public Enemy No 1, 1934; Satan's Mistress, 1935; Blackshirt the Audacious, 1936; Not Proven, 1935; Cardyce for the Defence, 1936; Blackshirt the Adventurer, 1936; Mystery on the Queen Mary, 1937; Blackshirt takes a Hand, 1937; Disappearance of Roger Tremayne, 1937; Racing Yacht Mystery, 1938; Blackshirt; Counter-Spy, 1938; The Man from Michigan, 1938; Body Unknown, 1939; Blackshirt Interferes, 1939; Poisoned Sleep, 1939; 13 in a Fog, 1940; Blackshirt Strikes Back, 1940; The Corporal Died in Bed, 1940; Seven Clues in Search of a Crime, 1941; Son of Blackshirt, 1941; Encore Allain, 1941; House with Crooked Walls, 1942; Lord Blackshirt, 1942; News Travels by Night, 1943; A Case for Solomon, 1943; Calling Lord Blackshirt, 1944; Work for the Hangman, 1944; Ten Trails to Tyburn, 1944; The Coming of Carew, 1945; A Case of Books, 1946; Without Malice, 1946; A Brief for O'Leary, 1947; No Clues for Dexter, 1948; And a Bottle of Rum, 1948; Tigers Have Claws, 1949; Cherchez la Femme; Dead Pigs at Hungry Farm, 1951; Lady in Black, 1952; Mr Whimset Buys a Gun, 1953; Suspense, 1953; The Way Out, 1954; So Sharp the Razor, 1955; Just an Ordinary Case, 1956; The Accidental Clue, 1957; The Long Night, 1958; Boomerang, 1959; Fog for a Killer, 1960; The Undetective, 1962; Almost Without Murder, 1963; Holiday for a Spy, 1964; Always Expect the Unexpected, 1965; The Devil was a Woman, 1966; Much Ado About Something, 1967; Never Mix Business With Pleasure, 1968; Some Geese Lay Golden Eggs, 1968; Blind Date for a Private Eye, 1969; The Quiet Ones, 1970; The Lady doth Protest, 1971; Yesterday's Tomorrow, 1972; Two and Two Make Five, 1973; Danger in the Channel, 1973; The D Notice, 1974; The Snatch, 1976; Two-Faced, 1977. *Address:* Gorse Field Cottage, Aldington Frith, near Ashford, Kent. *T:* Aldington 383. *Club:* Paternosters.

GRÆME, Maj.-Gen. Ian Rollo, CB 1967; OBE 1955; Secretary, National Ski Federation of Great Britain, since 1967; *b* 23 May 1913; *s* of late Col J. A. Græme, DSO, late RE; *m* 1941, Elizabeth Jean Dyas; two *d. Educ:* Boxgrove; Stowe; RMA Woolwich. King's Medal and Benson Memorial Prize, RMA, 1933. 2nd Lt RA 1933; pre-war service at regimental duty UK; War Service in Singapore, Java, India, Burma, Siam; psc 1942; Instructor Staff Coll., Quetta, 1944; CO 1st Burma Field Regt, 1945-46; OC, K Battery, RHA, 1949; jssc 1952; GSO1, HQ Northern Army Group, 1953-54; CO 27 Regt RA, 1955-57; Col GS Staff Coll., Camberley, 1957-59; idc 1960; Dep. Mil. Sec., WO, 1961-63; Dep. Dir Personnel Admin, WO, 1963-64; Dir Army Recruiting, 1964-67; Retd 1967. Mem. Royal Yachting Assoc., 1950-; Life Governor, Royal Life Saving Soc., 1956-; Life Mem., British Olympic Assoc., 1958-; Chm., Army Holiday Cttee for ski-ing, 1963-67; Council, Army Ski Assoc., 1958-; Mem. Council, Nat. Ski Fedn of GB, 1964-67 (Life Mem. Fedn). Mem. BIM, 1967. Gold Medal, Austrian Govt, 1972. *Recreations:* ski-ing, sailing, mountains. *Clubs:* Army and Navy, English-Speaking Union (Life Mem.); Ski Club of Great Britain, Army Ski Association, Alpbach Visitors Ski, White Hare, Garvock Ski (Pres. 1969-), Kandahar Ski; Ranelagh Sailing, Royal Artillery Yacht.

GRAESSER, Col Sir Alastair Stewart Durward, Kt 1973; DSO 1945; OBE 1963; MC 1944; TD, DL, JP; Honorary Vice President, National Union of Conservative and Unionist Associations, since 1976 (Chairman, 1974-76); President, Wales and Monmouth Conservative and Unionist Council, since 1972; Director, Development Corporation for Wales and Monmouth; *b* 17 Nov. 1915; *s* of Norman Hugo Graesser and Annette Stewart Durward; *m* 1939, Diana Aline Elms Neale; one *s* three *d. Educ:* Oundle; Gonville and Caius Coll., Cambridge. Director: Grosvenor Hotel Co Ltd; Municipal Life Assurance Ltd; Municipal General Assurance Ltd; Managing Trustee, Municipal Mutual Insurance Ltd; Member: Wales and Marches Postal Bd; CBI Regional Council for Wales (Past Chm.); Welsh Council. Pres. and Chm., E Flintshire Conservative and Unionist Assoc., 1959, etc; Pres., Wales and Monmouth Conservative Clubs Council, 1972-. Vice-Chm., Wales and Monmouth TA&VR Assoc.; Hon. Col, 3rd Bn Royal Welch Fusiliers (TA). High Sheriff of Flintshire, 1962; DL 1960, JP 1956, Clwyd (formerly Flints). *Recreation:* shooting. *Address:* The Rake, Rake Lane, Eccleston, Chester CH4 9JN. *T:* Chester 674712. *Clubs:* Bath; Hawks (Cambridge); Leander (Henley-on-Thames); Grosvenor (Chester).

GRAFFTEY-SMITH, Sir Laurence Barton, KCMG 1951 (CMG 1944); KBE 1947 (OBE 1932); *b* 16 April 1892; *s* of late Rev. Arthur Grafftey-Smith and late Mabel, *d* of Rev. Charles Barton, Cheselbourne, Dorset; *m* 1930, Vivien (marr. diss., 1937), *d* of G. Alexander Alderson; two *s* ; *m* 1946, Evgenia Owen, *d* of late P. H. Coolidge, Berkeley, Calif. *Educ:* Repton; Pembroke Coll., Cambridge. Student Interpreter, Levant Consular Service, 1914. HM Vice Consul, 1920; served at Alexandria, Cairo (Residency), Jeddah, Constantinople; Asst Oriental Sec. at the Residency, Cairo, 1925-35; HM Consul, Mosul, 1935-37; Baghdad, 1937-39; HM Consul-Gen. in Albania, 1939-40; attached British Embassy, Cairo, 1940; Chief Political Adviser, Diego Suarez, May 1942; Chief Political Officer, Madagascar, July 1942; Consul-Gen., Antananarivo, 1943; Minister to Saudi Arabia, 1945-47; High Comr for UK in Pakistan, 1947-51; retired from Govt service on 31 Dec. 1951; UK Rep. on Gov.-Gen.'s Commn, Khartoum, 1953-56. *Publications:* (with Godfrey Haggard) Visa Verses, 1915 (privately printed); Bright Levant, 1970; Hands to Play, 1975. *Address:* Broom Hill House, Coddenham, Suffolk. *Club:* Royal Automobile.

GRAFTON, 11th Duke of, *cr* 1675; **Hugh Denis Charles FitzRoy;** KG 1976; DL; Earl of Euston, Viscount Ipswich; Captain Grenadier Guards; *b* 3 April 1919; *e s* of 10th Duke of Grafton, and Lady Doreen Maria Josepha Sydney Buxton (*d* 1923), *d* of 1st Earl Buxton; *S* father, 1970; *m* 1946, Fortune (*see* Duchess of Grafton); two *s* three *d. Educ:* Eton; Magdalene Coll., Cambridge. ADC to the Viceroy of India, 1943-47. Mem. Historic Buildings Council for England, 1953-; Chairman: Soc. for the Protection of Ancient Buildings; Jt Cttee, Soc. for Protection of Ancient Buildings, Georgian Gp, Victorian Soc., and Civic Trust; National Trust East Anglian Regional Cttee; President: Council of British Soc. of Master Glass Painters; International Students Trust. Mem., Cathedrals Advisory Cttee; Trustee and Chm. Exec. Cttee, Historic Churches Preservation Trust; Royal Fine Art Commn, 1971-; Chm. Trustees, Sir John Soane's Museum; Vice-Chm. Trustees, Nat. Portrait Gallery. DL Suffolk, 1973. *Heir: s* Earl of Euston, *qv. Address:* Euston Hall, Thetford, Norfolk. *T:* Thetford 3282. *Club:* Boodle's.

GRAFTON, Duchess of; (Ann) Fortune FitzRoy, DCVO 1970 (CVO 1965); JP; Mistress of The Robes to The Queen since 1967; *o d* of Captain Eric Smith, MC, Lower Ashfold, Slaugham; *m* 1946, Duke of Grafton, *qv* ; two *s* three *d.* Lady of the Bedchamber to the Queen, 1953-66. SRCN Great Ormond Street, 1945; Mem. Bd of Governors, The Hospital for Sick Children, Great Ormond Street, 1952-66. JP County of London, 1949, W Suffolk, 1972. *Address:* Euston Hall, Thetford, Norfolk. *T:* Thetford 3282.

GRAFTON, NSW, Bishop of, since 1973; **Rt. Rev. Donald Norman Shearman;** *b* 6 Feb. 1926; *s* of late S. F. Shearman, Sydney; *m* 1952, Stuart Fay, *d* of late Chap. F. H. Bashford; three *s* three *d. Educ:* Fort St and Orange High Schools; St John's Theological College, Morpeth, NSW. Served War of 1939-45: air crew, 1944-46. Theological College, 1948-50. Deacon, 1950; Priest, 1951. Curate: of Dubbo, 1950-52; of Forbes, and Warden of St John's Hostel, 1953-56; Rector of Coonabarabran, 1957-59; Director of Promotion and Adult Christian Education 1959-62; Canon, All Saints Cathedral, Bathurst, 1962; Archdeacon of Mildura and Rector of St. Margaret's, 1963; Bishop of Rockhampton, 1963-71; Chairman, Australian Board of Missions, Sydney, 1971-73. *Address:* Bishopsholme, Grafton, NSW 2460, Australia. *T:* Grafton 42 2070.

GRAFTON, Peter Witheridge, CBE 1972; Partner, G. D. Walford & Partners, Chartered Quantity Surveyors, since 1949; *b* 19 May 1916; *s* of James Hawkins Grafton and Ethel Marion (*née* Brannan); *m* 1st, 1939, Joan Bleackley (*d* 1969); two *d* (and one *d* decd); 2nd, 1971, Margaret Ruth Ward; one *s. Educ:* Westminster City Sch.; Sutton Valence Sch.; Coll. of Estate Management. FRICS, FIArb. Served War of 1939-45, Queen's Westminster Rifles, Dorsetshire Regt and RE, UK and Far East (Captain). Mem. Council and Exec., RICS (Past Chm. Policy Review Cttee; Vice-Pres., 1974); Mem. and Past Chm., Quantity Surveyors Council (1st Chm., Building Cost Information Service); Past Mem. Council, Construction Industries Research and Information Assoc.; Past Mem. Research Adv. Council to Minister of Housing and Construction; Past Mem. Nat. Cons. Council for Building and Civil Engrg Industries and Mem., Agrément Bd; former Chm., Nat. Jt Consultative Cttee for Building Industry. Mem. Governing Bd, United Westminster Schs; Chm. of Governors, Sutton Valence Sch.; Past Chm., Old Suttonians Assoc. Contested (L) Bromley, 1959. *Publications:* numerous articles on techn. and other professional subjects. *Recreations:* golf (founder and Chm., Public Schs Old Boys Golf Assoc., Co-donor Grafton Morrish Trophy; past Captain of Chartered Surveyors Golfing Soc.); writing. *Address:* The Pines, Birch Hill, Addington, Surrey CR0 5HT. *T:* 01-654 5338. *Clubs:* Reform, East India India, Devonshire, Sports and Public Schools, Golfers; Addington Golf, Rye Golf, W Sussex Golf.

GRAHAM, family name of **Duke of Montrose.**

GRAHAM, Marquis of; James Graham; *b* 6 April 1935; *s* of 7th Duke of Montrose, *qv* ; *m* 1970, Catherine Elizabeth MacDonell, *d* of late Captain N. A. T. Young, and of Mrs Young, Ottawa; one *s* one *d. Educ:* Loretto. *Heir: s* Lord Fintrie, *qv. Address:* Auchmar, Drymen, Glasgow. *T:* 221.

GRAHAM, Rt. Rev. Andrew Alexander Kenny; *see* Bedford, Bishop Suffragan of.

GRAHAM, Andrew Guillemard; author and journalist; *b* 1 Feb. 1913; *s* of John Parkhurst Graham and Norah Madeleine (*née* Neal); unmarried. *Educ:* Uppingham Sch. (Rutland Schol.); New Coll., Oxford (BA). Served War with Welsh Guards, 1939-46; NW Europe campaign with 1st Bn, 1944-45; HQ, Guards Div., 1945-46. Sec., Conservative Club, St James's St., 1947-49; rejoined Welsh Guards, 1952; Asst Mil. Attaché, Brit. Legation, Saigon, 1952-54; Mil. Attaché (GSO1) Brit. Embassy, Beirut, 1955-57; Comptroller, Brit. Embassy, Paris, 1959-61. The Times wine correspondent, 1962-71. *Publications:* Interval in Indo-China, 1956; The Club, 1957; A Foreign Affair, 1958; Love for a King, 1959; Mostly Nasty, 1961; Sharpshooters at War, 1964; The Regiment, 1966; The Queen's Malabars, 1970. Regular Correspondent, The Times, 1962-71. *Recreation:* gardening. *Address:* c/o Coutts & Co., 440 Strand, WC2R 0QS. *Club:* Beefsteak.

GRAHAM, Angus, MA, FSA; Member of Royal Commission on Ancient Monuments (Scotland), 1960-74; *b* 1892; *yr s* of late R. C. Graham, Skipness, Argyll. *Educ:* Winchester Coll.; New Coll., Oxford. Served European War, 4th Highland LI, 1914-19. British Forestry Commission, 1920-22 (district officer); Price Bros and Co. Ltd, Quebec, 1922-25 (forester); Quebec Forest Industries Association, Ltd, 1925-33 (sec.-treasurer); Royal

Commission on Ancient Monuments (Scotland), 1935-57 (sec.). *Publications:* Forests in the National Development, 1923; Quebec Limit-Holders' Manual, 1932; The Golden Grindstone, 1935; Napoleon Tremblay, 1939; papers in Proc. Society of Antiquaries of Scotland, Jl Royal Society Antiquaries of Ireland, Jl of Forestry. *Address:* 1 Nelson Street, Edinburgh EH3 6LF. *T:* 031-556 1534. *Club:* New (Edinburgh).

GRAHAM, Admiral Sir Angus E. M. B. C.; *see* Cunninghame Graham.

GRAHAM, Antony Richard Malise; Director: Barrow Hepburn Group Ltd; British Tanners Products Ltd; *b* 15 Oct. 1928; *s* of late Col Patrick Ludovic Graham, MC, and late Barbara Mary Graham (*née* Jury); *m* 1958, Gillian Margaret, *d* of late L. Bradford Cook and of Mrs W. V. Wrigley; two *s* one *d*. *Educ:* Abberley Hall; Nautical Coll., Pangbourne. Joined Merchant Navy as an apprentice, 1945; left on obtaining Master Mariner's certif., 1955. Stewarts and Lloyds Ltd, 1955-60; PE Consulting Group Ltd, management consultants, 1960-72 (Regional Dir, 1970-72); Regional Industrial Dir (Under-Sec.), Yorks and Humberside, DoI, 1972-76. Contested (C) Leeds East, 1966. *Address:* 34 Sheffield Terrace, W8 7NA. *T:* 01-727 5091.

GRAHAM, Billy; *see* Graham, William F.

GRAHAM, Charles Spencer Richard, DL; *b* 16 July 1919; *s* and *heir* of Sir (Frederick) Fergus Graham, Bt, *qv*; *m* 1944, Isabel Susan Anne Surtees; two *s* one *d*. *Educ:* Eton. Served with Scots Guards, 1940-50, NW Europe (despatches) and Malaya. President, Country Landowners' Assoc., 1971-73. Mem., Nat. Water Council, 1973-. High Sheriff 1955, DL 1971, Cumbria (formerly Cumberland). *Address:* Crofthead, Longtown, Cumbria. *T:* Longtown 231. *Clubs:* Brooks's, Pratt's.

GRAHAM, Colin; Artistic Director: English Music Theatre, since 1975; Aldeburgh Festival, since 1969; stage director, designer, lighting designer, and author; *b* 22 Sept. 1931; *s* of Frederick Eaton Graham-Bonnalie and Alexandra Diana Vivian Findlay. *Educ:* Northaw Prep. Sch.; Stowe Sch.; RADA (Dip.). Dir of Productions, English Opera Gp, 1963-74; Associate Dir of Prodns, Sadler's Wells Opera/English National Opera, 1967-75. Principal productions for: English Music Theatre; Royal Opera, Covent Garden; Scottish Opera; New Opera Co.; Glyndebourne Opera; BBC TV; Brussels National Opera; Santa Fe Opera; Metropolitan Opera, New York; NYC Opera; dir. world premières of all Benjamin Britten's operas since 1958; of other contemp. composers. Theatre productions for: Old Vic Co.; Bristol Old Vic; Royal Shakespeare Co. Orpheus award (Germany) for best opera production, 1973 (War and Peace, ENO). *Publications:* A Penny for a Song (libretto for Richard Rodney Bennett), 1969; The Golden Vanity (libretto for opera by Britten), 1970; King Arthur (libretto for new version of Purcell opera), 1971; production scores for Britten's: Curlew River, 1969; The Burning Fiery Furnace, 1971; The Prodigal Son, 1973; contrib. Opera. *Recreations:* motor cycles, movies. *Address:* The Lion House, Orford, Suffolk IP12 2NR.

GRAHAM, David; *see* Graham, S. D.

GRAHAM, Rev. Douglas Leslie, MA (Dublin); retired; *b* 4 Oct. 1909; *s* of late Very Rev. G. F. Graham; *m* 1935, Gladys Winifred Ann, *y d* of J. W. Brittain, JP, Kilronan, Donnybrook, Co. Dublin; three *s*. *Educ:* Portora Royal Sch.; Dublin Univ. (BA); Munich Univ. Lectr in Classics, Dublin Univ., 1932-34; MA and Madden Prizeman, 1934; Asst Master, Eton Coll., 1934-41. Ordained, 1937. Served War as Temp. Chaplain, RNVR, 1941-45; HMS Trinidad, 1941; HMS King Alfred, 1942; HMS Daedalus, 1944; HMS Ferret, 1944; Headmaster, Portora Royal School, 1945-53; Headmaster, Dean Close Sch., 1954-68; Asst Master and Chaplain, Williston Acad., Easthampton, Mass, USA, 1968-72. Select Preacher to the Univs of Dublin, 1945, 1961 and 1965, and Oxford, 1956-57. FRSA. *Publications:* Bacchanalia (trans. from Greek Anthology), 1970; occasional articles on classical subjects. *Recreations:* books, birds and boxing. *Address:* Forest Cottage, West Woods, Lockeridge, near Marlborough, Wilts. *T:* Lockeridge 432.

GRAHAM, Edward; *see* Graham, T. E.

GRAHAM, Euan Douglas; Principal Clerk of Private Bills, House of Lords; *b* 29 July 1924; *yr s* of Brig. Lord D. M. Graham, CB, DSO, MC; RA. *Educ:* Eton; Christ Church, Oxford (MA). Served RAF, 1943-47. Joined Parliament Office, House of Lords, 1950; Clerk, Judicial Office, 1950-60; Principal Clerk of Private Bills, Examiner of Petitions for Private Bills, Taxing Officer, 1961-. *Address:* 122 Beaufort Mansions, Beaufort Street, SW3. *Clubs:* Brooks's, Beefsteak, Pratt's.

GRAHAM, Maj.-Gen. Frederick Clarence Campbell, CB 1960; DSO 1945; DL; *b* Ardencaple Castle, Helensburgh, Scotland, 14 Dec. 1908; *s* of Sir Frederick Graham, 2nd Bt, and Lady Irene Graham (*née* Campbell); *m* 1936, Phyllis Mary, *d* of late Maj.-Gen. H. F. E. MacMahon, CB, CSI, CBE, MC; three *s*. *Educ:* Eton Coll.; RMC Sandhurst. Commissioned Argyll and Sutherland Highlanders, 1929; served 1st and 2nd Bn Argyll and Sutherland Highlanders in China, India, UK and Palestine, 1929-39; Adjutant 1st Bn, 1937; War of 1939-45, served Palestine, N Africa, Crete, Syria, India, Italy; commanded 1st Bn Argyll and Sutherland Highlanders, 1944-end of war in Europe. Since 1945: GSO1, Home Counties District and Home Counties Div.; Joint Services Staff Coll.; Staff Coll., Camberley (Col); Comdr 61 Lorried Infantry Brigade (Brigadier); Asst Commandant, RMA Sandhurst; Dep. Comdr, Land Forces, Hong Kong; Adviser in recruiting, MoD; Comdr Highland District and 51st (Highland) Div., TA, 1959-62; retd from HM Forces, 1962. Col, The Argyll and Sutherland Highlanders, 1958-72. Col Comdt, The Scottish Div., 1968-69; Hon. Col, Argyll and Sutherland Highlanders of Canada, 1972. Mem. of Royal Company of Archers, The Queen's Body Guard for Scotland, 1958-. DL Perthshire, 1966. Mem., Stirling DC (Vice-Chm., 1977-). *Address:* Mackeanston House, Doune, Perthshire. *Club:* Caledonian.

GRAHAM, Sir (Frederick) Fergus, 5th Bt *cr* 1783; KBE 1956; HM Lieutenant, Cumberland, 1958-68; formerly Captain Irish Guards; *b* 10 March 1893; *er s* of Sir Richard Graham, 4th Bt, and Lady Cynthia Duncombe (*d* 1926), 3rd *d* of 1st Earl of Feversham; *S* father, 1932; *m* 1918, Mary Spencer Revell, CBE, *o c* of late Maj.-Gen. Raymond Reade, CB, CMG; one *s*. *Educ:* Eton; Christ Church, Oxford. BA 1914; MA 1920; is Lieut-Col late 6th Bn Border Regt (TA); formerly Hon. Col 4th Battalion Border Regt TA; TD; JP for Cumberland; Patron of 2 Livings. Served European War, Irish Guards SR, 1914-19 (wounded, despatches); MP (U) North Cumberland, 1926-35, (C) Darlington, 1951-Sept. 1959. *Heir: s* Major Charles Spencer Richard Graham, *qv*. *Recreation:* shooting. *Address:* Netherby, Longtown, Carlisle, Cumbria. *T:* Longtown 206. *Club:* Farmers'.

GRAHAM, George Boughen, QC 1964; *b* 17 July 1920; *s* of Sydney Boughen and Hannah Graham, Keswick, Cumberland; *m* Mavis, *o d* of late Frederick Worthington, Blackpool. *Educ:* Keswick Sch. Royal Signals, 1940-46. Barrister, Lincoln's Inn, 1950, Bencher, 1972. Chancellor, Diocese of Wakefield, 1959, Dio. of Sheffield, 1971. Member of Lloyd's, 1968. Comdr, Order of Merit (W Germany); Order of Aztec Eagle (Mexico). *Recreations:* walking and dining. *Address:* 24 Old Buildings, Lincoln's Inn, WC2A 3UJ. *T:* 01-242 2744; Brocklehurst, Keswick, Cumbria. *T:* Keswick 70042. *Clubs:* Athenæum; Derwent (Keswick).

GRAHAM, Gerald Sandford, MA, PhD, FRHistS; Rhodes Professor of Imperial History, London University, 1949-70, now Emeritus; *b* Sudbury, Ontario, 27 April 1903; *s* of Rev. H. S. Graham and Florence Marian Chambers; *m* 1929, Winifred Emily Ware (marr. diss. 1950); one *s*; *m* 1950, Constance Mary Greey, Toronto; one *s* two *d*. *Educ:* Queen's Univ., Canada; Harvard, 1926-27; Cambridge, 1927-29; Berlin and Freiburg-im-Breisgau, 1929-30; Instructor in History, and Tutor, Harvard Univ., 1930-36; successively Asst, Associate, and Prof. of History, Queen's Univ., 1936-46; Guggenheim Fellowship to US, 1941; RCNVR, 1942-45; Reader in History, Birkbeck Coll., Univ. of London, 1946-48. Mem., Inst. for Advanced Study, Princeton, 1952. Wilbur Knapp Vis. Prof., Univ. of Wisconsin, 1961; Vis. Prof. of Strategic Studies, Univ. of Western Ontario, 1970-72; Vis. Montague Burton Prof. of Internat. Relations, Univ. of Edinburgh, 1974. Hon. DLitt Univ. of Waterloo, Ont, 1973; Hon. LLD Queen's Univ., Ont, 1976. *Publications:* British Policy and Canada, 1774-1791, 1930; Sea Power and British North America, 1783-1820, 1941; Contributor to Newfoundland, Economic, Diplomatic and Strategic Studies, 1946; Empire of the North Atlantic, 1950 (2nd edn 1958); Canada, A Short History, 1950; The Walker Expedition to Quebec, 1711 (Navy Records Soc., and Champlain Soc.), 1953; The Politics of Naval Supremacy, 1965; contributor to Cambridge History of the British Empire, Vol. III, 1959; (with R. A. Humphreys) The Navy and South America, 1807-1823 (Navy Records Soc.), 1962; Britain in the Indian Ocean, 1810-1850, 1967; A Concise History of Canada, 1968; A Concise History of the British Empire, 1970; Tides of Empire, 1972; The Royal Navy in the American War of Independence, 1976. *Address:* Hobbs Cottage, Beckley, Rye, Sussex. *Clubs:* Athenæum, Royal Commonwealth Society.

GRAHAM, Gordon, PRIBA; Senior Partner, Architects Design Group, since 1958; President of the Royal Institute of British

Architects, since 1977; b Carlisle, 4 June 1920; s of late Stanley Bouch Graham and Isabel Hetherington; m 1946, Enid Pennington; three d . Educ: Creighton Sch.; Nottingham Sch. of Architecture. DipArch, RIBA, 1949. Served Royal Artillery, N Africa, Italy and NW Europe, 1940-46. Sen. Lectr, Nottingham Sch. of Architecture, 1949-61; RIBA Arthur Cates Prizeman, 1949; travelling scholar, South and Central America, 1953. Pres., Nottingham, Derby and Lincoln Soc. of Architects, 1965-66; RIBA: Chm., E Midlands Region, 1967-69; Mem. Council, 1967-73 and 1974; Vice-Pres., 1969-71; Hon. Sec., 1971-72 and 1975-76; Sen. Vice-Pres., 1976. Principal works in the field of industrial architecture; awards and commendations from RIBA, Civic Trust and Financial Times. Recreations: Rugby football, architecture. Address: Lockington Hall, Lockington, Derby DE7 2RH. Club: Reform.

GRAHAM, Air Vice-Marshal Henry Rudolph, CB 1958; CBE 1955; DSO 1941; DFC 1942; b 28 March 1910; s of Major Campbell Frederick Graham, late Cape Mounted Rifles and South African Mounted Rifles, and Frances Elizabeth Cheeseman; m 1949, Maisie Frances Butler; two s. Educ: Rondebosch; SA Trng Ship General Botha, S Africa. Union Castle Line, 1926-31; RAF, 1931-62. National Trust, 1966-69. Military Cross (Czechoslovakia), 1940. Recreations: cricket, golf, Rugby football. Address: The Country Club, PO Box 92, Plettenberg Bay, CP, South Africa. Clubs: Royal Air Force; Knysna Yacht (SA).

GRAHAM, Lt-Gen. Howard Douglas, OC 1967; CVO 1973; CBE 1946; DSO 1943 and Bar 1944; ED; CD; QC (Canada); retired as Lieutenant-General Canadian Army; b 1898. Served War of 1914-18: Canadian Infantry in France, Germany and Belgium; served War of 1939-45 (DSO and Bar, CBE), UK, France, 1940, Sicily and Italy; Senior Canadian Army Liaison Officer, London, and Army Adviser to the Canadian High Commissioner in London, 1946-48; Vice-Chief of Canadian General Staff, 1948-50; Gen. Officer Commanding Central Command, Canada, 1951-55; Chief of Canadian Gen. Staff, 1955-58; undertook, on behalf of Canadian Govt, during 1958, a comprehensive survey of all aspects of Canada's civil def. policy and programme. Acted as Canadian Sec. to the Queen, 1959 and 1967. Pres. (retd), Toronto Stock Exchange. Officer, US Legion of Merit; Chevalier Legion of Honour (France); Croix de Guerre with palm (France). Address: 33 Colonial Crescent, Oakville, Ont., Canada.

GRAHAM, Ian James Alastair, FSA; Assistant Curator, Peabody Museum of Archaeology, Harvard University; b 12 Nov. 1923; s of Captain Lord Alastair Graham, y s of 5th Duke of Montrose, and Lady Meriel Olivia Bathurst (d 1936), d of 7th Earl Bathurst; unmarried. Educ: Winchester Coll.; Trinity Coll., Dublin. RNVR (A), 1942-47; TCD 1947-51; Nuffield Foundn Research Scholar at The National Gallery, 1951-54; independent archaeological explorer in Central America from 1959. Occasional photographer of architecture. Publications: Splendours of the East, 1965; Great Houses of the Western World, 1968; Archaeological Explorations in El Peten, Guatemala, 1967; Corpus of Maya Hieroglyphic Inscriptions, vols 1 and 2, 1975; other reports in learned jls. Address: Chantry Farm, Campsey Ash, Suffolk. T: Wickham Market 746632; c/o Peabody Museum, Harvard University, Cambridge, Mass, USA. Club: White's.

GRAHAM, John, CB 1976; Fisheries Secretary, Ministry of Agriculture, Fisheries and Food, 1967-76; b 17 March 1918; s of late John Graham; m 1940, Betty Ramage Jarvie; two s three d. Educ: Fettes Coll., Edinburgh; Trinity Coll., Cambridge (Schol.). Classical Tripos, MA Cantab. Entered Post Office as Asst Principal, 1939; Min. of Food, 1940.

GRAHAM, John Alexander Noble, CMG 1972; HM Diplomatic Service; Deputy Under-Secretary of State, Foreign and Commonwealth Office, since 1977; b 15 July 1926; s and heir of Sir John Reginald Noble Graham, Bt, qv; m 1956, Marygold Ellinor Gabrielle Austin; two s one d. Educ: Eton Coll.; Trinity Coll., Cambridge. Army, 1944-47; Cambridge, 1948-50; HM Foreign Service, 1950; Middle East Centre for Arab Studies, 1951; Third Secretary, Bahrain 1951, Kuwait 1952, Amman 1953; Asst Private Sec. to Sec. of State for Foreign Affairs, 1954-57; First Sec., Belgrade, 1957-60, Benghazi, 1960-61; FO 1961-66; Counsellor and Head of Chancery, Kuwait, 1966-69; Principal Private Sec. to Foreign and Commonwealth Sec., 1969-72; Cllr (later Minister) and Head of Chancery, Washington, 1972-74; Ambassador to Iraq, 1974-77. Address: c/o Foreign and Commonwealth Office, SW1; Caerlaverock House, Glencaple, Dumfries. Club: Army and Navy.

GRAHAM, Maj.-Gen. John David Carew, CBE 1973 (OBE 1966); General Officer Commanding, Wales, since 1976; b 18 Jan. 1923; s of late Col J. A. Graham, late RE, and of Constance Mary Graham (née Carew-Hunt); m 1956, Rosemary Elaine Adamson; one s one d . Educ: Cheltenham Coll. psc 1955; jssc 1962. Commissioned into Argyll and Sutherland Highlanders, 1942 (despatches, 1945); served with 5th (Scottish) Bn, The Parachute Regt, 1946-49; British Embassy, Prague, 1949-50; HQ Scottish Comd, 1956-58; Mil. Asst to CINCENT, Fontainebleau, 1960-62; comd 1st Bn, The Parachute Regt, 1964-66; Instr at Staff Coll., Camberley, 1967; Regtl Col, The Parachute Regt, 1968-69; Comdr, Sultan's Armed Forces, Oman, 1970-72; Indian Nat. Defence Coll., New Delhi, 1973; Asst Chief of Staff, HQ AFCENT, 1974-76. Order of Oman, 1972. Recreations: photography, gardening. Address: Headquarters Wales, The Barracks, Brecon LD3 7EA. T: Brecon 3111.

GRAHAM, Prof. John Macdonald, CBE 1955; Professor of Systematic Theology, University of Aberdeen, 1937-71, retired; b 17 March 1908; s of Thomas Graham and Elizabeth Macdonald; m 1933, Jessie Huntley Carmichael; two s twin d. Educ: Allan Glen's Sch., Glasgow; University of Glasgow. MA. First Cl. Hons in Mental Philosophy, 1930; Ferguson Scholar in Philosophy, 1931. Minister of Radnor Park, Clydebank, 1933-37. Mem. of Aberdeen Town Council, 1947-64; Lord Provost of the City of Aberdeen, 1952-55 and 1961-64; DL 1956; Hon. DD Glasgow, 1959; Hon. LLD Aberdeen, 1964. FEIS 1964. Publication: Christianity, Democracy and Communism, 1958. Address: Ruchil House, Comrie, Perthshire. T: Comrie 307.

GRAHAM, Sir John (Moodie), 2nd Bt cr 1964; Director: John Graham (Dromore) Ltd, since 1966 (Chairman); Electrical Supplies Ltd, since 1967; Concrete (NI) Ltd, since 1967; Irish Terrazzo Ltd; Kwik-Mix Ltd; Ulster Quarries Ltd; Graham (Contracts) Ltd; G. H. Fieldhouse Plant (NI) Ltd; Fieldtrac Scotland Ltd; Sykes Pumps (NI) Ltd; b 3 April 1938; s of Sir Clarence Graham, 1st Bt, MICE, and Margaret Christina Moodie (d 1954); S father, 1966; m 1970, Valerie Rosemary, d of Frank Gill, Belfast; two d. Educ: Trinity Coll., Glenalmond; Queen's Univ., Belfast. BSc, Civil Engineering, 1961. Joined family firm of John Graham (Dromore) Ltd, Building and Civil Engineering Contractors, on graduating from University. Chm., Concrete Soc., NI, 1972-74; Vice-Pres., Concrete Soc. Pres., Northern Ireland Leukaemia Research Fund, 1967. Recreations: sailing, squash, water ski-ing, photography. Address: Sketrick Island, Killinchy, Co. Down. T: Killinchy 541449. Clubs: Strangford Lough Yacht; Dansk Yachtclub (Copenhagen).

GRAHAM, Hon. Sir (John) Patrick, Kt 1969; **Hon. Mr Justice Graham;** Judge of the High Court of Justice, Chancery Division, since 1969; Senior Patent Judge; b 26 Nov. 1906; s of Alexander Graham and Mary Adeline Cock; m 1931, Annie Elizabeth Newport Willson; four s. Educ: Shrewsbury; Caius Coll., Cambridge. Called to Bar, Middle Temple, 1930; read with Sir Lionel Heald, QC, MP; QC 1953. Served War of 1939-45: RAF (VR) and with SHAEF, demobilised, 1945, with rank of Group Capt. Dep.-Chm., Salop Quarter Sessions, 1961-69. Publication: Awards to Inventors, 1946. Recreations: golf, tennis, sailing. Address: Tall Elms, Radlett, Herts. T: Radlett 6307.

GRAHAM, Sir (John) Reginald (Noble), 3rd Bt of Larbert, cr 1906; VC 1917; OBE 1946; Major, Argyll and Sutherland Highlanders, TF and MGC; b 17 Sept. 1892; e s of Sir J. F. N. Graham, 2nd Bt; S father, 1936; m 1920, Rachel Septima, d of Col Sir Alexander Sprot, 1st and last Bt; one s one d. Educ: Cheam; Eton; Cambridge. Served European War (Mesopotamia and Palestine), 1914-18 (VC); Emergency Commission Sept. 1939 (Staff Capt.); Served on Staff at War Office, Essex Div. and Scottish Comd, temp. Lt-Col 1942-46 (OBE). Gentleman Usher of the Green Rod to the Most Noble Order of the Thistle, 1959-. Heir: s John Alexander Noble Graham, qv. Address: The Mailens, Gullane, East Lothian.

GRAHAM, Kathleen Mary, CBE 1958 (MBE 1945); d of late Col R. B. Graham, CBE, and Mrs M. G. Graham, London; unmarried. Educ: Cheltenham Ladies' Coll.; Univ. of London (Courtauld Inst. of Art). Courtauld Inst., Dept of Technology War-time Laboratory, 1940-41; Political Warfare Executive, 1942-45; entered HM Foreign Service, 1945; served in FO, 1946-49; Consul (Information) at San Francisco, Calif, 1949-53; served in FO, 1953-55; made Counsellor in HM Foreign Service in 1955 and appointed Dep. Consul-Gen. in New York, 1955-59; HM Consul-Gen. at Amsterdam, 1960-63; in FO, 1964-69, retired. Exec. Dir, 1970-73, a Governor, 1973-, E-SU. Recreations: music, history of art. Address: 16 Graham Terrace, SW1W 8JH. T: 01-730 4611.

GRAHAM, Kenneth, OBE 1971; Assistant General Secretary, Trades Union Congress, since 1977; Member (part-time), Manpower Services Commission, since 1974; *b* 18 July 1922; *er s* of Ernest Graham and Ivy Hutchinson, Cumberland; *m* 1945, Ann Winifred Muriel Taylor; no *c. Educ:* Workington Techn. Sch.; Leyton Techn. Coll.; Univ. of London (external). Engrg apprentice, 1938-42; Radar Research Unit, 1942-45; Air Trng Sch., qual. licensed engr, Air Registration Bd, 1947; employed in private industry, Mins of Aircraft Prodn and Supply, BOAC, and RN Scientific Service. Joined AEU, 1938: Mem. Final Appeal Court, Nat. Cttee, Divisional Chm., District Pres., etc, 1947-61; Tutor (part-time) in Trade Union Studies, Univ. of Southampton and WEA Jt Cttee for Adult Educn, 1958-61; TUC Organisation Dept, 1961-77, Head of TUC Organisation and Industrial Relations Dept, 1966-77. Member: Labour Utilisation Cttee, NEDC and Nat. Jt Adv. Council's Cttees on manpower, dismissals procedures and redundancy policies, 1964-68; Council, Inst. of Manpower Studies, 1975; Bd, European Foundn for Improvement of Living and Working Conditions, 1976. *Publications:* contrib. Job Satisfaction: Challenge and Response in Modern Britain, 1976. *Recreations:* music, military history. *Address:* 90 Springfield Drive, Ilford, Essex. *T:* 01-554 0839.

GRAHAM, Martha; dancer; choreographer; director and teacher of dancing at the Martha Graham School of Contemporary Dance in New York; *b* Pittsburgh, Pa; *d* of Dr and Mrs George Graham. *Educ:* privately, and with Ruth St Denis and Ted Shawn. First appeared in Xochitl, New York, 1920; first recital by pupils, 1926; danced lead in Stravinsky's La Sacre du Printemps, 1930; founded Dance Repertory Theatre, 1930; choreographer of 144 solo and ensemble productions inc. three films (A Dancer's World, 1957; Appalachian Spring, 1958; Night Journey, 1960). Foreign tours, 1954, 1955-56, 1958, 1962, 1963, 1967; performed and lectured in major cities of Europe, Middle East, Iron Curtain countries, and throughout the Orient; has given solo performances with leading orchestras of United States. Three by Martha Graham, TV, 1969. Teacher: Neighbourhood Playhouse; Juilliard Sch. of Music. In the last five years her sch. has taken students from over forty foreign countries. Guggenheim Fellow, 1932, 1939; holds many doctorates and awards, including the Capezio Award, 1959, and the Aspen Award in the Humanities, 1965. *Publication:* The Notebooks of Martha Graham, 1973; *relevant publication:* Martha Graham: Portrait of a Lady as an Artist, by LeRoy Leatherman, 1966. *Address:* Martha Graham School of Contemporary Dance, 316 East 63rd Street, New York, NY 10021, USA. *Club:* Cosmopolitan (New York).

GRAHAM, Sir Norman (William), Kt 1971; CB 1961; FRSE; Member, Council on Tribunals, since 1977; Secretary, Scottish Education Department, 1964-73, retired; *b* 11 Oct. 1913; *s* of William and Margaret Graham; *m* 1949, Catherine Mary Strathie; two *s* one *d. Educ:* High Sch. of Glasgow; Glasgow Univ. Dept of Health for Scotland, 1936; Private Sec. to Permanent Under-Sec. of State, 1939-40; Ministry of Aircraft Production, 1940; Principal Private Sec. to Minister, 1944-45; Asst Sec., Dept of Health for Scotland, 1945; Under-Sec., Scottish Home and Health Dept, 1956-63. Hon. DLitt Heriot-Watt, 1971; DUniv Stirling, 1974. *Recreations:* golf, gardening. *Address:* Suilven, Longniddry, East Lothian. *T:* Longniddry 52130. *Club:* New (Edinburgh).

GRAHAM, Hon. Sir Patrick; *see* Graham, Hon. Sir J. P.

GRAHAM, Peter; Parliamentary Counsel since 1972; *b* 7 Jan. 1934; *o s* of Alderman Douglas Graham, CBE, Huddersfield, and Ena May (*née* Jackson); *m* 1959; two *s. Educ:* St Bees Sch., Cumberland; St John's Coll., Cambridge (MA, LLB). Served as pilot in Fleet Air Arm, 1952-55. Called to Bar, Grays Inn, 1958; joined Parliamentary Counsel Office, 1959. *Recreation:* vintage motoring of all descriptions. *Address:* 6 Reidon Hill, Bisley, Surrey. *T:* Brookwood 2394. *Clubs:* Athenæum; Vintage Sports Car.

GRAHAM, Sir Ralph Wolfe, 13th Bt *cr* 1629; *b* 14 July 1908; *s* of Percival Harris Graham (2nd *s* of 10th Bt) (*d* 1954) and Louise (*d* 1934), *d* of John Wolfe, Brooklyn, USA; *S* cousin, 1975; *m* 1st, 1939, Gertrude (marr. diss. 1949), *d* of Charles Kaminski; 2nd, 1949, Geraldine, *d* of Austin Velour; two *s. Heir: s* Ralph Stuart Graham [*b* 5 Nov. 1950; *m* 1972, Roxanne, *d* of Mrs Lovette Gurzan]. *Address:* 134 Leisureville Boulevard, Boynton Beach, Fla 33435, USA.

GRAHAM, Sir Reginald; *see* Graham, Sir J. R. N.

GRAHAM, Sir Richard Bellingham, 10th Bt of Norton Conyers, *cr* 1662; OBE 1946; DL; Wing Commander, RAFVR;

Chairman, Yorkshire Television, since 1968; *b* 17 May 1912; *e s* of Sir Guy Graham, 9th Bt, and Katharine Noel (*d* 1966), *d* of Frank Stobart, Selaby, Darlington; *S* father, 1940; *m* 1939, Beatrice Mary, *o d* of late Michael Seymour Spencer-Smith, DSO; three *s. Educ:* Eton Coll.; Magdalene Coll., Cambridge. DL N Yorks (formerly NR Yorks), 1961; High Sheriff of Yorkshire, 1961. *Heir: s* James Bellingham Graham, *b* 8 Oct. 1940. *Address:* Norton Conyers, Melmerby, Ripon, North Yorks.

GRAHAM, Colonel Robert M.; *see* Mould-Graham.

GRAHAM, Dr Ronald Cairns; Chief Administrative Medical Officer, Tayside Health Board, since 1973; *b* 8 Oct. 1931; *s* of Thomas Graham and Helen Cairns; *m* 1959, Christine Fraser Osborne; two *s* one *d. Educ:* Airdrie Acad.; Glasgow Univ. MB, ChB Glasgow 1956; DipSocMed Edin. 1968; FFCM 1973. West of Scotland; house jobs, gen. practice and geriatric med., 1956-62; Dep. Med. Supt, Edin. Royal Infirmary, 1962-65; Asst Sen. Admin. MO, SE Regional Hosp. Bd, 1965-69; Dep. and then Sen. Admin. MO, Eastern Regional Hosp. Bd, 1969-73. *Recreation:* fishing. *Address:* 34 Dalgleish Road, Dundee DD4 7JT. *T:* Dundee 43146.

GRAHAM, Samuel Horatio, CMG 1965; OBE 1962; **Hon. Mr Justice Graham;** Puisne Judge, Supreme Court of the Commonwealth of the Bahamas, since 1973; *b* 3 May 1912; *s* of late Rev. Benjamin Graham, Trinidad; *m* 1943, Oris Gloria (*née* Teka); two *s* four *d. Educ:* Barbados; External Student, London Univ. BA (London) 1945; LLB (London) 1949. Teacher and journalist until called to Bar, Gray's Inn, 1949. Private practice as Barrister in Grenada, 1949-53; Magistrate, St Lucia, 1953-57; Crown Attorney, St Kitts, 1957-59; Attorney-General, St Kitts, 1960-62; Administrator of St Vincent, 1962-66; Puisne Judge, British Honduras, 1966-69; Pres., Industrial Court of Antigua, 1969-70. Mem., Council of Legal Educn, WI, 1971-. Chairman Inquiries into: Income Tax Reliefs; Coconut Industry, St Lucia, 1955; Legislators' Salaries, St Kitts, 1962. Acted Administrator of St Lucia, St Kitts and Dominica on various occasions. Acted Chief Justice, British Honduras, Feb.-May 1968. CStJ 1964. *Recreations:* cricket, bridge, swimming. *Address:* Supreme Court, PO Box N167, Nassau, Bahamas. *Clubs:* Royal Commonwealth Society (West Indian); St John's House; St Vincent Aquatic; Lyford Cay (Bahamas).

GRAHAM, (Stewart) David, QC 1977; *b* 27 Feb. 1934; *s* of Lewis Graham and Gertrude Graham; *m* 1959, Corinne Carmona; two *d. Educ:* Leeds Grammar Sch.; St Edmund Hall, Oxford (MA, BCL). Called to the Bar, Middle Temple, 1957; Harmsworth Law Scholar, 1958. Member: Council of Justice, 1976-; Bd of Deputies of British Jews, 1959-. *Publications:* (ed jtly) Williams on Bankruptcy, 1968; (ed) legal textbooks. *Recreations:* literature, music, travel. *Address:* (chambers) 3 Paper Buildings, Temple, EC4 7EU. *T:* 01-353 3721; (home) 133 London Road, Stanmore, Mddx. *T:* 01-954 3783.

GRAHAM, Stuart Twentyman, DFC 1943; FCIS, FIB; Director and Chief General Manager, Midland Bank Ltd, since 1974; *b* 26 Aug. 1921; *s* of late Twentyman Graham; *m* 1948, Betty June Cox; one *s. Educ:* Kilburn Grammar Sch. Served War, 1940-46: commissioned, RAF, 1942. Entered Midland Bank, 1938; Jt Gen. Manager, 1966; Asst Chief Gen. Manager, 1970. Director: Clydesdale Bank Ltd; Northern Bank Ltd. Member: Council, Inst. of Bankers; Industrial Develt Adv. Board, 1977-. *Recreations:* music, reading. *Address:* 14 Whitecroft Way, Beckenham, Kent BR3 3AG. *T:* 01-650 4786. *Clubs:* RAF Reserves, Overseas Bankers'.

GRAHAM, (Thomas) Edward; MP (Lab and Co-op) Enfield, Edmonton since Feb. 1974; a Lord Commissioner, HM Treasury, since 1976; *b* 26 March 1925; *m* 1950; two *s. Educ:* elementary sch.; WEA Co-operative College. BA Open Univ., 1976. Newcastle-on-Tyne Co-operative Soc., 1939-52; Organiser, British Fedn of Young Co-operators, 1952-53; Educn Sec., Enfield Highway Co-operative Soc., 1953-62; Sec., Co-operative Union Southern Section, 1962-67; Nat. Sec., Co-operative Party, 1967-74. *Address:* 90 First Avenue, Bush Hill Park, Enfield, Mddx EN1 1BP. *T:* 01-363 3013.

GRAHAM, Walter Gerald Cloete, CBE 1952; retired 1975; *b* 13 May 1906; *s* of late Lance Graham Cloete Graham, of HBM Consular Service in China; *m* 1937, Nellor Alice Lee Swan; one *s*; *m* 1949, Cynthia Anne, *d* of late Sir George Clayton East, Bt; one *s* one *d. Educ:* Malvern Coll.; The Queen's Coll., Oxford. Laming Travelling Fellow of Queen's, 1927-29. Entered Consular Service in China, 1928; served in Peking, Nanking, Shanghai, Mukden Chefoo and Tientsin; Consul: Port Said, 1942-44, Chengtu, 1944-45, Urumchi (Chinese Turkestan),

1945-47; Consul-General, Mukden, 1947-49, Peking, 1949-50; Counsellor, Foreign Office, 1951-52; Minister to Republic of Korea, 1952-54; Ambassador to Libya, 1955-59; Asia Adviser to Defence Intelligence Staff (formerly Jt Intell. Bureau), Min. of Defence, 1959-67; Res. Adviser, FCO Res. Dept, 1967-75. *Recreations:* cricket, golf, gardening. *Address:* Knabb's Farmhouse, Fletching, Uckfield, Sussex. *T:* Newick 2198. *Club:* MCC.

GRAHAM, Rear-Adm. Wilfred Jackson; Flag Officer, Portsmouth, since Oct. 1976; *b* 17 June 1925; *s* of William Bryce Graham and Jean Hill Graham (*née* Jackson); *m* 1951, Gillian Mary Finlayson; three *s* one *d*. *Educ:* Rossall Sch., Fleetwood, Lancs. Served War of 1939-45, Royal Navy: Cadet, 1943; specialised in gunnery, 1951; Comdr 1960; Captain 1967; IDC, 1970; Captain, HMS Ark Royal, 1975-76. *Recreations:* sailing, walking, skiing. *Address:* Lych Gate Cottage, Crondall, near Farnham, Surrey GU10 5PW. *T:* Aldershot 850 525. *Club:* Royal Naval Sailing Association.

GRAHAM, William, CB 1950; MBE 1920; Acting Secretary-General of the Intergovernmental Maritime Consultative Organisation (IMCO), 1961-63, Deputy Secretary-General, 1959-61; *b* 14 Dec. 1894; *s* of late A. Graham, Bradford, Yorks; *m* 1917, Elizabeth Young Warnock; one *s* one *d*. *Educ:* Bradford. Entered CS, 1911; served in Board of Trade until formation of Ministry of Shipping, 1939; Asst Secretary, Commercial Services Division, Ministry of Transport, 1940-46; Head of British Merchant Shipping Mission in Washington, DC, 1946; Under-Secretary, Ministry of Transport, 1946-59; Vice-Chairman, Maritime Transport Cttee, OEEC, 1948-59. *Address:* 115 Downs Court Road, Purley, Surrey. *T:* 01-660 1263.

GRAHAM, William Franklin, (Billy Graham); Evangelist; *b* Charlotte, NC, 7 Nov. 1918; *s* of William Franklin Graham and Morrow (*née* Coffey); *m* 1943, Ruth McCue Bell; two *s* three *d*. *Educ:* Florida Bible Institute, Tampa (ThB); Wheaton Coll., Ill (AB). Ordained to Baptist ministry, 1940; first Vice-Pres., Youth for Christ Internat., 1946-48; Pres., Northwestern Coll., Minneapolis, 1947-52; Evangelistic campaigns, 1946-; world-wide weekly broadcast, 1950-; many evangelistic tours of Great Britain, Europe, the Far East, South America and Australia. Chairman, Board of World Wide Pictures Inc. FRGS. Holds numerous honorary degrees in Divinity, Laws, Literature and the Humanities, from American universities and colleges; also varied awards from organisations, 1954-. *Publications include:* Peace with God, 1954; World Aflame, 1965; Jesus Generation, 1971; Angels—God's Secret Agents, 1976. *Recreations:* golf, jogging. *Address:* (office) 1300 Harmon Place, Minneapolis, Minnesota 55403, USA. *T:* 332-8081.

GRAHAM, Winston Mawdsley, FRSL; *b* Victoria Park, Manchester; *m* 1939, Jean Mary Williamson; one *s* one *d*. Chm., Soc. of Authors, 1967-69. Books trans. into 15 languages. *Publications:* some early novels (designedly) out of print, and are: Night Journey, 1941 (rev. edn 1966); The Forgotten Story, 1945; Ross Poldark, 1945; Demelza, 1946; Take My Life, 1947 (filmed 1947); Cordelia, 1949; Night Without Stars, 1950 (filmed 1950); Jeremy Poldark, 1950; Fortune is a Woman, 1953 (filmed 1956); Warleggan, 1953; The Little Walls, 1955; The Sleeping Partner, 1956 (filmed 1958); Greek Fire, 1957; The Tumbled House, 1959; Marnie, 1961 (filmed 1963); The Grove of Eagles, 1963; After the Act, 1965; The Walking Stick, 1967 (filmed 1970); Angell, Pearl and Little God, 1970; The Japanese Girl (short stories), 1971; The Spanish Armadas, 1972; The Black Moon, 1973; Woman in the Mirror, 1975; The Four Swans, 1976; The Angry Tide, 1977. BBC TV Series Poldark (the first four Poldark novels), 1975-76, second series (the last three Poldark novels), 1977. *Recreations:* golf, gardening, swimming. *Address:* Abbotswood House, Buxted, East Sussex. *T:* Buxted 3233. *Club:* Savile.

GRAHAM BRYCE, Dame Isabel, DBE 1968; Chairman: Oxford Regional Hospital Board, 1963-72; National Nursing Staff Committee, 1967-75; National Staff Committee, 1969-75; Member Board, British Transport Hotels, since 1962; Vice-President, Princess Christian College, Manchester, since 1953; Chairman, Goring and District Day Centre for the Elderly; *b* 30 April 1902; *d* of late Prof. James Lorrain Smith, FRS; *m* 1934, Alexander Graham Bryce, FRCS (*d* 1968); two *s*. *Educ:* St Leonards Sch., St Andrews; Edinburgh Univ. (MA). Investigator, Industrial Fatigue Research Board, 1926-27; HM Inspector of Factories, 1928-34; Centre Organiser, WVS, Manchester, 1938-39; Dir of Organization, Ontario Div., Canadian WVS, 1941-42; Tech. Adviser, American WVS, 1942-43; Res. Fellow Fatigue Lab. Harvard Univ., 1943-44; Nat. Council of Women: Chm., Manchester Br., 1947-50; Vice-Chm., Education Cttee, 1950-51. JP and Mem. Juvenile Court Panel,

Manchester City, 1949-55; Vice-Chairman: Assoc. of HMC's, 1953-55; Bd of Visitors, Grendon Prison, 1962-67. Member: Nurses and Midwives Whitley Council, 1953-57; General Nursing Council, 1956-61; Bd of Governors, Eastman Dental Hosp., 1957-63; Maternity and Midwifery Standing Cttee, 1957-72; Public Health Insp., Education Bd, 1958-64; Independent Television Authority, 1960-65 (Chm., General Advisory Council, 1964-65); Bd, ATV Network Ltd, 1968-72; Ancillary Dental Workers Cttee, 1956-68; Experimental Scheme for Dental Auxiliaries, 1958-69. *Publications:* (joint) reports on research into industrial psychological problems. *Address:* 2 St Leonard's Court, Reading Road, Wallingford OX10 9EY. *T:* Wallingford 35837. *Club:* VAD Ladies'.

GRAHAM-CAMPBELL, Rt. Rev. Archibald Rollo, CBE 1965; Assistant Bishop of Peterborough, since 1965; *b* 18 Feb. 1903; *s* of late Sir Rollo Frederick Graham-Campbell. *Educ:* Eton; King's Coll., Cambridge; Cuddesdon Theological Coll., 1st class Classical Tripos, Pt I, 1923; 1st class Classical Tripos Pt II, 1924; 2nd class Theological Tripos, Pt II, 1925; BA 1924; MA 1929; Deacon, 1926; Priest, 1927; Curate of St John, Middlesbrough, 1926-30; Assistant Master, Eton Coll., 1930-37; Vicar of St Paul, King Cross, 1937-42; Fellow, Dean and Chaplain of King's Coll., Cambridge, 1942-48; Examining Chaplain to Bishop of St Albans and to Bishop of Lincoln, 1946-48; Bishop of Colombo, 1948-64; Rector of Kislingbury with Rothersthorpe, 1965-68. Hon. Canon of Peterborough, 1967-. *Address:* 4 Penfold Drive, Great Billing, Northampton. *T:* Northampton 890498. *Clubs:* MCC, United Oxford & Cambridge University.
See also D. J. Graham-Campbell.

GRAHAM-CAMPBELL, David John, MA Cantab; Liaison Officer to Schools, Aberdeen University, since 1972-76; *b* 18 Feb. 1912; *s* of late Sir R. F. Graham-Campbell; *m* 1940, Joan Sybil, *d* of late Major H. F. Maclean; three *s*. *Educ:* Eton Coll.; Trinity Coll., Cambridge (Exhibitioner). Assistant Master, Eton Coll., 1935-64; Warden, Trinity Coll., Glenalmond, 1964-72. Served with 2nd Bn KRRC and on the staff, 1939-45 (Lt-Col). *Publication:* Writing English, 1953. *Recreations:* fishing, gardening, walking. *Address:* 17 Muirton Bank, Perth, Perthshire.
See also Rt Rev. A. A. R. Graham-Campbell, Baron Maclean.

GRAHAM-DIXON, Anthony Philip, QC 1973; *b* 5 Nov. 1929; *s* of Leslie Charles Graham-Dixon, *q v*; *m* 1956, Margaret Suzanne Villar; one *s* one *d*. *Educ:* Westminster School; Christ Church, Oxford. MA (1st Cl. Hon. Mods, 1st Cl. Lit. Hum.). RNVR, 1953-55, Lieut (SP). Called to the Bar, Inner Temple, 1956; Member of Gray's Inn, 1965-. Mem. Council, Charing Cross Hosp. Medical School, 1976-. *Publication:* (mem. adv. bd) Competition Law in Western Europe, 1976. *Recreations:* music (especially opera), gardening, tennis. *Address:* 31 Hereford Square, SW7. *T:* 01-373 1461; Masketts, Nutley, Uckfield, East Sussex. *T:* Nutley 2719.

GRAHAM-DIXON, Leslie Charles, QC 1950; retired 1956; *b* 17 June 1901; *m* 1926, Dorothy Rivett; two *s*. *Educ:* Merchant Taylors' Sch.; St John's Coll., Oxford. Called to the Bar, 1925, Inner Temple. Western Circuit. *Address:* 34 Cadogan Place, SW1. *T:* 01-235 5943.
See also A. P. Graham-Dixon.

GRAHAM DOW, R.; *see* Dow, R. G.

GRAHAM-GREEN, Graham John, TD 1945; Chief Taxing Master of the Supreme Court, since 1972 (Master, 1953-72); *b* 16 Dec. 1906; *m* 1933, Eirene Mary Baston; one *d*. *Educ:* Dulwich. Admitted solicitor, 1929; Partner Kingsford, Dorman & Co., 1935-52; and Director of Companies. Served HAC, 1924-33; RA (TA), 1935-45. Freeman of City of London, 1945; Member of Solicitors Company, 1945; Co-Founder of Catholic Marriage Advisory Council, 1946. *Publications:* Cordery's Law Relating to Solicitors (5th edn), 1961, Supplements 1962, 1963, 1965 and 1966; (6th edn), 1968, Supplements 1970, 1974; Criminal Costs and Legal Aid, 1965, 3rd edn 1973, etc. *Recreations:* riding, travelling. *Address:* Far Forest, Maresfield Park, East Sussex. *T:* Nutley 210. *Club:* Army and Navy.

GRAHAM HALL, Jean; *see* Hall, J. G.

GRAHAM-HARRISON, Francis Laurence Theodore, CB 1962; Deputy Under-Secretary of State, Home Office, 1963-74; *b* 30 Oct. 1914; *s* of late Sir William Montagu Graham-Harrison, KCB, KC, and Lady Graham-Harrison, *d* of Sir Cyril Graham, 5th and last Bt, CMG; *m* 1941, Carol Mary St John, 3rd *d* of late Sir Francis Stewart, CIE; one *s* three *d*. *Educ:* Eton; Magdalen

Coll., Oxford. Entered Home Office, 1938. Private Secretary to Parliamentary Under-Secretary of State, 1941-43; Asst Private Secretary to Prime Minister, 1946-49; Secretary, Royal Commission on Capital Punishment, 1949-53; Asst Secretary, Home Office, 1953-57; Asst Under-Secretary of State, Home Office, 1957-63. Trustee, Tate Gallery, 1975-. *Address:* 37 Steele's Road, NW3. *T:* 01-722 9618.

GRAHAM-MOON, Sir P. W. G.; *see* Moon.

GRAHAM SMITH, Stanley, CBE 1949; *b* 18 Jan. 1896; *s* of late George and Minnie Elizabeth Graham Smith; *m* 1929, Mrs Blanche Violet Horne (*d* 1974), widow (*née* Venning); one *s*. *Educ:* Strand Sch., King's Coll., London. Entered Civil Service, 1914 (Admiralty). Served European War as pilot in Royal Naval Air Service, Dec. 1916-Jan. 1919. Rejoined Admiralty, 1919. Private Secretary to Accountant-General of the Navy, 1922-32; Private Secretary to Civil Lord of Admiralty, 1932-35; Head of Air Branch, Admiralty, 1941-49; Under Secretary (Naval Staff), Admiralty, 1950-56; retired from Civil Service, 1956.

GRAHAM-TOLER, family name of the **Earl of Norbury.**

GRAHAM-VIVIAN, (Richard) Preston, MVO 1961; MC; Norroy and Ulster King of Arms, 1966-71, retired; *b* 10 Aug. 1896; 2nd *s* of late Sir Richard James Graham, Bt, and Lady Cynthia Duncombe; assumed additional surname of Vivian by Royal Licence, 1929; *m* 1921, Audrey Emily, *o c* of late Major Henry Wyndham Vivian and late Lady Maude Clements (who *m* 2nd, Christopher Foulis Roundell, CBE; he *d* 1958); one *s* one *d*. *Educ:* Eton; Trinity Coll., Cambridge (BA). Served European War, 1915-19, as Lieut in 21st and 7th Bns KRRC (twice wounded, prisoner, MC). Bluemantle Pursuivant of Arms, 1933-47; Windsor Herald of Arms, 1947-66; Earl Marshal's Secretary, 1954-61. FZS (Life). Hon. FSG; Vice-Pres., Irish Genealogical Res. Soc., 1968-. OStJ, 1949. *Address:* Wealden House, Warninglid, Haywards Heath, West Sussex. *T:* Warninglid 272. *Club:* Travellers'.

GRAHAME-SMITH, Prof. David Grahame; Professor of Clinical Pharmacology, University of Oxford, since 1972; Hon. Director, Medical Research Council Unit of Clinical Pharmacology, Radcliffe Infirmary, Oxford; Fellow of Corpus Christi College, Oxford, since 1972; *b* 10 May 1933; *s* of George E. and C. A. Smith; *m* 1957, Kathryn Frances, *d* of Dr F. R. Beetham; two *s*. *Educ:* Wyggeston Grammar Sch., Leicester; St Mary's Hosp. Medical Sch., Univ. of London. MB, BS (London) 1956; MRCS, LRCP 1956; MRCP 1958; PhD (London) 1966; FRCP 1972. House Phys., Paddington Gen. Hosp., London, 1956; House Surg., Battle Hosp., Reading, 1956-57. Captain, RAMC, 1957-60. Registrar and Sen. Registrar in Medicine, St Mary's Hosp., Paddington, 1960-61; H. A. M. Thompson Research Scholar, RCP, 1961-62; Saltwell Research Scholar, RCP, 1962-65; Wellcome Trust Research Fellow, 1965-66; Hon. Med. Registrar to Med. Unit, St Mary's Hosp., 1961-66; MRC Travelling Fellow, Dept of Endocrinology, Vanderbilt Univ., Nashville, Tennessee, USA, 1966-67; Sen. Lectr in Clinical Pharmacology and Therapeutics, St Mary's Hosp. Med. Sch., Univ. of London, 1967-71; Hon. Cons. Physician, St Mary's Hosp., Paddington, 1967-71. Mem., Cttee on Safety of Medicines, 1975. *Publications:* papers on biochemical, therapeutic and med. matters in scientific jls. *Recreations:* horse riding, jazz. *Address:* Romney, Lincombe Lane, Boars Hill, Oxford. *T:* Oxford 735889.

GRAHAMSTOWN, Bishop of, since 1974; **Rt. Rev. Kenneth Cyril Oram;** *b* 3 March 1919; *s* of Alfred Charles Oram and Sophie Oram; *m* 1943, Kathleen Mary Malcolm; three *s* one *d*. *Educ:* Selhurst Grammar Sch., Croydon; King's Coll., London; Lincoln Theol Coll. BA Hons English, 1st Cl. AKC. Asst Curate: St Dunstan's, Cranbrook, 1942-45; St Mildred's, Croydon, 1945-46; Upington with Prieska, S Africa, 1946-48; Rector of Prieska and Dir of Prieska Mission District, 1949-51; Rector of Mafeking, 1952-59; Dir of Educn, dio. Kimberley and Kuruman, 1953-62; Archdeacon of Bechuanaland, 1953-59; Dean and Archdeacon: of Kimberley, 1960-64; of Grahamstown, 1964-74. *Recreations:* music, walking. *Address:* Bishopsbourne, PO Box 162, Grahamstown, South Africa. *T:* 2500. *Club:* Albany (Grahamstown).

GRAINER, Ron; composer for stage and screen; *b* Atherton, Australia, 11 Aug. 1922; *s* of Ronald Albert and Margaret Grainer; *m* 1966, Jennifer Marilyn Dodd; one *s*. *Educ:* St Joseph's Coll., Nudgee, Brisbane; Sydney Conservatorium. *Compositions include:* musicals: Robert and Elizabeth, 1964; On the Level, 1966; Sing a Rude Song, 1970; *incidental music for stage:* Andorra, Nat. Theatre, 1964; Come As You Are, 1970; *film scores:* Some People; Live Now, Pay Later; Dock Brief;

Terminus; The Caretaker; Night Must Fall; A Kind of Loving; The Moonspinners; The Finest Hours; To Sir with Love; Lock up your Daughters; Before Winter Comes; The Omega Man; Cat and Mouse; *TV themes and incidental music:* Steptoe and Son; Maigret; Comedy Playhouse; Dr Who; Panorama; That Was The Week That Was; Boy Meets Girl; Man in a Suitcase; Thief; Paul Temple; For the Love of Ada; The Train Now Standing; South Riding. *Recreations:* humane farming, swimming. *Address:* Apartado 37, Albufeira, Algarve, Portugal. *Clubs:* Rotary, Vegetarian Soc.

GRAINGER, Leslie, CBE 1976; BSc, FIM; MInstF; Chairman: National Coal Board (Coal Products) Ltd, since 1977; National Coal Boar (IEA Services) Ltd, since 1977; *b* 8 August 1917. Mem. for Science, NCB, 1966-77. *Address:* National Coal Board, Hobart House, SW1. *T:* 01-235 2020.

GRAINGER-STEWART, Brig. Thomas, CB 1952; MC 1917; TD 1934 (3 bars); DL; retired as Deputy Secretary, Scottish Education Department; *b* 12 Jan. 1896; *s* of late Alexander Arthur Grainger-Stewart and of late Emily Francis Adam; *m* 1931, Pansy Gertrude Kemp (*d* 1976), *d* of late J. T. Salvesen, shipowner, Leith; no *c*. *Educ:* Edinburgh Academy; Edinburgh Univ. Called to Scottish Bar, 1921; Secretary, Educational Endowments (Scotland) Commn, 1929-36; Asst Sec., Scottish Education Dept, 1937-46; Under-Secretary, 1947-48; Deputy Secretary, 1949-59. Served European War, 1914-18, with 16th and 17th (Service) Battalions, The Royal Scots, 1914-19; France and Flanders, 1916-19, 2 Lt to Captain. Joined 7th/9th (Highlanders) Bn, The Royal Scots, TA, 1920; comd the Bn, 1932-38; Colonel 1936; Brigadier 1939; War of 1939-45, comd 155th (East Scottish) Infantry Bde, TA, 1939-42 (France, 1940); ADC to King George VI, 1943, and to Queen Elizabeth II, 1952-53. Hon. Colonel, 7th/9th (Highlanders) Bn, The Royal Scots, TA, 1955-60. Joined HM's Body Guard for Scotland, the Royal Company of Archers, 1931; Brigadier, 1940; Ensign, 1950; Lieutenant, 1953; Captain, 1965. DL County of City of Edinburgh, 1960. Member Scottish Cttee of Arts Council of Great Britain, 1961-66; Member Restrictive Practices Court, 1961-64. *Recreations:* archery, swimming, gardening. *Address:* Easter Belmont, 1 Easter Belmont Road, Edinburgh EH12 6EX. *T:* 031-337 6920.

GRANADO, Donald Casimir, TC 1970; Manager, Valpark Shopping Plaza; *b* 4 March 1915; *m* 1959, Anne-Marie Faustin Lombard; one *s* two *d*. *Educ:* Trinidad. Gen. Sec., Union of Commercial and Industrial Workers, 1951-53; Sec./Treas., Fedn of Trade Unions, 1952-53; Elected MP for Laventille, Trinidad, 1956 and 1961; Minister of: Labour and Social Services, 1956-61; Health and Housing, and Dep. Leader House of Representatives, 1961-63. Ambassador to Venezuela, 1963-64; High Comr to Canada, 1964-69; Ambassador to Argentina and to Brazil, 1965-69; High Comr to London, 1969-71, and Ambassador to France, Germany, Belgium, Switzerland, Holland, Luxembourg and European Common Market, 1969-71. Led Trinidad and Tobago delegn to UN, 1965; led govt delegn and went on govt business to various parts of the World. First Gen. Sec., People's National Movement. Chm., Valsayn Residents' Assoc. Vice-Pres., Trinidad & Tobago Bridge League. Reads and writes French and Spanish. *Recreations:* cricket, soccer, chess, bridge and golf; music (tape-recording), photography, writing. *Address:* 20 Grove Road, Valsayn Park, Trinidad.

GRANARD, 9th Earl of, *cr* 1684; **Arthur Patrick Hastings Forbes,** AFC, 1941; Bt 1628; Viscount Granard and Baron Clanehugh, 1675; Baron Granard (UK), 1806; Air Commodore late RAFVR; *b* 10 April 1915; *e s* of 8th Earl of Granard, KP, PC, GCVO, and Beatrice (*d* 1972), OBE, *d* of Ogden Mills, Staatsburg, Dutchess County, USA; *S* father, 1948; *m* 1949, Marie-Madeleine Eugènie, *y d* of Jean Maurel, Millau, Aveyron, formerly wife of late Prince Humbert de Faucigny Lucinge; two *d*. *Educ:* Eton; Trinity Coll., Cambridge. Served War of 1939-45 (despatches, AFC). Commandeur Légion d'Honneur; Croix de Guerre with Palm; Officer Legion of Merit, USA; Croix des Vaillants of Poland; Order of George I of Greece. *Heir: b* Hon. John Forbes, late Flt Lt RAF [*b* 8 Oct. 1920; *m* 1947, Joan, *d* of A. Edward Smith, Algoa, Westminster Road, Foxrock, Co. Dublin; one *s* three *d*]. *Address:* 11 rue Louis de Savoie, Morges, Switzerland. *Club:* White's.
See also Marquess of Bute.

GRANBY, Marquis of; David Charles Robert Manners; *b* 8 May 1959; *s* and *heir* of 10th Duke of Rutland, *qv*.

GRAND, Keith Walter Chamberlain; FCIT; Chairman: Penarth Engineering Co.; Railway Benevolent Association; *b* 3 July 1900; *m* 1st, 1925, Alice M. (*d* 1969), *d* of late Henry Gates,

Brockville, Ont., Canada; one *d* (one *s* decd); 2nd, 1971, Enid M. Wheatley. *Educ:* Rugby. Joined GWR 1919; USA 1926-29; General Manager, British Railways, Western Region, 1948-59. Member (full-time) British Transport Commn, 1959-62; Member Coastal Shipping Advisory Cttee, 1959-62; Chm., Coast Lines, 1968-71. *Recreation:* golf. *Address:* Queen Anne Flat, Little Sodbury Manor, Chipping Sodbury, near Bristol. *Clubs:* Carlton, MCC; Royal Mid-Surrey Golf (Richmond).

GRANDI, Count (di Mordano) *cr* 1937, **Dino;** retired; President Chamber of Fasci and Corporazioni, Italy, 1939-43; late Member of the Chamber of Deputies and of the Fascist Grand Council; *b* Mordano (Bologna), 4 June 1895; *m* 1924, Antonietta Brizzi; one *s* one *d*. Graduated in Law at the University of Bologna, 1919; volunteered for the war and was promoted to Captain for merit and decorated with silver medal, bronze medal, and three military crosses for valour; journalist and political organiser, after the war led the Fascist movement in the North of Italy and took part in the March on Rome as Chief of the General Staff of the Quadrunvirato; elected member of the Chamber of Deputies, 1921, 1924, 1929, 1934, and 1939; member of the General Direction of the Fascist Party Organisation, 1921-23-24; Deputy President of the Chamber of Deputies, 1924; Italian Delegate to the IV, V, International Labour Conference, 1922, 1923; Under-Secretary of State for the Interior, 1924; Under Secretary of State for Foreign Affairs, 1925-29; Italian Delegate, Locarno Conference, 1925; to Conferences for Settlement of War Debt, Washington, 1925 and London, 1926; and Hague Conference on War Debts, 1929; Head of Italian Delegation, London Naval Conference, 1930; Italian Delegate, Danubian Conference, London, 1932; Head of Italian Delegation, Geneva Disarmament Conference, 1932; Minister of Foreign Affairs, 1929-32; Permanent Italian Delegate to the Council of the League of Nations, 1925-32; Italian Ambassador in London, 1932-39; Keeper of the Seal and Minister of Justice, Italy, 1939-43; Head of Italian Delegation to London Naval Conference, 1936; Italian Representative to London Session of Council of League of Nations, 1936; at London Meeting of Locarno Powers, 1936; and on the London International Cttee for Non-Intervention in Spain, 1936, 1937, 1938, 1939. *Publications:* Origins of Fascism, 1929; Italian Foreign Policy, 1931; The Spanish War in the London Committee, 1939; The Frontiers of the Law, 1941, etc. *Recreations:* book collecting, riding, gardening, mountaineering. *Address:* I-41030 Albareto Di Modena, Italy.

GRANDY, Marshal of the Royal Air Force Sir John, GCB 1967 (KCB 1964; CB 1956); KBE 1961; DSO 1945; RAF; Governor and Commander-in-Chief, Gibraltar, since 1973; *b* Northwood, Mddx, 8 Feb. 1913; *s* of late Francis Grandy and Nellie Lines; *m* 1937, Cecile Elizabeth Florence Rankin, CStJ, *yr d* of Sir Robert Rankin, 1st and last Bt; two *s*. *Educ:* University College Sch., London. Joined RAF 1931. No 54 (Fighter) Sqdn, 1932-35; 604 (Middx) Sqdn., RAuxAF, 1935-36; Adjt and Flying Instructor, London Univ. Air Sqdn, 1937-39; Comd No 249 (Fighter) Sqdn during Battle of Britain; Staff Duties, HQ Fighter Comd, and Wing Comdr Flying RAF Coltishall, 1941; commanded: RAF Duxford, 1942 (First Typhoon Wing); HQ No 210 Group, No 73 Op Training Unit, and Fighter Conversion Unit at Abu Sueir, 1943-44; No 341 Wing (Dakotas), SE Asia Comd, 1944-45; DSO 1945, despatches 1943 and 1945. SASO No 232 Gp, 1945; *psc* 1946; Dep. Dir Operational Training, Air Min., 1946; Air Attaché, Brussels, 1949; Comd Northern Sector, Fighter Comd, 1950; Air Staff HQ Fighter Comd, 1952-54; Comdt, Central Fighter Estab., 1954-57; *idc* 1957; Comdr, Task Force Grapple (British Nuclear Weapon Test Force), Christmas Is., 1957-58; Assistant CAS (Ops), 1958-61; Commander-in-Chief, RAF, Germany and Comdr, Second Allied TAF, 1961-63; AOC-in-C, Bomber Command, 1963-65; C-in-C, British Forces, Far East, and UK Mil. Adviser to SEATO, 1965-67; Chief of the Air Staff, 1967-71. Air Cdre 1956; Air Vice-Marshal 1958; Air Marshal 1962; Air Chief Marshal 1965; Marshal of the RAF 1971. A Pres., Officers' Assoc., 1973-; Vice-President: Nat. Assoc. of Boys Clubs; Officers Pensions Soc. Ltd; Mem., Management Cttee, RNLI. Trustee: RAF Church, St Clement Danes; Imperial War Museum, 1970-. PMN 1967. Hon. Liveryman, Haberdashers' Co., 1968. Freeman, City of London, 1968. KStJ 1974. *Address:* The Convent, Gibraltar. *Clubs:* White's, Pratt's, Royal Air Force; Royal Yacht Squadron (Cowes).

GRANER, Most Rev. Lawrence L., CSC, DD, BA; *b* Franklin, Pa, USA, 3 April 1901; *s* of W. D. Graner. *Educ:* Holy Cross Seminary, Notre Dame, Indiana, USA; Notre Dame Univ.; Holy Cross Coll., Washington, DC, USA. BA (Notre Dame), 1924; member of congregation of Holy Cross, 1921; priest, 1928; missionary, diocese of Dacca, 1928-45; delegate to Gen.-Chapter of the Congregation of Holy Cross, 1945; Vicar-General of Dacca, 1937-45; member of Provincial Council of Congregation

of Holy Cross; War of 1939-45, Chaplain to US Air Forces; Bishop of Dacca, 1947-50; Archbishop of Dacca, 1950-67. *Address:* Corby Hall, Notre Dame, Indiana 46556, USA.

GRANGE, Kenneth Henry, RDI, FSIA; industrial designer; in private practice since 1958; Partner, Pentagram Design Partnership, since 1972; *b* 17 July 1929; *s* of Harry Alfred Grange and Hilda Gladys (*née* Long). *Educ:* London. Technical Illustrator, RE, 1948-50; Design Asst, Arcon Chartered Architects, 1948; Bronek Katz & Vaughn, 1950-51; Gordon Bowyer & Partners, 1951-54; Jack Howe & Partners, 1954-58. RDI 1969; FSIA 1959. 7 CoID Awards; Duke of Edinburgh Award for Elegant Design, 1963. *Recreations:* tennis, ski-ing. *Address:* 61 North Wharf Road, W2 1LA; Acrise Cottage, Christchurch Hill, NW3. *Club:* Reform.

GRANGER, Stewart; (James Lablache Stewart); actor (stage and films); *b* London, 6 May 1913; *s* of late Major James Stewart, RE, and Frederica Lablache; *m* 1st, Elspeth March (marr. diss., 1948); two *c*; 2nd, 1950, Jean Simmons, *qv* (marr. diss., at Nogales, Arizona, 1960); one *d*; 3rd, 1964, Viviane Lecerf. *Educ:* Epsom Coll. Began training as doctor but decided to become an actor. Studied at Webber-Douglas School of Dramatic Art; played at Little Theatre, Hull, and with Birmingham Repertory Company; appeared at Malvern Festivals, 1936-37; first London appearance as Captain Hamilton in The Sun Never Sets, Drury Lane, 1938; appeared on London stage, 1938-39; joined Old Vic Company, 1939; Dr Fleming in Tony Draws a Horse, Criterion, 1940; George Winthrop in A House in the Square, St Martin's, 1940; toured, 1940; served War of 1939-45, Army, 1940-42 (invalided). Toured, 1942; succeeded Owen Nares as Max de Winter in Rebecca, Lyric, 1942. Began film career in 1938, and has appeared in many films, including: The Man in Grey, The Lamp Still Burns, Fanny by Gaslight, Blue for Waterloo, The Love Story, The Madonna of the Seven Moons, Cæsar and Cleopatra, The Magic Bow, Captain Boycott, Blanche Fury, Saraband for Dead Lovers, Woman Hater, Adam and Evelyne, King Solomon's Mines, Soldiers Three, Light Touch, Wild North, Scaramouche, Young Bess, Salome, Beau Brummell, Footsteps in the Fog, Green Fire, Bhowani Junction, The Little Hut, North to Alaska, Swordsman of Siena, The Secret Invasion, Flaming Frontier, The Trygon Factor. *Address:* PO Box 115, Estepona, Málaga, Spain.

GRANIT, Prof. Ragnar Arthur, Commander, Order of Nordstjernan, Sweden, 1964; Professor Emeritus, since 1967, Karolinska Institutet, Stockholm; *b* 30 Oct. 1900; *s* of Arthur W. Granit and Albertina Helena Granit (*née* Malmberg); *m* 1929, Baroness Marguerite (Daisy) Bruun; one *s*. *Educ:* Swedish Normallyceum; Helsingfors University. MagPhil 1923, MD 1927. Prof. of Physiology, Helsingfors, 1937; Prof. of Neurophysiology, Stockholm, 1940; Dir of Dept of Neurophysiology, Medical Nobel Inst., 1945; retired, 1967. President, Royal Swedish Acad, Science, 1963-65. Lectures: Silliman, Yale, 1954; Sherrington, London, 1967; Liverpool, 1971; Murlin, Rochester, NY 1973; Hughlings Jackson, McGill, 1975. Visiting Professor: Rockefeller Univ., NY, 1956-66; St Catherine's Coll., Oxford, 1967; Pacific Medical Center, San Francisco, 1969; Fogarty Internat. Foundn, Nat. Inst. of Health, Bethesda, USA, 1971-72, 1975. Hon. MD: Oslo, 1951; Loyola, 1969; Pisa, 1970; Hon. DSc: Oxford, 1956; Hong Kong, 1961; Catedr. Hon., Lima, Santiago, Bogotá, 1958. Retzius Gold Medal, 1957; Donders Medal, 1957; Jahre Prize (Oslo), 1961; III Internat. St Vincent Prize, 1961; Nobel Prize for Medicine (jointly), 1967; Sherrington Medal, 1967; Purkinje Gold Medal, 1969. For. Mem., Royal Soc., 1960; Nat. Acad. Sci., Washington, 1968; Hon. Mem., Amer. Acad. of Arts and Sciences. Mem. and Hon. Mem. of several learned societies. Cross of Freedom (Finland), 1918. *Publications:* Sensory Mechanisms of the Retina, (UK) 1947 (US 1963); Receptors and Sensory Perception, (US) 1955; Charles Scott Sherrington: An Appraisal, (UK) 1966; Basis of Motor Control, (UK) 1970; Regulation of the Discharge of Motoneurons (UK), 1971; The Purposive Brain; Ung Mans Väg till Minerva, 1941. *Recreations:* sailing, island life, gardening. *Address:* The Medical Nobel Institute, Karolinska Institutet, S-104 01 Stockholm 60, Sweden.

GRANT, family name of **Baron Strathspey.**

GRANT, Alexander Ludovic, TD 1940; DL; JP; Director, Barclays Bank Ltd, 1945-73 (Chairman, Manchester and Liverpool Local Boards, 1945-73; Local Director, Liverpool, 1930, Manchester, 1940); Director, Barclays Bank (DCO), 1948-72; *b* 26 March 1901; *s* of late John Peter Grant, of Rothiemurchus, Aviemore, Inverness-shire, and late Lady Mary Grant, *d* of 3rd Earl Manvers; *m* 1946, Elizabeth Langley, *widow* of Capt. J. G. F. Buxton, Grenadier Guards, and *d* of late

Major Robert Barbour, Bolesworth Castle, Tattenhall, Cheshire; two *d. Educ:* Winchester; New Coll., Oxford (MA). Entered Barclays Bank Ltd, 1925; General Manager, Union Bank of Manchester, 1938-39 (Union Bank of Manchester was absorbed by Barclays Bank, 1940). Served Lovat Scouts, 1920-40 (Major 1935), and with Cheshire Home Guard, 1940-45. High Sheriff of Cheshire, 1956; DL Cheshire, 1963. *Recreations:* shooting, fishing, gardening. *Address:* Marbury Hall, Whitchurch, Salop. *T:* Whitchurch 3731. *Clubs:* Pratt's, MCC.

GRANT, Alexander (Marshall), CBE 1965; Artistic Director, National Ballet of Canada, since 1976; *b* Wellington, New Zealand, 22 Feb. 1928; *s* of Alexander and Eleather Grant. *Educ:* Wellington Coll., NZ. Arrived in London, Feb. 1946, to study with Sadler's Wells School on Scholarship given in New Zealand by Royal Academy of Dancing, London; joined Sadler's Wells Ballet (now Royal Ballet Company), Aug. 1946. Dir, Ballet for All (touring ballet company), 1971-76 (Co-director, 1970-71). Danced leading rôles in following: Mam'zelle Angot, Clock Symphony, Boutique Fantasque, Donald of the Burthens, Rake's Progress, Job, Three Cornered Hat, Ballabile, Cinderella, Sylvia, Madame Chrysanthème, Façade, Daphnis and Chloé, Coppélia, Petrushka, Ondine, La Fille Mal Gardée, Jabez and the Devil, Perséphone, The Dream, Jazz Calendar, Enigma Variations, Sleeping Beauty (Carabosse); film, Tales of Beatrice Potter (Peter Rabbit and Pigling Bland). *Recreations:* gardening, cinephotography. *Address:* National Ballet of Canada, 157 King Street East, Toronto, Ont M5C 1G9, Canada.

GRANT, Alexander Thomas Kingdom, CB 1965; CMG 1949; MA; Fellow of Pembroke College, Cambridge, 1966-73, now Fellow Emeritus; *b* 29 March 1906; *s* of late Harold Allan Grant and Marie F. C. Grant; *m* 1930, Helen Frances, *d* of late Dr and Mrs H. Newsome, Clifton, Bristol. *Educ:* St Olave's Sch.; University Coll., Oxford (Scholar in Modern History). Research on international financial problems at RIIA, 1932-35. Leverhulme Research Fellow, 1935-37. Lectr in Dept of Polit. Econ., UCL, 1938-39. Joined HM Treasury, 1939; Under-Sec., 1956; Under Sec., ECGD, 1958-66. UK member on Managing Board of European Payments Union, 1952-53; Secretary of Faculty of Economics, Cambridge, 1966-71; Senior Research Officer, Dept of Applied Economics, 1971-73. *Publications:* Society and Enterprise, 1934; A Study of the Capital Market in Post-War Britain, 1937; The Machinery of Finance and the Management of Sterling, 1967; The Strategy of Financial Pressure, 1972; Economic Uncertainty and Financial Structure, 1977; miscellaneous articles. *Address:* 66 Gough Way, Cambridge. *T:* Cambridge 63119. *Club:* United Oxford & Cambridge University.

GRANT, Allan Wallace, OBE 1974; MC 1941; TD 1947; Chairman, Ecclesiastical Insurance Office Ltd, since 1975; *b* 2 Feb. 1911; *s* of late Henry Grant and late Rose Margaret Sheppard; *m* 1939, Kathleen Rachel Bamford; one *d. Educ:* Dulwich Coll. LLB Hons (London). FCII. Eccles. Insurance Office, 1929; Chief Officer, 1952; Dir, 1966. Served War of 1939-45: Major, 2 i/c, 3rd Co. of London Yeomanry (Sharpshooters), N Africa, Sicily, Italy, NW Europe. Pres., Sharpshooters Assoc. Called to Bar, Gray's Inn, 1948. President: Insurance Inst. of London, 1966-67; Chartered Insce Inst., 1970-71; Insce Charities, 1973-74; Insce Orchestral Soc., 1973-74; Chairman: Insce Industry Training Council, 1973-75; Clergy Orphan Corp., 1967-; Governors, St Edmund's Sch., Canterbury and St Margaret's Sch., Bushey, 1967-; Coll. of All Saints, Tottenham, 1967-76; Governor, St Mary's Sch., Wantage, 1967-; Mem., Policyholders Protection Bd, 1975-; Treasurer: Historic Churches Preservation Trust, 1977-; Soc. for Advancing Christian Faith, 1977-. Assistant, Coopers' Co. Hon. DCanL Lexington, 1975. *Recreations:* golf, travel. *Address:* Fulham Palace (EIO Wing), Bishops Avenue, SW6 6EA. *T:* 01-736 0251. *Clubs:* City Livery; Richmond Golf.

GRANT, Andrew Francis Joseph, CB 1971; BSc, CEng, FICE; Member, Civil Service Appeal Board, since 1972; *b* 25 Feb. 1911; *er s* of Francis Herbert and Clare Grant; *m* 1934, Mary Harrison; two *s* two *d. Educ:* St Joseph's Coll., Beulah Hill; King's Coll., London. Asst Civil Engr with Contractors on London Underground Rlys, 1931; Port of London Authority, 1935; entered Civil Engineer-in-Chief's Dept, Admiralty, and posted to Singapore, 1937; Suptg Civil Engr, Durban, 1942; Civil Engr. Adviser, RN Home Air Comd, 1947; Suptg Civil Engr, Malta, 1951; Asst Dir, Navy Works, 1959; Fleet Navy Works Officer, Mediterranean, 1960; Director for Wales, MPBW, 1963; Regional Director, Far East, 1966; Dir, Home Regional Services, DoE, 1968-71. *Recreations:* painting, golf, travel. *Address:* The Lodge, Herington Grove, Hutton Mount, Shenfield, Essex. *T:* Brentwood 216486. *Club:* Civil Service.

GRANT, Anthony; *see* Grant, J. A.

GRANT, Sir Archibald, 13th Bt, *cr* 1705; *b* 2 Sept. 1954; *e s* of Captain Sir Francis Cullen Grant, 12th Bt, and of Lady Grant (Jean Margherita, *d* of Captain Humphrey Douglas Tollemache, RN); *S* father, 1966. *Heir: b* Francis Tollemache Grant, *b* 18 Dec. 1955. *Address:* House of Monymusk, Aberdeenshire. *T:* Monymusk 220.

GRANT, Brian; *see* Grant, H. B.

GRANT, Cary; actor; Director, Fabergé Inc.; *b* Bristol, 18 Jan. 1904; *s* of Elias Leach and Elsie Kingdom; became US citizen, 1942; *m* 1st 1934, Virginia Cherill (marr. diss., 1934); 2nd, 1942, Barbara Hutton (marr. diss., 1945); 3rd, 1949, Betsy Drake; 4th, 1965, Diane Cannon (marr. diss., 1968); one *d. Educ:* Fairfield Academy, Somerset. Started acting, New York, 1921; appeared in: Golden Dawn; Polly; Boom Boom; Wonderful Night; Street Singer; Nikki. *Films include:* Arsenic and Old Lace; None but the Lonely Heart; The Bishop's Wife; The Bachelor and the Bobby Soxer; Mr Blandings Builds His Dream House; To Catch a Thief; The Pride and the Passion; An Affair to Remember; Indiscreet; North by North-West; Operation Petticoat; A Touch of Mink; Charade; Father Goose; Walk, Don't Run. *Recreation:* riding.

GRANT, Rt. Rev. Charles Alexander; *see* Northampton, Bishop of, (RC).

GRANT, Hon. Sir Clifford (Harry), Kt 1977; Hon. Mr Justice Grant; Chief Justice of Fiji, since 1974; *b* England, 12 April 1929; *m* 1962, Karen Ann Ferguson. *Educ:* Montclair, NJ, USA; Harrison Coll., Barbados; Liverpool Coll.; Liverpool Univ. (LLB (Hons) 1949). Solicitor, Supreme Court of Judicature, 1951; Comr for Oaths, 1958; in private practice, London; apptd to HM Overseas Judiciary, 1958; Magistrate, Kenya, 1958, Sen. Magistrate, 1962; transf. to Hong Kong, Crown Solicitor, 1963; Principal Magistrate, 1965; transf. to Fiji, Sen. Magistrate, 1967; admitted Barrister and Solicitor, Supreme Court of Fiji, 1969; Chief Magistrate, 1971; Judge of Supreme Court 1972. Pres., Fiji Court of Appeal, and Chm., Judicial and Legal Services Commn; sole Comr, Royal Commn on Crime, 1975 (report published 1976). Sometime Actg Governor-General, 1973-1977. Fiji Independence Medal, 1970. *Recreations:* photography, literature, music. *Address:* Supreme Court, Suva, Fiji. *T:* Suva 211335.

GRANT, Prof. Colin King, MA, DPhil; Professor of Philosophy in the University of Durham, since 1959; *b* 22 March 1924; *s* of Edward Harold Stewart Grant and Leila Ellen Grant (née King); *m* Alison Stoddart Wallace, MB, MRCS, DMRT, DCH; two *s. Educ:* Clayesmore Sch.; Wadham Coll., Oxford. First Class Philosophy, Politics and Economics, 1944; Pollard Student of Wadham Coll., 1944-46; DPhil 1950. Assistant in Moral Philosophy Dept, Univ. of Glasgow, 1946-49; Lecturer in Philosophy, Univ. of Nottingham, 1949-59. Vis. Lectr, Univ. of Chicago, 1950-51; Visiting Professor: Univ. of Maryland, 1964; Univ. of Bergen, 1967. *Publications:* articles in Mind, Philosophy, Proc. of Aristotelian Society, etc. *Recreations:* travel, reading. *Address:* 202 Gilesgate, Durham.

GRANT, Derek Aldwin, DSO 1944; QC 1962; His Honour Judge Grant; a Circuit Judge (formerly an Additional Judge of the Central Criminal Court), since 1969; *b* 22 Jan. 1915; *s* of late Charles Frederick Grant; *m* 1954, Phoebe Louise Wavell-Paxton; one *s* three *d. Educ:* Winchester Coll.,; Oriel Coll., Oxford. Called to Bar 1938. Served in RAF, 1940-46 (King's Commendation, DSO). Master of the Bench, Inner Temple, 1969. Deputy Chairman, East Sussex County Sessions, 1962-71; Recorder of Salisbury, 1962-67, of Portsmouth, 1967-69. *Address:* Carters Lodge, Handcross, West Sussex. *Club:* Travellers'.

GRANT, Douglas Marr Kelso; Sheriff of South Strathclyde, Dumfries and Galloway (formerly of Ayr and Bute), since 1966; *b* 5 April 1917; *s* of John Marr Grant, JP, and Helen (née Kelso), Glasgow; *m* 1952, Audrey Stevenson Law; two *s* two *d. Educ:* Rugby; Peterhouse, Cambridge. Entered Colonial Admin. Service, Uganda Protectorate, 1939. Army Service, 1940-46; Kenya Regt, 7 Bn King's African Rifles; Military Admins. of Ethiopia, Madagascar, Tripolitania, Malaya; GSO2, Civil Affairs, Cairo, Delhi, London. Called to Bar, Gray's Inn, 1945; transferred Colonial Legal Service, 1946; Judicial and Legal Dept, Malaya, 1946-57 (Legal Adviser, Government of Johore, 1953-55); retired from Colonial Service, 1957. Admitted to Faculty of Advocates and Scottish Bar, 1959; Junior Counsel to Secretary of State under Private Legislation Procedure (Scotland) Act, 1936, 1961-66. Hon. Sheriff-Substitute: of

Lothians and Peebles, 1962; of Lanarkshire, 1963. Commissioner 1973; Mem., Detention Appeal Tribunal (NI Emergency Provisions Act 1973), 1974. *Recreation:* shooting. *Address:* Drumellan House, Maybole, Ayrshire. *T:* Maybole 82279. *Club:* Royal Over-Seas League (Edinburgh).

GRANT, Duncan Alistair Antoine, RBA, ARCA; Head of Printmaking Department, Royal College of Art, since 1970; *b* London, 3 June 1925; *s* of Duncan and Germaine Grant; *m* 1949, Phyllis Fricker; one *d. Educ:* Froebel, Whitehill, Glasgow; Birmingham Sch. of Art; Royal Coll. of Art. Joined staff of RCA, 1955. *One Man Shows* at the following galleries: Zwemmer; Piccadilly; AIA; Ashgate; Bear Lane, Oxford; Midland Group, Nottingham; Balclutha; Ware, London; 46, Edinburgh; Editions Alecto. *Works in the collections of:* V&A Museum; Min. of Works; LCC (now GLC); Arts Council; Carlisle Art Gall.; Ferens Art Gall., Hull; The King of Sweden; Dallas Museum; Cincinnati; Boston; Museum of Modern Art, New York; Chicago Art Inst.; Lessing J. Rosenwald Collection; Beaverbrook Foundn, Fredericton, NB; Vancouver Art Gall.; Victoria Art Gall. *Group Exhibitions* in Bahamas, Canada, Europe, S America, USA and UK. Awarded Silver Medal, Internat. Festival of Youth, Moscow, 1957. *Address:* 13 Redcliffe Gardens, SW10 9BG. *T:* 01-352 4312.

GRANT, Dr Duncan James Corrowr, RDI; Painter; *b* Rothiemurchus, Inverness, 1885; *s* of Major Bartle Grant and Ethel Grant; unmarried. *Educ:* St Paul's Sch. Studied at Westminster School of Art, Slade School, in Italy and in Paris, under Jacques Emile Blanche. Original Member London Artists' Association, Member of Camden Town Group and of London Group. Retrospective exhibitions, Tate Gallery, D'Offay Gallery, and Scottish Nat. Gall. of Modern Art, 1975. Made RDI, 1941, for printed textiles. Dr, Univ. of the Arts, 1921. *Address:* Charleston, Firle, East Sussex.

GRANT, Edward; Lord Mayor, City of Manchester, May 1972-May 1973; *b* 10 Aug. 1915; *s* of Edward and Ada Grant; *m* 1942, Winifred Mitchell. *Educ:* Moston Lane Sch.; Manchester High Sch. of Commerce. City Councillor, Manchester, 1950- (Alderman, 1970); Hosp. Administrator, Manchester AHA (T) North Dist (formerly NE Manchester HMC), 1948-75, now retired. *Recreations:* swimming, reading, gardening. *Address:* 14 Rainton Walk, New Moston, Manchester M10 0FR. *T:* 061-681 4758.

GRANT, Brig. Eneas Henry George, CBE 1951; DSO 1944 and Bar, 1945; MC 1936; JP; DL; retired; *b* 14 Aug. 1901; *s* of late Col H. G. Grant, CB, late Seaforth Highlanders and late Mrs Grant, Balnespick, Inverness-shire; *m* 1926, Lilian Marion, *d* of late S. O'Neill, Cumberstown House, Co. Westmeath; one *s* (and *er s,* Lieut Seaforth Highlanders, killed in action, Korea, 1951). *Educ:* Wellington Coll., Berks; RMC, Sandhurst. 2nd Lieut Seaforth Highlanders, 1920; Adjt Lovat Scouts, 1928-33; served in Palestine, 1936; War of 1939-45; France 1940; France and Germany, 1944-45. Lieut-Colonel 1942 (Subs. 1947); Colonel 1944 (Subs. 1948); Brigadier 1944 (Subs. 1952); Bde Commander, 1944-49; Comdr Gold Coast District, 1949-52. Col Comdt Gold Coast Regt, 1949-52; Deputy Commander, Northumbrian District, 1952-55; retired 1955. JP Inverness-shire, 1957. DL Inverness-shire, 1958. Chairman Inverness-shire TA and Air Force Association, 1961-65. *Recreations:* country pursuits. *Address:* Inverbrough Lodge, Tomatin, Inverness-shire. *Club:* Highland (Inverness).

GRANT, Sir Ewan G. M.; *see* Macpherson-Grant.

GRANT, Maj.-Gen. Ferris Nelson, CB 1967; Deputy Chairman, School for Visually Handicapped; *b* 25 Dec. 1916; *s* of late Lieut-Gen. H. G. Grant and of Mrs N. L. B. Grant *(née* Barker); *m* 1940, Patricia Anne *(née* Jameson); one *s* one *d. Educ:* Cheltenham Coll. Joined Royal Marines, 1935. Capt., HMS Suffolk, 1940-42; US Marine Corps Staff Coll., Major, 1943; Staff of SACSEA, Lt-Col 1943; Army Staff Coll., Camberley, 1946; 45 Commando, 1947; Chief Instructor, Commando Sch., 1949; CO 41 Commando, Korea, 1950; jssc, 1951; Bde Major, Commando Bde, 1952; Instructor, USMC Staff Coll., 1958; CO Amphibious Trng Unit, 1960; CO Depot RM, 1961; CO Infantry Trng Centre, 1963; Comdr, Plymouth Group, Royal Marines, 1965-68, retired. Legion of Merit (US). *Recreations:* sailing, gardening, painting; Past Pres. RN Boxing Assoc. *Address:* Little Burrow Farmhouse, Broadclyst, Exeter, Devon. *Clubs:* Army and Navy; Royal Yacht Squadron, Royal Naval Sailing Association.

GRANT, Frank, CB 1953; OBE 1939; former Under-Secretary, Ministry of Agriculture and Fisheries; *b* 1890; *s* of late J. F. Grant, Evesham; *m* 1926, Eileen, *d* of late T. H. Carey; one *s* one

d. Address: 9 Harefield Gardens, Middleton-on-Sea, Bognor Regis, West Sussex. *T:* Middleton-on-Sea 3511.

GRANT, George; MP (Lab) Morpeth, since 1970; *b* 11 Oct. 1924; *m* 1948, Adeline *(née* Conroy), Morpeth; one *s* four *d. Educ:* Netherton Council Sch. and WEA. Member Bedlingtonshire UDC, 1959-70 (Chm. for two years). Member: Labour Party, 1947-; NUM (Chm., 1963-70). PPS to Minister of Agriculture, 1974-76. *Recreations:* sport, gardening. *Address:* House of Commons, SW1; 30 Sheepwash Bank, Choppington, Northumberland. *Clubs:* Working Men's, in the Bedlington and Ashington area.

GRANT, Gordon, CB 1956; Secretary, Trade Marks, Patents and Designs Federation, 1970-73; *b* 13 Oct. 1907; *o s* of Harry Wykeham and Blanche Grant; *m* 1932, Lilian, *d* of William Gunner, two *d. Educ:* Christ's Hosp. Asst Traffic Supt, GPO, 1926; Principal Min. of Supply, 1939; Min. of Labour, 1940; Prin. Private Sec. to Rt Hon. Ernest Bevin, 1942-44; Asst Sec., 1944; Sec. Catering Wages Commission, 1944-45; idc 1949; Under Sec., Min. of Materials, 1951-54; Under Sec., Board of Trade, 1954-58; Comptroller-Gen., Patents, Designs and Trade Marks, 1958-69. *Address:* 4 Camborne House, Camborne Road, Sutton, Surrey. *T:* 01-643 2582.

GRANT, (Hubert) Brian; His Honour Judge Brian Grant; a Circuit Judge of Sussex and Kent (formerly Judge of County Courts since 1965); *b* 5 Aug. 1917; *m* 1946, Jeanette Mary Carroll; one *s* three *d. Educ:* Trinity Coll., Cambridge (Sen. Schol.). 1st cl. hons, Law Tripos, 1939; MA. War service, 1940-44: Commandos, 1942-44. Called to Bar, Gray's Inn, 1945 (Lord Justice Holker Senior Scholar). Mem., Law Reform Cttee, 1970-73. Vice-Chm., Nat. Marriage Guidance Council, 1970-72; Member: E Sussex Probation Cttee, 1973-; E Sussex Community Service Cttee, 1976-. *Publications:* Marriage, Separation and Divorce, 1946; Family Law, 1970. *Recreations:* travel and collecting books.

GRANT, Maj.-Gen. Ian Hallam L.; *see* Lyall Grant.

GRANT, Isabel Frances, MBE 1959; LLD (Edinburgh); *d* of late Colonel H. G. Grant, CB, late the Seaforth Highlanders; *g d* of late Field Marshal Sir Patrick Grant, KCB, GCMG; unmarried. *Educ:* privately. Founder of the Highland Folk Museum at Kingussie. *Publications:* Everyday Life on an Old Highland Farm, 1922; Social and Economic Development of Scotland before 1603, 1929; In the Tracks of Montrose, 1931; Everyday Life in Old Scotland, 1933; Social and Economic History of Scotland, 1934; Lordship of the Isles, 1935; Highland Folk Ways, 1961; Angus Og of the Isles, 1969. *Recreations:* reading, needlework. *Address:* 22 Lennox Row, Edinburgh EH5 3JW.

GRANT, Rt. Rev. James Alexander; Bishop Coadjutor, Diocese of Melbourne, since 1970; *b* 30 Aug. 1931; *s* of late V. G. Grant, Geelong. *Educ:* Trinity College, Univ. of Melbourne (BA Hons); Melbourne College of Divinity (BD). Deacon 1959 (Curate, St Peter's, Murrumbeena), Priest 1960; Curate, West Heidelberg 1960, Broadmeadows 1961; Leader Diocesan Task Force, Broadmeadows, 1962; Domestic and Examining Chaplain to Archbishop of Melbourne, 1966; Chairman, Brotherhood of St Laurence, 1971- (Director, 1969); Chaplain, Trinity Coll., Univ. of Melbourne, 1970-75, Fellow, 1975-. *Publications:* (with Geoffrey Serle) The Melbourne Scene, 1957; Perspective of a Century-Trinity College, 1872-1972, 1972. *Recreation:* historical research. *Address:* Trinity College, Parkville, Victoria 3052, Australia.

GRANT, James Currie, CBE 1975; Editor, The Press and Journal, Aberdeen, 1960-75, Associate Editor, 1975-76, retired; *b* 5 May 1914; *s* of Alexander Grant, Elgin; *m* 1940, Lillias Isabella Gordon; one *d. Educ:* Elgin Academy. With the Northern Scot, Elgin, 1930-36; joined The Press and Journal, as reporter, 1936; served with Royal Artillery, 1940-46; Sub-editor, The Press and Journal, 1946, Dep. Chief Sub-Editor, 1947-53, Asst Editor, 1953-56, Dep. Editor, 1956-60. Chm., Editorial Cttee, Scottish Daily Newspaper Soc., 1972-75. *Recreations:* social work, gardening. *Address:* 42 Fonthill Road, Aberdeen AB1 2UJ. *T:* 22090.

GRANT, Sir James Monteith, KCVO 1969; Lord Lyon King of Arms since 1969; Secretary to the Order of the Thistle, since 1971; Writer to the Signet; *b* 19 Oct. 1903; *m* 1st, 1935, Agnes Winifred Comrie Lorimer *(d* 1955); 2nd, 1958, Yvonne Margaret Wilkinson; one *d. Educ:* The Edinburgh Academy; Univ. of Edinburgh. MA, LLB Edinburgh; WS 1927. Carrick Pursuivant, 1946; Marchmont Herald, 1957. FSA (Scot). KStJ 1970 (OStJ 1967). Grand Officer (Class II), Order of the Polar Star, Sweden, 1977. *Address:* 40 Corstorphine Road, Edinburgh

EH12 6HS. *T:* 031-337 1209. *Clubs:* New, Scottish Arts (Edinburgh).

GRANT, James Shaw, CBE 1968 (OBE 1956); Chairman, Crofters' Commission, since 1963; Member, Highlands and Islands Development Board, since 1970; *b* 22 May 1910; *s* of William Grant and Johanna Morison Grant, Stornoway; *m* 1951, Catherine Mary Stewart; no *c. Educ:* Nicolson Inst.; Glasgow Univ. Editor, Stornoway Gazette, 1932-63; Mem., Crofters' Commn, 1955-63. Dir, Grampian Television, 1969-. Mem. Scottish Adv. Cttee, British Council, 1972. Governor, Pitlochry Festival Theatre, 1954-, Chairman, 1971-; Chm., Harris Tweed Assoc. Ltd, 1972-. FRAgSs 1973. Has written several plays. *Recreations:* golf, photography. *Address:* Ardgrianach, Inshes, Inverness. *T:* Inverness 31476. *Clubs:* Royal Over-Seas League; Highland (Inverness).

GRANT, Joan, (Mrs Denys Kelsey); *b* 12 April 1907; *d* of John Frederick Marshall, CBE; *m* 1st, 1927, Arthur Leslie Grant; one *d*; 2nd, 1940, Charles Robert Longfield Beatty; 3rd, 1960, Denys Edward Reginald Kelsey, MB, MRCP. Is engaged in psychotherapy as well as in writing. *Publications:* Winged Pharaoh, 1937; Life as Carola, 1939; Eyes of Horus, 1942; The Scarlet Fish and other Stories, 1942; Lord of the Horizon, 1943; Redskin Morning, 1944; Scarlet Feather, 1945; Vague Vacation, 1947; Return to Elysium, 1947; The Laird and the Lady, 1949; So Moses Was Born, 1952; Time out of Mind (autobiography), 1956; A Lot to Remember, 1962; (with Dr Kelsey) Many Lifetimes, 1969. *Address:* c/o A. P. Watt & Son, 26-28 Bedford Row, WC1.

GRANT, Rear-Adm. John, CB 1960; DSO 1942; *b* 13 Oct. 1908; *s* of late Maj.-Gen. Sir Philip Grant, KCB, CMG, and of late Annette, Lady Grant, Park Lodge, East Lulworth, Dorset; *m* 1935, Ruth Hayward Slade; two *s* two *d. Educ:* St Anthony's, Eastbourne; RN Colls, Dartmouth and Greenwich. Midshipman, HMS Queen Elizabeth, 1926; Sub-Lieut, HMS Revenge, 1930; Lieut, HMS Kent, China Station, 1932; specialised in anti-submarine warfare, 1933-39; Staff Officer Convoys, Rosyth, 1940; in comd HMS Beverley, 1941-42 (DSO); Trng Comdr, HMS Osprey, 1942, and subseq. in HMS Western Isles; in comd HMS Philante, 1943; Trng Comdr, HMS Osprey, 1944; in comd HMS Opportune, Fame and Crispin, 1945-47; Joint Staff Coll., 1947; Executive Officer, HMS Vernon; Capt. 1949; Dep. Dir Torpedo Anti-Submarine and Mine Warfare Div., Naval Staff, Admiralty, 1949-51; in comd HMS Cleopatra, 1952-53; Imperial Defence Coll., 1954; in comd HMS Vernon, 1955-57; on staff of Chief of Defence Staff, Min. of Defence, 1957-59; Rear-Adm., 1959; Flag Officer Commanding Reserve Fleet, 1959-60; retired list, 1961. Rank Organisation, 1961-65; Director, Conference of the Electronics Industry, 1965-71. *Address:* 4 Priors Barton, Kingsgate Road, Winchester, Hants.

GRANT, (John) Anthony; MP (C) Harrow Central since 1964; Solicitor and Company Director; *b* May 1925; *m* Sonia Isobel; one *s* one *d. Educ:* St Paul's Sch.; Brasenose Coll., Oxford. Admitted a Solicitor, 1952; Past Chm., Young Conservatives; Liveryman, Worshipful Company of Solicitors; Freeman, City of London; Warden, Guild of Freemen. Army 1943-48, Third Dragoon Guards (Capt.). Opposition Whip, 1966-70; Parly Sec., Board of Trade, June-Oct. 1970; Parliamentary Under-Secretary of State: Trade, DTI, 1970-72; Industrial Develt, DTI, 1972-74; a Vice-Chm., Conservative Party Organisation, 1974-76. Member: Council of Europe; WEU. *Recreations:* Rugby, cricket, swimming; Napoleonic history. *Address:* House of Commons, SW1.

GRANT, John Douglas; MP (Lab) Islington Central, since 1974 (Islington East, 1970-74); Parliamentary Under-Secretary of State, Department of Employment, since 1976; *b* 16 Oct. 1932; *m* 1955, Patricia Julia Ann; two *s* one *d. Educ:* Stationers' Company's Sch., Hornsey. Reporter on various provincial newspapers until 1955; Daily Express, 1955-70 (Chief Industrial Correspondent, 1967-70). Contested (Lab) Beckenham, 1966; Chm., Bromley Constituency Labour Party, 1966-70. Chm., Labour and Industrial Correspondents' Group, 1967. Opposition Front Bench Spokesman for policy on broadcasting and the press, 1973-74; Parly Sec., CSD, March-Oct. 1974; Parly Under-Sec. of State, ODM, 1974-76. *Publications:* Member of Parliament, 1974; articles in The Times, Observer, Sun, News of the World, Evening News, Evening Standard, Labour Weekly, Tribune, Socialist Commentary. *Recreations:* tennis, swimming, watching soccer. *Address:* 16 Magpie Hall Lane, Bromley, Kent. *T:* 01-467 0227.

GRANT, John James, CBE 1960; Director, University of Durham Institute of Education, 1963-77; *b* 19 Oct. 1914; *s* of John and Mary Grant; *m* 1945, Jean Graham Stewart; two *s. Educ:* Shawlands Academy, Glasgow; Univ. of Glasgow (MA, EdB). Supply teaching, Glasgow, 1939-40. Served War: UK, India, Burma, 1940-46. Mod. Lang. Master, High Sch. of Glasgow, 1946-48; Lectr in Educn, Univ. of Durham, 1948-52; Vice-Principal, Fourah Bay Coll., Sierra Leone, 1953-55, Principal, 1955-60; Principal, St Cuthbert's Soc., Univ. of Durham, 1960-63. Hon. DCL Durham, 1960. *Recreations:* golf, theatre, gardening. *Address:* Tithe Barn, Shincliffe, Durham. *T:* Durham 64728. *Club:* National Liberal.

GRANT, Captain John Moreau, CBE 1944; Royal Canadian Navy, retired; *b* 22 July 1895; *s* of late Hon. MacCallum Grant and Laura MacNeil Parker; *m* 1923, Jocelyn Clare Weaver-Bridgman; one *d. Educ:* Heidelberg Coll., Germany; RCN Coll., Halifax, NS. *Address:* 601 Transit Road, Victoria, British Columbia, Canada. *T:* 598-2138.

GRANT, Keith Wallace; Director, Design Council, since 1977; *b* 30 June 1934; *s* on Randolph and Sylvia Grant; *m* 1968, Deanne (*née* Bergsma); one *s* one *d. Educ:* Trinity Coll., Glenalmond; Clare Coll., Cambridge (MA). Account Exec., W. S. Crawford Ltd, 1958-62; General Manager: Covent Garden Opera Co., later Royal Opera, 1962-73; English Opera Group, 1962-73; Sec., Royal Soc. of Arts, 1973-77. *Address:* 43 St Dunstan's Road, W6. *T:* 01-748 8122. *Club:* Garrick.

GRANT, Sir (Kenneth) Lindsay, CMT 1969; Kt 1963; OBE 1956; ED 1944; Director, T. Geddes Grant Ltd (Chairman, 1946-64); Chairman, Vice-Chairman, or Director of numerous other companies; *b* Trinidad, 10 Feb. 1899; *s* of T. Geddes Grant (Canadian); *m* 1923, (Edith) Grace Norman; no *c. Educ:* Queen's Royal College, Trinidad; Maritime Business Coll., Halifax, NS. Served European War: (3rd Trinidad Contingent, 1916-17, 5th BWI Regt, 1917, RFC, 1917) 2nd Lieut; (RAF 1917-19) Flying Officer; War of 1939-45: (Trinidad Volunteers) Major, 2nd in Comd, 1944-45. Joined T. Geddes Grant Ltd, 1919; Manager, Office Appliances Dept, 1921; Director, 1927; Chm. and Man. Dir, 1946 (retd as Man. Dir, Sept. 1962; Chm. until 1964). Past and present activities: Church (Elder, Greyfriars); Boy Scouts; Cadets; Social Service. *Recreations:* none now; played cricket, Association football, tennis, golf. *Address:* (office) T. Geddes Grant Ltd, Box 171, Port of Spain, Trinidad. *T:* 54890; (nome) 50 Ellerslie Park, Maraval, Trinidad. *T:* 25202, Port of Spain. *Clubs:* Royal Commonwealth Society (West Indian), Royal Over-Seas League, (Hon. Life) MCC (all London); Union, Country, Queen's Park Cricket, etc (Trinidad).

GRANT, Sir Lindsay; see Grant, Sir K. L.

GRANT, Michael, CBE 1958 (OBE 1946); MA, LittD (Cambridge); *b* 21 Nov. 1914; *s* of late Col Maurice Harold Grant and of Muriel, *d* of C. Jörgensen; *m* 1944, Anne Sophie Beskow, Norrköping, Sweden; two *s. Educ:* Harrow Sch.; Trinity Coll., Cambridge. Porson Prizeman, First Chancellor's Classical Medallist, Craven Student; Fellow Trinity Coll., Cambridge, 1938-49. Served War of 1939-45, Army, War Office, 1939-40, Actg Capt.; first British Council Rep. in Turkey, 1940-45; Prof. of Humanity at Edinburgh Univ., 1948-59; first Vice-Chancellor, Univ. of Khartoum, 1956-58; Pres. and Vice-Chancellor of the Queen's Univ. of Belfast, 1959-66; Pres., 1953-56, and Medallist, 1962, Royal Numismatic Soc.; Huntington Medallist, American Numismatic Soc., 1965. J. H. Gray Lectr, Cambridge, 1955; Donnellan Lectr, Trinity Coll., Dublin, 1962; FSA. Chairman: National Council for the Supply of Teachers Overseas, 1963-66. President: Virgil Soc., 1963-66; Classical Assoc., 1977-78. Mem., Milan Acad. of Sciences and Letters; Chm., Commonwealth Conf. on Teaching of English as 2nd Language at Makerere, Uganda, 1961. Hon. LittD Dublin, 1961; Hon. LLD QUB, 1967. *Publications:* From Imperium to Auctoritas, 1946; Aspects of the Principate of Tiberius, 1950; Roman Anniversary Issues, 1950; Ancient History, 1952; The Six Main Aes Coinages of Augustus, 1953; Roman Imperial Money, 1954, repr. 1973; Roman Literature, 1954; translation of the Annals of Tacitus, 1956; Roman Readings (ed), 1958; Roman History from Coins, 1958; translations from Cicero, 1960, 1969, 1971, 1975; The World of Rome, 1960; Myths of the Greeks and Romans, 1962; Birth of Western Civilization (ed), 1964; The Civilizations of Europe, 1965; The Gladiators, 1967; The Climax of Rome, 1968; The Ancient Mediterranean, 1969; Julius Caesar, 1969; The Ancient Historians, 1970; The Roman Forum, 1970; Nero, 1970; Cities of Vesuvius, 1971; Herod the Great, 1971; Roman Myths, 1971; Cleopatra, 1972; (ed) Greek Literature in Translation, 1973; The Jews in the Roman World, 1973; The Army of the Caesars, 1974; The Twelve Caesars, 1975; The Fall of the Roman Empire, 1976; Saint Paul, 1976; Jesus, 1977. *Address:* Le Pitturacce, Gattaiola, Lucca, Italy. *Club:* Athenæum.

GRANT, Sir Patrick Alexander Benedict, 14th Bt *cr* 1688; Chieftain of Clan Donnachy; *b* 5 Feb. 1953; *e s* of Sir Duncan Alexander Grant, 13th Bt, and of Joan Penelope, *o d* of Captain Sir Denzil Cope, 14th Bt; *S* father, 1961. *Educ:* St Conleth's Coll., Dublin; The Abbey Sch., Fort Augustus. *Heir: b* Denzil Mohun Bede Grant [*b* 19 April 1955; *m* 1976, Nicola, *d* of A. T. Savill]. *Address:* Doire-nan-Guibhais, Duncanston, Conon Bridge, Ross-shire; 27 Crestway, Roehampton, SW15. *T:* 01-788 6250.

GRANT, Prof. Peter John, MA, PhD, MIMechE, FInstP; Professor of Nuclear Power, Imperial College of Science and Technology, London, since 1966; *b* London, 2 July 1926; *s* of Herbert James Grant; *m* Audrey, *d* of Joseph Whitham; one *s.* *Educ:* Merchant Taylors' Sch.; Sidney Sussex Coll., Cambridge. BA 1947, MA, PhD 1951. Research in Nuclear Physics at Cavendish Laboratory, 1947-50; Lectr in Natural Philosophy, Univ. of Glasgow, 1950-55; Chief Physicist, Atomic Energy Div., GEC Ltd, 1956-59; Reader in Engineering Science, Imperial Coll. of Science and Technology, 1959-66. *Publications:* Elementary Reactor Physics, 1966; Nuclear Science, 1971; papers on radioactivity, nuclear reactions, physics of nuclear reactors. *Address:* 49 Manor Road South, Esher, Surrey. *T:* 01-398 2001. *Club:* Athenæum.

GRANT, Ronald Thomson, OBE; FRS 1934; MD, FRCP, DPH; formerly physician on staff of Medical Research Council; Consultant Physician Emeritus, Guy's Hospital; *b* 5 Nov. 1892. *Educ:* Glasgow Univ. *Publications:* articles in scientific journals. *Address:* Farley Green Cottage, Shophouse Lane, Albury, Guildford, Surrey GU5 9EQ. *T:* Shere 2164.

GRANT, Air Vice-Marshal Stanley Bernard, CB 1969; DFC 1942; bar to DFC 1943; RAF; *b* 31 May 1919; *s* of late Harry Alexander Gwatkin Grant and Marjorie Gladys Hoyle; *m* 1948, Barbara Jean Watts (*d* 1963); one *s* one *d*; *m* 1965, Christiane Marie Py (*née* Bech); one step *s* two step *d*. *Educ:* Charterhouse; RAF Coll., Cranwell. Joined RAF, 1937; War of 1939-45; service in UK, Malta, Egypt and Italy. Air Ministry, 1946-47; Flying Training Command, 1948-54; Fighter Command, 1955-56; SEATO, Bangkok, 1957-59; Fighter Command, 1960-61; idc course, 1962; NATO, Fontainebleau, 1963-64; Directing Staff, IDC, 1965-68; Comdr, British Forces, Gulf, 1968-69; retired 1970. *Address:* 14 rue des Cordeliers, 83170 Brignoles, France. *Club:* Royal Air Force.

GRANT, Prof. Willis, DMus, Hon. RAM, FRCO, ARCM; Stanley Hugh Badock Professor of Music, 1958-72, and Dean of Faculty of Arts, 1968-70, Bristol University; now Emeritus Professor; *b* Bolton, 1 May 1907; *o s* of Herbert Grant; *m* Grace Winifred, *d* of C. A. Baker, Moseley, Birmingham. *Educ:* Astley Bridge Sch.; privately. Studied music with several teachers including Sir Edward C. Bairstow, York Minster; Organist and Choirmaster, All Souls' Parish Church, Bolton, 1929-31; Asst Organist, Lincoln Minster, 1931-36; Music Master, South Park High Sch., 1931-36; conducted Gate Burton Choral Soc., 1932-35; Extra-mural lectr for the University of Nottingham, 1936-37; Organist and Master of the Choristers, Birmingham Cathedral, 1936-58; Tutor in Special Music Course for Teachers at Sheffield City Training Coll., 1938-39; Conductor, Birmingham Bach Soc., 1938-58 (now Hon. Life Mem.); Lecturer in Music, Sheffield Univ., 1934-47; Extra-mural lecturer for WEA and Sheffield Univ., 1938-47; Dir of Music, King Edward's Sch., Birmingham, 1948-58; Extra-mural lectr for Birmingham Univ., 1956-58. Rep. of RSCM for Birmingham Dio., 1936-58. Pres. Birmingham Organists Assoc., 1950-55 (now Hon. Life Mem.); Mem., Management and Music Advisory Cttees of City of Birmingham Symphony Orchestra, 1950-58; Special Comr, RSCM, 1953-; Mem. Musical Adv. Board, 1952-55; Mem. Council: RCO; Incorporated Soc. of Musicians, 1956-59, 1960-(Mem. Exec. Cttee, 1958-; Pres., 1974-75); President: Music Masters' Assoc., 1958; Incorporated Assoc. of Organists, 1964-66; Bristol Bach Choir; Incorporated Soc. of Musicians, 1974-75; Chairman: Bristol Opera Co. Mem. Management Cttee, Western Orchestral Soc.; Music Panel, SW Arts Assoc.; Governor: Newton Park Coll., Bath; Birmingham Univ., 1973-. Served with HM Forces, RASC, 1941-42; AEC Major, lecturing on music in India Comd, 1942-46. *Publications:* An Album of Songs; Music in Education. *Recreations:* photography, gardening. *Address:* The Old Rectory, Compton Martin, Somerset BS18 6JP. *T:* West Harptree 350.

GRANT-FERRIS, family name of **Baron Harvington.**

GRANT-SUTTIE, Sir (George) Philip; *see* Suttie, Sir G. P. G.

GRANTCHESTER, 2nd Baron *cr* 1953; **Kenneth Bent Suenson-Taylor,** QC 1971; a Recorder of the Crown Court, since 1975; President, Value-added Tax Tribunals, since 1972; Chairman, Licensed Dealers' Tribunal, since 1976; *b* 18 Aug. 1921; of 1st Baron Grantchester, OBE, and of Mara Henriette (Mamie), *d* of late Albert Suenson, Copenhagen; *S* father, 1976; *m* 1947, Betty, *er d* of John Moores; three *s* three *d*. *Educ:* Westminster School; Christ's College, Cambridge (MA, LLM). Lieut RA, 1941-45. Called to the Bar, Middle Temple, 1946; admitted *ad eundem* by Lincoln's Inn, 1947. Lecturer in Company Law, Council of Legal Education, 1951-72. *Heir: e s* Hon. Christopher John Suenson-Taylor, *b* 8 April 1951. *Address:* The Gate House, Coombe Wood Road, Kingston Hill, Surrey. *T:* 01-546 9088.

GRANTHAM, Bishop Suffragan of, since 1972; **Rt. Rev. Dennis Gascoyne Hawker;** *b* 8 Feb. 1921; *o s* of Robert Stephen and Amelia Caroline Hawker; *m* 1944, Margaret Hamilton, *d* of Robert and late Daisy Henderson; one *s* one *d*. *Educ:* Addey and Stanhope Grammar Sch.; Queens' Coll., Cambridge (MA); Cuddesdon Theological Coll., Oxford. Lloyds Bank, 1939-40. Served War, Commissioned Officer, Royal Marines, 1940-46 (War Substantive Major). Deacon, 1950; Priest, 1951; Asst. Curate, St Mary and St Eanswythe, Folkestone, 1950-55; Vicar, St Mark, South Norwood, 1955-60; St Hugh's Missioner, Dio. Lincoln, 1960-65; Vicar, St Mary and St James, Gt Grimsby, 1965-72; Canon and Prebendary of Clifton, in Lincoln Cath., 1964-; Proctor in Convocation, 1964-74. *Address:* Fairacre, Barrowby High Road, Grantham, Lincs NG31 8NP. *T:* Grantham 4722. *Club:* United Oxford & Cambridge University.

GRANTHAM, Sir Alexander (William George Herder), GCMG 1951 (KCMG 1945; CMG 1941); *b* 15 March 1899; *s* of F. W. Grantham and A. von Herder; *m* 1st, 1925, Maurine Samson (*d* 1970), San Francisco; no *c*; 2nd, 1972, Mrs. M. E. Lumley. *Educ:* Wellington; RMC, Sandhurst; Pembroke Coll., Cambridge, MA. Gazetted 18th Hussars, 1917; Colonial Administrative Service, Hong Kong, 1922; called to Bar, Inner Temple, 1934; attended Imperial Defence Coll., 1934; Colonial Sec., Bermuda, 1935-38; Colonial Sec., Jamaica, 1938-41; Chief Sec., Nigeria, 1941-44; Governor, Fiji, and High Commissioner for Western Pacific, 1945-47; Governor Hong Kong, 1947-57. Hon. Fellow, Pembroke Coll., Cambridge. Hon. LLD Hong Kong Univ. *Address:* 90 Piccadilly, W1. *Club:* Cavalry and Guards.

GRANTHAM, Adm. Sir Guy, GCB 1956 (KCB 1952; CB 1942); CBE 1946; DSO 1941; retired; Governor and Commander-in-Chief of Malta, 1959-62; *b* 9 Jan. 1900; *s* of late C. F. Grantham, The Hall, Skegness, Lincs; *m* 1934, Beryl Marjorie, *d* of late T. C. B. Mackintosh-Walker, Geddes, Nairn; two *d*. Served War of 1939-45 (despatches, twice, DSO, CB, CBE); Chief of Staff to C-in-C, Mediterranean, 1946-48; Naval ADC to the King, 1947-48; Flag Officer (Submarines), 1948-50; Flag Officer, Second-in-Command, Mediterranean Fleet, 1950-51; Vice-Chief of Naval Staff, 1951-54; Comdr-in-Chief, Mediterranean Station, and Allied Forces, Mediterranean, 1954-57; Comdr-in-Chief, Portsmouth, Allied Comdr-in-Chief, Channel and Southern North Sea, 1957-59; First and Principal Naval ADC to the Queen, 1958-59. Retired list, 1959. Hon. Freeman of Haberdashers' Company. Mem., Commonwealth War Graves Commn 1962-70 (Vice-Chm. 1963-70). Governor and Mem. Administrative Board, Corps of Commissionaires, 1964-. *Address:* Stanleys, Hatch Lane, Liss, Hants. *T:* Liss 2135.

GRANTHAM, Roy Aubrey; General Secretary, Association of Professional, Executive, Clerical & Computer Staff (APEX), since 1970; a Director, Chrysler UK Ltd, since 1977; *b* 12 Dec. 1926; *m* 1964; two *d*. *Educ:* King Edward Grammar Sch., Birmingham. APEX: Midland area Organiser, 1949; Midland area Sec., 1959; Asst Sec., 1963. Exec. Member: European Movement; Labour Cttee for Europe; Confedn of Shipbuilding and Engineering Unions. Member: Royal Commn on Environmental Pollution, 1976-; CNAA, 1976-. *Publication:* Guide to Grading of Clerical and Administrative Work, 1968. *Recreations:* walking, reading, chess. *Address:* 18 The Grange, Shirley, Croydon CR0 8AP. *T:* 01-777 6154.

GRANTHAM, Mrs Violet Hardisty; Member of Newcastle upon Tyne City Council, 1937-74; Alderman of City, 1951-58; *o d* of Thomas Taylor, BSc, and Sarah Taylor; *m* John Grantham (*d* 1945) (formerly Sheriff of Newcastle upon Tyne, and Lord Mayor, 1936-37). *Educ:* privately. Dir of Private Companies. Lady Mayoress of Newcastle upon Tyne, 1936-37 and 1949-50; Sheriff of Newcastle upon Tyne, 1950-51 (first woman to hold this office); Lord Mayor, 1952-53 and 1957 (first woman to hold this office); Mem. Newcastle upon Tyne HMC, 1948-72; Founder Mem., and Mem. of Cttee, Percy Hedley Home for Spastic Children. Trustee: St Mary the Virgin Hosp. Trust (Chm.); Mary Magdalene and Holy Jesus Hosp. Trust (Vice-Chm.). Formerly Northern Area Chm. of Women's Junior Air

Corps; formerly Pres. Newcastle upon Tyne Branch of Royal College of Nursing; active in Townswomen's Guilds and other women's organisations. Freeman, City and Co. of Newcastle upon Tyne, 1968. *Address:* 4 Grange Road, Fenham, Newcastle upon Tyne 4. *T:* 33816.

GRANTLEY, 7th Baron, *cr* 1782; **John Richard Brinsley Norton,** MC 1944; Baron of Markenfield, 1782; a Member of Lloyd's; Director, Leslie & Godwin Ltd; *b* 30 July 1923; *o s* of 6th Baron and Jean Mary (*d* 1945), *d* of Sir David Alexander Kinloch, CB, MVO, 11th Bt; *S* father 1954; *m* 1955, Deirdre Mary Freda, *e d* of 5th Earl of Listowel, *qv*; two *s*. *Educ:* Eton; New Coll., Oxford. Served War of 1939-45, 1942-45, in Italy as Capt. Grenadier Guards (MC). *Heir: s* Hon. Richard William Brinsley Norton, *b* 30 Jan. 1956. *Address:* 53 Lower Belgrave Street, SW1; Markenfield Hall, Ripon, North Yorks. *Clubs:* White's, Pratt's.

GRANVILLE, family name of **Baron Granville of Eye.**

GRANVILLE, 5th Earl, *cr* 1833; **Granville James Leveson Gower,** MC 1945; Viscount Granville, 1815; Baron Leveson, 1833; Major Coldstream Guards (Supplementary Reserve); Vice-Lord-Lieutenant, Islands Area of the Western Isles, since 1976; *b* 6 Dec. 1918; *s* of 4th Earl Granville, KG, KCVO, CB, DSO, and Countess Granville, GCVO; *S* father, 1953; *m* 1958, Doon Aileen, *d* of late Hon. Brinsley Plunket and of Mrs V. Stux-Rybar, Luttrellstown Castle, Co. Dublin; two *s* one *d*. *Educ:* Eton. Served throughout War, 1939-45, Tunisia and Italy (twice wounded, despatches, MC). DL Inverness, 1974. *Heir: s* Lord Leveson, *qv*. *Address:* 49 Lyall Mews, SW1. *T:* 01-235 1026; Callernish, Sollas, North Uist, Outer Hebrides, Inverness-shire. *T:* Bayhead 213.

GRANVILLE OF EYE, Baron *cr* 1967, of Eye (Life Peer); **Edgar Louis Granville;** *s* of Reginald and Margaret Granville; *b* Reading, 12 Feb. 1899; *m* 1943, Elizabeth *d* of late Rev. W. C. Hunter; one *d*. *Educ:* High Wycombe, London and Australia. Served as officer in AIF, Gallipoli, Egypt and France. Capt. RA, 1939-40. MP (L) Eye Div. of Suffolk, 1929-51; Hon. Sec., Liberal Agricultural Group, House of Commons, 1929-31; Hon. Sec. Foreign Affairs Group, Vice-Pres. National League of Young Liberals; Chm., Young Liberals Manifesto Group; Parliamentary Private Sec. to Sir Herbert Samuel, first National Government, 1931; Parliamentary Private Sec. to Sir John Simon, National Government, 1931-36; Mem. of Inter-Departmental Cttee for the World Economic Conference, 1933. *Recreations:* cricket, football, ski-ing. *Address:* 112 Charlton Lane, Cheltenham, Glos.

GRANVILLE, Sir Keith, Kt 1973; CBE 1958; FCIT; *b* 1 Nov. 1910; *m* 1st, 1933, Patricia Capstick; one *s* one *d*; 2nd, 1946, Truda Belliss; one *s* four *d*. *Educ:* Tonbridge Sch. Joined Imperial Airways as Trainee, 1929 and served Italy, Tanganyika, Southern and Northern Rhodesia, Egypt, India. BOAC: Manager African and Middle East Div., 1947; Commercial Dir, 1954; Dep. Managing Dir, 1958-60; Mem. Bd, 1959-72; Dep. Chm., 1964-70; Man. Dir, 1969-70; Chm. and Chief Exec., 1971-72; Mem. Bd, BEA, 1971-72; British Airways Board: Mem., 1971-74; Dep. Chm., 1972-74; Chairman: BOAC Associated Companies Ltd, 1960-64; BOAC Engine Overhaul Ltd, 1971-72; International Aeradio Ltd, 1965-71 (Dep.-Chm., 1962-65). Mem. Bd, Maplin Development Authority, 1973-74. President: Inst. of Transport, 1963-64; IATA, 1972-73. Hon. FRAeS. *Address:* Speedbird, 1837 Château d'Oex, Switzerland. *T:* (029) 4 76 03.

GRANVILLE SLACK, George; *see* Slack, G. G.

GRANVILLE-SMITH, His Honour Stuart Hayne, OBE 1946; a Circuit Judge (formerly Judge of County Courts), 1947-75; *b* 7 May 1901; *s* of Granville Smith, Master of the Supreme Court of Justice, 1900-25, and Nellie Claire Mead; *m* 1935, Elisabeth Mary Woodcock (*d* 1976); one *s* one *d*. *Educ:* Marlborough Coll.; Oriel Coll., Oxford. Called to Bar, Inner Temple, 1925; Midland Circuit; North London Sessions. Prosecuting Counsel for Post Office, Midland Circuit, 1932. Served War of 1939-45, on active service with RAF 1940-46 (Wing Comdr); Control Office and Control Commission for Germany, 1946-47.

GRANVILLE-WEST, Baron, *cr* 1958 (Life Peer), of Pontypool, in the County of Monmouthshire; **Daniel Granville West;** Senior Partner in the firm of D. Granville West, Chivers & Morgan, Newbridge and Pontypool; *b* 17 March 1904; *s* of John West, Newbridge, Monmouthshire, and Elizabeth West (*née* Bridges); *m* 1937, Vera (JP Monmouthshire, 1956), *d* of J. Hopkins, Pontypool; one *s* one *d*. Admitted a Solicitor, 1929. Served War of 1939-45: Royal Air Force Volunteer Reserve, Flight Lt. MP

(Lab) Pontypool Div. of Monmouthshire, July 1946-58. PPS to Home Sec., 1950-51. Mem. of Abercarn Urban District Council, 1934-38 and of Monmouthshire County Council, 1938-47. *Address:* Brynderwen, Abersychan, Pontypool, Gwent. *T:* Talywain 236.

GRASAR, Rt. Rev. William Eric; *see* Shrewsbury, Bishop of, (RC).

GRASS, Günter Wilhelm; German writer and artist; *b* Danzig, 16 Oct. 1927; *m* 1954, Anna Schwarz; three *s* (inc. twin *s*) one *d*. *Educ:* Volksschule and Gymnasium, Danzig; Düsseldorf Kunstakademie; Hochschule für Bildende Künste. Lecture Tour of US, 1964, and many other foreign tours. Member: Akademie der Künste, Berlin; Deutscher PEN, Zentrum der Bundesrepublik; Verband Deutscher Schriftsteller; Amer. Academy of Arts and Sciences. Prizes: Lyric, Süddeutscher Rundfunk, 1955; Gruppe 47, 1959; Bremen Literary, 1959 (zurückgezogen); Literary, Assoc. of German Critics, 1960; Meilleur livre étranger, 1962; Georg-Büchner, 1965; Theodor-Heuss, 1969. *Publications:* novels: Die Blechtrommel, 1959 (The Tin Drum, 1962); Katz und Maus, 1961 (Çat and Mouse, 1963); Hundejahre, 1963 (Dog Years, 1965); Örtlich Betäubt, 1969 (Local Anaesthetic, 1970); *poetry:* Die Vorzüge der Windhühner, 1956; Gleisdreieck, 1960; Ausgefragt, 1967; *poetry in translation:* Selected Poems, 1966; Poems of Günter Grass, 1969; *drama:* Hochwasser, 1957 (Flood, 1968); Noch zehn Minuten bis Buffalo, 1958 (Only Ten Minutes to Buffalo, 1968); Onkel, Onkel, 1958 (Onkel, Onkel, 1968); Die bösen Köche, 1961 (The Wicked Cooks, 1968); Die Plebejer proben den Aufstand, 1966 (The Plebeians rehearse the Uprising, 1967); Davor, 1969; *prose:* Uber das Selbstverständlische, 1968; (Speak Out!, 1969); Aus dem Tagebuch einer Schnecke, 1972 (From the Diary of a Snail, 1974); Dokumente zur politischen Wirkung, 1972. *Address:* Niedstrasse 13, Berlin 41, Germany.

GRATTAN, Donald Henry; Controller, Educational Broadcasting, BBC, since 1972; *b* St Osyth, Essex, 7 Aug. 1926; *s* of Arthur Henry Grattan and Edith Caroline Saltmarsh; *m* 1950, Valmai Dorothy Morgan; one *s* one *d*. *Educ:* Harrow Boys Grammar Sch.; King's Coll., Univ. of London. BSc 1st Cl. Hons, Mathematics Dip. in Radio-Physics. Jun. Scientific Officer, TRE, Gt Malvern, 1945-46; Mathematics Teacher, Chiswick Grammar Sch., 1946-50; Sen. Master, Downer Grammar Sch., Mddx, 1950-56. BBC: Sch. Television Producer, 1956-60; Asst Head, Sch. Television, 1960-64; Head of Further Educn, Television, 1964-70; Asst Controller, Educnl Broadcasting, 1970-72. Member: Open Univ. Council; Council for Educnl Technology; European Broadcasting Union Working Party on Educn; Venables' Cttee on Continuing Educn, 1976-. Burnham Medal of BIM for services to Management Educn, 1969. *Publications:* Science and the Builder, 1963; Mathematics Miscellany (jt, BBC), 1966; numerous articles. *Recreations:* education (formal and informal), planning and organizing, people. *Address:* Delabole, Gossmore Close, Marlow, Bucks. *T:* Marlow 73571.

GRATTAN-BELLEW, Sir Arthur (John), Kt 1959; CMG 1956; QC (Tanganyika), 1952; *b* 23 May 1903; *s* of Sir Henry (Christopher) Grattan-Bellew, 3rd Bt, and Lady Sophia Forbes, *d* of 7th Earl of Granard, KP; *m* 1931, Freda Mary Mahony; one *s* one *d*. *Educ:* Downside Sch.; Christ's Coll., Cambridge (BA). Called to Bar, Lincoln's Inn, 1925; practised in London until 1935, Legal Service, Egyptian Govt, 1936-38; Colonial Legal Service, Malaya, 1938-41. Military Service, 1941-45 (POW 1942-45). Colonial Legal Service; Malaya, 1946-48; Attorney-General: Sarawak, 1948-52; Tanganyika, 1952-56; Chief Sec., Tanganyika, 1956-59; Legal Adviser's Dept, Foreign and Commonwealth Office, retired. Chm., Bellew, Parry and Raven Gp of companies. *Address:* Pledgdon Green, Henham, near Bishop's Stortford, Herts.

GRATTAN-BELLEW, Sir Henry Charles, 5th Bt, *cr* 1838; *b* 12 May 1933; *s* of Lt-Col Sir Charles Christopher Grattan-Bellew, 4th Bt, MC, KRRC and Maureen Peyton, *niece* and adopted *d* of late Sir Thomas Segrave, Shenfield, Essex; *S* father, 1948; *m* 1st, 1956, Naomi Ellis (marr. diss.), *yr d* of late Dr Charles Cyril Morgan, Chester; 2nd, Gillian; one *d*. *Educ:* St Gerard's, Bray, Co. Wicklow; Ampleforth Coll., York. *Heir: c* Patrick Edward Grattan-Bellew, *b* 26 Sept. 1934.

GRATTAN-COOPER, Rear Admiral Sidney, CB 1966; OBE 1946; *b* 3 Dec. 1911; *s* of Sidney Cooper; *m* 1940, Felicity Joan Pitt; two *s*. *Educ:* privately. Entered RN 1936; served in war of 1939-45; Chief of Staff Flag Officer (Air) Home, 1957-59; Staff of Supreme Allied Cdr Atlantic (NATO), 1961-63; Dep. Controller (Aircraft) RN, Min. of Aviation, 1964-66; retired 1966. *Recreations:* golf, swimming. *Address:* Hursley, St James, Cape, S Africa. *Club:* Army and Navy.

GRATTIDGE, Captain Harry, OBE 1940; retired 31 Dec. 1953, as Commodore, Cunard Line; *b* 30 Dec. 1890; *s* of George Grattidge and Nellie Tildesley; *m* 1917, Dorothy K. Sale (marriage dissolved), Plymouth; one *s. Educ:* Stafford Grammar Sch. Joined Cunard Line as Junior Officer, 1914; in command SS Ascania, 1943-44. After comdg various other ships became Capt. of Queen Mary, 1949-52; Queen Elizabeth, 1952-53. Lecture tour in USA, 1957. *Publication:* Captain of the Queens. *Address:* 41 Dudley Court, Upper Berkeley Street, W1H 7PH. *Club:* County Conservative (Stafford).

GRATWICK, John; Vice-Chairman, Empire Stores (Bradford) Ltd, since 1974; Chairman: Fattorini & Sons Ltd, since 1974; Guild Sound and Vision Ltd, since 1976; Director: Export Finance Consultant Ltd, since 1972; R. Kelvin Watson Ltd, since 1974; George Bassett (Holdings) Ltd, since 1977; Deputy Chairman, Lake & Elliot Ltd, since 1977; Chairman, Strategy Ltd, since 1974; Member (part-time), Monopolies and Mergers Commission, 1969-76; *b* 23 April 1918; *s* of Percival John and Kathleen Mary Gratwick; *m* 1944, Ellen Violet Wright; two *s* two *d. Educ:* Cranbrook Sch., Kent; Imperial Coll., Univ. of London. Asst Production Manager, Armstrong Siddeley, 1941-45; Director, Urwick, Orr & Partners Ltd, 1959, Man. Dir, 1968, Vice-Chm., 1971; Chm., Diebold Europe SA, 1972-77. Member: Economic Develt Cttee for the Clothing Industry, 1967-; Senate of Univ. of London, 1967-; Univ. of London Careers Adv. Bd, 1962-; Chm., Management Consultants Assoc., 1971-72. Governor, Cranbrook Sch., Kent, 1972; Trustee, Foundn for Business Responsibilities. Liveryman, Worshipful Co. of Farriers. *Recreations:* golf, sailing, photography, philately. *Address:* Silver Howe, Nuns Walk, Virginia Water, Surrey. *T:* Wentworth 3121. *Clubs:* National Liberal; Wentworth (Surrey).
See also Stephen Gratwick.

GRATWICK, Stephen, QC 1968; *b* 19 Aug. 1924; *s* of late Percival John Gratwick, Fawkham, Kent; *m* 1954, Jocelyn Chaplin, Horton Kirby, Kent; four *d. Educ:* Charterhouse, Balliol Coll., Oxford. Oxford 1942-44; Signals Research and Develt Estab., 1944-47. BA (Physics) 1946; MA 1950. Called to Bar, Lincoln's Inn, 1949, Bencher, 1976. *Recreations:* sailing, ski-ing, tennis, swimming, making and mending things. *Address:* 11 South Square, Gray's Inn, WC1R 5EU. *Clubs:* Ski Club of Great Britain; Little Ship.
See also John Gratwick.

GRAVE, Walter Wyatt, CMG 1958; MA (Cambridge); Hon. LLD (Cambridge and McMaster); Hon. Fellow of Fitzwilliam College, Cambridge; *b* 16 Oct. 1901; *s* of late Walter and Annie Grave; *m* 1932, Kathleen Margaret, *d* of late Stewart Macpherson; two *d. Educ:* King Edward VII Sch., King's Lynn; Emmanuel Coll., Cambridge (Scholar); Fellow of Emmanuel Coll., 1926-66, 1972-; Tutor, 1936-40; University Lecturer in Spanish, 1936-40; Registrary of Cambridge Univ., 1943-52; Principal of the University Coll., of the West Indies, Jamaica, 1953-58; Censor of Fitzwilliam House, Cambridge, 1959-66; Master of Fitzwilliam Coll., Cambridge, 1966-71. Temporary Administrative Officer, Ministry of Labour and National Service, 1940-43. *Address:* 18 Luard Road, Cambridge. *T:* 47415.

GRAVES, family name of Baron Graves.

GRAVES, 8th Baron, *cr* 1794; **Peter George Wellesley Graves;** Actor; *b* 21 Oct. 1911; *o s* of 7th Baron Graves; *S* father, 1963; *m* 1960, Vanessa Lee. *Educ:* Harrow. First appeared on London stage in 1934, and has subsequently played many leading parts. Mem. Windsor repertory co., 1941. Has appeared in films since 1940. *Recreation:* lawn tennis. *Heir: kinsman,* Evelyn Paget Graves [*b* 17 May 1926; *m* 1957, Marjorie Ann, *d* of late Dr Sidney Ernest Holder; two *s* two *d*]. *Address:* c/o Messrs Coutts & Co., 440 Strand, WC2. *Club:* All England Lawn Tennis.

GRAVES, Robert Ranke; writer; Hon. Fellow, St John's College, Oxford; *b* London, 1895; *s* of late Alfred Perceval and Amy Graves; *m* 1st, Nancy, *d* of late Sir Wm Nicholson; one *s* two *d* (and one *s* killed in Burma); 2nd, Beryl, *d* of late Sir Harry Pritchard; three *s* one *d. Educ:* Charterhouse; St John's Coll., Oxford (Hon. Fellow, 1971). Served in France with Royal Welch Fusiliers; Prof. of English Literature, Egyptian Univ., 1926. Clarke Lecturer at Trinity Coll., Cambridge, 1954. Arthur Dehon Little Memorial Lecturer, Massachusetts Institute of Technology, 1963. Professor of Poetry, Univ. of Oxford, 1961-66. Books (over 137) and manuscripts, on permanent exhibition, at Lockwood Memorial Library, Buffalo, NY. Bronze Medal for Poetry, Olympic Games, Paris, 1924; Gold Medal for Poetry, Cultural Olympics, Mexico, 1968; Gold Medal of Nat. Poetry Soc. of America, 1960; Queen's Gold Medal for Poetry, 1968.

Adoptive son of Deyá village, Mallorca, 1968, where resident since 1929. *Publications:* Goodbye to All That, An Autobiography, 1929 (revised 1957); But it Still Goes on, 1930; The Real David Copperfield, 1933; I, Claudius, 1934 (awarded Hawthornden and James Tait Black Memorial Prizes for 1934); Claudius the God, 1934; Antigua Penny Puce, 1936; T. E. Lawrence to his Biographer, 1938; Count Belisarius, 1938 (awarded Stock Prize, 1939); Sergeant Lamb of the Ninth, 1940; The Long Week End: A Social History (with Alan Hodge), 1940; Proceed, Sergeant Lamb, 1941; Wife to Mr Milton, 1943; The Reader Over Your Shoulder (with Alan Hodge), 1943; The Golden Fleece, 1944; King Jesus, 1946; The White Goddess, 1947; Collected Poems, 1948; Seven Days in New Crete, 1949; The Common Asphodel (Collected Essays on Poetry), 1949; The Isles of Unwisdom, 1949; Occupation: Writer, 1950; Poems and Satires, 1951; The Nazarene Gospel Restored (with Joshua Podro), 1953; The Greek Myths, 1955 (new edn, Greek Myths and Legends, 1968); Homer's Daughter, 1955; The Crowning Privilege, 1955; Adam's Rib, 1955; Catacrok (stories), 1956; Jesus in Rome (with Joshua Podro), 1957; They hanged my saintly Billy, 1957; (ed) English and Scottish Ballads, 1957; Steps, 1958; Collected Poems, 1959; The Penny Fiddle, 1960; More Poems, 1961; Oxford Addresses, 1962; New Poems, 1962; (with Raphael Patai) Hebrew Myths: Genesis, 1964; Collected Short Stories, 1964; Man Does, Woman Is (poems), 1964; Mammon and the Black Goddess, 1964; Hebrew Myths: Genesis (with Rafael Patai), 1965; Ann at High Wood Hall, 1965; Collected Short Stories, 1965; Love Respelt, 1965; Majorca Observed, 1965; Collected Poems, 1965; Seventeen Poems Missing from Love Respelt, 1966; Two Wise Children, 1967; Colophon, 1967; Poetic Craft and Principle, 1967; The Poor Boy who followed his Star, 1968; Poems 1965-68, 1968; The Crane Bag and other disputed subjects, 1968; Beyond Giving, 1969; Poems 1968-1970, 1970; The Song of Songs (with lithographs by Hans Erni), 1971; The Green-Sailed Vessel, 1971; All Things to all Men (play), 1971; Poems: abridged for dolls and princes, 1971; Poems 1970-72, 1972; Difficult Questions: Easy Answers, 1973; Timeless Meeting, 1973; At the Gate, 1974; Collected Poems 1975, 1975; *translations:* The Golden Ass, 1949; Alarcón's Infant with the Globe, 1956; Galvan's The Cross and the Sword, 1956; George Sand's Winter in Majorca, 1957; Suetonius's Twelve Cæsars; Lucan's Pharsalia; Homer's Anger of Achilles, 1959; Terence's Comedies, 1962; Rubaiyyat of Omar Khayaam (with Omar Ali-Shah), 1967. *Address:* c/o A. P. Watt & Son, 26/28 Bedford Row, WC1.

GRAVESON, Prof. Ronald Harry, CBE 1972; QC 1966; Barrister-at-Law; Professor of Private International Law (formerly of Law), since 1947 and Head of the Department of Laws, King's College, University of London; *b* 2 Oct. 1911; *o s* of Harry Graveson, Sheffield; *m* 1937, Muriel, *o d* of John Saunders, Sheffield; one *s* two *d. Educ:* King Edward VII Sch., Sheffield. LLB 1932, LLM 1933, LLD 1955 Sheffield; SJD Harvard 1936; PhD London 1941; LLD London 1951; Gregory Scholar in International Law of Harvard Univ.; Solicitor (Hons), 1934. Asst Lecturer in Law, King's Coll., University of London, 1938-40. Army, 1940-46 (Driver, RE; Lieut-Col RASC, G5 Div. SHAEF). Called to Bar, Gray's Inn, 1945; Bencher, 1965; Reader in English Law, University Coll., Univ. of London, 1946-47; Dean of the Faculty of Laws, Univ. of London, 1951-54, 1971-74, and KCL, 1951-58, 1959-63, 1966-70. Visiting Professor: Harvard Law Sch., 1958-59; NY Univ. Law Sch., 1959. Chm., UK, National Cttee of Comparative Law, 1955-57; Deputy Chm. of Convocation of Univ. of London, 1955-59 and Mem. of the Senate, 1958-69; Member: the Senate of the Inns of Court, 1967-69; Council of Legal Educn, 1965-70; Review Body on pay of doctors and dentists, 1971-; Cttees of Inquiry into Pay of Nurses and Midwives and of Professions supplementary to Medicine, 1974-75; Pres., Harvard Law Sch. Assoc. of the UK, 1959-61. Consultant Editor of the Law Reports and the Weekly Law Reports, 1970-75. Pres. International Association of Legal Science (UNESCO), 1960-62. Assoc. Mem. Inst. of International Law; Pres., Soc. of Public Teachers of Law, 1972-73; Corr. Member: Rome Inst. for the Unification of Private Law; Internat. Acad. of Comparative Law. FKC 1962. LLD (*hc*) Ghent, 1964; Uppsala, 1977; Dr Juris (*hc*) Freiburg, 1969. JP St Alban's City, 1961-66. Rep. HM Govt at Cttee of Council of Europe and at 8th, 9th, 10th and 11th Sessions of Hague Conf. of Private Internat. Law. Commandeur de l'Ordre de la Couronne de Chêne, 1964; Comdr, Order of Oranje Nassau, 1970; Order of National Merit, France, 1970; Grand Cross of Order of Merit, German Federal Republic, 1975. *Publications:* English Legal System, 1939; Conflict of Laws, 1948 (7th edition 1974); Cases on the Conflict of Laws, 1949; The Comparative Evolution of Principles of the Conflict of Laws in England and the USA 1960; General Principles of Private International Law, 1964; (jtly) The Conflict of Laws and International Contracts, 1951; Status in the Common Law, 1953; (jtly) A Century of Family Law, 1957; Law: An Introduction, 1967; (jtly) Unification of the International Law of Sale, 1968; Problems of Private International Law in Non-unified Legal Systems, 1975; Comparative Conflict of Laws, 1976; One Law, 1976; Jt Editor, International and Comparative Law Quarterly, 1955-61; various articles, notes or reviews since 1936 in English and foreign law reviews. Contributor to various collective volumes including essays in honour of British and foreign colleagues; Apollo; Connoisseur. *Recreations:* walking, works of art, international friendship. *Address:* 2 Gray's Inn Square, Gray's Inn, WC1R 5AA. *T:* 01-242 8492; Castle Hill Farm House, Bakewell, Derbys. *Clubs:* Athenæum, Royal Commonwealth Society.

GRAY, 22nd Lord, *cr* 1445; **Angus Diarmid Ian Campbell-Gray;** *b* 3 July 1931; *s* of Major Hon. Lindsay Stuart Campbell-Gray, Master of Gray, MC (*d* 1945), and Doreen (*d* 1948), *d* of late Cyril Tubbs, Thedden Grange, Alton, Hants; *S* grandmother 1946; *m* 1959, Patricia Margaret, *o d* of late Capt. Philip Alexander and of Mrs Alexander, Kilmorna, Lismore, Co. Waterford; one *s* three *d. Heir: s* Master of Gray, *qv. Address:* Airds Bay House, Taynuilt, Argyll. *Clubs:* Carlton, MCC.

GRAY, Master of; Hon. Andrew Godfrey Diarmid Stuart Campbell-Gray; *b* 3 Sept. 1964; *s* and *heir* of 22nd Lord Gray, *qv.*

GRAY, Air Vice-Marshal Alexander, CB 1944; MC; RAF retired; *b* 8 Sept. 1896. Deputy Air Commander, RAF Component, Eastern Air Command, South-East Asia Command, 1944; Dir of Flying Training, Air Ministry, 1945; Air Officer Commanding, Air Headquarters, Iraq, 1947; retired, 1949. *Address:* 8 Greenwood Avenue, Ferndown, Dorset.

GRAY, Alexander Stuart, FRIBA; Consultant to Watkins, Gray, Woodgate International, 1968-75; *b* 15 July 1905; *s* of Alexander and Mary Gray; *m* 1932, Avis, *d* of John Radmore, Truro; one *s* two *d. Educ:* Mill Hill Sch. Articled to R. S. Balgarnie Wyld, ARIBA; studied at Central Sch. of Arts and Crafts; Royal Academy Schools (Bronze Medal), 1928; Silver Medal and Travelling Studentship, 1932; Gold Medal and Edward Stott Trav. Studentship (Italy), 1933); Brit. Instn Schol., 1929. Lectr on Arch. subjects at Central Sch. of Arts and Crafts, Brixton Sch. of Bldg, and Hammersmith Sch. of Bldg, 1936-39; Lectr on Hosp. Planning at King Edward VII Hosp. Fund Colleges, 1950-. In partnership with W. H. Watkins won architectural comp. for new St George's Hosp., Hyde Park Corner, London (partnership 1939-68); before retirement Architect with partners to: Radcliffe Infirmary, Oxford, United Bristol Hospitals, Royal Free Hospital, Guy's Hospital, London Hospital, Eastman Dental Hospital, St Mary's, Manchester, and other hosps in London and the provinces; also in West Indies, where they were responsible for banks, and commercial buildings as well; hospitals for Comptroller of Development and Welfare in BWI, 1941-46; rebuilding of centre of Georgetown, British Guiana, after the fire of 1945, including new GPO, Telecommunications Building, etc. In Nigeria, University Coll. Hosp., Ibadan, and other works, also in Qatar (Persian Gulf), etc. *Publications:* various papers read at confs on Hosp. Planning with special ref. to designing for the tropics, and contrib. Tech. Jls. *Address:* 1 Temple Fortune Hill, NW11. *T:* 01-458 5741. *Clubs:* Arts, Old Millhillians.

GRAY, Andrew Aitken, MC 1945; Chairman, Wellcome Foundation Ltd, 1971-77; *b* 11 Jan. 1912; *s* of John Gray and Margaret Eckford Gray (*née* Crozier); *m* 1939, Eileen Mary Haines; three *s. Educ:* Wyggeston School, Leicester; Christ Church, Oxford. Served Royal Engineers, 1939-46 (MC, despatches). Unilever Ltd, 1935-52. Dir, Wellcome Foundation Ltd, 1954, Dep. Chm., 1967; Chm. and Man. Dir, Cooper, McDougall & Robertson, 1963-70. Chm., Herts AHA, 1974-77. Comdr, Orden del Mérito Agricola. *Recreations:* fishing, gardening, theatre. *Address:* Rainhill Spring, Stoney Lane, Bovingdon, Herts. *T:* Hemel Hempstead 833277. *Club:* East India, Devonshire, Sports and Public Schools.

GRAY, Anthony James; management consultant; *b* 12 Feb. 1937; *o s* of Sir James Gray, CBE, MC, FRS; *m* 1963, Lady Lana Mary Gabrielle Baring (*d* 1974); one *s* one *d. Educ:* Marlborough Coll.; New Coll., Oxford. C. T. Bowring & Co. (Insurance) Ltd, 1959-64; Investment Analyst, de Zoete & Gorton, 1965-67; Research Partner, James Capel & Co., 1967-73. Member, London Stock Exchange, 1971-73. Dep. Dir, Industrial Development Unit, Dept of Industry, 1973-75; Adviser, Special Industry Problems, Dept of Industry, 1975-76. Mem., Foundries EDC, 1977-. *Recreations:* golf, fishing, music. *Address:* Offham House, Offham, West Malling, Kent ME19 5NH. *Club:* Garrick.

GRAY, Basil, CB 1969; CBE 1957; MA; FBA 1966; Keeper of Oriental Antiquities, British Museum, 1946-69, Acting Director and Principal Librarian, 1968; *b* 21 July 1904; *s* of late Surgeon-Major Charles Gray and Florence Elworthy, *d* of Rev. H. v. H. Cowell; *m* 1933, Nicolete, *d* of late Laurence Binyon, CH; two *s* two *d* (and one *d* decd). *Educ:* Bradfield; New Coll., Oxford. British Academy excavations in Constantinople, 1928; entered British Museum (Printed Books), 1928; transferred to sub-Dept of Oriental Prints and Drawings, 1930; in charge of Oriental Antiquities (including Oriental Prints and Drawings) from 1938; Dep. Keeper, 1940. Mem. of Art Panel of the Arts Council, 1952-57, and 1959-68; President: Oriental Ceramic Soc., 1962-65, 1971-74, 1977-78; 6th Internat. Congress of Iranian Art and Archaeology, Oxford, 1972. Mem., Reviewing Cttee on Export of Works of Art, 1971-; Chm., Exhibn cttee, The Arts of Islam, Hayward Gallery, 1976. A Visitor of Ashmolean Museum, Oxford, 1969-. Sir Percy Sykes Meml Medal, 1978. *Publications:* Persian Painting, 1930; Persian Miniature Painting (part author), 1933; Chinese Art (with Leigh Ashton), 1935; The English Print, 1937; Persian Painting, New York, 1940; Rajput Painting, 1948; (joint) Commemorative Catalogue of the Exhibition of the Art of India and Pakistan, 1947-48, 1950; Treasures of Indian Miniatures in the Bikanir Palace Collection, 1951; Early Chinese Pottery and Porcelain, 1953; Japanese Screen-paintings, 1955; Buddhist Cave paintings at Tun-huang, 1959; Treasures of Asia; Persian Painting, 1961; (with D. E. Barrett) Painting of India, 1963; An Album of Miniatures and Illuminations from the Bâysonhori Manuscript of the Shâhnâmeh of Ferdowsi, 1971; The World History of Rashid al-Din, a study of the RAS manuscript, 1977; (ed) Faber Gallery of Oriental Art and Arts of the East Series. *Address:* Dawber's House, Long Wittenham, Oxon OX14 4QQ. *Club:* Savile.

GRAY, Charles Herbert, FRCS; Hon. Consultant Orthopædic Surgeon, Royal Free Hospital; formerly Consulting Orthopædic Surgeon, British Postgraduate Medical School, Hammersmith Hospital, and Connaught Hospital, Walthamstow. *Educ:* Victoria University, Manchester. BSc; MB, ChB (hons) 1932; MRCS, LRCP, 1932; FRCS, 1935. Temp. Lt-Col, Royal Army Medical Corps. Hunterian Prof., Royal College of Surgeons, 1946, 1949. Formerly, Fracture and Orthopædic Registrar, Middlesex Hosp.; Surg. Registrar, Royal Nat. Orthopaedic Hospital. Fellow: British Orthopaedic Assoc.; Hunterian Soc.; Membre Société Internationale de Chirurgie, Orthopédie et Traumatologie. *Publications:* various articles in medical jls. *Address:* 8 Upper Wimpole Street, W1. *T:* 01-580 5307; 16 Hamilton Close, NW8.

GRAY, Charles Horace, MD (London), DSc, FRCP, FRIC, FRCPath; Visiting Professor, Division of Clinical Chemistry, MRC Clinical Research Centre, Harrow; Emeritus Professor of Chemical Pathology in the University of London (Professor, at King's College Hospital Medical School, 1948-76); Consulting Chemical Pathologist, King's College Hospital District (Consultant, 1938-76); *b* 30 June 1911; *s* of Charles H. Gray and Ethel Hider, Erith, Kent; *m* 1938, Florence Jessie Widdup, ARCA, *d* of Frank Widdup, JP, Barnoldswick, Yorks; two *s. Educ:* Imperial Coll. and University Coll., London; University Coll. Hospital Medical Sch. Demonstrator in Biochemistry, University Coll., London, 1931-36; Bayliss-Starling Scholar in Physiology and Biochemistry, 1932-33; Visiting Teacher in Biochemistry, Chelsea Polytechnic, 1933-36; Demonstrator and Lecturer in Physiology, University Coll., 1935-36; Graham Scholar in Pathology, UCH Medical Sch., 1936-38; Pathologist in Charge Sector Biochemical Laboratory, Sector 9, Emergency Health Service, 1939-44. Mem. Clinical Res. Bd of Med. Res. Council, 1964-68; Chairman: MCB Exams Cttee, 1971-73; Steroid Reference Collection and Radioactive Steroid Synthesis Steering Cttee, MRC, 1973-76; Regional Scientific Cttee, SE Thames RHA. Member: Cttee of Management, Inst. of Psychiatry, 1966-73; Council, RCPath (Chm., Specialist Adv. Cttee in Chemical Pathology); Assoc. of Biochemists (Pres. 1969-71). *Publications:* The Bile Pigments, 1953; Clinical Chemical Pathology, 1953, 1959, 1963, 1965, 1968, 1971, 1974, 1977. The Bile Pigments in Health and Disease, 1961; (Editor) Laboratory Handbook of Toxic Agents; (Joint Editor) Hormones in Blood, 1961, 1967; contributions to medical and scientific journals. *Recreations:* music and travel. *Address:* Barn Cottage, Linden Road, Leatherhead, Surrey KT22 7JF. *T:* Leatherhead 72415; 34 Cleaver Square, SE11. *T:* 01-735 9652; Owls Mount, Portland, Dorset. *T:* Portland 820574. *Club:* Athenæum.

GRAY, David, CBE 1977 (OBE 1964); QPM 1960; HM Chief Inspector of Constabulary for Scotland since 1970; *b* 18 Nov. 1914; *s* of William Gray and Janet Borland; *m* 1944, Mary Stewart Scott; two *d. Educ:* Preston Grammar Sch. Chief Constable: Greenock, 1955-58; Stirling and Clackmannan, 1958-

69. *Recreations:* fishing, shooting, golf. *Address:* Kingarth, 42 East Barnton Avenue, Edinburgh EH4 6AQ. *T:* 031-336 6342. *Club:* Bruntsfield (Edinburgh).

GRAY, David; Secretary-General, International Lawn Tennis Federation, since Aug. 1976; *b* 31 Dec. 1927; *s* of David Reginald Gray and Beatrice Gladys (*née* Goodyear); *m* 1962, Margaret Clare Emerson; three *s* one *d*. *Educ:* King Edward VI Grammar Sch., Stourbridge; Birmingham Univ. (BA Hons English). Journalist: Evening Telegraph, Blackburn, 1951-53; News Chronicle, 1953-54. Guardian: Manchester Guardian/Guardian, 1954-76; Midlands Correspondent, 1955-56; Lawn Tennis Correspondent, 1956-76; Sports Editor, 1961-68. *Publications:* contrib. to Oxford Companion to Sport and other sports ref. books. *Recreations:* theatre, hill climbing. *Address:* 50 Luttrell Avenue, SW15 6PF. *T:* 01-788 4809. *Clubs:* Queen's, Players' Theatre.

GRAY, Dulcie; *see* Denison, D. W. C.

GRAY, Prof. Edward George, FRS 1976; Professor of Anatomy (Cytology), University College, London, since 1968; *b* 11 Jan. 1924; *s* of Will and Charlotte Gray; *m* 1953, May Eine Kyllikki Rautiainen; two *s*. *Educ:* University Coll. of Wales, Aberystwyth (BSc, PhD). Anatomy Dept, University Coll., London: Lectr, 1958; Reader, 1962. *Recreations:* violin playing, water colouring, gardening. *Address:* 58 New Park Road, Newgate Street, Hertford SG13 8RF. *T:* Cuffley 2891.

GRAY, Francis Anthony; Secretary and Keeper of the Records of the Duchy of Cornwall, since 1972; *b* 3 Aug. 1917; *s* of late Major F. C. Gray; *m* 1947, Marcia, *d* of late Major Hugh Wyld; one *s* two *d*. *Educ:* Marlborough; Magdalen Coll., Oxford. Treas., Christ Church, Oxford, 1952-72, Emeritus Student, 1972. Mem., Agricultural Adv. Council, 1963-68; Mem. Council, Royal Coll. of Art, 1967-73. *Recreation:* travel. *Address:* 10 Buckingham Gate, SW1; Temple House, Upton Scudamore, Warminster, Wilts. *T:* Warminster 2747. *Club:* Travellers'.

GRAY, Geoffrey Leicester, CMG 1958; OBE 1953; Secretary for Local Government, N Borneo (now Sabah), 1956-61, retired; *b* 26 Aug. 1905; *s* of late Leonard Swainson Gray, Resident Magistrate of Kingston, Jamaica, and of late Marion Scotland, Vale Royal, Kingston, Jamaica; *m* 1932, Penelope Miles (*d* 1971), MBE 1962, *o c* of late Philip Henry Townsend, OBE and late Gwenyth Gwendoline Roberts. *Educ:* Latymer Upper Sch. Cadet, North Borneo Civil Service, under British North Borneo (Chartered) Co., 1925; after qualifying in Malay and Law, served in various admin. posts, 1925-30; studied Chinese in Canton, 1931; attached Secretariat for Chinese Affairs and Educ. Dept, Hong Kong, 1931; Dist Officer, Jesselton, Supt, Govt Printing Office, and Editor, British North Borneo Herald and Official Gazette, 1932-35; Dist Officer, Kudat, 1935; Under-Sec., 1935-38; Govt Sec. Class 1b and *ex-officio* MLC, 1938-46; Additional Sessions and High Court Judge, 1938-46; interned by Japanese, 1941-45; Class 1a, 1946; accredited to HQ Brit. Mil. Admin (Brit. Borneo) at Labuan, 1946; assimilated into HM Colonial Admin. Service (later HM Overseas Service) on cession of North Borneo to the Crown, 1946; Actg Dep. Chief Sec., 1946; Protector of Labour and Sec. for Chinese Affairs, 1947; Resident, E Coast, in addition, 1947; Mem. Advisory Council, 1947-50; Comr of Immigration and Labour, 1948-51; Official MLC and MEC, 1950-61; Actg Fin. Sec., 1951-52; Dep. Chief Sec., Staff Class, 1952-56; represented North Borneo at Coronation, 1953; Chm., Bd of Educn and Town and Country Planning Bd, 1956-61; Actg Chief Sec. (intermittently), 1952-60; administered Govt, 1958, 1959; acted as High Comr, Brunei, 1959; retd, 1961. Life Associate, N Borneo and UK Branches, CPA, 1961. Chm., Borneo Mission Assoc., 1961-76; Commissary for Bp of Jesselton (later Sabah), 1961. Elected Incorporated Mem. of SPG (Mem., Standing Cttee, 1964-66; Mem., East Asia and Pacific Sub-Cttees, 1964-69; Mem. USPG Council, 1965, Mem. Gen. Cttee, 1966; Mem. Overseas Cttee, Grants and Budget Groups, 1969. *Address:* 1 Laburnum Cottages, Yapton, Arundel, Sussex BN18 0DX. *T:* Yapton 551770. *Clubs:* Royal Commonwealth Society, Travellers'.

GRAY, George Charles, DMus (Cantuar) 1968; FRCO 1920; FRSCM 1967; Organist and Master of the Music, Leicester Cathedral, 1931-69; Conductor of Leicester Bach Choir, 1931-69; Senior Lecturer in Music, Leicester College of Education, 1946-76; Lay Canon of Leicester Cathedral, 1942; Examiner, Trinity College of Music, 1958; *b* 1897; *s* of late Charles Wilson Gray and Alice Gray; *m* 1925, Gladys Gofton (*d* 1972), York; two *s* one *d* (and one *d* decd). *Educ:* Rotherham Grammar Sch. MusB (Dunelm) 1927. Articled pupil of late Sir Edward Bairstow at York Minster, 1919-22; Lafontaine Prize winner,

Royal Coll. of Organists, 1920, also winner, Worshipful Company of Musicians Silver Medal, 1922; Organist and Choirmaster successively of S Michael-le-Belfry, York, S Martin's, Leeds, and Alnwick Parish Church; Conductor of Alnwick Choral Union, and Wooler Choral Union Organist and Choirmaster, St Mary le Tower, Ipswich, 1926; Founder and Conductor of Ipswich Bach Choir 1927-30; Conductor of Ipswich Choral Society, 1928-30; Extra-mural Lecturer in Musical Appreciation at Vaughan Coll., Leicester, 1931-51; Lecturer in Singing, University Coll., 1931-58. Pres. Cathedral Organists' Assoc., 1968-70. Hon. MusM Leicester, 1965. *Recreation:* cricket. *Address:* 8 Knighton Court, Knighton Park Road, Leicester LE2 1ZB. *T:* 705167. *Club:* Rotary.

GRAY, Gilbert, QC 1971; a Recorder of the Crown Court, since 1972; *b* 25 April 1928; *s* of late Robert Gray, JP, Scarborough, and of Mrs Elizabeth Gray; *m* 1954, Olga Dilys Gray (*née* Thomas), BA, JP; two *s* two *d*. *Educ:* Scarborough Boys' High Sch.; Leeds Univ. (LLB). Pres., Leeds Univ. Union. Called to the Bar, Gray's Inn, 1953. *Recreation:* sailing. *Address:* Beckdale House, Scalby, Scarborough, North Yorks; 5 Kings Bench Walk, Temple, EC4; 2 Park Square, Leeds LS1 2NE. *Clubs:* City (York); Leeds (Leeds); Scarborough Sailing.

GRAY, His Eminence Cardinal Gordon; *see* St Andrews and Edinburgh, Archbishop of, (RC).

GRAY, Gordon; Chairman Emeritus, National Trust for Historic Preservation; *b* 30 May 1909; *s* of Bowman and Nathalie Lyons Gray; *m* 1938, Jane Boyden Craige (*d* 1953); four *s*; *m* 1956, Nancy Maguire Beebe; three step *d*. *Educ:* Woodberry Forest Sch., Woodberry Forest, Va; University of N Carolina, Chapel Hill, NC; Yale Law Sch., New Haven, Conn. Admitted to NY Bar, 1934, and associated with Carter, Ledyard & Milburn, 1933-35; with Manly, Hendren & Womble, Winston-Salem, NC, 1935-37; admitted to North Carolina Bar, 1936; Pres., Piedmont Publishing Company, 1937-47. N Carolina Senate, 1939, 1941, 1945. Enlisted in US Army as private, 1942; Capt., 1945. Asst Sec. of Army, 1947; Under-Sec. of Army, 1949; Sec. of Army, 1949; Special Asst to the President, USA, April-Nov. 1950; Dir, Psychological Strategy Board, July-Dec. 1951. Pres. of Univ. of N Carolina, Feb. 1950-Nov. 1955; Asst Sec. of Defense, International Sec. Affairs, US, 1955-57; Dir, Office of Defense Mobilization, 1957-58; Special Asst to President, USA, for National Security Affairs, 1958-61; Mem., President's Foreign Intelligence Adv. Bd, 1961-77. Chm., Summit Communications, Inc.; Director: R. J. Reynolds Industries Inc.; American Security Bank; Media General, Inc.; Trustee: Brookings Instn, 1961-75; Federal City Council. Pres., Kensington Orchids Inc. Holds several Hon. degrees. *Address:* 1224 30th Street NW, Washington, DC 20007, USA; (Office) 1616 H Street NW, Washington, DC 20006, USA. *Clubs:* Alibi, Chevy Chase, Burning Tree, Metropolitan (all Washington); The Brook (New York).

GRAY, Rear-Adm. Gordon Thomas Seccombe, CB 1964; DSC 1939; *b* 20 Dec. 1911; *s* of late Rev. Thomas Seccombe Gray and Edith Gray; *m* 1939, Sonia Moore-Gwyn; one *s* one *d*. *Educ:* Nautical Coll., Pangbourne. Entered RN, 1929; Sub-Lieut and Lieut, Mediterranean Fleet, 1934-36, ashore Arab revolt in Palestine (despatches); 1st Lieut, HMS Stork, 1939, Norwegian campaign (despatches, DSC); Comd HMS Badsworth, 1942-43 (despatches); Comd HMS Lamerton, 1943-45 (despatches). After the War comd destroyers Consort, Contest and St Kitts; JSSC, 1948; Comdr 1949; Directing Staff, RN Staff Coll., Greenwich, 1950; Exec. Officer, cruiser HMS Glasgow, 1951-53; Capt. 1953; Naval Deputy to UK Nat. Military Representative, at SHAPE; Capt. of 5th Frigate Sqdn, and Comd HMS Wakeful and HMS Torquay, 1956-59; Asst Chief of Staff to C-in-C Eastern Atlantic Command, 1959-61; in comd of Naval Air Anti-Submarine Sch. at Portland and Chief Staff Officer to Flag Officer Sea Trng, 1961-62; Senior Naval Instructor, Imperial Defence Coll., 1963-65, retd. *Recreation:* yachting. *Address:* Hollies, Wispers, Midhurst, West Sussex.

GRAY, Hamish; *see* Gray, J. H. N.

GRAY, Harold James, CMG 1956; *b* 17 Oct. 1907; 2nd *s* of late John William Gray and of Amelia Frances (*née* Miller); *m* 1928, Katherine Gray (*née* Starling); one *d*. *Educ:* Alleyn's Sch.; Dover County Sch.; Queen Mary Coll., London Univ. (MSc, LLB); Gray's Inn; Harvard University, USA (Master of Public Administration). Customs and Excise Dept, 1927; Asst Examiner, Patent Office, 1930, Examiner, 1935; Industries and Manufactures Dept, Board of Trade, 1938; Ministry of Supply, 1939; Asst Sec., Min. of Supply, 1942. transf. to Bd of Trade, 1946; Commercial Relations and Exports Dept, Board of Trade, 1950; Under-Sec., 1954; UK Senior Trade Comr and Economic and Commercial Adviser to High Commissioner in Australia, 1954-58; United Kingdon Senior Trade Commissioner and Economic Adviser to the High Commissioner in the Union of South Africa, 1958-60; Dir, National Association of British Manufacturers, 1961-65; Dir of Legal Affairs, CBI, 1965-72. FRSA; Mem. Inst. of Physics; Commonwealth Fund Fellowship, 1949-50. Chm., NUMAS (Management Services) Ltd. *Publications:* Electricity in the Service of Man, 1949; Economic Survey of Australia, 1955; Dictionary of Physics, 1958; (jtly) New Dictionary of Physics, 1975. *Recreations:* golf, swimming, riding. *Address:* Oaken Wood, Red Hill, Wateringbury, Kent ME18 5LD. *Club:* East India, Devonshire, Sports and Public Schools.

GRAY, Hugh, BSc(Soc), PhD; Lecturer in South Asia Politics, School of Oriental and African Studies, since 1970; *b* 19 April 1916; *s* of William Marshall Kemp Gray; *m* 1954, Edith Esther (*née* Rudinger); no *c. Educ:* Battersea Gram. Sch.; London Sch. of Economics. Army Service (Intelligence Corps), 1940-45. UNRRA, 1945-48; Internat. Refugee Organisation, 1948-52; Social Worker, 1952-57; Student on Leverhulme Adult Schol. at LSE, 1957-60; Fellow in S Asian Studies, SOAS, 1960-62; Lectr in Sociology with ref. to S Asia, SOAS, University of London, 1962-66; MP (Lab) Yarmouth, 1966-70; contested (Lab): Cheltenham, Feb. 1974; Norfolk South, Oct. 1974. *Publications:* various articles on Indian politics in Jl of Commonwealth Studies, Asian Survey, etc. *Recreations:* ski-ing, skating, theatre, ballet. *Address:* 22 Bridstow Place, W2. *Club:* Reform.

GRAY, Ian; MA; Managing Director and Chief Executive, Welsh Development Agency, since 1976; Member: Development Corporation for Wales, since 1976; Design Council Wales Advisory Committee; *b* 29 Aug. 1926; *er s* of late Henry Gray and Elizabeth Cowan Gray; *m* 1954, Vaudine Angela Harrison-Ainsworth; one *s* one *d. Educ:* Royal High Sch., Edinburgh; Univ. of Edinburgh (MA Econ.). War Service with Royal Scots and Indian Army, 1944-45 (2nd Lieut). Joined BoT, 1948; Private Sec. to successive Parly Secs, 1951-52 and to Pres., 1952-54; British Trade Comr, Wellington, 1954-56; Principal British Trade Comr, Cape Town, 1957-60; BoT, London, 1961-67; BoT Controller for Wales, Cardiff, 1967-69; Dir, Min. of Technology Office for Wales, 1970; Dir for Wales, DTI, 1971; Skelmersdale Develt Corporation: Gen. Manager, 1972-73; Man. Dir, 1973-76. Member: Ormskirk District HMC, 1972-74; Lancs AHA, 1973-76. *Recreations:* photography, carpentry, making and drinking wine. *Address:* Welsh Development Agency, Treforest Industrial Estate, Treforest, Mid Glamorgan. *T:* Treforest 2666. *Club:* Cardiff and County.

GRAY, James Hector Northey, (Hamish Gray); MP (C) Ross and Cromarty since 1970; *b* 28 June 1927; *s* of J. Northey Gray, Inverness, and Mrs. E. M. Gray; *m* 1953, Judith Waite Brydon, BSc, Helensburgh; two *s* one *d. Educ:* Inverness Royal Academy. Served in Queen's Own Cameron Hldrs, 1945-48. An Asst Govt Whip, 1971-73; a Lord Comr, HM Treasury, 1973-74; an Opposition Whip, 1974-Feb. 1975; Opposition spokesman on Energy, Feb. 1975-. Member, Inverness Town Council, 1965-70. *Recreations:* golf, walking, family life. *Address:* The Cedars, Drummond Road, Inverness. *Clubs:* St Stephen's; Highland (Inverness).

GRAY, John; see Gray, R. J.

GRAY, Rev. Prof. John; Professor of Hebrew, University of Aberdeen, since 1961; *b* 9 June 1913; *s* of James Telfer Gray; *m* Janet J. Gibson; five *c. Educ:* Kelso High Sch.; Edinburgh Univ. (MA, BD, PhD). Colonial Chaplain and Chaplain to Palestine Police, 1939-41; Minister of the Church of Scotland, Kilmory, Isle of Arran, 1942-47; Lectr in Semitic Languages and Literatures, Manchester Univ., 1947-53; Lectr in Hebrew and Biblical Criticism, University of Aberdeen, 1953-61. Mem., Soc. for Old Testament Study. *Publications:* The Kr Text in the Literature of Ras Shamra, 1955 (2nd edn 1964); The Legacy of Canaan, 1957 (2nd edn 1965); Archæology and the Old Testament World, 1962; The Canaanites, 1964; Kings I and II: a Commentary, 1964 (new edn, 1970); Joshua, Judges and Ruth, 1967; A History of Jerusalem, 1969; Near Eastern Mythology, 1969; contribs to various Bible Dictionaries, memorial volumes and learned journals. *Recreations:* beekeeping, gardening, trout-fishing. *Address:* Inverawe, Persley, Aberdeen AB2 8AQ. *T:* Bucksburn 2729.

GRAY, Sir John (Archibald Browne), Kt 1973; MA, MB, ScD; FRS 1972; Member, External Scientific Staff, Marine Biological Association Laboratories, Plymouth, since 1971; *b* 30 March 1918; *s* of late Sir Archibald Gray, KCVO, CBE; *m* 1946, Vera Kathleen Mares; one *s* one *d. Educ:* Cheltenham Coll.; Clare Coll., Cambridge (Hon. Fellow, 1976); University Coll.

Hospital. BA 1939; MA 1942; MB, BChir 1942; ScD 1962. Service Research for MRC, 1943-45; Surg. Lieut, RNVR, 1945-46; Scientific Staff of MRC at Nat. Inst. for Med. Research, 1946-52; Reader in Physiology, University Coll., London, 1952-58; Prof. of Physiology, University Coll., London, 1959-66; Medical Research Council: Second Sec., 1966-68; Sec., 1968-77; Dep. Chm., 1975-77. QHP 1968-71. FIBiol; FRCP 1974. *Publications:* papers, mostly on sensory receptors and sensory nervous system, in Jl of Physiology, etc. *Recreations:* painting, sailing, tennis. *Address:* Seaways, North Rock, Kingsand, near Plymouth PL10 1NG. *T:* Plymouth 822745.

GRAY, Air Vice-Marshal John Astley, CB 1945; CBE 1943; DFC; GM; retired; *b* 1899. *Educ:* Framlingham Coll. Served European War, 1917-19; War of 1939-45. Air Vice-Marshal 1944; AOC 91 (B) Gp, 1944-46; AOC RAF Mission to Greece, 1947-48; SASO, HQ Transport Comd, 1949-51; AOA, HQ ME Air Force, 1951-54; retired, 1954. *Address:* Bittern, Thorpeness, Suffolk. *Club:* Royal Air Force.

GRAY, John Magnus, CBE 1971 (MBE 1945); ERD 1946; Chairman, Northern Ireland Electricity Service, since 1974 (Deputy Chairman, 1973-74); *b* 15 Oct. 1915; *o s* of Lewis Campbell Gray, CA and Ingeborg Sanderson Gray (*née* Ross), Glasgow; *m* 1947, Patricia Mary, OBE 1976, *widow* of Major Aubrey D. P. Hodges and *d* of John Norman Eggar and Emma Frances Eggar (*née* Garrett), Epsom and Godalming; one *d. Educ:* Horris Hill, Newbury; Winchester College. Served RA, 1939-46 (Major). Joined Wm Ewart & Son Ltd, Linen Manufrs, Belfast, 1934; Dir 1950; Man. Dir 1958-72. Chairman: Irish Linen Guild, 1958-64; Central Council, Irish Linen Industry, 1968-74 (Mem.), 1957; Vice-Chm., 1966-68); Linen Industry Standards Cttee of BSI, 1969-74; Belfast Br., RNLI, 1970-76; Member: Council of Belfast T&AFA, 1948-68; Council of Belfast Chamber of Commerce, 1955-59; Gen. Synod of Church of Ireland, 1955-; Councils of FBI and CBI, 1956-74; NI Legal Aid Cttee, 1958-59; Export Council for Europe, 1964-70; Northern Ireland Adv. Council for BBC, 1968-72; Design Council, 1974-; Asst Comr for Commn on Constitution, 1969-73. Captain, Royal Co. Down Golf Club, 1963. *Recreations:* golf, gardening. *Address:* Blairlodge, Dundrum, Newcastle, Co. Down BT33 0NF. *T:* Dundrum 271. *Clubs:* Army and Navy; Ulster (Belfast).

GRAY, Vice-Adm. Sir John (Michael Dudgeon), KBE 1967 (OBE 1950); CB 1964; *b* Dublin, 13 June 1913; British; *m* 1939, Margaret Helen Purvis; one *s* one *d. Educ:* RNC, Dartmouth. HMS Nelson, 1931; Midshipman, HMS Enterprise, 1932-33; Sub-Lieut, HMS Devonshire, 1934; specialised in Gunnery, 1938. Served War of 1939-45; HMS Hermes; HMS Spartan; with US in Anzio; 8th Army in Italy; French Army in France (despatches). HMS Duke of York, 1945, Comdr 1947; Naval Adviser, UK Mission, Japan, 1947-50 (OBE Korean War); HMS Swiftsure, 1950, Capt. 1952; HMS Lynx, 1956; HMS Victorious, 1961; Rear-Adm. 1962; Dir-Gen. of Naval Trng, Min. of Def., 1964-65 (Admiralty, 1962-64); Vice-Adm. 1965; C-in-C, S Atlantic and S America, 1965-67. Sec., Oriental Ceramic Soc., 1974-. *Recreations:* squash, tennis, athletics (represented RN in 220 and 440 yds). *Address:* 55 Elm Park Gardens, SW10. *T:* 01-352 1757. *Club:* Naval and Military.

GRAY, Prof. John Richard; Professor of African History, University of London, since 1972; *b* 7 July 1929; *s* of Captain Alfred William Gray, RN and of Christobel Margaret Gray (*née* Raikes); *m* 1957, Gabriella, *d* of Dr Camillo Cattaneo; one *s* one *d. Educ:* Charterhouse; Downing Coll., Cambridge (Richmond Scholar). BA Cantab 1951; PhD London 1957. Lectr, Univ. of Khartoum, 1959-61; Res. Fellow, Sch. of Oriental and African Studies, London, 1961-63, Reader, 1963-72. Vis. Prof., UCLA, 1967. Editor, Jl African History, 1968-71; Chm., Africa Centre, Covent Garden, 1967-72. Order of St Silvester, 1966. *Publications:* The Two Nations: aspects of the development of race relations in the Rhodesias and Nyasaland, 1960; A History of the Southern Sudan, 1839-1889, 1961; (with D. Chambers) Materials for West African History in Italian Archives, 1965; (ed, with D. Birmingham) Pre-Colonial African Trade, 1970; (ed) The Cambridge History of Africa, vol. 4, 1975. *Recreation:* things Italian. *Address:* 39 Rotherwick Road, NW11 7DD. *T:* 01-458 3676.

GRAY, Rt. Rev. John Rodger, VRD 1956; Minister at Dunblane Cathedral, since 1966; Moderator of the General Assembly of the Church of Scotland, 1977-78; *b* 9 Jan. 1913; *s* of John Charles Gray, Hartlea, Coatbridge, and Jeannie Gilmour Rodger; *m* 1952, Dr Sheila Mary Whiteside; three *s. Educ:* High Sch. of Glasgow; Glasgow Univ. (MA 1934); Yale Univ. (BD 1938); Princeton Univ. and Seminary (ThM 1939). Pres., Glasgow Univ. Union, 1934-35. Commonwealth Fund Fellow,

Yale, 1937-39; Asst Minister, Barony of Glasgow, 1939-41; Chaplain: RN, 1941-46; RNVR, 1946-63; Minister, St Stephen's, Glasgow, 1946-66. Hastie Lectr in Theol., Glasgow Univ., 1947-50; Lectr in Theol., Glasgow Sch. of Study and Trng, 1948; Lectr, Princeton Inst. of Theol., 1949 and 1968. Convener, Church and Nation Cttee, Gen. Assembly of Church of Scotland; Mem., Religious Adv. Cttees, BBC, IBA, and STV. *Publications:* The Political Theory of John Knox, 1939; articles, sermons, and book revs in Expository Times, Gen. Practitioner, and Princeton Sem. Jl. *Recreations:* broadcasting, television. *Address:* The Cathedral Manse of Dunblane, Dunblane, Perthshire FK15 OAQ. *T:* Dunblane 822205. *Clubs:* Caledonian; New (Edinburgh).

GRAY, Rt. Rev. Joseph; Titular Bishop of Mercia and Auxiliary Bishop of Liverpool, (RC), since 1969; *b* 20 Oct. 1919; *s* of Terence Gray and Mary Gray (*née* Alwill). *Educ:* St Patrick's Coll., Cavan, Eire; St Mary's Seminary, Oscott, Birmingham; Dunboyne House, St Patrick's Coll., Maynooth, Eire; Pontifical Univ. of St Thomas Aquinas, Rome. Priest, 1943; Asst Priest, Sacred Heart, Aston, Birmingham, 1943-48; Dunboyne House, 1948-50 (Licentiate in Canon Law, 1950); Sec. to Archbp of Birmingham, 1950-55. Diocesan Chancellor, Birmingham, 1951-69; Pontifical Univ., 1959-60 (Doctorate in Canon Law, 1960); Vicar-Gen., Birmingham, 1960-69; Parish Priest, St Michael's, Birmingham, 1955-69. Papal Chamberlain, 1960; Domestic Prelate, 1966. Episcopal Ordination, Cathedral of Christ the King, Liverpool, Feb. 1969. Pres., Nat. Liturgical Commn for England and Wales, 1975-. *Recreations:* music, reading, travel. *Address:* Martland House, Spencer Road, Wigan, Lancashire. *T:* Wigan 42740.

GRAY, Margaret Caroline, MA Cantab; Headmistress, Godolphin and Latymer School, 1963-Dec. 1973; *b* 25 June 1913; *d* of Rev. A. Herbert Gray, DD, and Mrs Gray (Mary C. Dods, *d* of Principal Marcus Dods of New Coll., Edinburgh). *Educ:* St Mary's Hall, Brighton; Newnham Coll., Cambridge. Post graduate fellowship to Smith Coll., Mass, USA, 1935-36. Asst History mistress, Westcliff High Sch. for Girls, 1937-38; Head of History Dept, Mary Datchelor Girls' Sch., Camberwell, 1939-52; Headmistress, Skinners' Company's Sch., Stamford Hill, 1952-63. Chm., Nat. Advisory Centre on Careers for Women, 1970-. *Recreations:* gardening, motoring, walking. *Address:* 15 Fitzwilliam Avenue, Kew, Richmond, Surrey. *T:* 01-940 4439.

GRAY, Mary Elizabeth, CBE 1946 (OBE 1942); WRVS Administrator, Midland Region, 1949-71; resigned as County Commissioner, Gloucestershire Girl Guides (1949-61); *b* 19 May 1903; *d* of late Edward Wilmot Butler and Ethel Margaret Gray. *Educ:* Lanherne House, Dawlish; Switzerland. Joined WVS 1938; WVS Administrator, Eastern Counties Region 4, 1938-44; Deputy Vice-Chm., WVS, 1944; WVS Administrator SEAC and FE, 1944-48. *Recreations:* dog breeding, gardening. *Address:* Maisey Cottage, Gilberts End, Hanley Castle, Worcs.

GRAY, Milner Connorton, CBE 1963; RDI 1938; FSIA; AGI; MInstPack; Founder Partner and Senior Consultant, Design Research Unit; Past Master, Faculty of Royal Designers for Industry; Past President, Society of Industrial Artists and Designers; Past Master Art Workers' Guild; *b* 8 Oct. 1899; *s* of late Archibald Campbell Gray and Katherine May Hart, Eynsford, Kent; *m* 1934, Gnade Osborne-Pratt; no *c*. *Educ:* studied painting and design, London Univ., Goldsmiths' Coll. Sch. of Art. Head of Exhibitions Branch, Ministry of Information, 1940-41, and Adviser on Exhibitions, 1941-44; Senior Partner in Industrial Design Partnership, 1934-40; Principal, Sir John Cass Coll. of Art, 1937-40; on Visiting Staff: Goldsmiths' Coll. Sch. of Art, London Univ., 1930-40; Chelsea Sch. of Art, 1934-37; Royal Coll. of Art, 1940; Founder Mem., Soc. of Industrial Artists, 1930, Hon. Sec., 1932-40, Pres., 1943-48 and 1968; Member of Council: Design and Industries Assoc., 1935-38; RSA, 1959-65; Artists Gen. Benevolent Instn, 1959-; Adviser to BBC "Looking at Things" Schs Broadcasts, 1949-55. Member: Min. of Education Nat. Adv. Cttee on Art Examinations, 1949-52; Nat. Adv. Council on Art Education, 1959-69; Royal Mint Adv. Cttee, 1952-. Mem. Council, RCA, 1963-67; Mem. Court 1967-, Senior Fellow, 1971. British Pres., Alliance Graphique Internationale, 1963-71. Consultant Designer: BR Bd for BR Corporate Identity Prog., 1963-67; (jointly) to Orient Line, SS Oriana, 1957-61; Ilford Ltd, 1946-66; Internat. Distillers and Vintners, 1954-; Watney Mann Group, 1956-; British Aluminium Co., 1965-; ICI, 1966-; Min. of Technology, 1970-. Governor: Central Sch. of Art and Design, 1944-46; Hornsey Coll. of Art and Design, 1959-65. Hon. Des. RCA, 1963; Hon. DA Manchester, 1964. Served in 19th London Regt, and Royal Engineers, attached Camouflage Sch., 1917-19. Gold Medal, Soc. of Ind. Artists and Designers, 1955.

Publications: The Practice of Design (jointly), 1946; Package Design, 1955; (jtly) Lettering for Architects and Designers, 1962; articles, lectures and broadcasts on various aspects of design. *Address:* 8 Holly Mount, Hampstead, NW3 6SG. *T:* 01-435 4238; Felix Hall, Kelvedon, Essex. *Clubs:* Arts, Garrick.

GRAY, Nicol; *see* Gray, W. N.

GRAY, Prof. Peter, MA, PhD, ScD (Cantab); FRS 1977; CChem, FRIC; Professor and Head of Department of Physical Chemistry, University of Leeds, since 1965; *b* 25 Aug. 1926; *er s* of late Ivor Hicks Gray and Rose Ethel Gray; *m* 1952, Barbara Joan Hume, PhD, 2nd *d* of J. B. Hume, London; two *s* two *d*. *Educ:* Newport, High Sch.; Gonville and Caius Coll., Cambridge. Major Schol., 1943; Prizeman, 1944, 1945 and 1946, Gonville and Caius Coll.; BA 1st cl hons Nat. Sci. Tripos, 1946; Dunlop Res. Student, 1946; Ramsay Mem. Fellow, 1949-51; PhD 1949; Fellow, Gonville and Caius Coll., 1949-53; ICI Fellow, 1951; ScD 1963. University Demonstrator in Chem. Engrg, University of Cambridge, 1951-55; Physical Chemistry Dept, University of Leeds: Lectr, 1955; Reader, 1959; Prof., 1962; Chm., Bd of Combined Faculties of Science and Applied Science, 1972-74. Vis. Prof., Univ. of BC, 1958-59; Univ. of W Ont., 1969. Mem. Council: Faraday Soc., 1965 (Vice-Pres., 1970; Treasurer, 1973); Chemical Soc., 1969. Meldola Medal, Royal Inst. Chem., 1956; Marlow Medal, Faraday Soc., 1959. *Publications:* papers on phys. chem. subjects in scientific jls. *Recreation:* hill walking. *Address:* 4 Ancaster Road, Leeds LS16 5HH. *T:* Leeds 752826.

GRAY, Maj.-Gen. (Reginald) John, CB 1973; Chief Medical Officer, British Red Cross Society, since 1974; *b* 26 Nov. 1916; *s* of late Dr Cyril Gray and Frances Anne Higgins, Higginsbrook, Co. Meath; *m* 1943, Esme, *d* of late G. R. G. Shipp; one *s* one *d*. *Educ:* Rossall Sch.; Coll. of Medicine, Univ. of Durham. MB, BS. Commissioned into RAMC, 1939; served War of 1939-45 in India; later Burma, NW Europe, Egypt, Malta, BAOR. Comd of 9 (Br.) CCS, 1945; Asst Dir-Gen., AMS, WO, AMD3, 1954-57; comd of David Bruce Mil. Hosp., Mtarfa, 1957-60; 14 Field Amb., 4 Guards Bde, 1960-63; Brit. Mil. Hosp., Rinteln, 1963-64; The Queen Alexandra Mil. Hosp., Millbank, 1964-67; Asst Dir-Gen., AMS, Min. of Defence AMD1, 1967-69; Dep Dir-Gen., AMS, 1969-71. QHS 1970-73; DMS, UK Land Forces, 1972-73, retired. Col Comdt, RAMC, 1977-. Mem., Casualty Surgeons Assoc., 1976-. FRSM; FMedSoc. Lond; FFCM 1972. CStJ 1971 (OStJ 1957). *Recreations:* gardening, wine making, d-i-y slowly. *Address:* 11 Hampton Close, Wimbledon, SW20 0RY. *T:* 01-946 7429.

GRAY, Robin, (Robert Walker Gray), CB 1977; Deputy Secretary, Department of Trade, since 1975; *b* 29 July 1924; *s* of Robert Walker Gray and Dorothy (*née* Lane); *m* 1955, Shirley Matilda (*née* Taylor); two *s* one *d*. *Educ:* Headstone Council Sch.; Pinner Park Council Sch.; John Lyon Sch., Harrow; Birkbeck Coll., Univ. of London; London Sch. of Economics. BScEcons 1946; Farr Medal in Statistics. Air Warfare Analysis Section of Air Min., 1940-45; BoT, 1947; UK Delegn to OEEC, 1950-51; BoT, 1952-66; Commercial Counsellor, British High Commn, Ottawa, 1966-70; Under-Secretary: DTI, 1971-74; Dept of Prices and Consumer Protection, 1974-75; Dep. Sec., DoI, 1975. *Recreations:* fishing, growing rhododendrons, target shooting. *Address:* Tansy, Brook Road, Wormley, Godalming, Surrey GU8 GU8 5UA. *T:* Wormley 2486.

GRAY, Roger Ibbotson, QC 1967; a Recorder of the Crown Court, since 1972; *b* 16 June 1921; *o s* of late Arthur Gray and of Mary Gray (*née* Ibbotson), Seaford, Sussex; *m* 1952, Anne Valerie, 2nd *d* of late Capt. G. G. P. Hewett, CBE, RN; one *s*. *Educ:* Wycliffe Coll.; Queen's Coll. Oxford. 1st cl. hons Jurisprudence, Oxon, 1941. Commissioned RA, 1942; served with Ayrshire Yeomanry, 1942-45; Normandy and NW Europe, 1944-45; GSO3 (Mil. Ops), GHQ, India, 1946. Pres. of Oxford Union, 1947. Called to Bar, Gray's Inn, 1947; South-Eastern Circuit. Contested (C) Dagenham, 1955. *Publication:* (with Major I. A. Graham Young) A Short History of the Ayrshire Yeomanry (Earl of Carrick's Own) 151st Field Regiment, RA, 1939-46, 1947. *Recreations:* cricket, reading, talk. *Address:* 34 Halsey Street, SW3. *T:* 01-589 0221. *Clubs:* Carlton, MCC.

GRAY, Simon James Holliday; Lecturer in English, Queen Mary College, University of London, since 1965; *b* 21 Oct. 1936; *s* of Dr James Davidson Gray and Barbara Cecelia Mary Holliday; *m* 1965, Beryl Mary Kevern; one *s* one *d*. *Educ:* Westminster; Dalhousie Univ.; Trinity Coll., Cambridge (MA). Trinity Coll., Cambridge: Sen. Schol., Research Student and Harper-Wood Trav. Student, 1960; Supervisor in English, 1960-63; Sen. Instructor in English, Univ. of British Columbia, 1963-64. *Publications: novels:* Colmain, 1963; Simple People, 1965; Little

Portia, 1967; (as Hamish Reade) A Comeback for Stark, 1968; *plays:* Wise Child, 1968; Sleeping Dog, 1968; Dutch Uncle, 1969; The Idiot, 1971; Spoiled, 1971; Butley, 1971; Otherwise Engaged, 1975 (voted Best Play, 1976-77, by NY Drama Critics Circle); Plaintiffs and Defendants, 1975; Two Sundays, 1975; Dog Days, 1976. *Recreations:* squash, watching cricket and soccer, tennis, swimming. *Address:* c/o Clive Goodwin, 79 Cromwell Road, SW7. *T:* 01-370 4435.

GRAY, Stephen Alexander Reith; Director, United Kingdom Provident Institution, since 1973; *b* 18 June 1926; *er s* of late Alexander Reith Gray and Catherine Mary Thompson. *Educ:* Winchester Coll.; Trinity Coll., Cambridge. Stewarts & Lloyds Ltd, 1950-53; John Summers & Sons Ltd, 1953-68; BSC: Member for Engineering, 1968-70; Man. Dir, Strip Mills Div., 1970-72. Member: Clwyd AHA, 1973-; Wales Health Tech. Services Organisation, 1973-. High Sheriff of Flints, 1972. *Address:* Lower Soughton, Northop, Mold, Clwyd. *T:* Northop 203. *Club:* Leander.

GRAY, Sylvia Mary, CBE 1975 (MBE 1952); Chairman, National Federation of Women's Institutes, 1969-74; *b* 10 July 1909; *d* of Henry Bunting and Mary Elizabeth Gray. *Educ:* Wroxall Abbey. Chm., Bay Tree Hotels Ltd, 1946-. Mem., Witney RDC, 1943-54 (Vice-Chm. 1950-54); Chm., Oxon Fedn Women's Insts, 1951-54; Member: Nat. Fedn Women's Insts Exec. Cttee, 1955, Hon. Treas. 1958; Keep Britain Tidy Group Exec., 1967, Vice-Chm., 1974; Post Office Users' Nat. Council, 1969; National Trust, 1971, Chm., S Midlands Regional Cttee, 1975; IBA Advertising Standards Adv. Cttee, 1972; Council for European Architectural Heritage, 1972; Nat. Consumer Council, 1975-77; Redundant Churches Cttee, 1976-. *Recreation:* reading. *Address:* Bay Tree Hotel, Burford, Oxon. *T:* Burford 3137. *Club:* Naval and Military.

GRAY, Prof. Thomas Cecil, CBE 1976; MD, FRCS, FRCP, FFARCS; FFARACS (Hon.); FFARCSI (Hon.); JP; Professor of Anæsthesia, The University of Liverpool, 1959-76, now Emeritus; Dean of Postgraduate Medical Studies, 1966-70, of Faculty of Medicine, 1970-76; *b* 11 March 1913; *s* of Thomas and Ethel Gray; *m* 1937, Marjorie Kathleen (*née* Hely); one *s* one *d. Educ:* Ampleforth Coll.; University of Liverpool. General Practice, 1937-39. Hon. Anaesthetist to various hospitals, 1940-47. Active Service, Royal Army Medical Corps, 1942-44. Demonstrator in Anæsthesia, University of Liverpool, 1942, 1944-46; Reader in Anæsthesia, University of Liverpool, 1947-59; Hon. Cons Anæsthetist: United Liverpool Hosps, Royal Infirmary Branch; Liverpool Thoracic Surgical Centre, Broadgreen Hosp.; Mem. Bd, Faculty of Anæsthetists, RCSEng, 1948-69 (Vice-Dean, 1952-54; Dean, 1964-67). Member Council: RCS, 1964-67; Assoc. of Anæsthetists of Great Brit. and Ire., 1948-67 (Hon. Treas. 1950-56; Pres. 1957-59); ASME, 1972-76; FRSocMed (Mem. Council, 1958-61; Pres. Anæsthetic Section, 1955-56; Mem. Council, Sect. of Med. Educn, 1969-72); Chm. BMA Anæsthetic Group, 1957-62; Mem., Liverpool Regional Hosp. Board, 1968-74 (Chm., Anæsthetic Adv. Cttee, 1948-70; Chm., Med. Adv. Council, 1970-74); Mem., Merseyside RHA, 1974-77; Mem., Bd of Governors, United Liverpool Hosp., 1969-74; Mem. Clinical Res. Bd, Med. Res. Council, 1965-69; Hon. Civilian Consultant in Anæsthetics to the Army at Home (Guthrie Medal 1977). Hon. Consultant to St John's Ambulance; Member Council, Order of St John for Merseyside; Asst Dir-Gen., St John Ambulance, 1977-; Treas., Med. Defence Union, 1977-; Chm., Bd of Governors, Linacre Center for Study of Ethics of Health Care. Examiner in FFARCS, 1953-70; FFARCSI 1967-70: Dip. Vet. Anæsth., RCVS, 1968-76. Hon. Member: Sheffield and East Midlands Soc. of Anæsthetists; Yorks Soc. of Anæsthetists; Austrian Soc. of Anæsthetists; Soc. Belge d'Anesthesie et de Reanimation; Argentinian and Brazilian Socs of Anesthesiologists; Australian and Malaysian Socs of Anæsthetists; Assoc. of Veterinary Anæsthetists. Hon. Corresp. Member: Sociedade das Ciencias Medical di Lisboa; W African Assoc. of Surgeons. Henry Hill Hickman Medal, RSM; Clover Lecturer and Medallist, RCS of England, 1953; Simpson-Smith Memorial Lecturer, W London Sch. of Med., 1956; Jenny Hartmann Memorial Lectr, University of Basle, 1958; Eastman Lectr, University of Rochester, NY, 1958; Sims Commonwealth Travelling Prof., 1961; Sir James Young Simpson Memorial Lectr, RCS Edinburgh, 1967. JP City of Liverpool, 1966. Medallist, University of Liège. *Publications:* Consultant Ed. British Journal of Anæsthesia; Jt Ed., Modern Trends in Anæsthesia, Jt Ed., General Anæsthesia. Many contrib. gen. med. press and specialist jls. *Recreations:* music, golf, amateur dramatics. *Address:* Dalkey, Burbo Bank Road North, Liverpool L23 8TA. *T:* 051-924 5805. *Club:* West Lancs Golf.

GRAY, Vernon Foxwell, CIE 1936; *b* Singapore, 1 Sept. 1882; *s* of Alfred Thomas Gray and Jane Ann Foxwell; *m* 1st, 1919, Bertha Marie (*d* 1928), *d* of late James Walter Champion Stevens; one *d* ; 2nd, 1929, Marian Agnes Conley (*d* 1931), *d* of late Col Peter Burke; 3rd, 1937, Frances Buckland (*d* 1957), *d* of late Arthur Newman. *Educ:* Solihull Sch. Chm. and Pres., Punjab Chamber of Commerce, 1920-27 and 1938-39; Mem. of Punjab Legislative Council, 1923-29; Sole Representative Associated Chambers of Commerce of India-Ceylon at 10th Congress Assoc. Chambers of Commerce of Empire, in London, 1924; late Dir R. J. Wood and Co., Ltd, India; late Dir of John Bolton and Co., Ltd, Manchester; Jubilee Medal, 1935; Coronation Medal, *Recreations:* formerly: riding, fishing, tennis, golf. *Address:* Whittam, Hartley Road, Altrincham, Cheshire WA14 4AZ. *T:* 061-928 4374.

GRAY, Sir William, 2nd Bt, *cr* 1917; DL; late Yorkshire Regiment; *b* 18 Aug. 1895; *o s* of 1st Bt and Kate, *d* of late C. T. Casebourne, CE; *S* father, 1924; *m* 1st, 1929, Josephine (*d* 1943), *d* of William Henry Eveleigh; one *s* (and *er s* decd); 2nd, 1947, Mrs Beryl Henshaw, *d* of Alfred Stott, Liverpool. *Educ:* Loretto Sch., Edinburgh. Served European War, 1914-18, as Capt. Yorks Regt (despatches; wounded, prisoner); High Sheriff of Co. Durham, 1938-39. *Recreations:* shooting, fishing. *Heir: g s* William Hume Gray, *b* 26 July 1955. *Address:* Orchard Cottage, Egglestone, Barnard Castle, Durham. *T:* Cotherstone 228.

GRAY, William John, CB 1976; FRCPsych; Member of the Parole Board, Home Office, London, 1976-77; *b* 9 Jan. 1911; *m* 1942, Norma Margaret Morrison; two *d. Educ:* Wishaw High Sch.; Glasgow Univ. (MB, ChB). Dep. Medical Supt, Glengall Hosp., Ayr, 1939-42. Served War: Major, RAMC (Specialist Psychiatrist), 1942-47; Corps Psychiatrist and Staff Officer, Italy, 1943-45. SMO, Wakefield, Maidstone and Liverpool Prisons, 1947-62. Nuffield Travelling Fellowship, in six European countries, 1957. First Medical Supt and Governor, HM Prison, Grendon, 1962-75; Sen. PMO and Asst Under-Sec. of State, Home Office, 1971-75. *Publications:* several articles on med. and psychiatric treatment and med. care and protection of prisoners. *Recreations:* angling, bridge, gardening. *Address:* 88 Crosshill Terrace, Wormit, Newport on Tay, Fife DD6 8PS. *T:* Wormit 355. *Club:* Civil Service.

GRAY, William Macfarlane, OBE 1961; JP; FCCA; FCIS; Senior Partner Macfarlane Gray & Co., Stirling, 1934-71, Consultant, 1971-75; Hon. Sheriff for Stirling and Clackmannan since 1964; *b* 28 March 1910; *s* of Peter M. Gray and Isabella Bain Macfarlane; *m* 1938, Muriel Agnes Elizabeth Lindsay, *d* of James R. Lindsay, Glasgow; two *d. Educ:* The High Sch. of Stirling. Provost of Royal Burgh of Stirling, 1958-64; Nat. Pres., Assoc. of Certified and Corporate Accountants, 1954-56; Chm. Stirling Festival of the Arts Cttee, 1958-67; Chm. Stirlingshire Savings Cttee, 1959-76; Member: Court, Univ. of Stirling, 1968-72; Executive Cttee, Scottish Council (Development and Industry), 1961-75; Scottish Tourist Board, 1963-64; Council, National Trust for Scotland, 1962-74; Chairman: PO Advisory Cttee for Stirlingshire and Clackmannan; of Trustees, Smith Art Gallery and Museum, Stirling, 1958-64; Sponsoring Cttee for University of Stirling, 1963-65. Member: South of Scotland Electricity Board, 1961-66; Independent Television Authority (Chm. Scottish Adv. Cttee), 1964-70; Nat. Savings Cttee for Scotland, 1969-; Exec. Cttee, British Council (Chm. Scottish Adv. Cttee), 1970-76. Hon. Freeman: Royal Burgh of Stirling, 1964; Ville de Saint Valery-en-Caux, 1960. Hon. DUniv. Stirling, 1968. KStJ. *Recreations:* golf, bowling. *Address:* 12 Park Avenue, Stirling FK8 2QR. *T:* Stirling 4776. *Club:* Stirling and County.

GRAY, (William) Nicol, CMG 1948; DSO 1944, Bar, 1945; KPM 1951; FRICS; *b* 1 May 1908; *e s* of late Dr W. Gray, Westfield, West Hartlepool; *m* 1st, 1953, Jean Marie Frances Backhouse (marr. diss. 1966), *o c* of Lieut-Col G. R. V. Hume-Gore, MC and Mrs W. Lyne-Stephens, and *widow* of Major Sir John Backhouse, Bt, MC; two *d* ; 2nd, 1967, Margaret Clare Galpin, *widow* of Commander Walter Galpin, RN. *Educ:* Trinity Coll., Glenalmond. Royal Marines, 1939-46; GSO II RM Div., no I (Experimental) WOSB; Mil. Instructor, HMS Dorlin; CO 45 RM Commando; Comdt, RM Octu; Inspector-Gen., Palestine Police, 1946-48; Commissioner of Police, Federation of Malaya, 1948-52. Agent to the Jockey Club, Newmarket, 1953-64. Administrator, MacRobert Trusts, 1970-74. Trustee, Duke of Edinburgh's Award Scheme. OStJ. *Address:* Ettrickshaws, Selkirk TD7 5JP. *T:* Ettrick Bridge 218. *Clubs:* Boodle's; New (Edinburgh).

GRAY, Sir William (Stevenson), Kt 1974; JP; Chairman, Scottish Development Agency, since 1975; *b* 3 May 1928; *m* 1958, Mary Rodger; one *s* one *d. Educ:* Glasgow Univ., BL. Solicitor and

Notary Public. Chairman: Scottish Special Housing Assoc., 1966-72; Scotland W Industrial Promotion Gp, 1972-75; Irvine New Town Develt Corp., 1974-76; World of Property Housing Trust Scottish Housing Assoc. Ltd, 1974-; Clyde Tourist Assoc., 1972-75; Glasgow Arts Centres, 1975-; Third Eye Centre, 1975; Scottish Assoc. for Care and Resettlement of Offenders, 1975-; The Oil Club, 1975-. Member: Bd of Dirs, Glasgow Citizens' Theatre, 1970-75 (Vice-Pres., 1975-); Convention of Royal Burghs, 1971-75; Exec., Scottish Council (Develt and Industry), 1971-75; Lower Clyde Water Bd, 1971-72; Scottish Opera Bd, 1971-72; Nat. Trust for Scotland, 1971-72; Scottish Nat. Orchestra Soc., 1972-75; Court, Glasgow Univ., 1972-75; Clyde Port Authority, 1972-75; Adv. Council for Energy Conservation, 1974-; Scottish Adv. Cttee on JPs, 1975-; Scottish Economic Council, 1975-; Governor, Glasgow School of Art, 1961-75; Vice Pres., Charles Rennie Mackintosh Soc., 1974-. Mem., Glasgow Corporation, 1958-75, Chm., Property Management Cttee, 1964-67; Magistrate, City of Glasgow, 1961-64; Hon. Treasurer, City of Glasgow, 1971-72; Lord Provost, City of Glasgow and Lord Lieutenant, County of the City of Glasgow, 1972-75. JP Co. of City of Glasgow, 1965; DL Co. of City of Glasgow, 1971; DL City of Glasgow, 1976. Hon. LLD Strathclyde, 1974. *Recreations:* sailing, theatre. *Address:* 13 Royal Terrace, Glasgow G3 7NY. *T:* 041-332 8877.

GRAY DEBROS, Mrs E.; *see* Fox, W. M.

GRAYSON, Prof. Cecil, MA; Serena Professor of Italian Studies in the University of Oxford, and Fellow of Magdalen College, since 1958; *b* 5 Feb. 1920; *s* of John M. Grayson and Dora Hartley; *m* 1947, Margaret Jordan; one *s* three *d. Educ:* Batley Grammar Sch.; St Edmund Hall, Oxford. Army service (UK and India), 1940-46 (Major); First Class Hons (Mod. Langs), 1947; Univ. Lectr in Italian, Oxford, 1948; Lectr at St Edmund Hall, 1948; Lectr at New Coll., 1954. Corresp. Fellow, Commissione per i Testi di Lingua, Bologna, 1957; Mem., Accademia Letteraria Ital. dell' Arcadia, 1958; Corresp. Mem., Accademia della Crusca, 1960; Accademia delle Scienze, Bologna, 1964; Accademia dei Lincei, 1967; Istituto Veneto di Scienze, Lettere ed Arti, 1977; Barlow Lecturer, University Coll., London, 1963; Resident Fellow, Newberry Library, Chicago, 1965; Visiting Professor: Yale Univ., 1966; Berkeley, Calif, 1969, 1973; Perth, WA, 1973. An editor of Italian Studies. Premio Internazionale Galileo (storia della lingua italiana), 1974; Serena Medal for Italian Studies, British Academy, 1976. Comdr, Order of Merit, Italy, 1975. *Publications:* Early Italian Texts (with Prof. C. Dionisotti), 1949; Opusculi inediti di L. B. Alberti, 1954; Alberti and the Tempio Malatestiano, 1957; Vincenzo Calmeta, Prose e Lettere edite e inedite, 1959; A Renaissance Controversy: Latin or Italian?, 1960; L. B. Alberti, Opere volgari, I, 1960, II, 1966, III, 1973; L. B. Alberti e la prima grammatica volgare, 1964; Cinque saggi su Dante, 1972; (trans.) The Lives of Savonarola, Machiavelli and Guicciardini by Roberto Ridolfi, 1959, 1963, 1967; (ed) selected works of Guicciardini, 1964; (ed and trans.) L. B. Alberti, De pictura, De statua, 1972; articles in Bibliofilia, Burlingon Mag., English Misc., Giorn. Stor. d. Lett. Ital., Ital. Studies, Lettere Italiane, Lingua Nostra, Rassegna d. Lett. Ital., Rinascimento, The Year's Work in Mod. Languages. *Recreation:* music. *Address:* 11 Norham Road, Oxford. *T:* 57045.

GRAYSON, Sir Ronald Henry Rudyard, 3rd Bt of Ravens Point, *cr* 1922; *b* 15 Nov. 1916; *s* of Sir Denys Henry Harrington Grayson, 2nd Bt, and Elsie May (*d* 1973), *d* of Richard Davies Jones; *S* father 1955; *m* 1st, 1936, Babette Vivienne (marriage dissolved, 1944), *d* of Count Vivien Hollender; 2nd, 1946, Dorothy Vera Hoare, *d* of Charles Serrel. *Educ:* Harrow Sch. Engineering apprenticeship Grayson, Rollo & Clover Docks Ltd, 1934. Dir, 1940-49; Emigrated to Australia, 1953. Served War of 1939-45, RAF. *Heir: uncle* Rupert Stanley Harrington Grayson, writer [*b* 22 July 1897; *m* 1st, 1919, Ruby Victoria, *d* of Walter Henry Banks; 2nd, 1950, Vari Colette, *d* of Major Henry O'Shea]. *Recreations:* books, travel. *Address:* 22 Kimberly Street, Vaucluse, Sydney, New South Wales, Australia.

GRAYSTON, Rev. Prof. Kenneth, MA; Professor of Theology, Bristol University, since 1965; Pro-Vice-Chancellor, Bristol University, since 1976; *b* Sheffield, 8 July 1914; *s* of Ernest Edward and Jessie Grayston; *m* 1942, Elizabeth Alison, *d* of Rev. Walter Mayo and Beatrice Aste, Elsfield, Oxon.; no *c. Educ:* Colfe's Grammar Sch., Lewisham; Universities of Oxford and Cambridge. Ordained Methodist Minister, 1942; Ordnance Factory Chaplain, 1942-44; Asst Head of Religious Broadcasting, BBC, 1944-49; Tutor in New Testament Language and Literature, Didsbury Coll., 1949-64; Special Lecturer in Hellenistic Greek, Bristol Univ., 1950-64; Dean, Faculty of Arts, Bristol Univ., 1972-74. Select Preacher to Univ. of Cambridge, 1952, 1962, to Univ. of Oxford, 1971; Sec.

Studiorum Novi Testamenti Societas, 1955-65; Chairman: Theolog. Adv. Gp, British Council of Churches, 1969-72; Christian Aid Scholarships Cttee, 1973-. *Publications:* The Epistles to the Galatians and to the Philippians, 1957; The Letters of Paul to the Philippians and the Thessalonians, 1967; (contrib. in): A Theological Word Book of the Bible, 1950; The Teacher's Commentary, 1955; The Interpreter's Dictionary of the Bible, 1962, etc. (Contrib. to): Expository Times, New Testament Studies, Theology, London Quarterly and Holborn Review, etc. *Recreation:* travel. *Address:* 11 Rockleaze Avenue, Bristol BS9 1NG. *T:* Bristol 683872.

GREATBATCH, Sir Bruce, KCVO 1972 (CVO 1956); Kt 1969; CMG 1961; MBE 1954; Head of the British Development Division in the Caribbean, since 1974; *b* 10 June 1917; *s* of W. T. Greatbatch; unmarried. *Educ:* Malvern Coll.; Brasenose Coll., Oxford. Appointed Colonial Service, 1940, Northern Nigeria. War Service with Royal W African Frontier Force, 1940-45, rank of Major, Burma Campaign (despatches). Resumed Colonial Service, Northern Nigeria, 1945; Resident, 1956; Sec. to Governor and Executive Council, 1957; Senior Resident, Kano, 1958; Sec. to the Premier of Northern Nigeria and Head of Regional Civil Service, 1959; Dep. High Comr, Nairobi, Kenya, 1963; Governor and C-in-C, Seychelles, and Comr for British Indian Ocean Territory, 1969-73. KStJ 1969. *Recreations:* shooting, gardening, *Address:* British Development Division, Carlisle House, PO Box 167, Bridgetown, Barbados; c/o National Westminster Bank Ltd, Cornmarket Street, Oxford. *Club:* East India, Devonshire, Sports and Public Schools.

GREAVES, Maj.-Gen. Charles Granville Barry, CB 1947; CBE 1945 (OBE 1941); late Royal Engineers; *s* of late Charles Gregory Heritage Greaves, Inverness; *m* 1926, Maud Frances Mary, *d* of late Frank Euting, Durban, S Africa; two *s* (and one *s* decd). *Educ:* Inverness Royal Academy; RMA Woolwich. Commissioned RE 1920. Dir of Movements, War Office, 1949-53; retired 1953; American Bronze Star, 1945. *Address:* Devon Lodge, 15 Kimbolton Avenue, Bedford. *T:* 53368.

GREAVES, Prof. Harold Richard Goring; Professor of Political Science in the University of London 1960-75, now Emeritus; *s* of Harold Frederick Greaves, Derbyshire, and Beatrice Violet (*née* Heather); unmarried. *Educ:* London Sch. of Economics, University of London; Graduate Institute, Geneva. Taught at the London Sch. of Economics and Political Science from 1930; previously worked in business, a bank, and free lance journalism. Visiting Professor, Columbia Univ., New York, 1959-60; Literary Editor, Political Quarterly. Contested (Lab) Camborne, Cornwall, 1935. War-time service BBC and RIIA. *Publications:* The League Committees and World Order, 1931; The Spanish Constitution, 1933; Reactionary England, 1936; Raw Materials and International Control, 1936; The British Constitution, 1938; Federal Union, 1940; The Civil Service and the Changing State, 1947; The Foundations of Political Theory, 1958; Democratic Participation and Public Enterprise (Hobhouse Memorial Lecture), 1964; contrib. to Political Quarterly, Political Science Quarterly, Modern Law Review, The Civil Service in Britain and France, etc. *Address:* The Forge, Stoke by Clare, Suffolk. *Club:* Reform.

GREAVES, Prof. Robert William; Professor of History, University of Kansas, since 1968; *b* 27 May 1909; *s* of William Atkins Greaves and Olive Greaves (*née* Whatnall), Leicester; *m* 1955, Rose Louise Coughlin, Kansas City, Kansas, USA. *Educ:* Alderman Newton's Sch., Leicester; Merton Coll., Oxford (Exhibr, Harmsworth Schol.). BA, 1st cl. Mod. History, 1930; 2nd cl. PPE, 1931; MA 1934; DPhil 1936. Temp. Lectr, Queen's University of Belfast, 1935; Asst in History, Bedford Coll., London, 1935-39. Temp. Admin Officer, HM Treasury, 1940-42, Min. of Production, 1942-45; Asst Private Sec. to Chancellor of Exchequer, 1942, to Minister of Production, 1942-43. Bedford Coll., University of London: Lectr in History, 1945-50; Reader in History, 1950-62; Prof. of Modern History, 1962-68; Head of Dept of History, 1962-68; Vice-Princ., 1964-65. Birkbeck Lectr in Eccles. History, Trinity Coll., Cambridge, 1963-64. Vis. Professor: University of Kansas, 1965-66; University of Toronto, 1967-68. Hon. Sec., Royal Historical Society, 1955-58. *Publications:* The Corporation of Leicester 1689-1836, 1939, 2nd edn 1970; The First Ledger Book of High Wycombe, 1957; Autobiography and Court Papers of Archbishop Secker (in preparation); contrib. to Victoria County History of Leicestershire and to New Cambridge Modern History; articles and reviews in English Historical Review, Jl Eccles. History, History, etc. *Address:* 1920 Hillview Road, Lawrence, Kansas 66044, USA. *T:* 913-842-9161. *Clubs:* Reform, Royal Commonwealth Society.

GREAVES, Sir (William) Western, KBE 1974 (CBE 1960); *b* 29 Dec. 1905; *s* of late John Greaves, solicitor and late Mary Beatrice Aked, Bingley; *m* 1933, Marjorie Nahir Wright, *d* of late Leslie Wright, Alticry, Scotland; one *s* three *d. Educ:* Worcester Cathedral Choir Sch.; Ripon Sch. Hon. Chm. of Bd of Governors, Northlands Asociación Civil de Beneficencia (girls' sch.); Pres., La Rueda Finance Co.; Pres., Roca SA, wool exporters, retd 1972; Vice-Pres., UBY Co., plastics, retd 1973; Dir, Caledonia Argentina Insce, retd 1972; Vice-Pres., Chymen Aike, sheep ranch, retd 1972; Dir, Tenant Argentina, exporters, retd 1973 (all of Argentina). Chm., British Community Council, 1958-60 and 1971-73, Argentina. Associate, British Hosp. and British and American Benevolent Soc., British Soc. Trust (all Buenos Aires). *Recreations:* golf, riding (jumping). *Address:* La Rueda, c/o Tortugas Country Club, Tortuguitas, FCGB, Province of Buenos Aires, Argentina. *T:* Garin 329. *Clubs:* Canning, Royal Over-Seas League; English (Buenos Aires); Tortugas Country (director); Argentine Republic.

GREBENIK, Eugene, CB 1976; MSc (Economics); Principal of the Civil Service College, 1970-76; Deputy Secretary, Civil Service Department, 1972-76; Joint Editor, Population Studies; Consultant, Office of Population Censuses and Surveys, since 1977; *b* 20 July 1919; *s* of S. Grebenik; *m* 1946, Virginia, *d* of James D. Barker; two *s* one *d. Educ:* abroad; London Sch. of Economics. Statistician, Dept of Economics, Univ. of Bristol, 1939-40; London Sch. of Economics: Asst. 1940-44 and Lecturer, 1944-49, in Statistics (on leave, 1944-46; served in RN, 1944; Temp. Statistical Officer, Admiralty, 1944-45; Secretariat, Royal Commn on Population, 1945-46); Reader in Demography, Univ. of London, 1949-54; Research Sec., Population Investigation Cttee, 1947-54; Prof. of Social Studies, Univ. of Leeds, 1954-69. Mem., Impact of Rates Cttee, Ministry of Housing, 1963-64. Social Science Research Council: Statistics Cttee, 1966-69; Cttee on Social Science and Government, 1968-72; Population Panel, 1971-73; Member: Cttee on Governance of London Univ., 1970-72; Council, Royal Holloway Coll., Univ. of London, 1971-. Sec.-Treasurer, Internat. Union for Scientific Study of Population, 1963-73. Hon. Fellow, LSE, 1969. *Publications:* (with H. A. Shannon) The Population of Bristol, 1943; (with D. V. Glass) The Trend and Pattern of Fertility in Great Britain; A Report on the Family Census of 1946, 1954; various articles in statistical and economic journals. *Address:* Little Mead, Tite Hill, Egham, Surrey TW20 0NH. *T:* Egham 2994.

GRECH, Herbert F., CVO 1954; *b* 18 May 1899; *m* 1923, Alice Machell (*d* 1969); two *d* (one *s* decd). *Educ:* St Aloysius' Coll., Malta. Served in Army, 1917-20, Lieut King's Own Malta Regt of Militia. Malta Police Force, 1920-54; Commissioner of Police, Malta, 1951-54; retired 1954. *Address:* Flat 1, 27 Creche Street, Sliema, Malta. *T:* Sliema 30086. *Club:* Union (Malta).

GREEN, Alan, CBE 1974; Chairman: Walmsley (Bury) Group since 1970; Beloit Walmsley Ltd; Director: Scapa Group Ltd; Wolstenholme Bronze Powders Ltd (Vice-Chairman); Porritts & Spencer (Asia) Ltd, since 1969; Local Director, Barclays Bank, Manchester District, since 1969; *b* 29 Sept. 1911; *s* of Edward and Emily Green; *m* 1935, Hilda Mary Wolstenholme; three *d. Educ:* Brighton Coll. Schoolmaster, 1931-35; joined Scapa Dryers Ltd, Blackburn, 1935. Army Service, 1940-45. Formerly: Dir of Scapa Dryers Ltd, 1945; Vice-Chm. of Scapa Dryers Ltd, 1956; Dir of Scapa Dryers Inc., 1955; Dir of companies associated with Walmsley (Bury) Group, 1950; Chm. of Walmsley Operating Companies, 1954. Contested (C) Nelson and Colne, 1950-51; MP (C) Preston S, 1955-64, 1970-Feb. 1974; Parly Sec., Min. of Labour, 1961-62; Minister of State, BoT, 1962-63; Financial Sec. to the Treasury, 1963-64. Mem., Australia Cttee, BNEC, 1968-72; frequent business visits to Northern and Western Europe and North America. *Recreations:* cricket, golf, tennis, gardening, history. *Address:* The Stables, Sabden, near Blackburn, Lancs. *T:* Padiham 71528. *Clubs:* Reform, Royal Automobile.
See also D. C. Waddington.

GREEN, Prof. Albert Edward, FRS 1958; MA, PhD, ScD (Cambridge); Sedleian Professor of Natural Philosophy, University of Oxford, 1968-77; Fellow of Queen's College, Oxford, since 1968; *m* 1939, Gwendoline May Rudston. *Educ:* Jesus Coll., Cambridge Univ. (Scholar). PhD 1937; MA 1938; ScD 1943. Formerly: Lecturer in Mathematics, Durham Colls, University of Durham; Fellow of Jesus Coll., Cambridge, 1936; Prof. of Applied Mathematics, University of Newcastle upon Tyne, 1948-68. *Address:* Mathematical Institute, 24-29 St Giles, Oxford.

GREEN, Anthony Eric Sandall, ARA 1971; Member, London Group, 1964; Artist (Painter); *b* 30 Sept. 1939; *s* of late Frederick Sandall Green and Marie Madeleine (*née* Dupont); *m* 1961, Mary Louise Cozens-Walker; two *d. Educ:* Highgate Sch., London; Slade Sch. of Fine Art, University Coll. London. Henry Tonks Prize for drawing, Slade Sch., 1960; French Govt Schol., Paris, 1960; Gulbenkian Purchase Award, 1963; Harkness Fellowship, in USA, 1967-69. Has exhibited in: London, New York, Haarlem, Rotterdam, Stuttgart, Hanover, Helsingborg, Malmö, Tokyo. Paintings in various public collections, including: Tate Gallery; Olinda Museum, Brazil; Baltimore Mus. of Art, USA; Nat. Mus. of Wales; Gulbenkian Foundn; Arts Council of Gt Brit.; Contemporary Art Soc.; Frans Hals Mus., Holland; Boymans-van Bevningen Mus., Holland; Ulster Mus., Belfast; Ikeda Mus., Tokyo. Exhibit of the Year award, RA, 1977. *Recreations:* travelling, family life. *Address:* 17 Lissenden Mansions, Highgate Road, NW5. *T:* 01-485 1226.

GREEN, Arthur Eatough, CIE 1946; OBE 1937; MC 1917; MSc (Leeds); FICE; JP; Chief Engineer, Public Works Department, Bihar, India, retired; *b* 16 Dec. 1892; *s* of late William Green; *m* 1929, Frances Margaret, *d* of late Col William Henry Savage, CMG; two *s* one *d. Educ:* King's Sch., Pontefract; Leeds Univ. Served European War, 1914-18, in 5th Bn West Yorks Regt and RE. Appointed to PWD, India, 1919; served province of Bihar and Orissa, 1919-42; Chief Engineer and Sec. to Govt of Orissa, in PWD, 1942-44, to Govt of Bihar, 1944-47. JP Co. Antrim, 1964. *Recreation:* fishing. *Address:* Drumawillin House, Ballycastle, Co. Antrim, N Ireland. *T:* Ballycastle 62349

GREEN, Arthur Edward Chase, MBE (mil.) 1955; TD; FRICS; DL; Property Adviser, J. H. Schroder Wagg & Co., since 1972; Director, Schroder Properties Ltd; *b* 5 Nov. 1911; *s* of Harry Catling and Sarah Jane Green, Winchmore Hill, London; *m* 1941, Margaret Grace, *yr d* of John Lancelot and Winifred Churchill, Wallington, Surrey; one *s* two *d. Educ:* Merchant Taylors' Sch.; Coll. of Estate Management. HAC, 1932-: commnd, 1939; Adjt 11 (HAC) Regt RHA, 1941-42; Western Desert, ME; PoW 1942; despatches 1945; Territorial Efficiency Medal; Court of Assistants, HAC, 1946-76, Treasurer, 1966-69, Vice-Pres., 1970-72; Metropolitan Special Constabulary, HAC Div., 1937-39 and 1946-74 (Long Service Medal and bar). Surveyor, Legal and General Assce Soc., 1934-46, Chief Estates Surveyor, 1946-71. Mem., Cttee of Management, Pension Fund Property Unit Trust; Advr on Policy, Post Office Staff Superannuation Fund; Mem., Chancellor of the Exchequer's Property Adv. Panel, 1975-; Chm., Arnolds Centre Shop Properties Ltd; Director: Lock Estate Ltd; Franey & Co. Ltd. Mem., TA&VR Assocs for City of London, to 1977, and for Greater London. President: Camden and Islington Corps, St John Ambulance, 1974-75, No 7 Corps, City of London and Hackney, 1975-. Governor: Bridewell Royal Hosp.; Corpn of the Sons of the Clergy; City of London Sch.; Queenswood Sch. Founder-Trustee, Brunswick Boys' Club Trust. City of London Court of Common Council (Bread Street Ward), 1971-; Liveryman: Merchant Taylors' Co.; Gunmakers' Co. DL Greater London, 1967- (Representative DL for London Borough of Islington). *Recreations:* shooting, gardening, travel, photography. *Address:* 173 Cromwell Tower, Barbican EC2Y 8DD. *T:* 01-628 4724; Mariners, The Common, Southwold, Suffolk. *T:* Southwold 3410. *Clubs:* City Livery, Guildhall.
See also Very Rev . J . H . Churchill .

GREEN, Father Benedict; *see* Green, Rev. H. C.

GREEN, Benny; free-lance writer; *b* 9 Dec. 1927; *s* of David Green and Fanny Trayer; *m* 1962, Antoinette Kanal; three *s* one *d. Educ:* Clipstone Street Junior Mixed; subsequently uneducated at St Marylebone Grammar Sch. Mem., West Central Jewish Lads Club (now extinct). Saxophonist, 1947-60 (Most Promising New Jazz Musician, 1953); Jazz Critic, Observer, 1958-; Literary Critic, Spectator, 1970-; Film Critic, Punch, 1972-; frequent radio and TV appearances, 1955-. Artistic Dir, New Shakespeare Co., 1973-; Mem., BBC Archives Cttee, 1976. Book and lyrics, Boots with Strawberry Jam, Nottingham Playhouse, 1968; revised libretto, Showboat, Adelphi Theatre, London, 1972; co-deviser: Cole, Mermaid, 1974; Oh, Mr Porter, Mermaid, 1977. *Publications:* The Reluctant Art, 1962; Blame it on my Youth, 1967; 58 Minutes to London, 1969; Drums in my Ears, 1973; I've Lost my little Willie, 1976; Swingtime in Tottenham, 1976; (ed) Cricket Addict's Archive, 1977. *Recreation:* cricket. *Address:* c/o BBC, Broadcasting House, Portland Place, W1.

GREEN, Rev. Canon Bryan Stuart Westmacott, BD; DD (*hc*); Canon Emeritus of Birmingham Cathedral since 1970 (Hon. Canon, 1950-70); *b* 14 Jan. 1901; *s* of late Hubert Westmacott Green and late Sarah Kathleen Green (*née* Brockwell); *m* 1926, Winifred Annie Bevan; one *s* one *d. Educ:* Merchant Taylors' Sch.; London Univ. BD 1922; Curate, New Malden, 1924-28;

Staff of Children's Special Service Mission, 1928-31; Chap., Oxford Pastorate, 1931-34; Vicar of Christ Church, Crouch End, 1934-38; Vicar of Holy Trinity, Brompton, 1938-48; Rector of Birmingham, 1948-70. Conducted evangelistic campaigns: Canada and America, 1936, 1944, and 1947-77; Australia and New Zealand, 1951, 1953, 1958, 1974; West Africa, 1953; S Africa, 1953, 1955, 1956, 1957, 1959 and 1960; Ceylon, 1954, 1959. DD Hon. St John's Coll. Winnipeg, 1961. *Publications:* The Practice of Evangelism, 1951; Being and Believing, 1956; Saints Alive, 1959. *Recreation:* golf. *Address:* West Field, Southern Road, Thame, Oxon OX9 2EP. *T:* Thame 2026. *Club:* National.

GREEN, Prof. Cecil Alfred, MD, PhD, DPH Edinburgh; FRCPath; FInstBiol; Professor of Bacteriology, University of Newcastle upon Tyne, 1963-74; Director of Department of Microbiology, Royal Victoria Infirmary, Newcastle upon Tyne, 1947-74; *b* 5 Nov. 1908; *s* of George Alfred Green and Anne Bell; *m* 1940, Jemina Stewart Scott; one *s* one *d.* *Educ:* Dunfermline High Sch.; Edinburgh Univ. MB, ChB Edinburgh, 1932, and Vans Dunlop Scholar; Crichton Research Fellow, Edinburgh Univ., 1933-35; Lecturer in Bacteriology, Dept of Bacteriology, Edinburgh Univ., 1935-38; Bacteriologist to Edinburgh Royal Infirmary; Empire Rheumatism Council Research Scholar, 1938-39. Professor of Bacteriology, University of Durham, 1960-63; MD Gold Medal (Edinburgh) 1941. Surg. Comdr, RNVR, 1939-45. *Publications:* articles in med. jls on researches into and control of infectious diseases. *Address:* The Red House, Jesmond Park East, Newcastle upon Tyne.

GREEN, Prof. Dennis Howard; Professor of Modern Languages, University of Cambridge, since 1966; Fellow of Trinity College, Cambridge, since 1949; Head of the Department of Other Languages since 1956; *b* 26 June 1922; *s* of Herbert Maurice Green and Agnes Edith Green (*née* Fleming); *m* 1972, Margaret Parry. *Educ:* Latymer Upper Sch., London; Trinity Coll., Cambridge; Univ. of Basle. Univ. of Cambridge, 1940-41 and 1945-47; Univ. of Basle (Dr Phil.), 1947-49; Military service (RAC), 1941-45; Univ. Lecturer in German, St Andrews, 1949-50; Research Fellowship, Trinity Coll., Cambridge (first year held *in absentia*), 1949-52; Univ. Asst Lectr in German, Cambridge, 1950-54; Teaching Fellowship, Trinity Coll., Cambridge, 1952-66; Visiting Professor: Cornell Univ., 1965-66; Auckland Univ., 1966; Yale Univ., 1969; ANU, Canberra, 1971; UCLA, 1975; Univ. of Pennsylvania, 1975; Univ. of WA, 1976. *Publications:* The Carolingian Lord, 1965; The Millstätter Exodus: a crusading epic, 1966; (with Dr L. P. Johnson) Approaches to Wolfram von Eschenbach, 1977; Reviews and articles in learned journals. *Recreations:* walking and foreign travel. *Address:* Trinity College, Cambridge; 7 Archway Court, Barton Road, Cambridge. *T:* Cambridge 58070.

GREEN, Rev. Canon (Edward) Michael (Bankes); Rector of St Aldate with Holy Trinity, Oxford, since 1975; Principal, St John's College, Nottingham (until July 1970 The London College of Divinity), 1969-75; Canon Theologian of Coventry, 1970-76; *b* 20 Aug. 1930; British; *m* 1957, Rosemary Wake (*née* Storr); two *s* two *d.* *Educ:* Clifton Coll.; Oxford and Cambridge Univs. BD Cantab 1966. Exeter Coll., Oxford, 1949-53 (1st cl. Lit. Hum.); Royal Artillery (Lieut, A/Adjt), 1953-55; Queens' Coll., Cambridge, 1955-57 (1st cl. Theol. Tripos Pt III; Carus Greek Testament Prize; Fencing Blue), and Ridley Hall Theol Coll., 1955-57; Curate, Holy Trinity, Eastbourne, 1957-60; Lectr, London Coll. of Divinity, 1960-69, Principal, 1969. Member: Doctrine Commission of the Church, 1968-; Church Unity Commn, 1974-. Leader of missions, overseas and in UK. *Publications:* Called to Serve, 1964; Choose Freedom, 1965; The Meaning of Salvation, 1965; Man Alive, 1967; Runaway World, 1968; Commentary on 2 Peter and Jude, 1968; Evangelism in the Early Church, 1970; Jesus Spells Freedom, 1972; New Life, New Lifestyle, 1973; I Believe in the Holy Spirit, 1975; You Must Be Joking, 1976; (ed) The Truth of God Incarnate, 1977. contribs to various jls. *Recreations:* family, countryside pursuits, cricket, squash, fly fishing. *Address:* St Aldate's Rectory, 40 Pembroke Street, Oxford. *T:* Oxford 49423.

GREEN, Sir (Edward) Stephen (Lycett), 4th Bt, *cr* 1886; CBE 1964; DL, JP; Chairman, East Anglian Regional Hospital Board, 1959-74; *b* 18 April 1910; *s* of Sir E. A. Lycett Green, 3rd Bt, and Elizabeth Williams; *S* father, 1941; *m* 1935, Constance Mary, *d* of late Wm H. S. Radcliffe; one *d.* *Educ:* Eton; Magdalene Coll., Cambridge. Called to Bar, Lincoln's Inn, 1933. Served War of 1939-45 (Major, RA). CC 1946-49, JP 1946, DL 1961, High Sheriff 1973, Norfolk; Dep. Chairman Norfolk QS, 1948-71. Chairman: King's Lynn Hospital Management Cttee, 1948-59; Assoc. of Hosp. Management Cttees, 1956-58; Cttee of Inquiry into Recruitment, Training and Promotion of

Administrative and Clerical Staff in Hospital Service, 1962-63; Docking RDC, 1950-57. *Recreations:* shooting, reading. *Heir:* *b* Lt-Col Simon Lycett Green, TD, Yorks Dragoons Yeomanry [*b* 11 July 1912; *m* 1st, 1935, Gladys (marr. diss. 1971), *d* of late Arthur Ranicar, JP, Springfield, Wigan; one *d*; 2nd, 1971, Mary, *d* of late George Ramsden]. *Address:* Ken Hill, Snettisham, King's Lynn. *TA:* Snettisham, Norfolk. *T:* Snettisham 202; 60 Pont Street, SW1. *T:* 01-589 5958. *Clubs:* White's, Pratt's; Norfolk (Norwich); Allsorts (Norfolk).

GREEN, Ernest, CBE 1950; JP; LLD, MA; *b* 28 Jan. 1885; *s* of Horatio E. Green, Engineer; *m* 1911, Emma, 3rd *d* of John T. Wilde, cutlery manufacturer, Sheffield; no *c.* *Educ:* elementary sch. Organising Sec. (Yorks) Clerical Workers Union, 1916-23; Yorks District Sec., Workers' Educational Association, 1923-29; National Organising Sec., 1929-34; General Sec., 1934-50; Hon. Treasurer, 1951-62. Member: Civil Service Arbitration Tribunal, 1949-63; Management Cttee of Workers' Travel Assoc., 1934-64. JP Surrey, 1933; Hon. MA, Manchester, 1937; Hon. LLD Leeds, 1952. *Publications:* Education for a New Society; Adult Education-why this apathy?, 1954; contributor to Year Book of Education, and leading educational journals. *Recreation:* gardening. *Address:* Guardian Court, Flat 7, Wells Promenade, Ilkley, Yorks.

GREEN, Geoffrey; His Honour Judge Green; a Circuit Judge (formerly a Judge of County Courts), since 1969; Member, Parole Board, since 1976; *b* 10 Sept. 1918; *s* of Arthur Green, Ombersley, Worcs; *m* 1955, Olive Mary Elizabeth Batchelor; two *s* one *d.* *Educ:* Worcester Royal Grammar Sch.; Hertford Coll., Oxford. Served in RA and Indian Mountain Artillery, 1939-46 (despatches); Major. Barrister, Lincoln's Inn, 1947. Dep. Chm., Herefordshire QS, 1966-71. Chm., Agricultural Land Tribunal, West Midlands Area, 1965-69; Chm., Industrial Tribunals, 1965-68. *Recreation:* golf. *Address:* 239 Wells Road, Malvern Wells, Worcs WR14 4HF. *T:* Malvern 4020.

GREEN, Geoffrey Hugh, CB 1977; Deputy Under-Secretary of State (Policy), Procurement Executive, Ministry of Defence, since 1975; *b* 24 Sept. 1920; *o* *s* of late Duncan M. and Kate Green, Bristol; *m* 1948, Ruth Hazel Mercy; two *d.* *Educ:* Bristol Grammar Sch.; Worcester Coll., Oxford (Exhibr), 1939-41, 1945-47 (MA). Served with Royal Artillery (Ayrshire Yeomanry): N Africa and Italy, 1942-45 (Captain). Entered Min. of Defence, Oct. 1947; Principal, 1949; Asst Sec., 1960; Asst Under-Sec. of State, 1969; Dep. Under-Sec. of State, 1974. *Recreations:* travel, music, walking. *Address:* 47 Kent Avenue, Ealing, W13 8BE.

GREEN, Sir George (Ernest), Kt 1963; Chairman of Eagers Holdings Ltd; *b* 1892; *s* of Jabez Green, Brisbane, and Catherine Genevieve, *d* of T. Crouin; *m* Ailsa Beatrice, *d* of Charles George Rools Crane. *Educ:* Maryborough Grammar Sch. Pres., Royal National Agricultural and Industrial Assoc. of Qld, 1955-61. *Address:* 35 Markwell Street, Hamilton, Brisbane, Qld 4007, Australia.

GREEN, Major George Hugh, MBE; MC 1945; TD and 3 bars; Vice-Lieutenant of Caithness, 1973-77; Headmaster, Crossroads School; *b* 21 Oct. 1911; *s* of George Green, The Breck, John O'Groats; *m* 1936, Isobel Elizabeth Myron; two *s.* *Educ:* Wick High Sch.; Edinburgh Univ. (MA). Headmaster of small rural school in Caithness, 1933. Commnd into Seaforth Highlanders, TA, 1935; served War of 1939-45 with 5th Seaforths in 51st (H) Div., N Africa and NW Europe; retd from TA, 1962. DL Caithness 1965. *Recreations:* gardening, bee-keeping. *Address:* Tjaldur, Halkirk, Caithness. *T:* Halkirk 639. *Club:* Highland Brigade (Inverness).

GREEN, Graham John G.; see Graham-Green.

GREEN, Hon. Guy Stephen Montague; Hon. Mr Justice Green; Chief Justice of Tasmania, since 1973; Member, Faculty of Law, University of Tasmania, since 1974; *b* 26 July 1937; *s* of Clement Francis Montague Green and Beryl Margaret Jenour Green; *m* 1963, Rosslyn Mary Marshall; two *s* two *d.* *Educ:* Launceston Church Grammar Sch.; Univ. of Tasmania. Alfred Houston Schol. (Philosophy) 1958; LLB (Hons) 1960. Admitted to Bar of Tasmania, 1960; Partner, Ritchie & Parker Alfred Green & Co (Launceston), 1963; Pres., Tasmanian Bar Assoc., 1968-73 (Vice-Pres., 1966-68). Magistrate 1971-73. Mem.-at-Large, Appellate Court Judges' Section, World Assoc. of Judges, 1976-. Chairman: Tasmanian Cttee, Duke of Edinburgh's Award Scheme in Australia, 1975-; Sir Henry Baker Meml Fellowship Cttee, 1973-; Tasmanian Regional Cttee, Winston Churchill Meml Trust, 1975-; Dir, Winston Churchill Meml Trust, 1975-; Vice Patron: Art Soc. of Tasmania, 1974-; Royal Agricultural Soc. of Tasmania, 1974-. *Recreations:* walking, chess, music;

food and wine. *Address:* Judges' Chambers, Public Buildings, Franklin Square, Hobart, Tasmania 7000. *Clubs:* Launceston (Launceston, Tas.); Tasmanian, Athenæum (Hobart).

GREEN, Henry Rupert, CBE 1960; MA; Legal Senior Commissioner of Board of Control, 1953-60, later Ministry of Health; *b* 29 Dec. 1900; *o s* of late Henry Green, JP, solicitor, and Margaret Helen Green, Stockport, Cheshire; *m* 1937, Marie Elizabeth Patricia Bailey; three *s* one *d. Educ:* Charterhouse; Hertford Coll., Oxford (Exhibitioner). Barrister, Lincoln's Inn, 1926; practised on Northern Circuit, 1926-36; Commissioner of Board of Control, 1936. War of 1939-45: commissioned RAF, 1940; served as Operations Staff Officer, Malta, 1941-43; released, 1944. Pres. Governors, St Mary's Sch. for Girls, Gerrards Cross. *Publications:* title: Persons Mentally Disordered (Pts 2 and 3), Halsbury's Laws of England, 3rd Edn, 1960; title: Persons of Unsound Mind, Halsbury's Statutes (Burrows Edn), 1950 and similar title: Encyclopædia of Court Forms, 1949. *Recreation:* carpentry. *Address:* The Square House, Latchmoor Grove, Gerrards Cross, Bucks. *T:* Gerrards Cross 82316.

GREEN, Hon. Howard Charles, PC (Canada); QC (BC); LLD (University of British Columbia); *b* Kaslo, BC, 5 Nov. 1895; *s* of Samuel Howard and Flora Isabel Green; *m* 1st, 1923, Marion Jean (decd), *d* of Lewis Mounce, Vancouver; two *s*; 2nd, 1956, Donna Enid, *d* of Dr D. E. Kerr, Duncan, BC. *Educ:* High Sch., Kaslo; University of Toronto (BA); Osgoode Hall Law Sch. Served European War, 1915-19. Called to Bar of British Columbia, 1922; elected to Federal Parliament, 1935; Minister of Public Works and Govt House Leader, 1957-59; Acting Minister of Defence Production, 1957-58; Canadian Sec. of State for External Affairs, 1959-63. Is a Progressive Conservative. *Address:* 4160 W 8th Avenue, Vancouver, British Columbia, Canada. *Club:* Terminal City (Vancouver, BC).

GREEN, Rev. Humphrey Christian, (Father Benedict Green, CR); Principal, College of the Resurrection, Mirfield, since 1975; *b* 9 Jan. 1924; *s* of late Rev. Canon Frederick Wastie Green and of Margaret Susan Beltt Green (*née* Gosling). *Educ:* Dragon Sch., Oxford; Eton (King's Scholar); Merton Coll., Oxford (Postmaster). BA 1949, MA 1952. Served War, RNVR, 1943-46. Deacon 1951, priest 1952; Asst Curate of Northolt, 1951-56; Lectr in Theology, King's Coll., London, 1956-60. Professed in Community of the Resurrection (taking additional name of Benedict), 1962; Vice-Principal, Coll. of the Resurrection, 1965-75. Associate Lectr in Dept of Theology and Religious Studies, Univ. of Leeds, 1967-. *Publications:* The Gospel according to Matthew (New Clarendon Bible), 1975; contrib.: Towards a Church Architecture (ed P. Hammond), 1962; The Anglican Synthesis (ed W. R. F. Browning), 1964; theological jls. *Address:* College of the Resurrection, Mirfield, W Yorks WF14 0BW. *T:* Mirfield 493362.

GREEN, (James) Maurice (Spurgeon), MBE, TD, MA; Editor, The Daily Telegraph, 1964-74 (Deputy Editor, 1961-64); *b* 8 Dec. 1906; *s* of Lieut-Col James Edward Green, DSO; *m* 1st 1929, Pearl (*d* 1934), *d* of A. S. Oko, Cincinnati, USA; 2nd, 1936, Janet Grace, *d* of Maj.-Gen. C. E. M. Norie, CB, CMG, DSO; two *s. Educ:* Rugby Sch. (scholar); University Coll., Oxford (scholar, 1st Class, Honour Mods and Lit. Hum.). Editor of The Financial News, 1934-38; Financial and Industrial Editor of The Times, 1938-39 and 1944-53 (served in Royal Artillery, 1939-44); Asst Editor, 1953-61. Pres., Inst. of Journalists, 1976-77. *Recreations:* books, music, fishing. *Address:* 15 Sloane Avenue, SW3. *T:* 01-584 1649. *Club:* Reform.

GREEN, John Dennis Fowler; Executive Committee, Council for the Protection of Rural England (Chairman Gloucestershire Branch); Executive Committee, Land Settlement Association; *b* 9 May 1909; *s* of late Capt. Henry and Amy Gertrude Green, Chedworth, Glos; *m* 1946, Diana Judith, JP, *y d* of late Lt-Col H. C. Elwes, DSO, MVO, Colesbourne, Glos. *Educ:* Cheltenham Coll.; Peterhouse, Cambridge. President of the Union. Called to the Bar, Inner Temple, 1933; BBC, 1934-62; established agricultural broadcasting, 1935; Special Agric. Mission to Aust. and NZ, 1945-47; Controller, Talks Div., 1956-61. Pres. National Pig Breeders Assoc., 1955-56; Chm., Agricultural Adv. Council, 1963-68. Chm., Cirencester and Tewkesbury Conservative Assoc., 1964-69. *Publications:* Mr Baldwin: A Study in Post War Conservatism, 1933. Articles and broadcasts on historical and agricultural subjects. *Recreations:* forestry, field sports. *Address:* The Manor, Chedworth, Cheltenham. *T:* Fossebridge 233. *Clubs:* Bath, Buck's, Farmers'.

GREEN, John Michael, CB 1976; Commissioner, since 1971, Deputy Chairman, since 1973, Board of Inland Revenue; *b* 5 Dec. 1924; *s* of late George Green and of Faith Green; *m* 1951, Sylvia (*née* Crabb); one *s* one *d. Educ:* Merchant Taylors' Sch., Rickmansworth; Jesus Coll., Oxford (MA (Hons)). Served War, Army, RAC, 1943-46. Entered Inland Revenue as Asst Principal, 1948; served in HM Treasury, as Principal, 1956-57; Asst Sec., 1962; Under Sec., Bd of Inland Revenue, 1971. *Recreation:* gardening. *Address:* 5 Bylands, White Rose Lane, Woking, Surrey. *T:* Woking 72599. *Club:* Reform.

GREEN, Julian Hartridge; Writer; Member of Académie Française, 1971; *b* Paris, France, 6 Sept. 1900. *Educ:* Lycée Janson, Paris; Univ. of Virginia. Member: Acad. de Bavière, 1950; Royal Acad. of Belgium, 1951; Amer. Acad. of Arts and Sciences. Prix Harper, Prix Bookman, Prix de Monaco, 1951; Grand Prix National des Lettres, 1966; Grand Prix, Académie Française, 1970. *Publications:* Mont-Cinere, 1925; Le Voyageur sur la Terre, 1926; Adrienne Mesurat, 1927; Leviathan, 1929; Suite Anglaise; L'Autre Sommeil, 1930; Epaves, 1932; Le Visionnaire, 1934; Minuit, 1936; Journal, 1928-35, 2 vols 1938-39 (published in England as Personal Record, 1928-1939, 1940); Varouna, 1940; Memories of Happy Days, 1942; Journal, 1940-43, 1946; Si j'étais vous..., 1947; Journal, 1943-45, 1949; Moira, 1950; Sud, 1953; L'Ennemi, 1954; Journal, 1949-1954, 1955; Le Malfaiteur, 1956; L'Ombre, 1956; Le Bel Aujourd'hui, 1958; Chaque Homme dans sa Nuit, 1960; Partir avant le jour, 1963; Mille Chemins ouverts, 1964; Terre lointaine, 1966; Vers l'invisible, 1967; L'Autre, 1971; Ce qui reste de jour, 1972; Œuvres Complètes: Vol. I, 1972; Vol. II and Vol. III, 1973; Vol. IV and Vol. V, 1974. *Address:* c/o Plon, 8 rue Garancière, Paris 5e, France.

GREEN, Leslie William, CVO 1974; MBE 1953; Director; Brenard Press Ltd; Heathrow Airport, London; *b* 1 July 1912; *y s* of late George Green and of Jane E. Green; *m* 1938, Alice Robertshaw; one *s* one *d. Educ:* Moseley Grammar Sch., Birmingham; City of Birmingham Commercial Coll. Cert AIB; FCIT. Accountant Officer, RAF, 1940-46 (Flt-Lt); Asst Airport Man., Heathrow, 1946-47; Airport Man., Croydon, 1947-50; Dep. Airport Man., Heathrow, 1950-55; Airport Man., Heathrow, 1955-62; Admin. Dir, London Airports, 1962-65; Gen. Man., Gatwick, 1965-71; Gen. Man., Heathrow, 1971-73; Special Projects Dir, British Airports Authority, 1973-75. *Recreations:* golf, gardening, watching cricket. *Address:* Oakwood, Old Oak Avenue, Chipstead, Surrey. *T:* Downland 53903. *Clubs:* MCC; (Pres.) Chipstead and Coulsdon Cricket; Chipstead Golf.

GREEN, Rt. Rev. Mark; *see* Aston, Bishop Suffragan of.

GREEN, Dame Mary Georgina, DBE 1968; BA; Head Mistress, Kidbrooke School, SE3, 1954-73; Chairman, BBC London Local Radio Council, since 1973; *b* 27 July 1913; *er d* of late Edwin George Green and Rose Margaret Green (*née* Gibbs). *Educ:* Wellingborough High Sch.; Westfield Coll., University of London (Hon. Fellow, 1976). Assistant Mistress: Clapham High Sch., 1936-38; Streatham Hill and Clapham High Sch., 1938-40; William Hulme's Sch., Manchester, 1940-45; Head Mistress, Colston's Girls' Sch., Bristol, 1946-53. Member: Central Advisory Council for Education (Eng.), 1956-63; Church of England Board of Education, 1958-65; Council King George's Jubilee Trust, 1963-68; Court of Governors, London Sch. of Economics and Political Science, 1964-; Royal Commission on Trade Unions and Employers' Assocs, 1965-68; Council, City University, 1969-; Cttee of Inquiry into Nurses' Pay, 1974; Press Council, 1976-; Review Body on Doctors' and Dentists' Remuneration, 1976-; General Optical Council, 1977-; Dep. Chm., E-SU, 1976-. A Governor: BBC, 1968-73; Royal Ballet Sch., 1969-72; Centre for Educnl Develt Overseas, 1970-74; Rachel McMillan Coll. of Educn, 1970-73; E-SU, 1974-. *Address:* 45 Winn Road, SE12 9EX. *T:* 01-857 1514.

GREEN, Maurice; *see* Green, J. M. S.

GREEN, Rev. Canon Michael; *see* Green, Rev. Canon E. M. B.

GREEN, Paul Eliot, LittD; Writer; *b* 17 March 1894; *s* of William Archibald Green and Betty Lorine Byrd; *m* 1922, Elizabeth Atkinson Lay; one *s* three *d. Educ:* Buie's Creek Academy; University of North Carolina; Cornell Univ. Editor of The Reviewer, a literary quarterly, 1925; winner of Pulitzer Prize for best American Play, 1927, In Abraham's Bosom; Guggenheim Fellow for study abroad, 1928-30; Member, National Institute of Arts and Letters. Hon. Degrees from various Univs. *Publications: plays:* The Lord's Will and other Plays, 1925; Lonesome Road (one-act plays), 1926; The Field God and In Abraham's Bosom, 1927; In the Valley and Other Plays, 1928; The House of Connelly and Other Plays, 1931; Roll Sweet Chariot, 1935; Shroud my Body Down, 1935; Hymn to the

Rising Sun, 1936; Johnny Johnson, 1937; The Lost Colony (symphonic drama), 1937; Out of the South (The Life of a People in Dramatic Form), 1939; The Enchanted Maze, 1939; Native Son (co-author), 1941; The Highland Call (with music), 1941; The Common Glory (symphonic drama), 1948; Peer Gynt (modern adaptation of Ibsen's play), 1951; Wilderness Road (symphonic drama), 1956; The Founders (symphonic drama), 1957; Wings for to Fly (three Negro plays), 1959; The Confederacy (symphonic drama), 1959; The Stephen Foster Story (symphonic drama), 1960; Five Plays of the South, 1963; The Sheltering Plaid, 1965; Cross and Sword (symphonic drama), 1966; Texas (symphonic drama), 1967; Sing All a Green Willow (play with music), 1969; Trumpet in the Land (symphonic drama), 1972; The Honeycomb (folk drama), 1972; Drumbeats in Georgia (symphonic drama), 1973; Louisiana Cavalier (symphonic drama), 1976; We the People (symphonic drama), 1976; The Lone Star (symphonic drama), 1977; numerous screen plays; *novels:* The Laughing Pioneer, 1932; This Body the Earth, 1935; *miscellaneous:* Wide Fields (short stories), 1928; The Lost Colony Songbook, 1938; Salvation on a String (stories), 1946; Dog on the Sun (stories), 1949; The Hawthorn Tree (essays), 1943; Forever Growing (essay), 1945; The Common Glory Songbook, 1951; Dramatic Heritage (essays), 1953; Drama and the Weather (essays), 1958; Plough and Furrow (essays), 1963; Texas Songbook, 1967; Words and Ways (stories), 1968; Home to My Valley (stories), 1970; Land of Nod and other Stories (stories), 1976. *Recreations:* music and farming. *Address:* Old Lystra Road, Chapel Hill, North Carolina 27514, USA. *T:* 919-933-8581.

GREEN, Brig. Percy William Powlett, CBE 1960 (OBE 1956); DSO 1946; *b* 10 Sept. 1912; *er s* of late Brig.-Gen. W. G. K. Green, CB, CMG, DSO, Indian Army; *m* 1943, Phyllis Margery Fitz Gerald May, *d* of late Lieut-Col A. H. May, OBE; one *s* one *d*. *Educ:* Wellington Coll.; RMC. Commnd Northamptonshire Regt, 1932; Op. NW Frontier, India, 1936-37; BEF 1939-40; Lt-Col Comdg 2nd W Yorks Regt, 1945-46; Burma, 1944-45; Lt-Col Comdg 1 Malay Regt, 1946-47; Comd 4th King's African Rifles, 1954-56; Op. against Mau Mau; Col, Gen. Staff, War Office, 1956-57; Chief of Staff (Brig.) E Africa Comd, 1957-60; DDMI, War Office, 1961-63; Chief of Staff, N Ireland Command, 1963-65; Dep. Comdr, Aldershot District, 1965-67; retired, 1967. ADC to the Queen, 1965-67. Dep. Colonel, Royal Anglian Regt, 1966-76. *Recreations:* field sports. *Address:* Grudds, South Warnborough, Basingstoke, Hants. *T:* Long Sutton 472. *Club:* Army and Navy.

GREEN, Prof. Peter Morris; author and translator since 1953; Professor of Classics, University of Texas at Austin, since 1972; *b* 22 Dec. 1924; *o c* of late Arthur Green, CBE, MC, LLB, and of Olive Slaughter; *m* 1st, 1951, Lalage Isobel Pulvertaft (marr. diss.); two *s* one *d*; 2nd, 1975, Carin, Margreta, *y d* of G. N. Christensen, Saratoga, USA. *Educ:* Charterhouse; Trinity Coll., Cambridge. Served in RAFVR, 1943-47: overseas tour in Burma Comd, 1944-46. 1st Cl. Hons, Pts I and II, Classical Tripos, 1949-50; MA and PhD Cantab 1954; Craven Schol. and Student, 1950; Dir of Studies in Classics, 1951-52; Fiction Critic, London Daily Telegraph, 1953-63; Literary Adviser, The Bodley Head, 1957-58; Cons. Editor, Hodder and Stoughton, 1960-63; Television Critic, The Listener, 1961-63; Film Critic, John o'London's, 1961-63; Mem. Book Soc. Cttee, 1959-63. Former Mem. of selection cttees for literary prizes: Heinemann Award, John Llewellyn Rhys, W. H. Smith £1000 Award for Literature. Translator of numerous works from French and Italian, including books by Simone de Beauvoir, Fosco Maraini, Joseph Kessel. FRSL 1956; Mem. Council, Royal Society of Literature, 1958-63 (resigned on emigration). In 1963 resigned all positions and emigrated to Greece as full-time writer. Vis. Prof. of Classics: Univ. of Texas, 1971-72; UCLA, 1976. *Publications:* The Expanding Eye, 1953; Achilles His Armour, 1955; Cat in Gloves (pseud. Denis Delaney), 1956; The Sword of Pleasure (W. H. Heinemann Award for Literature), 1957; Kenneth Grahame, 1859-1932: A Study of his Life, Work and Times, 1959; Essays in Antiquity, 1960; Habeas Corpus and other stories, 1962; Look at the Romans, 1963; The Laughter of Aphrodite, 1965; Juvenal: The Sixteen Satires (trans.), 1967; Armada from Athens: The Failure of the Sicilian Expedition, 415-413 BC, 1970; Alexander the Great: a biography, 1970; The Year of Salamis, 480-479 BC, 1971; The Shadow of the Parthenon, 1972; The Parthenon, 1973; A Concise History of Ancient Greece, 1973; Alexander of Macedon 356-323 BC: a historical biography, 1974; Ovid: The Erotic Poems (trans.), 1978. *Recreations:* travel, swimming, spear-fishing, lawn tennis, table-tennis, squash racquets, amateur archæology, avoiding urban life. *Address:* c/o Department of Classics, University of Texas, Waggener Hall 123, Austin, Texas 78712, USA. *T:* 512 471-5742. *Club:* Savile.

GREEN, Maj.-Gen. Robert Leslie Stuart; Vice President, The Ordnance Board, since 1976; *b* 1 July 1925; *s* of Leslie Stuart Green and Eliza Dorothea Andrew; *m* 1952, Nancy Isobel Collier; two *d*. *Educ:* Chorlton Sch. 2nd Bn Black Watch, India, 1944-46; 6 Airborne Div., Palestine, 1946; 2 Parachute Bde, UK and Germany, 1946-47; 1st Bn HLI, UK, ME and Cyprus, 1947-56; ptsc 1959; jssc 1962; 1st Bn Royal Highland Fusiliers, UK, Germany and Gibraltar, 1959-69, Comd 1967-69; staff apptmt 1970; Military Dir of Studies, RMCS, 1970-72; Sen. Military Officer, Royal Armament Res. and Develt. Estabt, 1973-75. Governor, CARE for the Mentally Handicapped. *Recreations:* rough shooting, painting, music and sailing. *Address:* Williams & Glyn's Bank, 43 Curzon Street, Mayfair, W1. *Club:* Naval and Military.

GREEN, Roger (Gilbert) Lancelyn; author; *b* 2 Nov. 1918; *s* of Major G. A. L. Green, MC, RFA, and H. M. P. Sealy; *m* 1948, June, *d* of S. H. Burdett, Northampton; two *s* one *d*. *Educ:* Dane Court Sch., Surrey; Liverpool Coll.; privately; Merton Coll., Oxford (MA, BLitt). Part-time professional actor, 1942-45; Dep. Librarian, Merton Coll., Oxford, 1945-50; William Nobel Research Fellow in Eng. Lit., Liverpool Univ., 1950-52; Andrew Lang Lectr, Univ. of St Andrews, 1968. Editor, Kipling Journal, 1957-. Mythopoeic Schol. Award (USA), 1975. *Publications:* The Lost July, and other poems, 1945; Tellers of Tales, 1946, rev. edn 1965; The Searching Satyrs, 1946; Andrew Lang: a critical biography, 1946; The Sleeping Beauty, and other tales, 1947; The Singing Rose, and other poems, 1947; From the World's End: a fantasy, 1948, repr. USA 1971; Beauty and the Beast, and other tales, 1948; Poulton-Lancelyn: the story of an ancestral home, 1948; The Story of Lewis Carroll, 1949; The Wonderful Stranger, 1950; The Luck of the Lynns, 1952; A. E. W. Mason: a biography, 1952; The Secret of Rusticoker, 1953; King Arthur and his Knights of the Round Table, 1953, 8th edn 1967; The Diaries of Lewis Carroll, 1953; Fifty Years of Peter Pan, 1954; The Theft of the Golden Cat, 1955; The Adventures of Robin Hood, 1956, 6th edn 1966; Mystery at Mycenae, 1957; Two Satyr Plays (Penguin Classics), 1957; Into Other Worlds: space flight in fiction from Lucian to Lewis, 1957; Old Greek Fairy Tales, 1958; The Land Beyond the North, 1958; The Land of the Lord High Tiger, 1958; Tales of the Greek Heroes, 1958, 8th edn 1973; The Tale of Troy, 1958, 10th edn 1973; Lewis Carroll, 1960; The Saga of Asgard, 1960, 3rd edn as Myths of the Norsemen, 1970; J. M. Barrie, 1960; The True Book About Ancient Greece, 1960; The Luck of Troy, 1961, 4th edn 1973; Mrs Molesworth, 1961; Ancient Greece, 1962; Andrew Lang, 1962; The Lewis Carroll Handbook, 1962; Once, Long Ago, 1962; C. S. Lewis, 1963; Authors and Places, 1963; Ancient Egypt, 1963; Tales of the Greeks and Trojans, 1964; Tales from Shakespeare, 2 vols, 1964-65; A Book of Myths, 1965; Tales the Muses Told, 1965; Myths from Many Lands, 1965; Kipling and the Children, 1965; Andrew Lang: the greatest bookman of his age (Indiana Bookman), 1965; Folk Tales of the World, 1966; Sir Lancelot of the Lake, 1966; Tales of Ancient Egypt, 1967; Stories of Ancient Greece, 1968; Jason and the Golden Fleece, 1968; The Tale of Ancient Israel, 1969; St Andrew's Church, Bebington: a short history, 1969; The Book of Dragons, 1970; Kipling: the critical heritage, 1971; The Book of Magicians, 1973; (with Walter Hooper) C. S. Lewis: a biography, 1974; Holmes, this is Amazing: essays in unorthodox research, 1975; The Book of Other Worlds, 1976; The Tale of Thebes, 1977. *Recreations:* book collecting, Greece Ancient and Modern, Greek and Roman theatre. *Address:* Poulton Hall, Poulton-Lancelyn, Bebington, Wirral, Merseyside L63 9LN. *T:* 051-334 2057. *Clubs:* Lansdowne, Arts, Players, National Book League.

GREEN, Roger James N.; see Northcote-Green.

GREEN, Sam, CBE 1960; Chairman: Dula (ISMA) Ltd, since 1969; Green & Associates Ltd, since 1970; Spear Bros Ltd, since 1970; Director: British Legion Poppy Factory, Richmond, since 1964; British Legion Industries, since 1967; *b* Oldham, Lancs, 6 Feb. 1907; *s* of Fred Green; *m* 1942, Dr Lilly (*née* Pollak); one *d*. *Educ:* Manchester Coll. of Technology. Apprentice, Platt Bros, Oldham, 1920-34; Designer and Development Engr, British Northrop Automatic Loom Co., Blackburn, 1934-39 (invented 4-colour loom); Chief Engr, Betts & Co., London, 1939-42; Works Manager, Morphy-Richards Ltd, St Mary Cray, Kent, 1942-44; General Works Manager, Holoplast Ltd, New Hythe, near Maidstone, 1944-47; Industrial Adviser, Industrial and Commercial Finance Corp., London, 1947-52; Managing Dir of Remploy Ltd, 1952-64; Chm. and Man. Dir, Ralli Bros (Industries) Ltd, 1964-69; Chm., Industrial Advisers to the Blind, 1964-74; Director: J. E. Lesser Group Ltd, 1969-74; New Day Holdings Ltd, 1972-74. Chm., Inst. of Patentees and Inventors, 1975 (Vice-Chm., 1961). FRSA 1962. CEng; FIEE; FIProdE. *Recreations:* reading, gardening, cycling, walking, golf. *Address:* Holly Lodge, 39 Westmoreland Road, Bromley,

Kent. *T:* 01-460 3306. *Clubs:* Reform, Directors', Pickwick (oldest Bicycle Club).

GREEN, Sir Stephen; *see* Green, Sir E. S. L.

GREEN, Thomas Charles, CB 1971; Chief Charity Commissioner, 1966-75; *b* 13 Oct. 1915; *s* of late Charles Harold Green and late Hilda Emma Green (*née* Thomas); *m* 1945, Beryl Eva Barber, *widow* of Lieut N. Barber; one *d* (and one step *d*). *Educ:* Eltham Coll.; Oriel Coll., Oxford. Entered Home Office, 1938. Served with RAF, 1940-45. Asst Secretary: Home Office, 1950-64; Charity Commn, 1964-65. UK representative on UN Commn on Narcotic Drugs, 1957-64. Nuffield Travelling Fellowship, 1959-60. *Recreations:* gardening, photography. *Address:* Silver Birch Cottage, Burntwood Road, Sevenoaks, Kent. *T:* Sevenoaks 52933.

GREEN, Rev. Vivian Hubert Howard, DD, FRHistS; Fellow and Tutor in History, Lincoln College, Oxford, since 1951, and Sub-Rector, since 1970 (Senior Tutor 1953-62, 1974-77); Chaplain, 1951-69; acting Rector, 1972-73); *b* 18 Nov. 1915; *s* of Hubert James and Edith Eleanor Playle Green; unmarried. *Educ:* Bradfield Coll., Berks; Trinity Hall, Cambridge (Scholar). Goldsmiths' Exhibnr; 1st Cl. Hist. Tripos, Parts I and II; Lightfoot Schol. in Ecclesiastical Hist.; Thirlwall Medal and Prize, 1941; MA 1941; MA Oxon by incorp., 1951; DD Cambridge, 1958; DD Oxon by incorp., 1958. Gladstone Research Studentship, St Deiniol's Library, Hawarden, 1937-38; Fellow of St Augustine's Coll., Canterbury, 1939-48; Chaplain, Exeter Sch. and St Luke's Training Coll., Exeter, 1940-42; Chaplain and Asst Master, Sherborne Sch., Dorset, 1942-51. Deacon, 1939; Priest, 1940. Select Preacher, Oxford, 1959-60. *Publications:* Bishop Reginald Pecock, 1945; The Hanoverians, 1948; From St Augustine to William Temple, 1948; Renaissance and Reformation, 1952; The Later Plantagenets, 1955; Oxford Common Room, 1957; The Young Mr Wesley, 1961; The Swiss Alps, 1961; Martin Luther and the Reformation, 1964; John Wesley, 1964; Religion at Oxford and Cambridge (historical survey), 1964; The Universities, 1969; Medieval Civilization in Western Europe, 1971; A History of Oxford University, 1974; contributor to: Dictionary of English Church History (ed Ollard, Crosse and Bond); The Oxford Dictionary of the Christian Church (ed Cross). *Address:* Lincoln College, Oxford. *T:* Oxford 43658; Calendars, Burford, Oxford. *T:* Burford 3214.

GREEN, Lt.-Gen. Sir (William) Wyndham, KBE 1945; CB 1942; DSO 1918; MC 1916 and bar 1917; *b* 1887; *s* of Captain Percy Green, The Buffs; *m* 1st, 1916, Madge Bellairs (decd); one *d*; 2nd, 1924, Primrose, *d* of A. Townshend Cobbold, OBE; one *d* (one *s* decd). Served European War, 1914-18 (despatches, MC with bar, DSO, Croix de Guerre); NW Frontier, 1930 (despatches); Bt Lieut-Col, 1929; Lieut-Col 1935; Col 1937; Maj.-Gen. 1941; Acting Lieut-Gen. 1945. Chief Instructor (Equipments), School of Artillery, 1937-38; Commandant, Military Coll. of Science, Woolwich, 1938; 2nd in Comd Gibraltar, 1941-42; GOC AA Div. and Gps, 1942-45; GOC-in-C, AA Command, 1945-46; retired, 1946, as Lt-Gen. Vice-Chm., Kent T & AFA, 1948-52, Chm., 1952-54; Vice-Pres., 1954-56; Hon. Col 410 Coast Regt RA (Kent) TA, 1949-56; Chm. Canterbury Diocesan Bd of Finance, 1953-61. Col Commandant RA, 1947-52, DL Kent, 1949. A Governor Dover Coll., 1959-72. Polonia Restituta 3rd Class, 1943. *Address:* Little Gables, New Romney, Kent. *T:* New Romney 2137. *Clubs:* Army and Navy; Band of Brothers.

GREEN-PRICE, Sir Robert (John), 5th Bt, *cr* 1874; *b* 22 Oct. 1940; *o s* of Sir John Green-Price, 4th Bt, and Irene Marion (*d* 1954), *d* of Major Sir (Ernest) Guy Lloyd, 1st Bt, *qv*; *S* father, 1964. *Educ:* Shrewsbury. Army Officer, 1961-69; Captain, RCT, retd. ADC to Governor of Bermuda, 1969-72. *Heir:* kinsman John Chase Green-Price, *b* 27 June 1947. *Address:* Gwernaffel, Knighton, Powys. *T:* Knighton 580.

GREENACRE, Brigadier Walter Douglas Campbell, CB 1952; DSO 1945; MVO 1927; late Welsh Guards; Extra Equerry to the Queen since 1952 (to King George VI, 1936-52); *b* Durban, S Africa, 20 March 1900; *er s* of late Walter Greenacre, OBE, Durban; *m* 1928, Gwendolen Edith, *d* of late Lieut-Col L. R. Fisher-Rowe; three *s* two *d*. *Educ:* Leys Sch., Cambridge. Equerry to Prince of Wales, 1924-26; Extra Equerry to Prince of Wales, 1926-36; Welsh Guards, 1918-47; raised 3rd Bn Welsh Guards, 1941; commanded: 2nd Armoured Bn Welsh Guards, 1941-43; Col 5th Guards Armoured Bde, 1943-44; Brig. (temp.), 1944; 6th Guards Armoured Bde, NW Europe, 1944-45; 6th Guards Brigade, 1945-47, BAOR; Schleswig-Holstein Sub Area, 1947-48; 128 Inf. Bde TA, 1948-49; 17th Infantry Bde & Dist, MELF, 1950-52; Col, Gen. Staff, 1947; Brigadier, 1951; retired pay, 1952. *Recreations:* shooting, golf. *Address:* Rendham

Barnes, Saxmundham, Suffolk. *T:* Rendham 467. *Clubs:* White's, Pratt's.

GREENALL, family name of **Baron Daresbury.**

GREENAWAY, Alan Pearce, JP; Chairman, since 1976 and Joint Managing Director, since 1951, Daniel Greenaway & Sons Ltd (Vice-Chairman, 1965-76); *b* 25 Nov. 1913; *yr s* of Sir Percy Walter Greenaway, 1st Bt, and Lydie Amy (*d* 1962), *er d* of James Burdick; *m* 1948, Patricia Frances, *yr d* of Ald. Sir Frederick Wells, 1st Bt; one *s* one *d. Educ:* Canford. Served in King's Liverpool Regt during War of 1939-45, reaching rank of Captain. Liveryman: Worshipful Co. of Merchant Taylors; Worshipful Co. of Stationers and Newspaper Makers (Under-Warden 1971-72, Upper Warden, 1972-73, Master 1973-74). Mem. Court of Common Council for Ward of Bishopsgate, 1952-65; Sheriff for the City of London, 1962-63; JP, Co. London, 1964; Alderman, Lime Street Ward, City of London, 1965-72. Officer, l'Ordre de la Valeur Camerounaise, 1963; Commandeur, l'Ordre de Leopold Class III, 1963; Commander, Royal Order of the Phoenix, 1964. *Recreations:* golf, fishing, swimming. *Address:* The Doone, Byfleet Road, Cobham, Surrey; Greenaway House, 132 Commercial Street, EC1 6NF. *T:* 01-247 4343. *Clubs:* City Livery (Vice-Pres. 1971-72, Pres., 1972-73), Royal Automobile, United Wards; St George's Hill Golf.

GREENAWAY, Sir Derek (Burdick), 2nd Bt *cr* 1933; CBE 1974; TD; JP; DL; First Life President, Daniel Greenaway & Sons Ltd, 132 Commercial Street, E1, since 1976 (Chairman, 1956-76); *b* 27 May 1910; *er s* of Sir Percy Walter Greenaway, 1st Bt and Lydie Amy (*d* 1962), *er d* of James Burdick; *S* father 1956; *m* 1937, Sheila Beatrice, *d* of late Richard Cyril Lockett, 58 Cadogan Place, SW1; one *s* one *d. Educ:* Marlborough. Served in Field Artillery during War of 1939-45; Hon. Col: 44 (HC) Signal Regt (Cinque Ports) TA, 1966; 36th (Eastern) Signal Regt (V), 1967-74. Joint Master, Old Surrey and Burstow Foxhounds, 1958-66. Chm. Sevenoaks Constituency C & U Assoc., 1960-63; Pres. 1963-66; Vice Pres., 1966-. Asst Area Treasurer, SE Area Nat. Union of Cons. Assocs, 1966-69, Area Treasurer, 1969-75, Chm. 1975-. Master, Stationers' and Newspapermakers Co., 1974-75. JP County of Kent, 1962-; High Sheriff, 1971, DL 1973, Kent. FRSA. Life Mem., Assoc. of Men of Kent and Kentish Men. *Recreations:* hunting, shooting. *Heir:* s John Michael Burdick Greenaway [*b* 9 Aug. 1944. Late Lieut, The Life Guards; Director, Daniel Greenaway & Sons Ltd]. *Address:* Dunmore, Four Elms, Edenbridge, Kent. *T:* Four Elms 275. *Clubs:* Carlton, City of London, MCC.
See also A. P. *Greenaway,* H. F. R. *Sturge.*

GREENAWAY, Frank, MA, PhD; FRIC, FSA, FMA; Keeper, Department of Chemistry, The Science Museum, since 1967; Reader in the History of Science, Davy-Faraday Research Laboratory of the Royal Institution, since 1970; *b* 9 July 1917; 3rd *s* of late Henry James Greenaway; *m* 1942, Margaret (Miranda), 2nd *d* of late R. G. Heegaard Warner and *widow* of John Raymond Brumfit; two *s* three *d. Educ:* Cardiff High Sch.; Jesus Coll., Oxford (Meyricke Exhibitioner); University Coll. London. MA Oxon, PhD London. Served War of 1939-45, RAOC, as Inspecting Ordnance Officer, 1940-41 (invalided). Science Master: Bournemouth Sch., 1941-42; Epsom Gram. Sch., 1942-43; Research Labs, Kodak Ltd, 1944-49; Asst Keeper, Science Museum, 1949; Dep. Keeper, 1959; Keeper, 1967. Mem. Council: Brit. Soc. for the Hist. of Science, 1958-68, 1974- (Vice-Pres. 1962-65); Museums Assoc., 1961-70, 1973-76 (Hon. Editor, 1965-70). Chm., Cttee of Visitors, Royal Instn, 1964-65; Mem. Brit. Nat. Cttee of Internat. Council of Museums, 1956-58 and 1962-71; Membre Correspondant de l'Académie Internationale d'Histoire des Sciences, 1963. Member: Council, Soc. for Study of Alchemy and Early Chemistry, 1967- (Sec., 1967-74); History of Medicine Adv. Panel, The Wellcome Trust, 1968-74; Higher Educn Adv. Cttee, The Open Univ., 1970-73; British Nat. Cttee for Hist. of Sci., 1972-; British Nat. Cttee and Gen. Cttee, ICSU, 1972-; Sec.-Gen., Internat. Union of the Hist. and Philos. of Science (Hist. Div.), 1972-77; Vice-Pres., Commonwealth Assoc. of Museums, 1974-. Boerhaave Medal, Leyden Univ., 1968. *Publications:* Science Museums in Developing Countries, 1962; John Dalton and the Atom, 1966; (ed) Lavoisier's Essays Physical and Chemical, 1971; Editor, Royal Institution Archives, 1971-; Official Publications of the Science Museum; Papers on history of chemistry and on museology. *Recreations:* music, travel. *Address:* 135 London Road, Ewell, Epsom, Surrey. *T:* 01-393 1330. *Club:* Athenæum.

GREENAWAY, Sir Thomas Moore, Kt 1968; Hon. Consulting Physician, Royal Prince Alfred Hospital, since 1930; *b* 1 June 1902; *s* of T. C. Greenaway, Grafton, NSW; *m* 1927, Lavinia, *d*

of late G. H. Figtree, Wollongong, NSW; one s two d. *Educ:* N Sydney High Sch.; University of Sydney. MB, ChM, 1925; MRCP 1934; FRCP 1950. Foundn Fellow, RACP, 1938; Censor-in-Chief, 1952-56; Pres., RACP, 1960-62. Councillor, BMA (NSW Br.), 1944-48; Mem., NSW Med. Bd, 1963-73; Mem. Bd of Dirs, RPA Hosp., 1953-74. Lectr in Clinical Med., University of Sydney, 1940-62. Hon. Fellow, RACGP, 1968. *Publications:* contribs to various med. jls. *Recreation:* golf. *Address:* 231 Macquarie Street, Sydney, NSW 2000, Australia. *T:* 233-3420. *Club:* Australian (Sydney).

GREENBOROUGH, Hedley Bernard, (John Greenborough), CBE 1975; President, Confederation of British Industry, since 1978 (Deputy President, 1977-78); Managing Director and Deputy Chairman, Shell UK Ltd, since 1976; *b* 7 July 1922; *s* of William Greenborough and Elizabeth Marie Greenborough (*née* Wilson); *m* 1951, Gerta Ebel; one step s. *Educ:* Wandsworth School. War service: Pilot, RAF, later Fleet Air Arm, 1942-45; graduated Pensacola; Naval Aviator, USN, 1944. Joined Asiatic Petroleum Co., London, 1939; served with Shell Oil, Calif, 1946-47; Shell Brazil Ltd, Rio and Sao Paulo, 1948-57; Dep. Head, Lubricants Div., Shell Internat., London, 1958-60; Commercial Dir, later Exec. Vice-Pres., Shell Argentina Ltd, Buenos Aires, 1960-66; Area Coordinator, East and Australasia, Shell Internat., London, 1967-68; Man. Dir (Marketing), Shell-Mex and BP Ltd, 1969-71; Man. Dir and Chief Exec., 1971-75; Chm., UK Oil Pipelines Ltd, 1971-. Chairman: UK Oil Ind. Emergency Cttee, 1971-; UK Petroleum Ind. Adv. Cttee, 1971-77; Member: British Productivity Council, 1969-72; Inst. of Petroleum Council, 1970-73 (Pres. 1976-); Clean Air Council, 1971-75; Council, CBI, 1971-; CBI Econ. Policy Cttee, 1973-; CBI Finance Cttee, 1976-; Bd of Fellows, BIM, 1973- (Chm., 1976-); NEDC, 1977-; Vice-Chairman: British Chamber of Commerce in Argentina, 1962-66; British Road Fedn, 1969-75. President: Nat. Soc. for Clean Air, 1973-75; Incorporated Soc. of British Advertisers (ISBA), 1976-. Fellow, Inst. Petroleum; FBIM. Governor, Ashridge Management Coll., 1972- (Chm., 1977-). Liveryman, Co. of Distillers, 1975-. Freeman, City of London. *Recreations:* golf, travel, music. *Address:* 30 Burghley House, Oakfield, Somerset Road, Wimbledon Common, SW19. *T:* 01-946 0095. *Clubs:* Junior Carlton, MCC; Royal Wimbledon Golf.

GREENE, family name of **Baron Greene of Harrow Weald.**

GREENE OF HARROW WEALD, Baron *cr* 1974 (Life Peer), of Harrow; **Sidney Francis Greene,** Kt 1970; CBE 1966; Director, Trades Union Unit Trust, since 1970; General Secretary, National Union of Railwaymen, 1957-74; *b* 12 Feb. 1910; *s* of Frank James Greene and Alice (*née* Kerrod); *m* 1936, Masel Elizabeth Carter; three *d*. *Educ:* elementary. Joined Railway Service, 1924; appointed Union Organiser, 1944; Asst Gen. Sec., 1954. Mem., TUC Gen. Council, 1957-75 (Chm., 1969-70); Chm., TUC Economic Cttee, 1968-. Member: National Economic Development Council, 1962-75; Advisory Council, ECGD, 1967-70; part-time Member: Southern Electricity Board, 1964-; Nat. Freight Corp., 1973-; a Dir, Bank of England, 1970-. JP London, 1941-65. FCIT. *Recreations:* reading, gardening. *Address:* 26 Kynaston Wood, Boxtree Road, Harrow Weald, Mddx.

GREENE, Edward Reginald, CMG 1953; FRSA; art dealer; *b* Santos, Brazil, 26 Nov. 1904; *s* of late Edward Greene and of Eva Greene; *m* Irmingard Fischges. *Educ:* Bedales Sch.; St John's Coll., Cambridge (BA 1926). After Continental banking experience joined coffee merchant firm E. Johnston & Co. Ltd, 1927; has since travelled and traded in coffee, Brazil, USA, East Africa, Continent, Dir of Coffee, Ministry of Food, 1943, subsequently Dir of Raw Cocoa; resigned 1952. Hon. Vice-Pres., Brazilian Chamber of Commerce, 1968-. Mem., The Cambridge Soc. FRSA 1971. *Recreations:* painting, antiques. *Address:* Orbell House, Castle Hedingham, Essex. *T:* Hedingham 60298. *Clubs:* City of London, Garrick.

GREENE, Graham, CH 1966; Hon. LittD, Cambridge, 1962; Hon. Fellow of Balliol, 1963; Hon. DLitt, Edinburgh, 1967; Chevalier de la Légion d'Honneur, 1967; Shakespeare Prize, Hamburg, 1968; *b* 2 Oct. 1904; *s* of late Charles Henry Greene; *m* 1927, Vivien Dayrell-Browning; one *s* one *d*. *Educ:* Berkhamsted; Balliol Coll., Oxford. On staff of The Times, 1926-30; Literary Editor, The Spectator, 1940-41; department of Foreign Office, 1941-44. Director: Eyre & Spottiswoode Ltd, 1944-48; Bodley Head, 1958-68. *Publications:* Babbling April, 1925; The Man Within, 1929; The Name of Action, 1930; Rumour at Nightfall, 1931; Stamboul Train, 1932; It's a Battlefield, 1934; The Old School (Editor), 1934; The Bear Fell Free (limited edn), 1935; England Made Me, 1935; The Basement Room (short stories), 1935; Journey without Maps

(account of a journey through Liberia), 1936; A Gun for Sale, 1936; Brighton Rock, 1938; The Lawless Roads, 1939; The Confidential Agent, 1939; The Power and the Glory, 1940 (Hawthornden Prize for 1940); British Dramatists, 1942; The Ministry of Fear, 1943; Nineteen Stories, 1947; The Heart of the Matter, 1948; The Third Man, 1950; The End of the Affair, 1951; The Lost Childhood and other essays, 1951; Essais Catholiques, 1953; Twenty one Stories, 1954; Loser Takes All, 1955; The Quiet American, 1955; Our Man in Havana, 1958; A Burnt-Out Case, 1961; In Search of a Character, Two African Journals, 1961; A Sense of Reality, 1963; The Comedians, 1966; May we borrow your Husband? And other Comedies of the Sexual Life (short stories), 1967; Collected Essays, 1969; Travels with my Aunt, 1969; A Sort of Life, 1971; The Pleasure-Dome: the collected film criticism 1935-40, ed John Russell Taylor, 1972; Collected Stories, 1972; The Honorary Consul, 1973; Lord Rochester's Monkey, 1974; (ed) An Impossible Woman: the Memories of Dottoressa Moor of Capri, 1975; *plays:* The Living Room, 1953; The Potting Shed, 1957; The Complaisant Lover, 1959; Carving a Statue, 1964; The Return of A. J. Raffles, 1975; *for children:* The Little Train, 1947; The Little Fire Engine, 1950; The Little Horse Bus, 1952; The Little Steamroller, 1953; *film plays:* Brighton Rock, 1948; The Fallen Idol, 1948; The Third Man, 1949; Our Man in Havana, 1960; The Comedians, 1967. *Address:* c/o The Bodley Head, 9 Bow Street, WC2.
See also R. O. Dennys, *Sir Hugh Greene and Raymond Greene.*

GREENE, Graham Carleton; Managing Director, Jonathan Cape Ltd, since 1966, and Joint Chairman, Chatto, Bodley Head & Jonathan Cape Ltd, since 1970; *b* 10 June 1936; *s* of Sir Hugh Carleton Greene, *qv*, and Helga Mary Connolly; *m* 1957, Judith Margaret (marr. diss.), *d* of Rt Hon. Lord Gordon-Walker, *qv*; *m* 1976, Sally Georgina Horton, *d* of Sidney Wilfred Eaton. *Educ:* Eton; University Coll., Oxford (MA). Merchant Banking, Dublin, New York and London, 1957-58; Publishing: Secker & Warburg Ltd, 1958-62; Jonathan Cape, 1962- (Dir, 1962). Director: Chatto, Bodley Head & Jonathan Cape Ltd, 1969; Jackdaw Publications Ltd (Chm. 1964); Cape Goliard Press Ltd, 1967; Guinness Mahon Holdings Ltd, 1968; Australasian Publishing Co. Pty Ltd, 1969; Sprint Productions Ltd, 1971; Book Reps (New Zealand) Ltd, 1971; Chatto, Bodley Head & Cape Services Ltd (Chm. 1972); Guinness Peat Group Ltd, 1973; Grantham Book Storage Ltd (Chm. 1974); Triad Paperbacks Ltd, 1975; Chatto, Bodley Head and Jonathan Cape Australia Pty Ltd (Chm., 1977-). Mem. Council, Publishers Assoc., 1969- (Treas. 1975-77; Pres., 1977-79); Mem., Book Develt Council, 1970- (Dep. Chm., 1972-73); Member: Arts Council Working Party Sub-Cttee on Public Lending Right, 1970; Paymaster General's Working Party on Public Lending Right, 1970-72; Chm., Nat. Book League, 1974-76 (Dep. Chm., 1971-74); Mem. Gen. Cttee, Royal Literary Fund, 1975. *Address:* 11 Lord North Street, SW1P 3LA. *T:* 01-799 6808.

GREENE, Sir Hugh (Carleton), KCMG, KCMG 1964; OBE 1950; Chairman: The Bodley Head, since 1969; Greene, King & Sons Ltd, Westgate Brewery, Bury St Edmunds, since 1971; Member, Observer Editorial Trust, 1969-76; *b* Nov. 1910; *s* of late Charles Henry Greene; *m* 1934, Helga Guinness (marr. diss.); two *s*; *m* 1951, Elaine Shaplen (marr. diss.); two *s*; *m* 1970, Tatjana Sais. *Educ:* Berkhamsted; Merton Coll., Oxford (MA). Daily Telegraph Berlin staff, 1934; Chief Correspondent, 1938; expelled from Germany as reprisal, May 1939; Warsaw correspondent, 1939; after the outbreak of war reported events in Poland, Rumania, Bulgaria, Turkey, Holland, Belgium, and France. Joined BBC as head of German Service, 1940, after service in RAF; Controller of Broadcasting in British Zone of Germany, 1946-48; Head of BBC East European Service, 1949-50; Head of Emergency Information Services, Federation of Malaya, 1950-51; Asst Controller, BBC Overseas Services, 1952-55; Controller, Overseas Services, 1955-56; Chm. Federal Commn of Inquiry into Organisation of Broadcasting in Fed. of Rhodesia and Nyasaland, 1955; Dir of Administration, BBC, 1956-58; Dir, News and Current Affairs, BBC, 1958-59; Director-General, 1960-69; a Governor, BBC, 1969-71. Vice-Pres., European Broadcasting Union, 1963-69; Chm., European-Atlantic Action Cttee on Greece, 1971-74. Reported for Govt of Israel on Israel Broadcasting Authority, 1973; reported for Greek Govt on constitution of Greek broadcasting, 1975. FBIM, 1966. Hon. DCL E Anglia, 1969; DUniv Open Univ., 1973; DUniv York, 1973. *Publications:* The Spy's Bedside Book (with Graham Greene), 1957; The Third Floor Front, 1969; The Rivals of Sherlock Holmes, 1970; More Rivals of Sherlock Holmes: cosmopolitan crimes, 1971; The Future of Broadcasting in Britain, 1972; The Crooked Counties, 1973; The American Rivals of Sherlock Holmes, 1976. *Address:* Earl's Hall, Cockfield, near Bury St Edmunds, Suffolk.
See also R. O. Dennys, *Graham Greene, Graham C. Greene and Raymond Greene.*

GREENE, Ian Rawdon; Registrar to Dean and Chapter, St Patrick's Cathedral, Dublin, since 1973; *b* 3 March 1909; *o s* of Rawdon Greene and Marie Louise, Rahan, Bray, County Wicklow, Ireland; *m* 1937, Eileen Theodora Stack; one *d. Educ:* Cheltenham Coll.; Trinity Coll., Dublin (BA, LLB). Crown Counsel, Tanganyika, 1935; Resident Magistrate, Zanzibar, 1937. Military Service, Kenya, 1940-41. Sen. Resident Magistrate, Zanzibar, 1950; Actg Asst Judge, Zanzibar, on numerous occasions; Actg Chief Justice, Zanzibar, June 1954, and May-Oct. 1955; Judge-in-charge, Somaliland Protectorate, 1955; Chief Justice, Somaliland Protectorate, 1958-60, retired; Stipendiary Magistrate, North Borneo, 1961-64. Order of Brilliant Star of Zanzibar (4th Cl.), 1953. *Publications:* Jt Ed., Vols VI and VII, Zanzibar Law Reports. *Recreations:* cricket, golf, bridge, chess. *Address:* Malindi, Kilmacanogue, Co. Wicklow, Ireland. *T:* Dublin 867322. *Clubs:* The Victory (Services) Association; English (Zanzibar); Hargeisa (Somaliland); Friendly Brothers (Dublin).

GREENE, Sir (John) Brian; see Massy-Greene.

GREENE, Dame Judith; see Anderson, Dame Judith.

GREENE, Raymond; Chevalier of the Legion of Honour; Hon. Consultant Physician, Royal Northern Hospital, and Royal Free Hospital; Director, Heinemann Medical Books Ltd; *b* 17 April 1901; *s* of late Charles Henry Greene, MA, FRHistSoc; *m* 1934, Eleanor Craven, *d* of late Hamilton Gamble, St Louis, USA; one *s* one *d. Educ:* Berkhamsted; Pembroke Coll., Oxford (Theodore Williams Scholar in Medicine and Senior Open Scholar); Westminster Hospital (Scholar in Anatomy and Physiology), BA (Hons) Oxon. 1924, MA 1927, DM 1935; MRCP, 1943; FRCP 1954; held various appointments at Westminster Hospital, Queen Charlotte's Hospital, and Radcliffe Infirmary, Oxford. Mem. Kamet Expedition, 1931; Mem. Everest Expedition, 1933. Schorstein Research Fellow in Medical Science, University of Oxford, 1932-34; Senior Clinical Asst in charge of the Endocrine Clinic, Westminster Hosp., 1938-45; Physician: Metropolitan Hosp., 1945-54; Whittington Hosp., 1948-66. Formerly Chm., Nuffield Inst. of Comparative Medicine. Hunterian Professor, RCS of England, 1943 and 1956; Sandoz Lectr, Inst. of Neurology, 1972. Mem. British Pharmacopœia Commission, 1948-53; Vice-Pres., Royal Society of Medicine and Pres. Section of Endocrinology, 1953, Hon. Mem. 1973; Chm. Fourth Internat. Goitre Conf., 1960; Vice-Pres., Fifth Internat. Thyroid Conf., 1965; Vice-Pres., European Thyroid Assoc., 1966; Corresp. Mem., Amer. Thyroid Assoc.; Ex-Pres., Thyroid Club; Vice-Pres., Alpine Club, 1948-49; Hon. Mem., Oxford Univ. Exploration Club and Oxford Univ. Mountaineering Club. FZS (formerly Vice-Pres.). *Publications:* The Practice of Endocrinology, 1948; Myasthenia Gravis, 1969; Human Hormones, 1970; Sick Doctors, 1971; (jtly) Benign Enlargement of the Prostate, 1973; Moments of Being, 1974; many scientific and medical papers on the effects of great altitude and exposure to cold, and on endocrinology. *Recreations:* mountain climbing and travel. *Address:* 106 Harley Street, W1N 1AF. *T:* 01-935 3889; 10 Cheltenham Terrace, Chelsea, SW3 4RD. *T:* 01-730 1434. *Clubs:* Athenæum, Alpine. *See also* R. O. Dennys, Graham and Sir Hugh Greene.

GREENEWALT, Crawford Hallock; Director and Member of the Finance Committee, E. I. du Pont de Nemours & Co., Inc. (Chairman, 1967-74); Member, Board of Directors, Christiana Securities Co.; *b* Cummington Mass, 16 Aug. 1902; *s* of Frank Lindsay and Mary Hallock Greenewalt; *m* 1926, Margaretta Lammot du Pont; two *s* one *d. Educ:* William Penn Charter Sch.; Mass. Institute of Technology (BS). With E. I. du Pont de Nemours & Co., Inc. from 1922; Asst Dir Exptl Station, Central Research Dept, 1939; Dir Chem. Div., Industrial and Biochemicals Dept, 1942; Technical Dir, Explosives Department, 1943; Asst Dir, Development Dept, 1945; Asst Gen. Man. Pigments Dept, 1945-46; Vice-Pres., 1946; Vice-Pres. and Vice-Chm. Exec. Cttee, 1947; Pres., Chm. Exec. Cttee and Mem. Finance Cttee, 1948-62; Chm. Board, 1962-67; Chm. Finance Cttee, 1967-74; Member Board of Directors of various other organisations. Member: Amer. Acad. of Arts and Sciences, National Academy of Sciences, Amer. Philos. Soc.; Board of Trustees, Nat. Geographic Soc.; Carnegie Inst. of Washington, etc. Holds hon. degrees in Science, Engineering and Laws, and has various scientific awards and medals. *Publications:* The Uncommon Man, 1959; Hummingbirds, 1960; Bird Song: acoustics and physiology, 1969. *Recreation:* photography. *Address:* Greenville, Delaware 19807, USA; (office) Du Pont Building, Wilmington, Delaware 19898, USA. *Clubs:* Wilmington, Wilmington Country, Du Pont Country, Greenville Country (USA).

GREENFIELD, Prof. Archibald David Mant, CBE 1977; Dean of the Medical School and Professor of Physiology in the University of Nottingham, since 1966; *b* 31 May 1917; *s* of late A. W. M. Greenfield, MA, Parkstone, Dorset; *m* 1943, Margaret (*née* Duane); one *s* one *d. Educ:* Poole Grammar Sch.; St Mary's Hospital Medical Sch. BSc London, 1st class hons Physiology, 1937; MB, BS, 1940; MSc, DSc; FRCP. Dunville Prof. of Physiology in the Queen's Univ. of Belfast, 1948-64; Prof of Physiology in the Univ. of London, at St Mary's Hosp. Med. Sch., 1964-67. WHO Visiting Prof., India, 1960; Visiting Prof., Univ. of California, San Francisco Medical Center, 1962-63. Mem., Notts AHA (Teaching); Former Member: Sheffield RHB; Nottingham Univ. Hosp. Management Cttee. Member: Systems Bd, MRC; UGC, 1977-; Medical Acad. Adv. Cttee, Chinese Univ., Hong Kong. Mem., Physiological, Biochemical and Medical Research Societies. Chm., Editorial Bd, Monographs of the Physiological Soc. Sometime examiner in Oxford, Cambridge and 14 other Univs, RCS and RCSI. Hon. LLD. *Publications:* Papers in Lancet, Journal of Physiology, Clinical Science, and Journal of Applied Physiology. *Recreations:* sketching, bird watching, travel. *Address:* 25 Sutton Passeys Crescent, Nottingham NG8 1BX. *T:* Nottingham 782424.

GREENFIELD, Sir Cornelius (Ewen MacLean), KBE 1965 (MBE 1944); CMG 1956; Chairman, Rhodesian Banking Corporation Ltd; Member, Agricultural Marketing Authority, etc., Rhodesia; *b* 2 May 1906; *s* of Rev. C. E. Greenfield; *m* 1934, Brenda, *d* of E. M. Diaper; one *s* two *d.* Formerly Sec. to the Treasury, Rhodesia. Trustee, Automobile Assoc. of Rhodesia. *Recreation:* bowls. *Address:* Windsmoor, Hazeldean Road, Borrowdale, Salisbury, Rhodesia. *Club:* Salisbury (Salisbury).

GREENFIELD, Sir Harry, KBE 1974; Kt 1948; CSI 1946; CIE 1938; retired as Director, The Chartered Bank, 1973, and as Adviser, British-American Tobacco Co., 1974; *b* 2 Oct. 1898; *m* 1931, Hilda Adeline Wilkinson; one *s*. Served European War, Berks Yeomanry and Tank Corps in UK, France and Germany, 1916-19. In Civil Service in India, from 1919, retiring, 1947, as Chairman Central Board of Revenue, Govt of India. Delegate of India to Narcotics Commn of UN, 1946; Pres., Internat. Narcotics Control Board, Geneva, 1968-74; Pres., Permanent Central Narcotics Board, 1953-68 (Vice-Pres., 1948-52); Chm., Inst. for the Study of Drug Dependence, 1968-75; Mem. Cttee appointed to review Customs and Excise Organisation, 1951-53. Until 1974 associated with Internat. Chamber of Commerce for 20 years in furtherance of internat. trade. Governor, Polytechnic of Central London, 1970- (Regent Street Polytechnic, 1956-70); Chm. Council, The Leprosy Mission, 1962-74; Chm., Royal Society for India, Pakistan and Ceylon, 1963-75; Vice-Chm., Westminster Chamber of Commerce, 1963-65; Mem. Advisory Cttee Chelsea Sch. of Art, 1958-64. *Recreations:* gardening and fly-fishing. *Address:* Ruthven, Holmewood Ridge, Langton Green, near Tunbridge Wells, Kent. *Club:* Oriental.

GREENFIELD, Hon. Julius MacDonald, CMG 1954; Judge of the High Court of Rhodesia, 1968-74; *b* Boksburg, Transvaal, 13 July 1907; *s* of late Rev. C. E. Greenfield; *m* 1935, Florence Margaret Couper; two *s* one *d. Educ:* Milton Sch., Bulawayo; Universities of Capetown and Oxford. BA, LLB Cape; Rhodes Scholar, 1929; BA, BCL Oxon. Called to the Bar at Gray's Inn, 1933. QC 1948; practised at Bar in S Rhodesia, 1933-50; elected MP for Hillside, S Rhodesia, 1948, and appointed Minister of Internal Affairs and Justice, 1950; participated in London Conferences on Federation in Central Africa. MP Federal Parliament, in Umguza Constituency, 1953-63; Minister of Law, Federation of Rhodesia and Nyasaland, 1954-63; Minister for Home Affairs, 1962-63. *Publications:* Instant Crime, 1975; Instant Statute Case Law, 1977. *Address:* 17 Retzia Road, Hoheizen, Bellville 7530, South Africa. *T:* 978610. *Clubs:* Bulawayo, Salisbury (Rhodesia); City and Civil Service (Cape Town).

GREENHALGH, Jack; Vice-Chairman since 1974, and Managing Director since 1968, Cavenham Ltd; *b* 25 July 1926; *s* of Herbert Greenhalgh and Alice May (*née* Clayton); *m* 1951, Kathleen Mary Hammond; two *s* two *d. Educ:* Manchester Grammar Sch.; Trinity Coll., Cambridge (MA Hons). FBIM. Marketing Dept, Procter & Gamble Ltd, Newcastle upon Tyne, 1950-59; Marketing Dir, Eskimo Foods Ltd, Cleethorpes, 1959-64; Dir of Continental Ops, Compton Advertising Inc., NY, 1964-65; Man. Dir of various subsids, Cavenham Ltd, 1965-. *Recreations:* golf, sailing. *Address:* House on the Creek, Raymead Road, Maidenhead, Berks SL6 8NJ. *T:* Maidenhead 26765. *Clubs:* Wellington; Maidenhead Golf, Minchinhampton Golf.

GREENHAM, Peter George, RA 1960 (ARA, 1951); PRBA; RP; NEAC; Keeper of the Royal Academy Schools, since 1964; *b* 1909; *s* of George Frederick Greenham, MBE, civil servant; *m* 1964, Jane, *d* of late Dr G. B. Dowling, FRCP, and Mary Elizabeth Kelly; one *s* one *d. Educ:* Dulwich Coll.; Magdalen Coll., Oxford (Hist. Demy, BA); Byam Shaw Sch. of Art. *Publication:* Velasquez, 1969. *Recreation:* music. *Address:* c/o Royal Academy, Piccadilly, W1.

GREENHILL, family name of **Barons Greenhill** and **Greenhill of Harrow.**

GREENHILL, 2nd Baron, *cr* 1950, of Townhead; **Stanley E. Greenhill,** MD, DPH; Professor and Chairman, Department of Community Medicine, University of Alberta, Edmonton, Alberta, since 1959; *b* 17 July 1917; *s* of 1st Baron Greenhill and Ida Goodman; *S* father, 1967; *m* 1946, Margaret Jean, *d* of Thomas Newlands Hamilton, Ontario, Canada; two *d. Educ:* Kelvinside Academy, Glasgow; California and Toronto Univs. MD Toronto, DPH Toronto, FRCP(C), MFCM, FACP, FRSH, FRSM. British Information Services, 1941; RAF, 1944. Lecturer, Dept of Medicine, University of Alberta, 1952. WHO Consultant, 1973-74. *Publications:* contrib. medical journals. *Recreations:* photography, travel. *Heir:* *b* Hon. Malcolm Greenhill, *b* 5 May 1924. *Address:* 10223, 137th Street, Edmonton, Alta T5N 2G8, Canada. *T:* 403-452-4650; c/o 28 Gorselands, Newbury, Berks. *Club:* Faculty (Edmonton, Alta).

GREENHILL OF HARROW, Baron *cr* 1974 (Life Peer), of the Royal Borough of Kensington and Chelsea; **Denis Arthur Greenhill,** GCMG 1972 (KCMG 1967; CMG 1960); OBE 1941; HM Government Director: British Petroleum Co. Ltd, since 1973; British Leyland Ltd, since 1975; Member, Security Commission, since 1973; a Governor of the BBC, since 1973; *b* 7 Nov. 1913; *s* of James and Susie Greenhill, Loughton; *m* 1941, Angela McCulloch; two *s. Educ:* Bishop's Stortford Coll.; Christ Church, Oxford (Hon. Student 1977). Served War of 1939-45 (despatches thrice): Royal Engineers; in Egypt, N Africa, Italy, India and SE Asia; demobilised with rank of Col. Entered Foreign Service, 1946; served: Sofia, 1947-49; Washington, 1949-52; Foreign Office, 1952-54. Imperial Defence Coll., 1954; UK Delegation to NATO, Paris, 1955-57; Singapore, 1957-59; Counsellor, 1959-62; Minister, 1962-64, Washington DC; Asst Under-Sec. of State, FO, 1964-66; Dep. Under-Sec. of State, FO, 1966-69; Perm. Under-Sec. of State, FCO, and Head of the Diplomatic Service, 1969-73. Director: S. G. Warburg & Co.; Clerical Medical and General Assce; Wellcome Foundn Ltd; British-American Tobacco; Hawker Siddeley Group. Trustee, Rayne Foundn; Governor, Wellington Coll. *Address:* 25 Hamilton House, Vicarage Gate, W8. *T:* 01-937 8362. *Club:* Travellers'.

GREENHILL, Basil Jack, CMG 1967; FRHistS; FSA; Director, National Maritime Museum, Greenwich, since 1967; *b* 26 Feb. 1920; *o c* of B. J. and Edith Greenhill; *m* 1st, 1950, Gillian (*d* 1959), *e d* of Capt. Ralph Tyacke Stratton, MC; one *s*; 2nd, 1961, Ann, *d* of Walter Ernest Gifford; one *s. Educ:* Bristol Grammar Sch.; Bristol Univ. (T. H. Green Scholar). Served War of 1939-45: RNVR (Air Br.). Joined Commonwealth (subseq. Diplomatic) Service, 1946; served: Dacca, 1950-52; Peshawar, 1952-53; Karachi, 1953-54; UK Delegation, New York, 1954; Tokyo, 1955-58; UK Delegate to Conference on Law of the Sea, Geneva, 1958; British Deputy High Comr in E Pakistan, 1958-59; Ottawa, 1961-64; Commonwealth Office, 1965-66. Member: Cttee of Maritime Trust, 1970- (Mem., Council, 1977-); Ancient Monuments Bd for England, 1972-; Vice Pres., Soc. for Nautical Res., 1975-; First Pres., Internat. Congress of Maritime Museums, 1975-. Trustee, Royal Naval Museum, Portsmouth, 1973-. Governor, Dulwich Coll., 1974-; Chm., Dulwich Coll. Picture Gall. Cttee, 1977-. *Publications:* The Merchant Schooners, Vol. I, 1951, Vol. II, 1957, rev. edn, 1968; (ed and prefaced) W. J. Slade's Out of Appledore, 1959; Sailing For A Living, 1962; Westcountrymen in Prince Edward's Isle (with Ann Giffard), 1967 (Amer. Assoc. Award) (filmed 1975); The Merchant Sailing Ship: A Photographic History (with Ann Giffard), 1970; Women under Sail (with Ann Giffard), 1970; Captain Cook, 1970; Boats and Boatmen of Pakistan, 1971; (with Ann Giffard) Travelling by Sea in the Nineteenth Century, 1972; (with Rear-Adm. P. W. Brock) Sail and Steam, 1973; (with W. J. Slade) West Country Coasting Ketches, 1974; A Victorian Maritime Album, 1974; A Quayside Camera, 1975; (with L. Willis) The Coastal Trade: Sailing Craft of British Waters 900-1900, 1975; Archaeology of the Boat, 1976; (with Ann Giffard) Victorian and Edwardian Sailing Ships, 1976; (with Ann Gifford) Victorian and Edwardian Ports and Harbours, 1978; numerous articles and reviews on maritime history subjects. *Recreations:* writing, travel. *Address:* c/o National Maritime Museum, Greenwich, SE10. *Clubs:* Arts;

Royal Western Yacht (Plymouth); Karachi Yacht (Karachi). *See also C . S . R . Giffard .*

GREENING, Wilfrid Peter, FRCS; Consultant Surgeon to Royal Marsden Hospital since 1952; Consulting Surgeon, Charing Cross Hospital since 1975; Lecturer in Surgery to Charing Cross Hospital Medical School; *s* of Rev. W. Greening and M. M. Waller, Saxlingham, Norfolk; *m* 1st, 1939, Hilary Berryman (marr. diss., 1961); one *d*; 2nd, 1962, Susan Ann Clair Huber. *Educ:* St Edmund's Sch., Canterbury; King's Coll.; Charing Cross Hospital Medical Sch. MRCS 1937; LRCP 1937; FRCS 1939. Houseman and Surgical Registrar, Charing Cross Hosp., 1938. Served War of 1939-45 (despatches); Wing Comdr i/c Surgical Div., RAFVR, 1943. Surgical Registrar, Gordon Hospital, 1946; Consultant Surgeon: Woolwich Hospital, 1948; Bromley and District Hospital, 1947-66. *Publications:* contributions to medical literature. *Recreations:* fishing, golf. *Address:* 7 Ulster Terrace, Regent's Park, NW1 4PJ. *T:* 01-935 2567. *Club:* Garrick.

GREENLEES, Ian Gordon, OBE 1963; MA; Director of the British Institute of Florence, since 1958; *b* 10 July 1913; *s* of Samuel Greenlees and Rosalie Stewart. *Educ:* Ampleforth Coll.; Magdalen Coll., Oxford. Reader in English Literature at University of Rome, 1934-36; supervisor of cultural centres of English for the British Council and Acting British Council Representative in Italy, 1939-40; Dir, British Institute, Rome, 1940; commissioned in Army, 1940; served in North African and Italian Campaigns, 1942-45, with rank of Major (despatches). Second Sec. (Asst Press Attaché) at British Embassy, Rome, Jan.-Dec. 1946; Asst British Council Representative, Italy, May 1947-Sept. 1948; Deputy British Council Representative, Italy, 1948-54. Medaglia d'Argento ai Benemeriti della Cultura (Italy), 1959; Cavaliere Ufficiale, 1963, Commendatore, 1975, dell' Ordine del Merito della Repubblica Italiana. *Publication:* Norman Douglas, 1957. *Recreations:* swimming, walking, and talking. *Address:* Via Santo Spirito 15, Florence, Italy. *T:* Florence 291978; Casa Mansi, Via del Bagno 20, Bagni di Lucca. *T:* 0583 87522. *Clubs:* Athenæum; Leonardo da Vinci, Union (Florence).

GREENOCK, Lord; Charles Alan Andrew Cathcart; *b* 30 Nov. 1952; *s* and *heir* of 6th Earl Cathcart, *qv. Educ:* Eton. Commnd Scots Guards, 1972-75. *Address:* 14 Eaton Mews South, SW1. *Club:* Cavalry and Guards.

GREENOUGH, Mrs P. B.; *see* Sills, Beverly.

GREENSLADE, Brigadier Cyrus, CBE 1940; psc; *b* 13 May 1892; *s* of late William Francis Greenslade and R. B. Greenslade, St Mary Church, Torquay; *m* 1917, Edith Margaret Johnson (*d* 1975); one *d. Educ:* Blundell's Sch., Tiverton. 2nd Lieut Devonshire Regt 1914; Capt. South Staffordshire Regt; Major York and Lancaster Regt; Lieut-Col North Staffordshire Regt; Brevets of Major and Lieut-Col; Instructor at Staff Coll., Camberley, 1932-35; GSO2 Army HQ, India, 1936-37; Col. 1936; Brigadier 1940; served European War, 1914-18, France, Salonica; 1919, The Baltic States (despatches, OBE); War of 1939-45, War Office as AQMG and Dir of Quartering; France, as Dep. QMG (CBE); 2 Corps HQ as DA&QMG. Combined Ops Training Centre as 2nd i/c to Vice-Adm. and Chief Instructor; Middle East, Comdr Eritrea Area and Comdr 2nd Bde Sudan Defence Force, 1942-44 (despatches); Palestine, as Comdr Southern Palestine Area, 1944-46; retd pay, 1946. Dep. Chief, Displaced Persons Operation, UNRRA, Germany and Paris, 1946-47; International Refugee Organisation, Geneva HQ, 1947-48; Chief UK Officer, IRO, 1948-51. Exec. Officer, Royal Commonwealth Society for the Blind, 1953-59. Legion of Merit, USA (Commander). *Recreation:* fishing. *Address:* The Annexe, Briar Cottage, Sandy Lane, Long Crendon, Bucks. *T:* Long Crendon 208171. *Clubs:* Athenæum, Naval and Military.

GREENSLADE, Rev. Stanley Lawrence, DD; FBA 1960; Canon of Christ Church and Regius Professor of Ecclesiastical History, Oxford University, 1960-72; Emeritus Student of Christ Church, Oxford, 1972; *b* 14 May 1905; *s* of late William Greenslade and Alice Sear; *m* 1929, Phyllis Dora Towell; one *s* one *d. Educ:* Christ's Hosp.; Hertford Coll., Oxford (Open Classical Scholar, Class I, Hon. Classical Mods, Lit. Hum. II, Theology I); Wycliffe Hall, Oxford. Curate of St Mary's, Beeston, Leeds, 1929-30; Fellow, Chaplain, and Tutor in Theology, St John's Coll., Oxford, 1930-43; Lightfoot Prof. of Divinity, Univ. of Durham, 1943-50; Van Mildert Prof. of Divinity, Univ. of Durham, 1950-58; Ely Prof. of Divinity, Cambridge Univ., 1958-59; Fellow of Selwyn Coll., Cambridge, 1958-59. Senior Denyer-Johnson Scholar (Oxford Univ.), 1933. Canon of Durham, 1943-58; Examining Chaplain to Bishop of Durham, 1943-58; to Bishop of Bradford, 1956-61; to Bishop of

Chelmsford, 1933-43; to Bishop of Leicester, 1932-47. Ecumenical activities incl. Mem. of Faith and Order Cttee of WCC and of Anglican-Methodist, Anglican-Presbyterian, Anglican-Lutheran and Anglican-Orthodox Conversations. Hon. DD Edinburgh. *Publications:* The Work of William Tindale, 1938; The Christian Church and the Social Order, 1948; Schism in the Early Church, 1953; Church and State from Constantine to Theodosius, 1954; Early Latin Theology, 1956; ed The Cambridge History of the Bible: The West from the Reformation to the Present Day, 1963; Shepherding the Flock, 1967; introd. to facsimile The Coverdale Bible 1535, 1975. *Recreations:* music, bibliography. *Address:* Homestall, Church Lane, South Moreton, Didcot, Oxon OX11 9AF. *T:* Didcot 812088.

GREENSMITH, Edward William, OBE 1972; FCGI, FIMechE, BScEng; Chairman, Executive Board of the British Standards Institution, 1970-73, Deputy President since 1973; *b* 20 April 1909; *m* 1937, Edna Marjorie Miskin (*d* 1971); three *s*; *m* 1972, Margaret Boaden Miles. ICI, Engrg Adviser, 1964-71. Dir (non-executive), Peter Brotherhood Ltd, 1970-. *Publications:* contribs: Chemistry Ind., 1957, 1959. *Recreations:* sailing, gardening. *Address:* Battle Hill, Tanners Lane, Burford, Oxford OX8 4NA. *T:* Burford 2304.

GREENSMITH, Edwin Lloydd, CMG 1962; *b* 23 Jan. 1900; *s* of Edwin Greensmith; *m* 1932, Winifred Bryce; two *s* two *d*. *Educ:* Victoria Univ., Wellington, NZ. MCom (Hons), 1930. Accountant; Solicitor. Chief Accountant, Ministry of Works, New Zealand, to 1935; then Treasury (Accountant), 1955-65). Chm., NZ Wool Commn, 1965-72. *Recreations:* tennis, gardening. *Address:* Lowry Bay, Wellington, NZ. *T:* 683240. *Club:* Wellington (Wellington NZ).

GREENWAY, family name of **Baron Greenway.**

GREENWAY, 4th Baron *cr* 1927; **Ambrose Charles Drexel Greenway**; Bt 1919; marine photographer; *b* 21 May 1941; *s* of 3rd Baron Greenway and of Cordelia Mary, *d* of late Major Humfrey Campbell Stephen; *S* father, 1975. *Educ:* Winchester. *Recreations:* ocean racing and cruising, swimming. *Heir: b* Hon. Mervyn Stephen Kelvynge Greenway, *b* 19 Aug. 1942. *Address:* c/o House of Lords, SW1. *Clubs:* House of Lords Yacht; Royal London Yacht (Cowes); Royal Fowey Yacht, Island Sailing.

GREENWELL, Captain Sir Peter (McClintock), 3rd Bt *cr* 1906; TD; DL; formerly 98th (Surrey and Sussex Yeomanry) Field Regiment (TA); *b* 23 May 1914; *s* of 2nd Bt and Anna Elizabeth (*d* 1957), *e d* of late Adm. Sir Francis Leopold McClintock, KCB; *S* father, 1939; *m* 1940, Henrietta, 2nd *d* of late Peter and Lady Alexandra Haig-Thomas; two *s* one *d*. *Educ:* Winchester; Trinity Coll., Cambridge (BA). Served War of 1939-45 (despatches, 1946, prisoner). Chm., Ransomes, Sims and Jefferies Ltd, 1969-. Trustee, Royal Agric. Soc. (Dep. Pres., 1971). JP Suffolk, resigned, 1958; High Sheriff of Suffolk, 1966; DL Suffolk, 1973. *Heir: s* Edward Bernard Greenwell [*b* 10 June 1948; *m* 1974, Sarah Louise, *yr d* of late Lt-Col P. M. G. Anley; one *d*]. *Address:* Butley Abbey Farm, Woodbridge, Suffolk. *T:* Orford 233.

GREENWOOD, family name of **Viscount Greenwood** and of **Baron Greenwood of Rossendale.**

GREENWOOD, 2nd Viscount, *cr* 1937 of Holbourne; **David Henry Hamar Greenwood,** Baron, *cr* 1929; Bt, *cr* 1915; *b* 30 Oct. 1914; *e s* of 1st Viscount Greenwood, PC, KC, LLD, and Margery (*d* 1968), 2nd *d* of late Rev. Walter Spencer, BA; *S* father 1948; unmarried. *Educ:* privately and at Bowers Gifford. Agriculture and Farming. *Heir: b* Hon. Michael George Hamar Greenwood, *b* 5 May 1923. *Recreations:* shooting and reading. *Address:* 6 Picaterre, Alderney, Channel Islands.

GREENWOOD OF ROSSENDALE, Baron *cr* 1970 (Life Peer), of East Mersea, Essex; **Arthur William James Greenwood, (Anthony Greenwood),** PC 1964; DL; Member, Commonwealth Development Corporation, since 1970; Director, Britannia Building Society, since 1972 (formerly Leek, Westbourne and Eastern Counties Building Society) (Chairman, 1974-76); company director and consultant; *b* Leeds, 14 Sept. 1911; *s* of late Rt Hon. Arthur Greenwood, PC, CH; *m* 1940, Gillian Crawshay Williams; two *d*. *Educ:* Merchant Taylors' Sch.; Balliol Coll., Oxford (MA). President Oxford Union, 1933. National Fitness Council, 1938-39; Ministry of Information in UK, Russia and Middle East, 1939-42; Intelligence Officer in RAF (Flight Lieut), 1942-46; Allied Reparation Commission, Moscow, Potsdam Conference, Allied Reparation Conference, Paris, 1945; Organising Cttee, Inter-Allied Reparation Agency, 1945-46. Mem. Hampstead Borough Council, 1945-49. MP

(Lab), Heywood and Radcliffe, 1946-50, Rossendale, 1950-70. Vice-Chairman: Parly Labour Party, 1950, 1951; Parly Cttee of Labour Party, 1951-52 and 1955-60; Vice-Chm., Nat. Exec. Cttee of Labour Party, 1962-63, Chm., 1963-64 (Mem., 1954-70); Sec. of State for Colonial Affairs, Oct. 1964-Dec. 1965; Minister of Overseas Development, Dec. 1965-Aug. 1966; Minister of Housing and Local Government, 1966-70. Chm., Labour Parly Assoc., 1960-71; Mem., Central Lancashire New Town Develt Corp., 1971-76; Chm., UK Housing Assoc., 1972-; Dep. Chm., Housing Corp., 1974-; Pres., Housing Centre, 1975-; Chairman: Local Govt Trng Bd, 1975-; Local Govt Staff Commn, 1972-76; President: British Trust for Conservation Volunteers, 1974-; Socialist Educational Assoc., 1963-72; Cremation Soc., 1970-; River Thames Soc., 1971-; Pure Rivers Soc., 1971-76; River Stour Trust, 1977; Urban District Councils Assoc., 1971-72; London Soc., 1971-76; Josephine Butler Soc., 1971-76; Assoc. of Metropolitan Authorities, 1974-; Vice-President: Building Societies Assoc., 1971-; RSPCA; Adv. Bd on Redundant Churches, 1975-; British Rheumatic Assoc.; Central Council for Rehabilitation; British Council for Rehabilitation; Mem., Cttee of Inquiry on Rehabilitation of Disabled Persons, 1953; Chm., British Council for Rehabilitation of Disabled, 1975-. Pro-Chancellor, Univ. of Lancaster, 1972-. JP London, 1950; DL Essex 1974. *Address:* 38 Downshire Hill, Hampstead, NW3; The Old Ship Cottage, East Mersea, Essex. *Clubs:* Savile, Royal Automobile.

GREENWOOD, Allen Harold Claude, CBE 1974; JP; Deputy Chairman, British Aerospace, since 1977 (Member, Organizing Committee, 1976-77); Chairman, British Aircraft Corporation, 1976 (Deputy Chairman, 1972-75); *b* 4 June 1917; *s* of Lt-Col Thomas Claude Greenwood and Hilda Letitia Greenwood (*née* Knight). *Educ:* Cheltenham Coll.; Coll. of Aeronautical Engineering. Joined Vickers-Armstrongs Ltd, 1940; served RNVR (Fleet Air Arm), 1942-52 (Lt-Cmdr); rejoined Vickers-Armstrongs Ltd, 1946, Dir, 1960; British Aircraft Corp., 1962, Dep. Man. Dir, 1969. Pres., Assoc. of European Aerospace Companies, 1974-76. Vice-Chm., 1973, Chm., 1976, Remploy Ltd. Life Mem. Council, Cheltenham Coll. and St John's Sch., Leatherhead. Pres., Soc. of British Aerospace Companies, 1970-72. Mem. Council, Cranfield Inst. of Technology, 1973. JP Surrey 1962. *Address:* British Aerospace, Brooklands Road, Weybridge KT13 0RN. *T:* Weybridge 45522. *Clubs:* Athenæum, Royal Automobile.

GREENWOOD, Brig. Harold Gustave Francis, CBE 1942; MC; retired; *b* 15 Nov. 1894; *s* of late Lieut-Col H. S. Greenwood, VD, Kingston, Canada, and Matilda, *d* of Sir Henri Joly de Lotbinière, KCMG; *m* 1928, Gwyneth Francis, *d* of late E. B. Lemon, Winnipeg and late Mrs Ogilvie, Victoria, Canada; one *d*. *Educ:* Bishops Coll. Sch., Lennoxville, Canada; RMC, Canada. Served European War, 1914-18 (despatches twice, MC); NW Frontier Province, India, 1923-24 (despatches twice, Bt Major); lately Brigadier Engineer Staff, GHQ, India; and Chief Engineer 11th Army Group, SE Asia Command; retired pay, 1947. *Address:* c/o Lloyds Bank Ltd, Pall Mall, SW1; 3 Highlands Road, Buckingham, Bucks MK18 1PN.

GREENWOOD, Jack Neville; General Manager, Stevenage Development Corporation, since 1976; *b* 17 March 1922; *s* of Daniel Greenwood and Elvina Stanworth; *m* 1947, Margaret Jane Fincher; two *s* two *d*. *Educ:* Harrow County Sch. Mem., Chartered Inst. of Public Finance and Accountancy. RAF, 1941-46. Ruislip Northwood UDC, 1938-49; Southall Borough Council, 1949-50; Stevenage Develt Corp., 1950-, Chief Finance Officer, 1967-76. *Recreation:* gardening. *Address:* Woodfield, Rectory Lane, Stevenage, Herts. *T:* Stevenage 52851.

GREENWOOD, James Russell, MVO 1975; HM Diplomatic Service; *b* 30 April 1924; *s* of J. and L. Greenwood, Padiham; *m* 1957, Mary Veronica, *d* of late Dr D. W. Griffith and Dr Grace Griffith, Bures; one *s*. *Educ:* RGS, Clitheroe; Queen's Coll., Oxford. Army Service, 1943-47. BA, MA (Oxon) 1949; Foreign Office, 1949; subseq. service in Bangkok, 1950-52; Tokyo and Osaka, 1952-54; London, 1955-58; Rangoon, 1958-61; Rome, 1961-63; Bangkok, 1964-68; Counsellor (Information), Tokyo, 1968-73; Consul-General, Osaka, 1973-77. Order of Sacred Treasure (3rd cl.) Japan, 1975. *Recreations:* travel, golf, cricket. *Address:* c/o Foreign and Commonwealth Office, SW1. *Clubs:* United Oxford & Cambridge University, MCC.

GREENWOOD, Joan; Actress; Theatre, Films, Radio, Television; *b* 4 March 1921; *d* of late Earnshaw Greenwood, Artist; *m* 1960, André Morell; one *s*. *Educ:* St Catherine's Sch., Bramley, Surrey. First professional stage appearance in Le Malade Imaginaire, 1938; since then has appeared in: Little Ladyship; The Women; Striplings; Damaged Goods; Heartbreak House; Hamlet; Volpone; A Doll's House; Frenzy; Young

Wives' Tale; The Confidential Clerk (New York); Peter Pan 1951; The Moon and the Chimney, 1955; Bell, Book and Candle, 1955; Cards of Identity, 1956; Lysistrata, 1957-58; The Grass is Greener, 1959; Hedda Gabler, 1960, 1964; The Irregular Verb to Love, 1961; Oblomov (later Son of Oblomov), 1964; Fallen Angels, 1967; The Au Pair Man, 1969; The Chalk Garden, 1971; Eden End, 1972; In Praise of Love, 1973. Acted at Chichester Festival, 1962. *Films include:* They Knew Mr Knight, Latin Quarter, Girl in a Million, Bad Sister, The October Man, Tight Little Island, Bad Lord Byron, Train of Events, Flesh and Blood, Kind Hearts and Coronets, The Man in the White Suit, Young Wives Tale, Mr Peek-a-Boo, The Importance of Being Earnest, Monsieur Ripois, Father Brown, Moonfleet, Stage Struck, Tom Jones, The Moonspinners. *Recreations:* reading, ballet, music, painting. *Address:* c/o National Westminster Bank, 1 Brompton Square, SW3.

GREENWOOD, John Arnold Charles, OBE 1943; Director: Sun Alliance & London Insurance Group, 1971-77 (Chief General Manager, 1971-77); *b* 23 Jan. 1914; *o s* of late Augustus George Greenwood and Adele Ellen O'Neill Arnold; *m* 1940, Dorothy Frederica Pestell; two *d*. *Educ:* King's College Sch., Wimbledon. FCII; FRES. Joined Sun Insce Office Ltd, 1932; posted India, 1937-47; served War of 1939-45, TA, 36th Sikh Regt and AA&QMG 4th Indian Div. (Lt-Col, OBE, despatches); subseq. various appts: a Gen. Man., Sun Alliance & London, 1965; Dep. Chief Gen. Man., 1969. Morgan Owen Medal, 1939. *Publications:* papers on insurance, entomology. *Recreations:* entomology, writing, gardening. *Address:* The Thatches, Forest Road, Pyrford, Woking, Surrey. *T:* Byfleet 47714.

GREENWOOD, Prof. John Neill, DSc, MMetE; Emeritus Professor, University of Melbourne, since 1965; *b* St Helens, 12 Dec. 1894; *s* of late Ellen and Walter Greenwood; *m* 1934, Winifred, *d* of Katherine and James Borrie; two *s* one *d*. *Educ:* St Helen's Technical Sch. Victoria University, Manchester, 1st class hons metallurgy, 1913-16; Chief Research Asst, Sir W. G. Armstrong Whitworth & Co. (Openshaw), 1916-19; MSc, by thesis, 1917; Chief of Research Dept, Sam. Fox & Co., Ltd, 1919-24; Prof. of Metallurgy, Melbourne Univ., 1924-46. DSc 1922; MMetE (Melbourne), 1931; designing pilot plant for wrought tungsten for Australian Ministry of Munitions, 1942-44; Research Prof. of Metallurgy, 1946-59 (Sen. Prof. of Univ. from 1956), retd; Prof. (personal chair) and Dean of Faculty of Applied Sciences, 1960-64, retd. Past-Pres. and Mem. of Council, 1933-44, Australian Inst. Mining and Metallurgy. Royal Commissioner, King's Bridge Failure, 1962-63. Hon. Life Mem. Victorian Coll. of Optometry, 1964. Hon. DApSc Melbourne, 1968; Hon. DEng Monash, 1974. Silver Medal, Aust. Inst. Metals, 1958; Bronze Medal, Aust. Inst. Mining and Metallurgy, 1961. *Publications:* Glossary of metallographic terms; various original researches in metallurgy and pyrometry, in Journal Iron and Steel Inst., and Journal Institute of Metals, Faraday Soc., Birmingham Met. Soc., Staffs Iron and Steel Institute, Australasian Institute of Mining and Metallurgy. *Address:* 64 Wellington Street, St Kilda, Victoria 3182, Australia.
See also Prof. Norman N. Greenwood.

GREENWOOD, Prof. Norman Neill, MSc, DSc Melbourne; PhD; ScD Cambridge; FRIC; CChem; Professor and Head of Department of Inorganic and Structural Chemistry, University of Leeds, since 1971; *b* Melbourne, Vic., 19 Jan. 1925; *er s* of Prof. J. Neill Greenwood, *qv*; *m* 1951, Kirsten Marie Rydland, Bergen, Norway; three *d*. *Educ:* University High School, Melbourne; University of Melbourne; Sidney Sussex Coll., Cambridge. Laboratory Cadet, CSIRO Div. of Tribophysics, Melbourne, 1942-44; BSc Melbourne 1945, MSc Melbourne 1948; DSc Melbourne 1966. Masson Memorial Medal, Royal Australian Chem. Institute, 1945. Resident Tutor and Lecturer in Chemistry, Trinity Coll., Melbourne, 1946-48. Exhibn of 1851, Overseas Student, 1948-51; PhD Cambridge 1951; ScD Cambridge 1961. Senior Harwell Research Fellow, 1951-53; Lectr, 1953-60 Senior Lectr, 1960-61, in Inorganic Chemistry, Univ. of Nottingham; Prof. of Inorganic Chemistry, Univ. of Newcastle upon Tyne, 1961-71. Vis. Professor: Univ. of Melbourne 1966; Univ. of Western Australia, 1969; Univ. of Western Ontario, 1973; Tilden Lectr (Chem. Soc.), 1966-67; National Science Foundation Distinguished Vis. Prof., Michigan State Univ., USA, 1967; Univ. of W Ontario, 1973, International Union of Pure and Applied Chemistry: Mem., 1963-; Chm., Internat. Commn on Atomic Weights, 1969-75; Vice Pres. 1975-77, Pres., 1977-, Inorganic Chemistry Div. Chem. Soc. Award in Main Group Chemistry, 1975. Dr *hc* de l'Université de Nancy I, 1977. FRSA. *Publications:* Principles of Atomic Orbitals, 1964 (rev. edn 1968, 1973); Ionic Crystals, Lattice Defects, and Nonstoichiometry, 1968; (jointly) Spectroscopic Properties of Inorganic and Organometallic Compounds, vols I-IX, 1968-76;

WW 32

(with W. A. Campbell) Contemporary British Chemists, 1971; (with T. C. Gibb) Mössbauer Spectroscopy, 1971; Periodicity and Atomic Structure, 1971; (with B. P. Staughan and E. J. F. Ross) Index of Vibrational Spectra, vol. I, 1972, (with E. J. F. Ross) vol. II, 1975, vol. III, 1977; The Chemistry of Boron, 1973 (rev. edn 1975); numerous original papers and reviews in chemical jls and chapters in scientific monographs. *Recreations:* ski-ing, music. *Address:* Department of Inorganic and Structural Chemistry, The University, Leeds LS2 9JT.

GREENWOOD, Peter Bryan; His Honour Judge Greenwood; a Circuit Judge, since 1972. Called to the Bar, Gray's Inn, 1955. Dep. Chm., Essex QS, 1968-71. *Address:* 6 King's Bench Walk, Temple, EC4Y 7DR.

GREENWOOD, Robert; novelist and short-story writer; *b* Crosshills, Yorks, 8 March 1897; *m* 1932, Alice Ross; no *c*. *Publications:* novels: Mr Bunting, 1940; Mr Bunting at War, 1941; The Squad Goes Out, 1943; Wagstaff's England, 1947; Mr Bunting in the Promised Land, 1949; Good Angel Slept, 1953; O Mistress Mine, 1955; A Breeze in Dinglesea, 1957; A Stone from the Brook, 1960; Spring at the Limes, 1963; Summer in Bishop Street, 1965. Books published in England and/or USA and translated into Swedish, Spanish, German, French, Hebrew and Russian. Short stories published in England and USA. Adapted Bunting novels for the British film, Salute John Citizen. *Address:* Flat 1, 15 Bath Road, Felixstowe, Suffolk.

GREENWOOD WILSON, J.; *see* Wilson, John G.

GREESON, Surgeon Vice-Adm. Sir (Clarence) Edward, KBE 1950; CB 1945; retired; *b* 29 Nov. 1888; *s* of Rev. John Greeson; *m* 1st, 1911, Katharine Whyte (*d* 1959); one *d*; 2nd, 1959, Mrs Marion Meredith Edgecombe (*d* 1968); 3rd, 1969, Hon. Mrs Michael Scott. *Educ:* Aberdeen Grammar Sch.; Aberdeen Univ. (MB, ChB 1910; MD 1913). Surgeon, Royal Navy, 1914; Surgeon Capt., 1939; Surgeon Rear-Adm., 1945; Surgeon Vice-Adm., 1948. Served European War, 1914-19: battles of Heligoland Bight, Falkland Islands, Gallipoli; Shanghai Defence Force with 12th RM Bn, 1927; War of 1939-45: Fleet MO, Mediterranean Fleet, 1939-42; Battle of Matapan; Medical Dir-Gen. of the Navy, 1949-52; KHP 1946-52; QHP 1952; retd list, 1952. CStJ, 1948. *Address:* The Dell House, Alderney, CI.

GREET, Rev. Dr Kenneth Gerald; Secretary of the Methodist Conference since 1971; Chairman, World Christian Temperance Federation, 1962-72; *b* 17 Nov. 1918; *e s* of Walter and Renée Greet, Bristol; *m* 1947, Mary Eileen Edbrooke; one *s* two *d*. *Educ:* Cotham Grammar Sch., Bristol; Handsworth Coll., Birmingham. Minister: Cwm and Kingstone Methodist Church, 1940-42; Ogmore Vale Methodist Church, 1942-45; Tonypandy Central Hall, 1947-54; Sec. Dept of Christian Citizenship of Methodist Church, 1954-71; Member: Brit. Council of Churches, 1955-; World Methodist Council, 1957- (Chm., Exec. Cttee, 1976-); Chm. Exec. Temperance Council of Christian Churches, 1961-71. Rep. to Central Cttee, World Council of Churches, Addis Ababa, 1971, Nairobi, 1975; Beckly Lectr, 1962; Willson Lectr, Kansas City, 1966; Cato Lectr, Sydney, 1975. Hon. DD Ohio, USA. *Publications:* The Mutual Society, 1962; Man and Wife Together, 1962; Large Petitions, 1964; Guide to Loving, 1965; The Debate about Drink, 1969; The Sunday Question, 1970; The Art of Moral Judgement, 1970; When the Spirit Moves, 1975. *Recreations:* tennis, photography. *Address:* (office) 1 Central Buildings, Westminster SW1H 9NH. *T:* 01-930 7608; (residence) 16 Orchard Avenue, Shirley, Croydon CR0 8UA. *T:* 01-777 5376.

GREETHAM, (George) Colin; Headmaster, Bishop's Stortford College, since 1971; *b* 22 April 1929; *s* of late George Cecil Greetham and of Gertrude Greetham (*née* Heavyside); *m* 1963, Rosemary (*née* Gardner); two *s* one *d*. *Educ:* York Minster Song Sch.; St Peter's Sch., York; (Choral Scholar) King's Coll., Cambridge. BA (Hons) History Tripos Cantab, Class II, Div. I, 1952; Certif. of Educn (Cantab), 1953. *Recreations:* hockey, cricket, music, choral training. *Address:* Headmaster's House, Bishop's Stortford College, Bishop's Stortford, Herts. *T:* 54220.

GREEVES, Rev. Derrick Amphlet; Superintendent Minister, Salisbury Methodist Circuit, since 1974; *b* 29 June 1913; *s* of Edward Greeves, Methodist Minister; *m* 1942, Nancy (*née* Morgans); one *s* three *d*. *Educ:* Bolton Sch.; Preston Gram. Sch.; Manchester and Cambridge Univs, Manchester Univ. 1931-34 (BA); Cambridge Univ. (Wesley Hse), 1934-37 (MA). Entered Methodist Ministry, 1935; Barnet, 1937-39; Bristol, 1939-43. RAF Chaplain, 1943-47. S Norwood, 1947-52; Bowes Park, 1952-55; Westminster Central Hall, 1955-64; Guildford, 1964-69; Worcester, 1969-74. *Publications:* Christ in Me, a study of the Mind of Christ in Paul, 1962; A Word in Your Ear

(broadcast talks), 1970. *Address:* 12 Anderson Road, Salisbury, Wilts. *T:* Salisbury 24134.
See also Rev. F. Greeves.

GREEVES, Rev. Frederic, MA; LLD; Principal, 1949-67, and Randles Chair of Systematic Theology and Philosophy of Religion, 1946-67, Didsbury College; President, Methodist Conference, 1963-64; *b* 1 June 1903; *s* of Rev. Edward Greeves and Mabel Barnsley Greeves; *m* 1929, Frances Marion Barratt; one *s* one *d. Educ:* Merchant Taylors' Sch., Crosby; Manchester Univ. (BA); Didsbury Coll., Manchester; Cambridge Univ. Asst Tutor, Didsbury Coll., Manchester, 1924-28; Methodist Minister, Cheltenham, 1928-30; BA Cambridge, 1932 (MA 1936); Burney Prize, 1933; Minister, Cambridge, 1930-33; Epsom, 1933-39; Oxford, Chaplain to Methodists in Univ., 1939-46. Chm. West Regional Religious Adv. Council, BBC, 1952-57; Fernley-Hartley Lecture, 1956; Cato Lectr, 1960. Hon. LLD (Bristol), 1963. *Publications:* Jesus the Son of God, 1939; Talking about God, 1949; The Meaning of Sin, 1956; Theology and the Cure of Souls, 1960; The Christian Way, 1963. *Address:* 1 Westmorland House, Durdham Park, Bristol BS6 6XH. *T:* Bristol 311594.
See also Rev. D. A. Greeves.

GREEVES, John Ernest, CB 1966; Permanent Secretary, Ministry of Home Affairs for Northern Ireland, 1964-70, retired; *b* 9 Oct. 1910; *s* of late R. D. Greeves, Grange, Dungannon, Co. Tyrone; *m* 1942, Hilde Alexandra, *d* of E. Hülbig, Coburg, Bavaria; one *s* one *d. Educ:* Royal School, Dungannon. Entered Min. of Labour, NI, 1928; Asst Sec., 1956-62; Permanent Sec., 1962-64; subseq. Min. of Home Affairs. *Address:* 22 Downshire Road, Belfast BT6 9JL. *T:* 648380.

GREEVES, Maj.-Gen. Sir Stuart, KBE 1955 (CBE 1945; OBE 1940); CB 1948; DSO 1944; MC 1917; (ex-Indian Army) Deputy Adjutant General, India, until 1957, retired; *b* 2 April 1897; *s* of late J. S. Greeves; unmarried. *Educ:* Northampton Sch. Served European War, 1914-18 (MC and Bar); War of 1939-45 (DSO and Bar, CBE). *Recreation:* golf. *Address:* c/o Lloyds Bank, 6 Pall Mall, SW1; Flat 601, Grosvenor Square, College Road, Rondebosch, Cape Town, S Africa. *Club:* Naval and Military.

GREG, Barbara, RE 1946; *b* 30 April 1900; *d* of H. P. and J. E. Greg; *m* 1925, Norman Janes, *qv*; one *s* two *d. Educ:* Bedales. Studied at Slade Sch. of Fine Art. Has exhibited wood engravings in London, provincial and foreign exhibitions since 1926. ARE 1940. Books illustrated include A Fisherman's Log by Major Ashley Dodd, Enigmas of Natural History and More Enigmas of Natural History by E. L. Grant Watson, The Poacher's Handbook by Ian Niall, Fresh Woods, Pastures New, by Ian Niall. *Address:* 70 Canonbury Park South, Canonbury, N1. *T:* 01-226 1925.

GREGG, Humphrey P.; *see* Procter-Gregg.

GREGG, James Reali; *b* 16 Nov. 1899; *e s* of late James Gregg, OBE, JP, Carnmoney, Co. Antrim, N Ireland; *m* 1930, Nina Hamilton Smith, *d* of late William H. Smith, Upton Park, Templepatrick, N Ireland; no *c. Educ:* Royal Belfast Academical Institution; Lathrop Sch., Mo, USA; Hampden-Sidney Coll., Va; Harvard Coll., Harvard Univ.; St Catharine's Coll, Cambridge Univ. (MA). Called to Bar, King's Inn, Dublin, 1923; Gray's Inn, London, 1939; KC (Uganda) 1944. Chm., Court of Referees, NI, 1928; Nyasaland: Acting Attorney General, 1937-38; Uganda: Solicitor General, 1939, Attorney General, 1943; Puisne Judge, Nigeria, 1948; Judge of the Supreme Court, Hong Kong, 1953; Sen. Judge of Supreme Court of Hong Kong, 1959-61 (Acting Chief Justice, Hong Kong, Feb.-Nov. 1960); retired. *Recreation:* golf. *Address:* PO Box 91, Hermanus, Cape Province, South Africa. *Club:* Hong Kong (Hong Kong).

GREGG, Milton Fowler, VC 1918; OC 1967; CBE 1946; MC 1917, and Bar 1918; Canadian High Commissioner to Guyana, 1964-67, retired; *b* Mountain Dale, NB, Canada, 10 April 1892; *m* 1919, Amy Dorothy Alward, of Havelock, NB; one *d*; *m* 1964, Erica, widow of Kjeld Deichmann, Sussex, NB. *Educ:* Public Sch., New Brunswick; Provincial Normal Sch., Fredericton NB; Acadia Univ., Wolfville, NS (hon. MA). As a boy lived on a farm; enlisted as a private while at coll., 1914; went to France with 13th Batt. Royal Highlanders of Canada 1915 (wounded, Festubert); later obtained Commission in KORLR; transferred to Royal Canadian Regt; in France, 1917 (wounded, MC) (bar to MC, wounded, Cambrai, 1918, VC); Adjt; returned Canada, 1919; Major in Governor-General's Foot Guards; Dominion Treasurer Canadian Legion, BESL 1934-39; On outbreak of war, 1939 was posted 2nd in command

Royal Canadian Regt and proceeded to England with it 1939; Lieut-Col commanding West Nova Scotia Regt 1940; Commandant, Canadian OCTU, England, 1941; Col Commandant Officers' Training Centre, Canada, 1942; Brig. Commandant Canadian Sch. of Infantry, 1943. Minister of Fisheries, Canada, 1947-48; Minister of Veterans' Affairs, 1948-50; Minister of Labour, 1950, till defeated in General Election, 10 June 1957. United Nations Technical Assistance in Iraq, 1958-59; United Nations Children's Fund in Indonesia, 1960-63. Now with voluntary agencies related to internat. affairs, conservation, rural renewal, military and veterans' affairs. *Address:* Thorn Cottage, RR3, Fredericton, New Brunswick, Canada.

GREGOIRE, Most Rev. Paul; *see* Montreal, Archbishop of, (RC).

GREGOR, James Wyllie, CBE 1961; PhD, DSc, FRSE; Director, Scottish Plant Breeding Station, 1950-65; *b* 14 Jan. 1900; *s* of C. E. Gregor, Innerwick, East Lothian; *m* 1929, Mary Joanne Farquharson, *d* of A. Robertson Wilson, MD. *Educ:* St Mary's Sch., Melrose; Edinburgh Univ. *Publications:* scientific papers in various international journals. *Recreations:* various. *Address:* Old Mill House, Balerno, Midlothian. *T:* 031-449 3273.

GREGORY, Philip Herries, PhD, DSc London, DIC; FRS 1962; Head of Plant Pathology Department, Rothamsted Experimental Station, Harpenden, Hertfordshire, 1958-67; *b* Exmouth, Devon, 24 July 1907; *s* of late Rev. Herries Smith Gregory, MA and late Muriel Edith Gregory (*née* Eldridge), Hove, Sussex; *m* 1932, Margaret Fearn Culverhouse; one *s* one *d. Educ:* Brighton Technical Coll.; Imperial Coll. of Science and Technology, London. Research in medical mycology, Manitoba Med. Coll., 1931-34; Research plant pathologist, Seale-Hayne Agric. Coll., Newton Abbot, Devon, 1935-40; Rothamsted Experimental Station, Harpenden; Agric. Research Council Research Officer, 1940-47 (seconded for penicillin research to ICI, Manchester, 1945-46); Mycologist, Rothamsted Experimental Station, 1948-54; Prof. of Botany, University of London, Imperial Coll. of Science and Technology, 1954-58. Pres. British Mycological Soc., 1951. *Publications:* The Microbiology of the Atmosphere, 1961, 2nd edn, 1973; papers on mycology, plant pathology, and virology. *Address:* 11 Topstreet Way, Harpenden, Herts AL5 5TU.

GREGORY, Prof. Richard Langton, FRSE 1969; Professor of Neuropsychology and Director of Brain and Perception Laboratory, University of Bristol, since 1970; *b* 24 July 1923; *s* of C. C. L. Gregory, astronomer, and Patricia (*née* Gibson); *m* 1st, 1953, Margaret Hope Pattison Muir (marr. diss. 1966); one *s* one *d*; 2nd, 1967, Freja Mary Balchin. *Educ:* King Alfred Sch., Hampstead; Downing Coll., Cambridge, 1947-50. Served in RAF (Signals), 1941-46; Research, MRC Applied Psychology Research Unit, Cambridge, 1950-53; Univ. Demonstrator, then Lecturer, Dept of Psychology, Cambridge, 1953-67; Fellow, Corpus Christi Coll., Cambridge, 1962-67; Professor of Bionics, Dept of Machine Intelligence and Perception, Univ. of Edinburgh, 1967-70 (Chm. of Dept, 1968-70). Visiting Prof.: UCLA, 1963; MIT, 1964; New York Univ., 1966. Lectures: Eldridge Green, RCS, 1967; Royal Institution Christmas, 1967-68; Holm, UC Med. Sch., 1965; RSA Christmas, 1971; Charnock Bradley Meml, Edinburgh, 1975; R. I. Woodhull, 1976. CIBA Foundn Research Prize, 1956; Craik Prize for Physiological Psychology, St John's Coll., Cambridge, 1958; Waverley Gold Medal, 1960. FRMS 1961; FZS 1972; FRSA 1973. Manager of Royal Instn, 1971-74. Founder Editor, Perception, 1972; currently editing Oxford Companion to the Mind. *Publications:* Recovery from Early Blindness (with Jean Wallace), 1963; Eye and Brain, 1966, 3rd edn 1977; The Intelligent Eye, 1970; Concepts and Mechanisms of Perception, 1974; (ed jtly) Illusion in Nature and Art, 1973; articles in various scientific jls and patents for optical and recording instruments and a hearing aid; radio and television appearances. *Recreations:* punning and pondering. *Address:* Brain and Perception Laboratory, Department of Anatomy, The Medical School, University Walk, Bristol BS8 1TD. *Club:* Savile.

GREGORY, Roderic Alfred, CBE 1971; FRS 1965; George Holt Professor of Physiology, University of Liverpool, since 1948; *b* 29 Dec. 1913; *o c* of Alfred and Alice Gregory, West Ham, London; *m* 1939, Alice, *o c* of J. D. Watts, London; one *d. Educ:* George Green's Sch., London; University Coll. and Hospital, London. BSc Hons Physiology, 1934; MSc Biochemistry, 1938; MRCS, LRCP, 1939, FRCP 1977; PhD Physiology, 1942; DSc Physiology, 1949; Paul Philip Reitlinger Prize, 1938; Schafer Prize, 1939; Bayliss-Starling Scholar, 1935; Sharpey Scholar, 1936-39 and 1941-42; Rockefeller Fellow, 1939-41; Lecturer in Physiology, University Coll., London (Leatherhead), 1942-45;

Senior Lecturer in Experimental Physiology, University of Liverpool, 1945-48; Mem. Biolog. Res. Bd, MRC, 1965-71, Chm. 1969; Mem., MRC, 1967-71; a Vice-Pres., Royal Soc., 1971-73. Hon. Member: Amer. Gastroenterological Assoc., 1967; British Soc. of Gastroenterology, 1974. Inaugural Bengt Ihre Lecture and Anniversary Medal, Swedish Med. Soc., 1963; Lectures: Purser, TCD, 1964; Waller, Univ. of London, 1966; Meml Lecture, Amer. Gastroenterolog. Assoc., 1966; Ravdin, Amer. Coll. of Surgeons, 1967; Harvey, 1968; William Mitchell Banks, Liverpool Univ., 1970; Finlayson, RCPGlas, 1970; Bayliss-Starling, Physiological Soc. of GB, 1973. Baly Medal, RCP, 1965; John Hunter Medal, RCS, 1969; Beaumont Triennial Prize, Amer. Gastroenterological Assoc., 1976. Fellow, University Coll., London, 1965; Feldberg Foundn Prize, 1966. Hon. DSc, Univ. of Chicago, 1966. *Publications:* Secretory Mechanisms of the Gastro-intestinal Tract, 1962; various papers in Jl Physiol., Quart. Jl exp. Physiol. and elsewhere since 1935. *Recreation:* music. *Address:* University of Liverpool, PO Box 147, Liverpool L69 38X.

GREGORY, Ronald, QPM 1971; DL; Chief Constable of West Yorkshire Metropolitan Police, since 1974; *b* 23 Oct. 1921; *s* of Charles Henry Gregory and Mary Gregory; *m* 1942, Grace Miller Ellison; two *s. Educ:* Harris College. Joined Police Service, Preston, 1941. RAF (Pilot), 1942-44; RN (Pilot), 1944-46. Dep. Chief Constable, Blackpool, 1962-65; Chief Constable, Plymouth, 1965-68; Dep. Chief Constable, Devon and Cornwall, 1968-69; Chief Constable, West Yorkshire Constabulary, 1969-74. DL West Yorks, 1977. *Recreations:* golf, sailing. *Address:* Police Headquarters, Laburnum Road, Wakefield, West Yorkshire. *T:* Wakefield 75222.

GREGSON, family name of **Baron Gregson.**

GREGSON, Baron *cr* 1975 (Life Peer), of Stockport in Greater Manchester; **John Gregson,** AMCT, MBIM; Assistant Managing Director, The Fairey Co., since 1977 (Director 1976-77); Director: Fairey Engineering Ltd (Managing Director, 1974-77); Fairey Nuclear Ltd; Part-time Member, British Steel Corporation, since 1976. Joined Stockport Base Subsidiary, 1939; Fairey R&D team working on science of nuclear power, 1946; held overall responsibility for company's work on Trawsfynydd nuclear power station; appointed to Board, 1966. Mem. Council, Production Engineering Research Assoc.; Mem. Council, Univ. of Manchester Inst. of Science and Technology. *Address:* Fairey Engineering Limited, PO Box 41, Crossley Road, Heaton Chapel, Stockport, Cheshire SK4 5BD. *Club:* Reform.

GREGSON, Maj.-Gen. Guy Patrick, CB 1958; CBE 1953; DSO 1943 and Bar 1944; MC 1942; retired as General Officer Commanding 1st Division, Salisbury Plain District (1956-59); *b* 8 April 1906; *m*; one *s* one *d. Educ:* Gresham's Sch., Holt; RMA. 2nd Lieut RA, 1925. Served War of 1939-45 (despatches twice, MC, DSO and Bar, Croix de Guerre); Lt-Col 1942; Brig. 1950. Korea, 1953 (CBE). Regional Dir of Civil Defence, Eastern Region, 1960-68. *Address:* Bear's Farm, Hundon, Sudbury, Suffolk. *T:* Hundon 205. *Club:* Army and Navy.

GREGSON, Peter Lewis; Under Secretary, Department of Trade, since 1977; *b* 28 June 1936; *s* of late Walter Henry Gregson and of Lillian Margaret Gregson. *Educ:* Nottingham High Sch.; Balliol Coll., Oxford. Classical Hon. Mods, class I; Lit. Hum. class I; BA 1959; MA 1962. Nat Service, 1959-61; 2nd Lieut RAEC, attached to Sherwood Foresters. Board of Trade: Asst Principal, 1961; Private Sec. to Minister of State, 1963-65; Principal, 1965; Resident Observer, CS Selection Bd, 1966; London Business Sch., 1967; Private Sec. to the Prime Minister, 1968-72 (Parly Affairs, 1968-70; Econ. and Home Affairs, 1970-72); Asst Sec., DTI, and Sec., Industrial Development Adv. Bd, 1972-74; Under Sec., DoI, and Sec., NEB, 1975-77. *Recreations:* gardening, listening to music. *Address:* 36a Elwill Way, Park Langley, Beckenham, Kent BR3 2RZ. *T:* 01-650 5925.

GREGSON, William Derek Hadfield, CBE 1970; Assistant General Manager, Ferranti (Scotland) Ltd, since 1959, and Director, Ferranti EI, New York; Deputy Chairman, British Airports Authority, since 1975; *b* 27 Jan. 1920; *s* of William Gregson; *m* 1944, Rosalind Helen Reeves; three *s* one *d. Educ:* King William's Coll., IoM; Alpine Coll.; Villars; Faraday House Engrg College. DFH, CEng, FIEE, FBIM. Served with RAF, NW Europe, 1941-45 (Sqdn Ldr); Techn. Sales Man., Ferranti Ltd, Edinburgh, 1946-51; London Man., 1951-59. Chairman: BIM Adv. Bd for Scotland; Scottish Gen. Practitioners Res. Support Unit; Mem. Council: Electronic Engrg Assoc. (Pres. 1963-64); Soc. of British Aerospace Companies (Chm. Equipment Gp Cttee 1967); BEAMA (Chm. Industrial Control and Electronics Bd 1964; Chm., Measurement, Control and

Automation Conference Bd); BIM, 1975-; Member: Electronics EDC, 1965-75; Bd of Livingston New Town, 1968-76; Scottish Council (Develt and Industry); Scottish Council (CBI); Scottish Econ. Planning Council, 1965-71; Machine Tool Expert Cttee, 1969-70; Scottish Design Council; Scottish Telecommunications Bd, 1977-; Director: Edinburgh Chamber of Commerce; Scottish Nat. Orchestra. Comr, Northern Lighthouse Bd. *Recreations:* reading, collecting old silver, cabinet-making, automation in the home. *Address:* 44 Inverleith Place, Edinburgh EH3 5QB. *T:* 031-552 3713. *Club:* Royal Air Force.

GREIG, Henry Louis Carron, CVO 1973; Chairman: H. Clarkson & Co. Ltd, since 1973; H. Clarkson (Holdings) Ltd, since 1976; Director, James Purdey & Sons Ltd, since 1972; Gentleman Usher to the Queen, since 1962; *b* 21 Feb. 1925; *s* of late Group Captain Sir Louis Greig, KBE, CVO, DL; *m* 1955, Monica Kathleen, *d* of Hon. J. J. Stourton, *qv*; three *s* one *d. Educ:* Eton. Scots Guards, 1943-47, Captain. Joined H. Clarkson & Co. Ltd, 1948; Dir, 1954; Man. Dir, 1962. *Address:* Brook House, Fleet, Hants; Binsness, Forres, Moray. *Clubs:* White's; Royal Findhorn Yacht.

GREIG, Prof. James, MSc (London), PhD (Birmingham); William Siemens Professor of Electrical Engineering, University of London, King's College, 1945-70, now Emeritus Professor; *b* 24 April 1903; *s* of James Alexander Greig and Helen Bruce Meldrum, Edinburgh; *m* 1931, Ethel May, *d* of William Archibald, Edinburgh; one *d. Educ:* George Watson's Coll. and Heriot-Watt Coll., Edinburgh; University Coll., University of London. Experience in telephone engineering with Bell Telephone Company, Montreal, 1924-26; Mem. research staff, General Electric Company, London, 1928-33; Asst lectr, University Coll., London, 1933-36; Lectr, Univ. of Birmingham, 1936-39; Head of Dept of Electrical Engineering, Northampton Polytechnic, 1939-45. FIEE (Chm. Measurement Section, 1949-50; Mem. Council, 1955-58); Dean of the Faculty of Engineering, Univ. of London, 1958-62, and Mem. Senate, 1958-70; Mem. Court, Univ. of London, 1967-70. MRI; Fellow Heriot-Watt Coll., 1951; FRSE 1956; FKC 1963. Mem., British Assoc. for the Advancement of Science. Chm., Crail Preservation Soc., 1959-74. *Publications:* papers (dealing mainly with subject of electrical and magnetic measurements) to: Jl Inst. Electrical Engineers, The Wireless Engineer, and Engineering. *Address:* Inch of Kinnordy, Kirriemuir, Angus. *T:* Kirriemuir 2350. *Club:* Athenæum.

GREIG of Eccles, James Dennis, CMG 1967; Director, Population Bureau, Ministry of Overseas Development, since 1976; *b* 1926; *o s* of late Dennis George Greig of Eccles and Florence Aileen Marjoribanks; *m* 1st, 1952, Pamela Marguerite Stock (marr. diss., 1960); one *s* one *d*; 2nd, 1960 (marr. diss., 1967); one *s*; 3rd, 1968, Paula Mary Sterling. *Educ:* Winchester Coll.; Clare Coll., Cambridge; London Sch. of Economics. Military Service (Lieut, The Black Watch, seconded to Nigeria Regt), 1944-47. HMOCS: Administrative Officer, Northern Nigeria, 1949-55; Fedn of Nigeria, 1955-59; Dep. Financial Sec. (Economics), Mauritius, 1960-64; Financial Secretary, Mauritius, 1964-67; retired voluntarily on Mauritius achieving internal self-government, 1967. With Booker Bros. (Liverpool) Ltd, 1967-68; Head of Africa and Bureau, IPPF, 1968-76. *Recreations:* rough shooting, bowls, gardening, bridge. *Address:* 6 Beverley Close, Barnes, SW13. *T:* 01-876 5354; The Braw Bothy, Eccles, Kelso, Roxburghshire. *Club:* Hurlingham.

GREIG, Rear-Adm. Morice Gordon, CB 1963; DSC 1944; Chairman, Public Service Commission, Bermuda, since 1968; *b* 20 March 1914; *s* of late Gordon Eastley Greig, Malayan Civil Service, and late Elsie Challoner Greig (*née* Lake); *m* 1st; two *s* three *d*; 2nd, 1960, Stephanie Margaret; one step *d. Educ:* RNC, Dartmouth. Joined Royal Navy as Cadet, 1927. War of 1939-45: Western Approaches, Mediterranean (HMS Orion) and Combined Ops. Comdr, 1947-52, Admiralty, Staff Course, HMS Vigo, in command; Captain, 1952-61, Admiralty, course at IDC and HMS Girdle Ness, in command; Rear-Adm 1962-65, Chief of Staff and Dep. to Chm., Brit. Defence Staffs, Washington. Dir-Gen., Winston Churchill Memorial Trust, 1965-67. *Recreations:* painting, music, sailing. *Address:* Somerset Bridge, 9-20 Bermuda. *Club:* Army and Navy.

GREIG DUNBAR, Sir John; *see* Dunbar, Sir J. G.

GRENFELL, family name of **Barons Grenfell** and **St Just.**

GRENFELL, 3rd Baron *cr* 1902; **Julian Pascoe Francis St Leger Grenfell;** Special Representative of the World Bank to the United Nations, since 1974; *b* 23 May 1935; *s* of 2nd Baron Grenfell, CBE, TD, and of Elizabeth Sarah Polk, *o d* of late Captain Hon. Alfred Shaughnessy, Montreal, Canada; *S* father,

1976; *m* 1st, 1961, Loretta Maria (marr. diss. 1970), *e d* of Alfredo Reali, Florence, Italy; one *d*; 2nd, 1970, Gabrielle Katharina, *o d* of late Dr Ernst Raab, Berlin, Germany; two *d*. *Educ:* Eton; King's Coll., Cambridge. BA (Hons), President of the Union, Cambridge, 1959. 2 Lieut, KRRC (60th Rifles), 1954-56; Captain, Queen's Royal Rifles, TA, 1963; Programme Asst, ATV Ltd, 1960-61; frequent appearances and occasional scripts, for ATV religious broadcasting and current affairs series, 1960-64. Film and TV adviser, Encyclopaedia Britannica Ltd, 1961-64. Joined World Bank, Washington, DC, 1965; Chief of Information and Public Affairs for World Bank Group in Europe, 1970; Dep. Dir, European Office of the World Bank, 1973. *Recreations:* tennis, wine tasting. *Heir: cousin* Francis Pascoe John Grenfell, *b* 28 Feb. 1938. *Address:* Room 2435, The United Nations, New York, NY 10017, USA. *T:* (212) 754-6008. *Club:* Travellers', Royal Green Jackets.

GRENFELL, Andrée, (Mrs Roy Warden); President, Glemby International, UK and Europe, since 1976; Senior Vice President, Glemby International, USA, since 1976; *b* 14 Jan. 1940; *d* of Stephen Grenfell (writer) and Sybil Grenfell; *m* 1972, Roy Warden; two step *s*. *Educ:* privately. Man. Dir, Elizabeth Arden Ltd, UK, 1974-76; Director: Harvey Nichols Knightsbridge, 1972-74; Peter Robinson Ltd, 1968-72. Mem. Council, Inst. of Dirs, 1976; Fellow, BIM. *Recreations:* riding, dressage, wimming, yoga. *Address:* 45 Iverna Gardens, W8.

GRENFELL, Joyce Irene, OBE 1946; Actress and Writer (all own material, talks, articles, etc.); *b* 10 Feb. 1910; *d* of late Paul Phipps; *m* 1929, Reginald Pascoe Grenfell. *Educ:* Claremont, Esher, Surrey. Radio critic on the Observer 1936-39; Farjeon's Little Revue, 1939-40; Farjeon's Diversion, 1940-41; Farjeon's Light and Shade, 1942. Entertained troops, N Ireland, 1942; Welfare Officer, Can. Red Cross, 1941-43; entertained troops in hosps, Algiers, Malta, Sicily, Italy, Egypt, Trans-Jordania, Palestine, Syria, the Lebanon, Irak, Iran, India in 2 tours, 1944 and 1945. Noel Coward's Sigh No More, 1945-46; Tuppence Coloured, 1947-48; Penny Plain, revue, 1951-52. Films from 1949: Poets Pub, Stage Fright, Run for Your Money, The Happiest Days of Your Life, The Galloping Major, Laughter in Paradise, Pickwick Papers, Genevieve, The Million Pound Note, Forbidden Cargo, Belles of St Trinian's, The Good Companions, Here Comes the Bride, Blue Murder at St Trinian's, The Pure Hell of St Trinian's, The Americanization of Emily; Radio: We Beg to Differ, from Sept. 1949. Toured Canal Zone, entertaining troops, 1953. Joyce Grenfell Requests the Pleasure, Fortune Theatre, 1954, also Bijou Theatre, New York, 1955. Appeared on TV, New York, 1955. During 1956: concert tour, N Rhodesia; TV Series, BBC; TV and 20 concerts, USA; during 1957: tour of solo show; 4-week season, London; during 1958: Recital tour, Canada and USA; 3-week season, New York; during 1959: played 13 weeks solo engagement, Sydney, Australia; during 1960: toured USA, Canada, etc.; Seven Good Reasons, Scala Theatre, London; 6-week concert tour Great Britain; during 1962: solo show, Theatre Royal, Haymarket; 4-week concert tour, Great Britain; during 1963: Festival Performing Arts, TV, New York; concert tour (July-Oct.), Hong Kong, Singapore, Australia, New Zealand; during 1964: Two "Joyce Grenfell" (45 min.) shows for BBC2; concert tours of Switzerland and Canada; played in film The Yellow Rolls-Royce; during 1965: four-week season, Queen's Theatre, London; concert tour, England; two more (50 min.) solo programmes for BBC; during 1966: concert tour of Great Britain (7 weeks); tour of Australia, New Zealand; during 1967: concert tour of Great Britain (7 weeks); tour of Colls and Univs, USA; during 1968: concert tour GB; Solo BBC TV show; during 1969: Concert tour Hong Kong, Australia; solo BBC TV show; during 1970: Spring tour of England (8 weeks); concert tour, USA; Concert tour, GB, 1971; Face the Music, quiz, BBC2, 1971, 1972, 1973, 1974, 1975; four TV solo shows, BBC, 1972. President: Soc. of Women Writers and Journalists, 1957-; Time and Talents Settlement; Mem. Pilkington Cttee on Broadcasting, 1960-62. Council Mem., Winston Churchill Meml Trust, 1972-. Hon. Fellow: Lucy Cavendish Coll., Cambridge; Manchester Polytechnic. *Publications:* (with Sir Hugh Casson) Nanny Says, 1972; Joyce Grenfell Requests the Pleasure (autobiog.), 1976; contributions of light verse to Punch, of poetry to Observer, etc.; further contributions, light articles for various women's magazines. *Recreations:* listening to music; watching birds; finding wild flowers. *Address:* Flat 8, 34 Elm Park Gardens, SW10.

GRENFELL PRICE, Sir Archibald; *see* Price, Sir A. G.

GRENSIDE, John Peter, CBE 1974; Senior Partner, Peat, Marwick, Mitchell & Co., Chartered Accountants (Partner, since 1960); *b* 23 Jan. 1921; *s* of late Harold Cutcliffe Grenside and late Muriel Grenside; *m* 1946, Yvonne Thérèse Grau; one *s*

one *d*. *Educ:* Rugby School. ACA 1948, FCA 1960. War Service, Royal Artillery, 1941-46 (Captain). Joined Peat, Marwick, Mitchell & Co., 1948. Inst. Chartered Accountants: Mem. Council, 1966; Chm. of Parliamentary and Law Cttee, 1972-73; Vice-Pres., 1973-74; Dep. Pres., 1974-75; Pres., 1975-76; Chm., Overseas Relations Cttee, 1975-77; UK Rep. on Internat. Accounting Standards Cttee, Chm., 1976-. Jt Vice-Pres., Groupe d'Etudes des Experts Comptables de la CEE, 1972-75; Mem. Panel of Judges for Accountants' Award for Company Accounts, 1973-77; Trustee, Internat. Centre for Accounting Res., Lancaster Univ. *Publications:* various articles for UK and US accountancy jls. *Recreations:* travel, tennis. *Address:* 51 Cadogan Lane, SW1. *T:* 01-235 3722. *Clubs:* Athenæum, MCC, Queens', Hurlingham.

GRENVILLE; *see* Freeman-Grenville.

GRENVILLE, Prof. John Ashley Soames; Professor of Modern History, University of Birmingham, since 1969; *b* Berlin, 11 Jan. 1928; *m* 1st, 1960, Betty Anne Rosenberg (*d* 1974), New York; three *s*; 2nd, 1975, Patricia Carnie; one step *d*. *Educ:* Mistley Place and Orwell Park Prep. Sch.; Cambridge Techn. Sch.; corresp. courses; Birkbeck Coll.; LSE; Yale Univ. BA, PhD London; FRHistS. Postgrad. Schol., London Univ., 1951-53; Asst Lectr, subseq. Lectr, Nottingham Univ., 1953-64; Commonwealth Fund Fellow, 1958-59; Postdoctoral Fellow, Yale Univ., 1960-63; Reader in Modern History, Nottingham Univ., 1964-65; Vis. Prof., Queen's Coll., NY City Univ., 1964, etc; Prof. of Internat. History, Leeds Univ., 1965-69; Chm., British Univs History Film Consortium, 1968-71; Mem. Council: RHistS, 1971-73; List and Index Soc., 1966-71. Consultant, American and European Bibliographical Centre, Oxford and California and Clio Press, 1960-; Editor, Fontana History of War and Society, 1969-; Dir of Film for the Historical Assoc., 1975-. *Publications:* (with J. G. Fuller) The Coming of the Europeans, 1962; Lord Salisbury and Foreign Policy, 1964 (2nd edn 1970); (with G. B. Young) Politics, Strategy and American Diplomacy: studies in foreign policy 1873-1917, 1966 (2nd edn 1971); Documentary Films (with N. Pronay), The Munich Crisis, 1968; The End of Illusions: from Munich to Dunkirk, 1970; The Major International Treaties 1914-1973: a history and guide, 1974; Europe Reshaped 1848-78, 1975; Nazi Germany, 1976; contrib. various learned jls. *Recreation:* listening to music. *Address:* University of Birmingham, PO Box 363, Birmingham B15 2TT; 42 Selly Wick Road, Birmingham B29 7JA. *T:* 021-472 1273. *Club:* Athenæum.

GRENYER, Herbert Charles; Vice-President, London Rent Assessment Panel, since 1973; Deputy Chief Valuer, Board of Inland Revenue, 1968-73; *b* 22 Jan. 1913; *s* of Harry John Grenyer and Daisy Elizabeth Grenyer (*née* De Maid); *m* 1940, Jean Gladwell Francis; one *s* one *d*. *Educ:* Beckenham Grammar School. FRICS. Joined Valuation Office, 1938; District Valuer, Cardiff, 1948; Suptg Valuer, 1959; Asst Chief Valuer, 1964. *Recreations:* golf, gardening, listening to music. *Address:* Old Rickford, Worplesdon, Surrey. *T:* Worplesdon 2173. *Clubs:* Farnham Golf, Llanishen Golf.

GRESFORD JONES, Rt. Rev. Edward Michael, KCVO 1968; DD (Lambeth), 1950; Hon. Assistant Bishop of Monmouth, since 1970; *b* 21 Oct. 1901; *s* of Rt. Rev. Herbert Gresford Jones; *m* 1933, Lucy, *d* of R. Carr Bosanquet, Rock, Northumberland; three *d*. *Educ:* Rugby; Trinity Coll., Camb. Curate of St Chrysostom's, Victoria Park, Manchester, 1926-28; Chaplain of Trinity College, Cambridge, 1928-33; Vicar of Holy Trinity, South Shore, Blackpool, 1933-39; Rural Dean of the Fylde, 1938-39; Vicar of Hunslet, Leeds, 1939-42; Rector of St Botolph-without-Bishopsgate, 1942-50; Bishop Suffragan of Willesden, 1942-50; Bishop of St Albans, 1950-69; Lord High Almoner, 1953-70. Chairman of C of E Youth Council, 1942-50; Chm. of C of E Moral Welfare Council, 1951-61; Member of Council of Scouts' Assoc., 1955-76. Hon. Freedom of City of St Albans, 1969. *Recreations:* painting, bird watching and fishing. *Address:* Braeside, St Arvans, Chepstow, Gwent NP6 6EZ. *T:* Chepstow 2482.

GRESWELL, Air Cdre Jeaffreson Herbert, CB 1967; CBE 1962 (OBE 1946); DSO 1944; DFC 1942; RAF, retired; *b* 28 July 1916; *s* of William Territt Greswell; *m* 1939, Gwyneth Alice Hayes; one *s* three *d*. *Educ:* Repton. Joined RAF, 1935, Pilot. Served War of 1939-45, in Coastal Command, Anti-Submarine No. 217 Sqdn, 1937-41; No. 172 Sqdn, 1942; OC No. 179 Sqdn, Gibraltar, 1943-44. Air Liaison Officer, Pacific Fleet, 1946-47; Staff of Joint Anti-Submarine Sch., 1949-52; Staff of Flying Coll., Manby, 1952-54; Planning Staff, Min. of Defence, 1954-57; OC, RAF Station Kinloss, 1957-59; Plans HQ, Coastal Comd, 1959-61; Standing Group Rep. to NATO Council, Paris, 1961-64; Commandant, Royal Observer Corps, 1964-68. Sqdn

Ldr 1941; Wing Comdr 1942; Gp Capt. 1955; Air Cdre 1961. *Recreation:* croquet. *Address:* Picket Lodge, Ringwood, Hants.

GRESWELL, Richard Egerton, CMG 1963; MBE 1946; with Department of Transport, Taunton, Somerset; *b* 6 May 1916; *s* of late Ernest Arthur Greswell, Wayvile House, Bicknoller, Taunton, Som., and Grace Lillian (*née* Egerton); *m* 1948, Jean Patricia, *d* of Lieut-Col J. R. Hutchison, DSO; two *s* one *d.* *Educ:* Repton Sch.; Hertford Coll., Oxford (MA). HM's Overseas Civil Service in Northern Nigeria, 1938-63. War Service Royal West African Frontier Force (Artillery), East Africa and Burma Campaigns. Lt-Col, 1939-46. Sir John Hodsoll Award, 1966-67. *Publication:* Civil Defence and the County Council, 1967. *Recreations:* shooting, golf. *Address:* Wayvile House, Bicknoller, Taunton, Somerset. *T:* Stogumber 335. *Clubs:* Royal Commonwealth Society; Somerset County (Taunton).

GRETTON, family name of **Baron Gretton.**

GRETTON, 2nd Baron, *cr* 1944, of Stapleford; **John Frederic Gretton,** OBE 1950; *b* 15 Aug. 1902; *o s* of 1st Baron Gretton, PC, CBE, and Hon. Maud Helen de Moleyns, *y d* of 4th Baron Ventry; *S* father, 1947; *m* 1930, Margaret, *e d* of Capt. H. Loeffler; two *s* two *d.* *Educ:* Eton. MP (C) Burton Div. of Staffs, 1943-45. *Recreations:* yachting, shooting, travelling. *Heir: s* Hon. John Henrik Gretton [*b* 9 Feb. 1941; *m* 1970, Jennifer, *o d* of Edmund Moore, York; one *s* one *d*]. *Address:* Stapleford Park, Melton Mowbray. *T:* Wymondham (Leicestershire) 229; 77 Sussex Square, W2. *Club:* Carlton.

GRETTON, Vice-Adm. Sir Peter (William), KCB 1963 (CB 1960); DSO 1942; OBE 1941; DSC 1936; MA; Senior Research Fellow, University College, Oxford, since 1971; *b* 27 Aug. 1912; *s* of Major G. F. Gretton; *m* 1943, D. N. G. Du Vivier; three *s* one *d.* *Educ:* Roper's Preparatory Sch.; RNC, Dartmouth. Prize for Five First Class Certificates as Sub.-Lieut; Comdr 1942; Capt. 1948; Rear-Adm. 1958; Vice-Adm. 1961. Served War of 1939-45 (despatches, OBE, DSO and two Bars). Senior Naval Mem. of Directing Staff of Imperial Defence Coll., April 1958-60; Flag Officer, Sea Training, 1960-61; a Lord Commissioner of the Admiralty, Dep. Chief of Naval Staff and Fifth Sea Lord, 1962-63, retd. Domestic Bursar, University Coll., Oxford, 1965-71. Vice-Pres., Royal Humane Soc.; Testimonial of Royal Humane Society, 1940. *Publications:* Convoy Escort Commander, 1964; Maritime Strategy: A Study of British Defence Problems, 1965; Former Naval Person: Churchill and the Navy, 1968; Crisis Convoy, 1974. *Address:* 29 Northmoor Road, Oxford. *Club:* Army and Navy.

GREVE, Prof. John; Professor of Social Policy and Administration, University of Leeds, since 1974; *b* 23 Nov. 1927; *s* of Steffen A. and Ellen C. Greve; *m* Stella (*née* Honeywood); one *s* one *d.* *Educ:* elementary and secondary Schs in Cardiff; London Sch. of Economics (BSc(Econ)). Various jobs, incl. Merchant Navy, Youth Employment Service, and insurance, 1946-55; student, 1955-58; research work, then Univ. teaching, 1958-. Has worked in Norway at research institutes. Community Programmes Dept, Home Office, 1969-74; Prof. of Social Admin, Univ. of Southampton, 1969-74. Mem., Royal Commn on Distribution of Income and Wealth, 1974-. *Publications:* The Housing Problem, 1961 (and 1969); London's Homeless, 1964; Private Landlords in England, 1965; (with others) Comparative Social Administration, 1969, 2nd edn 1972; (with others) Housing, Planning and Change in Norway, 1970; (with others) Voluntary Housing in Scandinavia, 1971; (with others) Homelessness in London, 1971; various articles and papers, mainly on social problems, policies and administration, a few short stories. *Recreations:* walking, painting, listening to music, writing, good company. *Address:* c/o Department of Social Policy and Administration, University of Leeds, Leeds LS2 9JT.

GREVILLE, family name of **Baron Greville,** and of **Earl of Warwick.**

GREVILLE, 4th Baron, *cr* 1869; **Ronald Charles Fulke Greville;** *b* 11 April 1912; *s* of 3rd Baron and Olive Grace (*d* 1959), *d* of J. W. Grace, Leybourne Grange, Kent, and *widow* of Henry Kerr; *S* father 1952. *Educ:* Eton; Magdalen Coll., Oxford Univ. *Recreations:* music, travel, sport. *Heir:* none. *Address:* 75 Swan Court, Chelsea Manor Street, SW3; Cubberley, Ross-on-Wye, Herefordshire. *Clubs:* Bath; Hurlingham.

GREVILLE, Brig. Phillip Jamieson, CBE 1972; Commander, Fourth Military District, since 1977; *b* 12 Sept. 1925; *s* of Col S. J. Greville, OBE and Mrs D. M. Greville; *m* 1948, June Patricia Anne Martin; two *s* one *d* (and one *s* one *d* decd). *Educ:* RMC Duntroon; Sydney Univ. (BEng). 2/8 Field Co., 2nd AIF, New

Guinea, 1945; 1 RAR Korea (POW), 1951-53; Senior Instructor SME Casula, 1953-55; CRE, RMC Duntroon, 1955-58; Staff Coll., Camberley and Transportation Trng UK, 1959-61; Dir of Transportation AHQ, 1962-65; GSO1 1st Div., 1966; CE Eastern Comd, 1969-71; Comdr 1st Australian Logistic Support Group, Vietnam, 1971; Actg Comdr 1st Australian Task Force, Vietnam, 1971-72 (CBE); Dir of Transport, 1973-74; Dir Gen., Logistics, 1975-76. FCIT. *Publications:* A Short History of Victoria Barracks Paddington, 1969; The Central Organisation for War and its Application to Movements, Sapper series (RE Officers in Australia). *Recreation:* golf. *Address:* Flagstaff House, Keswick Barracks, SA 5035, Australia. *Club:* Royal Sydney Golf.

GREY, family name of **Earl Grey,** and of **Baron Grey of Naunton.**

GREY; see De Grey.

GREY, 6th Earl, *cr* 1806; **Richard Fleming George Charles Grey;** Bt 1746; Baron Grey, 1801; Viscount Howick, 1806; *b* 5 March 1939; *s* of late Albert Harry George Campbell Grey (Trooper, Canadian Army Tanks, who *d* on active service, 1942) and Vera Helen Louise Harding; *S* cousin, 1963; *m* 1st, 1966, Margaret Ann (marr. diss. 1974), *e d* of Henry Bradford, Ashburton; 2nd, 1974, Stephanie Caroline, *o d* of Donald Gaskell-Brown and formerly wife of Surg.-Comdr Neil Leicester Denham, RN. *Educ:* Hounslow Coll.; Hammersmith Coll. of Bldg (Quantity Surveying). Mem. Young Conservatives. *Recreations:* golf, sailing. *Heir: b* Philip Kent Grey [*b* 11 May 1940; *m* 1968, Ann Catherine, *y d* of Cecil Applegate, Kingsbridge, Devon; one *s*]. *Address:* 40 Compton Avenue, Mannamead, Plymouth, S Devon.

GREY OF NAUNTON, Baron, *cr* 1968 (Life Peer); **Ralph Francis Alnwick Grey,** GCMG 1964 (KCMG 1959, CMG 1955); GCVO 1973 (KCVO 1956); OBE 1951; Deputy Chairman, Commonwealth Development Corporation, since 1973; *b* 15 April 1910; *o s* of late Francis Arthur Grey and Mary Wilkie Grey (*née* Spence); *m* 1944, Esmé, CStJ, *widow* of Pilot Officer Kenneth Kirkcaldie, RAFVR, and *d* of late A. V. Burcher and Florence Burcher, Remuera, Auckland, New Zealand; two *s* one *d.* *Educ:* Wellington Coll., NZ; Auckland Univ. Coll.; Pembroke Coll., Cambridge. LLB (NZ). Barrister and Solicitor of Supreme Court of New Zealand, 1932; Associate to Hon. Mr Justice Smith, 1932-36; Probationer, Colonial Administrative Service, 1936; Administrative Service, Nigeria: Cadet, 1937; Asst Financial Sec., 1949; Administrative Officer, Class I, 1951; Development Sec., 1952; Sec. to Governor-Gen. and Council of Ministers, 1954; Chief Sec. of the Federation, 1955-57; Dep. Gov.-Gen., 1957-59; Gov. and C-in-C, British Guiana, 1959-64; Governor and C-in-C of The Bahamas, 1964-68, and of the Turks and Caicos Islands, 1965-68; Governor of N Ireland, 1968-73. Pres., Chartered Inst. of Secretaries, NI, 1970-. Mem., Bristol Regional Bd, Lloyds Bank Ltd, 1973-; Chm., Central Council, Royal Over-Seas League, 1976-. Mem. Council, Cheltenham Ladies' College. Hon. Bencher, Inn of Court of N Ireland. Hon. Freeman: City of Belfast, 1972; Lisburn, 1975. Hon. LLD QUB, 1971. GCStJ; Kt Comdr, Commandery of Ards, 1968-76. Bailiff of Egle. *Recreation:* golf. *Address:* Overbrook, Naunton, near Cheltenham, Glos. *T:* Guiting Power 263. *Clubs:* Travellers'; Ulster (Hon.).

GREY, Sir Anthony (Dysart), 7th Bt *cr* 1814; *b* 19 Oct. 1949; *s* of Edward Elton Grey (*d* 1962) (*o s* of 6th Bt) and of Nancy, *d* of late Francis John Meagher, Perth, WA; *S* grandfather, 1974; *m* 1970, Donna Daniels, museum curator. *Educ:* Guildford Grammar School, WA. *Recreations:* fishing, painting. *Address:* Van Riper Hopper House, 533 Berdan Avenue, Wayne, New Jersey 07470, USA. *T:* 201 6948169. *Club:* English-Speaking Union.

GREY, Beryl, (Mrs S. G. Svenson), CBE 1973; Prima Ballerina, Sadler's Wells Ballet, now Royal Ballet, 1942-57; Artistic Director, London Festival Ballet, since 1968; *b* London, 11 June 1927; *d* of Arthur Ernest Groom; *m* 1950, Dr Sven Gustav Svenson; one *s.* *Educ:* Dame Alice Owens Girls' Sch., London. Professional training: Madeline Sharp Sch., Sadler's Wells Sch. (Schol.), de Vos Sch. Début Sadler's Wells Co., 1941, with Ballerina rôles following same year in Les Sylphides, The Gods Go A'Begging, Le Lac des Cygnes, Act II, Comus. First full-length ballet, Le Lac des Cygnes on 15th birthday, 1942. Has appeared since in leading rôles of many ballets including: Sleeping Beauty, Giselle, Sylvia, Checkmate, Ballet Imperial, Donald of the Burthens, Homage, Birthday Offering, The Lady and the Fool. Film: The Black Swan (3 Dimensional Ballet Film), 1952. Left Royal Ballet, Covent Garden (as permanent Mem.) Spring 1957, to become free-lance ballerina. Regular guest appearances with Royal Ballet at Covent Garden and on

Continental, African, American and Far Eastern Tours. Guest Artist, London's Festival Ballet in London and abroad, 1958-64. First Western ballerina to appear with Bolshoi Ballet: Moscow, Leningrad, Kiev, Tiflis, 1957-58; First Western ballerina to dance with Chinese Ballet Co. in Peking and Shanghai, 1964. Engagements and tours abroad include: Central and S America, Mexico, Rhodesia and S Africa, Canada, NZ, Lebanon, Germany, Norway, Sweden, Denmark, Finland, Belgium, Holland, France, Switzerland, Italy, Portugal, Austria, Czechoslovakia, Poland, Rumania. Regular television and broadcasts in England and abroad. Dir-Gen., Arts Educational Trust, 1966-68; Governor: Dame Alice Owens Girls' Sch., London; Frances Mary Buss Foundn. Hon. DMus Leicester, 1970; Hon. DLitt City Univ., 1974. *Publications:* Red Curtain Up, 1958; Through the Bamboo Curtain, 1965. *Relevant publications:* biographical studies (by Gordon Anthony), 1952, (by Pigeon Crowle), 1952; Beryl Grey, Dancers of Today (by Hugh Fisher), 1955; Beryl Grey, a biography (by David Gillard), 1977. *Recreations:* music, painting, reading, swimming. *Address:* 78 Park Street, W1Y 3HP. *T:* 01-629 0477.

GREY, Charles Frederick, CBE 1966; miner; Independent Methodist Minister; *b* 25 March 1903; *m* 1925, Margaret, *d* of James Aspey. Mem. of Divisional Labour Exec. MP (Lab) Durham, 1945-70; Opposition Whip (Northern), 1962-64; Comptroller of HM Household, 1964-66, Treasurer, 1966-69. President: Independent Methodist Connexion, 1971; Sunderland and District Free Church Council; Mem., Univ. of Durham Council. Freeman of Durham City, 1971. Hon. DCL Durham, 1976. *Address:* 1A Moor House Gardens, Hetton-le-Hole, Tyne and Wear DH5 0AD. *T:* Hetton-le-Hole 2292.

GREY, Col Geoffrey Bridgman, CB 1977; CBE 1960; TD; DL; JP; Partner, Messrs D. G. Dawkins & Grey, Solicitors, Birmingham, since 1946; *b* 19 Oct. 1911; *s* of Alderman Samuel John Grey (formerly Lord Mayor of Birmingham) and Mrs Jessie Grey; *m* 1939, Betty Frances Mary (née Trimingham); two *d*. *Educ:* Mill Hill Sch., London; Brasenose Coll., Oxford Univ. (MA, BCL). Admitted solicitor, 1937. Commnd TA, S Staffs Regt, 1938; served War, 1939-45: European campaign with S Staffs, and York and Lancaster Regts; mentioned in despatches; Major 1943; TA, 1945-: Lt-Col 1950, Col 1954; comd 5th Bn S Staffs Regt, 1950-53; Hon. Colonel: 5th Bn S Staffs Regt, 1957-67; 5/6 (Territorial) Bn Staffs Regt (Prince of Wales), 1967-69; 5th Staffs Cadet Regt, 1963-; ADC, 1963-66; Chm., W Midland TA&VRA. Chm., Hazlemere Charity; Hon. Legal Adviser, W Midlands Baptist (Trust) Assoc. Pres., Birmingham Consular Assoc., 1965-67 (Vice-Pres., 1963-65); Hon. Consul for the Netherlands, 1959-; Vice-Consul for Belgium, 1965-. DL Staffs, 1954. Officer, Order of Orange Nassau, 1975. *Recreation:* photography. *Address:* 215 Bristol Road, Edgbaston, Birmingham B5 7UB. *T:* 021-440 3080. *Clubs:* Naval and Military; Edgbaston Priory (Birmingham).

GREY, John Egerton; Clerk Assistant and Clerk of Public Bills, House of Lords, since 1974; *b* 8 Feb. 1929; *s* of John Grey; *m* 1961, Patricia Hanna; two adopted *s*. *Educ:* Dragon Sch., Oxford; Blundell's; Brasenose Coll. Oxford. MA, BCL. Called to Bar, Inner Temple, 1954; practised at Chancery Bar, 1954-59. Clerk in Parliament Office, House of Lords, 1959; Clerk in Judicial Office, 1959-64; Chief Clerk, Public Bill Office, 1964-71; Chief Clerk, Cttees, 1971-74; Reading Clerk, June-Aug. 1974. *Recreation:* gardening. *Address:* 43 Half Moon Lane, SE24. *T:* 01-274 0468. *Club:* Arts.

GREY, Sir Paul (Francis), KCMG 1963 (CMG 1951); *b* 2 Dec. 1908; *s* of Lt-Col Arthur Grey, CIE, and Teresa (née Alleyne); *m* 1936, Agnes Mary, *d* of late Richard Weld-Blundell, Ince-Blundell Hall, Lancs; three *s*. *Educ:* Charterhouse; Christ Church, Oxford. Entered Diplomatic Service, 1933; served in Rome, 1935; Foreign Office, 1939; Rio de Janeiro, 1944; The Hague, 1945; Counsellor, Lisbon, 1949; Minister, British Embassy, Moscow, 1951-54; Assistant Under Sec., Foreign Office, Sept. 1954-57; HM Ambassador to Czechoslovakia, 1957-60; HM Ambassador to Switzerland, 1960-64. *Recreations:* shooting and fishing. *Address:* Hill House, Farley, Westerham, Kent.

GREY, Rex Burton; Director, Standard Telephones & Cables Ltd (Chairman, 1965-68); *b* El Paso, Texas, 27 Oct. 1920; *s* of Rex Grey and Georgie Mary (née Ferris); *m* 1942, Natalie C. Tandy; one *s*. *Educ:* Texas A and M Univ.; University of Houston; Harvard Univ. Gen. Electric, 1944-55; Texas Apparatus Co. (Pres. and owner), 1955-58; Manager, Controls and Automation Div., Dresser Industries, 1958-61; Man. Dir, Standard Telephones & Cables Ltd, 1961-65. Chairman: STC (South Africa); Supersonic (South Africa); Supersonic (Rhodesia); Supersonic (Zambia); ITT (Zambia); ITT (Maroc); Standard

Elec. (Iran); Standard Elec. (Turkey); SACT (Algeria); ITT (Nigeria); Creed & Co. Ltd; Pres., ITT Africa and Middle East; Vice-President: Internat. Telephone and Telegraph Corp.; ITT Europe; ITT Industries Europe; Director: Standard Telecommunication Labs; Commercial Cable Co. Ltd; Internat. Marine Radio Co. Ltd; Kolster-Brandes Ltd; Stanelco Industrial Services Ltd; Abbey Life Assurance Co. Ltd. *Recreations:* collecting antique guns, golf, hunting. *Address:* 10 Park Crescent, W1. *T:* 01-580 8266; 190 Strand, WC2.

GREY EGERTON, Sir (Philip) John (Caledon), 15th Bt, *cr* 1617; *b* 19 Oct. 1920; *er s* of Sir Philip Grey Egerton, 14th Bt; *S* father, 1962; *m* 1952, Margaret Voase (*d* 1971) (who *m* 1941, Sqdn Ldr Robert A. Ullman, *d* 1943), *er d* of late Rowland Rank. *Educ:* Eton. Served Welsh Guards, 1939-45. *Recreation:* fishing. *Heir:* *b* Brian Balguy Le Belward Egerton, *b* 5 Feb. 1925. *Address:* Little Oulton, Tarporley, Cheshire. *T:* Little Budworth 324. *Club:* Marylebone Cricket (MCC).

GREY-TURNER, Dr Elston, MC 1944; TD 1955; Secretary, British Medical Association, since 1976; *b* 16 Aug. 1916; *s* of late Prof. George Grey Turner, LLD, DCh, MS, FRCS, FRCSEd, FRACS, and late Alice Grey Schofield, BSc; *m* 1952, Lilias, *d* of late Col Sterling Charles Tomlinson, Hereford; two *s* one *d*. *Educ:* Winchester Coll.; Trinity Coll., Cambridge; St Bartholomew's Hosp. BA 1938, MA 1942, Cantab; MRCS, LRCP 1942. Ho. Surg., St Bart's Hosp., 1942. Served War in RAMC (N Af., Italy, Germany), 1942-46. Ho. Phys., Addenbrooke's Hosp., 1946; Asst Principal, Min. of Health, 1947-48; Jt Sec., Interdeptl Cttee on Rating of Site Values (Simes Cttee), 1948; Asst Sec., BMA, 1948, Under-Sec. 1960, Dep. Sec. 1964. Sec., Jt Emergency Cttee of the Professions, 1952; Local Sec., Gen. Assembly of World Med. Assoc., 1949; first World Conf. on Med. Educn, 1953; 19th World Med. Assembly, 1965; Sec.-Gen., Standing Cttee of Doctors of the EEC, 1976. Freeman, City of London, 1946; Lt-Col RAMC (TA), 1956; Col RAMC (TA), 1958; QHP, 1960-62; Carmichael Lectr, Royal Coll. of Surgeons in Ireland, 1971; Crookshank Lectr, Faculty of Radiologists, 1973. Mem., Court of Assistants, Soc. of Apothecaries of London, 1965- (Master, 1975-76); Hon. Col, 257 (Southern) Gen. Hosp., RAMC(V), 1973-. Dir, Provident Assoc. for Medical Care Ltd, 1976-; Mem. Council, Medical Insurance Agency Ltd, 1977-. Silver Jubilee Medal, 1977. OStJ 1961. *Publications:* articles in British and foreign med. jls. *Recreation:* gardener-handyman. *Address:* BMA House, Tavistock Square, WC1H 9JP. *T:* 01-387 4499; The Manor House, Petersham, Surrey TW10 7AG. *Club:* Carlton.

GRIBBLE, Rev. Canon Arthur Stanley, MA; Canon Residentiary and Chancellor of Peterborough Cathedral since 1967; *b* 18 Aug. 1904; *er s* of J. B. Gribble; *m* 1938, Edith Anne, *er d* of late Laurence Bailey; one *s*. *Educ:* Queens' Coll. and Westcott House, Cambridge (Burney Student); University of Heidelberg. Curate: St Mary, Windermere, 1930-33, Almondbury, 1933-36; Chaplain Sarum Theological Coll., 1936-38; Rector of Shepton Mallet, 1938-54. Examining Chaplain to Bp of Bath and Wells, 1947-54; Proctor in Convocation, diocese Bath and Wells, 1947-54; Rural Dean of Shepton Mallet, 1949-54; Prebendary of Wiveliscombe in Wells Cathedral, 1949-54; Principal, Queen's Coll., Birmingham, 1954-67; Recognised Lectr, Univ. of Birmingham, 1954-67. Hon. Canon, Birmingham Cathedral, 1954-67. Commissary for the Bishop of Kimberley and Kuruman, 1964-66. Examng Chaplain to Bishop of Peterborough, 1968-. Visiting Lectr, Graduate Theological Union, Berkeley, USA, 1970. *Recreation:* mountaineering. *Address:* Prebendal House, Minster Precincts, Peterborough. *T:* Peterborough 69441.

GRIBBLE, Leonard Reginald; Author; *b* 1 Feb. 1908; *s* of late Wilfred Browning Gribble and late Ada Mary Sterry; *m* 1932, Nancy Mason; one *d*. In 1928 wrote first detective story; literary adviser various London publishers; inaugurated The Empire Bookshelf series for the BBC; judge in two international novel competitions; has devised and written commercial radio programmes and commercial films; founder mem. Paternosters Club; in Press and Censorship Div. of Ministry of Information, 1940-45; co-founder Crime Writers Assoc., 1953. *Publications:* The Gillespie Suicide Mystery, A Christmas Treasury, 1929; The Jesus of the Poets, The Grand Modena Murder, 1930; Is This Revenge?, 1931; The Stolen Home Secretary, 1932; Famous Feats of Detection and Deduction, The Secret of Tangles, 1933; The Riddle of the Ravens, 1934; All The Year Round Stories (with Nancy Gribble), 1935; Riley of the Special Branch, The Case of the Malverne Diamonds, 1936; The Case-book of Anthony Slade, 1937; Tragedy in E flat, 1938; The Arsenal Stadium Mystery (filmed), 1939 and 1950; Heroes of the Fighting RAF, 1941; Death by Design (a film), 1942; Epics of the Fighting RAF, 1943; Heroes of the Merchant Navy, 1944;

Toy Folk and Nursery People (verse), 1945; Best Children's Stories of the Year (editor), 1946-50; Profiles from notable Modern Biographies (editor); Atomic Murder, 1947; Hangman's Moon, 1949; They Kidnapped Stanley Matthews, 1950; The Frightened Chameleon, 1951; Murder Out of Season, 1952; Famous Manhunts, 1953; Adventures in Murder, 1954; Triumphs of Scotland Yard, 1955; Death Pays the Piper, 1956; Famous Judges and their Trials, 1957; Great Detective Exploits, 1958; Don't Argue with Death, 1959; Hands of Terror, 1960; Clues that Spelled Guilty, 1961; When Killers Err, 1962; They Challenged the Yard, 1963; Heads You Die, 1964; Such Women are Deadly, 1965; Great Manhunters of the Yard, 1966; Strip Tease Macabre, 1967; Stories of Famous Conspirators, 1968; Famous Stories of Scientific Detection, 1969; Strange Crimes of Passion, 1970; They Got Away with Murder, 1971; Sisters of Cain, 1972; Programmed for Death, 1973; Such was Their Guilt, 1974; They Conspired to Kill, 1975; You Can't Die Tomorrow, 1976; Compelled to Kill, 1977; also writes fiction (some filmed) under several pseudonyms; translations in fourteen languages; contribs to Chambers's Encyclopædia, Encyclopedia Americana, DNB; book-reviews, feature articles, short stories and serials to various publications. *Recreations:* motoring abroad, watching things grow. *Address:* Chandons, Firsdown Close, High Salvington, Worthing, West Sussex. *T:* Worthing 61976.

GRIBBON, Maj.-Gen. Nigel St George, OBE 1960; Manging Director, Sallingbury Ltd, since 1977; Director, Gatewood Engines Ltd, since 1976; *b* Feb. 1917; *s* of late Brig. W. H. Gribbon, CMG, CBE; *m* 1943, Rowan Mary MacLeish; two *s* one *d. Educ:* Rugby Sch.; Sandhurst. King's Own, 1937-42; GSO3 10th Indian Div., 1942; Staff Coll. Quetta, 1943; Bde Major, 1st Parachute Bde, 1946; RAF Staff Coll., 1947; OC 5 King's Own, 1958-60; AMS WO, 1960-62; Comdr 161 Bde, 1963-65; Canadian Nat. Defence Coll., 1965-66; DMC MoD, 1966-67; ACOS NORTHAG, 1967-69; ACOS (Intelligence), SHAPE, 1970-72. Man. Dir, Partnerplan Public Affairs Ltd, 1973-75; Chm., Sallingbury Ltd, 1975-77. Member Council: British Atlantic Cttee; Canada-UK Chamber of Commerce; Wyndham Place Trust. Rear Commodore (Training) Little Ship Club; Member: Royal Yachting Assoc.; Army Sailing Assoc.; European Atlantic Gp. *Recreation:* sailing. *Address:* The Pump Cottage, Orford, Suffolk. *T:* Orford 413. *Clubs:* Army and Navy; Little Ship.

GRIDLEY, family name of **Baron Gridley.**

GRIDLEY, 2nd Baron, *cr* 1955; **Arnold Hudson Gridley;** *b* 26 May 1906; *er surv s* of 1st Baron Gridley, KBE, Culwood, Lye Green, Chesham, Bucks; *S* father, 1965; *m* 1948, Edna Lesley, *d* of late Richard Wheen of Shanghai, China; one *s* three *d. Educ:* Oundle. Overseas Civil Service, 1928-57: served in various Government Depts in Malaya; interned by Japanese in Changi Gaol, 1941-45; Dep.-Comptroller of Customs and Excise, Malaya, 1956. Chm., Centralised Audio Systems Ltd, 1968-. Mem. Council, HM Overseas Service Pensioners Assoc., 1966-; Govt Trustee, Far East (POW and Internee) Fund, 1973-; Mem., Somerset CC Rating Appeals Tribunal, 1966-; Governor, Hall Sch., Bratton Seymour, Som, 1970-. *Heir:* s Hon. Richard David Arnold Gridley, *b* 22 Aug. 1956. *Address:* Coneygore, Stoke Trister, Wincanton, Somerset. *T:* Wincanton 32209. *Club:* Royal Over-Seas League.

GRIER, Anthony MacGregor, CMG 1963; General Manager, Redditch Development Corporation, 1964-76; Member (C), Hereford and Worcester County Council, since 1977; *b* 12 April 1911; *e s* of late Very Rev. R. M. Grier, St Ninian's House, Perth, Scotland, and late Mrs E. M. Grier; *m* 1946, Hon. Patricia Mary Spens, *er d* of 1st Baron Spens, PC, KBE, QC; two *s* one *d. Educ:* St Edward's Sch.; Exeter Coll., Oxford. Colonial Administrative Service, Sierra Leone, 1935; attached to Colonial Office in London and Delhi, 1943-47; appointed to North Borneo, 1947; Development Sec., 1953; Under-Sec., 1956; Resident, Sandakan, 1963; retired, 1964. Chm., Sabah Electricity Board, 1956-64. Chm. of Governors, King's School, Worcester, 1976-. *Recreations:* tennis, golf, shooting. *Address:* Mulberry House, Abbots Morton, Worcester WR7 4NA. *T:* Inkberrow 792422. *Club:* East India, Devonshire, Sports and Public Schools.

See also *P . A . Grier*.

GRIER, Patrick Arthur, OBE 1963; HM Diplomatic Service; Counsellor and Head of Chancery, Berne, since 1974; *b* 2 Dec. 1918; *s* of late Very Rev. R. M. Grier, Provost of St Ninian's Cath., Perth, and Mrs E. M. Grier; *m* 1946, Anna Fraembs, *y d* of Hüttendirektor H. Fraembs, Rasselstein, Neuwied, Germany; one *d. Educ:* Lancing; King's Coll., Cambridge (MA 1946). Served War of 1939-45 with RA and Indian Mountain Artillery,

NW Frontier of India and Burma (Major). Kreis Resident Officer of Mönchen-Gladbach, 1946-47; Colonial Administrative Service, N Nigeria, 1947, later HMOCS; Clerk to Exec. Council, Kaduna, 1953-55; W African Inter-territorial Secretariat, Accra, 1955-57; Principal Asst Sec. to Governor of N Nigeria, 1957-59; Dep. Sec. to Premier, 1959-63; retired from HMOCS, 1963. CRO, 1963-64; First Sec., Canberra, 1964-66; Head of Chancery, Port of Spain, 1966-69; Dep. UK Permanent Rep. to Council of Europe, Strasbourg, 1969-74; Counsellor 1973. *Recreations:* tennis, ski-ing. *Address:* c/o Foreign and Commonwealth Office, SW1. *Clubs:* Junior Carlton, Royal Commonwealth Society; Ski Club of Great Britain.

See also *A . M . Grier*.

GRIERSON, Prof. Philip, MA, LittD; FBA 1958; FSA; Fellow, since 1935, Librarian, 1944-69, and President, 1966-76, Gonville and Caius College, Cambridge; Professor of Numismatics, University of Cambridge, since 1971 (Reader 1959-71); Professor of Numismatics and the History of Coinage, University of Brussels, since 1948; Hon. Keeper of the Coins, Fitzwilliam Museum, Cambridge, since 1949; Adviser in Byzantine Numismatics to the Dumbarton Oaks Library and Collections, Harvard University, at Washington, USA, since 1955; *b* 15 Nov. 1910; *s* of Philip Henry Grierson and Roberta Ellen Jane Pope. *Educ:* Marlborough Coll.; Gonville and Caius Coll., Cambridge (MA 1936, LittD 1971). University Lectr in History, Cambridge, 1945-59; Literary Dir of Royal Historical Society, 1945-55; Ford's Lectr in History, University of Oxford, 1956-57. Pres. Royal Numismatic Society, 1961-66. Corresp. Fellow, Mediaeval Acad. of America, 1972; Corresp. Mem., Koninklijke Vlaamse Acad., 1955; Assoc. Mem., Acad. Royale de Belgique, 1968. Hon. LittD (University of Ghent), 1958. *Publications:* Les Annales de Saint-Pierre de Gand, 1937; Books on Soviet Russia, 1917-42, 1943; Sylloge of Coins of the British Isles, Vol. I (Fitzwilliam Museum: Early British and Anglo-Saxon Coins), 1958; Bibliographie numismatique, 1966; English Linear Measures: a study in origins, 1973; (with A. R. Bellinger) Catalogue of the Byzantine Coins in the Dumbarton Oaks Collection and in the Whittemore Collection, vols 1, 2, 3, 1966-73; Numismatics, 1975; Monnaies du Moyen Age, 1976; The Origins of Money, 1977; Les monnaies, 1977; trans. F. L. Ganshof, Feudalism, 1952; editor: C. W. Previté-Orton, The Shorter Cambridge Medieval History, 1952; H. E. Ives, The Venetian Gold Ducat and its Imitations, 1954; Studies in Italian History presented to Miss E. M. Jamison, 1956. *Recreations:* squash racquets, science fiction. *Address:* Gonville and Caius College, Cambridge. *T:* Cambridge 312211.

GRIERSON, Sir Richard Douglas, 11th Bt *cr* 1685; *b* 25 June 1912; *o s* of Sir Robert Gilbert White Grierson, 10th Bt, and Hilda (*d* 1962), *d* of James Stewart, Surbiton, Surrey; *S* father 1957; unmarried. *Educ:* Imperial Service Coll., Windsor. Journalist. *Heir: cousin* Michael John Bewes Grierson [*b* 24 July 1921; *m* 1971, Valerie Anne, *d* of Russell Wright]. *Address:* 4 Modena Road, Hove BN3 5QG. *T:* Brighton 736355.

GRIERSON, Ronald Hugh; Director, General Electric Co., since 1968; *b* Nürnberg, Bavaria, 1921; *s* of E. J. Griessmann (name changed by Deed Poll in 1943); *m* 1966, Elizabeth Heather, Viscountess Bearsted, *er d* of Mrs G. Firmston-Williams; one *s. Educ:* Lycée Pasteur, Paris; Highgate Sch., London; Balliol Coll., Oxford. Served War 1939-45 (despatches). Staff Mem., The Economist, 1947-48; S. G. Warburg & Co., 1948-68 (Exec. Dir, 1958-68); Dep. Chm. and Man. Dir, IRC, 1966-67; Chm., Orion Bank, 1971-73; Dir-Gen., Industrial and Technological Affairs, EEC, 1973-74. Member of Council: CNAA; Betteshanger Sch.; RIIA; Chairman: Philharmonia Trust; EORTC Foundation. *Address:* General Electric Company, 1 Stanhope Gate, W1.

GRIEVE, Hon. Lord; William Robertson Grieve, VRD 1958; a Senator of the College of Justice in Scotland, since 1972; *b* 21 Oct. 1917; *o s* of late William Robertson Grieve (killed in action 1917) and of Mrs Grieve, Edinburgh; *m* 1947, Lorna St John, *y d* of late Engineer Rear-Adm. E. P. St J. Benn, CB; one *s* one *d. Educ:* Glasgow Academy; Sedbergh; Glasgow Univ. MA 1939, LLB 1946 (Glasgow); Pres. Glasgow Univ. Union, 1938-39. John Clark (Mile-end) Scholar, 1939. RNVR: Sub-Lt 1939; Lieut 1942; Lt-Comdr 1950; served with RN, 1939-46. Admitted Mem. of Faculty of Advocates, 1947; QC (Scot.) 1957. Junior Counsel in Scotland to Bd of Inland Revenue, 1952-57. Advocate-Depute (Home), 1962-64; Sheriff-Principal of Renfrew and Argyll, 1964-72; Procurator of the Church of Scotland, 1969-72; a Judge of the Courts of Appeal of Jersey and Guernsey, 1971. *Recreations:* golf, painting. *Address:* 20 Belgrave Crescent, Edinburgh EH4 3AJ. *T:* 031-332 7500. *Clubs:* New (Edinburgh); Hon. Company of Edinburgh Golfers.

GRIEVE, Christopher Murray, JP, Angus; (writes under pseudonym of Hugh McDiarmid); author and journalist; *b* Langholm, Dumfriesshire, 11 Aug. 1892; *m* 1st, Margaret Skinner; one *s* one *d*; 2nd, Valda Trevlyn; one *s. Educ:* Langholm Academy; Edinburgh Univ. One of the Founders of the Scottish Nationalist Party; Founder of Scottish Centre of PEN Club; regular contributor on literary, political, and general matters to many British and foreign newspapers and periodicals. Pres., Poetry Soc., 1976. Hon. Fellow, Modern Language Assoc. of America; Prof. of Literature to Royal Scottish Academy, 1974. Hon. LLD Edinburgh, 1957; Hon. RSA. *Publications:* Prose: Annals of the Five Senses, 1923; Contemporary Scottish Studies, 1926; Albyn, or the Future of Scotland, 1927; The Present Condition of Scottish Arts and Affairs, 1927; The Handmaid of the Lord (a novel, from the Spanish of Ramón Maria de Tenreiro), 1930; Scottish Scene, 1934; At the Sign of the Thistle, 1934; Scottish Eccentrics, 1936; The Scottish Islands, 1939; Lucky Poet (autobiography), 1943, repr. 1972; Poetry: Sangschaw, 1925; Penny Wheep, 1926; A Drunk Man looks at the Thistle, 1926; To Circumjack Cencrastus, 1930; Stony Limits and other poems, 1932; First Hymn to Lenin and other Poems, 1931; Second Hymn to Lenin and other Poems, 1935; The Birlinn of Clanranald (from the Scots Gaelic of Alexander MacDonald), 1935; Direadh, 1939; Golden Treasury of Scottish Poetry, 1940; Cornish Heroic Song for Valda Trevlyn, 1943; Speaking for Scotland (pub. USA only), 1946; A Kist of Whistles, 1952; R. B. Cunninghame Graham, a Centenary Study, 1955; In Memoriam James Joyce, 1957; The Battle Continues; Three Hymns to Lenin, 1957; Burns today and tomorrow, 1959; The Kind of Poetry I Want, 1961; Collected Poems (1920-61), 1962; The Company I've Kept; A Lap of Honour; Celtic Nationalism; The Uncanny Scot; A Clyack Sheaf; More Collected Poems, etc. Trans. The Threepenny Opera, Prince of Wales, 1972; Direadh, 1, 2, 3, 1974; Hugh MacDiarmid Anthology, 1974. *Recreation:* Anglophobia. *Address:* The Cottage, Brownsbank, by Biggar, Lanarkshire.

GRIEVE, Sir (Herbert) Ronald (Robinson), Kt 1958; FAMA 1968; Medical Practitioner; *b* 6 June 1896; 2nd *s* of Lieut Gideon James Grieve (killed in action, 1900) and Julia Australia Grieve (*née* Robinson), Sydney, Australia; *m* 1945, Florence Ross Timpson, formerly of Cheadle Heath, Cheshire; one *s* two *d. Educ:* Sydney Gram. Sch.; University of Sydney. Grad. in Medicine and Surgery. Resident Medical Officer, Newcastle Gen. Hosp., NSW, 1920-21; House Physician, Manchester Royal Infirmary, 1922-23; Hon. Clinical Asst in Medicine, Royal Prince Alfred Hospital, Sydney, 1941-47. Pres. BMA (NSW Branch), 1947; Mem. NSW Medical Board, 1938-63; Chm. Medical Benefits Fund of Australia, from inception, 1947-; Pres. Internat. Fedn of Voluntary Health Service Funds, 1968; Mem. Commonwealth of Australia Advisory Cttee on National Health Act, 1953-. MLC, NSW, 1933-34. *Recreations:* angling, the turf; formerly rowing and cricket (rep. Sydney Univ.). *Address:* Earlwood, Sydney, NSW 2206, Australia. *T:* LL 1514. *Clubs:* University, Old Sydneians, Australian Jockey (Sydney).

GRIEVE, Percy; see Grieve, W. P.

GRIEVE, Prof. Sir Robert, Kt 1969; MA, FRTPI, MICE, Professor Emeritus, University of Glasgow; *b* 11 Dec. 1910; *s* of Peter Grieve and Catherine Boyle; *m* 1933, Mary Lavinia Broughton Blackburn; two *s* two *d. Educ:* N. Kelvinside Sch., Glasgow; Royal Coll. of Science and Technology (now Univ. of Strathclyde), Glasgow. Trng and qual. as Civil Engr, eventually Planner. Local Govt posts, 1927-44; preparation of Clyde Valley Regional Plan, 1944-46; Civil Service, 1946-54; Chief Planner, Scottish Office, 1960-64. Prof. of Town and Regional Planning, Glasgow Univ., 1964-74; seconded as Chm., Highlands and Islands Develt Bd, 1965-70; retired from Chair, 1974. Director: Scottish Civic Trust; Patrick Geddes Meml Trust; Balnain Trust, Inverness; Cairngorm Sports Develt Co. Governor: Centre for Environmental Studies, 1972-75; Planning Exchange, 1973-76; Broadcasting Council for Scotland, BBC, 1974-; National Trust for Scotland, 1975-; Films of Scotland, 1975-; Member: Saltire Soc. Housing Award Panel, 1965-; North Sea Oil Panel, SSRC, 1975-; Hon. President: Scottish Rights of Way Soc.; New Glasgow Soc.; Inverness Civic Trust; Stewartry Mountaineering Club; Scottish Branch, RTPI; Pres., Scottish Mountaineering Council, 1975-; Former Vice-Pres., Internat. Soc. of Town and Regional Planners. Hon. Vice-Pres., Scottish Youth Hostels Assoc. Gold Medal, RTPI, 1974. Hon. DLitt Heriot-Watt; Hon. FRIAS. *Publications:* part-author and collaborator in several major professional reports and books; many papers and articles in professional and technical jls. *Recreations:* mountains, poetry. *Address:* Marchburn House, by Cairnryan, Wigtownshire. *T:* Cairnryan 250; 87 Bruntsfield Place, Edinburgh. *Clubs:* Scottish Arts (Edinburgh); Ours (Glasgow).

GRIEVE, Sir Ronald; see Grieve, Sir H. R. R.

GRIEVE, Thomas Robert, CBE 1968; MC 1944; Director: London and Provincial Trust Ltd, since 1970; Viking Resources Trust Ltd, since 1972; Oil and Associated Investment Trust, since 1971; Chairman, Hogg Robinson (Scotland) Ltd, since 1975; Member, Management Committee, Automobile Association, since 1971; Deputy Chairman, Hunterston Development Company Ltd, since 1973; Chairman, Newarthill Ltd, since 1977; *b* 11 Sept. 1909; *s* of Robert Grieve and Annie Craig (*née* Stark); *m* 1946, Doreen Bramley Whitehead; two *d. Educ:* Cargilfield and Fettes Coll., Edinburgh. Joined Anglo-Saxon Petroleum Co. Ltd, 1930; served in London, 1930-40. Commissioned 9th Highland Lt Inf. (TA), 1928, seconded Movement Control, Royal Engineers, 1943-45; served NW Europe, rank of Major. Vice-Pres. in charge of Operations, Shell Oil Co. of Canada, 1945; Exec. Asst to Regional Vice-Pres. of Shell Oil Co., Houston, Texas, 1949; Manager of Distribution and Supply Dept, Shell Petroleum Co. Ltd, London, 1951; Director: Shell-Mex and BP Ltd, Shell Refining Co. Ltd, Shell Co. UK Ltd, 1959-65; Shell International Petroleum Co. Ltd, 1963-65; Vice-Chm and Man. Dir, Shell-Mex and BP Ltd, 1965-71; Chm., United Kingdom Oil Pipelines Ltd, 1965-71; Chm., London Exec. Cttee, Scottish Council, 1971-77. *Recreations:* golf, travel. *Address:* 33 Park Close, Ilchester Place, W14 8NH. *T:* 01-602 3435. *Clubs:* Caledonian, MCC.

GRIEVE, William Percival, (W. Percy Grieve), QC 1962; MP (C) Solihull Division of Warwickshire since 1964; a Recorder, since 1972 (Recorder of Northampton, 1965-71); *b* 25 March 1915; *o s* of 2nd Lieut W. P. Grieve, the Middlesex Regt (killed in action, Ypres, Feb. 1915), Rockcliffe, Dalbeattie; *m* 1949, Evelyn Raymonde Louise, *y d* of late Comdt Hubert Mijouain, Paris, and of Liliane, *e d* of late Sir George Roberts, 1st and last Bt; one *s* one *d* (and one *s* decd). *Educ:* privately; Trinity Hall, Cambridge. Exhibitioner, Trinity Hall, 1933; Lord Kitchener Nat. Memorial Schol., 1934; BA 1937, MA 1940. Harmsworth Law Schol., 1937, called to Bar, 1938, Middle Temple; Bencher, 1969. Joined Midland Circuit, 1939. Commissioned the Middlesex Regt, 1939; Liaison Officer, French Mil. Censorship, Paris, 1939-40; Min. of Information, 1940-41; HQ Fighting France, 1941-43; Staff Capt. and Exec. Officer, SHAEF Mission to Luxembourg, 1944; Major and GSO2 Brit. Mil. Mission to Luxembourg, 1945; DAAG, BAOR, 1946. Asst Recorder of Leicester, 1956-65; Dep. Chm., Co. of Lincoln (Parts of Holland) QS, 1962-71. Mem. Mental Health Review Tribunal, Sheffield Region, 1960-64. Has served on Gen. Council of the Bar. Contested (C) Lincoln By-election, 1962. Member: House of Commons Select Cttee on Race Relations and Immigration, 1968-70; UK Delegn, Council of Europe (Chm., Procedure Cttee) and WEU, 1969; Hon. Vice-Pres., Franco-British Parly Relations Cttee (Chm., 1970-75); Chm., Luxembourg Soc., 1975. Member: Council, Officers' Assoc., 1969-; Council of Justice, 1971-; Council, Franco-British Soc., 1970; Council, Alliance Française, 1974. Officier avec Couronne, Order of Adolphe of Nassau; Chevalier, Order of Couronne de Chêne and Croix de Guerre avec Palmes (Luxembourg), 1945-46; Bronze Star (USA), 1945; Chevalier de la Légion d'Honneur, 1974; Commandeur de l'Ordre de Mérite (Luxembourg), 1976. *Recreations:* swimming, travel, the theatre. *Address:* 1 King's Bench Walk, Temple, EC4. *T:* 01-353 8436. *Clubs:* Hurlingham, Royal Automobile.

GRIEVE, William Robertson; see Grieve, Hon. Lord.

GRIEW, Prof. Stephen, PhD; Chairman, Department of Behavioural Science, University of Toronto Faculty of Medicine, since 1977; *b* 13 Sept. 1928; *e s* of late Harry and Sylvia Griew, London, England; *m* 1st, 1955, Jane le Geyt Johnson (marr. diss.); one *s* two *d* (and one *s* decd); 2nd, 1977, Eva Margareta Ursula, *d* of late Dr Johannes Ramberg and of Fru Betty Ramberg, Stockholm, Sweden; one step *s*. *Educ:* Univ. of London (BSc, Dip Psych); Univ. of Bristol (PhD). Vocational Officer, Min. of Labour, 1951-55; Univ. of Bristol: Research Worker, 1955-59; Lectr, 1959-63; Kenneth Craik Research Award, St John's Coll., Cambridge, 1960; Prof. of Psychology: Univ. of Otago, Dunedin, NZ, 1964-68 (Dean, Faculty of Science, 1967-68); Univ. of Dundee, 1968-72; Vice-Chancellor, Murdoch Univ., Perth, WA, 1972-77. Consultant, OECD, Paris, 1963-64; Expert, ILO, 1966-67; Mem., Social Commn of Rehabilitation Internat., 1967-75; Consultant, Dept of Employment, 1970-72; Vis. Prof., Univ. of Western Ont., London, Canada, 1970 and 1971. Vice-Pres., Australian Council on the Ageing, 1975-76. FBPsS 1960; Fellow, Gerontological Soc. (USA), 1969. *Publications:* handbooks and monographs on ageing and vocational rehabilitation, and articles in Jl of Gerontology and various psychological jls. *Recreations:* music, travel. *Address:* Department of Behavioural Science, Faculty of

Medicine, University of Toronto, Toronto, Canada M5S 1A8. *Club:* English-Speaking Union.

GRIFFIN, Adm. Sir Anthony (Templer Frederick Griffith), GCB 1975 (KCB 1971; CB 1967); Chairman, British Shipbuilders, since 1977 (Chairman-designate, Dec. 1975); *b* Peshawar, 24 Nov. 1920; *s* of late Col F. M. G. Griffin, MC, and B. A. B. Griffin (*née* Down); *m* 1943, Rosemary Ann Hickling; two *s* one *d. Educ:* RN Coll., Dartmouth. Joined RN, 1934; to sea as Midshipman, 1939; War Service in E Indies, Mediterranean, Atlantic, N Russia and Far East; specialised in navigation, 1944; Staff Coll., 1952; Imp. Defence Coll., 1963; comd HMS Ark Royal, 1964-65; Asst Chief of Naval Staff (Warfare), 1966-68; Flag Officer, Second-in-Command, Far East Fleet, 1968-69; Flag Officer, Plymouth, Comdr Central Sub Area, Eastern Atlantic, and Comdr Plymouth Sub Area, Channel, 1969-71; Controller of the Navy, 1971-75. Comdr 1951; Capt. 1956; Rear-Adm. 1966; Vice-Adm. 1968; Adm., 1971. Mem. Adv. Council, Science Policy Foundn, 1975-. FBIM. *Recreations:* sailing, skiing, riding, golf. *Address:* Candles Copse, Dunsfold Road, Cranleigh, Surrey. *T:* Cranleigh 3314.

GRIFFIN, Sir (Charles) David, Kt 1974; CBE 1972; Chairman, Nabalco Pty Ltd, since 1964; Deputy Chairman, Swiss Aluminium Australia Ltd; *b* 8 July 1915; *s* of Eric Furnival Griffin and Nellie Clarendon Griffin (*née* Devenish-Meares); *m* 1941, Jean Falconer Whyte; two *s. Educ:* Cranbrook Sch., Sydney; Univ. of Sydney (LLB and Gold Blue). 8th Aust. Div. 2nd AIF, 1940-45; POW Changi, Singapore, 1942-45. Associate to Sir Dudley Williams and Mem. Bar NSW, 1946-49; Solicitor, Sydney, 1949-64. Alderman, Sydney City Council, 1962-74, Chm. Finance Cttee, 1969-72; Lord Mayor of Sydney, 1972-73. Chairman: Australasian Petroleum Co. Pty Ltd, 1962-; Barclays Australia Ltd, 1976-; Vanguard Insurance Co. Ltd, 1977-; Director: Aetna Life of Aust. & NZ Ltd; Atlas Copco Aust. Pty Ltd; Robert Bosch (Aust.) Pty Ltd; Oil Search Ltd; Zellweger Aust. Pty Ltd; Man. Dir, Swiss Aluminium Mining Australia Ltd. Pres., NSW Inst. of Public Affairs; Mem. Council, Royal Agricl Soc.; Mem., Tertiary Educn Commn; Dir, Australian Elizabethan Theatre Trust; Trustee, Nat. Parks and Wildlife Foundn. *Publications:* The Happiness Box (for children); sundry verse and short stories. *Recreations:* golf, trout fishing. *Address:* 7 Mildura Street, Killara, NSW 2071, Australia. *T:* Sydney 498-2461. *Clubs:* Union, Elanora Country (Sydney); Royal Sydney Golf, Pine Valley Golf (NJ, USA).

GRIFFIN, Air Vice-Marshal Charles Robert, FRCS; Consultant Adviser in Orthopaedic Surgery, Royal Air Force, since 1971; Dean of Air Force Medicine, since 1976; *b* 15 May 1919; *s* of Charles Morgan Griffin and Sidney Weir Griffin; *m* 1961, Agnes Ray Turnbull; two *s. Educ:* Morgan's Sch., Castleknock, Co. Dublin; Trinity Coll., Dublin (BA, MB, BCh 1941). FRCS 1957. House Phys./Surg., Adelaide Hosp., Dublin, 1941-42; RAF Medical Br., 1942; served War: RAF stations Abingdon and Biggin Hill; N Africa, Malta and Italy with 72 Fighter (Spitfire) Sqdn and Desert Air Force Trng Wing; Comd and Air Min. appts, RAF Hosp., Wroughton, 1949; Surg. Registrar, Royal Postgrad. Hosp., Hammersmith, 1951; Canal Zone Egypt, Cyprus and Aden, 1952-56; RAF Hosp., Wroughton, 1957-58; Orthopaedic Registrar, Robert Jones and Agnes Hunt Orthopaed. Hosp., Oswestry, 1959-60; RAF Hosp., Wegberg, Germany, 1961-64; PM RAF Hosp., Halton, 1965-67; PA RAF Hosp., Wroughton, 1967-71; Central Med. Estabt, RAF, London, 1971-. QHS 1976-. CStJ 1972. *Publications:* contrib. ME section, The Medical History of the Second World War, Vol. III, 1955; contrib. Proc. RSM. *Recreations:* Rugger (from touch-line), fishing, gardening. *Address:* St Julian's Farm, South Marston, Wilts SN3 6RY. *T:* Stratton St Margaret 2367. *Club:* Royal Air Force.

GRIFFIN, Col Edgar Allen, CMG 1965; OBE 1943; ED 1945; Regional Director, Northern Region (Arras, France), Commonwealth War Graves Commission, 1969-72; *b* 18 Jan. 1907; 3rd *s* of Gerald Francis and Isabella Margaret Griffin; *m* 1936, Alethea Mary Byrne; two *s* two *d*. Retired from AMF, 1947; Australian Govt Nominee to Staff of War Graves Commn, 1947; Chief Admin. Officer, Eastern Dist (Cairo), 1947-54; UK Dist (London), 1954-58; Regional Dir, Southern Region (Rome), 1958-69. *Address:* 36 Pytchley Road, Kettering, Northants.

GRIFFIN, Mrs Francis D.; *see* Dunne, Irene.

GRIFFIN, Sir Francis (Frederick), Kt 1971; Director, Ryland Vehicle Group Ltd, since 1941; *b* 3 June 1904; *s* of James Cecil and Lucy Griffin; *m* 1936, Kathleen Mary Fitzgerald; one *d* (twin *d* and one adopted *s* decd). *Educ:* St Philip's Grammar Sch., Edgbaston. Nat. Deleg., W Midland Div., Motor Agents'

Assoc., 1948-54; Mem., Inst. of Motor Industry. Elected to Birmingham City Council, 1949 (Leader of Council, 1964-72). Chm., W Midland Planning Authority Conf., 1966-69; First Chm., W Midland Passenger Transp. Authority, 1969-72; Dir, Nat. Exhibn Centre, 1970-74, 1976-. Mem., Cons. Gp Metropolitan CC, 1973- (Chm., 1973-75). Freeman, City of Birmingham, 1970. *Publications:* Selling Municipal Houses, 1967; Selling More Council Houses, 1970. *Recreation:* politics. *Address:* 101 Metchley Lane, Harborne, Birmingham B17 0JH. *T:* 021-427 4554. *Club:* Conservative (Birmingham).

GRIFFIN, Sir John Bowes, Kt 1955; QC 1938; *b* 19 April 1903; *o s* of late Sir Charles Griffin; *m* Eva Orrell, 2nd *d* of late John Mellifont Walsh, Wexford; two *d. Educ:* Clongowes; Dublin Univ. (MA, LLD, First Cl. Moderatorship, Gold Medallist); Cambridge. Barrister-at-Law, Inner Temple, 1926. Administrative Officer, Uganda, 1927; Asst District Officer, 1929; Registrar, High Court, 1929; Crown Counsel, 1933; Actg Solicitor-Gen. and Attorney-Gen., various periods; Attorney-Gen., Bahamas, 1936 (Acting Governor and Acting Chief Justice, various periods); Solicitor-Gen., Palestine, 1939, Acting Attorney-Gen., various periods; Attorney-Gen., Hong Kong, 1946; Chief Justice of Uganda, 1952-56. Secretary: East Africa Law Officers Conference, 1933; Commission of Enquiry Admin. of Justice, East Africa, 1933; Chm. Prisons Enquiry, Bahamas, 1936; miscellaneous Bds and Cttees; Chairman: Tel Aviv Municipal Commn of Enquiry, Palestine, 1942; Review Cttees, Detainees (Defence and Emergency Regulations), Palestine, 1940-46. Retired, Dec. 1956; Actg Chief Justice, N Rhodesia, 1957; Chm. Commn of Enquiry Gwenbe Valley Disturbances, N Rhodesia, 1958; Speaker, Legislative Council, Uganda, 1958-62; Speaker, Uganda National Assembly, 1962-63, retd. Chairman: Public Service Commissions, 1963 and Constitutional Council, 1964, N Rhodesia; retd 1965. CStJ 1960. *Publications:* Revised Edn of Laws (Uganda), 1935; (joint) Hong Kong, 1950. *Address:* c/o Williams & Glyn's Bank Ltd, Holt's Branch, Kirkland House, Whitehall, SW1. *Clubs:* East India, Devonshire, Sports and Public Schools; Union (Malta).
See also A. J. Boase, M. H. M. Reid.

GRIFFIN, Kenneth James, OBE 1970; Special Adviser, Secretary of State for Industry, since 1974; Member, National Coal Board, since 1973; a Deputy Chairman, British Shipbuilders, since 1977 (a Deputy Chairman designate, 1976); *b* 1 Aug. 1928; *s* of late Albert Griffin and late Catherine (*née* Sullivan); *m* 1951, Doreen Cicely Simon; two *s* one *d. Educ:* Dynevor Grammar Sch., Swansea; Swansea Technical College. Area Sec., ETU, 1960; Dist Sec., Confedn of Ship Building Engrg Unions, 1961; Sec., Craftsmen Cttee (Steel), 1961; Mem., Welsh Council, 1968; Mem., Crowther Commn on Constitution (Wales), 1969; Joint Sec., No 8 Joint Industrial Council Electrical Supply Industry, 1969; Industrial Adviser, DTI, 1971-72; Co-ordinator of Industrial Advisers, DTI, 1972-74. *Recreations:* golf, music, reading. *Address:* 60 Woolaston Avenue, Lakeside, Cardiff. *T:* 0222 752184.

GRIFFIN, Rear-Adm. Michael Harold, CB 1973; Director of Dockyard Production and Support, 1972-77, retired; *b* 28 Jan. 1921; *s* of late Henry William Griffin and Blanche Celia Griffin (*née* Michael); *m* 1947, Barbara Mary Brewer; two *d. Educ:* Plymouth Junior Techn. Coll. CEng, FIMechE, MIMarE. Commnd, 1941; HMS Kent, 1942; HM Submarines Trusty, Tactician, Tally Ho, Alderney, 1944-50; Admty, 1950-52; HMS Eagle, 1952-54; staff C-in-C Portsmouth, 1954-57; HM Dockyard, Rosyth, 1957-60; Third Submarine Sqdn, 1960-62; Captain, 1962; HM Dockyard, Chatham, 1963-65; HMS St Vincent, 1966-69; Cdre Supt, Singapore, 1969-71. *Recreations:* yachting, cruising and racing; tennis, badminton; horology. *Address:* Rylston, Bannerdown Road, Batheaston, Bath, Avon. *T:* Bath 858379.

GRIFFIN, Paul, MBE 1961; MA Cantab; Principal, Anglo-World Language Centre, Cambridge, since 1976; *b* 2 March 1922; *s* of late John Edwin Herman Griffin; *m* 1946, Felicity Grace, *d* of Canon Howard Dobson; one *s* one *d. Educ:* Framlingham Coll.; St Catharine's Coll., Cambridge. Served War in Gurkhas, India, Burma, Malaya, 1940-46; North-West Frontier, 1941-43; Chindits, 1943-44. Asst Master and Senior English Master, Uppingham Sch., 1949-55; Principal, English Sch. in Cyprus, 1956-60; Headmaster, Aldenham Sch., 1962-74. Mem., Court of Corp. of Sons of the Clergy, 1973-. *Publications:* numerous articles, poems, and broadcast talks and plays. *Recreations:* sea angling, bridge. *Address:* Flat 5, 2 St Paul's Road, Cambridge. *T:* Cambridge 59897; 6 East Street, Southwold, Suffolk IP18 6EH. *T:* Southwold 3709.

GRIFFIN, Very Rev. Victor Gilbert Benjamin; Dean of St Patrick's Cathedral, Dublin, since 1969; *b* 24 May 1924; *s* of

Gilbert B. and Violet M. Griffin, Carnew, Co. Wicklow; *m* 1958, Daphne E. Mitchell; two *s. Educ:* Kilkenny Coll.; Mountjoy Sch., and Trinity Coll., Dublin. MA, 1st class Hons in Philosophy. Ordained, 1947; Curacy, St Augustine's, Londonderry, 1947-51; Curacy, Christ Church, Londonderry, 1951-57; Rector of Christ Church, Londonderry, 1957-69. Lecturer in Philosophy, Magee Univ. Coll., Londonderry, 1950-69. *Publications:* Trends in Theology, 1870-1970, 1970; Anglican and Irish, 1976; contrib. to New Divinity, 1970. *Recreations:* music, golf. *Address:* The Deanery, St Patrick's Cathedral, Dublin 8. *T:* Dublin 752451. *Club:* Friendly Brothers of St Patrick (Dublin).

GRIFFITH, Hon. Sir Arthur Frederick, Kt 1977; MLC; President, Legislative Council, Western Australia, since 1974; *b* Geraldton, 22 April 1913; *m* ; one *c. Educ:* public schs in Australia. Served War of 1939-45, RAAF (commnd from ranks). MLA for Canning, WA, 1950-53; MLC (Lib): Suburban, 1953-65; North Metropolitan, 1965-; Minister: for Mines, Housing and Justice, 1959-65; for Mines and Justice, 1965-71, Legislature of Western Australia; Leader of the Opposition, Legislative Council, 1958-59, 1971-74. *Address:* Office of the President, Legislative Council, Perth, Western Australia; 40 Tilton Terrace, City Beach, WA 6015, Australia.

GRIFFITH, Rev. Arthur Leonard; Minister, St Paul's Anglican Church, Toronto, since 1976; Lecturer in Homiletics, Wycliffe College, Toronto, since 1977; *b* 20 March 1920; *s* of Thomas Griffiths and Sarah Jane Taylor; *m* 1947, Anne Merelie Cayford; two *d. Educ:* Public and High Schs, Brockville, Ont; McGill Univ., Montreal (BA, McGill, 1942); United Theological Coll., Montreal (BD 1945; Hon. DD 1962); Mansfield Coll., Oxford, England, 1957-58. Ordained in The United Church of Canada, 1945; Minister: United Church, Arden, Ont, 1945-47; Trinity United Church, Grimsby, Ont, 1947-50; Chalmers United Church, Ottawa, Ont, 1950-60; The City Temple, London, 1960-66; Deer Park United Church, Toronto, 1966-75; ordained in Anglican Church 1976. *Publications:* The Roman Letter Today, 1959; God and His People, 1960; Beneath The Cross of Jesus, 1961; What is a Christian?, 1962; Barriers to Christian Belief, 1962; A Pilgrimage to the Holy Land, 1962; The Eternal Legacy, 1963; Pathways to Happiness, 1964; God's Time and Ours, 1964; The Crucial Encounter, 1965; This is Living!, 1966; God in Man's Experience, 1968; Illusions of our Culture, 1969; The Need to Preach, 1971; Hang on to the Lord's Prayer, 1973; We Have This Ministry, 1973; Ephesians: a positive affirmation, 1975; Gospel Characters, 1976. *Recreations:* music, drama, golf, fishing. *Address:* St Paul's Anglican Church, 227 Bloor Street East, Toronto M4W 1L8, Canada.

GRIFFITH, Edward Michael Wynne; Member of Agricultural Research Council since 1973; *b* 29 Aug. 1933; *e s* of Major H. W. Griffith, MBE; *m* Jill Grange, *d* of Major D. P. G. Moseley, Dorfold Cottage, Nantwich; two *s* (and one *s* decd). *Educ:* Eton; Royal Agricultural College. Regional Dir, National Westminster Bank Ltd, 1974-. High Sheriff of Denbighshire, 1969. Chm., Denbigh Div. Conservative Assoc.; Mem., Countryside Commn Cttee for Wales, 1972-; Mem., Min. of Agriculture Regional Panel, 1972. *Address:* Greenfield, Trefnant, Clwyd. *T:* Trefnant 633. *Club:* Boodle's.

GRIFFITH, Grosvenor Talbot; retired; Warden of Missenden Abbey, 1958-66; *b* 27 Jan. 1899; *s* of late Thomas Wardrop Griffith, CMG, and Louisa, *d* of late Grosvenor Talbot, JP, Leeds; *m* 1934, Hilda Mary, *d* of late Eric Nisbet, JP Ryton-on-Tyne; one *s* one *d. Educ:* Charterhouse; Trinity Coll., Cambridge. 1st Class Historical Tripos Pt 1 1921, 2nd Class Pt 2, 1922: RFA 1917-19; BEF France, 1918 (wounded Nov. 1918); Trinity Coll., Cambridge, 1919-23; Asst Master and Tutor Wellington Coll., 1923-34; called to Bar, Inner Temple, 1934; Headmaster, Oakham Sch., Rutland, 1935-57. Dep. Chm., Rutland Quarter Sessions, 1946-57; Chm. Rutland Magistrates, 1954-57. Mem. Governing Body English-Speaking Union, 1962-73; Governor, Dean Close Sch., 1966-. JP Bucks, 1962-66. *Publication:* Population Problems of Age of Malthus, 1926 (repr. 1967). *Recreation:* painting. *Address:* Old Swindon House, Swindon Village, Cheltenham. *T:* Cheltenham 25565. *Club:* English-Speaking Union.

GRIFFITH, Guy Thompson, FBA 1952; MA; Laurence Reader in Classics, Cambridge University, 1951- Sept. 1975; Fellow of Gonville and Caius College, 1931-75, Lecturer in Classics, 1937-75; *b* 7 Jan. 1908; *m* 1940, Josephine Marjorie Rainey; three *s* one *d. Educ:* The Leys Sch., and Gonville and Caius Coll., Cambridge. Served in RAFVR, 1941-45. Joint Editor Classical Quarterly, 1947-51. *Publications:* The Mercenaries of the Hellenistic World, 1935; (with Michael Oakeshott) A Guide to the Classics, 1936; The Greek Historians, in Fifty Years of

Classical Studies (ed M. Platnauer), 1954. Articles mostly on Greek History in periodicals. *Address:* 1 Springfield Road, Cambridge.

GRIFFITH, Hugh Emrys; Actor since 1938; *b* 30 May 1912; *s* of William and Mary Griffith, Marian Glas, Anglesey; *m* 1947, Adelgunde Margaret Beatrice von Dechend; no *c. Educ:* Llangefni Gram. Sch., Anglesey. Banking, 1929-37; Leverhulme Schol., RADA, 1938-39; Bancroft Gold Medallist, RADA, 1939; various West End Productions, 1939-40; 1st Bn Royal Welch Fusiliers, with service in the Far East, 1940-46. Stratford-upon-Avon Festival Season, 1946; Trinculo, Touchstone, Holofernes, First Witch, King of France, and Mephistophiles in Dr Faustus, Cardinal Montichelso in The White Devil, Duchess, 1947; The Playboy of the Western World and Machiavelli's Mandragola, Mercury, 1947 and 1948. The Comedy of Good and Evil, Arts, 1948; Swansea Festival, 1949, King Lear; also King Lear in Welsh, BBC 1949; Lyric and Duke of York's, 1950-51: Point of Departure (Anouilh's Eurydice), The Father, also the same part in New York. Stratford-upon-Avon Festival of Britain, 1951: John of Gaunt, Glendower, and Caliban. Andrew Deeson in Escapade, St James's and Strand, 1952-53; Bellman, in The Dark is Light Enough, Aldwych, 1954; General St Pé, in The Waltz of the Toreadors, Arts and Criterion, 1956-57; W. O. Gant in Look Homeward, Angel, Barrymore Theatre, New York, 1957-58; Count Cenci, in The Cenci, Old Vic, 1959; Azdak, in The Caucasian Chalk Circle, Aldwych, 1962; the Teacher in Andorra, Biltmore Theatre, New York, 1963; Falstaff, in Henry IV, Parts I and II, Stratford-upon-Avon Festival Season, 1964; Prospero in The Tempest, Nottingham Playhouse and European Tour for British Council. *Films include:* A Run for Your Money, The Galloping Major, The Titfield Thunderbolt, The Beggar's Opera, The Sleeping Tiger, Gone to Earth, Passage Home, The Good Companions, Lucky Jim, Ben Hur (American Oscar, 1959), Exodus, The Counterfeit Traitor, Mutiny on the Bounty, The Inspector, Term of Trial, Tom Jones, The Bargee, Hide and Seek, Oh Dad! Poor Dad! Mama's hung you in the Closet, and we're all feeling so sad, How to steal a Million, Danger Grows Wild, A Sailor from Gibraltar, Brown Eye-Evil Eye, Dare I Weep, Dare I Mourn, The Chastity Belt, The Fixer, Oliver!, Start the Revolution Without Me, Wuthering Heights, Cry of the Banshee, Dr Phibes, The Gingerbread House, Dr Phibes Rises Again, Canterbury Tales, What!, Lead Us not into Temptation, Luther, Final Programme, Craze, Take me High, The Cousin, Legend of the Werewolf, The Passover Plot, Casanova and Co., Joseph Andrews, The Last Remake of Beau Geste. Various broadcasts and TV incl. series Walrus and the Carpenter, 1965, Tchekov's The Proposal, Uncle Rollo, Clochemerle series, Owen MD, The Joke, A Legacy series, Grand Slam. Hon. DLitt, Univ. of Wales, 1965. *Recreation:* writing. *Address:* c/o International Creative Management, 22 Grafton Street, W1. *Club:* Garrick.

GRIFFITH, Prof. John Aneurin Grey, LLB London, LLM London; FBA 1977; Barrister-at-law; Professor of Public Law, London School of Economics and Political Science, University of London, since 1970; *b* 14 Oct. 1918; *s* of Rev. B. Grey Griffith and Bertha Griffith; *m* 1941, Barbara Eirene Garnet, *d* of W. Garnet Williams; two *s* one *d. Educ:* Taunton Sch.; LSE. British and Indian armies, 1940-46. Lectr in Law, UCW, Aberystwyth, 1946-48; Lectr in Law and Reader, LSE, 1948-59, Prof. of English Law, 1959-70. Mem., Marlow UDC, 1950-55, and Bucks CC, 1955-61. Vis. Prof. of Law, Univ. of California at Berkeley, 1966; Hon. Sec., Council for Academic Freedom and Democracy; Editor, Public Law, 1956-. *Publications:* (with H. Street) A Casebook of Administrative Law, 1964; Central Departments and Local Authorities, 1966; (with H. Street) Principles of Administrative Law, 5th edn, 1973; Parliamentary Scrutiny of Government Bills, 1974; (with T. C. Hartley) Government and Law, 1975; (ed) From Policy to Administration, 1976; articles in English, Commonwealth and American jls of law, public administration and politics. *Recreations:* drinking beer and writing bad verse. *Address:* London School of Economics and Political Science, Houghton Street, WC2. *Club:* Tatty Bogle.

GRIFFITH, John Eaton, CMG 1949; OBE 1941; *b* 1894; *s* of L. J. Griffith, Brondesbury; *m* 1921, Violet Godson (*d* 1958); two *d. Educ:* University Coll. RA., 1914-19, Egypt and France; retd disabled, 1919. 1920-50, UK Civil Service; Air Ministry; Ministry of Aircraft Production; Ministry of Production and Ministry of Fuel and Power; Principal Private Sec. to successive Ministers of Aircraft Production, Lord Beaverbrook and Lord Brabazon; Under-Sec., Ministry of Supply, 1949-50; retired, 1950. Chm. European Coal Organisation, 1946-47; Organising Cttee XIV Olympiad, 1948; Vice-Pres. International Lawn Tennis Federation; Vice-Pres. The Lawn Tennis Assoc.; Pres. Bucks Lawn Tennis Assoc. *Address:* St Martins, Grimm's Hill,

Great Missenden, Bucks. *T:* Gt Missenden 2244. *Clubs:* Junior Carlton; All England (Wimbledon).

GRIFFITH, Owen Glyn, OBE 1969; MVO 1954; Inspector, HM Diplomatic Service, since 1976; *b* 19 Jan. 1922; *s* of late William Glyn Griffith and Gladys Glyn Griffith (*née* Picton Davies); *m* 1949, Rosemary Elizabeth Cecil Earl; two *s*. *Educ:* Oundle Sch.; Trinity Hall, Cambridge. Commnd in Welsh Guards (twice wounded in N Africa), 1941-43; Colonial Service (later HMOCS), Uganda, 1944-63: District Officer, 1944-51; Private Sec. to Governor, 1952-54; Dist Comr, 1954-61; Perm. Sec., Min. of Commerce and Industry, 1961-63; Principal, CRO, 1963; 1st Sec. and Head of Chancery, British Embassy, Khartoum, 1965; 1st Sec. (Commercial), British Embassy, Stockholm, 1969; Dep. British High Comr, Malaŵi, 1973. *Recreations:* golf, fishing. *Address:* c/o Foreign and Commonwealth Office, SW1A 2AU; The Sundial, Marsham Way, Gerrards Cross, Bucks SL9 8AD. *Club:* Royal Commonwealth Society.

GRIFFITH, Patrick Waldron Cobham; Chairman, Turner & Newall Ltd, since 1976; *b* 26 April 1925; *s* of late Cyril Cobham Griffith and Louisa Ellen (*née* Mathews); *m* 1955, Sonia Pamela Clark; one *s* two *d*. *Educ:* Bryanston Sch. Fleet Air Arm, 1943-46. Worked for family company, Engineering Components Ltd, 1946-51; Mem., Aston Martin works team, 1951-55; Engineering Components Ltd: Sales Dir, 1955-58; Vice-Chm., 1959-68; Chm. and Man. Dir, 1968. Turner & Newall Ltd: Dir, 1968; Jt Man. Dir, 1972-74; Dep. Chm., 1974-76. Soc. of Motor Manufacturers & Traders: Chm. of Accessory & Components Cttee, 1974-76; Vice-Pres., 1976-; Mem. Council, 1974-. Vice-Chm., Slough Community Centre, 1966-72; Mem., Slough Social Fund, 1966-72; Chm., Slough Duke of Edinburgh Award Cttee, 1967-72. Won (with Peter Collins): Goodwood 9-hour race, 1952; RAC Tourist Trophy, 1953. *Recreations:* golf, gardening, swimming. *Address:* Turner & Newall Ltd, 20 St Mary's Parsonage, Manchester M3 2NL. *T:* 061-833 9272. *Clubs:* Bath, Royal Automobile, Naval; St James's (Manchester).

GRIFFITH, Stewart Cathie, CBE 1975; DFC 1944; TD 1954; Secretary, MCC, 1962-74; *b* 16 June 1914; *yr s* of H. L. A. Griffith, Middleton, Sussex; *m* 1939, Barbara Reynolds; one *s* one *d*. *Educ:* Dulwich Coll.; Pembroke Coll., Cambridge (MA). Asst Master, Dulwich Coll., 1937-39. Army, 1939-46. Glider Pilot Regt, Lieut-Col. Sec., Sussex County Cricket Club, 1946-50; Cricket Correspondent, Sunday Times, 1950-52; Asst Sec., MCC, 1952-62; Secretary: Internat. Cricket Conference, 1962-74; Cricket Council, 1969-74; Test and County Cricket Bd, 1969-73; Pres., Sussex CCC, 1975-77. *Recreations:* cricket, golf, real tennis, walking. *Address:* 7 Sea Way, Middleton, Sussex PO22 7RZ. *T:* Middleton-on-Sea 3000. *Clubs:* East India, Devonshire, Sports and Public Schools; MCC; Hawks (Cambridge), etc.

GRIFFITH-JONES, Sir Eric (Newton), KBE 1962; CMG 1957; QC (Kenya) 1954; Chairman, Commonwealth Development Corporation, since 1972 (Deputy Chairman, 1971-72); Chairman: The Guthrie Corporation Ltd and associated companies; Property Holdings (Pennine) Ltd; Director: Provident Mutual Life Assurance Association; Sutcliffe Mitchell (Insurances) Ltd; *b* 1 Nov. 1913; *s* of late Oswald Phillips Griffith-Jones and late Edith Sydney (*née* Newton); *m* 1946, Mary Patricia, *widow* of F. E. Rowland, and *d* of late Major W. T. Heagerty and of Mrs T. H. Holyoak; one *s* two *d* (and one *s* decd). *Educ:* Cheltenham Coll. Barrister-at-law, Gray's Inn, 1934; Advocate and Solicitor, Straits Settlements, and Johore, 1935; Crown Counsel, SS (Singapore), 1939; Mil. service, 1941-46. Capt., SS Volunteer Force (Efficiency Medal; POW 1942-45). Crown Counsel, Malayan Union, 1946; Federation of Malaya: Sen. Federal Counsel, 1948; Legal Adviser: Selangor, 1948-49, Perak, 1949-51. Actg Sol.-Gen. and Actg Attorney-Gen., 1951. Solicitor-Gen., Kenya, 1952-55. Dep. Speaker, Kenya Legislative Council, 1954-55; Attorney-Gen. and Minister for Legal Affairs, Kenya, 1955-61; Acting Chief Sec. Kenya, 1955-61 (occasions); Dep. Governor, 1961-63; Actg Governor (on occasions), 1959, 1961, 1962, 1963. Chm., Rubber Growers' Assoc. Ltd, 1970-71. Perak River Hydro-Electric Power Co. Ltd, 1973-76. Vice-Pres., Liverpool Sch. of Tropical Med., 1975-. FBIM. *Recreations:* tennis, golf, shooting and water ski-ing. *Address:* 33 Hill Street, W1A 3AR. *T:* 01-629 8484; 52-54 Gracechurch Street, EC3V 0BD. *T:* 01-626 5052; The Combe, Rogate, near Petersfield, Hants. *T:* Milland 466. *Clubs:* Sussex County Cricket, Liphook Golf; Nairobi and Karen Country (Kenya); Port Dickson (Malaysia).

GRIFFITH-JONES, (John) Mervyn (Guthrie), CBE 1977; MC 1943; His Honour Judge Griffith-Jones; Common Serjeant in

the City of London, since Oct. 1964; *b* 1 July 1909; *e s* of late John Stanley Griffith-Jones, JP; *m* 1947, Joan Clare Baker; two *s* one *d*. *Educ:* Eton; Trinity Hall, Cambridge. Called to the Bar, Middle Temple, 1932; Master of the Bench of the Middle Temple, 1958. Served War of 1939-45. Coldstream Guards in Western Desert, North Africa and Italy (despatches). One of the British Prosecuting Counsel at the trial of Major War criminals at Nuremberg, 1945-46; Counsel to the Crown at North London Sessions, 1946-50; one of the Counsel to the Crown at the Central Criminal Court, 1950-59, and First Senior, 1959-64. Recorder of Grantham, 1957; Recorder of Coventry, 1959; Chm., Norfolk QS, 1965-71; a Dep. Chm., City of London QS, 1969-71. Mem. Standing Cttee on Criminal Law Revision, 1958; Councillor, Westminster City Council, 1948-54. Liveryman, Glazier's Company; Lieutenancy, City of London. Mem. of the Pilgrims of Great Britain. One-man exhibitions of paintings, London, 1969, 1971, 1973, 1975, 1976. *Recreations:* painting, shooting, sailing. *Address:* 5 Blithfield Street, W8. *T:* 01-937 1105; Water Hall, Wighton, Wells, Norfolk. *T:* Walsingham 300. *Clubs:* MCC, White's, Pratt's.

GRIFFITH-WILLIAMS, Brig. Eric Llewellyn Griffith, CBE 1945; DSO 1918; MC and Bar; DL; psc; late RA; 5th *s* of late A. L. G. Griffith-Williams, Highfields, Marlow, Bucks; *b* 2 May 1894; *m* 1938, Delia (*d* 1964), *o c* of late Lt-Col H. S. Follett, CBE, Rockbeare Manor, Devon; one *d*. *Educ:* Tonbridge Sch.; RMA, Woolwich. Served European War, 1914-19; Bt. Lt-Col, 1937; War of 1939-45; Col 1940; Brig. 1940; retired pay, 1946. High Sheriff of Devonshire, 1966; DL Devon 1966. *Address:* Rockbeare Manor, Devon EX5 2LU. *Club:* Army and Navy.

GRIFFITHS, Rt. Rev. Ambrose; *see* Griffiths, Rt. Rev. M. A.

GRIFFITHS, Air Vice-Marshal Arthur, CB 1972; AFC 1964; Director General of Security (RAF), 1976-77 and Commandant-General RAF Regiment, 1975-77; *b* 22 Aug. 1922; *s* of late Edward and Elizabeth Griffiths; *m* 1950, Nancy Maud Sumpter; one *d*. *Educ:* Hawarden Grammar School. Joined RAF, 1940; war service with No 26 Fighter Reconnaissance Sqdn; post-war years as Flying Instructor mainly at CFS and Empire Flying Sch.; pfc 1954; comd No 94 Fighter Sqdn Germany, 1955-56; Dirg Staff, RCAF Staff Coll., Toronto, 1956-59; HQ Bomber Comd, 1959-61; comd No 101 Bomber Sqdn, 1962-64; Gp Captain Ops, Bomber Comd, 1964-67; comd RAF Waddington, 1967-69; AOA and later Chief of Staff, Far East Air Force, 1969-71; Head of British Defence Liaison Staff, Canberra, 1972-74. *Recreation:* golf. *Address:* 47 Murray Road, Northwood, Mddx. *T:* Northwood 27973. *Club:* Royal Air Force.

GRIFFITHS, Bruce (Fletcher), QC 1970; His Honour Judge Bruce Griffiths; a Circuit Judge, since 1972; *b* 28 April 1924; *s* of Edward Griffiths and Nancy Olga (*née* Fuell); *m* 1952, Mary Kirkhouse Jenkins, *y d* of late Judge George Kirkhouse Jenkins, QC; two *s* one *d*. *Educ:* Whitchurch Grammar Sch., Cardiff; King's Coll., London. RAF, 1942-47. LLB (Hons) London, 1951 (Jelf Medallist). Chm., Local Appeals Tribunal (Cardiff), Min. of Social Security, 1964-70; Vice-Chm., Mental Health Review Tribunal for Wales, 1968; Dep. Chm., Glamorgan QS, 1971; Comr of Assize, Royal Cts of Justice, London, 1971; Chancellor, Dio. of Monmouth, 1977-. Mem., Welsh Arts Council, Chm., Art Cttee; Purchaser, Contemp. Art Soc. for Wales, 1975-76. *Address:* 34 Park Place, Cardiff. *T:* 22454. *Clubs:* Bath; Cardiff and County (Cardiff).

GRIFFITHS, Edward; *b* 7 March 1929; Welsh; *m* 1954, Ella Constance Griffiths; one *s* one *d*. *Educ:* University Coll. of N Wales, Bangor. Industrial Chemist, 1951. Mem., Flintshire CC, 1964. MP (Lab) Brightside Div. of Sheffield, June 1968-Sept. 1974; contested (Ind Lab) Sheffield Brightside, Oct. 1974. *Recreation:* sport. *Address:* 8 Wheel Lane, Grenoside, Sheffield S30 3RN.

GRIFFITHS, Eldon Wylie, MA Cantab, MA Yale; MP (C) Bury St Edmunds, since May 1964; *b* 25 May 1925; *s* of Thomas H. W. Griffiths and Edith May; *m* 1949, Sigrid Griffiths; one *s* one *d*. *Educ:* Ashton Grammar Sch.; Emmanuel Coll., Cambridge. Fellow, Saybrook Coll., Yale, 1948-49; Correspondent, Time and Life magazines, 1949-55; Foreign Editor, Newsweek, 1956-63; Columnist, Washington Post, 1962-63; Conservative Research Department, 1963-64. Parly Sec., Min. of Housing and Local Govt, June-Oct. 1970; Parly Under-Sec. of State, DoE, and Minister for Sport, 1970-74; opposition spokesman on Europe, 1975-76. Chm., Anglo-Iranian Parly Gp. Consultant/Adviser, Nat. Police Federation; Pres., Assoc. of Public Health Inspectors, 1969-70. Director: Redman Heenan Ltd; Crane Fruehauf Ltd; Barber Greene Ltd. *Recreations:* reading, swimming, cricket. *Address:* Lynton Cottage, Ixworththorpe, Bury St Edmunds, Suffolk; 44 Carlisle Mansions, SW1.

GRIFFITHS, Gilbert, BA, LLB; Barrister-at-Law; a Deputy Circuit Judge, since 1974; *b* 21 July 1901; *s* of Harry Griffiths, Bilston, Staffs; *m* 1927, Bertha Verena, *d* of late Dan Gill, JP, Old Hill, Staffs; no *c. Educ:* King Edward's Sch., Birmingham; Trinity Hall, Cambridge. BA and LLB 1924; called to Bar, Inner Temple, 1925; joined Oxford Circuit. Recorder of Dudley, 1944-71; Asst Recorder of Birmingham, 1968-71; a Recorder of the Crown Court, 1972-74. *Recreation:* gardening. *Address:* 2 Fountain Court, Birmingham B4 6DR. *T:* 021-236 3882.

GRIFFITHS, Harold Morris; Counsellor (Economic), Washington, since 1975; *b* 17 March 1926; *s* of Rt Hon. James Griffiths, CH; *m* 1st, 1951, Gwyneth Lethby (*d* 1966); three *s* one *d*; 2nd, 1966, Elaine Burge (*née* Walsh); two *s. Educ:* Llanelly Grammar Sch.; London Sch. of Economics. Editorial Staff: Glasgow Herald, 1949-55; Guardian, 1955-67; Information Service, HM Treasury: Deputy Head, 1967-68, Head, 1968-72; Asst Sec., HM Treasury, 1972-75. *Address:* c/o Foreign and Commonwealth Office, SW1.

GRIFFITHS, Capt. Hubert Penry, OBE 1953; Assistant Commissioner, City of London Police, 1940-60; *b* 24 April 1894; *yr s* of late Henry Griffiths; *m* 1926, Beryl Rees, *o c* of late I. Newton Rees; one *s* (and one *s* one *d* decd). *Educ:* St Paul's Sch. Gazetted to 5th Special Res. Bn, Middlesex Regt, Oct. 1914; seconded to Nigeria Regt, Royal W African Frontier Force, 1915-20; served German W and E African Campaigns, 1915-18; Second in Command, 2nd Bn, 1918; served Egba Rising, 1918; Asst Comr, Nigeria Police, 1920, Commissioner, 1927; Actg Asst Inspector Gen., Northern Provinces, 1935-36; Police Div., Home Office, 1937; Actg Comr, City of London Police, 1952-53 and again for one year in 1954. Liveryman of Gold and Silver Wyre Drawers Company. OStJ 1952. Commander, Order of North Star (Sweden); Commander Star of Ethiopia. *Address:* 33 Seacliffe Avenue, Takapuna, Auckland 9, NZ. *Club:* City Livery.

GRIFFITHS, Sir Hugh; *see* Griffiths, Sir W. H.

GRIFFITHS, Islwyn Owen, QC 1973; a Recorder of the Crown Court, since 1972; *b* 24 Jan. 1924; *m* 1951, Pamela Norah Blizard. *Educ:* Swansea Grammar Sch.; Christ Church, Oxford (MA, BCL). Army (Royal Artillery), 1942-47; TA (RA), 1947-51; TARO, 1951. Called to Bar, Lincoln's Inn, 1953; Dep. Chm., Bucks QS, 1967-71. *Recreation:* sailing. *Address:* 72 Cheyne Court, SW3. *T:* 01-352 1704; 1 Harcourt Building, Temple, EC4. *T:* 01-353 9421. *Clubs:* Garrick; Royal Norfolk and Suffolk Yacht.

GRIFFITHS, Dr James Howard Eagle, OBE 1946; President, Magdalen College, Oxford, since 1968; *b* 6 Dec. 1908; *s* of Rev. James David Griffiths and Olive Arnold (*née* Chataway). *Educ:* Denstone Coll.; Magdalen Coll., Oxford (Demy). 1st cl. Natural Science (Physics), 1930; DPhil 1933; MA 1934. Sec., CVD (Admty), 1943-45. Magdalen Coll., Oxford: Fellow, 1934-68; Sen. Dean of Arts, 1947-50, 1956-60, 1965-66; Vice-Pres., 1951-52; University Demonstrator and Lectr in Physics, 1945-66; Reader in Physics, 1966-68; Vice-Chancellor, University of Malaya, Kuala Lumpur, 1967-68. C. V. Boys Prize, Physical Soc., London, 1951. Mem., Hebdomadal Council, Oxford, 1951-63, 1968-73; Mem., Hale Cttee on Univ. Teaching Methods. Hon. DEd, Univ. of Mindanao, Philippines, 1968. *Publications:* papers in Proc. Royal Soc., Proc. Phys. Soc. London and other physics jls. *Recreations:* music, wine. *Address:* Magdalen College, Oxford. *T:* Oxford 41781. *Club:* Leander (Henley-on-Thames).

GRIFFITHS, John Calvert, QC 1972; a Recorder of the Crown Court (sitting at Oxford), since 1972; Barrister-at-Law; *b* 16 Jan. 1931; *s* of Oswald Hardy Griffiths and Christina Flora Griffiths; *m* 1958, Jessamy, *er d* of Prof. G. P. Crowden and Jean Crowden; three *d. Educ:* St Peter's Sch., York (scholar); Emmanuel Coll., Cambridge (senr exhibnr) (BA 1st Cl. Hons 1955; MA 1960). Called to Bar, Middle Temple, 1956. Member, Executive Committee: General Council of the Bar, 1967-71; Senate of Inns of Court and the Bar, 1973-; Mem., Nat. Council of Social Service, 1974. Lieutenant, RE, 1949 (Nat. Service). *Recreations:* fishing, reading, gardening. *Address:* 2 Crown Office Row, Temple, EC4Y 7HJ. *T:* 01-353 9337. *Clubs:* Flyfishers', Hurlingham.

GRIFFITHS, John Edward Seaton, CMG 1959; MBE 1934; retired; *b* 27 Sept. 1908; *s* of A. E. Griffiths, MA, Cape Town; *m* 1937, Helen Parker, *d* of C. C. Wiles, MA, Grahamstown, SA; two *s* one *d. Educ:* South African Coll. Sch.; Cape Town Univ.; Selwyn Coll., Cambridge. Colonial Service (later HM Oversea Civil Service), Tanganyika, 1931-59; Asst Comr, East African Office, 1960-63; Director of Studies, Royal Inst. Public Administration, 1963-67; Administrative Training Officer, Govt of Botswana, 1967-73. *Publications:* articles in Tanganyika Notes and Records, Botswana Notes and Records and in Journal of Administration Overseas. *Recreations:* golf, photography. *Address:* c/o National Westminster Bank Ltd, 249 Banbury Road, Summertown, Oxford. *Clubs:* Royal Commonwealth Society; Mountain Club of South Africa (Cape Town).

GRIFFITHS, Lawrence; a Recorder of the Crown Court, since 1972; *b* 16 Aug. 1933; *s* of Bernard Griffiths and Olive Emily Griffiths (*née* Stokes); *m* 1959, Josephine Ann (*née* Cook); one *s* two *d. Educ:* Gowerton Grammar Sch.; Christ's Coll., Cambridge (MA). Called to Bar, Inner Temple, 1957; practised Swansea, 1958-; Mem. Wales and Chester Circuit; Prosecuting Counsel to Inland Revenue for Wales and Chester Circuit, 1969. *Address:* Peverell, 26 Hillside Crescent, Ffynone, Swansea. *T:* Swansea 59513; (chambers) Iscoed Chambers, 86 St Helens Road, Swansea. *T:* Swansea 52988. *Club:* Cardiff and County (Cardiff).

GRIFFITHS, Rt. Rev. (Michael) Ambrose, OSB; Abbot of Ampleforth, since 1976; *b* 4 Dec. 1928; *s* of Henry and Hilda Griffiths. *Educ:* Ampleforth Coll.; Balliol Coll., Oxford (MA, BSc Chemistry). Entered monastery at Ampleforth, 1950; theological studies at S Anselmo, Rome, 1953-56; ordained priest, 1957; Prof. of Theology at Ampleforth, 1963; Sen. Science Master, Ampleforth Coll., 1967; Inspector of Accounts for English Benedictine Congregation, 1971; Procurator (Bursar) at Ampleforth, 1972; Mem. Public School Bursars' Assoc. Cttee, 1975. *Recreations:* walking and Scouting. *Address:* Ampleforth Abbey, York YO6 4EN. *T:* Ampleforth 421.

GRIFFITHS, Sir Percival Joseph, KBE 1963; Kt 1947; CIE 1943; ICS (retired); formerly President, India, Pakistan and Burma Association; Director of various companies; *b* 15 Jan. 1899; *s* of late J. T. Griffiths, Ashford, Middx; *m* Kathleen Mary, *d* of late T. R. Wilkes, Kettering; three *s. Educ:* Peterhouse, Cambridge (MA). BSc London; entered Indian Civil Service, 1922; retired, 1937. Leader, European Group, Indian Central Legislature, 1946; Central Organiser, National War Front, India, and Publicity Adviser to Government of India; Mem. Indian Legislative Assembly, 1937. Hon. Fellow, SOAS, 1971. *Publications:* The British in India, 1947; The British Impact on India, 1952; Modern India, 1957; The Changing Face of Communism, 1961; The Road to Freedom, 1964; History of the Indian Tea Industry, 1967; Empire to Commonwealth, 1969; To Guard My People: the history of the Indian Police, 1971; A Licence to Trade: the History of English Chartered Companies, 1975. *Address:* St Christopher, Abbotts Drive, Wentworth, Virginia Water, Surrey. *Club:* Oriental.

GRIFFITHS, Peter Harry Steve; Senior Lecturer in Economic History, The Polytechnic, Portsmouth (formerly Portsmouth College of Technology), since 1967; *b* 24 May 1928; *s* of W. L. Griffiths, West Bromwich; *m* 1962, Jeannette Christine (*née* Rubery); one *s* one *d. Educ:* City of Leeds Training Coll. BSc (Econ.) Hons London, 1956; MEd Birmingham, 1963. Headmaster, Hall Green Road Sch., West Bromwich, 1962-64. Fulbright Exchange Prof. of Economics, Pierce Coll., Los Angeles, Calif, 1968-69. Chm., Smethwick Education Cttee; Leader, Conservative Group of Councillors in Smethwick, 1960-64. MP (C) Smethwick, 1964-66; Contested (C) Portsmouth N, Feb. 1974; Prospective Parly Cand. (C) Portsmouth N. *Publication:* A Question of Colour?, 1966. *Recreations:* motoring, writing. *Address:* 1 Gloucester Mews, Southsea, Hants. *Club:* Conservative (Smethwick).

GRIFFITHS, Sir Peter N.; *see* Norton-Griffiths.

GRIFFITHS, Sir Reginald (Ernest), Kt 1973; CBE 1965; Secretary, Local Authorities' Advisory Board, 1957-73; *b* 4 April 1910; *s* of Arthur Griffiths; *m* 1935, Jessica Lilian Broad; two *s. Educ:* St Marylebone Grammar Sch.; London Univ. (external). Asst Clerk, LCC, 1948-52; Dir of Estabs, LCC, 1952-57. Jt Sec., Police Council, 1957-72; Jt Sec., Nat. Jt Industrial Councils (Local Authorities), 1957-72; Mem., Nat. Industrial Relations Court, 1972-74. *Recreations:* gardening, golf. *Address:* 10 Woolbrook Park, Sidmouth, Devon. *T:* Sidmouth 4884.

GRIFFITHS, Richard Cerdin; Director, Inter-University Council for Higher Education Overseas, since 1970; *b* 21 Oct. 1915; *s* of James Griffiths, MBE, and Gwendolen Griffiths, Swansea; *m* 1944, Pamela de Grave Hetherington; three *s* one *d. Educ:* Swansea Grammar Sch.; Jesus Coll., Oxford (Exhibnr, Hon. Schol.). 1st Cl. Hons Maths Mods, 2nd Cl. Finals; MA. Entered Admiralty as Asst Principal, 1939; served Royal Navy (Ord. Seaman), 1940-41; British Admiralty Delegn, Washington, DC,

1941-43. Private Sec. to Sec. to Admiralty (Sir Henry Markham), 1943-44; transf. to Treasury, 1946; Private Sec. to Sec. of Treasury (Sir Edward Bridges), 1948-49; Asst Sec., 1949; Treasury Representative in Australia and New Zealand, 1952-53; Imperial Defence Coll., 1957; Sec., UK Delegn to Commonwealth Trade and Economic Conf., Montreal, 1958; Head of Arts and Science Div., 1958-63; Under-Sec., Treasury, 1963; Dep. Sec., UGC, 1963-70. Mem., UGC, Hong Kong; Mem. Council: S Pacific Univ., 1971-73; Queen Elizabeth Coll., Univ. of London; Hon. Sec., Civil Service Sports Council, 1961-71; Vice Chairman: Civil Service Lifeboat Fund; Hill Homes; Vice-Pres., Highgate Literary and Scientific Instn. Mem. Council, Hon. Soc. of Cymmrodorion. *Recreations:* cricket, sailing. *Address:* 2 St Albans Villas, NW5 1QU. *T:* 01-485 1862. *Clubs:* Athenæum; MCC.

GRIFFITHS, Roger Noel Price, MA Cantab; JP; Headmaster of Hurstpierpoint College, since 1964; *b* 25 Dec. 1931; *er s* of William Thomas and Annie Evelyn Griffiths; *m* 1966, Diana, *y d* of Capt. J. F. B. Brown, RN; three *d. Educ:* Lancing Coll.; King's Coll., Cambridge. Asst Master at Charterhouse, 1956-64. MA Oxon, by incorporation, 1960. *Recreations:* music, theatre, bowls. *Address:* Hurstpierpoint College, Hassocks, West Sussex BN6 9JS. *T:* Hurstpierpoint 833178. *Club:* East India, Devonshire, Sports and Public Schools.

GRIFFITHS, Trevor, BScEng, CEng, FIMechE, FIEE; registered professional engineer, State of California; Engineer Specialist, Bechtel Power Corporation, Norwalk, California; *b* 17 April 1913; *m* 1939, Evelyn Mary Colborn; one *d. Educ:* Bishop Gore Gram. Sch., Swansea; University Coll., London. Metropolitan Vickers Electrical Co. Ltd, 1934; Air Min., 1938; UKAEA, 1955; Min. of Power, 1960; Min. of Technology, 1969 (Chief Inspector of Nuclear Installations, 1964-71); Dep. Chief Inspector of Nuclear Installations, DTI, 1971-73. *Address:* 2025 Camino del Sol, Fullerton, Calif 92633, USA. *T:* (714) 992 0206.

GRIFFITHS, Trevor; playwright; *b* 4 April 1935; *s* of Ernest Griffiths and Anne Connor; *m* 1961, Janice Elaine Stansfeld; one *s* two *d. Educ:* Manchester Univ. BA (Hons) Eng. Lang. and Lit. Teaching, 1957-65; Educn Officer, BBC, 1965-72. *Publications:* Occupations, 1972, 2nd edn 1977; Sam Sam, 1972; The Party, 1974; Comedians, 1976; All Good Men, and Absolute Beginners, 1977; Through the Night, and Such Impossibilities, 1977; Thermidor, and The Wages of Thin, 1977. *Recreations:* soccer, music, chess. *Address:* c/o Clive Goodwin, 79 Cromwell Road, SW7. *T:* 01-370 4435. *Clubs:* Trades Council (Leeds); Bradford Labour (Manchester).

GRIFFITHS, Ward David; Part-time Member Board, British Steel Corporation, since 1970; *b* 9 Oct. 1915; *s* of David and Maud Griffiths; *m* 1940, Maisie Edith Williams; three *s* two *d. Educ:* elementary and technical schools. Steelworker, 1936-70. Br. Sec. and subseq. Exec. Mem., Iron and Steel Trades Assoc., 1960-68. Deleg., Tinplate Jt Industrial Council, 1965-68; Employee Dir, S Wales Gp and subseq. Strip Mills Div., British Steel Corp., 1968-70; Director: Grundy Auto Products Ltd, 1975-; Ruthner Continuous Crop Systems Ltd, 1976-. *Recreations:* motoring, Rugby football. *Address:* 18 Cambridge Gardens, Ebbw Vale, Gwent NP3 5HG. *T:* Ebbw Vale 303716. *Club:* Ernest Lever Works (Ebbw Vale).

GRIFFITHS, Hon. Sir (William) Hugh, Kt 1971; MC 1944; **Hon. Mr Justice Griffiths;** a Judge of the High Court of Justice, Queen's Bench Division, since 1971; *b* 26 Sept. 1923; *s* of late Sir Hugh Griffiths, CBE, MS, FRCS; *m* 1949, Evelyn, *d* of Col K. A. Krefting; one *s* three *d. Educ:* Charterhouse; St John's Coll., Cambridge. Commissioned in Welsh Guards, 1942; demobilised after war service, 1946. Cambridge, 1946-48. BA 1948. Called to the Bar, Inner Temple, 1949; QC 1964; Master of the Bench, Inner Temple, 1971. Recorder of Margate, 1962-64, of Cambridge, 1964-70; A Judge, National Industrial Relations Court, 1973-74. Mem., Bar Council, 1968-69. *Recreations:* golf, fishing. *Address:* 25 The Boltons, SW10. *T:* 01-370 1340. *Clubs:* Garrick; MCC; Hawks (Cambridge); Woking Golf.

GRIGG, John (Edward Poynder); political journalist; *b* 15 April 1924; *s* of 1st Baron Altrincham and Joan, *d* of 1st Baron Islington; *S* to father's barony, 1955, but did not apply for Writ of Summons to the House of Lords; disclaimed title, 31 July 1963; *m* 1958, Patricia, *d* of H. E. Campbell, *qv*; two *s* (adopted). *Educ:* Eton (Capt. of the Oppidans); New Coll., Oxford (Exhibitioner). MA, Modern History; Gladstone Memorial Prize. Served Grenadier Guards, 1943-45. Editor, National and English Review, 1954-60 (formerly Associate Editor); Columnist for The Guardian, 1960-67; has contrib. to many other papers. Governor, Nehru Meml Trust. Contested (C) Oldham West, 1951 and 1955. *Publications:* Two Anglican

Essays, 1958; The Young Lloyd George, 1973. *Heir:* (to disclaimed barony): *b* Hon. Anthony Ulick David Dundas Grigg [*b* 12 Jan. 1934; *m* 1965, Eliane de Miramon; two *s* one *d*]. *Address:* 32 Dartmouth Row, SE10. *T:* 01-692 4973. *Club:* Beefsteak.

GRIGGS, Norman Edward, CBE 1976; Secretary-General, The Building Societies Association, since 1963; Secretary-General, International Union of Building Societies and Savings Associations, since 1972; *b* 27 May 1916; *s* of late Archibald Griggs and Maud Griggs (*née* Hewing); *m* 1947, Livia Lavinia Jandolo; one *s* one step *s. Educ:* Newport Grammar Sch.; London Sch. of Econs and Polit. Science (BScEcon). FCIS. Accountancy Dept, County of London Electric Supply Co. Ltd, 1933-40; service in RE and RAPC, Middle East, 1940-46; Asst Sec., Glass Manufrs' Fedn, 1946-52; Sec., Plastics Inst., 1952-56; Asst Sec., Building Socs Assoc., 1956-61, Dep. Sec. 1961-63. *Recreation:* print addict. *Address:* Northmead, Holwell Road, Pirton, Hitchin, Herts. *T:* Pirton 216.

GRIGOROV, Mitko; Order of G. Dimitrov, 1964; Member, since 1971, Vice-President, since 1974, State Council of People's Republic of Bulgaria; *b* 9 Sept. 1920; *m* 1956, Stanka Stanoeva; one *d. Educ:* Sofia University. Mem. of Parliament from 1953, Minister without Portfolio, 1962-66; Bulgarian Ambassador to the Court of St James's, 1969-71. Mem., Editorial Board of magazine Problems of Peace and Socialism, 1966-69. *Recreation:* mountaineering. *Address:* c/o Durzhaven Suvet (State Council of Bulgaria), Dondoukov 2, Sofia, Bulgaria.

GRIGSON, Geoffrey; poet; *b* 2 March 1905; 7th *s* of late Canon W. S. Grigson, Pelynt, Cornwall and of Mary Beatrice Boldero; *m* 1st, Frances Galt (*d* 1937), St Louis, Missouri; one *d* ; 2nd, Berta Kunert (marr. diss.); one *s* one *d* ; 3rd, Jane Grigson, *qv , d* of G.S. McIntire, CBE; one *d* . Editor of New Verse, 1933-39; formerly on staff of Yorkshire Post, Morning Post (Literary Editor) and BBC. *Publications:* Several Observations, 1939; Under the Cliff and other poems, 1943; Henry Moore, 1943; The Isles of Scilly and other poems, 1946; Samuel Palmer, 1947; The Harp of Aeolus, 1947; Places of the Mind, 1949; The Crest on the Silver, 1950; William Barnes (Muses Library), 1950; John Clare (Muses Library), 1950; Essays from the Air, 1951; A Master of Our Time (Wyndham Lewis), 1951; Gardenage, 1952; Legenda Suecana (poems), 1953; Freedom of the Parish, 1954; The Englishman's Flora, 1955; Gerard Manley Hopkins, 1955; English Drawings, 1955; The Painted Caves, 1957; Art Treasures of the British Museum, 1958; The Three Kings, 1958; A Herbal of All Sorts, 1959; The Cherry Tree, 1959; English Excursions, 1960; Christopher Smart, 1961; The Shell Country Book, 1962; Collected Poems, 1963; Poems of Walter Savage Landor, 1964; (with Jane Grigson) Shapes and Stories, 1964; The Shell Country Alphabet, 1966; A Skull in Salop and Other Poems, 1967; Shapes and Adventures, 1967; Poems and Poets, 1968; A Choice of William Morris's Verse, 1968; Ingestion of Ice-Cream and Other Poems, 1969; Shapes and People, 1969; Notes from an Odd Country, 1970; (ed) Faber Book of Popular Verse, 1971; (ed) A Choice of Southey's Verse, 1971; Discoveries of Bones and Stones and Other Poems, 1971 (Duff Cooper Meml Prize 1972); (ed) Unrespectable Verse, 1971; Rainbows, Fleas and Flowers, 1971; Shapes and Creatures, 1972; Sad Grave of an Imperial Mongoose and Other Poems, 1973; (ed) Faber Book of Love Poems, 1973; (ed) Dictionary of English Plant Names, 1974; Angles and Circles and other Poems, 1974; The Contrary View, 1974; Britain Observed, 1975; (ed) Poet to Poet: Charles Cotton, 1975; (ed) Penguin Book of Ballads, 1975; The Goddess of Love, 1976; Faber Book of Epigrams, 1978; (ed) Faber Book of Nonsense Verse, 1978. *Address:* Broad Town Farm, Broad Town, Swindon, Wilts. *T:* Broad Hinton 259.

GRIGSON, Jane; Cookery Correspondent, Observer Colour Magazine, since 1968; *b* 13 March 1928; *d* of George Shipley McIntire, CBE, and Doris Berkley; *m* Geoffrey Grigson, *qv* ; one *d* . *Educ:* Casterton Sch., Westmorland; Newnham Coll., Cambridge. Editorial Assistant, Rainbird McLean Ltd, and Thames and Hudson Ltd, 1953-55; translator from Italian, 1956-67; cookery writer, 1967-. *Publications:* Charcuterie and French Pork Cookery, 1967; Good Things, 1971; Fish Cookery, 1973; English Food, 1974; The Mushroom Feast, 1975; Vegetables, 1978; contributing editor, World Atlas of Food, 1974; (translated) Of Crimes and Punishments, by Cesare Beccaria, 1964 (John Florio prize). *Address:* Broad Town Farmhouse, Broad Town, Swindon, Wiltshire. *T:* Broad Hinton 259.

GRILLER, Sidney Aaron, CBE 1951; Leader of Griller String Quartet since 1928; *b* London, 10 Jan. 1911; *s* of Salter Griller and Hannah (*née* Green); *m* 1932, Elizabeth Honor, *y d* of James Linton, JP, Co. Down, N Ireland; one *s* one *d. Educ:* Royal

Academy of Music. Toured British Isles, Holland, Germany, Switzerland, France, Italy, 1928-38; first concert tour in USA, 1939. Served RAF, 1940-45. Lecturer in Music, University of California, 1949; world tours, 1951, 1953. Prof. of Music: Royal Irish Acad. of Music, 1963; Royal Academy of Music, 1964. Worshipful Company of Musicians Medal for Chamber Music, 1944; FRAM, 1945; Mem. Royal Society of St George, 1955. *Address:* 63 Marloes Road, W8. *T:* 01-937 7067.

GRILLET, Alain R.; *see* Robbe-Grillet.

GRIMA, Andrew Peter; Jeweller by appointment to HM the Queen; Managing Director: H. J. Co. Ltd, since 1951; Andrew Grima Ltd, since 1966; *b* 31 May 1921; *s* of John Grima and Leopolda Farnese; *m* 1947, Helène Marianne Haller; one *s* two *d. Educ:* St Joseph's Coll., Beulah Hill; Nottingham Univ. Served War of 1939-45, REME, India and Burma, 1942-46 (despatches, 1945); commanded div. workshop. Director and jewellery designer, H. J. Co., 1947-. Exhibitions in numerous cities all over the world; designed and made prestige collection of watches, "About Time", 1970; exhibited at Goldsmiths' Hall. Opened shops in Sydney and New York, 1970; Zürich, 1971; Tokyo, 1973. Has donated annual Andrew Grima award to Sir John Cass Coll. of Art, 1963-. Duke of Edinburgh Prize for Elegant Design, 1966; 11 Diamond Internat. New York Awards, 1963-67. Freeman, City of London, 1964; Liveryman, Worshipful Co. of Goldsmiths, 1968. *Publications:* contribs to: International Diamond Annual, S Africa, 1970; 6 Meister Juweliere unserer Zeit, 1971. *Recreations:* paintings, sculpture, food and wine, campaign to rule out red tape. *Address:* 80 Jermyn Street, SW1. *T:* 01-839 7561. *Clubs:* Royal Automobile, Institute of Directors.

GRIME, Sir Harold (Riley), Kt 1959; DL; JP; Chairman and Editor-in-Chief of the West Lancashire Evening Gazette and associated newspapers; Editor of the Blackpool Gazette, 1926-62; *b* 12 May 1896; *s* of late Frederick Alexander Grime, JP, and late Fannie Grime (*née* Riley); *m* 1925, Mary (Mollie) Bowman (*d* 1970), *d* of late W. Powell Bowman, Leeds; two *d. Educ:* Arnold Sch., Blackpool; Bonn, Germany. East Lancs Regt, 1915-17; Indian Army, 1917-20. Yorkshire Evening Post and London Evening News, 1920-23. Dir, Press Association, 1942-51 (Chm. 1946-47); Dir, Reuters, 1945-47; Founder Mem., British Cttee, Internat. Press Inst., 1951; Chm., Guild of Editors (NW Region), 1957-58. Hon. Sec., Blackpool Victoria Hosp., 1938-48; Hon. Treas., Blackpool Conservative and Unionist Assoc., 1938-45; Dir, Blackpool Tower and Winter Gardens Cos., 1944-68 (Vice-Chm. 1953-68); Pres., Preston and District Chamber of Commerce, 1962-67. Mem., Gen. Advisory Council, BBC, 1960-64. Hon. Freeman of Blackpool, 1950. DL Lancs, 1968. JP for Blackpool, 1945-. *Publications:* The Silver Trumpet, 1942; Sand in My Shoes, 1950. *Address:* 24 Lowcross Road, Poulton-le-Fylde, Lancs.

GRIMES, Prof. William Francis, CBE 1955; DLitt, FSA; FMA; Director of the Institute of Archæology, and Professor of Archæology, University of London, 1956-73; *b* 31 Oct. 1905; *e s* of Thomas George Grimes, Pembroke; *m* 1st, 1928, Barbara Lilian Morgan (marr. diss., 1959); one *s* one *d*; 2nd, 1959, Audrey Williams (*née* Davies). *Educ:* University of Wales (MA); DLitt Wales, 1961. Asst Keeper of Archæology, National Museum of Wales, Cardiff, 1926-38; Asst Archæology Officer, Ordnance Survey, 1938-45; seconded to Min. of Works to record historic monuments on defence sites, 1939-45; Dir London Museum, 1945-56. Mem. Royal Commn on Ancient Monuments in Wales, 1948- (Chm., 1967-), and of Ancient Monuments Boards, England, 1954-77, Wales, 1959-; Mem. Royal Commn on Historical Monuments (England), 1964-. Sec. to Coun. for British Archæology, 1949-54, Pres. 1954-59, Vice-Pres., 1961-65, Treas., 1964-74; Pres. London and Middlesex Archæological Soc., 1950-59; Pres. Royal Archæological Institute, 1957-60 (Vice-Pres. 1951-57); Vice-President: Soc. of Antiquaries, 1953-57; Soc. for Medieval Archæology; Prehistoric Soc., 1958-61; Soc. for Roman Studies, 1973-; Hon. Dir of Excavations for the Roman and Mediæval London Excavation Council, 1946-; Chm., London Topographical Soc. 1961-73. Pres., Cambrian Archæological Assoc., 1963-64 (G. T. Clark Prize, 1946); Chm., Faculty of Archæology, History and Letters, British Sch. at Rome, 1963-66; President: Stanmore Archæological Soc., 1962-; Tenby Museum, 1969-; Field Studies Council, 1975- (Chm., 1966-75). *Publications:* Holt, Denbighshire, Legionary Works Depôt (Y Cymmrodor), 1930; Pre-history of Wales, 1951; (ed) Aspects of Archæology in Britain and Beyond, 1951; (with M. D. Knowles) Charterhouse, 1954; (with others) Brooke House, Hackney (London Survey, Vol. XXVIII), 1960; Excavations in Defence Sites, 1939-1945, I, 1960; The Excavation of Roman and Mediæval London, 1968; many papers in learned jls. *Address:* 29 Bryn Road, Swansea, West Glamorgan.

GRIMOND, Rt. Hon. Joseph; TD; PC 1961; LLD Edinburgh; MP (L) Orkney and Shetland since 1950; Leader of the Parliamentary Liberal Party, 1956-67, and May-July 1976; Director, The Manchester Guardian and Evening News Ltd, since 1967; Chancellor of University of Kent at Canterbury, since 1970; *b* 29 July 1913; *s* of Joseph Bowman Grimond and Helen Lydia Richardson; *m* 1938, Hon. Laura Miranda, *d* of late Sir Maurice Bonham Carter, KCB, KCVO, and Baroness Asquith of Yarnbury, DBE; two *s* one *d* (and one *s* decd). *Educ:* Eton; Balliol Coll., Oxford (Brackenbury Scholar). 1st Class Hons (Politics, Philosophy, and Economics). Called to the Bar, Middle Temple (Harmsworth Scholar), 1937. Served War of 1939-45, Fife and Forfar Yeomanry and Staff 53 Div. (Major). Contested Orkney and Shetland (Liberal), 1945. Dir of Personnel, European Office, UNRRA, 1945-47; Sec. of the National Trust for Scotland, 1947-49. Rector: Edinburgh Univ., 1960-63; Aberdeen Univ., 1969-72. Hon. LLD: Edinburgh, 1960; Aberdeen, 1972; Birmingham, 1974; Hon. DCL Kent, 1970. *Publications:* The Liberal Future, 1959; The Liberal Challenge, 1963; (with B. Neve) The Referendum, 1975; contributor: The Prime Ministers, 1976; My Oxford, 1977. *Address:* Old Manse of Firth, Kirkwall, Orkney.

GRIMSBY, Bishop Suffragan of, since 1966; **Rt. Rev. Gerald Fitzmaurice Colin, MA;** *b* 19 July 1913; *s* of Frederick Constant Colin and Jemima Fitzmaurice; *m* 1941, Iris Susan Stuart Weir; three *s* two *d. Educ:* Mountjoy Sch.; Trinity Coll., Dublin. MA (TCD) 1946. Deacon, 1936; Priest, 1937. St George's, Dublin, 1938; Chancellor's Vicar, St Patrick's Cathedral, Dublin, 1938; RAFVR, 1939-47; Vicar of Frodingham, Dio. of Lincoln, 1947-66; Canon of Lincoln Cathedral, 1960; Rural Dean of Manlake, 1960; Proctor in Convocation, 1960-65, 1966-70. *Recreation:* fishing. *Address:* 21 Westgate, Louth, Lincs.

GRIMSHAW, Maj.-Gen. Ewing Henry Wrigley, CB 1965; CBE 1957 (OBE 1954); DSO 1945; *b* 30 June 1911; *s* of Col E. W. Grimshaw; *m* 1943, Hilda Florence Agnes Allison; two *s* one *d. Educ:* Brighton Coll. Joined Indian Army, 1931. Served War of 1939-45, Western Desert and Burma (despatches twice). Transferred to Royal Inniskilling Fusiliers, 1947; Active Service in Malaya, Kenya and Suez, 1956 and Cyprus, 1958. GOC 44th Div. (TA) and Home Counties Dist, 1962-65. Col, The Royal Inniskilling Fusiliers, 1966-68; Dep. Col, The Royal Irish Rangers, 1968-73. *Address:* The Trellis House, Copford Green, near Colchester, Essex.

GRIMSTON, family name of **Baron Grimston of Westbury** and of **Earl of Verulam.**

GRIMSTON OF WESTBURY, 1st Baron, *cr* 1964; **Robert Villiers Grimston,** Bt *cr* 1952; BSc, ACGI; *b* 8 June 1897; *e s* of late Hon. Robert Grimston, Canon of St Albans; *m* 1923, Sybil, *e d* of late Sir Sigismund Neumann, Bt; three *s* two *d. Educ:* Repton; City and Guilds Engineering Coll., London Univ. Commissioned RGA (6″ Howitzers), 1916; served in Salonika and Palestine, 1916-19. MP (C) Westbury Div. Wilts, 1931-64; Junior Lord of the Treasury, 1937; Asst Whip (Unpaid), 1937; Vice-Chamberlain of HM's Household, 1938-39, Treasurer, 1939-42; Asst Postmaster-Gen., 1942-45; Parliamentary Sec., Ministry of Supply, 1945; Dep. Chm. of Ways and Means, 1962-64. Mem., UK Delegn to Gen. Assembly of UN, 1960. Pres. Urban District Councils Association, 1949-70. Comdr Parly Home Guard, 1941-42. *Heir:* *s* Hon. Robert Walter Sigismund Grimston [*b* 14 June 1925; *m* 1949, Hon. June Mary Ponsonby, *d* of 5th Baron de Mauley; two *s* one *d*]. *Address:* 4 Cadogan Square, SW1. *T:* 01-235 2340. *Club:* Carlton.

GRIMTHORPE, 4th Baron, *cr* 1886; **Christopher John Beckett,** Bt 1813; OBE 1958; DL; Deputy Commander, Malta and Libya, 1964-67; *b* 16 Sept. 1915; *e s* of 3rd Baron Grimthorpe, TD, and Mary Lady Grimthorpe (*d* 1962); *S* father, 1963; *m* 1954, Elizabeth Lumley, 2nd *d* of 11th Earl of Scarbrough, KG, PC, GCSI, GCIE, GCVO; two *s* one *d. Educ:* Eton. 2nd Lieut, 9 Lancers, 1936; Lt-Col, 9 Lancers, 1955-58; AAG, War Office, 1958-61; Brigadier, Royal Armoured Corps, HQ, Western Command, 1961-64. Col, 9/12 Royal Lancers, 1973-. ADC to the Queen, 1964-67. Director: Standard Broadcasting Corp. of Canada (UK), 1972-; Thirsk Racecourse Ltd, 1972-; Yorkshire Post Newspapers, 1973; Pres., London Metropolitan Region YMCA, 1972-. DL North Yorkshire, 1969. *Recreations:* travel, horse sports. *Heir:* *s* Hon. Edward John Beckett, *b* 20 Nov. 1954. *Address:* 87 Dorset House, Gloucester Place, NW1. *T:* 01-486 4374; Westow Hall, York. *T:* Whitwell-on-the-Hill 225. *Club:* Cavalry and Guards.

GRIMWOOD, Frank Southgate, BA; DPhil; ABPsS; *b* 14 July 1904; *s* of late Frank Grimwood, Ipswich and Newbury, and Rose Grimwood (*née* Lake), Bucklebury, Berks; *m* 1935, Mary

Habberley Price, MA Oxon; one s one d. *Educ:* Isleworth County High Sch.; Reading Univ. (Wantage Hall); The Queen's Coll., Oxford. DPhil Oxon; BA Hons University of Reading. Sub-Warden and Foreign Student Sec., SCM, 1929-30; Lecturer in Philosophy and Psychology, City Literary Institute, 1930-40; Welfare Officer (Oxon, Bucks, and Berks), Min. of Labour and Nat. Service, 1940-48. Advanced Student, The Queen's Coll., Oxford, 1948-56, including one year (1951) at Cuddesdon Theological Coll. (thesis on psychotherapy and religion). Lecturer and Tutor, Oxford Univ. Extra-Mural Delegacy, 1956-61; Warden and Director of Studies, Moor Park College, 1961-72; lecturing and tutoring groups for Nat. Marriage Guidance Council, 1965-70; Exec. Sec., Keble Coll., Oxford, Centenary Appeal, 1972-74. Private consultant psychotherapist. *Recreations:* painting, walking, biography. *Address:* 69A Jack Straw's Lane, Oxford OX3 0DW. *T:* Oxford 68535.

GRINDLE, Capt. John Annesley, CBE 1943; RN; JP; *b* 17 Sept. 1900; *s* of late George Annesley Grindle and late Eveleen Grindle; *m* 1925, Joyce Lilian Alton, *d* of J. W. A. Batchelor, Blackheath; two *s. Educ:* Pembroke Lodge, Southbourne; RN Colleges, Osborne and Dartmouth; Pembroke Coll., Cambridge; Midshipman, 1917; Comdr 1934; Captain 1941. Retired list, 1950. JP (Hants) 1952. *Recreation:* gardening. *Address:* Lark Hill, Portchester, Hants. *T:* Cosham 76067.

GRINDON, John Evelyn, CVO 1957; DSO 1945; AFC 1948; Group Captain, RAF retired; Metropolitan Police, New Scotland Yard (C4), since 1976; *b* 30 Sept. 1917; *s* of Thomas Edward Grindon (killed in action, Ypres, Oct. 1917), and Dora Eastlake. *Educ:* Dulwich College. Cadet at RAF Coll., Cranwell, 1935-37. Served in No 5 Group Bomber Command during War of 1939-45. Commanded The Queen's Flight, 1953-56; retired at own request 1959. Dir/Gen. Manager in printing/publishing, 1961-71. *Recreations:* music, sailing. *Address:* 1 Ovington Gardens, SW3. *T:* 01-589 8822. *Club:* Royal Air Force.

GRINDROD, Rt. Rev. John Basil Rowland; *see* Rockhampton, Bishop of.

GRINKE, Frederick, FRAM; Solo Violinist; Professor of Violin, Royal Academy of Music, London; *b* Winnipeg, Canada, 8 Aug. 1911; *s* of Arthur Grinke, Winnipeg; *m* 1942, Dorothy Ethel Sirr Sheldon; one *s. Educ:* Winnipeg; Royal Academy of Music, London (all prizes for solo and chamber music playing). Studied with Adolf Busch in Switzerland, with Carl Flesch in London and Belgium. Was leader and soloist with the Boyd Neel Orchestra for 10 years. Appeared regularly as Soloist with leading orchestras; has played in many countries in Europe also in America, Australia and New Zealand. Has appeared at Festivals: Edinburgh, Bath, Cheltenham, Three Choirs, Salzburg. Has taken part in many Promenade Concerts. A sonata was dedicated to him by Vaughan Williams; his sonata partner is Joseph Weingarten. Has made numerous recordings, including many works with the composers as pianists (such as Rubbra, Ireland, Berkeley, Benjamin). Has acted as mem. of the Jury for several international violin competitions. *Recreations:* music, cooking, wine, reading, the theatre. *Address:* Frog's Hall, Braiseworth, near Eye, Suffolk. *T:* Eye 483.

GRINT, Edmund Thomas Charles, CBE 1960; *b* 14 Feb. 1904; *e s* of Edmund Albert Grint; *m* 1930, Olive Maria, *d* of Albert Cheyne Sherras; one *s* two *d. Educ:* London Univ. (Dip. Econs). Joined ICI 1929; Commercial Dir, Nobel Div., 1946; Director: Billingham Div., 1952-61; Alkali Div., 1961-63; Mond Div., 1964. Dep. Chief Labour Officer, 1951; Chief Labour Officer, 1952-63; Gen. Manager Personnel, 1963-65. Chm., Nat. Dock Labour Board, 1966-69; Pres., Midland Iron and Steel Wages Bd, 1971. *Recreations:* golf, gardening. *Address:* Old Walls, Seal, Sevenoaks, Kent. *T:* Sevenoaks 61364.

GRISEWOOD, Harman Joseph Gerard, CBE 1960; Chief Assistant to the Director-General, BBC, 1955-64, retired; *b* 8 Feb. 1906; *e s* of late Lieut-Col Harman Grisewood and Lucille Cardozo; *m* 1940, Clotilde Margaret Bailey; one *d. Educ:* Ampleforth Coll., York; Worcester Coll., Oxford. BBC Repertory Co., 1929-33; Announcer, 1933-36; Asst to Programme Organiser, 1936-39; Asst Dir Programme Planning, 1939-41; Asst Controller, European Div., 1941-45; Actg Controller, European Div., 1945-46; Dir of Talks, 1946-47; Planner, Third Programme, 1947-48; Controller of the Third Programme, BBC, 1948-52; Dir of the Spoken Word, BBC, 1952-55. Member: Younger Cttee on Privacy, 1970-72; Lord Chancellor's Cttee on Defamation, 1971; Res. Officer, Royal Commn on Civil Liberty, 1973-75. Vice-Pres., European Broadcasting Union, 1953-54. Chm., The Latin Mass Soc., 1969. King Christian X Freedom Medal, 1946. Mem. Hon. Soc. of

Cymmrodorion, 1956. Knight of Magistral Grace, Sovereign and Military Order of Malta, 1960. *Publications:* Broadcasting and Society, 1949; The Recess, 1963 (novel); The Last Cab on the Rank, 1964 (novel); David Jones: Welsh National Lecture, 1966; One Thing at a Time (autobiography), 1968; The Painted Kipper, 1970. *Address:* c/o Coutts and Co., 10 Mount Street, W1Y 6DP.

GRIST, Ian; MP (C) Cardiff North since Feb. 1974; *b* 5 Dec. 1938; *s* of Basil William Grist, MBE and late Leila Helen Grist; *m* 1966, Wendy Anne (*née* White); two *s. Educ:* Repton Sch.; Jesus Coll., Oxford (Schol.). Plebiscite Officer, Southern Cameroons, 1960-61; Stores Manager, United Africa Co., Nigeria, 1961-63; Wales Information Officer, Conservative Central Office, 1963-74; Conservative Research Dept, 1970-74. *Recreations:* reading, listening to music, politics. *Address:* House of Commons, SW1A 0AA; 18 Tydfil Place, Roath, Cardiff.

GRIST, John Frank; Controller, English Regions BBC, 1972-77; *b* 10 May 1924; *s* of Austin Grist, OBE, MC, and Ada Mary Grist (*née* Ball); *m* Gilian, *d* of late Roger Cranage and Helen Marjorie Rollett; one *s* two *d. Educ:* Ryde Sch., IoW; London Sch. of Economics and Political Science (BSc Econ); Univ. of Chicago. RAF Pilot, 1942-46. BBC External Services, Talks Producer, Programme Organiser, Northern Region; Controller, Nat. Programmes, Nigerian Broadcasting Service, 1953-56; BBC TV Talks and Current Affairs at Lime Grove, 1957-72, Hd of Current Affairs Gp, 1967-72. Producer of political programmes; Editor of Gallery and of Panorama. *Address:* BBC, Broadcasting House, W1A 1AA.

GRIST, Prof. Norman Roy, FRCPEd; Professor of Infectious Diseases, University of Glasgow, since 1965; *b* 9 March 1918; *s* of Walter Reginald Grist and Florence Goodwin Grist (*née* Nadin); *m* 1943, Mary Stewart McAlister. *Educ:* Shawlands Acad., Glasgow; University of Glasgow, Postgrad. studies at Dept of Bacteriology, University of Liverpool, 1948-49; Virus Reference Lab., Colindale, London, 1951-52; Dept of Epidemiology, University of Michigan, 1956-57. BSc 1939; MB, ChB (Commendation), 1942; Mem. 1950, Fellow 1958, RCP, Edinburgh. Founder Mem., 1963, FCPath., 1967. Ho. Phys. Gartloch Hosp., 1942-43; RAMC, GDO 223 Fd Amb. and RMO 2/KSLI, 1943-46; Ho. Surg. Victoria Inf., Glasgow, 1946-47; Res. Phys, Ruchill Hosp., Glasgow, 1947-48; Research Asst, Glasgow Univ. Dept of Infectious Diseases, 1948-52; Lectr in Virus Disease, Glasgow Univ., 1952-62, and Regional Adviser in Virology to Scottish Western Reg. Hosp. Bd, 1960-74; Reader in Viral Epidemiology, Glasgow Univ., 1962-65. Consultant in Virus Diseases to WHO, 1967-. Bronze Medal, Helsinki Univ., 1973; Orden Civil de Sanidad, cat. Encomienda, Spain, 1974. *Publications:* Diagnostic Methods in Clinical Virology, 1974; numerous contribs. to British and international med. jls. *Recreations:* lazing, travelling, bird-watching. *Address:* 6A Sydenham Road, Glasgow G12 9NR. *T:* 041-339 5242. *Clubs:* Royal Automobile; Royal Scottish Automobile (Glasgow).

GROBLER, Richard Victor; Courts Administrator, Central Criminal Court, since 1977; *b* Umtali, S Rhodesia, 27 May 1936; *m* 1961, Julienne Nora de la Cour (*née* Sheath); one *s* three *d. Educ:* Bishop's, Capetown; Univ. of Cape Town (BA). Called to the Bar, Gray's Inn, 1961; joined staff of Clerk of the Court, Central Criminal Court, 1961; Dep. Clerk of the Court, 1970; Dep. Courts Administrator, 1972; Courts Administrator, Inner London Crown Court, 1974; Sec., Lord Chancellor's Adv. Cttee on Justices of the Peace for Inner London and Jt Hon. Sec., Inner London Br. of Magistrates' Assoc., 1974-77. Co-ordinator of Crown Courts Taxation in the South Eastern Circuit. Liveryman, Worshipful Company of Gold and Silver Wyre Drawers. *Recreations:* gardening, swimming, golf. *Address:* Central Criminal Court, Old Bailey, EC4M 7BS. *T:* 01-248 3277.

GROCOTT, Bruce Joseph; MP (Lab) Lichfield and Tamworth, since Oct. 1974; *b* 1 Nov. 1940; *s* of Reginald Grocott and Helen Grocott (*née* Stewart); *m* 1965, Sally Barbara Kay Ridgway; two *s . Educ:* Hemel Hempstead Grammar Sch.; Leicester and Manchester Univs. BA(Pol), MA(Econ). Admin. Officer, LCC, 1963-64; Tutor in Govt, Manchester Univ., 1964-65; Lectr and Sen. Lectr, Birmingham Polytechnic, 1965-72; Principal Lectr in Govt, North Staffordshire Polytechnic, 1972-74. Chm., Finance Cttee, Bromsgrove UDC, 1972-74. PPS to: Minister for Local Govt and Planning, 1975-76; Minister of Agriculture, 1976-. *Publications:* contribs to govt reports on local govt matters. *Recreations:* cricket, snooker, fiction writing. *Address:* House of Commons, SW1A 0AA. *T:* 01-239 3410. *Club:* Chasetown Working Men's.

GROHMAN, Vice-Adm. H. T. B.; see Baillie-Grohman.

GROMYKO, Andrei Andreevich, Order of Lenin (triple award); Minister of Foreign Affairs of the USSR, since 1957; Member of the Politburo, since 1973; *b* 6 July 1909; *m* Lydia D. Grinevich; one *s* one *d*. *Educ:* Agricultural Institute and Institute of Economics, Moscow. Scientific worker (senior), Acad. of Sciences USSR, 1936-39, also lecturing in Moscow Universities. Chief of American Division National Council of Foreign Affairs, 1939; Counsellor, USSR Washington Embassy, 1939-43; Ambassador to USA and Minister to Cuba, 1943-46; Soviet Representative on UN Security Council, 1946-48; Deputy Foreign Minister, 1946-49, 1953-54; 1st Deputy Minister of Foreign Affairs, 1949-52; Soviet Ambassador in London, 1952-53; First Deputy Foreign Minister in Moscow, 1954-57. Chm. of Delegates, Conference on Post-War Security, Dumbarton Oaks, USA, 1944. Hero of Socialist Labour, 1969. *Address:* Ministry of Foreign Affairs, 32-34 Smolenskaya-Sennaya Ploshchad, Moscow, USSR.

GRONCHI, Giovanni; Member of Senate of the Italian Republic; President of Italy, 1955-62; *b* Pontedera, 10 Sept. 1887; *s* of Sperandio Gronchi and Maria (*née* Giacomelli); *m* ; two *c*. *Educ:* Pisa Univ. Served European War of 1914-18 as a Volunteer. A founder of Italian Popular Party (Popolare), 1919; Head of Confederation of Christian Workers, 1919. Elected MP, 1919, and became Under-Sec. for Commerce and Industry, 1922; retired (parliamentary mandate), 1923-42; Minister for Industry, Commerce and Labour, 1944-45; Minister of Commerce, 1945. Elected to Constituent Assembly of Republic of Italy, 1946; Pres. Christian Democrat Parliamentary Group, 1946-48; Speaker, Chamber of Deputies, 1948-55. *Address:* Senato della Repubblica, Rome, Italy; Via Carlo Fea 7, Rome, Italy.

GRONHAUG, Arnold Conrad; Director of Mechanical and Electrical Engineering Services, Department of the Environment, since 1976; *b* 26 March 1921; *s* of late James Gronhaug, MBE, and Beatrice May Gronhaug; *m* 1945, Patricia Grace Smith; two *d*. *Educ:* Barry Grammar Sch.; Cardiff Technical Coll. CEng, FIEE, FCIBS. Electrical Officer, RNVR, 1941-46. Air Ministry Works Directorate, 1946-63: Area Mech. and Elec. Engr, AMWD Malaya, 1951-52; Air Min. Headquarters, 1952-60; Dep. Chief Engr, AMWD, RAF Germany, 1960-63; Sen. Mech. and Elec. Engr, Portsmouth Area MPBW, 1963-67; Jt Services Staff Coll., 1964-65; Suptg Engr, MPBW, 1967-71; Dir Defence Works (Overseas), MPBW, 1971-73; Dir of Social and Research Services, DoE, 1973-75; Dir of Engrng Services Develt, 1975-76. *Recreations:* music, photography, do-it-yourself. *Address:* 6 Pine Hill, Epsom, Surrey KT18 7BG. *T:* Epsom 21888.

GROOM, Sir (Thomas) Reginald, Kt 1961; Chartered Accountant; Partner, Peat, Marwick, Mitchell & Co, Brisbane, Qld; Commissioner, Australian National Airlines Commission, 1961-75; Director: Woodland Ltd (Chairman); Consolidated Rutile Ltd; Mount Isa Mines Holdings Ltd; P & O Australia Ltd; Elder Smith Goldsbrough Mort Ltd (Chairman Qld Board); Member of Commonwealth Banking Corporation Board, 1964-74, and of several private companies; *b* 30 Dec. 1906; *s* of Roy Graeme Groom and May Augusta Groom; *m* 1932, Jessie Mary Grace Butcher; two *s* one *d*. *Educ:* Brisbane Grammar Sch.; University of Qld (BA, BCom). Admitted to Institute of Chartered Accountants in Australia, 1932; in public practice, 1932-. Alderman, Brisbane City Council, 1943-; Lord Mayor of Brisbane, 1955-61. Commissioner, Qld Local Govt Grants Commn, 1977-. Dir, Australian Elizabethan Theatre Trust. *Recreations:* farming, fishing, golf. *Address:* 31 Jerdanefield Tower, Jerdanefield Road, St Lucia, Brisbane, Qld 4067, Australia. *T:* (home) 3711-983, (office) 221-9411. *Clubs:* Queensland, Johnsonian (Brisbane); Athenæum (Melbourne); Union (Sydney); Indooroopilly Golf.

GROOM, Air Marshal Sir Victor E., KCVO 1953; KBE 1952 (CBE 1945; OBE 1940); CB 1944; DFC 1918, and Bar, 1921; RAF retired; *b* 4 Aug. 1898; *e s* of late William E. Groom; *m* 1st, 1924, Maisie Monica Maule (*d* 1961); two *s* : 2nd, 1969, Mrs Muriel Constance Brown. *Educ:* Alleyns, Dulwich. Served European War, 1916-18 (DFC); Egypt, Iraq, 1919-22 (bar to DFC); RAF Staff Coll. (psa 1928); India, 1929-34; Bomber Command, 1936-41 (OBE); Directorate of Plans, Air Min., 1941-42; Head of RAF Staff planning the invasion under Chief of Staff to the Supreme Allied Commander, 1942-43; SASO 2nd Tactical Air Force, 1943-45; AOA Flying Trg Command, 1945-46; Dir-Gen. of Manning, Air Ministry, 1947-49; AOC 205 Group RAF, MEAF, 1949-51; C-in-C, MEAF, 1952; AOC-in-C, Technical Training Command, 1952-55, retired 1955. Officer Legion of Honour (France). *Address:* 8 Somerville House, Manor Fields, SW15. *T:* 01-788 1290. *Club:* Royal Air Force.

GROSBERG, Prof. Percy, PhD; CEng, MIMechE, FTI; Research Professor of Textile Engineering, since 1961, and Head of Department of Textile Industries, since 1975, University of Leeds; *b* 5 April 1925; *s* of late Rev. G. Grosberg and of Mrs P. Grosberg, Tel-Aviv; *m* 1951, Queenie Fisch; two *s* one *d*. *Educ:* Parktown Boys' High Sch., Johannesburg; Univ. of the Witwatersrand; Univ. of Leeds. BScEng, MScEng, PhD Witwatersrand; CEng, MIMechE 1965; FTI 1966. Sen. Res. Officer S African Wool Textile Res. Assoc., 1949-55; ICI Res. Fellow, 1955, Lectr in Textile Engrg, 1955-61, Univ. of Leeds. Warner Memorial Medal, 1968; Textile Inst. Medal, 1972. *Publications:* An Introduction to Textile Mechanisms, 1968; Structural Mechanics of Fibres, Yarns and Fabrics, 1969; papers on rheology of fibrous assemblies, mechan. processing of fibres, and other res. topics in Jl of Textile Inst., Textile Res. Jl, and other sci. jls. *Recreations:* music, gardening, travel. *Address:* 101 King Lane, Leeds LS17 5AX. *T:* Leeds 687478.

GROSS, Anthony; Painter, etcher; *b* 19 March 1905; *s* of Alexander Gross and Isabelle Crowley; *m* 1930, Marcelle Florenty; one *s* one *d*. *Educ:* Repton; Slade; Académie Julian. Exhibits London, Paris, New York, etc. Has also made films and illustrated books. Lives several months each year in France. *Address:* 115 King George Street, Greenwich, SE10 8PX.

GROSS, John Jacob; Editor, Times Literary Supplement, since 1974; *b* 12 March 1935; *s* of late Abraham Gross and Muriel Gross; *m* 1965, Miriam May; one *s* one *d*. *Educ:* City of London Sch.; Wadham Coll., Oxford. Editor, Victor Gollancz Ltd, 1956-58; Asst Lectr, Queen Mary Coll., Univ. of London, 1959-62; Fellow, King's Coll., Cambridge, 1962-65; Literary Editor, New Statesman, 1973. A Trustee, National Portrait Gall., 1977-. *Publications:* The Rise and Fall of the Man of Letters (1969 Duff Cooper Memorial Prize), 1969; Joyce, 1971. *Address:* 25 Platt's Lane, NW3 7NP. *T:* 01-435 6105.

GROSS, Solomon Joseph, CMG 1966; Under Secretary, Department of Industry, since 1974; *b* 3 Sept. 1920; *s* of late Abraham Gross; *m* 1948, Doris Evelyn (*née* Barker); two *d*. *Educ:* Hackney Downs Sch.; University Coll., London. RAF, 1941-46, Burma, India. Ministry of Supply, 1947; Attached OEEC, Paris, 1948-51; Raw Materials Dept, British Embassy, Washington, 1951-53; Board of Trade, 1954-57; British Trade Commr, Pretoria, SA, 1958-62; Principal British Trade Commr, Ghana, 1963-66; British Deputy High Commr, Ghana, 1966-67; Board of Trade, 1967-69; Minister, British Embassy, Pretoria, 1969-73. *Recreations:* squash, tennis, do-it-yourself. *Address:* 7 Northiam, N12. *T:* 01-445 3539. *Club:* Royal Automobile.

GROSSART, Angus McFarlane McLeod; Managing Director, Noble Grossart Ltd, Merchant Bankers, Edinburgh, since 1969; *b* 6 April 1937; 3rd *s* of William John White Grossart and Mary Hay Gardiner; unmarried. *Educ:* Glasgow Acad.; Glasgow Univ. (MA 1958, LLB 1960). CA 1962; Mem., Faculty of Advocates, 1963. Practised at Scottish Bar, 1963-69. Chairman: Scottish Investment Trust; Wright Dental Gp; Heron Motor Gp; Director: American Trust; Reed Shaw Osler; North Sea Assets; Pict Petroleum. Mem., Scottish Develt Agency, 1974-. Trustee, Scottish Civic Trust, 1974-; Dir, Scottish National Orchestra, 1973-. Formerly, Scottish Editor, British Tax Encyc., and British Tax Rev. *Recreations:* golfing, occasional skiing, open cars, art nouveau, early Scottish architecture, Scottish School paintings. *Address:* 48 Queen Street, Edinburgh EH2 3NR. *T:* 031-226 7011. *Clubs:* New, Honourable Company of Edinburgh Golfers (Edinburgh); Royal and Ancient (St Andrews).

GROSSCHMID-ZSÖGÖD, Prof. Géza (Benjamin), LLD; Professor of Economics, Duquesne University, Pittsburgh, USA, since 1955; *b* Budapest, Hungary, 29 Oct. 1918; *o s* of late Prof. Lajos de Grosschmid and Jolán, *o d* of Géza de Szitányi; *m* 1946, Leonora Martha Nissler, 2nd *d* of Otto Nissler and Annemarie Dudt; one *d*. *Educ:* Piarist Fathers, Budapest; Royal Hungarian Pázmány Péter Univ., Budapest (LLD 1943). With private industry in Hungary, 1943-44; Royal Hungarian Army, 1944-45; UNRRA, 1946-47; Duquesne University: Asst Prof. of Econs, 1948-52; Associate Prof., 1952-55; Dir, Inst. of African Affairs, 1958-70; Dir, African Language and Area Center, 1960-74; Academic Vice Pres., 1970-75. Ford Foundn Fellow, 1958; Fulbright-Hays Fellow, S Africa, 1965; attended Cambridge Colonial Conf., King's Coll., 1961. Director: World Affairs Council of Pittsburgh, 1974-; Afuture Fund of Philadelphia, 1976-. Mem., Bd of Visitors, Coll. of Arts and Sciences, Univ. of Pittsburgh; Governor, Battle of Britain Museum Foundn, 1977-. Kt of Malta, 1955 (Kt of Obedience, 1974, Comdr of Merit, 1956); Kt Comdr of St Gregory, 1968. Order of: Valour, Cameroon, 1967; Zaire, 1970; Equatorial Star, Gabon, 1973. *Publications:* (jtly) Principles of Economics, 1959; (trans. with

P. Colombo) The Spiritual Heritage of the Sovereign Military Order of Malta, 1958; contrib. Encyc. Britannica; articles in learned jls. *Recreations:* walking, golf, heraldry. *Address:* 3115 Ashlyn Street, Pittsburgh, Pa 15204, USA. *T:* (412) 331-7744. *Clubs:* Athenæum; Royal Forth Yacht (Edinburgh); Duquesne (Pittsburgh); Metropolitan, Army & Navy (Washington).

GROSVENOR, family name of **Baron Ebury,** and of **Duke of Westminster.**

GROSVENOR, Earl; Gerald Cavendish Grosvenor; commissioned Cheshire Yeomanry, 1973; *b* 22 Dec. 1951; *s* and *heir* of 5th Duke of Westminster, *qv. Educ:* Harrow. Pres., Chester Br., St George's Soc.; Vice-Pres., Cheshire Agricultural Soc.; Governor, Internat. Students' Trust; Vice-Pres., King's Sch., Chester; Pres., Chester and N Wales Chamber of Commerce. *Recreations:* shooting, fishing, tennis and flying. *Address:* Eaton, Chester, Cheshire. *T:* Chester 40022; 100 Eaton Square, W1. *T:* 01-235 4566. *Clubs:* Turf, MCC.

GROSVENOR, Mrs Beatrice Elizabeth Katherine, CBE 1952; United Kingdom Representative on the Executive Committee of the Programme of the United Nations High Commissioner for Refugees, 1959-60; *b* 6 Nov. 1915; *d* of late Lord Edward Grosvenor and late Lady Dorothy Charteris; *m* 1944 (marr. annulled, 1945), Major Richard Girouard. *Educ:* Holy Child Convent, Cavendish Square, W1. Served War of 1939-45 (despatches), with St John Ambulance Brigade; Asst Superintendent-in-Chief SJAB, 1946-52; Deputy Superintendent-in-Chief, 1952-59; County Pres. for Co. Cork, Eire, SJAB, 1960. DStJ 1958. *Address:* Kenmare House, Killarney, Co. Kerry. *T:* Killarney 41.

GROTRIAN, Sir John (Appelbe Brent), 2nd Bt, *cr* 1934; Director, United Newspapers; *b* 16 Feb. 1904; 2nd and *o* surv. *s* of Sir Herbert Brent Grotrian, 1st Bt, KC, JP, and Mary Lilian (*d* 1971), *d* of late Robert Adams, Barrister-at-law of Hamilton, Ont., Canada; *S* father 1951. *Educ:* Eton Coll.; Trinity Coll., Oxford. Served in War of 1939-45 (despatches). *Heir: nephew* Philip Christian Brent Grotrian [*b* 26 March 1935; *s* of Robert Philip Brent Grotrian (*d* on active service, 1945; *y s* of 1st Bt) and Elizabeth Mary Hardy-Wrigley; *m* 1960, Anne Isabel, *d* of Robert Sieger Whyte, Toronto, Canada; one *s*]. *Address:* Raughmere House, Lavant, Chichester, West Sussex. *T:* Chichester 527120; 40 Hamilton Terrace, NW8. *T:* 01-286 0762.

GROUES, Henri Antoine; *see* Pierre, Abbé.

GROUNDS, George Ambrose, CBE 1958; DSO 1917 (Bar 1918); TD 1933; DL; Retired; *b* 19 Nov. 1886; *s* of Frederick and Elizabeth Grounds; *m* 1950, Kathleen Burton Sale (*d* 1968). *Educ:* St Ives (Hunts) Gram. Sch.; Lowestoft Coll. Banking, 1903-45. Served European War, 1914-18, Royal Tank Corps, France (wounded); served War of 1939-45, RA; Lt-Col 1936. DL Lincs, 1951; Chm. Holland (Lincs) CC, 1963-67; Alderman HCC, 1961-74. *Address:* 16 Witham Bank West, Boston, Lincs. *T:* Boston 2772.

GROUNDS, Sir Roy (Burman), Kt 1969; LFRAIA; Hon. Fellow, AIA; Governing Director, Roy Grounds & Co. Pty Ltd, Architects, since 1963; *b* Melbourne, 18 Dec. 1905; *s* of Herbert Algernon Haslett and Maude Hawksworth (*née* Hughes); *m* 1940, Alice Bettine James; one *s* one *d* (and one *d* decd). *Educ:* Melbourne Grammar Sch.; Univ. of Melbourne. BArch Melbourne, 1947. Partner, Mewton & Grounds, 1932-38; Two Centenary Gold Medal awards for completed bldgs, 1935; practice in Europe and Melbourne, 1938-41. Commissioned RAAF, SW Pacific, 1941-45; Sen. Lectr in Architecture, Univ. of Melbourne, 1945-52; Sen. partner, Grounds, Romberg & Boyd, Architects, Melbourne, 1953-62. RVIA Arch. Award, 1954; RAIA Arch. Award (for Aust. Acad. of Science Bldg, Canberra), 1957; Pan-Pacific Architectural Citation of AIA, 1960; Sulman Award for Arch., 1961; RAIA Gold Medal, 1968. *Address:* 24 Hill Street, Toorak, Victoria 3142, Australia. *T:* 24-3110. *Club:* Commonwealth (Canberra).

GROUNDS, Stanley Paterson, CBE 1968; Charity Commissioner, 1960-69; *b* 25 Oct. 1904; 2nd *s* of late Thomas Grounds and Olivia Henrietta (*née* Anear), Melbourne, Australia; *m* 1932, Freda Mary Gale Ransford; twin *s* and *d*. *Educ:* Melbourne High Sch.; Queen's Coll., Melbourne Univ. (1st Cl. hons, MA). With Melbourne Herald, 1926-28; British Empire Producers' Organisation, London, 1928-33. Called to Bar, Middle Temple, 1933; at Chancery Bar, 1934-40. Served Royal Air Force, 1940-45 (Squadron Leader). Asst Charity Commissioner, 1946-58; Sec., Charity Commission, 1958-60. *Publications:* contrib. Encyclopædia of Forms and Precedents, Encyclopædia of Court Forms (on Charities), Halsbury's Laws of England, 3rd edn (on Charities). Articles in law jls. *Recreation:* other men's flowers. *Address:* St Helena, 19 Bell Road, Haslemere, Surrey GU27 3DQ. *T:* Haslemere 51230. *Club:* Army and Navy.

GROVER, Sir Anthony (Charles), Kt 1973; Chairman: Lloyd's Register of Shipping, 1963-June 1973; Lifeguard Assurance Ltd, 1964-76; *b* 13 Oct. 1907; *s* of F. J. Grover, Harrow, Middx; *m* 1931, Marguerite Beatrice Davies; one *s* one *d. Educ:* Westminster Sch. War of 1939-45 (despatches): joined Coldstream Guards, 1940; served in Italy, 1942-44; rose to rank of Major. Underwriting Mem. of Lloyd's, 1936- (Dep. Chm., 1958; Chm., 1959-60). Dep. Chm. and Treasurer, Lloyd's Register of Shipping, 1956-58, 1961-63. Comdr, Order of Leopold II, 1967; Comdr, Order of Oranje Nassau, 1968; Comdr, Order of Dannebrog, 1972. *Recreation:* golf. *Address:* Dial Cottage, Firbank Lane, St John's, Woking, Surrey. *T:* Woking 73928. *Clubs:* White's; Woking Golf; Royal St George's Golf (Sandwich); Honourable Company of Edinburgh Golfers; Swinley Forest Golf.

GROVER, Maj.-Gen. John Malcolm Lawrence, CB 1945; MC; *b* 6 Feb. 1897; *s* of late General Sir M. H. S. Grover, KCB, KCIE; *m* 1930, Betty Chune, *d* of late Maj.-Gen. L. Humphry, CB, CMG, Army Medical Service; one *s. Educ:* Winchester; RMC, Sandhurst. Commissioned King's Shropshire LI, 1914; served European War, 1914-18, France and Belgium (wounded thrice, MC and Bar); Operations NW Frontier, India, 1930-31; War of 1939-45, France and Belgium, 1939-40 (despatches); India and Assam, (Kohima-Imphal operations), 1942-44. Commanded 1st KSLI, 1938-39; GSO1 5th Div., 1940; 11th Inf. Brigade, 1940; 29th Independent Brigade Gp, 1941; 2nd Division, 1941-44; Dir of Army Welfare Services, War Office, 1944-48; retired, 1948. General Sec., Officers' Association, 1948-61. Col KSLI, 1947-55. Commissioner, Royal Hospital, Chelsea, 1957-66. OStJ 1961. *Address:* Bowmans, Crowborough, East Sussex. *Club:* Army and Navy.

GROVES, Sir Charles (Barnard), Kt 1973; CBE 1968 (OBE 1958); FRCM, Hon. RAM; conductor; General Music Director, English National Opera, since 1978; Associate Conductor, Royal Philharmonic Orchestra, since 1967; *b* 10 March 1915; *s* of Frederick Groves and Annie (*née* Whitehead); *m* 1948, Hilary Hermione Barchard; one *s* two *d. Educ:* St Paul's Cathedral Choir Sch.; Sutton Valence Sch.; Royal College of Music. Free lance accompanist and organist. Joined BBC, Chorus-Master Music Productions Unit, 1938; Asst Conductor BBC Theatre Orchestra, 1942; Conductor BBC Revue Orchestra, 1943; Conductor BBC Northern Orchestra, 1944-51; Dir of Music, Bournemouth Corporation, and Conductor, Bournemouth Municipal Orchestra, 1951-54; Conductor of Bournemouth Symphony Orchestra, 1954-61; Resident Musical Dir, Welsh National Opera Company, 1961-63; Musical Dir and Resident Conductor, Royal Liverpool Philharmonic Orchestra, 1963-77. President: Nat. Fedn of Music Socs; Nat. Youth Orchestra of GB, 1977-; Life Mem., RPO, 1976. FRCM 1961; Hon. RAM 1967; Hon. FTCL 1974; Hon. FGSM 1974; Hon. FRNCM, 1974. Conductor of the Year Award, 1968. Has toured Australia, New Zealand, South Africa, N and S America, Japan and Europe. Hon. DMus Liverpool, 1970. *Recreation:* English literature. *Address:* 12 Camden Square, NW1 9UY. *Club:* Athenæum.

GROVES, John Dudley, OBE 1964; Director of Information, Department of Health and Social Security, since 1977; *b* 12 Aug. 1922; *y s* of late Walter Groves; *m* 1943, Pamela Joy Holliday; one *s* two *d. Educ:* St Paul's Sch. Reporter, Richmond Herald, 1940-41; Queen's Royal Regt, 1941-42; commnd in 43rd Reconnaissance Regt, 1942; served in NW Europe, 1944-45 (despatches); Observer Officer, Berlin, 1945; Press Association (Press Gallery), 1947-51; Times (Press Gallery and Lobby), 1951-58; Head of Press Sect., Treasury, 1958-62; Dep. Public Relations Adviser to Prime Minister, 1962-64 (Actg Adviser, 1964); Chief Information Officer, DEA, 1964-68; Chief of Public Relations, MoD, 1968-77. *Publication:* (with R. Gill) Club Route, 1945. *Recreations:* walking, painting. *Address:* Mortimers, Manningford Bohune, Pewsey, Wilts.

GROVES, Ronald, MA, BSc Oxon; FRIC; Secretary, Sir Richard Stapley Educational Trust, since 1969; Trustee, King's College Hospital; Vice-Chairman Council, King's College Hospital Medical School; *b* 19 Aug. 1908; *s* of late John Ackroyd Groves and Annie Groves, Bradford, *m* 1939, Hilary Annot, *yr d* of late George Smith; two *s. Educ:* Bradford Grammar Sch.; Christ Church, Oxford. 1st Class Hons Nat. Sci. (Chemistry), 1931. Asst Master, Bradfield Coll., 1931-32; Worksop Coll., 1932-35; Senior Science Master and Housemaster, King's Sch., Canterbury, 1935-43; Bursar, 1937-43; Headmaster, Campbell

Coll., Belfast, 1943-54; Master, Dulwich Coll., 1954-66. Adviser, Jt Working Party of Governing Bodies' Assoc. and Headmasters' Conf., 1966-73. Chm., Food Standards Cttee, 1959-62. *Address:* 83 Cumnor Hill, Oxford. *Clubs:* Athenæum, MCC.

GROVES, Ronald Edward, CBE 1972; Chairman, since 1976 and Chief Executive, since 1973, International Timber Corporation Ltd; *b* 2 March 1920; *s* of Joseph Rupert and Eva Lilian Groves; *m* 1940, Beryl Doris Lydia Collins; two *s* one *d. Educ:* Watford Grammar School. Joined J. Gliksten & Son Ltd; served War of 1939-45, Flt-Lt RAF, subseq. Captain with BOAC; re-joined J. Gliksten & Son Ltd, 1946: Gen. Works Man. 1947; Dir 1954; Jt Man. Dir 1964; Vice-Chm. 1967; Dir, Gliksten (West Africa) Ltd, 1949; Vice-Chm., International Timber Corp. Ltd, 1970 (name of J. Gliksten & Son Ltd changed to International Timber Corp. Ltd, 1970 following merger with Horsley Smith & Jewson Ltd). President: Timber Trade Fedn of UK, 1969-71; London and District Sawmill Owners Assoc., 1954-56; Chm., Nat. Sawmilling Assoc., 1966-67. Chairman: Rickmansworth UDC, 1957-58, 1964-65 and 1971-72; W Herts Main Drainage Authority, 1970-74; Three Rivers District Council, 1977-78. *Recreations:* visiting theatre and opera; local community work. *Address:* 8 Pembroke Road, Moor Park, Northwood, Mddx. *T:* Northwood 23187.

GRUBB, Sir Kenneth (George), KCMG 1970 (CMG 1942); Kt 1953; Chairman, House of Laity, Church Assembly, 1959-70; *b* 9 Sept. 1900; *s* of Rev. H. P. Grubb and M. A. Crichton-Stuart; *m* 1st, 1926, Eileen Sylvia Knight (*d* 1932); 2nd, 1935, Nancy Mary Arundel; three *s* one *d. Educ:* Marlborough Coll. President: CMS, 1944-69; Cheltenham Training Colls, 1948-; Grubb Inst. of Behavioural Studies; Asia Christian Colls Assoc; Argentina Diocesan Assoc.; Chairman: Commission of Churches on Internat. Affairs, 1946-68; Missionary and Ecumenical Council, Church Assembly, 1964-67; Royal Foundation of St Katharine, 1957-77; Vice-President: Inst. of Race Relations, 1965-73; British Council of Churches, 1965-68. Vice-Pres. or Trustee of many other institutions including Inst. of Strategic Studies; a Church Commissioner, 1948-73; Hon. Fellow and Trustee, St Peter's Coll., Oxford. Missionary, 1923-28; Survey Application Trust, 1928-39, 1953-; Controller, in Ministry of Information, 1941-46; Sec.-Gen., Hispanic Council, 1946-53; Publicity Consultant, Rank Organisation, 1955-59. Director: Argentine Club Ltd; Craigmyle & Co. Ltd, and subsidiaries. United Kingdom Delegate: Unesco, 1954; Atlantic Congress, 1959. Hon. LLD Muhlenberg, Pa, 1961. *Publications:* numerous works on Latin America; World Christian Handbook, 1949, 1953, 1957, 1962, 1968; A Layman Looks at the Church, 1964; Crypts of Power (autobiography), 1971. *Address:* The Moot Farm Cottage, Downton, Salisbury, Wilts SP5 3JP. *T:* Downton 20433. *Clubs:* Canning, Naval and Military; Nikaean.

GRUBB, Violet Margaret, DSc London; retired; *b* Oxton, Notts, 1898; *o d* of Rev. H. Percy Grubb and M. A. Crichton-Stuart. *Educ:* Bournemouth High Sch.; Westfield Coll., University of London. BSc Hons London, 1920; DSc London, 1925; Asst Lecturer in Botany, Westfield Coll., 1923-25; Science teacher in I Fang Sch., Changsha, Central China and Lecturer in Hunan Provincial Univ., 1925-30; Lecturer in Dept of Botany, Westfield Coll., University of London, 1931-37; Headmistress, Westonbirt Sch., Tetbury, Glos, 1937-55; Principal, The Training Coll., Salisbury, 1955-62. Pres., Assoc. Head Mistresses of Boarding Schs, 1943-45. Chm., Assoc. of Independent and Direct Grant Schs, 1950-53; Member: Central Advisory Council for Education (England), 1956-59; Science Museum Advisory Council, 1957-64. *Publications:* Articles on Ecology and Reproduction of Marine Algæ and on distribution of Far Eastern Algæ, in scientific journals in England and abroad. *Address:* 28 Shady Bower Close, Salisbury, Wilts. *T:* Salisbury 28814. *Club:* Royal Over-Seas League.

GRUENBERG, Prof. Karl Walter; Professor of Pure Mathematics in the University of London, at Queen Mary College, since 1967; *b* 3 June 1928; *s* of late Paul Gruenberg and of Anna Gruenberg; *m* 1973, Margaret Semple; one *s* one *d. Educ:* Shaftesbury Grammar Sch.; Kilburn Grammar Sch.; Cambridge Univ. BA 1950, PhD 1954. Asst Lectr, Queen Mary Coll., 1953-55; Commonwealth Fund Fellowship, 1955-57 (at Harvard Univ., 1955-56; at Inst. for Advanced Studies, Princeton, 1956-57). Queen Mary College: Lectr, 1957-61; Reader, 1961-67; Prof., 1967-. Visiting Professor: Univ. of Michigan, 1961-62; Cornell Univ., 1966-67; Univ. of Illinois, 1972. *Publications:* Cohomological Topics in Group Theory, 1970; Relation Modules of Finite Groups, 1976; Linear Geometry (jtly with A. J. Weir), 2nd edn 1977; articles on algebra in various learned jls. *Address:* Department of Pure Mathematics, Queen Mary College (University of London), Mile End Road, E1 4NS. *T:* 01-980 4811.

GRUENTHER, Gen. Alfred M(aximilian); (Hon.) CB (UK) 1943; DSM (US) (with 2 Oak Leaf Clusters) 1943, 1945, 1956; US Army, retired; Director: Pan American World Airways; New York Life Insurance Co.; Dart Industries; Federated Department Stores; Member: The Business Council; Board of Trustees, Institute for Defense Analyses; President's Commission on an All-Volunteer Armed Force, since 1969; Editorial Board, Foreign Affairs Magazine, since 1959; *b* Nebraska, 3 March 1899; *s* of Christian M. Gruenther and Mary Shea; *m* 1922, Grace Elizabeth Crum; two *s. Educ:* Military Academy, West Point (BS). Commissioned, Field Artillery, 1918; routine peacetime assignments, including 8 years as instructor and asst professor chemistry and electricity at West Point; Deputy Chief of Staff, Allied Force Headquarters (London, North African Campaign, Algiers), 1942-43; Chief of Staff, Fifth Army (Italy), 1943-44; Chief of Staff, 15th Army Group (Italian Campaign), 1944-45; Dep. Comdr, US Forces in Austria, 1945; Dep. Comdt, Nat. War Coll. Washington, 1945-47; Dir Jt Staff, Jt Chiefs of Staff, 1947-49; Dep. Chief of Staff for Plans and Operations, Army Gen. Staff, 1949-51; Gen., US Army, 1951; Chief of Staff, SHAPE, 1951-53; Supreme Allied Commander, Europe, 1953-56; retd 1956. Member: Presidential Arms Control Gen. Adv. Cttee, 1966-69; Presidential Adv. Cttee on Foreign Assistance, 1965-69. Pres., American Red Cross, 1957-64. Chm., English-Speaking Union of US, 1966-68. Hon. Pres., World Bridge Federation. Several decorations, including Grand Cross of Légion d'Honneur, 1954, and Médaille Militaire, 1956. Hon. degrees from 38 universities including Harvard, Yale, Columbia, Dartmouth and Holy Cross. *Publications:* Famous Hands of the Culbertson-Lenz Match, 1932; Duplicate Contract Complete, 1933. *Address:* Cathedral Apartments, 4101 Cathedral Avenue, NW, Washington, DC 20016, USA.

GRUFFYDD JONES, Daniel; *see* Jones, D. G.

GRUGEON, John Drury; Leader of Kent County Council; *b* 20 Sept. 1928; *s* of Drury Grugeon and Sophie (*née* Pratt); *m* 1955, Mary Patricia (*née* Rickards); one *s* one *d. Educ:* Epsom Grammar Sch.; RMA, Sandhurst. Commissioned, The Buffs, Dec. 1948; served 1st Bn in Middle and Far East and Germany; Regimental Adjt, 1953-55; Adjt 5th Bn, 1956-58; left Army, 1960. Joined Save and Prosper Group, 1960. Chm., Finance Cttee, Assoc. of County Councils, 1976; Mem., Medway Ports Authority, 1977-. *Recreations:* cricket, shooting, local govt. *Address:* Sand Pett, Charing, Ashford, Kent TN27 0AT. *T:* Charing 2322. *Clubs:* MCC; Kent County CC.

GRUMMITT, J. H.; Principal, Royal Academical Institution, Belfast, 1940-59; *b* 29 Jan. 1901; *s* of Charles C. Grummitt and Annie E. Halliday; *m* 1931, Mary Christine Bennett; two *s* two *d. Educ:* Cheltenham; Caius Coll., Cambridge. Schs Sec., Student Christian Movement, 1923-28; Senior Classical Master, Ipswich Sch., 1929-30; Head of Classical Dept, Epsom Coll., 1930-33; Headmaster, Victoria Coll., Jersey, 1933-40. *Publication:* The Sacrament of Life, 1931. *Recreations:* music, bridge. *Address:* Clovelly, Holywood, Co. Down. *T:* H.2434.

GRUNDY, Air Marshal Sir Edouard (Michael FitzFrederick), KBE 1963 (OBE 1942); CB 1960; Chairman, Short Brothers and Harland, 1968-76; *b* 29 Sept. 1908; *s* of late Frederick Grundy and Osca Marah Ewart; *m* 1st, 1945, Lucia le Sueur (*née* Corder) (*d* 1973); three *s* (and one *d* decd); 2nd, 1975, Mrs Marie Louise Holder. *Educ:* St Paul's Sch.; RAF Coll., Cranwell. 56 (F) Sqdn 1928; 403 Flight FAA, 1929-31; Signals Specialist Course, 1932; RAF North Weald, 1933-36; RNZAF HQ, 1937-40; OC No 80 (S) Wing, 1941-42; CSO, NW African AF, 1942-43; CSO Mediterranean Allied Tactical Air Forces, 1943-44; CSO, RAF, Middle East, 1944-45; Commandant, Empire Radio Sch., 1945-46; Dep. Dir Air Staff Policy, Air Ministry, 1947-49; Air Adviser, Royal Norwegian AF, 1949-51; Dep. CSO, Supreme HQ Allied Powers Europe, 1951-52; idc 1953; Senior Air Staff Officer, Brit. Jt Services Mission in USA, 1954-55; Chm. NATO Military Agency for Standardisation, 1955-58; Air Officer i/c Administration, FEAF, 1958-61; Commandant-Gen. RAF Regt, 1961-62; Controller, Guided Weapons and Electronics, Ministry of Aviation, 1962-66; retired, 1966. Mem., Engineering Industries Council, 1975-. Pres., SBAC, 1975-76. FRAeS; FBIM. Chevalier, Royal Norwegian Order of St Olaf, 1953. *Recreations:* usual. *Address: c/o* Lloyds Bank Ltd, 6 Pall Mall, SW1. *Club:* Royal Air Force.

GRUNDY, Fred, MD; MRCP; DPH; Barrister-at-law; Assistant Director-General, World Health Organization, Geneva, 1961-66; retired; *b* 15 May 1905; *s* of Thomas Grundy, Manchester; *m* 1932, Ada Furnell Leppington, Hessle, Yorks; one *s* one *d. Educ:* Leeds and London Univs. MB, ChB (Hons), Leeds; MRCS, LRCP, 1927; DPH, RCPS, 1931; MD Leeds, 1933;

MRCP, 1951. Called to the Bar, Inner Temple, 1934. Resident hospital appts and gen. practice, 1927-31; Asst County Medical Officer, E Suffolk, 1931-34; Asst MOH to Borough of Willesden, 1934-35; Deputy MOH to Borough of Luton, 1935-37; MOH to Borough of Luton, 1937-49; Mansel Talbot Prof. of Preventive Medicine, Welsh Nat. Sch. of Medicine, 1949-61. *Publications:* A Note on the Vital Statistics of Luton, 1944; (with R. M. Titmuss) Report on Luton, 1945; Handbook of Social Medicine, 1945; The New Public Health, 1949; Preventive Medicine and Public Health: An Introduction for Students and Practitioners, 1951; papers on public health and scientific subjects. *Recreations:* mountaineering, yachting, golf, etc. *Address:* Galmington, Radyr, near Cardiff. *Club:* Yacht (Penarth).

GRUNDY, John Brownsdon Clowes, TD 1951; Officier d'Académie, 1937; MA, PhD; *b* 21 April 1902; *m* 1939, Carol Dorothea, *d* of Enid Pennington; two *s* three *d. Educ:* Emanuel Sch.; Fitzwilliam Hall, Cambridge (Exhibitioner); University Coll., London (research). Asst Master, St Paul's Sch., 1923-27; English Lektor, University of Göttingen, 1928; "The Connoisseur", 1928-29; Sen. Mod. Langs Master, Shrewsbury Sch., 1929-39. Served War of 1939-45, The Rangers (KRRC); principally in Gen. Staff (Intell.); Normandy-Germany, 1944; rank at release, temp. Col. First Rep. of Brit. Council in Finland, 1945-49; Dir, Brit. Institute, Cairo, 1949-50; head of mod. langs, Harrow Sch., 1950-53; Headmaster of Emanuel Sch., 1953-63; Head of Dept of Modern Languages, University Coll. of Sierra Leone, 1964-66. *Publications:* Tieck and Runge, 1929; Brush Up Your German, series, 1931-61; French Style, 1937; Life's Five Windows, 1968; various edns and translations of foreign texts. *Recreations:* antiquities, hills, foreign parts. *Address:* Llyn Du, Llansantffraid, Powys.

GRUNDY, R(upert) F(rancis) Brooks; consultant engineer; General Manager, Corby Development Corporation, 1950-68, and Industrial Projects Consultant to the Corporation, 1968-70; *b* 6 Sept. 1903; *s* of J. F. E. Grundy, fine art publisher, London and Emily Grundy (*née* Brownsdon); *m* 1938, Heather Mary, *d* of William and Mabel Thomas, Swansea; one *s* one *d. Educ:* Emanuel Sch., London; University Coll., London (BSc (Eng.)); Open Univ. (BA 1975). FICE, FIMunE. Municipal Engrg, 1922-44, at Croydon, Bournemouth, Swansea, Carlisle and Harrow; Borough Engr and Surveyor: Mansfield, 1944-45; Wallasey, 1945-49; Wandsworth, 1949-50. Mem., BBC Midlands Region Adv. Coun., 1966-68. *Publications:* Builders' Materials, 1930; Essentials of Reinforced Concrete, 1939, 1948; papers presented to ICE and IMunE. *Recreations:* golf, walking, reading. *Address:* The Mill House, Brigstock, Kettering, Northants. *T:* Brigstock 218.

GRÜNEBERG, Prof. Hans, FRS 1956; PhD Berlin, MD Bonn, DSc London; Professor of Genetics, University College, London, 1956-74, now Emeritus; *b* 26 May 1907; *o s* of late Dr Levi Grüneberg and late Mrs Else Grüneberg (*née* Steinberg), Wuppertal-Elberfeld, Germany; *m* 1st, 1933, Elsbeth (*d* 1944), *d* of late Hugo Capell; two *s*; 2nd, 1946, Hannah (*d* 1962), *d* of late Albrecht Blumenfeld. *Educ:* Städt. Gymnasium, Wuppertal-Elberfeld, Germany. Hon. Research Asst, University Coll., London, 1933-38; Moseley Research Student of Royal Society, 1938-42. Captain, RAMC, 1942-46. Reader in Genetics, University Coll., London, 1946-55. Hon. Dir, MRC Expmtl Genetics Res. Unit, 1955-72. *Publications:* The Genetics of the Mouse, 1943, 1952; Animal Genetics and Medicine, 1947; The Pathology of Development, 1963. Numerous papers in scientific jls. *Recreation:* foreign travel. *Address:* University College, Wolfson House, 4 Stephenson Way, NW1. *T:* 01-387 7050.

GRUNFELD, Prof. Cyril; Professor of Law, London School of Economics, since 1966; *b* 26 Sept. 1922; *o s* of Samuel and Sarah Grunfeld; *m* 1945, Phyllis Levin; one *s* two *d. Educ:* Canton High Sch., Cardiff; Trinity Hall, Cambridge (MA, LLB). Called to Bar, Inner Temple. British Army, 1942-45; Trinity Hall (Studentship), 1946-48; LSE: Asst, 1946-47; Asst Lectr, 1947-49; Lectr, 1949-56; Reader in Law, 1956—66; Pro-Dir, 1973-76; Convener, Legal Res. Fellow, 1976-. Vis. Research Fellow, ANU, 1970-71; Legal Adviser to Commn on Industrial Relations, 1971-74. Co-editor, Modern Law Review, British Jl of Industrial Relations and Industrial Law Jl. *Publications:* Modern Trade Union Law, 1966; The Law of Redundancy, 1971; contrib. to books and learned jls. *Recreations:* reading, walking. *Address:* London School of Economics and Political Science, Houghton Street, WC2A 2AE. *T:* 01-405 7686.

GRUNFELD, Henry; President, Mercury Securities Ltd (Chairman 1964-74), and S. G. Warburg & Co. Ltd (Chairman 1969-74), since 1974; *b* 1 June 1904; *s* of Max Grunfeld and Rosa Grunfeld (*née* Haendler); *m* 1931, Berta Lotte Oliven; one *s* one *d .* Manager: New Trading Co. Ltd, 1938; S. G. Warburg & Co.

Ltd, 1946; Dir, S. G. Warburg & Co. Ltd, 1951-74; *Address:* 30 Gresham Street, EC2P 2EB. *T:* 01-600 4555.

GRUNSELL, Prof. Charles Stuart Grant, CBE 1976; PhD; Professor of Veterinary Medicine, since 1957, University of Bristol; *b* 6 Jan. 1915; *s* of Stuart and Edith Grunsell; *m* 1939, Marjorie Prunella Wright; one *s* two *d. Educ:* Shanghai Public Sch.; Bristol Grammar Sch. Qualified as MRCVS at The Royal (Dick) Veterinary Coll., Edinburgh, 1937; FRCVS 1971. In general practice at Glastonbury, Som., 1939-48. PhD Edinburgh, 1952. Senior Lecturer in Veterinary Hygiene and Preventive Medicine, University of Edinburgh, 1952. Pro-Vice-Chancellor, Univ. of Bristol, 1974-77. Chm., Veterinary Products Cttee. Editor, Veterinary Annual. A Diocesan Reader. Defence Medal 1946. *Publications:* papers on the Erythron of Ruminants, on Vital Statistics in Veterinary Medicine, on Preventive Medicine, and on veterinary education. *Recreations:* squash, gardening. *Address:* Towerhead House, Banwell, near Weston-super-Mare, Avon. *T:* Banwell 2461.

GRYLLS, Rear-Adm. Henry John Bedford, CB 1956; *b* 24 Aug. 1903; *s* of late C. B. Grylls, CB, CBE, and late Mrs Grylls; *m* 1938, Ruth Ellison, *d* of late S. E. Minnis, CBE; one *s* one *d. Educ:* RN Colleges Osborne and Dartmouth. Midshipman, HMS Durban, 1921; Sub-Lieut 1924; Engineering Courses and Advanced Engineering Course, 1924-28; Lieut (E), HMS London, 1928-31; HM Dockyard, Chatham, 1931-34; Lieut-Comdr (E), HMS Rodney, 1934-37; Comdr (E) 1937; Engineer-in-Chief's Dept, Admiralty, 1938-41; Engineer Officer, HMS Duke of York, 1941-44; HM Dockyard, Devonport, 1944-45; Dockyard Dept, Admiralty, 1945-47; Capt. (E) 1946; Chief Engineer, HM Dockyard, Singapore, 1948-51; Asst Engineer-in-Chief, 1951-54; Rear-Adm. (E) 1954; Engineer Manager, HM Dockyard, Devonport, 1954-58, retired. *Address:* Penshurst, 6 Mornington Park, Wellington, Som. *T:* Wellington 2931.

GRYLLS, Michael; *see* Grylls, W. M. J.

GRYLLS, Rosalie G.; *see* Mander, Lady (Rosalie).

GRYLLS, (William) Michael (John); MP (C) North West Surrey, since 1974 (Chertsey, 1970-74); *b* 21 Feb. 1934; *s* of Brig. W. E. H. Grylls, OBE; *m* 1965, Sarah Smiles Justice, *d* of Captain N. M. Ford and of Lady (Patricia) Fisher, *qv*; one *s* one *d. Educ:* RN College, Dartmouth; Univ. of Paris. Lieut, Royal Marines, 1952-55. Mem., St Pancras Borough Council, 1959-62. Contested (C) Fulham, Gen. Elecs, 1964 and 1966; Mem., Select Cttee on Overseas Develt; Vice-Chm., Cons. Industry Cttee, 1975. Mem. GLC, 1967-70; Dep. Leader, Inner London Educn Authority, 1969-70; Chm., Further and Higher Educn, 1968-70; Mem., Nat. Youth Employment Council, 1968-70. *Recreations:* sailing, riding, gardening. *Address:* Walcot House, 139 Kennington Road, SE11. *Club:* Carlton.

GUAZZELLI, Rt. Rev. Victor; Auxiliary Bishop of Westminster (Bishop in East London) (RC), and Titular Bishop of Lindisfarne since 1970; *b* 19 March 1920; *s* of Cesare Guazzelli and Maria (*née* Frepoli). *Educ:* Parochial Schools, Tower Hamlets; English Coll., Lisbon. Priest, 1945. Asst, St Patrick's, Soho Square, 1945-48; Bursar and Prof. at English Coll., Lisbon, 1948-58; Westminster Cathedral: Chaplain, 1958-64; Hon. Canon, 1964; Sub-Administrator, 1964-67; Parish Priest of St Thomas', Fulham, 1967-70; Vicar General of Westminster, 1970. *Address:* The Lodge, Pope John House, Hale Street, E14. *T:* 01-987 4663.

GUBBINS, Major William John Mounsey, TD 1946; DL; *b* 23 Aug. 1907; *s* of late Col R. R. Gubbins, DSO, JP, The Old Hall, Rockcliffe, Carlisle; *m* 1932, Marjorie Mary, *d* of late T. O. Carter, The Place, Armathwaite, Cumberland; two *s. Educ:* Sherborne Sch. High Sheriff of Cumberland, 1959-60; DL of Cumberland, 1961-. *Recreations:* shooting, fishing, gardening. *Address:* Eden Lacy, Lazonby, Cumbria. *T:* Lazonby 337. *Club:* County (Carlisle).

GUDERLEY, Mrs C.; *see* Hyams, Daisy Deborah.

GUÐMUNDSSON, Guðmundur I., Comdr with Star, Order of the Falcon, 1957; Ambassador of Iceland to Sweden, since 1973, and concurrently to Finland and Austria; *b* 17 July 1909; *m* 1942, Rósa Ingólfsdóttir; four *s. Educ:* Reykjavík Grammar Sch.; Univ. of Iceland. Grad. in Law 1934. Practised as Solicitor and Barrister from 1934; Barrister to Supreme Court, 1939; Sheriff and Magistrate, 1945-56. Mem. Central Cttee, Social Democratic Party, 1940-65, Vice-Chm. of Party, 1954-65; Member of Althing (Parlt), 1942-65; Minister of Foreign Affairs, 1956-65; Minister of Finance, 1958-59; Chm., Icelandic Delegn to UN Conf. on Law of the Sea, Geneva, 1958 and 1960;

Mem. and Chm. of Board of Dirs, Fishery Bank in Reykjavík, 1957-65; Ambassador of Iceland: to UK, 1965-71, and concurrently to the Netherlands, Portugal and Spain; to United States, 1971-73, and concurrently to Argentina, Brazil, Canada, Mexico and Cuba. Establishment of Republic Medal, 1944. Hon. KBE; Grand Cross, Order of: White Rose (Finland); North Star (Sweden); Orange-Nassau (Netherlands); Chêne (Luxembourg); Southern Cross (Brazil); St Olav (Norway); Phoenix (Greece). *Address:* The Embassy of Iceland, Kommendörsg'atan 35, 11458 Stockholm, Sweden.

GUDMUNDSSON, Dr Kristinn; Commander of the Icelandic Falcon (1st Class); Ambassador of Iceland to the USSR, 1961-68; concurrently Ambassador at Bucharest (1964-68), Sofia (1965-68) and Budapest (1966-68); *b* 14 Oct. 1897; *s* of Gudmundur Sigfredsson and Gudrùn Einarsdòttir; *m* 1927, Elsa Alma Kalbow; one *d. Educ:* University of Reykjavik; Berlin and Kiel. Master, Akureyri Coll., 1929-44; Tax Dir, Akureyri, 1944-53; Minister for Foreign Affairs, Iceland, Sept. 1953-July 1956; Minister to the UK, 1956, subsequently Ambassador, until 1960; concurrently both at The Hague. Grand Cross: Dannebrog (Denmark); Vasa (Sweden); White Rose (Finland); St Olav (Norway); Verdienstorden (Germany); Crown of Oak (Luxembourg). *Publication:* Die dänischenglischen Handelsbeziehungen, 1931. *Address:* Grettisgata 96, Reykjavik, Iceland.

GUERISSE, Dr Albert Marie Edmond, GC 1946; DSO 1942 (under name of Patrick Albert O'Leary); medical officer; Major-General in the Belgian Army; Director-General, Medical Service, Belgian Forces; retired 1970; *b* Brussels, 5 April 1911; *m* 1947, Sylvia Cooper Smith; one *s. Educ:* in Belgium; Louvain; Brussels University. Medical Officer, Lieut, 1940; after Belgian capitulation embarked at Dunkirk and became, in Sept. 1940, Lieut-Comdr, RN; first officer of "Q" ship, HMS Fidelity (under name of P. A. O'Leary). Engaged on secret work in France from April 1941 until arrest by Gestapo in March 1943 (chief of an escape organisation). After 2 years in Concentration Camps returned to England. After demobilisation from RN rejoined Belgian Army (1st Lancers); joined Belgian Volunteer Bn, 1951, as Chief of Medical Service in Korea. Officier Légion d'Honneur, 1947; Medal of Freedom with golden palm, 1947; Officier Ordre Léopold, 1946, Grand Officier, 1970; French Croix de Guerre, 1945; Polish Croix de Guerre, 1944. *Address:* 100 avenue General Lartigue, 1200 Brussels, Belgium.

GUERITZ, Rear-Adm. Edward Findlay, CB 1971; OBE 1957; DSC 1942, and Bar, 1944; *b* 8 Sept. 1919; *s* of Elton and Valentine Gueritz; *m* 1947, Pamela Amanda Bernhardina Britton, *d* of Commander L. H. Jeans; one *s* one *d. Educ:* Cheltenham Coll. Entered Navy, 1937; Midshipman, 1938; served War of 1939-45 (wounded; DSC and Bar): HMS Jersey, 5th Flotilla, 1940-41; Combined Ops (Indian Ocean, Normandy), 1941-44; HMS Saumarez (Corfu Channel incident), 1946; Army Staff Coll., Camberley, 1948; Staff of C-in-C S Atlantic and Junior Naval Liaison Officer to UK High Comr, S Africa, 1954-56; Near East Operations, 1956 (OBE); Dep. Dir, RN Staff Coll., 1959-61; Naval Staff, Admty, 1961-63; idc 1964; Captain of Fleet, Far East Fleet, 1965-66; Dir of Defence Plans (Navy), 1967; Dir, Jt Warfare Staff, MoD, 1968; Admiral-President, Royal Naval Coll., 1968-70; Comdt, Jt Warfare Estabt, 1970-72. Lt-Comdr 1949; Comdr 1953; Captain 1959; Rear-Adm. 1969; retd 1973. Dep. Dir and Editor, RUSI. Pres., Soc. for Nautical Res.; Member Council: King George's Fund for Sailors; Marine Soc.; Seaman's Hosp. Soc. Chief Hon. Steward, Westminster Abbey. *Recreations:* history, reading. *Address:* 56 The Close, Salisbury, Wilts. *Club:* Army and Navy.

GUERNSEY, Lord; Charles Heneage Finch-Knightley; *b* 27 March 1947; *s* and *heir* of 11th Earl of Aylesford, *qv*; *m* 1971, Penelope Anstice, *y d* of Kenneth A. G. Crawley; twin *d. Educ:* Oundle, Trinity Coll., Cambridge. *Recreations:* shooting, fishing, Real tennis, cricket. *Address:* Rookwood, Packington Park, Meriden, near Coventry. *T:* Meriden 22573.

GUERNSEY, Dean of; *see* Cogman, Very Rev. F. W.

GUEST, family name of **Viscount Wimborne.**

GUEST; *see* Haden-Guest.

GUEST, Baron (Life Peer), *cr* 1961; **Christopher William Graham Guest,** PC 1961; a Lord of Appeal in Ordinary, 1961-71; *b* 7 Nov. 1901; *s* of Edward Graham and Mary Catherine Guest; *m* 1941, Catharine Geraldine Hotham; four *s* one *d. Educ:* Merchiston Castle; Cambridge (MA, LLB); Edinburgh (LLB). Called to Scots Bar, 1925, Inner Temple, 1929; Bencher, Inner Temple, 1961. 2nd Lieut Royal Artillery, TA, 1939; Major,

Judge Advocate General's Branch, War Office, 1942. QC, Scots Bar, 1945. Contested (U) Kirkcaldy Burghs, 1945; Advocate Depute, 1945; Pres. Transport Arbitration Tribunal, Scotland, 1947-55; Sheriff of Ayr and Bute, 1952-54; Trustee National Library of Scotland, 1952-57; Sheriff of Perth and Angus, 1954-55; Chm. Building Legislation Cttee, 1954-57; Chm. Scottish Agricultural Wages Board, 1955-61; Chm. Scottish Licensing Law Cttee, 1959-63. Dean of the Faculty of Advocates, 1955-57; a Senator of the College of Justice in Scotland, 1957-61. Hon. Fellow, Clare Coll., Cambridge, 1971. Hon. LLD Dundee, 1973. *Publication:* Law of Valuation in Scotland, 1930. *Address:* 3 Ainslie Place, Edinburgh. *T:* 031-225 5508; Woodend, Dirleton, E Lothian. *T:* Dirleton 276. *Clubs:* Buck's, Oriental.

GUEST, Prof. Anthony Gordon; Barrister-at-Law; Professor of English Law, King's College, University of London, since 1966; Reader in Common Law to the Council of Legal Education (Inns of Court), since 1967; *b* 8 Feb. 1930; *o s* of Gordon Walter Leslie Guest and Marjorie (*née* Hooper), Maidencombe, Devon; unmarried. *Educ:* Colston's Sch., Bristol; St John's Coll., Oxford (MA). Served Army and TA, 1948-50 (Lieut RA). Exhibr and Casberd Schol., Oxford, 1950-54; 1st cl. Final Hon. Sch. of Jurisprudence, 1954. Bacon Schol., Gray's Inn, 1955; Barstow Law Schol., 1955; called to Bar, Gray's Inn, 1956. University Coll., Oxford: Lectr, 1954-55; Fellow and Prælector in Jurisprudence, 1955-65; Dean, 1963-64; Travelling Fellowship to S Africa, 1957; Mem., Lord Chancellor's Law Reform Cttee, 1963-; Mem., Adv. Cttee on establishment of Law Faculty in University of Hong Kong, 1965; UK Deleg. to UN Commn on Internat. Trade Law, NY, Geneva and Vienna, 1968-77, to UN Conf. on Limitation of Actions, 1974; Mem., Board of Athlone Press, 1968-73; Mem. Governing Body, Rugby Sch., 1968-. *Publications:* (ed) Anson's Principles of the Law of Contract, 21st to 24th edns, 1959-75; Chitty on Contracts: (Asst Editor) 22nd edn, 1961, (Gen. Editor) 23rd and 24th edns, 1968-77; (ed) Oxford Essays in Jurisprudence, 1961; The Law of Hire-Purchase, 1966; (Gen. Editor) Benjamin's Sale of Goods, 1974; (ed jtly) Encylopedia of Consumer Credit, 1975; articles in legal jls. *Address:* 16 Trevor Place, SW7. *T:* 01-584 9260. *Club:* Garrick.

GUEST, Douglas Albert, CVO 1975; MA Cantab and Oxon; MusB Cantab; FRCM, Hon. RAM, Hon. FRCO; Hon. FRSCM; Organist and Master of the Choristers, Westminster Abbey, since 1963; Professor, Royal College of Music; Examiner to Associated Board of Royal Schools of Music; *b* 9 May 1916; 2nd *s* of late Harold Guest, Henley-on-Thames, Oxon.; *m* 1941, Peggie Florentia, *d* of late Thomas Falconer, FRIBA, Amberley, Gloucester; two *d. Educ:* Reading Sch.; Royal College of Music, London; King's Coll., Cambridge. Organ Scholar, King's Coll., Cambridge, 1935-39; John Stewart of Rannoch Scholar in Sacred Music, Cambridge Univ., 1936-39. Served War of 1939-45, Major, Royal Artillery (HAC) (despatches). Gazetted Hon. Major, April 1945. Dir of Music, Uppingham Sch., 1945-50; Organist and Master of the Choristers, Salisbury Cathedral, 1950-57. Conductor of Salisbury Musical Soc., 1950-57; Dir of Music St Mary's Sch., Calne, 1950-57; Master of the Choristers and Organist, Worcester Cathedral, 1957-63; Conductor Worcester Festival Chorus and Three Choirs Festival, 1957-63. Chm. Council of National Youth Orchestra of Great Britain, 1953-. *Recreations:* fly fishing, golf. *Address:* 8 Little Cloister, Westminster Abbey, SW1P 3PL. *T:* 01-222 6222. *Clubs:* Athenæum, Flyfishers'.

GUEST, Eric Ronald; Metropolitan Magistrate (West London), 1946-68; Barrister-at-Law; *b* 7 June 1904; *s* of late William Guest; *m* 1932, Sybil Blakelock; one *d. Educ:* Berkhamsted Sch.; Oriel Coll., Oxford. BA 1925 (1st Class Hons Sch. of Jurisprudence); BCL 1926; called to Bar, 1927; practised in London and on Oxford Circuit. Recorder of Worcester, 1941-46; served as Sqdn Leader with RAFVR, 1940-45. *Club:* Arts.

GUEST, George Howell, MA, MusB (Cantab); MusD (Lambeth), 1977; FRCO 1942; FRSCM 1973; Organist of St John's College, Cambridge, since 1951; Fellow, 1956; University Lecturer in Music, Cambridge University, since 1956; Special Commissioner, Royal School of Church Music, since 1953; Examiner to Associated Board of Royal Schools of Music, since 1959; Member of Council, Royal College of Organists, since 1964; Director of Studies in Music at St John's, Downing and Queens' Colleges; *b* 9 Feb. 1924; *s* of late Ernest Joseph Guest and late Gwendolen (*née* Brown); *m* 1959, Nancy Mary, *o d* of W. P. Talbot; one *s* one *d. Educ:* Friars Sch., Bangor; King's Sch., Chester; St John's Coll., Cambridge. Chorister: Bangor Cath., 1933-35; Chester Cath., 1935-39. Served in RAF, 1942-46. Sub-Organist, Chester Cath., 1946-47; Organ Student, St John's Coll., Cambridge, 1947-51; John Stewart of Rannoch Scholar in Sacred Music, 1948; University Asst Lectr in Music,

Cambridge, 1953-56; Prof. of Harmony and Counterpoint, RAM, London, 1960-61. Dir, Berkshire Boy Choir, USA, 1967, 1970. *Recreations:* watching Chester AFC; the Welsh language. *Address:* 9 Gurney Way, Cambridge. *T:* Cambridge 54932. *Club:* Athenæum.

GUEST, Henry Alan; Chief Executive, Civil Service Catering 'Organisation, since 1972; *b* 29 Feb. 1920; *m* 1947, Helen Mary Price; one *s* one *d. Educ:* Lindisfarne College. FHCIMA. War Service, 1940-46, France, India, Malaya; Captain RA. Supplies Man., J. Lyons & Co. Ltd, Catering Div., 1955; Rank Organisation, Theatre Div.: Dep. Controller, Catering, 1963; Controller, 1965; Group Catering Adviser, Associated British Foods, 1966. Mem. Royal Instn of Great Britain. *Publications:* papers on marketing and organisation in techn. jls and financial press. *Recreation:* swimming. *Address:* 14 Pensford Avenue, Kew, Surrey TW9 4HP.

GUEST, Ivor Forbes; Chairman, since 1969, Member, since 1965, Executive Committee of the Royal Academy of Dancing; Solicitor; *b* 14 April 1920; *s* of Cecil Marmaduke Guest and Christian Forbes Guest (*née* Tweedie); *m* 1962, Ann Hutchinson; no *c. Educ:* Lancing Coll.; Trinity Coll., Cambridge (MA). Admitted a Solicitor, 1949; Partner, A. F. & R. W. Tweedie, 1951-. Organised National Book League exhibn of books on ballet, 1957-58; Mem. Cttee, Soc. for Theatre Research, 1955-72; British Theatre Museum: Mem. Exec. Cttee, 1957-77 (Vice-Chm., 1966-77); Mem., Theatre Museum Adv. Council, 1974-. Editorial Adviser to the Dancing Times, 1963-; Sec., Radcliffe Trust, 1966-. *Publications:* Napoleon III in England, 1952; The Ballet of the Second Empire, 1953-55; The Romantic Ballet in England, 1954; Fanny Cerrito, 1956; Victorian Ballet Girl, 1957; Adeline Genée, 1958; The Alhambra Ballet, 1959; La Fille mal gardée, 1960; The Dancer's Heritage, 1960; The Empire Ballet, 1962; A Gallery of Romantic Ballet, 1963; The Romantic Ballet in Paris, 1966; Carlotta Zambelli, 1969; Dandies and Dancers, 1969; Two Coppélias, 1970; Fanny Elssler, 1970; The Pas de Quatre, 1970; Le Ballet de l'Opéra, 1976; The Divine Virginia, 1977. *Address:* 17 Holland Park, W11. *T:* 01-229 3780. *Clubs:* Garrick, MCC.

GUEST, Trevor George; Registrar of the Principal Registry of the Family Division of the High Court of Justice, since 1972; Barrister-at-Law; *b* 30 Jan. 1928; *m* 1951, Patricia Mary (*née* Morrison); two *d. Educ:* Denstone Coll., Uttoxeter, Staffs; Birmingham Univ. (LLB (Hons)). Called to the Bar, Middle Temple, 1953. *Recreations:* antiques, dogs, Church affairs. *Address:* The Old Rectory, Purleigh, Essex. *T:* Purleigh 375.

GUIDOTTI, Gastone, FRSA; Counsellor of State, Rome, since 1968; *b* 29 Sept. 1901; *m* 1931, Raffaellina Betocchi; one *d. Educ:* St Carlo's Coll., Modena and University of Siena, Italy. Head of Dept at Ministry of Foreign Affairs, Rome, 1935; First Sec., Belgrade; First Sec., Stockholm; Italian Rep. to Allied Govts, London, 1945; in charge of Italian Legation, Prague, 1945, Athens, 1946; Head of Liaison Office of Min. of Foreign Affairs with Allied Govt, Trieste, 1947; Gen. Dir of Polit. Affs, Italian Min. for For. Affs, Rome, and Mem. various Italian Delegns to Nato Confs, Coun. of Europe Meetings, etc, 1948; Head of Italian Representation to UNO, 1951; Italian Ambassador: Belgrade, 1955; Vienna, 1958; Bonn, 1961; UK, 1964-68. Holds foreign decorations including 4 grand crosses. *Recreations:* shooting, art collecting. *Address:* Via Ettore Petrolini 36, Rome, Italy; c/o Ministero degli Affari Esteri, Rome, Italy. *Clubs:* Unione (Florence), Circolo della Caccia (Rome).

GUILD, Surgeon Captain William John Forbes; CBE 1952; FRCS, MD; RN retd; House Governor, King Edward VII Convalescent Home for Officers, Osborne House, IoW, 1965-71; *b* 30 Aug. 1908; *s* of late William Guild and Jessie Guild, Dundee; *m* 1st, 1942, Joan (*d* 1957), *d* of Charles Innes, Hornsey; one *s* one *d*; 2nd, 1958, Jessie, *d* of John MacLennan, Mallaig. *Educ:* Harris Academy, Dundee; St Andrews Univ. MB, ChB 1930; MD (StA) 1936, FRCS (Ed.) 1941. Post-grad. House appts, Royal Infirmary, Dundee. Served RN Med. Service, 1933-65: Ophthalmic Specialist and Surgical Specialist; final appt as Med. Officer i/c RN Hosp., Gibraltar; ret. with rank of Surgeon Captain. Sen. Fellow, Assoc. of Surgeons; Mem., Faculty of Ophthalmologists. *Publications:* various papers on naval medical matters. *Recreations:* tennis, gardening, hill-walking. *Address:* The Manse, The Mall, Brading, Isle of Wight. *T:* Brading 316. *Club:* Royal Over-Seas League.

GUILDFORD, Bishop of, since 1973; **Rt. Rev. David Alan Brown;** *b* 11 July 1922; *s* of Russell Alan Brown and Olive Helen Brown (*née* Golding); *m* 1954, Elizabeth Mary Hele, BA, DipEd (London); two *s* one *d. Educ:* Monkton Combe Sch.; London

Coll. of Divinity; Sch. of Oriental and African Studies. Univ. of London: BD (1st Cl. Hons) 1946; MTh (Hebrew, Aramaic and Syriac), 1947; BA (1st Cl. Hons Classical Arabic), 1951. ALCD (1st Cl. Hons with distinction), 1948. Jun. Tutor, London Coll. of Divinity, 1947-49; Asst Curate, Immanuel, Streatham Common, 1948-51; Liskeard Lodge, CMS Training Coll., 1951-52; Missionary, CMS, 1952: District Missionary, Yambio, Sudan, 1952-54; Bishop Gwynne Coll., Mundri, Sudan, 1954-61 (Principal 1955); Canon Missioner, Khartoum Cathedral, and Bishop's Commissary (South), 1961-62; research studies at London, Khartoum and Amman Univs, 1962-65; Missionary, Dio. of Jordan, Lebanon and Syria, 1965-66; Asst Curate, St John the Evangelist, Bromley, 1966; Vicar of Christ Church, Herne Bay, 1967-73; Rural Dean of Reculver, 1972-73; Chairman: Canterbury Diocesan Council for Mission and Unity, 1972-73; British Council of Churches Working Party on Islam in Britain, 1974-; C of E Bd for Mission and Unity, 1977-. Warden, St Augustine's Coll., Canterbury, 1975-. *Publications:* A Manual of Evangelism, 1958; The Way of the Prophet, 1960; Preaching Patterns, 1961; A Catechism for Enquirers, Catechumens and Confirmation Candidates, 1961; Jesus and God, 1967; The Christian Scriptures, 1968; The Cross of the Messiah, 1969; The Divine Trinity, 1969; Mission is Living, 1972; A Guide to Religions, 1975; A New Threshold, 1976; God's To-morrow, 1977; contribs to Theology, New Fire. *Recreations:* gardening, reading, walking. *Address:* Willow Grange, Stringers Common, Guildford GU4 7QS. *T:* Guildford 73922. *Club:* Royal Commonwealth Society.

GUILDFORD, Dean of; *see* Bridge, Very Rev. A. C.

GUILFORD, 9th Earl of *cr* 1752; **Edward Francis North; Baron Guilford, 1683; JP; DL;** *b* 22 Sept. 1933; *s* of Major Lord North (*d* 1940) and Joan Louise (she *m* 2nd, 1947, Charles Harman Hunt), *er d* of late Sir Merrik Burrell, 7th Bt, CBE; *S* grandfather, 1949; *m* 1956, Osyth Vere Napier, *d* of Cyril Napier Leeston Smith, Trottiscliffe, near West Malling, Kent; one *s. Educ:* Eton. JP Dover and E Kent; DL Kent 1976. *Heir: s* Lord North, *qv. Address:* Waldershare Park, Dover, Kent. *T:* Kearsney 2244.
See also Major Hon. Sir Clive Bossom, Bt.

GUILLUM SCOTT, Sir John (Arthur), Kt 1964; TD 1945; Communar of Chichester Cathedral, since 1973; *b* 27 Oct. 1910; *e s* of late Guy H. Guillum Scott; *m* 1939, Muriel Elizabeth, *d* of late James Ross; one *d. Educ:* King's Sch., Canterbury. Queen Anne's Bounty, 1929-46; Asst Sec., Church Assembly, 1946-48, Sec., 1948-70; Sec.-Gen., General Synod of C of E, 1970-72. Inns of Court Regt TA, 1929-53; war service, 1939-45 (despatches); Lieut-Col commanding Inns of Court Regt, 1950-53; Bt Col, 1953. DCL (Lambeth) 1961. *Recreations:* gardening, field sports. *Address:* 2 The Chantry, Canon Lane, Chichester, West Sussex. *Club:* Royal Automobile.

GUILLY, Rt. Rev. Richard Lester, SJ; OBE 1945; *b* 6 July 1905; *s* of late Richard Guilly. *Educ:* Stonyhurst Coll.; Campion Hall, Oxford (Hons Mod. Hist.; BA, MA); Heythrop Coll. Entered Soc. of Jesus, 1924; Asst Master, Beaumont Coll., 1933-35; ordained 1938. Served War of 1939-45, Chaplain to the Forces: BEF (France), 1939-40; CF 3rd Cl. 1940; Senior RC Chaplain, N Ireland, 1 Corps District, AA Cmd, 2nd Army, 1940-45 (OBE, despatches). Superior of Soc. of Jesus in British Guiana and Barbados, 1946-54; Titular Bishop of Adraa and Vicar Apostolic of British Guiana and Barbados, 1954-56; Bishop of Georgetown, 1956-72. *Publications:* various articles on Church History, Christian Social Doctrine and Church in Guyana. *Address:* Villa Maria, St Peter, Barbados, WI.

GUINNESS, family name of **Earl of Iveagh** and **Baron Moyne.**

GUINNESS, Sir Alec, Kt 1959; CBE 1955; actor; *b* Marylebone, 2 April 1914; *m* 1938, Merula Salaman; one *s. Educ:* Pembroke Lodge, Southbourne; Roborough, Eastbourne. On leaving school went into Arks Publicity, Advertising Agents, as copywriter. First professional appearance walking on in Libel at King's Theatre, Hammersmith, 1933; played Hamlet in modern dress, Old Vic, 1938; toured the Continent, 1939. Served War of 1939-45; joined Royal Navy as a rating, 1941; commissioned 1942. Rejoined Old Vic, 1946-47. Hon. D Fine Arts Boston Coll., 1962; Hon. DLitt Oxon, 1977. *films include:* Oliver Twist, Kind Hearts and Coronets, The Lavender Hill Mob, The Bridge on the River Kwai (Oscar for best actor of the year, 1957); The Horse's Mouth; Tunes of Glory; Lawrence of Arabia; Murder by Death; Star Wars. *Plays include:* The Cocktail Party (New York); Hotel Paradiso, Ross, Dylan (New York); Wise Child; A Voyage Round My Father; Habeas Corpus; Yahoo (also devised, in collaboration); The Old Country, 1977. *Recreation:* fishing. *Address:* Kettlebrook Meadows, Steep Marsh, Petersfield, Hants. *Club:* Athenæum.

GUINNESS, Bryan; see Moyne, 2nd Baron.

GUINNESS, James Edward Alexander Rundell; Joint Chairman, Guinness Peat Group, since 1973 (Chairman, Guinness Mahon Holdings Ltd, 1968-72); b 23 Sept. 1924; s of late Sir Arthur Guinness, KCMG and Frances Patience Guinness, MBE (née Wright); m 1953, Pauline Mander; one s four d. Educ: Eton; Oxford. Served in RNVR, 1943-46. Joined family banking firm of Guinness Mahon & Co., 1946, Partner 1953. Dep. Chm., Public Works Loan Bd, 1977- (Comr, 1960-). Recreations: hunting, shooting, fishing. Address: 36 Phillimore Gardens, W8 7QF. T: 01-937 8877. Clubs: Brooks's, Pratt's; Royal Yacht Squadron (Cowes).

GUINNESS, John Ralph Sidney; Alternate UK Representative to the Law of the Sea Conference, since 1975; b 23 Dec. 1935; s of Edward Douglas Guinness and late Martha Letière (née Sheldon); m 1967, Valerie Susan North; two s one d. Educ: Rugby Sch.; Trinity Hall, Cambridge (BA Hons History, MA Hons). Union Discount Co. Ltd, 1960-61; Overseas Develt Inst., 1961-62; joined FO, 1962; Econ. Relations Dept, 1962-63; Third Sec., UK Mission to UN, New York, 1963-64; seconded to UN Secretariat as Special Asst to Dep. Under-Sec. and later Under-Sec. for Econ. and Social Affairs, 1964-66; FCO, 1967-69; First Sec. (Econ.), Brit. High Commn, Ottawa, 1969-72; seconded to Central Policy Rev. Staff, Cabinet Office, 1972-75; Counsellor, 1974. Recreation: iconography. Address: 9 Hereford Square, SW7 4TS. T: 01-373 8648. Club: Brooks's.

GUINNESS, Hon. Jonathan Bryan; Director: Leopold Joseph & Sons Ltd; Arthur Guinness Son & Co. Ltd; March Cars Ltd, etc; b 16 March 1930; s and heir of Baron Moyne, qv, and of Diana (née Mitford, now Lady Mosley); m 1st, 1951, Ingrid Wyndham (marr. diss. 1962); two s one d; 2nd, 1964, Suzanne Phillips (née Lisney); one s one d. Educ: Eton; Oxford (MA, Mod. Langs). Journalist at Reuters, 1953-56. Merchant Banker: trainee at Erlangers Ltd, 1956-59, and at Philip Hill, 1959-62; Exec. Dir, Leopold Joseph, 1962-64; Non-exec. Director: Leopold Joseph, 1964-; also of Arthur Guinness Son & Co. Ltd. CC Leicestershire, 1970-74; Chairman, Monday Club, 1972-74. Address: Osbaston Hall, Nuneaton, Warwickshire; 17 Kensington Square, W8. Clubs: Carlton, Beefsteak; Ibstock Working Men's.

GUINNESS, Sir Kenelm (Ernest Lee), 4th Bt, cr 1867; consultant; b 13 Dec. 1928; s of late Kenelm Edward Lee Guinness and of Mrs Josephine Lee Guinness; S uncle 1954; m 1961, Mrs Jane Nevin Dickson; two s. Educ: Eton Coll.; Massachusetts Institute of Technology, USA. Late Lieut, Royal Horse Guards. With IBRD, Washington, 1954-75. Heir: s Kenelm Edward Lee Guinness, b 30 Jan. 1962. Address: (home) 2814 35th Street NW, Washington, DC 20007, USA. T: FE7-3933. Club: Cavalry and Guards.

GUINNESS, Loel; see Guinness, T. L. E. B.

GUINNESS, Thomas Loel Evelyn Bulkeley, OBE 1942; late Irish Guards; s of late Benjamin S. Guinness; m 1st, 1927, Hon. Joan Yarde-Buller (from whom he obtained a divorce, 1936); one s decd; 2nd, 1936, Lady Isabel Manners (marr. diss., 1951), yr d of 9th Duke of Rutland; one s one d; 3rd, 1951, Gloria, d of Raphael Rubio, Mexico. Educ: Sandhurst. MP (U) City of Bath, 1931-45; Contested Whitechapel, 1929, and By-election, 1930; Group Captain Auxiliary Air Force Reserve. Served War of 1939-45: RAF (despatches five times). Comdr Order of Orange Nassau; Officer Legion of Honour, France; Croix de Guerre. Address: Villa Zanroc, Epalinges 1066, Vaud, Switzerland. Clubs: White's, Buck's, Turf, Beefsteak; Royal Yacht Squadron (Cowes).
See also Marquess of Dufferin and Ava.

GUIRINGAUD, Louis de; Grand Officier de la Légion d'Honneur, 1976; Minister for Foreign Affairs, France, since Aug. 1976; b 12 Oct. 1911; s of Pierre de Guiringaud and Madeleine de Catheu; m 1955, Claude Mony; one s. Educ: Lycée Buffon; Lycée Saint Louis; Université de Paris, Sorbonne; Ecole des Sciences politiques, Paris. Degrees in letters, law and political sciences. Joined Staff of Minister for Foreign Affairs, 1936; entered Diplomatic Service, 1938-; Attaché, Ankara, 1938-39. Served War of 1939-45: with French forces, 1939-40; assigned to French High Commn, Beirut, 1940-41; with Resistance in France, 1942; Special Asst to French Comr for Foreign Affairs, de Gaulle's Provisional Govt, Algiers, 1943-44; with French forces, Italy and France, 1944-45. First Sec., London, 1946-49; Political Dir, French High Commn in Germany, 1949-52; Consul-Gen., San Francisco, 1952-55; Dep. Rep. to UN Security Council, 1955-57; Amb. to Ghana, 1957; Dir, Dept of Moroccan and Tunisian Affairs, Min. for Foreign

Affairs, 1960; Dep. High Comr in Algeria, 1962; Gen.-Inspector, Diplomatic Posts, 1963-66; Amb. to Japan, 1966-72; Permanent Rep. to UN, 1972-76. Holds several other French and foreign decorations, incl. Grand Cross of Rising Sun. Address: Ministère des Affaires Etrangères, 37 Quai d'Orsay, 75007 Paris, France. T: 555-9540. Clubs: Jockey, Morfontaine (Paris).

GUISE, Sir John, GCMG 1975; KBE 1975 (CBE 1972); Governor-General, Papua New Guinea, 1975-77; b Papua, 29 Aug. 1914; m; five s four d. Served War, Australian New Guinea Administrative Unit. Royal Papuan Constabulary, 1946, Mem. contingent attending Queen Elizabeth's Coronation, London, 1953, Sgt Major, later transferred to Dept of Native Affairs for local govt and welfare duties, Port Moresby. Mem., 1st Select Cttee Political Develt, 1961-63, which drew up 1st House of Assembly, 1964; Chm., House of Assembly Select Cttee on Political and Constitutional Develt which drew up 1st Ministerial Govt for 2nd House of Assembly, 1968. Mem. for E Papua, Legislative Council, 1961-63; MHA, Milne Bay District, 1964-67; Speaker, Papua New Guinea House of Assembly, Minister for Interior, and later Deputy Chief Minister and Minister for Agriculture, Papua New Guinea, to 1975; unofficial leader of elected Members, Papua New Guinea House of Assembly, 1964-68. Delegate, S Pacific Conf., Pago Pago, 1962; Mem., Australian delegn to UN, 1962 and 1963; attended UNESCO Conf., Paris, Geneva, London, 1963. Prominent layman in Anglican Church affairs. Hon. LLD. KStJ 1976. Address: Lalaura Village, Cape Rodney, Central Province, Papua New Guinea.

GUISE, Sir John (Grant), 7th Bt cr 1783; Jockey Club Official since 1968; b 15 Dec. 1927; s of Sir Anselm William Edward Guise, 6th Bt and of Lady Guise (Nina Margaret Sophie, d of Sir James Augustus Grant, 1st Bt); S father, 1970. Educ: Winchester; RMA, Sandhurst. Regular officer, 3rd The King's Own Hussars, 1948-61. Recreations: hunting, shooting. Heir: b Christopher James Guise [b 10 July 1930; m 1969, Mrs Carole Hoskins Benson, e d of Jack Master; one s one d]. Address: Elmore Court, Gloucester. T: Hardwicke 293.

GUJADHUR, Hon. Sir Radhamohun, Kt 1976; CMG 1973; MLA Mauritius; Deputy Speaker, Legislative Assembly, Mauritius, since 1974 (and 1968-69); solicitor; Chairman, Consortium Cinematographique Maurice Ltée; Director, Trianon Estates Ltd; Managing Director of Companies; b Curepipe Road, Mauritius, 1909; m; eight c. Educ: Church of England Aided Sch., Curepipe; Curepipe De la Salle Sch., Port Louis; Royal Coll., Curepipe; St Xavier Coll., Calcutta. Mem. Municipal Council, 1943-47; Dep. Mayor, Port Louis, 1947; Mem. (nominated) Town Council, Curepipe, 1957-60 (Chm., 1963). Elected Mem. for constituency of Bon-Accord/Flacq, 1967. Address: Port Louis, Mauritius. Club: Mauritius Turf (Steward, 1970; Chm. 1974).

GULL, Sir Michael Swinnerton Cameron, 4th Bt, cr 1872; b 24 Jan. 1919; o s of 3rd Bt and Dona Eva Swinnerton (d 1973), e d of late Sir Thomas Swinnerton Dyer, 11th Bt; S father 1960; m 1950, Mrs Yvonne Bawtree, o d of Dr Albert Oliver Macarius Heslop, Cape Town; one s one d. Educ: Eton. Late Lieut, Scots Guards (SRO). Heir: s Rupert William Cameron Gull, b 14 July 1954. Address: 2 Harcourt Road, Claremont, Cape Town, S Africa.

GULLIVER, James Gerald; Chairman: James Gulliver Associates Ltd, since 1977; Alpine Holdings Ltd, since 1977; b 17 Aug. 1930; s of William Frederick and Mary Gulliver; m 1958, Margaret Joan (née Cormack); three s two d. Educ: Campbeltown Grammar Sch.; Univs of Glasgow and Harvard. Royal Navy (Short Service Commn), 1956-59; Dir, Concrete (Scotland) Ltd, 1960-61; Management Consultant, Urwick, Orr & Partners Ltd, 1961-65; Man. Dir, 1965-72, Chm., 1967-72, Fine Fare (Holdings) Ltd; Dir, Associated British Foods Ltd, 1967-72; Chm. and Chief Exec., Oriel Foods Ltd, 1973-76. FBIM; Fellow and Mem. Council, Inst. of Directors; Vice-Pres., Marketing Soc. Mem., Prime Minister's Enquiry into Beef Prices, 1973. FRSA. Freedom and Livery, Worshipful Co. of Gardeners. Guardian Young Businessman of the Year, 1972. Recreations: ski-ing, music, motoring. Address: Delamere House, Great Wymondley, Herts. T: Stevenage 68583. Club: Carlton.

GULLY, family name of Viscount Selby.

GUMMER, Ellis Norman, CBE 1974 (OBE 1960); Assistant Director-General (Administration), British Council, 1972-75; b 18 June 1915; o s of late Robert Henry Gummer, engr, and of Mabel Thorpe, Beckenham, Kent; m 1949, Dorothy Paton

Shepherd; two s. *Educ:* St Dunstan's Coll.; St Catherine's Society, Oxford. BLitt, MA. Library service: Nottingham Univ., 1939; Queen's Coll., Oxford, 1940-42; served War of 1939-45, Admty, 1942-45; British Council: East Europe Dept, 1945-50; Personnel Dept, 1950-52; Student Welfare Dept, 1952-59; Literature Group, 1959-61; Controller, Arts and Science Div., 1961-66; Controller, Finance Div., 1966-71. *Publication:* Dickens' Works in Germany, 1940. *Recreations:* books, topography, archaeology. *Address:* 9 Campden Street, W8 7EP. *T:* 01-727 4823.

GUMMER, John Selwyn; Director: Shandwick Publishing Co., since 1966; Siemssen Hunter Ltd, since 1973; Managing Director, EP Group of Companies, since 1975; *b* 26 Nov. 1939; *s* of Canon Selwyn Gummer and Sybille (*née* Mason); *m* 1977, Penelope Jane, *yr d* of John P. Gardner. *Educ:* King's Sch., Rochester; Selwyn Coll., Cambridge (Exhibr). BA Hons History 1961; MA 1971; Chm., Cambridge Univ. Conservative Assoc., 1961; Pres., Cambridge Union, 1962; Chm., Fedn of Conservative Students, 1962. Editor, Business Publications, 1962-64; Editor-in-Chief, Max Parrish & Oldbourne Press, 1964-66; BPC Publishing: Special Asst to Chm., 1967; Publisher, Special Projects, 1967-69; Editorial Coordinator, 1969-70. Consultant Publisher, EP Group, 1971-. Mem., ILEA Educn Cttee, 1967-70. Contested (C) Greenwich, 1964 and 1966; MP (C) Lewisham W, 1970-Feb. 1974. PPS to Minister of Agriculture, 1972; an additional Vice-Chm., Conservative Party, 1972-74; Prospective Parly Cand., Eye Div., Suffolk. *Publications:* (Jtly) When the Coloured People Come, 1966; The Permissive Society, 1971; (with L. W. Cowie) The Christian Calendar, 1974; (contrib.) To Church with Enthusiasm, 1969. *Address:* EP Group, East Ardsley, Wakefield, W Yorks. *T:* Wakefield 823971; Clarence House, Fressingfield, Suffolk, via Diss, Norfolk. *T:* Fressingfield 347.

GUN-MUNRO, Sir Sydney Douglas, Kt 1977; MBE 1957; Governor of St Vincent, West Indies, since 1977; *b* 29 Nov. 1916; *s* of Barclay Justin Gun-Munro and Marie Josephine Gun-Munro; *m* 1943, Joan Estelle Benjamin; two *s* one *d*. *Educ:* Grenada Boys' Secondary Sch.; King's Coll. Hosp., London (MB, BS Hons 1943); Moorfields Hosp., London (DO 1952). MRCS, LRCP 1943. House Surg., EMS Hosp., Horton, 1943; MO, Lewisham Hosp., 1943-46; Dist MO, Grenada, 1946-49; Surg., Gen. Hosp., St Vincent, 1949-71; Dist MO, Bequia, St Vincent, 1972-76. *Recreations:* tennis, boating. *Address:* Government House, St Vincent, West Indies. *T:* St Vincent 71917.

GUNDELACH, Finn Olav; a Vice-President, Commission of the European Communities, 1977 (Member, since 1973); *b* Velle, Denmark, 23 April 1925; *s* of Albert Gundelech and Jenny Hobolt; *m* 1953, Vibeke Rosenvinge; two *s*. *Educ:* Aarhus Univ. Sec., Danish Min. of For. Affairs, 1953-55; Permanent Rep. to UN, Geneva, 1955-59; Dir, Dept of Commercial Policy, GATT, 1959; Asst Gen. Sec., GATT, 1959, Asst Gen. Dir, 1965; Ambassador to EEC, 1967-72. Commander, Order of Dannebrog; Grand Cross (Brazil). *Publications:* articles in foreign trade jls. *Address:* Commission of the European Communities, Rue de la Loi 200, 1040 Brussels, Belgium.

GUNDRY, Rev. Canon Dudley William, MTh; Canon Residentiary and Chancellor of Leicester since 1963; Examining Chaplain to Bishop of Leicester; Proctor in Convocation, since 1970; *b* 4 June 1916; *e s* of late Cecil Wood Gundry and Lucy Gundry; unmarried. *Educ:* Sir Walter St John's Sch.; King's Coll., London. BD (1st cl. Hons) 1939, AKC (1st cl. Hons Theology) 1939, MTh 1941. Deacon, 1939; Priest 1940. Curate of St Matthew, Surbiton, 1939-44; Lectr in History of Religions, University Coll. of North Wales, Bangor, 1944-60; Mem. Senate and Warden of Neuadd Reichel, 1947-60; Dean of Faculty of Theology, 1956-60; Hon. Sec., British Section, Internat. Assoc. for History of Religions, 1954-60; Select Preacher, Trinity Coll., Dublin, 1957; Prof. and Head of Dept of Religious Studies, and Mem. of Senate, University Coll., Ibadan, 1960-63; Commissary to Bishop of Northern Nigeria, 1963-69; Rural Dean of Christianity, Leicester, 1966-74. Sometime Examining Chaplain to Bishops of Bangor and St Davids; Examiner to Universities of Leeds, London, Keele, St David's Coll., Lampeter, Gen. Ordination Examination. *Publications:* Religions: An Historical and Theological Study, 1958; Israel's Neighbours (in Neil's Bible Companion), 1959; The Teacher and the World Religions, 1968; many articles and signed reviews in theological and kindred journals. *Recreations:* motoring, ecclesiology. *Address:* 3 Morland Avenue, Leicester LE2 2PF. *T:* Leicester 704133. *Clubs:* Athenæum; Leicestershire (Leicester).

GUNLAKE, John Henry, CBE 1946; FIA; FSS; FIS; consulting actuary; *b* 23 May 1905; *s* of late John Gunlake, MRCS, LRCP,

and late Alice Emma Gunlake; unmarried. *Educ:* Epsom Coll. Institute of Actuaries: Fellow, 1933; Hon. Sec., 1952-54; Vice-Pres., 1956-59; Pres., 1960-62. A Statistical Adviser, Min. of Shipping, 1940-47. Member: Cttee on Econ. and Financial Problems of Provision for Old Age, 1953-54; Royal Commn on Doctors' and Dentists' Remuneration, 1957-60; Permanent Advisory Cttee on Doctors' and Dentists' Remuneration, 1962-70. *Publications:* Premiums for Life Assurances and Annuities, 1939. Contrib. to Jl of Inst. of Actuaries. *Recreations:* reading, music, walking. *Address:* 20 Belgrave Mews West, SW1. *T:* 01-235 7452. *Club:* Reform.

GUNN, John Angus Livingston; Under-Secretary, Department of the Environment, since 1976; *b* 20 Nov. 1934; *s* of late Alistair L. Gunn, FRCOG, and Alderman Mrs Sybil Gunn, JP, Chislehurst, Kent; *m* 1959, Jane, *d* of Robert Cameron, Wolverhampton; one *s* one *d* (and one *d* decd). *Educ:* Fettes Coll., Edinburgh (Foundationer); Christ Church, Oxford (Scholar). MA Oxford, 1st Cl. Hons in Classical Hon. Mod., 1955, and in final sch. of Psychology, Philosophy and Physiology, 1957; Passmore-Edwards Prizeman, 1956. National Service, commnd in S Wales Borderers (24th Regt), 1957-59. Entered Min. of Transport, 1959; Principal Private Sec. to successive Ministers of Transport (Rt Hon. Barbara Castle and Rt Hon. Richard Marsh), 1967-68; Asst Sec., MoT, DoE and Civil Service Dept, 1969-74; Under-Sec., Civil Service Dept, 1975. *Address:* Department of the Environment, 2 Marsham Street, SW1P 3EB.

GUNN, Prof. John Currie, CBE 1976; MA (Glasgow and Cambridge); FRSE, FIMA; Cargill Professor of Natural Philosophy, since 1949 and Head of Department, since 1973, University of Glasgow; *b* 13 Sept. 1916; *s* of Richard Robertson Gunn and Jane Blair Currie; *m* 1944, Betty Russum; one *s*. *Educ:* Glasgow Acad.; Glasgow Univ.; St John's Coll., Cambridge. Engaged in Admiralty scientific service, first at Admiralty Research Laboratory, later at Mine Design Dept, 1939-45; Research Fellow of St John's Coll., Cambridge, 1944; Lecturer in Applied Mathematics: Manchester Univ., 1945-46; University Coll., London, 1946-49. Member: SRC, 1968-72; UGC, 1974-. *Publications:* papers on mathematical physics in various scientific journals. *Recreations:* golf, music, chess. *Address:* 13 The University, Glasgow G12 8QG. *T:* 041-334 3042.

GUNN, Peter Nicholson; author; *b* 15 Aug. 1914; 2nd *s* of Frank Lindsay Gunn, CBE, and Adèle Margaret (*née* Dunphy); *m* 1953, Diana Maureen James; one *s*. *Educ:* Melbourne; Trinity Coll., Cambridge (MA). Served War 1939-45: Rifle Bde; POW 1942. Sen. Lectr, RMA, Sandhurst, 1949-54. *Publications:* Naples: a Palimpsest, 1961 (German trans. 1964, Italian trans. 1971); Vernon Lee: a Study, 1964; The Companion Guide to Southern Italy, 1969; My Dearest Augusta: a Biography of Augusta Leigh, Byron's half-sister, 1969; A Concise History of Italy, 1971; (ed) Byron's Prose, 1972; Normandy: Landscape with figures, 1975; Burgundy: Landscape with figures, 1976; Court of Magnificence: the Dukes of Urbino, 1976. *Address:* Hunt House, Whitaside, near Richmond, North Yorkshire. *T:* Gunnerside 386. *Club:* University Pitt (Cambridge).

GUNN, Thomson William, (Thom Gunn); *b* 29 Aug. 1929; *s* of Herbert Smith Gunn, and Ann Charlotte Gunn (*née* Thomson); unmarried. *Educ:* University Coll. Sch., Hampstead; Trinity Coll., Cambridge. British Army (National Service), 1948-50; lived in Paris six months, 1950; Cambridge, 1950-53; lived in Rome, 1953-54; has lived in California since 1954. Formerly Associate Prof., English Dept, University of Calif (Berkeley). *Publications:* Poetry from Cambridge, 1953; Fighting Terms, 1954; The Sense of Movement, 1957; My Sad Captains, 1961; Selected Poems (with Ted Hughes), 1962; Five American Poets (ed with Ted Hughes), 1962; Positives (with Ander Gunn), 1966; Touch (poems), 1967; Poems 1950-1966: a selection, 1969; Moly (poems), 1971; Jack Straw's Castle and other poems, 1976. *Recreations:* cheap thrills. *Address:* 1216 Cole Street, San Francisco, Calif 94117, USA.

GUNN, Sir William (Archer), KBE 1961; CMG 1955; JP; Australian grazier and company director; Chairman, International Wool Secretariat, 1961-73; *b* Goondiwindi, Qld, 1 Feb. 1914; *s* of late Walter and Doris Isabel Gunn, Goondiwindi; *m* 1939, Mary (Phillipa), *d* of F. B. Haydon, Murrurundi, NSW; one *s* two *d*. *Educ:* The King's Sch., Parramatta, NSW. Director: Rothmans of Pall Mall (Australia) Ltd; Grazcos Co-op. Ltd; Clausen Steamship Co. (Australia) Pty Ltd; Walter Reid and Co. Ltd; Gunn Rural Management Pty Ltd; Chairman and Managing Director: Moline Pastoral Co. Pty Ltd; Roper Valley Pty Ltd; Coolibah Pty Ltd; Mataranba Pty Ltd; Unibeef Australia Pty Ltd; Gunn Development Pty Ltd; Chairman:

Australian Wool Bd, 1963-72; Qld Adv. Bd, Develt Finance Corp., 1962-72; Member: Commonwealth Bank Bd, 1952-59; Qld Bd, Nat. Mutual Life Assoc., 1955-67; Reserve Bank Bd, 1959-; Aust. Meat Bd, 1953-66; Aust. Wool Bureau, 1951-63 (Chm. 1958-63); Aust. Wool Growers Council, 1947-60 (Chm. 1955-58); Graziers Federal Council of Aust., 1950-60 (Pres. 1951-54); Aust. Wool Growers and Graziers Council, 1960-65; Export Develt Council, 1962-65; Australian Wool Corp., 1973; Faculty of Veterinary Science, University of Qld, 1953-; Exec. Council, United Graziers Assoc. of Qld, 1944-69 (Pres., 1951-59; Vice-Pres., 1947-51); Aust. Wool Testing Authority, 1958-63; Council, NFU of Aust., 1951-54; CSIRO State Cttee, 1951-68; Chairman: The Wool Bureau Inc., New York, 1962-69; Trustee: Qld Cancer Fund; Australian Pastoral Research Trust, 1959-71. Coronation Medal, 1953; Golden Fleece Achievement Award (Bd of Dirs of Nat. Assoc. of Wool Manufrs of America), 1962; Award of Golden Ram (Natal Woolgrowers Assoc. of SA), 1973. *Address:* (home) 98 Windermere Road, Ascot, Qld 4007, Australia. *T:* Brisbane 268 2688; (office) Wool Exchange, 69 Eagle Street, Brisbane, Qld 4000. *T:* Brisbane 21 4044. *Clubs:* Queensland, Tattersalls, Queensland Turf (Brisbane); Union (Sydney); Australian (Melbourne).

GUNNING, John Edward Maitland, CBE 1960 (OBE 1945); Barrister-at-law; *b* 22 Sept. 1904; *s* of late John Elgee Gunning, Manor House, Moneymore, Co. Derry, and late Edythe, *er d* of T. J. Reeves, London; *m* 1936, Enid Katherine, *o d* of George Menhinick; two *s. Educ:* Harrow; Magdalene Coll., Cambridge. Called to Bar, Gray's Inn, 1933. Practised South Eastern Circuit, Central Criminal Court, North London Sessions, Herts and Essex Sessions. Joined Judge Advocate General's office, Oct. 1939. War of 1939-45: served BEF, France, 1939-40; N Africa, 1942-43; Italy, 1943-45 (despatches, OBE). Middle East, 1945-50; Deputy Judge Advocate Gen. with rank of Col, CMF, 1945, Middle East, 1946; Deputy Judge Advocate Gen. (Army and RAF): Germany, 1951-53, 1960-63, 1968-70; Far East, 1957-59, 1965-67; Senior Asst Judge Advocate Gen., 1965-70. *Recreations:* bridge, watching cricket, reading. *Address:* 31 Brunswick Court, Regency Street, SW1. *Clubs:* Travellers', MCC.

GUNNING, Sir Robert Charles, 8th Bt, *cr* 1778; gold-mine owner and farmer; *b* 2 Dec. 1901; *o s* of late Charles Archibald John Gunning and Beatrice Constance Purvis; *S* cousin 1950; *m* 1934, Helen Nancy, *d* of late Vice-Adm. Sir T. J. Hallet, KBE, CB; eight *s* two *d. Educ:* St Paul's Sch.; Leeds Univ. Business in the Sudan and Nigeria, 1924-33; prospecting and gold-mining in Nigeria, 1933-38; pegged first Nigerian lode gold-mine of the least importance, this in 1935 at Bin Yauri; served AA Command, 1939-46, temp. Capt. Emigrated to Alberta, 1948. Chairman: Peace River Hosp. Bd; Peace Region Mental Health Council. *Recreations:* gardening, cricket, and almost any ball game. *Heir: s* Lt-Comdr Charles Theodore Gunning, RCN [*b* 19 June 1935; *m* 1969, Sarah, *d* of Col Patrick Arthur Easton; one *d*]. *Address:* c/o Postmaster, Peace River, Alberta, Canada.

GUNSTON, Major Sir Derrick Wellesley, 1st Bt, *cr* 1938; MC; *b* 1891; *s* of late Major Bernard Hamilton Gunston, late 5th Dragoon Guards; *m* 1917, Evelyn (Gardenia), OBE 1944, *d* of Howard St George, Cam House, Campden Hill, W8; one *s. Educ:* Harrow; Trinity Coll., Cambridge. Pres. of the New Carlton Club at Cambridge; joined army at outbreak of war; second in command 1st Battalion Irish Guards at Armistice; War of 1939-45, Major 7th Bn Glos Regt; MP (C) Thornbury Division Glos, 1924-45; Parliamentary Private Sec. to Rt Hon. Sir Kingsley Wood, Parliamentary Sec. to the Ministry of Health in Conservative Government, 1926-29; Parliamentary Private Sec. to Rt Hon. Neville Chamberlain, Chancellor of the Exchequer, 1931-36, to Sir Edward Grigg, Joint Under-Sec. for War 1940-42. *Heir: s* Richard Wellesley Gunston [*b* 15 March 1924; *m* 1st, 1947, Elizabeth Mary (from whom he obtained a divorce, 1956), *e d* of Arthur Colegate, Hillgrove, Bembridge, IoW; one *d* ; 2nd, 1959, Mrs Joan Elizabeth Marie Coldicott, *o d* of Reginald Forde, Johannesburg; one *s*]. *Address:* Fram Cottage, Bembridge, IoW; 14 Pelham Crescent, SW7. *Clubs:* Carlton, Pratt's; MCC; Royal Yacht Squadron (Cowes); Bembridge Sailing (Bembridge, IoW).

GUNTER, Sir Ronald Vernon, 3rd Bt, *cr* 1901; Temporary Lieutenant RNVR; *b* 8 March 1904; *s* of Sir Nevill Gunter, 2nd Bt, and Clara Lydia, *widow* of John Pritchard-Barrett of Sydenham; *S* father, 1917; *m* 1st, 1925, Anne (who obtained a divorce, 1932, and *m* 2nd, 1939, William Johnston Dyson), *d* of C. Lovell Simmonds, St John's Coll. Park; two *d* ; 2nd, 1932, Dorothy Eleanor Johnston (marr. diss. 1950), *d* of H. E. Capes; 3rd, 1950, Mrs Vera Irene Wynn Parry (marr. diss. 1955), *d* of Sir Henry Philip Price, Bt; 4th, 1955, Phyllis Lesley Wallace, *d* of William St Clair Johnston. *Heir:* none. *Address:* Mill Hamlet Cottage, Sidlesham, Chichester, West Sussex PO20 7NB.

GUNTHER, Sir John Thomson, Kt 1975; CMG 1965; OBE 1954; MB, DTM&H Sydney; Vice-Chancellor, University of Papua and New Guinea, 1966-72; Assistant Administrator, Papua and New Guinea, 1957-66; formerly MEC and MLC, Papua and New Guinea; *b* 2 Oct. 1910; *s* of C. M. Gunther; *m* 1938; one *s* three *d. Educ:* King's Sch.; Sydney Univ. Dir of Public Health, Papua and New Guinea, 1949-56; Levers Pacific Plantations Pty Ltd, Brit. Solomon Is, 1935-37; Chm., Med. Bd (Mt Isa, Qld), investigating Plumbism, 1938-41; MO, RAAF, 1941-46; Malariologist, RAAF, 1943; CO 1 Trop. Research Fld Unit, 1944-45; Mem. S Pacific Commn Research Coun. (Chm. 1st meeting); Chm. Select Cttee on Polit. Develt for Papua and NG; Mem. Commn on Higher Educn, Papua and NG. *Publications:* reports to govt of Qld on Plumbism, 1939-40; reports to RAAF on Malaria and Scrub Typhus. *Recreation:* gardening. *Address:* Onkara Street, Buderim, Qld 4556, Australia. *Club:* University (Sydney).

GURD, Surg. Rear-Adm. Dudley Plunket, CB 1968; Medical Officer-in-Charge, Royal Naval Hospital, Malta, 1966-69; now in private practice; *b* 18 June 1910; *s* of Frederick Plunket Gurd and Annie Jane Glenn; *m* 1939, Thérèse Marie, *d* of John and Frances Delenda, Salonika,Greece; one *s* one *d. Educ:* Belfast Royal Academy; Queen's Univ., Belfast, MB, BCh, BAO (Hons) 1932; MD (High Commend) 1942; FRACS 1945; MCh 1959; FRCS (Eng.) 1964. Gilbert Blane Medal, 1943. Sen. Consultant and Adviser in Ophthalmology to the Navy, 1952; Warden, Ophthalmic Hosp. of St John, Jerusalem, Jordan, 1952-55. Joined RN as Surg. Lieut, 1934; Lieut-Comdr 1939; Comdr 1945; Capt. 1958; Rear-Adm. 1966; retired 1969; Served in Royal Naval Hosps at Malta, Barrow Gurney, Hong Kong, Plymouth and Haslar. QHS 1964. KStJ 1967. Hon. DSc QUB, 1969. Chevalier de l'Ordre Nationale du Viet-Nam, 1949; Gold Cross, Order of Holy Sepulchre, 1955. *Publications:* various contribs to ophthalmic literature. *Recreations:* interested in all kinds of sport and athletics, also in languages, religion and medical education. *Address:* Shanklin Lodge, Eastern Villas Road, Southsea, Hants. *T:* Portsmouth 31496. *Clubs:* Athenæum; Union (Malta).

GURDEN, Harold Edward; *s* of late Arthur William and late Ada Gurden; *m* Lucy Isabella Izon (*d* 1976); three *d.* Birmingham City Council, Selly Oak Ward, 1946-56; Pres. Birmingham and Dist Dairyman's Assoc., 1947-50; Chm. Soc. of Dairy Technology, Midland Div.; Pres.-Elect, Nat. Dairyman's Assoc., 1951; Chm., Northfield Div. Conservative Assoc., 1950-52. MP (C) Selly Oak Div. of Birmingham, 1955-Oct. 1974; Mem. of Speaker's Panel, House of Commons, 1966; Chm., Selection Cttee, House of Commons, 1970. Rector's Warden, St Margaret's Westminster, 1973-75. *Recreations:* bridge, golf, numismatics. *Address:* 53 Sussex Street, SW1.

GURDON, family name of **Baron Cranworth.**

GURDON, John Bertrand, DPhil; FRS 1971; Member of Staff, Medical Research Council Laboratory for Molecular Biology, Cambridge, since 1972; Fellow of Churchill College, Cambridge, since 1973; *b* 2 Oct. 1933; *s* of W. N. Gurdon, DCM, formerly of Assington Hall, Suffolk, and of late Elsie Marjorie (*née* Byass); *m* 1964, Jean Elizabeth Margaret Curtis; one *s* one *d. Educ:* Edgeborough; Eton; Christ Church, Oxford; BA 1956; DPhil 1960. Beit Memorial Fellow, 1958-61; Gosney Research Fellow, Calif. Inst. Technol., 1962; Departmental Demonstrator, Dept of Zool., Oxford, 1963-64; Lectr, Dept of Zoology, 1965-72; Research Student, Christ Church, 1962-72. Visiting Research Fellow, Carnegie Instn, Baltimore, 1965; Dunham Lectr, Harvard, 1971; Croonian Lectr, Royal Soc., 1976. Albert Brachet Prize (Belgian Royal Academy), 1968; Scientific Medal of Zoological Soc., 1968; Feldberg Foundn Award, 1975; Paul Ehrlich Award, 1977. *Publications:* Control of Gene Expression in Animal Development, 1974; articles in scientific jls, especially on nuclear transplantation. *Recreations:* skiing, squash, horticulture. *Address:* 4 The Cenacle, Hardwick Street, Cambridge; 19 Hids Copse Road, Cumnor Hill, Oxford. *Club:* British Ski.

GURNEY, Oliver Robert, MA, DPhil Oxon; FBA 1959; Shillito Reader in Assyriology, Oxford University, since 1945; Professor, 1965; Fellow of Magdalen College, 1963; *b* 28 Jan. 1911; *s* of Robert Gurney, DSc, and Sarah Gamzu, MBE, *d* of Walter Garstang, MD, MRCP; *m* 1957, Mrs Diane Hope Grazebrook (*née* Esencourt); no *c. Educ:* Eton Coll.; New Coll., Oxford. Served War of 1939-45, in Royal Artillery and Sudan Defence Force. Freeman of City of Norwich. For. Mem., Royal Danish Acad. of Sciences and Letters, 1976. *Publications:* The Hittites (Penguin), 1952; (with J. J. Finkelstein and P. Hulin) The Sultantepe Tablets, 1957, 1964; (with John Garstang) The Geography of the Hittite Empire, 1959; Ur Excavations, Texts,

VII, 1974; (with S. N. Kramer) Sumerian Literary Texts in the Ashmolean Museum, 1976; articles in Annals of Archæology and Anthropology (Liverpool), Anatolian Studies, etc. *Recreations:* lawn tennis, golf. *Address:* Bayworth Corner, Boars Hill, Oxford. *T:* Oxford 735322.

GUTCH, Sir John, KCMG 1957 (CMG 1952); OBE 1947; *b* 12 July 1905; *s* of late Clement Gutch, MA, King's Coll., Cambridge, and late Isabella Margaret Newton; *m* 1938, Diana Mary Worsley; three *s*. *Educ:* Aldenham Sch.; Gonville and Caius Coll., Cambridge. Classical scholar, 1924; 1st class Classical Tripos, Part I, 1926; 2nd class Classical Tripos, Part II, 1927; BA 1927; MA 1931. Cadet, Colonial Administrative Service, 1928; Asst District Commissioner, Gold Coast, 1928; Asst Colonial Secretary, Gold Coast, 1935; Asst Secretary, Palestine, 1936, Principal Asst Secretary, 1944, Under Sec., 1945; Asst Sec., Middle East Department, Colonial Office, 1947; Chief Secretary, British Administration, Cyrenaica, 1948; Adviser to the Prime Minister, Government of Cyrenaica, 1949; Chief Secretary, British Guiana, 1950-54; High Commissioner for Western Pacific, 1955-60. British Electric Traction Co. Ltd, 1961-69. Member: Governing Body, Aldenham School; Cttee of Management, Institute of Opthalmology. *Publications:* Martyr of the Islands: the life and death of John Coleridge Patteson, 1971; Beyond the Reefs: the life of John Williams, missionary, 1974. *Address:* Littleworth Cross, Seale, near Farnham, Surrey. *T:* Runfold 2081.

GUTHRIE, Rev. Donald Angus; Episcopal Chaplain to the University of Montana, Montana, USA, since 1977; *b* 18 Jan. 1931; *s* of Frederick Charles and Alison Guthrie; *m* 1959, Joyce Adeline Blunsden (*d* 1976); two *s* one *d*; *m* 1977, Lesley Josephine Boardman. *Educ:* Marlborough Coll.; Trinity Coll., Oxford (MA). Rector, St John's Church, Selkirk, 1963-69; Vice-Principal, Episcopal Theological Coll., Edinburgh, 1969-74; Priest-in-Charge, Whitburn Parish Church, Tyne and Wear, 1974-76; Provost, St Paul's Cathedral, Dundee, 1976-77. *Recreations:* walking, reading. *Address:* University of Montana, Missoula, Montana, USA.

GUTHRIE, Sir Giles (Connop McEacharn), 2nd Bt, *cr* 1936; OBE 1946; DSC 1941; JP; Merchant Banker; *b* 21 March 1916; *s* of Sir Connop Guthrie, 1st Bt, KBE, and late Eila, *d* of Sir Malcolm McEacharn of Galloway House, Wigtownshire; *S* father, 1945; *m* 1939, Rhona, *d* of late Frederic Stileman and Mrs Stileman, Jersey, CI; two *s* (and one *s* decd). *Educ:* Eton; Magdalene Coll., Cambridge. Winner with late C. W. A. Scott, of Portsmouth-Johannesburg Air Race, 1936; Served War of 1939-46 in Fleet Air Arm, Lieutenant Commander, 1943. Chairman and Chief Executive, BOAC, 1964-68; Mem. Bd, BEA, 1959-68; Chm., Air Transport Insurance Ltd, Bermuda, 1969-71; formerly: a Man. Dir, Brown Shipley & Co. Ltd; Dep. Chm., North Central Finance Ltd; Director: Prudential Assurance Co; Radio Rentals Ltd, and other cos. Governor, The London Hospital, 1965-68; a Vice-Chairman, 1968. JP West Sussex, 1955. *Recreations:* Conservation and Dendrology. *Heir:* *s* Malcolm Connop Guthrie [*b* 16 Dec. 1942; *m* 1967, Victoria, *o* *d* of late Brian Willcock and of Mrs Willcock, Belbroughton, Worcs; one *s* one *d*]. *Address:* Rozel, Jersey, Channel Islands. *Clubs:* MCC; Royal Yacht Squadron (Cowes).

GUTHRIE, Air Vice-Marshal Kenneth MacGregor, CB 1946; CBE 1944; CD 1948; retired; *b* 9 Aug. 1900; *s* of Rev. Donald and Jean Stirton Guthrie; *m* 1926, Catherine Mary Fidler; one *d*. *Educ:* Baltimore, USA; Montreal and Ottawa, Canada. RFC and RAF, 1917-19; RCAMC 1919-20; Canadian Air Board and RCAF since 1920. Asst Director of Military and Air Force Intelligence, General Staff, Ottawa, 1935-38; CO, RCAF Station, Rockcliffe, 1938-39; Senior Air Staff Officer, Eastern Air Command, 1939-41; CO, RCAF Station, Gander, Nfld, 1941; Air Officer i/c Administration, Western Air Command, 1942; Deputy Air Member Air Staff (Plans) AFHQ, Dec. 1942-44; AOC Northwest Air Command, RCAF, 1944-49. Retired, 1949. Legion of Merit (USA), 1946. *Recreations:* hunting, fishing, gardening. *Address:* 506, 9915-115 Street, Edmonton, Alberta T5K 1S5, Canada. *Clubs:* Garrison Officers' (Edmonton); Royal Vancouver Yacht (Vancouver).

GUTHRIE, Hon. Sir Rutherford (Campbell), Kt 1968; CMG 1960; *b* 28 Nov. 1899; *s* of late Thomas O. Guthrie, Rich Avon, Donald; *m* 1927, Rhona Mary McKellar, *d* of late T. McKellar; one *s* (and one *s* decd). *Educ:* Melbourne Church of England Grammar Sch.; Jesus Coll., Cambridge (BA). Farmer and grazier, Skipton, Victoria. Served European War of 1914-18 and War of 1939-45 (wounded, despatches): 9 Australian Div., Alamein. MP Ripon, Victoria, 1947-50; Minister for Lands and for Soldier Settlement, Australia, 1948-50. *Recreations:* fishing and golf. *Address:* Jedburgh Cottage, Howey Street, Gisborne,

Vic. 3437, Australia. *Clubs:* Melbourne, Naval and Military; Royal Melbourne Golf; Hawks, Pitt (Cambridge); Leander (Henley on Thames).

GUTHRIE, William Keith Chambers, LittD; FBA 1952; Master of Downing College, Cambridge, 1957-72, Hon. Fellow 1972; Laurence Professor of Ancient Philosophy, 1952-73; *b* 1 Aug. 1906; *s* of Charles Jameson Guthrie; *m* 1933, Adele Marion Ogilvy, MA; one *s* one *d*. *Educ:* Dulwich Coll.; Trinity Coll., Cambridge. Browne Scholar, 1927. Craven Student, 1928, Chancellor's Classical Medallist, 1929; Member of expeditions of American Society for Archaeological Research in Asia Minor, 1929, 1930 and 1932; Bye-Fellow of Peterhouse, 1930, Fellow, 1932-57, Hon. Fellow, 1957; University Proctor, 1936-37; Public Orator of the University, 1939-57; P. M. Laurence Reader in Classics, 1947-52; Intelligence Corps, 1941-45 (temp. Major 1945); Messenger Lecturer, Cornell Univ., 1957; James B. Duke Visiting Professor of Philosophy, Duke Univ., 1966; Raymond Prof. of Classics, State Univ. of New York at Buffalo, 1974. President, Classical Assoc., 1967-68. LittD Cambridge, 1959; Hon. DLitt: Melbourne, 1957; Sheffield, 1967. *Publications:* Monumenta Asiae Minoris Antiqua, IV (with W. M. Calder and W. H. Buckler), 1933; Orpheus and Greek Religion, 1935; Aristotle De Caelo, text, trans., introduction and notes (Loeb Classical Library), 1939; The Greek Philosophers, 1950; The Greeks and their Gods, 1950; F. M. Cornford, The Unwritten Philosophy (edited with a memoir by W. K. C. G.), 1950; Greek Philosophy: The Hub and the Spokes (Inaugural Lecture), 1953; In the Beginning: some Greek views of the origins of life and the early state of man, 1957; A History of Greek Philosophy, Vols 1-4, 1962-75; contributions to various classical journals. *Address:* 3 Roman Hill, Barton, Cambridge CB3 7AX. *T:* Comberton 2658.

GUTTERIDGE, Joyce Ada Cooke, CBE 1962; retired; *b* 10 July 1906; *d* of late Harold Cooke Gutteridge, QC, and late Mary Louisa Gutteridge (*née* Jackson). *Educ:* Roedean Sch.; Somerville Coll., Oxford. Called to the Bar, Middle Temple, Nov. 1938. Served in HM Forces (ATS), War of 1939-45. Foreign Office: Legal Assistant, 1947-50; Asst Legal Adviser, 1950-60; Legal Counsellor, 1960-61; Counsellor (Legal Adviser), UK Mission to the United Nations, 1961-64; Legal Counsellor, FO, 1964-66; re-employed on legal duties, FO, 1966-67. Hon. LLD, Western College for Women, Oxford, Ohio, 1963. *Publications:* The United Nations in a Changing World, 1970; articles in British Year Book of International Law and International and Comparative Law Quarterly. *Recreations:* reading, travel. *Address:* 8 Westberry Court, Grange Road, Cambridge CB3 9BG. *Clubs:* (Associate Lady Member) United Oxford & Cambridge University, University Women's.

GUTTMANN, Sir Ludwig, Kt 1966; CBE 1960 (OBE 1950); MD, FRCP, FRCS; FRS 1976; FRSA; Emeritus Consultant, Stoke Mandeville Hospital; Director: National Spinal Injuries Centre, Stoke Mandeville Hospital, Aylesbury, 1944-66; Stoke Mandeville Sports Stadium for the Paralysed and other Disabled, since 1969; Consultant to: Duchess of Gloucester House (Ministry of Labour) 1950; Star and Garter Home for Ex-Servicemen, Richmond (Vice-President, 1976); Chasely Home for Ex-Servicemen, Eastbourne; *b* 3 July 1899; *s* of Bernhard and Dorothea Guttman; *m* 1927, Else (*née* Samuel) (*d* 1973); one *s* one *d*. *Educ:* Breslau and Freiburg Universities (Germany). MD Freiburg, 1924; MRCP, 1947; FRCS, 1961; FRCP, 1962. Lecturer in Neurology, University of Breslau, 1930; Director, Dept of Neurology and Neuro-Surgery, Jewish Hospital, Breslau, 1933-39; Research Fellow, Dept of Surgery, Oxford Univ. (Senior Common Room, Balliol Coll.) 1939-43; Founder of Stoke Mandeville Games, 1948. First Albee Memorial Lecturer (Kessler Institute, New Jersey, USA), 1952; Ord. Professor (now Emeritus), Univ. of Cologne, Germany, 1954. FRSocMed; Member: British Assoc. of Neurologists, 1947; British Physiological Assoc., 1947; Hon. Member of Medical Societies. President: Med. International Society of Paraplegia, 1961-69; British Sports Association for the Disabled. 1962; International Sports Association for the Disabled, 1966. OStJ 1957. Hon. Freeman, Borough of Aylesbury, Bucks, 1962. Hon. DChir Durham, 1961; Hon. LLD Dublin, 1969; Hon. DSc Liverpool, 1971; Hon. FRCP(C). Commander de l'Ordre Oeuvre Humanitaire, France, 1952; First Recipient of Rehabilitation Prize, World Veterans Federation, 1954; Gold Medal for Verdiensten, Holland, 1958; Commendatore dell' ordine Al Merito, Italy, 1961; Officer, Order Oranje-Nassau, Holland, 1962; Grand Cross of Merit, Germany, 1962; Commandeur de l'Ordre de Léopold II, Belgium, 1963; Ordre du Mérite Combattant, France, 1963; Order of the Rising Sun, Japan, 1964; Order of Merit, Bavaria, 1971; Golden Star, Order of Merit, Germany, 1972; Olympic Gold Medal of Labour, Belgium Govt, 1972; Gold Medal, Dept. of Culture, Finland,

1975; Medaille d'Or du Sport et Jeunesse, France. *Publications:* Vol. VII Handbuch der Neurologie (Germany), 1936; Surgical Practice Vols 2 and 6, 1948 and 1949; Vol. Surgery, Official British Medical History of Second World War, 1953; Modern Trends in Diseases of the Vertebral Column, 1959; (ed) Neuro-Traumatology, vol. II, 1971; Spinal Cord Injuries: Comprehensive Management and Research, 1973. Editor International Journal, Paraplegia, 1962. *Recreations:* sport, photography, travelling. *Address:* Menorah, 26 Northumberland Avenue, Aylesbury, Bucks. *T:* Aylesbury 24901. *Club:* Athenæum.

GUY, Geoffrey Colin, CMG 1964; CVO 1966; OBE 1962 (MBE 1957); Governor and Commander in Chief, St Helena and its Dependancies, since 1976; *b* 4 Nov. 1921; *s* of late E. Guy, 14 Woodland Park Road, Headingley, Leeds, and of Constance Reed Guy (*née* Taylor); *m* 1946, Joan Elfreda Smith; one *s*. *Educ:* Chatham House Sch., Ramsgate; Brasenose Coll., Oxford. Served as Pilot, RAF, 1941-46, Middle East and Burma (Flight Lieut). Colonial Administrative Service, Sierra Leone: Cadet, 1951; District Commissioner, 1955; seconded Administrator, Turks and Caicos Islands, 1958-65; Administrator, Dominica, 1965-67, Governor, March-Nov. 1967; Sec., Forces Help Soc. and Lord Roberts' Workshops, 1970-73; Administrator, Ascension Island, 1973-76. *Recreations:* swimming, riding. *Address:* Plantation House, Island of St Helena; Tamarisk Cottage, Kirk Hammerton, York. *Clubs:* Royal Commonwealth Society, Royal Air Force.

GUY, Hon. James Allan, CBE 1968; JP; MEC; Senator, Australian Parliament, 1949 and 1951, retired 1956; *b* Launceston, Tas, 30 Nov. 1890; *s* of James Guy, Senator in Commonwealth Parliament, and Margaret McElwee; *m* 1st, 1916, Amy Louisa Adams (*d* 1951); one *s*; 2nd, 1952, Madge Kernohan. *Educ:* Tasmanian State Education. Member for Bass in Tasmania State Parliament, 1916-29; Chief Secretary and Minister for Mines, 1923-24; Chief Secretary and Minister for Railways, 1924-28; Deputy Premier, 1925-28; acting Premier, July 1926-Dec. 1926; Deputy Leader of the Opposition, June 1928-Sept. 1929. Member for Bass in Commonwealth Parliament, 1929-34; Asst Minister of State for Trade and Customs, 1932-34; Member for Wilmot, 1940-46; Government Whip, 1941-42; Opposition Whip, 1942-46. Represented Tasmanian Government at the opening of the Commonwealth Parliament at Canberra, May 1927; Member: Commonwealth Parliamentary Joint Cttee of Public Accounts, 1929-31; Commonwealth Parliamentary Standing Cttee on Broadcasting; Senate Standing Cttee on Regulations and Ordinances, 1950-55; Empire Parliamentary Delegation visiting Great Britain, Canada, and America, 1943; Temp. Chairman of Cttees, 1940. Life Title of "Honourable" conferred by King George VI, 1936. Alderman Launceston City Council, 1928-31. *Recreations:* motoring, bowling. *Address:* Cliffhaven, 3/10 Ozone Street, Cronulla, NSW 2230, Australia. *T:* Sydney 523.8940.

GUYANA, Bishop of; *see* West Indies, Archbishop of.

GUYATT, Prof. Richard Gerald Talbot, CBE 1969; Professor of Graphic Arts, Royal College of Art, since 1948, and Pro-Rector, since 1974; *b* 8 May 1914; *s* of Thomas Guyatt, sometime HM Consul, Vigo, Spain and Cecil Guyatt; *m* 1941, Elizabeth Mary Corsellis; one step *d*. *Educ:* Charterhouse. Freelance designer: posters for Shell-Mex and BP, 1935. War Service: Regional Camouflage Officer for Scotland, Min. of Home Security. Dir and Chief Designer, Cockade Ltd, 1946-48; Co-designer of Lion and Unicorn Pavilion, Festival of Britain, 1951; Consultant Designer to: Josiah Wedgwood & Sons, 1952-55, 1967-70; Central Electricity Generating Bd, 1964-68; British Sugar Bureau, 1965-68; W. H. Smith, 1970-. Vis. Prof., Yale Univ., 1955 and 1962. Ceramic Designs for Min. of Works (for British Embassies), King's Coll. Cambridge, Goldsmiths' Co. and Wedgwood commem. mugs for Coronation, 1953, Investiture, 1969 and Royal Silver Wedding, 1973. Designed silver medal for Royal Mint, Mint Dirs Conf., 1972, 700th Anniv. of Parlt stamp, 1965, and Postal Order forms, 1964 for Post Office; Silver Jubilee stamps, 1977. Exhibited paintings with London Group. Member: Stamp Adv. Cttee, 1963-74; Internat. Jury, Warsaw Poster Biennale, 1968; Bank of England Design Adv. Cttee, 1968-. Chm., Guyatt/Jenkins Design Group. FSIA; Hon. ARCA. *Publications:* articles in Architectural Review, Times, Graphis, Penrose Annual, Jl of RSA, etc. *Address:* Flat 1, 5 Onslow Square, SW7. *T:* 01-584 5398; Forge Cottage, Ham, Marlborough, Wilts. *T:* Inkpen 270.

GUYMER, Maurice Juniper, DL; JP; Metropolitan Stipendiary Magistrate, since 1967; *b* 29 Aug. 1914; *s* of Frank and Florence Mary Guymer. *Educ:* Northcliffe House, Bognor Regis; Westminster School. Admitted Solicitor, 1936. Served with

RAF, 1940-45. Chm., Inner London Juvenile Courts, 1967-76. Royal Borough of Kingston upon Thames: Council, 1953; Mayor, 1959-60 and 1960-61; Alderman, 1960-65; JP 1956. DL, Co. Surrey, 1960. Chm. Governing Body, Belmont Sch., Holmbury St Mary, 1977-. Chm., Kingston and Malden District Scout Council, 1962-76, Pres., 1976-. *Address:* Desborough Cottage, 132 Lower Ham Road, Kingston upon Thames, Surrey. *T:* 01-546 5529.

GWANDU, Emir of; Alhaji Haruna, (Muhammadu Basharu), CFR 1965; CMG 1961; CBE 1955; 18th Emir of Gwandu, 1954; Member, North Western State House of Chiefs, and Council of Chiefs; Member, and Chairman, Executive Council, State Self-Development Funds Council; President, former Northern Nigeria House of Chiefs, since 1957 (Deputy President 1956); *b* Batoranke, 1913; *m* 1933; fifteen *c*. *Educ:* Birnin Kebbi Primary Sch.; Katsina Training Coll. Teacher: Katsina Teachers Coll., 1933-35; Sokoto Middle Sch., 1935-37; Gusau Local Authority Sub-Treasurer, 1937-43; Gwandu Local Authority Treasurer, 1943-45; District Head, Kalgo, 1945-54. Member former N Reg. Marketing Board. *Recreations:* hunting, shooting. *Address:* Emir's Palace, PO Box 1, Birnin Kebbi, North Western State, Nigeria.

GWILLIAM, John Albert, MA Cantab; Headmaster of Birkenhead School, since Sept. 1963; *b* 28 Feb. 1923; *s* of Thomas Albert and Adela Audrey Gwilliam; *m* 1949, Pegi Lloyd George; three *s* two *d*. *Educ:* Monmouth Sch.; Trinity Coll., Cambridge. Assistant Master: Trinity Coll., Glenalmond, 1949-52; Bromsgrove Sch., 1952-56; Head of Lower Sch., Dulwich Coll., 1956-63. *Address:* The Lodge, Beresford Road, Birkenhead, Merseyside.

GWYNEDD, Viscount; David Richard Owen Lloyd George; *b* 22 Jan. 1951; *s* and *heir* of 3rd Earl Lloyd George of Dwyfor, *qv*. *Educ:* Eton. *Address:* 43 Cadogan Square, SW1; Brimpton Mill, near Reading, Berks.

GWYNN, Edward Harold, CB 1961; Deputy Under-Secretary of State, Ministry of Defence, 1966-72; retired 1972; *b* 23 Aug. 1912; *y s* of late Dr E. J. Gwynn, Provost of Trinity Coll., Dublin, and late Olive Ponsonby; *m* 1937, Dorothy, *d* of late Geoffrey S. Phillpotts, Foxrock, Co. Dublin; one *s* four *d*. *Educ:* Sedbergh School; TCD. Entered Home Office, 1936; Assistant Secretary, 1947; Assistant Under Secretary of State, 1956; Principal Finance Officer (Under-Secretary), Ministry of Agriculture, 1961-62; Deputy Under-Secretary of State, Home Office, 1963-66. *Recreations:* gardening, the countryside. *Address:* The Chestnuts, Minchinhampton, Glos. *T:* Nailsworth 2863.

GWYNNE-EVANS, Sir Ian William, 3rd Bt, *cr* 1913; Deputy Chairman, Real Estate Corporation of South Africa Ltd, since 1973 (Managing Director and Chairman, 1950-73); *b* 21 Feb. 1909; *er s* of Sir Evan Gwynne-Evans, 2nd Bt; *m* 1st, 1935, Elspeth Collins (marr. diss.); two *d*; 2nd, 1945, Monica Dalrymple. *Educ:* Royal Naval College, Dartmouth. Entered Royal Navy as Cadet, 1922; retired as Lieut, 1934. Served War, 1940-45, Lieut, Royal Navy. *Recreation:* bowls. *Heir:* *b* Francis Loring Gwynne-Evans [*b* 22 Feb. 1914; *m* 1st, 1937, Elisabeth Fforde (marr. diss., 1958), *d* of J. Fforde Tipping; two *s* one *d*; 2nd, 1958, Gloria Marie Reynolds; two *s* three *d*]. *Address:* 57 Eastwood Road, Dunkeld, Johannesburg, S Africa. *Clubs:* Garrick; Rand (Johannesburg).

GWYNNE JONES, family name of **Baron Chalfont.**

GWYNNE-JONES, Allan, DSO; RA; painter, etcher; *b* 27 March 1892; *s* of Ll. Gwynne-Jones; *m* 1937, Rosemary Elizabeth, *d* of H. P. Allan; one *d*. *Educ:* Bedales Sch. Abandoned study of law for painting; was a student at Slade School for a short time before the first European War, returned as student after war, 1919-23. Served European War, 1914-18: enlisted Army 1914, Public Schools Bn, commissioned 3rd East Surrey Regt (Reserve Bn) France, 1916; posted as 2nd Lt to 1st Cheshire Regt; awarded DSO, Somme, 1916; transferred to HM Welsh Guards, 1917 (wounded twice, despatches twice). Professor of Painting, Royal College of Art till 1930 when appointed Staff, Slade School, retired from Slade, 1959. Trustee of Tate Gallery, 1939-46. ARA 1955, RA 1965. Represented by pictures in the collections of HM The Queen and HM The Queen Mother, and in the Tate Gallery and the public galleries of Birmingham, Newcastle, Leeds, Oldham, Carlisle, Manchester, Sheffield, and Merthyr Tydfil, and the National Galleries of Wales, South Africa and Australia, and in the collections of the Arts Council and Contemporary Art Society; and by drawings, etchings and engravings in the British Museum, Victoria and Albert Museum, and National Museum of Wales; retrospective exhibn, Thomas Agnew, London, 1972. *Publications:* A Way of Looking at Pictures; Portrait Painters; Notes for art students; Introduction to Still-Life. *Address:* Eastleach Turville, near Cirencester, Glos. *T:* Southrop 214. *Club:* Athenæum.

GYÖRGYI, Albert S.; *see* Szent-Györgyi.

H

HABAKKUK, Sir John (Hrothgar), Kt 1976; FBA 1965; Vice-Chancellor, University of Oxford, 1973-77, a Pro Vice-Chancellor, since 1977; President, University College, Swansea, since 1975; Principal of Jesus College, Oxford, since 1967; *b* 13 May 1915; *s* of Evan Guest and Anne Habakkuk; *m* 1948, Mary Richards; one *s* three *d*. *Educ:* Barry County Sch.; St John's Coll., Cambridge (scholar and Strathcona student), Hon. Fellow 1971. Historical Tripos: Part I, First Class, 1935; Part II, First Class (with distinction), 1936; Fellow, Pembroke Coll., Cambridge, 1938-50, Hon. Fellow 1973; Director of Studies in History and Librarian, 1946-50. Temporary Civil Servant: Foreign Office, 1940-42, Board of Trade, 1942-46. University Lecturer in Faculty of Economics, Cambridge, 1946-50; Chichele Prof. of Economic History, Oxford, and Fellow of All Souls Coll., 1950-67. Visiting Lecturer, Harvard University, 1954-55; Ford Research Professor, University of California, Berkeley, 1962-63. Member: Grigg Cttee on Departmental Records, 1952-54; Advisory Council on Public Records, 1958-70; SSRC, 1967-71; Nat. Libraries Cttee, 1968-69. Chm., Cttee of Vice Chancellors and Principals of Univs of UK, 1976-77. Pres., RHistS, 1976-. Foreign Member: Amer. Phil. Soc.; Amer. Acad. of Arts and Sciences. Hon. DLitt: Wales, 1971; Cambridge, 1973; Pennsylvania, 1975. *Publications:* American and British Technology in the Nineteenth Century, 1962; Population Growth and Economic Development since 1750, 1971; articles and reviews. *Address:* The Lodgings, Jesus College, Oxford. *T:* Oxford 48140. *Club:* United Oxford & Cambridge University.

HABGOOD, Rt. Rev. John Stapylton; *see* Durham, Bishop of.

HACAULT, Most Rev. Antoine; *see* St Boniface, Archbishop of, (RC).

HACKER, Alan Ray; clarinettist; Professor, Royal Academy of Music, since 1960; *b* 30 Sept. 1938; *s* of Kenneth and Sybil Hacker; *m* 1959, Anna Maria Sroka; two *d*. *Educ:* Dulwich Coll.; Royal Academy of Music. FRAM. Joined LPO, 1958; founded Pierrot Players (with S. Pruslin and H. Birtwistle), 1965; revived basset clarinet and restored original text of Mozart's concerto and quintet, 1967; founded Matrix, 1971; Mem., Fires of London; founded Music Party for authentic performance of classical music, 1972; premieres of music by Birtwistle, Boulez, Feldman, Goehr, Maxwell Davies and Stockhausen. Revived the Baroque Clarinet (hitherto unplayed), 1975. Sir Robert Mayer Lectr, Leeds Univ., 1972-73. *Publications:* Scores of Mozart Concerto and Quintet, 1972; 1st edn of reconstructed Mozart Concerto, 1973. *Recreation:* social history. *Address:* 73 Brixton Water Lane, SW2 1QB.

HACKER, Prof. Louis M., MA (Columbia); Emeritus Professor of Economics, Columbia University, USA, 1967 (Economics Department, 1935; Dean of School of General Studies, 1952-58, Director, 1949-52; Professor of Economics, 1948-67); *b* 17 March 1899; *s* of Morris Hacker; *m* 1st, 1921, Lillian Lewis (*d* 1952); one *s* one *d*. ; 2nd, 1953, Beatrice Larson Brennan. *Educ:* Columbia Coll.; Columbia University. Assistant and contributing Editor of New International Encyclopædia, Social Science Encyclopædia, Columbia Encyclopædia; taught economics and history at University of Wisconsin, Ohio State University, Utah State Agricultural College, University of Hawaii, Yeshiva University, Penn State University, Univ. of Puget Sound, Army War College, National War College. Executive sec. American Academic Freedom Study; Editor, American Century Series; Chairman, Academic Freedom Cttee, American Civil Liberties Union, resigned 1968; Guggenheim Fellow, 1948, 1959; Relm Foundation Fellow, 1967. Harmsworth Professor of American History, Oxford Univ., 1948-49; Lecturer, Fulbright Conference on American Studies, Cambridge, 1952. Visiting Distinguished Professor of Economics, Fairleigh Dickinson, 1967-68. Fellow, Queen's Coll., Oxford, and MA (Oxon); Benjamin Franklin Fellow of

RSA; Hon. LLD Hawaii; Hon. LHD Columbia. Students Army Training Corps, 1918. *Publications:* (with B. B. Kendrick) United States since 1865, 1932, 4th edn 1949; The Farmer is Doomed, 1933; Short History of the New Deal, 1934; The US: a Graphic History, 1937; American Problems of Today, 1939; Triumph of American Capitalism, 1940; (with Allan Nevins) The US and Its Place in World Affairs, 1943; The Shaping of the American Tradition, 1947; New Industrial Relations (jointly), 1948; Government Assistance and the British Universities (jointly), 1952; (with H. S. Zahler) The United States in the 20th Century, 1952; Capitalism and the Historians (jointly), 1954; Alexander Hamilton in the American Tradition, 1957; American Capitalism, 1957; Larger View of the University, 1961; Major Documents in American Economic History, 2 vols, 1961; The World of Andrew Carnegie, Part 1, 1861-1901, 1968; The Course of American Economic Growth and Development, 1970; contributions to learned journals and reviews. *Recreations:* walking, bridge, travel. *Address:* 430 W 116th Street, New York, NY 10027, USA. *Clubs:* Athenæum (London); Faculty, Columbia University (New York); Pilgrims (USA).

HACKETT, Prof. Brian; Professor of Landscape Architecture, University of Newcastle upon Tyne, since 1967; *b* 3 Nov. 1911; *s* of Henry and Ida Adeline Mary Hackett; *m* 1942, Frederica Claire Grundy; one *s* two *d*. *Educ:* Grammar Sch., Burton-on-Trent; Birmingham Sch. of Architecture; Sch. of Planning for Regional Development, London. MA Dunelm, PPILA, RIBA, MRTPI. Professional experience, 1930-40; Flt-Lt, RAFVR, 1941-45; Lectr, Sch. of Planning for Regional Devlt, London, 1945-47; Univ. of Durham: Lectr in Town and Country Planning, 1947; Lectr in Landscape Architecture, 1948, Sen. Lectr, 1949-59; Vis. Prof. of Landscape Architecture, Univ. of Illinois, 1960-61; Reader in Landscape Arch., Univ. of Newcastle upon Tyne, 1962-66. Mem., Water Space Amenity Commn, 1973. Pres., Inst. of Landscape Architects, 1967-68; Hon. Corresp. Mem., Amer. Soc. of Landscape Architects, 1962. European Prize for Nature Conservation and Landscape Devlt, 1975. *Publications:* Man, Society and Environment, 1950; (jtly) Landscape Techniques, 1967; Landscape Planning, 1971; Steep Slopes Landscape, 1971; (jtly) Landscape Reclamation, 1971-72; numerous papers in internat. jls. *Recreation:* musical performance. *Address:* 46 High Street, Gosforth, Newcastle upon Tyne NE3 1LX. *T:* Newcastle upon Tyne 853380. *Club:* Royal Commonwealth Society.

HACKETT, Prof. Cecil Arthur, MA Cantab, Docteur de l'Université de Paris; Professor of French, University of Southampton, 1952-70, now Professor Emeritus; *b* 19 Jan. 1908; *s* of Henry Hackett and Alice Setchell; *m* 1942, Mary Hazel Armstrong. *Educ:* King's Norton Grammar Sch., Birmingham; University of Birmingham; Emmanuel Coll., Cambridge (Scholar and Prizeman). Assistant d'Anglais, Lycée Louis-le-Grand, Paris, 1934-36; Lecturer in French and English, Borough Road Coll., Isleworth, 1936-39. Served War of 1939-45: enlisted 1/8th Bn Middlesex Regt, 1939. Education Representative, British Council, Paris, 1945-46; Lecturer in French, University of Glasgow, 1947-52. Chevalier de la Légion d'Honneur. *Publications:* Le Lyrisme de Rimbaud, 1938; Rimbaud l'Enfant, 1948; An Anthology of Modern French Poetry, 1952, 4th edn 1976; Rimbaud, 1957; Autour de Rimbaud, 1967; (ed and introd) New French Poetry: an anthology, 1973; contributions to English and French Reviews. *Address:* Shawford Close, Shawford, Winchester, Hants. *T:* Twyford 713506.

HACKETT, Dennis William; publishing consultant; *b* 5 Feb. 1929; *s* of James Joseph Hackett and Sarah Ellen Hackett (*née* Bedford); *m* 1st, 1953, Agnes Mary Collins; two *s* one *d*; 2nd, 1974, Jacqueline Margaret Totterdell; one *d*. *Educ:* De La Salle College, Sheffield. Served with RN, 1947-49. Sheffield Telegraph, 1945-47 and 1949-54; Daily Herald, 1954; Odhams Press, 1954; Deputy Editor, Illustrated, 1955-58; Daily Express, 1958-60; Daily Mail, 1960; Art Editor, Observer, 1961-62; Deputy Editor, 1962, Editor, 1964-65, Queen; Editor, Nova, 1965-69; Publisher, Twentieth Century Magazine, 1965-72; Editorial Dir, George Newnes Ltd, 1966-69; Dir, IPC Newspapers, 1969-71; Associate Editor, Daily Express, 1973-74. Chm., Design and Art Directors' Assoc., 1967-68. FInstD. *Publication:* The History of the Future: Bemrose Corporation 1826-1976, 1976. *Recreations:* reading, squash. *Address:* 44 The Pryors, East Heath Road, Hampstead, NW3. *T:* 01-435 1368. *Club:* Royal Automobile.

HACKETT, Gen. Sir John Winthrop, GCB 1967 (KCB 1962; CB 1958); CBE 1953 (MBE 1938); DSO 1942 and Bar 1945; MC 1941; BLitt, MA Oxon; Principal of King's College, London, 1968-July 1975; *b* 5 Nov. 1910; *s* of late Sir John Winthrop

Hackett, KCMG, LLD, Perth, WA; *m* 1942 Margaret, *d* of Joseph Frena, Graz, Austria; one *d* (and two adopted step *d*). *Educ:* Geelong Grammar Sch., Australia; New Coll., Oxford, Hon. Fellow 1972. Regular Army, commissioned 8th KRI Hussars, 1931; Palestine, 1936 (despatches); seconded to Transjordan Frontier Force, 1937-39 (despatches twice); Syria, 1941 (wounded); Sec. Commn of Control Syria and Lebanon; GSO2 9th Army; Western Desert, 1942 (wounded); GSO1 Raiding Forces GHQ, MELF; Comdr 4th Parachute Brigade, 1943; Italy, 1943 (despatches); Arnhem, 1944 (wounded); Comdr Transjordan Frontier Force, 1947; idc 1951; DQMG, BAOR, 1952; Comdr 20th Armoured Bde, 1954; GOC 7th Armoured Div., 1956-58; Comdt, Royal Mil. Coll. of Science, 1958-61; GOC-in-C, Northern Ireland Command, 1961-63; Dep. Chief of Imperial Gen. Staff, 1963-64; Dep. Chief of the Gen. Staff, Ministry of Defence, 1964-66. Comdr-in-Chief, British Army of the Rhine, and Comdr Northern Army Gp, 1966-68. ADC (Gen.), 1967-68. Col. Commandant, REME, 1961-66; Hon. Col: 10th Bn The Parachute Regt, TA, 1965-67; 10th Volunteer Bn, The Parachute Regt, 1967-73; Oxford Univ. Officers Training Corps, 1967-; Col, Queen's Royal Irish Hussars, 1969-75. Mem., Lord Chancellor's Cttee on Reform of Law of Contempt, 1971-74; Mem., Disciplinary Tribunal, Inns of Court and Bar. Vis. Prof. in Classics, KCL, 1977-78. Lees Knowles Lectr, Cambridge, 1961; Basil Henriques Meml Lectr, 1970; Harmon Meml Lectr, USAF Acad., 1970. President: UK Classical Assoc., 1971; English Assoc., 1973-74. Hon. Liveryman, Worshipful Company of Dyers, 1975; Freeman of City of London, 1976. Hon. LLD: Queen's Univ. Belfast; Perth, WA, 1963; Exeter, 1977. FKC, 1968; Hon. Fellow St George's Coll., University of Western Australia, 1965. *Publications:* I Was a Stranger, 1977; articles and reviews. *Address:* Coberley Mill, Cheltenham, Glos. *T:* Coberley 207. *Clubs:* Cavalry and Guards, United Oxford & Cambridge University, White's.

HACKETT, Sir Maurice (Frederick), Kt 1970; OBE 1958; Chairman, NW Metropolitan Regional Hospital Board, 1965-74 (Member, 1949-74); *b* Wood Green, N22, 11 Nov. 1905; British; *m* 1924, Deborah Levene (*d* 1969); one *s. Educ:* Glendale Secondary Sch., Wood Green. Press Dept, Labour Party Headquarters, 1935-40. With Min. of Information, then Central Office of Information, 1940-65 (Head of Speakers' Sect.; Chief Reg. Officer, London SE Region; Head of Tours Divn); Chm., SE Region Economic Planning Council, 1966-71; Mem., Land Commn, 1969-71. 1st Nat. Chm., Labour Party League of Youth; Chm., Southgate, Sth Kensington, Barnet and Herts Federation Labour Parties. Mem., East Barnet UDC, 1942-46. Chairman: Barnet Group Hosp. Management Cttee, 1948-60; St Bernards Hosp. Management Cttee, 1960-62; SW Middx Hosp. Management Cttee, 1962-65; Mem., Gen. Nursing Council for England and Wales, 1969-73. *Recreations:* cinema, travel. *Address:* 2 Chesterfield House, South Grove, Highgate, N6. *T:* 01-348 2667.

HACKING, family name of **Baron Hacking.**

HACKING, 3rd Baron *cr* 1945, of Chorley; **Douglas David Hacking;** Bt 1938; Attorney and Counselor-at-Law of State of New York; *b* 17 April 1938; *er s* of 2nd Baron Hacking, and of Daphne Violet, *e d* of late R. L. Finnis; *S* father, 1971; *m* 1965, Rosemary Anne, *e d* of F. P. Forrest, FRCSE; two *s* one *d. Educ:* Aldro School, Shackleford; Charterhouse School; Clare College, Cambridge (BA 1961, MA 1968). Called to the Bar, Middle Temple, Nov. 1963 (Astbury and Harmsworth Scholarships). Served in RN, 1956-58; Ordinary Seaman, 1956; Midshipman, 1957; served in HMS Ark Royal (N Atlantic), 1957; HMS Hardy (Portland) and HMS Brocklesby (Portland and Gibraltar), 1958; transferred RNR as Sub-Lt, 1958, on completion of National Service; transf. List 3 RNR, HMS President, 1961; Lieut 1962; retired RNR, 1964. Barrister-at-Law, 1963-76; in practice, Midland and Oxford Circuits, 1964-75. Admitted to State and Federal Bar, New York State, 1975; with Simpson, Thacher and Bartlett, NYC, 1975-76. Member: Amer. Bar Assoc.; NY State Bar Assoc.; Bar Assoc. of City of New York. Pres., Assoc. of Lancastrians in London, 1971-72. Apprenticed to Merchant Taylors' Co., 1955, admitted to Freedom, 1962; Freedom, City of London, 1962. *Recreations:* squash, walking. *Heir: s* Hon. Douglas Francis Hacking, *b* 8 Aug. 1968. *Address:* Forrest Hill, Boxmoor, Herts HP3 0BD; c/o Lovell White and King, 21 Holborn Viaduct, EC1A 2DY; 375 Park Avenue, New York, NY 10022, USA. *Club:* MCC.

HACKNEY, Archdeacon of; *see* Timms, Ven. G. B.

HACKNEY, Arthur, RE 1960; RWS 1957 (VPRWS 1974-77); ARCA 1949; Head of Department (Printmaking), West Surrey College of Art and Design (Farnham Centre) (formerly Farnham School of Art), since 1968; *b* 13 March 1925; *s* of late

J. T. Hackney; *m* 1955, Mary Baker, ARCA; two *d. Educ:* Burslem Sch. of Art; Royal Coll. of Art, London. Served in Royal Navy, 1942-46. Travelling scholarship, Royal College of Art, 1949; part-time Painting Instructor, Farnham Sch. of Art, 1949, Lecturer, 1962; Head of Dept (Graphic), 1963-68. Work represented in Public Collections, including Bradford City Art Gallery, Victoria and Albert Museum, Ashmolean Museum, Wellington Art Gallery (NZ), Nottingham Art Gallery, Keighley Art Gallery (Yorks), Wakefield City Art Gallery, Graves Art Gallery, Sheffield, GLC, Preston Art Gallery, City of Stoke-on-Trent Art Gall., Kent Educn Cttee, Staffordshire Educn Cttee. Mem., Fine Art Bd, CNAA, 1975. *Address:* Woodhatches, Spoil Lane, Tongham, Surrey. *T:* Aldershot 23919. *Club:* Chelsea Arts.

HADDEN-PATON, Major Adrian Gerard Nigel, DL, JP; *b* 3 Dec. 1918; *s* of late Nigel Fairholt Paton, Covehithe, Suffolk; *m* 1951, Mary-Rose, *d* of Col A. H. MacIlwaine, DSO, MC, Troutbeck, S Rhodesia; two *s* (and two step *s*). *Educ:* Rugby; Worcester Coll., Oxford. 2nd Lt, 1st The Royal Dragoons, 1940; Adjutant, 1943-44; served 1940-45: Western Desert, Tunisia, Italy, France, Belgium, Holland, Germany and Denmark; (despatches); Maj. 1945. Instructor, RMA, Sandhurst, 1947-50; retired 1950. Mem. Estates Cttee of Nat. Trust, 1956, Properties Cttee, 1970, Finance Cttee, 1973; Mem. Exec. Cttee, 1959-73, and Finance Cttee, 1961-73 (Chm. 1962-68) of Country Landowners Association. Is an Underwriting Mem. of Lloyd's; Chm. Holland & Holland Ltd; Chm. Hertfordshire Agricultural Soc., 1961-69; Past Pres. Hertfordshire & Middlesex Trust for Nature Conservation. Chm. of Governors, Berkhamsted Sch. and Berkhamsted Sch. for Girls, 1973- (Governor 1950). JP 1951, DL 1962, Herts; High Sheriff, 1961. *Recreations:* shooting, forestry, gardening. *Address:* Rossway, Berkhamsted, Herts. *T:* Berkhamsted 3264. *Club:* Cavalry and Guards.

HADDINGTON, 12th Earl of, *cr* 1619; **George Baillie-Hamilton,** KT 1951; MC; TD; FRSE; FSAScot; LLD (Glasgow); Baron Binning, 1613; Scottish Representative Peer, 1922-63; HM Lieutenant County of Berwick, 1952-69; *b* 18 Sept. 1894; *s* of late Lord Binning; *e s* of 11th Earl, and Katharine Augusta Millicent (*d* 1952), *o c* of W. Severin Salting; *S* grandfather, 1917; *m* 1923, Sarah, *y d* of G. W. Cook, of Montreal; one *s* one *d. Educ:* Eton; Sandhurst. Served European War (Royal Scots Greys), 1915-18 (MC, wounded); late Major 19th (L and BH) Armoured Car Coy. Served European War of 1939-45; Wing Comdr RAFVR, 1941-45; Capt. Queen's Body Guard for Scotland, Royal Company of Archers, 1953-74. Pres. Soc. of Antiquaries of Scotland; Pres. Scottish Georgian Soc.; Chm. of Trustees, National Museum of Antiquities, Scotland; Trustee, National Library of Scotland. *Heir: s* Lord Binning, *qv. Address:* Mellerstain, Gordon, Scotland. *Club:* New (Edinburgh).

HADDON, Eric Edwin, CB 1965; CChem, FRIC; retired; Director, Chemical Defence Establishment, Ministry of Defence, 1961-68; *b* 16 March 1908; *s* of late William Edwin Haddon, York; *m* 1934, Barbara Fabian, York; no *c. Educ:* Archbishop Holgate's Grammar Sch., York; Queen Mary Coll., London Univ. BSc (Special) Chemistry, ARIC 1929; FRIC 1943. Joined Scientific Staff of Admiralty, 1929; Scientific Staff of War Dept, 1929; Sec., Scientific Advisory Council, Min. of Supply, 1945-52; Dir, Chemical Defence Research and Development, Min. of Supply, 1957-61. *Recreations:* electronics, gardening, bridge. *Address:* Knavesmire, St Leonards Road, Thames Ditton, Surrey KT7 0RX. *T:* 01-398 5944.

HADDON-CAVE, Charles Philip, CMG 1973; Financial Secretary, Hong Kong, since 1971; *b* 6 July 1925; *m* 1948, Elizabeth Alice May Simpson; two *s* one *d. Educ:* Univ. Tasmania; King's Coll., Cambridge. Entered Colonial Administrative Service, 1952: East Africa High Commn, 1952; Kenya, 1953-62; Seychelles, 1961-62; Hong Kong, 1962-. *Publication:* (with D. M. Hocking) Air Transport in Australia, 1951. *Address:* 45 Shouson Hill, Hong Kong. *T:* 530455; Colonial Secretariat, Hong Kong. *T:* 95406. *Clubs:* Oriental; Hong Kong, Hong Kong Country, Royal Hong Kong Jockey.

HADDOW, Prof. Alexander John, CMG 1959; DSc, MD, FRCPGlas, DTM&H; FRS 1972, FRSE; Administrative Dean, Faculty of Medicine, since 1970, and Professor of Administrative Medicine, University of Glasgow, since 1971; *b* 27 Dec. 1912; *s* of Alexander and Margaret Blackburn Haddow; *m* 1946, Margaret Ronald Scott Orr; two *s. Educ:* Hillhead High Sch., Glasgow; Glasgow Univ. Strang-Steel Research Scholar (zoology), Glasgow Univ., 1934-35; Medical Research Council Junior Research Fellow in Tropical Medicine, 1938-41. Entomologist, Yellow Fever Research Institute, Entebbe, 1942-45; Staff Mem., International Health Div., Rockefeller Foundation, 1945-49; Overseas Research Service, 1950-65;

Epidemiologist, East African Virus Research Institute, 1950-52; Acting Dir, 1952-53; Dir, 1953-65; Sen. Lectr in Epidemiology, Univ. of Glasgow, 1965-70, also Dir, Cancer Registration Bureau, W of Scotland Hosp. Region, 1966-70; Titular Prof. of Tropical Medicine, Glasgow Univ., 1970-71. Hon. Prof. of Medical Entomology, Makerere Coll., The University Coll. of East Africa, 1962-65. Mem. WHO expert panel on virus diseases, 1953. Trustee, Uganda National Parks, 1955-65; Life Honorary Park Warden, 1965-. Chalmers Gold Medal, Royal Soc. Tropical Medicine and Hygiene, 1957. Stewart Prize, BMA, 1962; Keith Prize, RSE, 1968. *Publications:* contributions to learned journals. *Address:* Faculty of Medicine, Glasgow University, Glasgow G12 8QQ. *T:* 041-339 8855.

HADDOW, Sir (Thomas) Douglas, KCB 1966 (CB 1955); FRSE; Chairman, North of Scotland Hydro-Electric Board, since 1973; *b* 9 Feb. 1913; *s* of George Haddow, Crawford, Lanarkshire; *m* 1942, Margaret R. S. Rowat (*d* 1969); two *s*. *Educ:* George Watson's Coll., Edinburgh; Edinburgh Univ.; Trinity Coll., Cambridge. MA (Edinburgh) 1932; BA (Cambridge) 1934. Department of Health for Scotland, 1935; Private Sec. to Sec. of State for Scotland, 1941-44. Commonwealth Fund Fellow, 1948. Secretary: Dept of Health for Scot., 1959-62; Scottish Develt Dept, 1962-64; Permanent Under-Sec. of State, Scottish Office, 1965-73. Mem. (pt-time), S of Scotland Electricity Bd, 1973-. Hon. LLD Strathclyde Univ., 1967; Hon. DLitt Heriot-Watt Univ., 1971. *Recreation:* golf. *Address:* The Coach House, Northumberland Street Lane SW, Edinburgh EH3 6JD. *T:* 031-556 3650; Castle View, Dirleton, East Lothian EH39 5EH. *T:* Dirleton 266. *Club:* Royal Commonwealth Society.

HADEN, William Demmery, TD, MA; Headmaster, Royal Grammar School, Newcastle upon Tyne, 1960-72, retired; *b* 14 March 1909; *s* of Reverend William Henry and Gertrude Haden, Little Aston; *m* 1939, Elizabeth Marjorie, *d* of R. S. Tewson, Chorley Wood; one *s* two *d*. *Educ:* Nottingham High Sch.; Wadham Coll., Oxford (2nd Class Lit. Hum.; MA 1934). English Master, Merchant Taylors' Sch., 1938-46; Headmaster, Mercers' Sch., 1946-59. War Service, 1940-45: served as Battery Comdr RA with Fourteenth Army throughout Burma Campaign (despatches twice); Administrative Commandant, Hmawbi Area, S Burma District, 1945. *Recreations:* games, gardening, listening to music. *Address:* 1 High Espley Cottages, Morpeth, Northumberland.

HADEN-GUEST, family name of **Baron Haden-Guest**.

HADEN-GUEST, 3rd Baron *cr* 1950, of Saling, Essex; **Richard Haden Haden-Guest;** *b* 1904; *s* of 1st Baron Haden-Guest, MC, and Edith (*d* 1944), *d* of Max Low; *S* brother, 1974; *m* 1st, 1926, Hilda (marr. diss. 1934), *d* of late Thomas Russell-Cruise; one *d*; 2nd, 1934, Olive Maria, *d* of late Anders Gotfrid Nilsson; one *s* decd; 3rd, 1949, Marjorie, *d* of late Dr Douglas F. Kennard. *Educ:* Bembridge. *Heir:* half-*b* Hon. Peter Haden Haden-Guest [*b* 1913; *m* 1945, Jean, *d* of late Dr Albert George Hindes; two *s* one *d*]. *Address:* Le Cèdre, Route des Fayards, Versoix, Geneva, Switzerland. *T:* Geneva 552761.

HADFIELD, (Ellis) Charles (Raymond), CMG 1954; *b* 5 Aug. 1909; *s* of Alexander Charles Hadfield, South Africa Civil Service; *m* 1945, Alice Mary Miller, *d* of Lt-Col Henry Smyth, DSO; one *s* one *d* (and one *s* decd). *Educ:* Blundell's Sch.; St Edmund Hall, Oxford. Joined Oxford University Press, 1936; Dir of Publications, Central Office of Information, 1946-48; Controller (Overseas), 1948-62. Mem., British Waterways Bd, 1962-66. *Publications:* British Canals, 1950, 5th edn 1974; The Canals of South Wales and the Border, 1960; The Canals of the East Midlands, 1966; The Canals of the West Midlands, 1966; The Canals of South West England, 1967; (with Michael Streat) Holiday Cruising on Inland Waterways, 1968; The Canal Age, 1968; The Canals of South and South East England, 1969; (with Gordon Biddle) The Canals of North West England, 1970; The Canals of Yorkshire and North East England, 1972; Introducing Inland Waterways, 1973; (with Alice Mary Hadfield) Introducing the Cotswolds, 1976; Waterways Sights to See, 1976. *Recreations:* writing; exploring canals. *Address:* 21 Randolph Road, W9 1AN. *T:* 01-286 4347.

HADFIELD, Esmé Havelock, FRCS; Consultant Ear, Nose and Throat Surgeon, High Wycombe, Amersham and Chalfont Hospitals; Associate Surgeon (Hon.), Ear, Nose and Throat Department, Radcliffe Infirmary, Oxford; *b* 1921; *o d* of late Geoffrey Hadfield, MD. *Educ:* Clifton High Sch.; St Hugh's Coll., Oxford; Radcliffe Infirmary Oxford. BA (Oxon.) 1942; BM, BCh Oxon 1945; FRCS 1951; MA Oxon. 1952. House Officer appts, Radcliffe Infirmary, Oxford, 1945; Registrar to ENT Dept, Radcliffe Infirmary, Oxford, 1948; Asst Ohren, Nase, Hals Klinik, Kantonspital, University of Zurich, 1949.

First Asst ENT Dept, Radcliffe Infirmary, Oxford, 1950. British Empire Cancer Campaign Travelling Fellow in Canada, 1953; Hunterian Prof., RCS, 1969-70. *Publications:* articles on ENT surgery in medical journals. *Recreation:* travel. *Address:* Linaver, Lane End, High Wycombe, Bucks. *T:* High Wycombe 881473.

HADFIELD, John Charles Heywood; author; Deputy Chairman, the Rainbird Publishing Group, Ltd; *b* 16 June 1907; 2nd *s* of H. G. Hadfield, Birmingham; *m* 1st, 1931, Phyllis Anna McMullen (*d* 1973); one *s*; 2nd, 1975, Joy Westendarp. *Educ:* Bradfield. Editor, J. M. Dent & Sons, Ltd, 1935-42; Books Officer for British Council in the Middle East, 1942-44; Dir of the National Book League, 1944-50; Organiser, Festival of Britain Exhibition of Books, 1951; Editor, The Saturday Book, 1952-73. *Publications:* The Christmas Companion, 1939; Georgian Love Songs, 1949; Restoration Love Songs, 1950; A Book of Beauty, 1952, rev. edn 1976; A Book of Delights, 1954, rev. edn 1977; Elizabethan Love Songs, 1955; A Book of Britain, 1956; A Book of Love, 1958; Love on a Branch Line, 1959; A Book of Pleasures, 1960; A Book of Joy, 1962; A Chamber of Horrors, 1965; (ed) The Shell Guide to England, 1970; (ed) Cowardy Custard, 1973. (With Miles Hadfield): The Twelve Days of Christmas, 1961; Gardens of Delight, 1964. *Recreations:* books, pictures, gardens. *Address:* Barham Manor, near Ipswich, Suffolk. *T:* Ipswich 830236. *Club:* Savile.

HADFIELD, Ven. John Collingwood; Archdeacon of Caithness, Rector of St John the Evangelist, Wick, and Priest-in-Charge of St Peter and the Holy Rood, Thurso, Caithness, since 1977; *b* 2 June 1912; *s* of Reginald Hadfield and Annie Best Hadfield (*née* Gribbin); *m* 1939, Margretta Mainwaring Lewis Matthews; three *s* three *d*. *Educ:* Manchester Grammar School; Jesus Coll., Cambridge (Exhibnr, BA 1st cl. Hons, Classical Tripos Pt 2 1934, MA 1938); Wells Theological College. Deacon 1935, priest 1936, Manchester; Curate of S Chad, Ladybarn, Manchester, 1935-44 (in charge from 1940); Vicar of S Mark, Bolton-le-Moors, Lancs, 1944-50; Vicar of S Ann, Belfield, Rochdale, Lancs, 1950-62; Surrogate, 1944-62; Proctor in Convocation for Dio. Manchester, 1950-62. Diocese of Argyll and The Isles: Rector of S Paul, Rothesay, Bute, 1962-64; Itinerant Priest, 1964-77; Canon of S John's Cathedral, Oban, 1965-77; Inspector of Schools, 1966-77; Synod Clerk, 1973-77. *Recreation:* music. *Address:* 4 Sir Archibald Road, Thurso, Caithness KW14 8HN. *T:* Thurso 2047.

HADHAM, John; *see* Parkes, Rev. J. W.

HADLEY, Dr George Dickinson; Emeritus Physician, Middlesex Hospital; *b* 30 June 1908; *s* of Laurence Percival Hadley and Norah Katherine Hadley (*née* Alabaster); *m* 1947, Jean Elinor Stewart; three *d*. *Educ:* King Edward VI Sch., Birmingham; Clare Coll., Cambridge. 1st Class Natural Sciences Tripos, Part I 1930, Part II 1931, Cambridge; MB, ChB Cantab 1934; MRCP 1937; MD Cantab 1939; Elmore Clinical Research Student, University of Cambridge, 1936-38; FRCP 1947. Major RAMC and Medical Specialist, 1939-45 (POW, Germany, 1940-45). Physician, Middlesex Hospital, 1946. Examiner in Medicine: Cambridge Univ., 1955-57; University of London, 1956-60; RCP, 1965-70. *Publications:* articles in various medical journals. *Recreations:* angling, 'cello playing, book-binding. *Address:* 59 Gloucester Crescent, NW1 7EG.

HADLEY, Sir Leonard Albert, Kt 1975; JP; Secretary, Unions of Workers, Wellington, NZ; *b* Wellington, 8 Sept. 1911; *s* of Albert A. Hadley, JP; *m* 1939, Jean Lyell (*d* 1966), *d* of E. S. Innes; one *s* one *d*. Mem., Nat. Exec., NZ Fedn of Labour, 1946-77; Dir, Reserve Bank of NZ, 1959-; Pres., Wellington Trustee Savings Bank, 1976 (Dep. Pres., 1973-76); Bd of Trustees since Bank's formation, 1964; Mem. Industrial Relns Council since formation, 1974 (and its predecessor, Industrial Adv. Council, 1953); Relieving Mem., Industrial Commn and Industrial Court, 1974 (and its predecessor, Arbitration Court, 1960); Member: NZ Immigration Adv. Council, 1964-; Periodic Detention Work Centre Adv. Cttee (Juvenile), 1964-, and Adult Centre, 1967- (both since formation); Absolute Liability Enquiry Cttee, 1963-, and Govt Cttees to review Exempted Goods, 1959 and 1962. Rep., NZ Fedn of Labour Delegns to ILO, Geneva, 1949 and 1966; Internat. Confedn of Free Trade Unions, 1949; Social Security Conf., Moscow, 1971; SE Asian Trade Union Conf., Tokyo, 1973; OECD Conf., Paris, 1974. Awarded Smith-Mundt Leader Study Grant in USA, 1953. JP 1967. *Recreations:* reading, music, outdoor bowls, Rugby, tennis, and sport generally. *Address:* (private) 3 Cheeseman Street, Wellington 2, New Zealand.

HADOW, Sir Gordon, Kt 1956; CMG 1953; OBE 1945; Deputy Governor of the Gold Coast (now Ghana), 1954-57; *b* 23 Sept.

1908; e s of late Rev. F. B. Hadow and Una Ethelwyn Durrant; m 1946, Marie, er d of late Dr L. H. Moiser; two s. Educ: Marlborough; Trinity Coll., Oxford. Administrative Service, Gold Coast, 1932; Dep. Financial Sec., Tanganyika, 1946; Under-Sec. Gold Coast, 1948; Sec. for the Civil Service, 1949; Sec. to Governor and to Exec. Council, 1950-54. Address: Little Manor, Coat, Martock, Somerset. Club: Athenæum.

HADOW, Sir (Reginald) Michael, KCMG 1971 (CMG 1962); HM Diplomatic Service, retired; Chairman, Anglo-Israel Association, since 1975; b 17 Aug. 1915; s of Malcolm McGregor Hadow and Constance Mary Lund; m 1976, Hon. Mrs Daphne Sieff. Educ: Berkhamsted Sch.; King's Coll., Cambridge. Selected for ICS, 1937; Private Sec. to HM Ambassador, Moscow, 1942; Under-Sec., External Affairs Dept, Delhi, 1946-47; transferred to Foreign Office, 1948; FO, 1948-52; Private Sec. to Minister of State, 1949-52; Head of Chancery, Mexico City, 1952-54; FO, 1955; Head of Levant Dept and promoted Counsellor, 1958; Counsellor, Brit. Embassy, Paris, 1959-62; Head of News Dept, FO, 1962-65; Ambassador to Israel, 1965-69; Ambassador to Argentina, 1969-72. Recreations: all field sports. Address: Anglo-Israel Association, 9 Bentinck Street, W1. Club: Travellers'.

HADRILL, John Michael W.; see Wallace-Hadrill.

HAENDEL, Ida; violinist; b Poland, 15 Dec. 1924; Polish parentage. Began to play at age of 3½; amazing gift discovered when she picked up her sister's violin and started to play. Her father a great connoisseur of music, saw in her an unusual talent and decided to abandon his own career as an artist (painter) to devote himself to his daughter; studied at Warsaw Conservatorium and finished with a gold medal at age of ten; also studied with such great masters as Carl Flesch and Georges Enesco. Has played in Europe, US, and Middle East with great conductors like Sir Henry Wood, Sir Thomas Beecham, Sir Malcolm Sargent, Klemperer, Szell, Molinari. During War of 1939-45 gave concerts for British and American troops, as well as concerts in factories. Publication: Woman with Violin (autobiog.), 1970. Address: 74 Upper Park Road, NW3. T: 01-722 2357.

HAFERKAMP, Wilhelm; Vice-President, Commission of the European Communities, since 1970; b Duisburg, 1 July 1923. Educ: Universität zu Köln. Head, Social Policy Dept, Deutscher Gewerkschaftsbund, 1950, Mem. Exec. Cttee and Head of Econ. Dept, 1962-67; Socialist Mem., Landtag of North Rhine-Westphalia, 1956-66, 1967; Mem., Combined Commn of European Communities, 1967-70. Address: 200 rue de la Loi, 1049 Brussels, Belgium. T: Brussels 735-00-40.

HAFFENDEN, Maj.-Gen. D. J. W.; see Wilson-Haffenden.

HAFFNER, Albert Edward, PhD; Chairman, North Eastern Gas Board, 1971-72 (Deputy Chairman, 1966-71); b 17 Feb. 1907; 4th s of late George Christian and late Caroline Haffner, Holme, near Burnley, Lancs; m 1934, Elizabeth Ellen Crossley, Cheadle Heath, Stockport; one s one d. Educ: Burnley Grammar Sch.; Royal College of Science; Imperial Coll., London; Technische Hochschule, Karlsruhe. BSc (1st Cl. Hons), ARCS, PhD, DIC, London. Burnley Gas Works, 1924-26; Gas Light & Coke Co, 1932-56; Research Chemist and North Thames Gas Bd; Gp Engr, Chief Engineer and later Bd Member, Southern Gas Bd, 1956-66. Past Pres., Instn Gas Engineers (Centenary Pres., 1962-63); Past Vice-Pres., Internat. Gas Union. CEng, MIChemE, FInstF, FInstPet. Publications: Contributor to: Proc. Roy. Soc., Jl Instn Gas Engrs, Instn Chem. Engrs, Inst. of Fuel, New Scientist; papers presented to Canadian Gas Assoc., French Chem. Soc., Japanese Gas Industry and at IGU Confs in USA, USSR and Germany, etc. Recreations: photography, travel, gardening, cabinetmaking. Address: Burnthwaite, Iwerne Courtney, near Blandford Forum, Dorset DT11 8QL. T: Child Okeford 749. Club: Anglo-Belgian.

HAGART-ALEXANDER, Sir C.; see Alexander.

HAGEN, Dr John P(eter), Presidential Certificate of Merit (US), 1947; DSM (US), 1959; Professor of Astronomy and Head of Department of Astronomy, Pennsylvania State University, 1967-75, now Emeritus; Director, Office of United Nations Conference, National Aeronautics and Space Administration, 1960-62 (Director, Vanguard Division, 1958-60); b 31 July 1908; s of John T. and Ella Bertha Hagen (née Fisher); m 1935, Edith W. Soderling; two s. Educ: Boston, Wesleyan, Yale and Georgetown Univs. Res. Associate, Wesleyan Univ., 1931-35; Supt Atmosphere and Astrophysics Div., US Naval Res. Lab., 1935-58; Dir, Project Vanguard, 1955-58. Lecturer, Georgetown Univ., 1949-. FRAS 1969; FIEEE; Fellow: Amer. Acad. of Arts

and Sciences; Amer. Assoc. for Advancement of Science. Hon. ScD: Boston 1958; Adelphi, Loyola, Fairfield, 1959; Mt Allison, 1960. Phi Beta Kappa. Publications: contrib. to Astrophysical Journal and to Proc. Inst. Radio Engrg; contributor to Encyclopædia Britannica. Address: 613 W Park Avenue, State College, Pa 16801, USA. T: 237-3031. Club: Cosmos (Washington, DC).

HAGEN, Victor W. Von; see Von Hagen.

HAGERTY, James C., (Jim Hagerty); b Plattsburg, 9 May 1909; s of James A. Hagerty; m 1937, Marjorie Lucas; two s. Educ: Blair Acad.; Columbia Univ. Joined staff of New York Times, 1934; Legislative Correspondent, 1938-42; Press Sec. to Governor Dewey, 1943-50; Sec. to Governor, 1950-52; Press Sec. to President Dwight D. Eisenhower, 1953-61; Vice-Pres., Corporate Relations, Amer. Broadcasting Cos Inc., 1961-74, retired 1974. Address: (home) 7 Rittenhouse Road, Bronxville, NY 10708, USA.

HAGGARD, William; see Clayton, Richard Henry Michael.

HAGGART, Most Rev. Alastair Iain Macdonald; see Edinburgh, Bishop of.

HAGGERSTON GADSDEN, Peter Drury; see Gadsden.

HAGGETT, Prof. Peter; Professor of Urban and Regional Geography, University of Bristol, since 1966; b 24 Jan. 1933; s of Charles and Elizabeth Haggett, Pawlett, Somerset; m 1956, Brenda Woodley; two s two d. Educ: Dr Morgan's Sch., Bridgwater; St Catharine's Coll., Cambridge (Exhib. and Scholar; MA, PhD). Asst Lectr, University Coll. London, 1956; Demonstrator and University Lectr, Cambridge, 1958; Fellow, Fitzwilliam Coll., 1964; Leverhulme Research Fellow (Brazil), 1959; Canada Council Fellow, 1977. Visiting Professor: Berkeley; Pennsylvania State; Western Ontario; Toronto; Monash, Australia. Member, SW Economic Planning Council, 1967-72. Governor, Centre for Environmental Studies, 1975-. Cullum Medal of American Geographical Soc., 1969; Meritorious Contribution Award, Assoc. of American Geographers, 1973. Publications: Locational Analysis in Human Geography, 1965; (ed jtly) Frontiers in Geographical Teaching, 1965; Models in Geography, 1967; (with R. J. Chorley) Network Analysis in Geography, 1969; Progress in Geography, vols 1-9, 1969-77; Regional Forecasting, 1971; (with A. D. Cliff and others) Elements of Spatial Structure, 1975; Geography: a modern synthesis, 1975; Processes in Physical and Human Geography: Bristol Essays, 1975; research papers. Recreations: natural history, cricket. Address: 5 Tun Bridge Close, Chew Magna, Somerset.

HÄGGLÖF, Gunnar, GCVO (Hon.), 1954; Swedish Diplomat; b 15 Dec. 1904; s of Richard Hägglöf and Sigrid Ryding, Stockholm, Sweden; m Anna, d of Count Folchi-Vici, Rome. Educ: Upsala Univ., Sweden. Entered Swedish Diplomatic Service, 1926; Minister without Portfolio, 1939. During War of 1939-45, led various Swedish delegns to Berlin, London, and Washington; Envoy to Belgian and Dutch Govts, 1944; Envoy in Moscow, 1946; permanent delegate to UN, 1947; Ambassador to Court of St James's, 1948-67; Ambassador to France, 1967-71. Delegate to Conf. for Constitution, European Council, 1949; delegate to Suez Confs, 1956; Mem. of Menzies Cttee to Cairo, 1956. Hon. DCL Birmingham, 1960. Publications: Diplomat, 1972; several books and essays in economics, politics and history. Recreations: ski-ing, swimming, reading and writing. Address: 9 rue de Marignan, 75008 Paris, France.

HAGUE, Prof. Douglas Chalmers; Professor of Managerial Economics, University of Manchester, since 1965; b Leeds, 20 Oct. 1926; s of Laurence and Marion Hague; m 1947, Brenda Elizabeth Fereday; two d. Educ: Moseley Grammar Sch.; King Edward VI High Sch., Birmingham; University of Birmingham. Assistant Tutor, Faculty of Commerce, Birmingham Univ., 1946; Assistant Lecturer, University College, London, 1947, Lecturer, 1950; Reader in Political Economy in University of London, 1957; Newton Chambers Professor of Economics, University of Sheffield, 1957-63. Visiting Professor of Economics, Duke Univ., USA, 1960-61; Head of Department of Business Studies, University of Sheffield, 1962-63; Professor of Applied Economics, University of Manchester, 1963-65. Director: Economic Models Ltd, 1970-; The Laird Gp, 1976-. Rapporteur to International Economic Association, 1953-; Member Working Party of National Advisory Council on Education for Industry and Commerce, 1962-63; Consultant to Secretariat of NEDC, 1962-63; Member: Treasury Working Party on Management Training in the Civil Service, 1965-67; EDC for Paper and Board, 1967-70; (part-time) N Western Gas

Board, 1966-72; Working Party, Local Govt Training Bd, 1969-70; Price Commn, 1973- (Dep. Chm., 1977); Director: Manchester School of Management and Administration, 1964-65; Centre for Business Research, Manchester, 1964-66. Member Council, Manchester Business School, 1964-; Chairman, Manchester Industrial Relations Society, 1964-66; President, NW Operational Research Group, 1967-69; British Chm., Carnegie Project on Accountability, 1968-72; Jt Chm., Conf. of Univ. Management Schools, 1971-73. Industrial Consultant. *Publications:* (with P. K. Newman) Costs in Alternative Locations: The Clothing Industry, 1952; (with A. W. Stonier) A Textbook of Economic Theory, 1953, 4th edn 1973; (with A. W. Stonier) The Essentials of Economics, 1955; The Economics of Man-Made Fibres, 1957; Stability and Progress in the World Economy (ed), 1958; The Theory of Capital (ed), 1961; Inflation (ed), 1962; International Trade Theory in a Developing World (ed) (with Sir Roy Harrod), 1965; Price Formation in Various Economies (ed), 1967; Managerial Economics, 1969; The Dilemma of Accountability in Modern Government (ed) (with Bruce L. R. Smith), 1970; Pricing in Business, 1971; (with M. E. Beesley) Britain in the Common Market: a new business opportunity, 1973; (with W. E. F. Oakeshott and A. A. Strain) Devaluation and Pricing Decisions: a case study approach, 1974; (with W. J. M. Mackenzie and A. Barker) Public Policy and Private Interests: the institutions of compromise, 1975; articles in economic and financial journals. *Recreations:* church organs, watching cricket and football. *Address:* 8 Knutsford Road, Wilmslow, Cheshire. *T:* Wilmslow 28898.

HAGUE, Harry; a Recorder of the Crown Court, since 1972; *b* 9 April 1922; *o c* of Harry Hague and Lilian (*née* Hindle), Stalybridge and Blackpool; *m* 1967, Vera, *d* of Arthur Frederick and Sarah Ann Smith, Manchester; two step *d. Educ:* Arnold Sch., Blackpool; Manchester and London Univs. LLB London. Army, 1941-44. Called to Bar, Middle Temple, 1946; Northern Circuit. Asst Recorder, Burnley, 1969-71. Contested (L): Blackburn East, 1950; Blackpool North, 1959, 1962 (bye-election) and 1964; Mem. Nat. Exec., Liberal Party, 1956-59 and 1962-64. *Recreations:* activities concerning animals, motoring, historical buildings. *Address:* 60 King Street, Manchester M2 4NA. *T:* 061-834 6876; Glenmore, 197 Victoria Road West, Cleveleys, Thornton-Cleveleys, Lancs. *T:* Cleveleys 2104.

HAHN, Prof. Frank Horace, FBA 1975; Professor of Economics, University of Cambridge, since 1972; Fellow of Churchill College, Cambridge, since 1960; *b* 26 April 1925; *s* of Dr Arnold Hahn and Maria Hahn; *m* 1946, Dorothy Salter; no *c. Educ:* Bournemouth Grammar School; London School of Economics. PhD London, MA Cantab. Univ. of Birmingham, 1948-60, Reader in Mathematical Economics, 1958-60; Univ. Lectr in Econs, Cambridge, 1960-67; Prof. of Economics, LSE, 1967-72; Frank W. Taussig Res. Prof., Harvard, 1975-76. Visiting Professor: MIT, 1956-57; Univ. of California, Berkeley, 1959-60. Fellow, Inst. of Advanced Studies in Behavioural Sciences, Stanford, 1966-67. Mem. Council for Scientific Policy, later Adv. Bd of Res. Councils, 1972-75. Fellow, Econometric Soc., 1962; Vice-Pres., 1967-68; Pres., 1968-69. Managing Editor, Review of Economic Studies, 1965-68. Foreign Hon. Mem., Amer. Acad. of Arts and Sciences, 1974. *Publications:* (with K. J. Arrow) General Competitive Analysis, 1971; The Share of Wages in the National Income, 1972; articles in learned journals. *Address:* 16 Adams Road, Cambridge. *T:* Cambridge 52560; 30 Tavistock Court, Tavistock Square, WC1. *T:* 01-387 4293.

HAIDER, Michael Lawrence; Chairman, Chief Executive Officer, and Chairman of Executive Committee, Standard Oil Co. (NJ), 1965-69, retired; *b* 1 Oct. 1904; *s* of Michael Haider and Elizabeth (*née* Milner). *Educ:* Stanford Univ. BS 1927. Chemical Engineer, Richfield Oil Co., 1927-29; Carter Oil Co., Tulsa, Okla., 1929-38 (Chief Engineer, 1935-38); Manager, Research and Engineering Dept, Standard Oil Development Co., 1938-45; Standard Oil Co. (NJ): Executive, Producing Dept, 1945-46; Deputy Co-ordinator of Producing Activities, 1952-54; Vice-President, 1960-61; Executive Vice-President, 1961-63; President and Vice-Chairman, Executive Cttee, 1963-65. Was with: Imperial Oil Ltd, Toronto, 1946-52 (Vice-President and Director, 1948-52); International Petroleum Co. Ltd (President and Director), 1954-59. President, American Institute of Mining and Metallurgical Engineers, 1952. *Publications:* (ed) Petroleum Reservoir Efficiency and Well Spacing, 1943; articles in technical journals. *Address:* (office) Room 1250, 1 Rockefeller Plaza, New York, NY 10020, USA; (home) Ocean Reef Club, Key Largo, Florida 33037, USA.

HAIG, family name of **Earl Haig.**

HAIG, 2nd Earl, *cr* 1919; **George Alexander Eugene Douglas Haig,** OBE 1966; Viscount Dawick, *cr* 1919; Baron Haig and 30th Laird of Bemersyde; is a painter; Member, Queen's Body Guard for Scotland; *b* March 1918; *o s* of 1st Earl and Hon. Dorothy Vivian (*d* 1939) (Author of A Scottish Tour, 1935), *d* of 3rd Lord Vivian; *S* father, 1928; *m* 1956, Adrienne Thérèse, *d* of Derrick Morley; one *s* two *d. Educ:* Stowe; Christ Church, Oxford. MA Oxon. 2nd Lieut Royal Scots Greys, 1938; retired on account of disability, 1951, rank of Captain; Hon. Major on disbandment of HG 1958; studied painting Camberwell School of Art; paintings in collections of Arts Council and Scottish Nat. Gallery of Modern Art. War of 1939-45 (prisoner). Member: Society of Scottish Artists; Royal Fine Art Commission for Scotland, 1958-61; Council and Executive Cttee, Earl Haig Fund, Scotland, 1950-65 and 1966-; Scottish Arts Council, 1969-75; President, Scottish Craft Centre, 1950-75. Member Council, Commonwealth Ex-Services League; Chairman, Officers' Association (Scottish Branch), 1977; Vice-President, Scottish National Institution for War Blinded; President Border Area British Legion, 1955-61; Chairman SE Scotland Disablement Advisory Cttee, 1960-73; Vice-Chairman, British Legion, Scotland, 1960, Chairman, 1962-65; Trustee, Scottish National War Memorial, 1961; Trustee, National Gallery of Scotland, 1962-72; Chairman: Berwickshire Civic Soc., 1971-73; Friends of DeMarco Gall., 1968-71. Berwickshire: DL 1953; Vice-Lieutenant, 1967-70. KStJ 1977. FRSA 1951. *Heir: s* Viscount Dawick, *qv. Address:* Bemersyde, Melrose, Scotland. *T:* St Boswells 2762. *Clubs:* Cavalry and Guards; New (Edinburgh).
See also Baron Astor of Hever, H. R. Trevor-Roper.

HAIG, General Alexander Meigs, Jr; Supreme Allied Commander Europe since 1974, and Commander-in-Chief, US European Command, since 1974; *b* 2 Dec. 1924; *m* 1950, Patricia Fox; two *s* one *d. Educ:* schs in Pennsylvania; Univ. of Notre Dame; US Mil. Acad., West Point (BS); Univs of Columbia and Georgetown (MA); Ground Gen. Sch., Fort Riley; Armor Sch., Fort Knox; Naval and Army War Colls. 2nd Lieut 1947; Far East and Korea, 1948-51; Europe, 1956-59; Vietnam, 1966-67; CO 3rd Regt, subseq. Dep. Comdt, West Point, 1967-69; Sen. Mil. Adviser to Asst to Pres. for Nat. Security Affairs, 1969-70; Dep. Asst to Pres. for Nat. Security Affairs, 1970-73; Vice-Chief of Staff, US Army, Jan.-July 1973, retd; Chief of White House Staff, 1973-74 when recalled to active duty. Awarded numerous US medals, badges and decorations; also Vietnamese orders and Cross of Gallantry; Medal of King Abd el-Aziz (Saudi Arabia). Hon. Dr Law, Niagara. *Recreations:* tennis, golf, squash, equitation. *Address:* SACEUR, B7010 SHAPE, Belgium. *T:* 065 444088, 065 444113.

HAIG, Mrs Mary Alison G.; *see* Glen Haig.

HAIGH, (Austin) Anthony (Francis), CMG 1954; retired as Director of Education and of Cultural and Scientific Affairs, Council of Europe, 1962-68; *b* 29 Aug. 1907; *s* of late P. B. Haigh, ICS, and Eliza (*d* 1963), *d* of George Moxon; *m* 1st, 1935, Gertrude (marr. diss. 1971), 2nd *d* of late Frank Dodd; two *s* two *d*; 2nd, 1971, Eleanore Margaret, *d* of late T. H. Bullimore and *widow* of J. S. Herbert. *Educ:* Eton; King's Coll., Cambridge. Entered Diplomatic Service, 1932; served in Foreign Office and at HM Embassies at Rio de Janeiro, Tokyo, Lisbon, Ankara, Cairo and Brussels; Head of Cultural Relations Department, Foreign Office, 1952-62. Chairman Cttee of Cultural Experts, Council of Europe, 1960-61; Chairman, Admin. Board, Cultural Fund of Council of Europe, 1961-62. *Publications:* A Ministry of Education for Europe, 1970; Congress of Vienna to Common Market, 1973; Cultural Diplomacy in Europe, 1974. *Address:* The Furnace, Crowhurst, near Battle, East Sussex. *Club:* Leander.

HAIGH, Clifford; Editor, The Friend, 1966-73; *b* 5 Feb. 1906; *yr s* of Leonard and Isabel Haigh, Bradford, Yorks; *m* 1st, 1934, Dora Winifred Fowler (*d* 1959); one *s* one *d*; 2nd, 1970, Grace Elizabeth Cross. Editorial Staff: Yorkshire Observer, 1924-27; Birmingham Post, 1928-46; The Times, 1947-61; Assistant Editor, The Friend, 1961-65. *Recreation:* walking. *Address:* 4 Chichester Road, Sandgate, Kent. *T:* Folkestone 38212.

HAIGHT, Gordon Sherman, PhD; Professor of English, Yale University, 1950, Emily Sanford Professor, 1966, Emeritus 1969; *b* 6 Feb. 1901; *s* of Louis Pease Haight and Grace Carpenter; *m* 1937, Mary Treat Nettleton. *Educ:* Yale Univ. BA 1923, PhD 1933. Master in English: Kent Sch., 1924-25; Hotchkiss Sch., 1925-30; taught English at Yale, 1931-69; Master of Pierson Coll., Yale Univ., 1949-53. Visiting Prof. of English: Columbia Univ., 1946-47; Univ. of Oregon, 1949. Guggenheim Fellow, 1946, 1953, 1960. Fellow Royal Society of Literature, Corres. Fellow British Academy. Member: Berzelius; Zeta Psi. *Publications:* Mrs Sigourney, 1930; George Eliot and

John Chapman, 1940, 1969; George Eliot, A Biography, 1968 (James Tait Black Award, Heinemann Award of Royal Society of Literature, Van Wyck Brooks Award, 1969; Amer. Acad. of Arts and Letters Award, 1970; Wilbur Cross Medal, Yale, 1977); Editor: Miss Ravenel's Conversion (J. W. De Forest), 1939, 1955; Adam Bede, 1948; The George Eliot Letters, 9 vols, 1954-78; Middlemarch, 1955; The Mill on the Floss, 1961; A Century of George Eliot Criticism, 1965; Portable Victorian Reader, 1971; contribs to various literary jls. *Recreations:* garden, water colours. *Address:* 145 Peck Hill Road, Woodbridge, Conn 06525, USA. *T:* 203-393-0689. *Clubs:* Yale, Century (New York); Elizabethan (New Haven).

HAILEY, Arthur; author; *b* 5 April 1920; *s* of George Wellington Hailey and Elsie Mary Wright; *m* 1st, 1944, Joan Fishwick (marr. diss. 1950); three *s*; 2nd, 1951, Sheila Dunlop; one *s* two *d*. *Educ:* English elem. schs. Pilot, RAF, 1939-47 (Flt-Lt). Emigrated to Canada, 1947; various positions in industry and sales until becoming free-lance writer, 1956. *Films:* Zero Hour, 1956; Time Lock, 1957; The Young Doctors, 1961; Hotel, 1966; Airport, 1970; The Moneychangers, 1976. *Publications:* (in all major languages): (with John Castle) Flight Into Danger, 1958; Close-Up (Collected Plays), 1960; The Final Diagnosis, 1959; In High Places, 1962; Hotel, 1965; Airport, 1968; Wheels, 1971; The Moneychangers, 1975. *Address:* (home) Lyford Cay, PO Box N7776, Nassau, Bahamas; (office) Seaway Authors Ltd, 1 Place Ville Marie, Suite 1609, Montreal H3B 2B6, Canada.

HAILSHAM, 2nd Viscount, *cr* 1929, of Hailsham; Baron, *cr* 1928 [disclaimed his peerages for life, 20 Nov. 1963]; *see under* Baron Hailsham of St Marylebone.

HAILSHAM OF SAINT MARYLEBONE, Baron *cr* 1970 (Life Peer), of Herstmonceux; **Quintin McGarel Hogg,** PC 1956; CH 1974; FRS 1973; Editor, Halsbury's Laws of England, 4th edition, since 1972; *b* 9 Oct. 1907; *er s* of 1st Viscount Hailsham, PC, KC, and Elizabeth (*d* 1925), *d* of Judge Trimble Brown, Nashville, Tennessee, USA, and *widow* of Hon. A. J. Marjoribanks; *S* father, 1950, as 2nd Viscount Hailsham, but disclaimed his peerages for life, 20 Nov. 1963 (Baron *cr* 1928, Viscount *cr* 1929); *m* 1944, Mary Evelyn, *d* of Richard Martin (of Ross), London, SW; two *s* three *d*. *Educ:* Eton (Schol.), Newcastle Schol.); Christ Church, Oxford (Scholar). First Class Hon. Mods, 1928; First Class Lit Hum, 1930; Pres., Oxford Union Soc., 1929. Served War of 1939-45: commissioned Rifle Bde Sept. 1939; served Middle East Forces, Western Desert, 1941 (wounded); Egypt, Palestine, Syria, 1942; Temp. Major, 1942. Fellow of All Souls Coll., Oxford, 1931-38, 1961-; Barrister, Lincoln's Inn, 1932; a Bencher of Lincoln's Inn, 1956, Treasurer, 1975; QC 1953. MP (C) Oxford City, 1938-50, St Marylebone, (Dec.) 1963-70; Jt Parly Under-Sec. of State for Air, 1945; First Lord of the Admiralty, 1956-57; Minister of Education, 1957; Dep. Leader of the House of Lords, 1957-60; Leader of the House of Lords, 1960-63; Lord Privy Seal, 1959-60; Lord Pres. of the Council, 1957-59 and 1960-64; Minister for Science and Technology, 1959-64; Minister with special responsibility for: Sport, 1962-64; dealing with unemployment in the North-East, 1963-64; higher education, Dec. 1963-Feb. 1964; Sec. of State for Education and Science, April-Oct. 1964; Lord Chancellor, 1970-74. Chm. of the Conservative Party Organization, Sept. 1957-Oct. 1959. Rector of Glasgow Univ., 1959-62. Pres. Classical Assoc., 1960-61. John Findley Green Foundation Lecture, 1960; Richard Dimbleby Lecture, 1976. Hon. Student of Christ Church, Oxford, 1962; Hon. FICE 1963; Hon. FIEE 1972; Hon. FIStructE 1960. Hon. Freeman, Merchant Taylors' Co., 1971. Hon. DCL: Westminster Coll., Fulton, Missouri, USA, 1960; Newcastle, 1964; Oxon, 1974; Hon. LLD: Cambridge, 1963; Delhi, 1972. *Publications:* The Law of Arbitration, 1935; One Year's Work, 1944; The Law and Employers' Liability, 1944; The Times We Live In, 1944; Making Peace, 1945; The Left was never Right, 1945; The Purpose of Parliament, 1946; Case for Conservatism, 1947; The Law of Monopolies, Restrictive Practices and Resale Price Maintenance, 1956; The Conservative Case, 1959; Interdependence, 1961; Science and Politics, 1963; The Devil's Own Song, 1968; The Door Wherein I Went, 1975; Elective Dictatorship, 1976. *Heir:* (*to disclaimed viscountcy*): *s* Hon. Douglas Martin Hogg [*b* 5 Feb. 1945; *m* 1968, Sarah, *d* of Baron Boyd-Carpenter, *qv*; one *s* one *d*]. *Recreations:* walking, climbing, shooting, etc. *Address:* House of Lords, SW1. *Clubs:* Carlton, Alpine, MCC.

HAILSTONE, Bernard, RP; painter; *b* 6 Oct. 1910; *s* of William Edward Hailstone; *m* 1934, Joan Mercia Kenet Hastings; one *s*. *Educ:* Sir Andrew Judd's Sch., Tonbridge. Trained at Goldsmiths' Coll. and Royal Academy Schs; Practising Artist, 1934-39; NFS, London (Fireman Artist), 1939-42; Official War Artist to Ministry of Transport, 1942-44; Official War Artist to

SEAC, 1944-45. Recent portraits include: HM Queen; Prince Charles and Princess Anne; Mrs Anne Armstrong, US Ambassador to UK; Pres. of USA, Jimmy Carter, 1977. *Recreation:* tennis. *Address:* 43a Glebe Place, Chelsea, SW3. *T:* 01-352 1309; 49 Roland Gardens, SW7. *T:* 01-373 2970. *Club:* Chelsea Arts.

HAIMENDORF, Christoph von F.; *see* Fürer-Haimendorf.

HAINE, Reginald Leonard, VC 1917; MC 1919; Captain HAC; *s* of late H. J. Haine, Clipsham, Ringley Avenue, Horley; *b* 10 July 1896; *m* 1923, Dora Beatrice, *er d* of late E. Holder, Monticello, South Border, Purley; one *d*. Lieut-Col Home Guard. *Address:* Dawslea Cottage, Hollist Lane, Midhurst, West Sussex.

HAINES, Sir Cyril (Henry), KBE 1962 (CBE 1953; MBE 1930); Chairman, South West London Rent Tribunal, 1962-66; *b* 2 March 1895; *s* of late Walter John Haines, OBE, formerly Deputy Chief Inspector of Customs and Excise; *m* 1934, Mary Theodora, *d* of late Rev. J. W. P. Silvester, BD, Hon. CF, Vicar of Wembley; two *d*. *Educ:* Hele's Sch., Exeter. Apptd to Scottish Education Dept, 1914. On active service with Army, 1915-19. Appt to Foreign Office, Dec. 1919. Called to Bar, Middle Temple, 1926. Asst Brit. Agent to Anglo-Mexican Revolutionary Claims Commn, 1928; Registrar, HM Supreme Court, for China, 1930 (acted as Asst Judge during absences from China of one of Judges); Asst Judge, HM Consular Court in Egypt, and, for Naval Courts, HM Consul at Alexandria, Egypt, 1943; Judge of HM Consular Court in Egypt, 1946. Indep. Referee for War Pension Appeals in Egypt, 1946; Asst Judge of HM Chief Court for the Persian Gulf, 1949-59, and Head of Claims Dept, Foreign Office, 1949-54; Judge of HM Chief Court for the Persian Gulf, 1959-61. Pres., Abbeyfield Orpington Soc., 1975- (Chm., 1962-75). *Address:* Wood Lea, The Glen, Farnborough Park, Orpington, Kent. *T:* Farnborough, Kent, 54507.

HAINES, Geoffrey Colton, OBE 1965; FCA, FSA; Member: Royal Masonic Benevolent Institution (Deputy Chairman, 1958-76); Board of Management, Royal Masonic Hospital; Fellow, The Royal Numismatic Society, (Hon. Treasurer, 1930-61); *b* Barrow-in-Furness, 18 Sept. 1899; *e surv. s* of late Harry Colton Haines, FCA, and Margaret Elizabeth Haines (*née* Barnes); *m* Olive (JP, Mayor of Wandsworth, 1956-57, Hon. Freeman 1969), *e surv. d* of late Philip Scott Minor, Solicitor, Manchester; one *d*. *Educ:* St Paul's Sch. Private and Officer Cadet, Inns of Court, OTC, 1917-18, 2nd Lieut The East Surrey Regt, 1919; Dep. Dist Warden, Putney, 1939-45; Bomb Reconnaissance Officer, Civil Defence, 1943-45; Asst Chief Warden, Civil Defence Corps, Wandsworth, 1954-55. Chief Executive Officer, London Association for the Blind, 1932-64, Vice-Pres., 1965; former Mem. of Executive Cttee of Royal National Institute for the Blind and other Charities for Blind Welfare; Hon. Mem., Nat. Assoc. of Industries for the Blind & Disabled Inc. (Chm. 1952-53). Hon. Mem., Cambridge Numismatic Soc. *Publications:* Revised, The Roman Republican Coinage (by late Rev. E. A. Sydenham), 1952; various papers to Numismatic Chronicle, etc. *Recreations:* archæology, Roman and Byzantine history and numismatics, travel, motoring, walking. *Address:* 31 Larpent Avenue, Putney, SW15 6UU. *T:* 01-788 0132.

HAINES, Joseph Thomas William; Member, Royal Commission on Legal Services, since 1976; Feature Writer, The Daily Mirror, since 1977; *b* 29 Jan. 1928; *s* of Joseph and Elizabeth Haines; *m* 1955, Irene Betty Lambert; no *c*. *Educ:* Elementary Schools, Rotherhithe, SE16. Parly Correspondent, The Bulletin (Glasgow) 1954-58, Political Correspondent, 1958-60; Political Correspondent: Scottish Daily Mail, 1960-64; The Sun, 1964-68; Dep. Press Sec. to Prime Minister, Jan.-June 1969; Chief Press Sec. to Prime Minister, 1969-70 and 1974-76, and to Leader of the Opposition, 1970-74. Mem. Tonbridge UDC, 1963-69, 1971-74. *Publication:* The Politics of Power, 1977. *Recreations:* heresy and watching football. *Address:* 7 Hazel Shaw, Tonbridge, Kent. *T:* 365919.

HAINSWORTH, Col John Raymond, CMG 1953; CBE 1945; retired; *b* 14 March 1900; *s* of William Henry Hainsworth, Keighley, Yorks; *m* 1925, Dora Marguerite Skiller, Rochester, Kent; one *s* one *d*. *Educ:* Taunton Sch.; RMA, Woolwich. Commissioned in Royal Engineers, 1919; posted to India, 1922. Served War of 1939-45 (despatches twice, CBE): Burma Campaign, 1942-45; apptd Dir of Works, GHQ, India, March 1945; seconded to Civil Employment in PWD, NWFP, India, 1946; Chief Engineer and Secretary to Government, PWD, NWFP, Pakistan, 1948-52; retired with rank of Col, 1952. *Recreations:* shooting, fishing. *Address:* 11 Butfield, Lavenham, Sudbury, Suffolk. *T:* Lavehham 604.

HAINWORTH, Henry Charles, CMG 1961; HM Diplomatic Service, retired; *b* 12 Sept. 1914; *o s* of late Charles S. and Emily G. I. Hainworth; *m* 1944, Mary, *yr d* of late Felix B. and Lilian Ady; two *d. Educ:* Blundell's Sch.; Sidney Sussex Coll., Cambridge. Entered HM Consular Service, 1939; HM Embassy, Tokyo, 1940-42; seconded to Ministry of Information (Far Eastern Bureau, New Delhi), 1942-46; HM Embassy, Tokyo, 1946-51; Foreign Office, 1951-53; HM Legation, Bucharest, 1953-55; NATO Defence Coll., Paris, 1956; Political Office, Middle East Forces (Nicosia), 1956; Foreign Office, 1957-61 (Head of Atomic Energy and Disarmament Dept, 1958-61); Counsellor, United Kingdom Delegation to the Brussels Conference, 1961-63; HM Minister and Consul-Gen. at British Embassy, Vienna, 1963-68; Ambassador to Indonesia, 1968-70; Ambassador and Perm. UK Rep. to Disarm. Conf., Geneva, 1971-74. *Recreations:* tennis, fishing. *Address:* c/o Barclays Bank Ltd, 50 Jewry Street, Winchester, Hants.

HAITINK, Bernard; Artistic Director and Permanent Conductor, Concertgebouw Orchestra, Amsterdam, since 1964; also Principal Conductor and Artistic Director, London Philharmonic Orchestra, since 1967; Musical Director, Glyndebourne Opera, since 1978; *b* Amsterdam, 4 March 1929. *Educ:* Amsterdam Conservatory. Studied conducting under Felix Hupke, but started his career as a violinist with the Netherlands Radio Philharmonic; in 1954 and 1955 attended annual conductors' course (org. by Netherlands Radio Union) under Ferdinand Leitner; became 2nd Conductor with Radio Union at Hilversum with co-responsibility for 4 radio orchs and conducted the Radio Philharmonic in public during the Holland Fest., in The Hague, 1956; conducted the Concertgebouw Orch. (as a subst. for Giulini), Oct. 1956; then followed guest engagements with this and other orchs in the Netherlands and elsewhere. Debut in USA, with Los Angeles Symph. Orch., 1958; 5 week season with Concertgebouw Orch., 1958-59, and toured Britain with it, 1959; apptd (with Eugen Jochum) as the Orchestra's permanent conductor, Sept. 1961; became sole artistic dir and permanent conductor of the orch., 1964; toured Japan and USSR, 1974; Japan, 1977. début at Royal Opera House, Covent Garden, 1977. Toured with London Philharmonic Orchestra: Japan, 1969; USA, 1970, 1971, 1976; Berlin, 1972; Holland, Germany, Austria, 1973; USSR, 1975; has been a guest conductor all over the world, including Glyndebourne Festival Opera 1972, 1973, 1975, 1976, 1977. Hon. RAM 1973. Bruckner Medal of Honour, 1970; Gold Medal, Internat. Gustav Mahler Soc., 1971. Chevalier de L'Ordre des Arts et des Lettres, 1972; Order of Orange Nassau, 1969; Officer, Order of the Crown (Belgium), 1977. *Address:* c/o London Philharmonic Orchestra Ltd, 53 Welbeck Street, W1M 7HE.

HAJNAL, John, FBA 1966; Professor of Statistics, London School of Economics, since 1975 (Reader, 1966-75); *b* 26 Nov. 1924; *s* of late Kálmán and of Eva Hajnal-Kónyi; *m* 1950, Nina Lande; one *s* three *d. Educ:* University Coll. Sch., London; Balliol Coll., Oxford. Employed by: Royal Commission on Population, 1944-48; UN, New York, 1948-51; Office of Population Research, Princeton Univ., 1951-53; Manchester Univ., 1953-57; London Sch. of Economics, 1957-. Vis. Fellow Commoner, Trinity Coll., Cambridge, 1974-75. Mem. Internat. Statistical Institute. *Publications:* The Student Trap, 1972; papers on demography, statistics, mathematics, etc. *Address:* London School of Economics and Political Science, Houghton Street, WC2A 2AE. *T:* 01-405 7686.

HAKEWILL SMITH, Maj.-Gen. Sir Edmund, KCVO 1967; CB 1945; CBE 1944; MC; psc; JP; Governor, Military Knights of Windsor since 1951; Deputy Constable and Lieutenant-Governor of Windsor Castle, 1964-72; *b* Kimberley, S Africa, 17 March 1896; *s* of George Cecil Smith and Mildred, 2nd *d* of J. B. Currey; *m* 1928, Edith Constance, *e d* of Brigadier-Gen. H. Nelson, DSO, Shovel, Somerset; one *d. Educ:* Diocesan Coll., South Africa; RMC Sandhurst. Commissioned into Royal Scots Fusiliers as 2nd Lieut, 1915; ADC to Governor of Bengal, 1921-22; Adjutant, 2nd RSF, 1927-30; Staff Coll., Quetta, 1930-32; Staff Capt., War Office, 1934-36. Employed Air Staff Duties, RAF, 1936-37; DAAG War Office, 1938-40. Comdr 5 Devons, March-June 1940; Comdr 4/5 RSF, 1940-41; Comd 157 Inf. Bde, 1941-42; Dir of Organisation, War Office (Maj.-Gen.), 1942-43; Comdr 155 Inf. Bde (Brig.), Feb.-Nov. 1943; Comdr 52nd Lowland Div. (Maj.-Gen.), 1943 till disbandment, 1946; Commander, Lowland District, 1946; retired pay, 1949. Served European War, 1915-18 (wounded twice, MC); War of 1939-45 (despatches, CBE, CB. Order of St Olaf, Order of Orange-Nassau). Col, The Royal Scots Fusiliers, 1946-57; Berks County Commandant, Army Cadet Force, 1952-57. Grand Officer of Order of Orange Nassau, 1947; Order of St Olaf, Second Class, 1947. *Address:* Mary Tudor Tower, Lower Ward, Windsor Castle, Berks.

HALABY, Najeeb Elias; President, Halaby International Corporation; Director: Chrysler Corporation; Bank America Corporation; Bank of America International; Atkins & Merrill; *b* 19 Nov. 1915; *s* of late Najeeb Elias Halaby and of Laura Wilkins Halaby; *m* 1946, Doris Carlquist; one *s* two *d. Educ:* Stanford Univ. (AB); Yale Univ. (LLB); Bonar Law Coll., Ashridge, (Summer) 1939. Called to the Bar: California, 1940; District of Columbia, 1948; NY, 1973. Practised law in Los Angeles, Calif, 1940-42, 1958-61; Air Corps Flight Instructor, 1940; Test pilot for Lockheed Aircraft Corp., 1942-43; Naval aviator, established Navy Test Pilot Sch., 1943; formerly Chief of Intelligence Coordination Div., State Dept; Foreign Affairs Advisor to Sec. of Defense; Chm., NATO Military Production and Supply Board, 1950; Asst Administrator, Mutual Security Economic Cooperation Administration, 1950-51; Dep. Sec. of Defense for Internat. Security, 1952-54; Vice-Chm., White House Advisory Group whose report led to formation of Federal Aviation Agency, 1955-56, Administrator of the Agency, 1961-65; Pan American World Airways: Director, 1965-73; Member, Executive Committee of Board, 1965-68; Senior Vice-President, 1965-68, President, 1968-71; Chief Executive, 1969-72; Chairman, 1970-72; Associate of Laurance and Nelson Rockefeller, 1954-57; Past Exec. Vice-Pres. and Dir, Servomechanisms Inc.; Sec.-Treas., Aerospace Corp., 1959-61; Pres., American Technology Corp. Member of Board: Planned Parenthood- World Population; Mem. Exec. Cttee, (Founder-Chm., 1971-73), US-Japan Econ. Council; Trustee: Aspen Inst., Aspen, Colo.; Internat. Executive Service Corps; Eisenhower Exchange Fellowships, Inc.; Amer. Univ. of Beirut. Monsanto Safety Award; FAA Exceptional Service Medal. Fellow, Amer. Inst. of Aeronautics and Astronautics. Hon. LLB: Allegheny Coll., Pa, 1967; Loyola Coll., LA, 1968. *Recreation:* golf. *Address:* 640 Fifth Avenue, New York, NY 10019, USA; Alpine, NJ 07620, USA. *Clubs:* Metropolitan, Chevy Chase (Washington); Bohemian Grove (California); University, River (NYC).

HALDANE, Archibald Richard Burdon, CBE 1968; *b* 18 Nov. 1900; *s* of late Sir William Haldane; *m* 1941, Janet Macrae Simpson-Smith; one *s* one *d. Educ:* Edinburgh Academy; Winchester Coll.; Balliol Coll., Oxford; Edinburgh University. LLB Edinburgh, 1926; WS 1926; DLitt Edinburgh, 1950. Dep. Chm., Trustee Savings Banks Assoc., 1959-61; Chm., Trustee Savings Banks Inspection Cttee, 1960-67; Vice-Pres., Trustee Savings Bank Assoc., 1971. Trustee, National Library of Scotland. *Publications:* By Many Waters, 1940; The Path by the Water, 1944; The Drove Roads of Scotland, 1950, repr. 1973; New Ways through the Glens, 1962, repr 1973; Three Centuries of Scottish Posts, 1971; By River, Stream and Loch, 1973. *Recreations:* fishing, walking. *Address:* Foswell, Auchterarder, Perthshire. *T:* Auchterarder 2610; 4 North Charlotte Street, Edinburgh. *T:* 031-225 4181. *Club:* New (Edinburgh).

HALE, family name of **Baron Hale.**

HALE, Baron *cr* 1972 (Life Peer), of Oldham; **(Charles) Leslie Hale;** *b* 13 July 1902; *s* of Benjamin George Hale, Managing Director of Stableford & Co. Ltd, Coalville, Leics; *m* 1926, Dorothy Ann Latham (*d* 1971); one *s* one *d. Educ:* Ashby-de-la-Zouch Boys' Grammar Sch. Articled to Evan Barlow, Solicitor, Leicester; practised in Coalville, Nuneaton and London. Mem. Leics County Council, 1925-50. Contested (L) S Nottingham, 1929. MP (Lab) for Oldham, Lancs. 1945-50, West Division of Oldham, 1950-Jan. 1968, resigned. Freedom of Oldham, 1969. *Publications:* Thirty Who Were Tried, 1955; John Philpot Curran, 1958; Blood on the Scales, 1960; Hanged in Error, 1961; Hanging in the Balance, 1962; None So Blind, 1963. *Recreation:* house painting. *Address:* 92 College Road, SE21.

HALE, Sir Edward, KBE 1952; CB 1942; Hon. LLD Leeds, 1959, Belfast, 1959, London, 1961; *b* 1895; *er s* of late Dr G. E. Hale, Eton; *m* 1930, Joan Latham (*d* 1971), *er d* of late Sir Alexander (Hon. Mr Justice) Bateson; two *d. Educ:* Tonbridge Sch.; Corpus Christi Coll., Oxford. MA; entered Treasury, 1921; Secretary to University Grants Cttee, 1951-57; Administrative Head, Historical Branch, Cabinet Office, 1958-60. *Address:* The Grange, Goring, Reading, Berks RG8 9EN.

HALE, Herbert Edward John, OBE 1970; HM Diplomatic Service; Consul-General, Stuttgart, since 1973; *b* 1 Jan. 1927; *s* of Herbert Frederick John Hale and Nora (*née* Smith); *m* 1951, Audrey Evelyn Barden; one *s* one *d. Educ:* Bec School. Admty, 1943-45; Fleet Air Arm, 1945-48; FO, 1948; UK Delegn to UN, NY, 1949; Consulate-General, NY, 1950 (Vice-Consul, 1951); Vice-Consul: Kansas City, 1953; Bremen, 1954; FO, 1957; UK Delegn to OECD, Paris, 1962 (1st Sec., 1963); Consul (Commercial), São Paulo, 1965-69; FCO, 1969, Head of Commodities Dept, 1971-72, Inspector, 1972-73. Officer

Cruzeiro do Sul (Brazil), 1968. *Recreations:* music, reading, golf. *Address:* c/o Foreign and Commonwealth Office, SW1; 6 Beresford Avenue, Tolworth, Surrey KT5 9LJ. *T:* 01-399 5649.

HALE, Prof. John Rigby, FBA 1977; Professor of Italian, University College London, since 1970; Chairman of Trustees, National Gallery, since 1974 (Trustee, 1973); *b* 17 Sept. 1923; *s* of E. R. S. Hale, FRCP, MD, and Hilda Birks; *m* 1st, 1952, Rosalind Williams; one *s* two *d*; 2nd, 1965, Sheila Haynes MacIvor; one *s*. *Educ:* Neville Holt Preparatory Sch.; Eastbourne Coll., Jesus Coll., Oxford. BA first cl. hons Mod. Hist., 1948; MA (Oxon) 1950. Served War, Radio Operator in Merchant Service, 1942-45. Commonwealth Fellow, Johns Hopkins and Harvard Univs, 1948-49; Fellow and Tutor in Modern History, Jesus Coll., Oxford, 1949-64. Editor, Oxford Magazine, 1958-59; Visiting Prof., Cornell Univ., 1959-60; Vis. Fellow, Harvard Centre for Renaissance Studies, I Tatti, 1963; Prof. of History, Univ. of Warwick, 1964-69; Vis. Prof., Univ. of California, Berkeley, 1969-70; Folger Library, Washington Fellowship, 1970. FSA 1962; FRHistS 1968; FRSA 1974. Socio Straniero, Accademia Arcadia, 1972; Chm., British Soc. for Renaissance Studies, 1973-76. *Publications:* England and the Italian Renaissance, 1954; The Italian Journal of Samuel Rogers, 1956; Machiavelli and Renaissance Italy, 1961; (trans. and ed) The Literary Works of Machiavelli, 1961; (ed) Certain Discourses Military by Sir John Smythe, 1964; The Evolution of British Historiography, 1964; (co-ed) Europe in the Late Middle Ages, 1965; Renaissance Exploration, 1968; Renaissance Europe 1480-1520, 1971; (ed) Renaissance Venice, 1973; Italian Renaissance Painting, 1977; Florence and the Medici: the pattern of Control, 1977; contributor: New Cambridge Modern History, vols 1, 2, 3; Past and Present; Studi Veneziani, Italian Studies, etc. *Recreation:* Venice. *Address:* Department of Italian, University College, Gower Street, WC1E 6BT. *T:* 01-387 7050; 26 Montpelier Row, Twickenham, Mddx TW1 2NQ. *T:* 01-892 9636. *Club:* Athenæum.

HALE, Comdr John William, DSO 1940; RN retired; *b* 30 March 1907; 4th *s* of late Warren Stormes Hale and late Cora Hale; *m* 1938, Ada Elizabeth Bowden; one *s* two *d*. *Educ:* Highgate Sch.; RN Coll., Dartmouth. Went to sea as midshipman in HMS Resolution, 1924; Lieut and joined Fleet Air Arm, 1929; Lieut Cdr 1937; at beginning of war of 1939-45, served in HMS Glorious and then HMS Illustrious; Commander, 1940; retired, 1957; Freeman of City of London; Past Master of Tallow Chandlers Company. Mem., Historic Houses Assoc. (opens Letheringham Water Mill and Gardens to public during the summer). *Recreation:* gardening. *Address:* Letheringham Mill, Woodbridge, Suffolk. *Club:* MCC.

HALE, Joseph; engineer; formerly Merchant Navy; *b* 28 Oct. 1913; *s* of J. Gordon Tyson Hale and M. Hale (*née* Johnston); *m* 1939, Annie Irene Clowes; one *s* one *d*. *Educ:* elementary and secondary technical schs. Mem. Bolton Town Council until 1950; Junior Whip to Labour Group; Chm. Bolton West Divisional Party, 1949; Mem. Amalgamated Engineering Union District Cttee, 1943-50. MP (Lab) Rochdale, 1950-51. *Recreations:* literature, music. *Address:* 30 Thorpe Street, Bolton, Lancs.

HALE, Kathleen, (Mrs Douglas McClean), OBE 1976; artist; illustrator and author of books for children; *b* 24 May 1898; *d* of Charles Edward Hale and Ethel Alice Aylmer Hughes; *m* 1926, Dr Douglas McClean (*d* 1967); two *s*. *Educ:* Manchester High Sch. for Girls; Manchester Sch. of Art; Art Dept (scholar) of University Coll., Reading; Central Sch. of Art; East Anglian Sch. of Painting and Drawing. Has exhibited paintings at: New English Art Club, London Group, Grosvenor Galleries, Vermont Gallery, Warwick Public Library Gallery; Gallery Edward Harvane, New Grafton Gallery, Parkin Gallery; metal groups and pictures at: Lefèvre Galleries; Leicester Galleries; Oxford Arts Council, Arts Centre. Mural for South Bank (Festival) Schs Section, 1951; Orlando Ballet for Festival Gardens, 1951; collab. with playwright, designed scenery and costumes, for Orlando Goes Camping, and, Orlando Buys a Cottage, Unicorn Theatre. *Publications:* The Orlando The Marmalade Cat Series, since 1938: Camping Holiday; Trip Abroad; Buys a Farm; Becomes a Doctor; Silver Wedding; Keeps a Dog; A Seaside Holiday; The Frisky Housewife; Evening Out; Home Life; Invisible Pyjamas; The Judge; Zoo; Magic Carpet; Country Peep-Show; Buys a Cottage; and The Three Graces; Goes to the Moon; and the Water Cats; Henrietta, the Faithful Hen, 1946; Puss-in-Boots Peep-Show, 1950; Manda, 1952; Henrietta's Magic Egg, 1973. TV and radio programmes. *Recreation:* painting. *Address:* Tod House, Forest Hill, near Oxford. *T:* Stanton St John 390.

HALE, Norman Morgan; Under Secretary, Department of Health and Social Security, since 1975; *b* 28 June 1933; *s* of late T. N. Hale and Mrs A. E. Hale, Evesham, Worcs; *m* 1965, Sybil Jean (*née* Maton); one *s* one *d*. *Educ:* Prince Henry's Grammar Sch., Evesham; St John's Coll., Oxford (MA). Min. of Pensions and National Insurance, 1955; Asst Sec., Nat. Assistance Bd, 1966; Min. of Social Security, 1966; CSD, 1970-72. *Address:* 64 Castle Avenue, Ewell, Epsom, Surrey. *T:* 01-393 3507.

HALES, Prof. Charles Nicholas, PhD, MD; MRCPath; FRCP; Professor of Clinical Biochemistry, University of Cambridge, since 1977; *b* 25 April 1935; *s* of Walter Bryan Hales and Phyllis Marjory Hales; *m* 1959, Janet May Moss; two *s*. *Educ:* King Edward VI Grammar Sch., Stafford; Univ. of Cambridge (BA 1956, MB, BChir, MA 1959, PhD 1964, MD 1971). MRCPath 1971; MRCP 1971, FRCP 1976. House Surgeon, UCH, 1959, House Physician, 1960; Stothert Res. Fellow, Royal Soc., 1963-64; Lectr, Dept of Biochem., Univ. of Cambridge, 1964-70; Clinical Asst, Addenbrooke's Hosp., Cambridge, 1961-68, Hon. Consultant in Clin. Biochem, 1968-70; Prof. of Med. Biochem., Welsh National Sch. of Medicine, Cardiff, and Hon. Consultant in Med. Biochem., University Hosp. of Wales, Cardiff, 1970-77. Consultant in Med. Biochem., South Glam Health Authority (T). *Recreations:* music, vegetable gardening. *Address:* Department of Clinical Biochemistry, Addenbrooke's Hospital, Hills Road, Cambridge CB2 2QR. *T:* Cambridge 45151.

HALEY, Philip William Raymond Chatterton, MBE 1956; HM Diplomatic Service, retired 1975; *b* 18 June 1917; 2nd *s* of late Joseph Bertram Haley and late Lilian Anne Chatterton Haley; *m* 1941, Catherine Skene Stewart, LRAM, LRCM; two *d*. *Educ:* Perse Sch.; London University. HM Services, 1940-47 in KOSB and on Gen. Staff; 2nd Lieut 1941, Lieut 1942, Captain 1943, Major 1945, Lt-Col 1946; Control Commn for Germany, 1947-56, serving also with Internat. Commn for the Saar. HM Diplomatic Service, 1956: Consul, Düsseldorf; Hamburg, 1959; 1st Sec., Bonn, 1961; Dep. Consul-General, Chicago, 1964; Consul, Johannesburg, 1967; Consul-Gen., Hanover, 1973. Croix de la Libération, 1946. *Recreations:* gardening, painting, senile delinquency. *Address:* Casa Iris No 10, San Patricio, Santa Ursula, Tenerife, Canary Isles.

HALEY, Sir William (John), KCMG, 1946; Hon. LLD Cambridge 1951, Dartmouth, New Hampshire, 1957, London, 1963, St Andrews, 1965; Hon. Fellow Jesus College, Cambridge 1956; FRSL; Commissioner of Appeal for Income Tax, Jersey, since 1971; Chairman: Barclaytrust, Channel Islands, since 1970; Barclaytrust International, since 1973; *b* Jersey, CI, 24 May 1901; *s* of Frank Haley, Bramley, Leeds, and Marie Sangan; *m* 1921, Edith Susie Gibbons; two *s* two *d*. *Educ:* Victoria Coll., Jersey. Joined Manchester Evening News, 1922; Chief Sub-Editor, 1925; Managing Editor, 1930; Dir Manchester Guardian and Evening News, Ltd, 1930; Jt Managing Dir, 1939-43; Dir Press Association, 1939-43; Dir Reuters, 1939-43; Editor-in-Chief, BBC, 1943-44; Dir-Gen., BBC, 1944-52; Editor of the Times, 1952-66; Dir and Chief Executive, The Times Publishing Co. Ltd, 1965-66; Chm., Times Newspapers Ltd, 1967; Editor-in-Chief, Encylopædia Britannica, 1968-69. Pres., Nat. Book League, 1955-62; Chm., Jersey Arts Council, 1976-. Chevalier Legion of Honour, 1948; Grand Officer, Order of Orange Nassau, 1950. *Address:* Beau Site, Gorey, Jersey, Channel Islands. *T:* Jersey Central 51068.
See also Prof. J. N. Hunt.

HALFORD, Maj.-Gen. Michael Charles Kirkpatrick, DSO 1946; OBE 1957; DL; *b* 28 Oct. 1914; *s* of Lieut-Col M. F. Halford, OBE, and Violet Halford (*née* Kirkpatrick); *m* 1945, Pamela Joy (*née* Wright); three *s*. *Educ:* Wellington Coll.; Trinity Coll., Cambridge. Commissioned Royal Guernsey Militia, 1932; 2nd Lieut York and Lancaster Regt, 1935; served Egypt and Palestine, 1936; France 1940; N Africa, Italy, France and Germany; comd Hallamshire Bn, York and Lancaster Regt, 1945, 1st Bn, 1954; Asst Army Instr, Imperial Defence Coll., 1957; comd 147 Inf. Bde (TA), 1960; GOC 43 (Wessex) Div./District, 1964-67; retd, 1967. Representative Col The York and Lancaster Regt, 1966-. DL Hants 1975. *Recreations:* shooting, golf. *Address:* Fairfields, Poulner Hill, Ringwood, Hants. *Club:* Army and Navy.

HALFORD-MacLEOD, Aubrey Seymour, CMG 1958; CVO 1965; HM Diplomatic Service, retired; Foreign Affairs Adviser to Scottish Council (Development and Industry), since 1971; *b* 15 Dec. 1914; *o s* of late Joseph and Clara Halford; changed name by deed poll from Halford to Halford-MacLeod, 1964; *m* 1939, Giovanna Mary, *o d* of late W. H. Durst; three *s* one *d*. *Educ:* King Edward's Sch., Birmingham; Magdalen Coll., Oxford. Entered HM Diplomatic (subseq. Foreign, now again Diplomatic) Service as Third Sec., 1937; Bagdad, 1939; Second

Sec., 1942; transferred to Office of Minister Resident in N Africa, 1943; First Sec., 1943; British mem. of Secretariat of Advisory Council for Italy, 1944; British High Commission in Italy, 1944; Asst Political Adviser to Allied Commission in Italy, Sept, 1944, Political Adviser, 1945; transferred to HM Foreign Office, 1946, Principal Private Sec. to Permanent Under-Sec.; Dep. Exec. Sec. to Preparatory Commission for Council of Europe, May 1949, and promoted Counsellor; Dep. Sec. Gen. of the Council of Europe, 1949-52; Counsellor, HM Embassy, Tokyo, 1953-55; in charge of HM Legation, Seoul, 1954; Counsellor at HM Embassy in Libya, 1955-57; HM Political Agent at Kuwait, 1957-59; HM Consul-Gen., Munich, 1959-65; HM Ambassador to Iceland, 1966-70. Dir, Scottish Opera, 1971-. Pres., Scottish Soc. for Northern Studies, 1973-76. Vice-Pres., Clan MacLeod Soc. of Scotland, 1976-. *Publication:* (with G. M. Halford) The Kabuki Handbook, 1956. *Recreations:* fishing, shooting, ornithology. *Address:* Mulag House, Ardvourlie, N Harris PA85 3AB. *T:* Harris 2054; 37 Buckingham Terrace, Edinburgh EH4 3AP. *T:* 031-332 4543; 1 Castle Street, Edinburgh EH2 3AJ.

HALIFAX, 2nd Earl of, *cr* 1944; **Charles Ingram Courtenay Wood,** Bt 1784; Baron Irwin, 1925; Viscount Halifax, 1866; Lord-Lieutenant of Humberside, since 1974 (for East Riding of Yorks, 1968-74); *b* 3 Oct. 1912; *e s* of 1st Earl of Halifax, KG, PC, OM, GCSI, GCMG, GCIE, TD, and Lady Dorothy Evelyn Augusta Onslow, CI, DCVO (*d* 1976); *S* father 1959; *m* 1936, Ruth (JP 1956 ER Yorks), *d* of late Captain Rt Hon. Neil James Archibald Primrose, MC, sometime MP; one *s* two *d*. *Educ:* Eton; Christ Ch., Oxford. 2nd Lieut Royal Horse Guards, 1934-37; War of 1939-45, Middle East, Captain. MP (U) York, 1937-45. Pro-Chancellor, Hull Univ., 1974-. High Steward of York Minster, 1970-. Mem. of Jockey Club; Senior Steward, 1950, 1959. Mem. of National Hunt Cttee; Joint Master, Middleton Foxhounds, 1946-; DL, E Riding of Yorks and Kingston upon Hull, 1955-68; JP, E Riding of Yorks, 1963-68; Chm., E Riding of Yorks CC, 1968-74. KStJ 1970. *Recreations:* hunting, shooting. *Heir: s* Lord Irwin, *qv*. *Address:* Garrowby, York YO4 1QD. *T:* Bishop Wilton 236; Swynford Paddocks, Six Mile Bottom, Newmarket. *T:* Six Mile Bottom 211. *Clubs:* Turf, White's.
See also Rt Hon. R. F. Wood.

HALIFAX (NS), Archbishop of, (RC), since 1967; **Most Rev. James Martin Hayes;** *b* 27 May 1924; *s* of late L. J. Hayes. *Educ:* St Mary's Univ., Halifax; Holy Heart Seminary, Halifax; Angelicum Univ., Rome. Asst, St Mary's Basilica, 1947-54; Chancellor and Sec. of Archdiocese of Halifax, 1957-65; Rector, St Mary's Basilica, 1963-65; Auxil. Bp of Halifax, 1965-66; Apostolic Administrator of Archdiocese of Halifax, 1966-67. Hon. Dr of Letters, St Anne's Coll., Church Point, NS; Hon. Dr of Sacred Theology, King's Coll., Halifax, NS. *Address:* 6541 Coburg Road, PO Box 1527, Halifax, Nova Scotia B3J 2Y3, Canada. *T:* 902-429-9388.

HALIFAX, Archdeacon of; *see* Alford, Ven. J. R.

HALL, family name of **Viscount Hall.**

HALL, 2nd Viscount, *cr* 1946, of Cynon Valley; **(William George) Leonard Hall;** Director of companies; *b* 9 March 1913; *s* of 1st Viscount Hall, PC, and Margaret, *d* of William Jones, Ynysybwl; *S* father, 1965; *m* 1st, 1935, Joan Margaret (*d* 1962), *d* of William Griffiths, Glamorganshire; two *d*; 2nd, 1963, Constance Ann Gathorne (*d* 1972), *d* of Rupert Gathorne Hardy, London; 3rd, 1975, Marie-Colette Bach, St Viatre. *Educ:* Christ Coll., Brecon; University Coll. Hospital. MRCS; LRCP. Asst MOH, Merthyr Tydfil, 1938-40. Surgeon Lt-Comdr, RNVR, 1940-46. Powell Duffryn Group, 1946-60; Dir of Investments, Africa, Asia and ME, Internat. Finance Corp. (affiliate of IBRD), 1962-64; Advisor for Special Projects, Internat. Finance Corp., 1963-64; Chm., Post Office, 1969-70. Liveryman, Hon. Co. of Carmen. *Recreations:* country activities. *Address:* Solvain, 41210 St Viatre, Loir et Cher, France. *T:* (54) 83 63 67.

HALL, Adam; *see* Trevor, Elleston.

HALL, Alfred Charles, CBE 1977 (OBE 1966); Deputy High Commissioner in Southern India, since 1975; *b* 2 Aug. 1917; *s* of Alfred Hall and Florence Mary Hall; *m* 1945, Clara Georgievna Strunina, Moscow; five *s* one *d*. *Educ:* Oratory Sch.; Polytechnic of Central London (Rothschild Prize; Local Govt Dip.). Served War, RA and Intell. Corps, 1939-43. LCC, 1934-39 and 1946-49; FO, with service in Saudi Arabia, Algeria, Egypt, Iran and USSR, 1943-46; FCO (formerly CRO and CO), with service in Pakistan, India, Nigeria, Canada and Australia, 1949-. *Publications:* freelance journalism and technical papers.

Recreations: music, reading, gardening, linguistics. *Address:* c/o Foreign and Commonwealth Office, SW1; White Cliff, St Margaret's Bay, Kent. *T:* Dover 852230.

HALL, Prof. Alfred Rupert, LittD; Professor of the History of Science and Technology, Imperial College of Science and Technology, University of London, since 1963; *b* 26 July 1920; *s* of Alfred Dawson Hall and Margaret Ritchie; *m* 1st, 1942, Annie Shore Hughes; two *d*; 2nd, 1959, Marie Boas. *Educ:* Alderman Newton's Boy's Sch., Leicester; Christ's Coll., Cambridge (scholar). LittD Cantab 1975. Served in Royal Corps of Signals, 1940-45. 1st cl. Historical Tripos Part II, 1946; Allen Scholar, 1948; Fellow, Christ's Coll., 1949-59, Steward, 1955-59; University Lectr, 1950-59. Medical Research Historian, University of Calif, Los Angeles, 1959-60, Prof. of Philosophy, 1960-61; Prof. of History and Logic of Science, Indiana Univ., 1961-63. FRHistS. Pres., British Soc. for History of Science, 1966-68; Vice-Pres., Internat. Acad. of the History of Science. Co-editor, A History of Technology, 1951-58. Corresp. Mem., Soc. for the History of Technology, 1970. Silver Medal, RSA, 1974. *Publications:* Ballistics in the Seventeenth Century, 1952; The Scientific Revolution, 1954; From Galileo to Newton, 1963; The Cambridge Philosophical Society: a history, 1819-1969, 1969. With Marie Boas Hall: Unpublished Scientific Papers of Isaac Newton, 1962; Correspondence of Henry Oldenburg, 1965-; (with Laura Tilling) Correspondence of Isaac Newton, vols 5-7, 1974-; (ed with Norman Smith) History of Technology, 1976-. Contributor to Isis, Annals of Science, etc. *Address:* Imperial College, Prince Consort Road, SW7. *T:* 01-589 5111; 2 Porchester Gardens, W2. *T:* 01-723 9558.

HALL, Sir Arnold (Alexander), Kt 1954; FRS 1953; MA; Chairman and Managing Director, Hawker Siddeley Group Ltd, since 1967 (Director, Hawker Siddeley Group, Nov. 1955-, Vice-Chairman, 1963-67); Chairman: Hawker Siddeley Diesels Ltd; Hawker Siddeley Electric Ltd; Hawker Siddeley Canada Ltd; High Duty Alloys Ltd; Director: Lloyds Bank; Phoenix Assurance; ICI; Onan Corporation, since 1976; *b* 23 April 1915; married. *Educ:* Clare Coll., Cambridge (Rex Moir Prize in Engineering, John Bernard Seely Prize in Aeronautics, Ricardo Prize in Thermodynamics). Res. Fellow in Aeronautics of the Company of Armourers and Brasiers (held at University of Cambridge), 1936-38; Principal Scientific Officer, Royal Aircraft Establishment, Farnborough, Hants, 1938-45; Zaharoff Prof. of Aviation, University of London, and Head of Dept of Aeronautics, Imperial Coll. of Science and Technology, 1945-51; Dir of the Royal Aircraft Establishment, Farnborough, 1951-55; Pres., Royal Aeronautical Society, 1958-59, Hon. Fellow, 1965; Dep. Pres., BEAMA, 1966-67, Pres., 1967-68; Vice-Pres., Engineering Employers' Fedn, 1968; President: Locomotive and Allied Manufacturers Assoc. of GB, 1968-69, 1969-70; SBAC, 1972-73. Member: Advisory Council on Scientific Policy, 1962-64; Air Registration Board, 1963-73; Electricity Supply Research Council, 1963-73; Advisory Council on Technology (Min. of Technology), 1965-67; Nat. Defence Industries Council, 1969-; Industrial Develt Adv. Bd, 1972-75; Dep. Chm., Engineering Industries Council, 1975-. Pro-Chancellor, Warwick Univ., 1964-70. Fellow, Imperial Coll. of Science and Technology, 1963-; Founder Fellow, Fellowship of Engineering, 1976 (Vice-Pres., 1977); For. Associate, US Nat. Acad. of Engrg, 1976-; Hon. Fellow, Clare Coll., Cambridge, 1967; Hon. ACGI; Hon. FRAeS; Hon. FAIAA; Hon. MIMechE, 1968; Hon. FIEE, 1975; Hon. DTech Loughborough 1976. Gold Medal, RAeS, 1962; Hambro Award (Business Man of the Year), 1975. *Address:* Hawker Siddeley Group Ltd, 18 St James's Square, SW1. *Club:* Athenæum.

HALL, Arthur Henderson, RWS 1970; RE 1961; MSIA; ARCA; painter, etcher, freelance illustrator; Head of School of Graphic Design, Kingston Polytechnic, 1965-71 (Senior Lecturer in charge, 1952-65); *b* 25 June 1906; *s* of Charles and Mary Hall; *m* 1942, Frances Bruce; one *s* one *d*. *Educ:* Sedgefield; Royal College of Art; British Sch., Rome. Prix de Rome, Engraving, 1931; Glass Designer for Webb & Corbett, 1933-36; Part-time Teacher, Kingston Sch. of Art, 1933-41; Part-time Teacher, London Central Sch. of Art, 1936-39. RAF, 1942-46. Teacher, London Central Sch. of Art, 1946-52; exhibits paintings and etchings at: RA, RWS, RE. *Publications:* numerous illustrations for children's books and books on gardening. *Recreations:* gardening, travel. *Address:* 15 Church Road, East Molesey, Surrey. *T:* 01-979 5681. *Club:* Nash House.

HALL, Arthur Herbert; Librarian and Curator, Guildhall Library and Museum, 1956-66, retired; Director of Guildhall Art Gallery, 1956-66; *b* 30 Aug. 1901; *y s* of Henry and Eliza Jane Hall, Islington, London; *m* 1927, Dorothy Maud (*née* Barton); two *s* one *d*. *Educ:* Mercers' Sch., Holborn, London. Entered Guildhall Library as junior asst, 1918; Dep. Librarian,

1943-56. Hon. Librarian, Clockmakers' and Gardeners' Companies, 1956-66. Served with RAOC, 1942-46. Chm. Council, London and Middlesex Archæological Soc., 1957-64, Vice-Pres., 1962-; Member: Council of London Topographical Soc., 1960-67; Exec. Cttee, Friends of Nat. Libraries, 1965-69. Hon. Sec., Middlesex Victoria County History Council; Enfield Archaeological Soc. (Hon. Sec., 1966-71); Master, 1974-75, Hon. Clerk, 1965-74, Asst Hon. Clerk, 1975-, Civic Guild of Old Mercers. Liveryman of the Clockmakers Co.; FLA 1930; FSA 1963. *Address:* 23 Uvedale Road, Enfield, Mddx. *T:* 01-363 2526.

HALL, Sir Basil (Brodribb), KCB 1977 (CB 1974); MC 1945; TD 1952; HM Procurator General and Treasury Solicitor, since 1975; *b* 2 Jan. 1918; *s* of late Alfred Brodribb Hall and of Elsie Hilda Hall, Woking, Surrey; *m* 1955, Jean Stafford Gowland; two *s* one *d. Educ:* Merchant Taylors' Sch. Articled Clerk with Gibson & Weldon, Solicitors, 1935-39; admitted Solicitor, 1942. Served War of 1939-45: Trooper, Inns of Court Regt, 1939; 2nd Lieut, 12th Royal Lancers, 1940; Captain, 27th Lancers, 1941; Major, 27th Lancers, 1942. Legal Asst, Treasury Solicitor's Dept, 1946; Sen. Legal Asst, 1951; Asst Treasury Solicitor, 1958; Principal Asst Solicitor, 1968; Dep. Treasury Solicitor, 1972. *Recreations:* military history, travel. *Address:* Woodlands, Danes Way, Oxshott, Surrey. *T:* Oxshott 2032. *Clubs:* Athenæum, Cavalry and Guards.

HALL, Very Rev. Bernard, SJ; Provincial of the English Province of the Society of Jesus, 1970-76; *b* 17 Oct. 1921. *Educ:* St Michael's Coll., Leeds; Heythrop Coll., Oxford. LicPhil, STL. Captain RA, 1941-46. Entered Society of Jesus, 1946; ordained priest, 1955. *Address:* Collegio S Roberto Bellarmino, Via del Seminario 120, 00186 Roma, Italy.

HALL, Betty, CBE 1977; Regional Nursing Officer, West Midlands Regional Health Authority, since 1974; *b* 6 June 1921; *d* of John Hall and Jane (*née* Massey), Eagley, Lancs. *Educ:* Bolton Sch.; Royal Infirm., Edinburgh (RGN); Radcliffe Infirm., Oxford and St Mary's Hosp., Manchester (SCM); Royal Coll. of Nursing (RNT). Nursed tuberculous patients from concentration camps, Rollier Clinic, Leysin, 1948-49; Ward Sister, Salford Royal Hosp., 1949-51; Sister Tutor, Royal Masonic Hosp., London, 1952-54; Principal Tutor, St Luke's Hosp., Bradford, 1954-61 (Mem. Leeds Area Nurse Trng Cttee); King Edward's Hosp. Fund Admin. Staff Coll., 1961-62; Work Study Officer to United Bristol Hosps, 1961-64; Asst Nursing Officer to Birmingham Regional Hosp. Bd, 1964-65, Regional Nursing Officer, 1966-74. Mem. W Mids Regional Nurse Trng Cttee. *Recreations:* reading, tapestry making, cricket. *Address:* 39 Minley Avenue, Harborne, Birmingham B17 8RP. *T:* 021-429 5167. *Club:* Naval and Military.

HALL, Catherine Mary, CBE 1967; FRCN; General Secretary, Royal College of Nursing of the United Kingdom, since 1957 (designate, 1956-57); *b* 19 Dec. 1922; *d* of late Robert Hall, OBE and of Florence Irene Hall (*née* Turner). *Educ:* Hunmanby Hall Sch. for Girls, Filey, Yorks. Gen. Infirmary, Leeds: nursing trng, 1941-44 (SRN); Ward Sister, 1945-47; sen. nursing appts, 1949-53; midwifery trng, Leeds and Rotherham, 1948 (SCM); travelling fellowship, US and Canada, 1950-51; student in nursing administration, Royal College of Nursing, 1953-54; Asst Matron, Middlesex Hosp., London, 1954-56. Part-time Member: CIR, 1971-74; British Railways Regional Bd for London and the South East, 1975-. Hon. Mem., Florida Nurses Assoc., 1973. FRCN 1976. OStJ 1977. Hon. DLitt City, 1975. *Address:* Peveril, Pilgrims' Way, Westhumble, Dorking, Surrey RH5 6AW. *T:* Dorking 2229.

HALL, Dr Cecil Charles, CB 1968; retired; Director, Warren Spring Laboratory, Ministry of Technology, 1964-68; *b* 10 May 1907; *s* of Frederick Harrington and Alice Hall; *m* 1950, Margaret Rose Nicoll; no *c. Educ:* Beckenham Gram. Sch.; London Univ. Jun. Chemist, S Metropolitan Gas Co., 1925-30: BSc 1st Hons Chem. (London), 1929; MSc (London), 1931. Jun. Asst, Fuel Research Stn, DSIR, 1930: PhD (London), 1934. Research in high pressure hydrogenation of coal tar and synthesis of oils and chemicals from coal by catalytic processes. Special Merit Promotion to Sen. Princ. Scientific Off., 1952; Dep. Chief Chemist, Fuel Res. Stn, DSIR, 1953; Dep. Dir, Warren Spring Lab., 1959. FRIC 1944; FInstF 1954. *Publications:* (with T. P. Hilditch) Catalytic Processes in Industrial Chemistry, 1937; numerous research and review papers in scientific and techn. jls dealing with chemistry of high pressure hydrogenation processes and with Fischer Tropsch synthesis. *Recreation:* gardening, specialising in iris growing and hybridising (Pres., British Iris Soc., 1967-70). *Address:* Tanglewood, Sollershott West, Letchworth, Herts. *T:* Letchworth 4339. *Clubs:* Civil Service; Rotary (Stevenage).

HALL, Christopher Myles; Director, Council for the Protection of Rural England, since 1974; *b* 21 July 1932; *s* of Gilbert and Muriel Hall; *m* 1957, Jennifer Bevan Keech; one *s* one *d. Educ:* New Coll., Oxford. 2nd cl. Hons PPE. Reporter and Feature-writer, Daily Express, 1955-58; Sub-editor and Leader-writer, Daily Mirror, 1958-61; Feature-writer and Leader-writer, Daily Herald/Sun, 1961-65; Special Asst (Information): to Minister of Overseas Develt, 1965-66; to Minister of Transport, 1966-68; Chief Information Officer, MoT, 1968; Sec., Ramblers' Assoc., 1969-74. Pres., The Holiday Fellowship, 1974-77; Vice-Chm., S Reg. Council of Sport and Recreation, 1976-; Hon. Sec., Chiltern Soc., 1965-68. *Publications:* (contrib.) Motorways in London, 1969; The Countryman's Britain; How to Run a Pressure Group, 1974; pamphlets; contrib. various jls. *Recreation:* walking in the countryside. *Address:* 16 South Hill Park, NW3 2SB; Shirburn Lodge Cottage West, Watlington, Oxford OX9 5HU. *Club:* United Oxford & Cambridge University.

HALL, Daniel George Edward, MA, DLit, FRHistS, FRAS; Professor Emeritus in the University of London since 1959; *b* 1891; *e s* of Daniel Hall of Offley, Hitchin, Herts, and Elinor Ann Field; *m* 1919, Helen Eugenie (*d* 1962), *o d* of late John Banks, Wynberg, SA; two *s* (and *e s* killed in action Nov. 1943) two *d. Educ:* Hitchin Grammar Sch.; King's Coll., Univ. of London. BA 1st Class Hons in Hist., Univ. of London, 1916; Gladstone Meml Prize and Inglis Studentship, KCL, 1915; Asst Lectr in History, KCL, 1916-17; MA 1918; DLit 1930; with the Lena Ashwell Concert Parties on the Western Front in 1916 and early 1917; Inns of Court OTC at Berkhampstead, 1917-19; Senior History Master: Royal Grammar Sch., Worcester, Jan.-July 1919; Bedales Sch., 1919-21; Prof. of History, Univ. of Rangoon, 1921-34; Headmaster of Caterham Sch., 1934-49; Prof. of Hist. of SE Asia, Univ. of London, 1949-59. Temp. Mem. Legislative Council of Burma, 1923-24; Corr. Mem. Indian Historical Records Commn, 1925; Mem. Panel of Additional Lectrs, SOAS, Univ. of London, 1940-49. Vis. Lectr, Johns Hopkins Univ. Sch. of Advanced Internat. Studies Summer Sch., Washington, DC, 1955. Visiting Professor: Cornell Univ. Dept Far Eastern Studies, 1959-60 and 1963; Univ. of Syracuse Summer Sch., 1963; Univ. of BC, 1964-65; Monash Univ., Vic, Aust., 1965; Univ. of BC, 1965-66; Cornell Univ., 1966, 1967-69, 1970-71, 1972; Univ. of Michigan, 1966; Univ. of BC, 1967. Royal Society of Arts Silver Medal, 1944. Hon. Fellow, SOAS, 1959. *Publications:* Imperialism in Modern History, 1923; A Brief Survey of English Constitutional History, 1925, rev. and enl., 1939; Early English Intercourse with Burma, 1587-1743, 1927, 2nd edn 1968; The Dalhousie-Phayre Correspondence, 1852-56, 1929; The Tragedy of Negrais, 1752-59, 1931; Studies in Dutch Relations, with Arakan, 1936; Dutch Trade with Burma in the 17th Century, 1939; Europe and Burma, 1945; Burma, 1950, rev. and enl., 1956, 1960; A History of South-East Asia, 1955, rev. and enl., 1964, 3rd edn 1968; Michael Symes: Journal of his second mission to Ava in 1802, 1955. Joint-author: a Handbook to the League of Nations for India, Burma and Ceylon, 1926; A High School British History, 1714-1930, 1935, rev. and enl., 1946; A Handbook of Oriental History, 1951; (ed) Historians of South-East Asia, 1961; Henry Burney: a political biography, 1974; articles in historical journals. *Recreation:* music. *Address:* 4 Chiltern Road, Hitchin, Herts. *T:* Hitchin 51662.

HALL, Rt. Rev. Denis Bartlett; *b* 9 April 1899; *s* of Frank Marshall Hall and Caroline Beatrice Hall (*née* Bartlett), both of Bristol. *Educ:* Tudor House Sch., Henleaze, Bristol; Bristol Grammar Sch.; Bristol Univ. (BA). RNVR, 1917-19. University of Bristol, 1919-23; Ridley Hall, Cambridge, 1923-24. Curate, St Gabriel's Sunderland, 1924-28; Chaplain, HMS Conway Sch. Ship, 1928-30; Vicar of Bishopston, Bristol, 1930-47; Asst Bishop on The Niger, 1947-57; Vicar of St Paul's, Thornton Heath, Surrey, 1957-61; Asst Bishop of Canterbury, 1960-61; Rector of Tormarton with W Littleton, Glos, 1961-66. *Address:* Cowlin House, 26 Pembroke Road, Clifton, Bristol BS8 3BB.

HALL, Denis C.; *see* Clarke Hall.

HALL, Denis Whitfield, CMG 1962; late Provincial Commissioner, Kenya; *b* 26 Aug. 1913; *s* of late H. R. Hall, Haslemere, Surrey; *m* 1940, Barbara Carman; two *s. Educ:* Dover College; Wadham Coll., Oxford. Dist Officer, Kenya, 1936; Personal Asst to Chief Native Comr, 1948; Senior Dist Comr, 1955; Provincial Comr, Coast Province, 1959. *Recreations:* sailing, tennis, walking, motoring. *Address:* Martins, Priory Close, Boxgrove, West Sussex. *Club:* Oxford University Yacht.

HALL, Air Vice-Marshal Donald Percy, CBE 1975; AFC 1963; Assistant Chief of Air Staff (Operational Requirements), since

1977; *b* 11 Nov. 1930; *s* of William Reckerby Hall and Elsie Hall; *m* 1953, Joyce (*née* Warburton); two *d*. *Educ:* Hull Grammar Sch.; Royal Air Force Coll., Cranwell. Entered Cranwell, 1949; flying appts until 1963; Staff, Germany, 1964-66; OC, No 111 Sqdn, 1966-68; Staff, IDC, 1968-70; OC, Empire Test Pilots Sch., 1970-73; OC, RAF Akrotiri, 1974-75; SASO, No 11 Gp, 1975-77; AOC No 11 Gp, 1977. *Recreations:* shooting, walking, swimming. *Address:* Manor House, Old Church Lane, Stanmore, Mddx HA7 2QZ. *Club:* Royal Air Force.

HALL, Sir Douglas (Basil), KCMG 1959 (CMG 1958); *b* 1 Feb. 1909; *s* of late Capt. Lionel Erskine Hall and late Jane Augusta Hall (*née* Reynolds); *b* and *heir-pres*. to Sir Neville Hall, 13th Bt, *qv*; *m* 1933, Rachel Marion Gartside-Tippinge; one *s* two *d* (and one *s* decd). *Educ:* Radley Coll.; Keble Coll., Oxford (MA). Joined Colonial Admin. Service, 1930; posted to N Rhodesia as Cadet; District Officer, 1932; Senior District Officer, 1950; Provincial Commr, 1953; Administrative Sec., 1954; Sec. for Native Affairs to Government of Northern Rhodesia, 1956-59, Acting Chief Sec. for a period during 1958; Governor and C-in-C, Somaliland Protectorate, 1959-60. JP Co. Devon, 1964, Chm., Kingsbridge Petty Sessional Div., 1971. *Publications:* various technical articles. *Recreation:* vintage cars. *Address:* Barnford, Ringmore, near Kingsbridge, Devon. *T:* Bigbury-on-Sea 401.

HALL, Ven. Edgar Francis, MA; Archdeacon of Totnes, 1948-62, Archdeacon Emeritus, 1962; Canon Residentiary of Exeter, 1934-62; Treasurer, Exeter Cathedral, 1951-62; *b* 14 Aug. 1888; *s* of Francis R. Hall, Oxford; *m* 1915, Anstice, *d* of Dr Louis Tosswill, Exeter; three *d*. *Educ:* Oxford High Sch.; Jesus Coll., Oxford (Scholar). Asst Master, Exeter Sch., 1911; Deacon 1914; Priest 1915; Curate of St James', Exeter, 1914; Chaplain of Exeter Sch., 1917; Vicar of Leusden, Devon, 1921; Diocesan Dir of Relig. Education, Exeter, 1934; Proctor in Convocation, 1944; Gen. Sec. Nat. Soc., 1943-47; Chm. Church of England Council for Education, 1949-58 (Sec. 1948-49). Retired, 1962. *Address:* Leusden Vicarage, Poundsgate, Newton Abbot, Devon.

HALL, Lady, (Edna); see Clarke Hall.

HALL, Edward, RP 1958; *b* 5 Feb. 1922; *s* of James and Elizabeth Hall; *m* 1946, Daphne Cynthia, (*née* Grogan); two *s* one *d*. *Educ:* Wyggeston Sch., Leicester. Leicester Coll. of Art, 1939-41; Royal Air Force, 1941-46; Wimbledon Sch. of Art, 1946-48; Slade Sch. of Fine Art, 1949-52. Since 1952, portrait painting; exhibits annually at Royal Academy; part-time teaching and lecturing in various London and provincial art schools, including Sir John Cass School of Art, Chelsea School of Art, Medway Coll. of Design. Hon. Treasurer, Royal Soc. of Portrait Painters, 1977-. *Recreations:* music, playing the piano. *Address:* 51 St George's Drive, SW1. *T:* 01-834 5366.

HALL, Maj.-Gen. Edward Michael, CB 1970; MBE 1943; DL; Commissioner, St John Ambulance, Cornwall, since 1971; *b* 16 July 1915; *s* of late Brig. E. G. Hall, CB, CIE; *m* 1948, Nina Diana (*née* McArthur); three *s*. *Educ:* Sherborne; RMA; Peterhouse, Cambridge. Commissioned RE, 1935; BA (Cantab) 1937. Served 1939-46, with Royal Bombay Sappers and Miners; Western Desert, India, Burma. CRE, 10th Armd and 3rd Inf. Div., 1957-59; Comd Training Bde, RE, 1962-63; Chief of Staff, Western Command, 1965-66; Military Deputy to Head of Defence Sales, 1966-70. Col Comdt, RE, 1973-76. DL Cornwall, 1971. CStJ 1977. *Recreation:* country pursuits. *Address:* Treworgey Manor, Liskeard, Cornwall.

HALL, Dr Edward Thomas; Professor, Research Laboratory for Archaeology and the History of Art, Oxford University, since 1975 (Director since 1954); Fellow of Worcester College, Oxford, since 1969; *b* 10 May 1924; *s* of Walter D'Arcy Hall, *qv*, and Ann Madelaine Hall; *m* 1957, Jenifer Louise de la Harpe; two *s*. *Educ:* Eton; Oxford Univ. BA 1948, MA 1953, DPhil 1953, Oxon; FPhysS. Mem. Hon. Scientific Cttee, National Gallery, 1971-; Trustee: British Museum, 1973-; National Gallery, 1977-. *Publications:* contrib. Archaeometry, various jls concerning science applied to archaeology. *Recreations:* the sea (above and under water), hot-air ballooning, making things. *Address:* Beenhams, Littlemore, Oxford. *T:* Oxford 777800; 11A Elm Park Lane, SW3 6DD. *T:* 01-352 5847.

HALL, Francis Woodall; HM Diplomatic Service; HM Consul-General, Alexandria, since 1971; *b* 10 May 1918; *s* of Francis Hall and Florence Adelaide Woodall; *m* 1951, Phyllis Anne Amelia Andrews; one *s* one *d*. *Educ:* Taunton School. Inland Revenue, 1936-40; Admty (Alexandria, Port Said, Haifa, Freetown), 1940-46; FO, 1946; Bahrain and Baghdad, 1949; Vice-Consul, Malaga, 1950; FO, 1952; 2nd Sec., Cairo, 1955;

Consul: Madrid, 1957; Zagreb, 1960; FO 1962; Consul, Stockholm, 1964; Head of Mombasa Office of British High Commn to Kenya, 1969. *Recreations:* music, walking, tennis. *Address:* Burton Cottage, Burton Lane, East Coker, Somerset; 4 Marlborough House, Qawra Road, Bugibba, Malta. *Clubs:* Union (Sliema); United Services (Marsa).

HALL, Sir (Frederick) John (Frank), 3rd Bt, *cr* 1923; *b* 14 Aug. 1931; *er s* of Sir Frederick Henry Hall, 2nd Bt, and Olwen Irene, *yr d* of late Alderman Frank Collis, Stokeville, Stoke-on-Trent, and Deganwy, Llandudno; *S* father, 1949; *m* 1st, 1956, Felicity Anne (marr. diss. 1960), *d* of late Edward Rivers-Fletcher, Norwich, and of Mrs L. R. Galloway; 2nd, 1961, Patricia Ann Atkinson (marr. diss., 1967); two *d*; re-married, 1967, 1st wife, Felicity Anne Hall; two *d*. *Heir:* *b* David Christopher Hall [*b* 30 Dec. 1937; *m* 1962, Irene, *d* of William Duncan, Aberdeen; one *s* one *d*]. *Address:* Carradale, 29 Embercourt Road, Thames Ditton, Surrey. *T:* 01-398 2801.

HALL, Frederick Thomas Duncan; Lord Mayor of Birmingham, May 1972-May 1973; *b* 12 Jan. 1902; *s* of Frederick James and Catherine Harriett Hall; *m* 1925, Irene Margaret Lawley; one *s*. *Educ:* Bourne Coll., Quinton, Birmingham. Chairman, Hall & Rice Ltd and associated cos. Member: West Bromwich Educn Cttee, 1933-46 (co-opted); Birmingham City Council, 1949-73 (Alderman, 1961); served Cttees: Educn, 1949-73 (Chm., 1966-69); Finance, 1966-73; Gen. Purposes, 1956-74; Jt Consultative, 1969-72 (Chm.); Allotments, 1949-66; West Midlands CC, 1974-. Governor: Birmingham Univ., 1967-73; Aston Univ., 1957-; Handsworth Grammar Sch., 1960-. Member: AMC (Educn) Cttee, 1967-72 (Vice-Chm., 1971-72); Assoc. of Educn Cttees Exec., 1968-72; Chm., Sandwell Ward Conservative Assoc., 1947-65; Pres., Handsworth Div. Conservative Assoc., 1973; Dir, Birmingham Repertory Theatre, 1970-73; formed Handsworth Historical Soc., 1951 (Chm., 1951-65). *Recreations:* hockey, golf, historical research. *Address:* 32 Englestede Close, Birmingham B20 1BJ. *T:* 021-554 6060. *Clubs:* Aberdovey Golf (Pres., 1967-); Sandwell Park Golf (Captain, 1948-49).

HALL, Maj.-Gen. Frederick William G.; see Gordon-Hall.

HALL, Rear-Adm. Geoffrey Penrose Dickinson, CB 1973; DSC 1943; Hydrographer of the Navy 1971-75; retired; *b* 19 July 1916; *er s* of late Major A. K. D. Hall and late Mrs P. M. Hall; *m* 1945, Mary Ogilvie Carlisle; two *s* one *d*. *Educ:* Haileybury. Served in American waters, 1935-37 and on Nyon Patrol during Spanish Civil War; joined surveying service, 1938, served in Indian Ocean until 1939 when transf. to minesweeping in Far East; hydrographic duties, home waters, Iceland, W Africa; navigational and minesweeping duties, Icelandic waters; transf. to Combined Ops, SE Asia; subseq. comd frigate, British Pacific Fleet; from 1947, hydrographic work: with RNZN, 1949-51; subseq. five comds i/c surveys at home and abroad; served ashore and in Atlantic, Indian Ocean, Antarctic waters (Cuthbert Peek Grant, RGS, for work in furtherance of oceanographical exploration); twice Asst Hydrographer; surveyed between S Africa and Iceland, 1965-67; Asst Dir (Naval), Hydrographic Dept, Taunton. Cadet 1934; Midshipman 1935; Sub-Lt 1938; Lieut 1939; Lt-Comdr 1945; Comdr 1953; Captain 1961; Rear-Adm. 1971. Pres., Hydrographic Soc., 1975. FRGS; FRICS. *Publications:* contribs to Nature, Deep Sea Research, Internat. Hydrographic Review. *Recreation:* country pursuits. *Address:* Legbourne Abbey, Louth, Lincs. *T:* Louth 2433. *Club:* Naval and Military.

HALL, Geoffrey Ronald, CEng, CChem, FRIC, SFInstF; Director, Brighton Polytechnic, since 1970; *b* 18 May 1928; *er s* of late Thomas Harold Hall, JP, and late Muriel Frances Hall, Douglas, IoM; *m* 1950, Elizabeth Day Sheldon; two *s* one *d*. *Educ:* Douglas High Sch., IoM; Univ. of Manchester (BSc). Research work in Nuclear Science and Engineering at AERE, Harwell, 1949-56; sabbatical at Oxford Univ., 1955; Colombo Plan Expert to Indian Atomic Energy Commn, 1956-58; Reader in Nuclear Technology, Imperial Coll., London, 1958-63; Prof. of Nuclear Technology, Imperial Coll., 1963-70. Pres., British Nuclear Energy Soc., 1970-71, 1976-; Mem. Council, Educn Cttee, and Pres., Inst. of Fuel, 1976-77; Mem. Admin. Bd, European Soc. for Engineering Educn; Founder Fellow, Fellowship of Engineering, 1976. *Publications:* papers related to nuclear science, fuels and engineering. *Recreations:* travel, caravanning. *Address:* 61 Sussex Court, Eaton Road, Hove, East Sussex.

HALL, George Edmund; HM Diplomatic Service; Assistant Under-Secretary of State, Foreign and Commonwealth Office, since 1977; *b* 29 Sept. 1925; *s* of late George Albert Hall and Phyllis Louise Hall (*née* Papps); *m* 1948, Margaret Patricia

Smith; two s. *Educ:* Highbury County Sch.; Trinity Hall, Cambridge (BA). Joined RAFVR 1943; served RAF Blind Landing Experimental Unit; demobilised as Flying Officer, 1947. Joined Foreign (subseq. Diplomatic) Service, 1950; Third Sec., Foreign Office, 1950-53; Third, Second and First Sec. (Commercial), Mexico City, 1953-58, FO, 1958-61; First Sec., Head of Chancery and First Sec. (Information), Lima, 1961-64; FO, 1964-69; Counsellor, Sept. 1968; Counsellor, Lisbon, 1969-72; Consul-General, São Paulo, 1973-77. Member: British-Mexican Soc. and Anglo-Peruvian Soc. (Exec. Cttee, 1965-69); Bd of Management, Inst. of Latin American Studies, London Univ., 1966-69. *Recreations:* reading, listening to music, swimming. *Address:* c/o Foreign and Commonwealth Office, SW1. *Club:* Buck's.

HALL, Harold George; His Honour Judge Hall; a Circuit Judge, since 1975; *b* 20 Sept. 1920; *s* of late Albert Hall and Violet Maud Hall (*née* Etherington); *m* 1950, Patricia Delaney; four *s* one *d. Educ:* Archbishop Holgate's Grammar Sch., York. RAF, 1940-46 (Flt-Lt). Called to Bar, Middle Temple, 1958; practised NE Circuit; Dep. Chm., WR Yorks QS, 1970; a Recorder, 1972-75. *Address:* 5 King's Bench Walk, Temple, EC4.

HALL, Harold Percival, CMG 1963; MBE 1947; Director of Studies, Royal Institute of Public Administration, since 1974; *b* 9 Sept. 1913; *s* of late Major George Charles Hall; *m* 1939, Margery Hall, *d* of late Joseph Dickson; three *s* (including twin *s*). *Educ:* Portsmouth Grammar Sch.; Royal Military College, Sandhurst. Commissioned Indian Army, 1933. Indian Political Service, 1937-47. Private Sec. to Resident, Central India States, 1937; Magistrate and Collector, Meerut, 1938-39. Military Service, 1938-43 (Major). Staff Coll., Quetta, 1941. Asst Political Agent, Loralai, 1943, Nasirabad, 1944; Dir, Food and Civil Supplies, and Dep. Sec., Revenue, Baluchistan, 1945-46; Principal, Colonial Office, 1947; Asst Sec. (Head of Pacific and Indian Ocean Dept), Colonial Office, 1955-62; Seconded to Office of UK Comr-Gen. for SE Asia, 1962-63; British Dep. High Comr for Eastern Malaysia, Kuching, Sarawak, 1963-64; Asst Sec., Colonial Office, 1965-66; Assistant Under-Secretary of State: Commonwealth Office, 1966-68; MoD, 1968-73. Mem. Governing Body, Sch. of Oriental and African Studies, 1971-74. *Recreations:* cricket, tennis, squash, golf. *Address:* 77 Moss Lane, Pinner, Middlesex.

HALL, (Harold) Peter; Legal Adviser and Solicitor, Crown Estate Commissioners, since Dec. 1976; Solicitor of Supreme Court; *b* 10 Dec. 1916; *s* of Arthur William Henry and Ethel Amelia Hall; *m* 1946, Tessibel Mary Mitchell (*née* Phillips); one *s* one *d. Educ:* Bristol Grammar Sch.; Bristol Univ. (LLB Hons). Articled to, and Asst Solicitor with, Burges Salmon & Co., Solicitors, Bristol, 1934-39. Served War of 1939-45: enlisted Somerset Light Inf., Dec. 1939; commnd in E Yorkshire Regt, 1940; service Home and Far East, 1940-45. Asst Provost Marshal (Major), Southern Army, India Command, 1945. Legal Branch, Min. of Agric., Fisheries and Food, 1946-66; Asst Legal Adviser, Land Commn, 1967-71; Asst Solicitor, Dept of the Environment, 1971-76. *Recreations:* reading, photography, walking. *Address:* Blue Cedars, Warren Road, Crowborough, East Sussex TN6 1QR. *T:* Crowborough 4003. *Club:* Army and Navy.

HALL, Prof. Henry Edgar; Professor of Physics, University of Manchester, since 1961; *b* 1928; *s* of John Ainger Hall; *m* 1962, Patricia Anne Broadbent; two *s* one *d. Educ:* Latymer Upper Sch., Hammersmith; Emmanuel Coll., Cambridge. BA 1952; PhD 1956. At Royal Society Mond Laboratory, Cambridge, 1952-58; Senior Student, Royal Commission for the Exhibition of 1851, 1955-57; Research Fellow of Emmanuel Coll., 1955-58; Lecturer in Physics, Univ. of Manchester, 1958-61. Simon Memorial Prize (with W. F. Vinen), 1963. Visiting Professor: Univ. of Western Australia, 1964; Univ. of Oregon, 1967-68; Cornell Univ., 1974. *Publications:* Solid State Physics, 1974; papers in scientific journals. *Recreations:* mountain walking, cinema-going. *Address:* The Physical Laboratories, The University, Manchester M13 9PL.

HALL, Prof. James Snowdon, CBE 1976; Professor of Agriculture, Glasgow University, and Principal, West of Scotland Agricultural College, since 1966; *b* 28 Jan. 1919; *s* of Thomas Blackburn Hall and Mary Milburn Hall; *m* 1942, Mary Smith; one *s* one *d. Educ:* Univ. of Durham (BSc Hons). FRAgSs, FInstBiol. Asst Technical Adviser, Northumberland War Agric. Exec. Commn, 1941-44; Lectr in Agriculture, Univ. of Newcastle upon Tyne, 1944-54; Principal, Cumbria Coll. of Agriculture and Forestry, 1954-66. *Address:* 26 Earls Way, Doonfoot, Ayr. *T:* Alloway 41162. *Clubs:* Farmers'; Royal Scottish Automobile (Glasgow).

HALL, Jean Graham, LLM (London); **Her Honour Judge Graham Hall;** a Circuit Judge (formerly Deputy Chairman, South-East London Quarter Sessions), since 1971; *b* 26 March 1917; *d* of Robert Hall and Alison (*née* Graham). *Educ:* Inverkeithing Sch., Fife; St Anne's Coll., Sanderstead; London Sch. of Economics. Gold Medal (Elocution and Dramatic Art), Incorporated London Acad. of Music, 1935; Teacher's Dipl., Guildhall Sch. of Music, 1937; Social Science Cert., London Sch. of Economics, 1937; LLB (Hons), London, 1950. Club Leader and subseq. Sub-Warden, Birmingham Univ. Settlement, 1937-41; Sec., Eighteen Plus (an experiment in youth work), 1941-44; Probation Officer, Hants, subseq. Croydon, 1945-51. Called to Bar, Gray's Inn, 1951. Metropolitan Stipendiary Magistrate, 1965-71. Pres., Gray's Inn Debating Soc., 1953; Hon. Sec., Soc. of Labour Lawyers, 1954-64; Pres., British Soc. of Criminology, 1971-74. Chm. Departmental Cttee on Statutory Maintenance Limits, 1966-68. Contested (Lab) East Surrey, 1955. *Recreations:* travel, congenial debate. *Address:* 2 Dr Johnson's Buildings, Temple, EC4. *Clubs:* University Women's.

HALL, Joan Valerie; *b* 31 Aug. 1935; *d* of Robert Percy Hall and Winifred Emily Umbers, Highfield, High Hoyland, Barnsley. *Educ:* Queen Margaret's Sch., York; Ashridge House of Citizenship. Contested (C) Barnsley, 1964 and 1966. MP (C) Keighley, 1970-Feb. 1974. PPS to Minister of State for Agriculture, Fisheries and Food, 1972-74. *Address:* Highfield, High Hoyland, Barnsley, South Yorks. *T:* Darton 2146.

HALL, Sir John; *see* Hall, Sir F. J. F.

HALL, Sir John, Kt 1973; OBE 1945; TD 1946; MP (C) Wycombe Division of Bucks, since Nov. 1952; chairman and director of companies in chemical and brewing industries; *b* 21 Sept. 1911; *m* 1935, Nancy, *er d* of late W. Hearn Blake; one *s* one *d.* Served War of 1939-45, RA, TA; Commissioned RAOC, 1940; Staff Coll., Camberley, 1941-42; various Staff appts, 1942-45; Lt-Col 1943. Mem. Grimsby Borough Council, 1946-48; contested (C) Grimsby, 1950, (C) East Fulham, 1951; PPS to Minister of Fuel and Power, 1956 and to Minister of Supply, 1957-59. Mem., Select Cttee on Public Acts, 1958-64; Vice-Chairman: Cons. Parly Trade and Industry Cttee, 1964-65; Finance Cttee, 1965-68, 1969-72, 1974- (Chm., 1973-74); Cons. Parly 1922 Cttee, 1970-; Mem., Select Cttee on Expenditure, 1970-72 (Chm. Sub-Cttee for DoE and Home Office); Chm., Select Cttee on Nationalised Industries, 1972-74. Treasurer, 1967, Vice-Chm., 1968-70, Chm., 1970-73, Inter-Parly Union (British Br.), and Vice-Chm., Internat. Executive. Mem. Order of Diplomatic Merit (Korea), 1975. *Address:* 41 Carlisle Mansions, Carlisle Place, SW1; Marsh, Great Kimble, Bucks. *Club:* Naval and Military.

HALL, John Anthony Sanderson, DFC 1943; QC 1967; a Recorder, since 1972 (Recorder of Swindon, 1971); *b* 25 Dec. 1921; *s* of late Rt Hon. W. Glenvil Hall, PC, MP, and late Rachel Ida Hall (*née* Sanderson); *m* 1st, Nora Ella Hall (*née* Crowe) (marr. diss. 1974); one *s* two *d*; 2nd, Elizabeth Mary Maynard. *Educ:* Leighton Park Sch.; Trinity Hall, Cambridge (BA). Served RAF, 1940-46, 85 Squadron and 488 (NZ) Squadron (Squadron Leader; DFC and Bar). Called to Bar, Inner Temple, 1948, Master of the Bench, 1975; Western Circuit; Dep. Chm., Hants Quarter Sessions, 1967. Member: Gen. Council of the Bar, 1964-68, 1970-74; Senate of the Four Inns of Court, 1966-68, 1970-74. *Recreations:* walking, sailing, fishing. *Address:* 2 Dr Johnson's Buildings, Temple, EC4. *Clubs:* Garrick; Hampshire (Winchester).

HALL, Sir John (Bernard), 3rd Bt *cr* 1919; Vice-President and Director, Bank of America International SA, Luxembourg, since 1977 (Administrator, 1974-77); Director: European Brazilian Bank Ltd; Fenchurch Steamship Corporation; *b* 20 March 1932; *s* of Lieut-Col Sir Douglas Hall, DSO, 2nd Bt, and Ina Nancie Walton, *d* of late Col John Edward Mellor, CB (she *m* 2nd, 1962, Col Peter J. Bradford, DSO, OBE, TD); *S* father, 1962; *m* 1957, Delia Mary, *d* of late Lieut-Col J. A. Innes, DSO; one *s* two *d. Educ:* Eton; Trinity Coll., Oxford (MA). Lieut, Royal Fusiliers (RARO). J. Henry Schroder Wagg & Co. Ltd, formerly J. Henry Schroder & Co, 1955-73 (Dir, 1967-73); Dir, The Antofagasta (Chili) and Bolivia Rly Co. Ltd, 1967-73. *Recreations:* travel, fishing. *Heir: s* David Bernard Hall, *b* 12 May 1961. *Address:* Penrose House, Patmore Heath, Albury, Ware, Herts SG11 2LT. *T:* Albury 255. *Clubs:* Boodle's, Lansdowne, Overseas Bankers'.

HALL, John Edward Beauchamp, CMG 1959; *b* 9 Dec. 1905; *s* of Henry William Hall, MA, and Emily (*née* Odam); *m* 1936, Jane Gordon (*née* Forbes); two *d. Educ:* Bradfield Coll., Berks; Worcester Coll., Oxford. Foundation Scholar, Bradfield Coll., 1919-24; Exhibitioner, Worcester Coll., Oxford, 1924-28.

Appointed to Colonial Administrative Service, Nigeria, 1930; Permanent Sec., Federal Government of Nigeria, 1958-60; retired, 1961. *Recreation:* gardening. *Address:* Meads, Stream Lane, Hawkhurst, Kent. *T:* Hawkhurst 2108.

HALL, Sir John Hathorn, GCMG 1950 (KCMG 1941; CMG 1935); DSO 1919; OBE 1931; MC; *b* 19 June 1894; *m* 1927, Torfrida Trevenen Mills; two *d. Educ:* St Paul's Sch.; Lincoln Coll., Oxford. Served European War, 1914-19 (despatches, MC, DSO, Croix de Guerre (Belgium)); Egyptian Civil Service, Ministry of Finance, 1919-21; Asst Principal, Colonial Office, 1921; Principal, 1927; seconded to Foreign Office, 1932; Chief Sec. to Govt of Palestine, 1933-37; British Resident, Zanzibar, 1937-40; Governor and C-in-C, Aden, 1940-44; Governor and C-in-C of Uganda, 1944-51; retd, 1951. Past Chm., Clerical, Medical & General Life Assurance Soc.; formerly Dir, Midland Bank Ltd and other cos. 1st Cl. Order of the Brilliant Star of Zanzibar; KStJ. *Address:* 128 Rivermead Court, Hurlingham, SW6 3SD. *Clubs:* Athenæum, Hurlingham.

HALL, Maj.-Gen. Kenneth, CB 1976; OBE 1962 (MBE 1958); Director of Army Education, 1972-76; *b* 29 July 1916; *s* of Frank Hall and Hannah Hall (*née* Clayton); *m* 1945, Celia Adelaide Elizabeth Francis; two *s. Educ:* Worksop Coll.; St John's Coll., Cambridge (BA). Served War of 1939-45: commissioned in Royal Tank Regt, 1940-49; transf. to Royal Army Educational Corps, 1949; War Office, 1945-52; HQ Malta Garrison, 1953-57; War Office, 1958-62; HQ Aldershot District, 1962-64; Chief Educn Officer, GHQ, MELF, 1965; Comdt Army Sch. of Educn, 1965-66; MoD, 1966-69; Comdt RAEC Centre, 1971-72. *Recreations:* boxing (Cambridge Univ. Blue, 1937-38-39), reading, golf. *Address:* 42 Exeter House, Putney Heath, SW15. *T:* 01-788 4794. *Clubs:* Army and Navy; Hawks (Cambridge).

HALL, Kenneth Lambert, CMG 1938; *b* 14 May 1887; *s* of late Thomas Lambert Hall, MRCS and *g g s* of William Hall of Arlington Manor, Bibury, Glos; *m* 1915, Mabel (*d* 1976), *d* of Towry Piper of Barnard Castle, Durham; one *s* decd. *Educ:* Hereford Sch.; Brasenose Coll., Oxford (Somerset Scholar). Entered Northern Nigerian Political Service as Asst Resident, 1912; Principal Asst Sec., Nigerian Secretariat, 1927; acting Dep. Chief Sec., 1927-30; Mem., Legislative Council, Nigeria; acting Sec., Southern Provinces, Nigeria, 1930; Chief Sec., Nyasaland, 1931-41; acting Governor and Comdr-in-Chief, Nyasaland on various occasions; Sec. Nyasaland Northern and Southern Rhodesia Inter-territorial Conference, 1941; retired, 1945. *Address:* St Luke's, 20 Linton Road, Oxford.

HALL, (Laura) Margaret; see MacDougall, Laura Margaret.

HALL, Michael Kilgour H.; see Harrison-Hall.

HALL, Sir Neville (Reynolds), 13th Bt *cr* 1687; retired; *b* 16 Feb. 1900; *s* of Captain Lionel Erskine Hall (*d* 1948) and Jane Augusta Hall (*d* 1949), *d* of late Thomas Leethem Reynolds; *S* brother, 1975; *m* 1957, Dorothy Maud, *d* of late William Lawrence Jones. *Educ:* Oundle; Royal Coll. of Science (ARCS); Keble Coll., Oxford (BSc). Demonstrator, Royal Naval Engineering Coll., Keyham, 1924-28; research at Oxford, 1928-31; Lecturer, Royal Naval Coll., Dartmouth, 1931-63. *Publications:* various scientific articles of no great importance. *Recreation:* designing and making clocks. *Heir: b* Sir Douglas Hall, *qv. Address:* Ash Cottage, Ash, Dartmouth, S Devon. *T:* Blackawton 288.

HALL, Sir Noel (Frederick), Kt 1957; Principal, Brasenose College, Oxford, 1960-73, Hon. Fellow 1973; *b* 23 Dec. 1902; *s* of late Cecil Gallopine Hall and late Constance Gertrude Upcher; *m* 1st, 1927, Edith Evelyn Pearl Haward (marr. diss. 1944); no *c*; 2nd, 1946, Elinor Hirschhorn Marks; one *s* one *d. Educ:* Royal Grammar Sch., Newcastle on Tyne; Bromsgrove Sch.; Brasenose Coll., Oxford. 1st Class hons Modern History, 1924; Senior Hulme Scholar, 1924-25; Certificate Social Anthropology, 1925; BA 1924; MA 1933. Commonwealth Fund Fellow in Economics, Princeton Univ., 1925-27, AM (Economics) Princeton, 1926; Lecturer in Political Economy, head of Dept of Political Economy, and Civil Service Tutor, University of London, University Coll., 1927-29; Senior Lecturer, 1929-35; Prof. of Political Economy in the University of London (University Coll.,) 1935-38; Sec. of Fellowship Advisory Cttee of Rockefeller Foundation for Social Sciences in Great Britain and Ireland, 1930-36; Dir, National Institute for Economic and Social Research, 1938-43; Mem. of International Commission for Relief of Child Refugees in Spain, 1939; Joint Dir, Ministry of Economic Warfare, 1940; Minister in charge of War Trade Department, British Embassy, Washington, 1941-43; Development Adviser West Africa, 1943-45; Principal of the Administrative Staff Coll., Greenlands, Henley-on-Thames,

1946-61. Ford Foundation Distinguished Visiting Prof., New York Univ., 1958 (University Medal, 1958). Hon. Associate, College of Advanced Technology, Birmingham, 1963. Hon. LLD Univ. of Lancaster, 1964. *Publications:* Measures of a National and International character for Raising Standards of Living (Report to Economic Committee of League of Nations, 1938); The Exchange Equalisation Account, 1935; Report on Grading Structure of Administrative and Clerical Staff in the Hospital Service, 1957; The Making of Higher Executives, 1958. *Recreations:* golf, bridge. *Address:* Homer End, Ipsden, Oxon. *T:* Checkendon 680294. *Club:* English-Speaking Union.

HALL, Peter; see Hall, H. P.

HALL, Prof. Peter Geoffrey; Professor and Head of Department of Geography, since 1968, Chairman, School of Planning Studies, since 1971, Dean of Urban and Regional Studies, since 1975, University of Reading; *b* 19 March 1932; *s* of Arthur Vickers Hall and Bertha Hall (*née* Keefe); *m* 1st, 1962, Carla Maria Wartenberg (marr. diss. 1966); 2nd, 1967, Magdalena Mróz; no *c. Educ:* Blackpool Grammar Sch.; St Catharine's Coll., Cambridge Univ. (MA, PhD). Asst Lectr, 1957, Lectr, 1960, Birkbeck Coll., Univ. of London; Reader in Geography with ref. to Regional Planning, London Sch. of Economics and Political Science, 1966. Vis. Prof., City and Regional Planning, Univ. of Calif., Berkeley, 1974. Member: SE Regional Planning Council, 1966-; Nature Conservancy, 1968-72; Transport and Road Research Laboratory Adv. Cttee on Transport, 1973-; Environmental Bd, 1975; SSRC, 1975- (Chm., Planning Cttee); EEC Expert Gp on New Tendencies of Social and Economic Develt, 1975-; Adv. Cttee on Trunk Road Assessment, 1977-. Mem., Editorial Bd, (and regular contributor to) New Society, 1965-; Exec. Cttee, (and Hon. Jl Editor), Regional Studies Assoc., 1967-; Exec. Cttee, Fabian Soc., 1964- (Chm. 1971-72); Governor, Centre for Environmental Studies, 1975-. FRGS; Hon. RTPI, 1975. *Publications:* The Industries of London, 1962; London 2000, 1963 (reprint, 1969); Labour's New Frontiers, 1964; (ed) Land Values, 1965; The World Cities, 1966; Containment of Urban England, 1973; Urban and Regional Planning, 1974; Europe 2000, 1976. *Recreations:* writing, reading, talking. *Address:* Department of Geography, University of Reading, Whiteknights, Reading RG6 2AF.

HALL, Sir Peter (Reginald Frederick), Kt 1977; CBE 1963; director of plays, films and operas; Director, National Theatre, since 1973; *b* Bury St Edmunds, Suffolk, 22 Nov. 1930; *s* of Reginald Edward Arthur Hall and Grace Pamment; *m* 1956, Leslie Caron (marr. diss., 1965); one *s* one *d*; *m* 1965, Jacqueline Taylor; one *s* one *d. Educ:* Perse Sch., Cambridge; St Catharine's Coll., Cambridge (MA Hons; Hon. Fellow, 1964). Dir, Arts Theatre, London, 1955-56 (directed several plays incl. first productions of Waiting for Godot, South, Waltz of the Toreadors); formed own producing company, International Playwrights' Theatre, 1957, and directed their first production, Camino Real; at Sadler's Wells, directed his first opera, The Moon and Sixpence, 1957. First productions at Stratford: Love's Labour's Lost, 1956; Cymbeline, 1957; first prod. on Broadway, The Rope Dancers, Nov. 1957. Plays in London, 1956-58: Summertime, Gigi, Cat on a Hot Tin Roof, Brouhaha, Shadow of Heroes; Madame de..., Traveller Without Luggage, A Midsummer Night's Dream and Coriolanus (Stratford), The Wrong Side of the Park, 1959; apptd Dir of Royal Shakespeare Theatre, Jan. 1960, responsible for creation of RSC as a permanent ensemble, and its move to Aldwych Theatre, 1960; Man. Dir at Stratford-on-Avon and Aldwych Theatre, London, 1960-68; Co-Dir, RSC, 1968-73; plays produced/directed for Royal Shakespeare Company: Two Gentlemen of Verona, Twelfth Night, Troilus and Cressida, 1960; Ondine, Becket, Romeo and Juliet, 1961; The Collection, Troilus and Cressida, A Midsummer Night's Dream, 1962; The Wars of the Roses (adaptation of Henry VI Parts 1, 2 and 3, and Richard III), 1963 (televised for BBC, 1965); Sequence of Shakespeare's histories for Shakespeare's 400th anniversary at Stratford: Richard II, Henry IV Parts 1 & 2, Henry V, Henry VI, Edward IV, Richard III, 1964; The Homecoming, Hamlet, 1965; The Government Inspector, Staircase, 1966; The Homecoming (NY), Macbeth, 1967; A Delicate Balance, Silence and Landscape, 1969; The Battle of the Shrivings, 1970; Old Times, 1971 (NY, 1971, Vienna, 1972); All Over, Via Galactica (NY), 1972; plays produced/directed for National Theatre: The Tempest, 1974; John Gabriel Borkman, 1975; No Man's Land, Happy Days, Hamlet, 1975; Tamburlaine the Great, 1976; No Man's Land (NY), Volpone, Bedroom Farce, 1977. *Films:* Work is a Four Letter Word, 1968; A Midsummer Night's Dream, Three into Two Won't Go, 1969; Perfect Friday, 1971; The Homecoming, 1973; Akenfield, 1974. *Opera:* at Covent Garden: Moses and Aaron, 1965; The Magic Flute, 1966; The Knot Garden, 1970; Eugene Onegin, Tristan and Isolde, 1971; at Glyndebourne: La

Calisto, 1970; Il Ritorno d'Ulisse in Patria, 1972; The Marriage of Figaro, 1973; Don Giovanni, 1977. Presenter, Aquarius (LWT), 1975-77. Associate Prof. of Drama, Warwick Univ., 1966-. Mem., Arts Council, 1969-73. DUniv York, 1966; Hon. Dr: Reading, 1972; Liverpool, 1974; Leicester, 1977. Tony Award (NY) for best director, 1966; Hamburg Univ. Shakespeare Prize, 1967. Chevalier de l'Ordre des Arts et des Lettres, 1965. *Recreation:* music. *Address:* The Wall House, Mongewell Park, Wallingford, Oxon.

HALL, Prof. Philip, FRS 1942; MA; Sadleirian Professor of Pure Mathematics, Cambridge University, 1953-67, now Emeritus (University Lecturer in Mathematics, 1933-51; Reader in Algebra, 1951-53); Fellow of King's College, Cambridge, 1927; *b* 11 April 1904. *Educ:* Christ's Hosp. Hon. Sec. London Mathematical Soc., 1938-41, 1945-48, Pres., 1955-57. Sylvester Medal, Royal Society, 1961; de Morgan Medal and Larmor Prize of the London Mathematical Soc., 1965. Hon. DSc: Tübingen, 1963; Warwick, 1977. Hon. Fellow, Jesus Coll. Cambridge, 1976. *Address:* 50 Impington Lane, Histon, Cambs.

HALL, Sir Robert de Zouche, KCMG 1953 (CMG 1952); MA; *b* 27 April 1904; *s* of late Arthur William Hall, Liverpool; *m* 1932, Lorna Dorothy (*née* Markham); one *s* one *d*. *Educ:* Willaston Sch.; Gonville and Caius Coll., Cambridge. MA, 1932; Colonial Administrative Service, Tanganyika, 1926; Provincial Comr, 1947; Senior Provincial Comr, 1950; Mem. for Local Government, Tanganyika, 1950-53. Governor, Comdr-in-Chief, and Vice-Adm., Sierra Leone, 1953-56. Hon. Sec. Vernacular Architecture Group, 1959-72, Pres., 1972-73; Chm. Governing Body, Somerset County Museum, 1961-73. *Publication:* (ed) A Bibliography on Vernacular Architecture, 1973. *Address:* 1 Lewis Street, Gisborne, New Zealand.

HALL, Robert King, PhD; international consultant, educator and executive; *b* Kewanee, Ill, 13 March 1912; *s* of Dr Nelson Hall and Nellie Jean Hyer; *m* 1938, Margaret Wheeler, Belmont, Mass; one *s* two *d*. *Educ:* Lake Forest Univ. (AB); Harvard Univ. (AM); Univ. of Chicago (AMEduc); Columbia Univ. (AM); Sch. of Asiatic Studies, NY (AM); Univ. of Michigan (PhD). Master: Cranbrook Sch. (Mich), 1936-40; Dir Research Milwaukee Country Day Schs, 1940-41; Asst Dir, Commn on Eng. Lang. Studies, Harvard Univ., 1941-43; Lt-Comdr, USNR, 1943-46; Assoc. Prof. Teachers Coll., Columbia Univ., 1947-50, Prof. of Comparative Education, 1950-55; Dir of Trng, Arabian Amer. Oil Co., Saudi Arabia, 1955-60. Hon. Lectr, Teachers Coll., Columbia Univ., 1955-57; Internat. Consultant, 1960-64; Sen. Advisor, Univ. of Petroleum and Minerals, Dhahran, 1964-. Vis. Prof. and Lectr, American and foreign Univs; special assignments in connection with education, in Japan, South America, Iran, Arabia; Jt Editor, Year Book of Education (London), 1952-57. Deleg. to numerous internat. educnl congresses. Holder of hon. degrees. *Publications:* Federal Control of Education in ABC Republics, 1942; The Teaching of English, 1942; Report of Latin-American Workshop, 1941; A Basic English for South America, 1943; Ingles Basico Para Brasil, 1943; Education for a New Japan, 1949; Kokutai no Hongi (with J. O. Gauntlett), 1949; Shūshin: The Ethics of a Defeated Nation, 1949; Educación en Crisis, 1950; Problemas de Educação Rural, 1950; Report of a Study of YMCA World Services Policy and Practices, 1962; A Strategy for the Inner City, 1963. Articles in English and foreign educnl jls; numerous monographs and consulting reports. *Recreation:* travel. *Address:* University of Petroleum and Minerals, Dhahran, Saudi Arabia.

HALL, Thomas William; Under-Secretary, Department of Transport, since 1976; *b* 8 April 1931; *s* of Thomas William and Euphemia Jane Hall; *m* 1961, Anne Rosemary Hellier Davis; two *d*. *Educ:* Hitchin Grammar Sch.; St John's Coll., Oxford (MA). Asst Principal, Min. of Supply, 1954; Principal: War Office, Min. of Public Building and Works, Cabinet Office, 1958-68; Asst Sec., Min. of Public Building and Works, DoE, 1968-70. *Recreations:* music, gardening, walking. *Address:* 43 Bridge Road, Epsom, Surrey KT17 4AN. *T:* Epsom 25900.

HALL, Trevor Henry, JP; Partner, V. Stanley Walker & Son, Chartered Surveyors, Leeds, Morley, Rothwell and Woodlesford, since 1945; *b* 28 May 1910; *o s* of H. Roxby Hall, Yorks; *m* 1937, Dorothy, *d* of late A. H. Keningley, Nostell; one *s* one *d*. *Educ:* Wakefield Sch.; Trinity Coll., Cambridge (Perrott Student); London Coll. of Estate Management; Univ. of Leeds. MA, PhD, FRICS. Served War of 1939-45, Army. Huddersfield Building Society: Chief Surveyor, 1935-39; Dir, 1958-; Vice-Pres., 1967-71; Pres., 1972-; Dep. Chm., 1974-, Dir, 1962-, Legal & General Assce Soc. (North Regional and Scottish Bds). Mem., Brotherton Cttee, Univ. of Leeds, 1967-; Pres., Leeds Library, 1969-. Cecil Oldman Meml Lectr in bibliography and textual

criticism, Univ. of Leeds, 1972. JP City of Leeds, 1959. *Publications:* The Testament of R. W. Hull, 1945; (with E. J. Dingwall and K. M. Goldney) The Haunting of Borley Rectory: A Critical Survey of the Evidence, 1956; A Bibliography of Books on Conjuring in English from 1580 to 1850, 1957; (with E. J. Dingwall) Four Modern Ghosts, 1958; The Spiritualists: The Story of William Crookes and Florence Cook, 1962; The Strange Case of Edmund Gurney, 1964; The Mystery of the Leeds Library, 1965; New Light on Old Ghosts, 1965; (with J. L. Campbell) Strange Things, 1968; Sherlock Holmes: Ten Literary Studies, 1969; Mathematical Recreations, 1633: An Exercise in 17th Century Bibliography, 1970; The Late Mr Sherlock Holmes, 1971; Old Conjuring Books: a bibliographical and historical study, 1972; The Card Magic of Edward G. Brown, 1973; Sherlock Holmes and His Creator, 1974; The Early Years of the Huddersfield Building Society, 1975; The Winder Sale of Old Conjuring Books, 1975; (with Percy H. Muir) Some Printers and Publishers of Conjuring Books and Other Ephemera, 1800-1850, 1976; Search for Harry Price, 1977. *Recreations:* walking, gardening, book collecting. *Address:* Carr Meadow, Thorner, Leeds, West Yorks. *T:* Leeds 892547. *Clubs:* Leeds (Leeds); Borough (Huddersfield).

HALL, Vernon F., CVO 1960; Anæsthetist, King's College Hospital, 1931-69, retired; *b* 25 Aug. 1904; *s* of Cecil S. and M. M. Hall; *m* 1935, C. Marcia Cavell; one *s* two *d*. *Educ:* Haberdashers' Sch.; King's Coll. Hosp., London. MRCS, LRCP, 1927; DA, 1938; FFARCS, 1948. Served War of 1939-45 in Army (Emergency Commission), 1942-46; Consultant Anæsthetist, India Command (Local Brig.), 1945; Dean, King's Coll. Hosp. Medical Sch., 1951-65. FKC 1958; Hon. FFARCS 1975. *Publications:* History of King's College Hospital Dental School, 1973; chapters on Anaesthesia—Rose & Carless, Surgery, etc. *Recreations:* riding, walking, reading and music. *Address:* Deercombe, Brendon, N Devon. *T:* Brendon 281.

HALL, Lieut-Col Walter D'Arcy, MC; *b* Australia, 10 Aug. 1891; *s* of late Thomas Skarratt Hall, of Weeting Hall, Brandon, Norfolk; *m* 1920, Ann Madelaine Brook (marr. diss.); two *s* one *d*; *m* 1957, Ruth Penelope Owen. *Educ:* Eton; Sandhurst. Joined 20th Hussars, 1911; served European War, 1914-19 (MC and Bar, Croix de Guerre avec Palme et Etoile); served War 1939-45. MP (U) Brecon and Radnor, 1924-29 and 1931-35. *Address:* Magnolia Cottage, Lower Woodford, Salisbury, Wilts SP4 6NQ. *Club:* Cavalry and Guards.
See also E . T . Hall .

HALL, Prof. William Bateman; Professor of Nuclear Engineering, University of Manchester, since 1959; *b* 28 May 1923; *s* of Sidney Bateman Hall and Doris Hall; *m* 1950, Helen Mary Dennis; four *d*. *Educ:* Urmston Grammar Sch.; College of Technology, Manchester. Engineering apprenticeship, 1939-44; Royal Aircraft Establishment, 1944-46; United Kingdom Atomic Energy Authority (formerly Dept of Atomic Energy, Min. of Supply), 1946-59: Technical Engineer, 1946-52; Principal Scientific Officer, 1952-56; Senior Principal Scientific Officer, 1956-58; Dep. Chief Scientific Officer, 1958. *Publications:* Reactor Heat Transfer, 1958; papers to scientific and professional institutions. *Recreations:* music, fell walking. *Address:* Maple Bank, Macclesfield Road, Alderley Edge, Cheshire. *T:* Alderley Edge 583034.

HALL, Brig. Sir William (Henry), Kt 1968; CBE 1962; DSO 1942; ED; Comptroller of Stores, State Electricity Commission of Victoria, 1956-70; Colonel Commandant, RAA Southern Command, since 1967; *b* 5 Jan. 1906; *s* of William Henry Hall, Edinburgh, Scotland; *m* 1930, Irene Mary, *d* of William Hayes; one *s* four *d*. *Educ:* Morgan Acad., Dundee; Melbourne Univ. Joined Staff of State Electricity Commn of Vic, 1924. Enlisted AIF, 1939: Capt. Royal Aust. Artillery, Palestine, Egypt; Syria, Papua, New Guinea, 1941 (Major); Aust. Dir of Armaments at AHQ, 1942 (Lt-Col); Dir of Armament at AHQ, 1945 (Col); CRA 3 Div. Artillery CMF, 1955-59 (Brig.). Chm., Anzac Day Commemoration Coun.; Dir, Royal Humane Society of Vic.; Chairman: Patriotic Funds Coun.; War Widows and Widowed Mothers' Trust; Discharged Servicemen's Employment Bd and Victorian Raffle Bd, 1969; RSL War Veterans' Trust; State Pres. Victorian Br., Returned Services League, 1964-74, Nat. Pres., Aust. Returned Services League, 1974. Assoc. Fellow, Aust. Inst. Management; Mem., Inst. of Purchasing and Supply (London). *Recreation:* golf. *Address:* Rosemont, 112 Kooyong Road, Caulfield, Vic. 3162, Australia; The Moorings, Flinders, Victoria 3929. *Clubs:* Naval and Military (Melbourne); Melbourne Cricket, Peninsula Country Golf, Flinders Golf.

HALL, William Telford, CSI 1947; CIE 1942; *b* 4 June 1895; *s* of John Hall, Edinburgh; *m* 1922, E. Winifred, *d* of late Col Sir George McCrae, DSO, DL; two *s* one *d*. *Educ:* George Heriot's

Sch. Served European War, 1914-18, Capt. Royal Irish Fusiliers and Machine Gun Corps, Salonica and France. Joined Indian Forest Service, 1921; Chief Conservator of Forests, United Provinces, India. *Address:* Rose Cottage, The Street, Effingham, Leatherhead, Surrey.

HALL, Willis; writer; *b* 6 April 1929; *s* of Walter and Gladys Hall; *m* 1973, Valerie Shute; one *s* (and three *s* by previous marriages). *Educ:* Cockburn High Sch., Leeds. TV plays include: The Villa Maroc; They Don't all Open Men's Boutiques; Song at Twilight; TV series: The Fuzz, 1977; (with Keith Waterhouse): The Upper Crusts, 1973; Billy Liar, 1974. *Publications:* (with Michael Parkinson) The A-Z of Soccer, 1970; Football Report, 1973; Football Classified, 1974; My Sporting Life, To See Such Sport, 1975; *children's books:* The Royal Astrologer, 1960; The Gentle Knight, 1967; The Incredible Kidnapping, 1975; The Summer of the Dinosaur, 1977; *plays:* The Long and the Short and the Tall, 1959; A Glimpse of the Sea, 1969; Kidnapped at Christmas, 1975; Walk on, Walk on, 1975; Stag Night, 1976; Christmas Crackers, 1976; (with Keith Waterhouse): Billy Liar, 1960; Celebration, 1961; All Things Bright and Beautiful, 1962; England Our England, 1962; Squat Betty and The Sponge Room, 1963; Say Who You Are, 1965; Whoops-a-Daisy, 1968; Children's Day, 1969; Who's Who, 1972; (musical) The Card, 1973; Saturday, Sunday, Monday (adaptation from de Filippo), 1973. *Address:* 64 Clarence Road, St Albans, Herts. *Club:* Garrick.

HALL-DAVIS, Alfred George Fletcher; MP (C) Morecambe and Lonsdale Division of Lancs since 1964; *b* 21 June 1924; *s* of late George Hall-Davis, BA, MB, and of Mrs J. B. Cowan; *m* 1956, Margaret Carr, *d* of George Rushworth, JP, Colne, Lancs; one *d. Educ:* Clifton Coll., Bristol. PPS, DES, 1970-73; an Asst Govt Whip, 1973-74. Dir, Bass Charrington Ltd. *Recreation:* walking. *Address:* House of Commons, SW1A 0AA.

HALL-THOMPSON, Major (Robert) Lloyd, ERD; TD; JP; *b* 9 April 1920; *s* of Lt-Col Rt Hon. S. H. Hall-Thompson, PC (NI), DL, JP, MP; *m* 1948, Alison F. Leitch, MSR; one *s* one *d. Educ:* Campbell Coll. Prep. Sch.; Campbell Coll. Royal School. Major, Royal Artillery, 1939-46; TA, 1946-56. Joined Unionist Party, 1938; Vice-Pres., Clifton Unionist Assoc. (Chm. 1954-57); MP (U) Clifton, 1969-73; Mem (U), N Belfast, NI Assembly, 1973-75 (Leader of the House, 1973-74); Chief Whip, NI Executive, 1973-74; Mem. (UPNI) for N Belfast, NI Constitutional Convention, 1975-76. Director of several companies. Formerly Mem. NI Hosps Authority (Past Vice-Chm. Finance and Gen. Purposes Cttee); Past Vice-Chm., Samaritan Hosp. Management Cttee; Life Governor, Samaritan Hosp.; Pres. and Trustee, North Belfast Working Men's Club; Trustee and Hon. Sec., Belfast Newsboys' Club and W. S. Armour Girls' Club; Vice-Pres., Cliftonville Football and Athletic Club; Founder, Trustee & Pres., Duncairn Friendship Assoc.; Life Mem., (Past Hon. Sec. and Hon. Treas.), Not Forgotten Assoc.; Life Mem., Royal Ulster Agric. Soc.; Freeman and Stewart, Down Royal Corp. of Horse Breeders; Mem. Cttee, NI Nurses Housing Assoc. *Recreations:* horse riding, hunting, racing, eventing, show jumping, breeding; golf, reading. *Address:* Maymount, Ballylesson, Belfast 8, Northern Ireland. *T:* Drumbo 327. *Club:* Ulster (Belfast).

HALLAM-HIPWELL, H.; *see* Vivenot, Baroness Raoul de.

HALLAND, Col Gordon Herbert Ramsay, CIE 1931; OBE 1918; HM Inspector of Constabulary for England and Wales, 1938; retired, 1953; *b* 1888; *e s* of late Rev. J. T. Halland, MA, Rector of Blyburgh, Kirton-in-Lindsey, Lincs; *m* 1st, 1916, Helen Claudine Blanche (*d* 1946), *o d* of late Maj.-Gen. J. M. Walter, CB, CSI, DSO; two *d*; 2nd, 1947, Baroness Sigrid von der Recke (*née* von Lutzau), Windau, Latvia. *Educ:* private; Royal Latin Sch., Buckingham. Science Master at Kirton Grammar Sch., Lincs, 1906-08; Entered Indian Police, 1908 and posted to Punjab; served Ambala, Lahore, Rohtak, Hoshiarpur, Rawalpindi, Lyallpur, and Amritsar Districts; on police duty with the King at Delhi Durbar, 1911; Served European War, 1914-18 in Army in India Reserve of Officers (Major and Gen. Staff Officer, 2nd Grade, Army Headquarters, India) (despatches, OBE); Principal, Punjab Police Training Sch., Phillaur, 1921-26; on police duty with Duke of Connaught at Delhi, 1921; on police duty with Prince of Wales at Delhi, 1922; Lt-Col, Army in India Reserve of Officers, 1927; attached Gen. Staff, Headquarters of Shanghai Defence Force and subsequently North China Command, 1927-30; Senior Superintendent of Police, Delhi, 1930-31; Hon. ADC to the Viceroy, 1930, with hon. rank of Col; Chief Constable of Lincs, 1931-34; Dep. Asst Commissioner in charge of the Metropolitan Police Coll., 1934-38; Inspector-Gen. of Police, Ceylon, 1942-44; services lent to Foreign Office, Aug. 1944-Oct. 1947, as

Inspector Gen. of Public Safety, CCG (British Element). Mem. County Council for Parts of Lindsey, Nov. 1953-March 1957. DL County of Lincoln, 1954-57. *Recreations:* gardening; (past) shooting, riding, polo, cricket, tennis. *Address:* Box Green House, Box, Stroud, Glos GL6 9HH. *T:* Nailsworth 2508. *Club:* Lincolnshire County.

HALLETT, Vice-Adm. Sir Cecil Charles; *see* Hughes Hallett.

HALLETT, Cecil Walter; retired as General Secretary, Amalgamated Engineering Union, 1957-64; *b* 10 Dec. 1899; *m*; two *s* two *d. Educ:* New City Road Elementary Sch., London. Messenger, Commercial Cable Co., 1913-15; apprentice fitter and turner, Gas Light and Coke Co., Becton, N Woolwich, 1916-18. HM Forces, 10th London Regt, 1918-19; journeyman fitter and turner, various firms, 1923-48; Asst Gen. Sec. AEU, 1948-57. Former Editor, AEU Monthly Jl and The Way. *Address:* 317 High Street South, Carterton, North Island, New Zealand.

HALLETT, Prof. George Edward Maurice, MDS; Professor of Children's Dentistry in the University of Newcastle upon Tyne (formerly King's College, University of Durham), 1951-77; Dean, Sutherland Dental School, 1960-77, and Hospital, 1970-77; *b* 30 July 1912; *s* of Edward Henry and Bertha Hallett; *m* 1936, Annetta Eva Grant Napier; three *d. Educ:* Birkenhead Institute; Liverpool Univ. (LDS, Gilmour Medal and other prizes). HDD RCSE 1939; FDS RCS 1948; MDS Durham, 1952; DOrth RCS, 1954; FDS RCSE 1960; FFD RCSI 1964. House Surgeon, Liverpool Dental Hosp., 1934-35; School Dental Officer, Doncaster CB, 1935-36, Notts, 1936-40; served War, 1940-46: Army Dental Corps, Major, despatches. University of Durham: Lecturer in Children's Dentistry, 1946, Reader, 1948; Lectr in Orthodontics, 1946. Examiner in Dental subjects, Universities of Dundee, Durham, Edinburgh and Glasgow; RCS of Eng., 1954-59; Consultant, United Teaching Hosps, Newcastle upon Tyne; Head of Dept of Child Dental Health, Dental Hosp., Newcastle upon Tyne, 1948. Mem. Dental Council, RCSE; Past President: Société Française d'Orthopedie Dento-Faciale; European Orthodontic Soc. (also former Editor; Hon. Life Mem.); North of England Odontological Soc.; Brit. Soc. for the study of Orthodontics; Newcastle Medico-Legal Soc.; former Mem., Newcastle RHB; Chm. Dental Advisory Cttee, RHB; Mem. Newcastle AHA (T); Mem. General Dental Council. Hon. Life Mem., British Dental Assoc. *Publications:* contribs to scientific and dental jls. *Recreations:* dilettantism in the glyptic arts, flying. *Address:* 63 Runnymede Road, Darras Hall, Ponteland, Newcastle upon Tyne NE20 9HJ. *T:* Ponteland 2646. *Club:* Newcastle Aero.

HALLETT, Victor George Henry; National Insurance Commissioner, since 1976; *b* 11 Feb. 1921; *s* of Dr Denys Bouhier Imbert Hallett; *m* 1947, Margaret Hamlyn. *Educ:* Westminster; Queen's Coll., Oxford (MA). Served War, 1939-45 (despatches 1946). Called to Bar, Inner Temple, 1949. Mem., Land Registration Rules Cttee, 1971-76; Conveyancing Counsel of the Court, 1971-76. *Publications:* Hallett's Conveyancing Precedents, 1965; (ed jtly) Key and Elphinstone's Conveyancing Precedents, 15th edn, 1952, and Prideaux's Precedents in Conveyancing, 25th edn, 1953. *Address:* Pump Cottage, Chyngton Road, Seaford, East Sussex. *T:* Seaford 892324. *Club:* Travellers'.

HALLIBURTON, Rev. Canon Robert John; Principal of Chichester Theological College, since 1975; Canon and Prebendary of Chichester Cathedral, since 1976; *b* 23 March 1935; *s* of Robert Halliburton and Katherine Margery Halliburton (*née* Robinson); *m* 1968, Jennifer Ormsby Turner; one *s* two *d* (and one *s* decd). *Educ:* Tonbridge Sch.; Selwyn Coll., Cambridge (MA); Keble Coll., Oxford (DPhil); St Stephen's House, Oxford. Curate, St Dunstan and All Saints, Stepney, 1961; Tutor, St Stephen's House, Oxford, 1967; Vice-Principal, St Stephen's House, 1971; Lectr, Lincoln Coll., Oxford, 1973. Select Preacher, Oxford Univ., 1976-77. Consultant, Anglican-Roman Catholic Internat. Commn, 1971-75. *Publications:* contrib. The Eucharist Today, ed. R. C. D. Jasper, 1974; articles in Studia Patristica, La Revue des Etudes Augustiniennes, Faith and Unity. *Recreations:* music, gardening, dog breeding. *Address:* Theological College, Chichester, West Sussex. *T:* Chichester 83369.

HALLIDAY, Edward Irvine, CBE 1973; RP 1952; RBA 1942; ARCA (London) 1925; President, Royal Society of Portrait Painters, since 1970; Past-President, Royal Society of British Artists; Vice-President and Chairman, Artists General Benevolent Institution, since 1965; President, Artists League of Great Britain, since 1975; *b* 7 Oct. 1902; *s* of James Halliday and Violet Irvine; *m* 1928, Dorothy Lucy Hatswell; one *s* one *d.*

Educ: Liverpool; Paris; Royal College of Art, London; British Sch. at Rome (Rome Scholar 1925). War of 1939-45: service with RAF Bomber Command until seconded for special duties with Foreign Office. Mural paintings in London and Liverpool. Posters of Western Highlands for British Railways. Principal Portraits include: The Queen, for various cities, regiments, etc.; The Queen and The Duke of Edinburgh, for SS Caronia; The Duke of Edinburgh, for Gordonstoun Sch., Baltic Exchange, the Press Club, and Nat. Defence Coll.; The Prince of Wales, for Air Support Comd, RAF, and Naval Club; Queen Elizabeth the Queen Mother; HRH Princess Alice, Countess of Athlone; Admiral of the Fleet the Earl Mountbatten of Burma; Countess Mountbatten of Burma; Pandit Nehru (painted in New Delhi); Sir Edmund Hillary; President Azikiwe (painted in Nigeria); Dr Kaunda (painted in Zambia); King Olaf of Norway. Conversation Pieces include: The Royal Family; The 5th Marquess of Salisbury with his brother and sisters; Undergraduates at Worcester Coll., Oxford, 1937 and 1952. Broadcasts on many subjects. Governor, Fedn of British Artists, 1970-. Gold Medal, Paris Salon, 1953, 1965. FRSA 1970. *Address:* 62 Hamilton Terrace, NW8. *T:* 01-286 7030. *Clubs:* Athenæum, Arts, Chelsea Arts.

HALLIDAY, Frank Ernest; author; *b* 10 Feb. 1903; *s* of James Herbert Halliday, Bradford, and Anne Louise Anderson, Scarborough; *m* 1927, Nancibel Beth Gaunt; one *s. Educ:* Giggleswick Sch.; King's Coll., Cambridge. Asst Master, Cheltenham Coll., 1929-48. Resident in St Ives as a writer, 1948-. Shakespeare Lectr, Stratford, Ont., 1964, and for British Coun. in Portugal and Spain, 1965. *Publications:* Five Arts, 1946; Shakespeare and his Critics, 1949 (rev. edn 1958); A Shakespeare Companion, 1952 (rev. edn 1964); Richard Carew of Antony, 1953; The Poetry of Shakespeare's Plays, 1954; The Legend of the Rood, 1955; Shakespeare in his Age, 1956; Shakespeare, A Pictorial Biography, 1956; The Cult of Shakespeare, 1957; A History of Cornwall, 1959; Indifferent Honest, 1960; The Life of Shakespeare, 1961; Unfamiliar Shakespeare, 1962; Meditation at Bolerium (Poems), 1963; A Concise History of England, 1964; A Cultural History of England, 1967; A Cornish Chronicle, 1967; Dr Johnson and his World, 1968; Chaucer and his World, 1968; Wordsworth and his World, 1969; Thomas Hardy: his life and work, 1972; The Excellency of the English Tongue, 1975; Robert Browning, 1976. *Recreations:* walking, swimming, music, archæology, and more than a recreation, the protection of St Ives. *Address:* 12 Barnaloft, St Ives, Cornwall. *T:* St Ives 6650.

HALLIDAY, Sir George Clifton, Kt 1967; Consultant Otolaryngologist, Royal Prince Alfred Hospital and Prince Henry Hospital (Consultant Surgeon, since 1960); *b* 22 April 1901; *s* of late Edward James Halliday, NSW; *m* 1927, Hester Judith Macansh; two *s* one *d. Educ:* The King's Sch., Parramatta; St Paul's Coll., Univ. of Sydney. MB, ChM Sydney Univ., 1925; FRCSE 1934; FRACS 1954. Surg., St George Hosp., 1935; Surg., Royal Prince Alfred Hosp., 1936; Lectr in Otolaryngology, Sydney Univ., 1948-61. Served in AAMC, Middle East, 1940-43 (Lt-Col). Hon. Mem., RSM, 1970; Corresp. Fellow, Amer. Laryngological Assoc., 1970. *Recreations:* tennis, cricket, golf. *Address:* 67 Cranbrook Road, Rose Bay, NSW 2029, Australia. *T:* FM 2280. *Clubs:* Union, Royal Sydney Golf, Elanora Country (all Sydney).

HALLIDAY, James; see Symington, D.

HALLIDAY, Prof. Michael Alexander Kirkwood; Professor of Linguistics in the University of Sydney, since 1976; *b* 13 April 1925; *s* of late Wilfrid J. Halliday and of Winifred Halliday (née Kirkwood). *Educ:* Rugby School; University of London. BA London; MA, PhD, Cambridge. Served Army, 1944-47. Asst Lectr in Chinese, Cambridge Univ., 1954-58; Lectr in General Linguistics, Edinburgh Univ., 1958-60; Reader in General Linguistics, Edinburgh Univ., 1960-63; Dir, Communication Res. Centre, UCL, 1963-65; Linguistic Soc. of America Prof., Indiana Univ., 1964; Prof. of General Linguistics, UCL, 1965-71; Fellow, Center for Advanced Study in the Behavioural Sciences, Stanford, Calif., 1972-73; Prof. of Linguistics, Univ. of Illinois, 1973-74; Prof. of Language and Linguistics, Essex Univ., 1974-75. Visiting Professor of Linguistics: Yale, 1967; Brown, 1971; Nairobi, 1972. Dr *hc* Nancy. *Publications:* The Language of the Chinese 'Secret History of the Mongols', 1959; (with A. McIntosh and P. Strevens) The Linguistic Sciences and Language Teaching, 1964; (with A. McIntosh) Patterns of Language, 1966; Intonation and Grammar in British English, 1967; A Course in Spoken English: Intonation, 1970; Explorations in the Functions of Language, 1973; Learning How To Mean, 1975; (with R. Hasan) Cohesion in English, 1976; contrib. System and Function in Language, ed G. Kress, 1976; articles in Jl of Linguistics, Word, Trans of Philological Soc., etc.

Address: Department of Linguistics, University of Sydney, NSW 2006, Australia.

HALLIDAY, Vice-Adm. Roy William, DSC 1944; Deputy Chief of Defence Staff (Intelligence), since 1978; *b* 27 June 1923; *m* 1945, Dorothy Joan Meech. *Educ:* William Ellis Sch.; University College Sch. Joined Royal Navy, 1941; served in Fleet Air Arm (fighter pilot) in World War II, in HMS Chaser, HMSs Victorious and Illustrious; test pilot, Boscombe Down, 1947-48; Comdg Officer 813 Sqdn (Wyverns, HMS Eagle), 1954; Army Staff Coll., Camberley; Comdr, 1958; Exec. Officer Coastal Forces Base (HMS Diligence), 1959; Sen. Officer 104th Minesweeping Sqdn, Far East Flt, in comd (HMS Houghton), 1961-62; Naval Asst to Chief of Naval Information, 1962-64; comdr (Air) HMS Albion, 1964-66; Captain, 1966; Dep. Dir Naval Air Warfare, 1966-70; HMS Euryalus in comd and as Captain D3 Far East Fleet and D6 Western Fleet, 1970-71; Commodore, 1971; Cdre Amphibious Warfare, 1971-73; Cdre Intelligence, Defence Intelligence Staff, 1973-75; Comdr British Navy Staff, Washington, Naval Attaché, and UK Nat. Liaison Rep. to SACLANT, 1975-78. ADC to the Queen, 1975. *Recreations:* gardening, walking. *Address:* Deputy Chief of Defence Staff (Intelligence), Ministry of Defence, Room 4139, Main Building, Whitehall, SW1A 2HB. *Club:* Army and Navy.

HALLINAN, Sir (Adrian) Lincoln, Kt 1971; DL; Barrister-at-law; a Recorder of the Crown Court, since 1972; Stipendiary Magistrate, South Glamorgan (Cardiff), since 1976; *b* 13 Nov. 1922; *e s* of Sir Charles Hallinan, *qv*; *m* 1955, Mary Parry-Evans, MA, BCL, *d* of Dr E. Parry-Evans, JP; two *s* two *d. Educ:* Downside. Lieut, Rifle Bde, 1942-47; TA, 1950-52 (Captain). Called to Bar, Lincoln's Inn, 1950; Wales and Chester Circuit. A Legal Mem., Mental Health Review Tribunal for Wales, 1966-76; Chm., Med. Appeals Tribunal, 1970-76. Cardiff CC, 1949-74 (serving on several educational and cultural cttees); Alderman, 1961-74; Lord Mayor of Cardiff, 1969-70. Contested (C), Aberdare, 1946, Cardiff West, 1951, 1959. Chm., Cardiff Educn Cttee, 1961-63 and 1965-70; Chm., Governing Body, Cardiff Coll. of Art, and Cardiff Coll. of Music and Drama, 1961-73; First Chm., Nat. Court of Governors, Welsh Coll. of Music and Drama, 1970; Chairman: Commemorative Collectors Soc.; S Wales Gp, Victorian Soc.; a Vice-Pres., Cardiff Business Club; Founder and Chm., Cardiff 2000-Cardiff Civic Trust, 1964-73, 1st Pres. 1973; Chm., Cardiff-Nantes Fellowship, 1961-68. Chevalier, Ordre des Palmes Academiques, 1965; Chevalier de la Légion d'Honneur, 1973. OStJ 1969. DL Glamorgan, 1969. *Recreations:* music, the arts, collecting. *Address:* 63 Cathedral Road, Cardiff CF1 9HE. *T:* Cardiff 20511; Sunny Hill, Newquay, Dyfed. *Club:* Cardiff and County (Cardiff).

HALLINAN, Sir Charles (Stuart), Kt 1962; CBE 1954; solicitor; *b* 24 Nov. 1895; *o s* of John Hallinan and Jane Hallinan (née Rees); *m* 1921, Theresa Doris Hallinan, JP (née Holman) (decd); three *s* one *d; m* 1966, Mme Paule Reboul, *er d* of Count Nicholas Debane, and *widow* of M. Gabriel Reboul. *Educ:* Monkton House Sch., Cardiff; Ratcliffe Coll., near Leicester; also privately. Solicitor, admitted 1919. Served European War, 1914-18, with Inns of Court OTC (Cav.) RFA and RFC; War of 1939-45: Comd 21st Bn (Glam.) Home Guard, Lt-Col. Deputy Lord Mayor of Cardiff, 1945-46, 1960-61, 1969-70, 1971-72, Lord Mayor, 1975-76; Past Chm., Cardiff Transport Cttee. Past Chm. and Life Vice-Pres., Wales Conservative Area Council; Patron, Wales Conservative Club Council; Life Vice-Pres. Assoc. of Cons. Clubs, England and Wales (Badge of Honour); Former Mem. Executive Cttee, Nat. Union of Conservative and Unionist Associations, and Mem. various local Cons. organisations; Pres., Cardiff W Young Conservatives; formerly Mem., Cardiff City Council and Alderman; Mem. Grand Council, Primrose League; Ruling Councillor, Ninian Stuart Habitation Primrose League; Pres., Cardiff West Conservative and Unionist Association; Contested (C) Central Div. Cardiff July 1945 and Cardiff W Div. Feb. 1950. Former Nat. Vice-Pres. Royal British Legion; now Patron, Wales. Past Pres., Cardiff and District Law Society; Vice-Pres., Cardiff Law Students Soc. Vice-President: Cardiff Business Club; BLESMA; Cardiff Central (OCA) Rifle Club; Past Captain, Cardiff Municipal Golfing Soc. Hon. Mem., Cardiff 2000; Hon. Rotarian, Cardiff. Past Member Court of Governors: Nat. Museum of Wales; Univ. of Wales; Ex-officio Mem., Court, UWIST; Governor, St Illtyd's Coll., Cardiff; Representative Governor for Cardiff and District Law Soc., Univ. of Wales; Chm. of Governors, Monkton House Cardiff Educn Trust Ltd. President: Old Monktonians Cardiff Assoc.; Salisbury Constitutional Club, Newport; Past Pres., S Wales Kennel Assoc.; Vice-Pres., The Rest (seaside) Convalescent Home, Porthcawl. Patron, S Wales Br., Soc. for Protection of Unborn Children. KCSG. OStJ. Hon. Citizen, Minneapolis City, Minn. *Address:* Twin Gables, 9 Cefn Coed Road, Cardiff. *T:* Cardiff 751252. *Clubs:* County (Cardiff);

Royal Porthcawl (Glam).
See also Sir A. L. Hallinan.

HALLINAN, Sir Eric, Kt 1955; *b* 27 Oct. 1900; *s* of Edward Hallinan, Midleton, Co. Cork, and Elizabeth, *d* of Maj.-Gen. Sir Thomas Dennehy; *m* 1936, Monica, *d* of George Waters, Midleton, Co. Cork; one *s* one *d. Educ:* Downside; Trinity Coll., Dublin. BA, LLB Dublin, 1924; Barrister-at-Law (King's Inns, 1923; Gray's Inn, 1927). Practised at Irish Bar, 1924-29. Colonial Administrative Service, Nigeria, 1930-36; Colonial Legal Service, Nigeria, 1936-40; Attorney-Gen., Bahamas, 1940-44; Puisne Judge: Trinidad, 1944-48; Nigeria, 1948-52; Chief Justice, Cyprus, 1952-57; Chief Justice of The West Indies, 1958-61; Justice of Appeal, Bahamas and Bermuda, 1966-68. LLD (*jure dig.*) Dublin, 1958. *Address:* Irlandaluz, El Cuartón, Tarifa (Cádiz), Spain. *Club:* Royal Commonwealth Society.

HALLINAN, Sir Lincoln; *see* Hallinan, Sir A. L.

HALLOWES, Odette Marie Celine, GC 1946; MBE 1945; Légion d'Honneur, 1950; Vice-President, Women's Transport Services (FANY); Member Royal Society of St George; housewife; *b* 28 April 1912; *d* of Gaston Brailly, Croix-de-Guerre, Médaille Militaire; *m* 1931, Roy Sansom (decd); three *d*; *m* 1947, late Captain Peter Churchill, DSO; *m* 1956, Geoffrey Macleod Hallowes. *Educ:* The Convent of Ste Thérèse, Amiens (France) and privately. Entered Special Forces and landed in France, 1942; worked as British agent until capture by Gestapo, 1943; sentenced to death June 1943; endured imprisonment and torture until 28 April 1945, when left Ravensbrück Concentration Camp (MBE, GC). Member: Military Medallists League (Vice-Pres.) Cttee, Victoria Cross and George Cross Assoc. Pres., 282 (East Ham) Air Cadet Sqdn. *Recreations:* reading, travelling, cooking, trying to learn patience. *Address:* West Mount, West Road, St George's Hill, Weybridge, Surrey KT13 0LZ. *Clubs:* FANY, Special Forces.

HALLOWS, Ralph Ingham, CMG 1973; MBE 1947; retired from Bank of England, 1973; *b* 4 May 1913; *s* of Ralph Watson Hallows, MA Cantab, TD, and Muriel Milnes-Smith; *m* 1939, Anne Lorna Bond; one *s* one *d. Educ:* Berkhamsted Sch. Indian Police Service, 1932; Indian Political Service, 1937; Indian Office/Commonwealth Relations Office, 1947; Kuwait Oil Co., 1948; Bank of England, 1954. Specialist Adv. to Select Cttee on Overseas Develt, 1974-. *Recreations:* golf, fishing, sailing. *Address:* Apple Tree Cottage, Thursley Road, Elstead, Surrey. *T:* Elstead 2284.

HALLPIKE, Charles Skinner, CBE 1958; FRS 1956; FRCP, FRCS; *b* 19 July 1900; *s* of Frank Robert Hallpike and Rosamund Helen Skinner; *m* 1935, Barbara Lee Anderson; two *s* one *d. Educ:* St Paul's Sch., W14; Guy's Hospital, SE1 (Entrance Schol. in Arts and Beaney Prizeman in Pathology); MB, BS London 1926; FRCS 1931; FRCP 1945. William J. Mickle Fellow, London Univ., 1941; Dalby Prizeman, 1943, Gamble Prizeman, 1934 and 1947, Hughlings Jackson Memorial Lecturer and Medallist, 1967, Royal Society of Medicine; Bárány Medallist, Univ. of Uppsala, 1958; Guyot Medallist, Univ. of Groningen, 1959. House Surg., Aural Depts Guy's Hosp. and Cheltenham Gen. Hosp., 1924-27; Bernhard Baron Research Fellow, Ferens Inst. of Otology, Middx Hosp., 1929; Duveen Travelling Student, Univ. of London, 1930; Rockefeller Travelling Fellow, 1931; Foulerton Research Fellow, Royal Society, 1934; Mem. Scientific Staff, Med. Research Council, 1940; Aural Physician and Dir of Otological Research Unit, of Medical Research Council, National Hosp. for Nervous Diseases, Queen Square, WC1, 1944-65, now Hon. Aural Physician; Dir of Research, Ferens Inst. of Otolaryngology, Middlesex Hosp., 1965-68. Mem. Collegium Otorhinolaryngologicum Amicitiae Sacrum (Shambaugh Prizeman, 1955); Hon. Fellow Royal Academy of Medicine, Ireland; FRSocMed (Hon. Sec. 1938, and Editorial Rep., 1946-52, Pres., 1965, Hon. Mem., 1970, Sect. Otol.); Mem. Flying Personnel Research Cttee, 1938-55. *Publications:* papers on otology, physiology, and pathology of the ear in Proc. Royal Society, Jl Physiology, Jl Pathology, Jl Laryngology and Otology, etc. *Address:* Fern Lodge, Ashurst Road, West Moors, Wimborne, Dorset BH22 0LS. *T:* Ferndown 874418.

HALLSTEIN, Walter; (Professor and Doctor); Grand Cross of Merit, Federal Republic of Germany; President, Commission of the European Economic Community, 1958-67; President, European Movement (international); *b* Mainz, Germany, 17 Nov. 1901; *s* of Jakob Hallstein and Anna Hallstein (*née* Geibel); unmarried. *Educ:* Humanistisches Gymnasium, Darmstadt and Mainz; Bonn, Munich and Berlin Univs. Doctorate of Law, University of Berlin. Prof, Rostock Univ., 1930-41; Prof., 1941-, Dir, 1941-44, Inst. for Comparative Law, Frankfort; Rector,

Frankfort Univ., 1946-48; Visiting Prof., Georgetown Univ., Washington, DC, USA; Pres., German Unesco activities, 1949-50; Head, German Schumanplan delegn, Paris, 1950; Staatssekretär: Federal Chancellery, 1950; German Foreign Office, 1951-58. Mem., Bundestag, 1969-72. Adviser, Action Cttee for the United States of Europe, 1969-. Holds eighteen hon. doctorates. Grand Cross of 26 foreign orders, etc.; International Charlemagne Prize of City of Aix-la-Chapelle, 1961; Robert Schuman Prize, 1969. *Publications:* Die Aktienrechte der Gegenwart, 1931; Die Berichtigung des Gesellschaftskapitals, 1942; Wiederherstellung des Privatrechts, 1946; Wissenschaft und Politik, 1949; United Europe-Challenge and Opportunity, 1962; Der unvollendete Bundesstaat, 1969; Europe in the Making, 1972; Die Europäische Gemeinschaft, 1973. *Recreation:* travelling. *Address:* 5439 Rennerod/Oberwesterwaldkreis, Germany; (office) D7 Stuttgart 1, Klopstockstrasse 29, Germany.

HALLSWORTH, Prof. Ernest Gordon, DSc, FRIC, FTS; Chairman, Land Resources Laboratories, Commonwealth Scientific and Industrial Research Organisation, Adelaide, since 1973 (Chief of Division of Soils, CSIRO, 1964-73); *b* 1913; *s* of Ernest and Beatrice Hallsworth, Ashton-under-Lyne, Lancs; *m* 1943, Elaine Gertrude Seddon (*d* 1970), *d* of R. C. Weatherill, Waverley, NSW; two *s* one *d* and one step *s*; *m* 1976, Merrily Ramly; one step *d. Educ:* Ashton Grammar Sch., Ashton-under-Lyne, Lancs; Univ. of Leeds. University of Leeds: First Cl. Hons in Agric. Chem., Sir Swire Smith Fellow, 1936; Asst Lectr in Agric. Chem., 1936; PhD 1939; DSc 1964. Lectr in Agric. Chem., Univ. of Sydney, 1939; Prof. of Soil Science, Univ. of West Australia, 1960-61; Prof. of Agric. Chem. and Head Dept Agric. Sci., Univ. Nottingham, 1951-64 (Dean, Faculty of Agric. and Hort., 1951-60). Pres. Lecturers' Assoc., Sydney Univ., 1946-49. Treas., Aust. Assoc. of Scientific Workers, 1943; Member: Science Advisory Panel, Australian Broadcasting Commn, 1949-51; Pasture Improvement Cttee, Australian Dairy Produce Bd (NSW), 1948-51; Chm. Insecticides and Fungicides Cttee, Australian Standards Inst., 1949-51. President: Internat. Soc. of Soil Science, 1964-68; Sect. 13, Aust. and NZ Assoc. for the Advancement of Science, 1976. Mem. Council, Flinders Univ., 1967-; Chief Scientific Liaison Officer (Aust.), London, 1971. Fellow, Aust. Acad. of Technol Scis, 1976. *Publications:* (Ed) Nutrition of the Legumes, 1958; (ed with D. V. Crawford) Experimental Pedology, 1964; (with others) Handbook of Australian Soils, 1968; contributions to: Aust. Jl Science, Jl Soc. Chem. Indust., Empire Jl Experimental Agric., Jl Agric. Science, Aust. Medical Jl, Jl Soil Science. *Recreations:* talking, pedology. *Address:* 30 Fowlers Road, Glen Osmond, SA 5064, Australia. *T:* 796318. *Clubs:* Farmers'; Commonwealth (Canberra).

HALLWARD, Bertrand Leslie, MA; *b* 24 May 1901; *er s* of late N. L. Hallward, Indian Educational Service, and Evelyn A. Gurdon; *m* 1926, Catherine Margaret, 2nd *d* of late Canon A. J. Tait; four *d. Educ:* Haileybury Coll. (Scholar); King's Coll., Cambridge (Scholar). Fellow of Peterhouse, 1923-39. Hon. Fellow 1956. Headmaster of Clifton Coll., 1939-48; Vice-Chancellor, Nottingham Univ., 1948-65. Hon. LLD: Sheffield, 1964; Nottingham, 1965. *Publications:* Chapters II, III, IV, and part of VII (the Second and Third Punic Wars) in Cambridge Ancient History, Vol. VIII, 1930; Editor of the Classical Quarterly, 1935-39. *Recreation:* gardening. *Address:* 52 Saxmundham Road, Aldeburgh, Suffolk. *T:* Aldeburgh 2667.
See also W. O. Chadwick, G. C. H. Spafford.

HALMOS, Prof. Paul; Professor of Sociology, The Open University, since 1974; *b* 19 Dec. 1911; *s* of Maurice Halmos and Ethel Soós; *m* 1st, 1937, Edith Halmos (*née* Molnár); one *s*; 2nd, 1972, Ena Edwards. *Educ:* Budapest, Hungary (Dr Jur 1935); London (BA 1945, PhD 1950). Lectr in Social Psychology, SW Essex Technical Coll., 1947-56; Lectr, Sen. Lectr, Tutor in Charge of Social Studies, Univ. of Keele, 1956-65; Prof. of Sociology, University Coll., Cardiff, Univ. of Wales, 1965-74. Distinguished Vis. Prof., Wayne State Univ., USA, 1972. *Publications:* Solitude and Privacy, 1952; Towards a Measure of Man, 1957; The Faith of the Counsellors, 1965; The Personal Service Society, 1970; The Personal and the Political, 1978; (ed) Sociological Review Monographs, 1958-74; (ed) Sociology and Social Welfare Series, 1966-. *Recreations:* philately, painting, mosaics. *Address:* The Open University, Walton Hall, Milton Keynes MK7 6AA.

HALPERN, Prof. Jack, FRS 1974; Louis Block Professor of Chemistry, University of Chicago, since 1962; *b* Poland, 19 Jan. 1925 (moved to Canada, 1929; USA 1962); *s* of Philip Halpern and Anna Sass; *m* 1949, Helen Peritz; two *d. Educ:* McGill Univ., Montreal. BSc 1946, PhD 1949. NRC Postdoc. Fellow, Univ. of Manchester, 1949-50; Prof. of Chem., Univ. of Brit.

Columbia, 1950-62 (Nuffield Foundn Travelling Fellow, Cambridge Univ., 1959-60); Prof. of Chem., Univ. of Chicago, 1962-71, Louis Block Prof., 1971-. Visiting Prof.: Univ. of Minnesota, 1962; Harvard Univ., 1966-67; California Inst. of Techn., 1969; Princeton Univ., 1970-71; Lectureships: 3M Lectr, Univ. of Minnesota, 1968; FMC Lectr, Princeton Univ., 1969; Du Pont Lectr, Univ. of Calif., Berkeley, 1970; Frontier of Chemistry Lectr, Case Western Reserve Univ., 1971; Venable Lectr, Univ. of N Carolina, 1973. Associate Editor: Jl of Amer. Chem. Soc.; Inorganica Chimica Acta; Mem. Editorial Bds: Accounts of Chemical Research; Jl of American Chemical Soc.; Jl of Catalysis; Catalysis Reviews; Jl of Coordination Chem.; Inorganica Chimica Acta; Inorganic Syntheses; Jl of Molecular Catalysis. Mem. Bd of Trustees, Gordon Research Confs, 1968-70; Chm., Gordon Conf. on Inorganic Chem., 1969; Chm., Amer. Chemical Soc. Div. of Inorganic Chem., 1971. Fellow, Amer. Acad. of Arts and Sciences, 1967. Holds several honours and awards, including: Amer. Chem. Soc. Award in Inorganic Chem., 1968; Chem. Soc. Award, 1976; Humboldt Award, 1977. *Publications:* Editor (with F. Basolo and J. Bunnett) Collected Accounts of Transition Metal Chemistry, vol. I, 1973, vol. II, 1977; contrib. articles on Catalysis and on Coordination Compounds to Encyclopaedia Britannica; numerous articles to Jl of Amer. Chemical Soc. and other scientific jls. *Recreations:* art, music. *Address:* Department of Chemistry, University of Chicago, Chicago, Illinois 60637, USA. *T:* (312) 753-8271. *Club:* Quadrangle (Chicago).

HALPIN, Most Rev. Charles A.; *see* Regina, Archbishop of, (RC).

HALPIN, Miss Kathleen Mary, CBE 1953 (OBE 1941); Chief Administrator, Regions, WRVS (formerly WVS), 1945-73; *b* 19 Nov. 1903; unmarried. *Educ:* Sydenham High Sch. (GPDST). Organising Sec., Women's Gas Council, 1935, and represented Gas Industry at International Management Congress, Washington, USA, 1936, Sweden, 1947. Appointed Chief of Metropolitan Dept, WVS, 1939; lent to Min. of Health and went to Washington as UK representative on Standing Technical Cttee on Welfare, UNRRA; Comr, Trainer, and Camp Adviser, Girl Guides Assoc., 1924-48; Comdt, BRCS, 1937-39; Mem. Council London Hostels Assoc., 1941-; Chm. Women's Gas Fedn, 1945-49, Pres., 1949-60. A Governor of St Bartholomew's Hospital, 1948-74; President Fedn of Soroptomist Clubs of Gt Britain and Ireland, 1959-60. Trustee, Fawcett Library. OStJ. *Recreations:* motoring, reading, theatre. *Address:* 7 Chagford House, Chagford Street, NW1 6EG. *T:* 01-262 6226.

HALSBURY, 3rd Earl of, *cr* 1898; **John Anthony Hardinge Giffard,** FRS 1969; Baron Halsbury, 1885; Viscount Tiverton, 1898; Consultant Director: The Distillers Co. Ltd; Chairman Committee of Institute of Cancer Research, Royal Cancer Hospital, since 1962; Chancellor of Brunel University, since 1966; Chairman, Meteorological Committee, since 1970; *b* 4 June 1908; *o s* of 2nd Earl and Esmé (*d* 1973), *d* of late James Stewart Wallace; *S* father, 1943; *m* 1st, 1930, Ismay Catherine, *er d* of late Lord Ninian Crichton-Stuart and Hon. Mrs Archibald Maule Ramsay; one *s*; 2nd, 1936, Elizabeth Adeline Faith, *o d* of late Major Harry Crewe Godley, DSO, Northamptonshire Regt and of late Mrs Godley, of Claremont Lodge, Cheltenham; two *d*. *Educ:* Eton. Man. Dir, Nat. Research Development Corporation, 1949-59; External Examiner, OECD, on mission to Japan, 1965. Chairman: Science Museum Advisory Council, 1951-65; Cttee on Decimal Currency, 1961-63; Review Body on Doctors' and Dentists' Pay, 1971-74; Deptl Cttee of Enquiry into pay of Nurses, Midwives and Professions Supplementary to Medicine, 1974-75; President: Institution of Production Engineers, 1957-59; Nat. Inst. of Industrial Psychol., 1963-75; Machine Tool Industry Res. Assoc., 1964-77; Member: Adv. Council to Cttee of Privy Council for Scientific Research, 1949-54; SRC, 1965-69; Computer Bd for Univs and Research Councils, 1966-69; Decimal Currency Bd, 1966-71; Nationalised Transport Advisory Council, 1963-67; Standing Commn on Museums and Galleries, 1960-76; MRC, 1973-; Cttee of Managers, Royal Institution, 1976-. A Governor: BBC, 1960-62; LSE, 1959-; UMIST, 1966- (formerly Mem. Council, Manchester Coll. of Sci. and Technol., 1956-65). Hon. FICE, 1975. Hon. DTech Brunel Univ., 1966; Hon. DUniv Essex, 1968. *Heir: s* Viscount Tiverton, *qv*. *Address:* 4 Campden House, 29 Sheffield Terrace, W8. *T:* 01-727 3035. *Clubs:* Athenæum, Royal Automobile.

HALSEY, Dr Albert Henry; Director, Department of Social and Administrative Studies, University of Oxford, since 1962; Professorial Fellow of Nuffield College, Oxford, since 1962; *b* 13 April 1923; *m* 1949, Gertrude Margaret Littler; three *s* two *d*. *Educ:* Kettering Grammar Sch.; London Sch. of Econs. BSc (Econ), PhD London, MA Oxon. RAF, 1942-47; student LSE,

1947-52; Research Worker, Liverpool Univ., 1952-54; Lectr in Sociology, Birmingham Univ., 1954-62. Fellow, Center for Advanced Study of Behavioral Sciences, Palo Alto, Calif, 1956-57; Vis. Prof. of Sociology, Univ. of Chicago, 1959-60. Adviser to Sec. of State for Educn, 1965-68; Chm. of CERI at OECD, Paris, 1968-70. Reith Lectr, 1977. Foreign Associate, Amer. Acad. of Educn. *Publications:* (jtly) Social Class and Educational Opportunity, 1956; (jtly) Technical Change and Industrial Relations, 1956; (with J. E. Floud) The Sociology of Education, Current Sociology VII, 1958; (jtly) Education, Economy and Society, 1961; Ability and Educational Opportunity, 1962; (with G. N. Ostergaard) Power in Co-operatives, 1965; (with Ivor Crewe) Social Survey of the Civil Service, 1969; (with Martin Trow) The British Academics, 1971; (ed) Trends in British Society since 1900, 1972; (ed) Educational Priority, 1972; Traditions of Social Policy, 1976; numerous articles and reviews. *Address:* 28 Upland Park Road, Oxford. *T:* Oxford 58625.

HALSEY, Rt. Rev. Henry David; *see* Carlisle, Bishop of.

HALSEY, Rev. John Walter Brooke, 4th Bt *cr* 1920 (but uses designation Brother John Halsey); *b* 26 Dec. 1933; *s* of Sir Thomas Edgar Halsey, 3rd Bt, DSO, and of Jean Margaret Palmer, *d* of late Bertram Willes Dayrell Brooke; *S* father, 1970. *Educ:* Eton; Magdalene College, Cambridge (BA 1957). Deacon, 1961, priest, 1962, Diocese of York; Curate of Stocksbridge, 1961-65; Brother in community of the Transfiguration, 1965-. *Heir: uncle* William Edmund Halsey [*b* 8 Jan. 1903; *m* 1931, Barbara Dorothea, *d* of late Charles Lindsay Orr Ewing; one *d* (one *s* decd)]. *Address:* Community of the Transfiguration, Manse Road, Roslin, Midlothian.

HALSEY, Reginald John, CMG 1957; BScEng; FCGI; DIC; CEng; FIEE; *b* 16 Dec. 1902; *s* of Edwin J. Halsey, Portsmouth; *m* 1930, Edna May Tonkin; one *d*. *Educ:* Secondary Sch. and HM Dockyard Sch., Portsmouth; Imperial Coll. of Science and Technology. Entered Post Office, 1927, and engaged on research in telecommunications; Asst Engineer-in-Chief, 1953-58; Dir of Research, 1958-64. Dir, Cable and Wireless Ltd., 1959-73. Chm., Adv. Cttee on Telecommunications, CGLI, 1957-. Hon. Mem., CGLI, 1972. Fellow of Imperial Coll., 1965. *Publications:* many scientific and engineering. *Address:* 12 Oakridge Avenue, Radlett, Herts WD7 8EP. *T:* Radlett 6488.

HALSTEAD, Ronald, CBE 1976; Chairman, Beecham Products, since 1967; Managing Director (Consumer Products), Beecham Group Ltd, since 1973; *b* 17 May 1927; *s* of Richard and Bessie Harrison Halstead; *m* 1968, Yvonne Cecile de Monchaux; two *s*. *Educ:* Lancaster Royal Grammar Sch.; Queens' Coll., Cambridge. MA, BSc, FRIC. Research Chemist, H. P. Bulmer & Co, 1948-53; Manufg Manager, Macleans Ltd, 1954-55; Factory Manager, Beecham Products Inc. (USA), 1955-60; Asst Managing Dir, Beecham Research Labs, 1960-62; Vice-Pres. (Marketing), Beecham Products Inc. (USA), 1962-64; Pres., Beecham Research Labs Inc. (USA), 1962-64; Chm., Food and Drink Div., Beecham Group Ltd, 1964-67. Mem. Egg Re-organisation Commn, 1967-68; Pres., Incorp. Soc. of Brit. Advertisers, 1971-73; Chairman: British Nutrition Foundn, 1970-73; Proprietary Assoc. of GB, 1968-; Vice-Chairman: Advertising Assoc., 1973-; Food and Drink Industries Council, 1973-76; Council Mem. and Exec. Cttee Mem., Food Manufrs' Fedn Inc., 1966- (Pres., 1974-76); Council Member: British Nutrition Foundn, 1967-; CBI, 1970-; BIM, 1972-; Bd Mem., Nat. Coll. of Food Technol., 1977-. Mem., Cambridge Univ. Appts Bd, 1969-73; Governor, Ashridge Management Coll., 1970-. FBIM, FInstM. *Recreations:* sailing, squash racquets, ski-ing. *Address:* 37 Edwardes Square, W8 6HH. *T:* 01-603 9010. *Clubs:* Hurlingham, Junior Carlton, Lansdowne, Royal Thames Yacht.

HALSTED, Maj.-Gen. John Gregson, CB 1940; OBE; MC; *b* 16 Aug. 1890; 2nd Lieut Loyal Regt, 1910; Capt., 1915; Bt Major, 1919; Major, 1928; Bt Lieut-Col, 1931; Lieut-Col, 1935; Col, 1937; Maj.-Gen., 1941; served European War, 1914-18 (wounded twice, despatches twice, Bt Major, MC); Palestine, 1936-39 (despatches, OBE); War of 1939-45 (CB), France 1939-40; MGA 1941; Vice-QMG, War Office, 1945; retired pay, 1946. *Address:* c/o Lloyds Bank, Woodbridge, Suffolk. *Club:* Naval and Military.

HAM, Rear-Adm. John Dudley Nelson, CB 1955; RN retired; *b* 7 Sept. 1902; *s* of Eng. Rear-Adm. John William Ham and Lily Frances Nelson; *m* 1927, Margery Lyne Sandercock; no *c*. *Educ:* Edinburgh House, Lee-on-Solent; RN Colleges, Osborne and Dartmouth. Junior Service, 1920-37; HMS Ramillies, HMS Ceres; staff of RN Engineering College; Destroyers; Commander, 1937; Engineer Officer, Yangtse, China, 1938-40;

served War of 1939-45: Chief Engineer, HMS Danae, 1940-41; Asst Dir Combined Operations Material, 1942; Chief Engineer, HMS Indomitable, 1945; Capt., 1946; Fleet Engineer Officer, Home Fleet, 1949; Staff Air Engineer Officer, 1951; Rear-Admiral, 1953; Dir of Aircraft Maintenance and Repair, 1953-55; Flag Officer Reserve Aircraft, 1955-57, retired. *Recreations:* golf, cabinet-making. *Address:* Green Lane Cottage, Lee-on-Solent, Hants. *T:* Lee-on-Solent 550660.

HAMBIDGE, Rt. Rev. Douglas Walter; *see* Caledonia, Bishop of.

HAMBLEDEN, 4th Viscount, *cr* 1891; **William Herbert Smith;** *b* 2 April 1930; *e s* of 3rd Viscount and Lady Patricia Herbert, DCVO 1953, *o d* of 15th Earl of Pembroke, MVO; *S* father 1948; *m* 1955, Donna Maria Carmela Attolico di Adelfia, *d* of late Count Bernardo Attolico and of Contessa Eleonora Attolico di Adelfia, Via Porta Latina, Rome; five *s*. *Educ:* Eton. *Heir: s* Hon. William Henry Bernard Smith, *b* 18 Nov. 1955. *Address:* The Manor House, Hambleden, Henley-on-Thames, Oxon. *TA:* Hambleden. *T:* Hambleden 335.
See also Baron Margadale .

HAMBLING, Sir (Herbert) Hugh, 3rd Bt, *cr* 1924; *b* 3 Aug. 1919; *s* of Sir (Herbert) Guy (Musgrave) Hambling, 2nd Bt; *S* father 1966; *m* 1950, Anne Page Oswald, Spokane, Washington, USA; one *s*. *Educ:* Wixenford Preparatory Sch.; Eton Coll. British Airways Ltd, 1937-39. RAF Training and Atlantic Ferry Command, 1939-46. British Overseas Airways: Montreal, 1948; Seattle, 1950; Manager, Sir Guy Hambling & Son, 1956. *Heir: s* Herbert Peter Hugh Hambling, *b* 6 Sept. 1953. *Address:* 1219 Evergreen Point Road, Bellevue, Washington 98004, USA. *T:* GL4 0905 (USA); Rookery Park, Yoxford, Suffolk, England. *T:* Yoxford 310.

HAMBRO, Charles Eric Alexander; Chairman, Hambros Bank Ltd, 1972; *b* 24 July 1930; *s* of late Sir Charles Hambro, KBE, MC, and Pamela Cobbold; *m* 1st, 1954, Evelyn (marr. diss., 1976), *d* of Sir Richard Cotterell, Bt, *qv* ; two *s* one *d* ; 2nd, 1976, Cherry Twiss, *d* of Sir John Huggins, GCMG, MC. *Educ:* Eton. 2nd Lieut Coldstream Guards, 1949-51; joined Hambros Bank Ltd, 1952: Man. Dir 1957; Dep. Chm. 1965; Vice-Chm., Guardian Royal Exchange Assurance; Chm., Hambro Corporation of Canada. Chm., Royal National Pension Fund for Nurses, 1968. *Recreations:* shooting, cricket, flying. *Address:* Dixton Manor, Gotherington, Cheltenham, Glos GL52 4RB. *T:* Bishops Cleeve 2011. *Clubs:* White's, MCC.

HAMBRO, Jocelyn Olaf, MC 1944; Chairman, Hambros Ltd, since 1970; Managing Director, Hambros Bank Ltd, 1947-72, and Chairman, 1965-72; Director: Phœnix Assurance Co. Ltd; Charter Consolidated Ltd; Diamond Development Co. Ltd; Christies; *b* 7 March 1919; *s* of late Ronald Olaf Hambro and late Winifred Martin-Smith; *m* 1st, 1942, Ann Silvia (*d* 1972), *d* of R. H. Muir; three *s*; 2nd, 1976, Margaret Elisabeth, *d* of late Frederick Bradshaw McConnel and *widow* of 9th Duke of Roxburghe. *Educ:* Eton; Trinity Coll., Cambridge. Coldstream Guards, 1939-45. Hambros Bank Ltd, 1945. *Recreations:* racing, shooting. *Address:* Redenham Park, Andover, Hants. *T:* Weyhill 2511; 16 Victoria Road, W8. *Clubs:* Jockey, Pratt's, White's.

HAMBURGER, Michael Peter Leopold, MA (Oxon); *b* Berlin, 22 March 1924; *e s* of late Prof. Richard Hamburger and Mrs L. Hamburger (*née* Hamburg); *m* 1951, Anne Ellen File; one *s* two *d*. *Educ:* Westminster Sch.; Christ Church, Oxford. Army Service, 1943-47; Freelance Writer, 1948-52; Asst Lectr in German, UCL, 1952-55; Lectr, then Reader in German, Univ. of Reading, 1955-64. Florence Purington Lectr, Mount Holyoke Coll., Mass, 1966-67; Visiting Professor, State Univ. of NY: at Buffalo, 1969; at Stony Brook, 1971; Vis. Fellow, Center for Humanities, Wesleyan Univ., Conn, 1970; Vis. Prof. Univ. of S Carolina, 1973; Regent's Lectr, Univ. of California, San Diego, 1973; Vis. Prof., Boston Univ., 1975-77. Bollingen Foundn Fellow, 1959-61, 1965-66. FRSL 1972. Corresp. Mem., Deutsche Akademie für Sprache und Dichtung, Darmstadt, 1973; Akademie der Künste, Berlin; Akad. der Schönen Künste, Munich. Translation Prizes: Deutsche Akademie für Sprache und Dichtung, Darmstadt, 1964; Arts Council, 1969; Arts Prize, Inter Nationes, Bonn, 1976; Medal, Inst. of Linguistics, 1977. *Publications: poetry:* Flowering Cactus, 1950; Poems 1950-1951, 1952; The Dual Site, 1958; Weather and Season, 1963; Feeding the Chickadees, 1968; Penguin Modern Poets, (with A. Brownjohn and C. Tomlinson) 1969; Travelling, 1969; Travelling, I-V, 1973; Ownerless Earth, 1973; Travelling VI, 1975; Real Estate, 1977; Moralities, 1977; *translations:* Poems of Hölderlin, 1943, rev. edn as Hölderlin: Poems, 1952; C. Baudelaire, Twenty Prose Poems, 1946, repr. 1968; J. C. F. Hölderlin, Selected Verse, 1961; G. Trakl, Decline, 1952; A.

Goes, The Burnt Offering, 1956; (with others) H. von Hofmannsthal, Poems and Verse Plays, 1961; (with C. Middleton) Modern German Poetry 1910-1960, 1962; (with others) H. von Hofmannsthal, Selected Plays and Libretti, 1964; B. Brecht, Tales from the Calendar, 1961; G. Büchner, Lenz, 1966; (with J. Rothenberg and the author) H. M. Enzensberger, The Poems of Hans Magnus Enzensberger, 1968; H. M. Enzensberger, Poems, 1966; H. M. Enzensberger, Poems For People Who Don't Read Poems, 1968; (with C. Middleton) G. Grass, Selected Poems, 1966; (with C. Middleton), G. Grass, The Poems of Gunter Grass, 1969; L. van Beethoven, Letters, Journals and Conversations, 1951, repr. 1967; J. C. F. Hölderlin, Poems and Fragments, 1967; P. Bichsel, And Really Frau Blum Would Very Much Like To Meet The Milkman, 1968; G. Eich, Journeys, 1968; N. Sachs, Selected Poems, 1968; Peter Bichsel, Stories for Children, 1971; Paul Celan, Selected Poems, 1972; (ed) East German Poetry, 1972; Peter Huchel: Selected Poems, 1974; German Poetry 1910-1975, 1977; Helmut Heissenbüttel: Texts, 1977; *criticism:* Reason and Energy, 1957; From Prophecy to Exorcism, 1965; The Truth of Poetry, 1970; Hugo von Hofmannsthal, 1973; Art as Second Nature, 1975; *autobiography:* A Mug's Game, 1973. *Recreations:* gardening, tennis, walking. *Address:* c/o Williams & Glyn's Bank Ltd, Kirkland House, Whitehall, SW1.
See also P. B. Hamlyn.

HAMBURGER, Sidney Cyril, CBE 1966; JP; Member, Supplementary Benefits Commission, 1967-77; Chairman, North Western Regional Health Authority, since 1973; *b* 14 July 1914; *s* of Isidore and Hedwig Hamburger; *m* 1940; three *s*. *Educ:* Salford Grammar Sch. Served in Army, 1940-46, Capt. Salford City Council: Mem., 1946-70; Alderman, 1961-70; Mayor of Salford, 1968-69. Chairman: NE Manchester Hosp. Management Cttee, 1970-74; Mem., Manchester Regional Hosp. Bd, 1966-74 (Chm. Finance Cttee). Mem., BBC NW Adv. Cttee, 1970-73. Pres. Council, Manchester-Salford Jews, 1962-65; Life-President: Manchester Jewish Homes for the Aged, 1965-; Zionist Central Council of Greater Manchester. JP Salford, 1957. *Recreation:* football. *Address:* 26 New Hall Road, Salford M7 0JU.

HAMER, Jean; *see* Rhys, Jean.

HAMER, John, MBE 1944; Secretary, Royal Horticultural Society, 1962-75; *b* 14 June 1910; 2nd *s* of late John and Katherine Hamer; *m* 1940, Marjorie Agnes Martin (*d* 1970); one *s* one *d*. *Educ:* University of Leeds (BA). Asst Master, 1932-39. War Service, 1939-46 (despatches, MBE): The Loyal Regt, Royal Tank Regt, Combined Operations, 1943-45; Lieut-Col; Controller of Supplies, Singapore, 1945. Joined Malayan Civil Service, 1946: District Officer, Jasin 1948, Klang 1952; British Adviser, Perlis, 1955; Deputy Chm., Rural Industrial Development Authority, Federation of Malaya, 1957; Ministry of Agriculture, 1958; State Sec., Penang, 1958-61. Joined Royal Horticultural Soc., 1961. *Recreation:* gardening. *Address:* Wildacres, Itchingfield, West Sussex RH13 7NZ. *T:* Slinfold 790467.

HAMER, Hon. Rupert James, ED; MLA; Premier of Victoria, Australia, also Treasurer and Minister of the Arts, since 1972; *b* 29 July 1916; *s* of H. R. Hamer, Wolverhampton, England; *m* 1944, April F., *d* of N. R. Mackintosh; two *s* two *d*. *Educ:* Melbourne Grammar and Geelong Grammar Schs; Trinity Coll., Univ. of Melbourne (LLM). Solicitor, admitted 1940. Served War of 1939-45: 5½ years, AIF, Tobruk, Alamein, NG, Normandy. Chief Sec. and Dep. Premier, Victoria, 1971-72; Minister for Immigration, 1962-64, for Local Govt, 1964-71; MLA (Lib.), Kew, Vic., 1971-; for E Yarra, 1958-71. CO, Vic. Scottish Regt, CMF, 1954-58. Pres., Keep Australia Beautiful Council. *Recreations:* tennis, golf, sailing. *Address:* 39 Monomeath Avenue, Canterbury, Victoria 3126, Australia. *Clubs:* Naval and Military; Royal Melbourne Golf.

HAMES, Jack Hamawi, QC 1972; a Recorder of the Crown Court, since 1977; *b* 15 June 1920; *s* of Elie and Edmee Hamawi; *m* 1949, Beryl Julia Cooper; two *s*. *Educ:* English School, Cairo; Queens' Coll., Cambridge (MA, LLB). Called to Bar, Inner Temple, 1948. *Publications:* Family Law, 1950; The Married Women's Property Act, 1872 (3rd edn 1971); contrib. to Solicitors' Jl. *Recreations:* squash, tennis, painting, music, poetry, history, literature. *Address:* 18 Castlemaine Avenue, South Croydon CR2 7HQ. *T:* 01-688 6326; 10 Old Square, Lincoln's Inn, WC2A 3SO. *T:* 01-405 0758. *Club:* Warlingham Squash.

HAMILL, Patrick; Chief Constable, Strathclyde Police, since 1977; *b* 29 April 1930; *s* of Hugh Hamill and Elizabeth McGowan; *m* 1954, Nellie Gillespie; four *s* one *d* . *Educ:* St

Patrick's High Sch., Dumbarton. Joined Dunbartonshire Constabulary, 1950; transf. to City of Glasgow Police, 1972; apptd Assistant Chief Constable: Glasgow, 1974; Strathclyde Police, 1975; attended Royal Coll. of Defence Studies Course, 1976. *Recreations:* walking, gardening, golf. *Address:* 173 Pitt Street, Glasgow G2 4JS. *T:* 041-204 2626.

HAMILTON, family name of **Duke of Abercorn,** and of **Barons Belhaven, Hamilton of Dalzell,** and **Holm Patrick.**

HAMILTON; *see* Baillie-Hamilton.

HAMILTON; *see* Douglas-Hamilton.

HAMILTON, 15th Duke of, *cr* 1643, Scotland, and **BRANDON,** 12th Duke of, *cr* 1711, Great Britain; **Angus Alan Douglas Douglas-Hamilton;** Premier Peer of Scotland; Hereditary Keeper of Palace of Holyroodhouse; *b* 13 Sept. 1938; *e s* of 14th Duke of Hamilton and Brandon, PC, KT, GCVO, AFC, and of Lady Elizabeth Percy, *er d* of 8th Duke of Northumberland, KG; *S* father, 1973; *m* 1972, Sarah, *d* of Sir Walter Scott, Bt, *qv*; two *d. Educ:* Eton; Balliol Coll., Oxford (BA). Engrg Flt Lieut RAF; retired, 1967. Flying Instructor, 1965; Sen. Commercial Pilot's Licence, 1967; Test Pilot, Scottish Aviation, 1971-72. KStJ 1975 (Prior, Order of St John in Scotland, 1975-). *Heir: b* Lord James (Alexander) Douglas-Hamilton, *qv*. *Address:* 8 Eccleston Mews, SW1. *T:* 01-235 7213; Lennoxlove, Haddington, E Lothian. *Clubs:* Naval and Military; New (Edinburgh).

HAMILTON, Marquess of; James Hamilton; company director; *b* 4 July 1934; *er s* of 4th Duke of Abercorn, *qv*; *m* 1966, Anastasia Alexandra, *e d* of Lt-Col Harold Phillips, Checkendon Court, Reading; one *s* one *d. Educ:* Eton Coll.; Royal Agricultural Coll., Cirencester, Glos. Joined HM Army, Oct. 1952; Lieut, Grenadier Guards. MP (UU) Fermanagh and South Tyrone, 1964-70. High Sheriff of Co. Tyrone, 1970. *Recreations:* shooting, water-ski-ing. *Heir: s* Viscount Strabane, *qv. Address:* Barons Court, Co. Tyrone, Northern Ireland. *T:* Newtown Stewart 215; 7 Upper Belgrave Street, SW1. *T:* 01-235 3161. *Clubs:* Turf, Royal Automobile.

HAMILTON OF DALZELL, 3rd Baron, *cr* 1886; **John d'Henin Hamilton,** MC 1945; JP; Lord Lieutenant of Surrey, since 1973 (Vice-Lieutenant, 1957-73); Chairman, Lord Chancellor's Advisory Committee on Legal Aid, since 1972; President, National Association of Probation Officers, 1964-74; a Lord-in-Waiting to the Queen, since 1968; *b* 1 May 1911; *s* of late Major Hon. Leslie d'Henin Hamilton, MVO, and Amy Cecile, *e d* of late Col Horace Ricardo, CVO; *S* uncle, 1952; *m* 1935, Rosemary Olive, *d* of late Major Hon. Sir John Coke, KCVO; two *s* one *d. Educ:* Eton; RMC, Sandhurst. Coldstream Guards, 1931-37 and 1939-45 (Major). Min. of Agriculture's Liaison Officer in South-East, 1960-64. Mem., Council on Tribunals, 1964-72; Chairman: Surrey Agricultural Exec. Cttee, 1958-68; Surrey Council of Social Service, 1960-73; Guildford Bench, 1968-; Guildford Cathedral Council, 1958-69. DL Surrey, 1957; JP Guildford, 1957. KStJ 1973. *Heir: s* Hon. James Leslie Hamilton [*b* 11 Feb. 1938; *m* 1967, Corinna, *yr d* of late Sir Pierson Dixon, GCMG, CB and of Lady Dixon; four *s*]. *Address:* Snowdenham House, Bramley, Guildford, Surrey. *T:* Bramley 2002.

HAMILTON, Adrian Walter, QC 1973; a Recorder of the Crown Court, since 1974; *b* 11 March 1923; *er s* of late W. G. M. Hamilton, banker, Fletching, Sussex and of late Mrs S. E. Hamilton; *m* 1966, Jill, *d* of S. R. Brimblecombe, Eastbourne; two *d. Educ:* Highgate Sch.; Balliol Coll., Oxford. BA 1st cl. Jurisprudence 1948, MA 1954. Served with RN, 1942-46: Ord. Seaman, 1942; Sub-Lt RNVR, 1943, Lieut 1946. Balliol Coll., 1946-48: Jenkyns Law Prize; Paton Mem. Student, 1948-49; Cassel Scholar, Lincoln's Inn, 1949; called to Bar, Lincoln's Inn, 1949 and Middle Temple; Mem., Senate of Inns of Court and the Bar, 1976-. *Recreations:* family, golf, sailing, gardening. *Address:* 63 Abbotsbury Road, W14 8EL. *T:* 01-603 0185. *Clubs:* Royal Automobile; Piltdown Golf.

HAMILTON, Rt. Rev. Alexander Kenneth; *see* Jarrow, Bishop Suffragan of.

HAMILTON, Anthony Norris; *b* 19 July 1913; 3rd *s* of Capt. Claude Hamilton, RD, RNR, and Kathleen Sophia Hamilton (*née* Mack); *m* 1942, Jean Philippa, 3rd *d* of Rev. David Railton, MC; one *s* three *d. Educ:* Kelly Coll.; Exeter Coll., Oxford. Asst Master Clifton Coll., 1935-40. Served War of 1939-45: commnd 6 Bn Argyll and Sutherland Highlanders, 1940; Gen. Staff, V Corps HQ, 1942, X Corps HQ 1943, VIII Army HQ, 1944. Ops Editor of VIII Army History of Italian Campaign, 1945. House

Master, Clifton Coll., 1946-48; Headmaster, Strathallan Sch., 1948-51; Headmaster, Queen Mary's Grammar Sch., Walsall, 1951-55; Headmaster, Hardye's Sch., Dorchester, 1955-74. *Recreations:* fishing, painting. *Address:* Foxbury, Gutch Common, Shaftesbury, Dorset.

HAMILTON, Sir (Charles) Denis, Kt 1976; DSO 1944; Editor-in-Chief, Times Newspapers Ltd, since 1967, Chairman since 1971, Chief Executive, 1967-70; *b* 6 Dec. 1918; *er s* of Charles and Helena Hamilton; *m* 1939, Olive, *yr d* of Thomas Hedley Wanless and Mary Anne Wanless; four *s. Educ:* Middlesbrough High Sch. Editorial Staff: Evening Gazette, Middlesbrough, 1937-38; Evening Chronicle, Newcastle, 1938-39; Editorial Asst to Viscount Kemsley, 1946-50; Editorial Dir, Kemsley (now Thomson) Newspapers, 1950-67; Editor of the Sunday Times, 1961-67. Director: Evening Gazette Ltd; Newcastle Chronicle and Journal Ltd; Times Newspapers Ltd; Thomson Organisation Ltd; Reuters, Ltd. Chm., British Cttee, Internat. Press Inst., 1972-; Member: Council, Newspaper Publishers' Association; Press Council; National Council for the Training of Journalists (Chm., 1957); BOTB, 1976-; Adv. Cttee on Appointment of Advertising Agents, 1976-; Trustee of British Museum, 1969-; British Library Bd, 1975-; Chm., British Museum Publications Ltd; Governor, British Inst. Florence, 1974-. Served War of 1939-45, TA, Durham Light Infantry; Lt-Col comdg 11th Bn Durham LI and 7th Bn Duke of Wellington's Regt. Hon. DLitt Southampton, 1975. Grande Officiale, Order of Merit (Italy), 1976. *Publications:* Jt Editor, Kemsley Manual of Journalism, 1952; Who is to own the British Press (Haldane Meml Lecture), 1976. *Recreation:* sailing. *Address:* 25 Roebuck House, Palace Street, SW1. *T:* 01-828 0410; Weston House, Nutbourne, Chichester, West Sussex. *T:* Emsworth 3351; (office) New Printing House Square, WC1X 8EZ. *Clubs:* Garrick, Grillions.

HAMILTON, Charles Keith Johnstone, MC; BA, BM Oxford; FRCP; Consulting Physician, Children's Department, Charing Cross Hospital; *b* 1890; *s* of late C. W. Hamilton, MD; *m* Christine Mary (*d* 1959), *y d* of late Ernest Durrant. *Educ:* privately; Lincoln Coll., Oxford; St Thomas' Hospital. Served European War 1914 in King Edward's Horse and Royal Field Artillery (wounded, MC); late Hon. Medical Dir Violet Melchett Infant Welfare Centre; late Consulting Paediatrician to LCC, and to Taunton and Somerset Hospital. John Temple Research Fellow, St Thomas' Hosp.; Mem., British Pædiatric Assoc. *Publications:* The Principles of Infant Nutrition (with K. Tallerman); Heart Disease in Childhood (with H. B. Russell); contributions to medical journals. *Recreations:* hunting, fishing, gardening. *Address:* Castle Farm, Exford, Som. *Club:* United Oxford & Cambridge University.

HAMILTON, Sir (Charles) William (Feilden), Kt 1974; OBE; inventor; Founder and Director, C. W. F. Hamilton & Co. Ltd and C. W. F. Hamilton Marine Ltd, Christchurch, New Zealand; *b* Ashwick Station, Fairlie, NZ, 26 July 1899; *s* of W. F. Hamilton; *m* 1923, Margery L., *d* of G. T. Wills, London; one *s* one *d. Educ:* Christ's Coll., New Zealand. Has owned Irishman Creek Station, Fairlie, 1921-; developing engineering, there, 1936; opened engrg works at Middleton, Christchurch, 1945. Inventor, in sphere of marine jet propulsion. Knighted for engineering services. *Recreations:* motor racing, jet boating, climbing. *Address:* c/o C. W. F. Hamilton & Co. Ltd, Box 709, Christchurch, New Zealand; Irishman Creek Station, Fairlie, New Zealand.

HAMILTON, Cyril Robert Parke, CMG 1972; Director: Rank Organisation and subsidiary companies, 1963-77; A. Kershaw & Sons Ltd, 1966-77; Rank Xerox Ltd, 1967-77; *b* 4 Aug. 1903; *s* of Alfred Parke and Annie Hamilton; *m* 1st, 1929, Cherie May Stearn (*d* 1966); one *s* one *d.*; 2nd, 1971, Betty Emily Brand. *Educ:* High Sch., Ilford; King's Coll., London Univ. Entered Bank of England, 1923, and retired as Deputy Chief Cashier, 1963, after career mainly concerned with internat. financial negotiations and Exchange Control. Vice-Chm., Standard and Chartered Banking Gp Ltd, 1969-74; Dep. Chm., Standard Bank, 1963-74; Director: Standard Bank of SA, 1963-74; Midland and International Banks, 1964-74; Banque Belge d'Afrique, 1969-74; Chairman: Malta International Banking Corp, 1969-74; Tozer Standard and Chartered Ltd, 1973-74. *Recreations:* golf, gardening. *Address:* Peat Moor, Harborough Hill, Pulborough, West Sussex. *T:* West Chiltington 2171. *Clubs:* Brooks's, Bath, MCC.

HAMILTON, Sir Denis; *see* Hamilton, Sir C. D.

HAMILTON, Dundas; *see* Hamilton, J. D.

HAMILTON, Sir Edward (Sydney), 7th and 5th Bt, *cr* 1776 and 1819; *b* 14 April 1925; *s* of Sir (Thomas) Sydney (Percival) Hamilton, 6th and 4th Bt, and Bertha Muriel, *d* of James Russell King, Singleton Park, Kendal; *S* father, 1966. *Educ:* Canford Sch. Served Royal Engineers, 1943-47; 1st Royal Sussex Home Guard, 1953-56. *Recreations:* Spiritual matters, music. *Address:* The Cottage, East Lavant, near Chichester, West Sussex PO18 0AL. *T:* Chichester 527414.

HAMILTON, Prof. George Heard; Director, Sterling and Francine Clark Art Institute, 1966-77, now Emeritus; Professor of Art, Williams College, Williamstown, Massachusetts, 1966-75, now Emeritus; Director of Graduate Studies in Art History, Williams College, 1971-75; *b* 23 June 1910; *s* of Frank A. Hamilton and Georgia Neale Heard; *m* 1945, Polly Wiggin; one *s* one *d*. *Educ:* Yale Univ. BA 1932; MA 1934; PhD 1942. Research Asst, Walters Art Gallery, Baltimore, 1934-36; Mem. Art History Faculty, Yale Univ., 1936-66 (Prof., 1956-66); Robert Sterling Clark Prof. of Art, Williams Coll., 1963-64. Slade Prof. of Fine Art, Cambridge Univ., 1971-72. FRSA 1973. LHD Williams Coll., 1977. *Publications:* (with D. V. Thompson, Jr) De Arte Illuminandi, 1933; Manet and His Critics, 1954; The Art and Architecture of Russia, 1954; Monet's Paintings of Rouen Cathedral, 1960; European Painting and Sculpture, 1880-1940, 1967; (with W. C. Agee) Raymond Duchamp-Villon, 1967; 19th and 20th Century Art: Painting, Sculpture, Architecture, 1970; Articles in Burlington Magazine, Gazette des Beaux-Arts, Art Bulletin, etc. *Recreations:* music, gardening. *Address:* Williamstown, Mass 01267, USA. *T:* (413) 458-8626. *Clubs:* Century Association (New York); Elizabethan (New Haven); Edgartown Yacht (Mass).

HAMILTON, Maj.-Gen. Godfrey John, CB 1966; CBE 1959 (OBE 1956); DSO 1935; *b* 31 March 1912; *s* of late Lieut-Col F. A. Hamilton, OBE, DL, JP, and of Mrs Hamilton, Osbaston, Monmouth; *m* 1st, 1937, Mary Penelope Colthurst; one *d* ; 2nd, 1942, Mary Margaret Kaye (novelist); two *d*. *Educ:* Radley Coll.; RMC, Sandhurst. Commnd, 1932; served in Guides Infantry, IA, 1932-48 (despatches): India, Burma and Malaya; Royal Irish Fusiliers (despatches twice): Palestine, Egypt, Germany, Korea, Kenya, N Ireland, Berlin. Chief, Joint Services Liaison Organization, BAOR, 1963-66. Retired, 1967. *Recreations:* fishing, painting. *Address:* The Old House, Boreham Street, near Hailsham, East Sussex. *Club:* Army and Navy.

HAMILTON, Graeme Montagu, TD; a Recorder of the Crown Court, since 1974; barrister-at-law; *b* 1 June 1934; *s* of late Leslie Montagu Hamilton and of Joan Lady Burbidge (Joan Elizabeth Burbidge, *née* Moxey). *Educ:* Eton; Magdalene Coll., Cambridge (MA). National Service, 4/7 Royal Dragoon Guards, 1953-55. Called to Bar, Gray's Inn, 1959; Mem., Senate of Inns of Court and Bar, 1975. TA City of London Yeomanry, Inns of Court and City Yeomanry, 1955-70. *Recreations:* sailing, shooting. *Address:* 35 Petersham Place, SW7 5PU. *T:* 01-584 3400; (professional) 2 Crown Office Row, Temple, EC4Y 7HJ. *Clubs:* Cavalry and Guards, Royal Thames Yacht, Royal Automobile.

HAMILTON, Hamish; Chairman, Hamish Hamilton, Ltd, Publishers, since 1931 (Managing Director, 1931-72); *b* Indianapolis, 15 Nov. 1900; *o s* of James Neilson Hamilton, and Suzanne van Valkenburg; *m* 1st, 1929, Jean Forbes-Robertson (marr. diss. 1933), *d* of Sir Johnston and Lady Forbes-Robertson; 2nd, 1940, Countess Yvonne Pallavicino, of Rome; one *s*. *Educ:* Rugby; Caius Coll., Cambridge (Medical Student, 1919). MA (Hons Mod. Langs), LLB. Travelled in USA, 1922-23; called to Bar (Inner Temple), 1925; London Manager Harper and Brothers, Publishers, 1926; founded Hamish Hamilton Ltd, 1931; served in Army, 1939-41 (Holland and France, 1940); seconded to American Division, Ministry of Information, 1941-45; Hon. Sec. Kinsmen Trust, 1942-56; founded Kathleen Ferrier Meml Scholarships, 1954; a Governor, the Old Vic, 1945-75; Member Council, English-Speaking Union; a Governor, British Institute, Florence. Chevalier de la Légion d'Honneur, 1953; Grande Ufficiale, Order of Merit (Italy), 1976. *Publications:* articles on publishing, Anglo-American relations and sport. Commemorative Anthologies: Decade, 1941, Majority, 1952. *Recreations:* music, the theatre, travel; formerly rowing (spare stroke Cambridge Eight, 1921; stroked Winning Crews Grand Challenge Cup, Henley, 1927 and 1928, and Olympic Eight, Amsterdam, 1928 (silver medal)), ski-ing, flying, squash. *Address:* 35 Cumberland Terrace, NW1. *T:* 01-935 3873. *Clubs:* Garrick; Leander, MCC.

HAMILTON, Rev. Herbert Alfred; *b* 16 June 1897; *s* of Alfred and Ada Elizabeth Hamilton; *m* 1st, 1929, Winifred Alice Johnson (*d* 1936); two adopted *s* ; 2nd, 1937, Phyllis Noella Pye

(*d* 1944); one *d* ; 3rd, 1944, Ellen Crossman Allen; one *s* one *d*. *Educ:* Merchant Taylors', Crosby; Manchester Univ.; Lancs Independent Coll. Ordained, 1924; Pastorates: Bolton, 1924-29; Birmingham, 1929-33; Sec. for Education and Youth Service, Congregational Union of England and Wales, 1933-45; Principal, Westhill Training Coll., Birmingham, 1945-54; Minister, Union Church, Brighton, 1954-63. Chm., Congregational Union of England and Wales, May 1961-62; Associate Gen. Sec., World Council of Christian Education, 1963-65; Asst Gen. Sec., World Council of Churches, 1965-66. Retired as consultant to the World Council of Christian Education, 1966. *Publications:* How to Say your Prayers, 1933; The Family Church, 1940; Church Youth Training, 1944; Conversation with God, 1955; contrib. to Expository Times, Times Educl Supplement, etc. *Recreations:* music, painting, conversation. *Address:* 22 Damian Way, Keymer, Hassocks, West Sussex.

HAMILTON, Brig. Hugh Gray Wybrants, CBE 1964 (MBE 1945); DL; General Manager, Corby Development Corporation, since 1968; *b* 16 May 1918; *s* of Lt-Col H. W. Hamilton, late 5th Dragoon Guards; *m* 1944, Claire Buxton; two *d*. *Educ:* Wellington Coll., Berks; Peterhouse, Cambridge; Royal Mil. Academy. Commissioned with Royal Engineers, 1938. War Service in BEF, BNAF, BLA, 1939-45. Post War Service in Australia, BAOR, France and UK. Instructor, Army Staff Coll., Camberley, 1954-56; Student, IDC, 1965; retired, 1968. DL Northants, 1977. *Recreations:* riding, sailing, farming. *Address:* Marston Trussell Hall, Market Harborough, Leics. *T:* Market Harborough 4209. *Club:* Army and Navy.

HAMILTON, Iain (Bertram); author and journalist; *b* 3 Feb. 1920; *s* of John Hamilton and Margaret Laird MacEachran; *m* 1944, Jean Campbell Fisher; one *s* one *d*. *Educ:* Paisley Grammar Sch. Editorial staff: Daily Record, 1944-45; The Guardian, 1945-52; The Spectator, 1952; Asst Editor, 1953, Associate Editor, 1954-56, The Spectator; Editor-in-Chief, 1957, Editorial Director, The Hutchinson group of publishing cos, 1958-62; Editor of The Spectator, 1962-63. Man. Dir, Kern House Enterprises Ltd, 1970-75; Dir of Studies, Inst. for Study of Conflict, 1975-77; Founder and Exec. Mem., British Irish Assoc. Has contrib. prose and verse to Radio, Daily Telegraph, Encounter, Illustrated London News, Interplay, The Times Educational and Literary Supplements, Spectator, World Review, Twentieth Century, Scots Review, Student of Edinburgh Univ. Former Art Critic of Public Opinion. *Publications:* Scotland the Brave, 1957; The Foster Gang (with H. J. May), 1966; Embarkation for Cythera, 1974; Arthur Koestler, 1978; *play:* The Snarling Beggar, 1951. *Recreation:* surviving. *Address:* 31 Highgate West Hill, N6. *T:* 01-340 8270; Kames, Tighnabruaich, Argyll. *T:* Tighnabruaich 481. *Club:* Garrick.

HAMILTON, Iain Ellis, BMus, FRAM; composer; pianist; Mary Duke Biddle Professor of Music (Chairman of the Department, 1966), Duke University, North Carolina, USA; *b* Glasgow, 6 June 1922; *s* of James and Catherine Hamilton. *Educ:* Mill Hill; Royal Academy of Music. Engineer (Handley Page Ltd), 1939-46; RAM (Scholar) 1947-51; BMus (London University), 1951. Lecturer at Morley Coll., 1952-58; Lecturer, London Univ., 1956-60. Prizes and awards include: Prize of Royal Philharmonic Society, 1951; Prize of Koussevitsky Foundation (America), 1951; Butterworth Award, 1954; Arnold Bax Gold Medal, 1956; Ralph Vaughan Williams Award, Composers' Guild of GB, 1975. FRAM, 1960. Chm. Composers' Guild, 1958; Chm. ICA Music Cttee, 1958-60. *Works:* 2 Symphonies; Sinfonia for two orchestras (Edinburgh Festival Commission); Concertos, for piano, clarinet, organ and violin; The Bermudas, for baritone, chorus and orchestra (BBC Commission); Symphonic Variations for string orchestra; Overture, Bartholomew Fair; Overture, 1912; Ecossaise for orchestra; Concerto for jazz trumpet and orchestra (BBC Commn); Scottish Dances; Sonata for chamber orchestra; 5 Love Songs for tenor and orchestra; (BBC Commission) Cantos for orchestra; Jubilee for orchestra; Arias for small orchestra; Circus for orchestra (BBC Commn); Epitaph for this World and Time: 3 choruses and 2 organs; Voyage for horn and orchestra; Alastor for orchestra; Amphion for violin and orchestra; Commedia for orchestra; Threnos for solo organ; Aubade and Paraphrase for solo organ; Clerk Saunders, a ballet; chamber works include: two String Quartets; String Octet; Sonatas for piano, viola, clarinet and flute; Flute Quartet; Clarinet Quintet; 3 Nocturnes for clarinet and piano; 5 Scenes for trumpet and piano; Sextet; Sonatas and Variants for 10 winds; Dialogues for soprano and 5 instruments; Nocturnes with Cadenzas for solo piano; 4 Border Songs and the Fray of Suport for unaccompanied voices; Opera: Agamemnon; Royal Hunt of the Sun; Pharsalia; The Catiline Conspiracy; Tamburlaine. Music for theatre and films. Hon.

DMus Glasgow, 1970. *Publications:* articles for many journals. *Address:* 40 Park Avenue, New York, NY 10016, USA.

HAMILTON, Ian; Editor, The New Review, since 1974; *b* 24 March 1938; *s* of Robert Tough Hamilton and Daisy McKay; *m* 1963, Gisela Dietzel; one *s. Educ:* Darlington Grammar Sch.; Keble Coll., Oxford (BA Hons). Editor, Review, 1962-72; Poetry and Fiction Editor, Times Literary Supplement, 1965-73; Lectr in Poetry, Univ. of Hull, 1972-. E. C. Gregory Award, 1963; Malta Cultural Award, 1974. *Publications:* (ed) The Poetry of War 1939-45, 1965; (ed) Alun Lewis: poetry and prose, 1966; (ed) The Modern Poet, 1968; The Visit (poems), 1970; A Poetry Chronicle, 1973; (ed) Robert Frost: selected poems, 1973; The Little Magazines, 1976. *Address:* Flat 6, 72 Westbourne Terrace, W2. *T:* 01-262 0650.

HAMILTON, James; MP (Lab) Bothwell since 1964; a Lord Commissioner of HM Treasury, and Vice-Chamberlain of the Household, since 1974; *b* 11 March 1918; *s* of George Hamilton and Margaret Carey; *m* 1945, Agnes McGhee; one *s* three *d* (and one *s* decd). *Educ:* St Bridget's, Baillieston; St Mary's, High Whifflet. District Councillor, 6th Lanarks, 1955-58; Lanarks County Council, 1958-64. National Executive Mem., Constructional Engrg Union, 1958-, Pres., 1968-; Chm., Trade Union Group, Parly Labour Party, 1969-. Asst Govt Whip, 1969-70; an Opposition Whip, 1970-74. *Recreations:* tennis, badminton, golf. *Address:* 12 Rosegreen Crescent, North Road, Bellshill, Lanarks.

HAMILTON, Prof. James; Professor of Physics, Nordic Institute for Theoretical Atomic Physics, since 1964; *b* 29 Jan. 1918; *s* of Joseph Hamilton, Killybegs, Co. Donegal and Jessie Mackay, Keiss, Caithness; *m* 1945, Glen, *d* of Charles Dobbs, Verwood, Dorset; two *s* one *d. Educ:* Royal Academical Institution, Belfast; Queen's Univ., Belfast; Institute for Advanced Study, Dublin; Manchester Univ. Scientific Officer, Admiralty, London, and South East Asia Command, 1943-45; ICI Fellow, Manchester Univ., 1945-48; Lectr in Theoretical Physics, Manchester Univ., 1948-49; University Lectr in Mathematics, Cambridge Univ., 1950-60. Fellow of Christ's Coll., Cambridge, 1953-60; Research Associate in Nuclear Physics, Cornell Univ., NY, 1957-58; Prof. of Physics, University Coll., London, 1960-64. Donegall Lectr, TCD, 1969. Foreign Mem., Royal Danish Acad. *Publications:* The Theory of Elementary Particles, 1959; (with B. Tromborg) Partial Wave Amplitudes and Resonance Poles, 1972; papers and articles on interaction of radiation with atoms, elementary particle physics, causality, and related topics. *Address:* Nordita, Blegdamsvej 17, 2100 Copenhagen, ø, Denmark. *T:* TRia 1616.

HAMILTON, James Arnot, CB 1972; MBE 1952; Permanent Under-Secretary of State, Department of Education and Science, since 1976; *b* 2 May 1923; *m* 1947, Christine Mary McKean; three *s. Educ:* University of Edinburgh (BSc). Marine Aircraft Experimental Estab., 1943: Head of Flight Research, 1948; Royal Aircraft Estab., 1952; Head of Projects Div., 1964; Dir, Anglo-French Combat Aircraft, Min. of Aviation, 1965; Dir-Gen. Concorde, Min. of Technology, 1966-70; Deputy Secretary: (Aerospace), DTI, 1971-73; Cabinet Office, 1973-76. *Publications:* papers in Reports and Memoranda series of Aeronautical Research Council, Jl RAeS, and technical press. *Address:* Pentlands, 9 Cedar Road, Farnborough, Hants. *T:* Farnborough 43254. *Club:* Athenæum.

HAMILTON, (James) Dundas; Deputy Chairman: Committee on Invisible Exports, since 1976; The Stock Exchange, 1973-76; *b* 11 June 1919; *o s* of late Arthur Douglas Hamilton and Jean Scott Hamilton; *m* 1954, Linda Jean, *d* of late Sinclair Frank Ditcham and Helen Fraser Ditcham; two *d. Educ:* Rugby; Clare Coll., Cambridge. Served War, Army (Lt-Col RA), 1939-46. Member, Stock Exchange, 1948; Partner, Fielding, Newson-Smith & Co., 1951; elected to Council of Stock Exchange, 1972. Director: Bluemel Bros Ltd; Richard Clay & Co. Ltd. Member: Council of Industrial Soc.; Soc. of Investment Analysts; Exec. Cttee, City Communications Orgn. *Publications:* The Erl King (radio play), 1949; Lorenzo Smiles on Fortune (novel), 1953; Three on a Honeymoon (TV series), 1956; Six Months Grace (play, jointly with Robert Morley), 1957; Stockbroking Today, 1968. *Recreations:* writing, swimming, skiing. *Address:* 45 Melbury Court, W8 6NH. *T:* 01-602 3157. *Clubs:* City of London; All England Lawn Tennis and Croquet.

HAMILTON, John Cole; see Cole-Hamilton.

HAMILTON, Adm. Sir John (Graham), GBE 1966 (KBE 1963; CBE 1958); CB 1960; National President, Institute of Marketing, 1972-75 (Director-General, 1968-72); *b* 12 July 1910; *s* of late Col E. G. Hamilton, CMG, DSO, MC, and Ethel

Marie (*née* Frith); *m* 1938, Dorothy Nina Turner, 2nd *d* of late Col J. E. Turner, CMG, DSO; no *c. Educ:* RN Coll., Dartmouth. Joined RN 1924; specialised in Gunnery, 1936. Served War of 1939-45: destroyers; on staff of Adm. Cunningham, Mediterranean; Gunnery Officer, HMS Warspite; Admiralty; SE Asia; Comdr, 1943 (despatches). In command, HMS Alacrity, Far East, 1946-48; Capt., 1949; Dep. Dir, Radio Equipment, 1950-51; in command, 5th Destroyer Squadron, 1952-53; Dir of Naval Ordnance, Admiralty, 1954-56; in command HMS Newfoundland, Far East, 1956-58; despatches, 1957; Rear-Adm., 1958; Naval Sec. to First Lord of the Admiralty, 1958-60; Vice-Adm., 1961; Flag Officer: Flotillas, Home Fleet, 1960-62; Naval Air Command, 1962-64; C-in-C Mediterranean, and C-in-C Allied Forces, Mediterranean, 1964-67; Adm. 1965. *Recreations:* walking, climbing, photography. *Address:* Chapel Barn, Abbotsbury, Dorset DT3 4LF. *T:* Abbotsbury 507.

HAMILTON, Maj.-Gen. John Robert Crosse, CB 1957; CBE 1950; DSO 1944; late RE; Fellow, Churchill College, Cambridge (Bursar, 1959-72); *b* 1 April 1906; *s* of late Major J. A. C. Hamilton, Fyne Court, Bridgwater, Somerset; *m* 1938, Rosamond Budd, *d* of late Richard Hancock, Hong Kong; one *s* one *d. Educ:* Radley; Royal Military Academy; Caius Coll., Cambridge. 2nd Lieut RE, 1925. Served War of 1939-45 (DSO), France, Belgium, Germany; acting Brig., 1947; Lt-Col 1948; Col, 1950; Maj.-Gen., 1956. Chief of Staff, HQ Malaya Command, 1955-56; Dir of Military Operations, War Office, 1956-59; retired, 1959. Col Comdt, RE, 1962-71. *Address:* Peas Hill End, Smith Gorge, Bridport, Dorset. *Club:* Naval and Military.

HAMILTON, Martha, (Mrs R. R. Steedman); Headmistress, St Leonards School, St Andrews, since 1970; *d* of Rev. John Edmund Hamilton and Hon. Lilias Maclay; *m* 1977, Robert Russell Steedman. *Educ:* Roedean Sch.; St Andrews Univ. (MA Hons Hist.); Cambridge Univ. (DipEd); Edinburgh Univ. (Dip. Adult Educn). Principal, Paljor Namgyal Girls' High School, Gangtok, Sikkim, 1959-66. Awarded Pema Dorji (for services to education), Sikkim, 1966. *Recreations:* ski-ing, photography. *Address:* St Leonards School, St Andrews, Fife. *T:* St Andrews 2126.

HAMILTON, Michael Aubrey; MP (C) Salisbury since Feb. 1965; *b* 5 July 1918; *s* of late Rt Rev. E. K. C. Hamilton, KCVO; *m* 1947, Lavinia, 3rd *d* of Col Sir Charles Ponsonby, 1st Bt, TD; one *s* three *d. Educ:* Radley; Oxford. Served War of 1939-45, with 1st Bn, Coldstream Guards. MP (C) Wellingborough Div. Northants, 1959-64; Asst Govt Whip (unpaid), 1961-62; a Lord Comr of the Treasury, 1962-64; UK Representative: UN Gen. Assembly, 1970; US Bicentennial Celebrations, 1976. *Address:* 27 Kylestrome House, Cundy Street, SW1. *T:* 01-730 1819; Lordington House, Chichester, Sussex.

HAMILTON, Myer A. B. K.; see King-Hamilton.

HAMILTON, North Edward Frederick D.; see Dalrymple Hamilton.

HAMILTON, Sir Patrick George, 2nd Bt, *cr* 1937; Chairman, Expanded Metal Co. Ltd; Director: Simon Engineering Ltd; Renold Ltd; Lloyds Bank Ltd; Possum Controls Ltd; *b* 17 Nov. 1908; *o s* of Sir George Clements Hamilton, 1st Bt, and Eleanor (*d* 1958), *d* of late Henry Simon and *sister* of 1st Baron Simon of Wythenshawe; *S* father, 1947; *m* 1941, Winifred Mary Stone (OBE 1957, MA), *o c* of Hammond Jenkins, Maddings, Hadstock, Cambs. *Educ:* Eton; Trinity Coll., Oxford (MA). First Managing Director and later Chairman of Tyresoles Ltd, 1934-53. Director of Propeller Production, Ministry of Aircraft Production, 1943-44. Chm., Advisory Cttee on Commercial Information Overseas, 1957-59. Dep. Chm., Export Publicity Council, 1960-63. Chm., Transport Users Consultative Cttee, NW Area, 1957-64; Mem., Central Transport Consultative Cttee, 1963-64. Treas., Fedn of Commonwealth Chambers of Commerce, 1962-64. Mem., ITA, 1964-69. Chm., Central Mddx Gp Hosp. Management Cttee, 1964-70. Trustee: Eleanor Hamilton Trust; Sidbury Trust; Disabled Living Foundn Trust. *Recreations:* gardening, travel. *Heir:* none. *Address:* 23 Cheyne Walk, SW3 5RD. *T:* 01-352 5577. *Club:* Carlton.

HAMILTON, Richard; painter; *b* 24 Feb. 1922; *s* of Peter and Constance Hamilton; *m* 1947, Terry O'Reilly (*d* 1962). *Educ:* elementary; Royal Academy Schs; Slade Sch. of Art. Jig and Tool draughtsman, 1940-45. Lectr, Fine Art Dept, King's Coll., Univ. of Durham (later Univ. of Newcastle upon Tyne), 1953-66. Devised exhibitions: Growth and Form, 1951; Man, Machine and Motion, 1955. Collaborated on: This is Tomorrow, 1956; 'an Exhibit', 1957; exhibn with D. Roth, ICA New Gall.,

1977. One man art exhibitions: Gimpel Fils, 1951; Hanover Gall., 1955, 1964, Robert Fraser Gall., 1966, 1967, 1969; Whitworth Gall, 1972; Nigel Greenwood Inc., 1972. Retrospective exhibitions: Tate Gallery, 1970 (also shown in Eindhoven and Bern); Guggenheim Museum, New York, 1973 (also shown in Cincinnati, Munich, Tübingen, Berlin); other exhibitions abroad include: Kassel, 1967, New York, 1967; Milan, 1968, 1969, 1971, 1972; Hamburg, 1969; Berlin, 1970, 1971, 1973. William and Noma Copley award, 1960; John Moores prize, 1969; Talens Prize International, 1970. *Address:* c/o Tate Gallery, Millbank, SW1P 4RG.

HAMILTON, Sir Richard Caradoc; *see* Hamilton, Sir Robert C. R. C.

HAMILTON, Richard Graham; a Recorder of the Crown Court, since 1974; Chancellor, Diocese of Liverpool, since 1976; *b* 26 Aug. 1932; *s* of Henry Augustus Rupert Hamilton and Frances Mary Graham Hamilton; *m* 1960, Patricia Craghill Hamilton (*née* Ashburner); one *s* one *d*. *Educ:* Charterhouse; University Coll., Oxford (MA). Called to Bar, Middle Temple, 1956. *Recreations:* reading, walking, films. *Address:* 15 Gwydrin Road, Liverpool L18 3HA. *T:* 051-722 5806. *Club:* Athenæum (Liverpool).

HAMILTON, Sir (Robert Charles) Richard (Caradoc), 9th Bt, *cr* 1647; *b* 8 Sept. 1911; *s* of Sir Robert Caradoc Hamilton, 8th Bt, and Irene Lady Hamilton (*née* Mordaunt) (*d* 1969); *S* father, 1959; *m* 1952, Elizabeth Vidal Barton; one *s* three *d*. *Educ:* Charterhouse; St Peter's Coll., Oxford (MA). Served in the Intelligence Corps, 1940-45. Schoolmaster at Ardingly Coll., Sussex, 1946-60. Owner, Walton Estate, Warwick. *Recreations:* dramatist; Real tennis. *Heir: s* Andrew Caradoc Hamilton, *b* 23 Sept. 1953. *Address:* Walton, Warwick. *T:* Stratford-on-Avon 840460.

HAMILTON, Robert William, FBA 1960; Keeper of the Ashmolean Museum, Oxford, 1962-72; Keeper of the Department of Antiquities, 1956-72; *b* 26 Nov. 1905; *s* of William Stirling Hamilton and Kathleen Hamilton (*née* Elsmie); *m* 1935, Eileen Hetty Lowick; three *s* two *d*. *Educ:* Winchester Coll.; Magdalen Coll., Oxford. Chief Insp. of Antiquities, Palestine, 1931-38; Dir of Antiquities, Palestine, 1938-48; Sec.-Librarian, British Sch. of Archæology, Iraq, 1948-49; Senior Lecturer in Near Eastern Archæology, Oxford, 1949-56. Fellow Magdalen Coll., Oxford, 1959-72. *Publications:* The Church of the Nativity, Bethlehem, 1947; Structural History of the Aqsa Mosque, 1949; Khirbat al Mafjar, 1959; (with others) Oxford Bible Atlas, 1974. *Address:* The Haskers, Westleton, Suffolk.

HAMILTON, Captain Sir Robert William Stirling-, 12th Bt, *cr* 1673; JP, DL; RN, retired; *b* 5 April 1903; *s* of Sir William Stirling-Hamilton, 11th Bt, and late Mabel Mary, *d* of Maj.-Gen. Tyndall; *S* father 1946; *m* 1930, Eileen, *d* of late Rt Rev. H. K. Southwell, CMG; one *s* two *d*. *Educ:* RNC, Dartmouth. Commodore, RN Barracks, Portsmouth, 1952-54, retired 1954. DL, Sussex, 1970-. *Heir: s* Bruce Stirling-Hamilton [*b* 5 Aug. 1940; *m* 1968, Stephanie, *e d* of Dr William Campbell; one *d*]. *Address:* Puriton Lodge, Hambrook, Chichester, West Sussex. *T:* West Ashling 363.

HAMILTON, Walter, MA; Hon. DLitt Durham; FRSL; Master of Magdalene College, Cambridge, since 1967; *b* 10 Feb. 1908; *s* of late Walter George Hamilton and Caroline Mary Stiff; *m* 1951, Jane Elizabeth, *o d* of Sir John Burrows, qv, Ridlands Cottage, Limpsfield Chart, Surrey; three *s* one *d*. *Educ:* St Dunstan's Coll.; Trinity Coll., Cambridge (Scholar). 1st Class Classical Tripos, Part I, 1927; Part II, 1929; Craven Scholar, 1927; Chancellor's Classical Medallist, 1928; Porson Prizeman and Craven Student, 1929. Fellow of Trinity Coll., 1931-35; Asst Lecturer, University of Manchester, 1931-32; Asst Master, Eton Coll., 1933-46, Master in Coll., 1937-46, Fellow, 1972-; Fellow and Classical Lecturer, Trinity Coll., 1946-50; Tutor, 1947-50; University Lectr in Classics, 1947-50; Head Master: of Westminster Sch., 1950-57; of Rugby Sch., 1957-66. Editor, Classical Quarterly, 1946-47. Chairman: Scholarship Cttee, Lord Kitchener Nat. Meml Fund, 1953-59, Exec. Cttee, 1967-77; Headmasters' Conference, 1955, 1956, 1965, 1966; Governing Body, Shrewsbury Sch., 1968-; Governing Bodies Assoc., 1969-74. Member: Exec. Cttee, British Council, 1958-70; Council of Senate of Cambridge Univ., 1969-74. *Publications:* A new translation of Plato's Symposium, 1951; Plato's Gorgias, 1960; Plato's Phaedrus and Letters VII and VIII, 1973; contributions to Classical Quarterly, Classical Review, etc. *Address:* Magdalene College, Cambridge; Ardbeg, Dervaig, Isle of Mull. *Club:* Athenæum.

HAMILTON, Sir William; *see* Hamilton, Sir C. W. F.

HAMILTON, William Aitken Brown, CMG 1950; *b* 3 June 1909; *e s* of Brown Hamilton, Milltimber, Aberdeenshire; *m* 1936, Barbara, *e d* of S. T. Gano, Belmont, Massachusetts, USA; one *s* (and one *s* decd). *Educ:* Aberdeen Grammar Sch.; Aberdeen Univ. 1st Class Hons Classics. Administrative Civil Service, Board of Education, 1931; Principal, 1936; Joint Sec., Athlone Cttee on Nursing Services, 1937-39; Ministry of Food, 1939-44; Asst Sec., 1943; Ministry of Education, 1944-49; Dir of Establishments and Under-Sec., 1946; Dir of Establishments and Asst Under-Sec. of State, CRO, 1949; Dir of Personnel, UN, 1959-62; Asst Under-Sec. of State, Commonwealth Office, 1962-67, retired. *Address:* Bonds, Bullingstone Lane, Speldhurst, Kent TN3 0JY. *T:* Speldhurst 164.

HAMILTON, William Winter; MP (Lab) Fife Central, since 1974 (Fife West, 1950-74); *b* 26 June 1917; *m* (wife died 1968); one *s* one *d*. *Educ:* Washington Grammar Sch., Co. Durham; Sheffield Univ. (BA, DipEd). Joined Lab. Party, 1936; contested W Fife, 1945; Chairman, H. of C. Estimates Cttee, 1964-70; Vice-Chm., Parly Labour Party, 1966-70; Mem., European Parlt, 1975-, Vice-Chm., Rules and Procedure Cttee, 1976- (Chm., 1975-76). School teacher; Mem. National Union of Teachers. Served War of 1939-45, Middle East, Capt. *Publication:* My Queen and I, 1975. *Address:* House of Commons, SW1.

HAMILTON-DALRYMPLE, Sir Hew; *see* Dalrymple.

HAMILTON FRASER, Donald; *see* Fraser.

HAMILTON-KING, Mrs Grace M.; Principal, Royal School of Needlework, 1950-66; *d* of late Canon Arthur West and of Mrs Louisa Oliver; *m* 1932, Edward Hamilton-King (decd). *Educ:* St Clair, Tunbridge Wells; Effingham House, Bexhill; Lytton House, London. London Academy of Music, 1922-23; Miss Kerr-Sander's Secretarial Coll., 1930-31; Temp. Administrative Officer, Home Office, 1941-45. Coronation Medal, 1953. *Address:* c/o Lloyds Bank, Pantiles Branch, 1 London Road, Tunbridge Wells, Kent.

HAMILTON-RUSSELL, family name of **Viscount Boyne.**

HAMILTON-SMITH, family name of **Baron Colwyn.**

HAMILTON-SPENCER-SMITH, Sir John; *see* Spencer-Smith.

HAMLEY, Donald Alfred; HM Diplomatic Service; Commercial Counsellor, British Embassy, Caracas, since 1973; *b* 19 Aug 1931; *s* of Alfred Hamley and Amy (*née* Brimacombe); *m* 1958, Daphne Griffith; two *d*. *Educ:* Devonport High Sch., Plymouth. Joined HM Foreign (subseq. Diplomatic) Service, 1949; Nat. Service, 1950-52; returned to FO; served in: Kuwait, 1955-57; Libya, 1958-61; FO, 1961-63; Jedda, 1963-65 and 1969-72; Rome, 1965-69; seconded to DTI, 1972-73. *Recreations:* tennis, golf, swimming, squash, choral singing. *Address:* c/o Foreign and Commonwealth Office, SW1A 2AL; 1 Forge Close, Bromley, Kent. *T:* 01-462 6696.

HAMLYN, Prof. David Walter; Professor of Philosophy, Birkbeck College, University of London, since 1964; *b* 1 Oct. 1924; *s* of late Hugh Parker Hamlyn and late Gertrude Isabel Hamlyn; *m* 1949, Eileen Carlyle Litt; one *s* one *d*. *Educ:* Plymouth Coll.; Exeter Coll., Oxford. BA (Oxon) 1948, MA 1949 (1st cl. Lit. Hum., 1st cl. Philosophy and Psychology, 1950). Research Fellow, Corpus Christi Coll., Oxford, 1950-53; Lecturer: Jesus Coll., Oxford, 1953-54; Birkbeck Coll., London, 1954-63, Reader, 1963-64. Mem. Council, Royal Inst. of Philosophy, 1968- (Exec., 1971-); Governor, Birkbeck Coll., 1965-69; Chm. Governors, Heythrop Coll., 1971-. Editor of Mind, 1972-. *Publications:* The Psychology of Perception, 1957 (repr. with additional material, 1969); Sensation and Perception, 1961; Aristotle's *De Anima*, Books II and III, 1968; The Theory of Knowledge, 1970 (USA), 1971 (GB); Experience and the Growth of Understanding, 1977; contrib. to several other books and to many philosophical and classical jls. *Recreations:* playing and listening to music. *Address:* 7 Burland Road, Brentwood, Essex CM15 9BH. *T:* Brentwood 214842; Department of Philosophy, Birkbeck College, Malet Street, WC1E 7HX. *T:* 01-580 6622.

HAMLYN, Paul (Bertrand); Founder and Chairman: Octopus Books (London, New York and Sydney), since 1971; Mandarin Publishers (Hong Kong), since 1971 (in association with Jardine, Matheson & Co., Hong Kong, since 1974); Co-founder (with David Frost) and Director, Sundial Publications, since 1973; Co-founder (with Doubleday & Co., New York) and

Director, Octopus International BV (Holland), since 1973; Director, News International, since 1971; *b* 12 Feb. 1926; 2nd *s* of late Prof. Richard Hamburger and Mrs L. Hamburger (*née* Hamburg); *m* 1st, 1952, Eileen Margaret (Bobbie) (marr. diss. 1969), *d* of Col Richard Watson; one *s* one *d*; 2nd, 1970, Mrs Helen Guest. *Educ*: St Christopher's Sch., Letchworth, Herts. Founder of Hamlyn Publishing Gp; Formed: Books for Pleasure, 1949; Prints for Pleasure, 1960; Records for Pleasure, Marketing long-playing classical records, and Golden Pleasure Books (jt co. with Golden Press Inc., NY), 1961; Music for Pleasure (with EMI), 1965. Paul Hamlyn Gp acquired by Internat. Publishing Corp, 1964; joined IPC Bd with special responsibility for all Corporation's book publishing activities; Butterworth & Co. acquired 1968; Director, IPC, 1965-70; Chm., IPC Books, controlling Hamlyn Publishing Gp, 1965-70 (formerly Chm., Paul Hamlyn Holdings Ltd, and associated Cos); Jt Man. Dir, News International Ltd, 1970-71. Mem. Council, ICA, 1977. *Address*: 64 Old Church Street, SW3. *T*: 01-352 8369.
See also M. P. L. Hamburger.

HAMMARSKJÖLD, Knut (Olof Hjalmar Åkesson); Director-General, International Air Transport Association, since 1966; *b* Geneva, 16 Jan. 1922; Swedish; *m*; four *s*. *Educ*: Sigtunaskolan; Stockholm Univ. Swedish Foreign Service, 1946; Attaché, Swedish Embassy, Paris, 1947-49; Foreign Office, Stockholm, 1949-51; Attaché, Swedish Embassy, Vienna, 1951-52; 2nd Sec., Moscow, 1952-54, 1st Sec, 1954-55; 1st Sec., Foreign Office, 1955-57; Head of Foreign Relations Dept, Swedish Civil Aero. Bd, 1957-59; Counsellor, Paris, also Dep. Head of Swedish Delegn to OEEC, 1959-60; Dep. Sec.-Gen., EFTA, Geneva, 1960-66; Minister Plenipotentiary. Hon. Fellow, Canadian Aeronautics and Space Inst.; Hon. Academician, Mexican Acad. of Internat. Law; Hon. FCIT (London). Comdr (1st cl.), Order of North Star (Sweden); Grand Officer, Order of Al-Istiqlal (Jordan); Commander: Order of Lion (Finland); Oranje Nassau (Netherlands); Order of Falcon (Iceland); Order of Black Star (France). *Publications*: articles on political, economic and aviation topics. *Recreations*: music, painting, ski-ing. *Address*: c/o IATA, 1000 Sherbrooke Street West, Montreal, PQ, Canada H3A 2R4. *T*: 844-6311; IATA, 26 Chemin de Joinville, PO Box 160, 1216 Cointrin-Geneva, Switzerland. *T*: 983366.

HAMMER, James Dominic George; HM Chief Inspector of Factories since 1975; *b* 21 April 1929; *s* of E. A. G. and E. L. G. Hammer; *m* 1955, Margaret Eileen Halse; two *s* one *d*. *Educ*: Dulwich Coll.; Corpus Christi Coll., Cambridge. BA Hons Mod. Langs. Joined HM Factory Inspectorate, 1953. *Address*: Health and Safety Executive, Regina House, 259 Old Marylebone Road, NW1 5RR. *T*: 01-723 1262.

HAMMERSLEY, Dr John Michael, FRS 1976; Reader in Mathematical Statistics, University of Oxford, and Professorial Fellow, Trinity College, Oxford, since 1969; *b* 21 March 1920; *s* of late Guy Hugh Hammersley and Marguerite (*née* Whitehead); *m* 1951, Shirley Gwendolene (*née* Bakewell); two *s*. *Educ*: Sedbergh Sch.; Emmanuel Coll., Cambridge. MA, ScD (Cantab); MA, DSc (Oxon). War service in Royal Artillery, Major, 1940-45. Graduate Asst, Design and Analysis of Scientific Experiment, Univ. of Oxford, 1948-55; Principal Scientific Officer, AERE, Harwell, 1955-59; Sen. Research Officer, Inst. of Economics and Statistics, Univ. of Oxford, 1959-69; Sen. Research Fellow, Trinity Coll., Oxford, 1961-69. FIMS 1959; FIMA 1964; Mem., ISI, 1961. Von Neumann Medal for Applied Maths, Brussels, 1966. *Publications*: (with D. C. Handscomb) Monte Carlo Methods, 1964, rev. edn 1966, repr. 1975, trans. as Les Méthodes de Monte Carlo, 1967; papers in scientific jls. *Recreation*: skiing. *Address*: Trinity College, Oxford. *T*: Oxford 49631.

HAMMERTON, Rolf Eric; His Honour Judge Hammerton; a Circuit Judge, since 1972; *b* 18 June 1926; *s* of Eric Maurice Hammerton and Dora Alice Hammerton (*née* Zander); *m* 1953, Thelma Celestine Hammerton (*née* Appleyard), JP; one *s* three *d*. *Educ*: Brighton, Hove and Sussex Grammar Sch.; Peterhouse, Cambridge (BA, LLB). Philip Teichman Prize, 1952; called to Bar, Inner Temple, 1952. *Recreation*: cooking. *Address*: The Shambles, 6 Onslow Road, Hove, East Sussex BN3 6TA. *T*: Hove 551874.

HAMMETT, Sir Clifford (James), Kt 1969; Chief Justice, Fiji, 1967-72; Acting Governor General of Fiji, 1971; Law Revision Commissioner, St Kitts, 1974; *b* 8 June 1917; *s* of late Frederick John and Louisa Maria Hammett; *m* 1946, Olive Beryl Applebee; four *s* one *d*. *Educ*: Woodbridge. Admitted Solicitor, 1939. Indian Army, 1st Punjab Regt, 1939, North Africa, 1940; captured at Singapore, 1942 (despatches); POW on Siam Railway, 1942-45. Magistrate, Nigeria, 1946-52. Called to the Bar, Middle Temple, 1948. Transferred to Fiji, 1952; Senior Magistrate, Fiji, 1954, Puisne Judge, 1955; conjointly Chief Justice, Tonga, 1956-68. *Recreation*: gardening. *Address*: c/o Lloyds Bank, 6 Pall Mall, SW1. *Club*: Naval and Military.

HAMMETT, Harold George; British Deputy High Commissioner, Peshawar, 1964-66; *b* 2 Aug. 1906; 2nd *s* of Arthur Henry Hammett; *m* 1st, 1936, Daphne Margaret Vowler; one *s*; 2nd, 1947, Natalie Moira Sherratt; one *s* one *d*. *Educ*: St Olave's; Clare Coll., Cambridge. Malayan Civil Service, 1928-57; retired from post of Resident Commissioner, Malacca, on Malayan Independence, 1957; Commonwealth Office (formerly CRO), 1958-66. *Recreations*: woodwork, gardening. *Address*: Hole Head, Holcombe, Dawlish, Devon. *T*: Dawlish 2114. *Clubs*: East India, Devonshire, Sports and Public Schools, Royal Commonwealth Society.

HAMMICK, Sir Stephen (George), 5th Bt, *cr* 1834; *b* 27 Dec. 1926; *s* of Sir George Hammick, 4th Bt; *S* father, 1964; *m* 1953, Gillian Elizabeth Inchbald; two *s* one *d*. *Educ*: Stowe. Royal Navy as Rating (hostilities only), 1944-48; RAC Coll., Cirencester, 1949-50; MFH Cattistock Hunt, 1961 and 1962. County Councillor (Dorset), 1958. Farmer, with 450 acres. *Recreations*: hunting, fishing, sailing. *Heir*: *s* Paul St Vincent Hammick, *b* 1 Jan. 1955. *Address*: Badgers, Wraxall, Dorchester. *T*: Evershot 343.

HAMMILL, Captain Charles Ford, CIE 1944; *b* 27 Nov. 1891; *s* of Capt. Tynte Ford Hammill, CB, RN; *m* 1933, Cynthia, *d* of late Adm. Sir Howard Kelly, GBE, KCB. Entered RNC, Osborne, 1904. Served in HMS Colossus, European War, 1914-18. Commanded HMS Enterprise, 1938, HMS Cornwall, 1939-41; Naval Attaché, Paris, 1934-37; Commodore, Senior Naval Officer Persian Gulf, 1942-44; Commodore in Charge Royal Naval Establishments, Durban, 1944-46; retired, 1943. *Address*: Bleak House, Slindon, Arundel, West Sussex. *T*: Slindon 281. *Club*: Naval and Military.

HAMMOND, Maj.-Gen. Arthur Verney, CB 1944; DSO 1943; Indian Army, retired; *b* 16 Oct. 1892; *s* of late Col Sir Arthur G. Hammond, VC, KCB, DSO; *m* 1919, Mary Ellen Eaton; two *d*; *m* 1947, E. Boyes Cooper. *Educ*: Streete Court; Wellington Coll.; Royal Military College, Sandhurst. 2nd Lieut 1911, attached R West Kent Regt; Joined QVO Corps of Guides (Cavalry), 1912; European War, 1914-18 (despatches); NW Persia, 1920-21; Staff Coll., Quetta, 1925-26; Brigade Major, 1928-32; commanded The Guides Cavalry, 1937-39; War Office, London, 1939-40 (Col on the Staff); Brigade Comd 1941-43; served in Burma, 1942-43 (DSO); Maj.-Gen. 1942; ADC to the King, 1942-43; Comdg Lucknow District, 1944-45; retired, 1947. *Address*: 2 Connaught Place, Dun Laoghaire, Eire.

HAMMOND, Catherine Elizabeth, CBE 1950; Colonel, WRAC (retired); *b* 22 Dec. 1909; *d* of late Frank Ernest Rauleigh Eddolls and late Elsie Eddolls (*née* Cooper); *m*; one *s* one *d*. *Educ*: Lassington House, Highworth, Wilts; Chesterville Sch., Cirencester, Glos. Joined ATS (TA) (FANY), 1938; Private, 7th Wilts MT Co. 1939; 2nd Subaltern 1940; Capt., 1942; Major, Commanding Devon Bn, 1942; Lieut-Col, Asst Dir ATS Oxford, 1943; Col, Dep. Dir ATS (later WRAC), Eastern Command 1947-50; Hon. Col 54 (East Anglia) Div./Dist WRAC/TA, 1964-67. Chm., WRAC Assoc., 1966-70. Chm., Highworth and District Br., RNLI, 1970-. Mem., Highworth Town Council, 1973-. *Recreations*: hockey—Army (women), 1947-48; all games; racing. *Address*: Red Down, Highworth, Wilts SN6 7SH. *T*: Highworth 762331.

HAMMOND, Dame Joan (Hood), DBE 1974 (CBE 1963; OBE 1953); CMG 1972; Australian operatic, concert, oratorio, and recital singer; *b* 24 May 1912; *d* of late Samuel Hood Hammond and Hilda May Blandford. *Educ*: Presbyterian Ladies Coll., Pymble, Sydney, Australia. Student of violin and singing at Sydney Conservatorium of Music; played with Sydney Philharmonic Orchestra for three years. Sports writer, Daily Telegraph, Sydney. Commenced public appearances (singing) in Sydney, 1929; studied in Europe from 1936; made operatic debut, Vienna, 1939; London debut in Messiah, 1938. World Tours: British Isles, USA, Canada, Australasia, Malaya, India, E and S Africa, Europe, Scandinavia, Russia, etc. Guest Artist: Royal Opera House, Covent Garden; Carl Rosa; Sadler's Wells; Vienna Staatsoper; Bolshoi, Moscow; Marinsky, Leningrad; Riga, Latvia; New York City Centre; Australian Elizabethan Theatre Trust; Netherlands Opera; Barcelona Liceo. Operatic roles: Aida, Madame Butterfly, Tosca, Salome, Otello, Thais, Faust, Don Carlos, Eugene Onegin, Invisible City of Kitej, La Traviata, Il Trovatore, La Bohème, Pique Dame, Manon, Manon Lescaut, La Forza del Destino, Fidelio, Simone Boccanegra, Turandot, Tannhauser, Lohengrin, Damnation of

Faust, Martha, Pagliacci, Der Freischutz, Oberon, Magic Flute, Dido and Aeneas; World Premieres: Trojan Women, Wat Tyler, Yerma; British Premiere, Rusalka. HMV Recording artist. Master Tutor in Voice, and Vocal Consultant, Victorian College of the Arts; Mem., Victorian Council of the Arts. Volunteer Ambulance Driver, London, War of 1939-45. Sir Charles Santley Award, Worshipful Co. of Musicians, 1970. Coronation Medal 1953. *Publication*: A Voice, A Life, 1970. *Recreations*: golf (won first junior Golf Championship of NSW, 1930 and 1931; NSW. LGU State Title, 1932, 1934, 1935; runner-up Australian Open Championship, 1933; Mem. first LGU team of Australia to compete against Gt Brit., 1935) (runner-up NSW State Squash Championship, 1934), yachting, swimming, tennis, writing, reading. *Address*: c/o Bank of New South Wales, Sackville Street, London, W1; Private Bag 101, Geelong Mail Centre, Victoria 3221, Australia. *Clubs*: New Century (London); Barwon Heads Golf (Victoria); Royal Sydney Golf, Royal Sydney Yacht Squadron (Sydney, Australia); Royal Motor Yacht (Dorset, England).

HAMMOND, John Colman, OBE 1959; MA; Retired as Headmaster, Harrison College, Barbados, WI (1949-65); *b* 24 Nov. 1906; *s* of late Ven. T. C. Hammond; *m* 1943, Majorie (*née* Cruse); one *s* one *d*. *Educ*: Rossall Sch.; Pembroke Coll., Cambridge (MA). Senior History Master, St John's Sch., Leatherhead, Surrey, 1929-46; House Master, 1934-46; Headmaster, Sompting Abbotts Sch., Sussex. 1947-49. Coronation Medal, 1953. *Recreation*: bridge. *Address*: 23 Riggindale Road, Streatham, SW16. *T*: 01-769 4541.

HAMMOND, Kay, (Dorothy Katharine); actress: *b* 18 Feb.; *d* of late Sir Guy Standing, KBE, and late Dorothy Plaskitt (professionally known as Dorothy Hammond); *m* 1st, 1932, Sir Ronald George Leon, 3rd Bt (marriage dissolved); two *s*; 2nd, 1946, Sir John Selby Clements, *qv*. *Educ*: The Lodge, Banstead, Surrey. Studied at Royal Academy of Dramatic Art. Among London appearances are: Beatrice in Nine Till Six, Arts and Apollo, 1930; Evergreen, Adelphi, 1930; Daphne Hibberd in Can the Leopard...?, Haymarket, 1931; Emmie in My Hat, New, 1932; Elsa Frost in Woman Kind, Phoenix, 1933; Elizabeth Rimplegar in Three-Cornered Moon, Westminster, 1934; Dorothy Wilson in Youth at the Helm, Globe, 1935; Hon. Ursula Maddings in Bees on the Boatdeck, Lyric, 1936; Diana Lake in French Without Tears, Criterion, 1936-38; Adeline Rawlinson in Sugar Plum, Criterion, 1939; Elvira in Blithe Spirit, Piccadilly, St James's and Duchess, 1941-44; Amanda in Private Lives (revival), Apollo, 1944-45; Lady Elizabeth Grey in The Kingmaker; Melantha in Marriage à la Mode, by John Dryden, St James's, 1946; Mrs Sullen in The Beaux' Stratagem, by George Farquhar, Phoenix and Lyric, 1949; Ann in Man and Superman, New, 1951; The Happy Marriage, Duke of York's, 1952; Eliza in Pygmalion, St James's, 1953-54; The Little Glass Clock, Aldwych, 1954-55; Lydia Languish in The Rivals, Saville, 1956; Millamant in The Way of the World, Saville, 1956; The Rape of the Belt, Piccadilly, 1957; Gilt and Gingerbread, Duke of York's, 1959; The Marriage-Go-Round, 1959. In numerous films, 1931-. *Address*: 4 Rufford Court, 109 Marine Parade, Brighton, East Sussex BN2 1AT. *T*: Brighton 63026.
See also Sir J. R. Leon, Bt.

HAMMOND, Prof. Nicholas Geoffrey Lemprière, CBE 1974; DSO 1944; FBA 1968; DL; Henry Overton Wills Professor of Greek, University of Bristol, 1962-73; a Pro-Vice-Chancellor, 1964-66; *b* 15 Nov. 1907; *s* of late Rev. James Vavasour Hammond, Rector of St Just-in-Roseland, Cornwall, and Dorothy May; *m* 1938, Margaret Campbell, *d* of James W. J. Townley, CBE, MIEE; two *s* three *d*. *Educ*: Fettes Coll. (schol.); Caius Coll., Cambridge (schol.). 1st Cl. Classical Tripos Pts I and II, dist. in Hist., Pt II; Montagu Butler Prize; Sandys Student; Pres. CU Hockey Club; Treas. Union Soc. Fellow Clare Coll., Cambridge, 1930; University Lectr in Classics, 1936; Junior Proctor, 1939; Sen. Tutor, Clare Coll., 1947-54 (Hon. Fellow, 1974); Headmaster, Clifton Coll., 1954-62. Johnson Prof., Wisconsin Univ., 1973-74; Mellon Prof., Reed Coll., Oregon, 1975-76; Brittingham Prof., Wisconsin Univ., 1977. Chm., Managing Cttee, British Sch. at Athens, 1972-75. Served War of 1939-45, as Lt-Col, campaigns in Greece, Crete, Syria, and Mem. Allied Mil. Mission, Greece, 1943-44 (despatches twice, DSO). Pres., Hellenic Soc., 1965-68. DL: Bristol, 1965; Cambridge, 1974. Officer, Order of the Phœnix, Greece, 1946. *Publications*: Memoir of Sir John Edwin Sandys, 1933; History of Greece, 1959, 2nd edn, 1967; Epirus, 1967; A History of Macedonia, Vol. 1, 1972; Studies in Greek History, 1973; The Classical Age of Greece, 1976; Migrations and Invasions in Greece, 1976; Editor: Clifton Coll. Centenary Essays, 1962; Cambridge Ancient History, new edn, vols I and II; Oxford Classical Dictionary, 2nd edn, 1970; articles and reviews in learned jls. *Address*: 3 Belvoir Terrace, Trumpington Road, Cambridge. *T*: Cambridge 57151.

HAMMOND, Stanley Alfred Andrew, CMG 1943; Adviser on Establishment, Organization and Training, Barbados, 1959-64, retired; *b* 24 Oct. 1898; *s* of Alfred Gauntlett Hammond; *m* 1946, Adèle Alice Viola, *d* of William Wallace Cathcart Dunlop. *Educ*: Bancrofts Sch.; Trinity Coll. Oxford. 2nd Lieut RE 1917; Superintendent of Education, Nigeria, 1922; Dir of Education, Jamaica, 1928; Senior Education Commissioner, West Indies, 1936; Educn Adviser to Comptroller for Development and Welfare, West Indies, 1940; Chief Adviser Development and Welfare Organization, West Indies, 1948. Commissioner, Enquiry into Organization of the Civil Service, Leeward Islands, 1951. Adviser with special Duties, Development and Welfare Organisation, West Indies, 1950-53; retired, 1953. Dir of Training, Barbados, 1956. *Address*: c/o Midland Bank Ltd, 52 Oxford Street, W1; Little Edgehill, St Thomas, Barbados, West Indies.

HAMMOND INNES, Ralph; author and traveller; *b* 15 July 1913; *s* of late William Hammond and Dora Beatrice Innes; *m* 1937, Dorothy Mary Lang. Staff of Financial News, 1934-40. Served Artillery, 1940-46. Mem. Council, Timber Growers' Organisation. Works regularly translated into numerous languages; many book club and paperback edns throughout the world. *Publications include*: Wreckers Must Breathe, 1940; The Trojan Horse, 1940; Attack Alarm, 1941; Dead and Alive, 1946; The Lonely Skier, 1947; The Killer Mine, 1947; Maddon's Rock, 1948; The Blue Ice, 1948; The White South (Book Society Choice), 1949; The Angry Mountain, 1950; Air Bridge, 1951; Campbell's Kingdom (Book Society Choice), 1952; The Strange Land, 1954; The Mary Deare (chosen by Literary Guild of America, Book Soc. Choice), 1956; The Land God Gave to Cain, 1958; Harvest of Journeys (Book Soc. Choice), 1959; The Doomed Oasis (chosen by Literary Guild of America, Book Soc. Choice), 1960; Atlantic Fury (Book Society Choice), 1962; Scandinavia, 1963; The Strode Venturer, 1965; Sea and Islands (Book Society Choice), 1967; The Conquistadors (Book of the Month and Literary Guild), 1969; Levkas Man, 1971; Golden Soak, 1973; North Star, 1974; The Big Footprints, 1977; *films*: Snowbound, Hell Below Zero, Campbell's Kingdom, The Wreck of the Mary Deare. *Recreations*: cruising and ocean racing, forestry. *Address*: Ayres End, Kersey, Ipswich IP7 6EB. *T*: Hadleigh (Suffolk) 3294. *Clubs*: Royal Ocean Racing, Royal Cruising.

HAMNETT, family name of **Baron Hamnett.**

HAMNETT, Baron *cr* 1970 (Life Peer), of Warrington; **Cyril Hamnett;** Chairman: Warrington New Town Development Corporation, 1969-77; Co-operative Press Ltd, 1953-77 (Director since 1947); Director, Nor-West Co-operative Society Ltd, 1946-73; *b* 20 May 1906; *e s* of James Henry Hamnett and Gertrude Hilton; *m* 1929, Elsie Cox (*d* 1970); one *d*. *Educ*: elementary and Manchester Technical School. Engineering Journalism, Editor and Publicity Officer to Union of Shop, Distributive & Allied Workers until 1952; Admin. Officer, 1953-66. Chm., Reynolds News and Sunday Citizen, 1953-67; Mem., Newspaper Proprietors' Assoc., 1953-67; Mem., British Press Council, 1956-65; Mem., Central Exec., Co-operative Union, 1953-74 (Chm. Parly Cttee, 1969-74); Manchester City Magistrate, 1950-76 (Chm. of Licensing Bench, 1962-65, 1968-76); Mem., Licensing Planning Cttee, 1960-77; Mem. of Tribunals. *Publications*: pamphlets and articles to magazines, newspapers, on industrial, trade union and co-operative subjects. Hon. Fellow, Manchester Polytechnic. *Recreation*: the pursuit of the unattainable. *Address*: 11 Bolton Avenue, Manchester M19 1RP. *T*: 061-432 4801. *Club*: Warrington Sports.

HAMNETT, Thomas Orlando; Chairman, Greater Manchester Council, 1975-1976, Vice-Chairman, 1976; *b* 28 Sept. 1930; *s* of John and Elizabeth Hamnett; *m* 1954, Kathleen Ridgway; one *s* five *d*. *Educ*: Stockport Jun. Techn. Sch. Sheetmetal craftsman, 1946-. Member, Manchester City Council, 1963 until re-organisation: Vice-Chm., Health Cttee, Chm. sub cttee on Staff on Cleansing Cttee, Mem. Policy and Finance Cttees; Mem. Transportation, and Recreation and Arts Cttees, Greater Manchester Council. *Recreations*: football, cricket, table tennis. *Address*: 199 Chapman Street, Gorton, Manchester M18 8WP. *T*: 061-223 3098. *Club*: Gorton Trades and Labour (Chm.).

HAMPDEN; see Hobart-Hampden.

HAMPDEN, 6th Viscount *cr* 1884; **Anthony David Brand;** *b* 7 May 1937; *s* of 5th Viscount Hampden and of Imogen Alice Rhys, *d* of 7th Baron Dynevor; *S* father, 1975; *m* 1969, Cara Fiona, *e d* of Claud Proby; two *s* one *d*. *Educ*: Eton. *Heir*: *s* Hon. Francis Anthony Brand, *b* 17 Sept. 1970. *Address*: Glynde Combe, Glynde, Lewes, Sussex. *Club*: White's.

HAMPSHIRE, Sir (George) Peter, KCMG 1967 (CMG 1963); HM Diplomatic Service, retired; *b* 1 Dec. 1912; *s* of late G. N. Hampshire and Marie Hampshire (*née* West); *m* 1956, Eve Buhler (*née* Rowell); no *c. Educ:* Repton; Oriel Coll., Oxford. Apptd to War Office, 1935; Control Office for Germany and Austria and Foreign Office (German Section), 1946-48; Office of UK High Commission, Ottawa, 1948-51; UK Dep. High Comr, Dacca, 1953-55; IDC, 1956; Counsellor, British Embassy, Buenos Aires, 1957-60; Asst Under-Sec. of State, CRO, 1961-64; DSAO, 1965-66; High Comr, Trinidad and Tobago, 1966-70. *Address:* Sorrels House, Dagworth, Stowmarket, Suffolk. *T:* Haughley 285. *Club:* Travellers'.

HAMPSHIRE, Margaret Grace, MA; JP; Principal of Cheltenham Ladies' College, since 1964; *b* 7 Sept. 1918; *o d* of Dr C. H. Hampshire, CMG, MB, BS, BSc, sometime Sec. of British Pharmacopœia Commission, and Grace Mary Hampshire. *Educ:* Malvern Girls' Coll.; Girton Coll., Cambridge. BA 1941; MA 1945. Entered Civil Service, Board of Trade, 1941. Joined Staff of Courtaulds, 1951. Head of Government Relations Department, 1959-64. Member: Board of Governors, University Coll. Hosp., 1961-64; Marylebone Borough Council, 1962-64; SW Regional Hosp. Board, 1967-70; Midlands Electricity Consultative Council, 1973-. JP Cheltenham, 1970. *Recreations:* music, reading, foreign travel. *Address:* The Ladies' College, Cheltenham, Glos.

HAMPSHIRE, Sir Peter; *see* Hampshire, Sir G. P.

HAMPSHIRE, Stuart Newton, FBA 1960; Warden of Wadham College, Oxford University, since 1970; *b* 1 Oct. 1914; *s* of G. N. Hampshire and Marie West; *m* 1961, Renee Ayer. *Educ:* Repton; Balliol Coll., Oxford. 1st Cl. Lit Hum, Oxford, 1936. Fellow of All Souls Coll., and Lectr in Philosophy, Oxford, 1936-40. Service in Army, 1940-45. Personal Asst to Minister of State, Foreign Office, 1945; Lectr in Philosophy, University Coll., London, 1947-50; Fellow of New Coll., Oxford, 1950-55; Domestic Bursar and Research Fellow, All Souls Coll., 1955-60; Grote Prof. of Philosophy of Mind and Logic, Univ. of London, 1960-63; Prof. of Philosophy, Princeton Univ., 1963-70. Fellow, Amer. Acad. of Arts and Sciences, 1968. Hon. DLitt Glasgow, 1973. *Publications:* Spinoza, 1951; Thought and Action, 1959; Freedom of the Individual, 1965; Modern Writers and other essays, 1969; Freedom of Mind and other essays, 1971; (ed jtly) The Socialist Idea, 1975; Two Theories of Morality, 1977; articles in philosophical journals. *Address:* Wadham College, Oxford.

HAMPSHIRE, Susan; actress; *b* 12 May 1942; *d* of George Kenneth Hampshire and June Hampshire; *m* 1967, Pierre Granier-Deferre (marr. diss. 1974); one *s* (one *d* decd). *Educ:* Hampshire Sch., Knightsbridge. Stage: Expresso Bongo, 'that girl' in Follow That Girl, Marion Dangerfield in Ginger Man, Fairy Tales of New York, Kate Hardcastle in She Stoops to Conquer, On Approval, Mary in The Sleeping Prince, Nora in A Doll's House, Katharina in The Taming of the Shrew, Peter in Peter Pan, Jeannette in Romeo and Jeannette, Rosalind in As You Like It, title rôle in Miss Julie, Elizabeth in The Circle, Ann Whitefield in Man and Superman. TV Serials: Andromeda (title rôle), Fleur Forsyte in The Forsyte Saga (Emmy Award for Best Actress, 1970), Becky Sharp in Vanity Fair (Emmy Award for Best Actress, 1973), Sarah Churchill, Duchess of Marlborough, in The First Churchills (Emmy Award for Best Actress, 1971), Glencora Palliser in The Pallisers. Films include: During One Night, The Three Lives of Thomasina, Night Must Fall, Wonderful Life, Paris in August, The Fighting Prince of Donegal, Monte Carlo or Bust, Rogan, David Copperfield, Living Free, A Time for Loving, Malpertius (E. Poe Prizes du Film Fantastique, Best Actress, 1972), Neither the Sea Nor the Sand, Roses and Green Peppers, Bang. *Recreations:* gardening, music, the study of antique furniture. *Address:* c/o Midland Bank Ltd, 92 Kensington High Street, W8 4SH. *T:* 01-937 0962.

HAMPSON, Prof. Elwyn Lloyd, MDS, FDSRCS; HDD RCSE; Professor of Operative Dental Surgery, University of Sheffield, since 1960; Consultant Dental Surgeon to Sheffield Area Health Authority; *b* 31 Jan. 1916; *s* of John and Mary Hampson; *m* 1940, Anne Cottrell; one *s* one *d. Educ:* Calday Grange Grammar Sch., W Kirby, Cheshire; Univ. of Liverpool. BDS with 1st Class Hons 1939; HDD RCSE 1944; FDSRCS 1949; MDS 1954; FDSE 1964. House surg., Liverpool Dental Hosp., 1939; Royal Army Dental Corps, 1941-45; Lecturer in Operative Dental Surgery, Edinburgh Dental Sch., 1945-47; Lecturer and later Senior Lecturer in Operative Dental Surgery, Univ. of Sheffield, 1947-60. *Publications:* Textbook of Operative Dental Surgery, 1973; many papers in scientific jls. *Recreation:* water colour painting. *Address:* 6 Chorley Place, Fulwood, Sheffield S10 3RS. *T:* Sheffield 302104.

HAMPSON, Dr Keith; MP (C) Ripon, since Feb. 1974; *b* 14 Aug. 1943; *s* of Bertie Hampson and Mary Elizabeth Noble; *m* 1975, Frances Pauline (*d* 1975), *d* of Mr and Mrs Mathieu Donald Einhorn. *Educ:* King James I Grammar Sch., Bishop Auckland, Co. Durham; Univ. of Bristol; Harvard Univ. BA, CertEd, PhD. Personal Asst to Edward Heath, 1966 and 1970 Gen. Elections and in his House of Commons office, 1968; Lectr in American History, Edinburgh Univ., 1968-74. *Recreations:* tennis, dancing, music. *Address:* House of Commons, SW1A 0AA. *T:* 01-219 4119. *Club:* Carlton.

HAMPSTEAD, Archdeacon of; *see* Pickering, Ven. F.

HAMPTON, 6th Baron *cr* 1874; **Richard Humphrey Russell Pakington;** Bt 1846; *b* 25 May 1925; *s* of 5th Baron Hampton, OBE, and Grace Dykes (*d* 1959), 3rd *d* of Rt Hon. Sir Albert Spicer, 1st Bt; *S* father, 1974; *m* 1958, Jane Elizabeth Farquharson, *d* of late T. F. Arnott, OBE, TD, MB, ChB; one *s* two *d. Educ:* Eton; Balliol Coll., Oxford. Observer in Fleet Air Arm, Sub-Lt (A) RNVR, 1944-47. Varied employment, mainly with advertising agencies, 1949-58; staff of Worcestershire Branch Council for the Protection of Rural England, 1958-71; staff of Tansley Witt & Co., Chartered Accts, Birmingham, 1971-73. *Publication:* (with his father, Humphrey Pakington) The Pakingtons of Westwood, 1975. *Heir:* s Hon. John Humphrey Arnott Pakington, *b* 24 Dec. 1964. *Address:* Palace Farmhouse, Upton-on-Severn, Worcester WR8 0SN. *T:* Upton-on-Severn 2512.

HAMPTON, Christopher James, FRSL 1976; playwright; *b* 26 Jan. 1946; *s* of Bernard Patrick Hampton and Dorothy Patience Hampton (*née* Herrington); *m* 1971, Laura Margaret de Holesch; two *d. Educ:* Lancing Coll.; New Coll., Oxford (BA). First play: When Did You Last See My Mother?, 1964 (perf. Royal Court Theatre, 1966; transf. Comedy Theatre; prod. at Sheridan Square Playhouse, New York, 1967). Resident Dramatist, Royal Court Theatre, Aug. 1968-70. *Plays:* Total Eclipse, Prod. Royal Court, 1968; The Philanthropist, Royal Court, 1970 (Evening Standard Best Comedy Award, 1970; Plays & Players London Theatre Critics Best Play, 1970), Ethel Barrymore Theatre, New York, 1971; Savages, Royal Court, 1973, Comedy, 1973, Mark Taper Forum Theatre, Los Angeles, 1974 (Plays & Players London Theatre Critics Best Play, Jt Winner, 1973; Los Angeles Drama Critics Circle Award for Distinguished Playwriting, 1974); Treats, Royal Court, 1976, Mayfair, 1976; Able's Will, BBC TV, 1977; *translations:* Marya, by Isaac Babel, Royal Court, 1967; Uncle Vanya, by Chekhov, Royal Court, 1970; Hedda Gabler, by Ibsen, Fest. Theatre, Stratford, Ont., 1970; A Doll's House, by Ibsen, Playhouse Theatre, New York, 1971, Criterion, London, 1973, Vivian Beaumont Theatre, New York, 1975; Don Juan, by Molière, Bristol Old Vic, 1972; Tales from the Vienna Woods, by Horváth, National Theatre, 1977. *Publications:* When Did You Last See My Mother?, 1967; Total Eclipse, 1969; The Philanthropist, 1970; Savages, 1974; Treats, 1976; *translations:* Isaac Babel, Marya, 1969; Chekhov, Uncle Vanya, 1971; Ibsen, Hedda Gabler, 1972; Ibsen, A Doll's House, 1972; Molière, Don Juan, 1972; Horváth, Tales from the Vienna Woods, 1977. *Recreations:* travel, cinema. *Address:* 2 Kensington Park Gardens, W11. *Club:* Dramatists'.

HAMSON, Prof. Charles John, QC 1975; Professor of Comparative Law, University of Cambridge, 1953-73; Fellow of Trinity College, since 1934; President, International Academy of Comparative Law, since 1966; Barrister-at-Law, Gray's Inn, Bencher, 1956, Treasurer, 1975; Corr. Mem. Institut de France (Acad. Sci. Mor. et Pol.), since 1961; Doctor *hc* Universities of Grenoble, Nancy, Poitiers, Bordeaux, Brussels, Montpellier, Strasbourg; Chevalier de la Légion d'Honneur; *b* 23 Nov. 1905; *er s* of Charles Edward Hamson (formerly of Constantinople), and of Thérèse Boudon; *m* 1933, Isabella, *y d* of Duncan Drummond and Grace Gardiner of Auchterarder; one *d. Educ:* Downside; Trinity Coll., Cambridge. Entrance and Sen. Scholar in Classics; Classical Tripos Part I 1925, Part II 1927 (distinction); Capt. CU Epée Team, 1928; Davison Scholar, Harvard Law Sch., 1928-29; Linthicum Foundation Prize (North-western Univ.) 1929; Yorke Prize, 1932; LLB 1934; LLM 1935. Asst Lecturer, 1932, Lecturer, 1934, Reader in Comparative Law, 1949; Chm. Faculty Board of Law, 1954-57. Editor, Cambridge Law Jl, 1955-74; Univ. Press Syndic, 1955-69; Library Syndic, 1966-73; Gen. Bd, 1966-69. Served War of 1939-45; commissioned in Army, 1940; detached for service with SOE; Battle of Crete, 1941; POW Germany, 1941-45. Hamlyn Lectures on Conseil d'Etat, 1954; Visiting Professor: University of Michigan Law Sch. (Ann Arbor), 1957; Paris Faculty of Law, 1959; Univ. of Pennsylvania, 1964; Auckland Univ., 1967; professeur associé, Paris II, 1973-74; Sherrill Lecturer, Yale Law Sch., 1960. Hon. Fellow, St Edmund's House, Cambridge, 1976. *Address:* 7 Cranmer Road, Cambridge. *T:* 50638.

HAMYLTON JONES, Keith; HM Diplomatic Service; HM Ambassador, to Costa Rica, since 1974, to Honduras, since 1975, and to Nicaragua, since 1976; *b* 12 Oct. 1924; *m* 1953, Eira Morgan; one *d*. *Educ:* St Paul's Sch.; Balliol Coll., Oxford (Domus Scholar in Classics, 1943); BA 1948; MA 1950. Welsh Guards, 1943; Italy, 1944 (Lieut); S France, 1946 (Staff Captain). HM Foreign (subseq. Diplomatic) Service, 1949; 3rd Sec., Warsaw, 1950; 2nd Sec., Lisbon, 1953; 1st Sec., Manila, 1957; Head of Chancery and HM Consul, Montevideo, 1962; Head of Chancery, Rangoon, 1967; Asst Head of SE Asia Dept, FCO, 1968; Consul-General, Lubumbashi, 1970-72; Counsellor, FCO, 1973-74. *Publication:* (as Peter Myllent) The Ideal World, 1972. *Recreations:* reading, writing, walking, music, tennis. *Address:* 71 Peel Street, Campden Hill, W8; Fairholm, Fairwarp, Uckfield, East Sussex; Cedar Cottage, Tinkers Lane, Blackboys, East Sussex.

HAN SUYIN, (Mrs Elizabeth Comber); doctor and author; (*née* Elizabeth K. Chow); *b* 12 Sept. 1917; *d* of Y. T. Chow (Chinese) and M. Denis (Belgian); *m* 1st, 1938, General P. H. Tang, (*d* 1947); one *d*; 2nd, 1952, L. F. Comber. *Educ:* Yenching Univ., Peking, China; Brussels Univ., Brussels, Belgium; London Univ., London, England. Graduated MB, BS, London (Hons) in 1948, since when has been a practising doctor. *Publications: as Han Suyin:* Destination Chungking, 1942; A Many Splendoured Thing, 1952; And the Rain My Drink, 1956; The Mountain Is Young, 1958; Cast but One Shadow and Winter Love, 1962; The Four Faces, 1963; China in the Year 2001, 1967; The Morning Deluge, 1972; Wind in the Tower, 1976; Lhasa, the Open City, 1977; *autobiography:* The Crippled Tree, 1965; A Mortal Flower, 1966; Birdless Summer, 1968. *Recreations:* botany, riding, swimming, lecturing. *Address:* c/o Jonathan Cape Ltd, 30 Bedford Square, WC1.

HANBURY, Lt-Col Hanmer Cecil, MVO 1953; MC 1943; JP; Vice Lord-Lieutenant (formerly Vice-Lieutenant) of Bedfordshire, since 1970; *b* 5 Jan. 1916; *yr s* of late Sir Cecil Hanbury, MP, FLS, and late Mrs Hanbury-Forbes, OBE, of Kingston Maurward, Dorchester, Dorset, and La Mortola, Ventimiglia, Italy; *m* 1939, Prunella Kathleen Charlotte, *d* of late Air Cdre T. C. R. Higgins, CB, CMG, DL, JP, Turvey House, Beds; one *s* one *d*. *Educ:* Eton; RMC, Sandhurst. 2nd Lieut Grenadier Guards, 1936; served 1939-45 with Grenadier Guards, France, Belgium, N Africa, Italy; Capt. 1943; Temp. Major, 1944; Major 1948; retired 1958. BRCS, Bedfordshire: Dir, 1959-71; Dep. Pres., 1972; Chm., Beds T&AVR Cttee, 1970-; Vice-Chm., E Anglia T&AVRA. DL 1958, JP 1959, Beds; High Sheriff, Beds, 1965. *Recreation:* shooting. *Address:* Turvey House, Turvey, Beds MK43 8EL. *T:* Turvey 227. *Clubs:* White's, Army and Navy, Pratt's.

HANBURY, Harold Greville, QC 1960; DCL; Vinerian Professor Emeritus of English Law, Oxford; Hon. Fellow, Lincoln College, Oxford; Hon. Master of the Bench, Inner Temple; *b* 19 June 1898; *s* of late Lt-Col Basil Hanbury and late Hon. Patience Verney; *m* 1927, Anna Margaret, *d* of late Hannibal Dreyer, Copenhagen, Denmark. *Educ:* Charterhouse; Brasenose Coll., Oxford (Scholar). Vinerian Law Scholar, 1921; Fellow of Lincoln Coll., Oxford 1921-49; Fellow of All Souls Coll., 1949-64; Vinerian Prof. of English Law, Oxford, 1949-64. Visiting Prof., Univ. of Ife, 1962-63; Dean of Law Faculty, Univ. of Nigeria, 1964-66. Barrister-at-Law, Inner Temple, 1922; Rhodes Travelling Fellow, 1931-32; Senior Proctor, Oxford Univ., 1933-34 and 1944-45. President: Bentham Club, UCL, 1954; Soc. of Public Teachers of Law, 1958-59. Chairman: Court of Inquiry into Provincial Omnibus Industry, 1954; Board of Inquiry into West Indian Airways, 1958; Tribunal for Industrials, Gibraltar, 1960; Independent Mem. Commns of Inquiry on Retail Distributive Trades, 1946; Minimum Wage Arbitrator in Nigeria, 1955. *Publications:* Essays in Equity, 1934; Modern Equity, 1935 (10th edn *sub nom*. Hanbury and Maudsley, 1976); Traité Pratique des Divorces et des Successions en Droit Anglais (with R. Moureaux), 1939 (2nd edn 1952); English Courts of Law, 1944 (4th edn by D. C. M. Yardley, 1967); Principles of Agency, 1952 (2nd edn, 1960); The Vinerian Chair and Legal Education, 1958; Biafra: a challenge to the conscience of Britain, 1968; articles in legal periodicals. *Recreations:* reading, aelurophily (Vice-Pres. Oxford and District Cat Club), formerly cricket, travelling. *Address:* Marlborough House, Falmouth, Cornwall. *T:* Falmouth 312154.

HANBURY, Sir John (Capel), Kt 1974; CBE 1969; Formerly Chairman, Allen and Hanburys Ltd, 1954-73 (Director, 1944); *b* 26 May 1908; *e s* of late Frederick Capel Hanbury; *m* 1935, Joan Terry Fussell; two *s* one *d* (and one *s* decd). *Educ:* Downside; Trinity Coll., Cambridge. Mem., Pharmacopoeia Commn, 1948-73; Chm., Central Health Services Council, 1970-76; Member, Standing Pharmaceutical Adv. Cttee, Dept of Health and Social Security; Pres. Assoc. of Brit. Pharmaceutical Industry, 1950-52; Chm., Assoc. of Brit. Chemical Manufacturers, 1961-63; Pres. Franco-British Pharmaceutical Commn, 1955. Vice-Chm., Essex AHA; Mem., Thames Water Authority. FRIC 1947; FPS 1955. Fellow, UCL, 1977. *Recreations:* horticulture, archæology. *Address:* Amwellbury House, Ware, Herts. *T:* Ware 2108. *Club:* United Oxford & Cambridge University.

HANBURY-TENISON, Airling Robin, MA, FLS, FRGS; farmer; Chairman, Survival International, since 1969; *b* 7 May 1936; *s* of Gerald Evan Farquhar Tenison and Ruth Julia Margarette Tenison, *d* of John Capel Hanbury, Pontypool; *m* 1959, Marika Hopkinson; one *s* one *d*. *Educ:* Eton; Magdalen Coll., Oxford (MA). Made first land crossing of South America at its widest point, 1958 (Mrs Patrick Ness Award, RGS, 1961); explored Tassili N'Ajjer, Tibesti and Aïr mountains in Southern Sahara, 1962-66; crossed S America in a small boat from the Orinoco to Buenos Aires, 1964-65; Geographical Magazine Amazonas Expedn, by Hovercraft, 1968; Trans-African Hovercraft Expedn (Dep. Leader), 1969; visited 33 Indian tribes as guest of Brazilian Govt, 1971; Winston Churchill Memorial Fellow, 1971; British Trans Americas Expedn, 1972; explored Outer Islands of Indonesia, 1973; Eastern Sulawesi, 1974; Sabah, Brunei, Sarawak, 1976; RGS Mulu (Sarawak) Expedn (Leader), 1977-78. Mem. Council, RGS, 1968-70, 1971-76. *Publications:* The Rough and the Smooth, 1969; A Question of Survival, 1973; A Pattern of Peoples, 1975; Report of a Visit to the Indians of Brazil, 1971; articles in: The Times, Spectator, Blackwood's Magazine, etc; articles and reviews in Geographical Magazine (numerous), Geographical Jl, Ecologist, Expedition, etc. *Recreations:* travelling, riding on Bodmin Moor, enjoying his wife's cooking. *Address:* Maidenwell, Cardinham, Bodmin, Cornwall PL30 4DW. *T:* Cardinham 224 and 282. *Club:* Kildare Street and University (Dublin).
See also R. Hanbury-Tenison.

HANBURY-TENISON, Richard; DL; *b* 3 Jan. 1925; *e s* of late Major G. E. F. Tenison, Lough Bawn, Co. Monaghan, Ireland, and Ruth, *o* surv. *c* of late J. C. Hanbury, JP, DL, Pontypool Park, Monmouthshire; *m* 1955, Euphan Mary, *er d* of late Major A. B. Wardlaw-Ramsay, 21st of Whitehill, Midlothian; three *s* two *d*. *Educ:* Eton; Magdalen Coll., Oxford. Served Irish Guards, 1943-47 (Captain, wounded). Entered HM Foreign Service, 1949: 1st Sec., Vienna, 1956-58; 1st Sec. (and sometime Chargé d'Affaires), Phnom Penh, 1961-63, and Bucharest, 1966-68; Counsellor, Bonn, 1968-70; Head of Aviation and Telecommunications Dept, FCO, 1970-71; Counsellor, Brussels, 1971-75; retired from Diplomatic Service, 1975. Pres., Monmouthshire Rural Community Council, 1959-75; Chm., Gwent Community Services Council; Pres., Gwent Local Hist. Council. DL 1973, High Sheriff 1977, Gwent. *Recreations:* shooting, fishing, conservation. *Address:* 30 Coleherne Court, SW5. *T:* 01-373 5714; Clytha Park, Abergavenny, Gwent. *T:* Gobion 300; Lough Bawn, Co. Monaghan. *Clubs:* Boodle's; Kildare Street and University (Dublin).
See also A. R. Hanbury-Tenison.

HANBURY-TRACY, family name of **Baron Sudeley.**

HANCOCK, Lt-Col Sir Cyril (Percy), KCIE 1946 (CIE 1941); OBE 1930; MC; *b* 18 Sept. 1896; *m* Joyce, *d* of F. R. Hemingway, ICS; three *s* one *d*. *Educ:* Wellington Coll.; RMC, Sandhurst. Commd Indian Army, 114th Mahrattas, 1914; ADC to GOC 1st Corps MEF (Gen. Sir Alexander Cobbe, VC), 1918; GSO 3 at GHQ Baghdad, 1919; transf. to Bombay Political Dept, 1920; Asst Pvte Sec. to Governor of Bombay (Lord Lloyd), 1921; Asst Pvte Sec. to Viceroy (Lord Reading), 1923; Sec., Rajkot Pol. Agency, 1925; Sec. to Resident for Rajputana, 1929; Prime Minister, Bharatpur State, Rajputana, 1932; Dep. Sec., Govt of India (Pol. Dept, i/c War Br.), 1939; Resident: Eastern States, Calcutta, 1941; Western India States and Baroda Rajkot, 1943. *Address:* Woodhayes, Firgrove Road, Yateley, Hants GU17 7NH. *T:* Yateley 873240. *Club:* MCC.
See also G. F. Hancock.

HANCOCK, David John Stowell; Under Secretary, HM Treasury, since 1975; *b* 27 March 1934; *s* of late Alfred George Hancock and Florence Hancock (*née* Barrow); *m* 1966, Sheila Gillian Finlay; one *s* one *d*. *Educ:* Whitgift Sch.; Balliol Coll., Oxford. Asst Principal, Bd of Trade, 1957; transf. to HM Treasury, 1959; Principal, 1962; Harkness Fellow, 1965-66; Private Sec. to Chancellor of the Exchequer, 1968-70; Asst Sec., 1970; Financial and Economic Counsellor, Office of UK Permanent Rep. to European Communities, 1972-74. *Recreations:* gardening, theatre. *Address:* 157 Rosendale Road, SE21 8HE. *T:* 01-670 3155. *Club:* Civil Service.

HANCOCK, Geoffrey Francis, CMG 1977; HM Diplomatic Service; Counsellor, Beirut, since Sept. 1973; *b* 20 June 1926; *s* of Lt-Col Sir Cyril Hancock, *qv* ; *m* 1960, Amelia Juana Aragon; one *s* one *d* . *Educ:* Wellington; Trinity Coll., Oxford. MA 1951. Third Sec., Mexico City, 1953; Second Sec., Montevideo, 1956; Foreign Office, 1958; Madrid, 1958; FO, 1960; MECAS, 1962; First Sec., Baghdad, 1964-67 and 1968-69; FCO, 1969-73. *Recreations:* music, sailing. *Address:* c/o Foreign and Commonwealth Office, Downing Street, SW1A 2AL.

HANCOCK, Prof. Sir Keith; see Hancock, Prof. Sir W. K.

HANCOCK, Maj.-Gen. Michael Stephen, CB 1972; MBE 1953; retired 1972; Planning Inspector, Department of the Environment, since 1972; *b* 19 July 1917; *s* of late Rev. W. H. M. Hancock and late Mrs C. C. Hancock (*née* Sherbrooke); *m* 1941, Constance Geraldine Margaret Ovens, *y d* of late Brig.-Gen. R. M. Ovens, CMG; one *s* one *d.* *Educ:* Marlborough Coll.; RMA, Woolwich. Commnd into Royal Signals, 1937; Comdr, Corps Royal Signals, 1st British Corps, 1963-66; Sec., Mil. Cttee, NATO, 1967-68; Chief of Staff, FARELF, 1968-70; VQMG, MoD, 1970-72. Col Comdt, Royal Signals, 1970-77. Chm., CCF Assoc., 1972-. CEng; FIEE; MBIM. *Recreation:* sailing. *Address:* Brakey Hill, Godstone, Surrey. *T:* Godstone 2273. *Club:* Army and Navy.

HANCOCK, Norman, CB 1976; CEng, FRINA; RCNC; Director of Warship Design, Ministry of Defence, 1969-76; *b* 6 March 1916; *o s* of Louis Everard Hancock, Plymouth; *m* 1940, Marie E., *d* of William E. Bow; two *s.* *Educ:* Plymouth Grammar Sch.; RNC Greenwich. Asst Constructor, AEW, Haslar, 1940; Constructor, Naval Construction Dept, 1944; British Services Observer (Constructor Comdr), Bikini, 1946. HM Dockyard, Singapore, 1949; Frigate design, Naval Construction Dept, 1952; Chief Constructor in charge of R&D, 1954; Prof. of Naval Architecture, RNC, Greenwich, 1957-62; Asst Dir of Naval Construction, in charge of Submarine Design and Construction, 1963-69. Liveryman, Worshipful Co. of Shipwrights; Mem. Council, RINA. *Recreations:* organ music, cabinet making, travel. *Address:* 41 Cranwells Park, Bath, Avon. *T:* Bath 26045. *Club:* Royal Commonwealth Society.

HANCOCK, Sir Patrick (Francis), GCMG 1974 (KCMG 1969; CMG 1956); HM Diplomatic Service, retired; Secretary, The Pilgrim Trust, since 1975; *b* 25 June 1914; *s* of late R. E. Hancock, DSO; *m* 1947, Beatrice Mangeot; one *s* one *d.* *Educ:* Winchester Coll.; Trinity Coll., Cambridge. Entered HM Foreign Service, 1937. Appointed Principal Private Sec., to Foreign Sec., 1955; Head of Western Dept, Foreign Office, 1956; Ambassador to Israel, 1959-62; Ambassador to Norway, 1963-65; Asst Under-Sec. of State, FO, 1965-68. Dep. Under-Sec. of State, FCO, 1968-69; Ambassador in Rome, 1969-74. Commander, Order of North Star, 1956. *Recreation:* salmon fishing. *Address:* 5 Shelley Court, Tite Street, SW3; The Old Vicarage, Affpuddle, Dorset. *T:* Puddletown 315.

HANCOCK, P(ercy) E(llis) Thompson, FRCP; Hon. Consultant Physician: The Royal Free Hospital; The Royal Marsden Hospital; Potters Bar and District Hospital; *b* 4 Feb. 1904; *s* of Frank Hancock; *m* 1932, Dorothy Barnes (*d* 1953); two *d* ; *m* 1955, Laurie Newton Sharp. *Educ:* Wellington Coll., Berks; Caius Coll., Cambridge; St Bartholomew's Hospital. MB 1937, BCh 1930, Cantab; FRCP 1944. Formerly: Senior Examiner in Medicine, Univ. of London; Dir of Dept of Clinical Res., Royal Marsden Hosp. and Inst. of Cancer Res. Member: Council, Imperial Cancer Res. Fund; Grand Council, British Empire Cancer Campaign for Research; Exec. Cttee, British Cancer Council; Chm., Clinical Res. Cttee; Mem. Exec. Cttee, Action on Smoking and Health. Hosp. Visitor, King Edward's Hosp. Fund for London; Mem., London Medical Appeals Tribunals, 1970-76. FRSocMed (Pres., Section of Oncology, 1974-75); Fellow, Assoc. Européene de Médecine Interne d'Ensemble. Hon. Member: American Gastroscopic Soc., 1958; Sociedad Chilena de Cancerología; Sociedad Chilena de Hematología; Sociedad Médica de Valparaíso. *Publications:* (joint) Cancer in General Practice; The Use of Bone Marrow Transfusion with massive Chemotherapy, 1960; (joint) Treatment of Early Hodgkin's Disease, 1967. *Recreations:* dining and wining. *Address:* 23 Wigmore Place, W1H 9DD. *T:* 01-935 6726; Is Morus, Santa Margherita di Pula, Cagliari, Sardinia.

HANCOCK, Sheila, OBE 1974; actress; *d* of late Enrico Hancock and late Ivy Woodward; *m* 1st, 1955, Alexander Ross (*d* 1971); one *d* ; 2nd, 1973, John Thaw; one *d* . *Educ:* Dartford County Grammar Sch.; Royal Academy of Dramatic Art. Acted in Repertory, Theatre Workshop, Stratford East, for 8 years. West End starring roles in: Rattle of a Simple Man, The Anniversary, A Delicate Balance (RSC), So What About Love?, Absurd Person Singular, Déjà Revue, The Bed Before Yesterday. Has starred in several successful revues; repeated stage role in film of The Anniversary. Appeared on Broadway in Entertaining Mr Sloane. Many Television successes, including her own colour spectacular for BBC2, and several comedy series. Awards: Variety Club, London Critics, Whitbread Trophy (for best Actress on Broadway). *Recreations:* reading, music, driving fast cars. *Address:* Tarlton, Glos.

HANCOCK, Air Marshal Sir Valston Eldridge, KBE 1962 (CBE 1953); CB 1958; DFC 1945; retired; grazier; *b* 31 May 1907; *s* of R. J. Hancock, Perth, W Australia; *m* 1932, Joan E. G., *d* of Col A. G. Butler, DSO, VD; two *s* one *d.* *Educ:* Hale Sch., Perth; RMC, Duntroon; psa; idc. Joined Royal Military College, Duntroon, 1925; transferred RAAF, 1929; Dir of Plans, 1940-41; commanded 71 (Beaufort) Wing, New Guinea, 1945; Commandant RAAF Academy, 1947-49; Deputy Chief of Air Staff, 1951-53; Air Mem. for Personnel, Air Board, 1953-54; Head of Australian Joint Services Staff, UK, 1955-57; Extra Gentleman Usher to the Royal Household, 1955-57; AOC 224 Group, RAF, Malaya, 1957-59; Air Officer Commanding Operational Command, 1959-61; Chief of Air Staff, Royal Australian Air Force, 1961-65. Commissioner-Gen., Australian Exhibit Organization Expo, 1967. Pres., Royal Commonwealth Soc., WA Branch. *Recreations:* literature and sport. *Address:* 108a Victoria Avenue, Dalkeith, WA 6009, Australia. *Club:* Weld (Perth).

HANCOCK, Prof. Sir (William) Keith, KBE 1965; Kt 1953; MA; FBA 1950; Emeritus Professor and Hon. Fellow; Professor of History, Australian National University, Canberra, 1957-65; *b* Melbourne, 26 June 1898; *s* of Archdeacon William Hancock, MA; *m* 1st, 1925, Theaden Brocklebank (*d* 1960); 2nd, 1961, Marjorie Eyre. Fellow of All Souls Coll., Oxford, 1924-30; Prof. of Modern History in the University of Adelaide, 1924-33; Prof. of History, Birmingham Univ., 1934-44; Chichele Prof. of Economic History, University of Oxford 1944-49; Dir, Institute of Commonwealth Studies, and Prof. of British Commonwealth Affairs in the University of London, 1949-56; Dir of the Research Sch. of Social Sciences, Australian National Univ., 1957-61; appointed to War Cabinet Offices as Supervisor of Civil Histories, 1941, thereafter editor of series. Fellow: Churchill Coll., Cambridge, 1964; St John's Coll., Cambridge, 1971-72. Hon. Fellow, Balliol Coll., Oxford; Corresp. Mem., Sch. of Oriental and African Studies. FAHA (1st Pres.) 1969. Hon. DLitt (Rhodes, Cambridge, Birmingham, Oxford, Cape Town, Melbourne, ANU, Adelaide, WA). Foreign Hon. Member: American Historical Association; American Academy of Arts and Sciences. Order of Merit of Republic of Italy. *Publications:* Ricasoli, 1926; Australia, 1930; Survey of British Commonwealth Affairs, 1937, 1940, and 1942; Politics in Pitcairn, 1947; (with M. M. Gowing) British War Economy, 1949; Country and Calling, 1954; War and Peace in this Century, 1961; Smuts: The Sanguine Years, 1870-1919, Vol. I, 1962; The Fields of Force, 1919-1950, Vol. II, 1968; Discovering Monaro, 1972; Professing History, 1976. *Address:* 49 Gellibrand Street, Campbell, Canberra, ACT 2601, Australia. *Club:* Athenæum.

HAND, Most Rev. Geoffrey David; see Papua New Guinea, Archbishop of.

HANDCOCK, family name of **Baron Castlemaine.**

HANDFIELD-JONES, Ranald Montagu, MC; Consulting Surgeon, St Mary's Hospital; Consulting General Surgeon, the Hospital for Women, Soho Square; Member Court of Examiners, RCS; Examiner in Surgery to Universities of London, Cambridge, Liverpool, Leeds and Manchester; *b* 12 May 1892; *s* of late C. R. Handfield-Jones, MD, and Alice Jervis; *m* 1920; three *s* one *d.* *Educ:* Epsom Coll.; St Mary's Hospital Medical Sch.; London Univ.; Epsom Scholarship to St Mary's Hosp.; Master of Surgery (University of London), MB, BS (Hons in Surgery and Midwifery, University Gold Medallist); FRCS; Hunterian Prof., RCS. Served European War in France, Oct. 1914-May 1918; prisoner of war, May-Nov. 1918. *Publications:* The Essentials of Modern Surgery (with A. E. Porritt), 5th edn, 1955; Surgery of the Hand, 2nd edn 1946; papers to medical journals. *Recreations:* entomology, cricket, golf, photography. *Address:* 9 Hurlingham Gardens, SW6. *T:* 01-736 5671.

HANDFORD, Stanley Alexander, MA Oxon; *b* Manchester, 1898; *s* of late Thomas Edward Handford, Harrogate; *m* 1923, Doris (*d* 1975), *d* of late James Henry Ollerhead, Oswestry. *Educ:* Bradford Grammar Sch.; Balliol Coll., Oxford (Classical Schol.); 1st class Hon. Classical Moderations and Craven Scholarship, 1920; Ireland Scholarship, 1921; 1st Class Literae

Humaniores and Charles Oldham Prize, 1922; Asst Lecturer in Classics, University Coll. of Swansea, 1922-23; Asst Lectr and Lectr, King's Coll., London, 1923-46; Reader, 1946-66. *Publications:* Revision of L. W. Hunter's Aeneas on Siegecraft, 1927; Xenophon's Anabasis, Books III and IV, 1928; The Latin Subjunctive, 1947; Caesar's Conquest of Gaul (Penguin Classics), 1951; Caesar's Gallic War, Books II and III, 1952; Fables of Aesop (Penguin Classics), 1954; Pocket Latin-English Dictionary, 1955; Sallust's Jugurthine War and Conspiracy of Catiline (Penguin Classics), 1963; Tacitus's Agricola and Germania (Penguin Classics), 1970. *Recreation:* music. *Address:* Hurstleigh, Elm Park Road, Pinner, Mddx HA5 3LE.

HANDLEY, Mrs Carol Margaret; Headmistress, Camden School for Girls, since 1971; *b* 17 Oct. 1929; *d* of Claude Hilary Taylor and Margaret Eleanor Taylor (*née* Peebles); *m* 1952, Eric Walter Handley, *qv*. *Educ:* St Paul's Girls' Sch.; University Coll., London (BA), Fellow 1977. Asst Classics Mistress: North Foreland Lodge Sch., 1952; Queen's Gate Sch., 1952; Head of Classics Dept, Camden Sch. for Girls, 1956; Deputy Headmistress, Camden Sch. for Girls, 1964. *Publications:* articles and book reviews for classical jls. *Recreations:* walking, riding, travel. *Address:* Camden School for Girls, Sandall Road, NW5 2DB. *T:* 01-485 3414.

HANDLEY, David John D.; see Davenport-Handley.

HANDLEY, Prof. Eric Walter; FBA 1969; Professor of Greek, University College, London, since 1968, and Director of the Institute of Classical Studies, University of London, since 1967; *b* 12 Nov. 1926; *s* of late Alfred W. Handley and A. Doris Cox; *m* 1952, Carol Margaret Taylor (see C. M. Handley). *Educ:* King Edward's Sch., Birmingham; Trinity Coll., Cambridge. Stewart of Rannoch Schol. and Browne Medal, 1945. Asst Lectr in Latin and Greek, University Coll. London, 1946, Lectr, 1949, Reader, 1961, Prof. of Latin and Greek, 1967-68. Cromer Greek Prize (jtly), 1958; Vis. Lectr on the Classics, Harvard, 1966; Vis. Mem., Inst. for Advanced Study, Princeton, 1971; Vis. Prof., Stanford Univ., 1977. Sec. Council Univ. Classical Depts, 1969-70, Chm., 1975-. *Publications:* (with John Rea) The Telephus of Euripides, 1957; The Dyskolos of Menander 1965; papers in class. jls, etc. *Recreations:* boating, hill-walking, travel. *Address:* University College London, Gower Street, WC1E 6BT. *T:* 01-387 7050. *Club:* United Oxford & Cambridge University.

HANDLEY, Richard Sampson, OBE 1946; Surgeon, The Middlesex Hospital, W1, since 1946, Surgeon Emeritus, 1974; *b* 2 May 1909; *e s* of late W. Sampson Handley; *m* 1st, 1942, Joan (*d* 1975), *d* of Dr Cyril Gray, Newcastle upon Tyne; one *s* one *d*; 2nd, 1976, Rosemary, *d* of Captain E. Dickinson, Reigate. *Educ:* Uppingham Sch.; Gonville and Caius Coll., Cambridge; The Middlesex Hospital. Entrance Schol., Middx Hosp., 1930; BA Cantab 1930 (Pts 1 and 2, Nat. Sci. Tripos); MRCS, LRCP and MA, MB, BCh Cantab, 1933; University Demonstrator of Anatomy, Cambridge, 1936; Asst Pathologist, 1937, and Surgical Registrar, 1939, Middx Hosp. FRCS 1938; Mem. Council, 1966, Vice-Pres., 1974, RCS; Hon. Sec. RSM, 1967-73, Pres., Surgery Section, 1971; Pres., Assoc. of Surgeons of GB and Ireland, 1973-74. Served, 1939-46 (despatches, OBE); Temp. Major RAMC and Surgical Specialist, serving with BEF, 1939, and MEF, 1940; Temp. Lieut-Col, RAMC, 1944, serving BLA. Late Examiner in Surgery, Cambridge Univ.; late Mem. Court of Examiners, RCS; late Hon. Sec., Assoc. of Surgeons of GB and Ireland. Hon. Member: Hellenic Surgical Soc.; Salonika Med. Soc. Hon. MD Salonika, 1976. *Publications:* papers and lectures on surgical subjects, especially with reference to malignant disease. *Recreations:* sailing, model-making. *Address:* Elmdon Cottage, Chalkpit Lane, Marlow, Bucks SL7 2JE. *T:* Marlow 6155; 107 Harley Street, W1. *T:* 01-486 1088.

HANDLEY, Vernon George, FRCM 1972; Musical Director and Conductor, Guildford Corporation, and Conductor, Guildford Philharmonic Orchestra and Choir, and Proteus Choir, since 1962; *b* 11 Nov. 1930; 2nd *s* of Vernon Douglas Handley and Claudia Lilian Handley, Enfield; *m* 1954, Barbara, *e d* of Kilner Newman Black and Joan Elfriede Black, Stoke Gabriel, Devon; one *s* one *d* (and one *s* decd). *Educ:* Enfield Sch.; Balliol Coll., Oxford (BA); Guildhall Sch. of Music. Conductor: Oxford Univ. Musical Club and Union, 1953-54; OUDS, 1953-54; Tonbridge Philharmonic Soc., 1958-61; Hatfield Sch. of Music and Drama, 1959-61; Prof. at RCM: for Orchestra and Conducting, 1966-72; for Choral Class, 1969-72. Guest Conductor from 1961: Bournemouth Symph. Orch.; Birmingham Symph. Orch.; Royal Philharmonic Orch.; London Philharmonic Orch.; BBC Welsh Orch.; BBC Northern Symph. Orch.; Royal Liverpool Philharmonic Orch.; Ulster Orch.; BBC Scottish Symphony Orch.; New Philharmonia Orch.; conducted London Symphony Orch. in internat. series, London, 1971; toured Germany, 1966.

Regular broadcaster and has made many records. Hon. RCM, 1970. Arnold Bax Mem. Medal for Conducting, 1962. *Recreations:* bird photography, old-fashioned roses. *Address:* Chatham, Cwmystwyth, Dyfed.

HANDLIN, Prof. Oscar; Carl H. Pforzheimer University Professor, Harvard University, since 1972; *b* 29 Sept. 1915; *m* 1937, Mary Flug; one *s* two *d*; *m* 1977, Lilian Bombach. *Educ:* Brooklyn Coll. (AB); Harvard (MA, PhD). Instructor, Brooklyn Coll., 1938-39; Harvard Univ.: Instructor, 1939-44; Asst Prof., 1944-48; Associate Prof., 1948-54; Prof. of History, 1954-65; Charles Warren Prof. of Amer. Hist., and Dir, Charles Warren Center for Studies in Amer. Hist., 1965-72; Harmsworth Prof. of Amer. History, Oxford Univ., 1972-73. Dir, Center for Study of History of Liberty in America, 1958-67; Chm., US Bd of Foreign Scholarships, 1965-66 (Vice-Chm. 1962-65). Hon. Fellow, Brandeis Univ., 1965. Hon. LLD Colby Coll., 1962; Hon. LHD: Hebrew Union Coll., 1967; Northern Michigan, 1969; Seton Hall Univ., 1972; Boston Coll., 1975; Hon. HumD Oakland, 1968; Hon. LittD Brooklyn Coll., 1972. *Publications:* Boston's Immigrants, 1790-1865, 1941; (with M. F. Handlin) Commonwealth, 1947; Danger in Discord, 1948; (ed) This Was America, 1949; Uprooted, 1951, 2nd edn 1972; Adventure in Freedom, 1954; American People in the Twentieth Century, 1954 (rev. edn 1963); (ed jtly) Harvard Guide to American History, 1954; Chance or Destiny, 1955; (ed) Readings in American History, 1957; Race and Nationality in American Life, 1957; Al Smith and his America, 1958; (ed) Immigration as a Factor in American History, 1959; John Dewey's Challenge to Education, 1959; (ed) G. M. Capers, Stephen A. Douglas, Defender of the Union, 1959; Newcomers, 1960; (ed jtly) G. Mittleberger, Journey to Pennsylvania, 1960; (ed) American Principles and Issues, 1961; (with M. F. Handlin) The Dimensions of Liberty, 1961; The Americans, 1963; (with J. E. Burchard) The Historian and the City, 1963; Firebell in the Night, 1964; A Continuing Task, 1964; (ed) Children of the Uprooted, 1966; The History of the United States, vol. 1, 1967, vol. 2, 1968; America: a History, 1968; (with M. F. Handlin) The Popular Sources of Political Authority, 1967; The American College and American Culture, 1970; Facing Life: Youth and the Family in American History, 1971; A Pictorial History of Immigration, 1972; (with M. F. Handlin) The Wealth of the American People, 1975. *Address:* 18 Agassiz Street, Cambridge, Mass 02140, USA. *Clubs:* St Botolph (Boston); Harvard (NY); Faculty (Cambridge, Mass).

HANDS, Terence David, (Terry Hands); Associate Director, Royal Shakespeare Company, since 1967; Consultant Director, Comédie Française, since 1975; *b* 9 Jan 1941; *s* of Joseph Ronald Hands and Luise Berthe Kohler; *m* 1st, 1964, Josephine Barstow (marr. diss. 1967); 2nd, 1974, Ludmila Mikael; one *d*. *Educ:* Woking Grammar Sch.; Birmingham Univ. (BA Hons Eng. Lang. and Lit.); RADA (Hons Dip.). Founder-Artistic Dir, Liverpool Everyman Theatre, 1964-66; Artistic Dir, RSC Theatregoround, 1966-67. Chevalier des Arts et des Lettres, 1973. *Director* (for Liverpool Everyman Theatre, 1964-66): The Importance of Being Earnest; Look Back in Anger; Richard III; The Four Seasons; Fando and Lis; *Artistic Director* (for RSC Theatregoround): The Proposal, 1966; The Second Shepherds' Play, 1966; The Dumb Waiter, 1967; Under Milk Wood, 1967; *directed for RSC:* The Criminals, 1967; The Latent Heterosexual, 1968; The Merry Wives of Windsor, 1968, 1975; Bartholomew Fair, 1969; Pleasure and Repentance, 1969; Pericles, 1969; Women Beware Women, 1969; Richard III, 1970; Balcony, 1971; Man of Mode, 1971; The Merchant of Venice, 1971; Murder in the Cathedral, 1972; Cries from Casement, 1973; Romeo and Juliet, 1973; The Bewitched, 1974; Henry IV, Parts 1 and 2, 1975; Henry V, 1975; Old World, 1976; Henry VI parts 1, 2 and 3, Coriolanus, 1977; *directed for Comédie Française:* Richard III, 1972 (Meilleur Spectacle de l'Année award); Pericles, 1974; Twelfth Night, 1976 (Meilleur Spectacle de l'Année award); Le Cid, 1977; *directed for Paris Opéra:* Verdi's Otello, 1976; *directed for Burg Theatre, Vienna:* Troilus and Cressida, 1977; *recording:* Murder in the Cathedral, 1976. *Publications:* trans. (with Barbara Wright) Genet, The Balcony, 1971; Pleasure and Repentance, 1976; (ed Sally Beauman) Henry V, 1976; contribs to Theatre 72, Playback. *Address:* c/o Royal Shakespeare Theatre, Stratford-upon-Avon, Warwicks CV37 6BB. *T:* Stratford-upon-Avon 3693.

HANDY, Gen. Thomas Troy, Hon. KBE 1945; DSC (US) 1918; DSM (US) 1945 (Oak Leaf Clusters, 1947 and 1954); Legion of Merit, 1945; formerly Deputy to General Ridgway (Supreme Allied Commander in Europe and Commander-in-Chief US European Command, 1952-53); *b* Tennessee, 11 March 1892; *s* of Rev. T. R. Handy and Caroline (*née* Hall); *m* 1920, Alma Hudson, Va; one *d*. *Educ:* Va Mil. Inst. (BS). Served European War, 1917-18 (DSC, French Croix de Guerre); War of 1939-45;

when US a belligerent, 1942, became Asst Chief of Staff, Ops Div.; Dep. Chief of Staff, US Army, 1944; Gen. 1945. Comdg-Gen. 4th Army, Texas, 1947; C-in-C all Amer. Troops in Europe (except in Austria and Trieste), 1949-52; retired 1954. Grand Officer, Legion of Honour, 1951. *Address:* 122 Brandon Drive East, San Antonio, Texas 78209, USA.

HANES, Prof. Charles Samuel, FRS 1942; FRSC 1956; Professor of Biochemistry, University of Toronto, 1951-68, now Emeritus; Hon. Fellow of Downing College, Cambridge; *b* 1903; *m* 1931, Theodora Burleigh Auret, Johannesburg; one *d. Educ:* University of Toronto (BA 1925); University of Cambridge, PhD Cantab 1929; ScD Cantab 1952. Lately Reader in Plant Biochemistry, University of Cambridge, and Director, Agricultural Research Council Unit of Plant Biochemistry; previously Dir of Food Investigation, Dept of Scientific and Industrial Research. Flavelle Medal, Royal Society of Canada, 1958. *Address:* Department of Biochemistry, University of Toronto, Toronto 5, Canada; 60 Beech Avenue, Apt 4, Toronto, Ont., Canada M4E 3H4.

HANGER, Hon. Sir Mostyn, KBE 1973; Chief Justice of Supreme Court of State of Queensland, 1971-77; *b* 3 Jan. 1908; *s* of Thomas Hanger; *m* 1936, Greta Lumley Robertson; three *s* one *d. Educ:* Gympie State High Sch.; Queensland Univ. BA 1929; LLM 1941. Admitted to Bar, 1930; QC 1950; Supreme Court Judge, 1953; Pres., Industrial Court, 1962-71; Actg Chief Justice, 1970-71. Served with RAAF in New Guinea, 1942-45 (Flt-Lt). *Recreations:* golf, orchids. *Address:* 73 Seventh Avenue, St Lucia, Brisbane, Qld 4067, Australia. *T:* 713393. *Clubs:* Queensland, United Services (Brisbane).

HANHAM, Sir Michael (William), 12th Bt *cr* 1667; DFC 1945; RAFVR; *b* 31 Oct. 1922; *s* of Patrick John Hanham (*d* 1965) and Dulcie, *yr d* of William George Daffarn and *widow* of Lynn Hartley; *S* kinsman, Sir Henry Phelips Hanham, 11th Bt, 1973; *m* 1954, Margaret Jane, *d* of W/Cdr Harold Thomas, RAF retd, and Joy (*née* MacGeorge); one *s* one *d. Educ:* Winchester. Joined RAF 1942, as Aircrew Cadet; served No 8 (Pathfinder) Gp, Bomber Command, 1944-45; FO 1945. At end of war, retrained as Flying Control Officer; served UK and India, 1945-46; demobilised, 1946. Joined BOAC, 1947, Traffic Branch; qualified as Flight Operations Officer, 1954; served in Africa until 1961; resigned, 1961. Settled at Trillinghurst Farmhouse and started garden and cottage furniture making business, 1963; now concerned also with management of Wimborne estate. *Recreations:* restoration of old houses (Vice-Chm. Weald of Kent Preservation Soc., 1972-74); preservation of steam railways; sailing. *Heir: s* William John Edward Hanham, *b* 4 Sept. 1957. *Address:* Deans Court, Wimborne, Dorset; Trillinghurst Farmhouse, Goudhurst, Cranbrook, Kent. *T:* Goudhurst 421. *Clubs:* Pathfinder; Hastings and St Leonards Sailing.

HANKEY, family name of **Baron Hankey.**

HANKEY, 2nd Baron *cr* 1939, of The Chart; **Robert Maurice Alers Hankey;** KCMG 1955 (CMG 1947); KCVO 1956; *b* 4 July 1905; *s* of 1st Baron Hankey, PC, GCB, GCMG, GCVO, FRS, and Adeline, *d* of A. de Smidt; *S* father, 1963; *m* 1st, 1930, Frances Bevyl Stuart-Menteth (*d* 1957); two *s* two *d*; 2nd, 1962, Joanna Riddall Wright, *d* of late Rev. James Johnstone Wright. *Educ:* Rugby Sch.; New Coll., Oxford. Diplomatic Service, 1927; served Berlin, Paris, London, Warsaw, Bucharest, Cairo, Teheran, Madrid, Budapest. HM Ambassador at Stockholm, 1954-60. Permanent UK Delegate to OEEC and OECD, and Chm., Economic Policy Cttee, 1960-65; Vice-Pres., European Inst. of Business Administration, Fontainbleau. Dir, Alliance Bldg Soc., 1970-. Member: Internat. Council of United World Colleges, 1966-; Council, Internat. Baccalaureat Foundn, Geneva, 1967-76. Pres., Anglo-Swedish Soc., 1969-75. Grand Cross of Order of the North Star (Sweden), 1954. *Recreations:* reading, tennis, ski-ing, music. *Heir: er s* Hon. Donald Robin Alers Hankey [*b* 12 June 1938; *m* 1st, 1963, Margaretha, *yr d* of H. Thorndahl, Copenhagen; 2nd, 1974, Eileen Désirée, *yr d* of Maj.-Gen. Stuart Battye, *qv*]. *Address:* Hethe House, Cowden, Edenbridge, Kent. *T:* Cowden 538.
See also Sir John Benn, Hon. H. A. A. Hankey.

HANKEY, Col George Trevor, OBE 1945; TD; late RAMC (TA); Consulting Dental and Oral Surgeon; *b* London, 15 March 1900; *er s* of J. Trevor Hankey, Lingfield, Surrey; *m* 1933, Norah (*d* 1939), *y d* of late R. H. G. Coulson, Tynemouth; (one *s* decd); *m* 1945, Mary Isobel, *d* of late R. H. G. Coulson, Tynemouth. *Educ:* Oakham Sch; Guy's Hosp. LDSEng, 1922; LRCP, MRCS 1925; elected FDS, RCS, 1948, FRCS 1977; Consultant Dental Surgeon, St Bartholomew's Hospital, 1928-65, retd; Consultant, The London Hosp. Dental Sch., 1928-66; Lectr in Oral Surg.,

University of London. Fellow, Royal Society of Medicine; Examr in Dental Surgery, RCS England, 1948-54; Examiner in Dental and Oral Surgery, University of London, 1948-56; Pres. Odontological Section, RSM 1957-58; Charles Tomes Lecturer, RCS, 1953; Mem. Bd Dent. Faculty RCS, 1958-73; Vice-Dean, 1966-67. John Tomes Prize, RCS, 1960, Mem. Bd Govs, London Hosp., 1954-63, and NE Metrop. Reg. Hosp. Bd, 1959-62; Fellow, Brit. Assoc. Oral Surgeons, Pres., 1963-64; Sprawson Lectr, 1967. Commissioned RAMC(TA), 1927; OC 141 Field Ambulance, 1939; OC 12 Gen. Hosp., 1952; Hon. Col 1957-62. Served War of 1939-45 (despatches, prisoner, OBE). Officer, Legion of Merit, USA, 1951. *Publications:* chapter on Mandibular Joint Disorders, in Surgical Progress, 1960; contrib. Brit. Dental Jl and British Jl of Oral Surgery; various communications on Oral Surgery and Pathology to Proc. Royal Society of Medicine. *Recreations:* golf, fishing. *Address:* 3 Harcourt House, 19a Cavendish Square, W1. *T:* 01-580 1141.

HANKEY, Hon. Henry Arthur Alers, CMG 1960; CVO 1959; HM Diplomatic Service, retired; *b* 1 Sept. 1914; *y s* of 1st Baron Hankey, PC, GCB, GCMG, GCVO, FRS; *m* 1941, Vronwy Mary Fisher; three *s* one *d. Educ:* Rugby Sch.; New Coll., Oxford. Entered HM Diplomatic Service, 1937; Third Sec., HM Embassy, Paris, 1939; Second Sec., Madrid, 1942; First Sec., Rome, 1946; Consul, San Francisco, 1950; First Sec., Santiago, 1953; promoted Counsellor and apptd Head of American Dept, Foreign Office, Sept. 1956; Counsellor, HM Embassy, Beirut, 1962-66; Ambassador, Panama, 1966-69; Asst Under-Sec. of State, FCO, 1969-74. Director: Lloyds Bank International, 1975-; Antofagasta (Chile) & Bolivia Railway Co. Ltd. *Recreations:* ski-ing, tennis, music. *Address:* Hosey Croft, Hosey Hill, Westerham, Kent. *T:* Westerham 62309. *Club:* United Oxford & Cambridge University.

HANKINSON, Cyril Francis James, Editor of Debrett's Peerage, 1935-62; *b* 4 Nov. 1895; *e s* of late Charles James Hankinson, MBE, JP (pen-name Clive Holland), of Ealing, W5, and formerly of Bournemouth, and late Violet, *d* of William Downs, CE; *m* 1942, Lillian Louise (*d* 1976), *d* of late Walter Herbert Read, FSI, 29 Castlebar Road, Ealing, W5; one *s. Educ:* Queen Elizabeth's Grammar Sch., Wimborne, Dorset. European War, 1915-19 with Kite Balloon Section RFC, France, Belgium and subsequently at Air Ministry; Asst Editor of National Roll of the Great War, 1919-21; Asst Editor of Debrett, 1921-35. *Publications:* My Forty Years with Debrett, 1963; A Political History of Ealing, 1972. Contributor to London, Commonwealth, and American Press, and to Encyclopaedia Britannica and Chambers's Encyclopaedia, of articles regarding Royal Family, Peerage, Heraldry, etc; also lectured and broadcast on these subjects. *Recreations:* reading biographies, watching cricket. *Address:* 13 Welsby Court, Eaton Rise, Ealing, W5. *T:* 01-997 5018. *Club:* MCC.

HANKINSON, Sir Walter Crossfield, KCMG 1948 (CMG 1941); OBE 1936; MC; *b* 1894; *y s* of late A. W. Hankinson; *m* 1936, Sheila, *d* of Dr Frederick Watson, Sydney. *Educ:* Manchester Grammar Sch.; Jesus Coll., Oxford. MA. Served European War, 1914-18 (MC); Colonial Office, 1920; transferred to Dominions Office, 1925; Acting Representative in Australia of HM Govt in the United Kingdom, 1931-32 and 1935-36; Principal Private Sec. to successive Secretaries of State for Dominion Affairs, 1937-39; Principal Sec., Office of High Commissioner for the United Kingdom in Canada, 1939-41; Principal Sec. to United Kingdom Representative to Eire, 1942-43; Dep. High Comr in Australia, 1943-47; Acting High Comr June 1945-June 1946; UK High Commissioner in Ceylon, 1948-51; British Ambassador to Republic of Ireland, 1951-55, retired. *Recreations:* bowls, gardening. *Address:* 25 Beauchamp Street, Deakin, Canberra, ACT 2600, Australia. *Club:* United Oxford & Cambridge University.

HANLEY, Denis Augustine; *b* 1903; *s* of late Edmund Hanley, Kintbury, Berks; *m* 1935, Kathleen Mary, *d* of J. P. Eyre, 56 York Terrace, Regent's Park; three *d. Educ:* Downside; Trinity Coll., Cambridge. MP (C) Deptford, 1931-35. Royal Naval Scientific Service, 1938-54. *Address:* Woodcombe, Oxbridge, Bridport, Dorset. *T:* Netherbury 343.

HANLEY, Gerald Anthony; author; *b* 17 Feb. 1916; *s* of Edward Michael Hanly and Bridget Maria Roche. *Publications:* Monsoon Victory, 1946; The Consul at Sunset, 1951; The Year of the Lion, 1953; Drinkers of Darkness, 1955; Without Love (Book Society Choice), 1957; The Journey Homeward (Book Society Choice), 1961; Gilligan's Last Elephant, 1962; See You in Yasukuni, 1969; Warriors and Strangers, 1971. *Recreations:* music, languages. *Address:* c/o Gillon Aitken, 17 Belgrave Place, SW1X 8BS.

HANLEY, Howard Granville, CBE 1975; MD, FRCS; Urologist, Royal Masonic Hospital London; Consulting Urologist, King Edward VII's Hospital for Officers, W1; Urological Consultant to the Army; Hon. Consulting Urologist, Royal Hospital, Chelsea; Dean of Institute of Basic Medical Sciences, Royal College of Surgeons; b 27 July 1909; s of F. T. Hanley; m 1939, Margaret Jeffrey; two s. Educ: St Bees Sch., Cumberland. MB 1932; MD 1934; FRCS 1937. Hunterian Prof., Royal College of Surgeons, 1955; Visiting Prof. of Urology: University of Calif, Los Angeles, 1958; Ohio State Univ., Columbus, 1961; University of Texas Southwestern Medical Sch., 1963; Tulane University, New Orleans, 1967; late Dean, Inst. of Urology, London Univ. Pres., Urological Section Royal Society of Medicine, 1964-65; Mem. Council, RCS, 1969. Fellow, Association of Surgeons of Great Britain and Ireland; Past Pres. (formerly Treasurer, Sec. and Vice-Pres.), British Assoc. Urological Surgeons; Sec., Hunterian Soc.; Hon. Librarian, Royal Society of Medicine. Member: Internat. Soc. Urology; German Urol. Soc.; Soc. Française d'Urologie; Med. Soc. London; Chelsea Clinical Soc. Corresp. Mem., Amer. Assoc. Genito-urinary Surgeons; Hon. Member: Mexican Urological Soc.; Western Sect. Amer. Urological Assoc. Liveryman, Worshipful Soc. of Apothecaries of London. Hon. FACS. Publications: Recent Advances in Urology, 1957; chapters in: British Surgical Practice, 1960; Modern Trends in Urology, 1960; A Text Book of Urology, 1960; contribs to jls on urology. Recreation: gardening. Address: 147 Harley Street, W1. T: 01-935 4444; Brandon House, North End Avenue, NW3. T: 01-458 2035. Club: Athenæum.

HANLEY, James; novelist, short story writer and playwright; b 1901. Publications: Men in Darkness (stories), 1931, New York, 1932; The Furys (novel), 1934; Stoker Bush (novel), 1935; The Maelstrom (novel), 1935; The Furys, New York, 1935; The Secret Journey, 1936; The Wall, 1936; Broken Water (an Autobiography), 1937; Grey Children (A Sociological Study), 1937; Half-an-Eye (stories), 1937; Hollow Sea (novel), 1938; Soldiers Wind (Essays), 1938; People Are Curious (stories), 1938; Between the Tides (Essays), 1939; Our Time is Gone (novel), 1940; The Ocean, 1941; No Directions (novel), 1943; At Bay (stories), 1943; Sailor's Song (novel), 1943; Crilley (stories), 1945; What Farrar Saw (novel), 1945; Winter Song (novel), 1950; A Walk in the Wilderness (stories), 1950; The Closed Harbour (novel), 1952; Don Quixote Drowned (essays), 1953; The Welsh Sonata (novel), 1954; Levine (novel), 1955; An End and a Beginning (novel), 1958; Say Nothing (novel), 1962; Plays One (play), 1968; Another World (novel), 1972; A Woman in the Sky (novel), 1973; A Dream Journey (novel), 1976. Recreations: fishing, music. Address: c/o David Higham Associates, 5/8 Lower John Street, Golden Square, W1R 4HA.

HANLEY, Sir Michael (Bowen), KCB 1974; attached Ministry of Defence; b 24 Feb. 1918; s of late Prof. J. A. Hanley, PhD, ARCS; m 1957, Lorna Margaret Dorothy, d of late Hon. Claude Hope-Morley. Educ: Sedbergh School; Queen's Coll., Oxford (MA). Served War of 1939-45. Address: c/o Ministry of Defence, SW1.

HANLON, John Austin Thomas, JP; a Recorder of the Crown Court, since 1972; b 18 Dec. 1905; s of late Thomas Peter Hanlon; m 1933, Marjorie Edith (Nesta), d of late John W. Waltham Taylor, Portsmouth. Educ: Portsmouth Grammar Sch. Joined Portsmouth Police, 1924; served through ranks CID, Det. Sgt, Det. Inspector; Dep. Chief Constable, Scarborough, 1934; Chief Constable, Leamington, 1938; Home Office Regional Comr's Staff, 1940; admitted student Gray's Inn, 1934; called to the Bar, 1944; practised NE Circuit. Deputy Chm. of Quarter Sessions: Co. Northumberland, 1955-65; Co. Durham, 1958-65; Chm., Co. Northumberland QS, 1965-71. Chm. of Traffic Comrs, Northern Traffic Area, 1953-75. JP Northumberland, 1954-. Recreations: athletics (British Team, Olympic Games, 1928; AAA 220 yds and 440 yds Champion, 1929; many internat. teams and events); fishing, shooting, motoring, music. Address: Hartburn, Morpeth, Northumberland. T: Hartburn 269. Club: Northern Counties (Newcastle upon Tyne).

HANMER, Sir John (Wyndham Edward), 8th Bt cr 1774; JP; b 27 Sept. 1928; s of Sir (Griffin Wyndham) Edward Hanmer, 7th Bt, and Aileen Mary (d 1967), er d of Captain J. E. Rogerson; S father, 1977; m 1954, Audrey Melissa, d of Major A. C. J. Congreve; two s. Educ: Eton. Captain (retired), The Royal Dragoons. JP Flintshire, 1971; High Sheriff of Clwyd, 1977. Recreation: shooting. Heir: s Wyndham Richard Guy Hanmer, b 27 Nov. 1955. Address: The Mere House, Hanmer, Whitchurch, Salop. T: Hanmer 383. Club: Cavalry and Guards.

HANNAH, Air Marshal Sir Colin Thomas, KCMG 1972; KCVO 1977; KBE 1971 (CBE 1954; OBE 1951); CB 1959; Governor of Queensland, 1972-77; b 22 Dec. 1914; s of late Thomas Howard Hannah; m 1939, Patricia, d of Harold Gordon; one d. Educ: Hale Sch., Perth; RAAF Coll. Served War of 1939-45; Dep. Dir, Armament, 1941-43; OC 6 Squadron, New Guinea, 1943-44; OC W Area, 1945-46; OC RAAF Amberley, 1949-51; DPS and DGP, 1951-54; IDC, 1955; Sen. ASO, RAF HQ FEAF, Singapore, 1956-59; Dir-Gen., Plans and Policy, 1959-61; DCAS, 1961-65; Operational Comd, RAAF, 1965-67; AOC, Support Comd, 1967-70; Chief of Air Staff, RAAF, 1970-72. ADC to HM The Queen, 1952-56. DGU 1975. KStJ 1972. Recreations: golf, fishing. Address: c/o National Bank of Australasia Ltd, 308/322 Queen Street, Brisbane, Queensland 4000, Australia. Clubs: Australian (Sydney); Queensland (Brisbane).

HANNAM, John Gordon; MP (C) Exeter, since 1970; b 2 Aug. 1929; s of Thomas William and Selina Hannam; m 1956, Wendy Macartney; two d. Educ: Yeovil Grammar Sch. Studied Agriculture, 1945-46. Served in: Royal Tank Regt (commissioned), 1947-48; Somerset LI (TA), 1949-51. Studied Hotel industry, 1950-52; Managing Dir, Hotels and Restaurant Co., 1952-61; Developed Motels, 1961-70; Chm., British Motels Fedn, 1967-74, Pres. 1974-; Mem. Council, BTA, 1968-69; Mem. Economic Research Council, 1967-. PPS to: Minister for Industry, 1972-74; Chief Sec., Treasury, 1974. Secretary: Cons. Parly Trade Cttee, 1971-72; Cons. Latin-American Gp; All-Party Disablement/Mobility Gp, 1974-; Cons. Arts and Amenities Cttee, 1974-; Chm., West Country Cons. Cttee, 1973-74; Vice-Chairman: Cons. Parly Energy Cttee, 1974-; Arts and Heritage Cttee, 1974-; Sports Cttee, 1974-; Chm., Cons. Cttee on Latin-America. Captain: Lords and Commons Tennis Club, 1975-; Lords and Commons Ski Club, 1977-; Cdre, House of Commons Yacht Club, 1975-. Mem., Snowdon working party on the disabled, 1975-76. Member: Glyndebourne Festival Soc.; Friends of Covent Garden. Pres., Exeter Chambers of Trade and Commerce. Recreations: music (opera), art (modern), sailing (anything), skiing (fast), Cresta tobogganing (foolish); county tennis and hockey (Somerset tennis champion, 1953). Address: Woodslea House, Brampford Speke, near Exeter, Devon. Clubs: All England Lawn Tennis, Ski of GB, Royal London Yacht.

HANNAM, Michael Patrick Vivian; HM Diplomatic Service; Consul General, Jerusalem, since 1976; b 13 Feb. 1920; s of Rev. Wilfrid L. Hannam, BD, and Dorothy (née Parker); m 1947, Sybil Huggins; one s one d. Educ: Westminster Sch. LMS Railway, 1937-40. Served in Army, 1940-46 (Major, RE). LMS Railway, 1946-50; Malayan Railway, 1950-60. FO, 1960-62; First Sec., British Embassy, Cairo, 1962-65; Principal British Trade Comr, Hong Kong, 1965-69 (and Consul, Macao, 1968-69); Counsellor, Tripoli, 1969-72; Counsellor (Economic and Commercial), Nairobi, 1972-73, Dep. High Commissioner, Nairobi, 1973-76. Recreations: music, swimming, tennis, photography. Address: Little Oaklands, Langton Green, Kent. T: Langton 2163. Clubs: Travellers', Royal Commonwealth Society; Lake (Kuala Lumpur); Turf (Cairo); Hong Kong, Country (Hong Kong).

HANNAN, William; insurance agent; b 30 Aug. 1906; m; one d. Educ: North Kelvinside Secondary Sch. MP (Lab) Maryhill, Glasgow, 1945-Feb. 1974; Lord Commissioner of HM Treasury, 1946-51; an Opposition Whip, Nov. 1951-53; PPS to Rt Hon. George Brown as First Sec. and Sec. of State for Economic Affairs, 1964-66, as Sec. of State for Foreign Affairs, 1966-68. Mem., British Delegation to Council of Europe. Town Councillor, Glasgow, 1941-45. Recreation: music. Address: 26 Balmoral Drive, Bearsden, Glasgow.

HANNAY, David Hugh Alexander; Counsellor, HM Diplomatic Service; Head of Energy Department, Foreign and Commonwealth Office, since 1977; b 28 Sept. 1935; s of Julian Hannay; m 1961, Gillian Rex; four s. Educ: Winchester; New Coll., Oxford. Foreign Office, 1959-60; Tehran, 1960-61; 3rd Sec., Kabul, 1961-63; 2nd Sec., FO, 1963-65; 2nd, later 1st Sec., UK Delegn to European Communities, Brussels, 1965-70; 1st Sec., UK Negotiating Team with European Communities, 1970-72; Chef de Cabinet to Sir Christopher Soames, Vice President of EEC, 1973-77. Recreations: travel, photography. Address: 3 The Orchard, Bedford Park, W4. T: 01-994 7004.

HANNAY, Lady Fergusson; see Leslie, Doris.

HANNEN, Mrs Nicholas; see Seyler, Athene.

HANNIGAN, James Edgar; Director of Housing 'B', Department of the Environment, since 1975; b 12 March 1928; s of James Henry and Kathleen Hannigan; m 1955, Shirley Jean

Bell; two d. Educ: Eastbourne Grammar Sch.; Sidney Sussex Coll., Cambridge (BA). Civil Service, 1951; Asst Sec., Housing Div., Min. of Housing and Local Govt, 1966-70; Asst Sec., Local Govt Div., DoE, 1970-72. Under Sec. 1972; Regional Dir for West Midlands, DoE, 1972-75; Chm., West Midlands Economic Planning Bd, 1972-75. Recreation: finding time. Address: 4 Pashley Road, Eastbourne, East Sussex.

HANNON, Ven. Arthur Gordon, MA, TCD; retired, with General Licence from the Bishop of Down and Dromore, 1960; b 16 April 1891; s of John Alexander Hannon and Martha Matilda, d of Rev. James Rice, BD, TCD; m 1923, Hilda Catherine Stewart-Moore Denny, g d of late Provost Traill of TCD; five s one d. Educ: Corrig Sch., Kingstown; Trinity Coll., Dublin; Honoursman Literature, Logic and Ethics, and Modern History (1st Class), Exhibitioner. Auditor of Coll. Theological Soc. TCD, represented Dublin Univ. in Athletics. Flour Milling Industry, 1911-13; Curate of Drumcondra and North Strand, Dublin, 1915-17; Head of Trinity Coll. Mission in Belfast, 1917-20; Rector of Ballymoney, 1920-24; Rector of Shankill Parish, Lurgan, 1924-40; Precentor of Dromore, 1924-32; Archdeacon of Dromore, 1933-40; Examining Chaplain to Bishop of Down, 1935-40; General Licence from Bishop of Down, 1940-54; Head of Community Relations Training Centre, 1940-54; Vicar of Kilbroney, Co. Down, 1954-60. Irish Representative, Congress of Europe, 1948. Chm., Churches' Industrial Council, 1959-61. Publications: The War and Foreign Missions, 1915; The Kingdom of God in Ireland, 1936. Address: Iderone, Mosside, Ballymoney, Co. Antrim, N Ireland.

HANSFORD, John Edgar; Under-Secretary, Defence Policy and Materiel Group, HM Treasury, since 1976; b 1 May 1922; s of Samuel George Hansford, ISO, MBE, and Winifred Louise Hansford; m 1947, Evelyn Agnes Whitehorn; one s. Educ: Whitgift Middle Sch., Croydon. Clerical Officer, Treasury, 1939. Served War of 1939-45: Private, Royal Sussex Regt, 1940; Lieutenant, Royal Fusiliers, 1943; served in: Africa, Mauritius, Ceylon, India, Burma, on secondment to King's African Rifles, demobilised, 1946. Exec. Officer, Treasury, 1946-50; Higher Exec. Officer, Regional Bd for Industry, Leeds, 1950-52; Exchange Control, Treasury, 1952-54; Agricultural Policy, Treasury, 1954-57; Sen. Exec. Officer, and Principal, Treasury, 1957-61; Principal, Social Security Div., Treasury, 1961-66; Public Enterprises Div., 1966-67; Overseas Develt Div., 1967-70; Asst Sec., Defence Policy and Materiel Div., Treasury, 1970-76; Under-Sec. in charge of Gp, 1976. Recreations: gardening, motoring. Address: 76 Nork Way, Banstead, Surrey SM7 1HW. T: Burgh Heath 57076.

HANSFORD JOHNSON, Pamela; see Johnson, P. H.

HANSON, Sir Anthony (Leslie Oswald), 4th Bt, cr 1887; b 27 Nov. 1934; s of Sir Gerald Stanhope Hanson, 2nd Bt, and Flora Liebe (d 1956), e d of late Lieut-Col W. A. R. Blennerhassett; S half-brother, 1951; m 1964, Denise Jane (Tuppence), e d of R. S. Rolph. Educ: Hawtrey's, Savernake, Wilts; Gordonstoun, Elgin, Morayshire. Career in Royal Navy until 1955; farming, 1956-. Recreation: hunting.

HANSON, Dr Bertram Speakman, CMG 1963; DSO 1942; OBE 1941; ED; b 6 Jan. 1905; s of William Speakman Hanson and Maggie Aitken Hanson; m 1932, Mayne, d of T. J. Gilpin; three s one d. Educ: St Peter's Coll., Adelaide; University of Adelaide (MB, BS). War Service: Comd 2/8 Aust. Field Amb., 1940-43; ADMS, 9 Aust. Div., 1943-44. Pres., SA Branch of BMA, 1952-53; Pres. College of Radiologists of Australasia, 1961-62; Member: Radiation Health Cttee of Nat. Health and Med. Research Coun., 1963-67; Radiological Advisory Cttee, S Aust., 1957-; Hon. Radiotherapist, Royal Adelaide Hospital, 1952-64; Pres., The Australian Cancer Soc., 1964-67; Chm., Exec. Board, Anti-Cancer Foundation, University of Adelaide, 1955-74; Mem. Council, International Union Against Cancer, 1962-74. FFR (Hon.) 1964; FAMA 1967; FRCR (Hon.) 1975. Publications: sundry addresses and papers in Med. Jl of Australia. Recreation: gardening. Address: 52 Brougham Place, North Adelaide, SA 5006, Australia. Clubs: Adelaide, Naval, Military and Air Force (Adelaide).

HANSON, Sir (Charles) John, 3rd Bt cr 1918; Member of the London Stock Exchange; b 28 Feb. 1919; o s of Major Sir Charles Edwin Bourne Hanson, 2nd Bt, and Violet Sybil (d 1966), 3rd d of late John B. Johnstone, Coombe Cottage, Kingston Hill, Surrey; S father 1958; m 1st, 1944, Patricia Helen (marr. diss. 1968), o c of late Adm. Sir (Eric James) Patrick Brind, GBE, KCB; one s one d; 2nd, 1968, Mrs Helen Yorke, d of late C. O. Trew. Educ: Eton; Clare Coll., Cambridge. Late Captain, The Duke of Cornwall's Light Infantry; served War of 1939-45. Heir: s Charles Rupert Patrick Hanson, b 25 June 1945.

Address: 7 Abingdon Gardens, Abingdon Villas, W8. T: 01-937 1297. Club: MCC.

HANSON, Derrick George; financial consultant; writer, director of companies; Director: Manufacturers Hanover Ltd, since 1977; Manufacturers Hanover Bank (Guernsey) Ltd, since 1977; Liverpool Building Society, since 1977; Phillips Group, Fine Art Auctioneers, since 1977; Senior Advisor (UK), Manufacturers Hanover Trust Company, since 1977; Barrister-at-Law; b 9 Feb. 1927; s of late John Henry Hanson and of Frances Elsie Hanson; m 1st, 1951, Daphne Elizabeth (née Marks) (decd); one s two d; 2nd, 1974, Hazel Mary (née Buckley). Educ: Waterloo Grammar Sch.; London Univ. (LLB (Hons)); Liverpool Univ. (LLM). Called to Bar, Lincoln's Inn, 1952. Joined Martins Bank Ltd, 1943; Martins Bank Ltd Advance Control, 1957; Asst Manager, Martins Bank Ltd, Liverpool City Office, 1959; Chief Trustee Manager, Martins Bank Ltd, 1963; Dir and Gen. Manager, Martins Bank Trust Co. Ltd, 1968; Dir and Gen. Manager, Barclays Bank Trust Co. Ltd, 1969-76; Chairman: Barclays Unicorn Ltd, 1972-76; Barclays Unicorn Internat. Ltd, 1974-76; Barclays Life Assce Co. Ltd, 1972-76; Director: Barclaytrust Management Ltd, 1971-76; Barclaytrust Internat. Ltd, 1972-76; Barclays Bank Ltd, Manchester Bd, 1976-77. Assessor, Cameron Tribunal regarding Bank Staff Relations, 1962; Dir, Oxford Univ. Business Summer Sch., 1971. Member: Commercial Property Cttee, British Property Fedn; NW Industrialists' Council, 1977-. George Rae Prize of Inst. of Bankers; FIB. Publications: Within These Walls: a century of Methodism in Formby, 1974; contribs to financial jls. Recreations: golf, gardening, music, hill-walking. Address: Tower Grange, Grange Lane, Formby, Liverpool L37 7BR. T: Formby 74040; 21 Old Buildings, Lincoln's Inn, WC2A 3UJ. T: 01-242 9365. Club: Formby Golf (Formby, Lancs).

HANSON, Frederick Horowhenua Melrose, CMG 1961; DSO 1943, and Bar 1945; OBE 1942; MM 1918; ED 1954; New Zealand Commissioner of Works, 1955-62, retired; Member of NZ Council for Technical Education; Chairman, NZ Defence Survey Committee, 1962; b Levin, New Zealand, 9 July 1896; s of Frederick Hanson; m 1924, Constance M., d of Edward Grindley. Educ: Wellington Coll.; Victoria Univ. Coll. Served European War, 1914-18 (MM), 1st NZEF, Wellington Regt. Educated and trained as civil engineer. With Public Works Dept, 1921-39. Served War of 1939-45 (despatches, DSO, bar, wounded thrice): 2 NZEF, CRE 2 NZ Div., CE 2 NZEF; Brig. NZ Chief Highways Engineer, 1946-49; Dep. Commissioner of Works, 1949-55. Territorial Mem. Army Bd, 1948-55. First Chm., NZ Nat. Roads Bd, 1954-55; Past Pres., NZ Instn of Engineers. FICE; FNZIE; MSINZ. Publications: on soil mechanics, foundations and road engineering. Recreations: shooting and fishing. Address: 17 Portland Crescent, Thorndon, Wellington 1, NZ. Club: United Services Officers' (Wellington, NZ).

HANSON, Sir James (Edward), Kt 1976; Chairman: Hanson Trust, since 1964; Hanson Transport Group, since 1973; b 20 Jan. 1922; s of late Robert Hanson, CBE and of Louisa Ann (née Rodgers); m 1959, Geraldine (née Kaelin); two s. Educ: public school. War Service 1939-46, 7th Bn Duke of Wellington's Regt. Dir (former Chm.), Trident Television. An Underwriting Mem. of Lloyds, 1951-. Trustee, D'Oyly Carte Opera Trust. Life Member: BHS; BSJA; Hunter Improvement Soc.; Yorks CCC. Liveryman, Saddlers' Co.; Freeman, City of London. FRSA. Recreations: riding (former MFH Grove and Rufford), sailing, photography. Address: 180 Brompton Road, SW3 1HF. T: 01-589 7070. Clubs: Brooks's; Huddersfield and Borough (Yorks); The Brook (NY); O'Donnell Golf (Calif.); Toronto (Canada); Royal Thames Yacht; Yacht Club de Monaco.

HANSON, Sir John; see Hanson, Sir Charles John.

HANSON, John Gilbert; Representative, British Council in Iran, since 1975, and Counsellor (Cultural) British Embassy, Tehran; b 16 Nov. 1938; s of Gilbert Fretwell Hanson and Gladys Margaret (née Kay); m 1962, Margaret Clark; three s. Educ: Manchester Grammar Sch.; Wadham Coll., Oxford (BA Lit. Hum. 1961, MA 1964). Asst Principal, WO, 1961-63; British Council: Madras, India, 1963-66; ME Centre for Arab Studies, Lebanon, 1966-68; Rep., Bahrain, 1968-72; Dep. Controller, Educn and Science Div., 1972-75. Recreations: books, music, sport, travel. Address: c/o The British Council, 10 Spring Gardens, SW1A 2BN. T: 01-930 8466. Clubs: Royal Commonwealth Society; Tehran (Tehran); Gymkhana (Madras).

HANSON, Rt. Rev. Richard Patrick Crosland, MA, DD; MRIA; Professor of Historical and Contemporary Theology, University of Manchester, since 1973; Assistant Bishop, Diocese of

Manchester, since 1973; *b* 24 Nov. 1916; *s* of late Sir Philip Hanson, CB, and late Lady Hanson; *m* 1950, Mary Dorothy, *d* of late Canon John Powell; two *s* two *d*. *Educ:* Cheltenham Coll.; Trinity Coll., Dublin. 1st Hons BA in Classics also in Ancient Hist., 1938; BD with Theol. Exhibn, 1941; DD 1950; MA 1961. Asst Curate, St Mary's, Donnybrook, Dublin, and later in Banbridge, Co. Down, 1941-45; Vice-Principal, Queen's Coll., Birmingham, 1946-50; Vicar of St John's, Shuttleworth, dio. Manchester, 1950-52; Dept of Theol., Univ. of Nottingham, Lectr, Sen. Lectr and Reader, 1952-62; Lightfoot Prof. of Divinity, Univ. of Durham, and Canon of Durham, 1962-64; Prof. of Christian Theology, Univ. of Nottingham, 1964-70; Hon. Canon of Southwell, 1964-70; Canon Theologian of Coventry Cathedral, 1967-70; Examining Chaplain to the Bishop of Southwell, 1968; Bishop of Clogher, 1970-73. *Publications:* Origen's Doctrine of Tradition, 1954; II Corinthians (commentary, Torch series), 1954; Allegory and Event, 1959; God: Creator, Saviour, Spirit, 1960; Tradition in the Early Church, 1962; New Clarendon Commentary on Acts, 1967; Saint Patrick: his origins and career, 1968; Groundwork for Unity, 1971; The Attractiveness of God, 1973; Mystery and Imagination: reflections upon Christianity, 1976; (ed, abridged and trans.), Justin Martyr's Dialogue with Trypho, 1963; contrib. to Institutionalism and Church Unity, 1963; The Anglican Synthesis, 1964; Vindications, 1966; (ed) Difficulties for Christian Belief, 1966; (co-ed) Christianity in Britain 300-700, 1968; (ed) Pelican Guide to Modern Theology, 1969-70; contribs to: A Dictionary of Christian Theology, 1969; Lambeth Essays on Ministry, 1969; Le Traité sur le Saint-Esprit de Saint Basile, 1969; Cambridge History of The Bible, vol. 1, 1970; articles in: Jl of Theol Studies, Vigiliae Christianae, Expository Times, Theology, Modern Churchman, The Times. *Recreations:* tennis, drama. *Address:* 24 Styal Road, Wilmslow, Cheshire SK9 4AG; Faculty of Theology, University of Manchester, Manchester M13 9PL.

HANTON, Alastair Kydd; Senior Director, Giro and Remittance Services, Post Office, since 1975; *b* 10 Oct. 1926; *er s* of late Peter Hanton and Maude Hanton; *m* 1956, Margaret Mary (*née* Lumsden); two *s* one *d*. *Educ:* Mill Hill Sch.; Pembroke Coll., Cambridge. Commonwealth Develt Corp., 1948-54; ICFC, 1954-57; Unilever, 1957-66; Rio Tinto-Zinc, 1966-68; Post Office, 1968-. *Recreation:* forestry. *Address:* 8 Gilkes Crescent, Dulwich Village, SE21 7BS. *T:* 01-693 2618.

HANWORTH, 2nd Viscount, *cr* 1936, of Hanworth; **David Bertram Pollock,** CEng, MIMechE, FIEE, FRPS, FIQA; Baron, *cr* 1926; Bt, *cr* 1922; Lt-Col Royal Engineers, retired; Barrister-at-Law (Inner Temple), 1958; *b* 1 Aug. 1916; *s* of Charles Thomas Anderson Pollock and Alice Joyce Becher; *S* grandfather, 1936; *m* 1940, Isolda Rosamond, *yr d* of Geoffrey Parker, of Cairo; two *s* one *d*. *Educ:* Wellington Coll.; Trinity Coll., Cambridge. (Mechanical Science Tripos, 1939). *Publications:* Amateur Carbro Colour Prints, 1950; Amateur Dye Transfer Colour Prints, 1956. *Recreations:* ski-ing, photography, gardening, canal cruising. *Heir: s* Hon. David Stephen Geoffrey Pollock [*b* 16 Feb. 1946; *m* 1968, Elizabeth Liberty, *e d* of Lawrence Vambe; two *d*]. *Address:* Folly Hill, Ewhurst, Cranleigh, Surrey.
See also Sir W. L. Farrer.

HAPPOLD, Prof. Frank Charles, PhD, DSc (Manchester); Professor of Biochemistry, University of Leeds, 1946-67, Emeritus Professor, 1967; *b* Barrow-in-Furness, 23 Sept. 1902; *s* of Henry Happold and Emma Happold (*née* Ley); *m* 1926, A. Margaret M. Smith, MA, Brighton; one *s* one *d*. *Educ:* privately; Barrow Gram. Sch.; University of Manchester. PhD (Manchester) 1927; DSc (Manchester) 1934. University of Leeds: Department of Bacteriology, 1926-36; Dept of Physiology, 1936-46; Dept of Biochemistry, 1946-67; Research Prof., University of Florida, 1958-59. First Chm., Fedn of European Biochem. Socs, 1964. Leverhulme Fellowship to Harvard Univ. Post Graduate Medical Sch., 1939; Visiting Prof., University of Ghana, 1967-70; Royal Soc. Vis. Prof., Univ. of Science and Technology, Kumasi, 1972. Co-founder with wife of International Tramping Tours, 1929. Diplôme d'Honneur, Fedn European Biochem. Socs, 1974. Bronze Medal, Ville de Paris, 1964. *Publications:* numerous scientific publications, mainly in Microbiological Chemistry and Enzymology. *Recreations:* gardening and travel. *Address:* Three Roods, Arnside, Carnforth LA5 0BB.

HARBERTON, 9th Viscount, *cr* 1791; **Henry Ralph Martyn Pomeroy;** Baron Harberton, 1783; *b* 12 Oct. 1908; *s* of 8th Viscount and late Mary Katherine, *o d* of A. W. Leatham, JP; *S* father 1956. *Educ:* Eton. *Heir: b* Lieut-Col Hon. Thomas de Vautort Pomeroy [*b* 19 Oct. 1910; *m* 1st, 1939, Nancy Ellen (marriage dissolved, 1946), *d* of late C. A. Penoyer; 2nd, 1950,

Pauline Stafford (*d* 1971), *d* of late Wilfred Sidney Baker, Stoke, Plymouth]. *Address:* 38 Thurloe Square, SW7. *T:* 01-589 6767.

HARBISON, Air Vice-Marshal William, CB 1977; CBE 1965; AFC 1956; Air Officer Commanding 11 Group, RAF, 1975-77; *b* 11 April 1922; *s* of W. Harbison; *m* 1950, Helen, *d* of late William B. Geneva, Bloomington, Illinois; two *s*. *Educ:* Ballymena Academy, N Ireland. Joined RAF, 1941; 118 Sqdn Fighter Comd, 1943-46; 263, 257 and 64 Sqdns, 1946-48; Exchange Officer with 1st Fighter Group USAF, 1948-50; Central Fighter Estabt, 1950-51; 4th Fighter Group USAF, Korea, 1952; 2nd ATAF Germany: comd No 67 Sqdn, 1952-55; HQ No 2 Group, 1955; psc 1956; Air Min. and All Weather OCU, 1957; comd No 29 All Weather Sqdn Fighter Comd, Acklington and Leuchars, 1958-59; British Defence Staffs, Washington, 1959-62; jssc 1962; comd RAF Leuchars Fighter Comd, 1963-65; ndc 1965-66; Gp Capt. Ops: HQ Fighter Comd, 1967-68; No 11 Group Strike Comd, 1968; Dir of Control (Ops), NATCS, 1968-72; Comdr RAF Staff, and Air Attaché, Washington, 1972-75. *Recreations:* flying, motoring. *Address:* c/o Lloyds Bank, Cox's & King's Branch, 6 Pall Mall, SW1. *Club:* Royal Air Force.

HARBORD, Rev. Derek (formerly Hon. Mr Justice Harbord); granted arms, 1967; *b* 25 July 1902; *yr s* of F. W. Harbord, Birkenhead, and Isabella (*née* Gardner), Sale; *m* Grace Rosalind (*d* 1969), *o d* of A. S. Fowles, Birmingham; two *s* one *d*. *Educ:* Mount Radford Sch., Exeter; Gray's Inn; St Michael's Theol Coll., Llandaff. Barrister-at-Law, 1925; Deacon, 1925; Priest, 1926; Curate, W Norwood, 1925-27; Streatham, 1927-29; Vicar, Stoke Lyne, 1929; Royal Army Chaplains Dept, 1929; Chaplain i/c Depot RAMC, Crookham, and V Lt Bde RA, Ewshott, 1929-30; Vicar, Hindolveston, 1930-33; Vicar, Good Shepherd, W Bromwich, 1933-35; resigned to become a Roman Catholic, 1935; reconciled with Anglican Communion and licensed to offic. Accra dioc., 1959-61; Rector of St Botolph-without-Aldgate with Holy Trinity, Minories, 1962-74; permission to officiate, dio. Rochester, 1974-. Practised at English Bar, 1935-40: Central Criminal Court, SE Circuit, Mddx and N London Sess; Sec., Bentham Cttee for Poor Litigants, 1937-40; AOER, 1938; HM Colonial Legal Service, 1940; Dist Magistrate and Coroner, Gold Coast, 1940-44; Registrar of High Court of N Rhodesia and High Sheriff of the Territory, 1944-46; Resident Magistrate and Coroner, N Rhodesia, 1946-53; Chm., Reinstatement in Civil Employment (Mining Industry) Cttee; Chm., Liquor Licensing Appeal Tribunal for N Rhodesia; a Judge of High Court of Tanganyika, and Mem. Ct of Appeal for E Africa, 1953-59; ret. 1959; admitted to Ghana Bar, 1959; Senior Lecturer, Ghana Sch. of Law, and Editor of Ghana Law Reports, 1959-61. *Publications:* Manual for Magistrates (N Rhodesia), 1951; Law Reports (N Rhodesia), 1952; Law Reports (Ghana), 1960. *Recreations:* 16 grandchildren. *Address:* Winterslow, Bayley's Hill, Sevenoaks, Kent TN14 6HS. *T:* Sevenoaks 52544. *Club:* Athenæum.

HARBORD-HAMOND, family name of **Baron Suffield.**

HARBOTTLE, Rev. Anthony Hall Harrison; Chaplain of the Royal Chapel, Windsor Great Park, since 1968; Chaplain to the Queen, since 1968; *b* 3 Sept. 1925; *y s* of Alfred Charles Harbottle, ARIBA, and Ellen Muriel, *o d* of William Popham Harrison; *m* 1955, Gillian Mary, *o d* of Hugh Goodenough; three *s* one *d*. *Educ:* Sherborne Sch.; Christ's Coll., Cambridge (MA); Wycliffe Hall, Oxford. Served War in Royal Marines, 1944-46. Deacon 1952, priest 1953; Asst Curacies: Boxley, 1952-54; St Peter-in-Thanet, 1954-60; Rector of Sandhurst with Newenden, 1960-68. Founder Mem., Kent Trust for Nature Conservation, 1954. FRES 1971. *Publications:* contribs to entomological jls, on lepidoptera. *Recreations:* butterflies and moths, nature conservancy, entomology, ornithology, philately, coins, Treasury and bank notes, painting, cooking, lobstering. *Address:* The Chaplain's Lodge, The Great Park, Windsor, Berks. *T:* Egham 2434.

HARCOURT, family name of **Viscount Harcourt.**

HARCOURT, 2nd Viscount, *cr* 1917; **William Edward Harcourt,** KCMG 1957; OBE 1945 (MBE 1943); Baron Nuneham, *cr* 1917; Chairman, Legal and General Assurance Society Limited, 1958-77; Chairman of Trustees: Rhodes Trust, since 1975; Oxford Preservation Trust, since 1958; Chairman, Board of Governors of Museum of London, since 1965; Vice-Lord-Lieutenant of Oxfordshire since 1963; Hon. Fellow, St Antony's College, Oxford; *b* 5 Oct. 1908; *o s* of 1st Viscount and Mary Ethel (*d* 1960), GBE, *o d* of late Walter H. Burns of New York and North Mymms Park, Hatfield; *S* father, 1922; *heir-pres.* to 10th Baron Vernon, *qv*; *m* 1st, 1931, Hon. Maud Elizabeth Grosvenor (marr. diss., 1942), *o d* of 4th Baron Ebury, DSO,

MC; two *d* (and one *d* decd); 2nd, 1946, Elizabeth Sonia (*d* 1959), *widow* of Capt. Lionel Gibbs, and *d* of late Sir Harold Snagge, KBE. *Educ:* Eton; Christ Church, Oxford, MA. Served War of 1939-45, with 63rd (Oxford Yeomanry) AT Regt RA and on staff. Man. Dir, Morgan Grenfell & Co. Ltd, 1931-68, Chm., 1968-73; Minister (Economic) HM Embassy, Washington, and Head of UK Treasury Delegation in USA, 1954-57; UK Exec. Dir of International Bank for Reconstruction and Development and of International Monetary Fund, 1954-57; Mem., Departmental (Radcliffe) Cttee on Working of Monetary and Credit Policy of United Kingdom, 1957-59 and of Departmental (Plowden) Cttee on Overseas Representational Services, 1962-64. *Address:* 23 Culross Street, W1. *T:* 01-629 6061; Stanton Harcourt, Oxon. *T:* Standlake 296.
See also Baron Ashburton, Hon. Mrs John Mulholland.

HARCUS, Rear-Adm. Ronald Albert, CB 1976; RN retired; Managing Director: RWO (Marine Equipment) Ltd; R. W. Owen Ltd; *b* 25 Oct. 1921; *s* of Henry Alexander Harcus and Edith Maud (*née* Brough); *m* 1946, Jean Heckman; two *s* two *d*. *Educ:* St Olave's Grammar Sch.; RNC Greenwich. FIMarE, MBIM. Entered Royal Navy, 1937; Comdr 1956; Captain 1964; Rear-Adm. 1974; served in HM Ships Nigeria, Jamaica, Ocean, Dainty (despatches, Korea, 1953); Fleet Marine Engr Officer Home Fleet, 1965-67; Dep. Dir Fleet Maintenance, 1968-69; Captain, HMS Sultan, 1971-72; attended Royal Coll. of Defence Studies, 1973; Asst Chief of Fleet Support, MoD (Navy), 1974-76. *Recreations:* fishing, sailing. *Address:* The Hollies, 18 Fountain Lane, Hockley, Essex. *T:* Hockley 3211.

HARDAKER, Alan, OBE 1971; General Secretary, Football League, since 1957; *b* 29 July 1912; *s* of John Hardaker and Emma Hardaker; *m* 1937, Irene Mundy; four *d*. *Educ:* Constable Street Elementary; Riley High Sch., Hull. Entered Town Clerk's Dept, Hull, 1929; Lord Mayor's Sec., Hull, 1936-39; war service in RNVR, 1939-46 (Lt-Comdr); Lord Mayor's Sec., Portsmouth, 1946-51; joined Football League staff, 1951. *Recreation:* fishing. *Address:* 317 Clifton Drive South, St Annes-on-Sea, Lancs FY8 1HN. *T:* St Annes 723014. *Clubs:* Variety; Shark Angling Club of Great Britain.

HARDEN, Donald Benjamin, CBE 1969 (OBE 1956); MA Cantab, MA Oxon, PhD Mich; FSA; Director of the London Museum, 1956-70; Acting Director of the Museum of London, 1965-70; *b* Dublin, 8 July 1901; *er s* of late John Mason Harden and Constance Caroline Sparrow; *m* 1st, 1934, Cecil Ursula (*d* 1963), *e d* of late James Adolphus Harriss; one *d*; 2nd, 1965, Dorothy May, *er d* of late Daniel Herbert McDonald. *Educ:* Kilkenny Coll.; Westminster Sch.; Trinity Coll., Cambridge; University of Michigan. Travelled in Italy and Tunisia, 1923-24; Senior Asst, Dept of Humanity, University of Aberdeen, 1924-26; Commonwealth Fund Fellow, University of Michigan, 1926-28; Asst University of Michigan Archæol Exped. to Egypt, 1928-29; Asst Keeper, Dept of Antiquities, Ashmolean Museum, Oxford, 1929-45; Keeper, Dept of Antiquities, and Sec., Griffith Institute, 1945-56. Temp. Civil Servant Ministries of Supply and Production, 1940-45. Vice-Pres. Soc. of Antiquaries of London, 1949-53, 1964-67; President: Council for British Archæology, 1950-54; Oxford Architectural and Historical Soc., 1952-55; Section H, British Assoc., 1955; London and Middlesex Archæol. Soc., 1959-65; Royal Archæol. Inst., 1966-69; Internat. Assoc. for History of Glass, 1968-74; Chm., Directors' Conf. (Nat. Museums), 1968-70; Hon. Sec. Museums Assoc., 1949-54, Chm. Educ. Cttee 1954-59, Pres. 1960; Hon. Editor, Soc. for Medieval Archæology, 1957-73, Pres., 1975-77; Mem. of Council, British School of Archæology in Iraq; Member: Ancient Monuments Board for England, 1959-74; Royal Commission on Historical Monuments (England), 1963-71; Trustee, RAEC Museum. Mem., German Archæol Inst. Leverhulme Fellowship for research on ancient glass, 1953. Gold Medal, Soc. of Antiquaries, 1977. *Publications:* Roman Glass from Karanis, 1936; (with E. T. Leeds) The Anglo-Saxon Cemetery at Abingdon, Berks, 1936; The Phoenicians, 1962, rev. edn 1971; (jointly) Masterpieces of Glass, British Museum, 1968; (ed) Dark-Age Britain, 1956. Numerous articles on archæology and museums. *Address:* 12 St Andrew's Mansions, Dorset Street, W1H 3FD. *T:* 01-935 5121. *Club:* Athenæum.

HARDEN, Major James Richard Edwards, DSO; MC; DL; JP; farmer; *b* 12 Dec. 1916; *s* of late Major J. E. Harden, DL, JP, Royal Irish Fusiliers, and L. G. C. Harden; *m* 1948, Ursula Joyce, *y d* of G. M. Strutt, Newhouse, Terling, Chelmsford, Essex; one *s* two *d*. *Educ:* Oriel House, St Asaph; Bedford Sch.; Sandhurst. Commissioned into Royal Tank Regt 1937; retired on agricultural release, 1947; MP (UU) for County Armagh, 1948-54. JP County Armagh, 1956, Cærnarvonshire, later Gwynedd, 1971; DL: Co. Armagh, 1946; Cærnarvonshire, later

Gwynedd, 1968; High Sheriff, Cærnarvonshire, 1971-72. *Recreations:* shooting, fishing. *Address:* Nanhoran, Pwllheli, Gwynedd LL53 8DL. *T:* Botwnnog 610.

HARDERS, Sir Clarence Waldemar, Kt 1977; OBE 1969; Secretary, Department of the Attorney-General of the Commonwealth, since 1970; *b* Murtoa, 1 March 1915; *s* of E. W. Harders, Dimboola, Vic; *m* 1947, Gladys, *d* of E. Treasure; one *s* two *d*. *Educ:* Concordia Coll., Unley, S Australia; Adelaide Univ. (LLB). Joined Dept of the Attorney-General, 1947; Dep. Sec., 1965-70. *Address:* Department of the Attorney-General, Canberra, ACT, Australia; 43 Stonehaven Crescent, Deakin, ACT 2600, Australia. *Clubs:* Commonwealth, National Press, Canberra Bowling (Canberra), Royal Automobile of Victoria.

HARDIE, Ven. Archibald George; Archdeacon of West Cumberland and Hon. Canon of Carlisle Cathedral since 1971; also Vicar of Haile, since 1970; *b* 19 Dec. 1908; *s* of late Archbishop Hardie and late Mrs Hardie; *m* 1936, Rosalie Sheelagh Hamilton (*née* Jacob); three *s* one *d*. *Educ:* St Lawrence Coll., Ramsgate; Trinity Coll., Cambridge (MA); Westcott House, Cambridge. Curate of All Hallows, Lombard St, EC, and London Sec. of Student Christian Movement, 1934-36; Chaplain, Repton Sch., 1936-38; Vicar of St Alban, Golders Green, London, NW11, 1938-44; OCF. Rector of Hexham Abbey, 1944-63; Vicar and Rural Dean of Halifax, 1963-71, and Hon. Canon of Wakefield Cathedral. *Recreations:* tilling the soil and chewing the cud. *Address:* The Vicarage, Haile, Egremont, Cumbria. *T:* Beckermet 336.

HARDIE, Archibald William, CBE 1974; Managing Director, Mitchell for Oils Ltd, since 1965; *b* 27 Feb. 1911; *s* of William Hardie and Janet Tait McCrae; *m* 1939, Helen Wightman Robertson; five *s*. *Educ:* Queen's Park Sch., Glasgow. FCCA. Man. Dir, Shell/BP Scotland, 1957-65. Chairman: Scottish Tourist Bd, 1967-71; Irvine Develt Corp., 1967-74. *Recreation:* golf. *Address:* 33 Cleveden Road, Glasgow G12 0PH. *T:* 041-339 5974; Steele Road Cottage, Newcastleton, Roxburghshire TD9 0SQ. *Club:* Royal and Ancient (St Andrews).

HARDIE, Sir Charles (Edgar Mathewes), Kt 1970; CBE 1963 (OBE 1943); chartered accountant; Partner in Dixon, Wilson, Tubbs & Gillett, since 1934, Senior Partner, since 1975; *b* 10 March 1910; *s* of Dr C. F. and Mrs R. F. Hardie (*née* Moore), Barnet, Herts; *m* 1st, 1937, Dorothy Jean (*née* Hobson) (*d* 1965); one *s* three *d*; 2nd, 1966, Mrs Angela Richli, *widow* of Raymond Paul Richli; 3rd, 1975, Rosemary Margaret Harwood. *Educ:* Aldenham Sch. Qualified as Chartered Accountant, 1932; practised in London, 1934-. War Service, 1939-44 (Col). Chairman: BOAC, 1969-70; Metropolitan Estate & Property Corp., 1964-71; White Fish Authority, 1967-73; Fitch Lovell Ltd, 1970-77; Director: British American and General Trust Ltd; British Printing Corp. Ltd (Chm., 1969-76); Royal Bank of Canada; Mann Egerton & Co. Ltd; Westminster Property Group Ltd. Deputy Chairman: NAAFI, 1953-72; AP Bank Ltd, 1974-75; Member: BEA Board, 1968-70; Council, Inst. of Directors. Governor, Aldenham Sch. Legion of Merit, USA, 1944. *Address:* The Old School House, Sturminster Newton, Dorset; 207 Cranmer Court, Whiteheads Grove, SW3 3HG.
See also C. J. M. Hardie.

HARDIE, (Charles) Jeremy (Mawdesley); Partner, Dixon Wilson & Co., since 1975; *b* 9 June 1938; *s* of Sir Charles Hardie, *qv*; *m* 1962, Susan Chamberlain (marr. diss. 1969); two *s* two *d*. *Educ:* Winchester Coll.; New Coll., Oxford (2nd Cl. Class. Hon. Mods, 1st Cl. Lit. Hum.); Nuffield Coll., Oxford (BPhil Econs). ACA 1965, Peat, Marwick, Mitchell & Co.; Nuffield Coll., Oxford, 1966-67; Jun. Res. Fellow, Trinity Coll., Oxford, 1967-68; Fellow and Tutor in Econs, Keble Coll., Oxford, 1968-75. Dir, National Provident Instn, 1972-; Member: Council, Advertising Standards Authority, 1972-; Monopolies and Mergers Commn, 1976-. *Recreation:* sailing. *Address:* 131 Gloucester Avenue, NW1. *T:* 01-586 3919.

HARDIE, Colin Graham; Official Fellow and Tutor in Classics, Magdalen College, Oxford, 1936-73; Public Orator of Oxford University, 1967-73; Hon. Professor of Ancient Literature, Royal Academy of Arts, since 1971; *b* 16 Feb. 1906; 3rd *s* of William Ross Hardie, Fellow of Balliol Coll. and Prof. of Humanity in Edinburgh Univ., and Isabella Watt Stevenson; *m* 1940, Christian Viola Mary Lucas; two *s*. *Educ:* Edinburgh Acad.; Balliol Coll., Oxford (Warner Exhibitioner and Hon. Scholar); 1st class Classical Moderations, 1926, and Lit Hum BA, 1928; MA, 1931; Craven Scholar, 1925; Ireland Scholar, 1925; Hertford Scholar, 1926; Gaisford Prize for Greek Prose, 1927; Junior Research Fellow of Balliol, 1928-29; Fellow and Classical Tutor, 1930-33; Dir of the British Sch. at Rome, 1933-36. *Publications:* Vitae Vergilianae antiquae, 1954; papers on

Virgil and Dante. *Recreation:* gardening. *Address:* Rackham Cottage, Greatham, Pulborough, Sussex. *T:* Pulborough 3170.

HARDIE, Jeremy; see Hardie, C. J. M.

HARDIE, John William Somerville, MA Cantab; Hon. DLitt; Principal, Loughborough College of Education, 1963-73; *b* 21 Aug. 1912; 2nd *s* of late Most Rev. W. G. Hardie, CBE, DD; *m* 1938, Evelyn Chrystal, 5th *d* of J. C. Adkins, Uppingham, Rutland; one *s* two *d. Educ:* St Lawrence Coll., Ramsgate; Trinity Coll., Cambridge. Second Cl. Hon. (Div. I) Modern and Medieval Lang. Tripos. Asst Master St Lawrence Coll., 1933-35; Asst Master Uppingham Sch., 1935-40; Headmaster Cornwall Coll., Montego Bay, Jamaica 1940-42; Headmaster Jamaica Coll., Kingston, Jamaica, 1943-46; Asst Master Blundell's Sch., 1946-47; Headmaster, Canford Sch., 1947-60; Headmaster-Elect, Hesarack Sch., Iran, 1960-61; consultant Voluntary Service Overseas, 1961; Managing Dir, The Broadcasting Company of Northern Nigeria Ltd (seconded by Granada TV Ltd), 1961-62; Head of Information and Research, The Centre for Educational Television Overseas, Nuffield Lodge, 1962-63. Chm., HMC Overseas Cttee, 1958-60. Mem. Council Loughborough Univ. of Technology, 1968-76; a Governor, St Luke's Coll., Exeter, 1974-. Hon. DLitt Loughborough, 1973. *Recreations:* hockey (Cambridge Univ. Hockey XI, 1931, 1932, Captain 1933; Welsh Hockey XI, 1931, 1932, Captain 1933-39), fishing, gardening, music, painting. *Address:* Blue Seas, Trelawney Road, St Mawes, Truro, Cornwall TR2 5BU.

HARDIE, Rt. Rev. William Auchterlonie, MA, BD. *Educ:* Univ. of Queensland. BA 1928, MA 1936, Univ. of Queensland; BD Melbourne Coll. of Divinity, 1931. Deacon, 1930; priest, 1931; Curate of Holy Trinity, Fortitude Valley, Brisbane, 1930-33; Chaplain Southport Sch., 1933-37; Rector of Holy Trinity, Woolloongabba, Brisbane, 1937-46; Warden of St John's Coll., Brisbane, 1946-50; Canon of St John's Cathedral and Examining Chaplain to the Archbishop of Brisbane, 1947-50; Archdeacon of Moreton, 1948-50; Dean of Newcastle, NSW, 1950-61; Bishop of Ballarat, 1961-75. Served War of 1939-45 as Chaplain, Royal Australian Air Force, 1941-44. *Address:* Lis Escop, South Street, Creswick, Vic. 3363, Australia.

HARDIE, William Francis Ross; President, Corpus Christi College, Oxford, 1950-69; Hon. Fellow, 1969; *b* 25 April 1902; *s* of late W. R. Hardie, Professor of Humanity, University of Edinburgh; *m* 1938, Isobel St Maur Macaulay; two *s. Educ:* Edinburgh Academy; Balliol Coll., Oxford. Fellow by Examination, Magdalen Coll., 1925; Fellow and Tutor in Philosophy, Corpus Christi Coll., Oxford, 1926-50. *Publications:* A Study in Plato, 1936; Aristotle's Ethical Theory, 1968; articles in philosophical journals. *Address:* Hogan, Frilford Heath, Abingdon, Oxon. *T:* Frilford Heath 390401.

HARDING, family name of **Baron Harding of Petherton.**

HARDING OF PETHERTON, 1st Baron *cr* 1958, of Nether Compton; **Field-Marshal Allan Francis, (John), Harding,** GCB 1951 (KCB 1944); CBE 1940; DSO 1941; MC; *b* 1896; *s* of late Francis E. Harding, Compton Way, S Petherton, Somerset; *m* 1927, Mary G. M., *d* of late Wilson Rooke, JP, Knutsford, Cheshire; one *s. Educ:* Ilminster Grammar Sch. Served European War, 1914-19, with TA and Machine Gun Corps (MC); Lieut Somerset Light Infantry 1920; Capt. 1923; psc 1928; Brigade Major British Force, Saar Plebiscite; Bt Major, 1935; Bt Lieut-Col 1938; Lieut-Col 1939; Brig. 1942; Maj.-Gen. 1942; Lieut-Gen. 1943; General, 1949; Field-Marshal, 1953. Served War of 1939-45 (despatches, CBE, DSO and two Bars, KCB). GOC CMF, 1946-47; GOC-in-C Southern Command, 1947-49; C-in-C, Far East Land Forces, 1949-51; Comdr-in-Chief, British Army of the Rhine, 1951-52; Chief of the Imperial Gen. Staff, 1952-55. Governor and Comdr-in-Chief, Cyprus, 1955-Nov. 1957. Director: Nat. Provincial Bank, 1957-69; Standard Bank, 1965-71; Williams (Hounslow) Ltd, 1962-74 (Chm. 1962-71); Plessey Co. Ltd, 1967-70 (Dir, 1962-75; Dep. Chm., 1964-67; Chm., 1967-70). ADC Gen. to King George VI, 1950-52, to the Queen, 1952-53. Col 6th Gurkha Rifles, 1951-61; Col Somerset and Cornwall LI (Somerset LI, 1953-60); Col, The Life Guards, and Gold Stick to the Queen, 1957-64. KStJ. Hon. DCL (Durham). *Recreation:* gardening. *Heir: s* Major Hon. John Charles Harding [*b* 12 Feb. 1928; *m* 1966, Harriet, *y d* of late Maj.-Gen. J. F. Hare, and Mrs D. E. Hare; one *s* one *d*]. *Address:* Lower Farm, Nether Compton, Sherborne, Dorset. *Clubs:* Army and Navy, Cavalry and Guards, Naval and Military.

HARDING, Ann; Retired Actress; *b* Fort Sam Houston, San Antonio, Texas, USA, 7 Aug. 1902; *d* of General George Grant Gatley; *m* 1937, Werner Janssen, Symphony Conductor (marr.

diss. 1963; Court restored Ann Harding as her legal name); one *d* from a former marriage. *Educ:* American public schs; Baldwin Sch., Bryn Mawr, Penna. First appearance as Madeline in Inheritors, with The Provincetown Players, New York; Tarnish, Trial of Mary Dugan, New York; Candida, London, 1937; Glass Menagerie, California, 1948; Garden District, New York, 1958. *Films include:* Holiday, East Lynne, Life of Vergie Winters, When Ladies Meet, The Fountain, Peter Ibbetson, Gallant Lady, Love From A Stranger (British picture), Mission to Moscow, Janie (Warners), Christmas Eve, It Happened on Fifth Avenue, The Man in the Grey Flannel Suit. *Recreations:* tennis, motoring, knitting, reading.

HARDING, Denys Wyatt, MA; Emeritus Professor of Psychology, University of London, since 1968; *b* 13 July 1906; *s* of Clement and Harriet Harding; *m* 1930, Jessie Muriel Ward; no *c. Educ:* Lowestoft Secondary Sch.; Emmanuel Coll., Cambridge. Investigator and Mem. of research staff, National Institute of Industrial Psychology, 1928-33; Asst (later Lecturer) in Social Psychology, London Sch. of Economics, 1933-38; Senior Lecturer in Psychology, University of Liverpool, 1938-45 (leave of absence for national service, 1941-44); part-time Lecturer in Psychology, University of Manchester, 1940-41 and 1944-45; Prof. of Psychology, Univ. of London, at Bedford Coll., 1945-68. Clark Lectr, Trinity Coll., Cambridge, 1971-72. Hon. Gen. Sec., British Psychological Soc., 1944-48. Mem. of editorial board of Scrutiny, a Quarterly Review, 1933-47. Editor, British Journal of Psychology (Gen. Section) 1948-54. *Publications:* The Impulse to Dominate, 1941; Social Psychology and Individual Values, 1953; Experience into Words: Essays on Poetry, 1963; Words into Rhythm, 1976; (ed with Gordon Bottomley) The Complete Works of Isaac Rosenberg, 1937; translated (with Erik Mesterton) Guest of Reality, by Pär Lagerkvist, 1936; various papers on psychology and literary criticism. *Address:* Ashbocking Old Vicarage, near Ipswich, IP6 9LG. *T:* Helmingham 347.

HARDING, Derek William; Secretary-General, British Computer Society, since 1976; *b* 16 Dec. 1930; *o s* of William Arthur Harding; *m* 1954, Daphne Sheila, *yr d* of Reginald Ernest Cooke; one *s* one *d. Educ:* Glendale Grammar Sch., London; Univ. of Bristol (BSc). FInstP, FIM. Develt Engr, Pye Ltd, 1954-56; Sen. Physics Master, Thornbury Grammar Sch., Bristol, 1956-60; Sen. Lectr in Physical Science, St Paul's Coll., Cheltenham, 1960-64; Asst Organiser, Nuffield Foundn Science Teaching Project, 1964-67; joined staff of Instn Metallurgists, 1967, Registrar-Sec., 1969-76. *Recreations:* sailing, music. *Address:* 16 Exeter Road, N14 5JY. *T:* 01-368 1463. *Club:* Athenæum.

HARDING, George William, CMG 1977; CVO 1972; HM Diplomatic Service; Ambassador to Peru, since 1977; *b* 18 Jan. 1927; *s* of late Lt Col G. R. Harding, DSO, MBE, and of Grace Henley (*née* Darby); *m* 1955, Sheila Margaret Ormond Riddel; four *s. Educ:* Aldenham; St John's College, Cambridge. Royal Marines, 1945-48. Entered HM Foreign Service, 1950; served in Singapore, 1951-52; Burma, 1952-55; Paris, 1956-59; Santo Domingo, 1960-63; Mexico City, 1967-70; Paris, 1970-74; FCO, 1974-76. *Address:* c/o Foreign and Commonwealth Office, SW1. *Clubs:* Garrick; Leander.

HARDING, Gerald William Lankester, CBE 1957; Fellow of University College, London; Director, Department of Antiquities, Hashemite Kingdom of Jordan, 1936-56; *b* 8 Dec. 1901; *s* of William Arthur Harding and Florence Maud Lankester. Excavating with Sir Flinders Petrie near Gaza, Palestine, 1926-32; Asst Dir, Wellcome Archæological Research Expedition to Near East at Tell Duweir (Lachish), Palestine, 1932-36. Star of Jordan, Second Class, 1952. *Publications:* (with E. Mackay) Bahrein and Hamamieh, 1928; (with E. Macdonald and J. L. Starkey) Beth Pelet II, 1930; (with others) Lachish I; (with O. Tufnell and C. H. Inge) Lachish II; Some Thamudic Inscriptions from Jordan, 1952; Four Tomb Groups from Jordan, 1953; The Antiquities of Jordan, 1959; Archæology in the Aden Protectorate, 1964; An Index and Concordance of Pre-Islamic Arabian Names and Inscriptions, 1971. Articles in Quarterly of the Dept of Antiquities of Palestine Annual of the Jordan Dept of Antiquities, Palestine Exploration Quarterly, etc. *Address:* POB 9788, Amman, Jordan.

HARDING, Sir Harold (John Boyer), Kt 1968; BSc, FCGI, DIC, FICE; Consulting Civil Engineer; individual practice since 1956; *b* 6 Jan. 1900; *s* of late Arthur Boyer Harding, Elvetham, Hants, and Helen Clinton (*née* Lowe); *m* 1927, Sophie Helen Blair, *d* of E. Blair Leighton, RI; two *s* one *d. Educ:* Christ's Hosp.; City and Guilds (Engrg) Coll.; Imperial Coll. of Science and Technology. Joined John Mowlem & Co. Ltd, Civil Engrg Contractors, 1922; Dir, John Mowlem & Co., 1950-56; Dir, Soil

Mechanics Ltd, 1949-56; Consultant to Channel Tunnel Study Group, 1958-70. Governor: Westminster Techn Coll., 1948-53; Northampton Engrg Coll., 1950-53; Imperial Coll., 1955-75. Mem., Building Res. Bd, 1952-55; Pres., ICE, 1963-64; Mem., Aberfan Disaster Tribunal, 1966-67; Vice-Pres., Parly and Scientific Cttee, 1968-72. James Forrest Lectr, ICE, 1952. Chm., British Tunnelling Soc., 1971-73. AMICE 1927; MICE 1939; FCGI 1952; Fellow, Imperial Coll. of Science and Technology, 1968. Hon. DSc City Univ., 1970. Prix Coiseau, Soc. des Ingénieurs Civils de France, 1964. *Publications:* numerous papers to ICE. *Recreations:* varied. *Address:* 37 Monmouth Street, Topsham, Exeter, Devon. *T:* Topsham 3281.

HARDING, Hugh Alastair, CMG 1958; Under-Secretary, Department of Education and Science, 1967-77; *b* 4 May 1917; 2nd *s* of late Roland Charles Harding, Norton-le-Moors, Staffordshire; *m* 1943, Florence Esnouf; one *s* one *d*. *Educ:* Rugby; Trinity Coll., Cambridge. Colonial Office, 1939; Asst Sec., 1950; Asst Sec., Treasury, 1961; Under-Sec., Treasury, 1962-64; Minister, UK Delegation to OECD, 1964-67. Served War of 1939-45, Army (Captain RA). *Address:* c/o National Westminster Bank, Town Hall Buildings, Tunstall, Stoke-on-Trent, Staffs.

HARDING, Mrs J. P.; *see* Manton, Sidnie M.

HARDING, John Philip, PhD; Keeper of Zoology, British Museum (Natural History), 1954-71, retired; *b* 12 Nov. 1911; *s* of Philip William and Eleanor Harding, Rondebosch, Cape Town; *m* 1937, Sidnie Manton, *qv*; one *s* one *d*. *Educ:* Torquay; University Coll., Exeter; University of Cincinnati; King's Coll., Cambridge. Ministry of Agriculture and Fisheries, 1936-37; British Museum (Natural History), 1937-71. Vis. Prof., Westfield Coll., Univ. of London, 1971-. *Publications:* scientific papers on Crustacea. *Recreations:* bee-keeping, mechanical devices, photography. *Address:* 88 Ennerdale Road, Richmond, Surrey. *T:* 01-940 2908.

HARDING, Maj.-Gen. Reginald Peregrine, CB 1953; DSO 1940; DL; late 5th Royal Inniskilling Dragoon Guards; *b* 3 July 1905; *s* of late John Reginald Harding, JP, and Elizabeth Margaret Harding; *m* 1941, Elizabeth Mary Baker (marr. diss. 1970); one *s* one *d*. *Educ:* Wellington Coll. Joined 5th Royal Inniskilling Dragoon Guards, 1925; served Palestine, 1938-39 (despatches); France and Flanders, 1940 (DSO); NW Europe, 1944 (Bar to DSO); Comdr N Midland District and 49 Armoured Div., Dec. 1951-55; Comdr, East Anglian District, 1955-58; retired, 1958. DL Essex, 1958. *Recreations:* steeplechasing, hunting, polo, fishing, shooting, racquets. *Address:* Abbots Croft, Chappel, Essex. *T:* Colchester 240232.

HARDING, Rosamond Evelyn Mary, PhD, LittD; *b* 1898; *d* of late W. A. Harding and Ethel Adela Harding, Madingley Hall, Cambs. *Educ:* Newnham Coll., Cambridge. PhD (Cambridge), 1931, LittD, 1941 (for research on subjects connected with music). Held Airplane Pilot's "A" Licence, 1936-39. *Publications:* A History of the Piano-Forte, 1933; edition of the Twelve Piano-Forte Sonatas of L. Guistini di Pistoia, 1732, 1933; Towards a Law of Creative Thought, 1936; Origins of Musical Time and Expression, 1938; An Anatomy of Inspiration, 3rd edn 1948 (corrected repr. of 2nd edn with new preface, 1967); edn of Il Primo Libro d'Intavolaura di Balli d'Arpicordo di Gio, Maria Radino, 1592, 1961; Matthew Locke: thematic catalogue, with calendar of the main events of his life, 1971; various articles in 4th and 5th edns, Grove's Dictionary of Music. *Address:* 24 Arthur Road, Wimbledon, SW19.

HARDING, Air Vice-Marshal Ross Philip, CBE 1968; Aviation Executive, Airwork Services Ltd, since 1976; *b* 22 Jan. 1921; *s* of P. J. Harding, Salisbury; *m* 1948, Laurie Joy Gardner; three *s*. *Educ:* Bishop Wordsworth Sch., Salisbury; St Edmund Hall, Oxford (MA). No 41 Sqdn Fighter Comd and 2 TAF, 1943-45; RAF Staff Coll., Andover, 1951; Air Min. (ACAS Ops), 1952-54; CO No 96 Sqdn, Germany, 1955-58; Directing Staff, RAF Staff Coll., Andover, 1958-60; CO Oxford Univ. Air Sqdn, 1960-62; Dep. Chief, British Mil. Mission, Berlin, 1963-65; CO RAF Valley, 1965-68; Senior Directing Staff (Air), Jt Services Staff Coll., 1968-69; Defence and Air Attaché, Moscow, 1970-72; Dir of Personal Services 1, MoD (Air), 1972-74; Senior RAF Member, RCDS, 1974-76. *Recreations:* ski-ing, shooting. *Address:* 8 Somerset Road, Salisbury, Wilts. *Club:* Royal Air Force.

HARDING, His Honour Rowe, LLD; DL; a Circuit Judge (formerly County Court Judge), 1953-76; Chairman, Swansea Porcelain Ltd, since 1976; *b* 10 Sept. 1901; *s* of late Albert Harding, Swansea, and of Elizabeth Harding; *m* 1933, Elizabeth Adeline, *d* of John Owen George, Hirwaun, S Wales; one *s* one *d*

(and one *s* decd). *Educ:* Gowerton County Sch.; Pembroke Coll., Cambridge. Qualified as solicitor, 1924; called to Bar, Inner Temple, 1928. Captain, Wales, Cambridge and Swansea Rugby football, 1924-28. Home Guard, 1940-44. Contested (Nat. L and C): Swansea East, 1945; Gower, 1950 and 1951. Mem., Swansea Town Council, 1945-48. Deputy Chairman, Quarter Sessions: Haverfordwest, 1945 (Chm., 1948-49): Breconshire, 1953 (Chm., 1955-71); Pembrokeshire, 1953 (Chm., 1971); Carmarthenshire, 1956-65; Glamorganshire, 1959-71; Chm., Radnorshire, QS, 1953-59. Dep. Chm., Local Tribunal for Conscientious Objectors in Wales, 1956-; Pres., Royal Institution of S Wales, 1960-61; Mem., Nat. Adv. Council on the Training of Magistrates, 1964; Chancellor: Diocese of St David's, 1949-; Diocese of Swansea and Brecon, 1974-; former Mem., Governing and Rep. Bodies of Church in Wales; Judge of the Provincial Court of Church in Wales, 1966-; Member: Council, Lampeter Coll.; Court of Governors, UC Swansea, 1956- (Council, 1957), Univ. of Wales, 1971-74; Chm., Welsh Regional Cttee, Cheshire Homes, 1961-63; Trustee, Cheshire Foundation, 1962-70. Vice-Pres., Welsh Rugby Union, 1953-56; Chm., Glamorgan County Cricket Club, 1959-76, Pres., 1977. DL Glamorgan, later West Glamorgan, 1970. Hon. LLD Wales, 1971. *Publications:* Rugby Reminiscences and Opinions, 1929; Rugby in Wales, 1970. *Recreations:* walking, gardening, watching Rugby football and cricket. *Address:* The Old Rectory, Ilston, Gower, near Swansea, West Glamorgan. *T:* Penmaen 243.

HARDING, Wilfrid Gerald, FRCP, PFCM, DPH; Area Medical Officer, Camden and Islington Area Health Authority (Teaching), since 1974; Consultant Physician in Community Medicine, University College Hospital, London, since 1971; Civil Consultant in Community Medicine to the RAF, since 1974; Hon. Lecturer, Department of Sociology, Bedford College, University of London, since 1969; President, Faculty of Community Medicine, Royal Colleges of Physicians of the UK, since 1975; *b* 17 March 1915; *s* of late Dr *hc* Ludwig Ernst Emil Hoffman and Marie Minna Eugenie (née Weisbach); *m* 1st, 1938, Britta Charlotta Haraldsdotter, Malmberg (marr. diss. 1970); three *s*; 2nd, 1973, Hilary Maxwell. *Educ:* Französisches Gymnasium, Berlin; Süddeutsches Landerziehungsheim, Schondorf, Bavaria; Woodbrooke Coll., Selly Oak, Birmingham; University Coll. London; University Coll. Hosp. Med. Sch. (interned twice in 1939 and 1940). MRCS, LRCP 1941; DPH London 1949; MRCP 1968; FFCM 1972; FRCP 1972. Ho. Phys. and Ho. Surg., UCH, 1941-42; Asst MOH, City of Oxford, 1942-43; RAMC, 1943-47, Field Units in NW Europe, 1 Corps Staff and Mil. Govt, Lt-Col (Hygiene Specialist). Public Health Officer, Ruhr Dist of Germany, CCG, 1947-48; London Sch. of Hygiene and Tropical Med., 1948-49; career posts in London public health service, 1949-64. Lectr in Public Health, Midwife Teachers Trng Coll., 1951-62; MOH, London Bor. of Camden, and Principal Sch. MO, ILEA, 1965-74. Chm. of Council, Soc. of MOH, 1966-71 (Pres. 1971-72); Chm., Prov. Bd of FCM, Royal Colls of Physicians of UK, 1971-72 (Vice-Pres., 1972-75, Pres., 1975-). Member: Central Health Services Council and Standing Med. Adv. Cttee, 1966-71 and 1975-; Standing Mental Health Adv. Cttee, 1966-71; Sub-cttees on Org. of Gp Practices, 1968-71, and on Med. Rehabilitation, 1968-72; Bd of Studies in Preventive Med. and Public Health, Univ. of London, 1965-; Council, UCH Med. Sch., 1965-; Ct of Govs and Bd of Management, London Sch. of Hyg. and Trop. Med., 1968-; Council for Educn and Trng of Health Visitors, 1965-; Public Health Laboratory Service Bd, 1972-. *Publications:* papers on public health and community med. in medical books and jls; Parkes Centenary Meml Lecture (Community, Health and Service), 1976. *Recreations:* watching river birds, music, wine. *Address:* 1 Mill Cottages, High Street, Farningham, Dartford DA4 0DW. *T:* Farningham 862733. *Club:* Athenæum.

HARDINGE, family name of Viscount Hardinge and Baron Hardinge of Penshurst.

HARDINGE, 4th Viscount *cr* 1846, of Lahore, and of King's Newton, Derbyshire; **Caryl Nicholas Charles Hardinge,** MBE 1946; Hon. Chairman, Greenshields Incorporated (investment dealers) and Greenshields Ltd; Chairman: Ritz-Carlton Hotel Co. of Montreal Ltd; Dale-Ross Holdings Ltd; Member: Montreal Stock Exchange; Canadian Stock Exchange; Toronto Stock Exchange; Director: The Jockey Club Ltd; Mt Royal Jockey Club Inc.; Electra Investments (Canada), Ltd; Holt, Renfrew & Co. Ltd; Phœnix Assurance Company; Markborough Properties Ltd; Trizec Corporation Ltd; International Atlantic Salmon Association; Acadia Life Insurance Co; *b* London, England, 25 Dec. 1905; *s* of 3rd Viscount Hardinge of Lahore, and Mary, Marchioness of Abergavenny (*d* 1954); *S* father 1924; *m*. 1928, Margaret Elizabeth Arnott, *d* of Hugh Fleming, Ottawa; one *s* two *d*.

Educ: Harrow, Served with 7th Queen's Own Hussars as Lieut and as ADC to Governor-Gen. of Canada, 1926-28. Partner, Kitcat & Aitken, London, 1931-51, and mem., London Stock Exchange. Served as Military Asst, with rank of Major, to Adjt-Gen. to the Forces, 1941-45. *Heir:* s Hon. (Henry) Nicholas (Paul) Hardinge [*b* 15 Aug. 1929; *m* 1955, Zoë Molson, Canada; three *s*]. *Address:* 1523 Summerhill Avenue, Montreal, Canada. *Clubs:* Turf; Toronto (Toronto); Mount Royal, Mount Bruno Country, Montreal Racket, St James's (Montreal); Lyford Cay (Nassau).

HARDINGE OF PENSHURST, 3rd Baron *cr* 1910; **George Edward Charles Hardinge;** *b* 31 Oct. 1921; *o* s of 2nd Baron Hardinge of Penshurst, PC, GCB, GCVO, MC, and Helen Mary Cecil; *S* father, 1960; *m* 1st, 1944, Janet Christine Goschen (marr. diss. 1962, she *d* 1970), *d* of late Lt-Col F. C. C. Balfour, CIE, CVO, CBE, MC; three *s* ; 2nd, 1966, Margaret Trezise; one *s*, and one step-*s*, now adopted. *Educ:* Eton; Royal Naval College, Dartmouth. RN 1940-47; subsequently in publishing. *Publication:* An Incompleat Angler, 1976. *Recreations:* reading, fishing, gardening. *Heir:* s Hon. Julian Alexander Hardinge, *b* 23 Aug. 1945. *Address:* Chalkfield, Friston, East Sussex. *T:* East Dean 3155. *Club:* Brooks's.
See also Lieut-Col J. F. D. Johnston.

HARDINGE, Sir Robert Arnold, 7th Bt *cr* 1801; *b* 19 Dec. 1914; *s* of Sir Robert Hardinge, 6th Bt and Emma Vera, *d* of Charles Arnold; *S* father, 1973. *Heir: kinsman* Nicholas William Hardinge [*b* 11 Oct. 1928; *m* 1973, Mrs Anne Curtis, *d* of Lt-Col W. T. Delamain].

HARDINGHAM, Sir Robert (Ernest), Kt 1969; CMG 1953; OBE 1947; Chief Executive, Air Registration Board, 1947-68; *b* 16 Dec. 1903; *s* of late Robert Henry Hardingham and Florence Elizabeth Hardingham; *m* 1929, I. Everett; one *s* one *d. Educ:* Farnborough; de Havilland Technical Coll. RAE Farnborough, 1918-21; de Havilland Aircraft Co., 1921-34; Air Min., 1934-37; Air Registration Board, 1937-68. Pres., Soc. of Licenced Aircraft Engineers and Technologists, 1968-72. Liveryman, Guild of Air Pilots and Navigators, 1966. CEng; FRAeS 1949 (Empire and Commonwealth Lecturer, 1952). Wakefield Gold Medal, RAeS, 1965; Silver Medal, Royal Aero Club, 1965. Cavaliere Ordino Merito della Repubblica Italiana. *Publications:* many technical papers. *Recreation:* golf. *Address:* Brackenwood, Dukes Kiln Drive, Gerrard's Cross, Bucks SL9 7HD. *T:* Gerrard's Cross 84490. *Club:* Naval and Military.

HARDMAN, Amy Elizabeth; Matron, The Royal Free Hospital, London, 1953-70; *b* 23 Dec. 1909; *d* of late Charlton James Hardman and Elizabeth Clark. *Educ:* Godolphin and Latymer Sch., Hammersmith; Rosebery Sch. for Girls, Epsom. General Training, St Bartholomew's Hosp., London, 1930-34 (SRN); Midwifery Training, Kingston County Hosp., 1937 (SCM); Asst Matron, Sister Tutor, Metropolitan Hosp., E8, 1937-42; Matron, The Guest Hospital, Dudley, Worcs, 1942-49; Matron, St Margaret's Hospital, Epping, 1949-53. *Publication:* An Introduction to Ward Management, 1970. *Address:* Apple Tree Cottage, Main Street, Northiam, Rye, East Sussex. *T:* Northiam 2319.

HARDMAN, David Rennie, MA, LLB; JP; Secretary, Cassel Educational Trust; Secretary, Stafford Cripps Memorial Appeal and Trustees; *b* 1901; *s* of David Hardman, MSc, and Isobel Rennie, Mansfield House University Settlement; *m* 1928, Freda Mary Riley; one *d* ; *m* 1946, Barbara, *er d* of late Herbert Lambert, Bath; one *s* one *d. Educ:* Coleraine Academical Instn; Christ's Coll., Cambridge. Mem. Railway Clerks' Assoc., 1919-21; Pres. Cambridge Union Soc., 1925; Contested (Lab) Cambridge Borough, 1929. Cambridge Borough Councillor and Cambridge County Councillor, 1937-46; late Chm. Cambs Education Cttee; JP Cambridge, 1941-47; MP (Lab) Darlington, 1945-51; Parl. Sec., Min. of Education, 1945-51; contested (Lab) Rushcliffe Div. of Notts, 1955; leader UK delegns UNESCO, Paris 1946, Mexico 1947, Beirut 1948, Paris 1949, Florence 1950, Paris 1951; Vice-Pres. Shaw Soc.; Pres., Holiday Fellowship, 1962-69. Visiting Prof. of English Literature, Elmira, New York, 1964-66. Barclay Acheson Prof. Internat. Studies, Macalester Coll., Minn, 1967. *Publications:* What about Shakespeare?, 1939; Poems of Love and Affairs, 1949; Telscombe: A Sussex Village, 1964. *Recreation:* gardening. *Address:* Bankyfield, Hurstpierpoint, West Sussex. *T:* Brighton 833194. *Club:* Savile.

HARDMAN, Air Chief Marshal Sir Donald; see Hardman, Sir J. D. I.

HARDMAN, Sir Henry, KCB 1962 (CB 1956); Governor and Trustee, Reserve Bank of Rhodesia, since 1967; *b* 15 Dec. 1905; *s*

of late Harry and late Bertha Hardman; *m* 1937, Helen Diana, *d* of late Robert Carr Bosanquet; one *s* two *d. Educ:* Manchester Central High Sch.; University of Manchester. Lecturer for Workers' Educational Association, 1929-34; Economics Tutor, University of Leeds, 1934-45; joined Ministry of Food, 1940; Deputy Head, British Food Mission to N America, 1946-48; Under-Sec., Ministry of Food, 1948-53; Minister, UK Permanent Delegation, Paris, 1953-54; Dep. Sec., Ministry of Agriculture, Fisheries and Food, 1955-60; Dep. Sec., Ministry of Aviation, 1960; Permanent Sec., 1961-63: Permanent Sec., Ministry of Defence, 1963-64; Permanent Under Sec. of State, Min. of Defence, 1964-66. Mem., Monopolies Commn, 1967-70 (Dep. Chm., 1967-68); Chm., Cttee of enquiry into the Post Office pay dispute, 1971; Consultant to CSD on dispersal of govt work from London, 1971-73 (report published, 1973). Chairman: Covent Garden Mkt Authority, 1967-75; Home-Grown Cereals Authority, 1968-77. Hon. LLD Manchester 1965. *Address:* 33 Durand Gardens, SW9 0PS. *T:* 01-582 1757. *Club:* Reform.

HARDMAN, James Arthur, MBE 1968; HM Diplomatic Service; Consul-General, Strasbourg, since 1975; *b* 12 Sept. 1929; *er s* of late James Sidney Hardman and Rachel Hardman; *m* 1953, Enid Mary Hunter; two *s. Educ:* Manchester Grammar Sch.; Manchester Univ. (BA Hons 1950). FCIS (FCCS 1964). Served in Intelligence Corps, 1951-53; Admiralty, 1953-54. HM Foreign Service, 1954; served: Tehran, 1955; FO, 2nd Sec., 1960; Bonn, 2nd, later 1st, Sec. (Comm.), 1962; Atlanta, Consul, 1967; New York, Consul (Comm.), 1970; FCO, Dep. Dir Diplomatic Service Language Centre, 1972. *Address:* c/o Foreign and Commonwealth Office, SW1. *Club:* Civil Service.

HARDMAN, Air Chief Marshal Sir (James) Donald Innes, GBE 1958 (OBE 1940); KCB 1952 (CB 1945); DFC; Royal Air Force retired; *b* 21 Feb. 1899; *s* of James Hardman, MA, Delph, Yorks; *m* 1930, Dorothy, *d* of William Ashcroft Thompson, JP, Larkenshaw, Chobham; two *s* one *d. Educ:* Malvern; Hertford Coll., Oxford. Served European War, 1916-19; joined RAF 1918; Wing Comdr, 1939; Air Commodore, 1941; Air Vice-Marshal, 1945; Air Officer i/c Administration, Air Comd, SE Asia, 1946-47; Asst Chief of Air Staff (Ops), 1947-49; Comdt RAF Air Staff Coll., 1949-51; AOC-in-C, Home Comd, 1951-52; Air Marshal 1952; Chief of Air Staff, RAAF, 1952-54; Air Chief Marshal, 1955; Air Mem. Supply and Organisation, 1954-57; retired, 1958. *Address:* Dolphin Cottage, St Cross Hill, Winchester, Hants. *Club:* Royal Air Force.
See also Sir W. J. F. North, Bt.

HARDWICK, Charles Aubrey, CMG 1971; QC (Australia); Vice-Patron, Benevolent Society of New South Wales, since 1973 (Director, 1947-73; Vice-President, 1958-61; President, 1961-73); *b* 29 July 1885; 2nd *s* of G. W. Hardwick, Rylstone, NSW; *m* 1922, Maisie Jean (*d* 1971), *er d* of David Fell, MLA, Sydney and Rout's Green, Bucks; three *s. Educ:* Rylstone Public Sch.; Univ. of Sydney (evening student). BA 1913, LLB 1915. NSW Dept of Attorney-General and of Justice, 1902-14; called to NSW Bar, 1915; KC 1934; Actg Judge, Supreme Court of NSW, 1939. Foundn Mem., NSW Inst. of Hospital Almoners, Treas. 1937-63; Dir, Prince Henry's Hosp., 1936-44; Vice-Chm., Metropolitan Hosps Contribution Fund, 1938-44. Mem., Sydney Cricket Ground, 1909-. *Recreation:* reading. *Address:* Wentworth Chambers, 180 Phillip Street, Sydney, NSW 2000, Australia; Box 2225, GPO, Sydney, NSW 2001. *T:* Sydney 28-3476 or 43-4825. *Clubs:* Australian, Australian Jockey (Life Mem.) (Sydney).

HARDWICK, Christopher, MD, FRCP; Physician Emeritus, Guy's Hospital, since 1976; *b* 13 Jan. 1911; *s* of Thomas Mold Hardwick and Harriet Taylor; *m* 1938, Joan Dorothy Plummer; two *s. Educ:* Berkhamsted Sch.; Trinity Hall, Cambridge; Middlesex Hospital. MRCS, LRCP 1935; MA (Cambridge) 1937; MD (Cambridge) 1940; FRCP 1947. House Physician, House Surgeon and Med. Registrar, Middlesex Hosp., 1935 and 1938-41; House physician and Registrar, Hosp. for Sick Children, Gt Ormond Street, 1936-38. Wing Comdr, Medical Specialist, RAF Med. Service, 1941-46. Physician, Guy's Hosp., 1946-76. Hon. Vis. Phys., Johns Hopkins Hosp., Baltimore, 1954. Mem. Council, RCP, 1965-68; Member: Assoc. of Physicians of Great Britain and Ireland; British Gastro-Enterological Soc.; Board of Governors, Guy's Hospital, 1967-74. Chm., British Diabetic Assoc., 1974-. *Publications:* contribs to medical literature. *Recreations:* gardening, reading. *Address:* The Red House, Calvert Crescent, Dorking, Surrey. *Club:* United Oxford & Cambridge University.

HARDWICK, Prof. James Leslie, MDS, MSc, PhD; FDSRCS; Professor of Preventive Dentistry, University of Manchester, since 1960; President, British Paedodontic Society; *b* 27 March

1913; *o s* of George Hardwicke and Mary Ann Hardwick; *m* 1954, Eileen Margaret Isobel Gibson; two *s* two *d*. *Educ:* Rugby Sch.; Birmingham Univ. MDS 1948, PhD 1950, Birmingham; FDSRCS 1954; MSc 1964. Private and hospital dental practice, 1935-39. Served War of 1939-45, Army Dental Corps. University of Birmingham: Lecturer, 1945-48, Sen. Lecturer, 1948-52, in Operative Dental Surgery; Reader in Dental Surgery, 1952-60. *Publications:* editor of and contributor to dental and other scientific journals and textbooks. *Address:* 167 Stanley Road, Cheadle Hulme, Cheshire SK8 6RF. *T:* 061-437 3555.

HARDWICKE, 10th Earl of, *cr* 1754; **Joseph Philip Sebastian Yorke;** Baron Hardwicke 1733; Viscount Royston 1754; *b* 3 Feb. 1971; *s* of Philip Simon Prospero Lindley Rupert, Viscount Royston (*d* 1973) and of Virginia Anne, *d* of Geoffrey Lyon; *S* grandfather, 1974. *Heir: cousin* Richard Charles John Yorke, *b* 25 July 1916. *Address:* 9 Fernshaw Road, SW10; The Mustique Company, St Vincent, West Indies.

HARDY; *see* Gathorne-Hardy.

HARDY, Alan; Member for Brent North, Greater London Council, since 1967; Chairman, Finance and Establishment Committee, since 1977; *b* 24 March 1932; *s* of John Robert Hardy and Emily Hardy; *m* 1972, Betty Howe. *Educ:* Hookergate Grammar Sch.; Univ. of Manchester; Inst. of Historical Res., Univ. of London (MA). Res. Asst to Sir Lewis Namier, History of Parliament Trust, 1955-56; Res. Officer and Dep. Dir, London Municipal Soc., 1956-63; Mem. British Secretariat, Council of European Municipalities, 1963-64. Mem. Bd, Harlow Develt Corp., 1968-. Contested Islington SW (C), 1966. *Publication:* Queen Victoria Was Amused, 1976. *Recreation:* exercising wife's dog. *Address:* 18 Meadowside, Cambridge Park, Twickenham, Mddx. *T:* 01-892 7968. *Club:* Guards' Polo.

HARDY, Sir Alister (Clavering), Kt 1957; FRS 1940; MA, DSc Oxon; FLS, FZS; Hon. Fellow of Exeter College, Oxford; Hon. Fellow of Merton College, Oxford (Fellow, 1946-63); Professor Emeritus, University of Oxford; *b* Nottingham, 10 Feb. 1896; *y s* of late Richard Hardy; *m* 1927, Sylvia Lucy, 2nd *d* of late Prof. Walter Garstang; one *s* one *d*. *Educ:* Oundle Sch.; Exeter Coll., Oxford. Lieut and Capt. 2/1 Northern Cyclist Bn, 1915-19; attached RE, Asst Camouflage Officer, Staff of XIII Army Corps, 1918; Christopher Welch Biological Research Scholar, 1920; Oxford Biological Scholar at the Stazione Zoologica, Naples, 1920; Asst Naturalist in Fisheries Dept, Min. of Agriculture and Fisheries, 1921-24; Chief Zoologist to the Discovery Expedition, 1924-28; Prof. of Zoology and Oceanography, University Coll., Hull, 1928-42; Regius Prof. of Natural History, University of Aberdeen, 1942-45; Linacre Prof. of Zoology, University of Oxford, 1946-61; Prof. of Zoological Field Studies, Oxford, 1961-63; Gifford Lectr, Univ. of Aberdeen, for 1963-65. Founder, and Dir 1969-76, Religious Experience Unit, Manchester Coll., Oxford. Scientific Medal of Zoological Soc., 1939. Hon. LLD Aberdeen; Hon. DSc: Southampton; Hull. Pierre Lecomte du Noüy Prize, 1968. *Publications:* The Open Sea, Part I, The World of Plankton, 1956; The Open Sea, Part II, Fish and Fisheries, 1958; The Living Stream, 1965; The Divine Flame, 1966; Great Waters, 1967; (with R. Harvie and A. Koestler) The Challenge of Chance, 1973; The Biology of God, 1975; Memoirs on Biological Oceanography. *Recreation:* water-colour sketching. *Address:* 7 Capel Close, Oxford OX2 7LA.

HARDY, Prof. Barbara Gladys; Professor of English Literature, Birkbeck College, University of London, since 1970; teacher and author; *d* of Maurice and Gladys Nathan; *m*; two *d*. *Educ:* Swansea High Sch. for Girls; University Coll. London. BA, MA. Subsequently on staff of English Dept of Birkbeck Coll., London; Prof. of English, Royal Holloway Coll., Univ. of London, 1965-70. Mem. Bd of Dirs, Athlone Press. *Publications:* The Novels of George Eliot, 1959; The Appropriate Form, 1964; George Eliot: Daniel Deronda (ed), 1967; Middlemarch: Critical Approaches to the Novel, 1967; The Moral Art of Dickens, 1970; (ed) Critical Essays on George Eliot, 1970; The Exposure of Luxury: radical themes in Thackeray, 1972; Tellers and Listeners: the narrative imagination, 1975; A Reading of Jane Austen, 1975; The Advantage of Lyric, 1977. *Address:* Birkbeck College, Malet Street, WC1E 7HX.

HARDY, Gen. Sir Campbell Richard, KCB 1957 (CB 1954); CBE 1951; DSO 1944 (and 2 Bars); RM retired; Director of the Coal Utilisation Council, 1960-70; *b* 24 May 1906; *s* of Major Frank Buckland Hardy, OBE; *m* 1931, Phyllis Cole Sutton; one *s* one *d*. *Educ:* Felsted Sch. 2nd Lieut RM, 1924; HMS Renown, 1927-

29; courses, 1929-30; HMS Rodney, 1930-31; Physical Training Officer, Portsmouth Div., RM, 1932-37; RNC Dartmouth, 1937-38; HMS Vindictive, 1938-39; served War of 1939-45; Adjt Ports Div., RM, 1939-40; RM Div., 1940-43; 46 Commando, RM, 1943-44; Comd 3 Commando Bde, 1944-45; Staff, RM Office, 1946-47; Chief Instructor, Sch. of Combined Ops, 1947-48; Comd 3 Commando Bde, 1948-51; CO Depot, RM, Deal, 1951; Chief of Staff Royal Marines, 1952-55; Commandant General of the Royal Marines, 1955-59; retired, 1959; Col Comdt, Royal Marines, 1961-66. *Address:* Bunch Lane House, Haslemere, Surrey. *T:* Haslemere 3177. *Club:* Army and Navy.

HARDY, David William; Senior Executive Director, Ocean Transport and Trading Ltd, since 1977; Director: Agricultural Mortgage Corporation; Globe Investment Trust Ltd; *b* 14 July 1930; 3rd *s* of late Brig. John H. Hardy, CBE, MC; *m* 1957, Rosemary, *d* of late Sir Godfrey F. S. Collins, KCIE, CSI, OBE; one *s* one *d*. *Educ:* Wellington Coll.; Harvard Business School (AMP). Chartered Accountant. Served 2nd RHA, 2/Lt, 1953-54. HM Govt Co-ordinator of Industrial Advrs, 1970-72; Gp Finance Dir, Tate & Lyle Ltd, 1972-77. Member: NEDC Cttee for Agriculture, 1970-72; Export Credit Guarantees Dept Adv. Council, 1973-; Co-opted Council of Inst. of Chartered Accountants, 1974-. Mem. Council, BIM, 1974- (Chm. Economic and Social Affairs Cttee, 1974-). *Address:* Everyndens, Lindfield, Haywards Heath, West Sussex. *T:* Lindfield 2551. *Club:* Naval and Military.

HARDY, Sir Harry, Kt 1956; JP; ATI; chartered textile technologist; *b* 10 Sept. 1896; *e s* of Friend and Elizabeth Ann Hardy, Rods Mills, Morley; *m* 1922, Remie (*d* 1955), *d* of Benjamin Siddle, Morley; *m* 1957, Mollie, *d* of Henry Dixon, Morley. *Educ:* Univ. of Leeds. Retired as chemical and fibre manufacturer. Lectr in Textiles, Dewsbury Technical Coll., 1920-35, Head of Textile Industries Dept, 1925-35; Lecturer in Textiles, Huddersfield Technical Coll., 1922-25; Examiner to City and Guilds of London Institute, 1941-44. Pres. Morley and District Textile Soc., 1936-; Founder Pres. Morley Musical Soc., 1943-58; Chm. Youth Employment Cttee, 1943-70; Chm. Local Employment Cttee, 1950-68; Founder Pres., Rotary Club of Morley, 1949-; Vice-Pres. Textile Inst., 1956-59; Liveryman, Cordwainers' Co., 1946-. Hon. Life Pres., Batley and Morley Conservative Assoc. (65 years active service). County Councillor, West Riding of Yorks, 1945-49, County Alderman, 1949-70; JP Borough of Morley, 1948-. Hon. Freeman, Borough of Morley, 1972. *Recreations:* education for textiles, science and technology of textiles; youth employment, music and the arts. *Address:* 45 The Roundway, Dartmouth Park, Morley, near Leeds. *T:* Morley 535150.

HARDY, Sir James (Douglas), Kt 1962; CBE 1955 (OBE 1953); Project Manager and Chief United Nations Adviser, UN Special Fund Public Service Reform and Training Project, Tehran, since 1968; *b* 8 June 1915; *s* of James Percy Hardy; *m* 1937, Robina, *d* of Robert Bookless; two *s*. *Educ:* Gonville and Caius Coll., Cambridge. ICS, 1937-47; Pakistan Civil Service, 1947-61. Dist and Sessions Judge and Dep. Comr, Punjab, up to 1952; Jt Sec. to Govt of Pakistan, 1953; served in: Min. of Communications, as Jt Sec. in charge, 1953-56; Cabinet Secretariat; Min. of Law. Apptd Jt Sec. in charge Estabt Div., President's Secretariat, 1959; promoted Sec., Govt of Pakistan President's Secretariat, 1960; retired, 1961. Ford Foundation representative, in N Africa, 1961-67. Star of Pakistan (SPk), 1961; Comdr Order of Tunisia, 1967. *Recreations:* riding, golf and motoring. *Address:* PO Box 1555, 10 Kh. Namdar, Elahieh, Shemiran, Tehran, Iran. *T:* Tehran 830744.

HARDY, Peter; MP (Lab) Rother Valley since 1970; *b* 17 July 1931; *s* of Lawrence Hardy and of Mrs I. Hardy, Wath upon Dearne; *m* 1954, Margaret Anne Brookes; two *s* (and one *s* decd). *Educ:* Wath upon Dearne Grammar Sch.; Westminster Coll., London; Sheffield Univ. Schoolmaster in S Yorkshire, 1953-70. Member: Wath upon Dearne UDC, 1960-70 (Chm. Council, 1968-69); Governing Body of Wath Grammar Sch. (Chm. of Governors, 1969-70). Pres., Wath upon Dearne Labour Party, 1960-68; contested (Lab): Scarborough and Whitby, 1964; Sheffield, Hallam, 1966. PPS to Sec. of State for the Environment, 1974-76; PPS to Foreign Sec., 1976-. Mem., NUPE. *Publications:* A Lifetime of Badgers, 1975; various articles on educational and other subjects. *Recreation:* watching wild life, notably badgers. *Address:* 53 Sandygate, Wath upon Dearne, Rotherham, South Yorkshire. *T:* Rotherham 874590. *Clubs:* Kennel; Rawmarsh Trades and Labour.

HARDY, Robert James; a Recorder of the Crown Court, since 1972; *b* 12 July 1924; *s* of James Frederick and Ann Hardy; *m* 1951, Maureen Scott; one *s* one *d*. *Educ:* Mostyn House Sch.; Wrekin Coll.; University Coll., London (LLB). Served, 1942-46,

Royal Navy, and Pilot, Fleet Air Arm. Called to Bar, 1950. *Recreation:* sailing. *Address:* Fallow Green, Overhill Lane, Wilmslow Park, Wilmslow, Cheshire. *T:* Wilmslow 28031; Betlem, Mallorca.

HARDY, Sir Rupert (John), 4th Bt, *cr* 1876; Lieutenant-Colonel Life Guards, retired; *b* 24 Oct. 1902; *s* of 3rd Bt and Violet Agnes Evelyn (*d* 1972), *d* of Hon. Sir Edward Chandos Leigh, KCB, KC; *S* father 1953; *m* 1930, Hon. Diana Joan Allsopp, *er d* of 3rd Baron Hindlip; one *s* one *d. Educ:* Eton; Trinity Hall, Cambridge. BA 1925. Joined The Life Guards, 1925; Major, 1940; retired, 1948, and rejoined as RARO, 1952; Lieut-Col comdg Household Cavalry Regt, 1952-56; ceased to belong to R of O, Dec. 1956; granted hon. rank of Lieut-Col. *Recreations:* hunting and shooting. *Heir: s* Richard Charles Chandos Hardy [*b* 6 Feb. 1945; *m* 1972, Venetia, *d* of Simon Wingfield Digby, *qv*]. *Address:* Barleythorpe House, Oakham, Rutland LE18 7EG. *Club:* Turf.
See also Sir Robert Black, Bt.

HARDY-ROBERTS, Brig. Sir Geoffrey (Paul), KCVO 1972; CB 1945; CBE 1944 (OBE 1941); JP; DL; Master of HM's Household, 1967-73; Extra Equerry to the Queen, since 1967; Secretary-Superintendent of Middlesex Hospital, 1946-67; *b* 1907; *s* of A. W. Roberts; *m* 1945, Eldred, *widow* of Col J. R. Macdonell, DSO. *Educ:* Eton; RMC Sandhurst. Regular Commission, 9th Lancers, 1926-37. Served War of 1939-45 (OBE, CBE, CB). Mem., West Sussex AHA, 1974-; Dep. Chm., King Edward VII Hospital, Midhurst, 1972-. JP 1960, DL 1964, West Sussex (formerly Sussex), High Sheriff, 1965, Sussex. Officer, Legion of Merit, 1945. *Address:* The Garden House, Coates, Pulborough, West Sussex RH20 1ES. *T:* Fittleworth 446. *Club:* Turf.

HARDYMAN, Norman Trenchard; Under-Secretary, Department of Education and Science, since 1975; *b* 5 Jan. 1930; *s* of late Rev. Arnold Victor Hardyman and late Laura Hardyman; *m* 1961, Carol Rebecca Turner; one *s* one *d . Educ:* Clifton Coll.; Christ Church, Oxford (Schol., MA). Asst Principal, Min. of Educn, 1955; Principal 1960; Private Sec. to Sec. of State for Educn and Science, 1966-68; Asst Sec. 1968. *Recreations:* walking, gardening, reading, photography. *Address:* 16 Rushington Avenue, Maidenhead, Berks. *T:* Maidenhead 24179.

HARE, family name of **Viscount Blakenham** and **Earl of Listowel.**

HARE, Hon. Alan Victor, MC 1942; Managing Director since 1971, and Chief Executive since 1975, Financial Times Ltd; *b* 14 March 1919; 4th *s* of 4th Earl of Listowel and Hon. Freda, *d* of 2nd Baron Derwent; *m* 1945, Jill Pegotty (*née* North); one *s* one *d. Educ:* Eton Coll.; New Coll., Oxford (MA). Army, 1939-45. Foreign Office, 1947-61; Industrial and Trade Fairs, 1961-63; Financial Times, 1963-. Chm., Throgmorton Publications, 1975; Dir, Pearson Longman Ltd, 1975-. Dep. Chm., Industrial and Trade Fairs Holdings, 1977- (Dir, 1977-); Mem., Press Council, 1975-. *Recreations:* walking, opera, swimming. *Address:* Flat 12, 53 Rutland Gate, SW7. *T:* 01-581 2184. *Clubs:* White's, Pratt's.
See also Viscount Blakenham.

HARE, Prof. Frederick Kenneth, PhD; FRSC 1968; Professor of Geography and Physics, University of Toronto, 1969-76; Director, Institute for Environmental Studies, since 1974; *b* Wylye, Wilts, 5 Feb. 1919; *s* of Frederick Eli Hare and Irene Smith; *m* 1st, 1941, Suzanne Alice Bates (marr. diss. 1952); one *s* ; 2nd, 1953, Helen Neilson Morrill; one *s* one *d. Educ:* Windsor Grammar Sch.; King's Coll., University of London (BSc); Univ. of Montreal (PhD). Lectr in Geography, Univ. of Manchester, 1940-41; War service in Air Min., Meteorological Office, 1941-45; Asst and Assoc. Prof. of Geography, McGill Univ., Montreal, 1945-52; Prof. of Geography and Meteorology, McGill Univ., 1952-64; Chm. of Dept, 1950-61; Dean of Faculty of Arts and Science, 1962-64; Prof. of Geography, Univ. of London (King's Coll.), 1964-66; Master of Birkbeck Coll., Univ. of London, 1966-68; Pres., Univ. of British Columbia, 1968-69. Vis. Centenary Prof., Univ. of Adelaide, 1974. FKC 1967. Sci. Advr, Dept of the Environment, Canada, 1972-73. Mem. Nat. Research Council of Canada, 1962-64; Chm. of Bd, Arctic Inst. of N America, 1963; Mem., NERC, 1965-68; Dir, Resources for the Future, 1968-; Mem., SSRC, Canada, 1974-. Chairman: Adv. Cttee on Canadian Demonstration Projects, 1974-75, for 1976 UN Conf. on Human Settlements; Special Prog. Panel on Ecoscis, NATO, 1975. President: Canadian Assoc. of Geographers, 1964; RMetS, 1967-68 (Vice-Pres., 1968-70); Fellow, Amer. Meteorological Soc., 1969; Hon. Fellow, Amer. Geographical Soc., 1963; Hon. Pres., Assoc. of Amer. Geographers, 1964. Hon. Life Mem., Birkbeck Coll., 1969. Hon.

LLD: Queen's (Canada) Univ., 1964; Univ. of W Ontario, 1968; Hon. DSc McGill, 1969; DSc *ad eund* . Adelaide, 1974. Meritorious Achievement Citation, Assoc. Amer. Geographers, 1961; President's Prize, RMetS (Can.), 1961, 1962; Patterson Medal, Can. Met. Service, 1973; Massey Medal, Royal Can. Geographical Soc., 1974. *Publications:* The Restless Atmosphere, 1953; On University Freedom, 1968; (with M. K. Thomas) Climate Canada, 1974; numerous articles in Quarterly Jl Royal Meteorological Soc., Geography, and other learned jls. *Recreation:* music. *Address:* Institute for Environmental Studies, University of Toronto, Toronto, Ont M5S 1AA, Canada. *Clubs:* Athenæum; McGill Faculty (Montreal) (Hon. Life Mem.); Toronto Faculty.

HARE, Kenneth; *see* Hare, F. K.

HARE, Prof. Patrick James; Grant Professor of Dermatology, University of Edinburgh, since 1968; *b* 18 Jan. 1920; *yr s* of John Henry Hare and Isabella McIntyre; *m* 1945, Mary, *yr d* of late Col A. H. Bridges, CB, CIE, DSO, and Dorothea Seth-Smith; two *s. Educ:* Westminster City Sch.; University Coll., London (Andrews Scholar); University Coll. Hosp. Med. Sch.; Johns Hopkins Univ. (Rockefeller Student). MB, BS, 1944; MD Johns Hopkins, 1944; RAMC 1945-48 (Burma, Singapore); Registrar, Dept of Dermatology, 1948; MRCP 1949; FRCP 1964; MRCPE 1968, FRCPE 1971. Travelling Fellow, Univ. of London, 1951 (Paris, Zürich); Consultant Dermatologist, UCH, 1951-68; Research worker and Senior Lecturer in Dermatology, UCH Med. Sch., 1952-59; MD London 1954; Cons. Dermatologist, Whittington Hosp., London, 1959-68. Mem., Jt Cttee for Higher Med. Trng, 1973- (Chm., Specialist Adv. Cttee (Dermatology), 1973-). Editor, British Journal of Dermatology, 1959-67. Sec. Sect. of Dermatology, Royal Society of Medicine, 1961-62. *Publications:* The Skin, 1966; Basic Dermatology, 1966; scientific and med. articles in various jls. *Recreations:* gardening, music. *Address:* Department of Dermatology, Royal Infirmary, Edinburgh. *T:* 031-229 2477, Ext. 2512; 7 East Castle Road, Edinburgh EH10 5AP. *T:* 031-229 3054.

HARE, Hon. Mrs Richard; *see* Gordine, Dora.

HARE, Rt. Rev. Richard; *see* Hare, Rt Rev. Thomas Richard.

HARE, Prof. Richard Mervyn, FBA 1964; White's Professor of Moral Philosophy and Fellow of Corpus Christi College, Oxford, since 1966; *b* 21 March 1919; *s* of late Charles Francis Aubone Hare and late Louise Kathleen (*née* Simonds); *m* 1947, Catherine, *d* of Sir Harry Verney, 4th Bt, DSO; one *s* three *d. Educ:* Rugby (Schol.); Balliol Coll., Oxford (Schol.). Commissioned Royal Artillery, 1940; Lieut, Indian Mountain Artillery, 1941; Prisoner of War, Singapore and Siam, 1942-45. 1st Lit. Hum. 1947. Fellow and Tutor in Philosophy, Balliol Coll., Oxford, 1947-66. Hon. Fellow, 1974. Visiting Fellow: Princeton, 1957; ANU, 1966; Wilde Lectr in Natural Religion, Oxford, 1963-66; Visiting Professor: Univ. of Michigan, 1968; Univ. of Delaware, 1974. Pres., Aristotelian Soc., 1972-73. Member: Nat. Road Safety Advisory Council, 1966-68; C of E Working Parties on Medical Questions, 1964-75. Hon. Fellow, Inst. of Life Scis, Hastings Center, 1974; For. Hon. Mem., American Acad. of Arts and Sciences, 1975. *Publications:* The Language of Morals, 1952; Freedom and Reason, 1963; Essays on Philosophical Method, 1971; Practical Inferences, 1971; Essays on the Moral Concepts, 1972; Applications of Moral Philosophy, 1972. *Recreations:* music, gardening. *Address:* Saffron House, Ewelme, Oxford.

HARE, Robertson; actor; *b* 17 Dec. 1891; *s* of Frank Homer Hare and Louisa Mary Robertson; *m* 1915, Irene Mewton (*d* 1969); one *d. Educ:* Margate Coll. Trained under Cairns James; first walked on as torch bearer in Sir John Martin Harvey's production of Oedipus Rex, Covent Garden, 1912; first big part Grumpy in the play of that name, 1914-16; joined the Army and served in France, 1917-18; opened with Tom Walls Leslie Henson management at Shaftesbury Theatre, 1922, in farce Tons of Money; continued association with this management when they transferred to Aldwych Theatre and remained there with the Ben Travers farces for eleven years; film work in parts created in the farces; teamed up with Alfred Drayton, 1936, in Vernon Sylvaine's Aren't Men Beasts, Strand Theatre, followed by Spot of Bother by same author, Ben Travers' two farces Banana Ridge and Spotted Dick, Sylvaine's Women Aren't Angels, Ben Travers' play She Follows Me About; with Alfred Drayton in Sylvaine's farce, Madame Louise, Garrick; with Ralph Lynn in Ben Travers' Outrageous Fortune, Winter Garden; with Alfred Drayton, then Arthur Riscoe, in Sylvaine's farce, One Wild Oat, Garrick, 1948 (filmed, 1951); with Arthur Riscoe in Sylvaine's farce, Will Any Gentleman?, Strand, 1950; with Ralph Lynn in Ben Travers' Wild Horses, Aldwych, 1952;

The Party Spirit, 1954; Man Alive, Aldwych, 1956; The Bride and the Bachelor, Duchess, 1956; Fine Fettle, Palace, 1959; The Bride Comes Back, Vaudeville, 1960-61; A funny thing happened on the way to the Forum, Strand, 1963; Oh Clarence!, Lyric, 1968. Has appeared in many films, from 1929. Author of Our Dear Relations (prod 1925), and (with Sydney Lynn) The Dark Room (prod 1927). BBC TV Series, All Gas and Gaiters, 1968-70. *Publication:* Yours Indubitably, 1957. *Recreations:* writing, swimming, golf. *Club:* Savage.

HARE, Ronald, MD (London); Emeritus Professor of Bacteriology in University of London since 1964 and Hon. Consulting Bacteriologist to St Thomas' Hospital since 1951; *b* 30 Aug. 1899; *s* of late Frederick Hare, MD, and Elizabeth Roxby Hare, Esh Winning, Co. Durham; *m* 1932, Barbara Thurgarland Wintle (*d* 1966); one *s. Educ:* Royal Masonic Sch.; Birkbeck Coll.; St Mary's Hosp., London. Scholar, Institute of Pathology and Research, 1925, and asst in Inoculation Dept, St Mary's Hospital, London, 1926-30; first asst in Research Laboratories, Queen Charlotte's Hospital, London, 1931-36; Research Associate in Connaught Laboratories, Univ. of Toronto, and Lectr in Dept of Hygiene and Preventive Medicine, 1936; has carried out extensive researches on the streptococci (Catherine Bishop Harman Prize of BMA and Nicholls Prize of Royal Society of Medicine); largely responsible for the planning and building of the penicillin plant set up in the University of Toronto by the Govt of Canada. Professor of Bacteriology, University of London, 1946-64. Mem. Council: Wright-Fleming Inst., 1952-60; Nuffield Inst. of Comparative Med., 1960-68; Fountains and Carshalton Gp Hospital Management Cttee, 1966-71. Pres., Pathology Sect., 1963-64, and Mem. Council, Royal Society of Medicine, 1965-68; Examr in Universities of: London, Malaya, Birmingham, West Indies, East Africa, Ibadan. *Publications:* Pomp and Pestilence, 1954; An Outline of Bacteriology and Immunity, 1956; Bacteriology and Immunity for Nurses, 1961; The Birth of Penicillin, 1970; many papers in scientific and medical jls. *Recreations:* water-colour painting, the history of pestilence. *Address:* Flat 3, 15 Warwick Square, SW1. *T:* 01-834 6038.

HARE, Sir Thomas, 5th Bt *cr* 1818; *b* 27 July 1930; *s* of Sir Ralph Leigh Hare, 4th Bt, and Doreen Pleasance Anna, *d* of late Sir Richard Bagge, DSO; *S* father, 1976; *m* 1961, Lady Rose Amanda Bligh, *d* of 9th Earl of Darnley; two *d. Educ:* Eton; Magdalene College, Cambridge (MA). ARICS. *Heir: cousin* Philip Leigh Hare [*b* 13 Oct. 1922; *m* 1950, Anne Lisle, *d* of Major Geoffrey Nicholson, CBE, MC; one *s* one *d*]. *Address:* Stow Bardolph, King's Lynn, Norfolk PE34 3HU.

HARE, Rt. Rev. Thomas Richard; *see* Pontefract, Bishop Suffragan of.

HARE DUKE, Rt. Rev. Michael Geoffrey; *see* St Andrews, Dunkeld and Dunblane, Bishop of.

HAREWOOD, 7th Earl of, *cr* 1812; **George Henry Hubert Lascelles;** Baron Harewood, 1796; Viscount Lascelles, 1812; Managing Director, English National Opera (formerly Sadler's Wells Opera), since 1972; *b* 7 Feb. 1923; *er s* of 6th Earl of Harewood, KG, GCVO, DSO, and HRH Princess Mary (Princess Royal; who *d* 28 March 1965); *S* father, 1947; *m* 1st, 1949, Maria Donata (marr. diss. 1967; she *m* 1973, Rt Hon. (John) Jeremy Thorpe, MP), *d* of late Erwin Stein; three *s*; 2nd, 1967, Patricia Elizabeth, *d* of Charles Tuckwell, Australia; one *s* and one step *s. Educ:* Eton; King's Coll., Cambridge (MA). Served War of 1939-45, Capt. Grenadier Guards (wounded and prisoner, 1944, released May 1945); ADC to Earl of Athlone, 1945-46, Canada. Editor of magazine "Opera" 1950-53; Royal Opera House, Covent Garden: a Dir, 1951-53; on staff, 1953-60; a Dir, 1969-72; Artistic Director: Edinburgh Internat. Festival, 1961-65; Leeds Festival, 1958-74; Artistic Advr, New Philharmonia Orch., London, 1966-76. Chm., Music Advisory Cttee of British Council, 1956-66; Chancellor of the Univ. of York, 1963-67; Member: Arts Council, 1966-72; Gen. Adv. Council of BBC, 1969-. President: English Football Assoc., 1963-72; Leeds United Football Club. Hon. LLD: Leeds, 1959; Aberdeen, 1966; Hon. DMus Hull, 1962. *Publication:* (ed) Kobbé's Complete Opera Book, 1953, rev. edn 1976. *Heir: s* Viscount Lascelles, *qv. Address:* Harewood House, Leeds LS17 9LG.

HARFORD, Sir James (Dundas), KBE 1956; CMG 1943; *b* Great Yarmouth, 7 Jan. 1899; *s* of late Rev. Dundas Harford, MA; *m* 1st, 1932, Countess Thelma, *d* of Count Albert Metaxa; one *s*; 2nd, 1937, Lilias Madeline, *d* of Major Archibald Campbell; two *d. Educ:* Repton; Balliol Coll., Oxford (Hon. Scholar, MA). Served European War, France and Belgium, 1917-19; Asst Master, Eton Coll., 1922-25; Administrative

Service, Nigeria, 1926; District administration, Bornu Province, 1926-29; Asst Sec., Nigerian Secretariat, 1930-34 and Clerk to Exec. and Legislative Councils; seconded to Colonial Office, 1934-36; Administrator of Antigua and Federal Sec. of the Leeward Islands, 1936-40; Administrator, St Kitts-Nevis, 1940-47; administered Government of Leeward Islands, on various occasions; seconded to Colonial Office, 1947-48; administered Government of Mauritius, on various occasions; Colonial Sec., Mauritius, 1948-53; Governor and Commander-in-Chief of St Helena, 1954-58. Conference Organiser, Commonwealth Institute, 1959-64. *Address:* Links Cottage, Rother Road, Seaford, East Sussex.

HARFORD, Sir (John) Timothy, 3rd Bt *cr* 1934; Director, Singer & Friedlander Ltd, since 1970 (Local Director, 1967-69); *b* 6 July 1932; *s* of Sir George Arthur Harford, 2nd Bt and Anstice Marion, *d* of Sir Alfred Tritton, 2nd Bt; *S* father, 1967; *m* 1962, Carolyn Jane Mullens; two *s* one *d. Educ:* Harrow Sch.; Oxford Univ.; Harvard Business Sch. Philip Hill Higginson Erlangers Ltd, 1960-63; Dir, Birmingham Industrial Trust Ltd, 1963-67. *Recreations:* wine and food, travel. *Heir: s* Mark John Harford, *b* 6 Aug. 1964. *Address:* South House, South Littleton, Evesham, Worcs. *T:* Evesham 830478. *Club:* Union (Birmingham).

HARGRAVE, John Gordon, FRSA; artist and writer; *b* 1894; *s* of Gordon Hargrave, landscape painter; *m* 1919, Ruth Clark (marr. diss. 1952); one *s*; *m* 1968, Gwendolyn Gray. *Educ:* Wordsworth's Sch., Hawkshead. Illustrated Gulliver's Travels, and the Rose and the Ring at the age of fifteen; chief cartoonist, London Evening Times, at the age of seventeen; joined the staff of C. Arthur Pearson Ltd, 1914; enlisted in RAMC, and served with 10th (Irish) Division in Gallipoli campaign (Suvla Bay Landing), and later in Salonika; invalided out, end of 1916; Art Manager, C. Arthur Pearson Ltd, 1917-20; founded the Kibbo Kift, 1920 (later Social Credit Party, The Green Shirts); Hon. Adviser to the Alberta Govt Planning Cttee, 1936-37; issued the Alberta Report, July 1937; invented the Hargrave Automatic Navigator for Aircraft, 1937; created animal character, "Bushy", for The Sketch, 1952. *Publications:* Lonecraft, 1913, and five other handbooks on camping and the outdoor life; At Suvla Bay, 1916; Harbottle, 1924; Young Winkle, 1925; And Then Came Spring, 1926; The Pfenniger Failing, 1927; The Confession of the Kibbo Kift, 1927; The Imitation Man, 1931; Summer Time Ends, 1935; Professor Skinner alias Montagu Norman, 1939; Words Win Wars, 1940; Social Credit Clearly Explained, 1945; The Life and Soul of Paracelsus, 1951; The Paragon Dictionary, 1953; The Suvla Bay Landing, 1964; The Facts of the Case concerning the Hargrave Automatic Navigator for Aircraft (privately pr.), 1969; special articles on Paracelsus, 1971, and L. Hargrave, inventor of the box-kite, in Encyclopaedia Britannica, 1974. *Recreation:* work. *Address:* 3 Rosemary Court, Fortune Green Road, Hampstead, NW6.

HARGREAVES, Alfred; *b* 15 Feb. 1899. Hon. Secretary West Derby (Liverpool) Labour Party, 1926; President Liverpool Trades Council and Labour Party, 1945. Mem., Liverpool City Council, 1928-50. MP (Lab) Carlisle, 1950-55. Min. of Transport's nominee on Mersey Docks and Harbour Board. Mem., Transport Salaried Staffs Assoc.; Chm., Liverpool, North Wales and Cheshire Divisional Council.

HARGREAVES, Eric Lyde; Emeritus Fellow since 1963 (Fellow, 1925, Tutor, 1930, Senior Tutor, 1937-56), Oriel College, Oxford; *b* 13 Oct. 1898; *s* of George Harrison and Emily Frances Hargreaves. *Educ:* St Paul's Sch.; Corpus Christi Coll., Oxford (Scholar). Wounded and taken prisoner, April 1918; 1st Class Lit. Hum., 1921; PhD London, 1924; University Lecturer in Economics, 1929-35, and 1954-59; Historian, Official History of Second World War (Civil Series), 1942-52; Fellow of Royal Economic and Royal Statistical Societies. *Publications:* Restoring Currency Standards, 1926; National Debt, 1930; (with M. M. Gowing) Civil Industry and Trade, 1952; essays and articles on economic subjects. *Recreation:* walking. *Address:* Oriel College, Oxford.

HARGREAVES, Prof. John Desmond; Professor of History, University of Aberdeen, since 1962; *b* 25 Jan. 1924; *s* of Arthur Swire Hargreaves and Margaret Hilda (*née* Duckworth); *m* 1950, Sheila Elizabeth (*née* Wilks); one *s* two *d. Educ:* Skipton Grammar Sch.; Bootham; Manchester Univ. War service, 1943-46. Asst Princ., War Office, 1947; Lectr in History: Manchester Univ., 1948-52; Fourah Bay Coll., Sierra Leone, 1952-54; Aberdeen Univ., 1954-62. Vis. Prof., Union Coll. Schenectady, New York, 1960-61; Univ. of Ibadan, 1970-71. Mem., Kidd Cttee on Sheriff Court Records, 1966; Mem., Scottish Records Adv. Council. Pres., African Studies Assoc. (UK), 1972-73. *Publications:* Life of Sir Samuel Lewis, 1958; Prelude to the

Partition of West Africa, 1963; West Africa: the Former French States, 1967; France and West Africa, 1969; West Africa Partitioned: Vol. I, The Loaded Pause, 1974; many articles and chapters in jls and collaborative volumes. Jt Editor, Oxford Studies in African Affairs. *Recreations:* inhabiting dilapidated shooting-lodge; hill-walking; occasional lawn tennis. *Address:* 146 Hamilton Place, Aberdeen. *T:* Aberdeen 26852. *Club:* Royal Commonwealth Society.

HARGREAVES, Brig. Kenneth, CBE 1956 (MBE (mil.) 1939); TD 1942; Lord-Lieutenant, West Yorkshire, since 1974 (West Riding of Yorkshire and City of York, 1970-74); President, Hargreaves Group Ltd, since 1974 (Managing Director, 1938-64, Chairman, 1964-74); Director: Lloyds Bank Ltd, 1965-73 (Chairman, Yorkshire Regional Board, 1967); Yorkshire Bank, since 1969; Sadler's Wells Trust Ltd, 1969; English National Opera Ltd, since 1975; *b* 23 Feb. 1903; *s* of late Henry Hargreaves, Leeds, and late Hope Hargreaves; *m* 1st, 1958, Else Margareta Allen (*d* 1968); one step *s* one step *d* (both adopted); 2nd, 1969, Hon. Mrs Margaret Packe; two step *d. Educ:* Haileybury Coll. Lieut-Col comdg 96th HAA Regt RA, 1939-41; Brig. comdg 3rd Ind. AA Bde, 1942-45; Hon. Col, several TA regiments, 1947-66; Vice-Pres., Yorks TAVR, 1970-. Mem., Royal Commn on Historical Monuments, 1971-. Pres., Queen's Silver Jubilee Appeal, W Yorks, 1977-. Chairman: Coal Industry Soc., 1933-34, Pres. 1973-75; Coal Trade Benevolent Assoc., 1958; British Railways (Eastern) Bd, 1970-73 (Dir, 1964-73). President: Chartered Inst. of Secretaries, 1956 (FCIS 1930); W Yorks Branch, BRCS, 1965-74, now Patron; St John Council (W Yorks), 1970-74, W and S Yorks, 1974-; Yorks Agricultural Soc., 1972-73; Haileybury Soc., 1974-75; Vice-Pres., Leeds Chamber of Commerce, 1946-47; Dep. Chm., Leeds Musical Festival, 1961-70; Mem. Court, University of Leeds, 1950-; Trustee, York Minster, 1970-; High Steward, Selby Abbey, 1974-. Contested: Pontefract, 1945; Keighley, 1950 and 1951; Hon. Treasurer, Yorks Provincial Area Conservative and Unionist Assoc., 1946-54; Governor, Swinton Conservative Coll., 1952-70; Lay Reader, Ripon Diocese, 1954-. Liveryman, Clothworkers' Co., 1938, Master, 1969-70. High Sheriff of Yorks, 1962-63; DL WR Yorks 1956-70. Hon. LLD Leeds Univ., 1970. KStJ 1970. *Recreations:* sailing, beagling. *Address:* Castle Garth, Wetherby, West Yorks. *T:* Wetherby 2413. *Clubs:* Army and Navy, Carlton; Royal Yorks Yacht.

HARGREAVES, Maj.-Gen. William Herbert, CB 1965; OBE 1945; FRCP; *b* 5 Aug. 1908; *s* of Arthur William Hargreaves; *m* 1946, Pamela Mary Westray; one *s* one *d. Educ:* Merchant Taylors' Sch.; St Bartholomew's Hospital. FRCP 1950; FRCPE 1965. Served War of 1939-45. Medical Liaison Officer to Surgeon-Gen., US Army, Washington, DC, 1946-48; Prof. of Medicine, Univ. of Baghdad, 1951-59; Physician to late King Faisal II of Iraq, 1951-58; Hon. Consulting Physician, Iraqi Army, 1953-59; Consulting Physician to the Army, 1960-65; retd 1965. Lectr in Tropical Medicine, Middlesex Hosp. Med. Sch., 1960-65, and London Hosp. Med. Sch., 1963-65; Hon. Consulting Physician, Royal Hosp., Chelsea, 1961-65; Chief Med. Advr, Shell Internat. Petroleum Co. Ltd, 1965-72. Examiner: RCP, 1964-66; Soc. Apothecaries, 1966-73. Mem. of Council, Royal Society of Medicine, 1966-69, Vice-Pres., Library (Scientific Research) Section, 1967-69. Counsellor, Royal Soc. of Tropical Med. and Hygiene, 1961-65; Member: Hosp. Cttee, St John's Ophthalmic Hosp., Jerusalem, 1968-71; Finance Cttee, RCP. OStJ 1965. Iraq Coronation Medal, 1953. *Publications:* The Practice of Tropical Medicine (with R. J. G. Morrison), 1965; chapters in: Textbook of Medicine (Conybeare), 16th edn 1975; Modern Trends in Gastro-Enterology (Avery Jones), 1951; Medicine in the Tropics (Woodruff), 1974; numerous articles in med. jls. *Recreations:* art and music. *Address:* Merestones, Mare Hill, Pulborough, West Sussex RH20 2DZ. *T:* Pulborough 3287.

HARINGTON, Gen. Sir Charles (Henry Pepys), GCB 1969 (KCB 1964; CB 1961); CBE 1957 (OBE 1953); DSO 1944; MC 1940; ADC (General) to the Queen, 1969-71; *b* 5 May 1910; *s* of Lt-Col H. H. Harington and Dorothy Pepys; *m* 1942, Victoire Marion Williams-Freeman; one *s* two *d. Educ:* Malvern; Sandhurst. Commissioned into 22nd (Cheshire) Regt, 1930. Served War of 1939-45: France and Belgium, 2nd Bn Cheshire Regt, 1939-40; CO, 1st Bn Manchester Regt and GSO1, 53 (W) Div., NW Europe, 1944-45. DS Staff Coll., 1946; GSO1 Mil. Mission Greece, 1948; CO 1st Bn The Parachute Regt, 1949; Mil. Asst to CIGS, 1951; SHAPE, 1953; Comdr 49 Inf. Bde in Kenya, 1955; idc 1957; Comdt Sch. of Infantry, 1958; GOC 3rd Div., 1959; Comdt, Staff Coll., Camberley, 1961; C-in-C Middle East, 1963; DCGS, 1966; Chief of Personnel and Logistics, to the three Services, 1968-71, retired; Col The Cheshire Regt, 1962-68. Col Comdt, Small Arms Sch. Corps, 1964-70; Col Comdt, The Prince of Wales Div., 1968-71. President:

Combined Cadet Force Assoc.; Milocarian Athletic Club. Chm. Governors, Star and Garter Home. Mem., London Bd, Northern Rock Building Soc. Knight Officer with swords, Order of Orange Nassau (Netherlands), 1945. *Recreations:* sailing, English watercolours. *Address:* 19 Rivermead Court, SW6. *Clubs:* Army and Navy, Hurlingham (Chm.).

HARINGTON, (Edward Henry) Vernon; a Recorder of the Crown Court, 1972-74; *b* 13 Sept. 1907; *er s* of late His Honour Edward Harington; *m* 1st, 1937, Mary Elizabeth (marr. diss. 1949), *d* of late Louis Egerton; one *d* (and one *d* decd); 2nd, 1950, Mary Johanna Jean, JP, *d* of late Lt-Col R. G. S. Cox, MC; two *d. Educ:* Eton. Called to Bar, Inner Temple, 1930. Private Sec. to Lord Chancellor and Dep. Serjeant-at-Arms, House of Lords, 1934-40; served with HM Forces, 1940-45 (Major, Coldstream Guards); WO, 1944-45; Austrian Control Commn, Legal Div., 1945; Asst Sec. to Lord Chancellor for Commns of the Peace, 1945; Dep. Judge Advocate, 1946; Asst Judge Advocate Gen., 1954-73. Dep. Chm., Herefordshire QS, 1969-71. Mem., Regional Agricl Wages Cttee (Chm., Hereford and Worcester and Warwicks and W Midlands Agricl Wages Cttee). JP Herefordshire, 1969-71. *Recreations:* shooting, fishing. *Address:* Woodlands House, Whitbourne, Worcester. *T:* Knightwick 437. *Club:* Cavalry and Guards.

HARINGTON, Maj.-Gen. John, CB 1967; OBE 1958; *b* 7 Nov. 1912; *s* of late Col Henry Harington, Kelston, Folkestone, Kent; *m* 1943, Nancy, *d* of Stanley Allen, Denne Hill, Canterbury; one *s. Educ:* Lambrook, Bracknell; Aldenham Sch.; RMA Woolwich. Commnd RA, 1933. Served War of 1939-45: BEF, 1939-40; Capt., RHA, France and Germany; Major 1943; 1st Airborne Corps; Lt-Col 1945. GSO1, British and Indian Div., Japan, 1946-47; CO 18th Regt RA, 1954-55; College Comdr, RMA, Sandhurst, 1956-57; Head of Defence Secretariat, Middle East, 1958-59; commanded 1st Artillery Brigade, 1960-61; BRA, Far East Land Forces, 1962; DMS (2), War Office, 1962-64 (Min. of Defence, 1964); Chief of Staff to C-in-C, Far East Comd, 1964-67, retired. *Recreations:* ski-ing, shooting, golf, tennis. *Address:* Harkaway, Goodworth Clatford, Andover, Hants. *Clubs:* Army and Navy, Ski Club of Great Britain.

HARINGTON, His Honour John Charles Dundas, QC 1957; a Judge of County Courts, later a Circuit Judge, 1958-73; *b* 27 June 1903; *yr s* of Sir Richard Harington, 12th Bt, and *heir-pres.* to Sir Richard Harington, 13th Bt, *qv; m* 1941, Lavender Cecilia, *d* of late Major E. W. Denny, Garboldisham Manor, Diss, Norfolk; two *s* one *d. Educ:* RN Colleges, Osborne and Dartmouth; Christ Church, Oxford. Called to Bar, 1928. Served War of 1939-45, RNVR, 1939-44. Recorder of Banbury, 1951-55; Recorder of New Windsor, 1955-58; Judge of County Courts (Hants Circuit), 1958-61. Herefordshire QS: Dep. Chm., 1953-57, Chm., 1957-71. *Recreations:* various. *Address:* Whitbourne Court, Worcester.

HARINGTON, Kenneth Douglas Evelyn Herbert; Metropolitan Magistrate since 1967; *b* 30 Sept. 1911; *yr s* of late His Honour Edward Harington; *m* 1st, 1939, Lady Cecilia Bowes-Lyon (*d* 1947), *er d* of 15th Earl of Strathmore; 2nd, 1950, Maureen Helen McCalmont, *d* of Brig.-Gen. Sir Robert McCalmont, KCVO, CBE, DSO; two *s. Educ:* Stowe. War of 1939-45: Served NW Europe (Major, Coldstream Guards). Hon. Attaché, British Legation, Stockholm, 1930-32; Barrister, Inner Temple, 1952; Acting Deputy Chm., Inner London and NE London Quarter Sessions, 1966-67. *Recreations:* shooting, fishing. *Address:* 21 Milner Street, SW3. *T:* 01-589 8951; Sotchers, Bury Gate, Pulborough, West Sussex. *T:* Fittleworth 227. *Club:* Cavalry and Guards.

HARINGTON, Sir Richard Dundas, 13th Bt *cr* 1611; *b* 16 Oct. 1900; *s* of 12th Bt and Selina Louisa Grace (*d* 1945), *d* of 6th Viscount Melville; *S* father, 1931. *Educ:* Eton. *Heir: b* John Charles Dundas Harington, *qv. Address:* c/o Coutts & Co., Bankers, 440 Strand, WC2.

HARINGTON, Vernon; *see* Harington, E. H. V.

HARINGTON HAWES, Derrick Gordon; Director General, International Hospital Federation, 1962-75; *b* 22 May 1907; *s* of late Col Charles Howard Hawes, DSO, MVO, Indian Army; *m* 1932, Drusilla Way; one *s* two *d. Educ:* Wellington Coll.; RMC Sandhurst. 14th Punjab Regt, IA, 1927-34; Indian Political Service, 1934-47; King Edward's Hospital Fund for London, 1949-62. *Address:* 42 Clarendon Road, W11. *Club:* Oriental.

HARKIN, Brendan; Chairman and Chief Executive, Labour Relations Agency, since 1977; *b* 21 April 1920; *s* of Francis and Catherine Harkin; *m* 1949, Maureen Gee; one *s* two *d. Educ:* St Mary's Christian Brothers' Primary and Grammar Schs, Belfast.

Apprentice Electrician, 1936. Asst Sec. 1953, Gen. Sec. 1955-76, NI Civil Service Assoc. (which after amalgamations became Public Service Alliance, 1971). Chm., Strathearn Audio Ltd, 1974-76; Deputy Chairman: NI Finance Corp., 1972-76; NI Development Agency, 1976. Mem., EEC Economic and Social Cttee, 1973-76. Pres., Irish Congress of Trade Unions, 1976. Regular television and radio broadcaster, and contributor to several publications, particularly on industrial relations. *Recreations:* theatre, music, reading. *Address:* 524 Antrim Road, Belfast, Northern Ireland.

HARKNESS, Sir Douglas (Alexander Earsman), KBE 1956 (CBE 1946); retired Civil Servant; Councillor, Clifton Ward, Belfast Corporation, 1967-73; *b* 12 Sept. 1902; *o c* of late George Wightman Harkness and Jane Earsman Harkness; *m* 1936, Annie, *o d* of late J. C. M. Blow and of Jane Sibbald Blow; one *s* one *d. Educ:* Newport (Mon.) High Sch.; University of Glasgow. 2nd Class Hons in History, 1922; 1st Class Hons in Economic Science, 1923; Reid Stewart Fellow, 1923-24. Min. of Agriculture, Northern Ireland, 1924; Lecturer in Agricultural Economics, Queen's Univ., Belfast, 1926; Asst Sec., Min. of Agriculture, 1936; Perm. Sec., 1948; Second Sec., Min. of Finance, 1952; Perm. Sec. to Min. of Finance, Northern Ireland, and Head of Northern Ireland Civil Service, 1953-61; Economic Adviser to the Government of Northern Ireland, 1961-63. LLD (*hc*) Queen's Univ. of Belfast, 1962. *Publications:* War and British Agriculture, 1941; A Tract on Agricultural Policy, 1945; Bolingbroke, 1957; various articles on economic and agricultural subjects. *Recreation:* golf. *Address:* 33 Knockdene Park, Belfast 5. *T:* 654051. *Club:* Ulster (Belfast).

HARKNESS, Lt-Col Hon. Douglas Scott, PC (Canada) 1957; GM 1943; ED 1944; Minister of National Defence, Canada, 1960-63; *b* 29 March 1903; *s* of William Keefer and Janet Douglas Harkness (*née* Scott); *m* 1932, Frances Elisabeth, *d* of James Blair McMillan, Charlottetown and Calgary; one *s. Educ:* Central Collegiate, Calgary; University of Alberta (BA). Served overseas in War (Italy and NW Europe), 1940-45; Major and Lt-Col, Royal Canadian Artillery; with Reserve Army, CO 41st Anti-Tank Regt (SP), Royal Canadian Artillery. MP (Calgary E) gen. elecs, 1945, 1949; Re-elected: (Calgary N) gen. elecs, 1953, 1957, 1958, 1962, 1963, 1965, (Calgary Centre) 1968, retired 1972; Min. for Northern Affairs and Nat. Resources and Actg Minister of Agric., June 1957; Minister of Agric., Aug. 1957; relinquished portfolios of Northern Affairs and Nat. Resources, Aug. 1957, of Agriculture, Oct. 1960. Mem. Alta Military Institute. Hon. LlD Calgary. *Address:* 716 Imperial Way SW, Calgary, Alta T2S 1N7, Canada. *T:* Calgary (403) 243-0825. *Clubs:* Ranchmen's, Calgary Petroleum (Calgary); Rideau (Ottawa).

HARKNESS, Rear-Adm. James Percy Knowles, CB 1971; *b* 28 Nov. 1916; *s* of Captain P. Y. Harkness, West Yorkshire Regt, and Gladys Dundas Harkness (*née* Knowles); *m* 1949, Joan, *d* of late Vice-Adm. N. A. Sulivan, CVO; two *d.* Dir-Gen., Naval Manpower, 1970; retired 1972. *Recreation:* sailing.

HARKNESS, Captain Kenneth Lanyon, CBE 1963; DSC 1940; Royal Navy; *b* 24 Aug. 1900; *s* of late Major T. R. Harkness, RA, and late Mrs G. A. de Burgh; *m* 1932, Joan Phyllis Lovell; one *d. Educ:* RN Colls, Osborne and Dartmouth; Cambridge Univ. Midshipman, HMS Bellerophon, 1917; Cambridge Univ., 1922; Qual. Gunnery, 1926; Comdr Admty, 1935; Sqdn Gunnery Off., 2nd Battle Sqdn, 1937; Comd HMS Winchelsea, 1938; Comd HMS Fearless, 1939-40; Capt. 1940; Chief of Intell. Service, Far East, 1940-42; Dep. Dir of Naval Ordnance, Admty, 1943-44; Comd HMS Ceylon, 1945; Comd HMS Sheffield, 1946; Chief of Staff to C-in-C Portsmouth, 1947; retired from RN, 1949. Civil Defence Officer, Portsmouth, 1949; Home Office, Asst Chief Staff Tng Off. (CD), 1952; Prin. Off., later Reg. Dir of CD, London Reg., 1954; Temp. seconded as CD Adviser, Cyprus, 1956; later Regional Dir of Civil Defence, London Region, 1954-65. *Recreation:* gardening. *Address:* Far Rockaway, Durford Wood, Petersfield, Hants GU31 5AW. *T:* Liss 3173. *Club:* Naval and Military.

HARLAND, Rt. Rev. Maurice Henry, MA, DD; *b* 17 April 1896; *s* of late Rev. William George Harland and late Clara Elizabeth Harland; *m* 1923, Agnes Hildyard Winckley, MBE 1967; two *d. Educ:* St Peter's Sch., York; Exeter Coll., Oxford (MA); Leeds Clergy Sch. DD (Lambeth) 1948. 2nd Lieut West Yorks Regt, 1914-15; 2nd Lieut R Field Artillery, 1915-16; Lieut Royal Flying Corps and afterwards RAF, 1916-19; Curate St Peter's, Leicester, 1922-27; Priest in Charge St Anne's Conventional District, 1927-33; Perpetual Curate of St Matthew's Holbeck, Leeds, 1933-38; Vicar of St Mary's, Windermere, 1938-42; Rural Dean of Ambleside; Vicar of Croydon, 1942-47; Archdeacon of Croydon, 1946-47; Hon. Canon of Canterbury, 1942-47; Bishop

Suffragan of Croydon, 1942-47; Bishop of Lincoln, 1947-56; Bishop of Durham, 1956-66, retired. Select Preacher, Oxford Univ., 1949-50. Pres., Edinburgh Sir Walter Scott Soc., 1940-50; Hon. Fellow, Exeter Coll., Oxford, 1950; Hon. DD Durham Univ., 1956. Introduced to House of Lords, 1954 and again in 1956 on becoming Bishop of Durham. *Recreations:* fishing, riding. *Address:* White Chimneys, Rookwood Road, West Wittering, near Chichester, West Sussex. *T:* West Wittering 2351.

HARLAND, Air Marshal Sir Reginald (Edward Wynyard), KBE 1974; CB 1972; with W. S. Atkins and Partners, Epsom, since 1977; *b* 30 May 1920; *s* of Charles Cecil Harland and Ida Maud (*née* Bellhouse); *m* 1942, Doreen Rosalind, *d* of late W. H. C. Romanis; three *s* two *d. Educ:* Summer Fields, Oxford; Stowe; Trinity Coll., Cambridge (MA). Served War of 1939-45: RAE Farnborough, 1941-42; N Africa, Italy and S France, 1942-45. Techn. trng, techn. plans and manning depts, Air Min., 1946-49; pilot trng, 1949-50; Chief Engrg Instructor, RAF Coll., Cranwell, 1950-52; Guided Weapon trng, RMCS Shrivenham, 1952-53; Thunderbird Project Officer: RAE Farnborough, 1953-55; Min. of Supply, 1955-56; psa 1957; Ballistic Missile Liaison Officer, (BJSM) Los Angeles, 1958-60; CO, Central Servicing Develt Estab., Swanton Morley, 1960-62; STSO, HQ No 3 (Bomber) Gp, Mildenhall, 1962-64; AO i/c Engrg, HQ Far East Air Force, Singapore, 1964-66; Harrier Project Dir, HQ Min. of Technology, 1967-68; idc 1969; AOC No 24 Group, RAF, 1970-72; AO Engineering, Air Support Command, 1972; AOC-in-C, RAF Support Command, 1973-77. Mem. Council, BIM, 1973; Pres., Soc. Environmental Engrs, 1974. CEng 1966; FIMechE 1967; FIEE 1964; FRAeS 1967; FBIM 1974; FIE (Singapore) 1967; MIE (Malaysia) 1966. *Publications:* occasional articles in Jl RAeS and other engrg jls. *Recreations:* sailing, bridge, reading. *Address:* Alabama, Chenies Road, Chorley Wood, Herts WD3 5LU. *Club:* Royal Air Force.

HARLAND, Sydney Cross, DSc (London); FRS 1943; FRSE 1951; FTI (Hon.) 1954; George Harrison Professor of Botany, Manchester University, 1950-58, retired, Emeritus Professor, 1958; Member, Agricultural Research Council, 1950-55; *b* 19 June 1891; *s* of Erasmus and Eliza Harland, Cliff Grange, Snainton, Yorks; *m* 1st, 1915, Emily Wilson Cameron; two *d*; 2nd, 1934, Olive Sylvia Atteck; one *s. Educ:* Municipal Secondary School, Scarborough; King's Coll., London. Asst Supt Agric., St Vincent, BWI, 1915; Asst for Cotton Research, Imp. Dept Agric. for West Indies, 1918; Head Botanical Dept, British Cotton Industry Res. Assoc., Manchester, 1920; Prof. Botany and Genetics, Imperial Coll. Trop. Agric., Trinidad, 1923; Chief Geneticist, Empire Cotton Growing Corp., Cotton Research Station, Trinidad, and Cotton Adviser to Comr of Agric., 1926; Gen. Adviser to State Cotton Industry of Sao Paulo, Brazil, 1935; Dir, Institute of Cotton Genetics, National Agricultural Soc., Peru, 1939-50. Mem., UNESCO Mission to Ecuador, 1962. President: Genetical Soc. of GB, 1953-56; Indian Cotton Congress, 1956; Fellow: Botanical Soc., Edinburgh, 1953; New England Inst. of Medical Res., 1963. Hon. Mem., Internat. Union for R&D, 1964. Hon. MSc Manchester, 1958; Hon. DSc West Indies, 1973. *Publications:* The Genetics of Cotton, 1939; also papers on cotton, cocoa, other tropical crops, and applied genetics. *Recreations:* travel, gardening, human genetics. *Address:* Cliff Grange, Snainton, Scarborough, Yorks. *T:* Snainton 549; Correo Nana, Carretera Central, Peru. *Club:* Athenæum.

HARLAND, Prof. William Arthur; Regius Professor of Forensic Medicine, University of Glasgow, since Oct. 1974; *b* 7 March 1926; *s* of Robert Wallace Harland and Elizabeth Montgomery Robb; *m* 1953, Brenda Foxcroft; three *s* one *d. Educ:* Methodist Coll., Belfast; Queen's Univ., Belfast. MB, BCh Belfast 1948, MD Belfast 1974; FRCP(C) 1959; PhD London 1964, FRCPath 1967, MRCPGlas 1971, FRCPGlas 1974. Demonstrator in Pathology, Emory Univ., 1951-53; Resident Pathologist, Presbyterian Hosp., NY, 1954; Dir of Labs, St Joseph's Hosp., Chatham, Ont, 1955-58; Assoc. Path., Jewish Gen. Hosp., Montreal, 1958-60; Sen. Lectr in Pathology, Univ. of West Indies, 1960-64; Path., MRC Atheroma Res. Unit, Western Infirmary, Glasgow, 1964-66; Sen. Lectr in Pathology, Univ. of Glasgow, 1966-74. *Publications:* various articles in sci. jls on thyroid diseases and on atherosclerosis. *Recreations:* bridge, bird-watching. *Address:* Department of Forensic Medicine, University of Glasgow, Glasgow G12 8QQ. *T:* 041-339 8855.

HARLECH, 5th Baron *cr* 1876; **William David Ormsby Gore**, PC 1957; KCMG 1961; *b* 20 May 1918; *e* surv. *s* of 4th Baron Harlech, KG, PC, GCMG, and Lady Beatrice Cecil (*see* Dowager Lady Harlech); *S* father, 1964; *m* 1st, 1940, Sylvia (*d* 1967), 2nd *d* of late Hugh Lloyd Thomas, CMG, CVO; one *s* three *d* (and one *s* decd); 2nd, 1969, Pamela, *o d* of Ralph F.

Colin, New York; one d. *Educ:* Eton; New Coll., Oxford. Joined Berks Yeomanry, 1939, Adjutant, 1942; Major (GS), 1945. MP (C) Oswestry Div. of Salop, 1950-61; Parliamentary Private Sec. to Minister of State for Foreign Affairs, 1951; Parliamentary Under-Sec. of State for Foreign Affairs, Nov. 1956-Jan. 1957; Minister of State for Foreign Affairs, 1957-61; British Ambassador in Washington, 1961-65. Dep.-Leader of the Opposition, House of Lords, 1966-67. Dep. Chm., Commn on Rhodesian Opinion, 1972. President: British Bd of Film Censors, 1965-; The Pilgrims (Soc. of UK, 1965-77); Trustee, The Pilgrim Trust, 1965- (Chm. 1974-); Chairman: Harlech Television; Kennedy Meml Trust; Papworth and Enham Village Settlements; European Movement, 1969-75. Dir, Commercial Bank of Wales, 1972-. Mem., Adv. Cttee, Kennedy Inst., Harvard. Trustee, Tate Gallery, 1971-; Governor, Yehudi Menuhin Sch. Hon. Chm., Shelter, 1969-73, Pres. 1973-; Chm., Nat. Cttee for Electoral Reform, 1976. Hon. Fellow, New Coll., Oxford, 1964. Hon. DCL, Univ. of Pittsburgh, 1962; Hon. LLD: Brown Univ., 1963; New York Univ., 1964; William and Mary Coll., 1965; Manchester, 1966. DL Salop, 1961. KStJ. *Publications:* Must the West Decline?, 1966; (jtly) Europe: the case for going in, 1971. *Heir:* s Hon. Francis David Ormsby Gore, b 13 March 1954. *Address:* 14a Ladbroke Road, W11. *T:* 01-229 6701; House of Lords, Westminster, SW1; Glyn, Talsarnau, Gwynedd. *T:* Harlech 338. *Club:* Pratt's.
See also Rt Hon. M. V. Macmillan, Sir A. L. Mayall, Baron Wardington.

HARLECH, Dowager Lady, DCVO 1947; **Beatrice Mildred Edith;** Extra Lady of the Bedchamber to the Queen Mother, since 1953; b 10 Aug. 1891; d of 4th Marquess of Salisbury, KG, GCVO; m 1913, 4th Baron Harlech, KG, PC, GCMG (d 1964); two s three d (and one s decd). *Address:* 14 Ladbroke Road, W11. *T:* 01-229 6679.
See also Baron Harlech.

HARLEY, Prof. John Laker, FRS 1964; FLS; MA, DPhil Oxon; Professor of Forest Science, and Fellow of St John's College, Oxford University, since 1969; b 17 Nov. 1911; s of late Charles Laker Harley and Edith Sarah (née Smith); m 1938, Elizabeth Lindsay Fitt; one s one d. *Educ:* Leeds Grammar Sch.; Wadham Coll., Oxford. Open Exhibition, Wadham Coll., 1930, Hon. Scholar 1933, Hon. Fellow, 1972; Christopher Welch Scholar, Oxford, 1933-37; Senior Student 1851 Exhibition, 1937-38. Departmental Demonstrator, Oxford, 1938-44. Served in Royal Signals, 1940-45: attached Operation Research Group No. 1, India, Lieut-Col GSO1. University Demonstrator, Oxford, 1945-62; Browne Research Fellow, Queen's Coll., Oxford, 1946-52; Official Fellow, Queen's Coll., Oxford, 1952-65; Reader in Plant Nutrition, Oxford Univ., 1962-65; Prof. of Botany, Sheffield Univ., 1965-69. Mem., ARC, 1970-. President: British Mycological Soc., 1967; British Ecological Soc., 1970-72. Editor, New Phytologist, 1961-. *Publications:* Biology of Mycorrhiza, 1969; scientific papers in New Phytologist, Annals of Applied Mycology, Annals of Botany, Biochemical Jl, Plant Physiology, Proc. Royal Soc., Jl of Ecology. *Recreation:* gardening. *Address:* The Orchard, Old Marston, Oxford OX3 0PQ.

HARLEY, Sir Stanley (Jaffa), Kt 1958; DL; President, Coventry Gauge & Tool Co. Ltd, since 1971 (Chairman and Managing Director, 1963-70); b 12 Nov. 1905; s of late Sir Harry Harley, CBE and Mrs Lydia Harley; m 1931, Rhona Townsend; two s one d. *Educ:* Wrekin Coll., Wellington, Salop; Birmingham Univ. Apprenticed to Coventry Gauge & Tool Co. Ltd, 1926; completed training at Coventry, on Continent, and in USA; Joint Man. Dir, Coventry Gauge & Tool Co. Ltd, 1935; Man. Dir, 1946, 1951; Dep. Chm. 1946; Chm. 1951; Dir, Tube Investments Ltd, 1969-71. Hon. Controller of Jigs, Tools and Gauges, Machine Tool Control, Min. of Supply and Min. of Production, 1940-46. Pro-Chancellor, Warwick Univ., 1973-. DL Co. Warwick, 1967. *Recreations:* golf, travel. *Address:* Sunnycrest, Ashorne, Warwick. *Clubs:* Royal Automobile; Drapers (Coventry).

HARLEY, Sir Thomas (Winlack), Kt 1960; MBE 1944; MC 1918; DL; Consultant with Simpson North Harley & Co., solicitors, Liverpool and London, admitted 1922; b 27 June 1895; o s of George Harley and Annie Thomson (née Macwatty); m 1924, Margaret Hilda, 2nd d of late Canon J. U. N. Bardsley; three s. *Educ:* Birkenhead Sch.; Eton. Served European War, 1914-19, France and Balkans, Major The King's Own Regt (despatches, MC); War of 1939-45, Major RA (TA); comd (HG) AA Battery (MBE). Mem., Liverpool Regional Hosp. Bd, 1947- (Chm., 1959-68). Mem. Board of Governors, United Liverpool Hosps, 1955-69; Pres., Bebington and Ellesmere Port Conservative Assoc., etc. DL Cheshire (formerly County of Chester), 1962. *Recreation:* gardening. *Address:* Hesketh Hey, Thornton Hough, Wirral, Merseyside L63 1JA. *T:* 051-336 3439. *Clubs:* Royal Over-Seas League; Royal Liverpool Golf.

HARLOCK, Maj.-Gen. Hugh George Frederick, CBE 1953; b 20 Aug. 1900; s of James Harlock, Camperdown, Victoria; m 1935, Florence Madge, d of W. C. Ewing, Sydney, NSW; one s one d. *Educ:* Wesley Coll., Melbourne; RMC Duntroon. Commnd Aust. Staff Corps, 1921; Regimental and Staff appts in Royal Australian Artillery, 1922-39; Aust. Imperial Force, 1940-47; Staff appts, AHQ, 1947-49; Aust. Army Rep., UK, 1950-52; Brig. i/c Admin., E Comd, 1953; Maj.-Gen. 1954; Gen. Officer Commanding, Northern Command, Australian Military Forces, 1954-57. *Address:* 2 Holmes Street, Toowong, Queensland 4066, Australia. *Club:* United Service (Brisbane).

HARMAN, Sir Cecil W. F. S. K.; see Stafford-King-Harman.

HARMAN, Ernest Henry, CBE 1973 (OBE 1961); Chairman, South Western Gas Region (formerly South Western Gas Board), 1964-73; b 1908; m 2nd, 1958, Dorothy Anne Parsons; (two d by 1st m). *Educ:* London Univ. BSc (Hons). Sec., 1936, Gen. Manager, 1944, Commercial Gas Co.; Gen. Manager, Sheffield and Rotherham Div., East Midlands Gas Board, 1949; Dep. Chm., East Midlands Gas Board, 1952. *Recreations:* tennis, motoring, music. *Address:* Little Orchard, 14 Mill Lane, Beckington, Bath BA3 6SN.

HARMAN, Gen. Sir Jack (Wentworth), KCB 1974; OBE 1962; MC 1943; Adjutant-General, Ministry of Defence (Army), since 1976; b 20 July 1920; s of late Lt.-Gen. Sir Wentworth Harman, KCB, DSO, and late Dorothy Harman; m 1947, Gwladys May Murphy (widow of Lt-Col R. J. Murphy), d of Sir Idwal Lloyd; one d and two step d. *Educ:* Wellington Coll.; RMC Sandhurst. Commissioned into The Queen's Bays, 1940, Bt Lt-Col, 1958; Commanding Officer, 1st The Queen's Dragoon Guards, 1960-62; commanded 11 Infantry Bde, 1965-66; attended IDC, 1967; BGS, HQ Army Strategic Command, 1968-69; GOC, 1st Div., 1970-72; Commandant, RMA, Sandhurst, 1972-73; GOC 1 (British) Corps, 1974-76. Col, 1st The Queen's Dragoon Guards, 1975-; Col Comdt, RAC, 1977-. *Address:* Sandhills House, Dinton, near Salisbury, Wilts. *T:* Teffont 288. *Club:* Cavalry and Guards.

HARMAN, Jeremiah LeRoy, QC 1968; b 13 April 1930; er s of late Rt Hon. Sir Charles Eustace Harman; m 1960, Erica Jane, e d of Hon. Sir Maurice Richard Bridgeman, qv; two s one d. *Educ:* Horris Hill Sch.; Eton Coll. Served Coldstream Guards and Parachute Regt, 1948-51; Parachute Regt (TA), 1951-55. Called to the Bar, Lincoln's Inn, 1954, Bencher, 1977; Mem., Bar Council, 1963-67. Director: Dunford & Elliott Ltd, 1972-; Brown Bayley Properties (Pty) Ltd (SA). *Recreations:* fishing, shooting, stalking, watching birds. *Address:* Great Shefford House, Newbury, Berks. *T:* Gt Shefford 212; Sra-na-Cloya, near Louisburgh, Co. Mayo; 9 Old Square, Lincoln's Inn, WC2. *T:* 01-405 0846.

HARMAN, John Bishop, FRCS, FRCP; Honorary Consulting Physician, since 1972; b 10 Aug. 1907; s of late Nathaniel Bishop Harman and of Katharine (née Chamberlain); m 1946, Anna Charlotte Malcolm Spicer; four d. *Educ:* Oundle; St John's Coll., Cambridge (Scholar); St Thomas's Hospital (Scholar). Fearnsides Scholar, Cantab, 1932; 1st Cl. Nat. Sci. Tripos Pt I, 2nd Cl. Pt II, Cantab; MA 1933; MD 1937; FRCS 1932; FRCP 1942. Physician: St Thomas' Hospital, 1938-72; Royal Marsden Hospital, 1947-72. Pres., Medical Defence Union. Late Lt-Col RAMC (despatches). *Publications:* contribs to medical literature. *Recreation:* horticulture. *Address:* 108 Harley Street, W1. *T:* 01-935 7822.

HARMAN, R. D. K.; see King-Harman.

HARMAN, Robert Donald, QC 1974; a Recorder of the Crown Court, since 1972; b 26 Sept. 1928; o s of late Herbert Donald Harman, MC; m 1st, 1960, Sarah Elizabeth (d 1965), o d of G. C. Cleverly; two s; 2nd, 1968, Rosamond Geraldine, JP, 2nd d of late Cmdr G. T. A. Scott, RN; two d. *Educ:* privately; St Paul's Sch.; Magdalen Coll., Oxford. Called to Bar, Gray's Inn, 1954; South-Eastern Circuit; a Junior Prosecuting Counsel to the Crown at Central Criminal Court, 1967-72; a Senior Treasury Counsel, 1972-74. *Recreations:* books, shooting, golf. *Address:* 2 Harcourt Buildings, Temple, EC4. *T:* 01-353 2112; 17 Pelham Crescent, SW7 2NR. *T:* 01-584 4304; Waldershare Cottage, Sandwich Bay, Kent. *T:* Sandwich 2760. *Clubs:* Garrick, Beefsteak, Pratt's; Royal St George's, Swinley Forest Golf.

HARMAR-NICHOLLS, family name of **Baron Harmar-Nicholls.**

HARMAR-NICHOLLS, Baron cr 1974 (Life Peer), of Peterborough, Cambs; **Harmar Harmar-Nicholls,** JP; Bt 1960; b

1 Nov. 1912; 3rd *s* of Charles E. C. Nicholls and Sarah Anne Nicholls, Walsall; *m* 1940, Dorothy Elsie, *e d* of James Edwards, Tipton; two *d*. *Educ:* Dorsett Road Sch., Darlaston; Queen Mary's Gram. Sch., Walsall. Mem. Middle Temple Inn of Court. Chairman: Nicholls and Hennessy (Hotels) Ltd; Malvern Festival Theatre Trust Ltd; Pleasurama, 1970-; Director: J. & H. Nicholls & Co., Paints, etc, 1945-; Radio Luxemburg (London) Ltd; Cannon Assurance Ltd, 1971-72; Mem. of Syndicate at Lloyd's. Mem. Darlaston UDC at age of 26 (Chm., 1949-50); County Magistrate, 1946. Vice-Chm. W Midland Fedn, Junior Imperial League, 1937; contested (C): Nelson and Colne, 1945; Preston by-election, 1946; MP (C) Peterborough Div. of Northants, 1950-Sept. 1974; PPS to Asst Postmaster-Gen., 1951-April 1955; Parly Sec., Min. of Agriculture, Fisheries and Food, April 1955-Jan. 1957; Parliamentary Sec., Min. of Works, 1957-60; Mem. Conservative Housing Cttee; Sec. of Parly Road Safety Cttee (Conservative); Jt Sec. All party Parly Group Empire Migration; Mem. Govt Overseas Settlement Board on migration to Commonwealth. War of 1939-45: volunteered as sapper, commnd Royal Engineers; served India and Burma. *Recreations:* gardening, reading, walking, theatre. *Address:* Abbeylands, Weston, Stafford. *T:* Weston 252. *Clubs:* St Stephen's, Constitutional; (Pres.) Unionist, City and Counties (Peterborough); Conservative (Darlaston); Unionist (Walsall).

HARMER, Cyril Henry Carrington; President, H. R. Harmer Ltd; Director, H. R. Harmer Inc., New York; *b* 17 Aug. 1903; *s* of Henry Revell Harmer and Edith Annie Harmer; *m* 1935, Elizabeth Boyd Baird; two *d*. *Educ:* Brighton Grammar Sch. Joined H. R. Harmer, 1921; Partner, 1927; Dir, 1946; Chm. and Man. Dir, 1967-76. Lieut RA, 1939-45; POW, 1941-45. FInstD; Roll of Distinguished Philatelists, 1969. *Publications:* (with R. E. R. Dalwick) Newfoundland Air Mails, 1953; contribs to philatelic jls. *Recreation:* bowls. *Address:* 20 Wildcroft Manor, SW15 3TS. *T:* 01-788 0710. *Clubs:* Hurlingham; Collectors (New York); Western Province Sports (Cape).

HARMER, Sir Dudley; *see* Harmer, Sir J. D.

HARMER, Sir Frederic (Evelyn), Kt 1968; CMG 1945; *b* 3 Nov. 1905; *yr s* of late Sir Sidney Frederic Harmer, KBE, FRS; *m* 1st, 1931, Barbara Susan (*d* 1972), *er d* of late Major J. A. C. Hamilton, JP, Fyne Court, Bridgwater, Som.; one *s* three *d*; 2nd, 1973, Daphne Shelton Agar. *Educ:* Eton; King's Coll., Cambridge. Wrangler, Maths Tripos Part II, 1926; Class 1, Div. 1, Econs Tripos Part II 1927; BA 1927; MA 1934. Entered Treasury, Oct. 1939; Temp. Asst Sec., 1943-45; served in Washington, March-June 1944 and again in Sept.-Dec. 1945 for Anglo-American economic and financial negotiations; resigned Dec. 1945. Dep. Chm., P&OSN Co., 1957-70. Chairman: Cttee of European Shipowners, 1965-68; Internat. Chamber of Shipping, 1968-71; HM Govt Dir, British Petroleum Co. Ltd, 1953-70. Hon. Fellow, LSE, 1970. *Recreations:* sailing, golf. *Address:* Tiggins Field, Kelsale, Saxmundham, Suffolk. *T:* Saxmundham 3156.

HARMER, Sir (John) Dudley, Kt 1972; OBE 1963; JP; farmer; *b* 27 July 1913; *s* of Ernest George William Harmer and Germaine Stuart Harmer (*née* Wells); *m* 1947, Erika Minder-Lanz, Switzerland; two *s*. *Educ:* Merchant Taylors' Sch.; Wye College. Certif. Agriculture. Mem. 1956, Dep. Chm. 1964-72, Kent Agric. Exec. Cttee; Mem., Kent CC Agric. and Smallholdings Cttee, 1958 (Chm. of Selection of Tenants and Loans Sub-Cttee); Vice-Chm. 1964-66, Chm. 1966-71, SE Area Conservative Provincial Council. Service connected with Home Guard, 1952-56: Hon. Major 1956. JP Kent, 1962. *Recreations:* gardening, travel. *Address:* Stone Hill, Egerton, Ashford, Kent. *T:* Egerton 241. *Club:* Royal Commonwealth Society.

HARMER, Michael Hedley, MA, MB Cantab, FRCS; Consulting Surgeon, Royal Marsden Hospital and Paddington Green Childrens Hospital (St Mary's Hospital); *b* 6 July 1912; *y s* of late Douglas Harmer, MC, FRCS, and May (*née* Hedley); *m* 1939, Bridget Jean, *d* of James Higgs-Walker, *qv*; one *s* one *d*. *Educ:* Marlborough; King's Coll., Cambridge; St Bartholomew's Hosp., London. Surgical Specialist, RAFVR, 1943-46. Bellman Snark Club, Cambridge, 1934-. Freeman of Norwich by Patrimony, 1935. *Publications:* (jt) A Handbook of Surgery, 1951; Aids to Surgery, 1962; (Jt Editor) Rose and Carless's Manual of Surgery, 19th edn, 1959; papers on the surgery and classification of malignant disease. *Recreations:* music, the country. *Address:* Perrot Wood, Graffham, Petworth, Sussex GU28 0NZ. *T:* Graffham 307.

HARMOOD-BANNER, Sir George Knowles, 3rd Bt, *cr* 1924; *b* 9 Nov. 1918; *s* of Sir Harmood Harmood-Banner, 2nd Bt, and Frances Cordelia (*d* 1975), *d* of late George Duberly, JP, Plansworth, Co. Durham; *S* father 1950; *m* 1947, Rosemary

Jane, *d* of Col M. L. Treston, CBE, FRCS, FRCOG, late IMS, and late Mrs Sheila Treston; two *d*. *Educ:* Eton; University of Cambridge. Served War of 1939-45: 2nd Lieut Royal Welch Fusiliers, 1942, attached to East African Engineers (SEAC); transferred RASC, 1945. *Recreations:* tennis, ski-ing and swimming. *Heir:* none. *Address:* c/o The Bank of Nova Scotia, 11 Waterloo Place, SW1.

HARMSWORTH, family name of **Viscount Rothermere** and **Baron Harmsworth.**

HARMSWORTH, 2nd Baron, *cr* 1939, of Egham; **Cecil Desmond Bernard Harmsworth;** painter; *b* 1903; *e s* of 1st Baron Harmsworth and Emilie Alberta (*d* 1942), *d* of William Hamilton Maffett, Finglas, Co. Dublin; *S* father, 1948; *m* 1926, Dorothy Alexander, *d* of late Hon. J. C. Heinlein, Bridgeport, Ohio, USA; one *d*. *Educ:* Eton Coll.; Christ Church, Oxford (MA); (in drawing) Académie Julian, Paris; (in painting) public galleries. Was successively newspaperman and book publisher before becoming a painter. Exhibitions: Galerie des Quatre-Chemins, Paris, 1933; Wildenstein Gall., London, 1938; Bonestell Gall., New York, 1944; Swedish Modern, Dallas, Texas, 1950; Messrs Roland, Browse & Delbanco, London, 1954. Has been regular contributor to Salon d'Automne and group exhibitions in Paris; has exhibited in many London and New York galleries, and at the Phillips Memorial Gallery, Washington, DC. Portraits of Norman Douglas, Havelock Ellis, Lord Inverchapel, James Joyce, Consuelo de Saint-Exupéry, Sir Osbert Sitwell, Swami Nikhilananda, etc. Chairman, Dr Johnson's House Trust. Served in British Information Services, New York, 1940-46. *Publications:* occasional prose and verse contributions to English, Irish, and US periodicals; drawings and paintings reproduced in US magazines. *Heir:* b Hon. Eric Beauchamp Northcliffe Harmsworth [*b* 28 Aug. 1905; *m* 1935, Hélène (*d* 1962), *d* of Col Jules-Raymond Dehove, Paris; one *s* one *d*; *m* 1964, Mrs Helen Hudson, London. *Educ:* Eton Coll.; Christ Church, Oxford (MA)]. *Address:* Lime Lodge, Egham, Surrey. *T:* Egham 379.

HARMSWORTH, Sir (Arthur) Geoffrey (Annesley), 3rd Bt *cr* 1918; FSA; Chairman, Harmsworth Press Ltd; President, West Country Publications Ltd; Director: Western Morning News Co. Ltd; Western Times Co. Ltd; Daily Mail & General Trust Ltd; F. Hewitt & Son (1927) Ltd; News Holdings Ltd; *b* 29 March 1904; *y s* of Sir Leicester Harmsworth, 1st Bt and late Annie Louisa Scott; *S* brother, 1962. *Educ:* Harrow. War Correspondent, 1939-40. Sqdn Leader RAFVR. *Publications:* The Maid of the Mountains, Her Story (with Miss José Collins), 1932; Abyssinian Adventure, 1935; I Like America, 1939; Northcliffe (with Reginald Pound), 1959. *Address:* White Cottage, Tealby, Lincoln.

HARMSWORTH, Sir Hildebrand Alfred Beresford, 2nd Bt, *cr* 1922; *b* 27 May 1901; *s* of 1st Bt and Kathleen Mary (*d* 1966), *d* of E. D. Berton, MB; *S* father, 1929; *m*; one *s* one *d*. *Educ:* Harrow. *Heir:* s Hildebrand Harold Harmsworth [*b* 5 June 1931; *m* 1960, Gillian Andrea, *o d* of William John Lewis; one *s* two *d*]. *Address:* Deepdene, Haslemere, Surrey. *T:* Haslemere 2092.

HARMSWORTH, St John Bernard Vyvyan; a Metropolitan Magistrate, since 1961; *b* 28 Nov. 1912; *e s* of Vyvyan George Harmsworth and Constance Gwendolen Mary Catt; *m* 1937, Jane Penelope, *er d* of Basil Tanfield Berridge Boothby; three *d*. *Educ:* Harrow; New Coll., Oxford. Called to the Bar, Middle Temple, 1937. Served in RNVR, Lieut-Comdr, Oct. 1939-Feb. 1946. *Recreations:* fly fishing, tennis. *Address:* 25 Whitelands House, SW3. *Clubs:* Boodle's, Pratt's, Beefsteak.

HARMSWORTH, Hon. Vere Harold Esmond; Chairman and Chief Executive, Associated Newspapers Group Ltd, since 1971; *b* 27 Aug. 1925; *s* and *heir* of Viscount Rothermere, *qv*; *m* 1957, Mrs Patricia Evelyn Beverley Brooks, *d* of John William Matthews, FIAS; one *s* two *d* (and one step *d*). *Educ:* Eton; Kent Sch., Conn, USA. With Anglo Canadian Paper Mills, Quebec, 1948-50; Associated Newspapers Ltd, 1951-; launched New Daily Mail, 1971, New Evening News, 1974. Dir, Reuters. Chm., Newsvendors' Benevolent Inst. Festival Appeal, 1963; Pres., Nat. Advertising Benevolent Soc., 1964; Festival Pres., 1966, Vice-Pres., 1967, Newspaper Press Fund; Chm., UK Section, Commonwealth Press Union, 1976; Pres., Printers Charitable Corp., 1974-76. Trustee, Vis-News. Pres., London Press Club, 1976. FRSA, FBIM. Comdr, Order of Merit (Italy). *Recreations:* painting, sailing, reading. *Address:* New Carmelite House, Carmelite Street, EC4. *Clubs:* Boodle's; Royal Yacht Squadron.

HARNDEN, Lt-Col Arthur Baker, CB 1969; BSc, CEng, FIEE, MBIM; Chairman, Appeals Tribunals, Supplementary Benefits

Commission, since 1970; *b* 6 Jan. 1909; *s* of Cecil Henry Harnden and Susan (*née* Baker); *m* 1st, 1935, Maisie Elizabeth Annie (*d* 1970), *d* of A. H. Winterburn, LRIBA; one *s*; 2nd, 1971, Jean Kathleen, *d* of H. F. Wheeler and *widow* of Eric J. Dedman; one step *s*. *Educ:* various state schools. Exec. Engr, GPO, 1933; Royal Corps of Signals, 1939-45; GSO1, WO, 1942; DCSO Antwerp, 1944, Hamburg 1945. Dir, London Telecommunications Region, GPO, 1962; Senior Dir, Operations, PO (Telecommunications), 1967-69. Principal, Comrie House Sch., Finchley, 1971-72. *Recreation:* painting. *Address:* Comrie, Dipley, Hartley Wintney, Hants. *T:* Hartley Wintney 3265.

HARPER, Alfred Alexander, MA, MD; Professor of Physiology, University of Newcastle upon Tyne, 1963-72; *b* 19 June 1907; *er s* of James and Elizabeth Harper. *Educ:* Aberdeen Grammar Sch.; Aberdeen Univ. Lecturer in Physiology, University of Leeds, 1935-36; Demonstrator in Physiology, St Thomas's Hosp., London, 1936-39; Lectr, later Reader, in Human Physiology, Univ. of Manchester, 1939-49; Prof. of Physiology, Univ. of Durham, 1949-63. *Publications:* papers in Jl of Physiology mostly on physiology of digestion. *Address:* Wellburn House, Benwell Lane, Newcastle upon Tyne NE15 6LX. *T:* Newcastle 748178.

HARPER, Sir Arthur (Grant), KCVO 1959 (CVO 1954); CBE 1954; JP; now retired; Chairman: Williams Development Holdings Ltd; Wareham Associates Ltd; Fund of New Zealand Services Ltd; Woolshed Restaurant Ltd; Director, Chartwell Regional Centre Ltd; *b* 16 July 1898; *s* of William John and Robina Harper; *m* 1925, Hilda Mary Evans; two *s* one *d. Educ:* Hastings High Sch. Entered NZ Civil Service, 1914; held various positions; Sec. for Internal Affairs, also Clerk of the Writs, NZ, 1948-58. Chief Electoral Officer, 1945-50; Dir of Royal Tours of NZ, 1953-54, 1956, 1958. Patron, Vice-Pres., Trustee or Mem. of several national and local voluntary organizations. JP 1949. *Recreations:* cricket and hockey, bowls (past); interested in most sports. *Address:* Flat 1, 50 Devonshire Road, Miramar, Wellington, NZ. *T:* 886-425. *Club:* United Services Officers' (Wellington).

HARPER, Bill; *see* Harper, F. A.

HARPER, Prof. Denis Rawnsley, CBE 1975; BArch, PhD, MSc Tech, FRIBA, MRTPI, FIOB, FIArb; building consultant; Professor of Building at the University of Manchester Institute of Science and Technology, 1957-74, now Emeritus; *b* 27 May 1907; *s* of James William Harper, Harrogate; *m* 1st, 1934, Joan Mary Coggin (*d* 1968); one *s* one *d*; 2nd, 1971, Dora Phylis Oxenham (widow). *Educ:* Harrogate Grammar Sch.; Univ. of Liverpool Sch. of Architecture. Asst Architect in Hosp. practice in London, 1930-38; RIBA Saxon Snell Prizeman, 1939; Lectr in Sch. of Architecture, University of Cape Town, 1939-49. In private practice (with Prof. Thornton White), in Cape Town, as architect and town planner, 1940-50; Associate Architect in BBC TV Centre, 1950-52; Chief Architect to Corby New Town, Northants, 1952-57. Hanson Fellow, The Master Builder Fedn of South Africa, 1972. Cttee Mem., CNAA; Past Pres., Inst. of Building. Mem., Summerland Fire Commn, 1973-74. *Publications:* various contribs to technical jls. *Recreations:* gardening, boating. *Address:* 89 Earls Barton Road, Great Doddington, Wellingborough, Northants. *T:* Wellingborough 223841.

HARPER, Donald John; Director-General, Performance and Cost Analysis, Procurement Executive, Ministry of Defence, since 1972; *b* 6 Aug. 1923; *s* of Harry Tonkin and Caroline Irene Harper; *m* 1947, Joyce Beryl Kite-Powell; two *d. Educ:* Purley County Grammar Sch. for Boys; Queen Mary Coll., London. 1st cl. BSc (Eng) 1943; CEng, MRAeS. Joined Aero Dept, RAE Farnborough, 1943; Scientific Officer, Spinning Tunnel, 1947-49; High Speed and Transonic Tunnel, 1950-59; Sen. Scientific Officer; Principal Scientific Officer, 1955; Dep. Head of Tunnel, 1958-59; Space Dept RAE, Satellite Launching Vehicles, 1960-62; Senior Principal Scientific Officer, MoD, Central Staff, 1963-65; Head of Assessment Div., Weapons Dept RAE, 1966-68; Dir of Project Time and Cost Analysis, MoD (PE), 1968-71. *Publications:* contrib. Aeronautical Res. Council reports and memoranda and techn. press. *Recreations:* music, especially choral singing; gardening; home improvement. *Address:* Minstrels, Hockering Road, Woking, Surrey. *T:* Woking 60541.

HARPER, Frank Appleby, (Bill), MBE 1954; Director of Establishments and Organisation, Department of Education and Science, since 1974; *b* 11 April 1920; *s* of F. S. and M. E. B. Harper; *m* 1st, 1943, Daphne Margaret (*née* Short) (*d* 1965); one *d*; 2nd, 1968, Mrs Jillian Kate Langstaff (*née* Brooks). *Educ:* grammar sch., Birmingham. Regular Army (Royal Engrs) until

joined Home Civil Service as Direct Entry Principal, 1964; Under-Sec. 1974. *Recreations:* home workshop; tentative classical guitar; atrocious golf. *Address:* Lochnell, Searle Road, Farnham, Surrey. *T:* Farnham (Surrey) 4127. *Club:* Royal Commonwealth Society.

HARPER, George Clifford; *b* 8 Aug. 1900; *s* of Charles George and Emily Harper, Newcastle upon Tyne; *m* 1925, Georgette Marie Aimée Guéry; two *d* (and one *s* decd). *Educ:* Shrewsbury Sch.; Christ Church, Oxford. Traffic Apprentice LNER; Asst Master at Stowe and Bedford; Headmaster of King Edward VI Sch., Southampton, until 1946; HM Inspector of Schools, 1947-60 (Metropolitan Divisional Inspector, 1952-60); Mem., Anglo-French Mixed Cultural Commn, 1954-60; Chm. and Dir, British Cttee for Interchange of Teachers with USA, 1960-65. Officier d'Académie. *Address:* 172 Coleherne Court, SW5 0DX. *T:* 01-373 4426.

HARPER, Heather (Mary), (Mrs E. J. Benarroch), CBE 1965; soprano; *b* 8 May 1930; *d* of late Hugh Harper, Belfast; *m* 1973, Eduardo J. Benarroch. *Educ:* Trinity Coll. of Music, London. Has sung mary principal roles incl. Arabella, Ariadne, Chrysothemis and Kaiserin, at Covent Garden, Glyndebourne, Sadler's Wells, Bayreuth, Teatro Colon (Buenos Aires), Edinburgh Fest., La Scala, NY Met, San Francisco and Frankfurt, and has sung at every Promenade Concert season since 1957; created the soprano role in Benjamin Britten's War Requiem in Coventry Cathedral in 1962; soloist at opening concerts: Maltings, Snape, 1967; Queen Elizabeth Hall, 1967. Toured USA, 1965, and USSR, 1967, with BBC SO; has toured USA annually, 1967-, and appears regularly at European music fests; has also sung in Asia, Middle East, Australia and S America. Has made many recordings, incl. works of Britten, Beethoven, Berg, Mahler and Verdi. FTCL; Hon. RAM, 1972. Hon. DMus, Queen's Univ., Belfast, 1966. Edison Award, 1971. *Recreations:* gardening, painting, cooking. *Address:* c/o 15 Lancaster Grove, Hampstead, NW3.

HARPER, John Mansfield; Senior Director, Planning and Provisioning, Post Office, since 1975; *b* 17 July 1930; *s* of late T. J. Harper and May (*née* Charlton); *m* 1956, Berenice Honorine, *d* of Harold Haydon; one *s* one *d. Educ:* Merchant Taylors' Sch.; St John's Coll., Oxford. 2nd Lieut Royal Corps of Signals, 1948-49. Asst Principal, Post Office, 1953; Private Sec. to Dir-Gen., 1956-58; Principal, 1958-66; Asst Sec., Reorganization Dept, 1966-69; Dir, North-Eastern Telecommunications Region, 1969-71; Dir, Purchasing and Supply, 1972-75. *Recreations:* music, gardening, electronics. *Address:* 34 Longfield Drive, Amersham, Bucks. *T:* Amersham 5443.

HARPER, Joseph, JP; MP (Lab) Pontefract and Castleford, since 1974 (Pontefract, March 1962-1974); Comptroller of HM Household, since 1974; *b* 17 March 1914; *m* 1939, Gwendoline Hughes; two *s* two *d. Educ:* Featherstone Elementary Sch. Started work at Sndydale Colliery, Yorks, 1928. Deleg. for Local Branch of NUM, 1943-62; served on Yorks area NUM Exec. Cttee, 1947-48 and 1950-52. Mem. Featherstone UDC, 1949-63 (Chm., 1955-56 and 1961-62); Chm. Featherstone Managers of Primary Schs and Governors of Secondary Sch., 1955-62; Vice-Chm. Divl Educn Executive, 1955-62; Mem. Osgoldcross Cremation Board, 1957-62; Mem. Pontefract and Castleford HMC, 1958-; an Asst Government Whip, 1964-66; a Lord Comr of the Treasury, 1966-70; an Opposition Whip, 1970-74. JP, WR Yorks, 1959. *Recreations:* music, watching Rugby League football. *Address:* House of Commons, SW1; 11 Bedford Close, Purston, Featherstone, near Pontefract, W Yorks.

HARPER, Norman Adamson; Chairman, Gemmological Association of Great Britain, since 1965; Founder-Director, Perry Greaves Ltd, 1964; Director: W. A. Perry & Co. Ltd, 1953; Gemmological Instruments Ltd, 1965; Managing Director, H. H. Bray Ltd; *b* 15 Oct. 1913; *s* of Andrew Adamson Harper, Newcastle-upon-Tyne; *m* 1st, 1935, Priscilla (*d* 1956), *d* of William George Hoverd; three *s* one *d*; 2nd, 1957, Brenda, *d* of Robert Watts one *s. Educ:* Rutherford Coll.; Durham Univ. Dip. Nat. Assoc Goldsmiths, 1946. FGA 1934; FRGS 1946; FInstD 1953. Chm., Nat. Assoc. of Goldsmiths, 1961-63; Guardian of Standard of Wrought Plate in Birmingham, 1963-; Sen. Lectr on Gemstones and Jewellery, City of Birmingham Sch. of Jewellery and Silversmithing, 1946-66; Founder, Course on Gem Diamonds for Jewellers, 1962. Freedom of Goldsmiths' Co. (Special Award), 1947; Freedom of City of London, 1947. Winner of Greenough Trophy, 1946. *Publications:* Introduction to Gemstones, 1955; Handbook on Gem Diamonds, 1965; articles in Jl of Gemmology, British Jeweller, Watchmaker and Jeweller, etc. *Recreations:* keyboard music, historical studies. *Address:* 9 Jury Street, Warwick CV34 4EH. *T:* Warwick 42791. *Clubs:* Athenæum, Naval and Military, Number Ten; Sutton Coldfield (Sutton Coldfield).

HARPHAM, Sir William, KBE 1966 (OBE 1948); CMG 1953; Director, Great Britain-East Europe Centre, 1967; *b* 3 Dec. 1906; *o s* of W. Harpham and N. Harpham (*née* Stout); *m* 1943, Isabelle Marie Sophie Droz; one *s* one *d. Educ:* Wintringham Secondary Sch., Grimsby; Christ's Coll., Cambridge. Entered Dept of Overseas Trade, 1929; transferred to Embassy, Brussels, 1931, Rome, 1934; Private Sec. to Parliamentary Sec. for Overseas Trade, 1936; seconded to League of Nations, 1937; reverted to Dept of Overseas Trade, 1939; served: Cairo, 1940-44; Beirut, 1944-47; appointed Counsellor (Commercial) at Berne, 1947; Head of Gen. Dept, Foreign Office, 1950-53; Dep. to UK Delegate to OEEC, 1953-56; Minister, British Embassy, Tokyo, 1956-59; Minister (Economic), Paris, 1959-63; Ambassador to Bulgaria, 1964-66; retd 1967. Order of Madara Horseman, Bulgaria, 1969; Order of Stara Planina, Bulgaria, 1976. *Address:* 9 Kings Keep, Putney Hill, SW15 6RA. *T:* 01-788 1383. *Clubs:* Travellers', Royal Automobile.

HARPLEY, Sydney Charles, ARA 1974; sculptor since 1956; *b* 19 April 1927; *s* of Sydney Frederick Harpley, electrical engr and cabinet maker, and Rose Isabel Harpley, milliner; *m* 1956, Sally Holliday (marr. diss. 1968), illustrator; two *s* one *d. Educ:* Royal Coll. of Art. ARCA 1956. Realist sculptor, portraits and figure; commnd Smuts Memorial, Cape Town, 1963; sculpture in collections of Nat. Gallery, NZ; Nat. Gallery, Cape Town; Paul Mellon, USA; Anton Rupert, SA; Princess Grace of Monaco; Fleur Cowles Meyer, London; S. & D. Josefowitz, Geneva; portrait of Edward Heath for Constitutional Club, 1973. *Recreations:* chess, music. *Address:* 15 Royal Crescent, W11. *T:* 01-602 0470. *Club:* Chelsea Arts.

HARRAP, George Paull Munro, CBE 1974; Chairman, George G. Harrap & Co. Ltd, since 1971; *b* 10 June 1917; *s* of George Steward and Kathleen Mary Harrap; *m* 1959, Alice Foyle. *Educ:* privately. Entered family firm, 1936. *Address:* Tile House, Stebbing Green, Essex. *T:* Stebbing 261; 60 Darwin Court, Gloucester Avenue, NW1 7BQ. *T:* 01-267 8571.

HARRER, Prof. Heinrich; author and explorer; (awarded title of Professor by President of Austrian Republic, 1964); *b* 6 July 1912; *m*; one *s*; *m* 1953, Margaretha Truxa (marr. diss. 1958); *m* 1962, Katharina Haarhaus. *Educ:* University of Graz, Austria (graduated in Geography, 1938). First ascent, Eiger North Wall, 1938; Himalayan Expedition, 1939; interned in India, 1939-44; Tibet, 1944-51; Himalayan Expedition, 1951; expeditions: to the Andes, 1953; to Alaska, 1954; to Ruwenzori (Mountains of the Moon), Africa, 1957; to West New Guinea, 1961-62; to Nepal, 1965; to Xingu Red Indians in Mato Grosso, Brazil; to Bush Negroes of Surinam (Surinam Expedn with King Leopold of Belgium), 1966; to the Sudan, 1970; to North Borneo (Sabah) (with King Leopold of Belgium), 1971; N-S crossing of Borneo, 1972; Valley of Flowers (Alaknanda), 1974; Andaman Islands, 1975; Zangkar-Ladakh, 1976. Austrian National Amateur Golf Champion, 1958; Austrian National Seniors Golf Champion, 1970. Pres., Austrian Golf Association, 1964. *Publications:* Seven Years in Tibet, 1953 (Great Britain, and numerous other countries); Meine Tibet-Bilder, 1953 (Germany); The White Spider, History of the North Face of the Eiger, 1958; Tibet is My Country: Biography of Thubten Jigme Norbu, *e b* of Dalai Lama, 1960 (Eng.); I Come from the Stone Age, 1964 (London); The Last 500, 1975; The Last Caravan, 1976. *Address:* Britschenstrasse 258, 9493-Mauren, Liechtenstein.

HARRIES, Rear-Adm. David Hugh, CB 1961; CBE 1952; RAN (retired); *b* 27 June 1903; *s* of David Henry Harries, Melbourne, Australia; *m* 1933, Margaret, *d* of Edric H. Stewart, Camden, New South Wales; two *s. Educ:* Melbourne Church of England Gram. Sch.; Royal Australian Naval College, Jervis Bay, NSW; 2nd Naval Mem., Aust. Naval Bd, 1952-53; Rear-Adm. 1954; Head of Australian Joint Service Staff, Washington, DC, USA, 1953-55; Flag Officer comdg HM Australian Fleet, 1956-58; retired 1960. US Legion of Merit, 1955. *Recreations:* golf, foreign languages. *Address:* 3 Grayland Place, Vaucluse, NSW 2030, Australia. *Clubs:* Union, Royal Sydney Golf (Sydney); Naval and Military (Melbourne).

HARRIMAN, Averell; see Harriman, William A.

HARRIMAN, (William) Averell; US Ambassador-at-Large, 1965-69; *b* 15 Nov. 1891; *s* of late Edward Henry Harriman and Mary Williamson Averell; *m* 1st, 1915, Kitty Lanier Lawrence (decd) two *d*; 2nd, 1930, Mrs Marie Norton Whitney; 3rd, 1971, Hon. Mrs Leland Hayward, *e d* of 11th Baron Digby, KG, DSO, MC, TD. *Educ:* Groton Sch., Yale Univ., BA 1913. Partner Brown Brothers Harriman & Co. since 1931, Limited partner since 1946; Chairman of the Board, Union Pacific Railroad Co. 1932-46; Mem. Business Advisory Council for the Dept of Commerce since 1933 (Chm., 1937-40). Vice-Pres. in Charge of Purchases and Supplies of Union Pacific Railroad Co., 1914-18; Chm. Board of Merchant Ship-building Corp., 1917-25; Chm. Board of W. A. Harriman & Co., Inc. (merged with Brown Brothers, 1931), 1920-30; Chm. Exec. Cttee Ill. Central Railroad Co., 1931-42; National Recovery Administration: Division Administrator of Div. II, Jan.-March 1934, Special Asst Administrator, March-May, 1934, Administrative Officer, Nov. 1934-June 1935; Associated with Industrial Materials Div., National Defense Advisory Commission, 1940; Chief, Materials Branch, Production Div., Office of Production Management, Jan.-March 1941; Pres. Roosevelt's Special Representative in Great Britain with rank of Minister, March 1941; Special Rep. of the Pres. and Chm. of the President's Special Mission to USSR with rank of Ambassador, 1941; US Representative in London of Combined Shipping Adjustment Board, 1942; Mem. London Combined Production and Resources Board, 1942; US Ambassador to USSR, 1943-46; to Britain, 1946; US Sec. of Commerce, 1946-48; US Special Representative in Europe under Economic Co-operation Act of 1948 (with rank of Ambassador) until 1950; US Rep. on N Atlantic Defence, Financial and Economic Cttee, 1949; Special Asst to Pres. Truman, 1950-51; Chm. NATO Commission on Defense Plans, 1951; Dir of Foreign Aid under Mutual Security Act, 1951-53; Governor, State of New York, Jan. 1955-Dec. 1958; US Ambassador-at-Large, Feb.-Dec. 1961 and 1965-69; Asst Sec. of State for Far Eastern Affairs, 1961-63; Under-Sec. for Political Affairs, 1963-65. US Representative, Vietnam Peace Talks, Paris, 1968-69. Democrat. *Publications:* Peace with Russia?, 1960; America and Russia in a Changing World, 1971; (with E. Abel) Special Envoy to Churchill and Stalin 1941-1946, 1975. *Address:* (residence) 3038 N Street, NW, Washington, DC 20007, USA.
See also *W. S. Churchill*.

HARRINGTON, 11th Earl of, *cr* 1742; **William Henry Leicester Stanhope;** Viscount Stanhope of Mahon and Baron Stanhope of Elvaston, Co. Derby, 1717; Baron Harrington, 1729; Viscount Petersham, 1742; late Captain RAC; *b* 24 Aug. 1922; *o s* of 10th Earl and Margaret Trelawney (Susan) (*d* 1952), *d* of Major H. H. D. Seaton; *S* father, 1929; *m* 1st, 1942, Eileen (from whom he obtained a divorce, 1946), *o d* of late Sir John Grey, Enville Hall, Stourbridge; one *s* one *d* (and one *d* decd); 2nd, 1947, Anne Theodora (from whom he obtained a divorce, 1962), *o d* of late Major Richard Arenbourg Blennerhassett Chute; one *s* two *d*; 3rd, 1964, Priscilla Margaret, *d* of Hon. A. E. Cubitt and Mrs Ronald Dawnay; one *s* one *d. Educ:* Eton; RMC, Sandhurst. Served War of 1939-45, demobilised 1948. Owns about 700 acres. Became Irish Citizen, 1965. *Heir: s* Viscount Petersham, *qv. Address:* Greenmount Stud, Patrickswell, Co. Limerick, Eire.
See also *Baron Ashcombe*.

HARRINGTON, Dr Albert Blair; Head of Civil Service Department Medical Advisory Service, since 1976; *b* 26 April 1914; *s* of late Albert Timothy Harrington and Lily Harrington; *m* 1939, Valerie White; one *d. Educ:* Brisbane Grammar Sch., Qld; Aberdeen Univ. MB, ChB 1938, MD 1944. House Phys., Woodend Hosp., Aberdeen, 1938-39; service in RAMC (Field Amb., Blood Transfusion Phys., Neurologist), 1940-45; MO (Head Injuries) and Dep. Supt, Stoke Mandeville Hosp., 1946-48; Med. Supt, Dunston Hill Hosp., Gateshead, 1948-50; SMO (Pensions), Cleveleys, 1950-53; Med. Supt, Queen Mary's Hosp., Roehampton, 1954-56; SMO, Dept of Health (Hosp. Bldg and later Regional Liaison Duties), 1956-68; PMO (Hosp. Bldg), Dept of Health, 1968-73; SPMO (Under-Sec.), DHSS, 1973-76. FFCM (Foundn Fellow) 1972. *Publications:* articles on Sjögren's Disease, paralytic poliomyelitis, and hospital planning and medical care. *Recreations:* gardening, country life; formerly tennis. *Address:* 59 Lauderdale Drive, Petersham, Richmond, Surrey TW10 7BS. *T:* 01-940 1345. *Club:* Athenæum.

HARRINGTON, Illtyd, JP; Member for Brent South, Greater London Council, since 1973; Deputy Leader of the Opposition, since 1977 (Deputy Leader of the Council, 1973-77); *b* 14 July 1931; *s* of Timothy Harrington and Sarah (*née* Burchell); unmarried. *Educ:* St Illtyd's RC Sch., Dowlais; Merthyr County Sch.; Trinity Coll., Caermarthen. Member: Paddington Borough Council, 1959-64; Westminster City Council, 1964-68 and 1971-, Leader, Lab. Gp, 1972-74; GLC, 1964-67; Alderman, GLC, 1970-73; Chm., Policy and Resources Cttee, GLC, 1973-77. JP Willesden 1968. First Chairman, Inland Waterways Amenity Adv. Council, 1968-71; Member: British Waterways Bd, 1974-; BTA, 1976-. Mem., Nat. Theatre Bd, 1975-; Pres., Grand Union Canal Soc., 1974. Patron, Westminster Cathedral Appeal, 1977. *Recreations:* a slave to local government; laughing, singing and incredulity. *Address:* 16 Lea House, Salisbury Street, NW8 8BJ. *T:* 01-402 6356. *Club:* Paddington Labour.

HARRIS, family name of **Barons Harris** and **Harris of Greenwich** and of **Earl of Malmesbury.**

HARRIS, 5th Baron (of Seringapatam and Mysore, and of Belmont, Kent, cr 1815); **George St Vincent Harris,** CBE 1972; MC; JP; DL; Vice-Lieutenant of Kent, 1948-72; b 3 Sept. 1889; e s of 4th Baron and Hon. Lucy Ada Jervis, CI (d 1930), d of 3rd Viscount St Vincent; S father, 1932; m 1918, Dorothy Mary (Order of League of Mercy), d of Rev. W. J. Crookes, late Vicar of Borden; one s. Educ: Eton; Christ Church, Oxford (MA). Capt. late Royal East Kent Imperial Yeomanry; served European War, 1914-18 (MC, wounded, despatches). Grand Master, Mark Master Masons of England, 1954-73; Grand Master, Masonic Knights Templar of England, 1947-73. Commissioner St John Amb. Brigade for Kent, 1940-45; Chm. Kent Police Authority, 1945-64; KStJ 1949. JP 1919, DL 1936, Kent. Heir: s Hon. George Robert John Harris, b 17 April 1920. Address: Belmont Park, Faversham, Kent. Clubs: Carlton, Beefsteak.

HARRIS OF GREENWICH, Baron cr 1974 (Life Peer), of Greenwich; **John Henry Harris;** Minister of State, Home Office, since 1974; b Harrow, Middlesex, 5 April 1930; s of Alfred George and May Harris; m 1952, Patricia Margaret Alstrom; one s one d. Educ: Pinner County Grammar Sch., Middlesex. Journalist on newspapers in Bournemouth, Leicester, Glasgow and London. National Service with Directorate of Army Legal Services, WO. Personal assistant to Rt Hon. Hugh Gaitskell when Leader of the Opposition, 1959-62; Director of Publicity, Labour Party, 1962-64; Special Assistant: to Foreign Secretary, 1964-65; to Rt Hon. Roy Jenkins as Home Secretary, 1965-Nov. 1967, and as Chancellor, Nov. 1967-1970. Staff of Economist newspaper, 1970-74. Eisenhower Exchange Fellow from UK, 1972. Mem. Council, Harlow, Essex, 1957-63; Chm. Council 1960-61, Leader of Labour Gp, 1961-63. Mem. Exec. Cttee, Britain in Europe, referendum campaign, 1975. Address: House of Lords, SW1. Clubs: Reform; Kent County Cricket.

HARRIS, Marshal of the Royal Air Force Sir Arthur Travers, 1st Bt, cr 1953; GCB 1945 (KCB 1942; CB 1940); OBE 1927; AFC 1918; b 13 April 1892; m 1st, 1916; one s two d; 2nd, 1938, Thérèse Hearne; one d. Served European War, 1914-19, 1st Rhodesian Regt, RFC, and RAF; India, 1921-22; Iraq, 1922-24; Egypt, 1930-32; Group Capt. 1933; Air Ministry, Dep. Dir of Plans, 1934-37; Air Commodore, 1937; AOC 4 Bomber Gp, 1937; Head of RAF Mission, USA and Canada, 1938; Air Vice-Marshal, 1939; Air Marshal, 1941; Air Chief Marshal, 1943; AOC, RAF Palestine and Transjordan, 1938-39; AOC, 5 Bomber Group, 1939-40; Deputy Chief of Air Staff, 1940-41; Head of Royal Air Force Delegation to USA, 1941; Commander-in-Chief Bomber Command 1942-45. Marshal of the RAF 1945. Managing Director South African Marine Corporation, 1946-53. Order of Suvorov (1st class) (Russia), 1944, Grand Cross Polonia Restituta (Poland), 1945, Chief Commander Legion of Merit (US), 1944; Grand Cross Order of the Southern Cross (Brazil), 1945; Grand Officier Légion d'Honneur, Croix de guerre avec palme (France), 1945; DSM (US), 1945. Freeman of Honiton and of Chepping Wycombe; Hon. LLD Liverpool, 1946. Heir: s Anthony Kyrle Travers Harris, b 18 March 1918. Address: The Ferry House, Goring-on-Thames, Oxfordshire RG8 9DX. Clubs: Army and Navy; Royal and Ancient (St Andrews); Bankers (New York); Nederlands (Cape Town).
See also R. J. Harris.

HARRIS, Rt. Rev. Augustine; Titular Bishop of Socia and Auxiliary Bishop of Liverpool, (RC), since 1965; b 27 Oct. 1917; s of Augustine Harris and Louisa Beatrice (née Rycroft). Educ: St Francis Xavier's Coll., Liverpool; Upholland Coll., Lancs. Ordained, 1942; Curate at: St Oswald's, Liverpool, 1942-43; St Elizabeth's, Litherland, Lancs, 1943-52; Prison Chaplain, HM Prison, Liverpool, 1952-65; Sen. RC Priest, Prison Dept, 1957-66; English Rep. to Internat. Coun. of Sen. Prison Chaplains (RC), 1957-66. Mem. Vatican Delegn to UN Quinquennial Congress on Crime, London, 1960 and Stockholm, 1965; Liaison between English and Welsh Hierarchy (RC) and Home Office, 1966-; Episcopal Moderator to Fédération Internationale des Associations Médicales Catholiques, 1967-; Episcopal Pres., Commn for Social Welfare (England and Wales), 1972-. Publications: articles for criminological works. Address: Beechville, Grassendale Park, Liverpool L19 0LS. T: 051-427 1400.

HARRIS, Sir Charles Herbert S.; see Stuart-Harris.

HARRIS, Sir Charles Joseph William, KBE 1961 (CBE 1927); Kt 1952; Private Secretary to successive Parliamentary Secretaries to Treasury, 1919-24, 1924-29 and 1931-61; retired

as Assistant Secretary, HM Treasury, 1961; b 1901; m 1924, Emily Kyle Thompson; one s two d. Educ: Christ Church Sch., Ramsgate; privately. Private Sec. to Conservative Chief Whip, 1924 and 1929-31. Freeman, City of London; Mem., Court of Assistants, Guild of Freemen of City of London; Liveryman, Scriveners' Company. Address: 3 Burcote Road, SW18. T: 01-874 8226. Club: City Livery.

HARRIS, Charles Reginald Schiller, MA, DPhil Oxon, PhD Princeton and Adelaide; FCIT; b 10 April 1896; e s of late Sir Charles Harris, GBE, KCB; m 1931, Lucia Marie Ghislaine, o d of late Dom José de Figueiredo de Pitinga and of late Mrs C. T. Terry; one d. Educ: Clifton Coll.; Corpus Christi Coll., Oxford (Scholar). 1st Class Lit. Hum., 1920; Senior Demy, Magdalen Coll., Oxon, 1920-21; Jane Eliza Procter Visiting Fellow, Princeton Univ., New Jersey, 1922-23; Fellow of All Souls Coll., Oxford, 1921-36; Editor of The Nineteenth Century and After, 1930-35; Leader Writer on the Staff of the Times, 1925-35, and the Economist, 1932-35; Dir-Gen., Buenos Aires Gt Southern and Western Railways, 1935-59; Dir, Entre Rios, Argentine North Eastern and Central Uruguay Railways, 1939-47. Commercial Counsellor HM Legation, Reykjavik, Iceland, 1940-42; Lieut-Col General List; Dir Property Control, AMGOT, Sicily, 1943, Allied Control Commission, Italy, 1944; Sec. to Adv. Gp of Experts on admin. personnel and budgetary matters, Preparatory Commn of UN, 1945; Historical Sect., Cabinet Office, 1945-58; Reader in Studies in the Humanities for Medical Students and Tutor of St Mark's Coll., Adelaide Univ., 1958-65. Vis Lectr, Lake Erie Coll., Ohio, 1973. Hon. Fellow, St Mark's Coll., Adelaide. Hon. DLitt Lake Erie Coll., 1973. Publications: Duns Scotus, 1927; Germany's Foreign Indebtedness, published under auspices of RIIA, 1935; vol. on Allied Administration of Italy, 1943-45, in the Official History of the Second World War, 1958; The Heart and the Vascular System in Ancient Greek Medicine, 1973. Recreation: fishing. Address: Rock House, Wheatley, Oxon. Club: Athenæum.

HARRIS, Colin Grendon, CMG 1964; HM Diplomatic Service, retired; b 25 Oct. 1912; m 1941, Adelaide Zamoiska (decd); m 1947, Monique Jacqueline Marcuse-Baudoux; four s two d. Educ: Rossall Sch.; Pembroke Coll., Cambridge. Entered Foreign (subseq. Diplomatic) Service, 1935; served Antwerp, Elisabethville, Leopoldville, Lisbon, Montevideo, Rio de Janeiro, Vienna, Tokyo, Oslo, retired 1969. Recreation: swimming. Address: 263 Avenue Defré, Brussels, Belgium.

HARRIS, David; Director, Commission of the European Communities, Directorate for Social and Demographic Statistics, since 1973; b 28 Dec. 1922; s of David and Margaret Jane Harris; m 1946, Mildred Alice Watson; two d. Educ: Bootle Grammar Sch.; LSE (BScEcon). FSS. Statistician, BoT, 1960; Statistician 1966 and Chief Statistician 1968, HM Treasury; Chief Statistician, Central Statistical Office, Cabinet Office, 1969. Recreations: tennis, swimming, economics. Address: 41 Boulevard Napoleon Ier, Luxembourg. T: Luxembourg 29876; 39 Greenhill Close, Camberley, Surrey. T: Camberley 20213.

HARRIS, Dame Diana R.; see Reader Harris.

HARRIS, Rev. Donald Bertram; Vicar of St Paul's, Knightsbridge, since 1955; b 4 Aug. 1904; unmarried. Educ: King's Coll. Choir Sch., Cambridge; Haileybury Coll.; King's Coll., Cambridge; Cuddesdon Coll., Oxford. Chorister, King's Coll. Choir, 1915-19; Choral Scholar, King's Coll., Cambridge, 1923-26; BA 1925; MA 1929; Ordained Deacon, 1927; Priest, 1928; Curate of Chesterfield Parish Church, 1927-31; St Mary the Less, Cambridge, 1931-36. Chaplain of King's Coll., Cambridge, 1932-33; Examg Chaplain to Bishop of Wakefield, 1932-36; Rector of Great Greenford, Middx, 1936-45; Archdeacon of Bedford 1946-55, and Rector of St Mary's Bedford, 1945-55, Life Governor, Haileybury and Imperial Service Coll., 1946-. Pres., Assoc. for Promoting Retreats, 1968-71. Address: St Paul's Vicarage, Wilton Place, SW1. T: 01-235 1810. Club: Royal Thames Yacht.

HARRIS, Dr Edmund Leslie, FRCP, FRCPE; Deputy Chief Medical Officer (Deputy Secretary), Department of Health and Social Security, since 1977; b 11 April 1928; s of late M. H. Harris and of Sylvia Harris; m 1959, Robina Semple (née Potter). Educ: Christian Brothers' Coll., Boksburg, S Africa; Univ. of Witwatersrand. MB, BCh 1952; MRCPE 1959, FRCPE 1971, MRCP 1959, FRCP 1975. Gen. practice, Benoni, S Africa, 1954; Registrar Tropical Medicine, Queen Mary's Hosp., Roehampton, 1956-58; Med. Registrar, Royal Surrey County Hosp., 1959; Sen. Med. Registrar, Gen. Hosp., Birmingham, 1960-61; Sen. Med. Adviser, Aspro-Nicholas, 1962-63; Med. and Veterinary Dir, Abbott Labs, 1964-68; Clinical Asst, West Kent Hosp., Maidstone, 1965-69; SMO,

Cttee on Safety of Drugs, DHSS, 1969-72; PMO, Cttee on Safety of Medicines and Medicines Commn, 1973; SPMO, Under-Sec., and Head of Medicines Div., DHSS, 1974-77. Adviser to WHO; Chm., Assoc. of Med. Advisers in Pharmaceutical Industry, 1966; Mem., Nat. Biol. Bd, 1975-; Dep. Chm., EEC Cttee on Proprietary Medicinal Products. Pres., Library Scientific Section, RSM, 1976-78. *Publications:* various, mainly on aspects of clinical pharmacology and control of medicines. *Recreations:* music, gardening, walking, photography. *Address:* Department of Health and Social Security, Alexander Fleming House, Elephant and Castle, SE1. *T:* 01-407 5522.

HARRIS, Euan Cadogan; Principal Assistant Solicitor, Ministry of Agriculture, Fisheries and Food, 1964-71; *b* 6 June 1906; *s* of late Charles Poulett Harris, MD and Violet Harris; *m* 1931, Brenda, *er d* of late William Turnbull Bowman, OBE and Jessie Bowman; two *d. Educ:* Epsom Coll.; Clare Coll., Cambridge. BA 1927; LLB 1928. Admitted Solicitor (Edmund Thomas Child Prize), 1930. Entered Legal Dept of Min. of Agric. and Fisheries, 1935; Asst Solicitor, 1949-64. *Recreations:* walking, swimming, gardening; reading, especially history. *Address:* 6 Newlands Road, Rottingdean, Sussex. *T:* Brighton 32019. *See also* A. K. *Rothnie.*

HARRIS, Frank; see Harris, W. F.

HARRIS, Frederic Walter, CBE 1972; Chairman, Marshall's Investments Ltd; *b* 6 March 1915; *s* of Alice and Walter Harris; *m* 1st, 1939, Betty Eileen Benson (*d* 1955); one *s* two *d*; 2nd, 1957, Joan Hope, *d* of David N. K. Bagnall, Overmist, Tadworth, Surrey. *Educ:* Belmont Coll. Streatham. Founded food-producing company as Dir, 1934; Joint Man. Dir of same company known as Marshall's Universal Ltd, 1939, Man. Dir, 1945-63, Chm. and Man. Dir, 1964-75, Pres., 1975- (company's capital now £1,151,310). MP (C), North Croydon, 1948-55, North West Croydon, 1955-70. Freeman of City of London; granted Freedom of Croydon, 1970; Liveryman of Basketmakers. *Address:* Wood Rising, The Ridge, Woldingham, Surrey. *T:* Woldingham 2365.

HARRIS, Geoffrey (Herbert); Chairman, Transport Users' Consultative Committee, since 1972 (Member, since 1961, Deputy Chairman, 1971-72); Chairman, London Transport Passengers' Committee, 1972-74; *b* 31 Jan. 1914; *s* of late W. Leonard Harris and late Sybil M. Harris; *m* 1945, Eve J. Orton; two *d. Educ:* Colchester Royal Grammar School. FCIS. Commercial Union Gp of Cos, 1932-37; Shell Gp of Cos, 1937-73; Manager Office Administration, London, 1963-73. Royal Artillery, 1937-45. *Recreations:* music, architecture, ski-ing, travel. *Address:* Garden End, Spinfield Lane, Marlow, Bucks. *T:* Marlow 72550. *Club:* East India, Devonshire, Sports and Public Schools.

HARRIS, Prof. Harry, FRCP; FRS 1966; Harnwell Professor of Human Genetics, University of Pennsylvania, since 1976; *b* 30 Sept. 1919; *m* 1948, Muriel Hargest; one *s. Educ:* Manchester Gram. Sch.; Trinity Coll., Cambridge. (MA, MD); FRCP 1973. Research Asst, Galton Laboratory, Dept of Eugenics, Biometry, and Genetics UC, London, 1947-50; Leverhulme Scholar, RCP, 1947-48; Lund Research Fellow, Diabetic Assoc., 1949; Lectr, Dept of Biochem., UC, London, 1950-53; Sen. Lectr, 1953-58, Reader in Biochem. Genetics, 1958-60, Dept of Biochem., The London Hosp. Med. Coll.; Prof. of Biochem., University of London, at King's Coll., 1960-65; Galton Prof. of Human Genetics, London Univ. at UCL, 1965-76. Hon. Lectr, 1950-55, Hon. Research Associate, 1955-60, Dept of Eugenics, Biometry, and Genetics, UCL; Hon. Dir, MRC Human Biochem. Genetics Res. Unit, 1962-76; Hon. Consulting Geneticist, UCH, 1966-76. Joint Editor: Annals of Human Genetics, 1965-; Advances in Human Genetics, 1970-. Nat. Research Coun. of Canada and Nuffield Foundation Vis. Lectr, British Columbia and McGill, 1967; Fogarty Scholar, Nat. Insts of Health, USA, 1972; Rock Carling Fellowship, Nuffield Provincial Hosps Trust, 1974. Lectures: Thomas Young, St George's Hosp. Med. Sch., 1966; De Frees, University Penna, 1966; Walter R. Bloor, Univ. Rochester, 1967; Langdon Brown, RCP, 1968; Sir William Jackson Pope, RSA, 1968; Darwin, Inst. Biol., 1969; Leonard Parsons, Birmingham Univ., 1969; Sidney Ringer, UCH Med. Sch., 1970; T. H. Huxley, Birmingham Univ., 1971; George Frederic Still, British Paediatric Assoc., 1971; L. S. Penrose Meml, Genetical Soc., 1973; Bicentennial, Coll. of Physicians of Pa, 1976. For. Associate, Nat. Acad. of Scis, USA, 1976. Hon. Dr Univ. René Descartes, Paris, 1976. William Allan Meml Award, Amer. Soc. of Human Genetics, 1968. *Publications:* An Introduction to Human Biochemical Genetics (Eugenics Laboratory Memoir Series), 1953; Human Biochemical Genetics, 1959; The Principles of Human Biochemical Genetics, 1970, 2nd edn 1975; Prenatal Diagnosis and Selective Abortion,

1975; (with D. A. Hopkinson) Handbook of Enzyme Electrophoresis in Human Genetics, 1976. *Address:* Apt G-610, Garden Court Apartments, 4631 Pine Street, Philadelphia, Pa 19143, USA. *T:* 215-476-6443.

HARRIS, Prof. Henry, FRCP; FRS 1968; Professor of Pathology, University of Oxford, since 1963; Hon. Director, Cancer Research Campaign, Cell Biology Unit, since 1963; Fellow of Lincoln College; *b* 28 Jan. 1925; *s* of late Sam and Ann Harris; *m* 1950, Alexandra Fanny Brodsky; one *s* two *d. Educ:* Sydney Boys' High Sch. and University of Sydney, Australia; Lincoln Coll., Oxford. Public Exhibnr, University of Sydney, 1942; BA Mod. Langs, 1944; MB BS 1950; Travelling Schol. of Austr. Nat. Univ. at Univ. of Oxford, 1952; MA; DPhil (Oxon.), 1954. Dir of Research, Brit. Empire Cancer Campaign, at Sir William Dunn Sch. of Pathology, Oxford, 1954-59; Visiting Scientist, Nat. Institutes of Health, USA, 1959-60; Head of Dept of Cell Biology, John Innes Inst., 1960-63; Vis. Prof., Vanderbilt Univ., 1968; Walker-Ames Prof., University of Washington, 1968; Foreign Prof., Collège de France, 1974. Member: ARC, 1968-; Council, European Molecular Biology Organization, 1974-76; Governor, European Cell Biology Organization, 1973-75. Lectures: Almroth Wright, 1968; Harvey, Harvey Soc. NY, 1969; Dunham, Harvard, 1969; Jenner Meml, 1970; Croonian, Royal Soc., 1971; Gwladys and Owen Williams, Liverpool Univ., 1971; Nat. Insts of Health, USA, 1971; Foundation, RCPath, 1973; Woodhull, Royal Instn, 1975; Wade Foundn, Southampton Univ., 1976. Foreign Hon. Mem., Amer. Acad. Arts and Sciences; Foreign Mem., Max-Planck Soc.; Corresp. Mem., Amer. Assoc. for Cancer Res. Hon. Fellow, Cambridge Philosophical Soc. Hon. FRCPath Aust. Hon. DSc Edinburgh, 1976. Feldberg Foundn Award, Ivison Macadam Meml Prize, RCSE, Prix de la Fondation Isabelle Decazes de Noüe for cancer research. *Publications:* Nucleus and Cytoplasm, 1968, 3rd edn, 1974; Cell Fusion, 1970; La Fusion cellulaire, 1974; papers on cellular physiology and biochemistry, in scientific books and jls. *Recreation:* history. *Address:* Sir William Dunn School of Pathology, South Parks Road, Oxford. *T:* Oxford 57321.

HARRIS, Lt-Gen. Sir Ian (Cecil), KBE 1967 (CBE 1958); CB 1962; DSO 1945; Partner and Manager, Ballykisteen Stud, Tipperary, and Owner, Victor Stud, Golden, Cashel, Tipperary; Chairman, Irish Bloodstock Breeders Association, 1977; *b* 7 July 1910; *y s* of late J. W. A. Harris, Victor Stud, Golden, Tipperary; *m* 1945, Anne-Marie Desmotreux; two *s. Educ:* Portora Royal Sch., Enniskillen, Northern Ireland; RMC, Sandhurst. 2nd Lt Royal Ulster Rifles, 1930; served War of 1939-45, NW Frontier of India, 1939 (despatches); comd 2nd Bn Royal Ulster Rifles, 1943-45; GSO1, 25 Ind. Div. and 7 Div. in Burma and Malaya, 1945-46 (despatches), India and Pakistan, 1946-47; AQMG Scottish Comd, 1949-51; comd 6th Bn Royal Ulster Rifles (TA), 1951-52; Chief of Staff, Northern Ireland, 1952-54; Comdr 1 Federal Infantry Bde, Malaya, 1954-57 (despatches); Dep. Dir of Staff Duties (A), WO, 1957-60; GOC Singapore Base District, 1960-62; Chief of Staff, Contingencies Planning, Supreme HQ, Allied Powers, Europe, 1963-66; GOC-in-C, then GOC, N Ireland, 1966-69. Colonel: Royal Ulster Rifles, 1962-68; Royal Irish Rangers, 1968-72. *Recreations:* riding and tennis. *Address:* Acraboy House, Monard, Co. Tipperary. *T:* Tipperary 51564. *Club:* Army and Navy.

HARRIS, Sir Jack A. S.; see Sutherland-Harris.

HARRIS, Sir Jack Wolfred Ashford, 2nd Bt, *cr* 1932; Chairman, Bing Harris & Co. Ltd, Wellington, NZ, since 1935; *b* 23 July 1906; *er s* of Rt Hon. Sir Percy Harris, 1st Bt, PC, and Frieda Bloxam (*d* 1962); *S* father 1952; *m* 1933, Patricia, *o d* of A. P. Penman, Wahroonga, Sydney, NSW; two *s* one *d. Educ:* Shrewsbury Sch.; Trinity Hall, Cambridge. BA (Cantab) History; then one year's study in Europe. Joined family business in New Zealand, 1929, and became director shortly afterwards. Past Pres. Wellington Chamber of Commerce. Served during War of 1939-45, for three years in NZ Home Forces. *Recreations:* gardening, fishing, swimming. *Heir:* *s* Christopher John Ashford Harris [*b* 26 Aug. 1934; *m* 1957, Anna, *d* of F. de Malmanche, Auckland, NZ; one *s* two *d*]. *Address:* Te Rama, Waikanae, near Wellington, NZ. *Clubs:* Royal Automobile; Wellington (Wellington); Northern (Auckland).

HARRIS, John Percival, DSC 1945; QC 1974; a Recorder of the Crown Court, since 1972; *b* 16 Feb. 1925; *o s* of Thomas Percival Harris and Nora May Harris; *m* 1959, Janet Valerie Douglas; one *s* two *d. Educ:* Wells Cathedral Sch.; Pembroke Coll., Cambridge. BA 1947. Served in RN, 1943-46: Midshipman, RNVR, 1944, Sub-Lt 1945. Called to Bar, Middle Temple, 1949, Bencher 1970. *Recreations:* golf, reading. *Address:* Tudor Court, Fairmile Park Road, Cobham, Surrey. *T:* Cobham 4756; 12 King's Bench Walk, Temple, EC4Y 7EL. *T:* 01-353 5892.

Clubs: Woking Golf, Royal Jersey Golf, Burnham and Berrow Golf.

HARRIS, Kenneth Edwin, MA, MD Cantab; FRCP; Senior Physician and Cardiologist, University College Hospital; Consulting Physician to the Republic of the Sudan in London; Consulting Physician Royal Chest Hospital; Senior Censor, Royal College of Physicians; Examiner in Medicine Universities of Cambridge, London and Bristol, and Conjoint Examining Board of England; *s* of late Dr Thomas Harris, MD, FRCP, Physician, Manchester Royal Infirmary, and late I. M. Harris (*née* Brockbank); *m* 1932, Edith I. L. Abbott, MB, BS (London), DPH(Eng.); no *c. Educ:* Shrewsbury Sch.; Gonville and Caius Coll. Cambridge; University Coll. Hospital. BA (Hons); Fellowes Silver Medal for Clinical Medicine; Liston Gold Medal for Surgery; Erichsen Prize for Practical Surgery. Liveryman, Apothecaries Soc.; Vice-Pres. of Cambridge Graduates Medical Club. Freeman of City of London. Mem., English-Speaking Union. *Publications:* Minor Medical operations (with E. I. L. Harris), 1938. Contributions to: Heart, Lancet, BMJ, 1929-. *Recreations:* philately, gardening, colour photography, foreign travel and architecture. *Address:* The White House, 4 Grand Avenue, Worthing, West Sussex BN11 5AN. *T:* Worthing 48056.

HARRIS, Leonard John; Counsellor, UK Representation to the EEC, Brussels, since 1976; *b* 4 July 1941; *s* of Leonard and May Harris; *m* 1965, Jill Christine Tompkins; one *s* two *d. Educ:* Westminster City Sch.; St John's Coll., Cambridge. BA 1964 (Eng. Lit.), MA 1967. HM Customs and Excise: Asst Principal, 1964; Private Sec. to Chairman, 1966-68; Principal, 1968; CS Selection Bd, 1970; HM Customs and Excise, 1971; Cabinet Office, 1971-74; First Sec., UK Rep. to EEC, 1974-76. *Recreations:* photography, music, cooking, eating. *Address:* 81 Highdown, Worcester Park, Surrey. *T:* 01-337 4564.

HARRIS, Brigadier Lewis John, CBE 1961 (OBE 1949; MBE 1943); Consultant to Federal Surveys and Mapping, Canada, since 1967; *b* 19 Dec. 1910; *e s* of late David Rees and of Cecilia Harris; *m* 1975, Thelma Opal, *d* of James Marshall Carr and Zettie Lou Witt, and *widow* of Lt-Col A. L. Nowicki, US Corps of Engineers. *Educ:* Christ Coll., Brecon; RMA, Woolwich; Pembroke Coll., Cambridge (Exhibitioner). Mech. Sci. Tripos, MA. Commissioned RE 1930; Triangulation of Jamaica, 1937-39; served War of 1939-45: British Expeditionary Force, 1939-40 (despatches); First Army in North Africa, 1942-43, AFHQ and American Seventh Army, Italy, 1944; Land Forces SE Asia, India, Burma and Malaya, 1944-46; Chief Instructor, Sch. of Mil. Survey, 1946-49; War Office, Geog. Section GS 1949-52; Ordnance Survey, 1952-53; Dir, Survey GHQ, Middle East, and GHQ, E Africa, 1953-55; Land Survey Adviser, Allied Forces, Mediterranean, 1954-55; Ordnance Survey of Great Britain, 1955-61; Dir, Map Production and Publication, 1956-59; Dir, Field Surveys, 1959-61; Dir of Mil. Survey, MoD and Chief of Geographical Section Gen. Staff, 1961-65. Brig. 1956. Hon. Col 135 Survey Engineer Regt, TA, 1965-67. Chm., Nat. Cttee for Cartography, Royal Society, 1961-67. Hon. Foreign Sec., Royal Geographical Soc., 1964-67; Vice-Pres., Internat. Cartographic Assoc., 1958-61. Hon. Vice-Pres., Army Rugby Union. FRGS, FRICS. *Publications:* various papers on cartography in learned jls. *Recreations:* outdoor sports, travelling. *Address:* PO Box 22123, 12410 Hound Ears Point, Fox Den, Knoxville, Tenn 37922, USA. *Clubs:* Naval and Military, MCC; Hawks (Cambridge); Royal Ottawa Golf; IZ, FF, BB.

HARRIS, Lyndon Goodwin, RI 1958; RSW 1952; RWA 1947; artist in oil, water-colour, stained glass, and etching; *b* 25 July 1928; *s* of late S. E. Harris, ACIS and Mary Elsie Harris. *Educ:* Halesowen Grammar Sch. Studied Art at: Birmingham Coll. of Art; Slade Sch. of Fine Art, 1946-50; University of London Inst. of Education, 1950-51; Courtauld Inst.; Central Sch. of Art and Crafts, London. Leverhulme Schol., Pilkington Schol., Slade Schol., and Slade Anatomy Prizeman; Dip. Fine Art (London) 1949; Courtauld Certificate, 1950; ATD 1951. *Works exhibited:* Paris Salon (Gold Medal, Oil Painting; Honourable Mention, Etching); RA (first exhibited at age of 13), RSA, RI, RSW, NEAC, RBA, RGI, RWA, and principal provincial galleries. *Works in permanent collections:* Ministry of Works; University Coll., London; Birmingham and Midland Inst.; City of Worcester; (stained glass) Gorsty Hill Methodist Church, Halesowen. *Recreation:* music (organ and pianoforte). *Address:* The Uplands, Waxland Road, Halesowen, West Midlands.

HARRIS, Margaret Frances, OBE 1975; Designer with English National Opera (formerly Sadler's Wells Opera), since 1961 (Resident Designer, 1961-76); Director, Theatre Design Course of the English National Opera (formerly Sadler's Wells), since 1966; *b* 28 May 1904; *d* of William Birkbeck Harris and

Kathleen Marion Carey. *Educ:* Downe House. In partnership with Elizabeth Montgomery and late Sophie Devine as firm of Motley, 1931-. Has designed many productions in London and New York of drama, opera and ballet: first notable production, Richard of Bordeaux, for John Gielgud, 1932; recently, sets and costumes for: Prokofiev's War and Peace, Coliseum, 1972; (with Elizabeth Montgomery) Unknown Soldier and His Wife, New London, 1973; A Family and a Fortune, 1975; Tosca, English Nat. Opera, 1976; Paul Bunyan, English Music Theatre, 1976. *Publications:* Designing and Making Costume, by Motley, 1965; Theatre Props, by Motley, 1976. *Address:* 40 Smith Square, SW1. *T:* 01-222 5431.

HARRIS, Martin Richard; Director, Reckitt and Colman Ltd, since 1977; *b* 30 Aug. 1922; *m* 1952, Diana Moira (*née* Gandar Dower); four *s. Educ:* Wellington Coll. FCA. Captain, RE, ME and Italy, 1941-46. Joined Price Waterhouse & Co., 1946, Partner, 1956-74; Dir Gen., Panel on Take-Overs and Mergers, 1974-77. Inst. of Chartered Accountants in England and Wales: Mem. Council, 1971-; Chm., Parly and Law Cttee, 1973-74; Mem., Accountants Internat. Study Gp, 1972-74. Mem., DTI's Companies Consultative Gp, 1972-74. US Silver Star 1945. *Recreations:* philately, antique furniture and china. *Address:* 76 Woodside, Wimbledon, SW19 7QL. *T:* 01-946 5756. *Clubs:* Carlton, MCC.

HARRIS, Maurice Kingston, CB 1976; formerly Secretary, Northern Ireland Ministry of Home Affairs, Jan. 1973, seconded to Northern Ireland Office, 1974-76; *b* 5 Oct. 1916; *s* of late Albert Kingston Harris and late Annie Rebecca Harris; *m* 1948, Margaret McGregor, *d* of Roderick Fraser McGregor; one *s* three *d. Educ:* The Perse Sch.; London Univ. 1st cl. Hons Mod. Langs, 1939. Served in Indian Army, 8th Punjab Regt, 1942-46. Colonial Office, 1946-47. Entered Northern Ireland Civil Service, 1947, and served in various Ministries. *Recreations:* music, walking. *Address:* 11 Kensington Gardens, Belfast BT5 6NP. *T:* Belfast 658348.

HARRIS, Noël H. V.; *see* Vicars-Harris.

HARRIS, Sir Percy W.; *see* Wyn-Harris.

HARRIS, Prof. Peter Charles, MD, PhD, FRCP; Simon Marks Professor of Cardiology, University of London, since 1966; Physician, National Heart Hospital; *b* 26 May 1923; *s* of David Jonathan Valentine and Nellie Dean Harris; *m* 1952, Felicity Margaret Hartridge; two *d. Educ:* St Olave's Grammar Sch.; Univ. of London. MB, BS (London) 1946; MRCP 1950; MD (Univ. medal) 1951; PhD 1955; FRCP 1965. House appts at King's Coll. Hospital, and elsewhere, 1946-55. Nuffield Fellow, Columbia Univ., New York, 1955-57; Lectr, Sen. Lectr and Reader in Medicine, Univ. of Birmingham, 1957-66; Dir, Inst. of Cardiology, Univ. of London, 1966-73. Hon. FACC, 1970. *Publications:* The Human Pulmonary Circulation (with D. Heath), 1962, 2nd edn 1977; articles to jls, etc, on cardio-pulmonary physiology and biochemistry. *Recreation:* chamber music. *Address:* 2 Beaumont Street, W1. *T:* 01-486 3043.

HARRIS, Philip; Principal, Monopolies and Mergers Commission, 1977; *b* Manchester, 15 Dec. 1915; *er s* of S. D. Harris and Sarah Chazan; *m* 1939, Sarah Henriques Valentine; three *d. Educ:* Manchester Grammar Sch.; Trinity Hall, Cambridge (Open Scholarship, BA 1st Cl (with dist.), Historical Tripos, MA 1970). Asst Principal, Board of Trade, 1938-40. Served War, 1940-45; Anti-Aircraft Command and Western Europe; 2nd Lieut RA, 1941; Lieut, 2/8th Lancs Fusiliers, 1944; Capt., 6th Royal Welch Fusiliers, 1945. Principal, Board of Trade, 1946; Asst Sec., Board of Trade, 1948-64; Asst Registrar, Office of the Registrar of Restrictive Trading Agreements, 1964-66, Principal Asst Registrar, 1966-73; Principal Asst Registrar, Fair Trading Div. I, DTI, 1973; Dir, Restrictive Trade Practices Div., Office of Fair Trading, 1973-76. Nuffield Travelling Fellowship, 1956-57 (study of Indian Industrial Development). UK Mem., EEC Adv. Cttee on Cartels and Monopolies, 1973-. Leader, UK Delgn to Internat. Cotton Advisory Cttee, 1960, 1963. *Recreation:* history. *Address:* 23 Court House Gardens, Finchley, N3. *T:* 01-346 3138. *Club:* Arts Theatre.

HARRIS, Phillip, FRCSE, FRCPE, FRCS(Glas); FRS(Ed); Deputy Director, and Consultant Neurosurgeon, Department of Surgical Neurology, Royal Infirmary and Western General Hospital, Edinburgh, since 1955; Lecturer, Member of Clinical Teaching Staff and Board of Studies, Edinburgh University, since 1949; Consultant Neurosurgeon, Spinal Unit, Edenhall Hospital, Musselburgh, since 1955; Assistant Editor, International Journal of Paraplegia, 1962; Member, MRC Brain Metabolism Unit, University of Edinburgh, since 1972; *b* Edinburgh, 28 March 1922; *s* of late Simon Harris, Edinburgh;

m 1949, Sheelagh Shèna (*née* Coutts); one *s* one *d*. *Educ:* Royal High Sch., Edinburgh; Edinburgh Univ.; Sch. of Med. of Royal Colls, Edinburgh. Medallist in Anatomy, Physiol., Physics, Materia Medica and Therapeutics, Med., Midwifery and Gynaec., and Surgery. LRCP and LRCSEd, LRFP and SG 1944; FRCSE 1948; MRCPE 1954; FRCPE 1959; FRCS(Glas) 1964 (*ad eundem*). Sydney Watson-Smith Lectr, RCPE, 1967; Honeyman-Gillespie Lectr, Edinburgh Univ., 1968; Visiting Prof.: Columbus, Ohio; Cincinnati, Ohio; Phoenix, Arizona; UCLA; Montreal Neurological Inst., Montreal; Guest Chief and Lectr in Univs in Canada, USA, Japan, Israel, Denmark. Corr. Mem., Amer. Assoc. of Neurolog. Surgeons; Hon. Mem., Scottish Paraplegia Assoc.; Chm., Epilepsy Soc. of Edinburgh and SE Reg.; Chm., Scottish Sports Assoc. for the Disabled; Founder Mem. and Mem. Council, Internat. Med. Soc. of Paraplegia; Founder, Scot. Assoc. Neurolog. Sciences; Mem. Council, Soc. Brit. Neurolog. Surgeons; Mem., Assoc. Surgns GB and Ire.; Chm. Exec. Cttee, Med. and Dent. Staff, Roy. Inf., Edinburgh (Mem. Bd of Management); Trustee and Dir, Scottish Trust for the Physically Disabled Ltd; Mem. Council, Royal High Sch., Edinburgh. FRSocMed (Mem. Council); FRS(Ed) 1967. *Publications:* Head and Brain, in Manual of Surgical Anatomy, 1964; (ed) Spinal Injuries, RCSE, 1965; Surgical Diathermy in Neurosurgery, in Surgical Diathermy, 1966; (ed jtly) Head Injuries, 1971; over 50 papers on Intracranial Aneurysms, Cervical Spondylosis, the Pituitary Gland, Cryosurgery, Head Injuries, Spinal Injuries, Med. Educn, New Instruments and Techniques in Neurosurgery, Muscle Spasm, Epilepsy. *Recreations:* sport, music, travelling. *Address:* 4/5 Fettes Rise, Edinburgh EH4 1QH. *T:* 031-552 8900. *Clubs:* Royal Scottish Automobile (Glasgow); University Staff (Edinburgh).

HARRIS, Ralph; General Director, Institute of Economic Affairs, since 1957; *b* 10 Dec. 1924; *m* 1949, Jose Pauline Jeffery; two *s* one *d*. *Educ:* Tottenham Grammar Sch.; Queens' Coll., Cambridge (Exhibr, Foundn Schol.). 1st Cl. Hons Econs, MA Cantab. Lectr in Polit. Economy, St Andrews Univ., 1949-56. Contested (C): Kirkcaldy, 1951; Edinburgh Central, 1955. Leader-writer, Glasgow Herald, 1956. Secretary: Wincott Foundn; Ross McWhirter Foundn. Mem. Council, Univ. Coll. at Buckingham; Dir, Churchill Press. Free Enterprise Award, 1976. *Publications:* Politics without Prejudice, a biography of R. A. Butler, 1956; Hire Purchase in a Free Society, 1958, 3rd edn 1961; (with Arthur Seldon) Advertising in a Free Society, 1959; Advertising in Action, 1962; Advertising and the Public, 1962; (with A. P. Herbert) Libraries: Free for All?, 1962; Choice in Welfare, 1963; Essays in Rebirth of Britain, 1964; Choice in Welfare, 1965; Right Turn, 1970; Choice in Welfare, 1970; Down with the Poor, 1971; (with Brendan Sewill) British Economic Policy 1970-74, 1975; Crisis '75, 1975; Catch '76, 1976; Freedom of Choice: consumers or conscripts, 1976; (with Arthur Seldon) Pricing or Taxing, 1976; Not from Benevolence, 1977; columnist in Truth, Statist, etc. *Recreations:* conjuring and devising spells against over-government. *Address:* 41 Parkgate Crescent, Hadley Wood, Barnet, Herts. *T:* 01-449 6212. *Clubs:* (Hon. Sec.) Political Economy, Mont Pelerin Society.

HARRIS, Richard Reader; *b* 4 June 1913; *s* of Richard Reader Harris; *m* 1940, Pamela Rosemary Merrick Stephens; three *d*. *Educ:* St Lawrence Coll., Ramsgate. Called to the Bar, 1941. Fire Service, 1939-45. MP (C) Heston and Isleworth, 1950-70. *Recreations:* squash, Tennis.

HARRIS, Robert; actor since 1922; *b* 28 March 1900; *s* of Alfred H. Harris and Suzanne Amelie (*née* Anstie). *Educ:* Sherborne; New Coll., Oxford. Has appeared in Shakespearean rôles with the Old Vic-Sadler's Wells Company and at Stratford-on-Avon, and in the West End (Hamlet, Oberon, Prospero, Angelo, Henry IV, King John, Shylock, Dr Faustus, J. Robert Oppenheimer). Other parts include: St Bernard, in The Marvellous History of St Bernard; Charles Tritton, in The Wind and The Rain; Eugene Marchbanks, in Candida; Orin Mannon, in Mourning Becomes Electra; Thomas More, in A Man for all Seasons (USA); Pope Pius XII in The Deputy (NY); 40 Years on (Canada); Prendergast, in Decline and Fall (film); Judge in Make No Mistake, Yvonne Arnaud, Guildford, 1971; Morta in Roma (film); Ransom (film); Love Among the Ruins (film). Television, verse reading, and radio plays (incl.: Old Jolyon in The Forsyte Saga; Prof. Gay in C. P. Snow's Strangers and Brothers (serial); Archdeacon Grantly in The Barchester Chronicles; The Mysterious Death of Charles Bravo). *Recreation:* travel. *Address:* 18 Pitt Street, W8. *T:* 01-937 8825. *Clubs:* Garrick, Chelsea Arts.

HARRIS, Dr Robert John Cecil; Director, Microbiological Research Establishment, Porton, since 1971; *b* 14 March 1922; *er s* of John Henry and Suzannah Harris; *m* 1946, Annette Constance Daphne Brading; one *s* one *d*. *Educ:* Maidstone Grammar Sch.; Imperial Coll of Science and Technology, London. PhD London; FRIC, FIBiol, FRCPath. Laura de Saliceto Student, London Univ., 1947-51; Research Fellow, British Empire Cancer Campaign (Inst. of Cancer Research), 1951-58; Head, Div. of Experimental Biology and Virology, Imperial Cancer Research Fund, 1958-68; Head, Dept of Environmental Carcinogenesis, Imperial Cancer Research Fund, 1968-71. Hon. DTech Brunel, 1973. *Publications:* Cancer: the nature of the problem, 1962, 3rd edn 1976; scientific papers in cancer jls. *Address:* 24 Harnwood Road, Salisbury, Wilts. *T:* Salisbury 29570. *Club:* Athenæum.

HARRIS, Sir Ronald (Montague Joseph), KCVO 1960 (MVO 1943); CB 1956; First Church Estates Commissioner, since 1969; *b* 6 May 1913; *o s* of late Rev. J. Montague Harris; *m* 1st, 1939, Margaret Julia Wharton (*d* 1955); one *s* three *d*; 2nd, 1957, Marjorie, *widow* of Julian Tryon, and *e d* of Sir Harry Verney, 4th Bt, DSO; one step *d* (one step *s* decd). *Educ:* Harrow; Trinity Coll., Oxford. India Office and Burma Office, 1936-38; Private Sec. to Sec. of Cabinet, 1939-43; India Office and Burma Office, 1944-47; Imperial Defence Coll., 1948; HM Treasury, 1949-52; Cabinet Office, 1952-55; Second Crown Estate Commissioner, 1955-60; Third Sec., HM Treasury, 1960-64; Sec. to Church Commissioners, 1964-68. Director: Yorks Insurance Co., 1966-69; Yorkshire General Life Assurance Co., 1969-; General Accident Fire and Life Assurance Corp. Ltd; Triplevest Ltd. Chairman: Benenden Sch. Council, 1971-; Friends of Yehudi Menuhin Sch., 1972- (Governor, 1976-). *Address:* Slyfield Farm House, Stoke D'Abernon, Cobham, Surrey. *Club:* Boodle's.

HARRIS, Rosemary Jeanne; author; *b* 1923; *yr d* of Marshal of the RAF Sir Arthur Harris, Bt, *qv*, and Barbara Kyrle Money. *Educ:* privately; Thorneloe Sch., Weymouth; St Martin's, Central and Chelsea Schs of Art. Red Cross Nursing Auxiliary, London, Westminster Div., from 1941. Student, 1945-48; picture restorer, 1949; student at Courtauld Inst. (Dept of Technology), 1950; Reader, MGM, 1951-52; subseq. full-time writer. Reviewer of children's books for The Times, 1970-73. Television play: Peronik, 1976. *Publications:* The Summer-House, 1956; Voyage to Cythera, 1958; Venus with Sparrows, 1961; All My Enemies, 1967; The Nice Girl's Story, 1968; A Wicked Pack of Cards, 1969; The Double Snare, 1975; Three Candles for the Dark, 1976; *for children:* The Moon in the Cloud, 1968 (Carnegie Medal); The Shadow on the Sun, 1970; The Seal-Singing, 1971; The Child in the Bamboo Grove, 1971; The Bright and Morning Star, 1972; The King's White Elephant, 1973; The Lotus and the Grail, 1974; The Flying Ship, 1974; The Little Dog of Fo, 1976; I Want to be a Fish, 1977; A Quest for Orion, 1978. *Recreations:* music, theatre, photography. *Address:* 33 Cheyne Court, Flood Street, SW3 5TR. *T:* 01-352 1721.

HARRIS, Prof. Roy; Professor of General Linguistics, University of Oxford, since Jan. 1978; Fellow of Worcester College, Oxford; *b* 24 Feb. 1931; *s* of Harry and Emmie J. Harris; *m* 1955, Rita Doreen Shulman; one *d*. *Educ:* Queen Elizabeth's Hospital, Bristol; St Edmund Hall, Oxford. MA, DPhil (Oxon), PhD (London). Lecteur, Ecole Normale Supérieure, Paris, 1956-57; Asst Lectr, 1957-58, Lectr, 1958-60, Univ. of Leicester; Exeter Coll., Oxford, 1960-76; Keble Coll., Oxford, 1960-67; Magdalen Coll., Oxford, 1960-76; New Coll., Oxford, 1960-67; Faculty of Medieval and Modern Languages, Oxford, 1961-76; Fellow and Tutor in Romance Philology, Keble Coll., Oxford, 1967-76; Prof. of the Romance Langs, Oxford Univ., 1976-77. *Publications:* Synonymy and Linguistic Analysis, 1973; contribs to Analysis, French Studies, Jl of Linguistics, Linguistics, Medium Ævum, Revue de linguistique romane, Theoria, Zeitschrift für romanische Philologie. *Recreations:* cricket, modern art and design. *Address:* 2 Paddox Close, Oxford OX2 7LR. *T:* Oxford 54256.

HARRIS, (Theodore) Wilson; *b* 24 March 1921; *m* 1st, 1945, Cecily Carew; 2nd, 1959, Margaret Whitaker (*née* Burns). *Educ:* Queen's Coll., Georgetown, British Guiana. Studied land surveying, British Guiana, 1939, and subseq. qualified to practise; led many survey parties (mapping and geomorphological research) in the interior; Senior Surveyor, Projects, for Govt of British Guiana, 1955-58. Came to live in London, 1959. Writer in Residence, Univ. of West Indies and Univ. of Toronto, 1970; Commonwealth Fellow, Leeds Univ., 1971; Vis. Prof., Univ. of Texas at Austin, 1972; Guggenheim Fellow, 1973; Henfield Fellow, UEA, 1974; Southern Arts Writer's Fellowship, 1976. *Publications:* Eternity to Season (poems, privately printed), 1954; Palace of the Peacock, 1960;

The Far Journey of Oudin, 1961; The Whole Armour, 1962; The Secret Ladder, 1963; Heartland, 1964; The Eye of the Scarecrow, 1965; The Waiting Room, 1967; Tradition, the Writer and Society: Critical Essays, 1967; Tumatumari, 1968; Ascent to Omai, 1970; The Sleepers of Roraima (a Carib Trilogy), 1970; The Age of the Rainmakers, 1971; Black Marsden, 1972; Companions of the Day and Night, 1975; Da Silva da Silva's Cultivated Wilderness, and Genesis of the Clowns, 1977. *Address:* c/o Faber and Faber, 3 Queen Square, WC1N 3AU.

HARRIS, Thomas Maxwell, FRS 1948; Professor of Botany, University of Reading, 1935-68, Professor Emeritus 1968; *b* 8 Jan. 1903; *s* of Alexander Charles Harris and Lucy Frances Evans; *m* 1928, Katharine Massey; one *s* three *d. Educ:* Bootham, York; Wyggeston Sch., Leicester; University Coll., Nottingham; Christ's Coll., Cambridge (scholar). Natural Science Tripos, Parts I and II, 1st Class Hons; London BSc, 1st Class Hons; ScD Cambridge; Mem. of Danish Expedition to E Greenland, 1926-27; Demonstrator in Botany, 1928; Fellow of Christ's Coll., 1928. Vice-Pres., Royal Society, 1960-61; President, Linnæan Soc., 1961-64; Vice-Pres., 1964. Trustee, Natural History Museum, 1963-73. *Publications:* communications to scientific journals on Palæobotany. *Recreation:* gardening. *Address:* Chusan, Farley Court, Farley Hill, near Reading, Berks; Department of Geology, The University, Reading, Berks.

HARRIS, Hon. Walter Edward, PC (Canada), QC (Canada); DCL; Director: Homewood Sanitarium Ltd; Victoria and Grey Trust Co.; *b* 14 Jan. 1904; *s* of Melvin Harris and Helen (*née* Carruthers); *m* 1933, Grace Elma Morrison; one *s* two *d. Educ:* Osgoode Hall, Toronto. Served War of 1939-45. First elected to House of Commons, Canada, 1940 (re-elected 1945, 1949, 1953), MP (Canada) until 1957. Parliamentary Asst to Sec of State for External Affairs, 1947; Parly Asst to Prime Minister, 1948; Minister of Citizenship and Immigration, 1950; of Finance, 1954-57. Mem. of the firm of Harris & Dunlop, Barristers, Markdale. *Address:* Markdale, Ontario, Canada.

HARRIS, (Walter) Frank; Financial Director, Dunlop (South Africa) Ltd, since 1972; *b* 19 May 1920; *m* Esther Blanche Hill; two *s* two *d. Educ:* King Edward's Sch., Birmingham; University of Nottingham. Served Royal Air Force, 1939-46. University, 1946-49. Ford Motor Company, 1950-65; Principal City Officer and Town Clerk, Newcastle upon Tyne, 1965-69. Comptroller and Dir, Admin, Massey-Ferguson (UK), 1969-71. *Recreations:* fell walking, gardening. *Address:* Acomb High House, Northumberland. *T:* Hexham 2844; PO Box 925, Durban, South Africa. *T:* 350202. *Club:* Reform.

HARRIS, William Barclay, QC 1961; *b* 25 Nov. 1911; *s* of W. Cecil Harris, Moatlands, E Grinstead, Sussex; *m* 1937, Elizabeth, 2nd *d* of Capt. Sir Clive Milnes-Coates, 2nd Bt, and of Lady Celia Milnes-Coates; one *s* two *d. Educ:* Harrow; Trinity Coll., Cambridge (MA). Served 1940-45: with Coldstream Guards, N Africa, Italy, Germany (despatches), Major. Barrister, Inner Temple, 1937. Chm., Rowton Hotels, 1965-. A Church Commissioner, 1966- (Chm., Redundant Churches Cttee, 1972-; Mem., Bd of Governors, 1972-). *Address:* Moatlands, East Grinstead, West Sussex. *T:* Sharpthorne 801228; 29 Barkston Gardens, SW5. *T:* 01-373 8793. *Clubs:* Athenæum, MCC, Brooks's.

HARRIS, Sir William (Gordon), KBE 1969; CB 1963; MA (Cantab); CEng; FICE; Partner, Peter Fraenkel & Partners, since 1973; *b* 10 June 1912; *s* of Capt. James Whyte Harris, Royal Naval Reserve, and Margaret Roberta Buchanan Forsyth; *m* 1938, Margaret Emily Harvie; three *s* one *d. Educ:* Liverpool Coll.; Sidney Sussex Coll., Cambridge. Mechanical Sciences Tripos and BA 1932, MA 1937. London Midland & Scottish Railway, 1932-35; Sudan Irrigation Dept, 1935-37; Joined Civil Engineer in Chief's Dept, Admiralty, 1937; Asst Civil Engineer in Chief, 1950; Deputy Civil Engineer in Chief, 1955; Civil Engineer in Chief, 1959; Dir-Gen., Navy Works, 1960-63; Dir-Gen. of Works, MPBW, 1963-65; Dir-Gen., Highways, MoT, later DoE, 1965-73. Chief British Delegate to: Perm. Internat. Assoc. of Navigation Congresses, 1969-; Perm. Internat. Assoc. of Road Congresses, 1970-73 (Vice-Pres., 1976-); Mem., Dover Harbour Bd, 1959- (Vice-Chm., 1975-); Chm., Construction Industry Manpower Bd, 1976-. Commonwealth Fund (of New York) Fellowship, 1950-51. A Vice-Pres., Instn Civil Engineers, 1971-74, Pres. 1974-75. Mem., Smeatonian Soc. of Civil Engineers. *Address:* 5 Moor Park Road, Northwood, Mddx. *T:* Northwood 25899.

HARRIS, Sir William (Woolf), Kt 1974; OBE 1961; JP; surveyor and company director; *b* London, 19 Aug. 1910; *e s* of Simon Harris and Fanny Harris, London; *m* 1952, Beverly Joyce, *y d* of Howard Bowden, Minneapolis, USA; one *s* two *d. Educ:* King's Coll.; Princeton Univ. Chm. of number of companies concerned with residential and industrial building construction. Chm., Bow Street Magistrates Court; Chm., Inner London Juvenile Courts; Dep. Chm., S Westminster Bench; Member: Inner London Sessions Appeals Court; London Probation Cttee and Home Office Juvenile Courts Consultative Cttee, 1955-72; a General Commissioner of Taxes; Vice-Pres. (former Chm.), Royal Soc. of St George (City of London); former jt Nat. Treas., Trades Adv. Council; Founder 1951, and Chm. until 1963, Addison Boys Club, Hammersmith; Conservative Party: Chairman: Nat. Union of Conservative Assocs, 1971-73; Party Conf., 1972; Standing Adv. Cttee on Candidates, 1971-73; Greater London Area, 1966-69 (Dep. Chm. 1963-66); former London Area, 1963 (Dep. Chm. 1961-63); Mem., Cons Party Adv. Cttee on Policy, 1965-75 and of other nat. adv. cttees; Mem., Nat. Exec. Cttee and Gen. Purpose Cttee, 1963-; Chm., S Battersea Conservative Assoc., 1956-63; former Pres. and Chm., Battersea Chamber of Commerce; Branch Chm., NSPCC, 1956-65; Founder and Nat. Chm., Leasehold Reform Assoc., 1956-67. Freeman, City of London; Liveryman, Basketmakers' Co.; High Sheriff of Greater London, 1971-72; JP Bow Street, 1952-. *Publications:* papers on problems of juvenile delinquency, child welfare, mental health and penal reform in various jls. *Recreations:* reading history, theatre, travel, listening to the wiseacres talk. *Address:* 165 Bickenhall Mansions, Gloucester Place, W1. *T:* 01-935 3752. *Clubs:* Carlton, St Stephen's, City Livery.

HARRIS, Wilson; *see* Harris, T. W.

HARRISON, (Alastair) Brian (Clarke); Director: Grindlay Brandts (Australia) Ltd; Agricultural Investments Australia Ltd; Commercial Bank of Australia Ltd (London Board); *b* 3 Oct. 1921; *s* of late Brig. E. F. Harrison, Melbourne; *m* 1952, Elizabeth Hood Hardie, Oaklands, NSW, Aust.; one *s* one *d. Educ:* Geelong Grammar Sch.; Trinity Coll., Cambridge. Capt. AIF. MP (C) Maldon, Essex, 1955-Feb. 1974; Parliamentary Private Secretary to: Min. of State, Colonial Office, 1955-56; Sec. of State for War, 1956-58; Min. of Agriculture, Fisheries and Food, 1958-60. Mem. Victoria Promotion Cttee (London); Mem. One Nation Gp which published The Responsible Society, and One Europe; toured USA on E-SU Ford Foundation Fellowship, 1959; Commonwealth Parliamentary Assoc. Delegations: Kenya and Horn of Africa, 1960; Gilbert and Ellice Islands, New Hebrides and British Solomon Islands Protectorate. Chm., Standing Conf. of Eastern Sport and Physical Recreation. *Recreations:* photography, gardening. *Address:* Green Farm House, Copford, Colchester, Essex. *Clubs:* Carlton, Pratt's; Melbourne (Australia).

HARRISON, Albert Norman, CB 1966; CVO 1955; OBE 1946; RCNC; Hon. FRINA; *b* 12 July 1901; *s* of William Arthur and Sarah Jane Harrison, Portsmouth, Hants; *m* 1941, Queenie Perpetua Parker, Luton, Beds; one *d. Educ:* Portsmouth; Royal Naval Coll., Greenwich. Asst Constructor, Royal Corps of Naval Constructors, 1926; Constructor, 1937; Principal Ship Overseer. Vickers-Armstrong, Barrow-in-Furness, 1936-39; Staff of RA (D), Home Fleet, 1940-41; Naval Constructor-in-Chief, Royal Canadian Navy, 1942-48; Chief Constructor, Admiralty, 1948-51; Asst Dir of Naval Construction, Admiralty, 1951-61; Dir of Naval Construction, Min. of Defence (N) (formerly Admiralty), 1961-66. *Address:* Whiteoaks, 126 Bloomfield Road, Bath, Avon. *T:* Bath 29145. *Club:* Bath and County (Bath).

HARRISON, Alexander, CBE 1955; CA; Vice-President, Trustee Savings Bank Association (Deputy-Chairman, 1947-59); *b* 26 Feb. 1890; *s* of John Harrison, CBE, LLD, FRSE, DL, and Helen Georgina Roberts; *m* 1931, Jean Muriel Small; one *s* three *d. Educ:* Merchiston Castle Sch. Chartered Accountant, 1914 (Distinction). Chm. Edinburgh Savings Bank, 1945-54. Mem. Edinburgh Town Council, 1946-48. Served European War, 1914-18; temp. Major, Royal Scots, attached Machine Gun Corps in France and Italy, FRSGS. Hon. Pres., Scottish Mountaineering Club. *Address:* 4 Whitehouse Terrace, Edinburgh EH9 2EU. *T:* 031-447 2898. *Clubs:* Alpine; New (Edinburgh).

HARRISON, Sir (Bernard) Guy, Kt 1951; late Chairman, Harrison & Sons, Ltd; *b* 2 July 1885; *s* of Bernard Bowles Harrison; *m* 1st, 1907, Cicely Ann (*d* 1957), *d* of late H. N. Vicat; one *s* one *d*; 2nd, 1958, Iris, *y d* of late E. R. C. Hall. *Educ:* Sevenoaks Sch. Pres. London Master Printers' Assoc., 1931-32; Pres. British Federation of Master Printers, 1933-34; Pres. Printing & Allied Trades Research Assoc., 1952-56; Chm., Joint Industrial Council (Printing & Allied Trades), 1939-45; Master of Stationers' Company, 1948-49. Governor, North

Western Polytechnic, 1947-57. Pres., Printers' Pension Corporation, 1959-60. *Publications:* occasional contribs to Astronomical and Ornithological Jls. *Recreations:* astronomy, ornithology, botany and entomology. *Address:* Beenleigh Manor, Habertonford, Totnes, Devon. *T:* Habertonford 234. *Club:* Athenæum.

HARRISON, Brian; *see* Harrison, A. B. C.

HARRISON, Rev. Cecil Marriott; Vicar of Aislaby, Diocese of York, since 1969; *b* 16 March 1911; *s* of late Tom Marriott Harrison, Davidson's Mains, Midlothian; *m* 1944, Phyllis Edith McKenzie. *Educ:* Westminster Sch.; Trinity Coll., Cambridge. 1st Class Classical Tripos Pt I, 1930; Pt II, 1932; BA 1932, MA 1936; Classical Sixth Form Master, Nottingham High Sch., 1932; Dulwich Coll., 1934; Charterhouse, 1936-47. Served War of 1939-45; Royal Signals, 1940-46; Headmaster of Felsted Sch., 1947-51; Headmaster, King's School, Peterborough, 1951-69. Deacon, 1966, Priest, 1967. *Address:* Aislaby Vicarage, Whitby, North Yorks. *T:* Whitby 810350. *Club:* Leander.

HARRISON, Prof. Charles Victor; Professor of Pathology, University of Ife, Nigeria, 1972-75; *b* Newport, Mon, 1907; *s* of Charles Henry Harrison, LDS, and Violet Harrison (*née* Witchell); *m* 1937, Olga Beatrice Cochrane; one *s* one *d. Educ:* Dean Close Sch., Cheltenham; University Coll., Cardiff; University Coll. Hosp., London. MB, BCh, BSc (Wales), 1929; MB, BS (London), 1929; MD (London), 1937; FCPath 1965; FRCP 1967. Demonstrator in Pathology, Welsh National School of Medicine, 1930; Asst Morbid Anatomist, British Postgraduate Medical Sch., 1935; Senior Lecturer, Liverpool Univ., 1939; Reader in Morbid Anatomy, Postgraduate Medical Sch. of London, 1946; Prof., Royal Postgrad. Med. Sch., Univ. of London, 1955-72. Hon. DSc Wales, 1972. Willie Seager Gold Medal in Pathology, 1927. *Publications:* (ed) Recent Advances in Pathology, 1973; various scientific papers in Jl of Pathology and Bacteriology, British Heart Journal, Jl Clin. Pathology, etc. *Recreations:* carpentry and gardening. *Address:* 8 Wattleton Road, Beaconsfield, Bucks HP9 1TS. *T:* Beaconsfield 2046.

HARRISON, Claude William, RP 1961; Artist; portrait painter and painter of conversation pieces, imaginative landscapes and murals, etc; *b* Leyland, Lancs, 31 March 1922; *s* of Harold Harrison and Florence Mildred Ireton; *m* 1947, Audrey Johnson; one *s. Educ:* Hutton Grammar Sch., Lancs. Served in RAF, 1942-46. Royal Coll. of Art, 1947-49; Studio in Ambleside, 1949-52. Exhibited since 1950 at: RA; RSA; Royal Society Portrait Painters; New English Art Club, etc. *Publication:* The Portrait Painter's handbook, 1968. *Recreation:* painting. *Address:* Easedale House, Grasmere, Cumbria. *T:* Grasmere 231.

HARRISON, Sir Colin; *see* Harrison, Sir R. C.

HARRISON, Sir Cyril (Ernest), Kt 1963; Chairman, English Sewing Cotton Co. Ltd, 1963-68 (Director 1942; Managing Director, 1948; Vice-Chairman 1952); a Deputy Chairman, Williams & Glyn's Bank, 1969-72 (Joint Deputy Chairman, Williams Deacon's Bank Ltd, 1961); former Director, The Royal Bank of Scotland; *b* 14 Dec. 1901; *s* of Alfred John Harrison, MIGasE, and Edith Harrison, Great Harwood, Lancs; *m* 1927, Ethel (*d* 1971), *d* of Edward Wood, FCA, JP, Burnley; two *s. Educ:* Burnley Grammar Sch. President: Manchester Chamber of Commerce, 1958-60; Cotton, Silk and Man-made Fibres Res. Assoc. Member: NW Electricity Bd, 1963-72; S Manchester Hosp. Management Cttee; Council, Manchester Business Sch.; Grand Council, CBI; Court of Govs, University of Manchester. Chm., Christie Hospital and Holt Radium Inst., 1959-61; Chm., NW Regional Council of FBI, 1957-59; Pres., FBI, 1961-63. Mem. National Economic Development Council, 1962-64. Chm., Bd of Governors, United Manchester Hospitals, 1967-74. Hon. MA, Victoria Univ. of Manchester, 1960. Comp. Textile Inst.; FBIM; FCIS. *Recreation:* golf. *Address:* 8 Harefield Drive, Holly Road South, Wilmslow, Cheshire. *T:* Wilmslow 22186.

HARRISON, Denis Byrne; JP; a Local Commissioner for Administration in England, since 1974, and Vice-Chairman of the Commission for Local Administration since 1975; *b* 11 July 1917; *y s* of late Arthur and Priscilla Harrison; *m* 1956, Alice Marion Vickers, *e d* of late Hedley Vickers. *Educ:* Birkenhead Sch.; Liverpool Univ. (LLM). Articled to late E. W. Tame, OBE (Town Clerk of Birkenhead). Admitted Solicitor, 1939; Asst Solicitor to Birkenhead Corp., 1939. Served War, 1939-46: 75th Shropshire Yeo. (Medium Regt) RA, Combined Ops Bombardment Unit; Staff Captain at HQ of OC, Cyprus. First Asst Solicitor, Wolverhampton Co. Borough, 1946-49; Dep. Town Clerk of Co. Boroughs: Warrington, 1949-57; Bolton,

1957-63; Sheffield, 1963-66; Town Clerk and Chief Exec. Officer, Sheffield, 1966-74. Mem., Advisory Council on Noise, 1970. Mem. Council, Univ. of Sheffield, 1975-. JP City of London, 1976. *Recreations:* foreign travel, music, ski-ing, golf. *Address:* Norfolk Lodge, Hollow Meadows, near Sheffield S6 6GH. *T:* Sheffield 303229; 108A Whitehall Court, SW1. *T:* 01-930 6394. *Clubs:* Sheffield (Sheffield); Lindrick Golf.

HARRISON, Maj.-Gen. Desmond, CB 1946; DSO 1940; FICE; Civil Engineer; *b* 11 Nov. 1896; *s* of R. J. Harrison, JP; *m* 1920; one *s* two *d. Educ:* Kilkenny Coll.; Mountjoy Sch., Dublin; RMA, Woolwich; Cambridge Univ. Temp. Maj.-Gen. 1944; Maj.-Gen. 1947; Comdt SME 1942; Engineer-in-Chief, SEAC, 1943; Director of Fortifications and Works, War Office, 1946; retired 1947. Mem. Overseas Food Corp., 1947; resigned 1949. Comdr Legion of Merit, USA. *Recreations:* golf, shooting, fishing. *Address:* 55 Hans Road, SW3. *T:* 01-584 4867. *Club:* Army and Navy.

HARRISON, Prof. Donald Frederick Norris, MD, MS, FRCS; Professor of Laryngology and Otology (University of London), at the Institute of Laryngology, Gray's Inn Road, WC1, since 1963; Surgeon, Royal National Throat, Nose and Ear Hospital; Civilian Consultant on ENT to RN; *b* 9 March 1925; *s* of Frederick William Rees Harrison, OBE, JP, and Florence, *d* of Robert Norris, Portsmouth, Hants; *m* 1949, Audrey, *o d* of Percival Clubb, Penarth, Glam.; two *d. Educ:* Newport High Sch., Mon.; Guy's Hosp. MD (London) 1960; MS (London) 1959; FRCS 1955. Ho. Surg., Guy's Hosp. and Royal Gwent Hospital, Newport; Surg. Registrar, Shrewsbury Eye and Ear Hosp.; Senior Registrar, Throat and Ear Dept, Guy's Hosp.; University Reader in Laryngology, Inst. of Laryngol. and Otol. Hunterian Prof., RCS, 1962; Chevalier Jackson Lectr, 1964; Erasmus Wilson Demonstrator, RCS, 1971; Yearsley Lectr, 1972; Wilde Lectr, 1972; Litchfield Lectr, 1973; Semon Lectr, 1974; Colles Lectr, RCSI, 1977. Mem. of Court of Examiners, RCS; Examr, NUI; External Examr, Univs of Melbourne, Sydney, Manchester, Liverpool, Glasgow and Cambridge; Fellow Medical Soc. London; Scientific Fellow, Royal Zoological Soc. of London; FRSM (Vice-Pres., Sect. of Laryngology; Mem. Council, Sect. of Oncology); Mem. BMA; Mem. Council: Brit. Assoc. of Otolaryngologists; Brit. Assoc. of Head and Neck Oncologists (Sec.); Former Chairman: Special Adv. Cttee on Human Communication; Bd Postgrad. Med. Studies, London Univ.; Chm., Centennial Conf., Laryngeal Cancer, 1974; Member: Council, Collegium Oto-Rhino-Laryngologium; Anatomical Soc. of Great Britain; Res. Cttee, Nat. Deaf Children's Soc. (Dep. Chm.); Cttee of Management, Institute of Cancer Research; Internat. Cttee for Cancer of Larynx; Chm., NE Thames Region Postgrad. Cttee. Editorial Board: Acta Otolaryngologica; Practica Oto-Rhino-Laryngologica; Annals of Oto-Rhino-Laryngology; Excerpta Medica (Sect. II); Otolaryngological Digest. Hon. Fellow: Acad. ENT, America, 1976; Triol. Soc., USA, 1977; Hon. FRACS, 1977. Hon. Member: NZ ENT Soc.; Jamaican ENT Soc.; Otolaryngological Soc., Australia; For. Mem., Internat. Broncho-œsophagological Soc.; Corresp. Member: Amer. Head and Neck Soc.; Soc. Française d'Otorhinolaryngologie; Otolaryngological Soc., Denmark; Amer. Acad. of Facial Plastic Reconstr. Surgery; Pacific Coast Oto-Ophthalmological Soc.; Amer. Laryngological Soc.; Yeoman, Soc. of Apothecaries. *Publications:* articles on familial hæmorrhagic telangiectases, meatal oseomata, cancer chemotherapy, head and neck surgery in learned jls; chapters in Text Books on Ent. and Gen. Surgery. *Recreations:* radio-controlled models, heraldry. *Address:* Institute of Laryngology and Otology, Gray's Inn Road, WC1. *T:* 01-837 8855; Springfield, Fisher's Farm, Horley, Surrey. *T:* Horley 4307.

HARRISON, Douglas Creese, DSc London, PhD Cantab, ARIC; Professor of Biochemistry, Queen's University, Belfast, 1935-67; *b* 29 April, 1901; *s* of Lovell and Lillian E. Harrison, MBE, JP; *m* 1926, Sylva Thurlow, MA, PhD, Philadelphia, USA; one *s. Educ:* Highgate Sch.; King's Coll., London; Emmanuel Coll., Cambridge. Keddey Fletcher-Warr Research Studentship, 1925-28; Lecturer at Sheffield Univ., 1926-35. *Publications:* various papers in the Biochemical Journal, Proc. Royal Society, Lancet, etc. *Address:* 4 Broomhill Park Central, Belfast. *T:* Belfast 665685.

HARRISON, Maj.-Gen. Eric George William Warde, CB 1945; CBE 1943; MC 1915; MA (hon.) Oxford; *b* 23 March 1893; *s* of Major W. C. Warde Harrison, Indian Army; *m* 1961, Mrs Roza M. Stevenson, *widow* of J. B. Stevenson (she *d* 1967). *Educ:* Royal Military Academy, Woolwich. Commissioned Royal Artillery, 1913; European War, France and Belgium, 1914-19, GSOII 58 Div. and III Corps (despatches four times, MC, Crown of Italy, Bt Major); Staff Coll. Camberley, 1925-26;

GSOII Lahore District, India, 1928-32; Major, 1932; Bt Lieut-Col 1934; Commanding Oxford Univ. OTC 1934-38; Lieut-Col 1939; Col 1939. War of 1939-45, CRA 12 Div., BRA Northern Ireland, CCRA 9 Corps, MGRA AFHQ, Comdr Surrey and Sussex District. War Service North Africa and Italy, 1943-45 (despatches, CBE, CB); Temp. Maj.-Gen. 1944; ADC to the King, 1945-46; retired pay, 1946. JP 1951, DL 1955, High Sheriff 1958, Cornwall. Chm. St Lawrence's Hospital Management Cttee, 1952-66. *Publications:* Riding, 1949; To Own a Dog, 1951. *Recreations:* shooting, fishing, gardening, painting; Rugby football Mother Country XV 1919, Army 1920; Athletics, represented England in 120 yds Hurdles, 1914 and 1920, Olympic Games, 1924; Master RA Harriers, 1920-24, Staff Coll. Drag 1925-26, Lahore Hounds 1928-31, South Oxon Foxhounds, 1935-38, North Cornwall Foxhounds, 1940-48. *Address:* Swallowfield Park, near Reading, Berks. *Club:* Army and Navy.

HARRISON, Ernest, CMG 1935; BSc; *b* 30 July 1886; *s* of Thomas Harrison and Louise Goodwin; *m* 1st, 1911, Annie Gladys Anyan (*d* 1920); 2nd, 1925, Josephine ffolliott Highett (*d* 1957); two *s* (and two killed on active service); 3rd, Helen Day Price. *Educ:* Holmes Chapel; Edinburgh Univ.; Ames, Iowa, USA. Lectr, Grootfontein Sch. of Agriculture, Cape Colony, 1910-12; Principal, Sch. of Agriculture, Cedara, Natal, 1913-17; Land Manager, S African Townships, Mining and Finance Corp., 1918-20; Dep. Dir of Agriculture, Kenya Colony, 1921-30; Dir of Agriculture, Tanganyika, 1930-37; Prof. of Agriculture, Imperial Coll. of Tropical Agriculture, Trinidad, BWI, 1938-43, 1943-47. Agricultural Consultant, Lima, Peru. *Address:* 876 Somenos Street, Victoria, BC, Canada.

HARRISON, Sir Francis Alexander Lyle, (Sir Frank Harrison), Kt 1974; MBE 1943; QC (NI); DL; President, Lands Tribunal for Northern Ireland, since 1964; *b* 19 March 1910; *s* of Rev. Alexander Lyle Harrison and Mary Luise (*née* Henderson), Rostrevor, Co. Down; *m* 1940, Norah Patricia (*née* Rea); two *d*. *Educ:* Campbell Coll., Belfast; Trinity Coll., Dublin. BA (Moderator in Legal Sci.), LLB (Hons). Called to Bar of NI, 1937. Served War: commissioned Gen. List, Oct. 1939; ADC to GOC, NI, 1939-40; Major, Dep. Asst Adjt-Gen., HQ, NI, 1941-45 (MBE). Apptd to determine Industrial Assurance disputes in NI, 1946-62; Counsel to Attorney-Gen., NI, 1946-48; KC 1948. Legal Adviser to Min. of Home Affairs, 1949-64; Sen. Crown Prosecutor, Co. Fermanagh, 1948-54; subseq. for Counties Tyrone, Londonderry and Antrim, 1954-64; Chm., Mental Health Review Tribunal, 1948-64; Counsel to the Speakers of House of Commons and Senate of NI, 1953-64; Mem. Statute Law Cttee, NI, 1953-64; Chm., Advisory Cttee under Civil Authorities Special Powers Acts (NI) 1922-61, 1957-62; Bencher, Inn of Court of NI, 1961; Chm., Shaftesbury Sq. Hosp. Management Cttee, 1964-73; Chm., Glendhu Children's Hostel, 1968-; Founder Mem., NI Assoc. of Mental Health, 1959-73; Mem. Exec. Cttee of Assoc. of Hosp. Management Cttees, NI, 1971-73; Boundary Comr under Local Govt (Boundaries) Act (NI), 1971. DL Co. Down, 1973. *Publications:* Report of Working Party on Drug Dependence, 1968; Recommendations as to Local Government Boundaries and Wards in Northern Ireland, 1972. *Recreations:* hybridisation of narcissi, country pursuits, social service. *Address:* Ballydorn Hill, Killinchy, Newtownards, Co. Down, Northern Ireland. *T:* Killinchy 541 250. *Clubs:* Ulster (Belfast); Strangford Lough Yacht.

HARRISON, Francis Anthony Kitchener; Assistant Director, Civil Service Selection Board, since 1967; *b* 28 Aug. 1914; *s* of late Fred Harrison, JP, and Mrs M. M. Harrison (*née* Mitchell); *m* 1955, Sheila Noëlle, *d* of late Lt-Col N. D. Stevenson and of Lady Nye; three *s* one *d*. *Educ:* Winchester; New Coll., Oxford. Asst Principal, India Office, Nov. 1937; 1st Sec., UK High Commn, New Delhi, 1949-51; Commonwealth Relations Office, 1951-56; Asst Sec., 1954; Dep. High Comr for the UK at Peshawar, 1956-59; Asst Sec., CRO, 1959-61; British Dep. High Comr, New Zealand, 1961-64; Asst Secretary: Cabinet Office, 1965-67. *Recreations:* golf, gardening. *Address:* Lea Farm, Bramley, near Guildford, Surrey. *T:* Bramley 3138. *Club:* Royal Commonwealth Society.

HARRISON, Francis Laurence Theodore G.; *see* Graham-Harrison.

HARRISON, Prof. Francis Llewelyn, FBA 1965; Professor of Ethnomusicology, University of Amsterdam, 1970-76, now Emeritus; *b* Dublin, 29 Sept. 1905; *s* of Alfred Francis and Florence May Harrison; *m* 1966, Joan Rimmer; (two *d* of a former marriage). *Educ:* St Patrick's Cathedral Gram. Sch., Dublin; Mountjoy Sch., Dublin; Trinity Coll., Dublin; Oxford Univ. MusB Dublin, 1926; MusD Dublin, 1929; MA, DMus Oxon, 1952; Hon. DLitt Queen's (Canada), 1974. Organist, St

Canice's Cath., Kilkenny, 1927; Prof. of Music: Queen's Univ., Kingston, Ontario, 1935; Colgate Univ., 1946; Washington Univ., St Louis, 1947; Lectr in Music, 1952, Sen. Lectr, 1956, Reader in History of Music, 1962-70, University of Oxford; Senior Research Fellow, Jesus Coll., 1965-70. Visiting Professor of Musicology: Yale Univ., 1958-59; Utrecht Univ., 1976-77; Vis. Prof. of Music, Princeton Univ., 1961, 1968-69; Vis. Mem., Inst. for Advanced Study, Princeton, 1957; Fellow of Center for Advanced Study in the Behavioral Sciences, Stanford, Calif, 1965-66. General Editor: Early English Church Music, 1961-73; Polyphonic Music of the Fourteenth Century, 1963-73. *Publications:* The Eton Choirbook (3 vols), 1956-61; Music in Medieval Britain, 1958; Collins Music Encyclopaedia (with J. A. Westrup), 1956; Musicology (with M. Hood and C. V. Palisca), 1963; European Musical Instruments (with J. Rimmer), 1964; Polyphonic Music of the Fourteenth Century, vol. V (Motets of French Provenance), 1969; Time, Place and Music, 1974; (with E. J. Dobson) Medieval English Songs, 1977; edns of music by William Mundy, John Sheppard and others; contribs to New Oxford History of Music, and to musical jls, etc. *Recreations:* travel, eating, model railways. *Address:* Keisersgracht 73, Amsterdam, Netherlands. *T:* (020) 25 48 32.

HARRISON, Fred Brian, FCA; Member, National Coal Board, since 1976; *b* 6 March 1927; *s* of Fred Harrison and Annie Harrison; *m* 1950, Margaret Owen; two *s*. *Educ:* Burnley Grammar Sch. FCA 1960. East Midlands Div., National Coal Board: Divnl Internal Auditor, 1953-55; Financial Accountant, No 3 Area, 1955-57, Cost Accountant, 1957-62; Chief Accountant, No 1 Area, 1962-67; Chief Accountant, N Derbyshire Area, NCB, 1967-68; Finance Dir, Coal Products Div., NCB, 1968-71, Dep. Man. Dir, 1971-73; Dep. Chief Exec., NCB (Coal Products) Ltd, 1973-76. *Recreations:* music, theatre. *Address:* 11 Birch Tree Walk, Watford, Herts. *T:* Watford 31967.

HARRISON, Sir Geoffrey (Wedgwood), GCMG 1968 (KCMG 1955; CMG 1949); KCVO 1961; HM Diplomatic Service, retired; *b* Southsea, 18 July 1908; *s* of late Lieut-Comdr Thomas Edmund Harrison, Royal Navy, and Maud, *d* of Percy Godman; *m* 1936, Amy Katharine, *d* of late Rt Hon. Sir R. H. Clive, PC, GCMG; three *s* one *d*. *Educ:* Winchester; King's Coll., Cambridge. Entered FO, 1932; served HM Embassy, Tokyo, 1935-37; HM Embassy, Berlin, 1937-39; Private Sec. to Parly Under-Sec., FO, 1939-41; First Sec., FO, 1941-45; Counsellor, HM Embassy, Brussels, 1945-47; Brit. Minister in Moscow, 1947-49; Head of Northern Dept, FO, 1949-51; Asst Under-Sec., FO, 1951-56; Ambassador: to Brazil, 1956-58; to Persia, 1958-63; Dep. Under-Sec. of State, FO, 1963-65; Ambassador to the USSR, 1965-68. Mem., West Sussex CC, 1970-77. Order of Homayoun (1st Class), 1959. *Recreations:* music, golf, gardening. *Address:* Timbers, Plummers Plain, near Horsham, Sussex. *T:* Handcross 400266; 6 Ormonde Gate, SW3.

HARRISON, George Anthony; solicitor; Chief Executive, Greater Manchester Council, since 1976; *b* 20 Aug. 1930; *s* of John and Agnes Catherine Harrison; *m* 1957, Jane Parry; two *s* one *d*. *Educ:* Roundhay Sch., Leeds; Trinity Coll., Cambridge (MA, LLB). Asst Solicitor, Wolverhampton, 1955-58; ICI, 1958-59; Dep. Town Clerk, Wallasey and Bolton, 1962-65; Town Clerk and Clerk of the Peace, Bolton, 1965-69; Dir-Gen., Greater Manchester Transport Exec., 1969-76. *Recreations:* music, squash, sailing. *Address:* 2 Clarebank, Chorley New Road, Bolton. *T:* Bolton 43545.

HARRISON, George Bagshawe, MA Cantab; PhD London; Emeritus Professor of English, University of Michigan, 1964 (Professor, 1949-64); *b* 14 July 1894; *s* of late Walter Harrison, Brighton; *m* 1919, Dorothy Agnes, *o d* of late Rev. Thomas Barker; one *d* (three *s* decd). *Educ:* Brighton Coll.; Queens' Coll., Cambridge (Classical Exhibitioner); 1st Class English Tripos, 1920. Commnd to 5th Bn The Queen's Royal Regt, and served in India and Mesopotamia, 1914-19; Staff Capt. 42nd Indian Infantry Brigade (despatches); War of 1939-45, RASC and Intelligence Corps, 1940-43. Asst Master, Felsted Sch., 1920-22; Senior Lecturer in English, St Paul's Training Coll., Cheltenham, 1922-24; Asst Lecturer in English Literature, King's Coll., University of London, 1924-27; Lecturer, 1927-29; Frederic Ives Carpenter Visiting Prof. of English, University of Chicago, 1929; Reader in English Literature, University of London, 1929-43; Head of English Dept and Prof. of English, Queen's Univ., Kingston, Ont., Canada, 1943-49; lectured at Sorbonne, 1933, in Holland, 1940; Alexander Lecturer, University of Toronto, Canada, 1947. Mem., Internat. Commn on English in the Liturgy. Hon. LittD Villanova, 1960, Holy Cross, 1961; Marquette, 1963; Hon. LLD Assumption, 1962. Campion Award for long and eminent service in cause of Christian literature, 1970. *Publications:* Shakespeare: the Man and his Stage (with E. A. G. Lamborn), 1923; Shakespeare's Fellows, 1923; John Bunyan: a Study in Personality, 1928; England in Shakespeare's Day; An Elizabethan Journal, 1591-94, 1928; A Second Elizabethan Journal 1595-98, 1931; A Last Elizabethan Journal, 1599-1603, 1933; Shakespeare at Work, 1933; The Life and Death of Robert Devereux, Earl of Essex, 1937; The Day before Yesterday (a Journal of 1936), 1938; Elizabethan Plays and Players, 1940; A Jacobean Journal, 1603-1606, 1941; A Second Jacobean Journal, 1607-1610, 1950; Shakespeare's Tragedies, 1951; Profession of English, 1962; The Fires of Arcadia, 1965, etc.; Editor: The Bodley Head Quartos, 1922-26; The New Readers' Shakespeare (with F. H. Pritchard); The Pilgrim's Progress and Mr Badman; The Church Book of Bunyan Meeting, 1928; Breton's Melancholike Humours, 1929; The Trial of the Lancaster Witches, 1612, 1929; The Earl of Northumberland's Advice to his son; translated and edited The Journal of De Maisse (with R. A. Jones), 1931; A Companion to Shakespeare Studies (with Harley Granville-Barker), 1934; The Letters of Queen Elizabeth, 1935; The Penguin Shakespeares, 1937-59; Contributor to The Road to Damascus, 1949; etc. *Address:* 36A Manson Street, Palmerston North, New Zealand. *T:* 75-895.

HARRISON, George Michael Antony; Chief Education Officer, City of Sheffield, since 1967; *b* 7 April 1925; *s* of George and Kathleen Harrison; *m* 1951, Pauline (*née* Roberts); two *s* one *d*. *Educ:* Manchester Grammar Sch.; Brasenose Coll., Oxford. MA (LitHum); DipEd. Military service, demobilised W/S Lieut, Parachute Regt, 1947. Asst Master, Bedford Modern Sch., 1951-53; Admin. Asst, W Riding CC, Education Dept, 1953-55; Asst Educn Officer, Cumberland CC Educn Dept, 1955-64; Dep. Educn Officer, Sheffield, 1965-67. *Recreations:* sailing, gardening, music. *Address:* Audrey Cottage, 83 Union Road, Sheffield S11 9EH. *T:* Sheffield 53783. *Club:* Royal Over-Seas League.

HARRISON, Sir Guy; see Harrison, Sir B. G.

HARRISON, Sir Harwood; see Harrison, Sir James Harwood.

HARRISON, Rear-Adm. Hubert Southwood, CBE 1951; DSC 1941; *b* Glasgow, 7 Aug. 1898; *s* of T. S. Harrison; *m* 1935, Beth Rowson Saynor (*d* 1962). *Educ:* Trinity Coll., Glenalmond. Cadet, RN, 1916; Midshipman, 1917; Sub-Lieut, 1918; Lieut (E), 1920; Lieut-Comdr (E), 1927; Comdr (E), 1930; Capt. (E), 1941; Rear-Adm. (E), 1948; Asst Dir of Dockyards, Admiralty, 1946-52; retired, 1952. *Recreations:* golf, sailing, fishing. *Address:* House in the Wood, Budock Vean, Falmouth. *T:* Mawnan Smith 337.

HARRISON, Maj.-Gen. Ian Stewart, CB 1970; Director-General, British Food Export Council, since 1970; *b* 25 May 1919; *s* of Leslie George Harrison and Evelyn Simpson Christie; *m* 1942, Winifred Raikes Stavert; one *s* one *d*. *Educ:* St Albans Sch. Commissioned, Royal Marines, 1937; service at sea, in Norway, Middle East, Sicily, BAOR, 1939-45; Staff Coll., Camberley (student), 1948; HQ 3rd Commando Bde, 1949-51 (despatches); Staff of Comdt-Gen., RM, 1951-52; Staff Coll., Camberley (Directing Staff), 1953-55; Commandant, RM Signal Sch., 1956-58; Joint Services Staff Coll. (Student), 1958; CO 40 Commando, RM, 1959-61; Dir, Royal Marines Reserves, 1962; Staff of Comdt-Gen., RM, 1963-64; Joint Warfare Estabt, 1965-67; British Defence Staff, Washington, DC, 1967-68; Chief of Staff to Comdt-Gen., RM, 1968-70, retired. ADC to HM the Queen, 1967-68. Mem. Bd, World Trade Centre Assoc. MBIM. *Recreations:* sailing, real tennis, lawn tennis, golf. *Address:* Manor Cottage, Runcton, Chichester, W Sussex. *T:* Chichester 85480. *Clubs:* MCC; Royal Yacht Squadron, Royal Naval Sailing Association, Royal Marines Sailing, Itchenor Sailing.

HARRISON, Sir (James) Harwood, 1st Bt *cr* 1961, of Bugbrooke; TD (2 bars) 1947; MA; MP (C) Eye Division of Suffolk since 1951; *b* 6 June 1907; *e s* of late Rev. E. W. Harrison, MA, Bugbrooke, Northampton; *m* 1932, Peggy Alberta Mary, *d* of late Lieut-Col V. D. Stenhouse, TD, JP, Minehead; one *s* one *d*. *Educ:* Northampton Grammar Sch.; Trinity Coll., Oxford. Hons degree (jurisprudence), 1928; MA 1946. Mem. Ipswich County Borough Council, 1935-46; Chm. Mental Hosp., 1938. Commissioned 4th Bn The Suffolk Regt, TA, 1935; Capt. 1939; Major 1940; captured (Singapore), 1942; on Burma Railway, 1943; Lieut-Col comdg 4th Suffolks, 1947; Bt-Col 1951; TARO 1951-65. Mil. Mem. Suffolk T & AFA, 1951-. Contested Eye Div. of Suffolk, 1950. Presented and sponsored Private Member's Bills: The Road Transport Lighting (Rear Lights) Act, 1953; The Road Traffic Act, 1964. PPS to Mr Harold Macmillan, Minister of Housing and Local Govt, 1953-54; Asst Whip, 1954-56; a Lord Commissioner of the Treasury, 1956-59; Comptroller of HM Household, 1959-61.

Pres., Nat. Union of Conservative and Unionist Assocs Eastern Area, 1963-66 (Chm. 1956-59, Vice-Chm. 1953-56); Chairman: Unionist Club, 1966-; Defence and External Affairs Sub-Cttee of Expenditure Cttee, 1971-; Brit. Br., IPU, 1973-74 (Vice-Chm., 1970; Treas., 1968). Pres. Ipswich and District Far East POW Fellowship, 1953. Chm., Cap Estate (St Lucia) Ltd; Dir of Chalwyns Ltd and other companies. Has lectured extensively in America, Europe and Africa. Patron, Lord of Manor and Land-Owner at Bugbrooke. *Recreation:* sailing. *Heir: s* Michael James Harwood Harrison [*b* 28 March, 1936; *m* 1967, Rosamund Louise, *d* of Edward Clive, Bishops Waltham; two *d*]. *Address:* Little Manor, Hasketon, Woodbridge, Suffolk. *T:* Woodbridge 242; 17 Tufton Court, Tufton Street, SW1. *T:* 01-799 6619. *Clubs:* Carlton, Crockford's, Pratt's; House of Commons Yacht (Commodore, 1969-70).

HARRISON, Jessel Anidjah; Chairman, Slimma Group Holdings Ltd, since 1973; *b* 28 May 1923; *s* of Samuel Harrison and Esta (*née* Romain); *m* 1st, 1943, Irene (*née* Olsberg) (marr. diss. 1956); one *s* one *d* ; 2nd, 1961, Doreen Leigh. *Educ:* Vernon House Preparatory Sch.; Brondesbury Coll.; Macauley Coll., Cuckfield, Sussex. Chairman: Slimma Ltd, 1964; Slimma (Wales) Ltd, 1971; Dir, Tootals Clothing Div. Chm., Clothing Export Council of Great Britain, 1973; Mem., British Overseas Trade Group for Israel. *Recreations:* golf, walking. *Address:* Springfields, 6 Madehurst Close, East Preston, Angmering, Sussex BN16 2TH. *T:* Rustington 5084. *Club:* Royal Automobile.

HARRISON, Surgeon Rear-Adm. John Albert Bews, QHP, FRCR; Dean of Naval Medicine and Medical Officer in charge of Institute of Naval Medicine, since 1977; *b* 20 May 1921; *s* of late Albert William Harrison and Lilian Eda Bews, Dover, Kent; *m* 1943, Jane (*née* Harris); two *s*. *Educ:* Queens' Coll., Cambridge; St Bartholomew's Hosp. MRCS, LRCP; DMRD; FRCR. After house appt, joined RNVR, 1947; served: HMS Sparrow, Amer. WI stn, 1950; RN Hosp., Plymouth, 1951; HMS Ganges, 1953; Admiralty Med. Bd and St Bartholomew's Hosp., 1955; Cons. Radiologist, RN Hosps, Hong Kong, Chatham, Malta, and Haslar, 1967; Adviser in Radiol. to Med. Dir Gen. (Naval), 1975; Dep. Med. Dir Gen., 1977. Surg. Comdr 1962; Surg. Captain 1970; Surg. Cdre 1975; Surg. Rear-Adm. 1977. Fellow: RSM; MedSocLond. OStJ 1975. QHP 1976. *Publications:* Hyperbaric Osteonecrosis et al, 1975; articles in med. press on sarcoidosis, tomography, middle ear disease, and dysbaric osteonecrosis. *Recreations:* fishing, cricket, countryman. *Address:* Alexandra Cottage, Swanmore, Hants SO3 2PB. *Club:* Naval and Military.

HARRISON, John Audley, CB 1976; a Director, Ministry of Defence, 1969-76; *b* 13 May 1917; *s* of John Samuel Harrison and Florence Rose (*née* Samways); *m* 1940, Dorothea Pearl (*née* West); two *s* one *d*. *Educ:* Caterham Sch., Surrey. Prudential Assce Co. Ltd, 1935-39. London Rifle Bde (TA), 1939-40; York and Lancaster Regt (emergency commn), 1940-46. Attached War Office (later MoD), 1946-76, retd, May 1976. *Recreations:* golf, bridge. *Address:* 23 Benfield Way, Portslade, Sussex. *T:* Brighton 418302. *Club:* Dyke Golf (Brighton).

HARRISON, John H.; see Heslop-Harrison.

HARRISON, Maj.-Gen. John Martin Donald W.; see Ward-Harrison.

HARRISON, Kathleen, (Mrs J. H. Back); leading character actress, stage and films; *d* of Arthur Harrison, MICE, Civil Engineer, and Alice Harrison; *m* 1916, John Henry Back; two *s* one *d*. *Educ:* Clapham High Sch. Trained at RADA. *Notable plays include:* Badger's Green, Prince of Wales Theatre, 1930; Night Must Fall, Duchess, 1935; The Corn is Green, Duchess, 1938; Flare Path, Apollo, 1942; The Winslow Boy, Lyric, 1946; All for Mary, Duke of York's, 1955; Nude with Violin, Globe, 1956; How Say You?, Aldwych, 1959; Watch it, Sailor!, Aldwych, 1960; The Chances, Chichester Festival, 1962; Norman, Duchess, 1963; title role in Goodnight Mrs Puffin, New Theatre, Bromley; Harvey, Richmond Theatre, 1971; She Stoops to Conquer, Young Vic, 1972; toured in All for Mary and Goodnight Mrs Puffin, 1970. *Films include:* In Which We Serve; The Huggett films; Alive and Kicking; The Winslow Boy; Bank Holiday; Holiday Camp; Barabbas; West 11; Scrooge. *TV includes:* Martin Chuzzlewit serial (Betsy Prig); title role in Mrs Thursday series; Waters of the Moon; The Coffee Lace; Spring and Autumn, 1973; The Defence, in Shades of Greene, 1975; Mrs Boffin, in Our Mutual Friend, 1976. *Address:* c/o International Creative Agency, Management, 22 Grafton Street, W1. *T:* 01-629 8080.

HARRISON, Kenneth Cecil, MBE 1945; FLA; City Librarian, Westminster, since 1961; *b* 29 April 1915; *s* of Thomas and Annie Harrison; *m* 1941, Doris Taylor; two *s*. *Educ:* Grammar Sch., Hyde. Asst, Hyde Public Library, 1931-36; Branch Librarian, Coulsdon and Purley Public Libraries, 1936-39; Borough Librarian: Hyde, 1939-47; Hove (also Curator), 1947-50; Eastbourne, 1950-58; Hendon, 1958-61. HM Forces, 1940-46; Commnd RMC Sandhurst, 1942; served with E Yorks Regt in Middle East, Sicily and NW Europe (wounded, 1944; Major 1944-46). President: Library Assoc., 1973; Commonwealth Library Assoc., 1972-75; Vice-Pres., Internat. Assoc. Metropolitan Libraries; Member: Central Music Library Council; Library Assoc. Council; MCC Arts and Library Cttee; British Council Libraries Advisory Panel; Chm. Jt Organising Cttee for Nat. Library Week, 1964-69. Hon. Sec., Westminster Arts Council, 1965-. British Council Consultant to Sri Lanka, 1974. Commonwealth Foundn Scholar, E and Central Africa, 1975. Has lectured on librarianship at European, Asian, US, and Brit. Univs and Library schools; C. C. Williamson Meml Lectr, Nashville, Tenn, 1969. Governor, Paddington Adult Educn Inst. Governor, Westminster College. Editor, The Library World, 1961-71. Knight, First Class, Order of the Lion (Finland), 1976. *Publications:* First Steps in Librarianship, 1950; Libraries in Scandinavia, 1961; The Library and the Community, 1963; Public Libraries Today, 1963; Facts at your Fingertips, 1964; British Public Library Buildings (with S. G. Berriman), 1966; Libraries in Britain, 1968; Public Relations for Librarians, 1973; (ed) Prospects for British Librarianship, 1976; contribs to many British and foreign jls. *Recreations:* reading, writing, travel, cricket, crosswords. *Address:* 50 West Hill Way, N20 8QS. *T:* 01-445 1298. *Clubs:* Royal Commonwealth Society, MCC.

HARRISON, Laurence, CMG 1952, retired; *b* 3 Oct. 1897; *s* of late George Henry Harrison; *m* 1st, 1923, Nellie Florence (Serving Sister of Order of St John; *d* 1963); one *d*; 2nd, 1969, Jenny Margaret Wallace Pritchard (*née* Duncan), Sandown, Johannesburg. *Educ:* St Dunstan's Coll.; Strand Sch. Served BEF France (RE), 1916-19. Entered Min. of Pensions, 1919; transf. to Dept of Overseas Trade, 1930; Asst Trade Commissioner, Johannesburg, 1937, Trade Commissioner (Grade II), 1945, Trade Commissioner (Grade I), New Delhi, 1947, Johannesburg, 1953-57. *Recreations:* horticulture, field natural history. *Address:* 3 Victoria Court, Barberton, 1300 East Transvaal, South Africa.

HARRISON, Lloyd Adnitt, CBE 1977; Chief Executive Officer, Greater Nottingham Co-operative Society Ltd, since 1969; *b* 15 March 1911; *s* of late Joseph Adnitt Harrison and Frances Louisa Harrison; *m* 1954, Mabel Pauline Hooley. *Educ:* Beeston Higher Sch., Notts; Co-operative Coll. Managing Sec., Nottingham Co-op. Soc. Ltd, 1965-69, and Admin. Officer, 1956-65. Director: Co-operative Insurance Soc. Ltd, 1973-; Co-operative Wholesale Soc. Ltd, 1968- (Chm., CWS, 1973-76). FBIM. *Recreations:* music, reading, walking, gardening, local radio (Chm. Local Radio Council, Nottingham). *Address:* 63 Parkside, Wollaton, Nottingham NG8 2NQ. *T:* Nottingham 256452.

HARRISON, Mrs Molly, MBE 1967; Curator, Geffrye Museum, 1941-69; *b* Stevenage, 1909; *d* of late Ethel and late Ernest Charles Hodgett; *m* 1940, Gordon Frederick Harrison; three *d*. *Educ:* Friends Sch., Saffron Walden; Convent in Belgium; Sorbonne. Teaching in various Schs, 1934-39; Asst to Curator, Geffrye Museum, 1939-41. FMA 1952; Member: Council Museums Assoc., 1953-56; Council of Industrial Design, 1958-61; Cttee of Management, Society of Authors, 1967. Lectr on varied educational topics. FRSA 1968. Editor, Local Search Series, 1969-. *Publications:* Museum Adventure, 1950; Picture Source Books for Social History, 1951, 1953, 1955, 1957, 1958, 1960 and 1966; Furniture 1953; Learning out of School, 1954; Food, 1954; Homes, 1960; Children in History, 1958, 1959, 1960, 1961; Your Book of Furniture, 1960; Shops and Shopping, 1963; How They Lived, 1963; Changing Museums, 1967; Hairstyles and Hairdressing, 1968; The English Home, 1969; People and Furniture, 1971; The Kitchen in History, 1972; Homes, 1973; Museums and Galleries, 1973; On Location: Museums, 1974; People and Shopping, 1975; Home Inventions, 1975; Homes in Britain, 1975; numerous articles and reviews. *Recreations:* writing, gardening. *Address:* The Coach House, Horse Leas, Bradfield, Berks. *T:* Bradfield 437.

HARRISON, Patrick Kennard; Secretary, Royal Institute of British Architects, since 1968; *b* 8 July 1928; *e s* of late Richard Harrison and Sheila Griffin; *m* 1955, Mary Wilson, *y d* of late Captain G. C. C. Damant, CBE, RN; one *d*. *Educ:* Lord Williams's Sch., Thame; Downing Coll., Cambridge (Exhbnr). Asst Principal, Dept of Health for Scotland, 1953; Private Sec. to Deptl Sec. and to Parly Secs, Scottish Office, 1958-60;

Principal, Scottish Develt Dept and Regional Develt Div., Scottish Office, 1960-68. *Address:* 63 Princess Road, NW1. *T:* 01-722 8508. *Clubs:* Reform; New (Edinburgh).

HARRISON, Rex Carey; Commendatore, Order of Merit of the Republic of Italy, 1967; actor; *b* 5 March 1908; *s* of William Reginald and Edith Carey Harrison; *m* 1st, 1934, Marjorie Noel Collette Thomas; one *s*; 2nd, 1943, Lilli Palmer (marr. diss. 1957); one *s*; 3rd, 1957, Kay Kendall (*d* 1959); 4th, 1962, Rachel Roberts (marr. diss. 1971); 5th, Hon. Elizabeth Rees Harris (marr. diss. 1976), *d* of 1st Baron Ogmore, PC, TD. *Educ:* Birkdale Preparatory Sch.; Liverpool Coll. Made first appearance on the stage at Liverpool Repertory Theatre, 1924; remained until 1927. Toured with Charley's Aunt playing Jack, 1927; also toured at intervals during subsequent years until 1935, and appeared with Cardiff Repertory, and in the West End. First appearance on London stage as Rankin in The Ninth Man, Prince of Wales Theatre, 1931; First appearance on New York stage at Booth Theatre, 1936, as Tubbs Barrow in Sweet Aloes. Played in French Without Tears at Criterion, 1936-37-38, and at Haymarket Theatre, 1939-41, in Design for Living (Leo) and No Time for Comedy (Gaylord Esterbrook). Volunteered RAFVR, 1941, and served till 1944. Released from Forces to make Blithe Spirit (film), and, 1945, Rake's Progress (film). Filmed in Hollywood, 1945-46-47. (Maxwell Anderson's) Anne of the Thousand Days, Schubert Theatre, NY, 1948-49 (Antoinette Perry Award, best actor); in The Cocktail Party, New Theatre, London, 1950; acted in and produced Bell, Book and Candle, Ethel Barrymore Theatre, NY, 1951, and Phœnix Theatre, London, 1954; in Venus Observed, Century Theatre, NY, 1952; directed and played in Love of Four Colonels, Schubert Theatre, NY, 1953; produced Nina, Haymarket Theatre, London, 1955; acted in: My Fair Lady (Henry Higgins), Mark Hellinger Theatre, NY, 1956-57 (Antoinette Perry Award, best actor), and Drury Lane, London, 1958-59; The Fighting Cock, Anta Theatre, NY, 1959; Platonov, Royal Court, 1960 (Evening Standard Award, best actor); August for the People, Edinburgh Festival, 1961, and Royal Court Theatre; The Lionel Touch, Lyric, 1969; Henry IV, Her Majesty's, 1974; Perrichon's Travels, Chichester, 1976; Caesar and Cleopatra, NY, 1977, etc. Began acting in films in 1929. Best known films: Storm in a Teacup, 1936; St Martin's Lane, 1937; Over the Moon, 1938; Night Train to Munich, Major Barbara, 1940-41; Blithe Spirit, 1944; I Live in Grosvenor Square, 1944; The Rake's Progress, 1945; (Hollywood, 1945) Anna and the King of Siam, 1946; The Ghost and Mrs Muir, 1947; The Foxes of Harrow, 1947; (Galsworthy's) Escape (in England), 1948; Unfaithfully Yours (in America), 1948; The Long Dark Hall, 1951; King Richard and the Crusaders, 1954; The Constant Husband, 1955; The Reluctant Debutante, 1958; Midnight Lace, 1960; The Happy Thieves, 1961; Cleopatra (Julius Caesar), 1962; My Fair Lady, 1964 (Academy Award, best actor); The Yellow Rolls Royce, 1965; The Agony and the Ecstacy, 1965; The Honey Pot, 1967; Doctor Dolittle, 1967; A Flea in her Ear, 1967; Staircase, 1968; The Prince and the Pauper, 1976; Man in the Iron Mask, 1977. *Publication:* Rex (autobiog.), 1974. *Recreations:* golf, yachting, fishing. *Address:* Beauchamp, St Jean Cap Ferrat, France. *Clubs:* Beefsteak, Green Room, Garrick; Players' (New York); Travellers' (Paris).

HARRISON, Prof. Richard John, MD, DSc; FRS 1973; Professor of Anatomy, Cambridge University, since 1968; Fellow of Downing College, Cambridge; *b* 8 Oct. 1920; *er s* of Geoffrey Arthur Harrison, MD, and late Theodora Beatrice Mary West; *m* Barbara, *o d* of James and Florence Fuller, Neston, Cheshire. *Educ:* Oundle; Gonville and Caius Coll., Cambridge (Scholar); St Bartholomew's Hosp. Medical Coll. LRCP, MRCS, 1944. House Surgeon, St Bartholomew's Hosp., 1944. MB, BChir, 1944; MA 1946; MD Cantab 1954. Demonstrator in Anatomy, St Bartholomew's Hosp. Medical Coll., 1944; Lectr in Anatomy, Glasgow Univ., 1946, DSc Glasgow 1948; Sen. Lectr, 1947, and Reader in Anatomy, 1950, Charing Cross Hosp. Medical Sch. (Symington Prize for research in Anatomy); Reader in charge of Anatomy Dept, London Hosp. Medical Coll., 1951-54; Prof. of Anatomy, University of London, at London Hosp. Medical Coll., 1954-68; Fullerian Prof. of Physiology, Royal Institution, 1961-67. Chm., Farm Animal Welfare Adv. Cttee, MAFF, 1974-. Pres., European Assoc. for Aquatic Mammals, 1974-76. FZS (Mem. Council, 1974-); FLS. *Publications:* Man the Peculiar Animal, 1958; (with J. E. King) Marine Mammals, 1965; Reproduction and Man, 1967; (with W. Montagna) Man, 2nd edn 1972; Functional Anatomy of Marine Mammals, vol. I, 1972, vol. II, 1974, vol. III, 1977; numerous papers on embryology, comparative and human anatomy. *Recreations:* marine biology, painting, golf. *Address:* The Beeches, 8 Woodlands Road, Great Shelford, Cambs. *T:* Shelford 3287. *Club:* Garrick.

HARRISON, Prof. Richard Martin, FSA; Professor of Archaeology, University of Newcastle upon Tyne, since 1972; *b* 16 May 1935; *s* of George Lawrance Harrison and Doris Waring (*née* Ward); *m* 1959, Elizabeth Anne Harkness Browne; one *s* three *d*. *Educ:* Sherborne Sch.; Lincoln Coll., Oxford (BA Greats 1958, MA 1961). FSA 1965. Scholar 1959, and Fellow 1960, Brit. Inst. of Archaeol., Ankara; Rivoira Scholar, Brit. Sch. at Rome, 1960; Controller of Antiquities, Provincial Govt of Cyrenaica, 1960-61; Lectr in Class. Archaeol., Bryn Mawr Coll., 1961-62; Glanville Res. Student, Lincoln Coll., Oxford, 1962-64; Newcastle upon Tyne University: Lectr in Roman and Romano-British History and Archaeol., 1964-68; Prof. of Roman Hist. and Archaeol., 1968-72; Vis. Fellow, Dumbarton Oaks, 1969. Dir, Excavations at Saraçhane (Istanbul), 1964-. Chm., Northern Soc. for Anatolian Archaeol., 1976. Corresp. Mem., German Archaeol. Inst., 1973. *Publications:* articles on Roman and Byzantine archaeol. in Anatolian Studies, Dumbarton Oaks Papers, Jl of Roman Studies. *Address:* 23 Linden Road, Gosforth, Newcastle upon Tyne NE3 4EY. *T:* Newcastle upon Tyne 850465.

HARRISON, Sir (Robert) Colin, 4th Bt, *cr* 1922; *b* 25 May 1938; *s* of Sir John Fowler Harrison, 2nd Bt, and Kathleen, *yr d* of late Robert Livingston, The Gables, Eaglescliffe, Co. Durham; *S* brother, 1955; *m* 1963, Maureen, *er d* of E. Leonard Chiverton, Garth Corner, Kirkbymoorside, York; one *s* two *d*. *Educ:* St Peter's Coll., Radley; St John's Coll., Cambridge. Commissioned with Fifth Royal Northumberland Fusiliers (National Service), 1957-59. Chm., Young Master Printers Nat. Cttee, 1972-73. *Heir:* *s* John Wyndham Fowler Harrison, *b* 14 Dec. 1972. *Address:* Keld Close, Hutton-le-Hole, York. *T:* Lastingham 329.

HARRISON, Prof. Ronald George; Derby Professor of Anatomy, University of Liverpool, since 1950; *b* 5 April 1921; *s* of James Harrison and Alice Hannah Harrison (*née* Edmondson); *m* 1945; two *s* one *d*; *m* 1966, Dr M. J. Hoey, Southport, Lancs; one *d*. *Educ:* Ulverston Grammar Sch.; Oxford Univ. BA Oxon, 1942; BM, BCh, Oxon 1944; MA Oxon, 1946; DM Oxon, 1949. Demy, Magdalen Coll., Oxford, 1939-42; Pres., OU Scientific Club, 1942. Junior Gynæcological House Surg., Nuffield Dept of Obstetrics and Gynæcology, Oxford, 1943; Gynæc. and Obst. House Surgeonships, Radcliffe Infirmary, Oxford, 1944-45; Demonstrator and Lecturer, Dept of Human Anatomy, Univ. of Oxford, 1945-49. Lectr in Anatomy, Ruskin Sch. of Drawing and Fine Art, 1946-50; Univ. Demonstrator, Dept of Human Anatomy, Univ. of Oxford, 1949-50; Lectr in Anatomy, Pembroke Coll., Oxford, 1950; Vis. Prof. of Egyptology, Univ. of Cairo, 1972. Sometime External Examr: RCS; RCSI; Univs of: Belfast, Birmingham, Glasgow, Leeds, London, Manchester, Oxford, TCD, Khartoum, Haile Sellassie I, Addis Ababa. First Celebrity Lectr, British Acad. Forensic Scis, 1970. BBC TV film, Tutankhamen Post-mortem, 1969; ITV film, Tutankhamen Kinship, 1973. Fellow: Eugenics Soc.; Zoological Soc. of London. Chm., Bd of Governors, Liverpool Coll. of Occupational Therapy, 1968; President: Inst. of Science Technology, 1972-76; Liverpool Univ. Med. Sciences Club, 1954-55. For. Corr. Mem., Royal Belgian Soc. of Obstetrics and Gynæcology, 1964-68. Pres., Rotary Club of Liverpool, 1971 (Vice-Pres., 1970). Kt of the Dannebrog (Denmark), 1977. *Publications:* A Textbook of Human Embryology, 1959, 1963; The Adrenal Circulation, 1960; Sex and Infertility, 1977; Chapters in Cunningham's Textbook of Anatomy, 1964, 1972; contrib. to various medical and scientific journals. Editor, Studies on Fertility, 1954-58. *Recreations:* riding, egyptology. *Address:* The Stables, Fernhill, Upper Brighton, Wallasey, Merseyside. *T:* 051-639 6327.

HARRISON, Theophilus George, OBE 1971; JP; Member, Greater Manchester Council, 1973-77 (Chairman, 1973-1974 and 1974-1975, Deputy Chairman, 1975-76); formerly General Secretary, National Association of Powerloom Overlookers; *b* 30 Jan. 1907; *s* of Alfred and Emma Harrison; *m* 1935, Clarissa Plevin; one *s* one *d*. Swinton and Pendlebury Borough Council: Mem., 1941-56; Alderman, 1956-74; Mayor, 1954-55; Chairman: Housing Cttee; Highways and Lighting Cttee; Mem., Div. Planning Cttee; Lancs CC: Mem. Educn Cttee, 1946- (Vice-Chm. 1951-53, Chm. 1953-); Vice-Chairman: Road Safety Cttee; Public Health and Housing Cttee; Chairman: Swinton and Pendlebury Youth Employment Cttee; Youth Adv. Cttee and Youth Centres; Mem., Div. Exec., Educn Cttee; Member: Gen. Council, Lancs and Merseyside Ind. Develt Corp.; N Counties Textile Trades Fedn Central Board; Swinton and Pendlebury Trades Council and Labour Party; Member: Manchester Reg. Hosp. Bd, 1961-; W Manchester HMC, 1957- (Chm. 1963-); Wrightington HMC, 1957-; Salford Community Health Council (Chm., Develt Cttee). Past Chm. or Mem. many other Co. or local organizations and cttees. Former Pres., SE Lancs and Cheshire Accident Prevention Fedn; Dir, RoSPA. JP 1949. *Recreations:* reading, Rugby League football (spectator); much of his political and public activities. *Address:* 271 Rivington Crescent, Bolton Road, Pendlebury, Swinton, Manchester M27 2TQ. *T:* 061-794 1112.

HARRISON, Rt. Hon. Walter, PC 1977; JP; MP (Lab) Wakefield, since 1964; Treasurer of HM Household and Deputy Chief Government Whip, since 1974; *b* 2 Jan. 1921; *s* of Henry and Ada Harrison; *m* 1948, Enid Mary (*née* Coleman); one *s* one *d*. *Educ:* Dewsbury Technical and Art Coll. Electrical Inspector and Electrical Foreman, Electricity Supply Industry, 1937-64. Asst Govt Whip, 1966-68; a Lord Comr of the Treasury, 1968-70; Dep. Chief Opposition Whip, 1970-74. West Riding CC, 1958-64; Alderman, Castleford Borough Council, 1959-66 (Councillor, 1952-59); JP West Riding Yorks, 1962. *Address:* House of Commons, SW1; 1 Milnthorpe Drive, Sandal, Wakefield, W Yorks. *T:* Wakefield 55550.

HARRISON, Prof. Wilfrid; Professor of Politics, University of Warwick, 1964-75, now Emeritus; *b* 30 May 1909; *s* of W. T. and Amy Harrison, Glasgow; *m* 1943, Elizabeth Sara, *d* of Rev. P. J. and Linda Sweeny, Ardagh, Co. Limerick; two *d*. *Educ:* Hyndland Sch., Glasgow; University of Glasgow (MA 1931); Queen's Coll., Oxford (BA 1933, MA 1937). Senior Demy of Magdalen Coll., Oxford, 1933; Lecturer in Politics, Queen's Coll., Oxford, 1935; Fellow of Queen's Coll., 1939-57, Dean, 1940; Prof. of Political Theory and Institutions, University of Liverpool, 1957-64; Pro-Vice-Chancellor, Univ. of Warwick, 1964-70. Temporary Civil Servant, Ministry of Supply, 1940-45. Editor of Political Studies, 1952-63. *Publications:* The Government of Britain, 1948; Conflict and Compromise, 1965; (ed) Bentham's Fragment on Government and Introduction to the Principles of Morals and Legislation, 1948; articles in Chambers's Encyclopædia and various journals. *Recreations:* piano; cooking. *Address:* 73 Coten End, Warwick.

HARRISON-CHURCH, Prof. Ronald James; Professor of Geography, University of London, at London School of Economics, since 1964; *b* 26 July 1915; *s* of late James Walter Church and late Jessie May Church; *m* 1944, Dorothy Violet, *d* of late Robert Colchester Harrison and late Rose Harrison; one *s* one *d*. *Educ:* Westminster City Sch.; Universities of London and Paris. BSc (Econ) 1936, PhD 1943, London. LSE: Asst Lectr, 1944-47; Lectr, 1947-58; Reader, 1958-64. Consultant to UN Economic Commn for Africa on large scale irrigation schemes, 1962. Visiting Professor: University of Wisconsin, 1956; Indiana Univ., 1965; Tel Aviv and Haifa Univs, 1972-73. Has lectured in many other univs in Brazil, US, Canada, West Africa, Belgium, France, Germany, Poland and Sweden. Mem. Council, Royal Afr. Soc.; Back Award, RGS, 1957. *Publications:* Modern Colonization, 1951; West Africa, 1957, 7th edn, 1974; Environment and Policies in West Africa, 1963, 2nd edn 1976; Looking at France, 1970, rev. repr. 1976; (jtly) Africa and the Islands, 1964, 4th edn, 1977; (jtly) An Advanced Geography of Northern and Western Europe, 1967, 2nd edn 1973; contrib to Geograph. Jl, W Africa, etc. *Recreations:* travel, television. *Address:* 8 Mannicotts, Welwyn Garden City, Herts. *T:* Welwyn Garden 23293.

HARRISON-HALL, Michael Kilgour; His Honour Judge Harrison-Hall; a Circuit Judge, since 1972; *b* 20 Dec. 1925; *s* of late Arthur Harrison-Hall, Oxford; *m* 1951, Jessie Margaret, *d* of late Rev. Arthur William Brown, Collingbourne Ducis, Wilts; two *s* two *d*. *Educ:* Rugby; Trinity College, Oxford. Called to Bar, Inner Temple, 1949. Dep. Chm., Warwickshire QS, 1968-71; a Recorder of the Crown Court, 1972. *Address:* Ivy House, Church Street, Barford, Warwick. *T:* Barford 272. *Clubs:* United Oxford & Cambridge University; Leander.

HARROD, Maj.-Gen. Lionel Alexander Digby, OBE 1969; Assistant Chief of Staff (Intelligence), SHAPE, since 1976; *b* 7 Sept. 1924; *s* of Frank Henry Harrod, CBE, and Charlotte Beatrice Emmeline (*née* David); *m* 1952, Anne Priscilla Stormont Gibbs; one *s* two *d*. *Educ:* Bromsgrove Sch. Grenadier Guards, 1944-63; Bde Major, 19 Bde, 1956-58; WO staff, 1959-60; CO 1 Welch, 1966-69; Brit. Def. Staff, Washington, 1969-70; Military Attaché, Baghdad, 1971; Staff HQ UKLF, 1972-73; Chief, Brit. Mission to Gp of Soviet Forces, Germany, 1974-76. Col, Royal Regt of Wales, 1977-. *Recreations:* sport, country life. *Address:* The Grange, Marnhull, Dorset. *T:* Marnhull, 256. *Clubs:* Army and Navy, Special Forces, MCC, Pratt's.

HARROD, Sir Roy (Forbes), Kt 1959; FBA 1947; Hon. Dr (Law), Poitiers; Hon. LLD Aberdeen; Hon. Dr (Laws) University of Pennsylvania; Hon. DLitt: Glasgow; Warwick; Stockholm; Hon. Student of Christ Church, since 1967; Hon. Fellow of Nuffield College; *b* 13 Feb. 1900; *s* of Henry Dawes

Harrod and Frances Marie Desirée Harrod; *m* 1938, Wilhelmine, *e d* of late Capt. F. J. Cresswell, The Norfolk Regt, and Lady Strickland, DBE; two *s*. *Educ:* Westminster Sch. (Scholar); New Coll., Oxford (Scholar), Hon. Fellow 1975; 1st class in Lit. Hum., 1921; 1st class in Modern History, 1922. Enlisted, Sept. 1918; Lecturer at Christ Church, 1922-24; Student, 1924-67; Junior Censor, 1927-29; Senior Censor, 1930-31; Mem. of the Hebdomadal Council of Oxford University, 1929-35; Bodleian Library Commission, 1930-31; University Lecturer in Economics, 1929-37 and 1946-52; Nuffield Reader in Economics, 1952-67. Visiting Professor for one term: Univ. of Pennsylvania, 1964, 1967, 1969, 1970; Univ. of Maryland, 1971; Claremont Grad. Sch., 1972. Pres. of Sect. F of Brit. Assoc., 1938; served under Lord Cherwell on Mr Churchill's private statistical staff in Admiralty, 1940, and in Prime Minister's office, at full time, 1940-42, and subsequently in advisory capacity; also statistical adviser to Admiralty, 1943-45; Vice-Pres., the Royal Economic Society (Mem., Council since 1933); Jt Editor, Economic Journal, 1945-61; Mem. of UN Sub-Commission on Employment and Economic Stability, 1947-50; Fellow of Nuffield Coll., 1938-47, and 1954-58; Hon. Fellow, 1958. Economic Adviser, International Monetary Fund, 1952-53; Sir George Watson Lecturer in American History, 1953; Bernard Harms Prize (Keil), 1966. Mem. Migration Board, Commonwealth Relations Office, 1953-66. Curator of Christ Church Pictures, 1956-64. Exec. Cttee of sponsors of East Anglia Univ., 1959-64; Pres. Royal Economic Soc., 1962-64; Mem., Royal Swedish Acad. of Science. *Publications:* International Economics, 1933 (revised edn, 1957, much revised 5th edn 1975); The Trade Cycle, an Essay, 1936; Britain's Future Population, 1943; A Page of British Folly, 1946; Are These Hardships Necessary? 1947; Towards a Dynamic Economics, 1948; The Life of John Maynard Keynes, 1951; And So It Goes On, 1951; Economic Essays, 1952, rev. edn 1972; The Dollar, 1953; The Foundations of Inductive Logic, 1956, 2nd edn 1974; Policy Against Inflation, 1958; The Prof. (A Personal Memoir of Lord Cherwell), 1959; Topical Comment, 1961; The British Economy, 1963; Reforming the World's Money, 1965; Towards a New Economic Policy, 1967; Dollar-Sterling Collaboration, 1968; Money, 1969; Sociology, Morals and Mystery, 1971; Economic Dynamics, 1973; papers in the Economic Journal, the Quarterly Journal of Economics, Economica, Mind, etc. *Address:* The Old Rectory, Holt, Norfolk. *T:* Holt 2204; 51 Campden Hill Square, W8. *T:* 01-727 8485.

HARROLD, Roy Mealham; Member, Press Council, since 1976; farmer, since 1947; *b* 13 Aug. 1928; *s* of John Frederick Harrold and Ellen Selena Harrold (*née* Mealham); *m* 1968, Barbara Mary, *yr d* of William and Florence Andrews; one *s* one *d*. *Educ:* Stoke Holy Cross Primary Sch.; Bracondale Sch., Norwich. County Chm., Norfolk Fedn of Young Farmers' Clubs, 1956-57; Mem., Nat. Council of Young Farmers, 1957-60; Mem. Council, Royal Norfolk Agric. Assoc., 1972-75. Lay Chm., Norwich East Deanery Synod, 1970-; Mem., Norwich Dio. Synod, 1970-; Mem., Norwich Dio. Bd of Patronage, 1970-. *Recreations:* music, opera, ballet. *Address:* Salamanca Farm, Stoke Holy Cross, Norwich NR15 8QJ. *T:* Framingham Earl 2322.

HARROP, Peter John; Deputy Secretary, Department of the Environment, since 1977; *b* 18 March 1926; *s* of late Gilbert Harrop; *m* 1975, Margaret Joan, *d* of E. U. E. Elliott-Binns, *qv*; one *s*. *Educ:* King Edward VII Sch., Lytham, Lancs; Peterhouse, Cambridge. MA (Hist. Tripos). Served RNVR, 1945-47 (Sub-Lt). Min. of Town and Country Planning, 1949; Min. of Housing and Local Govt, 1951; Dept of the Environment, 1970 (Chm., Yorks and Humberside Economic Planning Bd, and Regional Dir, 1971-73); Under Secretary: HM Treasury, 1973-76; DoE, 1976-77. *Recreations:* sailing, skiing. *Address:* 6 River House, The Terrace, Barnes, SW13. *Clubs:* Hurlingham, United Oxford & Cambridge University; Ski Club of Great Britain; Island Cruising (Salcombe).

HARROP, Maj.-Gen. William Harrington H.; *see* Hulton-Harrop.

HARROWBY, 6th Earl of, *cr* 1809; **Dudley Ryder;** Baron Harrowby, 1776; Viscount Sandon, 1809; Major, late RFA (TAR); *b* 11 Oct. 1892; *e s* of 5th Earl of Harrowby and Hon. Mabel Danvers Smith, DBE (*d* 1956), *y d* of late Rt Hon. W. H. Smith, MP, and 1st Viscountess Hambleden; *S* father 1956; *m* 1922, Lady Helena Blanche Coventry (*d* 1974), *e d* of late Viscount Deerhurst; two *s* one d. *Educ:* Eton; Christ Church, Oxford (BA). Asst Private Sec. to Viscount Milner, Sec. of State for the Colonies, Jan. 1919-Aug. 1920; MP (U) Shrewsbury Division of Salop, Nov. 1922-Nov. 1923, and Oct. 1924-May 1929; Parliamentary Private Sec. to Sir S. Hoare, Sec. of State for

Air, Dec. 1922-Nov. 1923; Alderman LCC, 1932-37, Mem. for Dulwich, 1937-40; served European War, Major RA, 1914-19 (wounded); served War of 1939-45. Col Commandant Staffs Army Cadet Force, 1946-50. DL Staffs, 1925; JP Staffs, 1929; Mem. of Royal Commission on Historical Manuscripts, 1935-66. Hon. DLitt Oxon, 1964. *Publications:* England at Worship; (joint) Geography of Everyday Things. *Heir: s* Viscount Sandon, *qv*. *Address:* Sandon Hall, Stafford; Burnt Norton, Campden, Gloucestershire. *Club:* Travellers'.

HARRY, Ralph Gordon, MChemA, CChem, FRIC; Scientific Adviser to A/S Persano: Medicinal-og Kosmetikfabrik, Farum, Copenhagen, Denmark, since 1973; *b* 25 June 1908; *s* of Jenkin Campbell Harry and Sarah Harrison; *m* 1938, Dorothy Mary Crafter; two *d*. *Educ:* Monkton House Sch., Cardiff; University Coll. of S Wales and Monmouthshire. Asst to Public Analyst, Cardiff (Inst. of Prev. Med.), 1934-37; Chief Chemist, J. Campbell Harry & Co., 1937-41; Manager, Toilet Research Dept, Unilever Ltd, 1941-47; Head, Cosmetic and Toilet Preparations Research Dept, Beecham Research, 1947-49; Chief Experimental Chemist, Maclean Gp of Companies, 1949-53; Chief Research and Develt Chemist and Dep. Chief Chemist (Pharmaceuticals and Cosmetics), Internat. Chemical Co. Ltd (American Home Products Corp.), 1954-73. Devised and published ultra-violet, infra-red, chemical and staining techniques to determine skin penetration; internationally recognised as pioneering recognition of cosmetics by medical profession and govt authorities thoughout world by his publications on post-mortem and living skin and acclaimed by leading dermatologists and cancer specialists. Rep., Gt Britain, Cttee of Honour, 2nd Symposium Internat. des Parfums, Synthetiques et Natural, et de Cosmetologie, Versailles, 1956. Premio Internazionale di Estetica e Cosmetologia 'Guiliana Brambilla', for outstanding contribs to the art and science of cosmetics, 1967. Fellow, RSocMed. Founder Vice-Chm., 1948-50, Hon. Mem., 1973, Soc. of Cosmetic Chemists. Co-patentee, several British, German, Greek, S American and Swiss patents. *Publications:* The Principles and Practice of Modern Cosmetics: Vol. 1, Modern Cosmeticology, NY 1940, Spanish edns 1954, 6th edn London 1973 (reprinted under title Harry's Cosmeticology); Vol. 2, Cosmetic Materials, their origin, uses and dermatological action, 1948, 2nd edn 1963; contrib. Chambers's Encycl., Br. Jl of Dermatology and Syphilis, The Analyst, Chem. & Ind., Paint Manufacture, Mnfg Chemist, Pharm. Jl, Jl of State Medicine (USA). *Recreations:* cine sound films (Double Star awards 16mm); 35mm technical photography (ARPS 1941); Hi-Fi sound. *Address:* 61 Kimberley Road, Penylan, Cardiff CF2 5DL. *T:* Cardiff 495075.

HARSCH, Joseph Close, CBE (Hon.) 1965; writer and broadcaster; columnist Christian Science Monitor, Boston; *b* Toledo, Ohio, 25 May 1905; *s* of Paul Arthur Harsch and Leila Katherine Close; *m* 1932, Anne Elizabeth Wood; three *s*. *Educ:* Williams Coll., Williamstown, Mass, (MA); Corpus Christi Coll., Cambridge (MA). Joined staff Christian Science Monitor, 1929; Washington corresp., then foreign corresp.; Asst Dir, Intergovt Cttee, London, 1939; Monitor Corresp. in Berlin, 1940, SW Pacific area, 1941 and 1942. Began radio broadcasting, 1943; Senior European Correspondent, NBC, 1957-65; Diplomatic Correspondent, NBC, 1965-67; Commentator, American Broadcasting Co., 1967-71; Chief Editorial Writer, Christian Science Monitor, 1971-74. *Publications:* Pattern of Conquest, 1941; The Curtain Isn't Iron, 1950. *Address:* c/o Christian Science Monitor, 1 Norway Street, Boston, Mass 02115, USA; Highland Drive, Jamestown, Rhode Island 02835, USA. *Clubs:* Garrick; Metropolitan, Cosmos (Washington, DC); Century (New York); St Botolph (Boston).

HART, Sir Byrne, Kt 1974; CBE 1968; MC; chartered accountant; *b* Brisbane, 4 Oct. 1895; *s* of F. McD. Hart; *m* 1922, Margaret H., *d* of D. Cramond; two *s*. *Educ:* Southport Sch.; Brisbane Grammar Sch. FCA. Served Wars of 1914-18 and 1939-45. Chairman: Utah Mining Australia Ltd; Wormald Bros (Qld) Pty Ltd; Hornibrook Highway Ltd; Castlemaine Perkins Ltd; Dep. Chm., Primary Mactaggarts Co-operative Assoc. Ltd. *Address:* 14 Gerald Street, Ascot, Brisbane, Queensland 4007. *Clubs:* Queensland, Queensland Turf (Brisbane); Union (Sydney).

HART, F(rancis) Dudley, FRCP; Physician, 1946-74, and Physician-in-charge Rheumatism Unit, Westminster Hospital, SW1, retired 1974; Physician, Hospital of St John and St Elizabeth, London; Consulting Physician: Westminster Hospital; Chelsea Hospital for Women; Consulting Rheumatologist, The Star and Garter Home for Disabled Sailors, Soldiers and Airmen, Richmond; lately Hon. Consulting Physician (Civilian) to the Army; *b* 4 Oct. 1909; *s* of Canon C. Dudley Hart and Kate Evelyn Bowden; *m* 1944, Mary

Josephine, *d* of late Luke Tully, Carrigaline, Co. Cork; one *s* two *d. Educ:* Grosvenor Sch., Nottingham; Edinburgh Univ. MB, ChB Edinburgh 1933, MD 1939; MRCP 1937, FRCP 1949. House physician and clinical asst, Brompton Hosp., 1937; Med. Registrar, Royal Northern Hosp., 1935-37; Med. Registrar, Westminster Hosp., 1939-42; Med. Specialist and Officer i/c Med. Div., RAMC, 1942-46. Mem., Cttee on Review of Medicines, 1975-. Ex-Pres. Heberden Soc.; Member: BMA; RSM, Assoc. of Physicians; Med. Soc. of London. Arris and Gale Lectr, RCS, 1955; Ellman Lectr, RCP, 1969; Stanley Davidson Lectr, Univ. of Aberdeen, 1970; Bradshaw Lectr, RCP, 1975. Executive Member: Arthritis and Rheumatism Council; Kennedy Inst. for Research into Rheumatism; Hon. Member: Ligue Française contre le Rheumatisme; American Rheumatism Association; Australian Rheumatism Association. *Publications:* (co-author) Drugs: actions, uses and dosage, 1963; (ed) French's Differential Diagnosis, 10th edn, 1973, 11th edn, 1977; (ed) The Treatment of Chronic Pain, 1974; Joint Disease: all the arthropathies, 1975; contributions to: Pye's Surgical Handicraft, 1939-72; Copeman's Textbook of the Rheumatic Diseases, 1964; Cortisone and ACTH, 1953; Miller's Modern Medical Treatment, 1962; Encyclopedia of General Practice, 1964; Chambers's Encyclopædia, 1964; Drug Treatment, 1976; articles on general medicine and rheumatism. *Recreations:* multi-track recording, travelling. *Address:* 24 Harmont House, 20 Harley Street, W1N 1AN. *T:* 01-935 4252; (private) 19 Ranulf Road, Hampstead, NW2. *T:* 01-794 2525.

HART, Sir Francis Edmund T.; *see* Turton-Hart.

HART, Frank Thomas, JP; *b* London, 9 Nov. 1911; *s* of late Samuel Black and Ada Frances Laura Hart; *m* 1938, Eveline Brenda Deakin, Leek, Staffs; three *s. Educ:* Gravesend and Sheerness Junior Technical Schs. Asst Sec., Buchanan Hospital, St Leonards-on-Sea, 1931-34; Sec., 1934-42; Sec., Central London Eye Hospital, 1942-44; Sec.-Superintendent, Princess Louise Hospital, 1944-48; Superintendent, Royal Infirmary, Sheffield, 1948-52; House Governor and Sec. to the Bd, Charing Cross Hospital, 1952-73; Hospital Manager, Zambia Medical Aid Soc., 1973-75. Mem. Tribunal set up by President of Zambia to hear applications for release from political detainees, 1973-75. Vice-Pres., League of Friends, Charing Cross Hosp.; Past Pres., Assoc. of Hosp. Secretaries; Past Pres. of the Hospital Officers' Club. DPA (London); Diploma of Economics (London). JP: Co. Mddx, 1955-65; Co. Surrey, 1965-. Mem., Worshipful Soc. of Apothecaries. *Publication:* (jointly) A Study of Hospital Administration, 1948. *Recreations:* all games, walking, reading. *Address:* 11 The Mount, St Leonards on Sea, East Sussex. *Clubs:* Forty; Sussex County Cricket.

HART, Sir George (Charles), KBE 1973; BEM 1971; JP 1967; company director, Auckland, New Zealand; Managing Director, British Hearing Aids NZ Ltd, Manufacturers of Universal Hearing Aids (chiefly electronic equipment); *m* Betty (née Thomas), Wales. Pioneered manufacture of hearing aids in New Zealand; researched, from 1930, into hearing defects; made what is believed to be the world's first electronic hearing aid; his firm exports to many countries. *Address:* British Hearing Aids NZ Ltd, Registered Office and Consulting Rooms, 171 Queen Street, Auckland, New Zealand; 355 Richardson Road, Mount Roskill, Auckland 4, NZ. *T:* 677418.

HART, George Vaughan; Consultant, Law Reform Division, Department of Justice, Dublin, since 1972; *b* 9 Sept. 1911; *e s* of George Vaughan Hart and Maude (née Curran); *m* 1949, Norah Marie, *d* of Major D. L. J. Babington; one *s* one *d. Educ:* Rossall; Corpus Christi Coll., Oxford. Called to Bar, Middle Temple, 1937. Served Royal Irish Fusiliers, 1940-45. Entered Home Office as Legal Asst, 1946; Principal Asst Legal Advr, 1967-72. Sec., Criminal Law Revision Cttee, 1959-72. *Recreations:* walking, bird-watching. *Address:* Annaghloy House, Castlebaldwin, Boyle, Co. Roscommon. *T:* Boyle 245. *Clubs:* Athenæum; Kildare Street and University (Dublin).

HART, Prof. Herbert Lionel Adolphus; FBA 1962; Principal, Brasenose College, Oxford, 1973-July 1978; Delegate of the Oxford University Press, 1960-74; *b* 18 July 1907; 3rd *s* of Simeon Hart and Rose (née Samson); *m* 1941, Jenifer, 3rd *d* of Sir John Fischer Williams, CBE, KC; three *s* one *d. Educ:* Cheltenham Coll.; Bradford Grammar Sch.; New Coll., Oxford (Hon. Fellow 1968). Open Classical Scholar, New Coll., Oxford, 1926; First Class Lit. Hum., 1929. Practised at the Chancery Bar, 1932-40. Served War of 1939-45, in War Office, 1940-45. Fellow and Tutor in Philosophy, New Coll., Oxford, 1945; University Lecturer in Philosophy, Oxford, 1948; Prof. of Jurisprudence, Oxford, 1952-68; Fellow, University Coll., Oxford, 1952-68, Res. Fellow 1969-73, Hon. Fellow, 1973; Sen. Res. Fellow, Nuffield Foundn, 1969-73. Visiting Professor:

Harvard Univ., 1956-57; Univ. of California, LA, 1961-62. Mem., Monopolies Commn, 1967-73. Pres., Aristotelian Soc., 1959-60; Vice-Pres., British Acad., 1976-77. Hon. Master of the Bench, Middle Temple, 1963. For. Mem., Amer. Acad. of Arts and Sciences, 1966. Hon. Dr of Law, Univ. of Stockholm, 1960; Hon. LLD: Univ. of Glasgow, 1966; Univ. of Chicago, 1966; Hon. DLitt, Univ. of Kent, 1969. Fellow, Accademia delle Scienze, Turin, 1964; Commonwealth Prestige Fellow (Govt of NZ), 1971. *Publications:* (with A. M. Honoré) Causation in the Law, 1959; The Concept of Law, 1961; Law Liberty and Morality, 1963; The Morality of the Criminal Law, 1965; Punishment and Responsibility, 1968; (ed, with J. H. Burns) Jeremy Bentham: An Introduction to the Principles of Morals and Legislation, 1970; (ed) Jeremy Bentham: Of Laws in General, 1970; articles in philosophical and legal journals. *Address:* Brasenose College, Oxford; 11 Manor Place, Oxford. *T:* 42402.

HART, Rt. Hon. Mrs Judith (Constance Mary), PC 1967; MP (Lab) Lanark Division of Lanarkshire since 1959; Minister for Overseas Development, since 1977; *d* of Harry Ridehalgh and late Lily Ridehalgh; *m* 1946, Anthony Bernard Hart, PhD, BSc, FRIC; two *s. Educ:* Clitheroe Royal Grammar Sch.; London School of Economics, London University (BA Hons 1945). Contested (Lab) Bournemouth West, 1951, and South Aberdeen, 1955. Jt Parly Under-Sec. of State for Scotland, 1964-66; Minister of State, Commonwealth Office, 1966-67; Minister of Social Security, 1967-68; Paymaster-General (in the Cabinet), 1968-69; Minister of Overseas Develt, 1969-70, 1974-75. Govt Co.-Chm., Women's Nat. Commn, 1969-70. Mem., Nat. Executive of Labour Party, 1969-; Chm., Labour Party Industrial Policy Sub-Cttee. *Publication:* Aid and Liberation, 1973. *Recreations:* theatre, gardening, spending time with her family. *Address:* 3 Ennerdale Road, Kew Gardens, Richmond-upon-Thames. *T:* 01-948 1989.

HART, Michael, MA; FRSA; Headmaster of European School, Mol, Belgium, since 1976; *b* 1 May 1928; *yr s* of late Dr F. C. Hardt; *m* 1956, Lida Dabney Adams, PhD (Wisconsin Univ.). *Educ:* Collège Français, Berlin; Landerziehungsheim Schondorf; Keble Coll., Oxford (Exhib.). 1st Cl. Hons History, 1951. Administrative Asst, UNRRA, 1945-47; Asst Master and Head of History, Sherborne Sch., 1951-56; Head of History, 1956-61, and Housemaster of School House, 1961-67, Shrewsbury Sch.; Headmaster of Mill Hill Sch., 1967-74; HM Inspector of Schs, DES, 1974-76. *Publications:* The EEC and Secondary Education in the UK, 1974; contrib. to Reader's Digest World Atlas and Atlas of British Isles. *Recreations:* travel, climbing. *Address:* European School, Europawijk 100, Mol, Belgium.

HART, P(hilip) M(ontagu) D'Arcy, CBE 1956; MA, MD (Cambridge), FRCP; Director, Tuberculosis Research Unit, Medical Research Council, 1948-65; *b* 25 June 1900; *s* of late Henry D'Arcy Hart and late Hon. Ethel Montagu; *m* 1941, Ruth, *d* of late Herbert Meyer and of Grete Meyer-Larsen; one *s. Educ:* Clifton Coll.; Gonville and Caius Coll., Cambridge; University Coll. Hospital. Dorothy Temple Cross Fellowship to USA, 1934-35; Consultant Asst Physician, UCH, 1934-37; Mem. Scientific Staff, MRC, 1937-65; Mem. Expert Cttee on Tuberculosis, WHO, 1947-64. Goldsmith Entrance Exhibnr, Filliter Exhibnr, Magrath Scholarship, Tuke Medals, UCH Medical Sch., 1922-25; Horton Smith MD Prize, Cambridge, 1930; Royal College of Physicians: Milroy Lecture, 1937; Mitchell Lecture, 1946; Weber-Parkes Prize, 1951; Marc Daniels Lecture, 1967; Stewart Prize, BMA, 1964. *Publications:* scientific papers on respiratory disease, and on epidemiological and microbiological subjects. *Address:* National Institute for Medical Research, Mill Hill, NW7. *T:* 01-959 3666; 37 Belsize Court, NW3. *Club:* Athenæum.

HART, Captain Raymond, CBE 1963; DSO 1945; DSC 1941, Bar 1943; Royal Navy; Director, Maritime World Ltd; *b* 24 June 1913; *o s* of late H. H. Hart, Bassett, Southampton; *m* 1945, Margaret Evanson, *o d* of Capt. S. B. Duffin, Danesfort, Belfast; two *s* one *d. Educ:* Oakmount Preparatory Sch.; King Edward VII Sch. Joined Merchant Navy, 1927; Joined Royal Navy, 1937; HMS Hasty, 2nd Destroyer Flotilla, 1939-42; in command: HMS Vidette, 1942-44 (despatches); HMS Havelock, 1944; Sen. Officer, 21st Escort Gp, 1944-45; served in HMS Vanguard during Royal Tour of S Africa, 1947. RN Staff Course, 1949-52; in command, HMS Relentless, 1952-53; Joint Services Staff Course, 1953-54. Staff C-in-C Allied Forces Mediterranean, as Liaison Officer to C-in-C Allied Forces Southern Europe, HQ Naples, Italy, 1954-56; in command, HMS Undine, and Capt. 6th Frigate Sqdn, 1957-58; Cdre Naval Drafting, 1960-62; retd from RN, 1963. Nautical Advr, British & Commonwealth Shipping Co., 1963-72; Fleet Manager, Cayzer, Irvine & Co. Ltd, 1972-76; Director: Union-Castle Mail

Steamship Co. Ltd; Clan Line Steamers Ltd, 1964-76; Cayzer, Irvine & Co. Ltd, 1966-76; British & Commonwealth Shipping Co. Ltd, 1966-76; Mem. Council: Missions to Seamen; Navy League Trust and Sea Cadet Assoc.; Mem. Cttee of Management of: Seamen's Hosp. Soc.; Marine Soc.; School of Navigation, Warsash. FRIN; FNI. Officer Order of Merit of Republic of Italy, 1958. *Recreations:* swimming, tennis, gardening, fishing. *Address:* Three Firs, Bramshott Chase, Hindhead, Surrey. *T:* Hindhead 4890.

HART, Thomas Mure, CMG 1957; *b* 1 March 1909; *s* of late Maxwell M. Hart and of Elizabeth Watson, Aiknut, West Kilbride; *m* 1936, Eileen Stewart Lawson; one *s* one *d*. *Educ:* Strathallan; Glasgow Univ.; Brasenose Coll., Oxford. Colonial Administrative Service, 1933; seconded Colonial Office, 1933-36; Malayan Civil Service, 1936; Dir of Commerce and Industry, Singapore, 1953; Financial Sec., Singapore, 1954; retired, 1959. Bursar, Loretto Sch., Musselburgh, 1959-69. *Recreation:* golf. *Address:* 44 Frogston Road West, Edinburgh EH10 7AJ. *T:* 031-445 2152. *Clubs:* Royal and Ancient (St Andrews); Honourable Company of Edinburgh Golfers.

HART, Rt. Rev. Mgr W. A.; *see* Dunkeld, Bishop of (RC).

HART-DAVIS, Sir Rupert (Charles), Kt 1967; author, editor and former publisher; Director of Rupert Hart-Davis, Ltd, Publishers, 1946-68; Vice-President, Committee of the London Library, since 1971 (Chairman 1957-69); *b* 28 Aug. 1907; *o s* of Richard Vaughan Hart-Davis and Sybil Mary Cooper, *er sister* of 1st Viscount Norwich; *m* 1st, 1929, Peggy Ashcroft (now Dame Peggy Ashcroft) (marr. diss.); 2nd, 1933, Catherine Comfort Borden-Turner (marr. diss.), *d* of Mary Borden and George Douglas Turner; two *s* one *d*; 3rd, 1964, Winifred Ruth (*d* 1967), *d* of C. H. Ware, Bromyard, and *widow* of Oliver Simon; 4th, 1968, June (*née* Clifford), *widow* of David Williams. *Educ:* Eton; Balliol Coll., Oxford. Student at Old Vic, 1927-28; Actor at Lyric Theatre, Hammersmith, 1928-29; office boy at William Heinemann Ltd, 1929-31; Manager of Book Soc., 1932; Dir of Jonathan Cape Ltd, 1933-40. Served in Coldstream Guards, 1940-45. Founded Rupert Hart-Davis Ltd, 1946. Hon. DLitt, Reading, 1964. *Publications:* Hugh Walpole: a biography, 1952; *edited:* George Moore: Letters to Lady Cunard, 1957; The Letters of Oscar Wilde, 1962; Max Beerbohm: Letters to Reggie Turner, 1964; A Catalogue of the Caricatures of Max Beerbohm, 1972; The Autobiography of Arthur Ransome, 1976. *Recreations:* reading, book-collecting, watching cricket. *Address:* The Old Rectory, Marske-in-Swaledale, Richmond, N Yorks. *Clubs:* Garrick, MCC.
See also Baron Silsoe.

HART DYKE, Sir Derek William, 9th Bt *cr* 1677; *b* 4 Dec. 1924; *s* of Sir Oliver Hamilton Augustus Hart Dyke, 8th Bt, and Millicent Zoë (*d* 1975), *d* of Dr Mayston Bond; *S* father, 1969; *m* 1st, 1953, Dorothy Moses, Hamilton, Ont (marr. diss. 1963); one *s* one *d*; 2nd, 1964, Margaret Dickson Elder, Ottawa (marr. diss. 1972). *Educ:* Harrow; Millfield. *Heir:* *s* David William Hart Dyke, *b* 5 Jan. 1955. *Address:* 80 Erie Avenue, Hamilton, Ontario L8N 2W6, Canada.

HARTFALL, Prof. Stanley Jack, TD 1942; BSc, MD; FRCP; Professor of Clinical Medicine, University of Leeds, 1948-64, now Emeritus; *b* 27 Feb. 1899; *m* 1931, Muriel Ann Hunter; two *s* (one *d* decd). *Educ:* University of Leeds; Guy's Hosp. House Surg. and House Physician. Resident Medical Officer, Leeds Gen. Infirmary, 1926-30; Medical Asst to Sir A. Hurst, Guy's Hosp., 1930-32; Leverhulme Research Scholar, Royal College of Physicians, London, 1932-33; Hon. Physician and Consulting Physician, Leeds Gen. Infirmary and Leeds Regional Hosp. Board, Harrogate Royal Bath Hosp., Dewsbury and District Gen. Hosp., Prof. of Therapeutics, University of Leeds, 1937. Lieut-Col RAMC (TA). *Publications:* numerous papers on pathological and clinical subjects, gastro-intestinal diseases, anaemias and blood diseases, arthritis and rheumatism. *Recreations:* cricket and tennis. *Address:* White Gables, Hill Farm Road, Playford, near Ipswich, Suffolk. *T:* Kesgrave 3784.

HARTHAN, John Plant, MA, FLA; Keeper of the Library, Victoria and Albert Museum, 1962-76; *b* 15 April 1916; *y s* of late Dr George Ezra Harthan, Evesham, Worcs, and Winifred May Slater. *Educ:* Bryanston; Jesus Coll., Cambridge; University Coll., London. Asst-Librarian, Southampton Univ., 1940-43; Royal Society of Medicine Library, 1943-44; Asst Under-Librarian, Cambridge Univ. Library, 1944-48; Asst-Keeper of the Library, Victoria and Albert Museum, 1948. FLA 1939. *Publications:* Bookbindings in the Victoria and Albert Museum, 1950 and 1961; co-editor, F.D. Klingender, Animals in Art and Thought, 1971; Books of Hours, 1977. *Recreations:* music, architecture, botany. *Address:* 20 Pelham Street, SW7.

HARTINGTON, Marquess of; Peregrine Andrew Morny Cavendish; *b* 27 April 1944; *s* of 11th Duke of Devonshire, *qv*; *m* 1967, Amanda Carmen, *d* of late Comdr E. G. Heywood-Lonsdale, RN, and of Mrs Heywood-Lonsdale; one *s* two *d*. *Educ:* Eton; Exeter Coll., Oxford. *Heir:* *s* Earl of Burlington, *qv*. *Address:* 15 Christ Church Road, SW14. *T:* 01-878 2272.

HARTLAND-SWANN, Julian Dana Nimmo; HM Diplomatic Service; Ambassador to the Mongolian People's Republic, since 1977; *b* 18 Feb. 1936; *s* of late Prof. J. J. Hartland-Swann and of Mrs Kenlis Hartland-Swann (*née* Taylour); *m* 1960, Ann Deirdre Green; one *s* one *d*. *Educ:* Stowe; Lincoln Coll., Oxford (History). Entered HM Diplomatic Service, 1960; 3rd Sec., Brit. Embassy, Bangkok, 1961-65; 2nd, later 1st Sec., FO, 1965-68; 1st Sec., Berlin, 1968-71; 1st Sec. and Head of Chancery, Vienna, 1971-74; FCO, 1975-77. *Recreations:* French food, sailing, music. *Address:* c/o Foreign and Commonwealth Office, SW1A 2AL.

HARTLEY, Arthur Coulton, CIE 1946; OBE 1943; ICS (retired); *b* 24 March 1906; *s* of late John Aspinall Hartley, Stream Mill, Chiddingly, Sussex; *m* 1943, Mrs Cecilie Leslie; one *s*. *Educ:* Cowley Grammar Sch.; Manchester Univ.; Balliol Coll., Oxford. Entered Indian Civil Service, 1929; Asst Magistrate, Comilla, Bengal, 1929-30; Subdivisional Magistrate, Sirajganj, Bengal, 1930-32; Asst Settlement Officer, Rangpur, Bengal, 1932-34; Settlement Officer, Rangpur, Bengal, 1934-37; Asst Sec. to Governor of Bengal, 1938-40; District Magistrate, Howrah, Bengal, 1940-43; Controller of Rationing, Calcutta, Bengal, 1943-45; Dir-Gen. of Food, Bengal, India, 1945-47. *Publication:* Report on Survey and Settlement Operations of Rangpur, 1938. *Recreations:* hill walking, painting. *Address:* Stream Mill, Chiddingly, Sussex.

HARTLEY, Brian Joseph, CMG 1950; OBE 1945 (MBE 1934); Project Manager, UNSF Survey of Northern Rangelands Project, Somalia, 1970-72; World Bank Consultant, Rangelands Projects Ethiopia, 1972-77; *b* 1907; *s* of late John Joseph Hartley, Tring, Herts; *m* 1951, Doreen Mary, *d* of Col R. G. Sanders; three *s* one *d*. *Educ:* Loughborough; Midland Agricultural Coll.; Wadham Coll., Oxford; Imperial Coll. of Tropical Agriculture, Trinidad. Entered Colonial Service; Agricultural Officer, Tanganyika, 1929; Aden Protectorate: Agricultural Officer, 1938; Agricultural Adviser, 1944; Dir of Agriculture, 1946-54; retd 1954; Chief, FAO(UN), mission in Iraq, 1955; Mem., Tanganyika Agricultural Corporation, 1956-62; Trustee, Tanganyika Nat. Parks, 1957-64; Mem., Ngorongoro Conservation Authority Advisory Board, 1963-64. UN (Special Fund) Consultant Team Leader: Kafue Basin Survey, N Rhodesia, 1960; Livestock Develt Survey, Somalia, 1966; Chief Livestock Adviser, FAO, Somalia, 1967-70. *Address:* Bryony Hill Farm, Winkleigh, Devon; Box 337, Malindi, Kenya.

HARTLEY, Prof. Brian Selby, PhD; FRS 1971; Professor of Biochemistry, Imperial College, University of London, since 1974; *b* 16 April 1926; *s* of Norman and Hilda Hartley; *m* 1949, Kathleen Maude Vaughan; three *s* one *d*. *Educ:* Queens' Coll., Cambridge; Univ. of Leeds. BA 1947, MA 1952, Cantab; PhD 1952, Leeds. ICI Fellow, Univ. of Cambridge, 1952; Helen Hay Whitney Fellow, Univ. of Washington, Seattle, USA, 1958; Fellow and Lectr in Biochemistry, Trinity Coll., Cambridge, 1964; Scientific Staff, MRC Laboratory of Molecular Biology, 1961-74. Hon. Mem., Amer. Soc. of Biological Chemists, 1977. British Drug Houses Medal for Analytical Biochemistry, 1969. *Publications:* papers and articles in scientific jls and books. *Recreations:* fishing, gardening. *Address:* Imperial College of Science and Technology, SW7 2AZ.

HARTLEY, Air Marshal Sir Christopher (Harold), KCB 1963 (CB 1961); CBE 1957 (OBE 1949); DFC 1945; AFC 1944; BA Oxon; Chairman, British Hovercraft Corporation, since 1974 (Deputy Chairman, 1970-74); *b* 31 Jan. 1913; *s* of late Brig.-Gen. Sir Harold Hartley, GCVO, CH, CBE, MC, FRS; *m* 1st, 1937, Anne Sitwell (marr. diss., 1943); 2nd, 1944, Margaret, *d* of Harold Watson; two *s*. *Educ:* Eton; Balliol Coll., Oxford (Williams Exhibnr); King's Coll., Cambridge. Zoologist on Oxford Univ. expeditions: to Sarawak, 1932; Spitsbergen, 1933; Greenland, 1937. Asst Master at Eton Coll., 1937-39. Joined RAFVR, 1938. Served War of 1939-45: 604 Sqdn, 256 Sqdn, Fighter Interception Unit, Central Fighter Establishment. Permanent Commission, 1945; AOC 12 Group, Fighter Command, 1959; ACAS (Operational Requirements), Air Min., 1961; DCAS, 1964-66; Controller of Aircraft, Min. of Aviation and Min. of Technology, 1966-70, retired. Chairman: FPT Industries Ltd, 1971-; Dir, Westland Aircraft Ltd, 1971-. *Recreations:* shooting, fishing, sailing. *Address:* 1 Osborne Court, Cowes, Isle of Wight. *Clubs:* Travellers', Royal London Yacht.

HARTLEY, Sir Frank, Kt 1977; CBE 1970; PhD London, CChem, FPS, FRIC; Vice-Chancellor, University of London, 1976-Sept. 1978; Dean of the School of Pharmacy, University of London, 1962-76; *b* 5 Jan. 1911; *s* of late Robinson King Hartley and Mary Hartley (*née* Holt); *m* 1937, Lydia May England; two *s. Educ:* Municipal Secondary (later Grammar) Sch., Nelson, Lancs; Sch. of Pharmacy (Fellow, 1977), University Coll. (Fellow, 1972), and Birkbeck Coll. (Fellow, 1970), University of London. Jacob Bell Schol., 1930, Silver Medallist in Pharmaceutics, Pharmaceut. Chem. and Pharmacognosy, 1932. Pharmaceutical Chemist, 1932, Demonstrator and Lectr, 1932-40, at Sch. of Pharmacy; 1st cl. hons BSc (Chem.), University of London, 1936, and PhD, 1941; Chief Chemist, Organon Laboratories Ltd, 1940-43; Sec., Therapeutic Research Corp., 1943-46; Sec., Gen. Penicillin Cttee (Min. of Supply), 1943-46; Dir of Research and Sci. Services, The British Drug Houses, Ltd, 1946-62; Chm. Brit. Pharmaceut. Conf, 1957, and of Sci. Adv. Cttee of Pharmaceut. Soc. of Great Britain, 1964-66; Mem. Council, 1955-58, 1961-64, Vice-Pres., 1958-60, 1964-65, 1967-69, Pres., 1965-67, of Royal Institute of Chemistry; Hon. Treasurer, 1956-61, Chm. 1964-68 of Chem. Council; Mem. 1953-, Vice-Chm. 1963-68, Chm. 1970-, of British Pharmacopoeia Commn, and a UK Deleg., 1964-, to European Pharmacopoeia Commn; Mem., 1970-, Vice-Chm., 1977-, Medicines Commn; Member: Poisons Bd (Home Office), 1958-66; Cttee on Safety of Drugs (Min. of Health), 1963-70; Cttee on Prevention of Microbiol Contamination of Medicinal Products, 1972-73; Chm., Panel on Grading of Chief Pharmacists in Teaching Hosps, 1972-74; Mem. Cttee of Enquiry on Contaminated Infusion Fluids, 1972; Chairman: Bd of Studies in Pharmacy, Univ. of London, 1964-68; Pharmacy Bd, CNAA, 1965-77; Collegiate Council, 1969-73; Mem., Academic Council, 1969-73. Co-opted Mem. Senate, 1968-76, ex officio Mem, 1976-, Senate Mem. of Court, 1970-76, ex officio Mem., 1976-, Dep. Vice-Chancellor, 1973-76, University of London; Member Council: St Thomas's Hosp. Medical Sch., University of London, 1968-; Royal Free Hosp. Med. Sch., 1970-; Member Bd of Governors: Royal Free Hosp. Gp, 1970-74; Kingston Polytechnic, 1970-75; British Postgrad. Med. Fedn, London Univ., 1972-; Royal Postgrad. Med. Sch., 1972-; Inst. of Basic Med. Sci, 1973-. Sir William Pope Memorial Lectr, RSA, 1962. Liveryman, Worshipful Soc. of Apothecaries of London. Charter Gold Medal, Pharm. Soc. of GB, 1974. *Publications:* papers on chem. and pharmaceut. research in Quarterly Jl of Pharmacy, Jl of Pharmacy and Pharmacology and Jl of Chem. Soc. Reviews and articles in sci. and tech. jls. *Recreations:* reading, gardening. *Address:* 146 Dorset Road, SW19 3EF. *T:* 01-542 7198. *Club:* Athenæum.

HARTLEY, Gilbert Hillard; His Honour Judge Hartley; a Circuit Judge (formerly Judge of County Courts), since 1967; *b* 11 Aug. 1917; *s* of late Percy Neave Hartley and late Nellie Bond (*née* Hillard); *m* 1948, Jeanne, *d* of late C. W. Gall, Leeds; one *s* two *d. Educ:* Ashville, Harrogate; Exeter Coll. Oxford. Called to Bar, Middle Temple, 1939. Served with Army, 1940-46. Recorder of Rotherham, 1965-67; Dep. Chm., WR of Yorkshire QS, 1965-71. *Address:* South Lawn, East Keswick, Leeds LS17 9DB.

HARTLEY, Ven. Peter Harold Trahair; Archdeacon of Suffolk, 1970-75, now Archdeacon Emeritus; Priest in Charge of Badingham with Bruisyard and Dennington; *b* 11 July 1909; *m* 1938, Ursula Mary Trahair; two *d. Educ:* Leys School; University of London (BSc 1935); Queen's College, Oxford (MA 1948); Cuddesdon Theological College. Deacon 1953, Priest 1954, Diocese of St Edmundsbury; Curate of Dennington and Badingham, 1953-55; Rector of Badingham, 1955, with Bruisyard, 1960, and Cransford, 1974; Rural Dean of Loes, 1967-70. *Publications:* papers in zoological journals. *Recreations:* natural history, naval and military history. *Address:* Pollards, Badingham, Woodbridge, Suffolk. *T:* Badingham 217.

HARTLEY, Richard Leslie Clifford, QC 1976; *b* 31 May 1932; *s* of late Arthur Clifford Hartley, CBE and late Nina Hartley. *Educ:* Marlborough Coll.; Sidney Sussex Coll., Cambridge (MA). Called to the Bar, Gray's Inn, 1956. *Recreations:* golf, tennis, horse racing. *Address:* 15 Chesham Street, SW1. *T:* 01-235 2420. *Clubs:* Garrick, MCC; Woking Golf, Rye Golf, St Enodoc Golf.

HARTLINE, Prof. Haldan Keffer; Professor of Biophysics, Rockefeller University, New York, 1953-74, now Emeritus; *b* Bloomsburg, Pa, 22 Dec. 1903; *s* of Daniel S. Hartline and Harriet F. Keffer; *m* 1936, Elizabeth Kraus; three *s. Educ:* Lafayette Coll. (BS); Johns Hopkins Univ. (MD), Nat. Res. Fellow, Medicine, Johns Hopkins Univ., 1927-29; Reeves Johnson Trav. Res. Schol., Universities of Leipzig and Munich, 1929-31; University of Pa; Fellow, Med. Physics, 1931-36; Asst Prof. Biophysics, Eldridge Reeves Johnson Foundn for Med. Physics, 1936-40; Assoc. Prof. Physiology, Cornell Univ. Med. Coll., NY, 1940-41; Asst Prof. Biophysics, Johnson Foundn, Univ. of Pennsylvania, 1941-42, Assoc. Prof. Biophysics, 1943-48, Prof. of Biophysics, 1948-49; Prof. Biophysics and Chm. of Dept, Johns Hopkins Univ., 1949-53. Mem., Nat. Acad. of Sciences; For. Mem., Royal Soc. (London). Hon. ScD: Lafayette Coll., 1959; Pennsylvania, 1971; Hon. Dr of Laws, Johns Hopkins Univ., 1969; Hon. Dr med Freiburg, 1971. William H. Howell Award (Physiol.), 1927; Howard Crosby Warren Medal, 1948; A. A. Michelson Award, 1964; Nobel Prize in Physiology or Medicine (jointly), 1967; Lighthouse Award, NY Assoc. for the Blind, 1969. *Publications:* contrib. Ratliff: Studies on Excitation and Inhibition in the Retina, 1974; articles in: Amer. Jl Physiol; Jl Gen. Physiol.; Jl Cell. Comp. Physiol.; Cold Spring Harbor Symposia on Quant. Biol.; Jl Opt. Soc. Amer.; Harvey Lectures; Science; Rev. Mod. Physics, etc. *Recreation:* mountain hiking. *Address:* Patterson Road, Hydes, Maryland 21082, USA. *T:* 301 592 8162.

HARTNELL, Air Vice-Marshal Geoffrey Clark, CBE 1955; RAAF, retired; *b* Melbourne, 15 April 1916; *s* of late F. B. Hartnell, Melbourne; *m* 1941, Joyce M., *d* of late J. T. Webster; two *s* one *d. Educ:* Wesley Coll. Cadet RAAF Pt Cook, 1936; service Aust., SW Pacific, UK, 1939-45; Air Staff RAAF HQ, 1946-50; CO RAAF Amberley, Qld, 1951-53; Dir of Air Staff Plans and Policy, RAAF HQ Melbourne, 1953-56; Senior Air Staff Officer, HQ Home Command, 1956-58; idc 1959; Officer Commanding RAAF Butterworth, 1960-62; Dir Gen. of Plans and Policy, Dept of Air, Canberra, 1960-63; Head, Australian Joint Services Staff and RAAF Representative, London, 1964-66; Extra Gentleman Usher to the Royal Household, 1964-66; Dir, Joint Service Plans, Dept of Defence, Canberra, 1966-68. Trustee, Australian War Memorial, Canberra. *Recreation:* woodwork. *Address:* 48 Endeavour Street, Red Hill, ACT 2603, Australia.

HARTNELL, Sir Norman, KCVO 1977 (MVO 1953); Dressmaker by appointment to HM the Queen, and to HM Queen Elizabeth the Queen Mother; Member Incorporated Society of London Fashion Designers (Chairman 1947-56); Ex-Vice-President Clothing Institute; *b* 12 June 1901. *Educ:* Magdalene Coll., Cambridge. Awarded Officier d'Académie by French Government, 1939; Royal Warrant, 1940; Neiman-Marcus Award, USA, for world influence on fashion, 1947. *Publications:* Silver and Gold (autobiography), 1955; Royal Courts of Fashion, 1971. *Recreations:* painting, riding, swimming. *Address:* 26 Bruton Street, Mayfair, W1.

HARTNETT, Sir Laurence (John), Kt 1967; CBE 1945; BBM (Singapore) 1974; FRSA; MIE (Australia); Industrial Adviser to Singapore Government; industrial consultant, chairman and director of a number of companies; *b* Woking, Surrey, 26 May 1898; *s* of John Joseph Hartnett, MD and Katherine Jane Hartnett; *m* 1925, Gladys Winifred, *d* of Charles Walter Tyler, Bexleyheath, Kent; three *d. Educ:* Kingston Grammar Sch.; Epsom Coll., England. Cadet, Vickers Ltd, England. Served European War, 1914-18, as Flt-Lieut and Flt Sub-Lieut, RNAS; War of 1939-45: Dir of Ordnance Production, Min. of Munitions, and Chm. Army Inventions Bd, Australia. Started own engrg and motor business; Man. Motor Dept, Guthrie & Co. Ltd, Singapore; Zone Man., General Motors, USA; Vice-Pres., General Motors Export Co., NY; Sales Man., General Motors, Nordeska, Sweden; Dir, Vauxhall Motors Ltd, England; Man. Dir, General Motors Holdens, Australia; Regional Dir of the overseas operations; Chm., Ambulance Design Cttee, 1967. Mem. Exec. and Past Pres., Aust. Industries Develt Assoc.; Trustee, Inst. of Applied Sciences, Vic.; Mem. Gov. Bd, Corps of Commissionaires. FAIM. *Publication:* Big Wheels and Little Wheels, 1964. *Recreations:* yachting, tennis. *Address:* Rubra, Mt Eliza, Vic. 3930, Australia. *T:* Melbourne 78-71271; Flat 4, 24 Hill Street, Toorak, Vic. 3142, Australia. *T:* Melbourne 245381. *Clubs:* Athenæum (Melbourne); Canadian Bay (Mt Eliza).

HARTOG, Harold Samuel Arnold; Knight, Order of the Netherlands Lion; KBE (Hon.) 1970; Advisory Director, Unilever NV, 1971-75; *b* Nijmegen, Holland, 21 Dec. 1910; *m* 1963, Ingeborg Luise Krahn. *Educ:* Wiedemann Coll., Geneva. Joined Unilever, 1931. After service with Dutch forces during War of 1939-45 he joined management of Unilever interests in France, and subseq. took charge of Unilever cos in the Netherlands; elected to Bds of Unilever, 1948; Mem. Rotterdam Group Management and responsible for Unilever activities in Germany, Austria and Belgium, 1952-60; subseq. Mem. Cttee for Unilever's overseas interests, in London; became, there, one of the two world co-ordinators of Unilever's foods interests,

1962; Chm., Unilever NV, 1966-71. *Recreations:* history of art; collecting Chinese pottery and porcelain. *Address:* Kösterbergstrasse 40B, 2000 2 Hamburg (Blankensee), Germany. *Clubs:* Dutch; Ubersee (Hamburg); Golf (Falkenstein).

HARTOPP, Sir John Edmund Cradock-, 9th Bt, *cr* 1796; TD; Director, Firth Brown Tools Ltd, 1961-76; *b* 8 April 1912; *s* of late Francis Gerald Cradock-Hartopp, Barbrook, Chatsworth, Bakewell, Derbyshire (kinsman of 8th Bt) and Elizabeth Ada Mary (*née* Stuart); *S* kinsman, Sir George Francis Fleetwood Cradock-Hartopp, 1949; *m* 1953, Prudence, 2nd *d* of Sir Frederick Leith-Ross, GCMG, KCB; three *d. Educ:* Summer Fields, Oxford; Uppingham Sch. Travelled in United States of America before joining at age of 18, Staff of Research Laboratories, Messrs Thos Firth & John Brown Ltd, Steel Makers, Sheffield, 1930; has since served in the Works and on the Commercial Staff; travelled in India and the Far East, 1948-49. War of 1939-45 (despatches twice); joined TA and served with Royal Engineers in UK; Norway, 1940; North Africa (1st Army), 1943; Italy, 1943-45; released, 1945, with rank of Major. Mem. Council: Machine Tool Research Assoc., 1965-70; Machine Tool Trades Assoc., 1970-73. *Recreations:* golf (semi-finalist English Golf Champ., 1935; first reserve, Eng. *v* France, 1935); cricket, tennis, motoring. *Heir:* cousin Lt-Comdr Kenneth Alston Cradock-Hartopp, MBE, DSC, RN [*b* 26 Feb. 1918; *m* 1942, Gwendolyn Amy Lilian Upton; one *d*]. *Address:* The Cottage, 27 Wool Road, Wimbledon Common, SW20. *Clubs:* East India, Devonshire, Sports, and Public Schools, MCC; Royal and Ancient (St Andrews).

HARTUNG, Ernst Johannes, DSc; Professor of Chemistry, University of Melbourne, 1928-53; Emeritus Professor since 1953; *b* Victoria, 23 April 1893; 2nd *s* of Carl August Ernst Hartung, Leipzig, and Ida Emilie, *d* of F. A. Hagenauer, Vic.; *m* 1922, Gladys, *d* of F. W. Gray, Glos; two *d. Educ:* Wesley Coll., Melbourne; University of Melbourne. BSc, 1913; DSc, 1919; Tutor in Chemistry, Trinity Coll., Melbourne, 1914; Lecturer and Demonstrator in Chemistry, University of Melbourne, 1919; Associate Prof., 1924; Winner of David Syme Scientific Research Prize, Australia, 1926; President of the Australian Chemical Institute, 1928. *Publications:* The Screen Projection of Chemical Experiments, 1953; Astronomical Objects for Southern Telescopes, 1968. Various scientific papers, including a series on Studies with the Micro-balance, and Studies in Membrane Permeability in Journal of Chemical Society, London, Transactions of Faraday Society, London. *Recreation:* astronomy. *Address:* Lavender Farm, Woodend, Victoria 3442, Australia.

HARTWELL, Baron, *cr* 1968 (Life Peer), of Peterborough Court in the City of London; **(William) Michael Berry,** MBE 1944; TD; Chairman and Editor-in-Chief of The Daily Telegraph and Sunday Telegraph; *b* 18 May 1911; 2nd *s* of 1st Viscount Camrose and Mary Agnes, *e d* of late Thomas Corns, London; *m* 1936, Lady Pamela Margaret Elizabeth Smith (*see* Lady Hartwell), *yr d* of 1st Earl of Birkenhead, PC, GCSI, KC; two *s* two *d. Educ:* Eton; Christ Church, Oxford (MA). 2nd Lieut 11th (City of London Yeo.) Light AA Bde, RA (TA), 1938; served War of 1939-45; Capt. and Major, 1940; Lieut-Col 1944 (despatches twice, MBE). Editor, Sunday Mail, Glasgow, 1934-35; Managing Editor, Financial Times, 1937-39; Chm. Amalgamated Press Ltd, 1954-59. *Publication:* Party Choice, 1948. *Address:* 18 Cowley Street, Westminster, SW1. *T:* 01-222 4673; Oving House, Whitchurch, near Aylesbury, Bucks. *T:* Whitchurch 307. *Clubs:* White's, Beefsteak; Royal Yacht Squadron.
See also Viscount Camrose.

HARTWELL, Lady; Pamela Margaret Elizabeth Berry; 2nd *d* of 1st Earl of Birkenhead, PC, GCSI, KC, and of Margaret, Countess of Birkenhead; *m* 1936, Hon. (William) Michael Berry (now Baron Hartwell, *qv*); two *s* two *d*. Member: Bd of Governors, English Speaking Union, 1971-; Adv. Council, V&A Museum, 1973-; British Section, Franco-British Council, 1977-; Chm., British Museum Soc., 1974-. *Address:* Oving House, Aylesbury, Bucks; 18 Cowley Street, Westminster, SW1.

HARTWELL, Benjamin James, OBE 1959; Clerk to Southport Borough Justices, 1943-73; *b* Southport, 24 June 1908; *s* of late Joseph Hartwell, Bucks, and late Margaret Ann Hartwell; *m* 1937, Mary (*née* Binns), Southport: one *s* one *d. Educ:* King George V Sch., Southport; London Univ. (LLM). Admitted a Solicitor of the Supreme Court, 1936; Hon. Sec. Justices' Clerks' Soc., 1947-59; Pres. Lancs and Cheshire Dist of Boys' Brigade, 1950-63; Chm. Council, Congregational Union of England and Wales, 1952-58; Chm. Congregational Union of England and Wales 1959-60. Mem. Home Secretary's Advisory Council on the Treatment of Offenders, 1955-63. *Address:* Mayfield, Longden Common Lane, Longden, near Shrewsbury SY5 8AQ. *T:* Dorrington 541.

HARTWELL, Sir Brodrick William Charles Elwin, 5th Bt, *cr* 1805; *b* 7 Aug. 1909; *s* of Sir Brodrick Cecil Denham Arkwright Hartwell, 4th Bt, and Joan Amy (*d* 1962), *o d* of Robert Milne Jeffrey, Esquimault, Vancouver; *S* father, 1948; *m* 1st, 1937, Marie Josephine, *d* of late S. P. Mullins (marriage dissolved 1950); one *s* ; 2nd, 1951, Mary Maude, MBE, *d* of J. W. Church, Bedford; one *d* decd. *Educ:* Bedford Sch. Sometime Pilot Officer RAF. Served War of 1939-45; Capt. Leics Regt, 1943. *Heir: s* Francis Antony Charles Peter Hartwell [*b* 1 June 1940; *m* 1968, Barbara Phyllis Rae, *d* of H. Rae Green; one *s*]. *Address:* Little Dale, 50 High Street, Lavendon, Olney, Bucks.

HARTWELL, Sir Charles (Herbert), Kt 1960; CMG 1954; *b* 1904; *m* 1st, 1931, Margaret Sheely (*d* 1942); 2nd, 1948, Mary Josephine Keane; one *s* decd. *Educ:* St John's Coll., Cambridge. Ceylon CS, 1927; Administrative Sec., Palestine, 1940; reverted to Ceylon Civil Service, 1942, and became Sec. to the Governor of Ceylon. Dir of Establishments, Kenya, 1947; Deputy Chief Sec. and Mem. for Education and Labour of Legislative Council of Kenya, 1952; Minister for Education, Labour and Lands, Kenya, 1955; Chief Sec., Uganda, 1955-60; retired from Colonial Service, July 1960; assumed duties as Chm. of Public Service Commission and Police Service Commission in Northern Rhodesia, Oct. 1960; retired, 1963; Ministry of Overseas Development, 1963-66; Adviser to the Government of Mauritius, 1966-67; Chm., Public Services Commn, Hong Kong, 1967-71; retired 1972. *Address:* 16 Clifton Place, Brighton, East Sussex. *Club:* East India, Devonshire, Sports and Public Schools.

HARTWELL, Eric; Vice-Chairman since 1972 and Joint Chief Executive since 1975, Trust Houses Forte Ltd; *b* 10 Aug. 1915; *m* 1st, 1937, Gladys Rose Bennett (marr. diss.); one *s* one *d* ; 2nd, 1952, Dorothy Maud Mowbray; one *s* one *d. Educ:* Mall Sch., Twickenham; Worthing High School. Fellow, Hotel Catering and Institutional Management Assoc. Electrical industry, 1932-37; Dir, Fortes & Co. Ltd, 1938; HM Forces, 1940-45; Jt Man. Dir, Forte Holdings Ltd, 1962; Dep. Man. Dir, Trust Houses Forte Ltd, 1970; Dep. Chief Exec., Trust Houses Forte Ltd, 1972-75. *Recreations:* yachting, painting, photography. *Address:* Tall Trees, 129 Totteridge Lane, N20 8NS. *T:* 01-445 2321. *Clubs:* National Sporting, River Emergency Service Association, Inner Magic Circle; Thames Motor Yacht.

HARTY, Maj.-Gen. Arthur Henry, CIE 1942; MB, BS, MRCS, LRCP, 1914; IMS, retired; *b* 13 Aug. 1890; *s* of T. Harty and M. E. Fowles; *m* 1919, Gladys Maud Davies; one *s* one *d* (and one *s* decd). *Educ:* Jamaica Coll., Jamaica; Queen's Univ., Kingston, Canada (MB, BS 1912). Joined Royal Navy as Surgeon, Aug. 1914; served in Grand Fleet and Mediterranean Fleet in European War; joined Indian Medical Service, 1919; Burma, 1920-23; Bombay Presidency and Sind 1923-42; Inspector-Gen., Civil Hospitals, Central Provinces, 1942-45; Maj.-Gen. 1946; Surgeon-Gen., Bombay, 1945-48. KHP, 1945-48. *Address:* c/o Grindlay's Bank Ltd, 13 St James's Square, SW1; 5 Gladstone Drive, Kingston 10, Jamaica, West Indies.

HARTY, Most Rev. Michael; *see* Killaloe, Bishop of, (RC).

HARUNA, Alhaji; *see* Gwandu, Emir of.

HARVATT, Thomas, CMG 1960; Secretary and Deputy Director, Council of Legal Education, 1934-68; *b* 5 Nov. 1901; *s* of Thomas Joseph Harvatt, Sheffield; *m* 1931, Nellie Adelaide, *d* of James Stephen Blythe, Sydenham; two *d. Educ:* King Edward VII Sch., Sheffield; University Coll., London; Inner Temple. Personal Asst to Dir of Educn, Sheffield, 1923-27; first Sec. for Educn, NALGO, 1927-34; Sec. to Council of Legal Education, 1934-68, and Dep. Dir of Inns of Court Sch. of Law, 1958-68; Mem. Cttee on Legal Education for Students from Africa, 1960. *Address:* 72 Old Lodge Lane, Purley, Surrey.

HARVEY, family name of **Barons Harvey of Prestbury** and **Harvey of Tasburgh.**

HARVEY OF PRESTBURY, Baron *cr* 1971 (Life Peer), of Prestbury in the County Palatine of Chester; **Arthur Vere Harvey,** Kt 1957; CBE 1942; FRAeS; *b* 31 Jan. 1906; *e s* of A. W. Harvey, Kessingland, Suffolk; *m* 1st, 1940, Jacqueline Anne (marr. diss., 1954), *o d* of W. H. Dunnett; two *s* ; 2nd, 1955, Mrs Hilary Charmian Williams. *Educ:* Framlingham Coll. Royal Air Force 1925-30; qualified as flying instructor; Dir of Far East Aviation Co. Ltd and Far East Flying Training Sch. Ltd, Hong-

Kong, 1930-35; Adviser to Southern Chinese Air Forces with hon. rank of Maj.-Gen., 1932-35; Sqdn Leader AAF, 1937, and founded 615 County of Surrey Squadron and commanded the Squadron in France, 1939-40 (despatches twice); Group Captain 1942; Air Commodore 1944. MP (C) Macclesfield Div. of Cheshire, 1945-71; Chairman Cons. Members' 1922 Cttee, 1966-70. Director: Film Corp. of America (UK) Ltd; Tradewinds Airways Ltd. Vice-Pres. British Air Line Pilots' Assoc., 1965. FRAeS. Hon. Freeman: Macclesfield, 1969; Congleton, 1970. Hon. DSc Salford, 1972. Comdr, Order of Oranje Nassau, 1969. *Recreations:* private flying (4th King's Cup Race, 1937), sailing. *Address:* Villa Wardija, Malta. *Clubs:* Buck's, Royal Air Force; Royal Yacht Squadron (Cowes).

HARVEY OF TASBURGH, 2nd Baron, *cr* 1954, of Tasburgh, Norfolk; **Peter Charles Oliver Harvey;** Bt 1868; Chartered Accountant; Director, English Transcontinental Ltd, Merchant Bankers; *b* 28 Jan. 1921; *er s* of 1st Baron Harvey of Tasburgh, GCMG, GCVO, CB, and Maud Annora (*d* 1970), *d* of late Arthur Watkin Williams-Wynn; *S* father, 1968; *m* 1957, Penelope Anne, *d* of Lt-Col Sir William Makins, 3rd Bt; two *d.* *Educ:* Eton; Trinity College, Cambridge. Served 1941-46 with Royal Artillery, Tunisia, Italy. Bank of England, 1948-56; Binder Hamlyn & Co., 1956-61; Lloyds Bank International Ltd (formerly Bank of London and South America), 1961-75. *Recreations:* sailing, music. *Heir: b* Hon. John Wynn Harvey [*b* 4 Nov. 1923; *m* 1950, Elena Maria-Teresa, *d* of late Marchese Giambattista Curtopassi, Rome; two *s* one *d*]. *Address:* 36 Lennox Gardens, SW1; Crownick Woods, Restronguet, Mylor, Cornwall. *Clubs:* Brooks's; Royal Cornwall Yacht, Royal Fowey Yacht.

HARVEY, Alan Frederick Ronald, OBE 1970; HM Diplomatic Service; Consul-General in Perth, Western Australia, since 1976; *b* 15 Dec. 1919; *s* of Edward Frederick and Alice Sophia Harvey; *m* 1946, Joan Barbara (*née* Tuckey); one *s.* *Educ:* Tottenham Grammar Sch. Air Ministry, 1936-40 (Civil Service appt). Served War, RAF, 1940-46. Air Min., 1946-49; Foreign Office, 1949-52 (on transfer to Diplomatic Service); HM Vice-Consul, Turin, 1953-55; Second Sec.: Rome, 1956; Tokyo, 1957-59; HM Consul (Information): Chicago, 1959-62; FO, 1963-65; First Sec. (Commercial): Belgrade, 1965-67; Tokyo, 1967-72; Commercial Counsellor: Milan, 1973-74; Rome, 1975-76. *Recreations:* tennis, golf. *Address:* c/o Foreign and Commonwealth Office, SW1; Farthings, Barnwood, Worth Park, Three Bridges, Sussex. *Club:* Royal Commonwealth Society.

HARVEY, Alexander, PhD, BSc, FInstP; Principal, University of Wales Institute of Science and Technology, 1946-68 (formerly Cardiff Technical College, later Welsh College of Advanced Technology); Pro-Vice-Chancellor, University of Wales, 1967-68; *b* 21 Sept. 1904; *s* of Andrew Harvey, Bangor, Co. Down; *m* 1933, Mona Anderson, Newcastle upon Tyne; one *s* two *d.* *Educ:* Gateshead Grammar Sch.; Armstrong (King's) Coll., Univ. of Durham. Commonwealth Fund Fellowship, Univ. of California, 1929-31; Scientific Asst, Adam Hilger Ltd, London, 1931-33; Asst Lecturer, Physics Dept, University of Manchester, 1933-34; Head of Physics Dept, Wigan and District Mining and Tech. Coll., 1934-42; Principal, Scunthorpe Tech. Sch., 1942-46. President: Assoc. of Principals of Technical Instns, 1957-58; South Wales Instn of Engineers, 1970-71; Chm. Council of Assoc. of Technical Instns, 1961-62. Hon. LLD Wales, 1970. *Publications:* Science for Miners, 1938; One Hundred Years of Technical Education, 1966; various papers on optical, spectroscopic and educational subjects. *Address:* 110 Pencisely Road, Llandaff, Cardiff. *T:* Cardiff 563795.

HARVEY, Arthur Douglas; Assistant Under-Secretary of State, Ministry of Defence, 1969-76; *b* 16 July 1916; *o s* of late William Arthur Harvey and Edith Alice; *m* 1940, Doris Irene Lodge; two *s.* *Educ:* Westcliff High Sch.; St Catharine's Coll., Cambridge. Wrangler, Maths Tripos, 1938. Entered War Office, 1938; served in Army, 1940-45; Princ. 1945; Registrar, Royal Military College of Science, 1951-54; Asst Sec. 1954; Under-Sec. 1969. *Address:* 36b Lovelace Road, Long Ditton, Surrey. *T:* 01-399 0587. *Club:* Royal Commonwealth Society.

HARVEY, Benjamin Hyde, OBE 1968; FCA; IPFA; DPA; General Manager, Harlow Development Corporation, 1955-73; *b* 29 Sept. 1908; *s* of Benjamin Harvey and Elizabeth (*née* Hyde); *m* 1938, Heather Frances Broome; one *d.* *Educ:* Stationers' Company's Sch. Local Govt, 1924-40; Treas., Borough of Leyton, 1940-47; Comptroller, Harlow Develt Corp., 1947-55. *Recreations:* books, sport. *Address:* 188 Hugh's Tower, Harlow, Essex. *T:* Harlow 24031; Brick House, Broxted, Essex. *T:* Henham 233. *Club:* Royal Automobile.

HARVEY, Prof. Brian Wilberforce; Professor of Property Law, University of Birmingham, since 1973; *b* 17 March 1936; *s* of Gerald and Noelle Harvey; *m* 1962, Rosemary Jane Brown; two *s* two *d.* *Educ:* Clifton Coll., Bristol; St John's Coll., Cambridge (Choral Schol., MA, LLM). Solicitor, 1961. Lectr, Birmingham Univ., 1962-63; Sen. Lectr, Nigerian Law Sch., 1965-67; Lectr, Sen. Lectr and Prof. of Law, QUB, 1967-73; Dir, Legal Studies, Univ. of Birmingham, 1973-76. Member: Statute Law Cttee (NI), 1972-73; Cttee on Legal Educn (NI), 1972-73; Jt Dir, Birmingham Vocational Trng (Law) Courses, 1973-; Governor, King Edward's Sch., Stourbridge, 1974-; Mem. Council, Worcester Three Choirs Festival, 1974-. Fellow, St Michael's Coll., Tenbury, 1975. *Publications:* Law of Probate Wills and Succession in Nigeria, 1968; (jtly) Survey of Northern Ireland Land Law, 1970; Settlements of Land, 1973; (ed) Vocational Legal Training in UK and Commonwealth, 1975; various articles in legal periodicals. *Recreations:* performing and listening to music, collecting books, squash, walking. *Address:* Mount Vernon, 5 Rainbow Hill Terrace, Worcester WR3 8NG. *T:* Worcester 22836.

HARVEY, Bryan Hugh; Visiting Professor, University of Aston in Birmingham, since 1972; *b* 17 Oct. 1914; *y s* of late Oliver Harvey and Ellen Harvey (*née* Munn); *m* 1941, Margaret, 2nd *d* of late E. G. Palmer; one *d.* *Educ:* King Edward VI Sch., Birmingham; Bristol Grammar Sch.; Corpus Christi Coll., Oxford; Harvard Univ. BA 1936; MA 1945; MSc 1953 (Industrial Hygiene). Printing industry until 1938, when joined Inspectorate of Factories. RAF, 1943-45, Aircraft and Armament Exper. Estabt; served in London, Manchester, Oldham, Bristol and Leeds areas, 1945-65; Dep. Chief Inspector, 1965; Chief Inspector, 1971-74. Dep. Dir Gen. (Dep. Sec.), Health and Safety Exec., 1975-76. Rockefeller Foundn Fellow, 1952-53; Hon. Lectr, Dept of Occupational Health, Univ. of Manchester, 1954-59. Chm., Adv. Cttee on major hazards, 1975-. Pres. British Occupational Hygiene Soc., 1976-77; FSA 1964; Hon. Fellow, Instn of Industrial Safety Officers, 1973. *Publications:* (with R. Murray) Industrial Health Technology, 1958; many articles in jls on industrial safety and hygiene, and industrial archaeology. *Recreations:* industrial archaeology, Georgian architecture, steam engines. *Address:* 2 Surley Row, Caversham, Reading, Berks RG4 8LY. *T:* Reading 479453. *Club:* Army and Navy.

HARVEY, Colin Stanley, MBE 1964; TD 1962; DL; a Recorder of the Crown Court, Western Circuit, since 1975; a Solicitor of the Supreme Court; *b* 22 Oct 1924; *s* of Harold Stanley and Lilian May Harvey; *m* 1949, Marion Elizabeth (*née* Walker); one *s* one *d.* *Educ:* Bristol Grammar Sch.; University Coll., Oxford (BA). Served 1939-45 war in Queen's Regt and RA, India, Burma, Malaya, Java. In private practice as a solicitor. Bt Lt-Col TAVR, 1973. DL Avon, 1977. *Recreations:* TAVR, riding, beagling. *Address:* 12 Southfield Road, Westbury-on-Trym, Bristol BS9 3BH. *T:* Bristol 625167. *Club:* Royal Commonwealth Society.

HARVEY, Ian Douglas, TD 1950; psc 1944; author; public relations consultant; free-lance journalist; Associate, Douglas Stephens Associates Ltd, Management Consultants; *b* 25 Jan. 1914; *s* of late Major Douglas Harvey, DSO, and of late Mrs Bertram Bisgood (*née* Dorothy Cundall); *m* 1949, Clare (legally separated), *y d* of late Sir Basil E. Mayhew, KBE; two *d.* *Educ:* Fettes Coll.; Christ Church, Oxford. Pres., Oxford Union Soc., 1936; BA, 1937; MA, 1941. Served War of 1939-45, Adjutant, 123 LAA Regt, RA, 1940; Bde Major, 38 AA Bde, RA, 1943; GSO2 (ops), HQ AA command, 1944; Staff Coll. Camberley, 1944; Bde Major 100 AA Bde, NW Europe, 1944; Lieut-Col Comdg 566 LAA Regt, RA (City of London Rifles) TA, 1947-50. Contested Spelthorne Div. of Mddx, 1945; MP (C) Harrow East, 1950-58; Sec., 1922 Cttee, 1955-56; Parly Sec., Min. of Supply, 1956-57; Jt Parly Under-Sec. of State, FO, 1957-58. Chm., Coningsby Club, 1946-47; Mem. of Council, Royal Borough of Kensington, 1947-52; Mem. of LCC for S Kensington, 1949-52; Rep. of LCC on County of London TA Assoc. 1949-52; Governor Birkbeck Coll., 1949-52; Deleg. Advertising Assoc. to Advertising Fedn of America Convention (Detroit), 1950; Chm. Press Relations Cttee of Internat. Advertising Conference (Great Britain), 1951; Member: Advertising Assoc.; Inst. of Public Relations; Parly Select Cttee for reform of the Army and Air Force Acts, 1952-54; Adv. Cttee on Publicity and Recruitment for Civil Defence, 1952-56; London Soc. of Rugby Union Football Referees; Rep. of Church Assembly on Standing Cttee of Nat. Soc., 1951-55; Vice-Pres., Campaign for Homosexual Equality. Director: W. S. Crawford Ltd, 1949-56; Colman, Prentis and Varley Ltd, 1962-63; Advertising Controller, Yardley of London Ltd, 1963-64 (Advertising Dir, 1964-66). Chm., London Old Fettesian Assoc., 1953-54; Sec., Iain Macleod Meml Trust, 1974-. *Publications:*

Talk of Propaganda, 1947; The Technique of Persuasion, 1951; Arms and To-morrow, 1954; To Fall Like Lucifer, 1971. *Recreations:* squash, cycling, swimming, tennis. *Address:* 28A Star Street, WC2 1QV. *T:* 01-723 0225. *Club:* Royal Automobile.

HARVEY, John Edgar; Director, Burmah Oil Trading Ltd, since 1974; Deputy Chairman, Burmah Castrol Europe Ltd, since 1970, and Director, subsidiary companies in Burmah Oil Group; *b* Londonderry, 24 April 1920; *s* of John Watt Harvey and Charlotte Elizabeth Harvey; *m* 1945, Mary Joyce Lane, BA, JP; one *s*. *Educ:* Xaverian Coll., Bruges, Belgium; Lyme Regis Grammar Sch. Radio Officer, in the Merchant Navy, 1939-45. Contested (C): St Pancras North, 1950; Walthamstow East, 1951; Mem. Nat. Exec. Cttee., Conservative Party, 1950-55; Chm., Woodford Conservative Assoc., 1954-56. MP (C) Walthamstow East, 1955-66. Mem., NSPCC Central Executive Cttee, 1963-68. Governor, Forest Sch., 1966-. Verderer of Epping Forest, 1970-. *Recreations:* various in moderation. *Address:* 43 Traps Hill, Loughton, Essex. *T:* 01-508 8753. *Clubs:* Carlton, City of London.

HARVEY, Prof. Leonard Patrick; Cervantes Professor of Spanish, King's College, University of London, since Oct. 1973; *b* 25 Feb. 1929; *s* of Francis Thomas Harvey and Eva Harvey; *m* 1954, June Rawcliffe; two *s*. *Educ:* Alleyn's Sch., Dulwich; Magdalen Coll., Oxford. 1st cl. hons BA Mod. Langs 1952; 2nd cl. Oriental Studies 1954; MA 1956; DPhil 1958. Lectr in Spanish, Univ. of Oxford, 1957-58; Univ. of Southampton, 1958-60; Queen Mary Coll., Univ. of London: Lectr, 1960-63; Reader and Head of Dept, 1963; Prof. of Spanish, 1967-73; Dean of Faculty of Arts, 1970-73. Vis. Prof., Univ. of Victoria, BC, 1966. *Publications:* articles in Al-Andalus, Bulletin of Hispanic Studies, Jl of Semitic Studies, Modern Philology, Revista de Filología Española, etc. *Address:* Tree Tops, Yester Park, Chislehurst, BR7 5DQ. *T:* 01-467 3565.

HARVEY, Prof. Leslie Arthur; Professor, 1946-69, and Head of Department of Zoology, University of Exeter, 1930-69; *b* 23 Dec. 1903; *s* of Arthur Harvey; *m* 1925, Christina Clare Brockway; one *s* one *d*. *Educ:* Bancroft's Sch.; Imperial Coll., London. ARCS 1923; BSc 1923; Beit Mem. Research Student, Imperial Coll., 1923-25; MSc 1925. Asst Lecturer, subsequently Lecturer in Zoology, University of Edinburgh, 1925-30. *Publications:* (with D. St Leger Gordon) Dartmoor, 1952; contributions to various learned journals, 1925-. *Recreations:* alpine gardening, bridge. *Address:* Benhams, The Garrison, St Mary's, Isles of Scilly. *T:* Scillonia 686.

HARVEY, Mary Frances Clare, MA; Headmistress, Badminton School, Westbury on Trym, Bristol, since Sept. 1969; *b* 24 Aug. 1927; *d* of Rev. Oliver Douglas Harvey, Highfield, Southampton. *Educ:* St Mary's Sch., Colchester; St Hugh's Coll., Oxford. BA Oxon, Final Honour Sch. of Mod. Hist., 1950; Diploma in Educn, 1951; MA 1954. History Mistress, St Albans High Sch., 1951; Head of History Dept, Portsmouth High Sch., GPDST, 1956; Headmistress, Sch. of St Clare, Penzance, 1962-69. *Recreations:* music, travel, reading, needlework. *Address:* 1 Great Brockeridge, Westbury on Trym, Bristol BS9 3TY. *T:* Bristol 628983.

HARVEY, Peter; Legal Adviser, Department of Education and Science, since 1977; *b* 23 April 1922; *o s* of Rev. George Leonard Hunton Harvey and Helen Mary (*née* Williams); *m* 1950, Mary Vivienne, *d* of John Osborne Goss and Elsie Lilian (*née* Bishop); one *s* one *d*. *Educ:* King Edward VI High Sch., Birmingham; St John's Coll., Oxford (MA, BCL). RAF, 1942-45. Called to the Bar, Lincoln's Inn, 1948. Entered the Home Office as a Legal Assistant, 1948; Principal Asst Legal Advr, 1971-77. *Publications:* contributor to Halsbury's Laws of England (3rd and 4th edns). *Recreations:* history, and walking. *Address:* Mannamead, Old Avenue, Weybridge, Surrey KT13 0PS. *T:* Weybridge 45133.

HARVEY, Rt. Rev. Philip James Benedict, OBE 1973; Auxiliary Bishop of Westminster (Bishop in North London) (RC), since 1977; *b* 6 March 1915; *s* of William Nathaniel and Elizabeth Harvey. *Educ:* Cardinal Vaughan Sch., Kensington; St Edmund's Coll., Ware, Herts. Ordained Priest, Westminster, 1939; Assistant Priest: Cricklewood, 1929-45; Kentish Town, 1945-46; Fulham, 1946-53; Asst Administrator, Crusade of Rescue, 1953-63, Administrator 1963-77. *Address:* 73 St Charles Square, W10 6EJ. *T:* 01-960 4029.

HARVEY, Rachel; *see* Bloom, Ursula.

HARVEY, Richard Jon Stanley, QC 1970; a Recorder of the Crown Court, since 1972; *b* 30 Aug. 1917; *s* of Nehemiah

Stanley Harvey, Home Civil Servant, and Alicia Margaret Harvey; *m* 1942, Yvonne Esther, *e d* of A. J. d'Abreu, FRCS, Waterford, Eire; no *c*. *Educ:* Newtown Sch., Waterford; Mountjoy Sch., Dublin; Trinity Coll., Dublin. 1st cl. sizarship in Irish, 1936; First Scholar of the House, History and Political Science, 1938; 1st cl. Moderatorship History and Political Science, 1940; Pres., Univ. Philosophical Soc., 1940-41; Founder Mem., Students Representative Council, 1941; LLB 1941. Royal Artillery, 1942-45; SUO Tonfanau RA OCTU, 1943; 2nd Lieut RA 1943, subseq. W/Subst. Lieut. Called to the Bar, Gray's Inn, 1947; Holker Scholar, 1947-48. Contested (C): Woolwich East, 1951 and 1952; Romford, 1955 and 1959. Gresham Prof. of Law, 1961-64. Received into Catholic Church, 1952. *Publications:* Harvey on Industrial Relations, 1971; contribs to learned jls; novels and other works written pseudonymously. *Recreations:* music, reading, gardening, swimming, walking, writing novels pseudonymously; formerly cricket and athletics (occasional mem. TCD 1st Cricket XI and Athletics 1st team, 1936-39). *Address:* 3 Raymond Buildings, Gray's Inn, WC1. *T:* 01-405 9420; Francis Taylor Building, Temple, EC4. *T:* 01-353 2182; The Barge, Great Walsingham, Norfolk. *T:* Walsingham 330. *Clubs:* Carlton, Sportsman, Newman Association, Catenian Association; Royal West Norfolk Golf.

HARVEY, Sir Richard Musgrave, 2nd Bt, *cr* 1933; Lieutenant-Commander, RN retired; *b* 1 Dec. 1898; *s* of Sir Ernest Musgrave Harvey, 1st Bt, KBE and Sophia (*d* 1952), *y d* of late Capt. Catesby Paget; *S* father 1955; *m* 1930, Frances Estelle, *er d* of late Lindsay Crompton Lawford, Montreal; one *s* one *d*. *Educ:* Royal Naval Colls, Osborne and Dartmouth. Heir: *s* Charles Richard Musgrave Harvey [*b* 7 April 1937; *m* 1967, Celia Vivien, *d* of G. H. Hodson; one *s*]. *Address:* Chisenbury Priory, Pewsey, Wilts.

HARVEY, Major Thomas Cockayne, CVO 1951; DSO 1945; Extra Gentleman Usher to the Queen, since 1952 (to King George VI, 1951-52); *b* 22 Aug. 1918; *s* of late Col John Harvey, DSO; *m* 1940, Lady Katharine Mary Coke, (Woman of the Bedchamber to Queen Elizabeth the Queen Mother, 1961-63), *yr d* of 3rd Earl of Leicester; one *s* two *d*. *Educ:* Radley; Balliol Coll., Oxford. Joined Scots Guards SRO, 1938. Served Norway, 1940, Italy, 1944; Private Sec. to the Queen, 1946-51. *Recreations:* golf, shooting, *Address:* 2 Catherine Wheel Yard, Little St James's Street, SW1. *T:* 01-499 6692; Warham House, Warham, Wells, Norfolk. *T:* Wells 457. *Clubs:* White's, Beefsteak.

HARVEY EVERS, H.; *see* Evers, H. H.

HARVEY-JAMIESON, H. M.; *see* Jamieson, H. M. H.

HARVIE ANDERSON, Rt. Hon. (Margaret) Betty, (Rt. Hon Betty Skrimshire), PC 1974; OBE 1955; TD 1959; DL; MP (C) East Renfrewshire since Oct. 1959; *d* of late T. A. Harvie Anderson, CB, Quarter and Shirgarton, and Mrs Harvie Anderson; *m* 1960, John Francis Penrose Skrimshire, MD, FRCP. *Educ:* St Leonard's Sch., St Andrews. CC, Stirlingshire, 1945-59; Leader, moderate group, Stirling CC, 1953-59; Member: Sec. of State for Scotland's Advisory Council on Education, 1955-59; Bd of Management Royal Scottish Nat. Instn; City of Glasgow T & AFA, 1949-51; Stirlingshire T & AFA, 1953-59; Exec. Cttee Princess Louise Scottish Hosp.; W Stirlingshire Unionist Assoc., 1938-54; Western Div. Council Scottish Unionist Assoc., 1939-59; convener Western Div. Council Women's Cttee, 1955-58; President: Scottish Young Unionists, 1955-58; St Leonard's Sch.; Chm. Scottish Assoc. of Mixed and Girls' Clubs, 1952-55. Company Comdr, ATS, 1938; Adj. Reception Depot, 1940; Sen. Comdr, Mixed Heavy Anti-Aircraft Regt, RA, 1942-43; Chief Comdr Mixed Heavy Anti-Aircraft Bde, 1943-46. Contested (C) W Stirlingshire, 1950 and 1951, Sowerby (Yorks), 1955; Member: Exec. Cttee, 1922 Cttee, 1962-70, 1974-; Chairman's Panel, House of Commons, 1966-70; Dep. Chm. of Ways and Means, House of Commons, 1970-73; Member: Historic Buildings Council for Scotland, 1966-; Royal Commission on Local Government in Scotland, 1966-69; Mr Speaker's Conf., 1966-68. DL Stirlingshire, 1973. *Address:* Quarter, by Denny, Stirlingshire. *T:* Denny 822271.

HARVIE-WATT, Sir George Steven, 1st Bt, *cr* 1945, of Bathgate; QC 1945; TD 1942 (with three Bars); DL; *b* 23 Aug. 1903; *s* of late James McDougal Watt of Armadale; *m* 1932, Bettie, *o d* of late Paymaster-Capt. Archibald Taylor, OBE, RN; two *s* one *d*. *Educ:* George Watson's Coll., Edinburgh; Glasgow Univ.; Edinburgh Univ. Called to Bar, Inner Temple, 1930; practised in London and on North Eastern Circuit. Commissioned RE TA 1924, 52nd (Lowland) Scottish Div., 1924-29; 56th (1st London) Div., 1929-38; Bt Major, 1935; Lt-Col Commanding 31st Bn RE TA, 1938-41; promoted Brig. to command 6th AA Bde, 1941;

Brig. Commanding 63rd AA Bde TA, 1948-50; Hon. Col 566 LAA Regt, 1949-62. ADC to King George VI, 1948-52; ADC to the Queen, 1952-58; MP (U) Keighley Div. of Yorks, 1931-35; (U) Richmond, Surrey, Feb. 1937-Sept. 1959; PPS to late Rt Hon. Euan Wallace when Parly Sec. to Board of Trade, 1937-38; Asst Government Whip, 1938-40; PPS to Rt Hon. Winston S. Churchill when Prime Minister, July 1941-July 1945; Hon. Treas. UK Branch of Commonwealth Parly Assoc., 1945-51; Mem. UK Deleg. to CPA Confs, Ottawa and Washington, 1949, Australia and New Zealand, 1950; Mem. of Borough Council, Royal Borough of Kensington, 1934-45. Formerly Mem. of City of London TA Association; TA Rep. Council of RUSI, 1948-57; DL: Surrey, 1942; Greater London, 1966; JP County of London, 1944-56. President: Consolidated Golf Fields Ltd, 1973- (Chief Executive, 1954-69, Dep. Chm., 1954-60, Chm., 1960-69); Printers' Pension Corp., 1956-57; Director: Midland Bank Ltd; Clydesdale Bank Ltd; Eagle Star Insce Co.; North British Steel Gp, and other cos; Formerly: Chm., Monotype Corp. Ltd; Director: Standard Bank Ltd; Great Western Rly Co. Member of Queen's Body Guard for Scotland, Royal Company of Archers; Hon. Freeman, City of London, 1976. FRSA 1973. Gold Medal, Inst. Mining and Metallurgy (for distinguished service to world-wide mining), 1969. *Heir:* s James Harvie-Watt [b 25 Aug. 1940; m 1966, Roseline, d of late Baron Louis de Chollet; one s one d]. *Recreation:* Territorial Army. *Address:* Earlsneuk, Elie, Fife. *T:* Elie 330506. *Clubs:* Caledonian (Chm. 1953-61, Vice-Pres. 1961-); Puffin's (Edinburgh).

HARVINGTON, Baron cr 1974 (Life Peer), of Nantwich; **Robert Grant Grant-Ferris,** PC 1971; Kt 1969; AE; Privy Chamberlain of the Sword and Cape to Popes Pius XII, John XXIII and Paul VI; b 30 Dec. 1907; s of late Robert Francis Ferris, MB, ChB; m 1930, Florence, d of Major W. Brennan De Vine, MC; one s one d. *Educ:* Douai Sch. Called to Bar, Inner Temple, 1937; joined RAuxAF, 1933, 605 (County of Warwick) Fighter Sqdn; Flight Comdr 1939-40; Wing Comdr, 1941; Air Efficiency Award, 1942. MP (C) North St Pancras, 1937-45; MP (C) Nantwich, Cheshire, 1955-Feb. 1974; PPS to Minister of Town and Country Planning (Rt Hon. W. S. Morrison, KC, MP), 1944-45; Temp. Chm. House of Commons and Chairman of Cttees, 1962-70; Chm. of Ways and Means and Dep. Speaker, House of Commons, 1970-74. Contested Wigan, 1935, North St Pancras, 1945, Central Wandsworth, 1950, 1951. Chm., Bd of Management, Hosp. of St John and St Elizabeth, 1963-70. Pres. Southdown Sheep Soc. of England, 1950-52, 1959-60, 1973; Pres. Nat. Sheep Breeders' Assoc., 1956-58; a Vice-Pres. Smithfield Club, 1964, Pres. 1970. Knight Grand Cross of Magistral Grace, the Sovereign and Military Order of Malta; holds Grand Cross of Merit with Star of same Order; Comdr, Order of Leopold II (Belgium), 1964. *Recreations:* hunting, golf, yachting (sometime Hon. Admiral, House of Commons Yacht Club). *Address:* La Vielle Maison, The Bulwarks, St Aubin, Jersey, Channel Islands. *Clubs:* Carlton; Royal Thames Yacht, Royal Yacht Squadron.

HARWOOD, Basil Antony, MA; QC 1971; Barrister-at-Law; a Master of the Supreme Court (Queen's Bench Division), 1950-70; Senior Master and Queen's Remembrancer, 1966-70; 2nd s of late Basil Harwood, DMus, Woodhouse, Olveston, Glos; m 1929, Enid Arundel, d of late Philip Grove, Quorn House, Leamington; two s. *Educ:* Charterhouse; Christ Church, Oxford (MA). Called to the Bar, Inner Temple, 1927. Served War of 1939-45 in Italy. Prosecuting Counsel to Post Office, Western Circuit, 1948-50. Pres. Medico-Legal Soc., 1967-69. *Address:* Woodstock House, Woodstock, Oxford.

HARWOOD, Elizabeth Jean, (Mrs J. A. C. Royle); international opera singer; b 27 May 1938; d of Sydney and Constance Harwood; m 1966, Julian Adam Christopher Royle; one s. *Educ:* Skipton Girls' High Sch.; Royal Manchester Coll. of Music. FRMCM, GRSM, LRAM. Kathleen Ferrier Memorial Schol., 1960; jt winner, Verdi Competition (Busetto), 1965. Principal operatic roles at Glyndebourne, Sadler's Wells, Covent Garden, Scottish Opera, principal opera houses in Europe incl. Salzburg and La Scala; toured Australia, 1965, with Sutherland-Williamson Internat. Opera Co. singing principal roles in Lucia de Lammermoor, La Sonnambula and L'Elisir d'Amore; début at NY Metropolitan Opera in Cosi Fan Tutte, 1975; took part in exchange visit to La Scala with Covent Garden Opera, 1976. Has made numerous recordings of oratorio and opera. *Recreations:* swimming, horse riding. *Address:* Masonetts, Fryerning, Ingatestone, Essex. *T:* Ingatestone 3024. *Club:* Oriental.

HASELDEN, Edward Christopher, CMG 1952; b 14 Aug. 1903; s of E. N. Haselden, Minieh, Upper Egypt; m 1929, Lily Jewett Foote; two d. *Educ:* Cheltenham Coll.; Pembroke Coll., Cambridge. Joined Sudan Political Service, 1925; Sudan Agent in Cairo, 1945-53; retired, 1953. Chm. of Anglo-Egyptian Aid Soc. Cttee, 1960. Order of the Nile (4th Class), 1936. *Address:* 14 Gilston Road, SW10. *Club:* Athenæum.

HASELDEN, Prof. Geoffrey Gordon; Brotherton Professor of Chemical Engineering, University of Leeds, since 1960; b 4 Aug. 1924; s of George A. Haselden and Rose E. (*née* Pleasants); m 1945, Eileen Doris Francis; three d. *Educ:* Sir Walter St John's Sch.; Imperial Coll. of Science and Technology. BScChemEng London 1944; ACGI; PhD (Eng) Chem Eng London, 1947; DScEng London, 1962; DIC; CEng; FIMechE; FIChemE; MInstR. Mem. Gas Research Bd, 1946-48; Lectr in Low Temperature Technology, Chemical Engrg Dept, 1948-57, Senior Lectr in Chemical Engrg, 1957-60, Imperial Coll. Chm., British Cryogenics Council, 1967-71. Pres., Commn A3, Internat. Inst. of Refrigeration, 1971-. Dir, Hall-Thermotank Products Ltd, 1968. *Publications:* Cyrogenic Fundamentals, 1971; research papers in Trans. Inst. Chem. Eng., etc. *Recreation:* Methodist lay preacher. *Address:* 12 High Ash Drive, Wigton Lane, Leeds LS17 8RA. *T:* Leeds 687047; The University, Leeds. *T:* Leeds 31751.

HASELDINE, (Charles) Norman; Joint Managing Director, Linden Marketing & Communications Ltd; b 25 March 1922; s of Charles Edward Haseldine and Lily White; m 1946, Georgette Elise Michelle Bernard; four s. *Educ:* Nether Edge Grammar Sch., Sheffield. Education Officer, Doncaster Co-operative Soc., 1947-57; PRO, Sheffield & Ecclesall Co-op. Soc., 1957-70. MP (Lab and Co-op) Bradford West, 1966-70; PPS to Minister of Power, 1968-69; PPS to Pres. Bd of Trade, 1969-70; Mem. Select Cttee on Nationalised Inds. *Recreation:* classical music. *Address:* 31 Roland Gardens, SW7; 115 Psalter Lane, Sheffield S11 8YR. *T:* Sheffield 585974.

HASELER, Dr Stephen Michael Alan; author and lecturer; Member of the Greater London Council, since 1973; b 9 Jan. 1942; m 1967, Roberta Alexander. *Educ:* London School of Economics. BSc(Econ), PhD. Contested (Lab) Saffron Walden, 1966; Maldon, 1970. Chairman: Labour Political Studies Centre, 1971-; General Purposes Cttee, GLC, 1973-75. *Publications:* The Gaitskellites, 1969; Social-Democracy—Beyond Revisionism, 1971; The Death of British Democracy, 1976. *Address:* 4 Carlton Mansions, Holland Park Gardens, W14. *T:* 01-602 3640. *Club:* Wood Green Labour.

HASELGROVE, Dennis Cliff, CB 1963; MA; Under Secretary, Department of the Environment, 1970-75; b 18 Aug. 1914; s of late H. Cliff Haselgrove, LLB, Chingford; m 1941, Evelyn Hope Johnston, MA, d of late R. Johnston, Edinburgh; one s. *Educ:* Uppingham Sch.; King's Coll., Cambridge. 1st Class, Classical Tripos, Parts I and II. Entered Ministry of Transport, Oct. 1937; Private Sec. to Permanent Sec., and Asst Priv. Sec. to Minister, 1941. Served in Intelligence Corps and 10th Baluch Regt, IA, 1941-45. Min. of Transport: Asst Sec., 1948; Under-Sec., 1957-70. Govt Delegate to: ILO Asian Maritime Conf., 1953; Internat. Conf. on Oil Pollution of the Sea, 1954, 1962; Internat. Lab. Conf. (Maritime Session), 1958; Internat. Conf. on Safety of Life at Sea, 1960. Imperial Defence Coll., 1955. *Recreations:* archæology, travel, philately. *Address:* 10 Church Gate, SW6 3LD. *T:* 01-736 5213.

HASELHURST, Alan Gordon Barraclough; MP (C) Saffron Walden, since July 1977; b 23 June 1937; s of John Haselhurst and Alyse (*née* Barraclough); m 1977, Angela (*née* Bailey). *Educ:* King Edward VI Sch., Birmingham; Cheltenham Coll.; Oriel Coll., Oxford. Pres., Oxford Univ. Conservative Assoc., 1958; Sec., Treas. and Librarian, Oxford Union Soc., 1959-60; Nat. Chm., Young Conservatives, 1966-68. MP (C) Middleton and Prestwich, 1970-Feb. 1974. Chm., Manchester Youth and Community Service, 1974-77. *Recreations:* squash, theatre, music. *Address:* House of Commons, SW1A 0AA. *Club:* MCC.

HASKARD, Sir Cosmo (Dugal Patrick Thomas), KCMG 1965 (CMG 1960); MBE 1945; b 25 Nov. 1916; o c of late Brig.-Gen. J. McD. Haskard, CMG, DSO; m 1957, Phillada, o c of Sir Robert Stanley, qv; one s. *Educ:* Cheltenham; RMC Sandhurst; Pembroke Coll., Cambridge (MA). Served War of 1939-45 (MBE); 2nd Lieut, TA (Gen. List), 1938; emergency Commn, Royal Irish Fusiliers, 1939; seconded KAR, 1941; served 2nd Bn, E Africa, Ceylon, Burma; Major 1944. Cadet, Tanganyika, 1940; transf. Nyasaland, 1946; Dist Comr, 1948; Provincial Commissioner, 1955; acting Secretary for African Affairs, 1957-58; Sec. for Labour and Social Development, 1961; Sec. for Local Government, 1962; Sec. for Natural Resources, 1963; Governor and C-in-C, Falkland Islands, and High Comr for the British Antarctic Territory, 1964-70. Served on Nyasaland-Mozambique Boundary Commission, 1951-52. Trustee, Beit Trust, 1976-. *Address:* Tragariff, Bantry, Co. Cork, Ireland.

HASKELL, Arnold Lionel, CBE 1954; Chevalier de la Légion d'Honneur, 1950; writer, lecturer, and journalist; Director, Royal Ballet School, 1946-65, Governor, since 1966; a Governor, The Royal Ballet since 1957; *b* 1903; *s* of late J. S. Haskell and Emmy Mesritz; *m* 1st, 1927, Vera Saitzoff (*d* 1968); two *s* one *d*; 2nd, 1970, Vivienne Marks. *Educ:* Westminster; Trinity Hall, Cambridge (MA). Mem., editorial staff, William Heinemann Ltd, 1927-32; joint founder of Camargo Soc., 1930; visited America with Russian Ballet, 1933-34; dance critic, Daily Telegraph, 1935-38; Founder the Vic-Wells Ballet Benevolent Fund, 1936; visited Australia, guest critic for Melbourne Herald and Sydney Daily Telegraph, 1936-37; Australia, 1938-39; toured Spain, Portugal and Germany for British Council, 1950-51, Italy, Yugoslavia and Greece, 1953, Germany and Italy, 1954, Italy 1955; visited USSR to study ballet and to lecture, 1960 and 1962, and as guest of Youth Organisation, 1967. Visited Cuba as guest of National Council of Culture, 1967, and lectured there for three months, 1968. Advised Dutch Government Commission on formation of a National ballet, 1954; Vice-Pres. jury, Varna dance competition, 1964, 1965, 1966 and 1970; Mem. jury, Internat. Ballet contest, Moscow, 1969 and 1973; Vice-Pres. Royal Academy of Dancing; Vice-Pres., Catholic Stage Guild; Governor, Trent Park Training Coll., 1953-58 and 1961; Council, Royal West of England Academy, 1961; Trustee, Holburne Menstrie Museum, 1970; Vice-Pres. and Trustee, Bath Preservation Trust. Hon. Member: Bath Inst. of Medical Engrg, 1971; Council, Bath Univ., 1971-76. Hon. DLitt Bath, 1974. *Publications:* Some Studies in Ballet, 1928; The Sculptor Speaks, 1932; Black on White, 1933; Balletomania, 1934; Diaghileff, 1935; Prelude to Ballet, Balletomane's Scrapbook, 1936; Dancing Round the World, 1937; Ballet Panorama, 1938; Ballet, a complete guide to appreciation, 1938; Balletomane's Album, 1939; Waltzing Matilda: a background to Australia, 1940; Australia, 1941; The Australians, 1943; The National Ballet, 1943; The Dominions-Partnership or Rift?, 1943; British Ballet, 1939-45; The Making of a Dancer, 1946; Ballet Vignettes, 1949; In His True Centre (autobiography), 1951; edited Ballet-to Poland in aid of Polish Relief Funds, 1940, and Ballet Annual, 1947-62; Saints Alive, 1953; co-edited Gala Performance, 1956; The Russian Genius in Ballet, 1962; Ballet Retrospect, 1964; What is Ballet, 1965; Heroes and Roses, 1966; Ballet Russe: the Age of Diaghilev, 1968; Infantilia, 1971; Balletomane at Large (autobiog.), 1972; Balletomania, Then and Now, 1976; contrib. Encyclopædia Britannica, British Journal of Aesthetics, Chambers's Encyclopædia and Annual Register. *Recreations:* travelling, opera-going, collecting sculpture, juvenilia. *Address:* 6A Cavendish Crescent, Bath, Avon BA1 2UG. *T:* Bath 22472. *Club:* Garrick.
See also F. J. H. Haskell.

HASKELL, Donald Keith; HM Diplomatic Service; Chargé d'Affaires and Consul-General, Santiago, Chile, since Dec. 1975; *b* 9 May 1939; *s* of Donald Eric Haskell and Beatrice Mary Haskell (*née* Blair); *m* 1966, Maria Luisa Soeiro Tito de Morais; one *s* one *d* (and one *s* one *d* decd). *Educ:* Portsmouth Grammar Sch.; St Catharine's Coll., Cambridge (BA 1961, MA 1964). Joined HM Foreign Service, 1961; served in: London, Lebanon, Iraq, Libya; HM Consul, Benghazi, 1969-70; First Sec., Tripoli, 1970-72; Foreign and Commonwealth Office, 1972-75. Foundation Medal, Soka Univ. of Japan, 1975. *Recreations:* rifle shooting, squash, wine and food. *Address:* c/o Foreign and Commonwealth Office, SW1A 2AL; Withens, Basingstoke Road, Alton, Hants GU34 1QH. *Club:* Hawks (Cambridge).

HASKELL, Francis James Herbert, FBA 1971; Professor of Art History, Oxford University and Fellow of Trinity College, Oxford, since October 1967; *b* 7 April 1928; *s* of Arnold Haskell, *qv*; *m* 1965, Larissa Salmina. *Educ:* Eton Coll.; King's Coll., Cambridge. Junior Library Clerk, House of Commons, 1953-54; Fellow of King's Coll., Cambridge, 1954-67; Librarian of Fine Arts Faculty, Cambridge Univ., 1962-67. Mem., British Sch. at Rome, 1971-. A Trustee, Wallace Collection, 1976-. *Publications:* Patrons and Painters: a study of the relations between Art and Society in the Age of the Baroque, 1963; Géricault (The Masters), 1966; An Italian Patron of French Neo-Classic Art, 1972; (ed jtly) The Artist and Writer in France, 1975; Rediscoveries in Art, 1975; articles in Burlington Mag., Jl Warburg Inst., etc; reviews in New Statesman, NY Review of Books, etc. *Recreation:* foreign travel. *Address:* 7 Walton Street, Oxford; Trinity College, Oxford OX1 2HG; 35 Beaumont Street, Oxford.

HASKELL, Peter Thomas, CMG 1975; PhD, FRES, FIBiol; Director, Centre for Overseas Pest Research, and Adviser on Pest Control, Ministry of Overseas Development since 1971; *b* 21 Feb. 1923; *s* of late Herbert James and Mary Anne Haskell; *m* 1946, Betty Jackson; one *s*. *Educ:* Portsmouth Grammar Sch.; Imperial Coll., London. BSc, ARCS, PhD. Asst Lectr, Zoology Dept, Imperial Coll., London, 1951-53; Lectr, 1953-55; Sen. Sci. Officer, Anti-Locust Research Centre, Colonial Office, 1955-57; Principal Sci. Officer, 1957-59; Dep. Dir, 1959-62; Dir, Anti-Locust Research Centre, Min. of Overseas Develt, 1962-71; Consultant, FAO, UN, 1962-; Consultant: UN Develt Programme, 1970-; WHO, 1973; OECD, 1975; UNEP, 1976; Agric. Adv. Panel, British Council, 1976; Professorial Res. Fellow, University Coll., Cardiff, 1971. Mem., Bd of Governors, Internat. Centre for Insect Physiology and Ecology, Kenya, 1972. Vis. Prof., Univ. of Newcastle, 1977. *Publications:* Insect Sounds, 1962; The Language of Insects, 1962; many papers and articles in scientific and literary jls. *Recreations:* sailing, gardening, reading. *Address:* 5 Alexandra Road, Kingston-upon-Thames, Surrey. *T:* 01-549 8157.

HASKINS, Sam, (Samuel Joseph); photographer; *b* 11 Nov. 1926; *s* of Benjamin G. Haskins and Anna E. Oelofse; *m* 1952, Elzabé van Heerden; two *s*. *Educ:* Helpmekaar Sch.; Witwatersrand Technical Coll.; Bolt Court Sch. of Photography. Freelance work: Johannesburg, 1953-68; London, 1968-. One-man Exhibitions: Johannesburg, 1953, 1960; Tokyo, 1970, 1973, 1976; London, 1972, 1976; Paris, 1973; Amsterdam, 1974. *Publications:* Five Girls, 1962; Cowboy Kate and other stories, 1964 (Prix Nadar, France, 1964); November Girl, 1966; African Image, 1967 (Silver Award, Internat. Art Book Contest, 1969); Haskins Posters, 1972 (Gold Medal, New York Art Directors Club, 1974); portfolios in most major internat. photographic magazines. *Recreations:* sculpting, books, music. *Address:* 9A Calonne Road, SW19 5HH.

HASLAM, Hon. Sir Alec (Leslie), Kt 1974; Judge of the Supreme Court of New Zealand, 1957-76, Senior Puisne Judge, 1973-76; *b* 10 Feb. 1904; *s* of Charles Nelson Haslam and Adeline Elsie Haslam; *m* 1933, Kathleen Valerie Tennent; two *s* two *d*. *Educ:* Waitaki Boys' High Sch.; Canterbury UC; Oriel Coll., Oxford. Rhodes Scholar 1927; 1st cl. hons LLM NZ; DPhil, BCL Oxon. Served with 10th Reinf. 2 NZEF, ME and Italy, 1943-46. Barrister and Solicitor, 1925; in private practice, 1936-57. Lectr in Law, Canterbury Univ., 1936-50 (except while overseas). Chm. Council of Legal Educn, 1962-75 (Mem. 1952); Mem., Rhodes Scholarship Selection Cttee, 1936-74; NZ Sec. to Rhodes Scholarships, 1961-74; Mem., Scholarships (Univ. Grants) Cttee, 1962-; Pres., Canterbury District Law Soc., 1952-53; Vice-Pres., NZ Law Soc., 1954-57; Mem., Waimairi County Council, 1950-56; Mem., NZ Senate, 1956-61. Sen. Lecturing Fellow, Univ. of Canterbury, 1977. Hon. LLD Canterbury, 1973. *Publication:* Law Relating to Trade Combinations, 1931. *Recreations:* reading, walking, swimming, bowls; formerly athletics (rep. Canterbury Univ. and Oriel Coll.) and rowing (rep. Oriel Coll.). *Address:* 22 Brackendale Place, Burnside, Christchurch 4, NZ. *T:* 588-589.

HASLAM, Rear Adm. David William, OBE 1964; Hydrographer of the Navy, since 1975; *b* 26 June 1923; *s* of Gerald Haigh Haslam and Gladys Haslam (*née* Finley). *Educ:* Ashe Prep. Sch., Etwall; Bromsgrove Sch., Worcs. FRGS, FRIN, FRICS, MNI. Special Entry Cadet, RN, 1941; HMS Birmingham, HMAS Quickmatch, HMS Resolution (in Indian Ocean), 1942-43; specialised in hydrographic surveying, 1944; HMS White Bear (surveying in Burma and Malaya), 1944-46; comd Survey Motor Launch 325, 1947; RAN, 1947-49; HMS Scott, 1949-51; HMS Dalrymple, 1951-53; i/c RN Survey Trng Unit, Chatham, 1953-56; HMS Vidal, 1956-57; comd, HMS Dalrymple, 1958; comd, HMS Dampier, 1958-60; Admty, 1960-62; comd, HMS Owen, 1962-64; Exec. Officer, RN Barracks, Chatham, 1964-65; Hydrographer, RAN, 1965-67; comd, HMS Hecla, 1968-70; Asst Hydrographer, MoD, 1970-72; comd, HMS Hydra, 1972-73; Asst Dir (Naval) to Hydrographer, 1974-75; sowc 1975. Lt-Comdr 1952; Comdr 1957; Captain 1965; Rear Adm. 1975. Pres., Hydrographic Soc., 1977-; Governor, Bromsgrove Sch., 1977-. *Publications:* The Journal of Navigation; Marine Policy. *Recreations:* most team games (Pres., English Schs Basketball Assoc.), supporting any youth organisations. *Address:* 183 Duffield Road, Derby DE3 1JB. *T:* Derby 57384; 30 Cranley Gardens, SW7 3RR. *T:* 01-370 2203/2914; 14 Cranmer Road, Taunton, Somerset.

HASLAM, (William) Geoffrey, DFC 1944; Chief General Manager, Prudential Assurance Co. Ltd, since 1974; *b* 11 Oct. 1914; *yr s* of late William John Haslam and late Hilda Irene Haslam; *m* 1941, Valda Patricia Adamson; two *s* one *d*. *Educ:* New Coll. and Ashville Coll., Harrogate. War Service with RAF, No 25 Sqdn (night fighters), 1940-46. Joined Prudential Assurance Co. Ltd, 1933: Dep. Gen. Manager, 1963; Gen. Manager, 1969. Chm., Industrial Life Offices Assoc., 1972-74; Chm., British Insurance Assoc., 1977-. *Recreation:* golf. *Address:* 6 Ashbourne Road, W5 3ED. *T:* 01-997 8164.

HASLEGRAVE, Herbert Leslie, WhSch (Sen.), MA Cantab, PhD London, MSc (Eng), CEng, FIMechE, FIEE, FIProdE; planning consultant; formerly Vice-Chancellor, Loughborough University of Technology; *b* 16 May 1902; *s* of late George Herbert Haslegrave and Annie (*née* Totty), Wakefield; *m* 1938, Agnes Mary, *er d* of Leo Sweeney, Bradford; one *d. Educ:* Wakefield Gram. Sch.; Bradford Technical Coll.; Trinity Hall Cambridge (Scholar). Rex Moir Prizeman, John Bernard Seeley Prizeman, Ricardo Prizeman, 1928; 1st Cl. Mechanical Sciences Tripos, 1928. English Electric Co. Ltd: Engineering Apprentice, 1918-23, Asst Designer, Stafford, 1928-30; Lecturer: Wolverhampton and Staffs, Technical Coll., 1931; Bradford Technical Coll., 1931-35; Head of Continuative Education Dept, Loughborough Coll., 1935-38; Principal: St Helens Municipal Technical Coll., 1938-43; Barnsley Mining and Technical Coll., 1943-46; Leicester Coll. of Technology, 1947-53; Loughborough Coll. of Technology, 1953-66. Bernard Price Lectr, SA Inst. of Electrical Engrs, 1971. Member of: Productivity Team on Training of Supervisors, visiting USA, 1951; Delegation on Education and Training of Engineers visiting USSR, 1956; Council, IMechE, 1965-66; Council, IEE, 1956-58. Chairman: Council, Assoc. of Technical Institutions, 1963-64; Cttee on Technician Courses and Examinations, 1967-69; Pres., Whitworth Soc., 1972-73. Hon. DTech Loughborough Univ. of Technology. *Publications:* various on engineering, education and management in proceedings of professional engineering bodies and educational press; chapter in Management, Labour and Community. *Recreations:* motoring, swimming, music. *Address:* 19 Lands Road, Brixham, Devon; 4 Capstan Square, E14 9EU.

HASLEGRAVE, John Ramsden, CBE 1975 (OBE (mil.) 1945); TD 1949; DL; Chief Executive, City of Portsmouth, 1974-77; *b* 15 April 1913; *s* of Col H. J. Haslegrave, CMG, TD, JP, and Mrs H. J. Haslegrave, OBE, MA; *m* 1957, Mary Kingswell; two *d. Educ:* Queen Elizabeth Grammar Sch., Wakefield; Peterhouse, Cambridge (MA, LLB). Solicitor 1938. Served War of 1939-45: 1/4 Bn KOYLI (TA), UK, Norway and Iceland; psc 1944; GSO2 WO; GSO1 GHQ Middle East; subseq. served with 4th Bn KOYLI TA, 1947-54, comdg, 1951-54; Col 150 Inf. Bde TA, 1958-60. Articled to Town Clerk, Chester, 1934-37; Dep. Town Clerk, Nuneaton, 1938-39, 1946-47; Asst Solicitor, Nottingham, 1947-49; Asst Town Clerk, Birmingham, 1949-52; Dep. Town Clerk, Leeds, 1952-60; Town Clerk and Chief Executive Officer, Portsmouth, 1960-74. Lay Canon, Portsmouth Cathedral; Governor, Portsmouth Grammar Sch. DL Hampshire 1975. *Recreations:* tennis, ski-ing, rugby football, golf, walking. *Address:* 27 Eastern Parade, Southsea, Portsmouth PO4 9RD. *T:* Portsmouth 32996; Blakehills Cottage, Troutbeck, Penrith, Cumbria. *Club:* Royal Automobile.

HASLEGRAVE, Neville Crompton; Town Clerk, 1965-74, and Chief Executive Officer, 1969-74, Leeds; Solicitor; *b* 2 Aug. 1914; *o s* of late Joe Haslegrave, Clerk of Council, and late Olive May Haslegrave; *m* 1943, Vera May, *o d* of Waldemar Julius Pedersen, MBE, and late Eva Pedersen; two *d. Educ:* Exeter Cathedral Choristers School; Leeds Univ. Asst Examr, Estate Duty Office, Bd of Inland Revenue, 1940-44; Asst Solicitor, Co. Borough of Leeds, 1944-46. Chief Prosecuting Solicitor, Leeds, 1946-51; Principal Asst Solicitor, Leeds, 1951-60; Dep. Town Clerk, Leeds, 1960-65. Pres., Leeds Law Soc., 1972-73. *Recreations:* music, walking. *Address:* Low House, Halton Gill, Skipton, N Yorks. *Club:* Headingley Taverners'.

HASLEWOOD, Prof. Geoffrey Arthur Dering; Professor of Biochemistry at Guy's Hospital Medical School, University of London, 1949-77; *b* 9 July 1910; *s* of N. A. F. Haslewood, Architect, and Florence (*née* Hughes); *m* 1943, B. W. Leeburn (*d* 1949); two *d*; *m* 1953, E. S. Blakiston, Geelong, Vic, Australia. *Educ:* St Marylebone Grammar Sch.; University Coll., London. Research on polycyclic aromatic hydrocarbons, etc, at Royal Cancer Hosp. (Free), 1933-35; Asst in Pathological Chemistry at British Postgraduate Med. Sch., 1935-39; Reader in Biochemistry at Guy's Hosp. Med. Sch., 1939-49. Mem., Zaire River Expedition, 1974-75. MSc 1932, PhD 1935, DSc 1946, London. FRIC 1946. *Publications:* Bile Salts, 1967; various articles and original memoirs in scientific literature, mainly on steroids in relation to evolution. *Recreation:* fishing. *Address:* 28 Old Fort Road, Shoreham-by-Sea, Sussex. *T:* Shoreham-by-Sea 3622.

HASLIP, Joan; author; *b* 27 Feb. 1912; *yr d* of late George Ernest Haslip, MD, original planner of the Health Service. *Educ:* privately in London and on the continent. Grew up in Florence. Sub-editor, London Mercury, 1929-39, contributed verse, reviews, etc; travelled extensively Europe, USA, Middle East; Editor, European Service, BBC, 1941-45 (Italian Section); lectured for British Council, Italy and Middle East; broadcast and contributed articles to BBC and various publications and newspapers. FRSL 1958. *Publications:* (several translated); Out of Focus (novel), 1931; Grandfather Steps (novel), 1932 (USA 1933); Lady Hester Stanhope, 1934; Parnell, 1936 (USA 1937); Portrait of Pamela, 1940; Lucrezia Borgia, 1953 (USA 1954); The Sultan, Life of Abdul Hamid, 1958, repr. 1973; The Lonely Empress, a life of Elizabeth of Austria, 1965 (trans. into ten languages); Imperial Adventurer, 1971 (Book of Month choice, USA, 1972); Catherine the Great, 1976. *Recreations:* travelling and conversation. *Address:* 5 Via di Doccia, Settignano, Firenze, Italy.

HASLUCK, Rt. Hon. Sir Paul, PC 1966; GCMG 1969; GCVO 1970; Governor-General of Australia, 1969-74; *b* 1 April 1905; *s* of E. M. C. Hasluck and Patience (*née* Wooler); *m* 1932, Alexandra Margaret Martin Darker, DStJ 1971; one *s* (and one *s* decd). *Educ:* University of Western Australia (MA). Journalist until 1938. Lectr in History, University of Western Australia, 1939-40; Australian Diplomatic Service, 1941-47; Head of Australian Mission to United Nations, 1946-47; Representative on Security Council, Atomic Energy Commn, General Assembly, etc. Research Reader in History, University of Western Australia, 1948. Official War Historian. Mem. (L) House of Representatives, 1949-69; Minister for Territories in successive Menzies Governments, 1951-63; Minister for Defence, 1963-64; Minister for External Affairs, 1964-69. Fellow, Aust. Acad. of Social Scis. Hon. Fellow, Aust. Acad. of Humanities. KStJ 1969. *Publications:* Black Australians, 1942; Workshop of Security, 1946; The Government and the People (Australian Official War History), vol. 1, 1951, vol. 2, 1970; Collected Verse, 1970; An Open Go, 1971; The Poet in Australia, 1975; A Time for Building: Australian administration in Papua New Guinea, 1976; Mucking About (autobiog.), 1977. *Recreations:* book collecting (Australiana). *Address:* 2 Adams Road, Dalkeith, WA 6009, Australia. *Clubs:* Weld (Perth); Claremont Football.

HASSALL, Joan, RE 1948; FSIA 1958; painter and wood engraver; *b* 3 March 1906; *d* of late John Hassall, RI, RWA, and late Constance Brooke-Webb. *Educ:* Parsons Mead, Ashtead; Froebel Educational Institute, Roehampton. Sec. to London Sch. of Art, 1925-27; studied Royal Academy Schs, 1928-33; studied Wood Engraving, LCC Sch. of Photo-engraving and Lithography. Teacher of Book Production (deputy), Edinburgh Coll. of Art, 1940; resumed her own work in London, chiefly wood engraving, 1945. Work represented in: British Museum, Victoria and Albert Museum and collections abroad. Designed the Queen's Invitation Card to her guests for Coronation, 1953. Master, Art Workers Guild, 1972 (Mem., 1964-); Bronze Medal, Paris Salon, 1973. *Publications:* first published engraving in Devil's Dyke, by Christopher Hassall, 1935; The Wood Engravings of Joan Hassall, 1960. Her engraved and drawn work appears in many classic and contemporary books of prose and poetry, and in advertising. *Recreations:* music, literature and printing. *Address:* Priory Cottage, Malham, Skipton, N Yorks BD23 4DD. *T:* Airton 356.

HASSALL, William Owen; Librarian to Earl of Leicester, Holkham, since 1937; Senior Assistant Librarian, Bodleian Library, Oxford, since 1938; *b* 4 Aug. 1912; *s* of Lt-Col Owen Hassall and Bessie Florence Hassall (*née* Cory); *m* 1936, Averil Grafton Beaves; three *s* one *d. Educ:* Twyford Sch., Hants; Wellington Coll., Berks; (Classical scholar) Corpus Christi Coll., Oxford. Hon. Mods, 1st cl. Modern History, 1936, DPhil 1941. Lent by RA to Min. Economic Warfare, 1942-46. Formerly: External Examnr in History, Univs of Bristol, Durham, Leicester and Oxford Insts of Educn (Trng Colls); Hon. Editorial Sec., British Records Assoc.; Mem. Council, Special Libraries and Information Bureaux. Hon. Sec., Oxfordshire Record Soc., 1947-76. FSA 1942; FRHistS. *Publications:* A Cartulary of St Mary Clerkenwell, 1949; A Catalogue of the Library of Sir Edward Coke, 1950; The Holkham Bible Picture Book, 1954; Wheatley Records, 956-1956, 1956; They saw it happen: an anthology of eye-witnesses' accounts for events in British history, 55BC-AD1485, 1957; Who's Who in History, vol. I, British Isles, 55BC-1485, 1960; (with A. G. Hassall) The Douce Apocalypse, 1961; How they Lived: an anthology of original accounts written before 1485, 1962; Index of Names in Oxfordshire Charters, 1966; History Through Surnames, 1967; The Holkham Library Illuminations and Illustrations in the Manuscript Library of the Earl of Leicester (printed for presentation to the Members of the Roxburghe Club), 1970; (with A. G. Hassall) Treasures from the Bodleian, 1975; contrib. to various learned publications. *Recreations:* lecturing; pioneering publication of medieval illuminations as colour transparencies; research on Holkham records. *Address:* Manor House, Wheatley, Oxford. *T:* Wheatley 2333.

HASSAN, Sir Joshua (Abraham), Kt 1963; CBE 1957; MVO 1954; QC (Gibraltar) 1961; JP; Chief Minister of Gibraltar, 1964-69, and since 1972; *b* 1915; *s* of late Abraham M. Hassan, Gibraltar; *m* 1945, Daniela (marr. diss. 1969), *d* of late José Salazar; two *d*; *m* 1969, Marcelle Bensimon; two *d*. *Educ:* Line Wall Coll., Gibraltar. Called to Bar, Middle Temple, 1939. HM Deputy Coroner, Gibraltar, 1941-64; Mayor of Gibraltar, 1945-50 and 1953-69; Mem. Executive Council, Chief Mem. Legislative Council, Gibraltar, 1950-64; Leader of the Opposition, Gibraltar House of Assembly, 1969-72. Chairman: Cttee of Management, Gibraltar Museum, 1952-65; Gibraltar Govt Lottery Cttee, 1955-70; Central Planning Commn, 1947-70. *Address:* 11/18 Europa Road, Gibraltar. *T:* A2295. *Clubs:* United Oxford & Cambridge University; Royal Gibraltar Yacht.

HASSEL, Prof. Odd; Knight of the Order of St Olav; Guldberg-Waage and Gunnerus Medals; Emeritus Professor of the University, Oslo; *b* 17 May 1897; *s* of Ernst August Hassel and Mathilde Klaveness. *Educ:* Oslo, Munich and Berlin Universities. Lectr, Oslo Univ., 1925, docent 1926, full Professor, 1934; Director, Department of Physical Chemistry of Univ. of Oslo, 1934-64. Hon. Fellow: Chemical Soc., London; Norwegian Chemical Soc., Oslo; Fellow of Academies in Oslo, Trondheim, Stockholm, Copenhagen, etc. Nobel Prize for Chemistry, 1969. Hon. Dr phil, Univ. of Copenhagen, 1950; Hon. Fil dr, Univ. of Stockholm, 1960. *Publications:* Kristallchemie, 1934, trans. English and Russian; about 250 scientific papers, chiefly on molecular structure problems. *Address:* Chemistry Department, University of Oslo, Blindern, Oslo 3, Norway; (home) Holsteinveien 10, Oslo 8. *T:* 232062.

HASSETT, Gen. Sir Francis (George), AC 1975; KBE 1976 (CBE 1966; OBE 1945); CB 1970; DSO 1951; MVO 1954; Chief of the Defence Force Staff, 1975-77, retired; *b* 11 April 1918; *s* of John Francis Hassett, Sydney, Australia; *m* 1946, Margaret Hallie Roberts, *d* of Dr Edwin Spencer Roberts, Toowoomba, Qld; one *s* two *d* (and one *s* decd). *Educ:* RMC, Duntroon, Australia. Graduated RMC, 1938. Served War of 1939-45, Middle East and South West Pacific Area (Lt-Col; despatches twice); CO 3 Bn Royal Australian Regt, Korea, 1951-52; Marshal for ACT Royal Tour, 1954; Comd 28 Commonwealth Bde, 1961-62; idc, 1963; DCGS, 1964-65; Head of Aust. Jt Services Staff, Australia House, 1966-67; GOC Northern Comd, Australia, 1968-70; Chm., Army Rev. Cttee, 1969-70; Vice Chief of Gen. Staff, Australia, 1971-73; CGS, Australia, 1973-75. Extra Gentleman Usher to the Queen, 1966-68. *Recreations:* fishing, boating. *Address:* 42 Mugga Way, Red Hill, Canberra, ACT 2603, Australia. *Clubs:* Commonwealth, Queensland.

HASTED, Maj.-Gen. William Freke, CB 1946; CIE 1943; CBE 1941; DSO 1937; MC; late Royal Engineers; *b* 28 Sept. 1897; *s* of late W. A. Hasted, Lindfield, Sussex; *m* 1920, Hella Elizabeth Mary (*d* 1961), *d* of Lieut-Col A. E. Cuming, Doneraile, Co. Cork; no *c*. *Educ:* Cheltenham Coll.; Cambridge Univ.; Royal Military Academy, Woolwich. First Commission, 1915; European war (2nd Division) 1916-18 (despatches, MC); Instructor RM Academy Woolwich, 1924-26; Instructor RMC of Canada, Kingston, Ont. 1926-30; OCRE South Irish Coast Defence, 1932-36; Bengal Sappers-Miners (Peshawar), 1936-37; Headquarters Northern Command, India, 1937; Waziristan Operations, 1937 (despatches twice, DSO); CRE Waziristan District, 1938-41; Waziristan Admadzai Operations, 1940 (despatches CBE); Deputy Chief Engineer, HQ Xth Army, 1941-42; Deputy Engineer-in-Chief (Air), GHQ, New Delhi, 1942-43; Chief Engineer 14 Army, 1944-45 (CB); Chief Engineer, Allied Land Forces SEAC, 1945-46; Engineer-in-Chief in India, 1946-47; late Controller of Aerodromes; retired pay, 1948. Pres., Loughborough Coll., Leics, 1951. Controller of Development, Kuwait, Persian Gulf, 1952; retired from Persian Gulf, 1954. *Recreations:* shooting, fishing, tennis; International Hockey, England, 1923; Hockey, Army and Combined Services, 1922-25. *Address:* c/o Lloyds Bank, Pall Mall, SW1.

HASTIE-SMITH, Richard Maybury; Under-Secretary, Ministry of Defence, since 1975; *b* 13 Oct. 1931; *s* of Engr-Comdr D. Hastie-Smith and H. I. Hastie-Smith; *m* 1956, Bridget Noel Cox; one *s* two *d*. *Educ:* Cranleigh Sch. (Schol.); Magdalene Coll., Cambridge (Schol.; BA). HM Forces, commnd Queen's Royal Regt, 1950-51. Entered Administrative Class, Home CS, War Office, 1955; Private Sec. to Permanent Under-Sec., 1957; Asst Private Sec. to Sec. of State, 1958; Principal, 1960; Asst Private Sec. to Sec. of State for Defence, 1965; Private Sec. to Minister of Defence (Equipment), 1968; Asst Sec., 1969; RCDS, 1974; Under-Sec., 1975. Governor: Cranleigh Sch.; St Catherine's Sch., Bramley. *Address:* 18 York Avenue, East Sheen, SW14. *T:* 01-876 4597. *Club:* University Pitt (Cambridge).

HASTINGS, family name of **Earl of Huntingdon.**

HASTINGS; *see* Abney-Hastings, family name of Countess of Loudoun.

HASTINGS, 22nd Baron, *cr* 1290; **Edward Delaval Henry Astley**, Bt 1660; *b* 14 April 1912; *s* of 21st Baron and Lady Marguerite Nevill (*d* 1975), *d* of 3rd Marquess of Abergavenny; *S* father 1956; *m* 1954, Catherine Rosaline Ratcliffe Coats, 2nd *d* of late Capt. H. V. Hinton; two *s* one *d*. *Educ:* Eton and abroad. Supplementary Reserve, Coldstream Guards, 1934; served War of 1939-45, Major 1945; farming in Southern Rhodesia, 1951-57. Mem. of Parliamentary delegation to the West Indies, 1958; a Lord in Waiting, 1961-62; Jt Parly Sec., Min. of Housing and Local Govt, 1962-64. Chairman: British-Italian Soc., 1957-62 (Pres., 1972-); Italian People's Flood Appeal, 1966-67; Governor: Brit. Inst. of Florence, 1959-; Royal Ballet, 1971-; Chm., Royal Ballet Benevolent Fund, 1966-; Pres., British Epilepsy Assoc., 1965-. Grand Officer, Order of Merit (Italy), 1968. *Heir: s* Hon. Delaval Thomas Harold Astley, *b* 25 April 1960. *Recreations:* riding, shooting, ballet, foreign travel. *Address:* Fulmodeston Hall, Fakenham, Norfolk. *T:* Thursford 231; Seaton Delaval Hall, Northumberland. *Clubs:* Brooks's, Army and Navy; Northern Counties (Newcastle); Norfolk County (Norwich).

HASTINGS, Archdeaconry; *see* Lewes and Hastings.

HASTINGS, Rev. Edward, MA, DD; *b* Kinneff, Kincardineshire, March 1890; *s* of late Rev. James Hastings, DD. *Educ:* Aberdeen Univ.; New Coll., Edinburgh. Ordained minister at Errol, Perthshire in 1921; resigned charge 1923 to undertake editorial work. *Publications:* The Speaker's Bible; The Local Colour of the Bible (with Rev. Dr Charles W. Budden); Joint-Editor of The Expository Times, 1922-65. *Address:* 11 King's Gate, Aberdeen AB2 6BL. *T:* Aberdeen 26048.

HASTINGS, Hubert De Cronin; Chairman, Architectural Press, 1927-74; Editor, Architectural Review, 1927-73; Editor, Architects' Journal, 1932-73; *b* 18 July 1902; *s* of Percy Hastings and Lilian Bass; *m* 1927, Hazel Rickman Garrard; one *s* one *d*. Royal Gold Medal for Architecture, 1971. *Address:* 9/13 Queen Anne's Gate, Westminster, SW1. *Clubs:* Arts, National, ICA.

HASTINGS, Michael; playwright; *b* 2 Sept. 1938; *s* of Max Emmanuel Gerald and Marie Katherine Hastings; *m* 1975, Victoria Hardie; one *s*. *Educ:* Imperial Service Coll., Windsor; Dulwich Coll.; Alleyn's Sch., Dulwich. Bespoke tailoring apprenticeship, Kilgour, French & Stanbury, London, 1953-56. FRGS. *Publications: plays:* Don't Destroy Me, 1956; Yes and After, 1957 (Arts Council Play Award, 1956); The World's Baby, 1962 (Enc. Britannica Award Medal, 1962); Lee Harvey Oswald: a far mean streak of indepence brought on by negleck, 1966; The Silence of Saint-Just, 1971; For the West (Uganda), 1977; *novels:* The Game, 1956; The Frauds, 1960; Tussy is Me, 1968 (Somerset Maugham Award, 1969); The Nightcomers, 1971; And in the Forest the Indians, 1975 (Arts Council Fiction Award, 1975); *poems:* Love me Lambeth, 1959; *stories:* Bart's Mornings and other Tales of Modern Brazil, 1975; *criticism:* Rupert Brooke, The Handsomest Young Man in England, 1967; Richard Burton: the erotic search, 1977; *for film and television:* for the West, 1963; Blue as his Eyes the Tin Helmet He Wore, 1966; The Search for the Nile, 1972 (Amer. Acad. of Arts and Scis 'emmy', 1972; St Christopher Medallion, 1975; British Screenwriters' Guild Award, 1975); The Nightcomers, 1972; Auntie Kathleen's Old Clothes, 1977. *Address:* c/o National Westminster Bank Ltd, Kensington High Street, W8.

HASTINGS, Stephen Lewis Edmonstone, MC 1944; MP (C) Mid-Bedfordshire since Nov. 1960; *b* 4 May 1921; *s* of late Lewis Aloysius MacDonald Hastings, MC, and of Edith Meriel Edmonstone; *m* 1st, 1948, Harriet Mary Elisabeth (marr. diss. 1971), *d* of Col Julian Latham Tomlin, CBE, DSO; one *s* one *d*; 2nd, 1975, Hon. Elisabeth Anne Lady Naylor-Leyland, *yr d* of late Viscount FitzAlan of Derwent and of Countess Fitzwilliam. *Educ:* Eton; RMC, Sandhurst. Gazetted Ensign, Scots Guards, 1939; served 2nd Bn, Western Desert, 1941-43 (despatches); SAS Regt, 1943. Joined Foreign Office, 1948. British Legation, Helsinki, 1950-52; British Embassy, Paris, 1953-58; First Sec., Political Office, Middle East Forces, 1959-60. Chm., European Supersonic Aviation Ltd; Director: Oxley Development; Dust Suppression Ltd. *Publication:* The Murder of TSR2, 1966. *Recreations:* fieldsports. *Address:* c/o House of Commons, SW1; 12A Ennismore Gardens, SW7. *Clubs:* Buck's, Pratts; Kandahar.

HASZELDINE, Prof. Robert Neville, FRS 1968; CChem, FRIC; MA Cantab, PhD Birmingham, PhD Cantab, DSc Birmingham,

ScD Cantab; Professor of Chemistry, since 1957, and Head of Department of Chemistry, 1957-76, Principal, since 1976, University of Manchester Institute of Science and Technology (Faculty of Technology, The University of Manchester); *b* Manchester, 3 May 1925; *s* of late Walter Haszeldine and late Hilda Haszeldine (*née* Webster); *m* 1954, Pauline Elvina Goodwin; two *s* two *d*. *Educ:* Stockport Grammar Sch.; University of Birmingham (John Watt Meml Schol., 1942); Sidney Sussex Coll., Cambridge; Queens' Coll., Cambridge. University of Cambridge: Asst in Research in Organic Chemistry, 1949; University Demonstrator in Organic and Inorganic Chemistry, 1951; Asst Dir of Research, 1956; Fellow and Dir of Studies, Queens' Coll., 1954-57, Hon. Fellow, 1976. Tilden Lectr, 1968; Vis. Lectr at universities and laboratories in the USA, Russia, Switzerland, Austria, Germany, Japan and France. Meldola Medal, 1953; Corday-Morgan Medal and Prize, 1960. *Publications:* numerous scientific publications in chemical jls. *Recreations:* mountaineering, gardening, natural history, good food, wine. *Address:* Windyridge, Lyme Road, Disley, Cheshire. *T:* Disley 2223; University of Manchester Institute of Science and Technology, Manchester M60 1QD. *T:* 061-236 3311.

HATFIELD, Hon. Richard Bennett; Premier of New Brunswick since 1970; MLA (Progressive C) Carleton County since 1961, New Brunswick; *b* 9 April 1931; single. *Educ:* Rothesay Collegiate Sch.; Hartland High Sch.; Acadia Univ.; Dalhousie Univ. BA Acadia 1952; LLB Dalhousie 1956. Admitted to Bar of NS, 1956. Joined law firm of Patterson, Smith, Matthews & Grant in Truro, NS, 1956; Exec. Asst to Minister of Trade and Commerce, Ottawa, 1957-58; Sales Man., Hatfield Industries Ltd, 1958-65. Leader of Opposition, 1968; Leader, PC Party of New Brunswick, 1969. Hon. LLD: Moncton, 1971; New Brunswick, 1972; St Thomas, 1973; Mount Allison, 1975. Hon. Chief, Micmac and Maliseet Tribes. Canada-Israel Friendship Award, 1973. *Address:* Office of the Premier, PO Box 6000, Fredericton, New Brunswick E3B 5H1, Canada. *T:* (506) 454-9724.

HATHERTON, 7th Baron *cr* 1835; **Thomas Charles Tasman Littleton,** TD 1953; *b* 6 Oct. 1907; *s* of 4th Baron Hatherton and Hester Edithe (*d* 1947), *d* of Thomas Tarrant Hoskins, MD, Tasmania; *S* brother, 1973; *m* 1933, Ann Scott, *o d* of late Lt-Comdr Thomas McLeod, RN; one *d*. *Educ:* St Edward's School. Commnd TA, 1934; served War of 1939-45; Captain TARO 1945, retd 1956. *Heir: cousin* Edward Charles Littleton, *b* 1950. *Address:* Walhouse, Hutton Henry, Castle Eden, Co. Durham. *Club:* Naval and Military.

HATTERSLEY, Alan Frederick, MA, DLitt; Professor Emeritus of History, University of Natal; Member Union Archives Commission, 1948-64; *b* 6 April 1893; *o s* of F. Kilvington Hattersley, Fairlawn, Harrogate. *Educ:* Leeds Grammar Sch.; Downing Coll., Cambridge. Professor of History and Political Science, University of Natal, 1923-53. Hon. DLitt (Natal), 1957. Fellow, Natal Soc., 1970. Civic honours conferred by Pietermaritzburg, 1972. *Publications:* A Short History of Western Civilisation 1927; A History of Democracy, 1930; South Africa (Home University Library), 1933; History Teaching in Schools, 1935; More Annals of Natal, 1936; Pietermaritzburg Panorama, 1938; Later Annals of Natal, 1938; Portrait of a Colony, 1940; The Natalians, 1940; Hilton Portrait, 1945; Journal of J. S. Dobie, 1945; The British Settlement of Natal, 1950; Carbineer, 1950; A Victorian Lady At the Cape, 1951; A Hospital Century, 1955; Oliver the Spy and Others, 1959; The First South African Detectives, 1960; The Convict Crisis and Growth of Unity, 1965; An Illustrated Social History of S Africa, 1969. *Recreation:* Emeritus Commissioner, Boy Scouts Association, South Africa. *Address:* Inglemoor House, 1 Sanders Road, Pietermaritzburg, S Africa. *TA:* Univcoll.

HATTERSLEY, Rt. Hon. Roy Sydney George, PC 1975; BSc (Econ.); MP (Lab) Sparkbrook Division of Birmingham since 1964; Secretary of State for Prices and Consumer Protection, since 1976; *b* 28 Dec. 1932; *s* of Frederick Roy Hattersley, Sheffield; *m* 1956, Molly, *d* of Michael Loughran, Consett, Co. Durham. *Educ:* Sheffield City Grammar Sch.; Univ. of Hull. Journalist and Health Service Executive, 1956-64; Mem. Sheffield City Council, 1957-65 (Chm. Housing Cttee and Public Works Cttee). PPS to Minister of Pensions and National Insurance, 1964-67; Jt Parly Sec., DEP (formerly Min. of Labour), 1967-69; Minister of Defence for Administration, 1969-70; Labour Party spokesman: on Defence, 1972; on Educn and Sci., 1972-74; Minister of State, FCO, 1974-76. Vis. Fellow, Inst. of Politics, Univ. of Harvard, 1971, 1972. Dir, Campaign for a European Political Community, 1966-67. *Publications:* Nelson, 1974; Goodbye to Yorkshire (essays), 1976. *Address:* House of Commons, SW1. *Club:* Reform.

HATTO, Prof. Arthur Thomas, MA; Head of the Department of German, Queen Mary College, University of London, 1938-77; *b* 11 Feb. 1910; *s* of Thomas Hatto, LLB and Alice Walters; *m* 1935, Margot Feibelmann; one *d*. *Educ:* Dulwich Coll.; King's Coll., London (Fellow, 1971); University Coll., London. BA (London) 1931; MA (with Distinction), 1934. Lektor für Englisch, University of Berne, 1932-34; Asst Lectr in German, KCL, 1934-38; Queen Mary Coll., University of London, 1938 (Head of Dept of German). Temp. Sen. Asst, Foreign Office, 1939-45; Part-time Lectr in German, University Coll., London, 1944-45; returned to Queen Mary Coll., 1945; Reader in German Language and Literature, University of London, 1946; Prof. of German Language and Literature, University of London, 1953. Governor, School of Oriental and African Studies, Univ. of London, 1960 (Foundn Day Lecture, 1970); Governor, QMC, Univ. of London, 1968-70. Chairman: London Seminar on Epic; Cttee 'A' (Theol. and Arts), Central Research Fund, Univ. of London, 1969. Fellow: Royal Anthropological Institute; Royal Asiatic Society (lecture: Plot and character in Kirghiz epic poetry of the mid 19th cent., 1976); Leverhulme Emeritus Fellow (heroic poetry in Central Asia and Siberia), 1977-. *Publications:* (with R. J. Taylor) The Songs of Neidhart von Reuental, 1958; Gottfried von Strassburg, Tristan (trans. entire for first time) with Tristran of Thomas (newly trans.) with an Introduction, 1960; The Niblungenlied: a new translation, with Introduction and Notes, 1964; editor of Eos, an enquiry by fifty scholars into the theme of the alba in world literature, 1965; articles in learned periodicals. *Recreations:* reading, gardening, walking. *Club:* The Confrères.

HATTON; *see* Finch Hatton, family name of Earl of Winchilsea.

HATTON, Frank; MP (Lab) Manchester, Moss Side, since 1974 (Manchester Exchange, June 1973-1974); *b* 25 Sept. 1921; *s* of James Hatton and Edith Latham; *m* 1949, Olive Kelly; two *s*. *Educ:* Manchester Central High School for Boys. Railway Clerk, 1939-51; Personnel Officer, Central Electricity Generating Board, 1951-73. Member: Manchester City Council, 1954-74 (Alderman, 1971-74); Manchester District Council, 1973-74; Chairman: Manchester Educn Cttee, 1962-67, 1971-74; Educn Cttee, Assoc. of Municipal Corporations, 1972-74; Local Authorities Higher Educn Cttee, 1972-74; Vice-Pres., Assoc. of Educn Cttees, 1973-74; Member: Cttee on Supply and Training of Teachers; Burnham Cttee. Chm., Manchester Polytechnic, 1972-74; Member of Council: Univ. of Manchester; Univ. of Manchester Inst. of Science and Technology; former Mem. Council, Open University; Governor, Cheadle Hulme Sch.; former Governor: Manchester Grammar Sch.; Chetham's Hosp. Sch. of Music. Mem. TGWU. Former Sec. and Agent, Manchester Exchange Constituency Labour Party; contested (Lab) Manchester (Moss Side), 1970. JP Manchester, 1965. *Address:* 50 Merston Drive, East Didsbury, Manchester M20 0WT; House of Commons, SW1.

HATTY, Hon. Sir Cyril (James), Kt 1963; director of companies; *b* 22 Dec. 1908; *o s* of James Hatty and Edith (*née* Russen); *m* 1937, Doris Evelyn, *o d* of James Lane Stewart and Mable Grace Stewart; two *s*. *Educ:* Westminster City Sch. Deputy Dir, O and M Division, UK Treasury, until Jan. 1947; emigrated to S Africa, in industry, Feb. 1947; moved to Bulawayo, in industry, Jan. 1948. MP for Bulawayo North, Sept. 1950-Dec. 1962; Minister of Treasury, Jan. 1954-Sept. 1962, also Minister of Mines, Feb. 1956-Dec. 1962. FCIS; Fellow, Inst. of Cost and Management Accountants; FBIM. *Publication:* Digest of SR Company Law, 1952. *Recreations:* painting, music. *Address:* Merton Park, Norton, Rhodesia. *T:* 74520. *Clubs:* Polytechnic, Salisbury, New (Salisbury).

HAUGHTON, Daniel Jeremiah; Chairman of the Board, Lockheed Aircraft Corporation, USA, 1967-76; *b* Dora, Walker County, Ala, 7 Sept. 1911; *s* of Gayle Haughton and Mattie Haughton (*née* Davis); *m* 1935, Martha Jean, *d* of Henry Oliver, Kewanee, Ill, a farmer; no *c*. *Educ:* Univ. of Alabama. BS degree in commerce and business administration, 1933. Lockheed Aircraft Corp., 1939-: first as systems analyst; Works Manager, Vega Aircraft Corp. (a subsidiary), 1943; General Manager, Lockheed-Georgia Co. (a div.), 1952-56; elected: a Lockheed Vice-Pres., 1952, Exec. Vice-Pres., 1956; a Dir, 1958; Pres. of Corp., 1961. Director: United Calif. Bank; South Calif. Edison Co.; Member of many professional societies; active in community and national affairs, including, 1967, Chm. of US Treasury Dept's industrial payroll savings bonds campaign. Chm., Nat. Multiple Sclerosis Soc.; Bd of Trustees, Nat. Security Industrial Assoc. Employer of the Year, Nat. Ind. Recreation Assoc., 1973; Management Man of the Year, Nat. Managing Assoc., 1966; Award of Achievement, Nat. Aviation Club, 1969; 16th Annual Nat. Transportation Award, Nat. Defense Transportation Assoc.; Tony Jennus Award, 1970;

Salesman of the Year, Sales and Marketing Assoc., Los Angeles, 1970. Hon. LLD: Univ. of Alabama, 1962; George Washington Univ., 1965; Hon. DSc (Business Admin) Clarkson Coll. of Tech., 1973; Hon. LLD Pepperdine Univ., 1975. *Recreation:* fishing. *Address:* 12956 Blairwood Drive, Studio City, Calif 91604, USA. *Clubs:* Capital City (Atlanta); California (Los Angeles).

HAUGHTON, Dr Sidney Henry, FRS 1961; FGS 1914; DSc; *b* 7 May 1888; *s* of Henry Charles Haughton and Alice Haughton (*née* Aves), London; *m* 1914, Edith Hoal, Cape Town; one *s* one *d. Educ:* Walthamstow Technical Institute; Trinity Hall, Cambridge. BA Cantab 1909; DSc Cape Town, 1921. Palæontologist, S African Museum, Cape Town, 1911, Asst Dir, 1914; Sen. Geologist, S African Geological Survey, 1920, Dir, 1934; Chief Geologist, S African Atomic Energy Board, 1948-54. Mem., at various times of Governmental Bds and Commns on Industrial Requirements, Fuel Research, Scientific and Industrial Research, Museums, University Finances. Hon. LLD Cape Town, 1948; Hon. DSc: Witwatersrand, 1964; Natal, 1967; Corresponding Mem., Geological Soc. Amer., 1948, etc. *Publications:* Stratigraphical Geology of Africa South of the Sahara, 1962; Geological History of Southern Africa, 1969; numerous, on geol., palæontolog. and geograph. subjects, in learned jls; rev. and ed Geology of South Africa, by A. L. Du Toit (3rd edn), 1954. *Recreations:* music, reading, walking; formerly: cricket, hockey, tennis. *Address:* Bernard Price Institute for Palaeontological Research, University of the Witwatersrand, Johannesburg, South Africa. *Club:* Country (Pretoria).

HAULFRYN WILLIAMS, John; *see* Williams, J. H.

HAUSER, Frank Ivor, CBE 1968; Director of Productions, Meadow Players, Oxford Playhouse, 1956-73; *b* 1 Aug. 1922; *s* of late Abraham and of Sarah Hauser; unmarried. *Educ:* Cardiff High Sch.; Christ Church, Oxford. Oxford, 1941-42; RA, 1942-45; Oxford, 1946-48. BBC Drama Producer, 1948-51; Director: Salisbury Arts Theatre, 1952-53; Midland Theatre Co., 1945-55. Formed Meadow Players Ltd, which re-opened the Oxford Playhouse, 1956; took Oxford Playhouse Co. on tour of India, Pakistan and Ceylon, 1959-60. Produced at Sadler's Wells Opera: La Traviata, 1961; Iolanthe, 1962; Orfeo, 1965; produced: at Oxford Playhouse: Antony and Cleopatra, 1965; Phèdre, 1966; The Promise, 1966; The Silent Woman, 1968; Pippa Passes, 1968; Uncle Vanya, 1969; Curtain Up, 1969; The Merchant of Venice, 1973; also: Il Matrimonio Segreto, Glyndebourne, 1965; A Heritage and its History, Phoenix, 1965; The Promise, Fortune, 1967; Volpone, Garrick, 1967; The Magic Flute, Sadler's Wells, 1967; Kean, Globe, 1971; The Wolf, Apollo, 1973; Cinderella, Casino, 1974; On Approval, Haymarket, 1975. *Recreation:* piano. *Address:* 5 Stirling Mansions, Canfield Gardens, NW6. *T:* 01-624 4690.

HAVELOCK, Sir Wilfrid (Bowen), Kt 1963; *b* 14 April 1912; *s* of late Rev. E. W. Havelock and Helen (*née* Bowen); *m* 1st, 1938, Mrs M. E. Pershouse (*née* Vincent) (marr. diss. 1967); one *s*; 2nd, 1972, Mrs Patricia Mumford, *widow* of Major Philip S. Mumford. *Educ:* Imperial Service Coll., Windsor, Berks. Elected to Kenya Legislative Council, 1948; Chairman, European Elected Members, 1952; Mem., Kenya Executive Council, 1952; Minister for Local Government, Kenya, 1954; Minister for Agriculture, Kenya, 1962-63. Dep. Chm., Agricl Finance Corp., Kenya, 1964-; Member: Nat. Irrigation Bd, 1974-; Hotels and Restaurant Authority, 1975-. Dir, Bamburi Portland Cement Co., 1974-. Chm., Kenya Assoc. of Hotelkeepers and Caterers, 1974, 1975, 1976. *Address:* PO Box 154, Malindi, Kenya. *Clubs:* Lansdowne (London); Mombasa, Muthaiga Country, Nairobi (Kenya).

HAVELOCK-ALLAN, Sir Anthony James Allan, 4th Bt *cr* 1858; film producer; *b* 28 Feb. 1905; *s* of Allan (2nd *s* of Sir Henry Havelock-Allan, 1st Bt, VC, GCB, MP), and Annie Julia, *d* of Sir William Chaytor, 3rd Bt; *S* brother, 1975; *m* 1939, Valerie Louise Hobson, *qv* (marr. diss. 1952), *d* of late Comdr Robert Gordon Hobson, RN; two *s*. *Educ:* Charterhouse; Switzerland. Artists and Recording Manager, Brunswick Gramophone Co., London and Vox AG, Berlin, 1924-29; entered films as Casting Dir and Producer's Asst, 1933; produced quota films for Paramount; produced for Pinebrook Ltd and Two Cities Films, 1938-40; Assoc. Producer to Noel Coward, 1941; with David Lean and Ronald Neame, formed Cineguild, 1942; Producer, Assoc. Producer or in charge of production for Cineguild, 1942-47; formed Constellation Films, independent co. producing for Rank Org. and British Lion, 1949; Mem. Cinematographic Films Council and Nat. Film Production Council, 1948-51; Mem. Home Office Cttee on Employment of Children in Entertainment; Chm. British Film Academy, 1952; formed with

Lord Brabourne and Major Daniel Angel British Home Entertainment to introduce Pay TV, 1958; Chm. Council of Soc. of Film and Television Arts (now BAFTA), 1962, 1963; Mem. Nat. Film Archive Cttee; a Gov. British Film Inst. and Mem. Institute's Production Cttee, 1958-65; Mem. US Academy of Motion Pictures Arts and Sciences, 1970. Films include: This Man is News, This Man in Paris, Lambeth Walk, Unpublished Story, From the Four Corners (documentary prod and dir), Brief Encounter (shared Academy script nomination), Great Expectations (shared Academy script nomination), Take my Life, Blanche Fury, Shadow of the Eagle, Never Take No for an Answer, Interrupted Journey, Young Lovers (dir Anthony Asquith), Orders to Kill (dir Anthony Asquith), Meet Me Tonight, The Quare Fellow, An Evening with the Royal Ballet (directed two ballets); (for television): National Theatre's Uncle Vanya, Olivier's Othello, Zeffirelli's Romeo and Juliet, David Lean's Ryan's Daughter. *Heir: s* Simon Anthony Henry Havelock-Allan, *b* 6 May 1944. *Address:* c/o Messrs Gorrie Whitson & Sons, 9 Cavendish Square, W1.

HAVERGAL, Henry MacLeod, OBE 1965; MA Oxon, BMus Edinburgh; FRCM; Hon. RAM; *b* 21 Feb. 1902; *er s* of Rev. Ernest Havergal; *m* 1st, 1926, Hyacinth (*d* 1962), *er d* of Arthur Chitty; two *s*; 2nd, 1964, Nina Davidson, Aberdeen. *Educ:* Choristers Sch., Salisbury; St Edward's Sch. and St John's Coll., Oxford. Dir of Music, Fettes Coll., Edinburgh, 1924-33; Haileybury Coll., 1934-36; Harrow Sch., 1937-45; Master of Music, Winchester Coll., 1946-53; Principal, Royal Scottish Academy of Music (later Royal Scottish Academy of Music and Drama), 1953-69, now Fellow; Dir, Jamaica Sch. of Music, 1973-75. Hon. DMus Edinburgh, 1958; Hon. LLD Glasgow, 1969. *Recreation:* fishing. *Address:* 2 Bellevue Terrace, Edinburgh EH7 4DU. *T:* 031-556 6525. *Clubs:* United Oxford & Cambridge University; New (Edinburgh).

HAVERS, Air Vice-Marshal Sir E. William, KBE 1946 (CBE 1941); CB 1944; *b* 15 Oct. 1887; *m* 1st, 1920, Blanche Mary Somerville Macey (*d* 1968); one *s* one *d*; 2nd, 1970, Mary Elizabeth Ritchie (despatches); Air Ministry, Industrial Whitley Council, 1921-23; Iraq, 1923-25; Coastal Command, 1926-28; RAF Staff Coll., 1929; Senior Equipment Staff Officer Air Defences, Great Britain, 1930-32; HQ Middle East, Egypt, 1932-34; Dir-Gen. of Equipment, Air Ministry, 1940-42; AOC No. 40 Group, RAF, 1943-46; retired 1946; Govt Missions in Middle East, HQ Cairo, 1946-48; Consultant to Ministry of Supply, 1952-53. District Comr S Wight Scouts, 1950-55. *Address:* Tenter Lodge, Waterside, Knaresborough, North Yorks. *T:* Harrogate 862312.

HAVERS, Rt. Hon. Sir (Robert) Michael (Oldfield), PC 1977; Kt 1972; QC 1964; MP (C) Merton, Wimbledon, since 1974 (Wimbledon, 1970-74); *b* 10 March 1923; 2nd *s* of Sir Cecil Havers, QC, and late Enid Snelling; *m* 1949, Carol Elizabeth, *d* of Stuart Lay, London; two *s*. *Educ:* Westminster Sch.; Corpus Christi Coll., Cambridge. Lieut RNVR, 1941-46. Called to Bar, Inner Temple, 1948; Master of the Bench, 1971. Recorder: of Dover, 1962-68; of Norwich, 1968-71; a Recorder, 1972; Chm., West Suffolk QS, 1965-71 (Dep. Chairman 1961-65). Chancellor of Dioceses of St Edmundsbury and Ipswich, 1965-73, of Ely, 1969-73. Solicitor-General, 1972-74; Shadow Attorney-General and Legal Adviser to Shadow Cabinet, 1974-. Chm., Lakenheath Anglo-American Community Relations Cttee, 1966-71. *Recreations:* golf, photography, reading. *Address:* (professional) 5 King's Bench Walk, Temple, EC4. *T:* 01-353 4713; (home) White Shutters, Ousden, Newmarket. *T:* Ousden 267; 6B Woodhayes Road, Wimbledon, SW19. *Clubs:* Garrick, Royal Automobile; Norfolk (Norwich); Royal Wimbledon Golf.
  See also Mrs A. E. O. Butler-Sloss.

HAVILAND, Denis William Garstin Latimer, CB 1957; MA; FBIM; FRSA; idc; Chairman and Managing Director, Staveley Industries Ltd, 1965-69 (Joint Managing Director and Deputy Chairman, 1964); *b* 15 Aug. 1910; *s* of late William Alexander Haviland and of Edyth Louise Latimer. *Educ:* Rugby Sch., St John's Coll., Cambridge (MA, exam. of AMInstT). LMS Rly, 1934-39. Army, RE (Col), 1940-46. Prin., Control Office for Germany and Austria, 1946; Asst Sec., 1947; transf. FO (GS), 1947; seconded to IDC, 1950; transf. Min. of Supply, 1951; Under Sec., 1953; Dep. Sec., 1959; trans. Min. of Aviation, 1959, Deputy Sec., 1959-64. Chm., Preparatory Commn European Launcher Develt Organisation, 1962-64. Director: Short Bros & Harland Ltd; Organised Office Designs; Consultant. Mem. Council, BIM, 1967-, Vice-Chm., 1973-74. Member: Management Studies Bd, CNAA; Ct, Cranfield Inst. of Technology. Liveryman, Co. of Coachmakers. *Address:* 113 Hampstead Way, NW11. *T:* 01-455 2638. *Club:* Bath.

HAVILLAND; see de Havilland.

HAWAII, Bishop of, (Episcopal Church in the USA); see Browning, Rt Rev. E. L.

HAWARDEN, 8th Viscount, cr 1791; **Robert Leslie Eustace Maude;** farming his own estate since 1952; b 26 March 1926; s of 7th Viscount Hawarden and Viscountess Hawarden (née Marion Wright (d 1974); S father 1958; m 1957, Susannah Caroline Hyde Gardner; two s one d. Educ: Winchester; Christ Church, Oxford. Cirencester Agricultural Coll., 1948-50. Served for a short time in the Coldstream Guards and was invalided out, 1945-46. Recreation: shooting. Heir: s Hon. Robert Connan Wyndham Leslie Maude, b 23 May 1961. Address: Wingham Court, near Canterbury, Kent. T: Wingham 222. Club: Farmers'.

HAWES, Derrick Gordon H.; see Harington Hawes.

HAWES, Maj.-Gen. Leonard Arthur, CBE 1940; DSO 1918; MC; MA (Hon.) Oxon; DL; Royal Artillery; b Throcking, Herts, 22 July 1892; s of C. A. Hawes, Uckfield, Sussex; m 1st, 1919, Gwendolen Mary (d 1970), d of D. H. Grimsdale, JP, Uxbridge, Middlesex; one d (one s decd); 2nd, 1972, Yolande, widow of Wyndham Robinson. Educ: Bedford; RM Academy, Woolwich. Lieut Royal Garrison Artillery, 1911; Capt., 1916; Temp. Major, 1917; Major, 1929; Bt Lieut-Col 1932; Lieut-Col and Col 1938; served European War, 1914-18 (wounded, CBE, DSO, MC, despatches, Order of Crown of Italy); served War of 1939-45; retired pay, 1945. DL West Sussex, 1977. Address: Old Manor House, West Harting, Petersfield, Hants. Club: Army and Navy.

HAWKE, family name of **Baron Hawke.**

HAWKE, 9th Baron, cr 1776, of Towton; **Bladen Wilmer Hawke;** b 31 Dec. 1901; s of 8th Baron and late Frances Alice, d of Col J. R. Wilmer, Survey of India; S father 1939; m 1934, Ina Mary, e d of late Henry Faure Walker, Highley Manor, Balcombe, Sussex; seven d. Educ: Winchester; King's Coll., Cambridge (MA). Bombay Company, India, 1923-38; Temp. Civil Servant, Ministry of Economic Warfare, 1940-43, War Office, 1943-45. Lord-in-Waiting to the Queen and Government Whip, House of Lords, 1953-57. Chm. Conservative Back Bench Peers Assoc., 1949-53; Executive Cttee, National Union Conservatives, 1950-53; Mem., House of Laity, Church Assembly, later Gen. Synod of C of E, 1955-75; Church Commissioner, 1958-73; Chm., Chichester Diocesan Board of Finance, 1962-72. Chm., Rhodesia Fairbridge Scholarship Fund. Director: Initial Services Ltd; Ecclesiastical Insurance Office, Ltd, 1961-77. Recreations: golf, gardening. Heir: b Squadron Leader Hon. (Julian Stanhope) Theodore Hawke, Auxiliary Air Force [b 19 Oct. 1904; m 1st, 1933, Angela Margaret Griselda (marr. diss., 1946), d of late Capt. Edmund W. Bury; two d; 2nd, 1947, Georgette Margaret, d of George S. Davidson; one s three d]. Address: Faygate Place, Faygate, Sussex. T: Faygate 252. Club: Carlton.

HAWKE, Robert James Lee; President, Australian Council of Trade Unions, since 1970; President, Australian Labor Party, since 1973; b 9 Dec. 1929; m 1956, Hazel Masterson; one s two d. Educ: Univ. of Western Australia (LLB, BA(Econ)); Oxford Univ. (BLitt). Research Officer and Advocate for Aust. Council of Trade Unions, 1958-69. Member: Governing Body of Internat. Labour Office; Board, Reserve Bank of Australia; Aust. Population and Immigration Council, 1976-. Recreations: tennis, cricket, reading. Address: 254 La Trobe Street, Melbourne, Vic 3000, Australia. T: 347 3966.

HAWKEN, Lewis Dudley; Commissioner of Customs and Excise since 1975; b 23 Aug. 1931; s of Richard and Doris May Evelyn Hawken; m 1954, Bridget Mary Gamble; two s one d. Educ: Harrow County Sch. for Boys; Lincoln Coll., Oxford (MA). Recreations: collecting Victorian books, tennis. Address: 19 Eastcote Road, Ruislip, Mddx. T: Ruislip 32405. Club: United Oxford & Cambridge University.

HAWKER, Albert Henry, CMG 1964; OBE 1960; b 31 Oct. 1911; s of late H. J. Hawker, Cheltenham and late Mrs G. A. Hawker, Exeter; m 1944, Margaret Janet Olivia, d of late T. J. C. Acton (ICS) and of Mrs M de C. Acton, BEM, Golden Furlong, Brackley, Northants; two s. Educ: Pate's Sch., Cheltenham. Served War of 1939-45: Bde Major 12th Bde, 1941-43; Staff Coll., Camberley, 1943-44; Lieut-Col Mil. Asst to CGS in India, 1944-46. RARO; Lieut-Col The Gordon Highlanders, 1946-61. Barclays Bank Ltd, Birmingham and Oxford Local Districts, 1929-39. Joined HM Overseas Civil Service, 1946; served in: Palestine, 1946-48; N Rhodesia, 1948-52; Zanzibar, 1952-64

(Development Sec., Admin. Sec., Perm. Sec. in Min. of Finance, Prime Minister's Office, Vice-President's Office and President's Office); retd, 1964. Director: Thomson Regional Newspapers Ltd, 1965-69; The Times Ltd and The Sunday Times Ltd, 1968-69; The Thomson Organization, 1969-77. Gold Cross, Royal Order of George I of Greece, 1948; Brilliant Star of Zanzibar, 1957. Recreations: sailing, cricket, tennis, golf, photography (Cdre, Zanzibar Sailing Club, 1955 and 1961). Address: (business) 4 Stratford Place, W1. T: 01-492 0321; Bowling Green Farm, Cottered, near Buntingford, Herts. T: Cottered 234. Clubs: Royal Commonwealth Society, Royal Yachting Association.

HAWKER, Rt. Rev. Dennis Gascoyne; see Grantham, Bishop Suffragan of.

HAWKER, Sir (Frank) Cyril, Kt 1958; Chairman: The Chartered Bank, 1973-74; The Standard Bank Ltd, 1962-74; Standard and Chartered Banking Group, 1969-74; The Bank of West Africa, 1965-73; Union Zairoise de Banques, 1969-74; Director, Head Wrightson & Co. Ltd, since 1962; Deputy-Chairman, Midland and International Banks, 1964-72; Hon. Treasurer and Chairman, Finance Committee, National Playing Fields Association, 1958-76; b 21 July 1900; s of late Frank Charley and Bertha Mary Hawker; m 1931, Marjorie Ann, d of late Thomas Henry and Amelia Harriett Pearce; three d. Educ: City of London Sch. Entered service Bank of England, 1920; Dep. Chief Cashier, 1944-48; Chief Accountant, 1948-53; Adviser to Governors, 1953-54; Executive Director, Bank of England, 1954-62. High Sheriff of County of London, 1963. President: MCC, 1970-71; Amateur Football Alliance; Hon. Vice-Pres., Football Assoc. Recreation: cricket. Address: Pounsley Lodge, Blackboys, near Uckfield, Sussex. T: Hadlow Down 250. Clubs: Athenæum, MCC.

HAWKER, Sir Richard (George), Kt 1965; MA Cantab; b 11 April 1907; s of late R. M. Hawker; m 1940, Frances C., d of late S. Rymill; two s two d (and one s decd). Educ: Geelong Grammar Sch.; Trinity Hall, Cambridge. Returned SA, 1929; took over management Bungaree Merino Stud, 1932. Mem. Blyth Dist Coun., 1936-42, 1946-70. War service: 9/23 Light Horse Regt, 1939-41; 1st Armoured Div., AIF, 1941-44. Member: Cttee SA Stud Merino Breeders Assoc., 1939-40, 1959- (Pres. 1962-63, 1963-64); Council, Aust. Assoc. of Stud Merino Breeders, 1962-71 (Pres., 1968-71); Australian Wool Industry Conf., 1963-65 (as nominee of Federal Graziers' Council). Chm., Roseworthy Agricultural Coll. Council, 1964-73. Director: Adelaide Steamship Co. Ltd, 1949 (Chm. 1952-73); Coal & Allied Industries, NSW, 1961-; (local bd in SA) Queensland Insurance Co. Ltd, 1955-74; Amalgamated Wireless (Australasia) Ltd, 1971-. Recreations: shooting, fishing. Address: Bungaree, Clare, SA 5453, Australia. T: Clare 2676. Clubs: Bath, Oriental; Australian (Sydney); Adelaide (SA).

HAWKES, (Charles Francis) Christopher, FBA, FSA; Professor of European Archaeology in the University of Oxford, and Fellow of Keble College, 1946-72, Professor Emeritus, since 1972; Hon. Fellow of Keble College, since 1972; Secretary, Committee of Research Laboratory for Archæology and History of Art, 1955-72; b 5 June 1905; o s of late Charles Pascoe Hawkes; m 1st, 1933, Jacquetta (from whom he obtained a divorce 1953) (see Jacquetta Hawkes), yr d of late Sir Frederick Gowland Hopkins, OM; one s; 2nd, 1959, Sonia Elizabeth, o d of late Albert Andrew Chadwick. Educ: Winchester Coll. (Scholar); New Coll. Oxford (Scholar). 1st in Classical Hon. Mods 1926, in Final Lit. Hum. 1928; BA 1928; MA 1931; entered British Museum, Dept. of British and Medieval Antiquities, 1928; Asst Keeper 1st Class, 1938; in charge of Prehistoric and Romano-British Antiquities, 1946. Principal in Ministry of Aircraft Production, 1940-45. Retired from British Museum, 1946. I/c Inst. of Archæology, Oxford, 1961-67, 1968-72. FBA, 1948; FSA 1932; Fellow of Royal Archæological Institute, Hon. Sec. 1930-35, and Hon. Editor of Archæological Journal, 1944-50; Pres., Prehistoric Soc., 1950-54; a National Sec. for Great Britain, 1931-48, Mem. of Permanent Council, 1948-71, and Mem. Cttee of Honour, 1971-, International Union of Prehistoric and Protohistoric Sciences; Hon. Sec. of Colchester Excavation Cttee and in joint charge of its excavations, 1930-62; in charge of, or associated with various excavations, 1925-64, on Roman and prehistoric sites, especially for the Hants Field Club, and near Oxford; conducted archæological expedns in N Portugal, 1958-59. Vis. Lectr, Univ. of Manchester, 1947-49; Lectures: Dalrymple, Univ. of Glasgow, 1948; George Grant McCurdy, Harvard Univ., 1953; Davies, Belfast, 1974; Myres Meml, Oxford, 1975; British Acad. at Rome, Accad. Naz. Lincei, 1975; Mortimer Wheeler, 1975; travelled in Europe as Leverhulme Research Fellow, 1955-58, and as Leverhulme Emeritus Fellow, 1972-73; Guest

Academician, Budapest, 1971; Guest Prof., Univ. of Munich, 1973-74; a Visitor, Ashmolean Museum, 1961-67. President: Section H., Brit. Assoc., 1957; Hants Field Club, 1960-63; Member: Council for British Archæology 1944-72 (Pres., 1961-64; Group 9 Convener, 1964-67); Ancient Monuments Board for England, 1954-69. Mem., German Archaeological Inst.; Corresp. Mem., RIA; Swiss Soc. for Prehistory. Editor of Inventaria Archæologica for Great Britain, 1954-76. Various British Acad. awards, 1963-; Hon. Dr Rennes, 1971; Hon. DLitt NUI, 1972. *Publications:* St Catharine's Hill, Winchester (with J. N. L. Myres and C. G. Stevens), 1931; Archæology in England and Wales, 1914-31 (with T. D. Kendrick), 1932; Winchester College: An Essay in Description and Appreciation, 1933; The Prehistoric Foundations of Europe, 1940, 1974; Prehistoric Britain (with Jacquetta Hawkes), 1943, 1947, 1957; Camulodunum: The Excavations at Colchester, 1930-39 (with M. R. Hull), 1947; (contrib. and ed with Sonia Hawkes) Archaeology into History, vol I, 1973; (contrib. and ed with P. M. Duval) Celtic Art in Ancient Europe, 1976; articles in encyclopædias, collaborative books, and many archæological journals; received complimentary vol. by British and foreign colleagues, 1971. *Recreations:* archæology, travelling, music. *Address:* Keble College, Oxford; 19 Walton Street, Oxford.

HAWKES, David, MA, DPhil; Research Fellow, All Souls College, Oxford, since 1973; *b* 6 July 1923; *s* of Ewart Hawkes and Dorothy May Hawkes (*née* Davis); *m* 1950, Sylvia Jean Perkins; one *s* three *d. Educ:* Bancroft's Sch. Open Scholarship in Classics, Christ Church, Oxford, 1941; Chinese Hons Sch., Oxford, 1945-47; Research Student, National Peking Univ., 1948-51. Formerly University Lecturer in Chinese, Oxford; Prof. of Chinese, Oxford Univ., 1959-71. Visiting Lecturer in Chinese Literature, Harvard Univ., 1958-59. *Publications:* Ch'u Tz'ŭ, Songs of the South, 1959; A Little Primer of Tu Fu, 1967; The Story of the Stone, 1973.

HAWKES, Jacquetta, OBE 1952; author and archaeologist; *b* 1910; *yr d* of Sir Frederick Gowland Hopkins, OM and Jessie Anne Stephens; *m* 1st, 1933, Christopher Hawkes (*see* Prof. C. F. C. Hawkes) (marr. diss. 1953); one *s*; 2nd, 1953, J. B. Priestley, *qv. Educ:* Perse Sch.; Newnham Coll., Cambridge. MA. Associate, Newnham Coll., 1951. Research and excavation in Great Britain, Eire, France and Palestine, 1931-40; FSA, 1940. Asst Principal, Post-War Reconstruction Secretariat, 1941-43; Ministry of Education, becoming established Principal and Sec. of UK National Commn for UNESCO, 1943-49; retired from Civil Service to write, 1949. John Danz Vis. Prof., Univ. of Washington, 1971. Vice-Pres. Council for Brit. Archæology, 1949-52; Governor, Brit. Film Inst., 1950-55. Archæological adviser, Festival of Britain, 1949-51. Mem., UNESCO Culture Advisory Cttee, 1966. *Publications:* Archæology of Jersey, 1939; Prehistoric Britain (with Christopher Hawkes), 1944; Early Britain, 1945; Symbols and Speculations (poems), 1948; A Land, 1951 (£100 Kemsley Award); Guide to Prehistoric and Roman Monuments in England and Wales, 1951; Dragon's Mouth, (play) (with J. B. Priestley); Fables, 1953; Man on Earth, 1954; Journey Down a Rainbow (with J. B. Priestley), 1955; Providence Island, 1959; Man and the Sun, 1962; Unesco History of Mankind, Vol. I, Part 1, 1963; The World of the Past, 1963; King of the Two Lands, 1966; The Dawn of the Gods, 1968; The First Great Civilizations, 1973; (ed) Atlas of Ancient Archaeology, 1975; The Atlas of Early Man, 1976; contrib. learned jls and national periodicals. *Recreation:* natural history. *Address:* Kissing Tree House, Alveston, Stratford-on-Avon, Warwicks; B3 Albany, W1.

HAWKES, Prof. John Gregory; Mason Professor of Botany, University of Birmingham, since 1967; *b* 27 June 1915; *s* of C. W. and G. M. Hawkes; *m* 1941, Ellen Barbara Leather; two *s* two *d. Educ:* Univ. of Cambridge. BA, MA, PhD, ScD. Botanist, Potato Res. Station of Commonwealth Agricultural Bureaux, 1939-48, 1951-52; Dir of Potato Research Project, Min. of Ag., Colombia, S America, 1948-51; Lectr and Sen. Lectr in Taxonomic Botany, 1952-61; Prof. of Taxonomic Botany (Personal Chair), 1961-67. *Publications:* The Potatoes of Argentina, Brazil, Paraguay, and Uruguay (with J. P. Hjerting), 1969; A Computer-Mapped Flora (with D. A. Cadbury and R. C. Readett), 1971; contribs to Jl Linnaean Soc.; also to various botanical and plant breeding jls. *Recreations:* walking, gardening, travel, art, archaeology. *Address:* Department of Plant Biology, University of Birmingham; (private) 66 Lordswood Road, Birmingham B17 9BY. *T:* 021-427 2944.

HAWKES, Prof. Leonard, FRS 1952; Head of Department of Geology, Bedford College, 1921-56; Professor Emeritus since 1956; Fellow of Bedford College; *b* 6 Aug. 1891; *s* of Rev. Philip Hawkes; *m* 1926, Hilda Kathleen, *d* of late L. V. Cargill; one *s. Educ:* Armstrong Coll.; Kristiania Univ. 1851 Exhibitioner,

1914. Served European War, 1914-18, Capt. RAMC, 1917-19 (despatches). Lecturer in Geology, Armstrong Coll., 1919-21. Sec., Geological Soc. of London, 1934-42 (Pres., 1956-58); Pres. Mineralogical Soc., 1954-57. Murchison Medallist, 1946. Wollaston Medallist, 1962. Geol. Soc. of London. *Publications:* papers dealing with geology of Iceland. *Address:* 26 Moor Lane, Rickmansworth, Herts. *T:* Rickmansworth 72955.

HAWKES, Raymond; Deputy Director, Naval Ship Production, since 1977; *b* 28 April 1920; *s* of Ernest Hawkes; *m* 1951, Joyce Barbara King; one *s* one *d. Educ:* RNC Greenwich. 1st cl. Naval Architecture, RCNC; CEng; FRINA. Ship design, Bath, 1942-45 and 1954-56; aircraft carrier research at RAE Farnborough, 1945-49; hydrodynamic research at A.E.W. (Admiralty Experiment Works) Haslar, 1949-54; Principal Admty Overseer, Birkenhead, 1956-58; ship prodn, Bath, 1958-62; Chief Cons. Design, assault ships, survey fleet, small ships and auxiliaries, 1962-69; Senior Officers War Course 1966; Asst Dir Warship Design and Project Man. for Through Deck Cruiser, 1969-72; Dep. Dir, Warship Design, 1972-77. *Recreation:* golf. *Address:* Wood Meadow, Beechwood Road, Combe Down, Bath. *T:* Combe Down 832885.

HAWKESBURY, Viscount; Luke Marmaduke Peter Savile Foljambe; *b* 25 March 1972; *s* and *heir* of 5th Earl of Liverpool, *qv.*

HAWKEY, Rt. Rev. Ernest Eric; *b* 1 June 1909; *s* of Richard and Beatrice Hawkey; *m* 1943, Patricia Spark. *Educ:* Trinity Grammar Sch., Sydney, NSW. Deacon, 1933; Priest, 1936. Curate: St Alban's, Ultimo, 1933-34; St Paul, Burwood, 1934-40; Priest-in-charge, Kandos, 1940-46, Rector, 1946-47; Aust. Bd of Missions: Actg Organising Sec., 1947-50; Organising Sec., 1950-68; Canon Residentiary, Brisbane, 1962-68; Bishop of Carpentaria, 1968-74. *Recreations:* music, gardening. *Address:* 2/12 Wellington Street, Clayfield, Queensland 4011, Australia. *T:* 622108.

HAWKING, Dr Stephen William, FRS 1974; Fellow of Gonville and Caius College, Cambridge; Professor of Gravitational Physics, Cambridge University, since 1977 (Reader, 1975-77); *b* 8 Jan. 1942; *s* of Dr F. and Mrs E. I. Hawking; *m* 1965, Jane Wilde; one *s* one *d. Educ:* St Albans Sch.; University Coll., Oxford (BA), Hon. Fellow 1977; Trinity Hall, Cambridge (PhD). Research Fellow, Gonville and Caius Coll., 1965-69; Fellow for distinction in science, 1969-; Mem. Inst. of Theoretical Astronomy, Cambridge, 1968-72; Research Assistant: Inst. of Astronomy, Cambridge, 1972-73; Dept of Applied Maths and Theoretical Physics, Cambridge Univ., 1973-75. Fairchild Distinguished Schol., Calif Inst. of Technol., 1974-75. (Jtly) Eddington Medal, RAS, 1975; Pius XI Gold Medal, Pontifical Acad. of Scis, 1975; Dannie Heinemann Prize for Math. Phys., Amer. Phys. Soc. and Amer. Inst. of Physics, 1976; William Hopkins Prize, Cambridge Philosoph. Soc., 1976; Maxwell Medal, Inst. of Physics, 1976; Hughes Medal, Royal Soc., 1976. *Publication:* (with G. F. R. Ellis) The Large Scale Structure of Space-Time, 1973. *Address:* 5 West Road, Cambridge. *T:* Cambridge 51905.

HAWKINS, Sir Arthur (Ernest), Kt 1976; BSc (Eng); CEng; FIMechE, FIEE; FBIM; Chairman 1972-77, Member, 1970-77, Central Electricity Generating Board; *b* 10 June 1913; *s* of Rev. H. R. and Louisa Hawkins; *m* 1939, Laura Judith Tallent Draper; one *s* two *d. Educ:* The Grammar Sch., Gt Yarmouth; City of Norwich Technical Coll. Served (prior to nationalisation) with Gt Yarmouth Electricity Dept, Central Electricity Bd and Islington Electricity Dept (Dep. Engr and Gen. Manager); Croydon Dist Manager of SE Elec. Bd, 1948; joined Brit. Electricity Authority as Chief Asst Engr in System Operation Br., 1951; Personal Engrg Asst to Chief Engr, 1954. With the CEGB since its formation in 1957, at first as System Planning Engr and then as Chief Ops Engr, 1959-64; Midlands Regional Dir, 1964-70. Mem., Nuclear Power Adv. Bd, 1973-. *Publications:* contrib. Jl of Management Studies; various papers to technical instns. *Recreations:* fell walking, swimming, motoring. *Address:* 61 Rowan Road, W6. *Club:* Royal Automobile.

HAWKINS, Clive David B.; *see* Black-Hawkins.

HAWKINS, Desmond, OBE 1963; BBC Controller, South and West, 1967-69; *b* 1908; *m* Barbara Hawkins (*née* Skidmore); two *s* two *d.* Novelist, critic and broadcaster, 1935-45; Literary Editor of New English Weekly and Purpose Quarterly; Fiction Chronicler of The Criterion; Features Producer, BBC West Region, 1946; Head of Programmes, 1955; founded BBC Natural History Unit, 1959. Hon. LLD Bristol, 1974. Silver Medal, RSPB, 1959; Imperial Tobacco Radio Award for best dramatisation, 1976. *Publications:* Poetry and Prose of John Donne, 1938; Hawk among the Sparrows, 1939; Stories, Essays and Poems of D. H. Lawrence, 1939; Lighter than Day, 1940; War Report, 1946; Sedgemoor and Avalon, 1954; The BBC Naturalist, 1957; Hardy the Novelist, 1965; Wild Life in the New Forest, 1972; Avalon and Sedgemoor, 1973; Hardy, Novelist and Poet, 1976. *Address:* 2 Stanton Close, Blandford Forum, Dorset DT11 7RT. *T:* Blandford 54954. *Club:* BBC.

HAWKINS, Air Vice-Marshal Desmond Ernest, CB 1971; CBE 1967; DFC and Bar, 1942; Deputy Managing Director, Services Kinema Corporation, since 1974; *b* 27 Dec. 1919; *s* of Ernest and Lilian Hawkins; *m* 1947, Joan Audrey (*née* Munro); one *s*. *Educ:* Bancroft Sch. Commissioned in RAF, 1938. Served War of 1939-45: Coastal Command and Far East, commanding 36, 230 and 240 Sqdns, 1940-46 (despatches). Commanded RAF Pembroke Dock, 1946-47 (despatches). Staff appts, 1947-50; RAF Staff Coll., 1950; Staff appts, 1951-55; commanded 38 Sqdn, OC Flg, RAF Luqa, 1955-57; jssc, 1957; Staff appts, 1958-61; SASO 19 Gp, 1961-63; commanded RAF Tengah, 1963-66; idc 1967; commanded RAF Lyneham, 1968; SASO, HQ, RAF Strike Command, 1969-71; Dir-Gen., Personal Services (RAF), MoD, 1971-74. *Recreations:* sailing, fishing. *Address:* c/o Barclays Bank, Bridgwater, Somerset. *Clubs:* Royal Air Force; Cruising Association.

HAWKINS, Prof. Eric William, CBE 1973; Director, Language Teaching Centre, University of York, since 1965; *b* 8 Jan. 1915; *s* of James Edward Hawkins and Agnes Thompson (*née* Clarie); *m* 1938, Ellen Marie Thygesen, Copenhagen; one *s* one *d*. *Educ:* Liverpool Inst. High Sch.; Trinity Hall, Cambridge (Open Exhibn). MA, CertEd, (Hon.) FIL. Asst Master, Royal Masonic Sen. Sch., 1937-40. War Service, 1st Bn The Loyal Regt, 1940-46 (despatches 1945); wounded N Africa, 1943; Adjt 1944; Major 1945. Asst Master, Liverpool Coll., 1946-49; Headmaster: Oldershaw Grammar Sch., Wallasey, 1949-53; Calday Grange Grammar Sch., Ches, 1953-65. Mem., Central Adv. Council for Educn (England) (Plowden Cttee), 1963-66; Governor, Centre for Information on Language Teaching and Research, 1968-75; Chm., Mod. Langs Cttee, Schools Council, 1968-74. Mem., Nat. Cttee for Commonwealth Immigrants, 1965-68; Trustee, Central Bureau for Educl Visits and Exchanges. Gold Medal, Inst. Linguists, 1971. *Publications:* (ed) Modern Languages in the Grammar School, 1961; (ed) New Patterns in Sixth Form Modern Language Studies, 1970; A Time for Growing, 1971; Le français pour tout le monde, vols 1-4, 1974-77. *Recreations:* walking, cello. *Address:* 44 East Lane, Shipton by Beningbrough, York YO6 1AH. *Club:* Royal Commonwealth Society.

HAWKINS, Frank Ernest; Chairman, 1959-73, and Managing Director, 1956-73, International Stores Ltd, Mitre Square, EC3; *b* 12 Aug. 1904; 2nd *s* of late George William and Sophie Hawkins; *m* 1933, Muriel, *d* of late Joseph and Isabella Sinclair; two *s* one *d*. *Educ:* Leyton County High Sch. Joined staff of International Stores Ltd as boy clerk, 1919; apptd: Asst Sec., 1934; Sec., 1935; Director, 1949; Managing Dir, 1956; Vice-Chm., 1958; Chairman, 1959. *Recreation:* golf. *Address:* Merton Court, Page's Croft, Wokingham, Berkshire. *Club:* East Berkshire Golf.

HAWKINS, Adm. Sir Geoffrey Alan Brooke, KBE *cr* 1952; CB 1949; MVO 1925; DSC 1917; *b* 13 July 1895; *e s* of late Capt. Hawkins, St Fentons, Baldoyle, Co. Dublin; *m* 1926, Lady Margaret Scott (*d* 1976), *d* of 7th Duke of Buccleuch; one *s* two *d*. *Educ:* Royal Naval Colls, Osborne and Dartmouth. Served European War, 1914-18 (DSC); War of 1939-45 (despatches). ADC to Governor-Gen. of South Africa, 1924-27; attached to staff of Prince of Wales, S African tour, 1925. Flag Officer, Malta, 1950-52; retired list, 1952. Attached to staff of Princess Royal, WI tour, 1960 and 1962. *Address:* Grafton Underwood, Kettering. *T:* Cranford 245. *Club:* Naval and Military.
See also A . A . Wall .

HAWKINS, Maj.-Gen. George Ledsam Seymour, CB 1943; MC; Indian Army, retired; *b* 13 May 1898; *s* of G. E. Hawkins, Apton Hall, Rochford, Essex; *m* 1921, Katharine Marian (*d* 1957), *d* of George Hancock, Templecombe, Somerset; one *d* (one *s* decd). Commd S Staffs Regt, Aug. 1914; trans. to RFA, 1915; served European War (MC), France and Belgium; trans. to Indian Army, 1925; served NWF (Waziristan), 1936-37 (despatches); Ordnance Consulting Offr, India Office, 1937-41; served World War II (CB), Dir of Ordnance Services, India; retd 1945. Col Comdt, IAOC, 1945-56; Reg. Dir, Southern Reg. Min. of Works, 1945-57. *Address:* The Cottage, Elsing Mill, Dereham, Norfolk.

HAWKINS, Sir Humphry (Villiers) Caesar, 7th Bt, *cr* 1778; MB, ChB; Medical Practitioner; *b* 10 Aug. 1923; *s* of Sir Villiers Geoffry Caesar Hawkins, 6th Bt and Blanche Hawkins, *d* of A. E. Hampden-Smithers; *S* father 1955; *m* 1952, Anita, *d* of C. H. Funkey, Johannesburg; two *s* two *d* (and one *d* decd). *Educ:* Hilton Coll.; University of Witwatersrand. Served War of 1939-45 with 6th SA Armoured Div. *Heir: s* Howard Cæsar Hawkins, *b* 17 Nov. 1956. *Address:* 41 Hume Road, Dunkeld, Johannesburg, S Africa. *Club:* Johannesburg Country.

HAWKINS, Paul Lancelot, TD 1945; MP (C) South West Norfolk since 1964; Partner in firm of Chartered Surveyors in rural practice; *b* 7 Aug. 1912; *s* of L. G. Hawkins and of Mrs Hawkins (*née* Peile); *m* 1937, E. Joan Snow; two *s* one *d*. *Educ:* Cheltenham Coll. Joined Family Firm, 1930; Chartered Surveyor, 1933. Served in TA, Royal Norfolk Regt, 1933-45; POW Germany, 1940-45. An Asst Govt Whip, 1970-71; a Lord Comr of the Treasury, 1971-73; Vice-Chamberlain of HM Household, 1973-74. Mem., Delegn to Council of Europe, 1976-. CC Norfolk, 1949-70, Alderman, 1968-70. *Recreations:* gardening, travel. *Address:* Stables, Downham Market, Norfolk. *Club:* Carlton.

HAWKINS, Rt. Rev. Ralph Gordon, CMG 1977; ThD; *b* St John's, Newfoundland, 1911; *s* of late Samuel J. and Alfreda Hawkins; *m* 1938, Mary Edna, *d* of late William James and Grace Leslie, Newport, Mon.; one *s* one *d* . *Educ:* Univ. Memorial Coll., St John's; St Boniface Coll., Warminster; Durham Univ. (Hatfield Coll.). BA, LTh 1934; deacon, 1935, priest, 1936, Bristol. Curate of St Anne's, Brislington, 1935-38; Rector of Morawa, 1938-43; Rector of Wembley-Floreat Park, 1943-49; Chaplain, RAAF, 1943-45; Rector of St Hilda's, N Perth, 1949-56; Canon of Perth, 1954; Archdeacon of Perth, 1957; Bishop of Bunbury, 1957-77. *Address:* 9 Cross Street, Bunbury, Western Australia 6230.

HAWKINS, Vice-Adm. Sir Raymond (Shayle), KCB 1965 (CB 1963); *b* 21 Dec. 1909; *s* of late Thomas Hawkins and Dorothy Hawkins, Bedford; *m* 1936, Rosalind, *d* of late Roger and Ada Ingpen; three *s* one *d*. *Educ:* Bedford Sch. Entered Royal Navy, 1927; HMS Iron Duke 1932; HMS Resolution, 1933; served with Submarines, 1935-43; HMS Orion, 1943. Asst Naval Attaché, Paris, 1954; Commanding Officer, HMS St Vincent, 1957; Rear-Adm., Nuclear Propulsion, 1959; Dir of Marine Engineering, 1961-63; Chief Naval Engineering Officer, 1962-63; Vice-Adm., 1964; a Lord Comr of the Admiralty, Fourth Sea Lord and Vice-Controller, 1963-64; Chief of Naval Supplies and Transport and Vice-Controller of the Navy, MoD, 1964-67; retd, 1967. *Recreations:* golf and gardening. *Address:* Hodshill, South Stoke, Bath, Avon. *T:* Combe Down 833021.

HAWKINS, Reginald Thomas, CBE 1949; *b* 13 May 1888; *s* of Robert William Hawkins; *m* 1914, Margaret T. (*d* 1972), *e d* of James Rennie Addison; one *d* (one *s* killed in action, RAF, 1944). *Educ:* Owen's Sch., Islington; Edinburgh Univ. (MA). Entered Civil Service, 1904; Scottish Education Dept, 1910. Served European War, 1914-18, with London-Scottish Regt in France, Salonika and Egypt. Asst Sec., Scottish Education Dept, 1939; Under-Sec., Scottish Education Dept, 1949-52; retired, 1952. Sec. to Advisory Council on Education in Scotland, 1935-38. *Publications:* articles on educational finance. *Address:* c/o Mrs Cameron, 65 Elwyn Road, March, Cambridgeshire. *T:* March 3258.

HAWKINS, Rev. Robert Henry; Canon of St George's Windsor, 1958-70; *b* 3 March 1892; *s* of Rev. Francis Henry Albert Hawkins and Mary Anna Ridley Hawkins (*née* Morris); *m* 1917, Margaret (*d* 1977), *e d* of Rev. T. A. Lacey, DD, Canon of Worcester; two *s* three *d*. *Educ:* Forest Sch., Essex; St Edmund Hall, Oxford. BA 1913, MA 1919. Served European War: commissioned 3rd S Staffs Regt, 1914; France and Salonika, 1915-17; RFC (Flight Comdr), 1917-19. Ordained Deacon, 1919, Priest, 1920; Vicar of: Maryport, Dio. Carlisle, 1923-27; St George, Barrow in Furness, 1927-34; Dalston, 1934-43; Vicar of St Mary, Nottingham, Rural Dean of Nottingham and Hon. Canon of Southwell, 1943-58. *Address:* Manormead, Tilford Road, Hindhead, Surrey. *T:* Hindhead 6493.

HAWKINS, William Francis Spencer, CB 1968; a Master of the Supreme Court (Chancery Division), 1933-Jan. 1969, Chief Master, 1959-Jan. 1969; *b* Richmond, Surrey, 13 Feb. 1896; *s* of Francis William Hawkins; *m* 1933, Eva Lilian, *d* of William Graham; one *s* one *d*. *Educ:* Rugby. Served European War, 1914-18: on active service, 1915-19, Salonika and British Army of the Black Sea, Signal Officer with 27th Div. Artillery and 80th Inf. Bde (despatches twice). Admitted a solicitor, 1921; Partner with Bird and Bird, Gray's Inn, 1928. Post Invasion Warden, War of 1939-45. Trustee United Law Clerks Soc., 1940-76. Pres.

of Wimbledon Hockey Club, 1952-60, and of Old Rugbeian Soc., 1957-59. Sometime Mem. Coulsdon and Purley, UDC and Council of the Magistrates Assoc. JP Surrey, 1947; Chm. Wallington Petty Sessions Div. Bench, Oct. 1958-60. *Address:* Rossley, Snowhill, Copthorne, Sussex RH10 3HA. *T:* Copthorne 712013.

HAWKSLEY, John Callis, CBE 1946; PhD, MD, FRCP; formerly Physician, University College Hospital and St Peter's, St Paul's and St Philip's Hospitals, London; *b* 30 Nov. 1903; *s* of late Joseph Hawksley, Great Yarmouth; *m* 1933, Margaret, *er d* of late Engineer Vice-Adm. Sir Reginald Skelton, KCB, CBE, DSO; two *s* two *d. Educ:* Dulwich Coll.; University Coll., London; University Coll. Hospital. Appts on resident staff, University Coll. Hosp., 1926-28; ship's surg., BISN Co., 1929; research appts, Birmingham Children's Hosp., 1930-32; Sebag-Montefiore Research Fellow, Hospital for Sick Children, Gt Ormond Street, 1933-34; Bilton Pollard Travelling Fellowship, University Coll. Hosp., 1935, devoted to work at Bispebjerg Hosp., Copenhagen; Asst Physician, University Coll. Hosp., 1936-39; Physician to University Coll. Hosp., 1940; retd, 1969. Temp. commission RAMC 1939; served with rank of Lieut-Col in MEF, 1941-44 (despatches); Consulting Physician, local Brig., with South East Asia Command, 1945. Fellow of University Coll., London, 1946; Dean of University Coll. Hosp. Med. Sch., 1949-54; Senior Vice-Pres., RCP, 1966. *Publications:* contributions to various medical journals. *Recreations:* mountaineering. *Address:* The Old Vicarage, East Kennett, Wilts. *T:* Lockeridge 237. *Club:* Alpine.

HAWLEY, Major Sir David Henry, 7th Bt, *cr* 1795; MA; FRICS; DL; late KRRC; Member of firm of Jas Martin & Co., Chartered Surveyors, Land Agents and Valuers, 8 Bank Street, Lincoln; *b* 13 May 1913; *e s* of Capt. Cyril Francis Hawley and Ursula Mary, *d* of Henry Percy St John; *S* uncle, 1923; *m* 1938, Hermione, 2nd *d* of late Col L. Gregson; one *s* two *d. Educ:* Eton; Magdalene Coll., Cambridge. Served Palestine, 1936-39 (medal and clasp), War of 1939-45 (prisoner, 1939-45 Star, despatches). Hon. Life Mem., Nat. Trust. DL 1952, High Sheriff, 1962-63, Lincs. *Heir: s* Henry Nicholas Hawley, *b* 26 Nov. 1939. *Address:* Tumby Lawn, Boston, Lincs PE22 7TA. *T:* Coningsby 42337.

HAWLEY, Donald Frederick, CMG 1970; MBE 1955; HM Diplomatic Service; British High Commissioner in Malaysia, since 1977; Barrister-at-law; *b* 22 May 1921; *s* of late F. G. Hawley, Berkhamsted, Herts and Mrs Hawley; *m* 1964, Ruth Morwenna Graham Howes, *d* of late Rev. P. G. Howes and of Mrs Howes, Charmouth, Dorset; one *s* three *d. Educ:* Radley; New Coll., Oxford (MA). Served in HM Forces, 1941. Sudan Political Service, 1944; joined Sudan Judiciary, 1947. Called to Bar, Inner Temple, 1951. Chief Registrar, Sudan Judiciary, and Registrar-Gen. of Marriages, 1951; resigned from Sudan Service, 1955; joined HM Foreign Service, 1955; FO, 1956: Political Agent, Trucial States, in Dubai, 1958; Head of Chancery, British Embassy, Cairo, 1962; Counsellor and Head of Chancery, British High Commission, Lagos, 1965; Vis. Fellow, Dept of Geography, Durham Univ., 1967; Counsellor (Commercial), Baghdad, 1968; HM Consul-General, Muscat, 1971; HM Ambassador to Oman, 1971-75; Asst Under Sec. of State, FCO, 1975-77. *Publications:* Handbook for Registrars of Marriage and Ministers of Religion, 1963 (Sudan Govt pubn); Courtesies in the Trucial States, 1965; The Trucial States, 1971; Oman and its Renaissance, 1977; Courtesies in the Gulf Area, 1977. *Recreations:* tennis, squash, sailing, book collecting; Hon. Sec., Sudan Football Assoc., 1952-55. *Address:* c/o Foreign and Commonwealth Office, SW1; West Pulridge, Little Gaddesden, near Berkhamsted, Hertfordshire. *T:* Little Gaddesden 3439. *Club:* Athenæum.

HAWORTH, Sir (Arthur) Geoffrey, 2nd Bt, *cr* 1911; MA; farmer; *b* 5 April 1896; *s* of Sir Arthur Haworth, 1st Bt, and Lily (*d* 1952), *y d* of late John Rigby, Altrincham; *S* father, 1944; *m* 1926, Emily Dorothea, *er d* of H. E. Gaddum, The Priory, Bowdon; two *s* two *d. Educ:* Rugby Sch.; New Coll., Oxford. Served European War, 1914-19, Lieut Queen's Own Royal West Kent Regiment and Machine Gun Corps (despatches). Chm., Hallé Concert Soc., 1965-. FRSA 1969. JP Chester, 1937-70. Hon. MA Manchester, 1972. *Recreation:* music. *Heir: s* Philip Haworth [*b* 17 Jan. 1927; *m* 1951, Joan Helen, *d* of late S. P. Clark, Ipswich; four *s* one *d*]. *Address:* The Red Brook, Lower Peover, Cheshire. *Club:* Farmers'.

HAWORTH, Very Rev. Kenneth William; Dean of Salisbury, 1960-71, Dean Emeritus, since 1971; *b* 21 Jan. 1903; *s* of William Bell and Helen Haworth; *m* 1937, Sybil Mavrojani; two *s* two *d. Educ:* Cheltenham Coll.; Clare Coll., Cambridge; Wells Theological Coll. Curate of St Giles, Willenhall, 1926; Domestic Chaplain 1931, Examining Chaplain, 1937, to Bp of Lichfield; Chaplain of Wells Theological Coll., 1938; CF (4th cl.), 1939; Rector of Stratton w. Baunton, Dio., Gloucester, 1943; Vice-Principal of Wells Theol. Coll., 1946, Principal, 1947-60; Prebendary of Combe II in Wells Cathedral, 1947-60; Exam. Chap. to Bishop of Bath and Wells, 1947; Proctor in Convocation, 1956-59; Exam. Chap. to Bishop of Salisbury, 1962. *Address:* The Common, Woodgreen, Fordingbridge, Hants. *T:* Breamore 239.

HAWORTH, Lionel, OBE 1958; FRS 1971; RDI; Director of Design, Rolls-Royce Ltd, Aero Division, Bristol, since 1968; *b* 4 Aug. 1912; *s* of John Bertram Haworth and Anna Sophia Ackerman; *m* 1956, Joan Irene Bradbury; one *s* one *d. Educ:* Rondebosch Boys' High Sch.; Univ. of Cape Town. Cape Town Corp's Gold Medal and schol. tenable abroad. BSc (Eng); CEng; FIMeche; FRAeS. Graduate Apprentice, Associated Equipment Co., 1934; Rolls-Royce Ltd, Derby: Designer, 1936; Asst Chief Designer, 1944; Dep. Chief Designer, 1951; Chief Designer (Civil Engines), 1954; Chief Engr (Prop. Turbines), 1962; Bristol Siddeley Engines Ltd: Chief Design Consultant, 1963; Chief Designer, 1964; Dir of Design, Aero Div., 1965. Brit. Gold Medal for Aeronautics, 1971; RDI 1976; Founder Fellow, Fellowship of Engineering, 1976. *Recreation:* sailing. *Address:* 10 Hazelwood Road, Sneyd Park, Bristol BS9 1PX. *T:* Bristol 683032.

HAWORTH, Robert Downs, DSc, PhD Victoria, BSc Oxon; FRS 1944; FRIC; Firth Professor of Chemistry, University of Sheffield, 1939-63, now Emeritus; *b* 15 March 1898; *s* of J. T. and Emily Haworth, Cheadle, Cheshire; *m* 1930, Dorothy, *d* of A. L. Stocks, Manchester; one *d. Educ:* Secondary Sch., Stockport; University of Manchester, Mercer Scholar, 1919; Beyer Fellow, 1920; 1851 Exhibition Scholar, 1921-23; 1851 Exhibition Sen. Student, 1923-25; Demonstrator in Organic Chemistry, Oxford, 1925-26; Lecturer in Chemistry, King's Coll., Newcastle upon Tyne, 1927-39. Visiting Prof. of Organic Chemistry, University of Madras, 1963-64. Davy Medal, Royal Society, 1956. Hon. DSc Sheffield, 1974. *Publications:* papers on organic chemistry in Journal of Chemical Society. *Address:* The University, Sheffield S3 7HF; 67 Tom Lane, Sheffield S10 3PA. *T:* Sheffield 302595.

HAWORTH, Hon. Sir William (Crawford), Kt 1969; Director of companies; *b* 15 April 1905; *s* of Edward Haworth; *m* 1927, Winifred Senior. *Educ:* Essendon; Melbourne Univ.; Victorian Pharmacy Coll. PhC 1925; MPS. War of 1939-45: Captain, 2nd AIF, 9th Div.; served in Egypt, Tobruk, Palestine and Syria; R of O 1944. Municipal Councillor, S Melbourne, 1923-38; Mem. Bd of Management, Victoria Infectious Diseases Hosp., 1936-38; Mem. Council, S Melbourne Technical Sch., 1939-62 (Pres., 1947-48) MLA for Albert Park, Vic Parliament, 1937-45; Minister for Health and Housing, Vic Govt, Oct.-Nov. 1945. MHR for Isaacs, Aust. Commonwealth Parliament, 1949-69. Mem., Jt Parly Cttee for Foreign Affairs, 1959-66; Leader of Aust. Delegn to Inter-Parly Union Conf., Warsaw, 1959 (Mem. IPU Council, 1959-60); Dep. Chm. of Cttees, 1960-69. *Recreation:* golf. *Address:* 11 Findon Avenue, North Caulfield, Vic 3161, Australia. *T:* 50 6008. *Clubs:* Australian (Melbourne); Amateur Sports, Naval and Military, West Brighton, Victoria Racing, Royal Automobile Club of Victoria, Kingston Heath Golf (Vic).

HAWSER, Cyril Lewis, QC 1959; a Recorder, since 1972 (Recorder of Portsmouth, 1969-71); *b* 5 Oct. 1916; *s* of Abraham and Sarah Hawser; *m* 1940, Phyllis Greatrex; one *s* one *d. Educ:* Cardiff High Sch.; Balliol Coll., Oxford (Williams Law Scholar; MA). Called to the Bar, 1938. Recorder of Salisbury, 1967-69. Mem. Council and Vice-Chm. of Exec. Cttee of Justice. *Recreations:* tennis, chess, conversation. *Address:* 39D Eaton Square, SW1. *T:* 01-235 6566.

HAWTHORNE, Prof. Sir William (Rede), Kt 1970; CBE 1959; FRS 1955; MA; ScD; FIMechE; FRAeS; Master of Churchill College, Cambridge, since 1968; Hopkinson and ICI Professor of Applied Thermodynamics, University of Cambridge, since 1951; Head of Department of Engineering, 1968-73; *b* 22 May 1913; *s* of William Hawthorne, MInstCE, and Elizabeth C. Hawthorne; *m* 1939, Barbara Runkle, Cambridge, Massachusetts, USA; one *s* two *d. Educ:* Westminster Sch.; Trinity Coll., Cambridge; Massachusetts Institute of Technology, USA. Development Engineer, Babcock & Wilcox Ltd, 1937-39; Scientific Officer, Royal Aircraft Establishment, 1940-44; British Air Commission, Washington, 1944; Dep. Dir Engine Research, Min. of Supply, 1945; Massachusetts Institute of Technology: Associate Prof. of Mechanical Engineering, 1946; George Westinghouse Prof. of Mechanical Engineering, 1948-51; Jerome C. Hunsaker Prof. of Aeronautical Engineering, 1955-

56; Vis. Inst. Prof., 1962-63; Mem. Corporation, 1969-74. A Vice-Pres., Royal Soc., 1970. Foreign Associate, US Nat. Acad. of Sciences, 1965. Chairman: Home Office Scientific Adv. Council, 1967-; Adv. Council for Energy Conservation, 1974-; Mem., Energy Commn, 1977-. Director: Dracone Developments Ltd, 1958-; Cummins Engine Co. Inc., 1974-. Governor, Westminster Sch., 1956-76. Hon. DEng Sheffield, 1976; Hon. FAIAA. For. Associate, US Nat. Acad. of Engrg, 1976. Medal of Freedom (US), 1947. *Publications:* papers in mechanical and aeronautical journals. *Address:* The Master's Lodge, Churchill College, Cambridge; Engineering Laboratory, Cambridge. *Club:* Athenæum.

HAWTON, Sir John (Malcolm Kenneth), KCB 1952 (CB 1947); *b* 18 Sept. 1904; *s* of John Francis Hawton; *m* 1935, Hilda Cawley; one *d. Educ:* Emanuel Sch.; St John's Coll., Cambridge (1st Class Classical Tripos, Foundation Scholar, Graves Prizeman). Barrister (Middle Temple); entered Ministry of Health, 1927; various duties in that Ministry, concerning local government, housing, water supply, private bill legislation, public health, wartime emergency services, also inception and running of National Health Service; Permanent Sec., Ministry of Health, 1951-60. Chm., British Waterways Board, 1963-68, Vice-Chm., 1968-74. Mem., Advertising Standards Authority, 1962-73. *Recreations:* erstwhile. *Address:* Roundway Cottage, The Roundway, Rustington, Sussex. *Club:* Reform.

HAWTREY, John Havilland Procter, CBE 1958; FICE; *b* 16 Feb. 1905; *e s* of late Edmond Charles Hawtrey and late Helen Mary Hawtrey (*née* Durand); *m* 1947, Kathleen Mary, *d* of late Captain M. T. Daniel, RN, Henley-on-Thames; one *s* one *d. Educ:* Eton; City and Guilds Engineering Coll., London (BSc 1927). Asst Engineer, later Dist Engineer, Burma Railways, 1927-47. Served War of 1939-45: with RE, 1940-46; Major 1942, in India and Burma, 1942-46 (despatches). Entered office of Crown Agents for Oversea Govts and Administrations, 1948: Chief Civil Engineer, 1956; Crown Agent and Engineer-in-Chief, 1965; retired, 1969. *Address:* 11 Curzon Avenue, Beaconsfield, Bucks. *T:* Beaconsfield 4220.
See also S. C. Hawtrey.

HAWTREY, Stephen Charles, CB 1966; Clerk of the Journals, House of Commons, 1958-72; *b* 8 July 1907; *s* of Edmond C. Hawtrey; *m* 1934, Leila Winifred, *e d* of late Lieut-Col Wilmot Blomefield, OBE; two *s* one *d. Educ:* Eton; Trinity Coll., Cambridge (MA). Asst Clerk, House of Commons, 1930; Senior Clerk, 1944. Temporarily attached: to Min. of Home Security, 1939; to Secretariat of Council of Europe, Strasbourg, France, at various sessions between 1950 and 1964. *Publication:* (With L. A. Abraham) A Parliamentary Dictionary, 1956 and 1964; 3rd edn (with H. M. Barclay), 1970. *Address:* 52 New Street, Henley-on-Thames, Oxon. *T:* Henley 4521. *Clubs:* United Oxford & Cambridge University, Railway.
See also J. H. P. Hawtrey.

HAY, family name of **Countess of Erroll, Earl of Kinnoull,** and of **Marquis of Tweeddale.**

HAY, Lord; Merlin Sereld Victor Gilbert Hay; Master of Erroll; *b* 20 April 1948; *s* and *heir* of Countess of Erroll, *qv* and of Sir Iain Moncreiffe of that Ilk, 11th Bt, *qv. Educ:* Eton; Trinity College, Cambridge. Page to the Lord Lyon, 1956. Lieut, Atholl Highlanders, 1974. *Address:* Easter Moncreiffe, Perthshire. *T:* Bridge of Earn 2338; Old Slains, Collieston, Aberdeenshire. *T:* 248. *Clubs:* Turf, White's, Pratt's; Puffin's (Edinburgh).

HAY, Sir (Alan) Philip, KCVO 1960 (CVO 1953); TD; Treasurer to the Duke of Kent and to Prince Michael of Kent; Director: Sotheby & Co.; National Mutual Life Association of Australasia; *b* 27 Feb. 1918; *y s* of late E. Alan Hay and of Mrs Hay, 72 Albert Hall Mansions, SW7; *m* 1948, Lady Margaret Katharine Seymour, DCVO (*d* 1975); three *s. Educ:* Harrow; Trinity Coll., Cambridge (BA). Herts Yeomanry, TA (135 Field Regt RA). 1939; prisoner, Singapore, 1942-45. Private Sec. to Princess Marina, Duchess of Kent, 1948-68. *Address:* Nottingham Cottage, Kensington Palace, W8. *T:* 01-937 5514. *Clubs:* Boodle's; All England Lawn Tennis.

HAY, Sir Arthur Thomas Erroll; 10th Bt of Park, *cr* 1663; ISO 1974; DiplArch; ARIBA 1935; retired Civil Servant; *b* 13 April 1909; *o s* of 9th Bt and Lizabel Annie (*d* 1957), *o d* of late Lachlan Mackinnon Macdonald, Skeabost, Isle of Skye; *S* father, 1923; *m* 1st, 1935, Hertha Louise (who was granted a divorce, 1942), *d* of late Herr Ludwig Stölzle, Nagelberg, Austria, and of H. E. Frau Vaugoin, Vienna; one *s*; 2nd, 1942, Rosemarie Evelyn Anne, *d* of late Vice-Adm. Aubrey Lambert and of Mrs Lambert. *Educ:* Fettes Coll., Edinburgh. Student of architecture, University of Liverpool, 1927-31; Diploma in

Architecture, Architectural Assoc., July 1934. Served War of 1939-45; 2nd Lieut RE 1943; Lieut 1944; service in Normandy, Belgium, Holland and Germany in 21 Army Group. *Heir: s* John Erroll Audley Hay, *b* 3 Dec. 1935. *Recreation:* golf. *Address:* c/o Lloyds Bank, Castle Street, Farnham, Surrey.

HAY, David Osborne, CBE 1962; DSO 1945; Secretary, Department of Aboriginal Affairs, since 1977; *b* 29 Nov. 1916; *2nd s* of late H. A. Hay, Barwon Heads, Victoria; *m* 1944, Alison Marion Parker Adams; two *s. Educ:* Geelong Grammar Sch.; Brasenose Coll., Oxford; Melbourne Univ. Joined Commonwealth Public Service, 1939. Australian Imperial Force, 1940-46: Major, 2nd Sixth Infantry Bn; served in Western Desert, Greece, New Guinea. Rejoined External Affairs Dept, 1947: Imp. Def. Coll., 1954; Minister (later Ambassador) to Thailand, 1955-57; High Comr in Canada, 1961-64; Ambassador to UN, New York, 1964-65; First Asst Secretary, External Affairs, 1966; Administrator of Papua and New Guinea, 1967-70; Sec., Dept of External Territories, Canberra, 1970-73; Defence Force Ombudsman, 1974-76. *Publication:* The Delivery of Services financed by the Department of Aboriginal Affairs, 1976. *Address:* 10 Hotham Crescent, Deakin, ACT 2600, Australia. *Clubs:* Australian, Melbourne, Naval and Military (Melbourne); Commonwealth (Canberra).

HAY, Prof. Denys, MA; FBA 1970; Professor of Medieval History, University of Edinburgh, since 1954; *b* 29 Aug. 1915; *s* of Rev. W. K. Hay and Janet Waugh; *m* 1937, Sarah Gwyneth, *d* of S. E. Morley; one *s* two *d. Educ:* Royal Grammar Sch., Newcastle upon Tyne; Balliol Coll., Oxford. 1st Cl. hons, Modern History, 1937; senior demy, Magdalen Coll., 1937. Temporary Lecturer, Glasgow Univ., 1938; Bryce Studentship, Oxford Univ., 1939; Asst Lecturer, University Coll., Southampton, 1939; RASC 1940-42; War Historian (Civil Depts), 1942-45; Lecturer in Medieval History, Edinburgh Univ., 1945, Vice-Principal, 1971-75. Literary Dir, RHistS, 1955-58; Lectures: Italian, British Acad., 1959; Wiles, QUB, 1960; Birkbeck, Trinity Coll., Cambridge, 1971-72; Visiting Prof., Cornell Univ., 1963; Senior Fellow, Newberry Library, Chicago, 1966; Trustee, Nat. Library of Scotland, 1966-; Pres., Historical Association, 1967-70; Mem., Reviewing Cttee on Export of Works of Art, 1976-. Editor, English Historical Review, 1958-65. Hon. For. Mem., Amer. Acad. of Arts and Scis, 1974. Hon. DLitt, Newcastle, 1970. *Publications:* Anglica Historia of P. Vergil, 1950; Polydore Vergil, 1952; From Roman Empire to Renaissance Europe, 1953 (The Medieval Centuries, 1964); ed. R. K. Hannay's Letters of James V, 1954; Europe: the emergence of an idea, 1957, new edn 1968; (ed) New Cambridge Modern History, Vol. I: The Renaissance, 1493-1520, 1957, new edn 1976; Italian Renaissance in its Historical Background, 1961, new edn 1976; Design and Development of Weapons (History of Second World War) (with M. M. Postan and J. D. Scott), 1964; Europe in the 14th and 15th Centuries, 1966; (ed with W. K. Smith) Aeneas Sylvius Piccolomini, *De Gestis Concilii Basiliensis,* 1967; (ed) The Age of the Renaissance, 1967; Annalists and Historians, 1977; Italian Church in the 15th Century, 1977; articles in historical journals. *Address:* 31 Fountainhall Road, Edinburgh EH9 2LN. *T:* 031-667 2886.

HAY, Sir Frederick Baden-Powell, 10th Bt of Alderston, *cr* 1703; *b* 24 June 1900; *s* of late Frederick Howard Hay; *S* uncle 1936; *m* 1935, Henrietta Margaret, *d* of Herbert William Reid; no *c. Recreations:* golf, turf, motoring. *Heir: b* Ronald Nelson Hay [*b* 9 July 1910; *m* 1940, Rita, *d* of John Munyard; one *s* one *d*]. *Address:* Haddington, 14/32 Mentone Parade, Mentone, Vic 3194, Australia. *T:* 550 3726. *Club:* Royal Caledonian (Melbourne).

HAY, Sir James B. D.; see Dalrymple-Hay.

HAY, Col James Charles Edward, CBE 1937; MC; TD; DL; Sheriff-Substitute of Lanarkshire at Glasgow, 1946-59, at Hamilton, 1959-61; solicitor; *b* 6 June 1889; *s* of late William Thomas Hay, solicitor, Hamilton; *m* 1929, Mary Buchanan Thomson; two *s. Educ:* Academy, Hamilton; Glasgow Univ. Hon. Col (late CO) 6th Battalion The Cameronians; late Comdr 156 (West Scottish) Infantry Bde; late Hon. Col 3rd (Lanarkshire) Army Cadet Bn; served European War, 1914-18; War of 1939-45 (despatches). Late Vice-Chm., Secretary, and Military Mem., Lanarkshire T&AFA. DL Co. of Lanark, 1933. *Recreations:* bowls, motoring, fishing. *Address:* 18 Lethame Road, Strathaven, Lanarkshire.

HAY, John Albert; Managing Director, Walport Group, since 1968; *b* 24 Nov. 1919; *er s* of Alderman J. E. Hay; *m* 1st, 1947, Beryl Joan (marr. diss. 1973), *o d* of Comdr H. C. Found, RN (retired); one *s* one *d*; 2nd, 1974, Janet May, *y d* of A. C. Spruce. *Educ:* Brighton, Hove and Sussex Grammar Sch. Solicitor admitted May 1945. Chairman: Brighton and Hove Young Conservatives, 1945-47; Sussex Federation of Young Conservatives, 1945-47; Young Conservative and Unionist Central Cttee, 1947-49; Conservative Party Housing and Local Govt Cttee, 1956-59; formerly Dir London Municipal Soc.; formerly Vice-Pres. Urban District Councils Assoc.; Hon. Sec. UK Council of the European Movement, 1965-66; Mem. of Exec. Cttee, Nat. Union of Conservative and Unionist Assoc., 1947-49 and 1950-51. Served War of 1939-45, in RNVR; temp. Sub-Lieut, RNVR, 1940-44; temp. Lieut, RNVR, 1944; invalided 1944. Member: British Delegn, Congress of Europe, 1948, and 1973; UK Delegns, Council of Europe and Western European Union, 1956-59. MP (C) Henley, Oxon, 1950-Feb. 1974; PPS to Pres. of BoT, 1951-56; Parly Sec., MoT, 1959-63; Civil Lord of the Admiralty, 1963-64; Parly Under-Sec. of State for Defence for the Royal Navy, April-Oct. 1964. Chm., British Section, Council of European Municipalities, 1971-76, Vice-Chm., 1976-77, Pres., 1977-. Mem. Court, Reading Univ., 1968-. Fellow, Royal Philharmonic Soc., 1976. *Recreations:* gardening, music, travel, historical study. *Address:* 62/66 Whitfield Street, W1. *T:* 01-580 8061.

HAY, Prof. John Duncan, MA, MD, FRCP; Professor of Child Health, University of Liverpool, 1957-74, now Professor Emeritus; *b* 6 Feb. 1909; *s* of late Prof. John Hay; *m* 1936, Jannett Ceridwen Evans; one *s* two *d. Educ:* Liverpool Coll.; Sidney Sussex Coll., Cambridge; Liverpool Univ. MB, ChB, 1st Cl. Hons, Liverpool, 1933; MA 1934, MB 1935, Cambridge; MD Liverpool, 1936; DCH London, MRCP 1939; FRCP 1951. Holt Fellowship in Pathology, Liverpool, 1935; Cons. Pædiatrician to: Royal Liverpool Children's Hospital, 1939-74; Royal Liverpool Babies' Hospital, 1939-61; Birkenhead Children's Hosp., 1937-54; Liverpool Maternity Hosp. 1946-74; Lancashire County Hosp., Whiston, 1942-51; Liverpool Open-Air Hospital, Leasowe, and Mill Road Maternity Hosp., 1947-74; Alder Hey Children's Hosp., 1957-74; Liverpool Education Cttee, 1951-72. Demonstrator in Pathology, University of Liverpool, 1935 and 1938; Asst Lectr in Clinical Pædiatrics, University of Liverpool, 1948-57. Brit. Paediatric Association: Treasurer, 1964-71; Pres., 1972-73; Hon. Mem., 1973-; President: Liverpool Med. Instn, 1972-73; Liverpool Paediatric Club, 1975-; Hon. Mem. Assoc. European Paediatric Cardiologists, 1975-. RAMC (Major and Lieut-Col), 1942-46. *Publications:* contribs to Archives of Disease in Childhood, British Heart Journal, BMJ, Lancet, Practitioner, Brit. Encyclopædia of Medical Practice, Medical Progress, 1957, Cardiovascular Diseases in Childhood. *Recreations:* music, fell walking. *Address:* Foenum Lodge, Oldfield Road, Heswall, Merseyside L60 6SN. *T:* 051-342 2607.

HAY, Noel Grant, QC (Nigeria) 1955; Attorney-General, Western Region, Nigeria, 1954-58, retired; *b* 21 Dec. 1910; *s* of William Grant Hay, Barrister, NZ, and Jessie Margaret Talboys; *m* 1937, Clare Morton. *Educ:* Otago Univ., Dunedin, New Zealand (BA; LLM Hons); Oxford Univ. Asst District Officer, Nigeria, 1937; Magistrate, Nigeria, 1939-42; Legal Dept, Nigeria, 1943-53; Senior Crown Counsel, 1949. Legal Sec., 1950. *Recreations:* golf, tennis, fishing. *Address:* 39B Kotare Street, Christchurch, New Zealand. *Club:* South Canterbury (Timaru).

HAY, Sir Philip; *see* Hay, Sir Alan Philip.

HAY, Lt-Gen. Sir Robert, KCIE 1947 (CIE 1942); MB, ChB Edinburgh 1912; DPH Glasgow 1928; DTM&H Liverpool, 1927; *b* 8 March 1889; *s* of late Robert Erskine Hay, The Kilt, Castlecary; *m* 1928, Mary Carnegie McAusland; two *d* (one *s* decd). *Educ:* George Watson's; Edinburgh Univ. RAMC SR, 1914; IMS 1917; late Dir-Gen. IMS; KHP, 1944-48; retired, 1948, KStJ 1948. Hon. FRCPE, 1969. *Address:* Little Rulwood, Denholm, Hawick, Roxburghshire. *T:* Denholm 302.

HAY, Maj.-Gen. Robert Arthur, CB 1970; MBE 1946; Commandant, Royal Military College, Duntroon, 1973-77; *b* 9 April 1920; *s* of Eric Alexander Hay and Vera Eileen Hay (*née* Whitehead); *m* 1944, Endree Patricia Hay (*née* McGovern); two *s* one *d. Educ:* Brighton Grammar Sch., Melbourne, Victoria; RMC Duntroon, ACT (graduated Dec. 1939). Lt-Col, 1945; Col, 1955; Col GS HQ Eastern Comd; Military Attaché, Washington, DC, 1956; Dir Administrative Planning, AHQ, 1959; Defence Representative, Singapore and Malaya, 1962; Brig., 1964; IDC London, 1965; Dir Military Ops and Plans, AHQ, 1966; Maj.-Gen., 1967; Dep. Chief of the General Staff, AHQ; Comdr, Australian Forces, Vietnam, 1969; Comdr, First Australian Div., 1970; Chief, Mil. Planning Office, SEATO, 1971-73. *Recreations:* tennis, golf. *Address:* 5 Borrowdale Street, Red Hill, ACT, Australia. *Clubs:* Melbourne Cricket, Naval and Military (Melbourne); Commonwealth, Royal Canberra Golf (Canberra); Tanglin (Singapore).

HAY, Robert Edwin, (Roy Hay), MBE 1970; VMH 1971; formerly Editor, Gardeners' Chronicle (1954-64); *b* 20 Aug. 1910; *o s* of late Thomas Hay, CVO, sometime Superintendent Central Royal Parks; *m* 1946, Elizabeth Jessie (*d* 1976), *d* of late Rev. H. C. Charter; two *d*; *m* 1977, Mrs Frances Perry. *Educ:* Marylebone Grammar Sch. Horticultural seed trade, 1928; Asst Editor, Gardeners' Chronicle, 1936; Editor, Royal Horticultural Soc.'s publications, 1939; Min. of Agriculture, 1940; Horticultural Officer, Malta, 1942; Controller of Horticulture and Seed Divs, British zone of Germany, 1945. Officier du Mérite Agricole: Belgium, 1956; France, 1959. *Publications:* Annuals, 1937; In My Garden, 1955; Gardening the Modern Way, 1962; (with P. M. Synge) The Dictionary of Garden Plants, 1969; (jtly) The Dictionary of Indoor Plants in Colour, 1975. *Recreation:* philately. *Address:* Hurtmore Farm House, Hurtmore, Godalming, Surrey. *Club:* Farmers'.

HAY DAVISON, Ian Frederic; *see* Davison, I. F. H.

HAYBALL, Frederick Ronald, CMG 1969; with Longman Group Ltd, Publishers, since 1969; *b* 23 April 1914; *s* of late Frederick Reuben Hayball and late Rebecca Hayball; *m* 1938, Lavinia Violet Palmer; one *s* one *d. Educ:* Alleyn's Sch., Dulwich. Accountant, Myers, Gondouin & Co. Ltd, 1932-39. Flying Officer, RAF, 1939-45. Foreign and Commonwealth Office, 1945-69 (Counsellor, retired). *Recreations:* cricket, angling, motoring. *Address:* 42 Theydon Park Road, Theydon Bois, Essex. *T:* Theydon Bois 2195. *Club:* RAF Reserves.

HAYCOCKS, Prof. Norman, CBE 1969; Professor of Education, University of Nottingham, 1946-73; Deputy Vice-Chancellor, University of Nottingham, 1962-66, Pro-Vice-Chancellor, 1969-73; *b* 17 Nov. 1907; *s* of late Aaron and Jessie Haycocks, Salop and Manchester; unmarried. *Educ:* Salford Grammar Sch.; Univs of Manchester (open Schol.), Paris and Grenoble. BA First Cl. Hons in French, Manchester, 1928 (Research Schol.), MA 1929 (by research, Mediaeval French). Lecturer Univ. of Grenoble, 1928-29; Asst Master, North Manchester Sch. (branch of Manchester Gram. Sch.), 1929-33; Lecturer in Education, University of Manchester, 1933-46. Chairman, Standing Conference of National Voluntary Youth Organisations, 1952-70; Mem. Schools Broadcasting Council, 1958-68, and Chm., Secondary I Programme Cttee, 1958-64; Governor, National Coll. for Training of Youth Leaders, 1960-70; Member: Youth Service Development Council, 1963-71; Television Research Cttee, 1963-; Adv. Cttee for Supply and Trng of Teachers, 1973-. Vice-Chm., Universities' Council for the Education of Teachers, 1967-69, Chm., 1969-73, Acad. Sec., 1973-. Vis. Prof. of Education, Univ. of East Anglia, 1976-. Hon. FCP, 1972. Hon. LLD Nottingham, 1974. Squadron Leader in Intelligence Branch of Royal Air Force, 1941-45 (despatches). *Publications:* articles and papers in educational journals. *Recreations:* theatre and gardening. *Address:* 109 Derby Road, Bramcote, Nottingham NG9 3GZ. *T:* Nottingham 255024. *Club:* National Liberal.

HAYCRAFT, Colin Berry; Chairman, Managing Director and controlling shareholder, Gerald Duckworth & Co. Ltd, publishers, since 1971; *b* 12 Jan. 1929; *yr s* of Major W. C. S. Haycraft, MC and Bar, 5/8 Punjab Regt (killed 1929), and Olive Lillian Esmée (*née* King); *m* 1957, Anna Margaret Lindholm; five *s* one *d* (and one *d* decd). *Educ:* Wellington Coll. (schol.); The Queen's Coll., Oxford (Open Schol. in Classics; 1st Cl. Classical Mods, 1st Cl. Lit.Hum., MA). Nat. service (army), 1947-49. Personal Asst to Chm., Cecil H. King, Daily Mirror Newspapers Ltd; Dir, Weidenfeld & Nicolson Ltd and Weidenfeld (Publishers) Ltd (original editor and subseq. Man. Dir, World University Library Ltd); joined Duckworth, 1968. Public Schs Rackets Champion (singles and pairs), 1946; Oxford blue for Squash Rackets (4 years, Captain OUSRC, Eng. internat.), Lawn Tennis (Devon Co. player) and Rackets. *Address:* 22 Gloucester Crescent, NW1 7DY.

HAYDAY, Sir Frederick, Kt 1969; CBE 1963; National Industrial Officer, National Union of General and Municipal Workers, 1946-71; Chairman, International Committee, Trades Union Congress; *b* 26 June 1912; *s* of late Arthur Hayday, MP for W Notts; *m.* Member: General Council of the Trades Union Congress, 1950-72 (Chairman, 1962-63, Vice-Chairman, 1964-69); IBA (formerly ITA), 1969-73; British Railways Board, 1962-76. Mem., Police Complaints Bd, 1977-. *Address:* 42 West Drive, Cheam, Surrey. *T:* 01-642 8928.

HAYDON, Dr Denis Arthur, FRS 1975; Reader in Surface and Membrane Biophysics, University of Cambridge, since 1974; Fellow and Director of Studies in Natural Sciences, Trinity Hall, Cambridge, since 1965; *b* 21 Feb. 1930; *s* of late Ernest George Haydon and Grace Violet (*née* Wildman); *m* 1958, Ann

Primrose Wayman; two s one d. *Educ:* Dartford Grammar Sch.; King's Coll., Univ. of London (BSc, PhD). MA Cantab. ICI Res. Fellow, Imperial Coll., London, 1956-58; Asst Dir of Res., Univ. of Cambridge, Dept of Colloid Science, 1959-70, and Dept of Physiology, 1970-74; Asst Tutor, Trinity Hall, 1968-73; Tutor for Natural Scientists, Trinity Hall, 1973-74. Chem. Soc. Award for Surface and Colloid Chem., 1976. *Publications:* (with R. Aveyard) An Introduction to the Principles of Surface Chemistry, 1973; papers on surface chemistry and membrane biophysics in Proc. Royal Soc., Trans Faraday Soc., Jl Chem. Soc. and other sci. jls. *Recreations:* climbing, sailing, music. *Address:* 23 Porson Road, Cambridge CB2 2ET. *T:* Cambridge 59826.

HAYDON, Walter Robert, CMG 1970; HM Diplomatic Service; Ambassador to the Republic of Ireland, since 1976; b 29 May 1920; s of Walter Haydon and Evelyn Louise Thom; m 1943, Joan Elizabeth Tewson; one s one d (and one d decd). *Educ:* Dover Grammar Sch. Served in Army in France, India and Burma, 1939-46. Entered Foreign Service, 1946; served at London, Berne, Turin, Sofia, Bangkok, London, Khartoum, UK Mission to UN (New York), Washington; Head of News Dept, FCO, 1967-71; High Comr, Malaŵi, 1971-73; Chief Press Sec., 10 Downing Street, 1973-74; High Comr, Malta, 1974-76. *Recreations:* walking, swimming, tennis. *Address:* c/o Foreign and Commonwealth Office, SW1; 7L Hyde Park Mansions, Cabbell Street, NW1. *Clubs:* Travellers', Royal Commonwealth Society.

HAYEK, Friedrich August von, FBA 1944; Dr Jur, DrScPol, Vienna; DSc (Econ.) London; b Vienna, 8 May 1899; s of late August von Hayek, Prof. of Botany at University of Vienna; certificate of naturalisation, 1938; m 1st, Hella von Fritsch (d 1960); one s one d; 2nd, Helene Bitterlich. *Educ:* University of Vienna. Austrian Civil Service, 1921-26; Dir, Austrian Institute for Economic Research, 1927-31; Lecturer in Economics, University of Vienna, 1929-31; Tooke Prof. of Economic Science and Statistics in University of London, 1931-50; Prof. of Social and Moral Science, University of Chicago, 1950-62; Prof. of Economics, Univ. of Freiburg i B, 1962-69. Hon. Fellow: LSE; Austrian Acad. of Scis; American Economic Assoc.; Hoover Inst. on War, Revolution and Peace; Argentine Acad. of Economic Sci. Dr jur *hc* Rikkyo Univ., Tokyo, 1964; Dr jur *hc* Univ. of Salzburg, 1974; Dr Lit. Hum. *hc* Univ. of Dallas, 1975; Hon. Dr Soc. Sci., Marroquia Univ., Guatemala, 1977. Nobel Prize in Economic Science (jtly), 1974. *Publications:* Prices and Production, 1931; Monetary Theory and the Trade Cycle, 1933 (German edition, 1929); Monetary Nationalism and International Stability, 1937; Profits, Interest, and Investment, 1939; The Pure Theory of Capital, 1941; The Road to Serfdom, 1944; Individualism and Economic Order, 1948; John Stuart Mill and Harriet Taylor, 1950; The Counter-revolution of Science, 1952; The Sensory Order, 1952; The Political Ideal of the Rule of Law, 1955; The Constitution of Liberty, 1960; Studies in Philosophy, Politics and Economics, 1967; Freiburger Studien, 1969; Law, Legislation & Liberty, vol. I: Rules and Order, 1973, Vol II: The Mirage of Social Justice, 1976; De-Nationalisation of Money, 1976; edited: Beiträge zur Geldtheorie, 1933; Collectivist Economic Planning, 1935; Capitalism and the Historians, 1954; and the works of H. H. Gossen, 1927; F. Wieser, 1929; C. Menger, 1933-36; and H. Thornton, 1939; articles in Economic Journal, Economica, and other English and foreign journals. *Address:* Urachstrasse 27, D-7800 Freiburg i Brg, West Germany. *Club:* Reform (London).

HAYES, Brian David, CB 1976; Deputy Secretary, Ministry of Agriculture, Fisheries and Food, since 1973; b 5 May 1929; s of late Charles and Flora Hayes, Bramerton, Norfolk; m 1958, Audrey Jenkins; one s one d. *Educ:* Norwich Sch.; Corpus Christi Coll., Cambridge. BA (Hist.) 1952, PhD (Cambridge) 1956. RASC, 1947-49. Joined Min. of Agriculture, Fisheries and Food, 1956; Asst Private Sec. to the Minister, 1958; Asst Sec., 1967; Under-Sec., Milk and Poultry Gp, 1970-73. *Recreations:* reading, caravanning, watching cricket. *Address:* 1 Wayside, SW14. *T:* 01-878 1905.

HAYES, Sir Claude (James), KCMG 1974 (CMG 1969); MA, BLitt; Chairman, Crown Agents for Oversea Governments and Administrations, 1968-74; b 23 March 1912; er s of late J. B. F. Hayes, West Hoathly, Sussex; m 1940, Joan McCarthy, yr d of Edward McCarthy Fitt, Civil Engineer; two s one d. *Educ:* Ardingly Coll.; St Edmund Hall, Oxford (Scholar); Sorbonne; New Coll., Oxford (Sen. Scholar). Heath Harrison Travelling Scholarship; Zaharoff Travelling Fellowship; Paget Toynbee Prize; MA, BLitt. Asst Dir of Examinations, Civil Service Commn, 1938. Captain RASC 1st Inf. Div. BEF, 1939; Major 1940, Combined Ops; Lieut-Col, 1942-45 (N Africa, Sicily, Italy, NW Europe). Dep. Dir of Examinations, Civil Service Commn,

1945; Dir and Comr, 1949, also Sec., 1955; Nuffield Foundn Fellowship, 1953-54, toured Commonwealth studying public service recruitment and management. Asst Sec., HM Treasury, 1957; British Govt Mem., Cttee on Dissolution of Central African Fedn, 1963; Under-Sec., HM Treasury, 1964-65; Prin. Finance Officer, Min. of Overseas Development, 1965-68. *Recreations:* travel; music; unaided gardening; antique furniture; 18th century bourgeois chattels; getting value for money from shops. *Address:* Prinkham, Chiddingstone Hoath, Kent. *T:* Cowden 335. *Club:* United Oxford & Cambridge University.

HAYES, Colin Graham Frederick, MA; RA 1970 (ARA 1963); Reader, Royal College of Art, since 1973; painter; b 17 Nov. 1919; s of Gerald Hayes and Winifred (née Yule); m 1949, Jean Westbrook Law; three d. *Educ:* Westminster Sch.; Christ Church, Oxford. Served Royal Engineers, 1940-45 (Middle East) (Capt.). Ruskin Sch. of Drawing, 1946-47. Tutor, and Sen. Tutor, 1971-73, RCA. Work in Collections: Arts Council; British Council; Carlisle Museum; etc. Hon. ARCA and Fellow, Royal College of Art, 1960. *Publications include:* Renoir, 1961; Stanley Spencer, 1963; Rembrandt, 1969; many articles on painting in jls. *Address:* 26 Cleveland Avenue, W4. *T:* 01-994 8762.

HAYES, Helen, (Mrs Charles MacArthur); actress; b Washington, DC 10 Oct. 1900; d of Francis Van Arnum Brown and Catherine Estelle Hayes; m 1928, Charles MacArthur (d 1956); one s one d. *Educ:* Sacred Heart Academy, Washington, DC. As actress has appeared in USA in stage plays, among others: Pollyanna, Dear Brutus, Clarence, Bab, Coquette, The Good Fairy, To the Ladies, Young Blood, Mary of Scotland, Victoria Regina, Ladies and Gentlemen, Twelfth Night, Harriet, Happy Birthday; The Wisteria Trees, 1950; Mrs McThing, 1952. First appearance in England in The Glass Menagerie, 1948. Is also radio actress. Has appeared in films: Farewell to Arms, The Sin of Madelon Claudet, Arrowsmith, The Son-Daughter, My Son John, Anastasia, Airport (Best Supporting Actress Award, 1971), etc. Awarded gold statuette by Motion Picture Academy of Arts and Sciences, 1932, as outstanding actress, based on performance in the Sin of Madelon Claudet; Hon. degrees: Smith Coll., Hamilton Coll., Columbia Univ., Princeton Univ., St Mary's Coll. *Publications:* A Gift of Joy, 1965; On Reflection, 1968; (with Anita Loos) Twice Over Lightly, 1971. *Address:* Nyack, New York, NY 10960, USA. *Clubs:* Cosmopolitan, River, etc.

HAYES, Most Rev. James Martin; *see* Halifax (NS), Archbishop of, (RC).

HAYES, Vice-Admiral Sir John (Osler Chattock), KCB 1967 (CB 1964); OBE 1945; Lord-Lieutenant of Ross and Cromarty, since 1977; b 9 May 1913; er s of late Major L. C. Hayes, RAMC and Mrs Hayes; m 1939, Hon. Rosalind Mary Finlay, o d of 2nd and last Viscount Finlay of Nairn; two s one d. *Educ:* RN Coll., Dartmouth. Entered RN, 1927. Served War of 1939-45; Atlantic, HMS Repulse, Singapore, Russian Convoys, Malta. The Naval Sec., 1962-64; Flag Officer: Flotillas, Home Fleet, 1964-66; Scotland and NI, 1966-68; retd. Comdr 1948; Capt. 1953; Rear-Adm. 1962; Vice-Adm. 1965. Chm., Cromarty Firth Port Authority, 1974-77. Mem., Queen's Body Guard for Scotland (Royal Company of Archers), 1969. Pres., Scottish Council, King George's Fund for Sailors, 1968. Dep. Chm. Bd of Governors, Gordonstoun Sch. King Gustav V of Sweden Jubilee Medal, 1948. *Recreations:* walking, music, writing. *Address:* Arabella House, by Tain, Ross and Cromarty. *T:* Nigg Station 273.

HAYES, John Philip; Chief Economic Adviser, Foreign and Commonwealth Office, since 1975; b 1924; s of late Harry Hayes and late Mrs G. E. Hayes (née Hallsworth); m 1956, Susan Elizabeth, d of Sir Percivale Liesching, GCMG, KCB, KCVO; one s one d. *Educ:* Cranleigh Sch.; Corpus Christi Coll., Oxford. RAFVR, 1943-46. Barnett Memorial Fellowship, 1948-49; Political and Economic Planning, 1950-53; OEEC, 1953-58; Internat. Bank for Reconstruction and Develt, 1958-64; Head, Economic Develt Div., OECD, 1964-67; Dir, World Economy Div., Economic Planning Staff, ODM, 1967-69; Dep. Dir Gen. of Economic Planning, ODM, later ODA, 1969-71; Dir, Econ. Program Dept, later Econ. Analysis and Projections Dept, IBRD, 1971-73; Dir, Trade and Finance Div., Commonwealth Secretariat, 1973-75. *Recreations:* music, lawn tennis. *Address:* 1 Elgar Avenue, Ealing, W5 3JU. *T:* 01-567 2426.

HAYES, John Trevor, MA Oxon, PhD London; FSA; Director of the National Portrait Gallery, London, since 1974; b 21 Jan. 1929; er s of late Leslie Thomas Hayes and late Gwendoline (née Griffiths), London. *Educ:* Ardingly; Keble Coll. Oxford (Open

Exhibr); Courtauld Inst. of Art, London; Inst. of Fine Arts, New York. Asst Keeper, London Museum, 1954-70, Dir, 1970-74; Commonwealth Fund Fellow, 1958-59 (NY Univ.); Vis. Prof. in History of Art, Yale Univ., 1969. *Publications:* London: a pictorial history, 1969; The Drawings of Thomas Gainsborough, 1970; Catalogue of Oil Paintings in the London Museum, 1970; Gainsborough as Printmaker, 1971; Rowlandson: Watercolours and Drawings, 1972; Gainsborough: Paintings and Drawings, 1975; various London Museum and Nat. Portrait Gall. pubns; numerous articles in The Burlington Magazine, Apollo and other jls. *Recreations:* music, walking, travel. *Address:* c/o The National Portrait Gallery, St Martin's Place, WC2H 0HE. *T:* 01-930 8511. *Clubs:* Athenæum, Beefsteak.

HAYES, Thomas William Henry; Adviser to the Director of Prisons, Botswana, since 1975; *b* 1 Aug. 1912; *s* of Henry Daniel and Joanna Hayes; *m* 1933, Alice Frances; one *s*. *Educ:* Central Foundation Sch., London; London Univ. After 3 years in teaching and 2 in industry joined Prison Service, 1937, as Borstal Housemaster. Served in RA, 1940-45. Dep. Gov. Rochester Borstal, 1945-48; Staff Officer, with Police and Prisons Mission to Greece, 1948-51; Governor, subseq. of Lewes Prison, Hatfield and Lowdham Grange Borstals, Ashford Remand Centre and Wormwood Scrubs Prison; Asst Dir of Borstals, Home Office, 1964-69; Regional Dir of Prisons, SW Region, 1969-72. *Recreations:* golf, contract bridge. *Address:* Barngate, Boot Lane, Dinton, near Aylesbury, Bucks. *T:* Stone (Bucks) 372. *Clubs:* Ellesborough Golf, Aylesbury Bridge.

HAYES, Prof. William, FRS 1964; FRSE 1968; FAA 1976; Professor and Head of the Department of Genetics, Research School of Biological Sciences, Australian National University, since 1974; *b* 18 Jan. 1913; *s* of William Hayes and Miriam (*née* Harris), Co. Dublin, Ireland; *m* 1941, Honora Lee; one *s*. *Educ:* College of St Columba, Rathfarnham, Co. Dublin; Dublin Univ. BA (1st Cl. Mods. Nat. Sci.) Dublin, 1936; MB, BCh, Dublin, 1937; FRCPI 1945; ScD, Dublin, 1949. Served in India as Major, RAMC, Specialist in Pathology, 1942-46. Lectr in Bacteriology, Trinity Coll., Dublin, 1947-50; Sen. Lectr in Bacteriology, Postgraduate Medical Sch. of London, 1950-57, later Hon. Senior Lectr; Dir, MRC Molecular Genetics Unit, 1957-68, Hon. Dir 1968-73; Prof. of Molecular Genetics, Univ. of Edinburgh, 1968-73. Hon. DSc: Leicester, 1966; NUI, 1973; Kent, 1973; Hon. LLD Dublin, 1970. *Publication:* The Genetics of Bacteria and their Viruses, 1964. *Recreations:* painting, reading or doing nothing. *Address:* Department of Genetics, Research School of Biological Sciences, Australian National University, Box 475, PO, Canberra, ACT 2601, Australia; 25 Canning Street, Ainslie, ACT 2602, Australia.

HAYHOE, Bernard John, (Barney), CEng, MIMechE; MP (C) Hounslow, Brentford and Isleworth, since 1974 (Heston and Isleworth, 1970-74); *b* 8 Aug. 1925; *s* of Frank Stanley and Catherine Hayhoe; *m* 1962, Anne Gascoigne Thornton, *o d* of Bernard William and Hilda Thornton; two *s* one *d*. *Educ:* State schools; Borough Polytechnic. Tool Room Apprentice, 1941-44; Armaments Design Dept, Ministry of Supply, 1944-54; Inspectorate of Armaments, 1954-63; Conservative Research Dept, 1965-70. PPS to Lord President and Leader of House of Commons, 1972-74. Hon. Sec., 1970-71, Vice-Chm., 1974, Cons. Parly Employment Cttee; Jt Hon. Sec., 1970-73, Vice-Chm., 1973-76, Cons. Gp for Europe; Vice-Chm., Cons. Party Internat. Office, 1973-; Mem., Select Cttee on Race Relations and Immigration, 1971-73; an additional Opposition Spokesman on Employment, 1974-. Governor, Birkbeck Coll., 1976-. *Address:* 20 Wool Road, SW20. *T:* 01-947 0037. *Club:* Conservative (Hounslow).

HAYHOE, Prof. Frank George James, MD, FRCP, FRCPath; Leukaemia Research Fund Professor of Haematological Medicine, University of Cambridge, since 1968; Fellow, Darwin College, Cambridge, since 1964; *b* 25 Oct. 1920; *s* of Frank Stanley and Catharine Hayhoe; *m* 1945, Jacqueline Marie Marguerite (*née* Dierkx); two *s*. *Educ:* Selhurst Grammar Sch.; Trinity Hall, Cambridge; St Thomas's Hospital Medical Sch. BA Cantab 1942; MRCS, LRCP 1944; MB, BChir Cantab 1945; MRCP 1949; MA Cantab 1949; MD Cantab 1951; FRCP 1965; FRCPath 1971. Captain RAMC, 1945-47. Registrar, St Thomas' Hosp., 1947-49. Elmore Research Student, Cambridge Univ., 1949-51; Lectr in Medicine, Cambridge Univ., 1951-68; Mem. Council of Senate, 1967-71. Mem., Bd of Governors, United Cambridge Hospitals, 1971-74; Mem., Cambs AHA, 1974-75. Langdon Brown Lectr, RCP, 1971. G. F. Götz Foundn Prize, Zürich Univ., 1974. *Publications:* (ed) Lectures in Haematology, 1960; Leukaemia: Research and Clinical Practice, 1960; Cytology and Cytochemistry of Acute Leukaemia, 1964; (ed) Current Research in Leukaemia, 1965; An Atlas of Haematological Cytology, 1969; Ultrastructure of Haemic Cells,

1973; Leukaemia, Lymphomas and Allied Disorders, 1976; contribs to med. and scientific jls, on haematological topics, especially leukaemia. *Address:* Department of Haematological Medicine, University of Cambridge. *T:* Cambridge 45171.
See also B. J. Hayhoe.

HAYMAN, Mrs Helene (Valerie); MP (Lab) Welwyn and Hatfield, since Oct. 1974; *b* 26 March 1949; *d* of Maurice Middleweek and Maude Middleweek; *m* 1974, Martin Hayman; one *s*. *Educ:* Wolverhampton Girls' High Sch.; Newnham Coll., Cambridge (MA). Pres., Cambridge Union, 1969. Worked with Shelter, Nat. Campaign for the Homeless, 1969; Camden Council Social Services Dept, 1971; Dep. Dir, Nat. Council for One Parent Families, 1974. Contested (Lab) Wolverhampton SW, Feb. 1974. *Address:* House of Commons, SW1A 0AA.

HAYMAN, John David Woodburn; His Honour Judge Hayman; a Circuit Judge, since 1976; *b* 24 Aug. 1918; *m*; two *s* four *d*. *Educ:* King Edward VII Sch., Johannesburg; St John's Coll., Cambridge (MA, LLB). Served with S African Forces, 1940-42. Called to the Bar, Middle Temple, 1945; sometime Lecturer in Law: University Coll. of Wales, Aberystwyth; Leeds Univ.; Cambridge Univ.

HAYMAN, Sir Peter (Telford), KCMG 1971 (CMG 1963); CVO 1965; MBE 1945; HM Diplomatic Service, retired; Chairman, Estates House Investment Trust; Governor, International Students House; Director, Delta Overseas; Adviser, Seatrade Publications; Member Executive Committee, International Grenfell Association; *b* 14 June 1914; *s* of C. H. T. Hayman, The Manor House, Brackley, Northants; *m* 1942, Rosemary Eardley Blomefield; one *s* one *d*. *Educ:* Stowe; Worcester Coll., Oxford. Asst Principal: Home Office, 1937-39; Min. of Home Security, 1939-41; Asst Priv. Sec. to Home Sec. (Rt Hon. Herbert Morrison, MP), 1941-42; Principal, Home Office, 1942. Served War, 1942-45, Rifle Bde, Major. Principal, Home Office, 1945-49; transf. to Min. of Defence as Personal Asst to Chief Staff Officer to the Minister, 1949-52; Asst Sec, Min. of Defence, 1950; UK Delegation to NATO, 1952-54; transf. to FO, 1954; Counsellor, Belgrade, 1955-58; seconded for temp. duty with Governor of Malta, 1958; Couns., Baghdad, 1959-61; Dir-Gen. of British Information Services, New York, 1961-64; Minister and Dep. Comdt, Brit. Milit. Govt in Berlin, 1964-66; Asst Under-Sec., FO, 1966-69; Dep. Under-Secretary of State, FCO, 1969-70; High Comr in Canada, 1970-74. *Recreations:* shooting, fishing, travel. *Address:* Uxmore House, Checkendon, Oxon. *T:* Checkendon 680 658. *Clubs:* Travellers', Army and Navy, MCC.

HAYMAN, Prof. Walter Kurt, FRS 1956; MA; ScD (Cambridge); Hon. ARCS (Imperial College); Professor of Pure Mathematics at the Imperial College of Science and Technology, London; *b* 6 Jan. 1926; *s* of late Franz Samuel Haymann and Ruth Therese (*née* Hensel); *m* 1947, Margaret Riley Crann, MA Cantab, *d* of Thomas Crann, New Earswick, York; three *d*. *Educ:* Gordonstoun Sch.; St John's Coll., Cambridge. Lecturer at King's Coll., Newcastle upon Tyne, 1947, and Fellow of St John's Coll., Cambridge, 1947-50; Lecturer, 1947, and Reader, 1953-56, Exeter. 1st Smiths prize, 1948, shared Adams Prize, 1949, Junior Berwick Prize, 1955; Senior Berwick Prize, 1964. Visiting Lecturer at Brown Univ., USA, 1949-50, at Stanford Univ., USA (summer) 1950 and 1955, and to the American Mathematical Soc., 1961. Co-founder with Mrs Hayman of British Mathematical Olympiad; Hon. Sec., Soc. for Protection of Science and Learning. *Publications:* Multivalent Functions (Cambridge, 1958) Meromorphic Functions (Oxford, 1964); Research Problems in Function Theory (London, 1967); Subharmonic Functions, vol I, 1976; papers in various mathematical journals. *Recreations:* music, travel. *Address:* Imperial College, Queen's Gate, SW7 2BZ. *T:* 01-589 5111.

HAYMAN, Rev. Canon William Samuel; Chaplain to The Queen's Household, 1961-73; *b* 3 June 1903; *s* of late Rev. William Henry Hayman, Rector of Leckford, and late Louise Charlotte Hayman; *m* 1930, Rosemary Prideaux Metcalfe; one *s* one *d*. *Educ:* Merchant Taylors' Sch.; St John's Coll., Oxford (MA). Deacon, 1926; Priest, 1927; Curate: St Matthew, Brixton, 1926-32; Wimbledon (in charge of St Mark), 1932-34; Vicar of Finstall, Worcs, 1934-38; Rector of Cheam, 1938-72. Hon. Canon of Southwark, 1952-60, Canon Emeritus, 1972. Rural Dean of Beddington, 1955-60; Archdeacon of Lewisham, 1960-72. *Recreations:* fly-fishing, photography, music, amateur operatics, scouting. *Address:* Wayside, Houghton, Stockbridge, Hants SO20 6LH. *T:* King's Somborne 264.

HAYNES, Denys Eyre Lankester; Keeper of Greek and Roman Antiquities, British Museum, 1956-76; *b* 15 Feb. 1913; 2nd *s* of late Rev. Hugh Lankester Haynes and late Emmeline Marianne

Chaldecott; *m* 1951, Sybille Edith Overhoff. *Educ:* Marlborough; Trinity Coll., Cambridge. Scholar, British School at Rome, 1936; Asst Keeper: Victoria and Albert Museum, 1937; British Museum, 1939-54 (released for war service, 1939-45); Dep. Keeper, British Museum, 1954. Geddes-Harrower Prof. of Greek Art and Archaeology, Univ. of Aberdeen, 1972-73. Chm., Soc. for Libyan Studies, 1974. Corr. Mem., German Archæological Inst., 1953; Ordinary Mem., 1957. Lectures: Burlington, 1976; Brown and Hayley, Univ. of Puget Sound, 1977. *Publications:* Porta Argentariorum, 1939; Ancient Tripolitania, 1946; Antiquities of Tripolitania, 1956; The Parthenon Frieze, 1958; The Portland Vase, 1964; Fifty Masterpieces of Classical Art, 1970; The Arundel Marbles, 1975. *Address:* Merle Cottage, Dean, near Charlbury, Oxon.

HAYNES, Edwin William George, CB 1971; Principal Executive Officer, Covent Garden Market Authority; *b* 10 Dec. 1911; *s* of Frederick William George Haynes and Lilian May Haynes (*née* Armstrong); *m* 1942, Dorothy Kathleen Coombs; one *s* one *d. Educ:* Regent Street Polytechnic Secondary Sch.; University of London (BA, LLM). Barrister-at-law, Lincoln's Inn, 1946. Estate Duty Office, Inland Revenue, 1930-39; Air Min., 1939; Min. of Aircraft Production, 1940; Min. of Supply, 1946; Min. of Aviation, 1959; Under-Sec., 1964; Under-Sec., DTI (formerly Min. of Technology), 1968-71. *Recreations:* tennis, cats. *Address:* 92 Malmains Way, Beckenham, Kent. *T:* 01-650 0224.

HAYNES, Sir George (Ernest), Kt 1962; CBE 1945; *b* 24 Jan. 1902; *e s* of Albert Ernest and Sarah Anne Haynes, Middlewich, Cheshire; *m* 1930, Kathleen Norris Greenhaigh; two *d. Educ:* Sandbach Sch.; Liverpool Univ. BSc 1922; school master and educational and social research, 1923-28; Warden of University Settlement, Liverpool, 1928-33; Dir, Nat. Council of Social Service, 1940-67; Mem., Lord Chancellor's Cttee: on Procedure of County Courts, 1948; on Legal Aid, 1944-45 (and Mem., Adv. Cttee, 1950-75); Chairman of Temp. Internat. Council for Educational Reconstruction of UNESCO, 1947-48; Mem. Colonial Office Advisory Cttee, on Social Development, 1947-63. President: Internat. Conf. of Social Work, 1948-56; National Birthday Trust; Standing Conf. for the Advancement of Counselling; Chairman: Preparatory Cttee, World Assembly of Youth, 1947-48; National Bureau for Co-operation in Child Care, 1963-68; Invalid Children's Aid Association, 1964-69; Rural Industries Loan Fund Ltd, 1949-68; Social Services Cttee, National Association for Mental Health, 1955-58; Standing Conference of British Organisations for Aid to Refugees, 1953-60; Council of British Assoc. of Residential Settlements, 1963-68; Adv. Council, Rural Industries Bureau, 1962-68; Exec. Cttee, British National Conference on Social Welfare, 1950-67; Social Science Cttee, Nat. Fund for Research into Crippling Diseases, 1968-72. Vice-Chm., Family Welfare Assoc., 1961-66. Mem. Council of Brit. Red Cross Soc., 1960-76; Vice-President: British Assoc. for Disability and Rehabilitation; Assoc. for Spina Bifida; Crown Trustee, City Parochial Foundation, 1965-75; Pres., Nat. Assoc. of Citizens Advice Bureaux; UK Delegate to UN Social Commission, 1962-66, and to UN Commn for Social Develt 1967. René Sand Memorial Award, 1958. *Address:* 103 Richmond Hill Court, Richmond, Surrey. *T:* 01-940 6304.

HAYNES, Ven. Peter; Archdeacon of Wells, Canon Residentiary and Prebendary of Huish and Brent in Wells Cathedral, since 1974; *b* 24 April 1925; *s* of Francis Harold Stanley Haynes and Winifred Annie Haynes; *m* 1952, Ruth Stainthorpe; two *s. Educ:* St Brendan's Coll., Clifton; Selwyn Coll., Cambridge (MA); Cuddesdon Theol Coll., Oxford. Staff of Barclays Bank, 1941-43; RAF, 1943-47. Deacon 1952, Priest 1953. Asst Curate, Stokesley, 1952-54; Hessle, 1954-58; Vicar, St John's Drypool, Hull, 1958-63; Bishop's Chaplain for Youth and Asst Dir of Religious Educn, Dio. Bath and Wells, 1963-70; Vicar of Glastonbury, 1970-74 (with Godney from 1972). Proctor in Convocation, 1976-. *Recreations:* sailing, model engineering. *Address:* 6 The Liberty, Wells, Somerset BA5 2SU. *T:* Wells 72224. *Club:* Sloane.

HAYNES, Rear-Adm. William Allen, CB 1968; OBE 1941; retired 1970; *b* 29 Sept. 1913; *s* of late Paymaster Capt. W. F. Haynes, Royal Navy and late Mrs M. W. Haynes (*née* Wilkinson); *m* 1964, Mary Theodosia Peploe; two *d. Educ:* Royal Naval Colleges, Dartmouth, Keyham and Greenwich. HMS Leander, 1935-36; HMS Glasgow, 1938-41; HM Dockyard, Chatham, 1941-44; HMS Gabbard, 1944-47; Admty i/c development of steam catapult, 1947-51; HMS Ceylon (Korean War), 1951-53; Apprentice Trng in HMS Fisgard, 1953-55; HM Dockyard, Chatham, 1955-60; Imp. Def. Coll., 1961; Dir of Naval Ship Production, 1962-67; Dir-Gen., Dockyards and Maintenance, 1967-69. Comdr 1947; Capt. 1958; Rear-Adm. 1966. *Recreations:* sailing, gardening. *Address:* Bowden House, Dartmouth, Devon. *T:* Stoke Fleming 234. *Club:* Royal Ocean Racing.

HAYNES DIXON, Margaret Rumer, (Rumer Godden); writer, playwright, poet; *b* 10 Dec. 1907; *d* of late Arthur Leigh Godden, Lydd House, Aldington, Kent, and Katherine Norah Hingley; *m* 1934, Laurence Sinclair Foster, Calcutta; two *d*; *m* 1949, James Haynes Dixon, OBE (*d* 1973). *Educ:* abroad and Moira House, Eastbourne. *Publications:* Chinese Puzzle, 1935; Lady and Unicorn, 1937; Black Narcissus (novel and play), 1938; Gypsy Gypsy, 1940; Breakfast with the Nikolides, 1941; Fugue in Time (novel and play), 1945; The River, 1946 (filmed, 1950); Rungli-Rungliot (biography), 1943; Candle for St Jude, 1948; In Noah's Ark (poetry), 1949; A Breath of Air, 1950; Kingfishers Catch Fire, 1953; Hans Christian Andersen (biography), 1955; An Episode of Sparrows, 1955 (filmed 1957); Mooltiki, 1957; The Greengage Summer, 1958 (filmed, 1961); China Court, 1961; The Battle of the Villa Florita, 1963 (filmed 1964); (with Jon Godden) Two Under the Indian Sun, 1966; The Kitchen Madonna, 1967; Swans and Turtles, 1968; In This House of Brede, 1969; (comp.) The Raphael Bible, 1970; The Tale of the Tales, 1971; The Old Woman Who Lived in a Vinegar Bottle, 1972; (with Jon Godden) Shiva's Pigeons, 1972; The Peacock Spring, 1975; children's books, incl. The Diddakoi, 1972 (Whitbread Award); published internationally (11 languages). *Address:* Rye, East Sussex.

HAYTER, 3rd Baron *cr* 1927 of Chislehurst, Kent; **George Charles Hayter Chubb,** KCVO 1977; CBE 1976; Bt 1900; Managing Director since 1941, Chairman since 1957 of Chubb & Son's Lock & Safe Co. Ltd; Director of Charles Early & Marriott (Witney) Ltd since 1952; *b* 25 April 1911; *e s* of 2nd Baron Hayter and Mary (*d* 1948), *d* of J. F. Haworth; *S* father, 1967; *m* 1940, Elizabeth Anne Rumbold, MBE 1975, JP; three *s* one *d. Educ:* Leys Sch., Cambridge; Trinity Coll., Cambridge (MA). Chairman: Royal Society of Arts, 1965-66; Management Cttee, King Edward's Hospital Fund for London, 1965-; Executives Assoc. of GB, 1960; Duke of Edinburgh's Countryside in 1970 Cttee. President: Canada-United Kingdom Chamber of Commerce, 1966-67; Royal Warrant Holders Association, 1967; Business Equipment Trades Association, 1954-55. Mem., CoID, 1964-71; Chairman: EDC International Freight Movement, 1972-; British Security Industry Assoc., 1973-. Worshipful Company of Weavers': Liveryman, 1934-; Upper Bailiff, 1961-62. *Publication:* Security offered by Locks and Safes (Lecture, RSA), 1962. *Heir:* s Hon. George William Michael Chubb, *b* 9 Oct. 1943. *Address:* Ashtead House, Ashtead, Surrey. *T:* Ashtead 73476.

HAYTER, Stanley William, CBE 1967 (OBE 1959); artist; *b* 27 Dec. 1901; *s* of William Harry Hayter and Ellen Mercy Palmer; *m* 1st, 1926, Edith Fletcher (marriage dissolved at Reno, Nevada, 1929); one *s* decd; 2nd, 1940, Helen Phillips (marr. diss., Paris, 1971); two *s. Educ:* Whitgift Middle Sch.; King's Coll., London. Chemist, Anglo-Iranian Oil Co., Abadan, Iran, 1922-25. Founded Atelier 17, Paris, 1927. Has exhibited since 1927 in various cities of Europe, America and Japan (incl. London: 1928, 1938, 1957, 1962, 1967). Paintings and prints in principal museums in Gt Britain, France, Belgium, Switzerland, Sweden, Italy, Canada, USA, Japan. Legion of Honour, 1951; Chevalier des Arts et Lettres, 1967. *Publications:* New Ways of Gravure, 1949 (New York also) (revised edn, 1966); Nature and Art of Motion, New York, 1964; About Prints, 1962. *Address:* 12 rue Cassini, 75 Paris 14e, France. *T:* 326 26.60.

HAYTER, Sir William Goodenough, KCMG 1953 (CMG 1948); Warden of New College, Oxford, 1958-76, now Hon. Fellow; *b* 1 Aug. 1906; *s* of late Sir William Goodenough Hayter, KBE; *m* 1938, Iris Marie, *d* of late Lieut-Col C. H. Grey (formerly Hoare), DSO; one *d. Educ:* Winchester; New Coll., Oxford. Entered HM Diplomatic Service, 1930; served Foreign Office, 1930; Vienna, 1931; Moscow, 1934; Foreign Office, 1937; China, 1938; Washington, 1941; Foreign Office, 1944 (Asst Under-Sec. of State, 1948); HM Minister, Paris, 1949; Ambassador to USSR, 1953-57; Deputy Under-Sec. of State, Foreign Office, 1957-58. Fellow of Winchester Coll., 1958-76. Trustee, British Museum, 1960-70. Hon. DL Bristol, 1976; Grosses Goldenes Ehrenzeichen mit dem Stern für Verdienste (Austria), 1967. *Publications:* The Diplomacy of the Great Powers, 1961; The Kremlin and the Embassy, 1966; Russia and the World, 1970; William of Wykeham, Patron of the Arts, 1970; A Double Life (autobiog.), 1974; Spooner, 1977. *Address:* Bassetts House, Stanton St John, Oxford. *T:* Stanton St John 598. *Club:* Brooks's.

HAYWARD, Sir Alfred, KBE 1961 (CBE 1960); retired; *b* England, 14 Jan. 1896; *s* of Thomas and Minnie Hayward, Sudbourne, Suffolk; *m* 1923, Margaret Fromm; one *s* two *d*. Came to New Zealand, 1911. Served European War, 1914-18, in France, 1916-18. Took up farming in Waikato district. Dir, NZ Co-op. Dairy Co., 1933-61. Chm., 1947-61; Deputy Chm., NZ

Dairy Board, 1958. JP 1957. *Address:* 42A Whittaker Street, Otumoetai, Tauranga, New Zealand.

HAYWARD, Sir Charles (William), Kt 1974; CBE 1970; Chairman and Joint Managing Director of Firth Cleveland Ltd and of constituent companies in Group at home and abroad at varying dates, 1936-73; *b* 3 Sept. 1892; *s* of John and Mary Hayward, Wolverhampton; *m* 1st, 1915, Hilda (*d* 1971), *d* of late John and Alexandra Arnold; one *s*; 2nd, 1972, Elsie Darnell, *d* of late Charles and Kate George. *Educ:* St John's School, Wolverhampton. Director of Electric and General Industrial Trusts Ltd, 1928, Chairman and Managing Director, 1932-73. Mem. of Post Office Advisory Council, 1952. Held Directorships since 1920 in various companies, public and private, including engineering, farming and horticulture. Chm. of Trustees The Hayward Foundn, 1961; Pres., Royal Wolverhampton Sch. Liveryman of Barbers' Company; Freeman of the City of London, 1938; Worshipful Company of Masons. Hon. Fellow, Keble Coll., Oxford, 1973. Hon. FRCS, 1970; Hon. Fellow, Inst. of Ophthalmology, 1967; Hon. LLD Birmingham, 1975. KStJ 1973. *Recreations:* yachting, collecting antiques and works of art. *Address:* Isle of Jethou, PO Box 5, Guernsey, CI. *T:* Guernsey 23844.
See also J . A . Hayward .

HAYWARD, Sir Edward (Waterfield), Kt 1961; grazier and company director, Australia; Chairman: John Martin & Co. Ltd; Coca Cola Bottlers Ltd, since 1948; Director: Finance Corporation of Australia, since 1955; Bennett & Fisher Ltd, since 1960; Bank of Adelaide; *b* 10 Nov. 1903; *s* of Arthur Dudley Hayward and Mary Anne Hayward; *m* 1972, Jean Katherine Bridges, *widow* of Ernest Bushby Bridges. *Educ:* St Peter's Coll., Adelaide, S Australia. Lt-Col, 2nd AIF, Middle East, New Guinea and Borneo (despatches: 1944 in New Guinea, 1945 in Borneo). Pres., Council of St John in South Australia (Chm. 1946). Purchased Silverton Park, Delamere, SA 1942, and established Border Leicester Stud and later Hereford Stud. KStJ 1960; Bronze Star Medal, USA, 1945. *Recreations:* polo (represented S Australia, Interstate, 1936-57); golf, swimming. *Address:* 100 Rundle Street, Adelaide, SA 5001, Australia. *T:* 23-0200; Carrick Hill, Springfield, SA 5062, Australia. *T:* 79-3886. *Clubs:* Adelaide, Naval, Military & Air Force, Royal Adelaide Golf, Adelaide Polo (Adelaide SA); Melbourne (Melbourne); Australian, Royal Sydney Golf (Sydney, NSW).

HAYWARD, Maj.-Gen. George Victor, BSc; CEng, FICE, FIMechE; Commandant, Technical Group, REME, 1971-73, retired; Colonel Commandant, REME, since 1973; *b* 21 June 1918; *e s* of late G. H. Hayward; *m* 1953, Gay Benson, *d* of late H. B. Goulding, MB, BCh, FRCSI; one *s* one *d. Educ:* Blundells; Birmingham Univ. (BSc). War of 1939-45: commissioned, 1940; transf. to REME, 1942; GSO1 REME Training Centre, 1958; Comdr, REME 2nd Div., 1960; Asst Mil. Sec., War Office, 1962; Col, RARDE, Fort Halstead, 1963; CO, 38 Central Workshop, 1965; Dep. Comdt, Technical Group, REME, 1966; Comdt, REME Training Centre, 1969. *Recreations:* sailing, skiing, shooting. *Address:* Chart Cottage, Chartwell, Westerham, Kent. *T:* Crockham Hill 253. *Club:* Army and Navy.

HAYWARD, Jack Arnold, OBE 1968; Chairman, Grand Bahama Development Co. Ltd and Freeport Commercial and Industrial Ltd, since 1976; *b* 14 June 1923; *s* of Sir Charles Hayward, *qv*; *m* 1948, Jean Mary Forder; two *s* one *d. Educ:* Northaw Prep Sch.; Stowe Sch., Buckingham. Joined RAF, 1941; flying training in Florida, USA; active service as officer pilot in SE Asia Comd, demobilised as Flt-Lt, 1946. Joined Rotary Hoes Ltd, 1947; served S Africa branch until 1950. Founded USA operations Firth Cleveland Gp of Companies, 1951; joined Grand Bahama Port Authority Ltd, Freeport, Grand Bahama Island, 1956. Hon. LLD Exeter, 1971. *Recreations:* promoting British endeavours, mainly in sport; watching cricket; amateur dramatics; preserving the British landscape, keeping all things bright, beautiful and British. *Address:* Seashell Lane (PO Box F-99), Freeport, Grand Bahama Island, Bahamas. *T:* Freeport 373-1528. *Clubs:* MCC, Royal Air Force, Durban Country (S Africa).

HAYWARD, Ven. John Derek Risdon; Vicar of Isleworth, since 1964; General Secretary, Diocese of London, since 1974; Archdeacon of Middlesex, 1974-75, now Archdeacon Emeritus; *b* 13 Dec. 1923; *s* of late Eric Hayward and of Barbara Olive Hayward; *m* 1965, Teresa Jane Kaye; one *s* one *d. Educ:* Stowe; Trinity Coll., Cambridge (BA 1956, MA 1964). Served War of 1939-45, Lieut 27th Lancers, Middle East and Italy, 1943-45 (twice wounded). Man. Dir, Hayward Waldie & Co., Calcutta (and associated cos), 1946-53. Trinity Coll., Cambridge, 1953-56, Westcott House, Cambridge, 1956-57. Asst Curate, St

Mary's Bramall Lane, Sheffield, 1957-58; Vicar, St Silas, Sheffield, 1959-63. Mem., General Synod, 1975. Bronze Star (US) 1945. *Recreations:* riding, skiing, sailing (when opportunity offers). *Address:* 61 Church Street, Isleworth, Mddx TW7 6BE. *T:* 01-560 6662. *Club:* Oriental.

HAYWARD, Sir Richard (Arthur), Kt 1969; CBE 1966; *b* 14 March 1910; *m* 1936, Ethel Wheatcroft; one *s* one *d. Educ:* Catford Central Sch. Post Office: Boy Messenger; Counter Clerk; Union of Post Office Workers: Assistant Secretary, 1947; Deputy General Secretary, 1951. Secretary General, Civil Service National Whitley Council (Staff Side), 1955-66; Chm., Supplementary Benefits Commn, 1966-69; Member, Post Office Board, 1969-71; Chairman: NHS Staff Commn, 1972-75; New Towns Staff Commn, 1976-; Member: Parole Board, England and Wales, 1975-; Solicitors' Disciplinary Tribunal, 1975-. UK Rep., Meeting of Experts on Conditions of Work and Service of Public Servants, ILO, 1963; overseas visits, inc. Israel, Mauritius, Canada, to advise on Trade Unionism in Public Services. Chm., Civil Service Sports Council, 1968-73, Life Vice-Pres., 1973; President: Civil Service Cricket Assoc., 1966-; Assoc. of Kent Cricket Clubs, 1970-; Pres., Civil Service Assoc. Football, 1974-. Governor, Guy's Hosp., 1949-72. *Recreations:* topography of Southwark, watching sport. *Address:* 10 Birchwood Avenue, Southborough, Tunbridge Wells, Kent TN4 0UD. *T:* Tunbridge Wells 29134. *Club:* MCC.

HAYWARD, Ronald George, CBE 1970; General Secretary of the Labour Party since 1972; *b* 27 June 1917; *s* of F. Hayward, small-holder, Oxon; *m* 1943, Phyllis Olive (*née* Allen); three *d. Educ:* Bloxham C of E Sch.; RAF Technical Schools, Halton, Cosford, Locking. Apprenticed Cabinet-maker, 1933-36. NCO, RAF: Technical Training Instructor, 1940-45. Labour Party: Secretary-Agent: Banbury Constituency, 1945-47; Rochester and Chatham Constituency, 1947-50; Asst Regional Organiser, 1950-59; Regional Organiser, 1959-69; National Agent, 1969-72. Vice-Pres., Nat. Union of Labour and Socialist Clubs. *Address:* 6 Carrick Court, Kennington Park Road, SE11. *Club:* The Wellesley (Cliftonville, Kent).

HAYWARD ELLEN, Patricia Mae; Executive Director, Bond Street Association and Regent Street Association; *b* 12 April 1919; *d* of Edric Allan Jordan and May Holdcraft; *m* 1st, 1945, Frederick Handel Hayward (*d* 1965); one *s*; 2nd, 1966, John Harold Ellen. *Educ:* Sydenham High School. Clerk, Securities Dept, National Provincial Bank, 1938-45; Export Dir, Perth Radios, 1955-60; Bond Street Assoc., 1961-; Regent Street Assoc., 1972-. Alderman, St Pancras Council, 1960-66 (Libraries/Public Health). Elected to Executive of Westminster Chamber of Commerce, 1971, Chm. City Affairs Cttee, 1971-75. FZS. *Recreations:* swimming, collecting first editions, press books and Meissen china. *Address:* 20 Chalcot Crescent, Regents Park, NW1 8YD. *T:* 01-722 4772. *Club:* Naval and Military.

HAYWOOD, Thomas Charles Stanley, OBE 1962; JP; Lieutenant of Leicestershire, since 1974 (Lord Lieutenant of Rutland, 1963-74); *b* 10 March 1911; *s* of late Charles B. Haywood, Woodhatch, Reigate, Surrey; *m* 1937, Anne, *d* of J. B. A. Kessler, London; two *s* one *d. Educ:* Winchester; Magdalene Coll., Cambridge. Served 1939-42 with Leics Yeomanry, Capt. 1940, Hon. Col, 1970-77. Chm. Trustees, Oakham Sch., 1964-. DL 1962, JP 1957, High Sheriff 1952, County of Rutland. *Address:* Gunthorpe, Oakham, Rutland. *T:* Manton 203. *Clubs:* Bath, MCC.

HAZAN, John Boris Roderick, QC 1969; JP; Barrister-at-Law; a Recorder of the Crown Court, since 1972; *b* 3 Oct. 1926; *s* of Selik and Eugenie Hazan. *Educ:* King's Coll., Taunton; King's Coll., Univ. of London. Called to Bar, Lincoln's Inn, 1948, Bencher 1977. Prosecuting Counsel to Inland Revenue, South Eastern Circuit, 1967-69. Dep. Chm., Surrey QS, 1969-71. Member: Criminal Law Revision Cttee, 1971-; Home Secretary's Policy Adv. Cttee on Sexual Offences, 1976-; Dept of Trade Inspector, Hartley Baird Ltd, 1973-76. JP Surrey, 1969. *Recreations:* music, opera, walking. *Address:* 4 Brick Court, Temple, EC4. *T:* 01-353 2725. *Club:* Savile.

HAZELL, Bertie, CBE 1962 (MBE 1946); District Organiser, National Union of Agricultural Workers, since 1937 and President, since 1966; *b* 18 April 1907; *s* of John and Elizabeth Hazell; *m* 1936, Dora A. Barham; one *d. Educ:* various elementary schs in Norfolk. Agricultural worker, 1921; apptd Sec. and Agent to E Norfolk Divisional Labour Party, Sept. 1933; Mem. W Riding of Yorks, War Agricultural Executive Cttee, 1939 (Chm. several of its Cttees, throughout war period). Contested (Lab) Barkston Ash Parliamentary Division, 1945 and 1950 Gen. Elections; MP (Lab) North Norfolk, 1964-70.

Chairman: E and W Ridings Regional Bd for Industry, 1954-64; N Yorks AHA, 1974-; Vice-Chm., Agricultural, Horticultural and Forestry Trng Bd, 1972-74; Member: E Riding Co. Agricultural Exec. Cttee, 1946-64; Agricultural Wages Board, 1946-; Leeds Regional Hosp. Board, 1948-74 (Chm. Works and Buildings Cttee); Potato Marketing Bd, 1970-. Magistrate, City of York, 1950-; Chairman: York and District Employment Cttee, 1963-74; N Yorks District Manpower Cttee, 1975-; Vice-Chm., Leeds Regional Hosp. Bd, 1967-74. Mem. Council, Univ. of E Anglia. *Recreation:* gardening. *Address:* 42 Fellbrook Avenue, Beckfield Lane, Acomb, York. *T:* York 78443.

HAZELL, Quinton, MBE 1961; Chairman, West Midlands Economic Planning Council, 1971-77; Chairman, Supra Group Ltd, since 1973; Director, Phoenix Assurance Co. Ltd, since 1968; *b* 14 Dec. 1920; *s* of late Thomas Arthur Hazell and Ada Kathleen Hazell; *m* 1942, Morwenna Parry-Jones; one *s. Educ:* Manchester Grammar School. Management Trainee, Braid Bros Ltd, Colwyn Bay, 1936-39; Royal Artillery, 1939-46; formed Quinton Hazell Ltd, 1946; Chm., 1946-73; Chm., Edward Jones (Contractors) Ltd, 1973-74. Mem., Welsh Adv. Cttee for Civil Aviation, 1961-67; Dir, Wales Gas Bd, 1961-65; Mem. Council, UC Bangor, 1966-68. *Recreations:* antiques, horology, water skiing. *Address:* Birdingbury Hall, Birdingbury, near Rugby, Warwicks. *T:* Leamington Spa 632650.

HAZI, Dr Vencel; Deputy Foreign Minister, Hungary, since 1976; *b* 3 Sept. 1925; *m* 1952, Judit Zell; one *d. Educ:* Technical Univ. and Univ. of Economics, Budapest. Entered Diplomatic Service, 1950; served in Min. of Foreign Affairs, Budapest, 1950; Press Attaché, Hungarian Legation, London, 1951-53; Counsellor, Legation, Stockholm, 1957-58; Ambassador: to Iraq, and to Afghanistan, 1958-61; to Greece, and to Cyprus, 1962-64; Head of Western Dept, Min. of For. Affairs, Budapest, 1964-68; Dep. For. Minister, Budapest, 1968-70; Ambassador to Court of St James's, 1970-76. Golden Grade of Order of Merit for Labour, 1962, and of Medal of Merit of Hungarian People's Republic, 1953; Grand Cordon of Order of Omayoum, 1st Class, Iran. *Recreations:* reading, music, swimming, chess. *Address:* Ministry for Foreign Affairs, Budapest, II Bem rkp 47, Hungary. *Club:* Opera Fans (Budapest).

HAZLERIGG, family name of **Baron Hazlerigg.**

HAZLERIGG, 2nd Baron, *cr* 1945, of Noseley; **Arthur Grey Hazlerigg,** Bt, *cr* 1622; MC 1943; DL, JP; *b* 24 Feb. 1910; *e s* of 1st Baron and Dorothy Rachel (*d* 1972), *e d* of John Henry Buxton, Easneye, Ware, Herts; *S* father 1949; *m* 1945, Patricia (*d* 1972), *e d* of late John Pullar, High Seat, Fields Hill, Kloof, Natal, SA; one *s* two *d. Educ:* Eton; Trinity Coll., Cambridge. BA 1932. Served War of 1939-45, Leics Yeomanry (MC); Major, 1941; served in Italy. DL Leics 1946; JP 1946. *Recreations:* golf, shooting. *Heir: s* Hon. Arthur Grey Hazlerigg, *b* 5 May 1951. *Address:* Noseley Hall, Leicester LE7 9EH. *Clubs:* Army and Navy, MCC.

HAZLEWOOD, Air Vice-Marshal Frederick Samuel, CB 1970; CBE 1967 (OBE 1960); AFC 1951 (Bar to AFC, 1954); retired; *b* 13 May 1921; *s* of Samuel Henry and Lilian Hazlewood; *m* 1943, Isabelle Mary (*née* Hunt); one *s. Educ:* Kimbolton Sch. Served War of 1939-45: joined RAF, 1939; ops with Bomber Command, 1941; MEAF and UK Coastal Command, 1940-45. CFS, 1948; Lancaster Units, 1948-53 (Sqdn Ldr); Staff Coll. course, 1955; Comdg Officer, No 90 Valiant Sqdn, 1958-61 (Wing Comdr); HQ, Bomber Comd, 1961-63; HQ, RAF, Germany, 1963-64 (Gp Capt.); OC, RAF, Lyneham, 1965-67; HQ, RAF, Germany, 1968-69 (Air Cdre); AOC and Commandant, Central Flying School, 1970-72; Dir of Personnel (Air), 1972; AOC 38 Gp, RAF, 1972-74; Comdt, Jt Warfare Estab., 1974-76. *Recreations:* golf, tennis, rough shooting. *Address:* Holly Ditch Farm, Calne, Wilts. *Club:* Royal Air Force.

HAZLEWOOD, Rt. Rev. John; *see* Ballarat, Bishop of.

HEAD, family name of **Viscount Head.**

HEAD, 1st Viscount *cr* 1960, of Throope; **Antony Henry Head;** PC 1951; GCMG 1963 (KCMG 1961); CBE 1946; MC 1940; *b* 1906; *s* of late Geoffrey Head; *m* 1935, Lady Dorothea Ashley-Cooper, *d* of 9th Earl of Shaftesbury, KP, PC, GCVO, CBE; two *s* one *d* (and one *d* decd). *Educ:* Eton; Royal Military Coll., Sandhurst, Adjt Life Guards, 1934-37; Staff Coll., 1939; Brigade Major 20th Gds Bde, 1940; Asst Sec. Cttee Imperial Defence, 1940-41; Guards Armd Div., 1941-42 (GSO2); representative with Directors of Plans for Amphibious Operations (Brigadier), 1943-45. MP (C) Carshalton Division of Surrey, 1945-60; Sec. of State for War, 1951-56; Minister of Defence, Oct. 1956-Jan.

1957. High Commissioner (first) of the United Kingdom in the Federation of Nigeria, 1960-63; High Commissioner to the new Federation of Malaysia, 1963-66. Trustee of the Thomson Foundation, 1967-75. Pres., RNIB, 1975- (Chm., 1968-75). Col Comdt, SAS Regt, 1968-76. Chm., Wessex Region, National Trust, 1970-76. *Recreations:* sailing, shooting. *Heir: s* Hon. Richard Antony Head [*b* 27 Feb. 1937; *m* 1974, Alicia, *er d* of Julian Salmond, Malmesbury. *Educ:* Eton; Royal Military Coll., Sandhurst]. *Address:* Throope Manor, Bishopstone, near Salisbury, Wilts.

HEAD, Adrian Herbert; His Honour Judge Head; a Circuit Judge since 1972; *b* 4 Dec. 1923; *s* of late Judge Head and Mrs Geraldine Head (*née* Pipon); *m* 1947, Ann Pamela, *d* of late John Stanning and late Mrs A. C. Lewin, of Leyland and Njoro, Kenya; three *s. Educ:* RNC Dartmouth (invalided, polio); privately; Magdalen Coll., Oxford (MA). Arden Scholar, Gray's Inn, 1947. Called to Bar, Gray's Inn, 1947 (subseq. ad eundem Inner Temple). Chm., Agricultural Land Tribunals (SE Region), 1971; Dep. Chm., Middlesex QS, 1971. Tredegar Memorial Lectr, RSL, 1948. *Publications:* The Seven Words and The Civilian, 1946; contrib. Essays by Divers Hands, 1953; Safety Afloat (trans. from Dutch of W. Zantvoort), 1965. *Recreations:* sailing, writing, trees. *Address:* Overy Staithe, Kings Lynn, Norfolk PE31 8JG. *T:* Burnham Market 312; 5 Raymond Buildings, Gray's Inn, WC1R 5BP. *T:* 01-405 7146. *Clubs:* Norfolk (Norwich); Royal Norfolk & Suffolk Yacht (Lowestoft); Royal Naval Sailing Association, Cruising Association.

HEAD, Alice Maud; *b* London; *b* 3 May 1886; *y d* of F. D. Head. *Educ:* privately; North London Collegiate Sch. for Girls. Editor of Woman at Home, 1909-17; Managing Director of the National Magazine Company, Ltd, and editor of Good Housekeeping, 1924-39; re-joined the firm of George Newnes Ltd, 1941-49; Director, Country Life Ltd, 1942-49. *Publications:* It Could Never Have Happened, 1939; contributions to various daily and weekly publications. *Recreations:* travelling, reading, theatre-going. *Address:* 22 Whitelands House, Chelsea, SW3. *T:* 01-730 1967. *Club:* PEN.

HEAD, Major Sir Francis (David Somerville), 5th Bt, *cr* 1838; late Queen's Own Cameron Highlanders; *b* 17 Oct. 1916; *s* of 4th Bt and Grace Margaret (*d* 1967), *d* of late David Robertson; *S* father, 1924; *m* 1st, 1950, Susan Frances (marr. diss. 1965), *o d* of A. D. Ramsay, OBE; one *s* one *d* ; 2nd, 1967, Penelope, *d* of late Wilfred Alexander. *Educ:* Eton; Peterhouse, Cambridge. BA 1937. Served War of 1939-45 (wounded and prisoner); retired 1951. *Heir: s* Richard Douglas Somerville Head [*b* 16 Jan. 1951. *Educ:* Eton; Magdalene Coll., Cambridge]. *Address:* 10 Fairway, Merrow, Guildford, Surrey. *Club:* Naval and Military.

HEAD, Mildred Eileen, OBE 1971; Senior Partner, Head & Woodward (furnishers); *b* 13 June 1911; *d* of Philip Strudwick Head and Katie Head. *Educ:* Sudbury Girls' Secondary Sch.; Chelsea Coll. of Physical Educn (Dipl.). MCSP. Teacher, Lectr and Organiser of Physical Educn, 1933-50; owner, director and partner in several furniture and drapery shops from 1950. Pres., Nat. Fedn of Business and Professional Women's Clubs of Gt Britain and N Ireland, 1966-69; Pres., Nat. Chamber of Trade, 1977- (Chm. Bd of Management, 1971-77). Mayor of Borough of Sudbury, 1970-71; Member: Price Commn, 1973-; Nat. Economic Cttee for Distributive Trades, 1974-; Retail Consortium, 1971-; Comr of Inland Revenue, 1959-; First Vice-Pres., Internat. Fedn of Business and Professional Women, 1974-. *Recreation:* theatre. *Address:* Rosebank, Ingrams Well Road, Sudbury, Suffolk CO1O 6RT. *T:* Sudbury 72185.

HEADFORT, 6th Marquis of, *cr* 1800; **Thomas Geoffrey Charles Michael Taylour;** Bt 1704; Baron Headfort, 1760; Viscount Headfort, 1762; Earl of Bective, 1766; Baron Kenlis (UK), 1831; *b* 20 Jan. 1932; *o s* of 5th Marquis and Elsie Florence (*d* 1972), *d* of J. Partridge Tucker, Sydney, NSW, and *widow* of Sir Rupert Clarke, 2nd Bt of Rupertswood; *S* father, 1960; *m* 1st, 1958, Hon. Elizabeth Nall-Cain (from whom he obtained a divorce, 1969), *d* of 2nd Baron Brocket; one *s* two *d* ; 2nd, 1972, Virginia, *d* of late Mr Justice Nable, Manila. *Educ:* Stowe; Christ's Coll., Cambridge (MA). 2nd Lieut Life Guards, 1950; acting Pilot Officer, RAFVR, 1952. Freeman, Guild of Air Pilots and Air Navigators, 1958. Piloted Prospector aircraft around Africa, 1960, etc. Associate, Royal Instn of Chartered Surveyors; Council, Royal Agricultural Society of England, 1961. Holds commercial pilot's licence. Underwriting Mem. of Lloyds. *Heir: s* Earl of Bective, qv. *Address:* Ellerslie, Crosby, Isle of Man. *T:* Marown 521; 1425 Figueroa Street, Paco, Manila, Philippines. *Clubs:* Cavalry and Guards; Kildare Street and University (Dublin); Ellan Vannin (Isle of Man); Manila Makati Sports (Philippines).

HEADLAM, Air Vice-Marshal Frank, CB 1965; CBE 1958 (OBE 1954); Head, Australian Joint Services Staff, London, 1968-71; *b* 15 July 1914; *s* of Malcolm Headlam, Oatlands, Tasmania; *m* 1940, Katherine Beatrice (marr. diss. 1956), *d* of P. S. Bridge, Victoria; one *s* one *d. Educ:* Clemes Coll., Hobart. Pilot Officer RAAF 1934. Served War of 1939-45 (SE Asia, Northern Australia). Gp Capt. 1942; Air Cdre 1953; Dir-Gen. of Plans, 1958; Mem. for Personnel Dept of Air, 1957 and 1959; Air Vice-Marshal 1961; Air Officer Commanding Operational Command, RAAF Penrith, NSW, 1961-62; Air Officer Commanding 224 Gp, Far East Air Force, 1962-64; Dep. Chief of Air Staff, RAAF, 1965-66; AOC Support Comd, RAAF, Melbourne, 1966-67. ADC to the Queen, 1954; Extra Gentleman Usher to the Queen, 1970-71. *Recreations:* tennis, golf, fishing, shooting. *Address:* 5 Thornton Street, Kew, Victoria, Australia. *Clubs:* Melbourne; Melbourne Cricket; Lawn Tennis Association of Victoria.

HEADLAM-MORLEY, Prof. Agnes, MA, BLit; Montague Burton Professor of International Relations, Oxford University, 1948-71; *b* 10 Dec. 1902; *o d* of late Sir James Wycliffe Headlam-Morley, CBE, Historical Adviser to the Foreign Office. *Educ:* Wimbledon High Sch., GPDST; Somerville Coll., Oxford. Fellow and Tutor, St Hugh's Coll., Oxford, 1932. Adopted Prospective Conservative Candidate, Barnard Castle Div. of Durham, 1936. Hon. Fellow: Somerville Coll., Oxford, 1948; St Hugh's Coll., Oxford, 1970; Mem., St Antony's Coll. Received into the Roman Catholic Church, 1948. *Publications:* The New Democratic Constitutions of Europe, 1929; Editor (with K. Headlam-Morley) of Studies in Diplomatic History by J. W. Headlam-Morley, 1930; Arthur Cayley Headlam (a memoir published in The Fourth Gospel as History by A. C. Headlam, 1948); Last Days, 1960; (ed) A Memoir of the Peace Conference of Paris 1919 by J. W. Headlam-Morley, 1972; essay on Gustav Stresemann in The History Makers, ed Sir John Wheeler-Bennett and Lord Longford, 1973. *Address:* 29 St Mary's Road, Wimbledon, SW19; St Hugh's College, Oxford. *T:* 01-946 6134.

HEADLAM-MORLEY, Kenneth Arthur Sonntag, OBE 1962; Secretary, The Iron and Steel Institute, 1933-67; *b* 24 June 1901; *o s* of late Sir James Headlam-Morley, CBE (who assumed additional surname of Morley by Royal Licence, 1917), Historical Adviser to the Foreign Office, and of Else, *y d* of late Dr August Sonntag, Lüneburg; *m* 1951, Lorna Dione, *d* of late Francis Kinchin Smith; three *s* two *d. Educ:* Eton; New Coll., Oxford (Schol.). Staff of Dorman, Long & Co Ltd, 1924; Secretary: Inst. of Metals, 1944-47; Instn of Metallurgists, 1945-48; Dep. Controller Chrome Ore, Magnesite and Wolfram Control, Foundry Bonding Materials Control and assoc. Controls of Min. of Supply, 1940-43. Hon. Life Member: Amer. Inst. of Mining and Metallurgical Engrs, 1955; Amer. Soc. for Metals, 1955. Hon. Member: l'Assoc. des Ingénieurs sortis de l'Ecole de Liège, 1955; Verein deutscher Eisenhüttenleute, 1955; Soc. Française de Métallurgie, 1956; The Indian Institute of Metals, 1963. Chevalier Order of Vasa (Sweden), 1954; Chevalier Order of the Crown (Belgium), 1955. *Recreation:* gardening. *Address:* Whorlton Hall, near Barnard Castle, Co. Durham. *T:* Whorlton 278. *Club:* Athenæum.

HEADLEY, 7th Baron *cr* 1797; **Charles Rowland Allanson-Winn;** Bt 1660 and 1776; retired; *b* 19 May 1902; *s* of 5th Baron Headley and Teresa (*d* 1919), *y d* of late W. H. Johnson; *S* brother, 1969; *m* 1927, Hilda May Wells-Thorpe; one *s* three *d. Educ:* Bedford School. *Recreations:* golf, fishing. *Heir: s* Hon. John Rowland Allanson-Winn, *b* 14 Oct. 1934. *Address:* Torton Top, Torton Hill Road, Arundel, West Sussex. *T:* Arundel 882569. *Club:* East India, Devonshire, Sports and Public Schools.

HEADLY, Derek, CMG 1957; lately Malayan Civil Service; Midlands Secretary, Independent Schools Careers Organisation (formerly Public Schools Appointments Bureau), since 1966; *b* 1908; *s* of L. C. Headly, The House-on-the-Hill, Woodhouse Eaves, Leics; *m* 1946, Joyce Catherine, *d* of C. F. Freeman; one *s* one *d. Educ:* Repton Sch.; Corpus Christi Coll., Cambridge (BA). Military Service, 1944-46, Lieut-Col, Special Ops Exec., Force 136 (despatches). Cadet, Malaya, 1931; served Muar, Trengganu, etc; Palestine, 1938-44; Resident N Borneo, 1949; ret. as Brit. Adv., Kelantan, 1957. Dir, Vipan & Headly Ltd, 1957-66. Mem. Melton and Belvoir RDC, 1958-67. Officer (Brother) Order of St John. *Recreations:* hunting, fishing, tennis, golf. *Address:* The Grange, Hoby, Melton Mowbray, Leics. *T:* Rotherby 214. *Club:* Special Forces.

HEAF, Peter Julius Denison, MD, FRCP; Consultant Physician, University College Hospital, since 1958; *b* 1922; *s* of late Prof. F. R. G. Heaf, CMG; *m* 1947, Rosemary Cartledge; two *s* two *d. Educ:* Stamford Sch., Lincs; University Coll., London, Fellow

1973. MB, BS 1946; MD London 1952; MRCP 1954; FRCP 1965. House Physician and Surg., also RMO, University Coll. Hosp., and Capt. RAMC, 1946-51; Research Asst, Brompton Hosp., 1953-54; Sen. Registrar, St Thomas' Hosp., 1955-58. *Publications:* papers on chest disease and pulmonary physiology, in Lancet, etc. *Recreations:* painting, sailing. *Address:* 16 Gordon Mansions, Torrington Place, WC1E 7HE. *T:* 01-580 6981.

HEAKES, Air Vice-Marshal Francis Vernon, CB 1944; Commander, Legion of Merit (US); RCAF retired; *b* 27 Jan. 1894; *s* of Frank R. Heakes, Architect, and Susie Pemberton Heakes; *m* 1920, Edna Eulalie Watson, BA; one *s* three *d. Educ:* University of Toronto. Canadian Expeditionary Force, Lieut 1916-17; RFC (seconded), 1917-18; RAF 1918-19; CAF 1919; CAF and RCAF since 1923; Air Mem. Permanent Joint Board, Canada and US; Dir Air Personnel, RCAF; Dir Plans & Operations; AOC, RCAF, Newfoundland; AOC Western Air Command, Canada. *Recreations:* sports, all kinds, writing prose and verse, oil painting, musical composition. *Address:* 1876 West 63rd Avenue, Vancouver, BC, Canada.

HEAL, Anthony Standerwick; Chairman, Heal & Son Holdings Ltd (formerly Heal & Son Ltd), since 1952; *b* 23 Feb. 1907; *s* of Sir Ambrose Heal and Lady Edith Florence Digby Heal; *m* 1941, Theodora Caldwell (*née* Griffin); two *s. Educ:* Leighton Park Sch., Reading. Joined Heal & Son Ltd 1929; Dir 1936. Chm. Council, London and S Eastern Furniture Manufrs Assoc., 1947-48; Master, Furniture Makers Guild (now Worshipful Co. of Furniture Makers), 1959-60; Mem. Council of Industrial Design, 1959-67; Mem. Council, City and Guilds of London Inst., 1969, Chm., Licentiateship Cttee, 1976-; Pres., Design and Industries Assoc., 1965; Chm. Indep. Stores Assoc., 1970-72. RSA Bi-Centenary Medal, 1964; Hon. FSIA, 1974; Order of White Rose of Finland, 1970; Chevalier (First Class) Order of Dannebrog, 1974. *Recreations:* vintage cars and steam engines. *Address:* Baylins Farm, Knotty Green, Beaconsfield, Bucks. *Clubs:* Vintage Sports Car, National Traction Engine.

HEALD, Rt. Hon. Sir Lionel Frederick, PC 1954; Kt 1951; QC 1937; JP; Air Commodore RAF (VR); *b* 7 Aug. 1897; *yr s* of late James Heald, Parrs Wood, Lancs; *m* 1st, 1923, Flavia, *d* of Lieut-Col J. S. Forbes; one *s* one *d*; 2nd, 1929, Daphne Constance, CBE 1976, *d* of late Montague Price; two *s* one *d. Educ:* Charterhouse; Christ Church, Oxford (Holford Exhibitioner). BALitt Hum 1920. Served RE (SR) 1915-19 (Italian Bronze Medal); RAF (VR), 1939-45. Borough Councillor (MR) St Pancras, 1934-37. Called to Bar, Middle Temple, 1923, Bencher, 1946; Junior Counsel to Board of Trade in technical matters, 1931-37; additional mem. of Bar Council, 1947. Contested (Nat C) SW St Pancras Div., 1945; MP (C) Chertsey, 1950-70. Governor, Middlesex Hospital, 1946-1953. JP Surrey, 1946. Attorney-Gen., 1951-54. *Address:* Chilworth Manor, Guildford, Surrey. *Club:* Garrick.
See also M . Heald.

HEALD, Mervyn, QC 1970; *b* 12 April 1930; *s* of Rt Hon. Sir Lionel Heald, *qv*; *m* 1954, Clarissa Bowen; one *s* three *d* (and one *s* decd). *Educ:* Eton College; Magdalene College, Cambridge. Called to the Bar, Middle Temple, 1954. *Recreations:* country pursuits. *Address:* Headfoldswood Farm, Loxwood, Sussex. *T:* Loxwood 752 248.

HEALD, Thomas Routledge; His Honour Judge Heald; a Circuit Judge (formerly County Court Judge), since 1970; *b* 19 Aug. 1923; *s* of late John Arthur Heald and Nora Marion Heald; *m* 1950, Jean, *d* of James Campbell Henderson; two *s* two *d. Educ:* Merchant Taylors' Sch.; St John's Coll., Oxford. Fish Schol., St John's Coll., Oxford, 1941; Lieut, RAC, 1943-45; BA (Jurisprudence) 1947; MA 1949. Called to Bar, Middle Temple, 1948; Midland Circuit; Prosecuting Counsel to Inland Revenue (Midland Circuit), 1965-70; Deputy Chairman, QS: Lindsey, 1965-71; Notts, 1969-71. Mem. Council, Nottingham Univ., 1974-. *Address:* Rebbur House, Nicker Hill, Keyworth, Nottingham NG12 5ED. *T:* Plumtree 2676.

HEALD, William; Member, Press Council, since 1967; News Editor, "Lancaster Guardian", Newspaper Series, 1955-75; *b* 16 March 1910; *s* of William Heald, OBE, and Elizabeth Ann Heald; *m* 1938, Elizabeth Elsie Mount; two *d. Educ:* Lancaster Royal Grammar Sch. Lancashire Evening Post, 1933-55. Mem. Exec. Council, Nat. Union of Journalists, 1955-; Nat. Pres., NUJ, 1963-64. *Address:* 74 Wyresdale Road, Lancaster LA1 3DY. *T:* Lancaster 63787. *Club:* Press.

HEALEY, Rt. Hon. Denis Winston, PC 1964; MBE 1945; MP (Lab) South East Leeds, Feb. 1952-55, Leeds East since 1955; Chancellor of the Exchequer, since 1974; *b* 30 Aug. 1917; *s* of late William Healey, Keighley, Yorks; *m* 1945, Edna May, *d* of Edward Edmunds, Coleford, Gloucestershire; one *s* two *d*. *Educ:* Bradford Grammar Sch.; Balliol Coll., Oxford. First Cl. Hons Mods 1938; Jenkyns Exhib. 1939; Harmsworth Sen. Schol., First Cl. Lit. Hum., BA 1940; MA 1945. War of 1939-45; entered Army, 1940; served N Africa, Italy. Major RE 1944 (despatches). Contested (Lab) Pudsey and Otley Div., 1945; Sec., International Dept, Labour Party, 1945-52. Mem. Parliamentary Cttee Labour Party, 1959-64. Secretary of State for Defence, 1964-70. Councillor, Royal Institute of International Affairs, 1948-60; Councillor, Institute of Strategic Studies, 1958-61; Mem. Brit. Delegn to Commonwealth Relations Conf., Canada, 1949; British Delegate to: Consultative Assembly, Council of Europe, 1952-54; Inter Parly Union Conf., Washington, 1953; Western European Union and Council of Europe, 1953-55. Mem. Exec. Fabian Soc., 1954-61. Member: Labour Party Nat. Exec. Cttee, 1970-75; Parly Cttee, Labour Party, 1970-. *Publications:* The Curtain Falls, 1951; New Fabian Essays, 1952; Neutralism, 1955; Fabian International Essays, 1956; A Neutral Belt in Europe, 1958; NATO and American Security, 1959; The Race Against the H Bomb, 1960; Labour Britain and the World, 1963. *Recreations:* travel, photography, music, painting. *Address:* House of Commons, SW1. *T:* 01-219 4503.

HEALEY, Sir Edward Randal C.; *see* Chadwyck-Healey.

HEALEY, Rt. Rev. Kenneth; an Assistant Bishop, Diocese of Lincoln since 1966; *b* 7 Aug. 1899; *s* of late Harry Healey; *m* 1925, Marjorie, *d* of late Harry Wright Palmer, Friday Bridge, Cambs; two *d*. *Educ:* Moulton Grammar Sch. Deacon, 1931; Priest, 1932; Asst Curate, Grantham, 1931; Rector of Bloxholm with Digby, 1935; and Vicar of Ashby de la Launde (in plurality), 1939; Rural Dean of Lafford North, 1938; Vicar of Nocton, 1943; Rector of Algarkirk, 1950-58; Archdeacon of Lincoln, 1951-58; Bishop Suffragan of Grimsby, 1958-65. Proctor in Convocation, 1945-70; Church Commissioner, 1952-72. Chm. (formerly Vice-Chm.) Lindsey and Kesteven Agricultural Wages Cttee, 1945-69. MA Lambeth, 1958. *Address:* Gedney Dyke, Spalding, Lincs. *T:* Long Sutton 362030.

HEANEY, Brig. George Frederick, CBE 1943; late Royal Engineers (retd); fruit grower; *b* 1 June 1897; 2nd *s* of late George Robert Heaney, Dublin; *m* 1929, Doreen Marguerite, *e d* of late Lieut-Col R. H. Hammersley-Smith, CBE; one *s* two *d* (and one *s* decd). *Educ:* St Lawrence; RMA Woolwich; Christ's Coll., Cambridge. 2nd Lieut RE 1916; European War in France, 1917-18 (wounded, despatches twice); apptd to Survey of India, 1921; in India and Burma, 1920-41; served in Persia-Iraq Forces, 1941-43 (CBE); D Survey, Allied Land Forces, SEAC, 1944-45; retired from Army, 1948; Surveyor-Gen. of India, 1946-51; Pres. Inst. of Surveyors (India), 1950-51; Managing Dir, North Essex Growers Ltd, 1963-64. *Address:* Milnthorpe, Chappel, near Colchester, Essex. *T:* Colchester 240234. *Club:* Army and Navy.

HEANEY, Leonard Martin, CMG 1959; Overseas Civil Service, retired; *b* 28 Nov. 1906; *s* of Alexander John and Lilian Heaney; *m* 1947, Kathleen Edith Mary Chapman; no *c*. *Educ:* Bristol Grammar Sch.; Oriel Coll., Oxford. Joined Colonial Service on leaving Oxford, 1929; served in Tanganyika, retiring as a Senior Provincial Commissioner, 1959. Military service with East African Forces in Abyssinia, Madagascar, Ceylon, Burma, 1940-45. *Recreations:* reading and golf. *Address:* Northwood, Burgundy Road, Minehead, Somerset. *T:* Minehead 3859.

HEANEY, Seamus Justin; Member of Irish Academy of Letters; Head of English Department, Carysfort College, Co. Dublin; *b* 13 April 1939; *s* of Patrick and Margaret Heaney; *m* 1965, Marie Devlin; two *s* one *d*. *Educ:* St Columb's College, Derry; Queen's University, Belfast. BA first cl. 1961. Teacher, St Thomas's Secondary Sch., Belfast, 1962-63; Lectr, St Joseph's Coll. of Educn, Belfast, 1963-66; Lectr, Queen's Univ., Belfast, 1966-72; free-lance writer, 1972-75; Lectr, Carysfort Coll., 1975-. *Publications:* Eleven Poems, 1965; Death of a Naturalist, 1966 (Somerset Maugham Award, 1967; Cholmondeley Award, 1968); Door into the Dark, 1969; Wintering Out, 1972; North, 1975 (W. H. Smith Award; Duff Cooper Prize). *Address:* c/o Faber & Faber, 3 Queen Square, WC1N 3RU.

HEANEY, Brig. Sheila Anne Elizabeth, CB 1973; MBE 1955; TD; Chairman, Women's Royal Voluntary Service, Scotland, since 1977; *b* 11 June 1917; 2nd *d* of late Francis James Strong Heaney, MA, MD, FRCSI, Liverpool and Anne Summers McBurney. *Educ:* Huyton Coll.; Liverpool University. BA 1938. Joined ATS, 1939, WRAC, 1949; Director, WRAC, and Hon. ADC to the Queen, 1970-73. *Address:* 41 Wardie Road, Edinburgh EH5 3LJ.

HEANLEY, Charles Laurence, TD 1950; FRCS; Consulting Surgeon; Member of Lloyd's; *b* 28 Feb. 1907; *e s* of Dr C. M. Heanley; *m* 1935; three *s*. *Educ:* Epsom Coll.; Downing Coll., Cambridge (Exhib., Schol.); London Hosp. BA Cambridge (Nat. Sci. Tripos) 1929, MA 1934; MRCS, LRCP 1932; MB, BCh Cambridge 1934; FRCS 1933; MRCP 1935. London Hosp., 1929; Surg. First Asst, 1936. Served War of 1939-45; France, Surgical Specialist, 17th Gen. Hosp., 1939-40; Surgeon Specialist, RAMC Park Prewitt Plastic Unit, 1941-42; India, OC No 3 British Maxillo-Facial Surgical Unit and Lieut-Col OC Surgical Div., 1942-45; Surg. in charge of Dept of Plastic Surg., London Hosp., 1946-64. Cons. Surg. Worthing Hosp., Bethnal Green Hosp., and Plastic Unit Queen Victoria Hosp., East Grinstead, 1945; Plastic Surg. London Hosp.; Hon. Cons. Plastic Surg. Royal National and Golden Square Hosps, 1969. *Publications:* varied medical articles. *Recreations:* swimming, archæology. *Address:* Vainona, St George, Woodmancote, Henfield, West Sussex BN5 9ST. *T:* Henfield 2947; 145 Heene Road, Worthing, West Sussex. *T:* Worthing 35344.

HEAP, Sir Desmond, Kt 1970; LLM, PPRTPI; solicitor; *b* 17 Sept. 1907; *o s* of late William Heap, Architect, Burnley, Lancs, and of Minnie Heap; *m* 1945, Adelene Mai, *o d* of late Frederick Lacey, Harrogate, and of Mrs F. N. Hornby; one *s* two *d*. *Educ:* The Grammar Sch., Burnley; Victoria University of Manchester. LLB Hons 1929; LLM 1936; Hon. LLD 1973; admitted, 1933; Hons Final Law Examination; Pres., Law Soc., 1972-73 (Mem. Council, 1954-, Chm. Law Reform Cttee, 1955-60, and Chm., Town Planning Cttee, 1964-70). Past Master, Worshipful Company of Solicitors; Liveryman of Worshipful Company of Carpenters. Mem., Court of Worshipful Co. of Chartered Surveyors; Legal Mem., RTPI (formerly TPI), 1935-, Mem. of Council, 1947-77, Pres., 1955-56; Assoc. Mem. Royal Institute of Chartered Surveyors, 1953-, Mem. of Council, 1957-; Mem. of Colonial Office Housing and Town Planning Adv. Panel, 1953-65; Prosecuting Solicitor, 1935-38 and Chief Asst Solicitor for City of Leeds, 1938-40; Dep. Town Clerk of Leeds, 1940-47; Lecturer in the Law of Town and Country Planning and Housing, Leeds Sch. of Architecture, 1935-47; Comptroller and City Solicitor to the Corporation of London, 1947-73. Mem. of Editorial Board of Journal of Planning and Environment Law, 1948-; Mem., Council on Tribunals, 1971-77. Dep. Pres., City of London Branch, British Red Cross Soc., 1956-76. Dir, Britannia Building Soc. Chm. of Governors, Hurstpierpoint Coll. FRSA (Mem. Council, 1974-). *Publications:* Planning Law for Town and Country, 1938; Planning and the Law of Interim Development, 1944; The Town and Country Planning Act, 1944, 1945; An Outline of Planning Law, 1943 to 1945, 1945; The New Towns Act, 1946, 1947; Introducing the Town and Country Planning Act, 1947, 1947; Encyclopædia of Planning, Compulsory Purchase and Compensation, Vol. 1, 1949; Heap on the Town and Country Planning Act, 1954, 1955; Encyclopædia of Town Planning Law, 1960; Introducing the Land Commission Act 1967, 1967; Encyclopædia of Betterment Levy, 1967; The New Town Planning Procedures, 1969; An Outline of Planning Law, 7th edn, 1977; How to Control Land Development, 1974; Lectures on tape: The Community Land Act, 1975; articles in legal jls. *Recreations:* swimming, fell walking, the amateur theatre. *Address:* Quarry House, Oak Hill Road, Sevenoaks, Kent. *T:* Sevenoaks 53688; (office) Coward Chance, Royex House, Aldermanbury Square, EC2V 7LD. *T:* 01-600 0808; Last, Suddards & Co., 128 Sunbridge Road, Bradford. *T:* Bradford 33571.*Clubs:* Athenæum, City Livery, Guildhall.

HEAP, Peter William; HM Diplomatic Service; Counsellor (Political and Economic), Caracas, since 1976; *b* 13 April 1935; *s* of Roger and Dora Heap; *m* 1960, Helen Cutting Wilmerding (marr. diss.); two *s* two *d*. *Educ:* Bristol Cathedral Sch.; Merton Coll., Oxford. Army, 1954-56. CRO, 1959; Third Sec., Dublin, 1960; Third and Second Sec., Ottawa, 1960; First Sec., Colombo, 1963-66; seconded to MoD, 1966-68; FO, 1968-71; Dep. Dir-Gen., British Information Services, New York, 1971-76. *Address:* c/o Foreign and Commonwealth Office, SW1A 2AL.

HEARN, David Anthony; General Secretary, Association of Broadcasting and Allied Staffs, since 1972; *b* 4 March 1929; *s* of James Wilfrid Laurier Hearn and Clara (*née* Barlow); *m* 1952, Anne Beveridge; two *s*. *Educ:* Trinity Coll., Oxford (MA). Asst to Gen. Sec., Assoc. of Broadcasting Staff, 1955; subseq. Asst Gen. Sec., then Dep. Gen. Sec.; Jt Gen. Sec., Amalgamated Film and Broadcasting Union; Sec., Fedn of Broadcasting Unions; *Address:* 4 Stocks Tree Close, Yarnton, Oxford OX5 1LU. *T:* Kidlington 4613.

HEARN, Rear-Adm. Frank Wright, CB 1977; Assistant Chief of Personnel and Logistics, Ministry of Defence, 1974-77; *b* 1 Oct. 1919; *s* of John Henry Hearn, Civil Servant, and Elsie Gertrude

Hearn; *m* 1st, 1947, Ann Cynthia Keeble (*d* 1964); two *d*; 2nd, 1965, Ann Christina June St Clair Miller. *Educ:* Abbotsholme Sch., Derbyshire. Joined RN, 1937; HMS Hood, 1937-39. Served War of 1939-45 in various HM Ships in Atlantic, Mediterranean and East Indies. Staff of CinC, Home Fleet, 1951-53; Sec. to Flag Officer, Submarines, 1954-56; after service in USA became Sec. to Dir of Naval Intell., 1958-60, when joined HMS Tiger as Supply Officer; Fleet Supply Officer, Western Fleet, 1962-64; subseq. service in Plans Div, MoD (Navy) and CSO (Admin.) to Flag Officer, Submarines; IDC 1969; commanded HMS Centurion in rank of Cdre, 1970-73; Chm., Review of Officer Structure Cttee, 1973-74. *Recreations:* golf, tennis, gardening, wine-making. *Address:* Hurstbrook Cottage, Hollybank Lane, Emsworth, Hants PO10 7UE. *T:* Emsworth 2149. *Club:* Royal Commonwealth Society.

HEARNSHAW, Prof. Leslie Spencer; Professor of Psychology, University of Liverpool, 1947-75, now Emeritus; *b* Southampton, 9 Dec. 1907; *o s* of late Prof. F. J. C. Hearnshaw, Prof. of History, King's Coll., London; *m* 1937, Gwenneth R. Dickins, Perth, Western Australia; one *s* three *d. Educ:* King's Coll. Sch., Wimbledon; Christ Church, Oxford; King's Coll., London. 1st Class Lit Hum, 1930; 1st Class Psychology Hons (London), 1932. Investigator, Nat. Institute of Industrial Psychology, London, 1933-38; Lecturer in Psychology, Victoria Univ., Coll., Wellington, NZ, 1939-47; Dir, Industrial Psychology Div., DSIR, Wellington, NZ, 1942-47; Mem. of Council, British Psychological Soc., 1949-57; Chm., Industrial Section, 1953-54; Pres., British Psychological Soc., 1955-56. Pres. Section J (Psychology), Brit. Assoc., 1954; Hon. Dir, Medical Research Council, Research Group into occupational aspects of ageing, 1955-59, 1963-70. Hobhouse Memorial Lecturer, 1966. Vice-Pres., International Assoc. of Applied Psychology, and Editor of its Journal, 1964-74. *Publications:* (with R. Winterbourn) Human Welfare and Industrial Efficiency, 1945; A Short History of British Psychology, 1840-1940, 1964; articles on industrial psychology and the psychology of thinking. *Address:* 1 Devonshire Road, West Kirby, Wirral L48 7HR. *T:* 051-625 5823.
See also C. T. C. Wall.

HEARST, Stephen; Controller, Radio 3, since 1972; *b* Vienna, Austria, 6 Oct. 1919; *m* 1948, Lisbeth Edith Neumann; one *s* one *d. Educ:* Vienna Univ.; Reading Univ. (Dip. Hort.); Brasenose Coll., Oxford (MA). Free lance writer, 1949-52; joined BBC as producer trainee, 1952; Documentary television: script writer, 1953-55; writer producer, 1955-65; Exec. Producer, Arts Programmes Television, 1965-67; Head of Arts Features, Television, 1967-71. *Publication:* Two Thousand Million Poor, 1965. *Recreations:* gardening, swimming, reading, listening to music. *Address:* c/o British Broadcasting Corporation, Broadcasting House, W1A 1AA.

HEARST, William Randolph, Jun.; journalist; Editor-in-Chief, The Hearst Newspapers, and Chairman of the Executive Committee, The Hearst Corporation; *b* NYC, 27 Jan. 1908; *s* of William Randolph Hearst and Millicent Veronica (*née* Willson); *m* 1st, 1928, Alma Walker (marr. diss., 1932); 2nd, 1933, Lorelle McCarver (marr. diss., 1948); 3rd, 1948, Austine McDonnell; two *s. Educ:* Collegiate Sch.; St John's Manlius Mil. Acad., Syracuse; Berkeley High Sch., Berkeley, Calif.; Hitchcock Mil. Acad., San Rafael, Calif; University of Calif. Began career with New York American, NYC, as a reporter, 1928; publisher, 1936-37; publisher, NY Journal-American, 1937-56; The American Weekly, 1945-56; War Correspondent, 1943-45. Member Boards: USO, NY; United Press International. *Address:* (home) 810 Fifth Avenue, New York, NY 10021, USA; (office) 959 Eighth Avenue, New York, NY 10019, USA. *Clubs:* Overseas Press, Marco Polo, Brook, Madison Square Garden (New York City); F Street, Sulgrave, National Press, Metropolitan, Burning Tree, International (Washington); Bohemian, Pacific Union (San Francisco); Tokyo Press; London Press.

HEATH, Barrie, DFC 1941; Group Chairman, Guest Keen & Nettlefolds Ltd, since 1975; Chairman, Guest Keen & Nettlefolds (UK) Ltd and Guest Keen & Nettlefolds (Overseas) Ltd, since 1974; Director, BHP/GKN Holdings Ltd (Australia), since 1975; Director (non-executive): Barclays Bank, since 1976; Barclays Bank UK Management Ltd, since 1975; Pilkington Brothers Ltd, since 1967; Smiths Industries Ltd, since 1970; *b* 11 Sept. 1916; *s* of George Heath and Florence Amina Heath (*née* Jones); *m* 1939, Joy Anderson; two *s. Educ:* Wrekin; Pembroke Coll., Cambridge. Trained with Rootes Securities Ltd, 1938-39; fighter pilot, RAF, 1939-45 (Wing Cmdr); Dir, Hobourn Aero Components, Rochester, 1946-50; Managing Dir, Powell Duffryn Carbon Products Ltd, 1950-60; Man. Dir, Triplex Safety Glass Co. Ltd, 1960-68, Chm., 1965-74; non-exec. Dir, GKN Ltd, 1972-74. Vice-President: Soc. of Motor Manufacturers and Traders, 1973- (Chm., Gen. Purposes Cttee); Engineering Employers' Fedn, 1975-; Inst. of Motor Industry, 1975-; Pres., German Chamber of Industry and Commerce in UK, 1977-; Founder Mem., Engineering Industries Council, 1975-; Chm., Commonwealth Games UK Jt Appeal Cttee, 1977-; Member: Appeal Council of the Queen's Silver Jubilee Appeal, 1976-; Industrial Democracy Cttee, 1975-77; British Overseas Trade Adv. Council, 1977-; BOTB, 1977-; Trustee: Nat. Motor Mus., 1975-; RAF Mus., 1976-. Freeman of City of London; Liveryman, Coachmaker and Coach Harness Makers' Co. *Recreations:* yachting, field sports. *Address:* GKN House, 22 Kingsway, WC2B 6LG. *T:* 01-242 1616 (Telex: 24911).

HEATH, Edward Peter, OBE 1946; an Executive Deputy Chairman, Inchcape & Co. Ltd, since 1975; Chairman, Anglo Thai Corporation Ltd, since 1975; Deputy Chairman, Bewac Motor Corporation Ltd, since 1970; *b* 6 June 1914; *m* 1953, Eleanor Christian Peck; one *s* three *d . Educ:* St Lawrence Coll., Ramsgate. Joined Borneo Co. Ltd, 1934; interned in Thailand, 1941-45. Gen. Manager, Borneo Co. Ltd, 1953-63; a Man. Dir, 1963-67; a Man. Dir, Inchcape & Co. Ltd, 1967-75. Director: Mann Egerton & Co. Ltd, 1973-; Dodwell & Co. Ltd, 1974-; Inchcape Far East Ltd, 1972-; Dep. Chairman: Hong Kong Assoc., 1975-; Anglo Thai Soc., 1975-. Order of White Elephant (5th Cl.) (Thailand); Officer, Order of Orange Nassau (Netherlands). *Recreations:* hunting, gardening, motoring. *Address:* Cooks Place, Albury, Guildford, Surrey GU5 9BJ. *T:* Shere 2698. *Club:* City of London.

HEATH, Rt. Hon. Edward Richard George, PC 1955; MBE 1946; MP (C) Bexley, Sidcup, since 1974 (Bexley, 1950-74); *b* Broadstairs, Kent, 9 July 1916; *s* of late William George and Edith Anne Heath. *Educ:* Chatham House Sch., Ramsgate; Balliol Coll., Oxford (Scholar; Hon. Fellow, 1969). Pres. Oxford Univ. Conservative Assoc., 1937; Chm. Federation of Univ. Conservative Assocs, 1938; Pres. Oxford Union, 1939; Oxford Union debating tour of American Univs, 1939-40; Pres. Federation of University Conservative and Unionist Associations, 1959-77, Hon. Life Patron, 1977. Served War of 1939-45 (despatches, MBE); in Army, 1940-46, in France, Belgium, Holland and Germany; gunner in RA, 1940; Major 1945. Lieut-Col comdg 2nd Regt HAC, TA, April 1947-Aug. 1951; Master Gunner within the Tower of London, 1951-54. Administrative Civil Service, 1946-47 resigning to become prospective candidate for Bexley. Asst Conservative Whip, Feb. 1951; Lord Commissioner of the Treasury, Nov. 1951, and Joint Deputy Govt Chief Whip, 1952, and Dep. Govt Chief Whip, 1953-55; Parliamentary Sec. to the Treasury, and Government Chief Whip, Dec. 1955-Oct. 1959; Minister of Labour, Oct. 1959-July 1960; Lord Privy Seal, with Foreign Office responsibilities, 1960-63; Sec. of State for Industry, Trade, Regional Development and Pres. of the Board of Trade, Oct. 1963-Oct. 1964; Leader of the Opposition, 1965-70; Prime Minister and First Lord of the Treasury, 1970-74; Leader of the Opposition, 1974-75. Chm., Commonwealth Parly Assoc., 1970-74. Mem. Council, Royal College of Music, 1961-70; Chm., London Symphony Orchestra Trust, 1963-70; Vice-Pres., Bach Choir, 1970-; Hon. Mem., LSO, 1974-. Smith-Mundt Fellowship, USA, 1953; Vis. Fellow, Nuffield Coll., Oxford, 1962-70, Hon. Fellow, 1970; Chubb Fellow, Yale, 1975. Lectures: Cyril Foster Meml, Oxford, 1965; Godkin, Harvard, 1966; Montagu Burton, Leeds, 1976; Edge, Princeton, 1976; Romanes, Oxford, 1976. Hon. DCL Oxon, 1971; Hon. DTech Bradford, 1971; Hon. LLD Westminster Coll., Salt Lake City, 1975; Dr *hc* Univ. of Paris, Sorbonne, 1976; Hon. Freeman, Musicians' Co., 1973. Freiherr Von Stein Foundn Prize; Estes J. Kefauver Prize 1971; Stresseman Gold Medal, 1971; Charlemagne Prize, 1963. Winner, Sydney to Hobart Ocean Race, 1969; Captain, Britain's winning Admiral's Cup Team, 1971. *Publications:* (joint) One Nation-a Tory approach to social problems, 1950; Old World, New Horizons (Godkin Lectures), 1970; Sailing: a course of my life, 1975; Music: a joy for life, 1976. *Recreations:* sailing, music. *Address:* House of Commons, SW1. *Clubs:* Buck's, Carlton; Royal Yacht Squadron.

HEATH, Maj.-Gen. Gerard William Egerton, CB 1949; CBE 1945; DSO 1945; MC 1916; retired; *b* 17 March 1897; *s* of late Maj.-Gen. Sir G. M. Heath, KCMG, CB, and Mary (*née* Egerton); *m* 1923, Hilda Mary, (*née* Houldsworth) (from whom he obtained a divorce, 1931); two *d*; *m* 1933, Gwendda Curtis (*née* Evans). *Educ:* Wellington Coll.; RMA Woolwich. Commissioned RA, 1915; served European War, 1915-18 (wounded); War of 1939-45 (despatches, 1940); CRA 43rd Div., 1942-44; CCRA 12 Corps, 1944-45; CCRA 1st Airborne Corps, 1945; Commandant Sch. of Artillery, Larkhill, 1945-47; GOC 1st Anti-Aircraft Group, 1947-49; GOC Troops, Malta, 1949-51. Pres. Regular Commissions Board, 1951-54, retired Nov. 1954. Col Comdt RA and Royal Malta Artillery, 1955, RHA

1957. *Recreations:* shooting and all forms of mounted sport. *Address:* Westbrook Farm, Avebury, Wilts. *T:* Avebury 248. *Club:* Naval and Military.

HEATH, Henry Wylde Edwards, CMG 1963; QPM; Commissioner of Police, Hong Kong, 1959-67, retired; *b* 18 March 1912; *s* of late Dr W. G. Heath and late Mrs L. B. Heath; *m* Joan Mildred Crichett; two *s* one *d. Educ:* Dean Close Sch.; HMS Conway. Probationer Sub-Inspector of Police, Leeward Islands, 1931; Asst Supt, Hong Kong, 1934; Superintendent, 1944; Asst Commissioner, 1950. Colonial Police Medal, 1953; QPM, 1957. *Recreations:* golf and sailing. *Clubs:* Hong Kong, Royal Hong Kong Golf (Hong Kong).

HEATH, Prof. John Baldwin; Professor of Economics, London Graduate School of Business Studies, since 1970; Economic Adviser, Civil Aviation Authority, since 1972; *b* 25 Sept. 1924; *s* of Thomas Arthur Heath and late Dorothy Meallin; *m* 1953, Wendy Julia Betts; two *s* one *d. Educ:* Merchant Taylors' Sch.; St Andrews Univ.; Cambridge Univ. RNVR, 1942-46. Spicers Ltd, 1946-50; Lecturer in Economics, Univ. of Manchester, 1956-64; Rockefeller Foundation Fellowship, 1961-62; Dir, Economic Research Unit, Bd of Trade, 1964-67; Dir, Economic Services Div., BoT, 1967-70. Mem., Mechanical Engrg EDC, 1971-76. *Publications:* articles in many learned jls on competition and monopoly, productivity, cost-benefit analysis. *Recreations:* music, walking. *Address:* 20 Denmark Avenue, SW19. *T:* 01-946 5474.

HEATH, John Moore, CMG 1976; HM Diplomatic Service; Consul-General, Chicago, since 1975; *b* 9 May 1922; *s* of Philip George and Olga Heath; *m* 1952, Patricia Mary Bibby; one *s* one *d. Educ:* Shrewsbury Sch.; Merton Coll., Oxford (MA). Served War of 1939-45, France, Belgium and Germany: commnd Inns of Court Regt, 1942; Capt. GSO3 11th Armoured Div., 1944-45 (despatches). Merton Coll., 1940-42, 1946-47. Entered Foreign Service, 1950; 2nd Sec., Comr-Gen.'s Office, Singapore, 1950-52; 1st Sec. (Commercial), Jedda, 1952-56; 1st Sec., FO, 1956-58; Nat. Def. Coll., Kingston, Ont., 1958-59; Head of Chancery and HM Consul, Brit. Embassy, Mexico City, 1959-62; Head of Chancery, Brit. Embassy, Kabul, Afghanistan, 1963-65; Counsellor and Head of Establishment and Organisation Dept, FCO (formerly DSAO), 1966-69; Counsellor (Commercial), Brit. Embassy, Bonn, 1969-74; Overseas Trade Advr, Assoc. of British Chambers of Commerce, on secondment, 1974. *Recreations:* walking, travel. *Address:* c/o Foreign and Commonwealth Office, SW1; 28 Caroline Terrace, SW1. *Club:* Naval and Military.

HEATH, Mark Evelyn; HM Diplomatic Service; Head of West African Department, Foreign and Commonwealth Office, and HM Ambassador to Chad, since 1975; *b* 22 May 1927; *s* of late Captain John Moore Heath, RN; *m* 1954, Margaret, *d* of late Sir (William) Lawrence Bragg, CH, OBE, MC, FRS; two *s* one *d. Educ:* Marlborough; Queens' Coll., Cambridge. Served in RNVR, 1945-48. Joined HM Foreign (subseq. Diplomatic) Service, 1950; served in: Djakarta, 1952-56; Copenhagen, 1956-58; FO, 1958-62; Sofia, 1962-64 (Chargé d'Affaires, 1963 and 1964); Ottawa, 1964-68; FO, later FCO, 1968, Head of Commodities Dept, 1970-71; Dep. Head, UK Delegn to OECD, 1971-74; seconded to Cabinet Office, 1974-75. Officer, Order of Dannebrog, 1957. *Address:* c/o Foreign and Commonwealth Office, SW1; 47 Arbrook Lane, Esher, Surrey KT10 9EG. *Club:* Athenæum.

HEATH, Air Marshal Sir Maurice (Lionel), KBE 1962 (OBE 1946); CB 1957; DL; Chief Hon. Steward, Westminster Abbey, 1965-74; Gentleman Usher to the Queen, since 1966; Appeal Director, Voluntary Research Trust National Appeal, King's College Hospital and Medical School, since 1977; *b* 12 Aug. 1909; *s* of Lionel Heath, Artist and Principal of the Mayo Sch. of Arts, Lahore, India; *m* 1938, Kathleen Mary *d* of Boaler Gibson, Bourne, Lincs; one *s* one *d. Educ:* Sutton Valence Sch.; Cranwell. Commissioned RAF, 1929; service with Nos 16 and 28 Squadrons; Specialist Armament duties, 1933-42; Chief Instructor, No 1 Air Armament Sch., 1942; Station Commander, Metheringham, No 5 Group, Bomber Comd, 1944 (despatches). Dep. to Dir-Gen. of Armament, Air Min., 1946-48; CO Central Gunnery Sch., 1948-49; Sen. Air Liaison Officer, Wellington, NZ, 1950-52; CO Bomber Comd Bombing Sch., 1952-53; idc, 1954; Dir of Plans, Air Min., 1955; Deputy Air Secretary, Air Ministry, 1955-57; Commander, British Forces, Arabian Peninsula, 1957-59; Commandant, RAF Staff Coll., 1959-61; Chief of Staff, HQ Allied Air Forces Central Europe, 1962-65, retd. Dir, Boyd and Boyd, Estate Agents, 1971-76. DL West Sussex, 1977. *Recreations:* sailing, golf and travel. *Address:* Broom Cottage, Sunset Lane, West Chiltington, Pulborough, Sussex RH20 2NY. *Club:* Royal Air Force.

HEATH, Oscar Victor Sayer, FRS 1960; DSc (London); Professor of Horticulture, University of Reading, 1958-69, now Emeritus; *b* 26 July 1903; *s* of late Sir (Henry) Frank Heath, GBE, KCB, and Frances Elaine (*née* Sayer); *m* 1930, Sarah Margery, *d* of Stephen Bumstead, Guestling, Hastings; two *s* one *d. Educ:* Imperial Coll., London (Forbes Medallist), Fellow, 1973. Asst Demonstrator in Botany, Imperial Coll., 1925-26; Empire Cotton Growing Corp. Sen. Studentship, Imperial Coll. of Tropical Agriculture, Trinidad, 1926-27; Plant Physiologist, Empire Cotton Growing Corp., Cotton Experiment Station, Barberton, S Africa, 1927-36; Research Student, Imperial Coll., London, 1936-39; Leverhulme Research Fellow, 1937-39; Research Asst, 1939-40, and Mem. of Staff, Research Inst. of Plant Physiology of Imperial Coll., Rothamsted, 1940-46, London, 1946-58; Sen. Principal Scientific Officer, 1948-58; Special Lectr in Plant Physiology, Imperial Coll., 1945-58; Dir, ARC Unit of Flower Crop Physiology, 1962-70; Mem. ARC, 1965-70; Leverhulme Emeritus Res. Fellow, 1970-72. *Publications:* chapters on physiology of leaf stomata in Encyclopædia of Plant Physiology (ed Ruhland) 1959, in Plant Physiology-a Treatise (ed Steward), 1959, and (with T. A. Mansfield) in Physiology of Plant Growth (ed Wilkins), 1969; The Physiological Aspects of Photosynthesis, 1969; Investigation by Experiment, 1970; Stomata, 1975; papers in scientific jls. *Address:* 10 St Peter's Grove, W6 9AZ. *T:* 01-748 0471.

HEATH-GRACIE, George Handel, BMus (Dunelm), 1932; FRCO 1915; Organist and Master of the Choristers, Derby Cathedral, 1933-57; Diocesan Choirmaster, 1936-57; Founder and Conductor, Derby Bach Choir, 1935; Special Commissioner, Royal School of Church Music, since 1951; *m* 1922, Marjory Josephine Knight. *Educ:* Bristol Grammar Sch.; Bristol Cathedral. Organist of various Bristol Churches, 1909-14; of St John's, Frome, 1914-15; Service with HM forces, 1915-19; Organist of St Peter, Brockley, SE, 1918-33; Conductor South London Philharmonic Soc., 1919-21; Broadcast Church Music Series, 1936-38; Music Dir, Derby Sch., 1938-44; Mem. panel of examnrs, Associated Bd of Royal Schs of Music, 1946-76; Sch. Music Adviser, Derbyshire Educn Cttee, 1944-57; Mem. Council, Incorporated Soc. of Musicians for SW England, 1964-67; Mem. Diocesan Adv. Cttee, to 1957; Mem., Artist selection panel, BBC, 1946-74. Extra-mural Lectr, University Coll., Nottingham; Festival Adjudicator and Lectr. Toured Canada and USA as adjudicator, lecturer and performer, 1949, return visit, 1953; travelled in Asia, and African Tour, 1959; Eastern Tour, Ceylon, Singapore, Malaya, 1960; Tour of W Indies, N and S America and New Zealand, 1966, and New Zealand, 1968. *Publications:* various Church Music and press articles. *Recreations:* gossip, grass-cutting, brewing, domestic repairs, and electrical engineering. *Address:* Shorms, Stockland, Honiton, Devon EX14 9DQ. *T:* Stockland 403. *Clubs:* Savage; Exeter and County; (Hon.) Kiwanis (Peterborough, Ont).

HEATH-STUBBS, John (Francis Alexander); poet; Lecturer in English Literature, College of St Mark and St John, Chelsea, 1963-73; *b* 1918; *s* of Francis Heath Stubbs and Edith Louise Sara (*née* Marr). *Educ:* Bembridge School; Worcester Coll. for the Blind, and privately; Queen's Coll., Oxford. English Master, Hall Sch., Hampstead, 1944-45; Editorial Asst, Hutchinson's, 1945-46; Gregory Fellow in Poetry, Leeds Univ., 1952-55; Vis. Prof. of English: University of Alexandria, 1955-58; University of Michigan, 1960-61. FRSL 1953. Queen's Gold Medal for Poetry, 1973. *Publications:* verse: Wounded Thammuz; Beauty and the Beast; The Divided Ways; The Swarming of the Bees; A Charm against the Toothache; The Triumph of the Muse; The Blue Fly in his Head; Selected Poems; Satires and Epigrams; Artorius; A Parliament of Birds; *drama:* Helen in Egypt; *Criticism:* The Darkling Plain; Charles Williams; The Pastoral; The Ode; The Verse Satire; *translations:* (with Peter Avery) Hafiz of Shiraz; (with Iris Origo) Leopardi, Selected Prose and Poetry; *edited:* Selected Poems of Jonathan Swift; Selected Poems of P. B. Shelley; Selected Poems of Tennyson; Selected Poems of Alexander Pope; (with David Wright) The Forsaken Garden; Images of Tomorrow; (with David Wright) Faber Book of Twentieth Century Verse; (with Martin Green) Homage to George Barker on his Sixtieth Birthday. *Recreation:* taxonomy. *Address:* 35 Sutherland Place, W2. *T:* 01-229 6367.

HEATHCOAT AMORY; family name of **Viscount Amory.**

HEATHCOTE, Brig. (Gilbert) Simon, CBE 1964 (MBE 1941); *b* 21 Sept. 1913; *s* of late Col R. E. M. Heathcote, DSO, Manton Hall, Rutland and Millicent Heathcote; *heir* to baronetcy of Earl of Ancaster, *qv*; *m* 1939, Patricia Margaret (*née* Leslie); one *s* one *d. Educ:* Eton; RMA Woolwich. Commnd RA, 1933, War Service in Europe, 1939-44; Comdr RA, 1960-62; Chief of Staff, Middle East Comd, 1962-64; retd. *Publications:* articles in service jls. *Recreations:* sailing, ski-ing, shooting. *Address:* Upton Dean, Upton, near Andover, Hants. *T:* Hurstbourne Tarrant 217. *Clubs:* Army and Navy, Royal Cruising.

HEATHCOTE, Sir Michael Perryman, 11th Bt, *cr* 1733; *b* 7 Aug. 1927; *s* of Leonard Vyvyan Heathcote, 10th Bt, and Joyce Kathleen Heathcote (*d* 1967); *S* father, 1963; *m* 1956, Victoria Wilford, *e d* of Comdr J. E. R. Wilford, RN, Retd; two *s* one *d.* *Educ:* Winchester Coll.; Clare Coll., Cambridge. Started farming in England, 1951, in Scotland, 1961. Is in remainder to Earldom of Macclesfield. *Recreations:* fishing, shooting and farming. *Heir:* *s* Timothy Gilbert Heathcote, *b* 25 May 1957. *Address:* Warborne Farm, Boldre, Lymington, Hants. *T:* Lymington 73478; Carie and Carwhin, Lawers, by Aberfeldy, Perthshire.

HEATHCOTE, Simon; *see* Heathcote, Gilbert S.

HEATHCOTE-DRUMMOND-WILLOUGHBY; family name of **Earl of Ancaster.**

HEATHCOTE-SMITH, Clifford Bertram Bruce, CBE 1963; acting Senior Clerk, Department of Clerk of House of Commons, 1973-77; HM Diplomatic Service, 1936-72; *b* 2 Sept. 1912; *s* of late Sir Clifford E. Heathcote-Smith, KBE, CMG; *m* 1940, Thelma Joyce Engström; two *s.* *Educ:* Malvern; Pembroke Coll., Cambridge. Entered Consular Service, 1936; served in China, 1937-44; Foreign Office, 1944-47; Political Adviser, Hong-Kong, 1947-50, Montevideo, 1951-56; Commercial Counsellor: Ankara, 1956-60; Copenhagen, 1960-64; Washington, 1964-65; Dep. High Comr, Madras, 1965-68; a Diplomatic Service Inspector, 1969-72. *Address:* Lampool Lodge, Maresfield, East Sussex. *T:* Nutley 2849.

HEATHER, Stanley Frank; Comptroller and City Solicitor since 1974; *b* 8 Jan. 1917; *s* of Charles and Jessie Heather; *m* 1946, Janet Roxburgh Adams, Perth; one *s* one *d.* *Educ:* Downhills Sch.; London Univ. Commnd Reconnaissance Corps, RAC, 1941; India/Burma Campaign, 1942-45. Admitted Solicitor, 1959. Asst Solicitor, City of London, 1963; Dep. Comptroller and City Solicitor, 1968. *Recreations:* golf, squash, fishing. *Address:* Kinnoull, 14 Morrell Avenue, Horsham, West Sussex. *T:* Horsham 60109; Guildhall, EC2P 2EJ. *Clubs:* City Livery; Ifield Golf and Country.

HEATON, David; Assistant Under Secretary of State, Home Office, since 1976; *b* 22 Sept. 1923; *s* of late Dr T. B. Heaton, OBE, MD; *m* 1961, Joan, *d* of Group Captain E. J. Lainé, CBE, DFC; two *s* one *d.* *Educ:* Rugby Sch. Served RNVR, 1942-46. HM Overseas Civil Service, Ghana, 1948-58; Cabinet Office, 1961-69; Home Office, 1969-. *Address:* 53 Murray Road, SW19 4PF. *T:* 01-947 0375.

HEATON, Very Rev. Eric William; Dean of Durham, since 1974; Moderator, General Ordination Examination, since 1971; *b* 15 Oct. 1920; *s* of late Robert William Heaton and Ella Mabel Heaton (*née* Brear); *m* 1951, Rachel Mary, *d* of late Rev. Charles Harold Dodd, CH, FBA; two *s* two *d.* *Educ:* Ermysted's, Skipton; (Exhibnr) Christ's Coll., Cambridge (MA). English Tripos, Part I; Theological Tripos, Part I (First Class). Deacon, 1944; Priest, 1945; Curate of St Oswald's, Durham, 1944-45; Staff Sec., Student Christian Movement in University of Durham, 1944-45; Chaplain, Gonville and Caius Coll., Cambridge, 1945-46; Dean and Fellow, 1946-53; Tutor, 1951-53; Bishop of Derby's Chaplain in University of Cambridge, 1946-53; Canon Residentiary, 1953-60, and Chancellor, 1956-60, Salisbury Cathedral; Tutor in Theology, Official Fellow and Chaplain, 1960-74, Senior Tutor, 1967-73, St John's College, Oxford. Chm. Council, Headington Sch., Oxford, 1968-74; Chm. Governors, High Sch., Durham, 1975-. Examining Chaplain to: Archbishop of York, 1951-56; Bishop of Portsmouth, 1947-74; Bishop of Salisbury, 1949-64; Bishop of Norwich, 1960-71; Bishop of Wakefield, 1961-74; Bishop of Rochester, 1962-74; Select Preacher: Cambridge University, 1948, 1958; Oxford Univ., 1958-59, 1967, 1971. Hon. Lectr, Univ. of Durham, 1975-. Hon. Fellow, Champlain Coll., Univ. of Trent, Ont, Canada, 1973-. *Publications:* His Servants the Prophets, 1949 (revised and enlarged Pelican edn, The Old Testament Prophets, 1958, 2nd rev. edn, 1977); The Book of Daniel, 1956; Everyday Life in Old Testament Times, 1956; Commentary on the Sunday Lessons, 1959; The Hebrew Kingdoms, 1968; Solomon's New Men, 1974; articles in Jl of Theological Studies, Expository Times, etc. *Address:* The Deanery, Durham DH1 3EQ. *T:* Durham 2500.

HEATON, Mrs Gwenllian Margaret, CBE 1946; TD; *b* 12 March 1897; *o c* of late Lieut-Col B. E. Philips, DL, JP, Rhual, Mold, Flintshire; *m* 1921, Commander H. E. Heaton, DL, JP, RN

(retd); two *s.* *Educ:* privately. Local service as VAD European War, 1914-18. Enrolled in Auxiliary Territorial Service Sept. 1938; embodied Aug. 1939 with rank of Senior Commander. Served on Staff at HQ Western Command, 1940-44 and HQ Eastern Command, 1944-45; Chief Commander 1941; Controller, 1942, with appointment as DDATS. Released with Age and Service Group July 1945. *Address:* Garregwen, Pantymwyn, Mold, Clwyd. *T:* Pantymwyn 234.

HEATON, Ralph Neville, CB 1951; *b* 4 June 1912; *s* of late Ernest Heaton; *m* 1939, Cecily Margaret Alabaster; three *s* one *d.* *Educ:* Westminster; Christ Church, Oxford. Formerly Deputy Secretary various Govt Depts, including Education, Transport, and Economic Affairs. Mem., GPDST Council. Commonwealth Fund Fellow, 1951-52. *Address:* 38 Manor Park Avenue, Princes Risborough, Bucks.

HEATON, Sir Yvo (Robert) Henniker-, 4th Bt *cr* 1912; *b* 24 April 1954; *s* of Sir (John Victor) Peregrine Henniker-Heaton, 3rd Bt, and of Margaret Patricia, *d* of late Lieut Percy Wright, Canadian Mounted Rifles; *S* father, 1971. *Heir:* *uncle* Peter Joseph Henniker-Heaton [*b* 9 May 1907; *m* 1934, Rose Maddock, *o d* of late Amyas Morse]. *Address:* 14 Woodville Road, Ealing, W5.

HEAUME, Sir Francis H. du; *see* du Heaume.

HEAVENER, Rt. Rev. Robert William; *see* Clogher, Bishop of.

HEAWOOD, Geoffrey Leonard; *s* of late Professor P. J. Heawood, OBE, DCL; *m* 1926, Norah Buchanan (*d* 1975), 2nd *d* of late Rt Rev. J. T. Inskip, DD; one *s* one *d.* *Educ:* Blundell's; Wadham Coll., Oxford (Math. Mods and Lit. Hum.). Capt. 4th Bn Wilts Regt; attached 1st Oxford and Bucks LI; Major, Home Guard. Tutor Knutsford Test Sch., 1919-22; London Sec. Student Christian Movement, 1922-24; Resident Tutor, King's Coll. Hostel, London, 1924-26; Asst Master Alleyns Sch., 1925-29; Headmaster County Sch. for Boys, Bromley, 1929-37; Headmaster Cheltenham Grammar Sch., 1937-53; Sec. of the Central Advisory Council for the Ministry (CACTM), 1953-60, General Sec., 1960-62; retired, 1962. *Publications:* Religion in School; Vacant Possession; Westminster Abbey Trinity Lectures, 1961; The Humanist-Christian Frontier. *Address:* North Cottage, Sheep Lane, Midhurst, West Sussex. *T:* Midhurst 4375.

HEBB, Prof. Donald Olding, FRSC 1959; FRS 1966; Professor of Psychology, 1947-72 (part-time appointment, 1972-74), and Chancellor, 1970-74, Professor Emeritus, 1975, McGill University (Chairman of Department, 1948-58; Vice-Dean of Biological Sciences, 1964-66); *b* 22 July 1904; *s* of Arthur Morrison Hebb and Mary Clara Olding; *m* 1st, 1931, Marion Isobel Clark (*d* 1933); 2nd, 1937, Elizabeth Nicholas Donovan (*d* 1962); two *d*; 3rd, 1966, Margaret Doreen Wright (*née* Williamson). *Educ:* Dalhousie Univ.; McGill Univ.; University of Chicago; Harvard Univ. PhD (Harvard), 1936. Taught in schools, Nova Scotia and Quebec, 1925-34; Instructor, Harvard Univ., 1936-37; Research Fellow, Montreal Neurological Inst., 1937-39; Lectr, Queen's Univ., 1939-42; Research Associate, Yerkes Labs of Primate Biology, 1942-47. Royal Soc. Vis. Prof., UCL, 1974. Hon. Res. Associate, Dalhousie Univ., 1977. Pres., Canadian Psychol Assoc., 1952; Pres., American Psychol. Assoc., 1960. Hon. DSc: Chicago, 1961; Waterloo, 1963; York, 1966; McMaster, 1967; St Lawrence, 1972; McGill, 1975; Hon. DHL, Northeastern, 1963; Hon. LLD: Dalhousie, 1965; Queen's, 1967; Western Ontario, 1968. *Publications:* Organization of Behaviour, 1949; Textbook of Psychology, 1958, 3rd edn 1972; papers in technical psychological jls. *Address:* RR1, Chester Basin, Nova Scotia B0J 1K0, Canada. *T:* (902) 275-4367.

HEBBLETHWAITE, Sidney Horace, CMG 1964; HM Diplomatic Service, retired; *b* 15 Nov. 1914; *s* of Sidney Horace Hebblethwaite and Margaret Bowler Cooke; *m* 1942, May Gladys Cook; two *d.* *Educ:* Reale Ginnasio-Liceo, Francesco Petrarca, Trieste, Italy; Pembroke Coll., Cambridge. Third Sec., FO, 1939; transferred to: Rome, 1939; FO, 1940; Lisbon, 1942; Second Sec. 1944; transferred to FO, 1945; Foreign Service Officer, 1948; 1st Sec. (Information), Athens, 1949; transferred to: Rome, 1951; FO, 1955; seconded to Treasury, 1957; transferred to Brussels, 1958; Counsellor: HM Embassy, Stockholm, 1958-62, Rangoon, 1962-65; Counsellor (Information), Washington, 1965-68; retired, in order to take up appt as HM Consul, Florence, 1970-74. *Recreations:* music, reading. *Address:* 10 Via San Egidio, Florence, Italy.

HEBDITCH, Maxwell Graham; Director, Museum of London, since 1977 (Deputy Director, 1974-77); *b* 22 Aug. 1937; *s* of late

Harold Hebditch, motor engr, Yeovil, and Lily (*née* Bartle); *m* 1963, Felicity Davies; two *s* one *d*. *Educ*: Yeovil Sch.; Magdalene Coll., Cambridge. MA, FSA, FMA. Field Archaeologist, Leicester Museums, 1961-64; Asst Curator in Archaeology, later Curator in Agricultural and Social History, City Museum, Bristol, 1965-71; Dir, Guildhall Mus., London, 1971-74. *Publications*: contribs to Britannia, Museums Jl, County Archaeological Jls. *Recreation*: archaeology. *Address*: Museum of London, London Wall, EC2Y 5HN. *T*: 01-600 3699.

HECKER, William Rundle, CBE 1963; MA, BSc, FKC; Headmaster of St Dunstan's College, Catford, 1938-67; *b* 1899; *s* of late W. J. Hecker, Margate, and Elizabeth, *d* of Richard Rundle, Hazelbeech, Northants; *m* 1925, Ione Murray, *d* of late J. P. Topping, MD; one *s*. *Educ*: Chatham House, Ramsgate; King's Coll., London. Served European War, 1914-18, in France; London Regt, 1917-19; Senior Science Master, Boston Gram. Sch., 1924-25; Asst Master, Epsom Coll., 1925-28; Headmaster of Tavistock Gram. Sch., 1928-31, Wilson's Gram. Sch., Camberwell, 1931-38. Pres. Incorporated Assoc. of Headmasters, 1951. Chm. Jt Cttee of the Four Secondary Assoc., 1958-59. *Recreations*: walking, gardening, travel. *Address*: 8 Brokes Crescent, Reigate, Surrey.

HECKLE, Arnold, CMG 1964; Chairman and President, Rubery Owen Canada Ltd; North American Director, The Rubery Owen Group of Companies; Director: Johnston Equipment Co. Ltd; Delta Benco Cascade Ltd; *b* 4 Dec. 1906; *s* of late James Allison Heckle; *m* 1954, Monique, *d* of late Alfred Choinière, Montreal. *Educ*: Padgate Sch., Lancs; Warrington Technical Coll. Entered Local Govt; subseq. Bd of Trade: Regional Controller, Midlands, 1941; Asst Sec., Bd of Trade; British Trade Comr, Johannesburg, 1957-60; Principal British Trade Comr, PQ, 1960-68. *Recreations*: fly-fishing, golf. *Address*: 35 Wynford Heights Crescent, Apartment 1403, Don Mills, Ontario, Canada.

HECTOR, Gordon Matthews, CMG 1966; CBE 1961 (OBE 1955); Deputy Secretary and Establishment Officer, Aberdeen University, since 1976; *b* 9 June 1918; *m* 1954, Mary Forrest, MB, ChB; *o d* of late Robert Gray, Fraserburgh, Aberdeenshire; one *s* two *d*. *Educ*: Edinburgh Academy; Lincoln Coll., Oxford. Military Service with East Africa Forces, 1940-45. Apptd Dist Officer, Kenya, 1946; Asst Sec., 1950; Sec. to Road Authority, 1951; Sec. to Govt of Seychelles, 1952; Acting Governor, 1953; Dep. Resident Comr and Govt Sec., Basutoland, 1956; Chief Sec., Basutoland, 1964; Deputy British Government Representative, Lesotho (lately Basutoland), 1965. Sec., Basutoland Constitutional Commn, 1957-58. Clerk to the Univ. Court, Aberdeen, 1967-76. Fellow of the Commonwealth Fund, 1939. Chm., Aberdeen Branches, Save the Children Fund and VSO; Mem. Bd of Governors, Oakbank D List Sch. *Recreations*: various. *Address*: 25 Albert Terrace, Aberdeen AB1 1XY. *T*: Aberdeen 27945. *Clubs*: Royal Over-Seas League; Nairobi (Kenya); Vincent's (Oxford).

HEDDY, Brian Huleatt; HM Diplomatic Service, retired; HM Consul-General in Durban, 1971-76; *b* 8 June 1916; *o s* of late Dr William Reginald Huleatt Heddy, Barrister-at-Law, and Ruby Norton-Taylor; *m* 1st, 1940, Barbara Ellen Williams (*d* 1965); two *s* one *d*; 2nd, 1966, Ruth Mackarness (*née* Hogan) (*d* 1967); (one step *s* two step *d*); 3rd, 1969, Horatia Clare Kennedy. *Educ*: St Paul's Sch.; Pembroke Coll., Oxford. Commissioned in 75th (Highland) Field Regt, Royal Artillery, Nov. 1939; served in France 1940; WA, 1943; War Office and France, 1944-45; Mem. of Gray's Inn. Entered Foreign Service, 1945. Appointed to Brussels, 1946; Denver, 1948; Foreign Office, 1952; Tel Aviv, 1953; UK Delegation to ECSC, Luxembourg, 1955; Foreign Office, 1959; promoted Counsellor, 1963; Consul-Gen. at Lourenço Marques, 1963-65; Head of Nationality and Consular Dept, Commonwealth Office, 1966-67; Head of Migration and Visa Dept, FCO, 1968-71. *Recreations*: tennis, golf. *Address*: Wynyards, Winsham, near Chard, Somerset. *T*: Winsham 260. *Clubs*: East India, Devonshire, Sports and Public Schools, MCC.

HEDGECOE, Prof. John, Dr RCA; FSIA; Professor of Photography, Royal College of Art, London, since 1965; *b* 24 March 1937; *s* of William Hedgecoe and Kathleen Don; *m* 1960, Julia Mardon; two *s* one *d*. *Educ*: Gulval Village Sch., Cornwall; Guildford Sch. of Art. Staff Photographer, Queen Magazine, 1957-72; Freelance: Sunday Times and Observer, 1960-70; most internat. magazines, 1958-; Portrait, HM the Queen, for British and Australian postage stamps, 1966; photographed The Arts Multi-Projection, British Exhibn, Expo Japan Show, 1970. Started Photography Sch. at RCA, 1965; Head of Dept and Reader in Photography, 1965-74; awarded Chair of Photography, 1975. Has illustrated numerous books, 1958-.

Exhibitions: London, Sydney, Toronto, Edinburgh, Venice; collection V&A Museum. *Publications*: Henry Moore, 1968 (prize best art book, world-wide, 1969); (co-author) Photography, Material and Methods, 1971-74 edns; Henry Moore, Energy in Space, 1973; The Book of Photography, 1976; Manual of Photographic Techniques, 1977; Colour Photography, 1978; The Thames, 1978. *Recreations*: sculpture, building, gardening. *Address*: Burgates, Little Dunmow, Essex CM6 3HT. *T*: Gt Dunmow 820328. *Club*: Chelsea Arts.

HEDGELAND, Air Vice-Marshal Philip Michael Sweatman, OBE 1957 (MBE 1948); CEng, FIEE; President of the Ordnance Board, Ministry of Defence, 1977-78; *b* 24 Nov. 1922; *s* of Philip and Margaret Hedgeland, Maidstone, Kent; *m* 1946, Jean Riddle Brinkworth, *d* of Leonard and Anne Brinkworth, Darlington, Co. Durham; two *s*. *Educ*: Maidstone Grammar Sch.; City and Guilds Coll., Imperial Coll. of Science and Technology, London. BSc(Eng), ACGI (Siemens Medallist). Served War: commnd into Technical Br., RAF, 1942; served as Radar Officer in Pathfinder Force and at TRE, Malvern. Radar Development Officer, Central Bomber Estabt, 1945-48; Radio Introduction Unit Project Officer for V-Bomber Navigation and Bombing System, 1952-57; Wing Comdr Radio (Air) at HQ Bomber Comd, 1957-60; jssc 1960; Air Ministry Technical Planning, 1961-62; Air Warfare Course, 1963; Dir of Signals (Far East), Singapore, 1963-65; commanded RAF Stanbridge (Central Communications Centre), 1966-67; SASO, HQ Signals Comd/90 Gp, 1968-69; IDC, 1970; MoD Procurement Exec., Project Dir for Airborne Radar, 1971-74; Vice-Pres., Ordnance Bd, 1975-76. *Recreations*: audio engineering, horticulture, amateur radio. *Address*: 16 Amersham Hill Gardens, High Wycombe, Bucks HP13 6QP. *T*: High Wycombe 25266. *Club*: Royal Air Force.

HEDGES, Anthony (John); Senior Lecturer in Music, University of Hull, since 1968; *b* 5 March 1931; *s* of late S. G. Hedges; *m* 1957, Delia Joy Marsden; two *s* two *d*. *Educ*: Bicester Grammar Sch.; Keble Coll., Oxford. MA, BMus, LRAM. National Service as solo pianist and arranger Royal Signals Band, 1955-57. Teacher and Lecturer, Royal Scottish Academy of Music, 1957-63. During this period became a regular contributor to Scotsman, Glasgow Herald, Guardian, Musical Times, etc. Lecturer in Music, Univ. of Hull, 1963. The Composers' Guild of Great Britain: Chm., Northern Br., 1966-67; Mem. Exec. Cttee of Guild, 1969-73; Chm. of Guild, 1972, Jt Chm., 1973. Member: Council, Central Music Library, Westminster, 1970; Council, Soc. for Promotion of New Music, 1974-; Music Bd, CNAA, 1974-77; Music Panel, Yorks Arts Assoc., 1974-75, Lincs and Humberside Arts Assoc., 1975-. From 1963 has written regularly for Yorkshire Post, and contributed to many jls, incl. Composer, Current Musicology, etc, and also broadcast on musical subjects. *Publications include*: (works): orchestral: Comedy Overture, 1962 (rev. 1967); Overture, October '62, 1962 (rev. 1968); Sinfonia Semplice, 1963; Expressions for Orchestra, 1964; Prelude, Romance and Rondo, strings, 1965; Concertante Music, 1965; Four Miniature Dances, 1967; A Holiday Overture, 1968; Variations on a theme of Rameau, 1969; Kingston Sketches, 1969; An Ayrshire Serenade, 1969; Four Diversions, strings, 1971; Celebrations, 1973; Symphony, 1972-73; Festival Dances, 1976; *choral*: Cantiones Festivalis, chorus and orch (various texts), 1960; Gloria, unaccompanied, 1965; Epithalamium, chorus and orch (Spencer), 1969; To Music, chorus and orch (various texts), 1972; Psalm 104, 1973; A Manchester Mass, chorus, orch. and brass band, 1974; A Humberside Cantata, 1976; Song Cycle, 1977; *chamber music*: Five Preludes, piano, 1959; Four Pieces, piano, 1966; Rondo Concertante, v, cl. hn, vc, 1967; Sonata for violin and harpsichord, 1967; Three Songs of Love, s, pf (from Song of Songs), 1968; String Quartet, 1970; Rhapsody, v, pf, 1971; piano sonata, 1974; *opera*: Shadows in the Sun (lib. Jim Hawkins), 1976; *miscellaneous*: Ballet music, The Birth of Freedom, 1961; songs and incidental music for The Good Woman of Setzuan (Brecht), 1962; film score, Young in Heart, 1963; Many anthems, part songs, albums of music for children, etc. *Recreations*: family life, reading, walking. *Address*: 13 Norfolk Street, Beverley HU17 7DN. *T*: Beverley 886529.

HEDGES, Sir John (Francis), Kt 1962; CBE 1958; solicitor in private practice; *b* 1917; *o s* of late Francis Reade Hedges and Nesta Violet (*née* Cavell); *m* 1957, Barbara Mary (*née* Ward), widow of Comdr Richard Scobell Palairet, RN; no *c*. *Educ*: St Andrew's, Eastbourne; Harrow. Commissioned Royal Signals, 1940; served India and SE Asia, TARO, 1950. Chm. Abingdon Conservative Assoc., 1948-60; Chm. Wessex Area, 1954-57 (Hon. Treas. 1960-67); Pres. Berks, Bucks and Oxon Justices' Clerks' Soc., 1955; Pres. Berks, Bucks and Oxon Inc. Law Soc., 1963; Chm. Turner's Court Sch. for Boys, 1955-75; Pres. League of Friends, Wallingford Hosps, 1953-73; Mem. Berks Exec.

Council, NHS, 1960-74 (Chm., 1971-74); Chm., Berkshire AHA, 1973-; Chm., Oxon Diocese Redundant Churches Uses Cttee, 1974-. Hon. Freeman, Borough of Wallingford, 1971. *Recreations:* shooting, gardening, music. *Address:* St Nicholas, High Street, Wallingford, Oxon OX10 0BW. *T:* Wallingford 36217. *Club:* Berkshire (Reading).

HEDLEY, Hilda Mabel, CB 1975; Under-Secretary, Department of Health and Social Security (formerly Ministry of Health), 1967-75; *b* 4 May 1918; *d* of late George Ward Hedley, Cheltenham, and late Winifred Mary Hedley (*née* Cockshott). *Educ:* Cheltenham Ladies' Coll.; Newnham Coll., Cambridge. Uncommon Languages Dept., Postal Censorship, 1940-42; Foreign Office, 1942-46; Min. of Health later DHSS, 1946-75. Sec. to Royal Commn on Mental Health, 1954-57. Nuffield Foundation Travelling Fellowship, 1960-61. Gen. Sec., Cheltenham Ladies' Coll. Guild, 1976-. *Recreations:* gardening, bird-watching. *Address:* The Anchorage, Castle Street, Winchcombe, Cheltenham GL54 5JA. *T:* Winchcombe 602314.

HEDLEY, Ronald; Director, Trent Polytechnic, Nottingham, since 1970; *b* 12 Sept. 1917; *s* of Francis Hedley, Hebburn, Co. Durham; *m* 1942; one *s* one *d. Educ:* Jarrow Grammar Sch.; Durham Univ. (MA, DipEd); Ecole Normale d'Instituteurs, Evreux. Various appts in teaching and educational administration, 1947-64. Dep. Dir of Education, Nottingham, 1964-70. Chm., Regional Acad. Bd, Regional Adv. Council for Further Educn in E Midlands, 1972-76; Member: Central Council for Educn and Trng in Social Work, 1971-; Nat Adv. Council for Educn for Ind. and Commerce, 1973-; Central Council for Educn and Trng of Health Visitors, 1972-; Cttee for Arts and Social Studies, CNAA, 1974-76; Personal Social Services Council, 1974-; Cttee on Recreation Management Training, 1977-. *Address:* 12 Grandfield Crescent, Radcliffe-on-Trent, Nottingham NG12 1AN *T:* Radcliffe-on-Trent 2584.

HEDLEY, Ronald Henderson, DSc, PhD; FIBiol; Director, British Museum (Natural History), since 1976; *b* 2 Nov. 1928; *s* of Henry Armstrong Hedley and Margaret Hopper; *m* 1957, Valmai Mary Griffith, New Zealand; one *s. Educ:* Durham Johnston Sch.; King's Coll., Univ. of Durham. Commissioned to Royal Regt of Artillery, 1953-55. Sen. Scientific Officer, British Museum (Natural History), 1955-61; New Zealand Nat. Research Fellow, 1960-61; Principal Scientific Officer, 1961-64; Dep. Keeper of Zoology, 1964-71; Dep. Dir, 1971-76. Vis. Lectr in Microbiology, Univ. of Surrey, 1968-75. Mem. Council, Fresh Water Biological Assoc., 1972-76; Trustee, Percy Sladen Meml Fund, 1972-; Pres., British Section, Soc. of Protozoology, 1975-; Mem. Council, Marine Biolog. Assoc., 1976-; Hon. Sec., Zoological Soc., London, 1977-. *Publications:* (ed with C. G. Adams) Foraminifera, vols 1-3, 1974; technical papers, mainly on biology, cytology and systematics of protozoa, 1956-. *Recreations:* gardening, sport. *Address:* British Museum (Natural History), Cromwell Road, SW7 5BD. *T:* 01-589 6323. *Club:* Athenæum.

HEDLEY-MILLER, Mrs Mary Elizabeth; Under-Secretary, HM Treasury, since 1973; *b* 5 Sept. 1923; *d* of late J. W. Ashe; *m* 1950, Roger Latham Hedley-Miller; one *s* two *d. Educ:* Queen's Sch., Chester; St Hugh's Coll., Oxford (MA). Joined HM Treasury, 1945; served in UK Treasury Delegn, Washington DC, 1947-49. *Recreations:* family, including family music; reading. *Address:* 108 Higher Drive, Purley, Surrey. *T:* 01-660 1837. *Club:* United Oxford & Cambridge University.

HEENAN, Maurice, CMG 1966; QC (Hong Kong) 1962; The General Counsel, United Nations Relief and Works Agency for Palestine Refugees in the Near East, since 1973; *b* NZ, 8 Oct. 1912; 2nd *s* of late David Heenan and of Anne Frame; *m* 1951, Claire, 2nd *d* of Emil Ciho, Trenčín, Bratislava, Czechoslovakia; two *d. Educ:* Canterbury Coll., University of New Zealand. Law Professional, LLB, Barrister and Solicitor of Supreme Court of New Zealand, Practised law in NZ, 1937-40. War of 1939-45; Major, 2nd NZEF; active service Western Desert, Libya, Cyrenaica and Italy, 1940-45 (despatches). Crown Counsel, Palestine, 1946-48. Solicitor-Gen., Hong Kong, 1961; HM's Attorney-Gen., Hong Kong, and *ex officio* MEC and MLC, Hong Kong, 1961-66; Dep.-Dir, Gen. Legal Dir., Office of Legal Affairs, Offices of the Sec.-Gen., UN, NY, 1966-73. *Recreations:* Rugby football, tennis, squash, ski-ing, golf. *Address:* Plane Trees, West Road, New Canaan, Conn 06840, USA. *Clubs:* Hong Kong; Country (New Canaan).

HEES, Hon. George H., PC (Canada) 1957; MP (Canada) (Progressive C) Northumberland, Ontario, since Nov. 1965 (Prince Edward-Hastings Riding); *b* Toronto, 17 June 1910; *s* of Harris Lincoln Hees, Toronto, and Mabel Good, New York; *m* 1934, Mabel, *d* of late Hon. E. A. Dunlop; three *d. Educ:* Trinity Coll. Sch., Port Hope, Ont; RMC, Kingston, Ont; University of Toronto; Cambridge Univ. Formerly Dir, George H. Hees & Son & Co. Served War of 1939-45: Royal Canadian Artillery, 1941-44; 3rd Anti-Tank Regt, Royal Canadian Artillery; Bde Major, 5th Infantry Bde, Holland (wounded); retd as Major. Contested (Prog. C) Spadina Riding, 1945. Minister of Transport, Canada, 1957-60; Minister of Trade and Commerce, 1960-63. Pres., Montreal and Canadian Stock Exchanges, 1964-65. Executive with George H. Hees Son & Co., Toronto; Director: Expo 67; Wood Green Community Centre. Hon. Dr of Laws, 1961. *Recreations:* reading, ski-ing, swimming, golf, tennis, riding, bridge; formerly boxing. *Address:* 7 Coltrin Place, Ottawa, Ontario, Canada; Rathbunwood, Cobourg, Canada. *Clubs:* Toronto Golf, Toronto Badminton and Racquet, Osler Bluff Ski (Toronto); Rideau, Royal Ottawa Golf (Ottawa); Mid-Ocean (Bermuda).

HEFFER, Eric Samuel; MP (Lab) Walton Division of Liverpool since 1964; *b* 12 Jan. 1922; *s* of William George Heffer and Annie Heffer (*née* Nicholls); *m* 1945, Doris Murray. *Educ:* Bengeo Junior Sch. and Longmore Senior Sch., Hertford. Served RAF, 1942-45. Pres. Liverpool Trades Council and Labour Party, 1959-60, 1964-65, and Vice-Pres., 1960 and 1964. Liverpool City Councillor, 1960-66. Member: Council of Europe, 1965-68; WEU, 1965-68 (served on political, social and financial cttees). Labour front bench spokesman on Industrial Relations, 1970-72; Minister of State, Dept of Industry, 1974-75. Mem., Lab Party Nat. Exec. Cttee, 1975-. *Publications:* (part author) The Agreeable Autocracies, 1961, (USA); (part author) Election 70, 1970; The Class Struggle in Parliament, 1973; articles in Tribune, Liverpool Daily Post, The Times, Guardian, New Statesmen, Spectator, New Outlook, Labour Voice, New Left Review, and in foreign jls. *Recreations:* hill-walking, mountaineering. *Address:* House of Commons, SW1.

HEGER, Prof. Robert; formerly First Conductor of State-Opera, Munich; *b* Strassbourgh, 19 Aug. 1886. *Educ:* Strassbourgh, Zürich, Lyon, Munich. Conductor at the Operas in Strassbourgh, Barmen; First Conductor at the Volks-opera in Vienna, 1911; Dir of the Opera in Nuremburg, 1912-19; First Conductor at the Munich Opera, 1919-25; First Conductor of the State Opera Vienna, 1925-33; Dir of the Concerts of the Soc. of Friends of Music, Vienna; Conductor at the State Opera, Berlin, 1933-45; Conductor at the Royal Opera in London, 1926-36. Formerly Pres., Hochschule für Musik, Munich. *Publications:* Trio for Piano; Ein Fest zu Haderslev, Opera; Concert for Violin, First Symphony; A Song of Peace, Chorus work; Second Symphony; Nine Songs; Verdi-Variations; Der Bettler Namenlos, Opera; Der Verlorene Sohn (the prodigal son), Opera: A serious Prelude and a Gay Fugue for Orchestra, op. 26; Lady Hamilton, Opera; Dramatic Overture, op. 28; Henry the Lion, Opera; A serious Symphonie (the third one) op. 30; Variations and Fugue on a Baroque theme for Orchestra, op. 32a; Chaconne and Fugue on a twelve-tone series, op. 35; 4 alte Marienlieder for a high soprano and orchestra, op. 42; Concerto for Violoncello and Orchestra, op. 43; Don Carlos-Variations, op. 44; Te Deum for 2 soli, choir and orchestra, op. 45. *Address:* Widenmayerstrasse 46 I, Munich, Germany.

HEGLAND, David Leroy, DFC 1944; Chairman: GKN Australia Ltd; Ajax GKN Holdings Pty Ltd; Director: GKN (Overseas) Ltd; Ajax Nettlefolds Pty Ltd; Kemtron Ltd; Galena; BHP-GKN Holdings Ltd; Massey-Ferguson Holdings (Australia) Ltd; Carlton and United Breweries Holdings Ltd; cattle grazier; *b* 12 June 1919; *s* of Lee and Jennie Hegland; *m* 1944, Dagmar Cooke; two *s* one *d. Educ:* Whitman Coll., Washington, USA (BA). Managing Director: GM International, Copenhagen, 1956-58; GM South African, Port Elizabeth, 1958-61; GM Holden's Pty Ltd, Melbourne, 1962-65; Chm. and Man. Dir, Vauxhall Motors Ltd, Luton, 1966-70; Director: General Motors Ltd, London, 1966-70; GMAC (UK) Ltd, Luton, 1966-70. Vice-Pres., SMMT. Mem., Industry Forum, Aust. Acad. of Science, 1972-. Mem., Delta Sigma Rho. FIMI. *Recreations:* tennis, golf, riding. *Address:* GKN Ltd, AMP Towers, Bourke & Williams, Melbourne, Victoria, Australia. *Clubs:* Royal & Ancient Golf (St Andrews); Melbourne, Victoria Racing (Melbourne); Albury (Albury, NSW).

HEIFETZ, Jascha; Commander, Legion of Honour, 1957; violinist, soloist; 1st Vice-President of American Guild of Musical Artists, Inc., New York City; Hon. Member: Society of Concerts of Paris Conservatoire; Association des Anciens Elèves du Conservatoire; Cercle International de la Jeunesse Artistique; Hon. Vice-President of Mark Twain Society, USA; Hon. President, Musicians' Fund of America; on music department staff, University of Southern California, Los Angeles; *b* Vilna, Russia, 2 Feb. 1901; father professional violinist and music teacher; *m* 1928, Florence Vidor; one *s* one *d* ; *m* 1947, Mrs

Frances Spiegelberg; one s. Educ: Music Sch. at Vilna; Petrograd Conservatory of Music under Professor Auer. Made his first public appearance at the age of 4½ when he played in Vilna Fantasie Pastorale; at 7 he played Mendelssohn Concerto before a full house in Kovno; entered Petrograd Conservatory when 10, and soon began to give concerts in Russia, Germany, Austro-Hungary, Scandinavia, and later met with a phenomenal success in the United States of America, 1917; from hence he proceeded to England; appeared as soloist with orchestras under Nikisch, Safonoff, Koussevitsky, Schneifoght, Stokowski, Toscanini, and others; toured Australia and New Zealand, 1921; Japan, China, Manchuria, Korea, 1923; tour of the World, 1925-27, including Europe, N Africa, S America, Mexico, India, Java, China, Australia, Philippines, etc; has made appearances in the Festival Hall, London, in recent years; his repertoire includes most of the classical and modern violin literature. Recreations: sailing, tennis, ping-pong (table tennis), motoring, aquatic sports, reading and dancing. Address: 1520 Gilcrest Drive, Beverly Hills, Calif 90210, USA. Clubs: Royal Automobile, Savage; Bohemian (New York); Newport Harbor Yacht (Newport); Beaux Arts, Inter-Allied (Paris).

HEILBRON, Hon. Dame Rose, DBE 1974; Hon. Mrs Justice Heilbron; a Judge of the High Court of Justice, Family Division, since 1974; b 19 Aug. 1914; d of late Max and Nellie Heilbron; m 1945, Dr Nathaniel Burstein; one d. Educ: Belvedere Sch., GPDST; Liverpool University, LLB 1st Class Hons, 1935; Lord Justice Holker Scholar, Gray's Inn, 1936; LLM 1937. Called to Bar, Gray's Inn, 1939, Bencher, 1968; joined Northern Circuit, Leader, 1973-74; QC 1949; Recorder of Burnley, 1956-71, a Recorder, and Hon. Recorder of Burnley, 1972-74. Mem., Bar Council, 1973-74. Hon. Fellow, Lady Margaret Hall, Oxford, 1976; Hon. LLD Liverpool, 1975. Hon. Col, WRAC(TA). Address: Royal Courts of Justice, Strand, WC2.

HEIM, Most Rev. Bruno Bernard, PhD, JCD; Apostolic Delegate to Great Britain since 1973; b Olten, Switzerland, 5 March 1911; s of Bernard and Elisabeth Heim-Studer. Educ: Olten, Engelberg and Schwyz; St Thomas of Aquino Univ.; Gregorian Univ.; Univ. of Fribourg; Papal Acad. of Diplomacy. Priest 1938; Vicar in Basle and Arbon, 1938-42; Chief Chaplain for Italian and Polish Internees in Switzerland, 1943-45; Sec., Papal Nunciature in Paris; Auditor at Nunciature in Vienna; Counsellor and Chargé d'affaires at Nunciature in Germany; titular Archbp of Xanthos, 1961; Apostolic Delegate to Scandinavia, 1961-69; Apost. Pro-Nuncio (Ambassador): to Finland, 1966-69; to Egypt, 1969-73; President of Caritas Egypt, 1969-73. Lauréat, French Acad.; Corresp. Mem., Real Academia de la Historia, Madrid, 1950; Mem. Council, Internat. Heraldic Acad.; Grand Cross: Order of Malta, 1950; Teutonic Order, 1961; Order of Finnish Lion, 1969; Order of St Maurice and Lazarus, 1973; (1st Class) Order of the Republic, Egypt, 1975; Gr. Officer Order of Holy Sepulchre; Orders of Merit: Germany, Italy, Austria; Officier Légion d'honneur, etc. Publications: Die Freundschaft nach Thomas von Aquin, 1934; Wappenbrauch und Wappenrecht in der Kirche, 1947; Coutumes et droit heraldiques de l'Eglise, 1949; L'oeuvre héraldique de Paul Boesch, 1973; contrib. Adler, Zeitschrift f. Heraldik und Genealogie, Heraldisk Tidskrift. Recreations: heraldry, heraldic painting, cooking, gardening. Address: 54 Parkside, SW19 5NF. T: 01-946 1410.

HEIN, Sir (Charles Henri) Raymond, Kt 1977; Chevalier de la Légion d'Honneur, 1950; QC 1956; Barrister-at-Law, in practice since 1925; Director of Companies; b 26 Sept. 1901; s of Jules Hein and Clémence de Charmoy; m 1928, Marcelle Piat; four s four d. Educ: Royal Coll., Mauritius (Scholar, 1920); Wadham Coll., Oxford. MA Oxon. Mem., Council of Govt, 1936-48; Mayor of Port Louis, 1948. Dir, 1937-, Pres., 1965-76, Mauritius Commercial Bank; Chairman: Swan Insurance Ltd, 1967-; Mauritius Life Assurance, 1972-; Anglo-Mauritius Assce Soc. Ltd, 1973-; New Mauritius Dock Co. Ltd, 1960-70 (Dir, 1937-70); Dir, Reinsurance Co. of Mauritius. Former President: Mauritius Chamber of Agric.; Mauritius Sugar Industry Res. Inst.; Mauritius Turf Club. Pres., Alliance Française, 1948-54. Former Pres., Bar Council. Publication: trans. Bernardin de St Pierre's Paul et Virginie, 1977. Recreations: music, gardening, ancient Greek literature. Address: Royal Road, Moka, Mauritius. T: 54-216; (chambers) Cathedral Square, Port Louis. T: 2-0327. Club: Mauritius Turf (Port Louis).

HEINE, Prof. Volker, FRS 1974; Professor of Theoretical Physics, University of Cambridge, since 1976; Fellow of Clare College, Cambridge, since 1960; b 19 Sept. 1930; m 1955, M. Daphne Hines; one s two d. Educ: Otago Univ. (MSc, DipHons); Cambridge Univ. (PhD). FInstP. Demonstrator, Cambridge Univ., 1958-63, Lectr 1963-70; Reader in Theoretical Physics, 1970-76. Vis. Prof., Univ. of Chicago, 1965-66; Vis. Scientist,

Bell Labs, USA, 1970-71. Publications: Group Theory in Quantum Mechanics, 1960; (jtly) Solid State Physics Vol. 24, 1970; articles in Proc. Royal Soc., Jl Physics, Physical Review, etc. Address: Cavendish Laboratory, Madingley Road, Cambridge CB3 0HE.

HEINZ, Henry John, II; Chairman, H. J. Heinz Company, since 1959 (President, 1941-59); b Sewickley, Pa, USA, 10 July 1908; s of Howard and Elizabeth Rust Heinz; m 1st, 1935, Joan Diehl (marr. diss. 1942); one s; m 1953, Drue English Maher. Educ: Yale (BA 1931); Trinity Coll., Cambridge. Salesman, H. J. Heinz Co., Ltd, London, 1932; with H. J. Heinz Co., Pittsburgh, Pa, Pres., 1941-59; Chm., 1959-; Dir or Officer, various subsidiaries of H. J. Heinz Co. in England, Canada, Australia and elsewhere. Commander, Royal Order of the Phœnix, Greece, 1950; Chevalier de la Légion d'Honneur, France, 1950; Comdr of Order of Merit, Italian Republic. Recreation: ski-ing. Address: (residence) Goodwood, Sewickley, Pa 15143, USA. Clubs: Buck's, White's; The Brook, River (New York); Duquesne, Rolling Rock, Allegheny Country, Laurel Valley Golf (Pittsburgh).

HEINZE, Prof. Sir Bernard (Thomas), Kt 1949; MA, LLD, MusDoc, FRCM; Degré Supérieur Schola Cantorum, Paris; Ormond Professor of Music, University of Melbourne, 1925-57; Director, State Conservatorium, NSW, 1957-66; Conductor Melbourne Philharmonic Society since 1928; Conductor under contract to ABC since 1947; b Shepparton, Vic, 1 July 1894; m 1932, Valerie Antonia, d of late Sir David Valentine Hennessy, of Melbourne; three s. Educ: St Patrick's Coll., Ballarat; Melbourne Univ. MA (Melbourne); LLD (Hon.) (Brit. Columbia); FRCM 1931. Won the Clarke Scholarship in 1912 and was sent to England to study at the Royal College of Music; studies interrupted by five years' service as an officer in the Royal Artillery; won the Gowland Harrison Scholarship, 1920; studied at the Schola Cantorum, Paris, under Vincent d'Indy and Nestor Lejeune; studied in Berlin under Willy Hess; returned to Australia, 1923; founded Melbourne String Quartette; Conductor: University Symphony Orchestra, 1924-32; Melbourne Symphony Orchestra, 1933-46. Mem., ABC Music Adv. Cttee; Chairman: Commonwealth Assistance to Australian Composers, 1967-; Music Adv. Cttee, Australian Council for the Arts, 1969-. Dir General for Music, Australian Broadcasting Co. 1929-32. Officier de la Couronne, Belgium, 1938; Polonia Restituta, 1973. Recreations: golf and philately. Address: 101 Victoria Road, Bellevue Hill, Sydney, NSW 2023, Australia. Clubs: Canada (Melbourne); Royal Sydney Golf, American (Sydney).

HEISBOURG, Georges; Ambassador of Luxembourg in Moscow, since 1974; b 19 April 1918; s of Nicolas Heisbourg and Berthe (née Ernsterhoff); m 1945, Hélène Pinet; two s one d. Educ: Athénée, Luxembourg; Univs of Grenoble, Innsbruck and Paris. Head of Govt Press and Information Office, Luxembourg, 1944-45; Attaché 1945-48, Sec. 1948-51, of Legation, London; Head of Internat. Organisations Section, Dir of Political Affairs, Min. of For. Affairs, Luxembourg, 1951-58; Luxembourg Ambassador to USA, Canada and Mexico, 1958-64; Perm. Rep. to UN, 1958-61; Luxembourg Ambassador: to Netherlands, 1964-67; to France, 1967-70; Perm. Rep. of Luxembourg to OECD, 1967-70; Sec. Gen., WEU, 1971-74. Chevalier, Nat. Order of Crown of Oak, 1958, Comdr, Order of Adolphe de Nassau, 1963, and Officer, Order of Merit, 1965, Luxembourg; also holds decorations from Austria, Belgium, France, Germany, Italy, Mexico, and the Netherlands. Recreations: tennis, swimming. Address: 3 Khruschevsky Pereuluk, Moscow, USSR.

HEISER, Terence Michael; Director of Housing Directorate 'A', Department of the Environment, since 1976; b 24 May 1932; s of David and Daisy Heiser; m 1957, Kathleen Mary Waddle; one s two d. Educ: Grafton Road Primary Sch., Dagenham; London Evacuee Sch., Sunninghill, Berks; Windsor County Boy's Sch., Berks; Birkbeck Coll., Univ. of London; BA (Hons English). Served in RAF (Radar Mechanic), 1950-52; joined Civil Service 1949, served with Colonial Office, Min. of Works, Min. of Housing and Local Govt; Principal Private Sec. to Sec. of State for the Environment, 1975-76; Under Sec., Housing, 1976. Recreations: reading, walking, talking. Address: 19 Sylvan Hill, Upper Norwood, SE19.

HEISKELL, Andrew; Chairman of Directors, Time, Inc., since 1960; b Naples, 13 Sept. 1915; s of Morgan Heiskell and Ann Heiskell (née Hubbard); m 1937, Cornelia Scott (marr. diss.); one s one d; m 1950, Madeleine Carroll (marr. diss.); one d; m 1965, Marian, d of Arthur Hays Sulzberger, and widow of Orvil E. Dryfoos. Educ: Switzerland; France; University of Paris. Science teacher, Ecole du Montcel, Paris, 1935. Life Magazine:

Science and Medicine Editor, 1937-39; Asst Gen. Manager, 1939-42; Gen. Manager, 1942-46; Publisher, 1946-60; Vice-Pres., Time, Inc., 1949-60. Director: Inter-American Press Assoc.; Center for Inter-American Relations; New York Urban Coalition; Nat. Urban Coalition; Internat. Executive Service Corps; Trustee, Bennington Coll.; Pres., Bd of Overseers, Harvard Coll. Wharton Sch. Alumni Soc., Univ. of Pennsylvania, Gold Medal Award of Merit, 1968. Hon. LLD: Shaw Univ., 1968; Lake Erie Coll., 1969; Hofstra Univ., 1972; Hobart and William Smith Colls, 1973; Hon. DLitt Lafayette Coll., 1969. *Address:* Time, Inc., Time and Life Building, Rockefeller Center, New York, NY 10020; 870 United Nations Plaza, New York, NY 10017; Darien, Conn, USA.

HEITLER, Prof. Walter Heinrich, PhD; FRS 1948; Professor of Theoretical Physics, University of Zürich, 1949-74; *b* 2 Jan. 1904; *m* 1942, Kathleen Winifred; one *s. Educ:* Universities of Berlin and Munich. Doctor's Degree, Munich, 1926; Privatdocent for Theoretical Physics, University of Göttingen, 1929-33; Research Fellow, University of Bristol, 1933-41; Professor of Theoretical Physics, 1941-49; Dir, School of Theoretical Physics, Dublin Institute for Advanced Studies, 1945-49. Hon. DSc, Dublin, 1954; Dr rer nat *hc*, Göttingen, 1969; Hon. DPhil Uppsala, 1973. Max Planck Medal, 1968; Marcel Benoist Prize, 1969. *Publications:* (with F. London) Theory of Chemical Bond, 1927; Quantum Theory of Radiation, 1936 (3rd edn 1954); Elementary Wave Mechanics, 1945 (2nd edn 1956); papers on Cosmic Rays, Meson theory, Quantum-electrodynamics; Der Mensch und die Naturwissenschaftliche Erkenntnis, 1961, 4th edn, 1966 (Eng. Trans. Man and Science, 1963); Naturphilosophische Streifzüge, 1970; Naturwissenschaft ist Geisteswissenschaft, 1972; Die Natur und das Göttliche, 1974, 3rd edn 1976 (Foundn for Western Thinking Lit. prize). *Recreations:* mountaineering, ski-ing. *Address:* The University, Zürich, Switzerland.

HELAISSI, Sheikh Abdulrahman Al-; Hon. GCVO; Saudi Arabian Ambassador to the Court of St James's, 1966-76; *b* 24 July 1922. *Educ:* Universities of Cairo and London. Secretary to Embassy, London, 1947-54; Under-Sec., Min. of Agriculture, 1954-57; Head of Delegn to FAO, 1955-61; Ambassador to Sudan, 1957-60; Representative to UN, and to various confs concerned with health and agriculture; Delegate to Conf. of Non-aligned Nations, Belgrade, 1961; Ambassador: Italy and Austria, 1961-66; UK and Denmark (concurrently), 1966-70. Versed in Islamic Religious Law. *Publication:* The Rehabilitation of the Bedouins, 1959. *Address:* c/o Ministry of Foreign Affairs, Riyadh, Saudi Arabia.

HELE, Desmond George K.; *see* King-Hele.

HELE, James Warwick; High Master of St Paul's School since 1973; *b* 24 July 1926; *s* of John Warwick Hele, Carlisle; *m* 1948, Audrey Whalley; four *d. Educ:* Sedbergh Sch.; Hertford Coll., Oxford; Trinity Hall, Cambridge (Schol., MA). 1st cl. hons History Tripos 1951. Asst Master, Kings College Sch., Wimbledon, 1951-55; Rugby School: Asst Master, 1955-73; Housemaster, Kilbracken, 1965-73; 2nd Master, 1970-73. *Recreations:* Rugby football (Oxford Univ. XV 1944), hill walking, Brathay Exploration Group. *Address:* The High Master's House, St Paul's School, Lonsdale Road, Barnes, SW13 9JT. *T:* 01-748 6420.

HELLINGS, Gen. Sir Peter (William Cradock), KCB 1970 (CB 1966); DSC 1940; MC 1943; DL; Chairman, SW Gas Consumers' Council, since 1973; *b* 6 Sept. 1916; *s* of Stanley and Norah Hellings; *m* 1941, Zoya, *d* of Col Bassett; one *s* one *d. Educ:* Naut. Coll., Pangbourne. Joined Royal Marines, 1935; Company Cmdr, 40 Commando, 1942; GSO 2, Commando Group, 1944; Comdr 41 and 42 Commandos, 1945-46; Brigade Major, 3 Commando Bde in Malaya, 1949-51; joined Directing Staff of Marine Corps Schs, Quantico, USA, 1954; Comdr 40 Commando, 1958; Brigade Comdr, 3 Commando Bde, 1959; Comdr Infantry Training Centre, Royal Marines, 1960; idc 1962; Dep. Dir, Joint Warfare Staff, 1963; Maj.-Gen., 1964; Chief of Staff to Commandant-Gen., RM, 1964; Group Comdr, HQ Portsmouth Group RM, 1967-68; Lt-Gen., 1968; Comdt-Gen., RM, 1968-71; General, 1970. Col Comdt, Royal Marines, 1977-. DL Devon 1973. *Recreations:* shooting, fishing. *Address:* The Leys, Milton Combe, Devon. *T:* Yelverton 3355.

HELLMAN, Lillian; playwright; *b* New Orleans, Louisiana, USA, 20 June 1907; *d* of Max Bernard Hellman and Julia Newhouse; *m* 1925, Arthur Kober (divorced). *Educ:* New York Univ.; Columbia Univ. Worked for Horace Liveright, Publishers, 1925-26. Hon. LLD Wheaton Coll., MA Tufts Univ.; Hon. LLD: Rutgers Univ., 1963, Brandeis Univ., 1965; Yale, 1974; Smith Coll., 1974; New York Univ., 1974; Franklin

and Marshall Coll., 1975; Columbia Univ., 1976; Creative Arts Award, Brandeis Univ.; Mem., National Academy of Arts and Letters (Gold Medal for Drama, 1964); Mem., American Academy of Arts and Sciences. Book reviews, Herald Tribune, wrote short stories. First produced play The Children's Hour, 1934. Wrote movie scenarios The Dark Angel, These Three (screen version of The Children's Hour), Dead End, The Little Foxes, North Star. *Publications:* plays produced: The Children's Hour, 1934; Days to Come, 1936; The Little Foxes, 1939; Watch on the Rhine, 1941; The Searching Wind, 1944; Another Part of the Forest, 1946; adapted from the French, Roblés' play, Montserrat, 1949; The Autumn Garden, 1951; adapted Anouilh's The Lark, 1955; adapted Voltaire's Candide as comic operetta, 1956; Toys in the Attic, 1960; adapted Blechman's novel How Much as play, My Mother, My Father and Me, 1963; edited: The Selected Letters of Anton Chekhov, 1955; (with introduction) Dashiell Hammett, The Big Knockover, 1966; (memoir) An Unfinished Woman, 1969 (National Book Award 1970); Pentimento, 1974; Scoundrel Time, 1976. *Address:* 630 Park Avenue, New York, NY 10021, USA.

HELLYER, Arthur George Lee, MBE 1967; FLS; Gardening Correspondent to the Financial Times; Editor of Amateur Gardening, 1946-67; Editor of Gardening Illustrated, 1947-56; *b* 16 Dec. 1902; *s* of Arthur Lee Hellyer and Maggie Parlett; *m* 1933, Grace Charlotte Bolt (*d* 1977); two *s* one *d. Educ:* Dulwich Coll. Farming in Jersey, 1918-21; Nursery work in England, 1921-29; Asst Editor of Commercial Horticulture, 1929; Asst Editor of Amateur Gardening, 1929-46. Associate of Hon. of Royal Horticultural Society; Victoria Medal of Honour in Horticulture. *Publications:* The Amateur Gardener, 1948; Amateur Gardening Pocket Guide, 1941; Amateur Gardening Popular Encyclopædia of Flowering Plants, 1957; Encyclopædia of Garden Work and Terms, 1954; Encyclopædia of Plant Portraits, 1953; English Gardens Open to the Public, 1956; Flowers in Colour, 1955; Garden Pests and Diseases, 1966; Garden Plants in Colour, 1958; Practical Gardening for Amateurs, 1935; Shrubs in Colour, 1966; Your Garden Week by Week, 1938; Your New Garden, 1937; Starting with Roses, 1966; Find out about Gardening, 1967; Gardens to Visit in Britain, 1970; Your Lawn, 1970; Carter's Book for Gardeners, 1970; All Colour Gardening Book, 1972; All Colour Book of Indoor and Greenhouse Plants, 1973; Picture Dictionary of Popular Flowering Plants, 1973; The Collingridge Encyclopaedia of Gardening, 1976; Shell Guide to Gardens, 1977. *Recreations:* gardening, photography, travelling. *Address:* Orchards, Rowfant, near Crawley, West Sussex. *T:* Copthorne 714838.

HELLYER, Hon. Paul Theodore, PC (Canada) 1957; FRSA 1973; Syndicated Columnist, Toronto Sun; *b* Waterford, Ont, Canada, 6 Aug. 1923; *s* of A. S. Hellyer and Lulla M. Anderson; *m* 1945, Ellen Jean, *d* of Henry Ralph, Toronto, Ont; two *s* one *d. Educ:* Waterford High Sch., Ont; Curtiss-Wright Techn. Inst. of Aeronautics, Glendale, Calif; University of Toronto (BA). Fleet Aircraft Mfg Co., Fort Erie, Ont. Wartime service, RCAF and Cdn Army. Propr Mari-Jane Fashions, Toronto, 1945-56; Treas., Curran Hall Ltd, Toronto, 1950 (Pres., 1951-62). Elected to House of Commons, 1949; re-elected, 1953; Parly Asst to Hon. Ralph Campney, Minister of Nat. Defence, 1956; Associate Minister of Nat. Defence, 1957; defeated in gen. elections of June 1957 and March 1958; re-elected to House of Commons in by-election Dec. 1958 and again re-elected June 1962, April 1963, Nov. 1965, June 1968, and Oct. 1972; defeated gen. election July 1974; Minister of National Defence, 1963-67; Minister of Transport, 1967-69, and Minister i/c Housing, 1968-69; resigned 1969 on question of principle relating to housing. Chm., Federal Task Force on Housing and Urban Develt, 1968. Served as a Parly Rep. to NATO under both L and C administrations. Joined Parly Press Gallery, Oct. 1974. Distinguished visitor, York Univ., 1969-70. Founder and Leader, Action Canada, 1971; joined Progressive Cons. Party, 1972; Candidate for leadership of Progressive Cons. Party Feb. 1976. *Publication:* Agenda: a Plan for Action, 1971. *Recreations:* philately, music. *Address:* 1982 Rideau River Drive, Ottawa, Ont, Canada. *T:* 238-5286. *Club:* Ontario.

HELMORE, Roy Lionel, JP; Principal, Cambridgeshire College of Arts and Technology, since 1977; *b* 8 June 1926; *s* of Lionel Helmore and Ellen Helmore (*née* Gibbins); *m* 1969, Margaret Lilian Martin. *Educ:* Montrose Academy; Edinburgh Univ. (BScEng). FIEE, MBIM. Crompton Parkinson Ltd, 1947-49; Asst Lectr, Peterborough Techn. Coll., 1949-53; Lectr, subseq. Sen. Lectr, Shrewsbury Techn. Coll., 1953-57; Head of Electrical Engrg and Science, Exeter Techn. Coll., 1957-61; Principal, St Albans Coll. of Further Education, 1961-77. Pres., Assoc. of Principals of Techn. Instns, 1972-73 (Hon. Sec. 1968-71); Member: Council, Assoc. of Colls for Further and Higher

Educn, 1974-; BBC Further Educn Adv. Council, 1967-73; Air Transport and Travel ITB, 1967-73; Technician Educn Council, 1973- (Vice-Chm.); Manpower Services Commn, 1974-; RAF Trng and Educn Adv. Cttee, 1976-; JP St Albans (now Herts), 1964. *Recreations:* gardening, travel, opera. *Address:* Chardingleye, 4 Plaistow Way, Great Chishill, Royston, Herts SG8 8SQ. *T:* Chrishall 570. *Club:* Royal Commonwealth Society.

HELMSING, Most Rev. Charles H.; Bishop (RC) of Kansas City-St Joseph, since 1962; *b* 23 March 1908; *s* of George Helmsing and Louise Helmsing (*née* Boschert). *Educ:* St Michael's Parochial Sch.; St Louis Preparatory Seminary; Kenrick Seminary. Sec. to Archbishop of St Louis, 1946-49; Auxiliary Bishop to Archbishop of St Louis, and Titular Bishop of Axum, 1949; first Bishop, Diocese of Springfield-Cape Girardeau, Mo, 1956-62. Member: Secretariat of Christian Unity, 1963-76; US Bishops Cttee for Ecumenical Affairs, 1964-76; Preparatory Cttee for Dialogue between Anglican Communion and Roman Catholic Church, 1966-67 (Chm., Roman Catholic Members); Chm., Special Cttee for Dialogue with Episcopal Church, US, 1964-76. Hon. Doctorates: Letters: Avila Coll. 1962; Humanities, Rockhurst Coll., 1963. Law: St Benedict's Coll. 1966. Order of Condor, Bolivia, 1966. *Address:* (Chancery Office) PO Box 1037, Kansas City, Missouri 64141, USA. *T:* (816), 756-1850.

HELPMANN, Sir Robert Murray, Kt 1968; CBE 1964; dancer, actor (stage and films); choreographer; producer; director; *b* 9 April 1909; *s* of James Murray Helpman, Mount Gambia, South Australia, and Mary Gardiner, Mount Shank, SA. *Educ:* Prince Alfred's Coll., Adelaide. First appeared under J. C. Williamson's Management, Australia, 1926-30; Premier Danseur, Sadler's Wells Ballet, 1933-50; Director, Australian Ballet, 1965-76; Artistic Dir, Adelaide Festival, 1970-. Guest dancer, Royal Opera House, 1958; guest artist, Sadler's Wells Royal Ballet, 1977. *Theatre:* Stop Press, Adelphi, 1936; Oberon, A Midsummer Night's Dream, Old Vic, 1937-38; Gremio, The Taming of the Shrew, 1939; title role, Old Vic prodn, Hamlet, New, 1944; Flamineo, The White Devil, 1947; Prince, He Who Gets Slapped, Duchess, 1947; Stratford-on-Avon, 1948 season: Shylock, King John and Hamlet; Sir Laurence Olivier's Shaw-Shakespeare Festival Season, 1951: Apollodorus, Caesar and Cleopatra; Octavius Caesar, Antony and Cleopatra; The Millionairess, New, 1952; Oberon, A Midsummer Night's Dream, Edinburgh Festival, USA and Canada, 1954; Old Vic Australian Tour, 1955: Petruchio, Taming of the Shrew; Shylock, Merchant of Venice; Angelo, Measure for Measure; Old Vic: Shylock, Merchant of Venice, 1956; Launce, The Two Gentlemen of Verona, 1957; Emperor, Titus Andronicus, 1957; Pinch, Comedy of Errors, 1957; King Richard, Richard III, 1957; Georges de Valera, Nekrassov, Edinburgh Festival and Royal Court, 1957; Sebastian, Nude with Violin, London and Australian Tour, 1958; *produced:* Madame Butterfly, Royal Opera Hse, Covent Gdn, 1950; Murder in the Cathedral, Old Vic, 1953; Coq d'Or, Royal Opera Hse, 1954, 1956, 1962; After the Ball, Globe, 1954; Antony and Cleopatra, Old Vic, 1957; The Marriage-Go-Round, Piccadilly, 1959; Duel of Angels: New York, 1960; Melbourne, 1961; Old Vic S American Tour, 1962; Peter Pan, Coliseum, 1972, 1973, 1974, Palladium, 1975; *choreographer:* Red Shoes (and Premier Danseur), 1948; Australia, 1964: Comus; Hamlet; The Birds; Miracle in the Gorbals; Adam Zero; The Soldier's Tale; Elektra; The Display; Yugen; Cinderella, Covent Gdn, 1965; Elektra, Australia, 1966; Sun Music, Australia; dir., Camelot, Drury Lane, 1964; *films include:* One of our Aircraft is Missing, Wyecroft in Caravan, Henry V (Bishop of Ely), Tales of Hoffmann, The Iron Petticoat, Big Money, Red Shoes, 55 Days in Pekin, The Soldier's Tale, The Quiller Memorandum, Chitty Chitty Bang Bang, Alice in Wonderland (Mad Hatter), Don Quixote, The Mango Tree. Has appeared on TV. Knight of the Northern Star (Sweden); Knight of the Cedar (Lebanon). *Address:* c/o Midland Bank Ltd, 70 St Martin's Lane, WC2.

HELSBY, family name of **Baron Helsby.**

HELSBY, Baron *cr* 1968 (Life Peer); **Laurence Norman Helsby,** GCB 1963 (CB 1950); KBE 1955; a Director: Rank Organisation, since 1968; Imperial Group, since 1968; Industrial and Commercial Finance Corporation, since 1972; Midland Bank, since 1968; Chairman, Midland Bank Trust Co., since 1970; *b* 24 April 1908; *s* of late Wilfred Helsby; *m* 1938, Wilmett Mary, *yr d* of late W. G. Maddison, Durham; one *s* one *d*. *Educ:* Sedbergh; Keble Coll., Oxford. Lecturer in Economics, University Coll. of the South West, 1930-31; Lecturer in Economics, Durham Colls in the University of Durham, 1931-45; Asst Sec., HM Treasury, 1946; Principal Private Sec. to the Prime Minister, 1947-50; Dep. Sec., Min. of Food, 1950-54; First

Civil Service Commissioner, 1954-59; Permanent Sec., Min. of Labour, 1959-62; Joint Permanent Sec. to the Treasury and Head of the Home Civil Service, 1963-68; Sec., Order of the British Empire, 1963-68. Hon. Fellow, Keble Coll., Oxford, 1959; Hon. LLD Exeter, 1963; Hon. DCL Durham, 1963. *Address:* Logmore Farm, Dorking, Surrey. *Club:* United Oxford & Cambridge University.

HELY, Brig. Alfred Francis, CB 1951; CBE 1945; DSO 1943; TD 1944; DL; Chief Dental Officer, Cheshire County Council, 1957-68; *b* 3 Aug. 1902; *s* of Alfred Francis Hely; unmarried. *Educ:* St Edward's Coll., Liverpool; Liverpool Univ. Qualified as a Dental Surg., 1923; in private practice, 1923-26. Liverpool Univ. OTC, 1921-25; Cadet Corporal, Duke of Lancaster's Own Imperial Yeomanry, 1925-26; 106 (Lancs Hussars), RHA, 1926-41 (comd, 1937-41); served War of 1939-45 (despatches twice); 60th Field Regt, RA, 1941-42; CRA 7 Ind. Div., 1942-45; Comd 7 Ind. Div. 1945 until end of hostilities in Burma (3 months); war service in Palestine, Western Desert, Greece, Crete, Syria, 1940-42, North-West Frontier, India, 1942, Burma, 1943-45. CRA 42 (Lancs) Inf. Div. (TA), 1947-50. DL County Palatine of Lancaster, 1951. *Recreations:* outdoor country pursuits. *Address:* Flat 2, Inchbroom, 21 Bidston Road, Birkenhead, Merseyside L43 2JY. *T:* 051-652 2132. *Club:* Army and Navy.

HELY, Air Commodore Arthur Hubert McMath, CB 1962; OBE 1945; Air Commodore Operations, HQ Maintenance Command, 1961-64, retired; *b* 16 Feb. 1909; *s* of Hamilton McMath Hely and Lubie Thrine Hely (*née* Jörgensen); *m* 1935, Laura Mary Sullivan, 6th *d* of Serjeant A. M. Sullivan, QC; two *s* two *d*. *Educ:* Mt Albert, Auckland, NZ; Auckland University Coll. Joined Royal Air Force, 1934; Staff Coll., 1942; HQ SACSEA, 1944, 1945; Joint Chiefs of Staff, Australia, 1946-48; Joint Services Staff Coll., 1948; Group Capt. 1950; HQ Fighter Command, 1953-56; HQ Far East Air Force, 1956, 1958; Air Ministry (acting Air Commodore), 1958; Air Commodore, 1959. *Recreations:* golf, painting. *Address:* Windrush, Harborough Hill, West Chiltington, West Sussex. *Clubs:* West Sussex Golf; RAF Changi Golf.

HELY-HUTCHINSON, family name of **Earl of Donoughmore.**

HEMINGFORD, 2nd Baron, *cr* 1943, of Watford; **Dennis George Ruddock Herbert,** MA; JP; Lieutenant of Cambridgeshire, 1974-75 (Lord Lieutenant of Huntingdon and Peterborough, 1968-74); Vice-President, Africa Bureau (Chairman, 1952-63); *b* 25 March 1904; *s* of 1st Baron Hemingford, PC, KBE; *S* father 1947; *m* 1932, Elizabeth McClare, *d* of late Col J. M. Clark, Haltwhistle, Northumberland; one *s* two *d*. *Educ:* Oundle; Brasenose Coll., Oxford. Master, Achimota Coll., Gold Coast, 1926-39; Headmaster, King's Coll., Budo, Uganda (CMS), 1939-47; Rector Achimota Training Coll., Gold Coast, 1948-51. Mem., London Government Staff Commission, 1963-65. JP Hunts, 1960-65, Huntingdon and Peterborough, 1965-74, Cambs, 1974. CC 1952, CA 1959, Chm. CC, 1961-65, Hunts; Alderman, Huntingdon and Peterborough CC, 1965-74, Vice-Chm., 1965-67, Chm., 1967-71. *Heir: s* Hon. Dennis Nicholas Herbert, *qv*. *Address:* The Coach House, Hemingford Abbots, Huntingdon. *T:* St Ives, Hunts, 62375. *Clubs:* Royal Commonwealth Society, National.

HEMINGWAY, Albert, MSc, MB, ChB; Emeritus Professor, University of Leeds (Professor of Physiology, 1936-67); *b* 1902; *s* of Herbert Hemingway, Leeds; *m* 1930, Margaret Alice Cooper; one *d*. *Educ:* University of Leeds. Demonstrator in Physiology, King's Coll., London, 1925; Senior Asst in Physiology, University Coll., London, 1926; Lecturer in Experimental Physiology, Welsh National Sch. of Medicine, 1927. Vis. Prof., Makerere University Coll., Uganda, 1968. Examiner in Physiology, Universities of St Andrews, Birmingham, Bristol, Cambridge, Durham, Glasgow, Liverpool, London, Manchester, Wales and RCS. Mem. various cttees of MRC on work and exercise physiology; Mem. Cttee, Physiological Soc. (Editor, Jl Physiology); Pres., Section I, British Assoc., 1959. *Publications:* original papers on the physiology of the circulation, exercise and the kidney in scientific and medical journals. *Recreations:* athletics, travel. *Address:* 4 Helmsley Drive, Leeds LS16 5HY. *T:* Leeds 785720.

HEMLOW, Prof. Joyce; Professor Emerita, McGill University, Montreal, Canada; author; *b* 30 July 1906; *d* of William Hemlow and Rosalinda (*née* Redmond), Liscomb, NS. *Educ:* Queen's Univ., Kingston, Ont (MA; Hon. LLD 1967); Harvard Univ., Cambridge, Mass (AM, PhD). Preceding a univ. career, period of teaching in Nova Scotia, Canada; lecturer in English Language and Literature at McGill Univ.; Prof. of English Language and Literature, McGill Univ., 1955-, now part-time.

FRSC 1960. Guggenheim Fellow, 1951-52, 1960-62 and 1966. Member: Phi Beta Kappa, The Johnsonians, and of other literary and professional organizations. Hon. LLD Dalhousie, 1972. James Tait Black Memorial Book Prize, 1958; Brit. Academy Award (Crawshay Prize), 1960. *Publications:* The History of Fanny Burney, 1958 (GB); (ed with others) The Journals and Letters of Fanny Burney (Madame d'Arblay), vols 1 and 2, 1972, vols 3 and 4, 1973, vols 5 and 6, 1976; articles in learned jls on Fanny Burney's novels and unpublished plays. *Address:* (home) Liscomb, Nova Scotia, Canada; The Crestwood, 3555 Atwater Avenue, Montreal, Canada. *Club:* English-Speaking Union (Canadian Branch).

HEMMING, Air Commodore Idris George Selvin, CB 1968; CBE 1959 (OBE 1954); retired; *b* 11 Dec. 1911; *s* of late George Hemming, Liverpool; *m* 1939, Phyllis, *d* of Francis Payne, Drogheda, Eire; two *s. Educ:* Chalford, Glos.; Wallasey, Cheshire. Joined RAF, 1928; served War of 1939-45, UK, India and Burma; Gp Capt. 1957; Air Cdre 1962; Dir of Equipment (Pol.) (RAF), MoD, 1962-66; Dir of Equipment (1) (RAF), MoD, Harrogate, 1966-68. *Recreations:* cricket, golf. *Address:* Ash House, St Chloe Green, Amberley, near Stroud, Glos GL5 5AP. *T:* Amberley 3581. *Club:* Royal Air Force.

HEMMING, John Henry; Joint Chairman, Municipal Journal Ltd, since 1976 (Director, since 1962; Deputy Chairman, 1967-76); Director and Secretary, Royal Geographical Society, since 1975; *b* 5 Jan. 1935; *s* of late Henry Harold Hemming, OBE, MC, and of Alice Louisa Weaver, OBE. *Educ:* Eton College; McGill University; Oxford University. Dep. Chm., Brintex Ltd, 1976- (Man. Dir, 1963-70). Member, Iriri River Expedition, Brazil, 1961. *Publications:* The Conquest of the Incas, 1970 (Robert Pitman Literary Prize, 1970, Christopher Award, NY, 1971); (jt) Tribes of the Amazon Basin in Brazil, 1972; Red Gold: The Conquest of the Brazilian Indians, 1976. *Recreations:* writing, travel. *Address:* 178-202 Great Portland Street, W1. *T:* 01-637 2400. *Clubs:* Travellers', Beefsteak, Geographical. *See also L . A . Service .*

HEMMINGS, David Leslie Edward; actor and director; engaged in entertainment industry since 1949; *b* 18 Nov. 1941; *m* 1st, 1960, Genista Ouvry; one *d*; 2nd, 1969, Gayle Hunnicutt (marr. diss. 1975); one *s*; 3rd, 1976, Prudence J. de Casembroot; two *s. Educ:* Glyn Coll., Epsom, Surrey. The Turn of the Screw, English Opera Group, 1954; Five Clues to Fortune, 1957; Saint Joan, 1957; The Heart Within, 1957; Men of Tomorrow, 1958; In the Wake of a Stranger, 1958; No Trees in the Street, 1959; Some People, 1962; Play it Cool, 1962; Live it Up, 1963; Two Left Feet, 1963; The System, 1964; Be my Guest, 1965; Eye of the Devil, 1966; Blow Up, 1966; Camelot, 1967; Barbarella, 1967; Only When I Larf, 1968; The Charge of the Light Brigade, 1968; The Long Day's Dying, 1968; The Best House in London, 1968; Alfred the Great, 1969; Fragment of Fear, 1970; The Walking Stick, 1970; Unman, Wittering & Zigo, 1971; The Love Machine, 1971; Voices, 1973; Don't Worry Momma, 1973; Juggernaut, 1974; Quilp, 1974; Profundo Rosso, 1975; Islands in the Stream, 1975; The Squeeze, 1976; Jeeves (musical), Her Majesty's, 1975. BBC TV, Scott Fitzgerald, 1975. Directed: Running Scared, 1972; The 14, 1973 (Silver Bear Award, Berlin Film Festival, 1973). *Recreation:* painting. *Address:* 94 Onslow Gardens, SW7. *Clubs:* Turf, Chelsea Arts, Magic Circle.

HEMP, Prof. William Spooner, MA, FRAeS; Stewarts and Lloyds Professor of Structural Engineering, Oxford University, since 1965; Professorial Fellow of Keble College, Oxford, since 1965; *b* 21 March 1916; *s* of late Rev. William James Hemp and Daisy Lilian Hemp; *m* 1938, Dilys Ruth Davies; one *s. Educ:* Paston Grammar Sch., North Walsham; Jesus Coll., Cambridge (Scholar, MA). Aeronautical Engineer, Bristol Aeroplane Co., 1938-46. Coll. of Aeronautics: Senior Lecturer, 1946-50; Prof. of Aircraft Structures and Aeroelasticity, 1950-65; Head of Dept of Aircraft Design, 1951-65; Dep. Principal, 1957-65. Mem. of various cttees of Aeronautical Research Council since 1948. Visiting Prof., Stanford Univ., Calif., 1960-61. *Publications:* Optimum Structures, 1973; research papers in the Theory of Structures, Solid Mechanics and Applied Mathematics. *Recreations:* mountain walking, music. *Address:* Department of Engineering Science, Park Road, Oxford. *T:* Oxford 59988.

HEMPHILL, 5th Baron *cr* 1906, of Rathkenny and Cashel; **Peter Patrick Fitzroy Martyn Martyn-Hemphill;** *b* 5 Sept. 1928; *o s* of 4th Baron Hemphill and Emily, *d* of F. Irving Sears, Webster, Mass; *S* father 1957; *m* 1952, Olivia Anne, *er d* of Major Robert Francis Ruttledge, MC, Cloonee, Ballinrobe, County Mayo; one *s* two *d*; assumed surname of Martyn in addition to Hemphill, 1959. *Educ:* Downside; Brasenose Coll., Oxford (MA). *Heir: s* Hon. Charles Andrew Martyn Martyn-Hemphill, *b* 8 Oct. 1954. *Address:* Tulira, Ardrahan, Co. Galway, Eire. *T:* Ardrahan 4.

Clubs: Royal Automobile, White's; Kildare Street and University (Dublin); County (Galway).

HEMSLEY, Thomas Jeffrey; free-lance opera and concert singer; *b* 12 April 1927; *s* of Sydney William Hemsley and Kathleen Annie Hemsley (*née* Deacon); *m* 1960, Hon. Gwenllian Ellen James, *d* of 4th Baron Northbourne, *qv*; three *s. Educ:* Ashby de la Zouch Grammar Sch.; Brasenose Coll., Oxford (MA). Vicar Choral, St Paul's Cathedral, 1950-51; Prin. Baritone, Stadttheater, Aachen, 1953-56; Deutsche Oper am Rhein, 1957-63; Opernhaus, Zurich, 1963-67; Glyndebourne, Bayreuth, Edinburgh Festivals, etc. Hon. RAM 1974. *Address:* 10 Denewood Road, N6. *T:* 01-348 3397.

HENBEST, Prof. Harold Bernard; Professor of Organic Chemistry at the Queen's University, Belfast, 1958-73; *b* 10 March 1924; *s* of A. Bernard Henbest and Edith Winifred Herbert; *m* 1948, Rosalind Eve Skone James; two *s* one *d. Educ:* Barking Abbey Sch.; Imperial Coll. of Science, London. Beit Research Fellow, 1947-48; Lectr, University of Manchester, 1948-56; Research Fellow, Harvard Univ., 1953-54; Vis. Prof., UCLA, 1954; Reader, KCL, 1956-57. *Publications:* Organic Chemistry (with M. F. Grundon), 1968; contribs to Jl of Chemical Soc. *Address:* 1 St Albans Gardens, Belfast, Northern Ireland.

HENDEL, Prof. Charles William; Professor Emeritus of Moral Philosophy and Metaphysics, Yale University; *b* 16 Dec. 1890; *s* of Charles William Hendel and Emma Stolz, American; *m* 1916, Elizabeth Phoebe Jones (*d* 1977); two *s. Educ:* Princeton Univ. LittB 1913; PhD 1917. United States Army, 1917-18, 2nd Lieut Infantry. Instructor, Williams Coll., 1919-20; Asst and Associate Prof., Princeton Univ., 1920-29; MacDonald Prof. of Moral Philosophy, McGill Univ., 1929-40; Chm. of Philosophy, 1929-40; Dean of Faculty of Arts and Science, 1937-40; Clarke Prof. of Moral Philosophy and Metaphysics, Yale Univ., 1940-59; Chm. of Dept, 1940-45 and 1950-59; Prof. Emeritus, 1959-. Gifford Lecturer, University of Glasgow, 1962-63. Hon. MA Yale, 1940. President: American Philosophical Assoc. (Eastern Div.), 1940; American Soc. for Political and Legal Philosophy, 1959-61. *Publications:* Studies in the Philosophy of David Hume, 1925 (2nd edn enlarged with Supplement, 1963); (jointly) Contemporary Idealism in America, 1932; Jean Jacques Rousseau, Moralist, 2 vols 1934 (2nd edn with Preface, 1963); Citizen of Geneva, 1937; Civilization and Religion, 1948; The Philosophy of Kant and our Modern World; John Dewey: Philosophy and the Experimental Spirit, 1959; many translations, joint authorships, and edns of philosophical works. *Recreations:* music; out-of-doors, in woods, fields and mountains. *Address:* The Brandon Inn, Brandon, Vermont 05733, USA. *T:* 247-5766.

HENDER, John Derrik; DL; Chief Executive, West Midlands Metropolitan County Council, since 1973; *b* 15 Nov. 1926; *s* of late Jessie Peter and late Jennie Hender; *m* 1949, Kathleen Nora Brown; one *d. Educ:* Great Yarmouth Grammar School. IPFA, FCA, FBIM. Deputy Borough Treasurer: Newcastle-under-Lyme, 1957-61; Wolverhampton County Borough, 1961-64; City Treas. 1965-69, Chief Exec. and Town Clerk 1969-73, Coventry County Borough. FBIM 1975. DL West Midlands, 1975. *Publications:* numerous articles relating to various aspects of local govt and related matters. *Recreation:* gardening. *Address:* West Midlands County Council, County Hall, 1 Lancaster Circus, Queensway, Birmingham B4 7DJ. *T:* 021-300 6000.

HENDERSON, family name of **Barons Faringdon** and **Henderson.**

HENDERSON, 1st Baron, *cr* 1945, of Westgate in the City and County of Newcastle upon Tyne; **William Watson Henderson,** PC 1950; Director, Alliance Building Society, 1955-75 (Chairman, 1966-72); journalist and political writer; *b* Newcastle upon Tyne, 8 Aug. 1891; *s* of late Rt Hon. Arthur Henderson, MP. *Educ:* Queen Elizabeth Grammar Sch., Darlington. Editorial Sec., Daily Citizen, 1912-14; Parliamentary Correspondent, Labour Press Dept, 1919-21; Lobby Correspondent, Daily Herald, 1919-21; Sec., Press and Publicity Dept, Labour Party, 1921-45; Private Sec. to Rt Hon. John Hodge, MP, Minister of Labour, 1917; Prospective Labour Candidate, Bridgwater Div. of Somerset, 1919-21; MP (Lab) Enfield, 1923-24 and 1929-31; Parliamentary Private Sec. to the Sec. of State for India, 1929-31; Personal Asst to Rt Hon. Arthur Greenwood, MP (Minister without Portfolio and Mem. of the War Cabinet), 1940-42; an additional mem. of the Air Council, 1945-47; a Lord in Waiting to the King, 1945-48; a Parly Under-Sec. of State, FO, 1948-51. A British Representative at Assembly of Council of Europe, 1954 and 1955; Labour Peers representative on Parliamentary Cttee of Parliamentary Labour Party, 1952-55. President: UN Parly Gp; Westminster Br., UNA. *Address:* 707 Collingwood House, Dolphin Square, SW1. *T:* 01-834 3800.

HENDERSON, Barry; *see* Henderson, J. S. B.

HENDERSON, Rt. Rev. Charles Joseph; Auxiliary Bishop in Southwark, (RC), since 1972; Titular Bishop of Tricala, since 1972; Parish Priest, St Mary's, Blackheath, since 1969; *b* 14 April 1924; *s* of Charles Stuart Henderson and Hanora Henderson (*née* Walsh). *Educ:* Mount Sion Sch., Waterford; St John's Seminary, Waterford. Priest, 1948; Curate, St Stephen's, Welling, Kent, 1948-55; English Martyrs, Streatham, SW16, 1955-58; Chancellor, RC Diocese of Southwark, 1958-70; Vicar General, RC Diocese of Arundel and Brighton, 1965-66; Episcopal Vicar for Religious, Southwark, 1968-73; Vicar General, RC Archdiocese of Southwark, 1969; Canon of Cathedral Chapter, 1972; Provost of Cathedral Chapter, 1973. Papal Chamberlain, 1960; Prelate of Papal Household, 1965. Freeman, City of Waterford, 1973. Kt Comdr of Equestrian Order of Holy Sepulchre, Jerusalem, 1973. *Recreation:* special interest in sport. *Address:* Park House, 6A Cresswell Park, Blackheath, SE3 9RD. *T:* 01-318 1094.

HENDERSON, Douglas Mackay, FRSE 1966; Regius Keeper, Royal Botanic Garden, Edinburgh, since 1970; *b* 30 Aug. 1927; *s* of Captain Frank Henderson and Adine C. Mackay; *m* 1952, Julia Margaret Brown; one *s* two *d*. *Educ:* Blairgowrie High Sch.; Edinburgh Univ. (BSc). Scientific Officer, Dept of Agriculture and Fisheries for Scotland, 1948-51. Royal Botanic Garden, Edinburgh, 1951-. *Publications:* British Rust Fungi (with M. Wilson), 1966; many papers on taxonomy of cryptogams. *Recreations:* music, art, hill walking, field natural history, sailing. *Address:* 12 Afton Terrace, Edinburgh EH5 3NG. *T:* 031-552 3457.

HENDERSON, Rt. Rev. Edward Barry, DSC 1944; DD (Lambeth) 1960; *b* 22 March 1910; 2nd *s* of late Dean of Salisbury, the Very Rev. E. L. Henderson; *m* 1935, Hester Borradaile Taylor; one *s* two *d*. *Educ:* Radley; Trinity Coll., Cambridge. Curate of St Gabriel's, Pimlico, 1934-36; Priest-in-charge, All Saints, Pimlico, 1936-39; Rector of Holy Trinity, Ayr, 1939-47; Chaplain, RNVR, 1943-44; Vicar of St Paul's, Knightsbridge, 1947-55; Rural Dean of Westminster, 1952-55; Bishop Suffragan of Tewkesbury, 1955-60; Bishop of Bath and Wells, 1960-75. Chm., Church of England Youth Council, 1961-69. Chaplain and Sub-Prelate, Order of St John of Jerusalem, 1961. Hon. Freeman, City of Wells, 1974. Hon. DLitt Bath, 1975. *Recreations:* fishing, golf, and sailing. *Address:* Hill Cottage, Ryme Intrinseca, near Sherborne, Dorset. *T:* Yetminster 894.

HENDERSON, Ven. Edward Chance, BD, ALCD; Archdeacon of Pontefract, since 1968; *b* 15 Oct. 1916; *s* of William Edward and Mary Anne Henderson; *m* 1942, Vera Massie Pattison; two *s* three *d*. *Educ:* Heaton Grammar Sch.; London University. Asst Curate, St Stephen, Newcastle upon Tyne, 1939-42; Organising Sec., CPAS, 1942-45; Vicar of St Mary of Bethany, Leeds, 1945-51; Priest i/c: Annley Hall, Leeds, 1948-51; St John, New Wortley, Leeds, 1949-51; Vicar of: All Souls, Halifax, 1951-59; Dewsbury, 1959-68; Darrington with Wentbridge, 1968-75. Examining Chaplain to Bishop of Wakefield, 1972-. *Address:* 12 Park Lane, Balne, Goole, North Humberside DN14 0EP. *T:* Goole 85284.

HENDERSON, Edward Firth, CMG 1972; HM Diplomatic Service, retired; *b* 12 Dec. 1917; *m* 1960, Jocelyn (*née* Nenk); two *d*. *Educ:* Clifton Coll.; BNC, Oxford. Served War of 1939-45 in Army (despatches); served in Arab Legion, 1945-47. With Petroleum Concessions Ltd, in Arabian Gulf, 1948-56; seconded to Foreign Service, 1956-59; established 1959; served in Middle East posts and in Foreign Office; Counsellor, 1969; Political Agent, Qatar, 1969-71, and Ambassador there 1971-74. Dir, M & G Securities Ltd, 1975-. *Address:* c/o Barclays Bank Ltd, 1 Pall Mall East, SW1. *Club:* Travellers'.

HENDERSON, Rear-Adm. Geoffrey Archer, CB 1969; retired; Administration Manager, National Mutual Life Assurance Society, since 1970; *b* 14 Aug. 1913; *s* of late Sir Charles James Henderson, KBE; *m* 1959 Pamela (Rachel), *d* of late Sir Philip Petrides; one *s* one *d*. *Educ:* Christ's Hosp. Entered RN, 1931. Served War of 1939-45; HMS Onslow, 1941-42 (despatches); Sec. to Asst Chief of Naval Staff (F), 1943-44. HMS Newfoundland, 1952-55; HMS Victorious, 1957-58; Cabinet Office, 1959-61; idc 1962; Director of Naval Officer Appointments (S), 1963-65; Commodore, RN Barracks, Portsmouth, 1965-66; ADC 1966; Naval Mem. of Senior

Directing Staff, Imperial Defence Coll., 1966-68; Chief Naval Supply and Secretariat Officer, 1968-70, and Dir, Management and Support Intelligence, MoD, 1969-70. *Address:* Pigeon's Green, St Mary's Platt, Sevenoaks, Kent TN15 8NL. *T:* Borough Green 882462.

HENDERSON, Rt. Rev. George Kennedy Buchanan; *see* Argyll and the Isles, Bishop of.

HENDERSON, Prof. George Patrick; Professor of Philosophy in the University of Dundee (formerly Queen's College, Dundee), since 1959, Dean, Faculty of Arts and Social Sciences, 1973-76; *b* 22 April 1915; *e s* of Rev. George Aitchison Henderson, MA, and Violet Margaret Mackenzie; *m* 1939, Hester Lowry Douglas McWilliam, BSc, *d* of Rev. John Morell McWilliam, BA. *Educ:* Elgin Academy; St Andrews Univ. (Harkness Scholar); Balliol Coll., Oxford. 1st Class Hons in Philosophy, University of St Andrews, 1936; Miller Prize and Ramsay Scholarship; MA 1936; Ferguson Scholarship in Philosophy, 1936; 2nd Class Lit Hum, University of Oxford, 1938; BA 1938. Asst in Logic and Metaphysics, University of St Andrews, 1938; Shaw Fellow in Mental Philosophy, University of Edinburgh, 1938. MA Oxon, 1943. Army Service, 1940-46; Royal Artillery (commissioned 1940, Adjutant 1942-43) and Gen. Staff (GSO 3 1945); served in UK, Italy and Greece. Lecturer in Logic and Metaphysics, University of St Andrews, 1945; Senior Lecturer, 1953. Corresp. Member: Acad. of Athens, 1973; Ionian Acad., 1975. Editor of the Philosophical Quarterly, 1962-72. *Publications:* The Revival of Greek Thought, 1620-1830, 1970; numerous articles and reviews in principal philosophical periodicals. *Recreations:* modern Greek studies, gardening. *Address:* Department of Philosophy, Dundee University, Dundee DD1 4HN.

HENDERSON, Sir Guy (Wilmot McLintock), Kt 1956; BA, LLB Cantab; QC (Uganda) 1949; Chief Justice of the Bahamas, 1951-60, retired; *b* 13 July 1897; *e s* of late Arthur James and Charlotte West Henderson; *m* 1930, Ann, *d* of late George and Elizabeth Dring-Campion; two *s* one *d*. *Educ:* Blundell's, Tiverton; Collegiate Sch., Wanganui, NZ; Trinity Coll., Cambridge. Served European War, 1914-18, Lieut RFA (SR). Barrister-at-Law, Inner Temple, 1923; private practice, Rangoon, Burma, 1924-29; professional clerk, prosecuting staff GPO, London, 1930-32; stipendiary and circuit magistrate, Bahamas, 1932-37; Crown Counsel, Tanganyika Territory, 1937-40; legal draftsman, Nigeria, 1940-45; dep. Chief Legal Adviser, British Military Administration, Malaya, 1945-46; Solicitor-Gen., Colony of Singapore, 1946-48; Attorney-Gen., Uganda Protectorate, 1948-51. *Address:* PO Box N 7776, Nassau, Bahamas.

HENDERSON, James Ewart, MA; Financial Consultant, Charles Stapleton & Co. Ltd, since 1973; Aviation Consultant, Hawker Siddeley Aviation Ltd, since 1973; free-lance Operational Research and Management Consultant, since 1975; Director, Lewis Security Systems, since 1976; *b* 29 May 1923; *s* of late Rev. James Ewart Henderson, MA, BD and Agnes Mary (*née* Crawford); *m* 1st, 1949, Alice Joan Hewlitt; one *d*; 2nd, 1966, Nancy Maude Dominy; two *s*. *Educ:* private sch.; Glasgow Univ.; Edinburgh Univ. Research on air rockets and guns, MAP, 1943-44; hon. commn in RAFVR, 1944-46; operational assessment of air attacks in Belgium, Holland and Germany, 2TAF, 1944-45; exper. research on fighter and bomber capability, and on the use of radar and radio aids: RAF APC Germany, 1945-46, Fighter Comd, 1946-49 and CFE, 1949-52; research on weapons effects and capability: Air Min., 1952-54, AWRE 1955, Air Min., 1955-58; Asst Scientific Adviser (Ops), Air Min., 1958-63; Dep. Chief Scientist (RAF), MoD, 1963-69; Chief Scientist (RAF) and Mem., Air Force Bd, 1969-73. *Publications:* technical papers on operational capability of aircraft and weapons; UK manual on Blast Effects of Nuclear Weapons. *Recreations:* flying, sailing, golf, opera, photography. *Clubs:* Naval and Military; Royal Scottish Automobile (Glasgow); Moor Park Golf.

HENDERSON, (James Stewart) Barry; management consultant; *b* 29 April 1936; *s* of James Henderson, CBE and Jane Stewart McLaren; *m* 1961, Janet Helen Sprot Todd; two *s*. *Educ:* Lathallan Sch.; Stowe Sch. Mem. British Computer Soc. Nat. Service, 1954-56; electronics and computer industries, 1957-65; Scottish Conservative Central Office, 1966-70; computer industry, 1971-74. MP (C) East Dunbartonshire, Feb.-Sept. 1974. Prospective Parly Cand. (C), Fife East, 1975-. *Address:* Midcraig, Wormit, Fife DD6 8RN. *T:* Gauldry 217.

HENDERSON, Sir James Thyne, KBE 1959; CMG 1952; *b* 18 Jan. 1901; *s* of late Sir Thomas Henderson; *m* 1930, Karen Margrethe Hansen; one *s* four *d*. *Educ:* Warriston, Moffat; Sedbergh Sch.; Queen's Coll., Oxford. Entered Diplomatic

Service, 1925, apptd to FO; transf. to Tehran, 1927; Athens, 1929; Helsinki, 1932, where acted as Chargé d'Affaires in 1932, 1933, 1934 and 1935; Foreign Office, 1935. First Sec., 1936; attached to Representative of Finland at the Coronation of King George VI, 1937; Tokyo, 1938; Santiago, 1941; Foreign Office, 1944; Stockholm, 1946, Chargé d'Affaires there in 1946 and 1947; Counsellor, 1947; Consul-Gen., Houston, 1949; HM Minister to Iceland, 1953-56; HM Ambassador to Bolivia, 1956-60, retired. *Recreation:* gardening. *Address:* 4 Merchiston Crescent, Edinburgh EH10 5AN. *T:* 031-229 1185. *Club:* Royal Automobile.

HENDERSON, Dame Joan; *see* Kelleher, Dame Joan.

HENDERSON, Prof. John Louis, MD, FRCPE; Professor of Child Health, University of Dundee, 1967-72, retired; *b* 25 March 1907; British; *m* 1st, 1938, Agnes Deneson McHarg, MB, ChB (*d* 1963); one *s* three *d*; 2nd, 1964, Helen Nea Carlisle Richards (*née* Attenborough). *Educ:* Leighton Park Sch., Reading; University of Edinburgh. Sen. Pres., Royal Medical Society, Edinburgh 1934-35; Lecturer, Dept of Child Health, University of Edinburgh, 1939-45; Rockefeller Travelling Fellow at Yale and Harvard, USA, 1946; Senior Lecturer, Dept of Child Health, University of Edinburgh, 1947-51; Physician, Royal Edinburgh Hosp. for Sick Children, 1948-51; Prof. of Child Health, University of St Andrews, 1951-67. Member: Scottish Health Services Council, 1953-62; GMC, 1968-; Chm. Standing Med. Adv. Cttee, Dept of Health for Scotland, 1956-62. *Publications:* Cerebral Palsy in Childhood and Adolescence, 1961; articles in medical journals. *Recreations:* golf, ornithology. *Address:* Dron, Invergowrie, by Dundee, DD2 5LH.

HENDERSON, Sir (John) Nicholas, GCMG 1977 (KCMG 1972; CMG 1965); HM Diplomatic Service; Ambassador to France, since 1975; *b* 1 April 1919; *s* of Prof. Sir Hubert Henderson; *m* 1951, Mary Barber (*née* Cawadias); one *d*. *Educ:* Stowe Sch.; Hertford Coll., Oxford (Hon. Fellow 1975). Mem. HM Diplomatic Service. Served Minister of State's Office, Cairo, 1942-43; Asst Private Sec. to the Foreign Sec., 1944-47; HM Embassy, Washington, 1947-49; Athens, 1949-50; Permanent Under Secretary's Dept, FO, 1950-53; HM Embassy, Vienna, 1953-56; Santiago, 1956-59; Northern Dept, FO, 1959-62; Permanent Under Secretary's Dept, 1962-63; Head of Northern Dept, Foreign Office, 1963; Private Sec. to the Sec. of State for Foreign Affairs, 1963-65; Minister in Madrid, 1965-69; Ambassador to Poland, 1969-72, to Federal Republic of Germany, 1972-75. *Publications:* Prince Eugen of Savoy (biography); various stories and articles in Penguin New Writing, Horizon, Apollo and History Today. *Recreations:* tennis, gardening, dogs. *Address:* 6 Fairholt Street, SW7. *T:* 01-589 4291; School House, Combe, near Newbury, Berks. *T:* Inkpen 330; c/o Foreign and Commonwealth Office, SW1. *Club:* Brooks's.

HENDERSON, John Stuart Wilmot; Director General of Ordnance Factories, Finance, Procurement and Administration, retired 1976; *b* 31 March 1919; *s* of Bruce Wilmot Henderson and Sarah (*née* Marchant); *m* 1941, Elsie Kathleen (*née* Rose); one *s* three *d*. *Educ:* Wade Deacon Grammar Sch., Widnes. Exec. Officer, Royal Ordnance Factories, 1938-39; served War of 1939-45: Royal Fusiliers, 1939-43; Intell. Corps, 1944-47; various appts in Ministries of Supply, Aviation, Technology and Defence, 1947-. *Recreations:* travelling, enjoying music, arguing. *Address:* Garth Down, Church Lane, Trottiscliffe, Kent. *T:* Fairseat 822863.

HENDERSON, Julia Juanita; Secretary-General, International Planned Parenthood Federation, since 1971; *b* 15 Aug. 1915; *d* of Frank and Agnes Henderson. *Educ:* Univs of Illinois (BA, MA) and Minnesota (PhD); Harvard Grad. Sch. of Public Admin. Research Asst, SSRC, 1938-39; Techn. Adviser, Unemployment Compensation Div., Social Security Bd, 1939-42; Lectr in Polit. Science, Wellesley Coll., 1942-44; United Nations: Mem. Secretariat on Organization and Budget Preparatory Commn of UN, London, 1945-46; Chief of Policy Div., Bureau of Finance, 1946-50; Dir, Div. of Social Welfare, Dept of Social Affairs, 1951-54; Dir, Bureau of Social Affairs, Dept of Econ. and Social Affairs, 1955-67; Assoc. Comr and Dir for Techn. Co-operation, 1967-71. Mem. Nat. Acad. of Public Admin; Mem. Council on Foreign Relations. Hon. LLD, Smith Coll., 1967; Hon. LittD, Rider Coll., 1969; Hon. DHum, Silliman Univ., 1975; Rene Sand Award, Internat. Council of Social Welfare, 1972. *Recreations:* music, theatre, golf, tennis. *Address:* Flat 3, 44 Cadogan Square, SW1. *T:* 01-584 7991. *Club:* United Oxford & Cambridge University.

HENDERSON, Keith, OBE; RWS; RSW; ROI; PS; *b* 1883; *er s* of George MacDonald Henderson and Constance Helen, *d* of

James Keith; *m* Helen (*d* 1972), *d* of Charles Knox-Shaw. *Educ:* Marlborough; Paris. Served Aug. 1914 to end of war (despatches twice). Pictures in Public Galleries, Manchester, Preston, Birmingham, Worthing, Newport, Leamington, Dublin, Glasgow, Aberdeen, Lancaster, Carlisle, Dundee, Swansea, Perth, Kirkaldy; many pictures and drawings in American and Canadian collections. War Artist to the Air Force, 1940. Each winter since 1971, off to the Equator to make studies of world's ever diminishing wild life. *Publications:* (also illustrator of) Letters to Helen; Palm-groves and Hummingbirds; Prehistoric Man; Burns by himself; Till 21 (autobiog.); The Labyrinth; The Romaunt of the Rose; The Conquest of Mexico; Green Mansions; No Second Spring; Buckaroo; Christina Strang; Highland Pack; Scotland before History, etc. *Address:* 9 St George's Terrace, Regent's Park, NW1 8XH.

HENDERSON, Kenneth David Druitt, CMG 1951; Secretary, Spalding Educational Trust and Union for the Study of Great Religions, since 1953; Vice-President, World Congress of Faiths, since 1966; *b* 4 Sept. 1903; *s* of late George Gilfillan Henderson, MA, MB, CM (Edinburgh); *m* 1935, Margery Grant, *d* of John Atkinson, Sydney, NSW; one *s* two *d*. *Educ:* Glenalmond; University Coll., Oxford. Entered Sudan Political Service, 1926; Dept Asst Civil Sec., 1938-44; Sec. to Governor-General's Council, 1939-44, to N Sudan Advisory Council, 1944; Principal Sch. of Administration and Police, Omdurman, 1944; Deputy-Governor, Kassala Province, Sudan, 1945; Asst Civil Sec., 1946-49; Governor, Darfur Province, Sudan, 1949-53. Officer, Order of the Nile, 1937. *Publications:* History of the Hamar Tribe, 1935; Survey of the Anglo-Egyptian Sudan, 1898-1944, 1945; The Making of The Modern Sudan, 1952; Sudan Republic, 1965; Account of the Parish of Langford, 1973; contribs to Chambers's Encyclopædia, Encyclopædia Britannica, and Encyclopædia Americana. *Address:* Orchard House, Steeple Langford, Salisbury, Wilts. *T:* Stapleford 388. *Club:* Athenæum.

HENDERSON, Air Vice-Marshal Malcolm, CB 1942; CIE 1938; CBE 1953; DSO 1916; RAF, retired; Director General, Over-Seas League, 1946-56; *b* 1 June 1891; 2nd *s* of late Lessels Henderson and *g s* of late George Malcolm, Dundee; *m* 1918, Elizabeth, *d* of late Frederick Craig, St Columb, North Cornwall; two *s* one *d* (and one *s* killed in action over France (Dunkerque), RAF, 1940). Served War of 1914-18 with Seaforth Highlanders, RFC and RAF; seriously wounded with 18 Sqdn RFC, losing leg by direct hit from AA. Comd 47 Sqdn, Egypt, 1922-25; RAF Staff Coll., 1926; IDC 1933; AOC: 14(F) Gp, 1940; 13 (F) Gp, 1942; 12 (F) Gp, 1945; retd 1946. Croix de Guerre with Palmes (France). *Address:* Beach House, Pevensey Bay, East Sussex.

HENDERSON, Sir Malcolm (Siborne), KCMG 1961 (CMG 1952); HM Diplomatic Service, retired; *b* 21 April 1905; *s* of late Lt-Col Kenneth Henderson; *m* 1933, Paula Elizabeth Wilms; two *d*. *Educ:* Winchester and privately. MA Edinburgh. Vice-Consul, Antwerp, 1927-30, Chicago, 1930-35, New York, 1935-42; Consul, Atlanta, 1942-44; Foreign Office, 1944-47; Counsellor (Commercial) and Consul-Gen., Lisbon, 1947-52; Land Commissioner, Hanover, 1952-55, and Consul-Gen., 1954-55; Ambassador: to Grand Duchy of Luxembourg, 1955-57; to Republic of Uruguay, 1957-61; to Austria, 1961-65. *Address:* 32 Cadogan Place, SW1X 9RX. *Club:* Travellers'.

HENDERSON, Sir Neville (Vicars), Kt 1975; CBE 1967; Founder of firm of Henderson & Lahey, Solicitors, Brisbane, 1924; retired to become consultant, 1971; grazier and company director, Australia; *b* 21 March 1899; *s* of John Cunningham Henderson, grazier, late of Brougham, Toowong, Brisbane, formerly of Goulburn, NSW, etc, and Ann Janet Henderson, *d* of Capt. Lachlan Macalister, 48th Regt; *m* 1934, Jean Hamilton Brownhill, *d* of David James Brownhill, Sydney, NSW; one *s* two *d*. *Educ:* Southport Sch., Southport, Qld; Univ. of Qld, Brisbane; Trinity Coll., Univ. of Melbourne, Vic. Final Hons Schol. in Law and Supreme Ct Prizeman (Melb.) 1922; BA, LLM (Melb.) 1922. Barrister and solicitor of Supreme Ct of Vic., 1923, and of High Ct of Aust., 1923; Solicitor of Supreme Ct of Qld, 1923; Notary Public, 1945. Mem. Council, Qld Law Assoc., 1926; assisted in drafting Act, 1927, and has taken part in Law Reform since that time; also Sec. Qld Law Soc. Incorp., 1928-54, and Clerk to Statutory Cttee of the Soc., 1928-31, also its delegate at Aust. Law Conf., Sydney (at which Law Council of Aust. was formed), 1932; Council, St John's Coll., Univ. of Qld, 1932-38; Sec., Law Council of Aust., 1939-40. Captain, AMF, 1932. Served War, 1940-44: Major, 1942, and apptd Dep. Asst Adj.-Gen., Northern Comd; assisted in organising course for rehabilitation of legal ex-Servicemen, and Hon. Lectr in Law of Life Ins., 1945. Sen. Partner, Henderson & Sons, Graziers, Mahrigong Station, Winton, Qld, 1950; Pres., Soc. of Notaries of Queensland, 1954-56; Founder and Governor, Henderson

Foundn (educnl and charitable instn), 1957. Man. Editor for Annotated Reprint of Qld Statutes (20 vols), 1962. Hon. Consul for Austria, Qld, 1957. Dist. Service Order in gold of Republic of Austria, Kt Cross First Cl., 1964. *Publications:* Estate Planning (Proc. of Second Commonwealth and Empire Law Conf., Ottawa, 1960), etc. *Address:* Glencraig, 63 Eldernell Avenue, Hamilton, Brisbane, Qld 4007, Australia. *T:* 268-3953. *Clubs:* Queensland, United Service, Queensland Turf, Tattersalls (all in Brisbane); Australasian Pioneers' (Sydney).

HENDERSON, Sir Nicholas; *see* Henderson, Sir J. N.

HENDERSON, Admiral Sir Nigel Stuart, GBE 1968 (OBE 1944); KCB 1962 (CB 1959); DL; Vice-Admiral of the United Kingdom, and Lieutenant of the Admiralty, since 1976; *b* 1 Aug. 1909; *s* of late Lt-Col Selby Herriott Henderson, IMS; *m* 1939, Catherine Mary Maitland; one *s* two *d. Educ:* Cheltenham Coll. Entered RN, 1927; served War of 1939-45 in HM Ships and as Fleet Gunnery Officer, Mediterranean; Comdr 1942; Capt. 1948; Naval Attaché, Rome, 1949-51; in comd HMS Protector, 1951; in comd RN Air Station, Bramcote, 1952; Imperial Defence Coll., 1954; in command HMS Kenya, 1955; Rear-Admiral, 1957; Vice-Naval Dep. to Supreme Allied Comdr, Europe, 1957-Dec. 1959; Vice-Adm. 1960; Dir-Gen. of Training, Admiralty, 1960-62; C-in-C Plymouth, 1962-65; Adm. 1963; Head of British Defence Staffs, Washington, and UK Rep., Mil. Cttee, NATO, 1965-68; Chm., Mil. Cttee, NATO, 1968-71; retired 1971. Rear-Admiral of the United Kingdom, 1973-76. Pres., Royal British Legion, Scotland, 1974-. DL Stewartry of Kirkcudbright, 1973. *Address:* Hensol, Mossdale, Castle Douglas, Kirkcudbrightshire. *T:* Laurieston 207.

HENDERSON, Patrick David; Professor of Political Economy, University College, London, since 1975; *b* 10 April 1927; *s* of late David Thomson Henderson and late Eleanor Henderson; *m* 1960, Marcella Kodicek; one *s* one *d. Educ.* Ellesmere Coll., Shropshire; Corpus Christi Coll., Oxford. Fellow and Tutor in Economics, Lincoln Coll., Oxford, 1948-65; Univ. Lectr in Economics, Oxford, 1950-65; Commonwealth Fund Fellow (Harvard), 1952-53; Junior Proctor, Oxford Univ., 1955-56; Economic Adviser, HM Treasury, 1957-58; Chief Economist, Min. of Aviation, 1965-67; Adviser Harvard Development Advisory Service (Athens and Kuala Lumpur), 1967-68; Vis. Lectr, World Bank, 1968-69; Economist, World Bank, 1969-75, Dir of Economics Dept 1971-72. Mem., Commn on Environmental Pollution, 1977-. *Publications:* India: the energy sector, 1975; (jointly) Nyasaland: The Economics of Federation, 1960; ed and contrib.: Economic Growth in Britain, 1965; contrib: The British Economy in the 1950's, 1962; Public Enterprise, 1968; Public Economics, 1969; Unfashionable Economics, 1970; The World Bank, Multilateral Aid and the 1970's, 1973; The Economic Development of Yugoslavia, 1975; articles in economic jls. *Address:* 3 Christchurch Hill, NW3. *T:* 01-435 5866.

HENDERSON, Peter, CB 1965; MD; Senior Principal Medical Officer, Ministry of Education, 1964-69; *b* 16 March 1904; *e s* of Peter and Margaret Henderson, Inverness; *m* 1933, Beatrice Chrissie Pashley, Bridlington, Yorks; no *c. Educ:* High Sch. and Royal Academy, Inverness; Aberdeen Univ. MB 1929; MD 1931; DPH London, 1932. Resident MO, Bradford City Sanatorium, 1929-30; House Physician, St Luke's Hospital, Bradford, 1930-31; Resident MO, Inst. of Ray Therapy, London, 1931-32; Asst MO, Somerset CC, 1933-35; Asst MO, St Helens, 1935-36; Dep. MOH, Leyton, 1936-39; MOH, Todmorden, 1939-40; MO, Min. of Educn, 1940-51, PMO, 1951-64. Consultant, WHO. Milroy Lectr, 1968. QHP 1962. *Publications:* various papers on the health and disabilities of children in BMJ, Lancet and Practitioner; contribs to The Theory and Practice of Public Health (ed W. Hobson), 1961, 4th edn 1974; chapter in The Humanist Outlook (ed A. J. Ayer), 1968; Disability in Childhood and Youth, 1974. *Recreation:* gardening. *Address:* Lythe Ghyll, Merrowcroft, Guildford, Surrey. *T:* Guildford 75353.

HENDERSON, Sir Peter (Gordon), KCB 1975; Clerk of the Parliaments since 1974; *b* 16 Sept. 1922; *m* 1950, Susan Mary Dartford; two *s* two *d. Educ:* Stowe Sch.; Magdalen Coll., Oxford (Demy). Served War, Scots Guards, 1942-44. Clerk, House of Lords, 1954-60; seconded to HM Treasury as Sec. to Leader and Chief Whip, House of Lords, 1960-63; Reading Clerk and Clerk of Public Bills, 1964-74; Clerk Asst, 1974. Mem., Cttee on Preparation of Legislation, 1973-74. *Address:* 16 Pelham Street, SW7 2NG; Helbeck Cottage, Brough, Kirkby Stephen, Cumbria CA17 4DD. *Clubs:* Boodle's, Pratt's.

HENDERSON, Ralph, CB 1959; OBE 1946; Director of Stores, Admiralty, 1955-60, retired; *b* 15 Aug. 1897; *s* of James Ralph

Henderson, Perth, Scotland (author, pen-name Sandy McNab); *m* 1923, Gladys Dunnett; two *s. Educ:* Perth Academy. Entered Civil Service, 1913. Served in Army, 1915-19, Lieut, Royal Field Artillery. Naval Store Officer, Naval Base, Singapore, 1939-42; Deputy Dir of Stores, Admiralty, 1944. French Croix de Guerre (with palm), 1918. *Recreation:* golf. *Address:* 18 Wykeham Court, Wykeham Road, Worthing, West Sussex. *T:* Worthing 203187.

HENDERSON, Robert Alistair; Chairman, Kleinwort, Benson Ltd, since 1975; President, Klescan Investments Ltd, since 1971; Chairman: Kleinwort, Benson Inc., since 1971; Kleinwort, Benson (Trustees) Ltd, since 1975; Cross Investment Trust Ltd, since 1969; Director: Equitable Life Assurance Society; Cadbury Schweppes Ltd; Fuji Kleinwort Benson Ltd; Hamilton Brothers Oil Co. (Gt Brit.) Ltd; Inchcape & Co. Ltd; Kleinwort, Benson Investment Trust Ltd; Kleinwort, Benson, Lonsdale Ltd; Sharps, Pixley Ltd; Asian & Euro-American Capital Corporation Ltd, Hong Kong; Asian & Euro-American Merchant Bankers (Malaysia) Berhad; PT Asian & Euro-American Capital Corporation Ltd, Thailand and Indonesia; Asian & Euro-American Merchant Bank Ltd, Singapore; *b* 4 Nov. 1917; *s* of Robert Evelyn Henderson and Beatrice Janet Elsie Henderson; *m* 1947, Bridget Elizabeth, *d* of late Col J. G. Lowther, CBE, DSO, MC, TD, and Hon. Lilah White, *er d* of 3rd Baron Annaly; two *s* one *d. Educ:* Eton; Magdalene Coll., Cambridge. Hons degree in History. Served War: 60th Rifles, 1940-45, Captain. Jessel Toynbee & Co. Ltd, 1945-48; Borneo Co. Ltd, 1948-51; Robert Benson, Lonsdale & Co. Ltd, 1951 (Dir, 1957); Dir, Kleinwort, Benson Ltd, 1961 (on merger of Robert Benson, Lonsdale & Co. Ltd with Kleinwort Sons & Co.; Vice-Chm., 1970-71, Dep. Chm., 1971-75). *Recreations:* gardening, shooting. *Address:* Ayot Bury, Ayot St Peter, Welwyn, Herts AL6 9BG. *T:* Welwyn 4360; 7 Royal Avenue, Chelsea, SW3 4QE. *T:* 01-730 1104. *Club:* Brooks's.

HENDERSON, Robert Brumwell; Deputy Chairman, Ulster Television Ltd, since 1977 (Managing Director, 1959); *b* 28 July 1929; *s* of late Comdr Oscar Henderson, CVO, CBE, DSO, RN, and of Mrs Henderson; *m*; two *d; m* 1970, Patricia Ann Davison. *Educ:* Brackenber House Sch., Belfast; Bradfield Coll., Berks; Trinity Coll., Dublin. BA (Hons) 1951, MA 1959. Journalism: London, Liverpool, Glasgow and Belfast, 1951-59. Chairman: British Regional Television Assoc., 1969-70; Cinematograph and Television Benevolent Fund, N Ire.; Publicity Assoc. of N Ire., 1959-60; Director: Independent Television News Ltd, 1964-68; Independent Television Publications Ltd, 1968-; Pres., Radio Industries Club of NI, 1972-; Member: Cttee to Review Higher Educn in NI, 1965; Council, NI Chamber of Commerce, 1963-67, 1977-; Appts Cttee of Trinity Coll., Dublin; Court of New University of Ulster; Council for Continuing Educn in NI, 1975-. Chm., NI Br., Inst. of Directors, 1974-. *Publication:* Midnight Oil, 1962. *Recreations:* reading, theatre and cinema, golf. *Address:* 5 Dorchester Park, Belfast BT9 6RH. *Club:* Bath.

HENDERSON, Roy (Galbraith), CBE 1970; FRAM; baritone; Teacher of Singing (private); Professor of Singing, RAM, London, 1940-74; *b* Edinburgh, 4 July 1899; *er s* of late Rev. Dr Alex. Roy Henderson, formerly Principal of Paton Coll., Nottingham; *m* 1926, Bertha Collin Smyth; one *s* two *d. Educ:* Nottingham High Sch.; Royal Academy of Music, London (Worshipful Company of Musicians Medal). Debut as baritone singer, Queen's Hall, London, 1925; has sung at all leading Festivals in England, Internat. Festival for contemporary music, Amsterdam, 1933; recitals at first two Edinburgh Festivals, 1947 and 1948; principal parts in all Glyndebourne Opera festivals, 1934-40, associated chiefly with works of Delius, Elgar and Vaughan Williams, and sang many first performances of contemp. music. Retired from concert platform, 1951, to devote his whole time to teaching (among his pupils was late Kathleen Ferrier). Conductor, Huddersfield Glee and Madrigal Soc., 1932-39; Founder and Conductor, Nottingham Oriana Choir, 1937-52. Conductor of Bournemouth Municipal Choir, 1942-53. Adjudicator at International Concours, Geneva, 1952, and Triennially, 1956-65. Mem. of the Jury of the International Muziekstad s'Hertogenbosch, Holland, 1955-62, 1965, and Barcelona, 1965. Master classes in singing: Royal Conservatory of Music, Toronto, 1956; Toonkunst Conservatorium, Rotterdam, 1957, 1958; s'Hertogenbosch, 1967. Awarded the Sir Charles Santley memorial by Worshipful Company of Musicians for distinguished services to the art of singing, 1958. *Publications:* contributed to: Kathleen Ferrier, ed Neville Cardus, 1954; Opera Annual, 1958. *Recreations:* fishing, gardening and cricket. *Address:* 85 Belsize Park Gardens, Hampstead, NW3. *T:* 01-722 3144.

HENDERSON, Rupert Albert Geary; Chairman: Australian Newsprint Mills Ltd, since 1960; Trustees of Reuters Ltd since 1961 (Trustee since 1952, Director, 1946-51); Amalgamated Television Services Pty Ltd, 1958-74; *b* 26 Feb. 1896; *s* of late Robert Geary Henderson and Isabel Henderson; *m* 1st, 1914, Helene, *d* of Thomas Mason; one *s*; 2nd, 1939, Hazel, *d* of Herbert Harris; one *d. Educ:* Glebe Public Sch., Sydney. Literary staff, The Sydney Morning Herald, 1915; London rep., 1923-26; Advertising Manager, Sydney Mail, 1927; Circulation Manager, Sydney Morning Herald, 1928; Sec. to Gen. Manager, 1934; Gen. Manager, 1938; Chm., Australian Associated Press Pty Ltd, 1940-49; Managing Director: John Fairfax & Sons Pty Ltd, 1949-56; John Fairfax Ltd, 1956-64; Associated Newspapers Ltd, 1954-64; Pres. Australian Newspaper Proprietors' Association, 1942-47 and 1951-58; Director, Australian Assoc. Press Pty Ltd. *Recreation:* grazier. *Address:* John Fairfax Ltd, 23 Hamilton Street, Sydney, NSW 2000, Australia. *TA:* Herald, Sydney. *T:* 20944.

HENDERSON, William Crichton; Advocate; Sheriff of Tayside, Central and Fife (formerly Stirling, Dunbarton and Clackmannan) at Stirling and Alloa, since 1972; *b* 10 June 1931; *s* of William Henderson, headmaster, and late Helen Philp Henderson (*née* Crichton); *m* 1962, Norma Sheila Hope Henderson (*née* Grant); two *d. Educ:* George Watson's Boys' Coll., Edinburgh; Edinburgh Univ. MA Edinburgh 1952, LLB Edinburgh 1954. Admitted Solicitor, 1954; Diploma in Administrative Law and Practice, Edinburgh, 1955; called to Scottish Bar, 1957; practised as Advocate, 1957-68; Sheriff of Renfrew and Argyll at Paisley, 1968-72. Chm., Supreme Court Legal Aid Cttee, 1967-68. *Recreations:* golf, photography, travel. *Address:* Woodcot, Dollar, Clackmannanshire. *T:* Dollar 2528; Old Station House, Lower Largo, Fife.

HENDERSON, Sir William (MacGregor), Kt 1976; FRS 1976; FRSE 1977; Secretary, Agricultural Research Council, since 1972; *b* 17 July 1913; *s* of late William Simpson Henderson and late Catherine Alice Marcus Berry; *m* 1941, Alys Beryl Goodridge; four *s. Educ:* George Watson's Coll., Edinburgh; Royal (Dick) Veterinary Coll., Edinburgh (MRCVS); Univ. of Edinburgh (BSc, DSc). Assistant, Dept of Medicine, Royal (Dick) Veterinary Coll., Edinburgh, 1936-38; Member Scientific Staff, Animal Virus Research Inst., Pirbright, 1939-56, Dep. Dir, 1955-56; Director, Pan American Foot-and-Mouth Disease Center, Rio de Janeiro, 1957-65; Head, Dept of Microbiology, ARC Inst. for Research on Animal Diseases, Compton, 1966-67, Director, 1967-72; Visiting Prof., Univ. of Reading, 1970-72. Corresp. Member: Argentine Assoc. of Microbiology, 1959; Argentine Soc. of Veterinary Medicine, 1965; Hon. Member, Brasilian Soc. of Veterinary Medicine, 1965; FRCVS, by election, 1973; Hon. DVMS Edinburgh, 1974; Hon. DVSc Liverpool, 1977; FIBiol. Orden de Mayo, Argentina, 1962. *Publications:* Quantitative Study of Foot-and-Mouth Disease Virus, 1949; contribs to scientific jls principally on foot-and-mouth disease. *Recreation:* gardening. *Address:* Yarnton Cottage, Streatley, Berks. *Club:* Athenæum.

HENDERSON-STEWART, Sir David (James), 2nd Bt *cr* 1957; *b* 3 July 1941; *s* of Sir James Henderson-Stewart, 1st Bt, MP, and of Anna Margaret (*née* Greenwell); *S* father, 1961; *m* 1972, Anne, *d* of Count Serge de Pahlen; three *s. Educ:* Eton Coll.; Trinity Coll., Oxford. *Heir: s* David Henderson-Stewart, *b* 2 Feb. 1973. *Address:* 3 Chepstow Crescent, W11 3EA. *T:* 01-221 6255. *Club:* Travellers'.

HENDREY, Mrs Graeme; see Lewis, Eiluned.

HENDRIE, Prof. Gerald Mills; Professor of Music, The Open University, since 1969; *b* 28 Oct. 1935; *s* of James Harold Hendrie and Florence Mary MacPherson; *m* 1962, Dinah Florence Barsham; two *s. Educ:* Framlingham Coll., Suffolk; Royal Coll. of Music; Selwyn Coll., Cambridge (MA, MusB, PhD). FRCO, ARCM. Director of Music, Homerton Coll., Cambridge, 1962-63; Lectr in the History of Music, Univ. of Manchester, 1963-67; Prof. and Chm., Dept of Music, Univ. of Victoria, BC, Canada, 1967-69; Reader in Music, subseq. Prof., The Open Univ., 1969-. *Publications:* Musica Britannica XX, Orlando Gibbons: Keyboard Music, 1962 (2nd rev. edn, 1967); The Chandos and Related Anthems of George Frideric Handel (3 vols and critical commentary for the Halle Handel Society's complete edn of Handel's works, in press since 1972); articles for Die Musik in Geschichte und Gegenwart; various others including musical compositions, recordings for TV, radio and disc. *Recreations:* history of architecture, gardening. *Address:* The Open University, Walton Hall, Milton Keynes, Bucks MK7 6AA. *T:* Milton Keynes 63280. *Club:* BBC.

HENDRY, (Alexander) Forbes, OBE 1957; MC 1940; TD 1947; DL; JP; *b* 24 Oct. 1908; *s* of late Alexander Hendry, Solicitor, Denny, and Catherine Ann Forbes; *m* 1939, Margaret Whitehead; one *s* two *d. Educ:* Stirling High Sch.; Univ. of Glasgow (MA, LLB). Admitted Solicitor, 1932; Town Clerk of Denny and Dunipace, 1934-59. Commissioned 7th Bn The Argyll and Sutherland Highlanders (TA), 1935. Served War of 1939-45 in France, Middle East, North Africa, Sicily and North West Europe; Lt-Col 1953; TARO 1956. Chairman and Managing Dir, Cannerton Brick Co. Ltd; Dep. Chm., Cruikshank & Co. Ltd, and Dir other companies. Contested (C) Lanarkshire North, 1955. MP (C) West Aberdeenshire, 1959-66. Mem., Parliamentary Delegn to Tunisia, 1961; Vice-Chm., Anglo-Tunisian Parliamentary Group, 1965; Mem., Executive Cttee, British Branch, Inter-Parly Union, 1963-65; Chairman: W Stirlingshire Cons. Assoc., 1968; Central and Southern Area, Scottish Cons. and Unionist Assoc., 1971; Local Govt Adv. Cttee, Scottish Cons. Party, 1971; Vice-Pres., Scottish Cons. and Unionist Assoc., 1972, Pres., 1974-75. Town Councillor, Burgh of Denny and Dunipace, 1969, Provost, 1971-74; DL Stirlingshire 1965, JP Stirlingshire 1971; Hon. Sheriff, Tayside Central and Fife, 1976. *Recreations:* gardening, politics, travelling. *Address:* Braes, Dunipace, Denny, Stirlingshire. *T:* Denny 822345. *Clubs:* Caledonian (Edinburgh); County (Stirling).

HENDRY, Prof. Arnold William; Professor of Civil Engineering, University of Edinburgh, since 1964; *b* 10 Sept. 1921; *s* of late Dr George Hendry, MB, ChB, Buckie, Scotland; *m* 1st, 1946, Sheila Mary Cameron Roberts (*d* 1966), Glasgow; two *s* one *d*; 2nd, 1968, Elizabeth Lois Alice Inglis, Edinburgh. *Educ:* Buckie High Sch.; Aberdeen Univ. Civil engineer with Sir William Arrol & Co. Ltd, Bridge builders and Engineers, Glasgow, 1941-43; Asst in Engineering, University of Aberdeen, 1943-46; Lecturer in Civil Engineering, 1946-49; Reader in Civil Engineering, Univ. of London, King's Coll., 1949-51; Prof. of Civil Engrg and Dean of Fac. of Engrg, Univ. of Khartoum, 1951-57; Prof. of Building Science, University of Liverpool, 1957-63. *Publications:* An Introduction to Photo-Elastic Analysis, 1948; (with L. G. Jaeger) The Analysis of Grid Frameworks, 1958; The Elements of Experimental Stress Analysis, 1964; about 100 papers and articles in professional and technical jls. *Recreation:* sailing. *Address:* Department of Civil Engineering, University of Edinburgh EH16 5TZ.

HENDRY, Forbes; see Hendry, A. F.

HENDY, Sir Philip, Kt 1950; *b* 27 Sept. 1900; *s* of Frederick James Roberts Hendy and Caroline Isobel Potts. *Educ:* Westminster School; Christ Church, Oxford. Lecturer and Asst to the Keeper, The Wallace Collection, London, 1923-27; lived in Florence, Italy, 1927-30; Curator of Paintings, Museum of Fine Arts, Boston, Mass, USA, 1930-33; Dir, City Art Gallery and Temple Newsam, Leeds, 1934-45; Slade Prof. of Fine Art, Oxford Univ., 1936-46; Director, National Gallery, London, 1946-67; Adviser, Israel Museum, Jerusalem, 1968-71. President: Internat. Council of Museums, 1959-65; ICOM Foundation, 1965-70. *Publications:* Hours in the Wallace Collection, 1926; The Isabella Stewart Gardner Museum, Catalogue of Paintings and Drawings, Boston, 1931, 2nd edn 1974; Matthew Smith (Penguin Modern Painters), 1944; Giovanni Bellini, 1945; Spanish Painting, 1946; The National Gallery, London, 1955; Masaccio (Unesco), 1957; Piero della Francesca and the Early Renaissance, 1968. *Address:* Whistlers Barn, Great Haseley, Oxford. *Club:* Athenæum.

HENHAM, John Alfred; Stipendiary Magistrate for South Yorkshire, since 1975; *b* 8 Sept. 1924; *s* of Alfred and Daisy Henham; *m* 1946, Suzanne Jeanne Octavie Ghislaine Pinchart (*d* 1972); two *s. Educ:* state schs; County Techn. Coll., Kent. Admitted solicitor, 1959 (Justices' Clerks' Soc. Prizeman). Asst to Justices' Clerks, Dartford, Doncaster and Walsall, 1940-60; RAF service, 1942-45; Clerk to Justices: Wednesbury Gp, 1960-61; Arundel and Worthing Divs, 1961-75. Mem. Council, Justices' Clerks' Soc., 1969-75; Mem., Lord Justice James Cttee, Dist of Criminal Business, 1973-75. *Publication:* Magistrates' Summary Jurisdiction: guide to sentencing powers, 1971, 3rd edn 1974. *Recreations:* gardening, fishing, shooting. *Address:* 7 Middlefield Croft, Dore, Sheffield S17 3AS; (office) Court House, Sheffield S3 8LW. *T:* Sheffield 77682, ext. 23. *Club:* Sheffield.

HENIG, Sir Mark, Kt 1965; Chairman: English Tourist Board; East Midlands Gas Consumers' Council (formerly Gas Consultative Council), since 1968; Deputy Chairman, National Gas Consumers' Council, since 1973; *b* 11 Feb. 1911; *e s* of Harry and Gertrude Henig; *m* 1937, Grace (*née* Cohen); one *s* one *d. Educ:* Wyggeston Grammar Sch., Leicester. Mem.

Leicester City Council, 1945-70, Alderman, 1958-70; High Bailiff, City of Leicester, 1965, Lord Mayor, 1967-68. Chm., Assoc. of Municipal Corporations, 1966-67. Member: Commn on the Constitution, 1969-73; Prime Minister's Cttee on Local Govt Rules of Conduct, 1973-74; Water Space Amenity Commn, 1973-. Chm., East Midlands Economic Planning Council, 1968-71. Vice-Chm., Leicester Theatre Trust, 1973-; Governor and Exec. Mem. Council, Royal Shakespeare Theatre. Dir, ATV Network Ltd, 1975-. Hon. LLD Leicester, 1977. *Address:* 35 Stanley Road, Leicester LE2 1RF. *T:* 708425. *Club:* Reform.
See also S. Henig.

HENIG, Stanley; Head of Division of Political Science, Preston Polytechnic, since 1976; *b* 7 July 1939; *s* of Sir Mark Henig, *qv*; *m* 1966, Ruth Beatrice Munzer; two *s. Educ:* Wyggeston Grammar Sch.; Corpus Christi Coll., Oxford. BA 1st Cl. Hons, 1961; MA 1965 Oxon. Teaching Asst, Dept of Politics, Univ. of Minnesota, 1961; Research Student, Nuffield Coll., 1962; Lecturer in Politics, Lancaster Univ., 1964-66. MP (Lab) Lancaster, 1966-70; Lectr in Politics, Warwick Univ., 1970-71; Lectr, Civil Service Coll., 1972-75. Governor, British Inst. of Recorded Sound, 1975-. Asst Editor, Jl of Common Market Studies, 1964-72, Editor, 1973-76. *Publications:* (ed) European Political Parties, 1969; External Relations of the European Community, 1971. *Recreation:* collector of old gramophone records. *Address:* 10 Yealand Drive, Lancaster LA1 4EW. *T:* 69624. *Club:* Europe House.

HENLEY, 7th Baron (Ire.), *cr* 1799; **Michael Francis Eden;** Baron Northington (UK) *cr* 1885; *b* 13 Aug. 1914; *er s* of 6th Baron Henley and Lady Dorothy Howard (*d* 1968), 3rd *d* of 9th Earl of Carlisle; *S* father, 1962; *m* 1st, 1943, Elizabeth, *d* of Sir A. L. Hobhouse (marriage dissolved by divorce, 1947); one *d*; 2nd, 1949, Nancy (marr. diss. 1975), *d* of Stanley Walton; two *s* three *d. Educ:* Eton; Balliol Coll., Oxford. Served War of 1939-45: Coldstream Guards, 1940-41; Household Cavalry, 1941-46. Pres., Liberal Party, 1966-67. Chm., CPRE, 1972-. *Heir:* s Hon. Oliver Michael Robert Eden, *b* 22 Nov. 1953. *Address:* Scaleby Castle, Carlisle. *Clubs:* Brooks's, Pratt's.

HENLEY, Sir Douglas (Owen), KCB 1973 (CB 1970); Comptroller and Auditor General, since 1976; *b* 5 April 1919; *s* of late Owen Henley and of Beatrice Mary Henley; *m* 1942, June Muriel Ibbetson; four *d. Educ:* Beckenham County Sch.; London Sch. of Economics (Hon. Fellow, 1974). BSc (Econ.), 1939; Gerstenberg Studentship and Leverhulme Res. Studentship (not taken up). Served Army, 1939-46; Queen's Own Royal West Kent Regt and HQ 12th Inf. Bde (despatches twice, 1945). Treasury, 1946; Treas. rep. (Financial Counsellor) in Tokyo and Singapore, 1956-59; Asst Under-Sec. of State, DEA, 1964-69, Dep. Under-Sec. of State, 1969; Second Permanent Sec., HM Treasury, 1972-76. *Address:* Walwood House, Park Road, Banstead, Surrey. *T:* Burgh Heath 52626.

HENLEY, Rear-Adm. Sir Joseph (Charles Cameron), KCVO 1963; CB 1962; *b* 24 April 1909; *e s* of Vice-Adm. J. C. W. Henley, CB; *m* 1934, Daphne Ruth (marr. diss. 1965), *d* of late A. A. H. Wykeham, of Pitt Place, Brighstone, IW; one *s* three *d*; *m* 1966, Patricia Sharp, MBE 1952, *d* of late Roy Eastman, Alberta, Canada. *Educ:* Sherborne. Joined Royal Navy, 1927. Served War of 1939-45, in HMS Birmingham and King George V. Capt., 1951, in command HMS Defender, 1954-55; Naval Attaché, Washington (as Commodore), 1956-57; Dir, Royal Naval Staff Coll., 1958; Chief of Staff, Mediterranean Station, 1959-61, as Commodore; Rear-Adm. 1960; Flag Officer, Royal Yachts and Extra Naval Equerry to the Queen, 1962-65; retd 1965. *Address:* 11a Hopewood Gardens, Darling Point, Sydney, NSW 2027, Australia. *Clubs:* Royal Yacht Squadron; Cruising Yacht (Australia); Royal Sydney Golf.

HENMAN, Philip Sydney; Founder of Transport Development Group Ltd; FCIT (MInstT, 1943). DUniv Surrey, 1974. Farmer. High Sheriff, Surrey, 1971-72. *Address:* Home Farm, Coldharbour Lane, Dorking, Surrey. *T:* Dorking 2310.

HENNELL, Rev. Canon Michael Murray; Residentiary Canon, Manchester Cathedral, since 1970; *b* 11 Sept. 1918; *s* of Charles Murray and Jessie Hennell; *m* 1950, Peggy Glendinning; four *s. Educ:* Bishops Stortford Coll. (Prep.); Royal Masonic Sch.; St Edmund Hall and Wycliffe Hall, Oxford. MA Oxon and, by incorporation, MA Cantab. Asst Curate: St Stephen's With St Bartholomew's, Islington, N1, 1942-44; All Saints, Queensbury, Middx, 1944-48; Tutor, Ridley Hall, Cambridge, 1948-51. St Aidan's Coll., Birkenhead: Sen. Tutor, 1951; Vice-Principal, 1952-59; Principal, 1959-63; Principal, Ridley Hall, Cambridge, 1964-70. Examining Chaplain to the Bishops of Derby and Manchester (Liverpool, 1964-75). Commissary to the Bishop on

the Niger, 1975-. *Publications:* John Venn and the Clapham Sect, 1958; ed and contrib., Charles Simeon, 1759-1836, 1959; contrib., The Anglican Synthesis, 1964; Popular Belief and Practice, 1972. *Address:* 21 Morville Road, Chorlton-cum-Hardy, Manchester M21 1UG.

HENNESSEY, Robert Samuel Fleming, CMG 1954; Assistant Research Director, Wellcome Foundation, 1967-70, retired; *b* 8 May 1905; *s* of late W. R. H. Hennessey and late Elizabeth Fleming; *m* 1930, Grace Alberta Coote; one *s* one *d. Educ:* St Andrew's Coll., Dublin; Dublin and London Universities. MD, FRCPI, DipBact, DTM&H. Pathologist, Uganda, 1929; Dep. Director (Laboratories), Palestine, 1944; Dep. Director, Medical Services, Palestine, 1946; Asst Medical Adviser, Colonial Office, 1947; Director of Medical Services, Uganda, 1949-55; Head of the Wellcome Laboratories of Tropical Medicine, London, 1956-58; Head of Therapeutic Research Division, Wellcome Foundation, 1958-66. *Publications:* papers on pathology in scientific jls. *Recreations:* golf, music, literature. *Address:* 51 Stone Park Avenue, Beckenham, Kent. *T:* 01-650 5336.

HENNESSY, family name of **Baron Windlesham.**

HENNESSY, Christopher; journalist; Chairman, Associated Catholic Newspapers (1912) Ltd, since 1970; *b* 29 Dec. 1909; *e s* of Daniel and Anne Hennessy; *m* 1942, Kathleen Margaret Cadley, Liverpool. *Educ:* St Edward's Coll., Liverpool. Served War of 1939-45 as Commissioned Officer in British and Indian Armies; commanded a Territorial Army Unit in the North-West, 1950-55. KCSG 1975. *Recreation:* travel. *Address:* Beech House, Montreal Road, Riverhead, Sevenoaks, Kent. *T:* Sevenoaks 54117.

HENNESSY, Denis William, OBE 1967; HM Diplomatic Service, retired; *b* 5 Dec. 1912; *s* of Daniel Hennessy and Rosina Gertrude Hennessy (*née* Griffiths); *m* 1937, Lorna McDonald Lappin; three *s* one *d. Educ:* private sch. Joined Foreign Office, 1930; served in the Foreign Office and in Prague, Washington, New York, Zürich, Bremen, Miami, Düsseldorf, Accra, and as Consul-Gen., Hanover; Counsellor, Bonn, 1969-72. *Address:* 6 Springside Avenue, Mount Pleasant, Western Australia 6153. *Club:* Travellers'.

HENNESSY, James Patrick Ivan, CMG 1975; OBE 1968 (MBE 1959); HM Diplomatic Service; Consul-General, Cape Town, since 1977; *b* 26 Sept. 1923; *s* of late Richard George Hennessy, DSO, MC; *m* 1947, Patricia, *o d* of late Wing Comdr F. H. Unwin, OBE; five *d* (one *s* decd). *Educ:* Bedford Sch.; Sidney Sussex Coll., Cambridge; LSE. Served RA, 1942-46 (Major). HM Overseas Service, Basutoland, 1948; Judicial Comr, 1953; Dist Comr, 1954-56; Jt Sec., Constitutional Commn, 1957-59; Supervisor of Elections, 1959; Sec. to Exec. Council, 1960; seconded to Office of High Comr, Cape Town/Pretoria, 1961-63; Perm. Sec., 1964; MLC, 1965; Sec. for External Affairs, Defence and Internal Security, 1967; Prime Minister's Office, 1968. Retired, later apptd after competitive exam to HM Diplomatic Service; FO, 1968-70; Montevideo, 1970; (Chargé d'Affaires 1971-72); FO, 1972-73; High Comr to Uganda and Ambassador, Rwanda, 1973-76. *Address:* c/o Foreign and Commonwealth Office, SW1A 2AL. *Clubs:* Naval and Military, Royal Commonwealth Society.

HENNESSY, Sir John Wyndham P.; *see* Pope-Hennessy.

HENNESSY, Sir Patrick, Kt 1941; Chairman: Ford Motor Co. Ltd, 1956-68; Henry Ford & Son Ltd, Cork, Eire, since 1955; *b* 18 April 1898; *s* of Patrick Hennessy, Ballyvodak House, Midleton, Co. Cork; *m* 1923, Dorothy Margaret (*d* 1949), *d* of Robert Davis, JP, Killaney Lodge, Boardmills, N Ireland; two *s* one *d*. Served European War, 1914-18, Royal Inniskilling Fus. Pres., Soc. of Motor Manufacturers & Traders, 1965 and 1966, Dep. Pres., 1967 and 1968. Formerly Mem. Adv. Council, Min. of Aircraft Production. *Address:* 4 Grafton Street, W1X 4RD; Larkmead, Theydon Bois, Essex. *T:* Theydon Bois 2139. *Club:* Royal Automobile.

HENNIKER, 7th Baron, *cr* 1800; **John Ernest De Grey Henniker-Major;** Bt 1765; Baron Hartismere (UK) 1866; sits in House of Lords as Baron Hartismere; formerly Land Agent for: Lord Mostyn (N Wales); W. D. Mackenzie (Henley-on-Thames; Sir Percy Loraine, Bt and Lord Henniker (Suffolk); *b* 18 Jan. 1883; *y s* of 5th Baron Henniker and Alice Mary (*d* 1893), *o d* of 3rd Earl of Desart; *S* brother 1956; *m* 1914, Molly (*d* 1953), *d* of late Sir Robert Burnet, KCVO; two *s. Educ:* Radley; Royal Agricultural College, Cirencester (Hons Diploma). Page of Honour to Queen Victoria, 1895-99; served in Army and RAF, 1914-19 (French Croix de Guerre). FLAS. *Heir:* s Hon. Sir John Patrick Edward Chandos Henniker-

Major, *qv. Address:* Thornham Hall, Eye, Suffolk. *T:* Mellis 207 and 314.

HENNIKER, Brig. Sir Mark Chandos Auberon, 8th Bt, *cr* 1813; CBE 1953 (OBE 1944); DSO 1945; MC 1933; DL; retired, 1958; *b* 23 Jan. 1906; *s* of late F. C. Henniker, ICS, and of Ada Russell (*née* Howell); *S* cousin (Lieut-Col Sir Robert Henniker, 7th Bt, MC) 1958; *m* 1945, Kathleen Denys (*née* Anderson); one *s* one *d. Educ:* Marlborough Coll.; Royal Military Academy, Woolwich; King's Coll., Cambridge. Royal Engineers, 1926; served India, 1928-34 (MC); Aldershot, 1937-39; BEF, 1939-40; North Africa, 1943; Sicily, 1943 (wounded); Italy, 1943 (OBE); NW Europe, 1944-45 (immediate award of DSO, Oct. 1944); India, 1946-47; Malaya, 1952-55 (CBE); Port Said, 1956 (despatches). Hon. Col, Parachute Engineer Regt (TA), 1959-68; Hon. Col, REME (TA), 1964-68. DL Gwent (formerly County of Mon), 1963. *Publications:* Memoirs of a Junior Officer, 1951; Red Shadow over Malaya, 1955; Life in the Army Today, 1957. *Recreations:* appropriate to age and rank. *Heir:* s Adrian Chandos Henniker [*b* 18 Oct. 1946; *m* 1971, Ann, *d* of Stuart Britton]. *Address:* c/o Lloyds Bank Ltd, Cox & King's Branch, 6 Pall Mall, SW1. *Club:* Athenæum.

HENNIKER-GOTLEY, Roger Alwyn, MA Oxon; Headmaster of Sebright School, 1938-63, retired; *b* 8 Feb. 1898; 3rd *s* of late Rev. George Henniker-Gotley and late Louisa Sarah Lefroy; *m* 1931, Helen Hope Campbell, *d* of late Rev. Gerald Campbell Dicker; two *s. Educ:* Cheltenham Coll.; Brasenose Coll., Oxford. Served European War, 1914-18, Lancashire Fusiliers. Asst Master and Housemaster, Stamford School, 1924-25; Asst Master and Housemaster, Worksop Coll., 1925-27; Asst Master and Senior English Master, Cranleigh Sch., 1927-38. *Recreations:* cricket, ornithology, gardening. *Address:* Little Orchard, Codford St Mary, Warminster, Wiltshire. *T:* Codford St Mary 239.

HENNIKER HEATON, Sir Yvo Robert; *see* Heaton.

HENNIKER-MAJOR, family name of **Baron Henniker.**

HENNIKER-MAJOR, Hon. Sir John (Patrick Edward Chandos), KCMG 1965 (CMG 1956); CVO 1960; MC 1945; Director, Wates Foundation, since 1972; *b* 19 Feb. 1916; *s* and *heir* of 7th Baron Henniker, *qv; m* 1946, Margaret Osla Benning (*d* 1974); two *s* one *d*; *m* 1976, Julia Marshall Poland (*née* Mason). *Educ:* Stowe; Trinity Coll., Cambridge. HM Foreign Service, 1938; served 1940-45, Army (Major, The Rifle Brigade). HM Embassy Belgrade, 1945-46; Asst Private Secretary to Secretary of State for Foreign Affairs, 1946-48; Foreign Office, 1948-50; HM Embassy, Buenos Aires, 1950-52; Foreign Office, 1952-60 (Counsellor and Head of Personnel Dept, 1953); HM Ambassador to Jordan, 1960-62; to Denmark, 1962-66; Civil Service Commission, 1966-67; Asst Under-Secretary of State, FO, 1967-68. Dir-Gen., British Council, 1968-72. Lay Mem., Mental Health Review Tribunal (Broadmoor), 1975. Trustee: City Parochial Foundn, 1973; London Festival Ballet, 1975. *Recreations:* gardening, bridge, ornithology. *Address:* Red House, Thornham Magna, Eye, Suffolk. *Club:* Special Forces.

HENNINGS, John Dunn, CMG 1968; HM Diplomatic Service; Assistant Under Secretary of State, Foreign and Commonwealth Office, since 1976; *b* 9 June 1922; *o c* of Stanley John and Grace Beatrice Hennings, Ipswich, Suffolk; *m* 1953, Joanna Anita, *er d* of J. Thompson Reed, Northampton; two *s. Educ:* Ipswich Sch.; University College, Oxford. Foreign Office and Berlin, 1947-49; Colonial Office, 1949-53; W African Inter-Territorial Secretariat, Accra, 1953-55; Colonial Office, 1955-60; Attaché for Colonial Affairs, British Embassy, Washington, DC, 1960-63; Commonwealth Relations Office, 1963; Counsellor, HM Diplomatic Service, 1965; Head, British High Commission, Residual Staff, Salisbury, Rhodesia, 1966-68; Counsellor and Head of Chancery, High Commn, Delhi, 1968-72; High Comr, Jamaica, and Ambassador (non-resident) to Haiti, 1973-76. Secretary, British Guiana Constitutional Commission, 1951. *Recreations:* reading, tennis, photography. *Address:* c/o Foreign and Commonwealth Office, Downing Street, SW1. *Club:* Travellers'.

HENNINGS, Richard Owen, CMG 1957; retired as Deputy Chief Secretary, Kenya (1960-63); *b* 8 Sept. 1911; *s* of W. G. Hennings; *m* 1939, Constance Patricia Milton Sexton; one *d. Educ:* Cheltenham; New Coll., Oxford. Newdigate Prize Poem, 1932. District Officer, Kenya, 1935; Political Officer, Ethiopia, 1941; Secretary for Agriculture, Kenya, 1953; Permanent Secretary, Ministry of Agriculture, Animal Husbandry and Water Resources, Kenya, 1956. Nominated Member of Kenya Legislative Council, 1960, and of East African Central Legislative Assembly, 1960. Hon. Editor, Ski Notes and Queries,

1964-71; Editor, Ski Survey, 1972-73. *Publications:* Arnold in Africa, 1941; African Morning, 1951; articles in The Geographical Magazine, Journal of African Administration, Corona, British Ski Year Book, Ski Notes and Queries. *Recreations:* ski-ing, tennis, gardening, reefing. *Address:* July Farm House, Great Chesterford, Saffron Walden, Essex. *Clubs:* Ski Club of Great Britain; Nairobi (Nairobi).

HENREY, Mrs Robert; authoress; *b* Paris, 13 Aug. 1906; maiden name Madeleine Gal; *m* 1928, Robert Selby Henrey, *o s* of Rev. Thomas Selby Henrey, Vicar of Old Brentford, Mddx, and Euphemia, *d* of Sir Coutts and Lady Lindsay of Balcarres; one *s. Educ:* Protestant Girls' Sch., Clichy; Convent of The Holy Family, Tooting, SW. *Publications:* autobiographical sequence in the following chronological order: The Little Madeleine, 1951, New York, 1953; An Exile in Soho, 1952; Julia, 1971; A Girl at Twenty, 1974; Madeleine Grown Up, 1952, New York 1953; Green Leaves, 1976; Madeleine Young Wife, New York 1954, London 1960; London under Fire 1940-45, 1969; A Month in Paris, 1954; Milou's Daughter, 1955, New York 1956; Her April Days, 1963; Wednesday at Four, 1964; Winter Wild, 1966; She Who Pays, 1969 (read in the above order these volumes make one consecutive narrative); *other books:* A Farm in Normandy, 1941; A Village in Piccadilly, 1943; The Incredible City, 1944; The Foolish Decade, 1945; The King of Brentford, 1946; The Siege of London, 1946; The Return to the Farm, 1947; London (with illustrations by Phyllis Ginger RWS) 1948, New York, 1949; A Film Star in Belgrave Square, 1948; A Journey to Vienna, 1950; Matilda and the Chickens, 1950; Paloma, 1951, New York, 1955; A Farm in Normandy and the Return, 1952; Madeleine's Journal, 1953; This Feminine World, 1956; A Daughter for a Fortnight, 1957; The Virgin of Aldermanbury (illustrations by Phyllis Ginger), 1958; Mistress of Myself, 1959; The Dream Makers, 1961; Spring in a Soho Street, 1962. *Recreations:* most feminine occupations: sewing, knitting, ironing, gardening. *Address:* c/o J. M. Dent & Sons, Aldine House, 26 Albemarle Street, W1X 4QY; Ferme Robert Henrey, 14640 Villers-sur-Mer, Calvados, France. *T:* Calvados (31) 87 03 88.

HENRI, Adrian Maurice; President, Liverpool Academy of Arts, since 1972; *b* Birkenhead, 10 April 1932; *s* of Arthur Maurice Henri and Emma Johnson; *m* 1957, Joyce Wilson. *Educ:* St Asaph Grammar Sch., N Wales; Dept of Fine Art, King's Coll., Newcastle upon Tyne, 1951-55. Hons BA Fine Art (Dunelm) 1955. Worked for ten seasons in Rhyl fairground, later as a scenic-artist and secondary school teacher; taught at Manchester then Liverpool Colls of Art, 1961-67. Led the poetry/rock group, Liverpool Scene, 1967-70; since then, freelance poet/painter/singer/songwriter/lecturer. Tour of USA, 1973; Bicentennial Poetry Tour of USA, 1976. *Exhibitions:* include: Biennale della Giovane Pintura, Milan, 1968; Pen as Pencil, Brussels, 1973; John Moores Liverpool Exhibns, 1962, 1965, 1974; Peter Moores Project, Real Life, Liverpool, 1977; John Moores Liverpool £2000 prize, 1972. *Major One -Man Shows:* ICA, London, 1968; ArtNet, London, 1975; Williamson Art Gall., Birkenhead, 1975; Retrospective 1960-76, Wolverhampton City Art Gall., 1976. Various recordings. *Publications:* Tonight at Noon, 1968; City, 1969 (out of print); Autobiography, 1971; *novel* (with Nell Dunn) I Want, 1972; World of Art Series: Environments and Happenings, 1974; The Best of Henri, 1975; *poems:* City Hedges 1970-76, 1977; *anthologies:* The Oxford Book of Twentieth Century Verse, 1973; The Liverpool Scene (ed Edward Lucie-Smith), 1967; Penguin Modern Poets No 10: The Mersey Sound, 1967, rev. and enlarged edn, 1974; British Poetry since 1945 (ed Edward Lucie-Smith: Penguin), 1970; *plays:* I Want a Guillaume Apollinaire Show (with Mike Kustow), 1968; Yesterday's Girl (a play with music for Granada TV), 1973. *Recreations:* watching Liverpool FC; visiting Shropshire and Normandy; old movies; SF, Gothic and crime novels. *Address:* 21 Mount Street, Liverpool L1 9HD. *T:* 051-709 6682; (literary agent) Deborah Rogers Ltd, 5-11 Mortimer Street, W1. *Clubs:* Private Chauffeurs', Peter Kavanagh's (Liverpool).

HENRION, Frederick Henri Kay, MBE 1951; RDI; PPSIA; General Consulting Designer for Industry and Commerce; Visiting Lecturer at Royal College of Art; *b* 18 April 1914; *m*; two *s* one *d*. Textile design in Paris, 1932-33; worked in Paris and London, 1936-39; designed Smoke Abatement Exhibition, Charing Cross Station, and worked on Glasgow Empire Exhibition, 1939, and New York World Fair, 1940-45. Design of all exhibitions for Ministry of Agriculture through Ministry of Information and exhibitions for Army Bureau of Current Affairs (WO), etc., 1943-45. Consultant Designer to US Embassy and US Office of War Information, 1945; Chief Cons. Designer to Sir William Crawford and Partners, 1946-47; Art Editor of Contact Publication, 1947-48; Art Director BOAC Publications, 1949-

51, and of Future Magazine, 1951; Designer, Festival of Britain pavilions (Agriculture and Natural History), 1950-51-54; Art Editor and Designer of the Bowater Papers, 1951-53; subseq. Cons. Designer for many firms. Posters for: GPO; BOAC; LPTB; Council of Industrial Design; exhibitions and permanent collections in Europe, USA and S America. One-man show, Designing Things and Symbols, at Institute of Contemporary Arts, 1960. Member Council and Vice-President, Society of Industrial Artists (President, 1961-63); Member: Council of Industrial Design, 1963-66; Advisory Council to Governors of London School of Printing; Council, CNAA (Chm. Bd of Graphic Design; Mem. Cttee of Art and Design); President: Alliance Graphique Internationale, 1962-67; ICOGRADA, 1968-70; Past Governor, Central School of Art; Outside Assessor, Scottish Schools of Art; Consultant Designer to: BTC; KLM Royal Dutch Airlines; British Olivetti Ltd; Tate & Lyle Ltd; The Postmaster General; BEA; Blue Circle Group; Courage, Barclay & Simonds Ltd; Financial Times; Volkswagen, Audi, NSU, Porsche, LEB, Penta Hotels, Braun AG. Co-ordinating graphics designer for British Pavilion, Expo 67. Master of Faculty, RDI, 1971-73; Head of Faculty of Visual Communication, London Coll. of Printing, 1976. Hon. Dip. Manchester, 1962. SIAD Gold Medal, 1976. *Publications:* Design Co-ordination and Corporate Image, 1967 (USA). Contributor to: Graphis, Gebrauchgraphik, Design Magazine, Architectural Review, Art and Industry, Penrose Annual, Format, Novum Gebrauchsgraphik, Design Magazine, The Designer, Print Magazine (USA). *Address:* 35 Pond Street, NW3 2PN. *T:* 01-435 7402.

HENRIQUES, Sir Cyril George Xavier, Kt 1963; QC (Jamaica); LLB; President, Court of Appeal, Jamaica, 1968-74; *b* Kingston, Jamaica, 5 July 1908; *s* of Cyril Charles Henriques and of Mrs Edith Emily Henriques; *m* Marjory Brunhilda (*née* Burrows); two *d. Educ:* St George's Coll., Jamaica; St Francis Xavier's Coll.; University College, London. Called to Bar, Inner Temple, 1936; Crown Counsel, Jamaica, 1939; Resident Magistrate, 1944; Attorney General, British Honduras, 1950; Puisne-Judge, Jamaica, 1955; appointment in British Honduras, 1956; Chief Justice of Supreme Court of Windward Islands and Leeward Islands, 1958; Judge of Appeal, Appeal Court of Jamaica, 1963-68. *Address:* 11 Jacks Hill Road, Kingston 6, Jamaica.
See also Mrs P. Crabbe.

HENRY, Hon. Sir Albert (Royle), KBE 1974; First Premier of the Cook Islands, since 1965 (re-elected 1968, 1972 and 1974); *b* 11 June 1907; *s* of Geoffrey Henry and Metua Grace; *m* Elizabeth, 2nd *d* of late Hugh McCrone Connal, Edinburgh; two *s* two *d. Educ:* St Stephen's Coll., Auckland, NZ. Land owner and plantation owner; school teacher, Cook Islands, 1924-36; Chief Clerk, Trading Co., 1937-42; joined Defence Force, 1940-43, no overseas service; Cook Islands Representative, Rugby, cricket and tennis, 1921-40; Official Sec., Cook Islands Progressive Assoc., 1947-64; Official Sec., Cook Islands Co-op. Soc., 1947-50. Hon. Dr of Laws, Univ. of Guam, 1968; Hon. Life Mem., Brazilian Cultural and Literary Union of Writers. *Recreation:* when not sleeping, is working. *Address:* Avarua, Rarotonga, Cook Islands.

HENRY, Cyril Bowdler, (C. Bowdler-Henry); Knight (First Class) Royal Norwegian Order of St Olav; Chevalier de la Légion d'Honneur; Officer of Order of Orange Nassau; Czechoslovak Military Medal of Merit (First Class); LRCP, MRCS, FDSRCS (Eng.); Vice-President Royal Society Medicine (President Sect. Odontology, 1954-55, Hon. Member, 1964); Life Governor, emeritus Hon. Consulting Surgeon, late Senior Surgeon and Lecturer in Oral Surgery, Royal Dental Hospital of London and Chairman of Governing Body of The London School of Dental Surgery (University of London), in Centenary Year of School's foundation; Member Board of Studies in Dentistry, and Examiner in Oral Surgery for Mastership in Dental Surgery, University of London; Life Governor Westminster Hospital; *b* Leire, Leics, 10 Oct. 1893; *s* of late Thomas Henry, Moorgate Park, Retford, and Rose Emily Bowdler, Shrewsbury; *m* 1920, Dorothy Mildred, 2nd *d* of late William Henry Bradley, Solicitor. *Educ:* King Edward VI's Grammar Sch., Retford; Sheffield Univ.; Royal Dental and Westminster Hospitals, and King's Coll., University of London. Lieut RAMC attached 22 CCS, BEF, 1915-16; House Physician, House Surgeon, Resident Obstetric Assistant, Westminster Hospital, 1917-20; in this post conducted deliveries for teaching ciné film on two cases of parturition (normal and breach presentation) (extracts in G. Drummond Robinson's Atlas of Normal Labour, 1921); Assistant Dental Surgeon, Metropolitan Hospital, 1919-22; Dental Surgeon, Westminster Hospital, 1922-29, Royal Dental Hospital, 1925-59. Oral Surgeon, EMS, Sept. 1939; gave services during Second World War as Hon. Oral Surgeon and Consulting Stomatologist to: Royal Norwegian

Armed Forces in UK; Royal Norwegian Min. of Social Welfare; Polish Min. of Labour and Social Welfare; Netherlands Army; Czechoslovak Armed Forces; Fighting French Forces; Armed Forces of Yugoslavia; Czechoslovak and Polish Red Cross Socs. Appointed to represent the Royal College of Surgeons at the IInd International Stomatological Congress (Bologna), 1935, and at the IXth International Dental Congress, Vienna, 1936. Arris and Gale Lectr, RCS, 1933-34; Hunterian Prof., RCS, 1935-36; Menzies Campbell Lectr (on dental history), RCS, 1962. A Governor, St George's Hosp., 1954-60. Hon. Fellow, British Assoc. of Oral Surgeons; Fellow, Harveian Soc. of London; Member: BMA; British Dental Assoc.; Hon. Mem., American Dental Soc. of London (President, 1960-61), etc. *Publications:* (with A. W. Marrett-Tims) Tomes' Dental Anatomy, 8th Edn; A Study of the Mandibular third molar tooth (with G. M. Morant), Biometrika, vol. 28, 1936; Chapters in a System of Dental Surgery by Sir Norman G. Bennett and in Post Graduate Surgery by Rodney Maingot; papers, lectures and reviews upon scientific subjects related to dental medicine, oral surgery, stomatology and dental history. *Address:* 62 Harley Street, W1. *T:* 01-580 1612.

HENRY, Sir Denis (Aynsley), Kt 1975; OBE 1962; QC Grenada 1968; barrister-at-law; Senior Partner, Henry, Henry & Bristol, St George's, Grenada, WI; *b* 3 Feb. 1917; *s* of Ferdinand H. Henry and Agatha May Henry; *m* 1966, Kathleen Carol (*née* Sheppard); two *s* three *d. Educ:* Grenada Boys' Secondary Sch.; King's Coll., London (LLB Hons). Called to Bar, Inner Temple (Certif. of Honour), 1939. In practice at Bar, Grenada, 1939-. Served three terms as nominated MLC, Grenada, 1952-65; Sen. nominated Mem. Exec. Council, 1956-65; Senator in First Parlt of Associated State of Grenada, 1966-67. Mem. Council, Univ. of West Indies, 1956-69. Pres. and Dir, Windward Islands Banana Growers Assoc., 1957-75; Pres., Commonwealth Banana Exporters Assoc., 1973-75; Chairman: Grenada Banana Co-operative Soc., 1953-75; Grenada Cocoa Assoc., 1973-75. Vice-Pres., Commonwealth Caribbean Society for the Blind, 1972-75; Mem. Exec., West India Cttee, London, 1972-75. *Recreations:* golf, swimming, tennis. *Address:* Mount Parnassus, St George's, Grenada, WI. *T:* 2370. *Clubs:* Royal Commonwealth Society; Grenada Golf, Richmond Hill Tennis (Grenada).

HENRY, Denis Robert Maurice, QC 1977; barrister-at-law; *b* 19 April 1931; *o s* of late Brig. Maurice Henry and of Mary Catherine (*née* Irving); *m* 1963, Linda Gabriel Arthur; one *s* two *d. Educ:* Shrewsbury; Balliol Coll., Oxford (MA). 2nd Lieut, KORR, 1950-51. Called to the Bar, Inner Temple, 1955. *Recreations:* history, golf. *Address:* Fountain Court, Temple, EC4 9DH. *T:* 01-353 7356.

HENRY, Sir James Holmes, 2nd Bt, *cr* 1922; CMG 1960; MC 1944; TD 1950; QC (Tanganyika) 1953, (Cyprus) 1957; Chairman, Foreign Compensation Commission, since 1977 (Commissioner, 1960-77); *b* 22 Sept. 1911; *er s* of Rt Hon. Sir Denis Stanislaus Henry, 1st Baronet, Cahore, Co. Londonderry, 1st Lord Chief Justice of Northern Ireland, and Violet (*d* 1966), 3rd *d* of late Rt Hon. Hugh Holmes, Court of Appeal, Ireland; *S* father, 1925; *m* 1st, 1941 (marriage terminated by divorce and rescript of Holy Office in Rome); 2nd, 1949, Christina Hilary, widow of Lieut-Commander Christopher H. Wells, RN, and *e d* of late Sir Hugh Holmes, KBE, CMG, MC, QC; three *d. Educ:* Mount St Mary's Coll., Chesterfield; Downside Sch.; University College, London. BA (Hons) Classics (1st Class), University Scholarships. Called to Bar, Inner Temple, 1934; practised, London, 1934-39. Served War of 1939-45, London Irish Rifles (wounded). Crown Counsel, Tanganyika, 1946; Legal Draftsman, 1949; jt comr, Revised Edn of Laws of Tanganyika (1947-49), 1950; Solicitor-General, 1952; Attorney-General, Cyprus, 1956-60. *Heir: b* Denis Valentine Henry [*b* 29 June 1917; *m* 1956, Elizabeth, *d* of Rowland Walker; one *s* two *d*]. *Address:* Kandy Lodge, 18 Ormond Avenue, Hampton-on-Thames, Mddx. *Clubs:* Travellers', Royal Commonwealth Society.

HENRY, Thomas Cradock, FDS, RCS; MRCS; LRCP; Consultant Dental Surgeon, Hospital for Sick Children, Great Ormond Street; Consultant Maxillo-Facial Surgeon, Royal Surrey County Hospital; Consultant Oral Surgeon, Italian Hospital, London; *b* 30 Dec. 1910; *s* of late Thomas Henry and Rose Emily Bowdler, Moorgate, Park Retford; *m* 1939, Claire Mary, 7th *c* of late R. A. Caraman, The Grange, Elstree; two *s. Educ:* King Edward VI Grammar Sch., Retford; King's Coll., University of London; Middlesex and Royal Dental Hospital; Saunders Scholar; qualified as Doctor, 1935. Formerly: House Physician, House Surgeon and Resident Anæsthetist St James's Hosp., London; Dental House Surgeon, St Bartholomew's Hosp.; Squadron Leader and Surgical Specialist, RAFVR, 1939-

46; Surgical Registrar, Plastic and Jaw Injuries Centre, East Grinstead, 1941-42; Surgeon in charge of Maxillo-Facial and Burns Unit, RAF Hosp., Cosford, 1942-46; Hunterian Prof., RCS, 1944-45. FRSocMed; Founder Fellow and Pres., British Assoc. of Oral Surgeons; Member: European Orthodontic Soc.; British Assoc. of Plastic Surgeons (Mem. Council); BMA. *Publications:* Fracture of the Facial Bones (chapter in Fractures and Dislocations in General Practice, 1949); Labial Segment Surgery (chapter in Archer's Oral Surgery, 1971); Melanotic Ameloblastoma (in Trans 3rd ICOS); numerous contrib. to leading medical and dental journals, including BMJ and Jl of Bone and Joint Surgery. *Recreations:* shooting and fishing. *Address:* Private Consulting Rooms, Mount Alvernia Nursing Home, Harvey Road, Guildford, Surrey. *T:* Guildford 67517; Fieldfares, Thursley, Surrey. *T:* Elstead 2279.

HENRY, Hon. Sir Trevor (Ernest), Kt 1970; Judge, Fiji Court of Appeal, since 1974; *b* 9 May 1902; *s* of John Henry and Edith Anna (*née* Eaton); *m* 1930, Audrey Kate Sheriff; one *s* one *d*. *Educ:* Rotorua District High Sch.; Univ. of New Zealand (Auckland). LLB 1925, LLM Hons 1926, NZ. Solicitor of Supreme Court of NZ, 1923, Barrister, 1925. Judge of the Supreme Court of NZ, 1955-77. *Recreation:* fishing. *Address:* 16 Birdwood Crescent, Parnell, Auckland 1, New Zealand. *Club:* Northern (Auckland).

HENRY, William Robert; Chairman, Coats Patons Ltd, since Oct. 1975; *b* 30 April 1915; *s* of William Henry and Sarah (*née* Lindsay); *m* 1947, Esther Macfayden; two *s* one *d*. *Educ:* Govan High Sch.; London Univ. Entered Company's service, 1934; Head of Financial Dept, 1953; Asst Accountant, 1957; Dir, J. & P. Coats Ltd (Parent Co.), 1966; Dep. Chm., Coats Patons Ltd, 1970. *Recreations:* sailing, gardening. *Address:* 2/9 Barcapel Avenue, Newton Mearns, Renfrewshire. *T:* 041-639 7290.

HENSBY, Frederick Charles, OBE 1973; HM Diplomatic Service; Counsellor and Head of Consular Department, Foreign and Commonwealth Office, 1976-77; *b* 7 Nov. 1919; *s* of late Charles Henry Hensby and Ivy Helen (*née* Lake); *m* 1946, Maud Joyce (*née* Stace). *Educ:* Hendon County Grammar Sch. Joined Foreign Office, 1937. Served War: Devonshire Regt, 1940-42; Intelligence Corps, 1942-46. Returned to FO, 1946; HM Embassy: Rio de Janeiro, 1947-50; Paris, 1950-52; FO, 1952-56; HM Vice Consul, Muscat, 1956-58; Sec. to Allied Kommandantura, Berlin, 1958-59; FO, 1960-62; First Sec. and Consul: Monrovia, 1962-64; Paris, 1965-66; Asst Head of Protocol Dept, FCO, 1967-69; First Sec., British High Commn, New Delhi, 1970-72; Asst Head, Immigration and Visa Dept, FCO, 1973-75. *Recreations:* gardening, bird-watching, golf. *Address:* c/o Foreign and Commonwealth Office, SW1; Giles Coppice, Woodsdale, Battle, Sussex TN33 0LS. *T:* Battle 2746. *Club:* Royal Commonwealth Society.

HENSHALL, Rt. Rev. Michael; *see* Warrington, Bishop Suffragan of.

HENSLEY, John; Secretary, Committee of Inquiry into Veterinary Profession, 1971-75; *b* 28 Feb. 1910; *s* of late Edward Hutton and Marion Hensley; *m* 1st, 1940, Dorothy Betty (*d* 1969), *d* of Percy George and Dorothy Coppard; one *s*; 2nd, 1971, Elizabeth, *widow* of Charles Cross and *d* of Harold and Jessie Coppard. *Educ:* Malvern; Trinity Coll., Cambridge (Chancellor's Classical Medal, MA). Entered Min. of Agriculture and Fisheries, 1933; Priv. Sec. to Chancellor of Duchy of Lancaster and Minister of Food, 1939; Priv. Sec. to Minister of Agriculture and Fisheries, 1945; Asst Sec., 1946; Under Sec., 1957; retired 1970. Member: Agricultural Research Council, 1957-59; Council, Nat. Inst. of Agricultural Botany, 1970-73. *Recreations:* genealogy, gardening. *Address:* 109 Markfield, Courtwood Lane, Addington, Croydon CR0 9HP. *T:* 01-657 6319.

HENSON, Ronald Alfred, MD, FRCP; Physician and Neurologist, The London Hospital, since 1949; Physician, National Hospitals for Nervous Diseases, Maida Vale Hospital, since 1952; *b* 4 Oct. 1915; *s* of Alfred and Nellie Henson, Chippenham, Wilts; *m* 1941, Frances, *d* of A. Francis and Jessie Sims, Bath; three *d*. *Educ:* King Edward VI Sch., Bath; London Hospital Medical Coll. Major, RAMC, 1940-46. Mem., Archbishops' Commission on Divine Healing, 1953-57. Dir of Studies, Institute of Neurology, University of London, 1955-64; Dir, Cancer Res. Campaign Neuropathological Res. Unit, London Hosp. Med. Coll., 1967-71. Hon. Consulting Neurologist, Royal Soc. Musicians, GB; formerly Mem. Board of Governors: The London Hosp.; Nat. Hosps for Nervous Diseases. President: Neurological Section, RSM, 1976-77 (Sec., 1956-58; Vice-Pres., 1974); Assoc. of British Neurologists, 1976-77 (Sec., 1964-68). Commonwealth Fellow 1964. Member:

Assoc. of Physicians of Great Britain and Ireland; British Neuropathological Soc.; Hon. Corresponding Mem. Amer. Neurological Assoc., 1966; Hon. Member: Canadian Neurological Soc., 1971; Belgian Neurological Soc., 1976. Chm., London Bach Soc. *Publications:* Music and the Brain (ed jtly), 1977; various contributions to the neurological literature. *Address:* 26 Stormont Road, Highgate, N6. *T:* 01-340 6092. *Clubs:* Athenæum, MCC.

HENTSCHEL, Christopher Carl, MSc; FLS, FZS, FIBiol; Principal, Chelsea College of Science and Technology, 1962-65, retired; *b* 4 July 1899; *s* of Carl and Bertha Hentschel; unmarried. *Educ:* St Paul's Sch. (Classical Scholar); King's Coll., London. Demonstrator, in Biology, St Bartholomew's Med. Coll., 1923-31; Chelsea Polytechnic, later Chelsea Coll. of Science and Technology: Lectr in Zoology, 1931-53; Head, Dept of Botany and Zoology, 1953-61; Vice-Principal, 1961-62. Mem. of Senate, University of London, 1956-64, 1966-70. Vice-Pres., Linnean Soc. of London, 1943-44, 1950-51, 1952-53; Formerly Governor: Sloane & Rutherford Schs, London; Paddington Technical Coll.; Pent Valley Sch., Folkestone. Hon. FChS. *Publications:* (with W. R. Ivimey Cook) Biology for Medical Students, 1932; papers on parasitic Protozoa. *Recreations:* motoring; continental travel. *Address:* Flat A, Dolphin House, 117 Sandgate High Street, Folkestone, Kent. *T:* Folkestone 38094. *Club:* Folkestone Rowing.

HENTY, Hon. Sir (Norman Henry) Denham, KBE 1968; Leader of the Government in the Senate, Australia, 1966-67; Minister for Supply, 1966-68; Senator for Tasmania 1950-68; Commissioner, Overseas Telecommunications, since 1968; *b* 13 Oct. 1903; *s* of Thomas Norman and Lily Henty; *m* 1930, Faith Gordon Spotswood; two *s* one *d*. *Educ:* Launceston Church Grammar Sch. Managing Director, T. Norman Henty Pty Ltd, 1937-50. Chm., Public Works Cttee, 1955-56; Minister for Customs and Excise, 1956-64; Minister for Civil Aviation, 1964-66. Alderman, Launceston City Coun., 1943-50; Mayor, City of Launceston, 1948-49. *Recreations:* golf, billiards. *Address:* 11 Beulah Gardens, Launceston, Tasmania 7250, Australia. *T:* Launceston 2-3031. *Clubs:* Tasmanian (Hobart); Launceston, Northern (Launceston); Commercial Travellers Association (Australia).

HENZE, Hans Werner; composer; *b* 1 July 1926; *s* of Franz Gebhard Henze and Margarete Geldmacher. *Educ:* Bünde i/W; Bielefeld i/W; Braunschweig. Studying music in Heidelberg, 1945; First Work performed (Chamber Concerto), at Darmstadt-Kranichstein, 1946; Musical Dir, Municipal Theatre, Constance, 1948; Artistic Dir of Ballet, Hessian States Theatre, Wiesbaden, 1950. Prof. of Composition, Acad. Mozarteum, Salzburg, 1961. Definite departure for Italy, living first in Forio d'Ischia, then Naples, then Castelgandolfo as a composer. Frequent international conducting tours. Member: German Acad. of Arts, E Berlin; Philharmonic Acad., Rome. Hon. DMus Edinburgh, 1970. Robert Schumann Prize, 1952; Prix d'Italia, 1953; Nordrhein-Westphalien Award, 1955; Berlin Prize of Artists, 1958; Great Prize for Artists, Hanover, 1962. *Publications:* a book of Essays; 6 symphonies; 7 full length operas, 3 one-act operas; 5 normal ballets and 5 chamber ballets; chamber music; choral works. *Address:* La Leprara, 00047 Marino, Roma, Italy.

HEPBURN, Audrey; actress; *b* Brussels, 4 May 1929; *d* of J. A. Hepburn; *m* 1st, 1954, Mel Ferrer (marr. diss. 1968); one *s*; 2nd, 1969, Dr Andrea Dotti; one *s*. Studied ballet in Amsterdam and in Marie Rambert's ballet sch. First stage part in musical production, High Button Shoes; first film appearance in Laughter in Paradise. Played leading rôles in Gigi (play), New York, 1951 (tour of America, Oct. 1952-May 1953); Ondine (play by Jean Giraudoux), 1954. *Films:* One Wild Oat, The Lavender Hill Mob; The Young Wives' Tale; The Secret People; Nous Irons à Monte Carlo; Roman Holiday, 1952; Sabrina Fair, 1954; War and Peace, 1956; Funny Face, 1957; Love in the Afternoon, 1957; The Nun's Story, 1958, also Green Mansions; The Unforgiven, 1960; Breakfast at Tiffany's, 1961; Paris When it Sizzles, 1962; Charade, 1962; My Fair Lady, 1964; How to Make a Million, 1966; Two for the Road, 1967; Wait Until Dark, 1968; Robin Hood and Maid Marion, 1975. *Address:* c/o Kurt Frings, 9440 Santa Monica Boulevard, Beverly Hills, Calif 90210, USA.

HEPBURN, Bryan Audley St John, CMG 1962; Financial Secretary, Sarawak, 1958-63; Member, Sarawak Legislative and Executive Councils, 1955-63; Member, Inter-Governmental Committee which led to establishment of Federation of Malaysia; *b* 24 Feb. 1911; *m* 1940, Sybil Isabel Myers; two *d*. *Educ:* Cornwall Coll., Jamaica. Jamaica Civil Service, 1930; Asst Sec., Colonial Service, 1944; Principal Asst Sec., Sarawak,

1947; Development Sec., 1951. Chm., Sarawak Develt Finance Corp., 1958-63; Chm., Sarawak Electricity Supply Co. Ltd, 1955-63; Dir, Malayan Airways Ltd, 1959-63; Dir, Borneo Airways Ltd, 1958-63; Dep. Chm., Malaysian Tariff Adv. Bd, 1963-65. Ministry of Overseas Development, 1966-73. *Recreations:* golf, swimming, fishing. *Address:* 7 Weald Rise, Haywards Heath, West Sussex. *Clubs:* Royal Over-Seas League; Royal Commonwealth Society; Sarawak (Sarawak).

HEPBURN, Katharine; actress; *b* 9 Nov. 1909; *d* of late Dr Thomas N. Hepburn and Katharine Houghton; *m* Ludlow Ogden Smith (marr. diss.). *Educ:* Hartford; Bryn Mawr College. First professional appearance on stage, Baltimore, 1928, in Czarina; first New York appearance, 1928, in Night Hostess (under name Katherine Burns), The Millionairess, New Theatre, London, 1952. Entered films, 1932; notable films: A Bill of Divorcement; Morning Glory; Little Women; The Little Minister; Mary of Scotland; Quality Street; Stage Door; The Philadelphia Story; Keeper of the Flame; Dragon Seed; Woman of the Year; Under-current; Without Love; Sea of Grass; Song of Love; State of the Union; Adam's Rib; The African Queen; Pat and Mike; Summer Madness; The Iron Petticoat; The Rainmaker; His Other Woman; Suddenly, Last Summer; Long Day's Journey into Night; Guess Who's Coming to Dinner; The Madwoman of Chaillot; The Lion in Winter; The Trojan Women; A Delicate Balance; Rooster Cogburn. *Stage:* Warrior's Husband; The Philadelphia Story; Without Love; As You Like It; Taming of the Shrew; Merchant of Venice; Measure for Measure, Australia, 1955; Coco, 1970; A Matter of Gravity, NY, 1976, tour, 1977. Academy Awards for performances in Morning Glory, Guess Who's Coming to Dinner, The Lion in Winter. Appears on TV. *Address:* PO Box 17-154, West Hartford, Conn 06117, USA.

HEPBURN, Surg. Rear-Adm. Nicol Sinclair, CB 1971; CBE 1968; Medical Officer, Department of Health and Social Security, since 1972; *b* 2 Feb. 1913; *s* of late John Primrose and Susan Hepburn, Edinburgh; *m* 1939, Dorothy Blackwood; two *s*. *Educ:* Broughton; Edinburgh Univ. MB, ChB 1935; DPH London, 1948; DIH London, 1952. Barrister-at-law, Gray's Inn, 1956. Joined RN, 1935; served during war in Atlantic and Pacific Stations; SMO, HM Dockyard: Plymouth, 1952; Portsmouth, 1955; Naval Medical Officer of Health: Portsmouth, 1959; Malta, 1962; Surg. Cdre and Dep. Med. Dir-Gen., 1966; Surg. Rear-Adm. 1969; MO i/c, RN Hosp., Haslar, 1969-72; retd. FRSM; FFCM 1973. *Address:* Mallows, 10 Chilbolton Avenue, Winchester, Hants SO22 5HD.

HEPBURN, Sir Ninian B. A. J. B.; *see* Buchan-Hepburn.

HEPBURN, Prof. Ronald William; Professor of Moral Philosophy, University of Edinburgh, since 1975 (Professor of Philosophy, 1964-75); *b* 16 March 1927; *s* of late W. G. Hepburn, Aberdeen; *m* 1953, Agnes Forbes Anderson; two *s* one *d*. *Educ:* Aberdeen Grammar Sch.; University of Aberdeen. MA 1951, PhD 1955 (Aberdeen). National service in Army, 1944-48. Asst, 1952-55, Lecturer, 1955-60, Dept of Moral Philosophy, University of Aberdeen; Visiting Associate Prof., New York University, 1959-60; Prof. of Philosophy, University of Nottingham, 1960-64. Stanton Lecturer in the Philosophy of Religion, Cambridge, 1965-68. *Publications:* (jointly) Metaphysical beliefs, 1957; Christianity and Paradox, 1958; chapters in: Collected Papers on Aesthetics, 1965; Christian Ethics and Contemporary Philosophy, 1966; British Analytical Philosophy, 1966; Hobbes and Rousseau, 1972; Education and the Development of Reason, 1972; Philosophy and the Arts, 1973; Contemporary British Philosophy, vol. IV, 1976; contrib. to learned journals; broadcasts. *Recreations:* music, hill-walking, photography. *Address:* Department of Philosophy, University of Edinburgh, David Hume Tower, George Square, Edinburgh EH8 9JX.

HEPBURNE-SCOTT, family name of Baron Polwarth.

HEPPEL, Richard Purdon, CMG 1959; HM Diplomatic Service, retired; Appeals Secretary for Bedfordshire, Buckinghamshire and Hertfordshire, Cancer Research Campaign, since 1970; *b* 27 Oct. 1913; 2nd *s* of late Engineer Rear-Admiral Walter George Heppel and Margaret, *d* of late Robert Stevens Fraser; *m* 1949, Ruth Theodora, *d* of late Horatio Matthews, MD; two *s* one *d*. *Educ:* Rugby Sch.; Balliol Coll., Oxford. Laming Travelling Fellow, Queen's Coll., 1935. Entered Diplomatic Service, 1936; Third Sec., Rome, 1939; Second Sec., Tehran, 1942; First Sec., Athens, 1944; Private Sec. to Min. of State, 1946; First Sec., Karachi, 1948, Madrid, 1951; Counsellor, HM Legation, Saigon, 1953-54; Ambassador to Cambodia, 1954-56; Minister at Vienna, 1956-59; Head of South East Asia Dept, Foreign Office, 1959; Head of Consular Dept, Foreign Office, 1961-63;

Imperial Defence Coll., 1960; Consul-Gen. at Stuttgart, 1963-69. Administrative Officer, The City Univ. Grad. Business Centre, 1969-70. Freeman, Skinners' Company, 1961, Liveryman 1969. *Address:* Barn Piece, Nether Winchendon, Bucks; Lacona 43, Isola d'Elba, Italy.

HEPPENSTALL, (John) Rayner; novelist, critic and criminal historian; *b* 27 July 1911; *s* of Edgar and Lizzie Heppenstall, Huddersfield, Yorks; *m* 1937, Margaret Harwood Edwards, Newport, Mon; one *s* one *d*. *Educ:* in Yorks (variously); Calais; University of Leeds; University of Strasbourg. Graduated (Modern Languages), 1933; schoolmaster, 1934; freelance author, 1935-39. Served War of 1939-45 Army (RA, Field, RAPC), 1940-45. Feature-writer and producer, BBC, 1945-65, Drama producer, 1965-67. *Publications:* First Poems, 1935; Apology for Dancing, 1936; Sebastian, 1937; The Blaze of Noon, 1939 (Arts Council Prize, 1966); Blind Men's Flowers are Green, 1940; Saturnine, 1943 (revised as The Greater Infortune, 1960); The Double Image, 1946; Poems, 1933-1945, 1946; The Lesser Infortune, 1953; Léon Bloy, 1954; Four Absentees, 1960; The Fourfold Tradition, 1961; The Connecting Door, 1962; The Woodshed, 1962; The Intellectual Part, 1963; Raymond Roussel: a critical guide, 1966; Portrait of the Artist as a Professional Man, 1969; The Shearers, 1969; A Little Pattern of French Crime, 1969; French Crime in the Romantic Age, 1970; Bluebeard and After, 1972; The Sex War and Others, 1973; Reflections on The Newgate Calendar, 1975; Two Moons, 1977; edited: Existentialism (G. de Ruggiero), 1946; Imaginary Conversations, 1948; Architecture of Truth, 1957; (with Michael Innes) Three Tales of Hamlet, 1950; translated: Atala and René (Chateaubriand), 1963; Impressions of Africa (Roussel) (with Lindy Foord), 1966; A Harlot High and Low (Balzac), 1970; When Justice Falters (Floriot), 1972. *Recreations:* variable. *Address:* Coach Cottage, 2 Gilford Road, Deal, Kent. *T:* Deal 63493.

HEPPENSTALL, Rayner; *see* Heppenstall, John R.

HEPPER, Anthony Evelyn; CEng; MIMechE; Chairman, Henry Sykes Ltd, since 1972; *b* 16 Jan. 1923; *s* of Lieut-Col J. E. Hepper; *m* 1970, Jonquil Francisca Kinloch-Jones. *Educ:* Wellington Coll., Berks. Royal Engrs, 1942-47 (retd as Hon. Maj.); Courtaulds Ltd, 1947-53; Cape Asbestos Co. Ltd 1953-57; Thomas Tilling Ltd, 1957-68 (Dir from 1963 until secondment); seconded as Industrial Adviser, DEA, 1966-67, and Mem., SIB, 1967; Chm., Upper Clyde Shipbuilders Ltd, 1968-71; Dir, Cape Industries Ltd, 1968-. *Recreation:* golf. *Address:* 70 Eaton Place, SW1. *T:* 01-235 7518.

HEPPLE, Prof. Bob Alexander; a Chairman of Industrial Tribunals (England and Wales), since 1977 (part-time, 1975-77); Hon. Professor of Comparative Social and Labour Law, University of Kent; *b* 11 Aug. 1934; *s* of Alexander Hepple and Josephine Zwarenstein; *m* 1960, Shirley Goldsmith; one *s* one *d*. *Educ:* Univ. of Witwatersrand (BA 1954, LLB *cum laude* 1957); Univ. of Cambridge (LLB 1966, MA 1968). Attorney, S Africa, 1958; Lectr in Law, Univ. of Witwatersrand, 1959-62; Advocate, S Africa, 1962-63. Left S Africa after detention without trial for anti-apartheid activities, 1963. Called to Bar, Gray's Inn, 1966; Lectr in Law, Nottingham Univ., 1966-68; Fellow of Clare Coll., Cambridge and Univ. Lectr in Law, 1968-76; Prof. of Comparative Social and Labour Law, Univ. of Kent, 1976-77. *Publications:* various books and articles on labour law, race relations, law of tort, etc; Founding Editor, Industrial Law Jl, 1972-77; Gen. Ed (jtly) Encyclopedia of Labour Relations Law, 1972-. *Recreation:* voluntary social services. *Address:* 5 Leycroft Close, Canterbury, Kent.

HEPPLE, (Robert) Norman, RA 1961 (ARA 1954); RP 1948; NEAC, 1950; *b* 18 May 1908; *s* of Robert Watkin Hepple and Ethel Louise Wardale; *m* 1948, Jillian Constance Marigold Pratt; one *s* one *d*. *Educ:* Goldsmiths' Coll.; Royal Acad. Schools. Figure subject and portrait painter. *Address:* (studio) 16 Cresswell Place, South Kensington, SW10; (home) 10 Sheen Common Drive, Richmond, Surrey. *T:* 01-878 4452. *Club:* Chelsea Arts.

HEPPLESTON, Prof. Alfred Gordon; Professor of Pathology, University of Newcastle upon Tyne (formerly Durham), 1960-77, now Emeritus Professor; *b* 29 Aug. 1915; *s* of Alfred Heppleston, Headmaster, and Edith (*née* Clough); *m* 1942, Eleanor Rix Tebbutt; two *s*. *Educ:* Manchester Grammar Sch. Chief Asst, Professorial Medical Unit, University of Manchester; Asst Lecturer in Pathology, Welsh Nat. Sch. of Medicine, Univ. of Wales, 1944-47; Dorothy Temple Cross Research Fellow, Univ. of Pennsylvania, 1947-48; Sen. Lectr in Pathology, Univ. of Wales, 1948-60. *Publications:* on pathological topics, largely in reference to pulmonary disorders.

Recreations: ornithology, cricket and music. *Address:* 6 Burnside Close, Ovingham, Northumberland NE42 6BS.

HEPTINSTALL, Leslie George; HM Diplomatic Service, retired; *b* 20 Aug. 1919; *s* of late Victor George Heptinstall and of Maud Maunder; *m* 1949, Marion Nicholls; one *d. Educ:* Thames Valley County Sch.; London Univ. (BSc Econ.). Served War of 1939-45: Capt., Royal Artillery; Middle East, Mediterranean, North-West Europe. Asst Principal, Colonial Office, 1948; Principal, 1951; seconded to West African Inter-Territorial Secretariat, Accra, 1955; Acting Chief Sec., 1958; Acting Administrator, W African Research Office, 1959; Principal, CRO, 1961; First Sec. on Staff of Brit. High Comr, Wellington, NZ, 1962-64; Brit. Dep. High Comr, Lahore, 1964-65; Head of South Asia Dept, ODM, 1966-68; Dep. Senior Trade Comr, Montreal, 1968-70; Internat. Coffee Orgn, 1971-73. *Recreations:* sailing, golf and tennis. *Address:* Brackenwood Cottage, Oxshott Road, Leatherhead, Surrey.

HEPWORTH, Rear-Adm. David, CB 1976; retired from RN, 1976; Head of Naval Support, Millbank Technical Services, since 1977; *b* 6 June 1923; *s* of Alfred Ernest Hepworth and Minnie Louisa Catherine Bennet Tanner (*née* Bowden); *m* 1st, 1946, Brenda June Case (marr. diss. 1974); one *s* one *d*; 2nd, 1975, Eileen Mary Macgillivray (*née* Robson). *Educ:* Banbury Grammar School. Boy Telegraphist, RN, 1939; HMS Ganges, 1939-40; served in Atlantic, Mediterranean and E Indies Fleets; commnd 1944; submarines and midget submarines, 1945-50; Home, Australian and Far East Stns, 1951-58; Sen. Officer Submarines Londonderry, 1959-61; CO HMS Ashanti, 1961-64; jssc 1964; Dep. Dir Undersea Warfare, MoD, 1964-66; idc 1967; CO HMS Ajax and Captain (D) 2nd Far East Destroyer Sqdn, 1968-69; Dir RN Tactical Sch. and Maritime Tactical Sch., 1969-71; Dir Naval Warfare, MoD, 1971-73; Staff of Vice-Chief of Naval Staff, 1973-76. Lt-Comdr 1952; Comdr 1958; Captain 1964; Rear-Adm. 1974. *Recreations:* tennis, gardening, music. *Address:* Darville House, Lower Heyford, Oxon. *T:* Steeple Aston 47460.

HERBECQ, Sir John (Edward), KCB 1977; Second Permanent Secretary, Civil Service Department, since 1975; *b* 29 May 1922; *s* of late Joseph Edward Herbecq and of Rosina Elizabeth Herbecq; *m* 1947, Pamela Filby; one *d. Educ:* High Sch. for Boys, Chichester. Clerical Officer, Colonial Office, 1939; Asst Principal, Treasury, 1950; Private Sec. to Chm., UK Atomic Energy Authority, 1960-62; Asst Sec., Treasury, 1964; Asst Sec., 1968, Under Sec., 1970, Dep. Sec., 1973, CSD. *Recreation:* Scottish country dancing. *Address:* Maryland, Ledgers Meadow, Cuckfield, Haywards Heath, West Sussex RH17 5EW. *T:* Haywards Heath 3387. *Club:* Royal Automobile.

HERBERT, family name of **Earls of Carnarvon, Pembroke,** and **Powis,** and **Baron Hemingford.**

HERBERT, Christopher Alfred, CB 1973; Under-Secretary, Ministry of Defence; *b* 15 June 1913; *s* of Alfred Abbot Herbert and Maria Hamilton (*née* Fetherston); *m* 1941, Evelyn Benson Scott (*née* Ross) (*d* 1972); one *s* one *d. Educ:* Mountjoy Sch., Dublin; Trinity Coll., Dublin (BA (Hons)). Indian Civil Service, 1937-47; Eastern Manager, May & Baker (India) Ltd, 1947-50. MoD. 1950-. *Recreations:* walking, gardening, reading. *Address:* 41 Woodcote Avenue, Wallington, Surrey. *T:* 01-647 5223. *Club:* East India, Devonshire, Sports and Public Schools.

HERBERT, Hon. (Dennis) Nicholas; Editorial Director, Westminster Press, since 1974; *b* 25 July 1934; *s* and *heir* of Baron Hemingford, *qv*; *m* 1958, Jennifer Mary Toresen Bailey, *d* of F. W. Bailey, Harrogate; one *s* three *d. Educ:* Oundle Sch.; Clare Coll., Cambridge (MA). Reuters Ltd, 1956-61; The Times: Asst Washington Corresp., 1961-65; Middle East Corresp., 1965-68; Dep. Features Editor, 1968-70; Editor, Cambridge Evening News, 1970-74. *Address:* Old Rectory, Hemingford Abbots, Huntingdon PE18 9AH. *T:* St Ives (Hunts) 66234. *Club:* Royal Commonwealth Society.

HERBERT, Lieut-Gen. Sir (Edwin) Otway, KBE 1955 (CBE 1944); CB 1946; DSO 1940; retired as General Officer Commanding-in-Chief, Western Command (1957-60); Colonel Commandant, Royal Artillery 1956-66; *b* 18 Nov. 1901; *s* of late Gustavus Otway Herbert; *m* 1925, Muriel Irlam Barlow; one *d. Educ:* Felsted Sch.; Royal Military Academy, Woolwich. Commissioned Royal Artillery, 1921: served war of 1939-45; BEF France and Belgium, 1939-40 (despatches, DSO); 1st Army, 78 Div., North Africa, 1942-43 (bar to DSO); 21 Army Group, 1943-45 (despatches, CBE, CB); GOC British Troops, Berlin, and British Commandant, Berlin, 1947-49; Dir Territorial Army and Cadets, War Office, 1949-52; GOC 44 (Home Counties) Div. and District, 1952-53; GOC-in-C, West

Africa Command, 1953-56. High Sheriff of Anglesey, 1964-65. Officer of Legion of Merit (USA); Knight Commander Orange Nassau (Netherlands); Commander of Leopold II (Belgium). *Recreations:* most outdoor sports available. *Address:* Llanidan House, Brynsiencyn, Anglesey. *T:* Brynsiencyn 393. *Club:* Army and Navy.

HERBERT, Major George, MBE; *b* 1892; *s* of William Herbert, York; *m* 1916, Elsie (*d* 1952), *d* of late G. E. Barton, York; one *s.* Served European War, France, 1914-19 (despatches, MBE) Major; Active Service, 1939-44 (despatches), Food Controller Gibraltar. MP (C) Rotherham, 1931-33; dir of companies. *Publications:* Trade Abroad, 1924; British Empire Ltd, 1926; The Call of Empire, 1927; 'Can Land Settlement Solve Unemployment?, 1934. *Recreations:* golf, fishing, cricket. *Address:* Hampden House, Duchy Road, Harrogate, North Yorks.

HERBERT, Hon. Nicholas; *see* Herbert, Hon. D. N.

HERBERT, Lieut-Gen. Sir Otway; *see* Herbert, Lieut-Gen. Sir E. O.

HERBERT, Prof. Robert Louis, PhD; Robert Lehman Professor of the History of Art, Yale University, since 1974; Slade Professor of Fine Art, University of Oxford, Jan.-Mar. 1978; *b* 21 April 1929; *s* of John Newman Herbert and Rosalia Harr Herbert; *m* 1953, Eugenia Randall Warren; one *s* two *d. Educ:* Wesleyan Univ., Middletown, Conn (BA 1951); Yale Univ. (MA 1954, PhD 1957). Fulbright Scholar, Paris, 1951-52; Faculty, Yale Univ., 1956-: Fellow, 1960-61 and 1968-69; Associate Prof., 1963; Prof., 1966; Departmental Chm., 1965-68. Guggenheim Fellow, 1971-72. Organizer of exhibitions: Barbizon Revisited, Boston Museum of Fine Arts and others, 1962-63; Neo-Impressionism, Solomon R. Guggenheim Mus., 1968; J. F. Millet, Musée Nationaux, Paris, and Arts Council, London, 1975-76. Chevalier, Ordre des Arts et des Lettres, 1976. *Publications:* Barbizon Revisited, 1962-63; Seurat's Drawings, 1963; The Art Criticism of John Ruskin, 1964; Modern Artists on Art, 1964; Neo-Impressionism, 1968; David, Voltaire, 'Brutus' and the French Revolution, 1972; J. F. Millet, 1975; articles in learned jls. *Address:* Department of the History of Art, Yale University, Box 2009, 56 High Street, New Haven, Conn 06520, USA. *T:* 436-1023.

HERBERT, Robin Arthur Elidyr, DL; JP; Deputy Chairman, Countryside Commission, since 1971; a Director: National Westminster Bank Ltd (Chairman, SW Regional Board); Leopold Joseph & Sons Ltd; Equity and Law Life Assurance, since 1977; *b* 5 March 1934; *s* of late Sir John Arthur Herbert, GCIE and Lady Mary Herbert; *m* 1960, Margaret Griswold Lewis; two *s* two *d. Educ:* Eton; Christ Church, Oxford (MA); Harvard Business School (MBA). ARICS. 2nd Lieut Royal Horse Guards, 1953-54; Captain Royal Monmouthshire RE, 1962-68. Mem. Council and Exec. Cttee, National Trust, and Chm. Cttee for Wales, 1969-. Mem. Council, RHS, 1971-74. DL 1968, JP 1964, High Sheriff 1972, Monmouthshire. *Recreations:* dendrology, walking. *Address:* Llanover, Abergavenny, Gwent. *T:* Nantyderry 880232. *Club:* Brooks's.

HERBERT, Walter Elmes, MRCS, LRCP 1928; LDS, RCS 1925; FDS, RCS 1948; FRSM; Professor of Conservative Dental Surgery, University of London, 1938-67, now Emeritus; Director of Department of Conservative Dental Surgery, Guy's Hospital Dental School, 1931-67; Lecturer in Operative Dental Surgery, 1933-67; *b* Sept. 1902; *s* of H. W. Herbert, Egham, Surrey; *m* 1933, Joyce Mary Griffith Clogg, MB, BS; one *s* one *d. Educ:* Queen' Coll., Taunton; Guy's Hospital Medical and Dental Schools (travelling Dental Scholar, 1928); North Western Univ., Chicago; Demonstrator in Operative Dental Surgery, Guy's Hospital, 1929-31; Univ. Reader in Conservative Dental Surgery, 1933-38. Vis. Prof. of Dentistry, Sch. of Dentistry, Nat. Univ. of Iran, Tehran, 1969-70. *Publications:* Operative Dental Surgery (with J. B. Parfitt), 4th edn 1939—7th edn 1955, (with W. A. Vale), 8th edn, 1962; Cancer of Stomach, in London, in Stockholm and in Amsterdam (jointly) Guy's Hospital Reports, 1939; The Training of the Dental Surgeon, 1962; and various contributions to British Dental Journal. *Recreations:* mountaineering, gardening. *Address:* Half Acre, 58 Kingswood Firs, Grayshott, Hindhead, Surrey. *T:* Hindhead 4563. *Club:* Alpine.

HERBERT, Walter William; *b* 24 Oct. 1934; *s* of Captain W. W. J. Herbert and Helen (*née* Manton); *m* 1969, Marie, *d* of Prof. C. A. McGaughey; one *d.* Trained as surveyor in RE; Egypt, 1953-54, demob. 1955; travelled in Middle East, 1955; Surveyor with Falkland Is Dependencies Survey; Hope Bay, Antarctica, 1955-58; travelled in S America, 1958-59; Mem. expedn to Lapland

and Spitzbergen, 1960; travelled in Greenland, 1960; Surveyor, NZ Antarctic Expedn, 1960-62; leader Southern Party; mapped 26,000 sq. miles of Queen Maud Range and descended Amundsen's route to Pole on 50th anniv.; led expedn to NW Greenland, 1966-67; dog-sledged 1,400 miles Greenland to Canada in trng for trans-Arctic crossing; led British Trans-Arctic Expedn, 1968-69, which made 3,800-mile first surface crossing of Arctic Ocean from Alaska via North Pole to Spitzbergen (longest sustained sledging journey in history of Polar exploration); led Ultima Thule expedn (filming Eskimos, Thule District), 1971-73; led expedn to Lapland, 1975; leading expedn to Greenland, 1977- (7,000 miles; first circumnavigation by dog sledge and skin boat). Hon. Mem., British Schools Exploring Soc.; Jt Hon. Pres., World Expeditionary Assoc. FRGS. Polar Medal 1962, and clasp 1969; Livingstone Gold Medal, RSGS, 1969; Founder's Gold Medal, RGS, 1970. *Publications:* A World of Men, 1968; Across the Top of the World, 1969; (contrib.) World Atlas of Mountaineering, 1969; The Last Great Journey on Earth, 1971; Polar Deserts, 1971; Eskimos, 1976; (contrib.) Expeditions the Expert's Way, 1977. *Recreation:* painting. *Address:* c/o Royal Geographical Society, SW7. *Club:* Lansdowne.

HERBERT-JONES, Hugh (Hugo) Jarrett, CMG 1973; OBE 1963; HM Diplomatic Service; Counsellor, Foreign and Commonwealth Office, since 1975; *b* 11 March 1922; *s* of late Dora Herbert-Jones (*née* Rowlands), and Captain Herbert-Jones; *m* 1954, Margaret, *d* of Rev. J. P. Veall; one *s* two *d*. *Educ:* Bryanston; Worcester Coll., Oxford. History Scholar. Commnd Welsh Guards, 1941; served NW Europe and Middle East; wounded 1944; demobilised 1946 (Major). Entered Foreign (later Diplomatic) Service, 1947; served: Hamburg, 1947; Berlin, 1949; Hong Kong, 1951; Phnom Penh, 1955; Saigon, 1956; Nairobi, 1959; Pretoria/Cape Town, 1963; FCO, 1966; Paris, 1973. *Recreations:* sailing, golf, music, spectator sports. *Address:* 30 Arterberry Road, Wimbledon, SW20 8AH. *T:* 01-946 9734; Prior's Hill, Park Road, Aldeburgh, Suffolk IP15 5ET. *T:* Aldeburgh 3335. *Clubs:* United Oxford & Cambridge University; MCC; London Welsh Rugby Football; Royal Wimbledon Golf; Aldeburgh Yacht.

HERBISON, Rt. Hon. Margaret McCrorie, PC 1964; Lord High Commissioner to the General Assembly of the Church of Scotland, 1970-71; *b* 11 March 1907. *Educ:* Dykehead Public Sch., Shotts; Bellshill Acad.; Glasgow Univ. Teacher of English and History in Glasgow Schs; MP (Lab) North Lanark, 1945-70; Jt Parly Under-Sec. of State, Scottish Office, 1950-51; Minister of Pensions and National Insurance, Oct. 1964-Aug. 1966, of Social Security, 1966-67. Chm., Select Cttee on Overseas Aid, 1969-. Member National Executive Cttee, Labour Party; Chm. Labour Party, 1957. Mem., Royal Commn on Standards of Conduct in Public Life, 1974-. Scotswoman of the Year, 1970. Hon. LLD Glasgow, 1970. *Recreations:* reading, gardening. *Address:* 61 Shottskirk Road, Shotts, Lanarkshire ML7 4AB. *T:* Shotts 21944.

HERCHENRODER, Sir (Marie Joseph Barnabe) Francis, Kt, *cr* 1953; QC; Assistant Legal Adviser, Commonwealth Office, retired, 1968; *b* 13 Feb. 1896; 3rd *s* of late Sir Alfred Herchenroder, KC and Lady Herchenroder (*née* Vinton); *m* 1923, Marie Charlotte Paule Geneve; two *d*. *Educ:* Royal College, Mauritius; Middle Temple, London. Called to the Bar, 1919; District Magistrate, Mauritius, 1923; Additional Substitute Procureur and Advocate General, Mauritius, 1934; Substitute Procureur and Advocate General, Mauritius, 1938; KC 1943; Puisne Judge, Supreme Court, Mauritius, 1944; Procureur and Advocate General, Mauritius, 1945; Chief Justice, Mauritius, 1949-60. Coronation Medals, 1937, 1953. *Address:* 11 Pelham Court, Chelsea, SW3. *T:* 01-584 3937.

HERD, Frederick Charles; Assistant Under-Secretary of State (Civilian Management, General), Ministry of Defence, 1970-75; *b* 27 April 1915. *Educ:* Strode's Sch., Egham; Sidney Sussex Coll., Cambridge. Asst Principal, Admiralty, 1937; Principal, 1941; Asst. Sec., 1950; Asst Under-Sec. of State, 1964. *Recreations:* music, lawn tennis, bridge. *Address:* 21 Cleveland Square, W2. *T:* 01-262 0920. *Clubs:* United Oxford & Cambridge University; Cumberland Lawn Tennis.

HERDON, Christopher de Lancy, OBE 1971; HM Diplomatic Service; Counsellor in British Embassy, Rome, since 1973; *b* 24 May 1928; *s* of Wilfrid Herdon and Clotilde (*née* Parsons); *m* 1953, Virginia Grace; three *s* two *d*. *Educ:* Ampleforth; Magdalen Coll., Oxford. Foreign Office, 1951; Vienna, 1953; 2nd Sec., Baghdad, 1957; Beirut, 1961; 1st Sec., Amman, 1962; FO, 1965; Aden, 1967; FCO, 1970. *Recreations:* painting, music, tennis, polo. *Address:* c/o Foreign and Commonwealth Office, SW1; Moses Farm, Lurgashall, Petworth, W Sussex GU28 9EP. *T:* North Chapel 323. *Club:* Reform.

HEREFORD, 18th Viscount *cr* 1550; **Robert Milo Leicester Devereux**; Bt 1611; Premier Viscount of England; *b* 4 Nov. 1932; *o s* of Hon. Robert Godfrey de Bohun Devereux (*d* 1934) and Audrey Maureen Leslie, DStJ 1963 (she *m* 2nd, 1961, 7th Earl of Lisburne, who *d* 1965), *y d* of late James Meakin, Westwood Manor, Staffs and of late Countess Sondes; *S* grandfather, 1952; *m* 1969, Susan Mary, *o c* of Major Maurice Godley, Ide Hill, Sevenoaks, Kent, and of Mrs Glen Godley, Spencer's Cottage, Little Haseley, Oxon; two *s*. *Educ:* Eton. Member: Royal Philharmonic Soc.; Royal Philharmonic Orchestra Assoc. OStJ. *Heir:* *s* Hon. Charles Robin de Bohun Devereux, *b* 11 Aug. 1975. *Address:* Haseley Court, Little Haseley, Oxford OX9 7LT. *T:* Great Milton 500. *Clubs:* Boodle's; House of Lords Yacht, Lloyd's Yacht.

HEREFORD, Bishop of, since 1973; **Rt. Rev. John (Richard Gordon) Eastaugh**; *b* 11 March 1920; *s* of Gordon and Jessie Eastaugh; *m* 1963, Bridget Nicola, *y d* of Sir Hugh Chance, *qv*; two *s* one *d*. *Educ:* Leeds Univ.; Mirfield. Curate of All Saints, Poplar, 1944; Rector: of W. Hackney, 1951; of Poplar, 1956; Commissary of Bp of Polynesia, 1962; Vicar of Heston, 1963; Archdeacon of Middlesex, 1966-73; Vicar of St Peter, Eaton Square, 1967-74. *Recreations:* theatre, music. *Address:* Bishop's House, The Palace, Hereford HR4 9BN.

HEREFORD, Dean of; *see* Rathbone, Very Rev. N. S.

HEREFORD, Archdeacon of; *see* Barfett, Ven. T.

HEREN, Louis Philip; Deputy Editor and Foreign Editor of The Times; *b* 6 Feb. 1919; *s* of William Heren and Beatrice (*née* Keller); *m* 1948, Patricia Cecilia O'Regan (*d* 1975); one *s* three *d*. *Educ:* St George's Sch., London. Army, 1939-46. Foreign Corresp. of The Times, 1947-; India, 1947-48; Israel and Middle East, 1948-50; Southeast Asian Corresp., 1951-53; Germany, 1955-60; Chief Washington Corresp. and American Editor, 1960-70. War Correspondent: Kashmir, 1947; Israel-Arab war, 1948; Korean war, 1950. Hannan Swaffer Award for Internat. Reporting, 1967; John F. Kennedy Memorial Award, 1968. *Publications:* New American Commonwealth, 1968; No Hail, No Farewell, 1970; Growing Up Poor in London, 1973; The Story of America, 1976. *Address:* Fleet House, Vale of Health, NW3. *T:* 01-435 0902. *Club:* Garrick.

HERFORD, Geoffrey Vernon Brooke, CBE 1956 (OBE 1946); MSc; FIBiol; Director of Pest Infestation Research, Agricultural Research Council, 1940-68, retired; *b* 1905; *s* of late Henry J. R. Herford, Hampstead; *m* 1933, Evelyn Cicely (*d* 1969), *d* of W. G. Lambert. *Educ:* Gresham's School, Holt; Magdalen College, Oxford (BA); Minnesota University (MSc). *Address:* Rose Cottage, Wells Road, Eastcombe, Stroud, Glos.

HERIOT, Alexander John, MS, FRCS, FDS; Surgeon, King's College Hospital; Postgraduate Regional Dean; *b* 28 May 1914; *s* of Robert Heriot; *m* 1940, Dr Christine Stacey (*d* 1958); two *s*; *m* 1959, Dr Cynthia Heymeson; one *s* one *d*. Major RAMC. *Address:* 261 Trinity Road, SW18.

HERITAGE, Prof. Robert, RDI, DesRCA, FSIA; Professor, School of Furniture Design, Royal College of Art, since 1974; *b* 2 Nov. 1927; *m* Dorothy; two *s* one *d*. *Educ:* Royal College of Art, RCA, 1950; freelance designer, 1951; Consultant Designer, Concord International, 1961; RDI 1963. *Recreations:* tennis, fishing. *Address:* 12 Jay Mews, Kensington Gore, SW7 2EP. *Club:* Chelsea Arts.

HERITAGE, Stanley James; Chairman, Yorkshire and Humberside Economic Planning Board, and Regional Director for Yorkshire and Humberside, Departments of the Environment and Transport, since 1977; *s* of late Albert Charles Heritage and Lizzie Victoria Heritage. *Educ:* Wallington High Sch. Ministry of Public Building and Works: Middle East Reg., 1965; HQ, 1967; Reg. Dir, Far East Reg., 1971; Reg. Planning Controller, NW Reg., DoE, 1972; Dir, NW Reg., PSA, 1974. *Recreation:* music. *Address:* 17 Woodville Court, Old Park Road, Roundhay, Leeds LS8 1JA. *T:* Leeds 662730. *Clubs:* Civil Service; Leeds (Leeds).

HERITAGE, Rev. Canon Thomas Charles; Canon Residentiary of Portsmouth Cathedral, 1964-76, now Canon Emeritus; *b* 3 March 1908; *s* of Thomas and Sarah Ellen Heritage; *m* 1934, Frances Warrington; twin *d*. *Educ:* The King's Sch., Chester; St Edmund Hall, Oxford. BA 1929; MA 1944; Diploma in Education (Oxford), 1930; ATCL 1931. Deacon, 1934; Priest, 1938. Curate of Christ Church, Chesterfield and Asst Master, Chesterfield Grammar Sch., 1934-38; Asst Master, Portsmouth Grammar Sch., 1938-64; Curate of St Mark, Portsmouth, 1938-40, St Christopher, Bournemouth, 1940-44; Chaplain of

Portsmouth Cathedral, 1945-64. Hon. Canon, 1958-64. Examining Chaplain to the Bishop of Portsmouth, 1965-. Warden, Portsmouth Diocesan Readers' Assoc., 1966. *Publications:* A New Testament Lectionary for Schools, 1943; The Early Christians in Britain (with B. E. Dodd), 1966. *Recreations:* music, the theatre, reading, travel. *Address:* 2 Braemar Rise, Salisbury, Wilts.

HERKLOTS, Geoffrey Alton Craig, CBE 1961; MSc, PhD; FLS; *b* Naini Tal, India, 10 Aug. 1902; *er s* of late Rev. Bernard Herklots, MA; *m* 1932, Iris, *yr d* of late Capt. Philip Walter, RN; two *s* one *d. Educ:* Trent Coll., Derbyshire; University of Leeds; Trinity Hall, Cambridge. Reader in Biology, University of Hong Kong, 1928-45; interned at Stanley Camp, Hong Kong, Jan. 1942-Aug. 1945; Secretary for Development, Hong Kong, 1946-48; Secretary for Colonial Agricultural Research, Colonial Office, London, 1948-53. Principal and Director of Research, Imperial College of Tropical Agriculture, Trinidad, 1953-60, retired 1961. Colombo Plan Botanical Adviser to HM Government of Nepal, 1961-63. Corresp. Member Zoological Society. *Publications:* Common Marine Food Fishes of Hong Kong, 1936, 1940; The Birds of Hong Kong, Field Identification and Field Note Book, 1946, 1952; Vegetable Cultivation in Hong Kong, 1941, 1947; The Hong Kong Countryside, 1951; Hong Kong Birds, 1953; Birds of Trinidad and Tobago, 1961; Vegetable Cultivation in South-East Asia, 1973; Flowering Tropical Climbers, 1976. Editor: Hong Kong Naturalist, 1930-41; Journal of Hong Kong Fisheries Research Station, 1940. *Recreations:* drawing, gardening, walking. *Address:* Vanners, Chobham, Woking, Surrey GU24 8SJ. *T:* Chobham (Woking) 8109. *Club:* Athenæum.

HERLIE, Eileen; actress; *b* 8 March 1920; *d* of Patrick Herlihy (Irish) and Isobel Cowden (Scottish); *m* 1st, 1942, Philip Barrett; 2nd, 1951, Witold Kuncewicz. *Educ:* Shawlands Academy, Glasgow. Varied repertoire with own company, 1942-44; Old Vic, Liverpool, 1944-45; Lyric Theatre, Hammersmith, 1945-46; Andromache in Trojan Women, Alcestis in Thracian Horses, Queen in Eagle has Two Heads, 1946-47; Gertrude in Hamlet (film), 1948; Medea, 1949; Angel with the Trumpet (film), 1949; Paula in The Second Mrs Tanqueray, Haymarket, 1950-51; Helen D'Oyly Carte in Gilbert and Sullivan (film), 1952; Mother in Isn't Life Wonderful? (film), 1952; John Gielgud Season, 1953; Mrs Marwood in The Way of the World; Belvidera in Venice Preserv'd; Irene in Sense of Guilt, 1953; Mrs Molloy in The Matchmaker, 1954; She Didn't Say No! (film), 1958; acted in George Dillon (New York), 1958; Take Me Along (New York), 1959; All America (New York), 1963; The Queen in Hamlet (New York), 1964; Halfway up the Tree, 1967; Emperor Henry IV, NY, 1973; Crown Matrimonial, 1973; The Seagull (film). *Recreations:* riding, reading, music. *Address:* c/o International Famous Agency, 1301 Avenue of the Americas, New York, NY 10019, USA.

HERMAN, Major Benjamin John, MVO 1974; Royal Marines; Commando Training Centre, Royal Marines, since 1976; *b* 30 Dec. 1934; *s* of B. E. Herman, MBE, Karachi, and Mary Robinson; *m* 1959, Vanessa Anne, *d* of Col J. M. Phillips, CBE, and Dulcie Farquharson; one *s* three *d. Educ:* Bedford Sch.; RN Staff Coll., Greenwich (psc). Joined Royal Marines, 1953; commissioned, 1954; 40 Commando RM; Regular Commission, 1955; 45 Commando, RM, 1957; Instr, Officers Trng Wing, 1959; ITC, RM, Actg Adjt, 1960; Instr, The Depot, RM, 1961; HMS Tartar, 1963; Marine Assistant and ADC to Comdt-Gen., RM, 1964; Adjt, Amphibious Trng Unit, RM, 1965; RN Staff Coll., 1966; Staff Officer, RM Barracks, Eastney, 1968; Company Comdr, 45 Commando, 1970; Equerry in Waiting to the Duke of Edinburgh, 1971-74; Private Sec. to Princess Anne, 1974-76; sowc 1976. MBIM. Order of the White Elephant (Thailand), 1972; Order of Pangkuan Negara, Defender of the Realm (Malaysia), 1972; Most Hon. Order of the Crown of Brunei, 1972. *Recreations:* tennis (Royal Navy), squash, Rugby football, model making, music. *Address:* 3 Oriental Road, Sunninghill, Ascot, Berks. *T:* Ascot 22380.

HERMAN, Josef; painter; *b* 3 Jan. 1911; *m* 1955, Eleanor Ettlinger; one *s* (one *d* decd). *Educ:* Warsaw. First exhibition, Warsaw, 1932; left for Belgium, 1938; arrived in Britain, June 1940; lived in: Glasgow, 1940-43; Ystradgynlais (mining village, Wales), 1944-53. Exhibitions include: Glasgow, 1942; Edinburgh, 1942; London, 1943; Roland, Browse and Delbanco Gallery, 1946-; British Council; Arts Council; (retrospective) Whitechapel Art Gallery, 1962; New Grafton Gallery, 1970. Work in permanent collections: Arts Council; British Council; National Museum, Cardiff; Contemporary Art Society; National Museum Bezalel, Jerusalem; National Gallery, Johannesburg; Tate Gallery, London; Victoria and Albert Museum, London; National Gallery, Melbourne; National Gallery, Ottawa;

National Gallery, Wellington, etc. Gold Medal, Royal National Eisteddfod, Llanelly, 1962; Contemporary Art Society prize, 1952 and 1953; prize, John Moore Exhibition, 1956; Trust House Award, 1962. *Publication:* Related Twilights (autobiog.), 1975. *Address:* 120 Edith Road, W14.

HERMANN, Alexander Henry Baxter; HM Diplomatic Service; Counsellor for Hong Kong Affairs, Washington, 1974-77; *b* 28 Dec. 1917; *m* 1944, Eudoksia Eugenia Domnina; one *d.* Joined Foreign Service, 1939; served 1942-55; Peking, Ahwaz, Chengtu, Chungking, Shanghai, Quito, Panama, Tamsui; Foreign Office, 1956; Commercial Counsellor and Consul-General, Rangoon, 1957-61; HM Consul-General at Marseilles, also to Monaco, 1961-65; Diplomatic Service Inspector, 1965-66; Counsellor, Hong Kong Affairs, Washington, 1967-70; Consul-General, Osaka, 1971-73. *Address:* 6 Church Farm Lane, Sidlesham, Sussex. *Club:* Oriental.

HERMES, Gertrude, RA 1971 (ARA 1963); RE; sculptor; wood engraver; Teacher of wood engraving, Royal Academy Schools, W1, until 1976; *b* Bickley, Kent, 1901; *m*; one *s* one *d. Educ:* Belmont, Bickley, Kent; Leon Underwood's Sch., London. Portrait Sculpture and decorative carving for buildings; wood engraving decorations for books; fountain and door furniture, Shakespeare Memorial Theatre, Stratford-on-Avon; Britannia Window, British Pavilion, Paris, 1937; 3 glass panels, British Pavilion, World's Fair, NY, 1939; Engravings for books, for: Cressett Press, Swan Press, Golden Cockerel Press, Penguin Books Ltd, etc.; member of: London Group; Society of Wood-engravers. *Recreations:* swimming and fishing. *Address:* 31 Danvers Street, Chelsea, SW3. *T:* 01-352 4006.

HERMON, Peter Michael Robert; Group Management Services Director, British Airways Board, since 1972; Member of Board: BOAC, since 1972; International Aeradio Ltd, since 1966; Chairman of Board, International Aeradio (Caribbean) Ltd, since 1967; *b* 13 Nov. 1928; British; *m* 1954, Norma Stuart Brealey; two *s* two *d. Educ:* Nottingham High Sch.; St John's and Merton Colls, Oxford. 1st cl. hons Maths Oxon. Leo Computers Ltd, 1955-59; Manager, Management and Computer Divs, Dunlop Co., 1959-65; Information Handling Dir, BOAC, 1965-68; Management Services Dir, BOAC, and Mem. Bd of Management, 1968-72. FCIT, FBCS. *Recreations:* hill walking, music. *Address:* The Hollies, Fireball Hill, Devenish Road, Sunningdale, Ascot, Berks. *T:* Ascot 23185.

HERMON-HODGE, family name of **Baron Wyfold.**

HERNIMAN, Ven. Ronald George; Archdeacon of Barnstaple since 1970, and Rector of Shirwell with Loxhore, since 1972; *b* 18 April 1923; *s* of George Egerton and Rose Herniman; *m* 1949, Grace Jordan-Jones; one *s* two *d. Educ:* Geneva; Bideford, Devon. Served RAF, 1941-46. Birkbeck Coll., London Univ., 1948-51 (BA); Oak Hill Theological Coll., 1951-53; Tutor, Oak Hill Coll., 1953-54; Asst Curate, Christ Church, Cockfosters, 1954-56; Dir of Philosophical Studies, Oak Hill, 1956-61; Rector of Exe Valley Group of Churches (Washfield, Stoodleigh, Withleigh, Calverleigh Oakford, Morebath, Rackenford, Loxbeare and Templeton), 1961-72. *Recreations:* sailing; making and mending things. *Address:* The Rectory, Shirwell, near Barnstaple, Devon. *T:* Shirwell 371.

HERON, Sir Conrad (Frederick), KCB 1974 (CB 1969); OBE 1953; Permanent Secretary, Department of Employment, 1973-76; *b* 21 Feb. 1916; *s* of Richard Foster Heron and Ida Fredrika Heron; *m* 1948, Envye Linnéa Gustafsson; two *d. Educ:* South Shields High Sch.; Trinity Hall, Cambridge. Entered Ministry of Labour, 1938; Principal Private Secretary to Minister of Labour, 1953-56; Under-Secretary, Industrial Relations Dept, 1963-64 and 1965-68, Overseas Dept, 1964-65; Dep. Under-Sec. of State, Dept of Employment, 1968-71; Dep. Chm., Commn on Industrial Relations, 1971-72; Second Permanent Sec., Dept of Employment, 1973. *Address:* Old Orchards, West Lydford, Somerton, Somerset. *T:* Wheathill 387.

HERON, (Cuthbert) George; His Honour Judge Heron; a Circuit Judge, since 1974; *b* 8 April 1911; *s* of late Lieut-Commander George Heron, RN, and late Kate Heron; *m* 1937, Maud Mary Josephine Hogan; one *s* one *d. Educ:* St Bede's Coll., Manchester; Manchester Univ. (LLB). Solicitor, 1934; called to Bar, Middle Temple, 1944; Oxford Circuit; Recorder of Lichfield, 1968-71; Hon. Recorder, 1972-; a Recorder of Crown Court, 1972-74. Served RAF, 1939-45 (Flt-Lieutenant). *Recreations:* reading, motoring, foreign travel. *Address:* 160 Wake Green Road, Moseley, Birmingham B13 9QD. *T:* 021-777 1960; Lamb Building, Temple, EC4. *Clubs:* Union, Worcestershire (Worcester).

HERON, Patrick, CBE 1977; painter; *b* 30 Jan. 1920; *e s* of T. M. and Eulalie Heron; *m* 1945, Delia Reiss; two *d*. *Educ*: St Ives, Cornwall; Welwyn Garden City; St Georges, Harpenden; Slade School. Art criticism in: New English Weekly, 1945-47; New Statesman and Nation, 1947-50; London correspondent, Arts (NY), 1955-58. John Power Lectr, Sydney Univ., 1973. One-man exhibitions: Redfern Gallery, London, 1947, 1948, 1950, 1951, 1954, 1956 and 1958; Waddington Galleries, London, 1959, 1960, 1963, 1964, 1965, 1967, 1968, 1970, 1973, and 1975; Rutland Gallery, London, 1975; Waddington Fine Arts, Montreal, 1970; Bertha Schaefer Gallery, NY, 1960, 1962 and 1965; Galerie Charles Lienhard, Zürich, 1963; Traverse Theatre Gallery, Edinburgh, 1965; São Paulo Bienal VIII, 1965 (Silver Medal) (exhibn toured S Amer., 1966); Harrogate Festival, 1970; Rudy Komon Gall., Sydney, 1970; Whitechapel Gallery, 1972; Bonython Art Gall., Sydney, 1973; Galerie le Balcon des Arts, Paris, 1977; Retrospective exhibitions: Wakefield City Art Gallery, Leeds, Hull, Nottingham, 1952; Richard Demarco Gallery, Edinburgh, 1967; Museum of Modern Art, Oxford, 1968; Kunstnernes Hus, Oslo, 1967. Twelve paintings shown at São Paulo Bienal II, Brazil, 1953-54. Carnegie International, Pittsburgh, 1961; British Art Today, San Francisco, Dallas, Santa Barbara, 1962-63; Painting and Sculpture of a Decade, 1954-64, Tate Gallery, 1964; British Painting and Sculpture, 1960-70, National Gallery of Art, Washington DC. Exhibited in group and British Council exhibitions in many countries; works owned by: Tate Gallery; Arts Council; British Council; V&A Museum; British Museum; Gulbenkian Foundation; Leeds City Art Gallery; Stuyvesant Foundation; National Portrait Gallery; Broadcasting House; Warwick Univ.; Wakefield City Art Gallery; Manchester City Art Gallery; Contemporary Art Society; Oldham Art Gallery; CEMA, N Ireland; Abbot Hall Art Gallery, Kendal; The Art Gallery, Aberdeen; National Gallery of Wales, Cardiff; Toronto Art Gallery; Montreal Museum of Fine Art; Vancouver Art Gallery; Toledo Museum of Art, Ohio; Smith College Museum of Art, Mass; Brooklyn Museum, NY; Albright-Knox Art Gallery, Buffalo, NY; University of Michigan Museum of Art; Boymans Museum, Rotterdam; Musée d'Art Contemporain, Montreal; Western Australian Art Gallery, Perth; Pembroke and Nuffield Colleges, Oxford; Stirling Univ.; Bristol City Art Gall.; Exeter Art Gallery; Exeter Univ. (Cornwall House); Plymouth City Art Gallery; Power Collection, Sydney; London Art Gall., London, Ont.; Hatton Art Gall., Newcastle Univ.; Southampton Art Gall.; Norwich Art Gall; also represented in Fitzwilliam Museum, Cambridge, and in municipal collections at Glasgow, Reading and Sheffield. Awarded Grand Prize by international jury, John Moores' 2nd Liverpool Exhibition, 1959. *Publications*: The Changing Forms of Art, 1955; Braque, 1958; contrib. The Guardian, Studio International. *Address*: Eagle's Nest, Zennor, near St Ives, Cornwall. *T*: St Ives 6921.

HERON, Raymond; Deputy Director, Propellants, Explosives and Rocket Motor Establishment, Ministry of Defence (Procurement Executive), since 1977; *b* 10 April 1924; *s* of Lewis and Doris Heron; *m* 1948, Elizabeth MacGathan; one *s* one *d*. *Educ*: Heath Grammar Sch., Halifax; Queen's Coll., Oxford (BA Physics). Shell Refining and Marketing Co., 1944-47; RN, Instructor Branch, 1947-52; Rocket Propulsion Estabt, Min. of Supply (later Min. of Technology), 1952-67; Cabinet Office, 1967; Asst Dir, Min. of Technology, 1967-73; Dep. Dir, Explosives Research and Development Estabt, MoD, 1973; Special Asst to Sec. (Procurement Exec.), MoD, 1973-74; Head of Rocket Motor Exec. and Dep. Dir/2, Rocket Propulsion Estabt, MoD (PE), 1974-76. *Publications*: articles in scientific and technical jls. *Recreations*: music, hill walking, golf. *Address*: 9 Grange Gardens, Wendover, Aylesbury, Bucks HP22 6HB. *T*: Wendover 622921. *Club*: Ashridge Golf.

HERON-MAXWELL, Sir Patrick Ivor, 9th Bt of Springkell, *cr* 1683; *b* 26 July 1916; *o s* of 8th Bt and Norah (*d* 1971), *d* of late Hon. Francis Parker; *S* father, 1928; *m* 1942, D. Geraldine E., *y d* of late C. Paget Mellor, Letchworth, Herts, and Victoria, BC; three *s*. *Educ*: Stowe. *Heir*: *s* Nigel Mellor Heron-Maxwell [*b* 30 Jan. 1944; *m* 1972, May Elizabeth Angela, *o d* of W. Ewing, Co. Donegal]. *Address*: 9 Cowslip Hill, Letchworth, Herts.

HERRICK, Very Rev. Richard William; Provost of Chelmsford Cathedral, since 1978 (Vice-Provost, 1962-77); Director of Chelmsford Cathedral Centre for Research and Training, since 1973; *b* 3 Dec. 1913; *s* of W. Herrick, Retford, Notts; *m* 1943, Ann L. Sparshott; two *s* one *d*. *Educ*: King Edward VI Sch., Retford; Leeds University; College of the Resurrection, Mirfield. Civil Servant, 1930-34. BA Leeds, 1937; Deacon, 1939; Priest, 1940; Curate of Duston, 1939-41; Curate of St Mark's, Portsea, 1941-47; Vicar of St Michael's, Northampton, 1947-57; Canon Residentiary of Chelmsford Cathedral, 1957-77; Director of Religious Education for the Diocese of Chelmsford, 1957-67;

Chm. of House of Clergy and Vice-Pres., Chelmsford Diocesan Synod, 1970; Dir of Laity Training, 1967-73; Proctor in Convocation and Mem. Gen. Synod, 1970-. *Address*: 208 New London Road, Chelmsford, Essex. *T*: Chelmsford 54318.

HERRIDGE, Geoffrey Howard, CMG 1962; Chairman, Iraq Petroleum Co. Ltd and Associated Companies, 1965-70, retired (Managing Director, 1957-63; Deputy Chairman, 1963-65); *b* 22 Feb. 1904; 3rd *s* of late Edward Herridge, Eckington, Worcestershire; *m* 1935, Dorothy Elvira Tod; two *s* two *d*. *Educ*: Crypt Sch., Gloucester; St John's Coll., Cambridge. Joined Turkish Petroleum Co. Ltd (later Iraq Petroleum Co. Ltd), Iraq, 1926; served in Iraq, Jordan, Palestine, 1926-47; General Manager in the Middle East, Iraq Petroleum Co. and Associated Companies, 1947-51; Executive Director, 1953-57; Member of London Cttee, Ottoman Bank, 1964. Chairman, Petroleum Industry Training Board, 1967-70. *Recreation*: sailing. *Address*: Flint, Sidlesham Common, Chichester, West Sussex. *T*: Sidlesham 357. *Club*: Oriental.

HERRIES, Lady (14th in line, of the Lordship *cr* 1490), of Terregles; **Anne Elizabeth Fitzalan-Howard;** *b* 12 June 1938; *e d* of 16th Duke of Norfolk, EM, KG, PC, GCVO, GBE, TD, and of Lavinia Duchess of Norfolk, *qv* ; *S* to lordship upon death of father, 1975. Racehorse trainer. *Recreations*: riding, golf, breeding spaniels. *Heir*: *sister* Lady Mary Katharine Fitzalan-Howard, *b* 14 Aug. 1940. *Address*: Everingham Park, York, Humberside. *T*: Holme-on-Spalding Moor 203.

HERRIES, Sir Michael Alexander Robert Young-, Kt 1975; OBE 1968; MC 1945; Chairman, Royal Bank of Scotland, since 1976 (Director since 1972; Vice-Chairman, 1974-75; Deputy Chairman, 1975-76); Joint Deputy Chairman, National and Commercial Banking Group Ltd (Director since 1976); Director: Matheson & Co. Ltd (Chairman, 1971-75); Jardine, Matheson & Co. Ltd; Scottish Widows' Fund and Life Assurance Society; Scottish Mortgage & Trust Co. Ltd; Williams and Glyn's Bank Ltd; Lloyds and Scottish Ltd; *b* 28 Feb. 1923; *s* of Lt-Col William Dobree Young-Herries and Ruth Mary (*née* Thrupp); *m* 1949, Elizabeth Hilary Russell (*née* Smith); two *s* one *d*. *Educ*: Eton; Trinity Coll., Cambridge (MA). Served KOSB, 1942-47; Temp. Captain, Actg Maj., Europe and ME; Adjt 5th (Dumfries and Galloway) Battalion and 1st Battalion TARO, 1949. Joined Jardine Matheson & Co. Ltd, 1948; served in Hong Kong, Japan and Singapore; Director, 1959; Managing Director, 1962; Chm. and Man. Dir, 1963-70; Chairman: Jardine Japan Investment Trust Ltd, 1972-76; Crossfriars Trust Ltd, 1972-76. Formerly Mem., Exec. Legislative Council, Hong Kong; Chm., Hong Kong Univ. and Polytechnics Grant Cttee, 1965-73. Member Council: London Chamber of Commerce and Industry; Missions to Seamen. Mem., Royal Company of Archers (Queen's Body Guard for Scotland), 1973-. Hon. LLD: Chinese Univ. of Hong Kong, 1973; Univ. of Hong Kong, 1974. *Recreations*: shooting, walking, swimming, tennis. *Address*: (office) Royal Bank of Scotland Ltd, 42 St Andrew Square, Edinburgh EH2 2YE. *T*: 031-556 9151; Spottes, Castle Douglas, Kirkcudbrightshire. *T*: Haugh of Urr 202; 30 Heriot Row, Edinburgh. *T*: 031-226 2711; 23 Eaton Place, SW1. *T*: 01-235 7869. *Clubs*: Caledonian, Farmers', City of London; New (Edinburgh).

HERRING, Cyril Alfred; Member, British Airways Board, since 1972 and Finance Director, since 1975; *b* Dulwich, 17 Jan. 1915; *s* of Alfred James Herring and Minnie Herring (*née* Padfield); *m* 1939, Helen (*née* Warnes); three *s*. *Educ*: Alleyn's Sch.; London School of Economics. BSc(Econ); FCMA; JDipMA; IPFA; FCIT. Chief Accountant, Straight Corporation Ltd, 1936-46; joined BEA, 1946; Chief Accountant, 1951-57; Personnel Director, 1957-65; Financial Director, 1965-71; Executive Board Member, 1971-74; Chief Executive, British Airways Regional Div., 1972-74; Chm. and Man. Dir, British Air Services Ltd, 1969-76; Chairman: Northeast Airlines Ltd, 1969-76; Cambrian Airways Ltd, 1973-76; London Rail Adv. Cttee, 1976-; CIPFA Public Corporations Finance Group, 1976-. Member Council: Chartered Inst. of Transport, 1971-74; Inst. of Cost and Management Accountants, 1967-77 (Vice-Pres., 1971-73, Pres., 1973-74); CBI, 1976- (Mem. Financial Policy Cttee, 1975-, Finance and General Purposes Cttee, 1977-). *Recreations*: flying, motoring, boating. *Address*: Cuddenbeake, St Germans, Cornwall. *Clubs*: Reform, Royal Aero.

HERRING, Lt-Gen. Hon. Sir Edmund Francis, KCMG 1949; KBE 1943 (CBE 1941); DSO 1919; MC; ED; QC; Lieutenant-Governor of Victoria, 1945-72; Chief Justice of Supreme Court of Victoria, 1944-64; Chancellor of Archdiocese of Melbourne, since 1941; *b* 2 Sept. 1892, Maryborough, Victoria; *s* of Edmund Selwyn Herring and Gertrude Stella Fetherstonhaugh; *m* 1922, Dr Mary Ranken Lyle (*see* Dame Mary Ranken Herring); three *d. Educ:* Melbourne Church of England Grammar Sch.; Trinity Coll., Melbourne Univ. (Rhodes Schol., Victoria, 1912); New Coll., Oxford (MA, BCL 1920), Hon. Fellow, 1949; Barrister, Inner Temple, 1920, Hon. Bencher 1963; called to Bar, Melbourne, 1921; KC 1936. King Edward's Horse, July-Dec. 1914; commnd RFA, Dec. 1914; BEF France and Macedonia, 1915-1919 (DSO, MC, despatches); Australian Citizen Forces, 1923-39; war of 1939-45 (CBE, KBE): AIF, 1939-44 (CRA 6th Div., 1939-41; commanded 6th Div., 1941-42; General Officer Commanding: Northern Territory Force, 1942; 2 Australian Corps, 1942; New Guinea Force, 1942-43; 1 Australian Corps, 1942-44; GMC 1 (Greece) 1941); DSC (USA) 1943. Dir Gen., Recruiting, Australia, 1950-51. Hon. Col. Melbourne Univ. Regt, 1950-. Chm. of Trustees, Shrine of Remembrance, Melbourne, 1945-; Mem. Bd, Australian War Memorial, Canberra, 1945-74, Chm., 1959-74; President: Toc H, Australia, 1947-; Boy Scouts Assoc. of Victoria, 1945-68; Australian Boy Scouts Assoc., 1959-. Vice-Pres., British and Foreign Bible Soc. London. Leader, Australian Coronation Contingent, 1953. Hon. DCL Oxford 1953; Hon. LLD Monash, 1973. KStJ 1953. *Recreation:* golf. *Address:* 226 Walsh Street, South Yarra, Vic. 3141, Australia. *T:* 261000. *Clubs:* Melbourne, Naval and Military, Australian (Hon. Mem.), Royal Melbourne Golf (Melbourne); Barwon Heads Golf.

HERRING, Dame Mary Ranken, DBE 1960; *b* 31 March 1895; *d* of late Sir Thomas Lyle, DSc, FRS and Lady Lyle, CBE; *m* 1922, Edmund Francis Herring (*see* Lieut-General Hon. Sir Edmund Francis Herring); three *d. Educ:* Toorak College and Melbourne University. MB, BS, Melbourne, 1921. Medical Officer, Ante-Natal Clinics, Prahran and South Melbourne, 1926-45; Mem. and Vice-Pres., Melbourne District Nursing Soc., 1931-57; Vice-President and President, AIF Women's Association, 1939-47; President, Council of Toorak Coll., 1948-71; Vice-Chairman, British Commonwealth Youth Sunday, 1947-59; Member and Patron: Children's Welfare Assoc. of Victoria; Spastic Children's Soc. of Victoria; Save the Children Fund; Victoria Family Council; Life Mem., Victorian Bush Nursing Assoc.; Chairman of Trustees, V. S. Brown Memorial Fund; Dep. President, Victoria League in Victoria, 1945-74; Dep. President, Red Cross in Victoria, 1945-74; Member Advisory Council on Child Welfare, 1956-61. CStJ, 1953. *Recreations:* gardening, golf. *Address:* 226 Walsh Street, South Yarra, Victoria 3141, Australia. *T:* 261000. *Clubs:* Lyceum, (Melbourne); Royal Melbourne Golf; Barwon Heads Golf.

HERRINGTON, Hugh Geoffrey, CBE 1954; *b* 28 Sept. 1900; *s* of Hugh William Herrington; *m* 1926, Olive, *d* of James Procter. *Educ:* Bablake Sch., Coventry, Warwickshire. Man. Dir, 1950-66, Dep. Chm., 1966-70, High Duty Alloys; Dir, Aluminium Wire & Cable Co., 1948-70; Dir, Hawker Siddeley, 1957-70. FRAES. *Address:* Two Wells, Skittle Green, Bledlow, Bucks. *T:* Princes Risborough 4534.

HERRIOT, James; *see* Wight, J. A.

HERROD, Donald, QC 1972; a Recorder of the Crown Court, since 1972; *b* 7 Aug. 1930; *o s* of Wilfred and Phyllis Herrod, Doncaster; *m* 1959, Kathleen Elaine Merrington, MB, ChB; two *d. Educ:* grammar schs, Doncaster and Leeds. Entered Army, 1948; commnd 1949. Called to Bar, 1956. *Recreations:* lawn tennis, golf, Association football. *Address:* Staircase House, Staircase Lane, Bramhope, Yorks LS16 9JD. *T:* Arthington 842697. *Club:* Leeds (Leeds).

HERRON, Very Rev. Andrew; Clerk to the Presbytery of Glasgow, since 1959; *b* 29 Sept. 1909; *s* of John Todd Herron and Mary Skinner Hunter; *m* 1935, Joanna Fraser Neill; four *d. Educ:* Glasgow Univ. (MA, BD, LLB). Minister: at Linwood, 1936-40, at Houston and Killellan, 1940-59; Clerk to the Presbytery of Paisley, 1953-59; Moderator of General Assembly of Church of Scotland, 1971-72. Convener: Gen. Admin Cttee; Business Cttee, Gen. Assembly, 1972-76; Gen. Trustee, Church of Scotland. Hon. DD St Andrews, 1975. *Publications:* Record Apart, 1974; Guide to the General Assembly of the Church of Scotland, 1976. *Address:* 36 Darnley Road, Glasgow G41 4NE. *T:* 041-423 6422. *Clubs:* Glasgow Art; Caledonian (Edinburgh).

HERRON, Henry, CBE 1975; Procurator-Fiscal, Glasgow, 1965-76, retired; *b* 6 May 1911; *s* of William and Jessie Herron; *m* 1942, Dr Christina Aitkenhead Crawford; one *s* two *d. Educ:* Hamilton Academy; Glasgow Univ. (MA, LLB). Solicitor. Depute Procurator-Fiscal, Glasgow, 1946; Procurator-Fiscal, Banff, 1946-51; Asst Procurator-Fiscal, Glasgow, 1951-55; Procurator-Fiscal, Paisley, 1955-65. *Recreations:* gardening, jurisprudence, criminology. *Address:* 51 Craw Road, Paisley. *T:* 041-889 3091.

HERRON, Shaun; Senior Leader Writer, Winnipeg Free Press, 1964-76 (Correspondent in USA, 1960-64); now lives in Ireland, Spain and Canada; *b* 23 Nov. 1912; *s* of late Thomas and Mary Herron, Carrickfergus, Co. Antrim, N Ireland; *m* ; two *s* two *d. Educ:* Belfast Royal Academy; Queen's Univ., Belfast; Edinburgh, and Princeton, New Jersey, USA. Ordained to Ministry of Scottish Congregational Churches, 1940; war service, 1941-44; Editor, British Weekly, 1950-58; Minister, United Church of Canada, 1958. Smith Lecturer, Union College, University of British Columbia, 1952; Cole Lecturer, Vanderbilt University, Nashville, Tenn., USA, 1956; Willson Lecturer, 1957, Oklahoma City University; Chancellor's Lecturer, Queen's Univ., Kingston, Ontario, 1959. Service with Toc H in Yorkshire and Wales. Has travelled intermittently, writing, as correspondent; broadcaster, etc. *Publications: novels:* Miro, 1968; The Hound and The Fox and The Harper, 1970; Through the Dark and Hairy Wood, 1972; The Whore-Mother, 1973; The Bird in Last Year's Nest, 1974; The MacDonnell, 1976; Chief of the Sheep, 1978. *Recreations:* travelling, writing. *Address:* c/o A. P. Watt and Son, 26/28 Bedford Row, WC1.

HERSCHELL, family name of **Baron Herschell.**

HERSCHELL, 3rd Baron, *cr* 1886; **Rognvald Richard Farrer Herschell;** late Captain Coldstream Guards; *b* 13 Sept. 1923; *o s* of 2nd Baron and Vera (*d* 1961), *d* of Sir Arthur Nicolson, 10th Bt, of that Ilk and Lasswade; *S* father, 1929; *m* 1948, Heather, *d* of 8th Earl of Dartmouth, CVO, DSO; one *d. Educ:* Eton. Page of Honour to the King, 1935-40. *Heir:* none. *Address:* Westfield House, Ardington, Wantage, Berks. *T:* East Hendred 224.

HERSEY, John; writer; *b* 17 June 1914; *s* of Roscoe M. and Grace B. Hersey; *m* 1st, 1940, Frances Ann Cannon (marr. diss. 1958); three *s* one *d* ; 2nd, 1958, Barbara Day Kaufman; one *d. Educ:* Yale Univ.; Clare Coll., Cambridge. Secretary to Sinclair Lewis, 1937; Editor Time, 1937-42; War and Foreign Correspondent, Time, Life, New Yorker, 1942-46. Mem. Council, Authors' League of America, 1946-70 (Vice-Pres., 1948-55, Pres., 1975-). Fellow, Berkeley Coll., Yale Univ., 1950-65; Master, Pierson Coll., Yale Univ., 1965-70, Fellow, 1965-. Writer in Residence, Amer. Acad. in Rome, 1970-71. Lectr, Yale Univ., 1971-75, Vis. Prof., 1975-76, Adjunct Prof., 1976-; Lectr, Salzburg Seminars in Amer. Studies, 1975; Vis. Prof., MIT, 1975. Chm., Connecticut Cttee for the Gifted, 1954-57; Member: Amer. Acad. Arts and Letters, 1953 (Sec., 1961-76); Nat. Inst. Arts and Letters, 1950; Council, Authors' Guild, 1946- (Chm., Contract Cttee, 1963-); Yale Univ. Council cttees on: the Humanities, 1951-56, and Yale Coll., 1959-69 (Chm., 1964-69); Vis. Cttee, Harvard Grad. Sch. of Educn, 1960-65; Nat. Citizens' Commn for the Public Schs, 1954-56; Bd of Trustees, Putney Sch., 1953-56; Trustee: Nat. Citizens' Council for the Public Schs, 1956-58; Nat. Cttee for the Support of the Public Schs, 1962-68. Delegate: to White House Conf. on Educn, 1955; to PEN Congress, Tokyo, 1958. Comr, Nat. Commn on New Technological Uses of Copyrighted Works, 1975-. Hon. Fellow, Clare Coll., Cambridge, 1967. Hon. MA Yale Univ., 1947; Hon. LLD Washington and Jefferson Coll., 1946; Hon. LHD New Sch. for Social Research, 1950; Hon. DHL Dropsie Coll., 1950; Hon. LittD: Wesleyan Univ., 1957; Clarkson Coll. of Technology, 1972. Pulitzer Prize for Fiction, 1945; Sidney Hillman Foundn Award, 1951; Howland Medal, Yale Univ., 1952. *Publications:* Men on Bataan, 1942; Into the Valley, 1943; A Bell for Adano, 1944; Hiroshima, 1946; The Wall, 1950; The Marmot Drive, 1953; A Single Pebble, 1956; The War Lover, 1959; The Child Buyer, 1960; Here to Stay, 1962; White Lotus, 1965; Too Far to Walk, 1966; Under the Eye of the Storm, 1967; The Algiers Motel Incident, 1968; The Conspiracy, 1972; The Writer's Craft, 1974; My Petition for More Space, 1974; The President, 1975; The Walnut Door, 1977. *Address:* 420 Humphrey Street, New Haven, Conn 06511, USA.

HERSHEY, Dr Alfred Day; Director, Genetics Research Unit, Carnegie Institution of Washington, 1962-74, retired; *b* 4 Dec. 1908; *s* of Robert D. Hershey and Alma (*née* Wilbur); *m* 1946, Harriet Davidson; one *s. Educ:* Michigan State Coll. (now Univ.). BS 1930; PhD 1934. Asst Bacteriologist, Washington Univ. Sch. of Medicine, St Louis Missouri, 1934-36; Instructor, 1936-38; Asst Prof., 1938-42; Assoc. Prof., 1942-50; Staff Mem., Dept of Genetics (now Genetics Research Unit), Carnegie Instn of Washington, 1950-. Albert Lasker Award, Amer. Public Health Assoc., 1958; Kimber Genetics Award, Nat. Acad. Sci., US, 1965. Hon. DSc, Chicago, 1967; Hon. Dr Med. Science, Michigan State, 1970. Nobel Prize for Physiology or Medicine (jtly), 1969. *Publications:* numerous articles in scientific jls or books. *Address:* Post Office Box 200, Cold Spring Harbor, New York 11724, USA. *T:* 516 692 6660.

HERTFORD, 8th Marquess of, *cr* 1793; **Hugh Edward Conway Seymour;** Baron Conway of Ragley, 1703; Baron Conway of Killultagh, 1712; Earl of Hertford, Viscount Beauchamp, 1750; Earl of Yarmouth, 1793; DL Warwick, 1959; formerly Lieutenant Grenadier Guards; *b* 29 March 1930; *s* of late Brig.-General Lord Henry Charles Seymour, DSO (2nd *s* of 6th Marquess) and Lady Helen Frances Grosvenor (*d* 1970), *d* of 1st Duke of Westminster; *S* uncle, 1940; *m* 1956, Comtesse Louise de Caraman Chimay, *o d* of late Lt-Col Prince Alphonse de Chimay, TD; one *s* three *d. Educ:* Eton. Chm., Hertford Public Relations Ltd, 1962-73. Chief interests are estate management (Diploma, Royal Agricultural Coll., Cirencester, 1956) and opening Ragley to the public. *Heir: s* Earl of Yarmouth, *qv. Address:* Ragley Hall, Alcester, Warwickshire. *T:* Alcester 2455. *Clubs:* hite's, Pratt's, Turf.

HERTFORD, Bishop Suffragan of, since 1974; **Rt. Rev. Peter Mumford;** *b* 14 Oct. 1922; *s* of late Peter Walter Mumford, miller, and of Kathleen Eva Mumford (*née* Walshe); *m* 1950, Lilian Jane, *d* of Captain George Henry Glover; two *s* one *d. Educ:* Sherborne School, Dorset; University Coll., Oxford; Cuddesdon Theological Coll. BA 1950, MA 1954 (Hons Theology). War Service, 1942-47, Captain, RA. Deacon, 1951; priest, 1952; Assistant Curate: St Mark, Salisbury, 1951-55; St Alban's Abbey, 1955-57; Vicar: Leagrave, Luton, 1957-63; St Andrew, Bedford, 1963-69; Rector of Crawley, Sussex, 1969-73; Canon and Prebendary of Ferring in Chichester Cathedral, 1972-73; Archdeacon of St Albans, 1973-74. Proctor in Convocation (St Albans), 1964-70 and 1974. *Address:* Hertford House, Abbey Mill Lane, St Albans, Herts. *T:* St Albans 66420.

HERVEY, family name of **Marquess of Bristol.**

HERVEY-BATHURST, Sir F.; *see* Bathurst.

HERWARTH von BITTENFELD, Hans Heinrich; Grand Cross (2nd Class), Order of Merit, Federal Republic of Germany, 1963; Hon. GCVO 1958; State Secretary, retired; Chairman, Aufsichtsrat of Unilever, Germany; *b* Berlin, 14 July 1904; *s* of Hans Richard Herwarth von Bittenfeld and Ilse Herwarth von Bittenfeld (*née* von Tiedemann); *m* 1935, Elisabeth Freiin von Redwitz; one *d. Educ:* Universities of Berlin, Breslau and Munich (Law and Nat. Econ.). Entered Auswärtiges Amt, Berlin, 1927; Attaché, Paris, 1930; Second Secretary and Personal Secretary to Ambassador, Moscow, 1931-39. Military Service, 1939-45. Oberregierungsrat, Regierungsdirektor, Bavarian State Chancellery, 1945-49; Ministerialdirigent and Chief of Protocol, Federal Government, 1950, Minister Plenipotentiary, 1952; German Ambassador to Court of St James's, 1955-61; State Secretary and Chief of German Federal Presidential Office, 1961-65; German Ambassador to Republic of Italy, 1965-69; Pres., Commn for Reform of German Diplomatic Service, 1969-71. Pres., Goethe Institut, Munich, 1971-77. *Recreations:* shooting, ski-ing, antiques. *Address:* Menzelstrasse 7, 8000 München 80, Germany.

HERZBERG, Charles Francis; Director of Corporate Development, Clarke Chapman Ltd, Group Headquarters Division, since 1975; *b* 26 Jan. 1924; *s* of Dr Franz Moritz Herzberg and Mrs Marie Louise Palache; *m* 1956, Ann Linette Hoare; one *s* two *d. Educ:* Fettes Coll., Edinburgh; Sidney Sussex Coll., Cambridge (MA). CEng, FIMechE, MIGasE. Alfred Herbert Ltd, 1947-51; Chief Engr and Dir, Hornflowa Ltd, Maryport, 1951-55; Chief Engr, Commercial Plastics Gp of Cos, and Dir, Commercial Plastics Engrg Co. at Wallsend on Tyne, North Shields, and Cramlington, Northumberland, 1955-66; Corporate Planning Dir, Appliance Div., United Gas Industries, and Works Dir, Robinson Willey Ltd, Liverpool, 1966-70; Man. Dir and Chief Exec., Churchill Gear Machines Ltd, Blaydon on Tyne, 1970-72; Regional Industrial Director, Dept of Industry, N Region, 1972-75. *Recreation:* shooting. *Address:* 3 Furzefield Road, Gosforth, Newcastle upon Tyne NE3 4EA. *T:* Newcastle upon Tyne 855202. *Club:* East India, Devonshire, Sports and Public Schools.

HERZBERG, Gerhard, CC (Canada), 1968; FRS 1951; FRSC 1939; Director, Division of Pure Physics, National Research Council of Canada, 1949-69, now Distinguished Research Scientist, National Research Council of Canada; *b* Hamburg, Germany, 25 Dec. 1904; *s* of late Albin Herzberg and Ella Herzberg; *m* 1929, Luise Herzberg, *née* Oettinger (*d* 1971); one *s* one *d*; *m* 1972, Monika Herzberg, *née* Tenthoff. *Educ:* Inst. of Technology, Darmstadt, Germany; Univ. of Göttingen, Germany; Univ. of Bristol, England. Lecturer, Darmstadt Inst. of Technology, 1930; Research Professor, Univ. of Saskatchewan, 1935; Prof. of Spectroscopy, Yerkes Observatory, Univ. of Chicago, 1945; Principal Research Officer, National Research Council of Canada, 1948. University Medal, Univ. of Liège, Belgium, 1950; President, RSC, 1966 (Henry Marshall Tory Medal, 1953). Joy Kissen Mookerjee Gold Medal of Indian Association for Cultivation of Science, 1954 (awarded 1957). Gold Medal of Canadian Association Phys., 1957; Bakerian Lecture, Royal Society, 1960; Faraday Lecture and Medal, Chem. Soc., 1970; Nobel Prize for Chemistry, 1971; Royal Medal, Royal Soc., 1971. Hon. Fellow: Indian Academy of Science, 1954; Indian Physical Society, 1957; Chemical Society of London, 1968. Hon. Member: Hungarian Academy of Sciences, 1964; Optical Society of America, 1968; Royal Irish Acad., 1970; Hon. Foreign Member American Academy Arts and Sciences, 1965; Foreign Associate, National Academy of Sciences, US, 1968. President, Canadian Association of Physicists, 1956; Vice-Pres., International Union of Pure and Applied Physics, 1957-63. Holds numerous hon. degrees, including Hon. ScD Cantab, 1972. *Publications:* Atomic Spectra and Atomic Structure, 1st edition (USA) 1937, 2nd edition (USA) 1944; Molecular Spectra and Molecular Structure: I, Spectra of Diatomic Molecules, 1st edition (USA), 1939, 2nd edition (USA), 1950; II, Infra-red and Raman Spectra of Polyatomic Molecules (USA), 1945; III, Electronic Spectra and Electronic Structure of Polyatomic Molecules (USA), 1966; The Spectra and Structures of Simple Free Radicals: an introduction to Molecular Spectroscopy (USA), 1971; original research on atomic and molecular spectra published in various scientific journals. *Address:* National Research Council, Ottawa, Ontario K1A 0R6, Canada. *T:* 99-22350; 190 Lakeway Drive, Ottawa, Ontario K1L 5B3, Canada. *T:* 746-4126.

HERZFELD, Gertrude, MB, ChB, FRCSE; retired; Vice-President: Scottish Society of Women Artists, since 1954; Edinburgh Cripple Aid Society, since 1956; Trefoil School for Physically Handicapped Children, since 1964; *b* 1890; *d* of late Michael Herzfeld. *Educ:* Private School; Edinburgh Univ. MB, ChB, Edinburgh, 1914; Dorothy Gilfillan Prize, 1914; FRCSE, 1920; Wm Gibson Scholarship, 1920-22; formerly House Surgeon, Royal Hospital for Sick Children and Chalmers Hospital, Edinburgh, 1914-17; Surgeon, attached RAMC Cambridge Hospital, Aldershot, 1917; senior House Surgeon, Bolton Infirmary, 1917-19; Consultant Surgeon: Bruntsfield Hospital for Women and Children, 1920-55; Royal Edinburgh Hospital for Sick Children, 1920-45; Surgeon, Edinburgh Orthopaedic Clinic, 1925-55; Univ. Lectr on Surgery of Childhood, 1920-45; Lectr, Edinburgh Sch. of Chiropody, 1924-28. Chairman, City of Edinburgh Div., BMA, 1960-62. Past Pres., Med. Women's Fedn. Hon. Mem., Fedn of University Women, Edinburgh Assoc. *Publications:* various articles on Surgical Conditions of Childhood in the British Medical Jl, Lancet, American Jl of Surgery, etc. *Recreations:* motoring, gardening. *Address:* Ashfield, 1 Chamberlain Road, Edinburgh 10. *T:* 031-229 8849. *Club:* Ladies Caledonian (Edinburgh).

HERZIG, Christopher; Under-Secretary, Department of Energy, since 1974; *b* 24 Oct. 1926; *s* of late L. A. Herzig and late Mrs Elizabeth Herzig (*née* Hallas); *m* 1952, Rachel Katharine Buxton; four *s* one *d. Educ:* Christ's Hosp.; Selwyn Coll., Cambridge (MA). Asst Principal, Min. of Fuel and Power, 1951-56; Principal, Min. of Supply, 1956-58; Min. of Aviation, 1959-61; Private Sec. to Lord President of the Council, 1961-64; Private Sec. to Minister of Technology, 1964-66; Asst Sec., Min. of Technology, 1966-70; Dept of Trade and Industry, 1970-71, Under-Sec., DTI, 1972-73. *Address:* Blatchford House, King's Road, Horsham, West Sussex. *T:* Horsham 65239.

HERZOG, Frederick Joseph, MC; Farmer; *b* 8 Dec. 1890; *s* of late F. C. Herzog, formerly of Mossley Hill, Liverpool; *m* 1918, Constance Cicely Broad; two *s* one *d. Educ:* Charterhouse; Trinity Coll., Cambridge. BA, Economics tripos, 1911. Served European War in Royal Artillery, 1914-19 (MC); retired with rank of Major. High Sheriff of Denbighshire, 1942; JP Denbighshire since 1946. *Recreations:* sketching, gardening. *Address:* The Grange, Ruthin, North Wales. *T:* Ruthin 2124.

HESELTINE, Michael Ray Dibdin; MP (C) Henley, since 1974 (Tavistock, 1966-74); *b* 21 March 1933; *s* of late Col R. D. Heseltine, Swansea, Glamorgan; *m* 1962, Anne Harding Williams; one *s* two *d. Educ:* Shrewsbury Sch.; Pembroke Coll., Oxford. BA PPE; Pres. Oxford Union, 1954. National Service (commissioned), Welsh Guards, 1959. Contested (C): Gower, 1959; Coventry North, 1964. Director of Bow Publications, 1961-65; Chm., Haymarket Press, 1966-70, 1974-. Vice-Chm., Cons. Parly Transport Cttee, 1968; Opposition Spokesman on Transport, 1969; Parly Sec., Min. of Transport, June-Oct. 1970; Parly Under-Sec. of State, DoE, 1970-72; Minister for Aerospace and Shipping, DTI, 1972-74; Opposition Spokesman on: Industry, 1974-76; Environment, 1976-. *Address:* 39 Connaught Square, W2; Thewford House, near Banbury, Oxon. *Clubs:* Carlton, Coningsby.

HESELTINE, William Frederick Payne, CVO 1969 (MVO 1961); Deputy Private Secretary to the Queen since 1977 (Assistant Private Secretary, 1972-77); *b* E Fremantle, W Australia, 17 July 1930; *s* of H. W. Heseltine; *m* 1st, Ann Elizabeth (*d* 1957), *d* of late L. F. Turner, Melbourne; 2nd, Audrey Margaret, *d* of late S. Nolan, Sydney; one *s* one *d. Educ:* Christ Church Grammar Sch., Claremont, WA; University of Western Australia (1st class hons, History). Prime Minister's dept, Canberra, 1951-62; Private Secretary to Prime Minister, 1955-59; Asst Information Officer to The Queen, 1960-61; Acting Official Secretary to Governor-General of Australia, 1962; Asst Federal Director of Liberal Party of Australia, 1962-64; attached to Household of Princess Marina for visit to Australia, 1964; attached to Melbourne Age, 1964; Asst Press Secretary to the Queen, 1965-67, Press Secretary, 1968-72. *Address:* St James's Palace, SW1. *Club:* Press.

HESKETH, 3rd Baron, *cr* 1935, of Hesketh, **Thomas Alexander Fermor-Hesketh,** Bt 1761; *b* 28 Oct. 1950; *s* of 2nd Baron and Christian Mary, *o d* of Sir John McEwen, 1st Bt of Marchmont; *S* father 1955; *m* 1977, Hon. Claire, *e d* of 3rd Baron Manton, *qv. Educ:* Ampleforth. *Heir: b* Hon. Robert Fermor-Hesketh, *b* 1 Nov. 1951. *Address:* Easton Neston, Towcester, Northamptonshire. *T:* Towcester 50445. *Club:* Turf.

HESKETH, (Charles) Peter Fleetwood Fleetwood-, TD 1943; DL; *b* 5 Feb. 1905; 2nd *s* of late Charles Hesketh Fleetwood-Hesketh, and late Anne Dorothea, *e d* of Sir Thomas Brocklebank, 2nd Bt; *m* 1940, Mary Monica, JP Lancs, 2nd *d* of Sir Ralph Cockayne Assheton, 1st Bt; one *d. Educ:* Eton. Studied architecture at London Univ. under Sir Albert Richardson, and at Architectural Association; Student RIBA and Registered Architect. Worked in office of late H. S. Goodhart-Rendel and later with Seely & Paget and other architects. Member of Lloyd's until 1975. Hon. district rep., for National Trust, 1947-68 (Mem., W Midlands Regional Cttee, 1972-); Member: Covent Gdn Conservation Area Adv. Cttee, 1972-; Archbp's Adv. Bd on Redundant Churches, 1973-; Soc. for Protection of Ancient Buildings; Westminster Soc.; Gen. Synod of Church of England, 1975-; Prayer Book Soc. (Founder Mem. and Trustee); Cttee of Incorporated Church Building Soc.; Council, Anglo-Rhodesian Soc., 1965- (Chm. Lancs and Cheshire Br., 1969-). Hon. Dist Rep., Georgian Group and other societies; Founder Mem., Victorian Society, Secretary, 1961-63 (Chm., Liverpool Gp, 1968-); Architectural Correspt, Daily Telegraph, 1964-67. Pres., Widnes, Cheshire, Div., Conservative Assoc., 1971-. Special Constable in London during Gen. Strike, 1926. 2nd Lieut DLO Yeomanry (Cavalry) 1926, Captain 1938. Served, 1939-45, with DLO Yeomanry; WO, MI (Liaison); in occupied France with 2nd SAS and Maquis; Monuments, Fine Arts and Archives (Austria). High Sheriff, Lancs., 1960-61; DL Lancs, 1961. A Burgess of Preston; Freeman of Hale. *Publications:* Guide to the Palace of Schönbrunn, 1945; Murray's Lancashire Architectural Guide, 1955; Lancs section of Collins's Guide to English Parish Churches, 1958 (ed. John Betjeman); Life of Sir Charles Barry, in Peter Ferriday's Victorian Architecture, 1963; 1790-1840 section of Ian Grant's Great Interiors, 1967; chapters in: Shell Guide to England (ed John Hadfield), 1970; The Country Seat (ed Howard Colvin and John Harris), 1970. Illustrated John Betjeman's Ghastly Good Taste, 1933, extended 1970. Contrib. articles and drawings to Country Life, etc. *Address:* The Manor House, Hale, near Liverpool. *T:* Hale 3116; 57 Great Ormond Street, WC1. *T:* 01-242 3672. *Clubs:* Travellers', MCC, Royal Automobile (Life Mem.).

HESKETH, Roger Fleetwood, OBE 1970; TD 1942; Vice Lord-Lieutenant of Lancashire, 1974-77 (Vice-Lieutenant, 1972-74); *b* 28 July 1902; *e s* of Charles Hesketh Fleetwood-Hesketh, DL; *m* 1952, Lady Mary Lumley, OBE, DStJ, *e d* of 11th Earl of Scarbrough, KG, PC, GCSI, GCIE, GCVO; one *s* two *d. Educ:* Eton; Christ Church, Oxford (MA). Called to the Bar, Inner Temple, 1928. MP (C) for Southport, 1952-59. High Sheriff, Lancs, 1947; DL 1950. JP 1950, Lancs; Mayor of Southport, 1950; Freeman of the Borough, 1966. Chairman, Lancashire Agricultural Executive Cttee, 1965-72. Trustee, Historic Churches Preservation Trust. Served War of 1939-45 (despatches, Bronze Star Medal, USA). Hon. Colonel, Duke of Lancaster's Own Yeomanry, 1956-67. *Address:* Meols Hall, Southport, Merseyside. *T:* Southport 28171; H4 Albany, Piccadilly, W1. *T:* 01-734 5320. *Clubs:* Travellers', Pratt's.

HESLOP-HARRISON, Prof. John, FRS 1970; MSc, PhD, DSc, FRSE, MRIA, FRSA, FLS; Royal Society Research Professor, University College of Wales, Aberystwyth, since 1977; Member, Agricultural Research Council, since 1977; *b* 10 Feb. 1920; *s* of late Prof. J. W. Heslop-Harrison, FRS; *m* 1950, Yolande, *d* of late Captain J. H. Massey, Burnley, Lancashire; one *s. Educ:*

Grammar School, Chester-le-Street, King's Coll. (University of Durham), Newcastle upon Tyne. MSc (Dunelm), PhD (Belfast), DSc (Dunelm). Radio Officer, Ministry of Supply, 1941-42; 2nd Lieut RAOC, 1942; Captain REME, 1942-45. Lecturer in Agricultural Botany, King's Coll., Univ. of Durham, 1945-46; Lecturer in Botany: Queen's Univ., Belfast, 1946-50; UCL, 1950-53; Reader in Taxonomy, UCL, 1953-54; Prof. of Botany, Queen's Univ., Belfast, 1954-60; Mason Prof. of Botany, Univ. of Birmingham, 1960-67; Prof. of Botany, Inst. of Plant Develt, Univ. of Wisconsin, 1967-71; Dir, Royal Botanic Gardens, Kew, 1971-76. Visiting Professor: (Brittingham) Univ. of Wisconsin, 1965; US Dept of Agriculture Institute of Forest Genetics, Rhinelander, Wis, 1968; Univ. of Massachusetts, Amherst, Mass, 1976-77; Lectures: Sigma Xi, Geneva, NY, 1969; William Wright Smith, Edinburgh, 1972; George Bidder, Soc. Exptl Biol., Leeds, 1973; Ghosh, Univ. of Calcutta, 1973; Kennedy Orton Meml, UCW, Bangor, 1974; Croonian, Royal Society, 1974; Amos Meml, E Malling, 1975; Holden, Univ. of Nottingham, 1976. Vice-President: Botanical Soc. of British Isles, 1972; Linnean Soc., 1973; President: Inst. of Biology, 1974-75; Sect. K, British Assoc. for Advancement of Science, 1974. Editor, Annals of Botany, 1961-67. Corresp. Mem., Royal Netherlands Botanical Soc., 1968; For. Fellow, Indian Nat. Sci. Acad., 1974; Mem., German Acad. of Science, 1975; For. Mem., American Botanical Soc., 1976-. Hon. DSc Belfast, 1971. Trail-Crisp Award, Linnean Soc., 1967; Univ. of Liège Medal, 1967; Erdtman Internat. Medal for Palynology, 1971; Cooke Award, Amer. Acad. of Allergy, 1974. *Publications:* New Concepts in Flowering-plant Taxonomy, 1953; (ed) Pollen: development and physiology, 1971; papers on botanical subjects in various British and foreign journals. *Recreations:* hill walking, photography and painting. *Address:* Old Post, Hatfield, near Leominster, Herefordshire; Welsh Plant Breeding Station, Plas Gogerddan, near Aberystwyth SY23 3EB.

HESS, Ellen Elizabeth, NDH; Administrator, Studley College Trust, since 1970; Principal, Studley College, Warwickshire, 1956-69; *b* 28 Dec. 1908; *d* of Charles Michael Joseph Hess and Fanny Thompson Hess (*née* Alder). *Educ:* Grammar School for Girls, Dalston; Royal Botanic Society, Regents Park. Lecturer in Horticulture, Swanley Horticultural College for Women, 1934-39; Agricultural Secretary, National Federation of Women's Institutes, 1939-46; Ellen Eddy Shaw Fellowship, Brooklyn Botanic Gardens, New York, USA, 1946-47; School of Horticulture, Ambler, Pa., USA, 1947-48; HM Inspector of Schools (Agriculture and Further Education), 1948-56. Veitch Meml Medal, RHS, 1967. *Recreations:* travel, photography, walking. *Address:* The Croft, 54 Torton Hill Road, Arundel, West Sussex BN18 9HH.

HESSE, Mary Brenda, MA, MSc, PhD; FBA 1971; Professor of Philosophy of Science, University of Cambridge, since 1975; Fellow of Wolfson College (formerly University College), Cambridge, since 1965; Vice-President, Wolfson College, since 1976; *b* 15 Oct. 1924; *d* of Ethelbert Thomas Hesse and Brenda Nellie Hesse (*née* Pelling). *Educ:* Imperial Coll., London; University Coll., London. MSc, PhD (London); DIC; MA (Cantab). Lecturer: in Mathematics, Univ. of Leeds, 1951-55; in Hist. and Philosophy of Science, UCL, 1955-59; in Philosophy of Science, Univ. of Cambridge, 1960-68; Reader in Philosophy of Sci., Cambridge Univ., 1968-75. Visiting Prof.: Yale Univ., 1961; Univ. of Minnesota, 1966; Univ. of Chicago, 1968. Stanton Lectr, Cambridge, 1977-. Editor, Brit. Jl for the Philosophy of Science, 1965-69. *Publications:* Science and the Human Imagination, 1954; Forces and Fields, 1961; Models and Analogies in Science, 1963; The Structure of Scientific Inference, 1974; articles in jls of philosophy and of the history and the philosophy of science. *Recreations:* walking, Roman roads. *Address:* Department of History and Philosophy of Science, Free School Lane, Cambridge CB2 3RH.

HESTON, Charlton; actor (films, stage and television), USA; *b* Evanston, Ill, 4 Oct. 1924; *s* of Russell Whitford Carter and Lilla Carter (*née* Charlton); *m* 1944, Lydia Marie Clarke (actress), Two Rivers, Wisconsin; one *s* one *d. Educ:* New Trier High Sch., Ill; Sch. of Speech, Northwestern Univ., 1941-43. Served War of 1939-45, with 11th Army Air Forces in the Aleutians. Co-Dir (with wife), also both acting, Thomas Wolfe Memorial Theatre, Asheville, NC (plays: the State of the Union, The Glass Menagerie, etc.). In Antony and Cleopatra, Martin Beck Theatre, New York, 1947; also acting on Broadway, 1949 and 1950, etc. *Films:* (1950-) include: Dark City, Ruby Gentry, The Greatest Show on Earth, Arrowhead, Bad For Each Other, The Savage, Pony Express, The President's Lady, Secret of the Incas, The Naked Jungle, The Far Horizons, The Private War of Major Benson, The Ten Commandments (Moses), The Big Country, Ben Hur (Acad. Award for best actor, 1959), The Wreck of the Mary Deare, El Cid, 55 Days at Peking, The Greatest Story Ever

Told, Major Dundee, The Agony and the Ecstacy, Khartoum, Will Penny, Planet of the Apes, Soylent Green, The Three Musketeers, Earthquake, Airport 1975, The Four Musketeers, The Last Hard Men, Battle of Midway, Two-Minute Warning, Gray Lady Down, The Prince and the Pauper. TV appearances, esp. in Shakespeare. Mem., Screen Actors' Guild (Pres., 1966-69); Mem., Nat. Council on the Arts, 1967-; Chm., Amer. Film Inst. and Center Theatre Group, LA. Is interested in Shakespearian roles. *Address:* c/o George Thomas, 1334 Lincoln No 130, Santa Monica, Calif 90401, USA.

HETHERINGTON, Alastair; *see* Hetherington, H. A.

HETHERINGTON, Arthur Carleton, CBE 1971 (MBE 1945); Secretary of Association of County Councils since 1974; *b* 13 Feb. 1916; *s* of late Arthur Stanley and Mary Venters Hetherington, Silloth, Cumberland; *m* 1941, Xenia, *d* of late Nicholas Gubsky, Barnes; three *s*. *Educ:* St Bees School. Admitted Solicitor 1938. Asst Solicitor: Peterborough, 1938-39; Stafford, 1939. Served Royal Artillery, 1939-46 (Hon. Lt-Col); Temp. Lt-Col 1944-46. Dep. Clerk of the Peace and Dep. Clerk of County Council: of Cumberland, 1946-52; of Cheshire, 1952-59; Clerk of the Peace and Clerk of County Council of Cheshire, 1959-64. Sec., County Councils Assoc., 1964-74. Mem., Departmental Cttee on Jury Service, 1963-64; Sec., Local Authorities Management Services and Computer Cttee, 1965-. *Recreations:* music, golf, family. *Address:* (home) 33 Campden Hill Court, W8 7HS; (office) 66A Eaton Square, SW1W 9BH. *T:* 01-235 5173. *Club:* Royal Automobile.

HETHERINGTON, Sir Arthur (Ford), Kt 1974; DSC 1944; Chairman, British Gas Corporation, 1973-76 (Member 1967, Deputy Chairman 1967-72, Chairman 1972, Gas Council); Chairman, Executive Board, British Standards Institution, since 1976; *b* 12 July 1911; *s* of late Sir Roger Hetherington and Lady Hetherington; *m* 1937, Margaret Lacey; one *s* one *d*. *Educ:* Highgate Sch.; Trinity Coll., Cambridge (BA). Joined staff of Gas Light & Coke Company, 1935. Served War, RNVR, 1941-45. North Thames Gas Board, 1949-55; joined staff of Southern Gas Board, 1955; Deputy Chairman, 1956; Chairman 1961-64; Chairman, E Midlands Gas Board, 1964-66. Hon. FIGasE. Hon. DSc London, 1974. *Address:* 32 Connaught Square, W2. *T:* 01-723 3128. *Clubs:* Athenæum; Royal Southampton Yacht. *See also* R. le G. Hetherington.

HETHERINGTON, Rear-Adm. Derick Henry Fellowes, CB 1961; DSC 1941 (2 Bars 1944, 1945); MA (Oxon), 1963; Domestic Bursar and Fellow of Merton College, Oxford, 1963-76; Emeritus Fellow, 1976; *b* 27 June 1911; *s* of Commander H. R. Hetherington, RD, Royal Naval Reserve, and Hilda Fellowes; *m* 1942, Josephine Mary, *d* of Captain Sir Leonard Vavasour, 4th Bt, RN; one *s* three *d* (and one *s* decd). *Educ:* St Neot's, Eversley, Hants; RNC Dartmouth. Cadet, HMS Barham, 1928-29; Midshipman-Comdr (HMS Effingham, Leander, Anthony, Wildfire, Kimberley, Windsor, Lookout, Royal Arthur, Cheviot), 1929-52; Captain 1950; Chief of Staff, Canal Zone, Egypt, 1950-52; Senior British Naval Officer, Ceylon, 1954-55; Captain (D) 4th Destroyer Squadron, 1956-57; Director of Naval Training, Admiralty, 1958-59; Flag Officer, Malta, 1959-61; retired 1961. Croix de Guerre (France) 1945. *Address:* Millway Lane, Appleton, Abingdon, Oxon.

HETHERINGTON, (Hector) Alastair; Controller, BBC Scotland, since 1975; *b* Llanishen, Glamorganshire, 31 Oct. 1919; *yr s* of late Sir Hector Hetherington and Lady Hetherington; *m* 1957, Miranda (separated 1976), *d* of Professor R. A. C. Oliver, *qv*; two *s* two *d*. *Educ:* Gresham's Sch., Holt; Corpus Christi Coll., Oxford (Hon. Fellow, 1971). Royal Armoured Corps, 1940-46. Editorial staff, The Glasgow Herald, 1946-50; joined Manchester Guardian, 1950, Asst Editor and Foreign Editor, 1953-56, Editor, 1956-75; Director: Guardian and Manchester Evening News Ltd, 1956-75; Guardian Newspapers Ltd, 1967-75. Member, Royal Commission on the Police, 1960-62. Vis. Fellow, Nuffield Coll., Oxford, 1973-. Trustee, Scott Trust, 1970-. Journalist of the Year, Nat. Press awards, 1970. *Recreations:* hill walking, golf. *Address:* 12 Kirklee Circus, Glasgow G12 0TW. *Club:* Athenæum.

HETHERINGTON, Roger le Geyt, CBE 1974 (OBE 1945); Consultant to and formerly Senior Partner of Binnie & Partners; *b* 20 Dec. 1908; *s* of late Sir Roger and Lady Hetherington; *m* 1945, Katharine Elise Dawson; one *d*. *Educ:* Highgate Sch.; Trinity Coll., Cambridge (MA). FICE, FIWES. Joined Binnie Deacon & Gourley (now Binnie & Partners), as pupil, 1930. Served War, RE, 1940-45. Taken into partnership, Binnie & Partners, 1947. Member, Central Advisory Water Committee, 1969-71. President, Institution of Civil Engineers, 1972-73. *Address:* 28 Denewood Road, Highgate N6 4AH. *T:* 01-340

4203. *Club:* United Oxford & Cambridge University. *See also* Sir A. F. Hetherington.

HETHERINGTON, Thomas Chalmers, (Tony), CBE 1970; TD; Director of Public Prosecutions, since 1977; *b* 18 Sept. 1926; *er s* of William and Alice Hetherington; *m* 1953, June Margaret Ann Catliff; four *d*. *Educ:* Rugby Sch.; Christ Church, Oxford. Served in Royal Artillery, Middle East, 1945-48; Territorial Army, 1948-67. Called to Bar, Inner Temple, 1952; Legal Dept, Min. of Pensions and Nat. Insce, 1953; Law Officers' Dept, 1962, Legal Sec., 1966-75; Dep. Treasury Solicitor, 1975-77. *Address:* Rosemount, Lingfield, Surrey. *T:* Lingfield 832742. *Club:* Athenæum.

HEUSTON, Prof. Robert Francis Vere, DCL Oxon 1970; Regius Professor of Laws, Trinity College, Dublin, since 1970; *b* Dublin, 17 Nov. 1923; *e s* of late Vere Douglas Heuston and of Dorothy Helen Coulter; *m* 1962, Bridget Nancy (*née* Bolland), widow of Neville Ward-Perkins; four step *c*. *Educ:* St Columba's Coll.; Trinity Coll., Dublin; St John's Coll., Cambridge. Barrister, King's Inns, 1947, Gray's Inn, 1951; Hon. Member, Western Circuit, 1966. Fellow, Pembroke Coll., Oxford, 1947-65 (Supernumerary Fellow, 1965-), Dean, 1951-57, Pro-Proctor, 1953; Professor of Law, Univ. of Southampton, 1965-70. Member, Law Reform Cttee (England), 1968-70, (Ireland), 1975-. Visiting Professor: Univ. of Melbourne, 1956; Univ. of British Columbia, 1960; Gresham Professor in Law, 1964-70. *Publications:* (ed) Salmond on Torts, 17th edn 1977, 16th edn 1973; Essays in Constitutional Law, 2nd edn 1964; Lives of the Lord Chancellors, 1964; various in learned periodicals. *Address:* Kentstown House, Brownstown, Navan, Ireland. *T:* Drogheda 25195. *Club:* United Oxford & Cambridge University.

HEWAN, Gethyn Elliot; Hon. Secretary, Surrey Golf Union, since 1977; *b* 23 Dec. 1916; *s* of late E. D. Hewan and Mrs L. Hewan; *m* 1943, Peggy (*née* Allen); one *s* two *d*. *Educ:* Marlborough Coll., Wilts; Clare Coll., Cambridge (Exhibitioner); Yale Univ., USA (Mellon Schol). BA Hons 1938; MA 1943, Cambridge. Served War of 1939-45 (despatches): Middle East; Capt. 3rd Regt RHA 1943; Staff Coll., Camberley, psc 1944; BMRA 51st Highland Div., 1944-45. Asst Master, Wellington Coll., 1946-50; Headmaster, Cranbrook Sch., Bellevue Hill, NSW, 1951-63; Acting Bursar, Marlborough Coll., Wilts, 1963; Asst Master, Winchester Coll., 1963-64, Charterhouse Sch., 1964-65; Headmaster, Allhallows Sch., Rousdon, 1965-74. Sec., NSW branch of HMC of Aust., 1956-63; Standing Cttee of HMC of Aust., 1958-63; Foundation Member, Aust. Coll. of Education, 1958; Exec. Cttee, Australian Outward Bound Foundation, 1958-63. *Recreations:* cricket (Cambridge blue, 1938), golf, fishing; formerly hockey (blue, 1936-37-38, Captain) and billiards (½-blue, 1938). *Address:* Little Hadlow, Worplesdon Hill, Woking, Surrey. *T:* Brookwood 2652. *Clubs:* MCC; I Zingari; Free Foresters; Oxford and Cambridge Golfing Society; Worplesdon Golf; Senior Golfers'.

HEWARD, Air Chief Marshal Sir Anthony Wilkinson, KCB 1972 (CB 1968); OBE 1952; DFC and bar; AFC; Air Member for Supply and Organisation, Ministry of Defence, 1973-76; *b* 1 July 1918; *s* of late Col E. J. Heward; *m* 1944, Clare Myfanwy Wainwright, *d* of late Maj.-Gen. C. B. Wainwright, CB; one *s* one *d*. Gp Captain RAF, 1957; IDC 1962; Air Cdre 1963; Dir of Operations (Bomber and Reconnaissance) MoD (RAF), 1963; Air Vice-Marshal 1966; Dep. Comdr, RAF Germany, 1966-69; AOA, HQ RAF Air Support Command, 1969-70; Air Marshal 1970; Chief of Staff, RAF Strike Command, 1970-72; AOC, No 18 (Maritime) Group, 1972-73; Air Chief Marshal, 1974. *Address:* Home Close, Donhead St Mary, near Shaftesbury, Dorset; 14 Trevor Street, SW7.

HEWARD, Edmund Rawlings; Master of the Supreme Court (Chancery Division), since 1959; *b* 19 Aug. 1912; *s* of late Rev. Thomas Brown Heward and Kathleen Amy Rachel Rawlings; *m* 1945, Constance Mary Sandiford, *d* of late George Bertram Crossley, OBE. *Educ:* Repton; Trinity Coll., Cambridge. Admitted a solicitor, 1937. Enlisted Royal Artillery as a Gunner, 1940; released as Major, DAAG, 1946. Partner in Rose, Johnson and Hicks, 9 Suffolk St, SW1, 1946. LLM 1960. *Publications:* Guide to Chancery Practice, 1962 (5th edn 1978); Matthew Hale, 1972; (ed) Part 2, Tristram and Coote's Probate Practice, 24th edn, 1973, 25th edn, 1977; (ed) Judgments and Orders in Halsbury's Laws of England, 4th edn; Lord Mansfield, 1978. *Address:* 36a Dartmouth Row, Greenwich, SE10 8AW. *T:* 01-692 3525. *Clubs:* United Oxford & Cambridge University, Travellers'.

HEWER, Christopher Langton, MB, BS (London); MRCP; Hon. FFARCS; Consulting Anæsthetist to St Bartholomew's

Hospital and to Hospital for Tropical Diseases, London; late Senior Anæsthetist, The Queen's Hospital for Children, Hackney Road; Seamen's Hospital, Royal Albert Dock; St Andrew's Hospital, Dollis Hill; late Anæsthetist to Queen Mary's Hospital, Roehampton, Ministry of Pensions, Brompton Chest Hospital and Anæsthetic Specialist RAMC; Examiner in Anæsthesia to Royal College of Surgeons of England and Royal College of Physicians; late Consultant Anæsthetist to West Herts Hospital, Hemel Hempstead, to Luton and Dunstable Hospital, and to Harpenden Hospital; *s* of Joseph Langton Hewer, MD, FRCS; *m* 1925, Doris Phœbe, *d* of H. D'Arcy Champney, MA, Bristol; two *s* one *d. Educ:* University Coll. Sch; St Bartholomew's Hospital. Junior Scholarship in Anatomy and Physiology in St Bartholomew's Hospital Medical Coll.; MB, BS London degree (distinction in Physiology), 1920; served as House Surgeon and Resident Anæsthetist at St Bartholomew's Hospital; FRSM; Sec. of the Anæsthetic Section of same, 1930 and 1931, Pres., 1936-37; late Vice-Pres. Assoc. of Anæsthetists of Great Britain and Ireland, and Editor Emeritus of the Association's Journal, Anæsthesia; Member Anæsthetics Cttee of MRC and RSM; Pres., Section of Anæsthetics, BMA, 1953; Hon. Member: Liverpool Soc. of Anæsthetists; Canadian Soc. of Anæsthetists; late Member Board of Faculty of Anæsthetists, RCS. Frederic Hewitt Lecturer, 1959. Henry Hill Hickman Medallist, 1966, John Snow Medallist, 1966. *Publications:* Anæsthesia in Children, 1922; (with H. E. G. Boyle) Practical Anæsthetics, 1923; (ed) Recent Advances in Anæsthesia and Analgesia, 1932, 12th edn 1976; Thoughts on Modern Anæsthesia, 1970; articles in medical journals and reports; Section on Anæsthesia in Post Graduate Surgery, edited by R. Maingot; formerly editor Section on Anæsthesia in Medical Annual. *Address:* 33 Stormont Road, Highgate, N6. *T:* 01-340 1388.

HEWER, Thomas Frederick, MD (Bristol); FRCP, FLS; Professor of Pathology, 1938-68, and Pro-Vice-Chancellor, 1966-68, University of Bristol; Professor Emeritus, 1968; *b* 12 April 1903; *s* of William Frederick Hewer and Kathleen Braddon Standerwick; *m* 1941, Anne Hiatt Baker, OBE 1977; two *s* two *d. Educ:* Bristol Gram. Sch.; University of Bristol. Commonwealth Fund Fellow and Asst Pathologist, Johns Hopkins Univ., USA, 1927-29; Bacteriologist Sudan Government, 1930-35; Sen. Lectr in Pathology, University of Liverpool, 1935-38. Chm., Bristol Br., English-Speaking Union, 1942-67, Vice-Pres., 1967-. Botanical explorer, FAO/UN, 1975-; consultant, WHO, investigating causation of cancer among Turkoman, NE Iran, making botanical exploration of desert E of Caspian Sea, 1976-. *Publications:* articles in medical and horticultural journals. *Recreations:* gardening and travel. *Address:* Vine House, Henbury, Bristol BS10 7AD. *T:* Bristol 503573. *Club:* English-Speaking Union.

HEWETSON, Gen. Sir Reginald (Hackett), GCB 1966 (KCB 1962; CB 1958); CBE 1945 (OBE 1943); DSO 1944; Adjutant-General, Ministry of Defence (Army), 1964-67; retired; *b* Shortlands, Kent, 4 Aug. 1908; *s* of late J. Hewetson, ICS, and E. M. M. Hackett-Wilkins; *m* 1935, Patricia Mable, *y d* of late F. H. Burkitt, CIE; one *s* one *d. Educ:* Repton; RMA, Woolwich. Regular Commission in RA, 1928; Service in India (including Active Service, 1930-32), 1929-35; RA depot and home stations, 1935-39; psc 1939; Staff Capt. RA 4 Div., 1938; Adjt 30 Fd Regt and Capt. 1939; France, Oct. 1939-Jan. 1940; 2nd war course at Staff Coll., Camberley, Jan.-April 1940; Brigade Major RA 43 (Wessex) Div. May-Sept. 1940. Temp. Major; various GSO2 jobs incl. instructor Senior Officers Sch., 1940-42; GSO1 (Lieut-Col) HQ L of C North Africa, Sept.-Nov. 1942; 78 Div. (in North Africa), 1942-43 (OBE); Lieut-Col Comdg Fd Regt in 56 (London) Div. in Italy, 1943-44 (DSO); BGS HQ 10 Corps, 1944-45; BGS, British Troops, Austria, 1945-47; Student, IDC, 1949; Dep. Dir Staff Duties, WO, 1950-52; CRA 2nd Infantry Div., BAOR, 1953-55; GOC 11th Armoured Div., March 1956; GOC, 4th Infantry Div. 1956-58; Commandant, Staff Coll., Camberley, 1958-61; Commander, British Forces, Hong Kong, Dec. 1961-March 1963; GOC-in-C, Far East Land Forces, 1963-64. Col Comdt, RA, 1962-73; Col Comdt, APTC, 1966-70; ADC (Gen.), 1966-67. Chm., Exec. Cttee, Army Benevolent Fund, 1968-. Gov. and Mem. Administrative Bd, Corps of Commissionaires, 1964. *Recreations:* cricket (Army and Kent 2nd XI MCC, IZ), hockey (Norfolk and RA), golf. *Address:* Cherry Orchard, Fairwarp, near Uckfield, East Sussex. *Clubs:* MCC, Army and Navy.

HEWETT, Sir John George, 5th Bt, *cr* 1813; MC 1919; Captain KAR; *b* 23 Oct. 1895; *e* surv. *s* of Sir Harold George Hewett, 4th Bt, and Eleanor (*d* 1946), *d* of Capt. Studdy, RN, and Mrs W. T. Summers; *S* father, 1949; *m* 1926, Yuilleen Maude, *o c* of Samuel F. Smithson, Lauriston, Camberley; two *s. Educ:* Cheltenham. Served European War, 1914-18, British East Africa, 1914-19.

Heir: er s Peter John Smithson Hewett, MM [*b* 27 June 1931; *m* 1958, Jennifer Ann Cooper, *o c* of Emrys Thomas Jones, Bexhill-on-Sea; two *s* one *d. Educ:* Bradfield Coll.; Jesus Coll., Cambridge. Called to the Bar, Gray's Inn, 1954; now a practising Advocate in Kenya. Kenya Regt attached Special Branch, Kenya Police, 1957]. *Address:* Ol'Morogi, Naivasha, Kenya.

HEWISH, Prof. Antony, MA, PhD; FRS 1968; Professor of Radioastronomy, University of Cambridge, since 1971 (Reader, 1969-71); Fellow of Churchill College since 1962; *b* 11 May 1924; *s* of Ernest William Hewish and late Frances Grace Lanyon Pinch; *m* 1950, Marjorie Elizabeth Catherine Richards; one *s* one *d. Educ:* King's Coll., Taunton; Gonville and Caius Coll., Cambridge (Hon. Fellow, 1976). BA (Cantab.) 1948, MA 1950, PhD 1952; Hamilton Prize, Isaac Newton Student, 1952. RAE Farnborough, 1943-46; Research Fellow, Gonville and Caius Coll., 1952-54; Asst Dir of Research, 1954-62; Fellow, Gonville and Caius Coll., 1955-62; Lectr in Physics, Univ. of Cambridge, 1962-69. Visiting Prof. in Astronomy, Yale, 1963; Prof. of the Royal Instn, 1977. Hon. DSc: Leicester, 1976; Exeter, 1977. Foreign Hon. Mem., Amer. Acad. of Arts and Sciences. Eddington Medal, Royal Astronomical Soc., 1969; Charles Vernon Boys Prize, Inst. of Physics and Physical Soc., 1970; Dellinger Gold Medal, Internat. Union of Radio Science, 1972; Michelson Medal, Franklin Inst., 1973; Hopkins Prize, Cambridge Phil Soc., 1973; Holweck Medal and Prize, Soc. Française de Physique, 1974; Nobel Prize for Physics (jtly), 1974. *Publications:* Papers in Proc. Royal Society, Phys. Soc., Mon. Not. Royal Astr. Soc., etc. *Recreations:* music, gardening, sailing. *Address:* Pryor's Cottage, Kingston, Cambridge. *T:* Comberton 2657.

HEWITT, family name of **Viscount Lifford.**

HEWITT, Cecil Rolph, (C. H. Rolph); Director, Statesman Publishing Co. Ltd, since 1965; *b* London, 23 Aug. 1901; *s* of Frederick Thompson Hewitt and Edith Mary Speed; *m* 1st, 1926, Audrey Mary Buttery (marr. diss., 1946); one *d*; 2nd, 1947, Jenifer Wayne, author and scriptwriter; one *s* two *d. Educ:* State schools. City of London Police, 1921-46 (Chief Inspector); editorial staff, New Statesman, 1947; editor The Author, 1956-60. Vice-Pres., Howard League for Penal Reform. Frequently broadcasts topical talks and documentaries. *Publications:* Crime and Punishment, 1950; Towards My Neighbour, 1950; On Gambling, 1951; Personal Identity, 1956; (Ed.) The Human Sum, 1957; Mental Disorder, 1958; Commonsense About Crime and Punishment, 1961; The Trial of Lady Chatterley, 1961; (with Arthur Koestler) Hanged by the Neck, 1961; All Those in Favour? (The ETU Trial), 1962; The Police and The Public, 1962; Law and the Common Man, 1967; Books in the Dock, 1969; Kingsley, 1973; Believe What You Like, 1973; Living Twice (autobiog.), 1974; Mr Prone, 1977; The Queen's Pardon, 1978; contributor to The Encyclopædia Britannica, Chambers's Encyclopædia, Punch, The Week-End Book, The New Law Journal, The Times Literary Supplement, The Author, The Nation (NY), daily and weekly press. *Recreations:* music, reading, and the contemplation of work. *Address:* Rushett Edge, Bramley, Surrey GU5 0LH. *T:* Bramley 3227.

HEWITT, Sir (Cyrus) Lenox (Simson), Kt 1971; OBE 1963; Chairman, Qantas Airways Ltd, since 1975 (Director since 1973); *b* 7 May 1917; *s* of Cyrus Lenox Hewitt and Ella Louise Hewitt; *m* 1943, Alison Hope (*née* Tillyard); one *s* three *d. Educ:* Scotch Coll., Melbourne; Melbourne Univ. (BCom). FASA, FCIS, LCA. Broken Hill Proprietary Co. Ltd, 1933-39; Asst Sec., Commonwealth Prices Br., Canberra, 1939-46; Economist, Dept of Post War Reconstruction, 1946-49; Official Sec. and Actg Dep. High Comr, London, 1950-53; Commonwealth Treasury: Asst Sec., 1953-55; 1st Asst Sec., 1955-62; Dep. Sec., 1962-66; Chm., Australian Univs. Commn, 1967; Secretary to: Prime Minister's Dept, 1968-71; Dept of the Environment, Aborigines and the Arts, 1971-72; Dept of Minerals and Energy, 1972-75. Lectr, Econs and Cost Accountancy, Canberra UC, 1940-49, 1954. Acting Chairman: Pipeline Authority, 1973-75; Petroleum and Minerals Authority, 1974-75; Chm., Petroleum and Minerals Co. of Aust. Pty Ltd, 1975-; Director: East/Aust. Pipeline Corp. Ltd, 1974-75; Jetabout Ltd, 1974-; Mary Kathleen Uranium Ltd, 1975-; Aust. Industry Develt Corp., 1975; Dep. Chm., Aust. Atomic Energy Commn, 1972-. *Recreations:* tennis, farming. *Address:* 9 Torres Street, Red Hill, Canberra, ACT 2603, Australia. *T:* 958679. *Clubs:* Brooks's; Melbourne (Melbourne); Union (Sydney).
See also *P . H . Hewitt.*

HEWITT, Rev. Canon George Henry Gordon; Residentiary Canon, Chelmsford Cathedral, since 1964; Chaplain to the Queen, since 1969; *b* 30 May 1912; *s* of Rev. G. H. Hewitt; *m*

1942, Joan Ellen Howden; two s one d. *Educ:* Trent Coll.; Brasenose, Oxford; Wycliffe Hall, Oxford. Asst Curate, St Clement, Leeds, 1936-39; Chaplain, Ridley Hall, Cambridge, 1939-41; Asst Curate, Leeds Parish Church, 1941-43; Religious Book Editor, Lutterworth Press, 1943-52; Diocesan Education Sec., Sheffield, 1952-58; Residentiary Canon, Sheffield Cathedral, 1953-58; Vicar of St Andrew, Oxford, 1958-64. *Publications:* Let the People Read, 1949; The Problems of Success: a history of the Church Missionary Society, 1910-1942, vol. I, 1971, vol. II, 1977. *Address:* 8 Rainsford Avenue, Chelmsford, Essex.

HEWITT, Harold; a Recorder of the Crown Court, since 1974; *b* 14 March 1917; *s* of George Truman Hewitt and Bertha Lilian Hewitt; *m* 1946, Doris Mary Smith; two *s*. *Educ:* King James I Grammar Sch., Bishop Auckland. Admitted solicitor (Hons), 1938; HM Coroner, S Durham, 1948. Chm. (part-time), Industrial Tribunal, 1975-. Member Council, Law Society, 1976-. *Recreations:* gardening, French literature, bird-watching. *Address:* Longmeadows, Etherley, Bishop Auckland, Co. Durham. *T:* Bishop Auckland 832386; Saltings Cottage, Bowness-on-Solway, Cumbria. *Club:* English-Speaking Union.

HEWITT, Harold; solicitor, consultant since 1973; *b* 1 Jan. 1908; *m* 1949, Jeannette Myers; one *d*. *Educ:* Bede Collegiate Sch., Sunderland; Armstrong Coll., Univ. of Durham. Solicitor, admitted 1930. Legal Adviser, High Commissioner for Austria, Allied Commission, 1946-49. Member, Law Society; Past Pres., Bexley and Dartford Law Soc. *Recreation:* social welfare work. *Address:* 121 Dorset House, Gloucester Place, NW1 5AQ. *Club:* Royal Automobile.

HEWITT, Sir John (Francis), KCVO 1971; CBE 1964; Trustee: Chevening Estate (Deputy Chairman); Dorneywood Trust; Attlee Memorial Foundation; Member, London Advisory Board, Norwich Union Insurance Group; Chairman, Michael Hooker & Associates Ltd; *b* 12 Nov. 1910; *o s* of late Rev. John Francis Hewitt, MA and of late Frances Hilda Hewitt, BLitt; *m* 1938, Betty Mida Pantin Dale-Glossop, *o d* of late Lieut-Col H. Dale-Glossop, MBE, and of Mrs T. E. Carew-Hunt; one *s* one *d*. *Educ:* St Lawrence Coll., Ramsgate and privately. London Stock Exchange, 1928; joined Board of Trade, 1941; Imperial Defence Coll., 1947; Board of Trade, 1948-57; HM Customs and Excise (International Div.), 1957-61; Secretary for Appointments to the Prime Minister, 1961-73, and Ecclesiastical Secretary to the Lord Chancellor, 1965-73. Chm., Ellison House (Probation Hostel) Camberwell, 1961-73. Vice-Pres., Age Action Year, 1976; Governor, St Michael's Sch., Limpsfield. *Address:* Little Heath, Limpsfield, Surrey. *T:* Limpsfield Chart 2205. *Club:* Travellers'.

HEWITT, Capt. John Graham, DSO, 1940; RN (retired); *b* 15 Oct. 1902; *s* of J. G. L. Hewitt, SM, Marton, NZ; two *s*; *m* 1947, Mrs Rooney, *widow* of Col J. J. Rooney, IMS. *Educ:* RN Colls, Osborne and Dartmouth. Midshipman, 1919; Comdr, 1936; commanded HMS Winchelsea, 1937, HMS Auckland, 1940-41; HMS Dauntless, 1941-42; Capt. 1942; HMS Royalist, 1944; HMS Frobisher, 1945-46; Second Naval Member of NZ Navy Board, 1947; Director Tactical Sch., Woolwich, 1949-52; retired list, 1952. Norwegian War Cross, 1942. *Recreation:* fishing. *Address:* 16 Royston Court, Kew Gardens, Richmond, Surrey.

HEWITT, Air Vice-Marshal Joseph Eric, CBE 1951 (OBE 1940); psa 1934; Royal Australian Air Force (retired); Member Panel of Military Experts, United Nations, since 1952; *b* 13 April 1901; *s* of late Rev. J. H. Hewitt, MA, BD and late Rose Alice Hewitt (*née* Harkness), Melbourne, Vic; *m* 1925, Lorna Pretoria (*d* 1976), *d* of late Alfred Eugene Bishop and late Joanne Bishop (*née* Prismall), Melbourne, Vic; three *d*. *Educ:* Scotch Coll., Melbourne; Royal Australian Naval Coll., Jervis Bay, NSW. Served in RAN, RN, RAAF and RAF, 1915-28; Cadet Midshipman, 1915; Midshipman, 1918; Sub-Lieut 1921; Lieut, 1922. Transferred to RAAF, 1928; Comdg Officer RAAF, HMAS Albatross, 1929-32; RAF Staff Coll., Andover, 1934; Asst Liaison Officer, Australia House, London, 1935; Comdg Officer, No 104 Sqdn, RAF, 1936-38; SASO, RAAF, Richmond, NSW, 1938-39; Sen. Admin. Staff Officer, Southern Area, HQ, 1939-40; DPS, HQ, RAAF, 1940-41; DCAS, RAAF, 1941; Director of Air Operations, Staff of C-in-C. Allied Command, NEI, Java, 1942; ACAS, 1942; Director of Allied Air Intelligence, SW Pacific Area, 1942 and 1944; AOC No 9 Op. Group, 1943 (Battle of Bismarck Sea, 1943); Air member for Personnel, RAAF, HQrs, 1945-48; Australian Defence Representative, London, 1949-51; Air Member for Supply and Equipment, Dept of Air, Melbourne, 1951-56, retired April 1956. Member, Council for Adult Education of Victoria, 1956-66. Manager, Education and Training, Internat. Harvester Co. (Aust.) Pty Ltd, 1956-66; Trustee, Services Canteens Trust

Fund, 1957-77. FAIM 1956. *Recreations:* swimming, gardening, reading. *Address:* Langate, 27 Canadian Bay Road, Mount Eliza, Vic 3930, Australia. *T:* 787 4944. *Club:* Naval and Military (Melbourne).

HEWITT, Sir Lenox; *see* Hewitt, Sir C. L. S.

HEWITT, Margaret, PhD; Reader in Social Institutions, University of Exeter, since 1970; *b* 25 Oct. 1928; *d* of Robert Henry Hewitt and Jessie Hewitt. *Educ:* Bedford Coll., London; London Sch. of Economics. BA Hons Sociology (1st Cl.) 1950, PhD Sociology 1953. Univ. of London Postgrad. Studentship in Sociology, 1950-52; Asst Lectr in Sociology, University Coll. of the South West, 1952-54; Lectr in Sociology, Univ. of Exeter, 1954-65, Sen. Lectr, 1965-70. Mem. Council, Univ. of Exeter, 1964-70; Governor: Bedford Coll., 1968-; St Luke's Coll., Exeter, 1969-. Member: Church Assembly, 1961-70; Gen. Synod of Church of England, 1970-; Standing Cttee of Gen. Synod, 1976-; Church Commn on Crown Appts, 1977-. Rep. of Univ. of London on Council of Roedean Sch., 1974-. *Publications:* Wives and Mothers in Victorian Industry, 1958; (with Ivy Pinchbeck) Children in English Society, Vol. I 1969, Vol. II 1973. *Recreation:* doing nothing. *Address:* 14 Velwell Road, Exeter, Devon EX4 4LE. *T:* Exeter 54150. *Club:* University Women's.

HEWITT, Sir Nicholas Charles Joseph, 3rd Bt *cr* 1921; *b* 12 Nov. 1947; *s* of Sir Joseph Hewitt, 2nd Bt and of Marguerite, *yr d* of Charles Burgess; *S* father, 1973; *m* 1969, Pamela Margaret, *o d* of Geoffrey J. M. Hunt, TD; two *s*. *Heir:* *s* Charles Edward James Hewitt, *b* 15 Nov. 1970. *Address:* The Forge, Hutton Buscel, Scarborough, North Yorks. *T:* West Ayton 2307.

HEWITT, Patricia Hope; General Secretary, National Council for Civil Liberties, since 1974; *b* 2 Dec. 1948; *d* of Sir (Cyrus) Lenox (Simson) Hewitt, *qv*, and Alison Hope Hewitt; *m* 1970, Julian Gibson-Watt (marr. diss. 1977). *Educ:* C of E Girls' Grammar Sch., Canberra; Australian Nat. Univ.; Newnham Coll., Cambridge. BA, AMusA (piano). Public Relations Officer, Age Concern (Nat. Old People's Welfare Council), 1971-73; Women's Rights Officer, Nat. Council for Civil Liberties, 1973-74; Trustee, Cobden Trust, 1974-; Mem., Sec. of State's Adv. Cttee on Employment of Women, 1977-. *Publications:* Your Rights (Age Concern), 1973, 4th edn 1976; Rights for Women (NCCL), 1975; Civil Liberties, the NCCL Guide (Pelican) (co-ed 3rd edn), 1977; The Privacy Report (NCCL), 1977. *Recreations:* reading, theatre, music, politics. *Address:* 2 Eton Hall, Eton College Road, NW3 2DW. *T:* 01-586 2936.

HEWITT, Richard Thornton, OBE 1945; Executive Director, the Royal Society of Medicine since 1952; Vice-President, The Royal Society of Medicine Foundation, Inc., New York, since 1969; *b* 1917; *yr s* of late Harold and Elsie Muriel Hewitt, Bramhall, Cheshire. *Educ:* King's Sch., Macclesfield; Magdalen Coll., Oxford (Exhibitioner). Served War, Lt-Col, infantry and special forces, 1939-46. Asst Registrary, Cambridge Univ., 1946. Incorporated MA, Magdalene Coll., Cambridge, 1946. Sec., Oxford Univ. Medical Sch., 1947-52. Hon. Fellow, Swedish Med. Soc., 1968. Liveryman, Worshipful Society of Apothecaries of London, 1954. Freeman of the City of London, 1954. *Recreations:* gentle golf and gardening, music. *Address:* 84 Dorset House, NW1. *T:* 01-935 4014; The White House, Iffley, Oxford. *T:* Oxford 779263. *Clubs:* Athenæum, MCC, Royal Automobile; Frewen (Oxford); Royal and Ancient (St Andrews).

HEWLETT, family name of Baron Hewlett.

HEWLETT, Baron *cr* 1972 (Life Peer), of Swettenham; **Thomas Clyde Hewlett,** Kt 1964; CBE 1959; MA; MIEx; Chairman since 1971, Managing Director since 1965, Anchor Chemical Co. Ltd (Export Director, 1950-61; Joint Managing Director, 1961-65; Deputy Chairman, 1968-71), and Chairman of subsidiary Cos; Chairman: Borg Warner Chemicals UK Ltd, since 1970; Burco Dean Ltd, since 1975; Chairman, North West Industrialists' Council, since 1971; *b* 4 Aug. 1923; *s* of late Thomas Henry Hewlett, JP (MP, Manchester Exchange, 1940-45); *m* 1949, Millicent, *d* of Sir John (William) Taylor, KBE, CMG; two *s*. *Educ:* Clifton; Magdalene Coll., Cambridge. Served War of 1939-45, Royal Marines (Lieut). BA 1948 (2nd Cl. Hons, Econs and Polit. Tripos); MA 1952. Pres., Cambridge Union, 1948; Chm., Cambridge Univ. Conservatives, 1948. Chm., NW Br. of Inst. of Export, 1961-66. Mem. Manchester City Council, 1949-56; President: Manchester and Salford Street Children's (Wood Street) Mission Management Cttee, 1972- (Chm. 1968-72); 2/230th Boy Scouts, 1957-70, Life Hon. Mem., 1970; 1st Wythenshawe Boy Scouts, 1958-67; Vice-Pres., City of Manchester County Scout Council, 1972; Mem. Youth Cttee,

Manchester City Council, 1959-65; Vice-Pres. Manchester Br. Cripples Aid Soc., 1963-; Mem. Manchester Cttee RNLI, 1964-; Vice-Chm., Manchester Naval Officers, 1974-; Pres., NW Br. Economic League, 1976-. President: Manchester Br. BIM, 1972-; PRI, 1975- (Pres. IRI, 1972-74). Pres., Altrincham and Sale Div. Young Conservs Assoc., 1961-69; Chairman: Altrincham and Sale Div. Cons. Assoc., 1954-61 (Vice-Pres. 1961); NW Area Young Conservs, 1951-53; Dep. Chm., Wythenshawe Div. Cons. Assoc., 1953-54; Vice-Chm. Nat. Young Conservs, 1953; Chm. Exec. Cttee, Nat. Union Cons. and Unionist Assocs, 1965-71 (Pres. NW Area, 1966-69, Chm. 1961-66); President: Cons. Political Centre, 1974-; Nat. Union of Cons. Party, 1976-. Pres., Northern Lawn Tennis Club, 1973; Mem. Council, Nat. Rifle Assoc., 1973. Trustee, Royal Exchange Theatre, 1974- (Jt Chm. Trust Appeal Cttee, 1974-). Manchester University: Mem. Cttee of Governors, 1966-; Mem. Court, 1976-; Governor, Clifton Coll., 1972- (Mem. Council, 1973-). JP Manchester, 1965-72. FPRI 1966; FBIM 1969. *Recreations:* gardening, photography. *Address:* Dane Edge, Swettenham, Congleton, Cheshire CW12 2LQ. *T:* Lower Withington 363; Anchor Chemical Co. Ltd, Clayton, Manchester M11 4SR. *T:* 061-223 2461-6. *Clubs:* Carlton, Cambridge Union.

HEXHAM AND NEWCASTLE, Bishop of, (RC), since 1975; **Rt. Rev. Hugh Lindsay;** *b* 20 June 1927; *s* of William Stanley Lindsay and Mary Ann Lindsay (*née* Warren). *Educ:* St Cuthbert's Grammar Sch., Newcastle upon Tyne; Ushaw Coll., Durham. Priest 1953. Asst Priest; St Lawrence's, Newcastle upon Tyne, 1953; St Matthew's, Ponteland, 1954; Asst Diocesan Sec., 1953-59; Diocesan Sec., 1959-69; Chaplain, St Vincent's Home, West Denton, 1959-69; Auxiliary Bishop of Hexham and Newcastle and Titular Bishop of Chester-le-Street, 1969-74. *Recreation:* walking. *Address:* Bishop's House, East Denton Hall, 800 West Road, Newcastle upon Tyne NE5 2BJ.

HEXHAM AND NEWCASTLE, Auxiliary Bishop of, (RC); *see* Swindlehurst, Rt Rev. O. F.

HEXT, Maj.-Gen. Frederick Maurice, CB 1954; OBE 1945; CEng; FIMechE; FIEE; *b* 5 May 1901; *s* of Frederick Robert Hext; *m* 1924, Kathleen Goulden; one *s. Educ:* Portsmouth Gram. Sch.; RMA, Woolwich. Commissioned RE 1921; served in India, 1925-28, and 1931-34; Instructor, Sch. of Military Engineering, 1939-42; served NW Europe Campaign (despatches) Comdr, REME, 53rd (Welsh) Div., and Dep. Dir of Mechanical Engineering, 12 Corps; DDME, 1 Corps, 1945-46; DDME, Burma Command, 1946-48; AAG, AG 21, War Office, 1949-51; DME, BAOR, 1951-53; Inspector of REME, 1953-56, retired 1956. Hon. Col 53 (Welsh) Inf. Div. REME, 1956-61. Maj.-Gen., 1953. Formerly Member Wessex RHB; Chm. Isle of Wight Group Hospital Management Cttee, 1961-72. FRSA. *Address:* Orchard Dene, Undercliff, St Lawrence, Isle of Wight. *T:* Niton 730387.

HEY, Donald Holroyde, DSc, PhD; FRS 1955; FRIC; Daniell Professor of Chemistry, University of London, 1950-71, now Emeritus Professor; President, Section B, British Association for the Advancement of Science, 1965; *b* Swansea, 1904; 2nd *s* of Arthur Hey, MusB, FRCO, LRAM, and Frances Jane Hey; *m* 1931, Jessie, MSc (Wales), *d* of Thomas and Katharine Jones; one *s* one *d. Educ:* Magdalen Coll. Sch., Oxford; University Coll., Swansea, BSc, MSc Wales; PhD London; DSc Manchester. Asst Lecturer in Chemistry, University of Manchester, 1928-30; Lecturer in Chemistry, University of Manchester, 1930-38; Lecturer in Chemistry, Imperial Coll. of Science and Technology, London, 1939-41; Dir of British Schering Research Institute, 1941-45; University Prof. of Chemistry at King's Coll., London, 1945-50; Asst Principal, King's Coll., 1962-68. Scientific Advr for Civil Defence, SE Region, 1952-58. Vice-Pres. of Chemical Soc. 1951-54 (Tilden Lectr, 1951, Pedler Lectr, 1970, Hon. Secretary, 1946-51, Vice-Pres., Perkin Div., 1971). Reilly Lectr, University of Notre Dame, Indiana, 1952; Visiting Prof. University of Florida, 1967. FKC; Fellow Imp. Coll. of Science and Technology, 1968; Hon. Fellow, Chelsea Coll., 1973. Member: Council, KCL; Adv. Council RMCS, 1961-73. Hon. DSc Wales, 1970. Defence Medal 1945. Intra-Science Res. Conf. Award and Medal, Santa Monica, Calif., 1968; Hon. Fellow, Intra-Science Res. Foundn, 1971. *Publications:* articles in scientific journals, mainly in Jl of Chem. Soc. *Recreations:* music, gardening. *Address:* 5 Wrayfield Avenue, Reigate, Surrey RH2 0NF. *T:* Reigate 47053.

HEY, Air Vice-Marshal Ernest, CB 1967; CBE 1963 (OBE 1954); CEng; Air Member for Technical Services, Department of Air, Canberra, 1960-72, retired; *b* Plymouth, Devon, 29 Nov. 1912; *s* of Ernest Hey, Terrigal, NSW; *m* 1936, Lorna, *d* of Sqdn Ldr A. Bennett, Melbourne; one *s* one *d. Educ:* Sydney Technical High

Sch.; Sydney University. RAAF cadet, 1934; served War of 1939-45; Dir Technical Services, 1947-54; AOC Maintenance Comd, 1956-57; Imp. Defence Coll., 1957; Liaison Air Material Comd, USAF, 1958-59. *Recreations:* painting, lawn bowls. *Address:* 36 Holmes Crescent, Campbell, Canberra, ACT 2601, Australia.

HEY, James Stanley, MBE 1945; DSc; retired; Research Scientist at Royal Radar Establishment, 1952-69; Chief Scientific Officer, 1966-69; *b* 3 May 1909; *s* of William Rennie Hey and Barbara Elizabeth Hey (*née* Matthews); *m* 1934, Edna Heywood. *Educ:* Rydal Sch.; Manchester Univ. BSc (Physics), 1930; MSc (X-ray Crystallography), 1931; DSc (Radio Astronomy and Radar Research), 1950. Army Operational Research Group, 1940-52 (Head of Estab., 1949-52). Hon. DSc: Birmingham, 1975; Kent, 1977. Eddington Medal, RAS, 1959. *Publications:* The Radio Universe, 1971; The Evolution of Radio Astronomy, 1973; research papers in scientific jls (RAS, Royal Society, Phys Soc., Philosophical Magazine, Nature, etc) including pioneering papers in radio astronomy. *Address:* 4 Shortlands Close, Willingdon, Eastbourne, Sussex BN22 0JE.

HEYCOCK, Baron *cr* 1967 (Life Peer), of Taibach; **Llewellyn Heycock,** CBE 1959; DL, JP; *b* 12 Aug. 1905; *s* of William Heycock and late Mary Heycock; *m* 1930, Olive Elizabeth (*née* Rees); one *s* (and one *s* decd). *Educ:* Eastern Sch., Port Talbot. Engine Driver, Dyffryn Yard Loco Sheds, Port Talbot. Glam CC, 1937-74 (Chm. 1962-63); Chm., West Glamorgan CC, 1973-75. Member: Council and Court, University of Wales; Council and Court, University Coll. of S Wales and Mon.; Chairman: Schools Museum Service for Wales; Celtic Sea Adv. Cttee; Exec. Cttee, Royal National Eisteddfod of Wales, Port Talbot, 1966; Chm., Welsh Jt Educn Cttee; President: Coleg Harlech; Assoc. of Educn Cttees, 1964-65; Nat. Assoc. of Div. Execs for England and Wales, 1954-55, 1965-66; Exec. Mem., County Councils Assoc.; Hon. Druid, Nat. Eisteddfod of Wales, 1963; Vice-Pres., Nat. Theatre Co. for Wales. Hon. LLD, University of Wales, 1963. Hon. Freedom of Port Talbot, 1961. CStJ. JP Glam; JP Port Talbot; DL Glam 1963. *Recreation:* Rugby football. *Address:* 1 Llewellyn Close, Taibach, Port Talbot, West Glam. *T:* Port Talbot 2565.

HEYCOCK, Air Cdre George Francis Wheaton, CB 1963; DFC 1941; JP; *b* 17 Sept. 1909; *s* of Rev. F. W. Heycock, MA, and Edith Rowlandson; *m* 1938, Betty Boyd; one *s. Educ:* Haileybury and Imperial Service Coll.; Cranwell Cadet Coll. Commnd in RAF, 1929; Flying Instructor at RAF Coll., Cranwell and Central Flying Sch., 111 Sqdn, Fleet Air Arm, 1935-37. Test Pilot, Farnborough, 1937-39. Command of 23 and 141 Sqdns, 1940-42. Dir of Ops, Indian Air Force, 1949; Command of RAF Syerston, 1950-52; Air Ministry, 1952-55; Chief of Staff, British Joint Services Mission (RAF Staff), Washington, and Air Attaché, Washington, 1955; Air Attaché, Paris, 1959-64. JP Northants, 1965. Comdr Légion d'Honneur. *Recreation:* golf. *Address:* The Manor House, Pytchley, Northants. *T:* Broughton 790269. *Clubs:* Buck's, Royal Air Force.

HEYERDAHL, Thor; author and anthropologist, since 1938; *b* 6 Oct. 1914; *s* of Thor Heyerdahl and Alison Heyerdahl (*née* Lyng); *m* 1st, 1936, Liv Coucheron Torp (*d* 1969); two *s*; 2nd, 1949, Yvonne Dedekam-Simonsen; three *d. Educ:* University of Oslo, 1933-36. Researches in the Marquesas Islands (Pacific), 1937-38; Researches among Coast Indians of Brit. Columbia, 1939-40. Active service Free Norwegian Army-Air Force parachute unit, 1942-45. Organised and led Kon-Tiki expedition, 1947. Continued research in USA and Europe, with authorship, 1948-. Chm. Bd, Kon-Tiki Museum, Oslo; organised and led Norwegian Archæological Expedition to the Galapagos Islands, 1953; experiments revealing tacking principles of balsa raft in Ecuador, 1953; field research, Bolivia, Peru, Colombia, 1954. Produced Galapagos film, 1955. Organised and led Norwegian Archæological Expedition to Easter Island and the East Pacific, 1955-56. Continued research, 1957-59. Made crossing from Safi, Morocco, to W Indies in papyrus boat, Ra II, 1970. Participation in: Internat. Congress of Americanists, 1952-; Pacific Science Congresses, 1961-, all with lectures subseq. publ. in Proc. Congress. Vice-President: World Assoc. of World Federalists, 1966-. Internat. Council, United World Colls, 1973. Mem., Royal Norwegian Acad. of Science, 1958; Fellow: New York Acad. of Sciences, 1960; Amer. Anthropological Assoc., 1966. Hon. Prof., Inst. Politecnico Nacional, Mexico, 1972; Hon. Dr Oslo Univ., 1961. Hon. Mem. Geog. Soc.: Peru, 1953; Norway, 1953; Brazil, 1954; USSR, 1964. Retzius Medal, Swedish Soc. for Anthropology and Geography, 1950; Mungo Park Medal, Royal Scottish Geographical Society, 1951; Prix Bonaparte-Wyse from Société de Géographie, Paris, 1951; Elish Kent Kane Gold Medal,

Geog. Soc. of Philadelphia, 1952; Vega Medal, Swedish Soc. of Anthropology and Geography, 1962; Lomonosov Medal, Moscow Univ., 1962; Royal Gold Medal, Royal Geog. Society, London, 1964; Oscar Prize for best documentary feature of 1951, Acad. of Motion Picture Arts and Sciences, 1952; Officer of El Order por Meritos Distinguidos, Peru, 1953; Gold Medal City of Lima; Gr.-Officer, Order Al Merito della Repubblica Italiana, Italy, 1965; Chevalier, Grand Cross, Knights of Malta, 1970; Comdr with Star, Order of St Olav, Norway, 1970; Order of Merit, Egypt, 1971; Royal Alaouites Order, Morocco, 1971; Hon. Citizen, Larvik, Norway, 1971; Kiril i Metodi Order, Bulgaria, 1972. Works trans. into numerous languages. *Publications:* Paa Jakt efter Paradiset, 1938; The Kon-Tiki Expedition, 1948; American Indians in the Pacific: the theory behind the Kon-Tiki expedition, 1952; (with A. Skjolsvold) Archæological Evidence of Pre-Spanish Visits to the Galapagos Islands, 1956; Aku-Aku: The Secrets of Easter Island, 1957; Co-editor (with E. N. Ferdon, Jr) Reports of the Norwegian Achæological Expedition to Easter Island and the East Pacific, Vol. I: The Archæology of Easter Island, 1961, vol. II: Miscellaneous Papers, 1965; Navel of the World (Chapter XIV) in Vanished Civilizations, 1963; Indianer und Alt-Asiaten im Pazifik: Das Abenteuer einer Theorie, 1966 (Vienna); Sea Routes to Polynesia, 1968; The Ra Expeditions, 1970; Chapters in Quest for America, 1971; Fatu-Hiva Back to Nature, 1974; Art of Easter Island, 1974; Zwischen den Kontinenten, 1975; Early Man and the Ocean, 1977; contrib. National Geographical Magazine, Royal Geographical Journal, The Geographical Magazine, Archiv für Völkerkunde, Ymer, Swedish Geogr. Year-book, South-western Journal of Anthropology, Russian Academy of Sciences Yearbook, American Antiquity, Antiquity (Cambridge); *relevant publication:* Senor Kon-Tiki, by Arnold Jacoby, 1965. *Recreations:* outdoor life, travelling. *Address:* Colla Micheri, Laigueglia, Italy.

HEYES, Sir Tasman (Hudson Eastwood), Kt 1960; CBE 1953; *b* 6 Nov. 1896; *s* of late Hudson Heyes and of Mary Heyes, Melbourne; *m* 1921, Ethel Brettell, *d* of late Archibald and Phoebe Causer, Melbourne; one *s* one *d*. *Educ:* Melbourne. Served European War, 1914-18, with 3rd Divisional Signal Co., AIF, France and Flanders, 1916-19. Attached to Historical Section, Cttee of Imperial Defence, London, and War Depts, Ottawa, Washington, and Wellington, 1924-28. Dir, Australian War Memorial, Canberra, 1939-42; Dept of Defence, Melbourne, 1942-46; Sec., Dept of Immigration, Australia, 1946-61. Mem., Australian Broadcasting Control Bd, 1963-68, retd. Former Mem., Immigration Planning Council. Nansen Medal, 1962. *Recreations:* gardening, golf, bowls. *Address:* Creswick, 536 Toorak Road, Toorak, Victoria 3142, Australia. *Club:* Melbourne.

HEYGATE, Sir George Lloyd, 5th Bt *cr* 1831; *S* father, 1976. *Heir: b* Richard John Gage Heygate.

HEYMAN, Allan, QC 1969; *b* 27 Feb. 1921; *e s* of late Erik Heyman and of Rita Heyman (*née* Meyer); *m* 1958, Anne Marie (*née* Castenschiold); one *d*. *Educ:* Stenhus Kostskole, Denmark; Univ. of Copenhagen. Master of Law (Univ. of Copenhagen), 1947. Called to Bar, Middle Temple, 1951, Bencher 1975. Pres., Internat. Lawn Tennis Fedn, 1971-74. Kt of Dannebrog (Denmark). *Recreations:* shooting, stalking, reading, music. *Address:* 1 New Square, Lincoln's Inn, WC2; Marshland House, Iken, Woodbridge, Suffolk. *Clubs:* Bath, Shikar; All England Lawn Tennis and Croquet.

HEYMAN, Sir Horace (William), Kt 1976; BSc; CEng, FIEE; Chairman, English Industrial Estates Corporation, 1970-77; Member, Supervisory Board, Hotelplan Genossenschaft, Zürich, since 1955; *b* 13 March 1912; *m* 1st, 1939; one *s* one *d*; 2nd, 1966, Dorothy Forster Atkinson. *Educ:* Ackworth Sch.; Darmstadt and Birmingham Univs. BSc hons, electrical engrg, 1936. Electricars Ltd, 1936-40; Metropolitan Vickers Ltd, Sheffield, 1940-45; Smith's Electric Vehicles Ltd and Subsids, 1945-64 (Man. Dir, 1949-64); Co-Founder, Sevcon Engineering Ltd, 1960; Vice-Pres., Battronic Corp., Philadelphia, 1960-64; Dir, Inghams Travel Gp, 1965-77; Export Marketing Adviser for Northern Region, BoT, 1969-70. Mem. Council, Soc. of Motor Manufrs and Traders, 1949-64 (Man. Cttee, 1952-64); Chm., Electric Vehicle Assoc. of Gt Britain, 1953-55. Witness at US Senate hearings on air and water pollution, 1967. Chairman: N Region Energy Conservation Group, 1973-77; NEDO Working Party on House Bldg Performance, 1976-; Mem. Council, Newcastle upon Tyne Polytechnic, 1974-. FIEE 1952; FRSA 1969. *Publications:* numerous in professional jls, on urban transport and food distribution. *Address:* Appletree House, Fellside, Whickham, Newcastle upon Tyne. *T:* Newcastle upon Tyne 885757. *Club:* National Liberal.

HEYMAN, Prof. Jacques, MA, PhD; FICE; FSA; Professor of Engineering, University of Cambridge, since 1971; Fellow of Peterhouse, 1949-51, and since 1955; Consultant Engineer, Ely Cathedral, since 1972; *b* 8 March 1925; *m* 1958, Eva Orlans; three *d*. *Educ:* Whitgift Sch.; Peterhouse, Cambridge. Senior Bursar, Peterhouse, 1962-64; University Demonstrator, Engineering Dept, Cambridge Univ., 1951, University Lectr, 1954, Reader, 1968. Vis. Professor: Brown Univ., USA, 1957-58; Harvard Univ., 1966. Mem., Council, ICE, 1960-63 and 1975-. Hon. DSc Sussex, 1975. James Watt Medal, 1973. *Publications:* The Steel Skeleton, vol. 2 (with Sir John Baker, M. R. Horne), 1956; Plastic Design of Portal Frames, 1957; Beams and Framed Structures, 1964, 2nd edn 1974; Plastic Design of Frames, vol. 1, 1969, vol. 2, 1971; Coulomb's Memoir on Statics, 1972; Equilibrium of Shell Structures, 1977; articles on plastic design and general structural theory. *Address:* Engineering Laboratory, Trumpington Street, Cambridge. *T:* Cambridge 66466.

HEYMANN, Prof. Franz Ferdinand, PhD; FInstP; Quain Professor of Physics, and Head of Department of Physics and Astronomy, University College, University of London, since 1975; *b* 17 Aug. 1924; *s* of Paul Gerhard Heymann and Magdalena Petronella Heymann; *m* 1950, Marie Powell. *Educ:* Univ. of Cape Town (BScEng with Distinction, 1944); Univ. of London (PhD 1953). FInstP 1966. Engr, Cape Town, 1944-45; Jun. Lectr in Engrg, Univ. of Cape Town, 1945-47; Special Trainee, Metropolitan Vickers, Manchester, 1947-50; University Coll. London: Asst Lectr in Physics, 1950-52; Lectr, 1952-60; Reader, 1960-66; Prof. of Physics, 1966-75. *Publications:* scientific papers on res. done mainly in fields of particle accelerators and elementary particle physics. *Recreations:* music, lapidary crafts, gardening. *Address:* Department of Physics and Astronomy, University College, Gower Street, WC1E 6BT; 59 The Gateway, Woking, Surrey. *T:* Woking 72304.

HEYMANSON, Sir (Sydney Henry) Randal, Kt 1972; CBE 1965 (OBE 1955); Chairman of the Board, American Australian Association, since 1966; *b* 18 April 1903; *s* of Frederick Heymanson and Elizabeth (*née* McDonnell). *Educ:* Melbourne C of E Grammar Sch.; Melbourne Univ. (MA Hons); London Univ. Australian Newspapers Service: European Corresp., 1928-40; Editor, NY, 1940-69; War Corresp., ETO; Editor and Publisher, Vital News, 1939-42; N American Rep., West Australian Newspapers, 1969-. Pres., Foreign Press Assoc., NY, 1942-43; Pres., Australian Soc. of NY, 1945-46. Exec. Vice-Pres. 1950-65, Pres. 1965-66, American Australian Assoc. *Recreations:* bibliomania, art collecting, travel. *Address:* 7 Mitchell Place, New York, NY 10017, USA. *Clubs:* Overseas Press, Dutch Treat (New York); National Press (Washington).

HEYS, Derek Isaac, CBE 1971; TD 1945; Senior Partner in Heys, Wall & Co, Freight Forwarders, 1949-73; Executive with Wingate & Johnston Ltd, Liverpool, since Jan. 1973; *b* 6 Aug. 1911; twin *s* of Isaac and Laura Heys; *m* 1936, Margaret Helena Ashcroft; one *s* one *d* (and one *s* decd). *Educ:* Birkenhead Sch. Late Lt-Col RA (TA). Pres., Internat. Fedn of Forwarding Agents' Assocs (FIATA), 1967-71; Nat. Chm., Inst. of Shipping and Forwarding Agents, 1962-63; Chm., Merseyside Chamber of Commerce and Industry, 1970-71; Chm., first Adv. Cttee of three, apptd by Dirs of Mersey Docks & Harbour Co. to represent interest of holders of Co.'s redeemable subordinated unsecured Loan Stock, 1974; Vice-President: Inst. of Freight Forwarders, 1965-; Assoc. of British Chambers of Commerce, 1975. Consul for Belgium in Liverpool, 1966-. *Recreation:* golf. *Address:* Greenfields, Telegraph Road, Caldy, Wirral, Merseyside. *T:* 051-625 8383. *Clubs:* Exchange (Liverpool); Royal Liverpool Golf (Hoylake).

HEYTESBURY, 6th Baron *cr* 1828; **Francis William Holmes à Court**; Bt 1795; *b* 8 Nov. 1931; *s* of 5th Baron Heytesbury and Beryl (*d* 1968), *y d* of late A. E. B. Crawford, LLD, DCL, Aston Clinton House, Bucks; *S* father, 1971; *m* 1962, Alison, *e d* of Michael Graham Balfour, CBE; one *s* one *d*. *Educ:* Bryanston; Pembroke College, Cambridge (BA 1954). *Heir: s* Hon. James William Holmes à Court, *b* 30 July 1967.

HEYWARD, Rt. Rev. Oliver Spencer; *see* Bendigo, Bishop of.

HEYWOOD, Francis Melville, MA; Warden of Lord Mayor Treloar College, 1952-69, retired 1969; *b* 1 Oct. 1908; 4th *s* of late Rt Rev. B. O. F. Heywood, DD; *m* 1937, Dorothea Kathleen, *e d* of late Sir Basil Mayhew, KBE; two *s* two *d*. *Educ:* Haileybury Coll. (Scholar); Gonville and Caius Coll. Cambridge (Scholar), 1st Class Hons, Classical Tripos, Part I, 1929; Part II, 1931; Rugby Football blue, 1928. Asst Master, Haileybury Coll., 1931-35; Fellow, Asst Tutor and Praelector, Trinity Hall, Cambridge, 1935-39; Master of Marlborough Coll., 1939-52.

Recreations: gardening, walking. *Address:* The Old Bakery, Catcott, near Bridgwater, Somerset. *T:* Chilton Polden 722627.

HEYWOOD, Geoffrey, MBE (mil.) 1945; JP; Consulting Actuary; Senior Partner, Duncan C. Fraser & Co., since 1952; *b* 7 April 1916; *s* of Edgar Heywood and Annie (*née* Dawson), Blackpool; *m* 1941, Joan Corinna Lumley; one *s* one *d. Educ:* Arnold Sch., Blackpool. Served War, 1940-46: Royal Artillery, N Africa, Italy, Greece; commissioned, 1941, Major, 1944; despatches, 1945. Refuge Assce Co Ltd, 1933-40; Duncan C. Fraser & Co. (Consulting Actuaries), 1946-. Pres., Manchester Actuarial Soc., 1951-53; Chm., Assoc. of Consulting Actuaries, 1959-62; Chm., Internat. Assoc. of Consulting Actuaries, 1968-72; Pres., Inst. of Actuaries, 1972-74 (Vice-Pres., 1964-67). Mem. Page Cttee to Review National Savings. Dep. Chm., Mersey Docks & Harbour Co.; Director: Liverpool Bd Barclays Bank; Barclays Bank Trust Co. Treas., Merseyside Youth Assoc. FFA 1939; FIA 1946. JP Liverpool 1962. *Publications:* contribs to Jl Inst. Actuaries. *Recreations:* golf, tennis, antiquarian horology. *Address:* Drayton, Croft Drive East, Caldy, Wirral, Merseyside. *T:* 051-625 6707. *Clubs:* Army and Navy, Royal Automobile.

HEYWOOD, Geoffrey Henry, CBE 1972; Consultant, Dunlop Heywood & Co., Chartered Surveyors, Manchester, since 1969 (Partner, 1930-69); Chairman, Skelmersdale Development Corporation, 1969-75; President, Manchester Rent Assessment Panel, 1965-74; *b* 22 Aug. 1903; *s* of late Henry Arthur Heywood, Christleton Lodge, Chester; *m* 1931, Magdeleine Jeanne Georgette Marie, *d* of late J. H. Herpin, Paris; one *s* one *d. Educ:* Repton School. FRICS. Mem. Council, RICS, 1950-70 (Pres. 1962-63). Mem., Skelmersdale Develt Corp., 1962-75 (Dep. Chm. 1962-69). *Recreation:* travelling. *Address:* 14 Alexandra Court, 171 Queen's Gate, SW7. *T:* 01-584 2695.

HEYWOOD, Very Rev. Hugh Christopher Lempriere, MA; Provost Emeritus of Southwell; *b* 5 Nov. 1896; *s* of late Charles Christopher Heywood; *m* 1920, Margaret Marion, *d* of Herbert Vizard; one *s* one *d. Educ:* Haileybury; Trinity Coll., Cambridge (Scholar and Stanton Student). Manchester Regt 1914-17 (wounded, despatches); 74th Punjabis IA 1917-23 (Staff Capt., 1919-22); Ordained, 1926; Curate of St Andrew's the Great, Cambridge, 1926-27; of Holy Cross, Greenford, 1927-28; Fellow and Dean, Gonville and Caius Coll., Cambridge, 1928-45; University Lecturer in Divinity, Cambridge, 1937-45; Provost of Southwell and Rector of S Mary, Southwell, 1945-69; Priest-in-charge of Upton, Diocese of Southwell, 1969-76. Examining Chaplain to Bishop of Southwark, 1932-41, and to Bishop of Southwell, 1941-69. Junior Proctor, Cambridge, 1934-35 and 1942-43. *Publications:* The Worshipping Community, 1938; On a Golden Thread, 1960. *Address:* The College of St Mark, Audley End, Saffron Walden, Essex.

HEYWOOD, Sir Oliver Kerr, 5th Bt, *cr* 1838; *b* 30 June 1920; *s* of late Maj.-Gen. C. P. Heywood, CB, CMG, DSO (2nd *s* of 3rd Bt) and late Margaret Vere, *d* of late Arthur Herbert Kerr; *S* uncle 1946; *m* 1947, Denise Wymondham, 2nd *d* of late Jocelyn William Godefroi, MVO; three *s. Educ:* Eton; Trinity Coll. Cambridge (BA). Served in Coldstream Guards, 1940-46 (despatches). Profession: artist. *Heir: s* Peter Heywood [*b* 10 Dec. 1947; *m* 1970, Jacqueline Anne, *d* of R. F. Hunt, Greenacre, Charlton Park Gate, Cheltenham; one *d*]. *Address:* Viner's Wood, Wickstreet, Stroud, Glos.

HEYWORTH, Peter Lawrence Frederick; Music Critic of The Observer since 1955; *b* 3 June 1921; *er s* of Lawrence Ormerod Heyworth and Ellie Stern. *Educ:* Charterhouse; Balliol Coll. Oxford. HM Forces, 1940-46; Balliol, 1947-50; University of Göttingen, 1950. Music critic of Times Educational Supplement, 1952-56; Record reviewer for New Statesman, 1956-58; Guest of the Ford Foundation in Berlin, 1964-65. *Publications:* (ed) Berlioz, romantic and classic: selected writings by Ernest Newman, 1972; (ed) Conversations with Klemperer, 1973. *Recreations:* wine and escape. *Address:* 32 Bryanston Square, W1H 7LS. *T:* 01-262 8906.

HEZLET, Vice-Admiral Sir Arthur Richard, KBE 1964; CB 1961; DSO 1944 (Bar 1945); DSC 1941; *b* 7 April 1914; *s* of late Maj.-Gen. R. K. Hezlet, CB, CBE, DSO; *m* 1948, Anne Joan Patricia, *e d* of late G. W. N. Clark, Carnabane, Upperlands, Co. Derry; two adopted *d. Educ:* RN College, Dartmouth. Comd HM Submarines: H44, Ursula, Trident, Thrasher and Trenchant, 1941-45; comd HMS Scorpion, 1949-50; Chief Staff Officer to Flag Officer (Submarines), 1953-54; Capt. (D), 6th Destroyer Squadron 1955-56; Dir, RN Staff Coll., Greenwich, 1956-57; comd HMS Newfoundland, 1958-59; Rear-Adm. 1959; Flag Officer (Submarines), 1959-61; Flag Officer, Scotland, 1961-62; Vice-Adm. 1962; Flag Officer, Scotland and Northern

Ireland, 1963-64; retired 1964. Legion of Merit (Degree of Commander) (US), 1945. *Publications:* The Submarine and Sea Power, 1967; Aircraft and Sea Power, 1970; The 'B' Specials, 1972; Electron and Sea Power, 1975. *Address:* Bovagh House, Aghadowey, Co. Derry, N Ireland. *Clubs:* Army and Navy, Royal Ocean Racing.

HIBBARD, Prof. Bryan Montague, MD, PhD; FRCOG; Professor of Obstetrics and Gynaecology, Welsh National School of Medicine, since 1973; Consultant Obstetrician and Gynaecologist, University Hospital of Wales; *b* 24 April 1926; *s* of Montague Reginald and Muriel Irene Hibbard; *m* 1955, Elizabeth Donald Grassie. *Educ:* Queen Elizabeth's Sch., Barnet; St Bartholomew's Hosp. Med. Coll., London (MD); PhD (Liverpool). MRCS. Formerly: Sen. Lectr, Liverpool Univ.; Consultant Obstetrician and Gynaecologist, Liverpool RHB. *Publications:* numerous contribs to world medical literature. *Recreations:* collecting 18th century drinking glasses, fell walking, coarse gardening. *Address:* The Clock House, Cathedral Close, Llandaff, Cardiff CF5 2ED. *T:* Cardiff 564565.

HIBBARD, Prof. Howard, PhD; Professor of Art History, Columbia University, since 1966; Slade Professor of Fine Art, University of Oxford, 1976-77; *b* 23 May 1928; *s* of Benjamin Horace Hibbard and Margaret Baker Hibbard; *m* 1951, Shirley Irene Griffith; three *d. Educ:* Univ. of Wisconsin (BA 1949, MA 1952); Columbia Univ.; Harvard Univ. (PhD 1958). Fulbright Fellow, Paris, 1949-50; Univ. Fellow, Columbia Univ., 1952-53; Harvard Prize Fellow, 1953-54; Fellow, Amer. Acad. in Rome, 1956-58; Vis. Instr, Univ. of Calif, 1958-59; Asst Prof., 1959-62, Associate Prof., 1962-66, Columbia Univ. Amer. Council of Learned Socs Fellow, Rome, 1962-63; Guggenheim Fellow, Rome, 1965-66 and 1972-73; Sen. Fellow, Nat. Endowment for Humanities, Rome, 1967; Vis. Dist. Scholar, City Coll., City Univ. of NY, 1973-74; Vis. Prof., Yale Univ., 1976. Fellow, Amer. Acad. of Arts and Sciences, 1969. Hon. MA Oxon 1977. Editor-in-Chief, Art Bulletin, 1974-78. *Publications:* The Architecture of the Palazzo Borghese, 1962; Bernini, 1965; Bernini e il barocco, 1968; (with J. Nissman) Florentine Baroque Art from American Collections, 1969; Carlo Maderno and Roman Architecture 1580-1630, 1972; Poussin: The Holy Family on the Steps, 1974; Michelangelo, 1975; Masterpieces of European Sculpture, 1977; contrib. Art Bull., Burlington Mag., Jl Soc. Architect. Historians. *Recreations:* gardening, cooking. *Address:* 176 Brewster Road, Scarsdale, NY 10583, USA. *T:* 914-725-3743; Via Alessandro Poerio 59, Villa dei Gerani, 00152 Rome, Italy. *T:* 5810783.

HIBBERD, (Andrew) Stuart, MBE; *b* 5 Sept. 1893; *y s* of late W. H. Hibberd, Canford Magna, Dorset; *m* 1923, Alice Mary, *e d* of late Lieut-Col Gerard Chichester, North Staffs Regt; no *c. Educ:* Weymouth Coll.; St John's Coll., Cambridge (MA). Served European War in 7th and 5th Batt. Dorset Regt; and 46th Punjabis IA; later 2/25th Punjabis IA; served in Gallipoli, Mesopotamia and Waziristan. Joined BBC, at Savoy Hill, 1924; on Headquarter Staff until retirement, 1951; for some years Chief Announcer. Fellow: Royal Society of Arts; Royal Society of St George. *Publication:* "This-is London", 1951. *Recreations:* gardening, music. *Address:* 2 West Field, Budleigh Salterton, Devon.

HIBBERD, Sir Donald (James), Kt 1977; OBE 1956; Chairman and Chief Executive, Comalco Ltd, since 1969; *b* 26 June 1916; *s* of William James Hibberd and Laura Isabel Hibberd; *m* 1942, Florence Alice Macandie; one *s* one *d. Educ:* Sydney Univ. (BEc). Commonwealth Dept of Trade and Customs, 1939-46; Exec. Asst, Commonwealth Treasury, 1946-53; Mem., Aust. Aluminium Production Commn, 1953-57; First Asst Sec., Banking Trade and Industry Br., Commonwealth Treasury, 1953-57; Exec. Dir, Commonwealth Aluminium Corp., 1957-61; Man. Dir, Comalco Industries Pty Ltd, 1961-69. Director: COR Ltd, 1949-51; G. E. Crane Hldgs Ltd, 1961-; Conzinc Rio Tinto of Aust. Ltd, 1962-71; Mem., Reserve Bank Bd, 1966-; Vice Chairman: Queensland Alumina Ltd, 1964-; Munich Reinsurance Co. of Aust. Ltd, 1970-; Chm., NZ Aluminium Smelters Ltd, 1969-. Pres., Aust. Mining Industry Council, 1972-73. Mem., Melbourne Univ. Council, 1967-. *Recreations:* golf, reading. *Address:* 193 Domain Road, South Yarra, Vic 3141, Australia. *T:* 264037. *Clubs:* Athenæum (Melbourne); Commonwealth (Canberra); Royal Melbourne Golf, Royal Canberra Golf, Frankston Golf.

HIBBERD, Prof. George, PhD; ARTC, CEng, FIMinE; FRSE; Dixon Professor of Mining, University of Glasgow, and Professor of Mining, University of Strathclyde, Glasgow, 1947-67, now Emeritus; *b* Muirkirk, NB, 17 May 1901; *e s* of Charles Hibberd and Helen Brown; *m* 1931, Marion Dalziel Robb Adamson; two *s* two *d. Educ:* Muirkirk Public Sch.; Royal Tech.

Coll., Glasgow. Walter Duncan Res. Scholar. Mining official, 1926-28; Coll. Lectr, 1928-46. Past Pres. Mining Inst. of Scotland. Mem. Council, Inst. Mining Engineers. *Publications:* A Survey of the Welsh Slate Industry; A Survey of The Caithness Flagstone Industry; numerous papers on mining and scientific subjects in technical press. (Jointly) A Survey of the Scottish Slate Industry and A Survey of the Scottish Free-Stone Quarrying Industry. *Recreations:* golf, gardening. *Address:* 120 Kings Park Avenue, Glasgow G44 4HS. *T:* 041-632 4608.

HIBBERD, Stuart; *see* Hibberd, A. S.

HIBBERT; *see* Holland-Hibbert, family name of Viscount Knutsford.

HIBBERT, Christopher, MC 1945; author; *b* 5 March 1924; *s* of late Canon H. V. Hibbert; *m* 1948, Susan Piggford; two *s* one *d.* *Educ:* Radley; Oriel Coll., Oxford (MA). Served in Italy, 1944-45; Capt., London Irish Rifles. Partner in firm of land agents, auctioneers and surveyors, 1948-59. Fellow, Chartered Auctioneers' and Estate Agents' Inst., 1948-59. Won Heinemann Award for Literature, 1962. FRSL. *Publications:* The Road to Tyburn, 1957; King Mob, 1958; Wolfe at Quebec, 1959; The Destruction of Lord Raglan, 1961; Corunna, 1961; Benito Mussolini, 1962; The Battle of Arnhem, 1962; The Roots of Evil, 1963; The Court at Windsor, 1964; Agincourt, 1964; (ed) The Wheatley Diary, 1964; Garibaldi and His Enemies, 1965; The Making of Charles Dickens, 1967; (ed) Waterloo: Napoleon's Last Campaign, 1967; (ed) An American in Regency England: The Journal of Louis Simond, 1968; Charles I, 1968; The Grand Tour, 1969; London: Biography of a City, 1969; The Search for King Arthur, 1970; (ed) The Recollections of Rifleman Harris, 1970; Anzio: the bid for Rome, 1970; The Dragon Wakes: China and the West, 1793-1911, 1970; The Personal History of Samuel Johnson, 1971; (ed) Twilight of Princes, 1971; George IV, Prince of Wales, 1762-1811, 1972; George IV, Regent and King, 1812-1830, 1973; The Rise and Fall of the House of Medici, 1974; (ed) A Soldier of the Seventy-First, 1975; Edward VII: a portrait, 1976; The Great Mutiny: India 1857, 1978. *Recreations:* gardening, travel, cooking. *Address:* 64 St Andrew's Road, Henley-on-Thames, Oxon.

HIBBERT, Eleanor; author; *b* London. *Educ:* privately. *Publications: as Jean Plaidy:* Together They Ride, 1945; Beyond The Blue Mountains, 1947; Murder Most Royal (and as The King's Pleasure, USA), 1949; The Goldsmith's Wife, 1950; Madame Serpent, 1951; Daughter of Satan, 1952; The Italian Woman, 1952; Sixth Wife, 1953, new edn 1969; Queen Jezebel, 1953; St Thomas's Eve, 1954; The Spanish Bridegroom, 1954; Gay Lord Robert, 1955; The Royal Road to Fotheringay, 1955, new edn 1968; The Wandering Prince, 1956; A Health Unto His Majesty, 1956; Here Lies Our Sovereign Lord, 1956; Flaunting Extravagant Queen, 1956, new edn 1960; Triptych of Poisoners, 1958, new edn 1970; Madonna of the Seven Hills, 1958; Light on Lucrezia, 1958; Louis the Wellbeloved, 1959; The Road to Compiegne, 1959; The Rise of the Spanish Inquisition, 1959; The Growth of the Spanish Inquisition, 1960; Castile For Isabella, 1960; Spain for the Sovereigns, 1960; The End of the Spanish Inquisition, 1961; Daughters of Spain, 1961; Katherine, The Virgin Widow, 1961; Meg Roper, Daughter of Sir Thomas More (for children), 1961; The Young Elizabeth (for children), 1961; The Shadow of the Pomegranate, 1962; The King's Secret Matter, 1962; The Young Mary, Queen of Scots, 1962; The Captive Queen of Scots, 1963; Mary, Queen of France, 1964; The Murder in the Tower, 1964; The Thistle and the Rose, 1965; The Three Crowns, 1965; Evergreen Gallant, 1965; The Haunted Sisters, 1966; The Queen's Favourites, 1966; The Princess of Celle, 1967; Queen in Waiting, 1967; The Spanish Inquisition, its Rise, Growth and End (3 vols in one), 1967; Caroline The Queen, 1968; Katharine of Aragon (3 vols in one), 1968; The Prince and the Quakeress, 1968; The Third George, 1969; Catherine de Medici (3 vols in one), 1969; Perdita's Prince, 1969; Sweet Lass of Richmond Hill, 1970; The Regent's Daughter, 1971; Goddess of the Green Room, 1971; Victoria in the Wings, 1972; Charles II (3 vols in one), 1972; The Captive of Kensington Palace, 1972; The Queen and Lord M, 1973; The Queen's Husband, 1973; The Widow of Windsor, 1974; The Bastard King, 1974; The Lion of Justice, 1975; The Passionate Enemies, 1976; The Plantagenet Prelude, 1976; The Revolt of the Eaglets, 1977; *as Eleanor Burford:* Daughter of Anna, 1941; Passionate Witness, 1941; Married Love, 1942; When All The World Was Young, 1943; So The Dreams Depart, 1944; Not In Our Stars, 1945; Dear Chance, 1947; Alexa, 1948; The House At Cupid's Cross, 1949; Believe The Heart, 1950; Love Child, 1950; Saint Or Sinner?, 1951; Dear Delusion, 1952; Bright Tomorrow, 1952; When We Are Married, 1953; Leave Me My Love, 1953; Castles in Spain, 1954; Hearts Afire, 1954; When Other Hearts, 1955; Two Loves In Her Life, 1955; Married in Haste, 1956;

Begin To Live, 1956; To Meet A Stranger, 1957; Pride of the Morning, 1958; Blaze of Noon, 1958; Dawn Chorus, 1959; Red Sky At Night, 1959; Night of Stars, 1960; Now That April's Gone, 1961; Who's Calling?, 1962; *as Ellalice Tate:* Defenders of The Faith, 1956 (under name of Jean Plaidy, 1970); Scarlet Cloak, 1957 (2nd edn, under name of Jean Plaidy, 1969); Queen of Diamonds, 1958; Madame Du Barry, 1959; This Was A Man, 1961; *as Elbur Ford:* The Flesh and The Devil, 1950; Poison in Pimlico, 1950; Bed Disturbed, 1952; Such Bitter Business, 1953 (as Evil in the House, USA 1954); *as Kathleen Kellow:* Danse Macabre, 1952; Rooms At Mrs Oliver's, 1953; Lilith, 1954 (2nd edn, under name of Jean Plaidy, 1967); It Began in Vauxhall Gardens, 1955 (2nd edn under name of Jean Plaidy, 1968); Call of the Blood, 1956; Rochester-The Mad Earl, 1957; Milady Charlotte, 1959; The World's A Stage, 1960; *as Victoria Holt:* Mistress of Mellyn, 1961; Kirkland Revels, 1962; The Bride of Pendorric, 1963; The Legend of the Seventh Virgin, 1965; Menfreya, 1966; The King of the Castle, 1967; The Queen's Confession, 1968; The Shivering Sands, 1969; The Secret Woman, 1971; The Shadow of the Lynx, 1972; On the Night of the Seventh Moon, 1973; The Curse of the Kings, 1973; The House of a Thousand Lanterns, 1974; Lord of the Far Island, 1975; The Pride of the Peacock, 1976; *as Philippa Carr:* The Miracle at St Bruno's, 1972; Lion Triumphant, 1974; The Witch from the Sea, 1975; Saraband for Two Sisters, 1976; Lament for a Lost Lover, 1977. *Address:* c/o Robert Hale Ltd, 45/47 Clerkenwell Green, EC1.

HIBBERT, Maj.-Gen. Hugh Brownlow, DSO 1940; *b* 10 Dec. 1893; *s* of late Adm. H. T. Hibbert, CBE, DSO; *m* 1926, Susan Louisa Mary Feilding (*d* 1975); one *s* one *d.* *Educ:* Uppingham; RMC, Sandhurst. Retired pay, 1946. *Address:* Albrighton Lodge, 54 High Street, Albrighton, near Wolverhampton.

HIBBERT, Reginald Alfred, CMG 1966; HM Diplomatic Service; Deputy Under-Secretary of State, Foreign and Commonwealth Office, since 1976; *b* 21 1922; *s* of Alfred Hibbert, Sawbridgeworth, Herts; *m* 1949, Ann Alun Pugh, *d* of late Sir Alun Pugh; two *s* one *d.* *Educ:* Queen Elizabeth's Sch., Barnet; Worcester Coll., Oxford. Served with SOE and 4th Hussars in Albania and Italy, 1943-45. Entered Foreign Service, 1946; served in Bucharest, Vienna, Guatemala, Ankara, Brussels; Chargé d'Affaires, Ulan Bator, 1964-66; Research Fellow, Leeds Univ., 1966-67; Political Adviser's Office, Singapore, 1967-69; Political Adviser to C-in-C Far East, 1970-71; Minister, Bonn, 1972-75; Asst Under-Sec. of State, FCO, 1975-76. *Address:* Frondeg, Pennal, Machynlleth, Powys SY20 9JX. *T:* Pennal 220. *Club:* Reform.

HICHENS, Mrs Mary Hermione, CBE 1950; ARRC; JP; County Councillor, Oxon, 1937-51, Chairman of Education Committee, 1946-57, Alderman, 1951-74; *b* 15 Oct. 1894; 3rd *d* of Gen. Rt Hon. Sir N. G. Lyttelton, GCB, GCVO; *m* 1919, William Lionel Hichens (Chm. of Cammell Laird; killed by enemy action, 1940); two *s* three *d* (and one *s* killed in action). *Educ:* Alexander Coll., Dublin. Served as Military Probationer QAIMNS in England, 1915; in France, 1916-19 (despatches, ARRC); Mem. of Royal Commission on the Geographical Distribution of the Industrial Population, 1937-39, signed Minority Report; Mem. of Consultative Panel on Post-War Reconstruction to Minister of Works and Buildings; Mem. of Departmental Cttee on Land Utilisation, 1941; Mem. of Departmental Cttee on Training of Teachers, 1942; Commissioner under the Catering Act, 1943-58. Member: County Councils Assoc., 1946-66; Oxon Agric. Exec. Cttee, 1956-61. JP Oxon 1934. *Address:* North Aston Hall, Oxford OX5 4JA. *T:* Steeple Aston 40200.

HICK, Prof. John Harwood; H. G. Wood Professor of Theology, University of Birmingham, since 1967; *b* 20 Jan. 1922; *s* of Mark Day Hick and Mary Aileen (Hirst); *m* 1953, (Joan) Hazel, *d* of F. G. Bowers, CB, CBE, and Frances Bowers; three *s* one *d.* *Educ:* Bootham Sch., York; Edinburgh Univ. (MA 1948 (1st cl. hons Philos); DLitt 1974); Oriel Coll., Oxford (Campbell-Fraser schol.; DPhil 1950); Westminster Coll., Cambridge. Friends' Ambulance Unit, 1942-45. Ordained, Presb. C of E, 1953; Minister, Belford Presb. Church, Northumberland, 1953-56; Asst Prof. of Philosophy, Cornell Univ., 1956-59; Stuart Prof. of Christian Philosophy, Princeton Theolog. Seminary, 1959-64; S. A. Cook Bye-Fellow, Gonville and Caius Coll., Cambridge, 1963-64; PhD by incorporation; Lectr in Divinity, Cambridge Univ., 1964-67. Guggenheim Fellow, 1963-64; Leverhulme Res. Fellow, 1976. Lectures: Mead-Swing, Oberlin Coll., USA, 1962-63; Mary Farnum Brown, Haverford Coll., USA 1964-65; James W. Richard, Univ. of Virginia, 1969; Distinguished Vis., Univ. of Oregon, 1969; Arthur Stanley Eddington Meml, 1972; Stanton, Cambridge Univ., 1974-77; Teape, Delhi and Madras, 1975; Ingersoll, Harvard, 1977; Hope, Stirling, 1977;

Younghusband, London, 1977; Mackintosh, East Anglia, 1978; Riddell, Newcastle, 1978-79. Visiting Professor: Banares Hindu Univ., 1971; Visva Bharati Univ., 1971. Visiting Fellow: British Acad. Overseas, 1974; Univ. of Ceylon, 1974. Hulsean Preacher, Cambridge Univ., 1969; Select Preacher, Oxford Univ., 1970. Chairman: Religious and Cultural Panel, Birmingham Community Relations Cttee, 1969-74; Coordinating Working Party, Statutory Conf. for Revision of Agreed Syllabus of Religious Educn, Birmingham, 1971-74; All Faiths for One Race, 1972-73; Pres., Soc. for the Study of Theology, 1975-76. Life Governor, Queen's Coll., Birmingham, 1972. Hon. TeolD Uppsala, 1977. *Publications:* Faith and Knowledge, 1957, 2nd edn 1966; Philosophy of Religion, 1963, 2nd edn 1973 (Spanish, Portuguese, Chinese, Japanese, Finnish and Swedish edns); (ed) Faith and the Philosophers, 1963; (ed) The Existence of God, 1963; (ed) Classical and Contemporary Readings in the Philosophy of Religion, 1963, 2nd edn 1970; Evil and the God of Love, 1966; (ed) The Many-Faced Argument, 1967; Christianity at the Centre, 1968; Arguments for the Existence of God, 1971; Biology and the Soul, 1972; God and the Universe of Faiths, 1973; (ed) Truth and Dialogue, 1974; Death and Eternal Life, 1976; (ed) The Myth of God Incarnate, 1977. *Address:* 70 Arthur Road, Birmingham B15 2UW. *T:* 021-454 6630.

HICKFORD, Lawrence David, CMG 1972; OBE 1957; JP; Member, New Zealand Dairy Board, since 1961; Chairman, Okato Dairy Co., New Zealand, since 1955 (Director, 1929-); Chairman or Director of Dairy Industries: Barbados, Trinidad and Jamaica, also Trinidad Processing Co.; farmer; *b* Taihape, NZ, 4 Nov. 1904; *s* of David and Emma Hickford; *m* 1927, Keitha May Wooldridge. Commissioned in TF, 1926; served in NZ Home Forces during War of 1939-45; Staff Captain in Mounted Rifles Bde; 2nd in Comd, Armoured Regt, rank Major. Farming at Okato, Taranaki, in partnership with C. G. Cocksedge, 1925-; 12,000 acres developed (dairying, sheep, beef and pigs). Chm. or Sec. numerous organisations in district, 1922-; still serving as Chm. Domain and Cemetery Bds, etc. Frequent overseas travel on business of Dairy Industry. Serves on many cttees of NZ Dairy Board; Dir, NZ Rennet Co., 1950-; Past Dir, Egmont Box Co. (liquidated); Dir, Nat. Dairy Assoc. of NZ for 23 yrs and Chm. for 10 yrs; on Exec. of Fedn of Taranaki Dairy Factories for over 30 yrs and Pres. for 14 years; Chm., Nat. Dairy Fedn of NZ for 10 years; Chm., Okato Veterinary Gp, embracing a number of Dairy Cos, 1945-; Mem., NZ Veterinary Services Council and NZ Animal Health Adv. Cttee; Mem. Taranaki CC, 1936- (Chm., 1951). Member: Airport Adv. Cttee, Hydatids Cttee, Pest Destruction, Fire Bd, Dist. Roads Council; Egmont Nat. Park Bd for 15 years, etc. Farmers' Union and Federated Farmers: Branch Chm. and Mem. Provincial Exec., 1925-61 (excl. some War yrs); Mem. Dominion Council for many years and Dominion Vice-Pres. for 2 yrs; elected Dominion Life Mem. 1961. Member and Patron of a number of Provincial Organisations. JP 1948-. *Address:* Dover Road, Okato, Taranaki, New Zealand.

HICKINBOTHAM, Rev. James Peter; Principal of Wycliffe Hall, Oxford, since 1970; *b* 16 May 1914; *s* of late F. J. L. Hickinbotham, JP and late Mrs Hickinbotham; *m* 1948, Ingeborg Alice Lydia Manger; two *s* one *d. Educ:* Rugby Sch.; Magdalen Coll., Oxford; Wycliffe Hall, Oxford. Deacon, 1937; priest, 1938; curate: St John, Knighton, Leicester, 1937-39; St Paul, S Harrow, 1940-42; Chaplain, Wycliffe Hall, Oxford, 1942-45; Vice-Principal, 1945-50. Prof. of Theology, University Coll. of the Gold Coast, 1950-54. Principal, St John's Coll. and Cranmer Hall, Durham, 1954-70. Examining Chaplain: to Bishop of Manchester, 1947-50; to Bishop of Leicester, 1948-53; to Bishop of Durham, 1955-70. Proctor in Convocation, 1957-70. Hon. Canon, Durham Cathedral, 1959-70. *Address:* 2 Norham Gardens, Oxford OX2 6QB. *T:* Oxford 57539.

HICKINBOTHAM, Sir Tom, KCMG 1953 (CMG 1951); KCVO 1954; CIE 1944; OBE 1939; Governor, The London Clinic, since 1959; *b* 27 April 1903; 2nd *s* of James Ryland Hickinbotham, MB, and Beatrice Elliot, *d* of Rev. Theophilus Sharp, MA. *Educ:* Royal Military Coll., Sandhurst. Entered Indian Army, 1923; served North West Frontier, 1924 (medal); posted to 5th Battalion Baluch Regiment, 1924; transferred to Indian Political Service, 1930; served in various appointments in Aden, 1931-32, 1933-35, and 1938-39; Political Agent, Bahrain, 1937, Muscat, 1939-41, Kuwait, 1941-43, Bahrain, 1943-45; Kalat, 1945-47; Chm. of the Aden Port Trust, 1948-51; Governor and Comdr-in-Chief of Colony and Protectorate of Aden, 1951-56, retired from Government Service. Director of various companies, 1956-73. Now lives in Scotland. *Publication:* Aden, 1958. *Recreation:* fishing. *Address:* Newburgh, Ettrick, Selkirk TD7 5HS. *Club:* Travellers'.

HICKLING, Rev. Colin John Anderson; Lecturer in New Testament Studies, King's College, University of London, since 1968; Priest in Ordinary to the Queen since 1974; *b* 10 July 1931; *s* of Charles Frederick Hickling, CMG, ScD, and of Marjorie Ellerington, *d* of late Henry Blamey. *Educ:* Taunton Sch.; Epsom Coll.; King's Coll., Cambridge; Chichester Theol Coll. BA 1953, MA 1957. Deacon 1957, Priest 1958. Asst Curate, St Luke's, Pallion, Sunderland, 1957-61; Asst Tutor, Chichester Theol Coll., 1961-65; Asst Priest Vicar, Chichester Cath., 1964-65; Asst Lectr in New Testament Studies, King's Coll., Univ. of London, 1965-68; Dep. Minor Canon, St Paul's Cath., 1969-; Dep. Priest in Ordinary to the Queen, 1971-74; Subwarden of King's Coll. Hall, 1969-. Boyle Lectr, 1973-76. *Publications:* (contrib.) Church without Walls, 1968; (contrib.) Catholic Anglicans Today, 1968; (ed jtly and contrib.) What About the New Testament?, 1975; (contrib.) St Paul: Teacher and Traveller, 1975; (contrib.) L'Evangile de Jean, 1977; reviews and articles. *Recreation:* music. *Address:* King's College Hall, Champion Hill, SE5 8AN. *T:* 01-733 2166.

HICKLING, Reginald Hugh, CMG 1968; PhD (London); Lecturer in South East Asian Law, School of Oriental and African Studies, London University; *b* 2 Aug. 1920; *er s* of late Frederick Hugh Hickling and Elsie May Hickling, Malvern, Worcs; *m* 1945, Beryl Iris (*née* Dennett); two *s* one *d* (and one *s* decd). *Educ:* Buxton Coll.; Nottingham Univ. RNVR, 1941-46. Dep. Solicitor, Evening Standard, London, 1946-50; Asst Attorney-Gen., Sarawak, 1950-55; Legal Adviser, Johore, 1956; Legal Draftsman, Malaya, 1957; Parly Draftsman, Malaya, 1959; Comr of Law Revision, Malaya, 1961; Commonwealth Office, 1964; Legal Adviser to High Comr, Aden and Protectorate of S Arabia, 1964-67; Maritime Law Adviser: Thailand, 1968-69; Malaysia, 1969; Ceylon, 1970; Attorney-General, Gibraltar, 1970-72. Vis. Prof., Dept of Law, Univ. of Singapore, 1974-76. *Publications:* The Furious Evangelist, 1950; The English Flotilla, 1954 (US as Falconer's Voyage, 1956); Sarawak and Its Government, 1955; Festival of Hungry Ghosts, 1957; An Introduction to the Federal Constitution, 1960; Lieutenant Okino, 1968. *Recreation:* not watching TV. *Address:* 1 Highfield Road, Malvern, Worcs. *T:* Malvern 62948.

HICKMAN, Sir (Alfred) Howard (Whitby), 3rd Bt, *cr* 1903; *b* 29 Jan. 1920; *s* of Major Sir Alfred Hickman, 2nd Bt, and Lilian Brenda, *o d* of late B. Howard Mander and Mrs Mander, of Trysull Manor, Wolverhampton; *S* father, 1947; *m* 1948, Mrs Margaret D. Thatcher, *o d* of Leonard Kempson; one *s. Educ:* Eton. *Heir: s* Richard Glenn Hickman, *b* 12 April 1949. *Address:* Shenley Cottage, Radlett, Herts. *T:* Radlett 6605.

HICKMAN, John Kyrle, CMG 1977; HM Diplomatic Service; Ambassador to Ecuador, since 1977; *b* 3 July 1927; *s* of late J. B. Hickman and Joan Hickman; *m* 1956, Jennifer Love; two *s* one *d. Educ:* Tonbridge; Trinity Hall, Cambridge. Served in RA, 1948-50. Asst Principal, WO, 1950; Principal, 1955; transf. to CRO, 1958; UK High Commn, Wellington, 1959-62; HM Diplomatic Service, 1965; British Embassy, Madrid, 1966; Counsellor and HM Consul-General, Bilbao, 1967; Dep. High Comr, Singapore, 1969-71; Head of SW Pacific Dept, FCO, 1971-74; Counsellor, Dublin, 1974-77. *Recreations:* ski-ing, golf. *Address:* c/o Foreign and Commonwealth Office, SW1; 3 Weltje Road, W6. *Club:* United Oxford & Cambridge University.

HICKMAN, Michael Ranulf; His Honour Judge Hickman; a Circuit Judge, since 1974; *b* 2 Oct. 1922; *s* of John Owen Hickman and Nancy Viola Hickman (*née* Barlow); *m* 1943, Diana Richardson; one *s* one *d. Educ:* Wellington; Trinity Hall, Cambridge. 2nd cl. Hons in Law. Served War, RAFVR, 1940-46. Cambridge Univ., 1946-48; called to Bar, Middle Temple, 1949. Actg Dep. Chm., Hertfordshire QS, 1965-72; a Recorder of Crown Court, 1972-74. *Recreations:* shooting, fishing, gun dog training. *Address:* The Acorn, Bovingdon, Herts. *T:* Hemel Hempstead 832226.

HICKS; see Joynson-Hicks.

HICKS, David (Nightingale); interior decorator, designer and author; Director of David Hicks Ltd; *b* 25 March 1929; 3rd surv. *s* of late Herbert Hicks (stockbroker and twice past Master Salter's Company) and late Mrs Hicks; *m* 1960, Lady Pamela Carmen Louise Mountbatten; one *s* two *d. Educ:* Charterhouse; Central School of Arts and Crafts, London. Interiors for: Helena Rubenstein; QE2; HRH the Prince of Wales; Govt of NSW; British Steel Corp.; Aeroflot Offices; Marquess of Londonderry; etc. Associate offices in: Bayonne, Brussels, Geneva, Johannesburg, Oslo, Paris, Tokyo. Designer of: fabrics, men's ties, carpets, tiles, furniture, sheets, etc. Master, Salters' Co., 1977-78. CoID (now Design Council) design award, 1970. *Publications:* David Hicks on Decoration, 1966; David Hicks on

Living—with taste, 1968; David Hicks on Bathrooms, 1970; David Hicks on Decoration—with fabrics, 1971; David Hicks on Decoration—5, 1972; David Hicks Book of Flower Arranging, 1976. *Recreations:* shooting, riding, preservation. *Address:* Britwell Salome, Oxfordshire OX9 5LJ. *T:* (office) 01-930 1991.

HICKS, Col Sir Denys (Theodore), Kt 1961; OBE 1950; TD 1943; DL; Member Council of The Law Society, 1948-69; *b* 2 May 1908; *s* of late Cuthbert Hicks, Bristol; *m* 1941, Irene Elizabeth Mansell Leach; four *d. Educ:* Clifton. Admitted a Solicitor of Supreme Court of Judicature, 1931. Served War of 1939-45; with RA in UK and on staff; Col 1953; Hon. Col, 266 (Gloucester Vol. Artillery) Bty RA (Vols), 1972-75. Vice-President of The Law Society, 1959, Pres., 1960; Chm., Internat. Bar Assoc., 1966-70, Pres., 1970-74, Hon. Life Pres., 1974. Dep. Chm., Horserace Betting Levy Board, 1961-76; Mem., Royal Commission on Assizes and QS, 1967. Hon. Member: Amer. Bar Assoc., 1960; Il Ilustre y Nacional Collegio de Abagados de Mexico, 1964; Virginia State Bar Assoc., 1966. DL Avon (formerly Glos), 1957. *Address:* Damson Cottage, Hunstrete, Pensford, Bristol BS18 4NY. *T:* Compton Dando 464; 12 Berkeley Square, Bristol BS8 1HD. *T:* 290221.

HICKS, Donald, OBE 1968; MSc (London), FIChemE, FRIC; Director-General, British Coal Utilisation Research Association, 1962-67; *b* 26 June 1902; *e s* of late Benjamin and Matilda Hicks; *m* May, *y d* of late William and Margaret Sainsbury, Shirenewton, Chepstow; no *c. Educ:* Pontypridd Grammar Sch.; Glamorgan Coll. of Technology. Chief Coal Survey Officer, DSIR, S Wales, 1930-45; Supt of Coal Survey Organisation, DSIR, 1946; Dir of Scientific Control, Nat. Coal Bd, 1947-58; Carbonisation and Scientific Dir and Mem. East Midland Divisional Bd of NCB, 1959-62; Dir of Operational Research and Dir of Pneumoconiosis Field Research, Nat. Coal Bd, 1949-62. *Publications:* Primary Health Care: a review, 1976; papers in various scientific and technical jls. *Recreations:* walking and reading. *Address:* 26 St Kingsmark Avenue, Chepstow, Gwent NP6 5LY. *T:* Chepstow 3147.

HICKS, Sir Edwin (William), Kt 1965; CBE 1956; Company Director and consultant; *b* 9 June 1910; *s* of late William Banks Hicks, Melbourne, Victoria; *m* 1st, 1937, Jean (*d* 1959), *yr d* of late Thomas MacPherson, Brighton, Victoria; four *s* one *d* ; 2nd, 1961, Lois, *o d* of Norman S. Swindon, Canberra; one *s* one *d. Educ:* Haileybury; Melbourne Grammar Sch.; Canberra Univ. Coll. (BCom 1947). Commonwealth Public Service Bd, 1929-31; Commonwealth Statistician's Branch, 1931-38; Trade and Customs Dept, 1938-48; Senior Inspector, then Actg Asst Comr Commonwealth Public Service Bd, investigating organisation and methods of Commonwealth Govt Depts, 1948-51; Secretary: Dept of Air, Commonwealth of Australia, 1951-56; Dept of Defence, 1956-68; Australia High Comr in NZ, 1968-71, retired from Public Service, 1971. Served 1942-45 with Royal Australian Air Force in South West Pacific Area. *Recreations:* formerly: cricket, football, tennis; now golf. *Address:* 73 Endeavour Street, Red Hill, ACT 2603, Australia.

HICKS, Lt-Col James Hamilton, OBE 1966; TD 1945; *b* 21 April 1909; *yr s* of late Major George Hicks, MC, TD, JP, and Elizabeth Young; *m* 1938, Roberta Kirk (*d* 1971), *y d* of late Thomas Boag, Greenock; no *c. Educ:* Pannal Ash Coll., Harrogate. 2nd Lieut RA, Territorial Army, 1929; Capt., 1934; Major, 1939; served in War of 1939-45, OC Bute Battery RA; POW (Germany), 1940-45; despatches, 1945; Lieut-Col, 1950. Chm. Buteshire T&AFA, 1950-62; County Cadet Commandant, Bute, 1950-53; DL, JP, Bute, 1949, Vice-Lieut, 1957-75. *Address:* 39 Crichton Road, Rothesay PA20 9JT. *T:* Rothesay 2612. *Club:* Royal Scottish Automobile (Glasgow).

HICKS, Sir John (Richard), Kt 1964; FBA 1942; Fellow of All Souls College, since 1952; *b* 1904; *s* of late Edward Hicks, Leamington Spa; *m* 1935, Ursula K. Webb (*see* U. K. Hicks). *Educ:* Clifton Coll.; Balliol Coll., Oxford. Lectr, London Sch. of Economics, 1926-35; Fellow of Gonville and Caius Coll., Cambridge, 1935-38, Hon. Fellow, 1971; Prof. of Political Economy, University of Manchester, 1938-46; Official Fellow of Nuffield Coll., Oxford, 1946-52; Drummond Prof. of Political Economy, University of Oxford, 1952-65; Member: Revenue Allocation Commn, Nigeria, 1950; Royal Commn on the Taxation of Profits and Income, 1951. Hon. Fellow, LSE, 1969. (Jtly) Nobel Memorial Prize for Economics, 1972. *Publications:* The Theory of Wages, 1932 (revised edn, 1963); Value and Capital, 1939; The Taxation of War Wealth (with U. K. Hicks and L. Rostas), 1941; The Social Framework, 1942 (4th edn, 1971); Standards of Local Expenditure (with U. K. Hicks), 1943; The Problem of Valuation for Rating (with U. K. Hicks and C. E. V. Leser), 1944; The Incidence of Local Rates in Great

Britain (with U. K. Hicks), 1945; The Problem of Budgeting Reform, 1948; A Contribution to the Theory of the Trade Cycle, 1950; (with U. K. Hicks) Report on Finance and Taxation in Jamaica, 1955; A Revision of Demand Theory, 1956; Essays in World Economics, 1960; Capital and Growth, 1965; Critical Essays in Monetary Theory, 1967; A Theory of Economic History, 1969; Capital and Time, 1973; The Crisis in Keynesian Economics, 1974. *Address:* All Souls College, Oxford. *Club:* Athenæum.

HICKS, Lady (John Richard); see Hicks, U. K.

HICKS, Reginald Jack; HM Diplomatic Service; Consul-General, Auckland, since 1973; concurrently Commissioner, Pitcairn Island; *b* 22 Jan. 1922; 3rd *s* of late Victor Hicks and Emily Hicks, Enfield; *m* 1946, Jean Sims; one *d. Educ:* Enfield Grammar Sch. HM Office of Works and Public Buildings, 1938. RAF (VR), 1941-46: Flying Instructor, US Army Air Corps, 1941-42, with subseq. service in Middle East and Burma (No 28 Sqdn); Flt-Lt. Min. of Works, 1946; Chief Clerk, New Delhi, 1951; seconded to Public Services Commn, Fedn of Rhodesia and Nyasaland, 1957; transf. to CRO, 1961; 1st Sec., Enugu, 1964-66; 1st Sec., Bathurst, 1966; 1st Sec. (Consular), New Delhi, 1966-69; Head of Parly Comr and Cttees Unit, FCO, 1969-73. *Recreations:* golf, travel. *Address:* c/o Foreign and Commonwealth Office, SW1A 2AL; 67 Hayes Lane, Kenley, Surrey. *Clubs:* Northern, Auckland (Auckland, NZ); Akarana Golf.

HICKS, Robert; MP (C) Bodmin, 1970-Feb. 1974 and since Oct. 1974; *b* 18 Jan. 1938; *s* of W. H. Hicks; *m* 1962, Maria Elizabeth Ann Gwyther; two *d. Educ:* Queen Elizabeth Grammar Sch., Crediton; University Coll., London; Univ. of Exeter. Taught at St Austell Grammar Sch., 1961-64; Lecturer in Regional Geography, Weston-super-Mare Technical Coll., 1964-70. An Asst Govt Whip, 1973-74; Mem., Select Cttee of House of Commons, European Secondary Legislation, 1973; Vice-Chm., Cons. Parly Cttee for Agriculture, 1972-73 (Chm., Horticultural Sub-Cttee), and 1974-. *Recreations:* cricket, gardening. *Address:* Parkwood, St Keyne, Liskeard, Cornwall. *T:* Liskeard 43195. *Club:* MCC.

HICKS, Thomas; see Steele, Tommy.

HICKS, Ursula Kathleen, (Lady Hicks); University Lecturer in Public Finance, Oxford, 1947-65; Fellow of Linacre College, since 1965; *b* 17 Feb. 1896; *d* of W. F. and I. M. Webb, Dublin; *m* 1935 Sir John Hicks, *qv. Educ:* Roedean; Somerville College, Oxford; London Sch. of Economics. Asst Lecturer, London Sch. of Economics, Oct. 1935 (resigned on marriage); Lecturer in charge of Dept of Economics, Liverpool University, 1941-46; Fiscal Comr, Uganda, 1962, Eastern Caribbean, 1962-63. Hon. Fellow, Inst. of Social Studies, The Hague, 1967; Hon. DSc (Econ.), Belfast, 1966. *Publications:* Finance of British Government, 1920-36, 1938; Taxation of War Wealth, 1941, Standards of Local Expenditure, 1943, The Problem of Valuation for Rating, 1944, and The Incidence of Local Rates, 1945 (with J. R. Hicks); Indian Public Finance, 1952 (UN); Finance and Taxation in Jamaica (with J. R. Hicks), 1955; Public Finance, 1955; British Public Finances, their Structure and Development, 1880-1952, 1954; Development from Below (Local Government and Finance in Developing Countries of the Commonwealth), 1961; Federalism and Economic Growth (with others), 1961; Report of Fiscal Commission Eastern Caribbean (Command Paper No 1991), 1963; Development Finance: Planning and Control, 1965; The Large City: A World Problem, 1974; articles in Economic Journal, Economica, Public Administration, etc. *Recreations:* painting, gardening. *Address:* Porch House, Blockley, Glos GL56 9BW. *T:* Blockley 210.

HICKS BEACH, family name of **Earl St Aldwyn.**

HICKSON, Geoffrey Fletcher, CBE 1973; MA; Secretary of Board of Extra-Mural Studies, University of Cambridge, 1928-67; Fellow of Fitzwilliam College, 1963-67; *b* 4 July 1900; *s* of late Professor S. J. Hickson, FRS; *m* 1934, Jane Margaret Amy, *er d* of late Dr W. R. Cazenove; two *s* one *d. Educ:* Uppingham Sch. (Scholar); Clare Coll., Cambridge (Archdeacon Johnson Exhib.). Historical Tripos, 1921 and 1922; Gladstone Prize, 1924. Asst Master, Highgate Sch., 1924. Asst Sec., Board of Extra-Mural Studies, Univ. of Cambridge, 1925. Mem. Council of Senate, 1947-62; Mem. Cambridge City Council, 1943-74; Chm. Cttee for Education, 1946-64; Mayor, 1947-49 and 1962-63; Alderman, 1952-74; Mem. Gen. Purposes Cttee, Assoc. of Municipal Corporations, 1956-74 (Dep. Chm., 1969-73); Chm., Non-County Boroughs Cttee for England and Wales, 1969-74. Chm. Central Cttee for Adult Education in HM Forces, 1957-60. Trustee of Uppingham Sch., 1957-77. Hon. Freeman, City of

Cambridge, 1974. *Recreations:* music and golf. *Address:* 16 Rathmore Road, Cambridge CB1 4AD. *T:* Cambridge 44472. *Club:* United Oxford & Cambridge University.

HIDAYATULLAH, M., OBE 1946; Chief Justice, Supreme Court of India, 1968-70; Acting President of India, 1969; *b* 17 Dec. 1905; *y s* of Khan Bahadur Hafiz M. Wilayatullah, ISO; *m* 1948, Pushpa Shah, *d* of A. N. Shah, ICS; one *s* (one *d* decd). *Educ:* Govt High Sch., Raipur; Morris Coll., Nagpur (Phillips Schol.; BA; Malak Gold Medal); Trinity Coll., Cambridge (MA); Lincoln's Inn; Bencher 1968. Nagpur High Court: Advocate, 1930-46; Govt Pleader, 1942-43; Advocate General, CP & Berar, 1943-46; Puisne Judge, 1946-54; Chief Justice, 1954-56; Chief Justice, Madhya Pradesh High Court, 1956-58; Puisne Judge, Supreme Court of India, 1958-68. Dean, Faculty of Law, Nagpur Univ., 1950-54; Mem., Faculty of Law, Sagar, Vikram and Aligarh Univs; Pres., Indian Law Inst., 1968-70; Pres., Internat. Law Assoc. (Indian Br.), 1968-70; Pres., Indian Soc. of Internat. Law, 1968-70; Mem., Internat. Inst. of Space Law, Paris; Internat. Coun. of Former Scouts and Guides (awarded Silver Elephant, bronze medal for gallantry); Exec. Coun., World Assembly of Judges; Advr, Council for World Peace through Law; rep. India at Internat. Confs at Bangkok, Helsinki, Durham, Geneva, Port of Spain, Belgrade, Venice, Canberra, Melbourne and Washington. Chancellor, Muslim Nat. Univ., New Delhi; Pro-Chancellor, Delhi Univ., 1968-70. Kt of Mark Twain. Hon. LLD: Univ. of Philippines, 1970; Ravishankar Univ., 1970; Rajasthan Univ., 1976. Medallion and plaque of Merit, Philconsa, Manila; Order of Jugoslav Flag with Sash, 1972. *Publications:* Democracy in India and the Judicial Process, 1966; The South-West Africa Case, 1967; Judicial Methods, 1969; (ed) Mulla's Mahomedan Law, 1972; A Judge's Miscellany, 1972; USA and India, 1977; numerous monographs and articles. *Recreations:* golf, bridge. *Address:* A-10 Rockside, 112 Walkeshwar Road, Bombay 6, India. *T:* 369798. *Clubs:* Delhi Gymkhana (New Delhi); Willingdon (Bombay).

HIDDEN, Anthony Brian, QC 1976; a Recorder of the Crown Court, since 1977; *b* 7 March 1936; *s* of late James Evelyn Harold Hidden, GM and of Gladys Bessie (*née* Brooks). *Educ:* Reigate Grammar Sch.; Emmanuel Coll., Cambridge (BA Hons 1957, MA 1960). 2nd Lieut, 1st Royal Tank Regt, Far East Land Forces, Hong Kong, 1958-59. Called to the Bar, Inner Temple, 1961; Mem., Hon. Soc. of Inner Temple, 1956-, and of Lincoln's Inn (*ad eundem*), 1973-. *Recreations:* reading, playing golf, watching football. *Address:* 8 New Square, Lincoln's Inn, WC2A 3QP. *T:* 01-242 4986.

HIDE, Dr Raymond, FRS 1971; Head of Geophysical Fluid Dynamics Laboratory (Chief Scientific Officer), Meteorological Office, Bracknell, since 1967; Hon. Professor: Department of Mathematics, University College, London University, since 1967; Department of Geophysics, University of Reading, since 1976; *b* 17 May 1929; *s* of late Stephen Hide and Rose Edna Hide (*née* Cartlidge); *m* 1958, (Phyllis) Ann Licence; one *s* two *d*. *Educ:* Percy Jackson Grammar Sch., near Doncaster; Manchester Univ.; Caius Coll., Cambridge. BSc 1st cl. hons Physics Manchester, 1950; PhD 1953, ScD 1969, Cantab. Res. Assoc. in Astrophysics, Univ. of Chicago, 1953-54; Sen. Res. Fellow, AERE Harwell, 1954-57; Lectr in Physics, Univ. of Durham (King's Coll., Newcastle), 1957-61; Prof. of Geophysics and Physics, MIT, 1961-67. Mem., NERC, 1972-75. Mem. Council: RAS, 1969-72 (Vice-Pres., 1970-72); Royal Meteorological Soc., 1969-72 and 1974-77 (Symons Meml Lectr, 1970; Pres., 1974-76). R. A. Fisher Meml Lectr, Inst. Physics, 1977. Fellow, Amer. Acad. of Arts and Sciences, 1964. Charles Chree Medal, Inst. Physics, 1975. *Publications:* papers in scientific jls. *Address:* 11 Clare Avenue, Wokingham, Berks. *T:* Bracknell 20242, ext. 2592.

HIEGER, Izrael, DSc (London); Biochemist, Royal Marsden Hospital, 1924-66; *b* Siedletz, Russian-Poland, June 1901; *s* of F. E. Hieger. *Educ:* Birkbeck Coll. and University Coll., London. With colleagues, Anna Fuller Memorial Prize for Cancer Research, 1939. *Publications:* One in Six: An Outline of the Cancer Problem, 1955; Carcinogenesis, 1961; papers on the discovery of cancer producing chemical compounds. *Address:* Chester Beatty Research Institute, Royal Marsden Hospital, Fulham Road, SW3.

HIGGINBOTTOM, Donald Noble; HM Diplomatic Service; Counsellor, Foreign and Commonwealth Office, since 1976; *b* 19 Dec. 1925; *s* of late Harold Higginbottom and Dorothy (*née* Needham); *m* 1950, Sarah Godwin. *Educ:* Calday Grange Grammar Sch., Cheshire; King's Coll., Cambridge (1st Cl. Hons Hist.); Yale Univ., USA (MA Hist.). Lectr in Humanities, Univ. of Chicago, 1951. Entered Foreign Office, 1953; Buenos Aires, 1955; Peking, 1958; Saigon, 1960; Phnom Penh, 1962;

Singapore, 1964; Bangkok, 1971; Buenos Aires, 1974. *Recreations:* electronic clocks, power boating. *Address:* c/o Foreign and Commonwealth Office, SW1A 2AL; 91 Dora Road, Wimbledon, SW19 7JT. *T:* 01-946 8890. *Clubs:* Travellers'; Yacht Club, Olivos (Buenos Aires).

HIGGINS, see Longuet-Higgins.

HIGGINS, Alec Wilfred, MBE 1944; MC 1940; TD 1945; DL, JP; Deputy Chairman of Lloyd's, 1975 and 1976; Chairman: Woods & Maslen Ltd, since 1963; Higgins & Doble, since 1962; *b* 1 Nov. 1914; *s* of Frederick Gladstone Higgins and late Beatrice Louisa Scriven; *m* 1939, Denise May Philcox; two *s* one *d*. *Educ:* Merton Court Sch., Sidcup; Sutton Valence Sch. Joined Woods & Maslen Ltd, 1937. Underwriting Mem. of Lloyd's, 1948 (Mem. Cttee, 1967-74 and 1975-); Mem. Cttee, Lloyd's Insce Brokers Assoc., 1960-63 and 1965-68 (Dep. Chm. 1965, Chm. 1966); Ex-officio Mem., Gen. Cttee, Lloyd's Register of Shipping, 1976; Chm., Insce Section, London Chamber of Commerce, 1963-64; Vice-Pres., Insce Inst. of London, 1967; Member: Council, Chartered Insce Inst., 1972; Insce Industry Trng Council, 1969; Export Guarantee Adv. Council, 1977-. Councillor, Chislehurst and Sidcup UDC, 1962-65 (Chm. Finance Rating and Gen. Purposes Cttee, 1962-65; Vice-Chm. of Council, 1964); Alderman, London Borough of Bexley, 1968-; JP Bexley, 1967; DL Greater London, 1973. *Recreations:* swimming, badminton. *Address:* Somersby, 12 Priestlands Park Road, Sidcup, Kent DA15 7HR. *T:* 01-300 3792. *Clubs:* City of London, Royal Automobile.

HIGGINS, Sir Christopher (Thomas), Kt 1977; Chairman, Peterborough Development Corporation, since 1968; *b* 14 Jan. 1914; *s* of late Thomas Higgins and Florence Maud Higgins; *m* 1936, Constance Joan Beck; one *s* one *d*. *Educ:* West Kensington Central Sch.; London Univ. Executive with Granada Group Ltd, 1939-54. Served War of 1939-45: with RA, 1940-46. Member: Acton Borough Council, 1945-65; GLC, 1964-67; Hemel Hempstead Develt Corp., 1947-52; Bracknell Develt Corp., 1965-68. Chm., North Thames Gas Consumers' Council, 1969-. *Recreations:* reading, gardening, walking; watching most sports. *Address:* Coronation Cottage, Wood End, Little Horwood, Milton Keynes, Bucks MK17 0PE. *T:* Winslow 2636.

HIGGINS, Frank; Member, National Bus Company, since 1974; *b* 30 Aug. 1927; *s* of Wilfred and Hilda Higgins; *m* 1948, Betty Pulford; one *s* one *d*. *Educ:* Hanley High Sch., Stoke-on-Trent; St Paul's Coll., Cheltenham. Teacher: Stoke-on-Trent, 1946; Notts, 1948-58; Organising Sec., Youth Gp, 1958-60; Teacher, Nottingham, Derby, 1960-73. Contested (Lab) Harborough 1966, Grantham 1970. Mem., Nottingham City Council, 1971 (Chm. Transportation Cttee, 1972-74); Mem., Notts CC, 1973-77 (Chm. Environment Cttee, 1973-77). *Recreations:* travelling, talking. *Address:* 216 Mansfield Road, Nottingham. *T:* Nottingham 603968.

HIGGINS, Rev. Canon John Denis P.; see Pearce-Higgins.

HIGGINS, John Patrick Basil, QC; **His Honour Judge Higgins;** County Court Judge, Northern Ireland, since 1971, for Armagh and Fermanagh, since 1976; *b* 14 June 1927; *e s* of late John A. and Mary Philomena Higgins, Magherafelt; *m* 1960, Bridget, *e d* of late Dr Matthew F. O'Neill, Hollingwood, Chesterfield; two *s* three *d*. *Educ:* St. Columb's Coll., Derry; Queen's Univ., Belfast (LLB). Called to Bar of N Ireland, 1948, Bencher, 1969-71; QC (N Ire.) 1967. Chairman: Mental Health Review Tribunal of NI, 1963-71; Legal Aid Adv. Cttee (NI), 1975-; Member: County Court Rules Cttee (NI), 1973-; Indictments Act Rules Cttee, 1974-; Statute Law Cttee of NI, 1975-. Chm., Voluntary Service, Belfast, 1975-. Member: Community Peace Conf., 1969; Bd of Management, St Joseph's Coll. of Educn, Belfast, 1969-; Bd of Governors, Dominican Coll., Portstewart, 1974-. *Address:* 2 Waterloo Park, Belfast, Northern Ireland. *T:* 777813.

HIGGINS, Prof. Peter Matthew; Professor of General Practice, Guy's Hospital Medical School, University of London, since 1974; *b* 18 June 1923; *s* of Peter Joseph Higgins and Margaret Higgins; *m* 1952, Jean Margaret Lindsay Currie; three *s* one *d*. *Educ:* St Ignatius' Coll., London; UCH, London. MB, BS; FRCP, FRCGP. House Phys., Medical Unit, UCH, 1947; RAMC, 1948-49; House Phys., UCH, St Pancras, 1950; Resident MO, UCH, 1951-52; Asst Med. Registrar, UCH, 1953; Gen. Practice, Rugeley, Staffs, 1954-66, and Castle Vale, Birmingham, 1966-68; Sen. Lectr, Guy's Hosp. Med. Sch., 1968-74. *Publications:* articles in Lancet, BMJ, Jl RCGP. *Recreations:* squash, swimming, sailing. *Address:* Wallings, Heathfield Lane, Chislehurst, Kent. *T:* 01-467 2756.

HIGGINS, Reynold Alleyne, LittD; FBA 1972; FSA; *b* Weybridge, 26 Nov. 1916; *er s* of late Charles Alleyne Higgins and of Marjorie Edith (*née* Taylor); *m* 1947, Patricia Mary, *d* of J. C. Williams; three *s* two *d. Educ:* Sherborne Sch.; Pembroke Coll., Cambridge (Scholar). First Cl., Classical Tripos pts I and II, 1937, 1938; MA, 1960; LittD, 1963. Served War: Queen Victoria's Rifles, KRRC, 1939-46 (Captain, PoW). Asst Keeper, Dept of Greek and Roman Antiquities, British Museum, 1947, Dep. Keeper, 1965-76, acting Keeper, 1976. Visiting Fellow, British School of Archaeology at Athens, 1969, Chm., Managing Cttee, 1975-. Corr. Mem., German Archaeological Inst. *Publications:* Catalogue of Terracottas in British Museum, vols I and II, 1954, 1959; Greek and Roman Jewellery, 1961; Greek Terracotta Figures, 1963; Jewellery from Classical Lands, 1965; Greek Terracottas, 1967; Minoan and Mycenaean Art, 1967; The Greek Bronze Age, 1970; The Archaeology of Minoan Crete, 1973; also articles and reviews in British and foreign periodicals. *Recreation:* travel. *Address:* Hartfield, Burstead Close, Cobham, Surrey. *T:* Cobham 3234.

HIGGINS, Terence Langley; MP (C) Worthing since 1964; *b* 18 Jan. 1928; *s* of Reginald Higgins, Dulwich; *m* 1961, Rosalyn, *d* of Lewis Cohen, London; one *s* one *d. Educ:* Alleyn's Sch., Dulwich; Gonville and Caius Coll., Cambridge. Brit. Olympic Team (athletics) 1948, 1952; BA (Hons) 1958. MA 1963; Pres. Cambridge Union Soc., 1958. NZ Shipping Co., 1948-55; Lectr in Economic Principles, Dept of Economics, Yale Univ., 1958-59; Economist with Unilever, 1959-64. Sec., Cons. Parly Finance Cttee, 1965-66; Opposition Spokesman on Treasury and Economic Affairs, 1966-70; Minister of State, Treasury, 1970-72; Financial Sec. to Treasury, 1972-74; Opposition Spokesman: on Treasury and Econ. Affairs, 1974; for Trade, 1974-76. Associate, Inst. of Chartered Shipbrokers. *Address:* 18 Hallgate, Blackheath Park, SE3. *Club:* Hawks (Cambridge).

HIGGON, Col Laurence Hugh, CBE 1958; MC 1916 and Bar 1917; *b* 3 Sept. 1884; 4th (and *o* surv.) *s* of late Capt. J. D. G. Higgon, RA, DL, JP, Scolton, Pembrokeshire; *m* 1922, Neda Kathleen C., *er d* of late Lieut-Col F. Rennick; two *d. Educ:* Cheltenham; RMA, Woolwich. Entered RA 1903; retired, 1927; comd 102nd (Pembroke Yeo.) Bde RA, 1930-35 (Bt Col); Hon. Col 1948; Hon. Comr Toc H in Wales, 1931. Rejoined RA (Lieut-Col), 1939. Home Guard, Pembs (Lieut-Col), 1942-45. DL, JP, Pembrokeshire; JP Haverfordwest. Served European War, 1914-19, France and Flanders (despatches twice, MC and Bar). Chm. Pembroke County War Memorial Hospital 1934-53; Mem. West Wales Hosps Management Cttee, 1948-53; Chm. Standing Joint Cttee, 1949-54; Chm., Pembroke TA Assoc., 1944-47; Lord Lieutenant, Pembrokeshire, 1944-54. OStJ. *Address:* Castle Corner, Manorbier, Dyfed. *T:* Manorbier 343. *Clubs:* Army and Navy; Pembroke County (Haverfordwest).

HIGGS, Brian James, QC 1974; a Recorder of the Crown Court, since 1974; Barrister-at-Law; *b* 24 Feb. 1930; *s* of James Percival Higgs and Kathleen Anne Higgs; *m* 1953, Jean Cameron DuMerton; two *s* three *d. Educ:* Wrekin Coll.; London Univ. Served RA, 1948-50. Called to Bar, Gray's Inn, 1955. Contested (C) Romford, 1966. *Recreations:* gardening, golf, wine, chess, bridge. *Address:* Navestock Woodhouse, Navestock Side, Brentwood, Essex. *T:* Coxtie Green 72032; 2 Harcourt Buildings, Temple, EC4Y 9DB. *T:* 01-353 2622.

HIGGS, Godfrey Walter, CBE 1960; Vice-President, Bahamas Senate, 1964-68; *b* 28 Sept. 1907; *yr s* of late Charles Roger Higgs; *m* 1937, Marion Suzanne (marr. diss.), *y d* of Roscoe Hagen, Rochester, NY; three *s*; *m* Eleanor Claire, *y d* of Charles Frederick Beckmann, New York City, USA. *Educ:* Queen's Coll., Taunton. Called to Bahamas Bar, 1929; English Bar, Inner Temple, 1933 (Profumo Prize); Deputy Speaker, House of Assembly, Bahamas, 1937-42; Mem. Executive Council and Leader for the Govt, Bahamas House of Assembly, 1942-45 and 1946-49; Member: Legislative Council, Bahamas, 1950-64; Senate, 1964-68. *Recreations:* yachting, swimming, golf, shooting, fishing, etc. *Address:* Stanley, PO Box N3247, East Bay Street, Nassau, Bahamas. *Clubs:* Royal Nassau Sailing, Lyford Cay (Nassau).

HIGGS, Rt. Rev. Hubert Laurence, MA Cantab; *b* 23 Nov. 1911; *s* of Frank William and Mary Ann Higgs; *m* 1936, Elizabeth Clare (*née* Rogers); one *s* one *d. Educ:* University Coll. Sch.; Christ's Coll., Cambridge; Ridley Hall, Cambridge. Curate: Holy Trinity, Richmond, 1935; St Luke's, Redcliffe Square, London, 1936-38; St John's, Boscombe (and Jt Sec. Winchester Youth Council), 1938-39. Vicar, Holy Trinity, Aldershot, 1939-45; Editorial Sec., Church Missionary Soc., 1945-52; Vicar, St John's, Woking, 1952-57 (Rural Dean, 1957); Archdeacon of Bradford and Canon Residentiary of Bradford Cathedral, 1957-65; Bishop Suffragan of Hull, 1965-76; RD of Hull, 1972-76.

Recreations: history, music-listening, gardening. *Address:* The Farmstead, Halesworth, Suffolk. *T:* Halesworth 2621.

HIGGS, Sir (John) Michael (Clifford), Kt 1969; solicitor; Partner, Higgs & Sons; *b* 30 May 1912; *s* of late Alderman A. W. Higgs, Cranford House, Stourton, Staffs; *m* 1st, 1936, Diana Louise Jerrams (*d* 1950); two *d*; 2nd, 1952, Rachel Mary Jones; one *s* one *d. Educ:* St Cuthberts, Malvern; Shrewsbury. LLB (Birmingham), 1932. Admitted solicitor, 1934. Served War of 1939-45 with 73 HAA Regt RA (TA), 1939-42; JAG Staff, 1942-46; demobilised, 1946, with rank of Lieut-Col. Mem. of Staffs County Council, 1946-49; MP (C) Bromsgrove Div. of Worcs, 1950-55; Mem. of Worcs CC, 1953-73 (Chm. 1959-73); Alderman, 1963; Chm., Hereford and Worcester CC, 1973-77. Mem. West Midlands Economic Planning Council, 1965-; Chm., W Midlands Planning Authorities' Conf., 1969-73. *Recreation:* tennis. *Address:* Pixham Cottage, Callow End, Worcester WR2 4TH. *T:* Worcester 830645. *Clubs:* Conservative (Birmingham); Worcestershire (Worcester).

HIGGS, Captain Michael Arnold, CB 1977; RN; *b* 16 Feb. 1927; *s* of Dr J. S. Higgs and Mrs Higgs; *m* 1950, Willie Doreen Stirling; three *s* two *d. Educ:* RNC, Dartmouth. Midshipman 1944; CO HMS Dundas, 1959; Exec. Officer, HMS Hampshire, 1961; Captain 1967; PSO to Royal Malaysian Navy, 1967-69; idc 1970; Captain (D1), Far East, 1971; Captain (F2), 1972; staff, Nat. Defence Coll., 1972-74; Captain, BRNC Dartmouth, 1974-76; apptd Flag Officer, Gibraltar, 1976; invalided 1976. *Recreations:* gardening, shooting. *Address:* Waltham House, Stroud, Petersfield, Hants. *T:* Petersfield 3991. *Club:* Army and Navy.

HIGGS, Sydney Limbrey, FRCS; Consulting Orthopædic Surgeon, St Bartholomew's Hospital; Hon. Consulting Surgeon, Royal National Orthopædic Hospital; Hon. Consulting Orthopædic Surgeon, North-East Metropolitan Regional Hospital Board; *b* 12 Sept. 1892; widower; one *d. Educ:* St John's Coll., Cambridge; St Bartholomew's Hospital. MB, BCh, MA, Cambridge, 1919; MRCS, LRCP 1917; FRCS 1922. Formerly: Regional Orthopædic Consultant, EMS; Surgeon, Queen Mary's Hospital, Roehampton; Hon. Consulting Orthopædic Surgeon to the Army, Eastern Command. Fellow British Orthopædic Association; Fellow Royal Society of Medicine. *Publications:* contributions to medical journals. *Address:* Phœnix, West Wittering, near Chichester, West Sussex. *Club:* Royal Yacht Squadron.

HIGGS-WALKER, James Arthur, MA Oxon; Headmaster of Sevenoaks School, 1925-54; *b* 31 July 1892; *s* of W. H. Higgs-Walker, Wychbury House, Hagley, Worcestershire; *m* 1917, Muriel Jessie, *e d* of Rev. Harold Earnshaw Smith, Himley Rectory, Staffs, and *g d* of Hon. Henley Eden; one *d. Educ:* Repton; St John's Coll., Oxford (Scholar). Served European War, Capt. in the Worcs Regt, in Egypt, Mesopotamia, Italy, 1914-19; House-Master and Chief History Master at Oundle Sch., 1919-25. *Publications:* European History, 1789-1815; Introduction to Eighteenth Century French Society; contributor to History and other periodicals. *Recreation:* member of Oxford University Authentics Cricket Club, and has played cricket for Worcs. *Address:* Long Barn, Chelwood Gate, Sussex.
See also M. H. Harmer.

HIGHAM, John Drew, CMG 1956; Member of Environment Secretary's Panel of Inspectors; *b* 28 Nov. 1914; *s* of Richard and Margaret Higham, Pendleton, Lancs; *m* 1st, 1936, Mary Constance Bromage (*d* 1974); three *d*; 2nd, 1976, Katherine Byard Pailing. *Educ:* Manchester Grammar Sch.; Gonville and Caius Coll., Cambridge (Scholar). Asst Principal, Admiralty, 1936; Asst Private Sec. to First Lord, 1939; Private Sec. to Parliamentary Sec. and Parliamentary Clerk, 1940; Principal, Admiralty, 1941; transferred to Colonial Office, 1946; Asst Sec. Colonial Office, 1948; seconded to Singapore as Under Sec., 1953, and as Dir of Personnel, 1955-57 (acted on various occasions as Chief Sec.); Asst Sec., Min. of Housing and Local Govt, 1965; Head of Development Control Div., DoE, 1970-74. Chevalier 1st Cl. Order of St Olaf (Norway), 1948. *Recreations:* history of art, gardening. *Address:* Avonside, Bredon, Tewkesbury, Glos. *T:* Bredon 72468; 6 Chalcot Gardens, NW3 4YB. *T:* 01-722 3157.

HIGHAM, Rear-Adm. Philip Roger Canning, CB 1972; Director, HMS Belfast Trust, since 1973; *b* 9 June 1920; *s* of Edward Higham, Stoke Bishop, Bristol; *m* 1942, Pamela Bracton Edwards, *er d* of Gerald Edwards, Southport, Lancs; two *s. Educ:* RNC Dartmouth. Cadet, 1937; Midshipman, 1938; Sub-Lt 1940; Lieut 1942; qual. Gunnery Officer, 1944; Second Gunnery Off., HMS Vanguard, Royal Tour of S Africa, 1947; psc 1948; Exper. Dept, HMS Excellent, 1951-52; Comdr, Devonport Gunnery Sch., 1953; Trials Comdr, RAE Aberporth,

1954-55; jssc 1956; Exper. Comdr, HMS Excellent, 1957-59; Admty (DTWP), 1960-61; Naval Attaché, Middle East, 1962-64; idc 1965; Dep. Chief Polaris Exec., 1966-68; Cdre i/c Hong Kong, 1968-70; Asst Chief of Naval Staff (Op. Requirements), 1970-72. *Recreations:* gardening, fishing. *Address:* Apple Tree Farm, Prinsted, Emsworth, Hants. *T:* Emsworth 2195. *Club:* Naval and Military.

HIGHET, Gilbert (Arthur); Anthon Professor of the Latin Language and Literature, Columbia University, New York, 1950-72, now Professor Emeritus; *b* 22 June 1906; *o s* of Gilbert Highet, Superintendent, Postal Telegraphs, Glasgow, and Elizabeth Gertrude Boyle; *m* 1932, Helen Clark, *o d* of Donald McInnes, Glasgow (*see* Helen MacInnes); one *s*. *Educ:* Hillhead High Sch., Glasgow; Glasgow Univ. (DLitt 1951); Balliol Coll., Oxford. Snell Exhibitioner and Hon. Schol., DLitt 1956. Fellow of St John's Coll., Oxford, 1932; Prof. of Greek and Latin, Columbia Univ., 1938-50; on leave for war service, 1941-46; with British mission in US and later in Mil. Govt, Germany (British Zone); commissioned, 1943; Lt-Col 1946. Became US citizen, 1951. Guggenheim Meml Fellow, 1951. Hon. Degrees: DLitt: Syracuse, 1960; Columbia, 1977; LHD: Case Inst. of Technology, 1952; Adelphi, 1964; Massachusetts, 1973. FRSL 1959. Mem. Bd of Judges, Book-of-the-Month Club, 1954-; Chm. Editorial Adv. Bd, Horizon, 1958-77. Wallace Award, Amer.-Scottish Foundn, 1973. *Publications:* The Classical Tradition: Greek and Roman Influences on Western Literature, 1949; The Art of Teaching, 1950; People, Places and Books, 1953; Juvenal the Satirist, 1954; The Mind of Man, 1954; A Clerk of Oxenford, 1954; Poets in a Landscape, 1957; Talents and Geniuses, 1957; The Powers of Poetry, 1960; The Anatomy of Satire, 1962 (Award of Merit, American Philological Association, 1963); Explorations, 1971; The Speeches in Vergil's Aeneid, 1972; The Immortal Profession, 1976; Translator of Werner Jaeger's Paideia: the Ideals of Greek Culture, 1939-44. Contributor: The Classical Review, The American Journal of Philology, etc. *Recreations:* two-piano duets, photography. *Address:* 15 Jeffreys Lane, East Hampton, New York 11937, USA. *Clubs:* Century (New York); Maidstone (East Hampton).

HIGHSMITH, Patricia; writer since 1942; *b* 19 Jan. 1921; *o c* of Jay Bernard Plangman and Mary Coates (of German and English-Scots descent respectively); name changed to Highsmith by adoption; unmarried. *Educ:* Barnard Coll., Columbia Univ., New York. For a year after univ. had a mediocre writing job; after that free-lance until publication of first novel. Lived in Europe and America alternately from 1951, and now has been some years in France. *Publications:* Strangers on a Train, 1950; The Blunderer, 1955; The Talented Mr Ripley, 1956; Deep Water, 1957; A Game for the Living, 1958; This Sweet Sickness, 1960; The Cry of the Owl, 1962; The Two Faces of January, 1964; The Glass Cell, 1965; A Suspension of Mercy, 1965; Plotting and Writing Suspense Fiction, 1966; Those Who Walk Away, 1967; The Tremor of Forgery, 1969; Eleven (short stories), 1970; Ripley Under Ground, 1971; A Dog's Ransom, 1972; Ripley's Game, 1974; The Animal-Lover's Book of Beastly Murder (short stories), 1975; Edith's Diary, 1977; Little Tales of Misogyny (short stories), 1977. *Recreations:* drawing, some painting, carpentering, snail-watching, travelling by train. *Address:* 77 Moncourt, France. *Club:* Detection.

HIGHTON, Rear-Adm. Jack Kenneth, CB 1959; CBE 1952; *b* 2 Sept. 1904; *s* of John Henry Highton and Kate (*née* Powers); *m* 1933, Eileen Metcalfe Flack; one *s* two *d*. *Educ:* Bedford Modern Sch. Joined Royal Navy, 1922; Captain 1951; Dir of Welfare and Service Conditions, 1955-57; Rear-Adm. 1957; Chief Staff Officer (Administration) to Commander-in-Chief, Plymouth, 1957-60; retired, 1960. *Recreations:* walking, sailing, gardening. *Address:* c/o National Westminster Bank Ltd, Woodbridge, Suffolk.

HIGMAN, Prof. Graham, FRS 1958; MA, DPhil; Waynflete Professor of Pure Mathematics, Oxford University, and Fellow of Magdalen College, Oxford, since Oct. 1960; *b* 1917; 2nd *s* of Rev. Joseph Higman; *m* 1941, Ivah May Treleaven; five *s* one *d*. *Educ:* Sutton Secondary Sch., Plymouth; Balliol Coll., Oxford. Meteorological Office, 1940-46; Lecturer, University of Manchester, 1946-55; Reader in Mathematics at Oxford Univ., 1955-60; Senior Research Fellow, Balliol Coll., Oxford, 1958-60. De Morgan Medal, London Mathematical Soc., 1974. *Publications:* papers in Proc. London Math. Soc., and other technical jls. *Address:* 64 Sandfield Road, Headington, Oxford. *T:* 62974.

HIGTON, Dennis John, CEng, FIMechE, FRAeS; Director-General of Military Aircraft Projects in Ministry of Defence (Under-Secretary), since 1976; *b* 15 July 1921; *s* of John William and Lillian Harriett Higton; *m* 1945, Joy Merrifield Pickett; one

s one *d*. *Educ:* Guildford Technical Sch.; RAE Farnborough Technical Sch. Mid-Wessex Water Co., 1937. RAE Engineering Apprentice, 1938-42; RAE Aerodynamics Dept (Aero Flight), 1942-52; learned to fly at No 1 EFTS RAF Panshangar, 1946; A&AEE Boscombe Down, Head of Naval Test and Supt of Performance, 1953-66; British Defence Staff, Washington DC, USA, 1966-70; MoD(PE) Anglo-French Helicopter Production, 1970-72; Director Aircraft Production, 1972-75; Mem., Fleet Air Arm Officers Assoc. *Publications:* research and memoranda papers mainly on aerodynamic flight testing. *Recreations:* beekeeping, skiing, sailing, gardening, squash, shooting. *Address:* Jasmine Cottage, Rollestone Road, Shrewton, Salisbury, Wiltshire SP3 4HG. *T:* Shrewton 276.

HILALY, Agha, HQA, SPk; Chairman, Board of Governors, Pakistan Institute of Strategic Studies, since 1973; *b* 20 May 1911; *s* of late Agha Abdulla; *m* 1938, Malek Taj Begum, *d* of Mirza Kazim, Bangalore; three *s*. *Educ:* Presidency Coll., Madras (MA); King's Coll., Cambridge (MA). Entered former ICS (Bengal cadre), 1936; Under-Sec., Govt of Bengal, 1939-41; Govt of India, 1941-47; entered Pakistan Foreign Service at time of Partition; Jt Sec., Min. of Foreign Affairs, 1951; Imp. Def. Coll., 1955; Ambassador to Sweden, Norway, Denmark and Finland, 1956; Delegate to UN Gen. Assembly, 1958; Ambassador to USSR and Czechoslovakia, 1959; High Commissioner in India and Ambassador to Nepal, 1961; High Commissioner for Pakistan in the UK and Ambassador to Ireland, 1963-66; Ambassador for Pakistan to the United States, 1966-71, also accredited to Mexico, Venezuela and Jamaica. Dir, State Bank of Pakistan, 1972-. Hilal-i-Quaid-i-Azam, Pakistan; Star of Pakistan; Grand Cross, Order of the North Star, Sweden; Grand Cross, Prabol Gurkha Dakshana Bahu (Nepal). *Recreations:* colour photography, shooting. *Address:* No 48 Fifteenth Street, Phase 5, Defence Housing Society, Karachi 6, Pakistan. *Clubs:* Travellers'; International (Washington); Sind (Karachi).

HILARY, David Henry Jephson; Assistant Under Secretary of State, Home Office, since 1975; *b* 3 May 1932; *s* of late Robert and Nita Hilary; *m* 1957, Phœbe Leonora, *d* of John J. Buchanan; two *s* two *d*. *Educ:* Tonbridge Sch.; King's Coll., Cambridge (Sandys Student 1954, Craven Student 1955; MA). Royal Artillery, 1953-54. Entered Home Office, 1956. *Recreations:* cricket, squash, bridge. *Address:* 17 Victoria Square, SW1. *Clubs:* RAC, MCC.

HILBORNE, Rev. Frederick Wilfred, CBE 1957; *b* 5 March 1901; *yr s* of Frank and Eleanor Hilborne; *m* 1929, Irene May Wheatland; one *s* one *d*. *Educ:* Eastbourne Coll.; Handsworth Theological Coll. Ordained into Ministry of Methodist Church, 1929. Commissioned in Royal Army Chaplains' Dept, 1929; served in Malta, 1932-35. War Service: BEF, 1939-40; MELF 1942; CMF, 1943-45. CF 3rd Class, 1939; CF 2nd Class, 1943; CF 1st Class, 1950. Appointed Dep. Chaplain-Gen. to the Forces and Hon. Chaplain to the Queen, 1953; relinquished both appointments and placed on retired pay, Dec. 1956. *Address:* 43 West Parade, Worthing, West Sussex BN11 5EF. *T:* Worthing 48204.

HILDER, Rev. Geoffrey Frank; Archdeacon of Taunton, 1951-71; Prebendary of Wells Cathedral, 1951-73; Provost of Western Division of Woodard Corporation, 1960-70; *b* 17 July 1906; *s* of Albert Thomas and Lilian Ethel Hilder; *m* 1939, Enid, *d* of Rev. F. E. Coggin. *Educ:* Uppingham Sch.; Lincoln Coll., Oxford; Inner Temple; Ely Theological Coll. Called to the Bar, 1930. Deacon, 1931; Priest, 1932; Rector of Ruardean, Glos., 1937-41; Vicar of St Stephen's, Cheltenham, 1941-48; Vicar of Hambridge, 1948-59. Prolocutor of Lower House of Convocation of Canterbury, 1955-70; Dir of Ecclesiastical Insurance Office Ltd, 1957-61. *Recreations:* music, gardening. *Address:* Church Races, Upton Cliffs, Bude, Cornwall. *T:* Widemouth Bay 345. *Club:* Athenæum.

HILDER, Rowland, RI 1938; painter; *b* Greatneck, Long Island, USA, 28 June 1905, British parents; *m* 1929, Edith Blenkiron; one *s* one *d*. *Educ:* Goldsmiths' Coll. Sch. of Art, London. Exhbn, Furneaux Gall., Wimbledon, 1974, 1976. PRI 1964-74. *Publications:* Illustrated editions of: Moby Dick, 1926; Treasure Island, 1929; Precious Bane, 1930; The Bible for To-day, 1940; The Shell Guide to Flowers of the Countryside (with Edith Hilder), 1955; (jointly) Sketching and Painting Indoors, 1957; Starting with Watercolour, 1966; Illustrative Biography, 1978. *Address:* 5 Kidbrooke Grove, Blackheath, SE3. *T:* 01-858 3072.

HILDITCH, Clifford Arthur; Director of Social Services, Manchester District Council, since April 1974 (Manchester City Council, 1970-74); *b* 3 Feb. 1927; *s* of late Arthur Clifford Hilditch and of Lilian Maud Hilditch (*née* Brockman); *m* 1953,

Joyce Hilditch (*née* Burgess); one *s*. *Educ:* Huntingdon Grammar Sch.; London Univ. Dip. in Applied Social Studies. Army Service, 1944-48 (commissioned into Indian Army, 1945). Service as an Administrative Officer, LCC (Welfare Services) until 1961; Manchester City Council: Dep. Chief Welfare Officer, 1962-64; Chief Welfare Officer, 1965-70. Hon. Fellow, Manchester Polytechnic, 1976. *Publications:* contributor to various hosp. and social services jls. *Recreations:* various. *Address:* 14 Priory Road, Wilmslow, Cheshire. *T:* Wilmslow 22109.

HILDRED, Sir William (Percival), Kt 1945; CB 1942; OBE 1936; Grand Officer, Order of Orange-Nassau, 1946; Commander Order of Crown of Belgium; MA; Director-General Emeritus International Air Transport Association (Director-General, 1946-66); *b* 13 July 1893; *s* of late William Kirk Hildred; *m* 1920, Constance Mary Chappell, MB, ChB; two *s* one *d*. *Educ:* Boulevard Sch., Hull; University of Sheffield. Served European War, 1st York and Lancaster Regt, 1914-17; entered Treasury, 1919; Finance Officer, Empire Marketing Board, 1926-34; Head of Special Measures Branch, Ministry of Agriculture and Fisheries, 1934-35; Deputy General Manager, Export Credits Guarantee Dept, 1935-38; Deputy Dir-Gen. of Civil Aviation, Air Ministry, 1938; Principal Asst Sec., Ministry of Aircraft Production, 1940; assisted in formation of RAF Ferry Command, Montreal, 1941; Director-Gen. of Civil Aviation, Ministry of Civil Aviation, 1941-46. Edward Warner Award of ICAO, 1965. Hon. LLD: Sheffield; McGill Univ.; FRSA. Hon. FRAeS. *Recreations:* cycling, music, carpentry. *Address:* Spreakley House, Frensham, Surrey. *Club:* Athenæum.

HILDRETH, Maj.-Gen. Sir (Harold) John (Crossley), KBE 1964 (CBE 1952; OBE 1945); *b* 12 June 1908; *s* of late Lt-Col H. C. Hildreth, DSO, OBE, FRCS, and late Mrs Hildreth; *m* 1950, Mary, *d* of late G. Wroe; two *s* three *d*. *Educ:* Wellington Coll., Berks; RMA, Woolwich. 2nd Lieut, RA, 1928; transferred to RAOC, 1935, as Captain; Major 1944; Lieut-Col 1948; Col 1952; Brig. 1958; Maj.-Gen. 1961. War Office: Col 1942-44; Brig. 1944-47; Inspector of Establishments, 1947-50; Controller of Army Statistics, 1950-51; Comdr RAOC, Ammunition Org., 1951-53; Comdr, Bicester, 1953-57; DOS, BAOR, 1957-60; Inspector, RAOC, War Office, 1960-61; Dir of Ordnance Service, War Office, 1961-64; retired, Dec. 1964. Man. Dir, Army Kinema Corp., 1965-70, Services Kinema Corp., 1970-75. Chm. Greater London Br., SS&AFA, 1977-. Col Commandant, RAOC, 1963-70. Legion of Merit (degree of Officer), USA. *Recreations:* shooting, sailing. *Address:* 59 Latymer Court, W6. *T:* 01-748 3107.

HILDRETH, (Henry) Jan (Hamilton Crossley); Director-General, Institute of Directors, since 1975; *b* 1 Dec. 1932; *s* of Maj.-Gen. Sir (Harold) John (Crossley) Hildreth, KBE, and late Mrs Joan Elise Hallett (*née* Hamilton); *m* 1958, Wendy Moira Marjorie, *d* of late Arthur Harold Clough, CMG; two *s* one *d*. *Educ:* Wellington Coll.; The Queen's Coll., Oxford. National Service in RA, BAOR, 1952-53; 44 Parachute Bde (TA), 1953-58. Oxford, Hon. Mods (Nat. Sci.), BA (PPE) 1956, MA. Baltic Exchange, 1956; Royal Dutch Shell Group, 1957: served Philippines (marketing) and London (finance); Kleinwort, Benson Ltd, 1963; NEDO, 1965; Member of Economic Development Cttees for the Clothing, the Hosiery and Knitwear, and the Wool Textile industries; Mem., London Transport Bd, subseq. LTE, 1968-72: main responsibilities Finance, Marketing, Corp. Plan, Data Processing, and Estates; Asst Chief Exec., John Laing & Son Ltd, 1972-74. A Governor, Wellington Coll., 1974-. FCIT. FRSA. *Recreations:* cross-country running, photography, water mills; and others. *Address:* 50 Ridgway Place, Wimbledon, SW19. *Club:* Vincent's (Oxford).

HILDYARD, Rev. Christopher, MVO 1966; MA; *b* 28 April 1901; *s* of Lyonel D'Arcy and Dora Hildyard. *Educ:* St George's, Windsor Castle; Repton; Magdalene Coll., Cambridge; Cuddesdon Theological Coll. Curate at Glass Houghton, West Yorks, 1925-27; Curate at Gisborough, North Yorks, 1927-28; Asst Minor Canon, Westminster Abbey, 1928-32; Minor Canon, Westminster Abbey, 1932-73; Chaplain of Westminster Hospital, 1937-58; Custodian, Westminster Abbey, 1945-55; Sacrist, Westminster Abbey, 1958-73. *Recreation:* painting. *Address:* 2 The Cloisters, Westminster, SW1. *T:* 01-222 4982.

HILDYARD, Sir David (Henry Thoroton), KCMG 1975 (CMG 1966); DFC 1943; HM Diplomatic Service, retired; *b* 4 May 1916; *s* of late His Honour G. M. T. Hildyard, QC, and Sybil, *d* of H. W. Hamilton Hoare; *m* 1947, Millicent (*née* Baron), widow of Wing Commander R. M. Longmore, OBE; one *s* one

d. *Educ:* Eton; Christ Church, Oxford. Served with RAF, 1940-46. Entered HM Foreign (subseq. Diplomatic) Service, 1948; Montevideo, 1950; Madrid, 1953; FO, 1957; Counsellor, Mexico City, 1960-65; Head of Economic Relations Dept, FO, 1965-68; Minister and Alternate UK Rep. to UN, 1968-70; Ambassador to Chile, 1970-73; Ambassador and Permanent UK Rep. to UN and other International Organisations, Geneva, 1973-76. *Recreations:* tennis, golf. *Address:* 10 The Little Boltons, SW10. *Club:* Hurlingham.

HILEY, Joseph; DL; *b* 18 Aug. 1902; *s* of Frank Hiley of Leeds; *m* 1932, Mary Morrison, *d* of Dr William Boyd; three *d*. *Educ:* West Leeds High Sch.; Leeds Univ., 1920-23. Formerly family business, Hiley Brothers, took over firm of J. B. Battye & Co. Ltd, 1924, Managing Dir 1927-59; Dir, Irish Spinners Ltd, 1952-74. Mem. of Lloyd's, 1966-. MP (C) Pudsey, Oct. 1959-Feb. 1974. Leeds City Councillor, 1930, Alderman, 1949, resigned, 1960; Lord Mayor of Leeds, 1957-58; President: West Leeds Conservative Assoc.; Leeds & District Spastics Soc.; Leeds YMCA; Central Yorks Scout Council; Past President: Hand-Knitting Assoc.; Leeds Chamber of Commerce; Chm., Northorpe Hall Trust. DL West Yorks, 1971. *Recreations:* cricket, theatre. *Address:* Elmaran, Layton Road, Horsforth, Leeds. *T:* Horsforth 4787. *Clubs:* Leeds (Leeds); Pudsey Conservative (Pudsey).

HILEY, Sir Thomas (Alfred), KBE 1966; Chartered Accountant, Australia, since 1932; *b* 25 Nov. 1905; *s* of William Hiley and Maria (*née* Savage); *m* 1929, Marjory Joyce (*née* Jarrott) (*d* 1972); two *s*. *Educ:* Brisbane Grammar Sch.; University of Qld. State Public Service, 1921; Public Accountancy, 1923; in practice (Public Accountant), 1925. Qld Parliament, 1944; Dep. Leader of Opposition, 1950; Treasurer of Qld and Minister for Housing, 1957; Treasurer, 1963; Deputy Premier, 1965; retired from Parliament, 1966. Pres., Inst. of Chartered Accts in Aust., 1946-47. Hon. MCom, University of Qld, 1960. *Recreations:* shooting, fishing, cricket. *Address:* Illawong, 39 The Esplanade, Tewantin, Qld 4565, Australia. *T:* 471-175. *Clubs:* Number 10 (London); Queensland (Brisbane).

HILGENDORF, Charles, CMG 1971; JP; farmer; *b* 1908; *s* of Prof. Frederick William Hilgendorf and Frances Elizabeth (*née* Murray); *m* 1936, Rosemary Helen Mackenzie; one *s* one *d*. *Educ:* Christ's College, Christchurch; Univ. of Canterbury, NZ (MA). Held various positions in Federated Farmers of NZ, 1946-61. Member: NZ Meat Producers Board, 1961- (Chm., 1972-); University Grants Cttee (of NZ), 1961- (Dep. Chm., 1970-). *Address:* Sherwood, Ashburton, NZ. *T:* Winchamore 643. *Clubs:* Farmers'; Christchurch, Wellington (both in New Zealand).

HILL, family name of **Marquess of Downshire, Baron Hill of Luton** and **Baron Sandys.**

HILL; see Clegg-Hill, family name of Viscount Hill.

HILL, 8th Viscount *cr* 1842; **Antony Rowland Clegg-Hill;** Bt 1726-27; Baron Hill 1814; *b* 19 March 1931; *s* of 7th Viscount Hill and Elisabeth Flora (*d* 1967), *d* of Brig.-Gen. George Nowell Thomas Smyth-Osbourne, CB, CMG, DSO; *S* father, 1974; *m* 1963, Juanita Phyllis, *d* of John W. Pertwee, Salfords, Surrey. *Educ:* Kelly Coll.; RMA, Sandhurst. Formerly Captain, RA. Freeman of Shrewsbury, 1957. *Heir:* cousin Peter David Raymond Charles Clegg-Hill [*b* 17 Oct. 1945; *m* 1973, Sharon Ruth Deane, Kaikohe, NZ; one *d*]. *Address:* House of Lords, SW1.

HILL OF LUTON, Baron, *cr* 1963 (Life Peer); **Charles Hill**, PC 1955; MA, MD, DPH, LLD; Chairman, National Joint Council for Local Authorities' Administrative, Professional, Technical and Clerical Services, since 1963; Chairman, Abbey National Building Society, since 1976 (Director since 1964); *b* 15 Jan. 1904; *s* of late Charles Hill and Florence M. Cook; *m* 1931, Marion Spencer Wallace; two *s* three *d*. *Educ:* St Olave's Sch.; Trinity Coll., Cambridge; London Hosp. Formerly: House Physician and Receiving Room Officer, London Hospital; London University Extension Lecturer in Biology; Deputy Medical Supt, Coppice Mental Hospital, Nottingham; Deputy MOH, City of Oxford; President: World Medical Assoc.; Central Council for Health Educn; Hon. Sec., Commonwealth Medical Conf. Sec., BMA, 1944-50; Chm., Chest, Heart and Stroke Assoc., 1974-. MP (L and C) Luton, 1950-63. Parly Sec., Min. of Food, 1951-April 1955; Postmaster-Gen., April 1955-Jan. 1957; Chancellor of the Duchy of Lancaster Jan. 1957-Oct. 1961; Minister of Housing and Local Government and Minister for Welsh Affairs, Oct. 1961-July 1962. Chm., Independent Television Authority, 1963-67; Chm. of Governors of the BBC, 1967-72; Chm. Laporte Industries Ltd, 1965-70. Hon. Fellow

Amer. Medical Assoc. *Publications:* What is Osteopathy? (jointly), 1937; Re-printed Broadcasts, 1941-50; Both Sides of the Hill, 1964; Behind the Screen, 1974. *Recreations:* golf and walking. *Address:* 5 Bamville Wood, East Common, Harpenden, Herts. *Club:* Reform.

HILL, Alan John Wills, CBE 1972; Managing Director, Heinemann Group of Publishers Ltd, since 1973; *b* 12 Aug. 1912; *s* of William Wills Hill; *m* 1939, Enid Adela Malin; two *s* one *d. Educ:* Wyggeston Sch., Leicester; Jesus Coll., Cambridge (Schol., MA). RAF, 1940-45: Specialist Armament Officer (Sqdn Ldr). Publishing Asst, Wm Heinemann Ltd, 1936-40; Dir, 1955; Jt Man. Dir, 1959-61; Chm. and Man. Dir, Heinemann Educational Books Ltd, 1961-; Chm., World's Work Ltd, 1973-; Pres., Heinemann Educational Books Inc. (USA), 1977. Chm., Soc. of Bookmen, 1965-68; Chm., Educational Publishers' Council, 1969-71; Member: Council, Publishers' Assoc., 1972-; Exec. Cttee, National Book League, 1973-; British Council Books Adv. Panel, 1973-; CNAA (Business Studies Panel), 1975-. Closely involved with Commonwealth literature and educn. *Publications:* (with R. W. Finn) And So Was England Born, 1939; History in Action, 1962; articles in jls. *Recreations:* tennis, swimming, mountain-walking. *Address:* 56 Northway, NW11 6PA. *T:* 01-455 8388; New House, Rosthwaite, Borrowdale, Cumbria. *Clubs:* Athenæum, Garrick, Royal Air Force, PEN.

HILL, Rev. Alexander Currie, CB 1957; Minister Emeritus of Portknockie, Banffshire; Principal Finance Officer, Board of Trade, 1958-64; *b* 23 Jan. 1906; *o s* of late Alexander Hill and Jeanie Currie; unmarried. *Educ:* George Heriot's Sch., Edinburgh; Univ. of Edinburgh; Univ. of Aberdeen (Faculty of Divinity); Christ's Coll., Aberdeen. Entered Administrative Class, Home Civil Service, 1928. Under-Sec., Board of Trade, 1950-58. *Address:* 62a Rubislaw Den North, Aberdeen AB2 4AN. *Clubs:* Reform; Royal Northern (Aberdeen).

HILL, (Arthur) Derek; artist, writer, and organiser of exhibitions; *b* Bassett, Hampshire 6 Dec., 1916; *s* of A. J. L. Hill and Grace Lilian Mercer. *Educ:* Marlborough Coll. Has designed sets and dresses for Covent Garden and Sadler's Wells. *One-man exhibitions:* Nicholson Gall., London, 1943; Leicester Galls, London, 1947, 1950, 1953 and 1956. *Organised exhibitions:* 1934 onwards: Dégas Exhibn for Edinburgh Fest. and Tate Gall., London, 1952; Landseer exhibn (with John Woodward) at Royal Academy, 1961, etc. Represented in exhibns, Europe and USA, 1957-; exhibns in New York, 1966 and 1969; retrospective exhibitions: Whitechapel Gall., London, 1961; Arts Council of NI, Belfast, 1970; Municipal Gall., Dublin, 1971. *Pictures owned by:* Tate Gall.; Nat. Gall. of Canada; Arts Council; Fogg Museum, Harvard; City Art Galleries of: Southampton, Birmingham, Bradford, Coventry, Carlisle, etc. FRGS. *Publications:* Islamic Architecture and Its Decoration (with Prof. Oleg Grabar), 1965; Islamic Architecture in North Africa (with L. Golvin), 1976; articles in Illustrated London News, Apollo, Burlington Magazine, etc. *Recreations:* gardening, travelling.

HILL, Sir Austin Bradford, Kt 1961; CBE 1951; FRS 1954; PhD (Econ.), 1926, DSc, 1929 (London); Emeritus Professor of Medical Statistics, London School of Hygiene and Tropical Medicine, University of London, and Hon. Director, Statistical Research Unit of Medical Research Council, 1945-61; Dean of the London School of Hygiene and Tropical Medicine, 1955-57, Honorary Fellow, 1976; *b* 8 July 1897; 3rd *s* of late Sir Leonard Erskine Hill, FRS; *m* 1923, Florence Maud, *d* of late Edward Salmon, OBE; two *s* one *d. Educ:* Chigwell Sch.; privately; University Coll., London. Flight Sub-Lieut in Royal Naval Air Service, 1916-18; on staff of Medical Research Council and its Industrial Health Research Board, 1923-33; Reader in Epidemiology and Vital Statistics, London Sch. of Hygiene and Tropical Medicine, 1933-45; seconded during the war to Research and Experiments Dept, Ministry of Home Security, 1940-42, and to Medical Directorate, RAF, 1943-45. Civil Consultant in Medical Statistics to RAF and mem. of Flying Personnel Research Cttee; Civil Consultant in Medical Statistics to RN, 1958-77; Mem., Cttee on Safety of Medicines, 1964-75; Pres. Royal Statistical Soc., 1950-52 (Hon. Sec. 1940-50); Gold Medallist, 1953; Pres. Section of Epidemiology, RSM, 1953-55, Section of Occupational Medicine, 1964-65; Member: Council, MRC, 1954-58; Cttee on Review of Medicines, 1975-; Fellow of University Coll., London; Hon. FRCP; Hon. FFCM; Hon. FIA; Hon FRSM; Hon. FAPHA; Hon. Fellow: Soc. of Community Medicine; Soc. of Occupational Medicine; Faculty of Medicine, University of Chile; Society for Social Medicine; Internat. Epidemiological Assoc.; Med. Research Club. Cutter Lecturer, Harvard, 1953; Harben Lecturer RIPH&H, 1957; Alfred Watson Memorial Lectr Inst. of Actuaries, 1962; Marc Daniels

Lectr RCP, 1963. Hon. DSc Oxford, 1963; Hon. MD Edinburgh, 1968. Galen Medallist, Soc. of Apothecaries, 1959; Harben Gold Medallist, 1961; Jenner Medallist, RSM, 1965; Heberden Medallist, Heberden Soc., 1965. *Publications:* Internal Migration and its Effects upon the Death Rates, 1925; The Inheritance of Resistance to Bacterial Infection in Animal Species, 1934; Principles of Medical Statistics, 1937, 10th edn 1977; Statistical Methods in Clinical and Preventive Medicine, 1962; reports to Industrial Health Research Board on industrial sickness and numerous papers in scientific journals, especially studies of cigarette smoking and cancer of the lung and of the clinical trial of new drugs. *Recreations:* travelling, gardening. *Address:* Green Acres, Little Kingshill, Great Missenden, Bucks. *T:* Gt Missenden 2380.

HILL, Christopher; *see* Hill, J. E. C.

HILL, Christopher Pascoe, CB 1964; CBE 1956; Charity consultant; *b* 6 July 1903; *s* of late Charles Pascoe Grenfell Hill; *m* 1st, 1926, Elizabeth Ridding Oldfield (*d* 1931), *d* of late Lieut-Col H. Oldfield, RMA; one *d* ; 2nd, 1934, Joan Elizabeth Smith, *d* of late R. W. Smith; two *s* one *d. Educ:* Merchant Taylors'; St John's Coll., Oxford, Galsford Prizeman, 1925. Entered Home Office, Asst Principal, 1925; Asst Sec., Ministry of Home Security, 1942; Home Office: Aliens Dept, 1943-47; Children's Dept, 1947-56; Asst Under-Sec. of State, 1957. Attached to Charity Commission, 1956, to prepare Charities Act, 1960; Chief Charity Commissioner, 1960-65; Sec. to Archbishop's Commission on Church and State, 1966-70. Vice Pres., Herts Council of Voluntary Service; Member: Exec. Cttee, Hertfordshire Soc.; Standing Conf. on Herts Countryside (Chm., 1967-76); Gen. Adv. Council of BBC; BBC and IBA Central Appeals Adv. Cttees (Chm.), 1969-74; Council, National Trust, 1969-73; Family Welfare Assoc. Inf. Cttee; Legal Bd, Church Assembly, 1966-70; Adv. Council, Christian Orgns Res. and Adv. Trust. Director: WRVS Trustees Ltd; Internat. Standing Conf. on Philanthropy, Geneva. UK correspondent, Foundation News, 1975-. King Haakon VII Liberty Cross, Norway. *Publications:* A Guide for Charity Trustees, 1966; UK section, Trusts and Foundations in Europe, 1972; UK section, Philanthropy in the Seventies, 1973; papers on delinquency and charity subjects in periodicals. *Recreations:* garden, painting, archæology, preserving Herts countryside. *Address:* The Grange, Therfield, Royston, Herts. *T:* Kelshall 358. *Club:* Athenæum.

HILL, Clifford Francis; HM Diplomatic Service; Consul-General, Durban, since 1977; *b* 27 Jan. 1930; *s* of William Bucknell Hill, Teignmouth, Devon; *m* 1953, Cicely Margaret Taylor; two *s* one *d. Educ:* Falmouth Grammar Sch.; Jesus Coll., Cambridge. RNVR, 1949-50. Entered Foreign (subseq. Diplomatic) Service, 1953; 3rd Sec. and Private Sec. to HM Ambassador, Tokyo, 1953-58; FO, 1959-60; 1st Sec., Office of Comr-Gen. for SE Asia, Singapore (later Office of Political Adviser, C-in-C Far East), 1960-64; seconded to CRO, 1964-66; 1st Sec., Information, Washington, 1966-69; FO, 1969-71; seconded to Home Office and subseq. NI Office for service in Belfast, 1971-73; Head of Cultural Exchange Dept, FCO, 1974-77. *Address:* c/o Foreign and Commonwealth Office, SW1.

HILL, Colin de Neufville, CMG 1961; OBE 1959; Business Manager, University of Sussex, since 1964; *b* 2 Jan. 1917; *s* of Philip Rowland and Alice May Hill; *m* 1950, Mary Patricia Carson Wilson; two *s. Educ:* Cheltenham Coll.; St Edmund Hall, Oxford. BA. hons in Mod. Langs, Oxford, 1938. Selected for appt to Colonial Service, 1938; Administrative Officer, Colonial Admin. Service, Eastern Nigeria, 1939; served with Provincial and Regional Administration, Eastern Nigeria, 1939-53; transferred to Tanganyika and apptd Sec. for Finance, 1954; Permanent Sec. to the Treasury, Tanganyika Government, 1959-64. *Recreations:* photography, gardening, music. *Address:* Mount Pleasant Farm, Barcombe, near Lewes, East Sussex.

HILL, Sir Cyril Rowley; *see* Hill, Sir (George) Cyril Rowley.

HILL, Prof. David Keynes, ScD; FRS 1972; Professor of Biophysics, Royal Postgraduate Medical School, University of London, since 1975; *b* 23 July 1915; *s* of Prof. Archibald Vivian Hill, CH, OBE, FRS, ScD, and late Margaret Neville, *d* of late Dr J. N. Keynes; *m* 1949, Stella Mary Humphrey; four *d. Educ:* Highgate Sch.; Trinity Coll., Cambridge. ScD Cantab 1965. Fellow, Trinity Coll., Cambridge, 1940-48; Physiologist on staff of Marine Biological Assoc., Plymouth, 1948-49; Sen. Lectr, 1949-62, Reader in Biophysics, 1962-75, Royal Postgrad. Med. Sch., London Univ. *Publications:* scientific papers in Jl Physiology. *Recreations:* gardening, walking. *Address:* Castlett Farm, Guiting Power, Cheltenham, Glos GL54 5UZ. *T:* Guiting Power 275; Royal Postgraduate Medical School, W12 0HS.

HILL, Sir Denis; see Hill, Sir John Denis Nelson.

HILL, Derek; see Hill, A. D.

HILL, Prof. Dorothy, CBE 1971; FRS 1965; FAA 1956; Research Professor of Geology, University of Queensland, 1959-72, now Emeritus Professor; President, Professorial Board, 1971-72, Member of Senate, since 1976; b 10 Sept. 1907; d of R. S. Hill, Brisbane; unmarried. Educ: Brisbane Girls' Grammar Sch.; Univs of Queensland and Cambridge. BSc (Qld) 1928, 1st Cl. Hons in Geol. and Univ. Gold Medal. Foundn Trav. Fellowship of Univ. of Queensland held at Newnham Coll., Cambridge, 1930-32; PhD Cantab 1932; Old Students' Res. Fellowship, Newnham Coll., Cambridge, 1932-35; Sen. Studentship (Exhibn of 1851) held at Cambridge, 1935-37; Coun. for Sci. and Indust. Res. Fellowship, held at Univ. of Queensland, 1937-42; DSc (Qld) 1942. WRANS, Second Off., 1942-45 (RAN Ops Staff). Univ. of Queensland: Lectr in Geol., 1946-56, Reader, 1956-59. Hon. Editor, Geol. Soc. of Aust., 1958-64; Mem. Council, Australian Acad. of Science, 1968-70, Pres. 1970; Pres., Geol Soc. of Aust., 1973-75. Lyell Medal, Geol. Soc. of London, 1964; Clarke Medal, Royal Society of NSW, 1966; Mueller Medal, ANZAAS, 1967; Foreign and Commonwealth Mem. Geol. Soc. London, 1967; Hon. Fellow, Geol Soc. of America, 1971. Hon. LLD Queensland, 1974. Publications: numerous, in geol and palæontol jls on fossil corals, archæocyatha, brachiopods, reef sediments and Australian geology and stratigraphy. Recreations: travel, reading. Address: University of Queensland, St Lucia, Brisbane, Qld 4067, Australia.

HILL, Rev. Canon Douglas George; Rector of Teversham, since 1974; Hon. Canon of Ely, since 1965; Examining Chaplain to the Bishop of Ely and Director of Studies in Ely Diocese, since 1965; b 1912; s of George and Edith Hill, Grimsby, Lincs; m 1944, Margaret Esther, d of late Judge Sir Gerald Hurst, QC; no c. Educ: St James' Choir Sch., Grimsby; Gonville and Caius Coll., Cambridge; Lincoln Theological Coll. Schol. Gonville and Caius Coll., 1931-35; John Stewart of Rannoch Schol. in Hebrew, 1932; 1st cl. Oriental Lang. Tripos pt 1, 1933, BA (1st cl. Oriental Lang. Tripos pt 2) 1934; 2nd cl. Theological Tripos pt 2 and Tyrwhitt Schol., 1935; MA 1938. Deacon, 1936, Priest 1937, Lincoln; Curate of: Louth with Welton-le-Wold, 1936-40; Crosby, Dio. of Lincoln, 1940-42; St Nicholas, Chislehurst, 1943-45; Vicar of Eynsford, Kent, Dio. of Rochester, 1945-56; Rector of Papworth Everard, Cambridge, Dio. of Ely, and Chaplain to Papworth Village Settlement and Hosp., 1956-60; Residentiary Canon of Ely Cathedral, 1960-65; Principal, Ely Theological Coll., 1960-64; Rector of Leverington, 1965-74. Recreations: travel and walking. Address: The Rectory, Teversham, Cambridge. T: Teversham 2220.

HILL, Douglas William, CBE 1965; DSc; b 3 March 1904; o s of Henry and Florence Mary Hill; m 1st, 1936, Margaret Eluned (d 1956), y d of Rev. O.M. Owen; one s; 2nd, 1958, Mabel Constance Prothero (d 1975), er d of James Belford. Educ: St George's Sch., Bristol; Univs of Bristol, Liverpool and Illinois, PhD Liverpool, 1926; DSc Bristol, 1936. Research Chemist, Boots Pure Drug Co. Ltd, 1927-30; Commonwealth Fund Fellow, Univ. of Illinois and Rockefeller Inst. for Med. Research, New York, 1930-33; Lectr in Organic Chemistry, UC Exeter and Special Lectr in Biochemistry, Bristol Univ., 1933-37; Asst to Dir, Shirley Inst., 1937-40; Min. of Supply, 1940-43; Combined Production and Resources Board, Washington DC, 1943-44; Dep. Dir, Shirley Inst., 1944-56; Director, 1956-69. Mem. Council RIC, 1948-60 (Chm., Manchester and Dist Sect., 1953-54); Mem. Council, Chemical Soc., 1947-50; Vice-Pres., Parly and Sci. Cttee, 1962-65; Chairman: Cttee of Dirs of Research Assocs, 1960-63; Cttee of Dirs of Textile Research, Assocs, 1964-66; Cttee on Mule Spinners' Cancer; Chm. of Governors, Royal Coll. of Advanced Technology, Salford, 1962-67; Chm. of Council and Pro-Chancellor, Univ. of Salford, 1967-75, Sen. Pro-Chancellor, 1976-; Member: UGC Cttee on Libraries, 1962-68, Cttee of Management, Science Policy Foundn; Chm., Perkin Centenary Trust; Dir, Shirley Developments Ltd, 1953-74. Chm., Macclesfield Div. Liberal Assoc., 1948-56. Bernard Dyer Memorial Medallist and Lectr, 1962; Mather Lectr, 1970. Hon. DSc Salford, 1969. Publications: Insulin: Its Production, Purification and Properties, 1936; Impact and Value of Science, 1944, 2nd edn, 1946; Co-operative Research for Industry, 1946; papers and articles in scientific jls, press and reviews. Recreations: sketching, travel, writing and lecturing. Address: 2 Marina Court, Tigne Sea Front, Sliema, Malta. T: 36132. Clubs: Athenæum; Malta Union.

HILL, Col (Edward) Roderick, DSO 1944; JP; Lord-Lieutenant of Gwent, since 1974 (HM Lieutenant for Monmouthshire,

1965-74); Chairman, Chepstow Race Course Co. Ltd, since 1964; b 1904; s of late Capt. Roderick Tickell Hill; m 1934, Rachel, e d of Ellis Hicks Beach, Witcombe Park, Glos; one s one d. Educ: Winchester; Magdalen Coll., Oxford. Gazetted to Coldstream Guards, 1926; served War of 1939-45, with regt (despatches, DSO); commanded 5th Bn and 1st Bn Coldstream Guards and Guards Training Bn; comd Regt, 1949-52. JP Co. Monmouth; High Sheriff of Monmouthshire, 1956; DL Monmouthshire, 1957; Vice-Lieut, 1963-65. Chm. of the Curre Hunt, 1959-65. Chm. of Governors, Monmouth Sch. and Monmouth Sch. for Girls, 1961-66; Chm. Chepstow RDC, 1962-63. Hon. Col, 104 Light AD Regt RA(V), 1967-69. Freeman and Liveryman, Haberdashers Co., 1969. Pres., Royal Welsh Agric. Soc., 1970-71. Pres., TA&VRA for Wales and Monmouthshire, 1971-74. Officer, Order of Orange-Nassau (with swords), 1946. KStJ 1972. Publication: (with the Earl of Rosse) The Story of the Guards Armoured Division, 1941-1945, 1956. Address: St Arvan's Court, Chepstow, Gwent. T: Chepstow 2091. Club: Cavalry and Guards.
See also Baron Raglan.

HILL, (Eliot) Michael; First Junior Prosecuting Counsel to the Crown, Central Criminal Court, since 1975; a Recorder of the Crown Court, since 1977; b 22 May 1935; s of Cecil Charles Hill and Rebecca Betty Hill; m 1965, Kathleen Irene (née Hordern); one s two d. Educ: Bancroft's Sch., Essex; Brasenose Coll., Oxford. Called to the Bar, Gray's Inn, 1958. South-Eastern Circuit. Second Prosecuting Counsel to Crown, Inner London Sessions, 1969, First Pros. Counsel to Crown, 1971; Fourth Jun. Pros. Counsel to Crown, Central Criminal Court, 1974, Third Jun. Pros. Counsel to Crown, 1974. Sec., Criminal Bar Assoc., 1973-75. Recreations: family, friends, riding, fishing and just living. Address: (chambers) 3 Temple Gardens, Temple, EC4Y 9AU. T: 01-353 1662.

HILL, Dame Elizabeth (Mary), DBE 1976; Emeritus Professor of Slavonic Studies, Cambridge; b 24 Oct. 1900. Educ: University and King's Colls, London. BA London 1924, PhD London 1928; MA Cantab 1937. War of 1939-45: Slavonic specialist, Min. of Information. University Lecturer in Slavonic, 1936-48; Prof. of Slavonic Studies, Univ. of Cambridge, 1948-68; Andrew Mellon Prof. of Slavic Languages and Literatures, Pittsburgh Univ., 1968-70. Fellow of University Coll., London; Fellow, Girton Coll., Cambridge. Address: 10 Croft Gardens, Cambridge.

HILL, Air Cdre Dame Felicity (Barbara), DBE 1966 (OBE 1954); Director of the Women's Royal Air Force, 1966-69; b 12 Dec. 1915; d of late Edwin Frederick Hill and late Mrs Frances Ada Barbara Hill (née Cocke). Educ: St Margaret's Sch., Folkestone. Joined WAAF, 1939; commnd, 1940; served in: UK, 1939-46; Germany, 1946-47; Far East Air Force, 1949-51; other appts included Inspector of WRAF, 1956-59; OC, RAF Hawkinge, 1959-60; OC RAF Spitalgate, 1960-62; Dep. Dir, 1962-65. Hon. ADC to the Queen, 1966-69. Address: Worcester Cottage, Mews Lane, Winchester, Hants. Club: Royal Air Force.

HILL, Sir Francis; see Hill, Sir J. W. F.

HILL, Sir (George) Cyril Rowley, 8th Bt cr 1779 of Brook Hall, Londonderry; journalist; b 18 Dec. 1890; o s of Sir George Rowley Hill, 7th Bt, and Alice Estelle Harley (d 1940), d of Edward Bacon, Eywood, Kington, Herefordshire; S father, 1954; m 1919, Edith Muriel, d of W. O. Thomas, Oakhurst, Liverpool, and Bryn Glas, Mold, North Wales. Educ: St Cyprian's, Eastbourne; Wellington Coll., and abroad. Heir: cousin George Alfred Rowley Hill [b 11 Oct. 1899; m 1st, 1924 (marr. diss. 1938); one s; 2nd, 1938; one s one d]. Address: 100a Leighton Avenue, Leigh-on-Sea, Essex. T: Southend-on-Sea 78046.

HILL, George Geoffrey David, CMG 1971; late Assistant Secretary, Department of the Environment (Head of International Transport Division, Ministry of Transport, 1964); b 15 Aug. 1911; o s of late William George Hill, JP; m 1935, Elisabeth Wilhelmina (née Leuwer); one d. Educ: Manchester Grammar Sch.; Gonville and Caius Coll., Cambridge (BA (Hons)). Entered Ministry of Transport as Asst Principal, 1934; Principal, 1941; Asst Sec., 1954; retired 1972. Recreations: bridge, languages. Address: 125 Ember Lane, Esher, Surrey. T: 01-398 1851.

HILL, George Raymond, GCA, FCIT, FHCIMA; Director, Bass Charrington Ltd; Chairman, Crest Hotels Ltd; b 25 Sept. 1925; s of George Mark and Jill Hill; m 1948, Sophie (née Gilbert); two d. Educ: St Dunstan's Coll., London. Royal Marines, 1943-46 (Lieut). Distillers Co. Ltd (Industrial Group), 1952-66; BP Chemicals Ltd, 1967-69; British Transport Hotels Ltd: Chief

Exec., 1970-76; Chm., 1974-76. Member Boards: British Railways (Scottish), and British Rail Hovercraft Ltd, 1972-76; Member: Hotel and Catering Industry Trng Bd; Civil Service Final Selection Bd; Vice-Chm. Bd, British Hotels Restaurants and Caterers Assoc. *Recreations:* music, theatre, works of art, country life. *Address:* 23 Sheffield Terrace, W8. *T:* 01-727 3986; The Paddocks, Upper Chedworth, Glos. *Club:* Honourable Artillery Company.

HILL, Gladys, MA, MD; FRCS, FRCOG; retired as Obstetrician and Gynæcologist, Royal Free Hospital (1940-59); *b* 28 Sept. 1894; *d* of late Arthur Griffiths Hill and Caroline Sutton Hill. *Educ:* Cheltenham Ladies' Coll.; Somerville Coll., Oxford; Royal Free Hosp. Med. Sch. MA Oxon, MD, BS London, FRCS 1936; FRCOG 1943. *Publications:* contribs to medical journals. *Recreations:* architecture, amateur dramatics, reading. *Address:* The Captain's Cottage, Bishops Lydeard, near Taunton, Som. *T:* Bishops Lydeard 432533.

HILL, Harold G.; *see* Gardiner-Hill.

HILL, Rt. Rev. Henry Gordon; *see* Ontario, Bishop of.

HILL, Sir Ian (George Wilson), Kt 1966; CBE 1945; TD; LLD; FRSE; MB; FRCPE; FRCP; Hon. Physician to HM The Queen in Scotland, 1956-70; Professor of Medicine, University of Dundee (formerly University of St Andrews), 1950-69, now Professor Emeritus; *b* 7 Sept. 1904; *s* of late A. W. Hill, JP, and of Mrs J. M. Hill, Edinburgh; *m* 1st, 1933, Audrey (*d* 1966), 2nd *d* of late G. W. Lavender, Stoke-on-Trent; one *s* one *d*; 2nd, 1968, Anna, *o d* of late M. W. Hill. *Educ:* George Watson's Coll., Edinburgh; Universities of Edinburgh, Michigan and Vienna. MB, ChB (Hons), Edinburgh, 1928; FRCPE 1933; FRCP 1956; Ettles Scholar, Allan Fellow, Shaw-Macfie-Lang Fellow, etc, Univ. of Edinburgh; Rockefeller Travelling Fellow, 1932-33; Lecturer in Medicine, University of Aberdeen, 1933-37; Lectr in Therapeutics, University of Edinburgh, 1937-49; Asst Physician, Edinburgh Royal Infirmary, 1938-50; Physician, Deaconess Hosp., Edinburgh, 1946-50. Served War of 1939-45, Officer i/c Med. Div., Mil. Hosps in UK, MEF and India, 1939-44; Consulting Physician, XIVth Army, Burma and ALFSEA, 1944-45; Col, Royal Army Medical Corps (TARO) retd; Hon. Col 2nd Scottish Gen. Hosp., 1947-58; Examr in Med., Univs Edinburgh, Glasgow, Birmingham, E Africa, Leeds, Singapore, Hong Kong; Vis. Prof. of Medicine: McGill Univ., 1967; Univ. of Teheran, 1970-71; Vis. Consultant in Medicine, Hong Kong, Malaya, Borneo, etc, 1956 and 1961; Hon. Consulting Physician, Scottish Comd (Army), 1965-70. Dean, Med. Faculty, Haile Selassie I Univ., Ethiopia, 1971-73. Lectures: Gibson, RCPE, 1949; Patel, Bombay, 1961; Walker, RCP and S Glasgow, 1962; Centennial, Univ. of Illinois, 1967; Carey Coombs, Univ. of Bristol, 1968; Wilson Meml, Univ. of Michigan, 1968. Former Senior Pres. Royal Medical Soc., Edinburgh; Pres., RCPE, 1963-66; Hon. Member: British Cardiac Soc. (Chm. 1962); Assoc. of Physicians of Great Britain and Ireland (Pres. 1962); Scottish Soc. of Physicians (Pres., 1967). Hon. Member: Cardiac and Endocrinological Socs of India; Cardiac Soc. of Hong Kong; Acad. Med., Singapore, 1966; Cardiological Soc., Colombia, 1968. Hon. FRACP 1966; Hon. FACP 1967. Hon. LLD Dundee, 1970. *Publications:* various contribs to scientific and medical books and journals, principally on cardiology. *Address:* Prior's Croft, 14 Nethergate, Crail KY10 3TY. *Clubs:* Flyfishers'; Crail Golfing Society.

HILL, Ian Macdonald, MS, FRCS; Consultant Thoracic Surgeon: St Bartholomew's Hospital, Lambeth, Southwark and Lewisham Area Health Authority (Teaching) (formerly SE Regional Hospital Board), since 1950; Greenwich District Health Authority, since 1976; *b* 8 June 1919; British; *m* 1944, Agnes Mary Paice; three *s* one *d*. *Educ:* Stationers' Company's Sch.; St Bartholomew's Hosp. Medical Coll. Undergrad. schols and medals, 1937-41; MB, BS (Hons) London, 1942; MRCS, LRCP 1942; FRCS 1944; MS London 1945. Demonstrator of Anatomy, St Bartholomew's, 1943; Surgical Chief Asst St Bart.'s Hosp., 1944; RAF Medical Branch, 1946; Wing Comdr i/c Surg. Div. No 1 RAF Gen. Hosp., 1947; Senior Registrar, Thoracic Surg. Unit, Guy's Hosp., 1948; Surgical Chief Asst, Brompton Hosp. and Inst. of Diseases of the Chest, 1950. Sub-Dean, St Bart's Hosp. Med. Coll., 1964-73. FRSocMed. Member: Soc. of Apothecaries; Soc. of Thoracic Surgeons; Thoracic and Cardiac Socs. Freeman of City of London. *Publications:* articles in professional jls, mainly relating to lung and cardiac surgery, 1942-61. *Recreations:* old cars, furniture, keyboard instruments; gardening and house care. *Address:* 98 Fox Lane, Palmers Green, N13 4AX. *T:* 01-886 7324; 152 Harley Street, W1N 1HH. *T:* 01-935 8868.

HILL, (Ian) Starforth, QC 1969; **His Honour Judge Starforth Hill**; a Circuit Judge, since 1974; *b* 30 Sept. 1921; *s* of late Harold Victor John Hill; *m* 1950, Bridget Mary Footner; one *s* two *d*. *Educ:* Shrewsbury Sch.; Brasenose Coll., Oxford (MA). 11th Sikh Regt, Indian Army, 1940-45, India, Africa, Italy (despatches). Called to Bar, Gray's Inn, 1949; Dep. Chm., Isle of Wight QS, 1968-71; Western Circuit; a Recorder of the Crown Court, 1972-74. *Address:* 1 Crown Office Row, Temple, EC4. *T:* 01-353 9272; Tulls Hill, Preston Candover, Hants RG25 2EW. *T:* Preston Candover 309. *Club:* Hampshire (Winchester).

HILL, Ivan Conrad, CBE 1960; Chairman: Illingworth, Morris & Co. Ltd, since 1976; Joshua Hoyle & Sons Ltd; Woolcombers Ltd; Winterbotham Strachan & Playne Ltd; Salts (Saltaire) Ltd; S. Schneider & Son Ltd; Chairman, Industrial Coal Consumers Council, since 1965; *b* 22 Jan. 1906; *s* of Wilfred Lawson Hill and Annie Jane (*née* England); *m* 1st, 1931, Alexandrina Ewart (marr. diss. 1962); four *d*; 2nd, 1963, Sheila Houghton. *Educ:* Oakham Sch.; St John's Coll., Cambridge. Exhibitioner and Open Scholar of St John's Coll. 1st cl. Hons Law Tripos Cantab 1928. Apptd Jt Man. Dir, Kelsall & Kemp Ltd, 1933. Chm. Wool Industries Research Assoc., 1950-53; Mem. Monopolies and Restrictive Practices Commn, and Monopolies Commn, 1951-63; Chm. British Rayon Research Assoc., 1956-61; Chairman, Samuel Courtauld & Co. Ltd, 1962-66. Liveryman, Weavers' Company, 1938-. *Recreations:* travel, architecture, sport. *Address:* Rookwoods, Sible Hedingham, Essex. *T:* Hedingham 60266.

HILL, Brig. James; *see* Hill, Brig. S. J. L.

HILL, James; *see* Hill, S. J. A.

HILL, Sir James Frederick, 4th Bt *cr* 1917; Chairman, Sir James Hill & Sons Ltd; Director, Huddersfield & Bradford Building Society; *b* 5 Dec. 1943; *s* of Sir James Hill, 3rd Bt and of Marjory, *d* of late Frank Croft; *S* father, 1976; *m* 1966, Sandra Elizabeth, *o d* of J. C. Ingram; one *s* three *d*. *Heir:* *s* James Laurence Ingram Hill, *b* 22 Sept. 1973. *Address:* Brookleigh, Burley Road, Menston, near Ilkley, West Yorks.

HILL, Sir (James William) Francis, Kt 1958; CBE 1954; DL; solicitor; company director; *b* 15 Sept. 1899; *s* of James Hill and Millicent (*née* Blinkhorn). *Educ:* City Sch., Lincoln; Trinity Coll., Cambridge. MA 1925, LLM 1926, LittD 1950 (Cambridge). 2nd Lieut KRRC, 1918. Admitted Solicitor, 1926. Senior partner Andrew and Co., Lincoln, Solicitors. Mem. Lincoln City Council, 1932-74 (Mayor, 1945-46); Hon. Freeman, Lincoln, 1961; Mem. Nottingham University Coll. Council, 1938-48; Pres. Nottingham Univ. Council, 1948-68; Pro-Chancellor, 1959-72; Chancellor, 1972-. Mem., Royal Commn on Local Govt in England, 1966-69. Chairman: Assoc. of Municipal Corporations, 1957-66; Municipal Mutual Insurance Ltd, 1972-; formerly Governor, Administrative Staff Coll.; President: European Conf. of Local Authorities, Strasbourg, 1966-68; International Union of Local Authorities, The Hague, 1967-71; Member: Historic Buildings Council, 1968-71; Adv. Board for Redundant Churches, 1969-75. Chm. of Governors: Lincoln Christ's Hosp. Foundation, Girls' High Sch., and Lincoln Sch., 1935-66. Hon. LLD Nottingham and Birmingham; Hon. DLitt Leicester. FSA, FRHistS (Hon. Vice Pres.). Contested (L) Peterborough, 1929, (C) Lincoln, 1950. DL Lincoln, 1974. *Publications:* Medieval Lincoln, 1948; Tudor and Stuart Lincoln, 1956; Georgian Lincoln, 1966; Victorian Lincoln, 1974; (ed) Banks Family Papers, 1952; contribs to historical and local govt jls. *Recreation:* local history. *Address:* The Priory, Lincoln. *T:* Lincoln 25759. *Club:* United Oxford & Cambridge University.

HILL, James William Thomas, (Jimmy); Managing Director, Jimmy Hill Ltd, since 1972; Soccer analyst to the BBC, since 1973; *m* 1st, 1950, Gloria Mary (marr. diss. 1961); two *s* one *d*; 2nd, 1962, Heather Christine; one *s* one *d*. *Educ:* Henry Thornton School, Clapham. Player, Brentford FC, 1949-52, Fulham FC, 1952-61; Gen. Manager, Coventry City FC, 1961-67, Managing Director, 1975-. London Weekend Television: Head of Sport, 1967-72; Controller of Press, Promotion and Publicity, 1971-72; Deputy Controller, Programmes, 1972-73. Mem., Sports Council, 1971-. Hon. Chm., The Professional Footballers Assoc., 1957-61. *Publications:* Striking for Soccer, 1961; Improve your Soccer, 1964. *Recreations:* golf, riding, tennis, soccer, bridge. *Address:* Jimmy Hill Ltd, 35 Ossington Street, W2 4LY. *Clubs:* The Sportsman, Queen's.

HILL, Jimmy; *see* Hill, James William Thomas.

HILL, John; City Treasurer of Liverpool since 1974; *b* 28 April 1922; *s* of William Hallett Hill and Emily Hill (*née* Massey); *m*

1952, Hilda Mary Barratt; one *s*. *Educ:* Merchant Taylors' Sch., Crosby; Liverpool Univ. (BCom); Inst. of Public Finance and Accountancy, 1954. City Treasury, Liverpool, 1949; apptd Asst City Treasurer, 1962. *Recreation:* music. *Address:* 325 Northway, Lydiate, Merseyside L31 0BW. *T:* 051-526 3699.

HILL, Sir (John) Denis (Nelson), Kt 1966; MB, BS; FRCP; DPM; Professor of Psychiatry, Institute of Psychiatry, since 1966; *b* 5 Oct. 1913; *s* of late Lieut-Col John Arthur Hill, Orleton Manor, near Ludlow; *m* 1st, 1938, Phoebe Elizabeth Herschel, *d* of Lieut-Col H. H. Wade; one *s* one *d*; 2nd, 1962, Lorna, *d* of J. F. Wheelan; one *s* one *d*. *Educ:* Shrewsbury Sch.; St Thomas' Hosp., London. Chief Asst, Dept Psychol Medicine, St Thomas' Hosp., 1938-44; Psychiatric Specialist, Emergency Medical Service, 1939-46; Physician and Lecturer in Psychological Medicine, King's Coll. Hosp., London, 1947-60; Senior Lecturer, Institute of Psychiatry, Maudsley Hosp., London, 1948-60; Hon. Physician, Maudsley Hosp., 1948-60; Prof. of Psychiatry, Middlesex Hosp. Medical Sch., London, 1961-66. Member: MRC, 1956-60; (Crown Representative) GMC, 1961-; Mem., Central Health Service Council, 1961-67; Pres. Psychiatry Sect., RSM, 1964-65. Lectures: Adolf Meyer, APA, 1968; Herman Goldman, NY Med. Coll., 1968; Vickers, MHRF, 1972; Maudsley, RCPsych, 1972. Rock Carling Fellow, 1969. *Publications:* Editor: Electro-encephalography: a symposium, 1950; contribs to textbooks on medical subjects and to scientific journals. *Address:* 71 Cottenham Park Road, Wimbledon, SW20; Orleton Manor, near Ludlow, Salop. *Club:* Athenæum.

HILL, John Edward Bernard; farming in Suffolk since 1946; *b* 13 Nov. 1912; *o s* of late Capt. Robert William Hill, Cambs Regt, and Marjorie Jane Lloyd-Jones, *d* of Edward Scott Miller; *m* 1944, Edith Laurd, widow of Comdr R. A. E. Luard, RNVR, and 5th *d* of late John Maxwell, Cove, Dunbartonshire; one adopted *d*. *Educ:* Charterhouse; Merton Coll., Oxford (MA). Various journeys; Middle East, Far East, India, USA, 1935-37; Far East, 1956-57; USA, 1958. Called to Bar, Inner Temple (Certificate of Honour), 1938. RA (TA), 1939; Air Observation Post Pilot, 1942; War Office, 1942; 651 (Air OP) RAF, Tunisia, 1942; wounded, 1943; invalided out, 1945. MP (C) South Norfolk, Jan. 1955-Feb. 1974; Mem. Parliamentary delegns: W Germany and Berlin, 1959; Ghana, 1965; IPU Conf., Teheran, 1966; CPA Conf., Uganda, 1967; Bulgaria, 1970; Council of Europe and WEU, 1970-72; Mem., European Parlt, 1973-74; Chm., Cons. Educn Cttee, 1971-73; Member: Select Cttee on Agriculture, 1967-69; Select Cttee on Procedure, 1970-71; Asst Govt Whip, 1959-60; a Lord Comr of the Treasury, 1960-64. Mem. East Suffolk and Norfolk River Board, 1952-62. Member: Governing Body, Charterhouse Sch., 1958; Langley Sch., Norfolk, 1962-77; GBA Cttee, 1966-; Council, Univ. of East Anglia, 1975-. *Recreations:* association football (Blue; Sec., OUAFC 1934); shooting, concerts, picture galleries. *Address:* Watermill Farm, Wenhaston, Halesworth, Suffolk. *T:* Blythburgh 207. *Club:* Garrick.

HILL, (John Edward) Christopher, FBA 1966; Master of Balliol College, Oxford, 1965-Sept. 1978; *b* 6 Feb. 1912; *m* 1st, 1944, Inez Waugh; one *d*; 2nd, 1956, Bridget Irene Sutton; one *s* one *d* (and one *d* decd). *Educ:* St Peter's Sch., York; Balliol Coll., Oxford. Fellow of All Souls Coll., Oxford, 1934; Asst Lectr, University Coll., Cardiff, 1936; Fellow and Tutor in Modern History, Balliol Coll., Oxford, 1938. Private in Field Security Police, commissioned Oxford and Bucks Light Inf., 1940, Major; seconded to Foreign Office, 1943. Returned to Balliol, 1945; University Lectr in 16th- and 17th-century history, 1959; Ford's Lectr, 1962. DLitt Oxford, 1965; Hon. DLitt: Hull, 1966; E Anglia, 1968; Hon. LittD Sheffield, 1967. For. Hon. Mem., Amer. Acad. of Sciences, 1973. *Publications:* The English Revolution 1640, 1940; (under name K. E. Holme) Two Commonwealths, 1945; Lenin and the Russian Revolution, 1947; The Good Old Cause (ed jointly with E. Dell), 1949; Economic Problems of the Church, 1956; Puritanism and Revolution, 1958; Oliver Cromwell, 1958; The Century of Revolution, 1961; Society and Puritanism in Pre-Revolutionary England, 1964; Intellectual Origins of the English Revolution, 1965; Reformation to Industrial Revolution, 1967; God's Englishman, 1970; Antichrist in 17th Century England, 1971; The World Turned Upside Down, 1972; ed, G. Winstanley, The Law of Freedom and other writings, 1973; Change and Continuity in Seventeenth Century England, 1975; Milton and the English Revolution, 1977; articles in learned journals, etc. *Address:* 21 Northmoor Road, Oxford. *T:* Oxford 58544.

HILL, John Frederick Rowland, CMG 1955; *b* 20 April 1905; *s* of Judge William Henry Hill; *m* 1930, Phyllys Esmé (*née* Fryer); one *s* two *d*. *Educ:* Pinewood Sch., Farnborough; Marlborough Coll.; Lincoln Coll., Oxford. BA Oxon, Hon. Sch.

Jurisprudence, 1927; Cadet Colonial Civil Service, Tanganyika, 1928; Asst District Officer, 1930; District Officer, 1940; Dep. Provincial Comr, 1947; Provincial Comr, 1948; Sen. Provincial Comr, 1950; Mem. for Communications, Works and Development Planning, Tanganyika Govt, 1951-56; Chm., Tanganyika Broadcasting Corp. and Dir of Broadcasting, 1956-57; Govt Liaison Officer, Freeport, Bahamas, 1957-58; Supervisor of Elections, Zanzibar, 1959-60. *Recreation:* golf. *Address:* Flat 3, 29 Powhiri Avenue, Whangarei, New Zealand. *Club:* Royal Commonwealth Society.

HILL, John Gibson, CB 1973; *b* 3 March 1910; *s* of Thomas Hill, Master Mariner, Islandmagee, Co. Antrim, and Anna Bella (*née* McMurtry); *m* 1944, Marian Fyffe Wilson, Belfast; one *s* one *d*. *Educ:* Royal Belfast Academical Instn; QUB (BA). Solicitor, 1934. Entered Civil Service, NI, 1935, Legal Asst, Min. of Finance; Dep. Principal, Assistance Bd, 1942; Min. of Home Affairs, NI: Dep. Principal, 1944; Principal, 1953; Asst Sec., 1960; Permanent Sec., 1970-73. *Recreations:* watching Rugby, yachting. *Address:* 7 York Avenue, Whitehead, Co. Antrim, Northern Ireland. *T:* Whitehead 3250. *Clubs:* Instonians Rugby; County Antrim Yacht.

HILL, Sir John McGregor, Kt 1969; BSc, PhD, FInstP; Chairman: United Kingdom Atomic Energy Authority since 1967; British Nuclear Fuels Ltd, since 1971; Radiochemical Centre Ltd, since 1975; *b* 21 Feb. 1921; *s* of John Campbell Hill and Margaret Elizabeth Park; *m* 1947, Nora Eileen Hellett; two *s* one *d*. *Educ:* King's Coll., London; St John's Coll., Cambridge. Flt Lieut, RAF, 1941. Cavendish Laboratory, Cambridge, 1946; Lecturer, London Univ., 1948. Joined UKAEA, 1950 (Mem. for Production, 1964-67). Member: Advisory Council on Technology, 1968-70; Nuclear Power Adv. Bd, 1973-; Energy Commn, 1977-. *Recreation:* golf. *Address:* Dominic House, Sudbrook Lane, Petersham, Surrey. *T:* 01-940 7221. *Club:* East India, Devonshire, Sports and Public Schools.

HILL, Sir John (Maxwell), Kt 1974; CBE 1969; DFC 1945; QPM; Chief Inspector of Constabulary, Home Office, 1972-75; *b* 25 March 1914; *s* of late L. S. M. Hill, Civil Servant, Plymouth; *m* 1939, Marjorie Louisa, *d* of late John Oliver Reynolds, Aylesbury, Bucks; one *s* one *d*. *Educ:* Plymouth Coll. Metropolitan Police Coll., Hendon, 1938-39; joined Metropolitan Police, 1933. Served with RAF, 1942-45. Dep. Comdr, New Scotland Yard, 1959; Metropolitan Police: Comdr, No 3 District, 1963, Comdr, No 1 District, 1964; HM Inspector of Constabulary, 1965; Asst Comr (Administration and Operations), 1966-68; Asst Comr (Personnel and Training), 1968-71; Dep. Comr, 1971-72. *Recreations:* walking, golf. *Address:* 23 Beacon Way, Banstead, Surrey. *T:* Burgh Heath 52771.

HILL, Michael; see Hill, E. M.

HILL, Michael William, CChem; Director, The British Library, Science Reference Library, since 1973; *b* 1928; *o s* of late Geoffrey William Hill, Ross on Wye and Torquay; *m* 1st, 1957, Elma Jack Forrest (*d* 1967); one *s* one *d*; 2nd, 1969, Barbara Joy Youngman. *Educ:* Nottingham High Sch.; Lincoln Coll., Oxford (BSc, MA). MRIC 1953; CChem. Research Chemist, Laporte Chemicals Ltd, 1953-56; Morgan Crucible Group: Laboratory Head, 1956; Asst Process Control Manager, 1958; Group Technical Editor, 1963. Asst Keeper, British Museum, 1964. Dep. Librarian, Patent Office Library, 1965; Keeper, Nat. Ref. Library of Science and Invention, 1968-73. Member: Exec. Cttee, Nat. Central Library, 1971-74; Council, Aslib, 1971-; EEC/CIDST Working Parties on Patent documentation, 1973-, and on Information for Industry, 1975-; Board, UK Chemical Inf. Service; Board, Chemical Soc. Library. Vice-Pres., IATUL, 1976. *Publications:* various articles in technological jls. *Address:* 137 Burdon Lane, Cheam, Surrey SM2 7DB. *T:* 01-642 2418. *Club:* United Oxford & Cambridge University.

HILL, Norman Hammond, MD (London), MRCP; Consulting Physician: Belgrave Hospital for Children; Metropolitan and Wembley Hospitals; *b* 10 March 1893; *s* of Lewis Gordon Hill and Amy Caroline Hammond; *m* 1938, Suzanne Mary, *y d* of Rev. H. S. Rees, Christchurch, Mon. *Educ:* Bradford Grammar Sch.; St Bartholomew's Hosp. MRCS, LRCP 1915. Served in Army, 1915-19, Capt. RAMC (TF); held appointment of House Surgeon, Chief Asst to a Medical Unit, and Casualty Physician St Bartholomew's Hosp. and House Physician and Senior Resident Medical Officer Metropolitan Hosp. *Publications:* articles on medical subjects to Lancet, British Medical Journal, Clinical Journal, and Medical Press and Circular. *Recreations:* golf, photography. *Address:* 22 Acacia Road, NW8. *T:* 01-722 7466.

HILL, Robert, ScD Cantab 1942; FRS 1946; biochemist; Member of Scientific Staff of Agricultural Research Council, 1943-66; *b* 2 April 1899; *s* of Joseph Alfred Hill and Clara Maud Jackson; *m* 1935, Amy Priscilla, *d* of Edgar Worthington; two *s* two *d*. *Educ:* Bedales Sch.; Emmanuel Coll., Cambridge (Scholar). Served European War, 1914-18: RE pioneer Anti-gas Dept, 1917-18. Emmanuel Coll., Cambridge, 1919-22; Senior Studentship (Exhibn of 1851), 1927; Beit Memorial Research Fellow, 1929; Senior Beit Memorial Research Fellow, 1935; Hon. Fellow of Emmanuel Coll., 1963. Royal Medal, Royal Society, 1963; 1st Award for photosynthesis, Soc. of American Plant Physiologists, 1963; Charles E. Kettering Research Award, 1963; Hon. Member: Amer. Soc. of Biological Chemists, 1964; Comité Internat. de Photobiologie, 1968; American Acad. Arts and Sciences, 1971; For. Associate, Nat. Acad. of Sciences, 1975; For. Mem., Accad. Nazionale dei Lincei, 1975. *Publication:* (with C. P. Whittingham) Photosynthesis, 1955. *Recreations:* growing plants and dyeing with traditional plant dyes, water-colour painting. *Address:* Department of Biochemistry, Tennis Court Road, Cambridge.

HILL, Sir Robert E.; *see* Erskine-Hill.

HILL, Roderick; *see* Hill, Colonel E. R.

HILL, Prof. Rodney, FRS 1961; PhD; ScD; Professor of Mechanics of Solids, University of Cambridge, since 1972 (Reader, 1969-72); Fellow, Gonville and Caius College, since 1972; *b* 11 June 1921; *o s* of Harold Harrison Hill, Leeds; *m* 1946, Jeanne Kathlyn, *yr d* of C. P. Wickens, Gidea Park; one *d*. *Educ:* Leeds Grammar Sch.; Pembroke Coll., Cambridge. MA, PhD, ScD Cambridge. Armament Research Dept, 1943-46; Cavendish Laboratory, Cambridge, 1946-48; British Iron and Steel Research Assoc., 1948-50; University of Bristol: Research Fellow, 1950-53, Reader, 1953; Univ. of Nottingham: Prof. of Applied Mathematics, 1953-62; Professorial Research Fellow, 1962-63; Berkeley Bye-Fellow, Gonville and Caius Coll., Cambridge, 1963-69. Hon. DSc Manchester, 1976. Editor, Jl of Mechanics and Physics of Solids, 1952-68. *Publications:* Mathematical Theory of Plasticity, 1950; Principles of Dynamics, 1964. *Address:* Dept of Applied Mathematics and Theoretical Physics, Cambridge.

HILL, (Stanley) James (Allen); company director; *b* 21 Dec. 1926; *s* of James and Florence Cynthia Hill; *m* 1958, Ruby Evelyn Ralph; two *s* three *d*. *Educ:* Regents Park Sch., Southampton; Southampton Univ.; North Wales Naval Training Coll. Former Pilot. Mem., Southampton City Council, 1966-70; Mem. Cttee, Southampton Conservative and Ratepayers Fedn. MP (C) Southampton Test, 1970-Sept. 1974; Prospective Parly Cand. (C) Southampton Test, 1975-; Sec., Cons. Parly Cttee on Housing and Construction, 1971-73. Mem., British Delegn to European Parlt, Strasbourg, and Chm., Regional Policy and Transport Cttee, 1973-75; Mem. Hon. Cttee for Europe Day, Council of Europe. *Recreations:* private aviation, farming. *Address:* 51 Oakley Street, SW3; Gunsfield Lodge, Melchet Park, Plaitford, Hants. *Clubs:* St Stephen's, British Light Aviation; Royal Southampton Yacht.

HILL, Brig. (Stanley) James (Ledger), DSO 1942, and Bars, 1944, 1945; MC 1940; Vice-Chairman, Powell Duffryn Ltd, 1970-76 (Director, 1961-76); Chairman, Pauls & Whites Ltd, 1973-76 (Director, since 1970); Director, Lloyds Bank Ltd, since 1972; *b* 14 March 1911; *s* of late Maj.-Gen. Walter Pitts Hendy Hill, CB, CMG, DSO, West Amesbury House, Wilts; *m* 1937, Denys, *d* of late E. Hubert Gunter-Jones, MC, JP, Gloucester House, Ledbury; one *d*. *Educ:* Marlborough; RMC Sandhurst. 2nd Bn, Royal Fusiliers, 1931-35; 2nd Bn, RF, BEF, 1939; DAAG, GHQ, BEF, 1940; comd 1st Bn, Parachute Regt, N Africa landing, 1942; comd 3rd Parachute Bde, 1943-45; took part in Normandy and Rhine crossing (wounded thrice); comdr 4th Parachute Bde (TA), 1947-48. Apptd to Bd of Associated Coal & Wharf Cos Ltd, 1948; Pres., Powell Duffryn Group of Cos in Canada, 1952-58. Legion of Honour (France), 1942; Silver Star (USA), 1945; King Haakon VII Liberty Cross (Norway), 1945. *Recreations:* fishing, birdwatching. *Address:* Strouds, Weston Patrick, near Basingstoke RG25 2NY. *T:* Basingstoke 81421. *Clubs:* Boodle's, Army and Navy; Island Sailing (IoW).

HILL, Starforth; *see* Hill, Ian S.

HILL, Susan Elizabeth, (Mrs Stanley Wells); novelist and playwright; *b* 5 Feb. 1942; *d* of R. H. and late Doris Hill; *m* 1975, Dr Stanley W. Wells; one *d*. *Educ:* grammar schs in Scarborough and Coventry; King's Coll., Univ. of London. BA Hons English 1963. FRSL 1972. Full-time writer of novels, plays and short stories, 1960-; literary critic, various jls, 1963-; numerous plays for BBC, 1970-. *Publications:* The Enclosure, 1961; Do me a Favour, 1963; Gentleman and Ladies, 1969; A Change for the Better, 1969; I'm the King of the Castle, 1970; The Albatross, 1971; Strange Meeting, 1971; The Bird of Night, 1972; A Bit of Singing and Dancing, 1973; In the Springtime of the Year, 1974; The Cold Country and Other Plays for Radio, 1975. *Recreations:* music, walking in the English countryside, friends, reading, broadcasting. *Address:* 19 West Street, Stratford-upon-Avon, Warwicks.

HILL, Victor Archibald Lord, MA; *b* 3 July 1905; *o s* of W. E. Hill; *m* 1938, Jean Melicent, *e d* of Dr D. N. Seth-Smith, Bournemouth; two *s*. *Educ:* Chigwell Sch.; Queen Mary Coll., London (Open Exhibr; Univ. Schol. in Classics; 1st cl. Hons BA); Hertford Coll., Oxford (Open Schol., 1st Cl. Hon. Mods, 3rd Cl. Lit. Hum.). MA (Oxon) 1934. Asst Master, Shrewsbury Sch., 1930-40, 1946-48; Headmaster, Allhallows Sch., 1948-65; Asst Master: Blundell's, 1965-66; Uppingham, 1966-67, 1968-69; Chigwell, 1969-70; Lectr in Classics, Exeter Univ., 1967-68. Served 1940-45, with KSLI and RA (Major). *Recreations:* music, travel, golf. *Address:* Beggars' Roost, Morchard Bishop, near Crediton, Devon. *T:* Morchard Bishop 315. *Club:* National Liberal.

HILL-NORTON, Admiral of the Fleet Sir Peter (John), GCB 1970 (KCB 1967; CB 1964); Chairman, Military Committee of NATO, 1974-77; *b* 8 Feb. 1915; *s* of Capt. M. J. Norton and Mrs M. B. Norton; *m* 1936, Margaret Eileen Linstow; one *s* one *d*. *Educ:* RNC Dartmouth. Went to sea, 1932; commnd, 1936; specialised in Gunnery, 1939; War of 1939-45: Arctic Convoys; NW Approaches; Admiralty Naval Staff. Comdr 1948; Capt. 1952; Naval Attaché, Argentine, Uruguay, Paraguay, 1953-55; comd HMS Decoy, 1956-57; comd HMS Ark Royal, 1959-61; Asst Chief of Naval Staff, 1962-64; Flag Officer, Second-in-Command, Far East Fleet, 1964-66; Dep. Chief of the Defence Staff (Personnel and Logistics), 1966; Second Sea Lord and Chief of Naval Personnel, Jan.-Aug. 1967; Vice-Chief of Naval Staff, 1967-68; C-in-C Far East, 1969-70; Chief of the Naval Staff and First Sea Lord, 1970-71; Chief of the Defence Staff, 1971-73. Liveryman, Shipwrights' Co., 1973; Freeman, City of London 1973. *Recreations:* golf, shooting, water ski-ing. *Address:* King's Mill House, South Nutfield, Surrey. *T:* Nutfield Ridge 3309. *Clubs:* Royal Thames Yacht, Royal Navy of 1765.

HILL-SMITH, Derek Edward, VRD 1958; His Honour Judge Hill-Smith; a Circuit Judge, since 1972; *b* 21 Oct. 1922; *s* of Charles Hill-Smith and Ivy (*née* Downs); *m* 1950, Marjorie Joanna, *d* of His Honour Montague Berryman, QC; one *s* one *d*. *Educ:* Sherborne; Trinity Coll., Oxford (MA). RNVR, 1942-46; Lt-Comdr RNR. Trinity Coll., Oxford, 1941-42 and 1946-47 (MA, Classics and Modern Greats); BEA, 1947-48; business, 1948-50; teaching, 1950-54; called to Bar, Inner Temple, 1954; Dep. Chm., Kent QS, 1970; Recorder, 1972. *Publications:* contrib. Law Guardian. *Recreations:* yacht-racing, the theatre, food and wine. *Address:* c/o National Westminster Bank, Grosvenor House, Park Lane, W1. *Clubs:* Garrick; Bar Yacht; Bar Lawn Tennis.

HILL-TREVOR, family name of **Baron Trevor.**

HILL-WOOD, Sir David (Basil), 3rd Bt *cr* 1921; stockbroker since 1956; Director, Guinness Mahon & Co., since 1977; former Director, Capel-Cure Myers Ltd; *b* 12 Nov. 1926; *s* of Sir Basil Samuel Hill Hill-Wood, 2nd Bt, and Hon. Joan Louisa Brand, *e d* of 3rd Viscount Hampden; *S* father, 1954; *m* 1970, Jennifer, 2nd *d* of late Peter McKenzie Strang, Adelaide; two *s* one *d*. *Educ:* Eton. Served in Army (Grenadier Guards), 1945-48. *Recreations:* cricket, shooting. *Heir:* *s* Samuel Thomas Hill-Wood, *b* 24 Aug. 1971. *Address:* Dacre Farm, Farley Hill, Reading, Berks. *T:* Eversley 733185; 58 Catheart Road, SW10. *T:* 01-352 0389. *Clubs:* White's; Melbourne (Melbourne).

HILL-WOOD, Sir Wilfred (William Hill), KCVO 1976; CBE 1946; Member, Directors' Advisory Cttee, Morgan, Grenfell & Co. Ltd, since 1967 (Managing Director, 1939-67); *b* 8 Sept. 1901; 2nd *s* of Sir Samuel Hill Hill-Wood, 1st Bt; *m* 1947, Diana Marian, *widow* of Wing Comdr Harry Manners Mellor, MVO, RAF, and *d* of Major Hugh Wyld. *Educ:* Eton; Trinity Coll., Cambridge. Director: Anglo-American Securities Corp. Ltd; North Atlantic Securities Corp. Ltd. *Address:* The House of Urrard, Killiecrankie, Perthshire; Flat 4, Cornwall Mansions, 33 Kensington Court, W8. *Club:* White's.

HILLABY, John; writer, naturalist and traveller; *b* 24 July 1917; *er s* of late Albert Ewart Hillaby, Pontefract, and Mabel Colyer; *m* 1st, 1940, Eleanor Riley, Leeds (marr. diss.); two *d*; 2nd, 1966, Thelma Gordon (*d* 1972), child analyst, *d* of Bernard Gordon, Montreal, and Jessie Kiewitsky. *Educ:* Leeds;

Woodhouse Grove, Yorkshire. Served RA, War of 1939-45. Local journalism up to 1939; magazine contributor and broadcaster, 1944-; Zoological Corresp., Manchester Guardian, 1949; European science writer, New York Times, 1951; biological consultant, New Scientist, 1953. Formerly a dir, Universities Fedn for Animal Welfare; Founder Pres., Backpackers Club. Has travelled on foot through parts of boreal Canada, Appalachian Trail, USA, Congo, traversed Ituri Forest and Mountains of the Moon (Ruwenzori), Sudan, Tanzania; three months foot safari with camels to Lake Rudolf, Kenya, and walked from Lands End to John o'Groats and from The Hague to Nice via the Alps. Woodward Lectr, Yale, 1973. TV series include: Hillaby Walks, Globetrotter, etc. FZS (scientific). *Publications:* Within The Streams, 1949; Nature and Man, 1960; Journey to the Jade Sea, 1964; Journey Through Britain, 1968; Journey Through Europe, 1972; Journey through Love, 1976. *Recreations:* talking, reading, music, walking alone; observing peculiarities of man, beast, fowl and flora. *Address:* 85 Cholmley Gardens, NW6. *T:* 01-435 4626; Rosedale-by-Pickering, North Yorkshire. *Club:* Savage.

HILLARD, His Honour Richard Arthur Loraine, MBE 1946; a Circuit Judge (formerly a County Court Judge), 1956-72; *b* 1906; *e s* of Frederick Arthur Hillard, Puriton Manor, Bridgwater, Som; *m* 1st, 1936, Nancy Alford (*d* 1964), *d* of Dr Alford Andrews, Cambridge; one *s* one *d*; 2nd, 1969, Monica Constance, *er d* of John Healey Carus, Darwen, and *widow* of Paul Hillard; one step *s* one step *d*. *Educ:* Worcester Royal Grammar Sch.; Christ Church, Oxford. Barrister, Gray's Inn, 1931; South-Eastern circuit. Served, 1940-45: Military Dept, Judge Advocate General's Office, 1941-45, Lt-Col 1945. Asst Reader and Lecturer, Council of Legal Education, 1945-55. Chm. Agricultural Land Tribunal, South Eastern Province, 1955. *Recreation:* gardening. *Address:* Oakchurch House, Staunton-on-Wye, Hereford. *T:* Moccas 345. *Club:* United Oxford & Cambridge University.

HILLARY, Sir Edmund, KBE 1953; Director, Field Educational Enterprises of Australasia Pty Ltd; Consultant to Sears Roebuck & Co., Chicago, on camping and outdoor equipment; author; lecturer; mountaineer; *b* 20 July 1919; *s* of Percival Augustus Hillary and Gertrude Hillary (*née* Clark); *m* 1953, Louise Rose (*d* 1975); one *s* one *d* (and one *d* decd). *Educ:* Auckland Grammar Sch., Auckland, New Zealand. Apiarist, 1936-43. RNZAF, navigator on Catalina flying boats in Pacific Area, 1944-45. Apiarist (in partnership with brother W. F. Hillary), 1951-70. Himalayan Expeditions: NZ Gawhal Expedition, 1951; British Everest Reconnaissance, 1951; British Cho Oyu Expedition, 1952; Everest Expedition, 1953; with Sherpa Tenzing reached summit of Mount Everest, May 1953 (KBE). Leader of NZ Alpine Club Expedition to Barun Valley, East of Everest, 1954. Appointed, 1955, leader of New Zealand Transantarctic Expedition; completed overland journey to South Pole, Jan. 1958. Expeditions in Everest region, 1960-61, 1963, 1964, 1965; built first hosp. for Sherpas in Everest Area, with public subscription and NZ doctor, 1966; led expedition to Antarctic for geological and mountaineering purposes incl. first ascent of Mt Herschel, 1967; expedition to E Nepal (explored Himalayan rivers with two jet boats; first ascent of 180 miles of Sun Kosi river from Indian border to Katmandu), 1968. Pres., New Zealand Volunteer Service Abroad, 1963-. Hon. LLD: Univ. of Victoria, BC, Canada, 1969; Victoria Univ., Wellington, NZ, 1970. Hubbard Medal (US), 1954; Star of Nepal 1st Class; US Gold Cullum Geographical Medal, 1954; Founder's Gold Medal, Royal Geographical Society, 1958; Polar Medal, 1958. *Publications:* High Adventure; East of Everest, 1956 (with George Lowe); The Crossing of Antarctica, 1958 (with Sir Vivian Fuchs); No Latitude for Error, 1961; High in the Thin Cold Air, 1963 (with Desmond Doig); School House in the Clouds, 1965; Nothing Venture, Nothing Win (autobiog.), 1975. *Recreations:* mountaineering, ski-ing, camping. *Address:* 278a Remuera Road, Auckland, SE2, New Zealand. *Clubs:* New Zealand Alpine (Hon. Mem.; Pres. 1965-67); Hon. Mem. of many other NZ and US clubs.

HILLER, Dame Wendy, DBE 1975 (OBE 1971); actress; *b* 1912; *d* of Frank Watkin and Marie Hiller, Bramhall, Cheshire; *m* 1937, Ronald Gow; one *s* one *d*. *Educ:* Winceby House, Bexhill. Manchester Repertory Theatre; Sir Barry Jackson's tour of Evensong; Sally Hardcastle in Love on the Dole, London and New York; leading parts in Saint Joan and Pygmalion at Malvern Festival, 1936. *Plays include:* Twelfth Night (war factory tour); Cradle Song (Apollo); The First Gentleman (Savoy); Tess of the d'Urbervilles (Piccadilly); The Heiress (Biltmore, NY, and Haymarket, London); Ann Veronica (Piccadilly); Waters of the Moon (Haymarket), 1951-53; The Night of the Ball (New), 1955; Old Vic Season, 1955-56; Moon for the Misbegotten (NY), 1957; Flowering Cherry

(Haymarket), 1958; Toys in the Attic (Piccadilly), 1960; Aspern Papers (NY), 1962; The Wings of the Dove (Lyric), 1963; The Sacred Flame (Duke of York's), 1967; When We Dead Awaken (Edinburgh Festival), 1968; The Battle of Shrivings (Lyric), 1970; Crown Matrimonial (Haymarket), 1972; John Gabriel Borkman, (National), 1975; Lies! (Albery), 1975; Waters of the Moon (Chichester), 1977. *Films:* Pygmalion; Major Barbara; I Know Where I'm Going; Outcast of the Islands; Separate Tables (Academy Award); Sons and Lovers; Toys in the Attic; A Man for All Seasons; David Copperfield; Murder on the Orient Express, etc. BBC TV: When We Dead Awaken, 1968; Peer Gynt, 1972; Clochemerle, 1973. *Address:* Spindles, Beaconsfield, Bucks.

HILLERY, Dr Patrick John; Uachtarán na hÉireann (President of Ireland), since Dec. 1976; *b* Miltown Malbay, 2 May 1923; *s* of Michael Joseph Hillery and Ellen (*née* McMahon); *m* 1955, Mary Beatrice Finnegan; one *s* one *d*. *Educ:* Miltown Malbay National Sch.; Rockwell Coll.; University Coll., Dublin. Mem. Health Council, 1955-57; MO, Miltown Malbay, 1957-59; Coroner for West Clare, 1958-59; Mem., Dáil, 1951-72; Minister: for Educn, 1959-65; for Industry and Commerce, 1965-66; for Labour, 1966-69; of Foreign Affairs, 1969-73; Comr for Social Affairs and a Vice-Pres., Commn of the European Communities, 1973-76. *Address:* Aras an Uachtaráin, Phoenix Park, Dublin 8, Ireland; Spanish Point, Co. Clare, Ireland.

HILLGARTH, Capt. Alan Hugh, CMG 1943; OBE 1937; RN, retired; *b* 7 June 1899; *s* of late Willmott Henderson Hillgarth Evans, MD, FRCS and Anne Frances Piercy; assumed surname of Hillgarth by deed poll, 1928; *m* 1st, 1929, Hon. Mary Sidney Katherine Almina Hope-Morley (marr. diss. 1946), 3rd *d* of 1st Baron Burghclere; one *s*; 2nd, 1947, Jean Mary (*d* 1975), *e d* of Frank Cobb; two *s* one *d*. *Educ:* Royal Naval Colls, Osborne and Dartmouth; King's Coll., Cambridge. Entered Royal Navy, 1912; Vice-Consul at Palma, 1932-37; Consul, 1937-39; Naval Attaché at Madrid, 1939-43; Chief of Intelligence Staff, Eastern Fleet, 1943-44; Chief of British Naval Intelligence, Eastern Theatre, 1944-46. *Publications:* various novels. *Recreation:* forestry. *Address:* Illannanagh House, Ballinderry, Co. Tipperary. *T:* Ballinderry 3. *Clubs:* Army and Navy, Garrick.

HILLIER, Arthur, OBE 1947; retired as Chairman and Managing Director, Sperry Gyroscope Co. Ltd (1938-59); Chairman: Industrial Products (Speco) Ltd since 1949; New Holland Machine Co. Ltd since 1954; *b* 2 Dec. 1895; *s* of Thomas Hillier and Ann Hillier (*née* Holland); *m* 1st, 1919, Rita Mary (*d* 1955), *d* of John Wakeley; two *d*; 2nd, 1956, Margaret Howard. *Educ:* Judd Sch., Tonbridge, Kent. Joined Sperry Gyroscope Co. Ltd as Asst Sec., 1916; Sec., 1920; Dir, 1922; Dir and Gen. Manager, 1933; Man. Dir, 1934. Freeman of City of London, 1930; Freeman and Liveryman of: Needlemakers' Company, 1930; Shipwrights' Company, 1951. FCIS 1937; FIN 1953 (was Founder Mem.); JP Middlesex, 1951; High Sheriff County of Middlesex, 1956-57. Comdr, Order of Orange Nassau (Netherlands), 1950; Officer, Legion of Honour (France), 1952; Commendatore, Order of Merit (Italy), 1955. *Recreation:* ancient history. *Address:* Cranmore, Little Forest Road, Bournemouth, Dorset. *T:* Bournemouth 765532. *Clubs:* Royal Automobile, City Livery.

HILLIER, Bevis; Editor, The Connoisseur, 1973-76; *b* 28 March 1940; *s* of J. R. Hillier and Mary Louise Hillier (*née* Palmer). *Educ:* Reigate Grammar Sch.; Magdalen Coll., Oxford (demy). Gladstone Memorial Prize, 1961. Editorial staff, The Times, 1963-68 (trainee, Home News Reporter, Sale Room Correspondent); Editor, British Museum Society Bulletin, 1968-70; Antiques Correspondent, The Times, 1970-; Guest Curator, Minneapolis Inst. of Arts, USA, 1971. FRSA 1967; *Publications:* Master Potters of the Industrial Revolution: The Turners of Lane End, 1965; Pottery and Porcelain 1700-1914, 1968; Art Deco of the 1920s and 1930s, 1968; Posters, 1969; Cartoons and Caricatures, 1970; The World of Art Deco, 1971; 100 Years of Posters, 1972; Introduction to A Boy at the Hogarth Press by Richard Kennedy, 1972; Austerity/Binge, 1975; (ed with Mary Banham) A Tonic to the Nation: The Festival of Britain 1951, 1976; contributor to The Connoisseur, Apollo, Trans English Ceramic Circle, Proc. Wedgwood Soc., etc. *Recreations:* piano; collecting; awarding marks out of ten for suburban front gardens. *Address:* Goldbeaters House, Manette Street, W1. *T:* 01-437 1972. *Clubs:* Beefsteak, Garrick.

HILLIER, Harold George, CBE 1971; Senior Director, Hillier Nurseries (Winchester) Ltd, since 1946; Horticulturalist (Nurseryman, Seedsman and Landscape Gardener); *b* 2 Jan. 1905; *s* of Edwin Lawrence and Ethel Marian Hillier; *m* 1934, Barbara Mary Trant; two *s* two *d*. *Educ:* Peter Symonds Sch., Winchester; King Edward's Grammar Sch., Southampton.

Nurseryman and Seedsman to Queen Elizabeth The Queen Mother. FLS; Hon. FRHS 1972 (a Vice-Pres., 1974). VMH 1957; Veitch Memorial Medal in Gold, 1962; Massachusetts Horticultural Society's Thomas Roland Medal, 1965. *Recreation:* horticulture. *Address:* Jermyns House, Ampfield, Romsey, Hants. *T:* Braishfield 68212.

HILLIER, Tristram Paul, RA 1967 (ARA 1957); painter and writer; *b* 11 April 1905; *s* of Edward Guy Hillier, CMG, and Ada Everett; *m* 1st, 1931, Irene Rose Hodgkins (marr. diss. 1935); two *s*; 2nd, 1937, Leda Millicent Hardcastle; two *d.* *Educ:* Downside; Christ's Coll., Cambridge. Studied at Slade Sch. and under André Lhôte, Paris. Has held nine one-man exhibitions in London at Lefevre Gall. (2) and Tooth's Gall. (7); other exhibitions: retrospective, Worthing Art Gall., 1960; Galerie Barreiro, Paris; Langton Gall., London, 1974; Pieter Wenning Gall., Johannesburg, 1975. Rep. by official purchases of pictures in following public collections: Tate Gall.; National Galleries of Canada, NSW, and Victoria; Ferens Art Gall., Hull; Contemporary Art Soc.; City Art Galleries: Manchester, Aberdeen, Leeds, Southampton, Nottingham, Belfast; Art Galleries of Toronto, Brisbane, Rochdale, Oldham, Kettering; Min. of Works (for Brit. Embassies Fund); Harris Museum, Preston; Chantrey Bequest. Served as Lieut RNVR, 1940-45. *Publication:* Leda and the Goose (autobiography), 1954. *Recreations:* riding, walking, swimming. *Address:* c/o Waddington & Tooth Galleries, 33 Cork Street, W1; Yew Tree Cottage, East Pennard, Shepton Mallet, Somerset. *T:* Ditcheat 284.

HILLIER-FRY, William Norman; HM Diplomatic Service; Consul-General, Hamburg, since 1974; *b* 12 Aug. 1923; *o s* of William Henry and Emily Hillier Fry; *m* 1948, Elizabeth Adèle Misbah; two *s* two *d.* *Educ:* Colfe's Grammar School, Lewisham; St Edmund Hall, Oxford (BA 1946). Served Army, 1942-45; commissioned, Loyal Regt, 1942. HM Foreign Service, 1946; served: Iran, 1947-52; Strasbourg (Delegation to Council of Europe), 1955-56; Turkey, 1956-59; Czechoslovakia, 1961-63; Counsellor, UK Disarmament Delegn, Geneva, 1968-71; Hd of ME Dept, ODA, 1971-74. *Recreations:* music, theatre. *Address:* c/o Foreign and Commonwealth Office, SW1.

HILLINGDON, 4th Baron *cr* 1886; **Charles Hedworth Mills;** Bt 1868; Captain, Life Guards; *b* 12 Jan. 1922; *er* and *o* surv. *s* of 3rd Baron and of Hon. Edith Mary Winifred, Cadogan (Edith, Lady Hillingdon, DBE), *e d* of Henry Arthur, Viscount Chelsea; *S* father 1952; *m* 1947, Lady Sarah Grey Stuart, 2nd *d* of 18th Earl of Moray; one *s* three *d.* *Educ:* Eton; Magdalen Coll., Oxford. 2nd Lieut Coldstream Guards, 1941; transferred Life Guards, 1942; Captain, 1943. *Heir: s* Hon. Charles James Mills, *b* 8 March 1951. *Address:* Messing Park, Kelvedon, Essex. *T:* Tiptree 364. *Club:* White's.

HILLIS, Arthur Henry Macnamara, CMG 1961; Comptroller General, National Debt Office, 1961-68; *b* 29 Dec. 1905; *s* of late John David Hillis, FRCS, Dublin; *m* 1936, Mary Francis; no *c.* *Educ:* Trinity Coll., Dublin. Called to Bar, Inner Temple, 1931. HM Treasury, 1941; Harkness Fund Fellow, USA, 1950-51; Minister (Treasury Adviser), UK Permanent Mission to United Nations, 1958-61; Under-Sec., Treasury, 1961. Mem., Internat. CS Commn (UN), 1974-. *Address:* 2 Hare Court, Temple, EC4. *T:* 01-353 3443. *Club:* Athenaeum.

HILLS, Edwin Sherbon, CBE 1971; FRS 1954; FAA; Professor of Geology, 1944-64, Research Professor, 1964-71, now Professor Emeritus, University of Melbourne; *b* Melbourne, 31 Aug. 1906; *s* of Edwin S. Hills, Melbourne; *m* 1932, Claire D. Fox; two *s* one *d.* *Educ:* Univs of Melbourne and London. DSc Melbourne; PhD London; FIC; DSc (Hon.) Dunelm; Foreign and Commonwealth FGS (Bigsby Medallist, 1951); David Syme Prize for Scientific Research (Melbourne), 1939. Dep. Vice-Chancellor, Univ. of Melbourne, 1962-71. Councillor, National Museum of Victoria; Trustee, Royal Soc. of Victoria. Fellow, Imperial Coll. of Science and Technology, London, 1968; Hon. Fellow Aust. Inst. of Geographers. *Publications:* Outlines of Structural Geology, 1940, new edn 1953; Physiography of Victoria, 1941, new edn 1975; Elements of Structural Geology, 1963, new edn 1971; (ed) Arid Lands: a Geographical Appraisal, 1966. *Address:* 25 Barry Street, Kew, Victoria 3101, Australia. *T:* 86-8572.

HILLS, Air Vice-Marshal Eric Donald, CB 1973; CBE 1968 (MBE 1941); SASO Maintenance Command, 1971-73, retired; *b* 26 Jan. 1917; *s* of late Henry James Hills; *m* 1945, Pamela Mary, *d* of late Col A. P. Sandeman, Cape Town; one *s* one *d.* *Educ:* Maidstone Grammar Sch. Joined RAF 1939; Group Captain 1962; Dir of Equipment 3 (RAF), 1968-69; Air Cdre 1969; Dir of Equipment (Policy) (RAF), MoD, 1969-71; Air Vice-Marshal

1971. *Recreations:* gardening, sport as spectator. *Address:* c/o National Westminster Bank Ltd, 3 High Street, Maidstone, Kent. *Club:* Royal Air Force.

HILLS, Lawrence Donegan; Director, Henry Doubleday Research Association, since 1954; *b* 2 July 1911; *s* of William Donegan and Mabel Annie Hills; *m* 1964, Mrs Hilda Cherry Brooke (*née* Fea). *Educ:* at home, owing to ill health. Took up horticulture on medical advice in 1927 and worked for many leading nurseries until 1940. Served War of 1939-45, RAF. Wrote first book, Miniature Alpine Gardening, in hospitals before invalided out on D-Day. Founded Henry Doubleday Research Assoc., 1954, and still Director-Secretary of this leading internat. body of gardeners and farmers without chemicals. Gardening Correspondent: Observer, 1958-66; Punch, 1966-70; Countryman, 1970; Associated Editor: Compost Science (USA); Ecologist, 1973. *Publications:* Miniature Alpine Gardening, 1944; Rapid Tomato Ripening, 1946; Propagation of Alpines, 1950; Alpines Without A Garden, 1953; Russian Comfrey, 1953; Alpine Gardening, 1955; Down To Earth Fruit and Vegetable Growing, 1960; Down to Earth Gardening, 1967; Lands of the Morning (Archaeology), 1970; Grow Your Own Fruit and Vegetables, 1971; Comfrey—Its Past, Present and Future, 1976; Organic Gardening, 1977. *Recreations:* reading, thinking, non-gardening writing. *Address:* 32 Convent Lane, Bocking, Braintree, Essex. *T:* Braintree 24083.

HILLYARD, Patrick Cyril Henry, OBE 1956; Head of Sound Light Entertainment BBC, 1952-64, retd Nov. 1964; *s* of Rev. Dr H. J. Hillyard and Louie Charlotte Robinson; *m* 1932, Ena Violet, *d* of late Rev. C. Porter-Brickwell; one *s.* *Educ:* The High Sch., Dublin. Studied stage production under Donald Calthrop. Stage directed and produced plays and musical comedies in England and America, including: A Midsummer Night's Dream, Twelfth Night, The Fake, Jolly Roger, No More Ladies, The Desert Song, Gay Divorce, On Your Toes, Lilac Time. Joined BBC Television Service as Dep. Productions Manager, 1937; Asst Dir of Variety, BBC, 1941; Actg Dir of Variety, BBC, 1946; Dir of Television Presentation, BBC, 1947; Head of Television Light Entertainment, BBC, 1948. *Recreations:* going to the theatre, golf, tennis and swimming. *Address:* c/o Barclays Bank, 15 Langham Place, W1.

HILTON, Conrad (Nicholson); Chairman: Hilton Hotels Corporation, since (formation of company) 1946; Hilton International Company since 1968; *b* 25 Dec. 1887; *s* of August Holver Hilton and Mary Laufersweiler; *m* 1925, Mary Barron; two *s* (and one *s* decd). *Educ:* St Michael's Coll., Santa Fé; New Mexico Mil. Inst.; New Mexico Sch. of Mines. MHR, New Mexico, 1912-13; Partner, A. H. Hilton & Sons, 1915. 2nd Lieut, US Army, 1917-19. Bought first hotel, Cisco, Texas, 1919; bought, sold and operated hotels, 1919-46; organized Hilton Hotels Corp., 1946; founded Hilton Internat. Co., 1948 (of which he is now Chm.); bought Waldorf-Astoria, 1949; bought Statler Hotel chain, 1954. Chm. of 2 companies, operating 155 hotels around the world. Holds several hon. doctorates; also knighthoods, etc in foreign Orders. *Publications:* Be My Guest, 1957; Inspirations of an Innkeeper, 1963. *Recreation:* golf. *Address:* 9990 Santa Monica Boulevard, Beverly Hills, Calif, USA. *T:* 277-6203. *Clubs:* Metropolitan (New York City); Chicago Athletic; Los Angeles Country; Bel Air Country.

HILTON, Sir Derek (Percy), Kt 1966; MBE 1945; *b* 11 April 1908; *o c* of Percy Hilton and Mary Beatrice Hilton (*née* Stott); *m* 1945, Joanna Stott, *er d* of late Sir Arnold Stott, KBE; three *d.* *Educ:* Rugby Sch.; Trinity Hall, Cambridge. Solicitor, 1932; subsequently private practice in Manchester. War of 1939-45, Manchester Regt; seconded to special operations executive, 1941. Mem. Council, Law Soc., 1951; Hon. Sec., Manchester Law Soc., 1950-59; Pres., Manchester Law Soc., 1957; Pres. of the Law Soc., 1965-66. Dir, Abbey National Building Soc., 1966-; Chm., Lancashire & Yorkshire Revisionary Interest Co. Ltd, 1956-77; Pres., Immigration Appeal Tribunal, 1970-. Norwegian Liberty Cross, 1945. *Recreations:* gardening, walking, fishing. *Address:* Eaves, Chapel-en-le-Frith, Stockport, Cheshire SK12 6UA. *T:* Chapel-en-le-Frith 2241. *Clubs:* Special Forces; St James's (Manchester).

HILTON, John Robert, CMG 1965; HM Diplomatic Service (appointed to Foreign Service, 1943), retired 1969; *b* 5 Jan. 1908; *s* of Oscar Hilton, MD, and Louisa Holdsworth Hilton; *m* 1933, Margaret Frances Stephens; one *s* three *d.* *Educ:* Marlborough Coll.; Corpus Christi Coll., Oxford (MA); Bartlett Sch. of Architecture; University Coll., London (Diploma). ARIBA. Dir of Antiquities, Cyprus, 1934-36; Architect to E. S. & A. Robinson Ltd and private practice, 1936-41. Capt. RE, 1941-43. Foreign Service, 1943; transferred to Istanbul, 1944; 2nd Sec., Athens, 1945; Foreign Office, 1947; 1st Sec., Istanbul, 1956;

Foreign Office, 1960. FRSA. *Publications:* articles in Architectural Review and other jls, Mind and Analysis; Memoir on Louis MacNeice (as appendix to his autobiography, The Strings are False), 1965. *Recreations:* philosophy, walking. *Address:* Hope Cottage, Nash Hill, Lacock, Wilts. *T:* Lacock 369.

HILTON, Col Peter, MC 1942 and Bars 1943 and 1944; DL; JP; Managing Director, James Smith (Scotland Nurseries) Ltd; *b* 30 June 1919; *er s* of Maj.-Gen. R. Hilton, *qv*; *m* 1942, Winifred, *d* of late Ernest Smith, Man. Dir Scotland Nurseries, Tansley; one *s* (and one *s* decd). *Educ:* Malvern Coll.; RMA Woolwich; psc. Commnd RA, 1939; BEF, 1939-40, 1st Div. Dunkirk; Western Desert, 1942-43, 7th Armd Div. Alamein (RHA Jacket 1942); Italy, 1943-44, 5th American Army, Adjt 3rd Regt RHA; Normandy, 1944, OC J Bty RHA (wounded Falaise Gap); Greece, 1946-49 (despatches 1948); Instructor Royal Hellenic Staff Coll.; Col RA 1949, retd; RARO; recalled Korean Emergency, 1950; TA Commn, 1951; CO 528 W Notts Regt, RA (TA), 1951-54; ACF Commn, 1962; Comdt Derbyshire ACF, 1962-66, Hon. Col 1972-77. Chm., Derbys War Pensions Cttee and Army Benevolent Fund; Comr no 3 Region, Comdr/Comr Derbys SJAB. Trustee: Derby New Theatre; Crich Meml Trust; Vice-Pres., British Heart Foundn, Derbs; Chm. of Governors, Anthony Gell Sch., Wirksworth. JP 1967, High Sheriff 1970-71, DL 1972, Derbs; Mem. Wirksworth Div. Derbs CC, 1967-77. FRHS. CStJ 1977 (OStJ 1970). Greek Order of Minerva, 1949. *Recreations:* ex-Service interests, local activities. *Address:* Alton Manor, Idridgehay, Derbs. *T:* Wirksworth 2435; James Smith (Scotland Nurseries) Ltd, Tansley, Matlock, Derbs DE4 5GF. *T:* Matlock 3036. *Club:* County (Derby).

HILTON, Prof. Peter John, MA, DPhil Oxon, PhD Cantab; Beaumont University Professor, Case-Western Reserve University, since 1972; *b* 7 April 1923; *s* of late Dr Mortimer Hilton and of Mrs Elizabeth Hilton; *m* 1949, Margaret (*née* Mostyn); two *s. Educ:* St Paul's Sch.; Queen's Coll., Oxford. Asst Lectr, Manchester Univ., 1948-51, Lectr, 1951-52; Lectr, Cambridge Univ., 1952-55; Senior Lecturer, Manchester Univ., 1956-58; Mason Prof. of Pure Mathematics, University of Birmingham, 1958-62; Prof. of Mathematics, Cornell Univ., 1962-71, Washington Univ., 1971-73. Visiting Professor: Cornell Univ., USA, 1958-59; Eidgenössische Techn. Hochschule, Zürich, 1966-67; Courant Inst., NY Univ., 1967-68. Mathematician-in-residence, Battelle Research Center, Seattle, 1970-. Chm., US Commn on Mathematical Instruction, 1971-74. Hon. Mem. Belgian Mathematical Soc., 1955. Silver Medal, Univ. of Helsinki, 1975. *Publications:* Introduction to Homotopy Theory, 1953; Differential Calculus, 1958; Homology Theory (with S. Wylie), 1960; Partial Derivatives, 1960; Homotopy Theory and Duality, 1965; (with H. B. Griffiths) Classical Mathematics, 1970; General Cohomology Theory and K- Theory, 1971; (with U. Stammbach) Course in Homological Algebra, 1971; (with Y.-C. Wu) Course in Modern Algebra, 1974; (with G. Mislin and J. Roitberg) Localization of Nilpotent Groups and Spaces, 1975; numerous research articles on algebraic topology, homological algebra and category theory in British and foreign mathematical journals. *Recreations:* travel, sport, reading, theatre, chess, bridge, broadcasting. *Address:* Battelle Research Center, 4000 NE 41st Street, Seattle, Washington 98105, USA.

HILTON, Maj.-Gen. Richard, DSO 1944; MC 1915; DFC and Bar, 1918; retired; *b* 18 Jan. 1894; 2nd *s* of John Edward Hilton, JP, Lambourn, Berks; *m* 1917, Phyllis Martha, *e d* of late Rev. S. H. Woodin, MA, Rector of Yarmouth, IoW; two *s. Educ:* Malvern; RMA Woolwich. Served European War, 1914-18, Western Front, in RA, RFC and RAF (wounded); commissioned 2nd Lieut, RGA, 1913; seconded to RFC, 1915; Lieut, 1915; Capt., 1917; Sqdn Comdr, 1918. Seconded to Tank Corps, 1922-23; Indian Mountain Artillery, 1924-30, 1934-38; Staff Capt., War Office, 1930-33; Major 1934; Bt Lt-Col 1937; Lt-Col 1939. War of 1939-45, BEF, 1939-40; Chief Instructor (Air), Sch. of Artillery, 1940; CRA 15th (Scottish) Div., 1941-44 (wounded); BGS to Allied Liberation Forces, Norway, 1945; Dep. Chief of British Mission to Soviet Zone of Germany, 1946-47; Military Attaché in Moscow, 1947-48; retd, 1948. Comdr, Order of St Olav, Norway, 1945. *Publications:* Military Attaché in Moscow, 1949; Nine Lives, 1955; The Indian Mutiny, 1957; The North-West Frontier, 1957; The Thirteenth Power, 1958; Imperial Obituary, 1968; contrib. to Blackwoods, Nineteenth Century and After, Service and other Journals. *Recreations:* languages, chess, world affairs, travel. *Address:* Buckingham Hotel, Buxton, Derbyshire SK17 9AS.
See also Col P. Hilton.

HILTON, Prof. Rodney Howard, FBA 1977; Professor of Medieval Social History, University of Birmingham, since 1963; *b* 1916; *s* of John James Hilton and Anne Hilton. *Educ:* Manchester Grammar Sch.; Balliol Coll. and Merton Coll., Oxford (BA, DPhil). Army, 1940-46; Lectr and Reader in Medieval History, Univ. of Birmingham, 1946-63. *Publications:* The Economic Development of Some Leicestershire Estates in the 14th and 15th Centuries, 1947; (with H. Fagan) The English Rising of 1381, 1950; (ed) Ministers' Accounts of the Warwickshire Estates of the Duke of Clarence, 1952; (ed) The Stoneleigh Leger Book, 1960; A Medieval Society, 1966; The Decline of Serfdom in Medieval England, 1969; Bondmen Made Free, 1973; The English Peasantry in the Later Middle Ages, 1975; (ed) Peasants, Knights and Heretics, 1976; articles and reviews in Past and Present, English Historical Review, Economic History Review, etc. *Recreations:* anti-Establishment politics; walking to visit historical monuments. *Address:* School of History, University of Birmingham, Birmingham B15 2TT. *T:* 021-472 1301.

HILTON, William (Samuel); Director, Master Builders' Federation, since 1969; National Director, Federation of Master Builders, since 1970; Managing Director, Trade Press (FMB) Ltd, since 1972; *b* 21 March 1926; *m* 1948, Agnes Aitken Orr; three *s. Educ:* Kyleshill, Saltcoats; Ardrossan Academy. Railway Fireman until 1949; Labour Party Agent to late Lord Kirkwood, 1949-52; Research and Education Officer for Building Trade Operatives, 1952-66. MP (Lab and Co-op) Bethnal Green, 1966- Feb. 1974. Mem. Agrément Bd for Building Industry, 1965-66; Mem. Economic Development Council for Building Industry, 1964-66. Editor, Builders Standard, 1954-66. *Publications:* Building by Direct Labour, 1954; Foes to Tyranny, 1964; Industrial Relations in Construction, 1968. *Address:* The Roost, 1 Mavelstone Close, Bromley, Kent.

HILTON-SERGEANT, Maj.-Gen. Frederick Cavendish, CB 1956; CBE 1955; retired 1957; Medical Adviser, British Red Cross, 1957-70; *b* 25 Feb. 1898; *s* of F. M. C. Sergeant, Liverpool; *m* 1929, Kathleen Margaret Howard, 2nd *d* of Howard J. Walker, Dalton Grange, Parbold; two *d. Educ:* Calday Sch.; Liverpool Univ. MB, ChB (Liverpool) 1921; DPH (Eng.) 1938; MFCM 1973; Leishman Prize, RAM Coll., 1932. 2nd Lieut, RFA, 1917-18; entered RAMC, 1923; served India, NW Frontier; China, Shanghai; and ME countries; Capt. 1926; Major 1934; Lieut-Col 1946; Brig. 1951; Maj.-Gen. 1953. Dep. Dir Hygiene, British Troops in Egypt and Ext. Examr in Preventive Medicine, Kasr-el-Aini Univ., Cairo, 1943-46; Dep. Dir Hygiene, W Comd, 1947-48; Prof. of Hygiene, RAM Coll., 1949; Comdt Army Sch. of Health, 1949-50; DDMS, Brit. troops in Egypt, 1951-52; DDMS, N Comd, 1953; Comdt and Dir of Medical Studies, Royal Army Medical Coll., 1953-57. QHP 1953-57. FRSM; FSocMOH. OStJ. *Publications:* contribs to Jl of RAMC. *Recreations:* ski-ing, sailing, tennis, golf. *Address:* Home Cottage, Quality Street, Merstham, Surrey. *T:* Merstham 3988.

HIM, George, PhD (Bonn); FSTD; AGI; RDI 1969-76; designer (freelance) and design consultant; Design Consultant to El Al Israel Airlines; Senior Lecturer, Leicester Polytechnic; *b* 4 Aug. 1900; *m* Shirley Elizabeth (*née* Rhodes). *Educ:* Warsaw, Moscow, Bonn, Leipzig. In practice, first in Germany, then in Poland, from 1928; in London, since 1937. Field of work: book illustration, publicity design, exhibitions; designed Festival Clock in Battersea Park, 1951; The Observer Masada Exhibition, 1966; Masada Exhibition, New York, Chicago, Washington, etc, 1967-69, other European cities, 1970-72; Chief Designer of Israel Pavilion, Expo 67, Montreal; designed covers for The New Middle East (monthly). Discoverer of the "County of Schweppshire" (with Stephen Potter) 1951-64. Retrospective exhibn, London Coll. of Printing, 1976. Work for TV. *Publications:* Israel, the Story of a Nation, 1957; children's books: Locomotive, 1937; The Little Red Engine, 1942 (with J. Lewitt); Squawky (with S. Potter), 1964; Folk Tales (with Leila Berg), 1966; Giant Alexander books (with F. Herrmann), 1964, 1966, 1971, 1972, 1975; Little Nippers (ed by Leila Borg), 1973, 1974; The Day with the Duke (with Ann Thwaite), 1969; Ann and Ben, 1974; The Adventures of King Midas (with Lynn Reid-Banks), 1976; illustrations to Zuleika Dobson, 1960; Plays for Puritans, 1966 (with Jim Rogerson) King Wilbur books. *Recreation:* work. *Address:* 37B Road, NW6 5JB. *T:* 01-624 6663.

HIMMELWEIT, Prof. Hilde T.; Professor of Social Psychology, London School of Economics, University of London, since 1964; *b* Berlin; *d* of S. Litthauer and Feodore Litthauer (*née* Remak); *m* 1940, Prof. F. Himmelweit (*d.* 1977), MD, FRCPEd; one *d. Educ:* Berlin; Hayes Court, Kent; Newnham Coll., Cambridge.

Degrees in Mod. Langs and Psych.; qual. Educational and Clinical Psychologist, 1943; PhD London 1945; Clin. Psychologist, Maudsley Hosp., 1945-48; joined LSE, 1949; Reader in Social Psychology, 1954. Dir Nuffield Television Enquiry, 1954-58; Visiting Professor: Univ. of Calif, Berkeley, 1959; Hebrew Univ., Jerusalem, 1974; Stanford Univ., Calif, 1975; Fellowship to Centre for Advanced Study of Behavioral Sciences, Stanford, Calif, 1967; Chm., Academic Adv. Cttee of Open Univ., 1969-74; FBPsS 1952; Member: Council, Brit. Psycholog. Soc., 1961-64; Editorial Bds, Brit. Jl of Soc. and Clin. Psychology, 1962-, Jl Communications Research, 1972-; Research Bd, Inst. of Jewish Affairs, 1970-; US SSRC Cttee on TV and Social Behaviour, 1973-; Annan Cttee on Future of Broadcasting, 1974-77; Trustee, Internat. Broadcasting Inst.; Adviser, House of Commons Select Cttee on ITA or IBA, 1972. DUniv Open, 1976. *Publications:* Television and the Child, 1958; articles and chapters on: rôle, structure and effects of broadcasting; personality theory and measurement; attitude development and change; socialization, rôle of school; societal influences on outlook and behaviour; study over time of voting behaviour, the dynamics of change in society. *Address:* London School of Economics, Houghton Street, WC2. *T:* 01-405 7686.

HIMSWORTH, Eric, CMG 1951; *b* 23 Nov. 1905; *s* of H. Himsworth and M. J. Macdonald; *m* 1941, Ethel Emily, *d* of Major Brook Pratt, DSO, Coldstream Guards; two *s. Educ:* Silcoates Sch., near Wakefield; Merton Coll., Oxford. MA, BCL Oxon; LLB, BSc (Econ.), DPA London. Colonial Administrative Service, 1928-55; Financial Sec., Malaya, 1952-55; UN Technical Assistance Administration, Nepal, 1956-64; IMF Financial Consultant, 1965-71. *Recreation:* travelling. *Address:* c/o Hongkong and Shanghai Banking Corporation, 9 Gracechurch Street, EC3.

HIMSWORTH, Sir Harold (Percival), KCB 1952; MD; FRS 1955; FRCP; Secretary, Medical Research Council, 1949-68, retired (Member and Deputy Chairman, 1967-68); *b* 19 May 1905; *s* of late Arnold Himsworth, Huddersfield, Yorks; *m* 1932, Charlotte, *yr d* of William Gray, Walmer, Kent; two *s. Educ:* King James' Grammar Sch., Almondbury, Yorks; University Coll. and University Coll. Hosp., London. Asst, Medical Unit, University Coll. Hosp., 1930; Beit Memorial Research Fellow, 1932-35; William Julius Mickle Fellow, University of London, 1935; Fellow of University Coll., London, 1936; Deputy Dir, Medical Unit, University Coll. Hospital, 1936; Goulstonian Lecturer, 1939; Oliver-Sharpey Lectr, 1949, RCP; Prof. of Medicine, Univ. of London and Dir of the Medical Unit, University Coll. Hospital, London, 1939-49; Mem. of Medical Research Council, 1948-49; Sydney Ringer Lecturer, 1949; Lowell Lecturer, Boston, Mass, 1947; Harveian Orator, Royal College of Physicians, 1962. Pres., Sect. of Experimental Medicine, Royal Society of Medicine, 1946-47. Chm., Bd of Management, London Sch. of Hygiene and Tropical Med., 1969-76. Prime Warden, Goldsmiths Co., 1975. Docteur *hc* Toulouse, 1950; Hon. LLD: Glasgow, 1953; London, 1956; Wales, 1959; Hon. DSc: Manchester, 1956; Leeds, 1968; Univ. of WI, 1968; Hon. ScD, Cambridge, 1964. New York Univ. Medallist, 1958; Conway Evans Prize, RCP, 1968. Member: Norwegian Med. Soc., 1954; Royal Soc. of Arts and Sciences, Göteborg, Sweden, 1957; Hon. Member: Med. Soc. of Sweden, 1949; Amer. Assoc. of Physicians, 1950; For. Mem., Amer. Philosoph. Soc., 1972; For. Hon. Member: Amer. Acad. of Arts and Sciences, 1957; Belgian Royal Acad. of Medicine, 1958 (For. corresp. Mem., 1955). Hon. FRCR 1958; Hon. FRCPE 1960; Hon. FRSM 1961; Hon. FRCS 1965; Hon. FRCPath 1969. *Publications:* The Development and Organisation of Scientific Knowledge, 1970; medical and scientific papers. *Recreation:* fishing. *Address:* 13 Hamilton Terrace, NW8. *T:* 01-286 6996. *Club:* Athenæum.

HINCHEY, Herbert John, CMG 1966; CBE 1955; Financial Adviser to Prime Minister of Mauritius, 1967-72; *b* 13 Feb. 1908; *s* of late Edward and late Mary A. Hinchey, Sydney, NSW; *m* 1944, Amy E., *d* of late William and late Caroline Beddows, Vuni Vasa Estate, Taveuni, Fiji; no *c. Educ:* Sydney Grammar Sch.; University of Sydney; London Sch. of Economics. Bank of New South Wales, Sydney and Brisbane, 1932-40; Colonial Administrative Service, later HMOCS, 1940-65; Financial Secretary: Western Pacific High Commn, 1948-52; Govt of Mauritius, 1952-57; E Africa High Commn/Common Services Organization, 1957-65. Sometime Member: Mauritius Legislative Coun.; E African Central Legislative Assembly; Chairman: E African Industrial Coun.; E African Industrial Research Bd; E African Currency Bd, etc. *Recreations:* photography, swimming, walking. *Address:* Avenue Lucien de Chazal, Vacoas, Mauritius. *Clubs:* Gymkhana (Mauritius); Corona, Nairobi (Nairobi).

HINCHINGBROOKE, Viscount; *see* Montagu, J. E. H.

HINCHLIFF, Rev. Canon Peter Bingham, MA, DD Oxon, PhD Rhodes; Chaplain and Fellow, Balliol College, Oxford, since 1972; *b* 25 Feb. 1929; *e s* of Rev. Canon Samuel Bingham Hinchliff and Brenda Hinchliff; *m* 1955, Constance, *d* of E. L. Whitehead, Uitenhage, S Africa; three *s* one *d. Educ:* St Andrew's Coll., Grahamstown, S Africa; Rhodes Univ., Grahamstown; Trinity Coll., Oxford. Deacon, 1952; Priest, 1953, in Anglican Church in S Africa; Asst in Parish of Uitenhage, 1952-55. Subwarden, St Paul's Theological Coll., Grahamstown, 1955-59; Lectr in Comparative Religion, Rhodes Univ., 1957-59; Prof. of Ecclesiastical History, Rhodes Univ., 1960-69; Canon and Chancellor, Grahamstown Cathedral, 1964-69; Sec., Missionary and Ecumenical Council of the General Synod (formerly the Church Assembly), 1969-72; Examng Chaplain to Bishop of Newcastle, 1973, to Bishop of Oxford, 1974-. Public Orator, Rhodes Univ., 1965; Hulsean Lectr, Cambridge Univ., 1975-76. Member: S African Jt Commn on Church Unity; Faith and Order Commn of World Council of Churches, etc. Provincial Hon. Canon, Cape Town Cathedral, 1959-; Hon. Canon, Grahamstown Cathedral, 1969-; Canon Theologian, Coventry Cathedral, 1972-. *Publications:* The South African Liturgy, 1959; The Anglican Church in South Africa, 1963; John William Colenso, 1964; The One-Sided Reciprocity, 1966; A Calendar of Cape Missionary Correspondence, 1967; The Church in South Africa, 1968; The Journal of John Ayliff, 1970; Cyprian of Carthage, 1974. Contributor to: Jl of Ecclesiastical History; Studia Liturgica, etc. *Recreations:* crossword puzzles, odd jobbery. *Address:* Balliol College, Oxford.

HINCHLIFFE, Sir (Albert) Henry (Stanley), Kt 1953; JP; DL; BA Oxon; Chairman Glazebrook Steel & Co. Ltd, Manchester, retired, 1971; Director, Barclays Bank, 1952-69, also Local Director, Manchester Board, 1943-70; *b* 10 May 1893; *s* of Edward Stanley Hinchliffe, Mucklestone, Market Drayton; *m* 1921, Vera, JP, *d* of Frederick Liddell Steel, Ranton Abbey, Staffs; three *d. Educ:* Cheltenham; Keble Coll., Oxford. Enlisted North Staffs Regt 1914; commissioned, 1915 (wounded Loos); Finance Dept, India, 1916-19; India Office, 1919-20. County Councillor Staffs, 1942-55. Dir Manchester Chamber of Commerce, 1938-72, Emeritus 1972; Pres., 1944-46; Pres., Assoc. of British Chambers of Commerce, 1950-52; Chm. UK Cttee, Federation of Commonwealth Chambers of Commerce, 1961-63; Leader of British side in UK, Canada Trade Conference, 1949, 1951, 1954, 1955. Dir LNER, 1944 until nationalisation; Mem., Manchester Joint Research Council (Chm., 1944-48). Governor of Manchester Grammar Sch., 1940-76. Member: Central Transport Consultative Cttee, 1944-51; Advisory Council, DSIR, 1949-54; Dollar Exports Advisory Council, 1951-52; National Research Development Corp., 1955-58; Management Cttee, St Mary's Hospitals, Manchester, 1926-59; Chm., Min. of Health Cttee on Cost of Prescribing, 1957-59; Member: (original) ITA, 1954-59; Court of Governors, Manchester Univ.; Finance Cttee, Keele Univ.; Trustee, John Rylands Library, 1952-72. JP Manchester 1942; High Sheriff 1944, DL 1946, Staffs. *Publications:* The Bar Sinister, 1935; contributor to Fortnightly Review and other periodicals. *Recreations:* ancient churches, country pursuits. *Address:* Mucklestone Old Rectory, Market Drayton, Salop. *TA* and *T:* Ashley 2188. *Clubs:* Lansdowne, MCC; St James's (Manchester).
See also D. W. Bazalgette.

HINCHLIFFE, Sir Henry; *see* Hinchliffe, Sir (A.) H. (S.).

HIND, Kenneth, ERD 1955; Senior Director, Employment and Industrial Relations, Post Office, since 1973; *b* 14 March 1920; *er s* of late Harry and Edith Hind; *m* 1942, Dorothy Walton; one *s. Educ:* Central Sec. Sch., Sheffield; Queens' Coll., Cambridge (Munro Schol.). Army, 1940-48: Major, REME. General Post Office: Asst Principal, 1948; Principal, 1950; Asst Sec., 1960; Dir, Radio and Broadcasting, 1967; Central Services, 1969; Senior Dir, 1971. *Recreations:* cricket, gardening. *Address:* 40 Wilbury Crescent, Hove, East Sussex BN3 6FJ. *T:* Brighton 779780.

HINDE, Sir Robert; *see* Hinde, Sir W. R. N.

HINDE, Prof. Robert Aubrey, FRS 1974; Royal Society Research Professor, University of Cambridge, since 1963; Fellow of St John's College, Cambridge, since 1958; *b* 26 Oct. 1923; *s* of late Dr and Mrs E. B. Hinde, Norwich; *m* 1st, 1948, Hester Cecily (marr. diss. 1971), *d* of late C. R. V. Coutts; two *s* two *d*; 2nd, 1971, Joan Gladys, *d* of F. J. Stevenson; two *d. Educ:* Oundle Sch.; St John's Coll., Cambridge; Balliol Coll., Oxford. Served Coastal Comd, RAF, Flt-Lt, 1941-45. Research

Asst, Edward Grey Inst., Univ. of Oxford, 1948-50; Curator, Ornithological Field Station (now sub-Dept of Animal Behaviour), Madingley, Cambridge, 1950-65; St John's Coll., Cambridge: Research Fellow, 1951-54; Steward, 1956-58; Tutor, 1958-63. Hon. Dir, MRC Unit on Develt and Integration of Behaviour, 1970-. Zoological Society's Scientific Medal, 1961. For. Hon. Mem., Amer. Acad. of Arts and Sciences, 1974; Hon. Fellow, Amer. Ornithologists' Union, 1977. Hon. ScD Univ. Libre, Brussels, 1974. *Publications:* Animal Behaviour: a synthesis of Ethology and Comparative Psychology, 1966; (ed) Bird Vocalizations: their relations to current problems in biology and pscyhology, 1969; (ed jtly) Short Term Changes in Neural Activity and Behaviour, 1970; Non-Verbal Communication, 1972; (ed jtly) Constraints on Learning, 1973; Biological Bases of Human Social Behaviour, 1974; (ed jtly) Growing Points in Ethology, 1976; sundry papers in biological and psychological journals. *Address:* Park Lane, Madingley, Cambridge. *T:* Madingley 430.

HINDE, Thomas; *see* Chitty, Sir Thomas Willes.

HINDE, Maj.-Gen. (Hon.) Sir (William) Robert (Norris), KBE 1956 (CBE 1948); CB 1955; DSO 1940 (and 2 Bars); *b* 25 June 1900; *s* of late Major H. Hinde, Fordlands, Northam, N Devon; *m* 1926, Evelyn Muriel Wright, *d* of late Capt. H. FitzHerbert Wright, Yeldersley Hall, Derby; one *s* three *d*. *Educ:* Wellington Coll.; RMC Sandhurst. 2nd Lieut 15th Hussars, 1919; served War of 1939-45: France, Belgium, 1939-40; Lt-Col 1940; Col 1944; comd 15/19th Hussars, 1940-42; comd 22nd Armd Bde, Libya, Italy, Normandy, 1943-44; Dep. Mil. Governor, Brit. Sector, Berlin, 1945-48; Dep. Comr, Land Niedersachsen, Hanover, 1949-51; Dist Comd, Cyrenaica, 1952-53; Maj.-Gen. 1957; Dir of Operations, Kenya, 1953-56; retd 1957. ADC 1950-56. Col 15th/19th Hussars, 1957-64. *Recreation:* fishing. *Address:* Shrewton House, Shrewton, Salisbury, Wilts. *T:* Shrewton 233. *Club:* Cavalry and Guards.
See also Earl Cawdor, Sir William Gordon Cumming, Bt.

HINDERKS, Prof. Hermann Ernst, MA, DrPhil; Professor of German in the Queen's University, Belfast, 1954-70; *b* 19 Dec. 1907; *s* of Elrikus Hinderks and Alma Charlotte Jane (*née* Hildebrand); *m* 1935, Ingeborg (*née* Victor); three *d*. *Educ:* Lichtwark Schule, Hamburg; Univs of Hamburg, Freiburg i.Br and Basle (MA, DrPhil 1938). Teacher St George's Cathedral Grammar Sch., Capetown, 1935-37; Head of German Dept, Rhodes University Coll., Grahamstown, S Africa, 1938-39; Lecturer in German, University of Cape Town, 1939-53. *Publications:* Friedrich Nietzsche, ein Menschenleben und seine Philosophie (with H. A. Reyburn and J. G. Taylor), 1st edn 1946, 2nd edn 1947 (Eng. version, Nietzsche, The Story of a Human Philosopher, 1948); Uber die Gegenstandsbegriffe in der Kritik der reinen Vernunft, 1948. *Recreations:* music and walking. *Address:* 8821 Gnotzheim, Spielberg 38, Mittelfranken, W Germany.

HINDLEY, Prof. Colin Boothman; Professor of Child Development since 1972, and Director of Centre for Study of Human Development since 1967, Institute of Education, London; *b* Bolton, 1923; *m* 1945; two *s*. *Educ:* Bolton Sch.; Manchester Univ.; University Coll., London. MB, ChB Manchester 1946; BSc London 1949 (1st cl. Psychol.). Asst Med. Officer, Hope Hosp., Salford; Res. Psychologist and subseq. Sen. Lectr, London Univ. Inst. of Educn, 1949-72; Head of Adolescent Development Dip. Course, 1968-. Psychol. Adviser, Internat. Children's Centre Growth Studies, Paris, 1954-; Editor, Jl of Child Psychol. and Psychiat., 1959-69; Mem. Council, Brit. Psychol. Soc., 1970-73; Mem. Cttee, Internat. Soc. for Study Behavioural Develt, 1969-75; Mem. Assoc. Child Psychol. and Psychiat. (Chm. 1967-68). FBPsS. *Publications:* chapters in Child Development: International Method of Study, ed Falkner, 1960; Learning Theory and Personality Development, in Psychosomatic Aspects of Paediatrics, ed Mackeith and Sandler, 1961; contribs to jls. *Address:* Department of Child Development, Institute of Education, Bedford Way, WC1H 0AL.

HINDLEY, Brig. Geoffrey Bernard Sylvester, CBE 1955 (OBE 1943); *b* 25 Oct. 1902; 2nd *s* of late Sir Clement D. M. Hindley, KCIE, and of Lady Hindley; *m* 1934, Ruth, *d* of late T. H. and Mrs Corfield; one *s* one *d*. *Educ:* Oundle Sch.; RMA Woolwich. Commissioned, 1923; NW Frontier (Ind. Gen. Service Medal and clasp), 1930; Staff Coll., 1937-38; Temp. Lt-Col 1941, subst. 1947; Temp. Col 1943, subst. 1947; Temp. Brig. 1943, Brig. 1952. Served War of 1939-45, Middle East, Sicily, Italy. Dep. Dir Staff Duties, WO, 1945-47; Comdr Gold Coast District and Comdt Gold Coast Regt, RWAFF, 1947-49; Comdr 15th AA Bde, 1949-52; Dep. QMG, HQ Northern Army Group and BAOR, 1953-56; retd 1956. General Manager: Hemel

Hempstead Development Corp., 1956-62; (Hemel Hempstead) Commission for the New Towns, April-Nov. 1962; Welwyn Garden City and Hatfield Development Corps, 1962-66; (Welwyn Garden City and Hatfield), for the Commission for the New Towns, 1966-67. *Recreations:* travel, philately, gardening. *Address:* 24 Eastport Lane, Lewes, East Sussex. *T:* Lewes 3432.

HINDLEY, Henry Oliver Rait; *b* 19 June 1906; 3rd *s* of late Sir Clement Hindley; unmarried. *Educ:* Oundle; Trinity Coll., Cambridge; Dundee School of Economics. Industrial Consultant, 1936-40; Treasury, 1940; Air Min., 1940-45: Dir-Gen., Brit. Air Commission, later British Supply Office, USA, 1945-46; Chairman: Northern Divisional Board of National Coal Board, Sept. 1946-47; Raw Cotton Commission, 1947-51. Canadian Civil Servant, 1961; Sec., Adv. Cttee on Broadcasting, 1965; Asst Under-Sec. of State, 1965-69; Dept of Communications, 1969-75. *Address:* 200 Rideau Terrace 1114, Ottawa, Ontario, K1M 0Z3, Canada.

HINDLEY-SMITH, David Dury, CBE 1972; Registrar, General Dental Council (formerly Dental Board of the UK), since 1947; *b* 20 Feb. 1916; *s* of late James Dury Hindley-Smith; *m* 1947, Dorothy Westwood Legge, *e d* of Arthur Collins and Mary Fielding; two *d*. *Educ:* Uppingham; King's Coll., Cambridge (MA); Paris and Vienna. Passed examination for Diplomatic Service, 1939. War Service: Artists' Rifles, 1939; commissioned Royal Fus., 1940; liaison officer to Gén. Leclerc, 1942, to Gén. de Gaulle's first administration, 1944; Acting Col. Vice-Chm., Surrey Assoc. of Youth Clubs, 1950-70 (Vice-Pres., 1970-); Executive Chm., Nat. Assoc. of Youth Clubs, 1970-74 (Vice-Pres., 1974-); Chm., Sembal Trust. *Address:* The Ark House, Whepstead, Bury St Edmunds, Suffolk. *T:* Horringer 351. *Club:* Boodle's.

HINDLIP, 5th Baron *cr* 1886; **Henry Richard Allsopp;** Bt 1880; *b* 1 July 1912; 2nd *s* of 3rd Baron Hindlip and Agatha (*d* 1962), 2nd *d* of late John C. Thynne; *S* brother, 4th Baron, 1966; *m* 1939, Cecily Valentine Jane, *o d* of late Lt-Col Malcolm Borwick, DSO, Hazelbech Hill, Northampton; two *s* one *d*. *Educ:* Eton; RMC Sandhurst. 2nd Lieut, Coldstream Guards, 1932; Major, 1941; retired, 1948. Served War of 1939-45; NW Europe, 1944. JP 1957, DL 1956, Wilts. Bronze Star Medal, USA, 1945. *Recreations:* travel, shooting. *Heir:* *s* Hon. Charles Henry Allsopp [*b* 5 Aug. 1940; *m* 1968, Fiona Victoria, *d* of Hon. William McGowan; one *s* one *d*]. *Address:* Vern Leaze, Calne, Wilts SN11 0NB. *T:* Calne 3229. *Clubs:* White's, Pratt's, Turf.
See also Sir R. J. Hardy, Bt.

HINDMARSH, Frederick Bell; Under-Secretary, Department of Health and Social Security, since 1973; *b* 31 Jan. 1919; *yr s* of Frederick Hindmarsh and Margaret May Hindmarsh; *m* 1947, Mary Torrance Coubrough; one *d*. *Educ:* County Grammar Sch., Acton. Clerical Officer, Min. of Health, 1936; Exec. Officer, 1937. Served war, Army, 1939-46. Min. of Pensions and Nat. Insurance and Min. of Social Security: Higher Exec. Officer, 1946; Sen. Exec. Officer, 1947; Chief Exec. Officer, 1951; Sen. Chief Exec. Officer, 1959; Prin. Exec. Officer, 1964; Asst Sec., DHSS, 1969. *Recreation:* music. *Address:* 3 Hawthorn Close, Nascot Wood Road, Watford, Herts WD1 3SB. *T:* Watford 36769.

HINDSON, William Stanley, CMG 1962; BScEng, MIM, FIMechE; *b* 11 Jan. 1920; *s* of late W. A. L. Hindson, Darlington; *m* 1944, Mary Sturdy (*d* 1961); one *s* one *d*; *m* 1965, Catherine Leikine, Paris, France; one *s*. *Educ:* Darlington Grammar Sch.; Coatham Sch., Redcar. With Dorman Long (Steel) Ltd, Middlesbrough, 1937-55; Metallurgical Equipment Export Co. Ltd and Indian Steelworks Construction Co. Ltd, 1956-62; Wellman Engineering Corp. Ltd, 1963-69; Cementation Co. Ltd, 1970-71; Humphreys & Glasgow, 1971-74; Chm., Dawnays Ltd, 1974-75. Engineering and metallurgical consultant, 1976-. Mem., Inst. of Directors. *Recreations:* chess, philately. *Address:* 36 Eresby House, Rutland Gate, SW7. *T:* 01-589 3194.

HINE, Air Cdre Patrick Bardon; Director of Public Relations (RAF), since 1975; *b* 14 July 1932; parents decd; *m* 1956, Jill Adèle (*née* Gardner); three *s*. *Educ:* Peter Symonds Sch., Winchester. Served with Nos 1, 93 and 111 Sqdns, 1952-60; Mem., Black Arrows aerobatic team, 1957-59; commanded: No 92 Sqdn, 1962-64; No 17 Sqdn, 1970-71; RAF Wildenrath, 1974-75. Queen's Commendation for Valuable Service in the Air, 1960. MBIM 1976. Winner, Carris Trophy, Hants, IoW and Channel Islands Golf Championship, and Brabazon Trophy, 1949; English Schoolboy Golf Internat., 1948-49; Inter-Services Golf, 1952-57. *Recreations:* golf, squash, caravanning, photography. *Address:* Belmont, Clappins Lane, Naphill, near

High Wycombe, Bucks. *T:* Naphill 2488. *Clubs:* Royal Air Force; Ashridge Golf.

HINES, Prof. Albert Gregorio; Professor of Economics, University of London, and Head of Department of Economics, Birkbeck College, since 1972; *b* 8 Oct. 1935; Jamaican; *m* 1962, June Rosemary Chesney Carcas (marr. diss. 1976); two *s* one *d*. *Educ:* Victoria Town Sch., Manchester; London Sch. of Economics, Univ. of London (BSc Econ). Asst Lectr, Univ. of Bristol, 1962-64; Lectr, University Coll. London, 1964-68; Prof. of Economics, Univ. of Durham, 1968-72. Vis. Prof., Massachusetts Inst. of Technology, 1971-72. Vice-Pres., Section F, British Assoc. for the Advancement of Science, 1970-71. Economist, Overseas Development Ministry, 1965-66. Mem., Gen. Adv. Council, BBC, 1974-; Chairman: Enquiry into Minority Arts in UK, 1975; Commn for Economic Stabilisation, Jamaica, 1975-. *Publications:* On the Reappraisal of Keynesian Economics, 1971; articles in: Economic Jl, Review of Economic Studies, Review of Economics and Statistics, Amer. Economic Review, The Times. *Recreations:* theatre, cinema, music, novels, cricket, walking. *Address:* Department of Economics, Birkbeck College, 7/15 Gresse Street, W1P 1PA. *Club:* National Liberal.

HINES, Sir Colin (Joseph), Kt 1976; OBE 1973; President: NSW Returned Services League Clubs Association, since 1971; NSW Branch, Returned Services League of Australia, since 1971; Deputy National President, Returned Services League of Australia, since 1974; *b* 16 Feb. 1919; *s* of J. Hines and Mrs Hines, Lyndhurst, NSW; *m* 1942, Jean Elsie, *d* of A. Wilson, Mandurama, NSW; two *s*. *Educ:* All Saints' Coll., Bathurst, NSW. Army, 1937-45. Farmer and grazier, 1946-71. Hon. Officer, Returned Services League of Aust., 1971-76. State Comr, Aust. Forces Overseas Fund, 1971-; Trustee, Anzac Meml Trust, 1971-. Chairman: War Veterans Homes, Narrabeen, 1971-; Clubs Mutual Services Ltd, 1972-. *Recreations:* rifle shooting, golf. *Address:* The Meadows, Lyndhurst, NSW 2741, Australia. *T:* Lyndhurst 17. *Club:* Imperial Services (Sydney, NSW).

HINES, Robert Henry; Metropolitan Stipendiary Magistrate, since 1976; *b* 14 Feb. 1931; *s* of late Harry Hines and Josephine Hines; *m* 1957, Shelagh Mary, *d* of Mathew McKernan; four *s*. *Educ:* St Edmund's Coll., Ware, Herts. Commnd Army, National Service, 1949-51. Called to the Bar, Lincoln's Inn, 1954; practised at Bar; joined Magistrates' Court's Service, Inner London, 1958; Chief Clerk, Bow Street Magistrates' Court, 1964-76. *Recreation:* music. *Address:* 39 Mount Park Crescent, W5 2RR. *T:* 01-997 2911.

HINES, (Vivian) Gerald, QC 1964; JP; **His Honour Judge Hines;** a Circuit Judge, Central Criminal Court, since 1972 (Chairman, North East London Quarter Sessions, 1965-68, Greater London Quarter Sessions (Middlesex Area), 1969, Greater London Quarter Sessions (Inner London), 1969-71); *b* 24 Dec. 1912; 2nd *s* of late John Hines and Lizzie Emily (*née* Daniells), Essex; *m* 1st, 1950, Janet Graham, MA (*d* 1957), *e d* of late John Graham, Wigtownshire; 2nd, 1960, Barbara, *y d* of late Herbert Gunton, Colchester. *Educ:* Earls Colne Grammar Sch. Admitted Solicitor, 1935; private practice, 1935-42; Clerk to Colchester Borough Justices, 1942; called to Bar, Inner Temple, 1943; South-Eastern Circuit. Dep. Chairman: Essex QS, 1955-67; County of London QS, 1965; Judge of the Central Criminal Court, 1968-69. Mem., Home Office Adv. Council on the Penal System, 1970-. Member: Council, Magistrates' Assoc., 1967-70; Standing Joint Cttee, Essex, 1962-65. Governor, New Coll., London, 1963-65; Member: Court of Essex Univ., 1966-; Council of Boy Scouts' Assoc., 1961-66; Essex CC, 1946-49. JP Essex, 1955, Greater London, 1965. Freeman, City of London, 1975. Liveryman, Fan Makers' Co., 1976. *Publications:* contrib. to Halsbury's Laws of England, 4th edn (Criminal Law Vol.); articles in British Jl of Criminology, The Magistrate and other jls. *Address:* Littlefield, Great Bentley, Colchester, Essex CO7 8QE. *T:* Great Bentley 250555; 3 Dr Johnson's Buildings, Temple, EC4Y 7BA. *T:* 01-583 2870. *Club:* City Livery.

HINGESTON, Brig. William Henry, CBE 1944; sugar cane planter; *b* 21 Nov. 1906; *s* of late Charles Sutherton and Elizabeth Leonore Hingeston, Transkei, South Africa; *m* 1936, Anne Emmett, *d* of late Mr Justice de Waal; one *s*. *Educ:* St Charles Coll., Pietermaritzburg. Cadet SA Military Coll., S Africa, 1929-30; (Lieut) Flying Instructor, SAAF, 1931-34; (Capt.) Adjt, SAAF, 1935; (Major and Lieut-Col) AAG, Defence Hqrs, Pretoria, 1936-40; OC Waterkloof Air Station, Pretoria, 1941; (Col) Senior Administrative Officer (Air), SAAF, Middle East Forces, 1941; Dep. General Officer Adminis. (Air), SAAF, Mediterranean and Mid-East Theatre, 1943; Dep. Adjt-Gen., UDF, 1945; Adjt-Gen., UDF, 1946; OC Witwatersrand Comd, 1948; OC Natal Comd, 1953; retd 1955.

Recreations: golf, bridge. *Address:* Box 22, Triangle, Fort Victoria, Rhodesia. *Club:* Johannesburg Country.

HINGLEY, Anthony Capper Moore, CVO 1954; *b* 28 Nov. 1908; *e s* of late Lieut-Col S. H. Hingley and Dorothy, *d* of Thomas Capper; *m* 1947, Ruth, *d* of late C. P. Andrews; two *s* one *d*. *Educ:* Rugby Sch.; Trinity Coll., Oxford (MA). Ceylon Civil Service, 1931-47; Asst Establishment Officer, Kenya, 1947-49; Chief Establishment Officer, Nyasaland, 1949-50; Sec. to Governor-Gen., Ceylon, 1950-54; Chief Establishment Officer, Nyasaland, 1954-60; seconded as Mem., Interim Federal Public Service Commn, Fedn of Rhodesia and Nyasaland, 1955-59; Establishments Adviser, Seychelles, 1965. *Recreations:* golf, bridge. *Address:* Copse Hill, West Hatch, Taunton, Som. *Clubs:* East India, Devonshire, Sports and Public Schools. Eccentric; Somerset County.

HINGSTON, Lt-Col Walter George, OBE 1964; psc; FRGS; Member, Marlborough and Ramsbury Rural District Council, 1970-74; *b* Radcliffe on Trent, Notts, 15 Feb. 1905; *s* of late Charles Hingston and late Mildred (*née* Pleydell Bouverie), Cotgrave, Nottingham; *m* 1939, Elizabeth Margaret, *d* of Brig. Sir Clinton Lewis, *qv*; two *d*. *Educ:* Harrow; RMC Sandhurst; and Staff Coll. 2nd Lieut, KOYLI, 1925; Nigeria Regt, RWAFF, 1931-36; 1st Punjab Regt, Indian Army, 1936. Served War of 1939-45: 4th Indian Div., North Africa, Eritrea (despatches); Dep. Dir Public Relations, GHQ India, 1942; Chief Information Officer to C-in-C, Ceylon, 1943; retired (invalided), 1945. Chief Information Officer, Dept of Scientific and Industrial Research, 1945-63; Editor, the Geographical Magazine, 1963-68. *Publications:* The Tiger Strikes, 1942; The Tiger Kills (with G. R. Stevens), 1944; Never Give Up, 1948. *Recreation:* fishing. *Address:* The Old Vicarage, Ramsbury, near Marlborough, Wilts. *Club:* Army and Navy.

HINKSON, Pamela; novelist, journalist, writer of travel books and children's books; *o d* of late H. A. Hinkson, author, Resident Magistrate, Ireland, and late Katharine Tynan Hinkson, poet and prose writer. *Educ:* privately, and by living in France and Germany. During War, 1939-45: worked for Ministry of Information; mem. of Cttee of Shamrock (Irish Service) Club in London; lectured in USA for British Information Service, on India, 1944. Lecture Tours to HM Forces overseas, 1946 and 1947. Lecture Tour to German audiences, Germany, 1947. *Publications:* include: Wind from the West, 1930; The Ladies' Road, 1932; The Deeply Rooted, 1935; Seventy Years Young (collaboration with Elizabeth, Countess of Fingall), 1937; Irish Gold, 1940; Indian Harvest, 1941; Golden Rose, 1944; The Lonely Bride, 1951; contributor to The Fortnightly, Cornhill, Spectator, New Statesman, Time and Tide, Observer, Sunday Times, Guardian, Country Life, etc. *Recreations:* friendship (with adults and children), country life, animals. *Address:* c/o Lloyds Bank, 112 Kensington High Street, W8.

HINSLEY, Prof. Francis Harry, OBE 1946; President, St John's College, since 1975 (Fellow, since 1944), and Professor of the History of International Relations in the University of Cambridge, since 1969; *b* 26 Nov. 1918; *s* of late Thomas Henry Hinsley, and of Emma Hinsley; *m* 1946, Hilary Brett, *d* of late H. F. B. Brett-Smith and of Helena Brett-Smith, Oxford; two *s* one *d*. *Educ:* Queen Mary's Grammar Sch., Walsall; St John's Coll., Cambridge. HM Foreign Office, war service, 1939-46; Research Fellow, St John's Coll., Cambridge, 1944-50; Lectr in History, Univ. of Cambridge, 1949-65; Tutor, St John's Coll., Cambridge, 1956-63; Editor, The Historical Journal, 1960-71; Reader in the History of International Relations, Univ. of Cambridge, 1965-69. Chm., Faculty Bd of History, Cambridge, 1970-72; Lees-Knowles Lectr on Military Science, Trinity Coll., 1970-71. UK Rep., Provisional Academic Cttee for European Univ. Inst., 1973-75. *Publications:* Command of the Sea, 1950; Hitler's Strategy, 1951; (ed) New Cambridge Modern History, Vol. XI, 1962; Power and the Pursuit of Peace, 1963; Sovereignty, 1966; Nationalism and the International System, 1973; (ed) British Foreign Policy under Sir Edward Grey, 1977. *Address:* St John's College, Cambridge. *T:* 61621; The Grove, Newnham, Cambridge. *T:* 50719.

HINSLEY, Prof. Frederick Baden; Professor of Mining and Head of Department of Mining Engineering, University of Nottingham, 1947-67, now Emeritus; *b* 20 May 1900; *m* 1932, Doris Lucy Spencer; three *s* two *d*. *Educ:* Coalville Technical Coll.; University of Birmingham. Lecturer and Vice-Principal, County Technical Coll., Worksop, 1932-39; Lecturer in Dept of Mining, University Coll., Cardiff, 1939-47. Pres. IMinE, 1968. Silver medal, Warwicks and S Staffs Inst. of Mining Engineers, 1940; Gold medal, South Wales Inst. of Engineers, 1946; Silver medal, Midland Counties Instn of Engineers, 1951; Douglas

Hay medal, 1955, Institution Medal, 1971, Instn of Mining Engineers; Van Waterschoot Van der Gracht medal, Royal Geol. and Mining Soc. of the Netherlands, 1962. *Publications:* contribs to: Proc. S Wales Inst. of Engineers; Proc. Nat. Assoc. of Colliery Managers; Trans Instn of Mining Engineers. *Recreations:* writing history of mining, gardening, reading. *Address:* 47 Ribblesdale Road, Sherwood, Nottingham. *T:* Nottingham 268981.

HINTON, family name of **Baron Hinton of Bankside.**

HINTON OF BANKSIDE, Baron *cr* 1965 (Life Peer); **Christopher Hinton,** OM 1976; KBE 1957; Kt 1951; FRS 1954; MA; Hon. FICE; Hon. FIMechE; Hon. FIEE; FIChemE; FRSA; *b* 12 May 1901; *s* of late Frederick Henry Hinton, Lacock, Wilts; *m* 1931, Lillian (*d* 1973), *d* of late Thomas Boyer; one *d*. *Educ:* Chippenham Grammar Sch.; Trinity Coll., Cambridge. Engineering apprenticeship, GWR Co., Swindon, 1917-23; Trinity Coll., Cambridge, 1923-26 (senior scholarship, 1st Class Hons Mech. Sciences Tripos, John Wimbolt Prize, Second Yeats Prize). ICI (Alkali), Northwich, 1926-40 (Chief Engineer, 1931-40); on loan from ICI to Ministry of Supply, 1940-46 (Dep. Dir-Gen. of Filling Factories, 1942-46); Dep. Controller Atomic Energy (Production), Min. of Supply, 1946-54; Mem. of Board for Engineering and Production, and Man. Dir (Industrial Gp), UKAEA, 1954-57; Chairman: Central Electricity Generating Board, 1957-64; Internat. Exec. Cttee of World Energy Conf., 1962-68; Dep. Chm., Electricity Supply Research Coun., 1965-; Special Adviser to the Internat. Bank for Reconstruction and Develt, 1965-70; Chancellor of Bath Univ., 1966-. President: CE1, 1976-; Fellowship of Engineering, 1976-. Hon. Fellow of Trinity Coll., Cambridge, 1957; Hon. Associate, Manchester Coll. of Science and Technology. Hon. DEng, Liverpool, 1955; Hon. DSc (Eng), London, 1956; Hon. ScD, Cambridge, 1960; Hon. LLD, Edinburgh, 1958; Hon. DSc: Oxford, 1957; Southampton, 1962; Durham, 1966; Bath, 1966. Albert Medal (RSA), 1957; Melchett Medal, Inst. of Fuel, 1957; Glazebrook Medal and Prize, 1966; Rumford Medal (Royal Soc.); Axel Johnson Prize, Roy. Swedish Acad. of Engrg; Wilhelm-Exner Medal, Österreichischer Gewerbeverein; Castner Medal, Soc. of Chem. Industries; James Watt Internat. Medal, IMechE. Pres., IMechE, 1966-67. Hon. Fellow: Metals Soc.; Instn of Gas Engineers; Inst. of Welding; Welding Soc.; Hon. MASME. For. Associate, Amer. Acad. of Engineering. Imperial Order of The Rising Sun (Japan), 1966. *Publication:* Engineers and Engineering, 1970. *Address:* Tiverton Lodge, Dulwich Common, SE21 7EW. *T:* 01-693 6447.

HINTON, Geoffrey Thomas Searle, CBE 1967; HM Diplomatic Service, retired; *b* 18 June 1918; *s* of Francis John Hinton and late Mabel Frances Hinton (*née* Minns); *m* 1942, Averin Dora Macalister; one *s* two *d*. *Educ:* Christ Coll., Brecon; Worcester Coll., Oxford (MA). Min. of Information, 1941; HM Forces, 1943-46; entered Foreign (subseq. Diplomatic) Service, 1946; served in: Cairo, 1947; Bangkok, 1957; Paris, 1966; Counsellor, FCO, 1970-76. *Recreations:* languages, place-names, narrow-gauge railways, cricket. *Address:* The Steps, Withington, Cheltenham, Glos. *T:* Withington 228. *Clubs:* Royal Commonwealth Society; Talyllyn Railway Preservation Society.

HINTON, Michael Herbert; partner in City chartered accountants; Alderman, Ward of Billingsgate, City of London, since 1971; *b* 10 Nov. 1934; *s* of Walter Leonard Hinton and Freda Millicent Lillian Hinton; *m* 1955, Sarah (*née* Sunderland); one *s* two *d*. *Educ:* Ardingly Coll. FCA. Liveryman: Farmers' Co., 1964; Wheelwrights' Co., 1971; Mem. Court of Common Council for Ward of Billingsgate, 1970-71; Clerk to Wheelwrights' Co., 1965-71; Sheriff, City of London, 1977-78. *Recreations:* cricket, collector, City of London interests. *Address:* 178 Burges Road, Thorpe Bay, Essex. *T:* Shoeburyness 2685. *Clubs:* Farmers, MCC, City Livery (Pres., 1976-77).

HINTON, Nicholas John; Director, National Council of Social Service, since 1977; *b* 15 March 1942; *s* of Rev. Canon Hinton and late Mrs J. P. Hinton; *m* 1971, Deborah Mary Vivian. *Educ:* Marlborough Coll., Wiltshire; Selwyn Coll., Cambridge (MA). Asst Dir, Northorpe Hall Trust, 1965-68; Nat. Assoc. for Care and Resettlement of Offenders, 1968-77, Dir, 1973-77. Member: Council, Howard League for Penal Reform; Central Council for Educn and Trng in Social Work; Bd of Governors, Volunteer Centre, 1973-75. Dir, Edington Music Festival, 1965-70. *Recreation:* music. *Address:* 26 Bedford Square, W1. *T:* 01-636 4066.

HINTON-COOPER, Harold, CIE 1945; ED 1943; retired; *b* 20 May 1891; *s* of Bernard Hinton-Cooper; *m* 1916, Winifred, *d* of late W. H. Lawson, JP, Swindon; one *s*. *Educ:* Deal Coll.; Swindon Technical Coll. Training on GWR, 1907-12; appointed

Asst Loco. Supt, Indian State Rlys, 1914; Dep. Chief Mechanical Engr, India, 1936-39; Chief Mechanical Engr, 1939-46; retd 1946. Afghan Medal, 1919; Coronation Medal, 1937. *Recreations:* golf, photography. *Address:* 49 Kenton Lane, Harrow, Mddx.

HINTZ, Orton Sutherland, CMG 1968; former Editor, The New Zealand Herald, Auckland, New Zealand, 1958-70; *b* 15 Nov. 1907; Trustee, Woolf Fisher Trust (educational); *s* of late Alfred and late Cora Hintz; *m* 1st, 1931, Flora Margaret McIver (*d* 1943); 2nd, 1965, Caroline Jean Crawford (*née* Hutchinson). *Educ:* Mt Albert Grammar Sch., Auckland; Auckland Univ. Joined NZ Herald Staff, 1925; Parly Corresp., 1935-38; War service, Naval Intelligence, 1941-46; Night Ed., NZ Herald, 1946; Assoc. Ed., NZ Herald, 1952; Dir, Wilson & Horton Ltd, 1961; Dir, NZ Press Assoc., 1962 (Chm., 1965-66); Reuters Trustee, 1964-68. Mem. Coun., Outward Bound Trust of NZ, 1961; Delegate, Commonwealth Press Conf., India and Pakistan, 1961. *Publications:* The New Zealanders in England, 1931; HMNZS Philomel, 1944; Trout at Taupo, 1955; (ed) Lord Cobham's Speeches, 1962; Fisherman's Paradise, 1975. *Recreations:* trout fishing (Pres. Lake Taupo Angling Fedn), cricket, Rugby football. *Address:* 36 Oregon Drive, Rainbow Point, Taupo, NZ. *T:* 1059M. *Clubs:* Flyfishers'; Anglers' (New York); Northern (Auckland).

HIPKIN, John; Director, Advisory Centre for Education, Cambridge, since 1974; *b* 9 April 1935; *s* of Jack Hipkin and Elsie Hipkin; *m* 1963, Bronwyn Vaughan Dewey; two *s* one *d*. *Educ:* Surbiton Grammar Sch. for Boys; LSE (BScEcon). Asst Teacher, 1957-65; Research Officer: King's Coll., Cambridge, 1965-68; Univ. of East Anglia, 1968-71; Sec., Schools Council Working Party on Whole Curriculum, 1973-74. *Publications:* (jtly) New Wine in Old Bottles, 1967; (ed jtly) Education for the Seventies, 1970; The Massacre of Peterloo (a play), 1968, 2nd edn 1974. *Recreations:* theatre, photography, history, modern music. *Address:* 82 Chesterton Road, Cambridge CB4 1ER. *T:* Cambridge 59574.

HIPPISLEY-COX, Peter Denzil John; solicitor and parliamentary agent; Senior Partner, Dyson, Bell & Co., London, since 1976; Chairman, Equity & Law Life Assurance Society, since 1977; *b* 22 May 1921; *s* of late Col Sir Geoffrey Hippisley Cox, CBE, and Lady Hippisley Cox; *m* 1st, 1948, Olga Kay (marr. diss. 1956); one *d*; 2nd, 1956, Frieda Marion Wood; two *d*. *Educ:* Stowe; Trinity Coll., Cambridge (MA). Served War, RAF (Signals), 1941-46 (Flt Lieut). Admitted a solicitor, 1949. Dir, Equity & Law Life Assurance Soc., 1965- (Dep. Chm. 1973). Member: Council, Law Soc., 1956-; Court, Drapers' Co., 1972-. Governor, Bancroft's Sch., 1975-. *Recreation:* music. *Address:* 95 Dovehouse Street, Chelsea, SW3 6JZ. *T:* 01-352 4608. *Club:* Carlton.

HIPWELL, Hermine H.; *see* Vivenot, Baroness R. de.

HIRSCH, Prof. Kurt August; Professor of Pure Mathematics, University of London, Queen Mary College, 1957-73, now Emeritus; *b* Berlin, 12 Jan. 1906; *s* of Dr Robert Hirsch and Anna (*née* Lehmann); *m* 1928, Elsa Brühl; one *s* two *d*. *Educ:* University of Berlin; University of Cambridge. Dr phil (Berlin), 1930; PhD (Cambridge), 1937. Asst Lecturer, later Lecturer, University Coll., Leicester, 1938-47; Lecturer, later Sen. Lecturer, King's Coll., Newcastle upon Tyne, 1948-51; Reader, University of London, Queen Mary Coll., 1951-57. Editor, Russian Mathematical Surveys. *Publications:* (with A. G. Kurosh) Theory of Groups, 3 vols, 3rd English edn 1971; (with F. R. Gantmacher) Theory of Matrices, 2 vols, English edn 1960; (with A. G. Kurosh) Lectures on General Algebra, English edn 1964; (with I. R. Shafarevich) Basic Algebraic Geometry, 1974; contribs to learned jls. *Recreations:* chess, gardening. *Address:* 101 Shirehall Park, NW4 2QU. *T:* 01-202 7902.

HIRSCH, Prof. Sir Peter (Bernhard), Kt 1975; MA, PhD; FRS 1963; Isaac Wolfson Professor of Metallurgy in the University of Oxford since 1966; Fellow, St Edmund Hall, Oxford, since 1966; *b* 16 Jan. 1925; *s* of Ismar Hirsch and Regina Hirsch (now Meyerson); *m* 1959, Mabel Anne Kellar (*née* Stephens), *widow* of James Noel Kellar; one step *s* one step *d*. *Educ:* Sloane Sch., Chelsea; St Catharine's Coll., Cambridge. BA 1946; MA 1950; PhD 1951. Reader in Physics in Univ. of Cambridge, 1964-66; Fellow, Christ's Coll., Cambridge, 1960-66. Has been engaged on researches with electron microscope on imperfections in crystalline structure of metals and on relation between structural defects and mechanical properties. Rosenhain Medal, Inst. of Metals, 1961; C. V. Boys Prize, Inst. of Physics and Physical Soc., 1962; Clamer Medal, Franklin Inst., 1970; Wihuri Internat. Prize, Helsinki, 1971; Royal Soc. Hughes Medal, 1973;

Metals Soc. Platinum Medal, 1976. Hon. Fellow, RMS, 1977. *Publications:* Electron Microscopy of Thin Crystals (with others), 1965; (ed) The Physics of Metals, vol. 2, Defects, 1975; numerous contribs learned jls. *Recreation:* bridge. *Address:* Department of Metallurgy and Science of Materials, Parks Road, Oxford OX1 3PH. *T:* Oxford 59981; 8 Lakeside, Oxford.

HIRSHFIELD, family name of **Baron Hirshfield.**

HIRSHFIELD, Baron *cr* 1967, of Holborn in Greater London (Life Peer); **Desmond Barel Hirshfield;** Joint Senior Partner, Stoy Horwath & Co., Chartered Accountants; Consultant, Stoy Hayward & Co.; Chairman, Horwath & Horwath (UK) Ltd; Director, European Operations, Horwath & Horwath International; Founder and Chairman, Trades Union Unit Trust Managers Ltd, since 1961; Deputy Chairman, MLH Consultants, since 1971; Founder and Director, Foundation on Automation and Human Development, since 1962; *b* 17 May 1913; *s* of late Leopold Hirshfield and Lily Hirshfield (*née* Blackford); *m* 1951, Bronia Eisen. *Educ:* City of London Sch. Chartered Accountant, 1939; Mem., Cttee on Consumer Credit, 1968-71; Dep. Chm., Northampton New Town Develt Corp., 1968-76; Member: Central Adv. Water Cttee, 1969-70; Top Salaries Review Body, 1975-; Admin. Trustee, Chevening Estate, 1970-; Pres., Brit. Assoc. of Hotel Accountants; Treasurer: UK Cttee of UNICEF, 1969-; Nat. Council for the Unmarried Mother and her Child, 1970-71. Pres., Norwood Charitable Trust, 1960-; Chm., Norwood Homes for Jewish Children, 1968-; Mem., Bd of Deputies of British Jews, 1955-67. Capt., British Team, World Maccabi Games, Prague, 1934. *Publications:* pamphlets and reports on The Accounts of Charitable Institutions; Avoidance and Evasion of Income Tax; Scheme for Pay as You Earn; Investment of Trade Union Funds; Organisations and Methods Reviews; articles in periodicals and newspapers. *Recreations:* travel, painting, caricaturing. *Address:* 54 Baker Street, W1M 1DJ. *T:* 01-486 5888. *Club:* Royal Automobile.

HIRST, David Cozens-Hardy, QC 1965; Barrister-at-Law; *b* 31 July 1925; *er s* of late Thomas William Hirst and of Margaret Joy Hirst, Aylsham, Norfolk; *m* 1951, Pamela Elizabeth Molesworth Bevan, *d* of Col T. P. M. Bevan, MC; three *s* two *d*. *Educ:* Eton; Trinity Coll., Cambridge. MA. Served 1943-47; RA and Intelligence Corps, Capt. 1946. Barrister, Inner Temple, 1951; Bencher, 1974; Vice-Chm. of the Bar, 1977-78. Member: Lord Chancellor's Law Reform Cttee; Gen. Council, Inns of Court and the Bar; Council on Tribunals; Cttee to review Defamation Act, 1952, 1971-. *Recreations:* shooting, lawn tennis, theatre and opera. *Address:* 1 Brick Court, Temple, EC4. *T:* 01-353 8845; Almond House, Hampton, Middx. *T:* 01-979 1666; Folly Cottage, Uploders, near Bridport, Dorset. *T:* Powerstock 284. *Clubs:* Boodle's, MCC.

HIRST, Geoffrey A. N., TD 1945; *b* 14 Dec. 1904; *s* of late Col E. A. Hirst, CMG, TD, Ingmanthorpe Hall, Wetherby, Yorks. *Educ:* Charterhouse; St John's Coll., Cambridge. Former Director: Samuel Webster & Sons Ltd; J. Hey & Co. Ltd; Hey & Humphries Ltd; Spinks (Caterers) Ltd; FBI: Mem. Grand Council and Executive Cttee, 1932-40, 1958-65; Mem. Economic Policy Cttee; Mem. Leeds Exec., 1930-46; East and West Riding Council and Exec., 1946-65, Vice-Chm., 1956, Chm., 1958-60. Mem. of Council, CBI: Mem., Economic Cttee, East and West Ridings and Humberside (Yorks) Regional Council, 1965-69. Leeds Chamber of Commerce: Mem. Council, 1932-; Junior Vice-Pres., 1948-49; Senior Vice-Pres., 1949-51; Pres., 1952-54; Mem. Council, Bradford Chamber of Commerce, 1950-70; Vice-Pres., Urban Dist Councils' Assoc., 1951-70; Mem., Nat. Advisory Council for Educn in Industry and Commerce, 1948-51; Chm., Yorks Regional Academic Bd, 1947-49; Mem., Leeds and Hull Academic Board, 1947-53 (Chm., 1949-50); Mem., Yorks Council for Further Educn, 1934-40 and 1949-51; Leeds Coll. of Technology: Mem. Bd of Governors, 1932-40; Vice-Chm., 1932-36 and 1938-40. Member: Leeds Nat. Service Cttee, 1938-40; UK Council of European Movement; Economic League, Central Council, 1934-67. Chm., W Yorks Regional Council and Exec., 1945-50; Mem., Nat. Council, Inst. of Marketing and Sales Management, 1932-35, 1960-62; Leeds Executive: Mem., 1930-; Chm., 1932-33; Pres., 1949-50; Vice-Pres. W Yorks Branch, English-Speaking Union. MP (C) Shipley Div., WR Yorks, 1950-70; Hon. Sec., Conservative Party's Parliamentary Trade and Industry Cttee, 1959-61, Vice-Chm., 1962, Chm., 1963-64. Member: Leeds Musical Festival Exec., 1934-54; Leeds Philharmonic Soc. Exec., 1930-39. FCS, FSS, FREconS, FInstMSM. Territl Army, 1924-32, rejoined, 1939; served War of 1939-45; Battery Comdr, second in Comd 69th Fd Regt, RA, 1939-44; attached to Staff, 21 Army Gp, 1945. *Publications:* various contribs to the Press. *Recreations:* travel, music. *Address:* Le Manoir, 1867 Glutières-sur-Ollon, Vaud, Switzerland. *T:* (025) 7.35.70. *Club:* Boodle's.

HIRST, Prof. John Malcolm, DSC 1945; PhD; FRS 1970; FIBiol; Director, Long Ashton Research Station, and Professor of Agricultural and Horticultural Science, Bristol University, since 1975; *b* 20 April 1921; *s* of Maurice Herbert Hirst and Olive Mary (*née* Pank); *m* 1957, Barbara Mary Stokes; two *d*. *Educ:* Solihull Sch.; Reading University. PhD London 1955. Royal Navy (Coastal Forces), 1941-46; Reading Univ. (BSc Hons Agric. Bot.), 1946-50; Rothamsted Exper. Stn., Harpenden, 1950-75, Hd of Plant Pathology Dept, 1967-75. Jakob Eriksson Gold Medal (Internat. Botanical Congress), 1959; Research Medal, RASE, 1970. *Publications:* papers in scientific jls mainly in Trans British Mycological Soc., Annals of Applied Biology, Jl of General Microbiology. *Address:* Long Ashton Research Station, Long Ashton, Bristol BS18 9AF. *T:* Long Ashton 2181.

HIRST, Prof. Paul Heywood; Professor of Education, University of Cambridge, and Fellow of Wolfson College (formerly University College), Cambridge, since 1971; *b* 10 Nov. 1927; *s* of late Herbert and Winifred Hirst, Birkby, Huddersfield. *Educ:* Huddersfield Coll.; Trinity Coll., Cambridge. BA 1948, MA 1952, Certif. Educn 1952, Cantab; DipEd 1955, London; MA Oxon (by incorporation), Christ Church, Oxford, 1955. Asst Master, William Hulme's Grammar Sch., Manchester, 1948-50; Maths Master, Eastbourne Coll., 1950-55; Lectr and Tutor, Univ. of Oxford Dept of Educn, 1955-59; Lectr in Philosophy of Educn, Univ. of London Inst. of Educn, 1959-65; Prof. of Educn, King's Coll., Univ. of London, 1965-71. Visiting Professor: Univ. of British Columbia, 1964, 1967; Univ. of Malawi, 1969. De Carpe Lectr, Univ. of Otago, 1976; Fink Lectr, Univ. of Melbourne, 1976. Mem. Council, Gordonstoun Sch.; Chm., Philosophy of Educn Soc. of GB. *Publications:* (with R. S. Peters) The Logic of Education, 1970; (ed with R. F. Dearden and R. S. Peters) Education and the Development of Reason, 1971; Knowledge and the Curriculum, 1974; Moral Education in a Secular Society, 1974; papers in: Philosophical Analysis and Education (ed R. D. Archambault), 1965; The Study of Education (ed J. W. Tibble), 1965; The Concept of Education (ed R. S. Peters), 1966; Let's Teach Them Right (ed C. Macy), 1969; also in Brit. Jl Educnl Studies, Jl Curriculum Studies, Proc. Philosophy of Educn Soc. *Recreation:* music, especially opera. *Address:* Wolfson College, Cambridge; Dept of Education, 17 Trumpington Street, Cambridge CB2 1PT. *T:* Cambridge 55271. *Club:* Athenæum.

HIRST, Prof. Rodney Julian, MA; Professor of Logic and Rhetoric, University of Glasgow, since 1961; *b* 28 July 1920; *s* of Rev. William Hirst and Elsie Hirst; *m* 1942, Jessica, *y d* of Charles Alfred Podmore; two *d*. *Educ:* Leeds Grammar Sch.; Magdalen Coll., Oxford. Demy, 1938-47; 1st Cl. Hons Classical Mods, 1940. War Service, 1940-45, mainly as REME Officer (Radar) at home and in Italy. First Class Hons Lit. Hum., Dec. 1947. Lectr in Logic and Metaphysics, St Andrews Univ., 1948; Glasgow University: Lectr, 1949, and Sen. Lectr, 1959, in Logic; Dean of Arts, 1971-73; Senate Assessor on Univ. Court, 1973-; Vice-Principal, 1976-. *Publications:* Problems of Perception, 1959; (co-author) Human Senses and Perception, 1964; Perception and the External World, 1965; Philosophy: an outline for the intending student, 1968; contribs to Encyclopedia of Philosophy and philosophical journals. *Address:* 179 Maxwell Drive, Glasgow G41 5AE. *T:* 041-427 3554.

HISCOCKS, Prof. Charles Richard, MA, DPhil; Professor of International Relations, University of Sussex, 1964-72, now Emeritus; *b* 1 June 1907; *y s* of F. W. Hiscocks; unmarried. *Educ:* Highgate Sch.; St Edmund Hall, Oxford; Berlin University. Asst Master, Trinity Coll. Sch., Port Hope, Ont, 1929-32; Bradfield Coll., 1936-39; Marlborough Coll., 1939-40. Served with Royal Marines, 1940-45, Lieut-Col; seconded to army for mil. govt duties in Germany, 1945; Brit. Council Rep. in Austria, 1946-49, S India, 1949-50; Prof. of Polit. Sci. and Internat. Relations, Univ. of Manitoba, 1950-64. UK Mem., UN Sub-Commn for Prevention of Discrimination and Protection of Minorities, 1953-62. Pres., Winnipeg Art Gall., 1959-60. Vis. Fellow, Princeton Univ., 1970-71; Fellow, Adlai Stevenson Inst. of Internat. Affairs, Chicago, 1971-72. Mem., Nat. Exec., UN Assoc., 1973-74, Vice-Pres., 1977-. *Publications:* The Rebirth of Austria, 1953; Democracy in Western Germany, 1957; Poland: Bridge for the Abyss?, 1963; Germany Revived, 1966; The Security Council: a study in adolescence, 1973. *Recreations:* music, art, riding. *Address:* Dickers, Hunworth, Melton Constable, Norfolk. *T:* Holt 2503. *Club:* Garrick.

HISS, Alger; Commercial printing since 1959 (manufacturing, 1957-59); *b* 11 Nov. 1904; *s* of Charles Alger Hiss and Mary L. Hughes; *m* 1929, Priscilla Fansler Hobson; one *s*. *Educ:* Johns Hopkins Univ. (AB 1926, Hon. LLD 1947); Harvard Univ. (LLB 1929). Sec. and law clerk to Supreme Court Justice

Holmes, 1929-30; law practice, 1930-33; asst to gen. counsel and asst gen. counsel, Agricultural Adjustment Admin., 1933-35; legal asst, special Senate cttee investigating munitions industry, 1934-35; special attorney, US Dept of Justice, 1935-36; asst to Asst Sec. of State, 1936; asst to Adviser on Political Relations, 1939; special asst to Dir, Office of Far Eastern Affairs, 1944; special asst to Dir, Office of Special Political Affairs, May 1944; Dep. Dir, Nov. 1944, Dir, 1945; accompanied Pres. Roosevelt and Sec. of State Stettinius to Malta and Yalta Conferences, Feb. 1945; exec. sec., Dumbarton Oaks Conversations, Aug.-Oct. 1944; sec.-gen., United Nations Conference on International Organization, San Francisco, 1945; Principal Adviser to US Delegation, Gen. Assembly of United Nations, London, 1946; elected Pres. and Trustee of Carnegie Endowment for Internat. Peace, Dec. 1946 (Pres. until 1949). Mem., Massachusetts Bar. Mem., Alpha Delta Phi, Phi Beta Kappa. *Publications:* The Myth of Yalta, 1955; In the Court of Public Opinion, 1957, new edn 1972; Holmes-Laski Letters (abridged edn), 1963. *Recreations:* tennis, swimming, ornithology. *Address:* c/o Davison-Bluth, 295 Lafayette Street, New York, NY 10012, USA. *T:* Worth 6-2492.

HITCH, Brian; HM Diplomatic Service; Counsellor, Algiers, since 1977; *b* 2 June 1932; *m* 1954, Margaret Kathleen Wooller; two *d. Educ:* Wisbech Grammar Sch. (FRCO, LRAM); Magdalene Coll., Cambridge. Joined FO, 1955; 3rd/2nd Sec., Tokyo, 1955-61; FO, 1961-62; 2nd/1st Sec., Havana, 1962-64; 1st Sec., Athens, 1965-68; 1st Sec. and Head of Chancery, Tokyo, 1968-72; Asst Head, Southern European Dept, FCO, 1972-73; Dep. Head, later Head, Marine and Transport Dept, FCO, 1973-75; Counsellor, Bonn, 1975-77. *Recreations:* chamber music, walking, Japanese studies. *Address:* British Embassy, 7 Chemin des Glycines, Algiers; (home) 1 Mount Ararat Road, Richmond, Surrey TW10 6PQ. *T:* 01-940 4737. *Club:* United Oxford & Cambridge University.

HITCHCOCK, Alfred Joseph; film producer-director; *b* 13 Aug. 1899; *s* of William and Emma Hitchcock; *m* 1926, Alma Reville; one *d. Educ:* St Ignatius Coll., London. Junior technician at Famous Players Lasky British Studios, 1920; Scenario writer, art dir, production manager, Gainsborough Pictures, 1923; Motion Picture Dir, 1925. Films include: The Lodger, Farmer's Wife, The Ring, Blackmail, Juno and the Paycock, Murder, Skin Game, Man Who Knew Too Much, Thirty-Nine Steps, Secret Agent, Sabotage, Young and Innocent, The Lady Vanishes, Jamaica Inn, Rebecca, Foreign Correspondent, Mr and Mrs Smith, Suspicion, Saboteur, Shadow of a Doubt, Lifeboat, Spellbound, Notorious, Paradine Case, Rope, Under Capricorn, Stage Fright, Strangers on a Train, I Confess, Dial M for Murder, Rear Window, To catch a Thief, The Trouble with Harry, The Wrong Man, Vertigo, North by Northwest, Psycho, The Birds, Marnie, Torn Curtain, Topaz, Frenzy, Family Plot. Television: Alfred Hitchcock Presents (1959-62), Alfred Hitchcock Hour (1963-65). Hon. DHumL, Columbia, 1972. Irving G. Thalberg Meml Award; Milestone Award, Producers' Guild, 1965; D. W. Griffith Award, Directors' Award, 1968; C. B. de Mille Award, 1972. Chevalier, Légion d'Honneur. *Address:* 10957 Bellagio Road, Bel Air, Los Angeles, California 90024, USA.

HITCHCOCK, Dr Anthony J. M.; Head of Research Policy (Transport) Division, Departments of the Environment and Transport, since 1975; *b* 26 June 1929; *s* of Dr Ronald W. Hitchcock and Hilda (*née* Gould); *m* 1953, Audrey Ellen (*née* Ashworth); one *s* two *d. Educ:* Bedales; Manchester Grammar Sch.; Trinity Coll., Cambridge; Univ. of Chicago. PhD, BA; MInstP; MCIT. Asst, Univ. of Chicago, 1951-52; AEA, 1953-67; Head of Traffic (later Transport) Dept, Transport and Road Res. Lab., 1967-75. *Publications:* Nuclear Reactor Control, 1960; articles in learned jls. *Recreation:* bridge. *Address:* Seal Point, Comeragh Close, Golf Club Road, Woking, Surrey GU22 0LZ. *T:* Woking 5219.

HITCHCOCK, Geoffrey Lionel Henry, CBE 1975 (OBE 1957); External Relations Consultant, Bell Educational Trust, Cambridge; *b* 10 Sept. 1915; *s* of late Major Frank B. Hitchcock, MC, and Mrs Mildred Hitchcock (*née* Sloane Stanley), Danbury, Essex; *m* 1950, Rosemary, *d* of Albert de Las Casas, Tiverton; two *s* one *d. Educ:* Oratory Sch., Caversham; Hertford Coll., Oxford (Exhibr, MA). British Council, April-Sept. 1939. Commnd London Rifle Bde, 1939; served with KAR in E Africa and SE Asia; Major 1943. Returned to British Council, 1946; served in London; Germany, 1950-54; Representative in Austria, 1954-59; Representative in Yugoslavia, 1962-67; Controller Home Div., British Council, 1970-73; Rep. of British Council in France and Cultural Counsellor, British Embassy, Paris, 1973-76. *Recreations:* racegoing, gardening. *Address:* c/o Barclays Bank Ltd, 2 High Street, Chelmsford, Essex CM1 1BG. *Club:* Travellers'.

HITCHCOCK, Prof. Henry-Russell; Adjunct Professor, Institute of Fine Arts, University of New York, since 1969; *b* 3 June 1903; *s* of Henry R. Hitchcock and Alice Whitworth Davis. *Educ:* Middlesex Sch., Concord, Mass, USA; Harvard Univ. MA 1927. Asst Prof. of Art, Vassar Coll., 1927-28; Asst, Assoc., Prof., Wesleyan Univ., 1929-48; Lectr in Architecture, Massachusetts Institute of Technology, 1946-48; Prof. of Art, Smith Coll., Mass, 1948-68; Prof. of Art, Univ. of Massachusetts, 1968. Dir, Smith Coll. Museum of Art, 1949-55; Lectr, Inst. of Fine Arts, New York Univ., 1951-57; Lectr in Architecture, Yale Univ., 1951-52, 1959-60, 1970, Cambridge Univ., 1962, 1964. Fellow Amer. Acad. of Arts and Sciences. Hon. Corr. Mem. RIBA; Franklin Fellow, RSA; Pres., Soc. of Architectural Historians, 1952-54; Fellow, Pilgrim Soc.; Founder-Mem., Victorian Soc.; Pres., Victorian Soc. in America, 1969-74. Hon. DFA New York Univ., 1969; Hon. DLitt Glasgow, 1973; Hon. DHL Pennsylvania, 1976. *Publications:* Modern Architecture, 1929, 2nd edn, 1970; J. J. P. Oud, 1931; The International Style (with Philip Johnson), 1932 (2nd edn 1966); The Architecture of H. H. Richardson, 1936 (3rd edn 1966); Modern Architecture in England (with others), 1937; Rhode Island Architecture, 1939 (2nd edn 1968); In the Nature of Materials, the Buildings of Frank Lloyd Wright, 1942 (2nd edn 1973); American Architectural Books, 1946; Painting towards Architecture, 1948; Early Victorian Architecture in Britain, 1954, 2nd edn 1972; Latin American Architecture since 1945, 1955; Architecture: Nineteenth and Twentieth Centuries, 1958 (new edn 1971); German Rococo: The Brothers Zimmermann, 1968; Rococo Architecture in Southern Germany, 1968; (with William Seale) Temples of Democracy, 1977. *Address:* 152 E 62nd Street, New York, NY 10021, USA. *T:* 758-6554.

HITCHENS, Ivon; *see* Hitchens, S. I.

HITCHENS, (Sydney) Ivon, CBE 1958; painter; *b* London, 3 March 1893; *o s* of Alfred Hitchens, painter and Ethel Margaret Seth-Smith; *m* 1935, Mary Cranford, *o d* of Rev. M. F. Coates, Hove; one *s. Educ:* Bedales; St John's Wood Art Schs; Royal Academy Schs. Member: 7 & 5 Soc.; London Group. One-man Exhibitions: Mayor Gallery, 1925; Arthur Tooth & Son, 1928; London Artists Assoc., 1929; Mansard Gallery, 1930; Lefevre Galleries, 1932, 1935, 1937; Leicester Galleries, 1940, 1942, 1944, 1947, 1949, 1950, 1952, 1954, 1957, 1959; Waddington Galleries, 1960, 1962, 1964, 1966, 1968, 1969, 1971, 1973, 1976; Poindexter, New York, 1966. Works purchased by Arts Council, and British Council; Stuyvesant Foundation; Ministry of Public Building and Works. Has also exhibited in New York World's Fair, 1939; UNESCO, Paris, 1946; British Painting since Whistler, National Gallery, 1940; Recent Tate Gallery Acquisitions, National Gallery, 1942; Tate Gallery Continental Exhibition, 1946-47; British Council Exhibitions; European Capitals, 1947, and Australia, 1949; Whitechapel Art Gallery, 1950; Contemporary Art Soc., The Private Collector, Tate Gallery, 1950, 1952. Purchase Prize, Arts Council Exhibition "50 painters for 1951"; British Council Hitchens and Nicholson Exhibition to Japan, 1953; Mural painting for Cecil Sharp House, London, 1954, Venezuela, 1955; twenty paintings in British Pavilion, XXVIII Biennale, Venice, 1956 (subseq. exhibited in Vienna and Munich, 1956, Paris and Amsterdam, 1957); Masters of British Painting, 1800-1950, Museum of Modern Art, New York, 1956; International Exhibition Brussels, 1958. Large landscape for Nuffield College, 1959; XI Premio, Lissone, Italy, 1959; 12th Exhibition International Assoc. art critics Exhibn, 1960; Exhibn British Paintings, 1720-1960, USSR, 1960. 3 Masters of Mod. Brit. Ptg; Arts Council, 1961; 20th Cent. Brit. Ptg: Brit. Council, Portugal, 1961; Kompas Sledelijk Museum, Eindhoven, Holland, 1962; Brit. Art Today, San Francisco, Dallas, Santa Barbara, 1962-63; Coll. E. LeBas, RA, 1963; Mural for Sussex Univ., 1963; Brit. Ptg in the "Sixties", Tate Gallery, 1963; Three British Painters, NZ, 1964; Ptg and Sculpture of a Decade, Gulbenkian Exhibn, 1964; The Bliss Travelling Collection. *Retrospective Exhibitions:* Temple Newsam, Leeds, 1945; Graves Art Gall., Sheffield, 1948; Tate Gallery, London, 1963; Southampton, 1964; Worthing Art Gall., 1966; Rutland Gall., London, 1972. *Represented in Public Collections of:* Leeds, Liverpool, Aberdeen, Wakefield, Shrewsbury, Salford, Hull, Manchester, Glasgow, Leicester, Bath, Birmingham, Bristol, Barnsley, Nottingham, Norwich, Southampton, Eastbourne, Newcastle upon Tyne, Huddersfield, Rochdale; also in Oxford and Cambridge Colls; Nat. Museum of Wales, Cardiff; Glynn Vivian Gall., Swansea; Victoria and Albert Museum, 1942; Cambridge, Fitzwilliam Museum; Tate Gall., 1938, 1941, 1942, 1959, 1965; Musée Nat. d'Art Moderne, Paris, 1957; Australian Nat. Galleries of Adelaide, Melbourne, Sydney; USA: Toledo Museum of Art and Albright Gall., Buffalo; Art Gall. of Seattle; Gothenberg Art Museum, Sweden; Nat. Gall., Oslo; Nat. Gall. of Canada, Ottawa; Art Gall. of Toronto; Nat. Gall. of New Zealand; Ashmolean Museum,

Oxford; the Queen's private collection of pictures; tapestry mural 10 ft × 20 ft, Chase Manhattan Bank, London. *Relevant Publications:* Penguin Modern Painters, by Patrick Heron, 1955; Ivon Hitchens, ed Alan Bowness, 1973. *Recreation:* streams. *Address:* Greenleaves, Petworth, Sussex.

HITCHIN, Prof. Aylwin Drakeford, CBE 1970; Boyd Professor of Dental Surgery, Director of Dental Studies, University of Dundee (formerly University of St Andrews), 1947-Dec. 1977 and Dean of Dundee Dental Hospital, 1947-73; Dental Consultant, Dundee Royal Infirmary, 1947-77; Civil Consultant Dental Surgeon to Royal Navy, 1957-77; *b* 31 Dec. 1907; *s of* Alfred Leonard Hitchin, FRPS, and Ruth Drakeford; *m* 1942, Alice Stella Michie; one *s* one *d. Educ:* Rutherford College, Newcastle upon Tyne; Durham University Coll. of Medicine. LDS (Dunelm) 1931, BDS 1932, MDS 1935; DDSc 1957; FDSRCS Edinburgh 1951; FFDRCS Ire 1964; FDSRCPS Glasgow 1967. Asst Hon. Dental Surgeon and Demonstrator of Dental Surgery, Newcastle upon Tyne Dental Hosp., 1932-36; Private Dental Practice, Newcastle upon Tyne, 1932-46 (except for 6 yrs with AD Corps during War of 1939-45); Dental Surgical Specialist, Scottish Command, 1943-45, with rank of Major. Chairman: Dental Educn Advisory Council, 1951-52; Dental Hosp. Assoc., 1959-60; Chm., Dental Cttee, Scot. Post-Grad. Med. Council; Member: Dental Cttee of MRC, 1966-72; Advisory Cttee on Medical Research (Scotland), 1967-71; Dental Adv. Cttee, Scottish Health Services Council, 1952-57, 1968-74; Convener, Dental Council, RCSE, 1971-74; Jt Cttee on Higher Training in Dentistry, 1969-74; East Scotland Regional Hosp. Bd, 1948-52; Dental Sub Cttee, UGC, 1969-73; Nominated Mem., Gen. Dent. Council, 1956-74; External Examiner Dental Subjects, Universities, Durham, Edinburgh, Queen's, Belfast, Dublin, Manchester, Liverpool, Birmingham, Leeds, Newcastle, Bristol, Wales, RCS in Ireland; Examiner, LDS, FDSRCS Edinburgh, FFDRCS Ire, and FDSRCPS Glasgow. William Guy Meml Lectr, RCSE, 1972; Founders and Benefactors Lectr, Univ. of Newcastle upon Tyne Dental Sch., 1973. President: Oral Surgery Club, 1956-57; Christian Dental Fellowship, 1966-69; Brit. Soc. Dental Radiology, 1961-63; Royal Odonto-Chir. Soc. of Scotland, 1969-70; Vice-Pres., Inter-Varsity Fellowship (Pres., 1966-67); Foundation Fellow of the British Assoc. of Oral Surgeons; Hon. Mem., Swedish Dental Soc. Comr, Dundee Presbytery and Synod of Angus and Mearns. Dr Odont (*hc*) Lund, 1977. *Publications:* contribs to dental periodical literature. *Address:* Kyleakin, 8 Cedar Road, Broughty Ferry, Dundee, Angus. *TA and T:* Dundee 77320.

HITCHINGS, Group Capt. John Phelp, CBE 1944; DL; Director, J. Cox & Co.'s Succrs Ltd, Bedminster, Bristol; *b* 2 Aug. 1899; *m* 1928, Gwendolyn Joyce Mary Newth; one *s* one *d. Educ:* Queen's Coll., Taunton. Served in RFC and RAF, 1917-18 and 1939-45; in business as Sole Leather Tanner, 1919-67. DL Avon 1974. *Recreation:* golf. *Address:* 19a The Avenue, Clifton, Bristol BS8 3HG. *T:* Bristol 36276.

HITCHINS, Francis Eric, CBE 1954; Member, Australian Wool Realization Commission, 1945-57; President Emeritus, Australian Wool and Meat Producers' Federation; sheep farming, Cranbrook, W Australia; *b* 15 Oct. 1891; *m* 1921, Bessie R. Paltridge; two *s* one *d.* Served European War, 1914-18, AIF, France. Inspector, Agric. Bank of W Australia, 1918-23; Land Valuer, Federal Taxation Dept, 1923-32; resumed sheep farming. Pres., Wool Sect., Primary Producers' Assoc. of WA; Pres., Australian Wool and Meat Producers' Fedn, 1941-52; Wool Grower Rep., Central Wool Cttee, War of 1939-45. Grower Rep., London Wool Confs, 1945 and 1950. *Publications:* Tangled Skeins: A Historic Survey of Australian Wool Marketing, 1956; Skeins Still Tangled: wool events 1952-72, 1972. *Address:* Pynup, Cranbrook, WA 6321, Australia. *T:* CB 12.

HITCHMAN, Sir (Edwin) Alan, KCB 1952 (CB 1948); Deputy Chairman, United Kingdom Atomic Energy Authority, 1964-66 (full-time Member, 1959); *b* 16 Nov. 1903; *s* of E. B. Hitchman, Newbury; *m* 1937, Katharine Mumford, *d* of Frank Hendrick, New York City; two *s. Educ:* St Bartholomew's Grammar Sch., Newbury; Downing Coll., Cambridge. Asst Principal, Ministry of Labour, 1926; Principal Private Sec. to Mr E. Brown, 1939, and to Mr E. Bevin, 1940, when Ministers of Labour; Principal Asst Sec., 1941; Under-Sec., 1946; transferred to HM Treasury, 1947; Dep. to Chief Planning Officer, 1948-49; Third Sec., HM Treasury, 1949-51; Perm. Sec. to Min. of Materials, 1951-52; Mem. Economic Planning Board, 1951-52; Chm. Agric. Improvement Council for England and Wales, 1952; Permanent Sec. to Min. of Agriculture and Fisheries, 1952-55, to Min. of Agriculture, Fisheries and Food, 1955-59. *Address:* 13 Wellington Square, Chelsea, SW3. *T:* 01-730 9359. *Club:* United Oxford & Cambridge University.

HIVES, family name of **Baron Hives.**

HIVES, 2nd Baron, *cr* 1950, of Duffield; **John Warwick Hives;** JP; *b* 26 Nov. 1913; *s* of 1st Baron Hives and of Gertrude Ethel (*d* 1961), *d* of John Warwick; *S* father, 1965; *m* 1st, 1937, Olwen Protheroe Llewellin (*d* 1972); no *c*; 2nd, 1972, Gladys Mary Seals. *Educ:* Manor School, Mickleover, Derby. JP Derbyshire, 1967. *Recreation:* shooting. *Heir: nephew* Matthew Peter Hives, *b* 25 May 1971. *Address:* Bendalls, Milton, Derby. *T:* Repton 3319. *Club:* Farmers'.

HOAD, Air Vice-Marshal Norman Edward, CVO 1972; CBE 1969; AFC 1951 and Bar, 1956; Senior RAF Member, Royal College of Defence Studies, since 1976; *b* 28 July 1923; *s* of Hubert Ronald Hoad and Florence Marie (*née* Johnson); two *s. Educ:* Brighton. Joined RAF, 1941, pilot trng, S Rhodesia; Lancaster pilot until shot down and taken prisoner in Germany, 1944; various flying and instructional duties, 1945-51; Sqdn Ldr 1951; OC No 192 Sqdn, 1953-55; psc 1956; Wing Comdr, HQ 2 ATAF, 1957-59; pfc 1960; OC No 216 Sqdn, 1960-62; jssc 1963; Gp Capt., MoD, 1963-65; idc 1966; Stn Comdr: RAF Lyneham, 1967, RAF Abingdon, 1968; Defence and Air Attaché, British Embassy, Paris, 1969-72; Dir, Defence Policy (A), 1972-74; Chief of Staff, 46 Gp, RAF Strike Comd, April-Oct. 1974; AOC No 46 Group, and Comdr, UK Jt Airborne Task Force, 1974-75. MBIM 1970. *Recreation:* oil painting. *Address:* Little Meadow, Stowupland, Stowmarket, Suffolk. *Club:* Royal Air Force.

HOAR, Hon. Ernest Knight, JP; *b* 20 Oct. 1898; *s* of Henry Knight Hoar and Sarah Ann Hoar, Luton, England; *m* 1924, Dorothy Helen Tomlin, Leicester, England; one *s. Educ:* Luton, England. Served European War, 1914-18, for 4½ years. Emigrated to Western Australia, 1922; entered Western Australian Parliament, 1943; Minister for Lands, Agriculture and Immigration, in the State Government, 1953-57; Agent-Gen. for Western Australia in London, 1957-65. Retired, 1965. *Recreation:* golf. *Address:* 61 Moreing Road, Attadale, WA 6156, Australia.

HOARE, Cecil Arthur, FRS 1950; DSc; FIBiol; *b* 6 March 1892; *m* Marie Leserson. *Educ:* XII St Petersburg Gymnasium; University of Petrograd (BSc 1917); University of London (DSc 1927). Fellow of Petrograd Univ., 1917-20; Lectr at Military Medical Academy, Petrograd, 1918-20; Researcher to Medical Research Council, 1920-23; Head of Protozoological Dept, Wellcome Laboratories of Tropical Medicine, London, 1923-57; Wellcome Research Fellow, 1957-70; Trypanosomiasis Research Institute, Uganda Medical Service, 1927-29; Acting Prof. of Medical Protozoology at London Sch. of Hygiene and Tropical Medicine, 1941-45; Recorder of "Protozoa" in Zoological Record, 1926-57; Mem., Expert Panel, WHO, 1957-73. Hon. Member: Soc. Protozool., USA; Brit. Soc. Parasitol.; Royal Soc. Trop. Med. and Hygiene; Société de Pathologie Exotique, Paris; For. Member: Société Belge de Médecine Tropicale; Soc. Protistol. Franç. G. Vianna Medal, Brazil. Acad. Sci., 1962; Patrick Manson Prize, 1963, Manson Medal, Royal Soc. Trop. Med., 1974. *Publications:* Handbook of Medical Protozoology, 1949; The Trypanosomes of Mammals, 1972; numerous papers dealing with the Protozoa. *Address:* 77 Sutton Court Road, W4 3EQ. *T:* 01-994 4838.

HOARE, Prof. Charles Antony Richard; Professor of Computation, Oxford University, since 1977; Fellow of Wolfson College, since 1977; *b* 11 Jan. 1934; *s* of Henry S. M. Hoare and Marjorie F. Hoare; *m* 1962, Jill Pym; two *s* one *d. Educ:* King's Sch., Canterbury; Merton Coll., Oxford (MA, Cert. Stats). Computer Div., Elliott Brothers, London, Ltd, 1959-68: successively Programmer, Chief Engr, Tech. Man., Chief Scientist; National Computer Centre, 1968; Prof. of Computer Science, QUB, 1968-77. *Publications:* Structured Programming (with O.-J. Dahl and E. W. Dijkstra), 1972; articles in Computer Jl, Commun. ACM, and Acta Informatica. *Recreations:* walking, swimming, reading, listening to music. *Address:* Programming Research Group, 45 Banbury Road, Oxford OX2 6PE. *T:* Oxford 58086.

HOARE, Rear-Adm. Dennis John, CB 1945; FIMechE; *b* 16 April 1891; *s* of late Herbert K. Hoare, Portsmouth; *m* 1919, Madeline (*d* 1975), *d* of T. Morris Prosser, JP, Newport, Mon.; two *s. Educ:* RNEC Keyham; RNC, Greenwich. HMS Collingwood, 1913-15, followed by service in HMS's Birkenhead, Goshawk and Glorious. Lecturer in Applied Mechanics at RNC Greenwich, 1919-24; then served in HM Ships Malaya and Shakespeare. Admiralty, 1926; HMS Exeter, 1930; later appointments included Fleet Engineer Officer, Mediterranean, Fleet Engineer Officer, Submarines, Asst Engineer-in-Chief, Superintendent Admiralty Engineering

Laboratory; retired July 1945. Dir of Research, British Internal Combustion Engine Research Assoc., 1945-58. Chevalier Order of Aviz (Portugal), 1921; Grand Officer, Order of Orange-Nassau (Netherlands), 1947. *Address:* Hall Cottage, Old Road, Ruddington, Nottingham NG11 6NF. *T:* Nottingham 216542.

HOARE, Rear-Adm. Desmond John, CB 1962; Vice President and Provost, United World Colleges, since 1969; *b* 25 June 1910; *s* of Capt. R. R. Hoare, OBE, Royal Navy; *m* 1941, Naomi Mary Gilbert Scott; one *s* two *d. Educ:* Wimbledon Coll.; King's Sch., Rochester. Joined RN, 1929; Engineering training, RNEC Keyham, 1930-33; Advanced engineering course, RNC Greenwich, 1934-36; HMS Exeter, 1936-39; Admiralty, 1939-41; HMS King George V, 1942-44; Admiralty, 1945-48; HMS Vanguard, 1949-51; HMS Condor (apprentice training), 1951-53; idc, 1955; Admiralty, 1956-59; Chief Staff Officer Technical to C-in-C Plymouth, 1960-62; retired, 1962. Headmaster, Atlantic Coll., 1962-69. Mem. Cttee, RNLI, 1969-. *Recreations:* sailing, power boats. *Address:* Bally Island House, Skibbereen, Cork, Ireland. *Club:* Royal Automobile.

HOARE, Sir Frederick (Alfred), 1st Bt, *cr* 1962; Kt 1958; Managing Partner of C. Hoare & Co., Bankers, of 37 Fleet Street, since 1947; Director: Messrs Hoare Trustees; Mitre Court Securities Ltd; The Trust Union Ltd; Mitre Court Cranes Ltd; Grimersta Estate Ltd; Tuscan Development Co.; Hoare's Bank Nominees Ltd; Trust Union Finance Ltd; Chairman, General Practice Finance Corporation, 1966-73; *b* 11 Feb. 1913; *s* of late Frederick Henry Hoare, 37 Fleet Street, EC4; *m* 1st, 1939, Norah Mary, OBE (*d* 1973), *d* of A. J. Wheeler; two *d* ; 2nd, 1974, Oonah Alice Dew, *d* of late Brig.-Gen. David Ramsay Sladen, CMG, DSO, and Isabel Sladen (*née* Blakiston-Houston). *Educ:* Wellington Coll. Clerk to C. Hoare & Co., 1931; Bankers' Agent, 1936, Managing Partner, 1947. Deputy Chairman: Nat. Mutual Life Assurance Soc., 1969-72; St George Assurance Co. Ltd, 1969-73. Common Councilman City of London, 1948; Alderman for Ward of Farringdon Without, 1950-71; Sheriff, City of London, 1956; Lord Mayor of London, 1961-62. Formerly one of HM Lieutenants for City of London; former Governor: Christ's Hosp.; Royal Bridewell Hosp.; Past Chm., St Bride's Institute; Mem., Court of Assistants and Prime Warden of Goldsmiths' Company, 1966-67. Pres., British Chess Federation, 1964-67; Past President: London Primary Schs Chess Assoc.; Cosmopolitan Banks Chess Assoc.; Upward Bound Young People's Gliding and Adventure Trust; Vice-Pres., Toc H. Trustee: Lady Hoare Thalidomide Appeal; Historic Churches Preservation Trust; Vice-Chm., Anglers' Co-operative Assoc.; Chm., John Eastwood Water Protection Trust Ltd; Member: Nat. Coun. of Social Service; Nat. Council, Noise Abatement Soc.; Chm., Family Welfare Assoc., 1961-68. Past Grand Deacon, United Grand Lodge of England. KStJ. Knight of Liberian Humane Order of African Redemption, 1962; Grand Officier de L'Ordre National de la République de Côte d'Ivoire, 1962. *Recreations:* chess, fishing, ornithology, photography, philately. *Heir:* none. *Address:* 34 Cadogan Square, SW1X 0JL. *Clubs:* Garrick, City Livery, Flyfishers'.

HOARE, John Michael; Administrator, Wessex Regional Health Authority, since 1973; *b* 23 Oct. 1932; *s* of Leslie Frank Hoare and Gladys Hoare; *m* 1963, Brita Hjalte; one *s* one *d . Educ:* Raynes Park; Christ's Coll., Cambridge (BA). Asst Sec., United Bristol Hosps, 1961; House Governor, St Stephen's Hosp., 1963; Asst Clerk, St Thomas' Hosp., 1965; Administrator, Northwick Park Hosp., 1967. Mem., Defence Medical Services Inquiry, 1971-73; Mem., Central Health Services Council, 1974. *Recreations:* reading, walking, music, squash. *Address:* 24 Clausentum Road, Winchester, Hants SO23 9QE. *T:* Winchester 4192.

HOARE, Marcus Bertram, CMG 1965; Hon. Mr Justice Hoare; Justice of Supreme Court of Queensland, since 1966; *b* 3 March 1910; *s* of John George and Emma Hoare; *m* 1936, Eileen Parker; four *s. Educ:* Brisbane Grammar Sch. Solicitor, 1933; Barrister-at-Law, 1944; QC (Australia) 1960. *Address:* 191 Laurel Avenue, Chelmer, Brisbane, Qld 4068, Australia. *T:* 379-4181. *Clubs:* Queensland, Johnsonian (Brisbane).

HOARE, Sir Peter Richard David, 8th Bt *cr* 1786; Director, N. Bentley Securities AG, Zürich, Investment Managers; *b* 22 March 1932; *s* of Sir Peter William Hoare, 7th Bt, and of Laura Ray, *o d* of Sir John Esplen, 1st Bt, KBE; *S* father, 1973; *m* 1961, Jane (marr. diss. 1967), *o d* of Daniel Orme. *Educ:* Eton. *Recreations:* travelling, shooting, skiing. *Heir: b* David John Hoare [*b* 8 Oct. 1935; *m* 1965, Mary Vanessa, *y d* of Peter Gordon Cardew; one *s*]. *Address: c/o* C. Hoare & Co., 37 Fleet Street, EC4. *Club:* Royal Automobile.

HOARE, Sir Timothy Edward Charles, 8th Bt *cr* 1784; *b* 11 Nov. 1934; *s* of Sir Edward O'Bryen Hoare, 7th Bt and of Nina Mary, *d* of late Charles Nugent Hope-Wallace, MBE; *S* father, 1969; *m* 1969, Felicity Anne, *o d* of Peter Boddington; one *s* twin *d. Educ:* Radley College; Worcester College, Oxford. *Heir: s* Charles James Hoare, *b* 15 March 1971. *Address:* 10 Belitha Villas, N1.

HOBAN, Brian Michael Stanislaus; Head Master of Harrow, since 1971; *b* 7 Oct. 1921; 2nd *s* of late Capt. R. A. Hoban; *m* 1947, Jasmine, 2nd *d* of J. C. Holmes, MC, Charterhouse, Godalming; one *s* one *d* (and one *d* decd). *Educ:* Charterhouse (Scholar); University Coll., Oxford (Sch.). 2nd Cl. Hon. Mods, 1947; 2nd Cl. Lit. Hum., 1949; BA 1949, MA 1957. Served War of 1939-45: Capt., Westminster Dragoons; NW Europe, 1944-45 (despatches); demobilised, Nov. 1945. Capt. Northants Yeomanry, TA, 1950-56. Asst Master: Uppingham Sch., 1949-52; Shrewsbury Sch., 1952-59; Headmaster, St Edmund's Sch., Canterbury, 1960-64; Head Master, Bradfield Coll., 1964-71. JP Berks, 1967-71. *Recreations:* music, cricket, golf, walking. *Address:* The Head Master's, Harrow-on-the-Hill, Mddx. *Clubs:* Athenæum; Vincent's (Oxford).

HOBART, Archbishop of, (RC), since 1955; Most Rev. Guilford Young, DD (Rome); *b* Sandgate, Queensland, 10 Nov. 1916. Ordained, Rome, 1939; Auxiliary Bishop of Canberra and Goulburn, 1948; Co-Adjutor Archbishop of Hobart, 1954; succeeded to See of Hobart, Sept. 1955. *Address:* Archbishop's House, 31 Fisher Avenue, Sandy Bay, Hobart, Tasmania 7005, Australia.

HOBART, Maj.-Gen. Patrick Robert Chamier, CB 1970; DSO 1945; OBE 1944; MC 1943; Lieutenant-Governor and Secretary, Royal Hospital, Chelsea, since 1973; *b* 14 Nov. 1917; *s* of Robert Charles Arthur Stanley Hobart and Elsie Hinds. *Educ:* Charterhouse; Royal Military Academy Woolwich; 2nd Lieut, Royal Tank Corps, 1937; served in war of 1939-45 (despatches 4 times); France, Western Desert, Tunisia, Italy, with 2nd Royal Tank Regt, BM 9th Armd Bde, GSO2 30 Corps, GSO1 7th Armd Div; NW Europe, GSO1 Guards Armd Div. and CO 1st RTR; CO 2nd RTR, BAOR and N Africa, 1958-60; Comdr, 20th Armoured Brigade, BAOR, 1961-63; Chief of Staff, 1 (British) Corps, BAOR, 1964-66; Dir Military Operations, MoD, 1966-68; Chief of Staff Army Strategic Command, 1968-70; Dir, RAC, 1970-72; retired. Col Comdt, Royal Tank Regt, 1968-, Representative Col Comdt, 1971-74. ADC to the Queen, 1961-66. *Address: c/o* Williams & Glyn's Bank Ltd, Kirkland House, Whitehall, SW1.

HOBART, Lt-Comdr Sir Robert (Hampden), 3rd Bt *cr* 1914; RN; *b* 7 May 1915; *o s* of Sir (Claud) Vere Cavendish Hobart, 2nd Bt, DSO, OBE and Violet Verve, MBE (*d* 1935), 2nd *d* of late John Wylie; *S* father 1949; *m* 1st, 1942, Sylvia (*d* 1965), *d* of H. Argo, Durban, Natal; three *s* one *d* ; 2nd, 1975, Caroline, widow of 11th Duke of Leeds. *Educ:* Wixenford; RN Coll., Dartmouth. Sub-Lieut, RN, 1935; Lieut-Comdr, 1945; served War of 1939-45 (wounded, two medals, four stars); retired, 1950. Contested (Nat Lib) Hillsborough Div. of Sheffield, 1945, (C and L) Itchen Div. of Southampton, 1950. *Heir: s* John Vere Hobart, *b* 9 April 1945. *Address:* Gatcombe Park, Newport, Isle of Wight. *Clubs:* Travellers', Royal London Yacht; Royal Yacht Squadron; Royal Southern Yacht, Royal Southampton Yacht, Bembridge Sailing.

HOBART-HAMPDEN, family name of Earl of Buckinghamshire.

HOBBS, Herbert Harry, CB 1956; CVO 1972; Director, Ancient Monuments and Historic Buildings, 1970-72, retired; *b* 7 Nov. 1912; *s* of late Bertie Hobbs and Agnes Dora (*née* Clarke); *m* 1937, Joan Hazel Timmins; two *s* one *d. Educ:* Bedford Sch.; Corpus Christi Coll., Oxford. Entered War Office, 1935; Comptroller of Lands and Claims, 1956-60; Asst Under-Sec. of State (Works), War Office, 1960-63; Under-Sec., MPBW, later DoE, 1963-72. Medal of Freedom with bronze palm (USA), 1946. *Recreation:* golf. *Address:* 9 Hemp Garden, Minehead, Som.

HOBBS, John Charles; Chief Insurance Officer, Department of Health and Social Security, 1971-76; *b* 28 May 1917; British; *m* 1961, Doris Gronow. *Educ:* Portsmouth Southern Grammar Sch.; Portsmouth Coll. of Technology. 1st cl. hons BSc and BSc (Spec.) Maths. Asst Principal, 1946; Principal, 1947; Asst Sec., 1957. *Recreations:* pianoforte, guitar, marquetry.

HOBBS, Maj.-Gen. Reginald Geoffrey Stirling, CB 1956; DSO 1942; OBE 1944; *b* 8 Aug. 1908; *e s* of late Brig.-Gen. Reginald Francis Arthur Hobbs, CB, CMG, DSO, Sutton Veny, Warminster, Wilts; *m* 1935, Mary Jameson, *d* of late Maj.-Gen.

Hugo De Pree, CB, CMG, DSO, Beckley, Rye, Sussex; one *d.* *Educ:* Wellington; RMA Woolwich. 2nd Lieut RA, 1928; Staff Coll., 1940; BEF, 1940; RHA Eighth Army, Western Desert, 1942-43; Staff, 21 Army Group NW Europe, 1944-45; Lieut-Col 1942; temp. Brig. 1947; Chief of Staff, Combined Ops, 1948; idc, 1949; CRA 1st Inf. Div., 1950-51; Comd 2 Inf. Bde, 1952; Maj.-Gen. 1955; Comdt, RMA Sandhurst, 1954-56; Near East, 1956; Dir of Royal Artillery, War Office, 1957-59; GOC 1 Div., 1959-60; Col Comdt, Royal Regt Artillery, 1963-68; Hon. Col, Essex Yeomanry, 1961-66; Pres., Regular Commissions Bd, 1961-62; Lieut-Governor and Sec., Royal Hospital, Chelsea, 1962-67. Order of White Lion 3rd Class, and Military Cross (Czechoslovakia), 1945; Officer of Legion of Honour and Croix de Guerre with Palm (France), 1958. *Recreation:* English Rugby International, 1932; Pres. of the Rugby Football Union, 1961-62. *Address:* Lerags House, Oban, Argyll. *T:* Oban 2450. *Club:* Army and Navy.

HOBBS, William Alfred, CB 1973; CBE 1965; Chief Valuer, Board of Inland Revenue, 1972-74; *b* 3 March 1912; *s* of A. V. Getland Hobbs; *m* 1937, Rose Winslade; one *s* one *d.* *Educ:* Brighton, Hove and Sussex Grammar Sch. Chartered Surveyor (FRICS). Private practice, 1928-38; joined Valuation Office, 1938; Dist Valuer (Maidstone), 1945; Superintending Valuer, 1950 (London, Manchester and Birmingham); Asst Chief Valuer, 1958; Dep. Chief Valuer, 1966-71. *Recreations:* fly-fishing, golf. *Address:* Bowcot Rise, Bowcot Hill, Headley, Hants. *T:* Headley Down 2025.

HOBDAY, Gordon Ivan; Chairman, The Boots Company Ltd, since 1973 (Managing Director, 1970-72); a Deputy Chairman, Price Commission, since 1977; President of the Council, Nottingham University, since 1973; *b* 1 Feb. 1916; *e s* of late Alexander Thomas Hobday and Frances Cassandra (*née* Meads); *m* 1940, Margaret Jean Joule; one *d.* *Educ:* Long Eaton Grammar Sch.; UC Nottingham. BSc, PhD London; FRIC. Joined Boots Co., 1939; Dir of Research, 1952-68; Dep. Man. Dir, 1968-70. *Recreations:* lawn tennis, handicrafts, gardening. *Address:* The Boots Co. Ltd, Nottingham NG2 3AA. *T:* Nottingham 56111. *Club:* Athenæum.

HOBDEN, Dennis Harry; *b* 21 Jan. 1920; *s* of Charles Hobden and Agnes Hobden (*née* Smith); *m* 1950, Kathleen Mary Hobden (*née* Holman) (marr. diss. 1970); two *s* two *d*; *m* 1977, Sheila Hobden (*née* Tugwell). *Educ:* elementary sch. Entered GPO, 1934. Served as Air Crew, RAF, 1941-46 (Flt Lieut). MP (Lab) Kemptown Div. of Brighton, 1964-70. Contested (Lab) Brighton, Kemptown, Feb. and Oct. 1974. Leader, Labour Gp, E Sussex CC; Dep. Leader, Labour Gp, Brighton Town Council. *Recreations:* politics, gardening, music, reading. *Address:* 3 Queens Park Terrace, Brighton, East Sussex BN2 2YA.

HOBDEN, Reginald Herbert, DFC 1944; HM Diplomatic Service; High Commissioner, Lesotho, since 1976; *b* 9 Nov. 1919; *s* of William Richard and Ada Emily Hobden; *m* 1945, Gwendoline Ilma Vowles; two *s* one *d.* *Educ:* Sir William Borlase's Sch., Marlow. Apptd Colonial Office, Dec. 1936. Served War of 1939-45 (despatches, DFC): RAFVR, Sept. 1940-Jan. 1946 (Sqdn Ldr). Returned to Colonial Office, 1946; seconded to Dept of Technical Co-operation, 1961; First Sec., UK Commn, Malta, 1962-64; HM Diplomatic Service, Nov. 1964: CRO until April 1968; Head of British Interests Section, Canadian High Commn, Dar es Salaam, April 1968; British Acting High Comr, Dar es Salaam, July-Oct. 1968, and Counsellor, Dar es Salaam, Oct. 1968-69; Counsellor (Economic and Commercial), Islamabad, 1970-75; Inst. of Develt Studies, Sussex Univ., 1975. *Recreations:* cricket, tennis, chess, bridge. *Address:* c/o Foreign and Commonwealth Office, SW1; 14 Belmont Close, Uxbridge, Mddx. *T:* Uxbridge 34754. *Club:* Royal Commonwealth Society.

HOBHOUSE, Sir Charles Chisholm, 6th Bt, *cr* 1812; TD; *b* 7 Dec. 1906; *s* of Sir Reginald A. Hobhouse, 5th Bt and Marjorie Chisholm Spencer (*d* 1967); *S* father, 1947; *m* 1st, 1946, Mary (*d* 1955), *widow* of Walter Horrocks, Salkeld Hall, Penrith; no *c*; 2nd, 1959, Elspeth Jean, *d* of T. G. Spinney, Mazagan, Morocco; one *s.* *Educ:* Eton. Commissioned North Somerset Yeomanry, 1926; Major 1940; Hon. Col 1966. *Recreations:* hunting, shooting. *Heir:* *s* Charles John Spinney Hobhouse, *b* 27 Oct. 1962. *Address:* The Manor, Monkton Farleigh, Bradford-on-Avon, Wilts. *T:* Bath 858558. *Clubs:* Brooks's, Cavalry and Guards, City of London.

HOBKIRK, Col Elspeth Isabel Weatherley, CBE 1951; TD 1952; WRAC (retired); Governor of HM Prison and of HM Borstal Institution, Greenock, 1955-69; also appointed Adviser to Scottish Home and Health Department on arrangements for Detention of Women and Girls in Scottish Penal Institutions,

1961, retired from Scottish Prison Service, Aug. 1969; *d* of late Brig.-Gen. C. J. Hobkirk, CMG, DSO, Cleddon Hall, Trellech, Mon. *Educ:* Sandecotes, Dorset; London Sch. of Art. JP Monmouthshire, 1938-49. Joined FANY, 1938; enrolled ATS, 1939; served War of 1939-45, Sen. Comdr, 1942; Chief Comdr, 1945; Controller and Dep. Dir ATS, HQ London District, 1946; Dep. Dir ATS, War Office, 1947-49; commissioned into Women's Royal Army Corps, 1949; Dep. Dir WRAC, War Office, 1949; Dep. Dir WRAC, HQ Eastern Command, 1950-52; Vice-Pres. Regular Commissions Bd, 1950-52; retired, 1952. Head Warden, Bristol Royal Hospital, 1952-54; Governor, HM Prison, Duke Street, Glasgow, 1954-55 (prison closed). Member: Govt Adv. Cttee on Drug Dependence, 1967-70; Parole Board for Scotland, 1970-73; (Chm.) Civil Service Commn Panel of Interviewers, 1969-73; Adv. Council on Social Work (Scotland), 1970-72; Emslie Cttee on Penalties for Homicide, 1970-72; Edinburgh Appeals Cttee, Campaign for Cancer Research, 1970-73; Bd of Dirs, St Columba's Hospice, 1977; an Hon. Sec., RUKBA, Edinburgh, 1974-75; Abbeyfield Edinburgh Exec. Cttee, 1975-76 (Chm. Extra Care House); Catholic Social Work Centre Exec. Cttee, 1974-. Hon. LLD Glasgow, 1976. *Recreations:* travel, painting, music, gardening; country pursuits generally. *Address:* 8 Moray Place, Edinburgh EH3 6DS.

HOBLER, Air Vice-Marshal John Forde, CB 1958; CBE 1943; *b* Rockhampton, Qld, Australia, 26 Sept. 1907; *s* of late L. E. Hobler, Rockhampton; *m* 1939, Dorothy Evelyn Diana Haines, Wilsford, Wilts; two *s* one *d.* *Educ:* Rockhampton, Qld. Served whole of War of 1939-45 in Bomber Command; commanded RAF Lossiemouth; Palestine, 1945; Staff Coll., 1946-48; Air Ministry, 1948-50; Comd Habbaniya, Iraq, 1950-52; HQ Flying Trg Comd, 1952-54; Air Ministry, 1954-56; AO i/c Administration, Middle East Air Force, 1956-58; Air Officer Commanding No 25 Gp, 1958-61; Air Officer i/c Administration, Far East Air Force, 1961-63, retd. *Address:* Paradise Point, Gold Coast, Qld 4216, Australia. *Club:* United Services (Brisbane).

HOBLEY, Brian; Chief Urban Archaeologist, City of London, since 1973; *b* 25 June 1930; *s* of William Hobley and Harriet (*née* Hobson); *m* 1953, Laurie Parkes; one *s* one *d.* *Educ:* Univ. of Leicester. BA Hons Leicester 1965, FSA 1969, AMA 1970. Field Officer, Coventry Corp., 1965; Keeper, Dept Field Archaeology, Coventry Museum, 1970. Lectr, Birmingham Univ. Extra-mural Dept, 1965-74. Mem. Council: Royal Archaeological Inst., 1972; Soc. for Promotion of Roman Studies, 1974. *Publications:* reports in learned jls incl. Proc. 7th, 8th and 9th Internat. Congresses of Roman Frontier Studies, Tel Aviv, Univ. Israel and Bucharest Univ., Rumania on excavations and reconstructions at The Lunt Roman fort, Baginton near Coventry and excavations in the City of London. *Recreation:* classical music. *Address:* Department of Urban Archaeology, Museum of London, 71 Basinghall Street, EC2V 5DT. *T:* 01-606 1933. *Club:* Octoberists.

HOBLEY, John William Dixon, CMG 1976; QC (Hong Kong); Attorney-General, Hong Kong, since 1973; *b* 11 June 1929; *s* of John Wilson Hobley and Ethel Anne Hobley; *m* 1953, Dorothy Cockhill; one *s* one *d.* *Educ:* University Sch., Southport, Lancs; Univ. of Liverpool (LLB). Called to the Bar, Gray's Inn, 1950; Northern Circuit, 1950-53; Hong Kong: Crown Counsel, 1953-62; Sen. Crown Counsel, 1962-65; Principal Crown Counsel, 1965-72; Attorney-Gen., Bermuda, 1972; Solicitor-Gen., Hong Kong, 1973. *Recreations:* music, bridge. *Address:* Attorney-General's Chambers, Central Government Offices, Hong Kong.

HOBMAN, David Burton; Director, Age Concern England (National Old People's Welfare Council), since 1970; *b* 8 June 1927; *s* of J. B. and D. L. Hobman; *m* 1954, Erica Irwin; one *s* one *d.* *Educ:* University College Sch.; Blundell's. Community work, Forest of Dean, 1954-56; British Council for Aid to Refugees, 1957; Nat. Council of Social Service, 1958-67; Visiting Lectr in Social Admin, Nat. Inst. for Social Work, 1967; Dir, Social Work Adv. Service, 1968-70. Vis. Prof., Sch. of Social Work, McGill Univ., Montreal, 1977. Member: BBC/ITA Appeals Adv. Council, 1965-69; Steering Cttee, Enquiry into Homelessness, Nat. Asstce Bd, 1967-68; Adv. Council, Nat. Corp. for Care of Old People, 1970-74; Metrication Bd, 1974-; Lord Goodman's Cttee Reviewing Law of Charity, 1975-76; Chairman: Social Welfare Commn Conf. of Bishops, 1968-71; Family Housing Assoc., 1969-70; Consultant, UN Div. of Social Affairs, 1968-69; Observer, White House Congress on Ageing, 1971-; Vice-Pres., Internat. Fedn on Ageing, 1974-; Governor: Cardinal Newman Comp. Sch., Hove, 1971-76 (Chm); Volunteer Centre, 1975-. *Publications:* A Guide to Voluntary Service, 1964, 2nd edn 1967; Who Cares, 1971; numerous papers, broadcasts. *Recreations:* caravanning, travel, pebble polishing. *Address:* 21 Withdean Crescent, Brighton, Sussex BN1 6WG. *T:* Brighton 503498. *Club:* Reform.

HOBSBAWM, Prof. Eric John Ernest, FBA 1976; Professor of Economic and Social History, Birkbeck College, University of London, since 1970; Professor-at-Large, Cornell University, since 1976; *b* 9 June 1917; *s* of Leopold Percy Hobsbawm and Nelly Grün; *m* 1962, Marlene Schwarz; one *s* one *d. Educ:* Vienna; Berlin; St Marylebone Grammar Sch.; Univ. of Cambridge (BA, PhD). Lectr, Birkbeck Coll., 1947; Fellow, King's Coll., Cambridge, 1949-55, Hon. Fellow, 1973; Reader, Birkbeck Coll., 1959. Hon. DPhil Univ. of Stockholm, 1970; Hon. Dr Hum. Let., Univ. of Chicago, 1976; Foreign Hon. Mem., American Academy of Arts and Sciences, 1971. *Publications:* Labour's Turning Point, 1948; Primitive Rebels, 1959; (pseud. F. Newton) The Jazz Scene, 1959; The Age of Revolution, 1962; Labouring Men, 1964; (ed) Karl Marx, Precapitalist Formations, 1964; Industry and Empire, 1968; (with G. Rudé) Captain Swing, 1969; Bandits, 1969; Revolutionaries, 1973; The Age of Capital, 1975; contribs to jls. *Recreation:* travel. *Address:* Birkbeck College, Malet Street, WC1. *T:* 01-580 6622.

HOBSON, Alec, CBE 1962 (OBE 1946); MVO 1955; *b* 29 Oct. 1899; *s* of Frederick Hobson, Esher, Surrey; *m* 1924, Elizabeth Josephine, *d* of Arthur Newman, Sudbury, Suffolk; one *s* (one *d* decd). Served Inns of Court and Royal West Surrey Regiments, 1918-19. Engaged in pedigree livestock improvement work, 1920-39; joint founder-partner Harry Hobson & Co. (pedigree livestock auctioneers), 1928. Domestic food production work for Min. of Agriculture, 1939-45. Sec., Royal Agricultural Soc. of England and of Nat. Agricultural Examinations Bds, 1946-61; Hon. Sec., Royal Agricultural Society of The Commonwealth, 1957-67. Founder Mem., Guild of Agricultural Journalists; Founder Pres., Nat. Soc. of Master Thatchers; Liveryman, Past Master, and Court of Assts, Worshipful Co. of Farriers; Freeman, Worshipful Co. of Farmers. *Recreations:* golf, gardening. *Address:* Clare Cottage, Oulton, Norwich NR11 6NX. *T:* Saxthorpe 362. *Clubs:* Travellers', Farmers'.

HOBSON, Basil; see Hobson, J. B.

HOBSON, Sir Harold, Kt 1977; CBE 1971; Dramatic Critic, The Sunday Times, 1947-76; *b* Thorpe Hesley, near Rotherham, 4 Aug. 1904; *o s* of late J. and Minnie Hobson; *m* 1935, Gladys Bessie (Elizabeth), *e d* of late James Johns; one *d. Educ:* privately; Oriel Coll., Oxford (Hon. Fellow, 1974). Asst Literary Editor, The Sunday Times, 1942-48; TV Critic, The Listener, 1947-51. Mem., National Theatre Bd, 1976-. Hon. DLitt Sheffield, 1977. Chevalier of the Legion of Honour. *Publications:* The First Three Years of the War, 1942; The Devil in Woodford Wells (novel), 1946; Theatre, 1948; Theatre II, 1950; Verdict at Midnight, 1952; The Theatre Now, 1953; The French Theatre of Today, 1953; (ed) The International Theatre Annual, 1956, 1957, 1958, 1959, 1960; Ralph Richardson, 1958; (with P. Knightly and L. Russell) The Pearl of Days: an intimate memoir of The Sunday Times, 1972; The French Theatre from 1830 onwards, 1977. *Recreations:* Lord's, contemporary French literature, bridge. *Address:* 905 Nelson House, Dolphin Square, SW1. *Clubs:* Beefsteak, Garrick, MCC.

HOBSON, (John) Basil, QC (Kenya, 1950; Nyasaland, 1953); His Honour Judge Hobson; a Circuit Judge (formerly Deputy Chairman, NE London Quarter Sessions), since 1968; *b* 1905; *s* of late J. D. Hobson, QC, Kenya, Trinidad, British West Indies, and late Cecilia (née Johnstone); *m* 1932, Ursula, *y d* of late William Collie, Trinidad; no *c. Educ:* Sherborne. Solicitor, 1929; Dep. Registrar, Supreme Court, Trinidad, 1936; admitted Middle Temple and called to Bar, 1938; Crown Counsel, Uganda, 1939. Served War of 1939-45, King's African Rifles, 1939-41; Dep. Judge-Advocate, East Africa Command, 1941-44; Solicitor-Gen., Kenya, 1947; MLC, Kenya, 1947-51; Chm., Labour Advisory Board, Kenya, 1948-49; Attorney-Gen., MEC and MLC, Nyasaland, 1951-57; acted Chief Justice, April-Nov. 1954; Dep. Chm., Essex QS, 1964-68. Chm. Commn on Fishing Industry, 1956; Chm. Select Cttee on Non-African Agriculture, 1957. *Recreation:* watching cricket. *Address:* 5 Essex Court, Temple, EC4. *T:* 01-353 8675. *Clubs:* MCC, XL.

HOBSON, Lawrence John, CMG 1965; OBE 1960; with British Petroleum Co. Ltd since 1966; *b* 4 May 1921; *er s* of late John Sinton Hobson and Marion Adelaide Crawford; *m* 1946, Patricia Fiona Rosemary Beggs (née Green); one step *s* (one *s* decd). *Educ:* Taunton Sch.; St Catharine's Coll., Cambridge. BA 1946, MA 1950. Served War, 1941-42. ADC and Private Sec. to Gov., Aden, 1942; Political Officer, 1944; Asst Chief Sec., 1956; Aden govt Student Liaison Officer, UK, 1960-62; Political Adviser to High Comr, Aden, 1963-66; retired from HMOCS, 1966. Mem., Newbury DC, 1973-. *Address:* Saffron House, Stanford Dingley, near Reading, Berks. *T:* Bradfield 536. *Club:* Bath.

HOBSON, Valerie Babette Louise, (Mrs Profumo); film and stage actress; *b* Larne, Ireland; *d* of Comdr R. G. Hobson, RN, and Violette Hamilton-Willoughby; *m* 1st, 1939, Anthony James Allan Havelock-Allan (marr. diss. 1952), *qv*; two *s*; 2nd, 1954, John Dennis Profumo, *qv*; one *s. Educ:* St Augustine's Priory, London; Royal Academy of Dramatic Art. Was trained from early age to become ballet dancer; first stage appearance at Drury Lane in Ball at the Savoy, aged 15. The King and I, Drury Lane, 1953. First film, Badgers Green; went to Hollywood and appeared in Werewolf of London, Bride of Frankenstein, The Mystery of Edwin Drood, etc; at 18 returned to England. Films include: The Drum, This Man is News, This Man in Paris, The Spy in Black, Q Planes, Silent Battle, Contraband, Unpublished Story, Atlantic Ferry, The Adventures of Tartu, The Years Between, Great Expectations, Blanche Fury, The Small Voice, Kind Hearts and Coronets, Train of Events, Interrupted Journey, The Rocking Horse Winner, The Card, Who Goes There?, Meet Me Tonight, The Voice of Merrill, Background, Knave of Hearts. *Recreations:* listening to music, writing, reading, painting.

HOBSON, Prof. William, BSc (1st Cl. Hons), MD (Dist.), DPH (Dist.), Leeds; MRCS; LRCP; Consultant in medical education, World Health Organisation, since 1971; *b* 5 Sept. 1911; *s* of William Hobson, The Langdales, Park Lane, Leeds; *m* 1937, Lucy Muriel Wilson; one *s* one *d*; *m* 1953, Heather McMahon Greer; one *d. Educ:* Fulneck; Bradford Grammar Sch.; Leeds Univ. Lecturer in Physiology and Hygiene, University of Leeds, 1936-38; Asst Sch. Medical Officer, Leeds, 1938-39; Asst County MO, Hants CC, 1939-40; Medical Officer of Health Borough of Lymington, Hants, 1940-42. Major, RAMC, 1942-46 (despatches). Senior Lecturer in Preventive Medicine, University of Bristol, 1946-48; Prof. of Social and Industrial Medicine, University of Sheffield, 1949-58; Chief, Educn and Training, WHO European Office, 1958-68; Chief of Staff Training, WHO HQ Geneva, 1968-71; Consultant, WHO Regional Office for E Mediterranean, Alexandria, 1971-72. WHO Visiting Prof. to India, 1957-58. Hon. Patron, Western Foundn of Vertebrate Zoology, Los Angeles, 1968. Commandeur de la Confrérie des Chevaliers de Tastevin de Bourgogne, 1963. *Publications:* The Health of the Elderly at Home (with J. Pemberton), 1955 (Ciba Foundn Prize, 1956); (ed) Modern Trends in Geriatrics, 1956; (ed) Theory and Practice of Public Health, 1961, 4th edn 1975 (trans. into Turkish and Italian), 1974; World Health and History, 1963; contribs to Jl of Hygiene, BMJ, Jl of Phys. Med., Jl of Social Med., Bristol Med. Chir. Jl, Jl Med. Chir. Soc., The Naturalist, etc. *Recreation:* ornithology. *Address:* Strand Cottage, Myrtleville, Co. Cork, Ireland.

HOCHHAUSER, Victor; impresario; *b* 27 March 1923; *m* 1949, Lilian Hochhauser (née Shields); three *s* one *d. Educ:* City of London Coll. Impresario for: David Oistrakh; Sviatoslav Richter; Mstislav Rostropovich; Gilels, Kogan; Bolshoi Ballet season at Covent Garden, 1963, 1969; Leningrad State Kirov Ballet, Covent Garden, 1961, 1966; Sunday Evening Concerts, Royal Albert Hall. *Recreations:* reading, swimming, sleeping. *Address:* 4 Holland Park Avenue, W11. *T:* 01-727 0781.

HOCHOY, Sir Solomon, TC 1969; GCMG 1962 (KCMG 1959; CMG 1957); GCVO 1966; OBE 1952; Governor-General and C-in-C of Trinidad and Tobago, 1962-72 (Governor, 1960-62); *b* Jamaica, 20 April 1905; *m* 1935, Thelma Edna Huggins; one adopted *d. Educ:* St Mary's Coll., Port-of-Spain, Trinidad. Trinidad Government: Clerk, 1928-44; Labour Officer, 1944-46; Deputy Industrial Adviser, 1946-49; Commissioner of Labour, 1949-55; Deputy Colonial Sec., 1955-56; Chief Sec., Trinidad and Tobago, 1956-60. KStJ 1961. *Recreation:* fishing. *Address:* Blanchisseuse, Trinidad. *Clubs:* Royal Commonwealth Society, Corona; Clipper (International).

HOCKADAY, Arthur Patrick, CB 1975; CMG 1969; Second Permanent Under Secretary of State, Ministry of Defence, since 1976; *b* 17 March 1926; *s* of late William Ronald Hockaday and of Marian Camilla Hockaday, *d* of Rev. A. C. Evans; *m* 1955, Peggy, *d* of H. W. Prince. *Educ:* Merchant Taylors' Sch.; St John's Coll., Oxford. BA (1st cl. Lit. Hum.) 1949, MA 1952. Apptd to Home Civil Service, 1949; Admty, 1949-62; Private Sec. to successive Ministers of Defence and Defence Secretaries, 1962-65; NATO Internat. Staff, 1965-69 (Asst Sec. Gen. for Defence Planning and Policy, 1967-69); Asst Under-Sec. of State, MoD, 1969-72; Under-Sec., Cabinet Office, 1972-73; Dep. Under-Sec. of State, MoD, 1973-76. *Recreation:* fell-walking. *Address:* 2 Toll-Gate Drive, Dulwich, SE21. *T:* 01-693 1773. *Club:* Naval and Military.

HOCKENHULL, Arthur James Weston, OBE 1966; HM Diplomatic Service, retired; *b* 8 Aug. 1915; *s* of late Frederick

Weston Hockenhull and late Jessie Gibson Kaye Hockenhull (*née* Mitchell); *m* 1955, Rachel Ann Kimber; two *d. Educ:* Clifton Coll.; Exeter Coll., Oxford. HM Overseas Civil Service; various appts in Far East, Cyprus and British Guiana, 1936-57. Interned by Japanese, in Singapore, 1942-45; First Sec., UK Commn, Singapore, 1958-63; Counsellor, British High Commn, Malaysia, 1964-68; Consul-Gen., Houston, 1969-74. *Recreations:* golf, gardening, swimming. *Address:* Church Cottage, Southmoor, Oxon. *Club:* United Oxford & Cambridge University.

HOCKER, Dr Alexander; Grosses Verdienstkreuz mit Stern des Verdienstordens der Bundesrepublic Deutschland, 1974; Director-General, European Space Research Organisation (ESRO), 1971-74; *m* 1940, Liselotte Schulze; five *s* one d. *Educ:* Univs of Innsbruck, Hamburg and Leipzig. Asst, Law Faculty, Leipzig Univ.; County Court Judge; Officer, Advanced Scientific Study Div., Min. of Educn, Hannover, 1947-49; Dep. of Sec.-Gen. of German Res. Assoc. (Deutsche Forschungsgemeinschaft), 1949-56; Ministerialrat and Ministerialdirigent (responsible for res., trng and sci. exchanges), Fed. Min. for Atomic Energy, 1956-61; Mem. Directorate, Nuclear Res. Centre (Kernforschungsanlage) Jülich, 1961-69; Sci. Adviser to Foundn Volkswagenwerk, 1969-71. German Deleg. to CERN, Geneva, 1952-61 (Chm. of Finance Cttee, 1960-61); Chm. of Legal, Admin. and Financial Working Gp of COPERS, 1961-63; Chm. of Council, ESRO, 1965-67 (Vice-Chm. 1964); Member: German Commn for Space Res., 1964-71. Kuratorium Max-Planck-Institut für Physik und Astrophysik, 1968-71; Max-Plank-Institut für Plasmaphysik, 1971-. *Publication:* (jtly) Taschenbuch für Atomfragen, 1968. *Address:* 53 Bonn-Bad Godesberg, Auguststrasse 63, Germany.

HOCKING, Frederick Denison Maurice; Cornwall County Pathologist; Consulting Biologist and Toxicologist, Devon River Board; late Consulting Pathologist, South-Western Regional Hospital Board; Acting Director Public Health Laboratory Service, Cornwall, and other hospitals in Cornwall; late Chemical Pathologist, Biochemist, and Assistant Pathologist, Westminster Hospital; Lecturer in General and Clinical Pathology, Westminster Hospital Medical School, University of London; *b* 28 Feb. 1899; *o s* of late Rev. Almund Trevosso Hocking and Gertrude Vernon Mary, *o d* of J. Parkinson; *m* 1st, 1927, Amy Gladys (*d* 1956), *y d* of A. T. Coucher; two *d*; 2nd, 1957, Kathleen, *e d* of Dr G. P. O'Donnell. *Educ:* High Sch., Leytonstone; City and Guilds of London Coll., Finsbury; Middlesex Hospital Medical Sch. RN Experimental and Anti-gas Station, 1917-18; Asst Laboratory Dir to the Clinical Research Assoc. MB, BS, BSc, MSc London, MRCS, LRCP, FRIC, FCS, FRMS; FRSA, MIBiol, FRSH. Associate of the City and Guilds of London Tech. Coll., Finsbury; Member: Pathological Soc. of Great Britain and Ireland; Association of Clinical Pathologists (Councillor, 1944-46); Society of Public Analysts; Medico-Legal Society; Brit. Assoc. in Forensic Medicine; Court, Univ. of Exeter (representing Royal Institute of Chemistry); Pres. South-Western Branch, British Medical Association, 1946; Chm. South-Western Branch, RIC, 1955-57; Mem. Council, RIC, 1959-62, 1965-68. Consulting Biologist, Devon River Bd. Mem. Brit. Acad. of Forensic Sciences; Mem. Soc. for Forensic Science. *Publications:* The Employment of Uranium in the Treatment of Malignant New Growths, British Empire Cancer Campaign International Conference, London, 1928; Disseminated Sclerosis (with Sir James Purves-Stewart), 1930; Seaside Accidents, 1958; Delayed Death due to Suicidal Hanging, 1961; Hanging and Manual Strangulation, 1966; Christmas Eve Crime in Falmouth (Murder in the West Country), 1975; The Porthole Murder: Gay Gibson (Facets of Crime), 1975; numerous scientific papers in medical journals, etc. *Recreations:* motoring, golf, sailing, hotels, good food. *Address:* Strathaven, Carlyon Bay, Cornwall.

HOCKING, Philip Norman; *b* 27 Oct. 1925; *s* of late Fred Hocking, FIOB; *m* 1950, Joan Mable, *d* of Horace Ernest Jackson, CBE, Birmingham; three *d. Educ:* King Henry VIII Sch., Coventry; Birmingham Sch. of Architecture. Dir, F. Hocking & Sons Ltd. Mem. Coventry City Council, 1955-60. Prominent Mem. Young Con. Movement. MP (C) Coventry South, 1959-64; PPS to Minister of State, FO, 1963-64. Contested Coventry S, 1964 and 1966. Chm., Conservative Back Benchers' Housing and Local Govt Cttee, 1962-64. *Recreations:* gardening and sailing. *Club:* Junior Carlton.

HOCKLEY, Sir Anthony Heritage F.; *see* Farrar-Hockley.

HOCKNEY, David; artist; *b* Bradford, 9 July 1937; *s* of Kenneth and Laura Hockney. *Educ:* Bradford Grammar Sch.; Bradford Sch. of Art; Royal Coll. of Art. Lecturer: Maidstone Coll. of Art, 1962; Univ. of Iowa, 1964; Univ. of Colorado, 1965; Univ.

of California, Los Angeles, 1966, Berkeley, 1967. One-man shows: Kasmin Ltd, London, 1963, 1965, 1966, 1968, 1969, 1970, 1972; Alan Gallery, New York, 1964-67; Museum of Modern Art, NY, 1964-68; Stedlijk Museum, Amsterdam, 1966; Whitworth Gallery, Manchester, 1969; Louvre, Paris, 1974; Galerie Claude Bernard, Paris, 1975; Nicholas Wilder, LA, 1976; Galerie Neundorf, Hamburg, 1977, etc; touring show of drawings and prints, Munich, Madrid, Lisbon, Teheran, 1977. Retrospective Exhibn, Whitechapel Art Gall., 1970. 1st Prize, John Moores Exhibn, Liverpool, 1967. Designer, The Rake's Progress, Glyndebourne, 1975. Film: A Bigger Splash, 1975. *Publications:* (ed and illustrated) 14 Poems of C. P. Cavafy, 1967; (illustrated) Six Fairy Tales of the Brothers Grimm, 1969; 72 Drawings by David Hockney, 1971; David Hockney by David Hockney, 1976. *Address:* c/o Kasmin Ltd, 10 Clifford Street, W1.

HODDER-WILLIAMS, Paul, OBE 1945; TD; publisher; Consultant Hodder & Stoughton Ltd, since 1975; *b* 29 Jan. 1910; *s* of late Frank Garfield Hodder Williams, sometime Dean of Manchester, and late Sarah Myfanwy (*née* Nicholson); *m* 1936, Felicity, 2nd *d* of late C. M. Blagden, DD, sometime Bishop of Peterborough; two *s* two *d. Educ:* Rugby; Gonville and Caius Coll., Cambridge (MA). Joined Hodder & Stoughton Ltd, 1931; Dir, 1936, Chm., 1961-75. Served with HAC (Major, 1942), 99th (London Welsh) HAA Regt RA (Lt-Col Comdg, 1942-45). *Recreations:* gardening, walking. *Address:* Court House, Exford, Minehead, Somerset. *T:* Exford 268.

HODDINOTT, Prof. Alun, DMus; Hon. RAM; Professor of Music, University College, Cardiff, since 1967; *b* 11 Aug. 1929; *s* of Thomas Ivor Hoddinott and Gertrude Jones; *m* 1953, Beti Rhiannon Huws; one *s. Educ:* University Coll. of S Wales and Mon. Lecturer: Cardiff Coll. of Music and Drama, 1951-59; University Coll. of S Wales and Mon, 1959-65; Reader, University of Wales, 1965-67. Member: BBC Music Central Adv. Cttee, 1971-; Welsh Arts Council, 1968-74; Member Council: Welsh Nat. Opera, 1972-75; Composers' Guild of GB, 1972-; Nat. Youth Orchestra, 1972-. Chm., Welsh Music Archive, 1977-. Artistic Dir, Cardiff Music Festival. Governor, Welsh Nat. Theatre, 1968-74. Walford Davies Prize, 1954; Arnold Bax Medal, 1957; John Edwards Meml Award, 1967. *Publications: symphonies:* 1955, 1962, 1968, 1969, 1973; *concertos for:* clarinet, 1951; oboe, 1954; harp, 1958; viola, 1958; piano, 1950, 1960, 1967; violin, 1961; organ, 1967; horn, 1969; *sonatas for:* piano, 1959, 1962, 1965, 1966, 1968, 1972; harp, 1964; clarinet, 1967; violin, 1969, 1970, 1971, 1976; cello, 1970; horn, 1971; *other compositions:* Nocturne, 1951; Welsh Dances, 1958, 2nd suite 1969, Investiture Dances 1969; 2nd Nocturne, 1959; Two Welsh Nursery Tunes, 1959; Sextet, 1960; Rebecca, 1962; Septet, 1962; Folk Song Suite, 1962; Sonatina, 1963; Variations, 1963; Medieval Songs, 1963; Divertimento, 1963; Danegeld, 1964; 4 Welsh Songs, 1964; Dives and Lazarus, 1965; String Quartet, 1965; Concerto Grosso, 1965; Variants, 1966; Night music, 1966; Suite for harp, 1967; Aubade, 1967; Roman Dream, 1968; Nocturnes and Cadenzas, 1968; Divertimenti for 8 instruments, 1968; Sinfonietta, 1968, no 2, 1969, no 3, 1970, no 4, 1971; Fioriture, 1968; An apple tree and a pig, 1968; Black Bart, 1968; Piano Trio, 1970; The Tree of Life, 1971; Motet, Out of the Deep, 1972; Ancestor Worship, cycle for high voice and piano, 1972; Piano Quintet, 1973; The Silver Swimmer, for voices and piano duet, 1973; The Beach of Falesá, opera, 1974; Ritornelli, 1974; The Magician, opera, 1975; Ynys Môn, cycle for tenor and piano, 1975; Landscapes, 1975; Voyagers, for male chorus, solo and orchestra, 1976; A Contemplation upon flowers, for soprano and orchestra, 1976; French Suite for orchestra, 1977; Italian Suite for recorder and guitar, 1977; Passaggio for orchestra, 1977; Sinfonia Fidei, 1977; What the old man does is always right, one act opera, 1977; and numerous other shorter works. *Address:* Maesawelon, Mill Road, Lisvane, Cardiff CF4 5UG. *Clubs:* Athenæum; Cardiff and County (Cardiff).

HODGART, Prof. Matthew John Caldwell; Professor of English, Concordia University, Montreal, Canada, since 1970; *b* 1 Sept. 1916; *s* of Matthew Hodgart (Major RE), MC, and Katherine Barbour Caldwell (*née* Gardner); *m* 1st, 1940, Betty Joyce Henstridge (*d* 1948); one *s* one *d*; 2nd, 1949, Margaret Patricia Elliott; one adopted *d. Educ:* Rugby Sch. (Scholar); Pembroke Coll., Cambridge (Scholar; BA 1938, MA 1945). Jebb Studentship, Cambridge, 1938-39. Served War, 1939-45: Argyll and Sutherland Highlanders and in Intelligence (mentioned in despatches). Cambridge University: Asst Lectr in English, 1945-49; Lectr in English, and Fellow of Pembroke Coll., 1949-64; Prof. of English, Sussex Univ., 1964-70. Vis. Professor: Cornell Univ., 1961-62 and 1969; Univ. of Calif, Los Angeles, 1977-78. Chevalier de la Légion d'honneur, and Croix de guerre, 1945. *Publications:* The Ballads, 1950; (with Prof. M. Worthington)

Song in the Work of James Joyce, 1959; Samuel Johnson, 1962; (ed) Horace Walpole, Memoirs, 1963; (ed) Faber Book of Ballads, 1965; Satire, 1969 (trans. various languages); A New Voyage (fiction), 1969; James Joyce, Student Guide, 1977; contrib. Rev. of English Studies, and TLS. *Recreations:* travel, study of architecture, photography. *Address:* 13 Montpelier Villas, Brighton BN1 3DG. *T:* Brighton 26993.

HODGE, Alan; Joint Editor of History Today since 1951; *b* 16 Oct. 1915; *s* of late Capt. T. S. Hodge, RD, RNR; *m* 1948, Jane, *d* of late Conrad Potter Aiken; two *d. Educ:* Liverpool Collegiate Sch.; Oriel Coll., Oxford. Asst Private Sec. to Minister of Information, 1941-45. Editor of The Novel Library (Hamish Hamilton), 1946-52. *Publications:* (with Robert Graves) The Long Week-End, 1940; The Reader Over Your Shoulder, 1943; (with Peter Quennell) The Past We Share, 1960. *Address:* 6 Lancaster Road, SW19. *T:* 01-946 4101.

HODGE, Alexander Mitchell, GC 1940; VRD; DL; Captain RNVR, retired; WS; Member of firm of Cowan & Stewart, WS, Edinburgh; Chairman, Standard Life Assurance Co.; *b* 23 June 1916; *y s* of James Mackenzie Hodge, Blairgowrie, Perthshire; *m* 1944, Pauline Hester Winsome, *o d* of William John Hill, Bristol; one *s* two *d. Educ:* Fettes Coll.; Edinburgh Univ. (MA 1936, LLB 1938). Joined RNVR, 1938; served with Royal Navy, 1939-45 (despatches, GC). Comdr RNVR, 1949, Capt. RNVR, 1953; CO of the Forth Div. RNVR, 1953-57. Chm., Edinburgh Dist Sea Cadet Cttee, 1959-63; Chm., Lady Haig's Poppy Factory, 1961-67; Mem. Council, Earl Haig Fund (Scotland), 1963-67; Chairman: Livingston New Town Licensing Planning Cttee, 1963-69; Edinburgh Western Gen. Hosp. Assoc. of Friends, 1962-68; Trustee and Mem. Cttee of Management: Royal Victoria Hosp. Tuberculosis Trust, 1964- (Pres., 1970-); Royal Edinburgh Inst. for Sailors, Soldiers and Airmen, 1964-71; Chm. General Comrs of Income Tax, Edinburgh South Div., 1967-; Pres., Edinburgh Chamber of Commerce, 1968-70; Dir, The Cruden Foundn, 1969-72; Governor, Fettes Coll., 1970-75. DL Edinburgh, 1972. *Address:* Springbank, Barnton, Midlothian. *T:* 031-336 3054. *Clubs:* Royal Automobile; New (Edinburgh).

HODGE, David, JP; Lord Provost of Glasgow, and Lord Lieutenant of County of City of Glasgow, since 1977; *b* 30 Sept. 1909; *s* of David Hodge and Sarah (*née* Crilly); *m* 1950; four *d. Educ:* St Mungo's Acad., Glasgow. Served War, RAF, 1940-46: air crew, Coastal Comd. On staff of Scottish Gas Bd, 1934-50; Prudential Assurance Co. Ltd, 1950-74, retd. Chm., Ruchill Ward and Maryhill Constituency for 20 yrs. Elected to Glasgow Corp., 1971; Magistrate, Corp. of Glasgow, 1972-74; Vice-Chm., Transport Cttee. Mem., City of Glasgow Dist Council, 1974: Chm., Licensing Court, Licensing Cttee, and Justices Cttee; Sec. of Admin; Council Rep., Convention of Scottish Local Authorities, 1974-77. JP Glasgow, 1975. *Recreations:* interested in all sports (former professional footballer; winner of tennis championships; former swimming and badminton coach); theatre, ballet, music. *Address:* 59 Hillend Road, Glasgow G22 6NY. *T:* 041-336 8727. *Clubs:* Royal Air Forces Association, Marist Centenary (Glasgow).

HODGE, John Dennis; Chief, R&D Plans and Programs Analysis Division, Department of Transportation, Washington, DC, since 1976; *b* 10 Feb. 1929; *s* of John Charles Henry Hodge and Emily M. Corbett Hodge; *m* 1952, Audrey Cox; two *s* two *d. Educ:* Northampton Engineering Coll., University of London (now The City Univ.). Vickers-Armstrong Ltd, Weybridge, England (Aerodynamics Dept), 1950-52; Head, Air Loads Section, Avro Aircraft Ltd, Toronto, Canada, 1952-59; Tech. Asst to Chief, Ops Div., Space Task Group, NASA, Langley Field, Va, USA, 1959; Chief, Flight Control Br., Space Task Group, NASA, 1961; Asst Chief of Flight Control, 1962, Chief, Flight Control Div., Flight Ops Directorate, NASA, MSC, 1963-68; Manager, Advanced Missions Program, NASA, Manned Spacecraft Centre, 1968-70; Dir, Transport Systems Concepts, Transport Systems Center, 1970; Vice-Pres., R&D, The Ontario Transportation Develt Corp., 1974—76. Hon. ScD, The City Univ., London, Eng., 1966; NASA Medal for Exceptional Service, 1967 and 1969; Dept of Transportation Meritorious Achievement Award, 1974. *Publications:* contribs to NASA publications and various aerospace jls. *Recreation:* reading. *Address:* 3443 Skyview Terrace, Falls Church, Va 22042, USA.

HODGE, John Ernest, CMG 1962; CVO 1956; QPM 1955; Inspector-General of Police, Republic of Nigeria, 1962-64; *b* 3 Nov. 1911; *s* of Rev. J. Z. Hodge, DD; *m* 1950, Margaret Henrietta, *d* of late Rev. Hugh Brady Brew, Wicklow; one *s* one *d. Educ:* Taunton Sch., Taunton, Som. Jamaica Constabulary, 1931-35; The Nigeria Police, 1935-64. Colonial Police Medal,

1953. Mem. East Lothian CC, 1972-75. OStJ 1961. *Recreation:* golf. *Address:* Netherlea, Dirleton, East Lothian, Scotland. *T:* Dirleton 272. *Clubs:* Royal Over-Seas League; North Berwick.

HODGE, Sir John Rowland, 2nd Bt *cr* 1921; MBE 1940; FRHS; company director; *b* 1 May 1913; *s* of Sir Rowland Hodge, 1st Bt, and Mabel (*d* 1923), *d* of William Edward Thorpe; *S* father, 1950; *m* 1936, Peggy Ann (marr. diss. 1939), *o d* of Sydney Raymond Kent; *m* 1939, Joan (marr. diss. 1961), *o d* of late Sydney Foster Wilson; three *d*; *m* 1967, Vivien Jill, *d* of A. S. Knightley; one *s* one *d. Educ:* Wrekin Coll.; Switzerland. Served War of 1939-45, RNVR; Lt-Comdr, RNVR, 1938; formerly Oxford and Bucks Light Infantry. Mem. Inst. of Directors. *Heir:* *s* Andrew Rowland Hodge, *b* 3 Dec. 1968. *Address:* Casa Toro, St Andrews, Malta. *T:* 37583. *Clubs:* British Racing Drivers, Naval, Royal Malta Yacht, Royal Yachting Association, Cruising Association.

HODGE, Sir Julian Stephen Alfred, Kt 1970; Merchant banker; Executive Chairman, Hodge Group Ltd (Managing Director, 1963-75); Chairman: Julian S. Hodge & Co. Ltd; Gwent Enterprises Ltd; Hodge Finance Ltd; Hodge Life Assurance Co. Ltd; Avana Group Ltd; Founder, Commercial Bank of Wales, 1971; *b* 15 Oct. 1904; *s* of late Alfred and Jane Hodge; *m* 1951, Moira (*née* Thomas); two *s* one *d. Educ:* Cardiff Technical Coll. Certified Accountant, 1930. Founded Hodge & Co., Accountants and Auditors. Founder and Trustee: The Jane Hodge Foundation, 1962-; Sir Julian Hodge Charitable Trust, 1964; Chm., Aberfan Disaster Fund Industrial Project Sub-Cttee. Member: Welsh Economic Council, 1965-68; Welsh Council, 1968; Council, Univ. of Wales Inst. of Science and Technology (Treasurer, 1968-76; Vice-Pres., 1976-); Foundation Fund Cttee, Univ. of Surrey; Management Cttee, Finance Houses Assoc. Pres., S Glamorgan Dist, St John Ambulance Bde. Governor, All Hallows (Cranmore Hall) Sch. Trust Ltd. FTII 1941. Hon. LLD Univ. of Wales, 1971. KStJ 1977 (CStJ 1972). *Publication:* Paradox of Financial Preservation, 1959. *Recreations:* golf, walking, reading, gardening. *Address:* (business) 31 Windsor Place, Cardiff CF1 3UR; (home) Ty Gwyn, Lisvane, Cardiff CF4 5SG. *Club:* Royal Automobile.

HODGE, Stephen Oswald Vere, CMG 1942; *b* 14 July 1891; *s* of late Rev. C. F. D. Hodge; *m* 1919, Margaret Mary Vere Neilson, *d* of W. Fitzroy Neilson; three *s. Educ:* Durham Sch.; Christ Church, Oxford. Served European War 1914-18, Lieut unattached list 1915-18 (despatches). Asst Dist Commissioner, Kenya, 1913; Sen. Dist Commissioner, 1935; MLC, Kenya, 1937-45; Provincial Comr, Kenya, 1939-46; retd, 1946. Provincial Comdt, Kenya Police Reserve, Rift Valley Prov., Kenya, 1952-53; Staff Officer to Prov. Comr, Rift Valley Prov., Kenya, 1953-54. *Address:* Sidai, PO Box 183, Nakuru, Kenya. *T:* Subukia 4Y10 (Kenya). *Clubs:* Royal Commonwealth Society; Muthaiga Country (Nairobi); Rift Valley Sports (Nakuru).

HODGES, C(yril) Walter; free-lance writer, book illustrator, theatrical historian and designer; *b* 18 March 1909; *s* of Cyril James and Margaret Mary Hodges; *m* 1936, Greta (*née* Becker); two *s. Educ:* Dulwich Coll.; Goldsmiths' Coll. Sch. of Art. Commenced as stage designer, 1929, then illustrator for advertising, magazines (esp. Radio Times) and children's books; began writing, 1937; served with Army, 1940-46 (despatches); has designed stage productions (Mermaid Theatre, 1951, 1964), permanent Elizabethan stage, St George's Theatre, 1976; exhibns (Lloyds, UK Provident Instn); mural decorations painted for Chartered Insce Inst., UK Provident Instn; Art Dir, Encyclopædia Britannica Films, 1959-61. Kate Greenaway Medal for illustration, 1965; Hons List, Hans Christian Andersen Internat. Award, 1966. *Publications:* Columbus Sails, 1939; The Flying House, 1947; Shakespeare and the Players, 1948; The Globe Restored, 1953 (rev. edn 1968); The Namesake, 1964; Shakespeare's Theatre, 1964; The Norman Conquest, 1966; Magna Carta, 1966; The Marsh King, 1967; The Spanish Armada, 1967; The Overland Launch, 1969; The English Civil War, 1972; Shakespeare's Second Globe, 1973; Playhouse Tales, 1974; The Emperor's Elephant, 1975; contrib. Shakespeare Survey. *Recreations:* listening to music, writing letters, visiting museums, driving the car. *Address:* 36 Southover High Street, Lewes, East Sussex. *T:* Lewes 6530.

HODGES, Rt. Rev. Evelyn Charles, DD; *b* Towlerton House, Co. Carlow, 8 Aug. 1887; *s* of Rev. W. H. Hodges; *m* 1927, Violet Blanche, *d* of George Hill Crawford, Dublin; one *s* one *d. Educ:* Rathmines; Mountjoy; Trinity Coll., Dublin (BA, Moderator, Large Gold Medal, 1910, MA 1913, BD 1923, 2nd Class Divinity Testimonium 1911, Higher Diploma on Education 1920). Curate Asst of Drumcondra and North Strand, Dublin, 1911-14; of Rathmines, Dublin, 1914-17;

Diocesan Inspector of Schs (Dublin, Glendalough and Kildare), 1917-24; Incumbent of Rathmines, 1924-28; Principal of Church of Ireland Training Coll (for Teachers), 1928-43; Canon of St Patrick's Cathedral, Dublin, 1934-43; Bishop of Limerick, Ardfert, and Aghadoe, 1943-60, retired. *Address:* 16 Stillorgan Park, Blackrock, Co. Dublin.

HODGES, Gerald; Director of Finance, City of Bradford Metropolitan Council, since 1974; *b* 14 June 1925; *s* of Alfred John Hodges and Gertrude Alice Hodges; *m* 1950, Betty Maire (*née* Brading); one *s* (and one *s* decd). *Educ:* King's Sch., Peterborough. IPFA. Accountancy Asst, Bexley Borough Council, 1941-48, and Eton RDC, 1948-49; Sen. Accountancy Asst, Newcastle upon Tyne, 1949-53; Chief Accountant, Hemel Hempstead, 1953-56; Dep. Treas., Crawley UDC, 1956-70; Treas., Ilkley UDC, 1970-74. *Publications:* occasional articles in Public Finance and Accountancy. *Recreations:* travelling, ornithology, reading. *Address:* 23 Victoria Avenue, Ilkley, West Yorks. *T:* Ilkley 607346.

HODGES, Air Chief Marshal Sir Lewis (Macdonald), KCB 1968 (CB 1963); CBE 1958; DSO 1944 and Bar 1945; DFC 1942 and Bar 1943; Deputy Commander-in-Chief, Allied Forces, Central Europe, 1973-76; retired 1976; *b* 1 March 1918; *s* of late Arthur Macdonald Hodges and Gladys Mildred Hodges; *m* 1950, Elizabeth Mary, *e d* of G. H. Blackett, MC; two *s. Educ:* St Paul's Sch.; RAF Coll., Cranwell. Bomber Command, 1938-44; SE Asia (India, Burma, Ceylon), 1944-45; Palestine, 1945-47; Air Ministry and Min. of Defence, 1948-52; Bomber Command, 1952-59; Asst Comdt, RAF Coll., Cranwell, 1959-61; AO i/c Admin., Middle East Comd, Aden, 1961-63; Imperial Def. Coll. 1963; SHAPE, 1964-65; Ministry of Defence, Asst Chief of Air Staff (Ops), 1965-68; AOC-in-C, RAF Air Support Comd, 1968-70; Air Mem. for Personnel, MoD, 1970-73. Air ADC to the Queen, 1973-76. Légion d'Honneur (French) 1950; Croix de Guerre (French) 1944. *Recreations:* sailing, shooting, fishing. *Address:* Allens House, Plaxtol, near Sevenoaks, Kent. *T:* Plaxtol 255; 181A Ashley Gardens, SW1. *T:* 01-834 5626. *Clubs:* Royal Air Force, Army and Navy.

HODGETTS, Robert Bartley; Under-Secretary, Department of Health and Social Security, since 1973; *b* 10 Nov. 1918; *s* of late Captain Bartley Hodgetts, MN and Florence Hodgetts (*née* Stagg); *m* 1st, 1945, A. K. Jeffreys; one *d*; 2nd, 1949, Frances Grace, *d* of late A. J. Pepper, Worcester; two *d. Educ:* Merchant Taylors' Sch., Crosby; St John's Coll., Cambridge (Scholar, BA). Served RNVR (A), 1940-45. Asst Principal, Min. of Nat. Insce, 1947; Principal 1951; Asst Sec. 1964. *Recreations:* watching cricket and Rugby football. *Address:* 9 Purley Bury Close, Purley, Surrey. *T:* 01-668 2827.

HODGINS, Ven. Michael Minden; Archdeacon of Hackney, 1951-71; Secretary of London Diocesan Fund, 1946-74; *b* 26 Aug. 1912; *yr s* of late Major R. Hodgins, Indian Army, and Margaret Hodgins (*née* Wilson); unmarried. *Educ:* Wellington; Cuddesdon Theological Coll. Deacon, 1939; Priest, 1940; Curate, S Barnabas, Northolt Park, 1939; Asst Secretary, London Diocesan Fund, 1943. MA Lambeth 1960. *Address:* 2 Pottery Close, Brede, Sussex. *Club:* Reform.

HODGKIN, Sir Alan (Lloyd), OM 1973; KBE 1972; FRS 1948; MA, ScD Cantab; Fellow of Trinity College, Cambridge, since 1936; John Humphrey Plummer Professor of Biophysics, University of Cambridge, since 1970; Chancellor, University of Leicester, since 1971; *b* 5 Feb. 1914; *s* of G. L. Hodgkin and M. F. Wilson; *m* 1944, Marion de Kay, *d* of late F. P. Rous; one *s* three *d. Educ:* Gresham's Sch., Holt; Trinity Coll., Cambridge. Scientific Officer working on Radar for Air Ministry and Min. of Aircraft Production, 1939-45. Lecturer and then Asst Dir of Research at Cambridge, 1945-52. Foulerton Research Prof., Royal Soc., 1952-69. Baly Medal, RCP, 1955; Royal Medal of Royal Society, 1958; Nobel Prize for Medicine (jointly), 1963; Copley Medal of Royal Society, 1965. Pres., Royal Society, 1970-75; Pres., Marine Biological Assoc., 1966-76. Foreign Member: Royal Danish Acad. of Sciences, 1964; Amer. Acad. of Arts and Sciences, 1962; Amer. Philosophical Soc.; Royal Swedish Acad. of Sciences; Member: Physiological Soc.; Leopoldina Acad., 1964; Pontifical Acad. of Sciences, 1968; Hon. MRIA, 1974; Hon. For. Mem., USSR Acad. of Scis, 1976. Fellow, Imperial Coll. London, 1972; Hon. FRSE, 1974; Hon. Fellow: Indian National Science Acad., 1972; Pharmaceutical Soc.; For. Assoc., Nat. Acad. of Scis, USA, 1974. Hon. MD: Berne 1956, Louvain 1958; Hon. DSc: Sheffield 1963, Newcastle upon Tyne 1965, E Anglia 1966, Manchester 1971, Leicester 1971, London 1971, Newfoundland 1973, Wales 1973, Rockefeller Univ., 1974, Bristol 1976; Oxford, 1977; Hon. LLD, Aberdeen 1973. *Publications:* scientific papers dealing with the Nature of Nervous conduction, Journ. Physiology, etc.

Recreations: travel, ornithology and fishing. *Address:* Physiological Laboratory, Cambridge; 25 Newton Road, Cambridge. *T:* Cambridge 59284.

HODGKIN, Prof. Dorothy Crowfoot, OM 1965; FRS 1947; Wolfson Research Professor, Royal Society, 1960-77; Fellow: Somerville College, Oxford; Wolfson College, Oxford, since 1977; Chancellor, Bristol University, since 1970; *b* 1910; *d* of late J. W. Crowfoot, CBE; *m* 1937, Thomas Hodgkin, *qv*; two *s* one *d. Educ:* Sir John Leman Sch., Beccles; Somerville Coll., Oxford. Pres., British Assoc. for the Advancement of Science, 1977-78. Fellow: Australian Academy of Science, 1968; Akad. Leopoldina, 1968. Foreign Member: Royal Netherlands Academy of Science and Letters, 1956; Amer. Acad. of Arts and Sciences, Boston, 1958, and other learned bodies. Hon. For. Mem., USSR Acad. of Scis, 1976. Hon. DSc Leeds and Manchester; Hon. ScD Cambridge and other Hon. degrees. Royal Medallist of the Royal Society, 1956; Nobel Prize for Chemistry, 1964; Copley Medal, Royal Soc., 1976. First Freedom of Beccles, 1965. *Publications:* various, on the X-ray crystallographic analysis of structure of molecules. *Recreations:* archæology, walking, children. *Address:* Crab Mill, Ilmington, Shipston-on-Stour, Warwicks. *T:* Ilmington 233.

HODGKIN, Eliot; artist and writer; *b* 19 June 1905; *o s* of Charles Ernest Hodgkin and Alice Jane Brooke; *m* 1940, Maria Clara (Mimi) Henderson (*née* Franceschi); one *s. Educ:* Harrow; Royal Academy Schs. Exhibited at Royal Academy and bought under Chantrey Bequest, for Tate Gallery: October, 1936; Undergrowth, 1943; Pink and White Turnips, 1972; One Man Shows: London Leicester Galleries, 1956; New York, Durlacher, 1958; London, Arthur Jeffress Gallery, 1959; New York, Durlacher, 1962; London, Reid Gallery, 1963; Agnew's, 1966. *Publications:* She Closed the Door, 1931; Fashion Drawing, 1932; 55 London Views, 1948; A Pictorial Gospel, 1949. *Address:* 9a Durham Place, SW3.

HODGKIN, Howard, CBE 1977; painter; Trustee, National Gallery; *b* 6 Aug. 1932; *m* 1955, Julia Lane; two *s. Educ:* Camberwell Sch. of Art; Bath Academy of Art. Taught at Charterhouse Sch., 1954-56; taught at Bath Academy of Art, 1956-66; occasional tutor, Slade Sch. of Art and Chelsea Sch. of Art. Vis. Fellow in Creative Art, Brasenose Coll. Oxford, 1976-77. A Trustee, Tate Gall., to 1977. One-man exhibitions include: Arthur Tooth & Sons, 1962, 1964, 1967; Kasmin Gallery, 1969, 1971, 1976; Arnolfini Gall., Bristol, 1970, 1975; Dartington Hall, 1970; Galerie Müller, Cologne, 1971; Kornblee Gall., NY, 1973; Museum of Modern Art, Oxford, Serpentine Gall., Turnpike Gall., Leigh, Lancs, Laing Art Gall., Newcastle upon Tyne, Aberdeen Art Gall., Graves Art Gall., Sheffield, Waddington Gall., 1976; Prizewinner, John Moores Exhibn, Liverpool, 1976. *Address:* c/o Kasmin Ltd, 10 Clifford Street, W1X 1RB. *T:* 01-437 1645.

HODGKIN, Thomas Lionel; lecturer and writer; Emeritus Fellow, Balliol College, Oxford; *b* 3 April 1910; *s* of late R. H. Hodgkin, Provost of Queen's Coll., Oxford, and D. F. Hodgkin, *d* of late A. L. Smith, Master of Balliol; *m* 1937, Dorothy Mary Crowfoot (*see* D. C. Hodgkin); two *s* one *d. Educ:* Winchester Coll. (Exhibitioner); Balliol Coll. (Schol.). Sen. Demy, Magdalen Coll., 1932-33; Asst Secretary, Palestine Civil Service, 1934-36; Education Officer, Cumberland Friends' Unemployment Cttee, 1937-39; Staff Tutor in North Staffs, Oxford University Tutorial Classes Cttee, 1939-45; Sec. to the Oxford University Delegacy for Extra-Mural Studies, and Fellow of Balliol, 1945-52; Visiting Lecturer: Northwestern Univ., Illinois, 1957; University Coll. of Ghana, 1958; Research Associate, Institute of Islamic Studies, McGill Univ., Montreal, 1958-61; Dir, Institute of African Studies, University of Ghana, 1962-65; Lecturer in Govt in New States, Univ. of Oxford, and Fellow of Balliol, 1965-70. MA Oxon. *Publications:* Nationalism in Colonial Africa, 1956; Nigerian Perspectives, 1960, 2nd edn 1975; African Political Parties, 1961; articles on African affairs. *Recreations:* birdwatching, conversation. *Address:* Crab Mill, Ilmington, Shipston-on-Stour, Warwicks. *T:* Ilmington 233.

HODGKINS, David John; Under-Secretary, Incomes Division, Department of Employment, since 1976; *b* 13 March 1934; *s* of Rev. Harold Hodgkins and Elsie McLauchlan; *m* 1963, Sheila Lacey; two *s. Educ:* Buxton Coll.; Peterhouse, Cambridge. BA 1956 (Hist. Tripos Pts I and II, Cl. 2 (1) and 1); MA 1960. Entered Min. of Labour as Asst Principal, 1956; Principal: Overseas Div., Min. of Lab., 1961-64; Safety, Health and Welfare Div., MoL, 1964-65; Treasury, 1965-68; Manpower and Productivity Services, Dept of Employment, 1968-70; Asst Secretary: Prices and Incomes Div., Dept of Employment, 1970-72; Industrial Relns Div., 1973-76. *Address:* Four Winds, Batchelors Way, Amersham, Bucks HP7 9AJ. *T:* Amersham 5207.

HODGKINSON, Very Rev. Arthur Edward; Provost of St Andrew's Cathedral, Aberdeen, since 1965; *b* 29 Oct. 1913; *s* of Arthur and Rose Hodgkinson. *Educ:* Glasgow High School; Edinburgh Theol College. LTh Durham 1942. Deacon 1939; Priest 1940. Curate, St George's, Maryhill, Glasgow, 1939-43; Choir Chaplain, 1943, and Precentor of St Ninian's Cath., Perth, 1944-47; Curate-in-Charge, St Finnian's, Lochgelly, 1947-52, and Rector, 1952-54; Rector, Holy Trinity, Motherwell, 1954-65; Commissary to Bp of St John's, 1961; Canon of St Mary's Cath., Glasgow, 1963-65. Hon. Canon of Christ Church Cathedral, Connecticut, 1965. *Recreations:* motoring, travel. *Address:* Cathedral House, 10 Louisville Avenue, Aberdeen AB1 6TX. *T:* Aberdeen 36984. *Club:* Royal Over-Seas League.

HODGKINSON, Sir Derek; *see* Hodgkinson, Sir W. D.

HODGKINSON, Commander Guy Beauchamp, DSO 1940; RN retired; *b* 11 Jan. 1903; *s* of Commander George Hodgkinson, RN retired, and Helen Blanche Raggett; *m* 1930, Beryl Margaret, *d* of Harry Langley; two *d. Educ:* St Hugh's Sch., Chislehurst; RN Colleges Osborne and Dartmouth. War of 1939-45 (despatches twice, DSO).

HODGKINSON, Terence William Ivan, CBE 1958; Director of the Wallace Collection, since 1974; *b* 7 Oct. 1913; *s* of late Ivan Tattersall Hodgkinson, Wells, Som, and of late Kathryn Van Vleck Townsend, New York (who *m* 2nd, 1929, Sir Gilbert Upcott, KCB; he *d* 1967); unmarried. *Educ:* Oundle Sch.; Magdalen Coll., Oxford. Served War of 1939-45 Major, Gen. Staff 1943. Joined staff of Victoria and Albert Museum (Dept of Architecture and Sculpture) 1946; Asst to the Dir, 1948-62; Secretary to the Advisory Council, 1951-67; Keeper, Dept of Architecture and Sculpture, 1967-74. *Publications:* (part author) Catalogue of Sculpture in the Frick Collection, New York, 1970; Catalogue of Sculpture at Waddesdon Manor, 1970; articles in Burlington Magazine, Bulletin and Yearbook of the Victoria and Albert Museum and for Walpole Society. *Recreation:* music. *Address:* 9 The Grove, N6.

HODGKINSON, Air Chief Marshal Sir (William) Derek, KCB 1971 (CB 1969); CBE 1960; DFC; AFC; *b* 27 Dec. 1917; *s* of late E. N. Hodgkinson; *m* 1939, Heather Goodwin, *d* of H. W. Goodwin, Southampton; one *s* one *d. Educ:* Repton. Commnd, 1937; No 220 Sqdn, 1938-40; POW Germany, 1942-45; OC No 210 Sqdn, 1947-49; RAF Staff Coll., 1951; Chief Instructor, Jt Austr. Anti Submarine Sch., Nowra, Austr., 1952-54; Directing Staff, Jt Services Staff Coll., 1954-57; OC No 240 Sqdn, 1957-58; OC RAF St Mawgan, 1960-61; ADC to the Queen, 1961-63; Staff of Chief of Defence Staff, 1961-63; Imp. Def. Coll., 1964; Comdt RAF Staff Coll., Andover, 1965; Asst Chief of the Air Staff, Operational Requirements, 1966-68; SASO, RAF Training Command, 1969-70; AOC-in-C, Near East Air Force, Commander British Forces Near East, and Administrator, Sovereign Base Area, Cyprus, 1970-73; Air Secretary, 1973-76; retired 1976. *Recreations:* cricket, fishing. *Address:* Frenchmoor Lodge, West Tytherley, Salisbury, Wilts. *Clubs:* Royal Air Force, MCC.

HODGSON, Arthur Brian, CMG 1962; Counsellor, British Red Cross Society, since 1976; *b* 24 Aug. 1916; *s* of late Major Arthur H. F. Hodgson, Westfields, Iffley, Oxford; *m* 1945, Anne Patricia Halse, *d* of late Lt-Col E. M. Ley, DSO, KRRC; two *s* two *d. Educ:* Edinburgh Academy; Eton Coll.; Oriel Coll., Oxford; Trinity Coll., Cambridge. Colonial Civil Service, Tanganyika Administration, 1939-62, retiring as Principal Sec. and Dir of Establishments. Dep. Dir-Gen., 1966-70, Dir-Gen., 1970-75, British Red Cross Society. *Recreations:* rowing, rifle shooting, gardening. *Address:* Chandlers, Furners Green, near Uckfield, Sussex TN22 3RH. *T:* Danehill 310. *Clubs:* Anglo-Belgian; Leander, MCC.

HODGSON, Hon. Sir Derek; *see* Hodgson, Hon. Sir W. D. T.

HODGSON, George Charles Day, CMG 1961; MBE 1950; lately an Administrative Officer, Nyasaland; retired from HMOCS, Nov. 1964; Secretary, Old Diocesans' Union, Diocesan College, Rondebosch, Cape, South Africa, since 1965; *b* 21 Sept. 1913; *s* of late P. J. Hodgson and of A. E. Joubert; *m* 1940, Edna Orde, *d* of late G. H. Rushmere; one *s. Educ:* Diocesan Coll., Rondebosch, Capetown, S Africa; Rhodes Univ., Grahamstown, S Africa; Cambridge Univ. Joined Colonial Administrative Service as Cadet, 1939. Military Service, 1940-42; Lieut, 1st Bn King's African Rifles. Returned to duty as Distr. Officer, Nyasaland, 1943; seconded for special famine relief duties in Nyasaland, 1949-50; Provincial Commissioner, 1952; Adviser on Race Affairs to Govt of Federation of Rhodesia and Nyasaland, 1958-59; Nyasaland Govt Liaison Officer to Monckton Commn, 1960; Permanent Sec., Ministry of Natural Resources and Surveys, Nyasaland, 1961-62; Permanent Sec., Ministry of Transport and Communications, Nyasaland, 1963-64. *Recreations:* Rugby football, cricket, golf. *Address:* Diocesan College, Rondebosch, Cape, South Africa; Maresfield Lowlands Avenue, Tokai, Cape, South Africa. *Clubs:* Royal Cape Golf, Western Province Cricket (Cape Town).

HODGSON, James; Senior Director of External Telecommunications, Post Office, since 1975 (Director, 1969-75); Director (non-executive), Cable and Wireless Ltd, since 1970; *b* 14 Oct. 1925; *s* of Frederick and Lucy Hodgson; *m* 1951, Patricia (*née* Reed); no *c. Educ:* Exeter Sch.; St John's Coll., Cambridge. Entered GPO, 1950; Private Sec. to Asst PMG, 1952-55 and to Dir Gen. GPO, 1955-56; seconded to Cabinet Office, 1961-63; Head of Telephone Operating Div. of GPO Headquarters, 1965-67; Vice-Director of External Telecommunications Executive, 1967-69. *Recreations:* travel, tennis, squash, archaeology. *Address:* 21 Keswick Heights, Keswick Road, Putney, SW15 2JR. *T:* 01-870 0186.

HODGSON, John Bury; Special Commissioner of Income Tax, since 1970; *b* 17 March 1912; *s* of Charles Hodgson and Dorothy Hope Hodgson; *m* 1948, Helen Sibyl Uvedale Beaumont. *Educ:* Derbyshire Grammar Sch.; Manchester Univ. Solicitor, 1942; Asst Solicitor of Inland Revenue, 1956-70. *Publications:* (contrib.) Halsbury's Laws of England; (Consulting Editor) Sergeant on Stamp Duties. *Recreations:* sailing, beekeeping. *Address:* 47 Cumberland Terrace, Regent's Park, NW1 4HP. *T:* 01-935 7010; Five Thorns Cottage, Brockenhurst, Hants. *T:* Brockenhurst 2653. *Clubs:* various yacht.

HODGSON, Maurice Arthur Eric; Deputy Chairman, ICI Ltd, since 1972; *b* 21 Oct. 1919; *s* of late Walter Hodgson and of Amy Hodgson (*née* Walker); *m* 1945, Norma Fawcett; one *s* one *d. Educ:* Bradford Grammar Sch.; Merton Coll., Oxford. MA, BSc; CEng, FIChemE. Joined ICI Ltd Fertilizer & Synthetic Products Gp, 1942; seconded to ICI (New York) Ltd, 1955-58; Head of ICI Ltd Technical Dept, 1958; Develt Dir, ICI Ltd Heavy Organic Chemicals Div., 1960, Dep. Chm., 1964; Gen. Man., Company Planning, ICI Ltd, 1966; Commercial Dir and Planning Dir, ICI Ltd, 1970; Director: Carrington Viyella Ltd, 1970-74; Imperial Chemicals Insce Ltd, 1970- (Chm. 1972). Vis. Fellow, Sch. of Business and Organizational Studies, Univ. of Lancaster, 1970-. FBIM 1972. *Recreations:* horse-racing, swimming, fishing. *Address:* Imperial Chemical Industries Ltd, Imperial Chemical House, Millbank, SW1P 3JF.

HODGSON, Prof. Phyllis; Professor of English Language and Mediæval Literature, Bedford College, University of London, 1955-72, retired; *b* 27 June 1909; *d* of late Herbert Henry Hodgson, MA, BSc, PhD, FRIC. *Educ:* Bolling Grammar Sch. for Girls, Bradford; Bedford Coll., University of London (BA); (Sen. Schol.) Lady Margaret Hall, Oxford (BLitt, DPhil). Tutor of St Mary's Coll., Durham Univ., 1936-38; Jex-Blake Fellow, Girton Coll., Cambridge (MA), 1938-40; Lecturer in English Language (Part-time), Queen Mary Coll., University of London, and Lecturer in English, Homerton Coll., Cambridge, 1940-42; Lecturer in English Language and Mediæval Literature, Bedford Coll., University of London, 1942-49; Reader in English Language in the University of London, 1949-55; External examiner for Reading Univ., 1955-57, 1961-63. Mem. Council of Early English Text Soc., 1959-; Chm., Bd of Studies in English, 1964-66. Sir Israel Gollancz Prize, British Academy, 1971. *Publications:* The Cloud of Unknowing (EETS), 1944, 1958; Deonise Hid Divinite (EETS), 1955, 1958; The Franklin's Tale, 1960; The Orcherd of Syon and the English Mystical Tradition (Proc. Brit. Acad. 1964), 1965; The Orcherd of Syon (EETS), 1966; Three 14th Century English Mystics, 1967; The General Prologue to the Canterbury Tales, 1969; articles in Review of English Studies, Modern Language Review, Contemporary Review, etc. *Recreations:* music, walking, travel. *Address:* 25 Barton Croft, Barton-on-Sea, New Milton, Hants BH25 7BT. *T:* New Milton 612 349.

HODGSON, Robin Granville; MP (C) Walsall North, since Nov. 1976; *b* 25 April 1942; *s* of Henry Edward and Natalie Beatrice Hodgson. *Educ:* Shrewsbury Sch.; Oxford Univ. (BA Hons 1964); Wharton Sch. of Finance, Univ. of Pennsylvania (MBA 1969). Investment Banker, New York and Montreal, 1964-67; Industry in Birmingham, England, 1969-72; Director, M. J. H. Nightingale & Co. Ltd, London EC2, 1972-. Contested (C) Walsall North, Feb. and Oct. 1974. *Recreations:* squash, theatre, riding. *Address:* Astley Abbotts, Bridgnorth, Salop. *T:* Bridgnorth 3122; 144 Campden Hill Road, W8. *T:* 01-221 5606.

HODGSON, Stanley Ernest, CBE 1974 (OBE 1966); retired; Education Adviser, British High Commission, New Delhi, 1971-77; *b* 11 July 1918; *s* of Harold Frederick Hodgson, MPS, and

Winifred Caroline (*née* Gale); *m* 1945, Joan Beryl (*née* Ballard); two *d*. *Educ:* Brentwood Grammar Sch.; London Univ. Teacher's Certif., London, 1941; BA Hons Russian, London, 1949. RA, 1941-46. British Council: India, 1949-54; Uganda, 1956-60; Reg. Rep., South India, 1965-68; Controller Estabts, 1969-71. *Recreations:* reading, gardening, walking. *Address:* Clarendon, Netherfield Road, Battle, East Sussex TN33 OHJ. *T:* Battle 2631. *Club:* Royal Commonwealth Society.

HODGSON, Thomas Charles Birkett, CVO 1970; OBE 1966; QPM 1969; Chief Constable, Thames Valley Constabulary, 1968-70; *b* 8 Dec. 1907; *s* of late Thomas Edward Birkett Hodgson, Preston, Lancs; *m* 1936, Gwyneth Cosslett Bowles, *d* of Ivor Willans Bowles, Llandaff, Cardiff; one *s* one *d*. *Educ:* St Peter's, York. Served with Lancashire Constabulary, 1927-55; Asst Chief Constable, Birmingham, 1955-59; Chief Constable, Berkshire, 1959-68. *Address:* Little Newnham, Sutton Veny, near Warminster, Wilts. *T:* Sutton Veny 254.

HODGSON, Thomas Edward Highton, CB 1958; Assistant Secretary, Office of Population Censuses and Surveys (formerly General Register Office), 1968-72; *b* 22 Aug. 1907; *e s* of late Sir Edward Hodgson, KBE, CB; *m* 1935, E. Catherine, *d* of T. Robin Hodgson; four *s*. *Educ:* Felsted Sch.; St John's Coll., Oxford. Asst Master, Felsted Sch., 1931; Board of Trade: Principal, 1941; Asst Sec., 1945; Asst Sec., Ministry of Materials, 1951; Under Secretary: Ministry of Supply, 1954; Ministry of Aviation, 1959; Ministry of Health, 1960-68. *Address:* 15 Church Street, Sudbury, Suffolk.

HODGSON, Hon. Sir (Walter) Derek (Thornley), Kt 1977; Hon. Mr Justice Hodgson; a Judge of the High Court of Justice, Queen's Bench Division, since 1977; *b* 24 May 1917; *s* of late Walter Hodgson, Whitefield, Manchester; *m* 1951, Raymonde Valda (*née* de Villiers) (*d* 1965); no *c*. *Educ:* Malvern Coll.; Trinity Hall, Cambridge. Scholar, Trinity Hall; Harmsworth Scholar, Middle Temple; 1st Cl. Law Tripos, Part II, 1938; 1st Cl. LLB, 1939. Served throughout War 1939-46, Royal Artillery; Burma 1942-45; released with rank of Captain, 1946. Called to Bar, Middle Temple, 1946 (Master of the Bench, 1967); QC 1961. Member: Senate of Inns of Court, 1966-69; Gen. Council of the Bar, 1965-69. Judge of the Salford Hundred Court of Record, 1965-71; a Law Comr, 1971-77; a Recorder of the Crown Court, 1972-77. Member: Lord Chancellor's Cttees on: Legal Educn, 1968-71; Contempt of Court, 1971-74; Butler Cttee on Mentally Abnormal Offenders, 1973-75. *Recreations:* fell walking, travel. *Address:* Royal Courts of Justice, Strand, WC2. *Clubs:* United Oxford & Cambridge University; Manchester, Tennis and Racquets (Manchester); Hawks (Cambridge).

HODGSON, William Donald John; General Manager, Independent Television News Ltd, since 1960, Director since 1973; *b* 25 March 1923; *s* of James Samuel Hodgson and Caroline Maud Albrecht; *m* 1946, Betty Joyce Brown; two *s* six *d*. *Educ:* Beckenham Grammar School. Served as pilot, RAF and Fleet Air Arm, 1942-46. Documentary and feature film editor (with Jean Renoir on The River, Calcutta), 1946-50; Organiser, Festival of Britain Youth Programme, 1950-51; Asst Sec., Central Bureau for Educational Visits and Exchanges, 1951-54; Asst Gen. Man., Press Assoc., 1954-60. *Recreations:* childcare, private flying, cricket, swimming. *Address:* 38 Park Road, Beckenham, Kent. *T:* 01-650 8959.

HODIN, Prof. Josef Paul, LLD; author, art historian, art critic; *b* 17 Aug. 1905; *s* of Eduard D. Hodin and Rosa (*née* Klug); *m* 1945, Doris Pamela Simms; one *s* one *d*. *Educ:* Kleinseitner Realschule and Neustädter Realgymnasium, Prague; Charles Univ., Prague; London Univ.; Art Academies of Dresden and Berlin. Press Attaché to Norwegian Govt in London, 1944-45; Dir of Studies and Librarian, Inst. of Contemporary Arts, London, 1949-54; Hon. Mem. Editorial Council of The Journal of Aesthetics and Art Criticism, Cleveland, 1955-; Mem. Exec. Cttee British Soc. of Aesthetics; Pres., British Section, AICA; Editor: Prisme des Arts, Paris, 1956-59; Quadrum, Brussels, 1956-66. 1st internat. prize for art criticism, Biennale, Venice, 1954. Hon. PhD Uppsala, 1969; Hon. Prof. Vienna, 1975. DSM 1st cl. Czechoslovakia, 1947; St Olav Medal, Norway, 1958; Comdr, Order of Merit, Italy, 1966; Grand Cross, Order of Merit, Austria, 1968; Order of Merit, 1st cl., Germany, 1969; Silver Cross of Merit, Austria, 1972. *Publications:* Monographs on Sven Erixson (Stockholm), 1940; Ernst Josephson (Stockholm), 1942, Edvard Munch (Stockholm), 1948, (Frankfurt a/M), 1951; Isaac Grünewald (Stockholm), 1949; Art and Criticism (Stockholm), 1944; J. A. Comenius and Our Time (Stockholm), 1944; The Dilemma of Being Modern (London), 1956, (New York), 1959; Henry Moore (Amsterdam, Hamburg), 1956, (London, New York), 1958, (Buenos Aires),

1963; Ben Nicholson (London), 1957; Barbara Hepworth (Neuchatel, London, New York), 1961; Lynn Chadwick (Amsterdam, Hamburg, London, New York), 1961; Bekenntnis zu Kokoschka (Mainz), 1963; Edvard Munch (Mainz), 1963; Oskar Kokoschka: A Biography (London, New York), 1966; Walter Kern (Neuchatel, London), 1966; Ruszkowski (London), 1967; Bernard Leach (London), 1967; Oskar Kokoschka: Sein Leben Seine Zeit (Mainz), 1968; Kafka und Goethe (Hamburg), 1968; Die Brühlsche Terrasse, Ein Künstlerroman, 1970; Emilio Greco, Life and Work (London, New York), 1971; Edvard Munch (London, New York, Oslo), 1972; Modern Art and the Modern Mind (London, Cleveland), 1972; Alfred Manessier (London, NY, Paris), 1972; Bernard Stern (London), 1972; Ludwig Meidner (Darmstadt), 1973; Hilde Goldschmidt (Hamburg), 1974; Paul Berger-Bergner, Leben und Werk (Hamburg), 1974; Die Leute von Elverdingen (Hamburg), 1974; Kokoschka und Hellas (Vienna), 1975; John Milne (London), 1977; contribs on literary and art subjects to internat. periodicals. *Address:* 12 Eton Avenue, NW3 3EH. *T:* 01-794 3609. *Clubs:* Arts, Pen.

HODKIN, Rev. Canon Hedley; Residentiary Canon, Manchester Cathedral, 1957-70, Canon Emeritus, since 1970; Sub-Dean, 1966-70; *b* 3 Jan. 1902; *s* of Walter and Elizabeth Hodkin; *m* 1932, Mary M., *d* of Dr J. A. Findlay; one *s* one *d*. *Educ:* University of Sheffield; Christ's Coll. and Westcott House, Cambridge. Curate of: Morpeth, 1935-38; St George's, Newcastle, 1938-40; Vicar of: St Luke's, Newcastle, 1940-47; Holy Trinity, Millhouses, Sheffield, 1947-57. Examining Chaplain: to Bishop of Newcastle, 1939-47; to Bishop of Sheffield, 1951-57; to Bishop of Manchester, 1957. Hon. Canon of Sheffield, 1955-57. Select Preacher, Cambridge, 1968. *Publication:* The Saving Name, 1954. *Recreation:* music. *Address:* 79 Folds Crescent, Sheffield S8 0EP. *T:* Sheffield 362155.

HODKINSON, William, CBE 1974 (OBE 1952); Part-time Member, British Gas Corporation, 1973-74; *b* 11 Aug. 1909; *s* of late William Hodkinson and late Ann Greenwood; *m* 1934, Ann, *d* of John Buxton; one *s*. *Educ:* St Anne's, Stretford; Salford Technical Coll. Stretford Gas Co.: Technical Asst, 1930-32; Asst Works Manager, 1932-35; UK Gas Corp. Ltd: Chief Technical Officer, 1935-39; Gen. Man., 1939-46; Tech. Dir and Gen. Man., 1946-49; North Western Gas Board (later North Western Gas Region): Chief Technical and Planning Officer, 1949-56; Dep. Chm., 1956-64; Chm., 1964-74. Pres., InstGasE, 1963-64. OStJ 1968. *Recreation:* golf. *Address:* 19 Harewood Avenue, Sale, Trafford, Cheshire. *T:* 061-962 4653.

HODSON, Baron (Life Peer), *cr* 1960, of Rotherfield Greys; **Francis Lord Charlton Hodson,** PC 1951; Kt 1937; MC; a Lord of Appeal in Ordinary, 1960-71; Member of Permanent Court of Arbitration at The Hague, 1949-73; *b* 1895; *s* of Rev. Thomas Hodson, MA, late Rector of Oddington, Glos, and Catherine Anne Maskew; *m* 1918, Susan Mary (*d* 1965), *d* of late Major W. G. Blake, DL; one *s* (and *er s* killed in Libya 23 Jan. 1942) one *d*. *Educ:* Cheltenham Coll.; Wadham Coll., Oxford (Hon. Fellow). 2nd Lieut 7th Bn Glos Regt, Sept. 1914; served in Gallipoli and Mesopotamia, 1915-17 (MC, Cavaliere of the Order of the Crown of Italy); retired as Captain, 1919; called to Bar, Inner Temple, 1921; Junior Counsel to Treasury (Probate), 1935; KC 1937; Judge of High Court of Justice (Probate Divorce and Admiralty Division), 1937-51; Bencher, Inner Temple, 1938; a Lord Justice of Appeal, 1951-60. Past Pres., Internat. Law Assoc., British Branch. *Address:* Rotherfield Greys, Oxon. *T:* Rotherfield Greys 303. *Clubs:* Brooks's; Huntercombe Golf (Henley-on-Thames).

HODSON, Prof. Cecil John, MB, BS London; FRCP; FRCR; DMRE; Professor of Uroradiology, School of Medicine, Yale University, since 1975; *b* 20 Dec. 1915; *s* of Dr J. E. Hodson and Kate Bassnett; *m* (marr. diss.); one *s*. *Educ:* Eastbourne Coll.; St Mary's Hosp., Paddington. Junior medical posts: St Mary's Hosp. and St Giles Hosp., Camberwell; Brompton Hosp.; Harefield Emergency Hosp. RAMC, 1942-46 (despatches); served in N Africa, Sicily, Italy and Greece; Major, Specialist in Radiology. Dep. Dir, X-Ray Dept, University Coll. Hosp., 1949; Dir, X-Ray Diagnostic Dept, UCH, 1960-70; Radiologist, Queen Elizabeth Hosp. for Children, 1948-70; Hon. Cons. Radiologist, Queen Alexandra Mil. Hosp., Millbank, 1963-70; Prof. of Radiology, Memorial Univ. of Newfoundland, 1970-75. Sec., Faculty of Radiologists, 1959-64, Vice-Pres., 1964-65. Baker Travelling Prof. of Royal Australasian College of Radiology, 1962. William Julius Mickle Fellow, University of London, 1966; FRSM. Member: The Renal Assoc.; Thoracic Soc.; British Paediatric Assoc.; Harveian Soc.; Medical Soc. of London. *Publications:* chapters in radiological textbooks; numerous contributions to medical journals. *Recreations:*

mountains, sailing, gardening. *Address:* School of Medicine, Yale University, New Haven, Conn 06520, USA; 720 Mt Carmel Avenue, Hamden, Conn 06518, USA. *Clubs:* Alpine Ski; United Hospitals Sailing; Royal Sussex Yacht.

HODSON, Donald Manly; *b* 10 Sept. 1913; 2nd *s* of late Prof. T. C. Hodson; *m* 1940, Margaret Beatson Bell, *er d* of late Sir Nicholas Beatson Bell, KCSI, KCIE; three *s* one *d. Educ:* Gresham's Sch.; Balliol Coll., Oxford. Editorial staff, the Economist, 1935; Leader writer, Financial Times, 1936; Asst Leader Page Editor, News Chronicle, 1937-38; Leader Page Editor, News Chronicle, 1939. BBC European Services: Sub-Editor, 1940; Chief Sub-Editor, 1942; Duty Editor, 1943; European Talks Editor, 1945; Asst Head of European News Dept, 1946; Head of European Talks and English Dept, 1948-51; Asst Controller, European Services, 1951-58; Controller, Overseas Services, 1958-68; Controller of Programmes, External Broadcasting, 1968-70; Dir of Programmes, External Broadcasting, 1971-73, retired. *Address:* Scotland House, Scotland Street, Stoke by Nayland, Suffolk. *T:* Nayland 262102. *Club:* Five Farthings.

HODSON, Prof. Frank, BSc London 1949; PhD Reading 1951; FGS; Professor of Geology in the University of Southampton since 1958; *b* 23 Nov. 1921; *s* of late Matthew and Gertrude Hodson; *m* 1945, Ada Heyworth; three *d. Educ:* Burnley Grammar Sch.; Reading Univ. Demonstrator, Reading Univ., 1947-49; Lecturer, Reading Univ., 1949-58. Dean, Faculty of Science, 1972-74, and 1976-, Public Orator, 1970-73, Univ. of Southampton. Mem., Southern Arts Council. Murchison Fund, Geol. Soc., 1962; Founder Mem. and first Hon. Sec., Palaeontol. Assoc., 1957. Pres. Sect. C (geology), British Assoc. for Adv. of Science, 1975; Mem., Mineralogical Soc. of GB. Hon. Mem. Geol. Soc. de Belg. *Publications:* geological papers in publications of learned societies. *Recreation:* book collecting. *Address:* Department of Geology, The University, Southampton SO9 5NH. *Club:* Athenæum.

HODSON, Henry Vincent; Editor, The Annual Register of World Events, since 1973; *b* 12 May 1906; *er s* of late Prof. T. C. Hodson; *m* 1933, Margaret Elizabeth Honey, Sydney; four *s. Educ:* Gresham's Sch.; Balliol Coll., Oxford. Fellow of All Souls Coll., Oxford, 1928-35; Staff of Economic Advisory Council, 1930-31; Asst Editor of the Round Table, 1931, Editor, 1934-39; Director, Empire Div., Ministry of Information, 1939-41; Reforms Commissioner, Govt of India, 1941-42; Principal Asst Sec., and later head of Non-Munitions Div., Min. of Production, 1942-45; Asst Editor, Sunday Times, 1946-50, Editor, 1950-61; Provost of Ditchley, 1961-71. Senior Partner, Hodson Consultants, 1971-. Consultant Editor: The International Foundation Directory, 1974-; The Business Who's Who, 1974-. *Publications:* Economics of a Changing World, 1933; (part) The Empire in the World, 1937; Slump and Recovery, 1929-37, 1938; The British Commonwealth and the Future, 1948; Twentieth Century Empire, 1948; Problems in Anglo-American Relations, 1963; The Great Divide: Britain-India-Pakistan, 1969; The Diseconomics of Growth, 1972; many articles in reviews, etc. *Address:* 23 Cadogan Lane, SW1X 9DP. *T:* 01-235 5509. *Club:* Brooks's.

HODSON, Joseph John, BDS; PhD; FRCPath; FDSRCS; Professor Emeritus, 1972; Professor of Oral Pathology, University of Sheffield, 1960-72; formerly Hon. Consultant in Oral Pathology to the United Sheffield Hospitals, and to Sheffield Regional Hospital Board; *b* 7 March 1912; *e s* of late Rev. J. J. Hodson, MA, and late Mrs A. Hodson, Birmingham; *m* 1937, Mary Alice, *d* of late John and Florence Whitman, Hull; one *s* one *d. Educ:* Birmingham Univ.; Royal College of Surgeons, Edinburgh. Dental Surgeon to Warwicks CC, 1938-41. War Service, Capt., Royal Army Dental Corps, 1941-45. University of Sheffield: Research Asst, 1947-49, Lectr, 1949-53, Sen. Lectr, 1953-60, in Oral Pathology. Howard Mummery Research Prize, BDA, 1952-57. *Publications:* various papers in Medical and Dental Jls covering research in oral tumours, dental and other diseases of the mouth. *Recreations:* music, gardening. *Address:* Fallowfield, 45 Warminster Road, Bathampton, Bath BA2 6XJ.

HODSON, Leslie Manfred Noel, CMG 1958; OBE 1953; QC 1943; retired as Advocate of the High Court of Southern Rhodesia (1929-63); now farming; *b* 2 Dec. 1902; *s* of late A. Hodson, JP, and Mrs Hodson; *m* 1927, Iona May Mackenzie (*d* 1972); two *s* one *d. Educ:* Boys' High Sch., Salisbury, Rhodesia; University of the Witwatersrand. City Councillor, Salisbury, Rhodesia, 1932-36; contested by-election, Hartley, 1937; MP for Salisbury Central, 1946 and 1948. First Chm. Rhodesia Univ. Assoc., 1945-53, of Inaugural Board, 1953, and of 1st Council, 1954-58, University Coll. of Rhodesia and Nyasaland, 1953-62.

MP Federal Assembly of Rhodesia and Nyasaland, 1953-62. Dep. Speaker Legislative Assembly, 1951, 1953. Hon. LLD Rhodesia, 1975. *Recreation:* journalism. *Address:* Tor Fell, Private Bag 451G, Salisbury, Rhodesia. *T:* Salisbury 2066073. *Club:* Salisbury.

HODSON, Rt. Rev. Mark Allin; an Assistant Bishop of London, with special responsibility for City of Westminster, since 1974; *b* 1907; *s* of Albert Edgar Hodson, Solicitor; *m* 1959, Susanna Grace, *e d* of late Arthur Hugh Lister, CMG. *Educ:* Enfield Grammar Sch.; University Coll., London (BA), Fellow, 1974; Wells Theological Coll. Ordained 1931; Asst Curate, St Dunstan, Stepney, 1931-35; Missioner St Nicholas, Perivale, 1935-40; Rector of Poplar, 1940-55. Officiating Curate-in-charge of All Hallows, E India Docks, 1942-52; St Stephen, Poplar, 1943-52; St Frideswide, Poplar, 1947-52; Prebendary of Newington in St Paul's Cathedral, London, 1951-55; Suffragan Bishop of Taunton, 1955-61, also Prebendary and Rector of St Michael and All Angels, Dinder, diocese of Bath and Wells, 1956-61; Bishop of Hereford, 1961-73. Exam. Chaplain to Bp of London, 1974-. Chaplain General, Guild of St Barnabas for Nurses, 1974-76; Pres., Retd Clergy Assoc., 1974-76. Foundn Governor, Enfield Grammar Sch. *Recreation:* travel. *Address:* 3 Vincent Square, SW1P 2LX. *T:* 01-828 4809. *Club:* Athenæum.

HODSON, Sir Michael (Robin Adderley), 6th Bt *cr* 1789; Captain, Scots Guards, retired; *b* 5 March 1932; *s* of Major Sir Edmond Adair Hodson, 5th Bt, DSO, and of Anne Elizabeth Adderley, *yr d* of Lt-Col Hartopp Francis Charles Adderley Cradock, Hill House, Sherborne St John; *S* father, 1972; *m* 1963, Katrin Alexa, *d* of late Erwin Bernstiel, Dinas Powis, Glamorgan; three *d. Educ:* Eton. *Heir:* *b* Patrick Richard Hodson [*b* 27 Nov. 1934; *m* 1961, June, *o d* of H. M. Shepherd-Cross; three *s*]. *Address:* Foxhill Farm, Bourton-on-the-Water, Gloucestershire.

HOEHNE, Most Rev. John; *see* Rabaul, Archbishop of, (RC).

HOFF, Harry Summerfield; *see* Cooper, William.

HOFFENBERG, Prof. Raymond; William Withering Professor of Medicine, University of Birmingham, since 1972; *b* 6 March 1923; *er s* of Benjamin and Dora Hoffenberg; *m* 1949; two *s. Educ:* Grey High Sch., Port Elizabeth; Univ. of Cape Town. MB, ChB 1948, MD, PhD, FRCP. Served with S African Armed Forces, N Africa and Italy, 1942-45. Sen. Lectr, Dept of Medicine, Univ. of Cape Town and Cons. Phys., Groote Schuur Hosp., 1955-67; CSIR (S Africa) Sen. Res. Fellow, 1954-55; Carnegie Corp. of NY Trav. Fellow, 1957-58; Cecil John Adams Trav. Fellow, 1957; Fellow, Univ. of Cape Town, 1966; banned by S African Govt, 1967; emigrated to UK, 1968. Sen. Scientist, MRC (UK), attached Div. of Biophysics, Nat. Inst. of Med. Res., 1968-70 and Clinical Res. Centre, Harrow, 1970-72; Cons. Phys. (Endocrinology), New End Hosp. and Royal Free Hosp. Med. Sch., London, 1968-70. Mem., West Midlands RHA. Member: Endocrine Soc. (SA) (Past Pres. and Chm.); Endocrine Soc. (UK); Endocrine Soc. (USA); Central and Exec. Cttee, Internat. Soc. for Endocrinology; Royal Soc. Med. (Council, Endocr. Sect., 1970-72, 1974-; Council, Med. Educn Sect., 1974-); London Thyroid Club; Med. Res. Soc.; Assoc. of Physicians, Europ. Thyroid Assoc.; Europ. Soc. for Clin. Investigation. Mem. Editorial Board: Clinical Science, 1968-72 (Chm. 1971-72); Clinical Endocrinology, 1971-; Jl of Endocrinology, 1974-. Governor, Warwick Schools Foundn Oliver-Sharpey Lectr, RCP, 1973. Past Mem. Nat. Council, S African Inst. of Race Relations; Past Chairman: World Univ. Service (SA); Defence and Aid Fund (SA); Adv. Bd to Nat. Union of S African Students (Hon. Vice-Pres. of Union, 1968-). *Publications:* chapters and scientific papers on various aspects of endocrinology and metabolism in med. and biochem. jls. *Recreations:* (largely nostalgic) reading, walking, gardening, golf, tennis, squash. *Address:* Dept of Medicine, Queen Elizabeth Hospital, Birmingham B15 2TH. *T:* 021-472 1311. *Club:* Athenæum.

HOFFMAN, Anna Rosenberg; Senior Partner, Anna M. Rosenberg Associates, public and industrial relations consultants, New York; *b* Budapest, Hungary, 19 July 1902; *d* of Albert Lederer and Charlotte Bacskal; *m* 1919, Julius Rosenberg; one *s*; *m* 1962, Paul Gray Hoffman (*d* 1974). Member: President's Commn on Income Maintenance Programs, 1968-; States Urban Action Center, 1967-; NY Urban Coalition, Inc. of Nat. Urban Coalition, 1967-; Mayor Lindsay's Cttee on Rent Control, 1967-; National Citizens' Commn for Internat. Cooperation; Bd of Directors, United Nations Assoc. of the United States of America, Inc.; Population Crisis Cttee; Franklin Delano Roosevelt Memorial Commission; Board of Trustees, Eleanor Roosevelt Memorial Foundation; Board of

Directors of World Rehabilitation Fund, Inc.; also Mem. of other Boards and Cttees, etc., in the United States. Formerly: Asst Sec. of Defense, USA, 1950-53; Regional Director of: War Manpower Commn, 1942-45; Social Security Admin., 1936-42; Office of Defense, Health and Welfare Services, 1941-42; Nat. Recovery Admin., 1934-35, Personal Representative of President Roosevelt, 1944, and of President Truman, 1945, to European Theatre of War; Sec. to President Roosevelt's Labor Victory Board, 1942-45; Member: US Nat. Commn for Unesco, 1946-50; Advisory Commn of the President on Universal Mil. Training, 1946-47; President Roosevelt's Industrial Relations Commn to Great Britain and Sweden etc.; Bd of Education, City of NY, 1961-63; Nat. Adv. Commn on Selective Service, 1966-67. Medal of Freedom, 1945 (first award by Gen. Eisenhower to a civilian); Medal for Merit, 1947; Dept of Defense Exceptional Civilian Service Award, 1953; Medallion of City of NY (for work on beautification of City), 1966. Holds Hon. Degrees in USA. *Publications:* chapter, Social Security and the National Purpose, in The Family in a World at War, 1942; article on history and status of American woman in business world, in The Great Ideas Today, 1966. *Recreations:* chiefly indoor gardening; collection of modern French art; antique china. *Address:* (office) 444 Madison Avenue, New York, NY 10022, USA; (home) 2 East 88 Street, New York, NY 10028, USA.

HOFFMAN, Dustin Lee; actor; *b* 8 Aug. 1937; *s* of Harry Hoffman and Lillian Hoffman; *m* 1969, Anne Byrne; two *d.* *Educ:* Santa Monica City Coll.; Pasadena Playhouse. Stage debut in Sarah Lawrence Coll. prodn, Yes is For a Very Young Man; Broadway debut, A Cook for Mr General, 1961; appeared in: Harry, and Noon and Night, Amer. Place Theatre, NY, 1964-65; Journey of the Fifth Horse, and Star Wagon, 1965; Fragments, Berkshire Theatre Festival, Stockbridge, Mass, 1966; Eh?, 1966-67; Jimmy Shine, Broadway, 1968-69. Dir, All Over Town, Broadway, 1974. Films: The Graduate, 1967; Midnight Cowboy, 1969; John and Mary, 1969, Little Big Man, 1971; Who Is Harry Kellerman and Why Is He Saying Those Terrible Things About Me?, 1971; Straw Dogs, 1972; Alfredo, Alfredo, 1972; Papillon, 1973; Lenny, 1974; All The President's Men, 1975; Marathon Man, 1976. Record: Death of a Salesman. Obie Award as best off-Broadway actor, 1965-66, for Journey of the Fifth Horse; Drama Desk, Theatre World, and Vernon Rice Awards for Eh?, 1966; Oscar Award nominee for The Graduate, Midnight Cowboy, and Lenny. *Address:* 315 E 65 Street, New York, NY 10021, USA. *T:* 472-3738.

HOFFMAN, Rev. Canon Stanley Harold, MA; Chaplain in Ordinary to the Queen, since 1976; Hon. Canon of Rochester Cathedral, since 1965; Diocesan Director of Education, Rochester, since 1965; Warden of Readers, since 1974; *b* 17 Aug. 1917; *s* of Charles and Ellen Hoffman, Denham, Bucks; *m* 1943, Mary Mifanwy Patricia, *d* of late Canon Creed Meredith, Chaplain to the Queen, and of Mrs R. Creed Meredith, Windsor; one *s* one *d.* *Educ:* The Royal Grammar Sch., High Wycombe, Bucks; St Edmund Hall, Oxford (BA 1939, MA 1943); Lincoln Theol Coll., 1940-41. Deacon, 1941; Priest, 1942; Curate: Windsor Parish Ch., 1941-44; All Saints, Weston, Bath, 1944-47; Chertsey (in charge of All SS), 1947-50; Vicar of Shottermill, Haslemere, Sy, 1951-64. Proctor in Convocation, Church Assembly, 1969-70; Exam. Chaplain to Bp of Rochester, 1973-. Member: Kent Educn Cttee, 1965-; Bromley Educn Cttee, 1967-; Kent Council of Religious Educn, 1965-; Archbps' Commn on Christian Initiation, 1970. Vice-Chm., Christ Church Coll., Canterbury. *Publications:* (pt-author): A Handbook of Thematic Material, 1968; Christians in Kent, 1972; Teaching the Parables, 1974; contrib. various pubns on Preaching and Religious Educn; numerous Dio. study papers. *Recreations:* music, walking (in love with Cornwall). *Address:* White Friars, Boley Hill, Rochester, Kent ME1 1TE. *T:* Medway 44087.

HOFFMANN, Leonard Hubert, QC 1977; barrister-at-law; *b* 8 May 1934; *s* of B. W. and G. Hoffmann; *m* 1957, Gillian Lorna Sterner; two *d.* *Educ:* South African College Sch., Cape Town; Univ. of Cape Town (BA); The Queen's Coll., Oxford (Rhodes Scholar; MA, BCL, Vinerian Law Scholar). Advocate of Supreme Court of S Africa, 1958-60. Called to the Bar, Gray's Inn, 1964. Stowell Civil Law Fellow, University Coll., Oxford, 1961-73. Member, Royal Commn on Gambling, 1976. *Publication:* The South African Law of Evidence, 1963 (3rd edn 1978). *Recreations:* opera, theatre. *Address:* 18 Heathhurst Road, NW3 2RX. *T:* 01-435 0476.

HOFFMEISTER, Maj.-Gen. Bertram Meryl, CB 1945; CBE 1944; DSO 1943; ED; *b* 15 May 1907; *s* of Flora Elizabeth Rodway and Louis George Hoffmeister; *m* 1935, Donalda Strauss; one *s* one *d.* *Educ:* Public Schs, Vancouver. Previous to war of 1939-45 employed by H. R. MacMillan Export Co. Ltd,

Vancouver, BC. 1st Lieut Seaforth Highlanders of Canada, 1927; Capt. 1934; Major 1939 and given command of a rifle Co. Served with Seaforth Highlanders in England as Co. Comdr, 1939-40; returned to Canada, 1942, to attend Canadian Junior War Staff Course; given Command of Seaforth Highlanders of Canada and commanded this Bn in assault on Sicily in July 1943 (DSO); Brig. Oct. 1943 and assumed command 2 Canadian Infantry Brigade (Bar to DSO battle of Ortona); Maj.-Gen. and commanded 5 Cdn Armoured Div. March 1944; operations on Hitler Line, May-June 1944 (2nd Bar to DSO, CBE); in NW Europe until conclusion of hostilities (CB). GOC Canadian Army Pacific Force, 1945. Gen. Manager, Canadian White Pine Co. Ltd, and MacMillan Industries Ltd (Plywood Div.), 1945-47; H. R. MacMillan Export Co. Ltd; Gen. Mgr Prod., 1947-49 and Vice-Pres. Prod., 1949; Pres., 1949-51; MacMillan & Bloedel Ltd; Pres. 1951-56; Chm. Bd, 1956-57. Agent-Gen. for British Columbia, 1958-61. Pres., Council of the Forest Industries of BC, Vancouver, 1961-71. Chm., Nat. Second Century Fund of BC, 1971-. *Recreations:* rugby, rowing, shooting, skiing. *Address:* 3040 Procter Avenue, West Vancouver, BC, Canada. *Clubs:* Vancouver, Capilano Golf and Country, Vancouver Rowing (Vancouver); Canadian.

HOFMEYR, Murray Bernard; Chairman and Managing Director, Charter Consolidated Ltd, since 1976; *b* 9 Dec. 1925; *s* of William and Margareta Hofmeyr; *m* 1953, Johanna Hendrika Hofmeyr (*née* Verdurmen); three *s* two *d.* *Educ:* BA (Rhodes), MA (Oxon). Joined Anglo American Corp., 1962; in Zambia, 1965-72; in England, 1972-. Exec. Dir, Anglo American Corp. of S Africa Ltd; Director: Minerals & Resources Corp. Ltd, and other cos in Anglo American Gp; Standard Chartered Bank Ltd; Selection Trust Ltd; Tara Exploration Ltd. *Recreations:* golf, tennis; Captain Oxford Univ. Cricket, 1951; played Rugby for England, 1950. *Address:* 42 Cumberland Terrace, NW1. *T:* 01-486 1021.

HOFSTADTER, Prof. Robert; Max H. Stein Professor of Physics, Stanford University, since 1971; Director, High Energy Physics Laboratory, Stanford University, 1967-74; *b* Manhattan, New York, NY, 5 Feb. 1915; *s* of Louis and Henrietta Hofstadter; *m* 1942, Nancy Givan, Baltimore, Md; one *s* two *d.* *Educ:* City Coll. of New York (BS *magna cum laude*); Princeton Univ. (MA, PhD). Instructor in Physics: University of Pennsylvania, 1940-41; City Coll., New York, 1941-42; Associate Physicist and Physicist, Nat. Bureau of Standards, Washington DC, 1942-43; Asst Chief Physicist, Norden Laboratories Corp., New York, 1943-46; Asst Prof., physics, Princeton Univ., 1946-50; Associate Prof., physics, Stanford Univ., 1950-54; Prof., physics, 1954-71. Mem. Bd Governors, Weizmann Institute of Science, Rehovoth, Israel, 1967-. Associate Editor: Physical Review, 1951-53; Investigations in Physics, 1951-; Review of Scientific Instruments, 1954-56; Reviews of Modern Physics, 1958-61. Has held various fellowships, Nobel Prize in Physics, 1961. Fellow American Physical Soc.; FPS (London); Mem. Italian Phys. Soc.; Sigma Xi; Phi Beta Kappa. Hon. LLD, City Univ. of NY, 1962; Hon. DSc: Gustavus Adolphus Coll., Minn, 1963; Carleton Univ., Ottawa, 1967; Seoul Nat. Univ., 1967; *Laurea* (*hc*), Padua, 1965; Dr Univ. (*hc*), Univ. of Clermont, 1967. *Publications:* (with Robert Herman) High Energy Electron Scattering Tables, 1960 (US); (ed) Nuclear and Nucleon Structure, 1963 (US); (co-ed with L. I. Schiff) Nucleon Structure (Proc. Internat. Conf. at Stanford Univ., 1963), 1964; numerous scientific papers on various aspects of molecular structure, solid state physics, nuclear physics and review articles on crystal counters, electron scattering and nuclear and nucleon structure. *Recreations:* skiing, photography. *Address:* Department of Physics, Stanford University, Stanford, California, USA.

HOG, Major Roger Thomas Alexander, MC; *b* 19 June 1893; *s* of late Steuart Bayley Hog, of Newliston; *m* 1937, Marjorie St Clair, *d* of Charles F. Wood. *Educ:* Winchester Coll.; RMA Woolwich. Served European War, 1914-19 and War of 1939-45, Royal Artillery, retired as Major. *Address:* Logie West, Crossford, Dunfermline, Fife. *T:* Dunfermline 23054. *Club:* New (Edinburgh).

HOGAN, Air Vice-Marshal Henry Algernon Vickers, CB 1955; DFC 1940; retired; *b* 25 Oct. 1909; *s* of late Lt-Col Edward M. A. Hogan, IA; *m* 1939, Margaret Venetia, *d* of late Vice-Adm. W. Tomkinson, CB, MVO; one *s* one *d.* *Educ:* Malvern Coll.; RAF Coll., Cranwell. Commissioned 1930. Served in Fighter Sqdns and Fleet Air Arm; Instructor CFS, 1936-37; Mem. RAF Long Distance Flight (Vickers Wellesleys) to Australia, 1938; commanded No 501 Sqdn throughout Battle of Britain; USA, 1941-43 (Arnold Scheme and RAF Delegation Washington); Asst Comdt, Empire CFS, 1944; commanded No 19 Flying Training Sch., RAF Coll., Cranwell, 1945; Staff Coll., 1946; Air

Ministry, 1947-48; SPSO, MEAF, 1949-50; commanded RAF, Wattisham 1951; Air Cdre 1953; Sector Comdr, Northern Sector, 1952-53; AOC No 81 Group, 1954; Air Vice-Marshal, 1956; AOC No 83 Group, 2nd ATAF, Germany, 1955-58; SASO, Flying Training Command, 1958-62. Led RAF Mission to Ghana, 1960, and Joint Services Mission to Ghana, 1961. Regional Dir, Civil Defence (Midland), 1964-68. USA Legion of Merit (Officer), 1945. *Recreation:* country pursuits. *Address:* Arbour Hill House, Ross-on-Wye, Herefordshire. *T:* 3333. *Club:* Royal Air Force.

HOGAN, Michael Henry; Chief Probation Inspector, Home Office, since 1972; *b* 31 May 1927; *s* of James Joseph Hogan and Edith Mary Hogan; *m* 1953, Nina Spillane (*d* 1974); one *s* three *d . Educ:* Ushaw Coll.; LSE. Certif. Social Sci., Certif. Mental Health. Asst Warden, St Vincent's Probation Hostel, 1949-50; London Probation Service: Probation Officer, Old Street, Stamford House, Tower Bridge Courts, 1953-59; Sen. Probation Officer, SE London Juvenile Ct, 1959-61; Home Office Inspectorate, 1961-. *Recreation:* golf. *Address:* 17 Beaufort Close, Reigate, Surrey RH2 9DG. *T:* Reigate 48556.

HOGAN, Hon. Sir Michael (Joseph Patrick), Kt 1958; CMG 1953; DSNB 1970; President, Courts of Appeal of the Bahamas, Bermuda, and Belize, and Member of that for Gibraltar; *b* 15 March 1908; *m* 1946, Patricia, *d* of late Thomas Galliford; no *c*. *Educ:* Belvedere Coll., Dublin; Stonyhurst Coll., Lancs; Trinity Coll., Dublin Univ. (BA, Gold Medal, 1st cl. hons; LLB). Admitted Solicitor, Ireland, 1930; admitted to Kenya Bar, 1931; called to Irish Bar (Kings Inns), 1936; Chief Magistrate, Palestine, 1936; Crown Counsel, 1937; Attorney-Gen., Aden, 1945; called to English Bar (Inner Temple), 1946; KC (Aden) 1946; Solicitor-Gen., Palestine, 1947; attached Foreign Office, 1949; Malaya: Solicitor-Gen., 1950, QC (Malaya) 1952; Attorney-Gen., Federation of Malaya, 1950-55; Chief Justice of Hong Kong, 1955-70, and of Brunei, 1964-70. British Mem., Anglo-Japanese Property Commission, 1960. Hon. LLD Dublin Univ., 1962. KSG 1970. *Publications:* revised edition of the Laws of Aden, 1948. *Recreations:* tennis, ski-ing, polo, golf. *Address:* 2 Carlyle Mansions, Cheyne Walk, SW3. *Clubs:* Athenæum; Kildare Street and University (Dublin); Royal Irish Yacht; Hong Kong, Hong Kong Country.

HOGARTH, (Arthur) Paul, ARA 1974; painter, illustrator and draughtsman; *b* Kendal, Cumbria, 4 Oct. 1917; *s* of Arthur Hogarth and Janet Bownass; *m* 1963, Patricia Douthwaite; one *s . Educ:* St Agnes Sch., Manchester; Coll. of Art, Manchester; St Martin's Sch. of Art, London. Travels in: Poland and Czechoslovakia, 1953; USSR and China, 1954; Rhodesia and S Africa, 1956; Ireland, with Brendan Behan, 1959; USA, 1961-76. Tutor of Drawing: Cambridge Sch. of Art, 1959-61; RCA, 1964-71; Associate Prof., Philadelphia Coll. of Art, 1968-69; Vis. Lectr, RCA, 1971-. Exhibitions: one-man, Leicester Gall., London, 1955; Agnews, London, 1957; Amer. Embassy, London, 1964; retrospective, Time-Life Bldg, London, 1968; World of Paul Hogarth, Arts Council, RCA Gall., 1970. Dr RCA, 1971. *Publications:* Defiant People, 1953; Looking at China, 1956; People Like Us, 1958; (illus.) Brendan Behan's Island, 1962; Creative Pencil Drawing, 1964 (4th edn 1970); (illus.) Brendan Behan's New York, 1964; (with Robert Graves) Majorca Observed, 1965; (with M. Muggeridge) London à la Mode, 1966; Artist as Reporter, 1967; (with A. Jacob) Russian Journey, 1969; Drawing People, 1971; Artists on Horseback, 1972; Drawing Architecture, 1973; Paul Hogarth's American Album, 1974; Creative Ink Drawing, 1974; Walking Tours of Old Philadelphia, 1976; Arthur Boyd Houghton, 1978; contrib. Graphis, Arts Rev., Design, Sports Illus., D. Tel. Mag., Illus. London News. *Recreation:* sailing. *Address:* c/o Leresche & Steele, 11 Jubilee Place, SW3 3TE. *T:* 01-352 4311. *Club:* Chelsea Arts.

HOGARTH, James, CB 1973; Under-Secretary, Scottish Home and Health Department, 1963-74, retired; *b* 14 Aug. 1914; *s* of George Hogarth; *m* 1940, Katherine Mary Cameron; two *s* one *d . Educ:* George Watson's, Edinburgh; Edinburgh Univ.; Sorbonne, Paris. Joined Dept of Health for Scotland as Asst Principal, 1938; Principal, 1944; Asst Sec., 1948; Under-Sec., 1963. *Publications:* Payment of the General Practitioner, 1963; translations from French, German, Russian, etc. *Recreation:* travel. *Address:* 6A Crawfurd Road, Edinburgh EH16 5PQ. *T:* 031-667 3878.

HOGARTH, Dr Margaret Cameron; formerly Chairman: Executive Committee, Central Council for District Nursing in London; Medical Advisory Committee Nursery School Association of Great Britain and Northern Ireland; Governor, Gipsy Hill Training College, Surrey County Council; Member Executive Committee, Children's Aid Society; a Vice-President of the Health Visitors Association; *b* 10 March 1885; *d* of Farquhar Macdonald, MA, Rector of Dingwall Academy, Ross-shire; *m* 1914, late Archibald Henry Hogarth, CBE, DCM, MA, MD Oxon, DPH; one *s. Educ:* Dingwall Acad.; Aberdeen Univ. Various Resident Hosp. appts, 1907-11, in London and Provinces, specialising in Obstetrics, Gynæcology, Eye and Ear and Child Diseases; Med. Supt, Eastby Sanatorium, Yorks; gen. practice, Colchester and London; Asst MOH and Dep. MOH, Bucks, 1911-12; Medical service under LCC, 1912-24; again with LCC, 1928-50 (Div. Med. Off., Principal Asst and Sen. MO); Ophthalmologist to two LCC eye clinics and, for a period, to LCC Schs for blind and blind and deaf children. Ext. Examr, Hygiene, to Goldsmiths' Trg Coll.; MO to certain Voluntary Maternity and Child Welfare centres and Ante-Natal Clinics. MO, Min. of Health, 1924-28; apptd Govt Rep. League of Nations Nutrition Cttee, 1936; Institute of Education, University of London: Ext. Examr Health Educ.; Mem. Health Educ. Panel, 1953-59; Lectr on Anatomy and Physiology to School of Dramatic Art and Speech Trg. *Publications:* various reports on specific subjects to LCC and Min. of Health; Public Health Reviews for Lancet; Survey of District Nursing in the Administrative County of London (publ. LCC); Medicine as a Career for Women (publ. Brit. Fedn University Women); Health in the Nursery School. *Recreations:* reading, picture galleries. *Address:* The Brook, 27 Stamford Brook Road, W6 0XJ.

HOGARTH, Paul; *see* Hogarth, A. P.

HOGBEN, Herbert Edward; retired; *b* 21 Dec. 1905; *s* of Herbert Edward Hogben; *m* 1929, Dorothy, *d* of Samuel Eastoe Pearson; three *d. Educ:* Borden Gram. Sch., Sittingbourne; King's Coll., London (BSc). Scientific Officer, Admiralty, 1927-; Princ. Scientific Officer, 1943; Sen. Princ. Sci. Off., 1952; Dep. Chief Sci. Off., 1961; Chief Sci. Off., Min. of Def. (Navy), 1965; Dep. Chief Scientist, Admiralty Surface Weapons Establishment, 1965-68; Scientific Adviser to Comdr, British Navy Staff, Washington, 1968-70. *Publications:* ASE monographs and technical notes, articles for Jl Inst. of Navigation. *Recreations:* gardening, travel. *Address:* 12 Portsdown Hill Road, Bedhampton, Havant PO9 3JX.

HOGG, family name of **Hailsham Viscountcy** and of **Baron Hailsham of Saint Marylebone.**

HOGG, Alexander Hubert Arthur, CBE 1973; Secretary, Royal Commission on Ancient Monuments in Wales and Monmouthshire, 1949-73; *b* 2 May 1908; *s* of A. F. Hogg; *m* 1943, Nellie, *d* of G. P. Henderson, MD; one *s* one *d. Educ:* Highgate Sch.; Sidney Sussex Coll., Cambridge (MA). Asst Engineer, Sir R. McAlpine & Sons, 1930-34; Junior Scientific Officer, Roads Research Laboratory, 1934-36; Lecturer, Engineering Dept, King's Coll., Newcastle upon Tyne, 1936-42; Temp. Experimental Officer, Admiralty Undex Works, Rosyth, 1942-45; ICI Fellowship, 1945-47; Lecturer Engineering Laboratory, University of Cambridge, 1947-49. FSA; FSAScot. Hon. DLitt Wales, 1974. Publications: Hill-Forts of Britain, 1975; papers in Philosophical Magazine and in Archæological periodicals. *Address:* Brynfield, Waun Fawr, Aberystwyth SY23 3PP. *T:* Aberystwyth 3479.

HOGG, George Robert Disraeli, CB 1955; CBE 1946; *b* 23 June 1894; *s* of John Hogg; *m* 1919, Daisy Winifred Martin (*d* 1976); two *d. Educ:* Westminster City Sch.; St John's Coll., Oxford. First Cl. Hons in Mathematics, 1916; BA 1919; Lecturer in Mathematics, Sir John Cass Technical Institute, 1919-20; entered Administrative Class, Home Civil Service and joined Dept of Scientific and Industrial Research, 1920; Under-Sec., 1950-57. Served European War, 1914-18, Army and Royal Air Force (meteorological officer, Lieut), 1916-19. *Recreations:* mathematical problems; chess. *Address:* 189 Sheen Lane, East Sheen, SW14 8LE. *T:* 01-876 3275.

HOGG, Vice-Adm. Sir Ian (Leslie Trower), KCB 1968 (CB 1964); DSC 1941, Bar to DSC 1944; *b* 30 May 1911; 3rd *s* of Col John M. T. Hogg, IA, and Elma (*née* Brand); *m* 1945, Mary G. J., *e d* of Col and Mrs Marsden; two *s. Educ:* Cheltenham Coll. Entered Royal Navy, 1929; specialised in Navigation, 1937; HMS Cardiff, 1939; HMS Penelope, 1940; HMAS Napier, 1941-43; HMS Mauritius, 1944-45; Master of the Fleet, 1946-47; British Admiralty Delegation, Washington, DC, 1948-49; HMS Sluys, in comd, 1950-51; Staff of C-in-C Med., 1952-53; Captain RN, Dec. 1953; Brit. Joint Staff, Washington, DC, 1955-57; idc 1958; Staff of Chief of Defence Staff, 1959-60; Cdre, Cyprus, 1961-62; Dir, Chief of Defence Staff's Commonwealth Exercise, 1962-63; Rear-Adm. 1963; Flag Officer, Medway, and Admiral Superintendent, HM Dockyard, Chatham, 1963-66; Vice-Adm. 1966; Defence Services Sec., 1966-67; Vice-Chief of the Defence Staff, 1967-70, retired. FRSA 1971. *Address:* The Old Mill, Wendover, Bucks. *T:* Wendover 623196. *Club:* Army and Navy.

HOGG, Sir John (Nicholson), Kt 1963; TD 1946; Deputy Chairman: Williams & Glyn's Bank Ltd, since 1970; Gallaher Ltd, since 1964; Director: The Prudential Assurance Co. Ltd; National & Commercial Banking Group Ltd; Honeywell Ltd; Chairman, Brown Harriman & International Banks Ltd; *b* 4 Oct. 1912; *o s* of late Sir Malcolm Hogg and of Lorna Beaman; *m* 1948, Barbara Mary Elisabeth, *yr d* of Capt. Arden Franklyn, Shedfield, Southampton and *widow* of Viscount Garmoyle (*d* of wounds, 1942); one *s* one *d. Educ:* Eton; Balliol Coll., Oxford. Joined Glyn, Mills and Co., 1934. Served War of 1939-45, with KRRC in Greece, Crete, Western Desert, Tunisia, NW Europe. Rejoined Glyn, Mills and Co. 1945, a Man. Dir., 1950-70, Dep. Chm. 1963-68, Chm. 1968-70. Fellow of Eton Coll., 1951-70. Mem. of Commonwealth War Graves Commission, 1958-64; A Trustee Imperial War Graves Endowment Fund, 1965. Sheriff County of London, 1960; Chm., Export Credits Guarantee Department's Adv. Council, 1962-67. Chm., Abu Dhabi Investment Bd, 1967-75. *Recreations:* cricket, tennis, fishing. *Address:* The Red House, Shedfield, Southampton. *T:* Wickham 832121. *Club:* Brooks's.

HOGG, Sir Kenneth Weir, 6th Bt, *cr* 1846; OBE 1946; Lieutenant-Colonel (retired); *b* 13 Sept. 1894; *s* of Guy Weir Hogg (*d* 1943); *S* to baronetcy of cousin, 4th Baron Magheramorne, 1957; *m* 1936, Hon. Aline Emily Partington, *o d* of 2nd Baron Doverdale. *Educ:* Haileybury; Christ Church, Oxford. Served in European War, 1914-18 and War of 1939-45; Irish Guards, 1915-33. *Recreations:* fishing, ski-ing. *Heir: cousin* Major Arthur Ramsay Hogg, MBE 1945 [*b* 24 Oct. 1896; *m* 1924, Mary Aileen Hester Lee, *d* of late P. H. Lee Evans; three *s* one *d*]. *Address:* 2 Curzon Place, Park Lane, W1. *Clubs:* White's, Portland.

HOGG, Brig. Oliver Frederick Gillilan, CBE 1943; pac; *b* 22 Dec. 1887; *s* of late Col Arthur Melvill Hogg, 6th Bombay Cavalry; *m* 1919, Ella Harold (*d* 1968), *d* of Arthur Harold Hallam, Shanghai; one *s. Educ:* Bedford Sch.; RMA, Woolwich. 2nd Lieut, RA 1907; Capt. 1914, Major, 1926; Lieut-Col 1934; Col 1935; Brig. 1939; retired, 1946; served European War (France) 1914-18 (1914 Star, British War and Victory Medals); Inspector of Danger Buildings, RGPF, 1915-16; Asst Supt RSAF, 1916-19; Asst Inspector Armaments Inspection Dept, 1921-25; Inspector AID, 1927-30; Mil. Asst to CSOF, 1933-36; War of 1939-45 (Defence and War Medals); Sec., Ordnance Board, 1936-39; Asst Master Gen. of the Ordnance, War Office, 1939; Dep. Dir of Military Administration, Ministry of Supply, 1939-41; Dir of Military Administration, Ministry of Supply, 1941-46; Leverhulme Research Fellow, 1950-51; FSA (Mem. Council, 1953-55); FRSA; FRGS; FRHistS; FAMS; Fellow, Soc. of Genealogists (Mem. Exec. Cttee, 1959-62); Mem., Soc. for Army Historical Research; Vice-Pres. Greenwich Conservative Assoc., 1957- (Hon. Treasurer, 1956-57); a Vice-Pres., Rescue. Order of Polonia Restituta, 3rd class. *Publications:* The History of the 3rd Durham Volunteer Artillery, 1860-1960, 1960; English Artillery 1326-1716, 1963; The Royal Arsenal: Its Background, Origin and Subsequent History, 2 vols, 1963; Further Light on the Ancestry of William Penn, 1965; Clubs to Cannon, 1968; Artillery: its origin, heyday and decline, 1970; The Woolwich Mess (2nd edn), 1971; historical and technical articles dealing with artillery and small arm subjects in Army Jls, etc.; Contrib. on artillery, engines of war and The Board of Ordnance, to Chambers's Encycl. *Recreations:* walking and boating. *Address:* 1 Hardy Road, Blackheath, SE3 7NS. *T:* 01-858 3306. *Club:* Naval and Military.

HOGG, Percy Herbertson, CBE 1965; retired; *b* 22 Dec. 1898; *s* of Andrew Herbertson Hogg, SCC, Edinburgh, and Mary Burrell Hogg; *m* 1925, Jean Kemp Selkirk; one *s* one *d. Educ:* Daniel Stewart's Coll., Edinburgh. Solicitor, Edinburgh, 1923-47; Dir, The Distillers Co. Ltd, 1952-65; Managing Dir, 1949-60, Chm., 1961-65, John Haig & Co. Ltd, Distillers. *Address:* 1 Northdown Road, Belmont, Surrey SM2 6DY. *T:* 01-642 4962.

HOGG, Rear-Adm. Peter Beauchamp, MIMechE; Head of British Defence Liaison Staff and Defence Adviser, Canberra, since 1977; *b* 9 Nov. 1924; *s* of Beauchamp and Sybil Hogg; *m* 1951, Gabriel Argentine Alington; two *s* two *d. Educ:* Connaught House, Weymouth; Bradfield Coll., Berks; Royal Naval Engineering Coll., Keyham. Lieut, HMS Sirius, 1947-49; Advanced Engrg Course, RNC Greenwich, 1949-51; HMS Swiftsure and HMS Pincher, 1951-53; Lt Comdr, Loan Service with Royal Canadian Navy, 1953-56; Staff of RN Engrg Coll., Manadon, 1956-58; Comdr (Trng Comdr), HMS Sultan, 1959-62; Marine Engr Officer, HMS Hampshire, 1962-64; JSSC, Latimer, 1964; Ship Dept, Bath, 1965-67; Captain, Ship Dept, Bath, 1968-69; CO, HMS Tyne, 1970-71; RCDS, 1972; CO, HMS Caledonia, 1973-74; Dir of Naval Recruiting, 1974-76. *Address:* British High Commission, Canberra, ACT 2600, Australia.

HOGG, Sir William Lindsay L.; *see* Lindsay-Hogg.

HOGGART, Richard; Warden, Goldsmiths' College, University of London, since 1976; *b* 24 Sept. 1918; 2nd *s* of Tom Longfellow Hoggart and Adeline Emma Hoggart; *m* 1942, Mary Holt France; two *s* one *d. Educ:* elementary and secondary schs, Leeds; Leeds Univ. (MA). Served 1940-46, RA; demobilised as Staff Capt. Staff Tutor and Sen. Staff Tutor, University Coll. of Hull and University of Hull, 1946-59; Sen. Lectr in English, University of Leicester, 1959-62; Prof. of English, Birmingham Univ., 1962-73, and Dir, Centre for Contemporary Cultural Studies, 1964-73; an Asst Dir-Gen., Unesco, 1970-75. Vis. Fellow, Inst. of Development Studies, Univ. of Sussex, 1975. Visiting Prof., University of Rochester (NY), USA, 1956-57; Reith Lectr, 1971. Member: Albemarle Cttee on Youth Services, 1958-60; Brit. Council Brit. Books Overseas Cttee, 1959-64; BBC Gen. Advisory Council, 1959-60 and 1964-; Youth Service Development Council, 1960-62; (Pilkington) Cttee on Broadcasting, 1960-62; Culture Adv. Cttee of the UK Nat. Commn for UNESCO; Arts Council, 1976- (Chm., Drama Panel, 1977-); New Statesman Bd, 1977; Chm., Adv. Council for Adult and Continuing Educn, 1977-. Governor, Royal Shakespeare Theatre. FRSL, 1957-63. Hon. DLitt Open Univ., 1973; Hon. Dr, Univ. of Bordeaux, 1975. Mem. Editorial Board, Universities Quarterly. *Publications:* Auden, 1951; The Uses of Literacy, 1957; W. H. Auden, 1957; W. H. Auden-A Selection, 1961; chap. in Conviction, 1958; chapter in Pelican Guide to English Literature, 1961; Teaching Literature, 1963; chapter in Of Books and Humankind, 1964; The Critical Moment, 1964; How and Why Do We Learn, 1965; The World in 1984, 1965; Essays by Divers Hands XXXIII; Guide to the Social Sciences, 1966; Technology and Society, 1966; Essays on Reform, 1967; Your Sunday Paper (ed), 1967; Speaking to Each Other: vol. I, About Society; vol. II, About Literature, 1970; Only Connect (Reith Lectures), 1972. Numerous introductions, articles, pamphlets and reviews. *Recreation:* pottering about the house and garden. *Address:* Goldsmiths' College, New Cross, SE14 6NW.

HOGGE, Maj.-Gen. Arthur Michael Lancelot; Deputy Master-General of the Ordnance, since 1977; *b* 4 Aug. 1925; *s* of late Lt-Col A. H. F. Hogge, Punjab Regt, Indian Army, and Mrs K. M. Hogge; *m* 1952, Gunilla Jeane Earley; two *s. Educ:* Wellington Coll.; Brasenose Coll., Oxford (war-time course). Commissioned, Oct. 1945; 6th Airborne Armoured Recce Regt and 3rd Hussars, Palestine, 1945-48; regimental appts, 3rd Hussars, BAOR, 1948-58; Queen's Own Hussars, BAOR, and Staff appts, 1958-65; comd Queen's Own Hussars, UK and Aden, 1965-67; Col GS, Staff Coll., 1969-71; Royal Coll. of Defence Studies, 1972; Dir of Operational Requirements, MoD, 1973-74, rank of Brig.; Dir Gen. Fighting Vehicles and Engineer Equipment, 1974-77. *Recreations:* sailing, horticulture. *Address:* c/o Lloyds Bank Ltd, Dorking, Surrey. *Club:* Cavalry and Guards.

HOGGER, Rear-Adm. Henry Charles, CB 1961; DSC 1942; *b* 27 June 1907; *s* of Henry George and Maria Jane Hogger; *m* 1935, Ethel Mary Kreiner (*d* 1973); two *s* one *d. Educ:* Portsmouth Grammar Sch. Entered Navy, Special Entry Cadet, 1925; specialised in Engineering at RNE Coll., Keyham and RN Coll., Greenwich. During War of 1939-45, served in HMS Kipling and Jervis, 1941-43. Chief Engineer, Hong Kong Dockyard, 1951-54; Asst Engineer-in-Chief, 1955-57; Manager, Engineering Dept, Portsmouth Dockyard, 1957; retired, 1961. Admiralty Regional Officer, Midlands, 1962; Dep. Head, Royal Naval Engineering Service, 1963-71; Dir, Production and Support Dockyards, 1970-72. *Recreation:* golf. *Address:* Broome, Upper Lansdown Mews, Bath, Avon. *T:* Bath 310108. *Clubs:* Royal Automobile, Army and Navy.

HOGUE, Oliver Alfred John, CVO 1954; literary staff, Mirror Newspapers, Sydney, 1962-75 and 1976; Associate News Editor, Daily Mirror, 1968-75; *b* 16 Sept. 1910; *s* of late Frank Arthur Hogue and Vida C. Hogue (*née* Robinson), Sydney; *m* 1st, 1936, Mary Barbour May (marr. diss., 1966); four *s*; 2nd, 1966, Mary Elizabeth Mofflin (*d* 1976), *d* of Solomon Merkel, Lithuania. *Educ:* Newcastle (NSW) High Sch. Literary staff, Newcastle Herald, 1930; War Correspondent in Australia, 1940-43; Press Sec. to Hon. J. A. Beasley, Australian Minister for Supply, 1943-45; Political Corresp. for Sydney Sunday Sun, Canberra, 1945-53; literary staff, Sydney Sun, 1954-62. Pres., C'wealth Parly Press Gall., 1947-49. Aust. Govt PRO for Australian visit of the Queen and Prince Philip, 1954. *Address:* 5 Hill Street, Roseville, NSW 2069, Australia. *T:* 41-6283. *Club:* Journalists' (Sydney).

HOGWOOD, Christopher Jarvis Haley; harpsichordist, musicologist and broadcaster; Director, Academy of Ancient Music, since 1973; *b* 10 Sept. 1941; *s* of Haley Evelyn Hogwood and Marion Constance Higgott. *Educ:* Cambridge Univ. (MA); Charles Univ., Prague. Harpsichord recordings. Editor of books and music. *Publication:* Music at Court (Folio Society), 1977. *Address:* 2 Claremont, Hills Road, Cambridge. *T:* Cambridge 63975; 25 Plough Way, SE16 2LS.

HOHLER, Henry Arthur Frederick, CMG 1954; HM Diplomatic Service, retired; Ambassador to Switzerland 1967-70; *b* 4 Feb. 1911; *e s* of late Lt-Col Arthur Preston Hohler, DSO; *m* 1st, 1932, Mona Valentine (*d* 1944), *d* of late Lieut-Col Arthur Murray Pirie, DSO; two *s*; 2nd, 1945, Eveline Susan, *d* of late Lieut-Col Hon. Neville Albert Hood, CMG, DSO; two *d.* *Educ:* Eton; Sandhurst. 2nd Lieut Grenadier Guards, 1931. 3rd Sec. in Foreign Office, 1934; Budapest, 1936; 2nd Sec., 1939; Foreign Office, 1941; 1st Sec., 1945; Berne, 1945; Helsinki, 1948; Moscow, 1949; Counsellor, 1950; Head of Northern Dept, Foreign Office, 1951; Minister in Rome, 1956; Ambassador in Saigon, 1960-63; Minister in Paris, 1963-65; Asst Under-Sec., Foreign Office, 1966-67. Liveryman, Grocers' Company. *Address:* 16 Egerton Terrace, SW3 2BT. *Club:* Boodle's.
See also T . S . Hohler.

HOHLER, Thomas Sidney, MC 1944; Chairman, King & Shaxson Ltd, since 1965 (Partner since 1946); Chairman of associated companies; *b* 1919; *s* of late Lt-Col Arthur Preston Hohler, DSO and late Mrs Stanley Barry, Long Crendon Manor, Bucks; *m* 1952, Jacqueline, *d* of late Marquis de Jouffroy d'Abbans, Chateau d'Abbans, Doubs, France; one *d.* *Educ:* Eton. 2nd Lieut SRO Grenadier Guards, 1939; Major 1944; served in: France, 1940; N Africa, 1942; Italy, 1943-44. Dir, Henry Sotheran Ltd; Chm., London Discount Market Assoc., 1972. Liveryman, Grocers' Co., 1956. *Recreations:* farming, shooting. *Address:* 59 Eaton Square, SW1W 9BG. *T:* 01-235 4751; Wolverton Park, Basingstoke, Hants. *T:* Kingsclere 298200. *Clubs:* Turf, City of London.
See also H. A. F. Hohler.

HOLBECHE, Brian Harry, CBE 1972; MA Cantab; Headmaster, King Edward's School, Bath, since 1962; *b* 1920; *s* of Ronald Harry Holbeche, Hillybroom, Essex; *m* 1945, Philippa, *d* of Rev. Canon Robert Hunter Jack; one *s* one *d.* *Educ:* Wyggeston Sch., Leicester; St Catharine's Coll., Cambridge (Scholar). Served War of 1939-45: Sub-Lt RNVR, Submarine Service, Middle East. Sen. English Master and Housemaster, St Peter's Sch., York, 1954-61. Pres., Headmasters' Assoc., 1970; Chairman: Direct Grant Cttee of Headmasters' Conf., 1972-73; Joint Four Secondary Schools' Assoc., 1974 (Vice-Chm., 1972-73); Jt Council of Heads, 1976. *Address:* Nelson House, Beechen Cliff, Bath, Avon. *Club:* East India, Sports and Public Schools.

HOLBROOK, Col Sir Claude Vivian, Kt 1938; CBE 1919; Officier, Légion d'Honneur; Royal Army Service Corps (retired); *b* 1886; 3rd *s* of late Col Sir Arthur R. Holbrook, KBE; *m* 1st, 1913, Katharine (*d* 1966), *d* of late C. F. Elston; two *s*; 2nd, 1967, Joan, *d* of late Theodore Petersen and *widow* of Capt. J. L. Elston, The Northants Regt. Served European War, 1914-19; also 1939-43. DL 1931-67, Warwicks. *Address:* Upper Durford, near Petersfield, Hants. *Club:* Royal Thames Yacht.

HOLBROOK, David Kenneth, MA; self-supporting author; *b* 9 Jan. 1923; *o s* of late Kenneth Redvers and late Elsie Eleanor Holbrook; *m* 1949, Margot Davies-Jones; two *s* two *d.* *Educ:* City of Norwich Sch.; Downing Coll., Cambridge (Exhibr). Intell., mines and explosives officer, ER Yorks Yeo., Armd Corps, 1942-44. Asst Editor, Our Time, 1948; Asst Editor, Bureau of Current Affairs, 1949; Tutor organiser, WEA, 1952-53; Tutor, Bassingbourn Village Coll., Cambs, 1954-61; Fellow, King's Coll., Cambridge, 1961-65; Sen. Leverhulme Res. Fellow, 1965; College Lectr in English, Jesus Coll., Cambridge, 1968-70. Compton Poetry Lectr, Hull Univ., 1969 (resigned); Arts Council Writer's Grant, 1970; Writer in Residence, Dartington Hall, 1970-73 (grant from Elmgrant Trust); Asst Dir English Studies, Downing Coll., Cambridge, 1973-75; Arts Council Writers Grant, 1976. *Publications:* Children's Games, 1957; Imaginings, 1961; English for Maturity, 1961; Iron, Honey, Gold, 1961; Llareggub Revisited, 1962; People and Diamonds, 1962; Against the Cruel Frost, 1963; Lights in the Sky Country, 1963; Thieves and Angels, 1963; English for the Rejected, 1964; The Secret Places, 1964; Visions of Life, 1964; The Quest for Love, 1965; Flesh Wounds, 1966; Object Relations, 1967; The Exploring Word, 1967; Children's Writing, 1967; (with Elizabeth Poston) The Cambridge Hymnal, 1967; (with John Joubert) The Quarry (opera), 1967; Plucking the Rushes, 1968; Old World New World, 1969; Human Hope and the Death Instinct, 1971; The Masks of Hate, 1972; Sex and Dehumanization, 1972; Dylan Thomas, The Code of Night, 1972; ed, The Case Against Pornography, 1972; The Pseudo-

revolution, 1973; English in Australia Now, 1973; Gustav Mahler and the Courage to Be, 1975; (with Christine Mackenzie) The Honey of Man, 1975; essay on Ted Hughes, in, The Black Rainbow, ed Peter Abbs, 1975; Sylvia Plath: poetry and existence, 1976; Lost Bearings in English Poetry, 1977; Chance of a Lifetime, 1977; A Play of Passion, 1977; Education, Nihilism and Survival, 1977; essay on The Need for Meaning, in, Human Needs and Politics, ed Ross Fitzgerald, 1977; essay on Magazines, in, Discrimination and Popular Culture, ed Denys Thompson; opera with Wilfred Mellers, The Borderline, perf. London 1958. *Recreations:* painting in oils, cooking, gardening. *Address:* Longacre, Stapleford, Cambridge. *T:* Shelford 2135.

HOLBURN, James; *b* 1 Dec. 1900; *s* of late Rev. James Holburn, Alyth, Perthshire; *m* 1931, Elizabeth Margaret (*d* 1972), *d* of late Rev. John McConnachie, DD, Dundee; three *s.* *Educ:* Harris Academy, Dundee; University of Glasgow (MA Hons). Editorial staff, the Glasgow Herald, 1921-34; joined The Times, 1934: asst correspondent and actg corresp. Berlin, 1935-39; correspondent Moscow, 1939-40; Ankara, 1940-41; War Correspondent, Middle East, 1941-42; Correspondent New Delhi, 1942-46; United Nations Headquarters, 1946-48; Diplomatic Corresp., 1948-51; Chief Corresp. Middle East, 1952-55; Editor, The Glasgow Herald, 1955-65. *Publications:* contributions to various periodicals. *Recreations:* golf, angling. *Address:* West Glenree, Alyth, Perthshire PH11 8DP. *T:* Alyth 526. *Club:* Western (Glasgow).

HOLCROFT, Sir Reginald Culcheth, 2nd Bt (2nd *cr*), *cr* 1921; TD; JP; *b* 6 April 1899; *s* of 1st Bt and Annie Gertrude (*d* 1929), *d* of late Rev. J. Coombes; *S* father, 1951; *m* 1st, 1928, Mary Frances (*d* 1963), *yr d* of late William Swire, CBE; two *s* two *d*; 2nd, 1965, Elizabeth, Countess of Bandon. *Educ:* Radley Coll.; RMC Sandhurst; Exeter Coll., Oxford. JP Salop 1934, High Sheriff, 1950. *Heir: s* Peter George Culcheth Holcroft [*b* 29 April 1931; *m* 1956, Rosemary Rachel, *yr d* of late G. N. Deas; three *s* one *d*]. *Address:* Wrentnall House, Pulverbatch, Shrewsbury, Salop. *Club:* Cavalry and Guards.

HOLDEN, Basil Munroe; Rector, Glasgow Academy, 1959-75, retired; *b* 10 Nov. 1913; *m* 1951, Jean Watters; two *s* two *d.* *Educ:* Queen Elizabeth's Grammar Sch., Blackburn; King's Coll., Cambridge (Foundation Scholar). BA 1935, Maths Tripos (Wrangler), MA 1939. Mathematical Master, Highgate Sch., 1937. Instructor Lieut RN, 1940. Head of Mathematical Dept, Oundle Sch., 1947; Housemaster, Oundle Sch., 1956. *Address:* Brackenburn Lodge, Manesty, Keswick, Cumbria CA12 5UG. *T:* Borrowdale 637.

HOLDEN, Sir David (Charles Beresford), KBE 1972; CB 1963; ERD 1954; *b* 26 July 1915; *s* of Oswald Addenbrooke Holden and Ella Mary Beresford; *m* 1948, Elizabeth Jean Odling; one *s* one *d.* *Educ:* Rossall Sch.; King's Coll., Cambridge. Northern Ireland Civil Service, 1937-76; Permanent Sec., Dept of Finance, NI, and Head of NI Civil Service, 1970-76; Dir, Ulster Office, 1976-77. Royal Artillery, 1939-46. *Address:* Falcons, Wilsford Cum Lake, Amesbury, Salisbury SP4 7BL. *T:* Amesbury 2493.

HOLDEN, Sir Edward, 6th Bt, *cr* 1893; Consultant Anæsthetist, Darlington & Northallerton Group Hospitals, 1957-74; *b* 8 Oct. 1916; *s* of Sir Isaac Holden Holden, 5th Bt, and Alice Edna Byrom (*d* 1971), *S* father, 1962; *m* 1942, Frances Joan, *e d* of John Spark, JP, Ludlow, Stockton-on-Tees; two adopted *s.* *Educ:* Leys Sch. and Christ's Coll., Cambridge (MA); St Thomas's Hosp. MRCS; LRCP 1942; BA Eng., 1946; FFA, RCS, 1958. Formerly Vis. Anæsth., Cumb. Infirm.; Carlisle; Cons. Anæsth. W Cumb. Hospital Group. *Recreations:* fishing and gardening. *Heir: b* Paul Holden [*b* 3 March 1923; *m* 1950, Vivien Mary Oldham; one *s* two *d*]. *Address:* Brigante, Stanwick-St-John, Richmond, N Yorks DL11 7RT. *T:* Piercebridge 474. *Club:* Farmers'.

HOLDEN, Sir John David, 4th Bt *cr* 1919; *b* 16 Dec. 1967; *s* of David George Holden (*d* 1971) (*e s* of 3rd Bt), and of Nancy, *d* of H. W. D. Marwood, Foulrice, Whenby, Brandsby, Yorks; *S* grandfather, 1976. *Heir: uncle* Brian Peter John Holden, *b* 12 April 1944. *Address:* Woodhouse Farm, Sutton-on-Derwent, York.

HOLDEN, Maj.-Gen. John Reid, CB 1965; CBE 1960 (OBE 1953); DSO 1941; *b* 8 Jan. 1913; 2nd *s* of late John Holden, MA, Edinburgh; *m* 1939, Rosemarie Florence, *d* of late William Henry de Vere Pennefather, Carlow; one *d.* *Educ:* Hamilton Academy; Glasgow Univ.; RMC, Sandhurst. 2nd Lieut Royal Tank Corps, 1937; Adjutant, 7th Royal Tank Regt, 1940-41 (despatches, DSO); Bde Major, 32nd Army Tank Bde, 1942; POW, 1942-45. GSO1, GHQ, Far ELF, Singapore, 1951-52 (OBE); CO 3rd Royal Tank Regt, BAOR, 1954-57; AAG, War

Office, 1958. Comdr, 7th Armoured Bde Group, BAOR, 1958-61 (CBE). Royal Naval War Coll., 1961. Chief of Mission, British Comdrs-in-Chief Mission to the Soviet Forces in Germany, 1961-63; GOC 43 (Wessex) Div. Dist, 1963-65; Dir, RAC, 1965-68, retired 1968. Col Comdt, RTR, 1965-68. Hon. Col, The Queen's Own Lowland Yeomanry, RAC, T&AVR, 1972-75. *Recreations:* books, gardening. *Address:* Woodhead of Dardarroch, Auldgirth, Dumfries. *T:* Dunscore 274.

HOLDEN, Kenneth Graham; Director: Williams & Glyn's Bank Ltd (Chairman, 1964-72, formerly as Williams Deacon's Bank Ltd); Yorkshire Bank Ltd; Trustees Corporation Ltd; The Industrial and General Trust Ltd; *b* 6 May 1910; *e s* of Norman Neill Holden; *m* 1937, Winifred Frances, *d* of Lt-Col T. F. S. Burridge; two *d. Educ:* Wellington Coll.; Pembroke Coll., Cambridge. Admitted Solicitor, 1935. Director: (and sometime Chm.) Hardman & Holden Ltd, Manchester, 1936-64; Royal Bank of Scotland Ltd, 1950-69; Geigy (Holdings) Ltd (later CIBA-Geigy (UK) Ltd), 1955-65; Borax Consolidated Ltd, 1961-64; Haden-Carrier Ltd, 1967-75; Manchester Ship Canal Co., 1968-74; National Commercial Banking Group Ltd, 1969-76. Part-time Mem., NW Gas Bd, 1965-72. Formerly Mem. Bd of Management (and sometime Jt Hon. Treasurer), Manchester Royal Infirmary. *Address:* 40 Lee Road, Aldeburgh, Suffolk. *T:* Aldeburgh 3159. *Club:* All England Lawn Tennis.

HOLDEN, Sir Michael (Herbert Frank), Kt 1973; CBE 1968; ED 1949; Chief Justice, Rivers State, Nigeria, 1970-76; *b* 19 May 1913; *s* of Herbert Charles Holden, solicitor, Bolton, Lancs, and Mary Clare Holden (*née* Timaeus); *m* 1941, Mabel, *d* of Harry Morgan, Cwt Blethyn, Usk, Monmouthshire, and Ethel Morgan (*née* Jones), Betllan Deg, near Usk; two *s* one *d. Educ:* Aldenham Sch., Elstree, Herts. Admitted solicitor, 1937; employed in Lagos, Nigeria, as Asst Solicitor to J. C. Ticehurst, Sept. 1937 to July 1940, when embodied in Nigeria Regt. Served War of 1939-45; demob. rank Captain, 1945. Private practice as solicitor in Jos, Northern Nigeria; apptd Magistrate, Sept. 1955; Chief Magistrate, 1960; Judge, 1961; Sen. Puisne Judge, Kano State, 1970. *Recreations:* photography, electronics, fishing. *Address:* Old Gore, Upton Bishop, Ross-on-Wye, Herefordshire. *T:* Upton Bishop 339.

HOLDEN, Patrick Brian, MA, FCIS; Director, Oriel Foods (Hatfield) Ltd, and Secretary, Oriel Foods Group, since 1975; Director, British and Foreign Food Brokers Ltd; *b* 16 June 1937; *s* of Reginald John and Winifred Isobel Holden; *m* 1972, Jennifer Ruth (*née* Meddings), MB, BS. *Educ:* Allhallows Sch. (Major Schol.); St Catharine's Coll., Cambridge (BA Hons Law 1960, MA 1963). FCIS 1965. Served Royal Hampshire Regt, 1955-57 (short service commn), seconded 1 Ghana Regt, RWAFF. Fine Fare (Holdings) Group: Company Sec. and Legal Asst, 1960-69; Legal and Develt Dir, 1965-69; Pye of Cambridge Gp, 1969-74; Dir, Pye Telecom. Ltd, 1972-74. Sec., New Town Assoc., 1974-75. MBIM. *Recreations:* squash, sailing. *Address:* Mulment House, Water Street, Cambridge CB4 1PA.

HOLDEN, Philip Edward; an Underwriting Member of Lloyd's since 1954; *b* 20 June 1905. *Educ:* King Edward VI Schs, Birmingham. Qualified, CA, 1929; Managing Dir Amalgamated Anthracite Collieries, from 1940. Past Chm., Amalgamated Anthracite Holdings Group of Cos. Has served on Exec. of Monmouthshire and S Wales Coal Owners Assoc., and as Chm. of its Commercial Cttee; also served on Exec. Bd of S Wales Coal Mines Scheme. Pres. Swansea Chamber of Commerce, 1952-53; Vice-Chm. Chamber of Coal Traders, 1953-65; Vice-Chm. Nat. Council of Coal Traders (Chm. 1953-65); Pres. Brit. Coal Exporters' Assoc., 1958-63; Mem. Industrial Coal Consumers' Council, 1958. A Dir of public and private cos (coal, shipping, manufactures, electronics, electro-chemical and general engineering, etc). *Recreations:* Pres. Swansea City AFC Ltd; Vice-Pres. Clyne Golf Club, Ltd. *Address:* La Maison Blanche, Jerbourg Road, St Martin, Guernsey, CI. *T:* Guernsey 37985. *Clubs:* Carlton, Royal Automobile; Bristol Channel Yacht (Swansea).

HOLDEN-BROWN, Derrick; Vice-Chairman, Allied Breweries Ltd, since 1975; *b* 14 Feb. 1923; *s* of Harold Walter and Beatrice Florence (*née* Walker); *m* 1950, Patricia Mary Ross Mackenzie; one *s* one *d. Educ:* Westcliff. Mem., Inst of Chartered Accountants of Scotland. Served War, Royal Navy, 1941-46, Lt RNVR, Coastal Forces. Chartered Accountant, 1948; Hiram Walker & Sons, Distillers, 1949; Managing Director: Cairnes Ltd, Brewers, Eire, 1954; Grants of St James's Ltd, 1960; Dir, Ind Coope Ltd, 1962; Chm., Victoria Wine Co., 1964; Dir, Allied Breweries Ltd, 1967, Finance Dir 1972. Dep. Chm., FDIC, 1974-76. *Recreations:* sailing, offshore cruising. *Address:* Copse House, Milford-on-Sea, Hants. *T:* Milford-on-Sea 2247.

Clubs: Carlton; Royal Lymington Yacht; Royal Naval Sailing Association.

HOLDER, Sir John (Eric Duncan), 3rd Bt, *cr* 1898; late Flight Lieutenant RAFVR; *b* 2 Aug. 1899; *s* of Sir Henry Holder, 2nd Bt, and Evelyn (*d* 1956), *d* of Sir Robert Ropner, 1st Bt; *S* father, 1945; *m* 1st, 1927, Evelyn Josephine (marr. diss.), *er d* of late William Blain; one *s* two *d*; 2nd, Marjorie Emily, *d* of late F. R. Markham. *Educ:* Uppingham; Brasenose Coll., Oxford (MA). *Heir: s* John Henry Holder, Royal Armoured Corps [*b* 12 March 1928; *m* 1960, Catharine Harrison, *yr d* of late Leonard Baker; two *s* (*twins*) one *d*]. *Address:* Mulberry House, 17 Johnsons Drive, Hampton, Middx TW12 2EQ.

HOLDER, Air Marshal Sir Paul (Davie), KBE 1965; CB 1964; DSO 1942; DFC 1941; Hon. Air Commodore, Royal Auxiliary Air Force, 1968; *b* 2 Sept. 1911; *s* of Hugh John and Frances Rhoda Holder; *m* 1940, Mary Elizabeth Kidd; two *s. Educ:* Bristol Univ.; University of Illinois, USA. Graduated Bristol Univ., 1931; MSc 1933; Robert Blair Fellow, 1934; PhD 1935. Vice-Pres., RAF Selection Board, 1947-48; Student, Administrative Staff Coll., Henley on Thames, 1949; CO, RAF, Shallufa, Egypt, 1950-51; CO, RAF, Kabrit, Egypt, 1952; Dep. Dir, Air Staff Policy, Air Min., 1953-55; Student, Imperial Defence Coll., 1956; AOC, Singapore, 1957; AOC, Hong Kong, 1958-59; ACAS (Trng), Air Min., 1960-62; AOC No 25 Gp, RAF Flying Trng Comd, 1963-64; AOC-in-C, RAF Coastal Comd, NATO Comdr Maritime Air, Channel Comd, and Comdr Maritime Air, Eastern Atlantic Area, 1965-68, retired 1968. Mem., Waverley District Council, 1976. FRAeS 1966. *Recreations:* golf, sailing, bridge. *Address:* Spring Cottage, Churt, Surrey. *T:* Frensham 2388. *Club:* Royal Air Force.

HOLDERNESS, Rt. Rev. George Edward, ERD (with 2 clasps) 1955; Dean of Lichfield since 1970; *b* 5 March 1913; 2nd *s* of A. W. Holderness, Roundhay, Leeds; *m* 1940, Irene Mary, *er d* of H. G. Hird, Bedale, Yorkshire; one *s* two *d. Educ:* Leeds Grammar Sch.; Keble Coll., Oxford (MA); Westcott House, Cambridge. Assistant Curate of Bedale, 1936-39; Chaplain and Asst Master, Aysgarth School, Bedale, 1939-47. CF (RARO), 1940; SCF, 81st W African Div., 1943; DACG, India Command, 1945. Vicar of Darlington, 1947-55; Hon. Canon of Durham Cathedral, 1954; Suffragan Bishop of Burnley, 1955-70; Rector of Burnley, 1955-70; Canon of Blackburn Cathedral, 1955-70. DACG, TA, Northern Command, 1951-55. *Recreations:* cricket, shooting, fishing. *Address:* The Deanery, Lichfield, Staffs. *Clubs:* MCC, Forty, Lord's Taverners', Farmers'.

HOLDERNESS, Sir Richard William, 3rd Bt, *cr* 1920; *b* 30 Nov. 1927; *s* of Sir Ernest William Elsmie Holderness, 2nd Bt, CBE, and Emily Carlton (*d* 1950), *y d* of late Frederick McQuade, Sydney, NSW; *S* father, 1968; *m* 1953, Pamela, *d* of Eric Chapman, CBE; two *s* one *d. Educ:* Dauntsey's Sch.; Corpus Christi Coll., Oxford. *Heir: s* Martin William Holderness, *b* 24 May 1957. *Address:* Rosetree House, Boxgrove, Chichester.

HOLDGATE, Martin Wyatt, PhD; Director General of Research, Department of the Environment, since 1976; *b* 14 Jan. 1931; *s* of Francis Wyatt Holdgate, MA, JP, and Lois Marjorie Bebbington; *m* 1963, Elizabeth Mary (*née* Dickason), widow of Dr H. H. Weil; two *s. Educ:* Arnold Sch., Blackpool; Queens' Coll., Cambridge. BA Cantab 1952; MA 1956; PhD 1955; FInstBiol 1967. Senior Scientist, Gough Is Scientific Survey, 1955-56; Lecturer in Zoology, Manchester Univ., 1956-57; Lecturer in Zoology, Durham Colleges, 1957-60; Leader, Royal Society Expedition to Southern Chile, 1958-59; Asst Director of Research, Scott Polar Research Institute, Cambridge, 1960-63; Senior Biologist, British Antarctic Survey, 1963-66; Sec., Working Gp on Biology, Scientific Cttee on Antarctic Res., 1964-68; Dep. Dir (Research), The Nature Conservancy, 1966-70; Director: Central Unit on Environmental Pollution, DoE, 1970-74; Inst. of Terrestrial Ecology, NERC, 1974-76. Hon. Professorial Fellow, UC Cardiff, 1976-. Member: NERC, 1976-; SRC, 1976-; ABRC, 1976-. Chairman: British Schools Exploring Society, 1967-; Young Explorer's Trust, 1972. *Publications:* Mountains in the Sea, The Story of the Gough Island Expedition, 1958; (Jt Ed) Antarctic Biology, 1964; (ed) Antarctic Ecology, 1970; (with N. M. Wace) Man and Nature in the Tristan da Cunha Islands, 1976; numerous papers in biological journals and works on Antarctic. *Address:* 35 Wingate Way, Trumpington, Cambridge. *Club:* Athenæum.

HOLDSWORTH, Albert Edward; His Honour Judge Holdsworth, QC; a Circuit Judge, since 1972; *b* 1909; *e s* of Albert Edward and Catherine Sarah Holdsworth; *m* 1st, 1941, Barbara Frances (*d* 1968), *e d* of Ernest Henry and Beatrice Maud Reeves; one *s*; 2nd, 1970, Brianne Evelyn Frances, *d* of

Arthur James and Evelyn Lock; two s. Educ: Sir George Monoux Sch., Walthamstow; Gonville and Caius Coll., Cambridge (Exhibitioner). Pres., Cambridge Union, 1932; Economics and Politics tripos; MA. Formerly journalist: Financial News, 1932-33; Special Correspondent, World Economic Conf., 1933; Yorkshire Post, 1933-46, Polit. Correspondent, later London Editor. Broadcasts for BBC on current affairs topics, 1935-56. Called to Bar, Middle Temple, 1936. Conservative Candidate Ipswich, 1951; moved resolution in favour of UK entry into European Common Market, Conservative Conf., Llandudno, 1962. Dep.-Chm., SW Metropolitan Mental Health Tribunal, 1962-65. QC 1969. Recreations: cinema, theatre, reading. Address: 2 Middle Temple Lane, Temple, EC4Y 9AA. T: 01-353 7926; West Gate, Sutton, Pulborough, West Sussex RH20 1PN. T: Sutton (West Sussex) 230. Club: Reform.

HOLDSWORTH, David, CBE 1976; QPM 1968; Chief Constable, Thames Valley Police, since 1970; b 10 May 1918; s of late Captain F. J. C. Holdsworth, DL, JP, The Mount, Totnes; m 1940, Diana Mary, d of Keith Hugh Williams, Kingsbridge, Devon. Educ: Sherborne; Metropolitan Police Coll., Hendon. Commnd Devonshire Regt, 1943; landed D Day, 1944; served in France, Belgium and Holland (wounded, despatches). Rejoined Metropolitan Police, 1945; Stn Inspector, Chelsea, 1945-52; Staff Officer, Police Coll., 1953-56; Asst Chief Constable, Wilts, 1956-64; Chief Constable, Oxon, 1964-68; Dep. Chief Constable, Thames Valley Police, 1968-70. District Comr, Boy Scouts' Assoc., Mid-Wilts, 1957-64; Chm., Exec. Cttee, Oxfordshire Scouts Assoc. Pres., Chief Constables' Club, 1976-77. Scouts Medal of Merit, 1975. Comdr, Order of Orange Nassau, 1972; Grosses Verdienstkreuz des Verdienstordens der Bundesrepublik Deutschland, 1972; Comdr, Order of Aztec Eagle, Mexico, 1973; Comdr, Order of Dannebrog, 1974; Médaille de Bayeux, 1974. Publication: The New Society: Development of Pop and Free Festivals in the Thames Valley Police Area, 1972-1975, 1975. Recreation: oil painting. Address: Chief Constable's Office, Police Headquarters, Kidlington, Oxford OX5 2NX. T: Kidlington 4343.

HOLDSWORTH, Mrs Mary, MA; Principal, St Mary's College, Durham University, 1962-74, Second Pro-Vice-Chancellor, 1973-74; b Voronezh, Russia, 24 Oct. 1908; d of late Col A. Zvegintzov, Chev. Gardes, Member of Duma, and Catherine Sverbeev; m 1940, Richard William Gilbert Holdsworth, Fellow, University College, Oxford, Flt-Lt RAFVR (killed on active service, 1942); one d. Educ: Cheltenham Ladies' Coll.; St Hugh's Coll., Oxford. Worked in banking and industry, 1931-37; College Sec., University College, Oxford, 1937-40; Air Ministry, 1942-43; Tutor for Education in the Forces, N Ireland, 1943-45; Secretary and Senior Research Officer, OU Institute of Commonwealth Studies, 1948-62. Member Royal Institute of International Affairs, 1961-. Publications: Turkestan in the 19th Century, 1959; Soviet African Studies, 1918-59 (annotated bibliography for RIIA), 1961; articles, reviews. Recreations: gardening, walking. Address: 125 High Street, Chalgrove 0X9 7SS.

HOLDSWORTH, Max Ernest, OBE 1944; TD; DL; MA; LLB; Barrister-at-Law; Deputy-Chairman, Court of Quarter Sessions, Gloucestershire, 1954-68; Recorder of Lichfield, 1939-68; Colonel (TA); b 6 Nov. 1895; o s of late M. F. Holdsworth. Educ: King Edward's Sch., Birmingham; Christ's Coll., Cambridge. Served European War, 1915-19; also in War of 1939-45; called to the Bar, Gray's Inn, 1922. DL Warwicks, 1945, Hereford and Worcester, 1974. Publication: Law of Transport, 1932. Address: 44 Britannia Square, Worcester. T: Worcester 23133. Club: Union and County (Worcester).

HOLE, George Vincer, CBE 1969; Chief Executive, British Airports Authority, 1965-72; b 26 Jan. 1910; s of George William Hole and Louisa Hole (née Vincer); m 1938, Gertraud Johanna Anna Koppe (Baroness von Broesigke); two s. Educ: Wilson's Grammar Sch., London; London Sch. of Economics. BSc (Econ.) 1933. Asst Auditor, Exchequer and Audit Dept, 1929; passed First Div. Exam., 1935; Under-Sec., 1958; Min. of Aviation, 1959-65; student Imperial Defence Coll., 1948; Chm. First Div. Assoc., 1949-50; Chm. OEEC Productivity Group, on Traffic Engineering and Control, in the United States, 1954; Chm. W European Airports Assoc., 1970; Member: Council, Internat. Bd of Airport Operators, 1970; Bd, Internat. Civil Airports Assoc. (Chm.); Bd, Airport Assocs Co-ordinating Council (first Chm.). FCIT. Hon. Treas., Caravan Club, 1960-66. Officer, Order of Orange Nassau, Netherlands, 1946; Officer, Order of the Crown, Belgium, 1946. Recreation: pottering. Address: 6 St Germans Place, Blackheath, SE3. T: 01-858 3917. Club: Reform.

HOLFORD, Rear-Adm. Frank Douglas, CB 1969; DSC 1944; Director General of Naval Manpower, Ministry of Defence, 1967-69, retired 1970; b 28 June 1916; y s of late Capt. C. F. Holford, DSO, OBE, and Ursula Isobel Holford (née Corbett); m 1942, Sybil Priscilla, d of late Comdr Sir Robert and Lady Micklem; two s. Educ: RN Coll., Dartmouth. Cadet, 1929, Midshipman, HMS Hood, 1933; Sub-Lieut, HMS Wolverine, 1937; Lieutenant: HMS Kent, 1938; HMS Anson, 1941; HMS Sheffield, 1943; Lieut-Comdr: HMS Excellent, 1945; HMS Triumph, 1948; Commander: Admlty, Naval Ordnance Dept, 1951; British Joint Services Mission, USA, 1953; HMS Excellent, 1955; Captain: Admlty, Dir Guided Weapons, 1957; Naval and Mil. Attaché, Buenos Aires, 1960; Staff C-in-C Portsmouth, 1962; Cdre-i-C Hong Kong, 1965. Rear-Adm. 1967. jssc 1947. Address: Great Down Cottage, Soberton, Hants. T: Droxford 448.

HOLFORD, Surgeon Rear-Adm. John Morley, CB 1965; OBE 1954; Senior Principal Medical Officer, Department of Health and Social Security, 1973-74, retired; b 10 Jan. 1909; o s of late Rev. W. J. Holford and Amy Finnemore Lello; m 1935, Monica Peregrine, d of late Preb. P. S. G. Propert; two s. Educ: Kingswood, Bath; Trinity Hall, Cambridge. MA, MB, Cantab; FRCP; joined RN 1935. War service in HMS Nelson, 1940-42; RN Hosp. Plymouth, 1942-44; consultant in Medicine to RN, 1954-66; Surgeon Capt., 1957; Surgeon Rear-Adm. 1963; Medical Officer in Charge, RN Hosp. Haslar, 1963-66. Retired, 1966. MO, Min. of Health, 1966, SMO, 1967, SPMO, 1973. Gilbert Blanc Medal, 1956; F. E. Williams Prize in Geriatric Medicine, RCP, 1972. CStJ 1964. Publications: Articles in medical journals. Recreations: chess (jt champion of South Africa, 1946), bridge. Address: c/o Lloyds Bank, 84 Park Lane, W1. Club: Army and Navy.

HOLGATE, Dr Sidney; Master of Grey College, University of Durham, since 1959; Chairman, Academic Advisory Committee, Open University, since 1975 (Member since 1969; Vice-Chairman, 1972-75); b Hucknall, Notts, 9 Sept. 1918; e s of late Henry and Annie Elizabeth Holgate; m 1942, Isabel Armorey; no c. Educ: Henry Mellish Sch., Nottingham; Durham Univ. Open Scholar, Hatfield Coll., Durham, 1937; Univ. Mathematical Scholarship, 1940; BA (1st Cl. Hons Mathematics) 1940; MA 1943; PhD 1945. Asst Master, Nottingham High Sch., 1941-42; Lecturer in Mathematics, University of Durham, 1942-46; Sec. of the Durham Colls, 1946-59; Pro-Vice-Chancellor, Univ. of Durham, 1964-69. Member: Schools Council Gen. Studies Cttee, 1967-70; Chm., BBC Radio Durham Council, 1968-72; Vice-Chm., BBC Radio Newcastle Council, 1972-74. Publications: mathematical papers in Proc. Camb. Phil. Soc. and Proc. Royal Soc. Recreations: cricket and other sports, railways, bridge. Address: Grey College, Durham DH1 3LG. T: Durham 69521.

HOLGATE, Surgeon Rear-Adm. (D) William, CB 1962; OBE 1951; Chief Dental Officer, Ministry of Health, 1961-71, and Ministry of Education and Science, 1963-71; b 6 July 1906; s of Anthony and Jane Holgate; m 1933, Inga Ommanney Davis; one s one d. Educ: Scarborough Coll.; Guy's Hospital. LDS, RCS Eng., 1927; FDS, RCS Eng., 1963. Royal Navy, 1928-61. Director of Dental Services, 1960. Address: Upalong, The Highway, Luccombe, Shanklin, Isle of Wight. Club: Savage.

HOLLAMBY, Edward Ernest, OBE 1970; FRIBA, FRTPI, FSIA; Director of Architecture, Planning and Development, Lambeth, since 1969; b 8 Jan. 1921; s of Edward Thomas Hollamby and late Ethel Mary (née Kingdom); m 1941, Doris Isabel Parker; one s two d. Educ: School of Arts and Crafts, Hammersmith; University Coll. London. DipTP London. Served RM Engrs, 1941-46. Architect, Miners' Welfare Commn, 1947-49; Sen. Architect, LCC, 1949-62; Borough Architect, Lambeth, 1963-65, Bor. Architect and Town Planning Officer, 1965-69. Works, 1949-, incl.: Christopher Wren and N Hammersmith Sec. Schs; Brandon Estate, Southwark; Housing at Elephant and Castle; study for Erith Township, Kent (prototype study for Thamesmead); pioneered rehabil. old houses, LCC Brixton Town Centre Develt Plan; housing schemes, Lambeth, 1965-, incl.: Lambeth Towers; Central Hill, Norwood; Stockwell; Brixton; flats, houses, old people's home, doctors' gp practice, Clapham. Area rehabil. and renewal schemes, Clapham Manor and Kennington; Norwood Libr. and Nettlefold Hall; schs for mentally retarded, Clapham and Kennington; rehabil. centre for disabled, Clapham; home for elderly, Kennington; offices for Tarmac, Brixton; recreation centre; prelim. study, Civic Centre, Brixton; holiday hotel for severely disabled, Netley, near Southampton. RIBA: Mem. Council, 1961-70, Hon. Treas., 1967-70; Mem., Historic Buildings Council; Chm., Assoc. London Borough Planning Officers; Founder Mem., William Morris Soc. Numerous design and Civic Trust awards. *Publications:* contrib. architectural and town planning jls. *Recreations:* travel, classical music, gardening. *Address:* Red House, Red House Lane, Upton, Bexleyheath, Kent DA6 8JF. *T:* 01-303 8808.

HOLLAND, Rt. Rev. Alfred Charles; Assistant Bishop, Diocese of Perth, Western Australia, since 1970; *b* 23 Feb. 1927; *s* of Alfred Charles Holland and Maud Allison; *m* 1954, Joyce Marion Embling; three *s* one *d*. *Educ:* Raine's Sch., London; Univ. of Durham (BA 1950, DipTh 1952). RNVR, 1945-47; Univ. of Durham, 1948-52; Assistant Priest, West Hackney, London, 1952-54; Rector of Scarborough, WA, 1955-70. President, Stirling Rugby Football Club, 1963-75 (Life Member, 1969). *Recreations:* reading, painting. *Address:* Law Chambers, Cathedral Square, Perth 6000, Western Australia. *T:* 257455, 859886 (home).

HOLLAND, Arthur David, CB 1973; TD 1947; Chief Highway Engineer, Department of the Environment, 1970-74; *b* 1 Nov. 1913; *o s* of Col. Arthur Leslie Holland, MC, TD, and Dora Helena Hassé; *m* 1938, Jean Moyra Spowart; two *s*. *Educ:* Malvern Coll.; University of Bristol (BSc(Eng)Hons). Asst Engineer, Great Western Railway Co, 1935-36; N Devon CC, 1936-37; Min. of Transport: Manchester, 1937-38; London, 1938-39. Served War: with RE, 1939-46; in Air Defence Gt Britain, 1939-42; with Middle East Forces, 1942-46, finally as Lt-Col RE (now Hon. Lt-Col), Sen. Staff Officer to Chief Engineer, Italy. Min. of Transport, Nottingham, 1946-47; Bridge Section, London, 1947-61; Divl Road Engr, E Midland Div., Nottingham, 1961-63; Asst Chief Engr (Bridges), 1963-65; Dep. Chief Engr, HQ London, 1965-70. FICE, FIStructE, FInstHE; Mem., Smeatonian Soc. of Civil Engrs. *Publications:* contribs to Proc. Instn of Civil Engineers and Instn of Highway Engineers. *Address:* Pine Tree Cottage, Pembroke Road, Woking, Surrey. *T:* Woking 62403.

HOLLAND, Sir Clifton Vaughan, (Sir John), Kt 1973; BCE; FTS, FIE(Aust), FAIM, FAIB; Chairman: John Holland (Holdings) Ltd, since 1962; John Holland Construction Group, since 1949; Process Plant Construction Pty Ltd, since 1949; Director: T&G Life Society, since 1972; Australia and New Zealand Banking Group, since 1976; *b* Melbourne, 21 June 1914; *s* of Thomas and Mabel Ruth Elizabeth Holland; *m* 1942, Emily Joan Atkinson; three *s* one *d*. *Educ:* Queen's Coll., Univ. of Melbourne (BCE). Junior Engineer, BP, 1936-39. Served War of 1939-45, RAE and 'Z' Special Force (Lt-Col). Construction Engr, BP Aust. 1946-49; Founder, John Holland Construction Group, 1949, Man. Dir 1949-72. Pres., Australian Fedn of Civil Contractors (Life Mem., 1971). Member: Rhodes Scholar Selection Cttee, 1970-73; Econ. Consultative Adv. Gp to the Treasurer, 1975-76; Mem. Bd, Royal Melbourne Hosp., 1963-; Nat. Chm., Outward Bound, 1973-74, Chm. Victorian Div., 1964-77; Councillor, Inst. of Public Affairs, 1970; Mem., Churchill Fellowship Selection Cttee, 1968-; Dir, Winston Churchill Meml Trust, 1976-; Chairman: La Trobe Centenary Commemoration Council, 1975-76; Matthew Flinders Bi-Centenary Council, 1973-75; History Adv. Council of Victoria, 1975-; Loch Ard Centenary Commemoration Cttee, 1976-; Dep. Chm., Queen's Silver Jubilee Appeal for Young Australians, 1977- (Chm., Victoria Appeal); Mem., Centenary Test Co-ordinating Cttee, 1976-77. Construction projects include: Jindabyne pumping station; Westgate Bridge; Tasman Bridge restoration. Foundation Fellow, Australian Acad. of Technological Scis. Peter Nicoll Russell Meml Medal, 1974. *Recreations:* golf, music, gardening, cricket. *Address:* 14 North Road, Brighton, Victoria 3186. *T:* 96.1558. *Clubs:* Australian, Naval and Military (Melbourne); Royal Melbourne Golf, Frankston Golf.

HOLLAND, David Cuthbert Lyall, CB 1975; Librarian of the House of Commons, 1967-76; *b* 23 March 1915; *yr s* of Michael Holland, MC, and Marion Holland (*née* Broadwood); *m* 1949, Rosemary Griffiths, *y d* of David Ll. Griffiths, OBE; two *s* one *d*. *Educ:* Eton; Trinity Coll., Cambridge (MA). War service, Army, 1939-46; PoW. Appointed House of Commons Library, 1946. Chm., Study of Parlt Gp, 1973-74. *Publications:* book reviews, etc. *Recreation:* book collecting. *Address:* The Barn, Milton Street, Polegate, East Sussex. *T:* Alfriston 870379. *Club:* Athenæum.

HOLLAND, David George, CMG 1975; a Deputy Chief, Overseas Department, Bank of England, since 1977; *b* 31 May 1925; *s* of late Francis George Holland and Mabel Ellen Holland; *m* 1954, Marian Elizabeth Rowles; two *s* one *d*. *Educ:* Taunton Sch.; Wadham Coll., Oxford. Inst. of Economics and Statistics, Oxford, 1949-63; Internat. Bank for Reconstruction and Development, Washington, DC, 1963-65; Min. of Overseas Development, 1965-67; Chief Economic Adviser, FCO, 1967-75;

a Dep. Chief, Economic Intelligence Dept, Bank of England, 1975-77. *Address:* 20 Woodside Avenue, Highgate, N6.

HOLLAND, Edgar William, CIE 1944; *b* 28 April 1899; *s* of Rev. Edgar Rogers Holland, MA, and Ellen Angela (*née* Jellicorse); *m* 1928, Doris Marjorie (*d* 1973), 2nd *d* of George Waverling Schoneman, late Postmaster-Gen., Bengal and Assam, and Hilda Edith (*née* Hope Ross). *Educ:* Rossall Sch.; Brasenose Coll., Oxford. Served in European War, 1914-18, in Royal Artillery, France, 1918. Entered Indian Civil Service, 1923, posted to Bengal Province; Commissioner of Commercial Taxes, 1941; Sec. to Government in Public Health Dept, 1943; Commissioner of Dacca Div., 1945; Chairman, Calcutta Improvement Trust, 1947; retired from ICS, 1948; Asst Governor HM Prison Service, 1951-56. *Recreations:* rowing, tennis, walking.

HOLLAND, Sir Jim Sothern, 2nd Bt, *cr* 1917; *b* 31 March 1911; *er s* of Sir R. Sothern Holland, 1st Bt, and Stretta Aimée Holland (*née* Price) (*d* 1949); *S* father, 1948; *m* 1937, Elisabeth Hilda Margaret, *o d* of Thomas Francis Vaughan Prickard, CVO; two *d*. *Educ:* Durnford; Marlborough; Trinity Coll., Oxon (MA). Central Mining and Investment, 1932-64; Dir, Price & Pierce Ltd, 1959-66; a Manager and Alternate Dir, Charter Consolidated Ltd, 1964-69. Joined TA 1939. City of London Yeomanry; TD 1950. Served War of 1939-45; 1942-44, ADC to Field-Marshal Viscount Gort, when Governor of Malta; Major RA, TA, 1946-48. *Recreations:* botany, stalking. *Heir:* *b* Guy Hope Holland, late Royal Scots Greys [*b* 19 July 1918; *m* 1945, Joan Marian, *o d* of late Capt. H. E. Street, 20th Hussars; two *d*. *Educ:* Christ Church, Oxford]. *Address:* Dderw, Rhayader, Powys. *T:* Rhayader 226. *Club:* Bath.

HOLLAND, Sir John; *see* Holland, Sir C. V.

HOLLAND, Rt. Rev. John Tristram, CBE 1975; *b* 31 Jan. 1912; *s* of Rt Rev. H. St B. Holland; *m* 1937, Joan Theodora Arundell, *d* of Dr R. Leslie Ridge, Carlton House, Enfield, Mddx; three *d*. *Educ:* Durham School; University College, Oxford; Westcott House, Cambridge. BA 1933, MA 1937, Oxford. Deacon, 1935; Priest, 1936; Curate of St Peter's, Huddersfield, 1935-37; Commissary to Bishop of Wellington, 1936-37; Vicar of Featherston, 1938-41; CF (2 NZEF), 1941-45; Vicar of: St Peter's, Upper Riccarton, 1945-49; St Mary's, New Plymouth, 1949-51; Bishop of Waikato, 1951-69; Bishop in Polynesia, 1969-75; Officiating Minister: Diocese of Canterbury, 1975-76; Diocese of Waiapu, 1976. *Address:* 12 Epsom Road, Mount Maunganui, New Zealand.

HOLLAND, Kenneth Lawrence, CBE 1971; QFSM 1974; HM's Chief Inspector of Fire Services since Sept. 1972; *b* 20 Sept. 1918; *s* of Percy Lawrence and Edith Holland; *m* 1941, Pauline Keith (*née* Mansfield); two *s* one *d*. *Educ:* Whitcliffe Mount Grammar Sch., Cleckheaton, Yorks. Entered Fire Service, Lancashire, 1937; Divisional Officer: Suffolk and Ipswich, 1948; Worcestershire, 1952; Dep. Chief Fire Officer, Lancashire, 1955. Chief Fire Officer: Bristol, 1960; West Riding of Yorkshire, 1967. Fellow, Instn Fire Engineers. OStJ 1964. Defence Medal; Fire Brigade Long Service and Good Conduct Medal. *Recreations:* motoring, golf, gardening. *Address:* Home Office (Fire Department), Queen Anne's Gate, SW1H 9AT. *T:* 01-213 3362. *Club:* St John House.

HOLLAND, Philip Welsby; MP (C) Carlton since 1966; *b* 14 March 1917; *s* of late John Holland, Middlewich, Cheshire; *m* 1943, Josephine Alma Hudson; one *s*. *Educ:* Sir John Deane's Grammar Sch. Northwich. Enlisted RAF 1936; commissioned 1943. Factory Manager, Jantzen Knitting Mills, 1946-47; Management Research, 1948-49; Manufacturers' Agent in Engineering and Refractories Products, 1949-60. Contested (C) Yardley Div. of Birmingham, Gen. Election, 1955; MP (C) Acton, 1959-64; PPS: to Minister of Pensions and Nat. Insurance, 1961-62; to Chief Sec. to Treasury and Paymaster-Gen., 1962-64; to Minister of Aviation Supply, 1970; to Minister for Aerospace, 1971; to Minister for Trade, 1972. Pres., Cons. Trade Union Nat. Adv. Cttee, 1972-74. Personnel Manager, The Ultra Electronics Group of Companies, 1964-66; Personnel Consultant to Standard Telephones and Cables Ltd, 1969-. Councillor, Royal Borough of Kensington, 1955-59. *Recreation:* travel. *Address:* 2 Holland Park Mansions, Holland Park Gardens, W14. *T:* 01-603 5640; Orston, Notts.

HOLLAND, Robert Einion, FIA; Chief General Manager, Pearl Assurance Co. Ltd, since 1977; *b* 23 April 1927; *s* of late Robert Ellis Holland and of Bene Holland; *m* 1955, Eryl Haf Roberts; one *s* two *d*. *Educ:* University Coll. of N Wales, Bangor (BSc). FIA 1957. Joined Pearl Assurance Co. Ltd, 1953; Dir, 1973. Chairman: Community Reinsurance Corp. Ltd, 1973-76;

Industrial Life Offices Assoc., 1976-; Aviation & General Insurance Co. Ltd, 1976-. Director: Pearl American Corp., 1972-; Monarch Insurance Co. of Ohio, 1977-. Mem., Welsh Develt Agency, 1976-. *Recreations:* golf and Welsh literature. *Address:* 55 Corkscrew Hill, West Wickham, Kent BR4 9BA. *T:* 01-777 1861.

HOLLAND, Stuart (Kingsley), Political Economist; *b* 25 March 1940; *y s* of Frederick Holland and May Holland, London; *m* 1976, Jenny Lennard; one *d*. *Educ:* state primary schs; Christ's Hosp.; Univ. of Missouri (Exchange Scholar); Balliol Coll., Oxford (Domus Scholar; 1st Cl. Hons Mod. History); St Antony's Coll., Oxford (Sen. Scholar; DPhil Econs). Econ. Asst, Cabinet Office, 1966-67; Personal Asst to Prime Minister, 1967-68; Res. Fellow, Centre for Contemp. European Studies, Univ. of Sussex, 1968-71, Assoc. Fellow and Lectr, 1971-. Vis. Scholar, Brookings Instn, Washington, DC, 1970. Special Adviser: Commons Expenditure Cttee, 1971-72; Minister of Overseas Develt, 1974-75. Res. Specialist, RIIA, 1972-74; Associate, Inst. of Develt Studies, 1974-. Consultant: Econ. and Social Affairs Cttee, Council of Europe, 1973; Open Univ., 1973. Rapporteur, Trades Union Adv. Cttee, OECD, 1977. Chm., Public Enterprise Gp, 1973-75. Member: Council, Inst. for Workers' Control, 1974-; Expert Cttee on Inflation, EEC Commn, 1975-76; UN Univ. Working Party on Socio-Cultural Factors in Develt, Tokyo, 1977. Lubbock Lectr, Oxford Univ., 1975; Tom Mann Meml Lectr, Australia, 1977. Mem., Labour Party, 1962-; Mem. sub-cttees (inc. Finance and Econ. Policy, Indust. Policy, EEC, Prices and Consumer Affairs, Public Sector, Pharmaceuticals, Multinationals), Nat. Exec. Cttee, Labour Party, 1972-; Prospective Parly Candidate (Lab), Vauxhall Div. of Lambeth, 1977. Associate Editor, European Economic Rev., 1970-. *Publications:* (jtly) Sovereignty and Multinational Corporations, 1971; (ed) The State as Entrepreneur, 1972; Strategy for Socialism, 1975; The Socialist Challenge, 1975; The Regional Problem, 1976; Capital versus the Regions, 1976; Uncommon Market, 1978; (ed) Beyond Capitalist Planning, 1978; contrib. symposia; articles in specialist jls and national and internat. press. *Recreation:* singing in the bath. *Address:* 35 Sussex Square, Brighton, E Sussex. *T:* Brighton 64639.

HOLLAND, Rt. Rev. Thomas; *see* Salford, Bishop of, (RC).

HOLLAND-HIBBERT, family name of **Viscount Knutsford.**

HOLLAND-MARTIN, Edward; Director: Racecourse Holdings Trust Ltd; The Steeplechase Co. (Cheltenham) Ltd; *b* 8 March 1900; *s* of late R. M. Holland-Martin, CB; *m* 1955, Dagny Mary MacLean, *yr d* of late Major J. M. Grant and late Mrs Horace Webber; one *d*. *Educ:* Eton; Christ Church, Oxford. Director: Bank of England, 1933-48; Bank of London and S America, 1948-70; Dep. Chm., BOLSA, 1951-70. Hon. Treasurer, 1928-71, Vice-Pres., 1971-, CPRE; Hon. Treasurer, Nat. Trust, 1948-68; Mem. Council, 1948, Hon. Treasurer, 1956-66, BHS. Sheriff of County of London, 1941; one of HM Lieutenants, City of London, 1933-. Mem. Jockey Club. *Address:* Overbury Court, near Tewkesbury, Glos GL20 7NP. *T:* Overbury 202; 28 St James's Place, SW1. *T:* 01-493 0937. *Club:* White's.

HOLLENDEN, 2nd Baron, *cr* 1912; **Geoffrey Hope Hope-Morley;** Past President of the Wholesale Textile Association; High Sheriff County of London, 1917; JP Kent; *b* 28 Jan. 1885; *e s* of 1st Baron and Laura M. (*d* 1945), *d* of Rev. G. Royds Birch; *S* father, 1929; *m* 1st, 1914, Hon. Mary Gardner (from whom he obtained a divorce, 1928), 3rd *d* of late Lord Burghclere; two *d*; 2nd, 1929, Muriel Ivy (*d* 1962), 3rd *d* of Sir John E. Gladstone, 4th Bt; 3rd, 1963, Mrs Violet Norris Howitt, *widow* of Frank Howitt, Harley Street, W1. *Educ:* Eton; Trinity Coll., Cambridge. Pres., Salmon and Trout Association. *Heir: nephew* Gordon Hope Hope-Morley, *qv.* *Address:* Ravensbourne, Stoke Fleming, near Dartmouth, Devon. *T:* Stoke Fleming 349.
See also Sir D. F. Muirhead.

HOLLENWEGER, Prof. Walter Jacob; Professor of Mission, University of Birmingham, since 1971; *b* 1 June 1927; *s* of Walter Otto and Anna Hollenweger-Spörri; *m* 1951, Erica Busslinger. *Educ:* Univs. of Zürich and Basel. Dr theol Zürich 1966 (and degrees leading up to it). Stock Exchange, Zürich, and several banking appts, until 1948. Pastor, 1949-57; ordained, Swiss Reformed Church, 1961. Study Dir, Ev. Acad., Zürich, 1964-65; Research Asst, Univ. of Zürich, 1961-64; Exec. Sec., World Council of Churches, Geneva, 1965-71. *Publications:* Handbuch der Pfingstbewegung, 10 vols, 1965/66; The Pentecostals, 1972 (also German and Spanish edns); (ed) Die Pfingstkirchen, 1971; Kirche, Benzin und Bohnensuppe, 1971; (ed) The Church for Others, 1967 (also German, Spanish and Portuguese edns); Pentecost between Black and White, 1975 (also German and Dutch edns); Evangelism Today, 1976 (also

German edn); Glaube, Geist und Geister, 1975. *Address:* Department of Theology, University of Birmingham, PO Box 363, Birmingham B15 2TT. *T:* 021-472 1301.

HOLLEY, Prof. Robert W., PhD; Resident Fellow, The Salk Institute, since 1968; *b* 28 Jan. 1922; *s* of Charles and Viola Holley, Urbana, Ill, USA; *m* 1945, Ann Dworkin; one *s*. *Educ:* Univ. of Illinois (AB); Cornell Univ. (PhD); Washington State Coll. Research Biochemist, Cornell Univ. Med. Coll., 1944-46; Instructor, State Coll. of Wash., 1947-48; Associate Prof. and Prof. of Biochem., Cornell Univ., 1948-57; Research Chemist, US Plant, Soil and Nut. Lab., ARS, USDA, 1957-64; Prof. of Biochem. and Molecular Biol., Biol. Div., Cornell Univ., 1964-75. Various awards for research, 1965-. Hon. DSc Illinois, 1970. Nobel Prize in Physiology or Medicine, 1968. *Publications:* many contribs to: Jl Amer. Chem. Soc., Science, Jl Biol. Chem., Arch. Biochem., Nature, Proc. Nat. Acad. Sci., etc. *Recreations:* family enjoys walks along ocean and trips to mountains. *Address:* The Salk Institute, PO Box 1809, San Diego, California 92112, USA. *T:* 453-4100 (ext. 341).

HOLLEY, (William) Stephen; DL; General Manager, Washington Development Corporation since 1965; *b* 26 March 1920; *m* 1947, Dinah Mary Harper; three *s*. *Educ:* King William's Coll. Student Accountant, 1937-39. War service, RA (TA), 1939-45 (Major). Colonial Service, and Overseas Civil Service, 1945-64; Mem. Legislature and State Sec., Head of Civil Service, Sabah, Malaysia, 1964. Mem., Planning Res. Cttee, Building Res. Station. Hon. ADK (Malaysia). DL Tyne and Wear, 1975. *Publications:* contribs to Sarawak Museum Jl and press articles on New Town Development. *Recreations:* gardening, theatre. *Address:* Ashfield House, 1 West Park Road, Cleadon, near Sunderland, Tyne and Wear. *T:* Boldon 2829. *Club:* Royal Commonwealth Society.

HOLLIDAY, Prof. Frederick George Thomas, CBE 1975; FRSE; Professor of Zoology, University of Aberdeen, since 1975; *b* 22 Sept. 1935; *s* of Alfred C. and Margaret Holliday; *m* 1957, Philippa Mary Davidson; one *s* one *d*. *Educ:* Bromsgrove County High Sch.; Sheffield Univ. BSc 1st cl. hons Zool. 1956; FIBiol 1970, FRSE 1971. Fisheries Research Trng Grant (Develt Commn) at Marine Lab., Aberdeen, 1956-58; Sci. Officer, Marine Lab., Aberdeen, 1958-61; Lectr in Zoology, Univ. of Aberdeen, 1961-66; Prof. of Biology, 1967-75, Dep. Principal, 1972, Acting Principal, 1973-75, Univ. of Stirling. Member: Scottish Cttee, Nature Conservancy, 1969; Council, Scottish Field Studies Assoc., 1970; Council, Scottish Marine Biol Assoc., 1967; Council, Freshwater Biol Assoc., 1969-72; NERC Oceanography and Fisheries Research Grants Cttee, 1971; Council, NERC, 1973-; Nature Conservancy Council, 1975- (Dep. Chm., 1976-77, Chm., 1977-); Scottish Economic Council, 1975-; Council, Marine Biol Assoc. UK, 1975-; Oil Develt Council for Scotland, 1976-; Bd of Governors, Rowett Res. Inst., 1976-. *Publications:* numerous on fish biology and wildlife conservation in Adv. Mar. Biol., Fish Physiology, Oceanography and Marine Biology, etc. *Recreations:* shooting, fishing, local history, gardening. *Address:* 142 Hamilton Place, Aberdeen. *T:* Aberdeen 55606. *Club:* Royal Commonwealth Society.

HOLLIDAY, Gilbert Leonard Gibson, CMG 1954; HM Ambassador to Morocco, 1965-69, retired; *b* 10 April 1910; *s* of late Rev. Andrew Barnes Holliday and late Violet Holliday (*née* White), Wigton, Cumberland; *m* 1934, Anita Lopez (*d* 1952); two *s*; *m* 1958, Jane Mary Wilkinson; one *s* two *d*. *Educ:* Rydal Sch.; Queen's Coll., Oxford. Laming Travelling Fellow, Queen's Coll., Oxford, 1931-32; served in Consular and Diplomatic Services at Buenos Aires, Valparaiso, Santiago, Katowice, Los Angeles, Foreign Office, New York, Warsaw, Paris, Berne and Stockholm; Ambassador to Laos, 1956-58; Foreign Office, 1958-60; Ambassador to Bolivia, 1960-64. *Recreation:* gardening. *Address:* (home) Notton Lodge, Lacock, Chippenham, Wilts SN15 2NF; (business) Notton Nurseries, 4 Notton, Lacock, Chippenham, Wilts SN15 2NF. *T:* Lacock 282.

HOLLIDAY, Dr Robin, FRS 1976; Head, Division of Genetics, National Institute for Medical Research, since 1970; *b* 6 Nov. 1932; *s* of Clifford and Eunice Holliday; *m* 1957, Diana Collet (*née* Parsons); one *s* three *d*. *Educ:* Hitchin Grammar Sch.; Univ. of Cambridge (BA, PhD). Member, Scientific Staff: Dept of Genetics, John Innes Inst., Bayfordbury, Herts, 1958-65; Division of Microbiology, Nat. Inst. for Med. Research, 1965-70. *Publications:* numerous scientific papers on mechanisms of genetic recombination, repair and cellular ageing. *Recreations:* biology other than genetics, sculpture. *Address:* National Institute for Medical Research, Mill Hill, NW7 1AA; Brick Kiln Cottage, Ashridge Road, Berkhamsted, Herts. *T:* Little Gaddesden 2483.

HOLLIGER, Heinz; oboist and composer; *b* Langenthal, Switzerland, 1939; *m* Ursula Holliger, harpist. *Educ:* Berne Conservatoire; Paris; Basle; studied with Cassagnaud, Veress, Pierlot and Boulez. Played with Basle Orch., 1959-63; teacher of oboe, Freiburg Music Acad., 1965-. Appeared at all major European music festivals. Has inspired compositions by Berio, Penderecki, Stockhausen, Henze, Martin and others. Compositions include: Der magische Tänzer, Trio, Dona nobis pacem, Pneuma, Psalm, Cardiophonie, Kreis, Siebengesang, H for wind quintet, string quartet Atembogen. Has won many international prizes, incl. Geneva Competition first prize, 1959, and Munich Competition first prize, 1961. *Address:* c/o Ingpen & Williams Ltd, 14 Kensington Court, W8 5DN.

HOLLINGS, Hon. Sir (Alfred) Kenneth, MC 1944; Hon. Mr Justice Hollings; Judge of the High Court of Justice, Family Division (formerly Probate, Divorce and Admiralty Division), since 1971; Presiding Judge, Northern Circuit, since 1975; *b* 12 June 1918; *s* of Alfred Holdsworth Hollings and Rachel Elizabeth Hollings; *m* 1949, Harriet Evelyn Isabella, *d* of W. J. C. Fishbourne, Brussels; one *s* one *d.* *Educ:* Leys Sch., Cambridge; Clare Coll., Cambridge. Law Qualifying and Law Tripos, Cambridge, 1936-39; MA. Served RA (Shropshire Yeomanry), 1939-46. Called to Bar, Middle Temple, 1947; Master of the Bench, 1971. Practised Northern Circuit; QC 1966; Recorder of Bolton, 1968; Judge of County Courts, Circuit 5 (E Lancs), 1968-71. Prosecuting Counsel for Inland Revenue, Northern Circuit, 1965-66. *Recreations:* walking, music. *Address:* Royal Courts of Justice, Strand, WC2; The Hermitage, Holmes Chapel, Cheshire. *T:* Holmes Chapel 33130; 35 Chelsea Towers, SW3. *T:* 01-352 0789. *Club:* Tennis and Racquets (Manchester).

HOLLINGS, Rev. Michael Richard, MC 1943; Parish Priest, St Anselm, Southall, Middlesex, since 1970; *b* 30 Dec. 1921; *s* of Lieut-Commander Richard Eustace Hollings, RN, and Agnes Mary (*née* Hamilton-Dalrymple). *Educ:* Beaumont Coll.; St Catherine's Society, Oxford (MA). St Catherine's, 1939; Sandhurst, 1941. Served War of 1939-45 (despatches): commnd Coldstream Guards, 1941; served N. Africa, Italy, Palestine, 1942-45; Major. Trained at Beda Coll., Rome, 1946-50. Ordained Rome, 1950; Asst Priest, St Patrick's, Soho Square, W1, 1950-54; Chaplain, Westminster Cathedral, 1954-58; Asst Chaplain, London Univ., 1958-59; Religious Adviser: ATV, 1958-59; Rediffusion, 1959-68; Thames Television, 1968. Member: Nat. Catholic Radio and TV Commn, 1968; Westminster Diocesan Schools Commn, 1970-; Southall Chamber of Commerce, 1971-; Oxford and Cambridge Catholic Educn Bd, 1971-; Executive, Council of Christians and Jews, 1971-; Lay Mem., Press Council, 1969-75; Exec., Ealing Community Relations Council, 1973-76; Nat. Conf. of Priests Standing Cttee, 1974-76. Chaplain: to Sovereign Military Order of Malta, 1957; to Roman Catholics at Oxford Univ., 1959-70; to Nat. Council of Lay Apostolate, 1970-74; to Catholic Inst. of Internat. Relations, 1971-. *Publications:* Hey, You!, 1955; Purple Times, 1957; Chaplaincraft, 1963; The One Who Listens, 1971; The Pastoral Care of Homosexuals, 1971; It's Me, O Lord, 1972; Day by Day, 1972; The Shade of His Hand, 1973; Restoring the Streets, 1974; I Will Be There, 1975; You Must Be Joking, Lord, 1975; The Catholic Prayer Book, 1976; Alive to Death, 1976; Living Priesthood, 1977; contrib. Tablet, Clergy Review, Life of the Spirit. *Recreations:* reading, walking, people. *Address:* St Anselm's Rectory, The Green, Southall, Mddx. *T:* 01-574 0167. *Club:* Athenæum.

HOLLINGSWORTH, Dorothy Frances, OBE 1958; Director-General, British Nutrition Foundation, since 1970; *b* 10 May 1916; *d* of Arthur Hollingsworth and Dorothy Hollingsworth (*née* Coldwell). *Educ:* Newcastle upon Tyne Church High Sch.; Univ. of Durham (BSc (2nd Cl. Hons Chemistry) 1937); Royal Infirmary, Edinburgh, Sch. of Dietetics (Dip. in Dietetics). Hosp. Dietitian, Royal Northern Hosp., London, N7, 1939-41; Govt Service, 1941-70: mainly at Min. of Food until its merger with Min. of Agric. and Fisheries, 1955, to form present Min. of Agric., Fisheries and Food. Principal Scientific Officer and Head of a Scientific Br., 1949-70 (Br. name was formerly Nutrition Br. and latterly Food Science Advice Br.). Chairman: British Dietetic Assoc., 1947-49; Internat. Cttee of Dietetic Assocs; 3rd Internat. Cong. Dietetics, 1961; Nutrition Panel, Food Gp, Soc. Chem. Ind., 1966-69 (Mem. Food Gp Cttee, 1969-72); Member: Nat. Food Survey Cttee, 1951-; Dietetics Bd, Council for Professions Supp. to Med., 1962-74; Cttee on Med. Aspects of Food Policy, 1970-; Physiological Systems and Disorders Bd, MRC, 1974-; Environmental Medicine Res. Policy Cttee, MRC, 1975-76; (Vice-Pres.) Inst. Food Sci. and Technol., 1970-; Council, Nutrition Soc., 1974-; (Dep. Chm.) Adv. Cttee on Protein, ODA, FCO, 1970-73; Jt ARC/MRC Cttee on Food and Nutrition Res., 1970-74; Royal Soc. British

Nat. Cttee for Nutritional Scis, 1970-; IBA Med. Adv. Panel, 1970-; Univ. of Reading Delegacy for Nat. Inst. for Res. in Dairying, 1973-. Institute of Biology: Mem. Council, 1964-69; Chm., Membership Cttee, 1967-69; Fellowship Cttee, 1970-73; Mem. Council, Internat. Union of Nutritional Scis, 1975-. FRIC 1956; State Registered Dietitian (SRD) 1963; Fellow of Inst. of Food Science and Technology, 1965; FIBiol 1968. *Publications:* The Englishman's Food, by J. C. Drummond and Anne Wilbraham (rev. and prod. 2nd edn), 1958; Hutchison's Food and the Principles of Nutrition (rev. and ed 12th edn with H. M. Sinclair), 1969; Nutritional Problems in a Changing World (ed, with Margaret Russell), 1973; (ed with E. Morse) People and Food Tomorrow, 1976; many papers in scientific jls. *Recreations:* talking with intelligent and humorous friends; appreciation of music, theatre and countryside; gardening. *Address:* 2 The Close, Petts Wood, Orpington, Kent BR5 1JA. *T:* Orpington 23168. *Clubs:* University Women's, Arts Theatre.

HOLLINGWORTH, John Harold; *b* 11 July 1930; *s* of Harold Hollingworth, Harborne, Birmingham; *m* 1968, Susan Barbara, *d* of J. H. Walters, Ramsey, IoM. *Educ:* Chigwell House Sch.; King Edward's Sch., Edgbaston. MP (C) All Saints Division of Birmingham, 1959-64. Chm., Edgbaston Div. Conservative Assoc., 1967; Vice-Chm., Birmingham Conservative Assoc., 1959-61, 1972- (Vice-Pres. 1960). *Publications:* contributions to political journals. *Recreations:* cricket, tennis. *Address:* Badge Court Cottage, Cooksey Green, Elmbridge, near Droitwich, Worcs. *T:* Cutnall Green 208.

HOLLINS, Rear-Adm. Hubert Walter Elphinstone, CB 1974; General Manager, Middle East Navigation Aids Service, Bahrain, since 1977; *b* 8 June 1923; *s* of Lt-Col W. T. Hollins; *m* 1963, Jillian Mary McAlpin; one *s* one *d.* *Educ:* Stubbington House; Britannia RNC Dartmouth. Cadet RN, 1937; Comdr 1957; Captain 1963; Rear-Adm. 1972; comd HM Ships Petard, Dundas, Caesar and Antrim; Flag Officer, Gibraltar, 1972-74; Admiral Commanding Reserves, 1974-77. MBIM. *Recreations:* fishing, shooting. *Address:* Roselands, Bucklebury, Berks. *T:* Bradfield 551; Middle East Navigation Aids Service, PO Box 66; Manama, Bahrain. *T:* Bahrain 8486.

HOLLIS, Anthony Barnard, QC 1969; a Recorder of the Crown Court, since 1976; *b* 11 May 1927; *er s* of late Henry Lewis Hollis and of Gladys Florence Hollis (*née* Barnard); *m* 1956, Pauline Mary (*née* Skuce); no *c.* *Educ:* Tonbridge Sch.; St Peter's Hall, Oxford. Called to Bar, Gray's Inn, 1951. *Recreation:* golf. *Address:* 1 King's Bench Walk, Temple, EC4. *T:* 01-353 4423. *Clubs:* Woking Golf; Royal St George's Golf (Sandwich).

HOLLIS, Rt. Rev. (Arthur) Michael; *b* 23 June 1899; *s* of late Right Rev. George Arthur Hollis, Bishop of Taunton; *m* 1935, Mary Cordelia, *d* of late Very Rev. Andrew Ewbank Burn, Dean of Salisbury. *Educ:* Leeds Grammar Sch.; Trinity Coll., Oxford (Scholar). Army, 1918-19; BA (2nd class Classical Hon. Mods) 1920; 1st class Litt. Hum., 1922; MA, 1924; BD, 1931; Leeds Clergy Sch., 1922; ordained deacon, 1923; priest, 1924; Curate S Andrew's, Huddersfield, 1923-24; Chaplain and Lecturer in Theology, Hertford Coll., Oxford, Fellow, 1926-31; Lecturer St Peter's Leeds, 1931; SPG Missionary, Bishop's Theological Seminary, Nazareth, diocese of Tinnevelly, India, 1931-37; Perpetual Curate of S Mary's Charlton Kings, diocese of Gloucester, 1937-42; CF 4th class (RARO) 1939-42; Bishop of Madras, 1942-47; Bishop in Madras, 1947-54; Moderator, Church of South India, 1948-54; Professor of Church History, United Theological Coll., Bangalore, 1955-60; Rector of Todwick, 1961-64; Second Assistant Bishop to the Bishop of Sheffield, 1963-66; Asst Bishop, Dio. of St Edmundsbury and Ipswich, 1966-75. Teaching, USA, 1960-61. *Publications:* Paternalism and the Church; The Significance of South India; Mission, Unity and Truth. *Address:* 72 Rembrandt Way, Bury St Edmunds, Suffolk.

HOLLIS, Daniel Ayrton, VRD; QC 1968; a Recorder of the Crown Court, since 1972; *b* 30 April 1925; *s* of Norman Hollis; *m* 1st, 1950, Gillian Mary Turner (marr. diss., 1961), *d* of J. W. Cecil Turner, Cambridge; one *s* one *d* ; 2nd, 1963, Stella Hydleman, *d* of Mark M. Gergel; one *s.* *Educ:* Geelong Grammar Sch., Australia; Brasenose Coll., Oxford. Served N Atlantic and Mediterranean, 1943-46. Lieut-Commander, RNVR. Called to Bar, Middle Temple, 1949; Bencher, 1975. Standing Counsel to Inland Revenue at Central Criminal Court and London Sessions, 1965-68; Dep. Chm., Kent QS, 1970-71. *Recreation:* travel. *Address:* Queen Elizabeth Building, Temple, EC4.

HOLLIS, Ven. Gerald; Archdeacon of Birmingham, since 1974; *b* Board, 1972-77; *s* of Canon Walter Hollis and Enid (*née* Inchbold); *m* 1946, Doreen Emmet Stancliffe; one *s* three *d.*

Educ: St Edward's Sch., Oxford; Christ Church, Oxford (MA); Wells Theological College. RNVR, 1940-45: on Staff RN Coll., Dartmouth, 1941-45. Curate: All Saints, Stepney, El, 1947-50; i/c St Luke's, Rossington, 1950-55; Rector, Armthorpe, 1955-60; Vicar of Rotherham and Rural Dean, 1960-74; Proctor in Convocation, dio. Sheffield, 1967-75; Hon. Canon Sheffield Cathedral, 1970. Mem. Gen. Synod, C of E, 1975-. *Publication:* Rugger: do it this way, 1946. *Recreation:* gardening. *Address:* Glengariff, 59 Salisbury Road, Moseley, Birmingham B13 8LB. *T:* 021-449 1642. *Club:* Vincent's (Oxford).

HOLLIS, Hugh; part-time Chairman for Civil Service Commission Appointments Board, 1972-77; *b* 25 July 1910; *s* of Ash and Emily Geraldine Hollis; *m* 1939, Muriel Bewick Hollis (*née* Nattrass); two *s. Educ:* Stockton Sec. Sch.; Constantine Techn. College. BSc Hons London; CChem; FRIC. Imperial Chemical Industries, 1928-36; Chemist, War Office, 1936-40; Principal Scientific Officer, Min. of Supply, 1940-56; Army Dept, MoD, 1956-71: Asst Dir Chemical Inspectorate; Dir 1963, title changed to Dir of Quality Assce (Materials), MoD, 1969-71 (CSO 1970), retired 1971. *Publications:* articles in Jl of Oil and Colour Chemists Assoc. and Inst. of Petroleum. *Recreations:* gardening, trout and salmon fishing. *Address:* Green Point, Fossebridge, Cheltenham, Glos. *T:* Fossebridge 463.

HOLLIS, Rt. Rev. Michael; *see* Hollis, Rt Rev. A. M.

HOLLIS, Rt. Rev. Reginald; *see* Montreal, Bishop of.

HOLLOM, Sir Jasper (Quintus), KBE 1975; Deputy Governor, Bank of England, since 1970; *b* 16 Dec. 1917; *s* of Arthur and Kate Louisa Hollom; *m* 1954, Patricia Elizabeth Mary Ellis. *Educ:* King's Sch., Bruton. Entered Bank of England, 1936; appointed Deputy Chief Cashier, 1956; Chief Cashier, 1962-66; Director, 1966-70. One of HM Lieutenants, City of London, 1970-. *Address:* Tiryns, Forest Road, Wokingham, Berks. *T:* Wokingham 781527.

HOLLOWAY, Derrick Robert Le Blond; Registrar of the Family Division, Principal Registry, since 1966; *b* 29 May 1917; *s* of Robert Fabyan Le Blond and Mary Beatrice Holloway; *m* 1942, Muriel Victoria Bower; one *s. Educ:* Brentwood; Univ. of London (LLB (Hons)). Principal Probate Registry, 1937. Served War of 1939-45: DCLI, RASC, Claims Commn. Sec., Cttee on Law of Intestate Succession, 1951; Sec., Cttee on Ancient Probate Records, 1953; Asst Sec., Royal Commn on Marriage and Divorce, 1952-56; Acting Registrar, Probate, Divorce and Admiralty Div., 1965. *Publications:* (ed jtly) Latey on Divorce (14th edn), 1952; Editor: Proving a Will (2nd edn), 1952; Obtaining Letters of Administration, 1954; Divorce Forms and Precedents, 1959; Probate Handbook, 1961, 4th edn 1976; Phillips' Probate Practice (6th edn), 1963; contrib. to Butterworths' Costs (4th edn), 1971. *Recreations:* marriage, gardening, foreign travel, music. *Address:* Brancaster, 15 Brookmans Avenue, Brookmans Park, Herts.

HOLLOWAY, Frank, FCA; Managing Director, Finance and Supplies, British Steel Corporation, since 1976; *b* 20 Oct. 1924; *s* of Frank and Elizabeth Holloway; *m* 1949, Elizabeth Beattie; three *d. Educ:* Burnage High Sch., Manchester. Served War, Royal Navy, 1943-46. Various senior finance appts in The United Steel Companies Ltd and later in British Steel Corp., 1949-72. Managing Dir, Supplies and Production Control, British Steel Corp., 1973-76. *Recreations:* cricket; owning and reading books. *Address:* 11 Copperfield Way, Chislehurst, Kent BR7 6RY. *T:* 01-467 9559.

HOLLOWAY, Gwendoline Elizabeth, BA Hons; *b* 9 April 1893. *Educ:* University of Bristol (Hall of Residence, Clifton Hill House). Asst Mistress at Harrogate College for Girls, 1917-26; Vice-Principal, Queen's Coll., 1926-31; Acting Principal, 1931-32; Principal, 1932-40; First woman to be appointed Principal of Queen's Coll.; Lady Principal of Alexandra Coll., Dublin, 1940-61; Headmistress, Lowther Coll., North Wales, 1961-63. President, Federation of Soroptimist Clubs of Great Britain and Ireland, 1948-49; Life Mem., Alumni Assoc., Univ. of Bristol (Pres. 1968-69). *Recreation:* walking.

HOLLOWAY, Prof. John, MA, DPhil, DLitt, LittD; Professor of Modern English, Cambridge, since 1972 (Reader, 1966-72); Fellow of Queens' College, 1955; *b* 1 Aug. 1920; *s* of George Holloway and Evelyn Astbury; *m* 1946, Audrey Gooding; one *s* one *d. Educ:* County Sch., Beckenham, Kent; New Coll., Oxford (Open History Scholar). 1st class Modern Greats, 1941; DPhil Oxon 1947; DLitt Aberdeen 1954; LittD Cambridge, 1969. Served War of 1939-45, commnd RA, 1942; subsequently seconded to Intelligence. Temporary Lecturer in Philosophy, New Coll., 1945; Fellow of All Souls Coll., 1946-60; John Locke

Scholar, 1947; University Lecturer in English, Aberdeen, 1949-54; University Lecturer in English, Cambridge, 1954-66; Sec., 1954-56, Librarian, 1964-66, Chm., 1970, 1971, English Faculty. FRSL 1956. Lecture Tour, Ceylon, India, Pakistan, 1958; Middle East, 1965; Byron Professor, University of Athens, 1961-63; Alexander White Professor, Chicago, 1965; Hinkley Prof., Johns Hopkins Univ., 1972. *Publications:* Language and Intelligence, 1951; The Victorian Sage, 1953; (ed) Poems of the Mid-Century, 1957; The Charted Mirror (Essays), 1960; (ed) Selections from Shelley, 1960; Shakespeare's Tragedies, 1961; The Colours of Clarity (essays), 1964; The Lion Hunt, 1964; Widening Horizons in English Verse, 1966; Blake, The Lyric Poetry, 1968; The Establishment of English, 1972; (ed with J. Black) Later English Broadside Ballads, 1975; The Proud Knowledge, 1977; contributions to journals; *verse:* The Minute, 1956; The Fugue, 1960; The Landfallers, 1962; Wood and Windfall, 1965; New Poems, 1970; Planet of Winds, 1977. *Recreation:* enjoyment. *Address:* Queens' College, Cambridge.

HOLLOWAY, John Edward, DSc; Hon. LLD, Hon. DCom; Director of Companies; *b* 4 July 1890; *s* of George John Holloway and Hester Maria Holloway (*née* Enslin); *m* 1913, Christina Maria Purchase (*d* 1967); one *s* three *d* (and one *d* decd). *Educ:* Stellenbosch Univ. (BA); London School of Economics. DSc (Econ) London, 1917, Hutchinson Research Medallist. Lecturer Grey University College, 1917-19; Lecturer and Professor Transvaal University College, 1919-25; Director Census and Statistics, 1925-33; Econ. Adviser to Treasury, 1934-37; Secretary for Finance, 1937-50; Chairman: Native Economic Commn, 1930-32; Customs Tariff Commn, 1934-35; Gold Mining Taxation Cttee, 1945; SW Africa Financial Commn, 1951; Univ. Finances Commn, 1951-53; Commn on Univ. Facilities for Non-Europeans, 1953; Member, SW Africa Commn, 1934-35; Transkeian Commn of Enquiry, 1962-63; Adviser Ottawa Conference, 1932, and Montreal Conference, 1958. World Economic Conference, 1933; Imperial Conference, 1937; Conferences of Finance Ministers, 1949, 1950, 1954; Delegate, Bretton Woods Conference, 1944; Leader S African Delegation: Conferences on Trade and Employment, Geneva, 1947, and Havana, 1948; formerly Alternate Governor IMF. Dir, Anglo-Alpha Cement; Consultant to Barclays National Bank; formerly Director: South African Marine Corporation; South African Iron and Steel Corporation, and other cos; Member Atomic Energy Board. Resigned from these boards when appointed Ambassador in Washington, July 1954; High Commissioner for The Union of South Africa in London, 1956-58. Former Vice-President, S African Foundation; Member of Council, University of Pretoria. *Publications:* Apartheid: a challenge, 1964; various articles, chiefly about gold in the monetary system and race relations in South Africa. *Recreations:* golf, bowls, fly-fishing. *Address:* 63 Fourth Street, Linden, Johannesburg, 2195, South Africa. *Clubs:* Civil Service (Cape Town); Pretoria Country (Pretoria, SA).

HOLLOWAY, Maj.-Gen. Robin Hugh Ferguson, CB 1976; CBE 1974; Director of Civil Defence, New Zealand; *b* Hawera, 22 May 1922; *s* of Hugh Ferguson Holloway and late Phyllis Myrtle Holloway; *m* 1947, Margaret Jewell, *d* of E. G. Monk, Temple Cloud, Somerset; one *s* two *d. Educ:* Hawera Technical High Sch.; RMC, Duntroon, Australia. Commnd NZ Staff Corps, 1942; served in 2nd NZEF, Solomon Is, Italy and Japan, 1943-47; qual. Air Observation Post Pilot, 1948-49; Staff Coll., Camberley, 1952; Jt Services Staff Coll., Latimer, 1958; Dir of Mil. Intelligence, 1959-61; Dep. Adjt Gen., 1962-63; Head, NZ Defence Liaison Staff, Singapore and Malaysia, 1964-65; ACDS, 1967-68; IDC, 1969; Comdr Northern Mil. Dist, and Comdr 1st Inf. Bde Gp, 1970; DCGS, 1971-73; CGS, 1973-76; R of O, March 1977. *Recreations:* gardening, golf. *Address:* 11 Joll Street, Karori, Wellington, New Zealand. *T:* Wellington 768120.

HOLLOWAY, Stanley, OBE 1960; Actor, Vocalist and Monologuist; *b* London, 1 Oct. 1890; *m* 1st, 1913; 2nd, 1939, Violet Marion Lane. Formerly seaside concert artist; first West End appearance as Capt. Wentworth in Kissing Time, Winter Garden, 1919; René in A Night Out, Winter Garden, 1920; original member of the Co-Optimists, and remained as one until disbandment, 1927; Bill Smith in Hit the Deck, London Hippodrome, 1927; Lieut Richard Manners in Song of the Sea, His Majesty's, 1928; Cooee, Vaudeville, 1929; appeared with the revived Co-Optimists, 1929, The Co-Optimists of 1930, London Hippodrome; Savoy Follies, Savoy, 1932; Here We Are Again, Lyceum, 1932; Eustace Titherley in Three Sisters, 1934; first appearance in pantomime, Prince of Wales's, Birmingham, 1934, as Abanazar in Aladdin, and has played same part each succeeding Christmas at Leeds, Golders Green, Edinburgh and Manchester; All Wave, Duke of York's, 1936; London Rhapsody, London Palladium, 1938; All The Best, season at Blackpool, 1938; Saville: in Up and Doing, 1940 and 1941 in

Fine and Dandy, 1942; Played First Gravedigger in Festival Production of Hamlet, New Theatre, 1951; Midsummer Night's Dream (with Old Vic at Edinburgh Festival, and subsequently Metropolitan Opera House, New York, followed by tour of USA and Canada); played Alfred Doolittle in New York production of My Fair Lady (musical version of Pygmalion), 1956-58 and in London production, Drury Lane, 1958-59; Burgess in Candida, Shaw Festival, Canada, 1970; Siege, Cambridge Theatre, 1972; William in You Never Can Tell, Shaw Festival, Canada, 1973; The Pleasure of His Company, tour of Australia and Hong Kong with Douglas Fairbanks Jnr, 1977. *Films:* Hamlet (Gravedigger), This Happy Breed, The Way Ahead, The Way to the Stars, Cæsar and Cleopatra, Champagne Charlie, The Perfect Woman, Midnight Episode, One Wild Oat, The Lavender Hill Mob, The Magic Box (Festival Film), Lady Godiva Rides Again, Meet Me To-night, The Titfield Thunderbolt, The Beggar's Opera, Meet Mr Lucifer, A Day to Remember, Fast and Loose, An Alligator Named Daisy, Jumping for Joy, No Trees in the Street, Alive and Kicking, No Love For Johnnie, On The Fiddle, My Fair Lady (Alfred Doolittle), Ten Little Indians, Mrs Brown You Have A Lovely Daughter, Run a Crooked Mile, Private Life of Sherlock Holmes, What's in it for Harry, The Flight of the Doves, Up the Front, Desperate Journey. TV series: Our Man Higgins, Hollywood, 1962-63; Thingamybob, London, 1968; TV film, Dr Jekyll and Mr Hyde, 1973. *Publication:* Wiv a Little Bit o' Luck (autobiography), 1967. *Address:* Pyefleet, Tamarisk Way, East Preston, Sussex.

HOLLOWOOD, A. Bernard, MSc(Econ); FRSA; Editor of Punch, 1957-68; author, economist and cartoonist; contributor of articles and drawings to Punch since 1942; Member of Punch Table since 1945; *b* 3 June 1910; 2nd *s* of Albert and Sarah Elizabeth Hollowood, Burslem, Staffordshire; *m* 1938, Marjorie Duncan, *d* of Dr W. D. Lawrie, Hartshill, Stoke-on-Trent; one *s* two *d. Educ:* Hanley High School; St Paul's Coll., Cheltenham; London University. Lecturer in Economics, School of Commerce, Stoke-on-Trent, and Loughborough Coll., 1932-43; lecturer to HM Forces; on staff of The Economist, 1944-45; Research Officer, Council of Industrial Design, 1946-47; Editor of Pottery and Glass, 1944-50; Pocket cartoonist of Sunday Times, 1957-60, The Times, Sunday Telegraph, etc. Broadcaster since 1939. Visiting Prof. at American Univs. Member, Court of Governors, London School of Economics. Hon. MA Keele, 1968. *Publications:* Direct Economics, 1943; Money is No Expense, 1946; An Innocent at Large, 1947; Britain Inside-Out, 1948; Scowle and Other Papers, 1948; Pottery and Glass, 1949; Poor Little Rich World, 1948; The Hawksmoor Scandals, 1949; Cornish Engineers, 1951; The Story of Morro Velho, 1954; Tory Story, 1964; Pont, The Story of Graham Laidler, 1969; Cricket on the Brain, 1970; Tales of Tommy Barr, 1970; Funny Money, 1975; Pamphlets and Papers on Economics. *Recreation:* village cricket (formerly county cricket: Staffordshire 1930-46). *Address:* Blackmoor Paddock, Haldish Lane, Shamley Green, Surrey. *T:* Bramley 2118.

HOLM PATRICK, 3rd Baron *cr* 1897; **James Hans Hamilton;** *b* 29 Nov. 1928; *s* of 2nd Baron and Lady Edina Ainsworth (*d* 1964), 4th *d* of 4th Marquess Conyngham; *S* father, 1942; *m* 1954, Anne Loys Roche, *o d* of Commander J. E. P. Brass, RN (retired); three *s. Heir: s* Hon. Hans James David Hamilton, *b* 15 March 1955. *Address:* Tara Beg, Dunsany, Co. Meath, Ireland.
See also Baron Swansea.

HOLMAN, Norman Frederick; *b* 22 Feb. 1914; *s* of late Walter John and Violet Holman, Taunton; *m* 1940, Louisa Young; one *s* two *d. Educ:* Huish's, Taunton. Entered Post Office as Exec. Officer, 1932; Higher Exec. Officer, 1942. Served in Royal Corps of Signals, 1942-46. Sen. Exec. Officer, 1950; Asst Accountant-Gen., 1953; Dep. Dir, 1956; Dir of Postal Finance, 1967; Dir of Central Finance and Accounts, PO, 1971-74. *Recreations:* bridge, tennis, The Observer crossword. *Address:* 29 Melbourne Avenue, Pinner, Mddx. *T:* 01-863 1669.

HOLMAN, Percy, BSc; Paper Merchant; *b* 5 April 1891; *s* of S. H. Holman; *m* 1918, Dorothy Anderson (*d* 1976); one *s* two *d. Educ:* Mill Hill Sch.; London School of Economics (London Univ.). Entered business 1913. Service in France with BRCS, 1915-18. Member Middlesex CC, 1928-31; Member Teddington UDC, 1928-34. Contested (Lab) Twickenham, 1931, 1932, 1934 and 1935; MP (Lab-Co-op) Bethnal Green, 1950-66, (Lab-Co-op) Bethnal Green South-West, 1945-50). *Recreation:* walking. *Address:* 3 Arundel Court, Wimbledon, SW19 4AF. *T:* 01-946 3497.

HOLMAN, Dr Portia Grenfell; Senior Physician in Psychological Medicine, Elizabeth Garrett Anderson Hospital, 1954-69, retired; *b* 20 Nov. 1903; *d* of Hon. William Arthur

Holman, KC, Premier of New South Wales, 1914-18, and Ada Augusta Kidgell. *Educ:* The Women's Coll., Sydney, NSW; Newnham Coll., Cambridge. Economics Tripos, 1923-26, BA Cantab, 1926. Research and lecturing at St Andrews Univ., 1927-33; MA Cantab 1923. Medical student, Cambridge and Royal Free Hospital, 1934-39. Consultant Psychiatrist to Twickenham Child Guidance Clinic, 1944, West Middlesex Hospital, 1945, Elizabeth Garrett Anderson Hospital, 1946. MD 1950; Burlingame Prize, 1952; FRCP 1961; FRCPsych 1971. Founder and first Chairman Association of Workers for Maladjusted Children, 1951. *Publications:* Bedwetting, 1954; Psychology and Psychological Medicine for Nurses, 1957; (with Amy Sycamore) Sebastians: hospital school experiment in therapeutic education, 1971; contributions to Journal of Mental Science. *Recreations:* mountain climbing, swimming. *Address:* 2 Prince Albert Road, NW1. *Club:* Royal Society of Medicine.

HOLMBERG, Eric Robert Reginald; Deputy Chief Scientist (Army), Ministry of Defence, since 1972; *b* 24 Aug. 1917; *s* of Robert and May Holmberg; *m* 1940, Wanda Erna Reich; one *s* one *d. Educ:* Sandown (Isle of Wight) Grammar Sch.; St John's Coll., Cambridge (MA); Imperial Coll., London (PhD). Joined Mine Design Department, Admiralty, 1940; Admiralty Gunnery Establishment, 1945; Operational Research Department, Admiralty, 1950; appointed Chief Supt Army Operational Research Group, 1956; Dir, Army Operational Science and Res., subseq. Asst Chief Scientist (Army), MoD, 1961-72. *Publications:* papers in Proc. Royal Astronomical Society. *Address:* 29 Westmoreland Road, Barnes, SW13. *T:* 01-748 2568.

HOLME, Maj.-Gen. Michael Walter, CBE 1966; MC 1945; *b* 9 May 1918; *s* of Thomas Walter Holme and Ruth Sangster Holme (*née* Rivington); *m* 1948, Sarah Christian Van Der Gucht; one *s* two *d. Educ:* Winchester College. Directing Staff, Staff Coll., Camberley, 1952-55; Comdr 1st Bn 3rd East Anglian Regt, 1960-62; Comdr Land Forces Persian Gulf, 1963-66; Chief of Staff, Western Comd, 1966-67; Divisional Brig., The Queen's Div., 1968-69; GOC Near East Land Forces, 1969-72, retired; Dep. Col, The Royal Anglian Regiment, 1970-77. *Recreations:* various. *Address:* c/o C. Hoare & Co., 37 Fleet Street, EC4; Glen Cottage, 145 Park Road, Camberley, Surrey. *Club:* Army and Navy.

HOLMER, Paul Cecil Henry, CMG 1973; HM Diplomatic Service; UK Deputy Permanent Representative to NATO, since 1976; *b* 19 Oct. 1923; *s* of Bernard Cecil and Mimi Claudine Holmer; *m* 1946, Irene Nora, *e d* of late Orlando Lenox Beater, DFC; two *s* two *d. Educ:* King's Sch., Canterbury; Balliol Coll., Oxford. Served in RA, 1942-46. Entered Civil Service, 1947; Colonial Office, 1947-49; transferred to HM Foreign Service, 1949; FO, 1949-51; Singapore, 1951-55; FO, 1955-56; served on Civil Service Selection Bd, 1956; FO, 1956-58; Moscow, 1958-59; Berlin, 1960-64; FO, 1964-66; Counsellor, 1966; Dep. High Comr, Singapore, 1966-69; Head of Security Dept, FCO, 1969-72; Ambassador, Ivory Coast, Upper Volta and Niger, 1972-75. Dir, African Develt Fund, 1973-75. *Address:* c/o Foreign and Commonwealth Office, SW1. *Club:* Travellers'.

HOLMES, David; Under Secretary, Department of Transport, since 1976; *b* 6 March 1935; *s* of late George A. Holmes and Annie Holmes; *m* 1963, Ann Chillingworth; one *s* two *d. Educ:* Doncaster Grammar Sch.; Christ Church, Oxford (MA). Asst Principal, Min. of Transport and Civil Aviation, 1957; Private Sec. to Jt Parly Sec., 1961-63; HM Treasury, 1965-68; Principal Private Sec. to Minister of Transport, 1968-70; Asst Sec., 1970. *Recreation:* music. *Address:* 15 The Orchard, Winchmore Hill, N21 2DN. *T:* 01-360 7134.

HOLMES, Sir (David) Ronald, Kt 1973; CMG 1969; CBE 1962 (MBE 1943); MC 1943; ED 1956; Chairman, Public Services Commission, Hong Kong, since 1971; *b* 26 Dec. 1913; *s* of late Louis James Holmes and late Emily Sutcliffe, Brighouse, W Yorks; *m* 1945, Marjorie Fisher, *d* of late Frank Hastings Fisher and Charlotte Fisher (*née* Gittins); two *s. Educ:* Bradford Grammar Sch.; Sidney Sussex Coll., Cambridge. Colonial Administrative Service, Hong Kong, 1938; various admin. posts. War service in Hong Kong and China, 1941-45, Major. Secretary for Chinese Affairs, Hong Kong, 1966; Secretary for Home Affairs, 1969-71. *Recreations:* reading, travel, golf. *Address:* 19 Severn Road, Hong Kong. *T:* Hong Kong 96966; San Luca, Gouvia, Corfu. *T:* Corfu 91411. *Clubs:* Hong Kong, Royal Hong Kong Golf, etc.

HOLMES, E(ric) M(ontagu) Price, CBE 1970; Manager, Legal Department, Beecham Group Ltd, 1946-74; Director, Magnet & Planet Building Society; *b* 26 Nov. 1909; *o s* of late Montagu Price Holmes, FSI, FAI and late Rose Holmes (*née* Chevens).

Educ: University College Sch., London; University Coll., Oxford (MA). Called to Bar, Inner Temple, 1933; Oxford Circuit. Served RA (TA), 1939-45; Major, GSO2, War Office. UNA: Chm. of Gen. Council, 1948-70; Chm., London Regional Council, 1947- (Pres. 1965); Chm. Exec. Cttee, 1970-72 and 1974-76, Vice-Chm., 1972-74; Pres., 1977. Delegate to World Fedn of UNAs, Marianske Lazne, Geneva, Warsaw, New York, Luxembourg, Moscow. Sec. to Governors, Ashridge Management Coll., 1962-74. Chm., St Marylebone Council of Churches, 1963-64. *Recreations:* reading, travel. *Address:* 42 St Stephens Close, Avenue Road, NW8 6DD. *T:* 01-722 0394. *Club:* Royal Over-Seas League.

HOLMES, Prof. Sir Frank (Wakefield), Kt 1975; JP; Chairman, New Zealand Planning Council, since 1977; *b* 8 Sept. 1924; *s* of James Francis Wakefield and Marie Esme Babette Holmes; *m* 1947, Nola Ruth Ross; two *s*. *Educ:* Waitaki Boys' Jun. High Sch. (Dux 1936); King's High Sch. (Dux 1941); Otago Univ.; Auckland University Coll. (Sen. Schol. 1948); Victoria University Coll. MA (1st Cl. Hons) 1949. Flying Officer, Royal NZ Air Force, 1942-45 (despatches). Economic Div., Prime Minister's and External Affairs Depts 1949-52; Lectr to Prof., Victoria Univ. of Wellington, 1952-67: Macarthy Prof. of Economics, 1959-67; Dean, Faculty of Commerce, 1961-63; Economics Manager, Tasman Pulp & Paper Co Ltd, 1967-70; Prof. of Money and Finance, Victoria Univ. of Wellington, 1970-77. Adviser, Royal Commn on Monetary, Banking and Credit Systems, 1955; Consultant, Bank of New Zealand, 1956-58 and 1964-67; Chm., Monetary and Economic Council, 1961-64 and 1970-72; Jt Sec., Cttee on Universities, 1959; Mem., NZ Council Educnl Research, 1965- (Chm. 1970-74); Chairman: Adv. Council on Educnl Planning and Steering Cttee, Educnl Develt Conf., 1973-74; NZ Govt Task Force on Economic and Social Planning, 1976. President: NZ Assoc. of Economists, 1961-63; Section G, ANZAAS, 1967; Central Council, Economic Soc. of Australia and NZ, 1967-68. Life Mem., VUW Students' Assoc., 1967. JP 1960. FRSA. *Publications:* Money, Finance and the Economy, 1972; pamphlets and articles on econs, finance, educn and internat. affairs. *Recreations:* camping, walking, swimming, tennis. *Address:* 16A Donald Crescent, Karori, Wellington 5, New Zealand. *T:* Wellington 768-779. *Club:* Wellington (Wellington).

HOLMES, Dr George Arthur; Fellow and Tutor, St Catherine's College, Oxford, since 1962; *b* 22 April 1927; *s* of late John Holmes and Margaret Holmes, Aberystwyth; *m* 1953, Evelyn Anne, *d* of late Dr John Klein and Audrey Klein; one *s* two *d* (and one *s* decd). *Educ:* Ardwyn County Sch., Aberystwyth; UC, Aberystwyth; St John's Coll., Cambridge (MA, PhD). Fellow, St John's Coll., Cambridge, 1951-54; Tutor, St Catherine's Society, Oxford, 1954-62; Mem., Inst. for Advanced Study, Princeton, 1967-68; Vice-Master, St Catherine's Coll., 1969-71. Jt Editor, English Historical Review, 1974-. *Publications:* The Estates of the Higher Nobility in Fourteenth-Century England, 1957; The Later Middle Ages, 1962; The Florentine Enlightenment 1400-1450, 1969; Europe: hierarchy and revolt 1320-1450, 1975; The Good Parliament, 1975; articles in learned jls. *Address:* St Catherine's College, Oxford.

HOLMES, George Dennis; Director-General and Deputy Chairman, Forestry Commission, since 1977; *b* 9 Nov. 1926; *s* of James Henry Holmes and Florence Holmes (*née* Jones); *m* 1953, Sheila Rosemary Woodger; three *d*. *Educ:* John Bright's Sch., Llandudno; Univ. of Wales (BSc (Hons)). Post-grad Research, Univ. of Wales, 1947; appointed Forestry Commission, 1948; Asst Silviculturist, Research Div., 1948; Asst Conservator, N Wales, 1962; Dir of Research, 1968; Comr for Harvesting and Marketing, 1973. FIFor; FIWSc. *Publications:* contribs to Forestry Commission pubns and to Brit. and Internat. forestry jls. *Recreations:* sailing, golf, walking. *Address:* Greskine, 7 Cammo Road, Barnton, Edinburgh EH4 8EF. *T:* 031-336 5502.

HOLMES, Brig. Kenneth Soar, CB 1963; CBE 1954; Managing Director, Posts, Postal Headquarters, 1971-72 (Senior Director, 1970-71); *b* 1912; *s* of W. J. Holmes, Ellesmere, Chaddesden Park Road, Derby; *m* 1936, Anne, *d* of C. A. Chapman, Leicester; one *s*. *Educ:* Bemrose Sch., Derby, and at Derby Technical Coll. Entered Post Office as Asst Traffic Superintendent (Telephones), 1930; Asst Surveyor, 1936; Principal, 1947; Asst Secretary, 1950. Served War of 1939-45 as Officer Commanding 43rd Division Postal Unit, with 21st Army Group and 2nd Army Headquarters, and as Asst Director of Army Postal Services, British Army of the Rhine. Director of: Army Postal Services, War Office, 1950-59; Mechanisation and Buildings, GPO, 1956-60; Postal Services, GPO, 1960-65; London Postal Region, 1965-70. Chairman Executive Cttee of Universal Postal Union, 1960-64. *Address:* 1 Wanderdown Road, Ovingdon, Brighton BN2 7BT. *T:* Brighton 37847.

HOLMES, Brigadier Leonard Geoffrey, CBE 1943; *b* 15 Jan. 1899; *s* of Lt-Col L. Holmes, TD; *m* 1940, Gladys May, *d* of Sir Robert James Black, 1st Bt; one *s*. *Educ:* Brighton Coll.; RMA, Woolwich. 2nd Lieut RA, Aug. 1916; European War, 1917-18; Staff Coll., Camberley, 1934-35; Middle East and North Africa, 1941-43; Brigadier 1949; retired 1953. *Address:* Headlams Well, Ipsden, Oxford.

HOLMES, Sir Maurice (Andrew), Kt 1969; Barrister-at-Law; *b* 28 July 1911; *o s* of Rev. A. T. Ellen Holmes; *m* 1935, Joyce Esther, *d* of late E. C. Hicks, JP, CC; no *c*. *Educ:* Felsted Sch., Essex. Served with RASC, 1941-45 (Major, despatches). Called to Bar, Gray's Inn, 1948; Practised at Bar, 1950-55. Director, 1955-60, Chairman, 1960-65, The Tilling Association Ltd; Chairman, London Transport Board, 1965-69. Circuit Administrator, South Eastern Circuit, 1970-74. Governor of Felsted School. *Recreations:* golf, music. *Address:* The Limes, Felsted, near Dunmow, Essex. *T:* Great Dunmow 820352. *Clubs:* Forty, MCC.

HOLMES, Maj.-Gen. Sir Noel Galway, KBE 1946 (CBE 1940); CB 1943; MC; *b* Galway, Ireland, 25 Dec. 1891; 4th *s* of late Capt. H. W. Holmes, Rockwood, Galway; *m* 1920, Mary, *er d* of late Sir Hugh Clifford, GCMG, GBE; one *s* one *d*. *Educ:* Bedford Sch. Joined Royal Irish Regt, 1912; India, 1912-14; served War of 1914-18, France (wounded, despatches four times. MC 1917, 1915 Star, War Medal, Victory Medal); Staff Course, Hesden, 1916, Cambridge, 1918; Bt Major, 1919; Temp. Lt-Col, AAQMG, Upper Silesia, 1921-22; trans. to East Yorkshire Regt, 1922; Staff Coll., 1926-27; Bde Major, Dover, 1929-31; GSO Southern Command, India, 1933-37; Bt Lt-Col, 1935; Commanded 1 Bn East Yorkshire Regt, 1938-39; served War of 1939-45 (Burma Star, Italy Star, France and Germany Medal, War Medal, Victory Medal); Maj.-Gen. JCO, MAFF and Dept of Agriculture and Fisheries for Scotland, Office, 1939-43; attended Chiefs of Staff confs, Washington, Quebec, Cairo, Teheran, Yalta and Potsdam; DQMG War Office, 1943-46; Commander Aldershot and Hampshire District, 1946; retired at own request, 1946; Chm., NE Divisional Coal Board (Yorkshire), 1946-57. Croix d'Officier of the Legion d'Honneur and Croix de Guerre with Palme, 1945; American Legion of Merit (Commander), 1946. *Recreations:* Davis Cup Lawn Tennis (Ireland), 1930; golf, shooting, etc. *Address:* Rockwood, Branksome Wood Road, Fleet, Hants GU13 8JU.

HOLMES, Sir Ronald; *see* Holmes, Sir D. R.

HOLMES, Sir Stanley, Kt 1974; DL; Chief Executive, Merseyside Metropolitan County Council, 1974-77; *b* 15 Dec. 1912; *s* of Stanley and Ethel Holmes, Liverpool; *m* 1939, Doris Elizabeth Burton; one *d*. *Educ:* Liverpool Collegiate School. Deputy Town Clerk, Liverpool, 1956, Town Clerk 1967; Chief Exec. and Town Clerk, 1969. DL County of Merseyside, 1974. Hon. LLD Liverpool, 1974. Kt 1st class Royal Norwegian Order of St Olaf, 1974. *Recreations:* people, places, paintings. *Address:* 44 Green Lane, Liverpool L18 6HD. *T:* 051-724 5432.

HOLMES, Sir Stephen (Lewis), KCMG 1950 (CMG 1942); MC 1918; MA; *b* 5 July 1896; *s* of late Basil Holmes and Isabella, *d* of Dr J. H. Gladstone, FRS; *m* 1922, Noreen, *o d* of late E. F. C. Trench, CBE, TD; one *s* one *d* (and one *s* decd). *Educ:* Westminster; Christ Church, Oxford. 2nd Lieut RGA (SR), 1915; served European War, France and Belgium, 1916-19 (MC, despatches twice, acting Major); entered Colonial Office, 1921; Principal, Dominions Office, 1928; Imperial Defence Coll., 1934; Senior Secretary, Office of High Commissioner for United Kingdom in Canada, 1936-39; Asst Sec., Dominions Office, 1939-43; Dominions Office representative, Washington, 1943-44; Deputy High Commissioner for the United Kingdom, Canada, 1944-46; Under Secretary, Board of Trade, 1946; Second Secretary, Board of Trade, 1947-51; Deputy Under-Secretary of State, Commonwealth Relations Office, 1951-52; High Commissioner for the UK in Australia, 1952-56. Master of the Leathersellers' Company, 1967-68. *Address:* Pinyons, Sandhurst, Hawkhurst, Kent. *Club:* Athenæum.

HOLMES, Prof. William; Professor of Agriculture, Wye College, University of London, since 1955; *b* Kilbarchan, Renfrewshire, 16 Aug. 1922; *s* of William John Holmes, Bank Manager; *m* 1949, Jean Ishbel Campbell, BSc; two *d*. *Educ:* John Neilson Sch., Paisley; Glasgow Univ.; West of Scotland Agricultural Coll. BSc (Agric), NDD, 1942; NDA (Hons), 1943; PhD Glasgow, 1947; DSc London, 1966. Asst Executive Officer, S Ayrshire AEC, 1943-44; Hannah Dairy Research Inst.: Asst in Animal Husbandry, 1944-47; Head of Department of Dairy and Grassland Husbandry, 1947-55. Member, Cttee on Milk Composition in the UK, 1958-60; Governor, Grassland Research Inst., 1960-75; Pres., British Grassland Soc., 1968-69;

Pres., British Soc. of Animal Production, 1969-70; Member: Adv. Technical Cttee, Univ. of W Indies, 1969-74; several technical cttees of ARC, JCO, MAFF and Dept of Agriculture and Fisheries for Scotland, 1960-. *Publications:* papers in technical agricultural journals. *Recreations:* gardening, beekeeping, travel, study of organizations. *Address:* Amage, Wye, Kent. *T:* Wye 812372. *Club:* Farmers'.

HOLMES à COURT, family name of **Baron Heytesbury.**

HOLMES SELLORS, Patrick John; see Sellors.

HOLMPATRICK; see Holm Patrick.

HOLROYD, Michael de Courcy Fraser; author; *b* London, 27 Aug. 1935; *s* of Basil Holroyd and Ulla (*née* Hall). *Educ:* Eton Coll.; Maidenhead Public Library. Saxton Memorial Fellowship, 1964; Bollingen Fellowship, 1966; Winston Churchill Fellowship, 1971. Chm., Soc. of Authors, 1973-74; Chm., Nat. Book League, 1976-77. FRSL 1968. *Publications:* Hugh Kingsmill: a critical biography, 1964 (rev. edn 1971); Lytton Strachey: The Unknown Years, 1967 (rev. edn 1971); Lytton Strachey: The Years of Achievement, 1968 (rev. edn 1971); A Dog's Life: a novel, 1969; The Best of Hugh Kingsmill, 1970; Lytton Strachey By Himself, 1971; Unreceived Opinions, 1973; Augustus John (2 vols), 1974, 1975; (with M. Easton) The Art of Augustus John, 1974; contribs to Times, Encounter, Spectator, etc. *Recreations:* listening to stories, avoiding tame animals, being polite, music, sleep. *Address:* c/o William Heinemann Ltd, 15 Queen Street, Mayfair, W1X 8BE. *T:* 01-493 4141.

HOLROYDE, Geoffrey Vernon; Director, Lanchester Polytechnic, since 1975; *b* 18 Sept. 1928; *s* of Harold and Kathleen Holroyde; *m* 1960, Elizabeth Mary, *d* of Rev. E. O. Connell; two *s* two *d*. *Educ:* Wrekin Coll.; Birmingham Univ. (BSc). ARCO. Royal Navy, 1949-54 and 1956-61; Welbeck Coll., 1954-56; English Electric, becoming Principal of Staff Coll., Dunchurch, 1961-70; British Leyland, Head Office Training Staff, 1970-71; Head, Sidney Stringer Sch. and Community Coll., Coventry, 1971-75. *Publications:* Managing People, 1968; Delegation, 1969; Organs of St Mary, Warwick, 1969. *Recreations:* music (organ and choir), canals, sailing, outdoor pursuits. *Address:* 5 Cape Road, Warwick. *T:* Warwick 42329.

HOLST, Imogen Clare, CBE 1975; musician; *b* 12 April 1907; *d* of Gustav Holst and Isobel (*née* Harrison). *Educ:* St Paul's Girls' Sch.; Royal Coll. of Music (ARCM). CEMA organiser, 1940-42; Dir of Music, Arts Centre, Dartington Hall, 1943-51; Musical Asst to Benjamin Britten, 1952-64; Conductor of Purcell Singers, 1953-67; Artistic Dir of Aldeburgh Festival, 1956-. FRCM 1966; Hon. Dr, Essex, 1968; Hon. DLitt Exeter, 1969; Hon. RAM, 1970. *Publications:* Gustav Holst: a biography, 1938, 2nd edn 1969; The Music of Gustav Holst, 1951, 2nd edn 1968; Tune, 1962; An ABC of Music, 1963; Bach, 1964; Britten, 1966; Byrd, 1972; Conducting a Choir, 1973; Holst, 1974; A Thematic Catalogue of Gustav Holst's Music, 1974. *Recreation:* walking. *Address:* 9 Church Walk, Aldeburgh, Suffolk IP15 5DU. *Club:* University Women's.

HOLT, Arthur Frederick; Chairman, Holt Hosiery Co. Ltd, Bolton, 1971-73; *b* 8 Aug. 1914; *m* 1939, Kathleen Mary, *d* of A. C. Openshaw, Turton, nr Bolton; one *s* one *d*. *Educ:* Mill Hill Sch.; Manchester Univ. Army Territorial Officer (5th Loyals), 1939-45; taken prisoner, Singapore, 1942-45; despatches twice, 1946. MP (L) Bolton West, 1951-64; Liberal Chief Whip, 1962-63. Pres., Liberal Party, Sept. 1974-Sept. 1975. *Recreation:* golf. *Address:* Harwood Lodge West, Harwood, near Bolton, Lancs. *T:* Bolton 21179. *Club:* Reform.

HOLT, Constance, CBE 1975; Area Nursing Officer, Manchester Area Health Authority (Teaching), 1973-77; *b* 5 Jan. 1924; *d* of Ernest Biddulph and of Ada Biddulph (*née* Robley); *m* 1975, Robert Lord Holt, OBE, FRCS. *Educ:* Whalley Range High Sch. for Girls, Manchester; Manchester Royal Infirmary (SRN); Queen Charlotte's Hosp., London; St Mary's Hosp., Manchester (SCM); Royal Coll. of Nursing, London Univ. (Sister Tutor Dipl.); Univ. of Washington (Florence Nightingale Schol., Fulbright Award). Nursing Officer, Min. of Health, 1959-65; Chief Nursing Officer: United Oxford Hosps, 1965-69; United Manchester Hosps, 1969-73. Pres., Assoc. of Nurse Administrators (formerly Assoc. of Hosp. Matrons), 1972-. Hon. Lectr, Dept of Nursing, Univ. of Manchester, 1972. *Publications:* articles in British and internat. nursing press. *Recreations:* reading, gardening, music. *Address:* High Bank, Didsbury, Manchester M20 8RQ.

HOLT, Herbert, RP; portrait painter; *b* 7 Aug. 1894; *s* of Henry A. Holt, stained-glass artist, and Alice Seddon, schoolmistress; *m* Nora Norbury; one *s*. *Educ:* Cowley Sch., St Helens; St Helens, Liverpool and Slade Art Schools. *Publication:* Portrait Painting in Oils, 1958. *Address:* 3 Bathurst Street, Blackburn, Lancs. *T:* Blackburn 61461. *Clubs:* Chelsea Arts; Artists', Liverpool, Liver Sketching (Liverpool).

HOLT, Jack; see Holt, John Lapworth.

HOLT, Sir James (Arthur), Kt 1960; Co-ordinator General of Public Works, Queensland, 1954-68, retired; director of companies since 1969; *b* 30 April 1899; *s* of James and Delia Holt; *m* 1932, Audrey May Benson; three *s* one *d*. *Educ:* Sydney High Sch.; Sydney Univ. (BE). Engineering draftsman, Sydney Harbour Bridge, 1922-27; Supervising Engineer, Sydney Harbour Bridge, 1927-32; Engineer-in-Charge, District Office, Department of Main Roads, NSW, 1933; Supervising Engineer, for design and construction contract for Story Bridge, Brisbane, 1934-40; Chief Engineer, Bridge Board, Queensland, 1940-49 (Engineer-in-charge, Allied Works Council, Cairns, 1943-44); Chief Engineer, Co-ordinator General's Dept, Queensland, 1949-53. Peter Nicol Russell Memorial Medal, Instn of Engineers, Australia, 1961, Hon. FIEAust, 1971. DEng (*hc*), University of Queensland, 1965. *Publications:* contributions to Journal of Institution of Engineers, Australia; papers on: The Story Bridge, Brisbane; The Fitzroy Bridge, Rockhampton. *Recreations:* bowls and surfing. *Address:* 11 Hawken Drive, St Lucia, Brisbane, Queensland 4067, Australia. *T:* 370 7707. *Clubs:* University of Queensland; St Lucia Bowls.

HOLT, Prof. James Clarke; Professor of History, University of Reading, 1966-78; Dean of Faculty of Letters and Social Sciences, 1972-76; Professor of Mediaeval History, Cambridge University, from Oct. 1978; *b* 26 April 1922; *s* of Herbert and Eunice Holt; *m* 1950, Alice Catherine Elizabeth Suley; one *s*. *Educ:* Bradford Grammar Sch.; Queen's Coll., Oxford (Hastings Schol.). MA 1947; 1st cl. Modern Hist.; DPhil 1952. Served with RA, 1942-45 (Captain). Harmsworth Sen. Schol., Merton Coll., Oxford, 1947; Univ. of Nottingham: Asst Lectr, 1949; Lectr, 1951; Sen. Lectr, 1961; Prof. of Medieval History, 1962. Mem., Adv. Council on Public Records, 1974-. Raleigh Lectr, British Acad., 1975. *Publications:* The Northerners: a study in the reign of King John, 1961; Praestita Roll 14-18 John, 1964; Magna Carta, 1965; The Making of Magna Carta, 1966; Magna Carta and the Idea of Liberty, 1972; papers in English Historical Review, Past and Present, Economic History Review, Trans Royal Hist. Soc. *Recreations:* mountaineering, cricket, fly-fishing. *Address:* Monksway, 77 Southcote Lane, Reading, Berks. *T:* Reading 53941. *Clubs:* National Liberal, MCC; Wayfarers' (Liverpool).

HOLT, Sir James (Richard), KBE 1977 (CBE 1972); Managing Director, Sino-British Ltd, since 1957; *b* 24 Dec. 1912; *s* of Albert Edward Holt and Margaret Anne Holt; *m* 1974, Jennifer May Squires; one adopted *s* one adopted *d*. *Educ:* Bishop Vesey's Grammar Sch. Manager, Meklong Railway Co., Ltd, 1938-41; interned, Bangkok, 1942-45; Dir, Sino-British Ltd, 1946-56. *Recreations:* racing, swimming. *Address:* 11 Soi Pranang, Rajvithi Road, Bangkok, Thailand. *T:* 2518071; 71 Belwell Lane, Four Oaks, Sutton Coldfield, West Midlands B74 4TS. *T:* 021-308 0932. *Clubs:* East India and Public Schools, Oriental, Royal Automobile; Royal Bangkok Sports (Bangkok, Thailand).

HOLT, Sir John Anthony L.; see Langford-Holt.

HOLT, Rear-Adm. John Bayley, CB 1969; Director: Premmit Ltd; Elint Engineering Ltd; *b* 1 June 1912; *s* of Arthur Ogden Holt and Gertrude (*née* Bayley); *m* 1940, Olga Esme Creake; three *d*. *Educ:* William Hulme Grammar Sch., Manchester; Manchester Univ. BScTech (hons) 1933. FIEE. Electrical Engineer with various cos and electric power undertakings, 1933-41. Joined RN; engaged on degaussing and minesweeping research and development, later on radar and electrical engineering, for Fleet Air Arm, 1941-48; served in HMS Cumberland on Gunnery Trials, Naval Air Stations, HQ and Staff appointments; comd HMS Ariel, 1961-63; subsequently Director of Naval Officer Appointments (Engineering Officers), and Dir-Gen. Aircraft (Naval), 1967-70, Ministry of Defence. Former Naval ADC to HM The Queen. Commander 1948; Captain 1958; Rear-Admiral 1967. Chm., Surrey Br., SS&AFA. *Recreations:* sailing, gardening, sacred music. *Address:* Rowley Cottage, Thursley, Godalming, Surrey. *T:* Elstead 2140. *Club:* Naval and Military.

HOLT, John Lapworth, (Jack Holt); Founder and Director of Jack Holt Ltd and Holt group of companies, designers and suppliers of small boats and their fittings (Managing Director, 1946-77); *b* 18 April 1912; *s* of Herbert Holt and Annie (*née* Dawson); *m* 1936, Iris Eileen Thornton; one *s* one *d*. *Educ:* St Peter's Sch., London; Shoreditch Techn. Inst. (Schol.). Joiner, boat builder and designer, 1929-46; formed Jack Holt Ltd, 1946; designed: first British post-war sailing dinghy class, Merlin; first British factory-made do-it-yourself boat building kit to construct Internat. Cadet, for Yachting World magazine; International Enterprise, National Solo and Hornet, Heron, Rambler, Diamond, Lazy E, GP14, Vagabond, Mirror Dinghy, Mirror 16, and Pacer. Techn. Adviser to Royal Yachting Assoc. dinghy cttee, 1950-. Jt winner (with Beecher Moore) of 12ft Nat. Championship, 1946 and Merlin Championships, 1946, 1947 and 1949; Merlin Silver Tiller series winner, 1954-56; won Solo Dutch Nat. Championships, 1962. *Recreation:* small boat sailing. *Address:* 16 Shottfield Avenue, East Sheen, SW14 8EA. *T:* 01-876 8074. *Clubs:* Ranelagh Sailing, Wraysbury Lake Sailing, Chichester Yacht, Aldenham Sailing, Carrum Yacht, Black Rock Sailing.

HOLT, John Michael, FRCP; Consultant Physician, Radcliffe Infirmary, Oxford, since 1968; Fellow of Linacre College, Oxford, since 1968; *b* 8 March 1935; *s* of Frank and Constance Holt; *m* 1959, Sheila Margaret Morton; one *s* three *d*. *Educ:* St Peter's Sch., York; Univ. of St Andrews. MA Oxon; MD St Andrews; MSc Queen's Univ. Ont. Registrar and Lectr, Nuffield Dept of Medicine, Radcliffe Infirmary, Oxford, 1964-66; Med. Tutor, Univ. of Oxford, 1967-73; Dir of Clinical Studies, Univ. of Oxford, 1971-76. Sec. to Editors, Quarterly Jl of Medicine, 1975-. *Publications:* papers on disorders of blood and various med. topics in BMJ, Lancet, etc. *Recreations:* sailing, riding. *Address:* Old Whitehill, Tackley, Oxon OX5 3AB. *T:* Tackley 241.

HOLT, Prof. John Riley, FRS 1964; Professor of Experimental Physics, University of Liverpool, since 1966; *b* 15 Feb. 1918; *er s* of Frederick Holt and Annie (*née* Riley); *m* 1949, Joan Silvester Thomas; two *s*. *Educ:* Runcorn Secondary Sch.; University of Liverpool. PhD 1941. British Atomic Energy Project, Liverpool and Cambridge, 1940-45. University of Liverpool: Lecturer, 1945-53, Senior Lecturer, 1953-56, Reader, 1956-66. *Publications:* papers in scientific journals on nuclear physics and particle physics. *Recreation:* gardening. *Address:* Rydalmere, Stanley Avenue, Higher Bebington, Wirral L63 5QE. *T:* 051-608 2041.

HOLT, Mary; Her Honour Judge Holt; a Circuit Judge, since 1977; *d* of Henry James Holt, solicitor, and of Sarah Holt (*née* Chapman); unmarried. *Educ:* Park Sch., Preston; Girton Coll., Cambridge (MA, LLB, 1st cl. Hons). Called to the Bar, Gray's Inn, 1949. Practised on Northern circuit. Former Vice-Chm., Preston North Conservative Assoc.; Member: Nat. Exec. Council, 1969-72; Woman's Nat. Advisory Cttee, 1969-70; representative, Central Council, 1969-71. MP (C) Preston N, 1970-Feb. 1974. Contested (C) Preston N, Feb. and Oct. 1974. *Publication:* 2nd edn, Benas and Essenhigh's Precedents of Pleadings, 1956. *Recreation:* walking. *Address:* The Law Courts, Birmingham; Rose Bank, 208 Garstang Road, Fulwood, Preston, Lancs PR2 4RD. *Clubs:* Constitutional, Royal Commonwealth Society.

HOLT, Prof. Peter Malcolm; FBA 1975; FRHistS; Professor of History of the Near and Middle East, University of London, since 1975; *b* 28 Nov. 1918; *s* of Rev. Peter and Elizabeth Holt; *m* 1953, Nancy Bury (*née* Mawle); one *s* one *d*. *Educ:* Lord Williams's Grammar Sch., Thame; University Coll., Oxford (Schol.) (MA, DLitt). Sudan Civil Service: Min. of Education, 1941-53; Govt Archivist, 1954-55. School of Oriental and African Studies, London, 1955-; Prof. of Arab History, 1964-75. FRHistS 1973. *Publications:* The Mahdist state in the Sudan, 1958, 2nd edn 1970; A Modern History of the Sudan, 1961, 2nd edn 1963; Historians of the Middle East (co-ed with Bernard Lewis), 1962; Egypt and the Fertile Crescent, 1966; Political and Social Change in Modern Egypt (ed), 1968; The Cambridge History of Islam (co-ed with Ann K. S. Lambton and Bernard Lewis), 1970; Studies in the History of the Near East, 1973; The Eastern Mediterranean Lands in the period of the Crusades, 1977; articles in: Encyclopaedia of Islam, Bulletin of SOAS, Sudan Notes and Records, Jl of African History, English Historical Rev., etc. *Address:* School of Oriental and African Studies, Malet Street, WC1E 7HP. *T:* 01-637 2388. *Club:* United Oxford & Cambridge University.

HOLT, Richard Anthony Appleby; Chairman: Hutchinson Ltd since 1959; Hutchinson Printing Trust since 1957; Hutchinson Publishing Group since 1965; *b* 11 March 1920; *s* of Frederick Appleby Holt and Rae Vera Franz (*née* Hutchinson); *m* 1945, Daphne Vivien Pegram; three *s* two *d*. *Educ:* Harrow Sch.;

King's Coll., Cambridge. Served War of 1939-45, commissioned 60th Rifles, 1941; demobilised, 1946 (Major). Admitted Solicitor, 1949. Chm. of Governors, Harrow Sch. *Recreation:* lawn tennis. *Address:* 21 Pelham Crescent, SW7. *T:* 01-589 8469. *Clubs:* Garrick, All England Lawn Tennis, MCC.

HOLT, Victoria; *see* Hibbert, Eleanor.

HOLT, Dame Zara (Kate); *see* Bate, Dame Z. K.

HOLT SMITH, Charles; *see* Smith, Charles H.

HOLTBY, Very Rev. Robert Tinsley; Dean of Chichester, since 1977; *b* 25 Feb. 1921; *o s* of William and Elsie Holtby, Thornton-le-Dale, Yorkshire; *m* 1947, Mary, *er d* of late Rt Rev. Eric Graham; one *s* two *d*. *Educ:* York Minster Choir Sch.; Scarborough Coll. and High School. St Edmund Hall, Oxford, 1939; MA (2nd Class Mod. Hist.), 1946; BD 1957. Choral Scholar, King's Coll., Cambridge, 1944; MA (2nd Class Theol.), 1952. Cuddesdon Theological Coll. and Westcott House, Cambridge, 1943-46. Deacon, 1946; Priest, 1947. Curate of Pocklington, Yorks, 1946-48. Chaplain to the Forces, 1948-52: 14/20th King's Hussars, Catterick; Singapore; Priest-in-charge, Johore Bahru. Acting Chaplain, King's Coll., Cambridge, 1952; Chaplain and Asst Master, Malvern Coll., 1952-54; Chaplain and Assistant Master, St Edward's Sch., Oxford, 1954-58; Canon Residentiary of Carlisle and Diocesan Dir of Educn, 1959-67, Canon Emeritus, 1967-; Gen. Sec., Nat. Soc. for Promoting Religious Education, 1967-77; Chaplain to the High Sheriff of Cumberland, 1964, 1966. Sec., Schs Cttee, Church of England Bd of Educn, 1967-74; Gen. Sec., Church of England Bd of Educn, 1974-77. *Publications:* Daniel Waterland, A Study in 18th Century Orthodoxy, 1966; Carlisle Cathedral Library and Records, 1966; Eric Graham, 1888-1964, 1967; Carlisle Cathedral, 1969. *Recreations:* music, walking, history. *Address:* The Deanery, Chichester, West Sussex PO19 1PX. *T:* Chichester 83286. *Club:* United Oxford & Cambridge University.

HOLTHAM, Mrs Carmen Gloria, JP; Organiser, Thurrock Citizens' Advice Bureau, Grays, Essex, since 1971; Member, Supplementary Benefits Commission, since 1976; *b* Kingston, Jamaica, 13 July 1922; *née* Bradshaw. *Educ:* Adventist Girls Sch.; Kingston Technical Coll., Kingston, Jamaica; London Univ. (Extra-Mural Course, Dip. Sociol.); NW London Polytech. (Cert. Office Management); SW London Polytech. (Cert. in Counselling); NE London Polytech. (Post Grad. Dip. Inf. and Advice Studies). Govt of Jamaica, 1942-57; United Jewish Appeal, NY, USA, 1958; Resident, England, 1959-; HM Factory Inspectorate, 1959; ILEA, 1959-64; Inst. of Med. Social Workers, 1964-66; Social Services Dept, London Borough of Camden, 1966; Willesden Citizens' Advice Bureau, London Bor. of Brent, 1967-70. Member: ILEA Sch. Care Cttee, 1963-67; Brent Community Relns Council, 1968-70; Brent Youth Service, 1969-70; British Caribbean Assoc., 1969-; Magistrates Assoc., 1969-; Grays Probation and After-Care Service, 1971; Thurrock Social Services for Elderly, 1971-; Bd of Governors, Treetops Sch., Grays, 1975-. JP Mddx (Highgate Magistrates' Court), 1969-71, Essex (Grays Magistrates' Court), 1972-. *Recreations:* reading, the theatre, ceramics. *Address:* 52 Davall House, Grays, Essex. *T:* Grays Thurrock 70838. *Club:* Friends International.

HOLTON, Michael; Assistant Secretary, Ministry of Defence, since 1976; *b* 30 Sept. 1927; 3rd *s* of late George Arnold Holton and of Ethel (*née* Fountain), Hampstead Garden Suburb, London; *m* 1951, Daphne Elizabeth Bache; one *s* two *d*. *Educ:* Finchley County Grammar Sch.; London Sch. of Economics. National Service, RAF, 1946-48; Min. of Food, 1948-54; Air Ministry, 1955-61; MoD, 1961-68; Sec., Countryside Commn for Scotland, 1968-70; Sec., Carnegie UK Trust, 1971-75. Sec., European Conservation Year Cttee for Scotland, 1970; Member: Consultative Cttee, Family Fund, 1973-75; Bd, Cairngorm Sports Develt Co., 1973-; Council, Soc. for Promotion of Nature Conservation, 1976-. Hon. Sec., RAF Mountaineering Assoc., 1952-54; Hon. Sec., British Mountaineering Council, 1954-59. *Publication:* Training Handbook for RAF Mountain Rescue Teams, 1953. *Address:* 43 Willifield Way, NW11 7XU. *T:* 01-455 5421. *Clubs:* Athenæum, Alpine; Himalayan (Bombay).

HOLTTUM, Richard Eric, MA; ScD; FLS; *b* Linton, Cambs, 20 July 1895; *s* of Richard Holttum; *m* 1927, Ursula, *d* of J. W. Massey, Saffron Walden; two *d*. *Educ:* Friends' Sch., Saffron Walden; Bootham Sch., York; St John's Coll., Cambridge (Foundation Scholar). Natural Sciences Tripos, Part 2 (Botany) Class 1, and Frank Smart Prize, 1920; Junior Demonstrator in Botany, Cambridge Univ., 1920-22; Assistant Director, Botanic Gardens, Singapore, 1922-25, Director, 1925-49. Professor of Botany, University of Malaya, 1949-54; President: Singapore

Gardening Society, 1937-39, 1947-53; Singapore Rotary Club, 1939-41; British Pteridological Society, 1960-63; Section K (Botany) British Association for the Advancement of Science, 1961. Editor, Series II (Pteridophyta), Flora Malesiana, 1959-. Hon. DSc, University of Malaya, 1949. Linnean gold medal, 1964; VMH 1972; has foreign gold medals, etc., for orchids. *Publications:* Orchids of Malaya, 1953; Gardening in the Lowlands of Malaya, 1953; Plant Life in Malaya, 1954; Ferns of Malaya, 1955; botanical and horticultural papers, especially on ferns and orchids. *Address:* 50 Gloucester Court, Kew Gardens, Richmond, Surrey. *T:* 01-940 6157.

HOLYOAKE, Rt. Hon. Sir Keith Jacka, PC 1954; GCMG 1970; CH 1963; Governor-General of New Zealand, since 1977; *b* 11 Feb. 1904; *s* of Henry Victor and Esther Holyoake; *m* 1935, Norma Janet Ingram; two *s* three *d. Educ:* Tauranga; Hastings; Motueka. President Golden Bay Rugby Union, 1930-33; Nelson Provincial Pres. Farmers' Union, 1930-41; Member Dominion Executive, Farmers' Union, 1940-50. Dominion Vice-Pres., 1940-50. President, NZ Hop Marketing Cttee, 1938-41; Member Exec.: NZ Tobacco Growers' Federation; NZ Fruit Exporters' Association. MP (Nat) (for Motueka, 1932-38, for Pahiatu, 1943-77); Dep. Leader Opposition, NZ, 1947; Cabinet, 1949; Dep. Prime Minister and Minister of Agriculture, Marketing and Scientific Research, 1949-57; Prime Minister and Minister for Maori Affairs, Sept.-Dec. 1957; Leader of Opposition, 1957-60; Prime Minister and Minister of Foreign Affairs (formerly of External Affairs), 1960-72; Minister of State, 1975-77. Farmer; Represented NZ farmers at World Conf. in London, 1946; Chairman FAO Conference, Rome, 1955; Member: SEATO meetings, 1962-; Conf. on Cambodia, Djakarta, 1970; Commonwealth Heads of Govt Conf., Singapore, 1971; Five-Power Conf. on Defence and Annual Ministerial Meeting of SEATO, London, 1971; S Pacific Forum, Canberra, 1972. Freeman, City of London, 1969. Hon. LLD: Victoria University of Wellington; Seoul Univ., Korea. *Recreations:* tennis, gardening. *Address:* 52 Aurora Terrace, Wellington, NZ. *T:* 44-797. *Clubs:* Ruahine (Dannevirke); Pahiatua (Pahiatua); Wellington, National (Wellington).

HOMAN, Philip John Lindsay; Director, Metrication Board, 1974-76; *b* 20 July 1916; *e s* of late Arthur Buckhurst Homan and Gertrude Homan; *m* 1940, Elisabeth Clemency Hobson; two *s* one *d. Educ:* Maidstone Grammar Sch.; LSE. Estate Duty Office, Inland Revenue, 1935-49. Served in RN, 1941-46. Board of Trade, 1949-69: Asst Sec., Controller, Midland Region, 1960; Principal Controller, Scotland, 1966; Min. of Technology, 1969-70; Under-Sec. and Dir, Office for Scotland, DTI, 1970-71; Under-Sec., Vehicles and Mechanical Engrg Products Div., later Mechanical Engrg Div., DTI, 1971-74. *Address:* Redlands, Kiln Lane, Stokenham, Kingsbridge, S Devon. *See also T. B. Homan.*

HOMAN, Rear-Adm. Thomas Buckhurst; Director General, Naval Personal Services, 1974-78; *b* 9 April 1921; *s* of late Arthur Buckhurst Homan and Gertrude Homan, West Malling, Kent; *m* 1945, Christine Oliver; one *d. Educ:* Maidstone Grammar Sch. RN Cadet, 1939; served War of 1939-45 at sea; Comdr 1958; Captain 1965; Defence Intell. Staff, 1965; Sec. to Comdr Far East Fleet, 1967; idc 1970; Dir Naval Officer Appts (S), 1971; Captain HMS Pembroke, 1973; Rear-Adm. 1974. *Recreations:* reading, theatre, golf, cooking. *Address:* 602 Hood House, Dolphin Square, SW1V 3NJ. *T:* 01-828 5904. *Club:* Army and Navy. *See also P. J. L. Homan.*

HOMANS, Prof. George Caspar; Professor of Sociology, Harvard University, since 1953; Professor of Social Theory, University of Cambridge, 1955-56; *b* 11 Aug. 1910; *s* of Robert Homans and Abigail (*née* Adams); *m* 1941, Nancy Parshall Cooper; one *s* two *d. Educ:* St Paul's Sch., Concord, New Hampshire; Harvard Univ. (AB). Harvard Univ.: Junior Fellow, 1934-39; Instructor in Sociology, 1939-41; Associate Professor of Sociology, 1946-53; Simon Visiting Professor, University of Manchester, 1953; Visiting Professor, University of Kent, 1967. Overseas Fellow, Churchill Coll., Cambridge, 1972. Pres., American Sociological Assoc., 1963-64; Mem., Nat. Acad. of Sciences, USA, 1972. Officer, US Naval Reserve (Lieut-Commander), 1941-45. *Publications:* Massachusetts on the Sea, 1930; An Introduction to Pareto, 1934; Fatigue of Workers, 1941; English Villagers of the 13th Century, 1941; The Human Group, 1950; Marriage, Authority and Final Causes, 1955; Social Behaviour, 1961, rev. edn 1974; Sentiments and Activities, 1962; The Nature of Social Science, 1967. *Recreations:* forestry, sailing. *Address:* 11 Francis Avenue, Cambridge, Mass 02138, USA. *T:* 617-547-4737. *Club:* Tavern (Boston, USA).

HOME; *see* Douglas-Home.

HOME, 14th Earl of [Disclaimed his peerages for life, 23 Oct. 1963]; *see under* Home of the Hirsel, Baron.

HOME OF THE HIRSEL, Baron *cr* 1974 (Life Peer), of Coldstream; Alexander Frederick Douglas-Home, KT 1962; PC 1951; DL; Chancellor, Order of the Thistle, since 1973; First Chancellor of Heriot-Watt University, 1966-77; *b* 2 July 1903; *e s* of 13th Earl of Home (*d* 1951), KT, and Lilian (*d* 1966), *d* of 4th Earl of Durham; *S* father, 1951, but disclaimed his peerages for life, 23 Oct. 1963; *m* 1936, Elizabeth Hester, 2nd *d* of late Very Rev. C. A. Alington, DD; one *s* three *d. Educ:* Eton; Christ Church, Oxford. MP (U) South Lanark, 1931-45; MP (C) Lanark Div. of Lanarkshire, 1950-51; Parliamentary Private Sec. to the Prime Minister, 1937-40; Joint Parliamentary Under-Sec., Foreign Office, May-July 1945; Minister of State, Scottish Office, 1951-April 1955; Sec. of State for Commonwealth Relations, 1955-60; Dep. Leader of the House of Lords, 1956-57; Leader of the House of Lords, and Lord Pres. of the Council, 1957-60; Sec. of State for Foreign Affairs, 1960-63; MP (U) Kinross and W Perthshire, Nov. 1963-Sept. 1974; Prime Minister and First Lord of the Treasury, Oct. 1963-64; Leader of the Opposition, Oct. 1964-July 1965; Sec. of State for Foreign and Commonwealth Affairs, 1970-74. Hon. Pres., NATO Council, 1973. Captain, Royal Co. of Archers, Queen's Body Guard for Scotland, 1973. Mem., National Farmers' Union, 1964. DL Lanarkshire, 1960. Hon. DCL Oxon., 1960; Hon. Student of Christ Church, Oxford, 1962; Hon. LLD: Harvard, 1961; Edinburgh, 1962; Aberdeen, 1966; Liverpool, 1967; St Andrews, 1968; Hon. DSc Heriot-Watt, 1966. Hon. Master of the Bench, Inner Temple, 1963; Grand Master, Primrose League, 1966; Pres. of MCC, 1966-67. Freedom of Selkirk, 1963; Freedom of Edinburgh, 1969; Freedom of Coldstream, 1972. Hon. Freeman, Skinners' Co., 1968. *Publication:* The Way the Wind Blows (autobiog.), 1976. *Address:* House of Lords, SW1; The Hirsel, Coldstream, Berwickshire. *T:* Coldstream 2345; Castlemains, Douglas, Lanarkshire. *T:* Douglas, Lanark 241. *See also Hon. D. A. C. Douglas-Home, Hon. William Douglas-Home, Duke of Sutherland, J. C. V. Wilkes.*

HOME, Captain Archibald John Fitzwilliam M.; *see* Milne Home.

HOME, Sir David George, 13th Bt, *cr* 1671; late Temp. Major Argyll and Sutherland Highlanders; *b* 21 Jan. 1904; *o s* of Sir John Home, 12th Bt and Hon. Gwendolina H. R. Mostyn (*d* 1960), *sister* of 7th Baron Vaux of Harrowden; *S* father, 1938; *m* 1933, Sheila, *d* of late Mervyn Campbell Stephen; two *s* two *d. Educ:* Harrow; Jesus Coll., Cambridge (BA 1925). Member Royal Company of Archers (HM Body Guard for Scotland). FSA (Scotland). *Heir: s* John Home [*b* 1 June 1936; *m* 1966, Nancy Helen, *d* of H. G. Elliott, Perth, Western Australia, and *widow* of Commander Ian Macgregor, RAN; one *s* one *d.*] *Address:* Winterfield, North Berwick, East Lothian. *Clubs:* Brooks's; New (Edinburgh); Royal and Ancient (St Andrews). *See also Sir D. P. M. Malcolm, Bt.*

HOME, Hon. William Douglas-; dramatic author; *b* Edinburgh, 3 June 1912; *s* of 13th Earl of Home, KT; *m* 1951, Rachel Brand (*see* Baroness Dacre); one *s* three *d. Educ:* Eton; New Coll., Oxford (BA). Studied at Royal Academy of Dramatic Art, and has appeared on the West End stage. Formerly Captain RAC. Contested (Progressive Ind) Cathcart Division of Glasgow, April 1942, Windsor Division of Berks, June 1942, and Clay Cross Division of Derbyshire (Atlantic Charter), April 1944, (Liberal) South Edinburgh, 1957. Author of the following plays: Great Possessions, 1937; Passing By, 1940; Now Barabbas, 1947; The Chiltern Hundreds, 1947; Ambassador Extraordinary, 1948; Master of Arts, 1949; The Thistle and the Rose, 1949; Caro William, 1952; The Bad Samaritan, 1953; The Manor of Northstead, 1954; The Reluctant Debutante, 1955; The Iron Duchess, 1957; Aunt Edwina, 1959; Up a Gum Tree, 1960; The Bad Soldier Smith, 1961; The Cigarette Girl, 1962; The Drawing Room Tragedy, 1963; The Reluctant Peer, 1964; Two Accounts Rendered, 1964; Betzi, 1965; A Friend in Need, 1965; A Friend Indeed, 1966; The Secretary Bird, 1968; The Queen's Highland Servant, 1968; The Grouse Moor Image, 1968; The Jockey Club Stakes, 1970; Lloyd George Knew My Father, 1972; At the End of the Day, 1973; The Bank Manager, 1974; The Dame of Sark, 1974; In The Red, The Kingfisher, Rolls Hyphen Royce, The Perch, 1977. *Address:* Drayton House, East Meon, Hants. *T:* East Meon 250. *Club:* Travellers'. *See also Baron Home of the Hirsel.*

HONE, Sir Brian (William), Kt 1970; OBE 1969; Chairman, Commonwealth Secondary Schools Libraries Committee, 1971-75; *b* 1 July 1907; *s* of Dr F. S. Hone, CMG, Adelaide; *m* 1933,

A. E. Boyce; three s one d. Educ: Prince Alfred Coll., Adelaide; Univs of Adelaide and Oxford. Asst Master, Marlborough Coll., Wilts, 1933-40; Headmaster, Cranbrook Sch., Sydney, 1940-50; Headmaster, Melbourne Church of England Grammar Sch., 1950-70. Chm., HMC of Independent Schools of Australia, 1954-57; Mem. Council: Monash Univ., 1959- (Dep. Chancellor, 1973-74); Australian Nat. Univ., 1960-75, etc. *Publications:* Cricket Practice and Tactics, 1937; (ed jtly) The Independent School, 1967. *Recreations:* tennis, walking. *Address:* 97 Sackville Street, Kew, Victoria 3101, Australia. *Club:* Melbourne (Melbourne).

HONE, Sir Evelyn (Dennison), GCMG 1965 (KCMG 1959; CMG 1953); CVO 1954; OBE 1946; *b* 13 Dec. 1911; 2nd s of late Arthur Rickman Hone, MBE, Salisbury, S Rhodesia, and late Olive Gertrude Fairbridge (*née* Scanlen); *m* 1946, Helen Joy Mellor; one s two d. *Educ:* Wellington Coll.; Rhodes Univ., S Africa; New College, Oxford Univ. Rhodes Scholar (Rhodesia), 1931; entered Colonial Service as Administrative Officer (cadet), Tanganyika Territory, 1935; Secretary to Government, Seychelles, 1944; Asst Secretary, Palestine, 1946; Colonial Secretary, British Honduras, 1948-53. Chief Secretary: Aden, 1953-57, N Rhodesia, 1957-59; Governor of Northern Rhodesia, 1959-64 (when the territory became the Republic of Zambia). Adviser, West Africa Cttee, 1967-75. Member: Central Council, Royal Over-Seas League, 1969-74; Council, Royal African Soc., 1971-; Pres., Zambia Soc., 1969. Hon. LLD, Rhodes Univ., 1964. *Address:* The Mill House, North Marston, Buckingham MK18 3PD.

HONE, Maj.-Gen. Sir (Herbert) Ralph, KCMG 1951; KBE 1946 (CBE Mil. 1943); MC; TD; GCStJ 1973; QC Gibraltar 1934, QC Uganda 1938; barrister-at-law; *b* 3 May 1896; s of late Herbert Hone and Miriam Grace (*née* Dracott); *m* 1st, 1918, Elizabeth Daisy, d of James Matthews (marr. diss. 1944); one s one d ; 2nd, 1945, Sybil Mary, *widow* of Wing Commander G. Simond; one s. *Educ:* Varndean Grammar Sch., Brighton; London Univ. LLB (Hons). Barrister-at-law, Middle Temple. Inns of Court OTC. Gazetted London Irish Rifles, 1915; Lieut, 1916; Captain, 1918; served with BEF, France, 1916 and 1917-18 (wounded, MC), Staff Captain, Ministry of Munitions, 1918-20; Major R of O (TA); Asst Treas., Uganda, 1920; called to Bar; practised and went South Eastern Circuit, 1924-25; Registrar, High Court, Zanzibar, 1925; Resident Magistrate, Zanzibar, 1928; Crown Counsel, Tanganyika Territory, 1930; acted Asst Legal Adviser to the Colonial and Dominions Offices, Jan.-Aug. 1933; Attorney-General, Gibraltar, 1933-36; Commissioner for the Revision of the laws of Gibraltar, 1934; King's Jubilee medal, 1935; Chm., Gibraltar Govt Commn on Slum Clearance and Rent Restriction, 1936; Coronation Medal, 1937; Acting Chief Justice, Gibraltar, on several occasions; Attorney-General, Uganda, 1937-43; Chairman, Uganda Government Cttee on Museum policy, 1938; Commandant, Uganda Defence Force, 1940; Chief Legal Adviser, Political Branch, GHQ, Middle East, 1941; Chief Political Officer, GHQ, Middle East, 1942-43; General Staff, War Office, 1943-45; Chief Civil Affairs Officer, Malaya, 1945-46; Maj.-Gen., 1942-46 (despatches twice, CBE (mil.)); Secretary-General to Governor-General of Malaya, 1946-48; Dep. Commissioner-General in SE Asia, 1948-49; Coronation Medal, 1953. Governor and C-in-C, North Borneo, 1949-54; Head of Legal Division, CRO, 1954-61. Resumed practice at the Bar, 1961. Retd TA with Hon. rank Maj.-Gen., 1956. GCStJ 1973; Mem. Chapter Gen. Order of St John, 1954-. Vice-Pres., Royal Commonwealth Society; Constitutional Adviser, Kenya Govt, Dec. 1961-Jan. 1962; Constitutional Adviser to Mr Butler's Advisers on Central Africa, July-Oct. 1962; Constitutional Adviser to South Arabian Government, Oct. 1965-Jan. 1966, and to Bermuda Government, July-Nov. 1966. Appeal Comr under Civil Aviation Licensing Act, 1961-71; Standing Counsel, Grand Bahama Port Authority, 1962-75. *Publications:* Index to Gibraltar Laws, 1933; revised edn of Laws of Gibraltar, 1935; revised edn of Laws of the Bahamas, 1965; Handbook on Native Courts, etc. *Recreations:* tennis, badminton and philately. *Address:* 1 Paper Buildings, Temple, EC4. *T:* 01-353 0165; 56 Kenilworth Court, Lower Richmond Road, SW15. *T:* 01-788 3367. *Clubs:* Athenæum, Royal Commonwealth Society.

HONE, Robert Monro, MA; Headmaster, Exeter School, since 1966; *b* 2 March 1923; s of late Rt Rev. Campbell R. Hone; *m* 1958, Helen Isobel, d of late Col H. M. Cadell of Grange, OBE; three d. *Educ:* Winchester Coll. (Scholar); New Coll., Oxford (Scholar). Rifle Brigade, 1942-45. Asst Master, Clifton Coll., 1948-65 (Housemaster, 1958-65). *Address:* Exeter School, Exeter. *T:* Exeter 73679.

HONEYCOMBE, Prof. Robert William Kerr; Goldsmiths' Professor of Metallurgy, University of Cambridge, since 1966;

President of Clare Hall, since 1973; *b* 2 May 1921; s of William and Rachel Honeycombe (*née* Kerr); *m* 1947, June Collins; two d. *Educ:* Geelong Coll.; Univ. of Melbourne. Research Student, Department of Metallurgy, University of Melbourne, 1941-42; Research Officer, Commonwealth Scientific and Industrial Research Organization, Australia, 1942-47; ICI Research Fellow, Cavendish Laboratory, Cambridge, 1948-49; Royal Society Armourers and Brasiers' Research Fellow, Cavendish Laboratory, Cambridge, 1949-51; Senior Lecturer in Physical Metallurgy, University of Sheffield, 1951-55; Professor, 1955-66. Fellow of Trinity Hall, Cambridge, 1966-73, Hon. Fellow, 1975. Pres., Instn of Metallurgists, 1977; Vice President: Metals Soc., 1977-; Royal Institution, 1977-. Visiting Professor: University of Melbourne, 1962; Stanford Univ., 1965; Monash Univ., 1974. Mem. Ct of Assts, Goldsmiths' Co., 1977-. Hon. DAppSc Melbourne, 1974. Rosenhain Medal of Inst. of Metals, 1959; Sir George Beilby Gold Medal, 1963; Ste-Claire-Deville Medal, 1971; Inst. of Metals Lectr and Mehl Medallist, AIME, 1976. *Publications:* The Plastic Deformation of Metals, 1968; papers in Proc. Royal Soc., Jl Inst. of Metals, etc. *Recreations:* gardening, photography, tennis. *Address:* Barrabool, 46 Main Street, Hardwick, Cambridge CB3 7QS. *T:* Madingley 501.

HONEYMAN, Prof. Alexander Mackie, MA, BLitt, PhD; Professor of Oriental Languages in University of St Andrews, 1936-67; Fellow of Royal Asiatic Society; *b* 25 Nov. 1907; s of late A. M. Honeyman, Cupar, Fife; *m* 1935, Cecilia Mary, 2nd d of late J. Leslie Milne, Edinburgh; one s one d (and one d decd). *Educ:* Universities of St Andrews, Edinburgh, London (School of Oriental Studies), Zürich and Chicago (Oriental Institute). 1st Class Hons Classics, 1929; BLitt in Ancient Languages, 1930; Guthrie Scholar, 1930, University of St Andrews; Commonwealth Fellow, New York and Chicago, 1932-34; PhD Chicago, 1934; Maclean Scholar of University of Glasgow, 1934-35, in Palestine, etc; Interim Lectr in Hebrew and Oriental Languages, Univ. of St Andrews, 1935-36. External Examiner to Univ. of Glasgow, 1941-44, 1946, 1951-54; Univ. of Edinburgh, 1946-48; Queen's Univ., Belfast, 1947-49; Univ. of Leeds, 1954-56, 1959; Univ. of London, 1959; Univ. of Brussels, 1972. Schweich Lecturer of British Academy, 1950; Leverhulme Fellowship, 1954. Travelled and excavated in S Arabia, 1950, 1954 and 1958. Trustee of National Library of Scotland, 1951-56; Mem. Council, Royal Asiatic Soc., 1952-56; Vice-Pres., British Branch, Hebrew Language Academy, 1954-. *Publications:* The Mission of Burzoe in the Arabic Kalilah wa-Dimnah, 1936; articles and reviews in archæological, philological and historical journals. *Address:* Cowan's Rigg, St Andrews, Fife, Scotland.

HONG KONG and MACAO, Bishop of, since 1966; Rt. Rev. John Gilbert Hindley Baker; *b* 10 Oct. 1910; and y s of late Arthur Ernest Baker, MRCS, LRCP, and Agnes Flora Baker (*née* Hindley), Bromley, Kent; *m* 1941, Martha Levering Sherman (*d* 1976), d of late Rev. Arthur Sherman, STD and Mrs Martha Sherman, Wuchang, China and Ohio, USA; two s two d. *Educ:* Westminster Sch.; Christ Church, Oxford. Deacon, 1935; Priest, 1936. SCM Sec., London, 1932-34; Dio. of Hong Kong and S China, 1935-; taught at Lingnan Univ., Canton, 1936-38; in Kunming, Yunnan, 1939-45; St John's Univ., Shanghai, 1947-49; Union Theol. Coll., Lingnan, 1949-51; Rector of Christ Church, Guilford, Conn., 1952-55; Gen. Sec., Church Assembly Overseas Coun., London, 1955-63; Vicar, St Nicholas Cole Abbey, London, 1955-66; Actg Dir, Christian Study Centre, Hong Kong, 1966. *Publications:* The Changing Scene in China, 1946 (US 1948); The Church on Asian Frontiers, 1963; contrib., All One Body, 1969. *Recreations:* walking, swimming, listening to music. *Address:* Bishop's House, 1 Lower Albert Road, Hong Kong. *T:* Hong Kong 265355. *Club:* Royal Commonwealth Society.

HONGLADAROM, Sunthorn; Knight Grand Cordon, Order of Crown of Thailand, and Order of White Elephant; Secretary-General, South-East Asia Treaty Organisation, 1972-77; Hon. Assistant Secretary-General, Thai Red Cross Society, since 1977; *b* 23 Aug. 1912; *m* 1937; five s one d. *Educ:* Trinity Coll., Cambridge. Asst Sec.-Gen. to Cabinet, 1946; Sec.-Gen., Nat. Economic Council, 1950; Ambassador to Fedn of Malaya (now Malaysia), 1957; Minister of Economic Affairs, 1959; Minister of Finance, 1960; Chairman of Boards of Governors; IBRD, IMF, IFC, and Internat. Development Assoc., 1961; Minister of Economic Affairs, 1966; Ambassador to UK, 1968-69, to USA, 1969-72. Hon. LLD, St John's Univ., NY, 1970. *Recreations:* golf, motoring. *Address:* Thai Red Cross Society, Chulalongkorn Memorial Hospital, Bangkok, Thailand. *Club:* Roehampton.

HONIG, Frederick; His Honour Judge Honig; a Circuit Judge (formerly a County Court Judge), since 1968; *b* 22 March 1912;

2nd s of late Leopold Honig; m 1940, Joan, o d of late Arthur Burkart. *Educ:* Berlin and Heidelberg Univs. LLD (Hons) Heidelberg, 1934. Barrister, Middle Temple, 1937. War service, 1940-47: Capt., JAG's Dept; Judge Advocate in civilian capacity, 1947-48; subseq. practised at Bar. *Publications:* (jtly) Cartel Law of the European Economic Community, 1963; contribs to Internat. Law Reports (ed. Lauterpacht) and legal jls, incl. Amer. Jl of Internat. Law, Internat. and Comparative Law Quarterly, Law Jl, Propriété Industrielle, etc. *Recreations:* foreign languages, country walking. *Address:* Lamb Building, Temple, EC4. *T:* 01-353 1612; 23 Shilling Street, Lavenham, Suffolk. *T:* Lavenham 565.

HONORÉ, Prof. Antony Maurice, DCL Oxon; FBA 1972; Regius Professor of Civil Law, University of Oxford, since 1971; Fellow of All Souls College, Oxford, since 1971; *b* 30 March 1921; *o s* of Frédéric Maurice Honoré and Marjorie Erskine (*née* Gilbert); *m* 1948, Martine Marie-Odette, 2nd *d* of Pierre Genouville, Le Chesnay, France; one *s* one *d. Educ:* Diocesan Coll., Rondebosch; Univ. of Cape Town; New Coll., Oxford. Rhodes Scholar, 1940. Union Defence Forces, 1940-45; Lieut, Rand Light Infantry, 1942. BCL 1948. Advocate, South Africa, 1951; called to Bar, Lincoln's Inn, 1952, Hon. Bencher, 1971. Lectr, Nottingham Univ., 1948; Rhodes Reader in Roman-Dutch Law, 1957-71, Fellow of Queen's Coll., Oxford, 1949-64, of New Coll., 1964-71. Visiting Professor: McGill, 1961; Berkeley, 1968. *Publications:* (with R. W. Lee) The South African Law of Obligations, 1950; (with R. W. Lee) The South African Law of Property etc, 1954; (with H. L. A. Hart) Causation in the Law, 1959; Gaius, 1962; The South African Law of Trusts, 2nd edn 1976. *Address:* All Souls College, Oxford. *T:* Oxford 22251.

HONOUR, (Patrick) Hugh; writer; *b* 26 Sept. 1927; *s* of late Herbert Percy Honour and Dorothy Margaret Withers. *Educ:* King's Sch., Canterbury; St Catharine's Coll., Cambridge (BA). Asst to Dir, Leeds City Art Gall. and Temple Newsam House, 1953-54. Guest Curator for exhibn, The European Vision of America, National Gall. of Art, Washington, Cleveland Museum of Art, and, as L'Amérique vue par l'Europe, Grand Palais, Paris, 1976. *Publications:* Chinoiserie, 1961 (2nd edn 1973); Companion Guide to Venice, 1965 (4th edn 1977); (with Sir Nikolaus Pevsner and John Fleming) The Penguin Dictionary of Architecture, 1966 (7th edn 1976); Neo-classicism, 1968 (4th edn 1977); The New Golden Land, 1976; (with John Fleming) The Penguin Dictionary of Decorative Arts, 1977. *Club:* Travellers'.

HONYWOOD, Col Sir William Wynne, 10th Bt *cr* 1660; MC; *b* 7 April 1891; 2nd *s* of Sir John William Honywood, 8th Bt of Evington; *S* brother, 1944; *m* 1923, Maud Naylor (*d* 1953) (who served in War of 1914-19 as special military probationer nurse), *d* of late William H. Wilson, Hexgreave Park, Southwell, Notts; one *s* two *d. Educ:* Downside. Joined 17th (DCO) Lancers, Aug. 1914; posted to RARO, 17th/21st Lancers, 1934; re-employed, Aug. 1939; Bt Major, Sept. 1939; Lieut-Col Pioneer Corps, 1940; Lieut-Col 8th Bn KSLI 1941; Chief Instructor, 210 Officer Cadet Training Unit, 1944; Col 1945; Deputy Dir Pioneers and Labour, Cyrenaica District, 1945-46; Comdt Royal Pioneer Corps Depôt, MEF, 1946-48. Served European War, 1914-19, in France, Belgium, and German East Africa (despatches thrice, MC); seconded to Air Ministry, Airship Pilot, 1918-19; Adjt Ceylon Mounted Rifles and Ceylon Planters Rifle Corps, 1928-31; War of 1939-45, served in France, 1939-40, and Middle East. *Heir: s* Filmer Courtenay William Honywood [*b* 20 May 1930; *m* 1956, Elizabeth Margaret Mary Cynthia Miller; two *s* two *d*]. *Address:* c/o Lloyds Bank Ltd, 6 Pall Mall, SW1.

HOOD, family name of **Viscounts Bridport** and **Hood.**

HOOD, 6th Viscount, *cr* 1796; **Samuel Hood,** GCMG 1969 (KCMG 1960; CMG 1953); Bt 1778; Baron 1782; Baron Hood (Great Britain), 1795; HM Diplomatic Service, retired; a Deputy Speaker and Deputy Chairman of Committees, House of Lords, since 1971; *b* 15 Oct. 1910; *s* of late Rear-Adm. Hon. Sir Horace Hood, KCB, DSO, MVO (3rd *s* of 4th Viscount), and late Ellen Touzalin; *S* uncle, 1933. *Educ:* Eton; Trinity Coll., Cambridge. Asst Private Sec. to Marquess of Zetland, Sec. of State for India, 1936-39; Private Sec. to Lord Macmillan, Sir John Reith and Mr A. Duff Cooper when Ministers of Information, 1939-41; served in the Foreign Office, 1942-47; mem. of the UK Delegns to meetings of Council of Foreign Ministers in London, Paris, New York and Moscow, 1945-47 and to the Peace Conf. in Paris, 1946; Dep. to Foreign Sec. for Austrian Peace Treaty, 1947; 1st Sec., HM Embassy, Madrid, 1947; Counsellor, HM Embassy, Paris, 1948; Asst Under-Sec. of State, Foreign Office, 1951; and British Representative, Council of Western European Union, 1956; HM Minister, Washington, 1957-62; Dep. Under-Sec. of State, FO, later FCO, 1962-69. Chm., Adv. Council, V&A Museum, 1975-. *Heir: b* Hon. Alexander Lambert Hood, *qv. Address:* 80 Eaton Square, SW1. *Clubs:* Brooks's, Travellers'; Swinley Forest Golf.
See also Baron Ashburton.

HOOD, Lt-Gen. Sir Alexander, GBE 1946 (CBE 1939); KCB 1943 (CB 1942); KCVO 1953; *b* 25 Sept. 1888; *s* of Alexander Hood, Trinity, Edinburgh; *m* 1st, Evelyn Dulcia, CStJ, *d* of George Ellwood, Kensington, W; 2nd, Mrs Helen Winifred Wilkinson, Hamilton, Bermuda. *Educ:* George Watson's Coll.; Edinburgh Univ. MB, ChB, 1910; MD 1931. House Surgeon Royal Infirmary, Edinburgh, 1910-11; Lieut RAMC, 1912. Served European War, 1914-18, in France and Belgium. Capt. 1915; Major 1924; Lieut-Col 1934; Col (Brevet) 1938, (Subst.) 1939; (despatches Palestine, 1939); Brig. 1940; Maj.-Gen. 1941; Lt-Gen. 1941. Sometime DDMS, British Forces in Palestine and Trans-Jordan; Dir-Gen., Army Medical Services, 1941-48; Chm. of Governors of Star and Garter Home for Disabled Sailors, Soldiers and Airmen, 1948; Governor and C-in-C, Bermuda, 1949-55. KHP 1941. Hon. degrees: FRCSE, 1942; FRCP, 1944; LLD Edinburgh, 1945; DCL Durham, 1946; FRFPSG, 1946. Hon. Freeman of Barbers' Company. Knight of Order of White Lion of Czechoslovakia, 1944; Knight of Order of Orange Nassau, 1945; Commander of Order of Crown of Belgium, 1945; Commander of American Legion of Merit, 1945. *Address:* Montalto, Baileys Bay, Bermuda. *Clubs:* Army and Navy; Royal and Ancient Golf.

HOOD, Hon. Alexander Lambert; Chairman, Tanganyika Concessions Ltd, since 1976; Director: J. Henry Schroder Wagg & Co., 1957-75; George Wimpey & Co. Ltd since 1957; Inveresk Group Ltd, 1966-74 (Chairman, 1967-74); *b* 11 March 1914; *s* of late Rear-Adm. Hon. Sir H. L. A. Hood, KCB, DSO, MVO, and late Ellen Floyd Touzalin; *b* and *heir-pres.* to 6th Viscount Hood, *qv; m* 1957, Diana Maud, CVO 1957, *d* of late Hon. G. W. Lyttelton; three *s. Educ:* RN Coll., Dartmouth; Trinity Coll., Cambridge; Harvard Business Sch. RNVR, 1939-45. Director: Petrofina (UK) Ltd; Union Miniere; Abbott Laboratories Inc. Part-time Mem., British Waterways Bd, 1963-73. *Address:* 67 Chelsea Square, SW3. *T:* 01-352 4952; Loders Court, Bridport, Dorset. *T:* Bridport 22983. *Club:* Brooks's.

HOOD, Clifford Firoved; Director Emeritus, Trans World Airlines; *b* Monmouth, Ill., 8 Feb. 1894; *s* of Edward Everett Hood; *m* 1917, Emilie R. Tener (decd); two adopted *s* decd; *m* 1943, Mary Ellen Tolerton. *Educ:* Univ. of Illinois (BS). Technical apprentice Packard Electric Co., Ohio, 1915, Sales Engineer, 1915-17; with American Steel and Wire Co., 1917-49; operating clerk, 1917; war service, 1st Lieut, US Army, 1917-19; foreman, Amer. Steel and Wire Co., 1919-25; asst superintendent, South Works, Worcester, Mass, 1925-27; superintendent, 1927-28; asst manager, subseq. manager, Worcester district, 1928-35; Vice-Pres. in charge of operations, 1935-37; Exec. Vice-Pres., 1937; Pres., 1938-49; Pres., Carnegie-Illinois Steel Corp., 1950; Exec. Vice-Pres. in charge operations, US Steel Co., 1951-52; Pres. US Steel Corporation, 1953; retired May 1959. Mem. Amer. Iron and Steel Inst. Holds several hon. degrees in law and engineering, from 1952. *Address:* One Royal Palm Way, Palm Beach, Florida 33480, USA. *Clubs:* Bath and Tennis, Seminole, Everglades, Beach (Palm Beach); Duquesne (Life member) (Pittsburgh).

HOOD, Douglas; see Hood, J. D.

HOOD, Maj.-Gen. Ernest Lionel Ouseley, CB 1976; Deputy Director-General of Army Medical Services, Ministry of Defence, 1973-76; *b* 3 July 1915; *s* of Lt-Col Ernest Frederick Hood, 7th Rajputs (The Duke of Connaught's Own) Indian Army, and Madeleine Ouseley (*née* Sherlock); *m* 1942, Helen McMillan Jackson; one *s* twin *d. Educ:* Cheltenham Coll.; Edinburgh Univ. MB, ChB, MFCM. Commissioned in RAMC, 1940. Served War of 1939-45, in NW Europe, India, Burma and Malaya. Served (post-war), in Pakistan, Egypt, France, W Germany, Singapore and Malaysia (Johore). Attended No 21 Staff Course, Staff Coll., Camberley, Jan.-Dec. 1950 (psc); DADMS, HQ 53 (Welsh) Infty Div., 1951-53; CO, 6 Field Amb., Tel-el-Kebir, Egypt, 1953-54; ADMS, HQ British Troops Egypt (Moascar), 1954-55; Officer in Charge and Chief Instr, Field Trng Sch., RAMC Field Trng Centre, Mytchett, Dec. 1955-58; Mil. Attaché to UK High Comr, Pakistan, 1959-60; ADMS, GHQ, FARELF, Singapore, 1960-62; CO, British Mil. Hosp., Hostert, W Germany, 1962-63; Col, 1963; ADMS, HQ 1st Div., BAOR, 1963-64; DDMS, HQ, BAOR, Nov. 1964-Oct. 1967; Asst Dir-Gen. (AMD2), MoD (Army), 1967-70; ADMS, HQ London Dist, 1970-71; DDMS, HQ 1st British Corps, W Germany, 1971-73. CStJ 1974. Brig. 1971; Maj.-Gen. 1973; QHP 1973. Col Comdt, RAMC, 1976-. *Recreations:* shooting, sailing. *Address:* The Willows, 6 Paddock Way, The Riding, Woking, Surrey GU21 5TB. *T:* Woking 60903. *Club:* British Medical Association.

HOOD, Sir Harold (Joseph), 2nd Bt *cr* 1922, of Wimbledon, Co. Surrey; TD; Circulation Director Catholic Herald; Circulation Director, Universe, 1953-60; *b* 23 Jan. 1916; *e s* of Sir Joseph Hood, 1st Bt, and Marie Josephine (*d* 1956), *e d* of Archibald Robinson, JP, Dublin; *S* father, 1931; *m* 1946, Hon. Ferelith Rosemary Florence Kenworthy, *o d* of 10th Baron Strabolgi and of Doris, Lady Strabolgi, 137 Gloucester Road, SW7; *two s two d* (and one *s* decd). *Educ:* Downside Sch. Mem. Editorial Staff, The Universe, 1936-39; Asst Editor, The Catholic Directory, 1950, Managing Ed., 1959-60; Editor, The Catholic Who's Who, 1952 Edition. 2nd Lieutenant 58th Middx Battalion RE (AA) (TA) 1939; Lieut RA, 1941. Kt of St Gregory (Holy See), 1964; Kt of Magistral Grace, SMO Malta, 1972. *Heir: s* John Joseph Harold Hood, *b* 27 Aug. 1952. *Address:* 31 Avenue Road, NW8 6BS. *T:* 01-722 9088. *Clubs:* Royal Automobile, MCC, Challoner.

HOOD, (James) Douglas, CBE 1956; Past Chairman and Managing Director: Wilson and Glenny Ltd, Hawick (1950-70); Simpson & Fairbairn Ltd (1962-70); Scottish Worsteds & Woollens Ltd (1962-70); Director: William McGeoch & Co. Ltd, Glasgow; William McGeoch & Co. (Northern) Ltd, Glasgow; *b* 24 May 1905; *s* of late George B. W. Hood; *m* 1931, Evelyn Mary, 2nd *d* of late Lachlan A. McGeoch, Glasgow; one *d. Educ:* Sedbergh Sch., Yorks. Attended Scottish Woollen Technical Coll., Galashiels; entered Scottish tweed trade, joining Wilson & Glenny Ltd, Hawick, 1923. Pres., Nat. Assoc. of Scottish Woollen Manufrs, 1948-51; Chm., Scottish Woollen Publicity Council (on its formation), 1957-64; Chm. Nat. Wool Textile Export Corp., 1958-70. Mem. Cttee, Soc. for welfare and teaching of the Blind, Edinburgh and SE Scotland. Guide dog owner. *Recreations:* music, walking and a reliance on Talking Books. *Address:* Silver Birches, Huntly Avenue, Melrose, Roxburghshire.

HOOD, (Martin) Sinclair (Frankland); Archaeologist; *b* 31 Jan. 1917; *s* of late Lt-Comdr Martin Hood, RN, and late Mrs Martin Hood, New York; *m* 1957, Rachel Simmons; one *s two d. Educ:* Harrow; Magdalen Coll., Oxford. British Sch. at Athens: student, 1947-48 and 1951-53; Asst Dir, 1949-51; Dir, 1954-62. Student, British Inst. Archaeology, Ankara, 1948-49. Geddes-Harrower Vis. Prof. of Greek Art and Archaeology, Univ. of Aberdeen, 1968. Took part in excavations at: Dorchester, Oxon, 1937; Compton, Berks, 1946-47; Southwark, 1946; Smyrna, 1948-49; Atchana, 1949-50; Sakca-Gozu, 1950; Mycenae, 1950-52; Knossos, 1950-51, 1953-55, 1957-61; Jericho, 1952; Chios, 1952-55. *Publications:* The Home of the Heroes: The Aegean before the Greeks, 1967; The Minoans, 1971; various excavation reports and articles. *Address:* The Old Vicarage, Great Milton, Oxford. *T:* Great Milton 202. *Club:* Athenæum.

HOOD, Roger Grahame; University Reader in Criminology and Fellow of All Souls College, Oxford, since 1973; *b* 12 June 1936; 2nd *s* of Ronald and Phyllis Hood; *m* 1963, Barbara Blaine Young; one *d. Educ:* King Edward's Sch., Five Ways, Birmingham; LSE (BSc Sociology); Downing Coll., Cambridge (PhD). Research Officer, LSE, 1961-63; Lectr in Social Admin, Univ. of Durham, 1963-67; Asst Dir of Research, Inst. of Criminology, Univ. of Cambridge, 1967-73; Fellow of Clare Hall, Cambridge, 1969-73. Member: Parole Bd, 1972-73; SSRC Cttee on Social Sciences and the Law, 1975-. Mem. Editorial Bd, British Jl of Criminology. *Publications:* Sentencing in Magistrates' Courts, 1962; Borstal Re-assessed, 1965; (with Richard Sparks) Key Issues in Criminology, 1970; Sentencing the Motoring Offender, 1972; (ed) Crime, Criminology and Public Policy: Essays in Honour of Sir Leon Radzinowicz, 1974; (with Sir Leon Radzinowicz) Criminology and the Administration of Criminal Justice: a bibliography, 1976. *Address:* 75 St Bernard's Road, Oxford. *T:* Oxford 56469.

HOOD, Col Sir Tom (Fielden), KBE 1967 (OBE 1944); CB 1959; TD 1944; DL; Chairman, Portman Building Society, since 1960; Director, National Employers' Mutual General Insurance Association Ltd (Chairman, 1970-76); *s* of late Tom Hood, AMICE, AMIMechE, and Emmeline Clayton Hood (*née* Fielden); *m* 1931, Joan, *d* of Richmond P. Hellyar; *two s. Educ:* Clifton Coll. ACA 1930, FCA 1938. Partner, Lawrence, Gardner & Co., Chartered Accountants, Bristol, 1931-57. 2nd Lieut RE (TA), 1923; CRE 61 Div., 1939-42; DCE Scottish Command, 1942-44; DCE Second Army, 1944-45; Col 1945. Chm., Commn of Enquiry into Port of Aden, 1963. Governor of Clifton Coll., 1954-; Mem. of Court of Univ. of Bristol, 1956-. DL Co. Gloucester, 1950-. *Recreation:* shooting. *Address:* Sion Cottage, Sion Hill, Bath BA1 2UL. *T:* Bath 25123. *Clubs:* Army and Navy; Bath and County (Bath).

HOOD, Sir William Acland, 8th Bt *cr* 1806 and 6th Bt *cr* 1809; *b* 5 March 1901; *s* of William Fuller-Acland-Hood (*d* 1933) and Elizabeth (*d* 1966), *d* of M. Kirkpatrick, Salt Lake City, USA; *S* to baronetcies of kinsman, 2nd Baron St Audries, 1971; *m* 1925, Mary, *d* of late Augustus Edward Jessup, Philadelphia; one *d* (one *s* decd). *Educ:* Wellington; RMA Woolwich; Univ. of California (MA). Naturalized American citizen, 1926. Formerly Lieutenant RE. Associate Professor, Los Angeles City College, retired. *Heir:* none. *Address:* SR2, Box 577, 29 Palms, California 92277, USA.

HOOD, William Francis, LLB (Lond); Master of the Supreme Court (Taxing Office), 1946-71; *b* 27 Sept. 1902; *s* of Wm Charles Reginald Hood, solicitor, and Margaret Frances, *d* of John McKissock, Glaick, Leswalt, Stranraer; *m* 1928, Gwendolen Lloyd, *d* of Rex Lloyd Turner, Croydon; two *d. Educ:* Haileybury (Schol.). Asiatic Petroleum Co. Ltd, 1921-23; solicitor (Hons), 1929; Partner Barnett Tuson Hood & Co., 117 Old Broad Street, EC2, 1936-46; RNVR 1941-45; Lieut-Comdr, 1945; Board of Management, Metropolitan Ear, Nose and Throat Hospital, 1945-47. Life Governor, Haileybury, 1972-; Editor Haileybury Register, 1962, 1974; Pres., Haileybury Soc., 1976-77. Pres., Brighton and Hove Musical Club, 1966-67, 1971-72. *Recreations:* travel, music, drama. *Address:* Poynings hurst, Slaugham, Sussex RH17 6AD. *T:* Handcross 400336.

HOOD PHILLIPS, Owen; *see* Phillips.

HOOFT, Willem Adolf Visser 't; *see* Visser 't Hooft.

HOOK, Rt. Rev. Ross Sydney; *see* Bradford, Bishop of.

HOOK, Prof. Sidney; Professor, Department of Philosophy, Graduate School of Arts and Science, New York University, 1939-72, now Emeritus Professor; Senior Research Fellow on War, Revolution and Peace, at Hoover Institution, Stanford University, since 1973; Founder of The New York University Institute of Philosophy; *b* 20 Dec. 1902; *s* of Isaac Hook and Jennie Halpern; *m* 1924; one *s* ; *m* 1935, Ann Zinken; one *s* one *d. Educ:* College of the City of New York; BS 1923; Columbia Univ. (MA 1926, PhD 1927); Columbia Univ. Fellowship in Philosophy, 1926-27; Guggenheim Research Fellowship in Philosophy for Study Abroad, 1928-29, 1953-; Ford Fellowship for the Study of Asian philosophy and culture, 1958. Teacher, New York City Public Schs, 1923-27; Instr in Philosophy, Washington Square Coll., New York Univ., 1927-32; Asst Prof., 1932-34; Assoc. Prof. and Chm. of Dept of Philosophy, 1933-39; Lectr, New Sch. for Social Research, NYC, 1931-. Vis. Prof., Univ. of California, 1950, Harvard Univ., 1961; Thomas Jefferson Memorial Lectr, Univ. of California at Berkeley, 1961; Regents Prof., Univ. of California at Santa Barbara, 1966; Vis. Prof., Univ. of California at San Diego, 1975. Fellow at Center for Advanced Study in the Behavioral Sciences, Stanford Univ., 1961-62. Butler Silver Medal for distinction in Philosophy, Columbia Univ., 1945. Organiser: conf. on Methods in Philosophy and Sci., conf. on Sci. Spirit and Dem. Faith, and Cttee for Cultural Freedom; Organiser and Co-Chm., Americans for Intellectual Freedom; President: Univ. Centers for Rational Alternatives; John Dewey Foundn (and Treasurer); Mem., American Philosophical Assoc. Vice-Pres., Eastern Div., 1958, Pres., 1959-60, Am. Assoc. Univ. Profs (past Council Mem.); Vice-President: Internat. Cttees for Academic Freedom; Council, Nat. Endowment for the Humanities. Hon. DHL: Univ. of Maine, 1960; Univ. of Utah, 1970; Hon LLD: Univ. of California, 1966; Rockford Coll., 1970; Univ. of Florida, 1971. Fellow: American Academy of Arts and Sciences, 1965; Nat. Acad. of Educn, 1968. *Publications:* The Metaphysics of Pragmatism, 1927; Towards the Understanding of Karl Marx, 1933; American Philosophy-To-day and To-morrow, 1935; From Hegel to Marx, 1936; Planned Society-Yesterday, To-day, To-morrow, 1937; John Dewey: An Intellectual Portrait, 1939; Reason, Social Myths and Democracy, 1940; The Hero in History, 1943; Education for Modern Man, 1946; Heresy, Yes-Conspiracy No, 1953; The Ambiguous Legacy; Marx and the Marxists, 1955; Common Sense and the Fifth Amendment, 1957; Political Power and Personal Freedom, 1959; The Quest for Being, 1961; The Paradoxes of Freedom, 1962; The Fail-Safe Fallacy, 1963; Religion in a Free Society, 1967; Academic Freedom and Academic Anarchy, 1970; Education and the Taming of Power, 1973; Pragmatism and the Tragic Sense of Life, 1975; Revolution, Reform and Social Justice, 1976; Editor of various works; contrib. numerous articles to philosophical journals. *Recreation:* gardening. *Address:* New York University, New York, NY 10003, USA. *T:* 212-598-3262; Hoover Institution, Stanford, Calif 94305, USA. *T:* 415-497-1501.

HOOK, Sheriff William Thomson; a Sheriff of Lothian and Borders at Linlithgow, since 1968 (of Renfrew and Argyll at

Greenock, 1956-68); *b* 6 Dec. 1918; *s* of Peter Dewar Hook, JP and Marianne Elizabeth Thomson; *m* 1947, Margaret, *d* of Robert Barr, Shadwell House, Leeds; one *s*. *Educ:* Edinburgh Acad.; Old Coll., Edinburgh (MA, LLB). Royal Northumberland Fusiliers, 1939-46 (despatches). Faculty of Advocates, 1948; Mem., College of Justice; Standing Jun. Counsel, Min. of Labour; a Chairman, Lothians Nat. Insce Tribunal; Mem. Cttee, Deaconess Hosp.; Mem., Probation and After Care Councils. Elder, West Kirk, Edinburgh. *Publication:* Gaelic Place Names of Bute. *Recreation:* Classical Association. *Address:* 10 Moray Place, Edinburgh. *Clubs:* New (Edinburgh); Royal Gourock Yacht.

HOOKER, Prof. Morna Dorothy; Lady Margaret's Professor of Divinity, University of Cambridge, since 1976; Fellow of Robinson College, Cambridge, since 1976; *b* 19 May 1931; *d* of Percy Francis Hooker, FIA, and Lily (*née* Riley). *Educ:* Univ. of Bristol (research schol.); Univ. of Manchester (research studentship). MA (Bristol, Oxford and Cambridge); PhD (Manchester). Research Fellow, Univ. of Durham, 1959; Lectr in New Testament Studies, King's Coll., London, 1961; Visiting Prof., McGill Univ., 1968; Lectr in Theology, Oxford, and Fellow, Linacre Coll., 1970-76; Lectr in Theology, Keble Coll., 1972-76; Visiting Fellow, Clare Hall, Cambridge, 1974. *Publications:* Jesus and the Servant, 1959; The Son of Man in Mark, 1967; (jt ed) What about the New Testament?, 1975; contribs to New Testament Studies, Jl of Theological Studies, Theology, etc. *Recreations:* Molinology, music. *Address:* Divinity School, St John's Street, Cambridge.

HOOKER, Sir Stanley (George), Kt 1974; CBE 1964 (OBE 1946); FRS 1962; DSc; DPhil; Technical Adviser to the Chairman, Rolls-Royce Ltd, since 1977; *b* 30 Sept. 1907; 5th *s* of William Harry and Ellen Mary Hooker; *m* 1st, 1936, Hon. Margaret Bradbury; one *d*; 2nd, 1950, Kate Maria Garth; one *d*. *Educ:* Borden Grammar Sch.; Imperial Coll., London; Brasenose Coll., Oxford. Scientific and Research Dept, Admiralty, 1935-38; Rolls Royce Ltd, 1938-48; Bristol Aero Engines, 1948-59. Apptd Chief Engr, Engine Div., Bristol Aeroplane Co. Ltd, 1951 and a Dir, 1952; Technical Dir (Aero), Bristol Siddeley Engines Ltd, 1959; Technical Dir, Bristol Engine Div. of Rolls-Royce Ltd, 1966-71; Gp Technical Dir, Rolls-Royce Ltd, 1971-77. FIMechE (Mem. Council, 1958-); FRAeS; Fellow, Imperial Coll. Hon. Prof., Peking Inst. of Aeronautical Scis, 1973. British Silver Medal for Aeronautics, awarded by RAeS, 1955; Diplôme Paul Tissandier, by Féd. Aero Internationale, 1955; Thulin Bronze Medal by Swedish Aero. Soc., 1960; Brit. Gold Medal for Aeronautics, by RAeS, 1961; James Clayton Prize (jointly), 1966; Gold Medal, RAeS, 1967; Churchill Gold Medal, Soc. of Engineers, 1968; Goddard Medal, Amer. Inst. of Aeronautics and Astronautics, 1969. *Address:* Rolls-Royce Ltd, PO Box 3, Filton, Bristol; Orchard Hill, Milbury Heath, Wotton-under-Edge, Glos. *Club:* Athenæum.
See also Sir John Barran, Bt.

HOOKWAY, Harry Thurston; Deputy Chairman and Chief Executive, The British Library Board, since 1973; *b* 23 July 1921; *s* of William and Bertha Hookway; *m* 1956, Barbara Olive, *o d* of late Oliver and Olive Butler; one *s* one *d*. *Educ:* Trinity Sch. of John Whitgift; London Univ. (BSc, PhD); FRIC. Various posts in industry, 1941-49; DSIR, 1949-65; Asst Dir, National Chemical Laboratory, 1959; Dir, UK Scientific Mission (North America), Scientific Attaché, Washington, DC, and Scientific Adviser to UK High Comr, Ottawa, 1960-64; Head of Information Div., DSIR, 1964-65; CSO, DES, 1966-69, Asst Under-Sec. of State, DES, 1969-73. Chm., UNESCO Internat. Adv. Cttee for Documentation, Libraries and Archives. Pres., Inst. of Information Scientists, 1973-76; Hon. FIInfSc. Dir, Arundel Castle Trustees Ltd, 1976-. Hon. LLD Sheffield, 1976. *Publications:* various contribs to jls of learned societies. *Recreations:* music, travel. *Address:* 35 Goldstone Crescent, Hove, East Sussex. *Club:* Athenæum.

HOOKWAY, Reginald John Samuel; Director of the Countryside Commission, since 1971; *b* 7 June 1920; *er s* of Charles and Florence Hookway, Bideford, Devon; *m* 1942, Ethel Lylie Ashford; one *s* two *d*. *Educ:* Bideford Grammar Sch.; University Coll. of the South West, Exeter (BSc). Served War, RE, 1940-46. Devon County Council: Research Officer, 1948-55; Asst County Planning Officer, 1955-58; Dep. County Planning Officer, Norfolk CC, 1958-64; Principal Planning Officer, Countryside Commn, 1965-69; Dep. Chief Planning Officer, Min. of Housing and Local Govt, 1969-71. FRTPI. *Publications:* a number of papers on rural and recreational planning. *Recreations:* walking, swimming. *Address:* 1 Albert Court, Albert Road, Cheltenham, Glos GL52 2TN.

HOOLAHAN, Anthony Terence, QC 1973; a Recorder of the Crown Court, since 1976; *b* 26 July 1925; *s* of late Gerald Hoolahan and of Val Hoolahan; *m* 1949, Dorothy Veronica Connochie; one *s* one *d*. *Educ:* Dorset House, Littlehampton, Sussex; Framlingham Coll., Suffolk; Lincoln Coll., Oxford (MA). Served War, RNVR, 1943-46. Oxford Univ., 1946-48. Called to Bar, Inner Temple, 1949. *Publication:* Guide to Defamation Practice (with Colin Duncan, QC), 2nd edn, 1958. *Recreations:* squash, swimming. *Address:* 1 Brick Court, Temple, EC4Y 9BY. *T:* 01-353 8845; Fair Lawn, Ormond Avenue, Richmond, Surrey TW10 6TN. *T:* 01-940 1194.

HOOLEY, Frank Oswald; MP (Lab) Sheffield, Heeley, 1966-70 and since Feb. 1974; *b* 30 Nov. 1923; *m* 1945, Doris Irene Snook; two *d*. *Educ:* King Edward's High Sch., Birmingham; Birmingham Univ. Admin. Asst, Birmingham Univ., 1948-52; Sheffield Univ.: Asst Registrar, 1952-65; Sen. Asst Registrar, 1965-66; Registrar, Fourah Bay Coll., Sierra Leone, 1960-62 (secondment from Sheffield); Sen. Admin. Asst, Manchester Poly., 1970-71; Chief Admin. Offr, Sheffield City Coll. of Educn, 1971-74. *Address:* House of Commons, SW1.

HOOLEY, Maj.-Gen. St John Cutler, CB 1958; CBE 1954; *b* 30 Sept. 1902; *s* of late S. P. Hooley, Tharston, Norfolk; *m* 1931, Molly Isobel, *d* of late Dr A. Scott-Turner, MRCS, LRCP, JP, London; one *d*. *Educ:* RMA, Woolwich. Royal Artillery, 2nd Lieut 1923; Captain RAOC, 1934; Dep. Dir Ordnance Services: AA Comd, 1945-46; British Mil. Mission, Greece, 1947-50; HQ Eastern Comd, 1950-52; Dir, Ordnance Services, HQ BAOR and Northern Army Gp, 1952-57; Brig. 1954, Maj.-Gen. 1957; Inspector RAOC, 1957-58; Comdt, Mechanical Transport Organisation, Chilwell, 1958-60, retired. Served War of 1939-45 in Norway, Middle East and India (despatches). *Recreations:* golf, travel, photography. *Address:* Storrington Cottage, Sea Avenue, Rustington, Sussex.

HOOPER, Sir Anthony (Robin Maurice), 2nd Bt *cr* 1962; Director, Couper Gallery; Assistant Manager, Schweppes Ltd, 1952; *b* 26 Oct. 1918; *o s* of Sir Frederic Collins Hooper, 1st Bt, and Eglantine Irene (Bland); *S* father, 1963; *m* 1970, Cynthia (marr. diss. 1973), *yr d* of Col W. J. H. Howard, DSO. *Educ:* Radley; New Coll., Oxford. Royal Artillery, 1939-41; Asst to Hubert Philips, News Chronicle, 1941-42; Political Research Centre, 1942-44; Actor (Liverpool, Windsor, Birmingham, Oxford, London, BBC), 1944-50; temp. Civil Servant, Cabinet Office, 1950-52. *Recreations:* music, conversation and people. *Club:* Savile.

HOOPER, Ven. Charles German, MA; Archdeacon of Ipswich, 1963-76, now Archdeacon Emeritus; *b* 16 April 1911; 2nd *s* of A. C. Hooper, Solicitor; *m* 1936, Lilian Mary, *d* of late Sir Harold Brakspear, KCVO; one *s* one *d*. *Educ:* Lincoln Coll., Oxford (MA 2nd cl. English). Curacies: Corsham, Wilts, 1934-36; Claremont, CP, South Africa, 1936-39; Rector, Castle Combe, Wilts, 1940; Chaplain, RAFVR, 1942-46 (despatches); Rector, Sandy, Beds, 1946-53; Vicar and Rural Dean, Bishop's Stortford, Herts, 1953-63; Rector of Bildeston, Suffolk, 1963-67; Rector of St Lawrence's and St Stephen's, Ipswich, 1967-74. Chaplain to Cutlers Co., Sheffield, 1964-65, to Drapers Co., 1972-73. *Recreations:* painting in water colours, sailing. *Address:* East Green Cottage, Kelsale, Saxmundham, Suffolk. *T:* Saxmundham 2702.
See also Baron Methuen.

HOOPER, Howard Owen, CB 1964; CMG 1952; Assistant Under Secretary of State, Ministry of Defence, 1964-71, retired; *b* 17 Oct. 1911; *s* of late R. H. Hooper and Mrs E. A. Hooper, St Stephen in Brannel, Cornwall; *m* 1937, Margaret Oliff, *d* of late S. H. and C. L. Marshall, Newbury. *Educ:* St Austell Grammar Sch.; Merton Coll., Oxford (Exhibitioner), BA 1933, MA 1963; DipEd Oxon 1934. Entered Civil Service, 1935; Asst Sec., British Supply Bd, N America, 1939-41; Sec. (UK), Combined Raw Materials Bd, Washington, 1946; Asst Sec., BoT, 1946; Mem., Trade Missions to Argentina and Brazil, 1947-49; Counsellor, Washington, 1951 (Dep. to UK Mem., Internat. Materials Conf.); Principal Estabt and Finance Officer, Min. of Materials 1952-54; Under-Secretary: BoT, 1954-55; Cabinet Office, 1955-58; Min. of Supply, 1958-59; WO, 1960-64. Comr, Queen Victoria Sch., Dunblane, 1965-71. Coronation Medal, 1953. *Publications:* contribs to Dictionary of National Biography. *Recreation:* history. *Address:* Englefield, Bridge Road, Cranleigh, Surrey. *T:* Cranleigh 3407. *Club:* Reform.

HOOPER, Sir Leonard (James), KCMG 1967 (CMG 1962); CBE 1951; idc; a Deputy Secretary, Cabinet Office, since 1973; *b* 23 July 1914; *m* 1951, Ena Mary Osborn. *Educ:* Alleyn's, Dulwich; Worcester Coll., Oxford. Joined Air Ministry, 1938, transferred Foreign Office, 1942; Imperial Defence Coll., 1953;

Dir, Govt Communications HQ, 1965-73. *Recreation:* sport. *Address:* 3c Carlisle Place, SW1. *T:* 01-834 5172. *Clubs:* Athenæum, Royal Automobile; New (Cheltenham).

HOOPER, Mrs Mia Lilly Kellmer; *see* Pringle, Dr M. L. K.

HOOPER, Sir Robin (William John), KCMG 1968 (CMG 1954); DSO 1943; DFC 1943; HM Diplomatic Service, retired; Special Representative of Foreign and Commonwealth Secretary, since 1976; Member, NATO Appeals Board, since 1976; *b* 26 July 1914; *s* of late Col John Charles Hooper, DSO, and late Irene Annie Palmer Hooper (*née* Anderson), Harewell, Faversham, Kent; *m* 1941, Constance Mildred Ayshford, *d* of late Lieut-Col Gilbert Ayshford Sanford, DSO, DL, Triley Court, Abergavenny, Mon; three *s. Educ:* Charterhouse; The Queen's Coll., Oxford. 3rd Sec., Foreign Office, 1938-40. Served War of 1939-45; on active service with RAF, 1940-44 (Wing-Comdr). Second Sec., HM Embassy, Paris, 1944-47; First Sec., HM Embassy, Lisbon, 1947-49; transferred to FO, 1949; Counsellor, 1950; Head of Personnel Dept, 1950-53; Counsellor, HM Embassy, Bagdad, 1953-56; Head of Perm. Under-Sec.'s Dept, FO, 1956-60; Asst Sec.-Gen. (Political), NATO, 1960-66; Ambassador to Tunisia, 1966-67; Ambassador to Southern Yemen, 1967-68; Dep. Sec., Cabinet Office, 1968-71; Ambassador to Greece, 1971-74. Chm., Anglo-Hellenic League, 1975-. Dir, Benguela Railway Co., 1976-. Chevalier, Legion of Honour, 1945. Croix de Guerre, 1939-45 (2 Palms), 1945. *Address:* F3, Albany, Piccadilly, W1; Brook House, Egerton, near Ashford, Kent. *Club:* Travellers'.

HOOSON, (Hugh) Emlyn, QC 1960; MP (L) Montgomeryshire, since 1962; a Recorder, since 1972 (Recorder of Swansea, 1971); *b* 26 March 1925; *s* of late Hugh and Elsie Hooson, Colomendy, Denbigh; *m* 1950, Shirley Margaret Wynne, *d* of late Sir George Hamer, CBE; two *d. Educ:* Denbigh Gram. Sch.; University Coll. of Wales; Gray's Inn (Bencher, 1968). Called to Bar, 1949; Wales and Chester Circuit (Leader, 1971-74); Dep. Chm., Flint QS, 1960-71; Dep. Chm., Merioneth QS, 1960-67, Chm., 1967-71; Recorder of Merthyr Tydfil, 1971. Leader, Welsh Liberal Party, 1966-. Vice-Chm. Political Cttee, North Atlantic Assembly, 1975-. Hon. Professorial Fellow, University Coll. of Wales, 1971. Farms Pen-y-banc farm, Llanidloes. *Address:* 1 Dr Johnson's Buildings, Temple, EC4. *T:* 01-353 7972; Summerfield, Llanidloes, Powys. *T:* Llanidloes 2298.

HOOTON, John Charles, CMG 1963; MBE 1945; QC (Bermuda) 1959; Under-Secretary (Legal), Advisory Division, HM Procurator-General and Treasury Solicitor's Department, 1974-77 (Assistant Solicitor, 1970-74); *b* 1912; *m* 1938, Jessica Patricia, *d* of R. J. Manning; two *s.* Served War of 1939-45; Lt-Col General List (despatches, Croix de Guerre, MBE). Palestine Police, 1932; Police, Gold Coast, 1937-49. Called to the Bar, Gray's Inn, 1949. Crown Counsel, Gold Coast, 1951-53 (Senior Asst Legal Sec., East African Common Services Organisation, 1953); Attorney-Gen., Bermuda, 1958-61; Legal Sec. to East African Common Services Organisation, 1961, retd from Org., 1962, re-apptd on contract, 1962-63; temp. Senior Asst, CO, 1963-64. *Address:* Dingleden House, Benenden, Kent. *Club:* Oriental.

HOOVER, Herbert William, Jr; President, 1954-66, and Chairman of the Board, 1959-66, The Hoover Company, North Canton, Ohio; *b* 23 April 1918; *s* of late Herbert William Hoover and Grace Hoover (*née* Steele); *m* 1941, Carl Maitland Good; one *s* one *d. Educ:* Choate Sch., Wallingford, Conn.; Rollins Coll. (AB). Served in US Army as 2nd Lieut, 1943-45. Offices held with Hoover Co.: Exec. Sales, 1941; Dir Public Relations, 1945; Asst Vice-Pres., 1948; Vice-Pres. Field Sales, 1952; Exec. Vice-Pres., 1953. The Hoover Co. Ltd, Canada: Pres., 1954; Dir, 1952; Hoover Ltd, England: Dir 1954, Chm. 1956. Hoover Inc., Panama: Dir and Pres., 1955; Hoover (America Latina) SA, Panama: Dir and Pres., 1955; Hoover Mexicana, Mexico: Dir and Pres., 1955; Hoover Industrial y Comercial SA, Colombia: Dir and Pres., 1960; Hoover Worldwide Corp., NY City: Pres. and Chm., 1960; Dir, S. A. Hoover, France, 1965. Dir, Harter Bank & Trust Co., Canton, Ohio. Past Regional Vice-Chm., US Cttee for the UN. Hon. LLD, Mount Union Coll., 1959. Bd of Trustees, Univ. of Miami. Chevalier Légion d'Honneur, France, 1965. *Address:* 70 Park Drive, Bal Harbour, Fla 33154, USA.

HOPE, family name of **Baron Glendevon, Marquess of Linlithgow** and **Baron Rankeillour.**

HOPE, Maj.-Gen. Adrian Price Webley, CB 1961; CBE 1952; *b* 21 Jan. 1911; *s* of late Adm. H. W. W. Hope, CB, CVO, DSO; *m* 1958, Mary Elizabeth, *e d* of Graham Partridge, Cotham Lodge, Newport, Pembrokeshire; no *c. Educ:* Winchester Coll.; RMC, Sandhurst. 2/Lt KOSB, 1931; Adjt, 1/KOSB, 1937-38; Staff

Capt. A, Palestine, Egypt, 1938-40; DAQMG (Plans) Egypt, 1940-41; Instructor, Staff Coll., 1941; AQMG, Egypt, Sicily, Italy, 1941-44; Col Asst Quartermaster, Plans, India, 1945; Brig., Quartermaster, SE Asia, 1946; Comdt Sch. of Military Admin., 1947-48; Instructor, jssc, 1948-50; DQMG, GHQ, MELF, 1951-53; Student, idc, 1954; Brig. Quartermaster (ops), War Office, 1955-57; BGS, HQ, BAOR, 1958-59; MGA, GHQ, FARELF, 1959-61; Dir of Equipment Policy, War Office, 1961-64; Dep. Master-Gen. of the Ordnance, Ministry of Defence, 1964-66; retd 1966. *Recreations:* tennis, golf. *Address:* Monks Place, Charlton Horethorne, Sherborne, Dorset. *Club:* Army and Navy.

HOPE, Sir Archibald (Philip), 17th Bt of Craighall, *cr* 1628; OBE 1945; DFC 1940; AE 1943; retired 1977; *b* 27 March 1912; *s* of 16th Bt and Hon. Mary Bruce, OBE, JP Midlothian, *e d* of 10th Lord Balfour of Burleigh; *S* father, 1924; *m* 1938, Ruth, *y d* of Carl Davis, Fryern, Storrington, Sussex; two *s. Educ:* Eton; Balliol Coll., Oxford. BA 1934; ACA 1939; FCA 1960; Mem. of Queen's Body Guard for Scotland (Royal Company of Archers). Served, RAFO, 1930-35; 601 (County of London) Sqdn AAF, 1935-39. Served War of 1939-45 (despatches twice, DFC, OBE). Wing Comdr (acting Group Capt.), AAF. Joined Airwork, 1945; Dir, 1951; resigned, June 1956; Dir, D. Napier & Son Ltd, 1956-61; Dir, Napier Aero Engines Ltd, 1961-68; Chief Exec., Napier Aero Engines Ltd, 1962-68; English Electric Co., 1968-70; Gp Treasurer, GEC Ltd, 1970-77. Mem., Airline Users Cttee, CAA, 1973-, Dep. Chm. 1974-. Chm., The Air League, 1965-68. FRAeS 1968. *Heir: s* John Carl Alexander Hope [*b* 10 June 1939; *m* 1968, Merle Pringle, *d* of Robert Douglas, Southside, Holbrook, Ipswich; one *s* one *d*]. *Address:* The Manor House, Somerford Keynes, near Cirencester, Glos GL7 6DL. *T:* Ashton Keynes 250. *Clubs:* Royal Air Force; New (Edinburgh); Nairobi (Nairobi).

HOPE, Bob, (Leslie Townes Hope), CBE (Hon.) 1976; Congressional Gold Medal, US, 1963; film, stage, radio, TV actor; *b* England, 29 May 1903; family migrated to US, 1907; *m* 1934, Dolores Reade; two adopted *s* two adopted *d. Educ:* Fairmont Gram. Sch. and High Sch., Cleveland, O. Started career as dance instructor, clerk, amateur boxer; formed dancing act for Fatty Arbuckle review. After Mid-West tours formed own Company in Chicago; toured New York and joined RKO Vaudeville and Keith Circuit; first important stage parts include: Ballyhoo, 1932; Roberta, 1933; Ziegfield Follies, 1935; first radio part, 1934. Entered films, 1938. *Films include:* Some Like It Hot; The Cat and the Canary; Road to Singapore; The Ghost Breakers; Road to Zanzibar; Star Spangled Rhythm; Nothing but the Truth; Louisiana Purchase; My Favorite Blonde; Road to Morocco; Let's Face It; Road to Utopia; Monsieur Beaucaire; My Favorite Brunette; They Got Me Covered; The Princess and the Pirate; Road to Rio; Where There's Life; The Great Lover; My Favorite Spy; Road to Bali; Son of Paleface; Here Come the Girls; Casanova's Big Night; The Seven Little Foys; The Iron Petticoat; That Certain Feeling; Beau James; The Facts of Life; Bachelor in Paradise; The Road to Hong Kong; Call Me Bwana; A Global Affair; Boy, Did I Get a Wrong Number!; Eight on the Run; How to Commit Marriage; Cancel My Reservation. *TV Series:* The Bob Hope Show, 1950-; numerous guest appearances. Four Royal Command Performances. Awarded 40 honorary degrees; more than a thousand awards and citations for humanitarian and professional services. *Publications:* They've Got Me Covered, 1941; I Never Left Home, 1944; This One's on Me, 1954; I Owe Russia $1200, 1963; Five Women I Love, 1966; The Last Christmas Show, 1974; Road to Hollywood, 1977. *Address:* Hope Enterprises Inc., 10,000 Riverside Drive, Suite 3, North Hollywood, Calif. 91602, USA.

HOPE, Sir (Charles) Peter, KCMG 1972 (CMG 1956); TD 1945; Ambassador to Mexico, 1968-72; *b* 29 May 1912; *s* of G. L. N. Hope and H. M. V. Riddell, Weetwood, Mayfield, Sussex; *m* 1936, H. M. Turner, *d* of late G. L. Turner, company director; three *s. Educ:* Oratory Sch., Reading; London and Cambridge Univs. BSc (Hons), ACGI. Asst War Office, 1938; RA, TA, 1939; served until 1946 (TD). Transferred to Foreign Office and posted HM Embassy, Paris, as Temp. First Sec., 1946; transferred to United Nations Dept, Foreign Office, 1950; to HM Embassy, Bonn, as Counsellor, 1953; Foreign Office Spokesman (Head of News Dept Foreign Office), 1956-59; Minister, HM Embassy, Madrid, 1959-62; Consul-General, Houston, USA, 1963-64; Minister and Alternate UK Rep. to UN, 1965-68. Mem., Acad. of International Law. Grand Cross, Order of the Aztec Eagle; Grand Officer, Order of Merito Militense. *Recreations:* shooting and fishing. *Address:* North End House, Heyshott, Midhurst, Sussex. *Club:* White's.

HOPE, Rev. Dr David Michael; Principal, St Stephen's House, Oxford, since 1974; *b* 14 April 1940. *Educ:* Nottingham Univ.

(BA Hons Theol.); Linacre Coll., Oxford (DPhil). Curate of St John, Tuebrook, Liverpool, 1965-70; Chaplain, Church of Resurrection, Bucharest, 1967-68; Vicar, St Andrew, Warrington, 1970-74. *Publication:* The Leonine Sacramentary, 1971. *Address:* St Stephen's House, Norham Gardens, Oxford OX2 6PZ. *T:* Oxford 55891.

HOPE, Sir James, 2nd Bt *cr* 1932; MM 1918; JP; farmer; *b* 2 May 1898; *s* of Sir Harry Hope, 1st Bt and Margaret Binnie Holms-Kerr; *S* father 1959. *Educ:* Fettes Coll. Served European War, 1916-19, with Black Watch (MM). District Chm., East Lothian Agricultural Executive Cttee, 1938-45. JP for East Lothian. *Heir: b* Robert Holms-Kerr Hope [*b* 12 April 1900; *m* 1928, Eleanor (*d* 1967), *d* of late Very Rev. Marshall Lang, DD, Whittingehame, East Lothian]. *Address:* Eastbarns, Dunbar, East Lothian. *T:* Innerwick 212. *Club:* New (Edinburgh).

HOPE, James Kenneth, CBE 1946; DL; MA (Hon.); Recorder of City of Durham, 1942-74; Clerk of the Peace of County of Durham, Clerk of Durham County Council, and County Registration Officer, 1937-61; County Controller of Civil Defence, 1942-61; Clerk of Durham County Magistrates' Courts Cttee, 1952-61; *b* 12 July 1896; *s* of late J. Basil Hope, OBE, JP, and of Amy L. Hope, Bedford; *m* 1928, Mary Joyce, *yr d* of late Lieut-Col Rouse Orlebar, JP, DL, Hinwick, Beds; three *d. Educ:* Bedford Sch. Served European War, 1915-19: Commissioned Officer, 1st Bn Bedfordshire Regt. Solicitor, 1922; Asst Solicitor, Beds County Council, 1922-27; Dep. Clerk of the Peace and of County Council, Durham, 1927-37; T&AFA, County of Durham, 1937-61. Pres., Durham County Assoc. of Parish Councils, 1963-69. DL, Co. Durham, 1944; High Sheriff of Durham, 1966. *Address:* West Park, Lanchester, Co. Durham. *T:* Lanchester 520339. *Club:* Durham County (Durham).
See also Viscount Pollington, Baron Vivian.

HOPE, Laurence Frank, OBE 1968; HM Diplomatic Service, retired; HM Consul General, Seattle, 1975-76; *b* 18 May 1918; *y s* of late Samuel Vaughan Trevylian Hope and late Ellen Edith Hope (*née* Cooler); *m* 1940, Doris Phyllis Rosa Hulbert; one *s* one *d. Educ:* County Grammar Sch., Lewes, Sussex. Served War, reaching rank of Major, in British Army (12th (2nd City of London Regt) Royal Fusiliers, TA and York and Lancaster Regt); Indian Army (7th Rajput Regt); Mil. Govt of Germany (Economic Div.), 1939-46. Bd of Trade, London, 1946-47; Asst Brit. Trade Comr, Pretoria, 1947-51; Cape Town, 1951-53; Bd of Trade, London, 1953-56; British Trade Comr, Sydney, 1956-60; Canberra, 1960-61; Lahore, 1961-63; Singapore, 1964; transferred to HM Diplomatic Service; Head of Commercial Section, Singapore, 1965-68; Counsellor (Economic and Commercial), Lagos, 1969-72; HM Consul-Gen., Gothenburg, 1972-75. *Recreations:* oil painting, chess, reading. *Address:* 22 Cranford Avenue, Exmouth, Devon EX8 2HU. *Club:* Oriental.

HOPE, Sir Peter; *see* Hope, Sir C. P.

HOPE-DUNBAR, Sir David, 8th Bt *cr* 1664; *b* 13 July 1941; *o s* of Sir Basil Douglas Hope-Dunbar, 7th Bt, and of his 2nd wife, Edith Maude Maclaren, *d* of late Malcolm Cross; *S* father, 1961; *m* 1971, Kathleen, *yr d* of late J. T. Kenrick; one *s* two *d. Educ:* Eton; Royal Agricultural College, Cirencester. Qualified: ARICS 1966. *Recreations:* fishing, shooting. *Heir: s* Charles Hope-Dunbar, *b* 11 March 1975. *Address:* Banks Farm, Kirkcudbright. *T:* Kirkcudbright 30424.

HOPE GILL, Cecil Gervase, MA; *b* 14 Dec. 1894; *s* of late Rt Rev. Charles Hope Gill and late Mary Hope Gill (*née* Thorp); *m* 1937, Kiti Colin, *e d* of Dr Alexander Campbell-Smith, Nelson, NZ. *Educ:* Windlesham House, Brighton; King William's Coll., IoM; Brighton Coll.; St John's Coll., Cambridge. Served in Royal Monmouthshire RE (Special Reserve), 1914-19 (wounded, despatches); Major 1919 (CRE Tournai); entered Levant Consular Service, 1920; served at Tangier (Vice-Consul), 1921; Casablanca, 1922; Saffi, 1923; Tetuan, 1923-25; Tangier (Asst Oriental Sec.), 1925-30; Jedda (Head of Chancery and Chargé d'Affaires), 1930-33; Alexandria (Consul), 1933-36; Addis Ababa, 1936; Imperial Defence Coll., 1937; Seattle, 1938-40; Baghdad (Asst Oriental Sec.), 1941; Léopoldville (Actg Consul-Gen.), 1941-42; Addis Ababa (First Sec.), 1942-44; Foreign Office, 1944-45; Tetuan (Consul-Gen.), 1945-52; retired from HM Foreign Service with rank of Consul-Gen., 1952. *Recreations:* travel, fruit growing, wine making, bee keeping, cinematography. *Address:* The High Threshing Floor, La Era Alta de Cotobro, Almuñécar (Granada), Spain. *T:* 958 630 628. *Cables:* Hopegill Almunecarspain. *Club:* Royal Automobile.

HOPE-JONES, Sir Arthur, KBE 1964; CMG 1956; Director of companies in UK and East Africa; Adviser to companies in these and other countries since 1960; *b* 26 May 1911; *s* of

William and Dinah Elizabeth Hope-Jones; *m* 1938, Lucile Owens, New York; one *s* one *d. Educ:* Kirkby Lonsdale; Christ's Coll., Cambridge (1st cl. hons Hist. Tripos); Columbia Univ., New York (Commonwealth Fund Fellow). Fellow of Christ's Coll., Cambridge, 1937-46. Served War, 1939-45 (TA Gen. List); seconded for duties at home and abroad; Economic Adviser in Persia to Anglo-Iranian Oil Co. Ltd (now BP), 1944-46; Economic Adviser Govt of Kenya, 1946-48; Mem., later Minister, for Commerce and Industry, Govt of Kenya, 1948-60; Member: Kenya Legislature, 1947-60; East African Legislative Assembly, 1955-60. Pres., Mesopotamia and Paiforce Dinner Club. *Publications:* Income Tax in the Napoleonic Wars, 1939; contribs to learned society and financial periodicals. *Recreations:* walking, fishing, reading. *Address:* 1 Buckland Court, Buckland, Betchworth, Surrey. *T:* Betchworth 2179; PO Box 43561, Nairobi, Kenya, East Africa. *Clubs:* East India; Muthaiga Country, Nairobi (Nairobi).

HOPE-JONES, Ronald Christopher, CMG 1969; HM Diplomatic Service, retired; *b* 5 July 1920; *s* of William Hope-Jones and Winifred Coggin; *m* 1944, Pamela Hawker; two *s* one *d. Educ:* Eton (scholar); King's Coll., Cambridge (scholar). Served with HM Forces, 1940-45. 3rd Sec., Foreign Office, 1946, Paris, 1947; 2nd Sec., Beirut, 1949; 1st Sec., FO, 1952; Head of Chancery and Consul, Quito, 1955; Commercial Sec., Budapest, 1959; Head of Chancery, 1960; FO, 1961, Counsellor, 1963; UK Rep. to Internat. Atomic Energy Agency, Vienna, 1964-67; FCO 1967; Head of Disarmament Dept, 1967-70; Head of N African Dept, 1970-71; Counsellor, Brasilia, 1972-73; Ambassador in La Paz, 1973-77. *Address:* Kingsmead, Prey Heath Road, Mayford, Woking, Surrey. *T:* Woking 62759.

HOPE-MORLEY, family name of Baron Hollenden.

HOPE-MORLEY, Gordon Hope; I. & R. Morley Ltd, 1933-67, retired as Chairman; *b* 8 Jan. 1914; *s* of late Hon. Claude Hope-Morley and Lady Dorothy Hope-Morley; *heir-pres.* to 2nd Baron Hollenden, *qv*; *m* 1945, Sonja Sundt, Norway; three *s. Educ:* Eton. War medals of 1939-45; King Haakon of Norway Liberation medal. *Address:* Hall Place, Leigh, Tonbridge, Kent. *T:* Hildenborough 832255. *Club:* Brooks's.
See also Sir Michael Hanley .

HOPE-WALLACE, (Dorothy) Jaqueline, CBE 1958; Member Board, Corby Development Corporation, since 1969; Commissioner, Public Works Loan Board, since 1974; *b* 1909; 2nd *d* of Charles Nugent Hope-Wallace and Mabel Chaplin. *Educ:* Lady Margaret Hall, Oxford. Entered Ministry of Labour, 1932; transferred to National Assistance Board, 1934; Asst Sec., 1946-58; Under-Sec., 1958-65; Under-Sec., Min. of Housing and Local Govt, 1965-69, retired. Commonwealth Fellow, 1952-53. Member Board: Governors, UCH, 1970-74; Inst. for Recorded Sound, 1971-74 (Chm. 1975); Nat. Corp. Care of Old People, 1973-; Chm., Friends of UCH, 1973-. *Recreations:* arts, travel, gardening. *Address:* 22 St Ann's Terrace, NW8.
See also P . A . Hope -Wallace

HOPE-WALLACE, Philip Adrian, CBE 1975; dramatic critic, The Guardian; *b* 6 Nov. 1911; *o s* of Charles Nugent Hope-Wallace and Mabel Chaplin. *Educ:* Charterhouse; Balliol Coll., Oxford; abroad. International Broadcasting Co., France, 1934; Public Relations, Gas Light & Coke Co., 1935-36; Correspondent, The Times, 1935-39; Press Officer, Air Ministry, 1939-45. Critic of music and drama to various journals; Time and Tide, 1945-49; The Listener; The Manchester Guardian (now The Guardian), 1946-. Broadcasting, journalism. Lectured at home and abroad. *Publications:* A Key to Opera, 1939; pamphlets on the drama, music, etc.
See also D. J. Hope-Wallace.

HOPETOUN, Earl of; Adrian John Charles Hope; Stockbroker; *b* 1 July 1946; *s* and *heir* of Marquess of Linlithgow, *qv; m* 1968, Anne, *e d* of A. Leveson, Hall Place, Hants; two *s. Educ:* Eton. Joined HM Navy, 1965. *Heir: s* Viscount Aithrie, *qv. Address:* Hopetoun House, South Queensferry, West Lothian; 36 Edwardes Square, W8. *Clubs:* Turf, White's.

HOPEWELL, John Prince; Consultant Surgeon (Urology), Royal Free Hospital, since 1957; *b* 1 Dec. 1920; *s* of Samuel Prince and Wilhelmina Hopewell; *m* 1959, Dr Natalie Bogdan (*d* 1975); one *s* one *d. Educ:* Bradfield Coll., Berks; King's Coll. Hosp., London. RAMC, 1945-48. Postgrad. education at King's Coll. Hosp. and Brighton, Sussex, and Hosp. for Sick Children, Gt Ormond Street. Formerly Cnslt Surgeon, Putney Hosp. and Frimley Hosp., Surrey. Past Chairman: Med. Cttee Royal Free Hosp.; N Camden Dist Med. Cttee. Founder Mem., British Transplantation Soc., 1972; Member: Internat. Soc. of Urology;

British Assoc. Urol. Surgeons. Hon. Mem., NY Section, AUA. Hunterian Prof., RCS, 1958. *Publications:* contribs to Surgical Aspects of Medicine, Modern Treatment Year Book, and various medical journals. *Recreations:* photography, travel. *Address:* 11 Harley House, Upper Harley Street, NW1. *T:* 01-935 5291.

HOPKIN, Sir Bryan; *see* Hopkin, Sir W. A. B.

HOPKIN, David Armand; Metropolitan Stipendiary Magistrate, since Aug. 1970; *b* 10 Jan. 1922; *s* of Daniel and Edmée Hopkin; *m* 1948, Doris Evelyn (*née* Whitaker); one *s* three *d*. *Educ:* St Paul's Sch., W Kensington; University Coll., Aberystwyth; Corpus Christi Coll., Cambridge (BA). Served in Army, 1942-47, Hon. Major, 1947. Member of Staff of Director of Public Prosecutions, 1950-70. *Recreations:* fencing, tennis; administrative steward, British Boxing Board of Control. *Address:* 8 Crane Grove, N7. *T:* 01-607 0349.

HOPKIN, Sir (William Aylsham) Bryan, Kt 1971; CBE 1961; Professor of Economics, University College Cardiff, since 1972 (on leave of absence, 1974-76); *b* 7 Dec. 1914; *s* of late William Hopkin and Lilian Hopkin (*née* Cottelle); *m* 1938, Renée Ricour; two *s*. *Educ:* Barry (Glam.) County Sch.; St John's Coll., Cambridge; Manchester Univ. Ministry of Health, 1938-41; Prime Minister's Statistical Branch, 1941-45; Royal Commn on Population, 1945-48; Econ. Sect., Cabinet Office, 1948-50; Central Statistical Office, 1950-52; Dir, Nat. Inst. of Econ. and Soc. Research, 1952-57; Sec., Council on Prices, Productivity, and Incomes, 1957-58; Dep. Dir, Econ. Sect., HM Treasury, 1958-65; Econ. Planning Unit, Mauritius, 1965; Min. of Overseas Devlt, 1966-67; Dir-Gen. of Economic Planning, ODM, 1967-69; Dir-Gen., DEA, 1969; Dep. Chief Econ. Adviser, HM Treasury, 1970-72; Head of Govt Economic Service and Chief Economic Advr, HM Treasury, 1974-77. Mem., Commonwealth Devel Corp., 1972-74. *Address:* Aberthin House, Aberthin, near Cowbridge, South Glamorgan. *T:* Cowbridge 2303.

HOPKINS, Alan Cripps Nind, MA Cantab, LLB Yale; Chairman, Wellman Engineering Corporation; *b* 27 Oct. 1926; *s* of late Rt Hon. Sir Richard V. N. Hopkins, GCB and Lady Hopkins; *m* 1st, 1954, Margaret Cameron (from whom divorced, 1962), *d* of E. C. Bolton, Waco, Texas, USA; one *s*; 2nd, 1962, Venetia, *d* of Sir Edward Wills, Bt, *qv*; twin *s*. *Educ:* Winchester Coll.; King's Coll., Cambridge; Yale University Law Sch., USA. BA Cantab 1947, MA 1950; LLB Yale 1952. Barrister, Inner Temple, 1948. MP (C and Nat L) Bristol North-East, 1959-66; PPS to Financial Sec. to Treasury, 1960-62. Dir, Dexion-Comino International Ltd. *Recreation:* travelling. *Address:* Hugditch, Ramsbury, near Marlborough, Wilts. *T:* Ramsbury 405; 59 Cadogan Place, SW1. *T:* 01-235 1846. *Club:* Brooks's.

HOPKINS, Anthony; actor since 1961; *b* Port Talbot, S Wales, 31 Dec. 1937; *s* of Richard and Muriel Hopkins; *m* 1st, 1968, Petronella (marr. diss. 1972); one *d*; 2nd, 1973, Jennifer, *d* of Ronald Lynton. *Educ:* Cowbridge, S Wales; RADA; Cardiff Coll. of Drama. London debut as Metellus Cimber in Julius Caesar, Royal Court, 1964; National Theatre, 1966-73: Juno and the Paycock, A Flea in Her Ear, 1966; The Dance of Death, The Three Sisters, As You Like It (all male cast), 1967; The Architect and the Emperor of Assyria, A Woman Killed with Kindness, Coriolanus, 1971; Macbeth, 1972; The Taming of the Shrew, Chichester, 1972; Equus, NY, 1974-75. Films: The Lion in Winter, 1967; The Looking Glass War, 1968; Hamlet, 1969; When Eight Bells Toll, 1971; Young Winston, 1972; A Doll's House, 1973; The Girl from Petrovka, 1973; All Creatures Great and Small, 1974; Dark Victory, 1975; Audrey Rose, 1976; A Bridge Too Far, 1976. Pierre Bezuhov in BBC TV serial, War and Peace, 1972; Doctor Kelno in Amer. TV film, QB VII; Bruno Hauptmann in The Lindbergh Kidnapping Case, Amer. TV, 1976. Best TV Actor Award, SFTA, 1973; Best Actor Award, NY Drama Desk, 1975; Outer Critics Circle Award, 1975; American Authors and Celebrities Forum Award, 1975; Emmy award, 1976. *Recreations:* reading and walking. *Address:* c/o Peggy Thomson, 7 High Park Road, Kew, Surrey.

HOPKINS, Antony, CBE 1976; composer and conductor; *b* 21 March 1921; *s* of late Hugh and of Marjorie Reynolds; adopted *c* of Major and Mrs T. H. C. Hopkins since 1925; *m* 1947, Alison Purves. *Educ:* Berkhamsted Sch.; Royal Coll. of Music. Won Chappell Gold Medal and Cobbett Prize at RCM, 1942; shortly became known as composer of incidental music for radio; numerous scores composed for BBC (2 for programmes winning Italia prize for best European programme of the year, 1952 and 1957). Composed music for many productions at Stratford and in West End. Dir, Intimate Opera Co., 1952-, and has written a

number of chamber operas for this group; *ballets:* Etude and Café des Sports, for Sadler's Wells; *films (music)* include: Pickwick Papers, Decameron Nights, Cast a Dark Shadow, Billy Budd; John and the Magic Music Man (narr. and orch.; Grand Prix, Besançon Film Festival, 1976). Regular broadcaster with a series of programmes entitled Talking about Music. Formerly Gresham Prof. of Music, City Univ. Hon. FRCM 1964. *Publications:* Talking about Symphonies, 1961; Talking about Concertos, 1964; Music All Around Me, 1968; Lucy and Peterkin, 1968; Talking about Sonatas, 1971; Downbeat, 1977. *Recreations:* motoring and motor sport. *Address:* Woodyard Cottage, Ashridge, Berkhamsted, Herts. *T:* Little Gaddesden 2257.

HOPKINS, Douglas Edward, DMus (London); FRAM, FRCO, FGSM; Professor, Royal Academy of Music, since 1937; Conductor, Stock Exchange Male Voice Choir, since 1956; *b* 23 Dec. 1902; *s* of Edward and Alice Hopkins; unmarried. *Educ:* St Paul's Cathedral Choir Sch.; Dulwich Coll.; Guildhall Sch. of Music (Ernest Palmer and Corporation Scholarships); Royal Academy of Music. Organist, Christ Church, Greyfriars, EC, 1921; Sub-Organist, St Paul's Cathedral, 1927; Master of the Music, Peterborough Cathedral, 1946; Organist, Canterbury Cathedral, 1953-55; Musical Dir, St Felix Sch., Southwold, 1956-65; Organist, St Marylebone Parish Church, 1965-71; Founder, and Dir 1962-74, Holiday Course for Organists; Organist, Royal Meml Chapel, RMA Sandhurst, 1971-76. Conductor of Handel Soc., 1928-33, and, since that, of various other musical societies. Liveryman, Worshipful Co. of Musicians. *Address:* 244 Mytchett Road, Mytchett, Camberley, Surrey GU16 6AF. *Club:* Savage.

HOPKINS, Admiral Sir Frank (Henry Edward), KCB 1964 (CB 1961); DSO 1942; DSC 1941; Commander-in-Chief, Portsmouth, 1966-67; retired, 1967; *b* 23 June 1910; *s* of late E. F. L. Hopkins and Sybil Mary Walrond; *m* 1939, Lois Barbara, *d* of J. R. Cook, Cheam, Surrey. *Educ:* Stubbington House; Nautical Coll., Pangbourne. Joined Navy as Cadet, 1927; served in HM Ships: London, Tiger, Whitehall, Vortigern, Winchester, Courageous, Furious, 1928-38; War of 1939-45 (despatches, 1941), in No 826 Fleet Air Arm Squadron (Formidable), 1940-41, and comd No 830 Sqdn, 1941-42, based on Malta; USS Hancock and USS Intrepid, American Pacific Fleet, 1944-45; took part in following operations: Dunkirk, air operations over Europe, Battle of Matapan, evacuation of Crete, bombardment of Tripoli, Malta, Battle of Leyte Gulf; Korean War, Theseus, 1950 (despatches); Capt., 1950; Dir of Air Warfare, Admiralty, comd Myngs, Tyrian, Grenville, and Ark Royal, 1954-58; comd RNC Dartmouth, 1958-60; Rear-Adm. 1960; Flag Officer: Flying Training, 1960-62; Aircraft Carriers, 1962-63; Vice-Adm. 1962; a Lord Comr of the Admiralty, Deputy Chief of Naval Staff and Fifth Sea Lord, 1963-64; Dep. Chief of Naval Staff, MoD, 1964-66; Adm. 1966. American Legion of Merit, 1948; Comdr, Order of Sword, Sweden, 1954. *Recreations:* sailing, golf. *Address:* Kingswear Court Lodge, Kingswear, S Devon. *Clubs:* Naval and Military, Royal Yacht Squadron; Royal Naval Sailing Assoc.; Britannia Yacht.

HOPKINS, Prof. Harold Horace, FRS 1973; Professor of Applied Optics, University of Reading, since 1967; Head of Department of Applied Optics, since 1977; *b* 6 Dec. 1918; *s* of William Ernest and Teresa Ellen Hopkins; *m* 1950, Christine Dove Ridsdale; three *s* one *d*. *Educ:* Gateway Sch., Leicester; Univs of Leicester and London. BSc, PhD, DSc, FInstP. Physicist, Taylor, Taylor & Hobson, 1939-42; Royal Engrs, 1942; Physicist: MAP, 1942-45; W. Watson & Sons, 1945-47; Research Fellow, then Reader in Optics, Imperial Coll., 1947-67. Pres., Internat. Commn for Optics, 1969-72. Hon. Dr.esSc Besançon. *Publications:* Wave Theory of Aberrations, 1951; papers in Proc. Royal Soc., Proc. Phys. Soc., Optica Acta, Jl Optical Soc. Amer. *Recreations:* keyboard music, sailing, languages. *Address:* 26 Cintra Avenue, Reading, Berks. *T:* Reading 81913.

HOPKINS, Col Harold Leslie, CIE 1946; OBE 1942; *b* 1897; *s* of Walter Hopkins, York; *m* 1927, Louise; one *s*. *Educ:* York. Served European War, 1914-18; War of 1939-45, in Europe, Middle East and India; Colonel, 1943. General Manager, Bombay Port Trust, 1944-45. Chief Docks Manager, Hull, 1956-59, retd. *Address:* 3 Westbourne Grove, Scarborough, North Yorks. *T:* Scarborough 72993.

HOPKINS, Prof. Harry Geoffrey, MSc, DSc London; MSc Manchester; Professor of Mathematics, since 1966, and Deputy Principal, since 1976, University of Manchester Institute of Science and Technology; *b* 14 April 1918; *s* of late Charles Thomas and late Violet Florence (*née* Johnson) Hopkins. *Educ:* Enfield Grammar Sch.; Harrow County Sch.; University Coll.,

London (Fellow, 1977). Scientific Officer, Structural and Mechanical Engrg Dept, RAE, Farnborough, 1940-45; Asst in Mathematics, Queen's Univ., Belfast, 1946; Lectr in Mathematics, Manchester Univ., 1946-52; Fulbright Scholar, 1951, and Vis. Prof. of Applied Mathematics, Brown Univ., Providence, RI, 1951 and 1952-54; Senior Principal Scientific Officer, Basic Research Div., Royal Armament R&D Estabt, Fort Halstead, 1954-59; Dep. Chief Scientific Officer (Appleton, Individual Merit Award), 1959-66; Senior Foreign Scientist Fellow (Nat. Science Foundn), Dept of Physics, Washington State Univ., Pullman, Washington, 1965-66. Editor, Jl of Mechanics and Physics of Solids, 1969-. UMIST: Mem. Ct, 1969-71; Mem. Council, 1974-76; Vice-Principal for Finance, 1974-77; Chm., Structure Sub-Cttee, 1976-77, Mem., Airframe Materials and Structures Sub-Cttee, 1977—, ARC. FIMA 1964; FRAS 1964; Mem. Acoustical Soc. of America, 1967; Mem. ASME 1967. *Publications:* theoretical research on the mechanics and physics of solids; contributed to: Deformation and Flow of Solids, 1956; Progress in Solid Mechanics, 1960; Progress in Applied Mechanics, 1963; Stress Waves in Anelastic Solids, 1964; Applied Mechanics Surveys, 1966; Engineering Plasticity, 1968; papers in Proc. and Phil. Trans Royal Soc., Jl Mech. and Phys. Solids, Rep. and Memo. Aero. Res. Council, and other math. and sci. jls. *Recreations:* music, alpine walking and photography, American history. *Address:* Department of Mathematics, University of Manchester Institute of Science and Technology, PO Box No 88, Sackville Street, Manchester M60 1QD. *T:* 061-236 3311.

HOPKINS, James S. R. S.; *see* Scott-Hopkins.

HOPKINS, John Collier Frederick, CMG 1962; DSc; AICTA; FIBiol; *b* 12 May 1898; *s* of late William and Edith Hopkins; *m* 1945, Elizabeth Callister, *d* of George and Helen Rothnie, Salisbury, Rhodesia; two *d. Educ:* Emanuel Sch.; King's Coll. and Imperial Coll., London (Vice-Pres., Univ. of London Boat Club, 1922); Imperial Coll. Trop. Agric., Trinidad. DSc (London) 1933; AICTA 1926. Hon. Artillery Co., 1916; RFC, 1916-18; RAF, 1918-19; Royal Rhodesia Regt, 1940-45. Agricultural Officer, Uganda, 1924. Mycologist, 1926, Senior Plant Pathologist, 1933, Chief Botanist and Plant Pathologist, 1946, S Rhodesia. Asst Editor, Commonwealth Mycological Inst, 1954, Dir and Editor, 1956-64. Pres., Rhodesia Scientific Assoc., 1930, 1940-42; Pres., Section C, S African Assoc. for the Advancement of Science, 1940; Chm., London Branch, Inst. Biology, 1961-64. *Publications:* Diseases of Tobacco in Southern Rhodesia, 1931; Common Veld Flowers, 1940; Tobacco Diseases, 1956; numerous papers in scientific journals. *Address:* Riverside, Glen Mona, Maughold, Isle of Man. *T:* Laxey 677.

HOPKINS, Rev. Canon Leslie Freeman; Canon Residentiary and Treasurer, Liverpool Cathedral, since 1964; *b* 1914; *o s* of Joseph Freeman and Mabel Hopkins, London; *m* 1940, Violet, *d* of Edgar Crick, Crayford; three *s* one *d. Educ:* City of London Sch. (Abbott Schol.); Exeter Coll., Oxford (Squire Schol. and Exhib.); Wells Theological Coll. BA 1937, 2nd Cl. Hon. Mods, 2nd Cl. Hons Theology; MA 1940; BD Oxon 1953. Deacon 1938, priest 1939; Curate of Crayford 1938, Nympsfield 1942; Priest-in-Charge, Holy Trinity, Charlton, 1942-45; Vicar of St Chrysostom's, Peckham, 1945-56; Surrogate, 1946-62; Vicar of All Saints, Battersea Park, 1956-62; Chief Inspector of Schools, Dio. of Southwark, 1954-62; Dir of Religious Education, Dio. of Liverpool, 1962-72; Chaplain of Josephine Butler Coll., 1962-72; Governor of Chester Coll., St Elphin's, Darley Dale and of Grammar Schs; Visiting Lectr in Religious Education; Mem. of Council: Guild of St Raphael, 1944-; USPG. Liveryman, Glass Sellers Co.; Freeman, City of London. *Publications:* contribs to press and Syllabuses of Religious Education. *Recreations:* architecture and music. *Address:* The Cathedral, Liverpool L1 7AZ. *T:* 051-709 6271. *Club:* Royal Commonwealth Society.

HOPKINS, Maj.-Gen. Ronald Nicholas Lamond, CBE 1943; Legion of Merit (US) 1944; psc; Australian Regular Army, retired; *b* 24 May 1897; *s* of Dr Wm F. Hopkins and Rosa M. B. Lamond; *m* 1926, Nora Frances Riceman; one *s. Educ:* Melbourne Grammar Sch.; RMC, Duntroon. Lieut Aust. Permt Forces, 1 Jan. 1918 and seconded 1st AIF; served with 6th Australian Light Horse Regt, Palestine, 1918; Staff Capt. 3rd Australian Light Horse Bde, 1919; Staff Coll., Quetta, 1927-28; attached Royal Tank Corps, England, 1937-38; 2nd AIF 1940; service in Middle East and New Guinea; Hon. ADC to Governor-Gen., 1943-45; late Dep. Chief of Gen. Staff (Australia). Chief Exec. Officer, Adelaide Festival of Arts, 1959-60. Hon. Fellow, St Mark's Coll., Univ. of Adelaide, 1977. *Addrrss:* 24 Wilsden Street, Walkerville, SA 5081, Australia. *Club:* Adelaide (Adelaide).

HOPKINSON, family name of **Baron Colyton.**

HOPKINSON, Albert Cyril, CBE 1970; FRIBA; consultant architect; *b* 2 Aug. 1911; *s* of Albert Hopkinson and Isaline Pollard (*née* Cox); *m* 1943, Lesley Evelyn Hill; one *s* one *d. Educ:* Univs of Sheffield and London. BA 1933; MA 1934. FRIBA 1949 (ARIBA 1934); Dipl. Town Planning and Civic Architecture, London, 1938. Min. of Public Building and Works, 1937-64; Dir of Works and Chief Architect, Home Office, 1964-75. *Recreations:* reading, walking. *Address:* 110b High Street, Berkhamsted, Herts. *T:* Berkhamsted 5256.

HOPKINSON, David Hugh; Editor, Birmingham Evening Mail, since 1974; Editor-in-Chief, Evening Mail series, since 1975; Director, Birmingham Post & Mail Ltd, since 1967; *b* 9 June 1930; *er s* of late C. G. Hopkinson; *m* 1952, Barbara Mary Lumb; three *s* one *d. Educ:* Sowerby Bridge Grammar Sch. Entered journalism on Huddersfield Examiner, 1950; Yorkshire Observer, 1954; Yorkshire Evening News, 1954; Evening Chronicle, Manchester, 1956; Chief Sub-Editor, Sunday Graphic, London, 1957; Asst Editor, Evening Chronicle, Newcastle upon Tyne, 1959; Chief Asst Editor, Sunday Graphic, 1960; Dep. Editor, Sheffield Telegraph, 1961, Editor, 1962-64; Editor, The Birmingham Post, 1964-73. Member: Guild of British Newspaper Editors; Lord Justice Phillimore's Cttee inquiring into law of contempt; International Press Institute; Associate Mem., Justice (British br. of Internat. Commn of Jurists). National Press Award, Journalist of the Year, 1963. *Address:* 63 Hampton Lane, Solihull, West Midlands. *T:* 021-705 1776.

HOPKINSON, Maj.-Gen. Gerald Charles, CB 1960; DSO 1945; OBE 1939; MC 1938; retired; *b* Wellington, Som, 27 May 1910; *s* of Capt. Charles Reginald Hopkinson; *m* 1938, Rhona Marion, *d* of Henry Turner, Farnham, Surrey; one *d. Educ:* Imperial Service Coll.; RMC Sandhurst. Second Lieut, Royal Tank Corps, 1930; served War of 1939-45 (India, Middle East, Italy and Europe); comd 1st RTR, Korea, 1952-53; 33rd Armoured Bde, BAOR, 1953-57; GOC 4th Div., BAOR, 1958-59; Dir, RAC, War Office, Oct. 1959-62. Lieut-Col 1952; Col 1953; Maj.-Gen. 1958. Order of the Crown and Croix de Guerre (Belgium). *Address:* Rosemount, Wrantage, Taunton, Somerset. *Club:* Army and Navy.

HOPKINSON, Giles; Under-Secretary, Department of the Environment, since 1976; *b* 20 Nov. 1931; *s* of late Arthur John Hopkinson, CIE, ICS, and of Eleanor (*née* Richardson); *m* 1956, Eleanor Jean Riddell; three *d. Educ:* Marlborough Coll.; Leeds Univ. (BSc). E. & J. Richardson Ltd, 1956-57; Forestal Land, Timber and Rly Co. Ltd, 1957-58; DSIR: Scientific Officer, 1958-61; Sen. Scientific Officer, 1961-64; Private Sec. to Perm. Sec., 1963-64; Principal, MoT, 1964-71; Asst Sec., DoE, 1971. *Recreations:* music, painting. *Address:* Digswell Water Mill, Digswell Lane, Welyn Garden City, Herts AL7 1SW. *Club:* Royal Commonwealth Society.

HOPKINSON, Col Henry Somerset Parnell, OBE 1944; DL; *b* 16 Oct. 1899; *s* of Col H. C. B. Hopkinson, CMG, CBE, and Hon. M. F. L. Parnell, *d* of 3rd Baron Congleton; *m* 1928, Josephine Marie de Gilibert Addison, *d* of Lieut-Col A. J. R. Addison, Royal Irish Rifles; one *d* (and one *d* decd). *Educ:* Winchester and RMC. 2nd Lt Rifle Brigade, 1919; Major, 1938; Staff Coll., 1933-34; Brig. 1945; served War of 1939-45, Palestine, Burma, India; retd 1948. County Councillor Monmouthshire, 1958-64; JP 1950, DL 1951, High Sheriff 1964, Gwent, formerly Monmouthshire. FSA, FSG. *Recreations:* shooting, foreign travel. *Address:* Llanfihangel Court, Abergavenny, Gwent. *T:* Crucorney 217. *Club:* Army and Navy.

HOPKINSON, (Henry) Thomas, CBE 1967; author, journalist; *b* 19 April 1905; 2nd *s* of late Archdeacon J. H. Hopkinson; *m* 1953, Dorothy, *widow* of late Hugh Kingsmill; (three *d* by previous marriages). *Educ:* St Edward's Sch., Oxford; Pembroke Coll., Oxford (Scholar). BA, 1927; MA, 1932. After working as a freelance journalist and in advertising and publicity, was appointed Asst Editor of the Clarion, 1934; Asst Editor, Weekly Illustrated, 1934-38; helped in preparation and launching of Picture Post; Editor, 1940-50; also edited Lilliput, 1941-46; Features Editor, News Chronicle, 1954-56; Editor, Drum Magazine, 1958-61. Dir for Africa of Internat. Press Inst., 1963-66. Senior Fellow in Press Studies, Univ. of Sussex, 1967-68. Vis. Prof. of Journalism, University of Minnesota, 1968-69. Dir, Course in Journalism Studies, UC Cardiff, 1971-75. *Publications:* A Wise Man Foolish, 1930; A Strong Hand at the Helm, 1933; The Man Below, 1939; Mist in the Tagus, 1946; The Transitory Venus (short stories), 1948; Down the Long Slide, 1949; Love's Apprentice, 1953; short life of George Orwell, 1953, in British Council series Writers and Their Work; The

Lady and the Cut-Throat (short stories), 1958; In the Fiery Continent, 1962; South Africa, 1964 (New York); (ed) Picture Post, 1938-1950, 1970; (with D. Hopkinson) Much Silence: the life and work of Meher Baba, 1974; stories in English and American magazines, and for radio. *Address:* 6 Marine Parade, Penarth, Cardiff. *T:* Cardiff 703354.

HOPKINSON, Prof. Ralph Galbraith; Senior Consultant, formerly Senior Partner, Ralph Hopkinson, Newton Watson and Partners, since 1967; *b* 13 Aug. 1913; *s* of late Ralph Galbraith Hopkinson and Beatrice Frances Wright; *m* 1938, Dora Beryl (*née* Churchill); two *s* (and one *s* decd). *Educ:* Erith Grammar Sch.; Faraday House. BSc (Eng), PhD, CEng, FIEE, FRPS. Research Engr, GEC, 1934-47, lighting and radar; Principal Scientific Officer, DSIR Building Research Stn, 1947-64 (Special Merit appointment, 1960); Haden-Pilkington Prof. of Environmental Design and Engrg, Univ. Coll. London, 1965-76, now Emeritus Prof. (Dean, Faculty of Environmental Studies, 1972-74); Hon. Research Fellow, Univ. Coll., London, 1977-. Work on: human response to buildings, leading to concept of environmental design by engr-physicists and architects in collab.; schools with Min. of Educn Develt Gp and on hosps with Nuffield Foundn, 1949-65; lighting design of new Tate Gallery extension and Stock Exchange Market Hall (Design Award of Distinction, Illum. Engrg Soc. of USA, 1974); visual and noise intrusion (urban motorways) for DoE, 1970; consultant, DoE Road Construction Unit. Pres., Illuminating Engrg Soc., 1965-66 (Gold Medallist, 1972; Hon. Mem., 1976); Mem., Royal Soc. Study Gp on Human Biology in the Urban Environment, 1972-74. Trustee, British Institution Fund, 1972-77. Hon. FRIBA, 1969. *Publications:* Architectural Physics: Lighting, 1963; Hospital Lighting, 1964; Daylighting, 1966; (with J. D. Kay) The Lighting of Buildings, 1969; Lighting and Seeing, 1969; The Ergonomics of Lighting, 1970; Visual Intrusion (RTPI), 1972; papers in Nature, Jl Optical Soc. of America, Jl Psychol., Illum. Eng, etc. *Recreations:* music, human sciences, boating, walking. *Address:* School of Environmental Studies, University College London, Wates House, 22 Gordon Street, WC1H 0QB. *Club:* Athenæum.

HOPKINSON, Thomas; *see* Hopkinson, H. T.

HOPLEY, Ven. Arthur; Archdeacon Emeritus; Archdeacon of Taunton, 1971-77; Prebendary of Milverton I, 1971-77; *b* 17 Oct. 1906; *o s* of Ernest Charles Hopley; *m* 1934, Marjorie Carswell Niven, *d* of John Niven; two *s*. *Educ:* Sir George Monoux Sch.; Wells Theological Coll. Asst Curate, St Mark's, Bath, 1941-44; Rector of Claverton, 1944-50; Vicar of Chard, 1950-62; Archdeacon of Bath, 1962-71; Prebendary of Yatton in Wells Cathedral, 1960-71. *Address:* The Old Parsonage, Angersleigh, Taunton, Somerset. *T:* Blagdon Hill 628.

HOPPE, Iver; Kt of Danish Dannebrog; Kt of Icelandic Falcon; Chairman and Chief Executive, Navalicon Ltd A/S, Denmark; *b* Denmark, 25 July 1920; *s* of Arthur Hans Knudsen Hoppe and Gerda (*née* Raun Byberg); *m* 1943, Ingeborg Lassen; one *d*. *Educ:* Aarhus Katedralskole; Copenhagen Univ. (Law Faculty), 1944. Acting Lecturer, Copenhagen Univ., 1946; Advocate to High Court and Court of Appeal, 1948; Jurisprudential Lecturer, Copenhagen Univ., 1952-58; study sojourn in Switzerland, 1949. A. P. Møller Concern, Copenhagen, 1955-71; Asst Dir, 1960; Man. Dir of Odense Steel Shipyard, Ltd, Odense and Lindø, 1964-71. Chm. A/S Svendborg Skibsvaerft, 1968-71; Mem. Bd of Dansk Boreselskab A/S and other cos until 1971; Man. Dir and Chief Exec., Harland and Wolff Ltd, Belfast, 1971-74; Member: Bd of Den Danske Landmandsbank A/S, 1970-72; Council of Danish National Bank, 1967-71; Bd of Danish Ship Credit Fund, 1965-71; Assoc. of Danish Shipyards, 1964-71; Assoc. of Employers within the Iron and Metal Industry in Denmark, 1967-71; Assoc. of Danish Industries, 1965-72; West of England Steam Ship Owners Protection and Indemnity Assoc., Ltd, 1960-66; Danish Acad. of Technical Sciences; Shipbuilders and Repairers Nat. Assoc. Exec. Council and Management Bd, 1971-74; British Iron and Steel Consumers' Council, 1971-74; Gen. Cttee, Lloyd's Register of Shipping; British Cttee, Det Norske Veritas; Amer. Bureau of Shipping, and other Danish and foreign instns. *Recreations:* reading, swimming, mountain walking, farming. *Address:* Malmmosegaard, Dyreborgvej 7, DK-5600 Faaborg, Denmark. *Club:* Travellers'.

HOPPER, Prof. Frederick Ernest, MDS, FDSRCS; FFDRCSIre; Professor of Dental Surgery and Dean of the School of Dentistry, University of Leeds, since 1959; Consultant Dental Surgeon, Leeds Area Health Authority, since 1959; Chairman, Board of Faculty of Medicine, University of Leeds, since 1975; *b* 22 Nov. 1919; *s* of Frederick Ernest Hopper, MPS and Margaret Ann Carlyle; *m* 1949, Gudrun Eik-Nes, LDSRCS,

d of Prost Knut Eik-Nes and Nina Eik-Nes, Trondheim, Norway; three *s*. *Educ:* Dame Allan's Sch., Newcastle upon Tyne; King's Coll., University of Durham. BDS (with dist.) 1943; FDSRCS 1948. House Surg., Newcastle upon Tyne Dental Hosp. and Royal Dental Hospital, 1943-44; served in EMS in Maxillo-Facial Centres at E Grinstead and Shotley Bridge, 1944-46; successively Lecturer, 1946, and Sen. Lecturer, 1956, in Periodontal Diseases, King's Coll., University of Durham; Lecturer in Dental Pharmacology and Therapeutics, 1947-59; Examiner in Dental subjects, Univs of Durham, Edinburgh, St Andrews, etc; Dental Surgeon in charge Parodontal Dept, Newcastle upon Tyne Dental Hosp., and Sen. Dental Surg., Plastic and Jaw Unit, Shotley Bridge, 1946-59; Cons. Dent. Surg., United Newcastle Hosps, 1955-59. Hon. Treas., Brit. Soc. of Periodontology, 1949-53, Pres. 1954. Member: General Dental Council; Brit. Dental Assoc.; Internat. Dental Fedn. *Publications:* contribs to med. and dental jls. *Recreations:* photography (still and ciné); golf. *Address:* School of Dentistry, Leeds LS1 3EU. *T:* 40111. *Clubs:* Savage; Alwoodley Golf (Leeds).

HOPPER, Prof. Robert John; Professor of Ancient History, University of Sheffield, 1955-75, now Emeritus; *b* 13 Aug. 1910; *s* of Robert and Alice Hopper, Cardiff, Glamorgan; *m* 1939, Henriette, *d* of Edward and Ella Kiernan, Timperley, Cheshire; no *c*. *Educ:* Mount Radford Sch., Exeter; University of Wales; Gonville and Caius Coll., Cambridge. Served Royal Welch Fusiliers and Intelligence Corps, 1941-45. Macmillan Student of British Sch. at Athens, 1935-37; Fellow of Univ. of Wales (in Athens and Rome), 1936-38; Lectr in Classics, UCW Aberystwyth, 1938-41 and 1945-47; Senior Lecturer in Ancient History, Univ. of Sheffield, 1947-55, Dean of Faculty of Arts, 1967-70. FRNS 1949; FSA 1951; Trustee of British Sch. of Archæology, Athens. Editor, The Annual. *Publications:* The Acropolis, 1971; The Early Greeks, 1976; Greek Trade and Industry, 1976; articles in classical and archæological periodicals. *Recreations:* numismatics; foreign travel. *Address:* 41 Barholm Road, Sheffield S10 5RR. *T:* Sheffield 302587. *Club:* National Liberal.

HOPTHROW, Brig. Harry Ewart, CBE 1946 (OBE 1940); Council Member, Solent Protection Society; *b* 13 Nov. 1896; *s* of Frederick Hopthrow; *m* 1925, Audrey Kassel (*d* 1975), *d* of J. Lewer; one *s* one *d*. *Educ:* Queen Elizabeth's Grammar Sch., Gainsborough; City Sch., Lincoln; Loughborough Coll. Served European War 1915-1918, RE, France and Flanders. Civil and Mechanical Engineer, ICI Ltd, 1925-36; Commanded 107 Co. RE, 1931-35, Major; Asst Dir of Works, GHQ, BEF, 1939-40, Lt-Col: served France and Flanders, 1939-40 and 1944; Dep. Chief Engineer: Home Forces, 1940-41, and Western Comd, 1941; Dir of Fortifications and Works, War Office, 1941-43; Dep. Controller Mil. Works Service, War Office, 1943-45; Asst Sec., ICI Ltd, 1945-58; Secretary and a Vice-Pres., Royal Institution, 1960-68. AMIMechE 1924, FIMechE 1933. Mem. Central Advisory Water Cttee (Min. of Housing and Local Govt), 1946-70; Mem. Cttee of Inquiry into Inland Waterways (Bowes Cttee), 1956-58; Vice-Chm. IoW River and Water Authority, 1964-73; UK Rep. to Council of European Industrial Fedns; Vice-Pres., Round Tables on Pollution, 1965-73. Officer of American Legion of Merit, 1946. *Recreation:* yachting. *Address:* Surrey House, Cowes, Isle of Wight. *T:* Cowes 2430. *Clubs:* Army and Navy; Royal Engineer Yacht; Royal London Yacht, Island Sailing (Cowes).

HOPWOOD, family name of **Baron Southborough.**

HOPWOOD, Brig. John Adam, CBE 1958; DSO 1943 (and Bar 1944); *b* 26 Jan. 1910; *s* of Ernest Hopwood and Constance Marion Adam; *m* Cressida Mona Browning, *d* of R. Campbell Browning, Armsworth, Alresford, Hants; no *c*. *Educ:* St David's, Reigate; Eton; RMC Sandhurst. Commissioned Black Watch, 1930; served with 1st Bn in India, 1931-35; ADC to Governor of Bengal, 1935-37; with 1st Bn Black Watch, and BEF in France, 1939-40; Staff Coll., 1940; Bde Major, 154 Inf. Bde, 1941; Second in Comd, 7th Bn Black Watch, N Africa and Sicily, 1942; comd 1st Bn Black Watch, Sicily and NW Europe, 1943-45; comd 154 and 156 Inf. Bdes, Germany, 1946; Mem. Training Mission to Iraq Army, Baghdad, 1946-48; attended jssc, Latimer, 1948; Liaison Appt, RAF Fighter Comd, 1949; comd 44 Parachute Bde (TA) London, 1950-53; Col i/c Admin., Hong Kong, 1953-55; comd 3 Inf. Bde, Canal Zone, UK, Cyprus, 1955-58; Vice-Pres., Regular Commissions Board, 1958-60, retd. Awarded Bronze Lion of Netherlands. *Recreations:* ornithology (MBOU), field sports, travel. *Address:* Gilletts Farm, Yarcombe, Honiton, Devon. *T:* Chard 3121. *Club:* Naval and Military.

HORAM, John Rhodes; MP (Lab) Gateshead West since 1970; Parliamentary Under-Secretary of State, Department of Transport, since 1976; *b* 7 March 1939; *s* of Sydney Horam, Preston. *Educ:* Silcoates Sch., Wakefield; Univ. of Cambridge. Market research officer, Rowntree & Co., 1960-62; leader and feature writer: Financial Times, 1962-65; The Economist, 1965-68; Jt Man. Dir, Commodities Res. Unit Ltd, 1968-70. Contested (Lab) Folkestone and Hythe, 1966. *Recreations:* playing tennis and squash. *Address:* 21 Valley Gardens, Gateshead NE9 5EB; 2 Howard House, Dolphin Square, SW1. *Club:* Saltwell Social (Gateshead).

HORAN, Rt. Rev. Forbes Trevor; *b* 22 May 1905; *s* of Rev. Frederick Seymour Horan and Mary Katherine Horan; *m* 1939, Veronica, *d* of late Rt Rev. J. N. Bateman-Champain, sometime Bishop of Knaresborough; two *s* two *d*. *Educ:* Sherborne and Trinity Hall, Cambridge. RMC Sandhurst, 1924-25; Oxford and Bucks Lt Infantry, Lieutenant, 1925-29; Trinity Hall, Cambridge, 1929-32; Westcott House, Cambridge, 1932-33; Curate, St Luke's, Newcastle upon Tyne, 1933-35; Curate, St George's, Jesmond, Newcastle upon Tyne, 1935-37; Priest-in-charge, St Peter's, Balkwell, 1937-40; RNVR. 1940-45; Vicar of St Chad's, Shrewsbury, 1945-52; Vicar of Huddersfield Parish Church, 1952-60; Bishop Suffragan of Tewkesbury, 1960-73. *Recreations:* gardening, walking. *Address:* 5 Hatherley Road, Cheltenham, Gloucestershire.

HORDER, family name of Baron Horder.

HORDER, 2nd Baron *cr* 1933, of Ashford in the County of Southampton; **Thomas Mervyn Horder;** Bt, of Shaston, 1923; *b* 8 Dec. 1910; *s* of 1st Baron Horder, GCVO, MD, FRCP, and Geraldine Rose (*d* 1954), *o d* of Arthur Doggett, Newnham Manor, Herts; *S* father, 1955. *Educ:* Winchester; Trinity Coll., Cambridge. BA 1932; MA 1937. Served War of 1939-45: HQ, RAF Fighter Comd, 1940-42 (despatches); Air HQ, India, 1942-44; Headquarters, South-East Asia Command, 1944-45; United Kingdom Liaison Mission, Tokyo, 1945-46; Chairman, Gerald Duckworth & Co. Ltd, 1948-70. *Publications:* various simple works for piano, clarinet, oboe, etc, 1960-62; (ed) The Orange Carol Book, 1962; Norfolk Dances for string orchestra, 1965; The Little Genius, 1966; Six Betjeman Songs, 1967; (ed) A Book of Love Songs, 1969; (ed) Ronald Firbank: memoirs and critiques, 1977. *Recreations:* music, idling. *Address:* Ashford Chace, Petersfield, Hants.

HORDERN, Michael Murray, CBE 1972; actor; *b* 3 Oct. 1911; *s* of Capt. Edward Joseph Calverly Hordern, CIE, RIN, and Margaret Emily (*née* Murray); *m* 1943, Grace Eveline Mortimer; one *d*. *Educ:* Brighton Coll. Formerly in business with The Educational Supply Assoc., playing meanwhile as an amateur at St Pancras People's Theatre. First professional appearance as Lodovico in Othello, People's Palace, 1937. Two seasons of repertory at Little Theatre, Bristol, 1937-39; War service in Navy, 1940-46; demobilised as Lieut-Comdr, RNVR. Parts include: Mr Toad in Toad of Toad Hall, at Stratford, 1948 and 1949; Ivanov in Ivanov, Arts Theatre, 1950. Stratford Season, 1952: Jacques, Menenius, Caliban. Old Vic Season, 1953-54: Polonius, King John, Malvolio, Prospero. "BB" in The Doctor's Dilemma, Saville, 1956; Old Vic Season, 1958-59: Cassius, Macbeth. Ulysses (Troilus and Cressida), Edinburgh Fest., 1962; Herbert Georg Beutler in The Physicists, Aldwych, 1963; Southman in Saint's Day, St Martin's, 1965; Relatively Speaking, Duke of York's, 1967; A Delicate Balance, Aldwych, 1969; King Lear, Nottingham Playhouse, 1969, National Theatre, 1970; Flint, Criterion, 1970; Jumpers, 1972 and 1976, Gaunt in Richard II, 1972, The Cherry Orchard, 1973, National Theatre; The Ordeal of Gilbert Pinfold, Manchester, 1977. Also many leading parts in films, radio and television. *Recreation:* fishing. *Address:* 24 Kelso Place, W8; Bagnor, Newbury, Berks. *Clubs:* Garrick; Flyfishers'.

HORDERN, Peter Maudslay; MP (C) Horsham and Crawley, since 1974 (Horsham, 1964-74); *b* 18 April 1929; British; *m* 1964, Susan Chataway; two *s* one *d*. *Educ:* Geelong Grammar Sch., Australia; Christ Church, Oxford, 1949-52 (MA). Mem. of Stock Exchange, London, 1957-74. Director: Petrofina (UK) Ltd, 1973-; Atlas Electric & General Trust, 1975-. Chm., Cons. Parly Finance Cttee, 1970-72; Member: Exec., 1922 Cttee, 1968-; Public Accts Cttee, 1970-. *Recreations:* golf, reading and travel. *Address:* 55 Cadogan Street, SW3.

HORLICK, Sir John (James Macdonald), 5th Bt *cr* 1914; Chairman, Folly Bridge Holdings Ltd, since 1971; Partner, Tournaig Farming Company; *b* 9 April 1922; *s* of Lt-Col Sir James Horlick, 4th Bt, OBE, MC, and Flora Macdonald (*d* 1955), *d* of late Col Cunliffe Martin, CB; *S* father, 1972; *m* 1948, June, *d* of Douglas Cory-Wright, CBE; one *s* two *d*. *Educ:* Eton; Babson Institute of Business Admin, Wellesley Hills, Mass, USA. Served War as Captain, Coldstream Guards. Dep. Chairman, Horlicks Ltd, retired 1971. *Recreations:* shooting, model soldier collecting. *Heir: s* James Cunliffe William Horlick, *b* 19 Nov. 1956. *Address:* Tournaig, Poolewe, Achnasheen, Ross-shire. *T:* Poolewe 250; Howberry Lane Cottage, Nuffield, near Nettlebed, Oxon. *T:* Nettlebed 641454. *Clubs:* Beefsteak, Bath; Highland (Inverness).

HORLOCK, Henry Wimburn Sudell; Director, Stepping Stone School, since 1962; *b* 19 July 1915; *s* of Rev. Henry Darrell Sudell Horlock, DD, and Mary Haliburton Laurie; *m* 1960, Jeannetta Robin, *d* of F. W. Tanner, JP. *Educ:* Pembroke Coll., Oxford (MA). Served Army, 1939-42; Ministry of Agriculture, 1942-60. Mem., Court of Common Council, City of London, 1969-; Sheriff, City of London, 1972-73; Liveryman, Saddlers Co., 1937-, Mem., Court of Assistants, 1968-, Master, 1976-77; Member: Parish Clerks' Co., 1966-; Court of Assistants, 1976-; Liveryman (Hon.), Plaisterers' Co., 1975-. Commander, Order of Merit, Federal Republic of Germany, 1972; Commander, National Order of the Aztec Eagle of Mexico, 1973. *Recreations:* travel, walking. *Address:* 33 Fitzjohn's Avenue, NW3 5JY. *T:* 01-435 9642. *Clubs:* Guildhall, City Livery, National.

HORLOCK, Prof. John Harold, FRS 1976; Vice-Chancellor, University of Salford, since 1974; Professor of Engineering, University of Salford, since 1976; *b* 19 April 1928; *s* of Harold Edgar and Olive Margaret Horlock; *m* 1953, Sheila Joy Stutely; one *s* two *d*. *Educ:* Edmonton Latymer Sch.; (Scholar) St John's Coll., Cambridge. 1st Class Hons Mech. Sci. Tripos, Pt I, 1948, Rex Moir Prize; Pt II, 1949; MA 1952; PhD 1955; ScD 1975. Design and Development Engineer, Rolls Royce Ltd, Derby, 1949-51; Research Fellow, St John's Coll., Cambridge, 1954-57; Univ. Demonstrator, 1952-56; University Lecturer, 1956-58, at Cambridge Univ. Engineering Lab.; Harrison Prof. of Mechanical Engineering and Head of Dept, Liverpool Univ., 1958-66; Prof. of Engineering, 1967-74, Dep. Head of Engineering Dept, 1969-73, Cambridge Univ. Professorial Fellow of St John's Coll., Cambridge, 1967-74. Visiting Asst Prof. in Mech. Engineering, Massachusetts Inst. of Technology, USA, 1956-57; Vis. Prof. of Aero-Space Engineering, Pennsylvania State Univ., USA, 1966. Dir, BICERA Ltd, 1964-65; Member: ARC, 1960-63, 1969-72; SRC, 1974-. Dir, Cambridge Water Co., 1971-74. CEng, FIMechE, FRAeS; Fellow, Fellowship of Engineering, 1977. Mem. ASME. Thomas Hawksley Gold Medal, IMechE, 1969. *Publications:* The Fluid Mechanics and Thermodynamics of Axial Flow Compressors, 1958; The Fluid Mechanics and Thermodynamics of Axial Flow Turbines, 1966; contribs to mech. and aero. engineering jls and to Proc. Royal Society. *Recreations:* music, cricket, golf. *Address:* University of Salford, Salford M5 4WT. *Clubs:* Athenæum, MCC.

HORN, Alan Bowes, CVO 1971; HM Diplomatic Service, retired; *b* 6 June 1917; *m* 1946, Peggy Boocock; one *s* one *d*. *Educ:* London Sch. of Economics. Served in Army, 1940-46. Joined Foreign Service, 1946; Vice-Consul, Marseilles, 1948-49; 2nd Sec., HM Embassy, Tel Aviv, 1949; promoted 1st Sec. and later apptd: London, 1951-53; New York, 1953-56; Helsinki, 1957-60; FO, 1960-63; Ambassador to the Malagasy Republic, 1963-67; Counsellor, Warsaw, 1967-70; Consul-General, Istanbul, 1970-73. *Address:* Oak Trees, Shere Road, Ewhurst, Cranleigh, Surrey.

HORN, Prof. Gabriel, MA, MD, ScD; Professor of Zoology, University of Cambridge, and Fellow of King's College, Cambridge, since 1978; *b* 9 Dec. 1927; *s* of late A. Horn and Mrs Horn; *m* 1952, Ann Loveday Dean Soper; two *s* two *d*. *Educ:* Handsworth Technical Sch. and Coll., Birmingham (Nat. Cert. in Mech. Engrg); Univ. of Birmingham (BSc Anatomy and Physiology; MD, ChB). MA, ScD Cantab. Served in RAF (Educn Br.), 1947-49. House appts, Birmingham Children's and Birmingham and Midland Eye Hosps, 1955-56; Univ. of Cambridge: Univ. Demonstrator in Anat., 1956-62; Lectr in Anat., 1962-72; Reader in Neurobiology, 1972-74; Fellow of King's Coll., 1962-74; Prof. and Head of Dept of Anat., Univ. of Bristol, 1974-77. Sen. Res. Fellow in Neurophysiol., Montreal Neurol Inst., McGill Univ., 1957-58; Vis. Prof. of Physiol Optics, Univ. of Calif, Berkeley, 1963; Vis. Res. Prof., Ohio State Univ., 1965; Vis. Prof. of Zool., Makerere University Coll., Uganda, 1966; Leverhulme Res. Fellow, Laboratoire de Neurophysiologie Cellulaire, France, 1970-71. Member: Biol Sciences Cttee, SRC, 1973-75; Jt MRC and SRC Adv. Panel on Neurobiol., 1971-72; Res. Cttee, Mental Health Foundn, 1973-; Council, Anatomical Soc., 1976-78. Kenneth Craik Award in Physiol Psychol., 1962. *Publications:* (ed with R. A. Hinde) Short-Term Changes in Neural Activity and Behaviour, 1970; contrib. scientific jls, mainly on topics in neurosciences.

Recreations: walking, music. *Address:* King's College, Cambridge. *T:* Cambridge 50411.

HORNBY, Sir Antony; *see* Hornby, Sir R. A.

HORNBY, Derrick Richard; Divisional Managing Director, Spillers International, since 1977; *b* 11 Jan. 1926; *s* of late Richard W. Hornby and Dora M. Hornby; *m* 1948, June Steele; two *s* one *d*. *Educ:* University Coll., Southampton (DipEcon). Early career in accountancy; Marketing Dir, Tetley Tea Co. Ltd, 1964-69; Man. Dir, Eden Vale, 1969-74; Chm., Spillers Foods Ltd, 1974-77. Pres., Food Manufrs Fedn Incorp.; Mem., Food and Drinks EDC. FBIM, FIGD, ACommA. *Recreation:* golf. *Address:* 26a Shawfield Street, Chelsea, SW3 4BD. *T:* 01-352 6862. *Clubs:* National Sporting; Wentworth (Surrey).

HORNBY, Frank Robert, CBE 1972 (MBE 1944); Chief Officer and Vice-Chairman, Council for National Academic Awards, 1964-72, retired; *b* 20 Aug. 1911; *yr s* of late Robert Wilson Hornby and Jane Hornby; *m* 1939, Kathleen Margaret, *yr d* of late Dr Sidney Berry and Helen Berry. *Educ:* Heversham Sch., Westmorland; Magdalene Coll., Cambridge. 1st Class Natural Sciences Tripos Pts 1 and 2. Schoolmaster, 1933-41. RAOC, 1941-46 (Lieut-Col). Asst Educn Officer, Nottingham Co. Borough, 1946-56; Sec., Nat. Coun. for Technological Awards, 1956-64. Hon. LLD CNAA, 1972. *Address:* 15 Williams Way, Radlett, Herts. *T:* Radlett 5083.

HORNBY, Prof. James Angus; Professor of Law in the University of Bristol since 1961; *b* 15 Aug. 1922; twin *s* of James Hornby and Evelyn Gladys (*née* Grant). *Educ:* Bolton County Grammar Sch.; Christ's Coll., Cambridge. BA 1944, LLB 1945, MA 1948 Cantab. Called to Bar, Lincoln's Inn, 1947. Lecturer, Manchester Univ., 1947-61. *Publications:* An Introduction to Company Law, 1957, 5th edn 1975; contribs to legal journals. *Recreations:* hill walking, chess. *Address:* The Faculty of Law, The University, Bristol. *Club:* United Oxford & Cambridge University.

HORNBY, Michael Charles St John; retired as Vice-Chairman, W. H. Smith & Son Ltd (1944-65); *b* 2 Jan. 1899; *e s* of C. H. St J. Hornby and Cicely Hornby; *m* 1928, Nicolette Joan, *d* of Hon. Cyril Ward, MVO; two *s* one *d*. *Educ:* Winchester; RMC Sandhurst; New Coll., Oxford. Joined Grenadier Guards, 1918; served in France and Germany. New Coll., Oxford, 1919-21. Entered W. H. Smith & Son, 1921. Prime Warden, Goldsmiths' Company, 1954-55. Chm., National Book League, 1959. *Recreations:* fox-hunting, shooting, cricket, gardening. *Address:* Pusey House, Faringdon, Oxon. *T:* Buckland 222. *Clubs:* White's, MCC.

See also Sir R. A. *Hornby, S. M. Hornby.*

HORNBY, Richard Phipps, MA; Director: J. Walter Thompson Co. Ltd; Halifax Building Society; *b* 20 June 1922; *e s* of late Rt Rev. Hugh Leycester Hornby, MC; *m* 1951, Stella Hichens; three *s* one *d*. *Educ:* Winchester Coll.; Trinity Coll., Oxford (Scholar). Served in King's Royal Rifle Corps, 1941-45. 2nd Cl. Hons in Modern History, Oxford, 1948 (Soccer Blue). History Master, Eton Coll., 1948-50; with Unilever, 1951-52; with J. Walter Thompson Co., 1952-63, 1964-. Contested (C) West Walthamstow: May 1955 (gen. election) and March 1956 (by-election); MP (C) Tonbridge, Kent, June 1956-Feb. 1974. PPS to Rt Hon. Duncan Sandys, MP, 1959-63; Parly Under-Sec. of State, CRO and CO, Oct. 1963-Oct. 1964. Member: BBC Gen. Adv. Council, 1969-74; Cttee of Inquiry into Intrusions into Privacy, 1970-72; British Council Exec. Cttee, 1971-74. *Recreations:* shooting, fishing, walking, riding and tennis. *Address:* 10 Hereford Square, SW7.

HORNBY, Sir (Roger) Antony, Kt 1960; President, Savoy Hotel Ltd, since 1977 (Vice-Chairman to Dec. 1976); Director, Connaught Hotel Co.; *b* 5 Feb. 1904; *s* of late C. H. St J. Hornby, Shelley House, Chelsea; *m* 1st, 1931, Lady Veronica Blackwood (marr. diss. 1940); one *d*; 2nd, 1949, Lily Ernst. *Educ:* Winchester Coll.; New Coll., Oxford. MA Oxon. Vice-Chm. King's Coll. Hosp., 1959-74. Served War of 1939-45, Grenadier Guards. A Trustee of the Wallace Collection, 1963-77; Chm., Nat. Art Collections Fund, 1970-75. *Recreation:* collecting pictures. *Address:* Claridge's Hotel, W1. *Clubs:* Garrick, MCC.

See also M. C. St J. *Hornby.*

HORNBY, Simon Michael; Director, W. H. Smith & Son (Holdings) Ltd, since 1974; *b* 29 Dec. 1934; *s* of Michael Hornby, *qv*; *m* 1968, Sheran Cazalet. *Educ:* Eton; New Coll., Oxford; Harvard Business Sch. 2nd Lieut, Grenadier Guards, 1953-55. Entered W. H. Smith & Son, 1958, Dir, 1965. Mem. Exec. Cttee, 1966-; Finance Cttee, 1970-; Council 1976-; National Trust; Mem. Adv. Council, Victoria and Albert

Museum, 1971-75; Trustee: British Museum, 1975-; Phoenix Trust, 1975-; Dep. Chm., Nat. Book League, 1976-. *Recreations:* gardening, golf. *Address:* 8 Ennismore Gardens, SW7 1LN. *T:* 01-584 1597; Lake House, Pusey, Faringdon, Oxon SN7 8QB. *T:* Buckland 659. *Club:* Garrick.

HORNE, Sir Alan Edgar, 2nd Bt *cr* 1929; MC; *b* 19 Sept. 1889; *s* of Sir Edgar Horne, 1st Bt, and Margery (*d* 1939), *d* of George Anderson May, Elford, Staffs; *S* father, 1941; *m* 1st, 1915, Henriette Kelly (*d* 1918); one *d*; 2nd, 1923, Roslyn (*d* 1961), *d* of John Brian Robinson; (one *s* decd). *Educ:* Eton; Magdalen Coll., Oxford. Served European War, 1914-19, in France and Balkans as Capt. Surrey Yeomanry and on Staff (despatches 4 times, MC, French Croix de Guerre); War of 1939-45, Basutoland and MELF, 1940-48, as Lt-Col Royal Pioneer Corps (African and Native Troops). *Heir: g s* Alan Gray Antony Horne, *b* 11 July 1948. *Address:* 1 The Paragon (Flat 4), Blackheath, SE3. *Clubs:* Cavalry and Guards, MCC.

HORNE, Alistair Allan; author, journalist, farmer and lecturer; *b* 9 Nov. 1925; *s* of late Sir (James) Allan Horne and Lady (Auriol Camilla) Horne (*née* Hay); *m* 1953, Renira Margaret Hawkins; three *d*. *Educ:* Le Rosey, Switzerland; Millbrook, USA; Jesus Coll., Cambridge (MA). Served War of 1939-45: RAF, 1943-44; Coldstream Gds, 1944-47; Captain, attached Intelligence Service (ME). Dir, Ropley Trust Ltd, 1948-77; Foreign Correspondent, Daily Telegraph, 1952-55. Founded Alistair Horne Res. Fellowship in Mod. History, St Antony's Coll., Oxford, 1969. Mem., Management Cttee, Royal Literary Fund, 1969-; Trustee, Imperial War Museum, 1975-. FRSL. Knight of Mark Twain. *Publications:* Back into Power, 1955; The Land is Bright, 1958; Canada and the Canadians, 1961; The Price of Glory: Verdun 1916, 1962 (Hawthornden Prize, 1963); The Fall of Paris: The Siege and The Commune 1870-71, 1965; To Lose a Battle: France 1940, 1969; Death of a Generation, 1970; The Terrible Year: The Paris Commune, 1971; Small Earthquake in Chile, 1972; A Savage War of Peace: Algeria 1954-62, 1977; contribs to books: Combat: World War I, ed Don Congdon, 1964; Impressions of America, ed R. A. Brown, 1966; Marshal V. I. Chuikov, The End of the Third Reich, 1967; Sports and Games in Canadian Life, ed N. and M. L. Howell, 1969; Decisive Battles of the Twentieth Century, ed N. Frankland and C. Dowling, 1976; The War Lords: Military Commanders of the Twentieth Century, ed Field Marshal Sir M. Carver, 1976; contribs various periodicals. *Recreations:* skiing, shooting, painting. *Address:* 24 Lansdowne Road, W11; Membury House, Ramsbury, Wilts. *Clubs:* Garrick, White's.

HORNE, Frederic Thomas; Master of the Supreme Court (Taxing Office) since 1967; *b* 21 March 1917; *y s* of Lionel Edward Horne, JP, Moreton-in-Marsh, Glos; *m* 1944, Madeline Hatton; two *s* two *d*. *Educ:* Chipping Campden Grammar Sch. Admitted a Solicitor (Hons), 1938. Served with RAFVR in General Duties Branch (Pilot), 1939-56. Partner in Iliffe Sweet & Co., 1956-67. *Recreations:* cricket, music. *Address:* Burfield Corner, 50 Dove Park, Chorleywood, Herts. *Club:* MCC.

HORNE, Maj.-Gen. Gerald Tom Warlters, CB 1949; CBE 1945 (OBE 1944); *b* 4 March 1898; *s* of late Thomas Warlters Horne and late Cornelia Horne (*née* Ellis); *m* 1921, Janetta Marie Graham; one *d* (and one *s* killed in action, 1944). *Educ:* Repton; RMA Woolwich. Commissioned 2nd Lieut Royal Regt of Artillery, 1917; served European War, 1914-18, transferred to Royal Army Ordnance Corps, 1925; Capt., 1925; Major, 1936; Staff Coll., 1938-39; War of 1939-45, BEF France, 1939-40; War Office, 1940-44; Italy, 1944-45; War Office, Dep. Dir Ordnance Services (Brig.), 1945-48; Maj.-Gen., 1948; Dir of Ordnance Services (War Office), 1948-51; retired, 1951. Bronze Medal for Valour (Italian), 1918. *Recreations:* golf and gardening. *Address:* 28 Smarts Heath Road, Mayford, Woking, Surrey.

HORNE, Prof. Michael Rex, MA, PhD, ScD Cantab; MSc (Manchester); CEng, FICE; FIStructE; Professor of Civil Engineering, University of Manchester, since 1960; *b* 29 Dec. 1921; *s* of late Rev. Ernest Horne, Leicester; *m* 1947, Molly, *d* of late Mark Hewett, Royston, Herts; two *s* two *d*. *Educ:* Boston (Lincs) Grammar Sch.; Leeds Grammar Sch.; St John's Coll., Cambridge. MA Cantab 1945; PhD Cantab 1950, ScD Cantab 1956. John Winbolt Prize for Research, Cambridge Univ., 1944. Asst Engineer, River Great Ouse Catchment Bd, 1941-45; Scientific Officer, British Welding Research Assoc., 1945-51; Asst Dir of Research in Engineering, 1951-56, Lectr in Engineering, 1957-60, Univ. of Cambridge. Instn of Civil Engineers, Telford Premiums, 1956, 1966. Chm., NW Branch, 1969-70, Vice-Pres., 1976-, IStructE; Mem., Merrison Cttee on Box Girders, 1970-73. Fellow, St John's College, Cambridge, 1957. Diploma, 1971, Bronze Medal, 1973, IStructE. *Publications:* (with J. F. Baker and J. Heyman) The Steel

Skeleton, 1956; (with W. F. Merchant) The Stability of Frames, 1965; The Plastic Theory of Structures, 1971; contribs on structures, strength of materials and particulate theory of soils to learned journals. *Recreations:* photography, wine-making, music. *Address:* 19 Park Road, Hale, Cheshire.

HORNER, Arthur William, CMG 1964; TD and clasp 1946; *b* 22 June 1909; *s* of Francis Moore and Edith Horner; *m* 1938, Patricia Denise (*née* Campbell); two *s* one *d. Educ:* Hardenwick; Felsted. Marine Insurance, 1926-39. Served War, 1939-46, Rifle Brigade; Lieut-Col; psc. Farming in Kenya, 1948-50. Colonial Administrative Service (later HM Overseas Civil Service), Kenya, 1950-64; Commissioner of Lands, 1955-61; Permanent Sec., 1961-64; Dir of Independence Celebrations, 1963; Principal, ODM, 1964-73; seconded Diplomatic Service, 1968-70, retired 1973. *Recreations:* music, gardening. *Address:* St Margaret's Cottage, Northiam, Rye, East Sussex.

HORNER, Hallam; *see* Horner, L. J. H.

HORNER, John; *b* 5 Nov. 1911; *s* of Ernest Charles and Emily Horner; *m* 1936, Patricia, *d* of Geoffrey and Alice Palmer; two *d. Educ:* elementary sch. and Sir George Monoux Grammar Sch., Walthamstow. Apprenticed Merchant Navy, 1927; Second Mate's Certificate, 1932. Joined London Fire Brigade, 1933; Gen. Sec. Fire Brigades Union, 1939-64; MP (Lab) Oldbury and Halesowen, 1964-70. Mem. Select Cttee on Nationalised Industries. *Publication:* Studies in Industrial Democracy, 1974. *Recreations:* walking, gardening, talking, listening to music, studying history and art. *Address:* Yew Tree, Howle Hill, Ross on Wye, Herefordshire. *T:* Ross on Wye 2932.

HORNER, (Lawrence John) Hallam, CBE 1973 (OBE 1959); Director, Chamber of Shipping of UK, 1966-72; *b* 14 June 1907; *o s* of late David Aitken Horner and Louise Stuart Black; *m* 1935, Kathleen Joan (*d* 1976), *o d* of late Charles D. Taite, Bowdon, Cheshire; two *d. Educ:* Malvern Coll.; Corpus Christi Coll., Oxford (MA). Served War of 1939-45, Royal Scots Fusiliers and Royal Armoured Corps (despatches). Admitted Solicitor (hons), 1931; Asst Solicitor, Cheshire CC, 1932-34; Rees & Freres, parly agents, 1934-51 (Partner, 1936); Sec., Canal Assoc., 1945-48; Parly Solicitor (later also 1975; Vice-Chm., Arthritis and Rheumatism Council for Research. Dock and Harbour Authorities' Assoc., 1946-51; Asst Gen. Man. *Club:* Special Forces. Agent, Chamber of Shipping of UK, 1951, Gen. *Publications:* A Full Life, 1960, new edn, 1974; Corps Commander, 1977; Editor, Famous Regiments Series. *Address:* Manor Oil Pollution of the Sea, 1952-66; Mem., City of London Coll. Shipping Adv. Cttee, 1966-72; Mem., Cttee of Management, British Ship Adoption Soc., 1968-72, FCIT (MInstT), 1970; Hon. FICS, 1972. Netherlands Bronze Cross, 1945. *Recreation:* watching birds. *Address:* Higher Woolcotts Farm, Brompton Regis, Dulverton, Somerset. *T:* Brompton Regis 237. *Club:* Reform.
See also Sir T. C. Spenser-Wilkinson.

HORNER, Mrs Sibyl Gertrude, CBE 1957; MB, BS; DPH Oxon; DIH; HM Senior Medical Inspector of Factories, 1957-61; *b* 18 Oct. 1895; 5th *d* of late Arthur Overton and Mary Overton, Forest Row, Sussex; *m* 1931, Bernard Stuart Horner, OBE; no *c. Educ:* London Sch. of Medicine and St Mary's Hosp., Paddington. MB, BS London 1919. HM Medical Inspector of Factories (Home Office), 1924; HM Dep. Senior Medical Inspector of Factories (Min. of Labour), 1948. Mem. Order of St John of Jerusalem. *Recreations:* horticulture, travel, walking. *Address:* Eaton Cottage, Esher, Surrey. *T:* Esher 63574.

HORNSBY, Harry Reginald, MBE 1944; *b* 19 Dec. 1907; *s* of Rev. E. F. Hornsby, Hon. CF; *m* 1946, Mary Elizabeth Whitley; no *c. Educ:* Bromsgrove Sch.; Brasenose Coll., Oxford. Asst Master, Christ's Hosp., Horsham, 1929-39; Headmaster, The King's Sch., Peterborough, 1939-51; Headmaster: Christ's Coll., Christchurch, NZ, 1951-63; St Paul's Sch., Hamilton, NZ, 1963-69; St Andrew's School, Nekualofa, Tonga, 1970-72. Lay Canon of Christchurch Cathedral, 1962-63; Mem. of Council, Univ. of Canterbury, NZ, 1962-63. War Service, 1940-45 (despatches): Gunner RA, 1940; commissioned Worcs Regt, 1941; served 3rd Queen Alexandra's Own Gurkha Rifles, 1941-45. Chm. Independent Schools Assoc. of New Zealand, 1960-63; Member: Outward Bound Trust of New Zealand, 1961-64; Council, Univ. of Waikato, 1965-68. Lay Canon of Waikato Cathedral, 1967, 1968, 1969. *Recreations:* all games, mountaineering, gardening. *Address:* 13 Bay View Road, Nelson, New Zealand.

HORNSBY-SMITH, family name of **Baroness Hornsby-Smith.**

HORNSBY-SMITH, Baroness *cr* 1974 (Life Peer), of Chislehurst; **Margaret Patricia Hornsby-Smith,** PC 1959; DBE 1961; *b* 17 March 1914; *o d* of F. C. Hornsby-Smith. *Educ:* Richmond. Ministry of Economic Warfare, 1941-45; Barnes Borough Council, 1945-49. MP (C) Kent, Chislehurst, 1950-66 and 1970-Feb. 1974; Parly Sec., Ministry of Health, 1951-57; UK delegate to Assembly of UN, 1958; Jt Parly Under-Sec. of State, Home Office, 1957-59; Jt Parly Sec., Min. of Pensions and Nat. Insurance, 1959-61. Led UK Parliamentary Delegation to Australasia, 1961, Kenya 1972. Pres., EAW, 1975; Vice-Chm., Arthritis and Rheumatism Council for Research. FRSA 1971. *Address:* 31 Stafford Mansions, Stafford Place, SW1E 6NL. *Club:* Special Forces.

HORNUNG, Lt-Col Sir John (Derek), KCVO 1976; OBE 1944; MC 1940; Lieutenant of the Queen's Bodyguard of the Yeomen of the Guard since 1971; Chairman, Sena Sugar Estates Ltd, since 1964; *b* 3 Jan. 1915; *er s* of late Lt-Col Charles Bernard Raphael Hornung. *Educ:* Eton. 2nd Lieut Irish Guards, 1936; served War of 1939-45, France and NW Europe; Lt-Col 1944; retd 1948. High Sheriff for Sussex, 1962; Exon Queen's Bodyguard of the Yeomen of the Guard, 1954-67, Clerk of the Cheque and Adjt, 1967-71. Steward of the Jockey Club, 1968-70. *Recreations:* breeding and racing thoroughbreds; shooting. *Address:* Ivorys, Cowfold, Horsham, West Sussex. *T:* Cowfold 240. *Clubs:* Jockey, White's, Cavalry and Guards.

HOROWITZ, Vladimir; pianist; *b* Kieff, Russia, 1 Oct. 1904; *s* of Samuel Horowitz and Sophie Bodik; *m* 1933, Wanda Toscanini. *Educ:* Kieff Conservatory; studied under Sergi Tarnowsky and Felix Blumenfeld. European Début, 1925; début with New York Philharmonic Orchestra, 1928. Soloist, New York Symphony Orchestra and other American orchestras. Winner 11 Grammy Awards. Royal Philharmonic Soc. Gold Medal, 1972. *Address:* c/o Shaw Concerts Inc., 1995 Broadway, New York, NY 10023, USA.

HORRIDGE, Prof. (George) Adrian, FRS 1969; FAA 1971; Professor of Neurobiology, Research School of Biological Sciences, Australian National University, ACT 2600, since 1969; *b* Sheffield, England, 12 Dec. 1927; *s* of George William Horridge and Olive Stray; *m* 1954, Audrey Anne Lightburne; one *s* three *d. Educ:* King Edward VII Sch., Sheffield. Fellow, St John's Coll., Cambridge, 1953-56; on staff, St Andrews Univ., 1956-60; Dir, Gatty Marine Laboratory, St Andrews, 1960-69. Vis. Fellow, Churchill Coll., Cambridge, 1976-77. ScD Cantab 1968. *Publications:* Structure and Function of the Nervous Systems of Invertebrates (with T. H. Bullock), 1965; Interneurons, 1968; (ed) The compound eye and vision of insects, 1975; contribs numerous scientific papers on behaviour and nervous systems of lower animals, to jls, etc. *Recreations:* optics, mathematics, marine biology, sailing, language, arts, boat construction in Indonesia. *Address:* PO Box 475, Canberra, ACT 2600, Australia. *T:* Canberra 494532.

HORROCKS, Lt-Gen. Sir Brian Gwynne, KCB 1949 (CB 1943); KBE 1945; DSO 1943; MC; a Director of Bovis Holdings since 1963; Gentleman Usher of the Black Rod, House of Lords, 1949-63; *b* 7 Sept. 1895; *o s* of late Col Sir William Heaton Horrocks, KCMG, CB; *m* 1928, Nancy, *d* of Brook and Hon. Mrs Brook Kitchin; one *d. Educ:* Uppingham; RMC Sandhurst. 2nd Lieut Middlesex Regt, 1914; served European War, France and Belgium, 1914, Russia, 1919 (wounded, MC); War of 1939-45 (wounded, DSO, CB, KBE); Comd 44 (HC Div.), 9 Armd Div., 13 Corps, 10 Corps in Egypt and Africa, 9 Corps Tunis, 30 Corps in BLA. GOC-in-C Western Comd, 1946; GOC-in-C British Army of the Rhine, 1948; retired, 1949. Hon. LLD (Belfast). *Publications:* A Full Life, 1960, new edn, 1974; Corps Commander, 1977; Editor, Famous Regiments Series. *Address:* Manor Farm, East Compton, Shepton Mallet, Somerset. *Club:* Naval and Military.

HORSBRUGH-PORTER, Sir Andrew (Marshall), 3rd Bt, *cr* 1902; DSO 1940; Col retired, 1953; *b* 1 June 1907; *s* of Sir John Horsbrugh-Porter, 2nd Bt, and Elaine Maud, *y d* of Thomas Jefferies; *S* father, 1953; *m* 1933, Annette Mary, *d* of late Brig.-Gen. R. C. Browne-Clayton, DSO, Browne's Hill, Carlow; one *s* two *d. Educ:* Winchester; RMC, Sandhurst. Subaltern 12th Royal Lancers, 1927; Capt., 1937; Acting Major, Sept. 1939; Temp. Major, Dec. 1939; Major, 1944; Lieut-Col, 1949. Served War of 1939-45 (DSO and Bar); commanded 27th Lancers, 1941-45; GSO1, Liaison attached to US Army, 1947; commanded 12th Royal Lancers, 1948-52; Military Adviser to UK High Commissioner, New Delhi, 1952. *Recreations:* watching polo and hunting. *Heir: s* John Simon Horsbrugh-Porter [*b* 18 Dec. 1938; *m* 1964, Lavinia Rose, *d* of Ralph Turton, Kildale Hall, Whitby, Yorks; one *s* two *d*]. *Address:* Manor Farm House, Salford, Chipping Norton, Oxon. *Club:* Cavalry and Guards.
See also Sir J. D. Barlow, Bt.

HORSEFIELD, John Keith, CB 1957; Historian, International Monetary Fund, 1966-69; *b* 14 Oct. 1901; *s* of Rev. Canon F. J. Horsefield, Bristol; *m* 1934, Lucy G. G. Florance. *Educ:* Monkton Combe Sch.; University of Bristol; MA 1948, DSc 1971; London Sch. of Economics. Lecturer, LSE, 1939; Min. of Aircraft Production, 1940; International Monetary Fund, 1947; Under-Sec., Min. of Supply, 1951; Dep. Asst Sec.-Gen. for Economics and Finance, NATO, 1952; Supply and Development Officer, Iron and Steel Bd, 1954; Dir of Finance and Accounts, Gen. Post Office, 1955-60; Chief Editor, International Monetary Fund, 1960-66. *Publications:* The Real Cost of the War, 1940; British Monetary Experiments, 1650-1710, 1960; The International Monetary Fund, 1945-1965, 1970; articles in Economica, etc. *Address:* 37 Clatterford Road, Carisbrooke, Newport, Isle of Wight PO30 1PA. *T:* Newport (IoW) 3675.

HORSFALL, Geoffrey Jonas, CBE 1967; Judge of the Grand Court of the Cayman Islands, West Indies, 1965-73, retired; *b* 22 Jan. 1905; *s* of late Major A. H. Horsfall, DSO, TD, Newcastle, NSW, Australia; *m* 1947, Robin, *y d* of late Curwin Maclure, Albury, NSW; one *s* two *d. Educ:* The King's Sch., Parramatta, NSW; Cheltenham Coll.; Keble Coll., Oxford. BA 1927; Barrister-at-Law, 1928, Gray's Inn; South-Eastern Circuit. Entered Colonial Legal Service, 1936, as Crown Counsel, Nigeria; Crown Counsel, Sierra Leone, 1943; Senior Magistrate, Fiji, 1947; Judicial Commissioner, British Solomon Islands Protectorate, 1953; Judge of the High Court, Zanzibar, 1958; Chief Justice of Zanzibar, 1964, but office abolished in Zanzibar revolution. *Recreations:* walking, gardening. *Address:* 78 Hawthorne Avenue, Chatswood, NSW 2067, Australia. *T:* 02-411-3892.

HORSFALL, Sir John (Musgrave), 3rd Bt *cr* 1909; MC 1946; TD 1949 and clasp 1951; JP; *b* 26 Aug. 1915; *s* of Sir (John) Donald Horsfall, 2nd Bt, and Henrietta (*d* 1936), *d* of William Musgrave; *S* father, 1975; *m* 1940, Cassandra Nora Bernardine, *d* of late G. E. Wright; two *s* one *d. Educ:* Uppingham. Major, Duke of Wellington's Regt. Director: Hayfield Textiles Ltd; Skipton Building Society; Worsted Spinners Federation Ltd. Mem. Skipton RDC, 1952-74; Pres. Skipton Divl Conservative Assoc. JP WR Yorks, 1959. *Recreation:* shooting. *Heir: s* Edward John Wright Horsfall [*b* 17 Dec. 1940; *m* 1965, Rosemary, *d* of Frank N. King; three *s*]. *Address:* Greenfield House, Embsay, Skipton, North Yorkshire. *T:* Skipton 4560. *Club:* Union (Bradford).

HORSFALL TURNER, Harold, CBE 1974; solicitor in private practice; Partner, Oswald Hickson Collier & Co., since 1974; *b* 1 June 1909; *s* of Stanley Horsfall Turner, Reader in Economics, Aberdeen University; *m* 1937, Eileen Mary Jenkins; two *s. Educ:* Rossall; The Queen's Coll., Oxford; Birmingham Univ. BA Oxford 1932, BCL Oxford 1934, LLB Birmingham 1935. Admitted Solicitor (with 1st Class Hons) 1936. Asst Solicitor, Dudley Corporation, 1936; Legal Asst, Inland Revenue, 1937; Sen. Legal Asst, Min. of National Insurance, 1945; The Law Society: Under-Sec., 1947; Second Secretary-Gen., 1964; Sec.-Gen., 1969-74. *Recreations:* boating, opera, photography. *Address:* 1 Old Palace Terrace, The Green, Richmond, Surrey. *T:* 01-948 1963. *Club:* Garrick.

HORSFIELD, Maj.-Gen. David Ralph, OBE 1962; FIEE; formerly Director, Rollalong Ltd; *b* 17 Dec. 1916; *s* of late Major Ralph B. Horsfield and Morah Horsfield (*née* Baynes); *m* 1948, Sheelah Patricia Royal Eagan; two *s* two *d. Educ:* Oundle Sch.; RMA Woolwich; Cambridge Univ. (MA). Commnd in Royal Signals, 1936; comd Burma Corps Signals, 1942; Instr, Staff Coll., 1944-45; comd 2 Indian Airborne Signals, 1946-47; Instr, RMA Sandhurst, 1950-53; comd 2 Signal Regt, 1956-59; Principal Army Staff Officer, MoD, Malaya, 1959-61; Dir of Telecommunications (Army), 1966-68; ADC to the Queen, 1968-69; Deputy Communications and Electronics, Supreme HQ Allied Powers, Europe, 1968-69; Maj.-Gen. 1969; Chief Signal Officer, BAOR, 1969-72; Col Comdt, Royal Signals, 1972-. *Recreations:* ski-ing (British Ski Champion, 1949), the visual arts. *Address:* Southill House, Cranmore, Shepton Mallet, Somerset. *T:* Cranmore 395. *Club:* Ski Club of Great Britain.

HORSFIELD, Brig. Herbert Eric, CBE 1943; MC (2 Bars); *b* 23 Aug. 1895; *s* of H. Horsfield; *m* 1924, Harriet Beatrice Mills; one *s* one *d. Educ:* Bradfield Coll., Berks; Royal Military Academy, Woolwich. Commissioned RE 1914; France and Flanders, 1915-19; India, Royal Bombay Sappers and Miners, 1920-30; Military Engineer Services, 1930-36; Aldershot, DCRE 1936-37; India, RB Sappers and Miners, 1937-38; Commandant RB Sappers and Miners, 1938-42; Chief Engineer, Eastern Army, 1942-43; Chief Engineer, 14th Army, 1943-44; Chief Engineer, Southern Army, 1945-46; Commandant RE Depot, 1946; Comdr Engineer Stores

Group, Long Marston; retired, 1948. John Mowlem & Co. Ltd, 1948-64. Councillor, Bognor Regis UDC, 1960-67 (Chm., 1964-65 and 1965-66). FRSA 1948-70. *Address:* St Julians, 34 Cross Bush Road, Felpham, Sussex. *T:* Middleton-on-Sea 2057. *Club:* Naval and Military.

HORSFORD, Maj.-Gen. Derek Gordon Thomond, CBE 1962 (MBE 1953); DSO 1944 and Bar 1945; *b* 7 Feb. 1917; *s* of late Captain H. T. Horsford, The Gloucestershire Regt, and Mrs V. E. Horsford, Bexhill-on-Sea; *m* 1948, Sheila Louise Russell Crawford; one *s* (and one step *s* two step *d*). *Educ:* Clifton Coll.; RMC, Sandhurst. Commissioned into 8th Gurkha Rifles, 1937; despatches 1943 and 1945; comd 4/1 Gurkha Rifles, Burma, 1944-45; transf. to RA, 1948; Instructor Staff Coll., 1950-52; transf. to King's Regt, 1950; GSO1, 2nd Infantry Div., 1955-56; comd 1st Bn, The King's Regt, 1957-59; AAG, AG2, War Office, 1959-60; Comdr 24th Infantry Brigade Group, Dec. 1960-Dec. 1962; Imperial Defence Coll., 1963; Brig., Gen. Staff, HQ, BAOR, 1964-66. Maj.-Gen. 1966; GOC: 50 (Northumbrian) Div./Dist, 1966-67; Yorks Dist, 1967-68; 17 Div./Malaya District, 1969-70; Maj.-Gen., Brigade of Gurkhas, 1969-71; Dep. Comdr Land Forces, Hong Kong, 1970-71, retired. Col, The King's Regt, 1965-70; Col, The Gurkha Transport Regt, 1973-. *Recreations:* travel, outdoor life. *Address:* St Mary's Cottage, Semley, Wilts. *Club:* Army and Navy.

HORSHAM, Bishop Suffragan of, since 1975; **Rt. Rev. Ivor Colin Docker;** *b* 3 Dec. 1925; *s* of Colonel Philip Docker, OBE, TD, DL, and Doris Gwendoline Docker (*née* Whitehill); *m* 1950, Thelma Mary, *d* of John William and Gladys Upton; one *s* one *d. Educ:* King Edward's High Sch., Birmingham; Univ. of Birmingham (BA); St Catherine's Coll., Oxford (MA). Curate of Normanton, Yorks, 1949-52; Lecturer of Halifax Parish Church, 1952-54; CMS Area Sec., 1954-59; Vicar of Midhurst, Sussex, 1959-64; RD of Midhurst, 1961-64; Vicar and RD of Seaford, 1964-71; Canon and Prebendary of Colworth in Chichester Cathedral, 1966-; Vicar and RD of Eastbourne, 1971-75; Proctor in Convocation, 1970-75. *Address:* Bishop's Lodge, Worth, Crawley, Sussex RH1O 4RT. *T:* Pound Hill 3051.

HORSHAM, Archdeacon of; *see* Kerr-Dineen, Ven. F. G.

HORSLEY, Air Marshal Sir (Beresford) Peter (Torrington), KCB 1974; CBE 1964; MVO 1956; AFC 1945; idc; psc; pfc; Chairman: Horsley Wood & Co. Ltd, since 1975; Horsley Wood Printing Ltd, since 1975; Director: M. L. Holdings Ltd; M. L. Aviation Ltd; Aeromaritime (UK) Ltd; *b* 26 March 1921; *s* of late Capt. Arthur Beresford Horsley, CBE; *m* 1st, 1943, Phyllis Conrad Phinney (marr. diss. 1976); one *s* one *d* ; 2nd, 1976, Ann MacKinnon, *d* of Gareth and Frances Crwys-Williams; two step *s* two step *d. Educ:* Wellington Coll. Joined Royal Air Force, 1940; served in 2nd TAF and Fighter Command. Adjt Oxford Univ. Air Sqdn, 1948; Commands: No 9 and No 29 Sqdns, RAF Wattisham, RAF Akrotiri. Equerry to Princess Elizabeth and to the Duke of Edinburgh, 1949-52; Equerry to the Queen, 1952-53; Equerry to the Duke of Edinburgh, 1953-56. Dep. Comdt, Jt Warfare Establishment, RAF Old Sarum, 1966-68; Asst CAS (Operations), 1968-70; AOC No 1 (Bomber) Gp, 1971-73; Dep. C-in-C, Strike Comd, 1973-75. Retired RAF, 1975. Croix de Guerre, 1944. Holds Orders of Christ (Portugal), North Star (Sweden), and Menelik (Ethiopia). *Publication:* (as Peter Beresford) Journal of a Stamp Collector, 1972. *Recreations:* ski-ing, philately. *Address:* c/o Barclays Bank Ltd, High Street, Newmarket.

HORSLEY, Colin, OBE 1963; FRCM; Pianist; Professor, Royal College of Music, London, and Royal Northern College of Music; *b* Wanganui, New Zealand, 23 April 1920. *Educ:* Royal College of Music. Debut at invitation of Sir John Barbirolli at Hallé Concerts, Manchester, 1943. Soloist with all leading orchestras of Great Britain, the Royal Philharmonic Soc. (1953, 1959), Promenade Concerts, etc. Toured Belgium, Holland, Spain, France, Scandinavia, Malta, Ceylon, Malaya, Australia and New Zealand. Festival appearances include Aix-en-Provence, International Contemporary Music Festival, Palermo, British Music Festivals in Belgium, Holland and Finland. Broadcasts frequently, and records for His Master's Voice. Hon. ARCM 1959; Hon. RAM; FRCM 1973. *Recreation:* gardening. *Address:* Tawsden Manor, Brenchley, Kent. *T:* Brenchley 2323.

HORSLEY, Sir Peter; *see* Horsley, Sir B. P. T.

HORSMAN, Malcolm; Director, Tozer Kemsley & Millbourn (Holdings) Ltd, since 1975; *b* 28 June 1933. Director, Slater Walker Securities Ltd, 1967-70; Chairman, Ralli International

Ltd, 1969-73; Director, The Bowater Corporation Ltd, 1972-77. Member: Study Group on Local Authority Management Structures, 1971-72; South East Economic Planning Council, 1972-74; Royal Commission on the Press, 1974-77. Member Council: Oxford Centre for Management Studies, 1973-; Birthright; Dep. Chairman Council: National Youth Theatre; Institute of Contemporary Arts Ltd. Visiting Fellow, Cranfield Institute of Technology/The School of Management, 1977-78. *Address:* 1 Gower Street, WC1E 6HA.

HORSTEAD, Rt. Rev. James Lawrence Cecil, CMG 1962; CBE 1956; DD (Hon.) 1956; Canon Emeritus of Leicester Cathedral; *b* 16 Feb. 1898; *s* of James William and Mary Leah Horstead; *m* 1926, Olive Davidson; no *c. Educ:* Christ's Hosp.; University and St John's Coll., Durham (Mathematical Scholar, Lightfoot Scholar). BA 2nd Cl. Maths Hons 1921; Theol. Hons 1923; MA 1924; Deacon, 1923; Priest, 1924; Curate St Margaret's Church, Durham, 1923-26; Sec. for Durham Student Christian Movement, 1923-26; Principal Fourah Bay Coll., 1926-36; Canon Missioner Diocese of Sierra Leone, 1928-36; Sec. Church Missionary Soc., Sierra Leone, 1926-36; Bishop of Sierra Leone, 1936-61; Archbishop of West Africa, 1955-61; Rector of Appleby Magna, 1962-68; Asst Bp, Diocese of Leicester, 1962-76. *Publication:* Co-operation with Africans, International Review of Missions, April 1935.

HORT, Sir James Fenton, 8th Bt *cr* 1767; *b* 6 Sept. 1926; *s* of Sir Fenton George Hort, 7th Bt, and Gwendolene, *d* of late Sir Walter Alcock, MVO; *S* father 1960; *m* 1951, Joan, *d* of late Edward Peat, Swallownest, Sheffield; two *s* two *d. Educ:* Marlborough; Trinity Coll., Cambridge. MA, MB, BCh, Cambridge, 1950. *Recreation:* fishing. *Heir: s* Andrew Edwin Fenton Hort, *b* 15 Nov. 1954. *Address:* 17 Portland Road, East Grinstead, West Sussex.

HORTON, Prof. Eric William; Professor of Pharmacology, University of Edinburgh, since 1969; Member, Governing Body, Inveresk Research International, Musselburgh, since 1971; *b* 20 June 1929; *e s* of Harold and Agnes Horton; *m* 1956, Thalia Helen, *er d* of late Sir George Lowe; two *s* one *d. Educ:* Sedbergh Sch.; Edinburgh Univ. BSc, MB, ChB, PhD, DSc, FRCPE. Mem. Scientific Staff, MRC, Nat. Inst. for Med. Res., London, 1958-60; Dir of Therapeutic Res. and Head of Pharmacology, Miles Labs Ltd, Stoke Poges, 1960-63; Sen. Lectr in Physiology, St Bartholomew's Hosp., London, 1963-66; Wellcome Prof. of Pharmacology, Sch. of Pharmacy, Univ. of London, 1966-69. Member: Adv. Cttee on Pesticides, MAFF, 1970-73; Biological Research and Cell Boards, MRC, 1973-75; Editorial Bd, British Jl of Pharmacology, 1960-66; Editorial Bd, Pharmacological Reviews, 1968-74. Hon. Treasurer, Brit. Pharmacological Soc., 1976-. Baly Medal, RCP, 1973. *Publications:* Prostaglandins, 1972; papers in various jls on peptides and prostaglandins. *Address:* 19 Blackford Road, Edinburgh EH9 2DT. *T:* 031-667 8125; 1 George Square, Edinburgh EH8 9JZ. *T:* 031-667 1011, ext. 2218.

HORTON, Maj.-Gen. Frank Cyril, CB 1957; OBE 1953; RM; *b* 31 May 1907; *s* of late Lieut-Comdr F. Horton, Royal Navy, and late Emma M. Hopper; *m* 1934, Jennie Ellaline Hammond: one *d. Educ:* Sir Roger Manwood's Sch. 2nd Lieut RM 1925; Lieut RM 1928; HMS Cumberland, China Station, 1928-29; HMS Royal Oak, Mediterranean Station, 1929-31; Captain RM, 1936; HMS Ajax, America and West Indies Station, 1936-37; Brevet Major, 1940; psc 1941; Actg Lieut-Col 1942; GSO1, Staff of Chief of Combined Operations, 1942-43; Comdg Officer, 44 (RM) Commando, SE Asia, 1943-44; Directing Staff, Army Staff Coll., 1945-46; Plans Div., Admiralty, 1946-48; Directing Staff, Jt Services Staff Coll., 1948-51; Comdt, Amphibious Sch., RM, 1951-52; idc 1953; Col GS, Staff of Comdt Gen., RM, 1954; Chief of Staff to Commandant Gen. Royal Marines, 1955-58; Maj. 1946; Lieut-Col 1949, Col 1953; Maj.-Gen. 1955; retired, 1958. County Civil Defence Officer, Essex, 1959; Regional Dir of Civil Defence, S Eastern Region, 1961-68. *Address:* Southland, Florance Lane, Groombridge, Sussex. *T:* Groombridge 355. *Club:* Royal Naval and Royal Albert Yacht (Portsmouth).

HORWOOD, Senator the Hon. Owen Pieter Faure; Member of South African Senate, since 1970; Minister of Finance, since 1975; Chancellor, University of Durban-Westville, since 1973; *b* 6 Dec. 1916; *e s* of late Stanley Ebden Horwood and of Anna Johanna Horwood (*née* Faure); *m* 1946, Helen Mary Watt; one *s* one *d. Educ:* Boys' High Sch., Paarl, CP; University of Cape Town (BCom). South African Air Force, 1940-42. Associate Prof. of Commerce, University of Cape Town, 1954-55; Prof. of Economics, University Coll. of Rhodesia and Nyasaland, 1956-57; Univ. of Natal: William Hudson Prof. of Economics, 1957-65; Dir of University's Natal Regional Survey; Principal and

Vice-Chancellor, 1966-70. Minister of Indian Affairs and Tourism, 1972-74; Minister of Economic Affairs, 1974-75. Formerly Director: Netherlands Bank of South Africa Ltd; Rembrandt Tobacco Corp. SA Ltd; Nat. Building Soc.; Trans-Natal Coal Corp.; Bonus Investment Corp. of S Africa; Netherlands Insurance Co. of SA Ltd. Financial Adviser to Govt of Lesotho. *Publications:* (jtly) Economic Systems of the Commonwealth, 1962; contribs to SA Jl of Economics, SA Bankers' Jl, Economica (London), Optima, etc. *Recreations:* cricket, gardening, sailing. *Address:* Private Bag X115, Pretoria, South Africa. *Clubs:* Durban (Durban); Kloof Country (Natal); Ruwa Country (Rhodesia); Western Province Cricket; Cape Town Cricket (Captain 1943-48).

HOSEGOOD, Philip James; Under-Secretary, Welsh Office, since 1976; *b* 9 Sept. 1920; *s* of George Frank and Madeleine Clarisse Hosegood; *m* 1948, Heather (*née* Roriston); two *d. Educ:* Heanor Grammar Sch.; correspondence courses. Joined Civil Service as Tax Officer, 1937; Exec. Officer, India Office, 1939. Served War, Army, 1941-46. Asst Principal, Min. of Civil Aviation, 1948; Principal, Min. of Civil Aviation, 1951 (later Min. of Transport); Asst Sec., Welsh Office, 1965. *Recreations:* music, outdoor activities. *Address:* 16 Rheidol Close, Llanishen, Cardiff CF4 5NQ. *T:* Cardiff 756445.

HOSFORD, John Percival, MS, FRCS; retired; Surgeon, Lecturer on Surgery, St Bartholomew's Hospital (1936-60); Surgeon, King Edward VII Hospital for Officers and Florence Nightingale Hospital; Consulting Surgeon to Hospitals at Watford, Leatherhead, Hitchin, St Albans and to the Foundling Hospital and Reedham Orphanage; *b* 24 July 1900; 2nd *s* of Dr B. Hosford, Highgate; *m* 1932, Millicent Sacheverell Violet Sybil Claud, *d* of late Brig.-Gen. C. Vaughan Edwards, CMG, DSO; one *s* one *d. Educ:* Highgate Sch.; St Bartholomew's Hosp. MB, BS (London) 1922; FRCS Eng. 1925; MS (London); University Gold Medal, 1925. Formerly Registrar St Bartholomew's Hosp. and of Royal National Orthopædic Hosp. Hunterian Prof., Royal College of Surgeons, 1932. Retired, Oct. 1960. Formerly: Mem. of Court of Examiners of Royal College of Surgeons; Examiner in Surgery at Universities of Oxford, London, Sheffield, Belfast; Fellow Assoc. of Surgeons (on Council) and Royal Society Med. *Publications:* numerous articles in medical and surgical journals and encyclopædias. *Recreations:* viniculture and gardening. *Address:* Carril, Reguengo, Portalegre, Portugal.

HOSIE, James Findlay, CBE 1972 (OBE 1955); a Director, Science Research Council, 1965-74; *b* 22 Aug. 1913; *m* 1951, Barbara Mary Mansell. *Educ:* Glasgow Univ. (MA Hons); St John's Coll., Cambridge (BA). Indian Civil Service, 1938-47; Principal, 1947-56, Asst Sec., 1956-58, Min. of Defence, London; Asst Sec. QMGF, War Office, 1958-61; Office of Minister for Science, later Dept of Educn. and Science, 1961-65. *Recreations:* bird-watching, gardening. *Address:* White Gables, West Street, Alfriston, Sussex. *T:* Alfriston 791.

HOSKING, Eric (John), OBE 1977; photographer, ornithologist, broadcaster; *b* 2 Oct. 1909; 3rd *s* of late Albert Hosking and Margaret Helen, *d* of William Steggall; *m* 1939, Dorothy, *d* of late Harry Sleigh; two *s* one *d. Educ:* Stationers' Company's Sch. London, N8. Hon. Fellow, Royal Photographic Society; a Vice-Pres., Royal Society for the Protection of Birds; Hon. Vice-Pres., London Natural History Soc.; a Vice-Pres., British Naturalists' Assoc.; Vice-President: Nature Photographic Society; British Ornithologists' Union; Chm., Photographic Advisory Cttee to Nature Conservancy. Scientific Fellow of Zoological Society; Fellow, Inst. Incorp. Photographers. Exhibited at Royal Photographic Society, 1932- (Council, 1950-56; Fellowship & Associateship Admissions Cttee, 1951-56 and 1960-65); Member: BOU, 1935-; Brit. Trust for Ornithology, 1938-; Cornell Laboratory of Ornithology, America, 1961-. Dir of Photography to Coto Doñana Expedn, Spain, 1956 and 1957; Leader of Cazoria Valley Expedition, Spain, 1959; Dir of Photography, British Ornithologists' Expedition to Bulgaria, 1960, to Hungary, 1961; other expeditions: Mountfort-Jordan, 1963; British-Jordan, 1965; Pakistan, 1966; World Wildlife Fund, Pakistan, 1967; Lindblad Galapagos Islands, 1970; Kenya and Rhodesia, 1972; Tanzania and Kenya, 1974. Photographic Editor: of New Naturalist, 1942-; of British Birds, 1960-76. RGS Cherry Kearton Award, 1968; RSPB Gold Medal, 1974; Zoological Soc. Silver Medal, 1975. *Publications:* Intimate Sketches from Bird Life, 1940; The Art of Bird Photography, 1944; Birds of the Day, 1944; Birds of the Night, 1945; More Birds of the Day, 1946; The Swallow, 1946; Masterpieces of Bird Photography, 1947; Birds in Action, 1949; Birds Fighting, 1955; Bird Photography as a Hobby, 1961; Nesting Birds, Eggs and Fledglings, 1967; An Eye for a Bird (autobiog.), 1970; Wildlife Photography, 1973. Illustrator of many books on natural history, by photographs. *Address:* 20 Crouch Hall Road, N8 8XH. *T:* 01-340 7703.

HOSKINS, Prof. William George, CBE 1971; FBA 1969; MA, PhD; *b* Exeter, 22 May 1908; *e s* of late William George Hoskins and Alice Beatrice Dymond; *m* 1933, Frances Jackson; one *s* one *d. Educ:* Hele's Sch., Exeter; University Coll., Exeter. Lectr in Economics, University Coll., Leicester, 1931-41; 1946-48; Central Price Regulation Cttee, 1941-45; Reader in English Local History, University Coll. (now Univ.) of Leicester, 1948-51; Reader in Econ. Hist., University of Oxford, 1951-65; Hatton Prof. of English History, University of Leicester, 1965-68, retired in despair, 1968; Emeritus Professor, 1968. BBC TV Series, Landscapes of England, 1976, 1977. Mem. Royal Commission on Common Land, 1955-58; Adv. Cttee on Bldgs of Special Architectural and Historical Interest (Min. of Housing and Local Govt), 1955-64; Vice-Pres. Leicestershire Archæol and Hist. Soc., 1952; Pres. Dartmoor Preserv. Assoc., 1962-76; Pres., British Agricultural History Soc., 1972-74; Leverhulme Res. Fellow, 1961-63; Leverhulme Emeritus Fellowship, 1970-71. Murchison Award, RGS, 1976. Hon. FRIBA, 1973. Hon. DLitt: Exon, 1974; CNAA, 1976. *Publications:* Industry, Trade and People in Exeter, 1935; Heritage of Leicestershire, 1946; Midland England, 1949; Essays in Leicestershire History, 1950; Chilterns to Black Country, 1951; East Midlands and the Peak, 1951; Devonshire Studies, (with H. P. R. Finberg), 1952; Devon (New Survey of England), 1954; The Making of the English Landscape, 1955; The Midland Peasant, 1957; The Leicestershire Landscape, 1957; Exeter in the Seventeenth Century, 1957; Local History in England, 1959; Devon and its People, 1959; Two Thousand Years in Exeter, 1960; The Westward Expansion of Wessex, 1960; Shell Guide to Rutland, 1963; The Common Lands of England and Wales (with L. Dudley Stamp), 1963; Provincial England, 1963; Old Devon, 1966; Fieldwork in Local History, 1967; Shell Guide to Leicestershire, 1970; History from the Farm, 1970; English Landscapes, 1973; The Age of Plunder, 1976. *Recreation:* parochial explorations. *Address:* 2 Lyndhurst Road, Exeter. *T:* 56604.

HOSKYNS, Sir Benedict (Leigh), 16th Bt, *cr* 1676; *b* 27 May 1928; *s* of Rev. Sir Edwyn Clement Hoskyns, 13th Bt, MC, DD and Mary Trym, *d* of Edwin Budden, Macclesfield; *S* brother 1956; *m* 1953, Ann Wilkinson; two *s* two *d. Educ:* Haileybury; Corpus Christi Coll., Cambridge; London Hospital. BA Cantab 1949; MB, BChir Cantab 1952. House Officer at the London Hospital, 1953. RAMC, 1953-56. House Officer at Royal Surrey County Hospital and General Lying-In Hospital, York Road, SE1, 1957-58; DObstRCOG 1958; in general practice, 1958-. *Heir: s* Edwyn Wren Hoskyns, *b* 4 Feb. 1956. *Address:* Harewood, Great Oakley, Essex. *T:* Ramsey 341.

HOSKYNS-ABRAHALL, Rt. Rev. Anthony Leigh Egerton; Honorary Assistant Bishop, diocese of Blackburn, since 1975; *b* 13 Oct. 1903; *s* of Bennet Hoskyns-Abrahall, CBE, and Edith Louise (*née* Tapp); *m* 1937, Margaret Ada Storey; two *s* one *d. Educ:* RNC Osborne and Dartmouth; Westcott House Theological Coll., Cambridge. Left RN, 1929; ordained, 1931; Curate, St Mary's Portsea, 1931-33; Chaplain, Shrewsbury Sch., 1933-36; Curate, St Wilfrid's, Harrogate, 1936-39; Chaplain, Tower of London, 1939; Chaplain, RNVR, 1939-45; Vicar, St Michael's, Aldershot, 1945-54; Rural Dean of Aldershot, 1949-54; Bishop Suffragan of Lancaster, 1955-74. Provost, Northern Chapter of Woodard Schools, 1964-77. *Recreations:* fishing, shooting, cricket. *Address:* Pedder's Wood, Scorton, near Preston, Lancs PR3 1BD. *T:* Garstang 2300. *Club:* MCC.

HOTBLACK, Maj.-Gen. Frederick Elliot, DSO 1917, MC; late Royal Tank Corps; *b* 1887; *s* of F. M. Hotblack, Norwich. Served European War, 1914-18 (DSO and bar, MC and bar, Legion of Honour, Order of St Anne, five times wounded); Brigade Major, 1st Rhine Brigade, 1921; General Staff Officer, War Office, 1927; Instructor Staff Coll., Camberley, 1932-35; Military Attaché, British Embassy, Berlin, 1935-37; General Staff, War Office, 1937-39; General Staff BEF Sept. 1939; Commander Division, 1939-40; ADC to the King, 1939; retired pay, 1941. Mem. Royal Tank Regimental Assoc. *Address:* 24 Emerson Court, Wimbledon Hill Road, Wimbledon SW19 7PQ.

HOTCHIN, Sir Claude, Kt 1967; OBE 1952; JP; Company Director and Grazier, Western Australia; Art Patron and Philanthropist since 1916; *b* 7 March 1898; *s* of John Robert Hotchin and Bertha Mary Hotchin (*née* Brown); *m* 1925, Doris May Clarkson; one *d. Educ:* Quorn and Broken Hill Public Schs; Hayward's Coll., Adelaide. District Comr, Boy Scouts, 1931-35; Foundation Mem., WA Soc. for Crippled Children, 1938 (Hon. Mem., 1954-); Member: Bd of Trustees, Public Library, Museum and Art, Gallery, of WA, 1948-60; Board of Western Australian Art Gallery, 1960-65 (also first Chm.); Senate, University of WA, 1951-69. Chm., Commonwealth Australia Jubilee Art Cttee for Western Australia, 1951. Chm., Friends of Royal Perth Hosp., 1969-75. Hon. LLD Univ. of WA, 1974. *Recreations:* golf, swimming, motoring, gardening. *Address:* Melville House, 5 Hotchin Avenue, Albany, Western Australia 6330. *T:* 95-1076. *Clubs:* Albany, Perth Rotary (Hon. Sec., 1931-34; Pres., 1935-36) (Perth, WA).

HOTHAM, family name of Baron Hotham.

HOTHAM, 8th Baron, *cr* 1797; **Henry Durand Hotham;** Bt 1621; *b* 3 May 1940; *s* of 7th Baron Hotham, CBE, and Lady Letitia Sibell Winifred Cecil, *er d* of 5th Marquess of Exeter, KG; *S* father, 1967; *m* 1972, Alexandra Stirling Home, *d* of late Maj. Andrew S. H. Drummond Moray; two *s* one *d. Educ:* Eton; Cirencester Agricultural Coll. Late Lieut, Grenadier Guards; ADC to Governor of Tasmania, 1963-66. *Heir: s* Hon. William Beaumont Hotham, *b* 13 Oct. 1972. *Address:* Dalton Hall, Dalton Holme, Beverley, Yorks; Scorborough Hall, Driffield, Yorks.

HOTHFIELD, 4th Baron, *cr* 1881; **Thomas Sackville Tufton;** Bt 1851; *b* 20 July 1916; *s* of Hon. Sackville Philip Tufton (*d* 1936; 2nd *s* of 1st Baron), and Winifred Mary Ripley Dalton (*d* 1970); *S* cousin, 1961. *Educ:* Eton; Cambridge Univ. *Heir: cousin* Lieut-Col George William Anthony Tufton, TD [*b* 28 Oct. 1904; *m* 1936, Evelyn Margarette Mordaunt; two *s* one *d*]. *Address:* House of Lords, SW1.

HOTSON, Leslie, LittD (Cambridge); FRSL; Shakespearean scholar and writer; *b* Delhi, Ont, Canada, 16 Aug. 1897; *s* of John H. and Lillie S. Hotson; *m* 1919, Mary May, *d* of Frederick W. Peabody. *Educ:* Harvard Univ. Sheldon Travelling Fellow, Harvard, 1923-24; Sterling Research Fellow, Yale, 1926-27; Associate Prof. of English, New York Univ., 1927-29; Guggenheim Memorial Fellow, 1929-31; Prof. of English, Haverford Coll., Pa, 1931-41; served War of 1939-45, 1st Lieut and Capt. Signal Corps, US Army, 1943-46; Fulbright Exchange Scholar, Bedford Coll., London, 1949-50; Research Associate, Yale, 1953; Fellow, King's Coll., Cambridge, 1954-60. *Publications:* The Death of Christopher Marlowe, 1925; The Commonwealth and Restoration Stage, 1928; Shelley's Lost Letters to Harriet, 1930; Shakespeare versus Shallow, 1931; I, William Shakespeare, 1937; Shakespeare's Sonnets Dated, 1949; Shakespeare's Motley, 1952; Queen Elizabeth's Entertainment at Mitcham, 1953; The First Night of Twelfth Night, 1954; Shakespeare's Wooden O, 1959; Mr W. H., 1964; Shakespeare by Hilliard, 1977. *Recreation:* boating. *Address:* Northford, Conn 06472, USA.

HOTTER, Hans; opera and concert singer; producer; *b* Offenbach, Germany; *m* 1936, Helga Fischer; one *s* one *d. Educ:* Munich. Concert career began in 1929 and opera career in 1930. Mem. of Munich, Vienna and Hamburg State Operas; guest singer in opera and concerts in all major cities of Europe and USA; concert tours in Australia; for the past 10 years, connected with Columbia Gramophone Co., England; guest singer, Covent Garden Opera, London, 1947-. Festivals: Salzburg, Edinburgh and Bayreuth. *Address:* Emil Dittlerstrasse 26, München-Solin, West Germany.

HOUBLON, Mrs Doreen A.; see Archer Houblon.

HOUCHEN, Harry Owen; Member of Board, for UK, Commercial Development (Pty) Ltd, Johannesburg; *b* 24 Sept. 1907; *s* of late Henry Houchen and Eliza Katherine, *d* of Burgoyne Owen; *m* 1935, Beatrix Elizabeth (*née* Ellett) (*d* 1976); one *s* one *d. Educ:* Canterbury Coll.; University of New Zealand. BE (Civil) 1932. From 1933 concerned with Transport and Civil Aviation, holding overseas appointments. Dir of Current Ops, BOAC, 1956; Man. Dir, Brookhirst Igranic Ltd, 1958; joined BTC as Gen. Man., BR Workshops, 1962; Member BR Bd for Mech. and Electr. Engrg and Workshops, 1964-69; Industrial Consultant, 1969-; Mem., Bd, Transportation Systems and Market Research Ltd, 1970-72. Order of Merit (1st cl.), Syria, 1956; Gold Medal of Merit, Lebanon, 1956. MRAeS 1936; FIMechE 1968 (MIMechE 1964). *Recreations:* travelling, yachting. *Address:* 21 Kylestrome House, Cundy Street, SW1. *T:* 01-730 4415; La Carolina, Aguilas, Prov. de Murcia, Spain. *Club:* Naval and Military.

HOUGH, George Hubert, CBE 1965; PhD; FRAeS; Managing Director, Hawker Siddeley Dynamics Ltd, since 1977; Deputy Chief Executive, Dynamics Group British Aerospace, since 1977; *b* 21 Oct. 1921; *m* ; one *s* two *d. Educ:* Winsford Grammar Sch.; King's Coll., London. BSc (Hons Physics), PhD; FIEE. Admiralty Signals Estabt, 1940-46. Standard

Telecommunication Laboratories Ltd (ITT), 1946-51 (as external student at London Univ. prepared thesis on gaseous discharge tubes); de Havilland Propellers Ltd: early mem. Firestreak team in charge of develt of guidance systems, 1951-59; Chief Engr (Guided Weapons), 1959; Chief Executive (Engrg), 1961; Dir, de Havilland Aircraft Co., 1962; Hawker Siddeley Dynamics Ltd: Technical Dir, 1963; Dep. Managing Dir, 1968. Dir, Sheepbridge Engrg Ltd. *Recreations:* sailing, golf. *Address:* Hemingstone, 54 The Drive, Rickmansworth, Herts. *T:* Rickmansworth 73502.

HOUGH, Prof. Graham Goulder; Praelector and Fellow of Darwin College, Cambridge, 1964-75, now Emeritus Fellow; Professor of English, 1966-75, now Emeritus, University Reader in English, 1965-66; *b* 14 Feb. 1908; *s* of Joseph and Clara Hough; *m* 1st, 1942, Rosamund Oswell; one *s* one *d*; 2nd, 1952, Ingeborg Neumann. *Educ:* Prescot Grammar Sch.; University of Liverpool; Queens' Coll., Cambridge. Lecturer in English, Raffles Coll., Singapore, 1930. Served War of 1939-45, with Singapore Royal Artillery (Volunteer), 1942-45. Professor of English, University of Malaya, 1946; Visiting Lecturer, Johns Hopkins Univ., 1950; Fellow of Christ's Coll., Cambridge, 1950 (Tutor, 1955-60); Visiting Prof. Cornell University, 1958. Hon. DLitt, Malaya, 1955; LittD, Cambridge, 1961. *Publications:* The Last Romantics, 1949; The Romantic Poets, 1953; The Dark Sun, 1957; Image and Experience, 1960; Legends and Pastorals, 1961; A Preface to the Faerie Queene, 1962; The Dream and the Task, 1963; An Essay on Criticism, 1966; Style and Stylistics, 1969. *Recreation:* travel. *Address:* The White Cottage, Grantchester, Cambridge. *T:* Trumpington 2227.

HOUGH, John Patrick; Secretary, Institute of Chartered Accountants in England and Wales, since 1972; *b* 6 July 1928; *s* of William Patrick Hough, MBE, Lt-Cmdr RN and Eva Harriet Hough; *m* 1956, Dorothy Nadine Akerman; four *s* one *d*. *Educ:* Purbrook High School. FCA, MIMC, FBCS. Articled M. R. Cobbett & Co., Portsmouth, 1950-53; Derbyshire & Co., 1953-54; Turquand Youngs & Co., 1954-57; Computer Specialist, IBM United Kingdom Ltd, 1957-61; Consultant 1961-62, Partner 1962-69, Robson Morrow & Co.; Dep. Sec., Inst. of Chartered Accountants in England and Wales, 1969-71. *Recreations:* music, food and wine. *Address:* 3 Talbot Place, Blackheath, SE3. *Clubs:* Travellers'; London Rowing.

HOUGH, Richard Alexander; writer; *b* 15 May 1922; *s* of late George and Margaret May Hough; *m* 1943, Helen Charlotte, *o d* of Dr Henry Woodyatt; four *d*. *Educ:* Frensham Heights. Served War, RAF Pilot, Fighter Command, home and overseas, 1941-46. Publisher, 1947-70: Bodley Head until 1955; Hamish Hamilton as Dir and Man. Dir, Hamish Hamilton Children's Books Ltd, 1955-70. Contrib. to: Guardian; Observer; Washington Post; NY Times; Encounter; History Today; New Yorker. Mem. Council, 1970-73, 1975-, Vice-Pres., 1977-, Navy Records Society. Chm., Auxiliary Hospitals Cttee King Edward's Hospital Fund, 1975. *Publications:* The Fleet that had to Die, 1958; Admirals in Collision, 1959; The Potemkin Mutiny, 1960; The Hunting of Force Z, 1963; Dreadnought, 1964; The Big Battleship, 1966; First Sea Lord: an authorised life of Admiral Lord Fisher, 1969; The Blind Horn's Hate, 1971; Captain Bligh and Mr Christian, 1972 (Daily Express Best Book of the Sea Award); Louis and Victoria: the first Mountbattens, 1974; One Boy's War: per astra ad ardua, 1975; (ed) Advice to a Grand-daughter (Queen Victoria's letters), 1975; The Great Admirals, 1977; Angels Fifteen (novel), 1978; numerous books for children under *pseudonym* Bruce Carter. *Recreations:* fell walking, riding, ornithology, travelling; special interest in maritime history. *Address:* 25 St Ann's Terrace, NW8 6PH. *T:* 01-722 3945; Town Foot, Troutbeck, Windermere, Cumbria. *T:* Ambleside 2417. *Clubs:* Garrick, MCC.

HOUGHTON, family name of **Baron Houghton of Sowerby.**

HOUGHTON OF SOWERBY, Baron *cr* 1974 (Life Peer), of Sowerby, W Yorks; **Arthur Leslie Noel Douglas Houghton,** PC 1964; CH 1967; *b* 11 Aug. 1898; *s* of John and Martha Houghton, Long Eaton, Derbyshire; *m* 1939, Vera Travis; no *c*. Sec., Inland Revenue Staff Fedn, 1922-60. Broadcaster in "Can I Help You?" Programme, BBC, 1941-64. Alderman LCC, 1947-49; Mem. Gen. Council, TUC, 1952-60. Chm., Staff Side, Civil Service National Whitley Council, 1956-58. MP (Lab) Sowerby, WR Yorks, March 1949-Feb. 1974; Chm. Public Accounts Cttee, 1963-64; Chancellor of the Duchy of Lancaster, 1964-66; Minister Without Portfolio, 1966-67. Chm., Parly Lab. Party, 1967-70, Nov. 1970-1974. Member: Commn on the Constitution, 1969-73; Royal Commn on Standards of Conduct in Public Life, 1974-. Chairman: Commonwealth Scholarships Commn, 1967-68; Young Volunteer Force Foundation, 1967-70 (Jt Vice-Chm. 1970-71); Chm., Teachers' Pay Inquiry, 1974;

Cttee on aid to Political Parties, 1975-76; Chm., Cttee on Security of Cabinet Papers, 1976. *Publication:* Paying for the Social Services, 2nd edn, 1968. *Address:* 110 Marsham Court, SW1. *T:* 01-834 0602; Becks Cottage, Whitehill Lane, Bletchingley, Surrey. *T:* Godstone 3340.

HOUGHTON, Albert Morley; retired 1972 as Under-Secretary, Department of Trade and Industry; *b* 26 June 1914; *m* 1939, Lallie Whittington Hughes; no *c*. *Educ:* Hamond's Grammar Sch., Swaffham, Norfolk; King's Coll., London Univ. Schoolmaster, 1937-39. Royal Navy, 1939-46. Entered Civil Service, Administrative class, 1946; Civil Service Selection Board, 1946-49; Ministry of Transport, 1949-65; UK Delegn to NATO 1954-56; Shipping Attaché to Comr Gen. for SE Asia, 1956-60; Under-Sec., and Hd of Electronics and Telecommunications Div., Min. of Technology, 1965-70. *Recreations:* reading, music, gardening. *Address:* High Beeches, North Pickenham, Swaffham, Norfolk. *T:* Holme Hale 489.

HOUGHTON, Rev. Alfred Thomas, MA, LTh; General Secretary Bible Churchmen's Missionary Society, 1945-66, Vice-President 1968; Hon. Canon, Diocese of Morogoro, Central Tanganyika, 1965; *b* Stafford, 11 April 1896; *s* of Rev. Thomas Houghton (Editor of the Gospel Magazine and Vicar of Whittington, Stoke Ferry, Norfolk) and Elizabeth Ann Houghton; *m* 1924, Coralie Mary, *d* of H. W. Green, and *g d* of Maj.-Gen. Green, Indian Army; two *s* four *d*. *Educ:* Clarence Sch. (now Canford Sch.); Durham Univ. (University Coll.); London Coll. of Divinity. BA Durham, 1923; MA Durham, 1929. Commissioned 2/5th PA Som LI, Burma, 1917; Staff Officer to Inspector of Infantry, South, AHQ India, 1918; Staff Capt., QMG's Br, AHQ India, 1919; demobilised, 1919; Deacon, 1921; Priest, 1922; Missionary Sch. of Medicine, 1923-24; Supt of BCMS Mission in Burma, 1924-40; Asst Bishop-Designate of Rangoon, 1940-44 (cancelled owing to Japanese occupation of Burma); Travelling Sec., Inter-Varsity Fellowship of Evangelical Unions, 1941-44, and Asst Sec., 1944-45. Pres. Missionary Sch. of Medicine, 1948-; Trustee Keswick Convention Council, 1948, and Chm., 1951-69; Chairman: Conference of British Missionary Socs, 1960; Church of England Evangelical Council, 1960-66; Pres. Mt Hermon Missionary Training Coll., 1960-71; Vice-President: Evangelical Alliance; Young Life Campaign; Lord's Day Observance Soc. *Publications:* Tailum Jan, 1930; Dense Jungle Green, 1937; Preparing to be a Missionary, 1956. *Address:* 14 Alston Court, St Albans Road, Barnet, Herts EN5 4LJ. *T:* 01-449 1741.

HOUGHTON, Arthur A., Jr; Chairman, Steuben Glass, since 1973 (President, 1933-73); *b* Corning, New York, USA, 12 Dec. 1906; *s* of Arthur Amory and Mabel Hollister Houghton; *m* 1973, Nina Rodale; one *s* three *d* of a previous marriage. *Educ:* St Paul's Sch.; Harvard Univ. Entered employment of Corning Glass Works, 1929; successively in manufacturing dept, in treasury dept, Asst to Pres., and Vice-Pres. Served War of 1942-45; Chm., Academic Planning Bd, US Army Air Forces Intelligence Sch. (Lieut-Col); Chm. and Pres., Wye Institute (Maryland). Dir, Corning Glass Works; formerly Director: US Steel Corporation; New York Life Insurance Company; Hon. Trustee: United States Trust Company; New York Public Library; Trustee Emeritus: Metropolitan Museum of Art; Pierpont Morgan Library; Mem., Bibliographical Socs of London, Oxford and Cambridge; Past President: Keats-Shelley Assoc. of America; Shakespeare Assoc. of America; Mem., Adv. Commn on the Arts, Bd of Governors, Fed. Reserve System. A Senior Fellow: Royal College of Art, London; RSA, London. Holds numerous hon. doctorates in Humanities, Law, Letters, Science, Literature and the Arts. Michael Friedsam Medal in Industrial Art. Officer Legion of Honour (France); Commandeur de l'Ordre des Arts et des Lettres. Assoc. CStJ. *Publication:* Design Policy Within Industry as a Responsibility of High-Level Management, 1951. *Address:* Wye Plantation, Queenstown, Maryland 21658, USA. *Clubs:* Century, Union, Harvard, Knickerbocker, Fifth Avenue (New York); Club of Odd Volumes (Boston); Philobiblon (Philadelphia).

HOUGHTON, Dr John, JP; Director, Teesside Polytechnic, since 1970; *b* 12 June 1922; *s* of George Stanley Houghton and Hilda (*née* Simpson); *m* 1951, Kathleen Lamb; one *s* one *d*. *Educ:* King Henry VIII Sch., Coventry; Hanley High Sch., Coventry Techn. Coll.; King's Coll., Cambridge; Queen Mary Coll., London Univ. BSc (hons) Engrg 1949; PhD 1952. CEng, MIMechE, FRAeS. Aircraft Apprentice, Sir W. G. Armstrong-Whitworth Aircraft Ltd, 1938-43; design and stress engr, 1943-46; student at univ. (Clayton Fellow), 1946-51; Lectr, Queen Mary Coll., London Univ., 1950-52; Sen. Lectr and Head of Aero-Engrg, Coventry Techn. Coll., 1952-57; Head of Dept of Mech. Engrg, Brunel Coll. Advanced Technology, 1957-61; Principal, Constantine Coll. of Technology, Middlesbrough,

1961-70. Freeman, City of Coventry, 1943. JP Middlesbrough, 1962. *Publications:* (with D. R. L. Smith) Mechanics of Fluids by Worked Examples, 1959; various research reports, reviews and articles in professional and learned jls. *Recreations:* keen sportsman (triple Blue), do-it-yourself activities, gardening, photography. *Address:* 14 Marton Moor Road, Nunthorpe, Middlesbrough, Cleveland. *T:* Middlesbrough 35263. *Club:* Middlesbrough Rotary.

HOUGHTON, Prof. John Theodore, FRS 1972; Professor of Atmospheric Physics, Oxford University, since 1976; Fellow of Jesus College, Oxford, since 1960; *b* 30 Dec. 1931; *s* of Sidney M. Houghton, schoolmaster and Miriam Houghton; *m* Margaret Edith Houghton (*née* Broughton), MB, BS, DPH; one *s* one *d*. *Educ:* Rhyl Grammar Sch.; Jesus Coll., Oxford (Scholar). BA hons Physics 1951, MA, DPhil 1955. Research Fellow, RAE Farnborough, 1954-57; Lectr in Atmospheric Physics, Oxford Univ., 1958-62; Reader, 1962-76. Mem., Astronomy, Space and Radio Bd, SRC, 1970-73 and 1976-; Chm., Meteorological Res. Cttee, Meteorological Office, 1975-; Mem. Jt Organising Cttee, Global Atmospheric Res. Programme, 1976-. Pres., RMetS, 1976-. Buchan Prize, RMetS, 1966. FInstP. *Publications:* (with S. D. Smith) Infra-Red Physics, 1966; The Physics of Atmospheres, 1977; papers in learned jls on atmospheric radiation, spectroscopy and remote sounding from satellites. *Address:* Lindfield, 1 Begbroke Lane, Begbroke, Oxford.

HOUGHTON, Maj.-Gen. Robert Dyer, CB 1963; OBE 1947; MC 1942; General Secretary, The Royal United Kingdom Beneficent Association, since 1968; *b* 7 March 1912; *s* of late J. M. Houghton, Dawlish, Devon; *m* 1940, Dorothy Uladh, *y* *d* of late Maj.-Gen. R. W. S. Lyons, IMS; two *s* one *d*. *Educ:* Haileybury Coll. Royal Marines Officer, 1930-64; Col Comdt, Royal Marines, 1973-76. *Recreations:* gardening, sailing, model engineering. *Address:* Vert House, Whitesmith, near Lewes, East Sussex. *Club:* Army and Navy.

HOUGHTON, Rev. Canon William Reginald; Canon Residentiary of Gloucester Cathedral, 1969-78; *b* 28 Sept. 1910; *s* of late William Houghton and late Elizabeth Houghton; unmarried. *Educ:* St John's Coll., Durham; Westcott House, Cambridge. BA (Durham) 1940; Dipl. in Th. (Durham) 1941; MA (Durham) 1943. Curate, St Clement, Leeds, 1941-43, Leeds Parish Church, 1943-47 (Senior Curate, 1945-47); Vicar of Beeston, Leeds, 1947-54. Surrogate, 1949-54. Public Preacher, Dio. Southwark, 1954-62; Asst Sec. South London Church Fund and Southwark Diocesan Board of Finance, 1954-56, Dep. Sec., 1956-60, Sec., 1960-61; Sec. Southwark Dio. Bd of Dilapidations, 1956-60; Canon Residentiary (Treas.) of Southwark Cathedral, 1959-62. Rector of St Mary de Crypt with St John the Baptist, Gloucester, 1962-69. *Recreations:* travel and reading. *Address:* Church Cottage, Diddlebury, Craven Arms, Salop SY7 9DH.

HOULDEN, Rev. Canon James Leslie; Lecturer in New Testament Studies, King's College, London University, since 1977; *b* 1 March 1929; *s* of James and Lily Alice Houlden. *Educ:* Altrincham Grammar Sch.; Queen's Coll., Oxford. Asst Curate, St Mary's, Hunslet, Leeds, 1955-58; Chaplain, Chichester Theological Coll., 1958-60; Chaplain Fellow, Trinity Coll., Oxford, 1960-70; Principal, Cuddesdon Theol Coll., later Ripon Coll., Cuddesdon, 1970-77. Hon. Canon of Christ Church Oxford, 1976-77. Mem., Liturgical Commn, 1969-76; Doctrine Commn of C of E, 1969-76. *Publications:* Paul's Letters from Prison, 1970; (ed) A Celebration of Faith, 1970; Ethics and the New Testament, 1973; The Johannine Epistles, 1974; The Pastoral Epistles, 1976; Patterns of Faith, 1977; reviews and articles in learned jls. *Address:* 33 Raleigh Court, Lymer Avenue, SE19. *T:* 01-670 6648.

HOULDSWORTH, Sir (Harold) Basil, 2nd Bt, *cr* 1956; Consultant Anæsthetist, Barnsley and District Hospitals, since 1954; *b* 21 July 1922; *s* of Sir Hubert Stanley Houldsworth, 1st Bt, QC and (Hilda Frances) Lady Houldsworth (*née* Clegg); *S* father 1956; *m* 1946, Norah Clifford Halmshaw; one *d*. *Educ:* Heckmondwike Grammar Sch.; Leeds Sch. of Medicine, MRCS, LRCP 1946; FFA RCS 1954; DA Eng. 1951. Junior Registrar Anæsthetist, Leeds Gen. Infirmary, 1946-48; Graded Specialist Anæsthetist, RAMC, 1948-50; Registrar Anæsthetist, Leeds General Infirmary and St James Hospital, Leeds, 1950-53; Senior Registrar, Sheffield City General Hospital, 1953-54. *Recreations:* theatre, ballet and gardening. *Heir:* none. *Address:* Shadwell House, Lundhill Road, Wombwell, near Barnsley, South Yorks. *T:* Wombwell 3191.

HOULDSWORTH, Sir Reginald (Douglas Henry), 4th Bt, *cr* 1887, OBE 1945; TD 1944; DL; landowner; *b* 9 July 1903; *s* of Sir Thomas Houldsworth, 3rd Bt, CBE; *S* father 1961; *m* 1934,

Margaret May, *d* of late Cecil Emilius Laurie; one *s* two *d*. *Educ:* Shrewsbury Sch.; Cambridge Univ. Hon. Col Ayrshire ECO Yeomanry, 1960-67; Commanded: Ayrshire Yeomanry, 1940-42; 4 Pack Mule Group, 1943-45. DL Ayrshire, 1970-. *Heir: s* Richard Thomas Reginald Houldsworth [*b* 2 Aug. 1947; *m* 1970, Jane, *o* *d* of Alistair Orr, Sydehead, Beith; two *s*]. *Address:* Kirkbride, Maybole, Ayrshire. *T:* Crosshill 202. *Clubs:* Cavalry and Guards; Western Meeting (Ayr); Prestwick (Prestwick).

HOULT, Norah; novelist and journalist; *b* Dublin; *d* of Powis Hoult and Margaret O'Shaughnessy. *Educ:* various boarding schools. *Publications:* Poor Women, 1928; Time, Gentlemen! Time!, 1929; Apartments to Let, 1931; Youth Can't be Served, 1933; Holy Ireland, 1935; Coming From the Fair, 1937; Nine Years is a Long Time, 1938; Four Women Grow Up, 1940; Smilin' on The Vine, 1941; Augusta Steps Out, 1942; Scene for Death, 1943; There Were No Windows, 1944; House Under Mars, 1946; Farewell, Happy Fields, 1948; Cocktail Bar, 1950; Frozen Ground, 1952; Sister Mavis, 1953; Journey into Print, 1954; A Death Occurred, 1954; Father Hone and the Television Set, 1956; Father and Daughter, 1957; Husband and Wife, 1959; Last Days of Miss Jenkinson, 1962; Poet's Pilgrimage, 1966; Only Fools and Horses Work, 1969; Not for Our Sins Alone, 1972; Two Girls in the Big Smoke, 1977. *Address:* Jonquil Cottage, Greystones, Co. Wicklow, Ireland. *Club:* United Arts (Dublin).

HOUNSFIELD, Godfrey Newbold, CBE 1976; FRS 1975; Senior Staff Scientist, Central Research Laboratories of EMI, Hayes, Mddx, since 1977 (Head of Medical Systems section, 1972-76; Chief Staff Scientist, 1976-77); *b* 28 Aug. 1919; *s* of Thomas Hounsfield, Newark, Notts. *Educ:* Magnus Grammar Sch., Newark; City and Guilds Coll., London (Radio Communications qualif.); Faraday House Electrical Engineering Coll. (Diploma); grad. for IEE. Volunteered for RAF, 1939; served 1939-46 (incl. period as Lectr at Cranwell Radar Sch.); awarded Certificate of Merit (for work done in RAF), 1945. Attended Faraday House, where he studied elec. and mech. engrg, 1947-51. Joined EMI Ltd, 1951, working initially on radar systems and, later, on computers; led design team for the first large, all transistor computer to be built in Great Britain, the EMIDEC 1100, 1958-59; invented the EMI-scanner computerised transverse axial tomography system for X-ray examination, 1969-72 (now used at Atkinson Morley's Hosp., Wimbledon, and leading hosps in the USA and European continent, which are buying the invention); the technique, as yet only applied to cranial examination, may soon be more widely used; the system has overcome obstacles to the diagnosis of disease in the brain which have continued since Röntgen's day (1895); it includes a patient-scanning unit; developer of a new X-ray technique (the EMI-scanner system) which won the 1972 MacRobert Award of £25,000 for the invention, and a Gold Medal for EMI Ltd. Dr Medicine (*hc*) Universität Basel, 1975; Hon. DSc: City, 1976; London, 1976; Hon. DTech Loughborough, 1976. Hon. FRCP 1976; Hon. FRCR 1976. Wilhelm-Exner Medal, Austrian Industrial Assoc., 1974; Ziedses des Plantes Medal, Physikalisch Medizinische Gesellschaft, Würzburg, 1974; Prince Philip Medal Award, CGLI, 1975; ANS Radiation Industry Award, Georgia Inst. of Technology, 1975; Lasker Award, Lasker Foundn, 1975; Duddell Bronze Medal, Inst. Physics, 1976; Golden Plate Award, Amer. Acad. of Achievement, 1976; Reginald Mitchell Gold Medal, Stoke-on-Trent Assoc. of Engrs, 1976; Churchill Gold Medal, 1976; Gairdner Foundn Award, 1976. *Publications:* contribs: New Scientist; Brit. Jl of Radiology. *Recreation:* mountain walking. *Address:* (home) South Airfield Farm, Winthorpe, near Newark, Notts. *T:* Newark 3637; EMI Central Research Laboratories, Shoenberg House, Trevor Road, Hayes, Mddx. *T:* 01-573 3888, ext. 2872.

HOUSDEN, Rt. Rev. James Alan George, BA; *b* Birmingham, England, 16 Sept. 1904; *s* of William James and Jane Housden; *m* 1935, Elfreda Moira Hennessey; two *s* one *d*. *Educ:* Essendon High School; University of Queensland; St Francis College. BA 1st class, Mental and Moral Philosophy, 1928; ThL 1st Class, 1929. Deacon, 1928; Priest, 1929. Curate, St Paul's Ipswich, Qld, 1928-30; Chaplain, Mitchell River Mission, 1930-32; Curate, All Souls' Cathedral, Thursday Island, 1932-33; Rector of Darwin, NT, 1933-37; Vicar of Coolangatta, Qld, 1936-40; Rector and Rural Dean, Warwick, 1940-46; Vicar of Christ Church, S Yarra, Melbourne, 1946-47; Bishop of Rockhampton, 1947-58; Bishop of Newcastle, NSW, 1958-72. *Recreation:* bowls. *Address:* 38 Maltman Street, Caloundra, Qld 4551, Australia. *Club:* Australian (Sydney, NSW).

HOUSE, Lt-Gen. Sir David (George), GCB 1977 (KCB 1975); CBE 1967; MC 1944; Gentleman Usher of the Black Rod,

House of Lords, since 1978; *b* 8 Aug. 1922; *s* of A. G. House; *m* 1947, Sheila Betty Darwin; two *d*. *Educ:* Regents Park Sch., London. War service in Italy; and thereafter in variety of regimental (KRRC and 1st Bn The Royal Green Jackets) and staff appts. Comd 51 Gurkha Bde in Borneo, 1965-67; Chief BRIXMIS, 1967-69; Dep. Mil. Sec., 1969-71; Chief of Staff, HQ BAOR, 1971-73; Dir of Infantry, 1973-75; GOC Northern Ireland, 1975-77. Colonel Commandant: The Light Division, 1974-77; Small Arms School Corps, 1974-77. *Address:* c/o Lloyds Bank Ltd, Cox's & King's Branch, 6 Pall Mall, SW1. *Club:* Army and Navy.

HOUSE, Donald Victor; Lay Member, Restrictive Practices Court, 1962-70, retired; *b* 31 Jan. 1900; *s* of Dr S. H. House, Liverpool; *m* 1925, Cicely May Cox-Moore; one *s* two *d*. *Educ:* Liverpool Coll. Lieut, Royal Garrison Artillery, 1918. Mem. (Fellow) Inst. of Chartered Accountants in England and Wales, 1922- (Mem. Council, 1942-62; Pres. 1954-55). Senior Partner, Harmood Banner & Co., 1946-62. Mem. Board of Governors, Guy's Hosp., 1955-74, and Chm. of Finance Cttee, 1957-74; Director: National Film Finance Corporation, 1954-70; Finance Cttee, Friends of the Poor and Gentlefolks Help, 1946-70; Mem., London Rent Assessment Panel, 1967-75. Hon. Sec., Herts Golf Union, 1964-75, now President; Mem. Council, English Golf Union. Dir of several public and other companies (to 1962); Chm., House Cttee enquiring into Northern Ireland shipping facilities. Special Constabulary Long Service Medal, 1943. *Recreations:* golf, amateur dramatics. *Address:* 8 Greyfell Close, Stanmore Hill, Stanmore, Mddx HA7 3DQ. *T:* 01-954 0525. *Clubs:* Royal Commonwealth Society; Sandy Lodge Golf, Porters Park Golf (Hon. Mem.).

HOUSE, Ven. Francis Harry, OBE 1955; MA; Officer Royal (Hellenic) Order of Phoenix, 1947; Archdeacon of Macclesfield since 1967; Rector of St James, Gawsworth, since 1967; *b* 9 Aug. 1908; *s* of late Canon William Joseph House, DD; *m* 1938, Margaret Neave; two *d*. *Educ:* St George's Sch., Harpenden; Wadham Coll., Oxford; Cuddesdon Theological Coll. Sec. of Student Christian Movement of Gt Britain and Ireland, 1931-34; Deacon, 1936; Priest, 1937. Asst Missioner, Pembroke Coll. (Cambridge) Mission, Walworth, 1936-37; Travelling sec. of World's Student Christian Federation, Geneva, 1938-40; Curate of Leeds Parish Church, 1940-42; Overseas Asst, Religious Broadcasting Dept, BBC, London, 1942-44; representative of World Student Relief in Greece, 1944-46; Sec. Youth Dept World Council of Churches, Geneva, and World Conference of Christian Youth, Oslo, 1946-47; Head of Religious Broadcasting BBC, London, 1947-55; Associate Gen. Sec. of the World Council of Churches, Geneva, 1955-62; Vicar of St Giles, Pontefract, 1962-67. Select Preacher, Cambridge Univ., 1949. Member: Gen. Synod of Church of England, 1970-; Gen. Synod's Commn on Broadcasting, 1971-73. *Publications:* articles contributed to: The Student Movement, The Student World, East and West, the Ecumenical Review, etc. *Address:* Gawsworth Rectory, Macclesfield, Cheshire. *T:* North Rode 201. *Club:* Travellers'.

HOUSE, Harry Wilfred, DSO 1918; MC; MA; Master of Wellington College, 1941-Aug. 1956; *b* Malvern, 26 Sept. 1895; 2nd *s* of late H. H. House, Acre End, Eynsham, Oxon; *m* 1926, Marjorie Stracey, *yr d* of late Arthur Gibbs, of Bramley, Surrey; two *s* one *d*. *Educ:* Lockers Park, Hemel Hempstead; Rugby Sch.; Queen's Coll., Oxford. Served in HM Forces on leaving Rugby in 1914; temp. 2nd Lieut 7th East Lancs Regt, Sept. 1914; served in France from July 1915 (wounded July 1916; MC; DSO); relinquished commission with rank of Temp. Major, March, 1919; total service in France 3 years 5 months; temp. appointment Colonial Office, March to Dec. 1919; matriculated Oxford Univ., Jan. 1920; 2nd Class Hon. Mods, March 1921; studied at the University of Paris, 1921-23; Fellow and Lecturer Queen's Coll., Oxford, 1923-41; Laming Resident Fellow, Queen's Coll., Oxford, 1924-41; Junior Proctor, Oxford Univ., 1931-32; Major, Oxford and Bucks Light Infantry, 1939-41; Military Asst to Quarter Master Gen., 1940-41. Supernumerary Fellow, Queen's Coll., Oxford, 1953. *Address:* The Old Rectory, Stutton, near Ipswich, Suffolk. *T:* Holbrook 205.

HOUSE, Prof. John William, MA; FRGS; Halford Mackinder Professor of Geography, University of Oxford, since 1974; Fellow of St Peter's College, Oxford, since 1974; *b* 15 Sept. 1919; *s* of John Albert House and Eveline (*née* Brunton), Bradford; *m* 1942, Eva (*née* Timm); two *s* two *d*. *Educ:* Bradford Grammar Sch.; Jesus Coll., Oxford (Open Exhibr). BA 1940, MA 1946. HM Forces, 1940-46, Major Intell. Corps; Médaille de la Reconnaissance Française 1944. Univ. of Durham: Lectr in Geography, 1946-58; Sen. Lectr, 1958-61; Reader, 1961-63; Leverhulme Research Fellow, 1957-58; Fulbright Prof., Univ. of Nebraska, 1962-63; Univ. of Newcastle upon Tyne: Reader in

Applied Geography, 1963-64; Prof., 1964-66; Prof. and Head of Dept, 1966-74. Mem., Northern Econ. Planning Council, 1966-74; Mem., Northern Pennines Rural Develt Bd, 1967-70. Murchison Award, RGS, 1970. *Publications:* Bellingham and Wark, 1952; Northumbrian Tweedside, 1956; Teesside at Mid Century, 1960; (ed) Northern Geographical Essays, 1966; Industrial Britain: the North East, 1969; (ed) The UK Space, 1974; papers on migration and mobility. *Recreations:* drama, gardening. *Address:* School of Geography, Mansfield Road, Oxford OX1 3TB. *T:* Oxford 41791.

HOUSEHOLD, Geoffrey Edward West, TD; Author; *b* 30 Nov. 1900; *s* of H. W. Household, MA, Barrister-at-Law; *m* 1942, Ilona M. J. Zsoldos-Gutmán; one *s* two *d*. *Educ:* Clifton Coll.; Magdalen Coll., Oxford. Mostly commerce in foreign capitals. *Publications: novels:* The Third Hour, 1937; Rogue Male, 1939; Arabesque, 1948; The High Place, 1950; A Rough Shoot, 1951; A Time to Kill, 1952; Fellow Passenger, 1955; Watcher in the Shadows, 1960; Thing to Love, 1963; Olura, 1965; The Courtesy of Death, 1967; Dance of the Dwarfs, 1968; Doom's Caravan, 1971; The Three Sentinels, 1972; The Lives and Times of Bernardo Brown, 1973; Red Anger, 1975; Hostage: London, 1977; *autobiography:* Against the Wind, 1958; *short stories:* The Salvation of Pisco Gabar, 1938; Tales of Adventurers, 1952; The Brides of Solomon, 1958; Sabres on the Sand, 1966; The Cats To Come, 1975; *for children:* The Spanish Cave, 1940; Xenophon's Adventure, 1955; Prisoner of the Indies, 1967; Escape into Daylight, 1976. *Recreation:* Atlantic Spain. *Address:* Church Headland, Whitchurch, Aylesbury, Bucks.

HOUSSEMAYNE du BOULAY, Roger William, CMG 1975; CVO 1972; HM Diplomatic Service; Vice Marshal of the Diplomatic Corps, since 1975; *b* 30 March 1922; *s* of Charles John Houssemayne du Boulay, Captain, RN, and Mary Alice Veronica, *née* Morgan; *m* 1957, Elizabeth, *d* of late Brig. Home, late RM, and of Lady Pile; one *d*, and two step *s*. *Educ:* Winchester; Oxford. Served RAFVR, 1941-46 (Pilot). HM Colonial Service, Nigeria, 1949-58; HM Foreign, later Diplomatic, Service, 1959; FO, 1959; Washington, 1960-64; FCO 1964-67; Manila, 1967-71; Alternate Director, Asian Development Bank, Manila, 1967-69, and Director, 1969-71; Counsellor and Head of Chancery, Paris, 1971-73; Resident Comr, New Hebrides, 1973-75. *Address:* Anstey House, near Buntingford, Herts.

HOUSTON, Aubrey Claud D.; *see* Davidson-Houston.

HOUSTON, Brig. David, CBE 1975 (OBE 1972); Military Attaché and Commander, British Army Staff, Washington, since 1977; *b* 24 Feb. 1929; *s* of late David Houston and Christina Charleson Houston (*née* Dunnett); *m* 1959, Jancis Veronica Burn; two *s*. *Educ:* Latymer Upper Sch. Commissioned, Royal Irish Fusiliers, 1949; served Korea, Kenya, BAOR, N Africa; Staff Coll., Camberley, 1961; commanded 1 Loyals and newly amalgamated 1st QLR, 1969-71; in comd 8th Inf. Bde, Londonderry, N Ireland, 1974-75; Mem. RCDS, 1976. *Recreations:* fishing, shooting, bird watching (feathered). *Address:* Inveroykel House, by Ardgay, Ross-shire IV24 3DP. *T:* Rosehall 255.

HOUSTON, James Caldwell, MD, FRCP; Physician to Guy's Hospital, since 1953; Dean of the Medical and Dental Schools, Guy's Hospital, since 1965; *b* 18 Feb. 1917; *yr s* of late David Houston and Minnie Walker Houston; *m* 1946, Thelma Cromarty Cruickshank, MB, ChB, 2nd *d* of late John Cruickshank, CBE; four *s*. *Educ:* Mill Hill Sch.; Guy's Hosp. Medical Sch. MRCS, LRCP 1939; MB, BS (London) 1940; MRCP 1944; MD 1946; FRCP 1956. Late Major RAMC; Medical Registrar, Guy's Hospital, 1946; Asst Ed., 1954, Jt Ed., 1958-67, Guy's Hosp. Reports; Member: Bd of Governors, Guy's Hosp., 1965-74; SE Metropolitan Regional Hosp. Bd, 1966-71; Lambeth, Lewisham and Southwark AHA (Teaching), 1974-; Court of Governors, London Sch. of Hygiene and Tropical Med., 1969-; Senate, Univ. of London, 1970; Bd of Faculty of Clinical Medicine, Cambridge Univ., 1975-; Special Trustee, Guy's Hosp., 1974-. Dir, Clerical, Medical & Gen. Life Assurance Soc., 1965; Vice-Pres., Medical Defence Union, 1970-. *Publications:* Principles of Medicine and Medical Nursing (jtly), 1956, 5th edn 1978; A Short Text-book of Medicine (jtly), 1962, 6th edn 1978; articles in Quart. Jl Med., Brit. Med. Bull., Lancet, etc. *Recreations:* golf, gardening. *Address:* 108 Harley Street, W1. *T:* 01-935 9338; 16 Hocroft Road, NW2. *T:* 01-435 3434; Cockhill Farm, Detling, Maidstone, Kent. *T:* Medway 31395.

HOUSTOUN-BOSWALL, Sir Thomas, 7th Bt, *cr* 1836; Chairman: Sir Thomas HB Properties Ltd; Continental Sales Agency Co. Ltd; Director: Tandridge Construction (Lingfield)

Ltd; Southern Television (Pty) Ltd; *b* 13 Feb. 1919; *s* of Major Sir Gordon Houstoun-Boswall, 6th Bt; *S* father 1961; *m* 1945, Margaret (marr. diss. 1970), *d* of George Bullen-Smith; one *s* one *d*; *m* 1971, Anne-Lucie, *d* of Pierre Naquet; one *d*. *Educ*: Windlesham House Sch.; Nautical Coll., Pangbourne. Fighter Pilot, RAFVR, 1939-45 (Middle East and UK). *Heir*: *s* Thomas Alford Houstoun-Boswall [*b* 23 May 1947; *m* 1971, Eliana, *d* of Dr John Pearse, New York; one *s*]. *Address*: Heath Grange, Lingfield, Surrey. *T*: Lingfield 833809.

HOVDE, Frederick Lawson; President's Medal for Merit (USA), 1948; President, Purdue University, 1946-71, now President Emeritus; *b* 7 Feb. 1908; *s* of Martin Rudolph Hovde and Julia Essidora Hovde (*née* Lawson); *m* 1933, Priscilla Louise Boyd; one *s* two *d*. *Educ*: University of Minnesota; Oxford Univ. Asst Dir Gen. Coll., University of Minnesota, 1932-36; Asst to Pres. and Exec. Sec. of Rochester Prize Scholarships, University of Rochester, 1936-41; Head, London Mission, Office of Scientific Research and Development, 1941-42; Exec. Asst to Chm., Nat. Defense Research Cttee, 1942-43; Chief, Rocket Ordnance Research Div., Nat. Defense Research Cttee, 1943-46. Hon. degrees: DSc: Hanover Coll., 1946; Case Inst. of Technology, 1948; Tri-State College, 1967; DEng Rose Polytechnic Inst., 1948; LLD: Wabash Coll., 1946; North Dakota Agricultural Coll., 1949; New York Univ., 1951; Michigan State Univ., 1955; Minnesota, 1956; Northwestern Univ., 1960; Notre Dame, 1964; Ball State Univ., 1965; Indiana State Univ., 1966; Indiana Univ., 1969; Purdue Univ., 1975; DHL Cincinnati, 1956; DCL Oxford, 1957; Dr *hc* University Rural do Estado de Minas Gerais, Brazil, 1965; DEd Valparaiso Univ., 1967; PdD Findlay Coll., 1961; DHum Northwood Inst., 1969. King's Medal for Service in the Cause of Freedom (Britain), 1948; President's Medal for Merit, USA, 1948; Washington Award, Western Soc. of Engineers, 1967; Gold Medal, Nat. Football Foundn and Hall of Fame, 1967; Theodore Roosevelt Award, Nat. Collegiate Athl. Assoc., 1970; Dist. Public Service Medal, Dept of Defense, 1970. Comdr, Order of the Southern Cross, Brazil, 1968. *Recreation*: golf. *Address*: 1701 Redwood Lane, Lafayette, Indiana 47905, USA. *T*: (office) 317-743-4266; (home) 317-447-0808. *Clubs*: Pauma Valley (Calif); Vincent's (Oxford, England).

HOVELL-THURLOW-CUMMING-BRUCE, family name of **Baron Thurlow,** and *see* Cumming-Bruce.

HOVEN, Helmert Frans van den; Chairman, Unilever N. V., since 1975; Vice-Chairman, Unilever Ltd, since 1975; *b* 25 April 1923; *m* 1950, Dorothy Ida Bevan; one *s*. *Educ*: Grammar and Trade schs in The Netherlands. Joined Unilever N. V., Rotterdam, 1938; transf. to Unilever Ltd, London, 1948, then to Turkey, 1951, becoming Chm. of Unilever's business there, 1958; Chm., Unilever's Dutch margarine business, Van den Bergh en Jurgens B. V., 1962; sen. marketing post, product gp, Margarine, Edible Fats and Oils, 1966; Mem. Bds of Unilever, and responsible for product gp, Sundry Foods and Drinks, 1970. *Recreations*: summer and winter sports in general. *Address*: c/o Unilever Ltd, Unilever House, EC4P 4BQ; Lower Farm, Effingham Common Road, Effingham, Leatherhead, Surrey KT24 5JG. *T*: Bookham 58665.

HOVING, Thomas; Director, The Metropolitan Museum of Art, 1967-77; *b* 15 Jan. 1931; *s* of Walter Hoving and Mary Osgood (*née* Field); *m* 1953, Nancy Melissa Bell; one *d*. *Educ*: Princeton Univ. BA Highest Hons, 1953; Nat. Council of the Humanities Fellowship, 1955; Kienbusch and Haring Fellowship, 1957; MFA 1958; PhD 1959. Dept of Medieval Art and The Cloisters, Metropolitan Museum of Art: Curatorial Asst, 1959; Asst Curator, 1960; Associate Curator, 1963; Curator, 1965; Commissioner of Parks, New York City, 1966; Administrator of Recreation and Cultural Affairs, New York City, 1967. Dir, IBM Americas-Far East Gp. Distinguished Citizen's Award, Citizen's Budget Cttee, 1967. Hon. Mem. AIA, 1967. Hon. LLD, Pratt Inst., 1967; Dr *hc*: Princeton; New York Univ. Middlebury and Woodrow Wilson Awards, Princeton. *Publications*: The Sources of the Ada Group Ivories (PhD thesis), 1959; Guide to The Cloisters, 1962; Metropolitan Museum of Art Calendar, 1966; The Chase and The Capture, 1976; Wyeth Catalogue, 1977; articles in Apollo magazine and Metropolitan Museum of Art Bulletin. *Recreations*: sailing, skiing, skating, tennis, bicycling. *Address*: 150 East 73rd Street, New York, NY 10021, USA.

HOW, Sir Friston (Charles), Kt 1958; CB 1948; *b* 17 Sept. 1897; *o c* of Charles Friston and Jane Ethel How, Leytonstone; *m* 1932, Ann Stewart, *e d* of late Alexander Chisholm Hunter, Aberdeen; no *c*. *Educ*: County High Sch. for Boys, Leyton; London Univ. Joined HAC, 1916; commissioned RM, 1917; served in France, 1917-18; demobilised 1919. Exchequer and Audit Dept, 1920;

HM Inspector of Taxes, 1920-37; Air Ministry, 1937-40; MAP, 1940-45; Ministry of Supply, 1946-53; Sec., Atomic Energy Office, 1954-59; retired, 1959; Member: Air Transport Advisory Council, 1960-61; Air Transport Licensing Bd, 1960-70. BSc (War) (London), 1917. Called to Bar, Middle Temple, 1927. *Address*: Desswood, Dess, Aboyne, Aberdeenshire. *T*: Kincardine O'Neil 246. *Club*: Royal Automobile.

HOWARD; *see* Fitzalan-Howard.

HOWARD, family name of **Earls of Carlisle, Effingham, Suffolk, and Wicklow,** and of **Barons Howard of Penrith** and **Strathcona.**

HOWARD DE WALDEN, 9th Baron *cr* 1597; **John Osmael Scott-Ellis,** TD; Baron Seaford, 1826; *b* 27 Nov. 1912; *s* of 8th Baron and Margherita, CBE 1920 (*d* 1974), *d* of late Charles van Raalte of Brownsea Island, Dorset; *S* father, 1946; *m* 1934, Countess Irene Harrach (*d* 1975), *y d* of Count Hans Albrecht Harrach; four *d*. *Educ*: Eton; Magdalene Coll., Cambridge (BA 1934, MA). Dir, Howard de Walden Estates Ltd (Chm.). Member of the Jockey Club (Senior Steward, 1957, 1964, 1976). *Heir*: (to Barony of Howard de Walden) four co-heiresses; (to Barony of Seaford) William Felton Ellis [*b* 27 Nov. 1912; *m* 1940, Edwina (*d* 1977), *d* of late Major R. E. Bond, Indian Army; one *s* one *d*]. *Address*: Avington Manor, Hungerford, Berks. *T*: Kintbury 229; Flat K, 90 Eaton Square, SW1. *T*: 01-235 7127. *Club*: Turf.
See also Capt. D. W. S. *Buchan of Auchmacoy*.

HOWARD OF PENRITH, 2nd Baron, *cr* 1930; **Francis Philip Howard,** DL; Captain late RA; *b* 5 Oct. 1905; *s* of 1st Baron and Lady Isabella Giustiniani-Bandini (*d* 1963) (*d* of Prince Giustiniani-Bandini, 8th Earl of Newburgh); *S* father, 1939; *m* 1944, Anne, *widow* of Anthony Bazley; four *s*. *Educ*: Downside; Trinity Coll., Cambridge (BA); Harvard Univ. Called to Bar, Middle Temple, 1931; served in War, 1939-42 (wounded). DL County of Glos, 1960. *Heir*: *s* Hon. Philip Esme Howard [*b* 1 May 1945; *m* 1969, Sarah, *d* of late Barclay Walker and of Mrs Walker, Perthshire; one *s* one *d*]. *Address*: Dean Farm, Hatherop, Glos.
See also Hon. Edmund B. C. *Howard*.

HOWARD, Alexander Edward, CBE 1972; Co-ordinating Officer Teaching Practice Organisation, Institute of Education, London University, since 1975; *b* 2 Aug. 1909; *o s* of Alexander Watson Howard and Gertrude Nellie Howard; *m* 1937, Phyllis Ada Adams; no *c*. *Educ*: Swindon Coll.; University Coll. and Westminster Coll., London Univ. BSc (London) 1930; Pt I, BSc (Econ.) 1934. Flt-Lieut, RAF, 1940-46. Asst Master, Sanford Boys' Sch., Swindon, 1931-34; Lectr in Maths, Wandsworth Techn. Coll., 1935-40; Maths Master, Wilson's Grammar Sch., 1946-48; Headmaster: Northfleet Sch. for Boys, Kent, 1948-51; Borough-Beaufoy Sch., London, 1951-54; Forest Hill Sch., London, 1955-63; Wandsworth Sch., 1963-74. Member: Naval Educn Adv. Cttee, 1966-; Army Educational Adv. Bd, 1957-74. Academic Council, RMA, 1970-75. FRSA 1970. *Publications*: The Secondary Technical School in England, 1955; Longman Mathematics Stages 1-5, 1962-67, new Metric edns, 1970-71; Teaching Mathematics, 1968; articles in Times Educational Supplement, The Teacher, Technology, Inside the Comprehensive Sch. *Recreations*: amateur theatre, old-time dancing, music, cricket, travel, rotary. *Address*: 19 Downsway, Sanderstead, Surrey CR2 0JB. *T*: 01-657 3399. *Club*: Surrey County Cricket.

HOWARD, Anthony Michell; Editor of the New Statesman, since 1972; *b* 12 Feb. 1934; *s* of Canon Guy Howard and Janet Rymer Howard; *m* 1965, Carol Anne Gaynor. *Educ*: Westminster Sch.; Christ Church, Oxford. Chm., Oxford Univ. Labour Club, 1954; Pres., Oxford Union, 1955. Called to Bar, Inner Temple, 1956. Nat. Service, 2nd Lieut, Royal Fusiliers, 1956-58; Political Corresp., Reynolds News, 1958-59; Editorial Staff, Manchester Guardian, 1959-61 (Harkness Fellowship in USA, 1960); Political Corresp., New Statesman, 1961-64; Whitehall Corresp., Sunday Times, 1965; Washington Corresp., Observer, 1966-69 and Political Columnist, 1971-72; Asst Editor, New Statesman, 1970-72. *Publications*: (contrib.) The Baldwin Age, 1960; (contrib.) Age of Austerity, 1963; (with Richard West) The Making of the Prime Minister, 1965. *Address*: 17 Addison Avenue, W11 4QS. *T*: 01-603 3749.

HOWARD, Sir Douglas Frederick, KCMG, *cr* 1953 (CMG 1944); MC; *b* 15 Feb. 1897; *s* of late John Howard Howard and of late Mrs Howard, Biddenham House, Bedford. *Educ*: Harrow. Served European War, 1915-18, France 1916 and 1918. Entered Diplomatic Service as 3rd Sec. Christiania, 1922; Bucharest, 1924; 2nd Sec., 1925; Rome, 1926; FO 1929. BA

1932. 1st Sec., 1934; Sofia, 1935; FO 1936; Madrid, 1939; Counsellor, FO, 1941; Madrid, 1945, where he was Chargé d'Affaires, Dec. 1946-Nov. 1949; Ambassador to Uruguay, 1949-53; HM Minister to the Holy See, 1953-57, retired. *Address:* Clophill House, Clophill, Bedford. *T:* Silsoe 60285. *Club:* Travellers'.

HOWARD, Hon. Edmund Bernard Carlo, CMG 1969; MVO 1961; HM Diplomatic Service, retired; *b* 8 Sept. 1909; *s* of 1st Baron Howard of Penrith, PC, GCB, GCMG, CVO, and Lady Isabella Giustiniani-Bandini (*d* of Prince Giustiniani-Bandini, 8th Earl of Newburgh); *m* 1936, Cécile Geoffroy-Dechaume; three *s* one *d* (and one *d* decd). *Educ:* Downside Sch.; Newman Sch., Lakewood, NJ; New Coll., Oxford. Called to the Bar, 1932; Sec., Trustees and Managers, Stock Exchange, 1937. Served in HM Forces, KRRC, 1939-45. Joined HM Diplomatic Service, 1947; served in: Rome, 1947-51; Foreign Office, 1951-53; Madrid, 1953-57; Bogotá, 1957-59; Florence, 1960-61; Rome, 1961-65; Consul-Gen., Genoa, 1965-69. Comdr, Order of Merit, Italy, 1973. *Publications:* Genoa: history and art in an old seaport, 1971 (Duchi di Galliera prize, 1973); trans The Aryan Myth, 1974. *Recreations:* travel, gardening, walking. *Address:* Jerome Cottage, Marlow Common, Bucks. *T:* Marlow 2129.

HOWARD, Sir Edward; see Howard, Sir H. E. de C.

HOWARD, Elizabeth Jane; novelist; *b* 26 March 1923; *d* of David Liddon and Katharine M. Howard; *m* 1st, 1942, Peter M. Scott; one *d*; 2nd, 1959, James Douglas-Henry; 3rd, 1965, Kingsley Amis, *qv. Educ:* home. Trained at London Mask Theatre Sch. Played at Stratford-on-Avon, and in repertory theatre in Devon; BBC, Television, modelling, 1939-46; Sec. to Inland Waterways Assoc., 1947; subsequently writing, editing and reviewing. John Llewellyn Rhys Memorial Prize for The Beautiful Visit, 1950; Book Critic, Queen Magazine, 1959-61. Hon. Artistic Dir, Cheltenham Literary Festival, 1962; Artistic co-Dir, Salisbury Festival of Arts, 1973. *Publications:* The Beautiful Visit, 1950; The Long View, 1956; The Sea Change, 1959; After Julius, 1965; Something in Disguise, 1969; Odd Girl Out, 1972; Mr Wrong, 1975; (ed) A Companion for Lovers, 1978. *Recreations:* music, gardening, enjoying all the arts, travelling, natural history. *Address:* Gardnor House, Flask Walk, NW3.

HOWARD, Francis Alex, (Frankie Howerd), OBE 1977; *b* 6 March 1922. *Educ:* Shooters Hill Sch., Woolwich, London. *Revues:* Out of this World, 1950; Pardon my French, 1953; Way Out in Piccadilly, 1966. *Plays:* Charlie's Aunt, 1955; Hotel Paradiso, 1957; A Midsummer Night's Dream (playing Bottom), 1958; Alice in Wonderland, 1960; A Funny Thing Happened on the Way to the Forum, 1963 (Critics' Award for Best Musical Actor, 1964); The Wind in the Sassafras Trees, Broadway, 1968; Simple Simon in Jack and the Beanstalk, Palladium, 1973; *films:* The Ladykillers, 1956; Runaway Bus, 1956; Touch of the Sun, 1956; Jumping for Joy, 1956; Further up the Creek, 1958; Carry On, Doctor, 1968; Carry on Up the Jungle, 1970; Up Pompeii, 1971; Up the Chastity Belt, 1972; Up the Front, 1972; The House in Nightmare Park, 1973. *TV Series:* Fine Goings On, 1959; Up Pompeii series for BBC, 1965, 1966, 1970-71; Up the Convicts, Australia, 1975; The Frankie Howerd Show, Canada, 1976. Royal Variety Performances, 1950, 1954, 1961, 1966. Variety Club of GB Award (Show Business Personality of the Year), 1966, 1971; Radio and TV Industries Award (Show Business Personality of the Year), 1971. *Recreations:* tennis, swimming, music, reading. *Address:* c/o RSO Management Ltd, 67 Brook Street, W1.

HOWARD, Frederick Richard, CB 1956; CMG 1950; lately Assistant Secretary, Air Ministry; *b* 7 June 1894; *m* 1920, Nellie Lewis. *Educ:* Strand Sch.; King's Coll., London; privately. Entered HM Civil Service, 1913, National Insurance Audit Dept. Served European War, 1914-18, in Civil Service Rifles, Aug. 1914-Jan. 1919; transferred to Air Ministry on release from Army, 1919; Private Sec. to successive Parliamentary Under-Secs of State for Air, 1937-39; Sec. to Riverdale Mission to Canada to plan Empire Air Training Scheme for Aircrew, 1939-40. *Recreations:* motoring, gardening, photography. *Address:* 22 Hadley Road, Enfield, Mddx.

HOWARD, George Anthony Geoffrey, DL; Chairman, Meat and Livestock Commission, 1974-77; *b* 22 May 1920; *o* surv. *s* of late Hon. Geoffrey Howard; *m* 1949, Lady Cecilia FitzRoy (*d* 1974), *d* of 8th Duke of Grafton; four *s. Educ:* Eton; Balliol Coll., Oxford. Served war of 1939-45: Green Howards, and attached Indian Army (wounded, Burma, 1945), Major 1945. RDC, Malton, 1946-74; CC, North Riding Yorks, 1947-55; Hon. NE Rep. for National Trust, 1948-58; Chm., York Georgian Soc., 1951-71 (Pres. 1971); Mem. Council, Country Landowners'

Assoc. 1951 (Chm.: Yorks Br., 1955-65, GP Cttee, 1956-61, Legal and Planning Cttee, 1961-68, Exec. Cttee, 1967-69; Pres. of Assoc., 1969-71). Member: National Parks Commn/Countryside Commn, 1966-74; Council, Royal Coll. of Art, 1968- (Sen. Fellow, RCA, 1974); Central Adv. Water Cttee, 1969-71; a Governor, BBC, 1972-. Mayor of the Company of Merchants of the Staple of England, 1964-65. Pres., Yorkshire Philosophical Soc., 1969-; Dep. Pres., Historic Houses Assoc., 1973-; DL, NR Yorks, 1971; Co-founder Agricultural Forum, 1971. FRAgSs 1972. *Address:* Castle Howard, York. *T:* Coneysthorpe 333; 18 Ennismore Mews, SW7. *T:* 01-589 7440. *Clubs:* White's, Brooks's, Pratt's.

HOWARD, Lt Comdr Hon. Greville (Reginald), VRD; RNR; *b* 7 Sept. 1909; 3rd *s* of 19th Earl of Suffolk and Berkshire; *m* 1945, Mary Ridehalgh; one *d. Educ:* Eton; RMC Sandhurst. Commissioned in King's Shropshire LI, 1930-35. London Manager of G. W. Joynson, Cotton Merchants and Brokers, 1935-39. Councillor Westminster City Council, 1937; Naval Service, War of 1939-45; destroyers commanded: HMS Viscount (temp.), 1943; HMS Sabre, 1943-44; HMS Nith, 1944. Rejoined Westminster City Council, 1945; Mayor of Westminster, 1946-47; Chm. Public Cleansing, Transport, Baths and Contracts Cttee, 1945 and 1947-49; Vice-Chm. Establishments Cttee, 1949; Vice-Chm. Refuse Sub-Cttee, Metropolitan Boroughs Standing Joint Cttee, 1947-49. MP (Nat L and C) St Ives Division of Cornwall 1950-66; retired, 1966. Hon. Overseas Director and European Consultant, Colour Processing Laboratories Ltd. Overseas Mem. Cttee of Management and Hon. Vice-Pres., Royal National Life-Boat Institution; Hon. Joint Pres., Nat. Assoc. of Inshore Fishermen; Hon. Pres., Fisheries Orgn Soc.; Vice-Chm. Sailing (Overseas), Sail Trng Assoc. *Recreations:* photography, sailing, bicycling, riding, fishing. *Address:* Redlynch, Brouch, near Mersch, Grand Duché de Luxembourg. *T:* 63560. *Clubs:* (supernumerary or overseas member of all) White's, Pratt's, Naval, Norwegian; Royal Yacht Squadron, Royal Norwegian Yacht, Royal Naval Sailing Assoc., Royal Cornwall Yacht.

HOWARD, Sir (Hamilton) Edward (de Coucey), 2nd Bt *cr* 1955; GBE 1972; Partner of Stockbroking Firm of Charles Stanley and Company; Chairman: Advance Electronics Ltd, 1959-74; LRC International Ltd; *b* 29 Oct. 1915; *s* of Sir (Harold Walter) Seymour Howard, 1st Bt, and Edith M. (*d* 1962), *d* of Edward Turner; *S* father 1967; *m* 1943, Elizabeth Howarth Ludlow; two *s. Educ:* Le Rosey, Rolle, Switzerland; Radley Coll., Abingdon; Worcester Coll., Oxford. Mem. of the Stock Exchange, London, 1946. Sheriff of the City of London, 1966 (Common Councillor, 1951; Alderman, 1963); Lord Mayor of London, 1971-72; one of HM Lieutenants, City of London, 1976-. Master of the Gardeners' Company, 1961. DSc City Univ., 1971. KStJ 1972. *Recreation:* gardening. *Heir: s* David Howarth Seymour Howard [*b* 29 Dec. 1945; *m* 1968, Valerie Picton, *o d* of Derek W. Crosse; one *s* two *d*. *Address:* Courtlands, Bishops Walk, Shirley Hills, Surrey. *T:* 01-656 4444. *Clubs:* City of London, City Livery, United Wards.

HOWARD, James Boag, CB 1972; Assistant Under-Secretary of State, Home Office, 1963-75; *b* 10 Jan. 1915; *yr s* of William and Jean Howard, Greenock; *m* 1943, Dorothy Jean Crawshaw; two *d. Educ:* Greenock High Sch.; Glasgow Univ. (MA, BSc; 1st cl. Hons Mathematics and Natural Philosophy). Asst Principal, Home Office, 1937; Private Sec. to Permanent Sec., Ministry of Home Security, 1940-41; Principal, 1941; Asst Sec., 1948. *Address:* 12 Windhill, Bishop's Stortford, Herts. *T:* Bishop's Stortford 51728. *Club:* Reform.

HOWARD, Sir John, Kt 1954; FICE; Chairman and Managing Director, John Howard and Co. Ltd, Civil Engineering Contractors; Chairman: John Howard & Co. (Holdings) Ltd; John Howard & Co. (Northern) Ltd; John Howard & Co. International Ltd; Howard Doris Ltd; Director, Steel Structures Ltd; *b* 17 Nov. 1901; *s* of John Golding Howard, Biddenham, Bedford; *m* 1931, Margaret Mary, *d* of Herbert Edward Kemp; three *s* one *d. Educ:* Bedford Sch. Chm., National Union of Conservative and Unionist Assocs, 1962. Chm., Harpur Trust, Bedford. Treasurer, Imperial Soc. of Knights Bachelor, 1968-. Hon. DSc Cranfield, 1971. *Recreations:* shooting, golf. *Address:* Crossland Fosse, Box End, Bedford. *T:* Bedford 854708; John Howard & Co. Ltd, Victory House, Meeting House Lane, Chatham, Kent. *T:* Medway 402040. *Clubs:* Carlton, Royal Automobile.

HOWARD, Mrs John E.; see Laski, Marghanita.

HOWARD, John Melbourne; Chartered Accountant; Director: H. Sichel & Sons Ltd; Epsom Glass Industries Ltd; a Partner in John Howard & Co. and A. J. Pickard & Co., both firms of

Chartered Accountants; *b* 10 Aug. 1913; *er s* of Harry Howard, Warlingham, Surrey; *m* 1948, Maisie Alexandra, *d* of Alexander Bartlett Gilbert. *Educ:* Whitgift Sch. ACA 1935; FCA 1945. Served in Royal Navy, 1941-45; commissioned in RNVR. MP (C) Test Division of Southampton, 1955-64; Parliamentary Private Secretary: to Financial Sec. to the Treasury, 1957-58; to Financial and Parliamentary Sec. to Admiralty and to Civil Lord, 1958-59; to Rt Hon. Edward Heath, MP, as Minister of Labour, 1959-60 and as Lord Privy Seal at the Foreign Office, 1960-63. *Recreation:* sailing. *Address:* Capel Manor House, Horsmonden, Kent. *Clubs:* Royal Automobile, Junior Carlton, Naval.

HOWARD, Leon Alexander L.; *see* Lee Howard.

HOWARD, Leonard Henry, RD 1941; retired; *b* 5 Aug. 1904; *m* 1st, 1938, Betty Scourse; one *s* one *d*; 2nd, 1960, Barbara Davies-Colley. *Educ:* Stubbington House Sch.; Nautical Coll., Pangbourne. Sea career in Royal Navy and P. & O.-Orient Lines (Merchant Navy), 1922-64; Commodore, P. & O.-Orient Lines, 1963-64 (now P. & O. Steam Navigation Co.), retired. *Recreations:* golf, gardening. *Address:* Port, Heyshott, Midhurst, W Sussex. *T:* Midhurst 2560. *Club:* Cowdray Park Golf.

HOWARD, Michael Eliot, CBE 1977; MC 1943; DLitt; FBA 1970; FRHistS; FRSL; Chichele Professor of the History of War in the University of Oxford, since 1977; *b* 29 Nov. 1922; *t s* of late Geoffrey Eliot Howard, Ashmore, near Salisbury, and of Edith Julia Emma, *o d* of Otto Edinger. *Educ:* Wellington; Christ Church, Oxford. BA 1946, MA 1948. Served War, Coldstream Guards, 1942-45. Asst Lecturer in History, University of London, King's Coll., 1947; Lecturer, 1950; Lecturer in War Studies, 1953-61; Prof. of War Studies, 1963-68; Fellow of All Souls Coll., Oxford, 1968-77. Vis. Prof. of European History, Stanford Univ., 1967. Ford's Lectr in English History, Oxford, 1971; Radcliffe Lectr, Univ. of Warwick, 1975; Trevelyan Lectr, Cambridge, 1977; FKC. Member: Council, Institute for Strategic Studies (Vice-Chm.); RIIA (Vice-Chm.); Chairman: RMA Academic Adv. Council, 1969-75; Army Educational Adv. Bd, 1966-71; Trustee, Imp. War Museum. Governor, Wellington Coll. Chesney Meml Gold Medal, RUSI, 1973. *Publications:* The Coldstream Guards, 1920-46 (with John Sparrow), 1951; Disengagement in Europe, 1958; Wellingtonian Studies, 1959; The Franco-Prussian War, 1961 (Duff Cooper Memorial Prize, 1962); The Theory and Practice of War, 1965; The Mediterranean Strategy in the Second World War, 1967; Studies in War and Peace, 1970; Grand Strategy, vol IV (in UK History of 2nd World War, Military series), 1971 (Wolfson Foundn History Award, 1972); The Continental Commitment, 1972; War in European History, 1976; (with P. Paret) Clausewitz On War, 1977; contributions to The New Cambridge Modern History. *Recreations:* music, weeding. *Address:* All Souls College, Oxford OX1 4AL. *Clubs:* Garrick, Beefsteak.

HOWARD, Michael Stockwin; Director, Cantores in Ecclesia, since 1964; Director of Music, St Marylebone Parish Church, since 1972; Co-founder (with George Newson) and Artistic Director, Rye Spring Music, 1976; Musical Director, Rye Spring Opera, and Principal Conductor, Dushkin Chamber Ensemble, since 1977; *b* London, 14 Sept. 1922; *er s* of late Frank Henry Howard (viola, Internat. String Quartet, Foundn principal, Beecham's Philharmonic) and Florence Mabel Howard; *m* 1969, Janet Margaret Cazenove (*née* Lawford). *Educ:* Ellesmere; Royal Acad. of Music; privately. Dir of Music, Ludgrove Sch.; Founder, Renaissance Society, and conductor, Renaissance Singers, 1944-64; Organist and Master of the Choristers, Ely Cath., 1953-58; Dir of Music, St George's Sch., Harpenden, 1959-61; Asst, Music Presentation, BBC, 1968-77. Freelance organist, harpsichordist, conductor, broadcaster and writer. ARAM 1976. Prix Musicale de Radio Brno, 1967; Gustave Charpentier Grand Prix du Disque, 1975. Recordings with essays include: Tallis/Byrd 1575 Cantiones Sacrae, 1969; Tallis at Waltham Abbey, 1974; Palestrina's The Garden of Love, 1974. *Publications:* The Private Inferno (autobiog.), 1974; contrib. Musical Times, Monthly Musical Record, Dublin Review, Listener, EMG Monthly Letter. *Recreations:* steam railway traction, village fairgrounds. *Address:* 50 Church Square, Rye, East Sussex. *Club:* Savage.

HOWARD, Very Rev. Richard Thomas, MA; Provost of Coventry Cathedral, 1933-58; Provost Emeritus since 1958; *b* 1884; *m* Ethel Marjorie Corfield (*d* 1977); two *s* three *d*. *Educ:* Weymouth Coll.; Jesus Coll., Cambridge (Rustat Scholar; 23rd Wrangler, First-Class in the Theological Tripos); Ridley Hall. Ordained, 1908; Chaplain of Jesus Coll., Cambridge, 1908-12; went out to St John's Coll., Agra, under the Church Missionary Soc., 1912; Vice-Principal, St Paul's Divinity Sch., Allahabab,

1913-18; Principal of St Aidan's Coll., Birkenhead, 1919-29; Vicar of Luton, 1929-33; Archdeacon of Coventry, 1941-46. Proctor in Convocation for Diocese of St Albans, 1931, and Coventry Cathedral Chapter, 1933. *Address:* Homelands Nursing Home, Cowfold, Sussex RH13 8AJ.

HOWARD, Robin Jared Stanley, CBE 1976; Director-General, Contemporary Dance Trust Ltd, since 1966; *b* 17 May 1924; *s* of Hon. Sir Arthur Howard, KBE, CVO, DL, and of Lady Lorna Howard. *Educ:* Eton; Trinity Coll., Cambridge (MA). Served War, 1942-45, Lieut, Scots Guards. Called to Bar, Inner Temple. Hon. Dir, Internat. Service Dept, United Nations Assoc., 1956-64. *Recreations:* sleep. *Address:* 7 Sandwich Street, WC1H 9AB. *Club:* MCC.

HOWARD, Rev. Canon Ronald Claude; Headmaster, Hurstpierpoint College, 1945-64; *b* 15 Feb. 1902; 2nd *s* of Henry H. and Florence Howard, The Durrant, Sevenoaks. *Educ:* Sidney Sussex Coll., Cambridge; Westcott House, Cambridge. Ordained, 1926; Curate of Eastbourne, 1926-28; Chaplain, Bradfield Coll., 1928-30; Asst Master, Tonbridge Sch., 1930-37; Asst Master, Marlborough Coll., 1937, Chaplain there, 1938-43; Chaplain and Asst Master, Radley Coll., 1943-45. Canon of Chichester, 1957; Communar of Chichester Cathedral, 1964-67. Canon Emeritus, 1969. *Recreations:* painting, collecting water-colours. *Address:* 26 Victoria Court, Hove, East Sussex.

HOWARD, Trevor Wallace; actor; *b* 29 Sept. 1916; father English, mother Canadian; *m* 1944, Helen Mary Cherry. *Educ:* Clifton Coll. Shakespeare Festival, Stratford-on-Avon, 1936 and 1939. Served War in Army, 1940-43, 1st Airborne Division. Played in the Recruiting Officer and Anna Christie, 1944; Old Vic Season, 1947-48, Petruchio in the Taming of the Shrew. *Films include:* Brief Encounter, 1945; The Third Man, 1949; An Outcast of the Islands, 1951; The Heart of the Matter, 1953 (Acad. award); Lovers of Lisbon (French); Cockleshell Heroes, 1955; The Key, Roots of Heaven, 1958; Sons and Lovers, 1960 (Acad. nomination); Mutiny on the Bounty, 1962; Von Ryan's Express, 1965; Father Goose, 1965; The Liquidator, 1966; The Charge of the Light Brigade, 1968; Ryan's Daughter, 1970; Mary Queen of Scots, 1971; The Offence, 1973; A Doll's House, 1973; 11 Harrowhouse, 1974; Hennessy, 1975; Conduct Unbecoming, 1975; Count of Monte Cristo, 1976 (Acad. nomination); The Last Remake of Beau Geste, 1977. *Plays include:* The Devil's General, 1953; Lopahin in The Cherry Orchard, Lyric, 1954; Two Stars for Comfort, Garrick, 1962; The Father, Piccadilly, 1964; waltz of the Toreadors, Haymarket, 1974; Scenario, Toronto, 1977. TV: The Invincible Mr Disraeli, 1963 (Acad. Award); Napoleon at St Helena, 1966 (Acad. nom.). *Recreations:* cricket, travel. *Address:* Rowley Green, Arkley, Herts. *Club:* MCC.

HOWARD, Sir Walter Stewart, Kt 1963; MBE 1944; DL; *b* 1888; *y s* of late Henry Blunt Howard; *m* 1917, Alison Mary Wall, *e d* of late Herbert F. Waring, Farningham Hill, Kent. *Educ:* Wellington; Trinity Coll., Cambridge. Vice-Chm., Warwicks CC, 1955 (Chm., 1956-60); Chm. Whiteley Village Trust, 1952-62; Governor: King Edward VI Sch., Birmingham; Warwick Sch.; Pres., Association of Education Cttees, 1962-63. Trustee of Shakespeare's birthplace. JP 1931, CC 1939, CA 1948, DL 1952, Warwicks. *Recreation:* foreign travel. *Address:* Barford, Warwick. *T:* Barford 208. *Club:* United Oxford & Cambridge University.

HOWARD, William Brian; Joint Managing Director, Marks & Spencer Ltd, since 1976; *b* 16 July 1926; *s* of William James and Annie Howard; *m* 1952, Audrey Elizabeth (*née* Jenney); one *s* one *d*. *Educ:* Revoe Junior Sch., Blackpool; Blackpool Grammar Sch.; Manchester Univ. (BA (Hons) Mod. Hist., Economics and Politics); Harvard Graduate Business Sch., 1973. Royal Signals, 1944-47. Marks & Spencer Ltd: Trainee, 1951; Deptl Manager, 1953; Merchandiser, 1954; Executive, 1966; Alternate Dir, 1972; Dir, 1973; Dir in Charge Food Div., 1974. A Church Comr, 1977-. Mem. Council, St George's House, Windsor; Governor, St Peter's Sch., Rickmansworth, 1970. *Address:* 79 The Drive, Chorleywood, Herts WD3 4DY. *T:* Rickmansworth 75725.

HOWARD, William McLaren, QC 1964; a Recorder, since 1972; Judge Advocate of the Fleet, since 1973; *b* 27 Jan. 1921; 3rd *s* of William George Howard and Frances Jane (*née* McLaren). *Educ:* Merchant Taylors' Sch. Entered RN as Cadet, 1938. Served at sea throughout War of 1939-45; Lieut 1942; resigned commission, 1946. Called to the Bar, Lincoln's Inn, 1947, Bencher, 1972; joined Inner Temple (*ad eundem*), 1960; Dep. Chm., Norfolk QS, 1967-71; Recorder of Ipswich, 1968-71. Mem., Bar Council, 1965-69 (also Mem., Bar Council Special Cttee on Sentencing and Penology). Pres., Norfolk Central

North Area, St John's Ambulance Bde, 1969-75; Vice-Pres., Norfolk Assoc. for Care and Resettlement of Offenders. Mem., British Acad. Forensic Sci. *Address:* 3 King's Bench Walk, Temple, EC4. *T:* 01-353 0431. *Club:* Garrick.

HOWARD-DOBSON, Gen. Sir Patrick John, KCB 1974 (CB 1973); Quartermaster General, since 1977; *b* 12 Aug. 1921; *s* of Canon Howard Dobson, MA; *m* 1946, Barbara Mary Mills; two *s* one *d. Educ:* King's Coll. Choir Sch., Cambridge; Framlingham College. Joined 7th Queen's Own Hussars, Egypt, Dec. 1941; served in: Burma, 1942; Middle East, 1943; Italy, 1944-45; Germany, 1946; psc 1950; jssc 1958; comd The Queen's Own Hussars, 1963-65 and 20 Armoured Bde, 1965-67; idc 1968. Chief of Staff, Far East Comd, 1969-72; Comdt, Staff Coll., Camberley, 1972-74; Military Secretary, 1974-76. Col Comdt, ACC, 1976-. Virtuti Militari (Poland), 1945; Silver Star (US), 1945. *Recreations:* sailing, golf, ski-ing. *Address:* The Cottage, Benington, near Stevenage, Herts. *Club:* Cavalry and Guards.

HOWARD-DRAKE, Jack Thomas Arthur; Assistant Under-Secretary of State, Home Office, since 1974; *b* 7 Jan. 1919; *o s* of Arthur Howard and Ruby (*née* Cherry); *m* 1947, Joan Mary, *o d* of Hubert and Winifred Crook; one *s* two *d. Educ:* Hele's Sch., Exeter. Asst Inspector, Ministry of Health Insurance Dept, 1937-39 and 1946-47. Served War, RA, 1939-46 (Major, despatches). Colonial Office: Asst Principal, 1947; Principal, 1949; Private Sec. to Sec. of State, 1956-62; Asst Sec., 1962; Asst Sec., Cabinet Office, 1963-65; Asst Sec., Home Office, 1965-72; Asst Under-Sec. of State, NI Office, 1972-74. *Recreations:* gardening, bird watching, golf. *Address:* Ashmore, 13 Warren View, Shorne, Gravesend, Kent DA12 3EJ. *T:* Shorne 2390.

HOWARD-JOHNSTON, Rear-Admiral Clarence Dinsmore, CB 1955; DSO 1942; DSC 1940; naval historian; *b* 13 Oct. 1903; *m* 1955, Paulette, *d* of late Paul Helleu. *Educ:* Royal Naval Colls Osborne and Dartmouth. Midshipman, 1921; Commander, 1937; Capt., 1943; Rear-Adm., 1953; Dir of Studies, Greek Naval War Coll., Athens, 1938-40; Dir Anti-U-Boat Div., Admiralty, 1943-45; Naval Attaché, Paris, 1947-50; apptd Naval ADC to the Queen, 1952; Chief of Staff to Flag Officer Central Europe, 1953-55; retired RN 1955. Inventor of simple hydraulic mechanisms; commended by Lords Comrs of the Admiralty for invention and devejt of anti-submarine training devices including Johnston Mobile A/S target, 1937. Order of Phœnix (Greece), 1940; Legion of Merit (USA), 1945. *Recreations:* fishing, pisiculture, hill-walking, gardening. *Address:* 45 Rue Emile Ménier, 75116 Paris, France. *Clubs:* White's, Naval and Military, (Naval Member) Royal Yacht Squadron; Jockey (Paris).

HOWARD-JONES, Maj.-Gen. Leonard Hamilton, CB 1959; CBE 1945 (OBE 1942); *b* 4 April 1905; *s* of late Hubert Stanley Howard-Jones, Maindee Park, Newport, Mon; *m* 1st, 1934, Irene Lucy Gillespie (*d* 1944); 2nd, 1945, Violet, *d* of Sidney Alfred Butler, and *widow* of Lieut-Col Francis John Leland; one *s* one *d. Educ:* Imperial Service Coll.; Cardiff Univ. (BSc Eng). Served War of 1939-45 (despatches; OBE; CBE). Commandant REME Training Centre, 1953-57; Inspector, Royal Electrical and Mechanical Engineers, War Office, 1957-60. MIMechE; AMIEE. *Address:* Rifle Range Farm, Fleet Road, Hartley Wintney, Hants RG27 8ED. *T:* Hartley Wintney 2358.

HOWARD-VYSE, Lt-Gen. Sir Edward (Dacre), KBE 1962 (CBE 1955); CB 1958; MC 1941; DL; *b* 27 Nov. 1905; *s* of late Lieut-Col Cecil Howard-Vyse, JP, Langton Hall, Malton, Yorks; *m* 1940, Mary Bridget, *er d* of late Col Hon. Claude Henry Comaraich Willoughby, CVO; two *s* one *d. Educ:* Wellington Coll., Berks; RMA. 2nd Lieut, Royal Artillery, 1925; served War of 1939-45: British Expeditionary Force, France, 1939-40; Lieut-Col, 1941; Mediterranean Expeditionary Force, 1941-44; In command 1st Royal Horse Artillery, Central Mediterranean Force, 1944-45. Brigadier, 1949; CRA 7th Armoured Division, BAOR, 1951-53; Commandant, Sch. of Artillery, 1953; Maj.-Gen., 1957; Maj.-Gen., Artillery, Northern Army Group, 1956-59; Dir, Royal Artillery, War Office, 1959-61; GOC-in-C, Western Command, 1961-64; retired, 1964. Lieut-Gen., 1961. Col Comdt: RA 1962-70; RHA 1968-70. Vice-Pres., Army Cadet Force Assoc., 1974-; Chm., 1964-74; Vice-Pres., Nat. Artillery Assoc., 1965-. DL E Riding of Yorks and Kingston upon Hull, 1964, Vice-Lieut, 1968-74; DL N Yorkshire, 1974-. *Recreations:* foxhunting and fishing; British Olympic Equestrian Team, 1936. *Address:* Langton House, Malton, North Yorks. *Club:* Army and Navy.

HOWARTH, David Armine; author; *b* 18 July 1912; *s* of Dr O. J. R. Howarth and Mrs E. K. Howarth. *Educ:* Tonbridge Sch.; Trinity Coll., Cambridge. BBC Talks Asst etc, 1934-39. War

Correspondent, 1939-40; RNVR, 1940-45. Knight 1st class, Order of St Olav (Norway), 1955; Cross of Freedom (Norway) 1945. *Publications:* The Shetland Bus, 1951; We Die Alone (also under title Escape Alone), 1955; The Sledge Patrol, 1957; Dawn of D-Day, 1959; The Shadow of the Dam, 1961; The Desert King, A Biography of Ibn Saud, 1964; The Golden Isthmus, 1966; A Near Run Thing: the Day of Waterloo, 1968; Trafalgar: The Nelson Touch, 1969; Sovereign of the Seas, 1974; The Greek Adventure, 1976; 1066, The Year of the Conquest, 1977; *fiction:* Group Flashing Two, 1952; One Night in Styria, 1953; *for children:* Heroes of Nowadays, 1957; Great Escapes, 1969. As Editor: My Land and My People (by HH The Dalai Lama), 1962. *Address:* Wildlings Wood, Blackboys, Sussex. *T:* Hadlow Down 233.

HOWARTH, Elgar; freelance musician; *b* 4 Nov. 1935; *s* of Oliver and Emma Howarth; *m* 1958, Mary Bridget Neary; one *s* two *d. Educ:* Manchester Univ. (MusB); Royal Manchester Coll. of Music (ARMCM 1956; FRMCM 1970). Royal Opera House, Covent Garden (Orchestra), 1958-63; Royal Philharmonic Orchestra, 1963-69; Mem., London Sinfonietta, 1968-71; Mem., Philip Jones Brass Ensemble, 1965-76; freelance conductor, 1970-; Musical Director, Grimethorpe Colliery Brass Band, 1972-. *Publications:* various compositions mostly for brass instruments. *Address:* 27 Cromwell Avenue, N6.

HOWARTH, Prof. Leslie, OBE 1955; FRS 1950; FRAeS; BSc, MA, PhD; Henry Overton Wills Professor of Mathematics, University of Bristol, 1964-76, now Emeritus; *b* 23 May 1911; *s* of late Fred and Elizabeth Ellen Howarth; *m* 1934, Eva Priestley; two *s. Educ:* Accrington Grammar Sch.; Manchester Univ.; Gonville and Caius Coll., Cambridge. Mathematical tripos, 1933; Smith's Prize, 1935; PhD, 1936. Berry-Ramsey Research Fellow, King's Coll., Cambridge, 1936-45; Lecturer in Mathematics in the University of Cambridge, 1936-49; Fellow of St John's Coll., Cambridge, 1945-49; Prof. of Applied Mathematics, University of Bristol, 1949-64; Adams Prize, 1951. Worked at External Ballistics Dept, Ordnance Board, 1939-42, and at Armament Research Dept, 1942-45. *Publications:* (ed) Modern Developments in Fluid Dynamics: High Speed Flow; papers on aerodynamics. *Address:* 10 The Crescent, Henleaze, Bristol BS9 4RW. *T:* Bristol 62 6346.

HOWARTH, Robert Lever; Senior Lecturer in General Studies, Wigan College of Technology; Leader, Labour Group, Bolton Metropolitan Borough; *b* 31 July 1927; *s* of James Howarth and Bessie (*née* Pearson); *m* 1952, Josephine Mary Doyle; one *s* one *d. Educ:* Bolton County Grammar Sch.; Bolton Technical Coll. Draughtsman with Hawker Siddeley Dynamics. MP (Lab) Bolton East, 1964-70. Lectr in Liberal Studies, Leigh Technical Coll., 1970-76. *Recreations:* gardening, reading, walking, films. *Address:* 11 Kinloch Drive, Bolton, Lancs. *T:* Bolton 44121.

HOWARTH, Thomas Edward Brodie, MC 1945; TD; Fellow and Senior Tutor, Magdalene College, Cambridge, since 1973; *b* 21 Oct. 1914; *e s* of Frank Fielding Howarth; *m* 1943, Margaret Teakle; two *s* one *d* (and one *s* decd). *Educ:* Rugby Sch.; Clare Coll., Cambridge (Scholar, MA, 1st cl. Hons Parts I and II, History Tripos). Asst Master, Winchester Coll., 1938-39, 1946-48; Headmaster King Edward's Sch., Birmingham, 1948-52; Second Master, Winchester Coll., 1952-62; High Master, St Paul's School, 1962-73. Served War of 1939-45, King's (Liverpool) Regt; Brigade Major, HQ Mersey Garrison; Brigade Major 207 Infantry Bde; NW Europe, June 1944; Personal Liaison Officer to C-in-C 21st Army Group. Trustee, Imperial War Museum, 1964-; Governor: St John's Sch., Leatherhead; Charterhouse Sch.; Rugby Sch. Mem., Public Schs Commission, 1966. Chm., Headmasters' Conference, 1969. *Publications:* Citizen-King, 1961; Culture, Anarchy and the Public Schools, 1969. *Recreation:* golf. *Address:* Magdalene College, Cambridge. *Clubs:* Athenæum, Savile.

HOWAT, Prof. Henry Taylor, CBE 1971; MSc (Manch.); MD, FRCP, FRCPE; Professor of Gastroenterology, University of Manchester, 1972-76, now Emeritus; Physician, Manchester Royal Infirmary, 1948-76; *b* 6 May 1911; *s* of late Adam Howat, MA, and late Henrietta Howat, Pittenweem, Fife; *m* 1940, Rosaline, *o d* of late Miles Green, Auckland, NZ; two *s* one *d. Educ:* Cameron Public Sch. and Madras Coll., St Andrews; Univ. of St Andrews. MB, ChB (St And) 1933; MD with Hons and Univ. Gold Medal (St And), 1960; MRCP 1937, FRCP 1948; MRCPE 1961, FRCPE 1965. Resident MO, Manchester Royal Infirmary, 1938-40. Served War, MEF and BLA; RMO, Physician Specialist, Officer in charge of Med. Div., Mil. Hosps, 1940-45; temp. Lt-Col, RAMC. Univ. of Manchester: Asst Lectr in Applied Physiology, 1946-48; Lectr in Med., 1948-69 (Chm., Faculty of Med., 1968-72); Reader, 1969-72; Physician, Ancoats Hosp., Manchester, 1946-62. United Manchester Hospitals,

1948-: Chm., Med. Exec. Cttee, 1968-73; Mem., Bd of Governors, 1966-74. President: European Pancreatic Club, 1965; British Soc. of Gastroenterology, 1968-69; Assoc. of Physicians of GB and Ire., 1975-76; Manchester Med. Soc., 1975-76. Hon. MD, Univ. of Louvain, Belgium, 1945. Medallist, J. E. Purkyně Czechoslovak Med. Soc., 1968. *Publications:* (ed) The Exocrine Pancreas, 1972; articles on gastrointestinal physiology and disease. *Recreation:* golf. *Address:* 19 Manor Road, Cheadle Hulme, Cheadle, Cheshire SK8 7DQ. *T:* 061-485 3146; 40 High Street, Pittenweem, Fife. *T:* Pittenweem 325. *Club:* Athenæum.

HOWD, Mrs Isobel; Regional Nursing Officer, Yorkshire Regional Health Authority, since 1973; *b* 24 Oct. 1928 (*née* Young); *m* 1951, Ralph Howd. SRN, RMN, BTA Cert. Matron, Naburn Hosp., York, 1960-63; Asst Regional Nursing Officer, Leeds Regional Hosp. Bd, 1963-70; Chief Nursing Officer, South Teesside Hosp. Management Cttee, 1970-73. *Address:* Yew Tree Cottage, Upper Dunsforth, York YO5 9RU. *T:* Boroughbridge 2534. *Club:* Naval and Military.

HOWE, 6th Earl, *cr* 1821; **Edward Richard Assheton Penn Curzon,** CBE 1961; DL; JP; Baron Howe, 1788; Baron Curzon, 1794; Viscount Curzon, 1802; Lieutenant-Commander RNVR; President, Chesham and Amersham Conservative Association, since 1972; *b* 7 Aug. 1908; a godson of King Edward VII; *o s* of 5th Earl Howe, PC, CBE, VD; *S* father, 1964; *m* 1st, 1935, Priscilla (whom he divorced, 1942), *o c* of Lieut-Col Sir Archibald Weigall, 1st Bt, KCMG; 2nd, 1946, Gay, *e d* of late Stephen Frederick Wakeling, Durban, South Africa; two *d.* *Educ:* Eton; Corpus Christi Coll., Cambridge. RNVR, 1928-46; war service in Atlantic and Pacific, 1940-46. Mem. (MR) LCC for South Battersea, 1937-46. Commissioner of Bucks St John Ambulance Bde, 1953-55; President: S Bucks Cons. and Unionist Assoc., 1965-72; St John Ambulance, Bucks; IRTE. Trustee, King William IV Naval Asylum. JP 1946, DL 1960, Bucks. Alderman, Buckinghamshire, 1958, County Councillor, 1973-, Vice-Chm., Bucks County Council, 1976-. President: Brit. Automobile Racing Club; Inst. of Road Safety Officers; Vice-Chm., RAC; Member: RAC Cttee; RAC Competitions Council; RNLI Cttee of Management. CStJ. *Recreations:* motoring, cricket, shooting, golf. *Heir: cousin* (Chambré) George (William Penn) Curzon (George Curzon, actor) [*b* 19 Oct. 1898; *m* 1st, 1927, Louise Merrill Rowe (*d* 1942); 2nd, 1950, Jane Victoria (marr. diss., 1965), *d* of late M. M. Fergusson, Toronto; one *s* one *d.* Comdr RN retd]. *Address:* Penn House, Amersham, Bucks. *T:* Holmer Green 3366; 20 Pitts Head Mews, W1. *T:* 01-499 4706. *Club:* Naval.

HOWE, Allen; Circuit Administrator, Wales and Chester Circuit, Lord Chancellor's Department, since Oct. 1974; *b* 6 June 1918; *s* of late Frank Howe and Dora Howe, Monk Bretton, Yorks; *m* 1952, Katherine, *d* of late Mr and Mrs Griff Davies, Pontypridd; two *d.* *Educ:* Holgate Grammar Sch., Barnsley. Served with E Yorks Regt and RWAFF, 1939-46, France, Africa, India and Burma (Major). HM Colonial Admin. Service, Gold Coast, 1946-55 (Sen. Dist Comr). Called to Bar, Middle Temple, 1953; practised Wales and Chester Circuit, 1955-59; Legal Dept, Welsh Bd of Health, 1959-65; Legal Dept, Welsh Office, 1965-74. *Recreations:* golf, gardening, walking. *Address:* 2 Orchard Drive, Whitchurch, Cardiff CF4 2AE. *T:* Cardiff 66626. *Clubs:* Cardiff and County; Radyr Golf.

HOWE, Elspeth Rosamund Morton, (Lady Howe), JP; Deputy Chairman, Equal Opportunities Commission, since 1975; Chairman, Southwark North Juvenile Court, since 1970; *b* 8 Feb. 1932; *d* of late Philip Morton Shand and Sybil Mary (*née* Sissons); *m* 1953, Rt Hon. Sir Geoffrey Howe, *qv*; one *s* two *d.* *Educ:* Bath High Sch.; Wycombe Abbey. Vice-Chm., Conservative London Area Women's Adv. Cttee, 1966-67, also Pres. of the Cttee's Contact Gp, 1973-77; Mem., Conservative Women's Nat. Adv. Cttee, 1966-71. Member: Lord Chancellor's Adv. Cttee on appointment of Magistrates for Inner London Area, 1965-75; Lord Chancellor's Adv. Cttee on Legal Aid, 1971-75; Parole Board, 1972-75. Co-opted Mem., ILEA, 1967-70; Mem., Briggs Cttee on Nursing Profession, 1970-72. Governor: Wycombe Abbey, 1968-; Froebel Educn Inst., 1968-75; Cumberlow Lodge Remand Home, 1967-70. Has served as Chm. or Mem. several sch. governing bodies in Tower Hamlets and on cttee of Inner London Pre-School Playgroups Assoc. and London Adventure Playgroups Assoc.; Pres., Peckham Settlement, 1976-. JP Inner London Juvenile Court Panel, 1964. *Publication:* Under Five (a report on pre-school education), 1966. *Address:* c/o Barclays Bank, 4 Vere Street, W1.
See also B . M . H . Shand .

HOWE, Sir Geoffrey; *see* Howe, Sir R. E. G.

HOWE, Prof. Geoffrey Leslie, TD 1962 (Bars 1969 and 1974); Professor of Oral Surgery, Royal Dental Hospital, London School of Dental Surgery, since 1967, and Dean of the School since 1974; *b* 22 April 1924; *e s* of late Leo Leslie John Howe, Maidenhead, Berks; *m* 1947, Heather Patricia Joan Hambly; one *s.* *Educ:* Royal Dental and Middlesex Hospitals. LDS RCS 1946; LRCP, MRCS 1954; FDS RCS 1955; MDS Dunelm, 1961; FFD RCSI 1964. Dental and Medical Sch. Prizeman; Begley Prize, RCS, 1951; Cartwright Prize, RCS, 1961. Dental Officer, Royal Army Dental Corps, 1946-49. House appointments, etc., Royal Dental and Middlesex Hospitals, 1949-55. Registrar in Oral Surgery, Eastman Dental Hosp. (Institute of Dental Surgery), 1955-56; Senior Registrar in Oral Surgery, Plastic and Oral Surgery Centre, Chepstow, Mon, 1956; Senior Registrar in Oral Surgery, Eastman Dental Hospital, 1956-59; Professor of Oral Surgery, University of Newcastle upon Tyne (formerly King's Coll., University of Durham), 1959-67; Cons. Oral Surgeon, United Newcastle upon Tyne Hosps, 1959-67; Chm., Central Cttee for Hosp. Dental Services, 1971-73; Chm., Council, BDA, 1973- (Vice-Chm., 1971-73). Hon. Col Comdt, RADC, 1975-. FRSM. OStJ. *Publications:* The Extraction of Teeth, 1961, 2nd edn 1970; Minor Oral Surgery, 1966, 2nd edn 1972; (with F. I. H. Whitehead) Local Anaesthesia in Dentistry, 1972; contribs to: Medical Treatment Yearbook, 1959; Modern Trends in Dental Surgery, 1962, and to numerous medical and dental journals. *Recreations:* sailing; Territorial Army Volunteer Reserve (lately Col, OC 217 (L) Gen. Hosp. RAMC (V), graded Cons. Dental Surgeon RADC, TAVR). *Address:* c/o Royal Dental Hospital, Leicester Square, WC2H 7BF. *T:* 01-930 8831; 70 Croham Manor Road, South Croydon, Surrey CR2 7BF. *T:* 01-686 4201. *Clubs:* Savage, Oral Surgery.

HOWE, Prof. G(eorge) Melvyn; Professor of Geography, University of Strathclyde, since 1967; *b* Abercynon, 7 April 1920; *s* of Reuben and Edith Howe, Abercynon; *m* 1947, Patricia Graham Fennell, *d* of Edgar and Miriam Fennell, Pontypridd; three *d.* *Educ:* Caerphilly Grammar Sch.; UCW Aberystwyth. BSc 1940; BSc 1st cl. hons Geog. and Anthrop., 1947; MSc 1949; PhD 1957; DSc 1974. Served with RAF, 1940-46: Meteorological Br., 1940-42; Intell. (Air Photographic Interpretation) Br., 1942-46, in Middle East Commnd 1942. Lectr, later Sen. Lectr, in Geography, UCW Aberystwyth, 1948; Reader in Geog., Univ. of Wales, 1964. Vis. Prof. (Health and Welfare, Canada), 1977. Mem. Council: Inst. of British Geographers; RSGS; Mem. Medical Geography Cttee, RGS; British Rep. on Medical Geog. Commn of IGU; Member: Adv. Cttee on Meteorology for Scotland; Nat. Cttee for Geography. FRGS; FRSGS; FRMetS. Gill Memorial Award, RGS, 1964. *Publications:* Wales from the Air, 1957, 2nd edn 1966; (with P. Thomas) Welsh Landforms and Scenery, 1963; National Atlas of Disease Mortality in the United Kingdom, 1963, 2nd edn 1970; The Soviet Union, 1968; The USSR, 1971; Man, Environment and Disease in Britain, 1972, 2nd edn 1976; (ed and contrib.) Atlas of Glasgow and the West of Scotland, 1972; (contrib.) Wales (ed E. G. Bowen), 1958; (contrib.) Modern Methods in the History of Medicine (ed E. Clarke), 1970; (ed with J. A. Loraine, and contrib.) Environmental Medicine, 1973; (contrib.) Environment and Man (ed J. Lenihan and W. W. Fletcher), 1976; (ed and contrib.) A World Geography of Human Diseases, 1977; articles in geographical, meteorological, hydrological and medical jls. *Recreation:* travel. *Address:* Hendre, 29 Birnam Crescent, Bearsden, Glasgow. *T:* 041-942 7223.

HOWE, Jack, RDI 1961; FRIBA 1953; FSIA 1955; Architect and Industrial Designer; *b* 24 Feb. 1911; *s* of Charles Henry and Florence Eleanor Howe; *m* 1960, Margaret Crosbie Corrie; one *s* one *d* (by former marriage). *Educ:* Enfield Grammar Sch.; Polytechnic Sch. of Architecture. Asst to E. Maxwell Fry, 1933-37; Chief Asst to Walter Gropius and Maxwell Fry, 1937-39; Drawing Office Manager to Holland, Hannan & Cubitts Ltd for Royal Ordnance Factories at Wrexham and Ranskill, 1939-43; Associate Partner, Arcon, 1944-48; private practice, 1949; Partnership with Andrew Bain, 1959-76. Architectural work includes: Highbury Quadrant Primary School, (LCC); Windmill House, Lambeth (LCC Housing Scheme); Television Research Lab. for AEI Ltd; Kodak Pavilion, Brussels Exhibn, 1958; Official Architects for British Trade Fair, Moscow, 1961; Industrial Designs include: Diesel Electric Locomotives and Express Pullman Trains; also Rly equipment. Industrial Design Consultant to various large firms and to BR Board. Mem. Design Index Cttee and Street Furniture Cttee, Design Council (formerly CoID), 1956-; Member: Cttee on Traffic Signs, Min. of Transport, 1962, 1963; Nat. Council for Diplomas in Art and Design. FSIA (Pres. 1963-64); Master of Faculty, RDI, 1975-77. Duke of Edinburgh's design prize, 1969. *Publications:* articles for various architectural and design jls. *Recreations:* music, tennis. *Address:* 4 Leopold Avenue, Wimbledon, SW19. *T:* 01-946 7116.

HOWE, Rt. Rev. John William Alexander; Secretary General, Anglican Consultative Council, since 1971; *b* 1920. *Educ:* Westcliff High Sch.; St Chad's Coll., Durham Univ. BA 1943; MA, BD 1948. Ordained, 1943; Curate, All Saints, Scarborough, 1943-46; Chaplain, Adisadel Coll., Gold Coast, 1946-50; Vice-Principal, Edinburgh Theological Coll., 1950-55; Hon. Chaplain, St Mary's Cathedral, Edinburgh, 1951-55; Bishop of St Andrews, Dunkeld and Dunblane, 1955-69. Hon. Canon, St Mary's Cath., Glasgow, 1969; Exec. Officer of the Anglican Communion, 1969-71. Hon. DD General Theological Seminary, NY, 1974. *Address:* 32 Eccleston Street, SW1W 9PY. *T:* 01-730 5271.

HOWE, Josephine Mary O'C.; *see* O'Connor Howe.

HOWE, Rt. Hon. Sir (Richard Edward) Geoffrey, PC 1972; Kt 1970; QC 1965; MP (C) Surrey East, since 1974 (Reigate, 1970-74); *b* 20 Dec. 1926; *er s* of late B. E. Howe and Mrs E. F. Howe, JP (*née* Thomson), Port Talbot, Glamorgan; *m* 1953, Elspeth Rosamund Morton Shand (*see* Lady Howe); one *s* two *d*. *Educ:* Winchester Coll. (Exhibitioner); Trinity Hall, Cambridge (Scholar, MA, LLB). Lieut Royal Signals 1945-48. Chm. Cambridge Univ. Conservative Assoc., 1951; Chm. Bow Group, 1955; Managing Dir, Crossbow, 1957-60, Editor 1960-62. Called to the Bar, Middle Temple, 1952; Bencher, 1969; Mem. General Council of the Bar, 1957-61; Mem. Council of Justice, 1963-70. Director: Sun Alliance & London Insce Co. Ltd, 1974-; AGB Research Ltd, 1974-; EMI Ltd, 1976-. Dep. Chm., Glamorgan QS, 1966-70. Contested (C) Aberavon, 1955, 1959; MP (C) Bebington, 1964-66. Sec. Conservative Parliamentary Health and Social Security Cttee, 1964-65; an Opposition Front Bench spokesman on labour and social services, 1965-66; Solicitor-General, 1970-72; Minister for Trade and Consumer Affairs, DTI, 1972-74; opposition front bench spokesman on social services, 1974-75, on Treasury and economic affairs, 1975-. Member: (Latey) Interdeptl Cttee on Age of Majority, 1965-67; (Street) Cttee on Racial Discrimination, 1967; (Cripps) Cons. Cttee on Discrimination against Women, 1968-69; Chm. Ely Hospital, Cardiff, Inquiry, 1969. Mem. Council of Management, Private Patients' Plan, 1969-70; an Hon. Vice-Pres., Consumers Assoc., 1974-. *Publications:* various political pamphlets for Bow Group and Conservative Political Centre. *Address:* c/o Barclays Bank, Cavendish Square Branch, 4 Vere Street, W1.

HOWE, Sir Robert George, GBE 1949; KCMG 1947 (CMG 1937); *b* Derby, 19 Sept. 1893; *s* of H. Howe; *m* 1919, Loveday Mary Hext (*d* 1970); one *s*. *Educ:* Derby Sch.; St Catharine's Coll., Cambridge. Third Sec. at Copenhagen, 1920; Second Sec., 1920; Belgrade, 1922; Rio de Janeiro, 1924; First Sec., 1926; Bucharest, 1926; Foreign Office, 1930; Acting Counsellor at Peking, 1934; Counsellor, 1936; Minister in Riga, 1940; Minister in Abyssinia, 1942-45; Asst Under-Sec. of State, Foreign Office, 1945; Governor-Gen. of the Sudan, 1947-55; retired 1955. JP Cornwall, 1955-68. *Recreation:* riding. *Address:* Cowbridge, Lostwithiel, Cornwall.

HOWELL, David Arthur Russell; MP (C) Guildford since 1966; *b* 18 Jan. 1936; *s* of Colonel A. H. E. Howell, DSO, TD, DL and Beryl Howell, 5 Headfort Place, SW1; *m* 1967, Davina Wallace; one *s* two *d*. *Educ:* Eton; King's Coll., Cambridge. BA 1st class hons Cantab, 1959. Lieut Coldstream Guards, 1954-56. Joined Economic Section of Treasury, 1959; resigned, 1960. Leader-Writer and Special Correspondent, The Daily Telegraph, 1960; Chm. of Bow Gp, 1961-62; Editor of Crossbow, 1962-64; contested (C) Dudley, 1964; a Lord Comr of Treasury, 1970-71; Parly Sec., CSD, 1970-72; Parly Under-Sec.: Dept of Employment, 1971-72; NI Office, March-Nov. 1972; Minister of State: NI Office, 1972-74; Dept of Energy, 1974. Dir of Conservative Political Centre, 1964-66. Trustee, Federal Trust for Educn and Research. Jt Hon. Sec., UK Council of European Movement, 1968-70. *Publications:* (co-author) Principles in Practice, 1960; Report of the Chatham House Conference on International Trade, 1964; The Conservative Opportunity, 1965; various pamphlets and articles. *Recreations:* travel, books. *Address:* House of Commons, SW1. *Club:* Buck's.

HOWELL, Rt. Hon. Denis Herbert, PC 1976; MP (Lab) Small Heath since 1961; Minister of Department of the Environment (responsible for environment, water resources and sport), since 1974; *b* 4 Sept. 1923; *s* of Herbert and Bertha A. Howell; *m* 1955, Brenda Marjorie, *d* of Stephen and Ruth Wilson, Birmingham; three *s* one *d*. *Educ:* Gower Street Sch.; Handsworth Grammar Sch., Birmingham. Mem., Birmingham City Council, 1946-56; Hon. Sec. Birmingham City Council Labour Group, 1950-55 (served Catering Establishment, General Purposes, Health and Watch Cttees); Chm. Catering Cttee, 1952-55; Health (Gen. Purposes) Sub-Cttee for setting up of first smokeless zones. MP (Lab) All Saints Div., Birmingham, 1955-Sept. 1959; Jt Parly

Under-Sec. of State, Dept of Educn and Science (with responsibility for sport), 1964-69; Minister of State, Min. of Housing and Local Govt (with responsibility for sport), 1969-70; Opposition Spokesman for Local Govt and Sport, 1970-74. Member: Dudley Road Hosp. Group Management Cttee, 1948-64; the Albemarle Cttee on the Youth Service; Management Cttee, City of Birmingham Symphony Orchestra, 1950-55. Governor, Handsworth Grammar Sch. Chairman: Birmingham Assoc. of Youth Clubs, 1963-64; Birmingham Settlement, 1963-64; Sports Council, 1965-70; Youth Service Develt Council, 1964-69 (report: Youth and Community Work in the 70's); Central Council of Physical Recreation, 1973-74. Pres., Assoc. of Professional, Exec. Clerical and Computer Staffs (APEX) (formerly CAWU), 1971-. Football League Referee, 1956-70. *Publication:* Soccer Refereeing, 1968. *Recreations:* sport, theatre, music. *Address:* 33 Moor Green Lane, Moseley, Birmingham B13 8NE. *Clubs:* Reform; Warwickshire County Cricket (Birmingham); Birmingham Press.

HOWELL, Dorothy, FRAM; Professor of Harmony and Composition, Royal Academy of Music, 1924-70, retired; *b* Handsworth, Birmingham, 1898. *Educ:* Royal Academy of Music. *Publications:* Symphonic Poem, Lamia; various works for Piano, Violin, etc. *Address:* Studley, Malvern Wells, Worcs.

HOWELL, Air Vice-Marshal Evelyn Michael Thomas, CBE 1961; CEng, FRAeS; Manager, International Operations, Van Dusen Air Inc., Minneapolis, USA, since 1972; *b* 11 Sept. 1913; *s* of Sir Evelyn Berkeley Howell, KCIE, CSI; *m* 1st, 1937, Helen Joan, *o d* of late Brig. W. M. Hayes, CBE, FRICS (marr. diss. 1972); one *s* three *d*; 2nd, 1972, Rosemary, *e d* of I. A. Cram, CEng, MICE; one *s* one *d*. *Educ:* Downside Sch.; RAF Coll., Cranwell. Commissioned, 1934; Dir of Air Armament Research and Devt, Min. of Aviation, 1960-62; Comdt, RAF Techn. Coll., 1963-65; SASO, HQ Technical Training Command RAF, 1966-67; retired, 1967. Gen. Manager, Van Dusen Aircraft Supplies Co., Oxford, 1967-72. Mem. Livery of Clothworkers' Co., 1938. *Recreations:* swimming, rifle shooting, tennis, boating. *Address:* c/o Lloyds Bank Ltd, 6 Pall Mall, SW1Y 5NH. *Club:* Royal Air Force.

HOWELL, Gwynne Richard; Principal Bass, Royal Opera House, since 1971; *b* Gorseinon, S Wales, 13 June 1938; *s* of Gilbert and Ellaline Howell; *m* 1968, Mary Edwina Morris; two *s*. *Educ:* Pontardawe Grammar Sch.; Univ. of Wales, Swansea (BSc); Manchester Univ. (DipTP); MRTPI 1966. Studied singing with Redvers Llewellyn while at UCW; pt-time student, Manchester RCM, with Gwilym Jones, during DipTP trng at Manchester Univ.; studied with Otakar Kraus, 1968-72. Planning Asst, Kent CC, 1961-63; Sen. Planning Officer, Manchester Corp., 1965-68, meanwhile continuing to study music pt-time and giving public operatic performances which incl. the rôle of Pogner, in Die Meistersinger; as a result of this rôle, apptd Principal Bass at Sadler's Wells, 1968; also reached final of BBC Opera Singers competition for N of Eng., 1967. In first season at Sadler's Wells, sang 8 rôles, incl. Monterone and the Commendatore; appearances with Hallé Orch., 1968 and 1969; covered rôle of Arkel in Pelleas and Melisande, Glyndebourne and Covent Garden, 1969; sang Goffredo, in Il Pirato, with Montserrat Caballe, 1969. Royal Opera House, Covent Garden: rôles include: début as First Nazarene in new prodn of Salome, conducted by Solti, 1969-70 season; the King, in Aida; Timur, in Turandot; Mephisto, in Damnation of Faust; Prince Gremin, in Eugene Onegin; High Priest, in Nabucco; Reinmar, in new prodn of Tannhauser, with Colin Davis, 1973-74 (later rôle, Landgraf); Colline, in La Boheme; Pimen, in Boris Godunov; Ribbing, new prodn of Un ballo in maschera, with Claudio Abbado; Padre Guardiano, in La forza del destino; Hobson, new prodn of Peter Grimes, 1975; new rôle of Sparafucile, in Rigoletto, 1975-76 season; Ramfis in Aida, 1977. Sang the Monk and King Philip, in Don Carlos, also Pogner, with Eng. Nat. Opera, 1974-75, and King Philip and Sarastro, 1975-76. As well as appearances in operatic rôles in this country and W Europe, performances of sacred music, notably the Verdi Requiem, Missa Solemnis (this with Giulini, 1972-73), Mozart Requiem, St Matthew and St John Passions, in Royal Fest. Hall, and at Prom. Concerts, etc, also in France, Austria, W Germany and USA (Amer. début with Chicago Symph. Orch., 1974). Has recorded for BBC radio and TV and for major recording companies. *Recreations:* tennis, squash, Rugby enthusiast, gardening. *Address:* 197 Fox Lane, N13. *T:* 01-886 1981.

HOWELL, Rt. Rev. Kenneth Walter, MA; Minister of St John's, Downshire Hill, Hampstead, since 1972; an Assistant Bishop, Diocese of London, since 1976; *b* 4 Feb. 1909; *s* of Frederick John and Florence Sarah Howell; *m* 1937, Beryl Mary Hope (*d* 1972), *d* of late Capt. Alfred and Mrs Hope, Bedford; two *s* one *d*. *Educ:* St Olave's; St Peter's Hall, Oxford; Wycliffe Hall,

Oxford. Curate of St Mary Magdalene, Peckham, 1933-37; Chaplain of Paraguayan Chaco Mission, 1937-38; Chaplain Quepe Mission, Chile, 1938-40; Superintendent of South American Missionary Society's Mission to Araucanian Indians in S Chile, 1940-47; Vicar of Wandsworth, 1948-63, Rural Dean, 1957-63; Chaplain, Royal Hosp. and Home for Incurables, Putney, 1957-63; Hon. Canon of Southwark, 1962-63; Bishop in Chile, Bolivia and Peru, 1963-71. *Address:* 64 Pilgrim's Lane, Hampstead, NW3 1SN.

HOWELL, Maj.-Gen. Lloyd, CBE 1972; Director of Army Education, since 1976; *b* 28 Dec. 1923; *s* of Thomas Idris Howell and Anne Howell; *m* 1st, 1945, Hazel Barker (*d* 1974); five *s* three *d*; 2nd, 1975, Elizabeth June Buchanan Husband (*née* Atkinson); two step *s*. *Educ:* Barry Grammar Sch.; University Coll. of S Wales and Monmouthshire (BSc); Royal Military Coll. of Science. CEng, MRAeS. Commissioned RA, 1944; Field Regt, RA, E Africa, 1945-46; Staff, Divl HQ, Palestine, 1946-47; Instr, RMA Sandhurst, 1949-53; TSO II Trials Estabt, 1954-57; SO II (Educn), Divl HQ, BAOR, 1957-59; DS, Royal Mil. Coll. of Science, 1960-64; SEO, Army Apprentices Coll., 1964-67; Headmaster/Comdg, Duke of York's Royal Mil. Sch., 1967-72; Col (Ed), MoD (Army), 1972-74; Chief Educn Officer, HQ UKLF, 1974-76. *Recreations:* gardening, golf, Rugby administration, reading. *Address:* Wanborough House, Lower Wanborough, near Swindon, Wilts. *T:* Wanborough 237. *Club:* Army and Navy.

HOWELL, Paul Philip, CMG 1964; OBE 1955; Fellow of and Director of Development Studies at Wolfson College, Cambridge; Director of Cambridge University Course on Development; *b* 13 Feb. 1917; *s* of Brig.-Gen. Philip Howell, CMG (killed in action, 1916) and Mrs Rosalind Upcher Howell (*née* Buxton); *m* 1949, Bridgit Mary Radclyffe Luard; two *s* two *d*. *Educ:* Westminster Sch.; Trinity Coll., Cambridge (Sen. Schol., MA); Christ Church, Oxford (MA, DPhil). Asst District Comr, Sudan Polit. Service, 1938; commnd in Sudan Defence Force, ADC to Gov.-Gen., 1940; Overseas Enemy Territory Administration, Eritrea, 1941; Asst District Comr, Zeraf Valley, 1942; District Comr, Central Nuer, 1944; District Comr, Baggara, Western Kordofan, 1946; Chm., Jonglei Investigation Team, 1948; Chm. (Dep. Gov.), Southern Development Investigation, 1953; Asst Chief Sec., Uganda Protectorate, 1955; Sen. Asst Sec., Min. of Natural Resources, 1955; Perm. Sec., Min. of Corporations and Regional Communications, 1957; Perm. Sec. Min. of Commerce and Industry, 1959; Chm., E African Nile Waters Co-ordinating Cttee, 1956-61; seconded to FO and Min. of Overseas Development; Head of Middle East Develt Div., Beirut, 1961-69. Member: Bd of Governors, Inst. of Development Studies, 1971-; Council, Overseas Development Inst., 1972-. *Publications:* A Manual of Nuer Law, 1954; (ed) The Equatorial Nile Project and its Effects in the Anglo-Egyptian Sudan, 1954; (ed) Natural Resources and Development Potential in the Southern Sudan, 1955. *Recreations:* fishing and country pursuits. *Address:* Wolfson College, Cambridge. *T:* Cambridge 53951; 4 Marlborough Court, Grange Road, Cambridge. *T:* Cambridge 62601; Burfield Hall, Wymondham, Norfolk. *T:* Wymondham 3389. *Clubs:* Travellers', Royal Commonwealth Society.

HOWELL, Ralph Frederic; MP (C) North Norfolk since 1970; *b* 25 May 1923; *m* 1950, Margaret (*née* Bone); two *s* one *d*. *Educ:* Diss Grammar Sch., Norfolk. Navigator/Bomb-aimer, RAF, 1941-46; farming near Dereham, Norfolk, 1946-; Dir, Mid-Norfolk Farmers Trading Co., 1963-. Mem., European Parlt, Strasbourg, 1974. *Address:* Wendling Grange, Dereham, Norfolk. *T:* Wendling 247. *Clubs:* Carlton, Farmers'; Norfolk (Norwich).

HOWELLS, Anne, (Mrs Ryland Davies), FRMCM (ARMCM); opera, concert and recital singer; *b* 12 Jan. 1941; *d* of Trevor William Howells and Mona Hewart; *m* 1966, Ryland Davies, *qv*. *Educ:* Sale County Grammar Sch.; Royal Manchester Coll. of Music. Three seasons (Chorus), with Glyndebourne, 1964-66; at short notice, given star rôle there, in Cavalli's L'Ormindo, 1967; rôles, there, also include: Dorabella in Cosi fan Tutte; Cathleen in (world première of) Nicholas Maw's Rising of the Moon, 1970; also the Composer in Ariadne; Diana in Calisto. Royal Opera House, Covent Garden: under contract for three years, 1969-71, where rôles included: Lena in (world première of) Richard Rodney Bennett's Victory; Rosina in Barber of Seville; Cherubino in Marriage of Figaro. Currently, 1973-, Guest artist with Royal Opera House. Recitals in Brussels and Vienna; operatic guest performances in Chicago and Geneva, 1972-73; Metropolitan Opera, NY, 1975; La Scala, 1976; Salzburg Festival, 1976. *Recreations:* cinema, reading. *Address:* Milestone, Broom Close, Esher, Surrey. *T:* Esher 64527.

HOWELLS, Christopher John; HM Diplomatic Service; Counsellor, Foreign and Commonwealth Office, since 1975; *b* 2 March 1933; *s* of Rev. Brinley Howells; *m* 1959, Jane Hayes; two *s* one *d*. *Educ:* Oakham Sch.; Merton Coll., Oxford (1st Cl. Hons Mod. Hist.). Royal Leicestershire Regt; Royal West African Frontier Force. Joined HM Diplomatic Service, 1958; Hong Kong, 1959; Third Sec., Peking, 1960; Foreign Office, 1962; First Sec., Vienna, 1965; MoD, 1967; Asst Political Adviser, Hong Kong, 1969; Counsellor and Head of Chancery, Warsaw, 1973. *Address:* c/o Foreign and Commonwealth Office, SW1. *Clubs:* Athenæum; Hong Kong (Hong Kong).

HOWELLS, Geraint Wyn; MP (L) Cardigan since Feb. 1974; *b* 15 April 1925; *s* of David John Howells and Mary Blodwen Howells; *m* 1957, Mary Olwen Hughes Griffiths; two *d*. *Educ:* Ponterwyd Primary Sch.; Ardwyn Grammar School. Farmer; Vice-Chm., British Wool Marketing Bd, 1971-; Man. Dir, Wilkinson & Stanier Ltd, Meat Wholesalers, Manchester. *Recreations:* walking, sport. *Address:* Glennydd, Ponterwyd, Ceredigion, Dyfed. *T:* Ponterwyd 258.

HOWELLS, Gilbert Haywood, FRCS; *b* 23 Aug. 1897; *s* of Henry Haywood and Hannah Elizabeth Howells; *m* 1926, Dorothy Mary Jones (*d* 1977); no *c*. *Educ:* Newport High Sch.; University Coll., Cardiff; St Thomas' Hosp. MB, BS London 1923; FRCS 1928. Consulting Surgeon: Royal National Ear Nose and Throat Hospital; (ENT), St George's Hosp.; (ENT), Moorfields Eye Hosp.; King Edward VII Hosp., Windsor; Upton Hosp., Slough; Fellow Royal Society of Medicine and British Association of Otolaryngologists; Mem. BMA; late Corresp. Mem. Société Française d'Otorhin. *Publications:* sundry articles in medical journals. *Address:* Breydon, South Park Drive, Gerrards Cross, Bucks. *T:* Gerrards Cross 3368.

HOWELLS, Herbert Norman, CH 1972; CBE 1953; DMus Oxon; MusDoc *hc* Cantab; FRCO; FRCM; Hon. RAM; composer; King Edward Professor of Music, University of London, Emeritus 1962; Professor of Composition at Royal College of Music; Director of Music, St Paul's Girls' School, Brook Green, 1936-62; sometime Editor RCM Magazine; Master, Worshipful Company of Musicians, 1959 (first John Collard Fellow; elected to John Collard Life Fellowship, 1959); *b* 17 Oct. 1892; *y s* of late Oliver Howells and Elizabeth Burgham; *m* 1920, Dorothy (*d* 1975), *y d* of late William Goozee; one *d* (one *s* decd). *Educ:* Lydney Grammar Sch.; Gloucester Cathedral; RCM. Became pupil of Sir Herbert Brewer, Gloucester Cathedral, 1905; Open Schol. in Composition at RCM, 1912; studied there under Stanford, Parratt, Parry, Charles Wood, and Walford Davies till 1917; succeeded to the Grove Scholarship, 1915, and became Bruce Scholar, 1916; first work heard in London was the Mass produced by Sir Richard Terry at Westminster Cathedral, 1912; was for short time sub-organist at Salisbury Cathedral. President: RCO, 1958-59; Incorporated Soc. of Musicians, 1952; Plainsong and Mediæval Soc. Hon. MusD Cambridge, 1961; Hon. Fellow RSCM, 1963; Hon. Fellow, St John's Coll., Cambridge, 1962. *Publications:* Sir Patrick Spens; Sine Nomine (Chorus and Orchestra) Procession; Puck's Minuet; Piano Concerto; Elegy for Strings; Concerto for Strings; Lady Audrey's Suite; Phantasy Quartet; Piano Quartet; Rhapsodic Quintet (Clar. and Str.); First and Third Sonatas for violin and pianoforte; Lambert's Clavichord; In Green Ways, five songs for Soprano and Orchestra; Peacock Pie song-cycle; Sonata for Organ; Hymnus Paradisi for Sopr., Ten., Chor. and Orchestra; Missa Sabrinensis for 4 solo voices, Chorus and Orchestra; Pageantry (Suite for Brass Band); A Kent Yeoman's Wooing Song for 2 Soli, Choir and Orchestra; Four Organ Rhapsodies; Six Psalm Preludes; Music for a Prince (for HRH Prince Charles); Introit (composed for Coronation Service, 1953); Inheritance (commissioned by The Arts Council of Great Britain for A Garland for the Queen, 1953); An English Mass, 1955 (for Chorus and Orch.); Howell's Clavichord (20 pieces); Missa Aedis Christi (for Christ Church, Oxford); Missa, Collegium Regale (for King's Coll., Cambridge); Three Figures (suite for Brass Band); Sequence for St Michael (commnd by St John's Coll., Cambridge); Coventry Antiphon (commnd for Coventry Cath.); Stabat Mater for Tenor, Chorus and Orchestra (commnd by the London Bach Choir); The Coventry Mass. *Recreations:* seeking quiet; English literature. *Address:* 3 Beverley Close, Barnes, SW13. *T:* 01-876 5119. *Club:* Savile.

HOWERD, Frankie; *see* Howard, F. A.

HOWES, Henry William, CMG 1951; OBE 1948; MA, MSc, PhD London; lecturer, author; *b* 1896; *e s* of late William and Laura Howes, Norwich; *m* 1923, Clarisse Vera, *y d* of late James Charles Bond, Rattlesden, Suffolk; one *d*. *Educ:* Bracondale and Grammar Schs, Norwich; Univs of London and Wales. Served

European War, 1914-18, Royal Marines, 1915-17. Teaching in Essex and Middlesex, 1921-30, and in Polytechnics and Institutes, 1927-36; Principal, Norwich City Coll. and Sch. of Art, 1936-44; Mem. of Exec. of Eastern Counties Cttee for Adult Educn. In HM Forces, 1940-44; first Dir of Educn, Gibraltar, 1944-49, City Councillor, 1945-49; Dir-Gen. of Education, Ceylon, 1949-54; Hon. Educn Adviser, Ceylon Army, 1951-; Mem. Court and Council, University of Ceylon, 1949-54. Educational Adviser, Caribbean, for Unesco, 1954; Educational Adviser, Odhams, 1956-57; Dir of Education, British Honduras, 1958-60; Mem. Council, University Coll. of West Indies, 1958-60; Adviser on Secondary Education, British Honduras, 1960; Unesco Adviser on Adult and Youth Education, Dominica, West Indies, 1962. Overseas Educational Adviser, Harrap's, 1963-67; Hon. Historical Adviser to Govt of Gibraltar, 1964-72. Hon. Life Mem., Ceylon Nat. Assoc. for Prevention of Tuberculosis. Chevalier of Order of Crown (Belgium), 1937; Officer of Order of Leopold II (Belgium), 1970; Kt Comdr, Order of Alfonso X, el Sabio (Spain), 1966; Kt of Order of St Gregory the Great, 1957; Officer of Order of Palmes Académiques (France), 1976. *Publications:* Bruges, 1935; Santiago de Compostela and its Prehistoric Origin, 1936; The Story of Gibraltar, 1948; The Gibraltarian:-The Origin and Development of Population in Gibraltar since 1704, 1951; Presenting Modern Britain, 1965; We Go to Spain, 1967. *Recreation:* Spanish and Flemish studies. *Address:* 11 Franklins Road, Stevenage, Herts. *T:* Stevenage 2512.

HOWES, Rear-Adm. Peter Norris, CB 1966; DSC 1941; Private Secretary to Lord Mayor of London, 1968-72; *b* 1 July 1916; *s* of Percy Groom Howes; *m* 1952, Priscilla Hamilton, *d* of Maj.-Gen. G. W. E. Heath, *qv* ; three *s* one *d. Educ:* St Peter's Court, Broadstairs; Royal Naval College, Dartmouth. Served in HM Ships Hood, Furious, Fortune, Albury, Aberdeen, Westminster, Adamant, Newcastle, Liverpool; commanded 6th Motor Gunboat Flotilla; HMS Chaplet; HMS Mercury; Dartmouth Training Sqdn; HMS Devonshire; specialised as Communications Officer, 1942; Senior Aide-de-Camp to Viceroy of India, 1947; Naval Asst to First Sea Lord, 1955-58; Flag Officer, Middle East Station, 1964-66. *Publication:* The Viceregal Establishments in India, 1948. *Recreations:* riding, shooting, fishing, photography. *Address:* Sutton Parva House, Heytesbury, Wilts. *T:* Sutton Veny 333. *Club:* White's.

HOWES, Sally Ann; actress (stage, film and television); *b* 20 July; *d* of late Bobby Howes; *m* 1958, Richard Adler (marr. diss.); *m* 1969, Andrew Maree (marr. diss.). *Educ:* Glendower, London; Queenswood, Herts; privately. *Films include:* Thursday's Child; Halfway House; Dead of Night; Nicholas Nickleby; Anna Karenina; My Sister and I; Fools Rush In; History of Mr Polly; Stop Press Girl; Honeymoon Deferred; The Admirable Crichton; Chitty, Chitty Bang Bang. First appeared West End stage in (revue) Fancy Free, at Prince of Wales's, and at Royal Variety Performance, 1950. *Stage Shows include:* Caprice (musical debut); Paint Your Wagon; Babes in the Wood; Romance by Candlelight; Summer Song; Hatful of Rain; My Fair Lady; Kwamina, NY; What Makes Sammy Run?, NY; Brigadoon (revival), NY City Center, 1962; Sound of Music, Los Angeles and San Francisco, 1972; Lover, St Martin's; The King and I, Adelphi, 1973, Los Angeles and San Francisco, 1974. Has appeared on television: in England from 1949 (Short and Sweet Series, Sally Ann Howes Show, etc); in USA from 1958 (Dean Martin Show, Ed Sullivan Show, Mission Impossible, Marcus Welby MD); Play of the Week; Panel Shows: Hollywood Squares; Password; Bell Telephone Hour; US Steel Hour, etc. *Recreations:* reading, riding, theatre. *Address:* c/o Kramer and Reiss, 9100 Sunset Boulevard, Los Angeles, Calif 90069, USA.

HOWICK OF GLENDALE, 2nd Baron *cr* 1960; **Charles Evelyn Baring;** a Managing Director, Baring Brothers & Co. Ltd, since 1969; *b* 30 Dec. 1937; *s* of 1st Baron Howick of Glendale, KG, GCMG, KCVO, and of Lady Mary Cecil Grey, *er d* of 5th Earl Grey; *S* father, 1973; *m* 1964, Clare Nicolette, *y d* of Col Cyril Darby; one *s* three *d. Educ:* Eton; New Coll., Oxford. Director: The London Life Association Ltd, 1972-; Swan Hunter Group Ltd, 1972-. Member: Exec. Cttee, Nat. Art Collections Fund, 1973-; Council, Friends of Tate Gall., 1973-. *Heir: s* Hon. David Evelyn Charles Baring, *b* 26 March 1975. *Address:* Howick, Alnwick, Northumberland. *T:* Longhoughton 624; 52 Chepstow Villas, W11. *T:* 01-229 2640. *Club:* Brooks's.
See also Sir E. H. T. Wakefield.

HOWIE, Sir James (William), Kt 1969; MD (Aberdeen); FRCP, FRCPGlas; FRCPath; Director of the Public Health Laboratory Service, 1963-73; *b* 31 Dec. 1907; *s* of late James Milne Howie and Jessie Mowat Robertson; *m* 1935, Isabella Winifred Mitchell, BSc; two *s* one *d. Educ:* Robert Gordon's Coll., Aberdeen; University of Aberdeen. University

lectureships in Aberdeen and Glasgow, 1932-40; Pathologist, RAMC, 1941-45 (served Nigeria and War Office); Head of Dept of Pathology and Bacteriology, Rowett Research Institute, Aberdeen, 1946-51; Prof. of Bacteriology, University of Glasgow, 1951-63. Mem. Agricultural Research Council, 1957-63. Convener, Medical Research Council Working Party on Sterilisers, 1957-64; Pres., Royal College of Pathologists, 1966-69 (Vice-Pres., 1962-66); President: BMA, 1969-70; Assoc. of Clinical Pathologists, 1972-73. QHP, 1965-68. Hon. ARCVS 1977; Honorary Member: Pathological Soc. of GB and Ireland, 1977; ACP, 1977. Hon. LLD Aberdeen, 1969. *Publications:* various publications in medical and scientific periodicals, particularly on bacteriology and nutrition. *Recreations:* golf, music. *Address:* Knockmalloch, Newtonmore, Inverness-shire. *T:* Newtonmore 348.

HOWIE, Prof. John Mackintosh; Regius Professor of Mathematics, University of St Andrews, since 1970; Dean, Faculty of Science, since 1976; *b* 23 May 1936; *s* of Rev. David Y. Howie and Janet McD. Howie (*née* Mackintosh); *m* 1960, Dorothy Joyce Mitchell Miller; two *d. Educ:* Robert Gordon's Coll., Aberdeen; Univ. of Aberdeen; Balliol Coll., Oxford. MA, DPhil, DSc, FRSE. Asst in Mathematics: Aberdeen Univ., 1958-59; Glasgow Univ., 1961-63; Lectr in Mathematics, Glasgow Univ., 1963-67; Visiting Asst Prof., Tulane Univ., 1964-65; Sen. Lectr in Mathematics, Stirling Univ., 1967-70. Mem., Cttee to Review Examination Arrangements (Dunning Cttee), 1975-77; Chm., Scottish Central Cttee on Mathematics, 1975-. *Publications:* An Introduction to Semigroup Theory, 1976; articles in British and foreign mathematical jls. *Recreation:* music. *Address:* Mathematical Institute, North Haugh, St Andrews, Fife KY16 9SS. *T:* St Andrews 4317.

HOWIE, Thomas McIntyre; Principal, Paisley College of Technology, since 1972; *b* 21 April 1926; *m* 1951, Catherine Elizabeth Logan; three *s. Educ:* Paisley Coll. of Technology; Strathclyde Univ. BSc (Eng); CEng, FICE. Civil Engrg Asst, Clyde Navigation Trust, 1947-50; Paisley Coll. of Technology: Lectr in Civil Engrg, 1950-55; Sen. Lectr in Civil Engrg, 1955-58; Head, Dept of Civil Engrg, 1958-72; Vice-Principal, 1970-72. *Recreation:* golf. *Address:* Dunscore, 38 Main Road, Castlehead, Paisley PA2 6AW. *T:* 041-889 5723. *Club:* Caledonian.

HOWIE, William; civil engineer, journalist; *b* Troon, Ayrshire, 2 March 1924; *er s* of Peter and Annie Howie, Troon; *m* 1951, Mairi Margaret, *o d* of Martha and late John Sanderson, Troon; two *s* two *d. Educ:* Marr Coll., Troon; Royal Technical Coll., Glasgow (BSc, Diploma). MP (Lab) Luton, Nov. 1963-70; Asst Whip, 1964-66; Lord Comr of the Treasury, 1966-67; Comptroller, HM Household, 1967-68. A Vice-Chm., Parly Labour Party, 1968-70. Mem., Instn of Civil Engineers, 1951; Member: Council, Instn of Civil Engineers, 1964-67; Governing Body, Imperial Coll. of Science and Technology, 1965-67; Council, City Univ., 1968-. *Recreations:* opera, watching football, trying to find time to play golf. *Address:* 34 Temple Fortune Lane, NW11 7UL. *T:* 01-455 0492. *Clubs:* Luton Trades Unionists, Luton Labour; Seretse.

HOWITT, Anthony Wentworth; Senior Executive Partner, Peat, Marwick, Mitchell & Co., Management Consultants, since 1957; Member, Price Commission, since 1973; *b* 7 Feb. 1920; *o s* of late Sir Harold Gibson Howitt, GBE, DSO, MC, and late Dorothy Radford; *m* 1951, June Mary Brent. *Educ:* Uppingham; Trinity Coll., Cambridge (MA). FCA, FCMA, JDipMA, FBIM, FIMC, FBCS. Commissioned RA; served in UK, ME and Italy, 1940-46 (Major). With Peat, Marwick, Mitchell & Co., Chartered Accountants, 1946-57. Member Council: Inst. of Management Consultants, 1964-77 (Pres., 1967-68); Inst. of Cost and Management Accountants, 1966-76 (Pres., 1972-73); Management Consultants Assoc., 1966- (Chm., 1976); British Consultants Bureau, 1968-75 (led mission to Far East, 1969). Mem., Devlin Commn of Inquiry into Industrial Representation, 1971-72. Member: Bd of Fellows of BIM, 1973-76; Adv. Panel to Overseas Projects Gp, 1973-76. Mem., Court of Assistants, Merchant Taylors' Co., 1971-. *Publications:* papers and addresses on professional and management subjects. *Recreations:* fox-hunting, tennis, golf. *Address:* Peat, Marwick, Mitchell & Co., 1 Puddle Dock, EC4V 3PD. *T:* 01-236 8000. *Clubs:* Army and Navy; MCC; Harlequins.

HOWITT, W(illiam) Fowler, DA (Dundee), FRIBA; Partner in Firm of Cusdin Burden and Howitt, Architects, since 1965; *b* Perth, Scotland, May 1924; *s* of late Frederick Howitt, Head Postmaster, Forfar; *m* 1951, Ann Elizabeth, *o d* of late A. J. Hedges, Radipole, Dorset; three *s* one *d. Educ:* Perth Academy. Royal Marines, 1943-46. Sch. of Architecture, Dundee, 1948; RIBA Victory Scholar, 1949. Asst Louis de Soissons, London (housing and flats), 1949-52; Prin. Asst to Vincent Kelly, Dublin (hosps & offices), 1952-55; Architect to St Thomas' Hosp. (Hosp. rebuilding schemes, flats, offices), 1955-64. Present projects include: Grosvenor Road Site Develt and New Royal Victoria Hosp., Belfast; phase 3, New Site Develt for Addenbrooke's Hosp. Cambridge; extns Princess Alexandra Hosp., Harlow; Tralee Hosp.; Faculty of Medicine, Univ. of Riyad, S Arabia. *Recreations:* reading, golf, childish pursuits. *Address:* 1-4 Yarmouth Place, Piccadilly, W1Y 8JQ. *T:* 01-493 8913; (home) 32 Gloucester Road, Teddington, Mddx TW11 0NU. *T:* 01-977 5772.

HOWKINS, John, MD, FRCS; Gynæcological Surgeon to St Bartholomew's Hospital, 1946-69 (Hon. Consultant Gynæcologist since 1969), to Hampstead General Hospital 1946-67 (Hon. Consultant Gynæcologist, since 1968), and to Royal Masonic Hospital, 1948-73; *b* 17 Dec. 1907; *m* 1940, Lena Brown; one *s* two *d. Educ:* Shrewsbury Sch.; London Univ. Arts Scholar, Middlesex Hospital, 1926; MRCS, LRCP, 1932; MB, BS, London, 1933; FRCS, 1936; MS London, 1936; MD (Gold Medal) London, 1937; MRCOG 1937, FRCOG 1947. House Surgeon and Casualty Surgeon, Middlesex Hosp., 1932-34; RMO Chelsea Hosp. for Women, 1936; Gynæcological Registrar, Middlesex Hosp., 1937-38; Resident Obstetric Surg., St Bartholomew's Hosp., 1938 and 1945; Temp. Wing-Comdr, RAFVR Med. Br., 1939-45. Hunterian Prof., RCS 1947. William Meredith Fletcher Shaw Lectr, RCOG, 1975. Sometime Examiner in Midwifery to Univs of Cambridge and London, RCOG, Conjoint Bd of England. Chm., Council Ski Club of Great Britain, 1964-67 (Hon. Life Member, 1968, Trustee, 1969-). *Publications:* Shaw's Textbook of Gynæcology, 1956 (8th edn 1962); Shaw's Textbook of Gynæcological Surgery, 3rd edn, 1967; (jointly) Bonney's Textbook of Gynæcological Surgery, 1963, 8th edn 1974. *Recreations:* ski-ing, salmon fishing and sheep farming. *Address:* Caen Hen, Abercegir, Machynlleth, Powys, Wales. *Club:* Ski Club of Great Britain.

HOWLAND, Lord; Andrew Ian Henry Russell; *b* 30 March 1962; *s* and *heir* of Marquess of Tavistock, *qv.*

HOWLAND, Robert Leslie, MA; Fellow of St John's College, Cambridge, since 1929; University Lecturer in Classics, 1934-72; Warden of Madingley Hall, 1965-75 (Senior Tutor, 1956-65, President, 1963-67); *b* 25 March 1905; *s* of Robert and Mary Howland; *m* 1930, Eileen, *d* of Robert Reid Tait; two *s* one *d. Educ:* Shrewsbury Sch.; St John's Coll., Cambridge. Mem. of Cambridge Univ. Athletic Team, 1925-28; Mem. of British National Athletic Team, 1927-39 (Capt. 1934-35), and British Olympic Team, 1928. Holder of English native record for putting the weight, 1930-48. *Publications:* papers in classical journals. *Address:* St John's College, Cambridge. *Clubs:* United Oxford & Cambridge University; Achilles; Hawks (Cambridge).

HOWLETT, Jack, CBE 1969; MA Oxon, PhD Manchester; MIEE, FSS, FIMA; Consultant to International Computers Ltd, since 1975; *b* 30 Aug. 1912; *s* of William Howlett and Lydia Ellen Howlett; *m* 1939, Joan Marjorie Simmons; four *s* one *d. Educ:* Stand Grammar Sch., Manchester; Manchester Univ. Mathematician, LMS Railway, 1935-40 and 1946-48; mathematical work in various wartime research estabts, 1940-46; Head of Computer Group, Atomic Energy Research Estabt, Harwell, 1948-61; Dir, Atlas Computer Lab., Chilton Didcot, Berks, 1961-75 (under SRC, 1965-75). Chm., Nat. Cttee on Computer Networks, 1976-. Fellow by special election, St Cross Coll., Oxford, 1966. *Publications:* reviews and gen. papers on numerical mathematics and computation. *Recreations:* hill walking, music. *Address:* 20B Bradmore Road, Oxford OX2 6QP. *T:* Oxford 52893. *Clubs:* New Arts, Savile.

HOWSAM, Air Vice-Marshal George Roberts, CB 1945; MC 1918; RCAF, retired: also retired from Federal Emergency Measures Organization, 1962 (Coordinator, Alberta Civil Defence, 1950-57) and from business; *b* 29 Jan. 1895; *s* of Mary Ida and George Roberts Howsam, Port Perry, Ont; *m* 1st, 1918, Lillian Isobel (*d* 1970), *d* of Mary and William Somerville, Toronto; one *s*; 2nd, 1972, Marion Isobel Garrett, *d* of Clarence Albert Mitchell and Mary Blanche McCurdy, New Brunswick and Nova Scotia. *Educ:* Port Perry and Toronto. Joined Canadian Expeditionary Force, March 1916 and RFC 70 Sqdn and 43 Sqdn, 1917-18; served as fighter pilot France and Belgium, 1917-18 (wounded twice, MC); with Army of Occupation in Germany; returned to Canada, 1921; RCAF photographic survey, NW Canada; RAF Staff Coll., England, 1930 (psa); Senior Mem., RCAF 1st Aerobatic Team (Siskin) Display, Cleveland, USA, 1929; Staff Mem. CGAO Operations at AFHQ, 1931-32; SASO MD2 Toronto, 1933-36; OC 2 Army Co-operation Sqdn, Ottawa, 1937; Dir of Training for RCAF, Ottawa, 1938-40; England and France, 1940; later in 1940,

SASO, No 4 Training Command, Regina; commanded No 11 Service Flying Training Sch., Yorkton, 1941; AOC No 4 Training Command, Calgary, 1942-44, also AOC Air Staging Route to Alaska, 1942-43 (thereby holding double command for two years); Chm. Organisation Cttee, Air Force HQ, Ottawa, 1945; retired 1946. Dominion Dir The Air Cadet League of Canada, 1946-47; Alberta Chm. RCAF Assoc., 1958-59. Canadian Deleg. to Emergency Measures NATO Assembly, Paris, Oct. 1960. Legion of Merit in Degree of Comdr (US), 1945; Order of White Lion (Czecho-Slovakia), 1946; Commandeur de l'ordre de la Couronne (Belgium), 1948. *Publications:* Rocky Mountain Foothills Offer Great Chance to Gliders (Calgary Daily Herald), 1923; Industrial and Mechanical Development: War (Canadian Defence Qtly Prize Essay), 1931. *Recreations:* gardening, writing, shooting. *Address:* 2040 Pauls Terrace, Victoria, BC, Canada; c/o Bank of Montreal, Government Street, Victoria, BC. *Clubs:* Union, Canadian, Victoria Golf (Victoria, BC); Empire (Toronto); Ranchmen's (Calgary).

HOWSON, Rear-Adm. John, CB 1963; DSC 1944; *b* 30 Aug. 1908; *s* of late George Howson and Mary Howson, Glasgow; *m* 1937, Evangeline Collins; one *s* one *d. Educ:* Kelvinside Academy, Glasgow; Royal Naval College, Dartmouth, 1922-25; Lieut, 1930; specialised in gunnery, 1934; Gunnery Officer, HMS Furious, 1936-38; served War of 1939-45 (despatches, DSC); HMS Newcastle, 1939-41; HMS Nelson, 1943-44; Comdr 1945; Fleet Gunnery Officer, British Pacific Fleet, 1947-48; Staff of C-in-C, Far East Stn, 1948-49; Exec. Officer, HMS Superb, 1949-50; Capt. 1951; served on Ordnance Bd, 1950-52; Comdg Officer, HMS Tamar, 1952-54; at SHAPE, 1955-57; Chief of Staff to C-in-C, Plymouth, 1958-61; Rear-Adm. 1961; Comdr, Allied Naval Forces, Northern Europe, 1961-62; Naval Dep. to C-in-C Allied Forces, Northern Europe, 1963-64. Regional Officer, N Midlands, British Productivity Council, 1964-71. FRSA. *Recreations:* walking, sailing. *Address:* Osborne House, 14 Yorke Road, Dartmouth, Devon TQ6 9HN. *T:* Dartmouth 2854. *Club:* Naval and Military.

HOY, Rev. David, SJ; *b* 1 March 1913; *s* of Augustine Hilary Hoy and Caroline Lovelace. *Educ:* Mount St Mary's Coll. Entered Society of Jesus, 1931. Senior English Master, Wimbledon Coll., 1947, Asst Head Master, 1957-59. Rector of St Robert Bellarmine, Heythrop, Chipping Norton, 1959-64; Rector of Stonyhurst College, 1964-71; Superior of Farm St Church, 1972-75. *Recreation:* walking. *Address:* 114 Mount Street, W1.

HOYER-MILLAR, Dame Elizabeth, DBE 1960 (OBE 1952); DL; Director, Women's Royal Naval Service, 1958-61; Hon. ADC to the Queen, 1958-61; *b* 17 Dec. 1910; *o d* of late Robert Christian Hoyer Millar, Craig, Angus, Scotland, and Muriel (*née* Foster). *Educ:* privately. VAD 1939-41; joined WRNS, 1942. JP 1968-76, DL 1971, Angus. *Recreations:* needlework, gardening, country pursuits. *Address:* The Croft, Hillside, Angus. *T:* Hillside 304.

HOYLE, Eric Douglas Harvey, JP; MP (Lab) Nelson and Colne, since Oct. 1974; *b* 17 Feb. 1930; *s* of late William Hoyle and Leah Ellen Hoyle; *m* 1953, Pauline Spencer; one *s*. *Educ:* Adlington CofE Sch.; Horwich and Bolton Techn. Colls. Engrg apprentice, British Rail, Horwich, 1946-51; Sales Engr, AEI, Manchester, 1951-53; Sales Engr, Charles Weston Ltd, Salford, 1953-75. Mem., Manchester Regional Hosp. Bd, 1968-74; Mem., NW Regional Health Authority, 1974-75. Contested (Lab): Clitheroe, 1964; Nelson and Colne, 1970 and Feb. 1974. Pres., Assoc. of Scientific, Technical and Managerial Staffs, 1977-; Chm., ASTMS Parly Cttee, 1975-76. JP 1958. *Recreations:* sport, cricket, theatre-going, reading. *Address:* 30 Ashfield Road, Anderton, Chorley, Lancs; House of Commons, SW1A 0AA. *T:* 01-219 3498.

HOYLE, Prof. Sir Fred, Kt 1972; FRS 1957; MA Cantab; Hon. Research Professor, Manchester University; Visiting Professor of Astrophysics, California Institute of Technology, since 1958; Professor of Astronomy, Royal Institution of Great Britain, since 1969; *b* 24 June 1915; *s* of Ben Hoyle, Bingley, Yorks; *m* 1939, Barbara Clark; one *s* one *d. Educ:* Bingley Grammar Sch.; Emmanuel Coll., Cambridge. Mayhew Prizeman, Mathematical Tripos, 1936; Smith's Prizeman, Goldsmith Exhibnr, Senior Exhibnr of Royal Commn for Exhibn of 1851, 1938. Fellow, St John's Coll., Cambridge, 1939; University Lecturer in Mathematics, Cambridge, 1945-58; Plumian Prof. of Astronomy and Exptl Philosophy, Cambridge Univ., 1958-73; Dir, Inst. of Theoretical Astronomy, Cambridge, 1967-73. Staff Mem., Mount Wilson and Palomar Observatories, 1956-58. Andrew D. White Prof.-at-Large, Cornell Univ., 1973; Sherman Fairchild Scholar, California Inst. of Technology, 1974. Mem. SRC, 1968-72. Vice-Pres., Royal Society, 1970-71; Pres., Royal

Astronomical Soc., 1971-73. Hon. Mem., Amer. Acad. of Arts and Sciences, 1964; Foreign Associate, US Nat. Acad. of Sciences, 1969. Hon. Fellow, St John's Coll., Cambridge. Hon. ScD E Anglia, 1967; Hon DSc: Leeds 1969; Bradford 1975; Newcastle 1976. Royal Astronomical Soc. Gold Medal, 1968; UN Kalinga Prize, 1968; Bruce Gold Medal, Astronomical Soc. of Pacific, 1970; Royal Medal, Royal Soc., 1974. *Publications: astronomy:* Some Recent Researches in Solar Physics, 1949; The Nature of the Universe, 1950; A Decade of Decision, 1953; Frontiers of Astronomy, 1955; Astronomy, 1962; Of Men and Galaxies, 1964; Galaxies, Nuclei and Quasars, 1965; Man in the Universe, 1966; From Stonehenge to Modern Cosmology, 1972; Nicolaus Copernicus, 1973; Highlights in Astronomy, 1975; Astronomy Today, 1975; Ten Faces of the Universe, 1976; Stonehenge, 1977; *novels:* The Black Cloud, 1957; Ossian's Ride, 1959; (with J. Elliot) A for Andromeda, 1962; (with G. Hoyle) Fifth Planet, 1963; (with J. Elliot) Andromeda Breakthrough, 1964; October the First is Too Late, 1966; (with G. Hoyle) Rockets in Ursa Major, 1969; (with G. Hoyle) Seven Steps to the Sun, 1970; (with G. Hoyle) The Molecule Men, 1971; (with G. Hoyle) The Inferno, 1972; (with G. Hoyle) Into Deepest Space, 1974; (with G. Hoyle) The Incandescent Ones, 1977; *play:* Rockets in Ursa Major, 1962; *textbook:* (with J. V. Narlikar) Action at a Distance in Physics and Cosmology, 1974; Astronomy and Cosmology, 1975; scientific papers. *Address:* c/o The Royal Society, 6 Carlton House Terrace, SW1Y 5AG.

HOYLE, George, CMG 1954; retired; *b* 8 May 1900; 3rd *s* of George Harry and Mary Elizabeth Hoyle, Leeds; *m* 1936, Margaret Stewart, *d* of Ernest and Beatrice Reed, Bridlington; two adopted *s. Educ:* Leeds Grammar Sch.; The Queen's Coll., Oxford. Colliery Undermanager, 1930-33; Junior Inspector of Mines, 1933-41; Senior Inspector, 1941-50; Divisional Inspector, 1950-58; Dep. Chief Inspector, 1958-66. *Recreations:* collecting old glass, gardening. *Address:* 14 Arnold's Close, Hutton, Brentwood, Essex CM13 1EZ. *T:* Brentwood 226176.

HSIUNG, Shih I; author; President, Tsing Hua College, Hong Kong (Founder, and Director, since 1963); Hon. Secretary of China Society, London, since 1936 (Secretary 1934-36); Member of Universities China Committee, London, since 1935; *b* Nanchang, China, 14 Oct. 1902; *s* of Hsiung, Yuen-Yui and Chou, Ti-Ping; *m* 1923, Tsai, Dymia, (author of Flowering Exile, 1952); three *s* three *d. Educ:* Teachers' Coll., National Univ., Peking. Associate Manager of Chen Kwang Theatre, Peking, 1923; Managing Director of Pantheon Theatre, Shanghai, 1927; Special Editor of Commercial Press, Shanghai; Prof. at Agriculture Coll., Nanchang; Prof. at Min-Kuo Univ., Peking, till 1932. Chinese Delegate to International PEN Congress at Edinburgh, 1934; at Barcelona, 1935; at Prague, 1938; at London, 1941; at Zürich, 1947; Chinese Delegate to First Congress of International Theatre Institute at Prague, 1948; lectured on Modern Chinese and Classical Chinese Drama, University of Cambridge, 1950-53; Visiting Prof., University of Hawaii, Honolulu. Dean, College of Arts, Nanyang Univ., 1954-55; Man.-Dir, Pacific Films Co. Ltd, Hong Kong, 1955-; Dir, Konin Co. Ltd, Hong Kong, 1956-; Dir, Success Co. Ltd, Hong Kong, 1956; Chm., Bd of Dirs Standard Publishers, Ltd, Hong Kong, 1961-. *Publications:* various Chinese books including translations of Bernard Shaw, James Barrie, Thomas Hardy, Benjamin Franklin, etc; English Publications: The Money-God, 1934; Lady Precious Stream, 1934; The Western Chamber, 1935; Mencius Was A Bad Boy, 1936; The Professor From Peking, 1939; The Bridge of Heaven, 1941; The Life of Chiang Kai-Shek, 1943; The Gate of Peace, 1945; Changing China: History of China from 1840 to 1911, 1946; The Story of Lady Precious Stream, 1949; Chinese Proverbs, 1952; Lady on the Roof, 1959. *Recreation:* theatregoing. *Address:* 41 Buckland Crescent, NW3. *T:* 01-586 1979; 1620-21-23 Central Building, Hong Kong; Tsing Hua College, Kowloon, Hong Kong. *T:* Hong Kong 820305. *TA:* Dr Hsiung, Hong Kong.

HUANG, Rayson Lisung, DSc, DPhil; Vice-Chancellor, University of Hong Kong, since Sept. 1972; *b* 1 Sept. 1920; *s* of Rufus Huang; *m* 1949, Grace Wei Li; two *s. Educ:* Munsang Coll., Hong Kong; Univ. of Hong Kong (BSc); Univ. of Oxford (DPhil, DSc); Univ. of Chicago. DSc (Malaya) 1956. Demonstrator in Chemistry, Nat. Kwangsi Univ., Kweilin, China, 1943; Post-doctoral Fellow and Research Associate, Univ. of Chicago, 1947-50; Univ. of Malaya, Singapore: Lecturer in Chemistry, 1951-54; Reader, 1955-59; Univ. of Malaya, Kuala Lumpur: Prof. of Chemistry, 1959-69, and Dean of Science, 1962-65. Vice-Chancellor, Nanyang Univ., Singapore, 1969-72. Hon. CBE; JP. Hon. DSc Hong Kong, 1968. *Publications:* Organic Chemistry of Free Radicals, 1974 (London); about 50 research papers on chemistry of free radicals, molecular rearrangements, etc, mainly in Jl of Chem.

Soc. (London). *Recreation:* music. *Address:* The Lodge, 1 University Drive, Hong Kong. *T:* H-433697. *Club:* Hong Kong Country.

HUBBACK, David Francis, CB 1970; Special Advisor to the Expenditure Committee of the House of Commons, since 1976; *b* 2 March 1916; *s* of late Francis William and Eva Hubback; *m* 1939, Elais Judith, *d* of late Sir John Fischer Williams; one *s* two *d. Educ:* Westminster Sch.; King's Coll., Cambridge. Mines Dept, Bd of Trade, 1939. War of 1939-45: Army, 1940-44; Capt., Royal Signals; Western Desert, Sicily, Normandy; Cabinet Office, 1944. UK Delegn to OEEC, 1948; Treasury, 1950; Principal Private Sec. to Chancellor of the Exchequer, 1960-62; Under-Sec., Treasury, 1962-68, Board of Trade, 1969, DTI, 1970-71; Dep. Sec., DTI, later Dept of Trade, 1971-76. Mem., London Library Cttee, 1971-. *Recreations:* mountain walking, reading. *Address:* 5 Mount Vernon, Hampstead, NW3. *T:* 01-435 4512. *Club:* Reform.

HUBBARD, family name of **Baron Addington.**

HUBBARD, Charles Edward, CBE 1965 (OBE 1954); *b* 23 May 1900; *s* of Charles Edward Hubbard and Catherine Billing; *m* 1st, 1927, Madeleine Grace Witham (*d* 1961); one *s* ; 2nd, 1963, Florence Kate Hubbard. *Educ:* King Edward VII Grammar Sch., King's Lynn. Royal Gardens, Sandringham, Norfolk, 1916-20; Royal Gardens, Oslo, Norway, 1919. RAF, 1918-19. Royal Botanic Gardens, Kew, 1920-65: Student Gardener, 1920-22; Tech. Asst, 1922-27; Asst Botanist, 1927-30; Botanist, 1930-46; Prin. Sci. Officer, 1946-56; Sen. Prin. Sci. Officer 1956-59; Dep. CSO, 1959-65; Dep. Dir of Royal Botanic Gardens, Kew, 1959-65, and Keeper of Herbarium and Library there, 1957-65. Linnean Gold Medal, 1967; Veitch Gold Meml Medal, 1970. Hon. DSc Reading, 1960. *Publications:* Grasses, 1954, 1968; numerous pubns on the Gramineae (Grasses) in various botanical books and jls. *Recreations:* walking; natural history. *Address:* 51 Ormond Crescent, Hampton, Mddx TW12 2TJ. *T:* 01-979 6923.

HUBBLE, Prof. Sir Douglas (Vernon), KBE 1971 (CBE 1966); MD (London); FRCP; Emeritus Professor, University of Birmingham; *b* 25 Dec. 1900; *s* of Harry Edward Hubble and Agnes Kate (*née* Field); *m* 1928, Marie Arnott Bryce; three *d. Educ:* St Bartholomew's Hospital, London. Physician, Derbyshire Children's Hospital, 1932; Physician, Derbyshire Royal Infirmary, 1942; Prof. of Pædiatrics and Child Health, and Dir, Inst. of Child Health, Univ. of Birmingham, 1958-68; Dean, Faculty of Medicine, Univ. of Birmingham, 1963-68; Dean, Faculty of Medicine, Haile Selassie I Univ., 1969-71. Pres., Paediatric Section, Royal Society of Medicine, 1956; Mem., British Pharmocopoeia Commission 1958-68; Lectures: Burns, RFPS(G), 1957; Honeyman Gillespie, Univ. of Edinburgh, 1958; Langdon Brown, RCP, 1960; Felton Bequest Travelling, Royal Children's Hosp., Melbourne, Australia, 1961; Lawson Wilkins Meml, Johns Hopkins Univ., 1965; Lloyd Roberts Meml, Univ. of Manchester, 1966; Tisdall, Canadian Med. Assoc., 1967; Osler, Soc. of Apothecaries of London, 1968; Leonard Parsons Meml, Univ. of Birmingham, 1971; Osler Oration, RCP, 1974. Council Mem., RCP, 1960-62; Public Orator, University of Birmingham, 1962-66; Mem., Clinical Research Board, MRC, 1962-66; Pædiatric Consultant, Josiah Macy, Jr, Foundation, 1968-69; Chm. Council for Investigation of Fertility Control, 1963-68. Hon. Mem. Amer. Pediatric Soc., 1963. Pres. Lichfield Johnson Soc., 1956. Member: Tropical Med. Research Bd, MRC, 1965-69; GMC, 1965-69. Hon. Fellow, RSM, 1972. James Spence Gold Medal, British Paediatric Assoc., 1970; Dawson Williams Prize, BMA, 1972. *Publications:* contrib. to medical and literary journals. *Address:* Yonder Hill, Thirtover Cold Ash, Newbury, Berks. *T:* Thatcham 64177.

HUBRECHT, J. B., PhD Ultraj; MA Cantab; FRAS; *b* 13 April 1883; 2nd *s* of late Professor A. A. W. Hubrecht, Utrecht, Holland; *m* 1907, Jonkvrouwe Leonore van Alphen; two *s* three *d. Educ:* High Sch., Utrecht; University, Utrecht; Christ's Coll., Cambridge. Isaac Newton student, 1907; did research in Astrophysics at Solar Physics Observatory, Cambridge, 1907-12; lectured on Astrophysics, University of Manchester, 1913; entered Dutch Diplomatic Service, 1915; Attaché, London, 1915; Tokio, 1917; Foreign Office, The Hague, 1919; Second Sec., 1919; Washington, 1919; First Sec., 1923; Madrid, 1924; Counsellor, 1926; London 1927; Netherland Minister: Rio de Janeiro, 1930; Bucharest, 1934; Rome, 1937; handed his passports by Italian Govt upon Italy's entry into War, 1940; proceeded to Indonesia and was interned there for over two years by Japanese, 1941. *Publication:* The Solar Rotation by Spectroscopic Observations, 1915. *Recreations:* books, puzzles. *Address:* Hoofdstraat 185, Driebergen, Holland.

HUCKER, Ernest George, CBE 1972; Senior Director, Post Office, 1969-71; *b* Wembdon, Som, 20 March 1908; *s* of Albert Hucker; *m* 1934, Mary Louise Jowett; one *s* one *d. Educ:* Hele's Sch., Exeter. Post Office Telephones, 1929; Asst Surveyor of Posts, 1932-39; served War of 1939-45, Army: France, 1939-40; India, 1942-45 (Lt-Col); London Postal Region, 1946-52; Controller of Ops, 1952; Comdt PO Management Trng Centre, 1952-55; Chief Inspector of Postal Services, 1956-62; Asst Sec. 1962-63; Dep. Dir 1963-65, Dir 1965-69, Midland Region. Freeman, City of London, 1952. *Recreations:* music, gardening. *Address:* 6 Ratton Drive, Eastbourne, East Sussex BN20 9BJ. *T:* Eastbourne 51414.

HUCKFIELD, Leslie (John); MP (Lab) Nuneaton since March 1967; *b* 7 April 1942; *s* of Ernest Leslie and Suvla Huckfield; *m* Karolyn Schindler, *d* of Alfred and Phyllis Schindler. *Educ:* Prince Henry's Grammar Sch., Evesham; Keble Coll., Oxford; Univ. of Birmingham. Lectr in Economics, City of Birmingham Coll. of Commerce, 1963-67. Contested (Lab) Warwick and Leamington, 1966. PPS to Minister of Public Building and Works, 1969-70; Parly Under-Secretary of State, Dept of Industry, 1976-. Chairman: Lab. Party Transport Gp, 1974-76; Independent Adv. Commn on Transport, 1975-76; Pres., Worcs Fedn of Young Socialists, 1962-64; Mem., Birmingham Regional Hosp. Bd, 1970-72. *Publications:* various newspaper and periodical articles. *Recreation:* keep-fit enthusiast. *Address:* House of Commons, SW1A 0AA.

HUCKLE, Sir (Henry) George, Kt 1977; OBE 1969; Chairman: Agricultural (formerly Agricultural, Horticultural and Forestry Industry) Training Board since 1970; Home-Grown Cereals Authority, since 1977; *b* 9 Jan. 1914; *s* of George Henry and Lucy Huckle; *m* 1st, 1935, L. Steel (*d* 1947); one *s*; 2nd, 1949, Mrs Millicent Mary Hunter; one *d* and one step *d. Educ:* Latymer Sch.; Oxford Univ. (by courtesy of BRCS via Stalag Luft III, Germany). Accountant trng, 1929-33; sales management, 1933-39; RAF bomber pilot, 1940-41; POW, Germany, 1941-45; Shell Group, 1945-70: Man. Dir, Shellstar Ltd, 1965-70, retd. *Recreations:* golf, gardening, following daughter's interest in horse eventing. *Address:* The Warren, Cowesfield Green, Whiteparish, Salisbury, Wilts. *T:* Whiteparish 357. *Club:* Farmers'.

HUCKSTEP, Prof. Ronald Lawrie, CMG 1971; MD, FRCS, FRCSE, FRACS; Professor of Traumatic and Orthopaedic Surgery, since 1972, and Chairman, School of Surgery, since 1975, University of New South Wales; Chairman of Departments of Orthopaedic Surgery and Director of Accident Services, Prince of Wales and Prince Henry Hospitals, Sydney, Australia, since 1972; *b* 22 July 1926; *er s* of late Herbert George Huckstep and Agnes Huckstep (*née* Lawrie-Smith); *m* 1960, Margaret Ann, *e d* of Ronald Græme Macbeth, DM, FRCS; two *s* one *d. Educ:* Cathedral Sch., Shanghai, China; Queens' Coll., Cambridge; Mddx Hosp. Med. Sch., London. MA, MB, BChir(Cantab) 1952; MD(Cantab) 1957; FRCS (Edinburgh) 1957; FRCS 1958; FRACS (by election) 1973. Registrar and Chief Asst, Orthopaedic Dept St Bartholomew's Hosp., and various surgical appts Mddx and Royal Nat. Orthopaedic Hosps, London, 1952-60; Hunterian Prof., RCS of Eng., 1959-60. Makerere Univ. Coll., Kampala, Uganda: Lectr, 1960-62, Sen. Lectr, 1962-65 and Reader, 1965-67, in Orthopaedic Surgery, with responsibility for starting orthopaedic dept in Uganda; Prof. of Orthopaedic Surgery, Makerere Univ., Kampala, 1967-72. Became Hon. Cons. Orthopaedic Surgeon, Mulago and Mengo Hosps, and Round Table Polio Clinic, Kampala; Adviser on Orthopaedic Surgery, Ministry of Health, Uganda, 1960-72. Corresp. Editor: Brit. and Amer. Jls of Bone and Joint Surgery, 1965-72; Jl Western Pacific Orthopædic Assoc.; British Jl of Accident Surgery. Fellow, British Orthopaedic Assoc., 1967; Hon. Fellow, Western Pacific Orthopaedic Assoc., 1968. Irving Geist Award, 11th World Congress of Internat. Soc. for Rehabilitation of the Disabled (for direction of film, Polio in Uganda), 1969; Commonwealth Foundn Travelling Lectr for 1970. FRSM; Patron Med. Soc., Univ. of NSW; Chairman, Fellow or Mem. various med. socs and of assocs, councils and cttees concerned with orthopaedic and traumatic surgery and rehabilitation of physically disabled. *Publications:* Typhoid Fever and Other Salmonella Infections, 1962; A Simple Guide to Trauma, 1970, repr. 1972, 1974, Italian edn 1975, 2nd edn 1977; Poliomyelitis-A Guide for Developing Countries, 1975; various booklets, papers and films on injuries, orthopaedic diseases, and appliances. *Recreations:* photography, designing simple orthopaedic appliances and implants for cripples in developing and developed countries, swimming, travel. *Address:* Department of Orthopaedic Surgery, University of New South Wales, PO Box 1, Kensington, Sydney, NSW 2033, Australia. *T:* Sydney 3990111.

HUDDIE, Sir David (Patrick), Kt 1968; Senior Research Fellow, Imperial College, London, since 1971; *b* 12 March 1916; *s* of James and Catherine Huddie; *m* 1941, Wilhelmina Betty Booth; three *s. Educ:* Mountjoy Sch., Dublin; Trinity Coll., Dublin. Aero Engine Division, Rolls-Royce Ltd: Asst Chief Designer, 1947; Chief Development Engineer, 1953; Commercial Dir, 1959; General Manager, 1962; Dir, Rolls-Royce Ltd, 1961; Man. Dir, Aero Engine Div., 1965; Chm. Rolls-Royce Aero Engines Inc., 1969-70, retired. Hon. DSc Dublin, 1968. *Recreations:* gardening, shooting, fishing. *Address:* The Dower House, Winster, Derbyshire DE4 2DH. *T:* Winster 213; 60 Richmond Hill Court, Richmond, Surrey. *T:* 01-940 8255. *Club:* Athenæum.

HUDLESTON, Rt. Rev. (Ernest Urban) Trevor; *see* Stepney, Suffragan Bishop of.

HUDLESTON, Air Chief Marshal Sir Edmund C., GCB 1963 (KCB 1958; CB 1945); CBE 1943; Air ADC to the Queen, 1962-67, retired 1967; *b* 30 Dec. 1908; *s* of late Ven. C. Hudleston; *m* 1936, Nancye Davis; one *s* one *d. Educ:* Guildford Sch., W Australia; Royal Air Force Coll., Cranwell. Entered Royal Air Force 1927; served in UK until 1933; India, NWFP, 1933-37 (despatches); RAF Staff Coll., 1938; lent to Turkish Govt 1939-40; served Middle East and N Africa, Sicily, Italy, 1941-43 (despatches thrice); AOC 2nd TAF Group, Western Front, 1944; Imperial Defence Coll., 1946; Head of UK's military delegation to the Western Union Military Staff Cttee, 1948-50; AOC No 1 Group, Bomber Command, 1950-51; Deputy Chief of Staff, Supreme Headquarters, Allied Command, Europe, 1951-53; AOC No 3 Group, Bomber Command, 1953-56; RAF Instructor, Imperial Defence Coll., 1956-57; Vice-Chief of the Air Staff, 1957-62; Air Officer Commanding-in-Chief, Transport Command, 1962-63; Comdr Allied Air Forces, Central Europe, 1964-67. Dir, Pilkington Bros (Optical Div.). Comdr Legion of Merit (USA), 1944; Knight Commander Order of Orange-Nassau (Netherlands), 1945; Commander Order of Couronne, Croix de Guerre (Belgium), 1945; Officer, Legion of Honour, 1956, Croix de Guerre (France), 1957. *Recreations:* cricket, squash, tennis, shooting, etc. *Address:* The King's House, 2 Ingram Avenue, NW11. *Club:* Royal Air Force.

HUDSON, Rt. Rev. A(rthur) W(illiam) Goodwin, ThD; Vicar of St Paul's, Portman Square, W1, since 1965; *s* of Alfred and Anne Goodwin Hudson; *m* Dr Elena E. de Wirtz; one *s. Educ:* London Univ.; London Coll. of Divinity. Ordained Deacon, 1940; Priest, 1941. Curate of St Paul, Chatham, 1940-42; Hon. CF, 1942-45; Vicar of Good Easter, Essex, 1942-45; Diocesan Missioner, Chelmsford Diocese, 1943-45; Head Master, Windsor Sch., Santiago, 1945-48; Chaplain, Santiago, Chile, 1945-48; Vicar of St Mary Magdalene, Holloway, 1948-55 (with St James, 1953-55); Vicar of All Saints, Woodford Wells, 1955-60; Coadjutor Bishop and Dean of Sydney, 1960-65. Hon. Gen. Sec., S Amer. Missionary Soc., 1949-60; Hon. Sec., Spanish and Portuguese Church Aid Soc., 1950-55. *Recreations:* yachting, tennis; and profession! *Address:* St Paul's, Robert Adam Street, Portman Square, W1. *Clubs:* National; Army and Navy.

HUDSON, Sir Edmund (Peder), Kt 1963; FRSE 1948; Vice-President, Association of Agriculture; *b* 1 May 1903; *e s* of late Harold Hudson and Helen Ingeborg Olsen; *m* 1934, Bodil Catharina Böschen, Bergen, Norway; three *s. Educ:* Marlborough Coll.; King's Coll., Cambridge. Open Schol., 1922; Harold Fry Research Student, 1925; MA; Imperial Chemical Industries Ltd, Billingham, 1929-34; Scottish Agricultural Industries Ltd: Dir 1934; Asst Man. Dir, 1947, Managing Dir, 1957-62; Dir, Scottish Widows' Trust & Life Assurance Soc., 1961-76, Chm., 1967-69. Pres. Fertiliser Manufacturers' Assoc., 1948-49; Chairman: Assoc. of Chemical & Allied Employers, 1953-55; Scottish Technical Educn Consultative Council, 1959-71. Member: Pilkington Cttee on Broadcasting, 1960-62; Chancellor of Exchequer's Panel, Civil Service Arbitration Tribunal, 1963-68. Rector's Assessor, University Court, University of Edinburgh, 1961-63. Chairman: Napier Coll. of Science and Technology, Edinburgh, 1965-68; Academic Adv. Cttee, Heriot-Watt Univ., 1966-71. FBIM, 1960-72. Mem. Council, Outward Bound Trust, 1964-73. Hon. DSc Heriot-Watt Univ., 1966. *Address:* 35 Ravelston Dykes, Edinburgh EH12 6HG. *T:* 031-337 3457. *Clubs:* New, Royal Forth Yacht (Edinburgh).

HUDSON, Eleanor Erlund, RE 1946 (ARE 1938); RWS 1949 (ARWS 1939); ARCA (London) 1937; Artist; *b* 18 Feb. 1912; *d* of Helen Ingeborg Olsen, Brookline, Boston, USA, and Harold Hudson. *Educ:* Torquay; Dorking; Royal College of Art (Diploma 1937, Travelling Scholarship 1938). Mem. Chicago Print Soc. and Soc. of Artist Print-Makers. Studied and travelled in Italy summer 1939. Interrupted by war. Exhibited in London,

Provinces, Scandinavia, Canada, USA, etc.; works purchased by War Artists Advisory Council, 1942-43. *Recreations:* music, country life. *Address:* 6 Hammersmith Terrace, W6. *T:* 01-748 3778.

HUDSON, Eric Hamilton, FRCP; Hon. Consulting Physician: West London Hospital; London Chest Hospital; King Edward VII Hospital, Midhurst; Papworth Village Settlement; retired as: Consultant Physician, Manor House Hospital; Senior Medical Officer, Prudential Assurance Co.; *b* 11 July 1902; *s* of James Arthur and Edith Hudson; *m* 1st, 1940, Jessie Marian MacKenzie (*d* 1968); two *s* one *d*; 2nd, 1972, Nora Joan Pitman. *Educ:* Radley Coll.; Emmanuel Coll., Cambridge; Guy's Hosp., London. MRCS, LRCP, 1927; MA, MB, BCh Cantab, 1931; MRCP 1933, FRCP 1941. Late Wing Commander RAF, Officer in charge Medical Div., 1941-45. Late Examr in Medicine, RCP; Past Pres., W London Medico-Chirurgical Soc., 1959. *Publications:* Section on diagnosis and treatment of respiratory Tuberculosis, Heaf's Symposium of Tuberculosis, 1957; contrib. to Perry and Holmes Sellors Diseases of the Chest, 1964; contrib. to medical jls on diseases of the lungs. *Recreation:* fishing. *Address:* The Shieling, Highclere, near Newbury, Berks. *T:* Highclere 253574.

HUDSON, Sir Havelock (Henry Trevor), Kt 1977; Lloyd's Underwriter since 1952; Chairman of Lloyd's, 1975, 1976 and 1977 (Deputy Chairman, 1968, 1971, 1973); *b* 4 Jan. 1919; *er s* of late Savile E. Hudson and Dorothy Hudson (*née* Cheetham); *m* 1st, 1944, Elizabeth (marr. diss., 1956), *d* of Brig. W. Home; two *s*; 2nd, 1957, Cathleen Blanche Lily, *d* of 6th Earl of St Germans; one *s* one *d*. *Educ:* Rugby. Merchant Service, 1937-38. Served War of 1939-45: Royal Hampshire Regt (Major), 1939-42; 9 Parachute Bn, 1942-44. Member: Cttee Lloyd's Underwriters Assoc., 1963; Cttee of Lloyd's, 1965-68, 1970-73; Exec. Bd, Lloyd's Register of Shipping, 1967-. Vice-Pres., Chartered Insurance Inst., 1973-76, Dep. Pres., 1976-; Chm., Arvon Foundn, 1973-. Mem., Bd of Governors, Pangbourne Coll., 1976-. *Recreation:* shooting. *Address:* The Old Rectory, Stanford Dingley, Berkshire. *T:* Bradfield 346. *Clubs:* Boodle's, Royal Automobile.

HUDSON, Ian Francis, CB 1976; Deputy Secretary, Department of Employment, since 1976; *b* 29 May 1925; *s* of Francis Reginald Hudson and Dorothy Mary Hudson (*née* Crabbe); *m* 1952, Gisela Elisabeth Grettka; one *s* one *d*. *Educ:* City of London Sch.; New Coll., Oxford. Royal Navy, 1943-47. Customs and Excise, 1947-53; Min. of Labour, 1953-56, 1959-61, 1963-64; Treasury, 1957-58; Dept of Labour, Australia, 1961-63; Asst Sec., 1963; DEA, 1964-68; Under-Sec., 1967; Dept of Employment, 1968-73; Dep. Sec. 1973; Sec., Pay Board, 1973-74; Sec., Royal Commn on Distribution of Income and Wealth, 1974-76. *Recreation:* philately. *Address:* 29 Westwood Avenue, South Harrow, Mddx. *T:* 01-422 0927.

HUDSON, James Ralph, CBE 1976; FRCS; Surgeon, Moorfields Eye Hospital, since 1956; Ophthalmic Surgeon, Guy's Hospital, 1963-76; Hon. Ophthalmic Surgeon: Hospital of St John and St Elizabeth, since 1953; King Edward VII Hospital for Officers, since 1970; Teacher of Ophthalmology, Guy's Hospital, 1964-76, Institute of Ophthalmology, University of London, since 1961; Consultant Adviser in Ophthalmology, Department of Health and Social Security; *b* 15 Feb. 1916; *o s* of late William Shand Hudson and Ethel Summerskill; *m* 1946, Margaret May Oulpé; two *s* two *d*. *Educ:* The King's Sch., Canterbury; Middlesex Hosp. (Edmund Davis Exhibnr), Univ. of London; MRCS, LRCP 1939; MB, BS London 1940; DOMS (England) 1948; FRCS 1949. Res. Med. Appts, Tindal House Emergency Hosp. (Mddx Hosp. Sector), 1939-42. RAFVR Med. Service, 1942-46; Sqdn Ldr, 1944-46. Moorfields Eye Hosp., Clin. Asst, 1947, Ho. Surg., 1947-49; Sen. Resident Officer, 1949, Chief Clin. Asst, 1950-56; Middlesex Hosp., Clin. Asst Ophth. Outpatients, 1950-51; Ophth. Surg., W Middlesex Hosp., 1950-56, Mount Vernon Hosp., 1953-59. Civilian Consultant in Ophthalmology to RAF, 1970-. Examr in Ophthalmology (Dipl. Ophth. of Examg Bd of Eng., RCP and RCS, 1960-65; Mem. Court of Examrs, RCS, 1966-72). FRSocMed 1947 (Vice-Pres. Sect. of Ophthalmology, 1965); Member: Ophthal. Soc. UK, 1948 (Hon. Sec. 1956-58, Vice-Pres., 1969-71); Faculty of Ophthalmologists, 1950 (Mem. Council, 1960-; Hon. Sec. 1960-70; Vice-Pres., 1970-74; Pres., 1974-77; Rep. on Council of RCS, 1968-73); Soc. Française d'Ophtal., 1950- (membre délégue étranger, 1970-); Scientific Cttee Les Entretiens Annuels d'Ophtalmologie, 1970-; Hon. Mem. Aust. Coll. Ophthalmologists; Pilgrims of Gt Britain. Liveryman, Soc. of Apothecaries, and Freeman of City of London. *Publications:* (with T. Keith Lyle) chapters in Matthews's Recent Advances in the Surgery of Trauma; contrib. to chapters in Rob and Rodney Smith's Operative Surgery, 1969; articles in: Brit. Jl of

Ophthalmology; Trans Ophth. Soc. UK; Proc. Royal Soc. Med. *Recreations:* motoring, travel. *Address:* 36 Wimpole Street, W1M 7AE. *T:* 01-935 5038, 01-486 3236. *Club:* Garrick.

HUDSON, John Arthur, CB 1970; Deputy Under-Secretary of State, Department of Education and Science, since 1969; *b* 24 Aug. 1920; *s* of Francis Reginald Hudson and Dorothy Mary (*née* Crabbe); *m* 1960, Dwynwen Davies; one *s* one *d*. *Educ:* City of London Sch.; Jesus Coll., Oxford. Served Royal Corps of Signals, 1941-45 (despatches). Entered Board of Education, 1946. Mem., South Bank Theatre Bd, 1967-. *Recreations:* gardening, microscopy. *Address:* 30 Syke Cluan, Iver, Bucks. *T:* Iver 653690.

HUDSON, Prof. John Pilkington, CBE 1975 (MBE 1943); GM 1944 and Bar 1945; BSc, MSc, PhD; NDH; FIBiol; former Director, Long Ashton Research Station, and Professor of Horticultural Science, University of Bristol, 1967-75; *b* 24 July 1910; *o s* of W. A. Hudson and Bertha (*née* Pilkington); *m* 1936, Mary Gretta, *d* of late W. N. and Mary Heath, Westfields, Market Bosworth, Leics; two *s*. *Educ:* New Mills Grammar Sch.; Midland Agricultural Coll.; University Coll., Nottingham. Hort. Adviser, E Sussex CC, 1935-39. Served War of 1939-45, Royal Engineers Bomb Disposal (Major). Horticulturist, Dept of Agric., Wellington, NZ, 1945-48; Lecturer in Horticulture, University of Nottingham Sch. of Agric., 1948-50; Head of Dept of Horticulture, University of Nottingham, 1950-67 (as Prof. of Horticulture, 1958-67, Dean, Faculty of Agriculture and Horticulture, 1965-67); seconded part-time to Univ. of Khartoum, Sudan, to found Dept of Horticulture, 1961-63. Associate of Honour, Royal New Zealand Institute of Horticulture, 1948. Member: Horticultural Bd, Jt Cons. Orgn on Agriculture; Res. Adv. Cttee, Forestry Commn; Advisory Cttee on Agricultural Education (Chm.); Adv. Bd, ARC Weed Res. Orgn; Econ. Develt Cttee for Agriculture; Chm., Inst. of Biology, Div. of Agric. Sci. PP and Hon. Mem., Hort. Educn Assoc. Editor, Experimental Agriculture, 1965-. Hon. Fellow, RASE, 1977. Victoria Medal of Honour, RHS, 1977. *Publications:* (ed) Control of the Plant Environment, 1957; contributions on effects of environment on plant behaviour to scientific jls. *Recreations:* travel, theatre, music, gardening. *Address:* The Spinney, Wrington, Bristol.

HUDSON, Prof. Liam, MA, PhD; Professor of Psychology, Brunel University, since 1977; *b* 20 July 1933; *er s* of Cyril and Kathleen Hudson; *m* 1st, 1955, Elizabeth Ward; 2nd 1965, Bernadine Jacot de Boinod; three *s* one *d*. *Educ:* Whitgift Sch.; Exeter Coll., Oxford. Post-graduate and post-doctoral research, Psychological Laboratory, Cambridge, 1957-65, and King's Coll., Cambridge, 1965-68; Fellow, King's Coll., Cambridge, 1966-68; Prof. of Educnl Scis, Univ. of Edinburgh, 1968-77, and Dir, Res. Unit on Intellectual Develt, 1964-77. Mem., Inst. for Advanced Study, Princeton, 1974-75. *Publications:* Contrary Imaginations, 1966; Frames of Mind, 1968; (ed) The Ecology of Human Intelligence, 1970; The Cult of the Fact, 1972; Human Beings, 1975. *Recreations:* painting, sculpture, otherwise largely domestic. *Address:* 9 Marlow Mill, Marlow, Bucks.

HUDSON, Maurice William Petre; Hon. Consulting Anæsthetist: National Dental Hospital (University College Hospital); Westminster Hospital; St Mary's Hospital; Emeritus Consultant Anæsthetist, Princess Beatrice Hospital; Part-time Consultant Anæsthetist, Queen Mary's Hospital, Roehampton; *b* 8 Nov. 1901; *s* of late Henry Hudson, ARCA, and Anna Martha Rosa (*née* Petre); *m* 1922, Fredrica Helen de Pont; one *s* one *d* (and two *s* decd). *Educ:* Sherborne Sch.; St Thomas' Hosp. MB, BS London, 1925; MRCS, LRCP, 1924; DA England, 1936; FFARCS, 1948. Formerly: Resident House Surg., Resident Anæsthetist, and Clin. Asst, Nose and Throat Dept, St Thomas' Hosp. Fellow Assoc. Anæsthetists of Gt Brit. Mem. Royal Soc. Med. *Publications:* contrib. to med. jls. *Recreations:* swimming, photography. *Address:* 15 Harley Street, W1. *T:* 01-580 1850, 01-580 3977.

HUDSON, Lt-Gen. Sir Peter, KCB 1977; CBE 1970 (MBE 1965); Deputy Commander-in-Chief, United Kingdom Land Forces, since 1977; *b* 14 Sept. 1923; *s* of Captain William Hudson, late The Rifle Bde, and Ivy (*née* Brown); *m* 1949, Susan Anne Knollys; one adopted *s* one *d* and one adopted *d*. *Educ:* Wellingborough; Jesus Coll., Cambridge. Commnd into The Rifle Bde, 1944; psc 1954; comd company in Mau Mau and Malayan campaigns, 1955-57; jssc 1963; comd 3rd Bn The Royal Green Jackets, 1966-67; Regimental Col The Royal Green Jackets, 1968; Comdr 39 Infantry Bde, 1968-70; IDC 1971; GOC Eastern Dist, 1973-74; Chief of Staff, Allied Forces Northern Europe, 1975-77. *Recreations:* travel, fishing, most games. *Address:* HQ UKLF, Wilton, Salisbury, Wilts. *Clubs:* Naval and Military, MCC; Green Jackets; Free Foresters.

HUDSON, Peter Geoffrey; Under-Secretary, Department of Industry, since 1975; *b* 26 July 1926; *s* of late Thomas Albert Hudson and late Gertrude Hudson; *m* 1954, Valerie Mary, *yr d* of late Lewis Alfred Hart and late Eva Mary Hart; two *s. Educ:* King Edward VII Sch., Sheffield; Queen's Coll., Oxford (Hastings Scholar, MA). Gold Medallist, Royal Schs of Music, 1940. Sub-Lt RNVR, 1944-46. Min. of Transport, 1949; Private Sec. to Minister of Transport and Civil Aviation, 1951-53; Principal, Min. of Transport and Civil Aviation, 1953-57; Admin. Staff Coll., Henley, 1957; British Civil Air Attaché, SE Asia and Far East, 1958-61; Asst Sec., Overseas Policy Div. and Estabt Div., Min. of Aviation and BoT, 1963-68; Counsellor (Civil Aviation), British Embassy, Washington, 1968-71; Under-Sec., DTI, subseq. Dept of Trade, 1971-75. Governor, Coll. of Air Trng, Hamble, 1974-75. *Recreations:* music, travel. *Address:* Candle Hill, Raggleswood, Chislehurst, Kent. *T:* 01-467 1761.

HUDSON, Peter John; Deputy Under-Secretary of State (Finance and Budget), Ministry of Defence, since 1976; *b* 29 Sept. 1919; *o s* of late A. J. Hudson; *m* 1954, Joan Howard FitzGerald; one *s* one *d. Educ:* Tollington Sch.; Birkbeck Coll., London. Exchequer and Audit Dept, 1938; RNVR, 1940-46 (Lieut); Asst Principal, Air Min., 1947; Private Sec. to Perm. Under Sec. of State for Air, 1948-51; Asst Sec., 1958; Head of Air Staff Secretariat, 1958-61; Imperial Defence Coll., 1962; Head of Programme and Budget Div., MoD, 1966-69; Under-Sec., Cabinet Office, 1969-72; Asst Under-Sec. of State, MoD, 1972-75; Dep. Under-Sec. of State (Air), MoD, 1975-76. *Address:* Folly Hill, Haslemere, Surrey GU27 2EY. *T:* 2078. *Club:* Royal Air Force.

HUDSON, Rowland Skeffington, CMG 1946; *b* 1 April 1900; *s* of late Commander William Joseph Villiers Hudson, Royal Navy; *m* 1928, Jean Mallagh Fegan; two *s. Educ:* St Edward's Sch., Oxford. 2nd Lieut Royal Air Force, April 1918; Probationer, BSA Co., N Rhodesia, 1919; Asst Native Commissioner, N Rhodesia, 1922; Native Commissioner, 1925; Asst Chief Sec., 1936; Labour Commissioner, 1940; Provincial Commissioner, 1944; Sec. for Native Affairs, 1945; Mem. Royal Commission on land and population in East Africa, 1953; Commissioner, Provincial Devolution, N Region, Nigeria, 1956; Head of African Studies Branch, Colonial Office, 1949-61; Special Administrative Adviser, Barotseland, 1963-64; Head of Administrative Services Branch, Ministry of Overseas Development, 1964-65; retired, 1966. *Recreation:* gardening. *Address:* Wymarks, Horsham Road, Shermanbury, Horsham, Sussex. *T:* Partridge Green 710562.

HUDSON, Thomas Charles, CBE 1975; Chairman, ICL Ltd, since 1972; Chartered Accountant (Canadian); *b* Sidcup, Kent, 23 Jan. 1915; British parents; *m* 1944, Lois Alma Hudson (marr. diss. 1973); two *s* one *d. Educ:* Middleton High Sch., Nova Scotia. With Nightingale, Hayman & Co, Chartered Accountants, 1935-40. Served War, Royal Canadian Navy, Lieut, 1940-45. IBM Canada, as Sales Rep., 1946-51 (transf. to IBM, UK, as Sales Manager, 1951, and Managing Dir, 1954-65). Plessey Company: Financial Dir, 1967; Dir, 1969-76; Dir, ICL, 1968. Councillor for Enfield, GLC, 1970-73. *Recreations:* tennis, ski-ing, gardening. *Address:* Highgate House, Merton Lane, N6 6NA. *T:* 01-340 9018. *Clubs:* Carlton, American, Inst. of Directors; Montreal Amateur Athletic Assoc. (Montreal).

HUDSON, Rt. Rev. Wilfrid John, CBE 1973; AKC; Head of Brotherhood of St Paul since 1961; *b* 12 June 1904; *s* of late John William and late Bertha Mildred Hudson, Worthing, Sussex; unmarried. *Educ:* Brighton Coll.; King's Coll., London. AKC, first Cl. and Jelf Prize, 1931. Deacon 1931, Priest 1932, London. Curate of St Barnabas, Pimlico, 1931-36; Principal of Brotherhood of Good Shepherd, Dubbo, Diocese of Bathurst, and Examining Chaplain to Bishop of Bathurst, 1937-42; Curate of All Saints, Woodham, Surrey, 1942-43; Acting Curate of St Barnabas, Ealing, 1944; Rector of Letchworth, Diocese of St Albans, 1944-50; Bishop of Carpentaria, 1950-60; Bishop Coadjutor of Brisbane, 1961-73. Associate of Inst. of Chartered Accountants, 1928. *Address:* Brotherhood House, Dubbo, NSW 2830, Australia.

HUDSON, Sir William, KBE 1955; FRS 1964; MICE; Commissioner, Snowy Mountains Hydro-Electric Authority, Australia, 1949-67; *b* 27 April 1896; *s* of Dr James Hudson, Nelson, NZ; *m* 1927, Eileen, OBE 1959, *d* of John Trotter, Fairlie, NZ; two *d. Educ:* Nelson Coll., NZ; University of London; Post-graduate course in Hydro-Electric Engineering, Grenoble, France. BSc (1st Cl. Hons), Univ. of London; Diploma (with distinction) in Civil Engineering, University Coll., London; Head Medal for Civil Engineering, University Coll., London. Served European War, France, 1916-17. Civil Engineering and Contracting Dept, Armstrong-Whitworth & Co. Ltd, London, 1920-21; Public Works Dept, New Zealand, 1923-24; Armstrong-Whitworth & Co. Ltd, Arapuni Hydro-Electric Scheme, NZ, 1924-27; Public Works Dept, NSW, 1928; First Asst to Resident Engineer, Metropolitan Water, Sewerage and Drainage Board, Sydney, NSW, 1928-30; Sir Alexander Gibb & Partners, London, Engineer-in-charge of construction work, Galloway (Scotland) Hydro-Electric Scheme, 1931-36; Metropolitan Water, Sewerage and Drainage Board, Sydney: Resident Engineer in charge of construction, Woronora Dam, 1937; Inspecting Engineer and Chief Construction Engineer, 1938-43; Engineer-in-Chief, 1948-49. Coronation Medal, 1953. Australasian Engineer Award for 1957 and Kernot Memorial Medal for Distinguished Engineering Achievement in Australia, 1959. Fellow University Coll., London, 1961-; Hon. Fellow, Royal Inst. of Architects, Australia, 1968. Hon. Member: Australasian Inst. of Mining and Metallurgy, 1961; Instn of Engrs, Australia, 1962; Instn of Royal Engineers, 1968. Dr of Laws (*hc*) Australian National University, 1962; Hon. Dr of Engineering, Monash Univ., Melbourne, 1968. James Cook Medal (Royal Society NSW), 1966. *Recreation:* yachting. *Address:* 39 Flanagan Street, Garran, ACT 2605, Australia.

HUDSON, William Meredith Fisher, QC 1967; Barrister-at-law; *b* 17 Nov. 1916; *o s* of late Lt-Comdr William Henry Fisher Hudson, RN (killed in action, Jutland, 1916); *m* 1st, 1938, Elizabeth Sophie (marr. diss., 1948), *d* of late Reginald Pritchard, Bloemfontein, SA; one *s* one *d*; 2nd, 1949, Pamela Helen, *d* of late William Cecil Edwards, Indian Police; two *d. Educ:* Imperial Service Coll.; Trinity Hall, Cambridge. BA 1938; Harmsworth Law Scholar, 1939; MA 1940. Called to the Bar, Middle Temple, 1943, Bencher, 1972; South Eastern Circuit, 1945; Mem. of Central Criminal Court Bar Mess. Commissioned Royal Artillery (TA), 1939; served War of 1939-45, Eritrea and Sudan. Chm., Blackfriars Settlement, 1970-. *Recreations:* trains, travel, theatre; formerly athletics (Cambridge Blue, Cross Country half Blue; rep. England and Wales, European Student Games, 1938). *Address:* 5 King's Bench Walk, Temple, EC4. *T:* 01-353 4713; (home) 62 Erpingham Road, SW15. *T:* 01-788 6524. *Clubs:* Hurlingham; Achilles; Hawks (Cambridge).

HUDSON DAVIES, (Gwilym) Ednyfed; *see* Davies, G. E. H.

HUDSON-WILLIAMS, Prof. Harri Llwyd, MA; Professor of Greek in the University of Newcastle upon Tyne (formerly King's College, Newcastle upon Tyne, University of Durham), 1952-76 and Head of Department of Classics, 1969-76; *b* 16 Feb. 1911; *yr s* of late Prof. T. Hudson-Williams; *m* 1946, Joan, *er d* of late Lieut-Col H. F. T. Fisher; two *d. Educ:* University College of North Wales; King's Coll., Cambridge (Browne Medallist; Charles Oldham Scholar); Munich University. Asst Lectr in Greek, Liverpool Univ., 1937-40; Intelligence Corps, 1940-41; Foreign Office, 1941-45; Lectr in Greek, Liverpool Univ., 1945-50; Reader in Greek, King's Coll., Newcastle upon Tyne, 1950-52; Dean of the Faculty of Arts, 1963-66. *Publications:* contribs to various classical jls, etc. *Recreation:* gardening. *Address:* Toft Hill Cottage, Apperley Road, Stocksfield, Northumberland. *T:* Stocksfield 2341.

HUFTON, Prof. Olwen, (Mrs B. T. Murphy), PhD; Professor of Modern History, University of Reading, since 1975; *d* of Joseph Hufton and Caroline Hufton; *m* 1965, Brian Taunton Murphy; two *d. Educ:* Hulme Grammar Sch., Oldham; Univ. of London (BA 1959, PhD 1962). Lectr, Univ. of Leicester, 1963-66; Lectr, then Reader, Univ. of Reading, 1966-75. *Publications:* Bayeux in the Late Eighteenth Century, 1967; The Poor of Eighteenth Century France, 1974; articles in Past and Present, Eur. Studies Rev., and French Hist. Studies. *Address:* 40 Shinfield Road, Reading, Berks. *T:* Reading 81514.

HUGGETT, Mrs Helen K.; *see* Porter, Prof. H. K.

HUGGINS, family name of Viscount Malvern.

HUGGINS, Alan Armstrong; Hon. Mr Justice Huggins; Justice of Appeal, Hong Kong, since 1976; *b* 15 May 1921; *yr s* of late William Armstrong Huggins and Dare (*née* Copping); *m* 1950, Catherine Davidson, *d* of late David Dick; two *s* one *d. Educ:* Radley Coll.; Sidney Sussex Coll., Cambridge (MA). TARO (Special List), 1940-48 (Actg Major); Admiralty, 1941-46. Called to Bar, Lincoln's Inn, 1947. Legal Associate Mem., TPI, 1949-70. Resident Magistrate, Uganda, 1951-53; Stipendiary Magistrate, Hong Kong, 1953-58; Diocesan Reader, Dio. of Hong Kong and Macao, 1954; District Judge, Hong Kong, 1958-65. Chm., Justice (Hong Kong Br.), 1965-68; Judicial Comr, State of Brunei, 1966-; Judge of Supreme Court, Hong Kong, 1965-76. Hon. Life Governor, Brit. and For. Bible Soc. Liveryman, Leathersellers' Company. *Recreations:* boating, archery, amateur theatre, tapestry. *Address:* Courts of Justice, Hong Kong; Rock Hill, Warfleet, Dartmouth, Devon.

HUGGINS, Prof. Charles B.; Professor of Surgery, University of Chicago, since 1936; William B. Ogden Distinguished Service Professor since 1962; *b* Halifax, Canada, 22 Sept. 1901; *s* of Charles Edward Huggins and Bessie Huggins (*née* Spencer); citizen of USA by naturalization, 1933; *m* 1927, Margaret Wellman; one *s* one *d. Educ:* Acadia (BA 1920; DSc 1946); Harvard (MD 1924). University of Michigan: Interne in Surgery, 1924-26; Instructor in Surgery, 1926-27; Univ. of Chicago, 1927-: Instructor in Surgery, 1927-29; Asst Prof., 1929-33; Assoc. Prof., 1933-36; Prof., 1936-; Dir, Ben May Laboratory for Cancer Research, 1951-69. Chancellor, Acadia Univ., 1972. Alpha Omega Alpha, 1942; Mem. Nat. Acad. of Sciences, 1949; Mem. Amer. Philosophical Soc., 1962. Sigillum Magnum, Bologna Univ., 1964; Hon. Prof., Madrid Univ., 1956; Hon. FRSocMed (London), 1956; Hon. FRCSE 1958; Hon. FRCS 1959; Hon. FACS 1963. Hon. MSc, Yale, 1947; Hon. DSc: Washington Univ., St Louis, 1950; Leeds Univ., 1953; Turin Univ., 1957; Trinity Coll., Hartford, Conn., 1965; Wales, 1967; Univ. of California, Berkeley, 1968; Univ. of Michigan, 1968; Hon. LLD: Aberdeen Univ., 1966; York Univ., Toronto, 1968; Hon. DPS, George Washington Univ., 1967. Has given many memorial lectures and has won numerous gold medals, prizes and awards for his work on urology and cancer research, including Nobel Prize for Medicine (jtly), 1966. Holds foreign orders. *Address:* Ben May Laboratory for Cancer Research, University of Chicago, 950 East 59th Street, Chicago, Ill 60637, USA.

HUGGINS, Kenneth Herbert, CMG 1960; *b* 4 Dec. 1908; *s* of late Herbert John Huggins and Nelly Bailey; *m* 1934, Gladys E. Walker; one *s* one *d. Educ:* Hitchin Grammar Sch.; Tollington Sch.; University Coll., London. BSc London 1930; PhD Glasgow, 1940. Asst and Lecturer in Geography, Glasgow Univ., 1930-41; Ministry of Supply, 1941; Staff of Combined Raw Materials Board, Washington, 1942-46; Board of Trade, 1947; Staff of Administrative Staff Coll., Henley, 1954-55; Commercial Counsellor, British Embassy, Washington, 1957-60; UK Trade Commissioner, subsequently Consul-General, Johannesburg, 1960-62. Dir, British Industrial Develt Office, NY, 1962-68. *Publications:* atlases and articles in geographical journals. *Recreation:* retirement. *Address:* Sunrise, Lustrells Road, Rottingdean, East Sussex BN2 7DS. *T:* Brighton 31024.

HUGGINS, Peter Jeremy William; *see* Brett, Jeremy.

HUGH-JONES, Evan Bonnor, CB 1953; MC 1915; *b* 1890; *s* of Ll. Hugh-Jones, CBE, Wrexham; *m* 1st, 1918, Elsie M. Iggulden (*d* 1950); one *s* one *d*; 2nd, 1952, Maud, *widow* of Thomas Lundon, MP. *Educ:* Oundle; McGill Univ., Montreal. Major in Royal Engineers, European War (despatches twice, MC); Chief Engineer (Roads), Ministry of Transport 1949-54, retired. *Address:* 1 Clavering Walk, Cooden, Sussex. *T:* Cooden 4210.

HUGH-JONES, Wynn Normington, MVO 1961; Secretary-General of the Liberal Party, since 1977; *b* 1 Nov. 1923; *s* of Huw Hugh-Jones and May Normington; *m* 1958, Ann (*née* Purkiss); one *s* two *d. Educ:* Ludlow; Selwyn Coll., Cambridge (Scholar). Served in RAF, 1943-46. Entered Foreign Service (now Diplomatic Service), 1947; Foreign Office, 1947-49; Jedda, 1949-52; Paris, 1952-56; FO, 1956-59; Chargé d'Affaires, Conakry, 1959-60; Head of Chancery, Rome, 1960-64; FO, 1964-66, Counsellor, 1964; Consul, Elizabethville (later Lubumbashi), 1966-68; Counsellor and Head of Chancery, Ottawa, 1968-70; FCO, 1971, attached Lord President's Office; Cabinet Office, 1972-73; Director-Gen., E-SU, 1973-77. *Recreations:* golf, gardening. *Address:* 1 Poyle Road, Guildford, Surrey. *Clubs:* National Liberal, Foreign Affairs; Hindhead Golf.

HUGH SMITH, Lt-Col Henry Owen, MVO 1976; Commanding Officer The Blues and Royals, since 1978; *b* 19 June 1937; *s* of Lt-Comdr Colin Hugh Smith and late Hon. Mrs C. Hugh Smith. *Educ:* Ampleforth; Magdalene Coll., Cambridge. BA Hons 1961. Commnd Royal Horse Guards, 1957; Blues and Royals, 1969; psc 1969; served Cyprus and Northern Ireland (wounded); Equerry in Waiting to The Duke of Edinburgh, 1974-76. *Recreations:* riding, sailing. *Address:* 26 Stack House, Cundy Street, SW1. *Clubs:* Boodle's, Pratt's, Cavalry and Guards; Royal Yacht Squadron.

HUGHES, family name of **Baron Hughes.**

HUGHES, Baron, *cr* 1961, of Hawkhill (Life Peer); **William Hughes,** PC 1970; CBE 1956 (OBE 1942); DL; Chairman, East Kilbride and Stonehouse Development Corporation, since 1975;

President: Scottish Federation of Housing Associations, since 1975; Scottish Association for Mental Health, since 1975; Chairman, Royal Commission on Legal Services in Scotland, since 1976; Member, Council of Europe and Western European Union, since 1976; company director; *b* 22 Jan. 1911; *e s* of late Joseph and Margaret Hughes; *m* 1951, Christian Clacher, *o c* of late James and Sophia Gordon; two *d. Educ:* Balfour Street Public Sch., Dundee; Dundee Technical Coll. ARP Controller Dundee, 1939-43; Armed Forces, 1943-46; Commissioned RAOC, 1944; demobilised as Capt., 1946. Hon. City Treasurer, Dundee, 1946-47; Chairman, Eastern Regional Hospital Board, Scotland, 1948-60; Lord Provost of Dundee and HM Lieut of County of City of Dundee, 1954-60; Member: Dundee Town Council, 1933-36 and 1937-61; Court of St Andrews Univ., 1954-63; Council of Queen's Coll., Dundee, 1954-63; Cttee on Civil Juries, 1958-59; Cttee to Enquire into Registration of Title to Land in Scotland, 1960-62; Chm. Glenrothes Dev. Corp., 1960-64; Mem., North of Scotland Hydro-Electric Bd, 1957-64; Scottish Transport Council, 1960-64. Jt Parly Under-Sec. of State for Scotland, 1964-69; Minister of State for Scotland, 1969-70, 1974-75. Contested (Lab) E Perthshire, 1945 and 1950. Fellow, Inst. of Dirs. Hon. LLD St Andrews, 1960. JP County and City of Dundee, 1943-76; DL Dundee 1960. Chevalier, Légion d'Honneur, 1958. *Recreation:* gardening. *Address:* Muircroft, Auchterarder, Perthshire PH3 1JJ. *T:* Auchterarder 2646.

HUGHES, Albert Henry, OBE 1961; HM Diplomatic Service, retired; HM Ambassador to El Salvador, 1975-77; *b* 20 Sept. 1917; *s* of George Albert Hughes; *m* 1939, Nancy Russell; two *s* one *d. Educ:* The Judd Sch., Tonbridge, Kent. Appointed to the Foreign Office, 1935. War of 1939-45: Served in HM Forces, 1940-45, HM Vice-Consul, Rouen, France, 1949; HM Consul, Tehran, Iran, 1949-52; HM Consul, Philadelphia, USA, 1953-55; HM Consul, Bilbao, Spain, 1962-64; Counsellor (Administration) and HM Consul-General, Washington, 1964-68; Head of Finance Dept, FCO, and Finance Officer of the Diplomatic Service, 1968-71; HM Consul-General, Amsterdam, 1971-75. *Recreations:* reading, gardening, photography. *Address:* The Cottage, Matfield Green, near Tonbridge, Kent.

HUGHES, Andrew Anderson, MA; Chairman, Grampian Construction Ltd, since 1971; *b* 27 Dec. 1915; *s* of Alexander and Euphemia Hughes; *m* 1946, Margaret Dorothy Aikman; no *c. Educ:* Waid Academy; St Andrews Univ.; Marburg Univ.; Emmanuel Coll., Cambridge. Colonial Administrative Service, 1939; Private Sec. to Governor, Gold Coast, 1940-42; Colonial Office, 1946; Dept of Health for Scotland, 1947; Asst Sec., 1956; Under-Sec., 1964; Under-Sec., Scottish Development Dept, 1966-69; Man. Dir, Crudens Ltd, 1969-71. Mem. Scottish Tourist Bd, 1969-. Dir, Grampian Holdings Ltd, 1973-. *Recreation:* golf. *Address:* 9 Palmerston Road, Edinburgh EH9 1TL. *T:* 031-667 2353. *Clubs:* Royal Commonwealth Society, Caledonian; New (Edinburgh).

HUGHES, Major Arthur John, MC 1945; TD and Clasp 1950; DL; Chairman, Hertfordshire County Council, since 1977; *b* 29 June 1914; *s* of Arthur Hubert Hughes and Dorothy Maud Hughes; *m* 1946, Penelope Joan Parker; one *s* one *d. Educ:* Highgate Sch. Entered family business, Wm Hughes Ltd, 1931; Chm. and Man. Dir, 1951. Commnd, Mddx Regt, 1936; served War of 1939-45 (Lt-Col 1943) (despatches twice, MC); subst. Major, 1949. Mem., Hatfield RDC, 1955-58 and 1961-64; Herts CC: Councillor, 1958; Alderman, 1966-73; Vice-Chm., 1968-69, 1971-73, 1974-77 (Chm., 1973); Conservative Gp Leader, 1974. DL Herts, 1974. *Recreations:* golf, gardening, good food, good wine, grand-children. *Address:* The Vineyards, Welwyn, Herts AL6 9NE. *T:* Welwyn 4242.

HUGHES, Maj.-Gen. Basil Perronet, CB 1955; CBE 1944; *b* 13 Jan. 1903; *s* of late Rev. E. B. A. Hughes; *m* 1932, Joan Marion Worthington; two *s. Educ:* Eton Coll.; RMA, Woolwich. Commissioned RFA 1923; Staff Coll., 1935-36; Directing Staff, Staff Coll., 1940. Served NW Frontier of India, 1930-31 (medal and clasp); Mohmand, 1933 (clasp); War of 1939-45 (star and despatches). Formerly: Hon. Col 2nd (London) Bn, Mobile Defence Corps; Hon. Colonel 571 LAA Regt (9th Battalion The Middx Regt DCO) RA, TA. ADC to the Queen, 1952-54; GOC 4 Anti-Aircraft Group, 1954; Maj.-Gen. RA (AA), War Office, 1955-58; retired, 1958. Col Comdt RA 1961-63; Hon. Colonel: 5th Bn, The Middx Regt (DCO), TA, 1964-69; 10th Bn, The Queen's Regt (Mddx), T&AVR, 1970-71. *Publications:* British Smooth-Bore Artillery, 1969; The Bengal Horse Artillery 1800-1861, 1971; Firepower, 1974. *Address:* St Nicholas Close, Stour Row, near Shaftesbury, Dorset. *Club:* Leander.

HUGHES, Brodie; *see* Hughes, E. B. C.

HUGHES, Rt. Hon. Cledwyn; PC 1966; CH 1977; MP (Lab) Anglesey since 1951; b 14 Sept. 1916; er s of Rev. Henry David and Emily Hughes; m 1949, Jean Beatrice Hughes; one s one d. Educ: Holyhead Grammar Sch.; University Coll. of Wales, Aberystwyth (LLB). Solicitor, 1940. Served RAFVR, 1940-45. Mem. Anglesey County Council, 1946-52. Contested (Lab) Anglesey, 1945 and 1950. Chairman: Welsh Parliamentary Party, 1953-54; Welsh Labour Group, 1955-56; Parly Labour Party, Oct. 1974-(Vice-Chm., March-Oct. 1974). Member: Cttee of Public Accounts, 1957-64; Cttee of Privileges, 1974-. Vice-Pres., Britain in Europe, 1975. Minister of State for Commonwealth Relations, 1964-66; Sec. of State for Wales, 1966-68; Min. of Agriculture, Fisheries and Food, 1968-70; Opposition spokesman on Agriculture, Fisheries and Food, 1970-72. Mem. Parly. Delegn to Lebanon, 1957; represented British Govt at Kenya Republic Celebrations, 1964; led UK Delegn to The Gambia Independence celebrations, 1965; Mission to Rhodesia, July 1965; led UK Mission on Contingency Planning to Zambia, 1966; led Parliamentary Delegn to USSR, 1977. Member: County Councils' Assoc.; Pres., UCW, Aberystwyth, 1976-. Hon. Freedom of Beaumaris, 1972; Freeman, Borough of Anglesey, 1976. Hon. LLD Wales, 1970. Alderman, Anglesey CC, 1973. Publication: Report on Conditions in St Helena, 1958. Address: Swynol Le, Trearddur, Holyhead, Gwynedd. T: Trearddur 544. Club: Travellers'.

HUGHES, Sir David (Collingwood), 14th Bt cr 1773; heraldic sculptor; b 29 Dec. 1936; s of Sir Richard Edgar Hughes, 13th Bt and Angela Lilian Adelaide Pell (d 1967); S father, 1970; m 1964, Rosemary Ann Pain, MA, LLB (Cantab), d of Rev. John Pain; four s. Educ: Oundle and Magdalene College, Cambridge (MA). National Service, RN, 1955-57. United Steel Cos Ltd, 1960-65; Unicam Instruments Ltd (subsequently Pye Unicam Ltd), export executive, 1965-70, E Europe manager, 1970-73. Builder, 1974-76. Recreations: carpentry, music, shooting, fishing. Heir: s Thomas Collingwood Hughes, b 16 Feb. 1966. Address: The Berristead, Wilburton, Ely, Cambs. T: Ely 740770.

HUGHES, Prof. David Leslie, CBE 1977; PhD, FRCVS, DipBact; Professor of Veterinary Pathology, University of Liverpool, since 1955; b 26 Oct. 1912; s of John and Eva Hughes; m 1st, 1938, Ann Marjorie Sparks (d 1971) 2nd, 1974, Jean Mavis, yr d of C. B. Saul. Educ: Wycliffe Coll., Stonehouse; Royal Veterinary Coll., London (MRCVS). PhD Nottingham, 1959. Agricultural Research Council Studentship in Animal Health, 1934-37 (DipBact London, 1936); Research Officer, Veterinary Laboratory, Min. of Agriculture, 1937-38; Lecturer in Bacteriology, Royal Veterinary College, 1938-40; Second Scientific Asst, Agricultural Research Council's Field Station, Compton, 1940-46; Head of Veterinary Science Div., Research Dept, Boots Pure Drug Co. Ltd, 1948-55; Dean of Faculty of Veterinary Science, University of Liverpool, 1965-68; Warden, Roscoe Hall, Univ. of Liverpool, 1965-72; Pro-Vice-Chancellor, Univ. of Liverpool, 1975-. Mem., ARC, 1973-. FRCVS 1952; Mem. Council, RCVS, 1964-76 (Pres. 1974-75; Sen. Vice Pres., 1975-76); Pres., British Veterinary Assoc., 1963-64. Scientific Editor, Research in Veterinary Science. Publications: scientific articles in Veterinary Record, British Veterinary Journal, Journal of Comparative Pathology, Journal of Hygiene, etc. Recreations: gardening, painting and travel. Address: 12 Beech Court, Allerton Road, Liverpool L18 3JZ. T: 051-724 4431. Club: Farmers'.

HUGHES, David Morgan; His Honour Judge Morgan Hughes; a Circuit Judge, since Nov. 1972; b 20 Jan. 1926; s of late Rev. John Edward Hughes and Mrs Margaret Ellen Hughes; m 1956, Elizabeth Jane Roberts; one s two d. Educ: Beaumaris Grammar Sch.; LSE (LLB). Army, 1944-48: Captain, Royal Welch Fusiliers; attached 2nd Bn The Welch Regt; Burma, 1945-47. London Univ., 1948-51; Rockefeller Foundn Fellowship in Internat. Air Law, McGill Univ., 1951-52; called to Bar, Middle Temple, 1953; practised Wales and Chester Circuit; Dep. Chm., Caernarvonshire QS, 1970-71; a Recorder, Jan.-Nov. 1972; Dep. Chm., Agricultural Lands Tribunal, 1972. Recreations: tennis, cricket, gardening. Address: Bryn, Kelsall, Cheshire. T: Kelsall 51349.

HUGHES, Hon. Sir Davis, Kt 1975; Agent-General for New South Wales, in London, since 1973; b 24 Nov. 1910; m 1940, Joan Philip Johnson; one s two d. Educ: Launceston High Sch., Tasmania; Phillip Smith Teachers' Coll., Hobart, Tas. Teacher, Tasmania, incl. Friends' Sch., Hobart, 1930-35; Master, Caulfield Grammar Sch., Melbourne, 1935-40. Served War, Sqdn Ldr, RAAF, Australia and overseas, 1940-45. Dep. Headmaster, Armidale Sch., Armidale, NSW, 1946-49; Mayor of Armidale, 1953-56. MLA, NSW, 1950-53 and 1956-65; Minister for Public Works, NSW, 1965-73. Recreations: tennis, golf, fishing, racing. Address: 15 Chester Street, Belgravia, SW1.

T: 01-235 3933. Clubs: East India, Sports and Public Schools, City Livery; Sunningdale Golf, Denham Golf; Australasian Pioneers, Australian Golf (Sydney); Armidale (Armidale).

HUGHES, Desmond; see Hughes, F. D.

HUGHES, Rev. Edward Marshall, MTh, PhD (London); Vicar of St Mary's, Dover, since 1971; Rural Dean of Dover, since 1974; b London, 11 Nov. 1913; o s of late Edward William Hughes, Newhouse, Mersham, Ashford, Kent, and Mabel Frances (née Faggetter); descendant of Edward Hughes, b 1719, of Little Swanton, Mersham; unmarried. Educ: City of London Sch.; King's Coll., London; Cuddesdon Coll., Oxford. Deacon, 1936, Priest, 1937, Canterbury; Curate, St Martin's, Canterbury, 1936-41; Chaplain RAFVR 1941 (invalided Oct. 1941); Curate Bearsted, Kent, 1941-46; Vicar of Woodnesborough, Kent, 1946-52; Chap. St Bartholomew's Hosp., Sandwich, 1947-52; Off. Chap. RAF Station, Sandwich, 1948-52; Warden of St Peter's Theological Coll., Jamaica, 1952-61; Canon Missioner of Jamaica, 1955-61; Examining Chap. to the Bp of Jamaica, 1953-61; Hon. Chap. Jamaica, RAFA, 1954-61; Mem. Board of Governors Nuttall Memorial Hospital, Kingston, 1956-61, and St Jago High Sch., Spanish Town, 1957-61; Visiting Lecturer, McGill Univ., Canada, 1957; Hon. Lecturer, Union Theological Seminary, Jamaica, 1957-58; Visiting Lecturer, Séminaire de Théologie, Haiti, 1959; Acting Rector, St Matthew's Church, Kingston, and Chap. Kingston Public Hospital, 1959-60; JP (St Andrew, Jamaica), 1959-63; Commissary to Bishop of Jamaica, 1968-. Fellow (Librarian, 1962-65), St Augustine's Coll., Canterbury (Central Coll. of the Anglican Communion), 1961-65; Hon. helper, RAF Benevolent Fund, for Kent, 1961-65, for London (Croydon), 1965-71, for Kent, 1971-; Divinity Master, VI Forms, The King's Sch., Canterbury, 1962-63; Officiating Chap., Canterbury Garrison, 1963-64; Vicar of St Augustine's, S Croydon, 1965-71. Proctor in Convocation, Dio. Canterbury, 1966-75. Examining Chap. to Archbishop of Canterbury, 1967-76; Chaplain to the Queen, 1973-. Publications: various papers on theological education overseas. Recreations: cultivating Japanese bonsai, exercising the dogs. Address: The Vicarage, Taswell Street, Dover, Kent CT16 1SE. T: Dover 206842. Club: Royal Cinque Ports Yacht (Dover).

HUGHES, Prof. Sir Edward (Stuart Reginald), Kt 1977; CBE 1971; Chairman and Professor, Department of Surgery, Monash University, Alfred Hospital, since 1973; President, Royal Australasian College of Surgeons, since 1975; b 4 July 1919; s of Reginald Hawkins Hughes and Annie Grace Langford; m 1944, Alison Clare Lelean; two s two d. Educ: Melbourne C of E Grammar Sch.; Univ. of Melbourne. MB, BS 1943; MD 1945; MS 1946; FRCS 1946, FRACS 1950. Resident Medical Officer, Royal Melbourne Hosp., 1943-45, Asst Surgeon 1950-53, Surgeon 1954-74; Surgeon, Alfred Hosp., 1974. Consultant Surgeon to Australian Army, 1976. Royal Australasian College of Surgeons: Mem. Council, 1967; Chm. Exec. Cttee, 1971. Hon. FACS, 1971; Hon. FRCS(C), 1977. Publications: Surgery of the Anal Canal and Rectum, 1957; All about an Ileostomy, 1966, 3rd edn 1971; All about a Colostomy, 1970, 2nd edn 1977; Ano-Rectal Surgery, 1972. Recreations: tennis, racing. Address: 24 Somers Avenue, Malvern, Victoria 3143, Australia. T: 20.7688. Clubs: Melbourne, Melbourne Cricket, Athenæum, Victoria Racing, Victoria Amateur Turf (Melbourne).

HUGHES, Prof. Emmet John; Professor of Politics, Eagleton Institute, Rutgers University, since 1970; b 26 Dec. 1920; s of Judge John L. Hughes, Summit, NJ; m ; two d (one s two d by previous marriages). Educ: Princeton Univ. (AB summa cum laude); Columbia Univ. (Graduate Sch.). Press Attaché, American Embassy, Madrid, 1942-46. Chief of Bureau for Time and Life Magazines: Rome, 1947-48, Berlin, 1948, 1949; Articles Editor, for Life Magazine, New York, 1949-53. Administrative Asst to the President of the United States, 1953, Special European Correspondent, Life Magazine, 1953-57; Chief of Foreign Correspondents, Time and Life, 1957-60; Senior Advisor on Public Affairs to the Rockefeller Brothers, 1960-63; Newsweek columnist and editorial consultant, Washington Post Co., 1963-68; Special Asst to Governor of NY State, 1968-70. Publications: The Church and the Liberal Society, 1944; Report from Spain, 1947; America the Vincible, 1959; The Ordeal of Power, 1963; The Living Presidency, 1973; (with P. A. Reynolds) The Historian as Diplomat, 1977. Address: 90 Olden Lane, Princeton, NJ 08540, USA.

HUGHES, (Ernest) Brodie (Cobbett), FRCS; Professor of Neurosurgery, since 1948, and Dean of the Faculty of Medicine and Dentistry, since 1974, University of Birmingham; b 21 Sept. 1913; o s of E. T. C. Hughes, surgeon, and D. K. Cobbett, Richmond, Surrey; m 1971, Frances Wendy Alexander. Educ: Eastbourne Coll.; University Coll. and Hospital, London. MB,

BS London 1937, FRCS 1939, ChM Birmingham 1949; resident appointments, UC Hospital, and at National Hospital for Nervous Diseases, Queen Square, London. After various appointments in neurosurgery was appointed Neurosurgeon, Birmingham United Hospitals, 1947. *Publications:* The Visual Fields, 1955; various publications in medical journals on neurosurgery and on perimetry and visual fields in particular. *Recreations:* playing the oboe, fly-fishing for trout; unsuccessful attempts to paint and draw in oils, water-colour, pen-and-ink and other media. *Address:* 68 Wellington Road, Edgbaston, Birmingham BI5 2ET. *T:* 021-440 3427. *Club:* Athenæum.

HUGHES, Air Vice-Marshal (Frederick) Desmond, CB 1972; CBE 1961; DSO 1945; DFC and 2 bars, 1941-43; AFC 1954; Director, Trident Trust, since 1976; *b* Belfast, 6 June 1919; *s* of late Fred C. Hughes, company dir, Donaghadee, Co. Down, and late Hilda (*née* Hunter), Ballymore, Co. Donegal; *m* 1941, Pamela, *d* of late Julius Harrison, composer and conductor; two *s. Educ:* Campbell Coll., Belfast; Pembroke Coll., Cambridge (MA). Joined RAF from Cambridge Univ. Air Sqdn, 1939; Battle of Britain, No. 264 Sqdn, 1940; night fighting ops in Britain and Mediterranean theatre, 1941-43; comd No. 604 Sqdn in Britain and France, 1944-45; granted perm. commn, 1946; served in Fighter Comd, 1946-53; Directing Staff, RAF Staff Coll., 1954-56; Personal Staff Off. to Chief of Air Staff, 1956-58; comd. RAF Stn Geilenkirchen, 1959-61; Dir of Air Staff Plans, Min. of Def., 1962-64; ADC to the Queen, 1963; Air Officer i/c Administration, HQ Flying Training Command, RAF, 1966-68; AOC, No 18 Group, RAF Coastal Command, and Air Officer, Scotland and N Ireland, 1968-70; Comdt, RAF Coll., Cranwell, 1970-72; SASO Near East Air Force, 1972-74, retired. *Recreations:* fishing, sailing, music. *Address:* c/o Midland Bank Ltd, Sleaford, Lincs. *Club:* Royal Air Force.

HUGHES, Prof. George Morgan; Professor of Zoology, Bristol University, since 1965; Head of Research Unit for Comparative Animal Respiration, since 1970; *b* 17 March 1925; *s* of James Williams Hughes and Edith May Hughes; *m* 1954, Jean Rosemary, *d* of Rowland Wynne Frazier and Jessie Frazier; two *s* one *d. Educ:* Liverpool Collegiate Sch.; King's Coll., Cambridge (Scholar). Martin Thackeray Studentship, 1946-48, MA, PhD, ScD (Cantab); Frank Smart Prize, 1946. Cambridge Univ. Demonstrator, 1950-55, Lectr, 1955-65; successively Bye-Fellow, Research Fellow and Fellow of Magdalene Coll., Cambridge, 1949-65. Univ. of Bristol: Head of Dept of Zoology, 1965-70. Research Fellow, California Inst. of Technology, 1958-59; Visiting Lectr in Physiology, State Univ. of New York, at Buffalo, 1964; Vis. Prof., Duke Univ., 1969; Japan Society for the Promotion of Science Vis. Prof., Kochi, Kyoto, Kyushu and Hokkaido Univs, 1974. Mem., Internat. Cœlacanth Expdn, 1972. *Publications:* Comparative Physiology of Vertebrate Respiration, 1963; Physiology of Mammals and other Vertebrates (jt), 1965; (ed) several symposium vols; papers in Jl of Experimental Biology and other scientific jls, mainly on respiration of fishes. *Recreations:* travel, golf, photography; hockey for Cambridge Univ., 1945, and Wales, 1952-53. *Address:* 11 Lodge Drive, Long Ashton, Bristol BS18 9JF. *T:* Long Ashton 3402.

HUGHES, George Ravensworth, CVO 1943; *b* 16 June 1888; *s* of Thomas McKenny Hughes, formerly Professor of Geology at Cambridge Univ.; *m* 1917, Margaret (*d* 1967), *d* of His Honour Judge Graham; one *s* one *d. Educ:* Eton; Trinity Coll., Cambridge. Clerk of the Worshipful Company of Goldsmiths, 1938-53. *Publications:* The Plate of the Goldsmiths' Co. (with J. B. Carrington), 1926; The Goldsmiths' Company as Patrons of their craft, 1919 to 1953; Articles on Antique and Modern Silverwork. *Recreations:* music, gardening, and golf. *Address:* Plummers, Bishopstone, Seaford, East Sussex. *T:* Seaford 892958. *Club:* Athenæum.

HUGHES, Brig. Gerald Birdwood V.; *see* Vaughan-Hughes.

HUGHES, Glyn Tegai, MA, PhD; Warden of Gregynog, University of Wales, since 1964; National Governor for Wales, of the BBC, and Chairman of the Broadcasting Council for Wales, since 1971; *b* 18 Jan. 1923; *s* of Rev. John Hughes and Keturah Hughes; *m* 1957, Margaret Vera Herbert, Brisbane, Qld; two *s. Educ:* Newtown and Towyn County Sch.; Liverpool Institute; Manchester Grammar Sch.; Corpus Christi Coll., Cambridge (Schol., MA, PhD). Served War, Royal Welch Fusiliers, 1942-46 (Major). Lector in English, Univ. of Basel, 1951-53; Lectr in Comparative Literary Studies, Univ. of Manchester, 1953-64, and Tutor to Faculty of Arts, 1961-64. Contested (L) Denbigh Div., elections 1950, 1955 and 1959. Mem., Welsh Arts Council, 1967-76; Vice-Pres., N Wales Arts Assoc.; Chm., Undeb Cymru Fydd, 1968-70. *Publications:* Eichendorffs Taugenichts, 1961; Romantic German Literature,

1978; articles in learned journals and Welsh language periodicals. *Recreation:* book-collecting. *Address:* Gregynog, Newtown, Powys. *T:* Tregynon 295.

HUGHES, Guy Erskine, CMG 1949; *b* 7 March 1904; *s* of late Major C. G. E. Hughes, the Cheshire Regt, and Florence, *d* of late S. A. Waters, sometime of Royal Irish Constabulary; *m* 1930, June, *d* of Donald Spicer, Ghent; three *s* one *d. Educ:* Harrow Sch.; Trinity Coll., Cambridge. Messrs Mather & Platt, Ltd; apprentice engineer, 1925-28; ICI Ltd, 1928-35; Messrs Ed. Sharp & Sons, Ltd; Dir, 1935-39. Served War of 1939-45, in RNVR; demobilised as Temp. Comdr RNVR (Sp.), 1945. Chief, Food, Agriculture and Forestry, CCG, 1946; Overseas Food Corp., Urambo, 1950. Managing Dir, Imperial Chemical Industries (South Africa) Ltd, 1952-58; Managing Dir, African Explosives and Chemical Industries Ltd, 1958-66. *Recreation:* fly-fishing. *Address:* Waterbank, Norham, Berwick upon Tweed. *Clubs:* Boodle's; Rand, Country (Johannesburg).

HUGHES, (Harold) Paul; Director of Finance, British Broadcasting Corporation, since 1971; Director, Kleinwort Benson Farmland Trust (Managers) Ltd; *b* 16 Oct. 1926; *o s* of Edmund and Mabel Hughes; *m* 1955, Beryl Winifred Runacres; one *s* one *d. Educ:* Stand Grammar Sch., Whitefield, near Manchester. Certified Accountant. Westminster Bank Ltd, 1942-45; Royal Marines and Royal Navy, 1945-49; Arthur Guinness Son & Co. Ltd, 1950-58; British Broadcasting Corporation: Sen. Accountant, 1958-61; Asst Chief Accountant, Finance, 1961-69; Chief Accountant, Television, 1969-71. *Recreations:* music, walking. *Address:* 26 Downside Road, Guildford, Surrey. *T:* Guildford 69166.

HUGHES, Rear-Adm. Henry Hugh, CB 1966; Director of Naval Electrical Engineering, 1964; Chief Naval Engineer Officer, 1967-68; retired, 1968; *b* 9 March 1911; British; *m* 1939, Margaret (*née* Lycett); two *d. Educ:* Clydebank High Sch.; Glasgow Univ. (BSc Hons). English Electric Co. Ltd, 1932-42; Electrical Officer, RNVR, 1942-45; transf. to RN as Lieut-Comdr, 1945; Comdr 1947; Capt. 1956; Rear-Adm. 1964. HMS Vanguard, 1947-49; subsequently: various appts in Admty and Dockyards; in comd, HMS Collingwood; Dep. Dir of Electrical Engrg. *Recreation:* tennis. *Address:* Tigh Failté, Argyll Terrace, Tobermory, Isle of Mull, Scotland. *T:* Tobermory 06882432.

HUGHES, Rev. Henry Trevor, MA; *b* 27 Feb. 1910; *s* of late Rev. Dr H. Maldwyn Hughes; *m* 1946, Elizabeth Catherine Williams; one *s* one *d. Educ:* Perse Sch., Cambridge. National Provincial Bank, 1926-31; Wesley House, Cambridge, 1932-35 (2nd Class Hons Theol Tripos, 1935); Chaplain, Culford Sch., Bury St Edmunds, 1935-41; Chaplain, Royal Air Force, 1941-45 (despatches). Asst Minister, Central Hall, Westminster, 1945-46; Vice-Principal and Chaplain, Westminster College of Education, 1946-53, Principal, 1953-69; Minister, Attleborough Methodist Church, 1969-75. Incorporated MA, Oxford Univ. through Lincoln Coll., 1959. Co-opted Mem., Norfolk Educn Cttee; Governor: Culford Sch., Bury St Edmunds; Wymondham Coll. Select Preacher, University of Oxford, 1965; Methodist representative, British Council of Churches Preachers' Exchange with the USA, 1964. *Publications:* Prophetic Prayer, 1947; Teaching the Bible to Seniors, 1948; Teaching the Bible to Juniors, 1949; Why We Believe, 1950; The Piety of Jeremy Taylor, 1960; Faith and Life, 1962; Life Worth Living, 1965; pamphlets: Letters to a Christian, 1947; Teaching the Bible Today, 1957; contributor to London Quarterly Review. *Recreation:* painting. *Address:* 102 New Road, Hethersett, Norfolk NR9 3HQ. *T:* Norwich 811038.

HUGHES, Herbert Delauney, MA; Principal of Ruskin College, Oxford, since 1950; *b* 7 Sept. 1914; *s* of late Arthur Percy Hughes, BSc, and late Maggie Ellen Hughes; *m* 1937, Beryl Parker. *Educ:* Cheadle Hulme Sch.; Balliol Coll., Oxford (State and County Major Scholar). BA (Hons) in Modern History, 1936; Asst Sec., New Fabian Research Bureau, 1937-39; Organising Sec., Fabian Soc., 1939-46; Mem. Exec. Fabian Soc., 1946- (Vice-Chm. 1950-52, 1958-59, Chm. 1959-60, Vice-Pres., 1971-); MP (Lab) Wolverhampton (West), 1945-50; Parliamentary Private Sec. to Minister of Education, 1945-47; to Financial Sec. to War Office, 1948-50; Mem. Lambeth Borough Council, 1937-42. Governor of Educational Foundation for Visual Aids, 1948-56. Member: Civil Service Arbitration Tribunal, 1955-; Commonwealth Scholarship Commn, 1968-74; Cttee on Adult Educn, 1969-73. Vice-Pres., Workers' Educational Assoc., 1958-67, Dep. Pres., 1968-71, Pres., 1971-; Chm. Management Cttee, Adult Literacy Resource Agency, 1975-. Served War of 1939-45, with 6 Field Regt Royal Artillery. *Publications:* (part author) Democratic Sweden, 1937, Anderson's Prisoners, 1940, Six Studies in Czechoslovakia,

1947. Advance in Education, 1947; Towards a Classless Society, 1947; A Socialist Education Policy, 1955; The Settlement of Disputes in The Public Service, 1968; (jt author) Planning for Education in 1980, 1970. *Recreations:* walking and foreign travel. *Address:* Ruskin College, Oxford; Crossways, Mill Street, Islip, Oxford. *T:* Kidlington 6935.

HUGHES, Jack William; chartered surveyor; a Senior Partner, Jones, Lang, Wootton, International Real Estate Advisers, 1949-76; Chairman, Bracknell New Town Development Corporation, since 1971; *b* 26 Sept. 1916; 2nd *s* of George William Hughes and Isabel Hughes, Maidstone, Kent; *m* 1939, Marie-Theresa, *d* of Graham Parmley Thompson. *Educ:* Maidstone Grammar Sch.; Univ. of London. BSc (Est. Man.); FRICS. Served with Special Duties Br., RAF, 1940-46. Director: Housing Corporation (1974) Ltd, 1974-; MEPC and URPT, Public Property Cos; South Bank Estates; Brighton Marina Co. (Rep. Brighton Corp.); Mem. Cttee, Mercantile Credit Gp Property Div.; Mem. Cttee of Management, Charities Property Unit Trust, 1967-74; Chm., South Hill Park Arts Centre Trust, 1972-; Member: Adv. Gp to DoE on Commercial Property, 1974-; DoE Working Party on Housing Tenure, 1976-; British Rail Property Board, 1976-; Trustee, New Towns Pension Fund, 1975. Freeman, City of London, 1959-; Liveryman, Painter Stainers Guild, 1960-. *Publications:* (jtly) Town and Country Planning Act 1949 (RICS); (Chm. of RICS Cttee) The Land Problem: a fresh approach; techn. articles on property investment, develt and finance. *Recreations:* golf, travel, reading. *Address:* Challoners, Rottingdean, Sussex; Flat 11, 102 Rochester Row, SW1. *Clubs:* Buck's, Carlton, RAFVR.

HUGHES, John; *see* Hughes, R. J.

HUGHES, Very Rev. John Chester; Vicar of Bringhurst with Great Easton and Drayton, since 1977; *b* 20 Feb. 1924; *m* 1950, Sybil Lewis McClelland; three *s* two *d* (and one *s* decd). *Educ:* Dulwich Coll.; St John's Coll., Durham. Curate of Westcliffe-on-Sea, Essex, 1950-53; Succentor of Chelmsford Cathedral, 1953-55; Vicar of St Barnabas, Leicester, 1955-61; Vicar of Croxton Kerrial with Branston-by-Belvoir, 1961-63; Provost of Leicester, 1963-77. ChStJ 1974. *Address:* The Vicarage, Great Easton, Market Harborough, Leics LE16 8SX. *T:* Rockingham 279.

HUGHES, John Dennis; Tutor in Economics and Industrial Relations since 1957, and Vice Principal since 1970, Ruskin College, Oxford; *b* 28 Jan. 1927; *s* of John (Ben) Hughes and Gwendoline Hughes; *m* 1949, Violet (née Henderson); four *d*. *Educ:* Westminster City Sch.; Lincoln Coll., Oxford (MA). Lieut, RAEC, 1949-50. Extramural Tutor, Univs of Hull and Sheffield, 1950-57. Dep. Chm., Price Commn, 1977-. Dir, Trade Union Res. Unit, 1970-. Mem., Industrial Develt Adv. Bd, 1975-. *Publications:* Trade Union Structure and Government, 1968; (with R. Moore) A Special Case? Social Justice and the Miners, 1972; (with H. Pollins) Trade Unions in Great Britain, 1973; Industrial Restructuring: some manpower aspects, 1976; Fabian Soc. pamphlets. *Recreation:* cycling. *Address:* Rookery Cottage, Old Headington, Oxford. *T:* Oxford 63076.

HUGHES, Rt. Rev. John Richard Worthington P.; *see* Poole Hughes.

HUGHES, Rt. Rev. John Taylor, CBE 1975; *b* 12 April 1908; *s* of Robert Edward and Annie Hughes. *Educ:* Castle Hill Sch., Ealing; Uxbridge County Sch.; Bede Coll., University of Durham. Ordained 1931; Asst Chaplain and Tutor, Bede Coll., Durham, 1931-34; Lecturer, Bede Coll., 1934-35; Curate, St John's, Shildon Co. Durham, 1934-37; Vicar, St James, West Hartlepool, 1937-48; Canon Residentiary and Missioner of Southwark Cathedral. Warden of Diocesan Retreat House, Southwark, 1948-56; Bishop Suffragan of Croydon, 1956-77; Archdeacon of Croydon, 1967-77; Bishop to the Forces, 1966-75. Pres., Norman Houses. *Recreations:* music, reading. *Address:* 1 Burgate House, Burgate, Canterbury, Kent CT1 2HB. *T:* Canterbury 69351.

HUGHES, Prof. Leslie Ernest, FRCS, FRACS; Professor of Surgery, Welsh National School of Medicine, since 1971; *b* 12 Aug. 1932; *s* of Charles Joseph and Vera Hughes; *m* 1955, Marian Castle; two *s* two *d*. *Educ:* Parramatta High Sch.; Sydney Univ. MB, BS (Sydney); DS (Queensland), 1975; FRCS, 1959; FRACS, 1959. Reader in Surgery, Univ. of Queensland, 1965-71. Eleanor Roosevelt Internat. Cancer Fellow, 1970. *Publications:* numerous papers in medical jls, chiefly on immune aspects of cancer, and diseases of the colon. *Recreation:* music. *Address:* Department of Surgery, University Hospital of Wales, Heath Park, Cardiff CF4 4XW. *T:* Cardiff 755944.

HUGHES, Mark; *see* Hughes, W. M.

HUGHES, Paul; *see* Hughes, H. P.

HUGHES, Major Richard Charles, MBE 1951; TD 1945; Director, Federation of Commodity Associations, since 1973; *b* 24 Dec. 1915; *s* of late Frank Pemberton Hughes and of Minnie Hughes, Northwich. *Educ:* Wrekin Coll., Wellington, Telford. TA commn, 4/5th (E of C) Cheshire Regt, 1935; regular commn, 22nd (Cheshire) Regt, 1939. Served War of 1939-45: 2 i/c 5th, 2nd and 1st Bns 22nd (Cheshire) Regt. Palestine, 1945-47; S/Captain MS and DAAG Western Comd, 1948-51; Korea, 1954; GSO2 Sch. of Infantry, 1955-56; Sec. of Sch. of Inf. Beagles, 1955-56; retd pay, 1958. Apptd Sec. to Sugar Sssoc. of London, British Sugar Refiners Assoc. and Refined Sugar Assoc., 1958; formed British Sugar Bureau and apptd Sec., 1964-66. Hon. Treas., W Kensington Environment Cttee, 1974-75; Mem. Barons Keep Management Cttee, 1975. Director: Sugar Assoc. of London, 1975; Rdfined Sugar Assoc., 1976. Member: City Liaison Cttee, Bank of England and City EEC Cttee, 1975; City Adv. Panel to City Univ., and Adv. to City of London Polytechnic, 1975; City Communications Consultative Gp, 1976. *Recreations:* travel, sailing, golf, beagling, antiques. *Address:* 8 Barons Keep, Barons Court, W14 9AT. *T:* 01-603 0429. *Club:* Hurlingham.

HUGHES, Robert; MP (Lab) Aberdeen North since 1970; *b* Pittenweem, Fife, 3 Jan. 1932; *m* 1957, Ina Margaret Miller; two *s* three *d*. *Educ:* Robert Gordon's Coll., Aberdeen; Benoni High Sch., Transvaal; Pietermaritzburg Techn. Coll., Natal. Emigrated S Africa, 1947, returned UK, 1954. Engrg apprentice, S African Rubber Co., Natal; Chief Draughtsman, C. F. Wilson & Co. (1932) Ltd, Aberdeen, until 1970. Mem., Aberdeen Town Council, 1962-70; Convener: Health and Welfare Cttee, 1963-68; Social Work Cttee, 1969-70. Mem., AEU, 1952-. Contested (Lab) North Angus and Mearns, 1959. Member: Standing Cttee on Immigration Bill, 1971; Select Cttee, Scottish Affairs, 1971; introd Divorce (Scotland) Bill 1971 (failed owing to lack of time); Parly Under-Sec. of State, Scottish Office, 1974-75. Chm., Aberdeen City Labour Party, 1961-69. Founder Mem. and Aberdeen Chm., Campaign for Nuclear Disarmament; Vice-Chm., 1975-76, Chm., 1976-, Anti-Apartheid Movement; Member: Movement for Colonial Freedom, 1955- (Chm. Southern Africa Cttee); Scottish Poverty Action Group; Aberdeen Trades Council and Exec. Cttee, 1957-69; Labour Party League of Youth, 1954-57. *Recreation:* golf. *Address:* House of Commons, SW1; 23 Lisburne Road, Hampstead, NW3.

HUGHES, (Robert) John; Editor, The Christian Science Monitor, since 1970; *b* Neath, S Wales, 28 April 1930; *s* of Evan John Hughes and Dellis May Hughes (née Williams); *m* 1955, Vera Elizabeth Pockman; one *s* one *d*. *Educ:* Stationers' Company's Sch., London. Reporter, sub-editor, corresp. for miscellaneous London and S African newspapers and news agencies (Natal Mercury, Durban; Daily Mirror, Daily Express, Reuter, London News Agency), 1946-54; joined The Christian Science Monitor, Boston, USA, 1954: Africa Corresp., 1955-61; Asst Foreign Editor, 1962-64; Far East Corresp., 1964-70; Man. Editor, 1970. Nieman Fellow, Harvard Univ., 1961-62. Pulitzer Prize for Internat. Reporting, 1967; Overseas Press Club of America award for best daily newspaper or wire service reporting from abroad, 1970. *Publications:* The New Face of Africa, 1961; Indonesian Upheaval (UK as The End of Sukarno), 1967; articles in magazines and encyclopaedias. *Recreations:* reading, walking, raising Labrador retrievers. *Address:* One Norway Street, Boston, Mass 02115, USA. *T:* (617) 262-2300. *Clubs:* Foreign Correspondents', Hong Kong Country (Hong Kong); Overseas Press (New York); Harvard (Boston).

HUGHES, Air Marshal Sir Rochford; *see* Hughes, Air Marshal Sir S. W. R.

HUGHES, Royston John; MP (Lab) Newport, Mon, since 1966; *b* 9 June 1925; *s* of John Hughes, Coal Miner; *m* 1957, Florence Marion Appleyard; three *d*. *Educ:* Ruskin Coll., Oxford. Miner, Nine Mile Point Colliery, Mon., until 1944; served with HM Forces, 1944-47. Administrative Officer, Standard Motor Co. Ltd, Coventry, 1958-66. Mem. Coventry City Council, 1962-66; various offices in Transport and General Workers' Union, 1959-66. PPS to Minister of Transport, 1974-75; Chm., Parly Labour Party Sports Gp; Vice-Chairman: Labour Middle East Council; Welsh Labour Gp (Chm., 1975-76); Jt Chm., PLP Environment Gp. *Recreation:* follows Rugby football, Newport and Wales. *Address:* 34 St Kingsmark Avenue, Chepstow, Gwent. *T:* 3266. *Clubs:* United Service Mess (Cardiff); St Pierre (Chepstow); Pontllanfraith Workingmen's Social.

HUGHES, Air Marshal Sir (Sidney Weetman) Rochford, KCB 1967 (CB 1964); CBE 1955 (OBE 1942); AFC 1947; Chairman, Mazda Motors (NZ); Director: Reserve Bank NZ; NZ Steel; Dillingham Industries (NZ) Ltd; Lees Industries Ltd; General Accident Fire & Life (NZ); Leopard Brewery; Auckland Harbour Bridge Authority; Overseas National Airways (New York); *b* 25 Oct. 1914; *s* of late Capt. H. R. Hughes, Master Mariner, and late Mrs Hughes (*née* Brigham), Auckland, NZ; *m* 1942, Elizabeth, *d* of A. Duncum, Colombo, Ceylon; one *d*. *Educ*: Waitaki High School; Oamaru, NZ. Editorial Staff, NZ Herald, 1933-36; RNZ Air Force, 1937-38; RAF, Far East and Middle East, 1939-44 (despatches; Greek DFC); Chief Ops, USAF All Weather Centre, 1948-49; Air Min. and CO Farnborough, 1950-54; Imperial Defence Coll., 1955; CO RAF Jever, Germany, 1956-59; Air Mem. and Chm., Defence Res. Policy Staff, MoD, 1959-61; Air Officer Commanding No 19 Group, 1962-64; Dep. Controller Aircraft (RAF), Ministry of Aviation, 1964-66; Air Comdr, Far East Air Force, 1966-69, retd 1969. Air Adviser, Civil and Military, to Govt of Singapore, 1969-72; Comr, Northland Harbour Bd, 1974. Livery Guild of Air Pilots and Air Navigators; FRAeS. *Recreations*: yachting, motoring, photography. *Address*: Tirimoana, 14 Cliff Road, Torbay, Auckland, New Zealand. *Club*: Royal NZ Yacht Squadron.

HUGHES, Ted, OBE 1977; author; *b* 1930; *s* of William Henry Hughes and Edith Farrar Hughes; *m* 1956, Sylvia Plath (*d* 1963); one *s* one *d*; *m* 1970, Carol Orchard. *Educ*: Pembroke Coll., Cambridge Univ. Author of Orghast (performed at 5th Festival of Arts of Shiraz, Persepolis, 1971). Awards: first prize, Guinness Poetry Awards, 1958; John Simon Guggenheim Fellow, 1959-60; Somerset Maugham Award, 1960; Premio Internazionale Taormina, 1973; The Queen's Medal for Poetry, 1974. *Publications*: The Hawk in the Rain, 1957 (First Publication Award, NY, 1957); Lupercal, 1960 (Hawthornden Prize, 1961); Meet My Folks! (children's verse), 1961; The Earth-Owl and Other Moon People (children's verse), 1963 (US as Moon Whales, 1976); How the Whale Became (children's stories), 1963; (ed, jtly) Five American Poets, 1963; Selected Poems of Keith Douglas (ed, with Introduction), 1964; Nessie, The Mannerless Monster (children's verse story), 1964 (US as Nessie the Monster, 1974); Recklings, 1966; The Burning of the Brothel, 1966; Scapegoats and Rabies, 1967; Animal Poems, 1967; Wodwo, 1967 (City of Florence Internat. Poetry Prize, 1969); Poetry in the Making, 1967 (US as Poetry Is, 1970); The Iron Man (children's story) (US as The Iron Giant, 1968); (ed) A Choice of Emily Dickinson's Verse, 1968; Five Autumn Songs for Children's Voices, 1968; Adaptation of Seneca's Oedipus, 1969 (play, National Theatre, 1968); (libretto) The Demon of Adachigahara, 1969; The Coming of the Kings (4 plays for children), 1970 (US as The Tiger's Bones, 1974); Crow, 1970; A Few Crows, 1970; Crow Wakes, 1970; (ed) A Choice of Shakespeare's Verse, 1971 (US as With Fairest Flowers while Summer Lasts); Shakespeare's Poem, 1971; (with R. Fainlight and Alan Sillitoe) Poems, 1971; Eat Crow, 1971; Prometheus on His Crag, 1973; Spring Summer Autumn Winter, 1974; (libretto) The Story of Vasco, 1974; Cave-Birds (limited edn with illustrations by Leonard Baskin), 1975; Season Songs, 1976; Earth-Moon, 1976; Gaudete, 1977. *Address*: c/o Faber and Faber Ltd, 3 Queen Square, WC1.

HUGHES, Thomas Lewis, CBE 1943; *b* 27 July 1897; *s* of late R. D. Hughes; *m* 1927, Helen Mary Beynon; three *s*. *Educ*: Birkenhead Sch. Served European War, 1915-18 (France); Indian Army, 1918-22; Indian Civil Service, Burma, 1923-39; Political Sec. to Burma Chamber of Commerce, 1939-42; despatches; Sec. to Governor of Burma, 1942-46; Treasury, 1948-50. Mem. for Stoke Poges, Eton RDC, 1958-74. Hon. Sec. Stoke Poges Golf Club, 1955-62. *Address*: Redwood Cottage, Stoke Poges, Bucks. *T*: Farnham Common 2383. *Club*: East India, Devonshire, Sports and Public Schools.

HUGHES, Thomas Lowe; President and Trustee, Carnegie Endowment for International Peace, New York, Washington, Geneva, since 1971; *b* 11 Dec. 1925; *s* of Evan Raymond Hughes and Alice (*née* Lowe); *m* 1955, Jean Hurlburt Reiman; two *s*. *Educ*: Carleton Coll., Minn (BA); Balliol Coll., Oxford (Rhodes Schol., BPhil); Yale Law Sch. (LLB, JD). USAF, 1952-54 (Major). Member of Bar: Supreme Court of Minnesota; US District Court of DC; Supreme Court of US. Professional Staff Mem., US Senate Sub-cttee on Labour-Management Relations, 1951; part-time Prof. of Polit. Sci. and Internat. Relations, Univ. of Southern California, Los Angeles, 1953-54, and George Washington Univ., DC, 1957-58; Exec. Sec. to Governor of Connecticut, 1954-55; Legislative Counsel to Senator Hubert H. Humphrey, 1955-58; Admin. Asst to US Rep. Chester Bowles, 1959-60; Staff Dir of Platform Cttee, Democratic Nat. Convention, 1960; Special Asst to Under-Sec. of State, Dept of

State, 1961; Dep. Dir of Intelligence and Research, Dept of State, 1961-63; Dir of Intell. and Res. (Asst Sec. of State), 1963-69; Minister and Dep. Chief of Mission, Amer. Embassy, London, 1969-70; Mem., Planning and Coordination Staff, Dept of State, 1970-71. Chm., Nuclear Proliferation and Safeguards Adv. Panel, Office of Technology Assessment, US Congress; Chm., Bd of Editors, Foreign Policy Magazine; Sec., Bd of Dirs, German Marshall Fund of US; Dir, Arms Control Assoc. Chairman: Oxford-Cambridge Assoc. of Washington; US-UK Bicentennial Fellowships Cttee on the Arts. Member Bds of Visitors: Harvard Univ. (Center for Internat. Studies); Princeton Univ. (Woodrow Wilson Sch. of Public and Internat. Affairs); Georgetown Univ. (Sch. of Foreign Service); Bryn Mawr Coll. (Internat. Adv. Bd.); Univ. of Denver (Soc. Sci. Foundn). Member Bds of Trustees: Civilian Military Inst.; Amer. Acad. of Political and Social Sci. Member: Internat. Inst. of Strategic Studies; Amer. Assoc. of Rhodes Scholars; Amer. Political Sci. Assoc.; Amer. Bar Assoc.; Amer. Assoc. of Internat. Law; Amer. For. Service Assoc.; Internat. Studies Assoc.; Wqashington Inst. of Foreign Affairs. Arthur S. Flemming Award, 1965. Hon. LLD: Washington Coll., 1973; Carleton Coll., 1974. *Publications*: occasional contribs to professional jls, etc. *Recreations*: swimming, tennis, music, 18th century engravings. *Address*: 5636 Western Avenue, Chevy Chase, Md 20015, USA; Carnegie Endowment for International Peace, United Nations Plaza, 46th Street, New York, NY 10017. *T*: (301)6561420; (212)557-0703; 11 Dupont Circle NW, Washington, DC 20036. *T*: (202)797-6411. *Clubs*: Yale, Century Association, Council on Foreign Relations (New York); Cosmos (Washington).

HUGHES, Rt. Rev. Thomas Maurice; Assistant Bishop of Llandaff, 1961-70; *b* 17 April 1895; *s* of David and Jane Hughes, Conwil, Carmarthen; *m* 1926, Margaret, *d* of Rev. D. C. Morris, Vicar of Port Talbot; one *s* one *d*. *Educ*: St John's Coll., Ystradmeurig; St David's Coll., Lampeter; Keble Coll., Oxford (Hons Theol). Served European War, 1915-17: 29th and 9th RF (wounded). Asst Curate, Port Talbot, 1922; Minor Canon, Llandaff Cathedral, 1928; Vicar of Cadoxton Neath, 1931; Vicar of St Catherine, Cardiff, 1937; Rector and Rural Dean, Merthyr Tydfil, 1942. Canon of Llandaff Cathedral, 1943; Vicar of St John Baptist, Cardiff, 1946-61; Canon and Precentor of Llandaff Cathedral, 1946-61; Rural Dean of Cardiff, 1954-61; Archdeacon of Margam, 1961-65; Archdeacon of Llandaff, 1965-69. *Recreation*: gardening. *Address*: St Andrew, High Street, Llandaff. *T*: Cardiff 563212.

HUGHES, Sir Trevor Denby L.; *see* Lloyd-Hughes.

HUGHES, Trevor Poulton, CB 1974; CEng, FICE, FIMunE, FIWE; Director-General, Highways, Department of Transport, since 1977; *b* 28 Sept. 1925; *y s* of late Rev. John Evan Hughes, and of Mary Grace Hughes; *m* 1950, Mary Ruth, *o d* of late Dr Frank Walwyn; two *s*. *Educ*: Ruthin Sch. Served RE, 1945-48; Municipal engineering, 1948-57; Dep. Borough Engineer, Colwyn Bay, 1957-61; Min. of Transport, 1961-62; Min. of Housing and Local Govt: Engineering Inspectorate, 1962-70; Dep. Chief Engineer, 1970-71; Dir, 1971-72 and Dir-Gen., 1972-74, Water Engineering, DoE; Dep. Sec., DoE, 1974-77. Hon. FInstWPC; Hon. FIPHE. *Recreations*: golf, gardening. *Address*: 16 The Bridle Road, Purley, Surrey CR2 3JA. *T*: 01-668 3314.

HUGHES, William, CB 1953; Deputy Secretary, Department of Trade and Industry, 1970-71; *b* 21 Aug. 1910; *o s* of late William Hughes, Bishop's Stortford, Herts, and of Daisy Constance, *y d* of Charles Henry Davis; *m* 1941, Ilse Erna, *o d* of late E. F. Plohs; one *s* one *d*. *Educ*: Bishop's Stortford Coll.; Magdalen Coll., Oxford (demy). Board of Trade, 1933; Asst Sec., 1942; Under-Sec., 1948-63 (Sec., Monopolies and Restrictive Practices Commission, 1952-55); Second Sec., 1963-71. Consultant to British Overseas Trade Bd, 1972-73; Under-Sec., Prices Commn, 1973-75. *Recreation*: music. *Address*: 250 Trinity Road, SW18. *T*: 01-870 3652; Page's, Widdington, Essex. *Clubs*: Reform; Leander.

HUGHES, Maj.-Gen. (Retd) William Dillon, CB 1960; CBE 1953; MD; FRCP(I); DTM&H; Commandant, Royal Army Medical College, 1957-60; *b* 23 Dec. 1900; *s* of R. Hughes, JP; *m* 1929, Kathleen Linda Thomas; one *s*. *Educ*: Campbell Coll., Belfast; Queen's Univ., Belfast. MB, BCh, BAO, 1923; Lieut, RAMC, 1928; Officer i/c Medical Div. 64 and 42 Gen. Hosps, MEF, 1940-42; Officer i/c Medical Div. 105 Gen. Hosp., BAOR, 1944-46; Sen. MO, Belsen, 1945; consulting Physician, Far East Land Forces, 1950-53; ADMS, Aldershot Dist, 1954. Prof. in Tropical Medicine and Consulting Physician, RAM Coll., 1955-56; Vice-Pres., Royal Society of Tropical Medicine and Hygiene, 1959-60; Col Comdt RAMC, 1961-65. QHP 1957;

Mitchiner Medal, RCS, 1960. *Address:* Littleport Farm, Sedgeford, Norfolk.

HUGHES, William Henry; His Honour Judge Hughes; a Circuit Judge, since 1972; *b* 6 Jan. 1915; *s* of late William Howard Hamilton Hughes; *m* 1961, Jenny, *d* of Theodore Francis Turner, *qv*; one *d. Educ:* privately; Keble Coll., Oxford. Served War of 1939-45; AA & QMG, BEF, France and Belgium, N Africa, Italy (despatches, Croix de Guerre and palm); Staff Coll.; Lieut-Col 1944. Called to the Bar, Inner Temple, 1949. Deputy Chairman: Isle of Ely QS, 1959-63; Essex QS, 1961-63; London Sessions, 1962-63, 1968-71; a Metropolitan Magistrate, 1963-71. Formerly a Mem., General Council of the Bar. *Recreations:* books, wine, shooting, travel. *Address:* Old Wardour House, Tisbury, Wilts. *T:* Tisbury 431; 43 Woodsome Road, NW5. *Clubs:* Beefsteak, Garrick.
See also C. G. Turner.

HUGHES, Rt. Rev. William James, DD; Rector of Port Burwell, Ontario, Canada, since 1970; *m* 1958, Ada Maud Baker. *Educ:* College of Resurrection, Mirfield, University of Leeds (BA 1919). Hon. DD Leeds, 1947; DD Lambeth 1958. Deacon, 1921; Priest, 1922; Vicar of St Benedict, Bordesley, 1927-30; Rector of St George's Cathedral, Georgetown, Guiana, 1930-44; Sub-Dean, 1930-37; Dean, 1937-44; Bishop of British Honduras, 1944-45; Bishop of Barbados, 1945-51; resigned, 1951; Vicar of St George, Edgbaston, and Assistant Bishop of Birmingham, 1951-53; Hon. Canon, Birmingham Cathedral, 1952-53; Bishop of Matabeleland, 1953-61; Archbishop of Central Africa, 1957-61; Bishop of Trinidad and Tobago, 1961-70. Formerly MLC Barbados. Sub-Prelate, Order of St John of Jerusalem, 1958. *Publication:* Think Again, 1947. *Address:* PO Box 179, Port Burwell, Ontario, Canada.

HUGHES, (William) Mark; MP (Lab) Durham since 1970; *b* 18 Dec. 1932; *s* of late Edward Hughes, sometime Prof. of History at Durham, and Sarah (*née* Hughes), Shincliffe, Durham; *m* 1958, Jennifer Mary, *d* of Dr G. H. Boobyer; one *s* two *d. Educ:* Durham Sch.; Balliol Coll., Oxford (MA). BA Oxon 1956; PhD Newcastle 1963. Sir James Knott Research Fellow, Newcastle-upon-Tyne, 1958-60; Staff Tutor, Manchester Univ. Extra-Mural Dept, 1960-64; Lectr, Durham Univ., 1964-70. PPS to Chief Sec. of Treasury, 1974-75; Member: Select Cttee on Expenditure (Trade and Industry Sub-Cttee), 1970-74; Select Cttee on Parly Comr, 1970-75; Delegn to Consultative Assembly of Council of Europe and WEU; European Parlt, 1975-. Member: Exec. Cttee, British Council, 1974-; Gen. Adv. Council, BBC, 1976-. An Hon. Vice-Pres., BVA, 1976-. *Recreations:* varied and private. *Address:* Grimsdyke, Vicarage Road, Potten End, Berkhamsted, Herts.

HUGHES, William Reginald Noel, FRINA, RCNC; *b* 14 Dec. 1913; *s* of Frank George Hughes and Annie May Hughes (*née* Lock); *m* 1936, Doris Margaret (*née* Attwool); two *s* two *d. Educ:* Prince Edward Sch., Salisbury, Rhodesia; Esplanade House Sch., Southsea, Hants; Royal Dockyard Sch., Portsmouth; RN Coll., Greenwich. Constr Sub Lieut, Chatham, 1933; Constr Sub Lieut and Lieut, RN Coll., Greenwich, 1934; Admty, London, 1937; HM Dockyard, Chatham, 1938; Admty, Bath, 1940; Constr Comdr, Staff of C-in-C Home Fleet, 1944; HM Dockyard, Hong Kong, 1947; Admty, Bath, 1951; Chief Constr, HM Dockyard, Devonport, 1954; Admty, Bath, 1958; Admty Repair Manager, Malta, 1961; Manager, Constructive Dept, Portsmouth, 1964; Dep. Dir of Dockyards, Bath, 1967-70; Gen. Manager, HM Dockyard, Chatham, 1970-73. Chairman: Race Control Cttee for Whitbread Round the World Race; Southsea Yacht Signal Station, etc. *Recreations:* sailing, foreign travel, photography. *Address:* Capstan House, Tower Street, Old Portsmouth, Hants. *T:* Portsmouth 812997. *Clubs:* Little Ship; Royal Naval Sailing Association.

HUGHES HALLETT, Vice-Adm. (retd) Sir (Cecil) Charles, KCB 1954 (CB 1950); CBE 1942; Chairman: Gas Purification and Chemical Co. Ltd, 1958-60; Edwards High Vacuum International Ltd, 1964-68; Mount Row Holdings Ltd, 1962-68; Director: John Tysack & Partners Ltd, 1960-75; *b* 6 April 1898; *s* of Col W. Hughes Hallett and Clementina Mary Loch; *m* 1920, Eileen Louise Richardson; two *d.* (one *s* one *d* decd); *m* 1944, Joyce Plumer Cobbold; one *s* one *d. Educ:* Bedford; RN Colls, Osborne and Dartmouth; Emmanuel Coll., Cambridge. Went to sea as Midshipman in Aug. 1914; present at Dardanelles and Battle of Jutland: specialised in gunnery, 1921, in staff duties, 1933; Comdr 1932; Capt. 1939; Rear-Adm. 1949; Vice-Adm. 1952; retd Feb. 1955. Comdg destroyer 1934-35, anti-aircraft ship, 1940-42, aircraft carrier, 1944-46, during War of 1939-45 (despatches twice, CBE); present at operations against Japanese mainland, 1945. Dir of Administrative Plans and Joint Planning Staff, 1942-44; Dep. Chief of Naval Air Equipment, 1946-48;

Admiralty for Special Duty, 1948-50; Chief of Staff to C-in-C Home Fleet, 1950-51; Admiral, British Joint Services Mission, Washington, 1952-54; Personal Asst to Chm., Charterhouse Group, 1955-59. Younger Brother of Trinity House, 1938; Renter Warden, Co. of Glovers, 1967, Master, 1968. Fellow, British Inst. of Management. Legion of Merit, Degree of Officer (USA), 1945. *Address:* Glebe House, Odstock, Salisbury, Wiltshire SP5 4SB. *T:* Salisbury 23854.

HUGHES-MORGAN, Brig. Sir David (John), 3rd Bt *cr* 1925; CBE 1973 (MBE 1959); *b* 11 Oct. 1925; *s* of Sir John Hughes-Morgan, 2nd Bt and of Lucie Margaret, *d* of late Thomas Parry Jones-Parry; *S* father, 1969; *m* 1959, Isabel Jean, *d* of J. M. Lindsay; three *s. Educ:* RNC, Dartmouth. Royal Navy, 1943-46. Admitted solicitor, 1950. Commissioned, Army Legal Services, 1955; Brig., Legal Staff, HQ UKLF, 1976-. *Heir: s* Ian Parry David Hughes-Morgan, *b* 22 Feb. 1960. *Address:* c/o National Westminster Bank Ltd, Brecon.

HUGHES-STANTON, Blair Rowlands; Painter and Engraver; Member of The London Group; Member of Society of Wood Engravers; *b* 22 Feb. 1902. *Educ:* Colet Court, London; HMS Conway. Studied at Byam Shaw Sch., 1919-21, Royal Academy Schools and Leon Underwood Sch., 1921-24. Hon. Academician, Accademia Delle Arti Del Disegno, Florence, 1963. Made Decorations at Wembley, 1925, and Paris Exhibition, 1926. Produced numerous Books at Gregynog Press, Wales, 1930-33, and Illustrated Books for Golden Cockerel, Cresset Presses; also Allen Press, California. International Prize for Engraving at Venice Biennale, 1938. Represented with Engravings in British Museum, Victoria and Albert Museum, Whitworth Gall. (Manchester), etc. and Galls and Museums in Australia, Canada, New Zealand. *Recreation:* travel. *Address:* North House, Manningtree, Essex. *T:* Manningtree 2717.

HUGHES-YOUNG, family name of **Baron St Helens.**

HUGHESDON, Charles Frederick, AFC 1943; FRAeS; *b* 10 Dec. 1909; *m* 1937, Florence Elizabeth Dawson (actress, as Florence Desmond); one *s. Educ:* Raine's Foundation School. Entered insurance industry, 1927; learned to fly, 1932; Flying Instructor's Licence, 1934; commnd RAFO, 1934; Commercial Pilot's Licence, 1936; has Fixed Wing and Helicopter Licences; joined Stewart, Smith & Co. Ltd, 1936; Chief Test Pilot, General Aircraft, 1939-43; rejoined Stewart, Smith & Co. Ltd, 1946; Chm. and Dir, overseas cos in Matthews Wrighton Gp; Chairman: Tradewinds Airways; Bigland Holdings. Hon. Treas., Air League; Hon. Treas., RAeS, FRAeS 1971. Order of the Cedar, Lebanon, 1972. *Recreations:* flying (fixed wing and helicopter), shooting, horseracing, breeding of thoroughbred horses, riding, yachting, water ski-ing, farming. *Address:* Dunsborough Park, Ripley, Surrey. *T:* Ripley 3366; Flat 12, 5 Grosvenor Square, W1. *T:* 01-493 1494. *Clubs:* Royal Air Force, Royal Thames Yacht, Lloyd's Yacht; Bembridge Yacht; Royal Perth (Australia) Yacht.

HUGILL, John, QC 1976; a Recorder of the Crown Court, since 1972; *b* 11 Aug. 1930; *s* of John A. and Alice Hugill; *m* 1956, Patricia Elizabeth Hugill (*née* Welton); two *d. Educ:* Fettes; Trinity Hall, Cambridge (BA). 2nd Lieut, RA, 1949. Called to the Bar, Middle Temple, 1954; Assistant Recorder, Bolton, 1971. *Recreation:* yachting. *Address:* The Boundary House, Lower Withington, Cheshire. *T:* Marton Heath 368.

HUGILL, Michael James; Assistant Master, Westminster School, since 1972; *b* 13 July 1918; 2nd *s* of late Rear-Adm. R. C. Hugill, CB, MVO, OBE. *Educ:* Oundle; King's Coll., Cambridge, Exhibitioner, King's Coll., 1936-39; MA 1943. War Service in the RN; Mediterranean, Home and Pacific Fleets, 1939-46; rank on demobilisation, Lieut-Comdr. Mathematics Master, Stratford Grammar Sch., 1947-51; Senior Mathematics Master, Bedford Modern Sch., 1951-57; Headmaster, Preston Grammar Sch., 1957-61; Headmaster, Whitgift School, Croydon, 1961-70; Lectr, Inst. of Education, Keele Univ., 1971-72. *Address:* 42 Kersfield House, Kersfield Road, SW15. *Club:* Army and Navy.

HUGO, Lt-Col Sir John (Mandeville), KCVO 1969 (CVO 1959); OBE 1947; Gentleman Usher to the Queen, 1952-69, an Extra Gentleman Usher since 1969; *b* 1 July 1899; *s* of R. M. Hugo; *m* 1952, Joan Winifred, *d* of late D. W. Hill; two *d. Educ:* Marlborough Coll.; RMA, Woolwich, Commissioned RA, 1917; transf. to Indian Cavalry, 1925; Military Sec. to Governor of Bengal, 1938-40; rejoined 7th Light Cavalry, 1940; Military Sec. to Governor of Bengal 1946-47; Asst Ceremonial Sec., Commonwealth Relations Office, 1948-52; Ceremonial and Protocol Secretary, 1952-69. *Address:* The Cottages, Nizels, Hildenborough, Kent. *T:* Hildenborough 832359. *Club:* Army and Navy.

HUIJSMAN, Nicolaas Basil Jacques, CMG 1973; *b* 6 March 1915; *s* of Nikolaas Kornelis Huijsman, Amsterdam and Hendrika Huijsman (*née* Vorkink). *Educ:* Selborne Coll., E London, S Africa; Univ. of Witwatersrand (BCom); Gonville and Caius Coll., Cambridge (Econ. Tripos). Commnd Royal Scots Fusiliers, 1940; HQ 17 Inf. Bde, 1940; GS03, WO, 1941-42; psc 1942; GSO2, HQ of Chief of Staff to Supreme Cmdr (Des) and SHAEF, 1943-45 (despatches 1944); Controller of Press and Publications, Control Commn for Germany, 1945-48; Colonial Office, 1948-62; Principal Private Sec. to Sec. of State for Commonwealth Relations and Colonies, 1962-64; Asst Sec., Min. of Overseas Develt, 1964-70, and 1974-75, Overseas Develt Admin/FCO, 1970-74. Bronze Star, US, 1945. *Recreations:* Byzantine history, music, opera, painting. *Address:* 13 Regent Square, Penzance TR18 4BG. *Club:* Reform.

HULBERT, Dame Cicely; *see* Courtneidge, Dame Cicely.

HULBERT, Jack; actor, dramatic author, manager, producer; *b* Ely, 24 April 1892; *s* of Dr H. H. Hulbert; *m* Cicely Courtneidge (*see* Dame Cicely Courtneidge); one *d. Educ:* Westminster; Gonville and Caius Coll., Cambridge. First appearance on professional stage, in The Pearl Girl, Shaftesbury Theatre, 1913; played in: Bubbly and Hullo Paris in Paris, 1919; Bran Pie; Little Dutch Girl; Pot Luck. Produced: The Blue Train; prod. and played in: By the Way, London and New York; Lido Lady; Clowns in Clover; The House that Jack Built; Follow a Star; prod. Folly to be Wise. Spent 10 years in *films:* Ghost Train; Sunshine Susie; Jack's the Boy; Jack Ahoy; Bulldog Jack; Jack of all Trades; Falling for You, etc.; Produced and played in: Under your Hat; Something in the Air; Full Swing (Palace Theatre); prod. Under the Counter; prod. and played in Here come the Boys; prod. and played for TV: Here come the Boys; Cinderella; Dick Whittington; The Golden Year; played in Hulbert Follies; Housemaster; Smith; The Squeaker; The White Sheep of the Family; prod. Gay's the Word; played in: The Reluctant Debutante; The Bride Comes Back; The Spider's Web; Let's Be Frank; The Amorous Prawn; Dear Octopus, etc. Served European War, 1917-19. Commandant in Special Constabulary, 1940-57. *Publication:* The Little Woman's Always Right (autobiog.), 1975. *Address:* c/o Herbert de Leon Ltd, Fielding House, 13 Bruton Street, W1X 3JY.

HULL, Bishop Suffragan of, since 1977; **Rt. Rev. Geoffrey John Paul;** *b* 4 March 1921; *s* of Robert John Paul and Ethel Mary (*née* Arthur); *m* 1951, Pamela Maisie Watts; five *d. Educ:* Rutlish School, Merton; Queens' Coll., Cambridge (MA); King's Coll., London (MTh, AKC). Deacon 1948; Curate of Little Ilford, E12; priest 1949; Church of S India, from Oct. 1950. Chaplain, St John's Coll., Palayamkotta, 1950-52; Kerala United Theological Seminary, 1952-65 (Principal, 1962-65); Church Missionary Society, 1965-66; Residentiary Canon, Bristol Cathedral, (Director of Ordination Training, Examining Chaplain), 1966-71; Hon. Canon of Bristol, 1971-77; Warden, Lee Abbey, 1971-77. *Publications:* The Gospel according to St Mark, 1957, and St John's Gospel, 1965, both published by Christian Students' Library in India. *Address:* Hullen House, Woodfield Lane, Hessle, N Humberside. *T:* Hull 649019.

HULL, John Folliott Charles; Chairman, J. Henry Schroder Wagg & Co Ltd, since 1977; *b* 21 Oct. 1925; *er s* of Sir Hubert Hull, CBE, and of Judith, *e d* of P. F. S. Stokes; *m* 1951, Rosemarie Waring; one *s* three *d. Educ:* Downside; Jesus Coll., Cambridge (MA). 1st cl. hons Law. Captain, RA, 1944-48, served with Royal Indian Artillery. Called to Bar, Inner Temple, 1952. J. Henry Schroder Wagg & Co. Ltd, 1957-72, 1974- (a Man. Dir, 1961-72); Jt Dep. Chm., Schroders Ltd, 1977-; Dep. Chm., Land Securities Investment Trust, 1976-; Director: Lucas Industries Ltd, 1975-; Legal and General Assurance Soc., 1976-; Land Securities Investment Trust Ltd, 1976-. Dir-Gen., City Panel on Take-overs and Mergers, 1972-74; Chm., City Company Law Cttee, 1976-. Mem., Council, Manchester Business Sch. *Recreations:* reading political history and 19th century novelists, supporting Chelsea Football Club. *Address:* 33 Edwardes Square, W8. *T:* 01-603 0715. *Club:* MCC.

HULL, Field Marshal Sir Richard (Amyatt), GCB 1961 (KCB 1956; CB 1945); DSO 1943; DL; *b* 7 May 1907; *m* 1934, Antoinette Mary Labouchère de Rougemont; one *s* two *d. Educ:* Charterhouse; Trinity Coll., Cambridge (MA). Joined 17th/21st Lancers, 1928; Commanded 17/21st Lancers, 1941; Commanded 12th Infantry Bde, 1943; Commanded 26 Armd Bde, 1943; Comd 1st Armd Div., 1944; Cmd 5th Infantry Div., 1945; Commandant Staff Coll. Camberley, 1946-48; Dir of Staff Duties, War Office, 1948-50; Chief Army Instructor, Imperial Defence Coll., 1950-52; Chief of Staff, GHQ, MELF, 1953-54; General Officer Commanding, British Troops in Egypt, 1954-56; Dep. Chief of the Imperial Gen. Staff, 1956-58; Comdr-in-Chief,

Far East Land Forces, 1958-61; Chief of the Imperial Gen. Staff, 1961-64; ADC Gen. to the Queen, 1961-64; Chief of the Gen. Staff, Ministry of Defence, 1964-65; Chief of the Defence Staff, 1965-67. Constable of the Tower of London, 1970-75. Pres., Army Benevolent Fund, 1968-71; Dir, Whitbread & Co. Ltd, 1967-76. Col Comdt, RAC, 1968-71. DL Devon 1973; High Sheriff, Devon, 1975. Hon. LLD Exeter, 1965. *Address:* Beacon Downe, Pinhoe, Exeter. *Club:* Cavalry and Guards.
See also Maj.-Gen. H. R. Swinburn.

HULME, Bishop Suffragan of, since 1975; **Rt. Rev. David George Galliford;** *b* 20 June 1925; *s* of Alfred Edward Bruce and Amy Doris Galliford; *m* 1954, Enid May Drax; one *d. Educ:* Bede Coll., Sunderland; Clare Coll., Cambridge (Organ Scholar 1942, BA 1949, MA 1951); Westcott House, Cambridge. Served 5th Royal Inniskilling Dragoon Guards, 1943-47. Curate of St John Newland, Hull, 1951-54; Minor Canon of Windsor, 1954-56; Vicar of St Oswald, Middlesbrough, 1956-61; Rector of Bolton Percy and Diocesan Training Officer, 1961-70; Canon of York Minster, 1969; Canon Residentiary and Treasurer of York Minster, 1970-75. *Publications:* God and Christian Caring, 1973; Pastor's Post, 1975; (ed) Diocese in Mission, 1968. *Recreations:* pottery, music, painting in oils. *Address:* Hulme House, 31 Bland Road, Prestwich, Manchester. *T:* 061-773 1504. *Clubs:* Royal Over-Seas League; Manchester.

HULME, Hon. Sir Alan (Shallcross), KBE 1971; FCA; grazier; *b* 14 Feb. 1907; *s* of Thomas Shallcross Hulme and Emily Clara (*née* Hynes); *m* 1938, Jean Archibald; two *s* one *d. Educ:* North Sydney Boys' High School. Pres., Qld Div. of Liberal Party of Aust., 1946-49, 1962-63. Director: Chandlers (Aust.) Ltd, 1952-58; J. B. Chandler Investment Co. Ltd, 1962-63. Hon. Treas., King's Univ. Coll., 1944-49. Former Vice-Consul for Portugal in Brisbane. Mem., Commonwealth Parlt, Australia, 1949-72; Minister for Supply, 1958-61; acted as Minister: for Army, May-July 1959; for Air, Dec. 1960; Postmaster-General, 1963-72; Minister for Defence, 1965-66 and on subseq. occasions; Vice-Pres., Exec. Council, 1966-72. Member: House Cttee, 1950-58; Jt Cttee of Public Accounts, 1952-58; Chairman: Commonwealth Cttee on Rates of Depreciation, 1954-55; Commonwealth Immigration Planning Council, 1956-58. *Recreations:* gardening, bowls. *Address:* Alcheringa Droughtmaster Stud, Eudlo, Qld 4554. *T:* Palmwoods 459267. *Club:* Brisbane (Brisbane).

HULME, Alfred Clive, VC 1941; Transport Contractor, New Zealand, since 1945; *b* 24 Jan. 1911; *s* of Harold Clive Hulme, Civil Servant, and Florence Sarah Hulme; *m* 1934, Rona Marjorie Murcott; one *s* one *d. Educ:* Dunedin High Sch. New Zealand Military Forces, War of 1939-45 (VC). Formerly tobacco farming; water and metal divining successfully in New Zealand, Australia, South Africa, and England. *Recreations:* tennis, boating, landscape gardening. *Address:* RD6, Te Puke, Bay of Plenty, New Zealand. *Club:* Returned Services Association.

HULME, Geoffrey Gordon; Under-Secretary, Department of Health and Social Security, since 1974; *b* 8 March 1931; *s* of Alfred and Jessie Hulme; *m* 1956, Shirley Leigh Cumberlidge; one *s* one *d. Educ:* Daybrook Street Elem. Sch.; King's Sch., Macclesfield; Corpus Christi Coll., Oxford (MA, 1st Cl Hons Mod. Langs). Nat. Service, Intelligence Corps, 1949-50; Oxford, 1950-53; Asst Principal, Min. of Health, 1953-59; Principal, 1959-64; Principal Regional Officer, W Midlands, 1964-67; Asst Sec., 1967-74. *Recreations:* the usual things and collecting edible fungi. *Address:* 3 Woodhyrst Gardens, Kenley, Surrey CR2 5LX. *T:* 01-660 5713.

HULME, Dr Henry Rainsford; Chief of Nuclear Research, Atomic Weapons Research Establishment, 1959-73, retired; *b* 9 Aug. 1908; *s* of James Rainsford Hulme and Alice Jane Smith; *m* 1955, Margery Alice Ducker, *d* of late Sir James A. Cooper, KBE, and of Lady Cooper. *Educ:* Manchester Grammar Sch.; Gonville and Caius Coll., Cambridge; University of Leipzig. BA (Math. Tripos) 1929; Smiths' Prizeman, 1931; PhD (Cambridge) 1932; ScD (Cambridge) 1948. Fellow of Gonville and Caius Coll., Cambridge, 1933-38; Chief Asst Royal Observatory, Greenwich, 1938-45; on loan to Admiralty during war. Scientific Adviser Air Ministry, 1946-48. *Publications:* on Mathematical Physics and Astronomy in learned jls. *Recreations:* various. *Address:* Birch Row, Ramsdell, near Basingstoke, Hants.

HULME-MOIR, Rt. Rev. Francis Oag, AO 1976; ED 1949; Bishop to the Australian Armed Forces, since 1965, and Chaplain-General (CE), Australian Army, since 1974; *b* 30 Jan. 1910; *2nd s* of Alexander Hugh and Violet Beryl Hulme-Moir; *m* 1937, Ena Dorothy Smee; two *s* one *d. Educ:* Moore Theological Coll.; Sydney Univ. ThL, ACT, 1935. Deacon, 1936; Priest,

1937. Chaplain to Forces, 1936; Chaplain, AIF, 1939-45 (despatches, 1944); Dep. Asst Chaplain-Gen., 1942; Asst Chaplain-Gen., 1945; Senior Chaplain, NSW, 1946; Archdeacon of Ryde, 1947; Archdeacon of Cumberland, 1950; Bishop of Nelson, New Zealand, 1954-65; Coadjutor Bishop and Dean of Sydney, 1965-67; Coadjutor Bishop, Northern Region, 1968; Sen. Asst Bishop of Sydney, 1967-75. Senior Anglican Chaplain to all NZ Services, 1959-64; Chaplain to NSW Police Force, 1965. ChStJ 1975. *Recreations:* golf, gardening, fishing. *Address:* 15 Acacia Street, Collaroy Plateau, NSW 2098, Australia. *Clubs:* Union, Tattersall's, Australasian Pioneers (all Sydney); Royal Sydney Motor Yacht.

HULSE, Sir (Hamilton) Westrow, 9th Bt, *cr* 1739; Barrister-at-Law, Inner Temple; *b* 20 June 1909; *o s* of Sir Hamilton Hulse, 8th Bt, and Estelle (*d* 1933) *d* of late William Lorillard Campbell, of New York, USA; *S* father, 1931; *m* 1st, 1932, Philippa Mabel (marr. diss., 1937), *y d* of late A. J. Taylor, Strensham Court, Worcs; two *s*; 2nd, 1938, Amber (*d* 1940), *o d* of late Captain Herbert Stanley Orr Wilson, RHA, Rockfield Park, Mon; 3rd, 1945 (marr. diss.); 4th, 1954, Elizabeth, *d* of late Col George Redesdale Brooker Spain, CMG, TD, FSA. *Educ:* Eton; Christ Church, Oxford. Wing Comdr RAFVR, served 1940-45 (despatches). *Heir: s* Edward Jeremy Westrow Hulse [*b* 22 Nov. 1932; *m* 1957, Verity Ann, *d* of William Pilkington, Wardington House, Banbury, Oxon.; one *s* one *d*]. *Address:* Breamore, Hants. *TA:* Breamore. *T:* Breamore 233. *Clubs:* Carlton, Bath; Leander.

HULSE, Sir Westrow; *see* Hulse, Sir H. W.

HULTON, Sir Edward (George Warris), Kt 1957; Magazine publisher; writer; *b* 29 Nov. 1906; *s* of late Sir Edward Hulton, former proprietor of Evening Standard; *m* 1st, Kira (marr. diss.), *d* of General Goudime-Levkovitsch, Imperial Russian Army; no *c* ; 2nd, 1941, Princess Nika Yourivietch (marr. diss., 1966), 2nd *d* of Prince Serge Yourievitch, Russian Councillor of State, Chamberlain to His Imperial Majesty, Officier de la Légion d'Honneur (France), sculptor, and Helene de Lipovatz, *d* of Gen. de Lipovatz; two *s* one *d*. *Educ:* Harrow; Brasenose Coll., Oxford (open scholarship. Contested Leek Div. Staffs, as Unionist, 1929; Harwich Div., 1931. Called to Bar, Inner Temple; practised on South-Eastern Circuit; Chm. and Managing Dir of Hulton Publications Ltd. Pres., European Atlantic Group, 1969-70; Mem., British Atlantic Cttee; Vice-Pres., European League for Economic Co-operation; Mem. Nat. Council, British Council of the European Movement. FRSA. Liveryman and Freeman of Company of Stationers; Freeman of City of London. NATO Peace Medal, 1969. *Publications:* The New Age, 1943; When I Was a Child, 1952; Conflicts, 1966; contrib. various newspapers and books. *Recreation:* reading. *Address:* Flat 9, 24 Carlton House Terrace, SW1. *Clubs:* Athenæum, Beefsteak, Carlton, Garrick, Travellers', Buck's.

HULTON, Sir Geoffrey (Alan), 4th Bt, *cr* 1905; JP; DL; *b* 21 Jan. 1920; *s* of Sir Roger Braddyll Hulton, 3rd Bt and Hon. Marjorie Evelyn Louise (*d* 1970), *o c* of 6th Viscount Mountmorres; *S* father 1956; *m* 1945, Mary Patricia Reynolds. *Educ:* Marlborough. Entered Royal Marines, Sept. 1938; Lieut, 1940; sunk in HMS Repulse, Dec. 1941; prisoner-of-war, Far East, Feb. 1942-Aug. 1945; Captain, 1948; retired (ill-health), 1949. Owner of Hulton Park estate. Chief Scout's Commissioner. Pres., Westhoughton Divisional Conservative Association; President: Royal Lancs Agricultural Soc.; Bolton and District Agricultural Discussion Soc.; Vice-President: Country Landowners' Assoc. (Lancashire); Lancashire County Cricket Club. JP Lancs, 1955; DL Lancs, later Greater Manchester, 1974. KCSG 1966. *Recreations:* country pursuits. *Heir:* none. *Address:* The Cottage, Hulton Park, Over Hulton, Bolton, BL5 1BH. *T:* Bolton 651324. *Clubs:* Lansdowne, Royal Over-Seas League.

HULTON, John; *b* 28 Dec. 1915; *e s* of late Rev. Samuel Hulton, Knaresborough; *m* 1940, Helen Christian McFarlan; two *d*. *Educ:* Kingswood Sch., Bath; Hertford Coll., Oxford. Leeds City Art Gallery and Temple Newsam House (Hon. Asst), 1937-38. Served War, RA, 1939-46. Keeper at Brighton Art Gall., Museum and Royal Pavilion, 1946-48; British Council Fine Arts Dept, 1948; Dir, 1970-75; resigned to follow course in landscape design at Thames Polytechnic. Organised many art exhibns abroad. *Recreations:* looking at painting and sculpture; landscape and gardens. *Address:* 70 Gloucester Crescent, NW1 7EG. *T:* 01-485 6906. *Club:* Athenæum.

HULTON-HARROP, Maj.-Gen. William Harrington, CB 1959; DSO 1944; General Officer Commanding Catterick Area, 1959, retired; *b* 7 May 1906; *s* of Hugh de Lacy Hulton-Harrop and Delitia Mary (*née* Hulton); *m* 1937, Pamela Scholefield; one *d*.

Educ: Charterhouse; RMA Sandhurst. 2nd Lieut KSLI, 1926; served War of 1939-45, N Africa, Sicily, Italy and Palestine. Lieut-Col 1942; Brig. 1949; Maj.-Gen. 1957; Commander 50th Division (TA) and Northumbrian District, 1956. *Address:* The Old Forge, Vernham Dean, Andover, Hants; c/o Lloyds Bank, 6 Pall Mall, SW1.

HUMBLE, Prof. Joseph Graeme, CVO 1955; Professor of Haematology, Westminster Medical School, London University, since 1972 (Reader 1965-72); Hon. Consultant Haematologist, Westminster Hospital, since 1949; *b* 10 July 1913; 2nd *s* of late Wensley Taylor Humble and late Louisa Ann (*née* Witham), Mansfield, Notts; *m* 1942, Elsie May (Anne), *d* of late A. Hunt, Mendlesham, Suffolk; three *s* (and two *s* decd). *Educ:* Bedford Modern Sch.; Westminster Hosp. Med. Sch., University of London. MRCS, LRCP 1937, MRCP 1959, FRCPath 1955, FRCP 1970. Westminster Hospital: House Physician Children's Dept, 1937-38; Junior Asst Pathologist, 1938-39; Acting Asst Pathologist and Temp. Lecturer in Pathology and Bacteriology, 1939-46; Haematologist, 1946-49. Member: Royal Society of Medicine; London Med. Soc. *Publications:* Westminster Hospital 1716-1966: a history, 1966, 2nd edn, Westminster Hospital, 1716-1974, 1974; various articles in Med. Jls. *Recreations:* cricket, golf, history. *Address:* Tree Shadows, Roman Road, Dorking, Surrey. *T:* Dorking 5296.

HUME, Sir Alan (Blyth), Kt 1973; CB 1963; *b* 5 Jan. 1913; *s* of late W. Alan Hume; *m* 1943, Marion Morton Garrett; one *s* one *d*. *Educ:* George Heriot's Sch.; Edinburgh Univ. Entered Scottish Office, 1936. Under-Sec., Scottish Home Department, 1957-59; Asst Under-Sec. of State, Scottish Office, 1959-62; Under-Sec., Min. of Public Bldg and Works, 1963-64; Secretary, Scottish Develt Dept, 1965-73. Chairman: Ancient Monuments Bd, Scotland, 1973-; Edinburgh New Town Conservation Cttee, 1975-. *Recreations:* golf, fishing. *Address:* 12 Oswald Road, Edinburgh EH9 2HJ. *T:* 031-667 2440. *Clubs:* English-Speaking Union, Royal Commonwealth Society; New (Edinburgh).

HUME, Major Charles Westley, OBE 1962; MC; BSc; late Senior Examiner, Patent Office; Founder, Universities Federation for Animal Welfare; Scientific Intelligence Officer (CD), Finchley 1950-61; Fellow of Zoological Society; Hon. Life Member, British Deer Society; *b* 13 Jan. 1886; *s* of Charles William Hume (formerly a Pampas rancher), and Louisa, *d* of Captain Waldron Kelly, 26th Cameronians; *m* 1966, Margaret Pattison, MA. *Educ:* Christ's Coll., Finchley; Strand Sch.; Birkbeck Coll. (University of London). Served in France (Royal Engineers Signals) in European War of 1914-18, and afterwards in 47th Divisional signals, TA; 3rd Signal Training Centre, 1939-41; qualified as Instructor, Fire Control (radar), 1941; Signals Experimental Establishment, 1942; HQ staff for Army Operational Research Group under Controller of Physical Research and Signals Development, 1942-45. Editor to the Physical Society, 1919-40; as Hon. Sec. of the British Science Guild organised the campaign which issued in the Patents Act, 1932; founded (1926) the University of London Animal Welfare Soc. and (1939) Universities Federation for Animal Welfare; campaigned successfully for prohibition (1956) of gin traps. Citoyen d'Honneur de Meurchin, Pas-de-Calais, 1973-; medal 'en témoignage de reconnaissance, la Ville de Meurchin', 1970; Prés. d'Honneur de Meurchin Sect., Union Nat. des Anciens Combatants; Sòci dóu Felibrige, e de l'Escolo de la Targo, 1958-; Sòci d'Ounour di Cardelin de Maiano. *Publications:* The Status of Animals in the Christian Religion, 1956; Man and Beast, 1962; articles on religion, animal welfare, statistical analysis, patent law, Provence, and rabbit-control. *Address:* 2 Cyprus Gardens, Finchley, N3. *Club:* Athenæum.

HUME, His Eminence (George) Basil, Cardinal; *see* Westminster, Archbishop of, (RC).

HUME, James Bell; Under-Secretary, Scottish Home and Health Department, since 1977; *b* 16 June 1923; *s* of Francis John Hume and Jean McLellan Hume; *m* 1950, Elizabeth Margaret Nicolson. *Educ:* George Heriot's Sch., Edinburgh; Edinburgh Univ. MA Hons History. RAF, 1942-45. Asst Principal, Dept of Health for Scotland, 1947; Principal 1951; Jt Sec., Royal Commn on Doctors' and Dentists' Remuneration, 1958-59; Asst Sec. 1959; Nuffield Trav. Fellowship, 1963-64; Head of Edinburgh Centre, Civil Service Coll., 1969-73; Under-Sec., Scottish Education Dept, 1973-77. *Recreations:* dance music, gardening. *Address:* 24 Cherry Tree Gardens, Balerno, Edinburgh EH14 5SP. *T:* 031-449 3781. *Clubs:* Caledonian, Royal Commonwealth Society; New (Edinburgh).

HUME, John; *b* 18 Jan. 1937; *s* of Samuel Hume; *m* 1960, Patricia Hone; two *s* three *d*. *Educ:* St Columb's Coll., Derry; St Patrick's Coll., Maynooth, NUI (MA). Pres., Credit Union League of

Ireland, 1964-68; MP for Foyle, NI Parlt, 1969-73; Member (SDLP), Londonderry: NI Assembly, 1973-75; NI Constitutional Convention, 1975-76; Minister of Commerce, NI, 1974. Contested (SDLP) Londonderry, UK elections, Oct. 1974. *Address:* 6 West End Park, Derry, N Ireland. *T:* Londonderry 65340.

HUME, Thomas Andrew, CBE 1977; FSA, FMA; Director, Museum of London, 1972-77; *b* 21 June 1917; *o s* of late Thomas Hume, Burnfoot, Oxton, and late Lillias Dodds; *m* 1942, Joyce Margaret Macdonald; two *s* one *d. Educ:* Heaton Grammar Sch.; King's Coll., Univ. of Durham (BA Hons Hist.). Gladstone Prizeman, Joseph Cowen Prizeman. Curator: Kirkstall Abbey House Museum, Leeds, 1949-52; Buckinghamshire County Museum, Aylesbury, 1952-60; Dir, City of Liverpool Museums, 1960-72. Mem., Standing Commn on Museums and Galleries, 1977-. Past Pres., NW Fedn of Museums; Past Vice-Pres., Internat. Assoc. of Transport Museums; Past Chm., ICOM British Nat. Cttee. Soc. of Antiquaries: Mem. Finance Cttee and Exec. Cttee; Mem. Area Archæological Cttee, Greater London. *Publications:* contribs Thoresby Soc., Records of Bucks; Excavation reports and historical articles. *Recreations:* travel, gardening. *Address:* Homegarth, Church Lane, Whittington, King's Lynn, Norfolk.

HUME-WILLIAMS, Sir Roy Ellis, 2nd Bt, *cr* 1922; *b* 31 July 1887; *s* of Rt Hon. Sir Ellis Hume-Williams, 1st Bt, PC, KBE, KC; *S* father, 1947; *m* 1st, 1915, Norah (marr. diss., 1949, she *d* 1964), *y d* of late David Anderson, Sydney, NSW; 2nd, 1949, Frances Mary (Molly), *er d* of Major Arthur Groom, OBE, Warham Wells, Norfolk. *Educ:* Eton; Trinity Hall, Cambridge. Cons. Engineer, 1910-14. Served in European War, 1914-19; retired with rank of Captain, RASC. Schoolmaster, 1920-48. *Recreations:* cricket, hockey, tennis, golf, skating. *Heir:* none. *Address:* Ardlui, The Highlands, East Horsley, Surrey. *Clubs:* Royal Automobile, MCC; County (Guildford).

HUMMEL, Frederick Cornelius, MA, DPhil, BSc; Head of Forestry Division, Commission of the European Communities, since 1973; *b* 28 April 1915; *s* of Cornelius Hummel, OBE, and Caroline Hummel (*née* Riefler); *m* 1st, 1941, Agnes Kathleen Rushforth (marr. diss., 1961); one *s* (and one *s* decd); 2nd, 1961, Floriana Rosemary Hollyer; three *d. Educ:* St Stephan, Augsburg, Germany; Wadham Coll., Oxford. District Forest Officer, Uganda Forest Service, 1938-46; Forestry Commn, 1946-; Mensuration Officer, 1946; Chief, Management Sect., 1956; released for service with FAO as Co-Dir, Mexican Nat. Forest Inventory, 1961-66; Controller, Management Services, Forestry Commn, 1966-68, Comr for Harvesting and Marketing, 1968-73. *Publications:* several for Forestry Commn; papers in British, foreign and internat. forestry jls. *Recreations:* walking, ski-ing. *Address:* Commission of the European Communities, 200 rue de la Loi, 1040 Brussels, Belgium; Ridgemount, 8 The Ridgeway, Guildford, Surrey. *T:* Guildford 72383.

HUMPHREY, Arthur Hugh Peters, CMG 1959; OBE 1952; Hon. PMN (Malaya), 1958; Controller of Special Projects, Overseas Development Administration, Foreign and Commonwealth Office, 1961-71; Malayan Civil Service, 1934-60, retired; *b* 18 June 1911; *s* of late Arthur George Humphrey, Bank Manager; *m* 1948, Mary Valentine, *d* of late Lieut-Col J. E. Macpherson; three *d. Educ:* Eastbourne Coll.; Merton Coll., Oxford. Appointed Malayan Civil Service, 1934; Private Sec. to Governor of Straits Settlements and High Comr for Malay States, 1936-38; Resident, Labuan, 1940-42; interned by Japanese in Borneo, 1942-45; idc 1948; Sec. for Defence and Internal Security, Fedn of Malaya, 1953-57; Mem. of Federal Legislative and Executive Councils, 1953-56; Sec. to the Treasury, Federation of Malaya, 1957-59; Director of Technical Assistance, Commonwealth Relations Office, 1960-61; Controller of Special Projects, ODM, 1961. Official Leader, United Kingdom delegations at Colombo Plan conferences: Tokyo, 1960, and Kuala Lumpur, 1961. Coronation Medal, 1953. *Recreations:* music, tennis. *Address:* 14 Ambrose Place, Worthing, Sussex. *T:* Worthing 33339. *Club:* East India, Devonshire, Sports and Public Schools.

HUMPHREY, Frank Basil, CB 1975; Parliamentary Counsel since 1967; *b* 21 Sept. 1918; *s* of late John Hartley Humphrey and Alice Maud Humphrey (*née* Broadbent); *m* 1947, Ol'ga Černa, *y d* of late Frántišek Černý, Trenčín, Czechoslovakia; two *s. Educ:* Brentwood Sch.; St Catharine's Coll., Cambridge (Schol.). 2nd cl. hons Pt I. Mod. Langs Tripos, 1st cl. hons Pt II Law Tripos. Served RA, 1939-45: Adjt 23rd Mountain Regt and DAAG 4 Corps, India and Burma. Called to Bar, Middle Temple, 1946 (Harmsworth Schol.). Seconded as First Parly Counsel, Fedn of Nigeria, 1961-64, and as Counsel-in-charge at

Law Commn, 1971-72. *Recreations:* gardening, mountain walking, music. *Address:* The Yews, Rookery Close, Fetcham, Surrey KT22 9BG. *T:* Leatherhead 72619.

HUMPHREY, Senator Hubert Horatio, Jr; United States Senator from Minnesota (Democrat), 1949-64 and since 1970; Deputy President of the Senate, since 1977; Member Board, Encyclopædia Britannica, Inc., since 1969; *b* Wallace, South Dakota, USA, 27 May 1911; *s* of Hubert Horatio Humphrey; *m* 1936, Muriel Fay Buck; three *s* one *d. Educ:* Denver Coll. of Pharmacy; University of Minnesota (AB) and Louisiana State Univ. (AM). State Dir, War Production Training and Re-employment Div., 1941-42; Asst Regional Dir, War Manpower Commn, 1943; Professor of Political Science, Macalester Coll., Minnesota, 1943-44; Radio News Commentator, 1944-45; Mayor, City of Minneapolis, 1945-48; US Senate Asst Majority Leader, 1961-64; Vice-President of the US, 1965-69. Jt Prof., Macalester Coll. at St Paul and Univ. of Minnesota at Minneapolis, 1969-70. American delegate to UN, 1956-57. Member: Phi Beta Kappa; Delta Sigma Rho; Amer. Polit. Sci. Assoc. Holds many honorary degrees. Democrat. *Publications:* The Cause is Mankind, 1964; The War On Poverty, 1964; School Desegregation: Documents and Commentaries, 1964; The Political Philosophy of the New Deal, 1970; The Education of a Public Man, 1977. *Address:* Waverley, Minnesota 55390, USA; 350 North Street SW, Washington, DC 20024, USA.

HUMPHREY, Prof. John Herbert, CBE 1970; BA; MD; FRS 1963; FRCP 1971; Professor of Immunology, Royal Postgraduate Medical School, London University, since 1976; *b* 16 Dec. 1915; *s* of Herbert Alfred Humphrey and Mary Elizabeth Humphrey (*née* Horniblow); *m* 1939, Janet Rumney, *d* of Prof. Archibald Vivian Hill, CH, OBE, FRS, ScD, and late Margaret Neville, *d* of late Dr J. N. Keynes; two *s* three *d. Educ:* Winchester Coll.; Trinity Coll., Cambridge; UCH Med. Sch. Jenner Research Student, Lister Inst., 1941-42; Asst Pathologist, Central Middx Hosp., 1942-46; External Staff, Med. Research Council, 1946-49; Member: Scientific Staff, Nat. Inst. for Med. Research, 1949-76, Dep. Dir, 1961-76, Head of Div. of Immunology and Experimental Biology, 1957-76; Expert Cttee on Biological Standardization, WHO, 1955-70; Expert Cttee on Immunology, WHO, 1962-. Editor, Advances in Immunology, 1960-67; Asst Editor, Immunology, 1958-68. Mem. Council, Royal Society, 1967-69. Fellow, Winchester Coll., 1967; Hon. Prof., Middlesex Hosp. Med. Sch., 1970. *Publications:* Immunology for Students of Medicine (with Prof. R. G. White), 1963; contribs to Jls of immunology, biochemistry, physiology, etc. *Address:* 17 Mortimer Crescent, NW6 5NP. *T:* 01-624 9376; Topcliffe's Mill, Meldreth, Royston, Herts. *T:* Royston 60376.

HUMPHREY, William Gerald, MA Oxon and Cantab, DPhil Oxon; Assistant Secretary, University of Cambridge Appointments Board, 1962-68; Headmaster of The Leys School, Cambridge, 1934-58; Group personnel officer, Fisons Ltd, 1958-62; *b* 2 Aug. 1904; *e s* of late Rev. William Humphrey and Helen Lusher; *m* 1936, Margaret, *er d* of late William E. Swift, Cornwall, Conn., USA; one *s. Educ:* King Edward VII Sch., Sheffield; Queen's Coll., Oxford (Hastings Scholar, Taberdar, University Sen. Research Student); 1st Class Final Honour Sch. of Natural Science, 1926; DPhil, 1928; Commonwealth Fund Fellow, Harvard Univ., 1929-31; Senior Science Master, Uppingham Sch., 1932-34. Mem. Ministry of Agriculture Cttee on demand for Agricultural Graduates. *Publications:* The Christian and Education, 1940; Papers in Journal of the Chemical Soc. *Recreation:* mountain walking. *Address:* 14 Wingate Way, Trumpington, Cambridge. *T:* Trumpington 2296.

HUMPHREYS, Arthur Leslie Charles, CBE 1970; Director: ICL Ltd (Managing Director, 1968-72; Deputy Chairman, 1972-77); Data Recording Instrument Co. Ltd, since 1976; Cambridge Instrument Co. Ltd, since 1977; *b* 8 Jan. 1917; *s* of late Percy Stewart Humphreys and late Louise (*née* Weston); *m* 1st, 1943, Marjorie Irene Murphy-Jones (decd); two *s* one *d*; 2nd, 1975, Audrey Norah Urquhart (*née* Dunningham). *Educ:* Catford Grammar Sch.; Administrative Staff Coll., Henley. International Computers & Tabulators Ltd: Dir 1963; Dep. Man. Dir 1964; Man. Dir 1967. *Recreations:* table tennis, bridge, music. *Address:* 5 Islehurst Close, Summer Hill, Chislehurst, Kent BR7 5QU. *T:* 01-467 9474.

HUMPHREYS, Prof. Arthur Raleigh; Professor of English, University of Leicester, 1947-76; *b* 28 March 1911; *s* of William Ernest Humphreys and Lois (*née* Rainforth); *m* 1947, Kathryn Jane, *d* of James and Jessie Currie, Drumadoon, Isle of Arran. *Educ:* Grammar Sch., Wallasey, Ches; St Catharine's Coll., Cambridge; Harvard Univ., USA. Charles Oldham Shakespeare Schol., Cambridge, 1932; BA (Cambridge), 1933, MA 1936; Commonwealth Fund Fellow, Harvard, 1933-35; AM

(Harvard), 1935. Supervisor in English, Cambridge Univ., 1935-37; Lectr in English, Liverpool Univ., 1937-46. Served War of 1939-45, RAF Intelligence, 1940-42 (Flying Officer); British Council Lecturer in English, Istanbul Univ., 1942-45. Fellow Folger Shakespeare Library, Washington, DC, 1960, 1961, 1964; Vis. Fellow, All Souls Coll., Oxford, 1966. *Publications:* William Shenstone, 1937; The Augustan World, 1954; Steele, Addison, and their Periodical Essays, 1959; (ed) Henry IV, Part I, 1960, Part II, 1966; Melville, 1962; (ed) Joseph Andrews, 1962; (ed) Tom Jones, 1962; (ed) Amelia, 1963; (ed) Jonathan Wild, 1964; (ed) Melville's White-Jacket, 1966; Shakespeare, Richard II, 1967; (ed) Henry V, 1968; (ed) Henry VIII, 1971; Shakespeare, Merchant of Venice, 1973; contrib: From Dryden to Johnson (ed B. Ford), 1957; Alexander Pope (ed P. Dixon), 1972; Shakespeare's Art (ed M. Crane), 1973; Shakespeare: Select Bibliographical Guides (ed S. Wells), 1973, and to learned journals. *Address:* 144 Victoria Park Road, Leicester LE2 1XD. *T:* Leicester 705118.

HUMPHREYS, Christmas; *see* Humphreys, T. C.

HUMPHREYS, David Colin, CMG 1977; Assistant Under Secretary of State (Naval Staff), Ministry of Defence, since 1977; *b* 23 April 1925; *s* of Charles Roland Lloyd Humphreys and Bethia Joan (*née* Bowie); *m* 1952, Jill Allison (*née* Cranmer); two *s* one *d*. *Educ:* Eton Coll. (King's Scholar); King's Coll., Cambridge (MA). Air Min., 1949; Private Sec. to Sec. of State for Air, 1959-60; Counsellor, UK Delegn to NATO, 1960-63; Air Force Dept, 1963-69; IDC 1970; Dir, Defence Policy Staff, 1971-72; Asst Sec. Gen. (Defence Planning and Policy), NATO, 1972-76. *Address:* Rivendell, North Drive, Virginia Water, Surrey. *T:* Wentworth 2130.

HUMPHREYS, Emyr Owen; Author; *b* 15 April 1919; *s* of William and Sarah Rosina Humphreys, Prestatyn, Flints; *m* 1946, Elinor Myfanwy, *d* of Rev. Griffith Jones, Bontnewydd, Caerns; three *s* one *d*. *Educ:* University Coll., Aberystwyth; University Coll., Bangor. Gregynog Arts Fellow, 1974-75. *Publications:* The Little Kingdom, 1946; The Voice of a Stranger, 1949; A Change of Heart, 1951; Hear and Forgive, 1952 (Somerset Maugham Award, 1953); A Man's Estate, 1955; The Italian Wife, 1957; Y Tri Llais, 1958; A Toy Epic, 1958 (Hawthornden Prize, 1959); The Gift, 1963; Outside the House of Baal, 1965; Natives, 1968; Ancestor Worship, 1970; National Winner, 1971 (Welsh Arts Council Prize, 1972); Flesh and Blood, 1974; Landscapes, 1976. *Recreations:* rural pursuits. *Address:* 13 Fordd Llangors, Cyncoed, Caerdydd CF2 6PF.

HUMPHREYS, Maj.-Gen. George Charles, CB 1952; CBE 1948 (OBE 1945); *b* 5 Oct. 1899; *s* of late George Humphreys, formerly of Croft House, Croft-on-Tees, Co. Durham, and Caroline Huddart; *m* 1931, Doris Isabelle, *d* of late A. B. Baines, Shanghai; no *c*. *Educ:* Giggleswick Sch., Yorks; RMC Sandhurst. 2nd Lieut Royal Northumberland Fusiliers, 1918; Lieut 1920; Capt. 1930; Bt-Major, Major 1938; Lieut-Col 1946; Col 1947; Brig. 1951; Maj.-Gen, 1952. Served with 2nd Bn Royal Northumberland Fusiliers, Iraq, India and China, 1919-31, Adjt 1925-28 (Iraq medal and clasp, 1920); Bde Major, E Lancs and Border TA Bde, 1935-37; GSO2 Public Relations, War Office, 1938-39; War of 1939-45, in UK and Italy; GSO1 War Office, 1939-40; successively (Jan. 1941-May 1946), AA and QMG 55th Inf. Div., 1st and 3rd Armd Gps, 79th Armd Div., Col (Q) ops War Office, Col A/Q (BUCO) 21 Army Gp, Col A/Q, 1944-46; Dep. Chief Mil. Div. (Brig.), 1946, Allied Commn for Austria; Brig. i/c Admin Burma Comd, 1946-48; BGS, HQ Scottish Comd, 1948-51; Maj.-Gen. Adminstration, GHQ Middle East Land Forces, 1951-54; Military Adviser to Contractors for Canal Base (War Office, July 1954-31 May 1955); retired from Army, June 1955, and appointed General Manager, Suez Contractors Management Co. Ltd; appointed Chief Executive to Governing Body of Suez Contractors (Services) Ltd, Jan. 1956 until Liquidation of Suez enterprise, July 1957; Chief Organizer, Dollar Exports Council Conference, 1958. *Recreations:* reading, travel and shooting. *Address:* Lauriston Cottage, Old Green Lane, Camberley, Surrey. *T:* Camberley 21078.

HUMPHREYS, John Henry; Chairman, Industrial Tribunals (Ashford, Kent), since 1976; Legal Officer, Law Commission, since 1973; *b* 28 Feb. 1917; British; *m* 1939, Helen Mary Markbreiter; one *s* one *d*. *Educ:* Cranleigh School. Solicitor. Served with Co. of London Yeomanry, and Northampton Yeomanry, 1939-47; Treasury Solicitor Dept, 1947-73. *Recreations:* sailing, golf, gardening. *Address:* Gate House Cottage, Sandown Road, Sandwich, Kent. *Club:* Prince's (Sandwich).

HUMPHREYS, Sir Kenneth (Owens), Kt 1976; company director, Australia; *b* 22 Aug. 1918; *s* of Arthur Gerald Humphreys and Olive Stephens Humphreys *m* 1973, Gladys Mary Hill; two *s*. *Educ:* Sydney Technical High Sch. Accounting profession, then RAAF to 1945. Gen. Manager and Dir, Clyde Industries Ltd, 1948-55; Partner, Irish Young & Outhwaite, 1955-74; Chairman: Commonwealth Industrial Gases Ltd; International Pacific Corp. Ltd; United Telecasters Syd. Ltd; Director: Qantas Airways Ltd; Aust. Reinsurance Co. Ltd; Commercial Bank of Aust. Ltd. Executive Member: Australia-Japan Business Co-operation Cttee; Mem. Council, Univ. of New England. *Recreation:* cattle grazing. *Address:* 2 Cabarita Road, Avalon, NSW 2107, Australia. *T:* 918 2373. *Clubs:* Australian, Union (Sydney); Commonwealth (Canberra).

HUMPHREYS, Kenneth William, BLitt, MA, PhD; FLA; Librarian, European University Institute, Florence, since 1975; *b* 4 Dec. 1916; *s* of Joseph Maxmillian Humphreys and Bessie Benfield; *m* 1939, Margaret, *d* of Reginald F. Hill and Dorothy Lucas; two *s*. *Educ:* Southfield Sch., Oxford; St Catherine's Coll., Oxford. Library Asst, All Souls Coll., Oxford, 1933-36; Asst, Bodleian Library, 1936-50; Dep. Librarian, Brotherton Library, University of Leeds, 1950-52; Librarian, Univ. of Birmingham, 1952-75. Hon. Lectr in Palaeography, University of Leeds, 1950-52; Hon. Lectr in Palaeography, University of Birmingham, 1952-75; Hon. Sec., Standing Conf. of Nat. and University Libraries, 1954-69, Vice-Chm., 1969-71, Chm. 1971-73; Mem. Library Adv. Council for England, 1966-71; Mem. Council, Library Assoc., 1964-75, Chm. Council 1973; Chm. Exec. Cttee, West Midlands Regional Library Bureau, 1963-75; Chairman: Jt Standing Conf. and Cttee on Library Cooperation, 1965-75; Nat. Cttee on Regional Library Cooperation, 1970-75; Mem. Comité International de Paléographie, and Colloque International de Paléographie, 1955-; Pres., Nat. and University Libraries Section, Internat. Fedn of Library Assocs, 1968-69, Pres., University Libraries Sub-Section, 1967-73; Pres., Ligue des Bibliothèques Européennes de Recherche. Editor: Studies in the History of Libraries and Librarianship; Liber Bulletin; Associate Editor, Libri; Jt Editor, Series of Reproductions of Medieval and Renaissance Texts. Hon. LittD Dublin (Trinity Coll.), 1967. *Publications:* The Book Provisions of the Medieval Friars, 1964; The Medieval Library of the Carmelites at Florence, 1964; The Library of the Franciscans of the Convent of St Antony, Padua at the Beginning of the fifteenth century, 1966; The Library of the Franciscans of Siena in the Fifteenth Century, 1977; articles in library periodicals. *Recreation:* collection of manuscripts. *Address:* La Cicala, via delle Palazzine 10, Fiesole, Italy. *T:* Florence 59 89 46. *Clubs:* Athenæum; Kildare Street and University (Dublin).

HUMPHREYS, Sir Myles; *see* Humphreys, Sir R. E. M.

HUMPHREYS, Sir Olliver (William), Kt 1968; CBE 1957; BSc, FInstP, CEng, FIEE, FRAeS; *b* 4 Sept. 1902; *s* of late Rev. J. Willis Humphreys, Bath; *m* 1933, Muriel Mary Hawkins. *Educ:* Caterham Sch.; University Coll., London. Joined staff GEC Research Labs, 1925, Dir, 1949-61; Director 1953, Vice-Chm., 1963-67, GEC Ltd; Chm. all GEC Electronics and Telecommunications subsidiaries, 1961-66 and GEC (Research) Ltd, 1961-67. Mem. Bd, Inst. Physics, 1951-63 (Pres., 1956-58); Mem. Coun., IEE, 1952-55 (Vice-Pres., 1959-63; Pres., 1964-65); Faraday Lectr, 1953-54. Mem., BoT Cttee on Organisation and Constitution of BSI, 1949-50; Chm., BSI Telecommunications Industry Standards Cttee, 1951-63 (Mem. Gen. Coun., 1953-56; Mem. Exec. Cttee, 1953-60); Chm., Internat. Special Cttee on Radio Interference (CISPR), 1953-61; Chm., Electrical Res. Assoc., 1958-61; Chm., DSIR Radio Res. Bd, 1954-62; Pres., Electronic Engrg Assoc., 1962-64; Founder Chm., Conf. of Electronics Industry, 1963-67; Mem., Nat. ERC, 1963-67. Fellow UCL, 1963. Liveryman, Worshipful Co. of Makers of Playing Cards. *Publications:* various technical and scientific papers in proceedings of learned societies. *Recreations:* travel, walking, reading. *Address:* The Penthouse, Teak Close, Branksome Park, Poole, Dorset BH13 6JH. *T:* Bournemouth 766195. *Club:* Royal Motor Yacht.

HUMPHREYS, Sir (Raymond Evelyn) Myles, Kt 1977; JP; Alderman; The Rt Hon. the Lord Mayor of Belfast, since 1975; *b* 24 March 1925; *s* of Raymond and May Humphreys; *m* 1963, Joan Tate; two *s*. *Educ:* Skegoniel Primary Sch.; Londonderry High Sch.; Belfast Royal Acad. Research Engr, NI Transport Bd, 1946-55; Transport Manager, Nestle's Food Products (NI) Ltd, 1955-59; Director: Walter Alexander (Belfast) Ltd, 1959-; Quick Service Stations Ltd, 1971-; Member of Board: Ulster Transport Authority, 1966-69; NI Transport Holding Co. Ltd, 1967-74; Chm., NI Railways Co. Ltd, 1966-. Mem., Belfast City Council, 1964-; Chm., Belfast Corp. Housing Cttee, 1966-69; High Sheriff of Belfast, 1969; Dep. Lord Mayor, 1970. Chm., NI

Police Authority, Royal Ulster Constabulary, 1976-. Mem., Nat. Exec. Cttee of Nat. Housing and Town Planning Council, Nat. Vice-Chm., 1970-; Past Chairman: Bd of Visitors, HM Prison, Belfast; Chm., Bd of Management, Dunlambert Secondary Sch. Past-Pres., Belfast Junior Chamber of Commerce; Chairman: City Council Planning Cttee, 1973-75; City Council Town Planning and Environmental Health Cttee, 1973-75. Mem. Council, NI Chamber of Commerce and Industry; Chm., Ulster Tourist Develt Assoc.; Senator, Junior Chamber Internat.; Belfast Harbour Comr; Member: Senate, QUB; NI Housing Assoc. Ltd (Chm.); NI Tourist Bd; Council, Queen's Silver Jubilee Appeal. District Transport Officer, St John Ambulance Brigade, 1946-66. Freeman of City of London, 1976. MIRTE; OStJ. *Address:* Mylestone, Chichester Park, Belfast BT15 5DW. *T:* Belfast 771518. *Clubs:* Ulster Reform, Cliftonville Golf (both Belfast).

HUMPHREYS, Prof. Robert Arthur, OBE 1946; MA, PhD Cantab; Director, Institute of Latin-American Studies, University of London, 1965-74; Professor of Latin-American History in University of London, 1948-74, now Emeritus; *b* 6 June 1907; *s* of late Robert Humphreys and Helen Marion Bavin Lincoln; *m* 1946, Elisabeth, *er d* of late Sir Bernard Pares, KBE, DCL. *Educ:* Lincoln Sch.; Peterhouse, Cambridge (Scholar). Commonwealth Fund Fellow, Univ. of Michigan, 1930-32. Asst Lectr in American History, UCL, 1932, Lectr 1935; Reader in American History in Univ. of London, 1942-48; Prof. of Latin-American History, UCL, 1948-70. Research Dept, FO, 1939-45. Mem., UGC Cttee on Latin American Studies, 1962-64; Chairman: Cttee on Library Resources, Univ. of London, 1969-71; Management Cttee, Inst of Archæology, 1975-; Mem. Adv. Cttee, British Library Reference Div., 1975-. Governor, SOAS, 1965-. Pres., RHistS, 1964-68 (Hon. Vice-Pres., 1968). Lectures: Enid Muir Meml, Univ. of Newcastle upon Tyne, 1962; Creighton, Univ. of London, 1964; Raleigh, Brit. Acad., 1965. Corresp. Member: Argentine Acad. of History; Instituto Histórico e Geográfico Brasileiro; Academia Chilena de la Historia; Sociedad Chilena de Historia y Geografia; Instituto Ecuatoriano de Ciencias Naturales; Sociedad Peruana de Historia; Instituto Histórico y Geográfico del Uruguay; Academia Nacional de la Historia, Venezuela. Hon. DLitt: Newcastle, 1966; Nottingham, 1972; Hon. LittD Liverpool, 1972; DUniv Essex, 1973. Comdr, Order of Rio Branco, Brazil, 1972. Machado de Assis Medal, Academia Brasileira de Letras, 1974. *Publications:* British Consular Reports on the Trade and Politics of Latin America, 1940; The Evolution of Modern Latin America, 1946; Liberation in South America, 1806-1827, 1952; Latin American History: A Guide to the Literature in English, 1958; The Diplomatic History of British Honduras, 1638-1901, 1961; (with G. S. Graham), The Navy and South America, 1807-1823 (Navy Records Soc.), 1962; (with J. Lynch) The Origins of the Latin American Revolutions, 1808-1826, 1965; Tradition and Revolt in Latin America and other Essays, 1969; The Detached Recollections of General D. F. O'Leary, 1969; The Royal Historical Society, 1868-1968, 1969; Co-edited: (with A. D. Momigliano) Byzantine Studies and Other Essays by K. H. Baynes, 1955; (with Elizabeth Humphreys) The Historian's Business and Other Essays by Richard Pares, 1961; contrib. to The New Cambridge Modern History, vols VIII, IX and X. *Address:* 13 St Paul's Place, Canonbury, N1 2QE. *T:* 01-226 8930.

HUMPHREYS, (Travers) Christmas, QC 1959; a Circuit Judge (formerly an Additional Judge, Central Criminal Court), 1968-76; *b* London, 1901; *o* surv. *s* of late Rt Hon. Sir Travers Humphreys, PC; *m* 1927, Aileen Maude (*d* 1975), *d* of Dr Charles Irvine and Alice Faulkner of Escrick, Yorks and Tunbridge Wells. *Educ:* Malvern Coll.; Trinity Hall, Cambridge (MA, LLB). Called to the Bar, Inner Temple, 1924; Bencher, 1955. Junior Counsel to Treasury for certain Appeals, 1932; Junior Counsel to Treasury at Central Criminal Court, 1934; Recorder of: Deal, 1942-56; Guildford, 1956-68; Deputy Chairman: E Kent QS, 1947-71; Co. of Kent QS, 1962-71. Senior Prosecuting Counsel to the Crown at the Central Criminal Court, 1950-59; a Commissioner, 1962-68. Founding Pres. of Buddhist Lodge, London, 1924 (now Buddhist Society); Past Pres. The Shakespearean Authorship Soc.; Joint Vice-Chm. Royal India, Pakistan and Ceylon Society; a Vice-Pres. Tibet Soc., 1962. *Publications:* The Great Pearl Robbery of 1913, 1928; What is Buddhism?, 1928, and Concentration and Meditation, 1935; The Development of Buddhism in England, 1937; Studies in the Middle Way, 1940; Poems of Peace and War, 1941; Seagulls, and other Poems, 1942; Karma and Rebirth, 1943; Shadows and other Poems, 1945; Walk On, 1947; Via Tokyo, 1948; Zen Buddhism, 1949; Buddhism (Pelican books); The Way of Action, 1960; Zen Comes West, 1960; The Wisdom of Buddhism, 1960; Poems I Remember, 1960; A Popular Dictionary of Buddhism, 1962; Zen, A Way of Life,

1962; Sixty Years of Buddhism in England, 1968; The Buddhist Way of Life, 1969; Buddhist Poems, 1971; A Western Approach to Zen, 1972; Exploring Buddhism, 1974; The Search Within, 1977; pamphlets, articles, etc. *Recreations:* music, entertaining; Eastern philosophy and Chinese Art. *Address:* 58 Marlborough Place, NW8 0PL. *T:* 01-624 4987.

HUMPHREYS-DAVIES, (George) Peter, CB 1953; Deputy Secretary, Ministry of Agriculture, Fisheries and Food, 1960-67; *b* 23 June 1909; *e s* of late J. W. S. Humphreys-Davies, Southfields, Eastbourne; *m* 1935, Barbara, *d* of late Lieut-Col F. G. Crompton, White Court, Alfriston, Sussex; two *s* one *d*. *Educ:* Sherborne; New Coll., Oxford. Craven Scholar, 1931. Asst Principal, Admiralty, 1932; HM Treasury, 1934; Private Sec. to Prime Ministers, 1936-38; Under-Sec., HM Treasury, 1949-56; Deputy Sec., Ministry of Supply, 1956-60; Directing Staff, Imperial Defence Coll., 1954. *Address:* Weyhurst Farm, Rudgwick, Sussex. *T:* Rudgwick 2221.

HUMPHRIES, George James, CMG 1965; OBE 1954; *b* 23 April 1900. *Educ:* St James Sch., Tyresham; Magdalen Coll. Sch., Brackley; Reading Univ. Served War, 1939-46, Lieut-Col. Surveyor, Nigeria, 1928; Sen., 1945; Deputy Dir, Overseas Surveys, 1946; Dir and Surveys Adviser, Dept of Technical Co-operation, 1963; Dir and Surveys Adviser to Min. of Overseas Development, 1964. *Address:* Greenacre, Heath House Road, Worplesdon Hill, Woking, Surrey.

HUMPHRIES, Gerard William; barrister at law; a Recorder of the Crown Court, since 1974; a Chairman of the Medical Appeals Tribunal, since 1976; *b* 13 Dec. 1928; *s* of John Alfred Humphries and Marie Frances Humphries (*née* Whitwell), Barrow-in-Furness; *m* 1957, Margaret Valerie, *o d* of late W. W. Gelderd and of Margaret Gelderd (*née* Bell), Ulverston; four *s* one *d*. *Educ:* St Bede's Coll., Manchester; Manchester Univ. (LLB Hons). Called to Bar, Middle Temple, 1952; admitted to Northern Circuit, 1954; Asst Recorder of Salford, 1969-71. *Recreations:* tennis, squash, golf, music, caravanning. *Address:* 1 Dean's Court, Crown Square, Manchester M3 3JL. *T:* 061-834 4097/9487. *Club:* Northern Lawn Tennis.

HUMPHRIES, John Anthony Charles; Chairman, Water Space Amenity Commission, since 1973; *b* 15 June 1925; *s* of Charles Humphries; *m* 1951, Olga June, *d* of Dr Geoffrey Duckworth, MRCP; four *d*. *Educ:* Fettes; Peterhouse, Cambridge (1st Law). Served War, RNVR, 1943-46. Solicitor (Hons), 1951. Chm., Inland Waterways Assoc., 1970 (Vice-Pres., 1973); Mem. Inland Waterways Amenity Adv. Council, 1971; Adviser to HM Govt on amenity use of water space, 1972; Mem. Nat. Water Council, 1973. *Recreations:* inland waters, gardening. *Address:* 21 Parkside, Wimbledon, SW19. *T:* 01-946 3764. *Clubs:* RNVR, City.

HUMPIDGE, Kenneth Palmer, CMG 1957; *b* 18 Nov. 1902; *s* of James Dickerson Humpidge, Stroud; *m* 1938, Jill Mary Russell, *d* of Russell Pountney, Bristol; two *d*. *Educ:* Wycliffe Coll.; Univ. of Bristol. BSc (Engineering). Public Works Dept, Nigeria, 1926; Director of Public Works, Northern Region, Nigeria, 1948-54; Director of Federal Public Works, 1954-57; Min. of Transport, Nottingham and Cheltenham, 1958-69. FICE. *Address:* Corner Walls, Amberley, Stroud, Glos. *T:* Amberley 3212.

HUNLOKE, Henry, TD 1946; Lt-Col, Royal Wiltshire Yeomanry; *b* 1906; *o s* of late Major Sir Philip Hunloke, GCVO; *m* 1929, Lady Anne Cavendish (who obtained a divorce, 1945), *d* of 9th Duke of Devonshire, KG; two *s* one *d*; *m* 1945, Virginia Clive (who obtained a divorce, 1972); one *d* (and one *d* decd); *m* 1972, Ruth Holdsworth. MP (U) Western Div. of Derbyshire, 1938-44. Served War of 1939-45 in Middle East (despatches). *Address:* 267 The Green, East Grafton, near Marlborough, Wilts.

HUNN, Sir Jack (Kent), Kt 1976; CMG 1964; LLM; Retired as Secretary of Defence, New Zealand (1963-66); *b* 24 Aug. 1906; *m* 1932, Dorothy Murray; two *s*. *Educ:* Wairarapa Coll.; Auckland Univ. Public Trust Office, 1924-46; Actg Sec. of Justice, 1950; Public Service Comr, 1954-61; Actg Sec. of Internal Affairs and Dir of Civil Defence, 1959; Sec. for Maori Affairs and Maori Trustee, 1960-63. Reviewed Cook Islands Public Service, 1949 and 1954; Mem. NZ delegn to Duke of Edinburgh's Conf, 1956; Mem. UN Salary Review Cttee, 1956; reviewed organisation of South Pacific Commn, Noumea and Sydney, 1957, and of SEATO, Bangkok, 1959. Chairman: Wildlife Commission of Inquiry, 1968; Fire Safety Inquiry, 1969; Fire Service Council, 1973; Fire Service Commn, 1974. *Publication:* Hunn Report on Maori Affairs, 1960. *Address:* 17 Kereru Street, Waikanae, Wellington, New Zealand. *T:* 5033.

HUNNINGS, Dr Gordon; Professor and Head of the Department of Philosophy, University of Natal, Pietermaritzburg, since 1977; *b* 8 March 1926; *s* of late William Butters Hunnings and late Ellen Hunnings (*née* Robinson); *m* 1947, Jean Mary Hunnings (*née* Marland); one *s*. *Educ:* Christie Hospital & Holt Radium Inst., Manchester (MSRT); Univ. of Bristol (BA); University Coll., London (PhD). Radium Curator, Hogarth Radiotherapy Centre, Nottingham, 1948-61; Lectr in Philosophy, Univ. of Khartoum, 1966-69; Sen. Lectr in Philosophy, Univ. of Malaŵi, 1969-70; Prof. of Philosophy, Univ. of Malaŵi, 1970-73; Vice-Chancellor, Univ. of Malaŵi, 1973-77. *Publications:* various papers in sci. and philos. jls. *Recreations:* theology, music, films. *Address:* Department of Philosophy, University of Natal, PO Box 375, Pietermaritzburg, Republic of South Africa. *T:* 29531.

HUNSDON, Baron; *see* Aldenham, Baron.

HUNT; *see* Crowther-Hunt.

HUNT, family name of **Barons Hunt** and **Hunt of Fawley.**

HUNT, Baron, *cr* 1966, of Llanvair Waterdine (Life Peer); **(Henry Cecil) John Hunt;** Kt 1953; CBE 1945; DSO 1944; President: National Association of Probation Officers, since 1974; Royal Geographical Society, since 1977; *b* 22 June 1910; *s* of late Capt. C. E. Hunt, MC, IA, and E. H. Hunt (*née* Crookshank); *m* 1936, Joy Mowbray-Green; four *d*. *Educ:* Marlborough Coll.; RMC, Sandhurst. Commissioned King's Royal Rifle Corps, 1930; seconded to Indian Police, 1934-35 and 1938-40 (Indian Police Medal, 1940). War of 1939-45: Comd 11th Bn KRRC, 1944; Comd 11th Indian Inf. Bde, 1944-46. Staff Coll., 1946; Joint Services Staff Coll., 1949; GSO 1, Jt Planning Staffs, MELF, 1946-48; Western Europe C's-in-C Cttee, 1950-51; Allied Land Forces, Central Europe, 1951-52; Col, Gen. Staff, HQ I (British) Corps, 1952; Asst Comdt, The Staff Coll., 1953-56; retired, 1956; Hon. Brigadier. Dir, Duke of Edinburgh's Award Scheme, 1956-66. Rector, Aberdeen Univ., 1963-66. Personal Adviser to Prime Minister during Nigerian Civil War, 1968-70. Chairman: Parole Bd for England and Wales, 1967-74; Adv. Cttee on Police in N Ireland, 1969; Pres., Council for Volunteers Overseas, 1968-74; Mem., Royal Commn on the Press, 1974-77. Leader, British Expedition to Mount Everest, 1952-53. President: The Alpine Club, 1956-58; Climbers' Club, 1963-66; British Mountaineering Council, 1965-68; The National Ski Fedn, 1968-72. Hon. FRGS. Order 1st Class Gurkha Right Hand, 1953; Indian Everest Medal, 1953; Hubbard Medal (US), 1954; Founder's Medal, RGS, 1954; Lawrence Memorial Medal, RCAS, 1954; Hon. DCL Durham 1954; Hon. LLD: Aberdeen 1954; London 1954; City 1976. *Publications:* The Ascent of Everest, 1953; Our Everest Adventure, 1954; (with C. Brasher) The Red Snows, 1959. *Recreations:* mountaineering, ski-ing. *Address:* Highway Cottage, Aston, Henley-on-Thames. *Clubs:* Alpine, Ski Club of Great Britain.
See also Hugh Hunt.

HUNT OF FAWLEY, Baron *cr* 1973 (Life Peer), of Fawley in the County of Buckingham; **John Henderson Hunt;** CBE 1970; MA, DM Oxon, FRCP, FRCS, FRCGP; President, Royal College of General Practitioners, 1967-70; Consulting Physician, St Dunstan's, 1948-66; PMO, Provident Mutual Life Assurance Association, since 1947; Governor: Charterhouse School; Sutton's Hospital, Old Charterhouse; National Hospital, Queen Square; *b* 3 July 1905; *s* of late Edmund Henderson Hunt, MCh, FRCS, and Laura Mary Buckingham; *m* 1941, Elisabeth Ernestine, *d* of Norman Evill, FRIBA; two *s* two *d*. (and one *s* decd). *Educ:* Charterhouse School; Balliol College, Oxford; St Bartholomew's Hospital. Theodore Williams Scholar in Physiology, Oxford Univ., 1926; Radcliffe Scholar in Pharmacology, 1928. RAF Medical Service, 1940-45 (Wing Comdr). Hon. Cons. in Gen. Practice, RAF; President: Hunterian Soc., 1953; Gen. Practice Section, Royal Soc. Med., 1956; Harveian Soc., 1970; Chelsea Clinical Soc., 1971; Med. Soc. London, 1973-74; Soc. of Chiropodists, 1974; Vice-Pres. Brit. Med. Students' Assoc., 1956-; Hon. Sec. Council, Coll. of Gen. Practitioners, 1952-67; Med. Soc. of London, 1964-65; Mem. Council: RCS (co-opted), 1957-61; Med. Protection Soc., 1948-69; St Dunstan's, 1966-; Member: General Advisory Council, BBC, 1958-66; Med. Services Review Cttee, 1958-61; Med. Commn on Accident Prevention, 1967-. Hon. Fellow, Aust. Coll. Gen. Practitioners; Amer. Acad. of Family Physicians; Hon. Mem. and Victor Johnston Medallist, Coll. of Family Physicians of Canada. Lloyd Roberts Lecturer (Manchester), 1956; Albert Wander Lectr (RSM), 1968; Paul Hopkins Memorial Orator (Brisbane), 1969; James MacKenzie Lectr, 1972. Late House Surgeon, and Chief Assistant Medical Professorial Unit, St Bart's Hosp. and House Physician National

Hosp. Queen Square. *Publications:* (ed) Accident Prevention and Life Saving, 1965; various papers in medical journals; chapter on Raynaud's Phenomenon, in British Encyclopædia of Medical Practice, 1938 and 1948; chapter on Peripheral Vascular Disease, in Early Diagnosis, by Henry Miller, 1959. *Recreation:* gardening. *Address:* 82 Sloane Street, SW1. *T:* 01-245 9333; 26 Cadogan Place, SW1. *T:* 01-235 5566. *Clubs:* Royal Air Force, Caledonian, MCC.

HUNT, Arthur James, OBE 1971; FRTPI, FRICS; Chief Reporter for Public Inquiries, Scottish Office, since 1974; *b* 18 Nov. 1915; *s* of Edward Henry and Norah Hunt; *m* 1946, Fanny Betty Bacon; one *s* three *d*. *Educ:* Tauntons Sch., Southampton. Ordnance Survey, 1938-44; Planning Officer with West Sussex, Kent and Bucks County Councils, 1944-48; Asst County Planning Officer, East Sussex CC, 1948-52; Town Planning Officer, City of Durban, SA, 1953-61; Sen. and Principal Planning Inspector, Min. of Housing and Local Govt, 1961-68; Mem., Roskill Commn on the Third London Airport, 1968-70; Superintending Inspector, Dept of the Environment, 1971-74. *Recreations:* sailing, gardening, caravan touring. *Address:* 13 Laverockdale Loan, Colinton, Edinburgh EH13 0EZ. *T:* 031-441 4854.

HUNT, David James Fletcher, MBE 1973; MP (C) Wirral, since March 1976; *b* 21 May 1942; *s* of Alan Nathaniel Hunt and Jessie Edna Ellis Northrop Hunt; *m* 1973, Patricia Margery (*née* Orchard); one *s* one *d*. *Educ:* Liverpool Coll.; Montpellier Univ.; Bristol Univ. (LLB); Guildford Coll. of Law. Solicitor of Supreme Court of Judicature, admitted 1968. Chm., Bristol Univ. Conservatives, 1964-65; Nat. Vice-Chm., FUCUA, 1965-66; Chm., Bristol City CPC, 1965-68; Nat. Vice-Chm., YCNAC, 1967-69; Chm., Bristol Fedn of YCs, 1970-71; Chm., British Youth Council, 1971-74; Nat. YC Chm., 1972-73; Vice-Chm., Nat. Union of Cons. and Unionist Assocs, 1974-76. Contested (C) Bristol South, 1970, Kingswood, 1974. Member: South Western Economic Planning Council, 1972-76; Adv. Cttee on Pop Festivals. *Recreations:* cricket, walking. *Address:* 23 Cable Road, Hoylake, Wirral. *T:* 051-632 4033; 14 Cowley Street, Westminster, SW1. *T:* 01-222 7149.

HUNT, Sir David (Wathen Stather), KCMG 1963 (CMG 1959); OBE 1943; Chairman, Board of Governors, Commonwealth Institute, since 1974; *b* 25 Sept. 1913; *s* of late Canon B. P. W. Stather Hunt, DD, and late Elizabeth Milner; *m* 1st, 1948, Pamela Muriel Medawar; two *s*; 2nd, 1968, Iro Myrianthousi. *Educ:* St Lawrence Coll.; Wadham Coll., Oxford. 1st Class Hon. Mods. 1934; 1st Class Lit. Hum. 1936; Thomas Whitcombe Greene Prize, 1936; Diploma in Classical Archæology, 1937; Fellow of Magdalen Coll., 1937. Served 1st Bn Welch Regt and General Staff in Middle East, Balkans, North Africa, Sicily, Italy, 1940-46 (despatches 3 times, OBE, US Bronze Star); GSO1 18th Army Group, 1943; 15th Army Group, 1943-45; Col General Staff, Allied Force HQ, 1945-46; attached staff Governor-General Canada, 1946-47; released and granted hon. rank of Colonel, 1947. Principal, Dominions Office, 1947; 1st Secretary, Pretoria, 1948-49; Private Secretary to Prime Minister (Mr Attlee), 1950-51, (Mr Churchill) 1951-52; Asst Secretary, 1952; Deputy High Commissioner for UK, Lahore, 1954-56; Head of Central African Dept, Commonwealth Relations Office, 1956-59; Asst Under Secretary of State, Commonwealth Relations Office, 1959-60; accompanied the Prime Minister as an Adviser, on African tour, Jan.-Feb. 1960; Dep. High Comr for the UK in Lagos, Fedn of Nigeria, Oct. 1960-62; High Comr in Uganda, 1962-65; in Cyprus, 1965-67; in Nigeria, 1967-69; Ambassador to Brazil, 1969-73. Dep. Chm., Exim Credit Management and Consultants, 1974-. Mem. Appts Commn, Press Council, 1977-. Corresp. Mem., Brazilian Acad. of Arts, 1972. US Bronze Star 1945. *Publications:* A Don at War, 1966; On the Spot, 1975; articles in Annual of British School of Archæology at Athens and Journal of Hellenic Studies. *Recreations:* golf, history and sailing. *Address:* 16-18 Hatton Garden, EC1N 8AT. *T:* 01-405 6403; Old Place, East Wing, Lindfield, West Sussex RH16 2HU. *T:* Lindfield 2298. *Clubs:* Athenæum; Pen Clube do Brazil.

HUNT, Rear-Adm. Geoffrey Harry C.; *see* Carew Hunt.

HUNT, Col (George) Vivian, OBE 1943; TD 1943; MA 1926; LLB 1928; Senior Partner in Wake Smith and Company, solicitors, Sheffield, retired; *b* 30 July 1905; *er s* of John Edwin Hunt, Crabtree Meadow House, Hope, Derbyshire; *m* 1935, Sylvia Anne, *d* of John Stanley Tyzack, Oakholme House, Sheffield; three *s*. *Educ:* Malvern Coll.; King's Coll., Cambridge (MA, LLB Hons). Commissioned RA (TA) 1926. Lt-Col 1940; invented Hunt Trainer, 1940; took part in North African, Sicilian and Italian campaigns with 78th Infantry Diviision, 1942-44; reconnoitred and laid out original defences North-East of Beja, Tunisia, which subseq. became known as 'Hunt's Gap'; Col 1944; Hon Col 513 LAA Regt RA (TA), 1947-55; retired from TA, 1956. JP for City of Sheffield, 1956-70. *Recreations:* golf, gardening. *Address:* The Lodge, Woodvale Road, Sheffield S10 3EX. *T:* Sheffield 660017. *Club:* Sheffield (Sheffield).

HUNT, Gilbert Adams, CBE 1967; Chairman, Chrysler United Kingdom Ltd (formerly Rootes Motors Ltd), since 1973 (Managing Director, 1967-73, and Chief Executive Officer, 1967-76); *b* Wolverhampton, 29 Dec. 1914; *s* of late Harold William Hunt, MBE, St Helen's, IoW; *m* 1938, Sarah (marr. diss. 1946), *d* of Captain Wadman-Taylor; *m* 1946, Olive Doreen, *d* of late Maurice Martin O'Brien; no *c*; *m* 1975, Diane Rosemary, *d* of Eric O. Cook. *Educ:* Old Hall, Wellington; Malvern Coll., Worcester. Director, High Duty Alloys, Slough, 1950-54; Dir and Gen. Man., High Duty Alloys (Dir, HDA, Canada, Northern Steel Scaffold & Engrg Co., all subsids Hawker Siddeley Gp), 1954-60; Man. Dir, Massey-Ferguson (UK) Ltd; Jt Man. Dir, Massey-Ferguson-Perkins; Dir, Massey-Ferguson Holdings Ltd; Chm. and Man. Dir, Massey-Ferguson (Eire) Ltd; Chm., Massey-Ferguson (Farm Services) Ltd, 1960-67. Chm., Cttee for Industrial Technologies, DTI, 1972-. President: Agricultural Engrs Association Ltd, 1965; The Society of Motor Manufacturers and Traders Ltd, 1972-74. Freeman, City of London, 1968. CEng, CIMechE, FIProdE, MIBF. Hon. DSc Cranfield, 1973. *Recreations:* golfing, sailing. *Address:* 6 Lowndes Square, SW1. *Club:* Royal Thames Yacht.

HUNT, Hugh (Sydney), CBE 1977; MA; Professor of Drama, University of Manchester, 1961-73, now Emeritus; *b* 25 Sept. 1911; *s* of Captain C. E. Hunt, MC, and late Ethel Helen (née Crookshank); *m* 1940, Janet Mary (née Gordon); one *s* one *d*. *Educ:* Marlborough Coll.; Magdalen Coll., Oxford. BA Oxon 1934, MA Oxon 1961. Hon. MA Manchester 1965. Pres. of OUDS, 1933-34; Producer: Maddermarket Theatre, Norwich, 1934; Croydon Repertory and Westminster Theatres, 1934-35; Producer, Abbey Theatre, Dublin, 1935-38; produced The White Steed, Cort Theatre, NY. Entered HM Forces, 1939; served War of 1939-45, with Scots Guards, King's Royal Rifle Corps, and Intelligence Service; demobilised, 1945. Director of Bristol Old Vic Company, 1945-49; Director Old Vic Company, London, 1949-53; Adjudicator Canadian Drama Festival Finals, 1954; Executive Officer, Elizabethan Theatre Trust, Australia, 1955-60; Artistic Dir, Abbey Theatre, Dublin, 1969-71. Produced: The Cherry Orchard, 1948, Love's Labour's Lost, 1949, Hamlet, 1950, New Theatre; Old Vic Seasons, 1951-53: Twelfth Night, Merry Wives of Windsor, Romeo and Juliet, Merchant of Venice, Julius Caesar. Produced The Living Room, New York, 1954; in Australia, Medea, 1955, Twelfth Night, 1956, Hamlet, 1957, Julius Caesar, 1959; The Shaughaun, World Theatre Season, Dublin, 1968; Abbey Theatre Productions include: The Well of the Saints, 1969; The Hostage, 1970; The Morning after Optimism, 1971; Arrah-na-Pogue, 1972; The Silver Tassle, 1972; The Three Sisters, 1973; The Vicar of Wakefield, 1974; Sydney Opera House: Peer Gynt, 1975; The Plough and the Stars, 1977. *Publications:* Old Vic Prefaces; The Director in the Theatre; The Making of Australian Theatre; The Live Theatre; The Revels History of Drama in the English Language, vol. VII, sections 1 and 2; author or co-author of several Irish plays including The Invincibles and In The Train. *Address:* Cae Terfyn, Criccieth, Gwynedd LL52 0SA. *Club:* Garrick.
See also Baron Hunt.

HUNT, Prof. (Jack) Naylor, DSc, MD; FRCP; Professor of Physiology at Baylor College of Medicine, Houston, Texas, since 1977; *b* 29 April 1917; *s* of Charles Frank Hunt and Mary Anne Moss; *m* 1948, Claire, *d* of Sir William Haley, *qv*; no *c*. *Educ:* Royal Masonic School, Bushey; Guy's Hospital Medical School. Resident MO, Hertford British Hosp., Paris, 1940. Temp. Surgeon Lieutenant, RNVR, 1940-45. Dept of Physiology, Guy's Hospital Medical School, 1945-76, Prof. of Physiology, 1962-76. Mem. Senate, Univ. of London, 1974-76. Rockefeller Fellow, 1951; Arris and Gale Lecturer, 1951; Gillson Scholar, 1952. *Publications:* various papers on the alimentary tract. *Address:* Physiology Department, Baylor College of Medicine, Houston, Texas 77030, USA.

HUNT, John Francis, CBE 1964; Under-Secretary and Controller of Supply, Ministry of Health, 1965-68, retired, 1968; *b* 10 Sept. 1906; *s* of late John William Hunt and late Beatrice (née Cass); *m* 1933, Vera Mary (née Jenkins) (*d* 1976); three *s*. *Educ:* Sir John Talbot Grammar Sch., Whitchurch, Shropshire; Liverpool Univ.; London Univ. (External). BSc Liverpool, 1st cl. hons Mathematics, 1928; Derby Scholar, 1928-29; LLB London, 2nd cl. hons (External), 1946. Entered Civil Service (District Audit), 1929; Asst District Auditor, 1929; Sen. Asst 1938; Deputy, 1947; transf. to Accountant-General's Dept, Min. of Health, 1947;

Asst Acct-Gen., 1947; Deputy, 1951; Asst Secretary, 1958; Transf. to Supply Div., 1960. Mem. Surrey CC, Dorking North, 1970-77. *Recreations:* reading, walking. *Address:* Fourways, Reigate Road, Dorking, Surrey. *T:* Dorking 4493. *Club:* Royal Automobile.

HUNT, Sir John (Joseph Benedict), GCB 1977 (KCB 1973; CB 1968); Secretary of the Cabinet, since 1973; *b* 23 Oct. 1919; *er s* of Major Arthur L. Hunt and Daphne Hunt; *m* 1st, 1941, Hon. Magdalen Mary Lister Robinson (*d* 1971), *yr d* of 1st Baron Robinson; two *s* one *d*; 2nd, 1973, Madeleine Frances, *d* of Sir William Hume, CMG, FRCP, and *widow* of Sir John Charles, KCB, FRCP. *Educ:* Downside; Magdalene College, Cambridge (Hon. Fellow, 1977). Served Royal Naval Volunteer Reserve, 1940-46, Lieut; Convoy escort, Western Approaches and in Far East. Home Civil Service, Admin. Class, 1946; Dominions Office, 1946; Priv. Sec. to Parly. Under-Sec., 1947; 2nd Sec., Office of UK High Comr in Ceylon, 1948-50; Principal, 1949; Directing Staff, IDC, 1951-52; 1st Sec., Office of UK High Comr in Canada, 1953-56; Private Secretary to: Sec. of Cabinet and Perm. Sec. to Treasury and Head of Civil Service, 1956-58; Asst Secretary: CRO 1958; Cabinet Office, 1960; HM Treasury, 1962-67, Under-Sec., 1965; Dep. Sec., 1968 and First Civil Service Comr, Civil Service Dept, 1968-71; Third Sec., Treasury, 1971-72; Second Permanent Sec., Cabinet Office, 1972-73. *Recreation:* gardening. *Address:* Cabinet Office, Whitehall, SW1.

HUNT, John Leonard; MP (C) Bromley, Ravensbourne, since 1974 (Bromley, 1964-74); *b* 27 Oct. 1929; *s* of late William John Hunt and of Dora Maud Hunt, Keston, Kent; unmarried. *Educ:* Dulwich Coll. Councillor, Bromley Borough Council, 1953-65; Alderman, Bromley Borough Council, 1961-65; Mayor of Bromley, 1963-64. Contested (C) S Lewisham, Gen. Election, 1959. Chm., All-Party Cttee on UK Citizenship, 1968-; Jt-Chm., British-Caribbean Assoc., 1968-77; Vice-Chm., Indo-British Parly Gp; UK Rep. at Council of Europe and WEU, 1973-77. Vice-Chm., Conservative Greater London Members' Cttee. Mem., BBC Gen. Adv. Council, 1975-. Mem. of London Stock Exchange, 1958-70; Dir, Arthur Wareham Associates Ltd. *Recreations:* foreign travel and good food. *Address:* 94 Park West, Marble Arch, W2. *T:* 01-262 7733.

HUNT, John Maitland, MA, BLitt; Headmaster of Roedean since Jan. 1971; *b* 4 March 1932; *s* of Richard Herbert Alexander Hunt and Eileen Mary Isabelle Hunt (née Witt); *m* 1969, Sarah, *d* of Lt-Gen. Sir Derek Lang, *qv*; two *s*. *Educ:* Radley College; Wadham College, Oxford. BA 1956; BLitt 1959; MA 1960. Assistant Master, Stowe School, 1958-70 (Sixth Form tutor in Geography). *Publications:* various articles on fine arts and architecture. *Recreations:* estate management, fine arts, writing, travel. *Address:* Roedean School, Brighton, East Sussex BN2 5RQ. *T:* Brighton 680791. *Club:* English-Speaking Union.

HUNT, Sir Joseph (Anthony), Kt 1966; MBE 1951; FBIM; Chairman: The Hymatic Engineering Co. Ltd, since 1960 (General Manager, 1938-65); The Hydrovane Compressor Co. Ltd, since 1968 (Director since 1960); Porvair Ltd, since 1969; The Fairey Company Ltd, 1970-75; Huntleigh Group, since 1974; *b* 1 April 1905; *s* of Patrick and Florence Anne Hunt; *m* 2nd, 1960, Esme Jeanne, *d* of Albert Edward Langston; two *s* one *d*. *Educ:* St Gregory's Sch., Farnworth, Lancs; Salford Royal Tech. Coll.; Manchester Coll. of Technology. Dir, Chloride Electrical Storage Co. Ltd,, 1965-73, Dep. Man. Dir, 1969-71, Dir in charge Overseas Ops, Chloride Gp, 1966-71; Chm., Kellogg-American Inc., 1976-; Director: Inmont Corp., USA, 1973-77; Nicholas Mendes and Associates, 1976-; Aston Technical Services, 1976-; Micro Image Technology Ltd, 1976-; Flowtron Aire Ltd, 1976-; Setpoint Ltd, 1976-. Chairman: Economic Planning Council, West Midlands, 1965-67; Hunt Cttee on Intermediate Areas, 1967-69; Pro-Chancellor, Univ. of Aston in Birmingham, 1965-70, Mem. Council, 1971-; Member, Redditch Devel. Corp., 1964-76; Central Training Council, 1964-74; National Advisory Council on Education for Industry and Commerce, 1961-75, Chm., 1967-75; W Midlands Adv. Council for Further Education, 1960-; Pres., British Assoc. for Commercial and Industrial Educn, 1971- (Chm. Exec. Council, 1960-61, Vice-Pres., 1961-71); Vice-Pres., City and Guilds of London Inst., 1971-; Mem. Council, Birmingham Chamber of Commerce, 1956-74. Hon. ACT (Birmingham) 1950. Hon. DSc Aston; Hon. LLD Birmingham. *Publications:* contrib. to Technical Press: on Organisation, Management, Education and Training. *Recreations:* reading, architecture, theatre. *Address:* 16A Ampton Road, Edgbaston, Birmingham B15 2UJ. *T:* 021-455 0594.

HUNT, Prof. Naylor; see Hunt, J. N.

HUNT, Prof. Norman Charles, CBE 1975; Professor of Business Studies, University of Edinburgh, since 1967 (Prof. of Organisation of Industry and Commerce, 1953-66); *b* 6 April 1918; *s* of Charles Hunt and Charlotte (*née* Jackson), Swindon, Wilts; *m* 1942, Lorna Mary, 2nd *d* of Mary and William Arthur Mann, Swindon, Wilts; two *s. Educ:* Commonweal Sch.; Swindon Coll.; University of London (Sir Edward Stern Schol., BCom 1st cl. hons); PhD (Edinburgh). On Staff (Research Dept and Personal Staff of Chief Mechanical Engineer); former GWR Co., 1934-45. Lectr in Organisation of Industry and Commerce, University of Edinburgh, 1946-53; Dir of Studies in Commerce, 1948-53; Dean of Faculty of Social Sciences, 1962-64. Member: Departmental Cttee on Fire Service, 1967-70; Rubber Industry NEDC, 1968-71; UGC, 1969- (Vice-Chm. 1974-76); ODM Working Party on Management Educn and Training in Developing Countries, 1968-69; Bd of Governors (and Chm., Management Develt Cttee), Council for Technical Educn and Training in Overseas Countries, 1971-75; Police Adv. Bd for Scotland, 1971-75. Chairman: R. and R. Clark Ltd, 1967-70; William Thyne Ltd, 1967-70; Director: William Thyne (Holdings) Ltd, 1963-70; William Thyne (Plastics) Ltd, 1967-70. Hon. DLitt Loughborough, 1975. *Publications:* Methods of Wage Payment in British Industry, 1951; (with W. D. Reekie) Management in the Social and Safety Services, 1974; articles in economic and management jls on industrial organisation, industrial relations, and management problems. *Recreations:* photography, motoring, foreign travel. *Address:* 65 Ravelston Dykes Road, Edinburgh EH4 3NU.

HUNT, Gen. Sir Peter (Mervyn), GCB 1973 (KCB 1969; CB 1965); DSO 1945; OBE 1947; Chief of the General Staff, 1973-76; ADC (General) to the Queen, 1973-76; retired; *b* 11 March 1916; *s* of H. V. Hunt, Barrister-at-law; *m* 1940, Anne Stopford (*d* 1966), *d* of Vice-Adm. Hon. Arthur Stopford, CMG; one *s* one *d. Educ:* Wellington Coll.; RMC Sandhurst. Commissioned QO Cameron Highlanders, 1936; commanded 7 Seaforth Highlanders, 1944-45; graduated Command and Gen. Staff Coll., Ft Leavenworth, USA. 1948; Instructor, Staff Coll., Camberley, 1952-55; Instructor, Imperial Defence Coll., 1956-57; commanded 1 Camerons, 1957-60; Comdr 152 (H) Infantry Brigade, TA, 1960-62; Chief of Staff, Scottish Command, 1962-64; GOC, 17 Div., also Comdr, Land Forces, Borneo, and Major-Gen., Bde of Gurkhas, 1964-65; Comdt, Royal Military Academy, Sandhurst, 1966-68; Comdr, FARELF, 1968-70; Comdr Northern Army Gp and C-in-C, BAOR, 1970-73. Col Queen's Own Highlanders (Seaforth and Camerons), 1966-75; Col 10th Princess Mary's Own Gurkha Rifles, 1966-75. FBIM 1975. Chevalier of the Order of Leopold II and Croix de Guerre (Belgium), 1940 (awarded 1945). *Recreations:* philately, travel with a camera. *Address:* Rose Cottage, Portloe, Truro, Cornwall TR2 5R8. *Club:* Naval and Military.

HUNT, Philip Bodley; Director, Welsh Office Industry Department, 1975-76; *b* 28 July 1916; *s* of Bernard and Janet Hunt; *m* 1940, Eleanor Margaret Parnell; three *s* one *d. Educ:* Sedbergh Sch.; Christ Church, Oxford (MA). Joined Board of Trade, 1946; Trade Commissioner, Montreal, 1952; Principal Trade Commissioner, Vancouver, 1955; Commercial Counsellor, Canberra, 1957; returned Board of Trade, 1962; Dept of Economic Affairs, 1964-65; Director, London & SE Region, BoT, 1968; Dir, DTI Office for Wales, 1972-75. Chm., S Wales Marriage Guidance Council, 1974-; Dir, Develt Corporation for Wales. *Recreations:* gardening, music. *Address:* 93 Station Road, Llanishen, Cardiff CF4 5UU. *T:* Cardiff 750480.

HUNT, Ralph Holmes V.; *see* Vernon-Hunt.

HUNT, Reginald Heber, DMus; FRCO; FLCM; Chairman of Corporation, London College of Music (Director, 1954-64); *b* 16 June 1891; *m* 1917, Lilian Blanche Shinton (*d* 1956); one *s* one *d*; *m* 1959, Mary Elizabeth Abbott. FRCO 1915; DMus London, 1925. Served European War, including France, 1915-19; Dir of Music, Sir Walter St John's Sch., Battersea, 1927-45; Lectr in Music, Coll. of St Mark and St John, Chelsea, 1933-39; Organist various London churches, 1919-39; Organist Godalming Parish Church, 1940-50, and Dir Music, County Gram. Sch., 1945-52; composer and arranger, BBC Military Band, 1929-40. Mem. Performing Right Soc., 1929-. Sec. Union of Graduates in Music, 1948-50; Prof. and Examr, London Coll. of Music, 1947-; Mem. Senate, Univ. of London, 1951-64; Moderator in Music, General Certificate of Education, University of London, 1950-63. FLCM (Hon.) 1949; Editor, Boosey's Sch. Orchestra Series, 1928-40. Liveryman, Worshipful Co. of Musicians, 1961. *Publications* include: The Wondrous Cross (Passion setting), 1955; This Blessed Christmastide (Carol Fantasy), 1964; various church and organ works, incl. Communion Service in G, 1966, Fantasy on *O Quanta Qualia,*

Fantasy on a Ground, 1973; Album of Six Organ Pieces, 1977; Piano Sonatina in G, 1961; much Educational Music for Piano, Clarinet, Trumpet, Recorder, Sch. Orch., and many children's songs, incl. Fun with Tunes, 1969; More Fun with Tunes, 1972; *text-books* include: School Music Method, 1957; Elements of Music, 1959; First Harmony Book, 1962; Second Harmony Book, 1966; Elements of Organ Playing, 1966; Extemporization for Music Students, 1968; Transposition for Music Students, 1969; Harmony at the Keyboard, 1970. *Address:* 2 Oyster Bend, Three Beaches, Paignton, Devon. *T:* 557475. *Club:* Royal Automobile.

HUNT, Rex Masterman; HM Diplomatic Service; Counsellor, British High Commission, Kuala Lumpur, since 1976; *b* 29 June 1926; *s* of H. W. Hunt and Ivy Masterman; *m* 1951, Mavis Amanda Buckland; one *s* one *d. Educ:* Coatham Sch.; St Peter's Coll., Oxford (BA). Served with RAF, 1944-48; Flt Lt RAFO. Entered HM Overseas Civil Service, 1951; District Comr, Uganda, 1962; CRO, 1963-64; 1st Sec., Kuching, 1964-65; Jesselton, 1965-67; Brunei, 1967; 1st Sec. (Econ.), Ankara, 1968-70; 1st Sec. and Head of Chancery, Jakarta, 1970-72; Asst ME Dept, FCO, 1972-74; Counsellor, Saigon, 1974-75. *Recreations:* golf, flying, fishing. *Address:* c/o Foreign and Commonwealth Office, SW1A 2AH. *Club:* Royal Commonwealth Society.

HUNT, Richard Henry; Registrar of the High Court of Justice in Bankruptcy, since 1966; *b* 19 Jan. 1912; *s* of late Francis John and Lucy Beatrice Louise Hunt; *m* 1947, Peggy Ashworth Richardson; two *s. Educ:* Marlborough Coll.; Queen's Coll., Oxford. Called to Bar, 1936. Served with RA, 1939-45: Western Desert, Greece and Crete campaigns (PoW, Crete, 1941). Elected Bencher, Middle Temple, 1964. *Recreations:* foreign travel, languages. *Club:* Royal Ocean Racing.

HUNT, Richard William, DPhil; FBA 1961; Sub-Librarian and Keeper of Western Manuscripts, Bodleian Library, and Fellow of Balliol College, Oxford, 1945-75; *b* 11 April 1908; *m* 1942, Katharine Eva Rowland; three *s. Educ:* Haileybury Coll.; Balliol Coll., Oxford. Lecturer in Palaeography, Univ. of Liverpool, 1934; Lectr in Palaeography and Transmission of Classical Latin Texts, Univ. of Oxford, 1948-75; Sandars Reader in Bibliography, Cambridge Univ., 1959-60. *Publications:* articles in learned journals. *Address:* 45 Walton Street, Oxford. *T:* Oxford 57632.

HUNT, Robert Frederick, CBE 1974; DL; Chairman and Chief Executive, Dowty Group Ltd, since 1975; *b* 11 May 1918; *s* of late Arthur Hunt, Cheltenham and Kathleen Alice Cotton; *m* 1947, Joy Patricia Molly, *d* of late Charles Leslie Harding, Cheltenham; four *d. Educ:* Pates Grammar Sch., Cheltenham; N Glos Techn. Coll. Apprenticed Dowty Equipment Ltd, 1935; Chief Instructor to Co.'s Sch. of Hydraulics, 1940; RAF Trng Comd, 1940; Export Man., Dowty Equipment Ltd, 1946; Vice-Pres. and Gen. Man., 1949, Pres., 1954, Dowty Equipment of Canada Ltd; Dir, Dowty Gp Ltd, 1956, Dep. Chm., 1959-75. Chm., Bd of Trustees, Improvement District of Ajax, Ont., 1954; Dir, Ajax and Pickering Gen. Hosp., 1954; Chm., Cheltenham Hosp. Gp Man. Cttee, 1959; Chm., Glos AHA, 1974-; Pres., 1967-68, Treas., 1973, Vice-Pres., 1976, Pres., 1977-78, SBAC. CEng; FCASI 1976; FRAeS 1968. DL Glos, 1977. *Recreations:* family interests, gardening. *Address:* Dowty Group Ltd, Arle Court, Cheltenham, Glos. *T:* Cheltenham 21411. *Club:* New (Cheltenham).

HUNT, Roland Charles Colin, CMG 1965; HM Diplomatic Service, retired; Director, British National Committee, International Chamber of Commerce, 1973-76; *b* 19 March 1916; *s* of Colin and Dorothea Hunt, Oxford; *m* 1939, Pauline, 2nd *d* of late Dr J. C. Maxwell Garnett, CBE; three *s* two *d. Educ:* Rugby Sch. (scholar); The Queen's Coll., Oxford (scholar). Entered Indian Civil Service, 1938. Served in various districts in Madras as Sub-Collector, 1941-45; Joint Sec. and Sec., Board of Revenue (Civil Supplies), Madras, 1946-47; joined Commonwealth Relations Office, 1948; served on staff of United Kingdom High Commissioner in Pakistan (Karachi), 1948-50; Mem. UK Delegation to African Defence Facilities Conference, Nairobi, 1951; served in Office of UK High Comr in S Africa, 1952-55; Asst Sec., 1955; attached to Office of High Comr for Fedn of Malaya, Kuala Lumpur, 1956; Dep. High Commisioner for the UK in the Federation of Malaya, Kuala Lumpur, 1957-59; Imperial Defence Coll., 1960; Asst Sec., Commonwealth Relations Office, 1961; British Dep. High Comr in Pakistan, 1962-65; British High Commissioner in Uganda, 1965-67; Asst Under-Sec. of State, CO and FCO, 1967-70; High Comr, Trinidad and Tobago, 1970-73. *Recreations:* ball-games, piano-playing. *Address:* Charlton Lodge, near Banbury, Oxon. *T:* King's Sutton 437. *Club:* United Oxford & Cambridge University.

HUNT, Thomas Cecil, CBE 1964; DM Oxford, FRCP, MRCS; Consulting Physician: St Mary's Hospital, Paddington; Royal Masonic Hospital; King Edward VII Hospital for Officers; Examiner in Medicine, Royal College of Physicians and London University; Chairman, The Medical Sickness, Annuity & Life Assurance Society, since 1974; *b* 5 June 1901; *s* of Rev. A. T. G. Hunt; *m* 1930, Barbara, *d* of Egerton Todd, London; one *s* two *d. Educ:* St Paul's Sch.; Magdalen Coll., Oxford (Demy); 1st class hons final Physiology; Theodore Williams Scholarships Anatomy, 1922; Pathology, 1924; Demonstrator and Tutor Physiology, Oxford, 1924-25; Radcliffe Prize Pharmacology, 1924; University Scholar St Mary's Hosp., 1924; BM, BCh Oxford, 1926; Radcliffe Travelling Fellowship, 1927; Asst Medical Unit St Mary's, 1927-28; MRCP, 1928; Medical Registrar St Mary's Hosp., 1928-30; Mackenzie Mackinnon Res. Fellow, 1930-31; Mem. Assoc. of Physicians, Great Britain and Ireland, 1931; Fellow, Royal Soc. Medicine (Past Pres. Clinical Sect.); Senior Censor, RCP, 1956; 2nd Vice-Pres., RCP, 1967. Past President: British Soc. Gastro-enterology; London Medical Soc.; World Organisation Gastro-Enterology; Pres., Oxford Graduate Medical Club; Hon. Mem. Societies of Gastro-enterology, France, Belgium, Mexico, Nigeria, Switzerland and Sweden. Lt-Col 1940-44, Service West Africa, North Africa; Brig. RAMC, 1944-45; Consultant Persia Iraq Command. *Publications:* Peptic Ulcer, Brit. Ency. Med. Pract., 1938; various contribs to medical jls on digestive diseases. *Recreations:* books, gardening. *Address:* 53 Townshend Road, NW8 6LJ. *T:* 01-722 5324 (home); 01-935 4766 (professional). *Clubs:* Athenæum, MCC; Vincent's (Oxford).

HUNT, Vernon Arthur Moore, CBE 1958; farmer; *b* 27 Dec. 1912; *s* of late Cecil Arthur Hunt, RWS, MA, LLB and late Phyllis Clara Hunt (*née* Lucas); *m* 1949, Betty Yvonne Macduff; two *s* one *d. Educ:* Sherborne; Trinity Coll., Cambridge (BA); Coll. of Aeronautical Engrg (Pilot's Licence). Airline Pilot, 1938; Capt., BOAC, 1939-46; Min. of Civil Aviation: Dep. Dir of Ops, 1947; Dir of Control and Navigation, 1949; Dir of Control (Plans), Nat. Air Traffic Control Service, 1962-68; Chief Inspector of Accidents, DTI (formerly BoT), 1968-73. Mollison Trophy, 1939; George Taylor Gold Medal, RAeS, 1954. CEng; FRAeS 1956; FRIN (FIN 1956). *Publications:* contribs to RAeS and Inst. Navigation Jls. *Recreations:* sailing. *Address:* Foxworthy, Manaton, near Newton Abbot, Devon TQ13 9UY. *T:* Manaton 310. *Clubs:* Naval and Military; Hayling Island Sailing.

HUNT, Col Vivian; *see* Hunt, Col G. V.

HUNT, William Field, JP; MA; a Deputy Circuit Judge of the Crown Court, 1973-75; *b* 24 Oct. 1900; *s* of late Edwin James Hunt, JP, The Grange, Bescot, Walsall, and Charlotte Sheldon Field; *m* 1939, Helen Margaret (*d* 1961), *d* of late Dr Henry Malet, Wolverhampton; no *c. Educ:* Edgbaston Preparatory Sch., Birmingham; Rydal, Colwyn Bay; Exeter Coll., Oxford. On leaving school, 1919, went into an accountant's office, 1921 became a Bar Student of Inner Temple, to Oxford, called to Bar 1925, and joined Oxford Circuit. Chm., Court of Referees, 1930-72, and of Nat. Ins. Tribunals, Birmingham District; Chm., Industrial Tribunal, Birmingham Area, 1968-72; a Dep. Chm., Agric. Land Tribunal, W Midlands Area, 1960-75; Recorder of Bridgnorth 1941-45, of Newcastle-under-Lyme, 1945-71; a Recorder of the Crown Court, 1972. JP Worcestershire, 1956-72. Freeman of Borough of Newcastle. *Recreations:* music, travel. *Address:* 1 Fountain Court, Steelhouse Lane, Birmingham B4 6DR. *T:* 021-236 5721; 53 Ascot Road, Moseley, Birmingham B13 9EN. *T:* 021-449 2929; Windmill Cottage, Holberrow Green, Redditch, Worcs. *T:* Inkberrow 792275.

HUNT, Rt. Rev. William Warren, MA; *b* 22 Jan. 1909; *s* of Harry Hunt, Carlisle; *m* 1939, Mollie, *d* of Edwin Green, Heswall, Cheshire; four *d. Educ:* Carlisle Grammar School; Keble College, Oxford; Cuddesdon Theological College, Oxford. Deacon 1932; Priest 1933; Curate: Kendal Parish Church, 1932-35; St Martin-in-the-Fields, London, 1935-40. Chaplain to the Forces, 1940-44. Vicar, St Nicholas, Radford, Coventry, 1944-48; Vicar, Holy Trinity, Leamington Spa, 1948-57, and Rural Dean of Leamington; Vicar and Rural Dean of Croydon, 1957-65; Bishop Suffragan of Repton, 1965-Jan. 1977. Hon. Canon Canterbury Cathedral, 1957. *Recreations:* golf, vicarage lawn croquet (own rules); travel, reading. *Address:* 15 Lynch Down, Funtington, Chichester, West Sussex PO18 9LR. *T:* West Ashling 536. *Club:* Royal Over-Seas League.

HUNTER, Hon. Lord; John Oswald Mair Hunter, VRD; a Senator of the College of Justice in Scotland, since 1961; Chairman, Scottish Law Commission, since 1971; *b* 21 Feb. 1913; *s* of John Mair Hunter, QC(Scot) and Jessie Donald Frew;

m 1939, Doris Mary Simpson; one *s* one *d. Educ:* Edinburgh Acad.; Rugby; New Coll., Oxford (BA 1934, MA 1961); Edinburgh Univ. (LLB 1936, LLD 1975). Entered RNVR, 1933; served War 1939-45 (despatches); Lt-Comdr RNVR; retired list 1949. Called to Bar, Inner Temple, 1937; admitted to Faculty of Advocates, 1937; QC(Scot) 1951. Advocate Depute (Home), 1954-57; Sheriff of Ayr and Bute, 1957-61. Chairman: Deptl Cttee on Scottish Salmon and Trout Fisheries, 1961-64; Lands Valuation Appeal Court, 1966-71; Scottish Council on Crime, 1972-75; Dep. Chm., Boundary Commn for Scotland, 1971-76. Pres., Scottish Univs Law Inst., 1972-; Member: Scottish Records Adv. Council, 1966-; Statute Law Cttee, 1971-; Chm., Cttee, RNLI (Dunbar). Hon. Patron, Trinity Unit (Granton), Sea Cadet Corps. *Recreation:* angling. *Address:* Little Ruchlaw, Stenton, Dunbar, East Lothian. *T:* Stenton 250. *Club:* New (Edinburgh).

HUNTER, Adam; MP (Lab) Dunfermline, since 1974 (Dunfermline Burghs, 1964-74); miner; *b* 11 Nov. 1908; *m* ; one *s* one *d. Educ:* Kelty Public Elem. Sch. Joined Labour Party, 1933; Member: Exec. Cttee NUM (Scot. Area); Lochgelly Dist Council, 1948-52; Sec., Fife Co-op. Assoc. and Dist Council, 1947-64. Mem. Fife CC, 1961-64. Voluntary Tutor, Nat. Council of Labour Colls. *Recreation:* reading. *Address:* House of Commons, SW1; Whitegates Terrace, Kelty, Fife, Scotland.

HUNTER, Adam Kenneth Fisher; Sheriff of North Strathclyde at Paisley; *b* 1920; *o s* of late Thomas C. Hunter, MBE, AMIEE, and Elizabeth Hunter; *m* 1949, Joan Stella Hiscock, MB, ChB; one *s* two *d. Educ:* Dunfermline High Sch.; St Andrews Univ. (MA Hons); Edinburgh Univ. (LLB). Called to Bar, 1946; Chm. of the Supreme Court Legal Aid Cttee of the Law Society of Scotland, 1949-53; Standing Junior Counsel to HM Commissioners of Customs and Excise, 1950-53; Sheriff-Substitute, later Sheriff, of Renfrew and Argyll (subseq. N Strathclyde) at Paisley, 1953-. *Recreations:* photography, music, motor boating. *Address:* Ravenswood, Bridge of Weir, Renfrewshire. *T:* 612017.

HUNTER, Dr Alan, CBE 1975; Director, Royal Greenwich Observatory, 1973-75; *b* 9 Sept. 1912; *s* of late George Hunter and Mary Edwards; *m* 1937, W. Joan Portnell; four *s. Educ:* Imperial Coll. of Science and Technology. PhD, DIC; FRAS. Research Asst, Applied Mech. Dept, RNC, 1940-46; Royal Observatory, Greenwich: Asst, 1937-61; Chief Asst, 1961-67; Dep. Dir, 1967-73. Editor, The Observatory, 1943-49. Treas., Royal Astronomical Soc., 1967-76 (Sec. 1949-56, Vice-Pres. 1957, 1965, 1976); Pres., British Astronomical Assoc., 1957-59; Chm., Large Telescope Users' Panel, 1974-75 (sec. 1969-73). Liveryman, Worshipful Co. of Clockmakers, 1975. *Recreation:* gardening. *Address:* The Old Vicarage, Ashburnham, Battle, E Sussex TN33 9NU. *T:* Hastings 892472.
See also Donald Hunter , Prof . Louis Hunter .

HUNTER, Alastair; *see* Hunter, M. I. A.

HUNTER, Sir Alexander (Albert), KBE 1976; Speaker of the House of Representatives of Belize, since 1974; *b* Belize, British Honduras, 21 May 1920; *s* of Alexander J. Hunter and Laura Hunter (*née* Reyes); *m* 1947, Araceli Cayetana Marin S., Alajuela, Costa Rica; one *s* two *d . Educ:* St John's Coll. (Jesuit), Belize City; Regis Coll. (Jesuit), Denver, Colo; Queen's Univ., Kingston, Ont. In Accounting Dept, United Fruit Co., Costa Rica, 1940-41 and 1945-47. Served War, NCO, Radar Br., RCAF, 1942-45: active service in UK, Azores, Gibraltar, with 220 Sqdn Coastal Comd, RAF. Joined staff of James Brodie & Co. Ltd, as Accountant, 1947; Company Sec., 1948; Dir 1952-61; Consultant: James Brodie & Co. Ltd, 1975-; Anschutz Overseas Corp., Denver, Colo, 1975-. MLA (PUP), Fort George Divn, 1961; Minister of Natural Resources, Commerce and Industry, March 1961; MHR (PUP), Fort George, under new Constitution, 1965; Minister of Natural Resources and Trade, 1965-69; Minister of Trade and Industry, 1969-74; Mem., Constitutional Ministerial External Affairs Cttee, 1965-74. Represented Belize: Bd of Governors, Caribbean Develt Bank, 1969-74; Council of Ministers, CARIFTA, 1971-73; Council of Ministers, Caribbean Economic Community, 1973-74. Acted as Dep. Governor, Aug. 1975. Pres., Belize Br., CPA; Chairman: Standing Orders Cttee; Regulations Cttee; House Cttee. People's United Party: Treasurer and Mem. Central Party Council, 1961-74; Mem. Exec. Cttee, 1961-74; Chm. Fort George Divn, 1961-74. Hon. Vice-Consul of El Salvador, 1951-. Former Vice-Pres., Belize Chamber of Commerce; Member: Property Valuation Appeal Bd, 1960; Citrus Industry Investigation Cttee, 1960. Member: West India Cttee; Internat. Game Fish Assoc.; Belize Rifle Club; Nat. Geographic Soc. *Recreations:* pistol-shooting, hunting, light and heavy tackle salt-water fishing. *Address:* 6 St Matthew Street, Caribbean Shores, Belize City, Belize. *T:* 4482.

HUNTER, Alistair John; HM Diplomatic Service; Head of Personnel Services Dept, Foreign and Commonwealth Office, since 1976; *b* 9 Aug. 1936; *s* of Kenneth Clarke Hunter and Joan Tunks; *m* 1963; one *s* two *d*. *Educ:* Felsted; Magdalen Coll., Oxford. 1st Cl. Hons English. Royal Air Force, 1955-57; Oxford Univ., 1957-60; CRO, 1961-65; Private Sec. to Permanent Under-Sec., 1961-63; 2nd Sec., British High Commn, Kuala Lumpur, 1963-65; 1st Sec. (Commercial), British Office, Peking, 1965-68; seconded to Cabinet Office, 1969-70; FCO, 1970-73; 1st Sec., Rome, 1973-75; FCO, 1975-. *Address:* 40 Braxted Park, SW16. *T:* 01-764 6014.

HUNTER, Rt. Rev. Anthony George Weaver; Rector of Hexham, Diocese of Newcastle, since 1975; Assistant Bishop, Diocese of Newcastle, since 1976; *b* 3 June 1916; *s* of Herbert George Hunter and Ethel Frances Weaver; *m* 1948, Joan Isobel Marshall. *Educ:* Wanstead; Leeds Univ. (BA); Coll. of the Resurrection, Mirfield. Deacon, 1941; Priest, 1942; Curate of St George's, Jesmond, 1941-43; Orlando Mission Dist, 1943-47; Johannesburg Coloured Mission, 1947-48; Curate of St George's, Jesmond, 1948-49; Vicar of Ashington, 1949-60; Proctor in Convocation, 1959-60; Vicar of Huddersfield, 1960-68; Rural Dean of Huddersfield, 1960-68; Hon. Canon of Wakefield, 1962-68; Proctor in Convocation, 1962-68; Bishop of Swaziland, 1968-75. OStJ. *Recreations:* walking, gardening, travel. *Address:* The Rectory, Hexham, Northumberland NE46 3EW. *T:* Hexham 2031. *Club:* St John's.

HUNTER, Prof. Archibald Macbride, MA, BD, PhD Glasgow, Hon. DD Glasgow, DPhil Oxon; Professor of New Testament Exegesis (formerly Biblical Criticism) in Aberdeen University, 1945-71; Master of Christ's College, Aberdeen, 1957-71; *b* 16 Jan. 1906; *s* of late Rev. Archibald Hunter, Kilwinning, and Crissie Swan MacNeish; *m* 1934, Margaret Wylie Swanson; one *s* one *d*. *Educ:* Hutchesons' Grammar Sch., Glasgow; Universities of Glasgow, Marburg and Oxford. Minister in Comrie, Perthshire, 1934-37; Prof. of New Testament, in Mansfield Coll., Oxford, 1937-42; Minister in Kinnoull, Perth, 1942-45. Hastie Lecturer, Glasgow Univ., 1938; Lee Lecturer, 1950; Sprunt Lecturer (Richmond, Va), 1954. *Publications:* Paul and His Predecessors, 1940; The Unity of the New Testament, 1943; Introducing the New Testament, 1945; The Gospel according to St Mark, 1949; The Work and Words of Jesus, 1950; Interpreting the New Testament, 1951; Design for Life, 1953; Interpreting Paul's Gospel, 1954; The Epistle to the Romans, 1955; Introducing New Testament Theology, 1957; The Layman's Bible Commentary, Vol. 22, 1959; Interpreting The Parables, 1960; Teaching and Preaching the New Testament, 1963; The Gospel according to John, 1965; The Gospel according to St Paul, 1966; According to John, 1968; Bible and Gospel, 1969; Exploring the New Testament, 1971; The Parables Then and Now, 1971; Taking the Christian View, 1974; On P. T. Forsyth, 1974; The New Testament Today, 1974; Gospel and Apostle, 1975; Jesus Lord and Saviour, 1976; articles and reviews in theological journals. *Recreation:* fishing. *Address:* 3 Carwinshoch View, Ayr. *T:* Ayr 64403.

HUNTER, Rt. Rev. Barry Russell; *see* Riverina, Bishop of.

HUNTER, Dr Colin Graeme, DSC 1939; physician; *b* 31 Jan. 1913; *s* of Robert Hunter and Evelyn Harrison; *m* 1944, Betty Louise Riley; one *s* one *d*. *Educ:* Scots Coll., Univ. of Otago, New Zealand. MD 1958, DSc 1970. Christchurch Hosp. NZ, 1937-38; Royal Naval Medical Service, 1938-55; Univ. of Toronto, Canada, 1955-58; Shell Research Ltd, 1958-73. Fellow: RCP (Lond.); Roy. Coll. of Pathologists; etc; also Mem. many societies; Freeman of City of London. *Publications:* scientific papers in many jls devoted to chemical and radiation toxicology. *Recreations:* sailing, squash. *Address:* 193 The Gateway, Dover, Kent. *T:* Dover 2172. *Clubs:* Army and Navy; Royal Cinque Ports Yacht, Royal Naval Sailing Association.

HUNTER, David Stronach, QC 1971; a Recorder of the Crown Court, since 1975; *b* 5 Oct. 1926; *s* of late Robert John Hunter and late Jayne Evelyn Hunter; *m* 1959, Janet Muriel Faulkner; one *s* two *d*. *Educ:* Harrow Sch., Hertford Coll., Oxford (Baring Scholar); MA Jurisprudence. Called to Bar, Middle Temple, 1951. *Recreations:* golf, gardening, painting. *Address:* Court Lodge, Egerton, near Ashford, Kent. *T:* Egerton 249. *Club:* MCC.

HUNTER, Donald, CBE 1957; MD, FRCP; Consulting Physician to the London Hospital, 1927-63; Curator of Museum, London Hospital Medical College, 1933-63; Director, Department for Research in Industrial Medicine, MRC, London Hospital, 1943-63; Member World Health Organisation Expert Advisory Panel on Social and Occupational Health, Geneva; Member, Commission Permanente et Association Internationale pour la Médecine du Travail, Geneva; Founder Editor, British Journal of Industrial Medicine, 1944; *b* 11 Feb. 1898; *s* of late George Hunter; *m* Mathilde, *d* of late Rev. Gustave Bugnion, Lausanne; two *s* two *d*. *Educ:* London Hospital. Medical Registrar, London Hosp., 1923-25; Res. Fellow, Harvard Medical Sch. and Massachusetts General Hospital, Boston, 1926. Lectures: Goulstonian, RCP, 1930; Arris and Gale, RCS, 1931; Croonian, RCP, 1942; Cutter, Harvard, 1945; George Haliburton Hume, Newcastle, 1946; Frederick Price, QUB, 1949, and Trinity Coll., Dublin, 1956; Ernestine Henry, RCP, 1950; Maitland Oration, Sydney Hosp., 1950; McIlrath Guest Prof. in Medicine, Royal Prince Alfred Hospital, Sydney, Australia, 1950; Vis. Lectr, in Medicine, Univ. of Cape Town, 1953; Sir Arthur Sims Commonwealth Travelling Prof., 1955; Prosser White Orator, 1956; Schorstein Lectr, 1956; Harveian Orator, RCP, 1957; Sir Charles Hastings Lectr, 1958; Cai Holten Lectr, Aarhus, Denmark, 1966; John Ash Lectr, Birmingham, 1972. Hon. DSc Durham; Hon. DIH Soc. Apoth., London; Hon. FRCPI; Hon. Foreign Mem. American Acad. of Arts and Sciences. Lately Cons. in Occupational and Environmental Medicine, The Middlesex Hosp., WI; Res. Fellow in Occupational Health, Guy's Hosp., SE1. Ex-member: Pharmacopœia Commission; Industrial Health Research Board; Poisons Board; ex-Senior Censor, Royal College of Physicians; ex-President, Association Physicians Great Britain and Ireland. *Publications:* (with Dr R. R. Bomford) Hutchison's Clinical Methods, 15th edn, 1968; The Diseases of Occupations, 6th edn, 1977; Health in Industry, 1959; various contributions to medical and scientific journals. *Address:* 13 Hitherwood Drive, SE19 1XA.

See also A. Hunter, L. Hunter.

HUNTER, Sir (Ernest) John, Kt 1964; CBE 1960; DL; Executive Chairman, Swan Hunter Group Ltd, since 1972 (Chairman and Managing Director, 1957-72); Chairman, North East Broadcasting Company Ltd; *b* 3 Nov. 1912; 2nd *s* of George Ernest Hunter and Elsie Hunter (*née* Edwards); *m* 1st, 1937, Joanne Winifred Wilkinson; one *s*; 2nd, 1949, Sybil Malfroy (*née* Gordon); one *s* one step *d*. *Educ:* Oundle Sch.; Cambridge Univ.; Durham Univ. (BSc). Apprentice, Swan, Hunter and Wigham Richardson Ltd, 1930-31; St John's Coll., Cambridge Univ., 1931-32; Durham Univ. (BSc) 1932-35; Draughtsman, SH and WR Ltd, 1935-37; Asst Manager: Barclay, Curle & Co. 1937-39; SH and WR Dry Docks, 1939-41; Asst Gen. Manager, SH and WR Dry Docks, 1941-43, Gen. Manager, 1943-45; Dir, Swan Hunter and Wigham Richardson Ltd, 1945, Chm., 1957-66. Director: Dorman Long Swan Hunter (Pty) Ltd; Newcastle & Gateshead Water Co.; Common Bros Ltd; Midland Bank; Swan Hunter Africa (Pty) Ltd; Swan Hunter International Ltd. Chairman: N-E Coast Ship-repairers' Association, 1957-58; Tyne Shipbuilders' Association, 1956-57. Dry Dock Owners' and Repairers' Central Council, 1961-62; President: NEC Institution, 1958-60; Shipbuilding Employers' Fedn, 1956-57; British Employers' Confedn, 1962-64; Shipbuilders' and Repairers' Nat. Assoc., 1968-. Mem. NEDC, 1962-64. First Chm., Central Training Council, 1964-68. Mem. of Cttees connected with shipping and with youth. Liveryman, Company of Shipwrights; Freeman: of City of London (by redemption); of Borough of Wallsend, 1972. DL Northumberland, 1968. Hon. DSc Newcastle, 1968. *Publications:* contrib. to Trans NEC Instn. *Recreations:* golf and gardening. *Address:* The Dene, Stocksfield, Northumberland. *T:* Stocksfield 3124. *Clubs:* Garrick; Northern Counties (Newcastle upon Tyne).

HUNTER, Guy, CMG 1973; author and consultant; Overseas Development Institute since 1967; *b* 7 Nov. 1911; *s* of Lt-Col C. F. Hunter, DSO, and Mrs A. W. Hunter (*née* Cobbett); *m* 1941, Agnes Louisa Merrylees. *Educ:* Winchester Coll.; Trinity Coll., Cambridge. 1st cl. hons Classics, MA. Called to Bar, Middle Temple, 1935. Civil Defence, Regional Officer, Edinburgh and Principal Officer, Glasgow and W Scotland, 1939-43; Dir (Admin), Middle East Supply Centre, GHQ, Cairo, 1943-45; Dir, PEP, 1945-46; Warden, Urchfont Manor, Wilts, and Grantley Hall, Yorks, Adult Colleges, 1946-55; Dir of Studies, 1st Duke of Edinburgh's Conf., 1955-56; from 1957, research and consultancy for developing countries overseas, mainly E, W and Central Africa, India, Pakistan, SE Asia, Fiji. Launching and 1st Dir, East African Staff Coll., 1966; Inst. of Race Relations, 1959-66. Visiting Prof., Univ. of Reading, 1969-75. Member: Economic and Social Cttee, EEC, 1975-; Council for Internat. Develt (ODM), 1977-. Bd of Governors, Inst. of Develt Studies, Sussex Univ. *Publications:* Studies in Management, 1961; The New Societies of Tropical Africa, 1962; Education for a Developing Region, 1963; (ed) Industrialization and Race Relations, 1965; South East Asia: Race, Culture and Nation, 1966; The Best of Both Worlds, 1967; Modernising Peasant Societies, 1969; The Administration of Agricultural Development, 1970; (ed jtly) Serving the Small Farmer, 1974;

(ed jtly) Policy and Practice in Rural Development, 1976. *Recreations:* gardening, nature, travel. *Address:* The Miller's Cottage, Hartest, Bury St Edmunds, Suffolk. *T:* Hartest 334. *Clubs:* Travellers', English-Speaking Union.

HUNTER, Ian Bruce Hope, MBE 1945; Impresario; Chairman and Managing Director, Harold Holt Ltd; *b* 2 April 1919; *s* of late W. O. Hunter; *m* 1949, Susan, *d* of late Brig. A. G. Russell; four *d. Educ:* Fettes Coll., Edinburgh; abroad as pupil of Dr Fritz Busch and at Glyndebourne. Served War of 1939-45, Lieut-Col. Asst to Artistic Dir, Edinburgh Festival, 1946-48; Artistic Administrator, Edinburgh Festival, 1949-50; Artistic Dir, Edinburgh Festival, 1951-55. Director, Bath Festivals, 1948, 1955, 1958-68; Adviser, Adelaide Festivals, 1960-64; Artistic Director: Festivals of the City of London, 1962-; Brighton Festivals, 1967-; (with Yehudi Menuhin) Windsor Festival, 1969-72; Hong Kong Arts Festival, 1973-75; Malvern Festival, 1977-; Dir-General, Commonwealth Arts Festival, 1965. Dir, British Nat. Day Entertainment, Expo' 67. Member: Opera/Ballet Enquiry for Arts Council, 1967-69; Arts Administration Course Enquiry for Arts Council, 1970-71; Arts Council Trng Cttee, 1974-76; Chm., Entertainment Cttee, Queen's Silver Jubilee Appeal. Trustee, Chichester Festival Theatre Trust; Governor, Yehudi Menuhin Sch. R. B. Bennett Commonwealth Prize for 1966. Hon. Mem., Guildhall Sch. of Music and Drama. FRSA (Mem. Council, 1968-73, 1976-). *Recreations:* riding, gardening, sailing. *Address:* 134 Wigmore Street, W1. *T:* 01-935 2331. *Club:* Garrick.

HUNTER, Brig. Ian Murray, CVO 1954; MBE 1943; psc 1943; fsc (US) 1955; FAIM 1964; Chairman, Allied Rubber Products (Qld) Pty Ltd; *b* Sydney, Aust., 10 July 1917; *s* of late Dr James Hunter, Stranraer, Scotland; *m* 1947, Rosemary Jane Batchelor; two *s* two *d. Educ:* Cranbrook Sch., Sydney; RMC, Duntroon. Lieut Aust. Staff Corps, and AIF 1939; 2/1 MG Bn, 1939-40; T/Capt. 1940; Staff Capt., 25 Inf. Bde, 1940-41; Middle East Staff Coll., Haifa, 1941; DA QMG (1), HQ 6 Div., 1941-42; T/Major 1942; AQMG, NT Force (MBE), 1942-43; Staff Sch. (Aust.), 1943; Gen. Staff 3 Corps and Advanced HQ Allied Land Forces, 1943-44; Lieut-Col 1945; Instructor, Staff Sch., 1945; AQMG, and Col BCOF, 1946-47; AQMG, AHQ and JCOSA, 1947; AA & QMG, HQ, 3 Div., 1948-50; Royal Visit, 1949; Exec. Commonwealth Jubilee Celebrations, 1950-51; CO 2 Recruit Trg Bn, 1952; CO 4 RAR, 1953; Executive and Commonwealth Marshal, Royal Visit, 1952, and 1954; Command and Gen. Staff Coll., Fort Leavenworth, USA, 1954-55; Military Mission, Washington, 1955-56; Officer i/c Admin., N Comd, 1956-59; Comd 11 Inf. Bde, 1959-60; Command 2nd RQR 1960-62; Chief of Staff 1st Div., 1963; Commandant, Australian Staff Coll., 1963-65; Comdr, Papua New Guinea Comd, 1966-69; DQMG, Army HQ, 1969. *Recreations:* golf, squash, swimming, riding. *Address:* Garthland, 42 Charlton Street, Ascot, Brisbane, Queensland 4007, Australia; Finchley, Hargreaves Street, Blackheath, NSW 2785, Australia. *Clubs:* Australian (Sydney); Queensland (Brisbane); Royal Sydney Golf.

HUNTER, Sir John; *see* Hunter, Sir E. J.

HUNTER, Surg. Rear-Adm. (D) John, CB 1973; OBE 1963; Director of Naval Dental Services, Ministry of Defence, 1971-74; *b* 21 Aug. 1915; *s* of Hugh Hunter and Evelyn Marian Hunter (*née* Jessop), Hale, Cheshire; *m* 1947, Anne Madeleine Hardwicke, Friarmayne, Dorset; three *s* two *d. Educ:* Bowdon Coll., Cheshire; Manchester Univ. LDS 1939. Surg. Lieut (D) RNVR 1940; HMS Kenya and 10th Cruiser Sqdn, 1941-42; HMS Newcastle and HMS Howe, British Pacific Fleet, 1944-47; transf. to RN; HMS Forth on Staff of Rear-Adm. Destroyers, Mediterranean (Surg. Lt-Comdr), 1948-50; Dartmouth, Royal Marines; Surg. Comdr, Staff of Flag Officer Flotillas Mediterranean, 1956; service ashore in Admty, 1960-63; Surg. Captain (D), Staff of C-in-C Mediterranean, 1965-66; Staff of C-in-C Plymouth Comd, 1967-68; Fleet Dental Surgeon on Staff of C-in-C Western Fleet, 1969-70. QHDS 1971-74. FRSocMed. *Recreations:* ocean racing, cruising, shooting. *Address:* Horsewells, Newton Ferrers, Plymouth PL8 1AT. *T:* Plymouth 872254. *Clubs:* Royal Ocean Racing, Army and Navy; Royal Western Yacht.

HUNTER, John Murray, MC 1943; Commissioner for Administration and Finance, Forestry Commission, since 1976; *b* 10 Nov. 1920; *s* of Rev. Dr John Hunter and Frances Hunter (*née* Martin); *m* 1948, Margaret, *d* of late Stanley Cursiter, CBE, RSW, RSA, and Phyllis Eda (*née* Hourston); two *s* three *d. Educ:* Fettes Coll.; Clare Coll., Cambridge. Served Army, 1941-45: Captain, The Rifle Bde. Served in Diplomatic Service at Canberra, Bogotá, Baghdad, Prague, Buenos Aires and in FCO (Head of Consular Dept, 1966, and of Latin America Dept,

1971-73); idc 1961, sowc 1965, jssc (Senior Directing Staff), 1967-69. Sec., Forestry Commn, 1973-75. *Recreations:* music, golf; formerly Rugby football (Cambridge 1946, Scotland 1947). *Address:* 11 Glencairn Crescent, Edinburgh EH12 5BS. *Club:* Scottish Arts (Edinburgh).

HUNTER, John Oswald Mair; *see* Hunter, Hon. Lord.

HUNTER, Major Joseph Charles, CBE 1959; MC 1918; DL; Chairman Leeds Regional Hospital Board, 1955-63; *b* 1 Sept. 1894; *s* of W. S. Hunter, Gillingcastle, Yorks; *m* 1st, 1920, Cicely Longueville Heywood-Jones (marr. diss. 1930); one *s* two *d*; 2nd, 1934, Prudence Josephine Whetstone; two *s. Educ:* Harrow. Commissioned Yorkshire Hussars Yeo., 1912. Served European War, 1914-18, Europe; Regular Commission RA 1916; retired, 1920 (Major, R of O); War of 1939-45, in RA. Alderman W Riding of Yorks County Council, 1955-61 (Mem. 1947-55); DL W Riding of Yorks and York, 1959, N Yorkshire, 1974. *Address:* Havikil Lodge, Scotton, Knaresborough, N Yorks. *T:* Knaresborough 3400.

HUNTER, Prof. Laurence Colvin; Professor of Applied Economics, University of Glasgow, since 1970; Chairman, Post Office Arbitration Tribunal, since 1974; *b* 8 Aug. 1934; *s* of Laurence O. and Jessie P. Hunter; *m* 1958, Evelyn Margaret (*née* Green); three *s* one *d. Educ:* Hillhead High Sch., Glasgow; Univ. of Glasgow (MA); University Coll., Oxford (DPhil). Asst, Manchester Univ., 1958-59; National Service, 1959-61; Post-Doctoral Fellow, Univ. of Chicago, 1961-62; Univ. of Glasgow: Lectr, 1962; Sen. Lectr, 1967; Titular Prof., 1969. Member: Ct of Inquiry into miners' strike, 1972; Council, Advisory, Conciliation and Arbitration Service, 1974-; Royal Commn on Legal Services in Scotland, 1976-. *Publications:* (with G. L. Reid) Urban Worker Mobility, 1968; (with D. J. Robertson) Economics of Wages and Labour, 1969; (with G. L. Reid and D. Boddy) Labour Problems of Technological Change, 1970; (with A. W. J. Thomson) The Nationalised Transport Industries, 1973; (with R. B. McKersie) Pay, Productivity and Collective Bargaining, 1973; several articles in economic jls. *Recreations:* golf, painting. *Address:* 23 Boclair Road, Bearsden, Glasgow. *T:* 041-942 0793. *Club:* Royal Commonwealth Society.

HUNTER, Rt. Rev. Leslie Stannard, MA; DD Lambeth; Hon. LLD Sheffield; Hon. DCL Dunelm; Hon. DD Toronto, 1954; *b* 1890; *yr s* of late Rev. John Hunter, DD, Minister of the King's Weigh House Church, London, and Trinity Church, Glasgow, and Marion Martin; *m* 1919, Grace Marion (*d* 1975), *yr d* of late Samuel McAulay, JP, of Aylesby, Lincs. *Educ:* Kelvinside Academy; New Coll., Oxford. Pres. of the Oxford University Lawn Tennis Club, 1911-12; Asst Sec. of the Student Christian Movement of Great Britain and Ireland, 1913-20; Curate of St Peter's, Brockley, SE, 1915-18; served with YMCA, BEF, 1916, and the Army of Occupation, 1919; Mem. of the Army and Religion Inquiry Commission, 1917-19; Asst Curate of St Martin-in-the-Fields and Chaplain of Charing Cross Hospital, London, 1921-22; Residentiary Canon of Newcastle on Tyne, 1922-26 and 1931-39; Vicar of Barking, Essex, 1926-30; Archdeacon of Northumberland, 1931-39; Chm., Tyneside Council of Social Service, 1933-39; Chaplain to the King, 1936-39; Bishop of Sheffield, 1939-62; Chm. of Sheffield Hospitals Council, 1940-49. House of Lords, 1944-62. Foundation Mem., British Council of Churches; Select Preacher, Universities of: Oxford, Cambridge, Glasgow, Aberdeen, St Andrews and Edinburgh, various years; Birks Memorial Lecturer, McGill Univ., Montreal, 1951. Hon. Freeman of City of Sheffield, 1962. Comdr Order of the Dannebrog, 1952. *Publications:* John Hunter, DD: A Life, 1921; A Parson's Job: Aspects of Work in the English Church, 1931; Let Us Go Forward, 1944; Church Strategy in a Changing World, 1950; The Seed and the Fruit, 1953; A Mission of the People of God, 1961; (Editor and part author) A Diocesan Service Book, 1965; Scandinavian Churches, 1965; The English Church: a New Look, 1966. *Address:* 55 Sefton Road, Sheffield S10 3TP.

HUNTER, Prof. Louis, PhD, DSc (London); FRIC; retired as Professor of Chemistry and Head of Department of Chemistry, University of Leicester (previously University College) (1946-65); Professor Emeritus, 1966; *b* 4 Dec. 1899; *s* of late George Hunter and Mary Edwards; *m* 1926, Laura Thorpe (decd). *Educ:* East London College (subsequently Queen Mary College), University of London. Assistant Lecturer, University Coll. of North Wales, Bangor, 1920-25; Lecturer and Head of Dept of Chemistry, University Coll., Leicester, 1925, Prof. of Chemistry, 1946, and Vice-Principal, 1952-57, Pro-Vice-Chancellor, University of Leicester, 1957-60. Visiting Professor: Univ. of Ibadan, Nigeria, 1963, and Ahmadu Bello Univ., 1966. Mem. of Council: Chemical Soc., 1944-47, 1950-53, 1956-59; Royal Institute of Chemistry, 1947-50, 1961-64 (Vice-Pres., 1964-66;

Chm. E Midlands Section, 1938-40); Sec. Section B (Chemistry), British Assoc. for the Advancement of Science, 1939-51, Recorder, 1951-56, mem. of Council, 1956-60. Hon. Fire Observer, Home Office, 1942-54; Scientific Adviser for Civil Defence, N Midlands, 1951-75; Dep. Chm., 1939, Chm., 1952, Leicester Jt Recruiting Bd. *Publications:* mainly in Jl Chem. Soc. *Address:* Orchard Close, Gaulby, Leics LE7 9BB. *T:* Billesdon 449. *Clubs:* Savage; Rotary (Leicester).
See also A. Hunter, D. Hunter.

HUNTER, (Mark Ian) Alastair, MD, FRCP; Physician, St George's Hospital, SW1, 1946-76, now Emeritus; *b* 18 June 1909; *s* of Mark Oliver Hunter and Diana Rachel (*née* Jones); unmarried. *Educ:* Winchester Coll. (Entrance Exhibition); Trinity Coll., Cambridge. Qualified as Doctor, 1933. MD Cambridge, 1945; FRCP (London), 1947. Dean, St George's Hosp. Med. Sch., 1956-71. Asst Registrar, 1950-57, Censor, 1971-73, Vice-Pres. and Sen. Censor, 1974-75, RCP. Mem., GMC. Dep. Vice-Chancellor, Univ. of London, 1972-73. Medical Awards Administrator, Commonwealth Scholarship Commn, 1974-. Hon. Keeper, 20th Century Painting, Fitzwilliam Museum, Cambridge. *Publications:* medical subjects. *Recreations:* various. *Address:* 35 Medfield Street, Roehampton Village, SW15. *Clubs:* Royal Automobile, MCC.

HUNTER, Muir Vane Skerrett, QC 1965; Lt-Col (Hon.); MA Oxon; MRI; Barrister-at-Law; *b* 19 Aug. 1913; *s* of late Hugh Stewart Hunter, Home Civil Service; *m* 1939, Dorothea Eason (JP); *e d* of late Philip Eason Verstone; one *d. Educ:* Westminster Sch.; Christ Church, Oxford (Scholar). Called, Gray's Inn, 1938 (*ad eundem* Inner Temple, 1965); Holker Senior Scholar; Bencher, Gray's Inn, 1976. Served 1940-46: Royal Armoured Corps; General Staff Intelligence, GHQ (India), GSO 1 attd War and Legislative Depts, Govt of India; returned to the Bar, 1946; standing counsel (bankruptcy) to Bd of Trade, 1949-65; Dep. Chm., Advisory Cttee on Service Candidates, HO; Member: EEC Bankruptcy Adv. Cttee, Dept of Trade, 1973-76; Insolvency Law Review Cttee, Dept of Trade, 1977-; Founder-Chairman, N Kensington Neighbourhood Law Centre, 1969-71; Mem. Exec. Cttee and Council of "Justice". Amnesty International Observer: Burundi, 1962; Rhodesia, 1969; Turkey, 1972. Hon. Adviser, Conf. of Private Residents Assoc., 1974-76. Member: Council, Shakespeare Theatre Trust; Royal Shakespeare Theatre Centenary Appeal Cttee. *Publications:* Editor, Williams on Bankruptcy, 1958-; Emergent Africa and the Rule of Law, 1963; Jt editor: Halsbury's Laws (4th edn), Vol 3; Atkins' Forms, Vol 7. *Recreations:* theatre, travel. *Address:* 49 Hurlingham Court, SW6. *T:* 01-736 1757; (chambers) 3 Paper Buildings, Temple, EC4Y 7EU. *T:* 01-353 3721. *Club:* Hurlingham.

HUNTER, Philip Brown, TD; Chairman, John Holt & Co. (Liverpool) Ltd, 1967-71; *b* 30 May 1909; *s* of Charles Edward Hunter and Marion (*née* Harper); *m* 1937, Joyce Mary (*née* Holt); two *s* two *d. Educ:* Birkenhead Sch.; London University. Practised as Solicitor, 1933-. Chm., Guardian Royal Exchange Assurance (Sierra Leone) Ltd; Director: Cammell Laird & Co. Ltd, 1949-70 (Chm. 1966-70); John Holt & Co. (Liverpool) Ltd, 1951-71 (Exec. Dir, 1960); Guardian Royal Exchange; Guardian Assurance Co. Ltd, 1967; Royal Exchange (Nigeria) Ltd; Lion of Africa Insurance Co. Ltd; Enterprise Insurance Co. Ltd, Ghana. *Recreations:* sailing, gardening. *Address:* Highfield, Northop, Mold, Clwyd. *T:* Northop 221. *Club:* Caledonian.

HUNTER, Rita; prima donna; leading soprano, Sadler's Wells, since 1958; *b* 15 Aug. 1933; *d* of Charles Newton Hunter and Lucy Hunter; *m* 1960, John Darnley-Thomas; one *d. Educ:* Wallasey. Joined Carl Rosa, 1950. Debut: Berlin, 1970; Covent Garden, 1972; Metropolitan, NY, 1972; Munich, 1973. Sang Brünnhilde in first complete Ring cycle with Sadler's Wells, 1973; first perf. of Norma, NY Metropolitan, 1975. Has sung leading roles in Aida, Trovatore, Masked Ball, Cavalleria Rusticana, Lohengrin, Flying Dutchman, Idomeneo, Don Carlos. Many recordings, including complete Siegfried and complete Euryanthe. *Recreations:* sewing, oil painting, reading, gardening (Mem. Royal Nat. Rose Soc.), caravanning (Mem. Caravan Club). *Address:* The Cornerways, 70 Embercourt Road, Thames Ditton, Surrey. *T:* 01-398 7502. *Club:* White Elephant.

HUNTER, Sir Robert (Brockie), Kt 1977; MBE 1945; FRCP; DL; Vice-Chancellor and Principal, University of Birmingham, since 1968; *b* 14 July 1915; *s* of Robert Marshall Hunter and Margaret Thorburn Brockie; *m* 1940, Kathleen Margaret Douglas; three *s* one *d. Educ:* George Watson's Coll. MB, ChB Edinburgh, 1938; FRCPE 1950; FACP 1963; FRSEd 1964; FInstBiol 1968; FFCM 1975. Personal Physician, Field-Marshal Montgomery, NW Europe, 1944-45. Asst Dir, Edinburgh Post-

Graduate Bd for Medicine, 1947; Lectr in Therapeutics, University of Edinburgh, 1947; Commonwealth (Harkness) Fellow in Medicine, 1948; Lectr in Clinical Medicine, University of St Andrews, 1948; Dean of the Faculty of Medicine, 1958-62; Prof. of Materia Medica, Pharmacology and Therapeutics, University of St Andrews, 1948-67, and in University of Dundee, 1967-68; late Consultant Physician to Dundee General Hosps and Dir, Post-graduate Medical Education. Hon. Lectr in Physiology, Boston Univ. Sch. of Medicine, USA, 1950. Member: Clinical Res. Bd, MRC, 1960-64; GMC, 1962-68; Ministry of Health Cttee on Safety of Drugs, 1963-68; UGC, 1964-68 (Chm., Medical Sub-Cttee, 1966-68); West Midland RHA, 1974-; Chairman: Clinical Trials Sub-Cttee; DHSS Working Party on Medical Administrators in Health Service, 1970-72; DHSS Independent Scientific Cttee on Smoking and Health, 1973-; Med. Adv, Cttee of Cttee of Vice-Chancellors and Principals. Malthe Foundation Lecturer, Oslo, 1958. Editor, Quarterly Journal of Medicine, 1957-67. Fellow (ex-President) Royal Medical Society. Major, Royal Army Medical Corps. Gained Purdue Frederick Medical Achievement Award, 1958. Senior Commonwealth Travelling Fellowship, 1960; Vis. Professor of Medicine: Post-Graduate school, University of Adelaide, 1965; McGill Univ., 1968. DL West Midlands, 1975. Hon. LLD: Dundee, 1969; Birmingham, 1974. *Publications:* Clinical Science; contrib. to Br. Med. Journ., Lancet, Edinburgh Med. Journ., Quarterly Journ. of Medicine. *Recreation:* fishing. *Address:* 43 Edgbaston Park Road, Birmingham B15 2RS. *T:* 021-454 0925. *Club:* Athenæum.

HUNTER, William Hill, CBE 1971; CA; JP; Partner in McLay, McAlister & McGibbon, Chartered Accountants, since 1946; *b* 5 Nov. 1916; *s* of Robert Dalglish Hunter and Mrs Margaret Walker Hill or Hunter; *m* 1947, Kathleen, *d* of William Alfred Cole; two *s. Educ:* Cumnock Academy. Chartered Accountant, 1940. Served War: enlisted as private, RASC, 1940; commissioned RA, 1941; Staff Capt., Middle East, 1944-46. Director: Abbey National Building Soc. (Scottish Adv. Bd); City of Glasgow Friendly Soc.; J. & G. Grant Glenfarclas/Glenlivet Distillery. President: W Renfrewshire Conservative and Unionist Assoc., 1972-; Scottish Young Unionist Assoc., 1958-60; Scottish Unionist Assoc., 1964-65. Contested (U) South Ayrshire, 1959 and 1964. Vice-Chm., Salvation Army Adv. Bd in Glasgow, 1972-. JP Renfrewshire, 1970. *Recreations:* gardening, golf, swimming. *Address:* Armitage, Kilmacolm, Renfrewshire PA13 4PH. *T:* Kilmacolm 2444. *Club:* Royal Scottish Automobile.

HUNTER BLAIR, Sir James, 7th Bt, *cr* 1786; *b* 7 May 1889; *s* of Capt. Sir E. Hunter Blair, 6th Bt, and Cecilia (*d* 1951), *d* of late Sir W. Farrer; *S* father 1945; *m* 1st, 1917, Jean (*d* 1953), *d* of late T. W. McIntyre, Sorn Castle, Ayrshire; two *s*; 2nd, 1954, Mrs Ethel Norah Collins (*d* 1966). *Educ:* Wellington; Balliol Coll., Oxford (1st Hon. Mod., 2nd Greats); Christ's Coll., Cambridge (Forestry). Articled to solicitor, 1911-14; served with Seaforth Highlanders, 1915-19; District Officer with Forestry Commission, 1920-28. Forestry and Farming at Blairquhan, 1928-. *Publications:* articles on Forestry and cognate subjects in various journals. *Recreation:* collecting pictures. *Heir: s* Edward Thomas Hunter Blair [*b* 15 Dec. 1920; *m* 1956, Norma (*d* 1972), *d* of W. S. Harris; one adopted *s* one adopted *d. Educ:* Eton; Balliol Coll., Oxford]. *Address:* Milton, Maybole, Ayrshire. *Clubs:* United Oxford & Cambridge University; New (Edinburgh).

HUNTER JOHNSTON, David Alan; Director: Lindustries Ltd; British American & General Trust Ltd; Trans Oceanic Trust Ltd; Chairman, Association of Investment Trust Companies, since 1975; *b* 16 Jan. 1915; *s* of James Ernest Johnston and Florence Edith Johnston (*née* Hunter); *m* 1949, Philippa Frances Ray; three *s* one *d. Educ:* Christ's Hospital; King's Coll., London. Royal Ordnance Factories, Woolwich, 1936-39; S Metropolitan Gas Co., 1939-44; Min. of Economic Warfare (Economic and Industrial Planning Staff), 1944-45; Control Office for Germany and Austria, 1945-47; Sec. to Scientific Cttee for Germany, 1946; FO (German Section), Asst Head, German Gen. Economic Dept, 1947-49; HM Treasury, Supply, Estabt and Home Finance Divs, 1949-53. Central Bd of Finance of Church of England: Sec. (and Fin. Sec. to Church Assembly), 1953-59, and Investment Manager, 1959-65; concurrently, Dir, Investment Man. to Charities Official Investment Fund, 1963-65; a Man. Dir, J. Henry Schroder Wagg & Co. Ltd, 1965-74; Chm., Reserve Pension Bd, 1974-75; Dir, Clerical, Medical & General Life Assurance Soc., 1970-74. Mem., Monopolies Commn, 1969-73. Fellow of King's Coll., London, and Hon. Treas. of the Corporation, and Vice Chm. of the Delegacy. *Recreations:* (chief interests) family, theology, country life, music, architecture; a lay reader. *Address:* Sharpes Farm, Little

Hadham, Herts. *T:* Much Hadham 2687. *Clubs:* Farmers', City of London.

HUNTER SMART, William Norman, CA; Partner, Hays Allan, Chartered Accountants, since 1950; *b* 25 May 1921; *s* of William Hunter Smart, CA, and Margaret Thorburn Inglis; *m* 1948, Bridget Beryl Andreae (*d* 1974); four *s*. *Educ:* George Watson's Coll., Edinburgh. Served War, 1939-45; commnd 1st Lothians & Border Horse, 1941; Warwickshire Yeomanry, 1942; served Middle East and Italy; Adjutant-Captain, 1945, mentioned in despatches. Qualified as Chartered Accountant, 1948. Joined Hays, Akers & Hays, 1948. Chm., Assoc. of Scottish Chartered Accountants in London, 1972-73; Institute of Chartered Accountants of Scotland: Council Mem., 1970-75; Vice-Pres., 1976-78. *Recreations:* sailing, shooting, gardening. *Address:* Little Heath House, Limpsfield Chart, Oxted, Surrey RH8 0SZ. *T:* Limpsfield Chart 2117. *Clubs:* Gresham, Caledonian; Royal Motor Yacht (Poole).

HUNTER-TOD, Air Marshal Sir John (Hunter), KBE 1971 (OBE 1957); CB 1969; Head of Engineer Branch and Director-General of Engineering (RAF), 1970-73, retired; *b* 21 April 1917; *s* of late Hunter Finlay Tod, FRCS; *m* 1959, Anne, *d* of late Thomas Chaffer Howard; one *s*. *Educ:* Marlborough; Trinity Coll., Cambridge (MA). DCAe 1948. Commissioned, 1940; Fighter Command and Middle East, 1939-45. Group Capt. 1958; Air Cdre 1963. Dir, Guided Weapons (Air), Min. of Aviation, 1962-65; AOEng, RAF Germany, 1965-67; AOC No 24 Group, RAF, 1967-70; Air Vice-Marshal, 1968; Air Marshal, 1971. CEng. Hon. DSc Cranfield Inst. of Technol., 1974. *Recreation:* gardening. *Address:* Whitetop, Larch Avenue, Sunninghill, Berks. *T:* Ascot 22264. *Club:* Royal Air Force.

HUNTING, (Charles) Patrick (Maule), CBE 1975; TD 1952; FCA; Chairman of Hunting Group, 1962-74; *b* 16 Dec. 1919; *s* of late Sir Percy Hunting; *m* 1941, Diana, *d* of late Brig. A. B. P. Pereira, DSO, of Tavistock, Devon; two *s* two *d*. *Educ:* Rugby Sch.; Trinity Coll., Cambridge. BA (Hons) Mod. and Mediaeval Langs; MA 1975; ACA 1936, FCA 1960. Served Royal Sussex Regt, 1939-45: France and Belgium, 1940; 8th Army, Western Desert, 1942; also in Palestine and Persia; Staff Coll., Camberley (psc), 1945. Entered Hunting Group 1936, Dir, 1946, Vice-Chm., 1961; Director: Hunting Associated Industries Ltd (Chm., 1965-74); Hunting Gibson Ltd (Chm., 1970-74); Hunting Gp Ltd (Chm., 1972-74); Dir, Berry Wiggins & Co. Ltd. Mem. Council, Chamber of Shipping of UK, 1960 (Chm. Tramp Tanker Section, 1962); Mem. Court, 1970, Senior Warden, 1977-, Ironmongers' Company. *Recreations:* golf, fishing. *Address:* The Old House, Birch Grove, Horsted Keynes, Sussex RH17 7BT. *T:* Chelwood Gate 254. *Clubs:* Bath, MCC; Royal Ashdown Forest (Golf).

HUNTING, (Lindsay) Clive; Chairman, Hunting Group of Companies, since 1975; *b* 22 Dec. 1925; *s* of late Gerald Lindsay Hunting and Ruth (*née* Pyman); *m* 1952, Shelagh (*née* Hill-Lowe); one *s* one *d*. *Educ:* Loretto; Trinity Hall, Cambridge (MA). Royal Navy, 1944-47; Cambridge, 1947-50; joined Hunting Group, 1950, Dir 1952, Vice-Chm. 1962; Group comprises Hunting Gibson Ltd (Hunting & Son Ltd; Northern Petroleum and Bulk Freighters Ltd; E. A. Gibson & Co. Ltd; Hunting Painting Contractors Ltd; Gibson Petroleum Ltd, Canada; Pétrole et Affrètements, France); Hunting Associated Industries Ltd (Hunting Engineering Management Ltd; Hunting Surveys and Consultants Ltd; Field Aircraft Services Ltd; Halmatic Ltd; Field Industries Africa Ltd; Field Aviation Co. Ltd, Canada) and Hunting Group Ltd (Brazos Young Corporation, USA). Chairman: Donkin & Co. Ltd, 1952; Seabridge Shipping Ltd, 1977. Pres., British Independent Air Transport Assoc., 1960-62; Pres., Fedn Internationale de Transporte Aerien Privée, 1961-63; Chm., Air League, 1968-71; Pres., Air Educn and Recreation Organisation, 1970-. *Recreation:* yachting. *Address:* Fugelmere Grange, Fulmer, Bucks SL3 6HN. *T:* Fulmer 2213. *Clubs:* City Livery; Royal London Yacht.

HUNTING, Patrick; *see* Hunting, C. P. M.

HUNTINGDON, 15th Earl of, *cr* 1529; **Francis John Clarence Westenra Plantagenet Hastings,** MA; artist; *b* 30 Jan. 1901; *s* of 14th Earl and Margaret (*d* 1953), 2nd *d* of Sir Samuel Wilson, sometime MP for Portsmouth; *S* father, 1939; *m* 1st, 1925, Cristina (who obtained a divorce, 1943 and *m* 2nd, 1944, Hon. Wogan Philipps, who *S*, 1962, as 2nd Baron Milford, *qv*; she died 1953), *d* of the Marchese Casati, Rome; one *d*; 2nd, 1944, Margaret Lane, *qv*; two *d*. *Educ:* Eton; Christ Church, Oxford. MA Hons, History; Slade School, London Univ. Played Oxford Univ. Polo team. Prof., Sch. of Arts & Crafts, Camberwell, 1938. ARP Officer and Dep. Controller Andover Rural district, 1941-

45. Jt Parly Sec., Min. of Agriculture and Fisheries, 1945-50. Prof., Central Sch. of Arts & Crafts, London, 1950. A pupil of Diego Rivera; *Exhibitions:* Paris, London, Chicago, San Francisco; Evanston, Ill; Monterey, Calif; of Science, World's Fair, Chicago, 1933; Marx House, Buscot Park, Faringdon; Birmingham Univ.; Women's Press Club, London; Casa dello Strozzato, Tuscany; The Priory, Reading; Vineyards, Beaulieu, etc. Chm. of Cttee Soc. of Mural Painters, 1953-57. Pres., Solent Protection Soc., 1958-68. Mem., Wine Trade Art Soc. *Publications:* Commonsense about India; The Golden Octopus. *Heir:* cousin David Fox Godolphin Hastings [*b* 13 Dec. 1909; *m* 1945, Mary, *d* of late E. C. Jones, Llandovery, and *widow* of E. H. Power]. *Address:* Blackbridge House, Beaulieu, Hants. *Club:* Garrick.
See also W. L. Wyatt.

HUNTINGDON, Bishop Suffragan of, since 1972; **Rt. Rev. Eric St Quintin Wall;** *b* 19 April 1915; *s* of Rev. Sydney Herbert Wall, MA, and Ethel Marion Wall (*née* Wilkins); *m* 1942, Doreen Clare (*née* Loveley); one *s* one *d*. *Educ:* Clifton; Brasenose Coll., Oxford (MA); Wells Theol. College. Deacon, 1938; Priest, 1939; Curate of Boston, 1938-41; Chaplain, RAFVR, 1941-45; Vicar of Sherston Magna, 1944-53; Rural Dean of Malmesbury, 1951-53; Vicar of Cricklade with Latton, 1953-60; Hon. Chaplain to Bp of Bristol, 1960-66; Hon. Canon, Bristol, 1960-72; Diocesan Adviser on Christian Stewardship, Dio. Bristol, 1960-66; Proc. Conv., 1964-69; Vicar, St Alban's, Westbury Park, Bristol, 1966-72; Rural Dean of Clifton, 1967-72; Canon Residentiary of Ely, 1972-. *Recreation:* golf (occasional). *Address:* Whitgift House, Ely, Cambs. *T:* Ely 2137.

HUNTINGFIELD, 6th Baron *cr* 1796; **Gerard Charles Arcedeckne Vanneck;** Bt 1751; international civil servant with United Nations Secretariat, 1946-75; *b* 29 May 1915; *er s* of 5th Baron Huntingfield, KCMG, and Margaret Eleanor (*d* 1943) *o d* of late Judge Ernest Crosby, Grasmere, Rhinebeck, NY; *S* father, 1969; *m* 1941, Janetta Lois, *er d* of Capt. R. H. Errington, RN, Tostock Old Hall, Bury St Edmunds, Suffolk; one *s* three *d*. *Educ:* Stowe; Trinity College, Cambridge. *Heir:* *s* Hon. Joshua Charles Vanneck, *b* 10 Aug. 1954. *Address:* 1815 Clarens, Switzerland.
See also Hon. P. B. R. Vanneck.

HUNTINGTON-WHITELEY, Sir Hugo (Baldwin), 3rd Bt *cr* 1918; DL; Partner: Price Waterhouse & Co., Chartered Accountants; *b* 31 March 1924; *e* surv. *s* of Captain Sir Maurice Huntington-Whiteley, 2nd Bt, RN, and Lady (Pamela) Margaret Huntington-Whiteley (*d* 1976), 3rd *d* of 1st Earl Baldwin of Bewdley, KG, PC; *S* father, 1975; *m* 1959, Jean Marie Ramsay (JP 1973); two *d*. *Educ:* Eton. Served in Royal Navy, 1942-47. Chartered Accountant. Worcs: High Sheriff 1971; DL 1972. *Recreations:* music, travel. *Heir:* *b* (John) Miles Huntington-Whiteley, VRD, Lieut-Comdr RNR [*b* 18 July 1929; *m* 1960, Countess Victoria Adelheid Clementine Louise, *d* of late Count Friedrich Wolfgang zu Castell-Rudenhausen; one *s* two *d*]. *Address:* Ripple Hall, Tewkesbury, Glos. *T:* Upton-on-Severn 2431. *Club:* Brooks's.

HUNTLEY, Arthur Geoffrey; President, May Acoustics, Ltd, acoustical engineers; *b* 1897; *s* of Rev. A. H. Huntley, Hull; *m*; two *s*. *Educ:* Hereford Cathedral Sch. Commenced training as chemical engineer, 1913; commissioned to the Royal Engineers (TA), 1914; served in the Royal Engineers in France, Belgium, and India, 1914-19 (1914-15 Star, GS and allied ribbons, despatches, TD); Lieut-Col RA, retd; secured post with large contracting firm and studied sound, 1920; founded the May Construction Co. Ltd, to undertake the work of acoustical engineers and contractors, 1922; AMIStructE, 1921; Mem. of the Acoustical Soc. of America, 1931. *Publications:* Acoustics, Cantor Lectures, Royal Society of Arts, 1928, and other articles to the technical press; The Acoustics of Structures, paper before the Institute of Structural Engineers, 1925. *Recreation:* bridge. *Adress:* Hill House Farm, 1 School Lane, Netteswell, Harlow, Essex CM20 2QB.

HUNTLY, 12th Marquess of, *cr* 1599, Earl of, *cr* 1450; **Douglas Charles Lindsey Gordon;** Lord of Gordon before 1408; Earl of Enzie, Lord of Badenoch, 1599; Bt 1625; Baron Aboyne, 1627; Earl of Aboyne, Lord Strathavon and Glenlivet, 1660; Baron Meldrum, 1815; sits under creation of 1815; Premier Marquess of Scotland; Chief of House of Gordon; Gordon Highlanders; *b* 3 Feb. 1908; *s* of late Lieut-Col Douglas Gordon, CVO, DSO, and Violet Ida, *d* of Gerard Streatfeild; *S* great-uncle, 1937; *m* 1941, Hon. Mary Pamela Berry (marr. diss. 1965), *o d* of 1st Viscount Kemsley; one *s* one *d*; *m* 1977, Elizabeth Haworth Leigh, *d* of Lt Cdr F. H. Leigh. *Heir:* *s* Earl of Aboyne, *qv*. *Address:* Hollybrook, Ewhurst Road, Cranleigh, Surrey. *T:* Cranleigh 71500. *Club:* Army and Navy.
See also Lord Adam Gordon.

HURD, Hon. Douglas Richard, CBE 1974; MP (C) Mid-Oxon, since Feb. 1974; b 8 March 1930; e s of Baron Hurd (d 1966) and Stephanie Corner; m 1960, Tatiana Elizabeth Michelle, d of A. C. Benedict Eyre, Westburton House, Bury, Sussex; three s. Educ: Eton (King's Scholar and Newcastle Scholar); Trinity Coll., Cambridge (Major Scholar). Pres., Cambridge Union, 1952. HM Diplomatic Service, 1952-66; served in: Peking, 1954-56; UK Mission to UN, 1956-60; Private Sec. to Perm. Under-Sec. of State, FO, 1960-63; Rome, 1963-66. Joined Conservative Research Dept, 1966; Head of Foreign Affairs Section, 1968; Private Sec. to Leader of the Opposition, 1968-70; Political Sec. to Prime Minister, 1970-74; Opposition Spokesman on European Affairs, 1976. Publications: The Arrow War, 1967; (with Andrew Osmond) Send Him Victorious, 1968; The Smile on the Face of the Tiger, 1969; (with Andrew Osmond) Scotch on the Rocks, 1971; Truth Game, 1972; Vote to Kill, 1975. Recreation: writing thrillers. Address: 2 Mitford Cottages, Westwell, Burford, Oxon. Club: Travellers'.

HURFORD, Peter John; Master of the Music, Cathedral and Abbey Church of St Alban, since 1958; b 22 Nov. 1930; e c of H. J. Hurford, Minehead; m 1955, Patricia Mary Matthews; two s one d. Educ: Blundells Sch.; Royal Coll. of Music; Jesus Coll., Cambridge. MA, MusB Cantab, FRCO, FRSCM, ARCM. Music, Bablake Sch., Coventry and Conductor, Leamington Spa Bach Choir, 1956-57; Conductor, St Albans Bach Choir, 1958-; Founder and Chm. (now Artistic Dir), Internat. Organ Festival Soc., 1963; Mem. Council, RCO, 1963-; Artist-in-Residence, Univ. of Cincinnati, 1967-68; Vis. Prof. of organ, Univ. of Western Ontario, 1976-77; recital and lecture tours throughout Europe, USA, Canada, Australia and NZ from 1960. Has made eighteen LP records. Publications: Suite: Laudate Dominum; sundry other works for organ; Mass for Series III; sundry church anthems. Recreations: walking and silence. Address: 31 Abbey Mill Lane, St Albans, Herts. T: St Albans 51810.

HURLEY, Ven. Alfred Vincent, CBE 1945 (OBE 1944); TD 1944; Archdeacon of Dudley, 1951-68; Rector of Old Swinford, 1948-64; b 12 Jan. 1896; s of Alfred Walter and Phoebe Hurley, Reading; m 1929, Jenny Drummond, 2nd d of Henry John Sansom, Pennsylvania Castle, Portland, Dorset; one s three d. Educ: Queen's Sch., Basingstoke; Keble Coll., Oxford (MA); Cuddesdon Coll. Artists' Rifles, 1915; Royal Flying Corps, 1916-19. Curate, Armley, Leeds, 1922; Chaplain: Leeds Prison, 1923-24; Portland Borstal Instn, 1924; Dep. Gov. Portland Borstal Instn, 1928; Rector of Portland, 1931; Rural Dean of Weymouth, 1937; Canon and Preb. of Salisbury, 1939. Chaplain to Forces, 4th Dorsets, 1939; SCF, 42 East Lancs Div. 1940; Asst Chaplain General, 8th Army, 1944 (despatches); Dep. Chaplain General, South East Asia Allied Land Forces, 1945-46; Hon. Canon of Worcester, 1951-; Exam. Chap. to Bishop of Worcester, 1951-68. Address: Old House, 1st Marine Avenue, Barton-on-Sea, Hants. T: New Milton 610952.

HURLEY, Sir Hugh; see Hurley, Sir W. H.

HURLEY, Sir John Garling, Kt 1967; CBE 1959; FAIM; JP; Managing Director, Berlei United Ltd, Sydney, 1948-69; b Bondi, NSW, 2 Oct. 1906; s of late John Hurley, MLA, and late Annie Elizabeth (née Garling); m 1st 1929, Alice Edith Saunders (d 1975); three d; 2nd, 1976, Desolie M. Richardson. Educ: Sydney Techn. High Sch. With Berlei group of cos, 1922-69, incl. Berlei (UK) Ltd, London, 1931-36; Chm., William Adams Ltd, 1963-74 (Dep. Chm. 1974-76); Director: Manufacturers' Mutual Insurance Ltd, Sydney, 1954; Develt Finance Corporation Ltd, 1967-; Australian Fixed Trusts Ltd, 1970-; Royal North Shore Hosp. of Sydney, 1969-76. President: Associated Chambers of Manufactures of Austr. 1955-56; Chamber of Manufactures of NSW, 1955-57; Member: Techn. and Further Educn Adv. Council of NSW, 1958-76; Industrial Design Council of Australia, 1958-76 (Dep. Chm, 1970-); Council, Abbotsleigh Sch., 1960-66; Australian Advertising Standards Adv. Authority, 1974-; Councillor, Nat. Heart Foundn of Australia (NSW Div.), 1969-. Chm., Standing Cttee on Productivity, Ministry of Labour Adv. Coun., 1957; Leader of Austr. Trade Mission to India and Ceylon, 1957. Chm. and Trustee, Museum of Applied Arts and Sciences, NSW, 1958-76. Member: Royal Agricultural Soc.; Sydney Cricket Ground; Australian-American Assoc.; Australia-Britain Soc.; Nat. Trust of Australia. FAIM 1949. Recreations: swimming, bowls. Address: 1 Arnold Street, Killara, NSW 2071, Australia. Clubs: Australian (Sydney); Royal Sydney Yacht Squadron; Australasian Pioneers' (NSW); Warrawee Bowling.

HURLEY, Sir (Wilfred) Hugh, Kt 1963; Chief Justice, High Courts of Northern States of Nigeria, 1967-69; retired, 1969; b 16 Oct. 1910; s of Henry Hutchings Hurley and Elizabeth Louise (née Maguire); m 1940, Una Kathleen (née Wyllie); one s two d.

Educ: St Stephen's Green Sch., Dublin; Trinity Coll., Dublin. Barrister-at-Law (King's Inns, Dublin), 1935; Magistrate, Nigeria, 1940; Chief Registrar, Supreme Court, Nigeria, 1949; Puisne Judge, Supreme Court, Nigeria, 1953-55, Judge, 1955-57, Senior Puisne Judge, 1957-60 and Chief Justice, 1960-67, High Court, Northern Nigeria. Chm., Judicial Service Commn, Northern Nigeria, and Mem., Judicial Service Commission, Federation of Nigeria, 1960-63. Called to the Bar, Gray's Inn, 1976. Hon. LLD Ahmadu Bello Univ., Nigeria, 1968. Address: 27 Instow Road, Earley, Reading, Berks.

HURLL, Alfred William, CVO 1970; CBE 1955; Member of Council, The Scout Association, since 1948 (Chief Executive Commissioner, 1948-70); b 10 Sept. 1905; s of Charles Alfred Hurll; m 1933, Elsie Margaret, d of Frederick Sullivan; one s one d. Educ: Grammar Sch., Acton. Joined staff, The Scouts Assoc. HQ, 1921; Sec., Home Dept, 1935; Asst Gen. Sec., 1938; Gen. Sec., 1941. Publication: (co-author) BP's Scouts, 1961. Recreations: cricket, theatre. Address: 106 Montrose Avenue, Twickenham, TW2 6HD. T: 01-894 1957.

HURON, Bishop of, since 1974; **Rt. Rev. Theodore David Butler Ragg,** DD; b 23 Nov. 1919; s of late Rt Rev. Harry Richard Ragg and Winifred Mary Ragg (née Groves) m 1945, Dorothy Mary Lee; one s two d. Educ: Univ. of Manitoba; Trinity Coll., Univ. of Toronto (BA, LTh); General Synod (BD). Deacon, 1949; priest, 1950; Asst Curate, St Michae. and All Angels, Toronto, 1949; Rector: Nokomis, 1951; Wolseley, 1953; St Clement's, N Vancouver, 1955; St Luke's, Victoria, 1957; Bishop Cronyn Memorial, London, 1962; St George's, Owen Sound, 1967. Examining Chaplain to Bishop of Huron, 1964-67; Archdeacon of Saugeen, 1967; elected Suffragan Bishop of Huron, 1973, elected Bishop of Huron, 1974. Hon. DD: Huron Coll., London, Ont., 1975; Trinity Coll., Toronto, Ont., 1975. Recreations: woodworking, golf, camping Address: 4-220 Dundas Street, London, Ontario, Canada N6A 1H3. T: (office) (519) 434-6893. Clubs: London, London Hunt and Country (London, Ont.).

HURRELL, Anthony Gerald; Under-Secretary, Duchy of Lancaster, since 1977; b 18 Feb. 1927; s of late William Hurrell and Florence Hurrell; m 1951, Jean Wyatt; two d. Educ: Norwich Sch.; St Catharine's Coll., Cambridge. RAEC, 1948-50; Min. of Labour, 1950-53; Min. of Educn, 1953-64; Min. of Overseas Develt, 1964-; Asst Sec., 1966; Fellow, Center for International Affairs, Harvard, 1969-70; Head of SE Asia Develt Div., Bangkok, 1972-74; Under Secretary: Internat. Div. ODM, 1974-76; Central Policy Rev. Staff, Cabinet Office, 1976. Recreations: bird-ringing, bird-watching, digging ponds, music. Address: Benacre, Mill Road, Stock, Essex CM4 9LL. T: Stock 840254.

HURRELL, Col Geoffrey Taylor, OBE 1944; Lord-Lieutenant of Cambridgeshire, 1974-75 (of Cambridgeshire and Isle of Ely, 1965-74); b 12 March 1900; s of Arthur Hurrell and Emily Taylor; m 1934, Mary Crossman; one s one d. Educ: Rugby; Sandhurst. Gazetted 17th Lancers, 1918; Lieut-Col comdg 17th/21st Lancers, 1940; Col 1944 High Sheriff, Cambridgeshire and Huntingdonshire, 1963; JP Cambs 1952, DL 1958. KStJ 1972. Recreations: hunting, shooting. Address: Park House, Harston, near Cambridge. Club: Cavalry and Guards.

HURRELL, Ian Murray, MVO 1961; HM Diplomatic Service, retired; b 14 June 1914; s of Capt. L. H. M. Hurrell and Mrs Eva Hurrell; m 1939, Helen Marjorie Darwin; no c. Educ: Dover Coll. Anglo-Iranian Oil Co., 1932-34; Indian Police (United Provinces), 1935-47; entered HM Foreign (subseq. Diplomatic) Service, 1948; Vice-Consul, Shiraz, 1949-51; Consul, Benghazi, 1952; FO, 1952-53; 1st Sec., Quito, 1954 (Chargé d'Affaires, 1955); Bangkok, 1956-60; Tehran, 1960-64; Ankara (UK Delegn to CENTO), 1964-67; Ambassador, Costa Rica, 1968-72. Asst Sec. (Environment), RSA, 1974-. Imperial Order of the Crown (Iran). Recreations: rambling, photography, skin-diving, gardening, chess, etc. Address: Quarr House, Sway, Hants. Club: Royal Over-Seas League.

HURRY, Leslie; artist; b 10 Feb. 1909; s of Alfred George Hurry and Edith Louise Perry Butcher. Educ: St John's Wood Art Schs; Royal Academy Schools. Theatrical productions, settings and costumes: Hamlet Ballet, Sadler's Wells Co., 1942; Le Lac des Cygnes, Sadler's Wells Co., 1943 and 1952; La Scherzi della Sortie, Mercury Ballet, 1951; Hamlet, Old Vic, 1944; Turandot, Covent Garden Opera, 1947; Medea, Edinburgh Festival, 1948; Cymbeline, 1949, King Lear, 1950, Stratford Memorial Theatre; La Forza del Destino, Edinburgh Festival (Glyndebourne Opera), 1951; Tamburlaine, Old Vic, 1951; Living Room, Wyndhams, 1953; Venice Preserv'd, Lyric, Hammersmith; Der

Ring des Nibelungen, Covent Garden Opera; The Tempest, Old Vic; Richard II, Old Vic; Measure for Measure, Old Vic (Australian Tour); Tamburlaine (Toronto and New York); Timon of Athens (Old Vic Theatre); The Gates of Summer (Provinces); The Moon and Sixpence, Sadler's Wells Opera Co.; Richard II, Old Vic Co. (Amer. and Canadian Tour); Richard III, Old Vic; The Hidden King, Edinburgh Festival; Henry VI, Parts I, II, III, Old Vic; Cat on a Hot Tin Roof, Comedy Theatre; King Lear, Old Vic; Hamlet Ballet (revival); Tristan and Isolde, Covent Garden Opera; costumes and setting for Mary Stuart (Edinburgh Fest., Old Vic), 1958; The Cenci, Old Vic; Andrea Chénier, Sadler's Wells Opera; St Joan, Old Vic; Troilus and Cressida, Royal Stratford Theatre; The Duchess of Malfi, Aldwych; Hamlet, Stratford upon Avon; Becket, Aldwych; Mourning Becomes Electra, Old Vic; St Joan, American Tour and Old Vic; A Village Romeo and Juliet (Delius Festival) Sadler's Wells Opera Co.; The Tempest, Old Vic; Beggar's Opera, Royal Shakespeare Co., Aldwych; (costumes) Maggie May, King Lear, Julius Cæsar, Stratford, Ont.; Swan Lake, Royal Ballet Touring Co.; Nicholas Romanov, Manitoba Theatre Centre, Canada; Stratford Festival, Canada: Last of the Tsars; The Government Inspector; Albert Herring; A Midsummer Night's Dream; La Cenerentola; School for Scandal; Sadler's Wells Opera Co.: Fidelio; Queen of Spades; Hamlet (opera, Humphrey Searle), Royal Opera, Covent Garden; Scènes d'Amour, Royal Ballet; Pericles, Stratford, Ont; Caesar and Cleopatra, Shaw Festival Theatre, Niagara on the Lake, Canada, etc. Exhibitions: Wertheim, 1937; Redfern, 1941, 1942, 1945; Rowland Browse Delblanco, 1946-50; Paintings and Theatre Designs (auspices Nat. Gall., Canada); Theatre Designs, Arts Council, 1964; paintings, Mercury Gall. (one-man shows, 1969, 1972, 1975). *Works in galleries:* Victoria and Albert Museum; Birmingham City Art Gallery; Whitworth Art Gallery, Manchester; Brighton Art Gallery; Melbourne Art Gallery, Australia; among Recent Acquisitions, BM Dept of Prints and Drawings, 1967-72. *Publications:* (Theatre Design) Leslie Hurry, 1946; (Paintings and Drawings) Leslie Hurry, 1952. *Address:* The Bunting's, Hundon, near Clare, Suffolk. *T:* Hundon 269.

HURST, Sir Donald; see Hurst, Sir J. H. D.

HURST, Edward Weston, MD, DSc (Birmingham); FRCP, retired 1969; formerly Consultant Pathologist to Industrial Hygiene Research Laboratories, Imperial Chemical Industries Ltd, Macclesfield; *b* Birmingham, 1900; *s* of Edward William Hurst and Clarinda, *d* of Thomas Wem; *m* 1926, Phyllis Edith, *d* of J. G. Picknett, MA, Leicester; three *d*; *m* 1942, Barbara Ternent, *d* of W. T. Cooke, DSc, Adelaide; one *s* one *d*. *Educ:* King Edward's Sch., Birmingham; Birmingham Univ. BSc 1920; MB, ChB, 1922; Hons in Obstetrics and Gynæcology, Queen's and Ingleby Scholarships; Walter Myers Travelling Student, Univ. of Birmingham, 1923-24; MD, 1924; Postgraduate study and research work at National Hospital, Queen Square, London, 1923-25; Pathologist to Miller General Hospital for South-East London, 1926-28; Pathologist to Milbank Fund for Research on Poliomyelitis, 1928-32; DSc, 1932; MRCP, 1932; FRCP, 1940; Associate at Rockefeller Institute, Princeton, NJ, 1932-34; Mem. of Research Staff, Lister Institute of Preventive Medicine, London, 1932-36; Reader in Experimental Pathology, University of London, 1932-36; Dir of the Institute of Medical and Veterinary Science, Adelaide, 1936-43; Keith Sheridan Professor of Experimental Medicine, University of Adelaide, 1938-43; William Withering Lecturer, University of Birmingham, 1935; Sir Joseph Bancroft Orator, Qld Branch BMA, 1940; G. E. Rennie Memorial Lecturer, RACP, 1941. *Publications:* Numerous contributions to pathology and allied subjects in English and foreign journals. *Recreation:* photography. *Address:* 46 Vermont Close, Winchester Road, Bassett, Southampton SO1 7LT.

HURST, George; Staff Conductor, Western Orchestral Society, since 1973; *b* 20 May 1926; Rumanian father and Russian mother. *Educ:* various preparatory and public schs. in the UK and Canada; Royal Conservatory, Toronto, Canada. First prize for Composition, Canadian Assoc. of Publishers, Authors and Composers, 1945. Asst Conductor, Opera Dept, Royal Conservatory of Music, of Toronto, 1946; Lectr in Harmony, Counterpoint, Composition etc, Peabody Conservatory of Music, Baltimore, Md, 1947; Conductor of York, Pa, Symph. Orch., 1950-55, and concurrently of Peabody Conservatory Orch., 1952-55; Asst Conductor, LPO, 1955-57, with which toured USSR 1956; Associate conductor, BBC Northern Symphony Orchestra, 1957; Principal Conductor, BBC Northern Symphony Orchestra (previously BBC Northern Orchestra), 1958-68; Artistic Adviser, Western Orchestral Soc., 1969-73. Since 1956 frequent guest conductor in Europe, Israel, Canada, South Africa. *Publications:* piano and vocal music

(Canada). *Recreations:* yachting, horse-riding, chess. *Address:* 21 Oslo Court, NW8. *T:* 01-722 3088.

HURST, Harold Edwin, CMG 1932; MA, DSc Oxon; FInstP; Professional Associate, Institution of Water Engineers; Hydrological Adviser, Ministry of Irrigation, Egypt, retired; *b* 1 Jan. 1880; *s* of Charles Hurst, Wigston Magna, Leics; *m* 1st, Winifred, *d* of late Capt. A. B. Hawes; 2nd, Marguerite, *d* of late Dr G. C. B. Hawes, Pangbourne; two *s*. *Educ:* Alderman Newton's Sch., Leicester; Hertford Coll., Oxford. Lectr and demonstrator Oxford Univ. Electrical Laboratory, 1903-6; Joined Survey of Egypt, 1906; Dir-Gen., Physical Dept, Min. of Public Works, Egypt, 1919-46. Thrice awarded Telford Premium, and Telford Gold Medal, 1957, by Instn of Civil Engrs for work on the utilization of Nile waters; Order of the Nile 2nd Class; Order of Ismail 3rd Class; travelled extensively in the Nile Basin for purposes of hydrological reconnaissance. *Publications:* papers on physics, the measurement of water, the magnetic survey of Egypt, and the Nile Basin, 1931 onwards; The Nile, 1952, 1957; (with Black and Simaika) Long Term Storage, 1965. *Recreations:* mechanical work, fishing, shooting. *Address:* Sandford-on-Thames, Oxford OX4 4XZ. *T:* Oxford 777293. *Club:* Gezira Sporting (Cairo).

HURST, Henry Ronald Grimshaw; Overseas Labour Adviser, Foreign and Commonwealth Office, since 1976; *b* 24 April 1919; *s* of Frederick George Hurst and Elizabeth Ellen (*née* Grimshaw); *m* 1942, Norah Joyce, *d* of John Stanley Rothwell; one *s* one *d*. *Educ:* Darwen and Blackpool Grammar Schs; St Catharine's Coll., Cambridge (MA). Served War, Army, 1940-46. Colonial Service, 1946-70: Permanent Sec., Min. of Labour, Tanzania, 1962-64; Labour Adviser, Tanzania, 1965-68, and Malawi, 1969-70; Dep. Overseas Labour Adviser, FCO, 1970-76. *Recreations:* tennis, cricket, gardening, *Address:* 47 Pampisford Road, Purley, Surrey. *T:* 01-660 6480. *Club:* Civil Service.

HURST, His Honour Sir (James Henry) Donald, Kt 1954; retired as Judge of County Courts; *b* 1895; *er s* of late J. G. Hurst, KC, Recorder of Birmingham; *m* 1924, Laura Olive, *d* of late James Bannister, Leicester; two *d*. *Educ:* King Edward VI Sch., Birmingham; Wadham Coll., Oxford. Served European War, 1914-18, Argyll and Sutherland Highlanders (wounded). Judge of County Courts Circuit 23 (Coventry, Northampton, etc), 1937-41; Circuit 36 (Oxford, Reading, etc), 1941-62, and of Circuit 53 (Cheltenham, Tewkesbury, Northleach, etc), 1941-62; retd Oct. 1962. Chm. Oxfordshire QS, 1947-62, Dep. Chm., 1962-67. *Address:* Clare Park, Farnham, Surrey. *T:* Aldershot 850681. *Club:* National Liberal.

HURST, Leonard Henry, CBE 1949; *b* Shanghai, 22 April 1889; *y s* of late Richard Willett Hurst, HM Consular Service (China); *m* 1st, 1920, Annie (*d* 1922), *d* of Arthur Liley; 2nd, 1928, Olive Rose Madeline (*d* 1967), *widow* of Major R. M. F. Patrick. *Educ:* Tonbridge; Pembroke Coll., Cambridge. Entered Levant Consular Service, 1908; Vice-Consul at Sofia, 1914; Consul at Bengasi, 1924, at Port Said, 1926, and at Basra, 1932; Consul-Gen. at Rabat, 1936-40, at Istanbul, 1942-47, at Tunis, 1947-49; retired from HM Foreign Service, Nov. 1949; British Consul, Rhodes, 1953-1957; British Consul, Crete, 1957-58. *Recreations:* mountaineering, numismatics. *Address:* Brynglas, Llechryd, Cards. *T:* Llechryd 393.

HURST, Margery, OBE 1976; Joint Chairman, Brook Street Bureau of Mayfair Ltd (Managing Director, 1947-76); *b* 23 May 1913; *d* of late Samuel and Deborah Berney; *m* 1948, Eric Hurst, Barrister-at-law; two *d*. *Educ:* Brondesbury and Kilburn High Sch.; Minerva Coll. RADA. Joined ATS on Direct Commission, 1943 (1939-45 war medal); invalided out of the service, 1944. Commenced business of Brook St Bureau of Mayfair Ltd, 1946; founded Margery Hurst Schs and Colls for administrative and secretarial studies. Co-opted Mem. of LCC Children's Cttee, 1956. Started non-profit making social clubs for secretaries, called Society for International Secretaries, in London, 1960; now in New York, Boston and Sydney; awarded Pimm's Cup for Anglo-American friendship in the business world, 1962. Member: American Cttee, BNEC, 1967-70; Exec. Cttee, Mental Health Research Fund, 1967-72. One of first women elected Underwriting Mem. of Lloyds, 1970. *Publication:* No Glass Slipper (autobiog.), 1967. *Recreations:* tennis, swimming, drama, opera. *Address:* Brook Street House, 47 Davies Street, W1Y 2LN. *Clubs:* Royal Corinthian Yacht; Royal Lymington Yacht; Lloyds Yacht.

HURST, Dr Robert, CBE 1973; GM 1944; FRIC 1977; retired; *b* Nelson, NZ, 3 Jan. 1915; *s* of late Percy Cecil Hurst and late Margery Hurst; *m* 1946, Rachael Jeanette (*née* Marsh); three *s*. *Educ:* Nelson Coll.; Canterbury Coll., NZ (MSc); Cambridge

Univ. (PhD). Experimental Officer, Min. of Supply, engaged in research in bomb disposal and mine detection, 1940-45. Group Leader Transuranic Elements Group, AERE, Harwell, 1948-55; Project Leader, Homogeneous Aqueous Reactor Project, AERE, Harwell, 1956-57; Chief Chemist, Research and Development Branch, Industrial Group UKAEA, 1957-58; Director, Dounreay Experimental Reactor Establishment, UKAEA, 1958-63; Dir. of Res., British Ship Res. Assoc., 1963-76. *Publication:* Editor, 1958-63; Dir. of Res., British Ship Res. Assoc., 1963-76. *Publication:* Editor, Progress in Nuclear Engineering, Series IV (Technology and Engineering), 1957. *Recreations:* gardening, sailing. *Address:* 15 Elms Avenue, Parkstone, Poole, Dorset. *Club:* Athenæum.

HURSTFIELD, Joel, DLit (London); Astor Professor of English History, University College, London, since 1962; *b* 4 Nov. 1911; *m* Elizabeth Valmai Walters, Hirwaun, Glam; one *s* one *d. Educ:* Owen's Sch.; University Coll., London. BA; Pollard and Gladstone Prizes. Mem. Brit. Univs Debating Team (USA Tour), 1934. University of London Postgrad. Studentship, 1935-36; Asst Lectr (later Lectr) University Coll., Southampton, 1937-40; Asst Comr, Nat. Savings Cttee, 1940-42; Official Historian, Offices of War Cabinet, 1942-46. Lecturer: QMC, London, 1946-51; UCL, 1951-53; Reader in Mod. Hist., 1953-59, Prof. of Mod. Hist., 1959-62, Fellow, 1963-, University College London. Vis. Prof., USA, 1967; Public Orator, Univ. of London, 1967-71; Shakespeare Birthday Lectr, Washington, 1969; James Ford Special Lectr in History, Oxford, 1972; Sen. Res. Fellow, Folger Shakespeare Library, Washington, 1973; John Coffin Meml Lectr, Univ. of London, 1974; Andrew Mellon Senior Res. Fellow, Huntington Library, USA, 1977-78; A. H. Dodd Meml Lectr, University Coll., Bangor, 1978. *Publications:* Control of Raw Materials, 1953; The Queen's Wards, 1958; Elizabeth I and the Unity of England, 1960; The Elizabethan Nation, 1964; Freedom, Corruption and Government in Elizabethan England, 1973; (ed jtly) Elizabethan Government and Society, 1961; (ed) Tudor Times (English History in Pictures), 1964; (ed jtly) Shakespeare's World, 1964; (ed) The Reformation Crisis, 1965; (ed jtly) Elizabethan People: state and society, 1972: (ed) Historical Association Book of the Tudors, 1973; The Historian as Moralist: reflections on the study of Tudor England, 1975; articles and reviews in History, Eng. Hist. Rev., Econ. Hist. Rev., The Times, Guardian, Daily Telegraph, etc. *Recreations:* walking in cities, the theatre. *Address:* 7 Glenilla Road, Hampstead, NW3. *T:* 01-794 2891; Northwood Cottage, 98 Northwood Road, Tankerton, Kent. *Club:* Athenæum.

HURWITZ, Vivian Ronald; His Honour Judge Hurwitz; a Circuit Judge, since 1974; *b* 7 Sept. 1926; *s* of Alter Max and Dora Rebecca Hurwitz; *m* 1963, Dr Ruth Cohen, Middlesbrough; one *s* two *d. Educ:* Roundhay Sch., Leeds; Hertford Coll., Oxford (MA). Served RNVR: Univ. Naval Short Course, Oct. 1944-March 1945, followed by service until March 1947. Called to Bar, Lincoln's Inn, 1952, practised NE Circuit. A Recorder of Crown Court, 1972-74. *Recreations:* tennis, music (listening), art (looking at), sport—various (watching). *Address:* 2 Bentcliffe Drive, Leeds LS17 6QX. *T:* Leeds 687174. *Club:* Moor Allerton Golf.

HUSAIN, Mohammad Arshad, Sitara-i-Pakistan; *b* 9 Jan. 1910; *o s* of M. Afzal Husain; *m* Husanara, 3rd *d* of late Sir Fazl-e-Husain, KCSI, KCIE; one *s* one *d. Educ:* Govt Coll., Lahore; St Catharine's Coll., Cambridge; Middle Temple, London. Advertising Cons., Govt of India, 1943; Dir Publicity Govt of Pakistan, 1947; joined Pakistan Foreign Service, 1950; Dep. Sec., 1950-53; Chargé d'Affaires, Brussels, 1954-56, Jt Sec., 1957-59; Ambassador to Sweden, Denmark, Norway and Finland, 1959-61; Ambassador to USSR and Czechoslovakia, 1961-63; High Comr, New Delhi, 1963-68; Foreign Minister, Pakistan, 1968-69. *Address:* 51/3 Lawrence Road, Lahore, Pakistan. *Club:* Karachi (Karachi).

HUSBAND, Sir (Henry) Charles, Kt 1975; CBE 1964; BEng, DSc, FICE, PPIStructE, FIMechE, FAmSCE; Senior Partner, Husband & Co., Consulting Engineers, Sheffield, London and Colombo, since 1937; *b* 30 Oct. 1908; *s* of Prof. Joseph Husband, DEng, MICE and Ellen Walton Husband; *m* 1932, Eileen Margaret, *d* of late Henry Nowill, Sheffield; two *s* two *d. Educ:* King Edward VII Sch., Sheffield; Sheffield Univ. Asst to Sir E. Owen Williams, MICE, 1931-33; Engr and Surveyor to First Nat. Housing Trust Ltd, 1933-36; planning and construction of large housing schemes in England and Scotland; from 1936, designed public works at home and overseas incl. major road and railway bridges, drainage and water supply schemes; Princ. Techn. Officer, Central Register, Min. of Labour and Nat.

Service, 1939-40; Asst Dir, Directorate of Aircraft Prodn Factories, Min. of Works, 1943-45; designed first high altitude testing plant for continuous running of complete jet engines, 1946, also research estabs for Brit. Iron and Steel Res. Assoc., Prodn Engrg Res. Assoc. and other industrial organisations; designed and supervised construction of 250 ft diameter radio telescope, Jodrell Bank, and other large radio telescopes at home and abroad incl. steerable aerials for GPO satellite stn, Goonhilly Downs, Cornwall. Chm., Yorks Assoc. ICE, 1949; Pres., Instn Struct. Engrs, 1964-65; Chm., Adv. Cttee on Engrg and Metallurgy, University of Sheffield, 1962-65; Mem. Ct, University of Sheffield; Mem. Cons. Panel in Civil Engrg, Bradford Univ. (formerly Inst. of Technology), 1962-; Mem., Council of Engrg Instns, 1965-66; Chm., Assoc. of Consulting Engineers, 1967. Hon. DSc Manchester Univ., 1964; Hon. DEng Sheffield Univ., 1967. Sir Benjamin Baker Gold Medal, ICE, 1959; (first) Queen's Gold Medal for Applied Science, Royal Society, 1965; Wilhelm Exner Medal for Science and Technology, University of Vienna, 1966; Instn Gold Medal, IStructE, 1974; James Watt Medal, ICE, 1976. *Publications:* contributions to British and foreign engrg jls. *Recreations:* sailing, walking. *Address:* Okenhold, School Green Lane, Sheffield S10 4GP. *T:* 303395. *Clubs:* Royal Thames Yacht, St Stephen's, Royal Automobile; Sheffield (Sheffield).

HUSKISSON, Alfred, OBE 1951; MC 1917, and Bar 1918; Director of S. Simpson and of Simpson (Piccadilly), 1940-74 (Dep. Chm. 1959-64; Managing Director Simpson (Piccadilly), 1940-59, S. Simpson Ltd, 1942-59); *b* 27 June 1892; *s* of Joseph Cliffe and Martha Huskisson; *m* 1st, 1922, Constance (marr. diss.), *d* of late Arthur Frederick Houfton, Nottingham; one *s* one *d*; 2nd, 1972, Sheila Mary Bullen Huskisson. *Educ:* privately. Served European War, 1914-18 (despatches); granted rank of Major, 1920. Managing Dir William Hollins & Co., Nottingham, 1929-38. Mem. Allies Welcome Cttee, 1943-50. Life Member: Overseas League, 1943; National Playing Fields Assoc. 1952. Hon. Treas. Abbey Div., Westminster Conservative Assoc., 1945-54; No 1 Assoc. Mem. Variety Club of Gt Brit., 1950-; Chm. Wholesale Clothing Manufacturers Assoc., 1952; Pres. Appeal Cottage Homes, Linen and Woollen Drapers, 1953; Master of the Worshipful Co. of Woolmen, 1952-53, 1964-65; Past Pres. The Piccadilly and St James's Assoc. (Chm. 1950-53); Vice-Pres. Westminster Philanthropic Soc. (Chm. 1956); Vice-Chm. Machine Gun Corps Officers' Club, 1960; Member: Grand Council of FBI, 1953-65; British Olympic Assoc. Appeals Cttee, 1955-56; British Empire & Commonwealth Games Appeal Cttee, 1958; British Olympic Assoc. Appeals Cttee, 1959-60; Export Council for Europe, 1960-66; Empire & Commonwealth Games UK Industrial Appeal Cttee, 1961; Chm. various Westminster and other appeals in the past. *Recreation:* golf. *Address:* 3 Edenhurst, 21 Grosvenor Road, Bournemouth, Dorset BH4 8BQ. *Clubs:* Simpson Services, Lord's Taverners (Pres. 1954, 1955); British Sportsman's, Isle of Purbeck Golf.

HUSKISSON, Robert Andrews; Chairman, Lloyd's Register of Shipping, since 1973 (Deputy Chairman, 1972-73); *b* 2 April 1923; *y s* of Edward Huskisson and Mary Huskisson (*née* Downing); *m* 1969, Alice Marian Swaffin. *Educ:* Merchant Taylors' Sch.; St Edmund Hall, Oxford. Served Royal Corps of Signals, 1941-47 (Major). Joined Shaw Savill & Albion Co. Ltd 1947; Dir 1966-72; Dep. Chief Exec., 1971-72; Director: Overseas Containers Ltd, 1967-72; Container Fleets Ltd, 1967-72; Cairn Line of Steamships Ltd, 1969-72. President: British Shipping Fedn, 1971-72 (Chm. 1968-71); International Shipping Fedn, 1969-73; Chm., Hotels and Catering EDC, 1975-. *Recreations:* golf, gardening, music. *Address:* Lanterns, Luppitt Close, Hutton Mount, Brentwood, Essex. *Clubs:* Vincent's (Oxford); Thorndon Park Golf.

HUSSEIN bin Onn, Datuk, SPMJ 1972; SPDK 1974; SIMP 1975; PIS 1968; MP for Sri Gading, since 1974; Prime Minister of Malaysia, since 1976; *b* Johore Bharu, 12 Feb. 1922; *s* of late Dato' Onn bin Jaafar and of Datin Hajjah Halimah binte Hussein; *m* Datin Suhailah; two *s* four *d. Educ:* English Coll., Johore Bharu; Military Acad., Dehra Dun, India. Called to the Bar, Gray's Inn. Cadet, Johore Mil. Forces, 1940; commnd Indian Army; served Egypt, Syria, Palestine, Persia, Iraq, and GHQ, New Delhi; seconded to Malayan Police Recruiting and Trng Centre, Rawalpindi; returned to Malaya with liberation forces, 1945; Comdt, Police Depot, Johore Bharu; demobilised. Joined Malay Admin. Service; served in Selangor State; Officer i/c Kampong (village) guards, Johore, in Communist emergency, 1948. Entered politics; National Youth Leader and Sec.-Gen., United Malays Nat. Org. (UMNO), 1950; Member: Fed. Legislative Council; Johore Council of State; Johore State Exec. Council; left UMNO when his father Dato' Onn bin Jaafar resigned from the organisation in 1951. Studied law in England;

in practice, Kuala Lumpur, 1963. Rejoined UMNO, 1968; MP for Johore Bharu Timor, 1969; Minister of Educn, 1970-73; Dep. Prime Minister, 1973-76; Minister of Trade and Industry, 1973-74; Minister of Finance, and Minister of Coordination and Public Corporations, 1974-76. Chairman: Commonwealth Parly Assoc., Malaysia, 1975-76; Inter Parly Union Malaysia Gp. President: Malayan Assoc. for the Blind; Kelab Golf Negara, Subang. *Recreation:* golf. *Address:* Prime Minister's Office, Jalan Dato' Onn, Kuala Lumpur.

HUSSEY, Prof. Joan Mervyn, MA, BLitt, PhD; FSA; FRHistS; Professor of History in the University of London, at Royal Holloway College, 1950-74, now Emeritus. *Educ:* privately; Trowbridge High Sch.; Lycée Victor Duruy, Versailles; St Hugh's Coll., Oxford. Research Student, Westfield Coll., London, 1932-34; Internat. Travelling Fellow (FUW), 1934-35; Pfeiffer Research Fellow, Girton, 1934-37; Gamble Prize, 1935. Asst Lectr in Hist., Univ. of Manchester, 1937-43; Lectr in Hist., 1943-47, Reader in Hist., 1947-50, at Bedford Coll., Univ. of London. Visiting Prof. at Amer. Univ. of Beirut, 1966; Pres., Brit. Nat. Cttee for Byzantine Studies, 1961-71; Vice-Pres., Internat. Cttee for Byzantine Studies, 1966-. Governor, Girton Coll., Cambridge, 1935-37; Mem. Council, St Hugh's Coll., Oxford, 1940-46; Mem. Council, Royal Holloway Coll., 1966-; Hon. Fellow, St Hugh's Coll., Oxford, 1968. *Publications:* Church and Learning in the Byzantine Empire 867-1185, 1937 (repr. 1961); The Byzantine World, 1957, 3rd edn 1966; Cambridge Medieval History IV, Pts I and II: ed and contributor, 1966-67; The Finlay Papers, 1973; reviews and articles in Byzantinische Zeitschrift, Byzantinoslavica, Trans Roy. Hist. Soc., Jl of Theological Studies, Enc. Britannica, Chambers's Enc., New Catholic Enc., etc. *Address:* 16 Clarence Drive, Englefield Green, Egham, Surrey TW20 0NL.

HUSSEY, Very Rev. John Walter Atherton; Dean of Chichester, 1955-77; *b* 15 May 1909; *yr s* of Rev. Canon John Rowden and Lilian Mary Hussey. *Educ:* Marlborough Coll.; Keble Coll., Oxford (MA); Cuddesdon Coll., Oxford. Asst Curate, S Mary Abbots, Kensington, 1932-37; Vicar of S Matthew, Northampton, 1937-55; Canon of Peterborough Cathedral, 1949-55; Master of S John's Hosp., Weston Favell, 1948-55; Rural Dean of Northampton, 1950-55. Chm. Diocesan Art Council. Mem., Redundant Churches Fund, 1969-. Hon. FRIBA. Hon. DLitt Sussex, 1977. *Recreation:* enjoying the arts. *Address:* 5 Trevor Street, SW7. *T:* 01-584 7865.

HUSSEY, Marmaduke James; Chief Executive Managing Director, Times Newspapers Ltd; *b* 1923; *s* of late E. R. J. Hussey, CMG and Mrs Christine Hussey; *m* 1959, Lady Susan Katharine Waldegrave (*see* Lady Susan Hussey); one *s* one *d.* *Educ:* Rugby Sch.; Trinity Coll., Oxford (Scholar, MA). Served War of 1939-45, Grenadier Guards, Italy. Joined Associated Newspapers, 1949, Dir 1964; Man. Dir, Harmsworth Publications, 1967-70; joined Thomson Organisation Exec. Bd, 1971. A Rhodes Trustee, 1972-. *Address:* 86 Chelsea Park Gardens, SW3. *T:* 01-352 1042. *Club:* Brooks's.

HUSSEY, Lady Susan Katharine, CVO 1971; Woman of the Bedchamber to the Queen, since 1960; *b* 1 May 1939; 5th *d* of 12th Earl Waldegrave, KG, *qv*; *m* 1959, Marmaduke James Hussey, *qv*; one *s* one *d. Address:* 86 Chelsea Park Gardens, SW3. *T:* 01-352 1042.

HUSTON, John; film director and writer; *b* Nevada, Missouri, 5 Aug. 1906; *s* of Walter Huston and Rhea Gore; *m* 1st, 1946, Evelyn Keyes; 2nd, 1949, Enrica Soma (*d* 1969); one *s* one *d.* Became an Irish Citizen, 1964. At beginning of career was reporter, artist, writer and actor at various times. Formerly: Writer for Warner Bros Studios, 1938; Director for Warner Bros 1941; Writer and Dir, Metro-Goldwyn-Mayer, 1949. Dir of several Broadway plays. Films directed or produced include: The Maltese Falcon; Key Largo; The Treasure of Sierra Madre; The Asphalt Jungle; The African Queen; Moulin Rouge; Beat the Devil; Moby Dick; Heaven Knows, Mr Allison; The Barbarian and the Geisha; The Roots of Heaven; The Unforgiven; The Misfits; Freud; The Night of the Iguana; The Bible... In the Beginning; Reflections in a Golden Eye; Sinful Davey; A Walk with Love and Death; The Kremlin Letter; Fat City; The Life and Times of Judge Roy Bean; The Mackintosh Man; The Man who would be King. Served US Army 1942-45, Major; filmed documentaries of the War. Hon. LittD Trinity Coll., Dublin, 1970. *Recreation:* foxhunting. *Address:* c/o Jess S. Morgan & Co. Inc., 6300 Wilshire Boulevard, 1100 Los Angeles, Calif 90048, USA.

HUTBER, Patrick; City Editor, The Sunday Telegraph, since 1966; *b* 18 May 1928; *s* of Hubert Anderson Mackintosh Hutber, OBE and Edith Mary (*née* Bull); *m* 1959, Josephine Mary

Robbie; one *s* three *d. Educ:* Ealing County Grammar Sch.; New Coll., Oxford (Galsworthy Scholar; MA). Sec. and Librarian, Oxford Union Soc., 1951. Special trainee, J. Lyons, 1952; Inst. of Bankers 1954; Financial Times, 1957-63 (Commercial Editor, 1959; "Lex", 1961); founded, as free-lance contrib., "Questor" column, Daily Telegraph, 1964; Financial Dir, Link Information Services, 1965. Chm. of Trustees, Soc. of Clinical Psychiatrists Res. Fund, 1975-; Mem. Council of Management, University Coll. at Buckingham, 1976-. Financial Journalist of the Year Award, 1972. *Publications:* The Decline and Fall of the Middle Class, 1976; (ed) What is Wrong with Britain?, 1978. *Recreations:* gardening, riding, music (esp. opera). *Address:* The Old Rectory, Drayton Parslow, Milton Keynes, Bucks. *T:* Mursley 241. *Club:* Garrick.

HUTCHINGS, Andrew William Seymour, CBE 1973; General Secretary, Assistant Masters Association, since 1939; *b* 3 Dec. 1907; *o s* of William Percy and Mellony Elizabeth Louisa Hutchings; unmarried. *Educ:* Cotham Sch., Bristol; St Catharine's Coll., Cambridge (MA). Asst Master: Downside Sch., 1929-30; Methodist Coll., Belfast, 1930-34; Holt Sch., Liverpool, 1934-36; Asst Sec., Asst Masters Assoc., 1936-39; Hon. Sec., Jt Cttee of Four Secondary Assocs, 1939-; Sec.-Gen. 1954-65, Pres. 1965-71 and 1972-73, Internat. Fedn of Secondary Teachers; Mem. Exec. Cttee, World Confedn of Organisations of Teaching Profession, 1954-; Mem. Secondary Schs Examination Council, 1939- and subseq. of Schools Council; Mem. Norwood Cttee on Curriculum and Examinations in Secondary Schs, 1941-43; Chm. Teachers' Panel, Burnham Primary and Secondary Cttee, 1965-; Chm. Nat. Foundn for Educnl Research in England and Wales, 1973-. FEIS 1963; FCP 1975. *Publications:* educnl and professional articles and memoranda for Asst Masters Assoc. *Recreation:* breeding and showing Great Danes (Mem. Kennel Club). *Address:* Danemead, Knowle Lane, Cranleigh, Surrey. *T:* Cranleigh 2840.

HUTCHINGS, Arthur James Bramwell; Professor of Music, University of Exeter, 1968-71, now Emeritus; *b* Sunbury on Thames, 14 July 1906; *s* of William Thomas Hutchings, Bideford, N Devon, and Annie Bramwell, Freckleton, Lytham, Lancs; *m* 1940, Marie Constance Haverson; one *d.* Formerly schoolmaster and organist; contributor to musical periodicals, critic and reviewer; served with RAF in SEAC; Prof. of Music, University of Durham, 1947-68, now Emeritus. Mem., Editorial Cttee, The English Hymnal, 1954-. Mem. Bd of Governors of Trinity Coll. of Music, 1947-. BA, BMus, PhD London; Hon. FTCL, FRSCM, Hon. RAM. Compositions include: works for strings, comic operas and church music. *Publications:* Schubert (Master Musicians Series), 1941, 4th edn 1973; Edmund Rubbra (contribution to Penguin Special, Music of Our Time), 1941; Delius (in French, Paris), 1946; A Companion to Mozart's Concertos, 1947; Delius, 1947; The Invention and Composition of Music, 1954; The Baroque Concerto, 1960, 3rd edn 1973; Pelican History of Music, Vol 3 (The 19th Century), 1962; Church Music in the Nineteenth Century, 1967; Mozart (2 vols), 1976. Contributions to: Die Musik in Geschichte und Gegenwart, 1956; The Mozart Companion, 1956; New Oxford History of Music, 1962; The Beethoven Companion, 1970; Grove's Dictionary of Music and Musicians, 6th edn, 1975. *Address:* 8 Rosemary Lane, Colyton, Devon EX13 6NJ. *T:* Colyton 542.

HUTCHINGS, Geoffrey Balfour, CMG 1946; Formerly Senior Partner in Lovell, White & King, Solicitors, 1 Serjeants' Inn, EC4; *b* 24 Feb. 1904; 2nd *s* of late Charles Graham Hutchings, Seaford, Sussex; *m* 1st, 1928, Dorothy Guest (*d* 1967), *o d* of late Rev. J. Guest Gilbert; one *s* one *d*; 2nd, 1969, Mrs Stella Graham. *Educ:* Giggleswick Sch., Yorks. Served with 1/4 Bn South Lancs Regt, Sept. 1939-41; Principal Dir of Salvage and Recovery, Ministry of Supply, 1941-44; Dir-Gen. of British Ministry of Supply Commission, North West Europe, 1944-45; resumed professional practice, 1945. *Recreation:* golf. *Address:* Dunaverty Lodge, Southend by Cambeltown, Argyll. *T:* Southend 634.

HUTCHINS, Frank Ernest, CEng, FIEE, FIMarE; RCNC; Deputy Director of Electrical Engineering (Procurement Executive), Ministry of Defence (Navy Dept), Bath, since Nov. 1973; *b* 27 Sept. 1922; *s* of Sidney William Hutchins and Eleanor Seager; *m* 1946, Patricia Mary Wakeford-Fullagar; one *d. Educ:* Sir Joseph Williamson's Mathematical Sch., Rochester, Kent; Royal Dockyard Sch., Chatham; Royal Naval Coll., Greenwich. BSc(Eng) 1st cl. Hons London. Member, Royal Corps of Naval Constructors (formerly Royal Naval Engineering Service); Asst Electrical Engr, Admiralty, Bath, 1945-49; Asst Staff Electrical Officer, BJSM, Washington DC, USA, 1949-51; Electrical Engr, Admiralty, Bath, 1951-63; Suptg Elec. Engr, Weapon

Development and Ship Design, MoD (Navy), Bath, 1963-65; HM Dockyard, Devonport: Dep. Elec. Engrg Manager, 1965-68; Dep. Production Manager, 1968-69; Productivity Manager, 1969-70; attended Senior Officers' War Course, RN War Coll., Greenwich, 1970-71; Asst Director Naval Ship Production (Procurement Executive), MoD (Navy), Bath, 1971-73. MBIM. *Recreations:* sketching, carpentry, gardening. *Address:* Bonnie Banks, Ralph Allen Drive, Bath BA2 5AE. *T:* Combe Down 833462. *Club:* Royal Western Yacht (Plymouth).

HUTCHINS, Captain Ronald Edward, CBE 1961; DSC 1943; RN; *b* 7 Jan. 1912; *s* of Edward Albert Hutchins and Florence Ada (*née* Sharman); *m* 1937, Irene (*née* Wood); two *s*. *Educ:* St John's (elem. sch.), Hammersmith; TS Mercury, Hamble, Hants (C. B. Fry); RN Coll., Greenwich. Royal Navy, 1928-61; Computer Industry, 1961-75; company director, 1964-75. *Recreations:* walking, gardening. *Address:* Silvergarth, Badgers Hill, Virginia Water, Surrey GU25 4SA. *T:* Wentworth 2622.

HUTCHINSON; *see* Hely-Hutchinson.

HUTCHINSON, Rev. Canon Archibald Campbell, MA; Chaplain at Cossham Hospital, Bristol, 1950-63, and at Glenside Hospital, 1950-63; retired; Assistant Priest, St Peter's Church, Henleaze, Bristol, 1964-74; *b* 9 Feb. 1883; *s* of Ven. Archdeacon Arthur Blockey Hutchinson; *m* 1912, Constance Clara Auden Stratton (*d* 1950), Newport, Isle of Wight; no *c*; *m* 1951, Dorothy May White, Sherborne, Dorset. *Educ:* St Lawrence Coll., Ramsgate; Corpus Christi Coll., Cambridge. Ordained, 1906; Curate of S John's, Carisbrooke, IoW; joined the Japan Mission of the CMS, 1909; formerly Lecturer at the Fukuoka Divinity Sch.; Lecturer for one year at The Central Theological Coll., Tokyo; Mem. of the Standing Cttee Diocese of Kyushu; Sec. of the CMS, Japan Mission; Hon. Canon of the Cathedral at Fukuoka in the diocese of Kyushu; left Japan, Dec. 1940; Asst Priest, St Andrew's Church, Halfway Tree, Jamaica, 1941-45; Asst Priest, St James' Church, Bristol, 1945-50. *Address:* 120 Howard Road, Westbury Park, Bristol BS6 7XA. *T:* Bristol 45740.

HUTCHINSON, Arthur Edward; a Recorder of the Crown Court, since 1974; *b* 31 Aug. 1934; *s* of late George Edward Hutchinson and Kathleen Hutchinson; *m* 1967, Wendy Pauline Cordingley, one *s* two *d*. *Educ:* Silcoates Sch.; Emmanuel Coll., Cambridge (MA). Commissioned, West Yorkshire Regt, 1953; served in Kenya with 5th Fusiliers, 1953-54. Called to Bar, Middle Temple, 1958; joined NE Circuit, 1959. *Recreations:* cricket, gardening, music. *Address:* 6 Park Square, Leeds LS1 2LW. *T:* Leeds 459763.

HUTCHINSON, Sir Arthur (Sydney), KBE 1953; CB 1946; CVO 1937; *idc*; *b* 21 March 1896; 2nd and *o* surv. *s* of late Sir Sydney Hutchinson, formerly Dir General of Telegraphs in India; *m* 1933, Charis Lyle, *d* of late Christopher Bathgate, Liverpool; no *c*. *Educ:* St Paul's Sch.; New Coll., Oxford. Army, 1916-18 (wounded); entered Home Office, 1919; Deputy Under-Sec. of State, 1948-57; retired, 1957. *Address:* Fairmead, Warren Road, Crowborough, East Sussex. *T:* Crowborough 61616. *Club:* United Oxford & Cambridge University.

HUTCHINSON, Rear-Adm. Christopher Haynes, CB 1961; DSO 1940; OBE 1946; RN retired; *b* 13 March 1906; 2nd *s* of late Rev. Canon Frederick William Hutchinson; *m* 1941, Nancy Marguerite Coppinger. *Educ:* Lydgate House Prep. Sch., Hunstanton; Royal Naval Colleges, Osborne and Dartmouth. Naval Cadet RNC Osborne, Sept. 1919; served largely in submarines; served War of 1939-45, commanding submarine Truant which sank German cruiser Karlsruhe, 9 April 1940 (despatches, DSO); Staff Officer, British Pacific Fleet 1945 (OBE); Qualified RN Staff Coll. (1946) and Joint Services Staff Coll. (Directing Staff); Commanding 3rd Submarine Flotilla, 1950-52; Senior Naval Adviser to UK High Commissioner, Australia, 1952-54; Captain, RN Coll., Greenwich, 1954-56; Commodore, 1st Class, Chief of Staff Far East Station, 1956-59; Director-General of Personal Services and Officer Appointments, 1959-61; retired, 1962. *Recreation:* shooting. *Address:* Gillhurst, Warninglid, near Haywards Heath, Sussex. *T:* Warninglid 259.

HUTCHINSON, Prof. George William, MA, PhD, Cantab; Professor of Physics, Southampton University, since 1960; *b* Feb. 1921; *s* of George Hutchinson, farmer, and Louisa Ethel (*née* Saul), Farnsfield, Notts; *m* 1943, Christine Anne (marr. diss. 1970), *d* of Matthew Rymer and Mary (*née* Proctor), York; two *s*. *Educ:* Abergele Grammar Sch.; Cambridge. MA 1946, PhD 1952, Cantab. State Schol. and Schol. of St John's Coll., Cambridge, 1939-42. Research worker and factory manager in cotton textile industry, 1942-47; Cavendish Lab., Cambridge,

1947-52; Clerk-Maxwell Schol. of Cambridge Univ., 1949-52; Nuffield Fellow, 1952-53, and Lecturer, 1953-55, in Natural Philosophy, University of Glasgow; Research Assoc. of Stanford Univ., Calif, 1954. Lecturer, 1955, Sen. Lectr, 1957, in Physics, University of Birmingham. Duddell Medal, Physical Soc., 1959. FPhysS; FRAS; FRSA. *Publications:* papers on nuclear and elementary particle physics, nuclear instrumentation and cosmic rays. *Recreations:* music, volley-ball, sailing. *Address:* Physical Laboratory, University of Southampton SO9 5NH. *T:* Southampton 559122.

HUTCHINSON, Jeremy Nicolas, QC 1961; Vice-Chairman, Arts Council of Great Britain, since 1977 (Member, since 1974); *b* 28 March 1915; *o s* of late St John Hutchinson, KC; *m* 1st, 1940, Dame Peggy Ashcroft (marr. diss. 1966); one *s* one *d*; 2nd, 1966, June Osborn. *Educ:* Stowe Sch.; Magdalen Coll., Oxford. Called to Bar, Middle Temple, 1939, Bencher 1963. RNVR, 1939-46. Practised on Western Circuit, N London Sessions and Central Criminal Court. Recorder of Bath, 1962-72; a Recorder of the Crown Court, 1972-76. Member: Cttee on Immigration Appeals, 1966-68; Cttee on Identification Procedures, 1974-76. *Address:* Queen Elizabeth Building, Temple, EC4. *T:* 01-583 9744. *Club:* MCC.

HUTCHINSON, Sir Joseph (Burtt), Kt 1956; CMG 1944; ScD Cantab; FRS 1951; Drapers' Professor of Agriculture, Cambridge, 1957-69, now Emeritus; Fellow, St John's College; *b* 21 March 1902; *s* of L. M. and Edmund Hutchinson; *m* 1930, Martha Leonora Johnson; one *s* one *d*. *Educ:* Ackworth and Bootham Schs; St John's Coll., Cambridge. Asst Geneticist, Empire Cotton Growing Corporation's Cotton Research Station, Trinidad, 1926-33; Geneticist and Botanist, Institute of Plant Industry, Indore, Central India, 1933-37; Geneticist, Empire Growing Corporation's Cotton Research Station, Trinidad, and Cotton Adviser to the Inspector-General of Agriculture, BWI, 1937-44. Chief Geneticist, Empire Cotton Growing Corp., 1944-49; Dir of its Cotton Research Station, Namulonge, Uganda, 1949-57. Chm. of Council of Makerere Coll., University Coll. of East Africa, 1953-57; Hon. Fellow, Makerere Coll., 1957. Pres., British Assoc., 1965-66; Foreign Fellow, Indian Nat. Science Acad., 1974. Royal Medal, Royal Society, 1967. Hon. DSc: Nottingham, 1966; East Anglia, 1972. *Publications:* The Genetics of Gossypium, 1947; Genetics and the Improvement of Tropical Crops, 1958; Application of Genetics to Cotton Improvement, 1959; Farming and Food Supply, 1972; (ed) Evolutionary Studies in World Crops, 1974; The Challenge of the Third World, 1975; numerous papers on the genetics, taxonomy, and economic botany of cotton. *Address:* Huntingfield, Huntingdon Road, Cambridge. *T:* Cambridge 76272.

HUTCHINSON, Ormond, CMG 1974; Chairman of Directors, Hutchinson Motors Ltd, Ford Dealers, Christchurch, New Zealand (retd as Managing Director, 1973); Director, The Colonial Motor Co. Ltd, Wellington, NZ; *b* 12 April 1896; *s* of Alexander Gilbert and Katherine Hutchinson; *m* 1945, Joan Margery Hutchinson; one *s*. *Educ:* Wellington, NZ. Served European War, 1914-18, with NZ Artillery (Messines, 1917, Passchendaele, 1917; two service medals). Joined Colonial Motor Co. (sole rights importing and distributing all Ford products in NZ); he became the Company's regular caller of motor dealers in South Island, using the model T; subseq. Manager, Timaru plant, and came to Christchurch as Manager of a dealership, 1924. Colonial Motor Company controls over 20 motor dealers throughout New Zealand. Vice-President: New Zealand Trotting Conf. (Past Pres. and Life Mem., New Brighton Trotting Club); Sumner Lifeboat Inst.; Mount Pleasant Yacht Club; New Brighton Power Boat Club. *Address:* 44 Cannon Hill Crescent, Christchurch 8, New Zealand. *T:* Christchurch, NZ 843-423. *Clubs:* Canterbury, Midland (Past Pres. and Life Mem.) (Christchurch, NZ).

HUTCHINSON, Patricia Margaret; HM Diplomatic Service; Consul-General, Geneva, since 1975; *b* 18 June 1926; *d* of Francis Hutchinson and Margaret Peat. *Educ:* abroad; St Paul's Girls' Sch.; Somerville Coll., Oxford (PPE, MA). ECE, Geneva, 1947; Bd of Trade, 1947-48; HM Diplomatic Service, 1948: 3rd Sec., Bucharest, 1948-50; Foreign Office, 1950-52; 2nd (later 1st) Sec., Berne, 1955-58; 1st Sec. (Commercial), Washington, 1958-61; FO, 1961-64; 1st Sec., Lima, 1964-67 (acted as Chargé d'Affaires); Dep. UK Permanent Rep. to Council of Europe, 1967-69; Counsellor: Stockholm, 1969-72; UK Delegn to OECD, 1973-75. *Recreations:* music, reading. *Address:* c/o Foreign and Commonwealth Office, SW1.

HUTCHINSON, Richard Hampson; His Honour Judge Hutchinson; a Circuit Judge, since 1974; *b* 31 Aug. 1927; *s* of late John Riley Hutchinson and May Hutchinson; *m* 1954,

Nancy Mary (née Jones); two s three d. Educ: St Bede's Grammar Sch., Bradford; UC Hull. LLB London. National Service, RAF, 1949-51. Called to Bar, Gray's Inn, 1949; practised on NE Circuit, 1951-74. Recorder: Rotherham, 1971-72; Crown Court, 1972-74. Recreations: reading, conversation. Address: 3 Mansfield Court, Newland Park, Hull. T: Hull 46704.

HUTCHINSON, Hon. Sir Ross, Kt 1977; DFC 1944; Speaker, Legislative Assembly, Western Australia, 1974-77; MLA (L) Cottesloe, 1950-77; b 10 Sept. 1914; s of Albert H. Hutchinson and Agnes L. M. Hutchinson; m 1939, Amy Goodall Strang; one s one d. Educ: Wesley Coll. RAAF, 1942-45. School teacher, 1935-49. Chief Sec., Minister for Health and Fisheries, 1959-65; Minister for Works and Water Supplies, 1965-71. Australian Rules Football, former Captain Coach; East Fremantle, East Perth and South Fremantle; Captain Coach, WA, 1939. Recreations: tennis, reading. Address: 42 Griver Street, Cottesloe, WA 6011, Australia. T: 312680. Club: Royal King's Park Tennis (Perth, WA).

HUTCHINSON, William James, TD; Chief Executive, County of Avon, since 1974 (Town Clerk and Chief Executive Officer, Bristol County Borough, 1969-74); b 12 Dec. 1919; s of William James Hutchinson and Martha Allan Hutchinson (née Downie); m 1944, Barbara Olive Benaton; one s one d. Educ: Brighton Hove and Sussex Grammar School. Admitted Solicitor, 1947. Bury County Borough Council, 1947-49; Bristol CBC, 1949-. Recreations: gardening, walking, theatre. Address: 32 Woodland Grove, Coombe Dingle, Bristol BS9 2BB. T: 683415.

HUTCHISON, A(lan) Michael Clark; MP (C) Edinburgh South since May 1957; b 26 Feb. 1914; y s of late Sir George A. Clark Hutchison, KC, MP, of Eriska, Argyll; m 1937, Anne, yr d of Rev. A. R. Taylor, DD, of Aberdeen; one s one d. Educ: Eton; Trinity Coll., Cambridge. Called to Bar, Gray's Inn, 1937. War of 1939-45 (despatches); served AIF, Middle East and Pacific theatres, psc. Mem. Australian Mil. Mission, Washington, USA, 1945-46. Entered Colonial Admin. Service, 1946, and served as Asst Dist Comr in Palestine till 1948; thereafter as Political Officer and Asst Sec. in Protectorate and Colony of Aden; resigned, 1955. Contested (C) Motherwell Div. of Lanarks, 1955. Parliamentary Private Secretary to: Parliamentary and Financial Sec. to the Admiralty, and to the Civil Lord, 1959; the Lord Advocate, 1959-60; Sec. of State for Scotland, 1960-62. Scottish Conservative Members' Committee: Vice-Chm., 1965-66, 1967-68; Chm., 1970-71. Introduced as Private Mem.'s Bills: Solicitors (Scotland) Act; Wills Act; Succession (Scotland) Act. Recreations: reading, Disraeliana. Address: (home) 16 Maunsel Street, SW1P 2QL. T: 01-828 1108; (office) 19 Newington Road, Edinburgh EH9 1QR. T: 031-667 5783. Club: New (Edinburgh). See also Lieut-Comdr Sir G. I. C. Hutchison.

HUTCHISON, Bruce; see Hutchison, W. B.

HUTCHISON, Hon. Sir Douglas; see Hutchison, Hon. Sir J. D.

HUTCHISON, Douglas; see Hutchison, J. D.

HUTCHISON, Lt-Comdr Sir (George) Ian Clark, Kt 1954; DL; Royal Navy, retired; Member of the Queen's Body Guard for Scotland, Royal Company of Archers; b 4 Jan. 1903; e s of late Sir George Clark Hutchison, KC, MP, Eriska, Argyllshire; m 1926, Sheena (d 1966), o d of late A. B. Campbell, WS; one d. Educ: Edinburgh Academy; RN Colleges, Osborne and Dartmouth. Joined Navy as Cadet, 1916; Lieut, 1924; Lieut-Comdr 1934; specialised in torpedoes, 1929; emergency list, 1931; Mem., Edinburgh Town Council, 1935-41; Chm., Public Assistance Cttee, 1937-39; contested Maryhill Div. of Glasgow, 1935; rejoined Navy Sept. 1939; served in Naval Ordnance Inspection Dept, 1939-43; MP (U) for West Div. of Edinburgh, 1941-59. Mem. National Executive Council of British Legion (Scotland), 1943-51; Governor of Donaldson's Sch. for the Deaf, Edinburgh, 1937-75; Mem. Cttee on Electoral Registration, 1945-46; Mem. Scottish Leases Cttee, 1951-52. DL County of City of Edinburgh, 1958. Recreations: golf, fishing, walking, philately. Address: 16 Wester Coates Gardens, Edinburgh EH12 5LT. T: 031-337 4888. Club: New (Edinburgh). See also A. M. C. Hutchison, J. V. Paterson.

HUTCHISON, Lt-Comdr Sir Ian Clark; see Hutchison, Sir G. I. C.

HUTCHISON, Isobel Wylie, Hon. LLD; FRSGS; JP; d of Thomas Hutchison, Carlowrie, West Lothian, and Jeanie Wylie; unmarried. Educ: Rothesay House Sch., Edinburgh; Studley Horticultural Coll. for Women. Plant-collecting in Arctic regions, Greenland, Alaska, and Aleutian Islands for the Royal Horticultural Society, Royal Herbarium of Kew, and the British Museum. Publications: verse: Lyrics from West Lothian, The Northern Gate, How Joy was Found, The Calling of Bride; novel: Original Companions; travel: On Greenland's Closed Shore; North to the Rime-Ringed Sun; Arctic Nights Entertainments; Stepping Stones from Alaska to Asia, 1937, republished 1943 under title The Aleutian Islands. Recreations: sketching, walking, botany, etc. Address: Carlowrie, Kirkliston, West Lothian. T: 031-333 3209.

HUTCHISON, Hon. Sir (James) Douglas, Kt 1959; Judge of Supreme Court of New Zealand, 1948-66, retired; b 29 Sept. 1894; s of Sir James Hutchison; m 1st, 1924, Mary Bethea Johnston (d 1943); two s two d; 2nd, 1954, Mary Elizabeth Averill. Educ: Otago Boys' High Sch.; Otago Univ.; Victoria University Coll. (now Victoria Univ. of Wellington). Served European War, 1914-18, with 1st NZEF in Gallipoli and France; War of 1939-45, DAAG, Southern Military District, NZ. Practised Carterton, 1920-24, Christchurch, 1924-48. Recreations: golf, tramping. Address: Main Road North, Paraparaumu, NZ. Clubs: Wellington, Canterbury (NZ).

HUTCHISON, Prof. James Holmes, CBE 1971 (OBE 1945); FRCP 1947; FRCPE 1960; FRCPGlas 1962; MD (Hons) 1939 (Glasgow); FRSE 1965; Professor of Paediatrics, University of Hong Kong, since 1977; b 16 April 1912; s of Alexander Hutchison and Catherine Holmes; m 1940, Agnes T. A. Goodall; one s one d. Educ: High Sch. of Glasgow; University of Glasgow. Qualified MB, ChB (Glasgow) 1934; Resident Hosp. Posts, 1934-36; Royal Hosp. for Sick Children, Glasgow: McCunn Research Schol., 1936-38; Asst Vis. Phys., 1938-39; Physician in charge of Wards, 1947-61; also Consulting Pædiatrician, Queen Mother's Hospital, Glasgow; Leonard Gow Lectr on Med. Diseases of Infancy and Childhood, 1947-61, Samson Gemmell Prof. of Child Health, 1961-77, Univ. of Glasgow. Dean, Fac. of Medicine, Univ. of Glasgow, 1970-73. President: Royal College of Physicians and Surgeons of Glasgow, Nov. 1966-Nov. 1968. British Paediatric Assoc., 1969-70; Assoc. of Physicians of GB and Ireland, 1973-74. Hon. FACP 1968. RAMC, Major and Lieut-Col, 1939-45. Publications: Practical Pædiatric Problems, 1964, 5th edn 1978; Rickets, in British Encyclopædia of Medical Practice, 2nd edn, 1952; Disorders of Storage, Obesity and Endocrine Diseases; chapters 50-57, in Pædiatrics for the Practitioner, 1953 (ed Gaisford and Lightwood); Hypothyroidism, in Recent Advances in Pædiatrics, 1958 (ed Gairdner), 2nd edn 1975; chapter chapter in Emergencies in Medical Practice (ed C. Allan Birch); chapter in Textbook of Medical Treatment (ed Davidson, Dunlop and Alstead); chapter in Endocrine and Genetic Diseases of Childhood (ed L. I. Gardner), 1969, 2nd edn 1976; Thyroid section in Paediatric Endrocrinology (ed D.Hubble), 1969; chapter in Textbook of Pædiatrics (ed J. O. Forfar and G. C. Arneil), 1973; many contributions to medical journals. Recreations: golf, country dancing (Scottish), motoring. Address: Department of Paediatrics, Queen Mary Hospital, Hong Kong; 21 Victoria Park Gardens North, Glasgow G11 7EJ. T: 041-339 1791. Clubs: Caledonian; College (University of Glasgow); Royal Scottish Automobile.

HUTCHISON, Sir James Riley Holt, 1st Bt, cr 1956; DSO 1945; TD; JP; s of late Thomas Holt Hutchison, Shipowner, and Florence Riley; m 1928, Winefryde Eleanor Mary, d of late Rev. R. H. Craft; one s (one d decd). Educ: Harrow; France. Shipowner, 1912. Served with Lanark Yeomanry and 17th Cavalry, Indian Army, throughout war, 1914-18; Hon. Col Lanarkshire Yeomanry, 1948-58. Dir of companies (Ailsa Shipbuilding Co. Ltd and others); President: Westminster Chamber of Commerce, 1963; Associated British Chambers of Commerce, 1960-62 (Dep.-Pres. 1958); UK Council of European Movement, 1955; Mem. Export Council for Europe, 1960; Nat. Pres. Incorporated Sales Managers' Assoc., 1949-51; Parl. Chm. Dock and Harbour Authorities Assoc. Served France, N Africa and on Staff, 1939-45. MP (U) Glasgow Central, 1945-50, Scotstoun Div. of Glasgow, Oct. 1950-Sept. 1959. Pres. Assembly of WEU, 1957-59. Parl. Under-Sec. of State and Financial Sec., War Office, 1951-54, and Vice-Chm. HM Army Council. JP Perthshire. Hon. LLD Glasgow, 1973. Chevalier Legion of Honour, 1945; Croix de Guerre; OStJ 1972. Publication: That Drug Danger, 1977. Recreations: writing, music, shooting, games. Heir: s Peter Craft Hutchison [b 5 June 1935; m 1966, Virginia, er d of John M. Colville, Gribloch, Kippen, Stirlingshire; one s]. Address: Rossie, Forgandenny, Perthshire. T: Bridge of Earn 265; 32 Moore Street, SW3 2QW. Clubs: Cavalry and Guards; Western (Glasgow).

HUTCHISON, James Seller; Chairman, The British Oxygen Co. Ltd and Associated Companies, 1950-72 (Director, 1940-72); b 15 Oct. 1904; s of late R. F. Hutchison, Glasgow; m Kathleen, d of late William Maude, Leeds; two d. *Educ:* Greenock Academy; Glasgow Univ. Chartered Accountant, 1928. *Recreations:* golf, gardening. *Address:* Shenfield House, Orchard Way, Esher, Surrey.

HUTCHISON, (Joseph) Douglas, CBE 1972; MC 1944; TD 1952; Director, Ranks Hovis McDougall Ltd, since 1956; Member, Agricultural Research Council, since 1973; *b* 3 April 1918; *s* of late John K. Hutchison, Kinloch, Collessie, Fife and late Ethel Rank, OBE; unmarried. *Educ:* Loretto; Clare Coll., Cambridge. BA Agric. 1939. Served Fife and Forfar Yeomanry, 1939-46 (Major); comd Regt, 1951-53. Director: R. Hutchison & Co. Ltd, 1951-73; Ranks Ltd (later RHM), 1956. Pres., Nat. Assoc. British and Irish Millers, 1963-64 and 1974-75; Pres., Research Assoc. Flour Millers and Bakers, 1967-72; Chm., Game Conservancy, 1970-75. *Recreations:* shooting, gardening, music. *Address:* Bolfracks, Aberfeldy, Perthshire. *Club:* New (Edinburgh).

HUTCHISON, Sir Kenneth; *see* Hutchison, Sir W. K.

HUTCHISON, Michael, QC 1976; a Recorder of the Crown Court, since 1975; *b* 13 Oct. 1933; *s* of Ernest and Frances Hutchison; *m* 1957, Mary Spettigue; two *s* three *d*. *Educ:* Lancing; Clare College, Cambridge (MA). Called to Bar, Gray's Inn, 1958. *Address:* Hare Dene, Albury, Guildford, Surrey GU5 9DB. *T:* Shere 2240.

HUTCHISON, Sir Peter, 2nd Bt, *cr* 1939; *b* 27 Sept. 1907; *er s* of Sir Robert Hutchison, 1st Bt, MD, CM, and Lady Hutchison (then Dr and Mrs Robert Hutchison); *S* father 1960; *m* 1949, Mary-Grace (*née* Seymour); two *s* two *d*. *Educ:* Marlborough; Lincoln Coll., Oxford. Admitted as a Solicitor, 1933. Dep.-Clerk of the Peace and of the CC, E Suffolk, 1947-71, Clerk of the Peace, 1971. *Recreations:* walking, gardening, reading. *Heir: s* Robert Hutchison, *b* 25 May 1954. *Address:* Melton Mead, near Woodbridge, Suffolk. *T:* Woodbridge 2746. *Club:* Ipswich and Suffolk (Ipswich).

HUTCHISON, Robert Edward; Keeper, Scottish National Portrait Gallery, since 1953; *b* 4 Aug. 1922; *y s* of late Sir William Hutchison; *m* 1946, Heather, *d* of late Major A. G. Bird; one *s* one *d*. *Educ:* Gresham's Sch., Holt. Served War, 1940-46, Infantry and RA; Asst Keeper, Scottish National Portrait Gallery, 1949. Hon. MA Edinburgh, 1972. *Publication:* (with Stuart Maxwell) Scottish Costume 1550-1850, 1958. *Address:* North House, Firth Home Farm, Roslin, Midlothian. *T:* Penicuik 75118.

HUTCHISON, Sidney Charles, CVO 1977 (MVO 1967); Secretary, Royal Academy of Arts, since 1968; *b* 26 March 1912; *s* of Henry Hutchison; *m* 1937, Nancy Arnold Brindley; no *c*. *Educ:* Holloway Sch., London; London Univ. (Dip. in Hist. of Art, with Dist.). Joined staff of Royal Academy, 1929. Served War of 1939-45: Royal Navy, rising to Lieut-Comdr (S), RNVR. Librarian of Royal Academy, 1949-68, also Sec. of Loan Exhibitions, 1955-68. Secretary: E. A. Abbey Meml Trust Fund for Mural Painting, 1960-; Incorporated E. A. Abbey Scholarships Fund, 1965-; E. Vincent Harris Fund for Mural Decoration, 1970-; British Institution Fund, 1968-; Chantrey Trustees, 1968-; Associate Mem., ICOM, 1964-. Lectr in the History of Art, for Extra-Mural Dept of Univ. of London, 1957-67. Gen. Comr of Income Tax, 1972-. Governor, Holloway Sch., 1969-. Organist and Choirmaster of St Matthew's, Westminster, 1933-37. FRSA 1950; FSA 1955; FMA 1962. Officer, Polonia Restituta, 1971; Chevalier, Belgian Order of the Crown, 1972; Grand Decoration of Honour (silver), Austria, 1972. *Publications:* The Homes of the Royal Academy, 1956; The History of the Royal Academy, 1768-1968, 1968; articles for Walpole Society, Museums Jl, Encyclopædia Britannica, Apollo, etc. *Recreations:* music, travel, golf. *Address:* 60 Belmont Close, Mount Pleasant, Cockfosters, Herts EN4 9LT. *T:* 01-449 9821. *Club:* Arts.

HUTCHISON, Prof. Terence Wilmot; Professor of Economics, University of Birmingham since 1956; Dean of the Faculty of Commerce and Social Science, 1959-61; *b* 13 Aug. 1912; *m* 1935, Loretta Hack; one *s* two *d*. *Educ:* Tonbridge Sch.; Peterhouse, Cambridge. Lector, Univ. of Bonn, 1935-38; Prof., Teachers' Training Coll., Bagdad, 1938-41. Served Indian Army, in intelligence, in Middle East and India, 1941-46; attached to Govt of India, 1945-46. Lecturer, University Coll., Hull, 1946-47; Lecturer, 1947-51 and Reader, 1951-56, London Sch. of Economics. Visiting Professor: Columbia Univ., 1954-55; Univ. of Saarbrücken, 1962; Yale Univ., 1963-64; Dalhousie Univ., 1970; Keio Univ., Tokyo, 1973; Univ. of WA, 1975; Visiting Fellow: Univ. of Virginia, 1960; Aust. Nat. Univ., Canberra, 1967. Mem. Council, Royal Economic Soc., 1967-72.

Publications: The Significance and Basic Postulates of Economic Theory, 1938 (2nd edn 1960); A Review of Economic Doctrines 1870-1929, 1953; Positive Economics and Policy Objectives, 1964; Economics and Economic Policy 1946-66, 1968; Knowledge and Ignorance in Economics, 1977; Keynes *v* the Keynesians, 1977; articles, reviews in jls. *Address:* 75 Oakfield Road, Birmingham B29 7ED. *T:* 021-472 2020.

HUTCHISON, (William) Bruce, OC 1967; Editorial Director, Vancouver Sun; *b* 5 June 1901; *s* of John and Constance Hutchison; *m* 1925, Dorothy Kidd McDiarmid; one *s* one *d*. *Educ:* Public and high schs, Victoria, BC. Political writer: Victoria Times, 1918; Vancouver Province, 1925; Vancouver Sun, 1938; editor, Victoria Times, 1950-63; associate editor, Winnipeg Free Press, 1944. Hon. LLD University of British Columbia, 1951. *Publications:* The Unknown Country, 1943; The Hollow Men, 1944; The Fraser, 1950; The Incredible Canadian, 1952; The Struggle for the Border, 1955; Canada: Tomorrow's Giant, 1957; Mr Prime Minister, 1964. *Recreations:* fishing, gardening. *Address:* 810 Rogers Avenue, Victoria, BC, Canada. *T:* Granite 9-2269. *Club:* Union (Victoria).

HUTCHISON, Sir (William) Kenneth, Kt 1962; CBE 1954; FRS 1966; FInstChemE; Hon. FInstGasE; Consultant; *b* 30 Oct. 1903; *s* of late William Hutchison; *m* 1929, Dorothea Marion Eva, *d* of late Commander Bertie W. Bluett, Royal Navy; one *d*. *Educ:* Edinburgh Academy; Corpus Christi Coll., Oxford. Joined staff of Gas, Light and Coke Co. as Research Chemist, 1926; seconded to Air Ministry as Asst Dir of Hydrogen Production, 1940, Dir, 1942; Dir of Compressed Gases, 1943; Controller of By-Products, Gas, Light and Coke Co., 1945, and a Managing Dir of the Company from 1947; Chm., South Eastern Gas Board, 1948-59; Deputy Chm., Gas Council, 1960-66; Chm., International Management and Engineering Group, 1967-69; Dir, Newton Chambers & Co. Ltd, 1967-73. President: Institution of Gas Engineers, 1955-56; British Road Tar Assoc., 1953-55; Inst. of Chem. Engineers, 1959-61; Soc. of British Gas Industries, 1967-68; Nat. Soc. for Clean Air, 1969-71. *Publications:* papers in Proc. Royal Society and other jls, 1926-. *Recreations:* sailing, golf. *Address:* 2 Arlington Road, Twickenham Park, Mddx. *T:* 01-892 1685. *Clubs:* Athenæum; Royal Cruising.

HUTCHISON, Prof. William McPhee; Personal Professor in Parasitology, University of Strathclyde, since 1971; *b* 2 July 1924; *s* of William Hutchison and Ann McPhee; *m* 1963, Ella Duncan McLaughland; two *s*. *Educ:* Eastwood Secondary Sch.; Glasgow Univ. BSc, PhD, DSc; FLS, FIBiol FRSE. Glasgow Univ. Fencing Blue, 1949; Ford Epée Cup Glasgow Univ. Fencing Champion, 1950. Strathclyde Univ.: Asst Lectr, 1952; Lectr, 1953; Sen. Lectr, 1969. Robert Koch Medal, 1970. *Publications:* contrib. Trans Royal Soc. Trop. Med. and Hygiene, BMJ, Acta Path. Microbiol. Scand. *Recreations:* general microscopy, woodwork, collection of zoological specimens. *Address:* 597 Kilmarnock Road, Newlands, Glasgow G43 2TH. *T:* 041-637 4882.

HUTSON, Sir Francis (Challenor), Kt 1963; CBE 1960; Senior Partner, D. M. Simpson & Co., Consulting Engineers, Barbados, 1943-70, retired; *b* 13 Sept. 1895; *s* of Francis and Alice Sarah Hutson; *m* 1st, 1925, Muriel Allen Simpkin (*d* 1945); two *s* one *d*; 2nd, 1947, Edith Doris Howell. *Educ:* Harrison Coll., Barbados; Derby Technical Coll., Derby. Resident Engineer, Booker Bros, McConnell & Co. Ltd, British Guiana, 1920-30; Consulting Engineer, Barbados, 1930-35; D. M. Simpson & Co., 1935-70. MLC, 1947-62, MEC, 1958-61, Barbados; PC (Barbados), 1961-70. FIMechE. *Recreation:* bridge. *Address:* Fleetwood, Erdison Hill, St Michael, Barbados. *T:* 93905. *Clubs:* Bridgetown, Royal Barbados Yacht, Savannah, (all in Barbados).

HUTSON, Maj.-Gen. Henry Porter Wolseley, CB 1945; DSO 1917; OBE 1919; MC; *b* 22 March 1893; *s* of late Henry Wolseley Hutson, Wimbledon, SW19; *m* 1922, Rowena, *d* of Surg.-Gen. Percy Hugh Benson, IA; two *s* one *d*. *Educ:* King's Coll. Sch.; RMA; 2nd Lieut RE, 1913; Capt. 1917; Major, 1929; Lieut-Col 1937; Col 1939; Temp. Brig. 1940; Maj.-Gen. 1944. Employed with Egyptian Army, 1920-24; under Colonial Office (Road Engineer Nigeria), 1926-28; Chief Instructor, Field Works and Bridging, Sch. of Military Engineering, 1934-36; Chief Engineer, Forestry Commn, 1947-58. MICE; MBOU; Chm., British Trust for Ornithology. Served European War, 1914-18, France, Belgium, Egypt and Mesopotamia (wounded, despatches thrice, DSO, OBE, MC); War of 1939-45 (despatches); retired pay, 1947. *Address:* The Koppies, 23 Hoskins Road, Oxted, Surrey. *T:* Oxted 2354.

HUTSON, John Whiteford, OBE 1966; HM Diplomatic Service; Counsellor (Commercial), Moscow, since 1976; *b* 21 Oct. 1927; *s* of John Hutson and Jean Greenlees Laird; *m* 1954, Doris Kemp; one *s* two *d*. *Educ:* Hamilton Academy; Glasgow Univ. (MA (Hons)). HM Forces, 1949-51; Foreign Office, 1951; Third Secretary, Prague, 1953; FO, 1955; Second Sec., Berlin, 1956; Saigon, 1959; First Sec., 1961; Consul (Commercial) San Francisco, 1963-67; First Sec. and Head of Chancery, Sofia, 1967-69; FCO, 1969; Counsellor, 1970; Baghdad, 1971-72; Inspector, FCO, 1972-74; Head, Communications Operations Dept, FCO, 1974-76. *Recreations:* hill-walking, photography. *Address:* c/o Foreign and Commonwealth Office, SW1.

HUTT, Sir (Alexander McDonald) Bruce, KBE, *cr* 1956 (OBE 1943); CMG 1949; Administrator, East Africa High Commission, 1954-59; *b* 9 Feb. 1904; *s* of late John Hutt; *m* 1929, Margaret Helen, *er d* of late George Murray, Hill Crest, Natal, SA; two *s*. *Educ:* St Andrew's Coll., Grahamstown, S Africa; University Coll., Oxford (BA). Entered Tanganyika Administrative Service as Cadet, 1926; Asst Dist Officer, 1928; Private Sec. and ADC, 1933; Asst Sec., Secretariat, 1935-37; Dist Officer, 1938; Dep. Provincial Commissioner, 1944; Provincial Commissioner, 1946; Dep. Chm., Development Commission, 1946; Acting Chief Sec. and Governor's Deputy, 1948-49; Mem. for Development and Works, Tanganyika, 1949-50; Deputy Chief Sec., 1950-51; Chief Sec., Tanganyika, 1951-54. Acting Governor, Tanganyika, 1953. *Publications:* (jointly) Anthropology in Action, 1935; first editor, Tanganyika Notes and Records. *Recreations:* golf, swimming, fishing, and shooting. *Address:* PO Box 33, Hill Crest, Natal, South Africa. *Clubs:* Royal Commonwealth Society; Vincent's (Oxford).

HUTT, Prof. William Harold; Distinguished Visiting Professor of Economics, University of Dallas, Texas, 1971-76; Professor of Commerce and Dean of the Faculty of Commerce, University of Cape Town, 1931-64; Professor Emeritus since 1965; *b* 3 Aug. 1899; *s* of William Hutt and Louisa (*née* Fricker); *m* 1946, Margarethe Louise Schonken. *Educ:* LCC Schs; Hackney Downs Sch.; London Sch. of Economics, University of London. Personal Asst to Chm., Benn Bros Ltd, and Manager, Individualist Bookshop Ltd, 1924-28; Senior Lecturer, University of Cape Town, 1928-30. Visiting Professor of Economics at various Univs and Colls in USA, 1966-69; Vis. Research Fellow, Hoover Instn, Stanford Univ., Calif., 1969-71; Distinguished Vis. Prof. of Economics, Calif. State Coll., 1970-71. *Publications:* The Theory of Collective Bargaining, 1930, 2nd edn, 1975; Economists and the Public, 1936; The Theory of Idle Resources, 1939; Plan for Reconstruction, 1943; Keynesianism-Retrospect and Prospect, 1963; The Economics of the Colour Bar, 1964; Politically Impossible?, 1971; The Strike-Threat System, 1973; A Rehabilitation of Say's Law, 1975; contrib. Individual Freedom: a symposium of articles 1934-75 (ed Klingaman and Pejovich), 1976; numerous articles in economic jls and symposia. *Recreations:* mountaineering, watching football and cricket. *Address:* c/o Standard Bank Ltd, ABC Branch, Adderley Street, Cape Town, South Africa. *Club:* Civil Service (Cape Town).

HUTTER, Prof. Otto Fred, PhD; Regius Professor of Physiology, University of Glasgow, since 1971; *b* 29 Feb. 1924; *s* of Isak and Elisabeth Hutter; *m* 1948, Yvonne T. Brown; two *s* two *d*. *Educ:* Chajes Real Gymnasium, Vienna; Bishops Stortford Coll., Herts; University Coll., London (BSc, PhD). Univ. of London Postgrad. Student in Physiology, 1948; Sharpey Scholar, UCL, 1949-52; Rockefeller Travelling Fellow and Fellow in Residence, Johns Hopkins Hosp., Baltimore, 1953-55; Lectr, Dept of Physiology, UCL, 1953-61; Hon. Lectr, 1961-70. Visiting Prof., Tel-Aviv Univ., 1968, 1970; Scientific Staff, Nat. Inst. for Medical Research, Mill Hill, London, 1961-70. *Publications:* papers on neuromuscular and synaptic transmission, cardiac and skeletal muscle, in physiological jls. *Address:* Institute of Physiology, University of Glasgow, Glasgow G12 8QQ. *T:* 041-339 8855.

HUTTON, Air Vice-Marshal Arthur Francis, CB 1955; CBE 1948; DFC 1935; FRAeS; FIMechE; *b* 9 Dec. 1900; *s* of Rev. A. W. Hutton; *m* 1927, Florence Strickland Oxley; one *s* two *d*. *Educ:* Queen Elizabeth's Gram. Sch., Darlington; Armstrong Coll., Newcastle; St Catharine's Coll., Cambridge (BA). Commissioned RAF 1924; DIC 1931; Officer Comdg No 28 Squadron, 1936; Officer Comdg No 52 Wing, 1939; Sen. Tech. Staff Officer, Far East, 1946; Dir of Engineering, Air Ministry, 1949; Sen. Tech. Staff Officer, Coastal Command, 1951; AOC No 43 Group, 1952; SASO Technical Training Command, 1953; Dir-Gen. of Engineering, Air Ministry, 1955-58, retd. Technical Consultant, Negretti & Zambra Ltd, 1959-61. MIMechE 1952. *Recreations:* shooting, golf. *Address:* Lower Berrick Farm, Berrick Salome, Oxford. *T:* Stadhampton 891065.

HUTTON, (David) Graham, OBE 1945; economist, author; *b* 13 April 1904; *er s* of late David James and Lavinia Hutton; *m* 1st, Magdalene Ruth Rudolph, Zürich (marr. diss. 1934); 2nd, Joyce Muriel Green (marr. diss. 1958); three *d*; 3rd, Marjorie, *d* of late Dr and Mrs David Bremner, Chicago. *Educ:* Christ's Hospital; London Sch. of Economics; French and German Univs. Gladstone Meml Prizeman, London Univ., 1929; Barrister-at-Law, Gray's Inn, 1932; Research Fellowship and teaching staff, LSE, 1929-33, Hon. Fellow 1971; Asst Editor, The Economist, 1933-38; FO and Min. of Information, 1939-45. *Publications:* Nations and the Economic Crisis, 1932; The Burden of Plenty (as ed. and contributor, 1935); Is it Peace?, 1936; Danubian Destiny, 1939; Midwest at Noon, 1946; English Parish Churches, 1952; We Too Can Prosper, 1953; All Capitalists Now, 1960; Inflation and Society, 1960; Mexican Images, 1963; Planning and Enterprise, 1964; Politics and Economic Growth, 1968; (with Olive Cook) English Parish Churches, 1976; essays in various collections, learned periodicals, etc. *Recreations:* ecclesiology, music, travel. *Address:* 38 Connaught Square, W2 2HL. *T:* 01-723 4067. *Cables:* Hutec, London, W2. *Clubs:* Reform, English-Speaking Union.

HUTTON, Gabriel Bruce; a Recorder of the Crown Court, since 1972; *b* 27 Aug. 1932; *y s* of Robert Crompton Hutton, *qv*; *m* 1st, 1963, Frances Henrietta Cooke (*d* 1963); 2nd, 1965, Deborah Leigh Windus; one *s* two *d*. *Educ:* Marlborough; Trinity Coll., Cambridge (BA). Called to Bar, Inner Temple, 1956; Dep. Chm., Glos QS, 1971. *Recreations:* hunting (Chm., Berkeley Hunt), shooting, fishing. *Address:* Chestal House, Dursley, Glos. *T:* Dursley 3285. *Club:* Gloucester (Gloucester).

HUTTON, Graham; *see* Hutton, D. G.

HUTTON, (Hubert) Robin; Director of Banking, Insurance and Financial Institutions, in the Commission of the European Communities, Brussels, since 1973; *b* 22 April 1933; *e s* of Kenneth Douglas and Dorothy Hutton; *m* 1st, 1956, Valerie Riseborough (marr. diss. 1967); one *s* one *d*.; 2nd, 1969, Deborah Berkeley; two step *d*. *Educ:* Merchant Taylors' Sch.; Peterhouse, Cambridge (Scholar). MA Cantab 1960. Royal Tank Regt, 1952-53 (commnd). Economic Adviser to Finance Corp. for Industry Ltd, 1956-62; economic journalist and consultant; Dir, Hambros Bank Ltd, 1966-70; Special Adviser: to HM Govt, 1970-72; Min. of Posts and Telecommunications, 1972-73. Chm., Cttee of Inquiry into Public Trustee Office, 1971. *Recreations:* cricket, ski-ing, gardening, travel. *Address:* Church Farm, Athelington, Eye, East Suffolk. *T:* Worlingworth 361. *Club:* MCC.

HUTTON, James Brian Edward, QC (NI) 1970; Senior Crown Counsel in Northern Ireland, since 1973; *b* 29 June 1931; *s* of James and Mabel Hutton, Belfast; *m* 1975, Mary Gillian, *o d* of J. R. W. Murland, Saintfield, Co. Down; one *d*. *Educ:* Shrewsbury Sch.; Balliol Coll., Oxford (1st Cl. final sch. of Jurisprudence); Queen's Univ. of Belfast. Called to Northern Ireland Bar, 1954; Bencher, Inn of Court of Northern Ireland, 1974; called to English Bar, 1972. Junior Counsel to Attorney-General for Northern Ireland, 1969; Legal Adviser to Min. of Home Affairs, Northern Ireland, 1973. *Address:* Bar Library, Royal Courts of Justice (Ulster), Belfast. *Club:* Ulster (Belfast).

HUTTON, John Campbell; artist; *b* New Zealand, 8 Aug. 1906; *s* of Colin Campbell Hutton and Penrhyn Florence Olive Hutton (*née* Fleming). *Educ:* Wanganui Collegiate School, NZ. Studied law until age of 25 and then abandoned it for art, in which he is self-taught; came to England as an artist in 1935 and worked extensively as a mural painter. Mural paintings for Festival of Britain, 1951, orient liners Orcades and Orsova, Buckingham Palace, Southampton liner terminal, etc. In engraved glass, Dunkirk War Memorial window in France; Guildford Cathedral. Has developed a special technique for large-scale engraving of his designs on glass which has been used for the Great Glass Screen which forms the West Front of new Coventry Cathedral; large screen in engraved glass, Plymouth Civic Centre; engraved glass panels; Shakespeare Centre, Stratford upon Avon; new Nat. Lib. and Archives, Ottawa; Civic Centre, Newcastle upon Tyne; Nat. Art Gall. of NZ, Wellington; glass engraving represented in: Victoria and Albert Museum, London; National Museum of Scotland, Edinburgh; Thanksgiving Chapel, Dallas, Texas, USA; Corning Museum of Glass, New York. One man exhibn, Commonwealth Inst. Art Gallery, 1969; touring retrospective exhibn, NZ, 1972-73. Designs also in stained glass and mosaic. *Recreation:* playing the Spanish guitar. *Address:* The Studio Barn, Oxford Road, Clifton Hampden, Abingdon, Oxon OX14 3EW. *T:* Clifton Hampden 7490.

HUTTON, Sir Leonard, Kt 1956; professional cricketer, retired 1956; Director, Fenner International (Power Transmission) Ltd; *b* Fulneck, near Pudsey, Yorks, 23 June 1916; *s* of Henry Hutton; *m* 1939, Dorothy Mary Dennis, *d* of late G. Dennis, Scarborough; two *s*. First played for Yorks, 1934. First played for England *v* New Zealand, 1937; *v* Australia, 1938 (century on first appearance); *v* South Africa, 1938; *v* West Indies, 1939; *v* India, 1946. Captained England *v* India, 1952; *v* Australia, 1953; *v* Pakistan, 1954; *v* Australia, 1954. Captained MCC *v* West Indies, 1953-54. Made record Test score, 364, *v* Australia at the Oval, 1938; record total in a single month, 1294, in June 1949; has made over 100 centuries in first-class cricket. Hon. Mem. of MCC, 1955 (first Professional to be elected). A selector, MCC, 1975-77. Served War of 1939-45: in RA and APTC. *Publications:* Cricket is my Life, 1950; Just my Story, 1956. *Recreation:* golf. *Address:* 1 Coombe Neville, Warren Road, Kingston-on-Thames, Surrey KT2 7HW. *T:* 01-942 0604.

HUTTON, Maurice, PhD, FIMA; Rector, Sunderland Polytechnic, 1969-76; *b* 4 Nov. 1914; *s* of William and Sarah Hutton; *m* 1939, Barbara Stark; one *s* one *d. Educ:* Univ. of Durham (BA, PhD). North Manchester High Sch., 1937-41; Oldham Technical Coll., 1941-44; Sunderland Technical Coll.: Lectr, 1945-53; Head of Dept, 1953-61; Vice-Principal, 1958-61; Principal, 1961-68. Comdr, Royal Norwegian Order of St Olav, 1966. *Publication:* (jt) Engineering Mathematics, 1959. *Recreations:* gardening, walking, working. *Address:* 17 Newlands Avenue, Sunderland SR3 1XW. *T:* Sunderland 285643.

HUTTON, Sir Noël (Kilpatrick), GCB 1966 (KCB 1957; CB 1950); QC, 1962; *b* 27 Dec. 1907; *s* of late William Hutton and of late Mrs D. M. Hutton, Whiteacre, Kippington, Sevenoaks; *m* 1936, Virginia Jacomyn, *d* of Sir George Young, 4th Bt, MVO; two *s* two *d. Educ:* Fettes Coll. (Scholar); University Coll., Oxford (Scholar, Hon. Fellow, 1973). OUBC crew 1930. Called to the Bar, Lincoln's Inn, 1932; entered Parly Counsel Office, 1938; First Parly Counsel, 1956-68. Governor, Alleyn's College (Chm., Estates Bd, 1973-75); Chm., Trusteeship Bd, Nat. Soc. for Mentally Handicapped Children. *Recreations:* music, golf, motoring. *Address:* Greenacre, Steeple Aston, Oxon OX5 3RT. *T:* Steeple Aston 40386. *Clubs:* Athenæum; Leander.

HUTTON, Maj.-Gen. Reginald Antony, CIE 1947; DSO 1944, and Bar 1945; OBE 1942; DL; *b* 18 April 1899; *s* of Charles Antony and Laura Beatrice Hutton, Earls Colne, Essex; *m* 1934, Margaret Isabel, *d* of Mark Feetham; two *d. Educ:* Haileybury and RMC, Sandhurst. Commissioned 1917, 2nd KEO Gurkha Rifles; Staff Coll., Camberley, 1934-35; Bde Major, 1938; GSO1 1940; Deputy Dir Military Intelligence, 1941; Bde Commander, 1944; Chief of Staff, 1 Corps, 1946. Served European War, 1914-18, General Service, 1917-18; 3rd Afghan War, 1919; Mahsud and NWF, 1919-20; Mohmand-Bajaur, 1933; Waziristan and NWF, 1938-40; War of 1939-45: (despatches 1940); Western Desert, Crete, Somaliland, Abyssinia, and Eritrea, 1940-42; Burma and Malaya, 1944-46; Chief of the General Staff, Pakistan Army, 1947-51; retired list, 1951. DL, Devon, 1962. *Address:* The Haven, Newton Ferrers, Devon. *T:* Newton Ferrers 325. *Club:* Naval and Military.

HUTTON, Robert Crompton; Recorder of Reading 1951-70 (of Oswestry, 1937-51); Chairman of Gloucestershire Quarter Sessions, 1943-70 (deputy Chairman, 1941-43); Chairman, Agricultural Land Tribunal, South Eastern Area, 1959-70; *b* 8 Aug. 1897; *s* of late Stamford Hutton, OBE; *m* 1927, Elfreda Bruce; three *s* one *d. Educ:* Winchester; Trinity Coll., Cambridge. Served European War, 1914-19, with 2/1 Royal Gloucestershire Hussars and Signals. Called to Bar, Inner Temple, 1923. TA, Royal Corps of Signals, 56th (1st London) Divl Signals, 1926-30. *Address:* 2 Harcourt Buildings, Temple, EC4; Harescombe Grange, Glos. *T:* Painswick 813260.
See also G. B. Hutton.

HUTTON, Robin; *see* Hutton, H. R.

HUTTON, Lt-Gen. Sir Thomas, KCIE 1944; CB 1941; MC; idc; psc; *b* 27 March 1890; *e s* of W. H. Hutton, JP, Clevedon, Som; *m* 1921, Isabel (CBE 1948; she died 1960), *d* of James Emslie, Edinburgh. *Educ:* Rossall; Royal Military Academy, Woolwich. 2nd Lieut Royal Artillery, 1909; Capt. 1915; Bt Major 1918; Major 1927; Bt Lt-Col 1927; Col 1930; Maj.-Gen. 1938; Lieut-Gen. 1941; served European War, 1914-18 (wounded thrice, despatches four times, Bt Major, Legion of Honour, French and Italian War Crosses, MC and Bar); Palestine, 1936; GSO3, 1918; Bde-Major, 1918-19; Asst Military Sec., 1919-20; DAAG, War Office, 1923-24; GSO2 E Command, 1924-26; Military Asst to CIGS 1927-30; GSO1, Military Operations, 1933-36; GSO1, 1st

Division, 1936-38; GOC Western Independent District, India, 1938-40; Deputy Chief of General Staff, Army Headquarters, India, 1940-41; Chief of the General Staff, India, 1941; GOC Burma, 1942; Sec. War Resources and Reconstruction Cttees of Council (India), 1942-44; retired pay, 1944; Officiating Sec., Viceroy's Executive Council; Sec., Planning and Development Dept, 1944-46; Regional Officer, Ministry of Health, 1947-49; General Manager, Anglo-American Council on Productivity, 1949-53; Dir, British Productivity Council, 1953-57. Chm. Organisation and Methods Training Council, 1957-64. Colonel Commandant RA, 1942-52. *Address:* 5 Spanish Place, W1. *T:* 01-935 8831. *Club:* Army and Navy.

HUTTON, Maj.-Gen. Walter Morland, CB 1964; CBE 1960; DSO 1943; MC 1936 and bar, 1942; MA (by decree, 1967); FIL (Arabic); Fellow, 1967-72 and Home Bursar, 1966-72, Jesus College, Oxford; *b* 5 May 1912; *s* of Walter Charles Stritch Hutton and Amy Mary Newton; *m* 1945, Peronelle Marie Stella Luxmoore-Ball; two *s* one *d. Educ:* Parkstone Sch.; Allhallows Sch.; RMC Sandhurst. Commissioned into Royal Tank Corps, 1932; served in Palestine, 1936 (MC); 1st Class Army Interpreter in Arabic, 1937; War of 1939-45: Western Desert, Alamein and N Africa (comdg 5 RTR); Italy (comdg 40 RTR); Comdt, Sandhurst, 1944-45; Instructor, Staff Coll., Camberley, 1949-51; BGS, Arab Legion, 1953-56; Imperial Defence Coll., 1957; Deputy Comd (Land), BFAP (Aden), 1957-59; Dir of Administrative Plans, War Office, 1959-60; Dir-Gen. of Fighting Vehicles, 1961-64; Chief Army Instructor, Imperial Defence Coll., 1964-66. Mem., Bd of Governors, United Oxford Hosps, 1969-72. *Address:* c/o Williams & Glyn's Bank, Kirkland House, Whitehall, SW1.

HUTTON, William, CBE 1962; FRSE; Solicitor; retired; Member Council, Law Society of Scotland, 1962-67; *b* 2 Feb. 1902; *e s* of late John Hutton, MPS, Brechin; *m* 1932, Marjorie Elizabeth, MStJ, *d* of late John Philip Gibb, Director of Raimes, Clark & Co. Ltd, Leith; one *s* one *d. Educ:* Brechin High Sch.; Edinburgh Univ., MA 1925, LLB (dist.) 1927, Thow Schol. 1927. Legal experience with Tait & Crichton, WS and Davidson & Syme, WS; admitted Solicitor, 1928; Legal Asst to Dept of Health for Scotland and Asst Draftsman to Scottish Office, 1929-32; Town Clerk of Kirkcaldy, 1932-39; Sen. Depute Town Clerk of Edinburgh, 1939-48; Dep. Chm. former SW Scotland Electricity Bd, 1948-55; Deputy Chm. South of Scotland Electricity Board, 1955-63. Comp. IEE, 1949-63. Notary Public, 1958; FRSE 1960; JP (Glasgow), 1960-64. *Address:* 21 Craiglockhart Loan, Edinburgh EH14 1JR. *T:* 031-443 3530.

HUTTON-WILLIAMS, Derek Alfred, MBE 1947; CEng, FIMechE; Director-General, Royal Ordnance Factories (Whitehall), 1969-75; *b* 26 April 1914; *s* of William Hutton-Williams and Violet Woodfall Hutton-Williams; *m* 1948, Yvonne Irene Anthony; one *s* three *d. Educ:* Oundle Sch.; London Univ. BSc, ACGI; FIMechE, MIEE; grad. NATO Defence Coll., Paris. Pupil, Winget Ltd, Rochester, 1935; Techn. Asst, Royal Arsenal, Woolwich, 1938; Asst to Director, Small Arms and Fuzes, Ordance Factories, 1939; Manager, Royal Ordnance Factory, Theale, Berks, 1942; Dep.-Dir, Housing Supplies, Ministry of Supply, 1945; Partner, Hutton-Williams and Partners (Industrial Consultant), 1946; Supt, Royal Ordnance Factory, Maltby, Yorks, 1949; NATO Defence Coll., 1957; Asst Dir, Guided Weapons Production, Min. of Aviation, 1958; Dir, Inspectorate of Armaments, 1959; Dir, Royal Small Arms Factory, Enfield, 1964. *Recreations:* gardening; recognising and accepting the inevitable; admiring craftsmanship. *Address:* The School House, Palgrave, near Diss, Norfolk.

HUWS JONES, Robin; *see* Jones, R. H.

HUXHAM, Henry William Walter, CB 1967; CBE 1960; Legal Staff of Law Commission, since Oct. 1967; *b* 10 Feb. 1908; *s* of late William Henry Huxham; *m* 1st, 1934, Mabel Marion (*d* 1949), *d* of W. T. Swain; 2nd, 1950, Winifred Annie, *d* of G. W. Rogers; one *d. Educ:* LLB London, 1930; admitted Solicitor, 1933; joined Solicitor's Dept, Min. of Labour, 1934; Solicitor to Min. of Labour, Aug. 1962-Oct. 1967. Chm., Civil Service Legal Soc., 1952, 1953. *Address:* 21 Holyoake Walk, East Finchley, N2 0JX. *T:* 01-883 3196.

HUXLEY, Sir Andrew Fielding, Kt 1974; FRS 1955; MA Cantab; Royal Society Research Professor, in Department of Physiology, University College London, since 1969 (Jodrell Professor 1960-69); *b* 22 Nov. 1917; *s* of late Leonard Huxley and Rosalind Bruce; *m* 1947, Jocelyn Richenda Gammell Pease; one *s* five *d. Educ:* University College Sch.; Westminster Sch.; Trinity Coll., Cambridge (MA). Operational research for Anti-Aircraft Command, 1940-42, for Admiralty, 1942-45. Fellow,

1941-60, and Dir of Studies, 1952-60, Trinity Coll., Cambridge; Hon. Fellow, Trinity Coll., 1967; Demonstrator, 1946-50, Asst Dir of Research, 1951-59, and Reader in Experimental Biophysics, 1959-60, in Dept of Physiology, Cambridge Univ.; Herter Lectr, Johns Hopkins Univ., 1959; Jesup Lectr, Columbia Univ., 1964; Alexander Forbes Lectr (Grass Foundation), 1966; Croonian Lectr, Royal Society, 1967; Review Lectr on Muscular Contraction, Physiological Soc., 1973; Hans Hecht lectr, Univ. of Chicago, 1975; Sherrington Lectr, Liverpool, 1977. Fullerian Prof. of Physiology and Comparative Anatomy, Royal Institution, 1967-73. Pres., BAAS, 1976-77. Foreign Hon. Mem., American Academy of Arts and Sciences, 1961; Mem., Leopoldina Academy, 1964; For. Mem. Danish Acad. of Sciences, 1964-. Nobel Prize for Physiology or Medicine (jointly), 1963; Copley Medal, Royal Soc., 1973. Hon. MD University of the Saar, 1964; Hon. DSc: Sheffield, 1964; Leicester, 1967; London, 1973; St Andrews, 1974; Aston, 1977. *Publications:* papers in the Journal of Physiology, etc. *Recreations:* walking, shooting. *Address:* Manor Field, Grantchester, Cambridge. *T:* Trumpington 2207.

HUXLEY, Anthony Julian; author, free-lance writer and photographer; *b* 2 Dec. 1920; *s* of Sir Julian Huxley, FRS; *m* 1st, 1943, Priscilla Ann Taylor; three *d*; 2nd, 1974, Alyson Ellen Vivian, *d* of late Beavan Archibald. *Educ:* Dauntsey's Sch.; Trinity Coll., Cambridge (MA). Operational Research in RAF and Min. of Aircraft Production, 1941-47; Economic Research in BOAC, 1947-48; with Amateur Gardening, 1949-71 (editor, 1967-71). *Publications:* (trans.) Exotic Plants of the World, 1955; (trans. and adapted) Orchids of Europe, 1961; (gen. editor) Standard Encyclopedia of the World's Mountains, 1962; (gen. editor) Standard Encyclopedia of Oceans and Islands, 1962; Garden Terms Simplified, 1962, 1971; Flowers in Greece: an outline of the Flora, 1964; (with O. Polunin) Flowers of the Mediterranean, 1965; (gen. ed.) Standard Encyclopedia of Rivers and Lakes, 1965; Mountain Flowers, 1967; (ed) Garden Perennials and Water Plants, 1971; (ed) Garden Annuals and Bulbs, 1971; House Plants, Cacti and Succulents, 1972; (ed) Deciduous Garden Trees and Shrubs, 1973; (ed) Evergreen Garden Trees and Shrubs, 1973; Plant and Planet, 1974; (ed) The Financial Times Book of Garden Design, 1975; (with W. Taylor) Flowers of Greece and the Aegean, 1977; (ed) The Encyclopedia of the Plant Kingdom, 1977. *Recreations:* photography, wild flowers, travel, gardening. *Address:* 50 Villiers Avenue, Surbiton, Surrey KT5 8BD. *T:* 01-399 1479.

HUXLEY, Elspeth Josceline, (Mrs Gervas Huxley), CBE 1962; JP; *b* 23 July 1907; *d* of Major Josceline Grant, Njoro, Kenya; *m* 1931, Gervas Huxley (*d* 1971); one *s*. *Educ:* European Sch., Nairobi, Kenya; Reading Univ. (Diploma in Agriculture); Cornell Univ., USA. Asst Press Officer to Empire Marketing Board, London, 1929-32; subsequently travelled in America, Africa and elsewhere; Mem. BBC Gen. Advisory Council, 1952-59; UK Independent Mem., Monckton Advisory Commission on Central Africa, 1959. *Publications:* White Man's Country; Lord Delamere and the Making of Kenya, 2 vols, 1935; Red Strangers (novel), 1939; Three detective stories; Atlantic Ordeal, 1943; Race and Politics in Kenya (with Margery Perham), 1944; The Walled City (novel), 1948; The Sorcerer's Apprentice (travel), 1948; I Don't Mind If I Do (light novel), 1951; Four Guineas (travel), A Thing to Love, 1954; The Red Rock Wilderness, 1957; The Flame Trees of Thika, 1959; A New Earth, 1960; The Mottled Lizard, 1962; The Merry Hippo, 1963; Forks and Hope, 1964; A Man from Nowhere, 1964; Back Street New Worlds, 1965; Brave New Victuals, 1965; Their Shining Eldorado: A Journey through Australia, 1967; Love Among the Daughters, 1968; The Challenge of Africa, 1971; Livingstone and his African Journeys, 1974; Florence Nightingale, 1975; Gallipot Eyes, 1976. *Recreation:* resting. *Address:* Green End, Oaksey, near Malmesbury, Wilts. *TA:* Oaksey, Malmesbury. *T:* Crudwell 252.

HUXLEY, Prof. George Leonard; Professor of Greek, Queen's University of Belfast, since 1962; *b* Leicester, 23 Sept. 1932; *s* of Sir Leonard Huxley, *qv*; *m* 1957, Davina Best; three *d*. *Educ:* Blundell's Sch.; Magdalen Coll., Oxford. 2nd Mods, 1st Greats, Derby Scholar 1955. Commnd in RE, 1951. Asst Dir, British School at Athens, 1956-58. Fellow of All Souls Coll., 1955-61; Vis. Lectr, Harvard Univ., 1958 and 1961; External Examiner: Trinity Coll., Dublin, 1969-71; St Andrew's Univ., 1973-76; Lancaster Univ., 1977-. Mem. of Exec., NI Civil Rights Assoc., 1971-72. Member: Managing Cttee, British Sch. at Athens, 1967-77; Irish Nat. Cttee Greek and Latin Studies, 1972- (Chm., 1976-). FSA; MRIA. Cromer Greek Prize, British Acad., 1963. *Publications:* Achaeans and Hittites, 1960; Early Sparta, 1962; The Early Ionians, 1966; Greek Epic Poetry from Eumelos to Panyassis, 1969; (ed with J. N. Coldstream) Kythera, 1972; Pindar's Vision of the Past, 1975; articles on Hellenic and Byzantine subjects. *Recreation:* siderodromophilia. *Address:* 48 Marlborough Park North, Belfast, N Ireland BT9 6HJ. *Club:* Athenæum.

HUXLEY, Mrs Gervas; *see* Huxley, Elspeth J.

HUXLEY, Hugh Esmor, MBE 1948; FRS 1960; MA, PhD; ScD; Deputy Chairman, Medical Research Council Laboratory of Molecular Biology, Cambridge; *b* 25 Feb. 1924; *s* of late Thomas Hugh Huxley and Olwen Roberts, Birkenhead, Cheshire; *m* 1966, Frances Fripp, *d* of G. Maxon, Milwaukee; one *d*, and two step-*s* one step-*d*. *Educ:* Park High Sch., Birkenhead; Christ's Coll., Cambridge (Exhibitioner and Scholar). Natural Science Tripos, Cambridge, 1941-43 and 1947-48 (Pt II Physics); BA 1948, MA 1950, PhD 1952. Served War of 1939-45, Radar Officer, RAF Bomber Command and Telecommunications Research Establishment, Malvern, 1943-47; Mem. Empire Air Armaments Sch. Mission to Australia and NZ, 1946. Research Student, Med. Research Council Unit for Molecular Biology, Cavendish Lab., Cambridge, 1948-52; Commonwealth Fund Fellow, Biology Dept, Massachusetts Inst. of Technology, 1952-54; Research Fellow, Christ's Coll., Cambridge, 1953-56; Mem. of External Staff of Med. Res. Council, and Hon. Res. Associate, Biophysics Dept, University Coll., London, 1956-61. Ziskind Vis. Prof., Brandeis Univ., 1971; Lectures: Harvey Soc., New York, 1964-65; Hooke, Univ. of Texas, 1968; Dunham, Harvard Med. Sch., 1969; Croonian, Royal Soc., 1970; Mayer, MIT, 1971; Penn, Pennsylvania Univ., 1971; Carter-Wallace, Princeton Univ., 1973; Adam Muller, State Univ. of NY, 1973. Fellow: King's Coll., Cambridge, 1961-67; Churchill Coll., Cambridge, 1967-. Member: Council, Royal Soc., 1973-; President's Adv. Bd, Rosentiel Basic Med. Scis Center, Brandeis Univ., 1971-; Scientific Adv. Council, European Molecular Biol. Lab., 1976-. Feldberg Foundation Award for Experimental Medical Research, 1963; William Bate Hardy Prize (Camb. Phil. Soc.) 1965; Louisa Gross Horwitz Prize, 1971; Internat. Feltrinelli Prize, 1974; Baly Medal, RCP, 1975. Mem., German Acad. of Science, Leopoldina, 1964; Foreign Hon. Mem., Amer. Acad. of Arts and Sciences, 1965; Hon. For. Mem., Danish Acad. of Sciences, 1971. Hon. Dr of Science: Harvard Univ., 1969; Chicago Univ., 1974; Univ. of Pennsylvania, 1976. *Publications:* contrib. to learned jls. *Recreations:* ski-ing, sailing. *Address:* Churchill College, Cambridge. *T:* Cambridge 61200; 7 Chaucer Road, Cambridge. *T:* Cambridge 56117.

HUXLEY, Sir Leonard (George Holden), KBE 1964; MA, DPhil Oxon; PhD Adelaide; FAA; Emeritus Professor, University of Adelaide; Vice-Chancellor, The Australian National University, 1960-Dec. 1967; *b* London, UK, 29 May 1902; *s* of George H. and Lilian S. Huxley; *m* 1929, Ella M. C., *d* of F. G. and E. Copeland; one *s* one *d*. *Educ:* The Hutchins Sch., Hobart; University of Tasmania; New Coll., Oxford. Rhodes Scholar, Tas., 1923; Jessie Theresa Rowden Scholar, New Coll., 1927; Scott Scholar, University of Oxford, 1929. Scientific staff, CSIR, Sydney, 1929-31; Head of Dept of Physics, University Coll. Leicester, 1932-40; Principal Scientific Officer, Telecommunications Research Estabt, MAP, 1940-46; Reader in Electromagnetism, University of Birmingham, 1946-49; Elder Prof. of Physics, University Adelaide, 1949-60; Mem. Executive, CSIRO, 1960; Mem. Council, University of Adelaide, 1953-60; Mem. Council, Aust. Nat. Univ., 1956-59; Foundation FAA, 1954 (Sec., Physical Sciences, 1959-62); Chm. Australian Radio Research Board, 1958-64; Chm. National Standards Commission, 1953-65; Chm. Radio Frequency Allocation Cttee, 1960-64; Mem. Nat. Library Council, 1961-72; Mem. Bd, US Educnl Foundn in Austr., 1960-65; Australian Deleg. on Cttee on Space Research, (COSPAR), 1959-60. First President Aust. Inst. of Physics, 1962-65. Mem., Queen Elizabeth II Fellowships Cttee, 1963-66; Chm., Gen. Coun. Encyclopædia Britannica Australia Awards, 1964-74; Chm. Bd, Aust./Amer. Educl Foundn, 1965-69; Trustee, Aust. Humanities Res. Council, 1968-70; Mem. Council, Canberra Coll. of Advanced Educn, 1968-74. DSc (*hc*), Tas. *Publications:* Wave Guides, 1949; (with R. W. Crompton) The Diffusion and Drift of Electrons in Gases, 1974; numerous scientific papers on gaseous Electronics, the ionosphere, upper atmosphere and related subjects. *Address:* 19 Glasgow Place, Hughes, Canberra, ACT 2605, Australia. *Club:* Commonwealth (Canberra).
See also Prof. G. L. Huxley.

HUXLEY, Michael Heathorn; *b* 9 Aug. 1899; *s* of Henry Huxley and Sophy Stobart; *m* 1926, Ottilie de Lotbinière Mills; one *s* one *d* (and one *s* decd). *Educ:* Rugby. Entered Diplomatic Service, 1922; served in Tehran and Washington and in the Foreign Office; Second Secretary, 1925; First Sec., 1934; resigned in order to launch and edit The Geographical Magazine, 1934; recalled for war service by Foreign Office, Sept, 1939; resumed editorial work, 1945; resigned editorship, 1959. *Address:*

Buckhold, Lodsworth, near Petworth, West Sussex. *Club:* National Liberal.

HUXLEY, Prof. Peter Arthur, PhD; FIBiol; Agricultural Research Adviser/FAO, Agricultural Research Centre, Tripoli, Libya, since 1977; *b* 26 Sept. 1926; *s* of Ernest Henry Huxley and Florence Agnes (*née* King); *m* 1954, Betty Grace Anne Foot (separated); three *s* one *d.* *Educ:* Alleyn's Sch.; Edinburgh Univ.; Reading Univ. (BSc, PhD). FIBiol 1970. RNVR, 1944-46. Asst Lectr to Sen. Lectr, Makerere University Coll., Uganda, 1954-64; Dir of Res., Coffee Res. Foundn, Kenya, 1965-69; Prof. of Horticulture, Univ. of Reading, 1969-74; Prof. of Crop Science, Univ. of Dar es Salaam/FAO, 1974-76. FRSA. *Publications:* approx. 70 pubns in agric., horticult., meteorol and agricl botany jls. *Recreations:* winemaking, gardening and listening to music. *Address:* c/o National Westminster Bank, 49 South Street, Dorchester, Dorset.

HUXSTEP, Emily Mary, CBE 1964; BA London: Headmistress of Chislehurst and Sidcup Girls' Grammar School, Kent, 1944-66; *b* 15 Sept. 1906; *d* of George T. and Nellie M. Huxstep (*née* Wood). *Educ:* Chatham Girls' Grammar Sch.; Queen Mary Coll. Headmistress, Hanson Girls' Grammar Sch., Bradford, Yorks, 1938-44. Hon. DCL Kent, 1974. *Address:* 23 Homewood Crescent, Chislehurst, Kent. *T:* 01-467 3690.

HUXTABLE, Rev. (William) John (Fairchild), DD; Executive Officer, Churches' Unity Commission, since 1975; *b* 25 July 1912; *s* of Rev. John Huxtable and Florence Huxtable (*née* Watts); *m* 1939, Joan Lorimer Snow; one *s* two *d.* *Educ:* Barnstaple Gram. Sch.; Western Coll., Bristol; Mansfield and St Catherine's Colls, Oxford. BA Bristol 1933; BA Oxon 1937, MA 1940. Minister: Newton Abbot Congreg. Church, 1937-42; Palmers Green Congreg. Church, 1942-54; Princ., New Coll., University of London, 1953-64. Chm., 1962-63, Sec., 1964-66, Minister Sec., 1966-72, Congregational Union of England and Wales; Jt Gen. Sec., United Reformed Church, 1972-74; Moderator, United Reformed Church, 1972-73. Vice-President: British Coun. of Churches, 1967-71; World Alliance of Reformed Churches, 1970-77; Vice-Moderator, Free Church Federal Council, 1975-76, Moderator, 1976-77; Member: Central Cttee, World Council of Churches, 1968-75; Jt Cttee of Translation of New English Bible, 1948-. Vice-Pres. Council, St Dunstan's, 1973-. Hon. DD: Lambeth, 1973; Aberdeen, 1973. *Publications:* The Ministry, 1943; (ed) John Owen's True Nature of a Gospel Church, 1947; (ed jtly) A Book of Public Worship, 1948; The Faith that is in Us, 1953; The Promise of the Father, 1959; Like a Strange People, 1961; Church and State in Education (C. J. Cadoux Meml Lect.), 1962; The Bible Says (Maynard Chapman Lects), 1962; Preaching the Law, (Joseph Smith Meml Lect.), 1964; The Preacher's Integrity (A. S. Peake Meml Lect), 1966; Christian Unity: some of the issues (Congreg. Lects), 1966; contribs to symposia: The Churches and Christian Unity, 1962; From Uniformity to Unity, 1962; A Companion to the Bible, 1963; Renewal of Worship, 1965; Outlook for Christianity, 1967; contrib. to Christian Confidence, 1970; also contribs to Congreg. Quarterly, Theology, London Quarterly and Holborn Review, and Proc. Internat. Congreg. Council. *Recreation:* reading. *Address:* 10 Gerard Road, Harrow, Mddx. *T:* 01-907 1420. *Club:* Royal Commonwealth Society.

HUYGHE, René; Grand Officier de la Légion d'Honneur; Member of the Académie Française since 1960; Hon. Professor of Psychology of Plastic Arts, Collège de France (Professor, 1950-76); Hon. Head Keeper, Musée de Louvre; Director, Museum Jacquemart-André, Paris, since 1974; *b* Arras, Pas-de-Calais, France, 3 May 1906; *s* of Louis Huyghe and Marie (*née* Delvoye); *m* 1950, Lydie Bouthet; one *s* one *d.* *Educ:* Sorbonne; Ecole du Louvre, Paris. Attached to Musée du Louvre, 1927; Asst Keeper, 1930; Head Keeper, Départment des Peintures. Dessins, Chalcographie, 1937. Mem. of Council, Musées Nationaux, 1952 (Vice-Pres. 1964, Pres. 1975); Pres. Assoc. internationale du Film d'Art, 1958. Holds foreign decorations. Praemium Erasmianum, The Hague, 1966. *Publications:* Histoire de l'Art contemporain: La Peinture, 1935; Cézanne 1936 and 1961; Les Contemporains, 1939 (2nd edn, 1949); Vermeer, 1948; Watteau, 1950; various works on Gauguin, 1951, 1952, 1959; Dialogue avec le visible, 1955 (trans. Eng.); L'Art et l'homme, Vol. I, 1957, Vol. II, 1958, Vol. III, 1961 (trans. Eng.); Van Gogh, 1959; Merveilles de la France, 1960; L'Art et l'Ame, 1960 (trans. Eng.); La peinture française aux XVIIe et XVIIIe Siècles, 1962; Delacroix ou le combat solitaire, 1963 (trans. Eng.); Puissances de l'Image, 1965; Sens et Destin de l'Art, 1967; L'Art et le monde moderne, Vol. I, 1970, Vol. II, 1971; Forces et Formes, 1971; La Relève du réel, 1974; La Relève de l'imaginaire, 1976; Ce que je crois, 1976. *Address:* 3 rue Corneille, Paris 75006, France. *Club:* Union interalliée (Paris).

HYAMS, Daisy Deborah, (Mrs C. Guderley), OBE 1974; Managing Director, Tesco (Wholesale) Ltd, since 1965; *b* 25 Nov. 1912; *d* of Hyman Hyams and Annie Burnett; *m* 1936, Sidney Hart; no *c*; *m* 1975, C. Guderley. *Educ:* Coborn Grammar Sch. for Girls, Bow. FGI. Joined Tesco, 1931. Director: Tesco (Wholesale) Ltd, 1955; Tesco Stores Ltd, 1961; Tesco (Holdings) Ltd, 1970. *Recreations:* travel, reading. *Address:* 10 Noblefield Heights, Great North Road, Highgate, N2 0NX. *T:* 01-348 1591.

HYATALI, Hon. Sir Isaac Emanuel, Kt 1973; TC 1974; Chief Justice and President of the Court of Appeal, Trinidad and Tobago, since 1972; *b* 21 Nov. 1917; *s* of late Joseph Hyatali and Mrs Hyatali; *m* 1943, Audrey Monica Joseph; two *s* one *d.* *Educ:* Naparima Coll., San Fernando; Gray's Inn and Council of Legal Education, London. Called to Bar, Gray's Inn. 1947. Private practice at the Bar, 1947-59; Judge, Supreme Court, 1959-62; Justice of Appeal, 1962-72; Pres., Industrial Court, 1965-72. Chm., Arima Rent Assessment Bd, 1953-59; Chm., Agricultural Rent Bd (Eastern Counties), 1953-59. Chairman: Agricultural Wages Council, 1958-59; Oil and Water Bd, 1959-62. Trinidad and Tobago Editor of West Indian Law Reports, 1961-65. Member: World Assoc. of Judges; British Inst. of Internat. and Comparative Law; Hon. Mem., World Peace through Law Center. *Recreations:* gardening, tennis, cricket, reading, social work. *Address:* (office) Chief Justice's Chambers Port-of-Spain, Trinidad-and-Tobago; (home) 12 Prada Street, S. Clair, Port-of-Spain. *T:* 62/32417. *Club:* (Hon. Mem.) Union Park Turf (Trinidad).

HYATT KING, Alexander; *see* King, A. H.

HYDE, Lord; George Edward Laurence Villiers; *b* 12 Feb. 1976; *s* and *heir* of 7th Earl of Clarendon, *qv*.

HYDE, Francis Edwin; Chaddock Professor of Economic History, University of Liverpool, 1970-75, now Emeritus (Chaddock Professor of Economics, 1948-70); *b* 18 July 1908; *s* of Walter Henry Hassall Hyde and Charlotte Ann Sharp; *m* 1st, 1935, Marian Rosa (*d* 1967), *d* of Thomas Abercromby Welton and Rosa Sheppard; one *d*; 2nd, 1970, Anne Elizabeth Evans. *Educ:* Wolverton Grammar Sch.; University of Liverpool; University of London; Harvard Coll., USA. BA, First Cl. Hons in History (Liverpool), 1929; MA (Liverpool), 1931; PhD (Econ.) London Sch. of Economics, 1931. Commonwealth Fund Fellow, 1931-33; Gladstone Memorial Fellow and University Fellow, 1929-31; Houblon-Norman Fellow, 1948; FRHistS. Lecturer in Economics and Economic History, 1934-48; Dean, Faculty of Arts, 1949-53, Pro-Vice-Chancellor, 1960-64, Univ. of Liverpool. Board of Trade, 1941-45; Pres., Liverpool Economic and Statistical Soc.; Chm., University Press of Liverpool; Hon. Treasurer Joint Matriculation Board, 1955-66; Mem. University Council, 1957-75. Editor of Business History. *Publications:* Mr Gladstone at the Board of Trade, 1934; The Import Trade of the Port of Liverpool, 1946; Economic History of Buckinghamshire, 1948; Stony Stratford, 1948; Blue Funnel: A History of Alfred Holt & Co., 1956; (with others) A New Prospect of Economics, 1958; Harrisons of Liverpool, 1830-1939, 1966; Shipping Enterprise and Management, 1967; (with Dr Sheila Marriner) The Senior: John Samuel Swire 1825-98, 1967; Liverpool and the Mersey, 1971; Far Eastern Trade, 1973; Cunard and the North Atlantic, 1975; reviews and articles in Economic Journals. *Recreations:* walking and rock climbing. *Address:* Heather Cottage, Village Road, West Kirby, Merseyside. *T:* 051-625 7632.

HYDE, H(arford) Montgomery, MA Oxon, DLit Belfast, FRHistS; FRSL; MRIA; author and barrister; *b* Belfast, 14 Aug. 1907; *o s* of late James J. Hyde, JP, Belfast, and Isobel Greenfield Montgomery; *m* 1st, 1939, Dorothy Mabel Brayshaw (from whom he obtained a divorce, 1952), *e d* of Dr J. Murray Crofts, CBE, Disley, Cheshire; 2nd, 1955, Mary Eleanor (marr. diss., 1966), *d* of Col L. G. Fischer, IMS; 3rd, 1966, Rosalind Roberts, *y d* of Comdr J. F. W. Dimond, RN. *Educ:* Sedbergh (Scholar); Queen's Univ. Belfast (Emily Lady Pakenham Scholar); 1st Class Hons Modern History, 1928; Magdalen Coll., Oxford (Open History Exhibitioner); 2nd Class Hons Jurisprudence, 1930; Harmsworth Law Scholar, Middle Temple, 1932. Called to Bar, Middle Temple, 1934; joined NE Circuit; Extension Lecturer in History, Oxford Univ., 1934; Private Sec. to Marquess of Londonderry, 1935-39; Asst Censor, Gibraltar, 1940; commissioned in Intelligence Corps, 1940; Military Liaison and Censorship Security Officer, Bermuda, 1940-41; Asst Passport Control Officer, New York, 1941-42; with British Army Staff, USA, 1942-44; Major, 1942; attached Supreme HQ Allied Expeditionary Force, 1944; Allied Commission for Austria, 1944-45; Lt-Col 1945; Asst Editor, Law Reports, 1946-47; Legal Adviser, British Lion Film Corp.

Ltd, 1947-49; MP (U) North Belfast, 1950-59; UK Delegate to Council of Europe Consultative Assembly, Strasbourg, 1952-55; Hon. Col Intelligence Corps (TA), NI, 1958-61; Professor of Hist. and Polit. Sci., University of the Punjab, Lahore, 1959-61; RAF Museum Leverhulme Research Fellowship, 1971-75. Active in campaign for abolition of capital punishment; has travelled extensively in Russia, The Far East, West Indies, Mexico, and South America. *Publications:* The Rise of Castlereagh, 1933; The Russian Journals of Martha and Catherine Wilmot (with the Marchioness of Londonderry), 1934; More Letters from Martha Wilmot, Impressions of Vienna (with the Marchioness of Londonderry), 1935; The Empress Catherine and Princess Dashkhov, 1935; Air Defence and the Civil Population (with G. R. Falkiner Nuttall), 1937; Londonderry House and Its Pictures, 1937; Princess Lieven, 1938; Judge Jeffreys, 1940, new edn, 1948; Mexican Empire, 1946; A Victorian Historian, 1947; Privacy and the Press, 1947; John Law, 1948, new edn 1969; The Trials of Oscar Wilde, 1948, 3rd edn 1973; Mr and Mrs Beeton, 1951; Cases that changed the Law, 1951; Carson, 1953; The Trial of Craig and Bentley, 1954; United in Crime, 1955; Mr and Mrs Daventry, a play by Frank Harris, 1957; The Strange Death of Lord Castlereagh, 1959; The Trial of Roger Casement, 1960, 2nd edn 1964; The Life and Cases of Sir Patrick Hastings, 1960; Recent Developments in Historical Method and Interpretation, 1960; Simla and the Simla Hill States under British Protection, 1961; An International Crime Case Book, 1962; The Quiet Canadian, 1962; Oscar Wilde: the Aftermath, 1963; Room 3603, 1964; A History of Pornography, 1964; Norman Birkett, 1964; Cynthia, 1965; The Story of Lamb House, 1966, 2nd edn 1975; Lord Reading, 1967; Strong for Service: The Life of Lord Nathan of Churt, 1968; Henry James At Home, 1969; The Other Love, 1970; Their Good Names, 1970; Stalin, 1971; Baldwin: the unexpected Prime Minister, 1973; Oscar Wilde, 1975; The Cleveland Street Scandal, 1976; British Air Policy between the Wars, 1976; Neville Chamberlain, 1976; Crime has its Heroes, 1976; Solitary in the Ranks, 1977; chapter 12 (The Congress of Vienna) in the Cambridge History of Poland, etc. *Recreations:* criminology, music. *Address:* Westwell House, Tenterden, Kent. *T:* Tenterden 3189. *Clubs:* Garrick, Beefsteak; Dormy House (Rye); Grolier (New York).

HYDE, William Leonard, FBS; Director and Chief General Manager, Leeds Permanent Building Society; Member of Council, Building Societies Association; Member, National House Builders Council; Regional Director, Lloyds Bank Ltd; Local Director, Royal Insurance Co. Ltd. *Recreations:* golf, walking. *Address:* 5 Burn Bridge Road, Harrogate, Yorks. *T:* Harrogate 871748. *Clubs:* RAC; Pannal Golf.

HYDE-PARKER, Sir R. W.; *see* Parker.

HYDE-SMITH, Marisa; *see* Robles, Marisa.

HYDE WHITE, Wilfrid; *b* 12 May 1903; *s* of William Edward White, Canon of Gloucester and Ethel Adelaide (*née* Drought); *m* 1927, Blanche Hope Aitken; one *s* ; *m* 1957, Ethel Korenman (stage name Ethel Drew); one *s* one *d*. *Educ:* Marlborough. First appeared in London in Beggar on Horseback, Queen's Theatre, 1925; successful appearances include: Rise Above It, Comedy; It Depends What You Mean, Westminster; Britannus in Cæsar and Cleopatra, St James's, London, and Ziegfield, New York; Affairs of State, Cambridge; Hippo Dancing, Lyric; The Reluctant Debutante, Cambridge, and Henry Miller's Theatre, New York (nominated for Tony award, 1956); Not in the Book, Criterion; Miss Pell is Missing, Criterion; The Doctor's Dilemma, Haymarket; Lady Windermere's Fan, Phoenix; Meeting at Night, Duke of York's; The Jockey Club Stakes, Duke of York's, and Cort Theatre, NYC (nominated for Tony award for best actor, 1973); The Pleasure of his Company, Phoenix; Rolls Hyphen Royce, Shaftesbury. *Films include:* The 3rd Man, The Browning Version, Golden Salamander, The Million Pound Note, Libel, Two Way Stretch, North West Frontier, Let's Make Love, His and Hers, On the Double, Ada, The Castaways, Crooks Anonymous, On the Fiddle, Aliki, My Fair Lady, 10 Little Indians, The Liquidator. *Address:* 67157 Santa Barbara Drive, Palm Springs, Calif 92262, USA. *T:* (714) 327-3276. *Clubs:* Green Room, Buck's.

HYLTON, 5th Baron, *cr* 1866; **Raymond Hervey Jolliffe,** ALAS; DL; *b* 13 June 1932; *er s* of 4th Baron Hylton and of the Dowager Lady Hylton, *d* of late Raymond Asquith and *sister* of 2nd Earl of Oxford and Asquith, *qv* ; *S* father, 1967; *m* 1966, Joanna Ida Elizabeth, *d* of late Andrew de Bertodano; three *s* one *d*. *Educ:* Eton (King's Scholar); Trinity Coll., Oxford (MA). Lieut R of O, Coldstream Guards. Asst Private Sec. to Governor-General of Canada, 1960-62; Trustee, Shelter Housing Aid Centre 1970-76; Chairman: Catholic Housing Aid

Soc., 1972-73; Nat. Fedn of Housing Assocs, 1973-76; Vice-Pres., Age Concern (Nat. Old People's Welfare Council), 1971-77; Pres., SW Reg. Nat. Soc. for Mentally Handicapped Children, 1976. Mem., Frome RDC, 1968-72. DL Somerset, 1975. *Heir: s* Hon. William Henry Martin Jolliffe, *b* April 1967. *Address:* Ammerdown, Radstock, Bath.

HYLTON-FOSTER, family name of Baroness Hylton-Foster.

HYLTON-FOSTER, Baroness, *cr* 1965, of the City of Westminster (Life Peer); **Audrey Pellew Hylton-Foster;** President and Chairman, London Branch, British Red Cross Society, since 1960; Convenor, Cross Bench Peers, since 1974; *b* 19 May 1908; *d* of 1st Viscount Ruffside, PC, DL (*d* 1958), and Viscountess Ruffside (*d* 1969); *m* 1931, Rt Hon. Sir Harry Hylton-Foster, QC (*d* 1965); no *c*. *Educ:* St George's, Ascot; Ivy House, Wimbledon. *Recreations:* gardening, trout fishing. *Address:* The Coach House, Tanhurst, Leith Hill, Holmbury St Mary, Dorking, Surrey RH5 6LU. *T:* Dorking 6575.

HYMAN, Joe; Chairman, John Crowther Group Ltd, since 1971; Underwriting member of Lloyd's; *b* 14 Oct. 1921; *yr s* of late Solomon Hyman and of Hannah Hyman; *m* 1st, 1948, Corinne I. Abrahams (marriage dissolved); one *s* one *d* ; 2nd, 1963, Simone Duke; one *s* one *d*. *Educ:* North Manchester Gram. Sch. Has been in Textiles, 1939-; Chm., Viyella International, 1962-69. Trustee, Pestalozzi Children's Village Trust, 1967-; Governor, LSE. FRSA 1968; FBIM. Comp. TI. *Recreations:* music, golf, gardening. *Address:* Lukyns, Ewhurst, Surrey; 24 Kingston House North, Prince's Gate, SW7. *Club:* Royal Automobile.

HYND, Henry; *b* Perth, Scotland, 4 July 1900; *s* of Henry Hynd; *m*, 1st, 1925, Phyllis Jarman (marr. diss. 1971); one *d* ; 2nd, 1971, Mrs Anne Nadine Scott. *Educ:* Perth Academy. Railway Clerk, 1915-20; Trade Union Official, 1920-45; Member Hornsey Borough Council, 1939-52; MP (Lab) for Central Hackney, 1945-50, for Accrington, 1950-66; Parliamentary Private Sec. to First Lord of the Admiralty, Dec. 1945-46 and to Min. of Defence, 1946-50. Hon. Pres., London Perthshire Assoc. JP Middlesex. Commander of Belgian Order of the Crown and Officer of Luxembourg Order of the Oak Crown. *Recreations:* travelling, bowls. *Address:* 31 Alford House, Stanhope Road, N6 5AL. *T:* 01-340 3308.

HYND, Ronald; choreographer; *b* 22 April 1931; *s* of William John and Alice Louisa Hens; *m* 1957, Annette Page, *qv* ; one *d*. *Educ:* erratically throughout England due to multiple wartime evacuation. Joined Rambert School, 1946; Ballet Rambert, 1949; Royal Ballet (then Sadlers Well's Ballet), 1952, rising from Corps de Ballet to Principal Dancer, 1959; danced Siegfried (Swan Lake), Florimund (Sleeping Beauty), Albrecht (Giselle), Poet (Sylphides), Tsarevitch (Firebird), Prince of Pagodas, Moondog (Lady and Fool), Tybalt (Romeo), etc; produced first choreography for Royal Ballet Choreographic Group followed by works for London Festival Ballet, Royal Ballet, Dutch National Ballet and Munich Ballet; Dir, Munich Ballet, 1970-73. *Ballets include:* Le Baiser de la Fée, 1968, new production 1974; Pasiphaë, 1969; Dvorak Variations, 1970; Wendekreise, 1972; In a Summer Garden, 1972; Das Telefon, 1972; Mozartiana, 1973; Charlotte Brontë, 1974; Mozart Adagio, 1974; Galileo (film), 1974; Orient/Occident, 1975; La Valse, 1975; Valses Nobles et Sentimentales, 1975; The Merry Widow, 1975; L'Eventail, 1976; The Nutcracker (new version for Festival Ballet), 1976. *Recreation:* the gramophone. *Address:* 51 Sutherland Place, W2 5BY. *T:* 01-229 1020.

HYND, Mrs Ronald; *see* Page, Annette.

HYSLOP, Dr James Morton; Principal and Vice-Chancellor, Rhodes University, 1963-76; *b* Dumbarton, 12 Sept. 1908; *s* of William Hyslop; *m* 1935, Helen Margaret, *d* of W. W. Hyslop, Glasgow; one *d*. *Educ:* High Sch. of Glasgow; Univ. of Glasgow (MA, DSc); Christ's Coll., Cambridge (BA, PhD). War Service as Flt-Lt, RAF, mainly in Middle East, 1941-45. Lectr, Univ. of Glasgow, 1933-41 and 1945-47; Prof. of Maths, Univ. of the Witwatersrand, 1947-60; Principal, Royal Coll., Nairobi (now University Coll., Nairobi), 1960-63. Hon. LLD: Glasgow, 1967; Rhodes, 1976. Coronation Medal, 1953. *Publications:* Infinite Series, 1941; Real Variable, 1960; papers in learned jls on mathematical topics. *Recreations:* golf, bowls. *Address:* 36 Grand Street, Port Alfred, South Africa. *Clubs:* Port Elizabeth, Albany (Grahamstown).

HYSLOP, James Telfer, OBE 1968; HM Diplomatic Service, retired; Consul General, Detroit, 1971-76; *b* 21 Sept. 1916; *s* of Mr and Mrs John J. Hyslop; *m* 1942, Jane Elizabeth Owers; one *s* one *d*. *Educ:* Queen Elizabeth's Grammar Sch., Hexham. Royal Navy, 1939-46. Entered Diplomatic Service, 1948; served at: Baltimore, 1948; Valparaiso, 1951; Amman, 1954; Tegucigalpa, 1958; San Francisco, 1961; Johannesburg, 1964; Bogota, 1968. *Recreations:* reading, music. *Address:* 12 Quay Walls, Berwick-on-Tweed. *Club:* Naval.

HYSLOP, Robert John M.; *see* Maxwell-Hyslop.

HYTNER, Benet Alan, QC 1970; a Recorder of the Crown Court, since 1972; *b* 29 Dec. 1927; *s* of Maurice and Sarah Hytner, Manchester; *m* 1954, Joyce, *er d* of Bernard and Vera Myers, Manchester; three *s* one *d. Educ:* Manchester Grammar Sch.; Trinity Hall, Cambridge (Exhibr). MA. National Service, RASC, 1949-51 (commnd). Called to Bar, Middle Temple, 1952. Mem., Gen. Council of Bar, 1969-73. *Recreations:* fell walking, music, theatre, reading. *Address:* 5 Essex Court, Temple, EC4.

HYTTEN, Torleiv, CMG 1953; Vice-Chancellor, University of Tasmania, 1949-57, retired; *b* Drammen, Norway, 17 Feb. 1890; *s* of late E. O. Hytten, Tönsberg, Norway; *m* 1922, Margaret Frances (*née* Compton); one *s* (and one *s* decd). *Educ:* Tönsberg; University of Tasmania. MA, 1st Cl. Hons Economics. Went to Australia, 1910; Journalist, 1920-26; University of Tasmania: Lecturer in Economics, 1926; Professor of Economics, 1929-35; Dir of Tutorial Classes, 1928-32. Economic Adviser: Tasmanian Govt 1929-35; Bank of NSW, 1935-49. Conducted case for Tasmanian Govt before Commonwealth Public Accts Cttee, 1930-31, before Commonwealth Grants Commn, 1933-34. Chm. Tasmanian State Employment Council, 1932; Delegate 16th Assembly, League of Nations, 1935; Chm. Aust. Nat. Cttee, Internat. Chamber of Commerce, 1949; Mem., Commonwealth Bank Bd, 1954-59. Conducted enquiry into Transport Problems in Qld, 1958. Knight 1st Class, Order of St Olav (Norway), 1951; Chevalier, Order of the Crown (Belgium), 1957. *Publications:* articles to Economic Record and similar periodicals, principally on economics of transport, and banking. *Address:* Forestgait, 22 King's Gate, Aberdeen AB9 2YL. *T:* Aberdeen 28473.

I

IBBOTSON, Lancelot William Cripps, CBE 1971 (MBE 1948); General Manager of Southern Region, British Railways, and Chairman, Southern Railway Board, 1968-72; *b* 10 Feb. 1909; *s* of William Ibbotson, FRCS and Mrs Dora Ibbotson (*née* Chapman), London; *m* 1931, Joan Marguerite Jeffcock; one *s* one *d. Educ:* Radley Coll. Traffic Apprentice, LNER, 1927; Chief Clerk to Dist. Supt, Newcastle, 1939; Asst Dist Supt, York, 1942; Dist Supt, Darlington, 1945; Asst to Operating Supt, Western Region, 1950; Asst Gen. Man., Western Region, 1959; Chief Operating Officer, British Railways, 1963; Gen. Man., Western Region, BR, and Chm., Western Railway Board, 1966-68. Gen. Man., A. Pearce, Partners & Assoc., 1975-; Chm., APPA Thermal Exchanges Ltd, 1976-. *Recreations:* foreign travel, photography. *Address:* Monks Well House, Waverley, Farnham, Surrey. *T:* Runfold 2328. *Club:* Royal Automobile.

IBIAM, Sir (Francis) Akanu, GCON 1963; KCMG 1962; KBE 1951 (OBE 1949); LLD, DLit; medical missionary; *b* Unwana, Afikpo Division, Nigeria, 29 Nov. 1906; *s* of late Ibiam Aka Ibiam and late Alu Owora; *m* 1939, Eudora Olayinka Sasegbon (*d* 1974); one *s* two *d. Educ:* Hope Waddell Training Instn Calabar; King's Coll., Lagos; University of St Andrews, Scotland. Medical Missionary with the Church of Scotland Mission, Calabar, Nigeria, 1936; started and built up new Hosp. in Abiriba, Bende Div., under Calabar Mission, 1936-45; Medical Supt, CSM Hosp., Itu, 1945-48; CSM Hosp., Uburu, 1952-57. MLC, Nigeria, 1947-52; MEC, 1949-52; retd from Politics, 1953; Principal, Hope Waddell Training Instn, Calabar, 1957-60; (on leave) Governor, Eastern Nigeria, 1960-66; Adviser to Military Governor of Eastern Provinces, 1966. Founder (1937) and former Pres., Student Christian Movement of Nigeria, now Hon. President; Trustee: Presbyterian Church of Nigeria, 1945-; Queen Elizabeth Hosp., Umuahia-Ibeku, 1953-; Scout Movement of Eastern Nigeria, 1957-; Mem. Bd of Governors: Hope Waddell Trg Instn, Calabar, 1945-60; Queen Elizabeth Hosp., 1950-60; Mem. Provl Council of University Coll., Ibadan, 1948-54; Mem. Privy Council, Eastern Nigeria, 1954-60; Pres., Christian Council of Nigeria, 1955-58; Mem. Calabar Mission Council, 1940-60 (now integrated with Church); Mem. Admin. Cttee of Internat. Missionary Council, 1957-61; Chm. Provisional Cttee of All Africa Churches Conf., 1958-62; Chairman: Council of University of Ibadan, Nigeria, 1958-60; Governing Council of Univ. of Nigeria, Nsukka, 1966;

a Pres. of World Council of Churches, 1961; a Pres. of All Africa Church Conf., 1963; Pres., World Council of Christian Educn and Sunday Sch. Assoc.; Chm. Council, United Bible Socs, 1966-72, Vice-Pres. 1972-; Founder and Pres., Bible Soc. of Nigeria, 1963-74, Patron 1974. Presbyterian Church of Nigeria: Mem. Educ. Authority, 1940-; Mem. Missionaries' Cttee, Med. Bd, and Standing Cttee of Synod; Advanced Training Fund Management Cttee of Synod; Elder, 1940-. Upper Room Citation, 1966. Hon. DSc Ife, 1966. Golden Cross with crown, Order of Orthodox Knights of Holy Sepulchre, Jerusalem, 1965; Golden Star Medal (1st degree), Order of Russian Orthodox Church, 1965. *Recreation:* reading. *Address:* 41a Colliery Avenue, Enugu, Nigeria.

IBRAHIM, Sir Kashim, GCON 1963; KCMG 1962; CBE 1960 (MBE 1952); Governor of Northern Nigeria, 1962-66; Chancellor, Lagos University, since 1976; *b* 10 June 1910; *s* of Mallam Ibrahim Lakkani; *m* 1st, 1943, Halima; 2nd, 1944, Khadija; 3rd, 1957, Zainaba; four *s* three *d* (and two *d* decd). *Educ:* Bornu Provincial Sch.; Katsina Teachers' Trng Coll. Teacher, 1929-32; Visiting Teacher, 1933-49; Educ. Officer, 1949-52. Federal Minister of Social Services, 1952-55; Northern Regional Minister of Social Develt and Surveys, 1955-56; Waziri of Bornu, 1956-62. Advr to Military Governor, N Nigeria, 1966-. Chm. Nigerian Coll. of Arts, Science and Technology, 1958-62; Chancellor, Ibadan Univ., 1967-75; Chm. Provisional Council of Ahmadu Bello Univ. Hon. LLD: Ahmadu Bello, 1963; Univ. of Ibadan; Univ. of Nigeria (Nsukka); University of Lagos. *Publications:* Kanuri Reader Elementary, I-IV; Kanuri Arithmetic Books, I-IV, for Elementary Schs and Teachers' Guide for above. *Recreations:* walking, riding, polo playing.

IDALOVICI, Mme Heinric; *see* Oldenbourg-Idalovici, Zoé.

IDDESLEIGH, 4th Earl of, *cr* 1885; **Stafford Henry Northcote;** Bt 1641; Viscount St Cyres, 1885; *b* 14 July 1932; *er s* of 3rd Earl of Iddesleigh and of Elizabeth, *er d* of late F. S. A. Lowndes and late Marie Belloc; *S* father, 1970; *m* 1955, Maria Luisa Alvarez-Builla y Urquijo (Condesa del Real Agrado in Spain), *d* of late Don Gonzalo Alvarez-Builla y Alvera and of Viscountess Exmouth, *widow* of 9th Viscount Exmouth; one *s* one *d. Educ:* Downside. 2nd Lieut, Irish Guards, 1951-52. Kt SMO Malta. *Heir: s* Viscount St Cyres, *qv. Address:* Shillands House, Upton Pyne Hill, Exeter, Devon EX5 5EB. *T:* Exeter 58916. *Club:* Royal Yacht Squadron (Cowes).

IEVERS, Frank George Eyre, CMG 1964; Postmaster-General, East Africa, 1962-65, retired; *b* 8 May 1910; *s* of Eyre Francis and Catherine Ievers; *m* 1936, Phyllis Robinson; two *s. Educ:* Dover Coll. Asst Traffic Supt, Post Office, 1933; Traffic Supt, East Africa, 1946; Telecommunications Controller, 1951; Regional Dir, 1959. *Recreations:* golf, photography. *Clubs:* Nairobi (Kenya); Sudan (Khartoum).

IEVERS, Rear-Adm. John Augustine, CB 1962; OBE 1944; *b* 2 Dec. 1912; *s* of Eyre Francis Ievers, Tonbridge, Kent; *m* 1937, Peggy G. Marshall; one *s* two *d. Educ:* RN Coll., Dartmouth. CO Naval Test Squadron, Boscombe Down, 1945-47; RN Staff Coll., 1948-49; HMS Ocean, 1949; HMS Glory, 1949-50; HMS Burghead Bay, 1951-52; CO, RN Air Station, Lossiemouth, 1952-54; Dep. Dir Naval Air Warfare Div., 1954-57; Captain Air, Mediterranean, 1957-60; Deputy Controller Aircraft, Min. of Aviation, 1960-63; retd, 1964. *Recreation:* golf. *Address:* 4 Woodlands Rise, North Ferriby, North Humberside. *T:* Hull 631424.

IFE, HH Aderemi I, The Oni of Ife since 1930; **Sir Titus Martins Adesoji Tadeniawo Aderemi;** PC (Western Nigeria) 1954; KCMG 1962 (CMG 1943); KBE 1950; Governor, Western Region, Nigeria, 1960-63; President House of Chiefs, Western Nigeria, 1954-60; Chairman, Council of Obas and Chiefs, Western Nigeria, since 1966; Member, Western House of Chiefs, since 1951; *b* Ife, 1889; Akui House of Ife Royal family; *m* 1910 (polygamous marriage); several *c. Educ:* CMS Sch., Ife. Joined staff of govt railway construction, 1909; Civil Service, 1910; resigned, and started trading and motor transport business, 1921. Founded Oduduwa Coll. (first secondary sch. for boys in Ife Division), 1932. Mem. House of Assembly, Western Nigeria, 1946-. MLC, Nigeria, 1947-; Mem., Nigerian House of Representatives, 1951-54; Central Minister without Portfolio, 1951-55. Mem. Nigeria Cocoa Marketing Board, 1947-; Dir Nigerian Produce Marketing Company Ltd, 1947-. Visited England, July-Oct. 1948; attended meetings connected with cocoa industry; delegate to African Conference, London, 1948; led Nigerian Delegation to Coronation, 1953; delegate to Conference for revision of Nigerian Constitution, in London, July-Aug. 1953, and at Lagos, Jan. 1954; delegate to Nigerian

Constitutional Confs, London, May-June 1957, Sept.-Oct. 1958. Hon. LLD University of Ife, 1967. *Recreations:* cricket and tennis; hunting game (before accession to the throne). *Address:* The Afin (Palace), Ife, Nigeria, West Africa.

IGNATIEFF, George, CC 1973; Vice-Chancellor and Provost, University of Trinity College, Toronto, since 1972; *b* 16 Dec. 1913; *s* of Count Paul N. Ignatieff and Princess Natalie Mestchersky; *m* 1945, Alison Grant; two *s. Educ:* St Paul's, London; Lower Canada Coll., Montreal; Jarvis Coll., Toronto; Univs of Toronto and Oxford. Rhodes Schol., Ont, 1935; BA Toronto 1935; BA Oxon 1938, MA 1960. Dept of External Affairs, Ottawa, 1940; 3rd Sec., London, 1940-44; Ottawa, 1944-45; Adviser, Canadian Delegn, UN Atomic Energy Commn, 1946; UN Assembly, 1946-47; Alt Rep., UN Security Council, 1948-49; Councillor, Canadian Embassy, Washington, DC, 1948-53; Imp. Def. Coll., London, 1953-54; Head of Defence Liaison Div., External Affairs, Ottawa, 1954-55; Canadian Ambassador to Yugoslavia, 1956-58; Dep. High Comr, London, 1959-60; Asst Under-Sec. of State for External Affairs, Ottawa, 1960-62; Perm. Rep. and Canadian Ambassador to NATO, 1962-65; Canadian Perm. Rep. and Ambassador to UN: NY, 1965-68; to Cttee on Disarmament, Geneva, 1968-71; to UN and other Internat. Organisations, Geneva, 1970-71. Chm., Bd of Trustees, Nat. Museums of Canada Corp., 1973. Hon. Fellow, St John's Coll., Winnipeg, 1973. Hon. LLD: Toronto, 1969; Brock, 1969; Guelph 1970; Saskatchewan, 1973; York, 1975; Hon. DCL Bishop's, 1973; Hon. DLitt: Victoria, BC, 1977; Toronto, 1977. *Address:* University of Trinity College, Toronto, Ontario, M5S 1H8, Canada. *Club:* Brooks's.

IKERRIN, Viscount; David James Theobald Somerset Butler; *b* 9 Jan. 1953; *s* and *heir* of 9th Earl of Carrick, *qv* ; *m* 1975, Philippa V. J., *yr d* of Wing Commander L. V. Craxton. *Educ:* Downside.

IKIN, Rutherford Graham; Headmaster of Trent College, 1936-68; *b* 22 Jan. 1903; *s* of late Dr A. E. Ikin, formerly Dir of Education, Blackpool; *m* 1936, Elizabeth Mary Mason; two *d. Educ:* King Edward VI Sch., Norwich; King's Coll., Cambridge (Choral Scholar). BA 1925; MA 1928; Asst Master at King's Sch., Ely, 1926-29; History Master and House Master, St Bees Sch., 1929-36. *Publications:* A Pageant of World History; The Modern Age; The History of the King's School, Ely. *Address:* Eden Bank, Top Lane, Whatstandwell, Matlock, Derbyshire. *T:* Ambergate 2582. *Club:* East India, Devonshire, Sports and Public Schools.

ILCHESTER, 9th Earl of, *cr* 1756; **Maurice Vivian de Touffreville Fox-Strangways;** Lord Ilchester of Ilchester, Somerset, and Baron Strangways of Woodsford Strangways, Dorset, 1741; Lord Ilchester and Stavordale, and Baron of Redlynch, 1747; Group Captain, Royal Air Force, retired 1976; *b* 1 April 1920; *s* of 8th Earl of Ilchester and Laure Georgine Emilie (*d* 1970), *d* of late Evanghelos Georgios Mazaraki, sometime Treasurer of Suez Canal Company; *S* father, 1970; *m* 1941, Diana Mary Elizabeth, *e d* of late George Frederick Simpson, Cassington, Oxfordshire. *Educ:* Kingsbridge Sch. CEng; MRAeS; FINucE; Fellow, Soc. of Engineers (Pres., 1974); MBIM; FRSA. *Recreations:* most sports, outdoor activities, enjoyment of the arts. *Heir: b* Hon. Raymond George Fox-Strangways [*b* 11 Nov. 1921; *m* 1941, Margaret Vera, *d* of late James Force, North Surrey, BC; two *s*]. *Address:* Farley Mill, Westerham, Kent TN16 1UB. *T:* Westerham 62314. *Clubs:* Brooks's, Royal Air Force.

ILERSIC, Prof. Alfred Roman; Professor of Social Studies, Bedford College, University of London, since 1965; *b* 14 Jan. 1920; *s* of late Roman Ilersic and Mary (*née* Moss); *m* 1944, Patricia Florence Bertram Liddle (marr. diss. 1976); one *s* one *d* ; *m* 1976, June Elaine Browning. *Educ:* Polytechnic Sec. Sch., London; London Sch. of Economics, Lectr in Econs, University Coll. of S West, Exeter, 1947-53; Lectr in Social Statistics, Beford Coll., 1953; Reader in Economic and Social Statistics, Bedford Coll., London, 1963. Mem., Cost of Living Adv. Cttee, 1970-. Chm., Inst. of Statisticians, 1968-70. Hon. Mem., Rating and Valuation Assoc., 1968. *Publications:* Statistics, 1953; Government Finance and Fiscal Policy in Post-War Britain, 1956; (with P. F. B. Liddle) Parliament of Commerce 1860-1960, 1960; Taxation of Capital Gains, 1962; Rate Equalisation in London, 1968; Local Government Finance in Northern Ireland, 1969. *Recreations:* listening to music, walking. *Address:* 4 Dewhurst House, Winnett Street, W1. *Club:* Reform.

ILIFFE, family name of **Baron Iliffe.**

ILIFFE, 2nd Baron, *cr* 1933, of Yattendon; **Edward Langton Iliffe;** Vice-Chairman of the Birmingham Post and Mail Ltd, 1957-74; Director of the Coventry Evening Telegraph and of the Cambridge News; *b* 25 Jan. 1908; *er s* of 1st Baron Iliffe, GBE, and Charlotte Gilding (*d* 1972); *S* father 1960; *m* 1938, Renée, *er d* of René Merandon du Plessis, Mauritius. *Educ:* Sherborne; France; Clare Coll., Cambridge. Served, 1940-46, with RAFVR (despatches). Governor, Royal Shakespeare Theatre, Stratford-on-Avon; Trustee, Shakespeare's Birthplace; Mem. Council, Univ. of Warwick, 1965-71; Pres., Internat. Lawn Tennis Club of Gt Britain, 1965. High Sheriff of Berks, 1957. Hon. Freeman, City of Coventry. *Heir: n* Robert Peter Richard Iliffe [*b* 22 Nov. 1944; *m* 1966, Anne, twin *d* of Comdr Arthur Skipwith; three *s* one *d* (incl. twin *s* and *d*)]. *Address:* 38 St James's Place, SW1. *T:* 01-493 1938; The Manor House, Yattendon, near Newbury, Berks. *T:* Hermitage 201579. *Clubs:* Carlton; Royal Yacht Squadron.

ILLINGWORTH, Sir Charles (Frederick William), Kt 1961; CBE 1946; Regius Professor of Surgery, University of Glasgow, 1939, Emeritus, 1964; Hon. Surgeon to the Queen, in Scotland, 1961-65; Extra Surgeon since 1965; *b* 8 May 1899; *s* of John and Edith Illingworth; *m* 1928, Eleanor Mary Bennett (*d* 1971); four *s. Educ:* Heath Grammar Sch., Halifax; Univ. of Edinburgh. Graduated Medicine, 1922. 2nd Lieut, RFC 1917. FRCSE 1925; FRCSGlas, 1963. Hon. FACS, 1954; Hon. FRCS, 1958; Hon. FRCSI, 1964; Hon. FRCS (Canada), 1965; Hon. Fellow, Coll. Surg. S Africa, 1965. DSc (Hon.): University of Sheffield, 1962; University of Belfast, 1963; Hon. LLD (Glasgow, Leeds) 1965. *Publications:* (jtly) Text Book of Surgical Pathology, 1932; Short Text Book of Surgery, 1938; Text Book of Surgical Treatment, 1942; Monograph on Peptic Ulcer, 1953; The Story of William Hunter, 1967; The Sanguine Mystery, 1970; University Statesman: Sir Hector Hetherington, 1971; various contributions to surgical literature, mainly on digestive disorders. *Address:* 57 Winton Drive, Glasgow G12 0QB. *T:* 041-339 3759.

ILLINGWORTH, David Gordon, MD, FRCPE; Surgeon Apothecary to HM Household at Holyrood Palace, Edinburgh, since 1970; Lecturer in General Practice Teaching Unit, Edinburgh University, since 1965; *b* 22 Dec. 1921; *yr s* of Sir Gordon Illingworth; *m* 1946, Lesley Beagrie, Peterhead; two *s* one *d. Educ:* George Watson's Coll.; Edinburgh University. MB, ChB Edinburgh, 1943; MRCPE 1949; MD (with commendation) 1963; FRCPE 1965; FRCGP 1970. Nuffield Foundn Travelling Fellow, 1966. RN Medical Service, 1944-46; medical appts, Edinburgh Northern Hosps Group, 1946-. Hon. Sen. Lectr in Rehabilitation Studies, Dept of Orthopaedic Surgery, Edinburgh Univ., 1977-. Mem., Cancer Planning Group, Scottish Health Service Planning Council, 1976-. *Publications:* contribs to BMJ, Jl of Clinical Pathology, Gut, etc. *Recreations:* golf, gardening. *Address:* 19 Napier Road, Edinburgh EH10 5AZ. *T:* 031-229 2392. *Club:* University (Edinburgh).

ILLINGWORTH, Leslie Gilbert; Political Cartoonist, Punch and Daily Mail; *b* Barry, Glam, 2 Sept. 1902; 2nd *s* of Richard Frederick Illingworth and Helen, *d* of Alexander MacGregor; unmarried. *Educ:* Barry County School; Royal College of Art; Slade School, London Univ. Political Cartoonist, Western Mail, Cardiff, 1921; first contributed to Punch, 1927; Free-lance Artist, 1926-39; joined Daily Mail, 1939; joined Punch as Junior Cartoonist, 1945. *Recreation:* gardening. *Address:* Silverdale, Robertsbridge, East Sussex. *T:* Robertsbridge 154. *Clubs:* Chelsea Arts, Royal Automobile.

ILLINGWORTH, Rear-Adm. Philip Holden Crothers, CB 1969; *b* 29 Nov. 1916; *s* of late Norman Holden Illingworth, Woking; *m* 1944, Dorothy Jean, *d* of George Wells, Southbourne; three *s* three *d. Educ:* RN Coll., Dartmouth, RNEC. Joined RN 1930, Rear-Adm. 1967. Dep. Controller of Aircraft, Min. of Technology, 1969, MoD, 1971-72; retd 1973. *Address:* Manor House, Marston Magna, Somerset. *T:* Marston Magna 294. *Club:* Naval and Military.

ILLINGWORTH, Raymond, CBE 1973; cricketer; Captain, Leicestershire County Cricket Club, since 1969; *b* 8 June 1932; *s* of late Frederick Spencer Illingworth and of Ida Illingworth; *m* 1958, Shirley Milnes; two *d. Educ:* Wesley Street Sch., Farsley, Pudsey. Yorkshire County cricketer; capped, 1955. Captain MCC, 1969. Toured: West Indies, 1959-60; Australia twice (once as Captain), 1962-63 and 1970-71. Played in 66 Test Matches (36 as Captain). *Publications:* Spinners Wicket, 1969; The Young Cricketer, 1972. *Recreations:* golf, bridge. *Address:* 386 Bradford Road, Stanningley, Pudsey, West Yorkshire LS28 7TQ. *T:* Pudsey 78137.

ILLINGWORTH, Ronald Stanley; Professor of Child Health, University of Sheffield, 1947-Sept. 1975; *b* 7 Oct. 1909; *s* of late H. E. Illingworth, ARIBA, ARPS, Fairleigh, Skipton Road, Ilkley; *m* Dr Cynthia Illingworth, MB, BS, FRCP, Consultant in Paediatric Accident and Emergency, Children's Hosp., Sheffield; one s two d. Educ: Clifton House Sch., Harrogate; Bradford Grammar Sch. MB, ChB Leeds, 1934; MRCS, LRCP, 1934; MD Leeds, 1937; MRCP, 1937; DPH Leeds (distinction), 1938; DCH (RCP and S), 1938; FRCP 1947; FRPS, Fellow, Royal Society Medicine; Mem. BMA; Hon. Member: British Paediatric Assoc.; Swedish Pædiatric Assoc.; Finnish Pædiatric Assoc.; Academy of Pædiatricians of the USSR. West Riding County Major Scholar, 1928; Nuffield Research Studentship, Oxford, 1939-41; Rockefeller Research Fellowship, 1939 and 1946. Formerly Resident Asst, Hospital for Sick Children, Great Ormond Street, London, 1938-39; Medical Specialist and officer in charge of Medical Division (Lt-Col), RAMC, 1941-46. Asst to Prof. of Child Health, Univ. of London, 1946. Hon. DSc Univ. of Baghdad, Iraq, 1975; Hon. MD Sheffield, 1976. *Publications:* The Normal Child: some problems of his first five years, 1953 (6th edn, 1975; trans. Greek, 1966 and 1970, Spanish, 1969, Japanese, 1968); (with C. M. Illingworth) Babies and Young Children: Feeding, Management and Care, 1954, 6th edn, 1977; ed, Recent Advances in Cerebral Palsy, 1958; Development of Infant and Young Child, Normal and Abnormal, 1960, 6th edn, 1975 (trans. Japanese, 1966, French, 1977); An Introduction to Developmental Assessment in the First Year, 1962; The Normal Schoolchild: His Problems, Physical and Emotional, 1964; (with C. M. Illingworth) Lessons from Childhood: some aspects of the early life of unusual men and women, 1966 (Japanese trans., 1969); Common Symptoms of Disease in Children, 1967, 5th edn 1975 (trans. Greek and Spanish 1968, Italian 1974, Dutch 1977); Treatment of the Child at Home: a guide for family doctors, 1971 (Greek trans., 1975); Basic Developmental Screening, 1973; The Child at School: a Paediatrician's Manual for Teachers, 1974; various medical and photographic papers. *Recreations:* climbing, photography, philately, travel. *Address:* 8 Harley Road, Sheffield S11 9SD. *T:* 362774.

ILLSLEY, Prof. Raymond, PhD; Professor of Medical Sociology and Director, Institute of Medical Sociology, University of Aberdeen, since 1975; Honorary Director, MRC Medical Sociology Unit, since 1965; *b* 6 July 1919; *s* of James and Harriet Illsley; *m* 1948, Jean Mary Harrison; two *s* one *d*. *Educ:* St Edmund Hall, Oxford (BA 1948). PhD Aberdeen 1956. Served War, 1939-45: active service in GB and ME, 1939-42; PoW, Italy and Germany, 1942-45. Econ. Asst, Commonwealth Econ. Cttee, London, 1948; Social Res. Officer, New Town Develt Corp., Crawley, Sussex, 1948-50; Sociologist, MRC, working with Dept of Midwifery, Univ. of Aberdeen, as Mem., Social Med. Res. Unit and later Mem., Obstetric Med. Res. Unit, 1951-64; Prof. of Sociology, Univ. of Aberdeen, 1964-75, Head of Dept of Sociology, 1964-71. Vis. Prof., Cornell Univ., NY, 1963-64; Vis. Scientist, Harvard Univ., 1968; Sen. Research Scientist, National Sci. Foundn, Boston Univ., 1971-72; Vis. Prof., Dept of Sociology, Boston Univ., 1971-72, Adjunct Prof., 1972-. Chairman: Scottish TUC Inquiry on Upper Clyde Shipbuilders Ltd, 1971; Social Sciences Adv. Panel, Action for the Crippled Child, 1971-; Health Services Res. Cttee, Chief Scientist's Org., SHHD, 1976-. Member: Sec. of State's Scottish Council on Crime, 1972-; Exec. Cttee, Nat. Fund for Res. into Crippling Diseases, 1972-; Chief Scientist's Cttee, SHHD, 1973-; Health Services Res. Bd, DHSS, 1973-; Steering Cttee, WHO Task Force on Abortion, 1974-; EEC Cttee on Med. Res., 1974-; Adv. Gp, WHO's Expanded Res. Prog. on Human Reproduction, 1975-; SSRC, 1976- (Chm., Sociol. and Soc. Admin Cttee). Fellow, Eugenics Soc.; Member: Brit. Sociol Assoc.; Union Internat. pour l'étude sci. de la population; Social Med. Soc.; Internat. Sociol Assoc.; Soc. for Study of Human Biol. *Publications:* Mental Subnormality in the Community: a clinical and epidemiological study (with H. Birch, S. Richardson, D. Baird et al), 1970; articles in learned jls on reproduction, migration, social mobility, mental subnormality. *Recreation:* rough husbandry. *Address:* Mains of Kebbaty, Midmar, Inverurie, Aberdeenshire. *T:* (office) Aberdeen 23423, ext. 2420. *Club:* National Liberal.

ILOTT, Sir John (Moody Albert), Kt 1954; JP; President: J. Ilott Ltd; Golden Bay Cement Co. Ltd; *b* 12 Aug. 1884; *s* of John and Elizabeth Ilott (*née* Baldwin); *m* 1912, Hazel E. M. Hall; one *s* one *d* (and one *d* decd). *Educ:* Terrace Sch., Wellington Coll.; Victoria Univ. Employed J. Ilott Ltd, 1903-. President Emeritus, NZ Crippled Children Soc. (Inc); Mem., J. R. McKenzie Trust; Past Vice-Pres., Rotary Internat. Jubilee Medal, 1935; Coronation Medal, 1953. Hon. LLD Victoria Univ., 1964. *Recreation:* bowls. *Address:* Apartment 5, Broadwater, 214 Oriental Parade, Wellington, New Zealand. *Clubs:* Wellesley (Wellington); Wellington Golf (Life Mem.); Miramar Golf (Life Mem.), both Wellington.

IMBERT-TERRY, Major Sir Edward (Henry Bouhier), 3rd Bt, *cr* 1917; MC 1944; *b* 28 Jan. 1920; *s* of Col Sir Henry B. Imbert-Terry, 2nd Bt, DSO, MC, DL, and Dorothy Lady Imbert-Terry (*d* 1975); *S* father, 1962; *m* 1944, Jean (JP 1973), 2nd *d* of late A. Stanley Garton; two *s* two *d*. *Educ:* Eton Coll.; New Coll., Oxford. Coldstream Guards, 1940-51; retired as Major, 1951. *Recreation:* golf. *Heir: er s* Andrew Henry Bouhier Imbert-Terry [*b* 5 Oct. 1945; *m* 1972, Sarah Margaret Evans (marr. diss. 1974)]. *Address:* Mead Meadow House, near Chobham, Surrey. *T:* Chobham 8500. *Clubs:* Cavalry and Guards, MCC.

IMESON, Kenneth Robert, MA; Headmaster, Nottingham High School, 1954-70; *b* 8 July 1908; *s* of R. W. Imeson; *m* 1st, 1934, Peggy (*d* 1967), *d* of late A. H. Mann, Dulwich; two *d*; 2nd, Peggy, *widow* of Duncan MacArthur, *d* of late Harold Pow. *Educ:* St Olave's; Sidney Sussex Coll., Cambridge (Schol.). Mathematical Tripos, Part 1 1928; Part II 1930. Asst Master, Llandovery Coll., 1930-33; Sen. Mathematical Master, Watford Grammar Sch., 1933-44; Headmaster, Sir Joseph Williamson's Mathematical Sch., 1944-53; Mem. Council SCM in Schools, 1948-58; Council of Friends of Rochester Cathedral, 1947-53; Board of Visitors, Nottingham Prison, 1956-57; Teaching Cttee, Mathematical Association, 1950-58; Trustee, Nottingham Mechanics Institution, 1955-70; Court of Nottingham Univ., 1955-64, 1968-70; Member: Oxford and Cambridge Examinations Board, 1957-61, 1962-70; Council Christian Education Movement, 1965-69; Council, Arts Educational Schools, 1971-; Cttee, Notts CCC, 1969-72; London Diocesan Bd of Educn, 1971-76; Central Council of Physical Recreation, 1971-. Governor: Lady Margaret Sch., Parson's Green; Purcell Sch. of Music, 1975-. *Publications:* articles in Journal of Education. *Recreations:* cricket and other games; music. *Address:* 14 Stourcliffe Close, W1H 5AQ. *T:* 01-262 9488. *Clubs:* MCC, Yellowhammers Cricket, Forty.

IMMS, George, CB 1964; Member, Civil Service Appeals Board; Commissioner and Director of Establishments and Organisation, HM Customs and Excise, 1965-71; *b* 10 April 1911; *o s* of late George Imms; *m* 1938, Joan Sylvia Lance; two *s*. *Educ:* Grange High Sch., Bradford; Emmanuel Coll., Cambridge (Scholar). Joined HM Customs and Excise, 1933; Asst Sec., 1946; Commissioner, 1957-65. *Address:* 26 Lynceley Grange, Epping, Essex.

IMRAY, Colin Henry; HM Diplomatic Service; Commercial Counsellor, Tel Aviv, since 1977; *b* 21 Sept. 1933; *s* of late Henry Gibbon Imray and of Frances Olive Imray; *m* 1957, Shirley Margaret Matthews; one *s* three *d*. *Educ:* Highgate Sch.; Hotchkiss Sch., Conn; Balliol Coll., Oxford (2nd cl. Hons PPE). Served in Seaforth Highlanders and RWAFF, Sierra Leone, 1952-54. CRO, 1957; 3rd, later 2nd Sec., Canberra, 1958-61; CRO, 1961-63; 1st Sec., Nairobi, 1963-66; FCO, 1966-70; British Trade Comr, Montreal, 1970-73; Counsellor, Head of Chancery and Consul-Gen., Islamabad, 1973-77; RCDS, 1977. *Recreations:* travel, walking. *Address:* c/o Foreign and Commonwealth Office, SW1A 2AH. *Clubs:* United Oxford & Cambridge University, Royal Commonwealth Society.

IMRIE, Sir John Dunlop, Kt 1950; CBE 1942; JP; Chartered Accountant; *b* 16 Oct. 1891; *s* of late Alexander Imrie, Kinross; *m* 1953, Mary Isobel Rae Rowan. *Educ:* Dollar Academy; Edinburgh Univ. MA Edinburgh 1925; BCom Edinburgh 1923; FRSE 1943; City Chamberlain of Edinburgh, 1926-51; Hon. Financial Officer, Edinburgh Festival Society, 1945-51; Local Government Comr, Trinidad, BWI, 1951-53; Dir, Caledonian Insurance Co. Ltd, until 1965; Chairman: Wm Brown (Booksellers) Ltd; Edinburgh Bookshop Ltd; Scottish Bookshops Ltd; Past-Pres., Inst. Municipal Treasurers and Accountants; Hon. Governor Dollar Acad. Member: Scottish War Savings Cttee, 1940-64; Scottish Housing Advisory Cttee, 1942; Scottish Rating and Valuation Cttee, 1943; Cttee on Water Rating in Scotland, 1944; Cttee on Houses of National Importance, 1949; Hospital Endowments Commission, 1949; Cttee on Scottish Financial and Trade Statistics, 1950; Cttee on Economic and Financial Problems of Provision for Old Age, 1954; Historic Buildings Council for Scotland, 1954-58; South of Scotland Electricity Board, 1955-59; Public Works Loans Commission, 1956-65. *Publications:* Contributions to Local Government Finance, Public Administration, etc. *Address:* Invervar Lodge, Glenlyon, Aberfeldy, Perthshire, Scotland. *T:* Glenlyon 203.

INAYAT MASIH, Rt. Rev.; see Lahore, Bishop of.

INCE, Brigadier Cecil Edward Ronald, CB 1950; CBE 1946 (OBE 1941); *b* 5 March 1897; 3rd *s* of late C. H. B. Ince, Barrister-at-Law; *m* 1924, Leslie, *o d* of late Robert Badham, Secretary of Midland & GW Rly, Ireland; two *d*. *Educ:*

Sevenoaks. Regular Army; RA 1915, RASC 1919-49. Deputy Dir (Supplies), Middle East, 1940-42; War Office, 1943-47; Commandant RASC Trng Centre, 1947-49. Dir of Enforcement, subseq. Dir of Warehousing, Min. of Food and Agric., 1949-55. *Publications:* various military pamphlets and articles in Service publications. *Recreations:* mild golf, with progressive gardening. *Address:* Half-Acre, West Grove, Walton-on-Thames, Surrey. *T:* Walton-on-Thames 25035.

INCE, Wesley Armstrong, CMG 1968; Solicitor and Company Director; *b* 27 Nov. 1893; *s* of John and Christina Ince, Melbourne; *m* 1919, Elsie Maud Ince, *d* of Wm H. Smith, Melbourne; two *d. Educ:* Wesley Coll., Melbourne; Melbourne Univ. Admitted practice Barrister and Solicitor, 1917; Partner, Arthur Robinson & Co., 1919-67. Chm., Claude Neon Industries Ltd, 1932-70; Chm., Rheem Australia Ltd, 1937-67; Foundn Mem. Coun., Inst. of Public Affairs, 1942-; Foundn Mem., Australian-American Assoc., 1941- (Federal Pres., 1962-63, 1965-67); Chm., Petroleum Refineries (Aust.) Ltd, 1952-61; Director: International Harvester Co. of Australia Pty Ltd, 1945-74; Hoyts Theatres Ltd, 1934-; Dulux Australia Ltd, 1945-74. *Recreations:* golf, bowls, swimming. *Address:* 372 Glenferrie Road, Malvern, Vic 3144, Australia. *T:* 20 9516. *Clubs:* Athenæum, Victoria Racing (Melbourne); Royal Melbourne Golf, Melbourne Cricket.

INCH, Sir John Ritchie, Kt 1972; CVO 1969; CBE 1958; QPM 1961; Chief Constable, Edinburgh City Police, 1955-75; *b* 14 May 1911; *s* of James Inch, Lesmahagow, Lanarkshire; *m* 1941, Anne Ferguson Shaw; one *s* two *d. Educ:* Hamilton Academy; Glasgow Univ. (MA, LLB). Joined Lanarkshire Constabulary, 1931; apptd Chief Constable, Dunfermline City Police, 1943, and of combined Fife Constabulary, 1949. OStJ 1964. Comdr, Royal Order of St Olav (Norway), 1962; Comdr, Order of Al-Kawkal Al Urdini (Jordan), 1966; Cavaliere Ufficiale, Order of Merit (Italy), 1969; Comdr, Order of Orange-Nassau (Netherlands), 1971; Order of the Oak Crown Class III (Luxembourg), 1972. *Recreations:* shooting, fishing, golf. *Address:* Fairways, Whitehouse Road, Barnton, Edinburgh EH4 6DA. *T:* 031-336 3558. *Club:* Royal Scots (Edinburgh).

INCHCAPE, 3rd Earl of, *cr* 1929; **Kenneth James William Mackay;** Viscount Glenapp of Strathnaver, *cr* 1929; Viscount Inchcape, *cr* 1924; Baron Inchcape, *cr* 1911; Chairman: Inchcape & Co. Ltd, since 1958; P & O Steam Navigation Co., since 1973; Director: Standard Chartered Bank Ltd; Guardian Royal Exchange Assurance; British Petroleum Co. Ltd; President: General Council of British Shipping, 1976-77; Royal Society for India, Pakistan and Ceylon, 1970-76; Commonwealth Society for the Deaf; *b* 27 Dec. 1917; *e s* of 2nd Earl and Joan (*d* 1933), *d* of late Lord Justice Moriarty; *S* father 1939; *m* 1st, 1941, Mrs Aline Thorn Hannay (from whom he obtained a divorce, 1954), *widow* of Flying Officer P. C. Hannay, AAF, and *d* of Sir Richard Pease, 2nd Bt; two *s* one *d*; 2nd, 1965, Caroline Cholmeley, *e d* of Cholmeley Dering Harrison, Emo Court, Co. Leix, Eire, and Mrs Corisande Harrison, Stradbally, Co. Waterford; two *s* and one adopted *s*. *Educ:* Eton; Trinity Coll., Cambridge (MA). Served War of 1939-45: 12th Royal Lancers BEF France; Major 27th Lancers MEF and Italy. Chm., Council for Middle East Trade, 1963-65. Prime Warden: Shipwrights' Co., 1967; Fishmongers' Co., 1977-78. Freeman, City of London. *Recreations:* shooting, fishing, riding. *Heir: s* Viscount Glenapp, *qv. Address:* Quendon Park, Saffron Walden, Essex; Glenapp Castle, Ballantrae, Ayrshire. *Clubs:* Brooks's, Buck's, Turf, City, Oriental.
See also Baron Craigmyle, Baron Tanlaw.

INCHIQUIN, 17th Baron of, *cr* 1543; **Phaedrig Lucius Ambrose O'Brien;** Bt 1686; *b* 4 April 1900; 2nd *s* of 15th Baron of Inchiquin and Ethel Jane (*d* 1940), *d* of late Johnstone J. Foster, Moor Park, Ludlow; *S* brother, 1968; *m* 1945, Vera Maud, *d* of late Rev. C. S. Winter. *Educ:* Eton; Magdalen Coll., Oxford (MA); Imperial Coll., London Univ. Major (retd) Rifle Brigade; served War, 1940-45, attached E African Intelligence Corps, Somalia, Abyssinia, Madagascar (wounded, despatches). Farming and coffee planting, Kenya, 1922-36; Geologist, Anglo-American Corp., 1936-39 and 1946-54; Colonial Service, Overseas Geological Survey (retd), 1954-59. Consulting Geologist, 1960-67. *Heir: nephew* Conor Myles John O'Brien, *b* 17 July 1943. *Address:* Hanway Lodge, Richard's Castle, Ludlow, Salop. *T:* Richard's Castle 210; Thomond House, Co. Clare, Ireland. *Club:* Royal Automobile.

INCHYRA, 1st Baron *cr* 1961; **Frederick Robert Hoyer Millar,** GCMG 1956 (KCMG 1949; CMG 1939); CVO 1938; *b* 6 June 1900; *s* of late R. Hoyer Millar; *m* 1931, Elizabeth de Marees van Swinderen; two *s* two *d. Educ:* Wellington Coll.; New Coll., Oxford. Hon. Attaché, HM Embassy, Brussels, 1922; entered

HM Diplomatic Service, 1923; served as Third Sec. at Berlin and Paris, and as Second Sec. at Cairo; Asst Private Sec. to Sec. of State for Foreign Affairs, 1934-38; First Sec. at Washington, 1939; Counsellor, 1941-42; Sec., British Civil Secretariat, Washington, 1943; Counsellor, FO, 1944; Asst Under-Sec. 1947; Minister, British Embassy, Washington, 1948; UK Deputy, North Atlantic Treaty Organisation, 1950; UK Permanent Representative on NATO Council, 1952; UK High Commissioner in Germany, 1953-55; British Ambassador to Bonn, 1955-57; Permanent Under-Sec. of State, Foreign Office, 1957-61. *Recreation:* shooting. *Heir: s* Hon. Robert Charles Reneke Hoyer Millar [*b* 4 April 1935; *m* 1961, Fiona Sheffield; one *s* two *d*]. *Address:* 57 Eaton Place, SW1; *T:* 01-235 7675; Inchyra House, Glencarse, Perthshire. *Clubs:* Boodle's, Turf, Metropolitan (Washington).

INCLEDON-WEBBER, Lt-Col Godfrey Sturdy, TD 1943; DL; MA; *b* 1 July 1904; *er s* of William Beare Incledon-Webber, DL, JP, Braunton, Devon; *m* 1931, Angela Florence, *d* of Sir Pierce Lacy, 1st Bt; three *d . Educ:* Eton (1st classical schol. Radley, 1918); Magdalen Coll., Oxford (BA 1926, MA 1947). Joined Royal Devon Yeomanry Artillery, 1924; served in War of 1939-45 (Lieut-Col Comdg 136 Lt AA Regt RA, 1942-45). Partner, Cutler and Lacy, Stockbrokers, Birmingham, 1933-53; Man. Dir, British Trusts Assoc. Ltd, 1953-73; Director: United Dominions Trust Ltd, 1959-73; English Insurance Co. Ltd, 1955; Chm., Incledon Estate Co. Ltd, 1949. Alderman and JP, City of London, 1963-71; one of HM's Lieutenants of City of London; Sheriff, City of London, 1968-69; Master: Worshipful Co. of Clothworkers, 1975-76 (excused service); Worshipful Co. of Saddlers, 1961-62. Hereditary Freeman of Barnstaple (1925); Lord of the Manor of Croyde and Putsborough, Devon. DL Devon, 1969; High Sheriff, Devon, 1970-71. FRSA 1971. OStJ 1968. *Recreations:* shooting, and interested in most kinds of sport and games; represented Eton at rackets (Public School Rackets winning pair 1922) and cricket, 1922-23, Oxford Univ. at real tennis and squash rackets, 1925-26; mem. British Squash Rackets Team which toured USA and Canada, 1927, and won Lapham Trophy, USA, Canada and GB competing. *Address:* Buckland Manor, Braunton, N Devon. *T:* Braunton 812016. *Clubs:* White's, Carlton, City Livery.

INDORE, Ex-Maharaja of, GCIE 1918; **HH Tukoji Rao Holkar;** *b* 26 Nov. 1890; *S* as Maharaja of Indore, 1903, and as Premier Ruling Prince of Central India; *m* 1928, Nancy Miller (Maharanee Sharmishthabai Holkar); one *d*; abdicated in favour of his son (by a former marriage), 1926 (*s* Maharaja Sir Yeshwant Rao Holkar, GCIE, *d* 1961). *Educ:* Mayo Chiefs' Coll., Ajmere; Imperial Cadet Corps. Visited Europe, 1910; attended Coronation, 1911; again visited Europe, 1913 and 1921. *Recreations:* riding, shooting, lawn tennis. *Address:* Lal Bagh Palace, Indore, MP, India.

INGE-INNES-LILLINGSTON, Lt-Comdr George David, RNR, MA, DL; a Crown Estates Commissioner, since 1974; *b* 13 Nov. 1923; *s* of late Comdr H. W. Innes-Lillingston, RN, and of Mrs Innes-Lillingston, formerly of Lochalsh House, Balmacara, Kyle, Ross-shire; *m* 1st, 1946, Alison Mary (*d* 1947), *er d* of late Canon F. W. Green, MA, BD, Norwich; one *d*; 2nd, 1955, Elizabeth Violet Grizel Thomson-Inge, *yr d* of late Lt-Gen. Sir William Thomson, KCMG, CB, MC; two *s* one *d. Educ:* Stowe, Buckingham; Merton Coll., Oxford (MA Hons Agric.). Served War as Lieut RNVR, 1942-45. Member: Agricultural Land Tribunal, 1962-72; Minister's Agricultural Panel for W Midlands, 1972-76; Chairman: N Birmingham and District Hosps, 1968-72; Staffordshire Br., Country Landowners' Assoc., 1968-71, and Headquarters Exec. Cttee, 1977-; Dep. Chm., CLA, 1977-; Pres., Staffs Agricultural Soc., 1970-71. JP 1967-74, DL 1969-, Staffs; High Sheriff, Staffs, 1966. *Recreations:* yachting, shooting. *Address:* Thorpe Hall, Tamworth, Staffordshire B79 0LH. *T:* Newton Regis 224. *Clubs:* Turf, Farmers'; Royal Highland Yacht (Oban).

INGERSOLL, Ralph McAllister; Editor and Publisher, USA; *b* 8 Dec. 1900; *s* of Colin Macrae and Theresa (McAllister) Ingersoll; *m* 1st, 1925, Mary Elizabeth Carden (marr. diss. 1935; she *d* 1965); 2nd, 1945, Elaine Brown Keiffer (*d* 1948); two *s* ; 3rd, 1948, Mary Hill Doolittle (marr. diss., 1962); 4th, 1964, Thelma Bradford. *Educ:* Hotchkiss Sch., Lakeville, Connecticut, 1922. Mining Engineer; Reporter for The New Yorker (mag.), 1925, Managing Editor, 1926-29; Assoc. Editor, Fortune Magazine, 1930, Managing Editor, 1930-35; Vice-Pres. and General Manager, Time, Inc., publishing Time, Life, Fortune, etc. Publisher of Time Magazine, 1937-39; resigned to organise and finance company subsequently to publish PM (NY daily newspaper); Editor, PM, 1940-46. Enlisted as Private, Engr. Amphibian Command, US Army, 1942; advanced to Lt-

Col, Gen. Staff Corps; served overseas, 1943-45; in Africa, England, Italy, France, Belgium, Luxembourg and Germany, on staffs of Gen. Jacob Devers, Field-Marshal Montgomery, and Gen. Omar Bradley. Legion of Merit, Bronze Arrowhead for assault landing in Normandy, and 7 campaign stars; Officer of Order of Crown (Belgium); returned to Editorship of PM; resigned, 1946; Pres., The RJ Company, Inc., 1948-59, investments, principally newspapers, including Middletown (NY) Times Herald, Union Gazette, Port Jervis, NY; President and Director of numerous newspapers and publishing concerns, in RI, NY, NJ, Pa, Conn, NH and Mass; President: General Publications, Inc. (newspaper management), 1959-75; Ingersoll Publications Inc., 1975-; Director: Central Home Trust Co., Eliz., NJ, 1963-67; Public Welfare Foundn, Washington DC, 1970-74; Recording for the Blind Foundn, NY, 1973-74. *Publications:* Report on England, 1940; America is Worth Fighting For, 1941; Action on All Fronts, 1941; The Battle is the Pay-Off, 1944; Top Secret, 1946; The Great Ones, 1948; Wine of Violence, 1951; Point of Departure, 1961. *Address:* (home) Cornwall Bridge, Conn 06754, USA. *Club:* The Brook (NYC).

INGESTRE, Viscount; Charles Henry John Benedict Crofton Chetwynd Chetwynd-Talbot; farmer and stud owner; *b* 18 Dec. 1952; *s* and *heir* of 21st Earl of Shrewsbury and Waterford, *qv*; *m* 1974, Deborah, *o d* of Noel Hutchinson; one *d*. *Educ:* Harrow. Pres., Birmingham Agricultural Exhibition Soc. *Recreations:* hunting, racing, shooting. *Address:* Ivy House Farm, Drointon, near Stafford ST18 0LX.

INGHAM, John Henry, CMG 1956; MBE 1947; *b* 1910. *Educ:* Plumtree School, S Rhodesia; Rhodes University College, S Africa; Brasenose College, Oxford. Administrative Officer, Nyasaland, 1936; Secretary for Agricultural and Natural Resources, Kenya, 1947; Administrative Secretary, 1952; Senior Secretary, East African Royal Commission, 1953-55; Secretary for African Affairs, Nyasaland, 1956-60; MEC, Nyasaland, 1961. Minister of Urban Development, Malawi, 1961. Representative of Beit Trust and Dulverton Trust in Central Africa, 1962-77. *Address:* 18 Jameson Avenue, Salisbury, Rhodesia.

INGHAM, Prof. Kenneth, OBE 1961; MC 1946; Professor of History, University of Bristol, since 1967; *b* 9 Aug. 1921; *s* of Gladson and Frances Lily Ingham; *m* 1949, Elizabeth Mary Southall; one *s* one *d*. *Educ:* Bingley Grammar Sch.; Keble Coll., Oxford (Exhibitioner). Served with West Yorks Regt, 1941-46 (despatches), 1945). Frere Exhibitioner in Indian Studies, University of Oxford, 1947; DPhil 1950. Lecturer in Modern History, Makerere Coll., Uganda, 1950-56, Prof., 1956-62; Dir of Studies, RMA, Sandhurst, 1962-67. MLC (Uganda), 1954-61. *Publications:* Reformers in India, 1956; The Making of Modern Uganda, 1958; A History of East Africa, 1962; The Kingdom of Toro in Uganda, 1975; contrib. to Encyclopædia Britannica, Britannica Book of the Year. *Address:* The Woodlands, 94 West Town Lane, Bristol BS4 5DZ.

INGILBY, Sir Thomas (Colvin William), 6th Bt *cr* 1866; *b* 17 July 1955; *s* of Sir Joslan William Vivian Ingilby, 5th Bt, DL, JP, and of Diana, *d* of late Sir George Colvin, CB, CMG, DSO; *S* father, 1974. *Educ:* Aysgarth Sch., Bedale; Eton Coll. Student Teacher, Springvale School, Marandellas, Rhodesia, Sept. 1973-April 1974. Joined Army, May 1974, but discharged on death of father; now studying at Royal Agricultural Coll., Cirencester, to take over the estate. Asst Dir, Great Yorkshire Show, 1977. *Recreations:* cricket, tennis, fives, squash rackets, shooting. *Address:* Ripley Castle, Ripley, near Harrogate, North Yorkshire HG3 3AY. *T:* Harrogate 770186.

INGLE, Charles Fiennes; Barrister-at-law; a Recorder (formerly Recorder of Penzance), since 1964; *b* 30 April 1908; *s* of F. S. Ingle and M. A. Ingle, Bath; *m* 1933, Mary (*née* Linaker); one *s* one *d*. *Educ:* Oundle; Jesus Coll., Cambridge (MA). Called to Bar, Inner Temple, 1931; Western Circuit; Dep. Chm., Devon QS, 1963-71. Sqdn Ldr, RAFVR, 1940-45. *Recreations:* yachting, shooting. *Address:* West Soar, Malborough, Devon. *T:* Galmpton 334.

INGLEBY, 2nd Viscount, *cr* 1955, of Snilesworth; **Martin Raymond Peake;** Landowner; Director, Hargreaves Group Ltd, since 1960; *b* 31 May 1926; *s* of 1st Viscount Ingleby, and of Joan, Viscountess Ingleby; *S* father, 1966; *m* 1952, Susan, *d* of late Henderson Russell Landale; four *d* (one *s* decd). *Educ:* Eton; Trinity Coll., Oxford (MA). Called to the Bar, Inner Temple, 1956. Sec., Hargreaves Group Ltd, 1958-61. Administrative Staff Coll., 1961. CC Yorks (North Riding), 1964-67. Mem., N Yorks Moors Nat. Park Planning Cttee, 1968-. *Heir:* none. *Address:* Snilesworth, Northallerton, North Yorks DL6 3QD. *T:* Osmotherley 214.

INGLEFIELD, Sir Gilbert (Samuel), GBE 1968; Kt 1965; TD; MA, ARIBA, AADip; Director, Tubal Cain Foundry & Engineering Works Ltd; *b* 13 March 1909; 2nd *s* of late Adm. Sir F. S. Inglefield, KCB; *m* 1933, Laura Barbara Frances, *e d* of late Captain Gilbert Thompson, Connaught Rangers; two *s* one *d*. *Educ:* Eton; Trinity Coll., Cambridge. Architect; served War of 1939-45 with Sherwood Foresters, France, Far East. British Council Asst Rep. in Egypt, 1946-49 and in London, 1949-56. Alderman, City of London (Aldersgate Ward), 1959; Sheriff, 1963-64; Chm., Barbican Cttee, 1963-66; Lord Mayor of London, 1967-68; one of HM Lieutenants for City of London; Church Commissioner for England, 1962; Governor: Thomas Coram Foundation; Royal Shakespeare Theatre; London Festival Ballet Trust; Fedn of British Artists, 1972-; Trustee, London Symphony Orchestra; Chm., City Arts Trust, 1968-76; Member: Royal Fine Art Commission, 1968-75; Redundant Churches Fund, 1972-76. Dep. Kt Principal, Imp. Soc. of Knights Bachelor, 1972-. Master, Haberdashers' Co., 1972; Master, Musicians Co., 1974; Assistant, Painter Stainers Co. Chancellor of the Order of St John of Jerusalem, 1969-; GCStJ. FRSA; Hon. RBA; Hon. GSM; Hon. FLCM. DL Beds, 1973-77. Hon. DSc City Univ., 1967. Comdr Order of the Falcon (Iceland), 1963; Order of the Two Niles, Class III (Sudan), 1964. *Recreations:* music, travel. *Address:* 6 Rutland House, Marloes Road, W8 5LE. *T:* 01-937 3458. *Clubs:* Athenæum, City Livery.

INGLEFIELD, Col Sir John (Frederick) C.; *see* Crompton-Inglefield.

INGLEFIELD-WATSON, Captain Sir Derrick W. I.; *see* Watson.

INGLESON, Philip, CMG 1945; MBE 1926; MC 1918; President, Grampian Furniture Ltd (formerly Revel Industrial Products Ltd), 1973-74 (Chairman, 1958-72); retired; *b* 14 June 1892; *s* of William Frederick and Phoebe H. Ingleson; *m* 1921, Gwendoline, *o d* of Col R. Fulton, 1st KGVO Gurkha Rifles, IA; one *d*. *Educ:* Rossall Sch.; Queens' Coll., Cambridge (Senior Classical Scholar). Served European War (France), 1914-19, Royal Fusiliers and Staff Captain 198th Infantry Brigade 66 Div. (MC, despatches); joined Sudan Political Service, 1919; Governor Halfa Province 1931; Governor Berber Province, 1932; Governor Bahr-el-Ghazal Province, 1934; Governor Darfur Province, 1935-44; Ministry of Production, 1944; Board of Trade, 1945; UK Trade Commissioner in Queensland, 1949-53, and in Western Australia, 1954-56; Chm., Chair Centre Ltd, 1958-72. Order of the Nile, 4th Class, 1929; Order of the Nile, 3rd Class 1935. *Recreation:* travel. *Address:* 36 Campden Hill Court, W8. *T:* 01-937 8993. *Club:* Bath.

INGLEWOOD, 1st Baron, *cr* 1964; **William Morgan Fletcher-Vane,** TD; DL; *b* 12 April 1909; *s* of late Col Hon. W. L. Vane and Lady Katharine Vane; assumed name of Fletcher-Vane by deed poll, 1931; *m* 1949, Mary (late Sen. Comdr ATS (despatches), JP, Mem. LCC, 1949-52, Cumberland CC, 1961-74), *e d* of Major Sir Richard G. Proby, Bt, *qv*; two *s*. *Educ:* Charterhouse; Trinity Coll., Cambridge (MA). 2nd Lt 6 Bn Durham Light Infantry, 1928; served Overseas: 1940, France, with 50 (N) Div. (despatches); 1941-44, Middle East with Durham LI and on the Staff, Lt-Col, 1943. MP (C) for Westmorland, 1945-64; Parliamentary Private Sec. to Minister of Agriculture, 1951-54, to Joint Under-Sec. of State, Foreign Office, 1954-55, and to Minister of Health, Dec. 1955-July 1956; Joint Parliamentary Secretary: Min. of Pensions and National Insurance, 1958-60; Min. of Agriculture, Oct. 1960-July 1962. DL Westmorland 1946, Cumbria 1974; Landowner; Mem. Chartered Surveyors Institution; formerly Mem. of Historic Buildings Council for England; Leader of UK Delegation to World Food Congress (FAO) Washington, June 1963. Chm., Anglo-German Assoc., 1973- (Vice-Chm., 1966-73). Order of the Phoenix, Greece, 4th Class; Order of the Cedar, Lebanon. *Heir:* *s* Hon. William Richard Fletcher-Vane, *b* 31 July 1951. *Address:* Hutton-in-the-Forest, Penrith, Cumbria CA11 9TH. *T:* Skelton 207; 19 Stack House, Cundy Street, Ebury Street, SW1. *T:* 01-730 1559. *Club:* Travellers'.

INGLIS, Allan, CMG 1962; Director of Public Works, Hong Kong, retired; *b* 25 Feb. 1906; *m* 1936, Constance M. Maclachlan; two *d*. *Educ:* Royal High Sch., Edinburgh; Heriot-Watt Coll., Edinburgh. Chartered Civil Engineer (FICE). Joined Colonial Service, 1930; Engrg Surveyor, Singapore, SS, 1930; Asst Engr, 1935, Exec. Engr, 1939, Malaya. Served War of 1939-45, Major Royal Engineers. Sen. Exec. Engr, 1946, State Engr, 1953, Malaya. *Address:* 26 Cramond Road South, Edinburgh EH4 6AA. *T:* 031-336 1695. *Clubs:* Royal Over-Seas League; Royal Scots (Edinburgh).

INGLIS, Brian (St John), PhD; FRSL; journalist; *b* 31 July 1916; *s* of late Sir Claude Inglis, CIE, FRS, and late Vera St John Blood; *m* 1958, Ruth Langdon; one *s* one *d. Educ:* Shrewsbury Sch.; Magdalen Coll., Oxford. BA 1939. Served in RAF (Coastal Command), 1940-46; Flight Comdr 202 Squadron, 1944-45; Squadron Ldr, 1944-46 (despatches). Irish Times Columnist, 1946-48; Parliamentary Corr., 1950-53. Trinity Coll., Dublin: PhD 1950; Asst to Prof. of Modern History, 1949-53; Lectr in Economics, 1951-53; Spectator: Asst Editor, 1954-59; Editor, 1959-62; Dir, 1962-63. TV Commentator: What the Papers Say, All Our Yesterdays, etc., 1957-. *Publications:* The Freedom of the Press in Ireland, 1954; The Story of Ireland 1956; Revolution in Medicine, 1958; West Briton, 1962; Fringe Medicine, 1964; Private Conscience: Public Morality, 1964; Drugs, Doctors and Disease, 1965; A History of Medicine, 1965; Abdication, 1966; Poverty and the Industrial Revolution, 1971; Roger Casement, 1973; The Forbidden Game: the social history of drugs, 1975; The Opium War, 1976; Natural and Supernatural, 1977. *Address:* Garden Flat, 23 Lambolle Road, NW3.

INGLIS, Sir Brian Scott, Kt 1977; Managing Director (first Australian to be so), Ford Motor Co. of Australia Ltd, since 1970; *b* Adelaide, 3 Jan. 1924; *s* of late E. S. Inglis, Albany, WA; *m* 1953, Leila, *d* of E. V. Butler; three *d. Educ:* Geelong Church of England Grammar School; Trinity Coll., Univ. of Melbourne. Served War of 1939-45; Flying Officer, RAAF, 453 Sqdn, 1942-45. Director and Gen. Manufacturing Manager, Ford Motor Co. of Australia Ltd, 1963-70. *Address:* 10 Bowley Avenue, Balwyn, Victoria 3103, Australia. *Clubs:* Australian (Melbourne); Geelong (Geelong); Barwon Heads Golf.

INGLIS, Maj.-Gen. Sir Drummond, KBE 1945 (OBE 1939); CB 1944; MC 1916; *b* 4 May 1895; *s* of late Major Thomas Drummond Inglis, RA, Colchester; *m* 1st, 1919, Monica (*d* 1976), *d* of late Philip Percival Whitcombe, MB, London; one *s* (one *d* decd); 2nd, 1977, Joan Proudlove, *d* of Pieter Johannes Jacobus Vrint. *Educ:* Wellington Coll.; RMA, Woolwich. 2nd Lt RE 1914; served European War, 1914-19 (4th Class Order of White Eagle of Serbia with swords, Bt Major); Palestine, 1937-39 (despatches, OBE); War of 1939-45, France, Belgium, Holland, Germany; Chief Engineer, 21st Army Group, 1943-45 (Officer of the Legion of Honour, Croix de Guerre with palms, Knight Grand Officer of the Order of Orange Nassau with swords); retired pay, 1945; Col Comdt RE, 1955-60. *Address:* The Thatched Cottage, Chignal Smealey, near Chelmsford, Essex. *Club:* Army and Navy.

INGLIS, Maj.-Gen. George Henry, CB 1952; CBE 1950; JP; Vice-Lieutenant of Cumberland, 1969-74; *b* 22 Aug. 1902; *s* of late Col Henry Alves Inglis, CMG, Dalston, Cumberland; *m* 1940, Margaret Edith, *d* of C. H. Shaw, Ullswater. *Educ:* Ardvreck, Crieff; Wellington Coll.; RMA Woolwich. 2nd Lt RA 1922. Served War of 1939-45, France, SEAC, MELF (despatches Burma, 1946, Palestine, 1949), temp. Brig., 1944. Comdg 18 Trng Bde, Oswestry, 1948; Comdr 52 Lowland Div. TA and Lowland Dist, 1950-52; Maj.-Gen. 1951; Gen. Officer Commanding Nigeria District, 1953-56; retired, 1956. Chairman: Carlisle Diocesan Board of Finance, 1961-70; Cumbrian (formerly Carlisle & NW Counties) Trustee Savings Bank, 1967-73. Pres., NW Area, Royal British Legion, 1973-. JP Cumberland, 1958; High Sheriff of Cumberland, 1961; DL Cumberland, 1962. Col Comdt RA, 1960-67. *Address:* Crosby House, Crosby-on-Eden, Carlisle CA6 4QZ. *T:* Crosby-on-Eden 239. *Club:* Army and Navy.

INGLIS, Maj.-Gen. Sir (John) Drummond; *see* Inglis, Maj.-Gen. Sir Drummond.

INGLIS, Prof. Kenneth Stanley, DPhil; Professor of History, Australian National University, since 1977; *b* 7 Oct. 1929; *s* of S. W. Inglis; *m* 1st, 1952, Judy Betheras (*d* 1962); one *s* two *d* ; 2nd, 1965, Amirah Gust. *Educ:* Univ. of Melbourne (MA); Univ. of Oxford (DPhil). Sen. Lectr in History, Univ. of Adelaide, 1956-60; Reader in History, 1960-62; Associate Prof. of History, Australian National Univ., 1962-65; Prof., 1965-66; Prof. of History, Univ. of Papua New Guinea, 1966-72, Vice-Chancellor, 1972-75; Professorial Fellow in Hist., ANU, 1975-77. *Publications:* Hospital and Community, 1958; The Stuart Case, 1962; Churches and the Working Classes in Victorian England, 1963; The Australian Colonists, 1974. *Address:* History Department, Research School of Social Sciences, Australian National University, Canberra, ACT 2600, Australia.

INGLIS, Sheriff Robert Alexander; Sheriff of North Strathclyde (formerly Renfrew and Argyll) at Paisley, since 1972; *b* 29 June 1918; *m* 1950, Shelagh Constance St Clair Boyd (marriage dissolved, 1956); one *s* one *d. Educ:* Malsis Hall, Daniel Stewart's Coll.; Rugby Sch.; Christ Church, Oxford (MA); Glasgow Univ. (LLB). Army, 1940-46; Glasgow Univ., 1946-48; called to Bar, 1948. Interim Sheriff-Sub., Dundee, 1955; perm. appt, 1956; Sheriff of Inverness, Moray, Nairn and Ross and Cromarty, 1968-72. *Recreations:* golf, fishing, bridge. *Address:* 1 Cayzer Court, Ralston, Paisley, Renfrewshire. *T:* 041-883 6498.

INGLIS of Glencorse, Sir Roderick (John), 10th Bt *cr* 1703 (then Mackenzie of Gairloch); MB, ChB; *b* 25 Jan. 1936; *s* of Sir Maxwell Ian Hector Inglis of Glencorse, 9th Bt and Dorothy Evelyn (*d* 1970), MD, JP, *d* of Dr John Stewart, Tasmania; *S* father, 1974; *m* 1960, Rachel, *d* of Lt-Col N. M. Morris, Dowdstown, Ardee, Co. Louth; three *s* (incl twin *s*) one *d* . *Educ:* Winchester; Edinburgh Univ. (MB, ChB 1960). *Heir: s* Alastair Mackenzie Inglis, younger of Glencorse, *b* 28 July 1961. *Address:* 35 Villiers Drive, Pietermaritzburg, S Africa.

INGLIS-JONES, Nigel John; Barrister-at-Law; a Recorder of the Crown Court, since 1976; *b* 7 May 1935; 2nd *s* of Major John Alfred Inglis-Jones and Hermione Inglis-Jones; *m* 1965, Lenette Bromley-Davenport; two *s* two *d* . *Educ:* Eton; Trinity Coll., Oxford (BA). Nat. Service with Grenadier Guards (ensign). Called to the Bar, Inner Temple, 1959. *Recreations:* conversation, fishing. *Address:* 4 Sheen Common Drive, Richmond, Surrey. *T:* 01-878 1320. *Club:* MCC.

INGOLD, Cecil Terence, CMG 1970; DSc 1940; FLS; Professor of Botany in University of London, Birkbeck College, 1944-72; Vice-Master, Birkbeck College, 1965-70, Fellow, 1973; *b* 3 July 1905; *s* of late E. G. Ingold; *m* 1933, Leonora Mary Kemp; one *s* three *d. Educ:* Bangor (Co. Down) Grammar Sch.; Queen's Univ., Belfast. Graduated BSc, QUB, 1925; Asst in Botany, QUB, 1929; Lectr in Botany, University of Reading, 1930-37; Lecturer-in-charge of Dept of Botany, University Coll., Leicester, 1937-44; Dean of Faculty of Science, London Univ., 1956-60. Dep. Vice-Chancellor, London Univ., 1966-68, Chm. Academic Council, 1969-72. Chm., University Entrance and School Examinations Council, 1958-64; Vice-Chm., Inter-Univ. Council for Higher Educn Overseas, 1969-74. Chm., Council Freshwater Biolog. Assoc., 1965-74; Pres., Internat. Mycological Congress, 1971. Hooker Lectr, Linnean Soc., 1974. Hon. DLitt Ibadan, 1969; Hon. DSc Exeter, 1972. *Publications:* Spore Discharge in Land Plants, 1939; Dispersal in Fungi, 1953; The Biology of Fungi, 1961; Spore Liberation, 1965; Fungal Spores: their liberation and dispersal, 1971; papers in Annals of Botany, New Phytologist, and Transactions of British Mycological Soc. *Address:* Birkbeck College, Malet Street, WC1.

INGOLDBY, Eric, CIE 1943; *b* 7 Jan. 1892; *m* 1925, Zyvee Elizabeth Taylor (*d* 1954); two *s.* Served European War of 1914-18, RGA. Joined Indian State Railways, 1921; Chief Mechanical Engineer, GIP Railway, 1934; Dir Railway Board, India, 1935-40; Chief Controller of Standardisation, Railway Board, Govt of India, 1941-47; retired 1949; mem. firm of Rendel, Palmer and Tritton, consulting engineers, 1947-55. *Address:* 5 Lynne Court, Chesham Road, Guildford, Surrey. *T:* Guildford 70878.

INGRAM, Dr David John Edward, MA, DPhil; DSc Oxon 1960; FInstP; Principal, Chelsea College, London University, since 1973; *b* 6 April 1927; *s* of late J. E. Ingram and late Marie Florence (*née* Weller); *m* 1952, Ruth Geraldine Grace McNair; two *s* one *d. Educ:* King's Coll. Sch., Wimbledon; New Coll., Oxford. Postgraduate research at Oxford Univ., 1948-52; Research Fellow and Lectr, University of Southampton, 1952-57; Reader in Electronics, University of Southampton, 1957-59; Prof. and Head of Dept of Physics, Univ. of Keele, 1959-73; Dep. Vice-Chancellor, University of Keele, 1964-65, 1968-71. Mem., UGC, Physical Sciences Cttee, 1971-74. Member, Governing Body: Wye Coll., London Univ.; St Dunstan's Coll.; King's College Sch., Wimbledon; St George's Hosp. Medical Sch.; Royal Dental Sch. Hon. DSc (Clermont-Ferrand). *Publications:* Spectroscopy at Radio and Microwave Frequencies, 1955, 2nd edn, 1967; Free Radicals as Studied by Electron Spin Resonance, 1958; Biological and Biochemical Applications of Electron Spin Resonance, 1969; Radiation and Quantum Physics, 1973; Radio and Microwave Spectroscopy, 1976; various papers in Proc. Royal Soc., Proc. Phys. Soc., etc. *Recreations:* sailing, debating. *Address:* 17 Roedean Crescent, SW15. *T:* 01-876 1990. *Club:* Athenæum.

INGRAM, Sir Herbert, 3rd Bt *cr* 1893; Partner, Cazenove & Co., 1947-70, retired; *b* 18 April 1912; *s* of Sir Herbert Ingram, 2nd Bt and Hilda Vivian Lake (*d* 1968); *S* father, 1958; *m* 1935, Jane Lindsay, *d* of J. E. Palmer Tomkinson; one *s* three *d. Educ:* Winchester; Balliol Coll., Oxford. Served War of 1939-45 (despatches): Grenadier Guards and REME, Major. *Recreations:* golf, ski-ing. *Heir: s* Herbert Robin Ingram [*b* 13 Jan. 1939; *m* 1st, 1963, Shiela (marr. diss. 1971), *o d* of Charles

Peczenik and Mrs Edward Remington-Hobbs; one *s* one *d* ; 2nd, 1973, Sallie, *d* of Mr and Mrs F. H. Minoprio; one *s*]. *Address:* Hurst Lodge, near Reading, Berks. *T:* Twyford (Berks) 341088. *Club:* White's.

INGRAM, Dame Kathleen Annie; *see* Raven, Dame Kathleen.

INGRAM, Prof. R. P. W.; *see* Winnington-Ingram.

INGRAM, Prof. Vernon Martin, FRS 1970; Professor of Biochemistry, Massachusetts Institute of Technology, since 1961; *b* Breslau, 19 May 1924; *s* of Kurt and Johanna Immerwahr; *m* 1950, Margaret Young; one *s* one *d*. *Educ:* Birkbeck Coll., Univ. of London. PhD Organic Chemistry, 1949; DSc Biochemistry, 1961. Analytical and Res. Chemist, Thos Morson & Son, Mddx, 1941-45; Lecture Demonstrator in Chem., Birkbeck Coll., 1945-47; Asst Lectr in Chem., Birkbeck Coll., 1947-50; Rockefeller Foundn Fellow, Rockefeller Inst., NY, 1950-51; Coxe Fellow, Yale, 1951-52; Mem. Sci. Staff, MRC Unit for Molecular Biology, Cavendish Lab., Cambridge, 1952-58; Assoc. Prof. 1958-61, MIT; Lectr (part-time) in Medicine, Columbia, 1961-73; Guggenheim Fellow, UCL, 1967-68. Jesup Lectr, Columbia, 1962; Harvey Soc. Lectr, 1965. Member: Amer. Acad. of Arts and Sciences, 1964; Amer. Chem. Soc.; Chemical Soc.; Biochemical Soc.; Genetical Society. William Allen Award, Amer. Soc. for Human Genetics, 1967. *Publications:* Haemoglobin and Its Abnormalities, 1961; The Hemoglobins in Genetics and Evolution, 1963; The Biosynthesis of Macromolecules, 1965, new edn, 1971; articles on human genetics, nucleic acids and differentiation in Nature, Jl Mol. Biol., Jl Cell Biol., Develt Biol., Jl Biol Chem., etc. *Recreation:* music. *Address:* Massachusetts Institute of Technology, Massachusetts Avenue, Cambridge, Mass 02139, USA. *T:* 617-253-3706.

INGRAMS, family name of **Baroness Darcy de Knayth.**

INGRAMS, Richard Reid; Editor, Private Eye, since 1963; *b* 19 Aug. 1937; *s* of Leonard St Clair Ingrams and Victoria (*née* Reid); *m* 1962, Mary Morgan; one *s* one *d* (and one *s* decd). *Educ:* Shrewsbury; University Coll., Oxford. Joined Private Eye, 1962. *Publications:* (with Christopher Booker and William Rushton) Private Eye on London, 1962; Private Eye's Romantic England, 1963; (with John Wells) Mrs Wilson's Diary, 1965; Mrs Wilson's 2nd Diary, 1966; The Tale of Driver Grope, 1968; (with Barry Fantoni) The Bible for Motorists, 1970; (ed) The Life and Times of Private Eye, 1971; (as Philip Reid, with Andrew Osmond) Harris in Wonderland, 1973; (ed) Cobbett's Country Book, 1974; (ed) Beachcomber: the works of J. B. Morton, 1974; The Best of Private Eye, 1974; God's Apology, 1977. *Recreation:* editing Private Eye. *Address:* c/o Private Eye, 34 Greek Street, W1. *T:* 01-437 4017.

INGRESS BELL, P.; *see* Bell, Philip I.

INIGO-JONES, Captain Henry Richmund, CIE 1947; *b* 26 Aug. 1899; *s* of Rev. Ralph William Inigo-Jones, Kelston Park, Bath. Somerset; *m* 1st, 1925, Hester Rhoda (*d* 1948), *d* of late Herbert Smith, Great Ryburgh, Norfolk; one *s* one *d* ; 2nd, 1951, Maidie Cubitt (from whom he obtained a divorce, 1961), London, SW. *Educ:* Elstow Sch., Bedford; Thames Nautical Training Coll.; HMS Worcester. Joined Royal Indian Marine (which later became Royal Indian Navy), 1920; transferred to Royal Navy on Indian Independence, and loaned to Indian Navy; Commodore-in-charge, Bombay, until 1951, when retired. *Address:* c/o Grindlay's Bank Ltd, 13 St James's Square, SW1Y 4LF. *Club:* Naval.

INMAN, family name of **Baron Inman.**

INMAN, 1st Baron, *cr* 1946, of Knaresborough; **Philip Albert Inman,** PC 1947; JP County of London; President, former Chairman, Charing Cross Hospital; President, Charing Cross Hospital Medical School; Member of Council, King Edward's Hospital Fund; Patron, Independent Hospitals Association; director of publishing, hotel and industrial companies; an underwriting member of Lloyd's; *b* 12 June 1892; *s* of Philip Inman; *m* 1919, May Amélie, *o d* of Edward Dew, Harrow; one *d* (and one *s* decd). *Educ:* Harrogate; Leeds Univ. Former Chm. of BBC and of Central Bd of Finance of Church Assembly; Lord Privy Seal during 1947; Chm. Hotels Executive, British Transport, 1948-51; a Church Commissioner, 1946-57. Mem. of Court, Worshipful Co. of Needlemakers; Hon. FRSH. *Publications:* The Human Touch; The Silent Loom; The Golden Cup; Oil and Wine; Straight Runs Harley Street (Novel); No Going Back (Autobiography). *Recreations:* walking, reading, golf. *Address:* Knaresborough House, Warninglid, Haywards Heath, West Sussex RH17 5SN. *T:* Warninglid 225. *Club:* Athenæum.

INMAN, Herbert, CBE 1977; Regional Administrator, Yorkshire Regional Health Authority, 1973-77; *b* 8 Jan. 1917; *s* of Matthew Herbert Inman and Rose Mary Earle; *m* 1939, Beatrice, *d* of Thomas Edward Lee and Florence Lee; twin *s*. *Educ:* Wheelwright Grammar Sch., Dewsbury; Univ. of Leeds. FHA (Nat. Pres. 1968-69); DPA. Various hosp. appts, Dewsbury, Wakefield and Aylesbury, 1933-48; Dep. Gp Sec., Leeds (A) Gp HMC and Dep. Chief Admin. Officer, 1948-62; Gp Sec. and Chief Admin. Officer, Leeds (A) Gp HMC, 1962-70; Gp Sec. and Chief Admin. Officer, Leeds (St James's) Univ. HMC, 1970-73. *Publications:* occasional articles in Hospital and Health Services jls. *Recreations:* travel, gardening, Rugby football, cricket, swimming. *Address:* 7 Potterton Close, Barwick in Elmet, Leeds LS15 4DY. *T:* Leeds 812538.

INMAN, Peter Donald, CBE 1977; TD 1946; DL; Chief Executive/Clerk, Lancashire County Council, 1974-76; *b* 21 Oct. 1916; *s* of Robert and Sarah Inman, Bradford; *m* 1947, Beatrice Dallas; one *s* one *d*. *Educ:* Bradford Grammar Sch.; Leeds Univ. (LLB). Solicitor. Served War, 1939-45: KOYLI; France, India and Germany (Major). Asst Solicitor, Dewsbury, 1946; Lancashire County Council: Asst Solicitor, 1948; Dep. Clerk, 1951; Clerk, 1973-74. DL Lancs 1974; Clerk of Lieutenancy, Lancs, 1974. Hon. Treasurer, Lancs Youth Clubs Assoc., 1948-68, Vice-Pres. 1968. *Recreations:* golf, gardening. *Address:* 1 Marlborough Drive, Fulwood, Preston PR2 4UE. *T:* Preston 862361.

INMAN, Rt. Rev. Thomas George Vernon; *b* 1904; *s* of late Capt. William James Inman, RE, Durban; *m* 1st, 1935, Alma Coker (*d* 1970), *d* of late Advocate Duncan Stuart Campbell, Bulawayo, Rhodesia; three *s* one *d* ; 2nd, 1971, Gladys Marjory Hannah, MB, ChB (she *m* 1st, 1947, Charles William Lysaght (*d* 1969), *d* of late David Rees Roberts, Cape Town. *Educ:* Selwyn Coll., Cambridge; St Augustine's Coll., Canterbury, MA 1932. Deacon, 1930; priest, 1931; Asst Missioner, Wellington Coll. Mission, Walworth, 1930-33; Curate of Estcourt, Natal, 1933; Curate of St Paul, Durban, 1933-37, Vicar, 1937-51; Canon of Natal, 1944-51; Archdeacon of Durban, 1950-51; Bishop of Natal, 1951-74; retired, 1974. Dean, Province of S Africa, 1966-74. Chaplain and Sub-prelate, Order of St John of Jerusalem, 1953. Hon. DD Univ. of the South, Tenn., USA, 1958. *Address:* PO Box 726, Durban 4000, Natal, South Africa. *T:* 333486.

INNES, Sir Charles (Kenneth Gordon), 11th Bt *cr* 1686; *b* 28 Jan. 1910; *s* of Major Charles Gordon Deverell Innes (*d* 1953), and Ethel Hilda, *d* of George Earle; *S* 1973 to baronetcy of Innes of Coxton, dormant since the death of Sir George Innes, 8th Bt, 1886; *m* 1936, Margaret Colquhoun Lockhart, *d* of F. C. L. Robertson and *g d* of Sir James Colquhoun of Luss, 5th Bt; one *s* one *d*. *Educ:* Haileybury Coll., Herts. War Service, 1939-45, Royal Artillery; Captain, Ayrshire Yeomanry. *Recreations:* photography, music, art, gardening. *Heir:* *s* David Charles Kenneth Gordon Innes [*b* 17 April 1940; *m* 1969, Marjorie Alison, *d* of E. W. Parker; one *s* one *d*. *Address:* October Cottage, Haslemere, Surrey GU27 2LF.

INNES, Fergus Munro, CIE 1946; CBE 1951; Chairman, India General Navigation and Railway Co. Ltd; *b* 12 May 1903; *s* of late Sir Charles Innes; *m* 1st, Evangeline, *d* of A. H. Chaworth-Musters (marriage dissolved); two *d* ; 2nd, Vera, *d* of T. Mahoney; one *s* one *d*. *Educ:* Charterhouse; Brasenose Coll., Oxford. Joined Indian Civil Service, 1926; various posts in Punjab up to 1937; Joint Sec., Commerce Dept, Govt of India, 1944; Mem., Central Board of Revenue, 1947; retired, 1947; Adviser in Pakistan to Central Commercial Cttee, 1947-53; Sec., The West Africa Cttee, 1956-61. Company director. *Address:* Trilliums, Knowl Hill, The Hockering, Woking, Surrey. *T:* Woking 4626. *Club:* Oriental.

INNES, Hammond; *see* Hammond Innes, Ralph.

INNES of Edingight, Malcolm Rognvald; Baron of Crommey; Marchmont Herald, since 1971; *b* 25 May 1938; 3rd *s* of late Sir Thomas Innes of Learney, GCVO, LLD, and Lady Lucy Buchan, 3rd *d* of 18th Earl of Caithness; *m* 1963, Joan, *o d* of Thomas D. Hay, CA, of Edinburgh; three *s*. *Educ:* Edinburgh Acad.; Univ. of Edinburgh (MA, LLB). Falkland Pursuivant Extraordinary, 1957; Carrick Pursuivant, 1958; Writer to HM Signet, 1964; Lyon Clerk and Keeper of the Records, 1966. Mem., Queen's Body Guard for Scotland (Royal Company of Archers), 1971. FSA (Scot.); OStJ. *Recreations:* fishing, shooting, visiting places of historic interest. *Address:* 35 Inverleith Row, Edinburgh EH3 5QH. *T:* 031-552 4924; Edingight House, Banffshire. *T:* Knock 270. *Clubs:* New, Puffins (Edinburgh).

INNES, Maughan William; Controller Finance, National Research Development Corporation, since 1965; *b* 18 Nov. 1922; *s* of Leslie W. Innes and Bridget Maud (*née* Humble-Crofts); *m* 1950, Helen Mary, *d* of Roper Spyers; one *s* (and one *s* decd). *Educ:* Marlborough College. FCA; MBIM. RAF, 1941-46. Chartered Accountant, 1949; in Canada, 1953-60; with NRDC from 1965. *Recreations:* music, theatre. *Address:* Little Dawyck, Woodhurst Lane, Oxted, Surrey RH8 9HD. *T:* Oxted 2666. *Club:* MCC.

INNES, Michael; see Stewart, John I. M.

INNES, Sir Walter James, 15th Bt, *cr* 1628; *b* 8 Aug. 1903; *s* of late Hector Innes (6th *s* of 11th Bt) and Annie Jane, *d* of W. Fraser; *S* cousin 1950. *Heir:* kinsman Ronald Gordon Berowald Innes, OBE 1943 [*b* 24 July 1907; *m* 1st, 1933, Elizabeth Haughton (*d* 1958), *e d* of late A. Fayle, Merlin, Clonmel, Co. Tipperary; two *s* one *d*; 2nd, 1961, Elizabeth Christian, *e d* of late Lt-Col C. H. Watson, DSO. *Educ:* Harrow]. *Address:* Carlos Pellegrini 485, 4 piso, Dep. B., Buenos Aires, Argentina.

INNES, Lt-Col William Alexander Disney, JP; Vice Lord-Lieutenant of Banffshire, since 1971; *b* 19 April 1910; 2nd *s* of late Captain James William Guy Innes, CBE, DL, JP, RN, of Maryculter, Kincardineshire; *m* 1939, Mary Alison, *d* of late Francis Burnett-Stuart, Howe Green, Hertford; two *s. Educ:* Marlborough Coll., RMC, Sandhurst. Gordon Highlanders: 2nd Lieut, 1930; Captain 1938; Temp. Major 1941; Major, 1946; Temp. Lt-Col, 1951; retd, 1952. Served War of 1939-45: Far East (PoW Malaya and Siam, 1942-45). Chm., Banffshire T&AFA, 1959. DL 1959, JP 1964, Banffshire. *Recreations:* shooting, gardening. *Address:* The Old Manse of Marnoch, Huntly, Aberdeenshire AB5 5RS. *T:* Bridge of Marnoch 273.

INNES-KER, family name of Duke of Roxburghe.

INNES-WILSON, Col Campbell Aubrey Kenneth, CBE 1954 (OBE 1946, MBE 1943); *b* 20 June 1905; *s* of late Captain R. A. K. Wilson, KSLI; *m* 1939, Lorna Isabel, *d* of late Major G. P. Humphreys, Donaghmore House, Castlefinn, Co. Donegal; one *s. Educ:* Fettes; Royal Military Academy, Woolwich; St John's Coll., Cambridge. 2nd Lt, RE 1925. Joined Survey of India, 1929; Dir, Eastern Circle, Survey of India, 1946; Dep. Surveyor-Gen. of India, 1947; Surveyor Gen. of Pakistan, 1950-54. Served War of 1939-45; Iraq and Persia, 1941-43 (MBE); Burma, 1943-45 (OBE, despatches twice). FRICS; FRGS. *Address:* 41 Horsecastles Lane, Sherborne, Dorset DT9 6BU. *T:* Sherborne 2486.

INNESS, Air Cdre William Innes Cosmo, CB 1962; OBE 1954; DL; Commandant, Air Cadets, London and South East, since 1968; *b* 25 March 1916; *y s* of Henry Atkinson Inness; *m* 1942, Margaret Rose Nolan, *er d* of Lt-Col P. E. Nolan, MBE, Royal Signals; two *s. Educ:* Richmond Sch., Yorkshire. Commissioned, RAF Coll., 1936; India, 1936-39; Iraq, 1939-41; Bomber Command, Flt, Sqdn and Station Comdr and GP Capt., Plans, 1941-45. Air Ministry Directorate-Gen. of Personnel, Brit. Bombing Survey Unit, and Directorate of Staff Duties, 1946-48; Air Attaché, Teheran, 1948-51; Sen. Personnel Staff Officer, No. 23 Gp, 1951-54; RAF Flying Coll., 1954-55; Station Comdr, St Eval, 1955-57; Dep. Asst Chief of Staff (Plans), HQ Allied Forces, Mediterranean, 1957-59; Air Officer i/c Administration, Coastal Command, 1959-62; AOC Gibraltar, 1962-65; Dir Personal Services (Provost Marshal), RAF, 1965-68, retired 1968. ADC 1966-68. DL Greater London, 1973; Representative DL, Greenwich, 1974. Chevalier of the Military Order of Aviz (Portugal), 1956. *Recreation:* flying. *Address:* c/o National Westminster Bank Ltd, Market Place, Sutton-in-Ashfield, Nottingham. *Clubs:* Royal Air Force, City Livery.

INNISS, Hon. Sir Clifford (de Lisle), Kt 1961; Judge of the Court of Appeal of Belize since 1974; *b* Barbados, 26 Oct. 1910; *e s* of late Archibald de Lisle Inniss and Lelia Emmaline, *e d* of Elverton Richard Springer. *Educ:* Harrison Coll., Barbados; Queen's Coll., Oxford. BA (hons jurisprudence), BCL. Called to bar, Middle Temple, 1935. QC (Tanganyika) 1950, (Trinidad and Tobago) 1953; Practised at bar, Barbados; subseq. Legal Draughtsman and Clerk to Attorney-Gen., Barbados, 1938; Asst to Attorney General and Legal Draughtsman, 1941; Judge of Bridgetown Petty Debt Court, 1946; Legal Draughtsman, Tanganyika, 1947; Solicitor Gen., Tanganyika, 1949; Attorney-Gen., Trinidad and Tobago, 1953; Chief Justice, British Honduras, later Belize, 1957-72; Judge of the Courts of Appeal of Bermuda, the Bahamas, and the Turks and Caicos Is, 1974-75. *Recreations:* cricket, tennis, swimming. *Address:* 11 Oriole Avenue, Belmopan, Belize. *Clubs:* Royal Over-Seas League; Barbados Yacht; Kenya Kongonis (hon. mem.); Belize-Pickwick (Belize).

INSALL, Donald William, FSA, FRIBA, FRTPI; architect and planning consultant; Principal, Donald W. Insall & Associates, since 1958; *b* 7 Feb. 1926; *o s* of late William R. Insall and Phyllis Insall, Henleaze, Bristol; *m* 1964, Amy Elizabeth, BA, *er d* of Malcolm H. Moss, Nanpantan, Leics; two *s* one *d. Educ:* private prep; Bristol Grammar Sch.; Bristol Univ.; RA; Sch. of Planning, London (Dip. (Hons)); SPAB Lethaby Schol. 1951. FRIBA 1968, FRTPI 1973. Coldstream Guards, 1944-47. Architectural and Town-Planning Consultancy has included town-centre studies, civic and univ., church, domestic and other buildings, notably in conservation of historic towns and buildings; Medal (Min. of Housing and Local Govt), Good Design in Housing, 1962. Visiting Lecturer: RCA, 1964-69; Internat. Centre for Conservation, Rome, 1969-; Coll. d'Europe, Bruges, 1976-; Mem., Council of Europe Working Party, 1969-70; Nat. Pilot Study, Chester: A Study in Conservation, 1968; Consultant, Chester Conservation Programme (EAHY Exemplar). Member: Historic Buildings Council for England, 1971-; Grants Panel, EAHY, 1974; Nat. Cttee, ICOMOS; Council, RSA, 1976- (FRSA, 1948); Member Committee: SPAB; Jt Cttee SPAB, Georgian Gp, Victorian Soc. and Civic Trust. Hon. Sec., Conf. on Trng Architects in Conservation. RIBA: Banister Fletcher Medallist, 1949; Neale Bursar, 1955; Examnr, 1957; Competition Assessor, 1971. Conferences: White House (on Natural Beauty), 1965; IUA (on Architectural Trng), Pistoia, 1968; UNESCO, 1969. Lecture Tours: USA, 1964, 1972 (US Internat. Reg. Conf. on Conservation); Mexico, 1972; Yugoslavia, 1973; Canada, 1974; Argentina, 1976. European Architectural Heritage Year Medal (for Restoration of Chevening), 1973; Jubilee Medal, 1977. *Publications:* (jtly) Railway Station Architecture, 1966; (jtly) Conservation Areas 1967; The Care of Old Buildings Today, 1973; Historic Buildings: action to maintain the expertise for their care and repair, 1974; contrib. to Encyclopædia Britannica, professional, environmental and internat. jls. *Recreations:* visiting, photographing and enjoying places; appreciating craftsmanship; Post-Vintage Thoroughbred Cars (Mem., Rolls Royce Enthusiasts' Club). *Address:* 73 Kew Green, Richmond, Surrey TW9 3AH; (office) 19 West Eaton Place, Eaton Square, SW1X 8LT. *T:* 01-245 9888. *Club:* Athenæum.

INSCH, James Ferguson, CBE 1974; CA; Director, Guest Keen & Nettlefolds Ltd since 1964; Chairman, Birmid-Qualcast Ltd, since 1977 (Deputy Chairman, 1975-77); *b* 10 Sept. 1911; *s* of John Insch and Edina (*née* Hogg); *m* 1937, Jean Baikie Cunningham; one *s* two *d. Educ:* Leith Academy. Chartered Accountant (Scot.). Director, number of GKN companies, 1945-66; Guest Keen & Nettlefolds Ltd: Group Man. Dir, 1967; Gp Dep. Chm. and Man. Dir, 1968-74 (retd). Pres., Nat. Assoc. of Drop Forgers and Stampers, 1962-63 and 1963-64. *Recreations:* golf, fishing. *Address:* Watling House, Twatling Road, Barnt Green, Birmingham. *T:* 021-445 2517.

INSKIP, family name of Viscount Caldecote.

INSKIP, John Hampden, QC 1966; a Recorder (formerly Recorder of Bournemouth), since 1970; *b* 1 Feb. 1924; *s* of Sir John Hampden Inskip, KBE, and Hon. Janet, *d* of 1st Baron Maclay, PC; *m* 1947, Ann Howell Davies; one *s* one *d. Educ:* Clifton Coll.; King's Coll., Cambridge. BA 1948. Called to the Bar, Inner Temple, 1949; Master of the Bench, 1975. Mem. of Western Circuit; Dep. Chm., Hants QS, 1967-71. Mem., Criminal Law Revision Cttee, 1973-. *Address:* 3 Pump Court, Temple, EC4. *T:* 01-353 2441; Clerks, Bramshott, Liphook, Hants.

INVERFORTH, 3rd Baron *cr* 1919, of Southgate; **Andrew Charles Roy Weir;** Chairman and Governing Director, Andrew Weir & Co. Ltd, since 1971; *b* 6 June 1932; *e s* of 2nd Baron Inverforth and of Iris Beryl, *d* of late Charles Vincent; *S* father, 1975; *m* 1966, Elizabeth, *o d* of John W. Thornycroft, *qv*; one *s* one *d. Educ:* Malvern College. *Heir: s* Hon. Andrew Peter Weir, *b* 16 Nov. 1966. *Address:* 27 Hyde Park Street, W2. *T:* 01-262 5721. *Clubs:* City of London, Bath, Royal Automobile.

INVERNESS, Provost of (St Andrew's Cathedral); see Woods, Very Rev. J. M.

INVERURIE, Lord; Michael Canning William John Keith; Master of Kintore; *b* 22 Feb. 1939; *s* and *heir* of 12th Earl of Kintore, *qv*; assumed surname of Keith in lieu of Baird; *m* 1972, Mary Plum, *d* of late Sqdn Leader E. G. Plum, Rumson, NJ, and of Mrs Roy Hudson; one *s. Educ:* Eton; RMA Sandhurst. Lately Lieutenant, Coldstream Guards. ACII. *Heir: s* Master of Inverurie, *qv. Address:* Keith Hall, Inverurie, Aberdeenshire. *T:* Inverurie 20495. *Club:* Royal Northern (Aberdeen).

INVERURIE, Master of; Hon. James William Falconer Keith; *b* 15 April 1976; *s* and *heir* of Lord Inverurie, *qv*.

IONESCO, Eugène; Chevalier de la Légion d'Honneur, 1970; Officier des Arts et lettres, 1961; homme de lettres; Membre de l'Académie française, since 1970; *b* 13 Nov. 1912; *m* 1936, Rodica; one *d*. *Educ:* Bucharest and Paris. French citizen living in Paris. Ballet: The Triumph of Death, Copenhagen, 1972. *Publications:* (most of which appear in English and American editions) Théâtre I; La Cantatrice chauve, La Leçon, Jacques ou La Soumission, Les Chaises, Victimes du devoir, Amédée ou Comment s'en débarrasser, Paris, 1956; Théâtre II: L'Impromptu de l'Alma, Tueur sans gages, Le Nouveau Locataire, L'Avenir est dans les œufs, Le Maître, La Jeune Fille à marier, Paris, 1958. Rhinocéros (play) in Collection Manteau d'Arlequin, Paris, 1959, Le Piéton de l'air, 1962, Chemises de Nuit, 1962; Le Roi se meurt, 1962; Notes et Contre-Notes, 1962; Journal en Miettes, 1967; Présent passé passé présent, 1968; Jeux de Massacre (play), 1970; Macbett (play), 1972; Ce formidable bordel (play), 1974; The Hermit (novel), 1975; The Man with the Suitcase, 1975. Contrib. to: Avant-Garde (The experimental theatre in France) by L. C. Pronko, 1962; Modern French Theatre, from J. Giraudoux to Beckett, by Jean Guicharnaud, 1962; author essays and tales. *Relevant publications:* The Theatre of the Absurd, by Martin Esslin, 1961; Ionesco, by Richard N. Coe, 1961; Eugène Ionesco, by Ronald Hayman, 1972. *Address:* c/o Editions Gallimard, 5 rue Sébastien Bottin, Paris 7e, France.

IONESCU, Prof. George Ghita; Professor of Government, University of Manchester, since 1970; Editor, Government and Opposition, since 1965; *b* 21 March 1913; *s* of Alexandre Ionescu and Hélène Sipsom; *m* 1950, Valence Ramsay de Bois Maclaren. *Educ:* Univ. of Bucharest (Lic. in Law and Polit. Sci.). Gen. Sec., Romanian Commn of Armistice with Allied Forces, 1944-45; Counsellor, Romanian Embassy, Ankara, 1945-47; Gen. Sec., Romanian Nat. Cttee, NY, 1955-58; Dir, Radio Free Europe, 1958-63; Nuffield Fellow, LSE, 1963-68. Hon. MA(Econ) Manchester. *Publications:* Communism in Romania, 1965; The Politics of the Eastern European Communist States, 1966; (jtly) Opposition, 1967; (jtly) Populism, 1970; (ed) Between Sovereignty and Integration, 1973; Centripetal Politics, 1975; The Political Thought of Saint-Simon, 1976. *Recreations:* music, bridge, racing. *Address:* 36 Sandileigh Avenue, Manchester M20 9LW. *T:* 061-445 7726. *Club:* Athenæum.

IPSWICH, Bishop of; *see* St Edmundsbury.

IPSWICH, Archdeacon of; *see* Walsh, Ven. G. D. J.

IRBY, family name of **Baron Boston**.

IRELAND; *see* de Courcy-Ireland.

IRELAND, Frank, FCA; IPFA; Principal City Officer and Town Clerk, Newcastle upon Tyne, 1969-74; *b* 2 May 1909; *s* of C. A. Ireland, Clitheroe, Lancs; *m* 1935, Elsie Mary (*née* Ashworth); one *s* two *d*. *Educ:* Clitheroe Royal Grammar Sch.; Victoria Univ., Manchester BA (Com). Chartered Accountant, 1931; Hons, IMTA, 1936. Derby County Borough, 1933-37; Newcastle upon Tyne, 1937-74; City Treasurer, 1962-69. *Recreations:* music, photography. *Address:* 61 Kenton Road, Newcastle upon Tyne NE3 4NJ. *T:* Gosforth 856930.

IRELAND, Frank Edward, BSc, CChem; FRIC; CEng; FIChemE; SFInstF; HM Chief Alkali and Clean Air Inspector, since 1964; *b* 7 Oct. 1913; *s* of William Edward Ireland and Bertha Naylor; *m* 1941, Edna Clare Meredith; one *s* three *d*. *Educ:* Liverpool Univ. (BSc). CChem, FRIC 1945; CEng, FIChemE 1950; SFInstF 1956. Plant Superintendent, Orrs Zinc White Works, Widnes, Imperial Smelting Corp. Ltd, 1935-51; Prodn Man., Durham Chemicals Ltd, Birtley, Co. Durham, 1951-53; Alkali Inspector based on Sheffield, 1953-58; Dep. Chief Alkali Inspector, 1958-64. Pres., Inst. of Fuel, 1974-75; Vice Pres., Instn of Chem. Engrs, 1969-72. George E. Davis Gold Medal, Instn of Chem. Engrs, 1969. Founder Fellow, Fellowship of Engineering, 1976. *Publications:* Annual Alkali Reports, 1964-; papers to nat. and internat. organisations. *Recreations:* golf, gardening. *Address:* 59 Lanchester Road, Highgate, N6. *T:* 01-883 6060.

IRELAND, Ronald David, QC (Scotland) 1964; Sheriff of Lothian and Borders (formerly Lothians and Peebles) at Edinburgh, since 1972; Director, Scottish Courts Administration, since 1975; *b* 13 March 1925; *o s* of William Alexander Ireland and Agnes Victoria Brown. *Educ:* George Watson's Coll., Edinburgh; Balliol Coll., Oxford (Scholar); Edinburgh Univ. Served Royal Signals, 1943-46. BA Oxford, 1950, MA 1958; LLB Edinburgh, 1952. Passed Advocate, 1952; Clerk of the Faculty of Advocates, 1957-58; Prof. of Scots Law, 1958-71, Dean of Faculty of Law, 1964-67, Aberdeen Univ. Governor, Aberdeen Coll. of Education, 1959-64 (Vice-Chm., 1962-64). Comr. under NI (Emergency Provisions) Act, 1974-75. Member: Bd of Management, Aberdeen Gen. Hosps, 1961-71 (Chm., 1964-71); Departmental Cttee on Children and Young Persons, 1961-64; Cttee on the Working of the Abortion Act, 1971-74; Hon. Sheriff for Aberdeenshire, 1963-. Member: North Eastern Regional Hosp. Bd, 1964-71 (Vice-Chm. 1966-71); After Care Council, 1962-65; Nat. Staff Advisory Cttee for the Scottish Hosp. Service, 1964-65; Chm., Scottish Hosps Administrative Staffs Cttee, 1965-72. *Recreations:* music, bird-watching. *Address:* 6a Greenhill Gardens, Edinburgh EH10 4BW. *Clubs:* New (Edinburgh); University, Royal Northern (Aberdeen).

IREMONGER, Thomas Lascelles; *o s* of Lt-Col H. E. W. Iremonger, DSO, Royal Marine Artillery, and Julia St Mary Shandon, *d* of Col John Quarry, Royal Berks Regiment; *m* Lucille Iremonger, author and broadcaster; one *d*. *Educ:* Oriel Coll., Oxford. HM Overseas Service (Western Pacific), 1938-46. RNVR (Lt), 1942-46. MP (C) Ilford North, Feb. 1954-Feb. 1974, Redbridge, Ilford North, Feb.-Sept. 1974; PPS to Sir Fitzroy Maclean, Bt, CBE, MP, when Under-Sec. of State for War, 1954-57. Member: Royal Commn on the Penal System, 1964-66; Home Sec.'s Adv. Council on the Employment of Prisoners; Gen. Council, Institute for Study and Treatment of Delinquency. Underwriting Mem. of Lloyd s. *Publications:* Disturbers of the Peace, 1962; Money, Politics and You, 1963. *Recreations:* sailing, riding, shooting. *Address:* 34 Cheyne Row, SW3; The Giant's House, Newbourn, near Woodbridge, Suffolk.

IRENS, Alfred Norman, CBE 1969; Chairman, South Western Electricity Board, 1956-73; *b* 28 Feb. 1911; *s* of Max Henry and Guinevere Emily Irens; *m* 1934, Joan Elizabeth, *d* of John Knight, FRIBA, Worsley, Manchester; two *s*. *Educ:* Blundell's Sch., Tiverton; Faraday House, London. College apprentice, Metropolitan Vickers, Ltd, Manchester. Subsequently with General Electric Co., Ltd, until joining Bristol Aeroplane Co., Ltd, 1939, becoming Chief Electrical Engineer, 1943; Consulting Engineer to Govt and other organisations, 1945-56. Part-time mem., SW Electricity Bd, 1948-56. Past Chm. IEE Utilization Section and IEE Western Sub-Centre; Chairman: British Electrical Development Assoc., 1962-63; SW Economic Planning Council, 1968-71; British Electrotechnical Approvals Bd for Household Equipment, 1974-; Bristol Waterworks Co., 1975-. Director: Bristol Waterworks Co., 1967-; Avon Rubber Co. Ltd, 1973-. Hon. MSc, Bristol, 1957. *Recreations:* general outdoor activities. *Address:* Crete Hill House, Cote House Lane, Bristol BS9 3UW. *T:* Bristol 627471. *Club:* Constitutional (Bristol).

IRESON, Rev. Canon Gordon Worley; Warden, Community of the Holy Name, since 1974; *b* 16 April 1906; *s* of Francis Robert and Julia Letitia Ireson; *m* 1939, Dorothy Elizabeth Walker; two *s* one *d*. *Educ:* Edinburgh Theological Coll.; Hatfield Coll., Durham. Asst Curate of Sheringham, 1933-36 Senior Chaplain of St Mary's Cathedral, Edinburgh, with charge of Holy Trinity, Dean Bridge, 1936-37; Priest-Lecturer to National Soc., 1937-39; Diocesan Missioner of Exeter Diocese, 1939-46; Hon. Chaplain to Bishop of Exeter, 1941-46; Canon Residentiary of Newcastle Cathedral, 1946-58; Canon-Missioner of St Albans, 1958-73; Examining Chaplain to Bishop of Newcastle, 1949-. *Publications:* Church Worship and the Non-Churchgoer, 1945; Think Again, 1949; How Shall They Hear?, 1957; Strange Victory, 1970. *Recreation:* making and mending in the workshop. *Address:* St Mary's, Ranelagh Road, Malvern Link, Worcs WR14 1BQ.

IRISH, Sir Ronald (Arthur), Kt 1970; OBE 1963; Partner, Irish Young & Outhwaite, Chartered Accountants; Chairman, Rothmans of Pall Mall (Australia) Ltd; Director of other companies; *b* 26 March 1913; *s* of late Arthur Edward Irish; *m* 1960, Noella Jean Austin Fraser; three *s*. *Educ:* Fort Street High School. Pres., Inst. of Chartered Accountants in Australia, 1956-58 (Life Mem., 1974); Pres., Tenth Internat. Congress of Accountants, 1972; Chm., Manufacturing Industries Adv. Council, 1966-72; Life Mem., Australian Soc. of Accountants, 1972. *Publications:* Practical Auditing, 1935 Auditing, 1947, new edn 1972. *Recreations:* golf, swimming. *Address:* Cootharinga, Castle Hill, NSW 2154, Australia. *Clubs:* Australian, Union, Killara Golf (Sydney).

IRON, Air Cdre Douglas, CBE 1944; *b* 1 Aug. 1893; *s* of Captain John Iron, OBE, and Anne Iron; *m* 1917, Dorothy Bentham (from whom he obtained a divorce); one *d*; *m* 1930, Mrs P. V.

Sankey (from whom he obtained a divorce). *Educ:* Tudor Hall Sch., Hawkhurst. Prob. Flight Sub.-Lt RNAS Sept. 1914; Flight Lt May 1915; Acting Lt-Col GSO1 (Air) April 1918; permanent commission, RAF, as Flight Lt 1919. Sqdn Leader, 1924; Wing Comdr 1930; attended Royal Naval Staff Coll., 1935; Group Capt. 1937; Air Officer i/c Administration, 4 Training Command, RCAF, Canada, with rank of Air Commodore, Dec. 1943; Air Officer Commanding 51 Group RAF, 1944-45; retired, 1945. *Recreation:* fishing. *Club:* Army and Navy.

IRONMONGER, Sir (Charles) Ronald, Kt 1970; Personnel Officer, GEC Traction Ltd (formerly AEI) Attercliffe, since 1966; Leader, S Yorkshire County Council, since 1973; *b* 20 Jan. 1914; *s* of late Charles and Emily Ironmonger; *m* 1938, Jessie (*née* Green); one *s* one *d. Educ:* Huntsmans Gardens Elementary Sch., Firth Park Secondary Sch., Sheffield. Elected Sheffield City Council, Nov. 1945; Chairman, Water Cttee, 1951-66; Leader of City Council and Chairman, Policy Cttee, 1966-68, 1969-; Chm., S Yorks Local Govt Reorganisation Jt Cttee, 1972; elected S Yorkshire CC, 1973, Chm., Policy Cttee, 1973-. Vice-Chm., AMA, 1977-. *Recreations:* reading, sport. *Address:* 70 Chestnut Avenue, Sheffield S9 4AP. *T:* Sheffield 42329.

IRONSIDE, family name of **Baron Ironside.**

IRONSIDE, 2nd Baron, *cr* 1941, of Archangel and of Ironside; **Edmund Oslac Ironside;** International Research and Development Co., since 1968; *b* 21 Sept. 1924; *o s* of 1st Baron Ironside, Field Marshal, GCB, CMG, DSO, and Mariot Ysobel Cheyne; *m* 1950, Audrey Marigold, *y d* of late Lt-Col Hon. Thomas Morgan-Grenville, DSO, OBE, MC; one *s* one *d. Educ:* Tonbridge Sch. Joined Royal Navy, 1943; retd as Lt, 1952. English Electric Gp, 1952-63; Cryosystems Ltd, 1963-68; Dir, Gemini Computer Systems Ltd, 1973; Dep. Chm., Parly and Scientific Cttee, 1974. Mem., Organising Cttee, British Library, 1971-72. Pres., Electric Vehicle Assoc., 1976. Governor, Tonbridge Sch. and others; Mem. Ct, City Univ., 1971-. *Publication:* (ed) High Road to Command: the diaries of Major-General Sir Edmund Ironside, 1920-22, 1972. *Heir: s* Hon. Charles Edmund Grenville Ironside, *b* 1 July 1956. *Address:* Broomwood Manor, Chignal St James, Chelmsford, Essex. *T:* Chelmsford 440231. *Club:* Royal Ocean Racing.

IRONSIDE, Christopher, OBE 1971; FRBS; Artist and Designer; *b* 11 July 1913; *s* of Dr R. W. Ironside and Mrs P. L. Williamson (2nd *m*; *née* Cunliffe); *m* 1st, 1939, Janey (*née* Acheson) (marriage dissolved, 1961); one *d*; 2nd, 1961, Jean (*née* Marsden); one *s* two *d. Educ:* Central Sch. of Arts and Crafts. Served War of 1939-45, Dep. Sen. Design Off., Directorate of Camouflage, Min. of Home Security. In charge of Educn Sect., Coun. of Industrial Design, 1946-48; part-time Teacher, Royal College of Art, 1953-63. Paintings in public and private collections. *One-man shows:* Redfern Gall., 1941; Arthur Jeffries Gall., 1960. *Design work includes:* Royal Coat of Arms, Whitehall and decorations in Pall Mall, Coronation, 1953; coinages for Tanzania, Brunei, Qatar and Dubai; reverses for Decimal Coinage, UK and Jamaican; many medals, coins and awards; theatrical work (with brother, late R. C. Ironside); various clocks; coat of arms and tapestry for Leather Sellers' Hall; firegrate for Goldsmiths' Co. FSIA 1970; FRBS 1977. *Recreation:* trying to keep abreast of modern scientific development. *Address:* 22 Abingdon Villas, W8. *T:* 01-937 9418; Church Farm House, Smannell, near Andover, Hants. *T:* Andover 3909.

IRVINE, Rt. Hon. Sir Arthur (James), PC 1970; Kt 1967; QC 1958; MP (Lab) Edge Hill Division of Liverpool, since 1947; *b* 14 July 1909; *s* of late J. M. Irvine, KC, Sheriff of Renfrew and Bute; *m* 1937, Eleanor, *d* of late E. E. T. Morris, Petersfield, Hants; four *s. Educ:* Angusfield Sch., Aberdeen; Edinburgh Academy; Edinburgh Univ. (MA 1929); Oriel Coll., Oxford (BA 1931, MA 1957). Pres., Oxford Union, 1932; called to Bar, Middle Temple, 1935; also Mem. of Inner Temple; Sec. to Lord Chief Justice of England, 1935-40; UK delegate to Council of Europe, 1961-62; Master of the Bench, Middle Temple, 1965; Chm. House of Commons Select Cttee on Procedure, 1965; Solicitor-General, 1967-70. Recorder of Colchester, 1965-67. Hon. Fellow, Oriel Coll., 1969. Contested Kincardine and West Aberdeenshire (L), 1935 and 1939 (by-election). DAAG HQ Eastern Command, 1944; DAMS HQ Land Forces, Greece, 1944-45 (despatches). Contested (Lab) Twickenham, 1945 and South Aberdeen (by-election), 1946. *Address:* 20 Wellington Square, SW3. *T:* 01-730 3117; 4 Paper Buildings, Temple, EC4. *T:* 01-353 8408.

IRVINE, B(ryant) Godman; MP (C) Rye Division of East Sussex since 1955; a Deputy Chairman of Ways and Means, and a Deputy Speaker, since 1976; Barrister-at-law; Farmer; *b*

Toronto, 25 July 1909; *s* of late W. Henry Irvine and late Ada Mary Bryant Irvine, formerly of St Agnes, Cornwall; *m* 1945, Valborg Cecilie, *d* of late P. F. Carslund; two *d. Educ:* Upper Canada Coll.; St Paul's Sch.; Magdalen Coll., Oxford (MA). Sec. Oxford Union Soc., 1931. Called to Bar. Inner Temple, 1932. Chm. Agricultural Land Tribunal, SE Province, 1954-56. Mem. Executive Cttee, East Sussex NFU, 1947-; Branch Chm., 1956-58. Chm. Young Conservative Union, 1946-47; Prospective Candidate, Bewdley Div. of Worcs, 1947-49; contested Wood Green and Lower Tottenham, 1951. PPS to Minister of Education and to Parly Sec., Ministry of Education, 1957-59, to the Financial Sec. to the Treasury, 1959-60. Mem., Speaker's Panel of Chairmen, House of Commons, 1965-76; Jt Sec., Exec. Cttee, 1922 Cttee, 1965-68, Hon. Treasurer, 1974-76; Vice-Chm., Cons. Agric. Cttee, and spoke on Agriculture from Opposition Front Bench, 1964-70; Mem., House of Commons Select Cttee on Agriculture, 1967-69; Commonwealth Parliamentary Association: Hon. Treasurer, 1970-73; Mem., General Council, 1970-73; Mem., Exec. Cttee, UK Branch, 1964-; Jt Sec. or Vice-Chm., Cons. Commonwealth Affairs Cttee, 1957-66; Jt Sec., Foreign and Commonwealth Affairs Cttee, 1967- (Vice-Chm., 1973-); Chm., Cons. Horticulture Sub-Cttee, 1960-62; All Party Tourist and Resort Cttee, 1964-66; Pres., British Resorts Assoc., 1962-. Served War of 1939-45, Lt-Comdr RNVR, afloat and on staff of C-in-C Western Approaches and Commander US Naval Forces in Europe. Comp. InstCE, 1936-74. *Recreations:* ski-ing, travel by sea. *Address:* Great Ote Hall, Burgess Hill, West Sussex. *T:* Burgess Hill 2179; Flat 91, 24 John Islip Street, SW1. *T:* 01-834 9221; 2 Dr Johnson's Buildings, Temple, EC4. *Clubs:* Carlton, Pratt's, Naval; Dormy House (Rye).

IRVINE, Surg. Captain Gerard Sutherland, CBE 1970; RN retired; Medical Officer, Department of Health and Social Security, since 1971; *b* 19 June 1913; *s* of Major Gerard Byrom Corrie Irvine and Maud Andrée (*née* Wylde); *m* 1939, Phyllis Lucy Lawrie; one *s. Educ:* Imperial Service Coll., Windsor; Epsom Coll.; University Coll. and Hosp., London. MRCS, LRCP, MB, BS 1937; DLO 1940; FRCS 1967. Jenks Meml Schol. 1932; Liston Gold Medal for Surgery 1936. Surg. Sub-Lt RNVR 1935, Surg. Lt RNVR 1937; Surg Lt RN 1939; Surg. Lt-Comdr 1944; Surg. Comdr 1953; Surg. Capt. 1963. Served War of 1939-45 (1939-45 Star, Atlantic Star with Bar for France and Germany, Burma Star, Defence Medal, Victory Medal); subseq. service: Ceylon, 1946; Haslar, 1947-49 and 1957-60; Malta, 1953-56; HMS: Maidstone (Submarine Depot Ship), 1949-51; Osprey (T&A/S Trng Sch.), 1951-53; Collingwood, 1956-57; Lion, 1960-62; Vernon (Torpedo Sch.), 1962-63; Sen. Cons. in ENT, 1953-70; Adviser in ENT to Med. Dir-Gen. (Navy), 1966-70; Sen. MO i/c Surgical Div., RN Hosp. Haslar, 1966-70; QHS 1969-70; retd 1970. Member: BMA 1938; Sections of Otology and Laryngology, RSM, 1948-77 (FRSM 1948-77); British Assoc. of Otolaryngologists, 1945-71 (Council, 1968-70); S Western Laryngological Assoc., 1951-71; Hearing Sub-Cttee of RN Personnel Res. Cttee, 1947-70; Otological Sub-Cttee of RAF Flying Personnel Res. Cttee, 1963-70. OStJ 1969. *Publications:* numerous articles in various medical jls. *Recreations:* gardening, philately, do-it-yourself. *Address:* 9 Alvara Road, Alverstoke, Gosport PO12 2HY. *T:* Gosport 80342.

IRVINE, James Eccles Malise; His Honour Judge Irvine; a Circuit Judge (Circuit No 20 and Leicester Crown Court), since 1972; *b* 10 July 1925; *y s* of late Brig.-Gen. A. E. Irvine, CB, CMG, DSO, Wotton-under-Edge; *m* 1954, Anne, *e d* of late Col G. Egerton-Warburton, DSO, TD, JP, DL, Grafton Hall, Malpas; one *s* one *d. Educ:* Stowe Sch. (Scholar); Merton Coll., Oxford (Postmaster). MA Oxon. Served Grenadier Guards, 1943-46 (France and Germany Star); Hon. Captain Grenadier Guards, 1946. Called to Bar, Inner Temple, 1949 (Poland Prizeman in Criminal Law, 1949); practised Oxford Circuit, 1949-71; Prosecuting Counsel for Inland Revenue on Oxford Circuit, 1965-71; Dep. Chm., Glos QS, 1967-71. *Publication:* Parties and Pleasures: the Diaries of Helen Graham 1823-26, 1957. *Address:* 2 Harcourt Buildings, Temple, EC4.

IRVINE, Maj.-Gen. John, OBE 1955; Director of Medical Services, British Army of the Rhine, 1973-75; *b* 31 May 1914; *s* of late John Irvine and late Jessie Irvine (*née* McKinnon); *m* 1941, Mary McNicol, *d* of late Andrew Brown Cossar, Glasgow; one *d. Educ:* Glasgow High Sch.; Glasgow Univ. MB, ChB 1940. MFCM 1973. Commnd into RAMC, 1940; served War of 1939-45 (despatches and Act of Gallantry, 1944): Egypt, Greece, Crete, Western Desert, 1941-43; Sicily, Italy and Yugoslavia, 1943-45; served with British Troops, Austria, 1947-49; Korea, 1953-54 (OBE); Malaya, 1954-56 (despatches); Germany, 1958-61; Ghana, 1961; Germany, 1962-64; DDMS, HQ BAOR, 1968-69; DDMS, 1st British Corps, 1969-71; Dep. Dir-Gen., AMS, 1971-73. QHS 1972-75. OStJ 1971. *Recreations:* tennis, ski-ing.

Address: 12 Clare Avenue, Wokingham, Berkshire. *T:* Wokingham 786292.

IRVINE, John Ferguson; Permanent Secretary (Northern Ireland Civil Service), attached to Northern Ireland Office, since 1977; *b* 13 Nov. 1920; *s* of Joseph Ferguson Irvine and Helen Gardner; *m* 1945, Doris Partridge (*d* 1973); one *s* one *d. Educ:* Ardrossan Acad.; Glasgow Univ. (MA). RAF, 1941-46; Scottish Home Dept, 1946-48; NI Civil Service, 1948-66; Chief Exec., Ulster Transport Authority, 1966-68; Chief Exec., NI Transport Holding Co., 1968; NI Civil Service, 1969-; Dep. Sec., DoE, NI, 1974-76. Chm. Management Cttee, 1974-75, and Vice-Chm. General Council, 1975, Action Cancer; Chm., NI Marriage Guidance Council, 1976-. Select Vestry (Glebewarden) Church of Ireland, Gilnahirk. *Recreations:* dog breeding, football. *Address:* Collinholme, Ballyhanwood Road, Gilnahirk, Belfast. *T:* Belfast 654276.

IRVINE, Rev. Canon John Murray; Canon Residentiary, Prebendary of Hunderton, Chancellor and Librarian of Hereford Cathedral, and Director of Ordination Training in the Diocese of Hereford, since 1965; Warden of Readers, since 1976; *b* 19 Aug. 1924; *s* of Andrew Leicester Irvine and Eleanor Mildred (*née* Lloyd); *m* 1961, Pamela Shirley Brain; one *s* three *d. Educ:* Charterhouse; Magdalene Coll., Cambridge; Ely Theological Coll. BA 1946, MA 1949. Deacon, 1948; Priest, 1949; Curate of All Saints, Poplar, 1948-53; Chaplain of Sidney Sussex Coll., Cambridge, 1953-60; Selection Sec. of CACTM, 1960-65. *Address:* The Cathedral Close, Hereford HR1 2NG. *T:* Hereford 66193.

IRVINE, Norman Forrest, QC 1973; a Recorder of the Crown Court, since 1974; *b* 29 Sept. 1922; *s* of William Allan Irvine and Dorcas Forrest; *m* 1964, Mary Lilian Patricia Edmunds (*née* Constable); one *s. Educ:* High Sch. of Glasgow; Glasgow Univ. BL 1941. Solicitor (Scotland), 1943. Served War, 1942-45: Lieut Royal Signals, Staff Captain. HM Claims Commn, 1945-46; London Claims Supt, Provincial Insurance Co. Ltd, 1950-52. Called to Bar, Gray's Inn, 1955. *Recreations:* reading, piano, walking, swimming. *Address:* (chambers) 2 Garden Court, Temple, EC4Y 9BL. *Clubs:* MCC, Hurlingham.

IRVINE, Dr Robin Orlando Hamilton, FRCP, FRACP; Vice-Chancellor, University of Otago, Dunedin, New Zealand, since 1973; *b* 15 Sept. 1929; *s* of late Claude Turner Irvine; *m* 1957, Elizabeth Mary, *d* of late Herbert Gray Corbett; one *s* two *d. Educ:* Wanganui Collegiate Sch.; Univ. of Otago. Otago University Med. Sch., 1948-53; MB, ChB, 1953; MD (NZ), 1958; FRCP, FRACP. House Phys., Auckland Hosp., 1954; Dept of Medicine, Univ. of Otago: Research Asst, 1955; Asst Lectr and Registrar, 1956-57. Leverhulme Research Scholar, Middlesex Hosp., London, 1958; Registrar, Postgraduate Medical Sch., London, 1959-60; Isaacs Medical Research Fellow, Auckland Hosp., 1960-61; Med. Tutor and Med. Specialist, Auckland Hosp., 1962-63; Lectr, Sen. Lectr in Med., Univ. of Otago, 1963-67; Associate Prof., 1968; Clinical Dean and Personal Professor, Univ. of Otago Medical Sch., 1969-72. Consultant, Asian Development Bank, 1974-. Member: Otago Hosp. Bd, 1969-; Med. Educn Cttee of Med. Council of NZ, 1969-73; Social Council of Nat. Develt Council of NZ, 1971-74; Social Develt Council, 1974-; Commn for the Future, 1976-; NZ Planning Council, 1977-; Otago Polytech. Council, 1973-; Dunedin Teachers Coll. Council, 1973-; NZ Adv. Cttee, Nuffield Foundn, 1973-. Trustee McMillan Trust, 1973-. Hon. ADC 1969, and Hon. Physician 1970, to the Governor-General, Sir Arthur Porritt. Dr *hc* Edinburgh, 1976. *Publications:* various papers on high blood pressure, renal med. and medical educn. *Recreations:* walking, reading, music. *Address:* University Lodge, St Leonards, Dunedin, New Zealand. *T:* 87.241. *Club:* Fernhill (Dunedin).

IRVINE, Very Rev. Thomas Thurstan; Dean of the United Diocese of St Andrew's, Dunkeld and Dunblane, since 1959; Rector of St John's, Perth, since 1966; *b* 19 June 1913; 5th *s* of late William Fergusson Irvine; *m* 1943, Elizabeth Marian, er *d* of late Francis More, CA, Edinburgh; five *d. Educ:* Shrewsbury; Magdalen Coll., Oxford. BA 2nd Class History, 1934; Diploma in Theology, 1935; MA 1938. Cuddesdon Coll., 1937; deacon, 1938, priest, 1939, St Albans; Curate, All Saints, Hertford, 1938-40; Precentor, St Ninian's Cathedral, Perth, 1940-43; Priest in charge, Lochgelly, 1943-45; Rector of Bridge of Allan, 1945-47; Rector of Callander, 1947-66. Examining Chaplain to Bishop of St Andrews, 1950. *Recreations:* fishing, walking. *Address:* St John's Rectory, Dupplin Terrace, Perth. *T:* Perth 21379.

IRVINE, Prof. William Tait; Consultant Surgeon to the Libyan Government, since 1973; *b* 19 March 1925; *s* of George Irvine; *m* 1950, May Warburton; two *d. Educ:* by his father and at Univs

of Glasgow, McGill and Minnesota, USA. BSc 1944, MB, ChB, 1947, FRCSE 1950, FRCS 1952, ChM (Hons) 1956, MD (Hons) 1957. Archibald Fellow in Surgery, McGill Univ., 1954; Mayo Foundation Fellow, Mayo Clinic, USA, 1955; Lectr in Surgery, Univ. of Glasgow, 1956; Asst Surg., The London Hospital, E1, 1957-60; Prof. of Surgery, Univ. of London, at St Mary's Hosp., 1960-72. *Publications:* various papers on surgical subjects. Editor: Modern Trends in Surgery; Scientific Basis of Surgery. *Recreations:* walking, reading. *Address:* 12 Kildare Terrace, W2.

IRVINE SMITH, Thomas, OBE 1945; DL; *b* 27 Oct. 1908; er *s* of late Sir Thomas Smith and of Lady (Elsie) Smith (*née* Ledgard); *m* 1942, Mary Peters. *Educ:* Fettes Coll., Edinburgh; Oriel Coll., Oxford. MA 1935. War Service, 1941-45: commnd 8th Gurkha Rifles; GHQ, MEF; ME Supply Centre, 1943; Liaison Officer with Govt of India, 1944-45; Lt-Col 1945. Business in Cawnpore, India, 1931-47; Mem. London Stock Exchange, 1949-69. Surrey County Council: Mem., 1955-77; Alderman, 1965-74; Vice-Chm., 1969-72; Chm., 1972-74; 1st Chm. of re-constituted Council, 1973-75; Chm., Surrey Educn Cttee, 1965-72. Member: Court, London Univ., 1967-; Council, Surrey Univ., 1966- (Chm., 1975-); Council, Royal Holloway Coll., 1970-; Murray Cttee, London Univ., 1970-72; Governor: Ottershaw Sch., 1959- (Chm. 1961-72); Gordon Boys' Sch., 1965-. DL Surrey, 1973; High Sheriff, Surrey, 1976-77. *Recreation:* gardening. *Address:* Titlarks Hill Lodge, Sunningdale, Berks. *T:* Ascot 22334.

IRVING, Charles Graham; MP (C) Cheltenham, since Oct. 1974; Director of Public Relations, Dowty Group Ltd (30 companies), since 1947; Alderman, County and District Councillor; *b* 4 May 1926. *Educ:* Glengarth Sch., Cheltenham; Lucton Sch., Hereford. Mem. Cheltenham Borough Council, 1947-74 (Alderman 1959-May 1967, and Sept. 1967-74); Mem., Cheltenham DC, 1974-; Mem. Gloucestershire CC, 1948- (Chm., Social Services Cttee, 1974-); Mayor of Cheltenham, 1958-60 and 1971-72; Dep. Mayor, 1959-63; Alderman of Gloucestershire County, 1965-74; Contested (C): Bilston, Staffs, 1970; Kingswood, Glos, Feb. 1974; Member Cons. Parly Cttees: Aviation; Social Services; Mem., Select Cttee on Administration; Vice-Chm., All Party Cttee CHAR. Pres., Cheltenham Young Conservatives. Dir, Cheltenham Art and Literary Festival Co. (responsible for the only contemp. Festival of Music in England); Founder Mem., Univ. Cttee for Gloucestershire; Pres., Cheltenham and Dist Hotels' Assoc. Member: Bridgehead Housing Assoc. Ltd; Nat. Council for the Care and Resettlement of Offenders (Nat. Dep. Chm., 1974); (Chm.) NACRO Regional Council for South West; Nat. Council of St Leonard's Housing Assoc. Ltd; (Chm.) SW Midlands Housing Assoc. Ltd; SW Regional Hosp. Bd, 1971-72; Glos AHA, 1974-; (Chm.) Cheltenham and Dist Housing Assoc. Ltd, 1972; (Chm.) Cheltenham Dist Local Govt Re-Organisation Cttee, 1972; Founder and Chm., Nat. Victims Assoc., 1973; Chm., Stonham Housing Assoc., 1976-. Chairman: Irving Hotels Ltd; Hamill Toms Public Relations Co. Ltd; Irving Engineering Co. Mem. NUJ; MIPR 1964. Freedom, Borough of Cheltenham, 1977. *Publications:* pamphlets (as Chm. SW Region of NACRO and SW Midlands Housing Assoc. Ltd, 1970-73) include: Prisoner and Industry; After-care in the Community; Penal Budgeting; What about the Victim; Dosser's Dream—Planner's Nightmare. Pioneered Frontsheet (1st prison newspaper); reported in national papers, Quest, Social Services, Glos. Life, etc. *Recreations:* antiques, social work. *Address:* Drake House, Cheltenham, Glos. *T:* Cheltenham 23083. *Club:* Constitutional.

IRVING, Clifford; Chairman, Executive Council, Isle of Man Government, since 1977; Member, House of Keys, 1955-61 and since 1966; Acting Speaker, House of Keys, since 1971; *b* 24 May 1914; *s* of late William Radcliffe Irving and Mabel Henrietta (*née* Cottier); *m* 1941, Nora, *d* of Harold Page, Luton; one *s* one *d. Educ:* Isle of Man; Canada. Chairman: IOM Tourist Bd, 1971-; IOM Sports Council, 1971-. *Recreations:* powerboating, angling. *Address:* Highfield, Belmont Hill, Douglas, Isle of Man. *T:* Douglas 3652.

IRVING, David Blair; Chairman, London Electricity Board, 1956-68; *b* 9 Nov. 1903; *s* of late Mitchell B. Irving, Sorn, Ayrshire, and Mary Ross, Broadford, Isle of Skye; *m* 1933, Isabel Gibson; one *s. Educ:* Ayr Academy. BSc Hons (London), 1923. British Thomson-Houston Co. Ltd; trained Rugby; subseq. positions in London, Sheffield, Bombay and Calcutta. Joined Central Electricity Bd, 1932, and London Electricity Bd at Vesting Day, 1 April 1948: Chief Engineer, Irving-May 1953; Dep. Chm., 1953-56. MIEE, 1945; FIEE, 1966; Mem. Société des Ingénieurs Civils de France, 1949-70; Mem. Royal Institution, 1957-69. Chm., British Electrical Development Assoc., 1960-61; Chm., Power Division IEE, 1962-63. Governor, Ashridge

Management Coll., 1965-68. *Publications:* papers to British and internat. engineering and scientific bodies. *Recreation:* golf. *Address:* Nettlecombe, Poughill, Bude, North Cornwall. *T:* Bude 3496. *Club:* Caledonian.

IRVING, David J. M.; *see* Mill Irving.

IRVING, Rear-Adm. Sir Edmund (George), KBE 1966 (OBE 1944); CB 1962; Hydrographer of the Navy, 1960-66, retired; *b* 5 April 1910; *s* of George Clerk Irving, British North Borneo, and Ethel Mary Frances (*née* Poole), Kimberley, SA; *m* 1936, Margaret Scudamore Edwards (*d* 1974); one *s* one *d. Educ:* St Anthony's, Eastbourne; RN College, Dartmouth. Joined HMS Royal Oak, as Cadet and Midshipman, 1927; Sub-Lieut's Courses, 1930-31; HMS Kellett Surveying Service, Dec. 1931 (various surveying ships); HMS Franklin, in command, 1944; Hydrographic Dept, 1946; HMS Sharpshooter, in command, 1948; Hydrographic Dept, 1949; HMS Dalrymple, in command, 1950; HMS Vidal, in command, 1953; Hydrographic Dept, Asst Hydrographer, 1954; HMS Vidal, in command, Oct. 1956; Hydrographic Dept, Asst Hydrographer, 1959. Acting Conservator of the River Mersey, 1975-. ADC, 1960. Trustee, Nat. Maritime Museum, 1972-. FRGS; FRICS; FRSA. Patron's Medal, RGS, 1976. *Recreation:* golf. *Address:* Camer Green, Meopham, Kent. *T:* Meopham 813253. *Club:* Army and Navy.

IRVING, Prof. Harry Munroe Napier Hetherington; Professor of Inorganic and Structural Chemistry, University of Leeds, 1961-71, Professor Emeritus, since 1972; *b* 19 Nov. 1905; *s* of John and Clara Irving; *m* 1st, 1934, Monica Mary Wildsmith (*d* 1972); no *c*; 2nd, 1975, Dr Anne Mawby. *Educ:* St Bees Sch., Cumberland; The Queen's Coll., Oxford. BA 1927; First Class in Final Honour Sch. (Chemistry), 1928; MA, DPhil 1930; DSc 1958 (all Oxon); LRAM 1930. Univ. Demonstrator in Chemistry, Oxford, 1934-61; Lectr in Organic Chemistry, The Queen's Coll., 1930-34; Fellow and Tutor, St Edmund Hall, 1938-51; Vice-Principal, 1951-61; Emeritus-Fellow, 1961-. Mem. Chem. Soc. 1935- (Council, 1954, Perkin Elmer Award, 1974); Mem. Soc. for Analytical Chemists, 1950- (Council, 1952-57, 1965-67; Vice-Pres. 1955-57; Gold Medal, 1971); Fellow Royal Inst. of Chemistry, 1948- (Council, 1950-52, 1962-65; Vice-Pres. 1965-67). Has lectured extensively in America, Africa and Europe; broadcasts on scientific subjects. Hon. DTech Brunel Univ., 1970. *Publications:* (trans.) Schwarzenbach and Flaschka's Complexometric Titrations; Short History of Analytical Chemistry, 1974; numerous papers in various learned jls. *Recreations:* music, foreign travel, ice-skating. *Address:* 1 North Grange Mount, Leeds LS6 2BY.

IRVING, James Tutin, MA Oxon and Cantab, MD, PhD Cantab; Professor of Physiology in the School of Dental Medicine at Harvard University and the Forsyth Dental Center, 1961-68, Professor Emeritus, 1968, Visiting Lecturer in Oral Biology, 1973-77; *b* Christchurch, New Zealand, 3 May 1902; *m* 1937, Janet, *d* of Hon. Nicholas O'Connor, New York. *Educ:* Christ's Coll., New Zealand; Caius Coll., Cambridge; Trinity Coll., Oxford; Guy's Hospital. Double First Class Hons, Nat. Sci. Tripos, Cambridge, 1923-24; Scholar and Prizeman, Caius Coll., 1923; Benn. W. Levy and Frank Smart Student, 1924-26; Beit Memorial Fellow, 1926-28; Lecturer in Physiology, Bristol Univ., 1931, and Leeds Univ., 1934; Head of Physiology Dept, Rowett Research Inst., and part-time lecturer, Aberdeen Univ., 1936; Prof. of Physiology, Cape Town Univ., 1939-53, Fellow 1948; Professor of Experimental Odontology, and Dir of the Joint CSIR and Univ. of Witwatersrand Dental Research Unit, 1953-59; Prof. of Anatomy, Harvard Sch. of Dental Med., 1959-61. Visiting Professor: Univ. of Illinois Dental Sch. 1947 and 1956; Univ. of Pennsylvania, 1951; Univ. of California, 1956. Editor, Archives of Oral Biology, 1962-. AM (Hon.) Harvard. Late Hon. Physiologist to Groote Schuur Hosp.; Fellow Odont. Soc. S Africa. Hon. Life Mem. of New York Academy of Sciences. Mem. of Soc. of Sigma Xi. Hon. Mem. of Soc. of Omicron Kappa Upsilon. S African Medal for war services (non-military), 1948. Isaac Schour Meml Award for Res. in Anatomical Scis, 1972. *Publications:* Calcium Metabolism, 1957; Calcium and Phosphorus Metabolism, 1973; many papers in physiological and medical journals, chiefly on nutrition, and bone and tooth formation; also publications on nautical history. *Recreations:* music, gardening, nautical research. *Address:* Harvard School of Dental Medicine, 188 Longwood Avenue, Boston, Mass 02115, USA; Rockmarge, Prides Crossing, Mass 01965, USA. *Clubs:* Athenæum; Inanda (Johannesburg).

IRVING, Prof. John; Freeland Professor of Natural Philosophy, University of Strathclyde, Glasgow, since 1961; *b* 22 Dec. 1920; *s* of John Irving and Margaret Kent Aird; *m* 1948, Monica Cecilia Clarke; two *s. Educ:* St John's Grammar Sch.; Hamilton Academy; Glasgow Univ. MA (1st Class Hons in Maths and Nat. Phil.), Glasgow Univ., 1940; PhD (Mathematical Physics), Birmingham Univ., 1951. Lectr, Stow Coll., Glasgow, 1944-45; Lectr in Maths, Univ. of St Andrews 1945-46; Lectr in Mathematical Physics, University of Birmingham, 1946-49; Nuffield Research Fellow (Nat. Phil.), University of Glasgow, 1949-51; Sen. Lectr in Applied Maths, University of Southampton, 1951-59; Prof. of Theoretical Physics and Head of Dept of Applied Mathematics and Theor. Physics University of Cape Town, 1959-61. Dean of Sch. of Mathematics and Physics, Strathclyde Univ., 1964-69. *Publications:* Mathematics in Physics and Engineering, 1959 (New York); contrib. to: Proc. Physical Soc.; Philosophical Magazine, Physical Review. *Recreations:* gardening, motoring. *Address:* Department of Natural Philosophy, University of Strathclyde, John Anderson Building, 107 Rotten Row, Glasgow G4 0NG. *T:* 041-552 4400.

IRVING, Laurence Henry Forster, OBE; RDI 1939; *b* 11 April 1897; *s* of late H. B. Irving, actor and author; *m* 1920, Rosalind Woolner; one *s* one *d. Educ:* by Thomas Pellatt; Royal Academy Schools. Served in RNAS and RAF, 1914-19 (Croix de Guerre, France); rejoined RAF Oct. 1939; served on Staff of British Air Forces in France, 1940 (despatches), and in 2nd Tactical Air Force, France, Belgium, 1943-44. Dir of the Times Publishing Co., 1946-62. Exhibited pictures at Royal Academy; held four exhibitions at the Fine Art Soc., 1925, 1928, 1936, 1950, and at Agnew and Sons, 1957; Art Dir to Douglas Fairbanks, 1928 and 1929, for film productions of The Iron Mask and The Taming of the Shrew; has designed a number of stage and film productions, including Pygmalion, Lean Harvest, The Good Companions, Punchinello, The First Gentleman, Marriage à la Mode, Hamlet (Old Vic), 1950, Man and Superman, 1951; The Happy Marriage, 1952; Pygmalion, 1953; The Wild Duck, 1955; produced and designed film production of Lefanu's Uncle Silas. Master of Faculty, RDI, 1963-65. *Publications:* Windmills and Waterways, 1927; Henry Irving; The Actor and his World, 1951; The Successors, 1967; The Precarious Crust, 1971; edited and illustrated: The Maid of Athens; Bligh's narrative of The Mutiny of the Bounty; A Selection of Hakluyt's Voyages; illustrated: Masefield's Philip the King; Conrad's The Mirror of the Sea; St Exupery's Flight to Arras. *Address:* The Lea, Wittersham, Kent. *Club:* Garrick.
See also Sir Felix Brunner.

IRVING, Robert Augustine, DFC and Bar, 1943; Musical Director, New York City Ballet, New York, 1958; *b* 28 Aug. 1913; *s* of late R. L. G. Irving; unmarried. *Educ:* Winchester; New Coll., Oxford; Royal College of Music. Répétiteur, Royal Opera House, 1936; Music master, Winchester Coll., 1936-40. RA, 1940-41; RAF (Coastal Command), 1941-45. Associate Conductor, BBC Scottish Orchestra, 1945-48; Conductor, Royal Opera House (The Royal Ballet), 1949-58. Many recordings for HMV and Decca, with Philharmonia and Royal Philharmonic Orchestras, also public concerts with these orchestras and London Philharmonic Orchestra. Wrote music for film, Floodtide, 1948; for New York production of As You Like It, 1949. *Recreations:* racing, bridge, mountaineering. *Address:* c/o New York City Ballet, New York State Theatre, Columbus Avenue and 62nd Street, New York, NY 10023, USA. *Clubs:* Brooks's, Alpine.

IRVING, Rt. Hon. Sydney, PC 1969; DL; MP (Lab and Co-op) Dartford, 1955-70, and since Feb. 1974; *b* 1 July 1918; *s* of Sydney Irving, Newcastle upon Tyne; *m* 1942, Mildred, *d* of Chariton Weedy, Morpeth, Northumberland; one *s* one *d* (and one *s* decd). *Educ:* Pendower Sch., Newcastle upon Tyne; London School of Economics, University of London. BSc (Econ.); DipEd. War Service, 1939-46: West Yorks Regt, Major. Chairman Southern Regional Council of Labour Party, 1965-67. Alderman, Dartford Borough Council; Mem. North-West Kent Divisional Executive, Kent Education Cttee, 1952-74. Opposition Whip (S and S Western), 1959-64; Treasurer of the Household and Deputy Chief Government Whip, 1964-66; Dep. Chm. of Ways and Means, 1966-68; Chm. of Ways and Means, and Deputy Speaker, 1968-70; Chairman Select Committees: on Procedure, 1974-; on Direct Elections to EEC, 1976-; Chm., Manifesto Gp, 1976-; Member: Cttee of Privileges, 1974-; Select Cttee on Members' Interests, 1974-; Select Cttee on the Member for Walsall, 1975; Liaison Cttee, Parly Lab Party, 1976-. Mem. CPA delegations: to Hong Kong and Ceylon, 1958; to Council of Europe and WEU, 1963-64; to Canada, 1974; Leader All Party Delegn: to Malta, 1965; to Israel, 1975. Mem. Exec. Cttee, Council European Municipalities, 1972-. Chairman: Dartford Dist Council, 1973-74; Dartford and Darenth Hosp. Management Cttee, 1972-74; Mem., Kent County Jt Cttees Chairmen, 1975. Pres., Thames-side Assoc. of Teachers, NUT, 1955; Mem. Min. of Education's Adv. Cttee on Handicapped Children, 1957-67; a Dep. Pro-Chancellor, Univ. of Kent, 1968-71; Dir, Foundn Fund, Univ. of Kent, 1971-74. DL Kent, 1976. *Address:* 10 Tynedale Close, Dartford, Kent. *T:* 25105.

IRWIN, Lord; Charles Edward Peter Neil Wood; *b* 14 March 1944; *s* and *heir* of 2nd Earl of Halifax, *qv*; *m* 1976, Camilla, *d* of Col C. F. J. Younger, *qv*; one *s*. *Educ:* Eton; Christ Church, Oxford. Contested (C) Dearne Valley, Feb. and Oct. 1974. *Heir: s* Hon. James Charles Wood, *b* 24 Aug. 1977. *Address:* Garrowby, York; 29 Tregunter Road, SW10. *Club:* Turf.

IRWIN, Maj.-Gen. Brian St George, CB 1975; Director General, Ordnance Survey, 1969-77, retired; *b* 16 Sept. 1917; *s* of late Lt-Col Alfred Percy Bulteel Irwin, DSO, and late Eileen Irwin (*née* Holberton); *m* 1939, Audrey Lilla, *d* of late Lt-Col H. B. Steen, IMS; two *s*. *Educ:* Rugby Sch.; RMA Woolwich; Trinity Hall, Cambridge (MA). Commnd in RE, 1937; war service in Western Desert, 1941-43 (despatches); Sicily and Italy, 1943-44 (despatches); Greece, 1944-45; subseq. in Cyprus, 1956-59 (despatches) and 1961-63; Dir of Military Survey, MoD, 1965-69. Col Comdt, RE, 1977-. FRICS (Council 1969-70, 1972-76); FRGS (Council 1966-70; Vice-Pres., 1974-77). *Recreations:* sailing, gardening, genealogy. *Address:* 16 Northwood House, Swan Green, Lyndhurst, Hants SO4 7DT. *T:* Lyndhurst 3499. *Club:* Army and Navy.

IRWIN, Francis (Charles), QC 1974; a Recorder (formerly Recorder of Folkestone), since 1971; *b* 5 June 1928; *s* of late R. Stanley Irwin; *m* 1955, Rosalind Derry Wykes, *d* of late Canon W. M. Wykes, Sedgefield, Co. Durham; four *s* one *d*. *Educ:* Glasgow Academy; Queen's Coll., Oxford (Scholar, BA). Served in Army, 1946-48. Called to Bar, Middle Temple, 1953; SE Circuit. Prosecuting Counsel, GPO (SE Circuit), 1964-69; Dep. Chm., W Suffolk QS, 1967-71. Contested (C): Bridgeton Div. of Glasgow, 1950; Small Heath Div. of Birmingham, 1951. *Address:* Hill House, Pebmarsh, Halstead, Essex. *T:* Earls Colne 2586; 8 New Square, Lincoln's Inn, WC2A 3QP. *T:* 01-242 4986.

IRWIN, Ian Sutherland; Managing Director, Scottish Transport Group, since 1975; *b* Glasgow, 20 Feb. 1933; *s* of Andrew Campbell Irwin and Elizabeth Ritchie Arnott; *m* 1959, Margaret Miller Maureen Irvine; two *s*. *Educ:* Whitehill Sen. Secondary Sch., Glasgow; Glasgow Univ. BL; CA, IPFA, FCIT. Commercial Man., Scottish Omnibuses Ltd, 1960-64; Gp Accountant, Scottish Bus Gp, 1964-69; Gp Sec., Scottish Transport Gp, 1969-75; Scottish Bus Gp Ltd (and all subsids) and Caledonian MacBrayne Ltd (and all subsids): Exec. Dir, 1972-; Chm., 1975-; Director: Swan National (Scotland) Ltd, 1974; British Transport Advertising Ltd. Vice Pres., Confedn Brit. Road Passenger Transport, 1975-; Mem. Exec. Cttee, Scottish Road Passenger Transport Assoc., 1975-. Governor, British Transport Staff Coll. *Publications:* various papers. *Recreations:* cricket, squash, reading, gardening. *Address:* Baldornie, 4 Glenlockhart Bank, Edinburgh EH14 1BL. *T:* 031-443 2108. *Club:* Colinton Castle Sports.

IRWIN, Sir James (Campbell), Kt 1971; OBE 1945; ED 1947; psc; FRIBA, LFRAIA; Partner in Woods, Bagot, Laybourne-Smith & Irwin, Architects, Adelaide, 1930-74; *b* 23 June 1906; *s* of Francis James and Margaret Irwin; *m* 1933, Kathleen Agnes, *d* of G. W. Orr, Sydney; one *s* one *d*. *Educ:* Queen's Sch., N Adelaide; St Peter's Coll., Adelaide; St Mark's Coll., Univ. of Adelaide (Hon. Fellow, 1973). Served War, AIF, 1940-46; Lt-Col RAA. Col Comdt, RAA, 1966-71. Mem. Adelaide City Council, 1935-72 (except for war years); Lord Mayor of Adelaide, 1963-66; Mem. Nat. Capital Planning Cttee, Canberra, 1964-70. President: RAIA, 1962-63; Adelaide Festival of Arts, 1964-66 (Chm. 1964-73); SA Sch. of Art, 1966-72; Home for Incurables, 1966-; Pioneers Assoc. of S Australia, 1968-73. *Address:* 35 Barnard Street, North Adelaide, SA 5006, Australia. *T:* 2672839. *Clubs:* Adelaide, Naval Military and Air Force of SA (Adelaide).

IRWIN, John Conran; Keeper, Oriental Department, Victoria and Albert Museum, since 1970; *b* 5 Aug. 1917; *s* of late John Williamson Irwin; *m* 1947, Helen Hermione Scott (*née* Fletcher), *d* of late Herbert Bristowe Fletcher; three *s*. *Educ:* Canford Sch., Wimborne, Dorset. Temp. commission, Gordon Highlanders, 1939. Private Sec. to Gov. of Bengal, 1942-45; Asst Keeper, Victoria and Albert Museum, 1946; Exec. Sec., Royal Academy Winter Exhibition of Indian Art, 1947-48; UNESCO Expert on museum planning: on mission to Indonesia, 1956; to Malaya, 1962; Keeper, Indian Section, Victoria and Albert Museum, 1959-70. British Acad. Travelling Fellowship, 1974-75. Lectures: Birdwood Meml, 1972; Tagore Meml, 1973; Lowell Inst., Boston, Mass, 1974; guest lectr, Collège de France, 1976. FRSA 1972; FRAS 1946; FRAI 1977. *Publications:* Jamini Roy, 1944; Indian art (section on sculpture), 1947; The Art of India and Pakistan (sections on bronzes and textiles), 1951, Shawls, 1955; Origins of Chintz, 1970; (with M. Hall) Indian Painted and Printed Fabrics, 1972; Indian Embroideries, 1974; articles in Encyclopædia Britannica, Chambers's

Encyclopædia, Jl of Royal Asiatic Soc., Burlington Magazine, etc. *Recreations:* music, walking. *Address:* Ashford Chace, Steep, Petersfield, Hants GU32 1AB. *T:* Petersfield 4746.

ISAAC, Alfred James; Director of Home Regional Services, Department of the Environment, 1971-75; *b* 1 Aug. 1919; *s* of Alfred Jabez Isaac and Alice Marie Isaac (both British); *m* 1943, Beryl Marjorie Rist; one *s* two *d*. *Educ:* Maidenhead Grammar Sch. Post Office Engineering Dept, 1936-49. Served War, RAFVR, Flt Lt (pilot), Coastal Command, 1941-46. Min. of Works, Asst Principal, 1949; Regional Dir, Southern Region, 1960-67; Dir of Professional Staff Management, 1967. *Recreations:* amateur radio, cycling, fishing. *Address:* Nutkin Cottage, Chestnut Avenue, Wokingham, Berks RG11 2UU. *T:* Wokingham 783992. *Clubs:* Civil Service; Victoria.

ISAAC, Anthony John Gower; on secondment to HM Treasury, since 1976; *b* 21 Dec. 1931; *s* of Ronald and Kathleen Mary Gower Isaac; *m* 1963, Olga Elizabeth Sibley; one *s* two *d* (and two *d* decd). *Educ:* Malvern Coll.; King's Coll., Cambridge (BA). HM Treasury, 1953-70: Private Sec. to Chief Sec. to Treasury, 1964-66; Inland Revenue, 1971; Comr of Inland Revenue, 1973-76. *Recreations:* gardening, fishing. *Address:* Moonsfield, Brenchley, Kent. *T:* Brenchley 2810.

ISAAC, Maurice Laurence Reginald, MA; Headmaster, Latymer Upper School, Hammersmith, W6, since 1971; *b* 26 April 1928; *s* of late Frank and Lilian Isaac; *m* 1954, Anne Fielden; three *d*. *Educ:* Selhurst Grammar Sch., Croydon; Magdalene Coll., Cambridge. BA Hist. Tripos, 1950; MA 1955, Cambridge; Certif. in Educn, 1952. Asst Master: Liverpool Collegiate Sch., 1952-56; Bristol Grammar Sch., 1956-62; Head of History, Colchester Royal Grammar Sch., 1962-65; Headmaster, Yeovil Sch., 1966-71. *Publications:* A History of Europe, 1870-1950, 1960; contributor to The Teaching of History, 1965. *Address:* Latymer Upper School, Hammersmith, W6 9LR. *T:* 01-741 1851.

ISAAC, Prof. Peter Charles Gerald; Professor of Civil and Public Health Engineering, since 1964, and Head of Department of Civil Engineering, since 1970, University of Newcastle upon Tyne; Partner, J. D. & D. M. Watson (consulting engineers); *b* 21 Jan. 1921, *s* of Herbert George Isaac and Julienne Geneviève (*née* Hattenberger); *m* 1950, Marjorie Eleanor White; one *s* one *d*. *Educ:* Felsted Sch.; London and Harvard Universities. BSc(Eng), SM. Asst Engineer, GWR, 1940-45; Lecturer in Civil Engineering, 1946; Senior Lecturer in Public Health Engineering, 1953, Reader, 1960, Univ. of Durham; Dean of Faculty of Applied Science, Univ. of Newcastle upon Tyne, 1969-73. Mem., Working Party on Sewage Disposal, 1969-70. Chm., History of the Book Trade in the North, 1965-. Member of Council: ICE, 1968-71, 1972-75; Bibliographical Soc., 1970-74; IPHE, 1973- (Pres., 1977-78); Pres., Occupational Hygiene Soc., 1962-63. Trustee, Asian Inst. Technology, Bangkok, 1968-. Director: Thorne's Students' Bookshop Ltd, 1969-74; Environmental Resources Ltd, 1972-74. FICE, FIWES, FIPHE, FIWPC. Clemens Herschel Prize in Applied Hydraulics, 1952; Telford Premium, 1957. *Publications:* Electric Resistance Strain Gauges (with W. B. Dobie), 1948; Public Health Engineering, 1953; Trade Wastes, 1957; Waste Treatment, 1960; River Management, 1967; William Davison of Alnwick: pharmacist and printer, 1968; Farm Wastes, 1970; Civil Engineering-The University Contribution, 1970; Management in Civil Engineering, 1971; Davison's Halfpenny Chapbooks, 1971; (ed) The Burman Alnwick Collection, 1973; contribs to various learned and technical jls. *Recreations:* bibliography, printing, Roman engineering. *Address:* The University, Newcastle upon Tyne NE1 7RU. *T:* Newcastle 28511. *Clubs:* National Liberal, Royal Commonwealth Society; Royal Scottish Automobile (Glasgow).

ISAACS, family name of Marquess of Reading.

ISAACS, Dame Albertha Madeline, DBE 1974; former Senator, now worker for the community, in the Bahamas; *b* Nassau, Bahamas, 18 April 1900; *d* of late Robert Hanna and Lilla (*née* Minns); *m*; three *s* one *d*. *Educ:* Cosmopolitan High Sch. and Victoria High Sch., Nassau. Member: Progressive Liberal Party, Senator, 1968-72; also of PLP's Nat. Gen. Council, and of Council of Women. Has joined a Good Samaritan Group. *Address:* c/o Progressive Liberal Party, Head Office, Nassau Court, Nassau, Bahamas.

ISAACS, Rt. Hon. George Alfred, PC 1945; DL, JP; Chairman Kingston County Bench 1943-45; *b* London, 1883. Past Alderman, Borough of Southwark; Mayor of Southwark, 1919-21; contested North Southwark, 1918; Gravesend, 1922; MP (Lab) Gravesend, 1923-24, North Southwark, 1929-31 and

1939-50, Southwark, 1950-Sept. 1959. Parl. Priv. Sec. to Sec. of State for Colonies, 1924, to Sec. of State for Dominions, 1929-31, to First Lord of the Admiralty, 1942-45; Minister of Labour and Nat. Service, 1945-Jan. 1951; Minister of Pensions, Jan.-Oct. 1951. Served on Govt's Departmental Cttee on Coroners and Departmental Cttee on Workmen's Compensation; also Mem. of Royal Commission on Workmen's Compensation. Sec. of Nat. Soc. of Operative Printers and Assistants, 1909-49; Past Pres., Printing and Kindred Trades Federation; Chm., Trades Union Congress General Council, 1945; Pres., World Trade Union Conference, London, 1945; Liveryman of the Worshipful Company of Stationers. Hon. Freeman of Borough of Southwark, 1957. JP 1929, DL 1947, Surrey. *Publication:* The Story of the Newspaper Printing Press. *Address:* Mole Cottage, 166 Portsmouth Road, Cobham, Surrey.

ISAACS, Jeremy Israel; Director of Programmes, Thames Television, since 1974; *b* 28 Sept. 1932; *s* of Isidore Isaacs and Sara Jacobs; *m* 1958, Tamara (*née* Weinreich), Capetown; one *s* one *d*. *Educ:* Glasgow Acad.; Merton Coll., Oxford (MA). Television Producer, Granada TV (What the Papers Say, All Our Yesterdays), 1958; Associated-Rediffusion (This Week), 1963; BBC TV (Panorama), 1965; Controller of Features, Associated Rediffusion, 1967; Controller of Features, Thames TV, 1968-74; Producer, The World at War, Thames TV, 1974. Desmond Davis Award for outstanding creative contrib. to television, 1972; George Polk Meml Award, 1973. *Recreations:* reading, walking, listening to music, sleeping. *Address:* 66 Wavendon Avenue, W4 4NS.

ISAACS, Mrs Nathan; *see* Lawrence, E. M.

ISHAM, Sir Ian (Vere Gyles), 13th Bt *cr* 1627; *b* 17 July 1923; *s* of Lt-Col Vere Arthur Richard Isham, MC (*d* 1968) and Edith Irene (*d* 1973), *d* of Harry Brown; *S* cousin, Sir Gyles Isham, 12th Bt, 1976. Served War of 1939-45, Captain RAC. *Heir: b* Norman Murray Crawford Isham [*b* 28 Jan. 1930; *m* 1956, Joan, *d* of late Leonard James Genet; two *s* one *d*]. *Address:* 40 Turnpike Link, Croydon, Surrey CR0 5NX.

ISHERWOOD, Christopher; author; *b* High Lane, Cheshire, 26 Aug. 1904; *s* of Lt-Col Francis B. Isherwood and Kathleen Machell-Smith. *Educ:* Repton Sch.; Corpus Christi, Cambridge. Private Tutor in London, 1926-27; Medical Student, Kings, London, 1928-29; Teacher of English, Berlin, 1930-33; Journalism, etc. in London, 1934-36; Film-Script work for Gaumont-British; went to China with W. H. Auden, 1938; worked for Metro-Goldwyn-Mayer, 1940, American Friends Service Cttee, 1941-42; editor of Vedanta and the West, 1943. Became a US citizen, 1946; travelled in South America, 1947-48. Elected Mem. US Nat. Inst. of Arts and Letters, 1949. Guest Prof., Los Angeles State Coll., and at University of California, Santa Barbara, 1959-62; Regents' Prof., University of California, 1965-66. Brandeis Medal for Fiction, 1975. *Publications: fiction:* All the Conspirators, 1928; The Memorial, 1932; Mr Norris Changes Trains, 1935; Goodbye to Berlin, 1939 (I Am a Camera, play by John van Druten, perf. US 1951, and Cabaret, musical by Joe Masteroff, John Kander and Fred Ebb, perf. US 1966, both based on stories from Goodbye to Berlin); Prater Violet, 1945; The World in The Evening, 1954; Down There on a Visit, 1962; A Single Man, 1964; A Meeting by the River, 1967 (play, adapted from the novel, by C. I. and Don Bachardy, perf. US, 1972); The Berlin of Sally Bowles, 1975; *biography:* Ramakrishna and his Disciples, 1965; *autobiography:* Lions and Shadows, 1938; Kathleen and Frank, 1971; Christopher and His Kind, 1977; *plays:* The Dog Beneath the Skin (with W. H. Auden), 1935; Ascent of F6 (with W. H. Auden), 1937; On the Frontier (with W. H. Auden), 1938; *travel:* Journey to a War (with W. H. Auden), 1939; The Condor and the Cows, 1949; *miscellaneous:* Exhumations, 1966; *translation:* (with Swami Prabhavananda) The Bhagavad-Gita, 1944; (with Swami Prabhavananda) Shankara's Crest-Jewel of Discrimination, 1947; Baudelaire's Intimate Journals, 1947; (with Swami Prabhavananda) How to Know God: the Yoga Aphorisms of Patanjali, 1953. *Recreations:* usual. *Address:* 145 Adelaide Drive, Santa Monica, Calif 90402, USA.

ISHERWOOD, Rt. Rev. Harold, MVO 1955; OBE 1959; *b* 23 June 1907; *s* of James and Margaret Ellen Isherwood; *m* 1940, Hannah Mary Walters. *Educ:* Selwyn Coll., Cambridge; Ely Theol Coll. BA 1938, MA 1946. Deacon 1939; priest 1940; Curate of Beeston, Notts, 1939-43; Chaplain: Nat. Nautical Sch., Portishead, 1943-51; Helsinki and Moscow, 1951-54; Oslo, 1954-59; Brussels, 1959-70; Vicar General, Dio. Gibraltar and Jurisdiction of North and Central Europe, 1970-75; Canon of Gibraltar, 1971-74; Asst Bishop, Dio. Gibraltar, 1974-77; Auxiliary Bishop, 1977-. *Recreations:* music, cricket, Rugby and Association football, tennis. *Address:* St Faith's House, The Close, Chichester PO19 1QB.

ISLE OF WIGHT, Archdeacon of; *see* Carpenter, Ven. F. C.

ISLES, Maj.-Gen. Donald Edward, OBE 1968; Director-General of Weapons (Army), since 1975; Colonel, The Duke of Wellington's Regiment, since 1975; Colonel Commandant, The King's Division, since 1975; *b* 19 July 1924; *s* of Harold and Kathleen Isles; *m* 1948, Sheila Mary Stephens (formerly Thorpe); three *s* one *d*. *Educ:* Roundhay; Leeds Univ.; RMCS. MRAeS; MBIM. Italian campaign, with 1st Bn, Duke of Wellington's Regt, 1944-45; Palestine, Egypt, Sudan, Syria, with 1DWR, 1945-47; GSO2, HQ BAOR, 1955-58; Asst Mil. Attaché, Paris, 1963-65; CO, 1DWR, BAOR and UN Forces in Cyprus, 1965-67; AMS, MoD, 1968; Col GS, MoD, 1968-71; Col GS, Royal Armament Res. and Develt Estab., 1971-72; Dir of Munitions, Brit. Defence Staff Washington, 1972-75. *Recreations:* tennis, squash. *Address:* c/o Lloyds Bank Ltd, 6 Pall Mall, SW1. *Club:* Army and Navy.

ISMAY, Sir George, KBE 1947; CB 1939; *b* 1891; *s* of late George Ismay, Carlisle; *m* 1919, Jeanette May, *d* of John Lloyd, Tredegar, Mon; two *d*. *Educ:* private schools, Carlisle. Entered Treasury, 1911; Asst Sec., 1934; Sec. Macmillan Cttee on Finance and Industry, 1929-31; Comptroller and Accountant General, GPO, 1937; Asst Dir-General, 1942; Deputy Dir-Gen., General Post Office, 1947-52; Dir, Woolwich Equitable Building Society, 1952-72; served European War, 1915-19, in Queen's Westminster Rifles. *Address:* Newstead, 105 Golden Avenue, Angmering-on-Sea, West Sussex BN16 1QT. *T:* Rustington 2855.

ISMAY, Walter Nicholas; Managing Director, Worcester Parsons Ltd, since 1975; *b* 20 June 1921; *s* of John Ismay, Maryport, Cumberland. *Educ:* Taunton's Sch., Southampton; King's Coll., University of London (BSc). Royal Aircraft Establishment, 1939-40; Ministry of Supply, 1940-43; Served Army (Capt., General List), 1943-46; Imperial Chemical Industries, Metals Division, 1948-58 (Technical Dir, 1957-58); Dir, Yorkshire Imperial Metals, 1958-67; Dep. Chm. Yorkshire Imperial Plastics, 1966-67; Dep. Chm. and Man. Dir, Milton Keynes Develt Corp., 1967-71; McKechnie Britain Ltd, 1972-75. FIMechE. *Recreation:* sailing. *Address:* 72 Woodbourne, Augustus Road, Edgbaston, Birmingham B15 3PJ. *T:* 021-454 6564.

ISOLANI, Casimiro Peter Hugh Tomasi, CBE 1975 (OBE 1960; MBE 1945); MVO 1961; *b* 2 Sept. 1917; *s* of late Umberto Tomasi Isolani, Bologna, and late Georgiana Eleanor Lyle-Smyth, Great Barrow, Ches; *m* 1943, Karin Gunni Signe Zetterström, *d* of Henry Zetterström, Gothenburg; one *s*. *Educ:* Aldenham Sch.; Clare Coll., Cambridge (Sen. Foundn Schol.). Commnd RA 1940, Intell. Corps 1941; attached 1st Canadian Div., 1943 (Sicily, Italy landings); Psychol Warfare Br., 1944; GS1 (Civil Liaison, Liaison Italian Resistance), 1945; FO 1946; Vice-Consul, Bologna, 1946; Attaché, later 1st Sec. (Information), British Embassy, Rome, 1947-61; resigned Foreign Service; Dep. Dir, Inst. for Strategic Studies, 1961-63; rejoined Foreign Service; Regional Information Officer, Paris, 1963-72; Counsellor (Information), Brussels, 1972-77. *Address:* 44 Pont Street, SW1X 0AD. *T:* 01-584 1543. *Clubs:* Anglo Belgian; Cercle Royal Gaulois (Brussels).

ISPAHANI, Mirza Abol Hassan; Pakistan Ambassador to Afghanistan, since 1973; *b* 23 Jan. 1902; *s* of late Mirza Mohamed Ispahani and late Sakina Sultan; *m* 1st, 1930, Ameneh Sultan Shushtary; two *s* one *d*; 2nd, 1954, Ghamar Azimi. *Educ:* St John's Coll., Cambridge. Joined family business of M. M. Ispahani, 1925; was Dir of M. M. Ispahani Ltd, and other business undertakings; Pres., Muslim Chamber of Commerce, Calcutta; Leader, Indian Trade Delegation to Middle East, 1947. Elected to Calcutta Corporation, 1933; resigned to work for introduction of separate electorates in Calcutta Corp., 1935, re-elected, 1940, Dep. Mayor, 1941-42; Mem. Bengal Legislative Assembly, 1937-47; Mem. of All India Muslim League Working Cttee until end of 1947; Pakistan Constituent Assembly; represented Muslim League at New York Herald Tribune Forum, 1946; toured US as Personal Representative of Quaid-i-Azam, M. A. Jinnah; Ambassador of Pakistan to USA, 1947-52; Dep. Leader, Pakistan Delegn to UN, 1947; Leader Pakistan Delegn to Havana Conf. on Trade and Employment, 1947; Mem., Pakistan Delegn to UN (Jammu and Kashmir), 1947. High Comr for Pakistan in the UK, 1952-54; Minister of Industries and Commerce, 1954-55; Minister of Industries, Jan.-Aug. 1955; resigned and reverted to business; mem., Supreme Council, National Reconstruction Movement of Pakistan. Interested in sports, journalism and welfare work. *Publications:* 27 Days in China, 1960; Leningrad to Samarkand, 1961; Qaid-e-Azam Jinnah as I knew him, 2nd rev. edn, 1967; Quaid-e-Azam Mohammad Ali Jinnah—Ispahani Correspondence, 1936-48,

1977. *Recreations:* reading, writing. *Address:* 2 Reay Road, Karachi, Pakistan. *T:* 510665.

ISSERLIS, Alexander Reginald; Director of Investigations, Office of the Parliamentary Commissioner for Administration, since 1977; *b* 18 May 1922; *y s* of late Isaak Isserlis, Ilford, Essex; *m* 1949, Eleanor Mary Ord, *d* of late Prof. R. D. Laurie, Aberystwyth; two *d. Educ:* Ilford High Sch.; Keble Coll., Oxford. British and Indian Army, 1942-46. Entered Civil Service, 1947. Principal, Min. of Health, 1950; Principal Private Secretary: to Lord President of the Council and Minister for Science, 1960-61; to Minister of Housing and Local Govt, 1962; Asst Sec., Min. of Housing and Local Govt, 1963; Under-Secretary: Cabinet Office, 1969; Min. of Housing and Local Government, 1969-70; Principal Private Secretary to the Prime Minister, 1970; Asst Under-Sec. of State, Home Office, 1970-72; Dir, Centre for Studies in Social Policy, 1972-77. *Recreations:* walking and Wales. *Address:* 5 Hartland Road, Epping, Essex. *T:* Epping 73299. *Clubs:* Athenæum, Farmers'.

ISSIGONIS, Sir Alec (Arnold Constantine), Kt 1969; CBE 1964; RDI 1964; FRS 1967; Advanced Design Consultant, British Leyland (Austin-Morris) Ltd, since 1972; *b* Smyrna, 1906; British citizen. *Educ:* Battersea Polytechnic, London (Engrg Dip.). Draughtsman, Rootes Motors Ltd, 1933-36; Suspension Engineer, Morris Motors Ltd, 1936, subsequently Chief Engineer; Deputy Engineering Co-ordinator and Chief Engineer, British Motor Corporation, 1957-61; Technical Director, 1961; Dir of R&D, BMC later British Leyland (Austin-Morris) Ltd, 1961-72; designs include: Morris Minor, 1948; Mini-Minor and Austin Seven, 1959; Morris 1100, 1962. Leverhulme Medal, Royal Society, 1966. *Address:* British Leyland (Austin-Morris) Ltd, Longbridge, Birmingham.

ITHEL JONES, Rev. John; *see* Jones, Rev. J. I.

ITURBI, José; Grand Cross of Alphonso X the Wise, 1947; Grand Cross of Isabel the Catholic, 1975; Concert Pianist, Conductor, Composer; *b* Valencia, Spain, 28 Nov. 1895; *s* of Ricardo and Theresa Iturbi; *m* 1915, Maria Giner (*d* 1927); (one *d* decd). *Educ:* College and Academies at Valencia. Began to play piano at age of three; at seven, recognised as a child prodigy, was teaching pupils three and four times his age; graduated from Conservatory in Valencia and later was sent to Barcelona to study with Joaquin Malats. After graduating from Paris Conservatoire at age of 17½ with the highest Grand Prix, he became head of Piano Faculty at Geneva Conservatoire, a post once held by Liszt; American début, 1929. Regular conductor of Rochester Philharmonic, 1936-44; Guest Conductor New York Philharmonic, Philadelphia Orchestra, Detroit Symphony, Chicago, Dallas, Los Angeles, Atlanta, and all leading symphony orchestras of United States; also all leading symphony orchestras of England, France, Spain, Mexico, S America, S Africa, Holland, Belgium, Israel, Italy, Argentina, Uruguay, Venezuela, Peru, etc. He averaged 200 concerts a year. In several films. Member: Royal Acad. of Fine Arts San Fernando, Madrid; Royal Acad. of Fine Arts San Carlos, Valencia. Gold Medal of Labor, Spain, 1968; Pre-eminent Son of Valencia, 1971; Querado Gold Medal for the Arts, Spain, 1972; Gold Medal, Circle of Bellas Artes, Madrid; Colossal of Rhodes Award, Valencia, 1975; FFF Award of Spanish Press, 1976. Commandeur, Légion d'Honneur, 1976; Companion, Order of St Michael (Greece); Order of St George (Greece). *Recreation:* flying. *Address:* 915 North Bedford Drive, Beverly Hills, Calif 90210, USA.

IVAMY, Prof. Edward Richard Hardy; Professor of Law, University of London, since 1960; *b* 1 Dec. 1920; *o s* of late Edward Wadham Ivamy and late Florence Ivamy; *m* 1965, Christine Ann Frances, *o d* of William and Frances Culver; one *s. Educ:* Malvern Coll.; University Coll., London. Served War of 1939-45, RA: 67 Field Regt, N Africa, Italy and Middle East; 2nd Lieut 1942; Temp. Capt. 1945; Staff Capt., GHQ, Cairo, 1946. LLB (1st cl. hons) 1947; PhD 1953; LLD 1967. Barrister-at-law, Middle Temple, 1949. University Coll.: Asst Lectr in Laws, 1947-50; Lectr, 1950-56; Reader in Law, 1956-60; Dean of Faculty of Laws, 1964 and 1965; Fellow, 1969. Hon. Sec., Soc. of Public Teachers of Law, 1960-63; Hon. Sec., Bentham Club, 1953-58; Mem. Editorial Board: Jl of Business Law; Lloyd's Maritime and Commercial Law Quarterly. *Publications:* Show Business and the Law, 1955; (ed) Payne and Ivamy's Carriage of Goods by Sea, 7th edn 1963-10th edn, 1976; Hire-Purchase Legislation in England and Wales, 1965; Casebook on Carriage of Goods by Sea, 1965 (3rd edn, 1977); Casebook on Sale of Goods, 1966 (3rd edn 1973); (ed) Chalmers's Marine Insurance Act 1906 6th edn, 1966 (8th edn, 1976); General Principles of Insurance Law, 1966 (3rd edn 1975); (ed) Topham and Ivamy's Company Law, 13th edn, 1967

(15th edn 1974); Casebook on Mercantile Law, 1967 (2nd edn, 1972); Fire and Motor Insurance, 1968 (2nd edn 1973); Casebook on Insurance Law, 1969 (3rd edn, 1973); Marine Insurance, 1969 (2nd edn 1974); Casebook on Shipping Law, 1970; Casebook on Partnership, 1970; Casebook on Agency, 1971; Personal Accident, Life and Other Insurances, 1973; (ed) Underhill's Partnership (10th edn, 1975); contrib. to Encyclopædia Britannica, Chambers's Encyclopædia, Current Legal Problems, Jl of Business Law; Annual Survey of Commonwealth Law, 1967-76. *Recreations:* railways, cricket, tennis. *Address:* 143 Bishop's Mansions, SW6. *T:* 01-736 4736.

IVEAGH, 3rd Earl of, *cr* 1919; **Arthur Francis Benjamin Guinness;** Bt 1885; Baron Iveagh 1891; Viscount Iveagh 1905; Viscount Elveden 1919; Member, Seanad Eireann, since 1973; Co-Chairman, Arthur Guinness Son & Co., Ltd; *b* 20 May 1937; *o s* of Viscount Elveden (killed in action, 1945) and Lady Elizabeth Hare, *yr d* of 4th Earl of Listowel; *S* grandfather, 1967; *m* 1963, Miranda Daphne Jane, *d* of Major Michael Smiley, Castle Fraser, Aberdeenshire; two *s* two *d. Educ:* Eton; Trinity Coll., Cambridge. *Heir: s* Viscount Elveden, *qv*. *Address:* Farmleigh, Castleknock, Co. Dublin. *Clubs:* Carlton, White's; Royal Yacht Squadron (Cowes); Kildare Street and University (Dublin).

IVELAW-CHAPMAN, Air Chief Marshal Sir Ronald, GCB 1957 (KCB 1953; CB 1949); KBE 1951 (CBE 1943); DFC 1918; AFC 1930; *b* 17 Jan. 1899; *s* of late Joseph Ivelaw-Chapman, Cheltenham; *m* 1930, Margaret, *d* of late C. W. Shortt, Beckenham; one *s* one *d. Educ:* Cheltenham Coll. 2nd Lieut Royal Flying Corps, 1917; European War, 1917-18; at home, India, and Iraq, 1919-20; Kabul evacuations (awarded AFC); served War of 1939-45: in various executive and staff appointments, 1939-43; prisoner of war, 1944-45. AOC No. 38 Group, 1945-46; Directing Staff, Imperial Defence Coll., 1947-49; C-in-C Indian Air Force, 1950-51; AOC-in-C Home Command, 1952; Deputy Chief of the Air Staff, 1952-53; Vice Chief of the Air Staff, 1953-57; retired, 1957. Pres. Cheltonian Society, 1956-57; Dir of Resettlement, Ministry of Labour, 1957-61. Mem. of Observer Trust, 1957-66. Pres. of Council, Cheltenham Coll., 1968-72; Vice-Pres., RAF Escaping Society. *Publication:* (with Anne Baker) Wings over Kabul, 1976. *Recreation:* fishing. *Address:* Knockwood, Nether Wallop, Hants. *Club:* Royal Air Force.

IVENS, Michael William; Director, Aims for Freedom and Enterprise (formerly Aims of Industry), since 1971; *b* 15 March 1924; *s* of Harry Guest Ivens and Nina Ailion; *m*; five *s* one *d*. Dir, Foundn for Business Responsibilities, 1967; Jt Editor, Twentieth Century, 1967; Vice-Pres., Junior Hosp. Doctors Assoc., 1969; Director: Standard Telephone, 1970; Working Together Campaign, 1972-73. Message Received Ltd, 1977-. Member: Exec. Council, Income Tax Payers' Soc.; Appeal Cttee, Make Children Happy, 1977; Jt Founder and Mem. Council, Nat. Assoc. for Freedom. *Publications:* (poetry) Another Sky, 1963; Practice of Industrial Communication, 1963; (poetry) Last Waltz, 1964; Case Studies in Management, 1964; Case Studies in Human Relations, 1966; Case for Capitalism, 1967; (poetry) Private and Public, 1968; Industry and Values, 1970; Which Way?, 1970; (poetry) Born Early, 1975; Prophets of Freedom and Enterprise, 1975; Freedom Quotes, 1976. *Recreations:* campaigning, chess. *Address:* 5 Plough Place, Fetter Lane, EC4A 1AN. *T:* 01-353 0621. *Clubs:* Carlton, Wig and Pen.

IVES, Arthur Glendinning Loveless, CVO 1954 (MVO 1945); *b* 19 Aug. 1904; *s* of late Rev. E. J. Ives, Wesleyan Minister; *m* 1929, Doris Marion, *d* of Thomas Coke Boden; three *s* one *d. Educ:* Kingswood Sch.; Queen's Coll., Oxford (classical scholar); MA. George Webb Medley Junior Scholarship for Economics, Oxford Univ., 1926. London Chamber of Commerce, 1928-29; joined staff of King Edward's Hosp. Fund for London, 1929; Sec., 1938-60; retired 1960. Seriously injured in railway accident at Lewisham, Dec. 1957. A Governor of Kingswood Sch., 1954-72. *Publications:* British Hospitals (Britain in Pictures), 1948; Kingswood School in Wesley's Day and Since, 1970; contrib. to The Times, Lancet, etc, on hospital administration and allied topics. *Address:* The Cedars, Bordyke, Tonbridge, Kent. *Club:* Athenæum.
See also Rev. A. K. Lloyd.

IVES, Robert; a Recorder (formerly Recorder of Bury St Edmunds), since 1963; *b* 25 Aug. 1906; *o s* of Robert Ives; *m* 1931, Evelyn Harriet Hairby Alston (*d* 1965), *er d* of Rev. F. S. Alston; two *d*; *m* 1966, Vera Bowack, *widow* of Pilot Officer N. H. Bowack. *Educ:* privately; Gonville and Caius Coll., Cambridge (MA). Called to Bar, Gray's Inn, 1928. War Service, 1940-45: RASC and Judge Advocate General's Dept. Judge of Norwich Guildhall Court of Record, 1952-71; Dep. Chm.,

Norfolk QS, 1967-71. Chairman: Mental Health Review Tribunal (E Anglia Region), 1960-63; Agricultural Land Tribunal (Eastern Area), 1961-; Mem. panel of Chairmen of Medical Appeal Tribunals, 1969-. *Recreations:* farm, garden, photography. *Address:* Erpingham House, Erpingham, Norwich NR11 7QD. *T:* Hanworth 208. *Club:* Norfolk (Norwich).

IVINS, Prof. John Derek; Professor of Agriculture, University of Nottingham, since 1958; *b* Eccleshall, Staffs, 11 March 1923; *s* of Alfred Ivins and Ann Ivins (*née* Holland); *m* 1952, Janet Alice Whitehead, BSc; one *s* one *d*. *Educ:* Wolstanton County Grammar Sch., Newcastle, Staffs. BSc Reading 1944, MSc 1951; PhD Nottingham 1954. Technical Officer, Seed Production Cttee of Nat. Inst. of Agricultural Botany, 1944-46; Regional Trials Officer, Nat. Inst. of Agricultural Botany, 1946-48; Nottingham University: Lectr in Agriculture, 1948-58; Dean: Faculty of Agriculture and Horticulture, 1962-65; Faculty of Agricl Sci., 1976-; Deputy Vice-Chancellor, 1969-74. Mem., UK Seeds Exec., 1973-. Chm. Council, NIAB, 1974-75; Mem. UGC sub-cttee, Agriculture and Veterinary Studies, 1975-. FRAgS 1973. *Publications:* papers in technical and agricultural journals. *Recreations:* shooting, gardening. *Address:* University of Nottingham School of Agriculture, Sutton Bonington, near Loughborough. *T:* Kegworth 2386.

J

JACK, Hon. Sir Alieu (Sulayman), Kt 1970; Speaker, House of Representatives of the Republic of The Gambia, 1962-72, and since 1977; *b* 14 July 1922; *m* 1946, Yai Marie Cham; four *s* four *d* (and one *d* decd). *Educ:* St Augustine's Elementary School. Entered Gambia Civil Service, 1939; resigned and took up local appt with NAAFI, 1940-44; Civil Service, 1945-48; entered commerce, 1948; Man. Dir, Gambia National Trading Co. Ltd, 1948-72. Mem., Bathurst City Council, 1949-62. Minister for Works and Communications, The Gambia, 1972-77. Represented The Gambia Parlt at various internat. gatherings; Pres., CPA Gambia Branch. Comdr, National Order of Senegal, 1967; Comdr, Order of Merit of Mauritania, 1967; Commander, Order of Fed. Republic of Nigeria, 1970; Kt Grant Band, Liberia, 1977. Grand Comdr and Chancellor, National Order of The Gambia, 1972. *Recreation:* golf. *Address:* 29 Leman Street, Banjul, The Gambia; House of Representatives, The Republic of The Gambia. *T:* (home) 93.639, (office) 241. *Club:* Bathurst (Banjul).

JACK, Sir Daniel (Thomson), Kt 1966; CBE 1951; Hon. LLD Glasgow; MA; Chairman, Air Transport Licensing Board, 1961-70; David Dale Professor of Economics, University of Durham, King's College, Newcastle upon Tyne, 1935-61; Sub-Rector, King's College, 1950-55; *b* 18 Aug. 1901; *m* 1st, 1945, Nan (*d* 1949), *widow* of Prof. John Dall, Queen's Univ., Canada; 2nd, 1954, Elizabeth Witter Stewart (*d* 1970), Kingston, Ont. *Educ:* Bellahouston Academy, Glasgow; University of Glasgow. Asst to the Adam Smith Prof. of Political Economy, University of Glasgow, 1923-28; Lecturer in Political Economy, University of St Andrews, 1928-35. Asst Regional Controller, Northern Region, Ministry of Labour and National Service, 1941; Industrial Commissioner, Ministry of Labour, 1942; Labour Adviser to Govt of India, 1943; Chm. of Bd of Inquiry into proposed 40-hour week in Copper Mining Industry of N Rhodesia, 1950; Mem. Royal Commn on E Africa, 1953; Pres. Economics Sect., Brit. Assoc., 1952; Chm. Bd of Inquiry into sugar dispute in Trinidad, 1955; Special Investigator into wages dispute, Gibraltar, 1955; Visiting lecturer, University of the Witwatersrand, 1956; Chm. Courts of Inquiry into Shipbuilding and Engineering Wages Disputes, 1956; Economic Adviser, Urban African Affairs Commn, Southern Rhodesia, 1957; Chm. Court of Inquiry into London Airport dispute, 1958; Chm. Rural Transport Inquiry, 1959; UK Independent Mem., Monckton Advisory Commission on Central Africa, 1959; Chm. Court of Inquiry into Ford dispute, 1963. *Publications:* The Economics of the Gold standard, 1925; The Restoration of European Currencies, 1927; International Trade, 1931; The Crises of 1931, 1931; Currency and Banking, 1932; Studies in Economic Warfare, 1940; Economic Survey of Sierra Leone, 1958; Report on Industrial Relations in the Sisal Industry, 1959; Report on Wage Fixing Machinery in Tanganyika, 1959; (with others) Economic Survey of Nyasaland, 1959. Articles in various journals. *Address:* Austenmead, School Lane, Chalfont St Peter, Bucks. *T:* Gerrards Cross 85577.

JACK, Prof. Ian Robert James; Professor of English Literature, University of Cambridge, since 1976; Fellow of Pembroke College, Cambridge, since 1961; *b* 5 Dec. 1923; *s* of John McGregor Bruce Jack, WS, and Helena Cockburn Buchanan; *m* 1st, 1948, Jane Henderson MacDonald; two *s* one *d*; 2nd, 1972, Margaret Elizabeth Crone; one *s*. *Educ:* George Watson's Coll.; Univ. of Edinburgh; Merton Coll., Oxford. James Boswell Fellow 1946, MA 1947, Edinburgh; DPhil Oxon 1950; LittD Cantab 1973. Brasenose Coll., Oxford; Lectr in Eng. Lit., 1950-55; Sen. Res. Fellow, 1955-61; Cambridge Univ.: Lectr in English, 1961-73; Reader in English Poetry, 1973-76; Librarian, Pembroke Coll., 1965-75. Vis. Professor: Alexandria, 1960; Chicago, 1968-69; California at Berkeley, 1968-69; British Columbia, 1975; de Carle Lectr, Univ. of Otago, 1964; Warton Lectr in English Poetry, British Acad., 1967; Guest Speaker, Nichol Smith Seminar, ANU, 1976; numerous lecture-tours for British Council and other bodies. Pres., Charles Lamb Soc., 1970-; Vice-President: Johnson Soc., 1964-; Brontë Soc., 1973-. *Publications:* Augustan Satire, 1952; English Literature 1815-1832 (Vol. X, Oxf. Hist. of Eng. Lit.), 1963; Keats and the Mirror of Art, 1967; Browning's Major Poetry, 1973; (ed) Sterne: A Sentimental Journey, etc, 1968; (ed) Browning: Poetical Works 1833-1864, 1970; (ed with Hilda Marsden) Emily Brontë: Wuthering Heights, 1976; general editor, Brontë novels (Clarendon edn); contrib. TLS, etc. *Recreations:* collecting books, travelling hopefully. *Address:* Highfield House, High Street, Fen Ditton, Cambridgeshire CB5 8ST. *T:* Teversham 2697.

JACK, James, CBE 1967; JP; General Secretary, Scottish Trades Union Congress, 1963-75; Member: Scottish Postal Board, since 1972; Board of the Crown Agents, 1975-77; *b* 6 Dec. 1910; *s* of late Andrew M. Jack and Margaret Reid; *m* 1936; one *s*. *Educ:* Auchinraith Primary Sch., Blantyre; St John's Gram. Sch., Hamilton. Chm., Glasgow N and E Cttee, Manpower Services Commn, 1975-; Member: Scottish Economic Council, 1964-; Scottish Oil Develt Council, 1974-; Scottish Develt Agency, 1975-; Lanarkshire Health Bd, 1975-; Industrial Tribunals, 1975-; Employment Appeal Tribunal, 1976-. JP Lanark. *Address:* 7 Stonefield Place, Blantyre, Glasgow G72 9TH. *T:* Blantyre 823304.

JACK, Robert Barr; Partner, McGrigor, Donald & Co., Solicitors, Glasgow, since 1957; Member, Scottish Law Commission, since 1974; *b* 18 March 1928; *s* of Robert Hendry Jack and Christina Alexandra Jack; *m* 1958, Anna Thorburn Thomson; two *s*. *Educ:* Kilsyth Acad.; High Sch., Glasgow; Glasgow Univ. MA 1948, LLB 1951. Admitted a solicitor in Scotland, 1951. Mem. Council, Royal Faculty of Procurators in Glasgow, 1971-74; Mem., Company Law Cttee of Law Society of Scotland, 1971-. Non-exec. Dir, Brownlee & Co. Ltd, Timber Merchants, Glasgow, 1974-. Chm., Scottish Nat. Council of YMCAs, 1966-73 (Hon. Treas. 1963-65; Vice-Chm. 1965-66); Mem. Council of Management, 1971-, and Mem. Exec. Cttee, 1972-, Quarrier's Homes; Gen. Council of Glasgow Univ.: Mem. Business Cttee, 1969-; Convener, Cttee on Finance and Statistics, 1972-. *Publications:* lectures on various aspects of company law, and articles on the legal implications of current cost accounting. *Recreations:* golf, gentle badminton; a dedicated lover of Isle of Arran which serves as a retreat and restorative. *Address:* (home) 39 Mansewood Road, Glasgow G43 1TN. *T:* 041-632 1659; (office) 224 Ingram Street, Glasgow G1 1JP. *T:* 041-248 5981. *Clubs:* Western (Glasgow); Pollok Golf; Western Gailes Golf; (Captain 1973-75) Shiskine Golf and Tennis (Isle of Arran).

JACK, Hon. Sir Roy (Emile), Kt 1970; MP (Nat) for Rangitikei, New Zealand; Speaker of the House of Representatives, since 1976; barrister and solicitor, Jack, Riddet, Young & Partners; *b* New Plymouth, 12 Jan. 1914; *s* of John Bain Jack; *m* 1946, Frances Anne, *d* of Dr G. W. Harty; one *d*. *Educ:* Wanganui Collegiate Sch.; Victoria University of Wellington, NZ (LLB). Served War 1939-45, RNZAF. Judge's Associate, barrister and solicitor, 1935-38; entered practice as barrister and solicitor, Wanganui, 1946. Mem., Wanganui City Council, 1946-55; Dep. Mayor, 1947-55. MP: for Patea, 1954-63; for Waimarino, subseq. Rangitikei, 1963-; Deputy Speaker, House of Representatives, 1961-66, Speaker, 1967-72; Attorney General and Minister of Justice, Feb.-Nov. 1972. *Recreations:* music (especially violin), reading, skiing, flying, gliding. *Address:* Parliament House, Wellington, New Zealand. *T:* Wellington 738288; (private) 49 College Street, Wanganui, New Zealand. *T:* Wanganui 57640. *Club:* Wanganui.

JACKLIN, Anthony, OBE 1970; professional golfer; *b* 7 July 1944; *s* of Arthur David Jacklin; *m* 1966, Vivien; two *s* one *d*. Successes include: British Assistant Pro Championship, 1965; Pringle Tournament, 1967; Dunlop Masters, 1967; Greater

Jacksonville Open, USA, 1968; British Open Championship, 1969; US Open Championship, 1970; Benson & Hedges, 1971; British Professional Golfers Assoc., 1972; Gtr Jacksonville Open, 1972; Bogota Open, 1973 and 1974; Italian Open, 1973; Dunlop Masters, 1973; Scandinavian Open, 1975; Kerrygold International, 1976; English National PGA Championship, 1977. Life Vice-Pres., Professional Golfers' Assoc., 1970. *Publication:* Golf with Tony Jacklin, 1969. *Recreation:* shooting. *Address:* Chestnut Lea, St Mary, Jersey, CI. *Clubs:* Potters Bar Golf; Hon. Mem. of others.

JACKLING, Sir Roger William, GCMG 1976 (KCMG 1965; CMG 1955); HM Diplomatic Service, retired; *b* 10 May 1913; *s* of P. Jackling, OBE, and Lucy Jackling; *m* 1938, Joan Tustin; two *s* (and one *s* decd). *Educ:* Felsted. DPA, London Univ., 1932; Solicitor, Supreme Court, 1935; Actg Vice-Consul, New York, 1940; Commercial Sec., Quito, 1942; 2nd Sec., Washington, 1943; 1st Sec., 1945; transf. Foreign Office, 1947; seconded to Cabinet Office, 1950 (Asst Sec.); Counsellor (commercial), The Hague, 1951; Economic and Financial Adviser to UK High Commr, Bonn; and UK commercial rep. in Germany, 1953; Minister (Economic), British Embassy, Bonn, 1955; Counsellor, British Embassy, Washington, 1957-59; Asst Under-Sec. of State, FO, 1959-63; Dep. Permanent UK Rep. to United Nations, 1963-67 (with personal rank of Ambassador from 1965); Dep. Under-Sec. of State, FO, 1967-68; Ambassador to Federal Republic of Germany, 1968-72; Leader, UK Delegn to UN Conf. on Law of the Sea, 1973-75. Chm., Bd of Trustees, Anglo-German Foundn for Study of Industrial Society. *Recreations:* gardening, golf. *Address:* 37 Boundary Road, St John's Wood, NW8. *Club:* Travellers'.

JACKMAN, Air Marshal Sir Douglas, KBE 1959 (CBE 1943); CB 1946; RAF; idc 1948; Air Officer Commanding-in-Chief, Royal Air Force Maintenance Command, 1958-61, retired; *b* 26 Oct. 1902; twin *s* of late A. J. Jackman; *m* 1931, Marjorie Leonore, *d* of late A. Hyland, Kingsdown, Kent. *Educ:* HMS Worcester. Officer Royal Mail Line until 1926; joined RAF, 1926; served in Iraq, 1928-30, in No 55 Squadron; in UK with Wessex Bombing Area and at Cranwell until 1934; to Middle East Command in 1934 and served at Aboukir until 1938, when posted to HQ Middle East until 1943; with Mediterranean Air Command and Mediterranean Allied Air Forces HQ until 1944; HQ Balkan Air Force, 1944-45 (despatches five times, CB, CBE, Comdr Order George 1st of Greece with Swords, AFC [Greek]); Dir of Movements Air Ministry, 1946-47; Dir of Organization (forecasting and planning), Air Ministry, 1949-52; AOC No 40 Group, 1952-55; Dir-Gen. of Equipment, Air Ministry, 1955-58; Co-ordinator, Anglo-American Relations, Air Ministry, 1961-64. Mem., Natal Reg. Council, SA Red Cross. *Publication:* technical, on planning, 1942. *Recreations:* golf (Member: RAF Golfing Soc.; Seniors Golfing Soc., Natal); woodworking. *Address:* 136A Marriott Road, Durban, South Africa. *Clubs:* Royal Over-Seas League; Durban Country.

JACKMAN, Frank Downer, CMG 1964; Chairman, Bitumax Pty Ltd, 1968-72; Commissioner of Highways and Director of Local Government for South Australia, 1958-66; *b* 14 May 1901; *s* of Arthur Joseph and Adela Mary Jackman; *m* 1930, Elaine Jean Nairn; two *d. Educ:* Prince Alfred Coll.; University of Adelaide. BE (Civil Engrg) 1923; FSASM 1923. Joined Engineer-in-Chief's Dept, SA Govt, 1923; transferred to Highways and Local Govt Dept, 1929; Asst Engr, 1929-37; District Engr, 1937-49; Chief Engr, 1949-58. MIE Aust., 1940; FCIT (MinstT), 1963. *Recreations:* fishing, racing. *Address:* 7 Crompton Drive, Wattle Park, S Australia 5066.

JACKS, Hector Beaumont, MA; Headmaster of Bedales School, 1946-July 1962; *b* 25 June 1903; *s* of late Dr L. P. Jacks; *m* 1st, Mary (*d* 1959), *d* of Rev. G. N. Nuttall Smith; one *s* one *d* ; 2nd, Nancy, *d* of F. E. Strudwick. *Educ:* Magdalen Coll. Sch. and Wadham Coll., Oxford. Asst master, Wellington Coll., Berks, 1925-32; Headmaster of Willaston Sch., Nantwich, 1932-37; Second Master, Cheltenham Coll. Junior Sch., 1940-46. *Recreation:* gardening. *Address:* Applegarth, Spotted Cow Lane, Buxted, Sussex. *T:* Buxted 2296.

JACKSON, family name of **Baron Allerton** and **Baroness Jackson of Lodsworth.**

JACKSON OF LODSWORTH, Baroness *cr* 1976 (Life Peer), of Lodsworth, W Sussex; **Barbara Mary Jackson,** DBE 1974; author; President, Institute for Environment and Development, since 1973; *b* 23 May 1914; *o d* of Walter and Teresa Ward; *m* 1950, Comdr (now Sir) Robert Jackson, *qv* ; one *s. Educ:* Convent of Jesus and Mary, Felixstowe; Lycée Molière and the Sorbonne, Paris; die Klause, Jugenheim a/d/B, Germany; Somerville Coll., Oxford (Exhibitioner). Hons Degree in

Philosophy, Politics and Economics, 1935; Univ. Extension Lecturer, 1936-39; joined staff of The Economist, 1939, as an Asst Editor; Visiting Scholar, Harvard Univ., 1957-68; Carnegie Fellow, 1959-67; Schweitzer Prof. of Internat. Economic Develt, Columbia Univ., 1968-73. Governor of Sadler's Wells and the Old Vic., 1944-53; Governor of BBC, 1946-50; Mem., Pontifical Commn for Justice and Peace, 1967-. Pres., Conservation Soc., 1973. Hon. Doctorates: Fordham Univ. and Smith Coll., 1949; Columbia Univ., 1954; Kenyon Coll. and Harvard Univ., 1957; Brandeis Univ., 1961, and others. Hon. Fellow LSE, 1976. Hon. FRIBA, 1975. *Publications:* (as Barbara Ward) The International Share-Out, 1938; Turkey, 1941; The West at Bay, 1948; Policy for the West, 1951; Faith and Freedom, 1954; Interplay of East and West, 1957; Five Ideas that Change the World, 1959; India and the West, 1961; The Rich Nations and the Poor Nations, 1962; Spaceship Earth, 1966; Nationalism and Ideology, 1967; The Lopsided World, 1968; (ed) The Widening Gap, 1971; (with René Dubos) Only One Earth, 1972; The Home of Man, 1976. *Recreations:* music, reading. *Address:* The Pound House, Lodsworth, Sussex GU28 9DE.

JACKSON, Albert Leslie Samuel, JP; Member, Birmingham City Council, since 1952; Lord Mayor of Birmingham, 1975-1976; *b* 20 Jan. 1918; *s* of Bert Jackson and Olive Powell; *m* Gladys Burley; one *s* one *d . Educ:* Handsworth New Road Council Sch. War service, Radio Mechanic, RAF. Subseq. formed building company, 1952, of which he is now Man. Dir. JP 1968. *Recreations:* chess, angling. *Address:* 10 St Helier House, Manor Close, Melville Road, Birmingham B16 9NG. *T:* 021-558 2266 and 021-454 0849.

JACKSON, Brig. Alexander Cosby Fishburn, CVO 1957; CBE 1954 (OBE 1943); *b* 4 Dec. 1903; *s* of late Col S. C. F. Jackson, CMG, DSO, and Lucy B. Jackson (*née* Drake); *m* 1934, Margaret Hastings Hervey, Montclair, NJ, USA; one *s* (and one *s* decd). *Educ:* Yardley Court, Tonbridge; Haileybury Coll.; RMC Sandhurst. 2nd Lt, R Hants Regt, 1923; Brig. 1952; employed RWAFF, 1927-33; served in Middle East, 1940-45 (despatches twice, OBE); Dep. Dir of Quartering, War Office, 1945-48; Comdr Northern Area, Kenya, 1948-51; Comdr Caribbean Area, 1951-54; HBM Military Attaché, Paris, 1954-58. ADC to the Queen, 1955-58. Order of Kutuzov 2nd Class, USSR, 1944; Comdr Legion of Honour, France, 1957. *Recreation:* bowls. *Address:* Glenwhern, Grouville, Jersey.

JACKSON, Sir Anthony Henry Mather M.; see Mather-Jackson.

JACKSON, Maj.-Gen. Arthur James, BSc; CEng; FIEE; Military Deputy, Head of Defence Sales, Ministry of Defence, since 1975; *b* Barrow-upon-Humber, Lincs, 31 March 1923; *e s* of Comdr A. J. Jackson, RD, RNR, Barrow-upon-Humber; *m* 1948, Joan Marguerite, *d* of late Trevor Lyons Relton, MBE, Whyteleafe, Surrey; two *s* two *d . Educ:* Barton Sch.; RMCS. BSc London, 1951. Joined Royal Signals, 1944; commnd 1946; served Italy and British Embassy, Belgrade, 1946-47; Austria, WO, Staff Coll., Far East, RMCS, BAOR, 1948-64; GSO1, Defence Ops Requirements Staff, MoD, 1965-66; CO 4th Div. Signal Regt, BAOR, 1967-68; psc, ptsc, psc†; Comdr (Brigadier), 12 Signal Gp, 1969-71; Dir of Telecommunications (Army), 1972-73; Dep. Comdt and Sen. Military Dir of Studies, RMCS, 1974-75. *Recreations:* golf, shooting, gardening, organ music. *Address:* Roughwood House, Fleet, Hampshire; Tower Lodge, Brampford Speke, Devon. *Club:* Army and Navy.

JACKSON, Mrs (Audrey) Muriel W.; see Ward-Jackson.

JACKSON, Very Rev. Brandon Donald; Provost of Bradford Cathedral, since 1977; *b* 11 Aug. 1934; *s* of Herbert and Millicent Jackson; *m* 1958, Mary Lindsay, 2nd *d* of John and Helen Philip; two *s* one *d . Educ:* Stockport School; Liverpool Univ.; St Catherine's Coll. and Wycliffe Hall, Oxford (LLB, DipTh). Curate: Christ Church, New Malden, Surrey, 1958-61; St George, Leeds, 1961-65; Vicar, St Peter, Shipley, Yorks, 1965-77. Religious Adviser to Yorkshire Television, 1969-; Church Commissioner, 1971-73; Examining Chaplain to Bp of Bradford, 1974-; Governor, Harrogate College, 1974-; Member: Council of Wycliffe Hall, Oxford, 1971-; Marriage Commission, 1975-. *Recreations:* sport (cricket, squash), fell-walking, fishing. *Address:* Provost's House, Cathedral Close, Bradford BD1 4EG. *T:* Bradford 32023.

JACKSON, Colin; see Jackson, G. C.

JACKSON, Prof. Derek Ainslie, OBE; DFC; AFC; MA Cantab and Oxon; DSc Oxon; FRS 1947; Research Professor, Faculté des Sciences, Centre National de la Recherche Scientifique, 91-Orsay, Paris; *b* 23 June 1906; *s* of late Sir Charles James Jackson; *m* 1936, Hon. Pamela Freeman-Mitford (marr. diss., 1951), 2nd *d* of 2nd Baron Redesdale; *m* 1951, Janetta (marr. diss. 1956), *d* of Rev. G. H. Woolley, VC, OBE, MC; one *d*; *m* 1957, Consuelo Regina Maria (marr. diss., 1959), *d* of late William S. Eyre and *widow* of Prince Ernst Ratibor zu Hohenlohe Schillingsfürst; *m* 1968, Marie-Christine, *d* of Baron Georges Reille. *Educ:* Rugby, Trinity Coll., Cambridge. Formerly Prof. of Spectroscopy in the University of Oxford. Served War of 1939-45, Observer in RAFVR, 1940-45. Wing Comdr 1943. Officer Legion of Merit (USA); Chevalier, Légion d'Honneur, France. *Publications:* numerous papers in Proc. Royal Soc., Jl de Physique, Phys. Review, Zeitschrift für Physik. *Address:* 20 Avenue des Figuiers, Ouchy, Lausanne, Switzerland; 19 rue Auguste Vacquerie, 75116 Paris; Chalet Mariza, 3780 Gstaad, Switzerland.

JACKSON, Sir Donald (Edward), Kt 1953; *b* 1892; *e s* of late Joseph Waterton Jackson, OBE, JP, MLC; *m* 1937, Amy Beatrice, *e d* of late Walter Augustus Reynolds, British Guiana; one *d. Educ:* The Middle Sch., British Guiana. LLB University of London, 1926. Called to Bar, Middle Temple, 1927; practised at Bar, British Guiana; Acting Asst Attorney-Gen., 1933, 1936, and Senior Magistrate, 1936; Registrar of Deeds, of Supreme Court and of West Indian Court of Appeal, British Guiana, 1944; Actg Puisne Judge, various periods, 1945-49; Puisne Judge, Windward and Leeward Islands, 1949; Chief Justice of Windward and Leeward Islands, and Judge of West Indian Court of Appeal, 1950-57, retired. Speaker, Legislative Council, British Guiana, 1957-61; Justice of Appeal, Federal Supreme Court of the West Indies, 1961-62; Justice of Appeal, British Caribbean Court of Appeal, 1962-66. Mem. of Commission on the Unification of the Public Services in the British Caribbean Area, 1948-49; Chm., Labour Commn of Enquiry, St Lucia, 1950; Chm., Commission of Inquiry into the Nutmeg Industry of Grenada, 1951; Mem. Brit. Guiana Constitutional Commn, 1954; Chm. of Commn of Inquiry into causes of Cessation of Work in Sugar Industry, St Lucia, 1957; Chm. Constitutional Cttee for British Guiana, 1958-59; Chm., Commn to review Salaries and Structure of W Indies Federal Civil Service, and also to enquire into remuneration of Ministers and other members of W Indies Fed. Legislature, 1960; Mem., Mixed Commn on Venezuela-Guyana Border Dispute, 1966-70; Chm. Elections Commn, Guyana, 1966-; Mem. Boundaries Commn, Bermuda, 1967. KStJ 1972. Cacique's Crown of Honour, Guyana, 1970. *Address:* Georgetown, Guyana. *Clubs:* Corona (Life Mem.); The Georgetown.

JACKSON, Edward; *see* Jackson, J. E.

JACKSON, Edward Francis, MA; Director, Oxford University Institute of Economics and Statistics, and Professorial Fellow of St Antony's College, Oxford, since 1959; *b* 11 July 1915; *o s* of F. E. Jackson, schoolmaster, and Miriam Eveline (*née* Jevon); *m* 1st, 1942, Anne Katherine Cloake (marr. diss.); 2nd, 1954, Mrs Marion Marianne Marris (*d* 1972), *o c* of late Arthur Ellinger; two *s. Educ:* West Bromwich Grammar Sch.; Univ. of Birmingham; Magdalen Coll., Oxford. BCom Birmingham with 1st cl. hons, 1934; Magdalen Coll., Oxford (Demy): 1st in PPE, 1937; Jun. G. W. Medley Schol., 1935-36; Sen. Demy, 1937; Lecturer in Economics: New Coll., 1938; Magdalen Coll., 1939. Temp. Civil Servant in War Cabinet Offices, 1941-45; established Civil Servant (Central Statistical Office), 1945; Dep. Dir, Res. and Planning Div., UN Econ. Commn for Europe, 1951-56. University Lectr in Economic Statistics, Oxford, and Research Fellow of St Antony's Coll., Oxford, 1956-59. Mem. Transport Adv. Council, 1965. *Publications:* The Nigerian National Accounts, 1950-57 (with P. N. C. Obigbo), 1960; articles in economic journals. *Address:* Institute of Economics and Statistics, St Cross Building, Manor Road, Oxford; The Manor House, Brill, Aylesbury, Bucks. *T:* Brill 205. *Club:* Reform.

JACKSON, Eric Stead, CB 1954; *b* 22 Aug. 1909; *yr s* of Stead Jackson, Shipley Glen, Yorks; *m* 1938, Yvonne Renée, *o d* of Devereux Doria De Brétigny, Victoria, BC; one *s* one *d. Educ:* Bradford Grammar Sch.; Corpus Christi Coll., Oxford (Scholar). 1st Class Hons Math. Mods, Math. Finals and Nat. Sci. Finals, Jun. Math. schol., 1930; MA. Asst Principal, Air Ministry, 1932; Sec., British Air Mission to Australia and NZ, 1939; Private Sec. to Minister of Aircraft Production, 1942, and to Resident Minister in Washington, 1943; Sec., British Supply Council in N America, 1944; Dir-Gen. Aircraft Branch, Control Commission, Berlin, 1945; Dep. Pres. Economic Sub-Commission, 1947; British Head of Bizonal Delegation to OEEC, Paris, 1948; Under Sec., Ministry of Supply, 1950-56; Dir-Gen., Atomic Weapons, Ministry of Supply, 1956-59; Under-Secretary: Min. of Aviation, 1959-67; Min. of Technology, 1967-70; Dept of Trade and Industry, 1970-71. *Address:* 10 Ditchley Road, Charlbury, Oxfordshire. *T:* Charlbury 682.

JACKSON, Rt. Rev. Fabian Menteath Elliot; Assistant Bishop of Bath and Wells, 1950-67; Prebendary of Wells Cathedral since 1954; *b* 22 Nov. 1902; *s* of William Henry Congreve and Maud Helen Jackson; unmarried. *Educ:* Westminster Sch.; University of London; Ely Theological Coll. BA Hons Classics, London, 1925; Deacon, 1926; Priest, 1927; S Augustine's, Kilburn, 1926-38; Priest-in-Charge of S Barnabas, Northolt Park, 1938-43; Vicar of All Saints, Clifton, 1943-46; Bishop of Trinidad, 1946-49, resigned, 1949; Rector of Batcombe with Upton Noble, Somerset, 1950-67. *Address:* St Monica's Home, Westbury on Trym, Bristol BS9 3UN.

JACKSON, Francis Alan; Organist and Master of the Music, York Minster, since 1946; *b* 2 Oct. 1917; *s* of W. A. Jackson; *m* 1950, Priscilla, *d* of Tyndale Procter; two *s* one *d. Educ:* York Minster Choir Sch.; Sir Edward Bairstow. Chorister, York Minster, 1929-33; ARCO, 1936; BMus Dunelm 1937; FRCO (Limpus Prize), 1937; FRSCM, 1963; DMus Dunelm 1957. Organist Malton Parish Church, 1933-40. Served War of 1939-45, with 9th Lancers in Egypt, N Africa and Italy, 1940-46. Asst Organist, York Minster, 1946; Conductor York Musical Soc., 1947; Conductor York Symphony Orchestra, 1947. Pres. Incorp. Assoc of Organists, 1960-62; Pres., RCO, 1972-74. Hon. Fellow, Westminster Choir Coll., Princeton, NJ, 1970. *Publications:* Organ and Church Music, Songs, Monodramas. *Recreation:* gardening. *Address:* 1 Minster Court, York YO1 2JJ. *T:* York 53873.

JACKSON, Col Sir Francis (James) Gidlow, Kt, *cr* 1955; MC 1917; TD 1930; *b* 16 Sept. 1889; 2nd *s* of late Charles Gidlow Jackson, JP, CA; unmarried. *Educ:* Bilton Grange; Rugby. Admitted Solicitor, 1912; Served European War, 1914-19; Egypt, Gallipoli, France and Belgium. Served France, 1940. *Recreation:* fishing. *Address:* Domus, Enville Road, Bowdon, Cheshire. *Club:* The Manchester (Manchester).

JACKSON, Frederick Hume, OBE 1966; HM Consul-General, Düsseldorf, since 1975; *b* 8 Sept. 1918; *o s* of late Maj.-Gen. G. H. N. Jackson, CB, CMG, DSO, Rathmore, Winchcombe, Glos and Eileen, *d* of J. Hume Dudgeon, Merville, Booterstown, Co. Dublin; *m* 1950, Anne Gibson; three *s* one *d. Educ:* Winchester; Clare Coll., Cambridge (MA). Military service, 1939-46: GSO3 (Intelligence), HQ 1 Corps District; Colonial Service (Tanganyika), 1946-57; FO, 1957-60; Head of Chancery, Saigon, 1960-62; 1st Sec., Washington, 1962-67; Counsellor and Dep. Head, UK Delegn to European Communities, Brussels, 1967-69; UK Resident Representative, Internat. Atomic Energy Agency, 1969-75; UK Perm. Representative to UNIDO, 1971-75. *Recreations:* fishing, sailing, shooting, riding. *Address:* c/o Barclays Bank Ltd, St Nicholas Street, Scarborough, North Yorks; British Consulate-General, Düsseldorf, BFPO 34. *T:* Düsseldorf 434281. *Club:* Flyfishers'.

JACKSON, Sir Geoffrey (Holt Seymour), KCMG 1971 (CMG 1963); HM Diplomatic Service, retired; Member, BBC General Advisory Council, since 1976; *b* 4 March 1915; *s* of Samuel Seymour Jackson and Marie Cecile Dudley Ryder; *m* 1939, Patricia Mary Evelyn Delany; one *s. Educ:* Bolton Sch.; Emmanuel Coll., Cambridge. Entered Foreign Service, 1937; Vice-Consul, Beirut, Cairo, Bagdad; Acting Consul-Gen., Basra, 1946; 1st Sec., Bogotá, 1946-50; Berne, 1954-56; Minister, Honduras, 1956, HM Ambassador to Honduras, 1957-60; Consul-Gen., Seattle, 1960-64; Senior British Trade Commissioner in Ontario, Canada, 1964; Minister (Commercial), Toronto, 1965-69; Ambassador to Uruguay, 1969-72; kidnapped by terrorists and held prisoner for 8 months, Jan.-Sept. 1971; Dep. Under-Sec. of State, FCO, 1973. Pres., Assoc. of Lancastrians, 1974. *Publications:* The Oven-Bird, 1972; People's Prison, 1973; Surviving the Long Night, 1974. *Recreations:* golf, Latin-Americana. *Address:* 63B Cadogan Square, SW1. *Club:* Canning.

JACKSON, (George) Colin; MP (Lab) Brighouse and Spenborough, 1964-70, and since Feb. 1974; *b* 6 Dec. 1921; *s* of George Hutton and Agnes Scott Jackson. *Educ:* Tewkesbury Grammar Sch.; St John's Coll., Oxford. Called to the Bar, Gray's Inn, 1950. Lecturer, writer and broadcaster in Britain, America, throughout Africa and Asia. Chm., Parly Lab Party Foreign Affairs Gp. Chm., Council for Advancement of Arab-British Understanding. *Publication:* The New India (Fabian Soc.). *Recreation:* travel. *Address:* 2 Courtfield Gardens, SW5. *T:* 01-370 1992. *Club:* Savile.

JACKSON, Most Rev. George Frederic Clarence; Bishop-Ordinary to the Canadian Armed Forces, since 1977; *b* 5 July 1907; *s* of James Sandiford Jackson; *m* 1939, Eileen de Montfort Welborn; two *s* two *d. Educ:* University of Toronto. Deacon, 1934; Priest, 1935, Diocese of Niagara. Diocese of: Toronto,

1937-38; Chester, 1938-46; Niagara, 1946-58; Qu'Appelle, 1958-77. Hon. Canon, Christ Church Cathedral, Hamilton, Ontario, 1952; Dean of Qu'Appelle, 1958; Bishop of Qu'Appelle, 1960; Archbishop of Qu'Appelle and Metropolitan of Rupert's Land, 1970-77. DD (*hc*) 1959. *Recreations:* curling, gardening. *Address:* Fort Qu'Appelle, Saskatchewan, Canada.

JACKSON, Gerald Breck; Managing Director, NCB (Ancillaries) Ltd, since 1972; *b* 28 June 1916; *o s* of Gerald Breck Jackson and Mary Jackson, Paterson, NJ; *m* 1940, Brenda Mary, *o d* of William and Mary Titshall; one *s*. *Educ:* various schs in USA; Canford Sch., Dorset; Faraday House Engrg Coll. Graduate Trainee, Central Electricity Bd, 1938. HM Forces, RE, 1939-43. Various appts in HV transmission with CEB and BEA, 1943-55; Overhead Line Design Engr, BEA, 1955-61; Asst Regional Dir, CEGB, 1961-64; Chief Ops Engr, CEGB, 1964-66; Regional Dir, NW Region, CEGB, 1966-68; Dir Engineering, English Electric Co. Ltd, 1968-69; Sen. Exec., Thomas Tilling Ltd, and Dir subsid. cos, 1969-71; Man. Dir, John Mowlem & Co. Ltd, 1971-72. DFH, CEng, FIEE. *Publications:* Network for the Nation, 1960; Power Controlled, 1966. *Recreations:* photography, pen-and-ink drawing. *Address:* 23 Balliol House, Manor Fields, Putney Hill, SW15 3LL. *T:* 01-788 0583. *Club:* Roehampton.

JACKSON, Glenda; actress; *b* Birkenhead, 9 May 1936; *d* of Harry and Joan Jackson; *m* 1958, Roy Hodges (marr. diss. 1976); one *s*. *Educ:* West Kirby Co. Grammar Sch. for Girls; RADA. Actress with various repertory cos, 1957-63, stage manager, Crewe Rep.; joined Royal Shakespeare Co., 1963. *Plays:* All Kinds of Men, Arts, 1957; The Idiot, Lyric, 1962; Alfie, Mermaid and Duchess, 1963; Royal Shakespeare Co.: Theatre of Cruelty Season, LAMDA, 1964; The Jew of Malta, 1964; Marat/Sade, 1965, NY and Paris, 1965; Love's Labour's Lost, Squire Puntila and his Servant Matti, The Investigation, Hamlet, 1965; US, Aldwych, 1966; Three Sisters, Royal Ct, 1967; Fanghorn, Fortune, 1967; Collaborators, Duchess, 1973; The Maids, Greenwich, 1974; Hedda Gabler, Australia, USA, London, 1975; The White Devil, Old Vic, 1976; Stevie, Vaudeville, 1977; *films:* This Sporting Life, 1963; Marat/Sade, 1967; Negatives, 1968; Women in Love (Oscar Award, 1971), 1970; The Music Lovers, 1971; Sunday, Bloody Sunday, 1971; The Boyfriend, 1972; Mary, Queen of Scots, 1972; Triple Echo, 1972; Il Sorviso de Grande Tentatore (The Tempter), 1973; Bequest to the Nation, 1973; A Touch of Class (Oscar Award, 1974), 1973; The Maids, 1974; The Romantic Englishwoman, 1974; Hedda Gabler, 1975; The Incredible Sarah, 1976; *TV:* Elizabeth in Elizabeth R, 1971. Best film actress awards: Variety Club of GB, 1971 and 1975; NY Film Critics, 1971; Nat. Soc. of Film Critics, US, 1971. *Recreations:* cooking, gardening, reading Jane Austen. *Address:* c/o Peter Crouch Ltd, 191 Wardour Street, W1.

JACKSON, Gordon Noel, CMG 1962; MBE; HM Ambassador to Ecuador, 1967-70, retired; *b* 25 Dec. 1913; *m* 1959, Mary April Nettlefold, *er d* of late Frederick John Nettlefold and of Mrs Albert Coates; one *s* two *d*. Indian Political Service until 1947; then HM Foreign Service; Political Officer, Sharjah, 1947; transf. to Kuwait, Persian Gulf, 1949; transf. to Foreign Office, 1950; Consul, St Louis, USA, 1953; Foreign Service Officer, Grade 6, 1955; Consul-General: Basra, 1955-57; Lourenço Marques, 1957-60; Benghazi, 1960-63; HM Ambassador to Kuwait, 1963-67. *Publications:* Effective Horsemanship (for Dressage, Hunting, Three-day Events, Polo), 1967; (with C. E. G. Hope) The Encyclopædia of the Horse, 1973. *Address:* Lowbarrow House, Leafield, Oxfordshire. *Club:* Travellers'.

JACKSON, Harvey; Hon. Consulting Surgeon, The National Hospital, Queen Square; Hon. Consulting Neurosurgeon, Westminster Hospital; Hon. Neurological Surgeon, St Thomas' Hospital; Hon. Consulting Surgeon, Acton General Hospital, since 1930; *b* 16 Oct. 1900; *s* of Richard Barlow Jackson and Elizabeth Shepherd; *m* 1930, Freda Mary Frampton; one *s* one *d*. *Educ:* Royal Grammar School, Newcastle upon Tyne; Middlesex Hospital. Hon. Asst Surg., West London Hosp., 1935-38. Past Pres., West London Medico-Chirurgical Soc.; Past Pres., Soc. of Brit. Neurological Surgeons; Fellow of Assoc. of Surgeons; Hunterian Prof. RCS of England, 1947, 1951; Elsberg Lectr, Neurological Soc. of New York, 1960; Visiting Prof. in Neurosurgery, University of Cairo, Guest Lectr, Univ. of Cincinnati, 1959; Lectr, Neurological Soc. of Chicago, 1959; Guest Lectr, Univ. of Santiago de Compostela, Spain, 1969. Past President: Section of Neurology, RSM; Surrey Branch, BMA. *Address:* 56 Fairacres, Roehampton Lane, SW15 5LY.

JACKSON, Herbert, FRIBA; FRTPI; architect and planning consultant; in private practice since 1931; *b* 25 June 1909; *s* of John Herbert Jackson; *m* 1930, Margaret Elizabeth Pearson.

Educ: Handsworth Grammar Sch.; Birmingham Sch. of Architecture. RIBA Bronze Medal, 1928; RIBA Saxon Snell Prizeman, 1930. Mem. RIBA Council, 1956-58; Vice-Pres. RIBA 1960-62; Chm., RIBA Allied Socs Conf., 1960-62. Gov., Birmingham Coll. of Art; Chm. Birmingham Civic Soc., 1960-65; Pres. Birmingham and Five Counties Architectural Assoc., 1956-58; Pres. Royal Birmingham Society of Artists, 1960-62 (Prof. of Architecture, 1961). *Publications:* (jt) Plans (for Minister of Town and Country Planning): S Wales Plan, 1947; W Midlands and N Staffs Plan, 1948. *Recreations:* travelling, reading. *Address:* 14 Clarendon Square, Leamington Spa, Warwicks. *T:* Leamington 24078; 17 Welbeck Street, W1M 7PF. *T:* 01-486 2872/4.

JACKSON, Sir Hugh (Nicholas), 2nd Bt, *cr* 1913; late Lt R W Fusiliers; *b* 21 Jan. 1881; *s* of 1st Bt and Alice Mary (*d* 1900), *y d* of William Lambarde, JP, DL, of Beechmont, Sevenoaks, Kent; *S* father, 1924; *m* 1931, Violet Marguerite Loftus, *y d* of Loftus St George; one *s* one *d*. *Heir:* *s* Nicholas Fane St George Jackson, *qv*. *Address:* 38 Oakley Street, SW3.

JACKSON, Ian (Macgilchrist), BA Cantab, MB, BChir, FRCS, FRCOG; Obstetric and Gynæcological Surgeon, Middlesex Hospital, 1948; Gynæcological Surgeon: Chelsea Hospital for Women, 1948; King Edward VII Hospital for Officers, 1961; Royal Masonic Hospital, 1963; Consulting Gynæcologist, King Edward VII Hospital, Midhurst, 1959; Consultant Obstetrician and Gynæcologist, RAF, 1964; *b* Shanghai, 11 Nov. 1914; *s* of Dr Ernest David Jackson; *m* 1943 (marr. diss., 1967); two *s* one *d*; *m* 1970, Deirdre Ruth Heitz. *Educ:* Marlborough Coll.; Trinity Hall, Cambridge (scholar; double 1st cl. hons, Nat. Sci. tripos pts I, II). London Hospital: open scholarship, 1936; house appointments, 1939; First Asst, Surgical and Obstetric and Gynæcol Depts, 1940-43. Served as Surgical Specialist, RAMC, 1943-47 (Major); Parachute Surgical Team, 224 Para. Field Amb.; Mobile Surgical Unit, 3 Commando Brigade. Royal College of Obstetricians and Gynæcologists: Council, 1951-61, 1962-70; Hon. Sec., 1954-61; Chm., Examination Cttee, 1962-65, Hon. Treas., 1966-70; Hon. Librarian, RSM, 1969-75. Examiner for Univs of Cambridge, Oxford, and London, Conjoint Bd and RCOG. Mem., Court of Assts, Worshipful Soc. of Apothecaries, 1966, Senior Warden 1977, Master 1978. Order of the Star of Africa (Liberia), 1969; Grand Officer of Order of Istiqlal, Jordan, 1970. *Publications:* British Obstetric and Gynæcological Practice (jtly), 1963; Obstetrics by Ten Teachers (jtly), 1966, 1972; Gynæcology by Ten Teachers (jtly), 1971; numerous contribs to medical literature. *Recreations:* fishing, golf, photography. *Address:* 23 Springfield Road, NW8. *T:* 01-624 3580; 104 Harley Street, W1. *T:* 01-935 1801. *Club:* Garrick.

JACKSON, James Barry; *see* Barry, Michael.

JACKSON, (John) Edward, CMG 1977; HM Diplomatic Service; HM Ambassador to Cuba, since 1975; *b* 24 June 1925; *s* of late Edward Harry Jackson and of Mrs Margaret Jackson, Cambridge; *m* 1952, Evelyn Stainton Harris, *d* of late George James Harris, MC and of Mrs Friede Rowntree Harris, York; two *s* one *d*. *Educ:* Ardingly; Corpus Christi Coll., Cambridge. RNVR (Sub-Lt), 1943-46; joined Foreign (now Diplomatic) Service, 1947; FO, 1947-49; 3rd Sec., Paris, 1949-52; 2nd Sec., FO, 1952-56; Bonn, 1956-57; 1st Sec., Bonn, 1957-59; Guatemala City, 1959-62; FO, 1963-68; Counsellor, 1968; NATO Defence Coll., Rome, 1969; Counsellor (Political Adviser), British Mil. Govt, Berlin, 1969-73; Head of Defence Dept, FCO, 1973-75. *Recreations:* pictures, antiques, tennis, golf. *Address:* c/o Foreign and Commonwealth Office, SW1A 2AH; 17 Paultons Square, SW3. *T:* 01-352 8501. *Clubs:* Travellers'; Hurlingham.

JACKSON, Sir John Montrésor, 6th Bt, *cr* 1815; elected Member of London Stock Exchange, 1948; formerly engaged on development work for Ministry of Aircraft Production; formerly with BBC; *b* Buenos Aires, Argentina, 14 Oct. 1914; *o surv s* of Sir Robert Montrésor Jackson, 5th Bt, and Katherine, *y d* of late John Abrey, The Glen and Barden Park, Tonbridge; *S* father, 1940; *m* 1953, Mrs E. Beatty. *Educ:* Tonbridge Sch.; Clare Coll., Cambridge. BA, 1936; London Stock Exchange, 1937-39; at outbreak of war, 1939, embodied with Territorial Army, RA (AA); released on medical grounds, May 1940. *Recreations:* golf, swimming and rowing. *Heir: kinsman* Robert Jackson [*b* 16 March 1910; *m* 1943, Maria E. Casamayou; two *d*]. *Address:* Rose Cottage, Charing, Kent.

JACKSON, John Wharton, JP; *b* 25 May 1902; *s* of John Jackson and Mary Wharton; *m* 1928, Mary Rigg; two *d*. *Educ:* Shrewsbury. Formerly Chm., Jackson's (Hurstead) Ltd, Rochdale. High Sheriff of Radnorshire, 1944-45; JP County of Lancaster, 1952. *Recreation:* golf. *Address:* Brackens, Mottram St Andrew, near Macclesfield, Cheshire. *T:* Prestbury 89277.

JACKSON, Joseph, QC 1967; *b* 21 Aug. 1924; *s* of late Samuel Jackson and of Hetty Jackson; *m* 1952, Marjorie Henrietta (*née* Lyons); three *d. Educ:* Queens' Coll., Cambridge; University Coll., London. MA, LLB Cantab, LLM London. Barrister, 1947, Gibraltar Bar. Chm., Probate and Divorce Bar Assoc., 1968-69. Member: General Council of the Bar, 1969-73; Senate of the Inns of Court, 1975-; Matrimonial Causes Rules Cttee, 1969-73; Special Divorce Comr, 1969-70. Dept of Trade Inspector, Dowgate and General Investments Ltd, 1975-. *Publications:* English Legal History, 1951 (2nd edn 1955); Formation and Annulment of Marriage, 1951, 2nd edn, 1969; Rayden on Divorce, 5th edn (supp.) 1951 to 12th edn 1974; Matrimonial Finance and Taxation, 1972, 2nd edn, 1975; contrib. to Halsbury's Laws of England, Encyclopædia Britannica, Atkin's Encyclopædia of Court Forms, Law Quarterly Review, Modern Law Review, Canadian Bar Review, etc. *Recreations:* gardening, painting, ceramics. *Address:* Brook House, 28 Uxbridge Road, Stanmore, Mddx. *T:* 01-954 2039; 1 Mitre Court Buildings, Temple, EC4. *T:* 01-353 0434/2277/0137.

JACKSON, Prof. Kenneth Hurlstone, FRSE 1977; FBA 1957; FSAScot 1951; Professor of Celtic Languages, Literatures, History and Antiquities, Edinburgh University, since 1950; *b* 1 Nov. 1909; *s* of Alan Stuart Jackson and Lucy Hurlstone; *m* 1936, Janet Dall Galloway, of Hillside, Kinross-shire; one *s* one *d. Educ:* Whitgift Sch., Croydon; St John's Coll., Cambridge (Exhibitioner and Scholar). First Cl. Hons with Distinction, Classical Tripos, 1930 and 1931 (Senior Classic, 1931); BA 1931; First Cl. Hons with Distinction, Archaeology and Anthropology Tripos, 1932; Sir William Brown medals for Greek and Latin verse, 1930 (two), 1931; Allen Research Studentship, 1932-34; research in Celtic at University Colls of North Wales and Dublin. Fellowship at St John's Coll., and Faculty Lectr in Celtic, Cambridge Univ., 1934-39; MA 1935; LittD 1954; Lectureship, 1939, Assoc. Professorship, 1940-49, Professorship, 1949-50, Celtic Languages and Literatures, Harvard Univ. Hon. AM Harvard, 1940. Editor of the Journal of Celtic Studies, 1949-57. Corr. Fellow of Mediæval Acad. of America, 1951; Pres. of Scottish Anthropological and Folklore Soc., 1952-60; Vice-Pres. of Soc. of Antiquaries of Scotland, 1960-63; Vice-Pres., English Place-Name Soc., 1973-; Mem., Comité Internat. des Sciences Onomastiques, 1955-; Mem. Council for Name Studies in Great Britain and Ireland, 1961-; one of HM Commissioners for Ancient Monuments (Scotland), 1963-. War service in the British Imperial Censorship, Bermuda (Uncommon Languages), 1942-44; in the US censorship, 1944. Hon. DLitt Celt. Ireland, 1958; Hon. DLitt Wales, 1963; Hon. DUniv Haute-Bretagne, 1971. Hon. Mem. Mod. Language Assoc. of America, 1958; Hon. Mem. Royal Irish Academy, 1965; Assoc. Mem., Royal Belgian Acad. for Scis, Letters and Fine Arts, 1975. *Publications:* Early Welsh Gnomic Poems, 1935; Studies in Early Celtic Nature Poetry, 1935; Cath Maighe Léna, 1938; Scéalta ón mBlascaod, 1939; A Celtic Miscellany, 1951, repr. 1971; Language and History in Early Britain, 1953; Contribs to the Study of Manx Phonology, 1955; The International Popular Tale and Early Welsh Tradition, 1961; The Oldest Irish Tradition, 1964; A Historical Phonology of Breton, 1967; The Gododdin, 1969; The Gaelic Notes in the Book of Deer, 1972; articles on Celtic Languages, literature, history and folklore in Zeitschrift für Celtische Philologie, Etudes Celtiques, Bulletin of the Bd of Celtic Studies, Antiquity, Journal of Roman Studies, Folklore, Journal of Celtic Studies, Scottish Gaelic Studies, Speculum, Modern Philology, etc. *Recreation:* walking. *Address:* 34 Cluny Drive, Edinburgh EH10 6DX. *Club:* Edinburgh University Staff.

JACKSON, Laura (Riding), (Mrs Schuyler B. Jackson); *see* Riding, Laura.

JACKSON, Hon. Sir Lawrence, KCMG 1970; Kt 1964; BA, LLB; Judge, 1949-77, and Chief Justice, 1969-77, Supreme Court of Western Australia; Chancellor, University of Western Australia, since 1968; *b* Dulwich, South Australia, 27 Sept. 1913; *s* of L. S. Jackson; *m* 1937, Mary, *d* of T. H. Donaldson; one *s* two *d. Educ:* Fort Street High Sch., Sydney; University of Sydney. *Recreations:* swimming, golf. *Address:* 13 Cliff Way, Claremont, WA 6010, Australia. *Club:* Weld (Perth, WA).

JACKSON, Very Rev. Lawrence, AKC; Provost of Blackburn Cathedral, since 1973; *b* Hessel, Yorks, 22 March 1926; *s* of Walter and Edith Jackson; *m* 1955, Faith Anne, *d* of Philip and Marjorie Seymour; four *d. Educ:* Alderman Newton's Sch.; Leicester Coll. of Technology; King's Coll., Univ. of London (AKC 1950); St Boniface Coll., Warminster. Asst Curate, St Margaret, Leicester, and Asst Chaplain, Leicester Royal Infirmary, 1951-54; Vicar of: Wymeswold, Leicester, 1954-59; St James the Greater, Leicester, 1959-65; Coventry (Holy Trinity),

1965-73. Canon of Coventry Cath., 1967-73; Rural Dean of Coventry N., 1969-73. Sen. Chap.: Leicester and Rutland ACF, 1955-65; Warwickshire ACF, 1965-73; Chap., Coventry Guild of Freemen, 1968-73; Dio. Chap., CEMS, 1969-71. Dir, The Samaritans of Leicester, 1960-65; Pres., Coventry Round Table, 1968; Chm. Governors, Coventry Blue Coat Sch.; Governor: Barr's Hill Sch.; Bablake Sch. Rotarian. *Recreations:* music, archæology, architecture, countryside, after dinner speaking. *Address:* The Provost's House, Preston New Road, Blackburn BB2 6PS. *T:* Blackburn 52502. *Club:* Eccentric.

JACKSON, Margaret M.; MP (Lab) Lincoln, since Oct. 1974; Parliamentary Under-Secretary of State, Department of Education and Science, since 1976; *b* Jan. 1943. *Educ:* Notre Dame High Sch., Norwich; Manchester Coll. of Sci. and Technol. Formerly: student apprentice, AEI, Manchester; exptl officer, Manchester Univ.; Labour Party res. asst; political adviser, Minister for Overseas Develt, 1974. PPS to Minister for Overseas Develt, 1974-75; Asst Govt Whip, 1975-76. Contested (Lab) Lincoln, Feb. 1974. *Address:* House of Commons, SW1A 0AA.

JACKSON, Sir Michael (Roland), 5th Bt, *cr* 1902; MA; MIEE; FIEI; *b* 20 April 1919; *s* of Sir W. D. Russell Jackson, 4th Bt, and Kathleen (*d* 1975), *d* of Summers Hunter, CBE, Tynemouth; *S* father 1956; *m* 1st, 1942, Hilda Margaret (marr. diss. 1969), *d* of Cecil George Herbert Richardson, CBE, Newark; one *s* one *d*; 2nd, 1969, Hazel Mary, *d* of Ernest Harold Edwards. *Educ:* Stowe; Clare Coll., Cambridge. Served War of 1939-45; Flight-Lt, Royal Air Force Volunteer Reserve. *Heir: s* Thomas St Felix Jackson, *b* 27 Sept. 1946. *Address:* Dragon Cottage, Dragon's Green, Horsham, West Sussex.

JACKSON, Mrs Muriel W.; *see* Ward-Jackson.

JACKSON, Nicholas Fane St George; organist, harpsichordist and composer; Organist and Master of the Choristers, St David's Cathedral, since 1977; *b* 4 Sept. 1934; *s* and *heir* of Sir Hugh Jackson, Bt, *qv*; *m* 1972, Nadia Françoise Geneviève (*née* Michard). *Educ:* Radley Coll.; Wadham Coll., Oxford; RAM. LRAM; ARCM. Organist: St Anne's, Soho, 1963-68; St James's, Piccadilly, 1971-74; St Lawrence, Jewry, 1974-77. Organ recitals and broadcasts: Berlin, 1967; Paris, 1972, 1975; USA (tour), 1975; Minorca, 1977. Début as harpsichordist, Wigmore Hall, 1963; appeared frequently with Soho Concertante, Queen Elizabeth Hall, 1964-72. Recordings: Mass for a Saint's Day, 1971; organ and harpsichord music, incl. works by Arnell, Bach, Mozart and Walther. Liveryman, Drapers' Co., 1965. *Publications:* compositions: Mass for a Saint's Day, 1966; 20th Century Merbecke, 1967; 4 Images (for organ), 1971; Solemn Mass, 1977. *Recreations:* sketching, riding. *Address:* Organist's Lodgings, St Davids, Pembrokeshire. *T:* St Davids 364. *Club:* Bath.

JACKSON, Oliver James V.; *see* Vaughan-Jackson.

JACKSON, Peter (Michael); Senior Planning Officer, South Yorkshire County Council, since 1974; *b* 14 Oct. 1928; *s* of Leonard Patterson Jackson; *m* 1961, Christine Thomas. *Educ:* Durham Univ.; University Coll., Leicester. Lecturer, Dept of Sociology, University of Hull, 1964-66; Fellow, Univ. of Hull, 1970-72; Tutor, Open Univ., 1972-74. MP (Lab) High Peak, 1966-70. *Recreations:* numismatics, book collecting, ski-ing. *Address:* The Mill, Edale, Derbyshire.

JACKSON, Air Vice-Marshal Sir Ralph (Coburn), KBE 1973; CB 1963; Adviser in Insurance and Company Medicine; Honorary Civil Consultant in Medicine to RAF; Consultant Medical Referee: Confederation Life Insurance Co.; Victory Re-insurance Co.; Chief Medical Officer, City of Westminster Assurance Co.; *b* 22 June 1914; *s* of Ralph Coburn Jackson and Phillis Jackson (*née* Dodds); *m* 1939, Joan Lucy Crowley; two *s* two *d. Educ:* Oakmount Sch., Arnside; Guy's Hosp., London. MRCS 1937; FRCPE 1960 (MRCPE 1950); FRCP 1972 (MRCP 1968, LRCP 1937); FRSM. Qualified in Medicine Guy's Hosp., 1937; House Officer appts, Guy's Hosp., 1937-38; commnd in RAF as MO, Nov. 1938; served in France, 1939-40; Russia, 1941; W Africa, 1942-43 (despatches); Sen. MO, 46 Gp for Brit. Casualty Air Evac., 1944-45 (despatches). Med. Specialist, RAF Hosps Wroughton, Aden and Halton, 1946-52 (Consultant in Med., Princess Mary's RAF Hosp. Halton, 1952-63; RAF Hosp., Wegberg, Germany, 1964-66); Consultant Advr in Medicine, 1966-74; Sen. Consultant to RAF, 1971-75; Advr in Medicine to CAA, 1966-75; Chm., Defence Med. Services, Postgrad. Council, 1973-75. QHP 1969-75. MacArthur Lectr, Univ. Edinburgh, 1959. Member: Assurance Med. Soc.; Main Grants Cttee, RAF Benevolent Fund; Hon. Mem., Chiltern Med. Soc. Liveryman, Worshipful Soc. of Apothecaries;

Freeman, City of London. Lady Cade Medal, RCS, 1960. *Publications:* papers on acute renal failure, the artificial kidney and routine electrocardiography in various medical books and journals, 1959-1974. *Recreations:* ancient buildings, history of City of London. *Address:* Piper's Hill, Marwell, Westerham, Kent TN16 1SB. *T:* Westerham 64436; (office) 14-19 Leadenhall Street, EC3. *T:* 01-626 6732. *Clubs:* Royal Air Force, City Livery.

JACKSON, Col Richard John Laurence, CBE 1971; DL, JP; FRIBA, DipArch; Architect; Chairman: North Yorkshire County Council, since 1977; Langbaurgh East Petty Sessional Division since 1961; *b* 17 Oct. 1908; *s* of John Robert and Kathleen Emma Jackson; *m* 1936, Sara Alexander Wilson; one *s. Educ:* Scarborough Coll.; Liverpool Univ. Served War of 1939-45, Green Howards; Middle East, Western Desert, Libya, Tunisia, Sicily and Normandy invasions. Member: North Riding of Yorkshire CC, 1949-73 (Alderman, 1961-74); North Yorkshire CC, 1973-. JP 1951; DL North Riding, 1967. *Recreation:* angling. *Address:* Bridgeholme, Egton Bridge, Whitby, North Yorks. *T:* Grosmont 221.

JACKSON, Prof. Richard Meredith, FBA 1966; LLD; JP; Downing Professor of the Laws of England, 1966-70; Fellow, St John's College, Cambridge, since 1946; *b* 19 Aug. 1903; *s* of James Jackson, JP, Northampton and Jenny May Jackson (*née* Parnell); *m* 1st, Lydia Jibourtovitch (marr. diss.); 2nd, 1936, Lenli, *d* of Alexander Tie Ten Quee, Kingston, Jamaica; one *d* (and one *s* decd). *Educ:* Sidcot; Leighton Park; St John's Coll., Cambridge. Admitted solicitor, 1928. Cambridge Law Sch., LLD 1939; Home Office, 1941-45; Sec. Royal Commn on JPs, 1946-48; Reader in Public Law and Admin., Cambridge, 1950; Member: Royal Commn on Mental Health Services, 1954-57; Deptl Cttee on Children and Young Persons, 1956-60; Council of the Magistrates' Assoc., 1948-72 (Vice-Pres., 1972-). JP Cambs, 1942. *Publications:* History of Quasi-Contract in English Law, 1936; Machinery of Justice in England, 1940 (6th edn, 1972); Machinery of Local Government, 1958 (2nd edn, 1965); Enforcing the Law, 1967 (2nd edn, 1972); ed, 3rd edn, Justice of the Peace, by Leo Page, 1967; articles in learned jls. *Recreation:* yacht cruising. *Address:* St John's College, Cambridge. *T:* 61621; 10 Halifax Road, Cambridge. *T:* 58179. *Club:* Royal Cruising.

JACKSON, Comdr Sir Robert (Gillman Allen), KCVO 1962; Kt 1956; CMG 1944; OBE 1941; Under Secretary-General in charge of UN assistance to Zambia, since 1973, to Indo-China, since 1975, to Cape Verde Islands, since 1975, to São Tome and Principe, since 1977; Adviser to President of Liberia since 1962; Consultant to Volta River Authority, Ghana, since 1962 (Member of Board 1965-76); Member, IUCN Commission on Environmental Policy, Law and Administration, since 1972; Senior Consultant to McKinsey & Company since 1970; *b* 1911; *m* 1950, Barbara Ward (judicially separated) (*see* Baroness Jackson of Lodsworth); one *s.* RAN, 1929-37; transf. to Malta and RN, 1937; Chief Staff Officer to Gov. and C-in-C, Malta, 1940; Planning Malta Comd Defence Scheme; re-armament of the Fortress; devolt Co-ordinated Supply Scheme, 1940 (OBE); Dir-Gen., ME Supply Centre and Principal Asst to UK Minister of State, 1942-45; co-ordn civilian supply ops/mil. ops; devolt Aid to Russia Supply route: estab. anti-locust campaign, 1942 (CMG); AFHQ for special duties in Greece, 1944-45; transf. to HM Treasury, 1945; Sen. Dep. Dir-Gen. of UNRRA, 1945-47, and, in 1945, i/c of UNRRA's ops in Europe (inc. 8,500,000 displaced persons); supervised transfer of UNRRA's residual functions to WHO, FAO, and assisted in establishment of IRO (now UNHCR), and International Children's Emergency Fund, 1947 (UNICEF); services recognised by various governments in Europe and Asia; Asst Sec.-Gen. for Co-ordination in the UN, 1948; HM Treasury, for duties with Lord Pres. of Council, 1949; Perm. Sec., Min. of Nat. Development, Australia, 1950-52 (Snowy Mountains Scheme); Adviser to Govt of India on Development Plans, 1952, 1957 and 1962-63, and to Govt of Pakistan, 1952; Chm. of Preparatory Commission for Volta River multi-purpose project, Gold Coast, 1953-56; Chm., Development Commission, Ghana, 1956-61 (Kt); Organisation of Royal Tours in Ghana, 1959 and 1961(KCVO); Mem. Adv. Bd, Mekong Project, SE Asia, 1962-76; Special Consultant to Administrator, UNDP, 1963-72; Comr i/c, Survey of UN Devolt System, 1968-71; Under Sec.-Gen. i/c UN Relief Ops in Bangladesh, 1972-74. Member: Cttee, Fédération Mondiale des Villes Jumelées Cités Unies, 1972-; Internat. Jury, Prize of Institut de la Vie, 1972-. Hon. DL Syracuse. *Publications:* An International Development Authority, 1955; Report of the Volta River Preparatory Commission, 1956; A Study of the United Nations Development System, 1969. *Address:* United Nations, New York City, NY 10017, USA; Palais des Nations, Geneva, Switzerland. *Clubs:* Brooks's; Victoria (Jersey); Melbourne (Victoria).

JACKSON, Thomas; General Secretary, Union of Post Office Workers, since 1967; HM Government Director, British Petroleum Co. Ltd, since 1975; *b* 1 April 1925; *s* of George Frederick Jackson and Ethel Hargreaves; *m* 1947, Norma Burrow; one *d. Educ:* Jack Lane Elementary Sch. Boy Messenger, GPO, 1939; Royal Navy, 1943; Postman, 1946; Executive Mem., Union of Post Office Workers, 1955; Asst Sec., Union of Post Office Workers, 1964. Member: Gen. Council of TUC, 1967-; Press Council, 1973-; Annan Cttee on the Future of Broadcasting, 1974-77; CRE, 1977-; Court and Council, Sussex Univ., 1974-. Vice-Pres., WEA, 1977-. A Governor: BBC, 1968-73; NIESR, 1974-. *Recreations:* cooking, photography. *Address:* UPW House, Crescent Lane, Clapham Common, SW4 9RN. *T:* 01-622 9977.

JACKSON, Gen. Sir William (Godfrey Fothergill), GBE 1975 (OBE 1958); KCB 1971; MC 1940, and Bar, 1943; Military Historian, Cabinet Office, since 1977; *b* 28 Aug. 1917; *s* of late Col A. Jackson, RAMC, Yanwath, Cumberland, and of E. M. Jackson (*née* Fothergill), Brownber, Westmorland; *m* 1946, Joan Mary Buesden; one *s* one *d. Educ:* Shrewsbury; RMA, Woolwich; King's Coll., Cambridge, King's medal, RMA Woolwich, 1937. Commnd into Royal Engineers, 1937; served War of 1939-45: Norwegian Campaign, 1940; Tunisia, 1942-43; Sicily and Italy, 1943-44; Far East, 1945; GSO1, HQ Allied Land Forces SE Asia, 1945-48; Instructor, Staff Coll., Camberley, 1948-50; Instructor, RMA, Sandhurst, 1951-53; AA & QMG (War Plans), War Office, during Suez ops, 1956; Comdr, Gurkha Engrs, 1958-60; Col GS, Minley Div. of Staff Coll., Camberley, 1961-62; Dep. Dir of Staff Duties, War Office, 1962-64; Imp. Def. Coll., 1965; Dir, Chief of Defence Staff's Unison Planning Staff, 1966-68; Asst Chief of General Staff (Operational Requirements), MoD, 1963-70; GOC-in-C, Northern Command, 1970-72; QMG, 1973-76. Colonel Commandant: RE, 1971-; Gurkha Engrs, 1971-76; RAOC, 1973-; Hon. Col, Engineer and Rly Staff Corps, RE, TAVR, 1977-; ADC (Gen.) to the Queen, 1974-76. *Publications:* Attack in the West, 1953; Seven Roads to Moscow, 1957; The Battle for Italy, 1967; Battle for Rome, 1969; Alexander of Tunis as Military Commander, 1971; The North African Campaigns, 1975; Normandy '44, 1977; contribs to Royal United Service Instn Jl (gold medals for prize essays, 1950 and 1966). *Recreations:* fishing, writing, gardening. *Address:* Williams & Glyn's Bank Ltd, Holt's Branch, Whitehall, SW1. *Club:* Army and Navy.

JACKSON, William Theodore, CBE 1967 (MBE 1946); ARIBA; MRTPI; Director of Post Office Services, Ministry of Public Building and Works, 1969-71, retired; *b* 18 July 1906; *y s* of Rev. Oliver Miles Jackson and Emily Jackson; *m* 1932, Marjorie Campbell; one *s* two *d. Educ:* Cheltenham Gram. Sch. Chief Architect, Iraq Govt, 1936-38; Dir, Special Repair Service, Min. of Works, 1939-45; Min. of Public Building and Works, 1946-69; Dir, Mobile Labour Force; Dir of Maintenance; seconded to World Bank as Advr to Iran Technical Bureau of Plan organisation, 1956-57; Regional Dir; Dir, Regional Services; Dir, Headquarters Services, 1967-69. *Recreations:* gardening, painting. *Address:* Church Farm, Blyford, Halesworth, Suffolk. *T:* Blythburgh 455.

JACKSON, William Unsworth; Chief Executive, Kent County Council, since 1974; *b* 9 Feb. 1926; *s* of William Jackson and Margaret Esplen Jackson (*née* Sunderland); *m* 1952, Valerie Annette (*née* Llewellyn); one *s* one *d. Educ:* Alsop High Sch., Liverpool. Solicitor. Entered local govt service, Town Clerk's Office, Liverpool, 1942; Dep. County Clerk, Kent, 1970. *Recreations:* sailing, gardening, talking and walking. *Address:* 34 Yardley Park Road, Tonbridge, Kent. *T:* Tonbridge 351078.

JACOB, Ven. Bernard Victor; Archdeacon of Kingston-upon-Thames, since 1977; *b* 20 Nov. 1921; *m* 1946, Dorothy Joan Carey; one *s* two *d. Educ:* Liverpool Institute; St Peter's College (MA) and Wycliffe Hall, Oxford. Curate, Middleton, Lancs, 1950-54; Vicar, Ulverston, Lancs, 1954-59; Vicar, Bilston, Staffs, 1959-64; Warden of Scargill House, Yorks, 1964-68; Rector of Mortlake, 1968-77. *Recreations:* travel, reading, enjoying life. *Address:* 7 Cornwall Road, Cheam, Sutton SM2 6DT.

JACOB, Lt-Gen. Sir (Edward) Ian (Claud), GBE 1960 (KBE 1946; CBE 1942); CB 1944; DL; late RE, Colonel, retired and Hon. Lieutenant-General; Chairman, Matthews Holdings Ltd, 1970-76; *b* 27 Sept. 1899; *s* of late Field Marshal Sir Claud Jacob, GCB, GCSI, KCMG; *m* 1924, Cecil Bisset Treherne; two *s. Educ:* Wellington Coll.; RMA, Woolwich; King's Coll., Cambridge (BA). 2nd Lieut, Royal Engineers, 1918; Capt. 1929; Bt Major, 1935; Major, 1938; Bt Lt-Col, 1939; Col, 1943. Waziristan, 1922-23. Staff Coll., 1931-32; GSO3 War Office,

1934-36; Bde-Maj., Canal Bde, Egypt, 1936-38; Military Asst Sec., Cttee of Imperial Defence, 1938; Military Asst Sec. to the War Cabinet, 1939-46; retired pay, 1946. Controller of European Services, BBC, 1946; Dir of Overseas Services, BBC, 1947 (on leave of absence during 1952); Chief Staff Officer to Minister of Defence and Deputy Sec. (Mil.) of the Cabinet during 1952; Dir-Gen. of the BBC, 1952-60; Director: Fisons, 1960-70; EMI, 1960-73; Chm., Covent Garden Market Authority, 1961-66; a Trustee, Imperial War Museum, 1966-73. CC, E Suffolk, 1960-70, Alderman, 1970-74; CC Suffolk, 1974-77. JP Suffolk, 1961-69; DL Suffolk, 1964. US Legion of Merit (Comdr). *Address:* The Red House, Woodbridge, Suffolk. *T:* Woodbridge 2001. *Club:* Army and Navy.

JACOB, Prof. François; Croix de la Libération; Grand Officier de la Légion d'Honneur; Departmental Head, Pasteur Institute; Professor of Cellular Genetics, at the College of France, since 1964; *b* Nancy (Meurthe & Moselle), 17 June 1920; *m* 1947, Lysiane Bloch; three *s* one *d. Educ:* Lycée Carnot, France. D en M 1947; D ès S 1954. Pasteur Institute: Asst, 1950; Head of Laboratory, 1956. Mem., Acad. of Scis, Paris, 1977. Charles Léopold Mayer Prize, Acad. des Sciences, Paris, 1962; Nobel Prize for Medicine, 1965. Foreign Member: Royal Danish Acad. of Letters and Sciences, 1962; Amer. Acad. of Arts and Sciences, 1964; Nat. Acad. of Scis, USA, 1969; Royal Soc., 1973; Soc. Royale Belgique, 1973. Dr *hc* University of Chicago, 1965. *Publications:* La Logique du Vivant, 1971; various scientific. *Recreation:* painting. *Address:* 28 rue du Dr Roux, Paris 15, France.

JACOB, Frederick Henry; retired; Director, Ministry of Agriculture, Fisheries and Food's Pest Infestation Control Laboratory, 1968-77; *b* 12 March 1915; *s* of Henry Theodore and Elizabeth Jacob; *m* 1941, Winifred Edith Sloman; one *s* one *d. Educ:* Friars Sch., Bangor; UC North Wales. BSc, MSc, FIBiol. Asst Entomologist: King's Coll., Newcastle upon Tyne, 1942-44; Sch. of Agriculture, Cambridge, 1944-45; Adviser in Agric. Zoology, UC North Wales, 1945-46; Adv. Entomologist, Min. of Agriculture and Fisheries, Nat. Agric. Adv. Service, N Wales, 1946-50; Head of Entomology Dept, MAFF, Plant Pathology Lab., 1950-68. *Publications:* papers mainly on systematics of Aphididae in learned jls. *Recreations:* tennis, hill walking, rock climbing. *Address:* Llys y Gwynt, Llandegai, Bangor, Gwynedd LL57 4BG. *T:* Bangor 53863. *Clubs:* Farmers', Climbers; Wayfarers (Liverpool).

JACOB, Gordon (Percival Septimus), CBE 1968; DMus; FRCM; Hon. RAM; Composer; Professor of Theory, Composition, and Orchestration, Royal College of Music, retired 1966; Editor of Penguin Musical Scores, 1947-57; *b* 5 July 1895; 7th *s* of late Stephen Jacob, *m* 1st, 1924, Sidney Wilmot (*d* 1958), *er d* of Rev. A. W. Gray, Ipswich; 2nd, 1959, Margaret Sidney Hannah, *d* of C. A. Gray, Helions Bumpstead; one *s* one *d. Educ:* Dulwich Coll.; Royal College of Music. Served European War, 1914-18; UPS and Queen's Royal West Surrey Regt (Prisoner of War in Germany, April 1917-Dec. 1918); Studied composition at the Royal College of Music under the late Sir Charles V. Stanford; Conducting under Adrian Boult, and Theory under Herbert Howells. Compositions include Orchestral, Choral and Chamber music, many concertos for various instruments, works for Wind Orchestra and Brass Band, also orchestrations and arrangements. Holder of John Collard Fellowship (Worshipful Company of Musicians), 1943-46; Cobbett Medal for Services to Chamber Music, 1949. *Publications:* Orchestral Technique, a Manual for Students; How to Read a Score; The Composer and his Art; The Elements of Orchestration; most of the works alluded to above; also many other smaller compositions. Contributed to Chambers's Encyclopædia and Groves Dictionary of Music. *Recreations:* gardening, motoring, reading; interested in all forms of art, and in natural history. *Address:* 1 Audley Road, Saffron Walden, Essex CB11 3HW. *T:* 22406.

JACOB, Lieut.-Gen. Sir Ian; see Jacob, Lieut.-Gen. Sir E. I. C.

JACOB, Isaac Hai, (Jack), QC 1976; Senior Master of the Supreme Court, Queen's Bench Division, and Queen's Remembrancer, since 1975; Fellow of University College, London, 1966; *b* 5 June 1908; 3rd *s* of late Jacob Isaiah and Aziza Jacob; *m* 1940, Rose Mary Jenkins (*née* Samwell); two *s. Educ:* Shanghai Public Sch. for Boys; London Sch. of Economics; University Coll., London. LLB (1st class Hons), London; Joseph Hume Scholar in Jurisprudence, University Coll., London, 1928 and 1930; Arden Scholar, Gray's Inn, 1930; Cecil Peace Prizeman, 1930. Called to the Bar, Gray's Inn, Nov. 1930; Mem., Senate of Inns of Court and the Bar. Served in ranks from 1940 until commissioned in RAOC 1942; Staff Capt., War Office (Ord. I), 1943-45. Master, Supreme Court, Queen's Bench Div., 1957. Prescribed Officer for Election Petitions,

1975-. Hon. Lectr in Law, University Coll., London, 1959-74; Hon. Lectr in Legal Ethics, Birmingam Univ., 1969-72; Hon. Visiting Lecturer: Imperial Coll. of Science and Technology, 1963-64; Birmingham Univ., 1964-65; Bedford Coll., 1969-; Vis. Professor: Sydney Univ., 1971; Osgoode Hall Law Sch., York Univ., Toronto; of English Law, UCL, 1974-; Member: Lord Chancellor's (Pearson) Cttee on Funds in Court, 1958-59; Working Party on the Revision of the Rules of the Supreme Court, 1960-65; (Payne) Cttee on Enforcement of Judgment Debts, 1965-69; (Winn) Cttee on Personal Injuries Litigation, 1966-68. Vice-President: Assoc. of Law Teachers; Industrial Law Soc.; Governor, Central London Polytechnic; Member, Cttee of Management: Inst. of Judicial Admin; Brit. Inst. of Internat. and Comparative Law; Selden Soc. Hon. Freeman, City of London, 1976. Adv. Editor, Court Forms; Editor, Annual Practice, 1961-66; Gen. Editor, Supreme Court Practice, 1967-. *Publications:* Law relating to Hire Purchase, 1938; Chitty and Jacob's Queen's Bench Forms (19th, 20th and 21st edns); Bullen, Leake and Jacob's Precedents of Pleadings (12th edn); chapter on Civil Procedure including Courts and Evidence, in Annual Survey of Commonwealth Law, 1965-; contributed titles: Discovery, Execution (jtly), to Halsbury's Laws of England, 4th edn; Compromise and Settlement, Issues, Order 14 Proceedings, Stay of Proceedings, Third Party Procedure, to Court Forms. *Recreations:* walking, painting. *Address:* 16 The Park, Golders Green, NW11. *T:* 01-458 3832. *Clubs:* Reform, Royal Automobile; Hendon Golf.

JACOB, Rhoda Hannah, MA Cantab; FRSA; *b* 5 June 1900; *y d* of late Ernest S. and late Lydia J. Brooksby Jacob. *Educ:* Dulwich High School; Sydenham High School, GPDST; Girton Coll., Cambridge (Classical Tripos). Teacher: Queenswood, Clapham Park, 1922-25; Richmond County Sch. for Girls, 1926; Kensington High School, 1926-35; Headmistress: Harrogate Coll., Yorks, 1935-52; Falmouth County High Sch., Cornwall, 1957-65. Archaeological Research Sec. to Sir Charles Walston, 1925; Triple Blue (hockey, netball, tennis); Hockey, County and Territorial (Surrey and South of England). *Recreations:* motoring, reading, archaeology. *Address:* Tregarth, 16 Spernen Wyn Road, Falmouth, Cornwall TR11 4EH. *T:* Falmouth 313067.

JACOB, Very Rev. William Ungoed; Dean of Brecon Cathedral since 1967; Vicar of St Mary's, Brecon with Battle, since 1967; *b* 6 Oct. 1910; *s* of Wm and L. M. M. Jacob; *m* 1935, Ivy Matilda Hall; one *d. Educ:* Llanelly Gram. Sch.; Llandovery Coll.; Jesus Coll., Oxford; Wycliffe Hall, Oxford. BA 2nd cl. History, 1932; 2nd cl. Theology, 1933; MA 1937. Ordained deacon, 1934; priest, 1935; Curate of Holy Trinity, Aberystwyth, 1934-36; Lampeter, 1936-40; Vicar of Blaenau Ffestiniog 1940-51; Rector of Hubberston, 1951-55; Vicar of St Peter's, Carmarthen, 1955-67; Canon of St David's Cathedral, 1957-67. Rural Dean of Carmarthen, 1958-60; Archdeacon of Carmarthen, 1960-67. Pres., Council of Churches for Wales 1971-76 (Sec., 1960-65). Mem., Coun. for Wales and Mon, 1963-66. Gen. Sec. Church in Wales Prov. Council for Mission and Unity, 1967-73; Chm., Provincial Selection Panel, 1974. *Publications:* Meditations on the Seven Words, 1960; Three Hours' Devotions, 1965; A Guide to the Parish Eucharist, 1969. *Address:* The Deanery, Brecon, S Wales. *T:* Brecon 3310.

JACOBS, Arthur David; Editor, British Music Yearbook, formerly Music Yearbook, since 1971; Professor, Royal Academy of Music, since 1964; Critic, Audio and Record Review, now Hi-Fi News & Record Review, since 1964; record reviewer, Sunday Times, since 1968; *b* 14 June 1922; *s* of late Alexander S. and of Estelle Jacobs; *m* 1953, Betty Upton Hughes; two *s. Educ:* Manchester Grammar Sch.; Merton Coll., Oxford (MA). Music Critic, Daily Express, 1947-52; Associate Editor, Opera, 1962-71; Music Critic, Jewish Chronicle, 1963-75. Leverhulme Res. Fellow in Music, 1977-78. Centennial Lectr, Illinois Univ., 1967; Vis. Professor: Univ. of Victoria, BC, 1968; Univ. of California at Santa Barbara, 1969; Temple Univ., Philadelphia, 1970, 1971; UCLA, 1973; Univ. of Western Ontario, 1974; McMaster Univ., 1975. Hon. RAM 1969. *Publications:* Music Lover's Anthology, 1948; Gilbert and Sullivan, 1951; A New Dictionary of Music, 1958 (also Spanish and Swedish edns); Choral Music, 1963: libretto of opera One Man Show by Nicholas Maw, 1964; (with Stanley Sadie) Pan Book of Opera, 1966; A Short History of Western Music, 1972; (ed) Music Education Handbook, 1976; many opera translations; contrib. Musical Times, foreign jls, etc. *Recreations:* puns, swimming, ski-ing, theatre. *Address:* 53 Friars Avenue, N20 0XG. *T:* 01-368 3010.

JACOBS, David Lewis; radio and television broadcaster; *b* 19 May 1926; *s* of David Jacobs and Jeanette Victoria Jacobs; *m* 1st, 1949, Patricia Bradlaw (marr. diss. 1972); three *d* (one *s* decd);

2nd, 1975, Caroline Munro (*d* 1975). *Educ:* Belmont Coll.; Strand Sch. RN, 1944-47. First broadcast, Navy Mixture, 1944; Chief Announcer, Radio SEAC, Ceylon, 1944-47; Asst Stn Dir, Radio SEAC, 1947; News Reader, BBC Gen. Overseas Service, 1947, subseq. freelance. Major radio credits include: Book of Verse, Housewives' Choice, Journey into Space, Dateline London, Grande Gingold, Curioser and Curioser, Puffney Post Office, Follow that Man, Man about Town, Jazz Club, Midday Spin, Music Through Midnight, Scarlet Pimpernel, DJ Show, Pick of the Pops, Saturday Show Band Show, Melodies for You, Any Questions, Any Answers. TV credits incl.: Focus on Hocus, Vera Lynn Show, Make up your Mind, Tell the Truth, Juke Box Jury, Top of the Pops, Hot Line, Miss World, Top Town, David Jacobs' Words and Music, Sunday Night with David Jacobs, Little Women, There Goes that Song Again, Make a Note, Where are they Now, What's My Line, Who What or Where, Frank Sinatra Show, Mario Lanza Show, Walt Disney Christmas Show, Wednesday Show, Wednesday Magazine, Eurovision Song Contest, TV Ice Time, Twist, A Song for Europe, Ivor Novello Awards, Aladdin, Airs and Graces, There Goes That Song Again, Tell Me Another, Those Wonderful TV Times. Numerous film performances incl. Golden Disc, You Must Be Joking, It's Trad Dad, Stardust; former commentator, British Movietone News. 2 Royal Command Performances; 6 yrs Britain's Top Disc Jockey on both BBC and Radio Luxembourg; Variety Club of Gt Brit., BBC TV Personality of Year, 1960, and BBC Radio Personality of the Year, 1975. Vice-Pres., Stars Organisation for Spastics (Past Chm.); Mem. Council, RSPCA, 1969-77, Vice-Chm. 1975-76. *Publication:* (autobiog.) Jacobs' Ladder, 1963. *Recreations:* talking and listening. *Address:* 19 Launceston Place, W8 5RL.

JACOBS, Prof. John Arthur; Professor of Geophysics, since 1974, and Fellow, Darwin College, since 1976, University of Cambridge; *b* 13 April 1916; *m* 1st, 1941, Daisy Sarah Ann Montgomerie (*d* 1974); two *d*; 2nd, 1974, Margaret Jones. *Educ:* Univ. of London. BA 1937, MA 1939, PhD 1949, DSc 1961. Instr Lieut RN, 1941-46; Lectr, Royal Holloway Coll., Univ. of London, 1946-51; Assoc. Prof., Univ. of Toronto, 1951-57; Prof., Univ. of British Columbia, 1957-67; Dir, Inst. of Earth Sciences, Univ. of British Columbia, 1961-67; Killam Meml Prof. of Science, Univ. of Alberta, 1967-74; Dir, Inst. of Earth and Planetary Physics, Univ. of Alberta, 1970-74. FRSC 1958; Centennial Medal of Canada, 1967; Medal of Canadian Assoc. of Physicists, 1975. *Publications:* (with R. D. Russell and J. T. Wilson) Physics and Geology, 1959, 2nd edn 1974; The Earth's Core and Geomagnetism, 1963; Geomagnetic Micropulsations, 1970; A Textbook on Geonomy, 1974; The Earth's Core, 1975. *Recreations:* walking, music. *Address:* Department of Geodesy and Geophysics, Madingley Rise, Madingley Road, Cambridge CB3 0EZ. *T:* Cambridge 51686. *Club:* Naval.

JACOBS, Brig. John Conrad S.; *see* Saunders-Jacobs.

JACOBS, John Robert Maurice; Golf Consultant, Delapre Park Golf Complex; Golf Adviser/Commentator, Independent Television, since 1967; Golf Adviser, Golf World Magazine since 1962; Golf Instructor: Golf Digest Magazine Schools, since 1971; Golf Magazine Schools, US; *b* 14 March 1925; *s* of Robert and Gertrude Vivian Jacobs; *m* 1949, Rita Wragg; one *s* one *d*. *Educ:* Maltby Grammar School. Asst Professional Golfer, Hallamshire Golf Club, 1947-49; Golf Professional: Gezira Sporting Club, Cairo, 1949-52; Sandy Lodge Golf Club, 1952-64; John Jacobs Golf Centres at Sandown Park and Newcastle upon Tyne, 1964-. Tournament Dir-Gen., 1971-76, Advr to Tournament Div., 1976-, PGA. *Publications:* Golf, 1961; Play Better Golf, 1969; Practical Golf, 1973; John Jacobs Analyses the Superstars, 1974; contrib.: Golf World Magazine; Golf Digest Magazine; Golf Magazine (US); The Director. *Recreations:* shooting, fishing. *Address:* The Old Vicarage, Emery Down, Lyndhurst, Hants. *Clubs:* Lucayan Country (Grand Bahamas); Sandy Lodge Golf, New Forest Golf, Brockenhurst Golf, Bramshaw Golf, John Jacobs Golf Centres.

JACOBS, Hon. Sir Kenneth (Sydney), KBE 1976; Hon. Mr Justice Jacobs; Justice of High Court of Australia since 1974; *b* 5 Oct. 1917; *s* of Albert Sydney Jacobs and Sarah Grace Jacobs (*née* Aggs); *m* 1952, Eleanor Mary Neal; one *d*. *Educ:* Knox Grammar Sch., NSW; Univ. of Sydney (BA, LLB). Admitted to NSW Bar, 1947; QC 1958; Supreme Court of NSW: Judge, 1960; Judge of Appeal, 1966; Pres., Court of Appeal, 1972. *Publication:* Law of Trusts, 1958. *Recreations:* printing and bookbinding; gardening. *Address:* High Court of Australia, Darlinghurst, NSW 2010, Australia. *Club:* University (Sydney).

JACOBS, Sir Roland (Ellis), Kt 1963; formerly: Chairman: Executive Trustee & Agency Co. of South Australia Ltd; South Australian Brewing Co. Ltd.; Director, Mutual Hospital Association Ltd; *b* Adelaide, 28 Feb. 1891; *s* of late S. J. Jacobs, Adelaide; *m* 1st, 1917, Olga (decd), *d* of late A. M. Hertzberg; one *s* two *d*; 2nd, 1970, Esther Lipman Cook. *Educ:* Geelong Coll., Vic. Past Pres., RSPCA; Pres., Post Graduate Foundation in Medicine; former Mem. Bd of Management: Royal Adelaide Hosp.; Queen Elizabeth Hosp.; ex officio Mem. Council: Adelaide Chamber of Commerce (Pres., 1942-43); Crippled Children's Assoc. of SA (past Pres.); Aust. Adv. Council for Physically Handicapped; President, Meals on Wheels Inc.; Mem., Nat. Council, Aust. Boy Scouts Assoc. Hon. Life Member (formerly Director): Aust. Elizabethan Theatre Trust; Adelaide Festival of Arts. *Recreation:* bowls. *Address:* 2 Tusmore Avenue, Leabrook, SA 5068, Australia. *Club:* Adelaide (Adelaide).

JACOBS, Sir Wilfred (Ebenezer), Kt 1967; OBE 1959; QC 1959; Governor, Antigua, since 1967; *b* 19 Oct. 1919; 2nd *s* of William Henry Jacobs and of late Henrietta Jacobs (*née* Du Bois); *m* 1947, Carmen Sylva, 2nd *d* of late Walter A. Knight and Flora Knight (*née* Fleming); one *s* two *d*. *Educ:* Grenada Boys' Secondary Sch.; Gray's Inn, London. Called to Bar, Gray's Inn, 1946; Registrar and Additional Magistrate, St Vincent, 1946; Magistrate, Dominica, 1947, and St Kitts, 1949; Crown Attorney, St Kitts, 1952; Attorney-Gen., Leeward Is, 1957-59, and Antigua, 1960. Acted Administrator, Dominica, St Kitts, Antigua, various periods, 1947-60. MEC and MLC, St Vincent, Dominica, St Kitts, Antigua, 1947-60; Legal Draftsman and Acting Solicitor-Gen., Trinidad and Tobago, 1960. Barbados: Solicitor-Gen., and Actg Attorney-Gen., 1961-63; PC and MLC, 1962-63; Dir of Public Prosecutions, 1964; Judge of Supreme Court of Judicature, 1967. KStJ. *Recreations:* swimming, gardening, golf. *Address:* Governor's Residence, Antigua, West Indies. *Clubs:* United Oxford & Cambridge University, Royal Commonwealth Society (West Indian).

JACOBS-LARKCOM, Eric Herbert Larkcom, CBE 1946; *b* 21 Jan. 1895; *s* of Herbert Jacobs, Barrister-at-law; (assumed additional surname of Larkcom by Royal Licence, 1915); *m* 1933, Dorothy Primrose Kerr Tasker; two *d*. *Educ:* University Coll. Sch. Entered Royal Engineers from RMA, Woolwich, 1916; served European War, 1914-18, France, 1917-18 (wounded); Staff Coll., Camberley, 1930-31; served War of 1939-45, France 1939-40; China, 1942-45; Col, 1942; retired pay, 1946; i/c Harbin Consulate-Gen. (at Changchun), 1947-48; Consul-Gen. Kunming, 1948-49; Consul, Tamsui, Formosa, 1951-53; Consul, Chiengmai, 1954-58, retired. Mentioned in despatches, 1945, Chinese Cloud and Banner, 1945, American Bronze Star, 1946. *Address:* White Lodge, 12 Pedn Moran, St Mawes, Truro, Cornwall. *Clubs:* Naval and Military; Royal Cornwall Yacht.

JACOBSEN, Frithjof; Norwegian Ambassador to the Court of St James's and to Ireland, since 1975; *b* 14 Jan. 1914; *m* 1941, Elsa Tidemand Anderson; one *s* two *d*. *Educ:* Univ. of Oslo (Law). Entered Norwegian Foreign Service, 1938; Legation, Paris, 1938-40; Norwegian Foreign Ministry, London, 1940-45; held posts in Moscow, London, Oslo, 1945-55; Director-Gen., Political Affairs, Oslo, 1955-59; Norwegian Ambassador to: Canada, 1959-61; Moscow, 1961-66; Under-Sec. of State, Oslo, 1966-70; Ambassador to Moscow, 1970-75. *Address:* 10 Palace Green, W8. *T:* 01-937 2247.

JACOBSON, family name of Baron Jacobson.

JACOBSON, Baron *cr* 1975 (Life Peer), of St Albans; **Sydney Jacobson, MC** 1944; Editorial Director, International Publishing Corporation Newspapers, 1968-74, Deputy Chairman, 1973-74; *b* 26 Oct. 1908; *m* 1938, Phyllis June Buck; two *s* one *d*. *Educ:* Strand Sch., London; King's Coll., London. Asst Editor: Statesman, India, 1934-36; Lilliput Magazine, 1936-39. Served in Army, 1939-45. Special Correspondent, Picture Post, 1945-48; Editor, Leader Magazine, 1948-50; Political Editor, Daily Mirror, 1952-62; Editor, Daily Herald, 1962-64; Editor, Sun, 1964-65; Chairman, Odhams Newspapers, 1968. Member Press Council, 1969-75. *Recreations:* tennis, walking, reading. *Address:* 6 Avenue Road, St Albans, Herts. *T:* St Albans 53873.

JACQUES, family name of Baron Jacques.

JACQUES, Baron *cr* 1968 (Life Peer), of Portsea Island; **John Henry Jacques;** a Lord in Waiting (Government Whip), 1974-77; Chairman of the Co-operative Union Ltd, 1964-70; *b* 11 Jan. 1905; *s* of Thomas Dobson Jacques and Annie Bircham; *m* 1929, Constance White; two *s* one *d*. *Educ:* Victoria Univ., Manchester; Co-operative Coll. Sec-Man., Moorsley Co-operative Society Ltd, 1925-29; Tutor, Co-operative Coll., 1929-42; Accountant, Plymouth Co-operative Soc. Ltd, 1942-45;

Chief Executive, Portsea Island Co-operative Soc. Ltd, Portsmouth, 1945-65; Pres., Co-operative Congress, 1961. Pres., Retail Trades Education Council, 1971-75. *Publications:* Book-Keeping I, II and III, 1940; Management Accounting, 1966; Manual on Co-operative Management, 1969. *Recreations:* walking, snooker, gardening, West-Highland terriers. *Address:* 23 Hilltop Crescent, Cosham, Portsmouth, Hants. *T:* Cosham 75511. *Club:* Co-operative (Portsmouth).

JACQUES, Peter Roy Albert; Secretary, TUC Social Insurance and Industrial Welfare Department, since 1971; *b* 12 Aug. 1939; *s* of George Henry Jacques and Ivy Mary Jacques (*née* Farr); *m* 1965, Jacqueline Anne Sears; one *s* one *d*. *Educ:* Archbishop Temple's Secondary Sch.; Newcastle upon Tyne Polytechnic (BSc Sociology); Univ. of Leicester. Building labourer, 1955-58; market porter, 1958-62; Asst, TUC Social Insce and Industrial Welfare Dept, 1968-71. Member: Industrial Injuries Adv. Council, 1972; Nat. Insce Adv. Cttee, 1972; Health and Safety Commn, 1974; Royal Commn on the Nat. Health Service, 1976; EEC Cttee on Health-Safety, 1976. *Publications:* responsible for TUC pubns Health-Safety Handbook; Occupational Pension Schemes. *Recreations:* reading, yoga, karate, walking, camping, vegetable growing. *Address:* TUC, Congress House, Great Russell Street, WC1B 3LS. *T:* 01-636 4030.

JACQUOT, Général d'Armée Pierre Elie; Grand Cross of Legion of Honour, 1961; *b* 16 June 1902; *s* of Aimé Jacquot and Marie (*née* Renault); *m* 1929, Lucie Claire Mamet; one *d* (and one *s* killed in action, Algeria, 1962). *Educ:* Saint-Cyr Military Academy, France. Commissioned 30th Chasseur Bn, 1922; Foreign Legion Service, 1925-29; French École de Guerre, 1929-31, Belgian, 1931-33; Capt. 1933; posted to GHQ, Sept. 1939; Comdr 3rd Bn of 109th Inf. Regt, 1940; with André Malraux (alias Col Berger) organised French Resistance in the Corrèze, Dordogne and Lot areas, 1940-44; served in First French Army, 1944-45 (Alsace-Lorraine Bde); Brig.-Gen. 1946; Dep. Chief of Army Staff, 1947; Maj.-Gen. 1950; comd 8th Inf. Div., 1951-54; Lieut.-Gen. 1954; High Comr and C-in-C, Indo-China, 1955-56; C-in-C French Forces in Germany, 1956-59; Gen. 1957; Inspector-Gen. of French Land Forces, 1959-61; Commander-in-Chief, Allied Forces Central Europe, 1961-63; Cadre de Réserve, Dec. 1963. *Publications:* Essai de stratégie occidentale, 1953; La Stratégie périphérique devant la bombe atomique, 1954. *Address:* (Winter) 15 Avenue de Villars, Paris 7; (Summer) Vrécourt, 88 Contrexéville, France.

JAEGER, Prof. John Conrad, FRS 1970; MA Cantab, DSc Sydney; Emeritus Professor of Geophysics, 1973 (Professor of Geophysics, 1952-72, and Head of Department of Geophysics and Geochemistry, 1965-71), Australian National University, Canberra; *b* Sydney, 30 July 1907; *s* of Carl Jaeger, Stockton-on-Tees; *m* 1st, Sylvia Percival Rees (marr. diss.); 2nd, Martha Elizabeth, (Patty), *d* of George Clarke, Hobart. *Educ:* C of E Grammar Sch., Sydney; Universities of Sydney and Cambridge. Lectr in Mathematics, later Prof. of Applied Maths, Univ. of Tasmania, 1935-51. Hon. DSc Tasmania. *Publications:* (with H. S. Carslaw) Operational Methods in Applied Mathematics, 1941, 2nd edn 1948; (with H. S. Carslaw) Conduction of Heat in Solids, 1947, 2nd edn 1959; An Introduction to the Laplace Transformation, 1949, 3rd edn (with G. H. Newstead) 1969; Elasticity, Fracture and Flow with Engineering and Geological Applications, 1956, 3rd edn 1969; An Introduction to Applied Mathematics, 1951, 2nd edn (with A. M. Starfield), 1974; (with N. G. W. Cook) Fundamentals of Rock Mechanics, 1969, 2nd edn 1976. *Recreations:* farming, conservation of Australian antiquities. *Address:* Private Bag 5, Post Office, Sorell, Tasmania 7172, Australia.

JAEGER, Prof. Leslie Gordon; FRSE 1966; Academic Vice-President, Acadia University, Nova Scotia, since 1975; *b* 28 Jan. 1926; *s* of Henry Jaeger; *m* 1948, Annie Sylvia Dyson; two *d*. *Educ:* King George V Sch., Southport; Gonville and Caius Coll., Cambridge. Royal Corps of Naval Constructors, 1945-48; Industry, 1948-52; University College, Khartoum, 1952-56; Univ. Lectr, Cambridge, 1956-62; Fellow and Dir of Studies, Magdalene Coll., Cambridge, 1959-62; Prof. of Applied Mechanics, McGill Univ., Montreal, 1962-65. Regius Prof. of Engineering, Edinburgh Univ., 1965-66; Prof. of Civil Engineering, McGill Univ., 1966-70; Dean, Faculty of Engineering, Univ. of New Brunswick, 1970-75. *Publications:* The Analysis of Grid Frameworks and Related Structures (with A. W. Hendry), 1958; Elementary Theory of Elastic Plates, 1964; Cartesian Tensors in Engineering Science, 1965; various papers on grillage analysis in British, European and American Journals. *Recreations:* golf, curling, contract bridge. *Address:* 13 Locust Avenue, Wolfville, NS, Canada. *T:* 542-9601. *Club:* Halifax (Halifax, Canada).

JAFFÉ, (Andrew) Michael; Director, Fitzwilliam Museum, Cambridge, since 1973; Professor of the History of Western Art, since 1973; Fellow of King's College, Cambridge, since 1952; *b* 3 June 1923; *s* of Arthur Daniel Jaffé, OBE, and Marie Marguerite Strauss; *m* 1964, Patricia Ann Milne-Henderson; one *s* two *d*. *Educ:* Eton Coll.; King's Coll., Cambridge (MA); Courtauld Inst. of Art. Lt-Comdr, RNVR, retd. Commonwealth Fund Fellow, Harvard and New York Univ., 1951-53; Asst Lectr in Fine Arts, Cambridge, 1956; Prof. of Renaissance Art, Washington Univ., St Louis, 1960-61; Vis. Prof., Harvard Univ., Summer 1961; Lectr in Fine Arts, Cambridge, 1961; Reader in History of Western Art, Cambridge, 1968; Head of Dept of History of Art, Cambridge, 1970-73; a Syndic, Fitzwilliam Museum, 1971-73. Mem., Adv. Council, V&A Museum, 1971-76. Organiser (for Nat. Gall. of Canada) of Jordaens Exhibn, Ottawa, 1968-69; Vis. Prof., Harvard Univ., Fall 1968-69. FRSA 1969. *Publications:* Van Dyck's Antwerp Sketchbook, 1966; Rubens, 1967; Jordaens, 1968; Rubens and Italy, 1977; articles and reviews (art historical) in European and N American jls, etc. *Recreation:* viticulture. *Address:* Grove Lodge, Trumpington Street, Cambridge. *Clubs:* Athenæum, Turf; Beefsteak, University Pitt (Cambridge).

JAFFRAY, Alistair Robert Morton; Deputy Under-Secretary of State, Ministry of Defence, since 1975; *b* 28 Oct. 1925; *s* of Alexander George and Janet Jaffray; *m* 1953, Margaret Betty, *d* of H. A. Newman, Bath; two *s* one *d*. *Educ:* Clifton Coll.; Corpus Christi Coll., Cambridge. BA First Cl. Hons., Mod. Langs. Served War, RNVR, 1943-46. Apptd Home Civil Service (Admty), 1948; Private Sec. to First Lord of Admty, 1960-62; Private Sec. to successive Secretaries of State for Defence, 1969-70; Asst Under-Sec. of State, MoD, 1971-75. *Address:* Okeford, 10 Lynch Road, Farnham, Surrey. *T:* Farnham 6572.

JAFFRAY, Sir William Otho, 5th Bt, *cr* 1892; *b* 1 Nov. 1951; *s* of Sir William Edmund Jaffray, 4th Bt, and of Anne, *o d* of late Capt. J. Otho Paget, MC, Thorpe Satchville Hall, Leics; *S* father, 1953. *Address:* The Manor House, Priors Dean, Petersfield, Hants. *T:* Hawkley 226.

JAGAN, Cheddi, DDS; Guyanese Politician; Leader of Opposition in National Assembly; *b* March 1918; *m* 1943; one *s* one *d*. *Educ:* Howard Univ.; YMCA Coll., Chicago (BSc); Northwestern Univ. (DDS). Member of Legislative Council, British Guiana, 1947-53; Minister of Agriculture, Lands and Mines, May-Oct. 1953; Minister of Trade and Industry, 1957-61; (first) Premier, British Guiana, and Minister of Development and Planning, 1961-64. Hon. Pres., Guyana Agricl and General Workers' Union. *Publications:* Forbidden Freedom, 1954; Anatomy of Poverty, 1964; The West on Trial, 1966. *Recreations:* swimming, tennis. *Address:* Freedom House, 41 Robb Street, Georgetown, Guyana.

JAHN, Prof. Hermann Arthur, PhD; Professor of Applied Mathematics, University of Southampton, 1949-72; *b* 31 May 1907; *s* of Friedrich Wilhelm Hermann Jahn and Marion May Curtiss; *m* 1943, Karoline Schuler; one *s* one *d*. *Educ:* City Sch., Lincoln; University Coll., London; University of Leipzig. BSc (London) 1928, MSc (London) 1935, PhD (Leipzig) 1935. Davy Faraday Research Laboratory, Royal Instn, London, 1935-41. RAE, Farnborough, 1941-46; University of Birmingham, 1946-48. *Publications:* scientific papers relating mainly to Group Theory and Quantum Mechanics. *Address:* 93 Highfield Lane, Southampton. *T:* Southampton 555039.

JAHODA, Prof. Marie, (Mrs A. H. Albu), CBE 1974; DPhil; Senior Research Consultant to Science Policy Research Unit, University of Sussex, since 1971; *b* 26 Jan. 1907; *d* of Carl Jahoda and Betty Jahoda; *m* 1st, 1927, Paul F. Lazarsfeld; one *d*; 2nd, 1958, Austen Albu, *qv*. *Educ:* Univ. of Vienna (DPhil). Prof. of Social Psychology, NY Univ., 1949-58; Res. Fellow and Prof. of Psychol., Brunel Univ., 1958-65; Prof. of Social Psychol., Sussex Univ., 1965-73. Hon. DLit: Sussex, 1973; Leicester, 1973. *Publications:* Die Arbeitslosen von Marienthal, 1933 (Eng. trans. 1971); Research Methods in Human Relations, 1953; Current Concepts of Positive Mental Health, 1958; Freud and the Dilemmas of Psychology, 1977; (ed) World Futures: the great debate, 1977. *Recreations:* cooking, cello, chess. *Address:* 17 The Crescent, Keymer, Sussex BN6 8RB. *T:* Hassocks 2267.

JAKEWAY, Sir (Francis) Derek, KCMG 1963 (CMG 1956); OBE 1948; Chairman, Devon Area Health Authority, since 1974; Governor and Commander-in-Chief, Fiji, 1964-68; *b* 6 June 1915; *s* of Francis Edward and Adeline Jakeway; *m* 1941, Phyllis Lindsay Watson, CStJ; three *s*. *Educ:* Hele's Sch., Exeter; Exeter Coll., Oxford (BA Hons Mod. Hist.). Colonial Administrative Service, Nigeria, 1937-54, seconded to

Seychelles, 1946-49, to Colonial Office, 1949-51; Chief Sec., British Guiana, 1954-59; Chief Sec., Sarawak, 1959-63. KStJ 1964. *Address:* 78 Douglas Avenue, Exmouth, Devon. *T:* Exmouth 71342.

JAKOBOVITS, Rabbi Dr Immanuel; Chief Rabbi of the United Hebrew Congregations of the British Commonwealth of Nations, since 1967; *b* 8 Feb. 1921; *s* of Rabbi Dr Julius Jakobovits and Paula (*née* Wreschner); *m* 1949, Amelie Munk; two *s* four *d. Educ:* London Univ. (BA; PhD 1955); Jews' Coll. and Yeshivah Etz Chaim, London. Diploma, 1944; Associate of Jews' Coll. Minister: Brondesbury Synagogue, 1941-44; SE London Synagogue, 1944-47; Great Synagogue, London, 1947-49; Chief Rabbi of Ireland, 1949-58; Rabbi of Fifth Avenue Synagogue, New York, 1958-67. Hon. DD Yeshiva Univ., NY, 1975. *Publications:* Jewish Medical Ethics, 1959 (NY; 4th edn 1975); Jewish Law Faces Modern Problems, 1965 (NY); Journal of a Rabbi, 1966 (NY), 1967 (GB); The Timely and the Timeless, 1977; contrib. learned and popular jls in America, England and Israel. *Address:* Adler House, Tavistock Square, WC1. *T:* 01-387 1066.

JAKOBSON, Prof. Roman; Samuel Hazzard Cross Professor of Slavic Languages and Literatures and of General Linguistics, Harvard University, since 1949; Institute Professor, Massachusetts Institute of Technology, since 1957; *b* Moscow, 11 Oct. 1896; *s* of Osip Jakobson, engineer, and Anna (*née* Wolpert); *m* 1962, Dr Krystyna Pomorska; no *c. Educ:* Lazarev Inst. of Oriental Languages, Moscow (AB); Moscow Univ. (AM); Prague Univ. (PhD). Research Assoc., Moscow Univ., 1918-20; Prof. Masaryk University (Brno), 1933-39; Vis. lectr at Univs of Copenhagen, Oslo, Uppsala, 1939-41; Professor: Ecole Libre des Hautes Études, New York, 1942-46; Columbia Univ., 1943-49. Visiting Professor: Yale, 1967; Princeton, 1968; Brown, 1969-70; Brandeis, 1970; Louvain, 1972; Collège de France, 1972; New York, 1973; Bergen, 1976. Hon. MA Harvard, 1949; Hon. doctorates in Letters and Philosophy: Cambridge, 1960; Chicago, 1961; Oslo, 1961; Uppsala, 1963; Mich., 1963; Grenoble, 1966; Nice, 1966; Rome, 1966; Yale, 1967; Prague, 1968; Brno, 1968; Zagreb, 1969; Ohio 1970; Louvain 1972; Tel Aviv, 1975; Harvard, 1975; Columbia, 1976; in Sciences: New Mexico, 1966; Clark, 1969. Award of Amer. Council of Learned Socs, 1960; Medal, Slovak Acad. of Sci., 1968; Amer. Assoc. for the Advancement of Slavic Studies, 1970. Corresp. Mem., British Acad., 1974 and Mem. seven continental Academies; Hon. Member: Assoc. phonétique internationale, 1952; Finno-Ugric Soc., 1963, Acad. of Aphasia, 1969; Royal Soc. of Letters, Lund, 1972; Philological Soc. (London), 1974; Royal Anthropological Inst., 1974; Societas Scientiarum Fennica, 1977; Pres., Permanent Council for Phonetic Sciences, 1955-61; Linguistic Soc. of America, 1956. Vice-Pres., International Cttee of Slavicists, 1966-; Internat. Soc. of Phonetic Science, 1970-; Internat. Assoc. for Semiotic Studies, 1969-; Hon. Pres., Tokyo Inst. for Advanced Studies of Language, 1967-. Bicentennial Medal, Boston Coll., 1976. Chevalier, Légion d'Honneur, 1948. *Publications:* Remarques sur l'évolution phonologique du russe comparée à celles des autres langues slaves, 1929; Characteristics of the Eurasian Linguistic Affinity (in Russian), 1931; Beitrag zur allgemeinen Kasuslehre, 1936; Kindersprache, Aphasie und allgemeine Lautgesetze, 1941; (joint) La Geste du Prince Igor, 1948; (joint) Preliminaries to Speech Analysis, 1952; The Kernel of Comparative Slavic Literature, 1953; Studies in Comparative Slavic Metrics, 1952; (joint) Fundamentals of Language, 1956; Morphological Inquiry into Slavic Declension, 1958; Essais de linguistique générale, I, 1963, II, 1973; Studies on Child Language and Aphasia, 1971; Selected Writings, Vol. I (Phonological Studies), 1962, expanded, 1971; Vol. IV (Slavic Epic Studies), 1966; Vol. II (Word and Language), 1971; Vol. V (Verse, its masters and explorers), 1978; Questions de poétique, 1973; Main Trends in the Science of Language, 1973; Pushkin and His Sculptural Myth, 1975; Six leçons sur le son et le sens, 1976; Hölderlin, Klee, Brecht, 1976; (jtly) Yeats' 'Sorrow of Love' through the Years; *relevant publications:* To Honor Roman Jakobson, 1967; Bibliography of R. Jakobson's Writings, 1971. *Address:* Boylston Hall 301, Harvard University, Cambridge, Massachusetts 02138, USA. *T:* 8685619.

JALLAND, William Herbert Wainwright, JP; His Honour Judge Jalland; a Circuit Judge, Manchester, since 1975; *b* 1922; *o s* of Arthur Edgar Jalland, QC, JP and Elizabeth Hewitt Jalland; *m* 1945, Helen Monica, *o d* of John and Edith Wyatt; one *s* one *d. Educ:* Manchester Grammar Sch.; Manchester Univ. LLB 1949. Served War of 1939-45, HM Forces at home and abroad, 1941-46: Captain, King's Own Royal Regt, attached 8th Bn Durham LI. Called to Bar, Gray's Inn, 1950; practised Northern Circuit; part-time Dep. Coroner, City of Salford, 1955-65; part-time Dep. Recorder, Burnley, 1962-70; part-time Dep. Chm., Lancs County Sessions, 1970-71; Recorder, 1972; a Circuit Judge,

Liverpool and Merseyside, 1972-75. JP Lancs, 1970; Liaison Judge at Magistrates' Courts, Rochdale, Middleton and Heywood, 1974-. *Recreations:* rambling, camping, gardening, photography. *Address:* Broad Oak, Hollin Lane, Styal, Wilmslow, Cheshire. *Club:* Manchester (Manchester).

JAMES, family name of **Barons James of Rusholme, Northbourne** and **Saint Brides.**

JAMES OF RUSHOLME, Baron *cr* 1959, of Fallowfield (Life Peer); **Eric John Francis James,** Kt 1956; Chairman, Royal Fine Art Commission, since 1976 (Member, since 1973); *b* 1909; *yr s* of. F. W. James; *m* 1939, Cordelia, *d* of late Maj.-Gen. F. Wintour, CB, CBE; one *s. Educ:* Taunton's School, Southampton; Queen's Coll., Oxford (Exhibitioner and Hon. Scholar, 1927. Hon. Fellow, 1959). Goldsmiths' Exhibitioner, 1929; BA, BSc 1931; MA, DPhil 1933; Asst Master at Winchester Coll., 1933-45; High Master of Manchester Grammar Sch., 1945-62; Vice-Chancellor, Univ. of York, 1962-73. Mem. of University Grants Cttee, 1949-59; Chm. of Headmasters' Conference, 1953-54; Mem. Central Advisory Council on Education, 1957-61; Member: Standing Commission on Museums and Galleries, 1958-61; Press Council, 1963-67; SSRC, 1965-68; Chairman: Personal Social Services Council, 1973-76; Cttee to Inquire into the Training of Teachers, 1970-71. Hon. LLD: McGill, 1957; York, (Toronto) 1970; Hon. DLitt New Brunswick, 1974; DUniv York, 1974. Fellow, Winchester Coll., 1963-69. *Publications:* (in part) Elements of Physical Chemistry; (in part) Science and Education; An Essay on the Content of Education; Education and Leadership; articles in scientific and educational journals. *Address:* Penhill Cottage, West Witton, Leyburn, N Yorks.

JAMES, Anne Eleanor S.; see Scott-James.

JAMES, Anthony Trafford, PhD; Member of Executive Committee of Unilever Research Colworth/Welwyn Laboratory, also Head of Division of Biosciences, since 1972; *b* Cardiff, Wales, 6 March 1922; *s* of J. M. and I. James; *m* 1945, O. I. A. Clayton; two *s* one *d. Educ:* University College London.; Northern Polytechnic; University Coll. London (BSc, PhD). Fellow 1975; Harvard Business Sch. (AMP). MRC Junior Fellowship at Bedford Coll., Univ. of London (with Prof. E. E. Turner, subject: Antimalarials), 1945-47; Jun. Mem. staff, Lister Inst. for Preventive Med., London (with Dr R. L. M. Synge, Nobel Laureate, subject: Structure of Gramicidin S), 1947-50; Mem. scientific staff, Nat. Inst. for Med. Res., London (special appt awarded, 1961), 1950-62 (with Dr A. J. P. Martin, FRS, Nobel Laureate, 1950-56); Unilever Research Lab., Sharnbrook: Div. Manager and Head of Biosynthesis Unit, 1962-67; Head of Div. of Plant Products and Biochemistry, 1967-69; Gp Manager, Biosciences Gp, 1969-72. Industrial Prof. of Chemistry, Loughborough Univ. of Technology, 1966-71. Member: SRC, 1973-; Food Sci. and Technol. Bd, MAFF; Chm., Food Composition, Quality and Safety Cttee, MAFF. Has had various awards incl. some from abroad. *Publications:* New Biochemical Separations (ed A. T. James and L. J. Morris), 1964; Lipid Biochemistry—an introduction (M. I. Gurr and A. T. James), 1972. Mem. Editorial Adv. Bd, Eur. Jl of Biochem. *Recreations:* glass engraving, antique collecting, gardening. *Address:* Unilever Research Colworth/Welwyn Laboratory, Colworth House, Sharnbrook, Beds MK44 1LQ. *T:* Bedford 55251.

JAMES, Wing Comdr Sir Archibald, KBE 1945; MC; *b* 1893; *s* of late H. A. James, of Hurstmonceux Place, Sussex; *m* 1st, 1919, Bridget, *d* of late Murray Guthrie, MP, of Torosay Castle, Isle of Mull; one *s* one *d*; 2nd, 1940, Eugenia, *widow* of Patrick Stirling, younger, of Kippendavie; two *s. Educ:* Eton; Trinity Coll., Cambridge. 3rd Hussars, RFC and RAF, 1914-26. MP (U) Wellingborough Division of Northants, 1931-45. Parliamentary Private Sec. to R. A. Butler, India Office and Ministry of Labour, 1936-38; Board of Education, 1942; Hon. First Sec. British Embassy, Madrid, 1940-41. *Address:* Champions Farm, Thakeham, Pulborough, West Sussex. *T:* West Chiltington 3250. *Clubs:* Boodle's, Pratt's; Salisbury (Rhodesia).
See also D. P. James.

JAMES, Rev. Canon Arthur Dyfrig, MA; Vicar of Tilstone Fearnall, Cheshire, since 1956, and of Wettenhale, since 1969; Headmaster of Christ College, Brecon, 1931-56; Member of Governing Body of the Church in Wales, 1933-56; Hon. Chaplain to the Bishop of Swansea and Brecon, 1947-53; Canon of Hay in Brecon Cathedral, 1953-59, Hon. Canon, since 1959; *b* 24 May 1902; *s* of late Very Rev. H. L. James, DD; *m* 1936, Ann Pamela Mary, *d* of late J. S. Pincham; four *s. Educ:* Rossall; Jesus Coll., Oxford (Scholar), 1st Class Classical Moderations, 2nd Class Lit. Hum. Sixth Form Master, St Edward's Sch.,

Oxford, 1925-31; Select Preacher, Oxford, 1952-54; Chaplain to High Sheriff of Breconshire, 1944-45, 1946-47, 1949-51, 1955-57; Asst Inspector of Schools, Diocese of Chester, 1957; Exam. Chaplain to Bishop of Chester, 1958-68; Priest-in-charge of Wettenhall, 1958; part-time Lecturer in Classics, St David's Coll., Lampeter, 1961-62, 1966-68. *Address:* The Vicarage, Tilstone Fearnall, near Tarporley, Cheshire. *T:* Tarporley 2449.

JAMES, (Arthur) Walter; Principal, St Catharine's, Windsor, since 1974; *b* 30 June 1912; *s* of late W. J. James, OBE; *m* 1st, 1939, Elisabeth (marr. diss. 1956), *e d* of Richard Rylands Howroyd; one *d*; 2nd, 1957, Ann Jocelyn, *y d* of late C. A. Leavy Burton; one *d* and one adopted *s* two adopted *d*. *Educ:* Uckfield Grammar Sch.; Keble Coll., Oxford (Scholar); 1st Cl. Mod. Hist.; Liddon Student; Arnold Essay Prizeman. Senior Demy of Magdalen Coll., 1935; Scholar in Mediæval Studies, British School at Rome, 1935; Editorial staff, Manchester Guardian, 1937-46. NFS 1939-45. Contested (L) Bury, Lancs, 1945. Dep. Editor, The Times Educational Supplement, 1947-51, Editor, 1952-69; Special Advisor on Educn, Times Newspapers, 1969-71; also Editor, Technology, 1957-60. Reader in Journalism, Univ. of Canterbury, NZ, 1971-74. Member: BBC Gen. Advisory Council, 1956-64; Council of Industrial Design, 1961-66; Council, Royal Society of Arts, 1964; Cttee, British-American Associates, 1964; Governor, Central School of Art and Design, 1966. Woodard Lecturer, 1965. *Publications:* (Ed.) Temples and Faiths 1958; The Christian in Politics, 1962; The Teacher and his World, 1962; A Middle-class Parent's Guide to Education, 1964; (contrib.) Looking Forward to the Seventies, 1967. *Recreation:* fishing. *Address:* Cumberland Lodge, The Great Park, Windsor, Berks. *T:* Egham 2316. *Club:* National Liberal.

JAMES, Aubrey Graham Wallen; Deputy Chief Land Registrar, since 1975; *b* 5 Jan. 1918; *s* of Reginald Aubrey James and Amelia Martha James; *m* 1952, Audrey Elizabeth, *er d* of Dr and Mrs A. W. F. Edmonds; two *s*. *Educ:* Nantgyle Grammar Sch.; London Univ. (LLB 1939). Solicitor, 1940. Served Second World War, 1940-46, Major, Cheshire Regt. Legal Asst, HM Land Registry, 1948; Asst Land Registrar, 1954; Land Registrar, 1963; Dist Land Registrar, Nottingham, 1963. Chm., E Midlands Region, CS Sports Council, 1970-75. *Recreations:* gardening, motoring, golf; have played Rugby, cricket and tennis with enthusiasm and in latter years, have turned to admin of these and other sports. *Address:* 399 Woodborough Road, Nottingham NG3 5HE. *T:* Nottingham 604317. *Club:* Beeston Fields Golf (Notts).

JAMES, Basil; Special Commissioner, since 1963; *b* 25 May 1918; *s* of late John Elwyn James, MA (Oxon.), Cardiff, and Mary Janet (*née* Lewis), Gwaelodygarth, Glam; *m* 1943, Moira Houlding Rayner, MA (Cantab.), *d* of late Capt. Benjamin Harold Rayner, North Staffs Regt, and Elizabeth (*née* Houlding), Preston, Lancs; one *s* twin *d*. *Educ:* Llandovery Coll.; Canton High Sch., Cardiff; Christ's Coll., Cambridge (Exhibnr). Tancred Law Student, Lincoln's Inn, 1936; Squire Law Scholar, Cambridge, 1936. BA 1939; MA 1942. Called to Bar, Lincoln's Inn, 1940. Continuous sea service as RNVR officer in small ships on anti-submarine and convoy duties in Atlantic, Arctic and Mediterranean, 1940-45. King George V Coronation Scholar, Lincoln's Inn, 1946. Practised at Chancery Bar, 1946-63. Admitted to Federal Supreme Court of Nigeria, 1962. *Publications:* contrib. to Atkin's Court Forms and Halsbury's Laws of England. *Recreations:* music, gardening.

JAMES, Cecil; *see* James, T. C. G.

JAMES, Rt. Rev. Colin Clement Walter; *see* Wakefield, Bishop of.

JAMES, Cynlais Morgan, CMG 1976; HM Diplomatic Service; Minister, British Embassy, Paris, since 1976; *b* 29 April 1926; *s* of Thomas James and Lydia Ann James (*née* Morgan); *m* 1953, Mary Teresa, *d* of R. D. Girouard and Lady Blanche Girouard; two *d*. *Educ:* Trinity Coll., Cambridge. Service in RAF, 1944-47. Cambridge 1948-51. Entered Senior Branch of Foreign Service, 1951; Foreign Office, 1951-53; Third Sec., Tokyo, 1953-56; Second Sec., Rio de Janeiro, 1956-59; First Sec. and Cultural Attaché, Moscow, 1959-62; FO, 1962-65; Paris, 1965-69; promoted Counsellor, 1968; Counsellor and Consul-General, Saigon, 1969-71; Head of W European Dept, FCO, 1971-75; NATO Defence Coll., Rome, 1975-76. *Recreation:* tennis. *Address:* HM Embassy, 35 rue du Faubourg St Honoré, 75008 Paris, France.

JAMES, Dr David Gwynfor; Head of Meteorological Research Flight, Royal Aircraft Establishment, Farnborough, since 1971; *b* 16 April 1925; *s* of William James and Margaret May Jones; *m*

1953, Margaret Vida Gower; two *d*. *Educ:* Univ. of Wales, Cardiff (BSc, PhD). Joined Meteorological Office, 1950; Met. Res. Flight, Farnborough, 1951; Forecasting Res., Dunstable, 1953; Christmas Island, Pacific, 1958; Satellite Lab., US Weather Bureau, 1961; Cloud Physics Res., Bracknell, 1966; Met. Res. Flight, RAE, 1971. *Publications:* papers in Qly Jl Royal Met. Soc., Jl Atmospheric Sciences, Met. Res. Papers, and Nature. *Recreations:* golf, choral singing. *Address:* 38 Oak Tree Close, Virginia Water, Surrey. *T:* Wentworth 3433. *Club:* Wentworth (Virginia Water).

JAMES, David Pelham, MBE 1944; DSC 1944; MP (C) North Dorset since 1970; *b* 25 Dec. 1919; *s* of Sir Archibald James, *qv*; *m* 1950, Hon. Jaquetta Digby, *y d* of 11th Baron Digby, KG, DSO, MC, TD; four *s* two *d*. *Educ:* Eton; Balliol. Served before the mast, Finnish 4-m. barque Viking, 1937-38; Balliol Coll., Oxford, 1938-39. Served War of 1939-45, RNVR, 1939-46; PoW 1943; escaped from Germany to Sweden, 1944. Mem. Antarctic Exped., 1945-46; Polar Adviser, Film Scott of the Antarctic, 1946-48. Joined Burns & Oates Ltd, Publishers, 1951. MP (C) Kemp Town Division of Brighton, 1959-64; Council Mem., Outward Bound Trust, 1948-72; Trustee National Maritime Museum, 1953-65. Knight of Malta, 1962. *Publications:* A Prisoner's Progress, 1946; That Frozen Land, 1952; Scott of the Antarctic: The Film, 1950; The Life of Lord Roberts, 1954; (ed) Wavy Navy, 1948; (ed) Outward Bound, 1957; (ed) In Praise of Hunting, 1960. *Recreations:* gardening, stalking. *Address:* Malabar House, Child Okeford, Blandford, Dorset. *T:* Child Okeford 388. *Clubs:* Pratt's, St Stephen's.

JAMES, Dr David William Francis; Director, Polytechnic of Wales (formerly Glamorgan Polytechnic), since 1972; *b* 29 March 1929; *s* of Thomas M. and Margaret A. James, Merthyr Tydfil; *m* 1953, Elaine Maureen, *d* of Thomas and Gladys Hewett, Swansea; two *d*. *Educ:* Cyfarthfa Castle Sch., Merthyr Tydfil; Univ. of Wales (BSc); Univ. of London (PhD). Research Asst, Inst. of Cancer Research, Royal Marsden Hosp., 1950-54; Flying Officer, RAF, 1954-56; Research Officer, Imperial Chemical Industries (now Mond Div.), 1956-60; Lectr and Sen. Lectr, UC North Wales, Bangor, 1960-71; Dep. Principal, Glamorgan Polytechnic, 1971-72; Principal (now Dir), Glamorgan Polytechnic, 1972. Member: WJEC Techn. Educn Cttee, Techn. Examns Cttee and Management Adv. Cttee, 1972-75; SRC Cttee for Postgrad. Trng in Polytechnics; Mid-Glamorgan Further Educn Cttee; CNAA, 1976-; Court, Univ. of Wales; Court, Univ. of Wales Inst. of Science and Technology. FRSA. *Publications:* research papers in Jl Chem. Soc., Proc. Royal Soc., Proc. Inst. Phys., Brit. Jl App. Phys., Jl Sci. Inst., etc; several patents. *Recreations:* photography, marquetry, church work. *Address:* West House, 36 Palace Road, Llandaff, Cardiff. *T:* Cardiff 563380.

JAMES, Air Vice-Marshal Edgar, CBE 1966; DFC 1945; AFC 1948 (Bar 1959); Aviation Consultant; *b* 19 Oct. 1915; *s* of Richard George James and Gertrude (*née* Barnes); *m* 1941, Josephine M. Steel; two *s*. *Educ:* Neath Grammar School. Joined RAF, 1939; commnd; flying instr duties, Canada, until 1944; opl service with Nos 305 and 107 Sqdns, 1944-45. Queen's Commendation for Valuable Service in the Air (1943, 1944, 1956). Empire Flying Sch. and Fighter Comd Ops Staff, until Staff Coll., 1950. Ops Requirements, Air Min., 1951-53; 2nd TAF Germany, 1953-56; comd No 68 Night Fighter Squadron, 1953; CFE, 1956-58; HQ Fighter Comd Staff, 1958-59; Asst Comdt, CFS, 1959-61; CO, RAF Leeming, 1961-62; Dir Ops Requirements 1, Min. of Def. (Air Force Dept), 1962-66; Comdr British Forces, Zambia, Feb.-Sept. 1966. Dep. Controller of Equipment, Min. of Aviation, then Min. of Technology, 1966-69. Wing Comdr 1953; Gp Capt. 1959; Air Cdre 1963; Air Vice-Marshal 1967. FRAeS 1971. *Recreations:* sailing, golf. *Address:* Overstrand, Riverside Road, Newton Ferrers, Devon. *T:* Newton Ferrers 872685; 70 Burton Court, SW3. *T:* 01-730 8482. *Clubs:* Army and Navy, Royal Air Force; Royal Western Yacht.

JAMES, Edward Foster, CMG 1968; OBE 1946; Deputy Director-General, Confederation of British Industry, since 1976; *b* 18 Jan. 1917; *s* of late Arthur Foster James; *m* 1951, Caroline Warwick Bampfylde, *d* of Hon. Francis Warwick Bampfylde; one *s* two *d*. *Educ:* Chiswick Grammar Sch. Served HM Forces, 1939-46, India, Burma, Malaya, Indonesia; Lieut-Colonel (GSO1) (OBE, despatches twice). Joined HM Diplomatic Service, 1947; Rangoon, 1948; Hong Kong, 1951; Foreign Office, 1953; Rome, 1955; Foreign Office, 1958; Berlin, 1960; FO (later FCO), 1961-74. Exec. Dir, Inst. of Directors, 1975-76. *Address:* Springfield House, West Clandon, Guildford, Surrey. *T:* Guildford 222412. *Club:* Boodle's.

JAMES, Edwin Kenneth George; Chairman, PAG Films Ltd, since 1977; Chief Scientific Officer, Civil Service Department,

1970-76; *b* 27 Dec. 1916; *s* of late Edwin and Jessie Marion James; *m* 1941, Dorothy Margaret Pratt; one *d. Educ:* Latymer Upper Sch.; Northern Polytechnic. BSc London; FRIC. Joined War Office, 1938; Chem. Defence Exper. Stn, 1942; Aust. Field Exper. Stn, 1944-46; Operational Research Gp, US Army, Md, 1950-54; Dir, Biol and Chem. Defence, WO, 1961; Army (later Defence) Op. Res. Estab., Byfleet, 1965; HM Treasury (later Civil Service Dept), 1968. *Recreations:* film making, philately. *Address:* 5 Watersmeet Road, East Harnham, Salisbury, Wilts. *T:* Salisbury 4099. *Club:* Athenæum.

JAMES, (Eliot) Antony B.; *see* Brett-James.

JAMES, (Ernest) Gethin, FRICS; Director, Estate Surveying Services, Property Services Agency, since 1977; *b* 20 March 1925; *s* of Ernest Bertram James and Gwladys James; *m* 1949, Phyllis Jane, *d* of late Frederick Lloyd Rice and Kathleen Mary Rice. *Educ:* Christ Coll., Brecon; Coll. of Estate Management. FRICS 1954. Defence Land Agent: Colchester, 1968-69; Aldershot, 1969-72; Dep. Chief Land Agent, MoD, 1972-74, Chief Land Agent and Valuer, 1974-75; Asst Dir (Estates), PSA, London Reg., 1975-77. *Recreations:* living each day, riding, golf, work, shooting. *Address:* 9 Tredenham Close, Farnborough, Hants. *T:* Farnborough 511825. *Club:* Officers' (Aldershot).

JAMES, Evan Maitland; Steward of Christ Church, Oxford, 1963-July 1978 (Acting Steward, 1962-63); *b* 14 Jan. 1911; *er s* of late A. G. James, CBE, and late Helen James (*née* Maitland); *m* 1939, Joan Goodnow, *d* of late Hon. J. V. A. MacMurray, Norfolk, Conn., USA; one *s* two *d. Educ:* Durnford; Eton (Oppidan Scholar); Trinity Coll., Oxford. Served War of 1939-45: Ordinary Seaman, 1941; Lieut, RNVR, 1942. Clerk of the Merchant Taylors' Company, 1948-62. *Address:* Upwood Park, Besselsleigh, Abingdon, Oxon OX13 5QE. *T:* Frilford Heath 390535.

JAMES, Gethin; *see* James, E. G.

JAMES, Henry Leonard; Director-General, Central Office of Information, since 1974; *b* 12 Dec. 1919; *o s* of late Leonard Mark James and late Alice Esther Jones; *m* 1949, Sylvia Mary, *d* of late Rupert John George Bickell and of Edith Alice Bickell, Blockley, Glos. *Educ:* King Edward VI Sch., Birmingham. Entered Civil Service in Min. of Health, 1938; Founder Editor, The Window, Min. of Nat. Insce, 1948-51; Dramatic Critic and London Corresp. of Birmingham News, 1947-51; Press Officer, Min. of Pensions and Nat. Insce, 1951-55; Head of Films, Radio and Television, Admty, 1955-61; Head of Publicity and Dep. Chief Information Officer, Min. of Educn, 1961-63; Chief Press Officer, Min. of Educn, 1963-64; Dep. Public Relations Adviser to Prime Minister, 1964; Dep. Press Sec. to Prime Minister, 1964-68; Chief Information Officer, Min. of Housing and Local Govt, 1969-70; Press Sec., 10 Downing Street, 1970-71; Dir of Information, DoE, 1971-74. *Publication:* The Fringe of Darkness, 1955. *Recreations:* theatre, visual arts, golf. *Address:* 106 Corringway, W5 3HA. *T:* 01-997 3021.

JAMES, Prof. Ioan Mackenzie, FRS 1968; MA, DPhil; Savilian Professor of Geometry, Oxford University, since 1970; Fellow of New College, Oxford, since 1970; Editor, Topology, since 1962; *b* 23 May 1928; *o s* of Reginald Douglas and Jessie Agnes James; *m* 1961, Rosemary Gordon Stewart, Fellow of Oxford Centre for Management Studies; no *c. Educ:* St Paul's Sch. (Foundn Schol.); Queen's Coll., Oxford (Open Schol.). Commonwealth Fund Fellow, Princeton, Berkeley and Inst. for Advanced Study, 1954-55; Tapp Res. Fellow, Gonville and Caius Coll., Cambridge, 1956; Reader in Pure Mathematics, Oxford, 1957-69, and Senior Research Fellow, St John's Coll., 1959-69. Treasurer, London Math. Soc. 1970-. Gov., St Paul's Schs, 1970-. *Publications:* (ed) The Mathematical Works of J. H. C. Whitehead, 1963; The Topology of Stiefel Manifolds, 1976; sundry papers in mathematical jls. *Address:* Mathematical Institute, 24-29 St Giles, Oxford. *T:* Oxford 54295.

JAMES, Sir Jack; *see* James, Sir John H.

JAMES, John; Chairman, John James Group of Companies Ltd, Bristol; *b* 25 July 1906; *m* 1st (marr. diss.), one *s* two *d* (and one *d* decd); 2nd, Margaret Theodosia Parkes. *Educ:* Merchant Venturers, Bristol. *Recreations:* chess, swimming. *Address:* Tower Court, Ascot, Berks. *T:* Ascot 21094.

JAMES, John A.; *see* Angell-James.

JAMES, John Anthony, CMG 1973; FRACS; Visiting Neurosurgeon, Wellington Hospital Board, Wellington, NZ, since 1965; *b* 2 April 1913; *s* of Herbert L. James and Gladys E. Paton; *m* 1941, Millicent Ward, Australia; three *s* one *d. Educ:*

Melbourne Grammar Sch. (Church of England); Melbourne Univ. (MB, BS). Served War: Surgeon-Lieut, RANR, 1940-43. Neurosurgeon, Neurosurgical Unit, Dunedin Hosp., 1947-52; Dir, Neurosurgical Unit, Otago Univ.; Sen. Lectr in Neurosurgery, Otago Univ., 1951-64. *Publications:* contribs to surgical jls. *Address:* 136 Vipond Road, Whangaparaoa, New Zealand. *Club:* Wellington (Wellington, NZ).

JAMES, Sir John Hastings, (Sir Jack), KCVO 1970; CB 1953; Deputy Master and Comptroller of the Royal Mint, and *ex officio* Engraver of HM's Seals, 1957-70; *b* 4 June 1906; *s* of late C. F. James; *m* 1st, 1935, Lady Ann Florence Cole (marr. diss., 1950), *e d* of 5th Earl of Enniskillen; one *s*; 2nd, 1963, Lady Maryoth (marr. diss., 1971), *d* of late Lord Edward Hay, and *widow* of Sir Gifford Fox; 3rd, 1971, Heather, *d* of late Brig. C. A. Lyon, and *widow* of Stephen Potter. *Educ:* Gresham's Sch., Holt; Merton Coll., Oxford. Entered Admiralty, 1929; Imperial Defence Coll., 1938; Under Sec., Admiralty 1948-57; CStJ. *Recreations:* reading, fishing. *Address:* Flat 4, 84 Elm Park Gardens, SW10. *T:* 01-351 0394. *Club:* Turf.

JAMES, Prof. John Ivor Pulsford, MB, MS London; FRCS; FRCSE; George Harrison Law Professor of Orthopædic Surgery, Edinburgh University, since 1958; Consultant in Orthopædic Surgery to the Navy since 1956; *b* 19 Oct. 1913; *s* of late Stanley B. James and Jessica Heley; *m* 1968, Margaret Eiriol Samuel, MB, ChB; one *s* one *d. Educ:* Eggars Grammar Sch., Alton, Hants; University Coll. and Hosp., London, Hampshire County Schol., 1932-38; Ferrière Schol., University Coll., 1935; Goldsmid Schol., University Coll. Hosp., 1935; Magrath Schol., University Coll. Hosp., 1937; Rockefeller Fellowship, 1947-48; Consultant Orthopædic Surgeon, Royal National Orthopædic Hospital, 1946-58; Asst Dir of Studies, Institute of Orthopædics, University of London, 1948-58. Fellow Univ. Coll., London. Hunterian Prof., RCS, 1957; Pres., British Orthopædic Assoc. (Fellow); Past Pres., British Soc. for Surgery of the Hand; Mem. Société Internationale de Chirurgie Orthopédique et de Traumatologie; Corresp. Member: Amer. Orthopædic Assoc.; Austr. Orthopædic Assoc.; Scandinavian Orthopædic Assoc.; Hon. Member: Amer. Acad. of Orthopædic Surgeons; Dutch Orthopædic Assoc.; Assoc. for Orthopædic Surgery and Traumatology of Yugoslavia; Canadian Orthopædic Assoc.; New Zealand Orthopædic Assoc.; Hellenic Assoc. of Orthopædics and Traumatology; Société Française d'Orthopédie et de Traumatologie. Late Temp. Lieut-Col RAMC. Golden Star, Order of Service to the Yugoslav People, 1970. *Publications:* Scoliosis, 1967, 2nd edn 1976; articles relating to curvature of the spine and surgery of the hand in medical journals, etc. *Recreations:* sailing, fishing, gardening. *Address:* The Princess Margaret Rose Orthopædic Hospital, Edinburgh EH10 7ED; 2 Regent Terrace, Edinburgh EH7 5BN.

JAMES, John Richings, CB 1966; OBE 1956; Professor of Town and Regional Planning, University of Sheffield, since 1967; Pro Vice-Chancellor, 1970-75; *b* 27 Oct. 1912; 2nd *s* of late Henry James, Crook, County Durham, and Florence James; *m* 1946, Elizabeth Emily Frances, 2nd *d* of late Dr A. E. Morgan; five *d. Educ:* Wolsingham Grammar Sch.; King's Coll., London (BA); Inst. of Education. Schoolmaster, 1937-40; Naval Intelligence, 1940-45. Research Officer (Newcastle Regional Office), Min. of Town and Country Planning, 1946-49; Sen. Research Officer (London), Min. of Housing and Local Govt, 1949-58; Dep. Chief Planner, MHLG, 1958-61; Chief Planner, 1961-67. UK Rep. on UN Cttee for Housing, Building and Planning, 1967-; Mem., Peterborough Develt Corp., 1970-. FRTPI (MTPI 1962); Hon. FRIBA 1969. *Publications:* Greece (3 vols), 1943-45. Contrib. to Chambers's Encyclopædia (Greece and Greek Towns and Islands). Articles on Land Use: Royal Society of Arts Jl, Royal Geog. Society Jl, etc. *Address:* The University, Sheffield S10 2TN.

JAMES, John Wynford George, OBE 1950; FRAeS 1963; FCIT (MInstT 1954); Member of Board, BEA, 1964-74; Chairman: BEA Airtours, 1972-74; British Airways Helicopters, 1967-74; Gulf Helicopters Ltd, 1970-76; Deputy Chairman, International Aeradio Ltd, 1971-74 (Director, 1956); British Airways Group Air Safety Adviser, 1973-74; *b* 13 Feb. 1911; *s* of William George and Elizabeth James; *m* 1934, Bertha Mildred Joyce Everard; one *s* two *d. Educ:* Royal Grammar School, Worcester. Joined Imperial Airways as a pilot, 1933; Capt., Imperial Airways/BOAC, 1935-46; BEA Chief Pilot, 1946. Chm. BALPA, 1943-48; Mem. Bd, International Helicopters Ltd, 1965-. Governor, College of Air Training, 1959- (Chm. 1959-61, 1963-66, 1968-70). Liveryman, GAPAN, 1960. *Recreations:* golf, gardening, fishing. *Address:* Wynsfield, Mill Lane, Gerrards Cross, Bucks. *T:* Gerrards Cross 84038.

JAMES, Lionel Frederic Edward, CBE 1977 (MBE (mil.) 1944); Comptroller, Forces Help Society and Lord Roberts Workshops, since Nov. 1970; *b* 22 Feb. 1912; *s* of late Frederic James, Westmount, Exeter; *m* 1933, Harriet French-Harley; one *s* one *d. Educ:* Royal Grammar Sch., Worcester. Investment Co., 1933-39. Served War with Royal Engineers, 1939-46: BEF; Planning Staff, Sicilian Invasion; N Africa, Sicily, Greece and Italy (Major). Dep. Dir, Overseas Service, Forces Help Soc., 1946, Dir, 1948; Asst Sec. of Society, 1953, Company Sec., 1963. *Recreation:* restoration of antiques. *Address:* 122 Brompton Road, SW3.

JAMES, Noel David Glaves, OBE 1964; MC 1945; TD 1946; *b* 16 Sept. 1911; *o s* of late Rev. D. T. R. James, and Gertrude James; *m* 1949, Laura Cecilia (*d* 1970), *yr d* of late Sir Richard Winn Livingstone; two *s* (and one *s* decd). *Educ:* Haileybury Coll.; Royal Agricultural Coll., Cirencester (Gold Medal and Estate Management Prize). In general practice as a land agent, 1933-39. Served War, 1939-46 (MC, despatches); 68 Field Regt RA (TA), France, Middle East, Italy. Bursar, Corpus Christi Coll., Oxford, 1946-51; MA (Oxon.) 1946. Fellow, Corpus Christi Coll., Oxford, 1950-51; Land Agent for Oxford Univ., 1951-61; Estates Bursar and Agent for Brasenose Coll., 1959-61; Fellow, Brasenose Coll., Oxford, 1951-61; Agent for Clinton Devon Estates, 1961-76. President: Land Agents Soc., 1957-58; Royal Forestry Soc. of England and Wales and N Ireland, 1962-64; Member: Central Forestry Examination Bd of UK, 1951-75; Regional Advisory Cttee, Eastern Conservancy, Forestry Commn, 1951-61; Regional Advisory Cttee, SW Conservancy, Forestry Commission, 1962-75; Departmental Cttee on Hedgerow and Farm Timber, 1953; UK Forestry Cttee, 1954-59; Governor Wye Coll., Kent, 1955-61; Governor Westonbirt Sch., 1959-68. FLAS; FRICS (Diploma in Forestry and Watney Gold Medal). Gold Medal for Distinguished Service to Forestry, 1967; Royal Agricultural Coll. Bledisloe Medal for services to agriculture and forestry, 1970. *Publications:* Artillery Observation Posts, 1941; Working Plans for Estate Woodlands, 1948; Notes on Estate Forestry, 1949; An Experiment in Forestry, 1951; The Forester's Companion, 1955 (2nd edn, 1966); The Trees of Bicton, 1969; The Arboriculturalist's Companion, 1972; A Book of Trees (anthology), 1973; articles on forestry. *Recreations:* forestry, shooting. *Address:* Blakemore House, Kersbrook, Budleigh Salterton, Devon. *T:* Budleigh Salterton 3886. *Club:* Army and Navy.

JAMES, Norah C.; *d* of late John H. Cordner-James. *Educ:* Francis Holland Sch., Baker Street, London; Slade Sch. of Art, where she studied sculpture. Was an organising sec. to the Civil Service Clerical Assoc., Advertising and Publicity Manager to Jonathan Cape, publishers; wrote first novel in 1929; joined ATS as private; invalided out of the ATS, Nov. 1943. *Publications:* Sleeveless Errand, 1929 (published USA); Hail! All Hail! (limited edn), 1929; Shatter the Dream, 1930; To Be Valiant, 1930 (published USA); Wanton Ways, 1931; Tinkle the Cat, 1932; Hospital (USA as Nurse Ariadne), 1933; Jake the Dog, 1933; Jealousy, 1933; Mrs Piffy, 1934; Strap-hangers (USA as Sacrifice), 1934; Cottage Angles, 1935; The Lion Beat the Unicorn, 1935; Return (USA as Two Divided by One), 1935; By a Side Wind, 1936; Sea View, 1936; Women Are Born to Listen, 1937; Stars Are Fire, 1937; The House by the Tree, 1938; As High as the Sky, 1938; Mighty City, 1939; I Lived in a Democracy (autobiography), 1939; Gentlewoman, 1940; The Long Journey, 1941; The Hunted Heart, 1942; Two Selfish People, 1942; Enduring Adventure, 1944; One Bright Day, 1945; There Is Always Tomorrow, 1946; Father, 1946; Penny Trumpet, 1947; Brittle Glory, 1948; (with B. Beauchamp) Green Fingers and the Gourmet, 1949; Swift to Sever, 1949; Pay the Piper, 1950; Pedigree of Honey, 1951; Cooking with Cider, 1952; So Runs the River, 1952; A Summer Storm, 1953; Silent Corridors, 1953; Over the Windmill, 1954; Wed to Earth, 1955; Mercy in Your Hands, 1956; The Flower and the Fruit, 1957; The True and the Tender, 1958; Portrait of a Patient, 1959 (repr. as Tangled Destiny, 1961); The Shadow Between, 1959; The Uneasy Summer, 1960; Wind of Change, 1961; A Sense of Loss, 1962; Sister Veronica Greene, 1963; Bright Day Renewed, 1964; Small Hotel, 1965; Hospital Angles, 1966; Double Take, 1967; Point of Return, 1969; There is No Why, 1970; Ward of Darkness, 1971; The Doctor's Marriage, 1972; If Only, 1972; The Bewildered Heart, 1973; Love, 1975. *Address:* c/o National Westminster Bank, Swinton House Branch, 322 Gray's Inn Road, WC1.

JAMES, Philip Gaved, CBE 1969; *b* 24 Sept. 1904; *s* of Samuel T. G. James and Frances L. R. James (*née* Richards); unmarried. *Educ:* Amersham Gram. Sch.; London Sch. of Economics. Chartered Accountant. With professional accountancy firms, 1921-34; various posts, London Passenger Transport Bd (later London Transport Exec.), 1934-60; Chief Financial Officer,

1948-60; Chief Accountant, BTC, 1960-62; Financial Controller, Brit. Rlys Bd, 1962-65; Mem. Brit. Rlys Bd, 1965-69; part-time Mem. BR London Midland Bd, 1969-73. *Publications:* contribs to various professional accountancy jls. *Recreation:* gardening. *Address:* 48 Southampton Road, Lymington, Hants SO4 9GQ. *T:* Lymington 73942. *Club:* Reform.

JAMES, Prof. Philip Seaforth; Professor of English Law, University College at Buckingham, since 1975; *b* 28 May 1914; *s* of Dr Philip William James, MC, and Muriel Lindley James; *m* 1954. Wybetty, *d* of Claas P. Gerth, Enschede, Holland; two *s. Educ:* Charterhouse; Trinity Coll., Oxford (MA), Research Fellow, Yale Univ., USA, 1937-38. Called to the Bar, Inner Temple, 1939. Served War of 1939-45, in Royal Artillery, India, Burma (despatches). Fellow of Exeter Coll., Oxford, 1946-49; Prof. and Hd of Dept of Law, Leeds Univ., 1952-75. Visiting Prof. University of Louisville, Kentucky, USA, 1960-61, Univ. of South Carolina, 1972-73. Chm., Yorks Rent Assessment Panel, 1966-75; Assessor to County Court under Race Relations Acts. Pres., Soc. of Public Teachers of Law, 1971-72. Governor, Swinton Conservative College, 1970-. *Publications:* An Introduction to English Law, 1950; General Principles of the Law of Torts, 1959; Shorter Introduction to English Law, 1969; various articles, notes and reviews on legal and biographical subjects. *Recreations:* golf and gardening. *Address:* University College at Buckingham, Hunter Street, Buckingham MK18 1EG. *Club:* National Liberal.

JAMES, Richard Austin, MC 1945; Receiver for Metropolitan Police District, since 1977; *b* 26 May 1920; *s* of late Thomas Morris James, Headmaster of Sutton Valence Sch., and Hilda Joan James; *m* 1948, Joan Boorer; two *s* one *d. Educ:* Clifton Coll.; Emmanuel Coll., Cambridge. British American Tobacco Co., 1938; Royal Engrs, 1939-41; Queen's Own Royal W Kent Regt, 1941-46; Home Office, 1948; Private Sec. to Chancellor of Duchy of Lancaster, 1960; Asst Sec., 1961; Dep. Receiver for Metropolitan Police District, 1970-73; Asst Under-Sec. of State, Police Dept, Home Office, 1974-76. *Recreations:* cricket, squash. *Address:* Cedarwood, Redbrook Lane, Buxted, Sussex. *T:* Buxted 2364. *Clubs:* Athenæum, MCC.

JAMES, Robert Leoline, CBE 1971; MA, PhD; Head Master of Harrow, 1953-71; *b* 27 Sept. 1905; 2nd *s* of late Very Rev. H. L. James, DD; *m* 1939, Maud Eliot, *o c* of late W. M. Gibbons, OBE, LLD; two *s. Educ:* Rossall Sch.; Jesus Coll., Oxford (Scholar). 1st Class Hon. Classical Mods 1926, 1st Class Lit. Hum. 1928; Asst Master St Paul's Sch., 1928; Housemaster and Upper VIIIth classical master; Headmaster of Chigwell Sch., Essex, 1939-46; High Master of St Paul's Sch., 1946-53. Chm. of Council, Heathfield Sch., 1960. *Publication:* Cicero and Sulpicius, 1933. *Recreations:* fly-fishing and bird-watching. *Address:* 25 Blenheim Drive, Oxford. *Club:* East India, Devonshire, Sports and Public Schools.

JAMES, Robert Vidal R.; *see* Rhodes James.

JAMES, Stanley Francis; Head of Economics and Statistics Division 6, Departments of Industry, Trade and Prices and Consumer Protection, since 1977; *b* 12 Feb. 1927; *s* of H. F. James; unmarried. *Educ:* Sutton County Sch.; Trinity Coll., Cambridge. Maths Tripos Pt II; Dip. Math. Statistics. Research Lectr, Econs Dept, Nottingham Univ., 1951; Statistician, Bd of Inland Revenue, 1956; Chief Statistician: Bd of Inland Revenue, 1966; Central Statistical Office, 1968; Asst Dir, Central Statistical Office, 1970-72; Dir, Stats Div., Bd of Inland Revenue, 1972-77. *Recreations:* travel, theatre, gardening. *Address:* 10B Chesterford Gardens, NW3 7DE. *T:* 01-794 4626. *Club:* Royal Automobile.

JAMES, (Thomas) Cecil (Garside), CMG 1966; Assistant Under-Secretary of State, Ministry of Defence, since 1968; *b* 8 Jan. 1918; *s* of Joshua James, MBE, Ashton-under-Lyne; *m* 1941, Elsie Williams, Ashton-under-Lyne; one *s* two *d. Educ:* Manchester Grammar Sch.; St John's Coll., Cambridge. Prin. Priv. Sec. to Sec. of State for Air, 1951-55; Asst Sec., Air Min., 1955; Civil Sec., FEAF, 1963-66; Chief of Public Relations, MoD, 1966-68. *Recreation:* golf. *Address:* 4 Park View, Hatch End, Mddx.

JAMES, Thomas Garnet Henry, FBA 1976; Keeper of Egyptian Antiquities, British Museum, since 1974; *b* 8 May 1923; *s* of late Thomas Garnet James and Edith (*née* Griffiths); *m* 1956, Diana Margaret, *y d* of H. L. Vavasseur-Durell; one *s. Educ:* Neath Grammar Sch.; Exeter Coll., Oxford. 2nd Cl. Lit. Hum. 1947; 1st Cl. Oriental Studies 1950, MA 1948. Served War of 1939-45, RA; NW Europe; 2nd Lieut 1943; Captain 1945. Asst Keeper, Dept of Egyptian and Assyrian Antiquities, 1951; Dep. Keeper

(Egyptian Antiquities), 1974. Laycock Student of Egyptology, Worcester Coll., Oxford, 1954-60; Wilbour Fellow, Brooklyn Museum, 1964; Editor, Jl of Egyptian Archæology, 1960-70; Editor, Egyptological pubns of Egypt Exploration Soc., 1960-. Mem., German Archæological Inst., 1974. *Publications:* The Mastaba of Khentika called Ikhekhi, 1953; Hieroglyphic Texts in the British Museum I, 1961; The Hekanakhte Papers and other Early Middle Kingdom Documents, 1962; (with R. A. Caminos) Gebel es-Silsilah I, 1963; Egyptian Sculptures, 1966; Myths and Legends of Ancient Egypt, 1969; Hieroglyphic Texts in the British Museum, 9, 1970; Archæology of Ancient Egypt, 1972; Corpus of Hieroglyphic Inscriptions in the Brooklyn Museum, I, 1974; (contrib.) W. B. Emery: Great Tombs of the First Dynasty II, 1954; (contrib.) T. J. Dunbabin: Perachora II, 1962; (contrib.) Cambridge Ancient History, 3rd edn, 1973; (contrib.) Encyclop. Britannica, 15th edn, 1974; (ed English trans.) H. Kees: Ancient Egypt, 1961; articles in Jl Egyptian Arch., etc; reviews in learned jls. *Recreations:* music, wine and food. *Address:* 14 Turner Close, NW11 6TU. *T:* 01-455 9221.

JAMES, Thomas Geraint Illtyd, FRCS; Hon. Surgeon, Central Middlesex Hospital; Late Teacher of Surgery, Middlesex Hospital, and Hon. Surgical Tutor, Royal College of Surgeons of England; *b* 12 July 1900; *s* of late Evan Thomas and Elizabeth James, Barry; *m* 1932, Dorothy Marguerite, *o d* of late David John, Cardiff; two *s. Educ:* Barry, Glam; University Coll., Cardiff; Welsh National Sch. of Medicine; St Mary's Hosp., London; Guy's Hosp., London. BSc Wales, 1921, Alfred Sheen Prize in Anat. and Physiol.; MRCS, LRCP, 1924; MB, ChB, 1925, Maclean Medal and Prize in Obst. and Gynæcol.; FRCSE, 1927; FRCS, 1928; MCh Wales, 1932; FRSocMed; Fellow Association of Surgeons of Great Britain and Ireland; Mem., Internat. Soc. for Surgery; Corr. Mem. Spanish-Portuguese Soc. of Neurosurgery. Mem. Soc. of Apothecaries; Freeman of City of London. Formerly: Assoc. Examr University of London; Mem. and Chm., Court of Examiners RCS of England; Examr in Surgery, University of Liverpool; Ho. phys., Ho. surg. and Resident Surgical Officer, Cardiff Royal Infirmary; Clinical Asst St Mark's, St Peter's and Guy's Hosps, London; Asst to Neurosurg. Dept, London Hosp.; Mem., Management Cttee, Leavesden Gp of Hosps. *Publications:* in various jls on surg. and neurosurg. subjects. *Recreations:* literature, travelling. *Address:* 1 Freeland Road, W5. *T:* 01-992 2430.

JAMES, Walter; *see* James, Arthur Walter.

JAMES, Prof. Walter, CBE 1977; Professor of Educational Studies, Open University, since 1969; *b* 8 Dec. 1924; *s* of late George Herbert James and Mary Kathleen (*née* Crutch); *m* 1948, Joyce Dorothy Woollaston; two *s. Educ:* Royal Grammar Sch., Worcester; St Luke's Coll., Exeter; Univ. of Nottingham. BA 1955. School teacher, 1948-52; Univ. of Nottingham: Resident Tutor, Dept of Extra-Mural Studies, 1958-65; Lectr in Adult Educn, Dept of Adult Educn, 1965-69; Dean and Dir of Studies, Faculty of Educnl Studies, Open Univ., 1969-77. Mem., DES Cttee on Youth and Community Work in 70s, 1967-69; Mem., ILO Working Party on Use of Radio and TV for Workers' Educn, 1968; Consultant on Adult Educn and Community Develt to Govt of Seychelles and ODA of FCO, 1973. Expert on Council of Europe Cttee for Out-of-School Educn and Cultural Activities Working Party on Organisation, Content and Methods of Adult Education, 1973-; Chm., Nat. Council for Voluntary Youth Services, 1970-76; Member: Gen. Synod, C of E, 1970-75; Exec. Cttee, Nat. Council of Social Service, 1970-75; Univs' Council for Educn of Teachers, 1970-; Univs Council for Adult Educn, 1971-; BBC Further Educn Adv. Council, 1971-75; Exec. Cttee and Council, Nat. Inst. of Adult Educn, 1971-; Library Adv. Council for England, 1974-; Trustee: Young Volunteer Force Foundn, 1972-; Trident Educnl Trust, 1972-; Pres., Inst. of Playleadership, 1972-74; Adviser: to Office of Educn, WCC, 1974-76; on Social Planning to State of Bahrain, 1975. Chm., Religious Adv. Bd and HQ Advr on Spiritual Develt, Scout Assoc. Mem. Adv. Council, HM Queen's Silver Jubilee Appeal, 1976-. *Publications:* (with F. J. Bayliss) The Standard of Living, 1964; (ed) Virginia Woolf, Selections from her essays, 1966; (contrib.) Encyclopaedia of Education, 1968; (contrib.) Teaching Techniques in Adult Education, 1971; (contrib.) Mass Media and Adult Education, 1971; numerous TV programmes, articles and reviews on youth, adult and higher educn. *Recreation:* living. *Address:* Westfield, 91 Bromham Road, Bedford MK40 4BS. *T:* Bedford 54819.

JAMES, William Henry E.; *see* Ewart James.

JAMES, Prof. William Owen, MA, DPhil; FRS 1952; Fellow, Imperial College, 1969 (Senior Research Fellow, 1967-70); London University Professor of Botany, and Head of Department at Imperial College of Science and Technology,

1959-67, now Emeritus Professor; *b* 21 May 1900; *s* of William Benjamin James and Agnes Ursula (*née* Co.lins); *m* 1928, Gladys Macphail Redfern; two *d. Educ:* Tottenham Grammar Sch.; Universities of Reading and Cambridge. BSc (London); PhD (Cambridge); MA, DPhil Oxon. Research Institute of Plant Physiology, Imperial Coll., 1926-27. Demonstrator in Plant Physiology, Oxford, 1928-55; Reader in Botany, Oxford, 1946-58. Part owner and co-editor of the New Phytologist, 1931-61; Director of Oxford Medicinal Plants Scheme, 1940-52. Member: Vegetable Drugs Cttee of Ministries of Health and Supply, 1940-45; Central Garden Produce Cttee (Ministry of Agriculture). Chairman, Teaching of Biology Cttee, 1962-67. Hon. ARCS 1964. Foreign Member: Swedish Royal Academy of Science; Amer. Society of Plant Physiologists; Deutsche botanische Gesellschaft, and Leopoldina. *Publications:* Elements of Plant Biology, 1949; Introduction to Plant Physiology, 7th edn 1973 (German edn 1965, Spanish edn 1967, Hungarian edn 1969); Plant Respiration, 1953 (Russian edn 1956); Background to Gardening, 1957; Cell Respiration, 1971; (jt) Biology of Flowers, 1935; papers on plant respiration, nutrition, alkaloid synthesis, etc, in botanical and allied journals. *Recreations:* gardening, boating, Hi Fi and reading. *Address:* 14 Roedean Crescent, SW15 5JU. *T:* 01-876 3785.

JAMES, William Thomas, OBE 1943; formerly Director of numerous public companies both at home and cverseas, mainly associated with British Electric Traction, and also Chairman of many of these; Director, United Transport Co.; *b* 5 June 1892; *s* of Morgan James, JP, and Mary James, Maesycwmmer Hse, Maesycwmmer, Mon; unmarried. *Educ:* Lewis's Sch., Pengam, Glam. London and Provincial Bank, 1909. Joined family business, 1911-14. Served European War, Glam Yeomanry, 1914-18 (Meritorious Service Medal). Rejoined family business, 1919-22; pioneered road passenger transport in Monmouthshire Valleys, 1923; developed passenger road services in S Wales and Mon, 1923-43. Having sold financial interests in 1932 to British Electric Traction Co. Ltd, joined staff of BET in London as Executive Dir, 1943; Dir of BET, 1947. Chm., Public Transport Assoc., 1951, 1952. Mem. Cttee, set up by Government to consider Rural Bus Services. FCIT. *Recreation:* farming. *Address:* (private) Uplands, Ty-Gwyn Road, Cardiff. *Clubs:* Naval and Military; Cardiff and County (Cardiff); Chepstow; St Pierre Golf and Country.

JAMESON, Derek; Editor of the Daily Express, since 1977; *b* 29 Nov. 1929; *e s* of Mrs Elsie Jameson; *m* 1st, 1948, Jacqueline Sinclair (marr. diss. 1966); one *s* one *d*; 2nd 1971, Pauline Tomlin; two *s. Educ:* elementary Schools, Hackney. Office boy rising to Chief Sub-editor, Reuters, 1944-60; Editor, London American, 1960-61; features staff, Daily Express, 1961-63; Picture Editor, Sunday Mirror, 1963-65; Asst Editor, Sunday Mirror, 1965-72; Northern Editor, Sunday and Daily Mirror, 1972-76; Managing Editor, Daily Mirror, 1976-77. *Recreations:* opera, music, reading. *Address:* 43 Arundel Square, N7 8AP. *T:* 01-607 1110. *Club:* Press.

JAMESON, John Richard; Under-Secretary, Department of Education and Science, since 1973; *b* 18 Oct. 1930; *s* of John Harrison and Gwendoline May Jameson; *m* 1st, 1958, Wendy Rhodes (marr. diss. 1970); one *s* one *d*; 2nd, 1970, Karin Quick; one *d. Educ:* Giggleswick Sch.; Balliol Coll., Oxford. Min. of Educn, 1952-59 and 1961-64; Cabinet Office, 1959-61; DES, 1964-. *Address:* 3A New Ground Road, Aldbury, Tring, Herts. *T:* Aldbury Common 306.

JAMESON, (Margaret) Storm, MA; Hon. LittD (Leeds); Writer; *b* Whitby, Yorks; *d* of William Storm Jameson; *m* Prof. Guy Chapman, OBE, MC (*d* 1972); one *s. Educ:* Leeds Univ. *Publications:* Happy Highways, 1920; Modern Drama in Europe, 1920; The Lovely Ship, 1927; The Voyage Home, 1930; A Richer Dust, 1931; That was Yesterday; A Day Off; No Time Like the Present, 1933; Company Parade, 1934; Love in Winter, 1935; In the Second Year, 1936; None Turn Back, 1936; Delicate Monster, 1937; Civil Journey, 1939; Farewell Night, Welcome Day, 1939; Europe to Let, 1940; Cousin Honoré, 1940; The Fort, 1941; The End of this War, 1941; Then We Shall Hear Singing, 1942; Cloudless May, 1943; The Journal of Mary Hervey Russell, 1945; The Other Side, 1945; Before the Crossing, 1947; The Black Laurel, 1948; The Moment of Truth, 1949; Writer's Situation, 1950; The Green Man, 1952; The Hidden River, 1955; The Intruder, 1956; A Cup of Tea for Mr Thorgill, 1957; A Ulysses Too Many, 1958; A Day Off and other stories, 1959; Last Score, 1961; Morley Roberts: The Last Eminent Victorian, 1961; The Road from the Monument, 1962; A Month Soon Goes, 1963; The Aristide Case, 1964; The Early Life of Stephen Hind, 1966; The White Crow, 1968; (autobiography) Journey from the North, Vol. I 1969, Vol. II 1970; Parthian Words, 1970; There will be a Short Interval,

1972; (ed) A Kind of Survivor, autobiog. of Guy Chapman, 1975. *Recreation:* travelling. *Address:* c/o Macmillan & Co., 4 Little Essex Street, WC2.

JAMESON, Air Cdre Patrick Geraint, CB 1959; DSO 1943; DFC 1940 (and Bar 1942), psa; Royal Air Force, retired, 1960; *b* Wellington, NZ, 10 Nov. 1912; *s* of Robert Delvin Jameson, Balbriggan, Ireland, and Katherine Lenora Jameson (*née* Dick), Dunedin, NZ; *m* 1941, Hilda Nellie Haiselden Webster, *d* of B. F. Webster, Lower Hutt, NZ; one *s* one *d. Educ:* Hutt Valley High Sch., New Zealand. Commissioned in RAF, 1936. War of 1939-45 (despatches 5 times, DFC and Bar, DSO): 46 Squadron, 1936-40, 266 Sqaudron, 1940-41; Wing Commander Flying, Wittering, 1941-42; Wing Commander (Flying), North Weald, 1942-43; Group Capt. Plans, HQ No 11 Group, 1943-44; 122 Wing in France, Belgium, Holland, Germany and Denmark, 1944-45; Staff Coll., Haifa, 1946; Air Ministry, 1946-48; CFE, West Raynham, 1949-52; Wunsdorf (2nd TAF), 1952-54; SASO, HQ No II Group, 1954-56; SASO HQ RAF Germany (2nd TAF) 1956-59. Norwegian War Cross, 1943; Netherlands Order of Orange Nassau, 1945; American Silver Star, 1945. *Recreations:* fishing, shooting, sailing, golf. *Address:* 70 Wai-Iti Crescent, Lower Hutt, New Zealand. *Clubs:* Royal Air Force, Royal Air Force Reserves; Royal Air Force Yacht (Hamble); Hutt Golf; Hutt; Mana Cruising.

JAMESON, Storm; *see* Jameson, M. S.

JAMESON, Maj-Gen. Thomas Henry, CBE 1946 (OBE 1937); DSO 1919; RM, retired; *b* 10 Dec. 1894; *s* of Robert W. Jameson, JP, and Katherine Anne Jameson; *m* 1918, Barbara Adèle Bayley (*d* 1958); one *d. Educ:* Monkton Combe Sch., near Bath, Somerset. Commission in Royal Marines, 1913; served Belgium, France, Gallipoli (despatches) HMS Resolution, HMS Kent, 1914-18; Siberia, 1919 (DSO). War of 1939-45: staff of C-in-C Home Fleet, 15 RM Battalion, Admiralty; Commandant Plymouth, Jan. 1944 and Depot, Deal, June 1944; Commandant Portsmouth Division RM, 1944-46 (CBE); retired, 1946. *Address:* Flete House, Ermington, Devon. *T:* Holbeton 335.

JAMIESON, Major David Auldjo, VC 1944; Director, Australian Agricultural Company (Governor, 1952-76); Deputy Chairman, UK Branch, Australian Mutual Provident Society, since 1973, Director, since 1963; one of HM Body Guard, Hon. Corps Gentlemen-at-Arms, since 1968; *b* 1 Oct. 1920; *s* of late Sir Archibald Auldjo Jamieson, KBE, MC; *m* 1st, 1948, Nancy Elwes (*d* 1963), *y d* of Robert H. A. Elwes, Congham, King's Lynn; one *s* two *d* ; 2nd, 1969, Joanna, *e d* of Edward Woodall. *Educ:* Eton Coll. Commissioned Royal Norfolk Regt May 1939; served War of 1939-45 (VC); retired, 1948. *Recreations:* shooting, golf. *Address:* The Drove House, Thornham, Hunstanton, Norfolk. *T:* Thornham 206.

JAMIESON, Hon. Donald Campbell, PC (Can.); MP (Liberal); Secretary of State for External Affairs, Canada, since 1976; *b* St John's, Newfoundland, 30 April 1921; *s* of Charles Jamieson and Isabelle Bennett; *m* 1946, Barbara Elizabeth Oakley; one *s* three *d* . *Educ:* Prince of Wales Coll.; St John's, Newfoundland. Served War with Canadian Naval Special Services and United Service Org. Camp Shows. Regular broadcasts, 1941-46; news broadcasting nightly, 1946; Attaché, Parly Press Gallery, Ottawa, 1948; former Pres., Newfoundland Broadcasting Co. Ltd; also Dir of Broadcast News; Past Chm., Affiliates Sect. Network Advt Cttee, CBC. Pres., Canadian Assoc. of Broadcasters, 1961-65. With Dept of Rural Reconstruction; then Crosbie & Co. Ltd, fishery; Sales Manager, Coca Cola, Newfoundland. MP (Liberal), 1966-, St John's, Newfoundland; Minister: of Supply and Services, 1968-69; of Transport, 1969-72; of Regional Economic Expansion, 1972-75; of Industry, Trade and Commerce, Sept. 1975-76. Past Chm., financial campaign of Canadian Cancer Soc.; Past Director: Canadian Centennial Council; Nat. Theatre School. Hon. LLD: Memorial, 1970; Acadia; St Francis Xavier. *Publication:* The Troubled Air, 1966. *Recreations:* fishing, hunting, boating. *Address:* (office) House of Commons, Ottawa, Ont, Canada; (home) Swift Current, Newfoundland, Canada.

JAMIESON, Rt. Rev. Hamish Thomas Umphelby; *see* Carpentaria, Bishop of.

JAMIESON, Lt-Col Harvey Morro Harvey-, OBE 1969; TD; DL; WS; Member, Queen's Body Guard for Scotland (Royal Company of Archers), since 1934; *b* 9 Dec. 1908; *s* of late Major A. H. Morro Jamieson, OBE, RGA, Advocate, Edinburgh, and Isobel, *d* of late Maj.-Gen. Sir Robert Murdoch Smith, KCMG; *m* 1936, Frances, *o c* of late Col. J. Y. H. Ridout, DSO; three *s* ; assumed additional surname of Harvey, with authority of Lord Lyon King of Arms, 1958. *Educ:* Edinburgh Acad.; RMC

Sandhurst (Prize Cadetship); Edinburgh Univ. (BL). Commissioned 1st Bn KOSB, 1928; Capt. RARO 1938; Major RA (TA), 1939, to raise 291 HAA Battery RA (TA). Served War of 1939-45, Belgium, Holland and Germany, RA and Staff, Major and Lieut-Col; Comd 3rd Edinburgh HG Bn, 1954-57. France and Germany Star, General Service and Home Defence Medals; Jubilee Medals 1935 and 1977; Coronation Medals, 1937 and 1953. Secretary and Legal Adviser, Co. of Merchants of City of Edinburgh, 1946-71; former Mem., Cttee on Conveyancing Legislation and Practice (apptd by Sec. of State for Scotland, 1964). Mem. Council, Cockburn Assoc. (Edinburgh Civic Trust); a Manager, Edinburgh and Borders Trustee Savings Bank, 1957-77. Chairman, Scottish Committee: HMC, Assocs of Governing Bodies of Boys' and Girls' Public Schs, 1966-71. DL, County of the City of Edinburgh, 1968. *Publications:* The Historic Month of June, 1953; contrib. to Juridical Review, Scots Law Times and Yachting Monthly. *Address:* 4 Moray Place, Edinburgh EH3 6DS. *T:* 031-225 6914; Lechine Cottage, by Lochearnhead, Perthshire. *T:* Lochearnhead 248. *Club:* Royal Forth Yacht (Granton).

JAMIESON, Rear-Adm. Ian Wyndham, CB 1970; DSC 1945; Home Bursar and Fellow, Jesus College, Oxford, since 1972; *b* 13 March 1920; *s* of late S. W. Jamieson, CBE; *m* 1949, Patricia Wheeler, Knowle, Warwickshire; two *s* one *d. Educ:* RNC, Dartmouth. Served War of 1939-45: Anti Submarine Warfare Specialist, 1943. Comdr, 1953; Staff of RN Tactical Sch., 1953-56; HMS Maidstone, 1956-58; Dir, Jt Tactical Sch., Malta, 1958; Capt. 1959; Asst Dir, Naval Intelligence, 1959-61; Comd HMS Nubian and 6th Frigate Sqdn, 1961-64; Dir, Seaman Officers Appts, 1964-66; Comd Britannia RN Coll., Dartmouth, 1966-68; Rear-Adm. 1968: Flag Officer, Gibraltar, and Admiral Superintendent, HM Dockyard, Gibraltar; also NATO Comdr, Gibraltar (Mediterranean Area), 1968-69; C of S to C-in-C Western Fleet, 1969-71; retired. Hon. MA Oxon, 1973. *Recreations:* hockey (Scotland and Combined Services), cricket, golf, tennis. *Address:* Buckels, East Hagbourne, near Didcot, Oxfordshire. *Clubs:* Army and Navy, MCC.

JAMIESON, John Kenneth; Chairman of Board, Chief Executive Officer and Chairman of Management Committee, Exxon Corporation (formerly Standard Oil Co. (NJ)), 1969-75; *b* Canada, 28 Aug. 1910; *s* of John Locke and Kate Herron Jamieson; US citizen; *m* 1937, Ethel May Burns; one *s* one *d. Educ:* Univ. of Alberta; Massachusetts Inst. of Technology (BS). Northwest Stellarene Co. of Alberta, 1932; British American Oil Co., 1934; Manager, Moose Jaw Refinery; served War of 1939-45 in Oil Controller's Dept of Canadian Govt; subseq. Manager, Manufrg Dept, British American Oil Co.; joined Imperial Oil Co., 1948: Head of Engrg and Develt Div., Sarnia Refinery, 1949; Asst Gen. Man. of Manufrg Dept, 1950; on loan to Canadian Dept of Defence Production, 1951; Dir, Imperial Oil, 1952, Vice-Pres. 1953; Pres. and Dir International Petroleum Co., 1959; Vice-Pres., Dir and Mem. Exec. Cttee Exxon Co., USA (formerly Humble Oil & Refining Co.), 1961, Exec. Vice-Pres. 1962, Pres. 1963-64; Exec. Vice-Pres. and Dir 1964, Pres. 1965, Jersey Standard. Director: Exxon Corp.; The Equitable Life Assurance Soc. of US; Mercantile Texas Corp.; Crutcher Resources Inc. (Chm.). *Address:* 1100 Milam Building, Suite 4601, Houston, Texas 77002, USA. *Clubs:* Blind Brook (Port Chester); Augusta National Golf (Augusta); Houston Country (Houston); Rosedale (Toronto).

JAMIESON, Kenneth Douglas, CMG 1968; HM Diplomatic Service; seconded to Royal College of Defence Studies as Senior Civilian Member of Directing Staff, since 1977; *b* 9 Jan. 1921; *s* of late Rt Hon. Lord Jamieson, PC, KC, Senator of College of Justice in Scotland and Violet Rhodes; *m* 1946, Pamela Hall; two *s* one *d. Educ:* Rugby; Balliol Coll., Oxford. War Service: 5th Regt RHA, 1941-45; HQ, RA 7th Armoured Div., 1945-46. Joined Foreign Service, 1946; served in: Washington, 1948; FO, 1952; Lima, 1954; Brussels, 1959; FO, 1961; Caracas, 1963; Dir of Commercial Training, DSAO, 1968; Head of Export Promotion Dept, FCO, 1968-70; Minister and UK Dep. Permanent Representative, UN, NY, 1970-74; Ambassador to Peru, 1974-77. *Address:* 55 Victoria Road, W8.

JAMIL RAIS, Tan Sri Abdul, PMN; High Commissioner for Malaysia in the UK, 1967-71; *b* 14 Jan. 1912; *s* of Abdul Rais and Saodah; *m* ; four *s* six *d* (and one *s* decd). *Educ:* Clifford Sch.; Jesus Coll., Oxford. Joined Govt service, 1932; State Sec., Perlis, 1951-52; State Financial Officer, Selangor, 1954-55; State Sec., Selangor, 1955-56; Chief Minister, Selangor, 1957-59; Sec. to Treasury, 1961-64; Chief Sec. to Malaysian Govt and Sec. to Cabinet, 1964-67. *Recreations:* golf, tennis. *Address:* c/o Ministry of External Affairs, Kuala Lumpur, Malaysia.

JAMISON, James Hardie, OBE 1974; chartered accountant; Partner, Coopers & Lybrand (formerly Cooper Brothers & Co.), Chartered Accountants, since 1942; *b* 29 Nov. 1913; *s* of late W. I. Jamison; *m* 1940, Mary Louise, *d* of late W. R. Richardson; two *s* one *d. Educ:* Sydney Church of England Grammar Sch. Mem., Nat. Council, Aust. Inst. of Chartered Accountants, 1969-77, Vice Pres., 1973-75, Pres., 1975-76. *Recreation:* sailing. *Address:* 8 McLeod Street, Mosman, NSW 2088, Australia. *Clubs:* Australasian Pioneers' (Pres. 1970-72), Australian, Royal Sydney Yacht Squadron, Sydney Amateur Sailing (Sydney); Commonwealth (Canberra).

JAMISON, Dr Robin Ralph, FRS 1969, CEng, CChem, FRAeS, MRIC; Chief Technical Executive (Research), Rolls Royce (1971) Ltd (formerly Rolls Royce Ltd), Bristol Engine Division, 1971-75; *b* 12 July 1912; *s* of Reginald Jamison, MD, FRCS, and Eanswyth Heyworth; *m* 1937, Hilda Watney Wilson, Cape Town; two *s* two *d. Educ:* South African Coll.; Univ. of Cape Town. BSc, PhD. S African Govt research grant, 1936-37; research and development of aero engines, Rolls Royce Ltd, 1937-50; Head of Ramjet Dept, Bristol Siddeley Engines Ltd, 1950-62 (Asst Chief Engr, 1956); advanced propulsion res., 1962-65; Chief Engr, Res., 1965-71. Vis. Prof., Bath Univ. of Technology, 1969-73. Herbert Ackroyd-Stuart Prize, RAeS, 1958; Thulin Bronze Medal, Swedish Aero. Soc., 1960; Silver Medal of RAeS, 1965. *Publications:* papers in aeronautical and scientific jls. *Recreations:* sailing, gardening, music. *Address:* 2 The Crescent, Henleaze, Bristol BS9 4RN. *T:* Bristol 62-7083.

JANES, John Douglas Webster, CB 1975; Deputy Secretary, Northern Ireland Office, since 1974; *b* 17 Aug. 1918; *s* of late John Arnold Janes and Maud Mackinnon (née Webster); *m* 1943, Margaret Isabel Smith; one *s* two *d. Educ:* Southgate County Sch., Mddx; Imperial Coll. of Science and Technology. 1st cl. BSc (Eng) London, ACGI, DIC. Entered Post Office Engineering Dept, Research Branch, 1939. Served Royal Signals, RAOC, REME, 1939-45: War Office, 1941-45; Major. Min. of Town and Country Planning, 1947; Min. of Housing and Local Govt, 1951; seconded to Min. of Power, 1956-58; HM Treasury, 1960-63; Min. of Land and Natural Resources, 1964-66; Prin. Finance Officer and Accountant Gen., Min. of Housing and Local Govt, 1968-70; Prin. Finance Officer (Local Govt and Develt), DoE, 1970-73, Dep. Sec., 1973; Chief Executive, Maplin Develt Authority, 1973-74. *Recreations:* singing, do-it-yourself. *Address:* 136 Waterfall Road, N14 7JN. *T:* 01-886 2133.

JANES, Rev. Maxwell Osborne; Minister, Crowborough United (Methodist and United Reformed) Church, 1967-77, now Emeritus; *b* 14 May 1902; *s* of Harry Janes; *m* 1927, Mildred Bertha Burgess; one *s. Educ:* Kilburn Gram. Sch.; University Coll., London; New Coll., London. BA London; BD London. Ordained Congregational Minister, 1927. Minister at: Rectory Road Congreg. Ch., Stoke Newington, 1927-32; Above Bar Congreg. Ch., Southampton, 1932-45; Moderator of Southern Province, Congreg. Union of England and Wales, 1945-50; Gen. Sec., London Missionary Soc., 1950-66; Pres., Congregational Church in England and Wales, 1966-67; Cons. Sec., Congregational Coun. for World Mission, 1966-67. *Publication:* Servant of the Church, 1952. *Recreations:* gardening, philately. *Address:* Fen Place, Turner's Hill, Crawley RH10 4QE.

JANES, Maj.-Gen. Mervyn, CB 1973; MBE 1944; *b* 1 Oct. 1920; *o s* of W. G. Janes; *m* 1946, Elizabeth Kathleen McIntyre; two *d. Educ:* Sir Walter St John's Sch., London. Commnd 1942; served with Essex Yeo. (104 Regt RHA), 1942-46, Middle East and Italy; psc 1951; served with 3 RHA, 1952-53; 2 Div., BMRA, 1954-55; Chief Instructor, New Coll., RMAS, 1956-57; Batt. Comd, 3 RHA, 1958-60; Asst Army Instructor (GSO1), Imperial Defence Coll., 1961-62; comd 1st Regt RHA, 1963-65; Comdr, RA, in BAOR, 1965-67; DMS2 (MoD(A)), 1967-70; GOC 5th Division, 1970-71; Dir, Royal Artillery, 1971-73. Col Comdt, RA, 1973-. *Recreations:* music, egyptology, ornithology, tennis. *Address:* Beck Cottage, Woodgreen, Fordingbridge, Hants. *Club:* Army and Navy.

JANES, Norman Thomas, RWS, RE, RSMA; Painter, Etcher and Wood Engraver; *b* Egham, Surrey 1892; *s* of Arthur T. Janes and Ada Louise Croxson, *m* 1925, Barbara Greg, *qv*; one *s* two *d. Educ:* Slade Sch. (drawing and painting); Central Sch. of Arts and Crafts (etching); Royal Coll. of Art. Served in the London Irish Rifles and the Royal Irish Regt, 1914-19; France, 1915-17; RAF 1941-45; served in Middle East for three years (despatches). Exhibited from 1921 at Internat. Soc., Royal Academy, New English Art Club, Goupil Gallery, Society of Wood Engravers and principal provincial galleries; abroad at Florence, Venice, Prague, Chicago, Stockholm, Johannesburg, New York; works purchased for permanent collections of British

Museum, Victoria and Albert Museum, Imperial War Museum, London Museum, City of London, Manchester City Gallery, Whitworth Gallery (Manchester), Bradford, Brighton, National Gallery of New Zealand, New York Public Library, Brooklyn Museum, Cincinnati, Pasadena, Brisbane and others. One-man exhibitions: Beaux Arts Gallery, London, 1932 and 1945; Middlesbrough, 1962; Clifton, 1975. *Recreations:* books, garden. *Address:* 70 Canonbury Park South, N1. *T:* 01-226 1925.

JANION, Rear-Adm. Hugh Penderel; Flag Officer, Royal Yachts, since 1975; *b* 28 Sept. 1923; *s* of Engr Captain Ralph Penderel Janion, RN, and Mrs Winifred Derwent Janion; *m* 1956, Elizabeth Monica Ferard; one *s* one *d. Educ:* Malvern Link Sch., Worcs; Britannia RNC Dartmouth. Naval Cadet, 1937; Midshipman, 1941; Sub-Lt 1942; Lieut 1944; Lt-Comdr 1952; Comdr 1958; Captain 1966; Rear-Adm. 1975; ADC to the Queen, 1975; an Extra Equerry to the Queen, 1975-. Younger Brother, Trinity House, 1976-. CO, HMS Bristol, 1973-75. *Recreations:* sailing, gardening. *Address:* King's Hayes, Batcombe, Shepton Mallet, Somerset BA4 6HF. *T:* Upton Noble 300. *Clubs:* Royal Navy of 1765 and 1785; Royal Naval (Portsmouth).

JANNEH, Bocar Ousman S.; *see* Semega-Janneh.

JANNER, family name of **Baron Janner.**

JANNER, Baron *cr* 1970 (Life Peer), of the City of Leicester; **Barnett Janner,** Kt 1961; Solicitor; *b* 20 June 1892; *s* of late Joseph and Gertrude Janner, Barry, Glamorgan; *m* 1927, Elsie Sybil Cohen (*see* Lady Janner); one *s* one *d. Educ:* Barry County Sch.; University of S Wales and Mon (Cardiff Coll.) (County Scholarship). BA; Pres. of Students Representative Council; editor of University Magazine; served 1st World War in RGA, France and Belgium (gassed); ARP Warden in London, War of 1939-45. President: Board of Deputies of British Jews, 1955-64 (now Chm. Israel Cttee); Assoc. of Jewish Friendly Societies; Zionist Federation of Gt Britain and Ireland; Chm., Parly Anglo-Benelux Gp; Past Chm., Inter-Parly Union; Chm., Anglo-Israel Parly Gp. Chairman, Lords and Commons Solicitors Gp; Vice-Pres. and Mem. Exec. Cttee of Conf. on Jewish Material Claims against Germany Inc.; Member: Executive Cttee of Cttee for Jewish Claims on Austria; Exec., World Zionist Organisation; Exec. Bd of Deputies of British Jews; Vice-President: Assoc. of Jewish ex-Servicemen; Assoc. of Metropolitan Authorities; Chairman: Leaseholders' Assoc. of Great Britain, Parliamentary Water Safety Cttee. Contested Cardiff Central, 1929; Whitechapel and St George's, 1930 and 1935; MP (L) Whitechapel and St George's Division of Stepney, 1931-35; joined Labour Party, 1936; MP (Lab), West Leicester, 1945-50, North-West Div. of Leicester, 1950-70; Hon. Pres., NW Leicester Lab. party; former Mem., House of Commons Panel of Chairmen. Vice-President: World Maccabi Assoc.; British Maccabi. Mem. Society of Labour Lawyers; formerly Hon. Rents Adviser to Labour Party. Pres., Leicester Civic Soc. Life Governor, Cardiff Univ. FRSA; CIPM. Hon. LLD Leeds, 1957. Commander: Order of Leopold II (Belgium), 1963; Order of Orange Nassau of Netherlands, 1970. *Recreation:* reading. *Address:* 69 Albert Hall Mansions, SW7 2AG. *T:* 01-589 8222; Victoria House, Bloomsbury Square, WC1. *T:* 01-405 1311, 01-242 3258; The Jungle, Stone Road, Broadstairs, Kent. *T:* Thanet 61642.

See also Hon. G. E. Janner, Lord Morris of Kenwood.

JANNER, Lady; Elsie Sybil Janner, CBE 1968; JP; *b* Newcastle upon Tyne; *d* of Joseph and Henrietta Cohen; *m* 1927, Barnett Janner (*see* Baron Janner); one *s* one *d. Educ:* Central Newcastle High Sch.; South Hampstead High Sch.; Switzerland. Founder and first Hon. Club Leader, Brady Girls' Club, Whitechapel, 1925 (now Pres., Brady Clubs and Settlement). War of 1939-45: Captain, Mechanised Transp. Corps (Def. Medal). Chm., Bridgehead Housing Assoc., to acquire property for residential purposes for homeless ex-offenders, 1967-75; Chairman: Adv. Bd, Stonham Housing Assoc. (amalgamation of S Western Housing Assoc. and St Leonards Housing Assoc.), 1975-; Stonham Meml Trust; Mem., Stonham Housing Assoc. Finance and Policy Cttee. Magistrates Assoc.: Vice-Pres.; Hon. Treasurer, 1971-76; formerly Dep. Chm., Road Traffic Cttee, and Mem., Exec. Cttee; former Mem., Jt Standing Cttee, Magistrates Assoc. and Justices' Clerks Soc. JP, Inner London, 1936; contested (Lab), Mile End, LCC, 1947; a Visiting Magistrate to Holloway Women's Prison, 1950-62; Chm., Thames Bench of Magistrates, 1975; Mem., Juvenile Courts Panel, 1944-70 (Chm. 1960-70); Former Member: Inner London and NE London Licensing Planning Cttees; Inner London Licensing Compensation Cttee; Inner London Mem., Cttee of Magistrates. Vice-Pres., Assoc. for Jewish Youth; Hon. Vice-Pres., Fedn of Women Zionists of Gt Brit. and Ire.; Chm. Bd of

Deputies, British Jews Educn and Youth Cttee, 1943-66 (Mem. For. Affairs Cttee); Chm., United Jewish Educnl and Cultural Org. (internat. body to re-construct Jewish educn in countries of Europe which had been occupied by Germans), 1947-50; Jewish Youth Organisations Committee: Founder, Chm. and now Life Hon. Pres.; Mem., Central Council of Jewish Religious Educn. Trustee, Mitchell City of London Charity and Educnl Foundn; Mem., former Nat. Road Safety Adv. Council, 1965-68; Mem. Council and Exec., Inst. Advanced Motorists. Freeman, City of London, 1975. *Recreations:* swimming, grandchildren. *Address:* 69 Albert Hall Mansions, SW7 2AG. *T:* 01-589 8222; The Jungle, Stone Road, Broadstairs, Kent. *T:* Thanet 61642.
See also Hon. G.E. Janner, Lord Morris of Kenwood.

JANNER, Hon. Greville Ewan, MA Cantab; QC 1971; MP (Lab) Leicester West, since 1974 (Leicester North West, 1970-74); barrister-at-law; author, lecturer, journalist and broadcaster; *b* 11 July 1928; *s* of Baron Janner, *qv* and of Lady Janner, *qv*; *m* 1955, Myra Louise Sheink, Melbourne; one *s* two *d. Educ:* Bishop's Coll. Sch., Canada; St Paul's Sch. (Foundn Schol.); Trinity Hall, Cambridge (Exhbnr); Harvard Post Graduate Law School (Fulbright and Smith-Mundt Schol.); Harmsworth Scholar, Middle Temple, 1955. Southern Jr Champion, 100 yds, 1947. Nat. Service: Sgt, RA, BAOR, War Crimes Investigator. Pres., Cambridge Union, 1952; Chm., Cambridge Univ. Labour Club, 1952; Internat. Sec., Nat. Assoc. of Labour Students, 1952; Pres., Trinity Hall Athletic Club, 1952. Contested (Lab) Wimbledon, 1955. Chm., All-Party Parly Industrial Safety Gp; Founder, Trustee and former Chm., All-Party Parly Cttee for Homeless and Rootless People; Vice-Chm., All-Party Parly Cttee for Release of Soviet Jewry; Hon. Sec., All-Party Parly Retirement Gp; Jt Hon. Sec., Parly Anti-Arab Boycott Cttee. Vice-President: Assoc. for Jewish Youth; Assoc. of Jewish Ex-Servicemen; Sen. Vice-Pres., Board of Deputies of British Jews; Jt Chm., Israel Solidarity Cttee; Pres., Jewish Scouts Adv. Council; Mem., Governing Council and European Exec., World Jewish Congress; Pres., Trinity Hall Law Soc. Mem., Exec., Anglo-Israel Chamber of Commerce; Member: Nat. Union of Journalists; Brit. Acad. of Forensic Sciences; Howard League for Penal Reform; Soc. of Labour Lawyers; President: Braunstone Action Cttee; Aid for Alyn Hosp.; Leicester New Parks Festival; Leicester County Fencing Assoc.; Leicester Fabian Soc.; Leicester Ex-Boxers' Assoc.; Vice-President: Leicester Polio Fellowship; Leicester St Matthew's Community Centre; Leicester Rowing Club; Chm. of Managers, Brady Clubs, 1960; Founder and Vice-Pres., The Bridge in Britain; Mem. Hon. Adv. Bd, Internat. Commn for Human Rights; Founder Mem., Internat. Cttee for Human Rights in USSR; Chm., Slepak Charitable Trust. Dir, Jewish Chronicle Newspaper Ltd. Mem., Magic Circle, 1976. FIPM 1976. *Publications:* (as Ewan Mitchell): Farming and the Law, 1962; The Lawyer and His World, 1962; The Businessman's Lawyer and Legal Lexicon, 1962; The Retailer's Lawyer, 1963; All You Need To Know About The Law, 1963; Motorists: Know Your Law, 1964; You and the Law, 1964; The Personnel Manager's Lawyer and Employer's Guide to the Law, 1964; Your Office and the Law, 1964; Your Factory and the Law, 1965; The Sales Executive's Lawyer, 1966; Your Property and the Law, 1966; The Director's Lawyer, 1968; The Businessman's Guide to Speech-making and to the Laws and Conduct of Meetings, 1968; Coping With Crime, 1969; Letters of the Law: the Businessman's Encyclopedia of Draft Letters, 1970; The Businessman's Guide to Letterwriting and to the Law on Letters, 1970; The Businessman's Legal Lexicon, 1970; The Business and Professional Man's Lawyer, 1971; The Employer's Lawyer, 1971; Letters of Industrial Law, 1972; The Businessman's Guide to Travel, 1972; The Businessman's Guide to Commercial Conduct and the Law, 1972; The Manufacturer's Lawyer, 1973; The Director's and Company Secretary's Handbook of Legal Letters, 1973; The Merchandiser's Lawyer, 1973; The Transport Manager's Lawyer, 1974; The Director and Company Secretary's Handbook of Draft Contract Letters, 1975; The Employer's Guide to the Law on Health and Safety at Work, 1975; The Employer's Guide to the Law on Employment Protection and Sex and Race Discrimination, 1976; The Caterer's Lawyer, 1976; The Employer's Handbook of Draft Legal Letters, 1977. *Recreations:* relaxing with his family; swimming, skin-diving, magic. *Address:* (home) 2 Linnell Drive, NW11. *T:* 01-455 5157; (chambers) 1 Garden Court, Temple, EC4. *T:* 01-353 5524/4927; House of Commons, SW1. *T:* 01-219 3000, 01-219 4469.

JANVRIN, Vice-Adm. Sir (Hugh) Richard Benest, KCB 1969 (CB 1965); DSC 1940; *b* 9 May 1915; *s* of late Rev. Canon C. W. Janvrin, Fairford, Glos.; *m* 1938, Nancy Fielding; two *s. Educ:* RNC, Dartmouth. Naval Cadet, 1929; Midshipman, 1933; Sub-Lt, 1936; Lt, 1937; Qualified Fleet Air Arm Observer, 1938. Served War of 1939-45 (took part in Taranto attack, 1940). In

Command: HMS Broadsword, 1951-53; HMS Grenville, 1957-58; RNAS Brawdy, 1958; HMS Victorious, 1959-60. Imperial Defence Coll., 1961; Dir, Tactics and Weapons Policy, Admiralty, 1962-63; Flag Officer, Aircraft Carriers, 1964-66; Dep. Chief of Naval Staff, MoD, 1966-68; Flag Officer, Naval Air Comd, 1968-70; retired 1971. Lieut-Comdr, 1945; Comdr, 1948; Capt., 1954; Rear-Adm., 1964; Vice-Adm. 1967. *Recreation:* gardening. *Address:* Allen's Close, Chalford Hill, near Stroud, Glos. *T:* Brimscombe 2336.

JANZON, Mrs Bengt; *see* Dobbs, Mattiwilda.

JAQUES, Prof. Elliott; Professor of Sociology and Director of Institute of Organisation and Social Studies, Brunel University, since 1970; *b* 18 Jan. 1917; *m* 1953, Kathleen (*née* Walsh); one *d. Educ:* Univ. of Toronto (BA, MA); Johns Hopkins Med. Sch. (MD); Harvard Univ. (PhD). Qual. Psycho-analyst (Brit. Psycho-An. Soc.) 1951. Rantoul Fellow in Psychology, Harvard, 1940-41; Major, Royal Can. Army Med. Corps, 1941-45; Founder Mem., Tavistock Inst. of Human Relations, 1946-51; private practice as psycho-analyst and industrial consultant, 1952-65; Head of Sch. of Social Sciences, Brunel Univ., 1965-70. Adviser to BoT on organisation for overseas marketing, 1966-69; Mem. Management Study Steering Cttee on NHS Reorganisation, 1972. *Publications:* The Changing Culture of a Factory, 1951; Measurement of Responsibility, 1956; Equitable Payment, 1961; (with Wilfred Brown) Product Analysis Pricing, 1964; Time-Span Handbook, 1964; (with Wilfred Brown) Glacier Project Papers, 1965; Progression Handbook, 1968; Work, Creativity and Social Justice, 1970; A General Theory of Bureaucracy, 1976; articles in Human Relations, New Society, Internat. Jl of Psycho-Analysis, etc. *Recreations:* art, music, skiing. *Address:* Institute of Organisation and Social Studies, Brunel University, Uxbridge, Mddx. *T:* Uxbridge 56461.

JARDINE, Sir (Andrew) Rupert (John) Buchanan-, 4th Bt *cr* 1885; MC 1944; landowner and farmer; *b* 2 Feb. 1923; *s* of Sir John William Buchanan-Jardine, 3rd Bt and of Jean Barbara, *d* of late Lord Ernest Hamilton; *S* father, 1969; *m* 1950, Jane Fiona (marr. diss. 1975), 2nd *d* of Sir Charles Edmonstone, 6th Bt; one *s* one *d. Educ:* Harrow; Royal Agricultural College. Joined Royal Horse Guards, 1941; served in France, Holland and Germany; Major 1948; retired, 1949. Joint-Master, Dumfriesshire Foxhounds, 1950. JP Dumfriesshire, 1957. Bronze Lion of the Netherlands, 1945. *Recreations:* hunting, shooting, fishing. *Heir: s* John Christopher Rupert Buchanan-Jardine [*b* 20 March 1952; *m* 1975, Pandora Lavinia, *d* of Peter Murray Lee]. *Address:* Dixons, Lockerbie, Dumfriesshire. *T:* Lockerbie 2508. *Club:* MCC.

JARDINE, Christopher Willoughby, CB 1967; Assistant Secretary, Monopolies and Mergers Commission, 1975-76; *b* 5 Aug. 1911; *e s* of Judge Willoughby Jardine, KC; *m* 1940, Anne Eva Katharine, *er d* of Sir George Duckworth-King, 6th Bart; three *d. Educ:* Eton (Scholar); King's Coll., Cambridge (Scholar; 1st Cl. Hons. History); and in France and Germany. BoT, later DTI: Asst Principal, 1934; Principal, 1939; Asst Sec., 1945; Under-Sec., 1962; Adviser on Commercial Policy, 1962-64; Insurance and Companies Dept, 1964-72; Principal, Monopolies and Mergers Commn, 1972-75. *Address:* 8 St Loo Court, St Loo Avenue, SW3. *T:* 01-352 1246. *Club:* MCC.

JARDINE, Brig. Sir Ian (Liddell), 4th Bt *cr* 1916; OBE 1966; MC 1945; UK Land Forces, since 1973; *b* 13 Oct. 1923; *o s* of Maj.-Gen. Sir Colin Arthur Jardine, 3rd Bt; *S* father 1957; *m* 1948, Priscilla Daphne, *d* of Douglas Middleton Parnham Scott-Phillips, Halkshill, Largs, Ayrshire; two *s* two *d. Educ:* Charterhouse. Served War, 1942-45, Coldstream Guards (MC); 2nd Lieut, 1943; Major, 1950; Lt-Col 1964; Col 1968; Brig., 1969; Brig., GS, 1973-75, Brig., Inf., 1975-, UKLF. ADC to the Queen, 1976-. *Heir: s* Andrew Colin Douglas Jardine, *b* 30 Nov. 1955. *Address:* Coombe Place, Meonstoke, Southampton. *T:* Droxford 569. *Club:* Brooks's.

JARDINE, James Christopher Macnaughton; Sheriff of North Strathclyde (formerly Stirling, Dunbarton and Clackmannan) at Dumbarton, since 1969; *b* 18 Jan. 1930; *s* of James Jardine; *m* 1954, Vena Gordon Kight; one *d. Educ:* Glasgow Academy; Gresham House, Ayrshire; Glasgow Univ. (BL). National Service (Lieut RASC), 1950-52. Admitted as Solicitor, in Scotland, 1953. Practice as principal (from 1955) of Nelson & Mackay, and as partner of McClure, Naismith, Brodie & Co., Solicitors, Glasgow, 1956-69. Jun. Vice-Pres., Sheriffs' Assoc., 1976-. Sec., Glasgow Univ. Graduates Assoc., 1956-66; Mem., Business Cttee of Glasgow Univ. Gen. Council, 1964-67. *Recreations:* boating, enjoyment of good music. *Address:* Sheriff's Chambers, Dumbarton. *T:* Dumbarton 3266. *Club:* Glasgow University College (Glasgow).

JARDINE, John Frederick James; HM Consul-General, Johannesburg, since 1973; *b* 22 Dec. 1926; *s* of late James Jardine; *m* 1957, Pamela Joyce; four *s* two *d. Educ:* Rock Ferry High Sch., Birkenhead. RAF, 1945-48; Inland Revenue, 1948-55; BoT, 1955-58; British Trade Comr, Karachi, 1958-63; BoT, 1963-66; Midland Regional Controller, 1966-71; DTI, 1971-73; seconded to HM Diplomatic Service (Under-Sec.), 1973. *Recreations:* tennis, squash, sailing. *Address:* c/o Foreign and Commonwealth Office, SW1A 2AH. *Club:* Rand (Johannesburg).

JARDINE, Lionel Westropp, CIE 1939; late ICS; *b* 15 Feb. 1895; *s* of late Sir John Jardine, 1st Bt, KCIE, LLD, Godalming; *m* 1922, Marjorie Mildred Woods, Englefield Green, Surrey, one *s* two *d. Educ:* Charterhouse (Scholar); Wadham Coll., Oxford (Exhibitioner). Served European War, 1914-18 (despatches, wounded); Political Service, Mesopotamia, 1919-21 (general service medal and bar, Iraq); entered ICS, 1921; NW Frontier, 1924-31 (general service medal, 1931) and 1936-39; Finance Minister, Kashmir State, 1932; Dep. Commissioner, Peshawar, 1936; Revenue and Divisional Commissioner, N-WFP, India, 1938-43 and 1946; Resident for Baroda and the Gujerat States, India, 1943-44; left India, 1947, to join Dr F. N. D. Buchman in the work of Moral Re-armament. FRSA. *Address:* 6 Victoria Road, W8 5RD. *T:* 01-937 7074. *Club:* Naval and Military.

JARDINE, Michael James, CB 1976; Deputy Director of Public Prosecutions since 1974; *b* 20 Nov. 1915; *s* of Judge James Willoughby Jardine, KC; *m* 1939; two *s* one *d. Educ:* Eton; King's Coll., Cambridge (BA). Called to Bar, Middle Temple, 1937. Served War with Scots Guards, 1940-46: active service in North Africa and Italy. Legal Asst to Director of Public Prosecutions, 1946; Asst Solicitor, 1965; Asst Director of Public Prosecutions, 1969. *Recreation:* bridge.

JARDINE, Robert Frier, CMG 1928; OBE 1926; Third Class of the Order of Al Rafidain of Iraq, 1937; *b* 9 June 1894; *s* of late Robert Brown Jardine; *m* 1932, Averil (*d* 1975), *o d* of late H. O. Dickin; twin *s* (both Mems of 1960, 1964, 1968 British Olympic Yachting teams). *Educ:* Downing Coll., Cambridge. Commissioned Sept. 1914 from Cambridge Univ. OTC; served European War in Egypt, Gallipoli and Mesopotamia (despatches); in political charge of districts in Northern Iraq and Kurdistan, 1917-21; repatriated Assyrians to their original homes in Hakkiari, 1922; Political Officer to columns in Kurdistan, 1923; Mem. of HMG Delegation to Turkey and League of Nations upon Turkish frontier question, 1924; HM Assessor on League of Nations' Commission in connection with Turco-Iraq frontier, and upon other Commissions, 1925; Administrative Inspector, Mosul Province, 1925-28; Adviser to British Ambassador in Turkey for Tripartite Treaty, 1926; Frontier Commissioner, 1927; Administrative Inspector, Basra Province, 1928-33; Pres. of Commission for settlement of titles to land in Iraq, 1933-36; acted in various capacities in Palestine, 1936-48, including Dir of Settlement and Registration of titles to Land, Civil Aviation, Commissioner for Auqaf, Irrigation, Commissioner of Compensation for Rebellion and War Damages, 1945; Land Settlement and Water Commissioner; Advisory Councillor. During War of 1939-45 assisted with political advice as Lt-Col, Gen. Staff, Jerusalem Bureau. *Publications:* Grammar of Bahdinan Kurmanji (Kurdish), 1922; Gazetteer of Place Names in Palestine and Trans-Jordan, 1941. *Recreation:* yachting. *Address:* Walhampton March, Lymington, Hants. *T:* Lymington 72481. *Clubs:* Royal Lymington Yacht, etc.

JARDINE, Sir Rupert Buchanan-; *see* Jardine, Sir A. R. J. B.

JARDINE of Applegirth, Col Sir William Edward, 11th Bt of Nova Scotia, *cr* 1672; OBE 1966; TD; DL; JP; Chief of the Clan Jardine; late The KOSB; *b* 15 April 1917; *s* of Sir Alexander Jardine of Applegirth, 10th Baronet, and Winifred Mary Hamilton (*d* 1954), *d* of Major Young, Lincluden House, Dumfries; *S* father, 1942; *m* 1944, Ann Graham, *yr d* of late Lt-Col Claud Maitland, DSO, Gordon Highlanders, of Dundrennan and Cumstoun, Kirkcudbright; two *s.* Mem. of The Queen's Body Guard for Scotland, The Royal Company of Archers. Commnd KOSB 1939, retd as Major, 1960. Lt-Col Comd 4/5 KOSB (TA), 1963-67, Bt Col 1967. Chm., Dumfriesshire SSAFA. Mem., Dumfries CC, 1960-75, Chm. Roads Cttee, 1970-75; Mem., Annandale and Eskdale DC, 1975-. JP 1962, DL 1970, co. of Dumfries. *Heir:* *s* Alexander Maule Jardine, *b* 24 Aug. 1947. *Address:* Denbie, Lockerbie, Dumfriesshire. *T:* Carrutherstown 631. *Clubs:* Army and Navy; Puffin's (Edinburgh).

JARDINE PATERSON, Sir John (Valentine), Kt 1967; Director, McLeod Russel & Co. Ltd, London, since 1967; *b* 14 Feb. 1920; *y s* of late Robert Jardine Paterson, Balgray, Lockerbie, Dumfriesshire, and Constance Margaret Jardine Paterson (*née* Steel); *m* 1953, Priscilla Mignon, *d* of late Sir Kenneth Nicolson, MC; one *s* three *d. Educ:* Eton Coll.; Jesus Coll., Cambridge. Emergency commn, The Black Watch, RHR, 1939. Dir of Jardine Henderson Ltd, Calcutta, 1952-67 (Chm. 1963-67). Chm., Indian Jute Mills Assoc., 1963; Pres., Bengal Chamber of Commerce and Industry and Associated Chambers of Commerce of India, 1966. *Recreations:* golf, shooting. *Address:* Norton Bavant Manor, Warminster, Wilts. *T:* Sutton Veny 378. *Clubs:* Oriental; Bengal, Royal Calcutta Turf (Calcutta).

JARMAN, Rev. Canon Cyril Edgar; Canon Residentiary, Chester Cathedral, 1943-73, Vice-Dean, 1965-73; *b* 2 Dec. 1892; *s* of William and Annie Jarman, Cliftonville, Margate; *m* 1928, Alice Josephine, *d* of Canon Stockley, Wolverhampton, Chancellor of Lichfield Cathedral; two *d. Educ:* Holy Trinity Sch., Margate; The Theological Coll., Lichfield. Deacon, 1916, Lichfield, Priest, 1918; Curate, St James', Wednesbury, 1916-22; Curate St Peter's, Wolverhampton, 1922-25; Vicar, St Mary's, Shrewsbury, 1925-37; Vicar, Penkridge, 1937-43; Prebendary of Lichfield Cathedral, 1941-43. Proctor in Convocation, Lichfield, 1935-43; Examining Chaplain to Bishop of Chester, 1939-73; Chaplain to High Sheriff of Cheshire, 1955. *Recreations:* reading, walking. *Address:* The Flat, Croft House, Hazler Crescent, Church Stretton, Salop. *T:* Church Stretton 2506.

JARMAN, Air Cdre Lance Elworthy, DFC 1940; RAF (retired); Director, Engineering Industries Association, 1958-73, retired; *b* 17 Aug. 1907; *s* of Hedley Elworthy and Mary Elizabeth Jarman (*née* Chatterway-Clarke); *m* 1940, Elizabeth Evelyn Litton-Puttock; one *s* one *d. Educ:* Christchurch High Sch., NZ; Canterbury Coll., Univ. of NZ. Commissioned, RAF, 1929; No 12 Bomber Sqdn, Andover, 1930; No 14 Bomber Sqdn, Amman, 1931; Officers' Engineering Course, Henlow, 1932-35; RAF, Abukir, Atbara, Sudan, Cairo, 1935-38; Maintenance Command, 1938. Served War of 1939-45: Nos 214 and 9 Bomber Sqdns, 1939; Chief Flying Instructor, Nos 11-20 and 23 Operational Training Units, 1940; CO, No 27 OTU, Lichfield, 1941; SASO, No 93 Bomber Gp, 1942; CO, RAF Stations, Kidlington and Wyton, 1943; SASO, No 205 Gp, Italy, 1945, qualified as Pathfinder; OC RAF Stations, Oakington and Abingdon, 1947; Senior Officer Administration, RAF, No 42 Gp, 1949; OC, RAF Jet Training Stations, Full Sutton and Merryfield, 1951; Chief of Staff, Royal Pakistan Air Force, 1952; AO Defence Research Policy Staff, Cabinet Office, 1955; AOA, NATO, Channel and Atlantic Commands, 1957; retired from RAF, 1958. CEng, MIMechE, AFRAeS, MBIM, MAIE. *Publications:* Editor, Engineering Industries Jl. *Recreation:* sailing; lectr, offshore and ocean navigation; examr, RYA/DTI yachtmaster certificate. *Address:* Merryfield, 42 Murray Road, Northwood, Mddx. *T:* Northwood 24010. *Clubs:* Royal Air Force; Royal Ocean Racing; RAF Yacht (Hamble); Royal New Zealand Yacht Squadron.

JARRATT, Alexander Anthony, CB 1968; Chairman and Chief Executive, Reed International, since 1974 (Director, since 1970); Director: ICI; Goodyear (UK); ATV; Chairman, Industrial Society; *b* 19 Jan. 1924; *o s* of Alexander and Mary Jarratt; *m* 1946, Mary Philomena Keogh; one *s* two *d. Educ:* Royal Liberty Gram. Sch., Essex; University of Birmingham. War Service, Fleet Air Arm, 1942-46. University of Birmingham, BCom, 1946-49. Asst Principal, Min. of Power, 1949, Principal, 1953, and seconded to Treas., 1954-55; Min. of Power: Prin. Priv. Sec. to Minister, 1955-59; Asst Sec., Oil Div., 1959-63; Under-Sec., Gas Div., 1963-64; seconded to Cabinet Office, 1964-65; Secretary to the National Board for Prices and Incomes, 1965-68; Dep. Sec., 1967; Dep. Under Sec. of State, Dept of Employment and Productivity, 1968-70; Dep. Sec., Min. of Agriculture, 1970. Man. Dir, IPC, 1970-73; Chm. and Chief Executive, IPC and IPC Newspapers, 1974. Chm., Economic Cttee, CBI, 1972-74; Mem., NEDC. Chm., Henley Admin. Staff Coll.; Governor: London Business Sch.; Ashridge Management Coll.; Cranfield Inst. of Technol.; NIESR. FRSA. *Recreations:* reading, painting. *Address:* c/o Reed International Ltd, Reed House, 82 Piccadilly, W1. *Club:* Savile.

JARRETT, Sir Clifford (George), KBE 1956 (CBE 1945); CB 1949; Chairman: Tobacco Research Council, since 1971; Dover Harbour Board, since 1971; *b* 1909; *s* of George Henry Jarrett; *m* 1933, Hilda Alice Goodchild (*d* 1975); one *s* two *d. Educ:* Dover County Sch.; Sidney Sussex Coll., Cambridge. BA 1931. Entered Civil Service, 1932; Asst Principal, Home Office, 1932-34, Admiralty, 1934-38; Private Sec. to Parl. Sec., 1936-38; Principal Private Sec. to First Lord, 1940-44; Principal Establishments Officer, 1946-50; a Dep. Sec., Admiralty, 1950-61; Permanent Sec., Admiralty, 1961-64; Permanent Under-

Sec., Min. of Pensions and Nat. Insurance, later Min. of Social Security, later Dept of Health and Social Security, 1964-70. A Trustee, Nat. Maritime Museum, 1969-. *Address:* The Coach House, Derry Hill, Menston, Ilkley, W Yorks. *Club:* United Oxford & Cambridge University.

JARRETT, Norman Rowlstone, CMG 1946; BA Oxon; *b* 23 Aug. 1889; *s* of late Arthur E. Jarrett, Netherby Cottage, Anstye, Cuckfield, Sussex; *m* 1st, Doris Griffith; one *s* one *d*; 2nd, Violet (*d* 1972), *d* of Rev. W. H. Wilkinson, Warminster. *Educ:* Highgate Sch.; Exeter Coll., Oxford (2nd Class Lit Hum 1912). Cadet FMS Civil Service, 1912; various administrative appointments in Malayan Civil Service, 1913-37; British Adviser, Trengganu, 1937; Food Controller, Malaya, 1939-41; Acting British Resident, Selangor, 1941; interned by Japanese in Singapore, 1942-45; Sec., Assoc. of British Malaya, 1946-53. *Recreations:* gardening, music. *Address:* Anvil Cottage, Lye Green, near Crowborough, East Sussex TN6 1UU. *T:* Crowborough 4466.

JARRETT, Prof. William Fleming Hoggan, PhD; MRCVS, FRCPath, FRSE; Professor of Veterinary Pathology, University of Glasgow, since 1968; *b* 2 Jan. 1928; *s* of James and Jessie Jarrett; *m* 1952, Anna Fraser Sharp; two *d*. *Educ:* Lenzie Academy; Glasgow Veterinary Coll.; Univ. of Glasgow (PhD). Gold Medal, 1949; John Henry Steele Meml Medal, 1961; Steel Bodger Meml Schol. 1955. ARC Research Student, 1949-52; Lectr, Dept of Veterinary Pathology, Univ. of Glasgow Vet. Sch., 1952-53; Head of Hospital Path. Dept of Vet. Hosp., Univ. of Glasgow, 1953-61; Reader in Pathology, Univ. of Glasgow, 1962-65; seconded to Univ. of E Africa, 1963-64; Titular Prof. of Experimental Vet. Medicine, Univ. of Glasgow, 1965. *Publications:* various, on tumour viruses, leukaemia and immunology, in Advances in Veterinary Science and Comparative Medicine. *Recreations:* sailing, skiing, mountaineering, music. *Address:* Alreoch House, Blanefield, Stirlingshire G63 9AP. *T:* Blanefield 70332. *Clubs:* Royal Northern Yacht (Rhu), Clyde Cruising, West Highland Yacht, Glencoe Ski, Scottish Ski.

JARRING, Gunnar, PhD; Grand Cross, Order of the North Star, Sweden; Swedish Ambassador and Special Representative of the Secretary-General of the United Nations on the Middle East question since Nov. 1967; *b* S Sweden, 12 Oct. 1907; *s* of Gottfrid Jönsson and Betty Svensson; *m* 1932, Agnes, *d* of Prof. Carl Charlier, Lund; one *d*. *Educ:* Lund; Univ. of Lund (PhD). Family surname changed to Jarring, 1931. Associate Prof. of Turkish Langs, Lund Univ., 1933-40; Attaché, Ankara, 1940-41; Chief, Section B, Teheran, 1941; Chargé d'Affaires *ad interim:* Teheran and Baghdad, 1945; Addis Ababa, 1946-48; Minister: to India, 1948-51, concurrently to Ceylon, 1950-51; to Persia, Iraq and Pakistan, 1951-52; Dir, Polit. Div., Min. of Foreign Affairs, 1953-56; Permanent Rep. to UN, 1956-58; Rep. on Security Council, 1957-58; Ambassador to USA, 1958-64, to USSR, 1964-73, and to Mongolia, 1965-73. *Publications:* Studien zu einer osttürkischen Lautlehre, 1933; The Contest of the Fruits- An Eastern Turki Allegory, 1936; The Uzbek Dialect of Quilich, Russian Turkestan, 1937; Uzbek Texts from Afghan Turkestan, 1938; The Distribution of Turk Tribes in Afghanistan, 1939; Materials to the Knowledge of Eastern Turki (vols 1-4), 1947-51; An Eastern Turki-English Dialect Dictionary, 1964. *Address:* c/o Ministry of Foreign Affairs, Stockholm, Sweden.

JARROLD, (Herbert) John, CBE 1969; MA; JP; Chairman, Jarrold & Sons Ltd, since 1937; *b* 16 Feb. 1906; *s* of late T. H. C. Jarrold, and *g g g s* of John Jarrold, founder of Jarrold & Sons Ltd (1770); *m* 1st, 1932, Catherine Grace Elliott (*d* 1973); three *s*; 2nd, 1974, Joan, *widow* of Michael Pank. *Educ:* Norwich Sch.; Queens' Coll., Cambridge. Studied printing and bookbinding in Leipzig; joined Jarrold & Sons Ltd, 1927. Councillor, Norwich City Council, 1936-47; Sheriff of Norwich, 1947-49, Alderman, 1949-56. Pres., British Fedn of Master Printers, 1961-62; Chm., Printing, Packaging and Allied Trades Research Assoc., 1964; Pres., Norwich Incorporated Chamber of Commerce, 1965-67. JP Norwich 1949; Lord Mayor of Norwich, 1970-71. *Publications:* many articles on colour reproduction and printing. *Address:* 1A Church Avenue, Norwich NR2 2AQ. *T:* Norwich 54612. *Club:* National Liberal.

JARROW, Bishop Suffragan of, since 1965; Rt. Rev. Alexander Kenneth Hamilton, MA; *b* 11 May 1915; *s* of Cuthbert Arthur Hamilton and Agnes Maud Hamilton; unmarried. *Educ:* Malvern Coll.; Trinity Hall, Cambridge; Westcott House, Cambridge. MA 1941. Asst Curate of Birstall, Leicester, 1939-41; Asst Curate of Whitworth with Spennymoor, 1941-45. Chaplain, RNVR, 1945-47. Vicar of S Francis, Ashton Gate, Bristol, 1947-58; Vicar of S John the Baptist, Newcastle upon Tyne, 1958-65; Rural Dean of Central Newcastle, 1962-65. *Publication:* Personal Prayers, 1963. *Recreations:* golf, trout fishing. *Address:* Melkridge House, Gilesgate, Durham. *T:* Durham 3797. *Clubs:* Naval; Burnham and Berrow Golf.

JARVIS, Ven. Alfred Clifford, MA; Archdeacon of Lindsey, and Canon Residentiary of Lincoln Cathedral, 1960-71, Archdeacon Emeritus since 1971; *b* 6 Feb. 1908; *o s* of late A. W. Jarvis; *m* 1937, Mary Dorothea Chapple. *Educ:* Sudbury Grammar Sch.; Fitzwilliam House, Cambridge; Lichfield Theological Coll. Curate of Brightlingsea, 1931; permission to officiate Diocese of Ely, 1936; Vicar of Horningsea, 1937; Chaplain to Fulbourn Mental Hospital, 1937; Rector of Coddenham, 1944-55; Curate in charge of Hemingstone, 1949-52; Hon. Chaplain to Bishop of St Edmundsbury and Ipswich, 1954; Vicar of Elsfield and Beckley, and Curate in charge of Horton cum Studley, 1955-58. Archdeacon of Lincoln, Canon and Preb. of St Mary Crackpool in Lincoln Cathedral, and Rector of Algarkirk, 1958-60. Chaplain to High Sheriffs of Lincolnshire: Lord Worsley, 1964; Sir Anthony Thorold, Bt, 1968. Proctor in Convocation, 1961; Warden of Lincoln Diocesan Assoc. of Readers, 1960. *Recreations:* shooting and fishing. *Address:* 4 Pottergate, Lincoln. *T:* Lincoln 31600; Glebe Cottage, Brinkhill, by Louth, Lincolnshire. *Club:* Flyfishers'.

JARVIS, Mrs Doris Annie, CBE 1969; Headmistress, Tower Hamlets Comprehensive Girls' School, 1963-74; *b* 18 April 1912; *d* of William George Mabbitt (killed on active service, 1918) and Ada Marie Mabbitt; *m* 1940, George Harry Jarvis; one *s*. *Educ:* South Hackney Central Sch.; City of London Sch. for Girls; King's Coll., London (BSc); Furzedown Training Coll., London. Commenced teaching in Bethnal Green, E2, Sept. 1935; worked in E London schools and evacuation areas during War period; post-war, taught at Daniel Secondary Sch., E2; Emergency Training College Lecturer, Camden Trg Coll., 1949-50; Headmistress, Wilmot Secondary Girls' Sch., Bethnal Green, E2, 1950-63. *Recreations:* home affairs, reading, walking, gardening; furthering knowledge of education and social work in E London, generally. *Address:* 1a Tolmers Avenue, Cuffley, Herts. *T:* Cuffley 3780.

JARVIS, Eric William George, CMG 1961; Judge of the High Court, Rhodesia, since 1963; *b* 22 Nov. 1907; *s* of late William Stokes Jarvis and Edith Mary Jarvis (*née* Langley), both of Essex, England; *m* 1937, Eveline Mavis Smith; one *s* one *d*. *Educ:* Salisbury Boys High Sch. (now Prince Edward Sch.), Salisbury, R; Rhodes Univ., Grahamstown, SA. BA (Hons R Law); LLB; admitted as Advocate High Court of Southern Rhodesia, 1929; appointed Law Officer of Crown, 1934; KC (1949); Solicitor-Gen. for Southern Rhodesia, 1949-55; Attorney-Gen. for Southern Rhodesia, 1955-62. *Recreations:* tennis, golf, bowls. *Address:* (home) 680 Glenwood Drive, Glenwood Park, Greater Salisbury, Rhodesia. *T:* 4600419; (office) PO Box 8050, Causeway, Salisbury. *T:* 26113/4. *Club:* Salisbury (Salisbury, R).

JARVIS, Frederick Frank, (Fred Jarvis); General Secretary, National Union of Teachers; Member of General Council, Trades Union Congress, since 1974; *b* 8 Sept. 1924; *s* of Alfred and Emily Ann Jarvis; *m* 1954, Elizabeth Anne Colegrove, Stanton Harcourt, Oxfordshire; one *s* one *d*. *Educ:* Plaistow Secondary Sch., West Ham; Oldershaw Grammar Sch., Wallasey; Liverpool Univ.; St Catherine's Society, Oxford. Dip. in Social Science with dist. (Liverpool Univ.); BA (Hons) in Politics, Philosophy and Economics (Oxon), MA (Oxon). Contested (Lab) Wallasey, Gen. Elec., 1951; Chm., Nat. Assoc. of Labour Student Organisations, 1951; Pres., Nat. Union of Students, 1952-54 (Dep. Pres., 1951-52); Asst Sec., Nat. Union of Teachers, 1955-59; Head of Publicity and Public Relations, 1959-70; Dep. Gen. Sec., NUT, 1970-74 (apptd Gen. Sec. Designate, March 1974). *Publications:* The Educational Implications of UK Membership of the EEC, 1972. Ed, various jls incl.: 'Youth Review', NUT Guide to Careers; NUT Univ. and Coll. Entrance Guide. *Recreations:* swimming, golf, tennis, gardening, cinema, theatre. *Address:* 92 Hadley Road, New Barnet, Herts EN5 5QR. *Club:* Ronnie Scott's.

JASPER, Cyril Charles; County Treasurer, Hertfordshire County Council, since 1972; *b* 16 Oct. 1923; *s* of James Edward Jasper and Daisy (*née* Brown); *m* 1949, Vera Newington; three *s* two *d*. *Educ:* Brockley County Grammar Sch. DPA London 1950; CIPFA (double Hons) 1959; MBIM 1970. Comptroller's Dept, LCC, 1940-60; Asst County Treas., W Sussex CC, 1961-69; Dep. Co. Treas., Herts CC, 1970-72. Financial Adviser to Educn Cttee, Assoc. of County Councils, 1972-. Collins Gold Medal, CIPFA, 1959. *Publications:* contrib. local govt papers. *Recreations:* amateur dramatics, youth work, office holder in Methodist church. *Address:* Dovedale, 47 Walton Road, Ware, Herts SG12 9PF. *Club:* Hertford.

JASPER, Robin Leslie Darlow, CMG 1963; HM Diplomatic Service, retired; b 22 Feb. 1914; s of T. D. Jasper, Beckenham; m 1st, 1940, Jean (marr. diss.), d of late Brig.-Gen. J. K. Cochrane, CMG; one d; 2nd, 1966, Diana Speed (née West), two step d. Educ: Dulwich; Clare Coll., Cambridge. Apprentice, LNER Hotels Dept, 1936-39; Bursar, Dominion Students Hall Trust (London House), 1939-40; RAFVR (Wing Comdr), 1940-45; Principal, India Office (later Commonwealth Relations Office), 1945; concerned with resettlement of the Sec. of State's Services in India, 1947-48; British Dep. High Commissioner, Lahore, Pakistan, 1949-52; Adviser to London Conferences on Central African Federation, and visited Central Africa in this connection, 1952-53; Counsellor, HM Embassy, Lisbon, 1953-55; visited Portuguese Africa, 1954; Commonwealth Relations Office, 1955-60 (Head of Information Policy Dept, 1958-60); attached to the United Kingdom delegation to the United Nations, 1955 and 1956; British Dep. High Commissioner, Ibadan, Nigeria, 1960-64; Counsellor, Commonwealth Office, 1965-67; Consul-Gen., Naples, 1967-71, retired 1972. Recreations: tennis, Rugby fives, wind music, 17th Century Church Sculpture, claret. Address: Casa de los Algarrobos, Barrio de San Juan, Almuñecar, (Granada), Spain. T: 631526. Clubs: MCC, Jesters.

JASPER, Very Rev. Ronald Claud Dudley, DD; Dean of York, since 1975; b 17 Aug. 1917; o s of late Claud Albert and late Florence Lily Jasper; m 1943, Ethel, o d of David and Edith Wiggins; one s one d. Educ: Plymouth Coll.; University of Leeds; College of the Resurrection, Mirfield. MA (with distinction), 1940; DD 1961; DLitt 1976. FRHistS 1954. Curate of Ryhope, 1940-42; St Oswald's, Durham, 1942-43; Esh, 1943-46; Chaplain of University Coll., Durham, 1946-48; Vicar of Stillington, 1948-55; Succentor of Exeter Cathedral, 1955-60; Lecturer in Liturgical Studies: King's Coll., London, 1960-67, Reader, 1967-68; RSCM, 1965-69; Canon of Westminster, 1968-75; Archdeacon, 1974-75. Chm., Church of England Liturgical Commn, 1964-. Publications: Prayer Book Revision in England, 1800-1900, 1954; Walter Howard Frere: Correspondence and Memoranda on Liturgical Revision and Construction, 1954; Arthur Cayley Headlam, 1960; George Bell: Bishop of Chichester, 1967; A Christian's Prayer Book, 1972; (ed) The Renewal of Worship, 1965; (ed) The Calendar and Lectionary, 1967; (ed) The Daily Office, 1968; (ed) Holy Week Services, 1971; (ed) Initiation and Eucharist, 1972; (ed) The Eucharist Today, 1974; Prayers of the Eucharist, 1975; Pray Every Day, 1976; contribs to Church Quarterly Review, Jl of Ecclesiastical History, Church Quarterly, London Quarterly, Expository Times, Ecumenica. Recreations: reading, writing, television. Address: The Deanery, York.

JAUNCEY, Charles Eliot, QC (Scotland) 1963; Advocate; Judge of the Courts of Appeal of Jersey and Guernsey, since 1972; b 8 May 1925; s of late Capt. John Henry Jauncey, DSO, RN, Tullichettle, Comrie, and Muriel Charlie, d of late Adm. Sir Charles Dundas of Dundas, KCMG; m 1st, 1948, Jean (marr. diss. 1969), d of Adm. Sir Angus Cunninghame Graham, qv; two s one d; 2nd, 1973, Elizabeth (marr. diss. 1977), widow of Major John Ballingal, MC. Educ: Radley; Christ Church, Oxford; Glasgow Univ. BA 1947, Oxford; LLB 1949, Glasgow. Served in War, 1943-46, Sub-Lt RNVR. Advocate, Scottish Bar, 1949; Standing Junior Counsel to Admiralty, 1954; Kintyre Pursuivant of Arms, 1955-71; Sheriff Principal of Fife and Kinross, 1971-74; Hon. Sheriff-Substitute of Perthshire, 1962. Mem. of Royal Co. of Archers (Queen's Body Guard for Scotland), 1951. Mem., Historic Buildings Council for Scotland, 1971-. Recreations: shooting, fishing, genealogy. Address: Tullichettle, Comrie, Perthshire. T: 349; 11 Forres Street, Edinburgh 3. T: 031-225 4612. Clubs: New (Edinburgh); Royal (Perth).

JAWARA, Hon. Sir Dawda Kairaba, Kt 1966; MP, The Gambia; President of the Republic of The Gambia, since 1970; b Barajally, MacCarthy Island Div., 16 May 1924. Educ: Muslim Primary Sch. and Methodist Boys' Grammar Sch., Bathurst; Achimota Coll. (Vet. School); Glasgow Univ. Veterinary Officer, Kombo St Mary, 1954-60; Dipl. in Trop. Vet. Med., Edinburgh, 1957. Leader of People's Progressive Party, The Gambia, 1960; Minister of Education, 1960-61; Premier, 1962-63; Prime Minister, 1963-70. Grand Cross: Order of Cedar of Lebanon, 1966; Nat. Order of Republic of Senegal, 1967; Order of Propitious Cluds of China (Taiwan), 1968; Grand Officer, Order of Islamic Republic of Mauretania, 1967; Grand Cordon of Most Venerable Star of Knighthood, Pioneers of Republic of Liberia, 1968; Grand Comdr, Federal Republic of Nigeria, 1970; Grand Master, Order of the Republic of The Gambia, 1972; Hon. GCMG, 1974. Address: State House, Banjul, The Gambia.

JAY, Rt. Hon. Douglas Patrick Thomas, PC 1951; MP (Lab) Wandsworth, Battersea North, since 1974 (Battersea North, July 1946-1974); b 23 March 1907; s of Edward Aubrey Hastings Jay and Isobel Violet Jay; m 1st, 1933, Margaret Christian (marr. diss. 1972), e d of late J. C. Maxwell Garnett, CBE, ScD; two s two d; 2nd, 1972, Mary Lavinia Thomas, d of Hugh Lewis Thomas. Educ: Winchester Coll.; New Coll., Oxford (Scholar). First Class, Litteræ Humaniores; Fellow of All Souls' Coll., Oxford, 1930-37, and 1968-; on the staff of The Times, 1929-33, and The Economist, 1933-37; City Editor of the Daily Herald, 1937-41; Asst Sec., Ministry of Supply, 1941-43; Principal Asst Sec., BoT, 1943-45; Personal Asst to Prime Minister, 1945-46; Economic Sec. to Treasury, 1947-50; Financial Sec. to Treasury, 1950-51; President, BoT, 1964-67. Chairman: Common Market Safeguards Campaign, 1970-77; London Motorway Action Group, 1968-. Director: Courtaulds Ltd, 1967-70; Trades Union Unit Trust, 1967-; Flag Investment Co., 1968-71. Publications: The Socialist Case, 1937; Who is to Pay for the War and the Peace, 1941; Socialism in the New Society, 1962; After the Common Market, 1968. Address: 6 Hampstead Grove, NW3; Monument Cottage, Britwell Salome, Watlington, Oxford. T: Watlington 2615.
See also Peter Jay.

JAY, Rev. Canon Eric George; Professor of Historical Theology, Faculty of Divinity, McGill University, 1958-75, Emeritus, 1977; b 1 March 1907; s of Henry Jay, Colchester, Essex; m 1937, Margaret Hilda, d of Rev. Alfred W. Webb; one s two d. Educ: Colchester High Sch.; Leeds Univ. BA 1st Cl. Hons Classics, 1929; MA 1930; BD (London) 1937; MTh 1940; PhD 1951. Deacon, 1931; priest, 1932; Curate, St Augustine, Stockport, 1931-34; Lecturer in Theology, King's Coll., London, 1934-47; Curate, St Andrew Undershaft, City of London, 1935-40. Served War as Chaplain in RAFVR 1940-45. Rector, St Mary-le-Strand, 1945-47; Dean of Nassau, Bahamas, 1948-51; Senior Chaplain to the Archbishop of Canterbury, 1951-58; Principal, Montreal Diocesan Theological Coll., 1958-64; Dean, Faculty of Divinity, McGill Univ., 1963-70. Fellow of King's Coll., London, 1948; Canon of Montreal, 1960. Hon. DD: Montreal Diocesan Theolog. Coll., 1964; Trinity Coll., Toronto, 1975; United Theol Coll., Montreal, 1976. Publications: The Existence of God, 1946; Origen's Treatise on Prayer, 1954; New Testament Greek; an Introductory Grammar, 1958; Son of Man, Son of God, 1965; The Church: its changing image through twenty centuries, 1977. Recreations: reading "thrillers"; watching cricket, Rugby football. Address: 570 Milton Street, Montreal H2X 1W4, Canada.

JAY, Peter; Ambassador to the United States, since 1977; b 7 Feb. 1937; s of Rt Hon. Douglas Patrick Thomas Jay, qv; m 1961, Margaret Ann, d of Rt Hon. James Callaghan, qv; one s two d. Educ: Winchester Coll.; Christ Church, Oxford. MA 1st cl. hons PPE, 1960. President of the Union, 1960. Nuffield Coll., 1960. Midshipman and Sub-Lt RNVR, 1956-57. Asst Principal 1961-64, Private Sec. to Jt Perm. Sec. 1964, Principal 1964-67, HM Treasury; Economics Editor, The Times, 1967-77, and Associate Editor, Times Business News, 1969-77. Presenter, Weekend World (ITV Sunday morning series), 1972-77; The Jay Interview (ITV series), 1975-76. Wincott Meml Lectr, 1975. FRSA 1975; FRGS 1977. Political Broadcaster of Year, 1973; Harold Wincott Financial and Economic Journalist of Year, 1973; Royal TV Soc.'s Male Personality of Year (Pye Award), 1974; SFTA Shell Internat. TV Award, 1974; named by Time magazine among 150 future leaders of the world, 1973. Publication: The Budget, 1972. Recreation: sailing. Address: c/o Foreign and Commonwealth Office, SW1; 39 Castlebar Road, W5 2DJ. T: 01-998 3570; Elm Bank, Glandore, West Co. Cork. T: Leap 55. Clubs: Garrick; Royal Naval Sailing Association.

JAYAWARDANA, Brig. Christopher Allan Hector Perera, CMG 1956; CVO 1954; OBE 1944 (MBE 1941); ED 1936; JP; FLS; KStJ; b 29 March 1898; 4th s of Gate Mahandiram Herat Perera Jayawardana; m 1924, Sylvia Dorothy Samarasinhe, e d of Mudaliyar Soloman Dias Samarasinhe; one d (and one s decd). Educ: Trinity Coll., Kandy, Ceylon; Keble Coll., Oxford (MA). Sen. Asst Conservator of Forests, Ceylon (retd); Dep. Warden of Wild Life, Ceylon (retd), 1924-25; served War of 1939-45; OC 1st Bn the Ceylon LI, 1938-43; Chief Comr, Ceylon Boy Scouts' Association, 1949-54; Extra Aide de Camp to HE the Governor Gen. of Ceylon, 1949-; Equerry to HM the Queen, during Royal Visit to Ceylon, 1954; Hon. ADC to the Queen, 1954-. Awarded Silver Wolf, 1949. FLS, 1924. Carnegie Schol., 1931; Smith-Mundt Schol., 1951; KStJ, 1959 (CStJ, 1954). Diploma of Forestry. Recreations: rifle shooting, big game hunting, deep sea fishing, golf, tennis, riding, painting, camping, photography. Address: 12 Sukhastan Gardens, Ward Place, Colombo 7, Sri Lanka. T: (home) 91354; (office) 33131. Clubs: Corona; Sea Anglers' (Sri Lanka).

JAYES, Percy Harris, MB, BS, FRCS; Plastic Surgeon: St Bartholomew's Hospital, London, 1952-73; Queen Victoria Hospital, East Grinstead, 1948-73; Consultant in Plastic Surgery to the Royal Air Force, since 1960; Consultant Plastic Surgeon, King Edward VII Hospital for Officers since 1966; *b* 26 June 1915; *s* of Thomas Harris Jayes; *m* 1945, Kathleen Mary Harrington (*d* 1963); two *s* one *d*; *m* 1964, Aileen Mary McLaughlin; one *s* one *d*. *Educ:* Merchant Taylors' Sch.; St Bartholomew's Hosp. Resid. Plastic Surg., EMS Plastic Unit, East Grinstead, 1940-48; Surgeon in Charge, UNRRA Plastic Unit, Belgrade, 1946; Mem. Council, Brit. Assoc. Plastic Surgeons, 1954-64 (Pres., Assoc., 1960). *Publications:* contrib. British Journal of Plastic Surgery, Annals of Royal College of Surgeons and other journals. *Recreation:* tennis. *Address:* Barton St Mary, Lewes Road, East Grinstead. *T:* East Grinstead 23461; 149 Harley Street, W1N 2DE. *T:* 01-935 4444.

JAYETILEKE, Sir Edward (George Perera), Kt 1951; QC (Ceylon) 1938; *b* 11 Oct. 1888; *s* of John Gratiaen Perera Jayetileke and Maria Perera; *m* 1915, Grace Victoria Abeyesundere; one *s* three *d*. *Educ:* Royal College, Colombo. Called to the Ceylon Bar, 1910; Solicitor-Gen., 1939; Attorney-Gen., 1941; Puisne Justice, 1942; Senior Puisne Justice, 1949; Chm. Judicial Service Commission, 1950-51; Chief Justice, Ceylon, 1950-51. *Recreations:* racing, bridge, horticulture. *T:* 9440. *Clubs:* Ceylon Turf, Orient (Colombo); Galle Gymkhana (Galle).

JAYEWARDENE, Junius Richard; President of Sri Lanka, since 1978; *b* Colombo, 17 Sept. 1906; *s* of Justice E.W. and A.H. Jayewardene; *m* 1935, Eliana B. Rupesinghe; one *s*. *Educ:* Royal Coll., Colombo; Ceylon University Coll.; Ceylon Law Coll. Sworn Advocate of Supreme Court of Ceylon, 1932. Joined Ceylon Nat. Congress, later United Nat. Party, 1938; Hon. Sec., 1940-47; Hon. Treasurer, 1946-48, 1957-58; Vice-Pres., 1954-56, 1958-72; Sec., 1972-73; Pres., 1973-. Member: Colombo Municipal Council, 1940-43; State Council, 1943-47; House of Representatives, 1947-56, 1960-77 (Leader, 1953-56); Minister of: Agriculture and Food, 1953-56; Finance, 1947-52, 1952-53, 1960; Chief Opposition Whip, 1960-65; Minister of State and Parly Sec. to Prime Minister, Minister of Defence and External Affairs, and Chief Govt Whip, 1965-70; Leader of the Opposition, House of Representatives, 1970-72, Nat. State Assembly, 1972-77; Prime Minister, Minister of Defence, Planning and Economic Affairs, and Land Implementation, 1977. *Publications:* Some Sermons of Buddha, 1940; Buddhist Essays; In Council, 1946; Buddhism and Marxism, 1950, 3rd edn 1957; Selected Speeches. *Address:* President's House, Colombo, Sri Lanka.

JEAFFRESON, David Gregory; Secretary for Economic Services, Hong Kong Government, since 1976; *b* 21 Nov. 1931; *s* of Bryan Leslie Jeaffreson, MD, FRCS, MRCOG and Margaret Jeaffreson; *m* 1959, Elisabeth Marie Jausions; two *s* two *d* (and one *d* decd). *Educ:* Bootham Sch., York; Clare Coll., Cambridge (MA). 2nd Lieut, RA, 1950. Dist Officer, Tanganyika, 1955-58; Asst Man., Henricot Steel Foundry, 1959-60; Admin. Officer, Hong Kong Govt, 1961-; Dep. Financial Sec., 1972-76. *Recreations:* French history, music, photography, sailing and walking. *Address:* 64 Mount Nicholson, Hong Kong. *T:* 5-730551. *Club:* Royal Hong Kong Yacht.

JEANS, Isabel; Actress; *b* London; *d* of Frederick George Jeans; *m* 1st, Claud Rains (marr. diss.); 2nd, Gilbert Edward, *y s* of late Rt Rev. Henry Russell Wakefield, Bishop of Birmingham; no *c*. *Educ:* London. Made first appearance under Sir Herbert Tree's management at His Majesty's; first acting role was at the Garrick as Peggy in The Greatest Wish; went to United States with Granville Barker's Company, playing Titania in A Midsummer Night's Dream and Fanny in Fanny's First Play; on returning to England appeared in musical comedy and then joined the Everyman Repertory Company, playing Fanny, Raina in Arms and the Man, Hypatia in Misalliance, and Olivia in Twelfth Night, and also appeared in a number of Elizabethan and Restoration revivals by the Phœnix Society including Volpone, The Maid's Tragedy, The Jew of Malta, The Old Bachelor, and as Margery Pinchwife in The Country Wife; went to Holland to play Laura Pasquale in At Mr Beam's, and later played Yasmin in Hassan at His Majesty's and Lydia Languish in The Rivals at the Lyric, Hammersmith; since 1924 has appeared as Zelie in The Rat, Nell Gwynne in Mr Pepys, Lady Dare Bellingham in Conflict, Amytis in The Road to Rome, Estelle in Beauty, Crystal Wetherby in The Man in Possession, subsequently playing the same part in New York, Leslie in Counsel's Opinion, Mrs Jelliwell in Springtime for Henry, Lady Coperario in Spring 1600, Lucy Lockit in The Beggar's Opera, Lola in Full House, La Gambogi in The Happy Hypocrite, Alice Galvoisier in Mademoiselle, Susanna Venables in Second Helping, Lady Utterwood in Heartbreak House, Mrs Erlynne in Lady Windermere's Fan; went to New York, Jan. 1948, to play Lucia in Make Way for Lucia; since returning to London has appeared as Madame Arkadina in The Seagull; The Countess in Ardele; Florence Lancaster in The Vortex; Mrs Allonby in A Woman of No Importance; Lady Elizabeth Mulhammer in The Confidential Clerk (created rôle at Edinburgh Festival, 1953, and appeared in it finally at Paris Festival of Dramatic Art, 1954; made first appearance on Television, in this rôle, 1955); Sophie Faramond in the Gates of Summer. In 1957 created rôle of Aunt Alicia in the film Gigi; Duchess of Berwick in Lady Windermere's Fan, 1966; Mrs Malaprop in The Rivals, 1967; Lady Bracknell in The Importance of Being Earnest, Haymarket, 1968; Mme Desmortes in Ring Round the Moon, Haymarket, 1969; Dear Antoine, Piccadilly, 1971. Films and TV plays in Hollywood, Paris, Rome and Vienna. *Recreation:* reading historical biographies. *Address:* 66/24 John Islip Street, SW1.

JEBB, family name of **Baron Gladwyn.**

JEBB, Eglantyne Mary, CBE 1950; MA Oxon; Principal of the Froebel Educational Institute, Roehampton, Roehampton Lane, SW15, 1932-55; retired 1955; *b* 22 Dec. 1889; *d* of Rev. Heneage Horsley Jebb and Geraldine Croker Russell. *Educ:* Streatham Coll. for Girls; Lady Margaret Hall, Oxford; Class I, in Hons Sch. of English Language and Literature; trained at S Mary's Coll., Lancaster Gate, W, for London University Teachers' Diploma, 1912-13; Asst English Tutor, Somerville Coll., Oxford, 1913-19; English Lecturer, Education Dept, University of Birmingham, 1919-31; Visiting Lecturer Wellesley Coll., Mass, USA 1928-29. *Address:* Tansey, Wintergreen Lane, Winterbrook, Wallingford, Oxfordshire.

JEELOF, Gerrit; Chairman, and Managing Director, Philips Industries, UK, since 1976; *b* 13 May 1927; *m* 1951, Jantje Aleida Plinsinga; two *d*. *Educ:* Dutch Trng Inst. for Foreign Trade, Nijenrode. Philips Industries: Eindhoven, Holland, 1950-53; Spain and S America, 1963-65; Eindhoven, Holland, 1965-70; Varese, Italy, 1970-76. Commendatore nel Ordine al Merito della Repubblica Italiana, 1974. *Recreations:* sailing and golf. *Address:* Philips Industries, Arundel Great Court, 8 Arundel Street, WC2R 3DT. *T:* 01-836 4360. *Clubs:* Buck's, Royal Thames Yacht, American.

JEFFARES, Prof. Alexander Norman; MA, PhD, DPhil; FRSA 1963; FRSL 1965; Professor of English Studies, Stirling University, since 1974; *b* 11 Aug. 1920; *s* of late C. Norman Jeffares, Dublin; *m* 1947, Jeanne Agnès, *d* of late E. Calembert, Brussels; one *d*. *Educ:* The High Sch., Dublin; Trinity Coll., Dublin; Oriel Coll., Oxford. Lectr in Classics, Univ. of Dublin, 1943-44; Lector in English, Univ. of Groningen, 1946-48; Lectr in English, Univ. of Edinburgh, 1949-51; Jury Prof. of English Language and Literature, Univ. of Adelaide, 1951-56; Prof. of English Lit., Leeds Univ., 1957-74. Sec., Australian Humanities Res. Council, 1954-57; Corresp. Mem. for Great Britain and Ireland, 1958-70; Hon. Fellow, Aust. Acad. of the Humanities, 1970-. Mem., Scottish Arts Council, 1977-. Vice-Pres., Film and Television Council of S Aust., 1951-56; Chairman: Assoc. for Commonwealth Literature and Language Studies, 1966-68, Hon. Fellow, 1971; Internat. Assoc. for Study of Anglo-Irish Literature, 1968-70, Co-Chm., 1971-73, Hon. Life Pres., 1973-; Dir, Yeats Internat. Summer Sch., Sligo, 1969-71. Editor, A Review of English Literature, 1960-67; General Editor: Writers and Critics, 1960-73; New Oxford English Series, 1963-; Joint Editor, Biography and Criticism, 1963-73; Literary Editor, Fountainwell Drama Texts, 1968-75; Editor, Ariel, A Review of Internat. English Literature, 1970-72. Hon. DLitt Lille. *Publications:* Trinity College, Dublin: drawings and descriptions, 1944; W. B. Yeats: man and poet, 1949, rev. edn 1962; Seven Centuries of Poetry, 1955, rev. edn 1950; (with M. Bryn Davies) The Scientific Background, 1958; The Poetry of W. B. Yeats, 1961; (ed with G. F. Cross) In Excited Reverie: a centenary tribute to W. B. Yeats, 1965; Fair Liberty was All His Cry: a tercentenary tribute to Jonathan Swift 1667-1743, 1967; A Commentary on the Collected Poems of W. B. Yeats, 1968; (ed) Restoration Comedy, 4 vols, 1974; (with A. S. Knowland) A Commentary on the Collected Plays of W. B. Yeats, 1975; Yeats: the critical heritage, 1977; also: edns of works by Congreve, Farquhar, Goldsmith, Sheridan, Cowper, Maria Edgeworth, Disraeli, Whitman and Yeats; edns of criticisms of Swift, Scott and Yeats; various monographs on Swift, Goldsmith, George Moore, Yeats, Oliver St John Gogarty; contribs to learned jls. *Recreations:* drawing, motoring. *Address:* Department of English Studies, University of Stirling, Stirling. *Clubs:* Athenæum, Royal Commonwealth Society.

JEFFCOATE, Sir (Thomas) Norman (Arthur), Kt 1970; Professor of Obstetrics and Gynæcology, University of Liverpool, 1945-72, now Emeritus; Hon. Consultant Obstetrical and Gynæcological Surgeon, Liverpool United Teaching Hospitals and Liverpool Regional Hospital Board; *b* 25 March 1907; *s* of Arthur Jeffcoate and Mary Ann Oakey; *m* 1937, Josephine Lindsay; four *s. Educ:* King Edward VI Sch., Nuneaton; University of Liverpool. MB, ChB (Liverpool) 1st class Hons 1929; MD (Liverpool) 1932; FRCS (Edinburgh) 1932; MRCOG 1932; FRCOG 1939 (Vice-Pres., 1967-69; Pres. 1969-72). Hon. Asst Surgeon: Liverpool Maternity Hosp., 1932-45; Women's Hosp., Liverpool, 1935-45. Lectures: Blair-Bell Memorial, Royal College of Obst. and Gynaec. 1938; Sir Arcot Mudalier, Univ. of Madras, 1955; Margaret Orford, S African Coll. of Physicians, Surgeons and Gynaecologists, 1969; J. Y. Simpson, RCSE, 1976. Joseph Price Orator, Amer. Assoc. of Obstetricians and Gynaecologists, 1966. Sims Black Travelling Commonwealth Prof., 1958; Visiting Professor: New York State Univ., 1955; University of Qld, 1964; Univ. of Melbourne, 1964; Univ. of Texas, 1965; Hon. Visiting Obstetrician and Gynæcologist, Royal Prince Alfred Hospital, Sydney, Australia, 1955-. Chairman, Med. Advisory Council of Liverpool Regional Hosp. Bd, 1962-69; President: N of England Obst. and Gynaec. Soc., 1960; Sect. of Obst. and Gynaec., RSM, 1965-66; Liverpool Med. Inst., 1966-67; Vice-Pres. Family Planning Assoc., 1962-; Member: Gen. Med. Council, 1951-61; Clinical Research Bd, MRC, 1961-65; Clinical Trials Sub-Cttee of Safety of Drugs Cttee, 1963-69; Bd of Science and Educn, BMA, 1968-69; Standing Maternity and Midwifery Adv. Cttee, Dept of Health and Social Security (formerly Min. of Health), 1963-72 (Chm., 1970-72); Standing Med. Adv. Cttee and Central Health Services Council, Dept of Health and Social Security, 1969-72; Jt Sub-Cttee on Prevention of Haemolytic Disease of the Newborn, 1968-72 (Chm., 1969-72). Hon. FCOG(SA), 1972; Hon. FACOG, 1972; Hon. FRCS (C), 1973; Hon. Member: Amer. Gynec. Club; Amer. Gynec. Soc.; Amer. Assoc. Obst. and Gynec.; Central Assoc. Obst. and Gynec.; Assoc. Surg., Ceylon; Obst. and Gynaec. Socs of: Canada, Finland, Honolulu, Malta, Montreal, Panama, S Africa, Uruguay, Venezuela. Hon. LLD, TCD, 1971. Eardley Holland Gold Medal, RCOG, 1975. *Publications:* Principles of Gynæcology, 1957 (4th edn, 1975); communications to medical journals. *Address:* 6 Riversdale Road, Liverpool L19 3QW. *T:* 051-427 1448.

JEFFERSON, George Rowland, CBE 1969; Hon. BSc (London); CEng, MIMechE, FRAeS; FRSA; a Director, British Aerospace, and Chairman and Chief Executive, Dynamics Group, British Aerospace, since 1977 (Member, Organizing Committee, 1976-77); Chairman, British Aircraft Corporation (Guided Weapons Division), since 1968; Director, Hawker Siddeley Dynamics Ltd, since 1977; *b* 26 March 1921; *s* of Harold Jefferson and Eva Elizabeth Ellen; *m* 1943, Irene Watson-Brown; three *s. Educ:* Grammar Sch., Dartford, Kent. Engrg Apprentice, Royal Ordnance Factory, Woolwich, 1937-42; commnd RAOC, 1942; transf. REME, 1942; served 1942-45, Anti-Aircraft Comd on heavy anti-aircraft power control systems and later Armament Design Dept, Fort Halstead, on anti-aircraft gun mounting development; subseq. Mem. Min. of Supply staff, Fort Halstead, until 1952; joined Guided Weapons Div., English Electric Co. Ltd, 1952; Chief Research Engr, 1953; Dep. Chief Engr, 1958; Dir, English Electric Aviation Ltd, 1961 (on formation of co.); British Aircraft Corporation: Dir and Chief Exec., BAC (Guided Weapons) Ltd, 1963 (on formation of Corp.), Man. Dir, 1968-77; Dep. Man. Dir, 1964; Mem. Board, 1965-77; Man. Dir, BAC (Guided Weapons Div.), 1966-77; Chm., BAC (Anti-Tank), 1968-; Director: BAC (Australia) Pty Ltd, 1968-; British Scandinavian Aviation AB, 1968- Member Council: SBAC, 1965-; Electronic Engineering Assoc., 1968-72. *Address:* Gyffen, Gosmore Road, Hitchin, Herts. *Club:* Army and Navy.

JEFFERSON, Sir J. A. D.; *see* Dunnington-Jefferson.

JEFFERY, George Henry Padget, CMG 1965; FASA; Auditor General for South Australia, 1959-72; Chairman, Board of Trustees, Savings Bank of South Australia, 1972-76 (Trustee, 1965-76); *b* 6 June 1907; *s* of late George Frederick Jeffery and late Adelaide Jeffery (*née* Padget), Victor Harbour, S Aust.; *m* 1934, Jean Loudon Watt, *d* of late Thomas Watt, Adelaide; two *s. Educ:* Adelaide High Sch.; Victor Harbour High Sch.; University of Adelaide. Associate, University of Adelaide, 1933; Auditor, SA Public Service, 1936-40, Chief Inspector, 1940-51; Sec., Public Buildings Dept, 1951-53; Chief Executive, Radium Hill Uranium Project, 1953-59; Mem., SA Public Service Board, 1956-59. Pres., SA Div., Aust. Soc. of Accountants, 1965-67. Chm., Royal Commission of Enquiry into Grape Growing Industry, 1965. Member: Parly. Salaries Tribunal, 1966-; Royal Commn on State Transport Services, 1966-67; Cttee of Inquiry into S Australian Racing Industry, 1974-75. Dep. Chm., S Australian Egg Bd, 1973-. Mem., Bd of Management, Queen Victoria Hosp., 1972-76. FASA 1958. *Recreations:* bowls,

cricket. *Address:* 49 Anglesey Avenue, St Georges, South Australia 5064, Australia. *T:* 79-2929. *Clubs:* Commonwealth, SA Cricket Association, Glenunga Bowling (Adelaide).

JEFFERY, Lilian Hamilton, FBA 1965; FSA 1956; Fellow and Tutor in Ancient History, Lady Margaret Hall, Oxford, since 1952; *b* 5 Jan. 1915; 3rd *d* of late Thomas Theophilus Jeffery, MA Cantab, and Lilian Mary (*née* Hamilton). *Educ:* Cheltenham Ladies' Coll.; Newnham Coll., Cambridge. BA (Class. Tripos) 1936; MA 1941; Dipl. in Class. Archæology, 1937; DPhil (Oxon) 1951. Mem. British Sch. of Archæology, Athens, 1937-; Mem. Soc. for Promotion of Hellenic Studies, 1937-. Nurse in Military Hosp., 1940-41; WAAF (Intelligence), 1941-45. First Katherine McBride Vis. Prof., Bryn Mawr Coll., USA, 1971-72. Ed. Annual of British School at Athens, 1955-61. *Publications:* (collab.) Dedications from the Athenian Akropolis, 1948; The Local Scripts of Archaic Greece, 1961; (contrib.) A Companion to Homer, 1962; (contrib.) Perachora ii, 1964; Archaic Greece, 1976; articles in Jl of Hellenic Studies, Annual of Brit. Sch. at Athens, Hesperia, Amer. Jl of Philology, Historia, Philologus, etc. *Recreation:* drawing. *Address:* Lady Margaret Hall, Oxford.

JEFFORD, Barbara Mary, OBE 1965; Actress; *b* Plymstock, Devon, 26 July 1930; *d* of late Percival Francis Jefford and of Elizabeth Mary Ellen (*née* Laity); *m* 1953, Terence Longdon (marr. diss., 1961); *m* 1967, John Arnold Turner. *Educ:* Weirfield Sch., Taunton, Som. Studied for stage, Bristol and Royal Academy of Dramatic Art (Bancroft Gold Medal). Seasons at Stratford-on-Avon: 1950, 1951, 1953 (Australian and NZ tour with Shakespeare Meml Theatre Company), 1954; toured NZ with NZ Players' Company in The Lady's Not for Burning, 1954-55; in Tiger at the Gates, London and USA, 1955 and 1956; seasons at the Old Vic: 1956, 1957, 1958, 1959, 1960, 1961, 1962 (attended Baalbek Festival in Lebanon with Old Vic Co., 1957, and toured N America and Canada with same Co. 1958-59). Shakespearian roles include: Isabella in Measure for Measure, 1950 and 1957; Desdemona in Othello, 1953 and 1954; Rosalind in As You Like It, 1953 and 1959; Imogen in Cymbeline, 1956; Beatrice in Much Ado About Nothing, 1956; Portia in The Merchant of Venice, 1956, 1957, 1964, 1973; Queen Margaret in Henry VI, 1957; Viola in Twelfth Night, 1949, 1958, 1959 and 1961; Ophelia in Hamlet, 1958, 1959; Helena in A Midsummer Night's Dream, 1964; Cleopatra, 1965, 1966; Katharina in The Taming of the Shrew, 1971; Gertrude in Hamlet, 1976, 1977. Non-Shakespearian roles include: Andromache in Tiger at the Gates, 1955, 1956; Beatrice in the Cenci, 1959; Gwendolen Fairfax in The Importance of Being Earnest, 1959, 1960; Saint Joan, 1960; Lavinia in Mourning becomes Elektra, 1961; Lina in Misalliance, 1962; step-daughter in Six Characters in Search of an Author, 1963; Nan in Ride a Cock Horse, 1965; Lady Cicely in Captain Brassbound's Conversion, 1965; Phèdre, 1965; Maggie Harris in Fill the Stage with Happy Hours, 1966; Irma in The Balcony, 1967; Patsy Newquist in Little Murders, 1967; Woman in As You Desire Me, 1968; Hedda Gabler, 1971; Mother Vauzou in Mistress of Novices, 1973; Alice in Dear Brutus, 1973; Arkadina in The Seagull, 1975; Hesione Hushabye in Heartbreak House, 1975; Roxane in Cyrano de Bergerac, 1976; Zabina in Tamburlaine the Great, 1976; Tuetis in War Music, 1977; Cleopatra in All for Love, 1977. Recitals: Heroines of Shakespeare, 1963, toured Europe; Labours of Love, devised 1968, toured throughout world. Has appeared regularly since 1962 at Oxford Playhouse, Nottingham Playhouse, and Bristol Old Vic, at festivals in Aldeburgh, Bath, Chichester and Edinburgh; has toured extensively in UK, Europe, USA, Near East, Far East, Africa and Australia. *Films:* Ulysses, 1967; A Midsummer Night's Dream, 1967; The Shoes of the Fisherman, 1968; To Love a Vampire, 1970; Hitler: the last ten days, 1973. Has appeared in numerous television and radio plays; Canterbury Tales, TV serial, 1969. Silver Jubilee Medal, 1977. *Recreations:* music, swimming, gardening. *Address:* 46 Devonshire Close, W1.

JEFFORD, Vice-Adm. (Retd), James Wilfred, CB 1953; CBE 1951 (OBE 1941); *b* 22 March 1901; *o s* of James Harris Jefford; *m* 1926, Dorothy Kate Caswell; one *d. Educ:* HMS Worcester. Sub-Lieut, RIN, 1922; Commander, RIN, 1941; Captain RIN, 1946; Rear-Adm., 1947. Transferred to special list of Royal Navy and appointed Flag Officer commanding Royal Pakistan Navy, on inception of Pakistan, 1947; appointment upgraded to C-in-C, 1950; Vice-Admiral Royal Pakistan Navy, 1953; appointment terminated, 1953; Chm. Penang Harbour Board, 1955-57; Chm. Penang Port Commission, 1956-57; retired 1957. Served European War, 1914-18, as midshipman; War of 1939-45, commanding HMI Ships Indus and Godavari; various staff and shore appointments. *Address:* Pennyroyal, Willey Lane, Sticklepath, near Okehampton, Devon EX20 2NG.

JEFFREYS, family name of **Baron Jeffreys**.

JEFFREYS, 2nd Baron, *cr* 1952, of Burkham; **Mark George Christopher Jeffreys**; Major, Grenadier Guards; *b* 2 Feb. 1932; *er s* of Capt. Christopher John Darell Jeffreys, MVO, Grenadier Guards (*o s* of 1st Baron; killed in action, 1940) and of Lady Rosemary Beatrice Agar, *y d* of 4th Earl of Normanton; *S* grandfather, 1960; *m* 1st, 1956, Sarah Annabelle Mary (marr. diss., 1967), *o d* of Major Henry Claude Lyon Garnett; two *s* two *d*; 2nd, 1967, Anne Louise, *d* of Sir Shirley Worthington-Evans, 2nd Bt, and of Mrs Joan Parry; one *d*. *Educ:* Eton; RMA, Sandhurst. *Heir: s* Hon. Christopher Henry Mark Jeffreys, *b* 22 May 1957. *Address:* Saddlewood Manor, Leighterton, Tetbury, Glos. *Club:* White's.

JEFFREYS, Anthony Henry, CB 1961; *b* 13 Aug. 1896; *yr s* of late Major-Gen. H. B. Jeffreys, CB, CMG; *m* 1922, Dorothy Bertha, *d* of late Lieut-Col Edward Tufnell. *Educ:* Eton. Served War of 1914-18 (despatches; wounded); 2nd Lieut RFA, 1915; Lieut 'D' Battery RHA, 1917-19; Staff Captain, GHQ, France, and War Office, 1939-41. Entered Parliament Office, House of Lords, 1919; called to the Bar Inner Temple, 1924. Examiner of Petitions for Private Bills, 1941; Chief Clerk of Cttees and Private Bills and Taxing Officer, 1945; Reading Clerk, House of Lords, 1953; Clerk Asst of the Parliaments, 1959-61, retd. Chm., City of Westminster Boy Scouts' Assoc., 1953-60. *Address:* Doom Bar House, Trebetherick, Wadebridge, Cornwall PL27 6SA. *T:* Trebetherick 3380. *Club:* Lansdowne.

JEFFREYS, Sir Harold, Kt 1953; FRS 1925; MA Cambridge; DSc Durham; Fellow of St John's College, Cambridge, since 1914; Plumian Professor of Astronomy and Experimental Philosophy, 1946-58; *b* 22 April 1891; *o s* of R. H. and E. M. Jeffreys, Birtley, Durham; *m* 1940, Bertha, *d* of late W. A. Swirles and H. Swirles, Northampton. *Educ:* Armstrong Coll., Newcastle upon Tyne; St John's Coll., Cambridge. University Reader in Geophysics, 1931-46. Mathematical Tripos, 1913; Isaac Newton Student, 1914; Smith's Prize, 1915; Adams Prize, 1927; commended, 1923; Buchan Prize of Royal Meteorological Society, 1929. Gold Medal of Royal Astronomical Society, 1937; Murchison Medal of Geological Soc., 1939; Victoria Medal of RGS, 1942; Royal Medal of Royal Society, 1948; Ch. Lagrange Prize, Acad. Royal Sci., Belg., 1948; Bowie Medal, Amer. Geophys. Union, 1952; Copley Medal, Royal Society, 1960; Vetlesen Prize, 1962; Guy Medal, Royal Statistical Society, 1963; Wollaston Medal, Geological Soc., 1964; Pres., Royal Astronomical Soc., 1955-57; Pres. Internat. Seism. Assoc., 1957-60; For. Associate, US Nat. Acad. of Sciences; Accad. dei Lincei, Rome, Acad. Sci. Stockholm, New York Acad. Sci., Amer. Acad. of Arts and Sciences, Acad. Roy. de Belgique; Hon. FRS, NZ; Corresp. Member: Amer. Geophys. Union; Geolog. Soc. America; RIA; Hon. Member: Inst. of Mathematics; Amer. Seismological Soc. Hon. LLD Liverpool, 1953; Hon. ScD Dublin, 1956; Hon. DCL Durham, 1960; Hon. DSc, Southern Methodist Univ., Dallas, 1967. *Publications:* The Earth: Its Origin, History, and Physical Constitution, 1924, 1929, 1952, 1959, 1962, 1970, 1976; Operational Methods in Mathematical Physics, 1927, 1931; The Future of the Earth, 1929; Scientific Inference, 1931, 1937, 1957, 1973; Cartesian Tensors, 1931, 1953; Earthquakes and Mountains, 1935, 1950; Theory of Probability, 1939, 1948, 1962, 1967; Methods of Mathematical Physics (with B. Jeffreys), 1946, 1950, 1956, 1962; Asymptotic Approximations, 1962, 1968; papers on Astronomy, Geophysics, Theory of Scientific Method, and Plant Ecology. *Address:* 160 Huntingdon Road, Cambridge CB3 0LB.

JEFFREYS, Mrs Judith Diana; Assistant Director (Keeper), the Tate Gallery, since 1975; *b* 22 Sept. 1927. *d* of Prof. Philip Cloake, FRCP and Letitia Blanche (*née* MacDonald); *m* 1968, William John Jeffreys. *Educ:* Bedales; Courtauld Inst. of Art, Univ. of London (BA Hons History of Art). Tate Gallery: Asst Keeper, 1951-64; Publications Manager, 1960-65; Dep. Keeper, 1964-75. *Recreations:* renovation of country house, reading, music, gardening. *Address:* The Tate Gallery, Millbank, SW1. *T:* 01-828 1212.

JEFFREYS, Montagu Vaughan Castelman, CBE 1953; MA Oxon; Emeritus Professor, University of Birmingham; *b* 16 Dec. 1900; *s* of late Col F. V. Jeffreys, RE, and late Annie Augusta Jeffreys (*née* Barton); *m* 1941, Joan Sheila, *d* of late Col R. D. Marjoribanks; one *s* one *d*. *Educ:* Wellington Coll.; Hertford Coll., Oxford. Asst Master, Oundle Sch., 1924-27; Lecturer in Education, Armstrong Coll., Newcastle upon Tyne, 1927-32; Lecturer in Educ., University of London Institute of Education, 1932-39; Prof. of Educn in University of Durham, 1939-46. Prof. of Educn in University of Birmingham and Dir of University of Birmingham Inst. of Educn, 1946-64. Pres. Inst. of Christian Educn, 1958-63. Does occasional broadcasting. *Publications:*

Play Production: for Amateurs and Schools (3 edns), 1933 (with R. W. Stopford); History in Schools: The Study of Development, 1939; Education-Christian or Pagan, 1946; Kingdom of This World, 1950; Glaucon: an Inquiry into the Aims of Education (3 edns and 5 reprints), 1950; Beyond Neutrality, 1955; Mystery of Man, 1957; Revolution in Teacher Training, 1961; Personal Values in the Modern World, 1962 (rev. edns 1966, 1968); The Unity of Education, 1966; The Ministry of Teaching, 1967; John Locke, Prophet of Common Sense, 1967; Religion and Morality, 1967; You and Other People, 1969; Education: its nature and purpose, 1972; articles on educational and religious topics in various periodicals. *Address:* Skymers Minor, Minstead, near Lyndhurst, Hants.

JEFFRIES, Graham Montague; *see* Graeme, Bruce.

JEFFRIES, Lionel Charles; actor since 1949; screen writer since 1959, and film director since 1970; *b* 10 June 1926; *s* of Bernard Jeffries and Elsie Jackson; *m* 1951, Eileen Mary Walsh; one *s* two *d*. *Educ:* Queen Elizabeth's Grammar Sch., Wimborne, Dorset; Royal Academy of Dramatic Art (Dip., Kendal Award, 1947). War of 1939-45: commissioned, Oxf. and Bucks LI, 1945; served in Burma (Burma Star, 1945); Captain, Royal West African Frontier Force. Stage: (West End) *plays:* Carrington VC; The Enchanted; Blood Wedding; Brouhaha; *films:* Colditz Story; Bhowani Junction; Lust for Life; The Baby and The Battleship; Doctor at Large; Law and Disorder; The Nun's Story; Idle on Parade; Two Way Stretch; The Trials of Oscar Wilde; Fanny; The Notorious Landlady (Hollywood); The Wrong Arm of the Law; The First Men in the Moon; The Truth about Spring; Arrivederci Baby; The Spy with a Cold Nose; Camelot (Hollywood); Chitty, Chitty, Bang Bang; Eyewitness; Baxter (also dir.). Dir., The Water Babies, 1976. Wrote and directed: The Railway Children, 1970; The Amazing Mr Blunden, 1972 (Gold Medal for Best Screen Play, Internat. Sci. Fiction and Fantasy Film Fest., Paris, 1974). *Recreations:* swimming, painting, golf. *Address:* c/o ICM, 22 Grafton Street, W1. *T:* 01-629 8080.

JEFFS, Group Captain (George) James (Horatio), CVO 1960 (MVO 1943); OBE 1950; Aviation Consultant; *b* 27 Jan. 1900; *s* of late James Thomas Jeffs, Chilvers Coton, Warwicks; *m* 1921, Phyllis Rosina (*née* Bell); two *s* one *d*. *Educ:* Kedleston Sch., Derby. Served European War: RNAS, 1916-18; RAF, 1918-19. Air Ministry, 1919-23; Croydon Airport, 1923-34; Heston Airport, 1934-37; Air Ministry, 1937-39. Served War of 1939-45, RAF: Fighter, Ferry, and Transport Commands, Group Captain. Ministry of Transport and Civil Aviation, 1945; Airport Commandant, Prestwick, 1950-57; Airport Commandant, London Airport, 1957-60. Legion of Merit, USA, 1944. *Address:* Pixham Firs Cottage, Pixham Lane, Dorking, Surrey. *T:* 4084. *Club:* Naval and Military.

JEFFS, Julian, QC 1975; Barrister; a Recorder of the Crown Court, since 1975; *b* 5 April 1931; *s* of Alfred Wright Jeffs, Wolverhampton, and Janet Honor Irene (*née* Davies); *m* 1966, Deborah, *d* of Peter James Stuart Bevan; three *s*. *Educ:* Mostyn House Sch.; Wrekin Coll.; Downing Coll., Cambridge (MA). Royal Navy (nat. service), 1949-50. Sherry Shipper's Asst, Spain, 1956. Barrister, Gray's Inn, 1958, Inner Temple, 1971; Midland and Oxford Circuit. Laureat de l'Office International de la Vigne et du Vin (for 'Sherry'), 1962; Editor, Wine and Food, 1965-67; Mem., Cttee of Management, International Wine & Food Soc., 1965-67, 1971-; Chm., 1970-72, Vice-Pres., 1975-, Circle of Wine Writers. Glenfiddich book award, 1974. General Editor, Faber's Wine Series. *Publications:* Sherry, 1961 (2nd edn 1970); (ed with Robert Harling) Wine, 1966; (an editor) Clerk and Lindsell on Torts, 13th edn 1969 (14th edn 1975); The Wines of Europe, 1971; Little Dictionary of Drink, 1973. *Recreations:* writing, wine, walking, old cars, musical boxes, follies, Iberian things. *Address:* Francis Taylor Building, Temple, EC4. *T:* 01-353 5657; Church Farm House, East Ilsley, Newbury, Berks. *T:* East Ilsley 216. *Clubs:* Beefsteak, Garrick, Reform, Saintsbury.

JEFFS, Kenneth Peter; Counsellor, Defence Supply, Washington, DC, since 1976; *b* 30 Jan. 1931; *s* of Albert Jeffs and Theresa Eleanor Jeffs; *m* Iris Woolsey; one *s* two *d*. *Educ:* Richmond and East Sheen County Sch. jssc. National Service, RAF, 1949-51. Entered CS as Clerical Officer, Bd of Control, 1947; Air Min., 1952; Principal, 1964; JSSC, 1966-67; Private Secretary: to Under-Sec. of State (RN), MoD, 1969-71; to Minister of Defence, 1971-72; Asst Sec., Dir Defence Sales, MoD, 1972-75. *Recreation:* rowing. *Address:* 3564 Brandywine Street NW, Washington, DC 20008, USA. *T:* (202) 244-8604.

JEGER, Mrs Lena (May); MP (Lab) Camden, Holborn and St Pancras South, since 1974 (Holborn and St Pancras South, Nov.

1953-Sept. 1959 and 1964-74); *b* 19 Nov. 1915; *e d* of Charles and Alice Chivers, Yorkley, Glos; *m* 1948, Dr Santo Wayburn Jeger (*d* 1953); no *c. Educ:* Southgate County Sch., Middx; Birkbeck Coll., London University (BA). Civil Service: Customs and Excise, Ministry of Information, Foreign Office, 1936-49; British Embassy Moscow, 1947; Manchester Guardian London Staff, 1951-54, 1961-; Mem. St Pancras Borough Council, 1945-59; Mem. LCC for Holborn and St Pancras South, 1952-55. Mem., Nat. Exec. Cttee, Labour Party, 1968-. Mem., Chairmen's Panel, House of Commons, 1971-. Chm., Govt Working Party on Sewage Disposal, 1969-70. *Address:* c/o House of Commons, SW1; 9 Cumberland Terrace, Regent's Park, NW1.

JEHANGIR, Sir Hirji, 3rd Bt, *cr* 1908; *b* 1 Nov. 1915; 2nd *s* of Sir Cowasjee Jehangir, 2nd Bt, GBE, KCIE, and Hilla, MBE, *d* of late Hormarji Wadia, Lowji Castle, Bombay; *S* father, 1962; *m* 1952, Jinoo, *d* of K. H. Cama; two *s. Educ:* St Xavier Sch., Bombay; Magdalene Coll., Cambridge. Chairman: Jehangir Art Gallery, Bombay; United Asia Publications; Dir., Coorla Spinning and Weaving Mill. *Heir: s* Jehangir, *b* 23 Nov. 1953. *Address:* Readymoney House, Nepeansea Road, Bombay 400 006, India; 24 Kensington Court Gardens, W8. *Clubs:* Crockford's; Willingdon (Bombay).

JEJEEBHOY, Sir Jamsetjee, 7th Bt *cr* 1857; *b* 19 April 1913; *s* of Rustamjee J. C. Jamsetjee Jejeebhoy (*d* 1947), and Soonabai Rustomjee Byramjee Jejeebhoy (*d* 1968); *S* cousin, Sir Jamsetjee Jejeebhoy, 6th Bt, 1968, and assumed name of Jamsetjee Jejeebhoy in lieu of Maneckjee Rustomjee Jamsetjee Jejeebhoy; *m* 1943, Shirin Jehangir H. Cama; one *s* one *d. Educ:* St Xavier's Coll., Bombay (BA). Chairman: Sir Jamsetjee Jejeebhoy Charity Funds; Sir J. J. Parsee Benevolent Instn, and other allied charitable instns; Trustee: Sir J. J. Sch. of Arts; Byramjee Jejeebhoy Parsee Charitable Instn. *Heir: s* Rustom Jejeebhoy, *b* 16 Nov. 1957. *Address:* (residence) Beaulieu, 95 Worli Sea Face, Bombay 25, India. *T:* 453955; (office) Maneckjee Wadia Building, Mahatma Gandhi Road, Fort, Bombay 1. *T:* 273843. *Clubs:* Willingdon Sports, Royal Western India, Turf (Bombay).

JELF, Maj.-Gen. Richard William, CBE 1948 (OBE 1944); *b* 16 June 1904; *s* of late Sir Ernest Jelf, King's Remembrancer and Master of the Supreme Court; *m* 1928, Nowell, *d* of Major Sampson-Way, RM, Manor House, Henbury; three *s* one *d. Educ:* Cheltenham Coll.; RMA Woolwich. Commissioned Royal Artillery, 1924; Staff Coll., Quetta, 1936; Dep. Dir Staff Duties, War Office, 1946; Imperial Defence Coll., 1948; CRA 2nd Division, 1949; Dep. Chief, Organization and Training Div., SHAPE, 1951; Comdr 99 AA Bde (TA), 1953; Chief of Staff, Eastern Command, 1956; Maj.-Gen., 1957; Commandant, Police Coll., Bramshill, 1957-63; Dir of Civil Defence, Southern Region, 1963-68. ADC to the Queen, 1954. Served North-West Frontier, India (Loe Agra), 1934; NW Europe, 1939-45. Hon. Sec., Lyme Regis RNLI. *Recreation:* yachting. *Address:* Casella Maria, Clappentail Lane, Lyme Regis, Dorset. *T:* 3284.

JELLICOE, family name of Earl Jellicoe.

JELLICOE, 2nd Earl, *cr* 1925; **George Patrick John Rushworth Jellicoe,** PC 1963; DSO 1942; MC 1944; Viscount Brocas of Southampton, *cr* 1925; Viscount Jellicoe of Scapa, *cr* 1918; Director: S. G. Warburg & Co., since 1973; Tate & Lyle, since 1976; Smiths Industries; Morgan Crucible; *b* 4 April 1918; *o s* of Admiral of the Fleet, 1st Earl Jellicoe and late Florence Gwendoline, *d* of Sir Charles Cayzer, 1st Bt; godson of King George V; *S* father, 1935; *m* 1st, 1944, Patricia Christine (marr. diss., 1966), *o d* of Jeremiah O'Kane, Vancouver, Canada; two *s* two *d* ; 2nd, 1966, Philippa, *o d* of late Philip Dunne; one *s* two *d. Educ:* Winchester; Trinity Coll., Cambridge (Exhibnr). Hon. Page to King George VI; served War of 1939-45, Coldstream Guards, 1 SAS Regt (despatches, DSO, MC, Légion d'Honneur, Croix de Guerre, Greek Military Cross). Entered HM Foreign Service, 1947; served as 1st Sec. in Washington, Brussels, Baghdad (Deputy Sec. General Baghdad Pact). Lord-in-Waiting, Jan.-June 1961; Jt Parly. Sec., Min. of Housing and Local Govt, 1961-62; Minister of State, Home Office, 1962-63; First Lord of the Admiralty, 1963-64; Minister of Defence for the Royal Navy, April-Oct. 1964; Deputy Leader of the Opposition, House of Lords, 1967-70; Lord Privy Seal and Minister in Charge, Civil Service Dept, 1970-73; Leader of the House of Lords, 1970-73. Chairman: Brit. Adv. Cttee on Oil Pollution of the Sea, 1968-70; 3rd Int. Conf. on Oil Pollution of the Sea, 1968. A Governor, Centre for Environmental Studies, 1967-70; Pres., National Federation of Housing Societies, 1965-70. *Recreation:* ski-ing. *Heir: s* Viscount Brocas, *qv. Address:* Tidcombe Manor, Tidcombe, near Marlborough, Wilts. *T:* Oxenwood 225; 97 Onslow Square, SW7. *T:* 01-584 1551. *Club:* Brooks's.

See also Adm. Sir Charles Madden, Bt.

JELLICOE, Ann; *see* Jellicoe, P. A.

JELLICOE, Geoffrey Alan, CBE 1961; FRIBA (Dist TP); PPILA; FRTPI; formerly Senior Partner of Jellicoe & Coleridge, Architects; *b* London, 8 Oct. 1900; *s* of George Edward Jellicoe; *m* 1936, Ursula, *d* of late Sir Bernard Pares, KBE, DCL. *Educ:* Cheltenham Coll.; Architectural Association. Bernard Webb Student at British School at Rome; RIBA Neale Bursar. Pres., Inst. of Landscape Architects, 1939-49; Hon. Pres. Internat. Fed. of Landscape Architects; Mem. Royal Fine Art Commission, 1954-68; former Trustee of the Tate Gallery; Hon. Corr. Mem. American and Venezuelan Societies of Landscape Architects. Gardens for: Sandringham, Royal Lodge (Windsor), Ditchley Park, RHS central area, Wisley; Chequers; Chevening (Kent); Horsted Place (Sussex); Shute House (Wilts); Delta Works (W Bromwich); Hilton Hotel (Stratford-upon-Avon); Dewlish House, Dorchester; The Grange, Winchester; Town Plans for: Guildford, Wellington (Salop), Hemel Hempstead New Town. Arch. Cons. to N Rhodesian Govt, 1947-52. Housing for Basildon, Scunthorpe, LCC; Plymouth Civic Centre; Chertsey Civic Centre; Cheltenham Sports Centre; GLC Comprehensive Sch., Dalston; Durley Park, Keynsham; Grantham Crematorium and Swimming Pool; comprehensive plans for central area, Gloucester, and for Tollcross, Edinburgh; Kennedy Memorial, Runnymede; Plans for Sark, Isles of Scilly, and Bridgefoot, Stratford-upon-Avon. *Publications:* Italian Gardens of the Renaissance (joint), 1925; (with J. C. Shepherd) Gardens and Design, 1927; Baroque Gardens of Austria, 1931; Studies in Landscape Design, Vol. I 1959, Vol. II 1966, Vol. III 1970; Motopia, 1961; (with Susan Jellicoe) Water, 1971; The Landscape of Man, 1975. *Address:* 19 Grove Terrace, Highgate, NW5. *T:* 01-485 1823.

JELLICOE, (Patricia) Ann, (Mrs Roger Mayne); playwright and director; *b* 15 July 1927; *d* of John Andrea Jellicoe and Frances Jackson Henderson; *m* 1st, 1950, C. E. Knight-Clarke (marr. diss., 1961); 2nd, 1962, Roger Mayne; one *s* one *d. Educ:* Polam Hall, Darlington; Queen Margaret's, York; Central Sch. of Speech and Drama (Elsie Fogarty Prize, 1947). Actress, stage manager and dir, London and provinces, 1947-51; privately commnd to study relationship between theatre architecture and theatre practice, 1949; founded and ran Cockpit Theatre Club to experiment with open stage, 1952-54; taught acting and directed plays, Central Sch., 1954-56; Literary Manager, Royal Court Theatre, 1973-75. *Plays:* The Sport of My Mad Mother, Royal Court, 1958; The Knack, Arts (Cambridge), 1961, Royal Court, 1962, New York, 1964, Paris, 1967 (filmed, 1965); Shelley, Royal Court, 1965; The Rising Generation, Royal Court, 1967; The Giveaway, Garrick, 1969; Flora and the Bandits, Dartington Coll. of Arts, 1976; *plays for children:* You'll Never Guess!, Arts, 1973; Clever Elsie, Smiling John, Silent Peter, Royal Court, 1974; A Good Thing or a Bad Thing, Royal Court, 1974; *translations include:* Rosmersholm, Royal Court, 1960; The Lady from the Sea, Queen's, 1961; The Seagull (with Ariadne Nicolaeff), Queen's, 1963; Der Freischütz, Sadlers Wells, 1964. *Principal productions include:* The Sport of My Mad Mother (with George Devine), 1958; For Children, 1959; The Knack (with Keith Johnstone), 1962; Skyvers, 1963; Shelley, 1965; A Worthy Guest, 1974. *Publications:* (apart from plays) Some Unconscious Influences in the Theatre, 1967; (with Roger Mayne) Shell Guide to Devon, 1975. *Address:* c/o Margaret Ramsay Ltd, 14a Goodwin's Court, St Martin's Lane, WC2.

JELLINEK, His Honour Lionel, MC 1918; Judge of County Courts, Surrey, 1958-71; *b* 30 Nov. 1898; *s* of Robert Jellinek, Company Director, London, and Alice Jellinek (*née* Kennedy); *m* 1923, Lydia, *d* of Ernst Moller, merchant, Oslo; one *d. Educ:* Repton; Lincoln Coll., Oxford. Lieut RFA, 1917-19. Called to Bar, Middle Temple, 1923. Art Critic, Sunday Referee, 1926-27. Major RA, 1941-45. Deputy Chm., Essex Quarter Sessions, 1956-58; Chm. Agricultural Land Tribunal, South Eastern Region, 1956-58. Vice-Pres. and Chm. Guildford Symphony Orchestra, 1963. JP Essex 1956. King Haakon VII's Frihets Medal, 1945. *Recreation:* music, especially chamber music (viola). *Address:* Yellow Hammers, Shamley Green, Guildford, Surrey. *T:* Bramley 3421. *Club:* County (Guildford).

JENKIN, Rt. Hon. (Charles) Patrick (Fleeming), PC 1973; MA; MP (C) Redbridge, Wanstead and Woodford, since 1974 (Wanstead and Woodford, 1964-74); *b* 7 Sept. 1926; *s* of late Mr and Mrs C. O. F. Jenkin; *m* 1952, Alison Monica Graham; two *s* two *d. Educ:* Dragon Sch., Oxford; Clifton Coll.; Jesus Coll., Cambridge. MA (Cantab.) 1951. Served with QO Cameron Highlanders, 1945-48; 1st Class Hons in Law, Cambridge, 1951; Harmsworth Scholar, Middle Temple, 1951; called to the Bar, 1952. Distillers Co. Ltd, 1957-70. Member: Hornsey Borough

Council, 1960-63; London Coun. of Social Service, 1963-67. An Opposition front bench spokesman on Treasury, Trade and Economics, 1965-70; Jt Vice-Chm., Cons. Parly Trade and Power Cttee, 1966-67; Chm., All Party Parly Group on Chemical Industry, 1968-70; Financial Sec. to the Treasury, 1970-72; Chief Sec. to Treasury, 1972-74; Minister for Energy, 1974; Opposition front bench spokesman: on Energy, 1974-76; on Soc. Services, 1976-. Director: Tilbury Contracting Gp Ltd, 1974-; Royal Worcester Ltd, 1975-; Continental and Industrial Trust Ltd, 1975-. Governor: Westfield Coll., 1964-70; Clifton Coll., 1969-. Mem. Council, 1974-. *Recreations:* music, gardening, sailing. *Address:* House of Commons, SW1. *T:* 01-219 5174. *Club:* West Essex Conservative (Wanstead).

JENKIN, Mary Elizabeth, MBE 1945; *b* 8 Jan. 1892; *d* of Professor C. F. Jenkin and Mrs C. F. Jenkin. *Educ:* Norland Place Sch.; St Paul's Girls Sch.; Oxford High Sch.; Oxford University. Worked in the Intelligence Division, Admiralty, 1916-20. MA Oxon, 1921; held various secretarial posts and travelled in Egypt and India, 1921-27; joined BBC, 1927; Head of the BBC Children's Hour, 1950-53; retd 1953. *Recreations:* acting, painting, reading. *Address:* Southfield House, Painswick, Glos. *Club:* University Women's.

JENKIN, Rt. Hon. Patrick; see Jenkin, Rt Hon. C. P. F.

JENKIN, Sir William Norman Prentice, Kt 1947; CSI 1946; CIE 1931; KPM 1924; *b* 11 Aug. 1899; *m* 1924, Ayliffe Wansborough, *d* of Percy Stevens. *Educ:* Scottish Academy. Commnd RFC, 1917; joined Indian Police Service, 1919; Superintendent, 1927; late Deputy Dir, Intelligence Bureau, Home Department, Government of India; Dir of Intelligence, Malaya, 1950-51. *Address:* Seven, Oaks Road, Tenterden, Kent. *T:* Tenterden 2760.

JENKIN PUGH, Rev. Canon Thomas; see Pugh.

JENKINS, Arthur Robert, CBE 1972; JP; Chairman: Robert Jenkins & Co. Ltd, Rotherham, since 1958; Robert Jenkins (Holdings) Ltd, since 1968; *b* 20 June 1908; *s* of Edgar Jackson Jenkins and Ethel Mary Bescoby; *m* 1935, Margaret Fitton Jones; one *s* three *d*. *Educ:* Rotherham Grammar Sch.; Sheffield Univ. CEng, FIMechE. Chairman: British Welding Assoc., 1956-68; Tank and Industrial Plant Assoc., 1958-61; of Council, Welding Inst., 1968-71; of Council, Process Plant Assoc., 1971-75; Pres., Welding Inst., 1951-53 and 1973-75; Vice-Pres., British Mechanical Engrg Confedn, 1972-. Mem. Exec. Bd, BSI, 1974. JP 1948. *Recreation:* gardening. *Address:* The Friary, Tickhill, Doncaster, South Yorks. *T:* Doncaster 742356.

JENKINS, Lt-Col Charles Peter de Brisay, MBE 1960; MC 1945; Clerk, Worshipful Company of Goldsmiths, since 1975; *b* 19 Aug. 1925; *s* of late Brig. A. de B. Jenkins and of Mrs Elizabeth Susan Jenkins; *m* 1949, Joan Mary, *e d* of late Col and Mrs C. N. Littleboy, Thirsk; one *s*. *Educ:* Cheltenham Coll.; Selwyn Coll., Cambridge. Commnd RE, 1944; served in Italy, 1944-45; subseq. Hong Kong, Kenya and Germany; jssc 1960; Instructor, Staff Coll., Camberley, 1961-63; Comdr, RE 1st Div., 1965-67; retd 1967. Asst Clerk, Goldsmiths' Co., 1968. *Recreations:* swimming, tennis, gardening. *Address:* Goldsmiths' Hall, Foster Lane, EC2; Oak Hill, South Brent, Devon.

JENKINS, Christopher; see Jenkins, J. C.

JENKINS, Clive; see Jenkins, D. C.

JENKINS, David, CBE 1977; MA, JP; Librarian, National Library of Wales, since 1969; *b* 29 May 1912; *s* of late Evan Jenkins and Mary (*née* James), Blaenclydach, Rhondda; *m* 1948, Menna Rhys, *o d* of late Rev. Owen Evans Williams, Penrhyn-coch, Aberystwyth; one *s* one *d*. *Educ:* Ardwyn Grammar Sch., Aberystwyth; UCW, Aberystwyth. BA Hons Welsh Lit. 1936, MA 1948; W. P. Thomas (Rhondda) Schol. 1936; Sir John Williams Research Student, 1937-38. Served War of 1939-45, Army; Major, 1943; NW Europe. National Library of Wales: Asst, Dept MSS, 1939-48; Asst Keeper, Dept of Printed Books, 1949, Keeper, 1957, Sen. Keeper, 1962. Professorial Fellow, UCW Aberystwyth, 1971. Gen. Comr of Income Tax, 1968-; Chm., Mid-Wales HMC, 1969-70; Chm. Welsh Books Council, 1974- (Vice-Chm. 1971-74); Member: Court of Governors, Univ. of Wales; Nat. Museum of Wales; Ct and Council, UC Aberystwyth; Council, British Records Assoc.; BBC Archives Adv. Cttee, 1976-; Hon. Soc. of Cymmrodorion; Library Adv. Council (Wales); Pantyfedwen Trust, 1969-; Coll. of Librarianship Wales; Bd of Celtic Studies; Governor: Ardwyn Grammar Sch., 1963-72; Penweddig Compreh. Sch., 1973-. Editor: NLW Jl, 1968-; Jl Welsh Bibiliog. Soc., 1964-;

Ceredigion, Trans Cards Antiq. Soc., 1973-. JP Aberystwyth 1959: Chm. Llanbadarn Bench 1965-69; Vice-Chm., Aberystwyth Bench, 1975; Member: Dyfed Magistrates' Courts Cttee; Dyfed-Powys Police Authority, 1977-. Sir Ellis Griffith Meml Prize, Univ. of Wales, 1975. *Publications:* Cofiant Thomas Gwynn Jones, 1973 (biog.; Welsh Arts Council Prize, 1974); (ed) Sglodion Nenyddol Kate Roberts, 1977; articles in NLW Jl, Bull. Bd of Celtic Studies and many other jls; contrib. Dictionary of Welsh Biography. *Recreation:* walking. *Address:* Hengwrt, Llanbadarn Road, Aberystwyth, Dyfed. *T:* Aberystwyth 3577.

JENKINS, (David) Clive; General Secretary, Association of Scientific, Technical and Managerial Staffs, since 1970 (Joint General Secretary, 1968-70); Member of the General Council of the TUC, since 1974; *b* 2 May 1926; *s* of David Samuel Jenkins and Miriam Harris Jenkins (*née* Hughes); *m* 1963, Moira McGregor Hilley; one *s* one *d*. *Educ:* Port Talbot Central Boys' Sch.; Port Talbot County Sch.; Swansea Techn. Coll. (evenings). Started work in metallurgical test house, 1940; furnace shift supervisor, 1942; i/c of laboratory, 1943; tinplate night shift foreman, 1945; Mem., Port Talbot Cooperative Soc. Educn. Cttee, 1945; Branch Sec. and Area Treas., AScW, 1946; Asst Midlands Divisional Officer, ASSET, 1947; Transport Industrial Officer, 1949; Nat. Officer, 1954; Gen. Sec., ASSET, 1961-68. Metrop. Borough Councillor, 1954-60 (Chm. Staff Cttee, St Pancras Borough Coun.); Chm., Nat. Jt Coun. for Civil Air Transport, 1967-68; Member: NRDC, 1974-; Bullock Cttee on Industrial Democracy, 1975-; Wilson Cttee to Review the Functioning of Financial Institutions, 1977-. Editor, Trade Union Affairs, 1961-63. Sometime columnist, Tribune, Daily Mirror, Daily Record. *Publications:* Power at the Top, 1959; Power Behind the Screen, 1961; (with J. E. Mortimer) British Trade Unions Today, 1965; (with J. E. Mortimer) The Kind of Laws the Unions Ought to Want, 1968; (with B. D. Sherman) Computers and the Unions, 1977; (with B. D. Sherman) Collective Bargaining: what you always wanted to know about trade unions and never dared ask, 1977; also pamphlets and essays. *Recreations:* bargaining with employers, organising the middle classes; arguing for British withdrawal from EEC. *Address:* (home) 16 St Marks Crescent, NW1. *T:* 01-485 4509; (office) Jamestown Road, NW1. *T:* 01-267 4422.
See also T . H . Jenkins .

JENKINS, Canon David Edward; Director, William Temple Foundation, Manchester, since 1973; *b* 26 Jan. 1925; *er s* of Lionel C. Jenkins and Dora (*née* Page); *m* 1949, Stella Mary Peet; two *s* two *d*. *Educ:* St Dunstan's Coll., Catford; Queen's Coll., Oxford (MA). EC, RA, 1943-45 (Captain). Priest, 1954. Succentor, Birmingham Cath. and Lectr, Queen's Coll., 1953-54; Fellow, Chaplain and Praelector in Theology, Queen's Coll., Oxford, 1954-69; Dir, Humanum Studies, World Council of Churches, Geneva, 1969-73 (Consultant, 1973-75). Exam. Chaplain to Bps of Lichfield, 1956-69, Newcastle, 1957-69 and Bristol, 1958-; Canon Theologian, Leicester, 1966-. Bampton Lectr, 1966; Hale Lectr, Seabury-Western, USA, 1970; Moorhouse Lectr, Melbourne, 1972; Cadbury Lectr, Birmingham Univ., 1974; Lindsay Meml Lectr, Keele Univ., 1976. Jt Editor, Theology, 1976-. *Publications:* Guide to the Debate about God, 1966; The Glory of Man, 1967; Living with Questions, 1969; What is Man?, 1970; The Contradiction of Christianity, 1976; contrib. Man, Fallen and Free, 1969, etc. *Recreations:* music, reading, walking. *Address:* William Temple Foundation, Manchester Business School, Booth Street West, Manchester M15 6PB. *T:* 061-273 8228.

JENKINS, Dennis Frederick M.; see Martin-Jenkins.

JENKINS, Elizabeth. *Educ:* St Christopher School, Letchworth; Newnham College, Cambridge. *Publications:* The Winters, 1931; Lady Caroline Lamb, a Biography, 1932; Harriet (awarded the Femina Vie Heureuse Prize), 1934; The Phoenix' Nest, 1936; Jane Austen, a Biography, 1938; Robert and Helen, 1944; Young Enthusiasts, 1946; Henry Fielding (The English Novelists Series), 1947; Six Criminal Women, 1949; The Tortoise and the Hare, 1954; Ten Fascinating Women, 1955; Elizabeth the Great (biography), 1958; Elizabeth and Leicester, 1961; Brightness, 1963; Honey, 1968; Dr Gully, 1972; The Mystery of King Arthur, 1975. *Address:* 8 Downshire Hill, Hampstead, NW3. *T:* 01-435 4642.

JENKINS, Sir Evan Meredith, GCIE, *cr* 1947 (KCIE, *cr* 1944; CIE 1936); KCSI, *cr* 1945 (CSI 1941); *b* 2 Feb. 1896; *s* of late Sir John Lewis Jenkins, KCSI. *Educ:* Rugby; Balliol Coll., Oxford. Served European War, 1914-19; joined Indian Civil Service, 1920, and served in Punjab; Chief Commissioner, Delhi, 1937; Sec., Dept of Supply, 1940-43; Private Sec to the Viceroy and Sec. to the Governor-General (Personal), 1943-45; Governor of

the Punjab, 1946-47. *Address:* 24 Ashley Gardens, SW1. *Club:* Travellers'.
See also Sir Owain Jenkins.

JENKINS, Very Rev. Frank Graham; Dean of Monmouth and Vicar of St Woolos, since 1976; *b* 24 Feb. 1923; *s* of Edward and Miriam M. Jenkins; *m* 1950, Ena Doraine Parry; two *s* one *d*. *Educ:* Cyfarthfa Sec. Sch., Merthyr Tydfil; Port Talbot Sec. Sch.; St David's Coll., Lampeter (BA Hist); Jesus Coll., Oxford (BA Theol., MA); St Michael's Coll., Llandaff. HM Forces, 1942-46. Deacon 1950, priest 1951, Llandaff; Asst Curate, Llangeinor, 1950-53; Minor Canon, Llandaff Cathedral, 1953-60; CF (TA), 1956-61; Vicar of Abertillery, 1960-64; Vicar of Risca, 1964-75; Canon of Monmouth, 1967-76; Vicar of Caerleon, 1975-76. *Address:* The Deanery, Stow Hill, Newport, Gwent NPT 4ED. *T:* Newport 63338.

JENKINS, Gilbert Kenneth; Keeper, Department of Coins and Medals, British Museum, since 1965; *b* 2 July 1918; *s* of late Kenneth Gordon Jenkins and of Julia Louisa Jenkins (*née* Colbourne); *m* 1939, Cynthia Mary, *d* of late Dr Hugh Scott, FRS; one *s* two *d*. *Educ:* All Saints Sch., Bloxham; Corpus Christi Coll., Oxford. Open Classical Scholar (Corpus Christi Coll.), 1936; First Class Honour Mods, 1938. War Service in Royal Artillery, 1940-46 (SE Asia, 1944-46). BA, 1946. Asst Keeper, British Museum, 1947; Dep. Keeper, 1956. An Editor of Numismatic Chronicle, 1964-. Mem., German Archaeological Inst., 1967; Corresp. Mem., Amer. Numismatic Soc., 1958. Akbar Medal, Numismatic Soc. of India, 1966; Royal Numismatic Soc. Medal, 1975. *Publications:* Carthaginian Gold and Electrum Coins (with R. B. Lewis), 1963; Coins of Greek Sicily, 1966; Sylloge Nummorum Graecorum (Danish Nat. Museum), part 42, N Africa (ed), 1969; The Coinage of Gela, 1970; Ancient Greek Coins, 1972; articles in numismatic periodicals. *Recreations:* music, cycling. *Address:* 3 Beechwood Avenue, Kew Gardens, Surrey.

JENKINS, Sir Gilmour; *see* Jenkins, Sir Thomas G.

JENKINS, Prof. Harold, MA, DLitt; Professor Emeritus, University of Edinburgh; *b* 19 July 1909; *s* of late Henry and Mildred Jenkins, Shenley, Bucks; *m* 1939, Gladys Puddifoot; no *c*. *Educ:* Wolverton Grammar Sch.; University Coll., London. George Smith Studentship, 1930. Quain Student, University Coll., London, 1930-35; William Noble Fellow, University of Liverpool, 1935-36; Lecturer in English, University of the Witwatersrand, South Africa, 1936-45; Lecturer in English, University Coll., London, 1945-46, then Reader in English, 1946-54; Prof. of English, University of London (Westfield Coll.), 1954-67; Regius Prof. of Rhetoric and English Lit., Edinburgh Univ., 1967-71. Visiting Prof., Duke Univ., USA, 1957-58, Univ. of Oslo, 1974. Jt Gen. Editor, Arden Shakespeare, 1958-. *Publications:* The Life and Work of Henry Chettle, 1934; Edward Benlowes, 1952; The Structural Problem in Shakespeare's Henry IV, 1956; The Catastrophe in Shakespearean Tragedy, 1968; John Dover Wilson (British Acad. memoir), 1973; articles in Modern Language Review, Review of English Studies, The Library, Shakespeare Survey, Studies in Bibliography, etc. *Address:* 22 North Crescent, Finchley, N3 3LL.

JENKINS, Hugh Gater; MP (Lab) Wandsworth, Putney, since 1964; *b* 27 July 1908; *s* of Joseph Walter Jenkins and Florence Emily (*née* Gater), Enfield, Middlesex; *m* 1936, Marie (*née* Crosbie), *d* of Sqdn Ldr Ernest Crosbie and Ethel (*née* Hawkins). *Educ:* Enfield Grammar Sch. Personal exploration of employment and unemployment, and political and economic research, 1925-30; Prudential Assce Co., 1930-40. ROC, 1938; RAF: Fighter Comd, 1941; became GCI Controller (Flt Lt); seconded to Govt of Burma, 1945, as Dir Engl. Programmes, Rangoon Radio. Nat. Union of Bank Employees: Greater London Organiser, 1947; Res. and Publicity Officer; Ed., The Bank Officer, 1948; British Actors' Equity Assoc.: Asst Sec., 1950; Asst Gen. Sec., 1957-64. LCC: Mem. for Stoke Newington and Hackney N, 1958-65 (Public Control and Town Planning Cttees). Fabian Soc. lectr and Dir of Summer Schools in early post-war years; Chm., H. Bomb Campaign Cttee, 1954; CND, Aldermaston Marcher, 1957-63; Chm. Victory for Socialism, 1956-60; Mem. Exec. Cttee Greater London Labour Party. Contested (Lab): Enfield W, 1950; Mitcham, 1955. Minister for the Arts, 1974-76. Member: Arts Council, 1968-71; Drama Panel, 1972-74; Nat. Theatre Bd, 1976-; Vice-Chm., Theatres Trust, 1977-. *Publications:* Essays in Local Government Enterprise (with others), 1964. Various pamphlets; contrib. to Tribune, New Statesman, The Times, etc. Occasional broadcasts and lectures on communications, theatrical and political subjects. *Recreations:* reading, writing, talking, walking, viewing, listening and occasionally thinking. *Address:* 75

Kenilworth Court, Lower Richmond Road, Putney, SW15. *T:* 01-788 0371.

JENKINS, Mrs Inez Mary Mackay, CBE 1943; *b* 30 Oct. 1895; *c* of John Mackay Ferguson; *m* 1923, Frederick Cyril Jenkins; one *s*. *Educ:* Berkhamsted Sch. for Girls; St Hilda's Hall, Oxford. Gen. Sec., National Federation of Women's Institutes, 1919-29; Sec., English Folk Dance and Song Soc., 1931-39; Chief Administrative Officer Women's Land Army (England and Wales), 1939-48; Mem. Central Agricultural Wages Board for England and Wales, 1952-63. *Publication:* History of the Women's Institute Movement of England and Wales, 1953. *Recreations:* gardening, philately. *Address:* White Ends, Rotherfield Greys, Oxon. *T:* Rotherfield Greys 206.

JENKINS, Dr Ivor, CBE 1970; Group Director of Research, Delta Metal Co. Ltd, since 1973; Managing Director, since 1973, Deputy Chairman, since 1977, Delta Materials Research Ltd; *b* 25 July 1913; *m* 1941, Carolina Wijnanda James; two *s*. *Educ:* Gowerton Grammar Sch.; Univ. of Swansea. BSc, MSc, DSc. Bursar, GEC Research Labs, Wembley, 1934; Mem. Scientific Staff, GEC, 1935; Dep. Chief Metallurgist, Whitehead Iron & Steel Co., Newport, Mon, 1944; Head of Metallurgy Dept, 1946, Chief Metallurgist, 1952, GEC, Wembley; Dir of Research, Manganese Bronze Holdings Ltd, and Dir, Manganese Bronze Ltd, 1961-69; Dir of Research, Delta Metal Co., and Dir, Delta Metal (BW) Ltd, 1969-73. FIM 1948 (Pres. 1965-66); Fellow, Amer. Soc. of Metals, 1974; Pres., Inst. of Metals, 1968-69; Mem., Iron and Steel Inst., 1937- (Williams Prize, 1946). *Publications:* Controlled Atmospheres for the Heat Treatment of Metals, 1946; contribs to learned jls at home and abroad on metallurgical and related subjects. *Recreations:* music, gardening, swimming. *Address:* The Grange, Onehouse, Stowmarket, Suffolk. *T:* Stowmarket 3196. *Clubs:* Athenæum, Anglo Belgian.

JENKINS, (James) Christopher; Deputy Parliamentary Counsel, since 1975; *b* 20 May 1939; *s* of Percival Si Phillips Jenkins and Dela (*née* Griffiths); *m* 1962, Margaret Elaine Edwards, *yr d* of late Rt Hon. L. John Edwards, PC, OBE, MP and of Mrs D. M. Edwards; two *s* one *d*. *Educ:* the late Lewes County Grammar Sch.; Magdalen Coll., Oxford. Solicitor, 1965. Joined Office of Parly Counsel, 1967. *Address:* 24 Southwood Avenue, N6. *Club:* United Oxford & Cambridge University.

JENKINS, Mrs Jennifer; *see* Jenkins, Mrs M. J.

JENKINS, John George, CBE 1971; farmer; *b* 26 Aug. 1919; *s* of George John Jenkins, OBE, FRCS and Alice Maud Jenkins, MBE; *m* 1948, Chloe Evelyn (*née* Kenward); one *s* three *d*. *Educ:* Winchester; Edinburgh University. Farmed in Scotland, 1939-62; farmed in England (Cambs and Lincs), 1957-. Pres., NFU of Scotland, 1960-61; Chm., Agricultural Marketing Development Exec. Cttee, 1967-73. Director: Agricultural Mortgage Corporation Ltd; FMC Ltd; Childerley Estates Ltd. Compère, Anglia Television programme Farming Diary, 1963-. *Publications:* contrib. Proc. Royal Soc., RSA Jl, etc. *Recreations:* tennis, bridge, wine, music and the arts generally. *Address:* Childerley Hall, Dry Drayton, Cambridge CB3 8BB. *T:* Madingley 271. *Club:* Farmers'.

JENKINS, Ven. (John) Owen; *b* 13 June 1906; *m* 1939, Gwladys Margaret Clark Jones, *d* of Ven. D. M. Jones, sometime Archdeacon of Carmarthen. *Educ:* St David's Coll., Lampeter; Jesus Coll., Oxford. Deacon 1929, priest 1930; Curate of: Cwmamman, 1929-33; Llanelly, 1933-39; Vicar of Spittal with Trefgarn, 1939-48; TCF, 1943-46; Vicar of Llangadock, 1948-60; Canon of St David's, 1957-62; Rector of Newport, Pembs, 1960-67; Archdeacon of Cardigan, 1962-67; Archdeacon of Carmarthen and Vicar of Llanfihangel Aberbythick, 1967-74. Editor, St David's Dio. Year Book, 1954-63. *Address:* Morfa Gwyn, Aberporth, Cardigan SA43 2EN. *T:* Aberporth 810060.

JENKINS, (John) Robin; *b* Cambuslang, Lanarks, 11 Sept. 1912; *s* of late James Jenkins and of Annie Robin; *m* 1937, Mary McIntyre Wyllie; one *s* two *d*. *Educ:* Hamilton Academy; Glasgow Univ. (MA Hons). Teacher of English: Dunoon Grammar Sch.; Ghazi Coll., Kabul, 1957-59; British Institute, Barcelona, 1959-61; Gaya Coll., Sabah, 1963-68. *Publications:* Happy for the Child, 1953; The Thistle and the Grail, 1954; The Cone-Gatherers, 1955; Guests of War, 1956; The Missionaries, 1957; The Changeling, 1958; Some Kind of Grace, 1960; Dust on the Paw, 1961; The Tiger of Gold, 1962; A Love of Innocence, 1963; The Sardana Dancers, 1964; A Very Scotch Affair, 1968; The Holy Tree, 1969; The Expatriates, 1971; A Toast to the Lord, 1972; A Far Cry from Bowmore, 1973; A Figure of Fun, 1974. *Recreation:* travel. *Address:* Southview, 55 Mary Street, Dunoon, Argyll, Scotland. *T:* Dunoon 3497.

JENKINS, Leslie Augustus Westover, CBE 1971; Chairman, Forestry Commission, 1965-70; Chairman, National Industrial Fuel Efficiency Service, 1968-72, Director since 1954; *b* 27 May 1910; *s* of L. C. W. Jenkins; *m* 1936, Ann Barker (*née* Bruce), *d* of R. Hugh Bruce, St John, NB, Canada; no *c. Educ:* Lancing Coll. Chm. and Managing Dir, John Wright & Sons (Veneers) Ltd, 1956-59; Man. Dir, I. & R. Morley Ltd, 1959-63; Director: Restall Brown & Clennell Ltd, 1963; G. N. Haden & Sons Ltd, 1967; Haden-Carrier Ltd, 1971-; Airscrew-Weyroc, 1971. Member: Industrial Coal Consumers Council, 1947- (Dep. Chm., 1971-73); BNEC, 1964-73 (a Dep. Chm. 1966-73); Consultative Cttee, ECSC, 1973-; Vice-Pres., CBI, 1965-68, Mem. Council, 1968-74; Pres., Nat. Assoc. Brit. Manufacturers, 1963-65. FRSA 1972; MInstF 1959; FBIM 1966 (Mem. Bd, 1968-). *Publication:* Woodlands of Britain (RSA Cantor Lectures), 1971. *Recreations:* yachting, golf. *Address:* Lyneham Lodge, Hook Park, Warsash, Hants. *T:* Locks Heath 3366. *Clubs:* Royal Ocean Racing, Royal Southern Yacht.

JENKINS, Mrs (Mary) Jennifer; Chairman, Historic Buildings Council for England, since 1975; *b* 18 Jan. 1921; *d* of late Sir Parker Morris; *m* 1945, Rt Hon. Roy Harris Jenkins, *qv*; two *s* one *d. Educ:* Girton Coll., Cambridge. Chm., Cambridge Univ. Labour Club. With Hoover Ltd, 1942-43; Min. of Labour, 1943-46; Political and Economic Planning (PEP), 1946-48; part-time extra-mural lectr, 1949-61; part-time teacher, Kingsway Day Coll., 1961-67. Chm., 1965-76, Mem. Council, 1958-76, Consumers' Assoc.; Mem. Exec. Bd, British Standards Instn, 1970-73; Mem., Design Council, 1971-74; Sec., Ancient Monuments Soc., 1972-75. Chm., N Kensington Amenity Trust, 1974-77. Trustee, Wallace Collection, 1977-. JP London Juvenile Courts, 1964-74. *Address:* 33 Ladbroke Square, W11 3NB.

JENKINS, Michael Romilly Heald; Counsellor, HM Diplomatic Service; Head of European Integration Department (External), Foreign and Commonwealth Office, since 1977; *b* 9 Jan. 1936; *s* of Prof. Romilly Jenkins and Celine Juliette Haeglar; *m* 1968, Maxine Louise Hodson; one *s* one *d. Educ:* privately; King's Coll., Cambridge (Exhibr, BA). Entered Foreign (subseq. Diplomatic) Service, 1959; served in Paris, Moscow and Bonn; Deputy Chef de Cabinet, 1973-75, Chef de Cabinet, 1975-76, to Rt Hon. George Thomson, EEC; Principal Advr to Mr Roy Jenkins, Pres. EEC, Jan-Aug. 1977. *Publications:* Arakcheev, Grand Vizier of the Russian Empire, 1969; contrib. History Today. *Address:* c/o Foreign and Commonwealth Office, SW1A 2AH. *Club:* MCC.

JENKINS, Sir Owain (Trevor), Kt 1958; Director: Assam Trading (Holdings) Ltd; Calcutta Electric Supply Corporation, etc; *b* 1907; 5th *s* of late Sir John Lewis Jenkins, KCSI, ICS; *m* 1940, Sybil Léonie, *y d* of late Maj.-Gen. Lionel Herbert, CB, CVO. *Educ:* Charterhouse; Balliol Coll., Oxford. Employed by Balmer Lawrie & Co. Ltd, Calcutta, 1929; Indian Army, 1940-44; Man. Dir, Balmer Lawrie, 1948-58. Pres. of the Bengal Chamber of Commerce and Industry and Pres. of the Associated Chambers of Commerce of India, 1956-57. *Address:* Standlands, Petworth, West Sussex. *T:* Lodsworth 287. *Clubs:* Oriental; Bengal (Calcutta).
See also Sir Evan Jenkins.

JENKINS, Ven. Owen; *see* Jenkins, Ven. J. O.

JENKINS, Peter White; County Treasurer, Merseyside County Council, since 1973; *b* 12 Oct. 1937; *s* of John White Jenkins, OBE, and Dorothy Jenkins; *m* 1961, Joyce Christine Muter; one *s* one *d. Educ:* Queen Mary's Grammar Sch., Walsall; King Edward VI Grammar Sch., Nuneaton. CIPFA. Local govt service in Finance Depts at Coventry, Preston, Chester, Wolverhampton; Dep. Treasurer, Birkenhead, 1969-73. *Recreations:* squash-rackets, gardening, reading. *Address:* Rydal House, Golf Links Road, Prenton, Wirral, Merseyside L42 8LW. *T:* 051-608 1000.

JENKINS, Robert Christmas Dewar, JP; *b* 29 Sept. 1900; *s* of late J. Hamilton Jenkins; *m* 1927, Marjorie, *d* of late Andrew George Houstoun; three *d. Educ:* Latymer Upper Sch. Mem. Kensington Borough Council, 1927-68, Leader of Conservative Party of Royal Borough of Kensington, 1945-53; Mem. LCC for Kensington (S), 1934-49; Mayor of Kensington, 1939-45. MP (C) Dulwich Div. of Camberwell, 1951-64. JP County of London, 1946; Alderman of Kensington, 1947. Chairman, Royal Borough of Kensington and Chelsea, 1964. Hon. Freeman, Royal Borough of Kensington, 1964-. Served in Inns of Court OTC and KRRC, 1918-19. *Recreation:* phrenology. *Address:* 24 Albemarle, Wimbledon Parkside, SW19. *T:* 01-788 4722.

JENKINS, Robin; *see* Jenkins, J. R.

JENKINS, Rt. Hon. Roy Harris, PC 1964; President of the European Commission, since 1977; *b* 11 Nov. 1920; *o s* of late Arthur Jenkins, MP, and of Hattie Jenkins; *m* 1945, Jennifer Morris (*see* M. J. Jenkins); two *s* one *d. Educ:* Abersychan Grammar Sch.; Balliol Coll., Oxford, Hon. Fellow, 1969. Sec. and Librarian, Oxford Union Society; Chairman, Oxford Univ. Democratic Socialist Club; First Class in Hon. Sch. of Philosophy, Politics and Economics, 1941. Served War of 1939-45, in RA, 1942-46; Captain, 1944-46. Contested (Lab) Solihull Div. of Warwicks, at Gen. Election, 1945. Mem. of Staff of Industrial and Commercial Finance Corp. Ltd, 1946-48. Mem. Exec. Cttee of Fabian Soc., 1949-61; Chm., Fabian Soc., 1957-58; Mem. Cttee of Management, Soc. of Authors, 1956-60; Governor, British Film Institute, 1955-58; Dir of Financial Operations, John Lewis Partnership, 1962-64. MP (Lab): Central Southwark, 1948-50; Stechford, Birmingham, 1950-76; PPS to Sec. of State for Commonwealth Relations, 1949-50; Minister of Aviation, 1964-65; Home Sec., 1965-67, 1974-76; Chancellor of the Exchequer, 1967-70; Dep. Leader, Labour Party, 1970-72. UK Deleg. to Council of Europe, 1955-57. Vice-Pres., Inst. of Fiscal Studies, 1970-. Formerly: Dep. Chm. Federal Union; Pres., Britain in Europe, Referendum Campaign, 1975; Dep. Chm., Common Market Campaign; Chm., Labour European Cttee. A President: of United Kingdom Council of the European Movement; Labour Cttee for Europe. Pres., UWIST, 1975-. Trustee, Pilgrim Trust, 1973-. Hon. Foreign Mem., Amer. Acad. Arts and Scis, 1973. Hon. Fellow, Berkeley Coll., Yale, 1972. Hon. LLD: Leeds, 1971; Harvard, 1972; Pennsylvania, 1973; Dundee, 1973; Loughborough, 1975; Hon. DLitt: Glasgow, 1972; City, 1976; Hon. DCL Oxford, 1973; Hon. DSc Aston, 1977; DUniv Keele, 1977. Charlemagne Prize, 1972; Robert Schuman Prize, 1972. Order of European Merit (Luxemburg), 1976. *Publications:* (ed) Purpose and Policy (a vol. of the Prime Minister's Speeches), 1947; Mr Attlee: An Interim Biography, 1948; Pursuit of Progress, 1953; Mr Balfour's Poodle, 1954; Sir Charles Dilke: A Victorian Tragedy, 1958; The Labour Case (Penguin Special), 1959; Asquith, 1964; Essays and Speeches, 1967; Afternoon on the Potomac?, 1972; What Matters Now, 1972; Nine Men of Power, 1975; contrib. to New Fabian Essays, 1952; contrib. to Hugh Gaitskell, A Memoir, 1964. *Address:* 33 Ladbroke Square, W11. *T:* 01-727 5262; St Amand's House, East Hendred, Berks. *Clubs:* Athenæum, Brooks's.

JENKINS, Simon David; Editor, London Evening Standard, since 1977; *b* 10 June 1943; *s* of Dr Daniel Jenkins and Nell Jenkins. *Educ:* Mill Hill Sch.; St John's Coll., Oxford (BA Hons); Research Student, Univ. of Sussex, 1964-65. Country Life magazine, 1965; Research Asst, Univ. of London Inst. of Educn, 1966; News Editor, Times Educational Supplement, 1966-68; joined Evening Standard, 1968; wrote Living in London column, 1969-74; Features Editor, 1972-74; Insight Editor, Sunday Times, 1974-75; Dep. Editor, Evening Standard, 1976. Mem. Council, Bow Group, and Editor of Crossbow, 1968-70; Stockholm Working Party on the Human Habitat, 1973; Member: Cttee Save Britain's Heritage; Council, Inst. of Contemporary Arts; Management Cttee, Paddington Churches Housing Assoc. *Publications:* A City at Risk, 1971; Landlords to London, 1974; (ed) Insight on Portugal, 1975; various pamphlets and articles in political and architectural jls. *Recreations:* architecture, music, watching London change. *Address:* Evening Standard, Shoe Lane, EC4. *T:* 01-353 8000.

JENKINS, Very Rev. Thomas Edward; *b* 14 Aug. 1902; *s* of late David Jenkins, Canon of St David's Cathedral and Vicar of Abergwili, and of Florence Helena Jenkins; *m* 1928, Annie Laura, *d* of late David Henry, Penygroes, Carms; one *s. Educ:* Llandyssul Grammar Sch.; St David's Coll., Lampeter; Wycliffe Hall, Oxford. St David's Coll., Lampeter, BA 1922, BD 1932, Powys Exhibitioner, 1924; Welsh Church Scholar, 1921. Ordained, 1925; Curate of Llanelly, 1925-34; Rector of Begelly, 1934-38; Vicar: Christ Church, Llanelly, 1938-46; Lampeter, 1946-55 (Rural Dean, 1949-54); Canon, St David's Cathedral, 1951-57; Vicar of Cardigan, 1955-57; Dean of St David's, 1957-72. *Address:* 18 North Road, Cardigan, Dyfed.

JENKINS, Sir (Thomas) Gilmour, KCB 1948 (CB 1941); KBE 1944; MC; Vice-President, Royal Academy of Music; Chairman, London Philharmonic Society; Member, London Philharmonic Orchestra Council; Vice-Pres., Marine Society; *b* 18 July 1894; *s* of late Thomas Jenkins; *m* 1916, Evelyne Mary (*d* 1976), *d* of C. H. Nash; one *s* one *d. Educ:* Rutlish Sch.; London Univ.; BSc. Served European War, RGA (MC and bar); entered Board of Trade, 1919; Asst Sec., 1934; Government Delegate to Maritime Sessions of International Labour Conference Geneva, 1935 and 1936, and Copenhagen, 1945; Principal Asst Sec., Board of

Trade, 1937; Second Sec., Ministry of Shipping, 1939; Dep. Dir-Gen., Ministry of War Transport, 1941-46; Permanent Sec., Control Office for Germany and Austria, 1946-47; Joint Permanent Under-Sec. of State, Foreign Office, during 1947; Permanent Sec. to Ministry of Transport, 1947-53; Permanent Secretary to Ministry of Transport and Civil Aviation, 1953-59; Pres. Inst. of Marine Engineers, 1953-54; Pres. Institute of Transport, 1954-55: Pres., International Conference on Safety of Life at Sea, 1960; Pres., International Conference on Pollution of the Sea by Oil, 1954 and 1962; Pres., International Conference on Load Lines, 1966. Hon. FRAM. Grand Officer, Order of Orange Nassau (Netherlands); Comdr with Star, Order of St Olav (Norway); Knight Comdr, Order of George I (Greece); Comdr, Order of the Crown (Belgium). *Publication:* The Ministry of Transport and Civil Aviation, 1959. *Recreation:* music. *Address:* c/o Highams Chase, Goldhanger, Maldon, Essex. *T:* Maldon 88644.

JENKINS, Thomas Harris; General Secretary, Transport Salaried Staffs' Association, since 1977; *b* 29 Aug. 1920; *s* of David Samuel Jenkins and Miriam Hughes (*née* Harris); *m* 1946, Joyce Smith; two *d* . *Educ:* Port Talbot Central Boys' Sch.; Port Talbot County Sch.; Shrewsbury Technical Coll. (evenings); Pitmans Coll., London (evenings). Served War, RAMC, 1941-46 (Certif. for Good Service, Army, Western Comd, 1946). Railway clerk, 1937-41; railway/docks clerk, 1946-49. Full-time service with Railway Clerks' Assoc., subseq. re-named Transport Salaried Staffs' Assoc., 1949-: Southern Reg. Divl Sec., 1959; Western Reg. Divl Sec., 1963; LMR Divl Sec., 1966; Sen. Asst Sec., 1968; Asst Gen. Sec., 1970, also Dep. to Gen. Sec., 1973. TSSA Representative: to Cttee of Transport Workers in European Community, 1975; London and SE, and West and Wales Regional Adv. Cttees of Hotels and Catering Industry Trng Bd. Member: Labour Party, 1946-; Bd, Air Transport and Travel Industry Trng Bd, 1976-. *Recreations:* I am paid for my hobby, but enjoy watching cricket, athletics and Rugby football. *Address:* 23 The Chase, Edgware, Mddx. *T:* 01-952 5314. *Clubs:* MCC, Middlesex County Cricket.
   See also D . C . Jenkins .

JENKINS, Vivian Evan, MBE 1945; Director of Social Services, Cardiff City Council, 1971-74, retired; *b* 12 Sept. 1918; *s* of late Arthur Evan Jenkins and late Mrs Blodwen Jenkins; *m* 1946, Megan Myfanwy Evans; one *s* one *d. Educ:* UC Cardiff (BA). Dipl. Social Science. Army, 1940; commnd Royal Signals, 1943; served with 6th Airborne Div. as parachutist, Europe, Far East and Middle East, 1943-46 (Lieut). Child Care Officer, Glamorgan CC, 1949; Asst Children's Officer, 1951; Mem. Home Office Children's Dept Inspectorate, 1952. *Recreations:* Rugby football (former Captain of Univ. XV and Pontypridd RFC; awarded two Wales Rugby caps as schoolboy, 1933 and 1937); cricket, golf. *Address:* Ty Gwyn, 10 Y Parc, Groesfaen, near Pontyclun, Mid Glamorgan. *T:* Cardiff 890574. *Clubs:* Radyr Golf, (Vice-Pres.) Pontypridd Rugby Football.

JENKINS, Sir William, Kt 1966; JP; Agent in London for Government of Northern Ireland, 1966-70; *b* 25 July 1904; *m* 1942, Jessie May Watson, Otago, NZ; no *c. Educ:* Whitehouse Sch.; Belfast Coll. of Technology. Joined W. H. Brady & Co. Ltd, Bombay, 1931; became Sen. Dir; retd 1956. JP Bombay, 1946; Hon. Presidency Magistrate Bombay, 1948. Dir various joint cos in Bombay. Chairman: Gilbert-Ash (NI) Ltd; Old Bushmills Distillery Co. Ltd; Divisional Chm., Nationwide Building Soc.; Director: Belfast Banking Co.; Arthur Guinness Son & Co. (B) Ltd; Local Dir, Commercial Union Assurance Corp. Ltd. Entered Belfast Corp., 1957; JP Belfast, 1958; High Sheriff, Belfast, 1961; Dep. Lord Mayor, 1962; Lord Mayor of Belfast, 1964, 1965, 1966. Mem. Senate of N Ireland, 1963-66; Mem. Senate of Queen's Univ., 1963-66; Hon. Treas., Queen's Univ., 1965; first recipient of "Community Award" by New Ireland Soc. of Queen's Univ. for outstanding services to community during term as Lord Mayor. Mem. Council, 1967-70 (Chm. NI Br., 1967-75), Inst. of Directors. *Recreation:* golf. *Address:* Lismachan, 378 Belmont Road, Belfast, N Ireland. *Clubs:* Royal Automobile; Willingdon (Bombay); Ulster Reform (Belfast); Royal Belfast Golf, Fortwilliam Golf.

JENKINS, William Frank, CB 1949; CBE 1943; ARCO; *b* 14 May 1889; *m* 1923, Marjorie Newton-Jones. Called to Bar, Gray's Inn, 1922, Dir-Gen. Disposals, Ministry of Supply, 1946; Under-Sec. (Contracts) Ministry of Supply, 1947-53; Principal Finance Officer, UK Atomic Energy Authority, 1954-57, retired. *Address:* The Gateway, Forest Moor Road, Knaresborough HG5 8JY.

JENKINSON, Sir Anthony Banks, 13th Bt, *cr* 1661; *b* 3 July 1912; *S* grandfather, 1915; *s* of Captain John Banks Jenkinson (killed European War, Sept, 1914) and Joan, *o d* of late Col

Joseph Hill, CB (she *m* 2nd, 1920, Maj.-Gen. Algernon Langhorne, CB, DSO, who died 1945); *m* 1943, Frances, *d* of Harry Stremmel; one *s* two *d. Educ:* Eton; Balliol Coll., Oxford (Editor, The Isis, 1933-34). Foreign Correspondent, 1935-40: first British reporter to interview Mao Tse-tung in Yenan, NW China, Daily Sketch, 1938; Mediterranean Snoop Cruise Series, Daily Express, 1939; Caribbean Snoop Cruise, N American Newspaper Alliance & Reader's Digest, 1940; Editor, Allied Labour News Service, London and New York, 1940-46. Managing Director: Cayman Boats Ltd, Cayman Is, 1947-52; Morgan's Harbour Ltd, Port Royal, Jamaica, 1953-73; Director: Port Royal Co. of Merchants Ltd, 1965-; Spanish Main Investments Ltd, Grand Cayman, 1962-; Caribbean Bank (Cayman) Ltd, 1973-; Cayman Free Press Ltd, 1974-. *Publications:* America Came My Way, 1935; Where Seldom a Gun is Heard, 1937. *Recreations:* sailing, travel. *Heir: s* John Banks Jenkinson, *b* 16 Feb. 1945. *Address:* 491 South Church Street, Grand Cayman, West Indies. *Clubs:* United Oxford & Cambridge University; MCC; Bembridge Sailing; Cayman Islands Yacht.

JENKS, Sir Richard Atherley, 2nd Bt, *cr* 1932; *b* 26 July 1906; *er s* of Sir Maurice Jenks, 1st Bt, and Martha Louise Christabel, *d* of late George Calley Smith; *S* father 1946; *m* 1932, Marjorie Suzanne Arlette, *d* of late Sir Arthur du Cros, 1st Bt; two *s. Educ:* Charterhouse. Chartered Accountant, retired. *Heir: s* Maurice Arthur Brian Jenks [*b* 28 Oct. 1933; *m* 1962, Susan, *e d* of Leslie Allen, Surrey; one *d*]. *Address:* 42 Sussex Square, W2 2SP. *T:* 01-262 8356.

JENKYNS, Henry Leigh; Under-Secretary, Department of the Environment (formerly Ministry of Housing and Local Government), 1969-76; *b* 20 Jan. 1917; *y s* of H. H. Jenkyns, Indian Civil Service; *m* 1947, Rosalind Mary Home; two *s* one *d. Educ:* Eton and Balliol Coll., Oxford. War Service in Royal Signals; Lt-Col, East Africa Command, 1944. Treasury, 1945-66; Private Sec. to Chancellor, 1951-53. Treasury Representative in Australia and New Zealand, 1953-56; UK Delegation to OECD, Paris, 1961-63; Asst Under-Sec. of State, DEA, 1966-69; Chm., SE Economic Planning Bd, 1968-71. Mem., Southwark Diocesan Adv. Cttee for Care of Churches, 1977-. *Recreations:* music, garden, sailing, mending things. *Address:* 79 Blue House Lane, Limpsfield, Surrey. *T:* Oxted 3905. *Club:* United Oxford & Cambridge University.

JENNER, Ann Maureen; Ballerina, Royal Ballet, Covent Garden, since 1970; *b* 8 March 1944; *d* of Kenneth George Jenner and Margaret Rosetta (*née* Wilson). *Educ:* Royal Ballet Junior and Senior Schools. Joined Royal Ballet Co., 1961: Soloist 1964; Principal Dancer 1970. Roles include: Lise, Fille Mal Gardée, 1966; Swanhilda, Coppelia, 1968; Cinderella, 1969; Princess Aurora, Sleeping Beauty, 1972; Giselle, 1973; Gypsy, Deux Pigeons, 1974; White Girl, Deux Pigeons, 1976; Juliet, Romeo and Juliet, 1977; one-act roles include: Symphonic Variations, 1967; Firebird, 1972; Triad, 1973; Les Sylphides; Serenade; Les Patineurs, etc. *Address:* Royal Opera House, Covent Garden, WC2E 7QA. *T:* 01-240 1200.

JENNINGS, Sir Albert (Victor), Kt 1969; Founder and Chairman, A. V. Jennings Industries (Australia) Ltd, 1932, retired 1972; *b* 12 Oct. 1896; *s* of John Thomas Jennings; *m* 1922, Ethel Sarah, *d* of George Herbert Johnson; two *s. Educ:* Eastern Road, Sch., Melbourne. Served First World War, AIF. Council Mem., Master Builders Assoc., 1943-; Vice.Pres. Housing, Master Builders Fedn of Aust., 1970-71; Member: Commonwealth Building Research and Advisory Cttee, 1948-72; Manufacturing Industries Adv. Council to Australian Govt, 1962-; Decentralisation and Develt Adv. Cttee to Victorian State Govt, 1965-; Commonwealth of Aust. Metric Conversion Bd, 1970-72; Trustee, Cttee for Economic Develt of Australia. Fellow: Aust. Inst. of Building (Federal Pres., 1964-65 and 1965-66); UK Inst. of Building, 1971. Aust. Inst. of Building Medal 1970; Sir Charles McGrath Award for Services to Marketing, 1976. *Recreations:* swimming, golf. *Address:* Ranelagh House, Rosserdale Crescent, Mount Eliza, Victoria 3930, Australia. *T:* 7871350. *Clubs:* Commonwealth (Canberra); Melbourne, Savage (Melbourne).

JENNINGS, Audrey Mary; see Frisby, A. M.

JENNINGS, Christopher; see Jennings, R. E. C.

JENNINGS, (Edgar) Owen, RWS 1953 (ARWS 1943); RE 1970 (ARE 1944); ARCA London 1925; FRSA; Principal, School of Art, Tunbridge Wells, 1934-65; *b* Cowling, Yorks, 28 Dec. 1899; *s* of Wesley Jennings, JP and Ann Elizabeth Jennings (*née* Hardy); *m* 1929, May (*d* 1977), *d* of Arthur Cullingworth; one *s* one *d. Educ:* Sch. of Art, Skipton; Coll. of Art, Leeds; Royal

College of Art, London. Examr in Three Dimensional Design for Ministry of Education. Exhibited: Royal Academy, 1925-71; RWS, RE, NEAC, Paris Salon, New York, Chicago, Antwerp, Vienna. CEMA and Brit. Coun. Exhibns in England, China, Russia, Poland, etc. Works in: British Museum; London Museum; Victoria and Albert Museum; Albertina; Brooklyn Museum, New York; Art Inst., Chicago; Public Collections Leeds, Birmingham, Wakefield. Logan Prize Winner, Chicago International, 1930; Silver Medallist, City and Guilds of London Inst.; ATD 1926. Pres., Royal Water-Colour Society Art Club, 1966-70. *Publications:* contrib. to various art jls (line engravings, wood engravings, watercolours). *Relevant publication:* review by Adrian Bury, with illustrations, in Old Water-Colour Soc.'s Annual Volume, 1973. *Recreations:* reading, drawing. *Address:* Linton, 26 Wilman Road, Tunbridge Wells, Kent TN4 9AP. *T:* 20581. *Club:* Chelsea Arts.

JENNINGS, Elizabeth (Joan); Author; *b* 18 July 1926; *d* of Dr H. C. Jennings, Oxon. *Educ:* Oxford High Sch.; St Anne's Coll., Oxford. Asst at Oxford City Library, 1950-58; Reader for Chatto & Windus Ltd, 1958-60. *Publications:* Poems (Arts Council Prize), 1953; A Way of Looking, poems, 1955 (Somerset Maugham Award, 1956); A Sense of the World, poems, 1958; (ed) The Batsford Book of Children's Verse, 1958; Let's Have Some Poetry, 1960; Every Changing Shape, 1961; Song for a Birth or a Death, poems, 1961; a translation of Michelangelo's sonnets, 1961; Recoveries, poems, 1964; Robert Frost, 1964; Christianity and Poetry, 1965; The Mind Has Mountains, poems, 1966 (Richard Hillary Prize, 1966); The Secret Brother (poems for children), 1966; Collected Poems, 1967; The Animals' Arrival, poems, 1969 (Arts Council Bursary, 1969); (ed) A Choice of Christina Rossetti's Verse, 1970; Lucidities, poems, 1970; Relationships, 1972; Growing Points, poems, 1975; Seven Men of Vision, 1976; Consequently I Rejoice, poems, 1977; also poems and articles in: New Statesman, New Yorker, Botteghe Oscure, Observer, Spectator, Listener, Vogue, The Scotsman, etc. *Recreations:* travel, looking at pictures, the theatre, conversation. *Address:* c/o David Higham Associates Ltd, 5-8 Lower John Street, W1R 4HA. *Club:* Society of Authors.

JENNINGS, Henry Cecil; Chairman, Co-operative Wholesale Society Ltd, 1966-73; Chief Executive Officer, North Eastern Co-operative Society Ltd, 1970-73; *b* 2 Jan. 1908; *s* of late Alfred Ernest Jennings and Gertrude Sybil Jennings; *m* 1934, Winifred Evelyn Radford; one *s* decd. *Educ:* Gerard Street Sch., Derby. Inspector of Shops, Derby Co-operative Soc. Ltd, 1947-49; Blackburn Co-operative Soc. Ltd: Grocery Manager and Buyer, 1949-51; Gen. Man., 1951-54; Gen. Man., Darlington Co-operative Soc. Ltd, 1954-70. Dir of Co-operative Insurance Soc. Ltd, 1968-70; Chm., Associated Co-operative Creameries Ltd, 1968-70; Chm., Birtley Distributive Centre, 1964-70. Pres., Co-operative Congress, 1967. FRSA. *Recreations:* reading, gardening, travel. *Address:* 28 Gladelands Way, Corfe Lodge Park, Broadstone, Dorset BH18 9JB. *T:* Broadstone 696388.

JENNINGS, John Charles; *b* 10 Feb. 1903; *m* 1927, Berta Nicholson; one *s. Educ:* Bede Coll., Durham; King's Coll., Durham Univ. Headmaster. Contested (C), SE Derbyshire, 1950 and 1951. MP (C) Burton-on-Trent, Staffs, 1955-Feb. 1974; Chm., Cttees of House of Commons, 1964-74. *Recreation:* politics. *Address:* The Elms, Overseal, Burton-on-Trent, Staffs. *T:* Overseal 343.

JENNINGS, Owen; *see* Jennings, E. O.

JENNINGS, Paul (Francis), FRSL; writer; *b* 20 June 1918; *s* of William Benedict and Mary Gertrude Jennings; *m* 1952, Celia Blom; three *s* three *d. Educ:* King Henry VIII, Coventry, and Douai. Freelance work in Punch and Spectator began while still in Army (Lt Royal Signals); Script-writer at Central Office of Information, 1946-47; Copy writer at Colman Prentis Varley (advertising), 1947-49; on staff of The Observer, 1949-66. Trustee, New Philharmonia Trust. *Publications:* Oddly Enough, 1951; Even Oddlier, 1952; Oddly Bodlikins, 1953; Next to Oddliness, 1955; Model Oddlies, 1956; Gladly Oddly, 1957; Idly Oddly, 1959; I Said Oddly, Diddle I?, 1961; Oodles of Oddlies, 1963; The Jenguin Pennings, 1963; Oddly Ad Lib, 1965; I Was Joking, of Course, 1968; The Living Village, 1968; Just a Few Lines, 1969; It's An Odd Thing, But..., 1971; (ed) The English Difference, 1974; For children: The Hopping Basket, 1965; The Great Jelly of London, 1967; The Train to Yesterday, 1974; Britain As She Is Visit, 1976; And Now For Something Exactly the Same, 1977; The Book of Nonsense, 1977; I Must Have Imagined It, 1977. *Recreations:* madrigal singing and thinking about writing another vast serious book. *Address:* Hill House, Rectory Hill, East Bergholt, Suffolk.

JENNINGS, Percival Henry, CBE 1953; *b* 8 Dec. 1903; *s* of late Rev. Canon H. R. Jennings; *m* 1934, Margaret Katharine Musgrave, *d* of late Brig.-Gen. H. S. Rogers, CMG, DSO; three *d. Educ:* Christ's Hospital. Asst Auditor, N Rhodesia, 1927; Asst Auditor, Mauritius, 1931; Auditor, British Honduras, 1934; Dep. Dir of Audit, Gold Coast, 1938; Dep. Dir of Audit, Nigeria, 1945; Dir of Audit, Hong Kong, 1948; Dep. Dir-Gen. of the Overseas Audit Service, 1955; Dir-Gen. of the Overseas Audit Service, 1960-63, retd. *Recreation:* golf. *Address:* Littlewood, Lelant, St Ives, Cornwall. *T:* Hayle 753407. *Clubs:* Royal Commonwealth Society; West Cornwall Golf.

JENNINGS, Rev. Peter; General Secretary, Council of Christians and Jews, since 1974; *b* 9 Oct. 1937; *s* of Robert William Jennings and Margaret Irene Jennings; *m* 1963, Cynthia Margaret Leicester; two *s. Educ:* Manchester Grammar Sch.; Keble Coll., Oxford (MA); Hartley Victoria Methodist Theological Coll.; Manchester Univ. (MA). Ordained 1965. Minister: Swansea Methodist Circuit, 1963-67; London Mission (East) Circuit, and Tutor Warden, Social Studies Centre, 1967-74. *Recreation:* photography. *Address:* 21 Perkins Road, Barkingside, Essex IG2 7NJ. *T:* 01-554 5468. *Club:* Athenæum.

JENNINGS, Sir Raymond (Winter), Kt 1968; QC 1945; Master, Court of Protection, 1956-70; *b* 12 Dec. 1897; *o s* of late Sir Arthur Oldham Jennings and Mabel Winter; *m* 1930, Sheila (*d* 1972), *d* of Selwyn S. Grant, OBE; one *s* one *d. Educ:* Rugby; RMC, Sandhurst; Oriel Coll., Oxford (MA, BCL). Served 1916-19 in Royal Fusiliers. Called to Bar, 1922; Bencher of Lincoln's Inn, 1951. *Recreation:* fishing. *Address:* 14C Upper Drive, Hove, East Sussex BN3 6GN. *T:* Brighton 773361. *Club:* Athenæum.

JENNINGS, (Richard Edward) Christopher, MBE 1941; DL; Editor of The Motor, 1946-60; *b* 8 June 1911; *s* of late Lt-Col E. C. Jennings, CBE, DL; *m* 1937, Margaret, *d* of James A. Allan; one *s. Educ:* Repton. Served with Riley (Coventry) Ltd, 1931-37. Joined Temple Press as Midland Editor of The Motor, 1937-39. War of 1939-45: Lt Ordnance Mechanical Engineer, 1940; Capt. 1942; Major, 1943; Lt-Col, 1944; served in Western Desert (MBE), Greece, Crete, Syria and Northern Europe. High Sheriff of Carmarthenshire, 1957. DL Carmarthenshire, 1960. Gen. Comr of Income Tax, 1965-; Mem., Dyfed-Carmarthen Adv. Cttee for Gen. Comrs of Income Tax, 1974-. Director: Trust Houses Ltd, 1960-68; Buckley's Brewery Ltd, 1961-77; British Automatic Co. Ltd, 1962-68; Teddington Bellows Ltd, 1965-72. Pres. RNLI, Bury Port. *Publications:* (military) dealing with the fall of Greece and Crete, 1941. *Recreations:* sailing and motoring; interested in preservation of historic ships and vehicles. *Address:* Gelli-deg, Kidwelly, Dyfed SA17 4NA. *T:* Ferryside 201. *Clubs:* Brooks's; Royal Highland Yacht.

JENNINGS, Prof. Robert Yewdall, QC 1969; MA, LLB Cantab; Whewell Professor of International Law, University of Cambridge, since 1955; Fellow of Jesus College, Cambridge, since 1939; sometime President of Jesus College; Member, Institute of International Law; *b* 19 Oct. 1913; *o s* of Arthur Jennings; *m* 1955, Christine, *yr d* of Bernard Bennett; one *s* two *d. Educ:* Belle Vue Grammar Sch., Bradford; Downing Coll., Cambridge (Scholar; 1st Cl. Pts I & II, Law Tripos; LLB). Barrister-at-Law, Lincoln's Inn, Hon. Bencher, 1970; Joseph Hodges Choate Fellow, Harvard Univ., 1936-37; Whewell Scholar in Internat. Law, 1936; Asst Lectr in Law, London Sch. of Economics, 1938-39; Reader in Internat. Law, Council of Legal Educn, 1959-70. Served War: Intelligence Corps, 1940-46; Hon. Major, Officers' AER. Senior Tutor, Jesus Coll., 1949-55. Joint Editor: International and Comparative Law Quarterly, 1956-61; British Year Book of International Law, 1960-. *Publications:* The Acquisition of Territory, 1963; General Course on International Law, 1967; articles in legal periodicals. *Address:* Jesus College, Cambridge.

JENOUR, Sir (Arthur) Maynard (Chesterfield), Kt 1959; TD 1950; JP; Vice-Lord-Lieutenant of Gwent, since 1974 (Vice-Lieutenant of Monmouthshire, 1965-74); Chairman and Joint Managing Director: Aberthaw & Bristol Channel Portland Cement Co. Ltd (Director, 1929); T. Beynon & Co., Ltd (Director, 1938); Chairman, Ruthin Quarries (Bridgend) Ltd (Director 1947); Director: Associated Portland Cement Manufacturers Ltd, 1963-75; Blue Jacket Motel (Pty) Ltd, Australia, 1964; *b* 7 Jan. 1905; *s* of Brig.-Gen. A. S. Jenour, CB, CMG, DSO, Crossways, Chepstow and Emily Anna (*née* Beynon); *m* 1948, Margaret Sophie (who *m* 1927, W. O. Ellis Fielding-Jones, *d* 1935; three *d*), *d* of H. Stuart Osborne, Sydney, NSW. *Educ:* Eton. Entered business, 1924. Served War of 1939-45, in England and Middle East, Royal Artillery, Major. High Sheriff of Monmouthshire, 1951-52; Pres., Cardiff Chamber of Commerce, 1953-54; Chm. Wales & Mon.

Industrial Estates Ltd, 1954-60; Mem. Board, Development Corporation for Wales, 1958-. JP Mon 1946; DL Mon, 1960. KStJ 1969. *Recreations:* walking, gardening, shooting. *Address:* Stonycroft, 13 Ridgeway, Newport, Gwent. *T:* Newport 63802. *Clubs:* Naval and Military; Cardiff and County (Cardiff); Union (Sydney, NSW).

JEPHCOTT, Sir Harry, 1st Bt *cr* 1962; Kt 1946; MSc (London); FRIC; FPS; Hon. President, late Chairman, Glaxo Group Ltd; Director Metal Box Co. Ltd, 1950-64; *b* 15 Jan.. 1891; *s* of late John Josiah Jephcott, Redditch; *m* 1919, Doris Gregory, FPS; two *s. Educ:* King Edward's Grammar Sch., Camp Hill, Birmingham; West Ham Technical Coll., London. Called to Bar (Middle Temple), 1925. Chm. Council, Dept Scientific and Industrial Research, 1956-61; Pres. Royal Inst. of Chemistry, 1953-55; Chm. Assoc. of British Chemical Manufacturers, 1947-52, Pres. 1952-55. Mem. Advisory Council Scientific Policy, 1953-56; Chm. Cttee Detergents, 1953-55. Chm. School of Pharmacy, University of London, 1948-69. Hon. Fellow, School of Pharmacy, 1966. Governor London Sch. of Economics, 1952-68; Governor North London Collegiate Sch., 1957-. Hon. DSc (Birmingham), 1956. Hon. FRCGP 1960; Hon. FRSocMed 1961. *Heir: s* John Anthony Jephcott, BCom [*b* 21 May 1924; *m* 1949, Sylvia Mary, *d* of Thorsten Frederick Relling, Wellington, NZ; two *d*]. *Address:* Weetwood, 1 Cheney Street, Pinner, Mddx HA5 2TF. *T:* 01-866 0305. *Club:* Athenæum.

JEPHSON-JONES, Brig. Robert Llewellyn, GC 1940; Commandant Central Ordnance Depot, Branston, 1957-60, retired; *b* 7 April 1905; *s* of Rev. J. D. Jones, and Margaret Noble Jones (*née* Jephson); *m* 1934, Irene Sykes; one *d. Educ:* St Edmund's Sch., Canterbury; RMC, Sandhurst. Commissioned as 2nd Lieut Duke of Wellington's Regt, 1925; served in Singapore and India, 1926-30; served in Royal West African Frontier Force, Adjt, 1930-34; transferred to RAOC, 1936; served War, Malta, Palestine, Egypt, Sudan, Italy, 1939-44 (GC Malta); Col, 1943; Brig., 1954; Deputy Dir of Ordnance Services, Scottish Command, 1954-57. *Address:* 100 Twyford House, Fairways, Ferndown, Dorset. *Club:* Naval and Military.

JEPSON, Richard Pomfret, FRCS, FRACS; Professor of Surgery, Adelaide University, Australia, 1958-68; *b* 15 Feb. 1918; *s* of W. N. and L. E. Jepson, Whalley, Lancs; *m* 1951, Mary Patricia Herbert Oliver; five *d. Educ:* St Mary's Grammar Sch., Clitheroe, Lancs; Manchester Univ., BSc, MB, ChB. House Surgeon, Manchester Royal Infirmary, 1941-42; Neurosurgical specialist, Major, RAMC, 1942-46; Asst Lecturer, Lecturer and Reader in Surgery, University of Manchester, 1946-54; Prof. of Surgery, University of Sheffield, 1954-58. Hunterian Prof., RCS, 1951; Commonwealth Fund Fellowship, 1951; Research Fellow, Western Reserve Univ., Cleveland, Ohio, 1951-52. Hon. Surgeon: Queen Elizabeth Hosp., 1958-68; Royal Adelaide Hosp., 1958-68 (Hon. Vascular Surgeon, 1968-). *Publications:* articles in physiological and surgical journals. *Recreations:* varied. *Address:* 112 Barnard Street, N Adelaide, S Australia 5006, Australia. *Club:* Adelaide.

JEPSON, Selwyn; author and occasional soldier; *o s* of late Edgar Jepson. *Educ:* St Paul's Sch. War of 1939-45, Major, The Buffs, Military Intelligence and SOE. Editorial journalism, 1919. *Publications:* novels: The Qualified Adventurer, 1921; That Fellow MacArthur, 1922; The King's Red-Haired Girl, 1923; Golden Eyes, 1924; Rogues and Diamonds, 1925; Snaggletooth, 1926; The Death Gong, 1928; Tiger Dawn, 1929; I Met Murder, 1930; Rabbit's Paw, 1932; Keep Murder Quiet, 1940; Man Running, 1948; The Golden Dart, 1949; The Hungry Spider, 1950; Man Dead, 1951; The Black Italian, 1954; The Assassin, 1956; Noise in the Night, 1957; The Laughing Fish, 1960; Fear in the Wind, 1964; The Third Possibility, 1965; Angry Millionaire, 1968; Dead Letters, 1970; Letter to a Dead Girl, 1971; The Gill Interrogators, 1974; *short stories:* (with Michael Joseph) Heads or Tails, 1933; *stage play:* (with Lesley Storm) Dark Horizon, 1933; *screen plays:* Going Gay, 1932; For the Love of You, 1932; Irresistible Marmaduke, 1933; Monday at Ten, 1933; The Love Test, 1934; The Riverside Murders, 1934; White Lilac, Hyde Park Corner (Hackett), 1935; Well Done, Henry, 1936; The Scarab Murder, 1936; Toilers of the Sea (adapted and directed), 1936; Sailing Along, 1937; Carnet de Bal: Double Crime on the Maginot Line (English Version), 1938; *television plays:* Thought to Kill, 1952; Dialogue for Two Faces, 1952; My Name is Jones, 1952; Little Brother, 1953; Last Moment, 1953; Forever my Heart, 1953; Leave it to Eve (serial), 1954; The Interloper, 1955; Noise in the Night (USA), 1958; The Hungry Spider, 1964; The Peppermint Child, 1976; *radio serial:* The Hungry Spider, 1957; *radio plays:* The Bath that Sang, 1958; Noise in the Night, 1958; Art for Art's Sake, 1959; Small Brother, 1960; Call it Greymail, 1961; Dark Corners, 1963. *Recreation:* painting. *Address:* The Far House, Liss, Hants. *Club:* Savile.

JERITZA, Maria; Opera and Concert Star; *b* Brno, Czechoslovakia; *m* Irving Seery. *Educ:* Royal Academy of Music, Vienna. Debut, Vienna State Opera, 1918; with Metropolitan Opera Company, New York, and with Vienna State Opera, 1922-49. Recipient of the highest orders and decorations, from: HH the Pope; Republic of Austria; Republic of Italy; and Republic of France. *Publication:* Sunlight and Song. *Address:* c/o Maurice Feldman, Suite 1404, 745 Fifth Avenue, New York, NY 10022, USA.

JERMYN, Earl; Frederick William John Augustus Hervey; Governing Partner: Investment Motoring Company; Jermyn Shipping; Kaelow Galleries & Co. (London); Chairman, Kitala Ltd; Director, Estate Associates Ltd; *b* 15 Sept. 1954; *s* and *heir* of 6th Marquess of Bristol, *qv. Educ:* Harrow; Neuchâtel Univ. *Address:* 18 Brompton Square, SW3.

JEROME, Hon. James Alexander, PC (Can.); QC (Can.) 1976; MP; Speaker of the House of Commons, since 1974; lawyer, since 1958; *b* Kingston, Ont., 4 March 1933; *s* of Joseph Leonard Jerome and Phyllis Devlin; *m* 1958, Barry Karen Hodgins; three *s* two *d. Educ:* Our Lady of Perpetual Help Sch., Toronto; St Michael's Coll. High Sch., Toronto; Univ. of Toronto; Osgoode Hall. Alderman, Sudbury, Ont., 1966-67. MP, Sudbury, 1968-; Parly Sec. to President of Privy Council, 1970-74. Pres., Commonwealth Parly Assoc., 1976-. *Recreations:* golf, ski-ing, tennis, piano. *Address:* The Farm, Kingsmere, Quebec, Canada. *T:* 827-1914.

JERRAM, Rear-Adm. Sir Rowland Christopher, KBE 1945 (CBE 1937); DSO 1920; DL; RN, retired; *b* 20 Feb. 1890; *s* of late C. S. Jerram, Talland, Cornwall; *m* 1919, Christine E. M. (*d* 1961), *d* of late J. Grigg, Port Looe, Looe, Cornwall; two *s.* Entered RN, 1907; served 1914-18 war in HM Ships Iron Duke, Lion and Queen Elizabeth; Sec. to Adm. Sir Ernle Chatfield (later Lord Chatfield), 1919-40, as 4th Sea Lord; 3rd Sea Lord, C-in-C Home Fleet, C-in-C Med. Fleet; 1st Sea Lord; Chm. Commn on Defence of India; Minister for Co-ordination of Defence. Served in HMS Cleopatra, Med., 1942-43; Sec. to Combined Ops HQ, 1943; Comptroller HQ SACSEA, 1943-45; Head of Admlty Mission to Med., 1945, retd Dec. 1945. Comr, St John Ambulance Bde, Cornwall, 1949-58. DL Cornwall, 1958. KStJ. *Address:* Temple Garth, St Cleer, Cornwall.

JERSEY, 9th Earl of, *cr* 1697; **George Francis Child Villiers;** Viscount Grandison, 1620; Viscount Villiers and Baron Hoo, 1691; Chairman: Wallace Brothers Bank (Jersey) Ltd; Seaby (Overseas) Ltd; Jersey Island Semen Exports Ltd; Associated Hotels Ltd; Hotel L'Horizon Ltd; *b* 15 Feb. 1910; *e s* of 8th Earl and Lady Cynthia Almina Constance Mary Needham (who *m* 2nd, 1925, W. R. Slessor (*d* 1945); she died 1947), *o d* of 3rd Earl of Kilmorey; *S* father, 1923; *m* 1st, 1932, Patricia Kenneth (who obtained a divorce, 1937; she *m* 2nd, 1937, Robin Filmer Wilson, who *d* 1944; 3rd, 1953, Col Peter Laycock), *o d* of Kenneth Richards, Cootamundra, NSW, and of Eileen Mary (now *widow* of Sir Stephenson Kent, KCB); one *d* ; 2nd, 1937, Virginia (who obtained a divorce, 1946), *d* of James Cherrill, USA; 3rd, 1947, Maria Luciana, (Bianca), *er d* of late Enrico Mottironi, Turin, Italy; two *s* one *d.* Director: Jersey General Investment Trust Ltd; Jersey General Executor and Trustee Co. Ltd. *Heir: s* Viscount Villiers, *qv. Address:* Radier Manor, Longueville, Jersey, Channel Islands. *T:* (Jersey) Central 53102.

JERSEY, Dean of; *see* Goss, Very Rev. T. A.

JERVIS, family name of **Viscount St Vincent.**

JERVIS, Charles Elliott, OBE 1966; Editor-in-Chief, Press Association, 1954-65; *b* Liverpool, 7 Nov. 1907; *y s* of late J. H. Jervis, Liverpool; *m* 1931, Ethel Braithwaite, Kendal, Westmorland; one *d.* Editorial Asst, Liverpool Express, 1921-23; Reporter, Westmorland Gazette, 1923-28; Dramatic Critic and Asst Editor, Croydon Times, 1928-37; Sub-Editor, Press Assoc., 1937-47; Asst Editor, 1947-54. Pres., Guild of British Newspaper Editors, 1964-65; Mem. of the Press Council, 1960-65. *Address:* Orchard End, Cart Lane, Grange-over-Sands, Cumbria. *T:* 2335. *Club:* Press.

JESSEL, family name of **Baron Jessel.**

JESSEL, 2nd Baron, *cr* 1924, of Westminster; **Edward Herbert Jessel,** Bt, *cr* 1917; CBE 1963; a Deputy Speaker, House of Lords; Chairman, Associated Leisure Ltd, 1963-77; *b* 25 March 1904; *o s* of 1st Baron, CB, CMG, and Maud (*d* 1965), 5th *d* of late Rt Hon. Sir Julian Goldsmid, Bt, MP; *S* father 1950; *m* 1st, 1935, Lady Helen Maglona Vane-Tempest-Stewart (from whom he obtained a divorce, 1960), 3rd *d* of 7th Marquess of Londonderry, KG, PC, MVO; two *d* (one *s* decd); 2nd, 1960,

Jessica, *d* of late William De Wet and Mrs H. W. Taylor, Cape Town. *Educ:* Eton; Christ Church, Oxford (BA). Called to Bar, Inner Temple, 1926. Formerly Director: Textile Machinery Makers Ltd; Truscon Ltd; Westminster Trust. Chm., Assoc. of Indep. Unionist Peers, 1959-64. *Address:* 4 Sloane Terrace Mansions, SW1. *T:* 01-730 7843. *Clubs:* Garrick, White's.
See also Sir G. W. G. Agnew.

JESSEL, Sir Charles (John), 3rd Bt *cr* 1883; farmer; *b* 29 Dec. 1924; *s* of Sir George Jessel, 2nd Bt, MC, and Muriel (*d* 1948), *d* of Col J. W. Chaplin, VC; *S* father, 1977; *m* 1956, Shirley Cornelia, *o d* of John Waters, Northampton; two *s* one *d*. *Educ:* Eton; Balliol College, Oxford. Served War of 1939-45, Lieut 15/19th Hussars (despatches). JP Kent 1960. *Recreations:* gardening, shooting. *Heir: s* George Elphinstone Jessel, *b* 15 Dec. 1957. *Address:* South Hill Farm, Hastingleigh, near Ashford, Kent. *T:* Elmsted 325. *Club:* Cavalry and Guards.

JESSEL, Oliver Richard; *b* 24 Aug. 1929; *s* of Comdr R. F. Jessel, DSO, OBE, RN; *m* 1950, Gloria Rosalie Teresa (*née* Holden); one *s* five *d*. *Educ:* Rugby. Founded group of companies, 1954; opened office in City of London, 1960; Chm., London, Australian and General Exploration Co. Ltd., 1960-75; formed New Issue Unit Trust and other trusts, 1962-68; responsible for numerous mergers, incl. Johnson & Firth Brown Ltd, and Maple Macowards Ltd. *Address:* The Grange, Marden, Kent. *T:* Maidstone 831264. *Club:* Garrick.
See also T. F. H. Jessel.

JESSEL, Sir Richard (Hugh), Kt 1960; Chairman and Managing Director, Jessel Toynbee & Co. Ltd, Discount Brokers, 1943-60, retired; *b* 21 Feb. 1896; 2nd *s* of late Sir Charles James Jessel, 1st Bt; *m* 1st, 1923, Margaret Ella (*d* 1953), *d* of late Sir George Lewis, 2nd Bt; two *s* one *d*; 2nd, 1954, Daphne (*d* 1971), widow of Major T. G. Philipson, MC, the Life Guards, and *d* of late W. B. Gladstone; 3rd, 1972, Diana, widow of Lt-Col George Trotter, late Royal Scots Greys. *Educ:* Eton. Founded Jessel Toynbee & Co., 1922; Limited Co. (private), Chm., 1943; Public Co., 1946; Public Works Commissioner, 1949-60; Exports Credits Guarantee Dept Advisory Council, 1951-60 (Dep. Chm., 1959). Served European War, 1914-18, Lt 2/7 Bn Hants Regt; served War of 1939-45, with Ministry of Economic Warfare, 1939-41; Priority Officer, Air Ministry, 1941-44. *Recreations:* racing, gardening. *Address:* The White House, Steeple Morden, Royston, Herts SG8 0PE. *Clubs:* Brooks's, MCC.

JESSEL, Toby Francis Henry; MP (C) Twickenham since 1970; *b* 11 July 1934; *y s* of Comdr R. F. Jessel, DSO, OBE, DSC, RN, Lees Court, Matfield, Kent; *m* 1967, Philippa Brigid (marr. diss. 1973), *e d* of Henry C. Jephcott, Cottingham, Yorks; one *d* decd. *Educ:* Royal Naval Coll., Dartmouth; Balliol Coll., Oxford (MA). Sub-Lt, RNVR, 1954. Conservative Candidate: Peckham, 1964; Hull (North), 1966. Parly deleg. to India and Pakistan, 1971; Member: Council of Europe, 1976; WEU, 1976. Chm., South Area Bd GLC Planning and Transportation Cttee, 1968-70. (Co-opted) LCC Housing Cttee, 1961-65; Councillor, London Borough of Southwark, 1964-66; Mem. for Richmond-upon-Thames, GLC, 1967-73; Hon. Sec. Assoc. of Adopted Conservative Candidates, 1961-66; Jt Sec., Indo-British Parly Gp. Mem. Metropolitan Water Bd, 1967-70; Mem., London Airport Consultative Cttee, 1967-70. Mem. Council, Fluoridation Soc., 1976. Governor, Mary Datchelor Grammar Sch. 1962-. Whitworth Memorial Prize for Music, 1951. *Recreations:* music, gardening, croquet (Longworth Cup, Hurlingham, 1961), ski-ing. *Address:* Old Court House, Hampton Court, East Molesey, Surrey. *Club:* Hurlingham.
See also O. R. Jessel, A. Panufnik.

JESSOP, Thomas Edmund, OBE 1945; MC 1918; MA, BLitt; Hon. LittD (Dublin); Hon. DLitt (Hull); Fellow of the British Psychological Society, Foreign Fellow, Accademia Nazionale dei Lincei (Rome); Médaille d'honneur, Brussels University; Ferens Professor of Philosophy in the University of Hull, 1928-61, Professor Emeritus since 1961; *b* Huddersfield, 10 Sept. 1896; *s* of Newton Jessop; *m* 1930, Dora Anne Nugent Stewart (*d* 1965), MA (Glasgow). *Educ:* Heckmondwike Sch., Leeds Univ.; Oriel Coll., Oxford. Served with Duke of Wellington's West Riding Regt on the Western Front, 1916-18 (twice wounded); Asst Lecturer in Logic and Metaphysics, University of Glasgow, 1925-28; Chm. of E and N Yorks and North Lindsey Adult Education Cttee, 1936-37; Donnellan Lectr, Dublin, 1944; Dunning Trust Lectr, Kingston, Ontario 1948; Visiting Professor: Brussels Univ., 1953; Los Angeles State Coll., 1963; San Francisco State Coll., 1970. Vice-Pres. Methodist Conf., 1955; Member: of World Methodist Council Exec. (1956-66); of Editorial Bd of SCM Press; of Editorial Bd of Archives Internationales d'Histoire des Idées, of Council of Royal

Institute of Philosophy, of Institut International de Philosophie, and of Yorks Executive of Royal Society of St George; Chm. of Adult Religious Education Sub-Cttee of Brit. Council of Churches, 1948-61. *Publications:* Lugano and its Environs, 1924; Montreux and Lake of Geneva, 1925; Locarno and its Valleys, 1927; Bibliography of George Berkeley, Bishop of Cloyne, 1934, rev. and enl. edn 1974; The Philosophical Background, in France, Companion to French Studies, 1937; Berkeley's Principles of Human Knowledge, 1937; The Scientific Account of Man, in The Christian Understanding of Man, 1938; Bibliography of Hume and of Scottish Philosophy, 1938; part-translator of A Hundred Years of British Philosophy by R. Metz, 1938; Law and Love, a study of the Christian Ethic, 1940; Science and the Spiritual, 1942; The Treaty of Versailles, 1942; Effective Religion, 1944; Education and Evangelism, 1947; The Works of George Berkeley (joint ed.), 1948-57; The Freedom of the Individual in Society, 1948; Reasonable Living, 1948; Berkeley, Philosophical Writings selected and edited, 1952; Social Ethics, 1952; On Reading the English Bible, Peake Lecture, 1958; "Writers and their Work" (British Council): contrib. Berkeley, 1959, Hobbes, 1960; Introduction to Christian Doctrine, 1960; The Christian Morality (Cambridge Open Divinity Lectures), 1960; The Enduring Passion, 1961; Spinoza on Freedom of Thought, 1962; Berkeley, Antologia degli Scritti Filosofici, 1967; contribs to encyclopædias and philosophical periodicals. *Recreation:* gardening. *Address:* 73 Park Avenue, Hull. *T:* 442606.

JESSUP, Frank William, CBE 1972; Director, Department for External Studies, Oxford University, 1952-76; Fellow of Wolfson College, Oxford, since 1965; *b* 26 April 1909; *s* of Frederick William Jessup and Alice Sarah (*née* Cheeseman); *m* 1935, Dorothy Hilda Harris; two *s* one *d*. *Educ:* Gravesend Boys' Grammar Sch.; Univ. of London (BA, LLB); Univ. of Oxford (MA). Called to Bar, Gray's Inn, 1935. Dep. County Educn Officer, Kent, until 1952. Chairman: Library Adv. Council (England), 1965-73; British Library Adv. Council, 1976-; Oxon Rural Community Council, 1976-; Vice-Chm., Universities Council for Adult Educn, 1973-76. Pres., Kent Archaeol Soc., 1976-. Chm. of Governors, Rose Bruford Coll. of Speech and Drama, 1960-72. FSA; Hon. FLA. Hon. DCL Kent 1976. *Publications:* Problems of Local Government, 1949; Introduction to Kent Feet of Fines, 1956; A History of Kent, 1958, repr. 1974; Sir Roger Twysden, 1597-1672, 1965, etc; contrib. to Archæologia Cantiana, Studies in Adult Educn. *Recreations:* reading, music, gardening. *Address:* Striblehills, Thame, Oxon. *T:* Thame 2027.

JESSUP, Philip C.; United States teacher and lawyer; Judge of International Court of Justice, 1961-70; Teacher of International Law, Columbia University, 1925-61; Hamilton Fish Professor of International Law and Diplomacy, 1946-61; *b* 5 Jan. 1897; *s* of Henry Wynans and Mary Hay Stotesbury Jessup; *m* 1921, Lois Walcott Kellogg; one *s*. *Educ:* Hamilton Coll., Clinton, NY (AB 1919); Columbia Univ. (AM 1924, PhD 1927); Yale Univ. (LLB). US Army Exped. Forces, 1918. Asst to Pres., and Asst Cashier, First Nat. Bank of Utica, NY, 1919-21; Parker & Duryea Law Firm, New York, 1927-43. Asst Solicitor, Dept of State, 1924-25; Asst to Elihu Root, Conf. of Jurists, Permanent Court of International Justice, Geneva, 1929; Legal Adviser to American Ambassador to Cuba, 1930; Chief, Div. of Office of Foreign Relief, Dept of State, 1943; Associate Dir, Naval Sch. of Military Government and Administration, 1942-44; Asst Sec. Gen. UNRRA and Bretton Woods Confs, 1943-44; Asst on Judicial Organisation, San Francisco Conf. on UNO, 1945; US Dep. Rep. to Interim Cttee of Gen. Assembly and Security Council, UN, 1948; Deleg. Sessions: UN Gen. Assembly, 3rd, Paris-New York, 1948-49, 4th New York, 1949, 6th, Paris, Nov. 1951-Jan. 1952, 7th New York 1952. Ambassador at Large of USA, 1949-53. Trustee, Woodrow Wilson Foundn, 1948-57, Pres., 1957-58. Storrs Lectr, Yale Univ. Law Sch., 1956; Cooley Lectr, Michigan Univ. Law Sch., 1958; Blaustein Lectr, Columbia Univ., 1970; Sibley Lectr, Univ. of Georgia Law Sch., 1970. Mem. Curatorium, Hague Acad. of Internat. Law, 1957-68; Trustee: Carnegie Endowment for Internat. Peace, 1937-60; Hamilton Coll., 1949-61; Associate Rockefeller Foundation, 1960-61; Vice-Pres. Institut de droit international, 1959-60, 1974-75. Hon. Mem. Inter-American Institute of International Legal Studies, 1964-. Chairman: Chile-Norway Permanent Conciliation Commn, 1958-; Austro-Swedish Commn for Reconciliation and Arbitration, 1976-; Mem. Governing Council, Inst. for Unification of Private Law, 1964-67, Hon. Mem., 1967-. Hon. President: Amer. Soc. of Internat. Law, 1969-73; Amer. Branch, Internat. Law Assoc., 1970-73. Senior Fellow, Council on Foreign Relations (NYC), 1970-71. Member: Amer. Philosophical Soc.; Amer. Acad. of Arts and Scis. Hon. LLD: Western Reserve Univ.; Seoul Nat. Univ., Rutgers Univ., Middlebury Coll., Yale Univ., St Lawrence

Univ., Univ. of Michigan; Johns Hopkins Univ.; Brandeis Univ.; Columbia Univ.; Colby Coll.; Pennsylvania Univ.; Hon. LCD: Colgate Univ., Union Coll.; Hon. JD Oslo; Doc (*hc*) Univ. of Paris; Hon. LittD, Univ. of Hanoi. Hon. Mem., Academia Mexicana de Derecho International. Hungarian Cross of Merit, Class II; Oficial Ordem Nacional do Cruzeiro do Sul, Brazil; Grand Officer, Order of the Cedars, Lebanon; Manley O. Hudson Gold Medal of the American Soc. of International Law, 1964; Distinguished Service Award, Connecticut Bar Assoc., 1970; Wolfgang G. Friedmann Meml Award; Columbia Univ. Sch. of Law Alumni Assoc. Medal for Excellence, 1977; Graduate Faculties Alumni of Columbia Univ. Award for Excellence, 1977. *Publications:* The Law of Territorial Waters and Maritime Jurisdiction, 1927; United States and the World Court, 1929; Neutrality, Its History, Economics and Law, Vol. I, The Origins (with F. Deak), 1935; Vol. IV, Today and Tomorrow, 1936, repr. 1976; Elihu Root, 1938, repr. 1964; International Problem of Governing Mankind, 1947; A Modern Law of Nations, 1948 (trans. German, Korean, Thai); Transnational Law, 1956 (trans. Arabic, Portuguese, Spanish, Japanese); The Use of International Law, 1959; Controls for Outer Space (with H. J. Taubenfield), 1959; The Price of International Justice, 1971; The Birth of Nations, 1974. *Address:* Windrow Road, Norfolk, Conn 06058, USA. *Clubs:* Century (New York); Cosmos (Washington).

JEVONS, Dr Frederic Raphael; Vice-Chancellor, Deakin University, Australia, since 1976; *b* 19 Sept. 1929; *s* of Fritz and Hedwig Bettelheim; *m* 1956, Grete Bradel; two *s*. *Educ:* Langley Sch., Norwich; King's Coll., Cambridge (Major Schol.). 1st Cl. Hons Nat. Scis Pt II (Biochem) Cantab 1950; PhD Cantab 1953; DSc Manchester 1966. Postdoctoral Fellow, Univ. of Washington, Seattle, 1953-54; Fellow, King's Coll., Cambridge, 1953-59; Univ. Demonstrator in Biochem., Cambridge, 1956-59; Lectr in Biol Chem., Manchester Univ., 1959-66; Prof. of Liberal Studies in Science, Manchester Univ., 1966-75. Mem. Editorial Adv. Bds, R and D Management and Studies in Science Educn; Mem. Jt Matriculation Bd, 1969-75; Chm. Gen. Studies Cttee, Schools Council, 1974-75; Mem. Jt Cttee, SRC and SSRC; Chm., Grad. Careers Council of Australia, 1976-. Interviewer for Civil Service Commn on Final Selection Bds; Adviser to Leverhulme project on educnl objectives in applied science, Strathclyde Univ.; British Council tours in India, E Africa, Nigeria. *Publications:* The Biochemical Approach to Life, 1964, 2nd edn 1968 (trans. Italian, Spanish, Japanese, German); The Teaching of Science: education, science and society, 1969; (ed jtly) University Perspectives, 1970; (jtly) Wealth from Knowledge: studies of innovation in industry, 1972; (ed jtly) What Kinds of Graduates do we Need?, 1972; Science Observed: science as a social and intellectual activity, 1973; Knowledge and Power, 1976; numerous papers on biochem., history of science, science educn and science policy. *Recreations:* music, theatre, reading. *Address:* Deakin University, PO Box 125, Belmont, Geelong, Vic 3216, Australia.

JEWELL, Maurice Frederick Stewart, CBE 1954; JP; DL; *b* 15 Sept. 1885; *s* of Maurice Jewell and Ada Brown; *m* 1911, Elsie May Taylor (*d* 1974); one *s* five *d*. *Educ:* Marlborough Coll. Served European War, 1914-19, with Royal Field Artillery; Major 1916. JP 1926, DL 1947, Worcs. *Recreations:* formerly cricket (President of Worcs County Cricket Club until 1954). *Address:* Bramble End, Birdham, Chichester, West Sussex PO20 7QN. *T:* Chichester 512478. *Club:* Worcestershire (Worcester).

JEWELL, Prof. Peter Arundel, PhD, FIBiol; Mary Marshall and Arthur Walton Professor of Physiology of Reproduction in the University of Cambridge, since Oct. 1977; *b* 16 June 1925; *s* of Percy Arundel Jewell and Ivy Dorothea Enness; *m* 1958, Juliet Clutton-Brock; three *d*. *Educ:* Wandsworth Sch.; Reading Univ. (BSc Agric.); Cambridge Univ. (BA, MA, PhD). Lectr, Royal Veterinary Coll., 1950-60; Research Fellow, Zoological Soc. of London, 1960-66; Dir, Div. of Biological Sciences, Univ. of Biafra, 1966-67; Sen. Lectr and Dir of Conservation Course, University Coll. London, 1967-72; Prof. of Zoology, Royal Holloway Coll., 1972-77. Mem. ICA. *Publications:* Island Survivors: the Ecology of the Soay Sheep of St Kilda, 1974; scientific papers in Jl Animal Ecology, Jl Wildlife Management, Zool. Soc. Symposia, Jl Physiology, etc. *Recreations:* drinking real ale; safaris, watching wild animals; listening, saving rare breeds, theatre, keeping up with three daughters. *Address:* St John's College, Cambridge CB2 1TP.

JEWERS, William George, OBE 1976; Member for Finance, British Gas Corporation, since 1976; *b* 18 Oct. 1921; *s* of late William Jewers and Hilda Jewers (*née* Ellison); *m* 1955, Helena Florence Rimmer; one *s* one *d*. *Educ:* Liverpool Inst. High Sch. for Boys. Liverpool Gas Co., 1938-41. Served War: RAFVR Observer (Flying Officer), 1941-46: Indian Ocean, 265 Sqdn

(Catalinas), 1943-44; Burma 194 Sqdn (Dakotas), 1945. Liverpool Gas Co./NW Gas Bd, Sen. Accountancy Asst, 1946-52; W Midlands Gas Bd: Cost Acct, Birmingham and Dist Div., 1953-62; Cost Acct, Area HQ, 1962-65; Asst Chief Acct, 1965-66; Chief Acct, 1967; Dir of Finance, 1968; Gas Council, Dir of Finance, 1969-73; British Gas Corp., Dir of Finance, 1973-76. FCMA, FCCA, JDipMA, CompIGasE. *Publications:* papers and articles on gas industry jls. *Recreations:* music, reading, golf. *Address:* 17 South Park View, Gerrards Cross, Bucks SL9 8HN. *T:* Gerrards Cross 86169.

JEWKES, Gordon Wesley; HM Diplomatic Service; Head of Finance Department, Foreign and Commonwealth Office, and Finance Officer of the Diplomatic Service, since 1975; *b* 18 Nov. 1931; *er s* of late Jesse Jewkes; *m* 1954, Joyce (*née* Lyons); two *s*. *Educ:* Barrow Grammar Sch.; Magnus Grammar Sch., Newark-on-Trent. Colonial Office, 1948; served HM Forces, Army, 1950-52; Gen. Register Office, 1950-63; CS Pay Res. Unit, 1963-65; Gen. Register Office, 1965-68; transf. to HM Diplomatic Service, 1968; CO, later FCO, 1968-69; Consul (Commercial), Chicago, 1969-72; Dep. High Comr, Port of Spain, 1972-75. *Recreations:* music, travel, walking, boating. *Address:* c/o Foreign and Commonwealth Office, SW1A 2AL. *Club:* Royal Commonwealth Society.

JEWKES, John, CBE 1943; MA (Oxon); MCom; Economic Adviser, Arthur Guinness, Son and Co. Ltd; *b* June 1902; *m* 1929, Sylvia Butterworth; one *d*. *Educ:* Barrow Grammar Sch.; Manchester Univ. MCom. Asst Sec., Manchester Chamber of Commerce, 1925-26; Lecturer in Economics, University of Manchester, 1926-29; Rockefeller Foundation Fellow, 1929-30; Professor of Social Economics, Manchester 1936-46; Stanley Jevons Prof. of Political Economy, Manchester, 1946-48; Prof. of Economic Organisation, Oxford, and Fellow of Merton College, 1948-69, Emeritus Fellow 1969. Visiting Prof., University of Chicago, 1953-54; Visiting Prof., Princeton Univ., 1961. Dir, Economic Section, War Cabinet Secretariat, 1941; Dir-Gen. of Statistics and Programmes, Ministry of Aircraft Production, 1943; Principal Asst Sec., Office of Minister of Reconstruction, 1944; Mem. of Fuel Advisory Cttee, 1945; Independent Mem. of Cotton Industry Working Party, 1946; Mem. of Royal Commission on Gambling, Betting and Lotteries, 1949. Mem. of Royal Commission on Doctors' and Dentists' Remuneration, 1957-60; Dir, Industrial Policy Gp, 1969-74. Hon. DSc Hull, 1973. *Publications:* An Industrial Survey of Cumberland and Furness (with A. Winterbottom), 1931; Juvenile Unemployment (with A. Winterbottom), 1933; Wages and Labour in the Cotton Spinning Industry (with E. M. Gray), 1935; The Juvenile Labour Market (with Sylvia Jewkes) 1938; Ordeal by Planning, 1948; The Sources of Invention (with David Sawers and Richard Stillerman), 1958; The Genesis of the British National Health Service (with Sylvia Jewkes), 1961; Value for Money in Medicine (with Sylvia Jewkes), 1962; Public and Private Enterprise, 1965; New Ordeal by Planning, 1968. *Recreation:* gardening. *Address:* Entwood, Red Copse Lane, Boars Hill, Oxford.

JHABVALA, Mrs R(uth) Prawer; author; *b* in Germany, of Polish parents, 7 May 1927; *d* of Marcus Prawer and Eleonora Prawer (*née* Cohn); came to England as refugee, 1939; *m* 1951, C. S. H. Jhabvala; three *d*. *Educ:* Hendon County Sch.; Queen Mary Coll., London Univ. Started writing after graduation and marriage, alternating between novels and short stories; occasional original film-scripts, including: Shakespeare-wallah, 1965; The Guru, 1969; Bombay Talkie, 1971; Autobiography of a Princess, 1975; Roseland, 1977. *Publications:* novels: To Whom She Will, 1955; The Nature of Passion, 1956; Esmond in India, 1958; The Householder, 1960; Get Ready for Battle, 1962; A Backward Place, 1965; A New Dominion, 1973; Heat and Dust, 1975 (Booker Prize, 1975); *short story collections:* Like Birds, like Fishes, 1964; A Stronger Climate, 1968; An Experience of India, 1971; How I became a Holy Mother and other Stories, 1976. *Recreation:* writing film-scripts. *Address:* c/o John Murray, 50 Albemarle Street, W1. *T:* 228823. *See also* Prof. S. S. Prawer.

JILANI, Asaf; Editor, Daily Jang, London (first Urdu Daily in UK), since 1973; *b* 24 Sept. 1934; *s* of Abdul Wahid Sindhi and Noor Fatima Jilani; *m* 1961, Mohsina Jilani; two *s* one *d*. *Educ:* Jamia Millia, Delhi; Sindh Marrsa, Karachi; Karachi Univ. (BA, Economics and Persian). Sub-Editor, Daily Imroze, Karachi (Progressive Papers Ltd), 1952; Political Corresp., Daily Imroze, 1954; Special Corresp., Daily Jang, Karachi (posted in India), 1959-65; London Editor: Daily Jang (Karachi, Rawalpindi, Quetta); Daily News, Karachi, and Akhbar-Jehan, Karachi, 1965-73. *Recreations:* cricket, swimming, painting. *Address:* (office) 52 Hoxton Square, N1 9BG. *T:* 01-739 1698; (home) 23 Horsham Avenue, N12. *T:* 01-368 5697. *Clubs:* BBC; (Founder Mem.) Karachi Press (Karachi).

JILLETT, Dr Raymond Leslie, TD 1964; Medical Superintendent/Governor, HM Prison, Grendon, Grendon Underwood, since 1975; *b* 24 March 1925; *s* of Leslie George and Ethel Florence Jillett, London; *m* 1955, Mary Patricia (*née* Lewis); two *d*. *Educ:* Bec Sch., London; King's Coll., Univ. of London; King's Coll. Hosp. Med. Sch., London. MB, BS London 1949, DPM 1964, MRCPsych 1971; MBIM 1976. Various hosp. appts, 1949-62; Asst Psychiatrist, Exe Vale Hosp., Exeter, 1962-68. TA, 1954-66: various appts to regts and 128 Field Amb., RAuxAF, Sqdn/Ldr Med., 1967-. HM Prison Service: MO, 1968; Sen. MO, Wakefield Prison, 1975. Oxford Postgrad. Fellowship in Psychiatry, 1964. Divl Surg. and Area Staff Officer, St John Amb. Bde, 1955-60; County Staff Officer, Cadets, 1960-68 (Devon); Area Comr, N Bucks, 1969-; County Surgeon, 1977. OStJ 1970. *Publications:* articles in Lancet and Brit. Jl of Psychiatry. *Recreations:* theatre, dramatic and operatic production. *Address:* (home) Gwynfa, Stratford Road, Buckingham MK18 1TF; HM Prison, Grendon, Grendon Underwood, Aylesbury. *Club:* Royal Air Force.

JIMENEZ DE ARECHAGA, Eduardo, DrJur; President of the International Court of Justice, The Hague, since 1976 (Judge of the Court since 1970); *b* Montevideo, 8 June 1918; *s* of E. Jiménez de Aréchaga and Ester Sienra; *m* 1943, Marta Ferreira; three *s* two *d*. *Educ:* Sch. of Law, Univ. of Montevideo. Prof. of Internat. Law, Montevideo Law Sch., 1949-69; Under-Sec., Foreign Relations, 1950-52; Sec., Council of Govt of Uruguay, 1952-55; Mem., Internat. Law Commn of UN, 1961-69 (Pres., 1963); Cttee *Rapporteur*, Vienna Conf. on Law Treaties, 1968-69; Minister of the Interior, Uruguay, 1968. Inter-Amer. Bar Assoc. Book Award, 1961. *Publications:* Reconocimiento de Gobiernos, 1946; Voting and Handling of Disputes in the Security Council, 1951; Treaty Stipulations in Favour of Third States, 1956; Derecho Constitucional de las Naciónes Unidas, 1958; Curso de Derecho Internacional Público, 2 vols, 1959-61. *Address:* International Court of Justice, Peace Palace, The Hague, Netherlands; Casila de Correo 539, Montevideo, Uruguay.

JINKS, Prof. John Leonard, FRS 1970; Professor of Genetics and Head of Department of Genetics, since 1965, Dean, Faculty of Science and Engineering, 1972-75, Birmingham University; *b* 21 Oct. 1929; *s* of Jack and Beatrice May Jinks; *m* 1955, Diana Mary Williams; one *s* one *d*. *Educ:* Longton High Sch., Stoke-on-Trent; Univ. of Birmingham. BSc Botany 1950, PhD Genetics 1952, DSc Genetics 1964, Birmingham. ARC Research Student: Univ. of Birmingham, 1950-52; Carlsberg Labs, Copenhagen; Istituto Sieroterapico, Milan, 1952-53; Scientific Officer, ARC Unit of Biometrical Genetics, Univ. of Birmingham, 1953-59; Harkness Fellow, California Inst. of Technology, 1959-60; Principal Scientific Officer, ARC Unit of Biometrical Genetics, 1960-65; Hon. Lectr 1960-62, Reader 1962-65, Univ of Birmingham. Mem., SRC, 1975-. Editor of Heredity, 1960-75, Acting Editor, 1976-. FIBiol 1968. *Publications:* Extrachromosomal Inheritance, 1964; (jtly) Biometrical Genetics, 1971; Cytoplasmic Inheritance, 1976; (jtly) Introduction to Biometrical Genetics, 1977; numerous papers and chapters in books on microbial genetics, biometrical genetics and behavioral genetics. *Recreations:* piano, gardening. *Address:* 81 Witherford Way, Selly Oak, Birmingham B29 4AN. T: 021-472 2008.

JOB, Rev. Evan Roger Gould; Precentor and Sacrist of Westminster Abbey, since 1974; *b* 15 May 1936; 2nd *s* of Thomas Brian Job and Elsie Maud Job (*née* Gould), Ipswich; *m* 1964, Rose Constance Mary, *o d* of Stanley E. Gordon and late Audrey H. Gordon, Hooton, Wirral; two *s*. *Educ:* Cathedral Choir School and King's Sch., Canterbury; Magdalen Coll., Oxford; Cuddesdon Theol Coll. BA 1960, MA 1964; ARCM 1955. Deacon 1962, priest 1963. Asst Curate, Liverpool Parish Church, 1962-65; Vicar of St John, New Springs, Wigan, 1965-70; Precentor of Manchester Cath., 1970-74. *Publications:* contrib. Churchman. *Recreations:* gardening, piano. *Address:* 7 Little Cloister, Westminster Abbey, SW1P 3PL. T: 01-222 1386.

JOBERT, Michel; Officier de la Légion d'Honneur; Croix de Guerre (1939-45); Minister for Foreign Affairs, France, 1973-74; Founder, Mouvement des Démocrates, 1974; Editor, La Lettre de Michel Jobert, since 1974; *b* Meknès, Morocco, 11 Sept. 1921; *s* of Jules Jobert and Yvonne Babule; *m* Muriel Frances Green; one *s*. *Educ:* Lycée de Meknès; Dip. de l'Ecole libre des sciences politiques; Ecole nationale d'Administration. Cour des comptes: Auditor, 1949; Conseiller Référendaire, 1953. Member of Ministerial Cabinets: Finance, Work and Social Security, President of the Council, 1952-56; Director of the Cabinet of the High Commission of the Republic in French West Africa, 1956-58; Dir of Cabinet of Minister of State, 1959-61; Jt Dir, 1963-66, then Director, 1966-68, of the Prime Minister's Cabinet (Georges Pompidou); Pres., Council of Admin. of Nat. Office of Forests, 1966-73; Admin. of Havas, 1968-73; Secretary-Gen., Presidency of the Republic, 1969-73; Conseiller-maitre, Cour des comptes, 1971. *Publications:* Mémoires d'avenir, 1974; L'autre regard, 1975; Lettre ouverte aux femmes politiques, 1976; Parler aux Français, 1977. *Address:* 21 quai Alphonse-Le Gallo, 92100 Boulogne-sur-Seine, France.

JOBLING, Captain James Hobson, RN; Metropolitan Stipendiary Magistrate, since 1973; *b* 29 Sept. 1921; *s* of late Captain and Mrs J. S. Jobling, North Shields, Northumberland; *m* 1946, Cynthia, *o d* of late F. E. V. Lean, Beacon Park, Plymouth; one *s* one *d*. *Educ:* Tynemouth High Sch.; London Univ. (LLB Hons, 1971). Entered Royal Navy, 1940; awarded Gedge Medal and Prize, 1946; called to Bar, Inner Temple, 1955; Comdr, 1960; JSSC course, 1961-62; Dir, Nat. Liaison, SACLANT HQ, USA, 1962-65; Chief Naval Judge Advocate, in rank of Captain, 1969-72; retd, 1973. *Recreations:* gardening, walking. *Address:* Pinewell Lodge, Wood Road, Hindhead, Surrey. T: Hindhead 4426. *Club:* Naval and Military.

JOCELYN, family name of **Earl of Roden.**

JOCELYN, Viscount; Robert John Jocelyn; *b* 25 Aug. 1938; *e s* and *heir* of 9th Earl of Roden, *qv*; *m* 1970, Sara Caecilia, *d* of Brig. Hon. Andrew Dunlop, ID, DSO, Rhodesia, and Mrs Sheila Dunlop, London; one *d*. *Address:* The White House, Chaddleworth, Berks.

JOCELYN, Dr Henry David; Hulme Professor of Latin, University of Manchester, since 1973; *b* 22 Aug. 1933; *s* of late John Daniel Jocelyn and Phyllis Irene Burton; *m* 1958, Margaret Jill, *d* of Bert James Morton and Dulcie Marie Adams; two *s*. *Educ:* Canterbury Boys' High Sch.; Univ. of Sydney (BA); St John's Coll., Univ. of Cambridge (BA, PhD). Teaching Fellow in Latin, Univ. of Sydney, 1955; Scholar in Classics, British Sch. at Rome, 1957-59; Univ. of Sydney: Lectr in Latin, 1960-64; Sen. Lectr in Latin, 1964-66; Reader in Latin, 1966-70; Prof. of Latin, 1970-73. Visiting Lectr in Classics, Yale Univ., 1967; FAHA 1970. *Publications:* The Tragedies of Ennius, 1967 (corr. reprint 1969); (with B. P. Setchell) Regnier de Graaf on the Human Reproductive Organs, 1972; papers on Greek and Latin subjects in various periodicals. *Address:* 4 Clayton Avenue, Manchester M20 0BN. T: 061-434 1526.

JÖDAHL, Ole Erik, GCVO (Hon.) 1975; Swedish Ambassador to the Court of St James's, 1972-76; *b* 18 Nov. 1910; *s* of Oscar Jödahl and Elida Rapp; *m* 1934, Karin, *d* of Hadar Rissler and Signe Ouchterlony; two *s* one *d*. Journalist, editor and Foreign Affairs commentator in Swedish social democratic and co-operative periodicals and newspapers, 1933-45. Entered Swedish Foreign Service as Press Attaché, Helsinki, 1945, Moscow, 1945-48; Head, Foreign Min. Press and Information Dept, 1948-53; Envoy, Belgrade, 1953-56 (Mem. Neutral Nations Supervisory Commn Korea, 1954); Ambassador to Bonn, 1956-67; Sec.-Gen., Min. for Foreign Affairs, 1967-72. Grand Cross, Swedish Order of the North Star; Grand Cross, Order of Merit of Federal Republic of Germany; Grand Cross of Yugoslav Flag; Chevalier, French Legion of Honour, etc. *Publication:* contrib. The War 1939-45 (in Swedish), 1945-47. *Recreations:* mountain walking, reading. *Address:* Bastugatan 27, S-117 25 Stockholm, Sweden. *Club:* Travellers'.

JOEL, Hon. Sir Asher (Alexander), KBE 1974 (OBE 1956); Kt 1971; Member of Legislative Council of New South Wales since 1957; Company Director and Public Relations Consultant; *b* 4 May 1912; *s* of Harry and Phoebe Joel, London and Sydney; *m* 1st, 1937 (marr. diss. 1948); two *s*; 2nd, 1949, Sybil, *d* of Frederick Mitchell Jacobs; one *s* one *d*. *Educ:* Enmore Public Sch.; Cleveland Street High Sch., Sydney. Served War of 1939-45: AIF, 1942, transf. RAN; Lieut RANVR, 1943; RAN PRO staff Gen. MacArthur, 1944-45, New Guinea, Halmaheras, Philippines. Dir, Paynter & Dixon Industries Ltd; Man. Dir, Carpentaria Newspapers Pty Ltd; Chm., Mount Isa TV Pty Ltd; Dir, Sureguard Holdings Ltd; Nat. Pres., Anzac Mem. Forest in Israel; Dir, Royal North Shore Hosp. of Sydney, 1959-. Mem., Sydney Cttee (Hon. Dir, 1956-64); Hon. Dir and Organiser, Pageant of Nationhood (State welcome to the Queen), 1963; Exec. Mem., Citizens Welcoming Cttee visit Pres. Johnson, 1966; Chm., Citizens Cttee Captain Cook Bi-Centenary Celebrations, 1970; Dep. Chm., Citizens Welcoming Cttee visit Pope Paul VI to Australia, 1970; Chm., Sydney Opera Hse Official Opening Citizens Cttee, 1972; Dep. Chm., Aust. Govt Adv. Commn on US Bi-Centenary Celebrations, 1976. Fellow: Advertising Inst. of Austr. (Federal Patron); Public Relations Inst. of Austr.; Austr. Inst. Management; FInstD; Mem., Public Relations Soc. of America; Hon. Mem., Royal Australian Historical Soc., 1970; Mem., Sydney Opera House Trust. Hon.

Fellow, Internat. Coll. of Dentists, 1975. US Bronze Star, 1943; Ancient Order of Sikatuna (Philippines), 1975. *Recreations:* fishing, gardening. *Address:* 2 Ormiston Avenue, Gordon, NSW 2072, Australia. *T:* 4985913. *Clubs:* Australian Jockey, Sydney Turf, Tattersall's American, Imperial Service, Journalists, (Hon. Mem.) Australian Pioneers, Royal Agricultural Society (Sydney); Royal Sydney Yacht Squadron.

JOEL, Harry Joel; *b* 4 Sept. 1894; *o s* of Jack Barnato Joel, JP. *Educ:* Malvern Coll. Served European War 1914-18 with 15th Hussars. *Recreations:* racing and shooting. *Address:* 15 Grosvenor Square, W1; Sefton Lodge, Newmarket; Childwick Bury, St Albans, Herts. *Clubs:* Buck's; Jockey (Newmarket).

JOELSON, F(erdinand) Stephen; writer on African affairs since 1917; editor, author, broadcaster and publisher; *b* 3 Jan. 1893; *e s* of late George and Sarah Jane Joelson; *m* 1921, Florence Emily, *er d* of late William and Elizabeth Buchanan; one *d.* *Educ:* Cardiff High Sch.; privately, on Continent and in prisoner-of-war camps. Asst manager of rubber estate, E Africa, 1914; POW German E Africa, (Aug.) 1914-17; then Intelligence Officer, GHQ, Dar es Salaam; official interpreter in French, German and Swahili at mil. courts, and liaison officer with Belg. Mil. Mission, GHQ; invalided home; demobilised, 1920. Sec. to internat. businessman; resigned 1924 to found London weekly newspaper East Africa, renamed East Africa and Rhodesia, 1936, and Rhodesia and Eastern Africa, 1966, to mark sympathy with Rhodesian claim for independence. Actively edited journal throughout 43 years until Brit. Govt's imposition of sanctions compelled cessation of publication, 1967. Was Chm. East Africa, Ltd, and Africana, Ltd, which published the newspaper and many vols on Af. affairs. Also Chm., Gold Areas of East Africa, Ltd. Formerly: Gov., Commonwealth Inst.; Vice-Pres., Royal African Society (hon. life Mem. and medallist, 'for dedicated service to Africa'); Mem. Coun., Royal Commonwealth Soc.; Mem. Grand Council, Royal Over-Seas League, Chm. E African Gp; Mem. Cttee, Royal Commonwealth Soc. for the Blind; Mem. Overseas Cttee, Inst. of Journalists. Co-founder, with late L. S. Amery, Colonial League, formed to oppose German colonial claims. Rep. Govt of Tanganyika Territory on adv. cttee to E African Office in London, 1925-39; mem. London Cttee of Voice of Kenya throughout its existence. Twice Chm. E Africa Dinner Club, and mem. cttee 50 years. FJI; Founder Mem., Commonwealth Writers of Britain. Mem. Council, Anglo-Rhodesian Soc. *Publications:* Tanganyika Territory, 1920; Germany's Claims to Colonies, 1939; compiled Settlement in East Africa, 1927, Eastern Africa Today, 1928, Eastern Africa Today and Tomorrow, 1934, Rhodesia and Eastern Africa, 1958, etc. *Recreations:* reading, writing, book-collecting, travel, watching cricket, gardening, reflecting in a hot bath. *Address:* Westwood, Cotlands, Sidmouth, Devon. *T:* Sidmouth 4753. *Club:* Royal Commonwealth Society.

JOHANNESBURG, Bishop of, since 1974; **Rt. Rev. Timothy John Bavin;** *b* 17 Sept. 1935; *s* of Edward Sydney Durrance and Marjorie Gwendoline Bavin. *Educ:* Brighton Coll.; Worcester Coll., Oxford (2nd Cl. Theol., MA); Cuddesdon Coll. Curate, St Alban's Cathedral, Pretoria, 1961-64; Chaplain, St Alban's Coll., Pretoria, 1965-68; Curate of Uckfield, Sussex, 1969-71; Vicar of Good Shepherd, Brighton, 1971-73; Dean and Rector of Cathedral of St Mary the Virgin, Johannesburg, 1973-74. ChStJ 1975. *Recreations:* music, theatre, walking, gardening. *Address:* PO Box 1131, Johannesburg, Transvaal 2000, S Africa. *T:* 834-5181.

JOHANNESBURG, Assistant Bishop of; *see* Pickard, Rt Rev. S. C.

JOHANSON, Rev. Dr Brian; Minister of the City Temple, London, since 1976; *b* 8 March 1929; *s* of Bernard Johanson and Petra Johanson; *m* 1955, Marion Shirley Giles; one *s* two *d* . *Educ:* Univ. of South Africa (BA, DD); Univ. of London (BD). Parish Minister, S Africa, 1956-63; Sen. Lectr in Theology, 1964-69, Prof. of Theol., 1970-76, Univ. of SA; Vis. Res. Fellow: Princeton Theol Seminary, 1970; Univ. of Aberdeen, 1976. *Publications:* univ. pubns in S Africa; booklets; essays in collections; articles in theol jls. *Recreations:* wide-ranging interests incl. apiculture and cabinet making. *Address:* The City Temple, Holborn Viaduct, EC1. *T:* 01-583 5532.

JOHN, Arthur Walwyn, CBE 1967 (OBE 1945); FCA; Financial Consultant; Director: J. H. Sankey & Son Ltd, since 1965; Schroder Property Fund, since 1971; Stenhouse Holdings Ltd, since 1976; Chairman, Property Holding and Investment Trust Ltd, since 1976; *s* of Oliver Walwyn and Elsie Maud John; *m* 1949, Elizabeth Rosabelle, *yr d* of Ernest David and Elsie Winifred Williams; one *s* two *d.* *Educ:* Marlborough Coll. Mem. Institute of Chartered Accountants, 1934 (Mem. Council,

1965-). Asst to Commercial Manager (Collieries), Powell Duffryn Associated Collieries Ltd, 1936. Joined Army, 1939; served War of 1939-45: commissioned, 1940; War Office, 1941; DAQMG First Army, 1942, and HQ Allied Armies in Italy; AQMG Allied Forces HQ, 1944 (despatches, 1943, 1945). Chief Accountant, John Lewis & Co. Ltd, 1945; Dep. Dir-Gen. of Finance, National Coal Board, 1946; Dir-Gen. of Finance, 1955; Member, NCB, 1961-68; Chm., NCB Coal Products Divn, 1962-68. Dir, Unigate Ltd, 1969-75. Mem., Price Commn, 1976-. *Recreations:* golf, gardening. *Address:* Limber, Top Park, Gerrards Cross, Bucks SL9 7PW. *T:* Gerrards Cross 84811. *Club:* Army and Navy.

JOHN, Brynmor Thomas; MP (Lab) Pontypridd since 1970; Minister of State, Home Office, since 1976; *b* 18 April 1934; *s* of William Henry and Sarah Jane John; *m* 1960, Anne Pryce Hughes; one *s* one *d.* *Educ:* Pontypridd Boys' Grammar Sch.; University Coll., London. LLB Hons 1954. Articled, 1954; admitted Solicitor, 1957; National Service (Officer, Educn Br., RAF), 1958-60; practising Solicitor, Pontypridd, 1960-70. Parly Under-Sec. of State for Defence (RAF), MoD, 1974-76. *Recreation:* watching Rugby football. *Address:* House of Commons, SW1; Yale Haven, Church Village, Glam. *T:* Newtown Llantwit 2062.

JOHN, Admiral of the Fleet Sir Caspar, GCB 1960 (KCB 1956; CB 1952); Vice-President, Star and Garter Home, since 1973 (Chairman, 1967-72); First Sea Lord and Chief of Naval Staff, 1960-63; *b* 22 March 1903; *s* of late Augustus John, OM, RA; *m* 1944, Mary Vanderpump; one *s* two *d.* *Educ:* Royal Naval College, Dartmouth. Joined Royal Navy, 1916. Served War of 1939-45, Home and Mediterranean Fleets, Captain, 1941; Rear-Adm., 1951; Flag Officer, Commanding Third Aircraft Carrier Squadron and Heavy Squadron, 1951-52; Deputy Controller Aircraft, 1953-54; Vice-Adm. 1954; Flag Officer, Air, 1955-57; Admiral 1957; Vice-Chief of Naval Staff, 1957-60; Principal Naval ADC to the Queen, 1960-62; Admiral of the Fleet, 1962. Chm., Housing Corp., 1964-68; Mem., Govt Security Commn, 1964-73. *Address:* Weaver's Cottage, Dean Combe, Buckfastleigh, Devon TQ11 0LZ. *T:* Buckfastleigh 3424.

JOHN, David Dilwyn, CBE 1961; TD; DSc; Director, National Museum of Wales, Cardiff, 1948-68; *b* 20 Nov. 1901; *e s* of Thomas John, St Bride's Major, Glam; *m* 1929, Marjorie, *d* of J. W. Page, HMI, Wellington, Salop; one *s* one *d* *Educ:* Bridgend County Sch.; University Coll. of Wales, Aberystwyth. Zoologist on scientific staff, Discovery Investigations, engaged in oceanographical research in Antarctic waters, 1925-35; awarded Polar Medal. Appointed Asst Keeper in charge of Echinoderms at British Museum (Natural History), 1935; Deputy Keeper, 1948. Joined Territorial Army, 1936; promoted Major, RA, 1942. Hon. LLD Univ. of Wales, 1969. *Publications:* papers, chiefly on Echinoderms, in scientific journals. *Address:* 7 Cyncoed Avenue, Cardiff CF2 6ST. *T:* Cardiff 752499.

JOHN, DeWitt; Director, First Church of Christ, Scientist, Boston, since 1970; *b* 1 Aug. 1915; *s* of Frank in Howard John and Frances DeWitt; *m* 1942, Morley Marshall; one *s* one *d.* *Educ:* Principia Coll. (BA); University of Chicago (MA); Columbia (MS). Editorial Page Ed., St Petersburg (Fla) Times, 1938-39; Political Writer, Christian Science Monitor (Boston), 1939-42; US Navy, 1942-45 (Bronze Star); Editorial Staff, Christian Science Monitor, 1945-49; associated with Christian Science Cttee on Publication of First Church of Christ, Scientist, Boston, Mass, 1949-64 (Asst Man., 1954-62 ard Man. of Cttees on Publication, 1962-64); Editor, The Christian Science Monitor, 1964-70. Authorized teacher of Christian Science, 1964-. *Publication:* The Christian Science Way of Life, 1962. *Address:* Old Concord Road, Lincoln, Mass 01773, USA.

JOHN, Michael M.; *see* Morley-John, M.

JOHN, Robert Michael; HM Diplomatic Service; HM Ambassador to Panama, since 1974; *b* 7 May 1924; *s* of E. A. H. John; *m* 1952, Anne Phebe Clifford Smith; two *d.* *Educ:* Merchant Taylors' Sch., Sandy Lodge. Served Indian Army (9th Jat Regt), 1942-47. Entered HM Foreign (subseq. Diplomatic) Service, 1950; 2nd Sec., Comr-General's Office, Singapore, 1952-56; 1st Sec. (Commercial), British Embassy, Rio de Janeiro, 1956-60; FO, 1960-64; 1st Sec. (Commercial), subseq. Counsellor (Commercial), British Embassy, Warsaw, 1964-67; British Consul-General, Osaka, Japan, 1967-71; Rio de Janeiro: Minister (Commercial), 1971-72; Consul General and Dir of Trade Promotion, Brazil, 1972-74. *Recreations:* reading, gardening. *Address:* c/o Foreign and Commonwealth Office, SW1. *Club:* Travellers'.

JOHN, Sir Rupert (Godfrey), Kt 1971; Governor of St Vincent, 1970-76; Special Adviser, Commonwealth Development Corporation, since 1977; Member, Barclays Bank International Ltd Policy Advisory Committe (St Vincent), since 1977; Director, St Vincent Building and Loan Association, since 1977; Consultant, Metrocint General Insurance Co. Ltd (St Vincent), since 1977; *b* 19 May 1916; 2nd *s* of late Donelley John; *m* 1937, Hepsy, *d* of late Samuel Norris; three *s* one *d* (and one *s* decd). *Educ:* St Vincent Grammar Sch.; Univ. of London (BA, DipEd); Gray's Inn; New York University. First Asst Master, St Kitts/Nevis Grammar Sch., 1944; Asst Master, St Vincent Grammar Sch., 1944-52; private practice at Bar of St Vincent, 1952-58; Magistrate, Grenada, 1958-60; Actg Attorney-General, Grenada, 1960-62; Human Rights Officer, UN, 1962-69; Mem. Internat. Team of Observers, Nigeria, 1969-70; Senior Human Rights Officer, 1970. Has attended numerous internat. seminars and confs as officer of UN. KStJ 1971. *Publications:* St Vincent and its Constitution, 1971; papers in various jls. *Recreations:* cricket, walking, swimming. *Address:* PO Box 677, Cane Garden, St Vincent, West Indies. *Club:* Royal Commonwealth Society (West Indian).

JOHN CHARLES, Rt. Rev. Brother; *see* Vockler, Rt. Rev. J. C.

JOHNES, Herbert J. L.; *see* Lloyd-Johnes.

JOHNS, Alun Morris, MD, FRCOG; Hon. Consulting Gynæcological and Obstetric Surgeon, Queen Charlotte's Hospital, London; *m* 1927, Joyce, *d* of T. Willoughby, Carlton-in-Coverdale, Yorks; one *s* two *d. Educ:* Manchester Univ. MB, ChB 1923, MD Manchester (Commend) 1925; FRCOG 1947. Late Consulting Surgeon, Surbiton Hospital and Erith and Dartford Hospitals. Examiner Central Midwives Board; Fellow Royal Society of Medicine; Fellow Manchester Med. Soc.; Fellow Manchester Path. Soc. *Address:* Loosley Row, near Princes Risborough, Bucks. *T:* Princes Risborough 5298.

JOHNS, Glynis; actress; *b* Pretoria, South Africa, 5 Oct. 1923; *d* of Mervyn Johns and Alice Maude (*née* Steel-Payne); *m* 1st, Anthony Forwood (marr. diss.); one *s* ; 2nd, 1952, David Foster, DSO, DSC and Bar (marr. diss.); 3rd, 1960, Cecil Peter Lamont Henderson; 4th, 1964, Elliott Arnold. *Educ:* Clifton and Hampstead High Schs. First stage appearance in Buckie's Bears, Garrick Theatre, London, 1935. Parts include: Sonia in Judgement Day, Embassy and Strand, 1937; Miranda in Quiet Wedding, Wyndham's, 1938 and in Quiet Weekend, Wyndham's, 1941; Peter in Peter Pan, Cambridge Theatre, 1943; Fools Rush In, Fortune; The Way Things Go, Phœnix, 1950; The King's Mare, Garrick, 1966; Come as You Are, New, 1970; A Little Night Music, New York, 1973 (Tony award for best musical actress); Ring Round the Moon, Los Angeles, 1975; 13 Rue de l'Amour, Phœnix, 1976; Cause Célèbre, Her Majesty's, 1977. Entered films in 1937. *Films include:* Frieda, An Ideal Husband, Miranda, State Secret, No Highway, The Magic Box, Appointment with Venus, Encore, The Card, Sword and the Rose, Personal Affair, Rob Roy, The Weak and the Wicked, The Beachcomber, Mad About Men, Josephine and Men, The Court Jester, Loser Takes All, The Chapman Report, Mary Poppins. Also broadcasts; television programmes include: Mrs Amworth (USA); All You Need is Love; Across a Crowded Room. *Address:* c/o Clive Nicholas, 15 Berkeley Street, W1.

JOHNS, Peter Magrath; Secretary: Lawn Tennis Association, since 1973; All England Lawn Tennis Ground Ltd, since 1977; *b* 8 June 1914; *s* of late Robert Johns and Gladys Johns (*née* Booth); *m* 1949, Kathleen Joan Whitefield; two *s. Educ:* Mill Hill School. Served War of 1939-45; commnd 1940; demobilised 1946 (Captain). Asst Sec., LTA, 1955-73. *Recreations:* lawn tennis, real tennis. *Address:* 54 The Ridgeway, Friern Barnet, N11 3LJ. *T:* 01-368 4655. *Clubs:* All England Lawn Tennis, Old Millhillians, Queen's; Coolhurst Lawn Tennis, International Lawn Tennis Club of Great Britain.

JOHNSON; *see* Croom-Johnson.

JOHNSON, Alan Campbell; *see* Campbell-Johnson.

JOHNSON, Alan Woodworth, FRS 1965; MA, ScD, PhD, ARCS, DIC, FRIC; Professor of Chemistry and Hon. Director, Agricultural Research Council Unit of Invertebrate Chemistry and Physiology, University of Sussex, since 1968; Member, National Research Development Corporation, since 1976; *b* 29 Sept. 1917; *s* of late James William and Jean Johnson, Forest Hall, Newcastle upon Tyne; *m* 1941, Lucy Ida Celia (*née* Bennett); one *s* one *d. Educ:* Morpeth Grammar Sch., Northumberland; Rutherford Coll., Newcastle-upon-Tyne; Royal College of Science, London. Chemist, Swan, Hunter & Wigham Richardson, Ltd, 1934; Thos Hedley & Co. Ltd, 1935-

36; Royal Schol., Imperial Coll. of Science, 1937; BSc, ARCS; PhD, DIC 1940; Research Asst in Organic Chemistry, RCS, 1940-42; Research Chemist, ICI Dyestuffs Div., 1942-46; University of Cambridge: ICI Fellow, 1946-48; Asst Dir of Research in Organic Chemistry, 1948-53; Lecturer in Organic Chemistry, 1953-55; Sir Jesse Boot Prof. of Organic Chemistry and Head of Dept of Chemistry, University of Nottingham, 1955-68; Fellow and Steward, Christ's Coll., Cambridge, 1951-55. Member: ARC Adv. Cttee on Plants and Soils, 1966-71; SRC Chemistry Cttee, 1976; Enzyme Panel, 1976. Vis. Professor: University of Melbourne, 1960; University of Calif, Berkeley, 1962. Lectures: Tilden, Chemical Soc., 1953; Reilly, Univ. Notre Dame, Ind, USA, 1962; Simonsen, Chemical Soc., 1967; Pedler, Chemical Soc., 1974; Amer. Chem. Soc. W Coast Lectr, 1976. Member Council: Royal Society, 1966-67, 1971-73; Chemical Soc., 1955, 1957, 1970-; Hon. Sec. Chemical Society, 1958-65, Vice-Pres., 1965-68, Pres., 1977-78. Corday-Morgan Lecturer, India and Ceylon, 1963; Trustee, Uppingham Sch., 1961-66, 1970-. Fellow, Imperial Coll. of Science and Technology, 1972. Hon. DSc, Memorial Univ., Newfoundland. Meldola Medallist, RIC, 1946; first award for Synthetic Organic Chemistry, Chem. Soc., 1972. *Publications:* Chemistry of Acetylenic Compounds, Vol. I 1946, Vol. II 1950; numerous papers in chemical and biochemical journals. *Recreations:* tennis, philately. *Address:* School of Molecular Sciences, The University of Sussex, Falmer, Brighton, East Sussex. *T:* Brighton 66755.

JOHNSON, Anne Montgomrey; Matron, The Star and Garter Home for Disabled Sailors, Soldiers and Airmen, since 1975; *b* 12 June 1922; *y c* of late Frederick Harold Johnson and late Gertrude Le Quesne (*née* Martin). *Educ:* St John's, Bexhill-on-Sea; Queen Elizabeth Hosp. (SRN); Brompton Hosp. (BTA); Simpson Memorial Maternity Pavilion, Edinburgh (SCM). Asst Matron, Harefield Hosp., 1956-59; Dep. Matron, St Mary's Hosp., Paddington, 1959-62; Matron, Guy's Hosp., 1962-68; Mem. Directing and Tutorial Staff, King Edward's Hosp. Fund for London, 1968-71; Regional Dir, Help the Aged, 1971-73; Central Sec., Mothers' Union, 1973. Member: King's Fund Working Party, 'The Shape of Hospital Management 1980', 1966-67 (report publd 1967); Jt Cttee of Gen. Synod Working Party 'The Hospital Chaplain' (report publd 1974); Hosp. Chaplaincies Council, 1963-. *Recreations:* ornithology, straight theatre, travel. *Address:* Flat 2, Ancaster House, Richmond Hill, Richmond-on-Thames, Surrey TW10 6RR.

JOHNSON, Rev. Prof. Aubrey Rodway, PhD; Emeritus Professor of Semitic Languages, University College of South Wales and Monmouthshire, Cardiff; *b* Leamington Spa, 23 April 1901; *y s* of Frank Johnson, Baptist Minister, and Beatrice Mary Bebb; *m* 1947, Winifred Mary Rowley; two *d. Educ:* Newport (Mon) Intermediate Sch.; South Wales Baptist Coll., Cardiff; Universities of Wales (University Coll., Cardiff), London (King's Coll.), Oxford (University Coll.) and Halle-Wittenberg. PhD Wales, 1931; Fellow of the University of Wales, 1931-33; Asst Lecturer and subsequently Lecturer in Semitic Languages, University Coll. of South Wales and Mon, Cardiff, 1934-44, Prof., 1944-66. Dean, Faculty of Theology, University Coll., Cardiff, and Chm. of the Cardiff Sch. of Theology, 1944-65; Dean, Faculty of Theology, University of Wales, 1952-55. Haskell Lectr, Graduate Sch. of Theology, Oberlin, 1951. Pres., Soc. for Old Testament Study, 1956. FBA, 1951. Hon. DD Edinburgh, 1952; Hon. DTheol Marburg, 1963; Hon. teol dr Uppsala, 1968. Burkitt Medal of British Academy, 1961. *Publications:* The One and the Many in the Israelite Conception of God, 1942 (2nd edn, 1961); The Cultic Prophet in Ancient Israel, 1944 (2nd edn revised, 1962); The Vitality of the Individual in the Thought of Ancient Israel, 1949 (2nd edn revised, 1964); Sacral Kingship in Ancient Israel, 1955 (2nd edn revised, 1967); The Cultic Prophet and Israel's Psalmody, 1978. *Recreation:* gardening. *Address:* The Gate House, Alderley, Wotton-under-Edge, Gloucestershire. *T:* Wotton-under-Edge 2145.

JOHNSON, Carol Alfred, CBE 1951. Admitted a Solicitor, 1933 (Hons). Secretary of the Parliamentary Labour Party, 1943-59. MP (Lab) Lewisham S, Sept. 1959-Feb. 1974; Chairman: Britain and Italy Co-ordinating Cttee; History of Parliament Trust; Vice-Pres., Lab. Cttee for Europe; Member Standing Joint Cttee National Parks; Chm., Commons, Footpaths and Open Spaces Soc.; Mem. Council, National Trust; Trustee, William Morris Soc.; Governor, British Inst., Florence; Pres., Southern Region Ramblers Assoc. Comdr, Italian Order of Merit. *Address:* 19 Melior Court, Shepherds Hill, N6.

JOHNSON, Celia, (Mrs Peter Fleming), CBE 1958; Actress; *b* Richmond, Surrey, 18 Dec. 1908; *d* of John Robert Johnson, MRCS, LRCP, and Ethel Griffiths; *m* 1935, Peter Fleming (*d* 1971); one *s* two *d. Educ:* St Paul's Girls' Sch.; abroad. Studied at Royal Academy of Dramatic Art. First appearance on stage as Sarah in Major Barbara, Theatre Royal, Huddersfield, 1928; first London appearance as Currita in A Hundred Years Old, Lyric, Hammersmith; rôles include: Suzette in The Artist and the Shadow, Kingsway, 1930; Loveday Trevelyan in Debonair, Lyric, 1930; Elizabeth in The Circle, Vaudeville, 1931; Phyl in After All, Criterion, 1931. First New York appearance, as Ophelia in Hamlet, Broadhurst, 1931. Betty Findon in Ten Minute Alibi, Embassy and Haymarket, 1933; Anne Hargraves in The Wind and the Rain, St Martin's, 1933; Elizabeth Bennet in Pride and Prejudice, St James's, 1936; Mrs de Winter in Rebecca, Queen's, 1940; Jennifer in The Doctor's Dilemma, Haymarket, 1942; Olga in The Three Sisters, Aldwych, 1951; Laura Hammond in Its Never Too Late, Westminster, 1954; Sheila Broadbent in The Reluctant Debutante, Cambridge Theatre, 1955; Isobel Cherry in Flowering Cherry, Haymarket, 1957; Hilary in The Grass is Greener, St Martin's, 1958; Pamela Puffy-Picq in Chin-Chin, Wyndham's, 1960; Clare Elliot in The Tulip Tree, Haymarket, 1962; Helen Hampster in Out of the Crocodile, Phœnix, 1963; Aline in The Master Builder, National Theatre, 1964; Hay Fever, National Theatre, 1965, Duke of York's, 1968; The Cherry Orchard, Chichester Festival Theatre, 1966; Gertrude in Hamlet, Cambridge Theatre, 1971; The Kingfisher, Lyric, 1977. Played St Joan, Old Vic Season, 1948-49, and Viola on Italian tour with Old Vic, 1950. Has appeared in films, including: A Letter from Home; In Which We Serve; Dear Octopus; This Happy Breed; Brief Encounter; The Astonished Heart; I Believe in You; The Holly and the Ivy; The Captain's Paradise; A Kid for Two Farthings; The Good Companions; The Prime of Miss Jean Brodie. Address: Merrimoles House, Nettlebed, Oxon.

JOHNSON, Christopher Hollis, CBE 1958; DSc; PhD; Director, Explosives Research and Development Establishment, Waltham Abbey (Ministry of Aviation), 1959-64, retired; b Reading, Berks, 18 March 1904; s of Ernest G. and Agnes M. Johnson; m 1st, 1930, Irene Kathleen (née Gilbert) (d 1963), Farnham, Surrey; no c; 2nd, 1966, Mrs Vera G. Lester (widow); five step c. Educ: Reading Sch.; University Coll., London. BSc 1st Cl. Hons (Chemistry), 1925; PhD London, 1927; Ramsay Gold Medal, 1927; DSc London, 1940. Teaching Fellow, Univ. of California, Berkeley, 1927-29; Lectr in Physical Chemistry, Univ. of Bristol, 1930-37; Senior Lectr in Inorganic Chemistry, Univ. of Birmingham, 1937-41; Research Manager, Shell Petroleum Co., 1942-48. Min. of Supply, 1948-59: various posts, the last being: Director, Materials and Explosives Research, Shell-Mex House. Publications: contribs to Phil. Mag., Chemical Society, Faraday Society. Address: Foxwold, Silford Cross, Bideford, N Devon. T: Bideford 4232.

JOHNSON, Prof. David Hugh Nevil; Professor of International Law, Sydney University, since Jan. 1976; b 4 Jan. 1920; 2nd s of James Johnson and Gladys Mary (née Knight); m 1952, Evelyn Joan Fletcher. Educ: Winchester Coll.; Trinity Coll., Cambridge; Columbia Univ., New York. MA, LLB Cantab. Served Royal Corps of Signals, 1940-46. Called to Bar, Lincoln's Inn, 1950. Asst Legal Adviser, Foreign Office, 1950-53; Reader in Internat. Law, 1953-59, in Internat. and Air Law, 1959-60, Prof., 1960-Dec. 1975, Dean of Faculty of Laws, 1968-72, Univ. of London. Sen. Legal Officer, Office of Legal Affairs, UN, 1956-57. Registrar, the Court of Arbitration, Argentine-Chile Frontier Case, 1965-68. Publications: Rights in Air Space, 1965; articles in legal jls. Address: 91 Eastwood Avenue, Epping, NSW 2121, Australia.

JOHNSON, (Denis) Gordon, CBE 1969; Chairman, Geo. Bassett Holdings Ltd, since 1971 (Chairman and Managing Director, 1964-71); Chairman: Geo. Bassett & Co. Ltd, Sheffield, since 1955; W. R. Wilkinson & Co. Ltd, Pontefract, since 1961; N. V. de Faam, Holland, since 1964; Drakes Sweets Marketing Ltd, since 1966; Barratt & Co. Ltd, London, since 1968; b 8 Oct. 1911; s of late Percy Johnson; unmarried. Educ: Harrow; Hertford Coll., Oxford (MA). President: Cocoa, Chocolate and Confectionery Alliance, 1964-66; Confectioners' Benevolent Fund, 1967-68; Member: Food Manufacturing Economic Develt Cttee; Council of Confedn of British Industry; Yorks Electricity Bd; Council, Sheffield Univ.; Chm., S Yorks Industrialists' Council, 1976. Chm., Hallam Conservative Assoc., 1966-69, and 1973-76; Hon. Treas., City of Sheffield Conservative Fedn, 1969-73; Chm., Sheffield Cons. Assocs, 1976. Vis. Fellow, Sheffield Polytechnic. FBIM; Mem., Inst. of Directors. Publications: address to British Assoc. (Economics Section), 1964; contributor to: Business Growth (ed Edwards and Townsend), 1966; Pricing Strategy (ed Taylor and Wills), 1969. Recreations: philosophy, politics, economics; Pres., Sheffield and Hallamshire Lawn Tennis Club. Address: Geo. Bassett & Co. Ltd, PO Box 80, Sheffield S6 2AP. T: 349508; 5 Windsor Court, Bents Road, Sheffield S11 9RG. T: 367991; 7 Broadbent Street, W1. T: 01-629 1642. Club: Carlton.

JOHNSON, Dr Donald McIntosh, MA, MB, BCh Cambridge; MRCS, LRCP; Chairman and Managing Director of Johnson Publications Ltd; b 17 Feb. 1903; s of late Isaac Wellwood Johnson, Bury, Lancs, and Bertha Louise Hall; m 1st, 1928, Christiane Marthe Coussaert, Brussels; one s; 2nd, 1947, Betty Muriel Plaisted, Oxford; one s one d. Educ: Cheltenham Coll.; Gonville and Caius Coll., Cambridge; St Bartholomew's Hospital (Entrance Schol.). Qualified as doctor, 1926; barrister-at-law, 1930. Medical Officer, Cambridge University East Greenland Expedn, 1926; Casualty Officer, Metropolitan Hospital, 1926; House Physician, East London Hospital for Children, Shadwell, 1927; Medical Officer to Harrington Harbour Hosp., Internat. Grenfell Assoc., Labrador, 1928-29; General Practitioner, Thornton Heath, Croydon, 1930-37; a Demonstrator of Anatomy, Oxford Univ., 1937-39. Served War in RAMC (Capt. TA), 1939-45. Mem. Croydon Medical Board, Ministry of Labour and National Service, 1951-55; MP (C) Carlisle, 1955-63, (Independent C) 1963-64; first MP to raise parly debate on the Ombudsman. Publications: The End of Socialism, 1945; A Doctor Regrets, 1948; Bars and Barricades, 1952; Indian Hemp, a Social Menace, 1952; A Doctor Returns, 1956; A Doctor in Parliament, 1958; Welcome to Harmony, 1962; The British National Health Service: Friend or Frankenstein?, 1962; A Cassandra at Westminster, 1967; A Doctor Reflects, 1975. Recreations: golf, photography. Address: 55 Langley Park Road, Sutton, Surrey. T: 01-642 6530. Club: United Oxford & Cambridge University.

JOHNSON, Dorothy, CBE 1955; BA; HM Deputy Chief Inspector of Factories, Ministry of Labour, 1947-55, retired; b 20 Dec. 1890; e d of late Thomas and Emily Johnson. Educ: Leeds Univ. Health and Welfare Branch, Min. of Munitions, 1917-21; HM Inspector of Factories, Home Office, 1922; HM Superintending Inspector of Factories, 1942. Called to the Bar, Middle Temple, 1955. Address: Hylands Hotel, Filey, North Yorks.

JOHNSON, Prof. Douglas William John; Professor of French History, University College London, since 1968; b Edinburgh, 1 Feb. 1925; o s of John Thornburn Johnson and Christine Mair; m 1950, Madeleine Rébillard; one d. Educ: Royal Grammar Sch., Lancaster; Worcester Coll., Oxford (BA, BLitt); Ecole Normale Supérieure, Paris. Birmingham Univ.: Lectr in Modern History, 1949; Prof. of Modern History and Chm. of Sch. of History, 1963-68. Vis. Prof., Univs of Aix-en-Provence, Nancy, Paris, British Columbia, Toronto. Mem. Nat. Council, Historical Assoc.; Chm. Bd of Examrs in History, Univ. of London; Mem. CNAA. FRHistS. Publications: Guizot: Aspects of French History 1787-1874, 1963; France and the Dreyfus Affair, 1966; France, 1969; Concise History of France, 1970; The French Revolution, 1970; (General Editor) The Making of the Modern World. Recreations: music, French politics. Address: University College, Gower Street, WC1E 6BT; 29 Rudall Crescent, NW3 1RR.

JOHNSON, Eric Alfred George, CBE 1953; consulting engineer; Consultant to: Sir Murdoch MacDonald & Partners; Leonard & Partners. b 3 Sept. 1911; s of Ernest George Johnson and Amelia Rhoda Johnson; m 1936, Barbara Mary Robin; one d. Educ: Taunton's Sch., Southampton; UC Southampton. Grad. Engrg, 1931; joined A. P. I. Cotterell & Sons, 1932; served for periods with Great Ouse Catchment Board and Trent Catchment Board, 1933-37; joined Min. of Agriculture, 1937; Regional Engr, 1940; Dep. Chief Engr, 1945; Chief Engr, 1949, retired 1972. Has specialised in flood control and drainage engineering. Publications: papers in ICE and other professional jls. Recreations: travel, out-door life. Address: 94 Park Avenue, Orpington, Kent. T: Orpington 23802.

JOHNSON, Eric Seymour Thewlis, MC 1918; b 8 Sept. 1897; e s of Ernest Johnson, TD, MA, JP. Educ: Winchester; Royal Military College, Sandhurst. 2nd Lieut, 16th Lancers, 1916; Lieut 1918-20. Cattle ranching, British Columbia, 1923-30; trained race-horses under National Hunt Rules, in England, 1931-40. War of 1939-45: served with 51st Training Regiment, RAC, and RAC Depot; retired 1945, with rank of Major. MP (C) Blackley Division of Manchester, 1951-64. T: (club) 01-499 1261. Club: Cavalry and Guards.

JOHNSON, Prof. Francis Rea; Professor of Anatomy, London Hospital Medical College, since 1968; b 8 July 1921; s of Marcus Jervis Johnson and Elizabeth Johnson; m 1951, Ena Patricia Laverty; one s one d. Educ: Omagh Academy, N Ire.; Queen's Univ., Belfast. MB, BCh, BAO 1945, MD 1949. House appts, Belfast City Hosp., 1946; Demonstrator in Anatomy and Physiology, QUB, 1947-50; Lectr in Anatomy, Sheffield Univ., 1950-57; Reader in Anatomy, London Hosp. Med. Coll., 1957-64; Prof. of Histology, London Hosp. Med. Coll., 1964-68.

Publications: papers on histochemistry and ultrastructure of tissues and organs in various jls. *Recreations:* motoring, camping, gardening. *Address:* 11 Beacon Rise, Sevenoaks, Kent. *T:* Sevenoaks 53343.

JOHNSON, Air Vice-Marshal Frank Sidney Roland, CB 1973; OBE 1963; FBIM; Base Manager, British Aircraft Corporation RSAF, Khamis Mushayt, Saudi Arabia, since 1976; *b* 4 Aug. 1917; *s* of Major Harry Johnson, IA, and Georgina Marklew; *m* 1943, Evelyn Hunt; two *s. Educ:* Trinity County Secondary Sch., Wood Green. Enlisted, 1935; served in UK and India; commnd, 1943; Germany (Berlin Airlift), 1948; Western Union Defence Organisation, 1955-57; Directing Staff, RAF Staff Coll., 1958-60; comd 113 MU, RAF Nicosia, 1960-63; Chief Instructor Equipment and Secretarial Wing, RAF Coll. Cranwell, 1963-64; Dep. Dir MoD, 1965-66; idc 1967; Chief Supply Officer, Fighter and Strike Comds, 1968-70; Dir-Gen. of Supply, RAF, 1971-73; Supply Manager, BAC, Saudi Arabia, 1974-76. *Recreations:* golf, squash, hockey, cricket. *Address:* British Aircraft Corporation Ltd, PO Box 33, RSAF, Khamis Mushayt, Saudi Arabia; 9 Hazely, Tring, Herts. *T:* Tring 3266. *Club:* Royal Air Force.

JOHNSON, Maj.-Gen. Sir George Frederick, KCVO 1957; CB 1951; CBE 1949; DSO 1944; DL; *b* 28 Nov. 1903; *s* of F. P. and F. M. Johnson; *m* 1938, Lady Ida Ramsay, *d* of 14th Earl of Dalhousie; two *s* one *d. Educ:* Eton; King's Coll., Cambridge. Commissioned Scots Guards, 1925; psc 1935; GSO1 London District, 1939; served War of 1939-45; Comdr 3rd Bn Scots Guards, 1940; Comdr 201 Guards Brigade, Western Desert, 1942; Comdr 32 Guards Brigade, NW Europe, 1944-45; Lieut-Col commanding Scots Guards, 1944-47; Comdr 1st Guards Brigade, Palestine, 1947-48; Tripoli, 1948-49; Chief of Staff, Scottish Command, 1949-53; GOC, London District, 1953-57, retired. DL Cumberland, 1959; High Sheriff of Cumberland, 1966. *Recreations:* shooting, fishing, ornithology, entomology. *Address:* Castlesteads, Brampton, Cumbria. *T:* Brampton 2272. *Club:* Turf.

JOHNSON, Air Marshal George Owen, CB 1943; MC; retired 1947; *b* 24 Jan. 1896; *s* of late George Edward Johnson, Woodstock, Ontario, and late Mrs Johnson, Toronto 5, Ontario; *m* 1st, 1924, Jean Eleanor McKay (*d* 1968), Pembroke, Ont; two *d* ; 2nd, 1968, Sarah Jane Roberts, RRC. *Educ:* Woodstock, Ontario; RAF Staff Coll., Andover (1927); Imperial Defence Coll. (1937). Lieut, CSCI, Canada, 1913-16; RFC, and RAF 1917-19; Royal Canadian Air Force, 1920-47; AOC, Western Air Command, RCAF, Vancouver, BC, 1938-39; Deputy Chief of Air Staff, Ottawa, 1939-42; AOC, No 1 Training Command, RCAF, Toronto, 1942; AOC-in-C, Eastern Air Command, RCAF, Halifax, NS, 1943-45; AOC-in-C RCAF, Overseas, 1945-46. *Address:* 4675 Valley Drive, Apt 102, Vancouver, BC V6J 4B7, Canada.

JOHNSON, Gordon; *see* Johnson, D. G.

JOHNSON, H(arold) Daintree, MA, MD; MChir Cantab; FRCS; retired; Hon. Surgeon, Royal Free Hospital, 1947; Senior Lecturer in Surgery, Royal Postgraduate Medical School; lately Member of Court of Examiners, Royal College of Surgeons; Late Examiner in Surgery, University of London; *b* 26 May 1910; *s* of Sir Stanley Johnson, sometime MP, and Lady Johnson (*née* Edith Heather); *m* 1944, Margaret Dixon; one *s* (and one *s* decd). *Educ:* Westminster; Christ's Coll., Cambridge; St Thomas's Hospital. Leverhulme Scholarship in Surgical Research, RCS, 1948. Surgical Registrar, St Thomas's Hosp., 1941; Surg. First Asst, London Hosp., 1942; Surg. Specialist, 224 and 225 Parachute Field Ambs, 6th Airborne Div., RAMC, 1943-46; FRSM; Fellow, Assoc. of Surgeons of Gt Britain and Ireland; Mem., Brit. Soc. of Gastro-enterology; Corr. Mem., Surgical Research Soc. *Publications:* (ed) Surgical Aspects of Medicine, 1959; The Cardia and Hiatus Hernia, 1968; The Swollen Leg, 1975; chapters in: Techniques in British Surgery, 1950; Management of Abdominal Operations, 1953 and 1957; Operative Surgery, 1967; Surgery of the Stomach and Duodenum, 1969 (USA); papers on various surgical subjects in Brit. Med. J., Lancet, Brit. J. Surg., Gut, Gastroenterol. (USA), Surgery Gynæcology and Obstetrics (USA), Surgery (USA), American J. Surg. (USA), Annals of Surgery (USA), J. thorac. cardiovasc. Surg. (USA), etc; letters in Nature, Times and Guardian. *Recreations:* farming, research. *Address:* 5 Holly Terrace, Highgate Village, N6. *T:* 01-340 3050; Red House Farm, Sible Hedingham, Essex. *T:* Hedingham 201. *Club:* Elizabethan.

JOHNSON, Ven. Hayman; Archdeacon of Sheffield since 1963; a Canon Residentiary of Sheffield Cathedral, since 1975; Chaplain to HM The Queen since 1969; *b* 29 June 1912; *s* of late W. G.

Johnson, Exeter; *m* 1943, Margaret Louise Price; one *d. Educ:* Exeter Sch.; New Coll., Oxon. Chaplain, RAFVR, 1941-46; Chaplain and Vicar Temporal, Hornchurch, 1953-61; Examining Chaplain to Bishop of Sheffield, 1962. *Address:* 62 Kingfield Road, Sheffield S11 9AV. *T:* Sheffield 57782.

JOHNSON, Sir Henry (Cecil), KBE 1972 (CBE 1962); Kt 1968; Member, Greater London Regional Board, Lloyds Bank, since 1971; Chairman, MEPC Ltd, 1971-76; *b* 11 Sept. 1906; *s* of William Longland and Alice Mary Johnson, Lavendon, Bucks; *m* 1932, Evelyn Mary Morton; two *d. Educ:* Bedford Modern Sch. Traffic Apprentice L & NER, 1923-26; series of posts in Operating Dept; Asst Supt, Southern Area, L & NER, 1942; Chief Operating Supt of Eastern Region, BR, 1955; Asst Gen. Man., Eastern Region, Dec. 1955, Gen. Man., 1958; Gen. Man., London Midland Region, BR, 1962, Chm. and Gen. Man., 1963-67; Chm., BR Bd, 1968-71 (Vice-Chm., 1967). Dir, The Imperial Life Assurance Co. of Canada, 1972-. *Recreations:* golf, continuing interest in farming. *Address:* Rowans, Harewood Road, Chalfont St Giles, Bucks. *T:* Little Chalfont 2409. *Clubs:* MCC; Royal and Ancient (St Andrews).

JOHNSON, Henry Leslie, FTI; farmer; *b* 4 March 1904; *s* of Henry and Annie Letitia Johnson, formerly of Macclesfield, Cheshire; *m* 1939, Mabel Caroline Hawkins, Woking, Surrey; one *s* two *d. Educ:* Rugby. Joined Courtaulds Ltd, 1922; Dir, 1933-68; Managing Dir, 1935-47. Vice-Chm., Warwicks CC, 1974-75. Pres., Textile Institute, 1942 and 1943. Liveryman, Worshipful Co. of Farmers; Freeman, City of London, 1959. *Address:* Offchurch, Warwicks. *TA* and *T:* Leamington Spa 24293.

JOHNSON, Howard Sydney; solicitor; Director, Alliance Building Society, since 1970; *b* 25 Dec. 1911; *s* of Sydney Thomas Johnson; *m* 1939, Betty Frankiss, actress. *Educ:* Brighton; Highgate. Served War of 1939-45, Africa; invalided out as Major. Joined TA before the war. Mem. of Brighton Town Council, 1945-50. MP (C) Kemptown Div. of Brighton, 1950-Sept. 1959. *Address:* 2 Kelly Road, Hove, East Sussex. *T:* Brighton 504729; c/o Howard Johnson & McCabe, 37 East Street, Brighton BN1 1JD. *T:* Brighton 27173.

JOHNSON, Hugh Eric Allen; author and editor; *b* 10 March 1939; *s* of late Guy Francis Johnson, CBE and Grace Kittel; *m* 1965, Judith Eve Grinling; one *s* two *d. Educ:* Rugby Sch.; King's Coll., Cambridge (MA). Staff writer, Condé Nast publications, 1960-63; Editor, Wine & Food, and Sec., Wine and Food Soc., 1963-65; Wine Corresp., 1965-67, and Travel Editor, 1967, Sunday Times; Editor, Queen, 1968-70. Pres., Direct Sunday Times Wine Club, 1973-; Editorial Dir, Jl of RHS, 1975-. *Publications:* Wine, 1966 (rev. edn 1974); The World Atlas of Wine 1971, rev. edn 1977; The International Book of Trees, 1973; Hugh Johnson's Pocket Wine Book, 1977; articles on gastronomy, travel and gardening. *Recreations:* travelling, staying at home. *Address:* Saling Hall, Great Saling, Essex. *Club:* Garrick.

JOHNSON, James, BA, DPA; MP (Lab) Kingston upon Hull West since 1964; *b* 16 Sept. 1908; *s* of James and Mary Elizabeth Johnson; *m* 1937, Gladys Evelyn Green; one *d. Educ:* Duke's Sch., Alnwick; Leeds Univ. BA 1st Cl. Hons Geography, 1931; Diploma in Education, 1932; Diploma in Public Administration (London), 1944. FRGS. Schoolmaster: Queen Elizabeth Grammar Sch., Atherstone, 1931; Scarborough High Sch., 1934; Bablake Sch., Coventry, 1944. Lecturer, Coventry Tech. Coll., 1948-50. MP (Lab) Rugby Div. of Warwicks, 1950-59. Trade Union Advr, Kenya Local Govt Workers, 1959-60; Student Adviser, Republic of Liberia, 1960-64. Played soccer for British Univs and Corinthians. Grand Comdr Order of Star of Africa (Liberia), 1967. *Address:* 70 Home Park Road, SW19. *T:* 01-946 6224. *Clubs:* Royal Over-Seas League; Humber St Andrews Engineering Social and Recreation.

JOHNSON, Air Vice-Marshal James Edgar, (Johnnie Johnson), CB 1965; CBE 1960; DSO 1943 and Bars, 1943, 1944; DFC 1941 and Bar, 1942; DL; President, Johnnie Johnson Housing Trust, Ltd; Director of Companies in Canada, South Africa and UK; *m* Pauline Ingate; two *s. Educ:* Loughborough Sch.; Nottingham Univ. Civil Engr and Mem. of RAFVR until 1939; served with 616 Sqdn AAF, 1940-42; 610 Sqdn AAF, 1943; Wing Comdr Flying: Kenley, 1943; 127 Wing, 1944; Officer Comdg: 125 Wing (2nd TAF), 1944-45; 124 Wing (2nd TAF), 1945-46; RCAF Staff Coll., 1947-48; USAF (Exchange Officer), 1948-50; served Korea (with USAF), 1950-51; OC, RAF Wildenrath (2nd TAF), 1952-54; Air Ministry, 1954-57; Officer Commanding, RAF Cottesmore, Bomber Command, 1957-60; idc 1960; Senior Air Staff Officer, No 3 Group, Bomber Command, Mildenhall, Suffolk, 1960-63; AOC, Air Forces

Middle East, Aden, 1963-65; retired. DL Leicester, 1967. Order of Leopold, 1945, Croix de Guerre, 1945 (Belgium); Legion of Merit, 1950, DFC 1943, Air Medal, 1950 (USA). *Publications:* Wing Leader, 1956; Full Circle, 1964. *Recreations:* shooting, golf. *Address:* The Old Hall, Middle Hambleton, Oakham, Rutland LE15 8BG. *Club:* Royal Air Force.

JOHNSON, John Robin; His Honour Judge Johnson; a Circuit Judge, since 1973; *b* 27 Nov. 1927; *s* of Sir Philip Bulmer Johnson, Hexham, Northumberland; *m* 1958, Meriel Jean, *d* of H. B. Speke, Aydon, Corbridge; one *s* one *d. Educ:* Winchester; Trinity Coll., Cambridge. Called to Bar, Middle Temple, 1950. Dep. Chm., Northumberland QS, 1966-71; a Recorder of the Crown Court, 1972-73. *Address:* 60 Grainger Street, Newcastle upon Tyne NE1 5JP.

JOHNSON, John Rodney; HM Diplomatic Service; Counsellor, British High Commission, Lagos, since 1975; *b* 6 Sept. 1930; *s* of Edwin Done Johnson, OBE and Florence Mary (*née* Clough); *m* 1956, Jean Mary Lewis; three *s* one *d. Educ:* Manchester Grammar Sch.; Oxford Univ. (MA). HM Colonial Service, Kenya, 1955-64; Dist Comr, Thika, 1962-64; Administrator, Cttee of Vice-Chancellors and Principals of UK Univs, 1965; First Sec., FCO, 1966-69; Head of Chancery, British Embassy, Algiers, 1969-72; Dep. High Comr, British High Commn, Barbados, 1972-74. *Recreations:* climbing, reaching remote places, gardening. *Address:* British High Commission, Lagos, c/o Foreign and Commonwealth Office, SW1; Quantocks, Bachelors Way, Amersham, Bucks. *T:* Amersham 7324. *Clubs:* Travellers'; Climbers; Bridgetown (Barbados).

JOHNSON, Air Vice-Marshal Johnnie; *see* Johnson, James Edgar.

JOHNSON, Kenneth James, OBE 1966; Director, Dunlop Ltd, since 1975; *b* 8 Feb. 1926; *s* of Albert Percy Johnson and Winifred Florence (*née* Coole); *m* 1951, Margaret Teresa Bontoft Jenkins; three *s* two *d. Educ:* Rishworth School, near Halifax; Wadham Coll., Oxford; LSE; SOAS. Indian Army (14 Punjab Regt), 1945-47. Colonial Admin. Service, Nigeria, 1949-61, senior appts in Min. of Finance and Min. of Commerce and Industry; Head of Economic Dept, later Dir of Industrial Affairs, CBI, 1961-70; Courtaulds Ltd, 1970-73: Chm. and Man. Dir, various subsidiary cos. Dep. Chm., Pay Board, 1973-74. FRSA 1972; FIPM 1976. *Recreations:* reading, walking, bridge, music. *Address:* Woodgetters, Shipley, Horsham, West Sussex. *T:* Southwater 730481. *Clubs:* East India, Devonshire, Sports and Public Schools, Royal Commonwealth Society.

JOHNSON, Dame Monica; *see* Golding, Dame (Cecilie) Monica.

JOHNSON, Nevil; Nuffield Reader in the Comparative Study of Institutions, University of Oxford, and Professorial Fellow, Nuffield College, since 1969; *b* 6 Feb. 1929; *s* of G. E. Johnson and Doris Johnson, MBE, Darlington; *m* 1957, Ulla van Aubel; two *s. Educ:* Queen Elizabeth Grammar Sch., Darlington; University Coll., Oxford (BA PPE 1952, MA 1962). Army service, 1947-49. Admin. Cl. of Home Civil Service: Min. of Supply, 1952-57; Min. of Housing and Local Govt, 1957-62; Lectr in Politics, Univ. of Nottingham, 1962-66; Sen. Lectr in Politics, Univ. of Warwick, 1966-69. Chm. Board, Faculty of Social Studies, Oxford, 1976-78. Vis. Prof., Ruhr Univ. of Bochum, 1968-69. Mem. Exec. Council, Royal Inst. of Public Admin., 1965-. Hon. Editor, Public Administration, 1967-. *Publications:* Parliament and Administration: The Estimates Committee 1945-65, 1967; Government in the Federal Republic of Germany, 1973; In Search of the Constitution, 1977 (trans. German, 1977); articles in Public Admin, Political Studies, Parly Affairs, Ztschr. für Politik, Die Verwaltung, and Der Staat. *Recreations:* walking, swimming, gardening. *Address:* 50 Norman Avenue, Abingdon, Oxon OX14 2HL. *T:* Abingdon 20078.

JOHNSON, Pamela Hansford, (Rt. Hon. Lady Snow), CBE 1975; writer; *b* London, 29 May 1912; *d* of R. Kenneth and Amy Clotilda Johnson; *m* 1st, 1936, Gordon Stewart; one *s* one *d*; 2nd, 1950, (as Dr Charles Percy Snow), Baron Snow, *qv*; one *s. Educ:* Clapham County Secondary Sch. Mem. Société Européenne de Culture; Fellow of Center for Advanced Studies, Wesleyan Univ., Conn., 1961; FRSL. Fellow: Timothy Dwight Coll., Yale Univ.; Founders Coll., York Univ., Toronto. Hon. DLitt: Temple Univ., Philadelphia; York Univ., Toronto; Widener Coll., Chester, Pa; Hon. DHL Louisville, Kentucky. *Publications:* novels: This Bed Thy Centre, 1935; Too Dear For My Possessing, 1940; An Avenue of Stone, 1947; A Summer to Decide, 1948; Catherine Carter, 1952; An Impossible Marriage, 1954; The Last Resort, 1956; The Unspeakable Skipton, 1959; The Humbler Creation, 1959; An Error of Judgment, 1962;

Night and Silence Who is Here?, 1963; Cork Street, Next to the Hatter's, 1965; The Survival of the Fittest, 1968; The Honours Board, 1970; The Holiday Friend, 1972; The Good Listener, 1975; *criticism:* Thomas Wolfe, 1947; I. Compton-Burnett, 1953; *essays:* Important to Me, 1974; *plays:* Corinth House, 1948 (published 1954); Six Proust Reconstructions, 1958; *translation:* (with Kitty Black) Anouilh's The Rehearsal (Globe Theatre), 1961; *social criticism:* On Iniquity, 1967. *Address:* 85 Eaton Terrace, SW1.

JOHNSON, Patrick, OBE 1945; MA; *b* 24 May 1904; 2nd *s* of A. F. W. Johnson, JP, and F. E. L. Cocking; unmarried. *Educ:* RN Colls, Osborne and Dartmouth; Tonbridge Sch.; Magdalen Coll., Oxford. Fellow and Lecturer in Natural Science, Magdalen Coll., 1928-47, Dean, 1934-38, Vice-Pres., 1946-47. Flying Officer, RAFO, 1929-34; commissioned in RA (TA), 1938; served War of 1939-45, in Middle East and NW Europe, Lt-Col, Asst Dir of Scientific Research, 21st Army Group and comdg No. 2 operational research section. Dir of Studies, RAF Coll., Cranwell, 1947-52; Dean of Inst. of Armament Studies, India, 1952-55; Scientific Adviser to the Army Council, 1955-58; Asst Scientific Adviser, SHAPE, 1958-62; Head of Experimental Develt Unit, Educnl Foundn for Visual Aids, 1962-70. *Recreations:* rowing (rowed against Cambridge, 1927), sailing, shooting. *Clubs:* Reform; Leander.

JOHNSON, Paul (Bede); author; *b* 2 Nov. 1928; *s* of William Aloysius and Anne Johnson; *m* 1957, Marigold Hunt; three *s* one *d. Educ:* Stonyhurst; Magdalen Coll., Oxford. Asst Exec. Editor, Réalités, 1952-55; Editorial Staff, New Statesman, 1955, Dir, Statesman and Nation Publishing Co., 1965, Editor of the New Statesman, 1965-70. Mem., Royal Commn on the Press, 1974-77. *Publications:* The Suez War, 1957; Journey into Chaos, 1958; Left of Centre, 1960; Merrie England, 1964; Statesmen and Nations, 1971; The Offshore Islanders, 1972; (with G. Gale) The Highland Jaunt, 1973; Elizabeth I, 1974; A Place in History, 1974; Pope John XXIII, 1975 (Yorkshire Post Book of the Year Award, 1975); A History of Christianity, 1976; Enemies of Society, 1977. *Recreations:* mountaineering, painting. *Address:* Copthall, Iver, Bucks. *T:* Iver 653350.

JOHNSON, Sir Peter (Colpoys Paley), 7th Bt *cr* 1755; Director and Editor, Nautical Publishing Co. Ltd, since 1970; *b* 26 March 1930; *s* of Sir John Paley Johnson, 6th Bt, MBE, and of Carol, *d* of late Edmund Haas; *S* father, 1975; *m* 1st, 1956, Clare (marr. diss. 1973), *d* of Dr Nigel Bruce; one *s* two *d*; 2nd, 1973, Caroline Elisabeth, *d* of late Sir John Hocsoll, CB. *Educ:* Wellington Coll.; Royal Military Coll. of Science. Served RA, 1949; retired 1961, Captain. Director, Sea Sure Ltd, 1965-73. British Delegate, Internat. Offshore (Yachting) Council, 1970- (Chm. Internat. Technical Cttee, 1973-); Ocean Racing Correspondent, Yachting World, London, 1971-. *Publications:* Ocean Racing and Offshore Yachts, 1970, 2nd edn 1972; Boating Britain, 1973; Guinness Book of Yachting Facts and Feats, 1975. *Recreation:* sailing. *Heir: s* Colpoys Guy Johnson, *b* 13 Nov. 1965. *Address:* Dene End, Buckland Dene, Lymington, Hants SO4 9DT. *T:* Lymington 75921. *Clubs:* Royal Ocean Racing; Royal Southern Yacht (Hamble).

JOHNSON, Philip Cortelyou; architect, with own firm, since 1953; *b* Cleveland, Ohio, 8 July 1906; *s* of Homer H. Johnson and Louise Pope Johnson. *Educ:* Harvard (AB 1927, *cum laude*). Dir, Dept of Architecture, The Museum of Modern Art, New York, 1932-54, Trustee, 1958-; Graduate Sch. of Design, Harvard, 1940-43 (BArch). Has taught and lectured at: Yale Univ.; Cornell Univ.; Pratt Inst. (Dr Fine Arts, 1962). Mem. AIA (New York Chapter); Architectural League, NY. *Publications:* Machine Art, 1934; Mies van der Rohe, 1st edn 1947, 2nd edn 1953; (with Henry-Russell Hitchcock) The International Style, Architecture since 1922, 1932, new edn 1966; (with others) Modern Architects, 1932; Architecture 1949-65, 1966; contributor to Architectural Review. *Address:* (business) Philip Johnson, 375 Park Avenue, New York, NY 10022, USA. *T:* Plaza 1-7440; (home) Ponus Street, New Canaan, Conn. *T:* Woodward 6-0565. *Club:* Athenæum.

JOHNSON, Richard Stringer, CBE 1968 (MBE 1945); TD 1954; Chairman, North Thames Gas Board, 1964-70; *b* 18 Jan. 1907; *s* of Percy Harry and Josephine Johnson; *m* 1933, Isabel Alice, *d* of J. N. Hezlett, Coleraine, N Ireland; one *s* one *d. Educ:* Stationers' Company's Sch.; Gonville and Caius Coll., Cambridge. Admitted a Solicitor, 1930; joined Staff of Gas Light and Coke Company, 1935. Served War, RA (TA), 1939-45. Controller of Services, Gas Light and Coke Company, 1946; Dep. Chm., South Eastern Gas Board, 1949; Chm., East Midlands Gas Board, 1956-64. *Address:* Medbourne Manor, near Market Harborough, Leics. *T:* Medbourne Green 224. *Club:* United Oxford & Cambridge University.

JOHNSON, Robert Lionel; a Recorder of the Crown Court, since 1977; barrister-at-law; *b* 9 Feb. 1933; *er s* of Edward Harold Johnson, MSc, FRIC, and Ellen Lydiate Johnson, Cranleigh; *m* 1957, Linda Mary, *er d* of late Charles William Bennie and Ena Ethel Bennie, Egglescliffe; one *s* two *d*. *Educ:* Watford Grammar Sch. (1940-51); London Sch. of Econs and Polit. Science. 5th Royal Inniskilling Dragoon Guards, 1955-57, Captain; ADC to GOC-in-C Northern Comd, 1956-57; Inns of Court Regt, 1957-64. Called to the Bar, Gray's Inn, 1957; Jun. Counsel to Treasury in Probate Matters, 1975-. Legal Assessor, GNC, 1977-. Trustee: (and Founder Mem.) Council, Cystic Fibrosis Res. Trust, 1964-; Robert Luff Charitable Foundn, 1977-. *Publications:* (with James Comyn) Wills & Intestacies, 1970; Contract, 1975; (with Malcolm Stitcher) Atkin's Trade, Labour and Employment, 1975. *Recreations:* charitable work, gardening. *Address:* Queen Elizabeth Building, Temple, EC4Y 9BS. *T:* 01-583 7837; 18 Scarsdale Villas, W8 6PR. *T:* 01-937 5361; Forest Gate, Pluckley, Kent. *T:* Bethersden 370; Quinta da Saudade, Albufeira, Portugal. *T:* 010 351.82.56182.

JOHNSON, Robert White, CBE 1962; Director, Cammell Laird & Co. Ltd, 1946-70; Chairman: Cammell Laird & Co. (Shipbuilders and Engineers) Ltd, 1957-68; Cammell Laird (Shiprepairers) Ltd, 1963-68; *b* 16 May 1912; *s* of late Sir Robert (Stewart) Johnson, OBE; *m* 1950, Jill Margaret Preston; two *s* one *d*. *Educ:* Rossall Sch. Robt Bradford & Co. Ltd (Insurance Brokers), 1931-35. Served War of 1939-45, Provost Marshal's Dept, RAF, becoming Wing Comdr. Director: Patent Shaft & Axletree Co. Ltd, Wednesbury, Staffs, 1946-51; Metropolitan-Cammell Carriage and Wagon Co. Ltd, Birmingham, 1946-64; English Steel Corp. Ltd, Sheffield, 1949-51 and 1954-; North Western Line (Mersey) Ltd, 1964-70; Bradley Shipping Ltd, 1964-70; formerly Dir, Scottish Aviation Ltd; Coast Lines Ltd; Chm. of North West Tugs Ltd, Liverpool, 1951-66; Mem. Mersey Docks and Harbour Board, 1948-70; Pt-time Mem. Merseyside and North Wales Electricity Board, 1956-66; Chm., Merseyside Chamber of Commerce and Industry, 1972-74. Underwriting Mem., Lloyd's, 1937-. Pres., Shipbuilding Employers' Federation, 1958-59. *Recreations:* fishing, shooting, golf. *Address:* The Oaks, Well Lane, Heswall, Wirral, Merseyside L60 8NE. *T:* 051-342 3304.

JOHNSON, Sir Ronald (Ernest Charles), Kt 1970; CB 1962; JP; Secretary of Commissions for Scotland; Chairman, Civil Service Savings Committee for Scotland; *b* 3 May 1913; *o c* of Ernest and Amelia Johnson; *m* 1938, Elizabeth Gladys Nuttall; two *s* (and one *s* decd). *Educ:* Portsmouth Grammar Sch.; St John's Coll., Cambridge. Entered Scottish Office, 1935; Sec., Scottish Home and Health Dept, 1963-72. Chm., Scottish Hosp. Centre, 1964-72. Mem., Scottish Records Adv. Council; Chm., Fire Service Res. and Training Trust. Served RNVR on intelligence staff of C-in-C, Eastern Fleet, 1944-45. Pres., Edinburgh Bach Soc. JP Edinburgh, 1972. *Recreation:* church organ. *Address:* 14 Eglinton Crescent, Edinburgh EH12 5DD. *T:* 031-337 7733. *Club:* New (Edinburgh).

JOHNSON, Stanley, CBE 1970; FCA; FCIT; Managing Director, British Transport Docks Board, 1967-75; *b* 10 Nov. 1912; *s* of late Robert and Janet Mary Johnson; *m* 1940, Sheila McLean Bald; two *s* two *d*. *Educ:* King George V Sch., Southport. Served as Lieut (S) RINVR, 1942-45. Joined Singapore Harbour Board, 1939; Asst Gen. Man. 1952; Chm. and Gen. Man. 1958-59; Chief Docks Man., Hull Docks, 1962; Asst Gen. Man. 1963, Mem. and Dep. Man. Dir 1966, British Transport Docks Board. Chm. Major Ports Cttee, Dock and Harbour Authorities Assoc., 1971-72. Mem., Exec. Council, British Ports Assoc., 1973-75; Vice-Pres., Internat. Assoc. of Ports and Harbours, 1975. Vice-Pres., CIT, 1973-75. *Recreations:* walking, reading, travel. *Address:* The Red House, Bearswood End, Beaconsfield, Bucks. *T:* Beaconsfield 3440. *Club:* Naval and Military.

JOHNSON, Stanley Patrick; Head of Prevention of Pollution and Nuisances Division, Commission of the European Communities, since 1973; *b* 18 Aug. 1940; *s* of Wilfred Johnson and Irène (*née* Williams); *m* 1963, Charlotte Offlow Fawcett; three *s* one *d*. *Educ:* Sherborne Sch.; Exeter Coll., Oxford (Trevelyan Schol., Sen. Classics Schol.); Harkness Fellow, USA, 1963-64. MA Oxon 1963; Dip. Agric. Econs Oxon 1964. World Bank, Washington, 1966-68; Project Dir, UNA-USA Nat. Policy Panel on World Population, 1968-69; Mem. Conservative Research Dept, 1969-70; Staff of Internat. Planned Parenthood Fedn, London, 1971-73; Consultant to UN Fund for Population Activities, 1971-73; Mem. Countryside Commn, 1971-73. Newdigate Prize for Poetry, 1962. *Publications:* Life Without Birth, 1970; The Green Revolution, 1972; The Politics of the Environment, 1973; (ed) The Population Problem, 1973; *novels:* Gold Drain, 1967; Panther Jones for President, 1968; God Bless America, 1974. *Recreations:* writing, travel. *Address:* 37 Avenue de la Sapinière, Brussels 1180, Belgium; 174 Regents Park Road, NW1. *T:* 01-722 4022; Nethercote, Winsford, Minehead, Somerset. *T:* Exford 379. *Clubs:* Carlton, Savile.

JOHNSON, Sir Victor Philipse Hill, 6th Bt, *cr* 1818; *b* 7 May 1905; *s* of Hugh Walters Beaumont Johnson, Kingsmead, Windsor Forest, and Winifred Mena Johnson (*née* Hill, now W. M. Livingstone), Fern Lea, Southampton; *S* cousin, Sir Henry Allen Beaumont Johnson, 5th Bt, 1965; unmarried. *Educ:* Cheltenham Coll. Ranched in BC, Canada, 1926-38. Served with RAF, 1939-45. *Recreations:* gardening, playing at golf. *Heir:* kinsman Cyril Martin Hugh Johnson, *b* (posthumously) 15 Jan. 1905. *Address:* Beach House, 64 Sea Lane, Goring-by-Sea, Worthing, West Sussex. *T:* Worthing 43630.

JOHNSON, Walter Hamlet; MP (Lab) Derby South since 1970; *b* Hertford, 21 Nov. 1917; *s* of John Johnson; *m* 1945. *Educ:* Devon House Sch., Margate. Councillor, Brentford and Chiswick for 6 years. Nat. Treasurer, Transport Salaried Staffs' Assoc., 1965-. Joined Labour Party, 1945. Contested (Lab) Bristol West, 1955 and South Bedfordshire, 1959, in General Elections; also Acton (Lab), 1968, in by-election. An Assistant Govt Whip, 1974-75. Is particularly interested in welfare services, transport and labour relations. A Senior Executive, Staff Training, London Transport. Nat. Treasurer, Nat. Fedn of Professional Workers, 1965-; Pres., Transport Salaried Staffs' Assoc., 1977-. Governor, Ruskin Coll., Oxford, 1966-. *Recreation:* sport. *Address:* House of Commons, SW1; 10 Melton Street, NW1. *T:* 01-387 2101.

JOHNSON, Prof. William, DSc Manchester, MA Cantab; CEng, FIMechE; Professor of Mechanics, Cambridge University, since 1975; Professorial Fellow, Fitzwilliam College, Cambridge, since 1975; *b* 20 April 1922; *er s* of James and Elizabeth Johnson; *m* 1946, Heather Marie (*née* Thornber); three *s* two *d*. *Educ:* Central Grammar Sch., Manchester; Manchester Coll. of Science and Technology (BScTech); BSc London. Served War, Lt REME, UK and Italy, 1943-47. Asst Principal, Administrative Grade, Home Civil Service, 1948-50; Lecturer, Northampton Polytechnic, London, 1950-52; Lectr in Engineering, Sheffield Univ., 1952-56; Senior Lectr in Mechanical Engineering, Manchester Univ., 1956-60; Prof. of Mechanical Engrg, 1960-75, Chm. of Dept of Mechanical Engrg, 1960-69, 1971-73, Dir of Medical Engrg, 1973-75, UMIST. Hon. Sec., Yorks Br. of IMechE, 1953-56 (Chm., NW Br., 1974-75). Founder, and Editor, Internat. Jl Mech. Sciences, 1960-. Hon. DTech Bradford, 1976. T. Constantine Medal, Manchester Soc. of Engrs, 1962; Bernard Hall Prize (jt), IMechE, 1965-66 and 1966-67; James Clayton Fund Prize (jt), IMechE, 1972. *Publications:* Plasticity for Mechanical Engineers (with P. B. Mellor), 1962; Mechanics of Metal Extrusion (with H. Kudo), 1962; Slip Line Fields: Theory and Bibliography (with R. Sowerby and J. B. Haddow), 1970; Impact Strength of Materials, 1972; Engineering Plasticity (with P. B. Mellor), 1973; Lectures in Engineering Plasticity (with A. G. Mamalis), 1976; papers in mechanics of solids, metal forming and impact engineering. *Recreation:* landscape gardening. *Address:* Engineering Department, University of Cambridge, Cambridge CB2 1QA.

JOHNSON, His Honour Judge William; County Court Judge for County Tyrone since 1947; *b* 1 April 1903; *s* of late William Johnson CBE and Ellen Johnson. *Educ:* Portora Royal Sch., Enniskillen; Trinity Coll., Dublin; King's Inns, Dublin (Certif. of Honour). LLB (1st cl.) and BA (Sen. Mod. Legal and Polit. Sci.) TCD. Called to Irish Bar and Bar of N Ireland, 1924. Served War of 1939-45 (despatches); ADJAG, Actg Lt-Col. Lectr in Law, QUB, 1933-36; Chm. Court of Referees 1928-30, Dep. Umpire 1930-35, Umpire 1935-47, NI Unemployment Insce and Pensions Acts; QC (Northern Ireland) 1946; Sen. Crown Prosecutor, Co. Antrim, 1947. Chairman: Cttee on Law of Intestate Succession in NI, 1951; Cttee on Law of Family Provision in NI, 1953; Cttee on Examns for Secondary Intermediate Schs in NI, 1958; Vice-Chm., Jt Cttee on Civil and Criminal Jurisdictions in NI, 1971; Chief Comr for NI, Boy Scouts Assocs, 1955-65. *Recreations:* reading, walking, scouting. *Address:* 69 Somerton Road, Belfast. *Club:* Tyrone County (Omagh).

JOHNSON, Sir William Clarence, Kt 1957; CMG 1952; CBE 1945 (OBE 1939); HM Chief Inspector of Constabulary for England and Wales, 1962-63, retired; *b* 8 May 1899; *m* 1918, Louisa Mary Humphreys; no *c*. *Educ:* Willowfield, Eastbourne. RE, 1914-19; joined Police Service at Portsmouth in 1920 and served in various ranks until 1932 when as Superintendent CID was appointed Chief Constable of Plymouth; Asst Chief Constable of Birmingham, 1936; Chief Constable of

Birmingham, 1941-45; one of HM Inspectors of Constabulary, 1945-62; Inspector-Gen. of Colonial Police, 1948-51. Chm., Police Salaries Commission, Malta, 1960. *Address:* 114 Willingdon Park Drive, Hampden Park, Eastbourne, East Sussex. *T:* Eastbourne 51536.

JOHNSON, William Harold Barrett; Commissioner of Inland Revenue, 1965-76; *b* 16 May 1916; *s* of late William Harold Johnson and Mary Ellen (*née* Barrett); *m* 1940, Susan Gwendolen, *d* of Rev. H. H. Symonds; one *s* one *d. Educ:* Charterhouse; Magdalene Coll., Cambridge. Served in Royal Artillery, 1939-45. Entered Inland Revenue Dept, 1945. Vice-Pres., Cruising Assoc., 1974-77. *Recreations:* cruising under sail, gardening. *Address:* 45 Granville Park, Lewisham, SE13.

JOHNSON-FERGUSON, Sir Neil (Edward), 3rd Bt, *cr* 1906; TD; Lt-Col Royal Corps of Signals; Vice-Lieutenant, Dumfriesshire, since 1965; *b* 2 May 1905; *s* of Sir Edward Alexander James Johnson-Ferguson, 2nd Bt, and Hon. Elsie Dorothea McLaren (*d* 1973), *d* of 1st Baron Aberconway; *S* father 1953; *m* 1931, Sheila Marion, *er d* of late Col H. S. Jervis, MC; four *s. Educ:* Winchester; Trinity Coll., Cambridge (BA). Capt. Lanarks Yeomanry, TA, 1928; Major 1937; Major, Royal Signals, 1939; Lt-Col 1945. JP 1954, DL 1957, Dumfriesshire. American Legion of Merit. *Heir: s* Ian Edward Johnson-Ferguson [*b* 1 Feb. 1932; *m* 1964, Rosemary Teresa, *d* of C. J. Whitehead, The Old House, Crockham Hill, Kent; three *s*]. *Address:* Fairyknowe, Eaglesfield, Dumfriesshire.

JOHNSON-MARSHALL, Percy Edwin Alan, CMG 1975; RIBA; FRTPI; Professor of Urban Design and Regional Planning, University of Edinburgh, since 1964; Head of New Department of Urban Design and Regional Planning, since 1967; in practice as planning consultant since 1960; *b* 20 Jan. 1915; *s* of Felix William Norman Johnson-Marshall and Kate Jane Little; *m* 1944, April Bridger; three *s* four *d. Educ:* Liverpool Univ. Sch. of Architecture; Dip. in Arch.(Dist) (RIBA) RTPI; (RIBA) DisTP; MA (Edin). Planning Architect, Coventry, 1938-41; Served War: with Royal Engrs (India and Burma), 1942-46. Asst Regional Planner, Min. of Town and Country Planning, 1946-49; Gp Planning Officer, in charge of reconstr. areas gp, LCC, 1949-59 (Projects incl.: Lansbury and Stepney/Poplar South Bank, (jtly with City Corp.) Barbican Area, Tower Hill area, etc). Apptd Sen. Lectr, Dept of Architecture, Univ. of Edinburgh, 1959. Director: Architectural Research Unit, 1961-64; Planning Research Unit, 1962. Consultant on Human Settlements for UN Stockholm Conf. on Environment, 1972. Principal of Planning Consultancy, Percy Johnson-Marshall and Associates (Projects incl. Edin. Univ. Plan, Kilmarnock and Bathgate Town Centres, Porto Regional Plan, etc). *Publications:* Rebuilding Cities, 1966; contribs to technical jls. *Address:* Bella Vista, Duddingston Village, Edinburgh EH15 3PZ. *T:* 031-661 2019.
See also Sir S. A. W. Johnson-Marshall.

JOHNSON-MARSHALL, Sir Stirrat Andrew William, Kt 1971; CBE 1954; BArch, FRIBA; architect and industrial designer; partnership: Robert Matthew, Johnson-Marshall & Partners, 1956 (Architects for York and Bath Universities, etc.); *b* 1912; *s* of Felix William Norman Johnson-Marshall and Kate Jane Little; *m* 1937, Joan Mary Brighouse; two *s* one *d. Educ:* Liverpool Univ. Sch. of Architecture (BArch, 1st Cl. Hons). Served War of 1939-45: Royal Engineers. Dep. County Architect, Herts, 1945-48; Chief Architect, Min. of Education, 1948-56. Formerly: Mem. Council, RIBA; Part-time Dir, National Building Agency. Ex-Mem., Medical Research Council. *Publications:* papers to Building Research Congress, 1951, National Union of Teachers, 1951, British Architects Conference, 1953. *Recreation:* fishing. *Address:* 42/46 Weymouth Street, W1; 16 Great George Street, Bristol; Curtis Mill, Lower Kilcot, Glos.
See also P. E. A. Johnson-Marshall.

JOHNSON SMITH, Geoffrey; MP (C) East Grinstead since Feb. 1965; *b* 16 April 1924; *s* of J. Johnson Smith; *m* Jeanne Pomeroy, MD; two *s* one *d. Educ:* Charterhouse; Lincoln Coll., Oxford. Served War of 1939-45: Royal Artillery, 1942-47; Temp. Capt. RA, 1946. BA Hons, Politics, Philosophy and Economics, Oxford, 1949. Mem., Oxford Union Soc. Debating Team, USA, 1949. Information Officer, British Information Services, San Francisco, 1950-52; Mem. Production Staff, Current Affairs Unit, BBC TV, 1953-54; London County Councillor, 1955-58; Interviewer, Reporter, BBC TV, 1955-59. MP (C) Holborn and St Pancras South, 1959-64; PPS, Board of Trade and Min. of Pensions, 1960-63; Opposition Whip, 1965; Parly Under-Sec. of State for Defence for the Army, MoD, 1971-72; Parly Sec., CSD, 1972-74. A Vice-Chm., Conservative Party, 1965-71. Mem., IBA Gen. Adv. Council, 1975-. *Address:* House of Commons, SW1. *Club:* Travellers'.

JOHNSTON; *see* Lawson Johnston.

JOHNSTON, Hon. Lord; Douglas Harold Johnston, TD; a Senator of the College of Justice in Scotland since 1961; *b* 1907; *s* of late Joseph Johnston, Advocate, Aberdeen; *m* 1936, Doris Isobel, *d* of late James Kidd, MP; two *s* two *d. Educ:* Aberdeen Grammar Sch.; St John's Coll., Oxford; Edinburgh Univ. Called to Bar, Inner Temple, 1931; Scottish Bar, 1932; Advocate-Depute, 1945; QC (Scot.) 1947; Solicitor-Gen. for Scotland, 1947-51. MP (Lab) Paisley, 1948-61. Chm., Royal Fine Art Commission for Scotland, 1965-. Served War of 1939-45. Hon. FRIAS. *Address:* Dunosdale, Barnton, Edinburgh. *T:* 031-336 3102.

JOHNSTON, Alastair McPherson; *see* Dunpark, Hon. Lord.

JOHNSTON, Sir Alexander, GCB 1962 (CB 1946); KBE 1953; Deputy Chairman, Panel on Take-overs and Mergers, since 1970; *b* 27 Aug. 1905; *s* of Alexander Simpson Johnston and Joan Macdiarmid; *m* 1947, Betty Joan Johnston, *qv*; one *s* one *d. Educ:* George Heriot's Sch.; University of Edinburgh. Entered Home Office, 1928; Principal Asst Sec., Office of the Minister of Reconstruction, 1943-45; Under-Sec., Office of Lord Pres. of the Council, 1946-48; Dep. Sec. of the Cabinet, 1948-51; Third Sec., HM Treasury, 1951-58; Chm., Bd of Inland Revenue, 1958-68. Dep. Chm., Monopolies and Mergers Commn, 1969-76. Hon. DSc(Econ) London, 1977. *Address:* 18 Mallord Street, SW3. *T:* 01-352 6840. *Club:* Reform.

JOHNSTON, Most Rev. Allen Howard; *see* New Zealand, Primate and Archbishop of.

JOHNSTON, Betty Joan, (Lady Johnston), JP; Chairman, Girls' Public Day School Trust, since 1975; Deputy Parliamentary Counsel, Law Commission, since 1975; *d* of Edward and Catherine Anne Harris; *m* 1947, Sir Alexander Johnston, *qv*; one *s* one *d. Educ:* Cheltenham Ladies' Coll.; St Hugh's Coll., Oxford (1st Cl. Hons Jurisprudence). Called to Bar, Gray's Inn, 1940 (Certificate of Honour, Arden and Lord Justice Holker scholar). Parly Counsel Office, 1942-52. Vice-Chm., Direct Grant Schs Jt Cttee, 1975-; Dep. Chm., Assoc. of Governing Bodies of Girls Public Schools, 1977-; Member: Council, Queen's Coll., London; Council, Francis Holland Schs. JP Inner London 1966. *Address:* 18 Mallord Street, SW3. *T:* 01-352 6840.

JOHNSTON, Brian (Alexander), MC 1945; freelance broadcaster and commentator; *b* 24 June 1912; *s* of Lt-Col C. E. Johnston, DSO, MC; *m* 1948, Pauline, *d* of late Col William Tozer, CBE, TD; three *s* two *d. Educ:* Eton; New Coll., Oxford (BA). Family coffee business, 1934-39. Served War of 1939-45: in Grenadier Guards; in 2nd Bn throughout, taking part in Normandy Campaign, advance into Brussels, Nijmegen Bridge and Crossing of Rhine into Germany. Joined BBC, 1945, retired 1972; specialises in cricket commentary for TV and radio (BBC Cricket Corresp., 1963-72), interviews, ceremonial commentary (*eg* Funeral of King George VI, 1952; Coronation of Queen Elizabeth II, 1953; Wedding of Princess Margaret, 1960); Let's Go Somewhere feature in In Town Tonight, Down Your Way, Twenty Questions, etc. *Publications:* Let's Go Somewhere, 1952; Armchair Cricket, 1957; Stumped for a Tale, 1965; The Wit of Cricket, 1968; All About Cricket, 1972; It's Been a Lot of Fun, 1974. *Recreations:* cricket, golf, theatre and reading newspapers. *Address:* 98 Hamilton Terrace, NW8. *T:* 01-286 2991. *Clubs:* MCC, Cavalry and Guards.

JOHNSTON, Sir Charles (Collier), Kt 1973; TD; Chairman, Standex International Ltd (a wholly owned subsidiary of Standex International Corporation, USA); *b* 4 March 1915; *e s* of late Captain Charles Moore Johnston and Muriel Florence Mellon; *m* 1939, Audrey Boyes Monk, LLB; two *s. Educ:* Tonbridge Sch., Kent. Served War: HM Forces, Territorial, commissioned 1938; served throughout war, in RA, retd, 1946, rank Major. Managing Dir, 1948, Chm., 1951, and Managing Dir, 1951-76, of Standex International Ltd (formerly Roehlen-Martin Ltd), Engravers, of Ashton Road, Bredbury, Cheshire. Chm., Macclesfield Constituency Conservative Assoc., 1961-65; Hon. Treas., NW Conservatives and Mem. Conservative Bd of Finance, 1965-71; Chm., NW Area Conservatives, 1971-76; Chm., Exec. Cttee of Nat. Union of Conservative and Unionist Assocs, 1976- (Mem., 1965-). Chm., Bd of Trustees, Charity of Edward Mayes and Others, 1961- (founded in 1621 for the deserving poor of Manchester); General Commissioner of Income Tax for Div. of Salford, 1966-. *Recreations:* fly fishing, spectator sports, travelling. *Address:* Narrow Lane House, Adlington, near Macclesfield, Cheshire. *T:* Poynton 2675. *Clubs:* Army and Navy; St James's (Manchester).

JOHNSTON, Charles Hampton, QC (Scotland) 1959; MA, LLB; Sheriff Principal of South Strathclyde, Dumfries and Galloway, since 1977; *b* 10 April 1919; *s* of John Johnston and Johanna Johnston (*née* Hampton), Edinburgh; *m* 1950, Isobel Ross Young; one *s* one *d. Educ:* Royal High School, Edinburgh; University of Edinburgh. Served War of 1939-45, with 52nd (Lowland) and 51st (Highland) Divs, 1940-46; released with rank of Captain. Advocate, 1947; Chm. Scottish Liberal Party, 1955-56; Standing Junior Counsel, Min. of Works, 1956-59; Sheriff of Glasgow and Strathkelvin (formerly Lanarkshire) at Glasgow, 1962-77. MA 1940, LLB 1947, Editor, The Student, 1940, Edinburgh. *Publications:* (joint) Agricultural Holdings (Scotland) Acts, 1961, new edn 1970. *Recreation:* pottering about in the country. *Address:* Westgrange, 12A Grange Road, Bearsden, Glasgow G61 3PL. *T:* 041-942 0659. *Clubs:* Strathclyde University Staff, Western (Glasgow).

JOHNSTON, Sir Charles (Hepburn), GCMG 1971 (KCMG 1959; CMG 1953); Member of Council of Toynbee Hall, since 1974; Member of Lloyd's since 1962; *b* 11 March 1912; *s* of Ernest Johnston and Emma Hepburn; *m* 1944, Princess Natasha Bagration; no *c. Educ:* Winchester; Balliol Coll., Oxford (1st Class Hon. Mods, 1932, Lit. Hum., 1934). Entered Diplomatic Service, 1936; 3rd Sec., Tokyo, 1939; 1st Sec., Cairo, 1945, and Madrid, 1948; Counsellor, FO, 1951, and British Embassy, Bonn, 1955; HM Ambassador in Amman, 1956; Gov. and C-in-C, Aden, 1960-63; High Comr for Aden and Protectorate of South Arabia, 1963; Dep. Under-Sec. of State, Foreign Office, 1963-65; High Commissioner, Australia, 1965-71. KStJ 1961. *Publications:* The View from Steamer Point, 1964; Mo and Other Originals, 1971; The Brink of Jordan, 1972; Estuary in Scotland (poems), 1974. *Address:* 32 Kingston House South, SW7 1NF. *Clubs:* White's, Beefsteak.

JOHNSTON, Rear-Adm. Clarence Dinsmore H.; *see* Howard-Johnston.

JOHNSTON, David Alan H.; *see* Hunter Johnston.

JOHNSTON, (David) Russell; MP (L) Inverness since 1964; *b* 28 July 1932; *s* of late David Knox Johnston and Georgina Margaret Gerrie Russell; *m* 1967, Joan Graham Menzies; two *s. Educ:* Carbost Public Sch.; Portree High Sch.; Edinburgh Univ. (MA). Commissioned into Intelligence Corps (Nat. Service), 1958; subseq., Moray House Coll. of Educn until 1961; taught in Liberton Secondary Sch., 1961-63. Research Asst, Scottish Liberal Party, 1963-64. Chm., Scottish Liberal Party, 1970- (Vice-Chm., 1965-70), Leader, 1974-; Mem., UK Delegn to European Parlt, 1973-75 and 1976-, Vice Pres., Political Cttee, 1976-. Mem., Royal Commission on Local Govt in Scotland, 1966-69. *Publications:* (pamphlet) Highland Development, 1964; (pamphlet) To Be a Liberal, 1972. *Recreations:* reading, photography. *Address:* Glendruidh, by Inverness IV1 2AA. *T:* Inverness 36431. *Club:* Scottish Liberal (Edinburgh).

JOHNSTON, Denis; *see* Johnston, (William) Denis.

JOHNSTON, Douglas Harold; *see* Johnston, Hon. Lord.

JOHNSTON, Edward Alexander, CB 1975; Government Actuary, since 1973; *b* 19 March 1929; 2nd *s* of Edward Hamilton Johnston, DLitt, and Iris Olivia Helena May; *m* 1956, Veronica Mary, *d* of Lt-Col J. S. N. Bernays, MC; two *s* two *d. Educ:* Groton Sch., USA; Marlborough Coll.; New Coll., Oxford. BA 1952; FIA 1957; FSS, ASA, FIMA; Founder Fellow, Pensions Management Inst. Equity & Law Life Assce Soc., 1952-58; Govt Actuary's Dept: Asst Actuary, 1958; Actuary, 1961; Principal Actuary, 1970. *Recreations:* music, sailing. *Address:* 3 Pembroke Villas, Richmond TW9 1QF. *T:* 01-940 3301. *Club:* Reform.

JOHNSTON, Very Rev. Frederick Mervyn Kieran; Dean of Cork, 1967-71, retired; *b* 22 Oct. 1911; *s* of Robert Mills Johnston and Florence Harriet O'Hanlon; *m* 1938, Catherine Alice Ruth FitzSimons; two *s. Educ:* Grammar Sch., Galway; Bishop Foy Sch., Waterford; Trinity Coll., Dublin. BA 1933. Deacon, 1934; Priest, 1936; Curate, Castlecomer, 1934-36; Curate, St Luke, Cork, 1936-38; Incumbent of Kilmeen, 1938-40; Drimoleague, 1940-45; Blackrock, Cork, 1945-58; Bandon, 1958-67; Rector of St Fin Barre's Cathedral and Dean of Cork, 1967. *Address:* Ardkilly, Sandycove, Kinsale, Co. Cork.

JOHNSTON, Frederick Patrick Mair; Chairman, Johnston Newspaper Group, since 1973; Member of the Press Council, since 1973; *b* Edinburgh, 15 Sept. 1935; *e s* of late Frederick M. Johnston and of Mrs M. K. Johnston, Falkirk; *m* 1961, Elizabeth Ann Jones; two *s. Educ:* Morrison's Acad., Crieff; Lancing Coll., Sussex; New Coll., Oxford (MA, Mod. Hist.).

Commissioned in Royal Scots Fusiliers, 1955; served in E Africa with 4th (Uganda) Bn, KAR, 1955-56. Joined Editorial Dept of Liverpool Daily Post & Echo, 1959; joined The Times Publishing Co. Ltd, as Asst Sec., 1960; Company Sec., F. Johnston & Co. Ltd, 1969; Managing Dir, F. Johnston & Co. Ltd, 1973; Chm., Dunn & Wilson Gp Ltd, 1976. President: Young Newspapermen's Assoc., 1968-69; Forth Valley Chamber of Commerce, 1972-73; Scottish Newspaper Proprietors' Assoc., 1976; Chm., Central Scotland Manpower Cttee, 1976. *Recreations:* reading, travelling. *Address:* Broompark, Brightons, Falkirk FK2 0JY. *T:* Polmont 62550. *Club:* Royal Commonwealth Society.

JOHNSTON, Frederick William; *b* 22 Dec. 1899; *er s* of late Frederick and Janey Johnston, Terenure, Co. Dublin, Eire; *m* 1928, Eileen Milne, Dublin; one *d. Educ:* St Patrick's Cathedral Grammar Sch. and Mountjoy Sch., Dublin; Dublin Univ. Merchant Navy (2nd mate), 1915-21; entered Dublin Univ. and King's Inns, Dublin, 1922; BA, LLB (TCD), 1925; called to Irish Bar, 1925; Colonial Administrative Service, Uganda, 1926-32; Magistrate, Uganda, 1933-42; Judge of the Supreme Court, Gambia, 1942-47; Puisne Judge, Nigeria, 1947-50; retired 1950; called to English Bar (Middle Temple), 1951; re-appointed Puisne Judge, Nigeria, 1952, retired 1955. *Address:* Lagos, Peel Hall Lane, Ashton, Chester.

JOHNSTON, George Alexander, MA, DPhil; *b* Jamaica, 11 Nov. 1888; *e s* of Rev. Robert Johnston, BD; *m* 1919, Pauline Violet, *y d* of late Sir George Roche; one *s* one *d. Educ:* University of Glasgow (MA, 1st cl. Hons Classics and Philosophy, 1912; DPhil, 1918); University of Berlin. Lecturer in Moral Philosophy, St Andrews Univ., 1912-14; Lecturer in Moral Philosophy, Glasgow Univ., 1914-19; served in Macedonia, at the War Office, and GHQ, Palestine and Cairo, 1916-19; Ministry of Labour, 1919-20; International Labour Office, 1920-40; Vis. Prof. of Social Legislation; Columbia Univ., New York, 1931-32; Ministry of Labour, 1940-45; Asst Dir, ILO, 1945-48; Treasurer ILO, 1948-53; Chm. UN Joint Staff Pensions Board, 1951; Sec.-Gen., Govt Training Inst., Istanbul, 1954; Mem. UN Economic Mission to Viet-Nam, 1955-56; Dir ILO London Office, 1956-57. Officer of Order of Orange-Nassau (Netherlands). *Publications:* An Introduction to Ethics, 1915; Selections from the Scottish Philosophy of Common Sense, 1915; The Development of Berkeley's Philosophy, 1923; International Social Progress, 1924; Citizenship in the Industrial World, 1928; Berkeley's Commonplace Book, 1930; The International Labour Organisation: its work for social and economic progress, 1970; articles in periodicals and encyclopædias. *Address:* 4 Chemin des Clochettes, 1206 Geneva, Switzerland.

JOHNSTON, Henry Butler M.; *see* McKenzie Johnston.

JOHNSTON, Hugh Philip, CB 1977; Deputy Secretary, Property Services Agency, Department of the Environment, since 1974; *b* 17 May 1927; *s* of Philip Rose-Johnston and Dora Ellen Johnston; *m* 1949, Barbara Frances Theodoridi; one *s* three *d. Educ:* Wimbledon Coll.; Faraday House. DFH (Hons); FIEE, FCIBS. Air Ministry Works Dept: Asst Engr, 1951; Engr, 1956; Ministry of Public Buildings and Works: Prin. Engr, 1964; Asst Dir, 1969; Dir (Under-Sec.), Dept of Environment and Property Services Agency, Engrg Services Directorate, 1970. *Recreations:* motoring, music. *Address:* 9 Devas Road, Wimbledon, SW20 8PD. *T:* 01-946 2021.

JOHNSTON, Ian Henderson; Director, Military Vehicles and Engineering Establishment, Ministry of Defence, since 1976; *b* 29 April 1925; *s* of late Peter Johnston and Barbara Johnston (*née* Gifford); *m* 1949, Irene Blackburn; two *d. Educ:* George Heriot's Sch., Edinburgh; Edinburgh Univ. (BSc Eng); Imperial Coll., London (DIC Aeronautics). D. Napier & Sons, 1945-46; National Gas Turbine Estabt, 1947-64; Ramjet Project Officer, Min. of Aviation, 1964-66; Exchange Officer to Wright Patterson Air Force Base, Ohio, 1966-68; Asst Dir (Engine Develt), Min. of Technology, 1968-70; Dep. Dir, National Gas Turbine Estabt, 1970-73; Dir-Gen., Multi-Role Combat Aircraft, MoD (PE), 1973-76. *Publications:* papers on turbine research in Aeronautical Research Council Reports and Memoranda Series. *Recreations:* golf, bridge. *Address:* 49 Salisbury Road, Farnborough, Hants. *T:* Farnborough 41971.

JOHNSTON, Maj.-Gen. James Alexander Deans, OBE 1945; MC 1937; Director of Medical Services, BAOR, 1969-70, retired; *b* 28 Feb. 1911; *s* of Walter Johnston and I. C. Gilchrist; *m* 1940, Enid O. Eldridge; one *s* two *d. Educ:* Glasgow Univ. MB, ChB Glasgow, 1933. House Surgeon, Taunton and Somerset Hosp., 1933-34. Commnd into RAMC, 1934; served in India, 1935-40 (Quetta Earthquake, 1935; Mohmand Ops, 1935;

Waziristan Ops, 1936-37); served in NW Europe, 1944-45; SMO during and after liberation of Belsen Concentration Camp, April 1945; ADMS HQ Malaya Comd, 19 Ind. Div. and 2 Br. Inf. Div. in Far East, 1945-47; ADMS Southern Comd, UK, 1947-49; DDMS HQ MELF, 1949-52; ADMS 2 Div., and DDMS HQ BAOR, 1952-57; OC British Military Hosp., Dhekelia, Cyprus, 1957-61; ADG WO, 1961-64; Comdt, Depot and Training Establishment and HQ AER, RAMC, 1964-66; DMS, FARELF, 1966-69. Major 1943; Lt-Col 1948; Col 1957; Brig. 1964; Maj.-Gen. 1966. QHP 1967-70. *Recreations:* swimming, tennis, country pursuits. *Address:* Park Cottage, Ewhurst Lane, Northiam, East Sussex.

JOHNSTON, James Campbell, CBE 1972; Senior Partner, J. B. Were & Son, Stock and Share Brokers, since 1967 (Partner since 1947); Chairman: Capel Court Corporation Ltd, since 1969; Australian Foundation Investment Co., since 1967; *b* 7 July 1912; *s* of late Edwin and Estelle Johnston; *m* 1938, Agnes Emily, *yr d* of late Richard Thomas; two *s* one *d. Educ:* Prince Alfred Coll., Adelaide; Scotch Coll., Melbourne; University of Melbourne. Admitted to Inst. Chartered Accountants, Australia, 1933; joined J. B. Were & Son, 1935; Stock Exchange of Melbourne: Mem., 1947; Mem. Cttee, 1954; Chm., 1972. *Address:* 13 Monaro Road, Kooyong, Victoria 3144, Australia. *T:* 20 2842. *Clubs:* Melbourne, Australian, Athenæum, Victoria Racing, Royal Melbourne Golf (Melbourne).

JOHNSTON, James Osborne; Director of Social Work, Corporation of Glasgow, 1969-75; *b* 18 June 1921; British; *m* 1971, Rosemary Guiton; two *d* by a former *m. Educ:* Allan Glen's Sch., Glasgow. Post Office, 1938-40; RAF, 1940-46; Scottish Educn Dept, 1946-65; Scottish Home and Health Dept, 1965-67; Social Work Services Group, 1967-69. *Recreations:* walking, talking. *Address:* Sandybrae, Twynholm, Kirkcudbrightshire.

JOHNSTON, Sir John (Baines), KCMG 1966 (CMG 1962); KCVO 1972; British High Commissioner in Canada, 1974-78; *b* 13 May 1918; *e s* of late Rev. A. S. Johnston, Banbury, Oxon; *m* 1969, Elizabeth Mary, *d* of late J. F. Crace; one *s. Educ:* Banbury Grammar Sch.; Queen's Coll., Oxford (Eglesfield Scholar). Served War, 1940-46: Adjt 1st Bn Gordon Highlanders, 1944; DAQMG HQ 30 Corps District, 1945. Asst Principal, Colonial Office, 1947; Principal, 1948; Asst Sec., West African Council, Accra, 1950-51; UK Liaison Officer with Commission for Technical Co-operation in Africa South of the Sahara, 1952; Principal Private Sec. to Sec. of State for the Colonies, 1953; Asst Sec., 1956; Head of Far Eastern Dept, Colonial Office, 1956; transferred to Commonwealth Relations Office, 1957; Dep. High Commissioner in S Africa, 1959-61; British High Commissioner: in Sierra Leone, 1961-63; in the Federation of Rhodesia and Nyasaland, 1963, Rhodesia, 1964-65; Asst, later Dep. Under-Secretary of State, FCO, 1968-71; British High Comr in Malaysia, 1971-74. *Address:* c/o Midland Bank Ltd, 10 High Street, Banbury, Oxon. *Club:* United Oxford & Cambridge University.

JOHNSTON, Lt-Col John Frederick Dame, CVO 1977 (MVO 1971); MC 1945; Assistant Comptroller, Lord Chamberlain's Office, since 1964; *b* 24 Aug. 1922; *m* 1949, Hon. Elizabeth Hardinge, JP Windsor 1971, *d* of 2nd Baron Hardinge of Penshurst, PC, GCB, GCVO, MC, and of Helen, Lady Hardinge of Penshurst; one *s* one *d. Educ:* Ampleforth. Served in Grenadier Guards, 1941-64. Extra Equerry to the Queen, 1965-. *Address:* Adelaide Cottage, Windsor Home Park, Berks. *T:* Windsor 68286; Stone Hill, Newport, Pembs. *Clubs:* Pratt's, MCC; Swinley Forest Golf.

JOHNSTON, Kenneth Robert Hope; QC 1953; *b* 18 June 1905; *e s* of Dr J. A. H. Johnston, Headmaster of Highgate Sch., 1908-36, and Kate Winsome Gammon; *m* 1937, Dr Priscilla Bright Clark, *d* of Roger and Sarah Clark, Street, Somerset; one *s* three *d. Educ:* Rugby Sch.; Sidney Sussex Coll., Cambridge Univ.; Harvard Univ., USA. Called to the Bar, Gray's Inn, 1933; Bencher, 1958. RAFVR, 1939-45. *Address:* Nesfield, Three Gates Lane, Haslemere, Surrey. *T:* 3762. *Club:* MCC.

JOHNSTON, Margaret; *see* Parker, Margaret Annette McCrie J.

JOHNSTON, Michael Errington; Under-Secretary, Ministry of Agriculture, Fisheries and Food, 1970-76; *b* 22 Jan. 1916; *s* of late Lt-Col C. E. L. Johnston, RA, and late Beatrix Johnston; *m* 1938, Ida Brown; two *d. Educ:* Wellington; Peterhouse, Cambridge (Scholar). BA, 1st cl. Hist. Tripos, 1937; MA 1947. Served War of 1939-45, Rifle Bde (Capt., despatches), Asst Principal, Board of Education, 1938; Principal, 1946; Asst Sec., HM Treasury, 1952, Under-Sec., 1962-68; Under-Sec., Civil Service Dept, 1968-70. *Recreations:* painting and birdwatching.

Address: 3 The Terrace, Barnes, SW13. *T:* 01-876 5265.
See also P . M . Johnston .

JOHNSTON, Ninian Rutherford Jamieson, RSA 1965; architect and town planner in private practice since 1946; *b* 6 March 1912; *s* of John Neill Johnston and Agnes Johnston; *m* 1937, Helen, *d* of Robert Henry Jackson and Jean Patrick Jackson; one *s* two *d. Educ:* Allan Glen's Sch.; Glasgow Sch. of Architecture. Served with Army, 1939-45. BArch 1934; FRIAS 1935; FRTPI (MTPI 1946); FRIBA 1951. *Principal Works:* Pollokshaws Central Redevelopment Area; Woodside Central Redevelopment Area, Glasgow; Central Hospitals at Dumfries, Greenock and Rutherglen. Mem. Roy. Fine Art Commission for Scotland, 1969-76. *Recreations:* music, painting, gardening. *Address:* 18 Woodlands Terrace, Glasgow, G3 6DF. *T:* 041-332 9184. *Club:* Art (Glasgow).

JOHNSTON, Patrick Murdoch, CBE 1963; HM Diplomatic Service, retired; *b* 5 Oct. 1911; *s* of late Claude Errington Longden Johnston, Lt-Col, Royal Artillery, and Beatrix (*née* Peppercorn); *m* 1936, Beatrice Jean Davidson; one *d. Educ:* Wellington Coll.; Peterhouse, Cambridge. Entered HM Consular Service and appointed Probationer Vice-Consul, Paris, Nov. 1934; transferred to Hamburg, Nov. 1935, Valparaiso, 1936; Vice-Consul, Lima, Nov. 1938; Foreign Service Officer Grade 7 and appointed Consul, Ponta Delgada, Azores, 1945; Consul, Bremen, 1947; Head of Commonwealth Liaison Dept, Foreign Office, 1949; Consul, Denver, Colorado, Dec. 1951, Bordeaux, Nov. 1954; Ambassador to the Republic of Cameroun, 1960-61, to Nicaragua, 1962-63; Consul-Gen., Casablanca, 1963-69. *Recreations:* ski-ing, photography, caravanning, puttering. *Address:* Crown Cottage, Dorchester-on-Thames, Oxon. *T:* Warborough 467. *Club:* Civil Service.

JOHNSTON, Peter Hope, CMG 1966; Administrative Officer, Development Planning Unit, University College, London, since 1976; *b* 31 Oct. 1915; *s* of late Robert Hope Johnston; *m* 1949, Patricia Cullen; one *s* two *d. Educ:* Summerfields; St Paul's Sch.; Magdalen Coll., Oxford (Maj. Exhibr). BA Oxon. Mem. HMOCS. Joined Tanganyika Govt Service, 1938; District Officer in Provincial Administration, 1938-49; on special duty, African Land Settlement, 1949-51; on special duty, Sec., Special Comr, Constitutional Development, 1952; District Comr, Senior District Officer, 1952-58; Provincial Comr, 1958-62; Courts Integration Adviser, High Court of Tanganyika, 1962-65; retd voluntarily from service of Govt of Tanganyika (Tanzania), 1965. Principal, Min. of Overseas Develt, 1965-76. Editor, Jl of Administration Overseas. *Publications:* (ed jtly) The Rural Base for National Development, 1968; Prospects for Employment Opportunities in the Nineteen Seventies, 1971. *Address:* Bell House, Milton Avenue, near Dorking, Surrey. *T:* Dorking 5611. *Club:* Surrey County Cricket.

JOHNSTON, Robert Smith; *see* Kincraig, Hon. Lord.

JOHNSTON, Robert William Fairfield, CMG 1960; CBE 1954; MC 1917; TD 1936 (and three Bars, 1947); Assistant Secretary, Ministry of Defence, 1946-62; retired from the Civil Service, 1962; *b* 1 May 1895; *e s* of late Capt. Robert Johnston, Army Pay Dept and Royal Justice; *m* 1922, Agnes Scott, *o c* of late Peter Justice, Edinburgh; one *s*. Entered Civil Service, Dec. 1910: served in War Office, Bd of Trade, Min. of Labour, Home Office, Office of Minister without Portfolio, Min. of Defence, and seconded to FO, as Counsellor in UK Delegation in Paris to NATO and OEEC, 1953-61. Territorial Army, 1910-47; served European War, 1914-18, The Royal Scots (1st, 9th and 16th Battalions) in France, Flanders, Macedonia and Egypt; commissioned 1917; War of 1939-45, Lieut-Col, Comdg 8th Bn Gordon Highlanders, 1940-42, and 100th (Gordons) Anti-Tank Regt, RA, 1942-44, in 51st (Highland) and 2nd (British) Inf. Divs respectively; retired as Lieut-Col TA, Sept. 1947. *Address:* 8 Broad Avenue, Queen's Park, Bournemouth, Dorset.

JOHNSTON, Prof. Ronald Carlyle; Professor of Romance Philology and Medieval French Literature, Westfield College, London, 1961-74; *b* 19 May 1907; *m*; one *s* three *d. Educ:* Ackworth Sch., Yorks; Bootham Sch., York; Merton Coll., Oxford. Travel in France, Germany and Spain, 1929-30. MA Oxon; 1st Cl. Hons Mediaeval and Modern Languages, French, 1929; Docteur de l'Université de Strasbourg, 1935. Asst Master Uppingham Sch., 1930-35; Lectr in French Philology and Old Fr. Lit., Oxford, 1935-45; Fellow of Jesus Coll., Oxford, 1945-48; Professor of French Language and Literature, University of St Andrews, 1948-61. External examiner in French, Universities of Oxford, Cambridge, Edinburgh, Aberdeen, and Manchester. Officier d'Académie. Chevalier de la Légion d'Honneur. *Publications:* Les Poésies lyriques du troubadour Arnaut de Mareuil (Paris), 1935; The Crusade and Death of Richard I

(Anglo-Norman Text Soc.), 1961; The Versification of Jordan Fantosme, 1974; (with A. Ewert) Selected Fables of Marie de France, 1942; (with D. D. R. Owen) Fabliaux, 1957; Two Old French Gauvain Romances, part 1, 1972; (with Ana Cartianu) English trans. of Creangǎ's Poveşti şi Povestiri, 1973; reviews in Medium Aevum, Modern Language Review, French Studies, etc. *Recreations:* rough gardening, travel. *Address:* Taunton House, Freeland, Oxford. *T:* Freeland 881276.

JOHNSTON, Russell; *see* Johnston, D. R.

JOHNSTON, Sir Thomas Alexander, 13th Bt of Caskieben, *cr* 1626; Attorney-at-Law; partner in legal firm of Howell, Johnston, Langford, Finkbohner and Lawler, Alabama, USA; *b* 7 Sept. 1916; *s* of Sir Thomas Alexander Johnston, 12th Bt and of Pauline Burke, *d* of Leslie Bragg Sheldon, Mobile; *S* father, 1959; *m* 1941, Helen Torrey, *d* of Benjamin Franklin Du Bois; one *s* two *d. Educ:* University of Alabama (LLB). Mem., Alabama House of Representatives, 1941-49; Mem., Alabama State Senate, 1949-54; Pres., Mobile Co. Bar Assoc., 1963. Member: Alabama Constitution Revision Cttee, 1970-; Alabama Judicial Compensation Commn, 1976-. *Recreations:* hunting, fishing. *Heir:* *s* Thomas Alexander Johnston, *b* 1 Feb. 1956. *Address:* Howell, Johnston, Langford, Finkbohner and Lawler, Commercial Guaranty Bank Building, Mobile, Alabama, USA.

JOHNSTON, Thomas Lothian; author and consultant; *b* 9 March 1927; *s* of T. B. Johnston and late Janet Johnston; *m* 1956, Joan, *d* of E. C. Fahmy, surgeon; two *s* three *d. Educ:* Hawick High Sch.; Univs of Edinburgh and Stockholm. MA 1951, PhD 1955, Edinburgh. Served RNVR, 1944-47 (Sub-Lt). Asst Lectr in Polit. Economy, Univ. of Edinburgh, 1953-55, Lectr 1955-65; Res. Fellow, Queen's Univ., Canada, 1965; Prof. and Hd of Dept of Econs, Heriot-Watt Univ., 1966-76. Vis. Prof., Univ. of Illinois, 1962-63; Vis. Prof., Internat. Inst. for Labour Studies, Geneva, 1973. Sec., Scottish Econ. Soc., 1958-65; Member: Scottish Milk Marketing Bd, 1967-72; Nat. Industrial Relations Court, 1971-74; Scottish Cttee on Licensing Laws, 1971-73; Nat. Youth Employment Council, 1968-71; Scottish Telecommunications Bd, 1977-; Chm. Council, Fraser of Allander Inst., Univ. of Strathclyde, 1975-. Chm. of Wages Councils; Arbitrator; Overseas Corresp., Nat. Acad. of Arbitrators, USA. *Publications:* Collective Bargaining in Sweden, 1962; (ed and trans.) Economic Expansion and Structural Change, 1963; (jtly) The Structure and Growth of the Scottish Economy, 1971; articles in learned jls. *Recreations:* camping, gardening, walking. *Address:* 14 Mansionhouse Road, Edinburgh EH9 1TZ. *T:* 031-667 1439.

JOHNSTON, Rt. Rev. William; *see* Dunwich, Bishop Suffragan of.

JOHNSTON, (William) Denis; Writer, Broadcaster and Professor; *b* Dublin, 18 June 1901; *o s* of late Hon. William John Johnston, Judge of the Supreme Court; *m* 1st, 1928, Shelah Kathleen (marr. diss.), *d* of John William Richards, Dublin; one *s* one *d*; 2nd, 1945, Betty, *d* of John William Chancellor, Dublin; two *s. Educ:* St Andrew's Coll., Dublin; Merchiston, Edinburgh; Christ's Coll., Cambridge (MA, LLM 1926, Pres. of the Union); Harvard Univ., USA (Pugsley Scholar). Barrister Inner Temple and King's Inns, 1925 and Northern Ireland, 1926; Dir, Dublin Gate Theatre, 1931-36; joined British Broadcasting Corporation, 1936; BBC War Correspondent, Middle East, Italy, France and Germany, 1942-45 (despatches); Programme Dir, BBC Television Service, 1946-47. Professor in English Dept, Mount Holyoke Coll., Mass, 1950-60; Guggenheim Fellowship, 1955; Head of Dept of Theatre and Speech, Smith Coll., 1961-66; Visiting Lecturer: Amherst Coll., 1966-67; Univ. of Iowa, 1967-68; Univ. of California, Davis, 1970-71. Berg Prof., New York Univ., 1971-72; Arnold Prof., Whitman Coll., 1972-73. *Publications:* plays: The Old Lady says 'No!', 1929; The Moon in the Yellow River, 1931; A Bride for the Unicorn, 1933; Storm Song, 1934; The Golden Cuckoo, 1939; The Dreaming Dust, 1940; A Fourth for Bridge, 1948; Strange Occurrence on Ireland's Eye, 1956; The Scythe and the Sunset, 1958; operatic version of Six Characters in Search of an Author (comp. Hugo Weisgall), 1959; *autobiography:* Nine Rivers from Jordan, 1953, operatic version (comp. Hugo Weisgall), 1968; The Brazen Horn, 1976; *biographies:* In Search of Swift, 1959; J. M. Synge, 1965. *Recreation:* sailing. *Address:* 8 Sorrento Terrace, Dalkey, Co. Dublin. *Club:* Royal Irish Yacht (Kingstown).

JOHNSTON, William James; Town Clerk, Belfast City Council, since 1973; *b* 3 April 1919; *s* of late Thomas Hamilton Johnston and of Mary Kathleen Johnston; *m* 1943, Joan Elizabeth Nancye (*née* Young); two *d. Educ:* Portora Royal Sch., Enniskillen. FCA(Ire.). Professional accountancy, 1937-44; Antrim CC, 1944-68, Dep. Sec., 1951-68; Dep. Town Clerk, Belfast, 1968-73.

Mem. Bd, Arts Council of NI, 1974-; Member: Local Govt Staff Commn, 1974-; Public Service Trng Cttee, 1974- (Chm., 1974-). *Recreations:* golf, live theatre. *Address:* Flat 5, 8 Lansdowne Road, Belfast BT15 4DA. *T:* Belfast 771194; 47 Layde Road, Cushendall, Co. Antrim. *T:* Cushendall 211. *Club:* Ulster Reform (Belfast).

JOHNSTON, William Robert Patrick K.; *see* Knox-Johnston, Robin.

JOHNSTONE, VANDEN-BEMPDE-, family name of **Baron Derwent.**

JOHNSTONE, Prof. Alan Stewart; Professor of Radiodiagnosis, University of Leeds, 1948-68, now Emeritus; Director of Radiodiagnosis (General Infirmary, Leeds), United Leeds Hospitals, 1939-68; *b* 12 May 1905; *s* of Dr David A. and Margaret E. Johnstone, The Biggin, Waterbeck, Dumfriesshire; *m* 1934, Elizabeth Rowlett; one *s* one *d. Educ:* St Bees Sch.; Edinburgh Univ. Radiologist, Hammersmith Post-Graduate Hospital, 1935; Radiologist, Leicester Royal Infirmary, 1936-39. Baker Travelling Prof. in Radiology, Coll. of Radiologists of Australasia, 1959. Pres. Radiology Sect., Royal Society of Med., 1959-60; Pres. Thoracic Soc. of Great Britain, 1961-62. *Publications:* contributor to A Text Book of X-ray Diagnosis by British Authors; many in Br. Jl of Radiology, Jl of Faculty of Radiologists, Post Graduate Med. Jl, Edinburgh Med. Jl, Jl of Anatomy. *Recreations:* golf, fly fishing, chess. *Address:* 46 Stanford Road, Rondebosch, Cape Province, South Africa. *T:* Cape Town 613879.

JOHNSTONE, Air Vice-Marshal Alexander Vallance Riddell, CB 1966; DFC 1940; AE; DL; Vice-Chairman, Council, TA&VRA, since 1969; *b* 2 June 1916; *s* of late Alex. Lang Johnstone and Daisy Riddell; *m* 1940, Margaret Croll; one *s* two *d. Educ:* Kelvinside Academy, Glasgow. 602 (City of Glasgow) Sqdn, AAF, 1934-41; CO RAF Haifa, 1942; Spitfire Wing, Malta, 1942-43 (despatches, 1942); RAF Staff Coll., 1943; OC Fairwood Common, 1943-44; HQ AEAF, 1944; Air Attaché Dublin, 1946-48; OC RAF Ballykelly, 1951-52; OC Air/Sea Warfare Devel. Unit, 1952-54; SASO HQ No 12 Gp, 1954-55; Founder and First CAS Royal Malayan Air Force, 1957; OC Middleton St George, 1958-60; idc, 1961; Dir of Personnel, Air Min., 1962-64; Comdr, Air Forces, Borneo, 1964-65; AO Scotland and N Ireland, AOC No 18 Group, and Maritime Air Comdr N Atlantic (NATO), 1965-68. DL Glasgow, 1971. Johan Mengku Negara (Malaya), 1958. *Publications:* Television Series, One Man's War, 1964; Where No Angels Dwell, 1969; Enemy in the Sky, 1976. *Recreations:* golf, sailing. *Address:* 3 Drumlin Drive, Milngavie, Glasgow. *Clubs:* Royal Air Force; Royal Scottish Automobile (Glasgow).

JOHNSTONE, Mrs Dorothy (Christian Liddle), CBE 1955; European Affairs Adviser, BAT Industries Ltd, since 1976; *b* 5 April 1915; *d* of William Hacket, printer, Peterhead, and Ethel Mary Duncan; *m* 1946, James Arthur Johnstone, *qv*; one *s. Educ:* Peterhead Acad.; Aberdeen Univ. Dept of Health for Scotland, 1937; Home Office, 1939; HM Treasury, 1943; Asst Sec., HM Customs and Excise, 1957; Comr of Customs and Excise, 1964-76. Gwilym Gibbon Res. Fellow, Nuffield Coll., Oxford, 1973-74. *Publication:* A Tax Shall Be Charged (CS Studies series), 1975. *Address:* 63 Cottesmore Court, Stanford Road, W8. *T:* 01-937 8726.

JOHNSTONE, Sir Frederic (Allan George), 10th Bt of Westerhall, Dumfriesshire, *cr* 1700; *b* 23 Feb. 1906; *o s* of Sir George Johnstone, 9th Bt and Ernestine (*d* 1955), *d* of Col Porcelli-Cust; *S* father, 1952; *m* 1946, Doris, *d* of late W. L. Shortridge; two *s. Educ:* Imperial Service Coll. *Heir:* *s* George Richard Douglas Johnstone, *b* 21 Aug. 1948.

JOHNSTONE, James Arthur; Commissioner of Inland Revenue 1964-73; *b* 29 July 1913; *o s* of Arthur James Johnstone, solicitor, Ayr, and Euphemia Tennant (*née* Fullarton); *m* 1946, Dorothy C. L. Hacket (*see* Mrs Dorothy Johnstone); one *s. Educ:* Ayr Academy; Glasgow Univ.; St John's Coll., Cambridge. Entered Inland Revenue Dept, 1936. Sec., Royal Commission on Taxation of Profits and Income, 1952-55; Chm., Hong Kong Inland Revenue Ordinance Rev. Cttee, 1976. *Address:* 63 Cottesmore Court, Stanford Road, W8. *T:* 01-937 8726. *Club:* Reform.

JOHNSTONE, Kenneth Roy, CB 1962; CMG 1949; Deputy Director-General of the British Council, 1953-62, retired; Chairman, International Department, British Council of Churches, 1963-71; *b* 25 Sept. 1902; 2nd *s* of late Edward Henderson Johnstone and late Stella Fraser; *m* 1944, Mary Pauline, *d* of R. C. Raine. *Educ:* Eton; Balliol Coll., Oxford.

Entered HM Diplomatic Service, 1926; served in Warsaw, 1928, Oslo, 1930, Sofia, 1931, and London; seconded to British Council, 1936; resigned to join Welsh Guards, 1939; served War of 1939-45: France, 1940; North Africa, 1942; Staff in Middle East and Greece, 1943-45 (Col). Readmitted to Foreign Service, 1945, and rejoined British Council. Chm. Council, SSEES, London Univ., 1965-76. Gold Cultural Medal (Italy); Gold Cross of Order of King George I (Greece). *Publications:* translated: Ivo Andric, Bosnian Story, 1959, Devil's Yard, 1962; Djilas, Montenegro, 1963; Amandos, Introduction to Byzantine History, 1969; Zakythinos, The Making of Modern Greece, 1976; Prevelakis, The Tale of a Town, 1976. *Address:* 4 Priory Crescent, Lewes, East Sussex. *T:* Lewes 3738. *Club:* United Oxford & Cambridge University.

JOHNSTONE, Morris Mackintosh O.; *see* Ord Johnstone.

JOHNSTONE, Maj.-Gen. Ralph E.; *see* Edgeworth-Johnstone.

JOHNSTONE, R(obert) Edgeworth, DSc (London); FIChemE; FIMechE; FRIC; Lady Trent Professor of Chemical Engineering, University of Nottingham, 1960-67; *b* 4 Feb. 1900; *e s* of Lieut-Col Sir Walter Edgeworth-Johnstone, KBE, CB; *m* 1931, Jessie Marjorie, *d* of late R. M. T. Greig; two *s* one *d. Educ:* Wellington; RMA Woolwich; Manchester Coll. of Technology; University Coll., London. Fellow Salters' Inst. of Industrial Chem., 1926-27. Held various posts at home and abroad with Magadi Soda Co., Trinidad Leaseholds, Petrocarbon, APV Co., Min. of Supply (Royal Ordnance Factories) and UK Atomic Energy Authority. Vice-Pres., IChemE, 1951; Liveryman, Worshipful Co. of Salters, 1956. Council Medal, IChemE, 1969. *Publications:* Continuing Education in Engineering, 1969; (with Prof. M. W. Thring) Pilot Plants, Models and Scale-up Methods in Chemical Engineering, 1957; papers in scientific and engineering jls, especially on distillation, process development and engineering education. *Recreations:* music, philosophy. *Address:* 23 Surrenden Crescent, Brighton BN1 6WE. *T:* Brighton 556845. *Club:* Athenæum.

JOHNSTONE, Maj.-Gen. Robert Maxwell, MBE 1954; MC 1942; MA, MD, FRCPE; Assistant Director (Overseas), British Postgraduate Medical Federation, 1970-76; *b* 9 March 1914; *s* of late Prof. Emer. R. W. Johnstone, CBE; *m* 1958, Marjorie Jordan Beattie (*d* 1960). *Educ:* Edinburgh Acad.; Craigflower; Fettes Coll.; Christ's Coll., Cambridge; Univ. of Edinburgh. MRCPE 1940; FRCPE 1944; MD Edinburgh 1954; MRCP 1966. Resident House Phys. and Surg., Royal Infirmary, Edinburgh, 1938-39. Sen. Pres., Royal Med. Soc., 1938-39. RMO, 129 Fd Regt RA, 1938-41; Company Comdr, 167 Fd Amb., RAMC, 1941-43; Staff Coll., Haifa, 1943; CO, 3 Fd Amb., 1945-46. Adviser in Medicine: HQ, E Africa Comd, 1950-51; Commonwealth Forces Korea, 1954-55; Officer i/c Med. Division: Cambridge Mil. Hosp., 1955-57; QAMH, Millbank, 1957-59; Prof. of Med., Univ. of Baghdad and Hon. Cons. Phys., Iraqi Army, 1959-63; CO, BMH, Iserlohn, 1963-65; Cons. Phys., HQ, FARELF, 1965-67; Dep. Director of Med. Services: Southern Comd, 1967-68; Army Strategic Comd, 1968-69; retd; Postgrad. Med. Dean, SW Metropolitan Region, 1969-70. CStJ 1969. *Recreations:* music, golf, fishing. *Address:* c/o Royal Bank of Scotland, 4 Shandwick Place, Edinburgh; 12 Thistleworth Close, Osterley, Mddx. *Club:* Athenæum.

JOHNSTONE, Prof. Thomas Muir; Professor of Arabic, University of London, since 1970; *b* 18 Jan. 1924; *s* of Thomas Cunningham Johnstone and Margaret Connolly Johnstone (*née* Muir); *m* 1949, Bernice Jobling; two *s* three *d. Educ:* Grove Academy, Broughty Ferry; School of Economics, Dundee. BCom 1944, BA 1954, PhD 1962, London. ICI, Manchester, 1944-57; Lectr in Arabic, School of Oriental and African Studies, 1957; Reader in Arabic, Univ. of London, 1965. Travelled extensively in Eastern Arabia and Oman; Mem., Middle East Comd Expedn to Socotra, 1967. Hon. Mem., Bd of Trustees, Univ. of Sanaa, Yemen. Mem. Editorial Bd, Cambridge Hist. of Arabic Literature. *Publications:* Eastern Arabian Dialect Studies, 1967; Harsusi Lexicon, 1977; articles, mainly on Arabian dialects and folklore and modern South Arabian languages, in Bulletin of School of Oriental and African Studies, Jl of Semitic Studies, Mariner's Mirror, Geographical Jl, Jl of Arabic Literature, Arabian Studies and Encyclopaedia of Islam. *Address:* School of Oriental and African Studies, Malet Street, WC1E 7HP. *T:* 01-637 2388.

JOHNSTONE, William; Chairman: Meat and Livestock Commission, since 1977; British Agricultural Export Council, since 1977; *b* 26 Dec. 1915; *s* of late David Grierson Johnstone and Janet Lang Johnstone (*née* Malcolm); *m* 1942, Mary Rosamund Rowden; one *s* two *d. Educ:* Dalry High Sch.;

Glasgow Univ. (BScAgric). NDA, NDD. Farming appt in Scotland, 1936-38; Technical Officer, Overseas Dept of Deutches Kalisyndikat, Berlin, 1938-39; joined ICI Ltd, 1940; seconded to County War Agricl Exec. Cttees in SE England on food prodn campaigns, 1940-45; Reg. Sales Management, ICI, 1950-61; Commercial Dir, Plant Protection Ltd, 1961-63, Man. Dir, 1963-73; Dir, Billingham/Agricl Div., 1961-73; Dep. Chm., Plant Protection Div., 1974-77. Chm. Subsid. Cos: Solplant (Italy), 1967-73; Sopra (France), 1971-75; Zeltia Agraria (Spain), 1976-77; Vis. Dir, ICI (United States) Inc., 1974-77; retd from ICI, 1977. *Recreations:* gardening, travel, reading, agriculture. *Address:* Drayton Mill, East Meon, Petersfield, Hants GU32 1PW. *T:* East Meon 216. *Club:* Farmers'.

JOHORE, Sultan of, since 1959; **HH Ismail,** First Class of the Johore Family Order (DK); Hon. KBE 1937; Hon. CMG 1926; First Class Order of the Crown of Johore (SPMJ); First Class Order Sri Mangku Negara (SMN); *b* 28 Oct. 1894; *s* of Maj.-Gen. HH Sir Ibrahim, DK (Darjah Karabat), SPMJ (1st class Order of Crown of Johore), Hon. GCMG, Hon. KBE, Sultan of Johore (*d* 1959); *S* father, 1959; Coronation as Sultan, 1960. *Educ:* in England. Major Johore Military and Volunteer Forces. First Class Order of the Crown of Kelantan; also holds some foreign decorations. *Address:* Istana Bukit Serene, Johore Bahru, Johore, Malaysia.

JOICEY, family name of **Baron Joicey.**

JOICEY, 4th Baron, *cr* 1906; **Michael Edward Joicey;** Bt 1893; *b* 28 Feb. 1925; *s* of 3rd Baron Joicey and Joan (*d* 1967), *y d* of 4th Earl of Durham; *S* father, 1966; *m* 1952, Elisabeth Marion, *y d* of late Lieut-Col Hon. Ian Leslie Melville; two *s* one *d. Educ:* Eton; Christ Church, Oxford. *Heir: s* Hon. James Michael Joicey, *b* 28 June 1953. *Address:* Etal Manor. Berwick-upon-Tweed, Northumberland. *T:* Crookham 205. *Clubs:* Bath, Lansdowne; Northern Counties (Newcastle upon Tyne).

JOINT, Sir (Edgar) James, KCMG 1958 (CMG 1948); OBE 1941; FRGS; HM Ambassador to Republic of Colombia, 1955-60, retired; *b* 7 May 1902; *m* 1st, 1928, Lottie Kerse (*d* 1929); 2nd, 1937, Holly Enid Morgan; three *s. Educ:* Fairfield, Bristol; London Univ.; Gonville and Caius Coll., Cambridge. Entered HM Foreign Service, 1923; subseq. served at Mexico City, Montevideo, Beira, Milan, Santos, Léopoldville, Guatemala, San Salvador, Brussels, Buenos Aires and Rome, 1951-55. Chm., Anglo-Colombian Soc., 1960-70. Grand Cross of Boyacá, Colombia, 1960. *Address:* St Nicholas, Station Road, Chobham, Surrey. *T:* Chobham 8991.

JOLL, Prof. James Bysse, MA; FBA 1977; Stevenson Professor of International History, University of London since 1967; *b* 21 June 1918; *e s* of Lieut-Col H. H. Joll and Alice Muriel Edwards. *Educ:* Winchester; University of Bordeaux; New Coll., Oxford. War Service, Devonshire Regt and Special Ops Exec., 1939-45. Fellow and Tutor in Politics, New Coll., Oxford, 1946-50; Fellow, 1951-67, now Emeritus, and Sub-Warden, 1951-67, St Antony's Coll., Oxford. Vis. Mem., Inst. for Advanced Study, Princeton, 1954 and 1971; Vis. Prof. of History, Stanford Univ., Calif., 1958; Vis. Lectr in History, Harvard University, 1962. *Publications:* The Second International, 1955, rev. edn 1974; Intellectuals in Politics, 1960; The Anarchists, 1964; Europe since 1870, 1973; Gramsci, 1977. *Recreation:* music. *Address:* London School of Economics and Political Sc ence, Houghton Street, Aldwych, WC2. *T:* 01-405 7686.

JOLLIFFE, family name of **Baron Hylton.**

JOLLIFFE, Christopher, CBE 1971; Director, Leverhulme Trust Fund, 1976 (Acting Director, 1972); Director, Science Division, Science Research Council, 1969-72 (Director for University Science and Technology, 1965-69); *b* 14 March 1912; *s* of William Edwin Jolliffe and Annie Etheldreda Thompson; *m* 1936, Miriam Mabel Ash. *Educ:* Gresham's Sch., Holt; University Coll., London. Asst Master, Stowe Sch., 1935-37; Dept of Scientific and Industrial Research, 1937-65. *Address:* 8 Broomfield Road, Kew, Richmond, Surrey TW9 3HR. *T:* 01-940 4265. *Club:* Athenæum.

JOLLIFFE, William Orlando, IPFA, FCA; County Treasurer of Lancashire since 1973; *b* 16 Oct. 1925; *s* of late William Dibble Jolliffe and Laura Beatrice Jolliffe; *m* 1st (marr. diss.); one *s* one *d*; 2nd, 1975, Audrey (*née* Dale); one step *d. Educ:* Bude County Grammar Sch. Institute of Public Finance Accountant. Chartered Accountant (first place in final exam. of (former) Soc. of Incorporated Accountants, 1956). Joined Barclays Bank Ltd, 1941. Served War of 1939-45 (HM Forces, 1944-48). Subseq. held various appts in Treasurers' depts of Devon CC, Winchester City Council, Doncaster CB Council, Bury CB

Council (Dep. Borough Treas.), and Blackpool CB Council (Dep. 1959, Borough Treas., 1962). Mem. Council, Chartered Inst. of Public Finance and Accountancy, 1969-; Financial Adviser, ACC, 1976-; Mem. Council (Pres. 1974-75), Assoc. of Public Service Finance Officers, 1963-76; Chm., Officers' Side, JNC for Chief Officers of Local Authorities in England and Wales, 1971-76; Mem. Exec. Cttee (Pres. 1970-71), NW Soc. of Chartered Accountants, 1966-76; Chm., NW and N Wales Region of CIPFA, 1974-76; Mem., Soc. of County Treasurers (Mem. Exec. Cttee, 1977-); Hon. Treas.: Lancashire Playing Fields Assoc.; Rufford Old Hall Management Cttee (Nat. Trust). Financial Adviser to Assoc. of Municipal Corporations, 1969-74; Mem. (Govt) Working Party on Collab. between Local Authorities and the National Health Service, 1971-74. *Publications*: articles for Public Finance and Accountancy and other local govt jls. *Recreations*: living (i.e. working and playing). *Address*: 4 Whitewood Close, Lytham, Lancs FY8 4RN. *T*: Lytham 736201. *Clubs*: Royal Over-Seas League, Royal Automobile.

JOLLY, Anthony Charles; a Recorder of the Crown Court, since 1975; *b* 25 May 1932; *s* of Leonard and Emily Jolly; *m* 1962, Rosemary Christine Kernan; two *s* one *d*. *Educ*: Royal Naval Coll., Dartmouth; Balliol Coll., Oxford (Exhibnr history; 1st Hon. Sch. Jurisprudence; MA). Called to Bar, Inner Temple, 1954. *Recreations*: sailing, reading, stern sculling. *Address*: (home) Naze House, Freckleton, Lancs PR4 1UN. *T*: Freckleton 632 285; (chambers) 36 St Ann Street, Manchester M2 7LD. *T*: 061-832 6954.

JOLLY, Hugh R., MA, MD, FRCP, DCH; Physician in charge of Pædiatric Department, Charing Cross Hospital, London, since 1965; *b* 5 May 1918; *s* of late Canon R. B. Jolly; *m* 1944, Geraldine Mary Howard; two *s* one *d*. *Educ*: Marlborough Coll.; Sidney Sussex Coll., Cambridge; The London Hospital. MB, BChir (Cantab), 1942; MA (Cantab), 1943; MRCP 1948; DCH (England), 1949; MD (Cantab), 1951 (Raymond Horton-Smith Prize); FRCP 1965. House posts, London Hosp. and N Middlesex Hosp., 1943; Capt., RAMC (Dermatologist), 1944-47; Hosp. for Sick Children, Great Ormond Street, London, 1948-51; Prof. of Paediatrics, Univ. Coll., Ibadan, Nigeria, 1961-62; Vis. Prof. of Child Health, Ghana Med. Sch., 1965-67; Consultant Pædiatrician: Plymouth, 1951-60; Charing Cross Hosp., 1960-; Chailey Heritage, 1966-; Vis. Consultant, Liverpool Sch. of Tropical Medicine, 1969-; Member: Council, Western Cerebral Palsy Centre; Jt Cttee, Central and Scottish Health Councils on Vaccination and Immunization; Old Achimotan Assoc., Ghana. Examiner: Univ. of Glasgow; Univ. of Benin; Univ. of Riyadh; Univ. of Singapore. Vice-President: Health Visitor's Assoc.; FPA. Trustee, London Br., Assoc. for Spina Bifida and Hydrocephalus. President: Pæd. Sect., RSM; Kingston Br., Royal Coll. of Midwives. Mem., Adv. Bd, Parents' Centres, Australia. On Editorial Board of Brit. Jl Med. Educn. *Publications*: Sexual Precocity, 1955; Diseases of Children, 1964, 3rd edn 1976; Paul in Hospital, 1972; Common Sense about Babies and Children, 1973; Book of Child Care, 1975 (trans. into German and Dutch); contribs (on pædiatric subjects) to: Lancet, Archives Dis. Childr., BMJ, Jl Pediatrics, etc. *Recreations*: water ski-ing, gliding, giving gardening instructions to my wife. *Address*: The Garden House, Warren Park, Kingston Hill, Surrey. *T*: 01-942 7855.

JOLLY, Air Cdre Robert Malcolm, CBE 1969; Managing Director, Leonard Griffiths & Associates Ltd, since 1977; Director: Griffiths Professional Services Ltd, since 1975; ADABAS, since 1976; *b* 4 Aug. 1920; *s* of Robert Imrie Jolly and Ethel Thompson Jolly; *m* 1946, Josette Jacqueline (*née* Baindeky); no *c*. *Educ*: Skerry's Coll., Newcastle upon Tyne. Commnd in RAF, 1943; Air Cdre 1971; Dir of Personal Services, MoD, 1970-72; Dir of Automatic Data Processing (RAF), 1973-75, retd. Fellow British Computer Soc., 1972; FBIM, 1973. *Address*: 1 Felbridge Close, Streatham, SW16 2RH. *T*: 01-769 4088. *Club*: Royal Air Force.

JOLOWICZ, Prof. John Anthony; Professor of Comparative Law, University of Cambridge, since 1976; Fellow, Trinity College, Cambridge, since 1952; *b* 11 April 1926; *e s* of late Prof. Herbert Felix Jolowicz and Ruby Victoria Wagner; *m* 1957, Poppy Stanley; one *s* two *d*. *Educ*: Oundle Sch.; Trinity Coll., Cambridge (Scholar; MA 1st Cl. Hons Law Tripos 1950). Served HM Forces (commnd RASC), 1944-48. Called to the Bar, Inner Temple, 1952; Univ. of Cambridge: Asst Lectr in Law, 1955, Lectr, 1959; Reader in Common and Comparative Law, 1972. Professeur associé, Université de Paris 2, 1976. Editor, Jl of Soc. of Public Teachers of Law, 1962-. *Publications*: (ed) H. F. Jolowicz's Lectures on Jurisprudence, 1963; Winfield and Jolowicz on Tort, 1971, 10th edn 1975; (with M. Cappelletti) Public Interest Parties and the Active Role of the

Judge, 1975; contrib. to Internat. Encyc. of Comparative Law and to legal jls. *Address*: Trinity College, Cambridge CB1 1TQ. *T*: Cambridge 58201; West Green House, Barrington, Cambridge CB2 5SA. *T*: Cambridge 870495. *Clubs*: Royal Automobile; Leander (Henley-on-Thames).

JOLY de LOTBINIÈRE, Lt-Col Sir Edmond, Kt 1964; Chairman, Eastern Provincial Area Conservative Association, 1961-65, President, 1969-72; Chairman, Bury St Edmunds Division Conservative Association, 1953-72, President, 1972; *b* 17 March 1903; *er s* of late Brig.-Gen. H. G. Joly de Lotbinière, DSO; *m* 1st, 1928, Hon. Elizabeth Alice Cecilia Jolliffe (marr. diss. 1937); two *s*; 2nd, 1937, Helen Ruth Mildred Ferrar (*d* 1953); 3rd, 1954, Evelyn Adelaide (*née* Dawnay), *widow* of Lt-Col J. A. Innes, DSO. *Educ*: Eton Coll.; Royal Military Academy, Woolwich. 2nd Lieut Royal Engineers, 1923; served in India; RARO, 1928; re-employed, 1939. Served War of 1939-45: in Aden, Abyssinian Campaign and East Africa (despatches); Major 1941; Lieut-Col 1943; retired 1945. Chm. and Managing Dir of several private companies connected with the building trade. *Recreations*: shooting, golf, bridge. *Address*: Horringer Manor, Bury St Edmunds, Suffolk. *T*: Horringer 208. *Club*: Naval and Military.
See also S. J. de Lotbinière.

JOLY de LOTBINIÈRE, S.; *see* de Lotbinière.

JONES; *see* Armstrong-Jones, family name of Earl of Snowdon.

JONES; *see* Elwyn-Jones.

JONES; *see* Griffith-Jones.

JONES; *see* Gwynne Jones, family name of Baron Chalfont.

JONES; *see* Hope-Jones.

JONES; *see* Hugh-Jones.

JONES; *see* Lloyd Jones and Lloyd-Jones.

JONES; *see* Morris-Jones.

JONES; *see* Wynne-Jones.

JONES, family name of **Baron Maelor.**

JONES, Alan Payan P.; *see* Pryce-Jones.

JONES, A(lan) Trevor, MD; FRCP; DPH; Provost of The Welsh National School of Medicine, University of Wales, 1955-Sept. 1969, retired; *b* 24 Feb. 1901; *y s* of Roger W. Jones, MA, JP, Pengam, Glam.; *m* 1931, Gwyneth, *y d* of Edward Evans, Hammersmith; one *s* one *d*. *Educ*: Lewis' Sch., Pengam; University Coll., Cardiff; University Coll., London; University Coll. Hosp., London. MD London 1927; DPH 1929; FRCP 1953. Resident appts, University Coll. Hosp., 1925-28; Dep. Supt, Marylebone Hosp., London, 1928-30; Gen. practice and Hon. Mem. Hosp. Staff, Carmarthen, 1930-34; MOH Carmarthen; MO, Welsh Bd of Health, 1934; Hosp. Officer for Wales, 1937-47; Sen. Admin. MO, Welsh Regional Hosp. Bd, 1947-55; Univ. of Wales Rep., Gen. Med. Council, 1956-69; Vice-Chm., Bd of Govs, United Cardiff Hosps. Commonwealth Fund Travelling Fellow, 1963. Hon. LLD Wales, 1970. *Publications*: Maternal Mortality in Wales, 1937; Survey of Hospital Services of South Wales, 1945; New Medical Teaching Centre, Cardiff, 1966, new edn 1971; articles in medical and public health jls. *Recreations*: photography, gardening. *Address*: 86 Celyn Avenue, Cardiff CF2 6EQ. *T*: Cardiff 752481.

JONES, (Albert) Arthur; MP (C) Daventry, since 1974 (Northamptonshire South, Nov. 1962-1974); *b* 23 Oct. 1915; *s* of late Frederick Henry Jones; *m* 1939, Peggy Joyce (*née* Wingate); one *s* one *d*. *Educ*: Bedford Modern Sch. Territorial, Beds Yeomanry, RA, 1938; Middle East with First Armd Div., 1941; captured at Alamein, 1942; escaped as POW from Italy, 600 miles walk to Allied Territory. Mem. Bedford RDC, 1946-49; Mem. Bedford Borough Council, 1949-74, Alderman, 1957-74; Mayor of Bedford, 1957-58, 1958-59; Member: Beds CC, 1956-67; Central Housing Advisory Cttee, 1959-62; Internat. Union of Local Authorities; Chm., Local Govt Nat. Adv. Cttee, Cons. Central Office, 1963-73; UK Rep., Consultative Assembly, Council of Europe and Assembly of WEU, 1971-73. Mem., Speaker's panel of Chairmen, 1974-. Member: Select Cttee on Immigration and Race Relations, 1969-70; Select Cttee on Expenditure, 1974-; Chm., Environment Sub-Cttee, 1974-; Vice-Chm., Cons. Back-Bench Cttee for the Environment. Hon. Treas., Town and Country Planning Assoc.; Mem., Cttee of

Management, UK Housing Assoc.; Vice-President: Inland Waterways Assoc.; Assoc. of District Councils. Chm. Estates Cttee, Gov. Body of Harpur Charity. Contested (C) Wellingborough Div., 1955. *Address:* Moor Farm, Pavenham, Bedford; 1 Little Smith Street, Westminster, SW1.

JONES, Alec; *see* Jones, T. A.

JONES, Allan G.; *see* Gwynne-Jones.

JONES, Arthur; *see* Jones, (Albert) Arthur.

JONES, Arthur Davies; *b* 1897; *s* of late Evan Jones, JP, Trimsaran; *m* 1942, Rosemary, 2nd *d* of late Rev. Frank Long-Price, Clearbrook, Llanarthney. *Educ:* Mill Hill; Emmanuel Coll., Cambridge. High Sheriff Carmarthenshire, 1941-42. *Address:* Clearbrook Hall, Llanarthney, Dyfed.

JONES, Maj.-Gen. Sir Arthur Guy S.; *see* Salisbury-Jones.

JONES, Brig. Arthur Thomas C.; *see* Cornwall-Jones.

JONES, Rt. Hon. Aubrey, PC 1955; Director: Thomas Tilling Ltd, since 1970; Cornhill Insurance Company Ltd, since 1971 (Chairman, 1971-74); Inbucon International Ltd, since 1975; Black & Decker, since 1977; *b* 20 Nov. 1911; *s* of Evan and Margaret Aubrey Jones, Merthyr Tydfil; *m* 1948, Joan, *d* of G. Godfrey-Isaacs, Ridgehanger, Hillcrest Road, Hanger Hill, W5; two *s. Educ:* Cyfarthfa Castle Secondary Sch., Merthyr Tydfil; London School of Economics. BSc (Econ.) 1st Cl. Hons, Gladstone Memorial Prizewinner, Gerstenberg Post-grad. Schol., LSE. On foreign and editorial staffs of The Times, 1937-39 and 1947-48. Joined British Iron and Steel Federation, 1949; General Dir, June-Dec. 1955. Served War of 1939-45, Army Intelligence Staff, War Office and Mediterranean Theatre, 1940-46. Contested (C) SE Essex in General Election, 1945 and Heywood and Radcliffe (by-election), 1946; MP (U) Birmingham, Hall Green, 1950-65; Parliamentary Private Sec. to Minister of State for Economic Affairs, 1952, and to Min. of Materials, 1953; Minister of Fuel and Power, Dec. 1955-Jan. 1957; Minister of Supply, 1957-Oct. 1959. Mem., Plowden Cttee of Inquiry into Aircraft Industry, 1965-66. Chairman: Staveley Industries Ltd, 1964-65 (Dir 1962-65); Laporte Industries (Holdings) Ltd, 1970-72; Director: Guest, Keen & Nettlefolds Steel Company Limited, 1960-65; Courtaulds Ltd, 1960-63. Chm., Nat. Bd for Prices and Incomes, 1965-70; Vice-Pres., Consumers' Assoc., 1967-72; leading consultant to: Nigerian Public Service Commn, 1973-74; Iranian Govt, 1974-; Mem. Panel of Conciliators, Internat. Centre for Settlement of Investment Disputes, 1974-. Pres., Oxford Energy Policy Club, 1976-. Industrial Fellow Commoner, Churchill Coll., Cambridge, 1972; Hon. Fellow, LSE, 1959, Mem., Court of Governors, 1964. Hon. DSc Bath, 1968. *Publications:* The Pendulum of Politics, 1946; Industrial Order, 1950; The New Inflation: the politics of prices and incomes, 1973. *Address:* 4 Plane Tree House, Duchess of Bedford's Walk, W8 7QT. *Clubs:* Brooks's, American.

JONES, Barry; *see* Jones, Stephen B.

JONES, Maj.-Gen. Basil Douglas, CB 1960; CBE 1950; *b* 14 May 1903; *s* of Rev. B. Jones; *m* 1932, Katherine Holberton, *d* of Col H. W. Man, CBE, DSO; one *s* two *d. Educ:* Plymouth Coll.; RMC, Sandhurst. 2nd Lieut, Welch Regt, 1924; transferred to RAOC, 1935; Major 1939; served with Australian Military Forces in Australia and New Guinea, 1941-44; Temp. Brig. 1947; Brig. 1955; Maj.-Gen. 1958. ADC to the Queen, 1956-58; Inspector, RAOC, 1958-60, retired. Col Commandant, RAOC, 1963-67. *Recreation:* golf. *Address:* Churchfield, Sutton Courtenay, Abingdon, Oxon. *T:* Sutton Courtenay 261.

JONES, Benjamin George; Partner, Linklaters & Paines, Solicitors; *b* 18 Nov. 1914; *s* of Thomas Jones, Llanarth; *m* 1946, Menna, *d* of Rev. Evelyn Wynn-Jones, Holyhead; one *s* one *d. Educ:* Aberaeron County Sch.; UCW Aberystwyth. Chairman: Council for the Welsh Language, 1973-; Hon. Soc. of Cymmrodorion, 1973- (Dep. Sec., 1960-63, Sec., 1963-73). Contested (L) Merioneth, 1959. Mem. Gen. Adv. Council, BBC, 1970-. Vice-Pres., UCW Aberystwyth, 1975-; Mem. Court, Univ. of Wales. *Recreations:* walking, music, visiting art galleries. *Address:* 12 Thornton Way, NW11 6RY. *Club:* Reform.

JONES, Benjamin Rowland R.; *see* Rice-Jones.

JONES, Beti; Chief Adviser on Social Work, Scottish Office, since 1968; *b* 23 Jan. 1919; *d* of Isaac Jones and Elizabeth (*née* Rowlands). *Educ:* Rhondda County Sch. for Girls; Univ. of

Wales. BA (Hons) History, Teaching Diploma. Grammar Sch. teaching, 1941-43; S Wales Organiser, Nat. Assoc. of Girls' Clubs, 1943-47; Youth Officer, Educn Branch, Control Commission, Germany, 1947-49; Children's Officer, Glamorgan CC, 1949-68. Hon. Fellow, Dept of Social Administration, University Coll., Cardiff. *Recreations:* people and places. *Address:* 14 Royal Circus, Edinburgh EH3 6SR. *T:* 031-225 1548. *Clubs:* Royal Over-Seas League (London and Edinburgh).

JONES, Sir Brynmor, Kt 1968; PhD Wales and Cantab, ScD Cantab, FRIC; Vice-Chancellor, University of Hull, 1956-72; *b* Sept. 1903; *o c* of late W. E. Jones, Rhos, Wrexham; *m* 1933, Dora Jones. *Educ:* The Grammar School, Ruabon; University Coll. of North Wales, Bangor (Exhibitioner and Research Scholar); St John's Coll., Cambridge (Hon. Fellow, 1970); Sorbonne, Paris; Fellow, Univ. of Wales, 1928-31. Asst Demonstrator, Cambridge, 1930; Lecturer in Organic Chemistry, University of Sheffield, 1931-46; Leverhulme Research Fellowship, 1939; Mem. Extra-Mural Research Team, Min. of Supply, University of Sheffield, 1940-45; G. F. Grant Professor of Chemistry, University Coll. and University of Hull, 1947-56; Dean of Faculty of Science and Dep. Principal, 1949-52, Vice-Principal, 1952-54; Pro-Vice-Chancellor, 1954-56. Sometime Examiner for Univs of St Andrews, London, Leeds, Oxford, Manchester, Edinburgh and the Inst. of Civil Engineers. Dir, Yorkshire TV, 1970-72. Chairman: Nat. Council for Educational Technology, 1967-73; UGC and Min. of Educn's sub-cttee on Audio-Visual Aids (Report, HMSO, 1965); Academic Council, BMA; Univs Council for Adult Educn, 1961-65; Pres., Assoc. for Programmed Learning and Educational Technology, 1969-72; Chairman: Vis. Grants Cttee to Univ. of Basutoland, Bechuanaland Protectorate and Swaziland, 1965; Programme Cttee on Higher Educn, BBC Further Educn Adv. Council, 1967-70, Vice-Chm., 1970-72; Member: Kennedy Memorial Trust, 1964-74; GMC, 1964-74; DSIR Postgraduate Trng Awards Cttee, 1963-65; Univ. Science and Technology Bd (SRC), 1965-68; Brit. Cttee of Selection for Frank Knox Fellowships to Harvard Univ., 1962-72; Inter-Univ. Council (and Exec.) for Higher Educn, Overseas; Adv. Cttee, Planning Cttee and Council of Open Univ., 1967-72; Royal Commn on Higher Educn in Ceylon, 1969-70; University Council, Nairobi; Provisional Council of Univ. of E Africa and of University Coll., Dar es Salaam, 1961-64; Council of University Coll., Dar es Salaam, 1964-68; Provisional Council, Univ. of Mauritius, 1965-67; General Nursing Council, 1960-66; Acad. Adv. Cttee, Welsh Coll. of Advanced Technology 1964-67; East Riding Educn Cttee, 1956-74; Hull Chamber of Commerce and Shipping; Council of Chemical Soc., 1945-48, and 1953-56; Senior Reporter, Annual Reports of Chemical Soc., 1948; President: Hull Civic Soc.; Hull Lit. and Philosoph. Soc., 1955-57; Hull Bach Choir; E Riding Local History Soc. Vice-Chm., Beverley Minster Restoration Appeal. Mem., Court of Universities of Nottingham and Sheffield, 1956-72; Governor: Hymers Coll.; Pocklington Sch.; E Riding Coll. of Agriculture. Hon. FCP. Hon. LLD Wales, 1968, Leeds, 1974; Hon. DLitt Hull, 1972. *Publications:* numerous papers on Physical Organic and on Organic Chemistry, mainly on kinetics and mechanism of organic reactions and on mesomorphism, in Journal of Chemical Soc. and other scientific periodicals; articles and published addresses on new learning resources and Educational Technology. University of Sheffield Record of War Work, 1939-45. *Recreations:* music, photography and walking. *Address:* 46 Westwood Road, Beverley, North Humberside HU17 8EJ. *T:* Beverley 888125.

JONES, Cecil Artimus E.; *see* Evan-Jones.

JONES, Charles Ian McMillan; Headmaster of Bedford School, since Sept. 1975; *b* 11 Oct. 1934; *s* of Wilfred Charles Jones and Bessie Jones (*née* McMillan); *m* 1962, Jennifer Marie Potter; two *s . Educ:* Bishop's Stortford Coll.; St John's Coll., Cambridge. Certif. Educn 1959, MA 1962. 2nd Lieut RA, 1953-55. Head of Geog. Dept, Bishop's Stortford Coll., 1960-70, Asst to Headmaster, 1967-70; Vice-Principal, King William's Coll., IoM, 1971-75. Man., England Schoolboy Hockey XI, 1967-74; Man., England Hockey XI, 1968-69; Mem. IoM Sports Couuncil, 1972-75. *Publications:* articles in Guardian. *Recreations:* hockey (Captain Cambridge Univ. Hockey XI, 1959; England Hockey XI, 1959-64, 17 caps; Gt Britain Hockey XI, 1959-64, 28 caps), cricket (Captain IoM Cricket XI, 1973-75), squash, gardening. *Address:* School House, 15 Park Avenue, Bedford MK40 2LB. *T:* Bedford 52919. *Clubs:* MCC, East India, Devonshire, Sports and Public Schools; Hawks (Cambridge).

JONES, General Sir Charles (Phibbs), GCB 1965 (KCB 1960; CB 1952); CBE 1945; MC 1940; Governor of Royal Hospital, Chelsea, 1969-75; Chief Royal Engineer, 1967-72; *b* 29 June

1906; s of late Hume Riversdale Jones and Elizabeth Anne (née Phibbs); m 1934, Ouida Margaret Wallace; two s. Educ: Portora Royal School; Enniskillen, N Ireland; Royal Military Academy, Woolwich; Pembroke Coll., Cambridge. Commissioned in RE, 1925; service with Royal Bombay Sappers and Miners in India, 1928-34; Adjt of 42nd (EL) Divl Engineers (TA), 1934-39; student at Staff Coll., Camberley, 1939. War of 1939-45: service in BEF, France and Belgium, as Bde Major 127 Inf. Bde, 1940; Instructor at Staff Coll., Camberley, 1940-41; GSO1 at GHQ Home Forces, 1941-42; CRE Guards Armoured Div. in UK and in NW Europe, 1943-44; BGS XXX Corps in NW Europe, 1945. Chief of Staff, Malaya Comd, 1945-46; BGS HQ Western Comd, UK, 1946; idc, 1947; Comdr 2nd Inf. Bde, 1948-50; Dir of Plans, War Office, 1950; GOC 7th Armoured Div., BAOR, 1951-53; Comdt, Staff Coll., Camberley, 1954-56; Vice AG, WO, 1957-58; Dir, Combined Military Planning Staff, CENTO, 1959; GOC, 1st Corps 1960-62; GOC, Northern Comd, 1962-63; Master General of the Ordnance, 1963-66; ADC (General) to the Queen, 1965-67. A Governor, Corps of Commissionaires, 1969-. Col Comdt, RE, 1961-72; Hon. Col, Engineer and Rly Staffs Corps, RE, T&AVR, 1970-77. Order of Leopold, Croix de Guerre (Belgium), 1945. Recreations: golf and fishing. Address: Westwick, Rye, East Sussex. Clubs: Army and Navy; Dormy House (Rye).

JONES, Rev. Canon Cheslyn Peter Montague, MA; Principal of Pusey House, Oxford, since 1971; b 4 July 1918; e s of late Montague William and Gladys Muriel Jones; unmarried. Educ: Winchester Coll.; New Coll., Oxford. BA 1st cl. Hons Theology, 1939; Senior Demy, Magdalen Coll., 1940-41. Deacon 1941; Priest 1942. Curate of St Peter, Wallsend, 1941-43; St Barnabas, Northolt Park, 1943-46; at Nashdom Abbey, 1946-51; Chaplain, Wells Theological Coll., 1951-52; Librarian, Pusey House, Oxford, 1952-56; Chaplain, Christ Church Cathedral, Oxford, 1953-56; Principal, Chichester Theological Coll., and Chancellor, Chichester Cathedral, 1956-69, Canon Emeritus, 1971. Select Preacher: Oxford Univ., 1960 and 1977; Cambridge Univ., 1962; Sir Henry Stephenson Fellow, Univ. of Sheffield, 1969-70; Bampton Lectr, Oxford Univ., 1970. Publications: (ed) A Manual for Holy Week, 1967; contributions to: Studies in the Gospels, 1955; Studies in Ephesians, 1956; Thirty 20th century hymns, 1960; Christian Believing, 1976; (editor and contributor): For Better For Worse, 1977; The Study of Liturgy, 1977. Recreations: travel, music. Address: Pusey House, Oxford OX1 3LZ. T: Oxford 59519.

JONES, Sir Christopher L.; see Lawrence-Jones.

JONES, Clement; see Jones, John C.

JONES, Daniel, BEM 1945; MP (Lab) Burnley since Oct. 1959; b 26 Sept. 1908; m 1932, Phyllis, d of John Williams Maesteg, Glam.; two s one d. Educ: Ynyshir Council Sch.; NCLC. In coal-mines of Rhondda Valley for 12 years, 1920-32; unemployed for 4 years; in engineering as a SR Engineer, 1939-54; Aircraft Industry, 1939-45 (BEM; commended by Russian Embassy, 1945); Aircraft Official, part-time 1940-54, full-time 1954-59, AEU. Mem. British Legion and Ex-Servicemen's Clubs, London, Burnley and Rhondda Valley. Recreations: music and walking. Address: 124 Marsden Road, Burnley. T: Burnley 5638.

JONES, Daniel Gruffydd; Under-Secretary, Welsh Office, since 1975; b 7 Dec. 1933; o s of late Ifor Ceredig Jones and of Gwendolen Eluned Jones; m 1969, Maureen Anne Woodhall; three d. Educ: Ardwyn Grammar Sch., Aberystwyth; University Coll. of N Wales, Bangor (BA). Asst Principal, Min. of Housing and Local Govt, 1960; Private Sec. to Parly Sec., 1962-63; Principal, 1963; Private Sec. to Sec. of Cabinet, 1967-69; Asst Sec., 1969; Sec., Water Resources Bd, 1969-73; Asst Sec., DoE, 1973; Sec., Prime Minister's Cttee on Local Govt Rules of Conduct, 1973-74; Asst Sec., DoE, 1974-75. Address: c/o Welsh Office, Cathays Park, Cardiff CF1 3NQ. T: Cardiff 28066.

JONES, David A.; see Akers-Jones.

JONES, David Hugh; Artistic Director, Royal Shakespeare Company (Aldwych), since 1978; b 19 Feb. 1934; s of John David Jones and Gwendolen Agnes Langworthy (née Ricketts); m 1964, Sheila Allen; two s. Educ: Taunton Sch.; Christ's Coll., Cambridge (MA 1st Cl. Hons English). 2nd Lieut RA, 1954-56. Production team of Monitor, BBC TV's 1st arts magazine, 1958-62, Editor, 1962-64; joined RSC, 1964; Aldwych Co. Dir, 1968-72; Artistic Dir, RSC (Aldwych), 1975-77; Producer, Play of the Month, BBC TV, 1977-78. Productions for RSC incl. plays by Arden, Gorky, Granville Barker, Günter Grass, Graham Greene, Mercer, O'Casey, Shakespeare, and Chekhov. Dir.

prodns for Chichester and Stratford, Ontario, Festival Theatres. Dir, films for BBC TV, incl. biography of poet, John Clare, 1969, and adaptations of Hardy and Chekhov short stories, 1972 and 1973. Recreations: chess, reading modern poetry, exploring mountains and islands. Address: 26 Fitzjohn's Avenue, NW3. T: 01-435 4739.

JONES, Rev. David Ian Stewart; Headmaster of Bryanston School, since 1974; b 3 April 1934; s of Rev. John Milton Granville Jones and Evelyn Moyes Stewart Jones (formerly Chedburn); m 1967, Susan Rosemary Hardy Smith; twin s and d. Educ: St John's Sch., Leatherhead; Selwyn Coll., Cambridge (MA). Commnd Royal Signals, 1952-54. Curate at Oldham Parish Church, 1959-62; Vicar of All Saints, Elton, Bury, 1963-66; Asst Conduct and Chaplain of Eton Coll., 1966-70; Conduct and Sen. Chaplain of Eton Coll., 1970-74. Recreations: reading (theology, philosophy, politics), music, rowing (coaching). Address: Bryanston School, Blandford, Dorset DT11 0PX. T: Blandford 2411.

JONES, David Jeffreys, CMG 1969; Puisne Judge, High Court, Uganda, 1960-72; b 18 Oct. 1909; s of Thomas John and Gwendoline Jones, The Larches, Ystradgynlais, Swansea; unmarried. Educ: Maesydderwen Grammar Sch.; Middle Temple. Called to Bar, 1933; practised in London and Wales Circuit to 1938; Sec., Ffynone Estates Co., 1938-43; Asst. Trust Officer, Public Trustee Office, 1943-46; Legal Asst, Control Commission, Germany, 1946-48; Dep. Legal Adviser to Commissioner at Hamburg, 1948-50; Resident Magistrate, Uganda, 1950-55; Sen. Res. Magistrate, Actg Asst Judicial Adviser, and Chm. Traffic Appeals Tribunal, 1955-60; Acting Chief Justice, June-Oct. 1969; Mem., Judicial Service Commn, 1969-; Chm., Judicial Inquiry into two missing Americans, 1971. Awarded Internat. Constantinian Order, 1970. Recreations: reading, music, all kinds of sport. Address: The Larches, Ystradgynlais, Swansea SA9 1QL. T: Glantawe 842298. Club: Royal Over-Seas League.

JONES, David le Brun, CB 1975; Deputy Secretary, Cabinet Office, since 1976; b 18 Nov. 1923; s of Thomas John Jones and Blanche le Brun. Educ: City of London Sch.; Trinity Coll., Oxford. Asst Principal, Min. of Power, 1947; Principal, MOP, 1952; Asst Sec., Office of the Minister for Science, 1962; Asst Sec., MOP, 1963; Under-Sec., MOP, later Min. of Technology and DTI, 1968-73; Dep. Sec., DTI, later DoI, 1973-76. Recreations: walking, reading, chess. Address: 47 Grove End Road, NW8 9NB. Club: United Oxford & Cambridge University.

JONES, David M.; see Mansel-Jones.

JONES, Prof. David Morgan, MA; Professor of Classics in the University of London (Westfield College) since 1953; b 9 April 1915; m 1965, Irene M. Glanville. Educ: Whitgift Sch.; Exeter Coll., Oxford (Scholar). 1st Class, Classical Hon. Mods, 1936; 1st Class, Lit Hum, 1938; Derby Scholar, 1938; Junior Research Fellow, Exeter Coll., Oxford, 1938-40; Oxford Diploma in Comparative Philology, 1940; Lecturer in Classics, University Coll. of North Wales, 1940-48; Reader in Classics in the University of London (Birkbeck Coll.), 1949-53. Publications: papers and reviews in classical and linguistic journals. Address: 48 Corringham Road, NW11. T: 01-455 7350.

JONES, D(avid) Prys; Metropolitan Stipendiary Magistrate since 1969; b 7 May 1913; s of John William and Ethel Banks Jones; m 1940, Joan Wiltshire; one s two d. Educ: Wigan Grammar Sch.; Manchester Univ. LLB (Hons) 1934. Called to Bar, Gray's Inn, 1935; joined Northern Circuit, 1936. Commnd Manchester Regt (TA), 1939; JAG's Dept as Captain, Legal Staff and Major Dep. Judge Advocate, 1944-45. Joined Dir of Public Prosecutions Dept, 1946; Asst Dir of Public Prosecutions, 1966. Recreations: music, walking. Address: 23 Upfield, Croydon, Surrey. T: 01-656 9167.

JONES, Derek John Claremont; Secretary for the Environment, Government of Hong Kong, since 1976; b 2 July 1927; er s of Albert Claremont Jones and Mrs Jones (née Hazell); m 1st, 1951, Jean Cynthia Withams; one s two d; 2nd, 1970, Kay Cecile Thewlis; one s. Educ: Colston Sch., Bristol; Bristol Univ.; London Sch. of Economics and Political Science. Economic Asst, Economic Section, Cabinet Office, 1950-53; Second Sec., UK Delegn to OEEC/NATO, Paris, 1953-55; Asst Principal, Colonial Office, 1955-57; Principal, Colonial Office, 1957-66; First Secretary, Commonwealth Office, 1966-67; Counsellor (Hong Kong Affairs), UK Mission, Geneva, 1967-71; Dep. Economic Sec., Govt of Hong Kong, 1971-73; Sec. for Economic Services, Govt of Hong Kong, 1973-76. Recreations: reading, travel, conversation. Address: 82 Mount Nicholson Gap, Hong Kong.

JONES, Captain Desmond V.; see Vincent-Jones.

JONES, Rev. Prof. Douglas Rawlinson; Lightfoot Professor of Divinity, University of Durham, and Residentiary Canon of Durham Cathedral since 1964; *b* 11 Nov. 1919; *s* of Percival and Charlotte Elizabeth Jones; *m* 1946, Hazel Mary Passmore; three *s* two *d*. *Educ:* Queen Elizabeth's Hosp., Bristol; St Edmund Hall, Oxford; Wycliffe Hall, Oxford. Squire Scholar, 1938; BA 1941; MA 1945; deacon, 1942; priest, 1943. Curate of St Michael and All Angels, Windmill Hill, Bristol, 1942-45; Lectr, Wycliffe Hall, Oxford, 1945-50; Chaplain, Wadham Coll., Oxford, 1945-50; Lectr in Divinity, 1948-50; University of Durham: Lectr, 1951; Sen. Lectr, 1963. Mem., Gen. Synod of C of E, 1970-. *Publications:* Haggai, Zechariah and Malachi, 1962; Isaiah, 56-66 and Joel, 1964; Instrument of Peace, 1965; contrib. to: Peake's Commentary on the Bible, 1962; Hastings' Dictionary of the Bible, 1963; The Cambridge History of the Bible, 1963; articles in Jl of Theolog. Studies, Zeitschrift für die Alttestamentliche Wissenschaft, Vetus Testamentum, Theology, Scottish Jl of Theology. *Recreation:* carpentry. *Address:* 12 The College, Durham DH1 3EQ. *T:* Durham 64295.

JONES, Prof. Douglas Samuel, MBE 1945; FRS 1968; Ivory Professor of Mathematics, University of Dundee, since 1965; *b* 10 Jan. 1922; *s* of late J. D. Jones and B. Jones (*née* Streather); *m* 1950, Ivy Styles; one *s* one *d*. *Educ:* Wolverhampton Grammar Sch.; Corpus Christi Coll., Oxford. DSc Manchester 1957. Flt-Lt, RAFVR, 1941-45. Commonwealth Fund Fellow, MIT, 1947-48; Asst Lectr in Maths, University of Manchester, 1948-51; Lectr 1951-54, Research Prof. 1955, New York Univ.; Sen. Lectr in Maths, Univ. of Manchester, 1955-57; Prof. of Maths, Univ. of Keele, 1957-64. Vis. Prof., Courant Inst., 1962-63. Member: UGC, 1976-; Computer Bd, 1977-. FIMA 1964; FRSE 1967. Hon. DSc Strathclyde, 1975. Keith Prize, RSE, 1974. *Publications:* Electrical and Mechanical Oscillations, 1961; Theory of Electromagnetism, 1964; Generalised Functions, 1966; Introductory Analysis, vol. 1, 1969, vol 2, 1970; articles in mathematical and physical jls. *Recreations:* golf, walking, photography. *Address:* Department of Mathematics, The University, Dundee DD1 4HN. *T:* Dundee 23181.

JONES, Edgar Stafford, CBE 1960 (MBE 1953); *b* 11 June 1909; *s* of late Theophilus Jones; *m* 1938, Margaret Aldis, *d* of late Henry Charles Askew; one *s* one *d*. *Educ:* Liverpool Institute High Sch. Mem. of Local Government Service, 1925-34; joined Assistance Board, 1934. Seconded to Air Min., as Hon. Flt-Lt RAFVR, 1943; Hon. Sqdn-Ldr, 1945. Transferred to Foreign Office, 1946; transferred to Washington, 1949; Dep. Finance Officer, Foreign Office, 1953; Head of Finance Dept, Foreign Office, 1957 and Diplomatic Service Administration Office, 1965, retired 1968. *Address:* 27 Cole Park Gardens, Twickenham, Mddx. *T:* 01-892 5435. *Clubs:* London Welsh Rugby Football; Glamorgan Cricket.

JONES, Edmund Angus, CMG 1963; company director; Managing Director, 1954-65, Chairman, 1962-67, Mobil Oil Australia Ltd; *b* 8 Jan. 1903; *s* of Frederick E. Jones; *m* 1926, Elsie May Townley; two *s* one *d*. *Educ:* Christchurch Boys' High Sch., NZ; Harvard Business Sch. (Advanced Management Programme). Vacuum Oil Co. Pty Ltd, 1928, Salesman, Christchurch, NZ; Branch Manager, Christchurch, NZ, 1932; Asst Gen. Man., 1935, Gen. Man., 1939, Wellington, NZ; Dir, Melbourne, Australia, 1944; Area Consultant, Standard Vacuum, New York, USA, 1948; Dir, 1951, Man. Dir, 1954, Vacuum Oil Co. Pty Ltd, Melbourne, Australia. *Publications:* various articles on Management. *Recreations:* golf, gardening. *Address:* 61/546 Toorak Road, Toorak, Victoria 3142, Australia. *T:* 208181. *Clubs:* Athenæum (Melbourne), also Rotary, Royal Melbourne Golf, Victoria Racing (all Melbourne).

JONES, Edward; see Jones, J. E.

JONES, Air Marshal Sir Edward G.; see Gordon Jones.

JONES, Sir Edward Martin F.; see Furnival Jones.

JONES, Rt. Rev. Edward Michael G.; see Gresford Jones.

JONES, Edward Norton, CMG 1952; OBE 1940; *b* 28 Jan. 1902; *s* of Daniel Norton Jones; *m* 1940, Cecilia Lucy Shaen (*née* Hamersley). *Educ:* St Paul's Sch., W Kensington; Corpus Christi Coll., Cambridge (BA). Gold Coast: Asst District Comr, 1925; District Commissioner, 1932; Sec. for Social Services, 1943; Dir of Social Welfare and Housing, 1946; Chief Commissioner, Northern Territories, 1948; Sec. for Development and Chm. of Marketing and Development Corporations, 1950; Permanent Sec. to the Ministry of Defence and External Affairs, Gold Coast, 1952; Mem., Public Service Commission, Ghana, 1955-61. *Recreation:* golf. *Address:* Walden, Innhams Wood, Crowborough, East Sussex. *Club:* Royal Commonwealth Society.

JONES, Rt. Hon. Sir Edward (Warburton), PC (N Ireland) 1965; Kt 1973; **Rt. Hon. Lord Justice Jones**; Lord Justice of Appeal, Supreme Court of Judicature, N Ireland, since 1973 (Judge of the High Court of Justice in Northern Ireland, 1968-73); *b* 3 July 1912; *s* of late Hume Riversdale Jones and Elizabeth Anne (*née* Phibbs); *m* 1st, 1941, Margaret Anne Crosland Smellie (*d* 1953); three *s*; 2nd, 1953, Ruth Buchan Smellie; one *s*. *Educ:* Portora Royal School, Enniskillen, N Ireland; Trinity Coll., Dublin. BA (TCD), with First Class Moderatorship, Legal Science, and LLB (TCD) 1935; called to Bar of Northern Ireland, 1936; QC (N Ireland), 1948; called to Bar (Middle Temple), 1964. Junior Crown Counsel: County Down, 1939; Belfast, 1945-55. Enlisted, 1939; commissioned Royal Irish Fusiliers, 1940; Staff Coll., Camberley, 1943; AAG, Allied Land Forces, SEA, 1945; released with Hon. rank Lt-Col, 1946. MP (U) Londonderry City, Parliament of Northern Ireland, 1951-68; Attorney-Gen. for Northern Ireland, 1964-68. Chancellor: Dio. Derry and Raphoe, 1945-64; Dio. Connor, 1959-64; Dio. Clogher, 1973; Lay Mem. Court of Gen. Synod, Church of Ireland. Bencher, Inn of Court of NI, 1961. *Recreations:* golf, sailing. *Address:* The Lodge, Spa, Ballynahinch, Co. Down, N Ireland. *T:* Ballynahinch 2240; Craig-y-Mor, Trearddur Bay, Anglesey. *T:* Trearddur Bay 860406. *Club:* Army and Navy.

JONES, Eifion, CMG 1964; OBE 1953; Permanent Secretary, Ministry of Works, Northern Nigeria, 1959-66; Member, Northern Nigerian Development Corporation, 1959-66; retired; *b* Llanelly, Carmarthenshire, 10 June 1912; *s* of I. J. Jones and R. A. Jones (*née* Bassett); *m* 1944, Kathleen, *d* of Donald and E. J. MacCalman, Argyllshire. *Educ:* Llanelli Grammar Sch.; University Coll., Swansea. BSc (Wales). Executive Engineer, Nigeria, 1942; Senior Executive Engineer, 1951; Chief Engineer, 1954; Dep. Dir of Public Works, Nigeria, 1958. FICE 1957; FIWE 1957. *Recreations:* golf, gardening. *Address:* c/o Barclays Bank Ltd, Llanelli, Dyfed.

JONES, Elfryn; Chief Statistician, Royal Commission on the Distribution of Income and Wealth, since 1974. *b* 9 July 1913; *m* 1940, Vera Anne Owen; two *s*. *Educ:* Enfield Grammar Sch.; Institute of Actuaries. FIA 1942. Prudential Assurance Co. Ltd, 1930-42; Temp. Statistical Officer, Admiralty, 1942-46; Permanent statistical staff Admiralty, later MoD, 1946-74; Head of Naval Statistics, 1954-68; Asst Under-Sec. of State (Statistics), MoD, 1968-74. *Publications:* various papers on manpower planning in actuarial and operational research jls and in proceedings of NATO science confs. *Recreations:* chess, swimming, gardening. *Address:* 20 Nursery Gardens, Purley, Pangbourne, Berks. *T:* Pangbourne 2917.

JONES, Sir Emrys; see Jones, Sir W. E.

JONES, Prof. Emrys, MSc, PhD (Wales); FRGS; Professor of Geography, University of London, at London School of Economics, since 1961; *b* Aberdare, 17 Aug. 1920; *s* of Samuel Garfield and Anne Jones; *m* 1948, Iona Vivien, *d* of R. H. Hughes; two *d*. *Educ:* Grammar Sch. for Boys, Aberdare; University Coll. of Wales, Aberystwyth. BSc (1st Class Hons in Geography and Anthropology), 1941; MSc, 1945; PhD, 1947; Fellow of the University of Wales, 1946-47; Asst Lectr at University Coll., London, 1947-50; Fellow, Rockefeller Foundation, 1948-49; Lectr at Queen's Univ., Belfast, 1950-58, Sen. Lectr, 1958. O'Donnel Lectr, Univ. of Wales, 1977. Chm., Regional Studies Assoc., 1967-69; Mem. Council, RGS, 1973-; Consultant on urbanisation and planning. Victoria Medal, RGS, 1977. *Publications:* Hon. Editor, Belfast in its Regional Setting, 1952; (jointly) Welsh Rural Communities, 1960; A Social Geography of Belfast, 1961; Human Geography, 1964; Towns and Cities, 1966; Atlas of London, 1968; (ed jtly) Man and his Habitat, 1971; (contrib.) The Future of Planning, 1973; (with E. van Zandt) The City, 1974; Readings in Social Geography, 1975; (with J. Eyles) Introduction to Social Geography, 1977; articles in geographical, sociological and planning jls. *Recreations:* books, music. *Address:* 4 The Apple Orchard, Hemel Hempstead, Herts. *T:* Hemel Hempstead 52357.

JONES, Lady (Enid); see Bagnold, Enid.

JONES, Eric Kyffin, CBE 1962 (MBE 1948); Chairman, Welsh Board of Health, 1961-Aug. 1962; *b* 4 Dec. 1896; *s* of Hugh Kyffin Jones and Catherine Jane (*née* Williams); *m* 1920, Helen Roberta Patricia (*née* Montgomery); one *d*. *Educ:* St Margaret's, Liverpool. Home Office, Boy Clerk, 1912; Welsh Board of Health: Principal, 1948; Asst Sec., 1955; Chm. (Under-Sec.),

1961. OStJ 1964. *Address:* 10 Penydre, Rhiwbina, Cardiff. *T:* Cardiff 62421.

JONES, Sir Eric (Malcolm), KCMG 1957; CB 1953; CBE 1946; Director, Government Communications Headquarters, Foreign Office, 1952-60, retired; *b* 27 April 1907; *m* 1929, Edith Mary Taylor; one *s* one *d. Educ:* King's Sch., Macclesfield. Textile Merchant and Agent, 1925-40. RAFVR 1940-46, Civil Servant, 1946-60; Dir, Simon Engineering Ltd, 1966-77. Legion of Merit (US), 1946. *Recreations:* ski-ing, golf. *Address:* 24 Thorncliffe, Lansdown Road, Cheltenham, Glos. *T:* Cheltenham 52359.

JONES, Ernest Edward; Chairman, South Yorkshire County Council, 1975-76; *b* 15 Oct. 1931; *s* of William Edward Jones and Eileen Gasser; *m* 1955, Mary Armstrong; one *s* one *d. Educ:* Bentley Catholic Primary Sch., Doncaster; Sheffield De La Salle Coll.; Hopwood Hall Coll. of Educn, Middleton, Lancs; Manch. Univ. Sch. of Educn; Management Studies Unit, Sheffield Polytech. Min. of Educn Teaching Certif. (CertEd); Univ. Dipl. in Science Studies (DipSc); Dipl. in Educn Management (DEM). School Master, 1953-. Doncaster County Borough: Councillor, 1962-74 (Chm. Health Cttee, 1971-74; Chm. Social Services Cttee, 1972-73; served on 15 other cttees at various times). Mem. Nat. Health Exec. Council, 1964-74; Mem. Doncaster and Dist Water Bd, 1972-74; AMC (Social Services), 1972-74. South Yorkshire CC: Mem. 1973-77; Dep. Chm., 1973-75; Chm., Rec., Culture and Health Cttee, 1973-75. Member: Peak Park Planning Bd; Yorks Arts Assoc.; Yorks Regional Land Drainage Cttee; Univ. of Hull Educn Delegacy; MRSH; former Member: AMA; Yorks and Humberside Museums and Art Galleries Fedn; Yorks and Humberside Regional Sports Council; Yorks, Humberside and Cleveland Tourist Bd. *Recreations:* music and fine arts, general interest in sport, fell-walking, keen caravanner. *Address:* 11 Norborough Road, Doncaster, South Yorks DN2 4AR. *T:* Doncaster 66122.

JONES, Ernest Turner, CB 1953; OBE 1942; MEng; Hon. FAIAA; FRAeS; *b* 7 Jan. 1897; *m* 1921, Millicent Adie Manning; one *s* one *d. Educ:* University of Liverpool. Pilot and flying instructor, RFC/RAF, 1915-19. Aerodynamics Dept, Royal Aircraft Establishment, 1923-30; Marine Aircraft Experimental Establishment, Felixstowe, 1930-38; Chief Technical Officer, Aeroplane and Armament Experimental Establishment, Martlesham, 1938-39; Chief Supt, Aeroplane and Armament Experimental Establishment, Boscombe Down, 1939-47; Dir of Instrument Research and Development, Ministry of Supply, 1947-49; Principal Dir of Scientific Research (Air), 1949-55, Dir-Gen. Tech. Development (Air), 1955-58, Dep. Controller (Overseas Affairs), 1958-59, Min. of Supply. Pres. Royal Aeronautical Society, 1956-57. *Publications:* many Research Memoranda published by Aeronautical Research Council. Jl Royal Aeronautical Society (paper in Flight Testing Methods). *Address:* Cross Deep House, 102 Cross Deep, Strawberry Hill, Twickenham, Middx. *T:* 01-892 6208.

JONES, Evan David, CBE 1965; FSA 1959; Librarian of the National Library of Wales, 1958-69; *b* 6 Dec. 1903; *e s* of Evan Jones and Jane (*née* Davies), Llangeitho; *m* 1933, Eleanor Anne, *o d* of John Humphrey Lewis, master mariner, Aberystwyth; one *s. Educ:* Llangeitho Primary Sch.; Tregaron County Sch.; University Coll. of Wales, Aberystwyth. BA 1926, Hons Welsh, Class 1, History 2a; Sir John Williams Research Student, 1928-29. Archivist Asst, National Library of Wales, 1929-36; Dep. Keeper of MSS and Records, 1936-38, Keeper, 1938-58. Lecturer in Archive Administration, UCW, 1957-58. President: Cambrian Archæological Assoc., 1962-63; New Wales Union, 1965-67; Welsh Harp Soc., 1965-; Welsh Bibliographical Soc., 1968-; Cymdeithas Emynau Cymru, 1968-; Cymdeithas Bob Owen, 1976-; Pres., Union of Welsh Independents, 1974-75. Chairman: Governors of Welsh Sch., Aberystwyth, 1946-47; Executive Cttee, Urdd Gobaith Cymru, 1954-57; Cambrian Archæological Assoc., 1954-57; Cardigans. Congregational Quarterly Meeting, 1960; Undeb y Cymdeithasau Llyfrau, 1959-61; Welsh Books Centre, 1966-70; Welsh Books Council, 1968-70; Govs, Coll. of Librarianship, Wales, 1968-74 (Vice-Chm., 1964-68); Three Counties Congregational Assoc., 1972-73; Sec., Welsh Congregational Church, Aberystwyth, 1938-; Treasurer: New Wales Union, 1970-; Interdenominational Cttee on Welsh Lang., 1970-. Mem. Court of Governors: Nat. Museum of Wales, 1958-69; University of Wales, 1958-71; Member: Council of UCW; Congregational Memorial Coll., Swansea; Bala-Bangor Congregational Coll.; Union of Welsh Independents; Ancient Monuments Bd for Wales, 1970-; Council of Brit. Records Assoc., 1958-69; Pantyfedwen Trust, 1958-69; Council of Hon. Soc. of Cymmrodorion; National Eisteddfod Council; Broadcasting Council for Wales, 1966-71; Library Advisory Council (Wales), 1965-69; Hon. Mem. of the Gorsedd (also Examr). Hon. FLA 1973. Hon LLD Wales, 1972. Editor: NLW

Jl, 1958-69; Jl of Merioneth History and Record Soc.; DWB Supplements. *Publications:* Gwaith Lewis Glyn Cothi, 1953; Victorian and Edwardian Wales, 1972; Gwaith Lewis Glyn Cothi 1837-39, 1973; Ystyriaethau ar Undeb Eglwysig, 1974; articles in Archæologia Cambrensis, Bulletin of Board of Celtic Studies, and many other journals; contrib. Dictionary of Welsh Biography. *Recreations:* colour photography, walking, gardening. *Address:* Penllerneuadd, North Road, Aberystwyth SY23 2EE. *T:* Aberystwyth 7286.

JONES, Ewan Perrins W.; *see* Wallis-Jones.

JONES, Sir Ewart (Ray Herbert), Kt 1963; FRS 1950; DSc Victoria, PhD Wales, MA Oxon, FRIC; Waynflete Professor of Chemistry, University of Oxford, 1955-Sept. 1978; Fellow of Magdalen College; *b* Wrexham, Denbighshire, 16 March 1911; *m* 1937, Frances Mary Copp; one *s* two *d. Educ:* Grove Park Sch., Wrexham; University Coll. of North Wales, Bangor; Univ. of Manchester. Fellow of Univ. of Wales, 1935-37; Lecturer, Imperial Coll. of Science and Technology, 1938; Reader in Organic Chemistry, University of London, and Asst Prof., 1945; Sir Samuel Hall Prof. of Chemistry, The University, Manchester, 1947-55; Arthur D. Little Visiting Prof. of Chemistry, Massachusetts Institute of Technology, 1952; Karl Folkers Lecturer at Universities of Illinois and Wisconsin, 1957. Mem. Council for Scientific and Industrial Research, and Chm., Research Grants Cttee, 1961-65; Mem. SRC and Chm., Univ. Science and Technology Bd, 1965-69; Mem., Science Bd, 1969-72. Chemical Society: Tilden Lectr, 1949; Pedler Lectr, 1959; Award in Natural Product Chem., 1974. Meldola Medal, Royal Institute of Chemistry, 1940; Davy Medal, Royal Society, 1966. Fritzsche Award, American Chemical Soc., 1962. President: Chemical Soc., 1964-66; RIC, 1970-72. Fellow, Imperial Coll., 1967; Foreign Mem. Amer. Acad. of Arts and Sciences, 1967. Hon. DSc: Birmingham, 1965; Nottingham, 1966; New South Wales, 1967; Sussex, 1969; Salford, 1971; Wales, 1971; Hon. LLD Manchester, 1972. *Publications:* scientific papers in Jl of the Chem. Soc. *Address:* Dyson Perrins Laboratory, South Parks Road, Oxford. *T:* Oxford 57809; 6 Sandy Lane, Yarnton, Oxford. *T:* Kidlington 2581. *Club:* Athenæum.

JONES, Major Francis, CVO 1969; TD (3 clasps); MA, FSA; DL; Wales Herald Extraordinary since 1963; County Archivist, Carmarthenshire, 1958-74; *b* Trevine, Pembrokeshire, 5 July 1908; *s* of James Jones, Grinston, Pembs, and Martha Jones; *m* Ethel M. S. A., *d* of late J. J. Charles, Trewilym, Pembs; two *s* two *d. Educ:* Fishguard County Sch., Pembs. Temp. Archivist of Pembs, 1934-36; Archivist, Nat. Library of Wales, 1936-39. Lt 4th Bn Welch Regt (TA), 1931-39; trans. Pembrokeshire Yeomanry (RA, TA), 1939, Battery Captain; served War of 1939-45: RA (Field), N Africa (despatches), Middle East, Italy; Battery Comdr, and 2nd-in-comd of regt; GSO2 War Histories; Mil. Narrator, Hist. Section, Cabinet Office, 1945-58 (Compiled Official narrative of Sicilian and Italian Campaigns); Battery Comdr, The Surrey Yeomanry, QMR (RA, TA), 1949-56; Mil. Liaison Officer, Coronation, 1953; served on the Earl Marshal's staff, State Funeral of Sir Winston Churchill, 1965; Mem., Prince of Wales Investiture Cttee, 1967-69. Local Sec. and Mem., Cambrian Assoc.; Vice-Pres., Council, Hon. Sec. of Cymmrodorion; Member: Gorsedd, Royal National Eisteddfod of Wales; Court and Council, Nat. Library of Wales, 1967-; Council, Nat. Museum of Wales; Historical Soc. of the Church in Wales; Carmarthenshire Local History Soc.; Pembrokeshire Records Soc. (Vice-Pres.); Croeso '69 Nat. Cttee; Academie Internationale d'Heraldique; Heraldry Soc. Trustee, Elvet Lewis Memorial (Gangell), 1967-. Vice-Pres., Dyfed Local Councils, 1974-. DL Dyfed, 1965. Broadcaster (TV and sound radio). Hon. MA Univ. of Wales. CStJ. *Publications:* The Holy Wells of Wales, 1954; The History of Llangunnor, 1965; God Bless the Prince of Wales, 1969; The Princes and Principality of Wales, 1969; (jtly) Royal and Princely Heraldry in Wales, 1969; numerous articles on historical, genealogical and heraldic matters to learned jls. *Recreations:* genealogical research and heraldry, fly-fishing, study of ancient ruins. *Address:* Hendre, Springfield Road, Carmarthen. *T:* Carmarthen 7099.

JONES, Sir Francis Avery, Kt 1970; CBE 1966; FRCP; Consulting Physician, Gastroenterological Department, Central Middlesex Hospital (Physician, 1940-74); Consultant in Gastroenterology: St Mark's Hospital, since 1950; and to Royal Navy since 1950; *b* 31 May 1910; *s* of Francis Samuel and Marion Rosa Jones; *m* 1934, Dorothea Pfirter; one *s. Educ:* Sir John Leman Sch., Beccles; St Bartholomew's Hosp. Baly Research Scholarship, St Bart's, 1936; Julius Mickle Fellowship, University of London, 1952. Goulstonian Lecturer, Royal College of Physicians, 1947; Lumleian Lectr, RCP; Nuffield Lectr in Australia, 1952; First Memorial Lectr, Amer. Gastroenterological Assoc., 1954; Croonian Lectr, RCP, 1969.

Formerly Examiner: RCP; Univ. of London; Univ. of Leeds. Chairman: Emergency Bed Service, 1967-72; Med. Records Cttee, Dept of Health and Social Security; Medical Adv. Cttee, British Council, 1970; Member: Med. Sub-cttee, UGC, 1966-71; Brent and Harrow AHA, 1975-; Dep. Chm., Management Cttee, King Edward VII Hosp. Fund, 1959-; Mem. Council, Surrey Univ., 1975-. Pres., United Services Section, RSM, 1974-75 (formerly Pres., section of Proctology); 2nd Vice-Pres., RCP, 1972-73; Pres., Medical Soc. of London. Editor of Gut, 1965-70. Hon. Mem., Amer., Canadian, French, Scandinavian and Australian Gastroenterological Assocs. Master, Worshipful Co. of Barbers, 1977-78. Hon. MD Melbourne, 1952. Ambuj Nath Bose Prize, RCP, 1971. *Publications:* Clinical Gastroenterology (jt author), 2nd edn 1967; Editor of Modern Trends in Gastroenterology First and Second Series, 1952 and 1958; many articles on Gastroenterology in the Medical Press. *Recreation:* water-side gardening. *Address:* 149 Harley Street, W1N 2DE. *T:* 01-935 4444; 44 Cleveland Square, W2; Mill House, Nutbourne, Pulborough, West Sussex. *Club:* Athenæum.

JONES, Francis Edgar, MBE 1945; PhD, DSc; FRS 1967; FIEE, FRAeS; FInstP; Director: Philips Industries, 1973-76; Unitech Ltd, since 1974; *s* of Edgar Samuel Jones and Annie Maude Lamb; *m* 1942, Jessie Gladys Hazell; four *s* one *d. Educ:* Royal Liberty Sch., Romford; King's Coll., London. Demonstrator in Physics, King's Coll., London, 1938-39; at Min. of Aircraft Production Research Estab., finishing as Dep. Chief Scientific Officer, 1940-52; Chief Scientific Officer and Dep. Dir, RAE, Farnborough, 1952-56; Technical Dir, Mullard Ltd, 1956-62; Man. Dir, 1962-72; Chm., Associated Semiconductor Manufacturers Ltd, 1962-72. Chairman: Adv. Council on Road Research, 1966-68; Electronic Components Bd, 1967-69; Radio & Electronic Component Manufacturers Fedn, 1967-69; Electronic Valve & Semiconductor Manufacturers Assoc., 1968; Member: Inland Transport Research and Develt Council, 1969; Cttee on Manpower Resources for Sciences and Technology (Chm., Working Group on Migration, 1967); Council for Scientific Policy, 1965-70; Central Adv. Council for Science and Technology, 1966-70; Nat. Defence Industries Council, 1969-76; Council, IEE, 1965-69 (Vice-Pres. 1972); Council, Royal Society, 1968; Cttee of Enquiry into Research Assocs; (part-time) Monopolies and Mergers Commn, 1973-; Chairman: EDC for Mech. Engrg, 1973-76; Rank Prize Fund for Optoelectronics. Pres., Engineering Industries Assoc., 1977-. Fellow, King's Coll., London, 1968. Mem. Delegacy, KCL, 1976. Vis. Prof. of Electrical Engineering, University Coll., London, 1968-. Trustee: Anglo-German Foundn for the Study of Industrial Soc., 1973; Rank Prize Funds, 1977-. Hon. Fellow, Univ. of Manchester Inst. of Science and Technology, 1970. Hon. DSc: Southampton, 1968; Nottingham, 1968; Cranfield, 1976; DUniv Surrey, 1968; Hon. DTech Brunel, 1969; Duddell Premium, IEE, 1949; Glazebrook Medal and Prize, Inst. of Physics, 1971. *Publications:* (with R. A. Smith and R. P. Chasmar) The Detection and Measurement of Infrared-Radiation, 1956; articles in Proc. Royal Society, RAeS Jl, Jl IEE, Nature. *Address:* Wendacre, Burton's Way, Chalfont St Giles, Bucks HP8 4BP. *T:* Little Chalfont 2228. *Club:* Athenæum.

JONES, Prof. F(rank) Llewellyn-, CBE 1965; MA, DPhil, DSc Oxon; Principal, University College of Swansea, 1965-74 (Vice-Principal, 1954-56 and 1960-62; Acting Principal, 1959-60); Professor Emeritus, since 1974; *b* 30 Sept. 1907; *er s* of Alfred Morgan Jones, JP, Penrhiwceiber, Glamorgan; *m* 1938, Eileen, *d* of E. T. Davies, Swansea; one *s* (one *d* decd). *Educ:* West Monmouth Sch.; Merton Coll., Oxford. Science Exhibnr 1925; 1st Cl. Nat. Sci. physics, BA 1929; Research Scholar, Merton Coll., 1929, DPhil, MA, 1931; Senior Demy, Magdalen Coll., 1931; Demonstrator in Wykeham Dept of Physics, Oxford, 1929-32; Lecturer in Physics, University Coll. of Swansea, 1932-40; Senior Scientific Officer, Royal Aircraft Establishment, 1940-45; Prof. of Physics, Univ. of Wales, and Head of Dept of Physics, University Coll. of Swansea, 1945-65. Vice-Chancellor, Univ. of Wales, 1969-71. Member: Radio Research Board, DSIR, 1951-54; Standing Conference on Telecommunications Research, DSIR, 1952-55; Board of Institute of Physics, 1947-50; Council of Physical Society, 1951-58. Visiting Prof. to Univs in Australia, 1956; Supernumerary Fellow, Jesus Coll., Oxford, 1965-66, 1969-70; Hon. Professorial Res. Fellow, Univ. of Wales, 1974-; Leverhulme Emeritus Fellow, 1977-79. Regional Scientific Adviser for Home Defence, Wales, 1952-59, Chief Reg. Sci. Adv., 1959-72; Pres., Royal Institution of South Wales, 1958-60; Mem. of Council for Wales and Mon, 1959-63, 1963-; Dir (Part-time), S Wales Gp, BSC, 1968-70; Chm., Central Adv. Council for Education (Wales), 1961-64. Hon. LLD Wales, 1975. C. V. Boys' Prizeman, The Physical Soc., 1960; Ragnar Hohn Scientific Achievement Award, 6th Internat. Conf. on Electric Contact Phenomena, Chicago, 1972. *Publications:*

Fundamental Processes of Electrical Contact Phenomena, 1953; The Physics of Electrical Contacts, 1957; Ionization and Breakdown in Gases, 1957, 2nd edn 1966; The Glow Discharge, 1966; Ionization, Avalanches and Breakdown, 1966; papers in scientific jls on ionization and discharge physics. *Recreations:* railways, walking and gardening. *Address:* Brynheulog, 24 Sketty Park Road, Swansea. *T:* Swansea 22344. *Club:* Athenæum.

JONES, Fred, CBE 1966; Deputy Secretary, HM Treasury, since 1975; *b* 5 May 1920; *s* of late Fred Jones and Harriet (*née* Nuttall); *m* 1954, Joy (*née* Field); two *s. Educ:* Preston Grammar Sch.; St Catherine's Coll., Oxford. Economist, Trades Union Congress, 1951-59; Tutor in Economics and Industrial Relations, Ruskin Coll., Oxford, 1960-62; Economist, National Economic Development Office, 1962-64; Dept of Economic Affairs: Senior Economic Adviser, 1964-66; Asst Sec., 1966-68; Asst Under-Sec. of State, 1968-69; HM Treasury, Asst Under-Sec. of State, 1969-75. Mem., British Nat. Oil Corpn, 1977-. *Recreations:* walking, reading. *Address:* 63 Revell Road, Kingston-on-Thames, Surrey.

JONES, Prof. Gareth (Hywel); Fellow of Trinity College, Cambridge, since 1961; Downing Professor of the Laws of England, Cambridge University, since 1975; *b* 10 Nov. 1930; *o c* of late B. T. Jones, FRICS, and Mabel Jones, Tylorstown, Glam; *m* 1959, Vivienne Joy, *o d* of C. E. Puckridge, FIA, Debden Green, Loughton; two *s* one *d*. *Educ:* Porth County Sch.; University Coll. London (PhD); St Catharine's Coll., Cambridge (Scholar); Harvard Univ. (LLM). LLB London 1951; MA, LLB 1953, LLD 1972, Cantab. Choate Fellow, Harvard, 1953; Yorke Prize, 1960. Called to Bar, Lincoln's Inn, 1955 (Scholar); Hon. Bencher 1975. Lecturer: Oriel and Exeter Colls, Oxford, 1956-58; KCL, 1958-61; Trinity Coll., Cambridge: Lectr, 1961-74, Tutor, 1967, Sen. Tutor, 1972; Univ. Lectr, Cambridge, 1961-74. Vis. Professor: Harvard, 1966 and 1975; Chicago, 1976; California at Berkeley, 1967 and 1971; Indiana, 1971, 1975. *Address:* Trinity College, Cambridge CB2 1TQ. *T:* Cambridge 58201; 64 Cavendish Avenue, Cambridge CB1 4UT. *T:* Cambridge 45366.

JONES, Geoffrey; *see* Jones, John G.

JONES, Ven. Geoffrey G.; *see* Gower-Jones.

JONES, Geoffrey Rippon R.; *see* Rees-Jones.

JONES, Air Marshal Sir George, KBE 1953 (CBE 1942); CB 1943; DFC; RAAF; *b* 22 Nov. 1896; *m* 1st, 1919, Muriel Agnes (decd), *d* of F. Stone; one *s* (and one *s* decd); 2nd, 1970, Mrs Gwendoline Claire Bauer. Served Gallipoli and European War, 1914-18 (despatches, DFC); joined RAAF, 1921; Dir Personnel Services, RAAF, 1936-40; Dir of Training, 1940-42; Chief of Air Staff, 1942-52. Dir, Ansett Transport Industries Ltd. *Address:* Flat 10, 104 Cromer Road, Beaumaris, Victoria 3193, Australia. *Club:* Naval and Military (Melbourne).

JONES, Sir George B. T.; *see* Todd-Jones.

JONES, Prof. George William; Professor of Government, University of London, since 1976; *b* 4 Feb. 1938; *er s* of George William and Grace Annie Jones; *m* 1963, Diana Mary Bedwell; one *s* one *d*. *Educ:* Wolverhampton Grammar Sch.; Jesus Coll., Oxford; Nuffield Coll., Oxford. Oxf. BA 1960, MA 1965, DPhil 1965. Univ. of Leeds: Asst Lectr in Govt, 1963; Lectr in Govt, 1965; London Sch. of Economics and Political Science: Lectr in Political Science, 1966; Sen. Lectr in Polit. Sci., 1971; Reader in Polit. Sci., 1974. Sec., Polit. Studies Assoc. of the UK, 1965-68; Exec. Cttee of PSA, 1969-75; Exec. Council, Hansard Soc., 1968-70; Mem., Editorial Cttee of The London Journal, 1973-; Mem., Layfield Cttee of Inquiry into Local Govt Finance, 1974-76. *Publications:* Borough Politics, 1969; (with B. Donoughue) Herbert Morrison: portrait of a politician, 1973; contribs to Political Studies, Public Admin., Political Qly, Parliamentary Affairs, Jl of Admin. Overseas. *Recreations:* cinema, politics. *Address:* Department of Government, London School of Economics, Houghton Street, WC2A 2AE. *T:* 01-405 7686.

JONES, Geraint Iwan; *b* 16 May 1917; *s* of Rev. Evan Jones, Porth, Glam; *m* 1st, 1940, M. A. Kemp; one *d*; 2nd, 1949, Winifred Roberts. *Educ:* Caterham Sch.; Royal Academy of Music (Sterndale Bennett Scholar). National Gallery Concerts, 1940-44; played complete organ works of Bach in 16 recitals in London, 1946. Musical dir of Mermaid Theatre performances of Purcell's Dido and Aeneas with Kirsten Flagstad, 1951-53. Formed Geraint Jones Singers and Orchestra, 1951, with whom many Broadcasts, and series of 12 Bach concerts, Royal Festival Hall, 1955; series of all Mozart's piano concertos, Queen

Elizabeth Hall, 1969-70. Frequent European engagements, 1947- and regular US and Canadian tours, 1948-. Musical Director: Lake District Festival, 1960-; Kirckman Concert Soc., 1963-; Artistic Director: Salisbury Festival, 1973-77; Manchester Internat. Organ Festival, 1977-. Recordings as organist and conductor; Promenade Concerts; also concerts and recordings as harpsichordist, including sonatas with violinist wife, Winifred Roberts. Grand Prix du Disque, 1959 and 1966. *Recreations:* motoring, photography, antiques, reading. *Address:* The Long House, Arkley Lane, Barnet Road, Arkley, Herts.

JONES, Sir Glyn (Smallwood), GCMG 1964 (KCMG 1960, CMG 1957); MBE 1944; *b* 9 Jan. 1908; *s* of late G. I. Jones, Chester; *m* 1942, Nancy Madoc, *d* of J. H. Featherstone, CP, South Africa; one *d* (and one *s* decd). *Educ:* King's Sch., Chester; St Catherine's, Oxford Univ. (MA); Hon. Fellow, 1977. OUAFC 1928, 1929, 1930. HM Colonial Service (now HM Overseas Civil Service) N Rhodesia: Cadet, 1931; District Officer, 1933; Commissioner for Native Development, 1950; Acting Development Sec., 1956; Prov. Comr, 1956; Resident Comr, Barotseland, 1957; Sec. for Native Affairs, 1958; Minister of Native Affairs and Chief Comr, 1959; Chief Sec., Nyasaland, 1960-61, Governor, 1961-64; Governor-Gen. of Malawi, 1964-66. Advr on Govt Admin to Prime Minister of Lesotho, 1969-71; Dep. Chm., Lord Pearce Commn on Rhodesian Opinion, 1971-72. KStJ. *Recreations:* shooting, fishing, golf, tennis. *Address:* Little Brandfold, Goudhurst, Kent. *Clubs:* Athenæum, Royal Commonwealth Society, MCC; Chester City.

JONES, Griffith Winston Guthrie, QC 1963; a Recorder, 1972-74 (Recorder of Bolton, 1968-71); *b* 24 Sept. 1914; second *s* of Rowland Guthrie Jones, Dolgellau, Merioneth; *m* 1959, Anna Maria McCarthy (*d* 1969). *Educ:* Bootham Sch., York; University of Wales; St John's Coll., Cambridge. Called to the Bar, Gray's Inn, 1939. Dep. Chm., Cumberland QS, 1963-71. War service in Royal Artillery, 1940-46. *Recreations:* gardening, painting. *Address:* 7B Princes Park Mansion, Liverpool L8 3SA. *Club:* Athenæum (Liverpool).

JONES, (Gwilym) Wyn, CBE 1977; Governor, Montserrat, since 1977; *b* 12 July 1926; *s* of late Rev. John Jones, MA, BD, and Elizabeth (*née* Roberts); *m* 1951, Ruth (*née* Thomas); one *s* one *d*. *Educ:* Llanrwst Grammar Sch.; UCNW, Bangor (BA Hons); London Univ. Served RN, 1944-47. Cadet, Colonial Admin. Service, Gilbert and Ellice Islands, 1950; DO, DC and Secretariat in Tarawa, Line Islands, Phoenix Islands and Ocean Island, 1950-61; Solomon Islands, 1961; Asst Sec., 1961-67; Sen. Asst Sec., 1967-74; Dep. Chief Sec., 1974; Sec. to Chief Minister and Council of Ministers, 1974-77. *Recreation:* walking alone. *Address:* Government House, Plymouth, Montserrat. *T:* 2150; Hafod Wen, 67 Victoria Drive, Deganwy, Gwynedd. *T:* Deganwy 83377.

JONES, Prof. Gwyn, CBE 1965; Professor of English Language and Literature, University College of South Wales, Cardiff, 1965-75; *b* 24 May 1907; *s* of George Henry Jones and Lily Florence (*née* Nethercott); *m* 1928, Alice (*née* Rees). *Educ:* Tredegar Grammar School; University of Wales. Schoolmaster, 1929-35; Lecturer, University Coll., Cardiff, 1935-40; Prof. of Eng. Language and Lit., University Coll. of Wales, Aberystwyth, 1940-64. Dir of Penmark Press, 1939-. Mem. of various learned societies; Pres. of Viking Soc. for Northern Research, 1950-52; Mem. of Arts Council and Chm. of Welsh Arts Council, 1957-67. Hon. DLitt Wales, 1977. Fellow, Institut Internat. des Arts et des Lettres, 1960. Christian Gauss Award, 1973. Knight, Order of the Falcon (Iceland), 1963. *Publications:* A Prospect of Wales, 1948; Welsh Legends and Folk-Tales, 1955; *novels:* Richard Savage, 1935; Times Like These, 1936; Garland of Bays, 1938; The Green Island, 1946; The Flowers Beneath the Scythe, 1952; The Walk Home, 1962; *short stories:* The Buttercup Field, 1945; The Still Waters, 1948; Shepherd's Hey, 1953; Selected Short Stories, 1974; *translations:* The Vatnsdalers' Saga, 1942; The Mabinogion, 1948; Egil's Saga, 1960; Eirik the Red, 1961; The Norse Atlantic Saga, 1964; A History of the Vikings, 1968; Kings, Beasts and Heroes, 1972; (ed) Welsh Review, 1939-48; Welsh Short Stories, 1956; (ed with I. F. Elis) Twenty-Five Welsh Short Stories, 1971; The Oxford Book of Welsh Verse in English, 1977; contrib. to numerous learned journals. *Recreation:* animals. *Address:* Department of English, University College, Cardiff.

JONES, Gwyn Owain, MA, DSc Oxon; PhD Sheffield; FMA; Director, National Museum of Wales, 1968-77; *b* 29 March 1917; *s* of Dr Abel John Jones, OBE, HMI, and Rhoda May Jones, Cardiff and Porthcawl; *m* 1st, 1944, Sheila Heywood (marr. diss.); two *d*; 2nd, 1973, Elizabeth Blandino. *Educ:* Monmouth Sch.; Port Talbot Secondary Sch.; Jesus Coll.,

Oxford. Glass Delegacy Research Fellow of University of Sheffield, later mem. of academic staff, 1939-41; Mem. UK Government's Atomic Energy project, 1942-46; Nuffield Foundation Research Fellow at Clarendon Laboratory, Oxford, 1946-49; Reader in Experimental Physics in University of London, at Queen Mary Coll., 1949-53; Prof. of Physics in Univ. of London, and Head of Dept of Physics at Queen Mary Coll., 1953-68; Fellow of Queen Mary Coll. Visiting Prof. Univ. of Sussex, 1964. Mem. Court and Council, UWIST, 1968-74; Hon. Professorial Fellow, University Coll., Cardiff, 1969-. Yr Academi Gymreig (English Language Section) 1971; Gorsedd y Beirdd (Aelod er Anrhydedd) 1974; Governor, Commonwealth Institute, 1974-77. *Publications:* Glass, 1956; (in collab.) Atoms and the Universe, 1956; papers on solid-state, glass, low-temperature physics; *novels:* The Catalyst, 1960; Personal File, 1962; Now, 1965. *Address:* New House, St Hilary, Cowbridge, South Glamorgan. *T:* Cowbridge 3998.

JONES, Gwyneth, CBE 1976; a Principal Dramatic Soprano, Royal Opera House, Covent Garden, since 1963, Vienna State Opera, since 1966; *b* 7 Nov. 1936; *d* of late Edward George Jones and late Violet (*née* Webster). *Educ:* Twmpath Sec. Mod. Sch., Pontypool, Mon; Royal College of Music, London; Accademia Chigiana, Siena; Zürich Internat. Opera Studio; Maria Carpi Prof., Geneva. Zürich Opera House, 1962-63. Oratorio and recitals as well as opera. Guest Artiste: La Scala, Milan; Berlin State Opera; Munich State Opera; Bayreuth Festival; Tokyo; Zürich; Metropolitan Opera, New York; Paris; Marseilles; Monte Carlo; Geneva; Dallas; San Francisco; Los Angeles; Teatro Colon, Buenos Aires; Edinburgh Festival; Welsh National Opera; Rome; Hamburg; Maggio Musicale, Florence; Chicago. Numerous recordings, radio and TV appearances. ARCM. Hon. DMus Wales. *Address:* Box 380, 8040 Zürich, Switzerland.

JONES, G(wyneth) Ceris; Chief Nursing Officer, British Red Cross Society, 1962-70, retired; *b* 15 Nov. 1906; 2nd *d* of late W. R. Jones, OBE, JP, Tre Venal, Bangor, N Wales. *Educ:* Bangor County Sch. for Girls. State Registered Nurse; trained at Nightingale Training Sch., St Thomas' Hosp., 1927-31; Sister Tutor's Certificate, Univ. of London; Diploma in Nursing, Univ. of London. Sister Tutor, St Thomas' Hosp., 1936-39; served with QAIMNS Reserve, 1939-41; Sister-in-charge, Leys School Annexe to Addenbrooke's Hospital, Cambridge, 1941-43; Asst Matron, London Hospital, 1943-47; Matron, Westminster Hospital, 1947-51; London Hospital, 1951-61. Florence Nightingale Medal, Internat. Cttee, Red Cross, 1971. *Address:* Meadow Cottage, Scole Common, Diss, Norfolk IP21 4EY.

JONES, Gwynoro Glyndwr; Assistant Education Officer, Development Forward Planning, West Glamorgan County Council, since 1977; *b* 21 Nov. 1942; *s* of J. E. and A. L. Jones, Minyrafon, Foelgastell, Cefneithin, Carms; *m* 1967, A. Laura Miles; two *s* one *d*. *Educ:* Gwendraeth Grammar Sch.; Cardiff Univ. BSc Econ (Hons) Politics and Economics. Market Research Officer with Ina Needle Bearings Ltd, Llanelli, 1966-67; Economist Section, Wales Gas Bd, 1967-69; Public Relations Officer, Labour Party in Wales, March 1969-June 1970; Dir of Res., West Glam. CC, 1974-77. Member: TGWU, 1969-; INLOGOV Working Gp on Res. and Intelligence Units in Local Govt, 1975-; S Wales Standing Conf. Working Gp, 1975-; Council of European Municipalities, 1977-; Local Govt Exec. Cttee of European movement, 1977-. MP (Lab) Carmarthen, 1970-Sept. 1974; Member: House of Commons Expenditure Cttee, 1972-74; Standing Orders Cttee, 1972-74; Council of Europe and WEU, 1974; PPS to Home Sec., 1974. Vice-Pres., District Council Assoc., 1974. Pres., Nat. Eisteddfod of Wales, 1974. Political Educn Officer, Swansea Labour Assoc., 1976-. Co-ordinator, Wales in Europe campaign, 1975; Sponsor, Wales Lab and TU Cttee for Europe, 1975. *Publications:* The Record Put Straight (booklet), 1973; articles in Soc. Commentary, etc. *Recreations:* sport (played Rugby for both 1st and 2nd class teams). *Address:* 29 The Paddock, West Cross, Swansea.

JONES, Harry, FRS 1952; BSc, PhD Leeds, PhD Cantab; *b* 1905; *m* 1931, Frances Molly O'Neill; one *s* two *d*. *Educ:* University of Leeds; Trinity Coll., Cambridge. Lecturer at Bristol Univ., 1932-37; Reader in Mathematics, Imperial Coll., Univ. of London, 1938-46; Prof. of Mathematics, 1946-72, now Professor Emeritus; Head of Dept, 1955-70; Pro-Rector, 1970-72; Fellow, 1975. *Publications:* (with N. F. Mott) The Theory of the Properties of Metals and Alloys, 1936; Theory of Brillouin Zones and Electronic States in Crystals, 1960; various contributions to scientific journals on Theoretical Physics. *Address:* 41 Berwyn Road, Richmond, Surrey. *T:* 01-876 1931.

JONES, Sir Harry (Ernest), Kt 1971; CBE 1955; Agent in Great Britain for Northern Ireland, 1970-76; *b* 1 Aug. 1911; *m* 1935,

Phyllis Eva Dixon; one *s* one *d. Educ:* Stamford Sch.; St John's Coll., Cambridge. Entered Northern Ireland Civil Service, 1934; Min. of Commerce: Principal Officer 1940; Asst Sec. 1942; Perm. Sec. 1955; Industrial Development Adviser to Ministry of Commerce, 1969. FInstD. *Recreation:* fishing. *Address:* 51 Station Road, Nassington, Peterborough. *T:* Stamford 782675.

JONES, Rt. Rev. Haydn Harold; *see* Venezuela, Bishop of.

JONES, Henry Arthur, CBE 1974; MA; Vaughan Professor of Education and Head of the Department of Adult Education, University of Leicester, since 1967; *b* 7 March 1917; *er s* of Henry Lloyd Jones; *m* 1st, 1942, Molly (*d* 1971), 4th *d* of Richard Shenton; two *s* ; 2nd, 1972, Nancy Winifred (*née* Cox), *widow* of Lt R. B. B. Jack, RN. *Educ:* Chorlton Grammar Sch.; Manchester Univ. George Gissing Prizeman, Manchester Univ., 1936; Graduate Research Fellow, Manchester Univ., 1937, MA 1938. Served War of 1939-45 with Lancs Fusiliers and DLI, 1940-42. Sen. English Master, Chorlton Grammar Sch., 1942-47; Resident Staff Tutor, Manchester Univ., 1947-49; Asst Dir of Extra-Mural Studies, Liverpool Univ., 1949-52, Dep. Dir 1953-57; Principal, The City Literary Institute, 1957-67. Chairman: Assoc. for Adult Education, 1964-67; Adult Educn Cttee, IBA, 1973-77; Exec. Chm., Nat. Inst. of Adult Education; Vice-President: Educnl Centres Assoc.; Pre-retirement Assoc.; Member: Library Adv. Council, DES, 1965-68; Sec. of State's Cttee on Adult Educn, DES, 1968-72. Chm., Leics Consultative Cttee for Voluntary Orgns, 1974-. Editor, Studies in Adult Education, 1974-. *Publications:* contributes to educational and literary journals. *Address:* Nether House, Great Bowden, Market Harborough, Leics. *T:* Market Harborough 2846.

JONES, Sir Henry (Frank Harding), GBE 1972 (KBE 1965); MBE 1943); Kt 1956; Chairman of the Gas Council, 1960-71; Vice-Chairman, International Executive Council, World Energy Conference, 1970-73, Hon. Vice-Chm. since 1973 (Chairman, British National Committee, 1968-71); *b* 13 July 1906; *s* of Frank Harding Jones, Housham Tye, Harlow, Essex; *m* 1934, Elizabeth Angela, *d* of J. Spencer Langton, Little Hadham, Herts; three *s* one *d. Educ:* Harrow; Pembroke Coll., Cambridge (Hon. Fellow 1973). Served War of 1939-45 with Essex Regt and on staff: France and Belgium, 1939-40; India and Burma, 1942-45. Lieut-Col 1943; Col 1945; Brigadier 1945. Before nationalisation of gas industry was: Deputy Chairman, Watford and St Albans Gas Co., Wandsworth and District Gas Co.; Dir of South Metropolitan, South Suburban and other gas companies. Chm. East Midlands Gas Board, 1949-52; Dep. Chm. Gas Council, 1952-60. Chairman: Benzene Marketing Co., 1972-77; Benzole Producers Ltd, 1972-77. Mem., Royal Commn on Standards of Conduct in Public Life, 1974-76. Chm., EDC for Chemical Industry, 1972-75. Liveryman, Clothworkers' Co., 1928, Master 1972-73. Hon. MInstGasE (Pres. 1956-57); MICE; MIChemE; FRSA 1964. Hon. LLD Leeds, 1967; Hon. DSc: Leicester, 1970; Salford, 1971. *Recreations:* fishing, gardening. *Address:* Pathacres, Weston Turville, Aylesbury, Bucks. *T:* Stoke Mandeville 2274. *Clubs:* Athenæum, Bath, MCC.

JONES, Captain Henry Richmund I.; *see* Inigo-Jones.

JONES, Air Cdre Herbert George, CBE 1942; ACIS 1906; *b* 26 Nov. 1884; *s* of George Reuben Jones; *m* 1913, Clarisse Lisney West; one *s* one *d. Educ:* privately. Joined Royal Army Pay Corps, 1914; Royal Air Force, 1918. Served European War, 1914-18 (despatches twice); War of 1939-45 (despatches twice); retired Nov. 1944. Chartered Sec. *Address:* 5 Cotman Gardens, Edgware, Middlesex.

JONES, Sir Hildreth G.; *see* Glyn-Jones.

JONES, Rev. Prof. Hubert C.; *see* Cunliffe-Jones.

JONES, Rev. Hugh; *see* Jones, Rev. R. W. H.

JONES, Hugh Ferguson, OBE 1971; JP; Regional Manager, Lombard North Central Ltd, Bankers; *b* 14 June 1913; *s* of Isaac Jones and Isabella Jones (*née* Stewart); *m* 1942; one *s. Educ:* Alun Grammar Sch., Mold; City of Liverpool Technical Coll. Master Mariner (Foreign going), with Ellerman Hall Line, Liverpool, 1929-47. Elected to Cardiff City Council, 1952; Alderman 1967-74, Lord Mayor, 1971-72; Co. Councillor, New S Glamorganshire CC, 1973-. Dir. of Welsh National Theatre; Mem. Court of Governors, Univ. of Wales. Liveryman of Hon. Co. of Master Mariners and Freeman of City of London, 1968. JP Cardiff, 1957. *Recreations:* nautical education and marine studies, music and the arts, outdoor sports in general. *Address:* 160 Pencisely Road, Llandaff, Cardiff. *T:* Cardiff 561744.

JONES, Hugh (Hugo) Jarrett H.; *see* Herbert-Jones.

JONES, Humphrey Lloyd, CMG 1961; Secretary of the Ashmolean Museum, Oxford, 1962-76; *b* 5 April 1910; *s* of Arthur Davis Jones, London; *m* 1938, Edith, *d* of W. H. Tatham, Natal; one *s* two *d. Educ:* Westminster (King's Scholar); Christ Church, Oxford (MA). Colonial Administrative Service, Northern Rhodesia, Cadet, 1932; Dist Officer, 1934; Private Sec. to Gov., 1937; Asst Sec., 1948. In 1952: acted as Economic Sec.; MEC and MLC; Chm. Maize Control Bd; Chm. Cold Storage Control Bd; attended Commonwealth Economic Conf. in London as rep. of Northern Rhodesia Govt. Seconded to Federal Govt of Rhodesia and Nyasaland as Under-Sec., 1954; Administrative Sec., Govt of Northern Rhodesia, 1956; MLC; Chm. Whitley Council. Acted as Chief Sec. and Deputy for the Governor on a number of occasions. MEC and MLC, 1961; Minister of Labour and Mines and of Local Government and Social Welfare, Northern Rhodesia Govt, 1961; retired 1962. *Recreations:* travel and photography. *Address:* Bishops Mill, Lucerne Road, Oxford.

JONES, Prof. Ian C.; *see* Chester Jones.

JONES, Ian E.; *see* Edwards-Jones.

JONES, Ilston Percival Ll.; *see* Llewellyn Jones.

JONES, Ivan Ellis, CIE 1944; *b* 26 June 1903; *s* of James L. Jones, 9 Castleford Park, Rathmines, Dublin; *m* 1948, Anna, *d* of Peter MacNeil, Eoligarry, Barra; one *s* one *d. Educ:* The High Sch., Harcourt Street, Dublin; Trinity Coll., Dublin. Entered Indian Civil Service, 1927; Asst Commissioner in Punjab, 1927; Under-Sec. to Punjab Govt 1929; Deputy Commissioner (Shahpur, Hissar, Multan, Amritsar), 1931-39; Registrar, Co-operative Societies, Punjab, 1940; Dir Food Purchases, Punjab, 1944; Sec. to Govt Punjab Civil Supplies Dept, 1945; Comr Jullundur, 1947; retired from ICS, 1947. Asst Classics Master, Royal High School, Edinburgh, 1949; Principal Classics Master, John Watson's Sch., Edinburgh, 1958, retd 1973. *Address:* 9 Abbotsford Park, Edinburgh EH10 5DX. *T:* 031-447 7122.

JONES, Ivor R.; *see* Roberts-Jones.

JONES, Jack L.; *see* Jones, James Larkin.

JONES, Sir James (Duncan), KCB 1972 (CB 1964); Policy Adviser, School for Advanced Urban Studies, Bristol University, since 1976; *b* 28 Oct. 1914; *m* 1943, Jenefer Mary Wade; one *s. Educ:* Glasgow High Sch.; Glasgow Univ.; University Coll., Oxford. Admiralty, 1941; Ministry of Town and Country Planning: joined 1946; Prin. Priv. Sec.; 1947-50; Under-Sec., Min. of Housing and Local Govt, 1958-63; Sec., Local Govt Commn for England, 1958-61; Dep. Sec., Min. of Housing and Local Govt, 1963-66; Dep. Sec., Min. of Transport, 1966-70; Sec., Local Govt and Develt, DoE, 1970-72; Permanent Sec., DoE, 1972-75. Mem. Adv. Council, Science Policy Foundn, 1976-. Hon. FRIBA. *Recreations:* reading, looking at buildings, walking. *Address:* The Courtyard, Ewelme, Oxford OX9 6HP. *T:* Wallingford 39270. *Clubs:* Athenæum; Oxford Union.

JONES, James Idwal; Welsh Geographer; retired MP; *b* 30 June 1900; *s* of James and Elizabeth Bowyer Jones; *m* 1931, Catherine Humphreys; one *s* (one *d* decd). *Educ:* Ruabon Grammar Sch.; Normal Coll., Bangor. Certificated Teacher, 1922. BSc Econ., London Univ. (Externally), 1936. Headmaster, Grango Secondary Modern Sch., Rhosllanerchrugog, near Wrexham, 1938. MP (Lab) Wrexham Div. of Denbighshire, 1955-70. *Publications:* A Geography of Wales, 1938; An Atlas of Denbighshire, 1950; Atlas Hanesyddol o Gymru, 1952, new edn 1972 (A Welsh Historical Atlas of Wales); A Geographical Atlas of Wales, 1955; A Historical Atlas of Wales, 1955; A New Geography of Wales, 1960; J. R. Jones (Ramoth), 1967. *Recreations:* photography and landscape painting. *Address:* Maelor, Ponciau, Wrexham, Clwyd, Wales.

JONES, James Larkin, (Jack), MBE 1950; FCIT; General Secretary, Transport and General Workers' Union, 1969-78; Deputy Chairman, National Ports Council, since 1967; Member, TUC General Council, since 1968; *b* 29 March 1913; *m* 1938, Evelyn Mary Taylor; two *s. Educ:* elementary sch., Liverpool. Worked in engineering and docks industries, 1927-39. Liverpool City Councillor, 1936-39; served in Spanish Civil War; wounded Ebro battle, Aug. 1938; Coventry District Sec., Transport and General Workers' Union, also District Sec., Confedn of Shipbuilding and Engineering Unions, 1939-55; Midlands Regional Sec., Transport and General Workers' Union, 1955-63, Asst Executive Sec., 1963-69. Mem., Midland Regional Bd for

Industry, 1942-46, 1954-63; Chm., Midlands TUC Advisory Cttee, 1948-63. Coventry City Magistrate, 1950-63; Executive Chm., Birmingham Productivity Cttee, 1957-63; Member: Labour Party Nat. Exec. Cttee, 1964-67; Nat. Cttee for Commonwealth Immigrants, 1965-69; Mem. NEDC and numerous other joint industrial bodies; Mem. Council, Conciliation and Arbitration Service, 1974-. Chairman: Internat. Cttee, TUC, 1972-; Transport Industries Cttee, TUC, 1972-; Vice-Pres., ITF, 1974-; Executive Board Member: Internat. Confedn of Free Trade Unions; European Trade Union Confedn; Mem., BOTB, 1975-. Mem. Council, Industrial Soc., 1967. Dir, Tribune, 1968-. Vis. Fellow, Nuffield Coll., Oxford, 1970-. Dimbleby Lecture, BBC, 1977. *Recreation:* walking. *Address:* 74 Ruskin Park House, Champion Hill, SE5. *T:* 01-274 7067.

JONES, Ven. James William Percy; Archdeacon of Huntingdon, 1947-55, Canon Emeritus since 1955; *b* 22 April 1881; *s* of late Canon D. Jones; *m* 1917, Judith Efa Bonnor-Maurice (*d* 1959); one *s* one *d* (and one *s* killed in action). *Educ:* Oswestry; Pembroke Coll., Oxford, Queen's Coll., Birmingham, 1904; MA 1907. Hon. CF 1921. Curate: Perry Barr, 1905-08; Nassington with Yarwell, 1908-13 and 1914-15; Llanfechain, 1913-14; Market Harborough, 1915-16. Asst Dir of Religious Education, 1922-32; Rural Dean of Leightonstone, 1930-47; Exam. Chaplain to Bishop of Ely, 1941; Hon. Canon Ely Cathedral, 1941-47, Canon Emeritus, 1954; Vicar of Great Gidding and Little Gidding, 1916-57, with Steeple Gidding, 1926-57. *Recreation:* formerly golf. *Address:* Cae Hywel, Llansantffraid, Powys.

JONES, Jennifer, (Mrs Norton Simon); film actress (US); *b* Tulsa, Okla; *d* of Philip R. Isley and Flora Mae (*née* Suber); *m* 1st, 1939, Robert Walker (marr. diss. 1945); two *s*; 2nd, 1949, David O. Selznick (*d* 1965); one *d* decd; 3rd, 1971, Norton Simon. *Educ:* schools in Okla and Tex; Northwestern Univ., Evanston, Illinois; American Academy of Dramatic Arts, New York City. Films, since 1943, include: The Song of Bernadette; Since You Went Away; Cluny Brown; Love Letters; Duel in the Sun; We Were Strangers; Madame Bovary; Portrait of Jenny; Carrie; Wild Heart; Ruby Gentry; Indiscretion of an American Wife; Beat the Devil; Love is a Many-Splendoured Thing; The Barretts of Wimpole Street; A Farewell to Arms; Tender is the Night; The Idol; The Towering Inferno. Awards include: American Academy of Motion Pictures, Arts and Sciences Award, 1943; 4 other Academy nominations, etc. Medal for Korean War Work.

JONES, (John) Clement, CBE 1972; writer, broadcaster, technical adviser to developing countries; Executive Director (programming), Beacon Broadcasting, Wolverhampton, since 1974; *b* 22 June 1915; *o s* of Clement Daniel Jones; *m* 1939, Marjorie, *d* of George Gibson, Llandrindod Wells; three *s. Educ:* Ardwyn, Aberystwyth. Various journalistic positions: News Editor, Express and Star, Wolverhampton, 1955; Editor, 1960-71; Editorial Director, 1971-74. Pres., Guild of British Newspaper Editors, 1966-67, Hon. Life Vice-Pres., 1972. Member: Press Council, 1965-74; Adv. Bd, Thomson Foundn, 1965-; BBC W Midlands Adv. Council, 1971-75; (part-time) Monopolies and Mergers Commn, 1973-; W Midlands Arts Assoc., 1973-; Exec. Cttee, Soc. Internat. Develt, 1974-; Vice Chm., Lichfield Dio. Media Council, 1974-; Mem. Council, and Chm. Press Freedom Cttee, Commonwealth Press Union, 1975-. Founder Mem., Circle of Wine Writers, 1966; Vice-Chm., British Human Rights Trust, 1975-; Governor, British Inst. Human Rights, 1971-; Pres., Staffordshire Soc., 1971-74. FRSA. *Publication:* UNESCO World Survey of Media Councils and Codes of Ethics, 1976. *Recreations:* travel, gardening, bee keeping. *Address:* 17 Swallowdale, Wightwick Bank, Wolverhampton. *T:* Wolverhampton 763253. *Clubs:* Athenæum, Press.

JONES, John Cyril, CBE 1951; BSc; MICE, FIMechE; Adviser for Technical Education, Colonial Office and Ministry of Overseas Development, 1956-67; *b* 30 Oct. 1899; *s* of John Jones, Swindon, Wilts; *m* 1928, Doris Anne, *d* of A. Tanner, Swindon, Wilts; one *d. Educ:* The College, Swindon; Loughborough Coll., Leics. Design and Research asst, GWR Co., 1922-31; Head of Dept, Loughborough Coll., 1931-34; Principal: St Helen's Municipal Coll., 1934-37, Cardiff Tech. Coll., 1937-41, Royal Tech. Coll., Salford, 1941-44; Dir of Educn, The Polytechnic, Regent Street, W1, 1944-56; Adviser for Tech. Educn to Colonial Office, 1956-61, and Dept of Tech. Co-operation, 1961-64. Hon. Sec. Assoc. of Tech. Instns, 1944-56; Hon. Treas. Assoc. of Tech. Instns, 1956-67; Pres., Assoc. of Prins of Tech. Instns, 1951; Mem. Central Advisory Council for Education (Eng.), 1947-56; RAF Educ. Advisory Cttee, 1948-56; Advisory Cttee on Educ. in Colonies, 1953-56; Council for Overseas Colls

of Art, Science and Technology, and Council for Tech. Educ. and Training in Overseas Countries, 1949-69. Member: Fulton Commn on Education in Sierra Leone, 1954; Keir Commn on Technical Education in N Rhodesia, 1960. Mem. Council for External Students, University London, 1954-66. Mem. of Council, RSA, 1960-66. Dir Asian Study Tour of Vocational Educ. and Training in the USSR, 1961, 1963; International Bank for Reconstruction and Development Missions to: Pakistan, 1962, 1963; Morocco and Kenya, 1965; Jamaica and Tunisia, 1966; Zambia, Greece, and Guyana, 1968; Cameroun, Tchad, Gabon and Pakistan, 1969; Indonesia, 1970; Morocco, Jordan, Iraq, 1971; Algeria, Zambia, and Korea, 1972; Oman, 1973; Lesotho, Swaziland, Greece, Israel, Lebanon and Zaire, 1974; Morocco, 1975. Mem. International Commn on Tech. Educ. in Sudan, 1966. Officier d'Académie (France), 1950; elected Hon. Mem. City and Guilds of London Inst., 1964. *Publications:* papers on higher technological education and reports on development of technical education in various overseas countries. *Recreations:* books, music, and foreign travel. *Address:* 26 Grand Marine Court, Durley Gardens, Bournemouth BH2 5HS.

JONES, John Edward; His Honour Judge Jones; a Circuit Judge (formerly County Court Judge since 1969); *b* 23 Dec. 1914; *s* of Thomas Robert Jones, Liverpool; *m* 1945, Katherine Elizabeth Edwards, SRN, *d* of Ezekiel Richard Edwards, Liverpool; one *s* one *d. Educ:* Liverpool Institute High School. ACIS 1939-70; BCom London 1942; LLB London 1945. Called to Bar, Gray's Inn, 1945; Member of Northern Circuit, 1946; Dep. Chm., Lancs QS, 1966-69. Dep. Chm., Workmen's Compensation (Supplementation) and Pneumoconiosis and Byssinosis Benefit Boards, 1968-69. Governor, Aigburth Vale Comprehensive Sch., 1976. Welsh Presbyterian Church: Deacon, 1947; Liverpool Presbytery Moderator, 1971. JP Lancs, 1966. *Address:* India Buildings, Water Street, Liverpool.

JONES, Air Vice-Marshal John Ernest A.; *see* Allen-Jones.

JONES, John Ernest P.; *see* Powell-Jones.

JONES, John Eryl O.; *see* Owen-Jones.

JONES, (John) Geoffrey; His Honour Judge Geoffrey Jones; a Circuit Judge since 1975; *b* 14 Sept. 1928; *s* of Wyndham and Lilias Jones; *m* 1954, Sheila (*née* Gregory); three *s. Educ:* St Michael's Sch., Llanelli; St David's Coll., Lampeter; University Coll., London. LLB London 1955. Army service, 1946-48, commnd into RASC, 1947. Electrical wholesale business, 1948-52. Called to Bar, Gray's Inn, 1956; practised Leicester, 1958-70 and London, 1970-75. *Recreation:* golf. *Address:* 2 Clarendon Park Road, Leicester LE2 3AD. *T:* Leicester 706669.

JONES, Air Marshal Sir John Humphrey E.; *see* Edwardes Jones.

JONES, John Iorwerth, CBE 1977; retired; Lord Mayor of Cardiff, 1976-77; Member, Cardiff City Council, since 1958; *b* 22 Oct. 1901; *s* of David Nicholls Jones and Minnie Jones (*née* Rees); single. *Educ:* Carmarthen (public and private). Apprenticed Electrical Engineering, 1918-23. Chm., Cardiff Trades Council, 1960-67. Elected to Cardiff City Council, 1958; on reorganisation elected to new City Council and also to South Glamorgan County Council, May 1974; Dep. Lord Mayor, 1974-75; re-elected to City Council, 1976; re-elected to County Council, 1977. Mem., New Theatre Trust, 1965-. *Recreations:* Rugby fan; interested in opera, music. *Address:* 23 Howard Gardens, Cardiff CF2 1EF. *T:* Cardiff 494195. *Club:* Cardiff Athletic (Cardiff).

JONES, Rev. J(ohn) Ithel; Pastor, Collins Street Baptist Church, Melbourne, since 1970; *b* 1 Jan. 1911; *s* of David Jones and Elizabeth Catherine Jones; *m* 1938, Hannah Mary Rees. *Educ:* Cyfarthfa Castle Sch., Merthyr Tydfil; University Coll., Cardiff; S Wales Baptist Coll. BA (Wales) 1st cl. hons Philosophy and 2nd cl. hons Welsh; BD (Wales); MA (Wales), Theology. Pastorates: Porthcawl, 1936-40; Horfield, Bristol, 1940-50; Haven Green, Ealing, 1950-57; Principal, and Prof. of Theol. and the Philosophy of Religion, S Wales Baptist Coll., 1958-70. Moderator, Free Church Federal Coun. of England and Wales, 1963-64; Dean of Divinity for University of Wales, 1964-67; Pres., Baptist Union of Gt Britain and Ireland, 1967-68. Mem. for Wales on Panel of Religious Advisers, ITA and Welsh Cttee, ITA, 1966-69. Lecture tours in USA, Australia, New Zealand. Hon. DD, Eastern, Pa, 1966; Hon. LLD, Baylor, 1966. *Publications:* Colossians, in New Bible Commentary, 1953; Temple and Town, 1961; The Holy Spirit and Christian Preaching, 1967; Facing the New World, 1968. *Recreations:* golf, music, motoring. *Address:* Suite 43 Rockley Tower, 3 Rockley Road, South Yarra, Vic 3141, Australia.

JONES, Sir (John) Kenneth (Trevor), Kt 1965; CBE 1956; QC 1976; Legal Adviser to the Home Office, 1956-77; *b* 11 July 1910; *s* of John Jones and Agnes Morgan; *m* 1940, Menna, *d* of Cyril O. Jones; two *s. Educ:* King Henry VIII Grammar Sch., Abergavenny; University Coll. of Wales, Aberystwyth; St John's Coll., Cambridge. Called to the Bar, Lincoln's Inn, 1937. Served Royal Artillery, 1939-45. Entered the Home Office as a Legal Asst, 1945. Mem. of the Standing Cttee on Criminal Law Revision, 1959-. *Address:* 54 Westminster Gardens, SW1. *T:* 01-834 4950. *Club:* Athenæum.

JONES, John Morgan, CB 1964; CBE 1946; Secretary Welsh Department, Ministry of Agriculture, 1944-68; *b* 20 July 1903; *s* of late Richard and Mary Ellen Jones, Pertheirin, Caersws, Montgomeryshire; *m* 1933, Dorothy Morris, *yr d* of late David Morris Wigley, Llanbrynmair, Montgomeryshire, and of Margaret Anne Wigley, Machynlleth; no *c. Educ:* Newtown County Sch.; University Coll. of Wales, Aberystwyth. BA 1922; Hons in Econ. 1923, History 1924; MA 1926. Research Staff Dept of Agric. Economics, University Coll. of Wales, 1924-30; Marketing Officer, Min. of Agric. and Fisheries, 1930-35; Registrar Univ. Coll. of Wales, Aberystwyth, 1936; seconded to Min. of Agric. as Minister's Liaison Officer for mid- and south-west Wales, 1940; Chm. Cardigan War Agric. Exec. Cttee, 1943. Sec./Treas. Aberystwyth and Dist Old People's Housing Soc. Ltd, 1972-76. Life Governor and Mem. Council, UCW. Hon. LLD Wales, 1973. *Publications:* Economeg Amaethyddiaeth, 1930; articles on rural economics, mainly in Welsh Journal of Agriculture. *Address:* Maesnewydd, North Road, Aberystwyth. *T:* Aberystwyth 2507. *Club:* Farmers'.

JONES, Brig. John Murray R.; *see* Rymer-Jones.

JONES, Sir John Prichard; *see* Prichard-Jones.

JONES, Rev. Prebendary John Stephen Langton; Residentiary Canon and Precentor of Wells Cathedral, 1947-67, Prebendary, since 1967; *b* 21 May 1889; *m* 1921, Jeanne Charlotte Dujardin; three *s* one *d. Educ:* Dover College; Jesus College, Cambridge. Asst Curate of Halifax Parish Church, 1914; Asst Curate, Hambleden, Berks, 1919; Vicar of Yiewsley, Middx, 1921; Rector of W Lydford, Taunton, 1939-47. Proctor in Convocation for Bath and Wells, 1946-50.

JONES, Air Chief Marshal Sir John Whitworth, GBE 1954 (CBE 1945); KCB 1949 (CB 1942); psa; retd; *b* 28 Feb. 1896; *s* of Lt-Col Aylmer Jones; *m* 1917, Anne Brown; one *s* decd. *Educ:* Magdalen College Sch., Oxford; St Paul's Sch. Temporary Air Commodore, 1942; Acting Air Vice-Marshal, 1942; Air Cdre, 1943; Air Marshal, 1949; Air Chief Marshal, 1953; Asst Deputy Chief of Staff, SEAC, 1943-45; RAF Dir-Gen of Organisation, Air Ministry, 1945-47; AOC Air Headquarters, Malaya, 1948; Air Officer Commanding-in-Chief Technical Training Command, 1948-52; Mem. for Supply and Organisation, Air Council, 1952-54, retired 1954. Commander, Order of Crown (Belgium). *Address:* 6 Gonville House, Manor Fields, Putney Hill, SW15.

JONES, Joseph, CBE 1941; *b* 10 Jan. 1890; *s* of late David E. Jones, Llangollen, Denbighshire; *m* 1919, Gwladys M. (*d* 1961), *d* of Owen Davies, Llanmaes, St Fagans, near Cardiff; (one *d* decd). *Educ:* Llangollen; Cardiff. Joined Glamorgan Constabulary, 1911; Superintendent, 1932; Deputy Chief Constable, 1936; Chief Constable of Glamorgan, 1937-51. Officer Brother Order of St John; King's Police Medal for Distinguished Service, 1947. *Recreations:* bowls, shooting, etc. *Address:* Fron Esgyn, Fron Cysyllte, Llangollen, Clwyd.

JONES, Prof. Kathleen; Professor of Social Administration, University of York, since 1965; *b* 7 April 1922; *d* of William Robert Savage and Kate Lilian Barnard; *m* 1944, Rev. David Gwyn Jones (*d* 1976); one *s. Educ:* North London Collegiate Sch.; Westfield Coll., Univ. of London (BA, PhD). Research Asst in Social Administration, Univ. of Manchester, 1951-53, Asst Lectr 1953-55; Sen. History Teacher, Victoria Instn, Kuala Lumpur, 1956-58, also Asst Lectr in History, Univ. of Malaya (part-time); Lectr in Social Administration, Univ. of Manchester, 1958-62, Sen. Lectr 1962-65. Chm., Social Scis Cttee, UK Commn for UNESCO, 1966-69; Mem., Gen. Synod of C of E, 1975-; Member: Archbp's Commn on Church and State, 1966-71; Lord Gardiner's Cttee on NI, 1974-75; Archibishop's Commn on Marriage, 1976-. Pres., Assoc. of Psychiatric Social Workers, 1968-70. Hon. FRCPsych. 1976. *Publications:* Lunacy, Law and Conscience, 1955; Mental Health and Social Policy, 1960; Mental Hospitals at Work, 1962; The Compassionate Society, 1965; The Teaching of Social Studies in British Universities, 1965; A History of the Mental Health Services, 1972; Opening the Door: a study of new policies for the mentally handicapped, 1975; (ed) Year Book of Social Policy in Britain; (ed) International Library of Social Policy. *Address:* 3 Fulford Mews, York. *T:* York 31611. *Club:* University Women's.

JONES, Keith H.; *see* Hamylton Jones.

JONES, Keith M.; *see* Miller Jones.

JONES, Hon. Mrs Keith Miller; *see* Askwith, Hon. Betty E.

JONES, Sir Kenneth; *see* Jones, Sir J. K. T.

JONES, Hon. Sir Kenneth (George Illtyd), Kt 1974; Hon. Mr Justice Kenneth Jones; a Judge of the High Court, Queen's Bench Division, since 1974; *b* 26 May 1921; *s* of Richard Arthur Jones and late Olive Jane Jones, Radyr, Cardiff; *m* 1947, Dulcie (*d* 1977), *yr d* of Thomas William Thursfield and late Winifred Thursfield, Linthorpe, Middlesbrough; one *s* two *d. Educ:* Brigg Gram. Sch.; University Coll., Oxford (1939-41, 1945-46), MA; Treas., Oxford Union Society, 1941; served in Shropshire Yeo. (76th Medium Regt RA), 1942-45; Staff Captain, HQ 13th Corps, 1945 (despatches). Called to Bar, Gray's Inn, 1946; joined Oxford Circuit, 1947; QC 1962; Mem. Gen. Council of the Bar, 1961-65, 1968-69; Bencher, Gray's Inn, 1969-. Recorder of: Shrewsbury, 1964-66; Wolverhampton, 1966-71; the Crown Court, 1972; Dep. Chm., Herefordshire QS, 1961-71; a Circuit Judge, 1972-73. *Recreations:* golf, sailing. *Address:* Royal Courts of Justice, Strand, WC2A 2LL.

JONES, Maj.-Gen. Leonard Hamilton H.; *see* Howard-Jones.

JONES, Leonard Ivan S.; *see* Stranger-Jones.

JONES, Leslie, MA; JP; Secretary for Welsh Education, Welsh Office and Department of Education and Science, 1970-77; *b* Tumble, Carms, 27 April 1917; *y s* of late William Jones, ME and Joanna (*née* Peregrine); *m* 1948, Glenys, *d* of late D. R. Davies, Swansea; one *s* one *d. Educ:* Gwendraeth Valley Grammar Sch.; Univ. of Wales. Served with RN, 1940-46 (Lieut RNVR). UC Swansea, 1937-40 and 1946-47 (1st cl. hons Econs); Lectr in Econs, Univ. of Liverpool, 1947-51; Lectr and Sen. Lectr in Econs, UC Cardiff, 1952-65; Dir, Dept of Extra-Mural Studies, UC Cardiff, 1965-69. Mem., Ancient Monuments Bd for Wales, 1970-. Hon. Fellow, UC Cardiff, 1971. JP Cardiff 1966. *Publications:* The British Shipbuilding Industry, 1958; articles on maritime, coal, iron and steel industries; industrial economics generally. *Recreations:* walking, gardening. *Address:* 43 Cyncoed Road, Cardiff. *Clubs:* National Liberal, Naval.

JONES, Lewis C.; *see* Carter-Jones.

JONES, Martin, FRAgS; Professor Emeritus of Agricultural Botany, University of Newcastle upon Tyne (formerly King's College), since 1962; *s* of J. G. Jones, Ruel Issa, Bow-street, Cardiganshire; *m* 1927, Olwen Elizabeth Watkin; two *s. Educ:* University Coll. of Wales, Aberystwyth. Welsh Plant Breeding Station, Aberystwyth, 1920-28; Jealott's Hill Agric. Research Stn, Berks, 1928-37; North of Scotland Coll. of Agriculture, Aberdeen, 1937-47; Prof. of Agricultural Botany, King's Coll., Newcastle upon Tyne, 1947-62. Pres., Brit. Grassland Soc., 1951-52; Pres., Agric. Section of Brit. Assoc., Aberdeen, 1963. Chm. Scientific Advisory Cttee, Sports Turf Research Inst., Bingley, 1948-60. *Address:* Y Winllan, Antaron Avenue, Southgate, Aberystwyth. *T:* Aberystwyth 7781. *Club:* Farmers'.

JONES, Maude Elizabeth, CBE 1973; Deputy Director-General, British Red Cross Society, since 1970; *b* 14 Jan. 1921; 2nd *d* of late E. W. Jones, Dolben, Ruthin, North Wales. *Educ:* Brynhyfryd Sch. for Girls, Ruthin. Joined Foreign Relations Dept, Jt War Organisation BRCS and OStJ, 1940; Dep. Dir, Jun. Red Cross, BRCS, 1949; Dir, Jun. Red Cross, 1960; Dep. Dir-Gen. for Branch Affairs, BRCS, 1966. Member: Jt Cttee (and Finance and Gen. Purposes Sub-Cttee) OStJ and BRCS; Council of Nat. Council of Social Service; Council of FANY. Governor, St David's Sch., Ashford, Mddx. SSStJ 1959. *Recreations:* music, gardening, reading. *Address:* 8 Townshend Court, St John's Wood, NW8 7DP. *T:* 01-722 0902. *Clubs:* Anglo-Belgian, VAD.

JONES, Mervyn; *see* Jones, Thomas Mervyn.

JONES, Mervyn; author; *b* 27 Feb. 1922; *s* of Ernest Jones and Katharine (*née* Jokl); *m* 1948, Jeanne Urquhart; one *s* two *d. Educ:* Abbotsholme School; New York University. Assistant Editor: Tribune, 1955-59; New Statesman, 1966-68; Drama Critic, Tribune, 1959-67. *Publications:* No Time to be Young,

1952; The New Town, 1953; The Last Barricade, 1953; Helen Blake, 1955; On the Last Day, 1958; Potbank, 1961; Big Two, 1962; A Set of Wives, 1965; Two Ears of Corn, 1965; John and Mary, 1966; A Survivor, 1968; Joseph, 1970; Mr Armitage isn't back yet, 1971; Life on the Dole, 1972; Holding On, 1973; The Revolving Door, 1973; Strangers, 1974; Lord Richard's Passion, 1974; The Pursuit of Happiness, 1975; Scenes from Bourgeois Life, 1976; Nobody's Fault, 1977. *Address:* 10 Waterside Place, NW1. *T:* 01-586 4404.

JONES, Nigel John I.; *see* Inglis-Jones.

JONES, Norman Stewart C.; *see* Carey Jones.

JONES, Captain Oscar Philip, CVO 1952; OBE 1945; FRGS; FRAeS; *b* 15 Oct. 1898; *s* of Oscar Jones, Beckenham; *m* 1st, 1920, Olive Elizabeth Turner (decd); one *s* decd; 2nd, 1963, Kathleen Jacobs, ARAM, JP, Liverpool. *Educ:* Beckenham, Kent. Served European War, Royal Engineers, 1916-17; Royal Flying Corps and RAF, 1917-19. Berkshire Aviation Tours, 1920-22; Instone Airline, 1922-24; Imperial Airways, 1924-40; Brit. Overseas Airways Corporation, 1940-65; Senior Captain North Atlantic, 1946-55; Special Liaison Officer, BOAC, Worldwide Goodwill and Lecture tours, 1955-65. RAFO and RAFVR, 1924-54. Founder Mem. and Warden, Guild of Air Pilots, 1929 (Deputy Master 1934); Warden, 1954-58; Cumberbach Trophy, 1931; Master Pilot's Certificate, 1935; FAI Gliding Certificate "C", 1939; OC No. 2 ATA Pool, 1940; Flight Capt., Atlantic, 1941; Flight Capt., Landplanes, 1942-45; Air Efficiency Award, 1943; Wing Cmdr, RAFO, 1945. Mem. BOAC "25" Club (Pres. 1952), also Speedbird Club. Flew the Queen, when Princess Elizabeth, to Canada, 1951; Britannia Trophy Award, 1951. Guild Master Pilot's Certificate, 1954. Past Pres., Bull-Terrier Club. *Recreations:* swimming, dog judging (International), light aeroplane flying, riding. *Address:* Squirrels, Spinney Lane, Pulborough, West Sussex RH20 2NX. *T:* West Chiltington 3140. *Clubs:* Royal Air Force Reserves; Southern Aero (Shoreham); Scottish Flying; Tiger.

JONES, Sir Owen Haddon W.; *see* Wansbrough-Jones.

JONES, Penry; Deputy Head of Programme Services, IBA (formerly ITA), since 1971; *b* 18 Aug. 1922; *s* of Joseph William and Edith Jones; *m* Beryl Joan Priestley; two *d. Educ:* Rock Ferry High Sch.; Liverpool Univ. Gen. Sec., YMCA, Altrincham, 1940; Sec., SCM, Southern Univs, 1945; Industrial Sec., Iona Community, 1948; Religious Programmes Producer, ABC Television, 1958; Religious Programmes Officer of ITA, 1964; Head of Religious Broadcasting, BBC, 1967. *Recreations:* hill-walking, swimming, watching Rugby football. *Address:* 36 Queens Gate, SW7. *T:* 01-584 8029. *Club:* Reform.

JONES, Brig. Percival de Courcy, OBE 1953; Chief Secretary, The Royal Life Saving Society, 1965-75; *b* 9 Oct. 1913; *s* of P. de C. Jones, Barnsley; *m* 1st, 1947, Anne Hollins (marr. diss., 1951); one *s*; 2nd, 1962, Elaine Garnett. *Educ:* Oundle; RMC, Sandhurst. Commissioned KSLI 1933; Staff Coll., 1942; comd Northamptons, Burma, 1944-45; Staff Coll. Instructor, 1949-50; AA & QMG, 11th Armoured Div., 1951-53; comd 1st KSLI, 1953-55; AQMG, War Office, 1955-58; NATO Defence Coll., 1958-59; Bde Comdr, 1959-62; retd 1962. Mem., Aylesbury Vale DC, 1976-. *Recreation:* ski-ing. *Address:* Berry Cottage, Townsend Green, Haddenham, Bucks. *T:* Haddenham 291889.

JONES, Peter Trevor S.; *see* Simpson-Jones.

JONES, Philip (Mark), OBE 1977; Founder and Director, Philip Jones Brass Ensemble, since 1951; *b* 12 March 1928. *Educ:* Royal College of Music (ARCM). Principal Trumpet with Royal Opera House, Royal Philharmonic, London Philharmonic, Philharmonia, New Philharmonia and BBC Symphony Orchestras; Head of Dept of Wind and Percussion, Royal Northern Coll. of Music, 1975-77. FRNCM. *Publications:* Joint Editor, Just Brass series (for Chester Music London). *Recreations:* ski-ing, mountain walking. *Address:* 14 Hamilton Terrace, NW8 9UG. *T:* 01-286 9155.

JONES, Philip Asterley, LLB London; Solicitor; *b* 21 June 1914; *s* of Leonard Asterley Jones, St Albans; *m* 1941, Ruth Florence Davis; two *s* (and one *s* decd). *Educ:* Tonbridge Sch.; Law Society's Sch. of Law. Admitted as Solicitor, 1937. Mem. St Albans City Council, 1938. MP (Lab) Hitchin, 1945-50. Served War of 1939-45; Driver RASC Sept. 1939, DAQMG 1943 (despatches). Lecturer in Law at Law Soc., 1945-51; Consultant to Guildford Coll. of Law, on practical training, 1969-72; Dir, vocational trng courses, Birmingham, 1972-75; Hd of Dept of Law, City of Birmingham Polytechnic, 1975-77. Editor, Solicitors' Journal, 1956-68; Editor, Local Govt Chronicle,

1950-63, Legal Editor, 1963-69. *Publications:* (with Sir Rupert Cross) An Introduction to Criminal Law, 1948, 8th edn (with R. I. E. Card), 1976; Cases on Criminal Law, 1949, 5th edn 1973. *Address:* 17 Fugelmere Close, Harborne, Birmingham B17 8SE. *T:* 021-429 3235.

JONES, Sir Philip (Frederick), Kt 1971; Chairman of Directors, The Herald and Weekly Times Limited, Melbourne, Australia, since 1970, Vice-Chairman, 1966-70, and Director since 1957, General Manager, 1953-63 (retd); Chairman, West Australian Newspapers Ltd; Director: Queensland Press Ltd, since 1970; Advertiser Newspapers Ltd, since 1975; *b* 14 Aug. 1912; British; *s* of J. F. Jones, Napier, NZ; *m* 1942, Josephine N., *d* of H. Kirschlager; no *c. Educ:* Barker's Coll., Hornsby, NSW, Australia. Dept of Treasury to 1951; Sec., The Herald and Weekly Times Ltd, 1951-53. ACA, AASA. *Recreation:* golf. *Address:* 25 Griffith Street, New Farm, Queensland 4005, Australia. *Clubs:* Melbourne, Athenæum, Metropolitan Golf, VRC, VATC, Moonee Valley Racing (all in Melbourne).

JONES, Mrs Rachel (Marianne); *b* 4 Aug. 1908; *d* of John Powell Jones Powell, solicitor, Brecon, and Kathleen Mamie Powell; *m* 1935, Very Rev. William Edward Jones (*d* 1974); one *s* three *d. Educ:* Princess Helena Coll.; Bedford Coll., University of London. Subwarden, Time and Talents Settlement, Bermondsey, 1931-32; Member: Bd of Governors, Fairbridge Farm Sch., Western Australia, 1945-49; Council for Wales and Mon, 1959-66; Nat. Governor for Wales of BBC and Chm. of Broadcasting Council for Wales, 1960-65. Member: Governing Body of the Church in Wales; Court and Council of Nat. Museum of Wales; Pres., St David's Diocesan Mothers' Union, 1965-70. *Recreations:* music, gardening. *Address:* Caldey View, Penally, Tenby, Dyfed. *T:* Tenby 3112.

JONES, Ranald M. H.; *see* Handfield-Jones.

JONES, Raymond Edgar; HM Diplomatic Service; Consul-General, Genoa, since 1976; *b* 6 June 1919; *s* of Edgar George Jones, Portsmouth; *m* 1942, Joan Mildred Clark; one *s* two *d. Educ:* Portsmouth Northern Grammar Sch. Entered Admiralty service as Clerical Officer, 1936; joined RAF, 1941; commissioned, 1943; returned to Admty as Exec. Officer, 1946; transf. to Foreign Service, 1948; Singapore, 1949; Second Sec., Rome, 1950; Bahrain, 1952; Rio de Janeiro, 1955; Consul, Philadelphia, 1958; FO, 1961; First Sec., Copenhagen, 1963; Consul, Milan, 1965; Toronto (Dir of British Week), 1966; Dep. High Comr, Adelaide, 1967-71; FCO, 1971-76. *Recreations:* music, gardening. *Address:* Via XII Ottobre 2, I-16121 Genoa, Italy. *Club:* Royal Commonwealth Society.

JONES, Reginald Ernest, MBE 1942; Chief Scientific Officer, Ministry of Technology, 1965-69, retired; *b* 16 Jan. 1904; *m* 1933, Edith Ernestine Kressig; one *s* one *d. Educ:* Marylebone Gram. Sch.; Imperial Coll. of Science and Technology. MSc, DIC, FIEE. International Standard Electric Corp., 1926-33; GPO, 1933-65 (Asst Engr-in-Chief, 1957). Bronze Star (US), 1943. *Recreations:* music, gardening, walking. *Address:* 22 Links Road, Epsom, Surrey. *T:* Epsom 23625.

JONES, Reginald Victor, CB 1946; CBE 1942; FRS 1965; Professor of Natural Philosophy, University of Aberdeen, since 1946; *b* 29 Sept. 1911; *s* of Harold Victor and Alice Margaret Jones; *m* 1940, Vera, *d* of late Charles and Amelia Cain; one *s* two *d. Educ:* Alleyn's; Wadham Coll., Oxford (Exhibitioner), Hon. Fellow, 1968; Balliol Coll., Oxford. MA, DPhil, 1934; Skynner Senior Student in Astronomy, Balliol, 1934-36. Air Ministry: Scientific Officer, 1936; Air Staff, 1939; Asst Dir of Intelligence, 1941, Dir, 1946. Admiralty: seconded Adm. Res. Lab., 1938-39. Min. of Defence: Consultant, 1948-; Dir of Scientific Intelligence, 1952-53; Mem., Carriers Panel, 1962-63; Chm., Air Defence Working Party, 1963-64. DoE (formerly Min. of Labour): Physics Advisory Cttee, 1949-52. Min. of Fuel and Power: Chm., Safety in Mines Res. Advisory Bd, 1956-60 (Mem., 1950-56). Home Office: Scientific Adviser, Civil Defence, 1952-. Min. of Supply: Scientific Advisory Council, 1952-55; Chm., Infra-red Cttee, 1950-60. DSIR: Radio Research Bd, 1952-56; Scientific Grants Cttee, 1952-57; General Bd, Nat. Phys. Lab., 1951-57, 1961-66. War Office: Scientific Advisory Council, 1963-66. Min. of Aviation: Chm., Electronics Research Council, 1964-67 (Mem., 1960-64). Min. of Technology: Chm., Electronics Research Council, 1967-70; DTI: Advisory Council on Calibration and Measurement, 1966-74; Visiting Bd, Nat. Phys. Lab., 1966-69; Adv. Cttee for Research on Measurements and Standards, 1969-; Nuclear Safety Cttee, 1973-. Dept of Educn and Science: Cttee on Universities and Research Estabs, 1965-67; UGC Library Cttee, 1963-67. Royal Society: Chm., Paul Fund Cttee, 1962-; a Vice-Pres., 1971-72; British Nat. Cttee for Scientific Radio, 1961-65; British Nat. Cttee for History of

Science, 1966- (Chm., 1970-); Sectional Cttee for Physics, 1967-70 (Council, 1970-72). Gov., Dulwich Coll., 1966-. Consultant, CCG, 1948-54. Mem. and Chm., Research Adv. Council, BTC, 1949-63. Aberdeen Univ. Ct, 1956-60. Pres., Crabtree Foundation, 1958. Physics Cttee, Nuffield Foundation, 1962-66. Chm., Cttee on University Physics Depts, IPPS, 1962-64. BBC Gen. Adv. Council, 1964-67. Council, Soc. of Instrument Technology, 1966-68. Lectures: Poynting, 1961; Brunel, 1962; Kelvin, 1963; Da Vinci, 1963; York, 1964; Tizard, 1964; Joseph Payne, 1965; Cherwell-Simon, 1965; Lees Knowles, 1967-68; Ludwig Mond, 1967-68; Kelvin, IEE, 1969; Wilkins, Royal Society, 1969; Larmer, 1972; Bernal, 1973; Chester Beatty, 1974; Duke of Edinburgh, 1974; Chelsea, 1974; Tyndall, 1974; Hawksley, 1974; Vis. Lectr, Amer. Assoc. Advancement of Science, 1962. Rapporteur, European Convention on Human Rights, 1970. Pres., Sect. A, British Assoc., 1971. Jt Editor, Notes and Records of the Royal Society. NZ Govt Prestige Fellow, 1973. Festschrift, Ausschuss für Funkortung, 1955. Hon. DSc Strathclyde, 1969; DUniv York, 1976. US Medal of Freedom with Silver Palm, 1946; US Medal for Merit, 1947; BOIMA Prize, Inst. of Physics, 1934; Duddell Medal, Physical Soc., 1960; Parsons Medal, 1967; Hartley Medal, Inst. of Measurement and Control, 1972; Mexican Min. of Telecommunications Medal, 1973. *Publication:* Most Secret War, 1978. *Address:* Natural Philosophy Department, University of Aberdeen, Aberdeen AB9 2UE. *T:* Aberdeen 40241. *Clubs:* Athenæum; Royal Northern (Aberdeen).

JONES, Rhona Mary; Chief Nursing Officer, St Bartholomew's Hospital, 1969-74, retired; *b* 7 July 1921; *d* of late Thomas Henry Jones and late Margaret Evelyn King; single. *Educ:* Liverpool; Alder Hey Children's Hosp.; St Mary's Hosp., Paddington. RSCN 1943; SRN 1945; SCM 1948. Post-Registration Training, and Staff Nurse, Queen Charlotte's Hosp., 1946-48; Ward Sister, 1948-50, Departmental Sister, 1950-52, St Mary's Hosp., Paddington; General Duty Nurse, Canada, 1952-53; Asst Matron, Gen. Infirmary, Leeds, 1953-57; Dep. Matron, Royal Free Hosp., London, 1957-59; Matron, Bristol Royal Hosp., 1959-67; Matron and Superintendent of Nursing, St Bartholomew's Hosp., 1968-69. Chm., Bristol Branch, Royal Coll. of Nursing, 1962-65; Member: Standing Nursing Adv. Cttee, Central Health Services Council, 1963-74; Exec. Cttee, Assoc. Nurse Administrators (formerly Assoc. Hosp. Matrons for England and Wales), 1963-74; Area Nurse Trng Cttee, SW Region, 1965-67; NE Metropolitan Area Nurse Training Cttee, 1969-74; E London Group Hosp. Management Cttee, 1969-74. Vice-Pres., Bristol Royal Hosp. Nurses League. *Recreations:* reading, gardening, travel. *Address:* 26 Seaton Drive, Bedford MK40 3BG. *T:* Bedford 65868.

JONES, Air Vice-Marshal Richard Ian, CB 1960; AFC 1948; psa; pfc; *m* 1940, Margaret Elizabeth Wright. *Educ:* Berkhamsted Sch.; Cranwell. Group Captain, 1955; Air Commodore, 1960; Air Vice-Marshal, 1965. Senior Air Staff Officer, Royal Air Force, Germany (Second Tactical Air Force), Command Headquarters, 1959-63; Dir of Flying Training, 1963-64; AOC No 25 Group, RAF Flying Training Command, 1964-67; SASO, Fighter Command, 1967-68; AOC No 11 (Fighter) Gp, Strike Command, 1969-70. *Recreations:* golf, ski-ing. *Club:* Royal Air Force.

JONES, Maj.-Gen. Richard K.; see Keith-Jones.

JONES, Robert Garallt; Fellow in Creative Writing, University of Wales, 1976-77; *b* 11 Sept. 1934; *s* of Rev. R. E. Jones and Elizabeth Jones, Nefyn, Wales; *m* 1962, Susan Lloyd Griffith; two *s* one *d. Educ:* Denstone; University of Wales (University Student Pres., 1956-57). Sen. English Master, Sir Thomas Jones Sch., Amlwch, 1957-60; Lectr in Educn, University Coll., Aberystwyth, 1961-65; Prin., Mandeville Teachers' Coll., Jamaica, 1965-67; Warden and Headmaster, Llandovery Coll., 1967-76. Member: Gov. Body, Church in Wales, 1959-; Welsh Acad. (Yr Academi Gymreig), 1959-; Broadcasting Council for Wales; Welsh Arts Council; Univ. Council, Aberystwyth. FRSA. Editor of Impact (the Church in Wales quarterly). *Publications:* Ymysg Y Drain, 1959; Y Foel Fawr, 1960; Cwlwm, 1962; Yn Frawd I'r Eos, 1962; (ed) Fy Nghymru I, 1962; Nadolig Gwyn, 1963; Gwared Y Gwirion, 1966; The Welsh Literary Revival, 1966; Jamaican Landscape, 1969; Cysgodion, 1973; Jamaica, Y Flwyddyn Gyntaf, 1974; (ed) Poetry of Wales 1930-1970, 1975; Bardsey, 1976. *Recreations:* freelance TV interviewing, cricket, journalism, writing. *Address:* Lerry Dale, Dolybont, Borth, Aberystwyth, Wales.

JONES, Robert Gwilym L.; see Lewis-Jones.

JONES, Robert Hefin, CVO 1969; PhD; Assistant Secretary, Welsh Office, since 1972; *b* 30 June 1932; *s* of late Owen Henry

and Elizabeth Jones, Blaenau Ffestiniog. *Educ:* Ysgol Sir Ffestiniog; University Coll. of Wales, Aberystwyth (BSc); University of London (PhD). Asst Master, Whitgift Sch., 1957-63; HM Inspector of Schools (Wales), 1963; seconded to Welsh Office as Sec., Prince of Wales Investiture Cttee, and Personal Asst to the Earl Marshal, 1967; Principal, Welsh Office, 1969. *Recreations:* music, reading, cooking. *Address:* 34 The Grange, Llandaff, Cardiff. *T:* Cardiff 564573. *Club:* East India, Devonshire, Sports and Public Schools.

JONES, Brig. Robert Llewellyn J.; see Jephson-Jones.

JONES, Rev. (Robert William) Hugh; Moderator of the West Midland Province of the United Reformed Church (formerly of the Congregational Church in England and Wales), 1970-Aug. 1978; *b* 6 May 1911; *s* of Evan Hugh Jones and Sarah Elizabeth Salmon; *m* 1939, Gaynor Eluned Evans; one *s* one *d. Educ:* Chester Grammar Sch.; Univs of Wales and Manchester; Lancashire Independent College. BA Wales, History and Philosophy. Ordained, 1939; Congregational Church: Welholme, Grimsby, 1939-45; Muswell Hill, London, 1945-49; Warwick Road, Coventry, 1949-61; Petts Wood, Orpington, 1961-69; President, Congregational Church in England and Wales, 1969-70. Frequent broadcaster, radio and TV; Mem., BBC/ITA Central Religious Adv. Cttee, 1971-75. *Recreations:* drama, photography. *Address:* 8 Worcester Road, Kenilworth, Warwicks. *T:* Kenilworth 53624.

JONES, Robin Francis McN.; see McNab Jones.

JONES, R(obin) Huws, CBE 1969; Consultant, Joseph Rowntree Memorial Trust, since 1976 (Associate Director, 1972-76); *b* 1 May 1909; *m* 1944, Enid Mary Horton; one *s* two *d. Educ:* Liverpool Univ. Frances Wood Prizeman, Royal Statistical Society. Lectr, Social Science Dept, Liverpool Univ., 1937-39; Staff Tutor (City of Lincoln) Oxford Univ. Extra-mural Delegacy, 1939-47; Dir of Social Science Courses, University Coll., Swansea, 1948-61; Principal, Nat. Inst. for Social Work Training, 1961-72. Visiting Prof., University of Minnesota, 1964; Heath Clark Lectr, University of London, 1969; Neely Memorial Lectr, Cleveland, O, 1969. Member: Minister of Health's Long Term Study Group, 1965-69; Cttee on Local Authority and Allied Personal Social Services, 1965-68; NE Metropolitan Reg. Hosp. Bd, 1967-72; Central Council for Educn and Training in Social Work, 1971-72; Cttee, King's Fund Centre, 1970-75; Chief Scientist's Cttee, DHSS, 1971-; Chm., Consultative Cttee, The Family Fund; Pres., Internat. Assoc. of Schools of Social Work, 1976 (Hon. Treasurer, 1970-74). Hon. Fellow, Inst. of Social Welfare. *Publications:* The Doctor and the Social Services, 1971; contributions to journals. *Address:* Lambfold, High Lorton, Cockermouth, Cumbria. *T:* Lorton 619. *Club:* Savile.

JONES, Brigadier Ronald M.; see Montague-Jones.

JONES, Sir Samuel Bankole-, Kt 1965; legal consultant; Chairman, Sierra Leone Commercial Bank, since 1974; *b* 23 Aug. 1911; *s* of Samuel Theophilus Jones, Freetown, and Bernice Janet Jones; *m* 1922, Mary Alexandrina Stuart; three *s* two *d. Educ:* Methodist Boys' High Sch., Freetown; Fourah Bay Coll.; Durham Univ.; Middle Temple, London. MA, BCL, Diploma in Educn (Durham). Barrister-at-Law, 1938; private practice, 1938-49; Police Magistrate, Actg Solicitor Gen., 1949-58; Actg Puisne Judge, 1958-60; Puisne Judge, 1960-63; Chief Justice, Sierra Leone, 1963-65; Acting Governor Gen., Aug.-Nov., 1965; Pres., Court of Appeal, Sierra Leone, 1965-71. Chm., Fourah Bay Coll. Council, University Coll. of Sierra Leone, 1956-69; Chancellor, Univ. of Sierra Leone, 1969. Member: UNO Commn into death of its late Sec. Gen.; World Habeas Corpus Cttee, World Peace through World Center, 1968. Fellow, Internat. Soc. for Study of Comparative Public Law, 1969. Hon. DCL Durham, 1965. *Recreations:* reading, walking, gardening. *Address:* 8 Kingharman Road, Brookfields, Freetown, Sierra Leone, West Africa. *T:* 5061. *Clubs:* Royal Commonwealth Society (London); Freetown Reform (Freetown).

JONES, Sir Samuel (Owen), Kt 1966; FIREE (Aust.), FIE Aust.; Chairman, Standard Telephones & Cables Pty Ltd, 1968-76 (Managing Director, 1961-69); Chairman: Concrete Industries (Monier) Ltd, 1969-76; Austral Standard Cables Pty Ltd, 1967-69 and 1972-75; Export Finance and Insurance Corporation, 1975-77; Director, Overseas Corporation (Australia) Ltd, 1969-75; *b* 20 Aug. 1905; *s* of late John Henry Jones and Eliza Jones (*née* Davies); *m* 1932, Jean, *d* of late J. W. Sinclair; two *d. Educ:* Warracknabeal High Sch.; University of Melbourne. Engineering Branch, PMG's Dept, 1927-39. Lt-Col comdg Divisional Signal Unit, AIF abroad, 1939-41; CSO Aust. Home

Forces, 1941-42; Dir, Radio and Signal Supplies, Min. of Munitions, 1942-45. Technical Manager, Philips Electrical Industries Pty Ltd, 1945-50, Tech. Dir, 1950-61; Chairman: Telecommunication Co. of Aust., 1956-61; Australian Telecommunications Develt Assoc., 1967-70 (Mem., 1963-75); Consultative Council, Export Payments Insurance Corp, 1970-75; Director: Television Equipment Pty Ltd, 1960-61; Cannon Electric (Australia) Pty Ltd, 1964-68. National Pres., Aust. Inst. of Management, 1968-70; Councillor, Chamber of Manufactures of NSW, 1968-72; Member: Govt's Electronics and Telecommunications Industry Adv. Cttee, 1955-72; Export Develt Council, 1969-74; Council, Macquarie Univ., 1969-74; Council, Nat. Library of Australia, 1971-74; Australian Univs Commn, 1972-75. *Publications:* several technical articles. *Recreations:* bowls, fishing. *Address:* Apartment 11, 321 Edgecliff Road, Woollahra, NSW 2025, Australia; Mummuga Lodge, Dalmeny, NSW 2546. *Clubs:* Union, Royal Automobile of Australia, Royal Sydney Yacht Squadron (all in Sydney); Naval and Military (Melbourne).

JONES, Sir Simon (Warley Frederick) Benton, 4th Bt *cr* 1919; *b* 11 Sept. 1941; *o s* of Sir Peter Fawcett Benton Jones, 3rd Bt, OBE, and Nancy (*d* 1974), *d* of late Warley Pickering; *S* father, 1972; *m* 1966, Margaret Fiona, *d* of David Rutherford Dickson; two *s* two *d. Educ:* Eton; Trinity College, Cambridge (MA). JP for Lincolnshire (parts of Kesteven), 1971; High Sheriff, Lincs, 1977. *Heir: s* James Peter Martin Benton Jones, *b* 1 Jan. 1973. *Address:* Irnham Hall, Grantham, Lincs. *T:* Corby Glen 212.

JONES, (Stephen) Barry; BSc (Econ); MP (Lab) Flint East, since 1970; Parliamentary Under-Secretary of State for Wales, since 1974; *b* 1938; *s* of Stephen Jones and late Grace Jones, Mancot, Flintshire; *m* Janet Jones (*née* Davies); one *s . Address:* 30 Paper Mill Lane, Oakenholt, Flint. *T:* Flint 3430. *Clubs:* Connah's Quay Labour Party; Caergwrle Labour Party.

JONES, S(tuart) Lloyd; Chairman, Welsh Health Technical Services Organisation, 1973-76; *b* 26 Aug. 1917; *s* of Hugh and Edna Lloyd Jones, Liverpool; *m* 1942, Pamela Mary Hamilton-Williams, Heswall; one *s* three *d. Educ:* Rydal Sch.; Univ. of Liverpool. Solicitor, 1940; Dep. Town Clerk, Nottingham, 1950-53; Town Clerk of Plymouth, 1953-70; Chief Exec. Officer and Town Clerk of Cardiff, 1970-74. One of Advisers to Minister of Housing and Local Govt on Amalgamation of London Boroughs, 1962; Indep. Inspector, extension of Stevenage New Town, 1964; Member: Cttee on Public Participation in Planning, 1969; PM's Cttee on Local Govt Rules of Conduct, 1973-74. Pres., Soc. of Town Clerks, 1972. Distinguished Services Award, Internat. City Management Assoc., 1976. *Address:* High Dolphin, Dittisham, South Devon. *Clubs:* Cardiff and County; Royal Western Yacht Club of England (Plymouth).

JONES, Sydney, CBE 1971; PhD; Member of Board, British Railways, 1965-76, part-time, 1975-76 (Director of Research, BR Board, 1962-65); Chairman, Computer Systems and Electronics Requirement Board, Department of Industry, since 1975; *b* 18 June 1911; *s* of John Daniel Jones and Margaret Ann (*née* Evans); *m* 1938, Winifred Mary (*née* Boulton); two *s* one *d. Educ:* Cyfarthfa Castle Grammar Sch.; Cardiff Technical Coll.; Cardiff Univ. Coll.; Birmingham Univ. BSc 1st cl. hons (London) 1932; PhD (London) 1951. General Electric Co., Witton, 1933-36; teaching in Birmingham, 1936-40; Scientific Civil Service at HQ, RRE, Malvern, and RAE, Farnborough, 1940-58; Dir of Applications Research, Central Electricity Generating Board, 1958-61; Technical Dir, R. B. Pullin, Ltd, 1961-62. Chm., SIRA Inst. Ltd, 1970-. Chm., Transport Adv. Cttee, Transport and Road Res. Lab., 1972-. Governor, Malvern Girls' Coll. FIEE 1960; FIMechE 1965; FCIT 1971; Fellow, Fellowship of Engineering, 1977. Hon. DSc 1977. *Publications:* (jtly) Introductory Applied Science, 1942; papers on automatic control. *Recreations:* gardening, wine, photography, house design. *Address:* Uplands, 25 Graham Road, Malvern, Worcs WR14 2HU. *T:* Malvern 2566. *Club:* Athenæum.

JONES, Sydney T.; *see* Tapper-Jones.

JONES, Terence Leavesley; Under-Secretary, Department of the Environment, since 1974; *b* 24 May 1926; *s* of Reginald Arthur Jones and Grace Jones; *m* 1966, Barbara Hall; one *s . Educ:* Nottingham High Sch.; Jesus Coll., Cambridge (MA). RNVR, 1944-46 (Sub-Lt). Asst Inspector of Ancient Monuments, Min. of Works, 1949; Principal, 1957; Sec., Historic Buildings Council for England, 1961-67; Asst Sec., 1967. *Recreations:* music, archæology. *Address:* 6 Broughton Gardens, Highgate, N6 5RS. *T:* 01-348 3144. *Club:* Athenæum.

JONES, Thomas; *see* Jones, Tom.

JONES, Thomas E.; *see* Elder-Jones.

JONES, Thomas Glanville; a Recorder of the Crown Court, since 1972; *b* 10 May 1931; *s* of Evan James Jones and late Margaret Olive Jones; Welsh; *m* 1964, Valma Shirley Jones; three *s. Educ:* St Clement Dane's Grammar Sch.; University Coll., London (LLB). Called to Bar, 1958. Sec., Swansea Law Library Assoc., 1963; Exec. Mem., Swansea Festival of Music and the Arts, 1967; Chm., Guild for Promotion of Welsh Music, 1970; Chm., Jt Professional Cttees of Swansea Local Bar and Swansea Law Soc. and W. Wales Law Soc.; Mem., Grand Theatre Trust. *Recreations:* Welsh culture, Rugby, reading, music, poetry, gardening. *Address:* Angel Chambers, 94 Walter Road, Swansea SA1 5QA. *T:* Swansea 56123/4; Gelligron, 12 Eastcliff, Southgate, Swansea SA3 2AS. *T:* Bishopston 3118. *Club:* Ffynone (Swansea).

JONES, (Thomas) Mervyn, CBE 1961; Chairman, Civic Trust for Wales; *b* 2 March 1910; *s* of late Rev. Dr Richard Jones and Violet Jones, Llandinam; *m* 1st (marr. diss. 1960); one *s* one *d ;* 2nd, 1960, Margaret, *d* of Ernest E. Cashmore, Newport; one *s* one *d. Educ:* Newtown Co. Sch.; University Coll. of Wales, Aberystwyth (LLB); Trinity Hall, Cambridge (MA, LLM). Pres. Trinity Hall Law Soc., 1949. Asst Solicitor, Newport Corporation, Town Clerk, 1948; Chairman: Wales Gas Bd, 1948-70; Wales Tourist Bd, 1970-76; Wales Cttee, European Architectural Heritage Year (EAHY), 1975; Member: Board of Management, Welsh National Opera Company; Ashby Cttee on Adult Education, 1953-54; Tucker Cttee on Proceedings before Examining Justices, 1957-58; Council, University of Wales; Design Cttee Wales; Welsh Councils, 1965-. Pres., Industrial Assoc., Wales and Mon, 1959-60. FBIM; Hon. FSIA. *Publications:* Planning Law and the Use of Property; Requisitioned Land and War Works Act, 1945; various titles and articles in Local Govt books and journals. *Recreations:* playing at golf, helping to keep Wales beautiful. *Address:* Dyffryn, Ely Road, Llandaff, Cardiff. *T:* Cardiff 562070. *Club:* United Oxford & Cambridge University.

JONES, Thomas Philip; Deputy Secretary, Department of Energy, since 1976; *b* 13 July 1931; *s* of William Ernest Jones and Mary Elizabeth Jones; *m* 1955, Mary Phillips; two *s. Educ:* Cowbridge Grammar Sch.; Jesus Coll., Oxford (BA). 2nd Lieut, Royal Artillery, 1953-55; Asst Principal, Min. of Supply, 1955; Principal Min. of Aviation, 1959; on loan to HM Treasury, 1964-66; Principal Private Sec. to Minister of Aviation, 1966-67; Asst Sec., Min. of Technology, subseq. Min. of Aviation Supply, 1967-71; Under Secretary, DTI, 1971; Under Sec., Dept of Energy, 1974. *Recreations:* squash, reading. *Address:* 12 Broomwater West, Teddington, Middx. *T:* 01-977 6336.

JONES, Tom, CBE 1974 (OBE 1962); JP; Regional Secretary for Wales, Transport and General Workers' Union, 1969-73, retired (N Wales and Border Counties, 1953); Chairman, Appeals Tribunal North Wales, NHS Staff Commission, since 1974; Member of Industrial Tribunal for North Wales and North West England, since 1975; *b* 13 Oct. 1908; Welsh parents, father coalminer; *m* 1942, Rosa Jones (*née* Thomas); two *s* two *d. Educ:* Elem. Sch., Rhos, Wrexham; WEA Studies, Summer Schools. Coalminer, 1922-36 (having left sch. aged 14). Soldier, Spanish Republican Army (Internat. Bde), 1937-38 (captured by Franco Forces, 1938; PoW, 1940; sentenced to death by Franco Authorities, sentence commuted to 30 years imprisonment; released following representations by British Govt which involved a Trade Agreement; Knight of Order of Loyalty, Spanish Republic (Spanish Govt in Exile) 1974). Worked in Chem. Industry, 1941-44; became full-time Union Official of T&GWU, 1945; Hon. Sec., RAC of N Wales (TUC) for 20 years, retired. Member: Welsh Economic Council; Welsh Council (Vice-Chm.; reappointed 1971); Merseyside and N Wales Electricity Bd, 1976-; Court of Governors, Univ. of Wales; Prince of Wales Cttee; Treasurer, N Wales WEA; Governor, Coleg Harlech; Past Member: Welsh Industrial Estates Corp.; Welsh Bd for Industry. JP Flint, 1955. *Recreations:* reading, do-it-yourself hobbies, extra-mural activities. *Address:* 2 Blackbrook Avenue, Hawarden, Deeside, Clwyd. *T:* Hawarden 532365.

JONES, (Trevor) Alec; MP (Lab) Rhondda, since 1974 (Rhondda West, March 1967-1974); Parliamentary Under-Secretary of State, Welsh Office, since 1975; *b* 12 Aug. 1924; *m* 1950, Mildred M. Evans; one *s. Educ:* Porth County Grammar School; Bangor Normal Training Coll. Schoolteacher from 1949. PPS to Minister of Defence for Equipment, 1968-70, to Minister of State, DHSS, 1974; Parly Under-Sec. of State, DHSS, 1974-75. Sponsored Divorce Reform Act, 1969. *Address:* 58 Kenry Street, Tonypandy, Rhondda, Wales. *T:* Tonypandy 3472. *Club:* Ystrad Labour (Rhondda).

JONES, William Elwyn Edwards; *b* 1904; *s* of the Rev. Robert William Jones and Elizabeth Jane Jones, Welsh Methodist Minister; *m* 1936, Dydd, *d* of Rev. E. Tegla Davies; one *s* two *d. Educ:* Bootle Secondary Sch.; Festiniog County Sch.; University of Wales. BA (Wales), LLB (London). Admitted Solicitor, 1927; Clerk to the Justices, Bangor Div., Caernarvonshire, 1934. Town Clerk, Bangor, 1939-69. MP (Lab) Conway Div. of Caernarvonshire, 1950-51. Member: Nat. Parks Commn, 1966-68, Countryside Commn, 1968-71; Council and Court of Governors, and Treasurer, University Coll. of N Wales. CC Caernarvonshire, 1948-69. *Publications:* Press articles in Welsh and English. *Recreation:* walking. *Address:* 23 Glyngarth Court, Glyngarth, Menai Bridge, Gwynedd, N Wales. *T:* Glyn Garth 422.

JONES, Sir (William) Emrys, Kt 1971; BSc; Principal, Royal Agricultural College, Cirencester, 1973-July 1978; *b* 6 July 1915; *s* of late William Jones and Mary Ann (*née* Morgan); *m* 1938, Megan Ann Morgan (marr. diss., 1966); three *s*; *m* 1967, Gwyneth George. *Educ:* Llandovery Gram. Sch.; University Coll. of Wales, Aberystwyth. Agricultural Instr, Gloucester CC, 1940-46; Provincial Grassland Adv. Officer, NAAS, Bristol, 1946-50; County Agricultural Officer, Gloucester, 1950-54; Dep. Dir, 1954-57, Dir 1957-59, NAAS, Wales; Sen. Advisory Officer, NAAS, 1959-61; Dir, 1961-66; Dir-Gen., Agricultural Develt and Adv. Service (formerly Chief Agricl Advr), MAFF, 1967-73. Mem., Adv. Council for Agriculture and Horticulture in England and Wales, 1973-. Independent Chm., Nat. Cattle Breeders' Assoc., 1976-. Hon. LLD Wales, 1973; Hon. DSc Bath, 1975. *Recreations:* golf, shooting. *Address:* (until July 1978) Royal Agricultural College, Cirencester, Glos. *T:* Cirencester 2531; (from July 1978) The Draey, 18 St Mary's Park, Louth, Lincs. *Clubs:* Athenæum, Farmers'.

JONES, Sir William Lloyd M.; *see* Mars-Jones.

JONES, William Stephen, CBE 1965; Chairman: J. M. Jones & Sons (Holdings) Ltd, since 1969; J. M. Jones & Sons Ltd, since 1969; Southern Heating Ltd, since 1957; Berks, Bucks & Oxon Trading Co. Ltd, since 1955; Markham Developments Ltd, since 1969; Markham Developments (Investment) Ltd, since 1971; J. M. Jones Homes Ltd, since 1973; President, Markham Foncière SA, Paris, since 1972; *b* 26 Dec. 1913; *s* of John Markham and Alice Jones; *m* 1938, Joan Constance Reach; two *s. Educ:* Maidenhead. Joined J. M. J. Construction Group, 1931; Dir, 1943; Man. Dir, 1949; Chm., 1969. Member: Housing Corp., 1964-; Agrément Board. Dep. Chm., Ramsbury Building Soc. FIOB (Mem. Council, Inst. of Building); Pres., Nat. Fedn of Building Trades Employers, 1963. *Recreations:* reading, gardening, tennis. *Address:* Lychen Cottage, Littlewick Green, Berks SL6 3QR. *T:* Littlewick Green 2731. *Club:* Reform.

JONES, William Tinnion, MD; District Community Physician, Brent Health District; Senior Lecturer in Community Medicine, Middlesex Hospital Medical School, since 1975; *b* Maryport, Cumberland, 30 July 1927; *s* of late Ben and Mary Tinnion Jones; *m* 1950, Jennifer Provost Bland, MB; three *d. Educ:* St Bees Sch.; Edinburgh Univ.; London Sch. of Hygiene and Tropical Medicine. MB, ChB Edinburgh, 1950; MD Edinburgh, 1957; DPH London, 1955. Surg. Lt, RNZN (UN Forces, Korea), 1951-54; Med. Dir, Nuffield Industrial Health Survey, Tyneside, 1956-57; Asst MOH, Reading, 1955-56; Med. Adv., Birfield Ltd, 1957-63; Hubert Wyers Travelling Fellow, 1961; Med. Dir (founder) W Midlands Industrial Health Service, 1963-69; Tutor and Lectr in Industrial Health, Univ. of Birmingham, and London Sch. of Hygiene and Tropical Med., 1965-69; Dir-Gen., Health Educn Council, 1969-71; Physician i/c, Inf. and Adv. Service, TUC Centenary Inst. of Occupational Health, London Sch. of Hygiene and Tropical Med., 1971-75; Cons. Physician (Occupational Health), Gt Ormond Street Hosp. for Sick Children. *Publications:* articles in several med. jls. *Recreations:* the popular arts in their various forms. *Address:* 63 Crown Street, Harrow-on-the-Hill, Mddx. *T:* 01-864 1430; Central Middlesex Hospital, Acton Lane, NW10 7NS. *T:* 01-965 5733.

JONES, Wyn; *see* Jones, G. W.

JONES, Wynn Normington H., *see* Hugh-Jones.

JONES-PARRY, Ernest; Executive Director: International Sugar Council, 1965-68; International Sugar Organisation, since 1969; *b* 16 July 1908; *o s* of late John Parry and Charlotte Jones, Rhuddlan; *m* 1938, Mary Powell; two *s. Educ:* St Asaph; University of Wales; University of London. MA (Wales) 1932; PhD (London) 1934; FRHistS. Lecturer in History, University Coll. of Wales, 1935-40; Ministry of Food, 1941; Treasury, 1946-47; Asst Sec., Ministry of Food, 1948-57; Under Sec., 1957; Dir of Establishments, Ministry of Agriculture, Fisheries and Food, 1957-61. *Publications:* The Spanish Marriages, 1841-46, 1936; The Correspondence of Lord Aberdeen and Princess Lieven, 1832-1854 (2 vols), 1938-39; articles and reviews in History and English Historical Review. *Recreations:* reading, watching cricket. *Address:* 3 Sussex Mansions, Old Brompton Road, SW7. *T:* 01-589 7979. *Club:* Athenæum.

JONES-WILLIAMS, Dafydd Wyn, OBE 1970; MC 1942; TD 1954; DL; Commissioner for Local Administration for Wales (Local Ombudsman), since 1974; *b* 13 July 1916; *s* of late J. Jones-Williams, Dolgellau; *m* 1945, Rosemary Sally, *e d* of late A. E. Councell, Blaenau Hall, Rhydymain; two *d. Educ:* Dolgellau Grammar Sch.; UCW Aberystwyth (LLB). Served 1939-45 with HAC and X Royal Hussars (Western Desert). Formerly comdg 446 (Royal Welch) AB, LAA Regt, RA (TA). Solicitor, 1939. Clerk of County Council, Clerk of Peace, and Clerk to Lieutenancy, Merioneth, 1954-70; Circuit Administrator, Wales and Chester Circuit, 1970-74. Member: Hughes-Parry Cttee on Legal Status of Welsh Language, 1963-65; Nat. Broadcasting Council for Wales; Lord Chancellor's Adv. Cttee on Trng of Magistrates. Formerly: Mem., Nature Conservancy (Chm., Cttee for Wales); Chm., Merioneth and Montgomeryshire T&AFA. DL Merioneth, 1958. *Recreation:* golf. *Address:* Holly Cottage, Merthyr Mawr, near Bridgend, Mid Glam. *T:* Bridgend 56560; Bryncoedifor Cottage, Rhydymain, near Dolgellau, Gwynedd. *T:* Rhydymain 635. *Clubs:* Army and Navy; Royal St Davids Golf; Royal Porthcawl Golf.

JONZEN, Mrs Karin, FRBS; sculptor; *b* London (Swedish parents), 22 Dec. 1914; *d* of U. Löwenadler and G. Munck av Fulkila; *m* 1944, Basil Jonzen (*d* 1967); one *s*; *m* 1972, Åke Sucksdorff. Studied Slade Sch., 1932-36. Slade Dipl. and Scholarship, 1934; Rome Scholarship, 1939 Lectr, Camden Arts Centre, 1969-70. *Exhibitions:* Battersea Park Open Air Exhibn, 1948-51; Leicester Galls; Roland, Browse and Delbanco; Piccadilly Gall.; Royal Academy; Raymond and Raymond Gall., New York, 1970; O'Hana Gall., 1970-71; Grafton Gall., 1970-71; Fieldborne Gall., 1974; *Work in permanent collections:* V&A Museum, also Bradford, Brighton, Glasgow, Melbourne; *official purchases:* Arts Council; Selwyn Coll., Cambridge; Modern Schs in Leics, Cardiff and Hertford; Festival of Britain Exhibition; Southend Art Gall. and Museum. Carving on Guildford Cathedral, 1961; Leverhulme Res. Grant to travel in Greece and Italy, 1962; Life-size Bronze Figure for WHO HQ, New Delhi, 1963, and Bronze Torso for WHO at Geneva, 1965 (both gifts of British Govt); exhibited three works in City of London Festival, 1968 (Madonna and Child purchased for St Mary le Bow, Cheapside, 1969); life-size Bronze purchased by City of London Corp. for London Wall site, 1971; over life-size bronze group, Guildhall, 1972; portrait busts of Dame Ninette de Valois and Warwick Braithwaite, at Sadler's Wells, 1975; three-quarter life-size Pietà for Swedish Church, Marylebone. *Relevant publication:* Karin Jonzen: sculptor, introd. Carel Weight, 1976. *Recreation:* music. *Address:* The Studio, 6A Gunter Grove, SW10.

JOOSTE, Gerhardus Petrus; South African Secretary for External Affairs, 1956-66 (Secretary for Foreign Affairs, 1961); retired, 1966; Special Adviser (part-time) on Foreign Affairs to Prime Minister and Minister of Foreign Affairs, 1966-68; Chairman, State Procurement Board, 1968-71; *b* 5 May 1904; *s* of Nicolaas Jooste and Sofie Jooste (*née* Visser); *m* 1934, Anna van Zyl van der Merwe; one *s* one *d. Educ:* Primary and Secondary Schs, Winburg and Kroonstad; Rondebosch Boys High; Grey Coll., Bloemfontein; Pretoria Univ. Entered Union Public Service, 1924; Priv. Sec. to Hon. N. C. Havenga, Minister of Finance, 1929; Dept of External Affairs, 1934; Legation Sec. and Chargé d'Affaires *ad interim*, Brussels, 1937-40; Chargé d'Affaires to Belgian Government-in-Exile, 1940-41; transf. to Dept of External Affairs, Pretoria, as Head of Economic Div., 1941-46; Head of Political and Diplomatic Div. of the Dept, 1946-49; Ambassador to US and Permanent Delegate to UN, 1949-54; High Commissioner of the Union of South Africa in London, 1954-56. Mem., Commn of Enquiry regarding Water Matters, 1966-; Mem. (ex officio), Atomic Energy Bd, 1956-66. Mem., South African Acad. of Science and Arts. *Recreation:* bowls. *Address:* 851 Government Avenue, Arcadia, Pretoria, South Africa.

JOPE, Prof. Edward Martyn, FBA 1965; FSA 1946; MRIA 1973; Professor of Archæology, The Queen's University of Belfast, since 1963; Visiting Professor in Archaeological Sciences, University of Bradford, since 1974; *b* 28 Dec. 1915; *s* of Edward Mallet Jope and Frances Margaret (*née* Chapman); *m* 1941, Margaret Halliday; no *c. Educ:* Kingswood Sch., Bath; Oriel Coll., Oxford. Staff of Royal Commission on Ancient

Monuments (Wales), 1938; Biochemist, Nuffield and MRC Grants, 1940; Queen's Univ., Belfast: Lectr in Archæology, 1949; Reader, 1954. Mem. Ancient Monuments Adv. Coun. (NI), 1950; Mem. Royal Commission on Ancient Monuments (Wales), 1963-; Pres. Section H, British Assoc., 1965. Rhys Res. Fellow and Vis. Sen. Res. Fellow, Jesus Coll., Oxford, 1977-78. *Publications:* Early Celtic Art in the British Isles, 1977; (ed) Studies in Building History, 1961; papers in Biochem. Jl, Proc. Royal Society Med., Phil. Trans Royal Soc., Spectrochemica Acta, Trans. Faraday Soc., Proc. Prehistoric Soc., Antiquaries' Jl, Medieval Archæology, Oxoniensia, Ulster Jl of Archæology, Proc. Soc. of Antiquaries of Scotland, etc. *Recreation:* music. *Address:* Queen's University, Belfast BT7 1NN, N Ireland; 1 Chalfont Road, Oxford.

JOPLING, (Thomas) Michael; MP (C) Westmorland since 1964; farmer; *b* 10 Dec. 1930; *s* of Mark Bellerby Jopling, Masham, Yorks; *m* 1958, Gail, *d* of Ernest Dickinson, Harrogate; two *s*. *Educ:* Cheltenham Coll.; King's Coll., Newcastle upon Tyne (BSc Agric.). Mem., Thirsk Rural District Council, 1958-64; contested Wakefield (C), 1959; Mem. National Council, National Farmers' Union, 1962-64. Jt Sec., Cons. Parly Agric. Cttee, 1966-70; PPS to Minister of Agriculture, 1970-71; an Asst Govt Whip, 1971-73; a Lord Comr, HM Treasury, 1973-74; an Opposition Whip, March-June 1974; an opposition spokesman on agriculture, 1974-75, 1976-; Shadow Minister of Agriculture, 1975-76. Mem., UK Exec., Commonwealth Parly Assoc., 1974-. *Address:* Ainderby Hall, Thirsk, North Yorks. *T:* Sinderby 224; Pine Rigg, Windermere, Westmorland. *T:* Windermere 2590. *Clubs:* Carlton, Beefsteak.

JORDAN, Most Rev. Anthony, OMI; *b* Broxburn, West Lothian, Scotland, 10 Nov. 1901; Priest, July 1929; Consecrated Bishop, Sept. 1945; Vicar Apostolic of Prince Rupert, Canada, and Titular Bishop of Vada, 1945-55; Coadjutor, 1955, translated as Archbishop of Edmonton in 1964; retired, 1973. *Address:* 13101 Churchill Crescent, Edmonton, Alberta T5N 4H5, Canada.

JORDAN, David Harold, CMG 1975; MBE 1962; Director of Trade, Industry and Customs (formerly Commerce and Industry) and Member of Legislative Council, Hong Kong, since 1972; *b* Sunderland, 27 Oct. 1924; *er s* of late H. G. Jordan, OBE, and Gwendoline Rees; *m* 1st, 1951, Lorna Mary Holland (marr. diss.), *er d* of late W. R. Harvey; three *s* one *d*; 2nd, 1971, Penelope Amanda, *d* of Lt-Col B. L. J. Davy, OBE, TD; one *d*. *Educ:* Roundhay Sch., Leeds; Berkhamsted; Magdalen Coll., Oxford (1st Cl. Chinese), MA 1956. 9th Gurkha Rifles, Indian Army, 1943-47. Colonial Administrative Service (Hong Kong), 1951; Asst Sec. for Chinese Affairs, 1952-55; Colonial Secretariat, 1956-68: Asst Sec., 1956-60; Defence Sec., 1961-66. jssc 1960. Dep. Dir, Commerce and Industry, 1968-70; Dep. Economic Sec., 1970-71; Dep. Financial Sec., 1971-72. *Address:* 47 Sassoon Road, Hong Kong. *T:* 5-874817; Trade, Industry and Customs Department, Ocean Centre, Kowloon, Hong Kong. *T:* 3-677229. *Clubs:* Hong Kong; Royal Hong Kong Jockey.

JORDAN, Douglas Arthur, CMG 1977; Deputy Commissioner of Controls and Customs, Trade, Industry and Customs Department, Hong Kong, since 1977; *b* 28 Sept. 1918; *s* of late Arthur Jordan and Elizabeth Jordan; *m* 1st, 1940, Violet Nancy (*née* Houston); one *d*; 2nd, 1970, Constance Dorothy (*née* Wallis). *Educ:* East Ham Grammar Sch., London. HM Customs and Excise: Officer, 1938; Surveyor, 1953; Inspector, 1960; Asst Collector, Manchester and London, 1962-68; Sen. Inspector, 1968-69; Chief Investigation Officer, 1969-77. Freeman, City of London, 1964. *Recreations:* golf, music. *Address:* 7 Thakeham Close, Sydenham, SE26 6HN. *T:* 01-778 9874. *Clubs:* Wig and Pen, Press.

JORDAN, Henry; Under-Secretary, Department of Education and Science, 1973-75; *b* 1919; *s* of late Henry Jordan and Mary Ann Jordan (*née* Shields); *m* 1946, Huguette Yvonne Rayée; one *s*. *Educ:* St Patrick's High Sch., Dumbarton. Served War, RA, 1939-46. Home Civil Service, Post Office, 1936; Foreign Office, 1947; Central Land Board and War Damage Commn, 1949; Min. (later Dept) of Educn, 1957. *Address:* 72 Shearman Road, Lee Park, Blackheath, SE3 9HX. *T:* 01-318 0906.

JORDAN, Rev. Preb. Hugh; Curate of St James's, Hereford, and teaching at Hereford High School, 1969-72, retired; a Prebendary of St Paul's Cathedral, 1963-69, now Emeritus; *b* 29 Dec. 1906; *m* 1936, Elizabeth Hamilton Lamb, Dublin; two *s* one *d*. *Educ:* Trinity Coll., Dublin; Royal School, Cavan, Eire. School Teacher, 1924-29; Curate St Kevin's Church, Dublin, 1932-34; Gen. Sec. City of Dublin YMCA, 1934-39; Vicar: St Luke's, Eccleston, St Helens, Lancs, 1939-45; Penn Fields, Wolverhampton, 1945-49; Redland, Bristol (and Lecturer and Tutor, Tyndale Hall, Bristol), 1949-56; Principal, London Coll.

of Divinity, 1956-69. *Recreations:* formerly: hockey, soccer, cricket, tennis, athletics and boxing. *Address:* Boylefield Cottage, Clehonger, Hereford. *T:* Madley 579.

JORDAN, Air Marshal Sir Richard Bowen, KCB 1956 (CB 1947); DFC 1941; psa; RAF retired; *b* 7 Feb. 1902; *s* of late A. O. Jordan, Besford Ct, Worcestershire; *m* 1932, F. M. M. Haines; one *d*. *Educ:* Marlborough Coll.; RAF Coll., Cranwell. Joined RAF, 1921. Late AOC the RAF in India and Pakistan; Air Officer Commanding RAF Gibraltar, 1948-49; Commandant of the Royal Observer Corps, 1949-51; ADC to the King, 1949-51; Air Officer Commanding No. 25 Group, 1951-53; Dir-Gen. of Organisation, Air Ministry, 1953-55; Air Officer Commanding-in-Chief, Maintenance Command, 1956-58, retd. *Address:* The Long House, Ramridge Park, near Andover, Hants.

JORDAN, Prof. Wilbur Kitchener; Professor of History, Harvard University, 1946-72; Williams Professor of History and Political Science, Harvard University, 1965-72; now Emeritus Professor; *b* 15 Jan. 1902; *s* of William and Emma Shepard Jordan; *m* 1929, Frances Ruml. *Educ:* Oakland City Coll. (AB 1923); Harvard (AM 1928, PhD 1931). Instructor in History, Harvard Univ., 1931-37; Prof. of History, Scripps Coll., 1937-40; Prof. of History and Gen. Editor, University Press, University of Chicago, 1940-43; Pres., Radcliffe Coll., 1943-60. Sterling Fellow, Harvard Univ., 1930-31; Guggenheim Fellow, 1943. Corres. Fellow, British Acad., 1969. Hon. LHD, Bates Coll., 1944; Hon. DLitt: Oakland City Coll., 1960; Reed Coll., 1967; Hon. LLD: University of Vermont, 1962; Dartmouth Coll., 1966; Hon. LittD, Oxford Univ., 1964. *Publications:* The Development of Religious Toleration in England (4 vols), 1932-40, London; Men of Substance, 1942, Chicago; Philanthropy in England, 1480-1660, 1959, London; The Charities of London, 1480-1660, 1960, London; The Charities of Rural England, 1480-1660, 1961, London; The Social Institutions of Lancashire, 1962, Manchester; The Chronicle and Political Papers of King Edward VI, 1966 (Ithaca, NY and London); Edward VI: The Young King, 1968 (London); Edward VI: The threshold of power, 1970 (London) (Press faculty award, Harvard, 1971; Schuyler Prize, Amer. Hist. Assoc., 1972). *Address:* 3 Concord Avenue, Cambridge, Mass 02138, USA.

JORDAN MALKIN, Harold; *see* Malkin, H. J.

JORDAN-MOSS, Norman, CB 1972; CMG 1965; Deputy Secretary, HM Treasury, since 1976; *b* 5 Feb. 1920; *o s* of Arthur Moss and Ellen Jordan Round; *m* 1st, 1965, Kathleen Lusmore (*d* 1974); one *s* one *d*; 2nd, 1976, Philippa Rands; one *d*. *Educ:* Manchester Gram. Sch.; St John's Coll., Cambridge (MA). Ministry of Economic Warfare, 1940-44; HM Treasury, 1944-71; Asst Representative of HM Treas. in Middle East, 1945-48; Principal, 1948; First Sec. (Econ.), Belgrade, 1952-55; Financial Counsellor, Washington, 1956-60; Counsellor, UK Permanent Delegation to OECD, Paris, 1963-66; Asst Sec., HM Treasury, 1956-68, Under-Sec., 1968-71; Dep. Under-Sec. of State, DHSS, 1971-76. *Recreations:* music, theatre. *Address:* Milton Way, Westcott, Dorking, Surrey. *Club:* Travellers'.

JORISCH, Mrs Robert; *see* Lofts, Norah.

JOSEPH, Sir (Herbert) Leslie, Kt 1952; Vice-Chairman, Trust Houses Forte Ltd; *b* 4 Jan. 1908; *s* of David Ernest and Florence Joseph; *m* 1934, Emily Irene, *d* of Dr Patrick Julian Murphy, Cwmbach, Aberdare; two *d*. *Educ:* The King's Sch. Canterbury. Commissioned RE, 1940-46. Chairman: Assoc. Amusement Parks Proprietors Gt Brit., 1949, 1950, 1951; National Amusements Council, 1950-51; Amusement Caterers' Assoc., 1953, 1954; Housing Production Board for Wales, 1952-53. High Sheriff, Mid Glamorgan, 1975-76. *Recreations:* horticulture and ceramics. *Address:* Coedargraig, Newton, Porthcawl, Mid Glamorganshire. *T:* Porthcawl 2610.

JOSEPH, Rt. Hon. Sir Keith (Sinjohn), 2nd Bt, *cr* 1943; PC 1962; MP (C) Leeds North-East since Feb. 1956; *b* 17 Jan. 1918; *o c* of Sir Samuel George Joseph, 1st Baronet, and Edna Cicely, *yr d* of late P. A. S. Phillips, Portland Place, W1; *S* father 1944; *m* 1951, Hellen Louise, *yr d* of Sigmar Guggenheimer, NY; one *s* three *d*. *Educ:* Harrow; Magdalen Coll., Oxford. War of 1939-45, served 1939-46; Captain RA; Italian campaign (wounded, despatches). Fellow All Souls Coll., Oxford, 1946-60, 1972-; barrister, Middle Temple, 1946. Contested (C) Baron's Court, General Election, 1955. PPS to Parly Under-Sec. of State, CRO, 1957-59; Parly Sec., Min. of Housing and Local Govt, 1959-61; Minister of State at Board of Trade, 1961-62; Minister of Housing and Local Govt and Minister for Welsh Affairs, 1962-64; Sec. of State for Social Services, DHSS, 1970-74. Co-Founder and first Chm., Foundation for Management Education, 1959;

Founder and first Chm., Mulberry Housing Trust, 1965-69; Founder, and Chm. Management Cttee, Centre for Policy Studies Ltd, 1974-. Chm., Bovis Ltd, 1958-59; Dep. Chm., Bovis Holdings Ltd, 1964-70 (Dir, 1951-59); Director: Gilbert-Ash Ltd, 1949-59. Drayton Premier Investment Trust Ltd, 1975-. FIOB. Common councilman of City of London for Ward of Portsoken, 1946, Alderman, 1946-49. Liveryman, Vintners' Company. *Publication:* Reversing the Trend: a critical appraisal of Conservative economic and social policies, 1975. *Heir: s* James Samuel Joseph, *b* 27 Jan. 1955. *Address:* 23 Mulberry Walk, SW3 6DZ. *Club:* Carlton.

JOSEPH, Sir Leslie; *see* Joseph, Sir H. L.

JOSEPH, Maxwell; Chairman: Grand Metropolitan Ltd; Giltspur Ltd; Norfolk Capital Ltd; Truman Ltd; Director: Fraser Ansbacher Ltd; Watney Mann and Truman Holdings Ltd; Express Dairy Co. Ltd; Mecca Ltd; International Distillers & Vintners Ltd. *Recreations:* philately (Cape of Good Hope Gold Medallist), gardening. *Address:* 1 York Gate, Regents Park, NW1 4PU.

JOSEPHS, Wilfred; composer; *b* 24 July 1927; *s* of Philip Josephs and Rachel (*née* Block); *m* 1956, Valerie Wisbey; two *d*. *Educ:* Rutherford Coll. Boys' Sch.; Univ. of Durham at Newcastle (now Newcastle Univ.) (BDS Dunelm). Qual. dentistry, 1951. Army service, 1951-53. Guildhall Sch. of Music (schol. in composition, prizes), 1954; Leverhulme Schol. to study musical comp. in Paris with Maître Max Deutsch, 1958-59; Harriet Cohen Commonwealth Medal (for 1st quartet) and prizes; First Prize, La Scala, Milan, for Requiem, 1963. Abandoned dentistry completely and has since been a full-time composer, writing many concert works, many film and television scores and themes, incl. music for: The Great War, I, Claudius, Disraeli, Cider with Rosie, All Creatures Great and Small, Sister Dora, Swallows and Amazons, The Brontë Series, The Somerset Maugham Series, Horizon, Chéri, The Avenue, Love Story, A Place in Europe, The Inventing of America, The Norman Conquests, The Ghosts of Motley Hall, The House of Bernardo Alba, The Hunchback of Notre Dame, etc; also a television opera, The Appointment; one-act opera, Pathelin; children's musical, King of the Coast, which won the Guardian/Arts Council Prize, 1969. Vis. Prof. of Comp. and Composer-in-Residence at Univ. of Wisconsin-Milwaukee, 1970; similarly at Roosevelt Univ., Chicago, 1972. Whilst many film/television compositions have been commercially recorded, the composer's first disc of concert music is to be made in 1977/78 of his Symphonies Nos 7 and 3. Member: British Acad. of Film and Television Arts; Incorp. Soc. of Musicians; Council and Exec. Cttee, Soc. for Promotion of New Music; Exec. Cttee, Composers' Guild of GB. *Publications:* Requiem, Symphonies, 1-8, various sonatas, quartets etc. *Recreations:* writing music, tennis, swimming, reading, films. *Address:* Downshire Hill House, 50 Downshire Hill, Hampstead, NW3. *T:* 01-435 1530.

JOSEPHSON, Prof. Brian David, FRS 1970; Professor of Physics, Cambridge University, since 1974; Fellow of Trinity College, Cambridge, since 1962; *b* 4 Jan. 1940; *s* of Abraham Josephson and Mimi Josephson; *m* 1976, Carol Anne Olivier. *Educ:* Cardiff High School; Cambridge Univ. BA 1960, MA, PhD 1964, Cantab. FInstP. Asst Dir of Res. in Physics, 1967-72, Reader in Physics, 1972-74, Univ. of Cambridge. Vis. Faculty Mem., Maharishi European Res. Univ., 1975-. For. Hon. Mem., Amer. Acad. of Arts and Scis, 1974. Hon. DSc Wales, 1974. Awards: New Scientist, 1969; Research Corp., 1969; Fritz London, 1970; Nobel Prize for Physics, 1973. Medals: Guthrie, 1972; van der Pol, 1972; Elliott Cresson, 1972; Hughes, 1972; Holweck, 1973. *Publications:* research papers on physics and theory of intelligence. *Recreations:* mountain walking, ice skating. *Address:* Cavendish Laboratory, Madingley Road, Cambridge CB3 0HE. *T:* Cambridge 66477.

JOSKE, Sir Percy Ernest, Kt 1977; CMG 1967; **Hon. Mr Justice Joske;** Judge of the Australian Industrial Court, and of the Supreme Courts of the Australian Capital Territory, the Northern Territory of Australia and Norfolk Island, since 1960; *b* 5 Oct. 1895; *s* of Ernest and Evalyne Joske; *m* 1928, Mavis Connell (*d* 1968); one *s*; *m* 1969, Dorothy Larcombe. *Educ:* Wesley Coll., Melbourne; Melbourne Univ. (MA, LLM). John Madden Exhibitioner and First Class Final Honourman in Laws. QC (Australia) (KC 1944). Editor, Vic. Law Reports, 1936-56; Registrar: Dental Bd of Vic., 1939-58; Dietitians Registration Bd of Vic., 1942-58; Lecturer in Domestic Relations Law, Melbourne Univ., 1948-51. MHR for Balaclava, Australian Parl, 1951-60. Mem., Parly Standing Cttee on Foreign Affairs, Constitution Review, Privileges and Standing Orders; Aust. Deleg. to UN, 1955; Mem. Coun., ANU, 1956-60; Chm., Aust. Commonwealth Immigration Planning Coun.,

1959-60. Pres., Royal Life Saving Soc., Australia, 1951-. *Publications:* Remuneration of Commission Agents, 1924 (3rd edn 1957); Marriage and Divorce, 1924 (5th edn 1968); Procedure and Conduct of Meetings, 1936 (6th edn 1976); Insurance Law, 1933 (2nd edn 1948); Sale of Goods and Hire Purchase, 1949 (2nd edn 1961); Partnership, 1957 (2nd edn 1966); Local Government, 1963; Australian Federal Government, 1967 (3rd edn 1976); Commission Agency, 1975; Insurance, 1975; Family Law, 1976. *Recreations:* writing, gardening. *Address:* 119 The Boulevarde, Strathfield, NSW 2135, Australia. *T:* 642 3156. *Clubs:* Melbourne Cricket; Royal Sydney Yacht.

JOSLIN, Ivy Collin, BSc; late Headmistress, Francis Holland School, Clarence Gate, NW1; *b* 12 April 1900. *Educ:* Skinners' Company's Sch., London; University Coll., London. Science Mistress, Howell's Sch., Denbigh, 1922-24; Physics Mistress, Southend-on-Sea High Sch., 1924-29; Science Mistress, St Stephen's High Sch., Clewer, 1929-30; Mathematics Mistress, Dame Alice Owen's Sch., London, 1930-33; Headmistress, Derby High Sch., 1933-39; Headmistress, Newcastle on Tyne Church High Sch., 1943-45. *Publications:* Everyday Domestic Science (with P. M. Taylor), 1932; General Science, 1937; The Air Around Us, 1961; Water in the World, 1962; Electricity in Use, 1964. *Recreations:* bridge, chess. *Club:* University Women's.

JOSLIN, Maj.-Gen. Stanley William, CB 1951; CBE 1950 (MBE 1936); MA; FIMechE; Chief Inspector of Nuclear Installations, Ministry of Power, 1959-64, retired; *b* 25 March 1899; *m* 1939, Eva Hudson (*d* 1976); one *d*. *Educ:* Hackney Downs Sch.; Royal Military Academy Woolwich; Cambridge Univ. Commissioned 2nd Lieut, Royal Engineers, 1918; served: Germany, 1918-19; India, 1920-23; Nigeria, 1926-28; Singapore, 1937-39; War of 1939-45; NW Europe, 1944-49; transferred to REME, 1943; Maj.-Gen., 1950; Dir of Mechanical Engineering, War Office, 1950-53; retired, 1954. UK Atomic Energy Authority, 1954-59. *Recreations:* walking, music. *Address:* Southern Cottage, Maresfield Park, Uckfield, East Sussex TN22 2HD. *T:* Uckfield 2933.

JOSLING, John Francis; writer on legal subjects; Principal Assistant Solicitor of Inland Revenue, 1965-71; *b* 26 May 1910; *s* of John Richard Josling, Hackney, London, and Florence Alice (*née* Robinson); *m* 1935, Bertha Frearson; two *s* two *d*. *Educ:* Leyton Co. High Sch. Entered a private Solicitor's office, 1927; articled, 1937; admitted as Solicitor, 1940. Served War of 1939-45 (war stars and medals): RA, 1940-45; JAG's Br, 1945-46. Entered office of Solicitor of Inland Revenue, 1946; Sen. Legal Asst, 1948; Asst Solicitor, 1952. Mem., Law Society. Coronation Medal, 1953. *Publications:* Oyez Practice Notes on Adoption of Children, 1947, 8th edn 1977; Execution of a Judgment, 1948, 5th edn 1974; (with C. Caplin) Apportionments for Executors and Trustees, 1948, 3rd edn 1963; Change of Name, 1948, 11th edn 1977; Naturalisation, 1949, 3rd edn 1965; Summary Judgment in the High Court, 1950, 4th edn 1974; Periods of Limitation, 1951, 4th edn 1973; (with L. Alexander) The Law of Clubs, 1964, 3rd edn 1975; contribs to: Simon's Income Tax (2nd edn); Halsbury's Laws of England vol. 20 (3rd edn); Pollard's Social Welfare Law, 1977; (ed) Caplin's Powers of Attorney, 1954, 4th edn 1971; (ed) Wilkinson's Affiliation Law and Practice, 1971, 4th edn 1977; (ed) Summary Matrimonial and Guardianship Orders, 3rd edn 1973; many contribs to Solicitors' Jl and some other legal jls. *Recreations:* music and musical history; Victorian novels; Georgian children and Elizabethan grand-children. *Address:* Proton, Farley Way, Fairlight, Sussex. *T:* Pett 2501.

JOSSET, Lawrence; RE 1951 (ARE 1936); ARCA; free-lance artist; *b* 2 Aug. 1910; *s* of Leon Antoine Hyppolite and Annie Mary Josset; *m* 1960, Beatrice, *d* of William Alford Taylor. *Educ:* Bromley County Sch. for Boys; Bromley and Beckenham Schs of Art; Royal College of Art (diploma). Engraver's Draughtsman at Waterlow and Son Ltd, Clifton Street, 1930-32; Art Master at Red Hill Sch., East Sutton, near Maidstone, Kent, 1935-36. Mem. of Art Workers' Guild. *Publications:* Mezzotint in colours; Flowers, after Fantin-Latour, 1937; The Trimmed Cock, after Ben Marshall, 1939; Brighton Beach and Spring, after Constable, 1947; Carting Timber and Milking Time, after Shayer, 1948; The Pursuit, and Love Letters, after Fragonard, 1949; Spring and Autumn, after Boucher, 1951; A Family, after Zoffany, 1953; Master James Sayer, 1954; HM The Queen after Annigoni, commissioned by the Times, 1956, and plates privately commissioned after de Lazlo, James Gunn and Oswald Birley. *Recreations:* outdoor sketching, cycling, etc. *Address:* The Cottage, Pilgrims Way, Detling, near Maidstone, Kent.

JOST, H. Peter, CBE 1969; DSc; CEng; FIMechE; FIProdE; Managing Director, since 1955, and Chairman, since 1973, K. S. Paul Products Ltd; Director, Stothert & Pitt Ltd, 1971; Director of overseas companies; *b* 25 Jan. 1921; *o s* of late Leo and Margot Jost; *m* 1948, Margaret Josephine, *o d* of late Michael and of Mrs Sara Kadesh, Norfolk Is, S Pacific; two *d. Educ:* City of Liverpool Techn. Coll.; Manchester Coll. of Technology. Apprentice, Associated Metal Works, Glasgow and D. Napier & Son Ltd, Liverpool; Methods Engr, K & L Steelfounders and Engrs Ltd, 1943; Chief Planning Engr, Datim Machine Tool Co. Ltd, 1946; Gen. Man. 1949, Dir 1952, Trier Bros Ltd; Lubrication Consultant: Richard Thomas & Baldwins Ltd, 1960-65; August Thyssen Hütte AG 1963-66; Chairman: Bright Brazing Ltd, 1969-76; Peppermill Brass Foundry Ltd, 1970-76; Centralube Ltd, 1974-77 (Man. Dir, 1955-77); Associated Technology Gp Ltd, 1976-; Engineering & General Equipment Ltd, 1977-; Dir, Williams Hudson Ltd, 1967-75. Chairman: Lubrication Educn and Res. Working Gp, DES, 1964-65; Cttee on Tribology, DTI, 1966-74; Industrial Technologies Management Bd, DTI, 1972-74; Dep. Chm., Cttee for Industrial Technologies, DTI, 1972-74; Member: Adv. Council on Technology, 1968-70; Cttee on Terotechnology, 1971-72. Hon. Associate, Manchester Coll. of Science and Technology, 1962; Univ. of Salford: Privy Council's Nominee to Ct, 1970; Mem. Council, 1974. Mem. Council: IProdE, 1973- (Vice-Pres., 1975-77, Pres., 1977-; Chm., Technical Policy Bd and Mem., Exec. Policy Cttee, 1974); IMechE, 1974 (Mem. Technical Bd, 1975); Mem. External Affairs Cttee, CEI, 1974-; Pres., Internat. Tribology Council, 1973-. Fellow, American Soc. Mechanical Engrs, 1970. Chm., Manchester Technology Assoc. in London, 1976-. Hon. MIPlantE, 1969; Hon. Member: Société Française de Tribologie, 1972; Gesellschaft für Tribologie, 1972; Amer. Soc. of Manufacturing Engrs, 1977. Hon. DSc Salford, 1970. Sir John Larking Medal 1944, Derby Medal 1955, Liverpool Engrg Soc.; Hutchinson Meml Medal 1952, Silver Medal for Best Paper 1952-53, IProdE. *Publications:* Lubrication (Tribology) Report of DES Cttee, 1966 (Jost Report); The Introduction of a New Technology, Report of DTI Cttee, 1973; various papers in Proc. IMechE, Proc.IProdE, technical jls, etc. *Recreations:* music, opera, gardening, riding. *Address:* Hill House, Wills Grove, Mill Hill, NW7. *T:* 01-959 3355. *Club:* Athenæum.

JOUGHIN, Michael, CBE 1971; JP; DL; Chairman, Scottish Agricultural Development Council; farmer since 1952; *b* 26 April 1926; *s* of John Clague Joughin and May Joughin; *m* 1948, Lesley Roy Petrie; one *s* one *d. Educ:* Kelly Coll., Tavistock. Lieut, Royal Marines, 1944-52, RM pilot with Fleet Air Arm, 1946-49. Pres., NFU of Scotland, 1964-66. Chm. of Governors: N of Scotland Coll. of Agriculture, 1969-72; Blairmore Prep. Sch., 1966-72; Chairman: N of Scotland Grassland Soc., 1970-71; Elgin Market Green Auction Co., 1969-70; Chm., N of Scotland Milk Marketing Bd, 1974- (Vice-Chm., 1968-74); Governor: Rowett Research Inst., 1968-74; Scottish Plant Breeding Inst., 1969-74; Animal Diseases Research Assoc., Moredun Inst., 1969-74; Member: Intervention Bd for Agric. Produce, 1972-76; Econ. Develt Council for Agriculture, 1967-70; Agric. Marketing Develt Exec. Cttee, 1965-68; Scottish Constitutional Cttee, 1969-70; British Farm Produce Council, 1965-66. FRAgS 1975. JP Moray, 1965; DL Moray, 1974. *Recreation:* sailing. *Address:* Wester Manbeen, Elgin, Moray. *T:* Elgin 7082. *Clubs:* New, Caledonian (Edinburgh); Royal Naval Sailing Assoc., Royal Marines Sailing, Royal Findhorn Yacht, Goldfish.

JOWETT, Very Rev. Alfred, CBE 1972; Dean of Manchester since 1964; *b* 29 May 1914; *s* of Alfred Edmund Jowett; *m* 1939, Margaret, *d* of St Clair Benford; one *s* three *d. Educ:* High Storrs Grammar Sch., Sheffield; St Catharine's Coll., Cambridge; Lincoln Theological Coll. BA 1935; Certif. Educn 1936; MA 1959. Deacon 1944; Priest 1945. Curate of St John the Evangelist, Goole, 1944-47; Sec., Sheffield Anglican and Free Church Council and Marriage Guidance Council, 1947-51; Vicar of St George with St Stephen, Sheffield, 1951-60; Part-time Lecturer, Sheffield Univ. Dept of Education, 1950-60; Vicar of Doncaster, 1960-64; Hon. Canon of Sheffield Cathedral, 1960-64. Select Preacher, Oxford Univ., 1964. Mem., Community Relations Commn, 1968-77 (Dep. Chm., 1972-77). Hon. Fellow, Manchester Polytechnic, 1972. *Publication:* (Part-author) The English Church: a New Look, 1966. *Recreations:* theatre, music, walking. *Address:* The Deanery, Prestwich, Manchester M25 8QF. *T:* 061-773 4301.

JOWETT, Ronald Edward, CBE 1969; MD, FRCS; Hon. Consultant Otolaryngologist, Sunderland and Durham Hospital Groups; *b* 5 March 1901; *s* of James and Emma Jowett, Halifax, Yorks; *m* 1929, Lilian Waring, Halifax; two *s. Educ:* Heath Sch., Halifax; Leeds Univ.; Leeds Med. Sch. MB, ChB (Hons) Leeds, 1922; Scattergood and Hardwick Prizes; MD Leeds, 1923; DLO,

RCP&S London, 1925, MRCP 1933; FRCS 1966. Otolaryngologist, Sunderland Hosp. Gp, 1925-71; Surgeon, Newcastle upon Tyne Throat, Nose and Ear Hosp., 1937-50. President: Regional Hospitals' Consultants and Specialists Assoc., 1951-53 and 1964-65; Newcastle upon Tyne and Northern Counties Med. Soc., 1955; N of England Otolaryngological Soc., 1955. Mem., Newcastle Regional Hosp. Bd, 1947-69 (Chm. of its Med. Adv. Cttee, 1953-69; Vice-Chm. of the Bd, 1967-69). FRSM. *Publications:* The Injured Workman (with G. F. Walker), 1933; contribs to: Med. Press and Circular, BMJ, Proc. Roy. Soc. Med., Jl of Mental Science, Jl of Laryngology and Otology, Den Norske Turistforenning. *Recreations:* making music, fishing. *Address:* 18 Brookfield, Westfield, Gosforth, Newcastle upon Tyne NE3 4YB. *T:* Gosforth 853551.

JOWITT, Edwin Frank, QC 1969; a Recorder of the Crown Court, since 1972; *b* 1 Oct. 1929; *s* of Frank and Winifred Jowitt; *m* 1959, Anne Barbara Dyson; three *s* two *d. Educ:* Swanwick Hall Grammar Sch.; London Sch. of Economics. LLB London 1950. Called to Bar, Middle Temple, 1951, Bencher 1977; Member Midland Circuit. Dep. Chm. Quarter Sessions: Rutland, 1967-71; Derbyshire, 1970-71. *Recreation:* fell walking. *Address:* 2 Crown Office Row, Temple, EC4. *T:* 01-353 1365; 7 Fountain Court, Steelhouse Lane, Birmingham B4 6DR.

JOY, Michael Gerard Laurie, CMG 1965; MC 1945; *b* 27 Oct. 1916; *s* of late Frank Douglas Howarth Joy, Bentley, Hants; *m* 1951, Ann Félise Jacomb; one *s* three *d. Educ:* Winchester; New Coll., Oxford. Served RA, 1940-46 (MC, wounded). Foreign Office, 1947; Private Sec. to Permanent Under Sec. of State, 1948-50; Saigon, 1950-53; Washington, 1953-55; IDC, 1956; Foreign Office, 1957-59; Counsellor, 1959; Addis Ababa, 1959-62; Stockholm, 1962-64; seconded to Cabinet Office, 1964-66; Foreign Office, 1966-68. *Recreation:* shooting. *Address:* Marelands, Bentley, Hants. *T:* Bentley 3288.

JOY, Peter, OBE 1969; HM Diplomatic Service; Counsellor, Foreign and Commonwealth Office, since 1973; *b* 16 Jan. 1926; *s* of late Neville Holt Joy and Marguerite Mary Duff Beith; *m* 1953, Rosemary Joan Hebden; two *s* two *d. Educ:* Downhouse Sch., Pembridge; New Coll., Oxford. Served with RAF, 1944-47. Entered Foreign (subseq. Diplomatic) Service, 1952; 1st Sec., Ankara, 1959; 1st Sec., New Delhi, 1962; FO, 1965; 1st Sec., Beirut, 1968. *Recreations:* shooting, fishing. *Address:* 12 Willow Road, Hampstead, NW3 1TJ. *T:* 01-435 3746; Carrick House, Eday, Orkney. *Club:* Travellers'.

JOYCE, Alec Houghton, CIE 1943; CBE 1952 (OBE 1938); *b* 5 March 1894; *m* 1917, Mary, 2nd *d* of late George Frederick Oates, Roundhay, Leeds; two *s.* Served European War, 1914-19, in France and Russia (Meritorious Service Medal); entered India Office, 1919; Joint Publicity Officer to the India and Burma Round Table Conferences, 1930-32; Personal Asst to the Prime Minister during Monetary and Economic Conference, 1933; on special duty in India and Burma, 1935 and in India, 1936-37. Seconded at various times to No. 10 Downing Street as Actg Chief Press Adviser. Paid official visits to USA and Canada, 1943; to India, 1943; again to India with Cabinet Delegation, 1946; and to USA and all Provs of Canada, 1951; on an official tour of Pakistan, India, and Ceylon, 1951-52; Head of Information Dept Commonwealth Relations Office (Asst Sec.), 1948-Nov. 1954, subseq. employed in charge of branch conducting liaison with UK, Commonwealth, and foreign Press and with BBC; retired, 1957. *Address:* 3 Kaye Moor Road, Sutton, Surrey. *Club:* East India, Devonshire, Sports and Public Schools.

JOYCE, Eileen; concert pianist; *b* Zeehan, Tasmania; *d* of Joseph and Alice Joyce, Western Australia. *Educ:* Loreto Convent, Perth, Western Australia; Leipzig Conservatoire. Studied in Germany under Teichmuller, and later, Schnabel. Concert début in London at Promenade Concerts under Sir Henry Wood. Numerous concert tours, radio performances and gramophone recordings. During War of 1939-45, played in association with London Philharmonic Orchestra, especially in blitzed towns and cities throughout Great Britain. Concerts with: all principal orchestras of the UK; Berlin Philharmonic Orchestra in Berlin; Conservatoire and National Orchestras, France; Concertgebouw Orchestra, Holland; La Scala Orchestra, Italy; Philadelphia Orchestra, Carnegie Hall, New York. Concert tours in: Australia, 1948; SA, 1950; Scandinavia and Holland, 1951; S Amer., Scandinavia and Finland, 1952; Jugoslavia, 1955; NZ, 1958; USSR, 1961; India, 1962; also performed harpsichord in several concerts Royal Albert Hall and Royal Festival Hall. Has contributed to sound tracks of films including: The Seventh Veil, Brief Encounter, Man of Two Worlds, Quartet, Trent's Last Case; appeared in films: Battle for Music, Girl in a Million,

Wherever She Goes (biographical). Hon. DMus Cantab, 1971. Address: Chartwell Farm, Westerham, Kent.

JOYCE, John H.; retired shipowner; b 6 Oct. 1906. Formerly: Chm., Elder Dempster Lines Ltd; Dep. Chm., Coast Lines Ltd; Director: Belgian Line; Nigerian National Shipping Line; Nigerian Airways; Liner Holdings Ltd, and associated cos; Chairman: Liverpool and London Steamship Protection and Indemnity Assoc. Ltd; Liverpool and London War Risks Insurance Assoc. Ltd; Liverpool Steamship Owners' Assoc., 1957; General Council of British Shipping, 1957. Address: Top Garden, Leicester Road, Ashby de la Zouch, Leics.

JOYNSON-HICKS, family name of **Viscount Brentford.**

JOYNT, Evelyn Gertrude, MBE 1967; Major (retired) WRAC; Director, World Bureau of World Association of Girl Guides and Girl Scouts, since 1971; b 5 Sept. 1919; 2nd d of late Rev. George Joynt, Dublin. Educ: Collegiate Sch., Enniskillen; Banbridge Academy. Joined ATS, 1942; transf. to WRAC, 1952; jsc, WRAC Staff Coll., 1954; served Middle East and Far East; OC Drivers and Clerks Training Wing, WRAC; DAQMG, Eastern Comd; retired 1967; Nat. Gen. Sec., YWCA of GB, 1968-71. Address: 223 Latymer Court, W6. T: 01-748 3449.

JUBB, Edwin Charles, CB 1942; OBE 1925; b 1883; s of Edwin Charles Jubb, Hull; m 1912, Emily Herbert (d 1964), d of late Charles Powell, Co. Limerick, one s one d (and one s decd). Educ: Rossall; Pembroke Coll., Cambridge. 14th Wrangler 1906; Second Class Hons Science Tripos, 1907; entered Civil Service, 1908; Dir of Navy Contracts Admiralty from 1936; retired 1947. Recreations: cricket and singing. Address: Warren House, Farnham Common, Bucks. T: Farnham Common 3952. Club: Royal Commonwealth Society.

JUDD, Eric Campbell, CBE 1974; MVO 1956; Chairman, West Africa Committee, since 1976; b St Thomas, Ont, 10 Aug. 1918; s of Frederick William Judd, PhmB (Canada), and Marjorie Katherine (née Bell); m 1947, Janet Creswell (née Fish); two s one d. Educ: Wellington, Canada; St Thomas Collegiate; Toronto Univ. Trainee Manager, Cities Service Oil Co., Canada, 1937-40. RCAF and RAF, 1940-45: Canada, N Atlantic Ferry Comd, Europe, Malta, Middle East, Far East, W Indies; retd Sqdn Ldr RCAF Reserve, 1945. Joined Unilever Ltd, 1946; United Africa Co. Ltd, Nigeria, 1946-60, Chm., 1957-60; Dir, UAC Ltd London, 1960, Man. Dir, 1968; Dep. Chm. and Jt Man. Dir, UAC International, 1969-77. Mem. House of Assembly, Western Nigeria, 1955-56; Chm., BNEC Africa, 1969-72; Chm., Adv. Gp Africa BOTB, 1972-74; Vice-Chm., West Africa Cttee, London, 1963-76. Recreations: golf, tennis, theatre, music, reading. Address: Amberway, 23 Townsend Lane, Harpenden, Herts AL5 3PY. T: Harpenden 2617. Club: Mid-Herts Golf.

JUDD, Frank Ashcroft; MP (Lab) Portsmouth North, since 1974 (Portsmouth West, 1966-74); Minister of State, Foreign and Commonwealth Office, since 1977; b 28 March 1935; s of Charles and Helen Judd; m 1961, Christine Elizabeth Willington; two d. Educ: City of London Sch.; London Sch. of Economics. Contested (Lab): Sutton and Cheam, 1959; Portsmouth West, 1964. Sec.-Gen., Internat. Voluntary Service, 1960-66. PPS: to Minister of Housing, 1967-70; to the Leader of the Opposition, 1970-72; Mem., Opposition's Front Bench Defence Team, 1972-74; Parliamentary Under-Secretary of State: for Defence (Navy), MoD, 1974-76; ODM 1976; Minister for Overseas Develt, 1976-77. Member: British Parly Delegn to Council of Europe and WEU, 1970-73; Mem., ASTMS. Publications: (jtly) Radical Future, 1967; Fabian International Essays, 1970; Purpose in Socialism, 1973; various papers and articles on current affairs. Recreation: walking. Address: House of Commons, SW1A 0AA; 84 Kingston Crescent, North End, Portsmouth. T: Portsmouth 60447.

JUDD, John Basil Thomas; HM Consul-General at Zagreb, 1961-65; retired; re-employed in the Foreign Office, 1966-69; b 12 May 1909; s of John Matthews Judd and Helena Beatrice Jenkins; m 1939, Cynthia Margaret Georgina, yr d of Sir Henry White-Smith, CBE; two s one d. Educ: The Leys; Downing Coll., Cambridge; Inner Temple (called to the Bar, 1931). Entered Levant Consular Service, 1932; Vice-Consul and 3rd Sec. at Jedda, 1936; Vice-Consul at Casablanca and Tangier, 1939-43; Consul at Tunis and Marseilles, 1943-46; Consul and 1st Sec. at Paris, 1946; Consul at Jerusalem, 1949; Foreign Office, 1951; Consul-Gen. at Valparaiso, 1953; Consul-Gen. and Counsellor, Cairo, 1955-57; Consul-Gen. at Basra, 1957-61. Recreations: fishing, theatre and opera. Address: 77 Siren Street, Senglea, Malta. Clubs: Royal Automobile, Brooks's; Union, Sports (Malta).

JUDD, Nadine; see Nerina, Nadia.

JUDGE, Edward Thomas, MA Cantab; Director: Dorman Long Vanderbill Corporation Ltd; BPB Industries Ltd; Pilkington Bros Ltd; ETJ Consultancy Services; Fibreglass Ltd; Zenith Electric Co. Ltd; Cleveland Scientific Institution; b 20 Nov. 1908; o s of late Thomas Oliver and Florence Judge (née Gravestock); m 1934, Alice Gertrude Matthews; two s. Educ: Worcester Royal Grammar Sch.; St John's Coll., Cambridge. Joined Dorman Long, 1930, and held various appts, becoming Chief Technical Engr, 1937; Special Dir, 1944; Chief Engr, 1945; Dir, 1947; Asst Man. Dir, Dorman Long (Steel) Ltd, 1959; Jt Man. Dir, 1960; Chm. and Gen. Man. Dir, Dorman Long & Co. Ltd, 1961-67. Chairman: Reyrolle Parsons Ltd, 1969-74 (Dep. Chm., 1968); A. Reyrolle & Co. Ltd, 1969-73; C. A. Parsons & Co. Ltd, 1969-73. Mem. Exec. and Develt Cttees of Brit. Iron & Steel Fedn; Rep. of Minister of Transport on Tees Conservancy Commn., 1951-66; part-time Mem. N Eastern Electricity Bd, 1952-62; Vice-Pres., Iron & Steel Inst., 1958. President: British Iron & Steel Federation, 1965, 1966, 1967; British Electrical Allied Manufacturers' Assoc. Ltd, 1970-71 (Dep. Pres., 1969-70). Bessemer Gold Medal, Iron and Steel Inst., 1967. Publications: technical papers. Recreation: fishing. Address: Wood Place, Aspley Guise, Milton Keynes MK17 8EP.

JUDGE, Harry George, MA Oxon, PhD London; Director, University of Oxford Department of Educational Studies, since 1973; Fellow of Brasenose College, since 1973; b 1 Aug. 1928; s of George Arthur and Winifred Mary Judge; m 1956, Elizabeth Mary Patrick; one s two d. Educ: Cardiff High Sch.; Brasenose Coll., Oxford. Asst Master, Emanuel Sch. and Wallington County Grammar Sch., 1954-59; Dir of Studies, Cumberland Lodge, Windsor, 1959-62; Head Master, Banbury Grammar Sch., 1962-67; Principal, Banbury Sch., 1967-73. Member: Public Schools Commission, 1966-70; James Cttee of Inquiry into Teacher Training, 1971-72; Educn Sub-Cttee, UGC. Chm., School Broadcasting Council, 1977. Member Governing Body: Cherwell Sch.; Marlborough Coll., Wilts. Publications: Louis XIV, 1965; School Is Not Yet Dead, 1974; contribs on educational and historical subjects to collective works and learned jls. Recreation: canals. Address: 2 Upland Park Road, Oxford.

JUDGE, Igor; a Recorder of the Crown Court, since 1976; b 19 May 1941; s of Raymond and Rosa Judge; m 1965, Judith Mary Robinson; one s two d. Educ: Oratory Sch., Woodcote; Magdalene Coll., Cambridge (Exhbnr, MA). Harmsworth Exhbn and Astbury Scholar, Middle Temple. Called to the Bar, Middle Temple, 1963. Recreations: history, music, cricket. Address: The Homestead, Crick, Northampton. T: Crick 822333.

JUKES, E(rnest) Martin, CBE 1975; QC 1954; Barrister-at-Law; Deputy Chairman, Health and Safety Commission, since 1974; a Chairman of Industrial Tribunals; b 5 Dec. 1909; s of Ernest and Hilda Gordon Jukes, Purley, Surrey; m 1931, Mary Kinloch (née Anderson); two s one d. Educ: Merchant Taylors' Sch.; St John's Coll., Oxford (MA). Called to the Bar, Jan. 1933; Mem. of the Bar Council, 1952-56 and 1964; Master of the Bench, Middle Temple, 1962; Judge of the Courts of Appeal for Guernsey and Jersey, 1964; Commissioner for Municipal Election Petitions, 1961. Dir-Gen., Engineering Employers Fedn, 1966-75. Member: Engineering Industry Training Bd, 1965-75; Council, CBI, 1965-75. Served War of 1939-45 as Lieut-Col RASC, in UK, France, Germany and Belgium (despatches). Address: 1 Essex Court, Temple, EC4. T: 01-353 0168. Clubs: Brooks's, Flyfishers'.

JUKES, John Andrew, CB 1968; Member, Central Electricity Generating Board, since 1977; b 19 May 1917; s of Captain A. M. Jukes, MD, IMS, and Mrs Gertrude E. Jukes (née King); m 1943, Muriel Child; two s two d. Educ: Shrewsbury Sch.; St John's Coll., Cambridge; London Sch. of Economics. MA in physics Cambridge, BSc (Econ.) London. FInstHE 1977. Cavendish Laboratory, Cambridge, 1939; Radar and Operational Research, 1939-46; Research Dept, LMS Railway, 1946-48; Economic Adviser, Cabinet Office and Treasury, 1948-54; British Embassy, Washington, DC, 1949-51; Economic Adviser to UK Atomic Energy Authority, 1954-64 and Principal Economics and Programming Office, UKAEA, 1957-64; appointed to Dept Economic Affairs as Dep. Dir-Gen., 1964; Dep. Under-Sec. of State, Dept of Economic Affairs, 1967; Dir Gen., Research and Economic Planning, MoT, 1969-70; Dir Gen., Economics and Resources, DoE, 1970-72; Dep. Sec. (Environmental Protection), DoE, 1972-74; Dir-Gen., Highways, DoE, 1974-76; Dept of Transport, 1976-77. Recreations: ski-ing, orienteering, gardening. Address: 38 Albion Road, Sutton, Surrey. T: 01-642 5018. Club: Royal Automobile.

JUKES, Richard Starr, CBE 1969; FCA; Director, BPB Industries Ltd, 1943-76 (Chairman, 1965-73); *b* 6 Dec. 1906; *s* of late Rev. Arthur Starr Jukes and Mrs Annie Florance Jukes; *m* 1935, Ruth Mary Wilmot; one *s* two *d*. *Educ*: St Edmund's, Canterbury. Mem. Inst. of Chartered Accountants, 1929. Gyproc Products Ltd: Sec./Accountant, 1934; Dir, 1939; The British Plaster Board (Holdings) Ltd: Dir, 1943; Jt Man. Dir, 1947; Man. Dir, 1954; Dep. Chm., 1962; Chm., 1965 (since Aug. 1965 the company has been known as BPB Industries Ltd). Mem. Council, Inst. of Directors. *Recreation*: golf. *Address*: White House, Watford Road, Northwood, Mddx. *T*: Northwood 24125. *Clubs*: Island Sailing; Moor Park Golf, Sandy Lodge Golf; Sundsvalls Golfklubb (Sweden); Hillside Golf (Rhodesia).

JUMA, Sa'ad; *b* Tafila, Jordan, 21 March 1916; *s* of Mohammed Juma; *m* 1959, Salwa Ghanem, Beirut; two *s* one *d*. *Educ*: Damascus Univ. (L'Essence in Law). Chief of Protocol, Min. of For. Affairs, 1949; Dir of Press, 1950; Sec. to Prime Minister's Office, 1950-54; Under-Sec., Min. of Interior, 1954-57; Governor of Amman, 1957-58; Under-Sec., Min. of For. Affairs, 1958-59; Ambassador: to Iran, 1959-61; to Syria, 1961-62; to USA, 1962-65; Minister of the Royal Court, 1965-67; Prime Minister, 1967; Ambassador to United Kingdom, 1969-70; Senator, 1970-75. Orders of El Nahda (1st Class) and Star of Jordan (1st Class); decorations from Syria, Lebanon, China, Italy, Libya, Malaysia and Ethiopia. *Publications*: Conspiracy and the Battle of Destiny, 1968; Hostile Society, 1970; God or Destruction, 1973; Sons of Snakes, 1973. *Recreations*: reading, music, bridge. *Address*: Jebel Amman, 4th Circle, Amman, Jordan. *T*: Amman 44111. *Clubs*: Travellers', Hurlingham.

JUNGIUS, Vice-Adm. Sir James (George), KBE 1977; Supreme Allied Commander Atlantic's Representative in Europe, since 1978; *b* 15 Nov. 1923; *s* of Major E. J. T. Jungius, MC; *m* 1949, Rosemary Frances Turquand Matthey; three *s*. *Educ*: RNC, Dartmouth. Served War of 1939-45: Midshipman, Sub-Lt and Lt, in Atlantic and Mediterranean; Commando Ops in Adriatic (despatches). Specialised in Navigation in 1946, followed by series of appts as Navigating Officer at sea and instructing ashore. Comdr, Dec. 1955; CO, HMS Wizard, 1956-57; Admlty, 1958-59; Exec. Officer, HMS Centaur, 1960-61; Captain, 1963; Naval Staff, 1964-65; CO, HMS Lynx, 1966-67; Asst Naval Attaché, Washington, DC, 1968-70; CO, HMS Albion, 1971-72; Rear-Adm., 1972; Asst Chief of Naval Staff (Operational Requirements), 1972-74; Vice-Adm., 1974; Dep. Supreme Allied Comdr Atlantic, 1975-77. MBIM. *Recreation*: fishing. *Address*: c/o National Westminster Bank, Southsea, Hants. *Clubs*: Naval and Military, MCC.

JUNGWIRTH, Sir (William) John, Kt 1957; CMG 1948; AASA; JP; retired as Permanent Head of Premier's Department, Melbourne, Victoria, 1962; *b* Melbourne, 10 Aug. 1897; British; *m* 1st, 1923, Ruth Powell (*d* 1938); one *s* one *d*; 2nd 1942, Edna Tamblyn; two *s*. *Educ*: Melbourne. Joined Victorian Public Service, 1915; Private Sec. to various Premiers, 1920-32; Permanent Head of Premier's Dept, 1934-62. Past President: YMCA; Methodist Men's Soc. of Victoria; Pres., Board of Management, Prince Henry's Hospital; Chairman: District Trustees, Independent Order of Rechabites; Healesville Wild Life Sanctuary. *Recreations*: bowls, reading. *Address*: 31 Bulleen Road, North Balwyn, Victoria 3104, Australia. *Club*: Royal Automobile of Victoria (Melbourne).

JUNOR, John; Editor, Sunday Express, since 1954; Chairman, Sunday Express, 1968; Director, Beaverbrook Newspapers, since 1960; *b* 15 Jan. 1919; *s* of Alexander Junor, Black Isle, Ross and Cromarty; *m* 1942, Pamela Mary Welsh; one *s* one *d*. *Educ*: Glasgow Univ. (MA Hons English). Lt (A) RNVR, 1939-45. Contested (L) Kincardine and West Aberdeen, 1945, East Edinburgh, 1948, Dundee West, 1951; Asst Editor, Daily Express, 1951-53; Dep. Editor, Evening Standard, 1953-54. Hon. LLD New Brunswick, 1973. *Recreations*: golf, tennis, sailing. *Address*: c/o Sunday Express, Fleet Street, EC4Y 2NJ. *Clubs*: Royal Southern Yacht; Royal and Ancient; Walton Heath.

JUPP, Clifford Norman, CMG 1966; *b* 24 Sept. 1919; *s* of Albert Leonard Jupp and Marguerite Isabel (*née* Day Winter); *m* 1945, Brenda (*née* Babbs); one *s* two *d*. *Educ*: Perse Sch., Cambridge; Trinity Hall, Cambridge. Armed Forces, 1940-46. Mem. of HM Foreign and Diplomatic Service, 1946-70; served in: Foreign Office, 1946; Beirut, 1947-49; New York, 1949-51; Foreign Office, 1951-53; Cairo, 1953-56; Kabul, 1956-59; Foreign Office, 1959-61; Brussels, 1961-63; Belgrade, 1963-66; seconded to BoT and Min. of Technology, 1967-70. With Burton Gp Ltd, 1970-72; Dir, British Textile Confedn, 1972-76. *Address*: Tigh nan Croitean, Kildatton, Isle of Islay, Argyll, Scotland.

JUPP, Hon. Sir Kenneth Graham, Kt 1975; MC 1943; **Hon. Mr Justice Jupp**; a Judge of the High Court, Queen's Bench Division, since 1975; Presiding Judge, North Eastern Circuit, since 1977; *b* 2 June 1917; *s* of Albert Leonard and Marguerite Isabel Jupp; *m* 1947, Kathleen Elizabeth (*née* Richards); two *s* two *d*. *Educ*: Perse Sch., Cambridge; University Coll., Oxford (Sen. Class. Schol., 1936; 1st Cl. Hon. Mods 1938); Lincoln's Inn (Cassel Schol.). Regimental Service in France, Belgium, N Africa and Italy, 1939-43; War Office Selection Board, 1943-46. Called to Bar, Lincoln's Inn, 1945, Bencher, 1973; QC 1966; Dep. Chm., Cambridge and Isle of Ely QS, 1965-71; a Recorder of the Crown Court, 1972-75. Chm., Independent Schs Tribunal, 1964-67; conducted MAFF inquiry into Wool Marketing Scheme, 1965; Chm., Public Inquiry into Fire at Fairfield Home, Nottingham, 1975. *Recreations*: sailing, music, language. *Address*: Royal Courts of Justice, Strand, WC2. *Club*: Garrick.

JURINAC, (Srebrenka) Sena; opera singer; Member of Vienna State Opera since 1944; *b* Travnik, Yugoslavia, 24 Oct. 1921; *d* of Ludwig Jurinac, MD, and Christine Cerv. *Educ*: High Sch.; Musical Academy. Made first appearance on stage as Mimi with Zagreb Opera, 1942. Frequent appearances at Glyndebourne Festivals, 1949-56, as well as at the Salzburg Festivals. Guest appearances at La Scala, Covent Garden, San Francisco, Teatro Colón. Principal parts include: Donna Anna and Donna Elvira in Don Giovanni; Elisabeth in Tannhauser; Tosca; Jenufa; Marie in Wozzeck; Marschallin in Der Rosenkavalier; Composer in Ariadne auf Naxos; Elisabeth in Don Carlos; Desdemona in Othello. *Film*: Der Rosenkavalier, 1962. Kammersängerin award, 1951; Ehrenkreuz für Wissenschaft und Kunst, 1961; Grosses Ehrenzeichen für Verdienste um die Republik Oesterreich, 1967. *Address*: c/o Vienna State Opera, Austria.

JURY, Archibald George, CBE 1961; FRIBA; FRIAS; City Architect, Glasgow, 1951-72, retired; *b* 23 June 1907; *s* of late George John Jury and Mabel Sophie Jury (*née* Fisher); *m* 1931, Amy Beatrice Maw; one *d*. *Educ*: Mount Radford, Exeter; SW School of Art. Architect to Council, Taunton, 1938-40, and 1945. Served War, 1940-45, with Corps of Royal Engineers (rank of Major). Chief Housing Architect, Liverpool, 1946-49; Dir of Housing, Glasgow, 1949-51; Dir of Planning, Glasgow, 1951-66. Organised the building of 100,000 houses, 100,000 school places and numerous civic buildings; responsible for the Glasgow Devpt Plan, 1960-80, and implementation of urban renewal programme and official architecture. Several Saltire Soc. awards for best-designed flats in Scotland. Chairman: Technical Panel, Scottish Local Authorities Special Housing Group, 1965-72; Technical Panel, Clyde Valley Planning Adv. Cttee, 1960-70; Pres., Glasgow Inst. of Architects, 1970-72. *Publications*: contrib. professional and technical journals. *Recreations*: fishing, gardening, painting. *Address*: Summerlea, Watchill Road, Lochmaben, Dumfriesshire.

K

KABERRY, Sir Donald, 1st Bt, *cr* 1960; TD 1946; DL; MP (C) North-West Division of Leeds since 1950; *b* 18 Aug. 1907; *m* 1940, Lily Margaret Scott; three *s*. *Educ*: Leeds Grammar Sch. Solicitor (Mem. of Council of The Law Society, 1950-55). Served War of 1939-45, in RA (despatches twice). Mem. Leeds City Council for 20 years, now Hon. Alderman. Asst Government Whip, 1951-April 1955; Parliamentary Sec., Board of Trade, April-Oct. 1955; Vice-Chm., Conservative Party, Oct. 1955-61; Member: Select Cttee Nationalised Industries, 1961- (Chm. Sub-Cttee C, 1974-); Speaker's Panel of Chairmen, 1974-. Chairman: Yorkshire Chemicals Ltd, 1964-77; W. H. Baxter Ltd; Pres., Yorks Area Council of Conservative Party, 1966- (Chm. 1952-56; Dep. Pres. 1956-65); Chm., Assoc. of Conservative Clubs, 1961-; Chairman: Bd of Governors, United Leeds Hosps, 1961-74; Leeds Teaching Hosps Special Trustee, 1974-; President: Headingly Branch, Royal British Legion; Leeds Dunkirk Veterans Assoc., 1973-; Treasurer, Leeds Poppy Day Appeal Fund, 1947-73. Pres., Incorporated Leeds Law Soc., 1952. DL York and West Yorks, 1974. *Heir*: *s* Christopher Donald Kaberry [*b* 14 March 1943; *m* 1967, Gaenor Elizabeth Vowe, *yr d* of C. V. Peake; two *s* one *d*. *Educ*: Repton Sch.]. *Address*: Beckfield, East Keswick, Leeds LS17 9DB. *T*: Collingham Bridge 3257. *Clubs*: Carlton, Constitutional; Leeds.

KADOORIE, Sir Lawrence, Kt 1974; CBE 1970; JP (Hong Kong); Partner, Sir Elly Kadoorie & Sons; Chairman: Sir Elly Kadoorie Successors Ltd; St George's Building Ltd; Director,

Sir Elly Kadoorie Continuation Ltd; also chairman and director of many other companies; *b* Hong Kong, 2 June 1899; *s* of Sir Elly Kadoorie, KBE, and Laura Kadoorie (*née* Mocatta); *m* 1938, Muriel, *d* of David Gubbay, Hong Kong; one *s* one *d*. *Educ*: Cathedral Sch., Shanghai; Ascham St Vincents, Eastbourne; Clifton Coll., Bristol; Lincoln's Inn. With his brother, Horace, founded New Territories Benevolent Soc. Is also Chairman: China Light & Power Co., Ltd, Schroders & Chartered Ltd, Hong Kong Carpet Manufacturers Ltd, Nanyang Cotton Mill Ltd and others. Mem. Council and Court, Univ. of Hong Kong. Fellow, Mem., Patron, Governor, Chm., etc, of numerous other assocs, cttees, etc. JP Hong Kong 1936; MEC 1954, MLC 1950, 1951, 1954, Hong Kong. Hon. LLD Univ. of Hong Kong, 1961; FInstD (London). KStJ (A) (UK) 1972. Solomon Schechter Award (USA), 1959; Ramon Magsaysay Award (Philippines), 1962; Officier de l'Ordre de Léopold (Belgium), 1966; Officier, Légion d'Honneur (France), 1975. *Recreations*: sports cars (Life Mem. Hong Kong AA), photography, Chinese works of art. *Address*: St George's Building, 24th floor, 2 Ice House Street, Hong Kong. *T*: 5-249221. *Clubs*: Royal Automobile; Hong Kong, Hong Kong Country, Royal Hong Kong Jockey, Jewish Recreation, American (Hong Kong); Travellers' Century (USA).

KADRI, Sibghat Ullah; barrister-at-law; *b* 23 April 1937; *s* of Haji Maulana Firasat Ullah Kadri and Begum Tanwir Fatima Kadri; *m* 1963, Carita Elisabeth Idman; one *s* one *d*. *Educ*: S. M. Coll., Karachi; Karachi Univ. Called to the Bar, Inner Temple, 1969. Sec. Gen., Karachi Univ. Students Union, 1957-58; jailed without trial, for opposing military regime of Ayub Khan, 1958-59; triple winner, All Pakistan Students Debates, 1960; Gen. Sec., Pakistan Students' Fedn in Britain, 1961-62, Vice Pres., 1962-63; Pres., Inner Temple Students Assoc., 1969-70. Producer and broadcaster, BBC Ext. Urdu Service, 1965-68, and Presenter, BBC Home Service Asian Prog., 1968-70. In practice at the Bar, 1969- (Head of Chambers, 11 King's Bench Walk). Vis. Lectr in Urdu, Holborn Coll., London, 1967-70. Org. Pakistani Def. Cttees during wave of 'Paki-bashing', 1970; active in immigrant and race-relations activities, 1970-; led Asian delegn to Prime Minister, June 1976; attended UN Conf., Migrant Workers in Europe, Geneva, 1975; led Pakistan delegn to 3rd Internat. Conf., Migrant Workers in Europe, Turin, 1977. Gen. Sec., Pakistan Action Cttee, 1973; Sec. Gen., Standing Conf. of Pakistani Orgs in UK, 1975-; Convenor, Asian Action Cttee, 1976. *Publications*: articles in ethnic minority press on immigration and race relations. *Recreations*: family and reading. *Address*: 11 King's Bench Walk, Temple, EC4Y 7EQ. *T*: 01-353 4931/2.

KAGAN, family name of **Baron Kagan.**

KAGAN, Baron *cr* 1976 (Life Peer), of Elland, W Yorks; **Joseph Kagan,** Kt 1970; Chairman of Gannex Group of Companies; *b* 6 June 1915; *s* of Benjamin and Miriam Kagan; *m* 1943, Margaret Stromas; two *s* one *d*. *Educ*: High School, Kaunas, Lithuania; Leeds University. BCom hons (Textiles). Founder of 'Gannex'-Kagan Textiles Limited, 1951, since when Chairman and Managing Director. *Recreation*: chess. *Address*: Barkisland Hall, Barkisland, Halifax, West Yorks. *T*: Elland 4121.

KAHN, family name of **Baron Kahn.**

KAHN, Baron, *cr* 1965 (Life Peer), of Hampstead; **Richard Ferdinand Kahn,** CBE 1946; FBA 1960; MA; Professor of Economics, Cambridge University, 1951-72; Fellow of King's College, Cambridge; *b* 10 Aug. 1905; *s* of late Augustus Kahn. *Educ*: St Paul's Sch. (Scholar); King's College, Cambridge (Scholar). Temporary Civil Servant in various Govt Depts, 1939-46. *Publications*: Selected Essays on Employment and Growth, 1973; articles on economic subjects. *Address*: King's College, Cambridge CB2 1ST. *T*: Cambridge 53311. *Club*: Royal Automobile.

KAHN-ACKERMANN, Georg; Secretary General, Council of Europe, since 1974; *b* 4 Jan. 1918; *m* 1945, Rosmarie Müller-Diefenbach; one *s* three *d*. *Educ*: in Germany and Switzerland. Served in Armed Forces, 1939-45. Press Reporter and Editor from 1946; Commentator with Radio Bavaria and wrote for newspaper, Abendzeitung, 1950. Author of several books, a publisher's reader, and mem. Exec. Cttee of Bavarian Assoc. of Journalists. Dir, VG WORT, Munich, 1972-74; Vice-Chm., Bd of Deutschlandfunk (Cologne). Mem., Social Democratic Party (SDP), from 1946, and of the German Federal Parliament, 1953-57, 1962-69 and 1970-74. Previous appts include: Vice-Pres., Western European Union Assembly, 1967-70; Chm., Political Commn of Western European Union, 1971-74; Vice-Pres., Consultative Assembly of Council of Europe until elected Secretary General in 1974. *Recreations*: horse-riding, ski-ing.

Address: Council of Europe, Strasbourg, France. *T*: Strasbourg 61.49.61.

KAHN-FREUND, Sir Otto, Kt 1976; FBA 1965; QC 1972; Professor of Comparative Law, University of Oxford, 1964-71; Emeritus Fellow, Brasenose College, 1971; *b* 17 Nov. 1900; *s* of Richard and Carrie Kahn-Freund; *m* 1931, Elisabeth (*née* Klaiss); one *d*. *Educ*: Goethe-Gymnasium, Frankfurt-am-Main; Universities of Frankfurt, Heidelberg, Leipzig, London. Doctor of Laws (Frankfurt) 1925, Master of Laws (London) 1935. Judge in German Courts, 1928-33. Barrister-at-Law (Middle Temple), 1936-; Hon. Bencher, Middle Temple, 1969. Asst Lecturer, Lecturer, and Reader in Law, 1935-61, Professor of Law, 1951-64, LSE. Arthur Goodhart Prof. of Legal Sci., and Professorial Fellow, Cambridge University, 1975-76; Hon. Fellow, Trinity Hall, Cambridge, 1977. Co-editor, Modern Law Review; Hon. Pres., Internat. Soc. for Labour Law and Social Legislation; Mem., Royal Commission on Trade Unions and Employers' Assocs, 1965-68. Doctor of Laws (*hc*): Bonn, 1968; Stockholm, 1969; Brussels, 1969; Paris, 1972; Leicester, 1973; Leuven, 1974; York (Canada), 1975; Cambridge, 1977. *Publications*: Law of Carriage by Inland Transport, 4th edn, 1965; (Co-editor) Dicey and Morris, Conflict of Laws, 9th edn 1973; English edn of Renner, Institutions of Private Law and their Social Functions, 1949; Co-author, The System of Industrial Relations in Great Britain, 1954; Co-author, Matrimonial Property Law, 1955; Co-author, Law and Opinion in England in the 20th Century, 1959; The Growth of Internationalism in English Private International Law, 1960; Labor Law and Social Security in: American Enterprise in the Common Market, 1960; Delictual Liability and the Conflict of Laws, 1968; Labour and the Law (Hamlyn Lectures), 1972; (jtly) A Source-Book on French Law, 1973; General Problems of Private International Law, 1975; numerous articles and notes in legal periodicals. *Recreations*: reading and walking. *Address*: Roundabouts, Shottermill, Haslemere, Surrey GU27 3PP. *T*: Haslemere 3774. *Club*: Athenæum.

KAISER, Philip M.; United States Ambassador to Hungary, since 1977; *b* 12 July 1913; *s* of Morris Kaiser and Temma Kaiser (*née* Sloven); *m* 1939, Hannah Greeley; three *s*. *Educ*: University of Wisconsin; Balliol Coll., Oxford (Rhodes Scholar). Economist, Bd of Governors, Fed. Reserve System, 1939-42; Chief, Project Ops Staff, also Chief, Planning Staff, Bd Economic Warfare and Foreign Econ. Admin., 1942-46; Expert on Internat. Organization Affairs, US State Dept., 1946; Exec. Asst to Asst Sec. of Labor in charge of internat. labor affairs, US Dept of Labor, 1947-49; Asst Sec. of Labor for Internat. Labor Affairs, 1949-53; mem., US Govt Bd of Foreign Service, Dept of State, 1948-53; US Govt mem., Governing Body of ILO, 1948-53; Chief, US delegn to ILO Confs, 1949-53; Special Asst to Governor of New York, 1954-58; Prof. of Internat. Relations and Dir, Program for Overseas Labor and Industrial Relations, Sch. of Internat. Service, American Univ., 1958-61; US Ambassador, Republic of Senegal and Islamic Republic of Mauritania, 1961-64; Minister, Amer. Embassy, London, 1964-69. Chm., Encyclopaedia Britannica International Ltd, 1969-75; Dir, Guinness Mahon Holdings Ltd, 1975-77. Member: US Govt Interdepartmental Cttee on Marshall Plan, 1947-48; Interdepartmental Cttee on Greek-Turkish aid and Point 4 Technical Assistance progs, 1947-49. *Recreations*: tennis, swimming, music. *Address*: American Embassy Budapest, 16 Boltzmanngasse, Vienna, Austria A-1090.

KALDOR, family name of **Baron Kaldor.**

KALDOR, Baron *cr* 1974 (Life Peer), of Newnham in the City of Cambridge; **Nicholas Kaldor,** MA; Hon. Dr (Dijon); FBA 1963; Professor of Economics in the University of Cambridge, 1966-75 (Reader in Economics, 1952-65); Fellow of King's College, Cambridge, since 1949; *b* Budapest, 12 May 1908; *s* of late Dr Julius Kaldor; *m* 1934, Clarissa Elisabeth Goldschmidt; four *d*. *Educ*: Model Gymnasium, Budapest; London Sch. of Economics. BSc (Econ.), 1st Class hons, 1930. Asst Lecturer, Lecturer and Reader in Economics, London Sch. of Economics, 1932-47; Rockefeller travelling Fellowship in US, 1935-36; Research Associate (part-time), Nat. Inst. of Economic and Social Research, 1943-45; Chief of Economic Planning Staff, US Strategic Bombing Survey, 1945; Dir, Research and Planning Division, Economic Commission for Europe, Geneva, 1947-49; Mem. of UN group of experts on international measures for full employment, 1949; Mem. of Royal Commission on Taxation of Profits and Income, 1951-55; Adviser on tax reform, Government of India, 1956; Economic Adviser, Economic Commission for Latin America, Santiago, Chile, 1956; Fiscal Adviser, Govt of Ceylon, 1958; Ford Visiting Research Prof., University of Calif., 1959-60; Fiscal Adviser, Government of Mexico, 1960; Economic Adviser, Govt of Ghana, 1961; Fiscal

Adviser, Govt of British Guiana, 1961, of Turkey, 1962, of Iran, 1966, of Venezuela, 1976; Visiting Economist, Reserve Bank of Australia, Sydney, 1963. Special Adviser to the Chancellor of the Exchequer, 1964-68 and 1974-76. Pres., Section F, British Assoc. for Advancement of Science, 1970. Hon. Member: Amer. Acad. of Arts and Scis; Amer. Econ. Assoc.; Royal Econ. Soc. of Belgium. Hon. Fellow, LSE, 1970. Pres., REconS, 1974-76. *Publications:* Quantitative Aspects of the Full Employment Problem in Britain (in Beveridge's Full Employment in a Free Soc.), 1944; (jointly) Statistical Analysis of Advertising Expenditure and Revenue of the Press, 1948; (part author) National and International Measures for Full Employment, 1950; An Expenditure Tax, 1955; Indian Tax Reform, 1956; Essays in Economic Stability and Growth, Essays in Value and Distribution, 1960; Capital Accumulation and Economic Growth (in The Theory of Capital), 1961; Ensayos sobre Desarrollo Económico (Mexico), 1961; Essays on Economic Policy, Vols I, II, 1964; Causes of the Slow Rate of Growth of the United Kingdom, 1966; Conflicts in Policy Objectives, 1971; Further Essays in Economic Theory, 1978; Further Essays in Applied Economics, 1978; Official Papers on Taxation, Vols I, II, 1978; papers in various economic jls. *Address:* King's College, Cambridge CB2 1ST; 2 Adams Road, Cambridge CB3 9AD. *T:* Cambridge 59282. *Club:* Reform.
See also M. J. Stewart.

KAN YUET-KEUNG, Sir, Kt 1972; CBE 1967 (OBE 1959); JP; Senior Unofficial Member of Executive Council, Hong Kong; Chairman, Bank of East Asia Ltd; *b* 26 July 1913; *s* of late Kan Tong Po, JP; *m* 1940, Ida; two *s* one d. *Educ:* Hong Kong Univ.; London Univ. BA Hong Kong 1934. Solicitor. Chm. of Council, Chinese Univ. of Hong Kong. Hon. LLD: Chinese Univ. of Hong Kong, 1968; Univ. of Hong Kong, 1973. Order of Sacred Treasure, 3rd Class, Japan. *Recreations:* tennis, swimming, golf. *Address:* Swire House, 11th Floor, Chater Road, Hong Kong. *T:* Hong Kong 238181.

KANE, Professor George; FBA 1968; William Rand Kenan Jr Professor of English in the University of North Carolina at Chapel Hill, since 1976; *b* 4 July 1916; *o s* of George Michael and Clara Kane; *m* 1946, Katherine Bridget, *o d* of Lt-Col R. V. Montgomery, MC; one *s* one d. *Educ:* St Peter's Coll.; British Columbia University; Toronto Univ.; University Coll., London (Fellow 1972). BA (University of BC), 1936; Research Fellow, University of Toronto, 1936-37; MA (Toronto), 1937; Research Fellow, Northwestern Univ., 1937-38; IODE Schol., for BC, 1938-39. Served War of 1939-45: Artists' Rifles, 1939-40; Rifle Bde, 1940-46 (despatches). PhD (London), 1946; Asst Lecturer in English, University Coll., London, 1946, Lecturer, 1948, Reader in English, 1953; Prof. of English Language and Literature and Head of English Dept, Royal Holloway College, London Univ., 1955-65; Prof. of English Language and Medieval Literature, 1965-76 and Head of English Dept, 1968-76, King's College, London, Prof. Emeritus, 1976, Fellow, 1976. Vis. Prof., Medieval Acad. of America, 1970, Corresp. Fellow, 1975; Fellow, Amer. Acad. of Arts and Scis. Member: Council, Early English Text Soc., 1969; Governing Body, SOAS, 1970-76; Council, British Acad., 1974-76. Sir Israel Gollancz Memorial Prize, British Acad., 1963; Chambers Memorial Lecturer, University Coll., London, 1965; British Academy Lectr, Accademia Nazionale dei Lincei, Rome, 1976; Public Orator, University of London, 1962-66. Gen. editor of London Edn of Piers Plowman. *Publications:* Middle English Literature, 1951; Piers Plowman, the A Version, 1960; Piers Plowman: The Evidence for Authorship, 1965; Piers Plowman: the B version, 1975; articles and reviews. *Recreation:* fishing. *Address:* Greenlaw Hall, Chapel Hill, North Carolina, USA. *Club:* Athenæum.

KANE, Jack, OBE 1969; DL; JP; Chairman, Consultative Council, South of Scotland Electricity Board, since 1977; Lord Provost of the City of Edinburgh and Lord Lieutenant of the County of the City of Edinburgh, 1972-75; *b* 1 April 1911; *m* 1940, Anne Murphy; one *s* two d. *Educ:* Bathgate Academy. Served War, 1940-46. Librarian, 1936-55; SE of Scotland Dist Sec., Workers' Educational Assoc., 1955-76. Chm., Board of Trustees for Nat. Galls of Scotland, 1975-; Mem., South of Scotland Electricity Bd, 1975-. JP Edinburgh, 1945; DL City of Edinburgh, 1976. Dr *hc* Edinburgh, 1976. Grand Officer, Order of the Oaken Crown (Luxembourg), 1972; Grand Cross of Merit (W Germany). *Recreations:* reading, walking. *Address:* 88 Thirlestane Road, Edinburgh EH9 1AS. *T:* 031-447 7757. *Club:* Newcraighall Miners' Welfare Inst.

KANSAS CITY, Bishop of, (RC); *see* Helmsing, Most Rev. Charles H.

KANTOROVICH, Prof. Leonid Vitalevich; Head of Department, Institute of Systems Research, Moscow, USSR, since 1976; mathematician, economist; *b* Leningrad, 19 Jan. 1912; *m* 1938, Natalja Vladimirovna Iljana; one *s* one d. *Educ:* Univ. of Leningrad, 1930. Instructor, Leningrad Inst. of Industrial Construction Engineering, 1930-34; Professor, 1934-39; Instructor, Leningrad Univ., 1932-34; Professor, 1934-41, 1945-60, Mathem. Inst., Acad. of Sciences (Leningrad Filial) (Head of Dept, 1945-60); Dep. Dir, Mathem. Inst., Siberian Branch, Acad. of Sciences of the USSR, 1960-71; Head of Research Lab., Inst. of Nat. Economy Control, Moscow, 1971-76. Corr. Mem., Acad. of Sciences of the USSR, 1958-64; Mem., 1964-. Foreign Member: Hungarian Acad. of Sciences, 1967; Acad. of Arts and Science, Boston, USA, 1969. Dr *hc*: Glasgow, 1966; Grenoble, 1967; Nice, 1969; Helsinki, 1970; Sorbonne, Paris, 1975; Vysoka Scola Econ. i Plan., Warsaw, 1975; Cambridge, 1976; Pennsylvania, 1976. State Prize, USSR, 1949; Lenin Prize, USSR, 1965; Nobel Prize for Economics, 1975. Order Sign of Honour, 1944; Order of Labour Red banner, 1949, 1950, 1975; Order of Lenin, 1967. *Publications:* Variatsionnoe iscislenie (Calculus of Variations), 1933; Priblizhennye metody vysshego analiza (Approximate Methods of Higher Analysis), 1936; Matematicheskie metody organizatsii i planirvaniya proizvodstva (Mathematical Methods of Organizing and Planning Production), 1939; Funktsional'nyi analiz v poluuporyadochennyh prosranstvah (Functional Analysis in Semiordered Spaces), 1950; Rascet ratsional'nogo raskroya promyshlennyh materialov (Calculation of Rational Cutting of Industrial Materials), 1951; Ekonomichesky rascet nailuchschego ispolzovaniya resursov (Economical Calculation of the Best Use of Resources), 1959; Funktsional'nyi analiz y normirovannyh prostranstvah (Functional Analysis in Normed Spaces), 1959; Optimal'nye rescheniya v ekonomike (Optimal Decisions in Economy), 1972; Essays in Optimal Planning, 1976; Funktsional'nyi Analiz (Functional Analysis), 1977. *Address:* Akademia Nauk, Leninsky Prospekt, 14, Moscow, USSR.

KANTOROWICH, Prof. Roy Herman, BArch (Witwatersrand), MA (Manchester); RIBA, FRTPI; Professor of Town and Country Planning, University of Manchester, since 1961; Dean of the Faculty of Arts, 1975-76; *b* Johannesburg, 24 Nov. 1916; *s* of George Kantorowich and Deborah (*née* Baranov); *m* 1943, Petronella Sophie Wissema (violinist, as Nella Wissema); one *s* two d. *Educ:* King Edward VII Sch., Johannesburg; University of Witwatersrand. BArch 1939; ARIBA 1940; MTPI 1965 (AMTPI 1946). Post-grad. studies in Housing and Planning, MIT and Columbia Univ., 1939-41; Planning Officer: Vanderbijl Park New Town, 1942-45; directing Cape Town Foreshore Scheme, 1945-48; private practice in Cape Town, in architecture and town planning, 1948-61. Pres., S African Inst. Town and Regional Planners, 1960. Formerly Town Planning Consultant to Cape Provincial Admin., and for many cities and towns in S Africa incl. Durban, Pretoria and Port Elizabeth; Cons. for New Town of Ashkelon, Israel, 1950-56. Member: NW Econ. Planning Coun. 1965-; Council (Chm., Educn Cttee), TPI, 1965-70; Planning Cttee, SSRC, 1969-73; Construction and Environment Bd, and Chm., Town Planning Panel, CNAA, 1971-75. Buildings include: Civic Centre, Welkom, OFS; Baxter Hall, University of Cape Town; Sea Point Telephone Exchange (Cape Province Inst. of Architects Bronze Medal Award); Architecture and Planning Building, Univ. of Manchester. FRSA 1972. *Publications:* Cape Town Foreshore Plan, 1948; (with Lord Holford) Durban 1985, a plan for central Durban in its Regional Setting, 1968; contribs to SAArch. Record, Jl RTPI and other professional jls. *Recreations:* music, tennis. *Address:* 3 Winster Avenue, Manchester M20 8YA. *T:* 061-445 9417. *Club:* Northern Lawn Tennis.

KAPITZA, Peter Leonidovich, FRS 1929; PhD Cantab; FInstP; Director of Institute for Physical Problems of Academy of Sciences of the USSR; Editor, Journal of Experimental and Theoretical Physics of Academy of Sciences, USSR; late Royal Society Messel Research Professor; late Director of the Royal Society Mond Laboratory; *b* Kronstadt, Russia, 26 June (old style) 1894; *s* of late Gen. Leonid Kapitza and Olga, *d* of Gen. J. Stebnitsckiy; *m* 1st, late Nadejda, *d* of Cyril Tschernosvitoff; 2nd, Anna, *d* of Professor A. N. Kryloff; two *s*. *Educ:* Secondary Sch., Kronstadt; Petrograd Politechnical Inst. (Faculty of Electrical Engrg). Lecturer, Petrograd Politechnical Inst., 1919-21; Clerk Maxwell Student, Cambridge Univ., 1923-26; Fellow, Trinity Coll., 1925 (Hon. Fellow, 1966). Asst Dir of Magnetic Research, Cavendish Laboratory, Cambridge, 1924-32; Cor. Mem. Acad. of Science of USSR, 1929; For. Mem., Council of French Physical Soc., 1935; Mem. Acad. of Science, USSR, 1939; Hon. Mem. Société des Naturalistes de Moscou, 1935; Fellow, Amer. Physical Soc., 1937; Hon. MInst. Met., 1943; Hon. Mem. and Franklin Medal of Franklin Inst., USA, 1944;

Foreign Member: Royal Acad. of Science, Sweden, 1966; Royal Netherlands Acad. of Sciences, 1969; Serbian Acad. of Sciences and Arts, 1971; Finnish Acad. of Science and Letters, 1974; For. Hon. Mem., Amer. Acad. of Arts and Sciences, 1968. Numerous Hon. Doctorates, Fellowships, etc, 1944-. Rutherford Memorial Lectr, 1969. Medal Liege Univ., 1934; State prize for Physics, 1941 and 1943; Faraday Medal of Electr. Engrs 1942. Order of Lenin, 1943, 1944, 1945, 1964, 1971, 1974; Moscow Defence Medal, 1944; Hero of Socialist Labour, 1945, 1974; Order of the Red Banner of Labour, 1954; Sir Devaprasad Sarbadhikari Gold Medal, Calcutta Univ., 1955; Kothenius Gold Medal of German Acad. of Naturalists, 1959; Lomonosov Gold Medal, Acad. of Sciences, USSR, 1959; Great Gold Medal, Exhibn of Economic Achievements USSR, 1962; International Niels Bohr Gold Medal of Dansk Ingeniørvorening, 1964; Rutherford Medal of Inst. of Physics and Physical Soc., England, 1966; Order of the Yugoslav Banner with Ribbon, 1967; Kamerlingh Onnes Gold Medal of Netherlands Soc. for Refrigeration, 1968; Simon Prize, Inst. Physics, 1973, etc. *Publications:* Collected Papers, 3 vols, 1964-67; various publications on physics, mainly on magnetism, cryogenics and high temperature plasma in scientific journals. *Recreation:* chess. *Address:* The Institute for Physical Problems, Vorobjevskoe Shosse 2, Moscow, 117334, USSR.

KAPLAN, Prof. Joseph; Professor of Physics, University of California at Los Angeles (UCLA), 1940-70, now Professor Emeritus; *b* 8 Sept. 1902; *s* of Henry and Rosa Kaplan, Tapolcza, Hungary; *m* 1933, Katherine Elizabeth Feraud; no *c.* *Educ:* Johns Hopkins University, Baltimore, Md, PhD 1927; National Research Fellow, Princeton Univ., 1927-28. University of Calif. at Los Angeles: Asst Prof. of Physics, 1928-35; Associate Prof., 1935-40; Prof., 1940-. Chief, Operations Analysis Section, Second Air Force, 1943-45 (Exceptional Civilian Service Medal, US Air Corps, 1947). Chm., US Nat. Cttee for Internat. Geophysical Year, 1953-64. Fellow: Inst. of Aeronautical Sciences, 1957; Amer. Meteorological Soc., 1970 (Pres., 1963-67). Mem. Nat. Acad. of Sciences, 1957; Hon. Mem., Amer. Meteorological Soc., 1967; Vice-Pres., International Union of Geodesy and Geophysics, 1960-63, Pres., 1963-; Hon. Governor, Hebrew Univ. of Jerusalem, 1968. Hon. DSc: Notre Dame, 1957; Carleton Coll., 1957; Hon. LHD: Yeshiva Univ. and Hebrew Union Coll., 1958; Univ. of Judaism, 1959. Exceptional Civilian Service Medal (USAF), 1960; Hodgkins Prize and Medal, 1965. Exceptional Civilian Service Medal, 1969; John A. Fleming Medal, Amer. Geophysical Union, 1970; Commemorative Medal, 50th Anniversary, Amer. Meteorological Soc., 1970; Special Award, UCLA Alumni Assoc., 1970. *Publications:* Across the Space Frontier, 1950; Physics and Medicine of the Upper Atmosphere, 1952; (co-author) Great Men of Physics, 1969; publications in Physical Review, Nature, Proc. Nat. Acad. of Sciences, Jl Chemical Physics. *Recreations:* golf, ice-skating, walking. *Address:* 1565 Kelton Avenue, Los Angeles, Calif 90024, USA. *T:* Granite 38839. *Club:* Cosmos (Washington, DC).

KAPP, Edmond X.; artist; *b* London, 5 Nov. 1890; *s* of late E. B. Kapp, London and Bella Wolff, New York; *m* 1st, 1922, Yvonne Cloud, writer; one *d* ; 2nd, 1932, Polia Chentoff, artist (*d* 1933); 3rd, 1950, Patricia Greene, writer. *Educ:* Owen's Sch., London; Paris; Berlin University; Christ's Coll., Cambridge (Scholar). BA. Served European War, 1914-19, BEF France; Lieut Royal Sussex Regt; Staff Capt. Spec. Appt Intelligence GHQ (M in D); first one-man shows of drawings and caricatures, Cambridge, 1912, London, 1919; Chief Master in painting, Maurice Sterne, Rome 1922-23; subseq. Exhibitions of paintings, drawings, lithographs at the Leicester Galleries and Wildenstein Gall., London; Brighton; Bath; Birmingham; Manchester; Bradford; Newcastle; Buffalo, USA; Toronto, Canada; UNESCO, Paris; Geneva; Monte Carlo, Milan, etc; Picasso sits for portrait and lithograph, 1938; represented in National Gallery Exhibition (British Art since Whistler), 1945; invited to exhibit *hors concours* 1st French Biennale Internat., Menton, 1951; Wakefield, York, Harrogate, 1957; invited by Whitechapel Art Gallery, London, to hold 50-year Retrospective Exhibition of paintings and drawings, 1961; Bear Lane Gallery (abstract paintings only), Oxford, 1962; Royal Festival Hall, 1968. Music into Art Programme, BBC TV, 1968. Works acquired by: British Museum; Victoria and Albert Museum; National Portrait Gallery; Imperial War Museum; London Museum; S London Art Gallery, Camberwell; Contemporary Art Soc., London; Perth Museum and Art Gallery, WA; Yale Law Sch. Library, USA (legal portraits as stained-glass windows); Bibliothèque Nationale, Paris; Tel-Aviv Gallery, Israel; Palais de la Paix, Geneva; Fitzwilliam Museum, Cambridge; Ashmolean, Oxford; Manchester; Whitworth (Manchester); Leeds; Birmingham; Bradford; Wakefield; Kettle's Yard Museum of Modern Art, Cambridge; and other provincial galleries; 240 drawings acquired by Barber Inst. of Fine Arts, Birmingham, 1969; also in

private collections made by Samuel Courtauld, Lord Clark, Sacha Guitry, Sir Hugh Walpole, Daniel de Pass, Jim Ede, Lord Goodman, etc.; 70 drawings, commnd by the London Philharmonic Orchestra, 1943, and exhibited London and provincial city Art Galleries. The Nations at Geneva, 1934-35, series of twenty-five portraits on the stone, commissioned by British Museum and Nat. Portrait Gallery and acquired for other collections; complete set of Original Lithographs acquired by Buffalo City (Albright) Art Gallery (USA), 1939. Commissioned as Official War Artist, 1940; as Official Artist to UNESCO, Paris, 1946-47 (20 portrait-drawings). Commissioned to make 8 portraits for Gonville and Caius and Christ's Colls., Cambridge and Merton Coll., Oxford, 1965-66, and Provost Lord Caccia for Eton College, 1975. Since 1960, apart from occasional portraits his painting has been exclusively abstract. *Publications:* Personalities, Twenty-four Drawings (Secker, 1919); Reflections, Twenty-four Drawings (Cape, 1922); Ten Great Lawyers (plates in colour), (Butterworth, 1924); Minims. Twenty-eight Abstract Drawings; with Yvonne Cloud, Pastiche: A Music-Room Book (Faber, 1925 and 1925); his work is reproduced in: Modern Drawings (by Campbell Dodgson); History of Caricature (by Bohun Lynch); Encycl. Britannica (XIII edn); From Sickert to 1948 (by John Russell); Things New and Old (by Max Beerbohm); Modern Caricaturists (by H. R. Westwood), etc. *Recreations:* music and nonsense. *Address:* 2 Steele's Studios, Haverstock Hill, NW3 4RN. *T:* 01-722 3174. *See also Helen Kapp.*

KAPP, Helen; Director, Abbot Hall, Kendal, 1961-67, retired; *b* London; *d* of late E. B. Kapp, London, and Bella Wolff, New York. *Educ:* Maria Grey Sch.; Slade Sch. of Art; University Coll., London; Paris. Painter and illustrator; one-man shows; London, 1939; Haifa, 1946; Wakefield, 1954; Guide-Lecturer for Arts Council (CEMA) 1940-45; Lecturer for War Office, 1946-48; Lecturer, Extra Mural Dept, London Univ., 1948-51; Dir City Art Gallery and Museum, Wakefield, 1951-61. *Publications:* Illustrated: (with Gerald Bullett) Seed of Israel, 1929; (with John Collier) The Scandal and Credulities of John Aubrey, 1931; (with E. S. Rohde): Vegetable Cultivation and Cookery, 1938; Rose Recipes, 1939; (with Basil Collier): Take 40 Eggs, 1938; Catalan France, 1939; (with Harold Morland) Satires and Fables, 1945; Toying with a Fancy, 1950; Wrote: Enjoying Pictures, 1975. *Recreations:* music, conversation and idleness. *Address:* 17 Carr Avenue, Leiston, Suffolk IP16 4JA. *T:* Leiston 830010. *See also Edmond Kapp.*

KAPPEL, Frederick R.; retired as Chairman of Boards, American Telephone & Telegraph Company and International Paper Company; Chairman, Board of Governors, US Postal Service; *b* Albert Lea, Minnesota, 14 Jan. 1902; *s* of Fred A. Kappel and Gertrude M. Towle Kappel; *m* 1927, Ruth Carolyn Ihm; two *d.* *Educ:* University of Minnesota (BSE). Northwestern Bell Telephone Company: various positions in Minnesota, 1924-33; Plant Engineer, Nebraska, S Dakota, 1934. Plant Operations Supervisor (Exec.) Gen. Staff, Omaha, Nebraska, 1937, Asst Vice-Pres. Operations, 1939, Vice-Pres. Operations and Dir, 1942. Amer. Telephone & Telegraph Co., NY: Asst Vice-Pres. (O & E), Vice-Pres. (Long Lines), Vice Pres. (O & E), 1949. Pres. Western Electric Co , 1954-56; Chm. and Chief Exec. Officer, Amer. Tel. & Tel. Co , 1956-67, Chm. Exec. Cttee, 1967-69; Chm. Bd, International Paper Co., 1969-71, Chm. Exec. Cttee 1971-74. Director: Amer. Telephone & Telegraph Co., 1956-70; Chase Manhattan Bank, 1956-72; Metropolitan Life Insurance Co., 1958-75; General Foods Corporation, 1961-73; Standard Oil Co. (NJ), 1966-70; Whirlpool Corp., 1967-72; Chase Manhattan Corp., 1969-72; Boys' Club of America; Acad. of Polit. Sciences, 1963-71; Member: Business Council (Chm., 1963-64); Advisory Board of Salvation Army, 1957-73; US Chamber of Commerce; various societies. Trustee: Presbyterian Hospital, 1949-74; Grand Central Art Galleries, Inc., 1957-70; Aerospace Corp., 1967-74; Tax Foundation, 1960-72. Trustee, University of Minnesota Foundation. Holds numerous hon. doctorates and awards, including: Cross of Comdr of Postal Award, France, 1962; Presidential Medal of Freedom, 1964. *Publications:* Vitality in a Business Enterprise, 1960; Business Purpose and Performance. *Recreation:* golf. *Address:* 343 West Royal Flamingo Drive, Sarasota, Fla 33577, USA. *Clubs:* Triangle, University, Economic (New York); Siwanoy Country (Bronxville); International (Washington); American Yacht (Rye, NY); Bird Key Yacht, Sarabay Country (Sarasota, Fla).

KARACHI, Archbishop of, (RC), since 1958; **His Eminence Cardinal Joseph Cordeiro;** *b* Bombay, India, 19 Jan. 1918. *Educ:* St Patrick's High School; DJ College, Karachi; Papal Seminary, Kandy, Ceylon. Priest, 1946; Asst Chaplain, St Francis Xavier's, Hyderabad, Sind, 1947; Asst Principal, St Patrick's High

School, Karachi, 1948; Student at Oxford, 1948; Asst Principal, St Patrick's High Sch., 1950; Principal, Grammar Sch., and Rector, Diocesan Seminary, Quetta, 1952. Cardinal, 1973. *Address:* St Patrick's Cathedral, Karachi 3, Pakistan. *T:* 515870.

KARAJAN, Herbert von; *see* Von Karajan.

KARANJA, Dr Josphat Njuguna; Vice-Chancellor, University of Nairobi, since 1970; *b* 5 Feb. 1931; *s* of Josphat Njuguna; *m* 1966, Beatrice Nyindombi, Fort Portal, Uganda; one *s* two *d.* *Educ:* Alliance High Sch., Kikuyu, Kenya; Makerere Coll., Kampala, Uganda; University of Delhi, India; Princeton Univ., New Jersey, USA (PhD). Lecturer in African Studies, Farleigh Dickinson Univ., New Jersey, 1961-62; Lecturer in African and Modern European History, University College, Nairobi, Kenya, 1962-63; High Comr for Kenya in London, 1963-70. *Recreations:* golf, tennis. *Address:* University of Nairobi, Box 30197, Nairobi, Kenya.

KARIMJEE, Sir Tayabali Hassanali Alibhoy, Kt 1955; Brilliant Star of Zanzibar (3rd Class); Jubilee Medal of Sultan of Zanzibar; *b* 7 Nov. 1897; *s* of Hassanali A. Karimjee and Zenubbai H. A. Karimjee; *m* 1917, Sugrabai Mohamedali Karimjee; one *d.* *Educ:* Zanzibar and Karachi. Pres., Indian National Association, Zanzibar, 1930 and 1942; Pres. Chamber of Commerce, Zanzibar, 1940 1941, 1942; Mem. Fighter Fund Cttee, 1940-43; Mem. Red Cross Cttee, 1940-45; MLC, Zanzibar, 1933-45. Chm. Board of Directors, Karimjee Jivanjee & Co. Ltd., Karimjee Jivanjee Estates Ltd, Karimjee J. Properties Ltd, International Motor Mart Ltd (Tanganyika), Karimjee Trading Co. (Bombay); Director, Karimjee Jivanjee & Co. (UK) Ltd, London. King George V Jubilee Medal, 1935; Coronation Medals, 1937 and 1953. *Address:* 234 E. I. Lines, Aziz Bhatti (NH) Road, Karachi 4, Pakistan. *Clubs:* Royal Commonwealth Society; Royal Over-Seas League; Karachi (Karachi); WIAA (Bombay).

KARK, (Arthur) Leslie; MA (Oxon); FRSA; Author, Barrister; Chairman: Lucie Clayton Secretarial College; Lucie Clayton Ltd; *b* 12 July 1910; *s* of Victor and Helena Kark, Johannesburg; *m* 1st, 1935, Joan Tetley (marr. diss., 1956); two *d*; 2nd, 1956, Evelyn Gordine (*see* E. F. Kark); one *s* one *d.* *Educ:* Clayesmore; St John's Coll., Oxford. Called to Bar, Inner Temple, 1932; Features Editor of World's Press News, 1933; Editor of Photography, 1934; Public Relations Officer to Advertising Association, 1935; Features Editor News Review, 1936-39; London Theatre Critic, New York Herald Tribune; News Editor, Ministry of Information, 1940. Served War of 1939-45, RAF, 1940-46; Air-gunner; Wing Commander in Command of Public Relations (Overseas) Unit; author, Air Ministry's official book on Air War, Far East. Short stories and novels translated into French. Swedish, German, Polish, etc. *Publications:* The Fire Was Bright, 1944; Red Rain, 1946; An Owl in the Sun, 1948; Wings of the Phœnix, 1949; On the Haycock, 1957. *Recreations:* fly-fishing, golf. *Address:* 9 Clareville Grove, SW7. *T:* 01-373 2621; Roche House, Sheep Street, Burford, Oxon. *T:* Burford 3007. *Club:* Savage.

KARK, Mrs Evelyn Florence, (*nom de plume* **Lucie Clayton**); Director; *b* 5 Dec. 1928; *d* of Emily and William Gordine; *m* 1956 (Arthur) Leslie Kark, *qv;* one *s* one *d.* *Educ:* privately and inconspicuously. Asst to Editor, Courier Magazine, 1950; became Head of model school and agency (assuming name of Lucie Clayton), 1952; founded Lucie Clayton Sch. of Fashion Design and Dressmaking, 1961, and Lucie Clayton Secretarial College, 1966. *Publication:* The World of Modelling, 1968. *Recreations:* talking, tapestry, cooking. *Address:* 9 Clareville Grove, SW7. *T:* 01-373 2621; Roche House, Burford, Oxfordshire. *T:* Burford 3007.

KARK, Mrs Nina Mary; *see* Bawden, N. M.

KARMEL, Alexander D., QC 1954; **His Honour Judge Karmel;** a Circuit Judge (Additonal Judge, Central Criminal Court, since 1968); *b* 16 May 1904; *s* of Elias Karmel; *m* 1937, Mary, *widow* of Arthur Lee and *d* of Newman Lipton; one *s.* *Educ:* Newcastle upon Tyne Royal Grammar Sch. Barrister-at-law, Middle Temple, 1932; Master of the Bench, 1962; Leader of Northern Circuit, 1966; Comr of Assize, Stafford, summer 1967; Recorder of Bolton, 1962-68. Mem., Bar Council, 1950-53, 1961-64. *Recreations:* croquet, golf. *Address:* Central Criminal Court, Old Bailey, EC4; 5 Essex Court, EC4. *T:* 01-236 4365. *Clubs:* Royal Automobile, Hurlingham.

KARMEL, David, CBE 1967; QC 1950; JP; a Recorder of the Crown Court, since 1972; *b* 1957; *s* of Joseph Michael Karmel; *m* 1943, Barbara, *d* of late Sir Montague Burton; one *d.* *Educ:* St Andrews College; Trinity Coll., Dublin. Called to Bar, Gray's

Inn, 1928; Mem. of the Northern Circuit; Master of the Bench, Gray's Inn, 1954, Treasurer 1970, Vice-Treasurer, 1971; Mem. Inner Temple; Mem. of the Bar of Northern Rhodesia. Enlisted King's Royal Rifle Corps, 1939; commissioned in 60th Rifles, Dec. 1940; Capt., 1942; Major, 1943; served War of 1939-45 (wounded), in 1st Bn Western Desert, Tunisia and Italy, 1941-44, and in Jugoslavia, with Mil. Mission 1944-45. Recorder of Wigan, 1952-62; Dep. Chm., Glos QS, 1970-71. Mem. Gen. Council of Bar, 1956-60. Steward, British Boxing Bd of Control. Mem. Industrial Disputes Tribunal; Chairman: Cttees of Investigation under Agric. Marketing Act, 1958; Truck Acts Cttee, 1959; Advisory Cttee on Service Candidates, 1963; Dep. Chm., Central Arbitration Cttee. Mem. indep. panel of Industrial Court, Mem. Cttee on Legal Education of Students from Africa, 1960. HQ Referee, NCB. JP County of Glos., 1963. *Recreations:* theatre, travelling. *Address:* 1 Brick Court, EC4. *T:* 01-353 0777; 108 Eaton Place, SW1. *T:* 01-235 6159; Domaine Vigne Groussière, 83880 Méounes-les-Montrieux, France. *T:* 94.48.97.21. *Clubs:* Beefsteak, Buck's, Travellers'; Travellers' (Paris).

KARMEL, Emeritus Prof. Peter Henry, AC 1976; CBE 1967; Chairman, Tertiary Education Commission, since 1977 (Chairman, Universities Commission, 1971-77); *b* 9 May 1922; *s* of Simeon Karmel; *m* 1946, Lena Garrett; one *s* five *d.* *Educ:* Caulfield Grammar Sch.; Univ. of Melbourne (BA); Trinity Coll., Cambridge (PhD). Research Officer, Commonwealth Bureau of Census and Statistics, 1943-45; Lectr in Econs, Univ. of Melbourne, 1946; Rouse Ball Res. Student, Trinity Coll., Cambridge, 1947-48; Sen. Lectr in Econs, Univ. of Melbourne, 1949; Prof. of Econs, 1950-62, Emeritus, 1965, Univ. of Adelaide; Principal-designate, Univ. of Adelaide at Bedford Park (subseq. Flinders Univ. of SA), 1961-66; Vice-Chancellor, Flinders Univ. of SA, 1966-71; Chancellor, Univ. of Papua and New Guinea, 1969-70 (Chm., Interim Council, 1965-69). Mem., SSRC, 1952-71; Mem. Council, Univ. of Adelaide, 1955-69; Vis. Prof. of Econs, Queen's Univ., Belfast, 1957-58; Mem. Commonwealth Cttee: on Future of Tertiary Educn, 1961-65; of Economic Enquiry, 1963-65; Member: Australian Council for Educnl Research, 1968-; Cttee of Enquiry into Educn in SA, 1969-70 (Chm.); Adv. Cttee of Cities Commn, 1972-74; Interim Cttee for Aust. Schools Commn, 1972-73 (Chm.); Cttee of Enquiry on Med. Schs, 1972-73 (Chm.); Cttee of Enquiry on Open Univ., 1973-74; Chairman: Australian Council, 1974-77; Cttee on Post-Secondary Educn in Tasmania, 1975-76. FACE 1969; FASSA 1971. Hon. LLD: Univ. of Papua and New Guinea, 1970; Univ. of Melbourne, 1975; Hon. LittD Flinders Univ. of SA, 1971; Hon. DLit, Murdoch Univ., 1975. *Publications:* Applied Statistics for Economists, 1957, 1962 (1970 edn with M. Polasek, 4th edn 1977), Portuguese edn, 1972; (with M. Brunt) Structure of the Australian Economy, 1962, repr. 1963, 1966; (with G. C. Harcourt and R. H. Wallace) Economic Activity, 1967 (Italian edn 1969); articles in Economic Record, Population Studies, Jl Royal Statistical Assoc., and other learned jls. *Address:* Tertiary Education Commission, Canberra, ACT, Australia. *T:* 496059.

KARP, David; novelist; *b* New York City, 5 May 1922; *s* of Abraham Karp and Rebecca Levin; *m* 1944, Lillian Klass; two *s.* *Educ:* College of The City of New York. US Army, 1943-46, S Pacific, Japan; College, 1946-48; Continuity Dir, Station WNYC, New York, 1948-49; free-lance motion picture-television writer and motion picture producer, 1949-; President: Leda Productions Inc., 1968-; Television-Radio Branch, Writers Guild of America West, 1969-71; Member: Editorial Bd, Television Quarterly, 1966-71, 1972-; Council, Writers Guild of America, 1966-73. Guggenheim Fellow, 1956-57. *Publications:* One, 1953; The Day of the Monkey, 1955; All Honorable Men, 1956; Leave Me Alone, 1957; The Sleepwalkers, 1960; Vice-President in Charge of Revolution (with Murray D. Lincoln), 1960; The Last Believers, 1964; short stories in Saturday Eve. Post, Collier's, Esquire, Argosy, The American, etc; articles and reviews in NY Times, Los Angeles Times, Saturday Review, Nation, etc. *Recreations:* photography, reading. *Address:* 1116 Corsica Drive, Pacific Palisades, Calif 90272, USA. *T:* 459-1623. *Club:* PEN (New York).

KARSAVINA, Tamara, (Mrs H. J. Bruce); President of the Licentiate Club of the Royal Academy of Dancing, since 1954; *b* 10 March 1885; *d* of Platon Karsavin and Anna (*née* Khomiakova); *m* 1915, H. J. Bruce; one *s.* *Educ:* Imperial Theatre Sch., St Petersburgh, Russia. Artist of the Marinsky Theatre, St Petersburgh, 1902-19, Prima Ballerina: Leading Dancer of Ballets Russes of Serge Diaghilev, 1909-22; guest artist, 1923-29. First London appearance (under name of Tamara Karsavina), in Divertissement, Coliseum, 1909; Armide, in Le Pavillon d'Armide, at first appearance of Imperial Russian Ballet at Covent Garden, 1911; in subsequent years danced frequently in England. Is resident in London. Fellow, Royal Acad. of Dancing. Gold Medal of Order of St Vladimir; Order of the Red Cross; Palmes Académiques; Order of the Emir of Bokhara. Holder of Royal Academy of Dancing Coronation Award for 1954. *Publications:* Theatre Street, 1930; Ballet Technique, 1956; Flow of Movement, 1962. *Recreations:* gardening, interior decoration.

KARSH, Yousuf, OC 1968; Portrait Photographer since 1932; *b* Mardin, Armenia-in-Turkey, 23 Dec. 1908; parents Armenian; Canadian Citizen; *m* 1939, Solange Gauthier (*d* 1961); *m* 1962, Estrellita Maria Nachbar. *Educ:* Sherbrooke, PQ Canada; studied photography in Boston, Mass., USA. Portrayed Winston Churchill in Canada's Houses of Parliament, 1941; King George VI, 1943; HM Queen (then Princess) Elizabeth and the Duke of Edinburgh, 1951; HH Pope Pius XII, 1951; also portrayed, among many others: Shaw, Wells, Einstein, Sibelius, Somerset Maugham, Picasso, Eden, Eisenhower, Tito, Eleanor Roosevelt, Thomas Mann, Bertrand Russell, Attlee, Nehru, Ingrid Bergmann, Lord Mountbatten of Burma, Augustus John; seven portraits used on postage stamps of six countries. One man exhibns: Men Who Make our World, Pav. of Canada, Expo. 67; Montreal Mus. of Fine Arts, 1968; Boston Mus. of Fine Arts, 1968; Corning Mus., 1968; Detroit Inst. of Arts, 1969; Corcoran Gall. of Art, Washington, 1969; Macdonald House, London, 1969; Seattle Art Museum; Japan (country-wide), and Honolulu, 1970; Men Who Make our World, Europe and USA, 1971, 1972, 1973, 1974, 1975; exhibn acquired in toto by: Museum of Modern Art, Tokyo; Nat. Gall. of Australia; Province of Alberta, Canada, 1975-76; numerous exhibns throughout US, 1971-75, 1976-77. Visiting Professor: Ohio Univ., 1967-69; Emerson Coll., Boston, 1972-73, 1973-74; Photographic Advisor, Internat. Exhibn, Expo '70, Osaka, Japan. Trustee, Photographic Arts and Scis Foundn, 1970. FRPS; Fellow Rochester Sci. Mus. RCA 1975. Holds eight hon. degrees. Canada Council Medal, 1965; Centennial Medal, 1967; Master of Photographic Arts, Prof. Photogrs of Canada, 1970; First Gold Medal, Nat. Assoc. Photog. Art, 1974. *Publications:* Faces of Destiny, 1947; (co-author) This is the Mass, 1958; Portraits of Greatness, 1959; (co-author) This is Rome, 1960; (co-author) This is the Holy Land, 1961; (autobiog.) In Search of Greatness, 1962; (co-author) These are the Sacraments, 1963; (co-author) The Warren Court; Karsh Portfolio, 1967; Faces of our Time, 1971; Karsh Portraits, 1976. *Recreations:* tennis, bird-watching, archæology, music. *Address:* (business) Chateau Laurier Hotel, Suite 660, Ottawa, Canada. *T:* AC 613-236-7181; (home) Little Wings, Box 1931, Prescott Highway, Ottawa. *Clubs:* Garrick; Rideau (Ottawa); Century, Dutch Treat (NY).

KASER, Michael Charles, MA; Reader in Economics, University of Oxford, and Professorial Fellow of St Antony's College since 1972; *b* 2 May 1926; *er s* of Charles Joseph Kaser and Mabel Blunden; *m* 1954, Elisabeth Anne Mary, *er d* of Cyril Gascoigne Piggford; four *s* one *d. Educ:* King's Coll., Cambridge (Exhibr). Foreign Service, London and Moscow, 1947-51; UN Secretariat, Econ. Commn for Europe, Geneva, 1951-63; Faculty Fellow, St Antony's Coll., Oxford, 1963-72. Vis. Prof. of Econs, Univ. of Michigan, 1966; Vis. Lectr, Cambridge Univ., 1967-68 and 1977-78; Vis. Mem. Faculty, Institut européen d'Administration des Affaires, Fontainebleau, 1958-. Convenor/Chm., Nat. Assoc. for Soviet and East European Studies, 1965-73. Governor, Plater Coll., Oxford. Member: Council and Exec. Cttee, Internat. Econ. Assoc.; Council, Royal Econ. Soc.; Editorial Boards: Economic Jl; Soviet Studies, Jl Industrial Economics, Oxford Rev. of Educn, CUP East European Monograph Series; Steering Cttee, Königswinter Anglo-German Confs (Chm., Oxford Organizing Cttee). *Publications:* Comecon: Integration Problems of the Planned Economies, 1965, 2nd edn 1967; (ed) Economic Development for Eastern Europe, 1968; (with J. Zieliński) Planning in East Europe, 1970; Soviet Economics, 1970; (ed, with R. Portes) Planning and Market Relations, 1971; (ed, with H. Höhmann and K. Thalheim) The New Economic Systems of Eastern Europe, 1975; (ed, with A. Brown) The Soviet Union Since the Fall of Khrushchev, 1975, 2nd edn 1977; Health Care in the Soviet Union and Eastern Europe, 1976; papers in economic jls and symposia. *Address:* 7 Chadlington Road, Oxford. *T:* Oxford 55581. *Club:* Reform.

KASSANIS, Basil, OBE 1977; DSc (London), FRS 1966; retired; Senior Principal Scientific Officer, Department of Plant Pathology, Rothamsted Experimental Station, Harpenden, Herts, 1961-77; *b* 16 Oct. 1911; *s* of Zacharias and Helen Kassanis; *m* 1952, Jean Eleanor Matthews; one *s* one *d. Educ:* University of Thessaloniki, Greece. Came to Rothamsted Experimental Station as British Council scholar, 1938; appointed to staff, 1943. Research Medal, Royal Agricultural Soc., 1965. *Publications:* scientific papers in various jls.

Recreation: sculpture (local exhibns). *Address:* 3 Rosebery Avenue, Harpenden, Herts AL5 2QT. *T:* 5739.

KASTLER, Alfred; French physicist; Director, Atomic Clock Laboratory, Centre national de la Recherche Scientifique, since 1958 (Member, Management Board); *b* 3 May 1902; *s* of Frédéric Kastler and Anna (*née* Frey); *m* 1924, Elise Cosset; two *s* one *d. Educ:* Lycée Bartholdi, Colmar; Ecole Normale Supérieure. Taught in Lycées, Mulhouse, Colmar, Bordeaux, 1926-31; Asst at Faculty of Sciences, Bordeaux, 1931-36; Lecturer, Faculty of Science, University of Clermont-Ferrand, 1936-38; Prof., Faculty of Sciences, Bordeaux, 1938-41; Prof. of Physics: Ecole Normale Supérieure, Paris, 1941-68; University of Louvain, Belgium, 1953-54. Member: Institut de France; Académie Royale Flamande; Polish Acad. of Science; Deutsche Akademie der Wissenschaften zu Berlin; Akademie Leopoldina; Indian Acad. of Science. Hon. Member: Société Française de Physique; Optical Soc. of America; Polish Soc. of Physics. Hon. Doctorates: Louvain, Pisa, Oxford, Edinburgh, Quebec, Jerusalem, Belgrade, Bucharest. Holweck Medal and Prize, Phys. Soc., 1954; Nobel Prize for Physics, 1966. Officier de la Légion d'Honneur; Grand Officier de l'Ordre National du Mérite. *Address:* 1 Rue du Val-de-Grâce, Paris 5e, France.

KASTNER, Prof. Leslie James, MA, ScD Cantab, FIMechE; Professor of Mechanical Engineering, King's College, University of London, 1955-76; Dean of Faculty of Engineering, University of London, 1974-76; *b* 10 Dec. 1911; *o s* of late Professor Leon E. Kastner, sometime Prof. of French Language and Literature, University of Manchester, and of Elsie E. Kastner; *m* 1958, Joyce, *o d* of Lt-Col Edward Lillington, DSO, Belstone, Devon. *Educ:* Dreghorn Castle Sch.; Colinton, Midlothian; Highgate Sch.; Clare Coll., Cambridge (Mechanical Science Tripos). Apprenticeship with Davies and Metcalfe, Ltd, Locomotive Engineers, of Romiley, Stockport, 1930-31 and 1934-36; Development Engineer, 1936-38; Osborne Reynolds Research Fellowship, University of Manchester, 1938; Lectr in Engineering, University of Manchester, 1941-46; Senior Lectr, 1946-48; Prof. of Engineering, University Coll. of Swansea, University of Wales, 1948-55. Mem. of Council, Institution of Mechanical Engineers, 1954. FKC 1974. Graduates' Prize, InstMechE, 1939; Herbert Ackroyd Stuart Prize, 1943; Dugald Clerk Prize, 1956. *Publications:* various research papers in applied thermodynamics and fluid flow. *Address:* 37 St Anne's Road, Eastbourne. *Club:* National Liberal.

KATENGA-KAUNDA, Reid Willie; Malaŵi Independence Medal, 1964; Malaŵi Republic Medal, 1966; *b* 20 Aug. 1929; *s* of Gibson Amon Katenga Kaunda and Maggie Talengeske Nyabanda; *m* 1952, Elicy Nyabanda; one *s* three *d* (and one *s* one *d* decd). *Educ:* Ndola Govt Sch., Zambia; Inst. of Public Administration, Malaŵi; Trinity Coll., Oxford; Administrative Staff Coll., Henley. Sec., Nkhota Kota Rice Co-op. Soc. Ltd, 1952-62; Dist. Comr, Karonga, Malaŵi, 1964-65; Sen. Asst Sec., Min. of External Affairs, Zomba, Malaŵi, 1966; MP and Parly Sec., Office of the President and Cabinet, Malaŵi, 1966-68; Dep. Regional Chm., MCP, Northern Region, 1967-68; Under Sec., Office of the President and Cabinet, 1968-69; High Comr in London, 1969-70; Perm. Sec., Min. of Trade, Industry and Tourism, 1971-72; High Comr in London, 1972-73, and concurrently to the Holy See, Portugal, Belgium, Holland and France. Dep. Chm., Ncheu and Mchinji Inquiry Commn, 1967. *Recreations:* reading, walking, cinema, Association football. *Address:* c/o Ministry of External Affairs, Lilongwe, Malaŵi.

KATER, Sir Gregory (Blaxland), Kt 1974; CEng; Chairman, The Commercial Banking Company of Sydney Ltd, Australia; *b* 15 May 1912; *s* of late Hon. Sir Norman William Kater; *m* 1937, Catherine Mary Ferris-Scott; two *s* one *d. Educ:* The King's Sch., Sydney, Aust.; Cambridge Univ., Eng. (MA). Chartered Electrical Engineer; Grazier. Chairman: Electrical Equipment of Australia Ltd, 1939; Mercantile & General Reinsurance Co. of Aust. Ltd and Mercantile & General Life Reassurance Co. of Aust. Ltd, both 1957; Oil Search Ltd (Dir 1950, Chm. 1957); Permanent Trustee Co. Ltd (Dir 1951, Chm. 1956); Metal Manufactures Ltd (Dir, 1963, Chm. 1976); CSR Ltd (Dir 1949, Chm. 1977). Director: H. E. Kater & Son Pty Ltd, Merino Stud, 1948; Vickers Australia Ltd, 1965; Vickers Cockatoo Docks Pty Ltd, 1972; W. R. Carpenter Holdings Ltd, 1970. Vice-Pres., NSW Soc. for Crippled Children, 1950. Liveryman, Worshipful Co. of Broderers, London. *Recreation:* golf. *Address:* 106 Victoria Road, Bellevue Hill, NSW 2023, Australia. *T:* 36 7295. *Clubs:* Junior Carlton, London; Australian, Royal Sydney Golf, Union (all of Sydney, Aust.).

KATILUNGU, Simon Chikwanda; Chairman, Zambia Airways Corporation, Lusaka, since 1969, and Managing Director since 1973; *b* 1 Nov. 1924; *m* 1952, Anna Chileshe Mwango; two *s* four *d. Educ:* Munali Secondary Sch. and Jan. H. Hofmeyr Sch. of Social Work, Johannesburg, SA. Sen. Social Research Asst, 1952-60; Librarian, 1960-61; Politician, 1961-64; High Comr for Zambia in London, 1964-67; Resident Sec., Public Service of Zambia, 1967-69. Chairman: Youth Council, Zambia, 1969-; Zambia AAA, 1969-73; Zambia Library Service Adv. Council, 1969-71; Pres., Assoc. of African Airlines, 1972-73 (Mem. Exec. Cttee, 1969-); Mem. Exec. Cttee, Lusaka Chamber of Commerce and Industry, 1971-. *Recreations:* theatre and table tennis. *Address:* (home) 24 J Mwilwa Road, Lusaka, Zambia; (office) City Airport, Haile Selassie Avenue, Lusaka, Zambia.

KATIN, Peter Roy; Concert Pianist; *b* 14 Nov. 1930; *m* 1954, Eva Zweig; two *s. Educ:* Henry Thornton Sch.; Westminster Abbey; Royal Academy of Music. First London appearance at Wigmore Hall, 1948. A leading Chopin interpreter. Performances abroad include most European countries, West and East, S and E Africa, Japan, Canada, USA, Hong Kong, India, New Zealand, Singapore, Malaysia. Recordings, Decca, Everest, Unicorn, HMV, Philips, Lyrita, MFP. Currently writing book about Chopin. Mem. Incorporated Soc. of Musicians (ISM). FRAM, ARCM. *Recreations:* reading, writing, fishing, tape recording. *Address:* c/o Tower Music, 125 Tottenham Court Road, W1P 9HN. *T:* 01-387 4206.

KATO, Tadao; Japanese Ambassador to the Court of St James's, since 1975; *b* 13 May 1916; *m* 1946, Yoko; two *s . Educ:* Tokyo Univ.; Cambridge Univ. Joined Japanese Diplomatic Service 1939; Singapore, 1952; London, 1953; Counsellor, Economic Affairs Bureau, Min. of Foreign Affairs, 1956-69; Counsellor, Washington, 1959-63 (Vis. Fellow, Harvard, 1959-60); Dep. Dir, Econ. Affairs Bureau, Min. of Foreign Affairs, 1963-66, Dir, 1966-67; Ambassador to OECD, 1967-70, to Mexico, 1970-74. 1st Class Order of Aztec Star, Mexico, 1972. *Recreations:* golf, goh. *Address:* 23 Kensington Palace Gardens, W8. *Clubs:* Sunningdale Golf; Koganei Golf, Abiko Golf (Japan).

KATSINA, Emir of; *see* Nagogo, Alhaji Hon. Sir Usuman.

KATZ, Sir Bernard, Kt 1969; FRS 1952; Professor and Head of Biophysics Department, University College, London, since 1952; *b* Leipzig, 26 March 1911; *s* of M. N. Katz; *m* 1945, Marguerite, *d* of W. Penly, Sydney, Australia; two *s. Educ:* University of Leipzig (MD 1934). Biophysical research, University Coll., London, 1935-39; PhD London, and Beit Memorial Research Fellow, 1938; Carnegie Research Fellow, Sydney Hospital, Sydney, 1939-42; DSc London, 1943. Served War of 1939-45 in Pacific with RAAF, 1942-45; Flt-Lt, 1943. Asst Dir of Research, Biophysics Research Unit, University Coll., London, and Henry Head Research Fellow (Royal Society), 1946-50; Reader in Physiology, 1950-51. Lectures: Herter, Johns Hopkins Univ., 1958; Dunham, Harvard Coll., 1961; Croonian, Royal Society, 1961; Sherrington, Liverpool Univ., 1967. A Vice-Pres., Royal Society, 1965, Biological Secretary and Vice-President, 1968-76. Mem., Agric. Research Coun., 1967-77. Fellow of University Coll., London. FRCP, 1968. Hon. DSc: Southampton, 1971; Melbourne, 1971. Feldberg Foundation Award, 1965; Baly Medal, RCP, 1967; Copley Medal, Royal Society, 1967; Nobel Prize (jtly) for Physiology and Medicine, 1970. For. Member: Royal Danish Academy Science and Letters, 1968; Accad. Naz. Lincei, 1968; Amer. Acad. of Arts and Sciences, 1969; For. Assoc., Nat. Acad. of Scis, USA, 1976; Hon. Mem., Japanese Pharmacol. Soc., 1977. *Publications:* Electric Excitation of Nerve, 1939; Nerve, Muscle and Synapse, 1966; The Release of Neural Transmitter Substances, 1969; papers on nerve and muscle physiology in Jl of Physiol., Proc. Royal Society, etc. *Address:* University College, WC1E 6BT.

KATZ, Milton; Director, International Legal Studies, and Henry L. Stimson Professor of Law, Harvard University, since 1954; *b* 29 Nov. 1907; *m* 1933, Vivian Greenberg; three *s. Educ:* Harvard Univ. AB 1927; JD 1931. Anthropological Expedition across Central Africa for Peabody Museum, Harvard, 1927-28; Mem. of Bar since 1932; various official posts, US Government, 1932-39; Prof. of Law, Harvard Univ., 1940-50; served War of 1939-45, with War Production Board and as US Executive Officer, Combined Production and Resources Board, 1941-43; thereafter Lt-Comdr, USNR, until end of war; Dep. US Special Representative in Europe with rank of Ambassador, 1949-50; Chief US Delegation, Economic Commission for Europe, and US Mem., Defense Financial and Economic Cttee under North Atlantic Treaty, 1950-51; Ambassador of the United States and US Special Representative in Europe for ECA, 1950-51; Associate Dir, Ford Foundation, 1951-54, and Consultant, 1954-66. Dir, Internat. Program in Taxation, 1961-63. Consultant, US Office of Technology Assessment, 1974-; Chm., Energy Adv. Cttee, 1975-. Fellow Amer. Acad. of Arts and

Sciences (Councilor); Trustee: Carnegie Endowment for Internat. Peace (Chm. Bd); World Peace Foundation (Exec. Cttee); Citizens Research Foundation (Pres.); Inter American Univ. Foundation; Brandeis Univ.; Case Western Reserve Univ.; International Legal Center (Chm. Bd); Director, Internat. Friendship League; Member: Corp., Boston Museum of Science; Cttee on Foreign Affairs Personnel, 1961-63; Case Inst. of Technology Western Reserve Univ. Study Commn, 1966-67; Panel on Technology Assessment, Nat. Acad. of Sciences, 1968-69; Cttee on Life Sciences and Social Policy, Nat. Research Council, 1968- (Chm.); Vis. Cttee for Humanities, MIT, 1970-73; Adv. Bd Energy Laboratory, MIT, 1974-. Sherman Fairchild Dist. Schol., Cal. Tech., 1974. John Danz Lectr, Univ. of Washington, 1974. Hon LLD Brandeis, 1972. Legion of Merit (US Army), 1945; Commendation Ribbon (US Navy), 1945. *Publications:* Cases and Materials on Administrative Law, 1947; Government under Law and the Individual (co-author and editor), 1957; The Law of International Transactions and Relations (with Kingman Brewster, Jr), 1960; The Things That are Caesar's, 1966; The Relevance of International Adjudication, 1968; The Modern Foundation: its dual nature, public and private, 1968; Man's Impact on the Global Environment (contrib, with others), 1970; (ed) Federal Regulation of Campaign Finance, 1972; Assessing Biomedical Technologies (with others), 1975; articles in legal, business and other jls. *Address:* (business) Harvard Law Sch., Cambridge, Mass, USA; (home) 6 Berkeley Street, Cambridge, Mass, USA.

KATZ, Mindru; concert pianist; *b* 3 June 1925; *s* of Bernard Katz and Olga Avramescu; single. *Educ:* Bucharest Royal Academy of Music (under Florica Musicescu). Gave first public recital, 1931; first concert with Bucharest Philharmonic Orchestra, 1947. Subsequently, concert tours in all the continents. Has made numerous recordings. Prizewinner, International Piano Competitions, Berlin, Prague, 1951 and Bucharest, 1953. Emeritus Artist, Rumania, 1953; First Class State Prize, Rumanian People's Republic, 1954. *Recreations:* mountaineering, chess, films, drawing. *Address:* c/o Ibbs & Tillett, 124 Wigmore Street, W1H OAX; 45 Hanassi Street, Nof-Yam, Israel. *T:* 932415.

KATZIN, Olga, Journalist; Pen-name Sagittarius; *b* London, 9 July 1896; *d* of John and Mathilde Katzin; *m* 1921, Hugh Miller, actor; two *s* one *d. Educ:* Privately. *Publications:* Troubadours, 1925; A Little Pilgrim's Peeps at Parnassus, 1927; Sagittarius Rhyming, 1940; London Watches, 1941; Targets, 1943; Quiver's Choice, 1945; Let Cowards Flinch, 1947; Pipes of Peace, 1949; Up the Poll, 1950; Strasbourg Geese and Other Verses, 1953; Unaida (with Michael Barsley), play, 1957; The Perpetual Pessimist (with Daniel George), 1963. *Address:* 23 Manor House, Marylebone Road, NW1.

KATZIR, Prof. Ephraim, PhD; President, State of Israel, since 1973; *b* Kiev, Ukraine, 16 May 1916; *s* of Yehuda Katchalski and Tsila Katchalski; *m* 1938, Nina Gotlieb; one *s* one *d . Educ:* Rehavia High Sch., Jerusalem; Hebrew Univ., Jerusalem (chemistry, botany, zool., bacteriol.; MSc *summa cum laude* 1937; PhD 1941). Settled in Israel with parents, 1922; involved in Labour youth movement; Inf. Comdr, Jewish Self-Defence Forces (Hagana). Asst, Dept of Theoretical and Macromolecular Chem., Hebrew Univ., 1941-45; Res. Fellow, Polytechnic Inst., and Columbia Univ., NY, 1946-48; Actg Head, Dept of Biophys., Weizmann Inst. of Science, Rehovot, Israel, 1949-51, Head 1951-73 (mem. founding faculty of Inst.); Chief Scientist, Israel Def. Min., 1966-68. Vis. Professor: (of Biophys.), Hebrew Univ., 1953-61; Rockefeller Univ., NY, and Univ. of Mich, Ann Arbor, 1961-65; Battelle Seattle Res. Center, Washington, 1971. Guest Scientist, Harvard Univ., 1957-59; Sen. Foreign Scientist Fellowship, Univ. of Calif, LA, 1964. Member: Bd of Governors, Hebrew Univ.; Biochem. Soc. of Israel; Israel Acad. of Sciences and Humanities; Israel Chem. Soc.; Council, Internat. Union of Biochem.; Scientific Adv. Panel, Ciba Foundn; AAAS; Assoc. of Harvard Chemists; Leopoldina Acad. of Science, Germany; World Acad. of Art and Science; New York Acad. of Science (Life Mem.). Centennial Foreign Fellow, Amer. Chem. Soc.; For. Associate, Nat. Acad. of Sciences of USA. For. Member: Royal Soc.; Amer. Philosoph. Soc. Hon. Member: Amer. Acad. of Arts and Sciences; Amer. Soc. of Biol Chemists; Harvey Soc. Hon. Prof., Polytechnic Inst. of New York, 1975. Hon. Dr: Hebrew Univ., 1973; Brandeis Univ., Univ. of Mich, and Hebrew Union Coll., 1975; Weizmann Inst. of Science, 1976. Tchernikhovski Prize, 1948; Weizmann Prize, 1950; Israel Prize in Nat. Sciences, 1959; Rothschild Prize in Nat. Sciences, 1961; Linderstrøm Lang Gold Medal, 1969; Hans Krebs Medal, 1972. Adv. Editor: (series) Molecular Biol., Biochem and Biophys.; Progress in Surface and Membrane Science; Jl of Life Sciences. Mem. Editorial Board: Biopolymers; Eur. Jl of Biochem.; Excerpta Medica; Analyt. Biochem.;

(series) Advances in Exper. Medicine and Biol. *Address:* President's Residence, 3 Hanassi Street, Jerusalem, Israel.

KAUFFMANN, C. Michael, MA, PhD; Keeper, Department of Prints & Drawings and Paintings, Victoria and Albert Museum, since 1975; *b* 5 Feb. 1931; *s* of Arthur and Tamara Kauffmann; *m* 1954, Dorothea (*née* Hill); two *s*. *Educ*: St Paul's Sch.; Merton Coll., Oxford (Postmaster); Warburg Inst., London Univ. (Jun. Research Fellow). Asst Curator, Photographic Collection, Warburg Inst., 1957-58; Keeper, Manchester City Art Gall., 1958-60; Asst Keeper, Dept of Prints & Drawings and Paintings, Victoria and Albert Museum, 1960-75, and Asst to the Director, 1963-66; Visiting Associate Prof., Univ. of Chicago, 1969. *Publications:* The Baths of Pozzuoli: medieval illuminations of Peter of Eboli's poem, 1959; The Legend of St Ursula, 1964; An Altar-piece of the Apocalypse, 1968; Victoria & Albert Museum: catalogue of foreign paintings, 1973; British Romanesque Manuscripts 1066-1190, 1975; exhibn catalogues; articles in art historical jls. *Address:* 53 Twyford Avenue, W3 9PZ. *T:* 01-992 6050.

KAUFMAN, Gerald Bernard; MP (Lab) Manchester, Ardwick, since 1970; Minister of State, Department of Industry, since 1975; *b* 21 June 1930; *s* of Louis and Jane Kaufman. *Educ:* Leeds Grammar Sch.; The Queen's Coll., Oxford. Asst Gen.-Sec., Fabian Soc., 1954-55; Political Staff, Daily Mirror, 1955-64; Political Correspondent, New Statesman, 1964-65; Parly Press Liaison Officer, Labour Party, 1965-70. Parly Under-Sec. of State, DoE, 1974-75, Dept of Industry, 1975. *Publications:* (jtly) How to Live Under Labour, 1964; (ed) The Left, 1966; To Build the Promised Land, 1973; *Recreations:* travel, going to the pictures. *Address:* 87 Charlbert Court, Eamont Street, NW8. *T:* 01-722 6264.

KAULBACK, Ronald John Henry, OBE 1946; *b* 23 July 1909; *er s* of late Lieutenant-Colonel Henry Albert Kaulback, OBE, and Alice Mary, *d* of late Rev. A. J. Townend, CF; *m* 1940, Audrey Elizabeth, 3rd *d* of late Major H. R. M. Howard-Sneyd, OBE; two *s* two *d*. *Educ:* Rugby; Pembroke Coll., Cambridge. In 1933 journeyed through Assam and Eastern Tibet with Kingdon Ward; returned to Tibet, 1935, accompanied by John Hanbury-Tracy, spending eighteen months there in an attempt to discover source of Salween River; 1938 spent eighteen months in Upper Burma hunting and collecting zoological specimens for the British Museum (Natural History); Murchison Grant of Royal Geog. Society, 1937. *Publications:* Tibetan Trek, 1934; Salween, 1938. *Recreations:* shooting, schnorkeling. *Address:* Ardnagashel House, Bantry, Co. Cork, Eire. *T:* Bantry 209. *Clubs:* Naval and Military, Special Forces.

KAUNDA, (David) Kenneth; President of Zambia, since Oct. 1964 (Prime Minister, N Rhodesia, Jan.-Oct. 1964); Chancellor of the University of Zambia since 1966; *b* 28 April 1924; *s* of late David Julizgia and Hellen Kaunda, Missionaries; *m* 1946, Betty Banda; seven *s* two *d*. *Educ:* Lubwa Training Sch.; Munali Secondary Sch. Teacher, Lubwa Training Sch., 1943-44, Headmaster, 1944-47; Boarding Master, Mufulira Upper Sch., 1948-49. African National Congress: District Sec., 1950-52; Provincial Organising Sec., 1952-53; Sec.-Gen., 1953-58; Nat. Pres., Zambia African Nat. Congress, 1958-59; Nat. Pres., United Nat. Independence Party, 1960; Chm., Pan-African Freedom Movement for East, Central and South Africa, 1962; Minister of Local Government and Social Welfare, N Rhodesia, 1962-63. Chm., Organization of African Unity, 1970. Hon. Doctor of Laws: Fordham Univ., USA, 1963; Dublin Univ., 1964; University of Sussex, 1965; Windsor Univ., Canada, 1966; University of Chile, 1966; Univ. of Zambia, 1974; DUniv York, 1966. *Publications:* Black Government, 1961; Zambia Shall Be Free, 1962; Humanist in Africa, 1966; Humanism in Zambia and its implementation, 1967; Letter to My Children. *Recreations:* music, table tennis, football, draughts, gardening and reading. *Address:* State House, PO Box 135, Lusaka, Zambia.

KAUNDA, Reid Willie K.; see Katenga-Kaunda.

KAUNTZE, Ralph, MBE 1944; MD; FRCP; Physician to Guy's Hospital, 1948-71, Consultant Physician Emeritus since 1971; Senior Consultant Physician: Commercial Assurance Co. Ltd; British & European Assurance Co.; European Assurance Co Ltd; *b* 5 June 1911; *s* of Charles Kauntze and Edith, *d* of Ralph Bagley; *m* 1935, Katharine Margaret, *yr d* of late Ramsay Moodie; two *s* one *d*. *Educ:* Canford Sch.; Emmanuel Coll., Cambridge; St George's Hosp., London. William Brown Sen. Schol., St George's Hosp. 1932; MRCS, LRCP 1935; MA, MB, BCh Cantab 1937; MRCP 1939; MD Cantab 1946; FRCP 1950. Served, 1939-45, RAMC, chiefly Mediterranean area, Lt-Col O i/c Med. Div. Asst Dir of Dept of Med., Guy's Hosp., 1947-48, Physician to Cardiac Dept, 1956-71; Cons. Phys. to High

Wycombe War Memorial Hosp., 1948-50; Dir Asthma Clinic, 1948-52, and of Dept of Student Health, 1950-63, Guy's Hosp.; Physician to Royal Masonic Hospital, 1963-76. Hon. Vis. Phys., Johns Hopkins Hosp., Baltimore, 1958. Examiner in Medicine: RCP; London Univ. Mem. Brit. Cardiac Soc.; Mem. Assoc. of Physicians. *Publications:* contrib. med. jls. *Recreations:* farming, walking. *Address:* Blewbury Manor, near Didcot, Oxon. *T:* Blewbury 850246.

KAVANAGH, P. J., (Patrick Joseph Gregory Kavanagh); writer; *b* 6 Jan. 1931; *s* of H. E. (Ted) Kavanagh and Agnes O'Keefe; *m* 1st, 1956, Sally Philipps (*d* 1958); 2nd, 1965, Catherine Ward; two *s*. *Educ:* Douai Sch.; Lycee Jaccard, Lausanne; Merton Coll., Oxford (MA). British Council, 1957-59; acting (stage, TV, films); journalism. *Publications:* poems: One and One, 1960; On the Way to the Depot, 1967; About Time, 1970; Edward Thomas in Heaven, 1974; novels: A Song and Dance, 1968; A Happy Man, 1972; *autobiog.:* The Perfect Stranger, 1966; *for children:* Scarf Jack, 1978. *Recreation:* walking. *Address:* Sparrowthorn, Elkstone, Cheltenham, Glos.

KAVANAGH, Patrick Bernard, CBE 1977; QPM 1974; Deputy Commissioner, Metropolitan Police, since 1977; *b* 18 March 1923; *s* of late Michael Kavanagh and late Violet Kavanagh (*née* Duncan); *m* Beryl, *er d* of late Lt-Comdr Richard Owen Williams, RNR and Annie (*née* McShiells); one *s* two *d*. *Educ:* St Aloysius Coll., Glasgow. Rifle Bde, 1941-43; Para. Regt, 1943-46 (Lieut). Manchester City Police (Constable to Supt), 1946-64; Asst Chief Constable, Cardiff City Police, 1964-69; Asst and Dep. Chief Constable, S Wales Constabulary, 1969-73; Asst Comr (Traffic), Metropolitan Police, 1974-77. *Recreations:* cricket, swimming, music, crosswords. *Address:* New Scotland Yard, Broadway, SW1. *T:* 01-230 1212.

KAY, Sir Andrew Watt, Kt 1973; Regius Professor of Surgery, University of Glasgow, since 1964; part-time Chief Scientist, Scottish Home and Health Department, since 1973; *b* 14 Aug. 1916; of Scottish parentage; *m* 1943, Janetta M. Roxburgh; two *s* two *d*. *Educ:* Ayr Academy; Glasgow Univ. MB, ChB (Hons) with Brunton Memorial Prize, 1939; FRCSEd 1947; FRFPSG 1956 (Pres. 1972-); FRCS 1960; FRCSGlas 1967; FRSE 1971; MD (Hons) with Bellahouston Gold Medal, 1944; Major Royal Army Medical Corps i/c Surgical Div., Millbank Military Hospital, 1946-48; ChM (Hons) 1949; Consultant Surgeon in charge of Wards, Western Infirmary, Glasgow, 1956-58; Asst to Regius Prof. of Surgery, Glasgow Univ., 1942-56; Prof. of Surgery, University of Sheffield, 1958-64. Sims Travelling Prof., Australasia, 1969; McLaughlin Foundn Edward Gallie Vis. Prof., Canada, 1970. Pres., Surgical Research Soc., 1969-71. Member: Royal Commission on Medical Education, 1965-68; MRC, 1967-71; Hon. Mem., The N Pacific Surgical Assoc. FRACS 1970; FRCSCan 1972; FCS(SoAf) 1972; Hon. Fellow: Norwegian Surgical Assoc., Belgian Surgical Soc.; Amer. Surg. Assoc., 1972; Hon. FACS, 1973. Hon. DSc: Leicester, 1973; Sheffield, 1975. Cecil Joll Prize, RCS, 1969; Gordon-Taylor Lectureship and Medal, 1970. *Publications:* (with R. A. Jamieson, FRCS) Textbook of Surgical Physiology, 1959 (2nd edn 1964); several papers in medical and surgical jls on gastroenterological subjects. *Recreation:* gardening. *Address:* Ormidale, Grange Avenue, Milngavie, Glasgow G62 8AQ. *T:* 041-956 3378.

KAY, Air Vice-Marshal Cyril Eyton, CB 1958; CBE 1947; DFC 1940; retired as Chief of Air Staff, with the rank of Air Vice-Marshal, RNZAF (1956-58); *b* 25 June 1902; *s* of David Kay and Mary, *d* of Edward Drury Butts; *m* 1932, Florence, *d* of Frank Armfield; two *d*. *Educ:* Auckland, NZ. Joined RAF, 1926, 5 years Short Service Commn; joined RNZAF, 1935, Permanent Commn. As Flying Officer: flew London-Sydney in Desoutter Light aeroplane, 1930 (with Flying Off. H. L. Piper as Co-pilot); first New Zealanders to accomplish this flight; also, as Flying Off. flew a De Havilland-Dragon Rapide (with Sqdn Ldr J. Hewett) in London-Melbourne Centenary Air Race, 1934; then continued over Tasman Sea to New Zealand (first direct flight England-New Zealand). Comdg Officer No 75 (NZ) Sqdn "Wellington" Bombers stationed Feltwell, Norfolk, England, 1940; Air Board Mem. for Supply, RNZAF, 1947; AOC, RNZAF, London HQ, 1950; Air Board Mem. for Personnel, 1953. *Publication:* The Restless Sky, 1964. *Recreation:* golf. *Clubs:* Royal Air Force; Officers' (Wellington, NZ).

KAY, Ernest, FRGS; Director-General, International Biographical Center, New York, since 1976; *b* 21 June 1915; *s* of Harold and Florence Kay; *m* 1941, Marjorie Peover; two *s* one *d*. *Educ:* Spring Bank Central Sch., Darwen, Lancs. Reporter, Darwen News, 1931-34; Ashton-under-Lyne Reporter, 1934-38; Industrial Corresp., Manchester Guardian and Evening News, 1938-41; The Star, London, 1941-47; London Editor,

Wolverhampton Express and Star, 1947-52, Managing Editor, 1952-54; Managing Editor, London Evening News, 1954-57; Editor and Publisher, John O'London's, 1957-61; Managing Editor, Time and Tide, 1961-67; Founder of Internat. Biographical Centre, Cambridge, and Dir-Gen., 1967-76. Chairman: Kay Sons and Daughter Ltd, 1967-77; Dartmouth Chronicle Group Ltd, 1968-77; Pres., Melrose Press Ltd, 1970-77. FRSA 1967; FRGS 1975. Hon. DLitt Karachi, 1967; Hon. PhD Hong Kong, 1976. Emperor Haile Selassie Gold Medal, 1971. Key to City of: Las Vegas, 1972; New York, 1975. Gold Medal, Ordre Supreme Imperial Orthodoxe, Constantinian de Saint-Georges (Greece), 1977. *Publications:* Great Men of Yorkshire, 1956, 2nd edn 1960; Isles of Flowers: the story of the Isles of Scilly, 1956, 3rd edn 1977; Pragmatic Premier: an intimate portrait of Harold Wilson, 1967; The Wit of Harold Wilson, 1967; Editor, Dictionary of International Biography, 1967-; Dictionary of Caribbean Biography, 1970-; Dictionary of African Biography, 1970-; Dictionary of Scandinavian Biography, 1972-; International Who's Who in Poetry, 1970-; World Who's Who of Women, 1973-; International Who's Who in Music, 1975-; International Authors and Writers Who's Who, 1976-; Women in Education, 1977-. *Recreations:* reading, writing, music, watching cricket, travel. *Address:* Orcheston, 11 Madingley Road, Cambridge CB3 0EG. *T:* Cambridge 63893. *Clubs:* Surrey CCC; Derbyshire CCC; Rolls Royce Owners'; National Arts (New York City).

KAY, Dr Harry, PhD; Vice-Chancellor, University of Exeter, since 1973; *b* 22 March 1919; *s* of late Williamson T. Kay; *m* 1941, Gwendolen Diana, *d* of Charles Edward Maude; one *s* one *d. Educ:* Rotherham Grammar Sch.; Trinity Hall, Cambridge (1938-39, 1946-51). Research with Nuffield Unit into Problems to Ageing, Cambridge, 1948-51; Psychologist of Naval Arctic Expedition, 1949. Lecturer in Experimental Psychology, Univ. of Oxford, 1951-59; Prof. of Psychology, Univ. of Sheffield, 1960-73. Visiting Scientist, National Institutes of Health, Washington, DC, 1957-58. Pro-Vice-Chancellor, University of Sheffield, 1967-71. Pres., British Psychological Soc., 1971-72. Hon. Director: MRC Unit, Dept of Psychology, Sheffield; Nat. Centre of Programmed Instruction for Industry, Sheffield. Member: SSRC, 1970-73; MRC, 1975-77 (Chm., Environmental Medicine Res. Policy Cttee, 1975-77); CNAA; Open Univ. Acad. Adv. Cttee; BBC Further Educn Adv. Cttee; Nuffield Foundn Social Studies Adv. Cttee; NATO Human Factors Panel, 1972-75. Vernon Prize, 1962. *Publication:* (with B. Dodd and M. Sime) Teaching Machines and Programmed Instruction, 1968. *Address:* The University, Exeter, Devon EX4 4QJ.

KAY, Humphrey Edward Melville, MD, FRCP, FRCPath; Haematologist, Royal Marsden Hospital, since 1956; *b* 10 Oct. 1923; *s* of late Rev. Arnold Innes and Winifred Julia Kay; *m* 1950, April Grace Lavinia Powlett; one *s* two *d. Educ:* Bryanston Sch.; St Thomas's Hospital. MB, BS 1945. RAFVR, 1947-49; junior appts at St Thomas's Hosp., 1950-56. Sec., MRC Cttee on Leukaemia, 1968-; Dean, Inst. of Cancer Research, 1970-72. Editor, Jl Clinical Pathology, 1972-. *Publications:* papers and chapters on blood diseases, etc. *Recreation:* natural history including gardening. *Address:* 15 Earls Court Gardens, SW5.

KAY, John Menzies, MA, PhD, CEng, FIMechE; Director, GSK Steel Developments Ltd, since 1976; *b* 4 Sept. 1920; *s* of John Aiton Kay and Isabel Kay (*née* Menzies). *Educ:* Sherborne Sch.; Trinity Hall Cambridge. University Demonstrator in Chemical Engineering, Cambridge University, 1948; Chief Technical Engineer, Division of Atomic Energy Production, Risley, 1952; Prof. of Nuclear Power, Imperial Coll. of Science and Technology, University of London, 1956; Dir of Engineering Development, Tube Investments Ltd, 1961; Chief Engineer, Richard Thomas & Baldwins Ltd, 1965; Dir-in-charge, Planning Div., BSC, 1968-70; Dir of Engrng, Strip Mills Div., BSC, 1970-76. Mem., Nuclear Safety Adv. Cttee, 1960-76. *Publications:* Fluid Mechanics and Heat Transfer, 1963; contribs to Proc. of Institution of Mechanical Engineers. *Recreations:* mountaineering, music. *Address:* Church Farm, St Briavels, near Lydney, Glos. *Clubs:* Alpine, United Oxford & Cambridge University.

KAY, Jolyon Christopher; HM Diplomatic Service; Economic Counsellor, Jedda, since 1974; *b* 19 Sept. 1930; *s* of Colin Mardall Kay and Gertrude Fanny Kay; *m* 1956, Shirley Mary Clarke; two *s* two *d. Educ:* Charterhouse; St John's Coll., Cambridge (BA). Chemical Engr, Albright and Wilson, 1954; UKAEA, Harwell, 1958; Battelle Inst., Geneva, 1961; Foreign Office, London, 1964; MECAS, 1965; British Interests Section, Swiss Embassy, Algiers, 1967; Head of Chancery and Information Adviser, Political Residency, Bahrain, 1968; FCO, 1970. *Recreations:* acting, skiing, croquet. *Address:* c/o Foreign

and Commonwealth Office, SW1; Double Doors, Blewbury, Oxfordshire. *T:* Blewbury 850240. *Clubs:* National Liberal; Harwell Croquet.

KAY, Maj.-Gen. Patrick Richard, CB 1972; MBE 1945; RM retired; Director of Naval Security, Ministry of Defence, since 1974; *b* 1 Aug. 1921; *y s* of late Dr and Mrs A. R. Kay, Blakeney, Norfolk; *m* 1944, Muriel Austen Smith; three *s* one *d. Educ:* Eastbourne Coll. Commissioned in Royal Marines, 1940; HMS Renown, 1941-43; 4 Commando Bde, 1944-45; Combined Ops HQ, 1945-48; Staff of Commandant-Gen., Royal Marines, 1948-50 and 1952-54; Staff Coll., Camberley, 1951; 40 Commando, RM, 1954-57; Joint Services Amphibious Warfare Centre, 1957-59; Plans Div., Naval Staff, 1959-62; CO, 43 Commando, RM, 1963-65; CO, Amphibious Training Unit, RM, 1965-66; Asst Dir (Jt Warfare) Naval Staff, 1966-67; Asst Chief of Staff to Comdt-Gen. RM, 1968; IDC, 1969; C of S to Comdt-Gen., RM, 1970-74, retired 1974. *Recreation:* golf. *Address:* Halfway, Church Lane, Ewshot, Farnham, Surrey.

KAY, Sydney Entwisle, CBE 1948 (MBE 1918); *b* 18 July 1888. *Educ:* Sutton Valence Sch.; Emmanuel Coll., Cambridge (First Class Hons Mediæval and Modern Languages Tripos). Vice-Consul in Consular Service, 1911; Consul at Stockholm, 1920; Consul-General: Lourenço Marques, 1933-39; Milan, 1939-40; Commercial Counsellor, Lisbon, 1940; Consul-Gen. at Marseilles, 1944; retired, 1948. *Address:* Residence Leclos de Cimiez, Bloc D2, 31 Avenue Cap de Croix, 06 Nice, France.

KAY, Very Rev. William, DSO 1919; MC, MA; Provost of Blackburn Cathedral, 1936-61; *e s* of William Henry Kay, Withnell, Chorley, Lancs; *m* Helen Nora (*d* 1974), *d* of late Edgar Brierley, Sandfield, Rochdale; four *d. Educ:* Hatfield Coll.; Durham Univ. Late 1st Batt. The Grenadier Guards, and 2nd Batt. The Manchester Regt. (MC and two bars, DSO); Vicar of Cresswell, Derbyshire, 1922-28; Rural Dean of Bolsover, 1928; Rector of Whitwell with Steetley, 1928-29; Vicar of Newark, 1929-36; Hon. Canon of Southwell, 1932-36; Rural Dean of Newark, 1933-36. *Address:* Woodruffe, Brockenhurst, Hants. *T:* 2196.

KAY-SHUTTLEWORTH, family name of **Baron Shuttleworth.**

KAYE, Danny, (Daniel Kominski); Actor (Stage, Film, TV, and Radio); *b* New York, NY, 18 Jan.; *s* of Jacob Kominski and Clara Nemorovsky; *m* 1940, Sylvia Fine, producer, lyricist and composer; one *d*. Official Permanent Ambassador-at-Large for UNICEF (first award for Internat. Distingushed Service). Scopus Laureate, 1977. Played in Straw Hat Review, Ambassador Theatre, New York City, 1939; Lady in the Dark, 1940; Let's Face It, 1941; appeared London Palladium, also provincial tour, Great Britain, 1949; London Palladium, 1955. Has had weekly television show (CBS), 1963-67. Instituted annual 'Look In' for Children, Metropolitan Opera, NYC. Since 1943 has appeared successfully in films, including: Up In Arms, 1943; Wonder Man, 1944; Kid from Brooklyn, 1945; The Secret Life of Walter Mitty, 1946; That's Life, 1947; A Song is Born, 1949; The Inspector-General, 1950; On the Riviera, 1951; Hans Christian Andersen, 1952; Knock on Wood, 1954; White Christmas, 1954; The Court Jester, 1956; Merry Andrew, 1957; Me And The Colonel, 1958; Five Pennies, 1959; On the Double, 1960; The Man from The Diner's Club, 1963; The Madwoman of Chaillot, 1968; *Play:* Two by Two, NY, 1970. *Address:* Box 750, Beverly Hills, Calif, USA.

KAYE, Col Douglas Robert Beaumont, DSO 1942 (Bar 1945); DL; JP; *b* 18 Nov. 1909; *s* of late Robert Walter Kaye, JP, Great Glenn Manor, Leics; *m* 1946, Florence Audrey Emma, *d* of late Henry Archibald Bellville, Tedstone Court, Bromyard, Herefordshire; one *s* one *d. Educ:* Harrow. 2nd Lieut Leicestershire Yeo., 1928; 2nd Lieut 10th Royal Hussars, 1931. Served War of 1939-45: Jerusalem, 1939-41; Cairo and HQ 30 Corps, 1941-42; Lieut-Col comdg 10th Royal Hussars, Africa and Italy, 1943-46 (despatches twice). Bde Major, 30 Lowland Armd Bde (TA), 1947-49; Lieut-Col comdg 16th/5th Queen's Royal Lancers, 1949-51; AA & QMG 56 London Armd Div. (TA), 1952-54; Col Comdt and Chief Instructor, Gunnery Sch., RAC Centre, 1954-56; retd 1956. Master of Newmarket and Thurlow Foxhounds, 1957-59. DL 1963, JP 1961, High Sheriff 1971, Cambridgeshire and Isle of Ely. Mem., Newmarket RDC, 1959-74 (Chm., 1972-74), E Cambridgeshire DC, 1974. *Recreations:* hunting, shooting. *Address:* Brinkley Hall, near Newmarket, Suffolk. *T:* Stetchworth 202. *Club:* Cavalry and Guards.

KAYE, Elaine Hilda; Headmistress, Oxford High School, GPDST, since 1972; *b* 21 Jan. 1930; *d* of late Rev. Harold Sutcliffe Kaye and Kathleen Mary (*née* White). *Educ:* Bradford

Girls' Grammar Sch.; Milton Mount Coll.; St Anne's Coll., Oxford. Assistant Mistress: Leyton County High Sch., 1952-54; Queen's Coll., Harley Street, 1954-59; South Hampstead High Sch., GPDST, 1959-65; Part-time Tutor, Westminster Tutors, 1965-67; Dep. Warden, Missenden Abbey Adult Coll., 1967-72. *Publications:* History of the King's Weigh House Church, 1968; History of Queen's College, Harley St, 1972; Short History of Missenden Abbey, 1973. *Recreations:* music, walking, conversation. *Address:* 20 Rowland Close, Wolvercote, Oxford OX2 8PW. *T:* Oxford 53917.

KAYE, Sir Emmanuel, Kt 1974; CBE 1967; Founder and Chairman of The Kaye Organisation Ltd, since 1966; Joint Founder and Governing Director (with J. R. Sharp, died 1965), of Lansing Bagnall Ltd, since 1943; *b* 29 Nov. 1914; *m* 1946, Elizabeth Cutler; one *s* two *d. Educ:* Richmond Hill Sch.; Twickenham Technical Coll. Founded J. E. Shay Ltd, Precision Gauge, Tool and Instrument Makers, and took over Lansing Bagnall & Co. of Isleworth, 1943; then founded Lansing Bagnall Ltd (all with late J. R. Sharp). Transf. to Basingstoke, 1949 (from being smallest manufr of electric lift trucks, became largest in Europe). Royal Warrant as supplier of Industrial Trucks to Royal Household, 1971; Queen's Awards for Export Achievement in 1969, 1970 and 1971 and only co. to win Queen's Awards for both Export Achievement and Technological Innovation, 1972; Design Council Award, 1974; winners of Gold and other Continental Awards. Chairmanships include: Industrial Modernisation Ltd, 1953-76; Lansing Bagnall International Ltd, Switzerland, 1957-; Fork Truck Rentals, 1961-; Lansing Leasing Ltd, 1962-; Elvetham Hall Ltd, 1965-; Lansing Bagnall AG, Switzerland, 1966-; Lansing GmbH, Germany, 1966-; Pool & Sons (Hartley Wintney) Ltd, 1967-; Hubbard Bros Ltd, 1969-; Regentruck Ltd, 1969-; Hawkington Ltd, 1972-; L. B. Components Ltd, 1973-77; Wigan Engineering Ltd, 1973-; Hadley Contract Hire Ltd, 1973-; Lansing Bagnall (Northern) Ltd, 1974-; Lansing Bagnall Inc., 1974-; Henley Forklift Gp, 1976-; Lansing Henley Ltd; 1977-; Lansing Ltd, 1977-. Worshipful Co. of Farriers, 1953; Freeman of City of London, 1954; founded Unquoted Companies' Gp, 1968; Member: CBI Taxation Cttee, 1970-; Council of Industry for Management Educn, 1970-; Export Guarantees Adv. Council, 1971-74; Inflation Accounting Cttee, 1974-75; CBI Wealth Tax Panel, 1974-; Queen's Award Review Cttee, 1975; CBI President's Cttee, 1976-; CBI Council, 1976-; Reviewing Cttee on Export of Works of Art, 1977-. Visiting Fellow, Univ. of Lancaster, 1970-. Governor: Girls' High Sch., Basingstoke, 1955-70; Queen Mary's Coll., Basingstoke, 1971-75. Trustee, Glyndebourne, 1977-. Fellow, Psionic Medical Soc., 1977-. *Recreations:* art, chess, music, ski-ing. *Address:* The Croft, Hartley Wintney, Hampshire RG27 8HT; 25 St James's Place, SW1 1NP.

KAYE, Geoffrey John; *b* 14 Aug. 1935; *s* of Michael and Golda Kaye; *m* 1968, Susan Ruth Pinkus; one *d. Educ:* Christ College, Finchley. Started with Pricerite Ltd when business was a small private company controlling six shops, 1951; apptd Manager (aged 18) of one of Pricerite Ltd stores, 1953; Supervisor, Pricerite Ltd, 1955; Controller of all stores in Pricerite Ltd Gp, 1958; Director, 1963; Chairman and Man. Dir, 1966-73. Mem. Cttee, British Assoc. Monte Carlo. *Recreations:* football, athletics, golf. *Address:* Apartment 19A, L'Estoril, Avenue Princesse Grace, Monte Carlo, Monaco. *Club:* Monte Carlo Country.

KAYE, Sir John Christopher L.; *see* Lister-Kaye.

KAYE, Sir Stephen Henry Gordon, 3rd Bt, *cr* 1923; *b* 24 March 1917; *s* of Sir Henry Gordon Kaye, 2nd Bt and Winifred (*d* 1971), *d* of late Walter H. Scales, Verwood, Bradford; *S* father 1956. *Heir:* brother David Alexander Gordon Kaye [*b* 26 July 1919; *m* 1st, 1942, Elizabeth (marr. diss. 1950), *o d* of Capt. Malcolm Hurtley, Baynards Manor, Horsham, Sussex; 2nd, 1955, Adelle, *d* of Denis Thomas, Brisbane, Queensland; two *s* four *d*]. *Address:* Mortimore's, New Buildings, Sandford, near Crediton, Devon EX17 4PP.

KAYLL, Wing Commander Joseph Robert, DSO 1940; OBE 1946; DFC 1940; DL; JP; *b* 12 April 1914; *s* of late J. P. Kayll, MBE, The Elms, Sunderland; *m* 1940, Annette Lindsay Nisbet; two *s. Educ:* Aysgarth; Stowe. Timber trader; joined 607 Sqdn AAF, 1934; mobilised Sept. 1939; Commanding Officer 615 Squadron, 1940; (prisoner) 1941; OC 607 Sqdn AAF 1946. DL Durham, 1956; JP Sunderland, 1962. Mem., Wear Boating Assoc. *Recreation:* yachting. *Address:* Hillside House, Hillside, Sunderland, Tyne and Wear. *T:* 283282. *Clubs:* Royal Ocean Racing; Sunderland Yacht; Royal Northumberland Yacht.

KAYSEN, Prof. Carl; David W. Skinner Professor of Political Economy, School of Humanities and Social Science, Massachusetts Institute of Technology, since 1977; *b* 5 March 1920; *s* of Samuel and Elizabeth Kaysen; *m* 1940, Annette Neutra; two *d. Educ:* Philadelphia Public Schs; Overbrook High Sch., Philadelphia; Pa, Columbia and Harvard Univs. AB Pa 1940; MA 1947, PhD 1954, Harvard. Nat. Bureau of Economic Research, 1940-42; Office of Strategic Services, Washington, 1942-43; Intelligence Office, US Army, 1943-45; State Dept, Washington, 1945. Dep. Special Asst to President, 1961-63. Harvard University, 1947-66: Teaching Fellow in Econs, 1947; Asst Prof. of Economics, 1950-55; Assoc. Prof. of Economics 1955-57; Prof. of Economics, 1957-66; Assoc. Dean, Graduate Sch. of Public Administration, 1960-66; Lucius N. Littauer Prof. of Political Economy, 1964-66; Jr Fellow, Soc. of Fellows, 1947-50, Actg Sen. Fellow, 1957-58, 1964-65; Syndic, Harvard Univ. Press, 1964-66; Dir, Inst. for Advanced Study, Princeton, NJ, 1966-76, Dir Emeritus, 1976. Sen. Fulbright Res. Schol., LSE, 1955-56. Trustee, Pennsylvania Univ., 1967-. *Publications:* United States *v* United Shoe Machinery Corporation, an Economic Analysis of an Anti-Trust Case, 1956; The American Business Creed (with others), 1956; Anti-Trust Policy (with D. F. Turner), 1959; The Demand for Electricity in the United States (with F. M. Fisher), 1962; The Higher Learning, The Universities, and The Public, 1969; numerous articles on economic theory and applied economics. *Recreations:* squash, tennis. *Address:* 200-219, Massachusetts Institute of Technology, Cambridge, Mass. 02139, USA.

KAZAN, Elia; author; independent producer and director of plays and films; *b* Constantinople, 7 Sept. 1909; *s* of George Kazan and Athena Sismanoglou; *m* 1st, 1932, Molly Thacher (*d* 1963); two *s* two *d*; 2nd, 1967, Barbara Loden. *Educ:* Williams Coll. (AB); 2 years postgraduate work in Drama at Yale. Actor, Group Theatre, 1932-39; first London appearance as Eddie Fuseli in Golden Boy, St James, 1938. Directed *plays:* Skin of Our Teeth, 1942; All My Sons, A Streetcar Named Desire, 1947; Death of a Salesman, 1949; Camino Real, Tea and Sympathy, 1953; Cat on a Hot Tin Roof, 1955; Dark at Top of the Stairs, JB, 1958; Sweet Bird of Youth, 1959; After the Fall, 1964; But For Whom Charlie, 1964; The Changeling, 1964; Four times won best stage Director of Year, 1942, 1947, 1948, 1949. Directed *films:* Streetcar named Desire, 1951; Viva Zapata, 1952; Pinky, 1949; Gentleman's Agreement, 1948 (won Oscar, best Dir); Boomerang, 1947; A Tree Grows in Brooklyn, 1945; On the Waterfront, 1954 (won Oscar, best Dir); East of Eden, 1954; Baby Doll, 1956; A Face in the Crowd, 1957; Wild River, 1960; Splendour in the Grass, 1962; America, America, 1964; The Arrangement, 1969; The Visitors, 1972; The Last Tycoon, 1977. Three times won Best Picture of Year from New York Film Critics, 1948, 1952, 1955. *Publications:* America, America (novel), 1963; The Arrangement (novel), 1967; The Assassins, 1972; The Understudy, 1974; magazine articles in New York Times, Theatre Arts, etc. *Recreation:* tennis. *Address:* (business) 850 Seventh Avenue, New York City, NY 10019, USA.

KEAN, Arnold Wilfred Geoffrey, CBE 1977; Secretary and Legal Adviser, Civil Aviation Authority, since 1972; *b* 29 Sept. 1914; *s* of late Martin Kean; *m* 1939, Sonja Irene, *d* of late Josef Andersson, Copenhagen; two *d. Educ:* Blackpool Gram. Sch.; Queens' Coll., Cambridge (Schol.). 1st cl. 1st div. Law Tripos, Pts I and II; Pres., Cambridge Union, 1935; Wallenberg (Scandinavian) Prize; Commonwealth Fund Fellow, Harvard Law Sch.; Yarborough-Anderson Schol., Inner Temple. Called to the Bar (studentship, certif. of honour, 1939). War of 1939-45, Legal staff of British Purchasing Commn and UK Treas. Delegn in N America. HM Treasury Solicitor's Dept, 1945; Princ. Asst Solicitor, 1964-72. Member: Legal Cttee, Internat. Civil Aviation Organisation, 1954-; Air Travel Reserve Fund Agency, 1975-; Leader, UK Deleg. at internat. confs on maritime, railway, atomic energy and air law. Tutor in Law, Civil Service Coll., 1963-. Air Law Editor, Jl of Business Law, 1970-. FRAeS. King Christian X Liberation Medal (Denmark), 1945. *Publications:* articles in legal periodicals. *Recreations:* music, stamps, gardening. *Address:* Tall Trees, South Hill Avenue, Harrow HA1 3NU. *T:* 01-422 5791.

KEANE, Major Sir Richard (Michael), 6th Bt *cr* 1801; farmer; *b* 29 Jan. 1909; *s* of Sir John Keane, 5th Bart, DSO, and Lady Eleanor Hicks-Beach (*d* 1960), *d* of 1st Earl St Aldwyn; *S* father, 1956; *m* 1939, Olivia Dorothy Hawkshaw; two *s* one *d. Educ:* Sherborne Sch.; Christ Church, Oxford. Diplomatic Correspondent to Reuters 1935-37; Diplomatic Corresp. and Asst to Editor, Sunday Times, 1937-39. Served with County of London Yeomanry and 10th Royal Hussars, 1939-44; Liaison Officer (Major) with HQ Vojvodina, Yugoslav Partisans, 1944; attached British Military Mission, Belgrade, 1944-45. Publicity Consultant to Imperial Chemical Industries Ltd, 1950-62.

Publications: Germany: What Next?, (Penguin Special), 1939; Modern Marvels of Science (editor), 1961. *Recreation:* fishing. *Heir:* s John Charles Keane, b 16 Sept. 1941. *Address:* Cappoquin House, Cappoquin, County Waterford, Eire. *T:* Cappoquin 11.

KEANE, Mrs Robert; Mary Nesta (*Nom de plume:* **M. J. Farrell**); b 20 July 1905; d of Walter Clarmont Skrine and Agnes Shakespeare Higginson; m; two d. *Educ:* Privately. (With John Perry) Spring Meeting (play perf. Ambassadors Theatre and New York, 1938); Ducks and Drakes (play perf. Apollo Theatre, 1941); Guardian Angel (play perf. Gate Theatre, Dublin, 1944); Treasure Hunt (play perf. Apollo Theatre, 1949). *Publications:* Young Entry; Taking Chances; Mad Puppettstown; Conversation Piece; Devoted Ladies; Full House; The Rising Tide; Two Days in Aragon, 1941; Loving Without Tears (novel), 1951; Treasure Hunt, 1952. *Address:* Dysert, Ardmore, Co. Waterford, Ireland. *TA:* Ardmore. *T:* Ardmore 5.

KEAR, Graham Francis; Under-Secretary, Petroleum Production Division, Department of Energy, since 1974; b 9 Oct. 1928; s of Richard Walter Kear and Eva Davies. *Educ:* Newport (St Julian's) High Sch., Mon; Balliol Coll., Oxford (BA). Min. of Supply, 1951-52 and 1954-57; UK Delegn to ECSC, 1953-54; Min. of Aviation, 1957-59 and 1960-63; NATO Maintenance Supply Agency, Paris, 1959-60; MoD, 1963-65; Cabinet Office, 1968-71; Min. of Aviation Supply/DTI, 1971-72; Fellow, Harvard Univ. Center for Internat. Affairs, 1972-73. *Recreation:* music. *Address:* 8 Branstone Court, Kew Road, Richmond, Surrey TW9 3LE. *T:* 01-940 7341. *Club:* United Oxford & Cambridge University.

KEARLEY, family name of **Viscount Devonport.**

KEARNEY, Sheriff Brian; Sheriff of Glasgow and Strathkelvin, since 1977; b 25 Aug. 1935; s of James Samuel and Agnes Olive Kearney; m 1965, Elizabeth Mary Chambers; two s one d. *Educ:* Largs Higher Grade; Greenock Academy; Glasgow Univ. (MA, LLB). Qualified solicitor, 1960; Partner, Biggart, Lumsden & Co., Solicitors, Glasgow, 1965. Sheriff of N Strathclyde at Dumbarton, 1974-77. *Address:* Sheriff's Chambers, Sheriff Court House, 149 Ingram Street, Glasgow G1 1EJ. *Club:* Royal Scottish Automobile (Glasgow).

KEARNS, Sir Frederick (Matthias), KCB 1975 (CB 1970); MC 1944; Second Permanent Secretary, Ministry of Agriculture, Fisheries and Food, since 1973; b 21 Feb. 1921; er s of G. H. and Ivy Kearns, Burnley; m 1946, Betty Broadbent; one d. *Educ:* Burnley Gram. Sch.; Brasenose Coll., Oxford; RMC Sandhurst. BA (Hons) 1941; MA 1947, Oxon. Commissioned Royal Fusiliers, 1942. Served 8th and 5th Armies, N Africa and Italy, 1942-46; Brigade Major, 167th Inf. Brigade, Trieste, 1946. Asst Principal, Ministry of Agriculture, 1948; Principal 1950; Asst Sec., Min. of Agriculture, Fisheries and Food, 1957; Regional Controller, Northern Region, 1957-60; Head of Finance Division, 1960-63; Head of External Relations Div., 1963-64; Under-Sec., External Relations, 1964-68; Meat and Livestock Group 1968-69; Deputy Secretary, 1969-73; on special assignment to UK Delegn for EEC Negotiations, 1970-72. *Recreations:* fishing, poetry. *Address:* 26 Brookway, Blackheath, SE3. *T:* 01-852 0747. *Club:* Reform.

KEARNS, Prof. Howard George Henry, OBE 1954; Professor of Agricultural and Horticultural Science, Bristol University 1957-67, now Emeritus; Dir, Long Ashton Research Station, 1957-67; b 13 May 1902; s of Henry Kearns and Elizabeth Anne Baker; m 1930, Molly Yvonne Cousins. *Educ:* St Paul's Sch., West Kensington; Downing Coll., Cambridge; Wye Coll., University of London. Lecturer in Zoology (Entomology), Bristol Univ., 1926-31; Advisory Entomologist, Long Ashton Research Station, 1931-32; Research Entomologist, 1933-; Reader in Entomology, Bristol Univ., 1950. Particular interests in applied biology, spray techniques and design of spray machinery for temperate and tropical crops. Mem. Ministry Overseas Development's Consultative Panel for Agriculture. *Publications:* contrib. to: Insecticides and Colonial Agricultural Development, 1954; Science and Fruit, 1953; Modern Commercial Fruitgrowing, 1956; articles in learned jls on various aspects of plant protection. *Recreations:* engineering, natural history, photography. *Address:* Clive Weare House, Clewer, Wedmore, Som. *T:* Cheddar 742165.

KEARON, Air Cdre Norman Walter, CMG 1974; CBE 1967 (OBE 1943); Chief Executive, British Aircraft Corporation, Saudi Arabia; Royal Air Force (retd). Served War of 1939-45 (OBE). Dept of the Air Member for Supply and Organisation, 1963; retired as Director, Directorate of Organisation, Royal Air Force, 1968. *Address:* c/o Midland Bank Ltd, Godalming, Surrey.

KEARTON, family name of **Baron Kearton.**

KEARTON, Baron cr 1970 (Life Peer), of Whitchurch, Bucks; **Christopher Frank Kearton;** Kt 1966; OBE 1945; FRS 1961; Chairman and Chief Executive, British National Oil Corporation, since 1976; Chairman, Electricity Supply Research Council since 1960 (Member, since 1964); part-time Member: UK Atomic Energy Authority, since 1955; Central Electricity Generating Board, since 1974; Director, Hill Samuel Group, since 1970; b 17 Feb. 1911; s of Christopher John Kearton and Lilian Hancock; m 1936, Agnes Kathleen Brander; two s two d. *Educ:* Hanley High Sch.; St John's Coll., Oxford. Joined ICI, Billingham Division, 1933. Worked in Atomic Energy Project, UK and USA, 1940-45. Joined Courtaulds Ltd, i/c of Chemical Engineering, 1946; Dir 1952; Dep. Chm., 1961-64; Chm., 1964-75. Visitor, DSIR, 1955-61, 1963-68. Chairman: Industrial Reorganisation Corp., 1966-68; Tropical Products Inst. Cttee, 1958-; East European Trade Council, 1975-77. Member: Windscale Accident Cttee, 1957; Special Advisory Group, British Transport Commn, 1960; Adv. Council on Technology, 1964-70; NEDC, 1965-71; Adv. Cttee, Industrial Expansion Bill, 1968-70 (Chm.); Central Adv. Council for Science and Technology; Cttee of Enquiry into Structure of Electricity Supply Industry, 1974-75; Offshore Energy Technology Bd, 1976-; Energy Commn, 1977-; Council, Royal Soc., 1970; Pres., Soc. of Chemical Industry, 1972-74 (Chm., Heavy Organic Chemical Section, 1961-62). President: RoSPA, 1973-; BAAS, 1978-79. Fellow, Imperial Coll. London, 1976; Hon. Fellow: St John's Coll., Oxford, 1965; Manchester Coll. of Sci. and Techn., 1966; Soc. of Dyers and Colourists, 1974. Comp. TI, 1965; Hon. MIChemE 1968; Hon. LLD Leeds, 1966; Hon. DSc: Bath, 1966; Aston in Birmingham, 1970; Reading, 1970; Keele, 1973; Ulster, 1975. FRSA 1970. *Address:* The Old House, Whitchurch, near Aylesbury, Bucks. *T:* Whitchurch 232. *Club:* Athenæum.

KEARTON, Prof. William Johnston, DEng, FIMechE, FRINA; Emeritus Professor, Liverpool University, since 1958; b 26 March 1893; s of Christopher and Dinah Kearton; m 1917, Janet Miller; one d decd. *Educ:* University of Liverpool. Commenced practical training with Vickers, Sons, and Maxim, at the Naval Construction Works, Barrow-in-Furness, 1909; Vickers Scholar, 1913. Lecturer in Engineering, Liverpool Univ., 1919-37; Senior Lecturer in Mechanical Engineering, Liverpool Univ., 1937-47; Dean of the Faculty of Engineering, Liverpool Univ., 1948-53; Harrison Prof. of Mechanical Engineering, Liverpool University, 1947-58, retd. *Publications:* Steam Turbine Theory and Practice, 1922; (Jt) Alignment Charts, 1924; Turbo-Blowers and Compressors, 1926; (Joint) Turbo-Gebläse und Kompressoren, 1929; Steam Turbine Operation, 1931; papers in Proc. Inst. of Mech. Engineers. *Recreations:* various. *Address:* 32 Popples Drive, Illingworth, Halifax, W Yorks. *T:* Halifax 246273.

KEATING, Donald Norman, QC 1972; a Recorder of the Crown Court, since 1972; b 24 June 1924; s of late Thomas Archer Keating and late Anne Keating; m 1945, Betty Katharine (née Wells) (d 1975); two s one d. *Educ:* Roan Sch.; King's Coll., London. BA History, 1948. RAFVR, 1943-46 (Flt Lt). Called to Bar, Lincoln's Inn, 1950. *Publications:* Law and Practice of Building Contracts, edns 1955, 1963, 1969, 1978; Guide to RIBA Forms, 1959; various articles in legal and other jls. *Recreations:* theatre, music, travel, walking. *Address:* 11 King's Bench Walk, Temple, EC4Y 7EQ. *T:* 01-353 9281.

KEATING, Henry Reymond Fitzwalter; author; b 31 Oct. 1926; s of John Hervey Keating and Muriel Marguerita Keating (née Clews); m 1953, Sheila Mary Mitchell; three s one d. *Educ:* Merchant Taylors' Sch.; Trinity Coll., Dublin. Journalism, 1952-60; Crime Reviewer for The Times, 1967-. Chm. Crime Writers' Assoc., 1970-71. *Publications:* Death and the Visiting Firemen, 1959; Zen there was Murder, 1960; A Rush on the Ultimate, 1961; The Dog it was that Died, 1962; Death of a Fat God, 1963; The Perfect Murder, 1964; Is Skin-Deep, Is Fatal, 1965; Inspector Ghote's Good Crusade, 1966; Inspector Ghote Caught in Meshes, 1967; Inspector Ghote Hunts the Peacock, 1968; Inspector Ghote Plays a Joker, 1969; Inspector Ghote Breaks an Egg, 1970; Inspector Ghote goes by Train, 1971; Inspector Ghote Trusts the Heart, 1972; The Underside, 1974 (paperback editions of all the preceding titles); The Strong Man, 1971; (ed) Blood on my Mind, 1972; Bats Fly Up for Inspector Ghote, 1974; A Remarkable Case of Burglary, 1975; Murder Must Appetize, 1976; Filmi, Filmi, Inspector Ghote, 1976; (ed) Agatha Christie: First Lady of Crime, 1977. *Recreation:* popping round to the post. *Address:* 35 Northumberland Place, W2 5AS. *T:* 01-229 1100.

KEATING, John; (Seán Céitinn; RHA; Hon. RA; Hon. RSA; Painter; b Limerick, 29 Sept. 1889; s of Joseph Keating and

Anne Hannan; *m* 1919, May, *d* of John Walsh, Eadstown, County Kildare; two *s. Educ:* St Munchin's Coll., Limerick. At twenty went to Dublin, having won a Scholarship in Art at the Dublin Metropolitan Sch. of Art; spent four years in Aran, off the west coast of Ireland; came back to Dublin and won the Taylor Scholarship in Painting; worked with Sir William Orpen in London until 1916; returned to Ireland in that year. *Recreations:* reading and idling. *Address:* Ait an Cuain, Ballyboden Road, Rathfarnham, Co. Dublin. *T:* 904957.

KEATING, Paul John Geoffrey; Irish Ambassador to the Court of St James's, since 1977; *b* 13 Aug. 1924; *s* of Joseph Hannan Keating and Mary Mercedes Joyce; *m* 1952, Teresa McGowan; one *s* one *d. Educ:* Presentation Coll., Glasthule; Trinity Coll., Dublin; Sorbonne, Paris. Entered Irish Foreign Service as Third Sec., 1949; Vice-Consul, New York, 1951; Sec., Irish Mission to UN, 1956; First Secretary: Dublin, 1960; London, 1962; Counsellor, London, 1964; Chief of Protocol, Dublin, 1967; Ambassador: Lagos, 1968; Bonn, 1970; Asst Sec. and Political Dir, Dept of Foreign Affairs, Dublin, 1972; Dep. Sec., 1973; Sec., 1974. Grand Officer, Order of Leopold II, Belgium, 1968. *Address:* Irish Embassy, 17 Grosvenor Place, SW1X 7HR. *T:* 01-235 2171. *Clubs:* Garrick, Travellers'; Kildare Street and University (Dublin).

KEATINGE, Sir Edgar (Mayne), Kt 1960; CBE 1954; *b* 3 Feb. 1905; *s* of late Gerald Francis Keatinge, CIE; *m* 1930, Katharine Lucile Burrell; one *s* one *d. Educ:* Rugby Sch.; School of Agriculture, S Africa. Diploma in Agriculture, 1925. S African Dept of Agriculture, 1926-29. Served War of 1939-45 with RA. Resigned with rank of Lieut-Col. West African Frontier Force, 1941-43; Commandant Sch. of Artillery, West Africa, 1942-43; CC West Suffolk, 1933-45. Parliamentary Candidate, Isle of Ely, 1938-44; MP (C) Bury St Edmunds, 1944-45; JP Wilts 1946; Chm. Wessex Area Nat. Union of Conservative Assocs, 1950-53; Mem. Panel, Land Tribunal, SW Area. Governor, Sherborne Sch., 1951-74. Mem. Council, Royal Africa Soc., 1970. *Recreations:* travel, shooting. *Address:* Teffont, Salisbury, Wilts SP3 5RG. *T:* Teffont 224. *Clubs:* Carlton, Boodle's.
See also Prof. W. R. Keatinge.

KEATINGE, Prof. William Richard; MA; MB, BChir; PhD; Professor of Physiology, London Hospital Medical College, since 1971; *b* 18 May 1931; *s* of Sir Edgar Keatinge, *qv*; *m* 1955, M. E. Annette Hegarty; one *s* two *d. Educ:* Upper Canada Coll.; Rugby Sch.; Cambridge Univ.; St Thomas's Hospital. House Phys., St Thomas's Hospital, 1955-56; Surg.-Lt RN (Nat. Service), 1956-58; Jun. Research Fellow and Dir of Studies in Medicine, Pembroke Coll., Cambridge, 1958-60; Fellow, Cardiovascular Research Inst., San Francisco, 1960-61; MRC appt Radcliffe Infirmary, Oxford, 1961-68; Fellow of Pembroke Coll., Oxford, 1965-68; Reader in Physiology, London Hosp. Med. Coll., 1968. *Publications:* Survival in Cold Water, 1969; chapters in textbooks of physiology and medicine; papers in physiological and medical jls on temperature regulation and on control of blood vessels. *Recreations:* ski-ing, archaeology. *Address:* London Hospital Medical College, Turner Street, E1.

KEAY, Ronald William John, CBE 1977 (OBE 1966); DPhil; FIBiol; Executive Secretary, The Royal Society, since 1977; *b* 20 May 1920; *s* of Harold John Keay and Marion Lucy (*née* Flick); *m* 1944, Joan Mary Walden; one *s* two *d. Educ:* King's College Sch., Wimbledon; St John's Coll., Oxford (BSc, MA, DPhil). Colonial Forest Service, Nigeria, 1942-62. Seconded to Royal Botanic Gardens, Kew, 1951-57; Dir, Federal Dept of Forest Research, Nigeria, 1960-62; Dep. Exec. Sec., The Royal Society, 1962-77. Pres., Science Assoc. of Nigeria, 1961-62; Vice-Pres., Linnean Soc., 1965-67, 1971-73, 1974-76; Pres., African Studies Assoc., 1971-72. Chm., Finance Cttee, Internat. Biological Programme, 1964-74; Treasurer, Scientific Cttee for Problems of the Environment, 1976-77. *Publications:* Flora of West Tropical Africa, Vol. 1, 1954-58; Nigerian Trees, 1960-64; papers on tropical African plant ecology and taxonomy, and science policy. *Recreations:* gardening, walking, natural history. *Address:* Flat 1 (Private), 6 Carlton House Terrace, SW1Y 5AG. *T:* 01-839 5260. *Club:* Athenæum.

KEDOURIE, Prof. Elie, FBA 1975; Professor of Politics in the University of London, since 1965; Editor, Middle Eastern Studies, since 1964; *b* 25 Jan. 1926; *er s* of A. Kedourie and L. Dangour, Baghdad; *m* 1950, Sylvia, *d* of Gourgi Haim, Baghdad; two *s* one *d. Educ:* Collège A-D Sasson and Shamash Sch., Baghdad; London Sch. of Economics; St Antony's Coll., Oxford (Sen. Scholar). BSc(Econ). Has taught at the London Sch. of Economics, 1953-. Visiting Lecturer: Univ. of California, Los Angeles, 1959; Univ. of Paris, 1959; Visiting Prof.: Princeton Univ., 1961-62; Monash Univ., Melb., 1967; Harvard Univ., 1968-69; Tel Aviv Univ., 1969. *Publications:* England and

the Middle East, 1956; Nationalism, 1960; Afghani and 'Abduh, 1966; The Chatham House Version, 1970; Nationalism in Asia and Africa, 1971; Arabic Political Memoirs, 1974; In the Anglo-Arab Labyrinth, 1976; (ed) The Middle Eastern Economy, 1977. *Address:* London School of Economics, Houghton Street, Aldwych, WC2A 2AE. *T:* 01-405 7686.

KEE, Robert; author and broadcaster; *b* 5 Oct. 1919; *s* of late Robert and Dorothy Kee; *m* 1st, 1948, Janetta, *d* of Rev. G. H. Woolley, VC; one *d* ; 2nd, 1960, Cynthia, *d* of Edward Judah; one *s* one *d* (and one *s* decd). *Educ:* Stowe Sch.; Magdalen Coll., Oxford (Exhibr, MA). RAF, 1940-46. Atlantic Award for Literature, 1946. Picture Post, 1948-51; Picture Editor, WHO, 1953; Special Corresp., Observer, 1956-57; Literary Editor, Spectator, 1957; Special Corresp., Sunday Times, 1957-58; BBC TV (Panorama, etc), 1958-62; Television Reporters International, 1963-64; ITV (Rediffusion, Thames, London Week-End, ITN, Yorkshire), 1964-. Alistair Horne Research Fellow, St Antony's Coll., Oxford, 1972-73. BAFTA Richard Dimbleby Award, 1976. *Publications:* A Crowd Is Not Company, 1947; The Impossible Shore, 1949; A Sign of the Times, 1955; Broadstrop In Season, 1959; Refugee World, 1961; The Green Flag, 1972; many translations from German incl. 0815, The Return of Gunner Asch, Officer Factory, etc. *Recreations:* Irish history, swimming, listening to music. *Address:* 81 Kew Green, Richmond, Surrey.
See also William Kee.

KEE, William; His Honour Judge Kee; a Circuit Judge, since 1972; *b* 15 Oct. 1921; *yr s* of Robert and Dorothy Kee; *m* 1953, Helga Wessel Eckhoff; one *s* three *d. Educ:* Rottingdean Sch.; Stowe Sch. Served War, Army, 1941-46: attached 9th Gurkha Rifles, Dehra Dun, 1943; Staff Captain, Bde HQ, 1945-46. Called to Bar, Inner Temple, 1948. Jt Chm., Independent Schools' Tribunal, 1971-72. *Publications:* (jt) Divorce Case Book, 1950; contributor to: titles in Atkin's Encyclopaedia of Court Forms; Halsbury's Laws of England. *Recreations:* listening to music, walking. *Address:* Oak Hill Cottage, Oak Hill Road, Sevenoaks, Kent TN13 1NP. *T:* 52737.
See also Robert Kee.

KEEBLE, (Herbert Ben) Curtis, CMG 1970; Deputy Under Secretary of State (Chief Clerk), Foreign and Commonwealth Office, since 1976; *b* 18 Sept. 1922; *s* of Herbert Keeble and Gertrude Keeble, BEM; *m* 1947, Margaret Fraser; three *d. Educ:* Clacton County High Sch.; London University. Served Royal Irish Fusiliers, 1942-47. Entered HM Foreign (subsequently Diplomatic) Service, 1947; served in Djakarta, 1947-49; Foreign Office, 1949-51; Berlin, 1951-54; Washington, 1954-58; Foreign Office, 1958-63; Counsellor and Head of European Economic Organisations Dept, 1963-65; Counsellor (Commercial), Berne, 1965-68; Minister, Canberra, 1968-71; Asst Under-Sec. of State, FCO, 1971-73; HM Ambassador, German Democratic Republic, 1974-76. *Recreations:* sailing, skiing, painting. *Address:* c/o Foreign and Commonwealth Office, SW1. *Club:* Travellers'.

KEEBLE, Major Robert, DSO 1940; MC 1945; TD 1946; Director: Associated Portland Cement Manufacturers Ltd, 1970-74; Aberthaw & Bristol Channel Portland Cement Co. Ltd; engaged in cement manufacture; Manager, Hull Savings Bank; *b* 20 Feb. 1911; *s* of late Edwin Percy and Alice Elizabeth Keeble; unmarried. *Educ:* King Henry VIII's Sch., Coventry. Commanded Royal Engineer Field Company; Territorial Army Commission, passed Staff Coll., Camberley, 1939; Freeman of City of London and Liveryman of Company of Fanmakers; served in War of 1939-45 (despatches twice, twice wounded, DSO, MC, 1939-45 Star, African Star, France-Germany Star and Defence Medal, TD). Member Institute Directors; Inst. Quarrying. Governor, Hull Univ. Hon. Brother, Hull Trinity House. *Recreations:* fired in rifle team winning Lord Wakefield Shield for TA, 1939; sailing. *Address:* 15 Fernhill Close, Kenilworth CV8 1AN. *T:* Kenilworth 55668. *Clubs:* Royal Automobile; Royal Yorkshire Yacht.

KEEBLE, Thomas Whitfield; HM Diplomatic Service, retired 1974; Senior Clerk (Acting), Committee Office, House of Commons, since 1976; *b* 10 Feb. 1918; *m* 1945, Ursula Scott Morris; two *s. Educ:* Sir John Deane's Grammar Sch., Cheshire; St John's Coll., Cambridge (MA); King's Coll., London (PhD). Served, 1940-45, in India, Persia, Iraq and Burma in RA (seconded to Indian Artillery), Captain. Asst Principal, Commonwealth Relations Office, 1948; Private Sec. to Parliamentary Under Sec. of State; Principal, 1949; First Sec., UK High Commn in Pakistan, 1950-53, in Lahore, Peshawar and Karachi; seconded to Foreign Service and posted to UK Mission to the United Nations in New York, 1955-59; Counsellor, 1958; Head of Defence and Western Dept, CRO,

1959-60; British Dep. High Comr in Ghana, 1960-63; Head of Econ. Gen. Dept, CRO, 1963-66; Minister (Commercial), British Embassy, Buenos Aires, 1966-67; Hon. Research Associate, Inst. of Latin American Studies, Univ. of London, 1967-68; Minister, British Embassy, Madrid, 1969-71; Head of UN (Econ. and Social) Dept, FCO, 1971-72, of UN Dept, 1972-74; Sen. Directing Staff (Civil), Nat. Defence Coll., Latimer, 1974-76. *Publications:* British Overseas Territories and South America, 1806-1914, 1970; articles in Hispanic reviews. *Recreations:* golf, Spanish literature, bird watching. *Address:* c/o National Westminster Bank Ltd, King's Parade, Cambridge. *Club:* United Oxford & Cambridge University.

KEEGAN, Denis Michael; Barrister; General Manager, Mercantile Credit Co. Ltd; *b* 26 Jan. 1924; *o s* of Denis Francis Keegan and Mrs Duncan Campbell; *m* 1st, 1951, Pamela Barbara (marr. diss.), *yr d* of late Percy Bryan, Purley, Surrey; one *s*; 2nd, 1961, Marie Patricia (marr. diss.), *yr d* of late Harold Jennings; one *s*; 3rd, 1973, Ann Irene, *d* of Norman Morris. *Educ:* Oundle Sch.; Queen's University, Kingston, Ontario, Canada (BA). Served RN Fleet Air Arm, 1944-46 (petty officer pilot). Called to Bar, Gray's Inn, 1950. Mem. Nottingham City Council, 1953-55, resigned. MP (C) Nottingham Sth, 1955-Sept. 1959. Formerly Dir, Radio and Television Retailers' Assoc. *Recreations:* reading, talking, music. *Address:* 95 Clare Court, Judd Street, WC1. *T:* 01-242 1234.

KEEL, Jonathan Edgar, CB 1956; retired; *b* 21 Feb. 1895; *s* of Wm Keel, JP and Elizabeth Keel; *m* 1927, Olga Constance Pointing (*d* 1975); one *s*. *Educ:* Middlesbrough High Sch. Inland Revenue as second division clerk, 1912; transferred to Tax Dept as Surveyor of Taxes, 1916; transferred to Air Ministry with rank of Principal, 1938; went to USA as Dir of Finance and Administration of British Air Commission, 1940; Asst Sec., 1941; Ministry of Aircraft Production, 1944; Under Sec., 1946; Under Sec., 1948; in charge of Safety and General Dept, 1948-53; UK Rep. on Coun. of Internat. Civil Aviation Org., Montreal, 1953-57; retd from Public Service, 1957. *Recreations:* gardening and golf. *Address:* 5 Redcroft Walk, Cranleigh, Surrey. *T:* Cranleigh 3282.

KEELE, Prof. Cyril Arthur; Emeritus Professor of Pharmacology, University of London; *b* 23 Nov. 1905; 2nd *s* of Dr David and Jessie Keele; *m* 1942, Joan Ainslie, *er d* of Lieut-Col G. A. Kempthorne; three *s*. *Educ:* Epsom Coll.; Middlesex Hospital Medical Sch. MRCS, LRCP 1927; MB, BS (London) 1928; MRCP 1929; MD London 1930; FRCP 1948; FFARCS 1958. Medical Registrar, Middlesex Hosp., 1930-32; Demonstrator and Lectr in Physiology, 1933-38; Lectr in Pharmacology, 1938-49; Reader in Pharmacology and Therapeutics, 1949-52, at Middlesex Hospital Medical Sch.; Prof. of Pharmacology and Therapeutics, Univ. of London, 1952-68; Dir, Rheumatology Res. Dept, Middlesex Hosp. Med. Sch., 1968-73. *Publications:* Recent Advances in Pharmacology (with Prof. J. M. Robson), 1956; Samson Wright's Applied Physiology, 12th edn (with Prof. E. Neil); (with Dr D. Armstrong) Substances producing Pain and Itch, 1964. Papers in scientific journals on the control of sweating, analgesic drugs and chemical factors producing pain. *Address:* 25 Letchmore Road, Radlett, Herts WD7 8HU.

KEELEY, Thomas Clews, CBE 1944; MA; physicist; Fellow of Wadham College, Oxford, 1924-61, now Emeritus Fellow; Sub-Warden, 1947-61, retired; *b* 16 Feb. 1894; *s* of T. F. Keeley, Erdington, Birmingham. *Educ:* King Edward's School, Birmingham; St John's Coll., Cambridge (Scholar). Royal Aircraft Establishment, 1917-19. Oxford from 1919. Fellow of the Institute of Physics. *Recreations:* photography, travel. *Address:* Wadham College, Oxford. *T:* 42564. *Club:* English-Speaking Union.

KEELING, (Cyril) Desmond (Evans), CB 1977; Secretary to the Price Commission, since 1975; *b* 13 April 1921; *s* of late Cyril F. J. Keeling, MC, and Susan Evans Keeling; *m* 1947, Megan Miles; one *d*. *Educ:* Southend High Sch., Peterhouse, Cambridge. Parts I and II, Economics, Cambridge, 1939-41 and 1945-46. Served 1941-45 in Infantry (wounded, despatches): Adjutant 5th Bn Wilts Regt, 1944-45. Research, LSE, 1946; Ministry of Works, 1947; Asst Sec., 1960; Dir, Treasury Centre for Administrative Studies, 1963-65; Under-Sec., Treasury, and Dir of Training, 1965-68; Under-Sec., Civil Service Dept, 1968-69, MAFF, 1970-74; Dep. Sec., 1975. Fellow-Commoner, Emmanuel Coll., Cambridge, Michaelmas 1969; Study at London Graduate Business Sch., 1970. Chm. Council, RIPA, 1977-. *Publications:* Management in Government, 1972; articles in public administration journals. *Recreation:* gardening. *Address:* Headlong Hill, Stokesheath Road, Oxshott, Surrey. *T:* Oxshott 2616. *Club:* United Oxford & Cambridge University.

KEELING, Sir John (Henry), Kt 1952; Director, Safeguard Industrial Investments Ltd, 1953-69 (Chairman, 1953-66); Vice-Chairman, Bowater Paper Corp. Ltd, 1945-67; Chairman, West Riding Worsted and Woollen Mills Ltd, 1944-62 (Director, 1962-68); *b* 18 Aug. 1895; *s* of John Henry Keeling and Mary, *d* of Edward P. Allis, Milwaukee, Wisconsin; *m* Dorothy *d* of Dr Morgan I. Finucane and Jane Sheridan; three *s* one *d*. *Educ:* Summerfields, St Leonards, and Oxford; Eton. Queen's Royal West Surrey Regt Territorials, 1914-18, when transferred to Coldstream Guards. In 1923 founded London and Yorkshire Trust Ltd (with Reginald E. Cornwall), past Dir and Chm., retd 1972. Min. of Aircraft Prod., 1940-45; Dir-Gen. Aircraft Distrib., 1943-45; Dep. Chm., BEA, 1947-65. *Address:* Hurst House, Sedlescombe, Sussex. *T:* 340; Grosvenor House, Park Lane, W1. *T:* 01-499 2987. *Club:* White's.

KEELY, Eric Philipps, CBE 1950; Director, National Sulphuric Acid Association Ltd, 1959-67; *b* 11 Aug. 1899; *s* of late Erasmus Middleton Keely, Nottingham; *m* 1942, Enid Betty Curtis; two *d*. *Educ:* Highgate Sch. Served European War, 1917-18, Lancashire Fusiliers; Ministry of Agriculture and Fisheries, 1930; Food (Defence Plans) Dept, Board of Trade 1937; Ministry of Food, 1939; seconded to Govt of India, 1943-44; Under-Sec., Ministry of Food, 1952; Under-Sec., Ministry of Agriculture, Fisheries and Food, 1955-59. *Address:* Wilderness Cottage, Oxted, Surrey. *T:* Oxted 3907. *Club:* Travellers'.

KEEN, Sir Bernard (A.), Kt 1952; FRS 1935; DSc; Fellow of University College, London; *b* 1890; *m* Elsie Isabelle Cowley (*d* 1956); two *s*. *Educ:* University Coll., London. Andrews Scholar, 1908; Trouton Research Scholar, 1911; Carey Foster Res. Prizeman, 1912; Soil Physicist, Rothamsted, 1913; Suffolk Regt (Gallipoli and Palestine), 1914-17; Research Dept, Woolwich Arsenal, 1918; returned to Rothamsted, 1919; Dir, Imperial Institute of Agricultural Research, India, 1930-31; Pres., Royal Meteorological Soc., 1938 and 1939; Vice-Pres., Institute of Physics, 1941-43; Cantor Lecturer, Royal Society of Arts, 1942; formerly Asst Dir and Head of Soil Physics Dept, Rothamsted Experimental Station, 1919-43; Scientific Adviser Middle East Supply Centre, Cairo, 1943-45; adviser on rural development, Palestine, 1946; Chm. of UK Govt Mission to W Africa on production of vegetable oils and oil seeds, 1946; adviser to E African Governments on agricultural policy and research needs, 1947; mem., Scientific Council for Africa, 1950-54; Chm. of Governors, E African Tea Research Inst., 1951-54. Broadcast talks to schools on science of agriculture and gardening, 1928-41; Dir, E African Agriculture and Forestry Research Organisation, 1947-55; Scientific Adviser, Baird and Tatlock (London) Ltd, 1955-63; mem., Scientific Panel Colonial Development Corp., 1955-63; Mem., Forest Products Res. Bd, DSIR, 1957-59. Travelled extensively in USA, S Africa, India, E and W Africa, Middle East, Bulgaria and Australia, to examine and report on the scientific, technical, and administrative problems in agriculture. *Publications:* The Physical Properties of the Soil, 1931; The Agricultural Development of the Middle East, 1946; various papers in scientific and agricultural journals. *Address:* Suite 5, Hotel Bristowe, Grange Road, Southbourne, Bournemouth BH6 3NY. *Club:* Athenæum.

KEEN, Patrick John, CMG 1968; MBE 1944; retired; *b* 30 June 1911; *s* of Brig. P. H. Keen, CB; *m* 1st, 1940, Joyce (*d* 1954), *d* of E. Seth-Ward; two *s* one *d* (and one *s* decd); 2nd, 1958, Anne Cunitia, *d* of Capt. J. A. A. Morris, RN. *Educ:* Haileybury Coll.; RMC Sandhurst. Hampshire Regt, 1931; Indian Political Service, 1936-47; served with 2/13th FF Rifles, 1939-43; HM Diplomatic Service, 1948-68; served in Afghanistan, Pakistan, Cyprus and British Guiana; retd, 1968. *Address:* Saxted House, Emsworth, Hants. *T:* Emsworth 2302.

KEENE, Air Vice-Marshal Allan L. A. P.; *see* Perry-Keene.

KEENE, Sir Charles (Robert), Kt 1969; CBE 1950; JP; Chairman, Kingstone Ltd; *b* 21 Sept. 1891; *s* of late Charles Edward Keene; *m* 1st, 1921, Ruth Stocks (*d* 1949); two *s* (one *s* decd); 2nd, 1952, Hetty Swann. Dep. Regional Comr (N Midland Region), 1941-44. Member, Leicester City Council, 1926-70: Alderman, 1945-70; Lord Mayor, 1953-54; Chairman: Town-Planning Cttee, 1942-53; Slum Clearance Cttee, 1952-62; Educn Cttee, 1953-62; High Bailiff, Leicester, 1935-36. Pro-Chancellor, Univ. of Leicester; Chairman: Governors of Leicester Colls of Art and Technology, 1927-69; City of Leicester Polytechnic, 1969-71 (Hon. Fellow 1970); Charles Keene Coll. of Further Education, 1961-70; Council of University of Leicester, 1928-72; Governors, Gateway Sch., 1928-68. JP Leicester 1940. Hon. Freeman, City of Leicester, 1962. Hon. LLD Leicester Univ., 1963. *Address:* Gaulby, Leicestershire. *T:* Billesdon 215.

KEENLEYSIDE, Hugh Llewellyn, CC (Canada) 1969; consultant; *b* 7 July 1898; *s* of Ellis William Keenleyside and Margaret Louise Irvine; *m* 1924, Katherine Hall Pillsbury, BA, BSc; one *s* three *d*. *Educ:* Langara School and Public Schools, Vancouver, BC; University of British Columbia (BA); Clark University (MA, PhD). Holds several hon. degrees in Law, Science. Instructor and Special Lecturer in History, Brown University, Syracuse Univ., and University of British Columbia, 1923-27; Third Sec., Dept of External Affairs, 1928; Second Sec., 1929; First Sec. and First Chargé d'Affaires, Canadian Legation, Tokyo, 1929; Dept of External Affairs and Prime Minister's Office, 1936; Chm, Board of Review to Investigate charges of illegal entry on the Pacific Coast, 1937; Sec., Cttee in charge of Royal Visit to Canada, 1938-39; Counsellor, 1940; Asst Under-Sec. of State for External Affairs, 1941-44; Mem. and Sec., Canadian Section, Canada-United States Permanent Jt Bd on Defence, 1940-44, Acting Chm., 1944-45; Member: North-West Territories Council, 1941-45; Canada-United States Joint Economic Cttees, 1941-44; Special Cttee on Orientals in BC; Canadian Shipping Board, 1939-41; War Scientific and Technical Development Cttee, 1940-45; Canadian Ambassador to Mexico, 1944-47; Deputy Minister of Resources and Development and Comr of Northwest Territories, 1947-50; Head of UN Mission of Technical Assistance to Bolivia, 1950; Dir-Gen., UN Technical Assistance Administration, 1950-58; Under-Sec. Gen. for Public Administration, UN, 1959. Chairman: BC Power Commn, 1959-62; BC Power and Hydro Authy, 1962-69. Vice-Pres. National Council of the YMCAs of Canada, 1941-45; Vice-Chm., Canadian Youth Commission, 1943-45; Head of Canadian Deleg. to UN Scientific Conf. on Conservation and Utilization of Resources, 1949. Life Mem., Asiatic Soc. of Japan; one of founders and mem. of first Board of Governors of Arctic Institute of North America; Vice-Chm., Board of Governors, Carleton Coll., 1943-50; Pres. Assoc. of Canadian Clubs, 1948-50; Mem. Bd of Trustees, Clark Univ., 1953-56; Mem. Senate, University of British Columbia, 1963-69. Hon. Life Mem., Canadian Association for Adult Education; Mem. Board of Governors, Canadian Welfare Council, 1955-69; Member: Canadian National Cttee of World Power Conference; Adv. Bd (BC), Canada Permanent Cos; Hon. Bd of Dirs, Resources for the Future; Dir, Toronto-Dominion Bank, 1960-70. Assoc. Comr General, UN Conf. on Human Settlements, 1975-76 (Hon. Chm. Canadian Nat. Cttee, 1974-77). Chancellor, Notre Dame Univ., Nelson, BC, 1969-. Dir and Fellow, Royal Canadian Geographic Soc. Haldane Medal, Royal Inst. of Public Administration, 1954; first recipient, Vanier Medal, Inst. of Public Administration of Canada, 1962. *Publications:* Canada and the United States, 1929, revised edn 1952; History of Japanese Education (with A. F. Thomas), 1937; International Aid: a summary, 1966; various magazine articles. *Recreations:* reading, outdoor sports, cooking, poker. *Address:* 3470 Mayfair Drive, Victoria, BC, Canada. *T:* 592-9331.

KEENLEYSIDE, Francis Hugh; *b* 7 July 1911; *s* of late Capt. Cecil A. H. Keenleyside and Gladys Mary (*née* Milne); *m* 1st, 1935, Margaret Joan, *d* of late E. L. K. Ellis; two *s* two *d*; 2nd, 1962, Joan Winifred (*née* Collins); one *d*. *Educ:* Charterhouse; Trinity Coll., Oxford. 1st class Hons in Philosophy, Politics and Economics, 1933, Whitehead Travelling Student. Entered Administrative Class, Home Civil Service, 1934; Principal Private Sec. to four successive Ministers of Shipping and War Transport, 1939-43; Asst Sec. in charge of Shipping Policy Div., 1943; Asst Manager, Union Castle, 1947; Dep. Leader, British delegation to Danube Conf., Belgrade, 1948; Gen. Manager, Union Castle, 1953; Asst Managing Dir, Union-Castle, 1956-60; Shipping Adviser, Suez Canal Users Assoc., 1957. Mem., Gen. Council of Chamber of Shipping, 1953-60; Editor, Alpine Journal, 1953-62. Chevalier (1st Cl.) of Order of St Olav (Norway), 1948; Officer of Order of George I (Greece), 1950; King Christian X Liberty Medal (Denmark), 1946. *Publications:* Peaks and Pioneers, 1975; contrib. to mountaineering jls, etc. *Recreation:* mountaineering. *Address:* c/o Credit Andorra, Sant Julia de Loria, Principality of Andorra. *Clubs:* Alpine; Salisbury.

KEENS, Philip Francis, CBE 1973 (OBE 1966); Member, Trustee Savings Bank Central Board, since 1976; Chairman: Trustee Savings Bank, South East, since 1975; Central Trustee Savings Bank Ltd, since 1972; Trustee Savings Bank Trustee Co. Ltd, since 1967; *b* 18 June 1903; *s* of Sir Thomas Keens; *m* 1st, 1930, Sylvia Irene Robinson (*d* 1970); one *s* one *d*; 2nd, 1974, Mrs Margaret Faith Warne. *Educ:* Tettenhall Coll., Staffs. Incorporated Accountant, 1925; Chartered Accountant, 1957. Partner, Keens, Shay, Keens & Co., London, 1926-67; Trustee, Luton Trustee Savings Bank, 1934 (Chairman, 1949-64); Dep. Chm., Trustee Savings Bank Assoc., 1966-76 (Chm. Southern Area, 1967); Chm., London South Eastern Trustee Savings Bank, 1964-76 (Vice-Chm., 1958-75). Past Master, Worshipful Co. of Feltmakers. *Recreation:* golf. *Address:* Kimpton Grange, near Hitchin, Herts. *T:* Kimpton 832205. *Clubs:* City Livery; The Club (St Austell, Cornwall).

KEEP, Charles Reuben; Managing Director, Tozer Kemsley & Millbourn (Holdings) Ltd, since 1973; Chairman or Director of subsidiary companies; President, Export Leasing Co. Ltd, Bermuda, since 1973; *b* 1932; *m*; one *d*. *Educ:* HCS, Hampstead. Joined Lloyds & Scottish Finance Ltd, 1956, Director, 1969; Man. Dir, International Factors Ltd, 1970; Dep. Man. Dir, Tozer Kemsley & Millbourn (Holdings) Ltd, 1972. *Address:* The Oaks, 20 Forest Lane, Chigwell, Essex IG7 5AE. *T:* 01-504 3897. *Clubs:* Gresham; Chigwell Golf.

KEEPING, Charles William James; artist, book designer and Fine Art Lecturer since 1952; Visiting Lecturer in Art, Croydon College of Art, since 1963; *b* 22 Sept. 1924; *s* of Charles Keeping and Eliza Ann Trodd; *m* 1952, Renate Meyer; three *s* one *d*. *Educ:* Frank Bryant Sch., Kennington; Polytechnic, Regent Street. Apprenticed to printing trade, 1938; served as telegraphist, RN, 1942-46; studied for Nat. Diploma of Design at Polytechnic, London, 1946-52; Vis. Lectr in Art, Polytechnic, 1956-63. Illustrated over 100 books, drawings for wall murals, television and advertising. MSIA. Certificate of Merit (for illustrations to The God Beneath the Sea) 1970, Library Assoc.; Certificate, Highly Commended, for Hans Andersen Medal, Rio de Janeiro, Internat. Bd on Books for Young People, 1974. *Publications:* Black Dolly, 1966; Shaun and the Carthorse, 1966; Charley Charlotte and the Golden Canary, 1967 (Kate Greenaway Medal); Alfie and the Ferryboat, 1968; Tinker Tailor, 1968 (a Francis Williams Meml Bequest prize-winner, 1972); Joseph's Yard, 1969 (Honour Book award) (also filmed for TV); Through the Window, 1970 (also filmed for TV); Spider's Web, 1973 (Bratislava cert.); Richard, 1973; Railway Passage, 1974 (Golden Apple, Bienalle Illustration Bratislava, 1975); Wasteground Circus, 1975; Cockney Ding Dong, 1975; The Wildman, 1976 (a Francis Williams prize-winner, 1977); Inter-City, 1977. *Recreations:* talking, walking, driving ponies. *Address:* 16 Church Road, Shortlands, Bromley BR2 0HP. *T:* 01-460 7679. *Club:* Nash House.

KEETON, George Williams, FBA 1964; Barrister-at-law; Principal, London Institute of World Affairs, 1938-52; President, since 1952; Leverhulme Fellow, 1971; *b* 22 May 1902; *o s* of John William and Mary Keeton; *m* 1st, 1924, Gladys Edith Calthorpe; two *s*; 2nd, Kathleen Marian Willard. *Educ:* Gonville and Caius Coll., Cambridge (Foundation Scholar in Law); Gray's Inn (Bacon Scholar). BA, LLB, with first class hons, 1923; MA, LLM, 1927; LLD 1932. Called to Bar, 1928; Editor, The Cambridge Review, 1924; Reader in Law and Politics, Hong Kong Univ., 1924-27; Senior Lecturer in Law, Manchester Univ., 1928-31; Reader in English Law, 1931-37, Prof. of English Law, 1937-69, Dean, Faculty of Laws, 1939-54, Vice-Provost, 1966-69, University Coll., London; Professor of English Law, Univ. of Notre Dame, 1969-71; Professor Associate, Brunel Univ., 1969-77. Distinguished Vis. Prof., Miami Univ., 1971-73. Mem. Exec. Cttee, American Judicature Soc., 1974-77. Hon. LLD: Sheffield 1966; Hong Kong 1972; Hon. DLitt Brunel, 1977. *Publications:* The Development of Extraterritoriality in China, 1928; The Austinian Theories of Law and Sovereignty (with R. A. Eastwood, LLD), 1929; The Elementary Principles of Jurisprudence, 1930, 2nd edn 1949; Shakespeare and his Legal Problems, 1930; The Problem of the Moscow Trial, 1933; The Law of Trusts, 1st edn 1934, 10th edn 1974; An Introduction to Equity, 1st edn 1938, 8th edn 1976; National Sovereignty and International Order, 1939; Making International Law Work (with G. Schwarzenberger, PhD), 1st edn 1939, 2nd edn 1946; The Speedy Return (novel), 1938; Mutiny in the Caribbean (novel), 1940; The Case for an International University, 1941; Russia and Her Western Neighbours (with R. Schlesinger), 1942; China, the Far East, and the Future, 1st edn 1942, 2nd edn 1949; A Liberal Attorney-General, 1949; The Passing of Parliament, 1952; Social Change in the Law of Trusts, 1958; Case Book on Equity and Trusts, 1958, 2nd edn 1974; Trial for Treason, 1959; Trial by Tribunal, 1960; Guilty but Insane, 1961; The Modern Law of Charities, 1962, 2nd edn 1971; The Investment and Taxation of Trust Funds, 1964; Lord Chancellor Jeffreys, 1964; The Norman Conquest and the Common Law, 1966; Shakespeare's Legal and Political Background, 1967; (with L. Sheridan) Equity, 1970; Government in Action, 1970; Modern Developments in the Law of Trusts, 1971; The Football Revolution, 1972; English Law: the judicial contribution, 1974; (with S. N. Frommel) British Industry and European Law, 1974; Keeping the Peace, 1976; (with L. A. Sheridan) Trusts in the Commonwealth, 1977; numerous contributions to periodicals. *Address:* Picts Close, Picts Lane, Princes Risborough, Bucks. *T:* 94.

KEEWATIN, Bishop of, since 1974; **Rt. Rev. Hugh James Pearson Allan,** DD; *b* 7 Aug. 1928; *s* of Hugh Blomfield Allan and Agnes Dorothy (*née* Pearson); *m* 1955, Beverley Edith Baker; one *s* three *d*. *Educ*: St John's Coll., Univ. of Manitoba (LTh 1955, BA 1957). Deacon 1954, priest 1955; Assistant: St Aidan's, Winnipeg, 1954; All Saints, Winnipeg, 1955; Missionary, Peguis Indian Reserve, 1956-60; Rector, St Mark's, Winnipeg, 1960-68; Hon. Canon, Diocese of Rupert's Land, 1967; Rector, St Stephen's Swift Current, Sask., 1968-70; Rural Dean of Cypress, 1968-70; Dean of Qu'Appelle and Rector of St Paul's Cathedral, Regina, Sask., 1970-74. Hon. DD, St John's Coll., Univ. of Manitoba, 1974. *Recreations*: ornithology, boating. *Address*: Bishopstowe, 15 Sylvan Street, Kenora, Ont. P9N 3W7. *T*: (home) 468-5655, (office) 468-7011.

KEGGIN, Air Vice-Marshal Harold, CB 1967; CBE 1962; LDS; Director of Dental Services, Royal Air Force, 1964-69, retired; *b* 25 Feb. 1909; *y s* of John and Margaret Keggin, Port Erin, Isle of Man; *m* 1935, Margaret Joy (*née* Campbell); one *s* two *d*. *Educ*: Douglas High Sch.; University of Liverpool. Dental Officer, RAF, commissioned, 1932; Flt Lieut 1934; Sqdn Ldr 1939; Wing Comdr 1942; Gp Capt. 1954; Air Cdre 1958; Air Vice-Marshal 1964. QHDS 1958-69. *Recreations*: golf, fishing. *Address*: Rosecroft, 7 Cotlands, Sidmouth, Devon EX10 8SP. *T*: Sidmouth 4790.

KEGIE, James, OBE 1967; FRTPI, FRICS, AIAS; Town Planning Consultant, and retired from local government, 1974; *b* 30 Sept. 1913; *s* of Henry Kegie and Mary Ann (May) Kegie; *m* 1st, 1939, Doreen (*d* 1969), *d* of Rev. Nicholas Martin Cuthbert and Mary Ann Cuthbert; two *s*; 2nd, 1974, Helen Ruth, *d* of Alfred Quinton Barton and Amy Elizabeth Barton. *Educ*: Gateshead-upon-Tyne Grammar Sch.; Coll. of Estate Management. Planning appts in private practice and local govt in Durham, W Sussex, Cheshire and Monmouthshire, 1929-45; County Planning Officer, Monmouthshire CC, 1945-74. Pres., Co. Planning Officers' Soc., 1968-69; Member: Exec. Council, Co. Planning Officers' Soc. 1948-74; Bd of Housing Corp., 1974; Countryside Commn, 1974; Welsh Cttee of Countryside Commn, 1974; Bd of Welsh Develt Agency, 1976; Management Cttee, Sch. of Advanced Urban Studies, Bristol Univ., 1974; Consultant to Nat. Trust on Structure Plans in Wales, 1974; Member: European Architectural Heritage Cttee for Wales, 1974; Bi-lingual Signs Cttee, Wales, 1972; Working Parties and Research Gps on Town and Country Planning, 1960-77; Bd of Civic Trust for Wales, 1970; Tech. Unit on Structure Plans (Chm.), Sports Council for Wales, 1977. *Publications*: County of Monmouth Development Plan, 1953; Minority Report, Bilingual Signs Cttee, 1972; contrib. Jl of RICS. *Recreations*: river and sea fishing, caravanning, motoring, walking, gardening; conservation of the countryside and built environment. *Address*: High Meadow, Christchurch, near Newport, Gwent NP6 1JJ. *T*: Caerleon 422141.

KEIGHLEY, Frank; Director, The Rank Foundation Ltd; Fellow of Institute of Bankers; *b* 19 March 1900; *e s* of late Wm L. Keighley; *m* 1926, Mary, *e d* of late J. K. Wilson; one *s*. *Educ*: Northern Institute, Leeds. Entered Union of London & Smiths Bank (which was amalgamated with National Provincial Bank in 1918) as Junior Clerk, 1915; retired, as Chief General Manager, Dec. 1961, and as Dir, Dec. 1969. *Address*: Little Court, 88 Fulmer Drive, Gerrards Cross, Bucks. *T*: Gerrards Cross 84117.

KEIGHLY-PEACH, Captain Charles Lindsey, DSO 1940; OBE 1941; RN retired; *b* 6 April 1902; *s* of late Admiral C. W. Keighly-Peach, DSO; *m* 1st, V. B. Cumbers; one *s* one *d*; *m* 2nd, Beatrice Mary Harrison (*d* 1974). *Educ*: RN Colleges, Osborne and Dartmouth. Midshipman, 1919; Sub-Lieut 1922; Lieut 1924; 3 Squadron, RAF, 1926; HMS Eagle (402 Sqdn), 1927; H/M S/M M2, 1929; HMS Centaur, 1930; Lieut-Cdr 1932; HMS Glorious (802 Sqdn), 1932; RN Staff Coll., Greenwich, 1934; SOO to RA Destroyers, 1935; HMS London, 1937; Commander, 1938; RN Air Station Lee-on-Solent, 1939; HMS Eagle, 1940-41; Naval Assistant (Air) to 2nd Sea Lord, 1941-44; Capt. 1943; RN Air Station, Yeovilton, 1944-45; Comdg HMS Sultan, Singapore, 1945-47; in command HMS Troubridge and 3rd Destroyer Flot. Med., 1947-49; Dir Captain, Senior Officer's War Course, RN, 1949-51; Asst Chief Naval Staff (Air) on loan to Royal Canadian Navy, 1951-53. *Recreations*: golf, gardening. *Address*: Hatteras, Hall Road, Brockdish, Diss, Norfolk IP21 5JY. *T*: Harleston 853136.

KEILLER, Brian Edwin, CMG 1961; Farmer (dairy and pig), 1930-59; now retired; *b* Bulls, NZ, 18 July 1901; *s* of E. Keiller, Bulls, NZ, and Muriel Kathrine Waitt; *m* 1932, Helena Maude Harcourt; two *s* one *d*. *Educ*: Wanganui Collegiate Sch., Wanganui, NZ. Dep. Chm. from its inception of Nat. Pig Industry Council, also Chm. Wellington Dist Pig Council (15 yrs), retd, 1953; original Mem. NZ Horse Soc., 1951; Mem. Council, Royal Agric. Society, 1942- (Chm. 1945-52); represented NZ Meat Bd, 1949; Hon. Life Mem. Royal Agric. Society of England; Treas., Manawatu Agric. and Pastoral Assoc., 1951- (Mem., 1933, Chm., 1942-51). Mem. Wellington Harbour Bd, 1947- (Chm. 1957-61); Pres. Harbours Assoc. of NZ, 1957-61. Chairman: Watson Bros Ltd; Everyday Products Pty Co., 1966; Dir, Barnard and Abraham Ltd. Pres. Wanganui Old Boys' Assoc., 1951-55 (centenary, 1954); Governor: Massey Agric. Coll., 1954-63; Mem, Exec. Cttee, Nga Taura Girls' Sch.; 1959- (former Chm.); Chm., Carnot Sch. for Girls, 1951-. Held various offices in Manawatu. War of 1939-45: Home Guard and Chm. Manawatu Primary Production Council. Coronation Medal, 1953. *Recreations*: golf (Chm. Greens Research Cttee of NZ Golf Council, retd 1956), ski-ing, fishing. *Address*: Atawhai-iti, 88 Te Awe Awe Street, Palmerston North, New Zealand. *T*: 80655. *Clubs*: Wellington, Wellington Racing (Life Mem.), Manawatu Racing (Life Mem.), Palmerston North.

KEIR, Mrs David; see Cazalet-Keir, T.

KEIR, Thelma C.; see Cazalet-Keir.

KEITH, family name of **Baron Keith of Kinkel** and of **Earl of Kintore.**

KEITH of KINKEL, Baron *cr* 1977 (Life Peer), of Strathtummel; **Henry Shanks Keith,** PC 1976; a Lord of Appeal in Ordinary, since 1977; *b* 7 Feb. 1922; *s* of late Baron Keith of Avonholm, PC (Life Peer); *m* 1955, Alison Hope Alan Brown; four *s* (including twin *s*) one *d*. *Educ*: Edinburgh Academy; Magdalen Coll., Oxford (MA); Edinburgh Univ. (LLB). War of 1939-45 (despatches); commnd Scots Guards, Nov. 1941; served N Africa and Italy, 1943-45; released, 1945 (Capt.). Advocate, Scottish Bar, 1950; Barrister, Gray's Inn, 1951, Bencher 1976; QC (Scotland), 1962. Standing Counsel to Dept of Health for Scotland, 1957-62; Sheriff of Roxburgh, Berwick and Selkirk, 1970-71; Senator of Coll. of Justice in Scotland, 1971-77. Chairman: Scottish Valuation Adv. Coun., 1972-76 (Mem., 1957-70); Dep. Chm., Parly Boundary Commn for Scotland, 1976; Member: Law Reform Cttee for Scotland, 1964-70; Cttee on Law of Defamation, 1971-74; Mem. Panel of Arbiters: European Fisheries Convention, 1964-71; Convention for Settlement of Investment Disputes, 1968-71. *Address*: House of Lords, SW1; Woodend, Strathtummel, Perthshire. *T*: Tummel Bridge 255.
See also G. O. Mayne.

KEITH, David; see Steegmuller, Francis.

KEITH, John Lucien, CBE 1951 (OBE 1943); *b* 22 May 1895; *s* of George Keith, Engineer and Director of S American Telephone Companies; unmarried. *Educ*: Ecole Closelet, Lausanne; Hertford Coll., Oxford (MA). British South Africa Co., N Rhodesia, 1918-25; District Officer, Colonial Service, N Rhodesia, 1925-38; Acting Dir of African Education, N Rhodesia, 1930-31; African Research Survey, Chatham House, 1938-39; Colonial Office, 1939; Dir of Colonial Scholars and head of Student Dept, Colonial Office, 1941-56. Adviser on Students' Affairs, W Nigeria Office, London, 1957-62; London Rep. of Univ. of Ife, Nigeria, 1962-72. Official missions to British West Africa, 1947, BWI, 1947, Malaya and Hong Kong, 1948, British East Africa and Mauritius, 1951, North America and British West Indies, 1954, British East and Central Africa, 1955, Ghana, 1957, Nigeria, 1960, and Zambia, 1964, for Independence celebrations. *Recreations*: travelling, talking books for the blind. *Address*: 49A Sea Road, Bexhill-on-Sea, East Sussex. *T*: Bexhill-on-Sea 215463. *Club*: Royal Commonwealth Society.

KEITH, Sir Kenneth (Alexander), Kt 1969; merchant banker; Chairman, Hill Samuel Group Ltd, since 1972 (Group Chief Executive, 1972-76); Chairman, Rolls Royce Ltd, since 1972; *b* 30 Aug. 1916; *er s* of late Edward Charles Keith, Swanton Morley House, Norfolk; *m* 1st, 1946, Lady Ariel Olivia Winifred Baird (marr. diss., 1958), 2nd *d* of 1st Viscount Stonehaven, PC, GCMG, DSO, and Countess of Kintore; one *s* one *d*; 2nd, 1962, Mrs Nancy Hayward (marr. diss. 1972), Manhasset, New York; 3rd, 1973, Mrs Marie Hanbury, Burley-on-the-Hill, Rutland. *Educ*: Rugby Sch. Trained as a Chartered Accountant. 2nd Lt Welsh Guards, 1939; Lt-Col 1945; served in North Africa, Italy, France and Germany (despatches, Croix de Guerre with Silver Star). Asst to Dir Gen. Political Intelligence Dept, Foreign Office, 1945-46. Chm., Philip Hill Investment Trust Ltd; Vice-Chm., 1974-, Dir, 1949-; Beecham Gp Ltd; Director, The Times Newspapers Ltd, and other companies; Vice-Chm., BEA, 1964-71. Member: NEDC, 1964-71; CBI/NEDC Liaison Cttee,

1974-; Defence Industries Council; Nat. Defence Industries Council; SBAC. Vice-Pres., Engrg Employers Fedn. Chairman: Economic Planning Council for East Anglia, 1965-70; Governor, Nat. Inst. of Economic and Social Research. Council Mem., Manchester Business Sch. FBIM. *Recreations:* shooting, golf, farming. *Address:* 80 Eaton Square, SW1W 9AP. *T:* 01-730 4000; The Wicken House, Castleacre, Norfolk. *T:* Castleacre 225. *Clubs:* White's; Pratt's; Racquet and Tennis (New York).

KEITH, Robert Farquharson, CB 1973; OBE 1948; Chief Registrar of Trade Unions and Employers' Associations from 1971 until repeal of Industrial Relations Act 1971 in 1974; *b* 22 June 1912; *s* of Dr Robert Donald Keith and Mary Lindsay (*née* Duncan), Turriff, Aberdeenshire; *m* 1958, Jean Abernethy (*née* Fisher); one *s. Educ:* Fettes; Caius Coll., Cambridge (Classical Scholar). Indian Civil Service, 1937-47; Dep. Comr, Upper Sind Frontier, 1945-47; Home Civil Service, Min. of Labour, later Dept of Employment, 1948; Under-Sec., Employment Services and Estabs Divs, 1965-71. *Address:* Parkhead, Auchattie, Banchory, Kincardineshire. *T:* Banchory 3166. *Club:* Caledonian.

KEITH, Trevor; Charity Commissioner since Oct. 1972; *b* 3 Sept. 1921; 2nd *s* of George Keith and May Mabel Keith (*née* Newman). *Educ:* Isleworth County Grammar School. Called to Bar, Lincoln's Inn, 1951. Entered Civil Service, Air Min., 1938; RAF, 1941-45; Air Min., 1946-48; Inland Revenue, Estate Duty Office, 1948-52; Charity Commn, 1952-. *Recreations:* cricket, travel, gastronomy. *Address:* 7 Lucastes Road, Haywards Heath, W Sussex.

KEITH-JONES, Maj.-Gen. Richard, CB 1968; MBE 1947; MC 1944; Manager, Management Development, Mardon Packaging International Ltd, 1969-75; *b* 6 Dec. 1913; *o s* of late Brig. Frederick Theodore Jones, CIE, MVO, VD; *m* 1938, Margaret Ridley Harrison; three *d. Educ:* Clifton Coll.; Royal Military Academy Woolwich. Commissioned into Royal Artillery, 1934; served in UK, 1934-42; 1st Airborne Div., 1943-44; War Office, 1944-47; Palestine and Egypt, 1st Regt RHA, 1947-49; Instructor Staff Coll., Camberley, 1949-52; Military Asst to F-M Montgomery, 1953-55; CO 4th Regt, RHA, 1955-57; Senior Army Instructor, JSSC, 1957-59; Dep. Comdr 17 Gurkha Div., Malaya, 1959-61; Student, Imperial Defence Coll., 1962-63; Military Adviser, High Comr, Canada, 1963-64; GOC 50 (Northumbrian) Div. (TA), 1964-66; Comdt, Jt Warfare Establishment, 1966-68; retd 1969. Col Comdt RA, 1970-; Hon. Col, 266 (Glos Vol. Artillery) Batt., RA, T&AVR, 1975-. *Recreations:* fishing, shooting, golf. *Address:* c/o Lloyd's Bank Ltd, Cox's & King's Branch, 6 Pall Mall, SW1; The White House, Brockley, Backwell, Bristol BS19 3AU. *Clubs:* Army and Navy, MCC.

KEITH-LUCAS, Prof. Bryan; Professor of Government, University of Kent at Canterbury, 1965-77, now Emeritus (Master of Darwin College, 1970-74); *b* 1 Aug. 1912; *y s* of late Keith Lucas, ScD, FRS, and Alys (*née* Hubbard); *m* 1946, Mary Hardwicke (Sheriff of Canterbury, 1971); one *s* two *d. Educ:* Gresham's Sch., Holt; Pembroke Coll., Cambridge. MA Cantab 1937, MA Oxon 1948. Solicitor, 1937. Asst Solicitor: Kensington Council, 1938-46; Nottingham, 1946-48. Served 1939-45 in Buffs and Sherwood Foresters, N Africa and Italy (Major, despatches); DAAG Cyprus, 1945-46. Sen. Lectr in Local Govt, Oxford, 1948-65; Faculty Fellow of Nuffield Coll., 1950-65, Domestic Bursar, 1957-65. Chm., Commn on Electoral System, Sierra Leone, 1954; Commn on local govt elections, Mauritius, 1955-56. Member: Roberts Cttee on Public Libraries, 1957-59; Commn on Administration of Lagos, 1963; Mallaby Cttee on Staffing of Local Govt, 1964-67; Local Govt Commn for England, 1965-66; Royal Commn on Elections in Fiji, 1975. Vice-Chm., Hansard Soc., 1976-. Chairman: Nat. Assoc. of Parish Councils, 1964-70 (Vice-Pres., 1970-; Pres., Kent Assoc., 1972-); Canterbury Soc., 1972-75; Pres., Kent Fedn of Amenity Socs, 1976-. City Councillor, Oxford, 1950-65. Hon. Fellow, Inst. of Local Govt Studies, Birmingham Univ., 1973. *Publications:* The English Local Government Franchise, 1952; The Mayor, Aldermen and Councillors, 1961; various articles on local govt. *Address:* 20 King Street, Canterbury, Kent. *T:* Canterbury 64336. *Club:* National Liberal.
See also David Keith-Lucas.

KEITH-LUCAS, David, CBE 1973; MA, DSc; FIMechE, FRAeS; Chairman, Airworthiness Requirements, since 1972; *b* 25 March 1911; *s* of late Keith Lucas, ScD, FRS, and Alys (*née* Hubbard); *m* 1942, Dorothy De Bauduy Robertson; two *s* one *d. Educ:* Gresham's Sch., Holt; Gonville and Caius Coll., Cambridge. BA (Mech Sci Tripos, 2nd Class Hons) 1933; MA 1956; FRAeS 1948; FIMechE 1949; FAIAA 1973, Hon. FAIAA 1974. Apprenticed 1933-35, design team 1935-39, C. A.

Parsons & Co. Ltd; Chief Aerodynamicist, Short Bros Ltd, 1940-49; Short Bros & Harland Ltd: Chief Designer, 1949-58; Technical Dir, 1958-64; Dir of Research, 1964-65; Dir, John Brown & Co., 1970-77; Cranfield Inst. of Technology (formerly Coll. of Aeronautics): Prof. of Aircraft Design, 1965-72; Pro-Vice-Chancellor, 1970-73; Prof. of Aeronautics and Chm. College of Aeronautics, 1972-76; Emeritus Prof., 1977. Member: Senate, Queen's Univ., Belfast, 1955-65; Council, Air Registration Board, 1967-; Commn on Third London Airport, 1968-70; Civil Aviation Authority, 1972-. President: RAeS, 1968; Engrg Section, British Assoc. for the Advancement of Science, 1972. Hon. DSc: Queen's Univ., Belfast, 1968; Cranfield Inst. of Technology, 1975. Gold Medal, RAeS, 1975. *Publications:* The Shape of Wings to Come, 1952; The Challenge of Vertical Take-Off (lects IMechE), 1961-62; The Role of Jet Lift (lect. RAeS), 1962; papers on aircraft design, vertical take-off, engrg economics, in engrg jls. *Recreations:* youth organisations, small boats. *Address:* Manor Close, Emberton, Olney, Bucks MK46 5BX. *T:* Bedford 711552. *Club:* Naval and Military.
See also B. Keith-Lucas.

KEKWICK, Prof. Ralph Ambrose, FRS 1966; Professor of Biophysics, University of London, 1966-71, now Emeritus; Member Staff, Lister Institute, 1940-71 (Head, Division of Biophysics, 1943-71); *b* 11 Nov. 1908; 2nd *s* of late Oliver A. and Mary Kekwick; *m* 1st, 1933, Barbara (*d* 1973), 3rd *d* of W. S. Stone, DD, New York; one *d*; 2nd, 1974, Dr Margaret Mackay, *er d* of J. G. Mackay, MB, BS, Adelaide, Australia. *Educ:* Leyton County High Sch.; University Coll., London (Fellow, 1971). BSc 1928; MSc 1936; DSc 1941. Bayliss-Starling Scholar, University Coll. London, 1930-31. Commonwealth Fund Fellow, New York and Princeton Univs, 1931-33. Lectr in Biochemistry University Coll. London, 1933-37. Rockefeller Fellow, University of Uppsala, Sweden, 1935; MRC Fellow, Lister Inst., 1937-40. Reader in Chemical Biophysics, University of London, 1954-66. Oliver Memorial Award for Blood Transfusion, 1957. *Publications:* MRC Special Report "Separation of protein fractions from human plasma" (with M. E. Mackay), 1954. Papers on physical biochemistry and haematology, mostly in Biochemical Jl and Brit. Jl of Haematology. *Recreations:* music, gardening and bird watching. *Address:* 31 Woodside Road, Woodford Wells, Essex IG8 0TW. *T:* 01-504 4264.

KELBURN, Viscount of; Patrick Robin Archibald Boyle; television director/producer; *b* 30 July 1939; *s* and *heir* of 9th Earl of Glasgow, *qv*; *m* 1975, Isabel Mary James. *Educ:* Eton; Paris Univ. National Service in Navy; Sub-Lt, RNR, 1959-60. Worked in Associated Rediffusion Television, 1961, since when has worked at various times for Woodfall Film Productions; Asst on Film Productions, 1962-64; Asst Dir in film industry, 1962-67; producer/director of documentary films, Yorkshire TV, 1968-70; freelance film producer, 1971-. *Recreations:* skiing, theatre. *Address:* 93 Hereford Road, W2. *T:* 01-727 9731.

KELF-COHEN, Reuben, CB 1950; Economics writer and consultant; Director and Secretary, Radio Industry Council, 1960-66; *b* Leeds, 29 Sept. 1895; *m* 1922, Edith Florence Kelf (*d* 1964); one *d. Educ:* Manchester Grammar Sch.; Wadham Coll., Oxford (Classical Scholar). Gaisford Greek Verse Prize, 1915; Lothian Historical Essay Prize, 1920; 1st Class Hons (History), 1920; 1st class Hons (Economics) London Univ., 1931. Served European War, 1914-18, Royal Field Artillery (wounded). Entered Bd of Educn, 1920; Tutorial Class Tutor, London Univ., 1924-39; Board of Trade, 1925-41; Petroleum Dept, 1941-42; Principal Asst Sec. (Gas and Electricity), Ministry of Fuel and Power, 1942-45; Under-Sec., Ministry of Fuel and Power, 1946-55; Dir, East Indian Produce Co. 1955-59. Vis. Lecturer: St Andrews Univ., 1970; University Coll., Aberystwyth, 1971. Freeman of the City of London; Liveryman of the Company of Horners. FRSA 1970. *Publications:* Knights of Malta, 1920; Nationalisation in Britain, 1958; Twenty Years of Nationalisation: The British Experience, 1969; British Nationalisation 1945-1973, 1974; articles on economic subjects. *Recreations:* bridge, bowls, sea voyages. *Address:* 14 Harold Road, Upper Norwood, SE19. *T:* 01-653 1086. *Club:* Savage.

KELL, Joseph; *see* Burgess, Anthony.

KELLAR, Alexander James, CMG 1961; OBE 1948; *b* 26 June 1905; *er s* of James Dodds Ballantyne Kellar and Florence Maud Kellar (*née* Coveney). *Educ:* George Watson's Coll.; Edinburgh Univ. (MA, LLB). Sen. Pres., Students' Representative Council; Pres., Nat. Union of Scottish Students, 1929-30; Commonwealth Fund Fellow, Yale (Mem. Elizabethan Club) and Columbia (AM Internat. Law and Relations); called to Bar, Middle Temple, 1936. Asst Sec., Brit. Employers' Confedn, 1938-41;

Employers' (Substitute) Delegate, Governing Body of ILO, 1940. Mem. Army Officers' Emergency Reserve, 1938. Attached War Office, 1941-65; ODM, 1970-73; English Tourist Bd, 1970-73. *Recreations:* riding, travel. *Address:* Grey Walls, Friston, Sussex. *Club:* Royal Automobile.
See also R. J. Kellar

KELLAR, Prof. Robert James, CBE 1968 (MBE 1943); MB, ChB, FRCSEd, FRCPEd, FRCOG; Professor of Obstetrics and Gynæcology, University of Edinburgh, 1946-74; *yr s* of James Dodds Ballantyne Kellar and Florence Maud Kellar (*née* Coveney). *Educ:* Univ. of Edinburgh; MB, ChB, 1931; MRCPEd, 1934, FRCSEd, 1935; FRCOG, 1945; FRCPEd, 1946. Univ. of Edinburgh: Annandale Gold Medal for Clinical Surgery, Wightman Prize for Clinical Medicine, Murchison Prize for Medicine (halved), Buchanan Prize for Midwifery and Diseases of Women, 1931, Simpson Prize for Obstetrics, 1932; Lister Prize for Surgery, 1934; Freeland Barbour Fellowship in Obstetrics; Leckie Mactier Research Fellow, 1934-35; Beit Memorial Research Fellow, 1935-37. Formerly: Reader in Obstetrics and Gynæcology, University of London, British Post-Graduate Medical Sch.; Asst, Obstetrical Unit, University Coll. Hosp.; Tutor in Clinical Gynæcology, House Surgeon Out-patients Department and to Prof. of Midwifery, Royal Infirmary, Edinburgh. Lt-Col, Royal Army Medical Corps; Officer in charge of a Surgical Div. (despatches, MBE). Mem. Council, RCOG, 1963. Hon. Fellow Amer. Assoc. of Obst. and Gynæcol. *Address:* 27 Hope Terrace, Edinburgh EH9 2AP.
See also A. J. Kellar.

KELLAS, Arthur Roy Handasyde, CMG 1964; HM Diplomatic Service, retired; High Commissioner in Tanzania, 1972-74; *b* 6 May 1915; *s* of Henry Kellas and Mary Kellas (*née* Brown); *m* 1952, Katharine Bridget, *d* of Sir John Le Rougetel, KCMG, MC; two *s* one *d*. *Educ:* Aberdeen Grammar Sch.; Aberdeen Univ.; Oxford Univ.; Ecole des Sciences Politiques. Passed into Diplomatic Service, Sept. 1939. Commissioned into Border Regt, Nov. 1939. War of 1939-45: Active Service with 1st Bn Parachute Regt and Special Ops, Af. and Gr, 1941-44 (despatches twice). Third Sec. at HM Embassy, Tehran, 1944-47; First Sec. at HM Legation, Helsingfors, 1948-50; First Sec. (press) at HM Embassy, Cairo, 1951-52; First Sec. at HM Embassy, Baghdad, 1954-58; Counsellor, HM Embassy, Tehran, 1958-62; Imperial Defence Coll., 1963-64; Counsellor, HM Embassy and Consul-Gen., Tel Aviv, 1964-65; Ambassador to Nepal, 1966-70, to Democratic Yemen, 1970-72. Pres., Britain-Nepal Soc., 1975-. *Recreations:* reading, riding, boxing. *Address:* Laurel Villa, Culworth, Banbury, Oxon OX17 2AZ. *T:* Sulgrave 558. *Club:* United Oxford & Cambridge University.

KELLAWAY, (Charles) William; Secretary and Librarian, Institute of Historical Research, University of London, since 1971; *b* 9 March 1926; *s* of late Charles Halliley Kellaway, FRS; *m* 1952, Deborah, *d* of late Sir Hibbert Alan Stephen Newton; one *s* two *d*. *Educ:* Geelong Grammar Sch.; Lincoln Coll., Oxford. BA Modern History, 1949, MA 1955. FLA, FRHistS, FSA. Asst Librarian, Guildhall Library, 1950-60; Sub-Librarian, Inst. of Historical Research, 1960-71. Hon. General Editor, London Record Society, 1964-. *Publications:* The New England Company, 1649-1776, 1961; (Joint Editor) Studies in London History, 1969; Bibliography of Historical Works Issued in UK, 1957-70, 3 vols, 1962, 1967, 1972; (ed jtly) The London Assize of Nuisance 1301-1431, 1973. *Address:* 2 Grove Terrace, NW5. *T:* 01-485 1741.

KELLEHER, Dame Joan, DBE 1965; Hon. ADC to the Queen, 1964-67; Director, Women's Royal Army Corps, 1964-67; *b* 24 Dec. 1915; *d* of late Kenneth George Henderson, Stonehaven; *m* 1970, Brig. M. F. H. Kelleher, OBE, MC, late RAMC. *Educ:* privately at home and abroad. Joined ATS, 1941; commissioned ATS, 1941; WRAC, 1949. *Recreations:* golf and gardening. *Address:* c/o Midland Bank, 123 Chancery Lane, WC2.

KELLER, Prof. Andrew, FRS 1972; Research Professor in Polymer Science, Department of Physics, University of Bristol, since 1969; *b* 22 Aug. 1925; *s* of Imre Keller and Margil Klein; *m* 1951, Eva Bulhack; one *s* one *d*. *Educ:* Budapest Univ. (BSc); Bristol Univ. (PhD). FInstP. Techn. Officer, ICI Ltd, Manchester, 1948-55; Bristol Univ.: Min. of Supply res. appt, 1955-57; Res. Asst, 1957-63; Lectr, 1963-65; Reader, 1965-69. High Polymer Prize, Amer. Phys. Soc., 1964; Swinburne Award, Plastics Inst., 1974. *Publications:* numerous papers in Jl Polymer Science, Progress Reports in Physics, Proc. Royal Soc., Macromol. Chem., etc. *Recreations:* outdoor sports, mountain walking, concerts. *Address:* 41 Westbury Road, Bristol BS9 3AU. *T:* Bristol 628526.

KELLER, René; Ambassador of Switzerland to Austria, since 1976; *b* 19 May 1914; *s* of Jacques Keller and Marie (*née* Geiser); *m* 1942, Marion (*née* Werder); one *s* two *d*. *Educ:* Geneva; Trinity Coll., Cambridge. Vice-Consul, Prague, 1941-45; 2nd Sec. of Legation, The Hague, 1947-50; 1st Sec., London, 1950-54; Head of News Dept, Berne, 1954-56; 1st Counsellor, Swiss Embassy, Paris, 1957-60; Ambassador to Ghana, Guinea, Liberia, Mali and Togo, 1960-62; Ambassador to Turkey, 1962-65; Head of Perm. Mission of Switzerland to Office of UN and Internat. Organisations, Geneva, 1966-68; Ambassador of Switzerland to UK, 1968-71; Head of Direction for International Organisation, Foreign Ministry of Switzerland, 1971-75. *Recreations:* golf, sailing. *Address:* Embassy of Switzerland, Prinz Eugen Strasse 7-9, A1030 Vienna, Austria. *Club:* Travellers'.

KELLER, Prof. Rudolf Ernst, MA Manchester; DrPhil Zürich; Professor of German Language and Medieval German Literature, University of Manchester, since 1960; *b* 3 Feb. 1920; *m* 1947, Ivy Sparrow; two *d*. *Educ:* Kantonsschule Winterthur, Switzerland; University of Zürich. Teacher at Kantonsschule Winterthur, 1944-46; Asst, 1946-47, Asst Lecturer, 1947-49, University of Manchester; Lecturer in German, Royal Holloway College, University of London, 1949-52; Sen. Lecturer, 1952-59, Reader in German, 1959-60, Dean of Faculty of Arts, 1968-70, Pro-Vice-Chancellor, 1976-79, University of Manchester. *Publications:* Die Ellipse in der neuenglischen Sprache als semantisch-syntaktisches Problem, 1944; Die Sprachen der Welt, 1955 (trans. Bodmer: The Loom of Language); German Dialects, Phonology and Morphology with Selected Texts, 1961; articles in learned periodicals. *Recreations:* reading, travel. *Address:* 11a Rathen Road, Manchester M20 9QJ. *T:* 061-445 6952.

KELLETT, Alfred Henry, CBE 1965; Chairman, South Western Areas, National Coal Board, 1967-69, retired; *b* 2 Aug. 1904; British; *m* 1934, Astrid Elizabeth (*née* Hunter); one *s* three *d*. *Educ:* Rossall Sch.; Universities of Cambridge and Birmingham. Man. Dir, Washington Coal Co. Ltd, 1940-47; Area Gen. Man., NCB Durham Div., 1950-59; Dep. Chm., Durham Div., 1960; Chm., South Western Div., NCB, 1961-67. CStJ. *Recreation:* travel. *Address:* Pent House, Benenden, Cranbrook, Kent.

KELLETT, Brian Smith; Chairman, since 1976, and a Managing Director, since 1968, Tube Investments Ltd; Chairman, British Aluminium Co. Ltd, since 1972; Director, Unigate Ltd, since 1974; *b* 8 May 1922; *s* of late Harold Lamb Kellett and Amy Elizabeth Kellett (*née* Smith); *m* 1947, Janet Lesly Street; three *d*. *Educ:* Manchester Grammar Sch.; Trinity Coll., Cambridge (MA). Wrangler and Sen. Scholar, 1942. Exper. Officer, Admty, 1942-46; Asst Principal, Min. of Transport, 1946-48; Sir Robert Watson-Watt & Partners, 1948-49; Pilkington Bros Ltd, 1949-55; joined Tube Investments Ltd, 1955, Dir 1965, Dep. Chm. and Chief Exec., 1974. Member: Royal Commn on Standards of Conduct in Public Life, 1974-76; PO Review Cttee, 1976-77. A Vice-Pres., Engineering Employers' Fedn, 1976-. Governor, London Graduate Sch. of Business Studies, 1976-. *Address:* 10 Elm Walk, NW3 7UP. *T:* 01-458 6723.

KELLETT, Sir Stanley Everard, 6th Bt *cr* 1801; *b* 1911; *s* of Francis Stanley Kellett (*d* 1955) (2nd *s* of 3rd Bt); *S* kinsman, Sir Henry de Castres Kellett, 5th Bt, 1966; *m* 1938, Audrey Margaret Phillips; one *s* one *d*. *Heir: s* Stanley Charles Kellett [*b* 5 March 1940; *m* 1st, 1962, Lorraine May (marr. diss. 1968), *d* of F. Winspear; 2nd, 1968, Margaret Ann, *d* of J. Bofinger]. *Address:* 33 Caroma Avenue, Kyeemagh, New South Wales 2216, Australia.

KELLETT-BOWMAN, (Mary) Elaine; MP (C) Lancaster, since 1970; Member, European Parliament, since 1975; *b* 8 July 1924; *d* of late Walter Kay; *m* 1st, 1945, Charles Norman Kellett (decd); three *s* one *d*; 2nd, 1971, Edward Thomas Kellett-Bowman, JP, MBA, DMS, AMBIM, *s* of late R. E. Bowman. *Educ:* Queen Mary Sch., Lytham; The Mount, York; St Anne's Coll., Oxford (post-graduate distinction in welfare diploma). Contested (C): Nelson and Colne, 1955; South-West Norfolk, March and Oct. 1959; Buckingham, 1964, 1966. Mem. Social Affairs and Regional Policy Cttees, European Parlt. Camden Borough Council: Alderman, 1968-74; Vice-Chm., Housing Cttee, 1968; Chm., Welfare Cttee, 1969. Called to Bar, Middle Temple, 1964. Lay Mem., Press Council, 1964-68. Governor, Culford Sch., 1963; Mem. Union European Women, 1956; Delegate to Luxemburg, 1958. No 1 Country Housewife, 1960; Christal MacMillan Law Prize, 1963. *Recreations:* gardening, stamp collecting. *Address:* House of Commons, SW1; 42 Schoolhouse Lane, Halton, Lancaster. *Club:* English-Speaking Union.

KELLEY, Mrs Joanna Elizabeth, OBE 1973; Assistant Director of Prisons (Women), 1967-74; *b* 23 May 1910; *d* of late Lt-Col William Beadon, 51st Sikhs; *m* 1934, Harper Kelley (*d* 1962); no *c. Educ:* Hayes Court; Girton Coll., Cambridge (MA). Souschargé, Dept of Pre-History, Musée de l'Homme, Paris, 1934-39; Mixed Youth Club Leader, YWCA, 1939-42; Welfare Officer, Admiralty, Bath, 1942-47; Prison Service, 1947-74; Governor of HM Prison, Holloway, 1959-66. FSA. Hon. Fellow Girton Coll., Cambridge, 1968. Hon. LLD Hull Univ., 1960. *Publication:* When the Gates Shut, 1967. *Recreation:* reading. *Address:* c/o Lloyds Bank Ltd, 6 Pall Mall, SW1.

KELLEY, Richard; MP (Lab) Don Valley Division of West Yorks since Oct. 1959; *b* 24 July 1904; *m* 1924; four *s* three *d. Educ:* Elementary Sch. Councillor, West Riding of Yorks County Council, 1949-59; a Trade Union Secretary for ten years. Mem. of the National Union of Mineworkers. *Address:* House of Commons, SW1; 23 St Lawrence Road, Dunscroft, Doncaster, W Yorks DN7 4AS.

KELLGREN, Prof. Jonas Henrik, FRCS, FRCP; Professor of Rheumatology, University of Manchester, 1953-76, now Emeritus; Dean, 1970-73; *b* 11 Sept. 1911; *s* of Dr Harry Kellgren and Vera (*née* Dumelunksen); *m* 1942, Thelma Marian Reynolds; four *d. Educ:* Bedales Sch.; University Coll., London. MB, BS, 1934; FRCS 1936; FRCP 1951. Junior clinical appointments, University Coll. Hosp., 1934-42 (Beit Memorial Fellow 1938-39); served War, 1942-46, as surgical and orthopædic specialist, RAMC; Mem. Scientific Staff, Med. Research Council, Wingfield Morris Orthopædic Hosp., Oxford, Chronic Rheumatism, University of Manchester, 1947. Pres. Heberden Soc., 1958-59. *Publications:* numerous articles in medical and scientific jls. *Recreation:* landscape painting. *Address:* 163 Palatine Road, Manchester M20 8GH. *T:* 061-445 1568.

KELLIHER, Sir Henry (Joseph), Kt 1963; Chairman and Managing Director (Founder), Dominion Breweries Ltd since 1929; *b* March 1896; *s* of Michael Joseph Kelliher; *m* 1917, Evelyn J., *d* of R. S. Sproule; one *s* four *d. Educ:* Clyde Sch. Dir, Bank of New Zealand, 1936-42. Founded League of Health of NZ Youth, 1934 (objective, Free milk scheme for NZ children, in which it succeeded); purchased Puketutu Island, 1938; established Puketutu Ayrshire Stud, 1940, Aberdeen Angus Stud, 1942, Suffolk Stud, 1946; Thoroughbred and Standard Bred Studs, 1969. Founded: Kelliher Art Trust, 1961; Kelliher Charitable Trust, 1963. KStJ 1960. *Publications:* New Zealand at the Cross Roads, 1936; Why your £ buys Less and Less, 1954. *Recreations:* gardening, riding. *Address:* Puketutu Island, Manukau Harbour, Auckland, New Zealand. *T:* 543733.

KELLOCK, Jane Ursula, JP; Member, Police Complaints Board, since 1977; *b* 21 Oct. 1925; *d* of late Arthur George Symonds and late Gertrude Frances Symonds; *m* 1967, Thomas Oslaf Kellock, *qv. Educ:* Priors Field Sch., Godalming. WRNS, 1943-45. Sec., Africa Bureau, London, 1957-67; Editor, Africa Digest, 1957-75; Board Member, Commonwealth Development Corporation, 1965-73. Former Mem., S Metropolitan Conciliation Cttee, Race Relations Bd. JP: Inner London, 1968-77; Nottingham City Bench, 1977. *Recreation:* travel. *Address:* 8 Huntingdon Drive, The Park, Nottingham NG7 1BW.

KELLOCK, Thomas Oslaf, QC 1965; **His Honour Judge Kellock;** a Circuit Judge, since 1976; *b* 4 July 1923; *s* of late Thomas Herbert Kellock, MA, MD, MCh Cambridge, FRCS LRCP; *m* 1967, Jane Ursula Kellock, *qv. Educ:* Rugby; Clare Coll., Cambridge. Sub-Lieut (Special Branch), RNVR, 1944-46. Called to the Bar, Inner Temple, 1949, Bencher, 1973. Admitted: Gold Coast (Ghana) Roll of Legal Practitioners, 1955; N Rhodesia (Zambia) Bar, 1956; Nigeria Bar, 1957; Ceylon (Sri Lanka) Roll of Advocates, 1960; Sierra Leone Bar, 1960; Malayan Bar, 1967; Fiji Bar, 1975. Has also appeared in courts of Kenya, Malaŵi, Pakistan, Jammu and Kashmir, Sarawak. Dir, Legal Div., Commonwealth Secretariat, 1969-72; a Recorder of the Crown Court, 1974-76. Constitutional Advr to HH Sultan of Brunei, 1975-76. Chm., Anti-Apartheid Movement, 1963-65; Contested (L) Torquay, 1949, S Kensington, 1966 and March 1968, Harwich, Oct. 1974. *Recreation:* travelling. *Address:* 8 Huntingdon Drive, The Park, Nottingham NG7 1BW. *T:* Nottingham 48304. *Club:* Reform.

KELLOW, Kathleen; see Hibbert, Eleanor.

KELLY, Dr Anthony, FRS 1973; Vice-Chancellor, University of Surrey, since 1975; *s* of late Group Captain Vincent Gerald French and Mrs Violet Kelly; *m* 1956, Christina Margaret (*née* Dunleavie); three *s* one *d. Educ:* Presentation Coll., Reading; Univs of Reading (Schol.) and Cambridge. BSc Reading 1949;

PhD 1953, ScD 1968, Cantab. Research Assoc., Univ. of Illinois, 1953-55; ICI Fellow, Univ. of Birmingham, 1955; Asst, Associate Prof., Northwestern Univ., 1956-59; Univ. Lectr, Cambridge, 1959-67; Founding Fellow, Churchill Coll., 1960; Dir of Studies, Churchill Coll., 1960-67; Supt, Div. of Inorganic and Metallic Structure, 1967-69, Dep. Dir, 1969-75, Nat. Physical Lab. (seconded to ICI, 1973-75). Member: SRC Cttee, 1967-72; Council, Inst. of Metals, 1969-74; Council, British Non-Ferrous Metals Res. Assoc., 1970-73; Engrg Materials Requirements Bd, DoI, 1973-75 (Chm., 1976-); Adv. Cttee, Community Ref. Bureau of EEC, 1973-75. William Hopkins Prize, 1967; Beilby Medal, 1967; A. A. Griffith Medal, 1974. *Publications:* Strong Solids, 1966, 2nd edn 1973; (with G. W. Groves) Crystallography and Crystal Defects, 1970; many papers in jls of physical sciences. *Recreations:* brewing, gardening, sailing. *Address:* Headley Cottage, Weston Green, Thames Ditton, Surrey. *Club:* Hardway Sailing (Gosport).

KELLY, Sir Arthur (John), Kt 1961; CBE 1950; *b* 17 Nov. 1898; *yr s* of John Kelly, Hodge Bower, Shropshire; *m* 1928, Florence Mary Smyth, *yr d* of John Smyth, Belfast. *Educ:* Bridgnorth; Shrewsbury. Served European War, 1917-19: RFC 12 Sqdn and RAF Army of Occupation, Germany. Temp. Asst, Min. of Labour, Whitehall, 1919-22; Asst Principal, Min. of Labour, N Ireland, 1922; Principal, Cabinet Offices, N Ireland, 1940; Asst Sec., 1941; seconded as N Ireland Govt Liaison Officer at Home Office, Whitehall, 1943; Permanent Sec., Min. of Labour N Ireland, 1956; Sec. to the Cabinet and Clerk of the Privy Council of Northern Ireland, 1957-63, retd. *Recreation:* golf. *Address:* 6 Cherryhill, Beechlands, Malone Road, Belfast. *Club:* Malone Golf (Belfast).

KELLY, Basil; see Kelly, J. W. B.

KELLY, Charles Henry; Chief Constable of Staffordshire, since 1977; *b* 15 July 1930; *s* of Charles Henry Kelly and Phoebe Jane Kelly; *m* 1952, Doris (*née* Kewley); one *s* one *d. Educ:* Douglas High Sch. for Boys, IOM; London Univ. LLB (Hons). Asst Chief Constable of Essex, 1972; Dep. Chief Constable of Staffordshire, 1976. *Recreations:* cricket, football. *Address:* Castanea, 31 High Park, Newport Road, Stafford ST16 1BL. *T:* Stafford 57717.

KELLY, Edward Ronald; Home Controller, Central Office of Information, since 1976; *b* 14 Oct. 1928; *s* of late William Walter Kelly and of Millicent Kelly; *m* 1954, Storm Massada. *Educ:* Honiton Sch. Journalist: Bath Evening Chronicle, 1952; East African Standard, 1953; Sunday Post, Kenya, 1954; Reuters, 1956; Central Office of Information, 1958-: Editor in Chief, Overseas Press Services Div., 1964; Asst Overseas Controller, 1968; Dir, Publications and Design Services Div., 1970. *Recreations:* fishing, fly-tying, carpentry. *Address:* The Coach House, Willinghurst, Shamley Green, near Guildford, Surrey GU5 0SU. *T:* Cranleigh 5461. *Club:* Flyfishers'.

KELLY, Rev. Canon John Norman Davidson, DD; FBA 1965; Principal of St Edmund Hall, Oxford, since 1951; Vice-Chancellor, Oxford University, Sept.-Oct. 1966 (Pro-Vice-Chancellor, 1964-66, 1972-78); *b* 13 April 1909; *s* of John and Ann Davidson Kelly. *Educ:* privately; Glasgow Univ.; Queen's Coll., Oxford (Ferguson Scholar; Hertford Scholar; 1st Cl. Hon. Mods, Greats and Theology; St Stephen's House. Deacon, 1934; priest, 1935; Curate, St Lawrence's, Northampton, 1934; Chaplain, St Edmund Hall, Oxford, 1935; Vice-Principal and Trustee, 1937. Select Preacher (Oxford), 1944-46, 1959, 1961, 1962; Speaker's Lectr in Biblical Studies, 1945-48; University Lecturer in Patristic Studies, 1948-76; Select Preacher (Cambridge), 1953; Chm. Cttee of Second Internat. Conf. on Patristic Studies, Oxford, 1955; Proctor in Convocation of Canterbury representing Oxford University, 1958-64; Chm. Archbishop's Commn on Roman Catholic Relations, 1964-68; accompanied Archbishop of Canterbury on his visit to Pope Paul VI, 1966; Mem., Academic Council, Ecumenical Theological Inst., Jerusalem, 1966-. In the War of 1939-45 did part-time work at Chatham House and collaborated in organizing the Oxford Leave Courses for United States, Allied, and Dominions Forces. Canon of Chichester and Prebendary of Wightring, 1948, Highleigh, 1964. Took lead in obtaining Royal Charter, new statutes and full collegiate status for St Edmund Hall, 1957. Mem. Governing Body: Royal Holloway Coll., London, 1959-69; King's Sch., Canterbury. Lectures: Paddock, General Theological Seminary, NY, 1963; Birkbeck, Cambridge, 1973. Hon. DD: Glasgow, 1958; Wales, 1971; Hon. Fellow, Queen's Coll., Oxford, 1963. *Publications:* Early Christian Creeds, 1950, 3rd edn 1972; Rufinus, a Commentary on the Apostles' Creed, 1955; Early Christian Doctrines, 1958, 5th edn 1977; The Pastoral Epistles, 1963; The Athanasian Creed, 1964; The Epistles of Peter and of Jude, 1969; Aspects of the Passion, 1970; Jerome, 1975. *Recreations:* motoring, cinema, travel. *Address:* Principal's Lodgings, St Edmund Hall, Oxford OX1 4AR. *T:* Oxford 41039. *Clubs:* Athenæum, Royal Automobile; Vincent's (Oxford).

KELLY, Rt. Hon. (John William) Basil, PC (NI) 1969; **Rt. Hon. Mr Justice Kelly;** Judge of the High Court of Justice in Northern Ireland, since 1973; *b* 10 May 1920; *o s* of late Thomas William Kelly and late Emily Frances (*née* Donaldson); *m* 1957, Pamela, *o d* of late Thomas Colmer and Marjorie Colthurst. *Educ:* Methodist Coll., Belfast; Trinity Coll., Dublin. BA (Mod.) Legal Science, 1943; LLB (Hons) 1944. Called to Bar: of Northern Ireland, 1944; Middle Temple, 1970; QC (N Ireland) 1958. Senior Crown Counsel: Co. Fermanagh, 1965-66; Co. Tyrone, 1966-67; Co. Armagh, 1967-68; MP (U) Mid-Down, Parliament of Northern Ireland, 1964-72; Attorney-Gen. for Northern Ireland, 1968-72. *Recreations:* golf, music. *Address:* Rock Cottage, Quintin Bay, Co. Down. *T:* Portaferry 247. *Club:* Ulster Reform (Belfast).

KELLY, Kenneth Linden; Secretary-General of the Automobile Association, 1954-63; *b* 5 Dec. 1913; *s* of Herbert Linden Kelly and Alice Maud Gray; *m* 1939, Betty Joan Roe; two *d. Educ:* Kingston Grammar School. Served War of 1939-45 in RAOC, Europe and Middle East; Actg Dep. Dir of OS Middle East Forces, 1945 (Col.). Chm., Governors of Kingston Grammar School, 1957-72. FRSA 1955. Royal Order of the Phœnix, Greece, 1963. *Address:* 172 Norbiton Hall, Kingston Upon Thames, Surrey. *T:* 01-549 2319. *Clubs:* Kingston Rowing (Vice-Pres.); Remenham (Henley).

KELLY, Richard Denis Lucien, MC 1944; a Recorder of the Crown Court, since 1972; *b* 31 Jan. 1916; *e s* of late Richard Cecil Kelly, OBE and Joan Maisie Kelly, Hyde Manor, Kingston, Sussex; *m* 1945, Anne Marie (marr. diss. 1954), *o d* of late James Stuart Anderson, Hinton House, Christchurch; one *d. Educ:* Marlborough Coll.; Balliol Coll., Oxford. Served Surrey and Sussex Yeomanry, 1939-40; Indian Mountain Artillery, India and Burma, 1941-45; Hon. Major, retd. Called to Bar, in absentia, Middle Temple, 1942; Midland and Oxford Circuit; Bencher, 1976. Blackstone Pupillage Prize, 1947; Harmsworth Law Scholar, 1948. Dep. Chm., Kesteven QS, and Dep. Recorder of Bedford, 1968. Alternate Chm., Burnham Cttee, 1973-. *Publications:* (abridgment) The Second World War, by Sir Winston Churchill, 1959; (with R. MacLeod) The Ironside Diaries 1939-40, 1962. *Recreations:* walking, history. *Address:* 3 Temple Gardens, Temple, EC4Y 9AU. *T:* 01-353 4949. *Club:* Garrick.

KELLY, Sir Theo, (William Theodore), Kt 1966; OBE 1958; JP; Chairman, Woolworths Ltd, Australia, since 1963 (Managing Director, 1945-70), and its subsidiary and associated companies; Chairman: Woolworths (NZ) Ltd (Director and General Manager, 1934-71); Woolworths Properties Limited; *b* 27 June 1907; *m* 1944, Nancy Margaret Williams; two *s* two *d.* War of 1939-45; RAAF, 1942-44, Wing Comdr. Dir, RAAF Canteen Services Bd, 1944-59. General Manager: Woolworths Ltd (NZ), 1932; Woolworths (Australia and NZ), 1945. Mem. Board, Reserve Bank of Australia, 1961-75; Chm., Computer Sciences of Australia Pty Ltd; Dep. Chm., Australian Mutual Provident Soc., 1967-. Life Governor, Royal Life Saving Soc.; Trustee, National Parks and Wildlife Foundn, 1969-. Mem. Board, Royal North Shore Hosp., 1969-77. Fellow, Univ. of Sydney Senate, 1968-75. FRSA 1971; FAIM 1967. JP NSW, 1946. *Recreation:* boating. *Address:* 73 Yarranabbe Road, Darling Point, Sydney, NSW 2027, Australia; (office) Woolworths Ltd, 540 George Street, Sydney, NSW. *Clubs:* Sydney Rotary, Royal Motor Yacht, American National, Australian Golf (all in Sydney).

KELLY, Sir William Theodore; *see* Kelly, Sir Theo.

KELSALL, William, OBE 1971; QPM 1969; Chief Constable of Cheshire, 1974-77; *b* 10 Jan. 1914. *Address:* Three Keys Cottage, Quarry Bank, Utkinton, Tarporley, Cheshire.

KELSEY, Mrs Denys E. R.; *see* Grant, Joan.

KELSEY, Emanuel; Solicitor and Parliamentary Officer to the Greater London Council, 1964-70; *b* 16 Feb. 1905; *s* of late Emanuel and Margaret Kelsey, Blyth, Northumberland; *m* 1934, Dorothy, *d* of late Alexander Mitchell-Smith, Bathgate, Scotland; one *s* one *d. Educ:* King Edward VI School, Morpeth. Legal Asst, Min. of Agric. and Fisheries, and Commissioners of Crown Lands, 1929; Sen. Asst, Parly Dept, LCC, 1931; Dep. Solicitor and Parly. Officer, LCC, 1962; Solicitor and Parly Officer, LCC, 1964. Hon. Solicitor to Royal Society for the Prevention of Accidents, 1964-70. *Recreation:* coping with retirement. *Address:* Monk's Rest, Arterberry Road, Wimbledon, SW20. *T:* 01-946 2564.

KELSEY, Maj.-Gen. John, CBE 1968; Director of Military Survey, 1972-77; *b* 1 Nov. 1920; *s* of Benjamin Richard Kelsey and Daisy (*née* Powell); *m* 1944, Phyllis Margaret, *d* of Henry Ernest Smith, Chingford; one *s* one *d. Educ:* Royal Masonic Sch.; Emmanuel Coll., Cambridge; Royal Mil. Coll. of Science. BSc. Commnd in RE, 1940; war service in N Africa and Europe; Lt-Col 1961; Col 1965; Dep. Dir Mil. Survey; Brig. Dir Field Survey, Ordnance Survey, 1968; Dir of Mil. Survey, Brig. 1972; Maj.-Gen. 1974. *Recreations:* Rugby football (played for Cambridge Univ., Richmond, Dorset, Wilts; Mem. RFU, 1965-66); sailing. *Address:* 33 Courtenay Place, Lymington, Hants. *T:* Lymington 3649.

KELSEY, Julian George; Fisheries Secretary, Ministry of Agriculture, Fisheries and Food, since 1976; *b* 1922; *s* of William and Charlotte Kelsey, Dulwich; *m* 1944, Joan (*née* Singerton); one *d.* Lord Chancellor's Dept, 1939; War Service, 1941-46: Captain, Lancs Fusiliers and RAC; SOE and Force 136; Exec. Officer, Central Land Board, 1948; Asst Principal, 1951, Under Sec., 1969, MAFF. *Address:* c/o Ministry of Agriculture, Fisheries and Food, Whitehall Place, SW1A 2HH.

KELSICK, Osmund Randolph, DFC 1944; President and Managing Director of Antigua Holdings Ltd (owning and operating The Blue Waters Beach Hotel); Antigua Land Development Co. Ltd; Chairman: Caribbean Consultants Ltd; Bottlers (Antigua) Ltd; Vigie Beach Hotel Ltd (St Lucia); Director: T. H. Kelsick Ltd (Montserrat); Caribbean Travel Association; Anguilla Beaches Ltd; *b* 21 July 1922; *s* of T. H. Kelsick; *m* 1950, Doreen Avis Hodge; one *s* (and one *s* decd); two step *d. Educ:* private preparatory sch.; Montserrat Grammar Sch.; Oxford Univ. (Devonshire Course). RAF, Fighter Pilot, 1940-46. ADC and Personal Sec. to Governor of the Leeward Islands, 1946-47; District Commissioner, Carriacou, 1947-51; Asst Chief Sec., Governor's Office, Grenada, 1951-52; Asst Administrator and Administrator, St Vincent, 1952-57. In 1956 seconded for short periods as Asst Trade Commissioner for British West Indies, British Guiana and British Honduras in UK, and Executive Sec. of Regional Economic Cttee in Barbados. Chief Sec., Leeward Islands, 1957-60. Past Pres., Caribbean Hotel Assoc. FRSA 1973. *Recreations:* fishing, gardening, tennis. *Address:* Blue Waters Beach Hotel, Antigua, Leeward Islands, West Indies. *Clubs:* Royal Commonwealth Society (West Indian); New (Antigua); Celebrity (Toronto).

KELWAY, Colonel George Trevor, CBE 1963; TD 1941; DL; JP; District Registrar, HM High Court of Justice in Pembrokeshire and Carmarthenshire, 1940-62; *b* 30 March 1899; *yr s* of late George Stuart Kelway, Milford Haven, Ch. de la Légion d'Honneur, Ch. de l'Ordre de Léopold, &c.; *m* 1931, Gwladys, *d* of late Joseph Rolfe, Goodig, Burry Port, Carm., formerly High Sheriff of Carmarthenshire; one *d. Educ:* Warminster; St Edmund Hall, Oxford. Served European War, 1914-18, and War of 1939-45; Comdg Pembrokeshire Hy. Regt RA (TA), 1927-35; formerly Hon. Col. Pembs Coast Regt, 424 and 425 (Pembs.) Regts RA (TA), and The Pembroke Yeomanry, 1943-58; Chm. Pembs T&AFA, 1945-60. Admitted a Solicitor, 1922. Dep. Chm., Pembs QS, 1960-71. Chm. Pembs Conservative Assoc., 1950-60; Pres. Wales & Mon Cons. Party, 1957 and 1961; Mem. Lloyd's, 1942-; an original Mem. Milford Haven Conservancy Bd, 1958-. DL 1948, JP 1957, Pembrokeshire; High Sheriff, 1958. Provincial Grand Master, S Wales (Western Div.). *Recreation:* golf. *Address:* Cottesmore, near Haverfordwest, Dyfed. *T:* Haverfordwest 2282. *Club:* Pembrokeshire County (Haverfordwest).

KEM (pseudonym of Kimon Evan Marengo); Political Cartoonist and Journalist; *b* Zifteta, Egypt, 4 Feb. 1906; 2nd *s* of Evangelo Tr. Marengo and Aristea, *d* of Capt. John Raftopoulo, Lemnos; *m* 1954, Una O'Connor; two *s. Educ:* privately, publicly and personally and from time to time attended such seats of learning as the Ecole des Sciences Politiques, Paris, Exeter Coll., Oxford, etc. Edited and Illustrated Maalèsh, a political weekly published simultaneously in Cairo and Alexandria, 1923-31; in summer of 1928 represented a group of Newspapers at International Press Conference, Cologne; has travelled extensively; a fluent linguist, has command of English, French, Greek, Italian, and Arabic and understands a few other languages. *Publications:* In French: Oua Riglak! 1926; Gare les Pattes! 1929; Alexandrie, Reine de la Méditerranée, 1928. In English: Toy Titans, International politics in verse and pictures, 1937; Lines of Attack, 1944. In Arabic: Adolf and his donkey Benito, 1940; now a free-lance, contributing to newspapers and periodicals all over the world. *Recreations:* swimming, riding, drawing, and castigating politicians. *Address:* 40 Grand Avenue, Southbourne, Bournemouth, Dorset.

KEMBALL, Prof. Charles, MA, ScD Cantab; FRS 1965; FRIC; MRIA; FRSE; Professor of Chemistry, Edinburgh University, since 1966; Dean of the Faculty of Science, 1975-78; *b* 27 March 1923; *s* of late Charles Henry and of Janet Kemball; *m* 1956, Kathleen Purvis, *o d* of late Dr and Mrs W. S. Lynd, Alsager, Cheshire; one *s* two *d. Educ:* Edinburgh Academy; Trinity Coll., Cambridge (Sen. Schol.). First Class Hons in Natural Sciences Tripos, Pt I, 1942, Pt II, 1943. Employed by Ministry of Aircraft Production in Dept of Colloid Science, University of Cambridge, 1943-46; Fellow of Trinity Coll., Cambridge, 1946-54 (Junior Bursar, 1949-51; Asst Lectr, 1951-54); Univ. Demonstrator in Physical Chemistry, 1951-54; Professor of Physical Chemistry, Queen's Univ., Belfast, 1954-66 (Dean of the Faculty of Science, 1957-60, Vice-Pres., 1962-65). Meldola Medal, 1951, Royal Inst. of Chemistry; Corday-Morgan Medal, 1958, Tilden Lectr, 1960, Surface and Colloid Chem. Award, 1972, Chemical Soc.; Ipatieff Prize, American Chemical Soc., 1962; Pres., RIC, 1974-76 (Vice-Pres., 1959-61); Vice-Pres., Faraday Soc., 1970-73. *Publications:* contributions to various scientific jls. *Recreation:* hill walking. *Address:* 5 Hermitage Drive, Edinburgh EH10 6DE. *Clubs:* Athenæum, English-Speaking Union.

KEMBALL, Brig. Humphrey Gurdon, CBE 1971 (OBE 1966); MC 1940; *b* 6 Nov. 1919; *s* of late Brig.-Gen. Alick Gurdon Kemball (late IA) and late Evelyn Mary (*née* Synge); *m* 1945, Ella Margery Emmeline (*née* Bickham); no *c. Educ:* Trinity Coll., Glenalmond; RMC, Sandhurst. Commissioned 1939, 1st Bn The Prince of Wales's Volunteers. Served War of 1939-45 (MC); Staff Coll., 1943. JSSC, 1956; commanded 1st Bn The Lancashire Regt (PWV), 1961-63; i/c Administration, HQ Federal Regular Army, Aden, 1964-66; Asst Dir, MoD, 1966-68; Mil. Attaché, Moscow, 1968-71; HQ British Forces, Near East, 1971-73; Dep. Comdr, SW District, 1973-74, retired. *Recreations:* fishing, travelling. *Address:* c/o Grindlay's Bank Ltd, 13 St James's Square, SW1. *Club:* Naval and Military.

KEMBALL-COOK, Brian Hartley, MA Oxon; Headmaster, Bedford Modern School, 1965-Aug. 1977; *b* 12 Dec. 1912; *s* of Sir Basil Alfred Kemball-Cook, KCMG, CB, and Lady Nancy Annie Kemball-Cook (*née* Pavitt); *m* 1947, Marian, *d* of R. C. R. Richards, OBE; three *s* one *d. Educ:* Shrewsbury Sch. (Sidney Gold Medal for Classics); Balliol Coll., Oxford (Scholar). First Class Classical Honour Mods, 1933; First Class, Litt. Hum., 1935. Sixth Form Classics Master, Repton Sch., 1936-40. Intelligence Corps, 1940-46 (despatches); Regional Intelligence Officer and Political Adviser to Regional Comr, Hanover, 1946; Principal, Min. of Transport, 1946-47. Sen. Classics Master, Repton Sch., 1947-56; Headmaster, Queen Elizabeth's Grammar Sch., Blackburn, 1956-65. Chm., Bedfordshire Musical Festival, 1967. Croix de Guerre with Palm, 1946. *Publications:* Ed. Shakespeare's Coriolanus, 1954; (contrib.) Education: Threatened Standards, 1972. *Recreations:* mountaineering, music. *Address:* 3 Ebble Mead, Bedford MK41 7TS. *T:* Bedford 52510. *Clubs:* Alpine, Climbers, Public Schools.

KEMBER, William Percy, FCA; Senior Director, Finance and Management Services, Post Office Telecommunications, since 1972; *b* 12 May 1932; *s* of late Percy Kember, Purley, and Mrs Q. A. Kember, Oxted, Surrey. *Educ:* Uppingham. Chartered Accountant. Various posts with Royal Dutch/Shell Group in Venezuela, 1958-63; British Oxygen Co., 1963-67; Coopers & Lybrand, 1967-72. Visitor, Royal Institution, 1977. *Recreations:* sailing, ski-ing. *Address:* 10 Broadlands Close, N6 4AF. *T:* 01-348 2643. *Clubs:* Royal Automobile, Ski Club of Great Britain.

KEMMER, Prof. Nicholas, FRS 1956; FRSE 1954; MA Cantab, DrPhil Zürich; Tait Professor of Mathematical Physics, University of Edinburgh, since 1953; *b* 7 Dec. 1911; *o s* of late Nicholas P. Kemmer and of late Barbara Kemmer (*née* Stutzer; later Mrs Barbara Classen); *m* 1947, Margaret, *o d* of late George Wragg and late Nellie (who *m* 2nd, C. Rodway); two *s* one *d. Educ:* Bismarckschule, Hanover; Universities of Göttingen and Zürich. DrPhil Zürich, 1935; Imperial Coll., London: Beit Scientific Research Fellow, 1936-38; Demonstrator, 1938; Fellow 1971. Mem. of UK Govt Atomic Energy Research teams in Cambridge and Montreal, 1940-46; University Lecturer in Mathematics, Cambridge, 1946-53 (Stokes Lecturer since 1950). Hughes Medal, Royal Society, 1966. J. Robert Oppenheimer Meml Prize (Univ. of Miami), 1975. *Publications:* The Theory of Space, Time and Gravitation, 1959 (trans. from the Russian of V. Fock, 1955); What is Relativity?, 1960 (trans from the Russian, What is the theory of Relativity?, by Prof. L. D. Landau and Prof. G. B. Rumer, 1959); Vector Analysis, 1977; papers in scientific jls on theory of nuclear forces and elementary particles. *Address:* 35 Salisbury Road, Edinburgh EH16 5AA. *T:* 031-667 2893.

KEMP, family name of Viscount Rochdale.

KEMP, Athole Stephen Horsford, OBE 1958 (MBE 1950); Secretary-General, Royal Commonwealth Society, since 1967; *b* 21 Oct. 1917; *o s* of late Sir Joseph Horsford Kemp, CBE, KC, LLD, and Mary Kemp; *m* 1940, Alison, *yr d* of late Geoffrey Bostock, FCA; two *s* one *d. Educ:* Westminster Sch.; Christ Church, Oxford (MA). War service, RA, 1939-46; POW Far East (Thailand-Burma Railway). Malayan CS, 1940-64. *Recreations:* gardening, walking rights of way, wine. *Address:* Lockey House, Langford, near Lechlade, Glos. *T:* Filkins 239.

KEMP, Charles, CMG 1957; CBE 1951; retired as UK Senior Trade Commissioner and Economic Adviser to UK High Commissioner in South Africa (1953-58); *b* Whitstable, Kent, 25 Oct. 1897; *e s* of late Capt. Alfred and Elizabeth Kemp; *m* 1924, Helen Beatrice Stowe (*d* 1957); one *s. Educ:* Christ's Hospital; London University. HM Office of Works, 1915; served European War (wounded 1917); rejoined HM Office of Works, 1917; Dept of Overseas Trade, 1918; Asst to UK Trade Comr in E Africa, 1920; Trade Comr Grade III, 1931; Winnipeg, 1935; Cape Town, 1937; Trade Comr, Grade II, 1942, Grade I and transferred to Johannesburg, 1946. *Address:* 57 Hedge Row, Brighton Beach, Durban, South Africa. *Clubs:* Royal Commonwealth Society; Pretoria (Pretoria); Durban (Durban).

KEMP, Charles Edward; retired as Headmaster of Reading School; *b* 18 Nov. 1901; *e s* of Frederick Kemp, Salford, Lancs; *m* 1927, Catherine Mildred, *e d* of W. H. Taggart, IOM; two *s. Educ:* Manchester Grammar School (Foundation Scholar); Corpus Christi Coll., Oxford (open Scholar), Goldsmith Exhibitioner, 1922; 1st Class Maths, 1923. Master, Manchester Grammar Sch., 1923-30; Master, Royal Naval Coll., Dartmouth, 1930-34; Headmaster: Chesterfield Sch., 1934-39; Reading Sch., 1939-66. *Address:* Maple House, Wantage Road, Streatley, Berks. *T:* Goring-on-Thames 2679.

KEMP, Rear-Adm. Cuthbert Francis, CB 1967; ADC 1965; Chief Service Manager, Westland Helicopters, 1968-69; *b* 15 Sept. 1913; *s* of A. E. Kemp, Willingdon; *m* 1947, Margaret Law, *d* of L. S. Law, New York; two *s. Educ:* Victoria Coll., Jersey. Joined RN, 1931; RN Engrg Coll., 1936. Served in HMS Ajax and Hood; Pilot, 1939. Served War of 1939-45: carriers and air stations at home and abroad; Naval Staff, Washington, 1945-47; Fleet Engr Officer, E Indies, 1950-52; qual. Staff Coll., 1956; Admty, 1957-59; qual. Canadian Nat. Defence Coll., 1962; Supt RN Aircraft Yard, Belfast, 1962-65; Rear-Adm., Engineering, Staff of Flag Officer, Naval Air Command, 1965, retd 1967. *Recreations:* cricket, squash, shooting. *Address:* Beech House, Marston Magna, Som. *T:* Marston Magna 563. *Clubs:* Army and Navy; Royal Naval and Royal Albert Yacht (Portsmouth).

KEMP, David Ashton McIntyre, QC 1973; a Recorder of the Crown Court, since 1976; *b* 14 Oct. 1921; *s* of late Sir Kenneth McIntyre Kemp and Margaret Caroline Clare Kemp; *m* 1st, 1949, Margaret Sylvia Jones (*d* 1971); 2nd, 1972, Maureen Ann Frances Stevens, widow. *Educ:* Winchester Coll.; Corpus Christi Coll., Cambridge. 1st cl. hons Law Cantab. Called to Bar, Inner Temple, 1948. *Publications:* (with M. S. Kemp) The Quantum of Damages, Personal Injuries Claims, 1954 (4th edn 1975); (with M. S. Kemp) The Quantum of Damages, Fatal Accident Claims, 1956 (4th edn 1975). *Recreations:* ski-ing, tennis, gardening. *Address:* 2 The Green, Wimbledon Common, SW19 5AZ. *T:* 01-946 1317. *Clubs:* Hurlingham, Ski Club of Great Britain.

KEMP, Rt. Rev. Eric Waldram; see Chichester, Bishop of.

KEMP, Air Vice-Marshal George John, CB 1976; *b* 14 July 1921; *m* 1943, Elspeth Beatrice Peacock; one *s* two *d.* Commnd RAF, 1941; served in night fighter sqdns with spell on ferrying aircraft to Middle East; served in Iraq, 1953-54 and Far East, 1960-61; Stn Comdr RAF Upwood, 1968-69; Dir of Manning RAF, 1970-71; Dir of Personnel (Policy and Plans) RAF, 1972; Dir-Gen. of Personnel Management, RAF, 1973-75. *Recreations:* many and various. *Address:* Courts Cottage, Forge Hill, Acrise, Folkestone, Kent CT18 8LJ. *T:* Elham 588. *Club:* Royal Air Force.

KEMP, Prof. Kenneth Oliver; Chadwick Professor of Civil Engineering and Head of Civil Engineering Department, University College London, since 1970; *b* 19 Oct. 1926; *s* of Eric Austen Kemp; *m* 1952, Josephine Gloria (*née* Donovan); no *c. Educ:* University Coll. London. BSc(Eng), PhD, MICE, MIStructE. Surveyor, Directorate of Colonial Surveys, 1947-49; Asst Engr, Collins and Mason, Consulting Engrs, 1949-54. University College London: Lectr, Sen. Lectr, Dept of Civil Engrg, 1954-69; Reader in Structural Engrg, 1969-70. *Publications:* papers in: Proc. Instn of Civil Engrs; The

Structural Engr; Magazine of Concrete Research; Internat. Assoc. of Bridge and Structural Engrg. *Recreation:* Norfolk. *Address:* Frenchmans, Duck Street, Wendens Ambro, Essex CB11 4JC. *T:* Saffron Walden 40966. *Club:* Athenæum.

KEMP, Sir Leslie (Charles), KBE 1957 (CBE 1948); BScEng; FICE, MIEE, ACGI; Vice-Chairman, General Development Corporation, Athens, since 1960; *b* 22 April 1890; *s* of John Charles Kemp, London; *m* 1st, 1918, Millicent Constance (marr. diss., 1959), *d* of late Thomas Maitland; two *s*; 2nd, 1961, Melina Enriquez. *Educ:* Forest Hill House School; London Univ. BScEng 1st Cl. Hons, 1910. Engineer with Fraser and Chalmers, Erith, 1910-14. Served as captain in RGA, France, 1914-19. Contract Engineer, English Electric Co., 1919-23; Technical Adviser, Power and Traction Finance Co., 1923-25; Midlands Branch Manager, English Electric Co., 1924-26; Man. Dir, Athens Piraeus Electricity Co., 1926-41; Manager, Asmara War (land plane repair) base, Asmara, Eritrea, 1942-43; Dep. Regional Dir, Middle East, BOAC, 1943-44; Vice-Chm and Managing Director, Athens Piraeus Electricity Co., 1944-55; Vice-Chm., Société Générale Héllenique, 1957-72. Citizen (Feltmaker) and Freedom of City of London, 1956. Cross of Commander of Royal Order of George I of Greece, 1951. *Recreations:* yachting and golf. *Address:* 12 Queen Amalia Avenue, Athens, Greece. *Clubs:* Junior Carlton, Royal Thames Yacht; Royal Yacht Squadron (Cowes); Royal Corinthian Yacht (Burnham-on-Crouch); Royal Hellenic Yacht (Greece).

KEMP, Oliver, CMG 1969; Director, British Steel Corporation Office, Brussels, since 1973; *b* 12 Sept. 1916; *s* of Walter Kemp; *m* 1940, Henrietta Taylor; two *s*. *Educ:* Wakefield Grammar Sch.; Queen's Coll., Oxford. MA Oxon (Lit. Hum.), 1939. Served in HM Forces, 1939-45. Apptd Adviser in HM Foreign Service, 1945; served in Moscow, Egypt, Indonesia, Yemen, Laos and Foreign Office, 1946-62. HM Chargé d'Affaires in Yemen, 1957-58; First Secretary and Head of Chancery in Laos, 1958-60. HM Ambassador to Togo (and Consul-General), 1962-65; Deputy Head of the United Kingdom Delegation to the European Communities, Luxembourg, 1965-67; Ambassador to Mongolia, 1967-68; FCO, 1968-70 and 1971-73 (European affairs); retd 1970. *Recreations:* music, reading, languages, golf, gardening, travel. *Address:* 7 Rue de la Fontaine, Genval, Belgium. *T:* 653 36 32; Hunmanby, Filey, N Yorks. *T:* Hunmanby 890051.

KEMP, Lt-Comdr Peter Kemp, OBE 1963; RN (retd); FSA, FRHistS; Head of Naval Historical Branch and Naval Librarian, Ministry of Defence, 1950-68; Editor of Journal of Royal United Service Institution, 1957-68; *b* 11 Feb. 1904; *e s* of Henry and Isabel Kemp; *m* 1st, 1930, Joyce, *d* of Fleming Kemp; 2nd, 1949, Eleanore, *d* of Frederick Rothwell; two *d* (and one *s* decd). *Educ:* Royal Naval Colleges, Osborne and Dartmouth. Served in submarines till 1928 (invalided); Naval Intelligence Division, 1939-45. Asst Editor, Sporting and Dramatic, 1933-36; Member: Editorial Staff, The Times, 1936-39 and 1945-50; Council of Navy Records Society; Editorial Adv. Board of Military Affairs (US). *Publications:* Prize Money, 1946; Nine Vanguards, 1951; HM Submarines, 1952; Fleet Air Arm, 1954; Boys' Book of the Navy, 1954; HM Destroyers, 1956; Famous Ships of the World, 1956; Victory at Sea, 1958; Famous Harbours of the World, 1958; (with Prof. C. Lloyd) Brethren of the Coast, 1960; History of the Royal Navy, 1969; The British Sailor: a social history of the lower deck, 1970; Escape of the Scharnhorst and Gneisenau, 1975; A History of Ships, 1978. Regimental Histories of: Staffordshire Yeomanry; Royal Norfolk Regiment; Middlesex Regiment; King's Shropshire Light Infantry; Royal Welch Fusiliers. Books on sailing. Children's novels. Edited: Hundred Years of Sea Stories; Letters of Admiral Boscawen (NRS); Fisher's First Sea Lord Papers, Vol. I (NRS), 1960, Vol. II (NRS), 1964; Oxford Companion to Ships and the Sea, 1976. *Recreations:* sailing, golf. *Address:* 51 Market Hill, Maldon, Essex. *T:* Maldon 52609. *Clubs:* West Mersea Yacht, Maldon Golf.

KEMP, Robert Thayer; Under Secretary, Export Credits Guarantee Department, since 1975; *b* 18 June 1928; *s* of Robert Kemp and Ada Kemp (*née* Thayer); *m* 1951, Gwendolyn Mabel Minty; three *s*. *Educ:* Bromley Grammar Sch.; London Univ. (BA (Hons) Medieval and Mod. History). Asst Secretary, Export Credits Guarantee Dept, 1970. *Recreations:* cricket, music, theatre. *Address:* c/o Export Credits Guarantee Department, Aldermanbury House, Aldermanbury, EC2P 2EL. *T:* 01-606 6699.

KEMP, Thomas Arthur, MD; FRCP; Physician, St Mary's Hospital, 1947-75, Paddington General Hospital 1950-75; *b* 12 Aug. 1915; *s* of late Fred Kemp and Edith Peters; *m* 1942, Ruth May Scott-Keat; one *s* one *d*. *Educ:* Denstone Coll.; St

Catharine's Coll., Cambridge (Exhibitioner); St Mary's Hospital, London (Scholar). MB, BChir 1940; MRCP 1941; FRCP 1949; MD 1953. Examiner in Medicine, Universities of London and Glasgow. FRSM (Jt Hon. Sec., 1961-67). Served in Middle East, 1944-47; Lt-Col RAMC Officer i/c Medical Division; Hon. Cons. Physician to the Army, 1972-75. Pres. Brit. Student Health Assoc., 1962-63; Chm. Brit. Student Tuberculosis Foundation, 1963-65. *Publications:* papers in medical journals. *Recreations:* games, especially Rugby football, Cambridge (1936), England (Captain 1948), Pres., Rugby Football Union, 1971-72. *Address:* 2 Woodside Road, Northwood, Mddx. *T:* Northwood 21068. *Club:* Hawk's (Cambridge).

KEMPE, John William Rolfe; Headmaster of Gordonstoun since 1968; *b* 29 Oct. 1917; *s* of late William Alfred Kempe and Kunigunda Neville-Rolfe; *m* 1957, Barbara Nan Stephen, *d* of Dr C. R. Huxtable, FRCS, MC, Sydney, Australia; two *s* one *d*. *Educ:* Stowe; Clare Coll., Cambridge (Exhibitioner in Mathematics). Served war of 1939-45, RAFVR Training and Fighter Command; CO 153 and 255 Night Fighter Squadrons. Board of Trade, 1945; Firth-Brown (Overseas) Ltd, 1946-47; Head of Maths Dept, Gordonstoun, 1948-51; Principal, Hyderabad Public Sch., Deccan, India, 1951-54; Headmaster, Corby Grammar School, Northants, 1955-67. Exploration and mountaineering, Himalayas, Peru, 1952-56; Member: Cttee, Mount Everest Foundation, 1956-62; Cttee, Brathay Exploration Group, 1964-73. FRGS. *Publications:* Articles in Alpine Jl, Geographical Jl, Sociological Review. *Address:* Gordonstoun School, Elgin, Moray. *Club:* Alpine.

KEMPFF, Wilhelm Walter Friedrich; pianist and composer; *b* Jüterbog, Berlin, 25 Nov. 1895. *Educ:* Viktoria Gymnasium, Potsdam; Berlin University and Conservatoire (studied under H. Barth and Robert Kahn). Professor and Director of Stuttgart Staatliche Hochschule für Musik, 1924-29, since when has made concert tours throughout the world. Has made numerous recordings. Mem. of Prussian Academy of Arts. Mendelssohn Prize, 1917; Swedish Artibus et Litteris Medal, etc. *Compositions include:* two symphonies; four operas; piano and violin concertos; chamber, vocal and choral works. *Publication:* Unter dem Zimbelstern, Das Werden eines Musikers (autobiog.), 1951. *Address:* 8193 Ammerland, Oberbayern, Germany; c/o Ibbs & Tillett, 124 Wigmore Street, W1.

KEMPNER, Prof. Thomas; Principal, Administrative Staff College, Henley-on-Thames, and Professor and Director of Business Studies, Brunel University, since 1972; *b* 28 Feb. 1930; *s* of late Martin and Rosa Kempner; *m* 1958, June Maton; three *d*. *Educ:* University Coll. London (BSc (Econ)). Asst Administrator, Hyelm Youth Hostels, 1948-49, and part-time, 1951-55; Research Officer, Administrative Staff Coll., Henley, 1954-59; Lectr (later Sen. Tutor) in Business Studies, Sheffield Univ., 1959-63; Prof. of Management Studies, Founder, and Dir of Management Centre, Univ. of Bradford, 1963-72. Member of various cttees, including: Social Studies and Business Management Cttees of University Grants Cttee, 1966-76; Management, Education and Training Cttee of NEDO, 1969-(Chm. of its Student Grants Sub-Cttee); Chm., Food Industry Manpower Cttee of NEDO, 1968-71; Jt Chm., Conf. of Univ. Management Schools, 1973-75. FBIM (Burnham Medal, 1970). Hon. DSc Cranfield, 1976. *Publications:* editor, author, and contributor to several books, including: Bradford Exercises in Management (with G. Wills), 1966; Is Corporate Planning Necessary? (with J. Hewkin), 1968; A Guide to the Study of Management, 1969; Management Thinkers (with J. Tillet and G. Wills), 1970; Handbook of Management, 1971; (with K. Macmillan and K. H. Hawkins) Business and Society, 1974; Models for Participation, 1976; numerous articles in Management jls. *Recreation:* travel. *Address:* Administrative Staff College, Henley-on-Thames, Oxon. *T:* Hambleden 454.

KEMPSTER, Michael Edmund Ivor, QC 1969; a Recorder of the Crown Court, since 1972; *b* 21 June 1923; *s* of late Rev. Ivor T. Kempster, DSO; *m* 1949, Sheila, *d* of Dr T. Chalmers, KiH, Inverness; two *s* two *d*. *Educ:* Mill Hill Sch.; Brasenose Coll., Oxford (Scholar, MA, BCL). Royal Signals, 1943-46. Called to Bar, Inner Temple, 1949; Profumo Prize; Bencher 1977. Mem., Govt Cttee on Privacy, 1971; Chm., London Univ. Disciplinary Appeals Tribunal. Governor, Mill Hill School. *Recreations:* fishing, hare-hunting. *Address:* 10 South Square, Gray's Inn, WC1R 5EW. *T:* 01-242 2902.

KEMSLEY, 2nd Viscount *cr* 1945, of Dropmore; **(Geoffrey) Lionel Berry**, DL; Bt 1928; Baron 1936; *b* 29 June 1909; *e s* of 1st Viscount Kemsley, GBE and Mary Lilian (*d* 1928), *d* of Horace George Holmes; *S* father, 1968; *m* 1933, Lady Helen Hay, OStJ, *e d* of 11th Marquess of Tweeddale; four *d*. *Educ:*

Marlborough; Magdalen Coll., Oxford. Served War of 1939-45. Capt. Grenadier Guards; invalided out of Army, 1942. MP (C) Buckingham Div. of Bucks, 1943-45. Dep. Chm., Kemsley Newspapers Ltd, 1938-59. Chm., St Andrew's Hospital, Northampton; Pres., Assoc. of Independent Hospitals. Mem. Chapter General, Order of St John. Master of Spectacle Makers' Co., 1949-51, 1959-61. CC Northants, 1964-70; High Sheriff of Leicestershire, 1967, DL 1972. FRSA; KStJ. *Heir: b* Hon. Denis Gomer Berry, TD [*b* 11 July 1911; *m* 1st, 1934, Rosemary Leonora de Rothschild (marr. diss., 1942); two *d*; 2nd, 1947, Mrs Pamela Grant, *d* of late Lord Richard Wellesley; one *s* one *d*]. *Address:* Thorpe Lubenham, Market Harborough, Leics. *T:* Market Harborough 2629. *Clubs:* Bath, Turf, Pratt's.
See also Hon. A. G. Berry.

KENDALL, Prof. David George, FRS 1964; MA Oxon; Professor of Mathematical Statistics, University of Cambridge, and Fellow of Churchill College, since Oct. 1962; *b* 15 Jan. 1918; *s* of Fritz Ernest Kendall and Emmie Taylor, Ripon, Yorks; *m* 1952, Diana Louise Fletcher; two *s* four *d. Educ:* Ripon GS; Queen's Coll., Oxford. Fellow Magdalen Coll., Oxford, and Lectr in Mathematics, 1946-62. Vis. Lectr, Princeton Univ., USA, 1952-53. Guy Medal in Silver of Royal Statistical Soc., 1955. Mem. Internat. Statistical Inst.; Mem. Council, Royal Society, 1968-69; President: London Mathematical Soc., 1972-74; Internat. Assoc. Statist. in Phys. Sci., 1973-75; Bernoulli Soc. for Mathematical Stats and Probability, 1975. Chm. Parish Reg. Sect., Yorks Archaeol. Soc., 1974-. Hon. D. de l'U. Paris (René Descartes), 1976. Weldon Meml Prize and Medal for Biometric Science, 1974; Sylvester Medal, Royal Soc., 1976. *Publications:* (jt ed) Mathematics in the Archaeological and Historical Sciences, 1971; (jt ed) Stochastic Analysis, 1973; (jt ed) Stochastic Geometry, 1974. *Address:* Churchill College, Cambridge.

KENDALL, Denis; *see* Kendall, W. D.

KENDALL, James; MA; DSc (Edinburgh); LLD (Glasgow); FRS 1927; Professor of Chemistry, University of Edinburgh, 1928-59, now Emeritus (Dean of the Faculty of Science, 1953-54 and 1957-59); Vice-President, British Association for the Advancement of Science, 1951; *b* Chobham, Surrey, 30 July 1889; *s* of William Henry Kendall and Rebecca Pickering; *m* 1st, 1915, Alice (*d* 1955), *d* of Thomas Tyldesley, Victoria, BC; one *s* two *d*; 2nd, 1955, Jane Bain, *d* of late Malcolm Steven, Auckingill, Caithness. *Educ:* Farnham Grammar Sch.; University of Edinburgh; Nobel Institute, Stockholm. Prof. of Chem., Columbia University New York City, 1913-26; Professor of Chem., Washington Square Coll., New York Univ., 1926-28; Dean of the Graduate Sch., New York Univ., 1927-28; Visiting Professor, Stanford Univ., 1919 and 1923; University of Calif, 1923; Pennsylvania State Coll., 1927; Chm., New York Section, American Chemical Soc., 1925; Hon. Member, American Institute of Chemists. Lieut, US Naval Reserve, 1917-19; Lieut-Comdr, 1924-26. Pres. Royal Society of Edinburgh, 1949-54 (General Sec., 1936-46). *Publications:* At Home among the Atoms, 1929; Breathe Freely!, 1938; Young Chemists and Great Discoveries, 1939; Great Discoveries by Young Chemists, 1953; Humphry Davy, Pilot of Penzance, 1954; Michael Faraday, Man of Simplicity, 1955; contributions to scientific journals in the field of inorganic and physical chemistry; revisions of chemistry textbooks of Alexander Smith. *Address:* 26 Lasswade Road, Eskbank, Midlothian EH22 3EE. *T:* 031-663 2146. *Clubs:* Chemists' (New York); New (Edinburgh).

KENDALL, Sir Maurice (George), Kt 1974; MA, ScD; FBA 1970; Director, World Fertility Survey, since 1972; Chairman, Scientific Control Systems (Holdings), 1971-72; Fellow: American Statistical Association; Econometric Society; Institute of Mathematical Statistics; London Graduate School of Business Studies; *b* 6 Sept. 1907; *s* of late John Roughton Kendall and Georgina Kendall; *m* 1st, 1933, Sheila Frances Holland Lester; two *s* one *d*; 2nd, 1947, Kathleen Ruth Audrey Whitfield; one *s. Educ:* Central Sch., Derby; St John's Coll., Cambridge (Wrangler 1929). Entered Administrative Class, Civil Service, 1930; Ministry of Agriculture, 1930-41; Statistician, Chamber of Shipping, 1941-49 and Jt Asst Gen. Manager, 1947-49; Professor of Statistics in the University of London 1949-61. Chm., Scientific Control Systems Ltd, 1967-71. Fellow, British Computer Soc.; ex-President: Royal Statistical Soc.; Operational Research Soc.; Inst. of Statisticians; Hon. Mem., Market Research Soc. Hon. Fellow, LSE, 1975. Gold Medal, Royal Statistical Society, 1968. DUniv: Essex, 1968; Lancaster, 1975. *Publications:* (with G. Udny Yule) An Introduction to the Theory of Statistics, 14th edn, 1950; (with Alan Stuart) The Advanced Theory of Statistics, vol. I, 1958, 3rd edn 1969; vol. II, 1961, 3rd edn 1973; vol. III, 1966, 3rd edn 1975; Contributions to Study of Oscillatory Time-Series, 1947; Rank Correlation

Methods, 1948, 4th edn 1970; (ed) The Sources and Nature of the Statistics of the United Kingdom, vol. 1, 1952, vol. 2, 1957; Exercises in Theoretical Statistics, 1954, 3rd edn 1968; (with W. R. Buckland) A Dictionary of Statistical Terms, 1955, 3rd edn 1971; A Course in Multivariate Analysis, 1957; A Course in the Geometry of n Dimensions, 1961; (with Alison G. Doig) A Bibliography of Statistical Literature, vol. 1, 1962, vol. 2, 1965, vol. 3, 1968; (with P. A. Moran) Geometrical Probability, 1963; (ed) Mathematical Model Building in Economics and Industry, first series, 1968, second series, 1970; (ed, with E. S. Pearson) Studies in the History of Probability and Statistics, 1970; (ed) Cost-benefit Analysis, 1971; (ed, with Alan Stuart) Selected Papers of George Udny Yule, 1971; Time-Series, 1973; Multivariate Analysis, 1975; (ed, with R. L. Plackett) Second Series of Studies in the History of Probability and Statistics, 1977; various papers on theory of statistics and applications to economics and psychology. *Recreations:* chess, gardening. *Address:* Grosvenor Gardens House, 35-37 Grosvenor Gardens, Victoria, SW1W 0BS. *T:* 01-828 4242; 1 Frank Dixon Close, SE21. *T:* 01-693 6076.

KENDALL, (William) Denis, PhD; FRSA; FIMechE; MIAE; Chartered Engineer; *b* Halifax Yorks, 27 May 1903; *yr s* of J. W. Kendall, Marton, Blackpool; *m* 1952, Margaret Hilda Irene Burden. *Educ:* Trinity Sch.; Halifax Technical Coll. MP (Ind.) Grantham Division of Kesteven and Rutland, 1942-50; Mem., War Cabinet Gun Bd, 1941-45 (decorated). Cadet in Royal Fleet Auxiliary; Asst to Chief Inspector, Budd Manufacturing Corp., Philadelphia, Pa, 1923; Dir of Manufacturing, Citroen Motor Car Co., Paris, 1929-38; Managing Director, British Manufacture and Research Co., Grantham, England (manufacturers of aircraft cannon and shells), 1938-45, and Consultant to Pentagon, Washington, on high velocity small arms. Executive Vice-Pres., Brunswick Ordnance Corp., New Brunswick, NJ, 1952-55 (also Dir and Vice-Pres. Ops, Mack Truck Corp.); President and Director: American MARC, Inc., 1955-61 (manufacturers of Diesel Engines, who developed and produced the world's first Diesel outboard engine, and also electric generators, etc), Inglewood, Calif; Dynapower Systems Corp. (Manufacturers of Electro-Medical equipment), Santa Monica, Calif, 1961-73; Pres., Kendall Medical International, Los Angeles, Calif, 1973-. Mem. President's Council, American Management Assoc. Mem. Worshipful Co. of Clockmakers, Freeman City of London, 1943; Governor of King's Sch., Grantham, 1942-52. Chevalier de l'Ordre du Ouissam Alouite Cherifien. Mason. Religious Society of Friends (Quakers). *Address:* 1319 North Doheny Drive, Los Angeles, Calif 90069, USA. *T:* Crestview 66506; 159 Abbotts Road, Mitcham, Surrey. *Clubs:* Royal Norfolk and Suffolk Yacht (Lowestoft); Riviera Country Club, Cave des Rois, United British Services (Los Angeles, Calif).

KENDALL, William Leslie; Secretary General of Staff Side, Civil Service National Whitley Council, since 1976; *b* 10 March 1923; *m* 1943, Irene Canham; one *s* one *d.* Clerk Insurance Cttee, 1937-41. RAF 1941-46. Entered Civil Service, 1947; Civil Service Clerical Association: held hon. posts; Asst Sec., 1952; Dep. Gen. Sec., 1963; Gen. Sec., CPSA (formerly CSCA), 1967-76. Sec., Civil Service Alliance, 1967; Governor, Ruskin Coll., 1967-76. Member: CS Nat. Whitley Council (Chm. Staff Side, 1973-75); Employment Appeal Tribunal, 1976-. *Recreations:* reading, the 18th century; Dr Johnson. *Address:* (home) 24 Hollman Gardens, SW16 3SJ. *T:* 01-764 7591; (office) 19 Rochester Row, SW1. *T:* 01-828 2727.

KENDALL-CARPENTER,   John   MacGregor   Kendall; Headmaster, Wellington School, since 1973; *b* 25 Sept. 1925; *s* of C. E. Kendall-Carpenter and late F. F. B. Kendall-Carpenter (*née* Rogers); *m* 1955, Iris Anson; three *s* two *d. Educ:* Truro Sch.; Exeter Coll., Oxford. Fleet Air Arm, Pilot RNVR, 1943-45. Oxford, 1947-51; Asst Master, Clifton Coll., 1951-61, and Housemaster, 1957-61; Headmaster: Cranbrook School, Kent, 1961-70; Eastbourne Coll., 1970-73. Member: Air Cadet Council, 1965-70; Air League Council, 1963-70; Schools Mem., Rugby Football Union Cttee. (Member or Captain: Oxford Univ. Rugby XV, 1948-50, England Rugby XV, 1948-54). *Recreations:* outdoor activities, church architecture. *Address:* Headmaster's House, South Street, Wellington, Som. *Clubs:* East India, Devonshire, Sports and Public Schools; Vincent's (Oxford).

KENDON, Donald Henry, CBE 1961; FIEE, FIMechE; Chairman Merseyside and North Wales Electricity Board, 1954-62, retired; *b* 9 Aug. 1895; *s* of Samuel and Ellen Susan Kendon; *m* 1923, Katharine Grace Honess; five *s. Educ:* Goudhurst, Kent; King's Coll., University of London. BSc (Eng.) Hons. Served European War, 1914-19, in RE and RAF. Electrical Engineer with Edmundson's Electricity Corp., Ltd, 1921-34;

General Manager: Cornwall Electric Power Co., 1934-39; Shropshire, Worcestershire and Staffordshire Electric Power Co., 1939-48; Dep. Chairman, Midlands Electricity Board, 1948-54; Member: Central Electricity Authority, 1956, 1957; Electricity Council. *Address:* Quedley, Flimwell, via Wadhurst, East Sussex.

KENDREW, Maj.-Gen. Sir Douglas (Anthony), KCMG 1963; CB 1958; CBE 1944; DSO 1943 (Bar 1943, 2nd Bar 1944, 3rd Bar 1953); Governor of Western Australia, 1963-73; *b* 22 July 1910; *er s* of Alexander John Kendrew, MC, MD, Barnstaple, North Devon; *m* 1936, Nora Elizabeth, *d* of John Harvey, Malin Hall, County Donegal; one *s* one *d*. *Educ:* Uppingham Sch. 2nd Lieut Royal Leicestershire Regt, 1931; Capt. 1939; Major 1941; served War of 1939-45: Bde Major, N Africa, 1942; comd 6th Bn York and Lancaster Regt. N Africa and Italy, 1943; Bde Comd. Italy, Middle East and Greece, 1944-46; Commandant, Sch. of Infantry, Rhine Army, 1946-48; Commandant Army Apprentice Sch., Harrogate, 1948-50; Chief of Staff, NID, 1950-52; Bde Comd. 29 Brit. Inf. Bde, Korea, 1952-53; idc 1954; Brig. Administration HQ Northern Comd, 1955; GOC Cyprus Dist, and Dir of Ops, 1956-58; Dir of Infantry, War Office, 1958-60; Head of British Defence Liaison Staff, Australia, 1961-63. Col, Royal Leicestershire Regt, 1963-64. Hon. Col, SAS Regt, RWAR Australia, 1965. Pres., Knights of the Round Table, 1975. Comr, Royal Hospital, Chelsea, 1974. Hon. LLD Univ. of WA, 1969. KStJ 1964. *Recreations:* Rugby football (played for England 10 times, Capt. 1935; toured NZ and Australia, 1930; Army XV, 1932-36); golf and fishing. *Address:* The Manor House, Islip, Northants. *T:* Thrapston 2325. *Club:* Army and Navy.

KENDREW, Sir John (Cowdery), Kt 1974; CBE 1963; ScD; FRS 1960; Director General, European Molecular Biology Laboratory, Heidelberg, since 1975; *b* 24 March 1917; *s* of late Wilfrid George Kendrew, MA, and Evelyn May Graham Sandberg. *Educ:* Dragon Sch., Oxford; Clifton Coll., Bristol; Trinity Coll., Cambridge (Hon. Fellow, 1972). Scholar of Trinity Coll., Cambridge, 1936; BA 1939; MA 1943; PhD 1949; ScD 1962. Min. of Aircraft Production, 1940-45; Hon. Wing Comdr, RAF, 1944. Fellow, Peterhouse, Cambridge, 1947-75 (Hon. Fellow, 1975); Dep. Chm., MRC Lab. for Molecular Biology, Cambridge, 1946-75. Reader at Davy-Faraday Laboratory at Royal Instn, London, 1954-68. Mem., Council for Scientific Policy, 1965-72 (Dep. Chm., 1970-72); Sec.-Gen., European Molecular Biology Conf., 1970-74. Chm., Defence Scientific Adv. Council, 1971-74; Pres., British Assoc. for Advancement of Science, 1973-74; Trustee, British Museum, 1974-. Pres., Internat. Union for Pure and Applied Biophysics, 1969-72; Sec. Gen. Internat. Council of Scientific Unions, 1974-; Trustee, Internat. Foundn for Science, 1975-. Hon. Mem., American Soc. of Biological Chemists, 1962; Foreign Hon. Mem., Amer. Acad. of Arts and Sciences, 1964; Leopoldina Academy, 1965; Foreign Assoc., Amer. Nat. Acad. of Sciences, 1972; Hon. Fellow: Inst. of Biology, 1966; Weizmann Inst., 1970. Lectures: Herbert Spencer, Univ. of Oxford, 1965; Crookshank, Faculty of Radiologists, 1967; Procter, Internat. Soc. of Leather Chemists, 1969; Fison Meml, Guy's Hosp., 1971. Hon. DSc: Univ. of Reading, 1968; Univ. of Keele, 1968; DUniv Stirling, 1974; Dr *honoris causa* Pécs, Hungary, 1975. (Jointly) Nobel Prize for Chemistry, 1962; Royal Medal of Royal Society, 1965. Editor in Chief, Jl of Molecular Biology, 1959-. *Publications:* The Thread of Life, 1966; scientific papers in Proceedings of Royal Society, etc. *Address:* EMBL, Postfach 10.2209, 69 Heidelberg, Germany. *T:* Heidelberg 6221-13497. *Club:* Athenæum.

KENDRICK, John Bebbington Bernard; Chief Inspector of Audit, Ministry of Housing and Local Government, 1958-65, retired; *b* 12 March 1905; 3rd *s* of late John Baker Kendrick and Lenora Teague, Leominster, Herefordshire; *m* 1932, Amelia Ruth, 4th *d* of late James Kendall, Grange-over-Sands; two *s*. *Educ:* Leominster Grammar Sch.; King's Sch., Chester; Queen's Coll., Oxford (MA). Called to Bar, Middle Temple. Asst District Auditor, 1926; Deputy District Auditor, 1946; District Auditor, 1953; Deputy Chief Inspector of Audit, 1958. *Recreation:* fell walking. *Address:* Green Acres, Old Hall Road, Troutbeck Bridge, Windermere, Cumbria LA23 1HF. *T:* Windermere 3705.

KENDRICK, Sir Thomas Downing, KCB 1951; FBA; FSA; Hon. DLitt (Durham and Oxford); Hon. LittD (Dublin); Hon. FRIBA; Director and Principal Librarian of British Museum, 1950-59, retired; *b* 1895; *m* 1st, 1922, Helen Kiek (*d* 1955); *m* 2nd, 1957, Katharine Elizabeth Wrigley. Keeper of Brit. Antiquities, Brit. Museum, 1938-50. Hon. Fellow Oriel Coll., Oxford. Mem. Royal Commn of 1851; Foreign Mem. Royal Swedish Acad. of Letters, History and Antiquities; Mem. German Archæological Inst. *Publications:* The Druids, 1927,

repr. 1966; Archæology of the Channel Isles, vol I, 1928; A History of the Vikings, 1930, repr. 1968; Anglo-Saxon Art to AD 900, 1938, repr. 1972; Late Saxon and Viking Art, 1949, repr. 1974; British Antiquity, 1950, repr. 1970; The Lisbon Earthquake, 1956; Saint James in Spain, 1960; Great Love for Icarus, 1962; Mary of Agreda, 1967. *Address:* Old Farm House, Organford, Poole, Dorset. *Club:* Athenæum.

KENEALLY, Thomas Michael; author; *b* 7 Oct. 1935; *s* of Edmond Thomas Keneally; *m* 1965, Judith Mary Martin; two *d*. Studied for NSW Bar. Schoolteacher until 1965; Commonwealth Literary Fellowship, 1966, 1968, 1972; Lectr in Drama, Univ. of New England, 1968-69. FRSL 1973. *Publications:* The Place at Whitton, 1964; The Fear, 1965, 2nd edn 1973; Bring Larks and Heroes, 1967, 2nd edn 1973; Three Cheers for the Paraclete, 1968; The Survivor, 1969; A Dutiful Daughter, 1971; The Chant of Jimmie Blacksmith, 1972; Blood Red, Sister Rose, 1974; Gossip from the Forest, 1975; The Lawgiver, 1975; Season in Purgatory, 1976; A Victim of the Aurora, 1977. *Recreations:* swimming, fishing, Rugby. *Address:* c/o Wm Collins Publishers, 14 St James's Place, SW1A 1PS. *T:* 01-493 5321.

KENILWORTH, 3rd Baron; *see* Siddeley, J. T. D.

KENNABY, Very Rev. Noel Martin; *b* 22 Dec. 1905; *s* of Martin and Margaret Agnes Kennaby; *m* 1st, 1933, Margaret Honess Elliman; 2nd, 1937, Mary Elizabeth Berry. *Educ:* Queens' Coll., Cambridge; Westcott House, Cambridge. BA 1928; MA 1932. Deacon 1929, priest 1930, Diocese of Guildford; Curate of Epsom, 1929-32; in charge of Christ Church, Scarborough, 1932-36; Vicar of St Andrew's, Handsworth, 1936-42; Tynemouth, 1942-47; Surrogate from 1942; Rural Dean of Tynemouth, 1943-47; Provost and Vicar of Newcastle upon Tyne, 1947-61; Rural Dean of Newcastle upon Tyne, 1947-61; Senior Chaplain to the Archbishop of Canterbury, 1962-64; Hon. Canon, Newcastle Cathedral, 1962-64; Dean of St Albans and Rector of the Abbey Church, 1964-73, Dean Emeritus, 1973. Commissary, Jamaica, 1950-67. *Publication:* To Start You Praying, 1951. *Address:* 60 Alexandra Road, Bridport, Dorset.

KENNAN, Prof. George Frost; Professor, Institute for Advanced Study, Princeton, NJ, 1956-74, now Professor Emeritus; *b* 16 Feb. 1904; *m* 1931, Annelise Sorensen; one *s* three *d*. *Educ:* Princeton Univ. (AB); Seminary for Oriental Languages, Berlin. Foreign Service of the USA; many posts from 1926-52; US Ambassador to the USSR, 1952-53; Institute for Advanced Study, Princeton, 1953-61; US Ambassador to Yugoslavia, 1961-63. George Eastman Vis. Prof., Oxford, 1957-58; Reith Lectr, BBC, 1957; Prof., Princeton Univ., 1963 and 1964. Hon. LLD: Dartmouth and Yale, 1950; Colgate, 1951; Notre Dame, 1953; Kenyon Coll., 1954; New School for Social Research, 1955; Princeton, 1956; University of Michigan and Northwestern, 1957; Brandeis, 1958; Wisconsin, 1963; Harvard, 1963; Denison, 1966; Rutgers, 1966; Marquette, 1972; Hon. DCL Oxford, 1969. Benjamin Franklin Fellow, RSA, 1968. President: Nat. Inst. of Arts and Letters, 1965-68; Amer. Acad. of Arts and Letters, 1968-72. Pour le Mérite (Germany), 1976. *Publications:* American Diplomacy, 1900-50, 1951 (US); Realities of American Foreign Policy, 1954 (US); Amerikanisch Russische Verhältnis, 1954 (Germany); Soviet-American Relations, 1917-20; Vol. I, Russia Leaves the War, 1956 (National Book Award; Pulitzer Prize 1957); Vol. II, The Decision to Intervene, 1958; Russia, the Atom and the West, 1958; Soviet Foreign Policy, 1917-1941, 1960; Russia and the West under Lenin and Stalin, 1961; On Dealing with the Communist World, 1964; Memoirs, vol. 1, 1925-1950, 1967 (National Book Award 1968; Pulitzer Prize 1968); Memoirs, vol. 2, 1950-1963, 1973; From Prague after Munich: Diplomatic Papers 1938-1940, 1968; Democracy and the Student Left, 1968; The Marquis de Custine and his 'Russie en 1839', 1972; The Cloud of Danger, 1977. *Club:* Century (New York City).

KENNARD, Sir George Arnold Ford, 3rd Bt *cr* 1891; Midland Representative for Cement Marketing Co.; *b* 27 April 1915; *s* of Sir Coleridge Kennard, 1st Bt; *S* brother, 1967; *m* 1st, 1940, Cecilia Violet Cokayne Maunsel (marr. diss. 1958); one *d*; 2nd, 1958, Jesse Rudd Miskin (marr. diss. 1974), *d* of Hugh Wyllie. *Educ:* Eton. Commissioned 4th Queen's Own Hussars, 1939; served War of 1939-45 (despatches twice), Egypt, Greece (POW Greece); comd Regt, 1955-58; retired, 1958. Joined Cement Marketing Co., 1967. *Recreations:* hunting, shooting, fishing. *Heir:* none. *Address:* Gogwell, Tiverton, Devon. *T:* Tiverton 2154. *Club:* Cavalry and Guards.

KENNAWAY, Sir John (Lawrence), 5th Bt, *cr* 1791; *b* 7 Sept. 1933; *s* of Sir John Kennaway, 4th Bt and Mary Felicity, *yr d* of late Rev. Chancellor Ponsonby; *S* father 1956; *m* 1961, Christina

Veronica Urszenyi, MB, ChB (Cape Town); one *s* two *d. Educ:* Harrow; Trinity Coll., Cambridge. *Heir: s* John Michael Kennaway, *b* 17 Feb. 1962. *Address:* Escot, Ottery St Mary, Devon EX11 1LU.

KENNEDY, family name of **Marquess of Ailsa.**

KENNEDY, Sir Albert (Henry), Kt 1965; Chairman, Securicor (Ulster) Ltd; Director: Styletype Printing Ltd, Glengormley, Co. Antrim; M. & W. Publications (Liverpool) Ltd; *b* 11 May 1906; *s* of Joseph and Catherine Kennedy; *m* 1st, 1931, Elizabeth Freeborn (decd); two *d*; 2nd, 1942, Muriel Lucile Hamilton (decd); one *d* (and one step-*s* one step-*d*). Joined Royal Ulster Constabulary, 1924; District Inspector, 1936; County Inspector, 1951; Deputy Commissioner, Belfast, 1954; Deputy Inspector General, 1957; Inspector General, Jan. 1961-Jan. 1969. Has studied police methods in N and S America, Africa, ME and various European countries. King's Police Medal, 1947. *Recreations:* reading, golf, light gardening; general interest in sporting activities. *Address:* Culmoray, Cultra Avenue, Cultra, Holywood, Co. Down, Northern Ireland. *T:* Holywood 2405. 9. *Clubs:* Royal Belfast Golf, Clandeboye Golf (Ulster).

KENNEDY, Alfred James, DSc (London), PhD (London), CEng, MIEE, FIMM, FIM, FInstP; Director, BNF Metals Technology Centre, Wantage (formerly The British Non-Ferrous Metals Research Association), since 1966; *b* 6 Nov. 1921; *m* 1950, Anna Jordan; no *c. Educ:* Haberdashers' Aske's Hatcham Sch.; University Coll., London (Fellow 1976). BSc (Physics) 1943. Commissioned R Signals, 1944; Staff Major (Telecommunications) Central Comd, Agra, India, 1945-46 and at Northern Comd, Rawalpindi, 1946-47; Asst Lectr in Physics, UCL 1947-50; Res. Fellow, Davy-Faraday Lab. of Royal Institution, London, 1950-51; Royal Society, Armourers' and Brasiers' Research Fellow in Metallurgy (at Royal Institution), 1951-54; Head of Metal Physics Sect., BISRA, 1954-57; Prof. of Materials and Head of Dept. of Materials, Coll. of Aeronautics, Cranfield, 1957-66. Institution of Metallurgists: Pres., 1976-77; a Vice Pres., 1971-74, 1975-76; Mem. Council, 1968-74, 1975-; Pres., Inst. of Metals, 1970-71 (Mem. Council, 1968-73; Fellow, 1973); Member: Metallurgy Cttee, CNAA, 1965-71; Council, The Metals Soc., 1974- (Platinum Medallist, 1977); Inst. of Physics, 1968-71; SRC, 1974-; Metall. and Mat. Cttee, SRC, 1970-75 (Chm. 1973-74); Engrg Bd, 1973-; Council of Env. Sci. and Eng., 1973-; Adv. Council for Applied R&D, 1976-. Fellow, Amer. Soc. Met., 1972. Pres., Brit. Soc. of Rheology, 1964-66; a Governor, Nat. Inst. for Agric. Engrg, 1966-74. *Publications:* Processes of Creep and Fatigue in Metals, 1962; The Materials Background to Space Technology, 1964; Creep and Stress Relaxation in Metals (English edn), 1965; (ed) High Temperature Materials, 1968; research papers and articles, mainly on physical aspects of deformation and fracture in crystalline materials, particularly metals. *Recreations:* music, painting. *Address:* Woodhill, Milton under Wychwood, Oxon. *T:* Shipton under Wychwood 830334. *Club:* Athenæum.

KENNEDY, Archibald E. C.; *see* Clark-Kennedy.

KENNEDY, Brig. Archibald Gordon M.; *see* Mackenzie-Kennedy.

KENNEDY, Sir Clyde (David Allen), Kt 1973; Chairman of Sydney (New South Wales) Turf Club, since 1972 (formerly Vice-Chairman); company director; Member, Totalisator Agency Board. *Address:* 13A/23 Thornton Street, Darling Point, NSW 2027, Australia. *Clubs:* Sydney Turf; Rugby; Tattersalls (all NSW).

KENNEDY, Daisy; Violinist (Australian); *b* Burra, South Australia, 1893; *d* of J. A. Kennedy, Headmaster, Norwood, Adelaide; *m* 1924, John Drinkwater (*d* 1937); one *d*; two *d* by former marriage to Benno Moiseiwitsch, CBE. *Educ:* Elder Scholar, University Conservatorium, Adelaide. Left Adelaide for Prague, 1908; studied with Prof. Sevcik; later entered Meisterschule, Vienna, under same Prof., and held a Scholarship during 2nd year; made début in Vienna, 1911, and in London at Queen's Hall with Prof. Sevcik the same year; played at principal concerts at Queen's Hall, (Royal) Albert Hall, and throughout United Kingdom; has given many recitals at Wigmore Hall, Æolian Hall, and Grotrian Hall since début; toured Australia and New Zealand, 1919-20; début in Æolian Hall, New York, Nov. 1920; second tour, 1925; has given first performances of many violin works in London; appeared in recitals and with orchestra in Prague, Vienna and Budapest, and also played on the Radio several times in each city 1931; formed the Kennedy Trio with Lauri and Dorothy Kennedy, 1932; recital in Egypt, 1933. *Address:* 208 Rivermead Court, Ranelagh Gardens, SW6. *T:* 01-736 4379.

See also T. Moiseiwitsch, H. M. Self.

KENNEDY, David Matthew; American Banker; Special Representative of the First Presidency of the Church of Jesus Christ of Latter-day Saints; *b* Randolph, Utah, 21 July 1905; *s* of George Kennedy and Katherine Kennedy (*née* Johnson); *m* 1925, Lenora Bingham; four *d. Educ:* Weber Coll., Ogden, Utah (AB); George Washington Univ., Washington, DC (MA, LLB); Stonier Grad. Sch. of Banking, Rutgers Univ. (grad.). Technical Asst to Chm. of Bd, Federal Reserve System, 1930-46; Vice-Pres. in charge of bond dept, Continental Illinois Bank and Trust Co., Chicago, 1946-53, full Vice-Pres., 1951, Pres., 1956-58, Chm. Bd and Chief Exec. Officer, 1959- (temp. resigned, Oct. 1953-Dec. 1954, to act as special Asst to Sec. of Treas., in Republican Admin.); after return to Continental Illinois Bank, still advised Treasury (also under Democrat Admin). Chm. of a Commission: (apptd by President Johnson) to improve drafting of Federal budget, 1967; (apptd by Mayor of Chicago) for Economic and Cultural Develt of Chicago, 1967. Again in Govt, when nominated to Nixon Cabinet, Dec. 1968; Secretary of the Treasury, 1969-70; Ambassador-at-large, USA, and Mem. President Nixon's Cabinet, 1970-73; US Ambassador to NATO, 1972. Director (past or present) of many corporations and companies including: Internat. Harvester Corp.; Abbott Laboratories; Swift & Co.; Pullman Co.; Nauvoo Restoration Inc.; Member of numerous organizations; Trustee: Univ. of Chicago; George Washington Univ.; Brookings Instn, etc. Holds hon. doctorates. *Address:* 3793 Parkview Drive, Salt Lake City, Utah 84117, USA. *Clubs:* Union League, Commercial Executives (Chicago); Old Elm Country (Fort Sheridan, Ill); Glenview Country, etc.

KENNEDY, Douglas Neil, OBE 1952 (MBE); Vice-President, English Folk Dance and Song Society; President, Folk Lore Society, 1964-65; *b* Edinburgh, 1893; *s* of John Henderson Kennedy and Patricia Grieve Thomson, *g s* of David Kennedy the Scottish singer; *m* 1st, 1914, Helen May Karpeles; two *s*; 2nd, 1976, Elizabeth Ann Ogden. *Educ:* George Watson's Coll., Edinburgh; Imperial College of Science. Served London Scottish prior to and during European War, 1914-18, and received his commission in that regiment; MBE for War services, and retired with the rank of Captain; served War of 1939-45, RAF, 1940-45. Demonstrator in the Department of Botany, Imperial Coll., 1919-24; Organising Dir, English Folk Dance Society (on the death of its founder Cecil J. Sharp), 1924. *Publications:* England's Dances, 1950; English Folk-dancing Today and Yesterday, 1964; other works relating to traditional dance and song. *Address:* Deck House, Waldringfield, Wood Bridge, Suffolk.

KENNEDY, Francis, CBE 1977 (MBE 1958); HM Consul-General, Atlanta, USA, since 1973; *b* 9 May 1926; *s* of late James Kennedy and of Mrs Alice Kennedy; *m* 1957, Anne O'Malley; two *s* two *d. Educ:* Univs of Manchester and London. HM Colonial Service, Nigeria, 1953-63; HM Diplomatic Service, 1964-. *Address:* Suite 912, 225 Peachtree Street NE, Atlanta, Ga, USA; 81 Downs Hill, Beckenham, Kent.

KENNEDY, (George) Michael (Sinclair); Northern Editor, The Daily Telegraph, since 1960, and Northern Music Critic since 1950; *b* 19 Feb. 1926; *s* of Hew Gilbert Kennedy and Marian Florence Sinclair; *m* 1947, Eslyn Durdle; no *c. Educ:* Berkhamsted School. Joined Daily Telegraph, Manchester, 1941; served Royal Navy (BPF), 1943-46; rejoined Daily Telegraph, Manchester, serving in various capacities on editorial staff; Asst Northern Editor, 1958. Mem. Council, Royal Northern Coll. of Music; Mem. Cttee, Vaughan Williams Trust, 1965- (Chm. 1977-); Trustee: Barbirolli Memorial Foundn, 1971; Elgar Foundn and Birthplace Trust, 1975. Hon. Mem., Royal Manchester Coll. of Music, 1971. Hon. MA Manchester, 1975. FJI 1967. *Publications:* The Hallé Tradition, 1960; The Works of Ralph Vaughan Williams, 1964; Portrait of Elgar, 1968; Portrait of Manchester, 1970; Elgar Orchestral Works, 1970; History of Royal Manchester College of Music, 1971; Barbirolli: Conductor Laureate, 1971; (ed) The Autobiography of Charles Hallé, 1973; Mahler, 1974; Richard Strauss, 1976; scripts for BBC, contrib. musical jls. *Recreations:* listening to music, watching cricket. *Address:* 3 Moorwood Drive, Sale, Cheshire M33 4QA. *T:* 061-973 7225. *Club:* Portico Library (Manchester).

KENNEDY, Lt-Col Sir (George) Ronald (Derrick), 7th Bt *cr* 1836; OBE 1975; HQ Dhekelia Garrison, since 1977; *b* 19 Nov. 1927; *s* of Sir Derrick Edward de Vere Kennedy, 6th Bt, and of Phyllis Victoria Levine, *d* of late Gordon Fowler; *S* father, 1976; *m* 1949, Noelle Mona, *d* of Charles Henry Green; one *s* one *d. Educ:* Clifton College. Regimental service in RA, 1947-58; Staff Coll., Camberley, 1959; staff duties, Aden, 1960-63; regimental duty, 1963-66; staff duties, MoD and HQ BAOR, 1966-71; Defence Attaché, Mexico City, Havana and El Salvador, 1971-

74; GSO 1, UK Delegn to Live Oak, SHAPE, 1974-77. *Recreations:* foreign travel, military history. *Heir:* s Michael Edward Kennedy, *b* 12 April 1956. *Address:* c/o Lloyds Bank, Newbury, Berks.

KENNEDY, Horas Tristram, OBE 1966; HM Diplomatic Service, retired; *b* 29 May 1917; *s* of George Lawrence Kennedy and Mary Dow; *m* 1953, Maureen Beatrice Jeanne Holmes (formerly Stevens) (*d* 1976); three *d* (one *s* decd). *Educ:* Oundle; King's Coll., Cambridge. History and Mod Langs, MA. Entered HM Consular Service, 1939; Vice-Consul, Valparaiso, Chile, 1939-46; Foreign Office, 1946-48; 1st Secretary: Belgrade, 1949-52; Buenos Aires, 1952-56; Berne, 1956-61; Santiago de Chile, 1961-67; Commercial Counsellor, Warsaw, 1967-70; Consul-Gen., Barcelona, 1971-73. *Recreations:* country walking, landscape painting. *Address:* Pomfrets, Burnham Overy, Norfolk. *T:* Burnham Market 496.

KENNEDY, James Cowie; Chief Officer of Greater London Council Parks Department since 1970; *b* 27 Dec. 1914; *e s* of Robert and Elizabeth Kennedy; *m* 1st, 1939, Eleanor Colman (*d* 1970); one *s* one *d* ; 2nd, 1972, Joan G. Cooper, Bristol. *Educ:* Bishops Stortford Coll.; Northern Polytechnic, London. Architect; Dipl. Arch. (N Poly.). Architectural private practice, 1932-37; War Dept, 1937-42; war service, 1942-47 (Private, subseq. Major RE); joined London County Council, 1947, Greater London Council, 1965. Member Exec. Cttee: Greater London and SE Sports and Recreation Council; National Playing Fields Assoc.; Internat. Fedn of Parks and Recreation Administration; Inst. of Parks and Recreation Administration, etc. *Publications:* articles in technical jls. *Recreations:* playing with children; enjoying food and drink; working for the Church. *Address:* 174 Clarence Gate Gardens, NW1 6AR.

KENNEDY, Prof. John (Stodart), FRS 1965; Deputy Chief Scientific Officer, Agricultural Research Council, 1967-77, and Professor of Animal Behaviour in the University of London, Imperial College Field Station, Ascot, 1968-77, now Professor Emeritus; *b* 19 May 1912; *s* of James John Stodart Kennedy, MICE, and Edith Roberts Kennedy (*née* Lammers); *m* 1st, 1936, Dorothy Violet Bartholomew (divorced, 1946); one *s* ; 2nd, 1950, Claude Jacqueline Bloch (*widow, née* Raphäel); one step *s* , one *s* one *d. Educ:* Westminster Sch.; University Coll., London. BSc (London) 1933; DSc (London) 1956. Locust investigator for Imperial Inst. of Entomology, University of Birmingham, 1934-36, Anglo-Egyptian Sudan, 1936-37; MSc (London) 1936; London Sch. of Hygiene and Trop. Med., 1937-38; PhD (Birmingham) 1938; Rockefeller Malaria Res. Lab., Tirana, Albania, 1938-39; Wellcome Entomolog. Field Labs, Esher, Surrey, 1939-42; Res. Officer, Middle East Anti-Locust Unit, 1942-44; Chem. Defence Exptl Station, Porton, Wilts, 1944-45; ARC Unit of Insect Physiology, Cambridge, 1946-67. Pres. Royal Entomological Society, 1967-69 (Hon. Fellow, 1974). *Publications:* numerous research papers and review articles on the biology of locusts, mosquitos and greenfly, and insect behaviour generally. *Address:* 3 The Glade, Woodend Drive, South Ascot, Berks. *T:* Ascot 20633.

KENNEDY, Ludovic Henry Coverley; writer and broadcaster; *b* Edinburgh, 3 Nov. 1919; *o s* of Captain E. C. Kennedy, RN (killed in action, 1939, while commanding HMS Rawalpindi against German battle-cruisers Scharnhorst and Gneisenau), and of Rosalind, *d* of Sir Ludovic Grant, 11th Bt of Dalvey; *m* 1950, Moira Shearer King (*see* Moira Shearer); one *s* three *d. Educ:* Eton; Christ Church, Oxford (MA). Served War, 1939-46: Midshipman, Sub-Lieut, Lieut, RNVR. Priv. Sec. and ADC to Gov. of Newfoundland, 1943-44. Librarian, Ashridge (Adult Education) Coll., 1949; Rockefeller Foundation Atlantic Award in Literature, 1950; Winner, Open Finals Contest, English Festival of Spoken Poetry, 1953; Editor, feature, First Reading (BBC Third Prog.), 1953-54; Lecturer for British Council, Sweden, Finland and Denmark, 1955; Belgium and Luxembourg, 1956; Mem. Council, Navy Records Soc., 1957-60. Contested (L) Rochdale, by-elec., 1958 and Gen. elec., 1959; Pres., Nat. League of Young Liberals, 1959-61; Mem., Lib. Party Council, 1965-67. Pres., Sir Walter Scott Club, Edinburgh, 1968-69. FRSA 1974-76. Columnist, Newsweek International, 1974-75. Chm., Royal Lyceum Theatre Co. of Edinburgh, 1977-. *TV and radio:* Introd. Profile, ATV, 1955-56; Newscaster, Independent Television News, 1956-58. Introducer of AR's feature On Stage, 1957; Introducer of AR's, This Week, 1958-59; Chm. BBC features: Your Verdict, 1962; Your Witness, 1967-70; Commentator: BBC's Panorama, 1960-63; Television Reporters Internat., 1963-64 (also Prod.). Introducer, BBC's Time Out, 1964-65, World at One, 1965-66; Presenter: Lib. Party's Gen. Election Television Broadcasts, 1966; The Middle Years, ABC, 1967; The Nature of Prejudice, ATV, 1968; Face the Press, Tyne-Tees, 1968-69, 1970-72; Against the Tide,

Yorkshire TV, 1969; Living and Growing, Grampian TV, 1969-70; 24 Hours, BBC, 1969-72; Ad Lib, BBC, 1970-72; Midweek, BBC, 1973-75; Newsday, BBC, 1975-76; Interviewer, Tonight, BBC, 1976-. *Films include:* The Sleeping Ballerina; The Singers and the Songs; Scapa Flow; Battleship Bismarck; Life and Death of the Scharnhorst; U-Boat War; Target Tirpitz; The Rise of the Red Navy; Lord Haw-Haw. *Publications:* Sub-Lieutenant, 1942; Nelson's Band of Brothers, 1951; One Man's Meat, 1953; Murder Story (play, with essay on Capital Punishment), 1956; play: Murder Story (Cambridge Theatre), 1954; Ten Rillington Place, 1961; The Trial of Stephen Ward, 1964; Very Lovely People, 1969; Pursuit: the chase and sinking of the Bismarck, 1974; A Presumption of Innocence: the Amazing Case of Patrick Meehan, 1975. Gen. Editor, The British at War, 1973-. *Recreations:* fishing, shooting, golf, backgammon. *Address:* c/o A.D. Peters, 10 Buckingham Street, WC2. *Club:* MCC.

KENNEDY, Michael; *see* Kennedy, G. M. S.

KENNEDY, Moira, (Mrs L. Kennedy); *see* Shearer, M.

KENNEDY, Paul Joseph Morrow, QC 1973; a Recorder of the Crown Court, since 1972; *b* 12 June 1935; *o s* of Dr J. M. Kennedy, Sheffield; *m* 1965, Virginia, twin *d* of Baron Devlin, *qv* ; two *s* two *d. Educ:* Ampleforth Coll.; Gonville and Caius Coll., Cambridge (MA, LLB). Called to Bar, 1960. *Address:* Rydal, 11A Kent Road, Harrogate HG1 2LE. *T:* Harrogate 502704.

KENNEDY, Sir Ronald; *see* Kennedy, Sir G. R. D.

KENNEDY, Thomas Alexander; Under-Secretary, Head of Economics and Statistics Division, Department of Energy, since 1974; *b* 11 July 1920; *s* of late Rt Hon. Thomas Kennedy, PC, and Annie S. Kennedy (*née* Michie); *m* 1947, Audrey (*née* Plunkett); one *s* two *d. Educ:* Alleyn's Sch., Dulwich; Durham Univ. (BA). Economist: Bd of Trade, 1950-52; Colonial Office, 1952-55; Lecturer in Economics at Makerere Coll., Uganda, 1955-61; Economist: Treasury, Foreign Office, DEA, 1961-67; Economic Director, NEDO, 1967-70; Under-Sec., DTI, 1970-74. *Address:* 342 Willoughby House, Barbican, EC2; 31 Greys Close, Cavendish, Suffolk. *T:* Glemsford 280754.

KENNEDY, Air Vice-Marshal Thomas Lawrie, AFC 1953 and Bar 1960; RAF; Commander, Northern Maritime Air Region, since 1977; *b* 19 May 1928; *s* of James Domoné Kennedy and Margaret Henderson Lawrie; *m* 1959, Margaret Ann Parker; one *s* two *d. Educ:* Hawick High Sch. RAF Coll., Cranwell, 1946-49; commissioned, 1949. Sqdn service, 1949-53; exchange service, RAAF, 1953-55; returned to UK, 1955; 27 Sqdn (Canberra), 1955-57; Radar Research Estabt, 1957-60; RAF Coll. Selection Bd, 1960-62; RN Staff Coll., Greenwich, 1962; HQ Middle East, 1962-64; CO, No 99 (Britannia) Sqdn, 1965-67; HQ Air Support Comd, 1967-69; CO, RAF Brize Norton, 1970-71; Dep. Comdt, RAF Staff Coll., 1971-73; Dir of Ops (AS) MoD, 1973-75; Royal Coll. of Defence Studies, 1976. *Recreations:* golf, sailing. *Address:* Bendameer House, Burntisland, Fife. *Club:* Royal Air Force.

KENNEDY, William Quarrier, FRS 1949; retired as Professor of Geology, University of Leeds (1945-67), now Emeritus; Founder and first Director of Research Institute of African Geology in the University of Leeds, 1955-67; *b* 30 Nov. 1903; *s* of John Gordon Kennedy and Peterina Webster; *m* 1st, 1933, Elizabeth Jane Lawson McCubbin; one *s* two *d* ; 2nd, 1962, Sylvia Margaret Greeves; one *s* one *d. Educ:* Glasgow High Sch.; Glasgow Univ.; University of Zürich. Geologist and senior geologist in the geological survey of Great Britain, 1928-45. Leader of the British Ruwenzori Expedition, 1951-52; Scientific Dir, Royal Society's expedition to Tristan da Cunha, 1962. Hon. Oppenheimer Research Fellow, Univ. of Leeds; Hon. Regent, St Salvator's Coll., Univ. of St Andrews. Clough Medal, 1966; Lyell Medal, 1967. *Publications:* various in scientific journals. *Address:* Loseberry, Kirkpark Road, Elie, Fife.

KENNEDY SHAW, W. B.; *see* Shaw.

KENNER, George Wallace, FRS 1964; PhD, ScD Cantab; MSc Manchester; Royal Society Research Professor, University of Liverpool, since 1977; *b* Sheffield, 16 Nov. 1922; *s* of Professor James Kenner, FRS; *m* 1951, Jillian Gervis, *d* of Angus K. Bird, Cambridge; two *d. Educ:* Manchester Grammar Sch.; Manchester Univ. Holder of DSIR Senior Award at Christ's Coll., Cambridge, 1944-46; Research Fellow of Trinity Hall, Cambridge, 1946-49; University Demonstrator, Cambridge, 1946-53; Rockefeller Foundation Fellow, Eidgenössische Technische Hochschule, Zürich, 1948-49; Staff Fellow of Trinity Hall, 1949-57; University Lecturer, 1953-57; Heath Harrison

Prof. of Organic Chemistry, Liverpool Univ., 1957-76. President: British Assoc., Section B, 1974; Chem. Soc. Perkin Div., 1974-76. Lectures: Tilden, Chem. Soc., 1955; Simonsen, 1972; Bakerian, Royal Society, 1976; Pedler, 1977. Meldola Medal, RIC, 1951; Corday-Morgan Medal, Chem. Soc., 1957. *Publications:* papers in Jl Chem. Soc. and Tetrahedron. *Recreations:* sailing, motorcycling, modern art. *Address:* The Robert Robinson Laboratories, Oxford Street, Liverpool L69 3BX. *T:* 051-709 6022.

KENNET, 2nd Baron *cr* 1935, of the Dene; **Wayland Hilton Young;** author; *b* 2 Aug. 1923; *s* of 1st Baron Kennet, PC, GBE, DSO, DSC, and of Kathleen (who *m* 1st, Captain Robert Falcon Scott, CVO, RN, and died 1947); *S* father 1960; *m* 1948, Elizabeth Ann, *d* of late Captain Bryan Fullerton Adams, DSO, RN; one *s* five *d. Educ:* Stowe; Trinity Coll., Cambridge; Perugia; Harvard. Served in RN, 1942-45. Foreign Office, 1946-47, and 1949-51. Rapporteur, Defence Cttee, Parliamentary Assembly, WEU, 1962-65; Parly Sec., Min. of Housing and Local Govt, 1966-70; Opposition Spokesman on Foreign Affairs and Science Policy, 1971-74. Chairman: Adv. Cttee on Oil Pollution of the Sea, 1970-74; CPRE, 1971-72; Internat. Parly Confs on the environment, 1972-; Dir, Europe Plus Thirty. Hon. FRIBA 1970. Editor of Disarmament and Arms Control, 1962-65. *Publications:* (as Wayland Young): The Italian Left, 1949; The Deadweight, 1952; Now or Never, 1953; Old London Churches (with Elizabeth Young), 1956; The Montesi Scandal, 1957; Still Alive Tomorrow, 1958; Strategy for Survival, 1959; The Profumo Affair, 1963; Eros Denied, 1965; Thirty-Four Articles, 1965; (as Wayland Kennet) Preservation, 1972; (ed) Existing Mechanisms of Arms Control, 1965; Fabian pamphlets on defence, disarmament, environment, multinational companies, etc. *Heir: s* Hon. William Aldus Thoby Young, *b* 24 May 1957. *Address:* 100 Bayswater Road, W2.

KENNEY, Prof. Edward John, FBA 1968; Kennedy Professor of Latin, University of Cambridge, since 1974; Fellow and Librarian of Peterhouse, Cambridge, since 1953; *b* 29 Feb. 1924; *s* of George Kenney and Emmie Carlina Elfrida Schwenke; *m* 1955, Gwyneth Anne, *d* of late Henry Albert Harris. *Educ:* Christ's Hospital; Trinity Coll., Cambridge. BA 1949, MA 1953. Served War of 1939-45: Royal Signals, UK and India, 1943-46; commissioned 1944, Lieut 1945. Porson Schol., 1948; Craven Schol., 1949; Craven Student, 1949; Chancellor's Medallist, 1950. Asst Lectr, Univ. of Leeds, 1951-52; University of Cambridge: Research Fellow, Trinity Coll., 1952-53; Asst Lectr, 1955-60, Lectr, 1966-70; Reader in Latin Literature and Textual Criticism, 1970-74; Director of Studies in Classics, Peterhouse, 1953-74, Tutor, 1956-62, Senior Tutor, 1962-65. Jt Editor, Classical Quarterly, 1959-65. James C. Loeb Fellow in Classical Philology, Harvard Univ., 1967-68; Sather Prof. of Classical Literature, Univ. of California, Berkeley, 1968. Pres., Jt Assoc. of Classical Teachers, 1977-79. For. Mem., Royal Netherlands Acad. of Arts and Scis, 1976. *Publications:* P. Ouidi Nasonis Amores etc (ed), 1961; (with Mrs P. E. Easterling) Ovidiana Graeca (ed), 1965; (with W. V. Clausen, F. R. D. Goodyear, J. A. Richmond) Appendix Vergiliana (ed), 1966; Lucretius, De Rerum Natura III (ed), 1971; The Classical Text, 1974; articles and reviews in classical jls. *Recreations:* cats and books. *Address:* Peterhouse, Cambridge CB2 1RD. *T:* Cambridge 50256.

KENNEY, Reginald; Principal, Harper Adams Agricultural College, 1962-77; *b* 24 Aug. 1912; *m* 1946, Sheila Fay De Sa; two *d. Educ:* King Edward VII School, Lytham St Anne's; Leeds Univ.; West of Scotland Agric. Coll. Warden and Lectr, Staffordshire Farm Inst. (now Staffordshire Coll. of Agriculture), 1937-38; Asst County Agric. Educn Officer, Beds CC, 1938-42 (seconded Beds WAEC, 1939-42); Lectr in Farm Management and Animal Husbandry, University of Reading, 1942-48; Principal, Dorset Farm Inst. (now Dorset Coll. of Agriculture), 1948-62. Hon. FRAgS. *Publication:* Dairy Husbandry, 1957. *Recreations:* travel, mountains. *Address:* Brackenside, Clive Avenue, Church Stretton, Salop. *Club:* Farmers'.

KENNEY, (William) John; United States lawyer; Partner, Cox, Langford & Brown; *b* Oklahoma, 16 June 1904; *s* of Franklin R. Kenney and Nelle Kenney (*née* Torrence); *m* 1931, Elinor Craig; two *s* two *d. Educ:* Lawrenceville Sch., New Jersey; Stanford Univ (AB); Harvard Law Sch. (LLB). Practised law in San Francisco, 1929-36; Head of oil and gas unit, Securities and Exchange Commission, 1936-38; practised law in Los Angeles, 1938-41; Special Asst to Under-Sec. of the Navy; Chm. Navy Price Adjustment Board, General Counsel, 1941-46; Asst Sec. of the Navy, 1946-47; Under-Sec. of the Navy, 1947-49; Minister in charge of Economic Cooperation Administration Mission to the UK, 1949-50; Deputy Dir for Mutual Security, resigned 1952.

Chairman: Democratic Central Cttee of DC, 1960-64; DC Chapter, American Red Cross. Director: Riggs National Bank; Merchants Transfer and Porter International; Trustee, George C. Marshall Foundn, Lexington, Va. *Address:* 78 Kalorama Circle, NW, Washington, DC 20008; (office) 21 Dupont Circle NW, Washington, DC 20036, USA. *Clubs:* California (Los Angeles); Alibi, Metropolitan, Chevy Chase (Washington).

KENNY, Dr Anthony John Patrick, FBA 1974; designated to take office as Master of Balliol College, Oxford, October 1978 (Fellow, 1964-78; Senior Tutor, 1971-72 and 1976-78); Lecturer, University of Oxford, 1965-Oct. 1978; *b* Liverpool, 16 March 1931; *s* of John Kenny and Margaret Jones; *m* 1966, Nancy Caroline, *d* of Henry T. Gayley, Jr, Swarthmore, Pa; two *s. Educ:* Gregorian Univ., Rome (STL); St Benet's Hall, Oxford (DPhil). Ordained priest, Rome, 1955; Curate in Liverpool, 1959-63; returned to lay state, 1963. Asst Lectr, Univ. of Liverpool, 1961-63; Lectr in Philosophy, Exeter and Trinity Colls, Oxford, 1963-64; Wilde Lectr in Natural and Comparative Religion, Oxford, 1969-72; jt Gifford Lectr, Univ. of Edinburgh, 1972-73. Visiting Professor: Univs of Chicago, Washington, Michigan, and Cornell, Stanford and Rockefeller Univs. Editor, The Oxford Magazine, 1972-73. *Publications:* Action, Emotion and Will, 1963; Responsa Alumnorum of English College, Rome, 2 vols, 1963; Descartes, 1968; The Five Ways, 1969; Wittgenstein, 1973; The Anatomy of the Soul, 1974; Will, Freedom and Power, 1975. *Address:* Balliol College, Oxford; 7 Mansfield Road, Oxford. *T:* Oxford 48766.

KENNY, Douglas Timothy, MA, PhD; President of the University of British Columbia, since 1975; Professor of Psychology, since 1965; *b* Victoria, BC, 1923; *m* ; two *c. Educ:* Univ. of British Columbia (BA 1945, MA 1947); Univ. of Washington (PhD). Dept of Psychology, Univ. of British Columbia, 1950, Head of Dept 1965-69; Dean of Faculty of Arts, 1970-75 (Acting Dean, 1969-70). Pres., Faculty Assoc., 1962. Pres., BC Psychological Assoc., 1961. Member: Canada Council, 1975-; Bd of Trustees, Vancouver Gen. Hosp., 1976-. *Publications:* articles in Canadian and US jls. *Address:* University of British Columbia, Vancouver, BC, V6T 1W5 Canada.

KENNY, Michael, ARA 1976; Sculptor and Lecturer at University of London, Goldsmiths' College and Slade School of Fine Art; *b* 10 June 1941; *s* of James Kenny and Helen (*née* Gordon); *m* 1968, Rosemary Flood (separated); one *s* one *d* and one step *d. Educ:* St Francis Xavier's Coll., Liverpool; Liverpool Coll. of Art; Slade Sch. of Fine Art (DFA London). Works in public collections of: Tate Gallery; Arts Council of GB; London Borough of Camden, etc, and private collections in England, Europe and America. Exhibited extensively in Gt Britain, Europe and S America. Member of Faculty of Sculpture, British School at Rome; Mem., Fine Art Bd of Council for Nat. Academic Awards. *Recreation:* ornithology. *Address:* 52 Bronsart Road, SW6 6AA. *T:* 01-385 8205. *Club:* Chelsea Arts.

KENNY, Sir Patrick (John), Kt 1976; FRCS, FRACS; Hon. Surgeon, St Vincent's Hospital and Lewisham Hospital, Sydney, since 1946; *b* 12 Jan. 1914; *s* of Patrick John Kenny and Agnes Margaret Carberry; *m* 1942, Beatrice Ella Hammond; two *s. Educ:* Marcellin Coll., Sydney; Sydney Univ. (MB, BS 1936, MS 1946). FRCS 1940; FRACS 1944. War Service, AIF, UK, ME and SWPA, 1940-46. Anderson Stuart Memorial Res. Fellow, Sydney Univ., 1938, Lectr in Surg. Anat., 1949-55. Royal Australasian Coll. of Surgeons: Councillor, 1959; Vice Pres., 1967-69; Pres., 1969-71. Pres., NSW Med. Bd, 1974. FRCPS(Hon) 1970. *Publications:* surgical treatises. *Recreations:* golf, gardening. *Address:* 13 David Street, Mosman, Sydney, NSW 2088, Australia. *T:* 960-2820. *Clubs:* Australian, Royal Sydney Golf (Sydney).

KENRICK, Brig. Harry Selwyn, CB 1945; CBE 1941; ED 1941; Superintendent-in-Chief, Auckland Hospitals, 1946-61; retired; *b* 7 Aug. 1898; *s* of late W. G. K. Kenrick, Stipendiary Magistrate, Auckland, NZ, and Beatrice Thom; *m* 1926, Lorna Winifred Dick; two *d. Educ:* Waitaki; Oamaru, NZ; Otago Univ., NZ; Edinburgh Univ. MB, ChB (NZ), 1924; FRCS (Edinburgh), 1926; practised as consulting Obstetrician and Gynæcologist in Auckland, NZ, 1928-39. Served as infantry officer with NZ Division in France, 1916-18 (wounded); maintained interest in Territorial work and on outbreak of war, 1939, appointed ADMS Northern Command; went overseas, 1940, in command of a NZ Field Ambulance; ADMS, NZ Division, 1940 (despatches for services in Greece and CBE for Service as Senior Medical Officer in Battle for Crete, also Greek Military Cross for this); formerly Col Commandant, RNZAMC and Hon. Surgeon to the Governor-General of NZ; DMS, NZEF (CB). *Address:* 37 Victoria Avenue, Remuera, Auckland, New Zealand. *Clubs:* Northern, Officers (Auckland, NZ).

KENSINGTON, 7th Baron *cr* 1776; **William Edwardes;** Baron Kensington (UK) 1886; Lieutenant-Colonel Guides Cavalry, Indian Army; *b* 15 May 1904; *s* of 6th Baron and Mabel Carlisle (*d* 1934), *d* of George Pilkington, Stoneleigh, Woolton; *S* father 1938. *Educ:* Eton; RMC. *Heir: n* Hugh Ivor Edwardes [*b* 24 Nov. 1933; *m* 1961, Juliet Elizabeth Massy Anderson; two *s* one *d*]. *Address:* Mardan, PO Bromley, Rhodesia. *Club:* Cavalry and Guards.

KENSINGTON, Suffragan Bishop of, since 1964; **Rt. Rev. Ronald Cedric Osbourne Goodchild;** *b* 17 Oct. 1910; *s* of Sydney Osbourne and Dido May Goodchild; *m* 1947, Jean Helen Mary (*née* Ross); one *s* four *d*. *Educ:* St John's School, Leatherhead; Trinity Coll. (Monk Schol.), Cambridge; Bishops' Coll., Cheshunt. 2nd Cl. Hist. Tripos Parts I and II, 1931, Dealtry Exhibn. 1932, 3rd Class Theol. Tripos, 1932, Asst Master, Bickley Hall Sch., Kent, 1932-34; Curate, Ealing Parish Church, 1934-37; Chap. Oakham Sch., 1937-42. Chap. RAFVR, 1942-46 (despatches), Warden St Michael's House, Hamburg, 1946-49; Gen. Sec. SCM in Schools, 1949-53; Rector St Helen's Bishopsgate with St Martin Outwich, 1951-53; Vicar of Horsham, Sussex, 1953-59; Surrogate and Rural Dean of Horsham, 1954-59; Archdeacon of Northampton and Rector of Ecton, 1959-64. Examiner, Religious Knowledge, Southern Univs Jt Bd, 1954-58; Examining Chaplain to Bishop of Peterborough, 1959. Chairman Christian Aid Dept, British Council of Churches, 1964. Mem. of Convocation, 1959. *Publication:* Daily Prayer at Oakham School, 1938. *Recreations:* tennis, golf, cricket, photography. *Address:* 19 Campden Hill Square, W8. *T:* 01-727 9818. *Club:* Royal Air Force.

KENSWOOD, 2nd Baron, *cr* 1951; **John Michael Howard Whitfield;** *b* 6 April 1930; *o s* of 1st Baron Kenswood; *S* father, 1963; *m* 1951, Deirdre Anna Louise, *d* of Colin Malcolm Methven, Errol, Perthshire; four *s* one *d*. *Educ:* Trinity Coll. Sch., Ontario; Harrow; Grenoble Univ.; Emmanuel Coll., Cambridge (BA). *Heir: s* Hon. Michael Christopher Whitfield, *b* 3 July 1955. *Address:* Manor Farm, Roch, Haverfordwest, Dyfed. *T:* Camrose 359.

KENT, Arthur William, CMG 1966; OBE 1950; Deputy Chairman and Chief Executive, United Transport Holdings (Pty) Ltd, Johannesburg; Joint Managing Director, United Transport Overseas Ltd; *b* 22 March 1913; *s* of Howard and Eliza Kent; *m* 1st, 1944, Doris Jane (*née* Crowe; marr. diss., 1958); one *s* one *d*; 2nd, 1958, Mary (*née* Martin). Deputy City Treasurer, Nairobi, 1946-48, City Treasurer, 1948-65. Chief Executive: United Transport Overseas Ltd, Nairobi, 1966-69; Transport Holdings of Zambia Ltd, 1969-71; Chm. and Dir of a number of cos owned by United Transport Overseas Ltd and other BET cos. FIMTA; FCA; FCIT. *Address:* (home) 31 Gleneagles Road, Hurlingham, Sandton, Transvaal, South Africa; (business) PO box 6149, 8th Floor, National Board House, 94 Pritchard Street, Johannesburg, South Africa. *T:* 23-1761. *Clubs:* East India, Devonshire, Sports, and Public Schools; Rand (Johannesburg); Muthaiga Country (Nairobi).

KENT, Rear-Adm. Derrick George, CB 1971; retired 1971; *b* May 1920; *s* of Eric William Kent and Doris Elizabeth Osborn; *m* 1943, Estelle Clare Firkins; two *d*. *Educ:* St Lawrence College, Ramsgate. Joined RN 1938; Midshipman, HMS Cumberland, 1939-40; Submarine Service, 1940; Comdr, HM Submarine Spark, in Far East, 1943-45; Captain, 1960; Commanded: HMS Diana, 1963; HMS Plymouth; 22nd Escort Squadron, Far East, 1963-64; Imperial Defence Coll., 1965; Captain (SM), Third Submarine Sqdn, HMS Maidstone, 1966-67; Comdr, Clyde Submarine Base, and HMS Neptune, 1967-68; Commodore, 1968; Comdr, Clyde, and Supt Clyde Submarine Base, 1968-69; Rear-Adm., 1969; Flag Officer, Malta, and NATO Commander, SE Mediterranean, 1969-71. *Address:* 73 Exeter House, Putney Heath, SW15. *Club:* Little Ship.

KENT, Dorothy Miriam; Under-Secretary, Department of Employment, since 1973; *d* of Donald Roy Thom, CBE, and Elsie Miriam Thom (*née* Rundell); *m* 1948, Eric Nelson Kent; one *s* two *d*. *Educ:* North London Collegiate Sch.; Somerville Coll., Oxford (Scholar). MA Hons History. Temp. wartime civil service posts, 1941-46; entered Min. of Labour, 1946; Principal, 1950; Asst Sec., 1964; Under-Sec., 1973. *Address:* 45 Lytton Grove, SW15 2HD. *T:* 01-788 0214.

KENT, Sir Harold Simcox, GCB 1963 (KCB 1954; CB 1946); QC 1973; Commissary to Dean and Chapter of St Paul's Cathedral, since 1976; *b* 11 Nov. 1903; *s* of late P. H. B. Kent, OBE, MC; *m* 1930, Zillah Lloyd; one *s* (one *d* decd). *Educ:* Rugby School; Merton Coll., Oxford. Barrister-at-law, 1928; Parliamentary Counsel to the Treasury, 1940; HM Procurator-General and Treasury Solicitor, 1953-63; Standing Counsel to Church

Assembly and General Synod, 1964-72; Vicar-General of the Province of Canterbury, 1971-76; Dean of the Arches Court of Canterbury and Auditor of the Chancery Court of York, 1972-76. Mem., Departmental Cttee to examine operation of Section 2 of Official Secrets Act, 1911, 1971-72. DCL Lambeth, 1977. *Address:* Oak Meadow, Broad Campden, Glos. *T:* Evesham 840421. *Club:* United Oxford & Cambridge University.

KENT, Paul Welberry, DSc; FRIC; JP; Master of Van Mildert College and Director of Glycoprotein Research Unit, Durham University, since 1972; Student Emeritus of Christ Church, Oxford; *b* Doncaster, 19 April 1923; *s* of Thomas William Kent and Marion (*née* Cox); *m* 1952, Rosemary Elizabeth Boutflower, *y d* of Major C. H. B. Shepherd, MC; three *s* one *d*. *Educ:* Doncaster Grammar Sch.; Birmingham Univ.; Jesus Coll., Oxford. BSc 1944, PhD 1947, Birmingham; MA 1952, DPhil 1953, DSc 1966, Oxon. Asst Lectr, subseq. ICI Fellow, Birmingham Univ., 1946-50; Vis. Fellow, Princeton Univ., 1948-49; Univ. Demonstrator in Biochem., Oxford, 1950-72; Lectr, subseq. Student, Tutor and Dr Lees Reader in Chem., Christ Church, 1955-72; Research Assoc., Harvard, 1967; Vis. Prof., Windsor Univ., Ont, 1971. Mem., Oxford City Council, 1964-72; Governor, Oxford Coll. of Technology, subseq. Oxford Polytechnic, 1964-72, Vice-Chm. 1966-69, Chm. 1969-70; Member: Cttee, Biochemical Soc., 1963-67; Chemical Council, 1965-70; Res. Adv. Cttee, Cystic Fibrosis Res. Trust, 1977-; Commn on Religious Educn in School. Sec., Foster and Wills Scholarships Bd, 1960-72; Pres., Soc. for Maintenance of the Faith, 1975-. JP Oxford, 1972. Hon. DLitt Drury Coll., 1972. Hon. Fellow, Canterbury Coll., Ont, 1976. Rolleston Prize, 1952; Medal of Société de Chemie Biologique, 1969; Verdienstkreuz (Bundesrepublik), 1970. *Publications:* Biochemistry of Amino-sugars, 1955; (ed) Membrane-Mediation Information, Vols I and II, 1972; (ed) International Aspects of the Provision of Medical Care, 1976; articles in sci. and other jls. *Recreations:* music, travel. *Address:* Master's House, Van Mildert College, Durham. *T:* Durham 65452; Briscoe Gate, Cotherstone, Barnard Castle, Co. Durham. *Club:* Athenæum.

KENT, Sir Percy Edward, (Sir Peter Kent), Kt 1973; DSc, PhD; FRS 1966; FGS; consultant geologist; Chairman, Natural Environment Research Council, 1973-77; *b* 18 March 1913; *s* of Edward Louis Kent and Annie Kate (*née* Woodward); *m* 1940, Margaret Betty Hood, JP (*d* 1974); two *d*; *m* 1976, Lorna Ogilvie Scott. *Educ:* West Bridgford Gram. Sch.; Nottingham Univ. 1st cl. hons BSc London 1934; PhD 1941; DSc 1959. RAFVR, 1941-46 (despatches, 1944). Legion of Merit (USA), 1946. Geologist to E African Archæological Expedn (L. S. B. Leakey), 1934-35. Joined Anglo Iranian Oil (later BP), 1936; responsible for geological survey work in UK, Iran, E Africa, Papua, Canada and Alaska, for BP, 1946-60; managerial duties in BP, 1960-65; Chief Geologist, BP Co. Ltd, 1966-71, Exploration Manager, 1971-73. Pres. Yorks Geol Soc., 1964-66; Chm., Petroleum Exploration Soc. of Great Britain, 1966-68; Member: Council, Royal Soc., 1968-70; Council for Science Policy, 1968-; Pres., Geological Soc., 1966-70. Adrian Vis. Fellow, Univ. of Leicester, 1967-70. Hon. DSc: Leicester, 1972; Durham, 1974. Murchison Medal, Geological Soc. of London, 1969; (jt) MacRobert Award, 1970; Royal Medal, Royal Soc., 1971; Sorby Medal, Yorkshire Geol. Soc., 1973. *Publications:* many papers on stratigraphy and structural geology, Britain and abroad. *Recreations:* walking, gardening, landscape painting, choral singing. *Address:* 38 Rodney Road, West Bridgford, Nottingham. *T:* Nottingham 23-13-55. *Club:* Geological Society Club.

KENT, Ronald Clive, CB 1965; Director (Administration), Institution of Civil Engineers, since 1976; *b* 3 Aug. 1916; *s* of Dr Hugh Braund Kent and Margaret Mary Kent; *m* 1965, Mary Moyles Havell; one step-*s* one step-*d*. *Educ:* Rugby Sch.; Brasenose Coll., Oxford. Air Ministry, 1939; Royal Artillery, 1940-45; Air Ministry, 1945-58; Asst Under-Sec. of State, Air Min., 1958-63, MoD, 1963-67; Dep. Under-Sec. of State, MoD, 1967-76. *Address:* 6 Cookes Lane, Church Road, Cheam, Surrey. *Club:* Royal Automobile.

KENT, Brig. Sidney Harcourt, OBE 1944; *b* 22 April 1915; *s* of Major Geoffrey Harcourt Kent, Hindhead; *m* 1945, Nina Ruth, *d* of Gen. Sir Geoffry Scoones, KCB, KBE, CSI, DSO, MC; one *s* one *d*. *Educ:* Wellington Coll.; RMC Sandhurst. 2nd Lieut KOYLI, 1935; Lt-Col 1944; Brig. 1944; GSO1 Eighth Army, 1944; BGS Allied Land Forces, SE Asia, 1944. Comd 128 Inf. Bde (TA), 1960-63. Manager and Sec., Turf Board, 1965; Gen. Manager, 1969, Chief Executive, 1973-76, The Jockey Club. *Recreations:* farming, travel. *Address:* The Old Vicarage, Kingsey, Aylesbury, Bucks. *T:* Haddenham 291411.

KENTNER, Louis; Concert Pianist and Composer; *b* Silesia, 19 July 1905; *s* of Julius and Gisela Kentner; *m* 1931, Ilona Kabos (marr. diss. 1945); *m* 1946, Griselda Gould, *d* of late Evelyn Suart; no *c. Educ:* Budapest, Royal Academy of Music (at age of 6) under Arnold Szekely, Leo Weiner, Zoltan Kodaly. Concert début Budapest at age of 15; awarded a Chopin prize, Warsaw, a Liszt prize, Budapest. Has given concerts in most European countries; toured South Africa, Far East, New Zealand, Australia, S America; 6 tours of USA; three tours of USSR. First world performance, Bartok 2nd Piano Concerto, Budapest, and first European performance, Bartok 3rd Piano Concerto, London, 1946; many first performances of Kodaly and Weiner's Piano works. Came to England, 1935; naturalised British, 1946; since residence in England played much modern British music. Played numerous troop concerts during War of 1939-45. Has made many gramophone recordings. Pres., Liszt Society. Hon. RAM 1970. *Publications:* Three Sonatinas for Piano, 1939; two essays in Liszt Symposium, 1967; The Piano, 1976. *Recreations:* reading, chess playing. *Address:* 1 Mallord Street, Chelsea, SW3.

KENWORTHY, family name of **Baron Strabolgi.**

KENWORTHY, Cecil; Registrar of Family Division (formerly Probate and Divorce Division), of High Court of Justice, since 1968; *b* 22 Jan. 1918; *s* of John T. and Lucy Kenworthy; *m* 1944, Beryl Joan Willis; no *c. Educ:* Manchester and Bristol Grammar Schools. Entered Principal Probate Registry, 1936. *Publications:* (co-editor) supplements to Rayden on Divorce, 1967, 1968; (co-editor) Tolstoy on Divorce, 7th edn, 1971. *Address:* 526 Ben Jonson House, Barbican, EC2.

KENWORTHY, Joan Margaret, BLitt, MA; Principal, St Mary's College, University of Durham, since 1977; *b* Oldham, Lancs, 10 Dec. 1933; *o d* of Albert Kenworthy and late Amy (*née* Cobbold). *Educ:* Girls Grammar Sch., Barrow-in-Furness; St Hilda's Coll., Oxford (BLitt, MA). Henry Oliver Beckit Prize, Oxford, 1955; Leverhulme Overseas Res. Scholar, Makerere Coll., Uganda, and E African Agriculture and Forestry Res. Org., Kenya, 1956-58; Actg Tutor, St Hugh's Coll., Oxford, 1958-59; Tutorial Res. Fellow, Bedford Coll., London, 1959-60; Univ. of Liverpool: Asst Lectr in Geography, 1960-63; Lectr, 1963-73; Sen. Lectr, 1973-77; Warden of Salisbury Hall, 1966-77 and of Morton House, 1974-77. IUC short-term Vis. Lectr, Univ. of Sierra Leone, 1975. Member: Council, African Studies Assoc. of UK, 1969-72; Council, Inst. of Brit. Geographers, 1976-78; Cttee, Merseyside Conf. for Overseas Students Ltd, 1976-77. Treasurer, Assoc. of Brit. Climatologists, 1976-79. *Publications:* (contrib.) Geographers and the Tropics, ed R. W. Steel and R. M. Prothero, 1964; (contrib.) Oxford Regional Economic Atlas for Africa, 1965; (contrib.) Studies in East African Geography and Development, ed S. Ominde, 1971; (contrib.) An Advanced Geography of Africa, ed J. I. Clarke, 1975; (contrib.) Rangeland Management and Ecology in East Africa, ed D. J. Pratt and M. D. Gwynne, 1977; articles in jls and encycs. *Recreation:* wildlife safaris. *Address:* 1 Elvet Garth, South Road, Durham DH1 3TP. *T:* Durham 3865.

KENYA, Archbishop of, since 1970; **Most Rev. Festo Habakkuk Olang';** Bishop of Nairobi; *b* 11 Nov. 1914; *m* 1937, Eseri D. Olang'; four *s* eight *d. Educ:* Alliance High School. Teacher, 1936-43; ordained 1945; consecrated Assistant Bishop of Mombasa in Namirembe Cathedral, by Archbishop of Canterbury, 1955; Bishop of Maseno, 1961. *Address:* PO Box 40502, Nairobi, Kenya. *T:* 28146.

KENYATTA, HE Hon. Mzee Jomo, CGH; MP; (First) President of the Republic of Kenya since Dec. 1964; Prime Minister, also Minister for Internal Security and Defence, and Foreign Affairs, Kenya, since 1963; *b* (approximately) 1889; *m* ; four *s* four *d. Educ:* Church of Scotland Mission, Kikuyu, Kenya; London School of Economics, Great Britain. General Sec., Kikuyu Central Assoc., 1922. Founded first African-owned journal, Mwigwithania, 1928; sent by Kenya Africans to Britain to press case for Independence; travelled extensively in Europe: represented Ethiopia at the League of Nations, briefly, during war; Pres., first Pan-African Congress, Manchester, Gt Britain, 1945; Pres., Kenya African Union, 1947-52; imprisoned and detained by British, 1952-61; elected *in absentia,* while in restriction at Lodwar, Pres., Kenya African National Union, 1960; MLC 1962; Minister of State for Constitutional Affairs and Economic Planning, 1962. Hon. LLD: University of E Africa, 1965; Manchester Univ., 1966. KStJ 1972. *Publications:* Facing Mt Kenya; Kenya, The Land of Conflict; My People of Kikuyu; Harambee. *Address:* PO Box 30510, Nairobi, Kenya. *T:* Nairobi 27411; Ichaweri, Gatundu, Kenya.

KENYON, family name of **Baron Kenyon.**

KENYON, 5th Baron, *cr* 1788; **Lloyd Tyrell-Kenyon,** CBE 1972; FSA; DL; Bt 1784; Baron of Gredington, 1788; Captain late Royal Artillery, TA; *b* 13 Sept. 1917; *o s* of 4th Baron and Gwladys Julia (*d* 1965), *d* of late Col H. R. Lloyd Howard, CB; *S* father, 1927; *m* 1946, Leila Mary, *d* of Comdr J. W. Cookson, RN, Strand Hill, Winchelsea, and widow of Lt Hugo Peel, Welsh Guards; three *s* one *d. Educ:* Eton; Magdalene Coll., Cambridge. BA (Cambridge), 1950. 2nd Lt Shropshire Yeo. 1937; Lt RA, TA, retired (ill-health) with hon. rank of Captain. Dir, Lloyds Bank Ltd, 1962- (Chm. North West Bd); President: University Coll. of N Wales, Bangor, 1947-; Nat. Museum of Wales, 1952-57. Trustee, Nat. Portrait Gall., 1953-, Chm., 1966-; Chairman: Wrexham Powys and Mawddach Hosp. Management Cttee, 1960-74; Clwyd AHA, 1974-; Friends of the Nat. Libraries, 1962-; Flint Agricultural Exec. Cttee, 1964-73. Member: Standing Commn on Museums and Galleries, 1953-60; Welsh Regional Hosp. Bd, 1958-63; Council for Professions Supplementary to Medicine, 1961-65; Royal Commn on Historical MSS, 1966-; Bd of Governors, Welbeck Coll. Chief Comr for Wales, Boy Scouts' Assoc., 1948-65. DL Co. Flint, 1948; CC Flint, 1946 (Chm., 1954-55). Hon. LLD Wales, 1958. *Heir: s* Hon. Lloyd Tyrell-Kenyon, [*b* 13 July 1947; *m* 1971, Sally Carolyn, *e d* of J. F. P. Matthews; two *s*]. *Address:* Gredington, Whitchurch, Salop SY13 3DH. *TA:* Hanmer 330. *T:* Hanmer 330. *Clubs:* Brooks's, Cavalry and Guards, Beefsteak.

KENYON, Alec Hindle, CEng, FIEE; Chairman, East Midlands Electricity Board, 1965-69, retired; *b* 11 June 1905; *s* of late William Kenyon, Accrington, Lancs; *m* 1932, Elizabeth Mary Wollaston; one *s* one *d. Educ:* Bootham Sch., York. Accrington Corp., Northampton Electric Light & Power Co., and North Eastern Electricity Supply Co.; Liaison Officer, North Eastern Electricity Board, 1948-59; Dep. Chm., East Midlands Electricity Board, 1959-64. Chm., North Eastern Centre, Instn of Electrical Engineers, 1955-56. *Recreations:* walking and gardening. *Address:* 8 Oakwood, Hexham, Northumberland.

KENYON, Clifford, CBE 1966; JP; farmer; *b* 11 Aug. 1896; *m* 1922, Doris Muriel Lewis, Herne Hill, London; three *s* two *d. Educ:* Brighton Grove Coll., Manchester; Manchester Univ. Joined Labour Party, 1922; Mem. Rawtenstall Council, 1923; Mayor, 1938-42, resigned from Council, 1945. MP (Lab) Chorley Div. of Lancs, 1945-70. JP Lancs, 1941. *Address:* Scarr Barn Farm, Crawshawbooth, Rossendale, Lancs. *T:* Rossendale 5703.

KENYON, Sir George (Henry), Kt 1976; DL; JP; Chairman: William Kenyon & Sons Ltd, since 1961; Tootal Ltd, since 1976; *b* 10 July 1912; *s* of George Henry Kenyon and Edith (*née* Hill); *m* 1938, Christine Dorey (*née* Brentnall); two *s* one *d . Educ:* Fulneck; Mostyn House; Radley (Scholar); Manchester Univ. (1st Cl. Hons Eng; Trevithick Scholar). Director: William Kenyon & Sons Ltd, 1942; Tootal Ltd, 1971; Williams & Glyn's Bank, 1972; Manchester Ship Canal, 1972. Gen. Comr, Inland Revenue, 1957-73. Manchester University: Chm. Bldgs Cttee, 1962-70; Treas., 1970-72; Chm. Council, 1972-. Hon. Treas., Civic Trust, NW, 1962-; Member: NW Adv. Cttee, Civil Aviation, 1967-72; Manchester Reg. Hosp. Bd, 1962-68; NW Reg. Econ. Planning Council, 1970-73; boys clubs, schs, local min. cttees, St John's Amb., 1943-. JP Cheshire, 1959; Chm., S Tameside Bench, 1974-; DL Chester, 1969; High Sheriff, Cheshire, 1973-74. *Recreations:* reading, talking, travel. *Address:* Limefield House, Hyde, Cheshire. *T:* 061-368 2012. *Club:* St James's (Manchester).

KENYON, Hugh; *b* 11 Jan. 1910; *s* of Thomas and Emily Kenyon; *m* 1941, Mary Winifred, *d* of Sir Peile Thompson, 4th Bt; one *s* one *d . Educ:* Rossall Sch.; St John's Coll., Oxford (MA). Oxford House, Bethnal Green, 1932-34; Prison Commn, 1934-68: Governor of Prisons, 1947-57; Nuffield Travelling Fellowship for Civil Servants (12 months study of penal system in Scandinavia), 1957; Asst Comr of Prisons, 1958-64; Director of Prison Administration, 1964-68; Inspection and Report on conditions in the prisons of the Bahamas, 1966; nine months lecturing, UN, Asia and Far East Inst., Tokyo, 1968 and 1972; Inspection and Report on prison system in Bermuda, 1970. *Recreations:* gardening, golf, music, philately. *Address:* Yarrowfield, Mayford, Woking, Surrey GU22 0SE. *T:* Woking 62870.

KENYON, Prof. John Philipps; G. F. Grant Professor of History, University of Hull, since 1962; *b* 18 June 1927; *s* of William Houston Kenyon and Edna Grace Philipps; *m* 1962, Angela Jane Ewert (*née* Venables); one *s* two *d . Educ:* King Edward VII Sch., Sheffield; Univ. of Sheffield (BA); Christ's Coll., Cambridge (PhD). Fellow of Christ's Coll., Cambridge, 1954-62; Lectr in Hist., Cambridge, 1955-62. Visiting Prof., Columbia

Univ., New York, 1959-60; Junior Proctor, Cambridge, 1961-62; John U. Nef Lectr, Univ. of Chicago, 1972; Ford's Lectr in English Hist., Oxford, 1975-76. *Publications:* Robert Spencer Earl of Sunderland, 1958; The Stuarts, 1958, 2nd edn 1970; The Stuart Constitution, 1966; The Popish Plot, 1972; Revolution Principles, 1977; contribs to various learned jls. *Recreation:* bridge. *Address:* Department of History, University of Hull, Hull HU6 7RX. *T:* Hull 46311.

KENYON, Dame Kathleen (Mary), DBE 1973 (CBE 1954); MA; DLitt, DLit, LHD, FBA; FSA; Principal of St Hugh's College, Oxford 1962-73; *b* 5 Jan. 1906; *e d* of late Sir Frederic G. Kenyon, GBE, KCB. *Educ:* St Paul's Girls' Sch.; Somerville Coll., Oxford. Asst at excavations, British Assoc's expedition to Zimbabwe, S Rhodesia, 1929, Verulamium, 1930-35, Joint Expedition to Samaria, Palestine, 1931-34; Dir, excavations at Jewry Wall site, Leicester, 1936-39, Viroconium, Salop, 1936-37, the Wrekin, Salop, 1939; Southwark, 1945-48; Breedon-on-the-Hill, Leics, 1946; Sutton Walls, Herefords, 1948-51; Sabratha, Tripolitania, 1948-49, 1951; Jericho, Jordan, 1952-58; Jerusalem, Jordan, 1961-67. Sec., University of London Inst. of Archæology, 1935-48; acting Dir, 1942-46; Sec., Council for British Archæology, 1944-49; Lecturer in Palestinian Archæology, University of London, Institute of Archæology, 1948-62; Dir, British Sch. of Archæology in Jerusalem, 1951-66. Divisional Comdt and Sec., Hammersmith Div., British Red Cross Soc., 1939-42; Dir, Youth Dept British Red Cross Soc., 1942-45. Norton Lecturer, Archæological Institute of America, 1959; Schweich Lecturer, British Academy, 1963; Haskell Lecturer, Oberlin Coll., Ohio, 1976. Hon. Fellow: Somerville Coll., 1960; St Hugh's Coll., Oxford, 1973. Trustee, British Museum, 1965-. Hon. DLitt Exon. *Publications:* Verulamium Theatre Excavations, 1935; Excavations at Viroconium, 1940; Excavations on the Wrekin, 1943; Excavations at the Jewry Wall Site, Leicester, 1948; Excavations at Breedon-on-the-Hill, Leicester, 1950; Beginning in Archæology, 1952; Excavations at Sutton Walls, Herefordshire, 1954; Digging Up Jericho, 1957; contributor to Samaria-Sebaste, 1, 1942 and 3, 1958; Excavations at Jericho I, 1960 and II, 1965; Archæology in the Holy Land, 1960; Amorites and Canaanites, 1967; Jerusalem: excavating 3,000 years of History, 1968; Royal Cities of the Old Testament, 1971; Palestine in the Time of the Eighteenth Dynasty, 1971; Digging up Jerusalem, 1974. *Recreation:* gardening. *Address:* Rose Hill, Erbistock, Wrexham, Clwyd. *T:* Overton-on-Dee 355. *Clubs:* University Women's, VAD Ladies.

KEOGH, Charles Alfred, FRCS; Hon. Consulting Surgeon, Ear, Nose and Throat Department, The London Hospital and Medical Coll. *Educ:* London Hosp. Comdr of Royal Norwegian Order of St Olaf, 1943. *Address:* 139 Harley Street, W1.

KEOHANE, Dr Kevin William, CBE 1976; Rector, Roehampton Institute of Higher Education, since Sept. 1976; *b* 28 Feb. 1923; *s* of William Patrick and Mabel Margaret Keohane; *m* 1949, Mary Margaret (Patricia) Ashford; one *s* three *d*. *Educ:* Borden Grammar Sch., Sittingbourne, Kent; Univ. of Bristol (BSc (1st Cl. Hons Physics), PhD. FInstP. War service, RAF, Radar Br. (Flt Lt). Research appts and Lectr in Anatomy, Univ. of Bristol, 1947-59; Chelsea College, London: Reader in Biophysics, 1959; Prof. of Physics and Head of Dept of Physics, 1965; Prof. of Science Educn and Dir, Centre for Science Educn, 1967-76; Vice-Principal, 1966-76. Royal Society Leverhulme Prof., Fed. Univ. of Bahia, Brazil, 1971; Vis. Prof., Chelsea College, 1977-. Mem., Academic Adv. Cttee, Open Univ., 1970-; Court, Univ. of Bristol, 1968-; University of London: Member: Academic Council, 1974-76; Extra-Mural Council, 1974-76; School Examinations Council, 1975-76. Dir, Nuffield Foundn Science Projects, 1966-; Member: Nat. Programme Cttee for Computers in Educn, 1974-; Royal Society/Inst. of Physics Educn Cttee, 1970-73; SSRC Educn Bd, 1971-74; BBC Further Educn Adv. Cttee, 1972-75. Manager, Royal Instn, 1972-75. Chairman: Science Div., Univ. of London Inst. of Educn, 1967-76; Formation Cttees: City of London Polytechnic, 1974-75; Goldsmiths' Coll., 1975-. Mem. Delegacy, Goldsmiths' Coll., 1974-; Chm. of Governors, Garnett Coll., 1974-; Governor: Philippa Fawcett and Digby Stuart Colls, 1973-76; Ursuline Convent Sch., Wimbledon, 1967-. Numerous overseas consultancies and visiting professorships; Academic Mem., British Assoc of Science Writers, 1971-; Editor, Jl of Physics Educn, 1966-69; Mem., Editorial Bd, Jl Curriculum Studies, and Studies in Sci. Educn. *Recreations:* Rugby (spectator) (President, Chelsea Coll. RFC, 1974-76), railways. *Address:* Roehampton Institute, Grove House, Roehampton Lane, SW15 5PJ. *T:* 01-878 5751; 3 Thetford Road, New Malden, Surrey. *T:* 01-942 6861. *Club:* Athenæum.

KEPPEL, family name of **Earl of Albemarle.**

KEPPEL-COMPTON, Robert Herbert, CMG 1953; *b* 11 Dec. 1900; *s* of late J. H. Keppel-Compton, Southampton; *m* 1930, Marjorie, *yr d* of late Rev. W. B. Preston; one *s* one *d*. *Educ:* Oakham Sch.; Sidney Sussex Coll., Cambridge. BA, LLB Cantab. Entered Colonial Administrative Service, 1923. Dep. Provincial Commissioner, 1945; Development Sec., 1946; Provincial Commissioner, Nyasaland, 1949-55; retired from Colonial Service, 1955. *Address:* Higher Leigh, Kingsbridge, Devon.

KER; *see* Innes-Ker, family name of **Duke of Roxburghe.**

KER, Douglas R. E.; *see* Edwardes-Ker.

KER, K(eith) R(eginald) Welbore, OBE 1964; HM Diplomatic Service, retired; Director, Anglo-German Association, 1971-73; *b* 8 Aug. 1913; *s* of late Reginald Arthur Ker and Morna, *d* of Welbore MacCarthy, sometime Bishop of Grantham; *m* 1954, Marisa (*née* Ummarino), formerly Lo Bianco; three *s* two *d* (one step *s* one step *d*). *Educ:* Malvern Coll. Business, 1932-39. Served in HM Army, 1939-46, Major 1945 (despatches). Apptd British Consul, Bolzano, 1946; Second Sec., Rio de Janeiro, 1948; transf. to Stockholm, 1950; to Singapore, 1951; acting Consul, Hanoi, 1952; First Sec., Belgrade, 1953-55; transf. to Rangoon, 1956; to Saigon, 1957; to FO, 1957; to Hamburg, 1958; to Bonn, 1959; HM Consul-Gen., Hanover, 1961-64; First Sec., 1965-67, Counsellor, 1967-69, Lisbon; Consul-General, Cape Town, 1970-73. *Recreations:* walking, travel, tennis, collecting water-colour drawings. *Address:* 39 Marryat Road, SW19. *T:* 01-946 6418. *Club:* Travellers'.

KER, Neil Ripley, FBA 1958; Reader in Palæography, Oxford University, 1946-68, Reader Emeritus since 1968; Fellow of Magdalen College, 1946-68, Honorary Fellow, since 1975; *b* 28 May 1908; *s* of Robert MacNeil Ker and Lucy Winifred Strickland-Constable; *m* 1938, Jean Frances, *d* of Brig. C. B. Findlay; one *s* three *d*. *Educ:* Eton Coll.; Magdalen Coll., Oxford. BLitt (Oxon), 1933; Lecturer in Palæography, Oxford, 1936-46; James P. R. Lyell Reader in Bibliography, Oxford, 1952-53; Sandars Reader in Bibliography, Cambridge, 1955. Sir Israel Gollancz Mem. Prize, British Acad., 1959; Edwards Lecturer, Glasgow, 1960; Gold Medallist, Bibliographical Soc., 1975. Hon. DLitt Reading, 1964; Hon. Dr Leyden, 1972; Hon. LittD Cambridge, 1975. Corresp. Fellow, Medieval Acad. of America, 1971; Corresp. Mem., Bayerische Akademie der Wissenschaften, 1977. *Publications:* Medieval Libraries of Great Britain, 1941 (2nd edn 1964); Pastedowns in Oxford Bindings, 1954; Catalogue of Manuscripts containing Anglo-Saxon, 1957; English Manuscripts in the Century after the Norman Conquest, 1960; Medieval Manuscripts in British Libraries: I, London, 1969; II, Abbotsford-Keele, 1977; Records of All Souls College 1437-1600, 1971; (ed) The Parochial Libraries of the Church of England, 1959; articles and reviews in Medium Aevum, etc. *Recreation:* hill walking. *Address:* 22 London Street, Edinburgh EH3 6NA.

KERANS, Comdr John Simon, DSO 1949; RN retired; *b* 30 June 1915; *m* 1946, Stephanie Campbell Shires; two *d*. *Educ:* RN Coll., Dartmouth. Cadet and Midshipman, HMS Rodney, Home Fleet, 1932-33; Midshipman and Sub-Lt HMS Cornwall, 1933-35; RN Coll., Greenwich, 1935-37; China Station, 1937-39. Served War of 1939-45: Staff, Chief of Intelligence Staff, Far East, Hong Kong and Singapore, 1939; HMS Naiad, Home and Medit. Stations, 1940-42; Staff Officer (Intelligence), Staff C-in-C, Medit. and Levant, 1942-43; 1st Lt, HMS Icarus, N Atlantic, 1943-44; Staff, C-in-C, Portsmouth, 1944; i/c HMS Blackmore (Lt-Comdr) 1944; Security Intelligence, Hong Kong, 1947; on loan to Malayan Police, Kuala Lumpur, 1948; Asst Naval Attaché, Nanking, 1949, joined frigate Amethyst after her attack by Communist forces (DSO), 1949; Comdr Dec. 1949; RN Staff Course, Greenwich, 1950; Head Far East Section, Naval Intelligence Admiralty, 1950-52; i/c HMS Rinaldo, 1953-54; Brit. Naval Attaché, Bangkok, Phnom Penh, Ventiane, Saigon and Rangoon, 1954-55; Sen. Officers' Technical Course Portsmouth, 1957; retired RN, 1958. MP (C) The Hartlepools, 1959-64; Civil Servant, Pensions Appeal Tribunals, 1969-. *Address:* 26 Riddlesdown Avenue, Purley CR2 1JG. *T:* 01-660 3614. *Club:* Littlehampton Sailing.

KEREMA, Archbishop of, (RC), since 1976; **Most Rev. Virgil Copas,** DD; Member of Religious Order of Missionaries of Sacred Heart (MSC); *b* 19 March 1915; *s* of Cornelius Copas and Kathleen (*née* Daly). *Educ:* St Mary's Coll. and Downlands Coll., Toowoomba, Queensland. Sec. to Bp L. Scharmach, Rabaul, New Britain, New Guinea, 1945-51; Religious Superior, Dio. of Darwin, Austr, 1954-60; Bishop of Port Moresby, 1960-66; Archbishop of Port Moresby, 1966-76. *Address:* Catholic Church, Box 90, PO Kerema, Gulf Province, Papua New Guinea, Oceania. *T:* Kerema 681079.

KERENSKY, Dr Oleg Alexander, CBE 1964; FRS 1970; Consultant, Freeman Fox & Partners, Consulting Engineers, since 1975 (Partner, 1955-75); *b* 16 April 1905; *s* of late Alexander F. Kerensky and Olga (*née* Baronovsky); *m* 1928, Nathalie (*d* 1969); one *s*; *m* 1971, Mrs Dorothy Harvey. *Educ:* Russia, later small private sch. in England; Northampton Engrg Coll. (now The City Univ.). FICE; FIStructE; FIHVE; FWeldI; Fellow, Fellowship of Engineering 1976. Jun. Asst, Oxford CC, 1926; Dorman Long & Co.: Asst Engr, Bridge Design Office, 1927-30, construction of Lambeth Bridge, 1930-32; Sen. Design Engr, Bridge Dept, 1932-37; Chief Engr and Sub-Agent: on construction of Wandsworth Bridge, Holloway Bros (London) Ltd, 1937-40; on Avonmouth Oil Jetty, 1940-43; Chief Engr, Mulberry Harbours, N Wales, 1943-45; Sen. Designer, Holloway Bros (London) Ltd, 1945-46; Principal Bridge Designer, Freeman Fox & Partners, 1946-55. Mem. Exec. Bd, BSI (Chm., Engrg Council); Chm., CIRIA. Mem. Council, City Univ. President: IStructE, 1970-71; IHVE, 1971-72. Hon. Fellow, Concrete Soc. Hon. Dr of Science, City Univ., 1967. Gold Medal, IStructE, 1977. *Publications:* numerous papers in learned jls. *Recreations:* bridge, croquet, swimming. *Address:* 27 Pont Street, SW1. *T:* 01-235 7173. *Clubs:* Athenæum, Hurlingham.

KERLE, Rt. Rev. Ronald Clive; Rector of St Swithun, Pymble, Diocese of Sydney, since 1976; *b* 28 Dec. 1915; *s* of William Alfred Ronald Kerle and Isabel Ada (*née* Turner); *m* 1940, Helen Marshall Jackson; one *s* one *d*. *Educ:* Univ. of Sydney (BA); Moore Theological Coll., Sydney. Sydney ACT, ThL 1937; BA 1942. Deacon 1939; Priest, 1940; Curate, St Paul's, Sydney, 1939; St Anne, Ryde, 1939-41; Rector, Kangaroo Valley, 1941-43; St Stephen, Port Kembla, 1943-47; Chaplain, AIF, 1945-47; Gen. Sec., NSW Branch, Church Missionary Society, 1947-54; Rector of Summer Hill, 1954-57; Archdeacon of Cumberland, 1954-60; Bishop Co-adjutor of Sydney, 1956-65; Bishop of Armidale, 1965-76. *Address:* Rectory, 11 Merrivale Road, Pymble, NSW 2073, Australia.

KERLEY, Sir Peter (James), KCVO 1972 (CVO 1952); CBE 1951; MD, FRCP, FRCR, DMRE; Emeritus Consultant, X-Ray Department, Westminster Hospital; Emeritus Consultant Adviser to Ministry of Health on radiology; Emeritus Consultant Radiologist to: King Edward VII Sanatorium, Midhurst; The National Heart Hospital; Ministry of Aviation; late Hon. Editor of the Journal of Faculty of Radiologists (now Clinical Radiology); Examiner in radiology: RCP; University of Leeds; Faculty of Radiologists, University of Liverpool; *b* Dundalk, Ireland, 27 Oct. 1900; *s* of Michael and Matilda Kerley; *m* 1929, Olivia MacNamee (*d* 1973), Enniskillen; two *d*. *Educ:* University Coll., Dublin (MB 1923 and MD 1932); University of Vienna (Diploma, 1924); Cambridge Univ. (DMRE 1925). Major RAMC 1939-44. President: Radiology Section, RSM, 1939-40; Faculty of Radiologists, 1952-55. FRSM; Hon. Fellow: Amer. Coll. of Radiology; Australasian Coll. of Radiology; Faculty of Radiologists of Ireland; Radiological Soc. of Chicago; Radiological Soc. of Toronto. Röntgen Award, 1944; Gold Medal, RCR, 1976. OStJ 1958. *Publications:* Recent Advances in Radiology, 4th edn; (with Shanks) A Text-Book of Radiology in 6 vols; also various articles on diseases of the Chest and Digestive Tract. *Recreation:* fishing. *Address:* 11 Wimpole Street, W1M 7AB. *T:* 01-580 1660; 9 Heath Rise, SW15. *Clubs:* White's, Travellers'; Royal Wimbledon Golf.

KERMACK, Stuart Grace, CBE 1955; *b* 11 April 1888; 2nd *s* of Henry Kermack, Advocate; *m* 1922, Nell P., *y d* of Thomas White, SSC; two *s* one *d*. *Educ:* Edinburgh Academy; Fettes Coll.; Edinburgh Univ. MA, LLB, Edinburgh Univ.; Scots Bar, 1911; served European War, RFA (TF) Capt., Gallipoli, Egypt, Palestine; Judge in Sudan, 1918-19; Judicial Service, Palestine, 1920-30; Lecturer in Jurisprudence, Edinburgh Univ., 1933-36; Sheriff-Substitute of Lanarkshire at Glasgow, 1936-55; Sheriff-Substitute of Renfrew and Argyll at Oban, 1955-62. King Haakon VII Liberty Cross, 1948. *Publications:* Criminal Procedure in Palestine, 1927; Law of Scotland: Sources and Juridical Organisation, 1933; Contributions to Juridical Review, Stair Society's Sources of Scots Law, etc. *Address:* c/o 14 Dundas Street, Edinburgh.
See also S. O. Kermack.

KERMACK, Stuart Ogilvy; Sheriff of Tayside, Central and Fife at Forfar and Arbroath, since 1971; *b* 9 July 1934; *s* of Stuart Grace Kermack, *qv*; *m* 1961, Barbara Mackenzie, BSc; three *s* one *d*. *Educ:* Glasgow Academy; Jesus Coll., Oxford; Glasgow Univ.; Edinburgh Univ. BA Oxon (Jurisprudence), 1956; LLB Glasgow, 1959. Elected to Scots Bar, 1959. Sheriff Substitute of Inverness, Moray, Nairn and Ross, at Elgin and Nairn, 1965-71. *Publications:* articles in legal journals. *Recreation:* tidying up. *Address:* 7 Little Causeway, Forfar, Angus. *T:* Forfar 4691.

KERMAN, Prof. Joseph Wilfred; Professor of Music, University of California at Berkeley, since 1974; *b* 3 April 1924; *m* 1945, Vivian Shaviro; two *s* one *d*. *Educ:* New York Univ. (AB); Princeton Univ. (PhD). Dir of Graduate Studies, Westminster Choir Coll., Princeton, NJ, USA, 1949-51; Music Faculty, Univ. of California at Berkeley, 1951-71 (Dep. Chm., 1960-63); Heather Prof. of Music, Oxford Univ., and Fellow of Wadham Coll., Oxford, 1972-74. Co-editor, 19th century Music. Guggenheim and Fulbright Fellowships; Visiting Fellow: All Souls Coll., Oxford, 1966; Society for the Humanities, Cornell Univ., USA, 1970; Clare Hall, Cambridge, 1971. Fellow, American Academy of Arts and Sciences. Hon. FRAM. Hon. DHL Fairfield Univ., 1970. *Publications:* Opera as Drama, 1956; The Elizabethan Madrigal, 1962; The Beethoven Quartets, 1967; A History of Art and Music (with H. W. Janson), 1968; (ed) Ludwig van Beethoven: Autograph Miscellany, 1786-99 (Kafka Sketchbook), 2 vols, 1970; Listen, 1972; (co-ed) Beethoven Studies, vol 1 1973, vol 2 1977; essays, in music criticism and musicology, in: Musical Quarterly, Hudson Review, San Francisco Chronicle, etc. *Address:* Music Department, University of California, Berkeley, Calif 94720, USA; 107 Southampton Avenue, Berkeley, Calif 94707.

KERMODE, Prof. (John) Frank, MA; FBA 1973; King Edward VII Professor of English Literature, University of Cambridge, and Fellow of King's College, Cambridge, since 1974; *b* 29 Nov. 1919; *s* of late John Pritchard Kermode and late Doris Pearl Kermode; *m* 1947, Maureen Eccles (marr. diss. 1970); twin *s* and *d*; *m* 1976, Anita Van Vactor. *Educ:* Douglas High Sch.; Liverpool Univ. BA 1940; War Service (Navy), 1940-46; MA 1947; Lecturer, King's Coll., Newcastle, in the University of Durham, 1947-49; Lecturer in the University of Reading, 1949-58; John Edward Taylor Prof. of English Literature in the University of Manchester, 1958-65; Winterstoke Prof. of English in the University of Bristol, 1965-67; Lord Northcliffe Prof. of Modern English Lit., UCL, 1967-74. Charles Eliot Norton Prof. of Poetry at Harvard, 1977-78. Co-editor, Encounter, 1966-67. FRSL 1958. Mem. Arts Council, 1968-71; Chm., Poetry Book Soc., 1968-76. For. Hon. Mem., Amer. Acad. of Arts and Scis. Hon. DHL Chicago, 1975. Officier de l'Ordre des Arts et des Sciences. *Publications:* (ed) Shakespeare, The Tempest (Arden Edition), 1954; Romantic Image, 1957; John Donne, 1957; The Living Milton, 1960; Wallace Stevens, 1960; Puzzles & Epiphanies, 1962; The Sense of an Ending, 1967; Continuities, 1968; Shakespeare, Spenser, Donne, 1971; Modern Essays, 1971; Lawrence, 1973; (ed, with John Hollander) Oxford Anthology of English Literature, 1973; The Classic, 1975; (ed) Selected Prose of T. S. Eliot, 1975; contrib. Review of Eng. Studies, Partisan Review, New York Review, New Statesman, etc. *Address:* King's College, Cambridge CB2 1ST. *T:* Cambridge 50411; 27 Luard Road, Cambridge. *T:* Cambridge 47398.

KERN, Karl-Heinz; Ambassador of German Democratic Republic to the Court of St James's since Dec. 1973; *b* 18 Feb. 1930; *m* 1952, Ursula Bennmann; one *s*. *Educ:* King George Gymnasium, Dresden; Techn. Coll., Dresden (chem. engrg); Acad. for Polit. Science and Law (Dipl. jur., post-grad. History). Leading posts in diff. regional authorities of GDR until 1959; foreign policy, GDR, 1959-62; Head of GDR Mission in Ghana, 1962-66; Head of African Dept, Min. of For. Affairs, 1966-71; Minister and Chargé d'Affaires, Gt Britain, 1973. Holds Order of Merit of the Fatherland, etc. *Recreations:* sport, reading, music. *Address:* 34 Belgrave Square, SW1X 8QB. *T:* 01-235 9941.

KERNOFF, Harry, RHA 1935; Professional Artist, Portrait, Landscape and Mural; *b* London, 9 Jan. 1900; *s* of Isaac Kernoff (Russian Jewish) and Katherine A'Barbanelle (Old Spanish Jewish Stock), family migrated to Dublin, May 1914. *Educ:* Elementary Sch., London; Metropolitan Sch. of Art, Dublin. All Ireland Taylor Art Scholarship, 1923; Exhibits yearly RHA, from 1926; 16 One-man Exhibitions in Dublin Yearly, 1926-58; 1 Ex. Gieves Gallery, London, 1931; One-man Show, White Gallery, 1938; 1 Ex. Castlebar, Co. Mayo, 1947; Exhibited Mural at Royal Academy, 1931, and in Paris, Chicago, New York, Amsterdam, Cork, Glasgow and Wales 1953, etc.; 80 small oils, Toronto, 1965. *Work in public collections:* 3 Pictures in Belfast Art Gallery (1 water colour, 2 woodcuts); 3 pictures in Nat. Art Gallery of Ireland; 2 Oil Paintings Municipal Gallery, Dublin (Street Scene, Brazen Head); 2 Oil Paintings Limerick Art Gallery; 2 Oil Paintings in Waterford Art Gall.; Oil Painting in Castlebar Gallery, 1947; 3 Oils in Killarney Art Gallery; 1 Oil in Monaco. Pictures in World's Fair, Glasgow, 1938; and World's Fair, New York, 1939; Oil, Killarney Landscape, in Irish Legation, Washington, 1959-63; Oil, Irish Volunteer, purchased by Irish Government, 1946; Oil, Turf-Girl, Tel-Aviv, 1950; Oil, Thomas Ashe, Teacher's Club, 1953; Oil, Berkeley Univ., Calif, USA, 1966; 3 Portraits, National Gall. of Ireland,

1968. 10 works, Arts Festival in Nova Scotia, 1957; Exhibitions: Ritchie Gall., (NS), Dublin, 1958 (oils, pastels, water colours); Lugano, 1964; Robertstown, Kildare, 1968 (40 portraits from James Joyce to Brendan Behan); Dublin, 1973; one-man exhbn, Dublin, 1974. Paintings in many private collections. Sold Portraits (in 1965) of: James Joyce (USA); W. B. Yeats (England); James Stephen; Brendan Behan; Oliver St John Gogarty (USA); Sean O'Casey, etc. Interested in Modern Movements in Art. Mem. Royal Dublin Society, 1947-. *Publications:* 1 Colour Reprod. in Twelve Irish Artists, 1940; Ltd Edn Book of Woodcuts (220 signed and numbered copies), 1942; Book of New Woodcuts (Ltd Edn 300 signed), 1944, (Ltd Edn 400 signed and numbered), 1951; Calendar for Egan's Tullamore, 1952; Calendar for Cherry-Tree, Dublin, 1955; Woodcuts in Ireland of the Welcomes, 1955; 12 Woodcuts in New Irish Poets, USA, 1948; Woodcuts in Bi-Cen. Guinness Harp, 1959; 6 Oils, Dublin Scenes, in Irish Tatler, 1959; (new 4 colour print, 16 ins × 16 ins) A Bird Never Flew on One Wing, 1961; New Colour Prints, Old Claddagh, Galway, 1962. Illustrated: Centenary Books, 1946-; Storyteller's Childhood, 1947; Tinker Boy, 1955. *Recreations:* swimming, verse. *Address:* 13 Stamer Street, Dublin 8, Ireland. *T:* Dublin 751675. *Clubs:* United Arts, Royal Dublin Society (Dublin).

KERR, family name of **Marquess of Lothian** and **Baron Teviot.**

KERR, Andrew Stevenson, CBE 1976; Chief Conciliation Officer, Advisory, Conciliation and Arbitration Service, since 1974; *b* 28 Aug. 1918; *s* of John S. Kerr and Helen L. Kerr; *m* 1946, Helen Reid Bryden; two *s* two *d*. *Educ:* Spiers' Sch., Beith, Ayrshire; Glasgow Univ. MA (Hons). Served Army, 1940-46. Entered Min. of Labour, 1947; general employment work in the Ministry, in Scotland, 1947-63; Industrial Relns Officer for Scotland, Min. of Labour, 1964-66; Dep. Chief Conciliation Officer, Min. of Labour, 1966-68; Chief Conciliation Officer, Dept of Employment, 1968-71; Controller (Scotland), Dept of Employment, 1972-74. *Recreations:* golf, history. *Address:* 11 Forest Way, Tunbridge Wells, Kent TN2 5HA. *T:* Tunbridge Wells 24858.

KERR, Archibald Brown, CBE 1968 (OBE 1945); TD; Hon. Consulting Surgeon, Western Infirmary, Glasgow (Surgeon, 1954-72); Member of Court, University of Glasgow; *b* 17 Feb. 1907; *s* of late Robert Kerr and Janet Harvey Brown; *m* 1940, Jean Margaret, *d* of late John Cowan, MBE; one *d*. *Educ:* High Sch. and University of Glasgow. BSc 1927; MB, ChB 1929; Hon. LLD, 1973; FRFPSGlas. 1933; FRCSEd 1934; FRCSGlas. 1962. Asst to Prof. Path. Glasgow Univ., 1931-33; Surg. to Out-Patients, West. Infirm. Glasgow, 1932-39. Served in 156 (Lowland) Field Amb. and as Surgical Specialist, Officer in Charge of Surgical Div. and Col Comdg No. 23 (Scottish) Gen. Hosp., 1939-45. Surg. to Royal Alexandra Infirmary, Paisley, 1946-54; Asst Surg., West. Infirm., Glasgow, 1945-54. Lectr in Clinical Surgery, Univ. of Glasgow, 1946-72. Pres. 1951-52, Hon. Mem. 1971, Royal Medico-Chirurgical Society of Glasgow; Pres., Royal College of Physicians and Surgeons of Glasgow, 1964-66. Mem., Western Regional Hosp. Bd. Periods on Council of RCPS Glasgow and RCS Edinburgh. *Publications:* The Western Infirmary 1874-1974, 1974; contribs to Med. and Surg. Jls. *Recreation:* golf. *Address:* 10 Iain Road, Bearsden, Glasgow G61 4LX. *T:* 041-942 0424. *Clubs:* College (University of Glasgow), Royal Scottish Automobile.

KERR, Clark; Chairman, Carnegie Council on Policy Studies in Higher Education, since 1974; *b* 17 May 1911; *s* of Samuel W. and Caroline Clark Kerr; *m* 1934, Catherine Spaulding; two *s* one *d*. *Educ:* Swarthmore Coll. (AB); Stanford Univ. (MA); Univ. of Calif., Berkeley (PhD). Actg Asst Prof., Stanford Univ., 1939-40; Asst Prof., later Assoc. Prof., Univ. of Washington, 1940-45; Prof., Dir, Inst. of Industrial Relations, Univ. of Calif, Berkeley, 1945-52; Chancellor, Univ. of Calif at Berkeley, 1952-58; Pres., Univ. of Calif, 1958-67, now Emeritus President. Chm., Carnegie Commn on Higher Educn, 1967-74. Govt service with US War Labor Board, 1942-45. Mem. Pres. Eisenhower's Commn on Nat. Goals, President Kennedy and President Johnson Cttee on Labor-Management Policy; Contract Arbitrator for: Boeing Aircraft Co. and Internat. Assoc. of Machinists, 1944-45; Armour & Co. and United Packinghouse Workers, 1945-47, 1949-52; Waterfront Employers' Assoc. and Internat. Longshoremen's and Warehousemen's Union, 1946-47, etc. Member: Amer. Acad. of Arts and Sciences; Royal Economic Society; Amer. Econ. Assoc.; Nat. Acad. of Arbitrators, etc. Phi Beta Kappa, Kappa Sigma. Trustee, Rockefeller Foundation, 1960-; Chm., Armour Automation Cttee, 1959-, Hon. LLD: Swarthmore, 1952; Harvard, 1958; Princeton, 1959; Notre Dame, 1964; Chinese Univ. of Hong Kong, 1964; Rochester, 1967; Hon. DLitt, Strathclyde, 1965; Hon. DHC, Bordeaux, 1962, etc.

Publications: Unions, Management and the Public (jt), 1948 (rev. edns 1960, 1967); Industrialism and Industrial Man (jtly), 1960 (rev. edns 1964, 1973); The Uses of the University, 1963 (rev. edn 1972); Labor and Management in Industrial Society, 1964 (rev. edn 1972); Marshall, Marx and Modern Times, 1969; contribs to American Economic Review, Review of Economics and Statistics, Quarterly Jl of Economics, etc. *Recreation:* gardening. *Address:* 8300 Buckingham Drive, El Cerrito, Calif 94530, USA. *T:* 5291910. *Club:* Bohemian.

KERR, Dr David Leigh; Director, War on Want, since 1970, Vice-Chairman, 1973-74, Chairman, 1974-77; *b* 25 March 1923; *s* of Myer Woolf Kerr and Paula (*née* Horowitz); *m* 1st, 1944, Aileen Saddington (marr. diss. 1969); two *s* one *d*; 2nd, 1970, Margaret Dunlop; one *s* two *d*. *Educ:* Whitgift Sch., Croydon; Middlesex Hosp. Med. Sch., London. Hon. Sec., Socialist Medical Assoc., 1957-63; Hon. Vice-Pres., 1963-72. LCC (Wandsworth, Central), 1958-65, and Coun., London Borough of Wandsworth, 1964-68. Contested (Lab) Wandsworth, Streatham (for Parlt), 1959; MP (Lab) Wandsworth Central, 1964-70. Family Doctor, Tooting, 1946-. Member: Royal Society of Medicine; Inter-departmental Cttee on Death Certification and Coroners. Governor, British Film Inst., 1966-71. *Recreations:* gardening, photography, squash. *Address:* 222 Norbury Avenue, Thornton Heath, Surrey CR4 8AJ. *T:* 01-764 7654.

KERR, Deborah Jane, (Deborah Kerr Viertel); Actress; *b* 30 Sept. 1921; *d* of Capt. Arthur Kerr-Trimmer; *m* 1st, 1945, Sqdn Ldr A. C. Bartley (marr. diss., 1959); two *d*; 2nd, 1960, Peter Viertel. *Educ:* Northumberland House, Clifton, Bristol. Open Air Theatre, Regent's Park, 1939, Oxford Repertory, 1939-40; after an interval of acting in films, appeared on West End Stage; Ellie Dunn in Heartbreak House, Cambridge Theatre, 1943; went to France, Belgium, and Holland for ENSA, playing in Gaslight, 1945. *Films:* Major Barbara, 1940; Love on the Dole, 1940-41; Penn of Pennsylvania, 1941; Hatter's Castle, 1942; The Day Will Dawn, 1942; Life and Death of Colonel Blimp, 1942-43; Perfect Strangers, 1944; I See a Dark Stranger, 1945; Black Narcissus, 1946; The Hucksters and If Winter Comes, 1947 (MGM, Hollywood); Edward My Son, 1948; Please Believe Me, 1949 (MGM, Hollywood); King Solomon's Mines, 1950; Quo Vadis, 1952; Prisoner of Zenda, Julius Caesar, Dream Wife, Young Bess (MGM), 1952; From Here to Eternity, 1953; The End of the Affair, 1955; The Proud and Profane, The King and I, 1956; Heaven Knows, Mr Allison, An Affair to Remember, Tea and Sympathy, 1957; Bonjour Tristesse, 1958; Separate Tables, The Journey, Count Your Blessings, 1959; The Sundowners, The Grass is Greener, The Naked Edge, The Innocents, 1961; The Chalk Garden, The Night of the Iguana, 1964; Casino Royale, 1967; Eye of the Devil, Prudence and the Pill, 1968; The Arrangement, 1970. *Stage:* Tea and Sympathy, NY, 1953; The Day After the Fair, London, 1972, tour of US, 1973-74; Seascape, NY, 1975; Candida, London, 1977. *Address:* Klosters, 7250 Grisons, Switzerland.

KERR, Desmond Moore, OBE 1970; HM Diplomatic Service; Deputy High Commissioner, Dacca, since 1976; *b* 23 Jan. 1930; *s* of late Robert John Kerr and Mary Elizabeth Kerr; *m* 1956, Evelyn Patricia South; one *s* two *d*. *Educ:* Methodist Coll., Belfast; Queen's Univ., Belfast. BA Hons (Classics and Ancient History). CRO, 1952; British High Commn, Karachi, 1956-59, Lagos, 1959-62; Second Sec., 1960; Commonwealth Office, 1962-66; First Sec., 1965; Dep. British Govt Rep., West Indies Associated States, 1966-70; FCO, 1970-76. *Address:* c/o Foreign and Commonwealth Office, SW1; 28 The Millbank, Ifield, Crawley, Sussex. *T:* Crawley 21462.
See also E. Kerr.

KERR, Donald Frederick, CVO 1961; OBE 1960; Manager, Government Press Centre, Foreign and Commonwealth Office, 1976; *b* 20 April 1915; *s* of Dr David Kerr, Cheshire; *m* 1942, Elizabeth Hayward; two *s* one *d*. *Educ:* Sydney High Sch.; University of Sydney (BEcon). Served RAF (Navigator), SEAC, 1942-46. Deputy Director: British Information Service, New Delhi, 1947-53; UK Information Service, Ottawa, 1953-55; UK Information Service, Toronto, 1955-56; Dir, UK Information Service in Canada, Ottawa, 1956-59; Dir, British Information Services in India, New Delhi, 1959-63; Controller (Overseas), COI, 1963-76; on secondment, Dir of Information, Commonwealth Secretariat, Sept. 1969-Sept. 1970. *Recreation:* golf. *Address:* 36 Murray Road, Wimbledon, SW19. *Clubs:* Royal Automobile; Royal Wimbledon Golf.

KERR, Dr Edwin; Chief Officer, Council for National Academic Awards, since 1972; *b* 1 July 1926; *e s* of late Robert John Kerr and Mary Elizabeth Kerr (*née* Ferguson); *m* 1949, Gertrude Elizabeth (*née* Turbitt); one *s* two *d*. *Educ:* Royal Belfast

Academical Instn; Queen's Univ., Belfast (BSc, PhD). FIMA, FBCS. Asst Lectr in Maths, QUB, 1948-52; Lectr in Maths, Coll. of Technology, Birmingham (now Univ. of Aston in Birmingham), 1952-55; Lectr in Maths, Coll. of Science and Technology, Manchester (now Univ. of Manchester Inst. of Science and Technology), 1956-58; Head of Maths Dept, Royal Coll. of Advanced Technology, Salford (now Univ. of Salford), 1958-66; Principal, Paisley Coll. of Technology, 1966-72. Mem. Adv. Cttee on Supply and Training of Teachers, 1973-. President: Soc. for Res. into Higher Educn, 1974-; The Mathematical Assoc., 1976-77. Hon. DUniv Open, 1977. *Publications:* (with R. Butler) An Introduction to Numerical Methods, 1962; various mathematical and educational. *Recreation:* gardening. *Address:* The Coppice, Kingfisher Lure, Loudwater, Chorleywood, Herts. *T:* Rickmansworth 77187.
See also *D* . *M* . *Kerr* .

KERR, Francis Robert Newsam, OBE 1962; MC 1940; JP; farmer since 1949; Vice Lieutenant of Berwickshire since 1970; *b* 12 Sept. 1916; *s* of late Henry Francis Hobart Kerr and Gertrude Mary Kerr (*née* Anthony); *m* 1941, Anne Frederica Kitson; two *s* one *d. Educ:* Ampleforth College. Regular Officer, The Royal Scots, 1937-49; TA 1952-63; retired as Lt-Col. Member: Berwickshire County Council, 1964-75; SE Scotland Regional Hosp. Bd, 1971-74; Borders Area Health Bd, 1973- (Vice-Chm.); Borders Reg. Council, 1974-; Post Office Users Nat. Council, 1972-73; Whitley (Nurses and Midwives) Council, 1970-. Sheriff of Berwick upon Tweed, 1974. *Recreations:* country pursuits. *Address:* Blanerne, Duns, Berwickshire. *T:* Cumledge 222. *Club:* Farmers'.

KERR, Rt. Hon. Sir John Robert, AK 1976 (AC 1975); PC 1977; GCMG 1976 (KCMG 1974; CMG 1966); GCVO 1977; Governor-General of Australia, 1974-77; *b* 24 Sept. 1914; *s* of late H. Kerr, Sydney; *m* 1st, 1938, Alison (*d* 1974), *d* of F. Worstead, Sydney; one *s* two *d* ; 2nd, 1975, Mrs Anne Robson, *d* of J. Taggart. *Educ:* Fort Street Boys' High Sch.; Sydney Univ. (LLB). Admitted NSW Bar, 1938. Served War of 1939-45: 2nd AIF, 1942-46; Col, 1945-46. Princ., Australian Sch. of Pacific Admin., 1946; Organising Sec., S Pacific Commn, 1946-47; QC (NSW) 1953; Mem. NSW Bar Coun., 1960-64; Vice-Pres., 1962-63, Pres., 1964, NSW Bar Assoc.; Vice-Pres., 1962-64, Pres. 1964-66, Law Coun. of Australia; Judge of Commonwealth Industrial Court and Judge of Supreme Court of ACT, 1966-72; Judge of Courts of Marine Inquiry, 1967-72; Chief Justice, Supreme Court, NSW, 1972-74; Lieutenant Governor, NSW, 1973-74. Deputy President: Trades Practices Tribunal, 1966-72; Copyright Tribunal, 1969-72; presided at 3rd Commonwealth and Empire Law Conf., Sydney, 1965; Pres., Industrial Relations Soc. of Australia, 1964-66; Pres., NSW Marriage Guidance Coun., 1961-62; Mem. Bd of Coun. on New Guinea Affairs, 1964-71; Mem. Med. Bd of NSW, 1963-66; Pres., Law Assoc. for Asia and Western Pacific, 1966-70. Hon. Life Mem., Law Soc. of England and Wales, 1965; Hon. Mem., Amer. Bar Assoc., 1967-. KStJ 1974. *Publications:* various papers and articles on industrial relations, New Guinea affairs, organisation of legal profession, etc. *Address:* c/o Australia House, The Strand, WC2B 4LA.

KERR, Hon. Sir Michael (Robert Emanuel), Kt 1972; Hon. Mr Justice Kerr; a Judge of the High Court of Justice, Queen's Bench Division, since 1972; *b* 1 March 1921; *s* of Alfred Kerr; *m* 1952, Julia, *d* of Joseph Braddock; two *s* one *d. Educ:* Aldenham Sch.; Clare Coll., Cambridge. Served War, 1941-45 (Pilot; Flt-Lt). BA Cantab (1st cl. Hons Law) 1947, MA 1952; called to Bar, Lincoln's Inn, 1948, Bencher 1968; QC 1961. Dep. Chm., Hants QS, 1961-71. Member: Bar Council, 1968-72; Senate, 1969-72. Mem. Vehicle and General Enquiry Tribunal, 1971-72. Governor, Aldenham Sch., 1959-. *Publications:* McNair's Law of the Air, 1953, 1965; articles and lectures on commercial law and arbitration. *Recreations:* travel, ski-ing, tennis (not real), music. *Address:* c/o Royal Courts of Justice, Strand, WC2A 2LL. *Clubs:* Garrick, Queen's.

KERR, Robert Reid, TD; MA, LLB; Sheriff of Tayside, Central and Fife (formerly Stirling, Dumbarton and Clackmannan) at Falkirk, since 1969; *b* 7 May 1914; *s* of James Reid Kerr, sugar refiner, and Olive Rodger; *m* 1942, Mona Kerr; three *d. Educ:* Cargilfield; Trinity Coll., Glenalmond; Oxford Univ.; Glasgow Univ. Sheriff-Substitute: of Inverness, Moray, Nairn and Ross and Cromarty at Fort William, 1952-61; of Aberdeen, Kincardine and Banff at Banff, 1961-69. SBStJ. *Address:* Kinnell House, Old Polmont, Falkirk FK2 0XZ.

KERR, Russell (Whiston); MP (Lab) Hounslow, Feltham and Heston, since 1974 (Middlesex, Feltham, 1966-74); Air Charter Executive; *b* 1 Feb. 1921; *s* of Ivo W. and Constance Kerr, Australia; *m* 1st, 1946, Shirley W. N. Huie; one *s* one *d* ; 2nd, 1960, Anne P. Clark (*née* Bersey) (*d* 1973); r.o *c. Educ:* Shore Sch., Sydney; University of Sydney. BEcon 1941. RAAF Aircrew, 1942-46; operational service with Bomber Comd Pathfinder Force, flying Lancaster Bombers over Germany (Flying Officer/Navigator). Returned to England to live, 1948. Contested (Lab): Horsham, Sussex, 1951; Merton and Morden, 1959; Preston North, 1964. Dir (unpaid), Trib.ne, 1969-; Chm., Tribune group of MPs, 1969-70. Nat. Exec Mem., ASTMS, 1964-; Chm., Select Cttee on nationalised industries, 1974-. *Publications:* articles in various radical and TU jls. *Recreations:* cricket, golf, walking, talking. *Address:* c/o House of Commons, SW1. *Clubs:* Feltham Ex-Servicemen's, Putney Workingmen's, Royal Mid-Surrey Golf.

KERR, Thomas Henry; Director, National Gas Turbine Establishment, since 1974; *b* 18 June 1924; *s* of late Albert Edward Kerr and Mrs Francis Jane Kerr (*née* Simpson); *m* 1946, Myrnie Evelyn Martin Hughes; two *d. Educ:* Magnus Grammar, Newark; University Coll., Durham Univ. BSc 1949; FRAeS; Diplôme Paul Tissendier 1957. RAFVR pilot, 1942-46. Aero Flight, RAE, 1949-55; Head of Supersonic Flight Group, 1955-59; Scientific Adviser to C-in-C Bomber Comd, High Wycombe, 1960-64; Head of Assessment Div., Weapons Dept, RAE, 1964-66; Dep. Dir and Dir of Defence Operational Analysis Estabt, 1966-70; Head of Weapons Research Gp, Weapons Dept, RAE, 1970-72; Dir Gen. Establishments Resources Programmes (C), MoD (PE), 1972-74. *Publications:* reports and memoranda of Aeronautical Research Council, lectures to RAeS and RUSI. *Recreations:* bridge, water ski-ing, tennis, badminton. *Address:* Bundu, 013 Kingsley Avenue, Camberley, Surrey GU15 2NA. *T:* Camberley 25961.

KERR, Sir William Alexander B., (Sir Alastair); *see* Blair-Kerr.

KERR, William Francis Kennedy, PhD, CEng, FIMechE; Principal, Belfast College of Technology, since 1969; *b* 1 Aug. 1923; *m* 1953, H. Adams; two *s. Educ:* Portadown Technical Coll. and Queen's Univ., Belfast. BSc (Hons) in Mech. Engineering, MSc, PhD. Teacher of Mathematics, Portadown Techn. Coll., 1947-48; Teacher and Sen. Lectr in Mech. Eng, Coll. of Techn., Belfast, 1948-55; Lectr and Adviser of Studies in Mech. Eng, Queen's Univ. of Belfast, 1955-62; Head of Dept of Mech., Civil, and Prod. Eng, Dundee Coll. of Techn., 1962-67; Vice-Principal, Coll. of Techn., Belfast, 1967-69. Member: Educn and Employment Cttee of NI Chamber of Commerce, 1969; NI Training Council, 1970; NI rep. on Council for Educnl Technology in UK, 1973; Chm., NI Cttee for Educnl Technology, 1973; Governor, Royal Belfast Academical Instn, 1969. *Publications:* contribs on environmental testing of metals, etc. *Recreations:* golf, motoring, reading. *Address:* 27 Maxwell Road, Bangor, Co. Down, Northern Ireland. *T:* Bangor 5303.

KERR-DINEEN, Ven. Frederick George; Archdeacon of Horsham, since 1975; Rector of Stopham with Hardham, since 1973; *b* 26 Aug. 1915; second *s* of late Henry John Dineen and adopted *s* of late Prebendary Colin Kerr; *m* 1951, Hermione Iris, *er d* of late Major John Norman MacDonald, (KEH); four *s* one *d. Educ:* Tyndale Hall, Clifton; St John's Coll., Durham. MA, LTh (Dunelm). Ordained, 1941; Curate: St Paul's, Portman Square, 1941-44; St John's, Weymouth, 1945-46; Vicar: St Michael's, Blackheath Park, 1946-53; Lindfield, 1953-62; Holy Trinity, Eastbourne, 1962-73; Archdeacon of Chichester, 1973-75; Proctor in Convocation, 1970-74. *Address:* The Rectory, Stopham, Pulborough, West Sussex. *T:* Fittleworth 333.

KERRIDGE, Sir Robert (James), Kt 1962; Managing Director, Kerridge Odeon; Director of over 50 companies; *b* 29 Oct. 1901; British; *m* 1922, Phyllis Elizabeth Roland; three *s* two *d. Educ:* Christchurch, NZ. Qualified in Accountancy, 1920; Principal, Kerridge Commercial Coll., 1920-29. Engaged in transport and newspaper business for a number of years. Acquired first theatre, 1920; subseq. numerous theatres, and controlling interest of NZ Theatres Ltd (W. R. Kemball); also took over: Fullers Theatre Corp. Ltd, John Fuller & Sons Ltd; J. C. Williamson Picture Corp. Ltd; company now directs well over 100 theatres and some merchandising companies. FRSA. CStJ. Cavaliere Dell'Ordine Al Merito Della Repubblica (Italy), 1958; International Order of the Lion. *Recreations:* farming, golf, fishing. *Address:* 1 Judge Street, Parnell 1, Auckland N2, NZ. *T:* 44091. *Club:* Auckland (New Zealand).

KERRIN, Very Rev. Richard Elual, MA; Dean of Aberdeen and Orkney, 1956-69; Rector of St John's Episcopal Church, Aberdeen, 1954-70, retired; *b* 4 July 1898; *s* of Rev. Daniel Kerrin and Margaret Kerrin; *m* 1925, Florence Alexandra, *d* of Captain J. Reid; one *s. Educ:* Robert Gordon's Coll., Aberdeen; University of Aberdeen (MA); Edinburgh Theological Coll.

(Luscombe Scholar). Ordained deacon, 1922; priest, 1923. Curate, Old St Paul, Edinburgh, 1922-25; Rector, Inverurie, 1925-37; Rector, Holy Trinity, Stirling, 1937-47; Rector, Fraserburgh, 1947-54; Canon of Aberdeen, 1954-56. *Address:* Elora, St Bryde's Road, Kemnay, Aberdeenshire AB5 9NB. *T:* Kemnay 480.

KERRY, Knight of; *see* FitzGerald, Sir G. P. M.

KERRY, Michael James, CB 1976; Solicitor to Departments of Trade, Industry and Prices and Consumer Protection, since 1973; *b* 5 Aug. 1923; *s* of Russell Kerry and Marjorie (*née* Kensington); *m* 1951, Sidney Rosetta Elizabeth (*née* Foster); one *s* two *d. Educ:* Rugby Sch.; St John's Coll., Oxford (MA). Served with RAF, 1942-46. Called to Bar, Lincoln's Inn, 1949. Joined BoT as Legal Asst, 1951; Sen. Legal Asst, 1959; Asst Solicitor, 1964; Principal Asst Solicitor, Dept of Trade and Industry, 1972. *Recreations:* golf, tennis, gardening. *Address:* South Bedales, Lewes Road, Haywards Heath, W Sussex. *T:* Scaynes Hill 303. *Club:* Piltdown Golf.

KERSHAW, family name of **Baron Kershaw.**

KERSHAW, 4th Baron, *cr* 1947; **Edward John Kershaw;** Chartered Accountant; *b* 12 May 1936; *s* of 3rd Baron and Katharine Dorothea Kershaw (*née* Staines); S father, 1962; *m* 1963, Rosalind Lilian Rutherford; one *s* two *d. Educ:* Selhurst Grammar Sch., Surrey. Entered RAF Nov. 1955, demobilised Nov. 1957. Admitted to Inst. of Chartered Accountants in England and Wales, Oct. 1964. *Heir: s* Hon. John Charles Edward Kershaw, *b* 23 Dec. 1971.

KERSHAW, Henry Aidan; His Honour Judge Henry Kershaw; a Circuit Judge, since 1976; *b* 11 May 1927; *s* of late Rev. H. Kershaw, Bolton; *m* 1960, Daphne Patricia, *widow* of Dr. C. R. Cowan; four *s. Educ:* St John's, Leatherhead; Brasenose Coll., Oxford (BA). Called to Bar, Inner Temple, 1953. Asst Recorder of Oldham, 1970-71; a Recorder of the Crown Court, 1972-76. Dep. Chm., Agricultural Land Tribunal, 1972-76. *Recreations:* golf, ski-ing, oil-painting. *Address:* Broadhaven, St Andrew's Road, Lostock, Bolton, Lancs. *T:* Bolton 47088.

KERSHAW, J(ohn) Anthony, MC 1943; MP (C) Stroud Division of Gloucestershire, since 1955; Barrister-at-Law; *b* 14 Dec. 1915; *s* of Judge J. F. Kershaw, Cairo and London, and of Anne Kershaw, Kentucky, USA; *m* 1939, Barbara, *d* of Harry Crookenden; two *s* two *d. Educ:* Eton; Balliol Coll., Oxford (BA). Called to the Bar 1939. Served War, 1940-46: 16th/5th Lancers. Mem. LCC, 1946-49; Westminster City Council, 1947-48. Parly Sec., Min. of Public Building and Works, June-Oct. 1970; Parliamentary Under-Secretary of State: FCO, 1970-73; for Defence (RAF), 1973-74. Mem. Exec. Cttee, British Council, 1974-. *Address:* The Tithe Barn, Didmarton, Badminton, Glos. *Club:* White's.

KERSHAW, Joseph Anthony; independent management consultant, since 1975; *b* 26 Nov. 1935; *s* of Henry and Catherine Kershaw, Preston; *m* 1959, Ann Whittle; three *s* two *d. Educ:* Ushaw Coll., Durham; Preston Catholic Coll., SJ. Short service commn, RAOC, 1955-58; Unilever Ltd, 1958-67; Gp Marketing Manager, CWS, 1967-69; Managing Director: Underline Ltd, 1969-71; Merchant Div., Reed International Ltd, 1971-73; Head of Marketing, Non-Foods, CWS, 1973-74; (first) Director, Nat. Consumer Council, 1975. *Recreations:* fishing, shooting, cooking; CPRE. *Address:* Westmead, Meins Road, Blackburn, Lancs BB2 6QF. *T:* Blackburn 55915.

KERSHAW, Philip Charles Stones; His Honour Judge Kershaw; a Circuit Judge (formerly Deputy Chairman, Lancashire Quarter Sessions), since 1961; *b* 9 April 1910; *s* of Joseph Harry and Ethel Kershaw; *m* 1935, Michaela Raffael; one *s* one *d. Educ:* Stonyhurst Coll.; Merton Coll., Oxford. Called to the Bar, Gray's Inn, 1933; practised Northern Circuit until Aug. 1939. Served in Army, 1939-45 (Major). Resumed practice, 1945-61. *Address:* Fountain House, East Beach, Lytham, Lancs. *T:* Lytham 736072. *Club:* Portico Library (Manchester).

KERSHAW, Raymond Newton, CMG 1947; MC; *b* 3 May 1898; *s* of G. W. Kershaw, Wahroonga, Sydney, Australia; *m* 1925, Hilda Mary, *d* of W. J. Ruegg, JP; two *s* one *d. Educ:* Sydney High Sch.; Sydney Univ.; New Coll., Oxford; Sorbonne. Served European War, 1914-18, with AIF in France, 1917-18 (MC); Rhodes Scholar for NSW, 1918; Mem. of Secretariat, League of Nations, Geneva, 1924-29; Adviser to the Governors, Bank of England, 1929-53; Member: E African Currency Bd, 1932-53; W African Currency Bd, 1943-53, Palestine Currency Bd, 1943-52, Burma Currency Board, 1946-52; Adviser to Commonwealth Development Finance Co., 1953-55; a Gen. Comr of Income Tax

for City of London, 1956-65; a London Director: Commercial Banking Co. of Sydney, 1956-66 (Chm., London Bd, 1964-66); Bank of NZ, 1955-68 (Chm. London Bd, 1963-68); Australian Mutual Provident Soc., 1955-70. *Address:* Warren Row, near Wargrave, Berks. *T:* Littlewick Green 2708.

KERSHAW, Mrs W. J. S.; *see* Paling, Helen Elizabeth.

KERSHAW, Prof. William Edgar, CMG 1971; VRD; Professor of Biology, University of Salford, 1966-76, now Emeritus Professor; Advisor in Tropical Medicine to Manchester Area Health Authority, since 1976; *Educ:* Manchester University. MB, ChB, 1935; MRCS LRCP, 1936; DTM&H Eng. 1946; MD 1949; DSc 1956. Chalmers Memorial Gold Medal, Royal Society of Tropical Medicine and Hygiene, 1955. Formerly: Surgeon Captain, RNR; Demonstrator in Morbid Anatomy, Manchester Univ.; Leverhulme Senior Lectr in Med. Parasitology, Liverpool Sch. of Trop. Med. and Liverpool Univ.; Walter Myers and Everett Dutton Prof. of Parasitology and Entomology, Liverpool Univ., 1958-66. Hon. Lectr, Dept of Bacteriology, Univ. of Manchester, 1977-. *Address:* Mill Farm, Hesketh Bank, Preston PR4 6RA. *T:* Hesketh Bank 4299.

KERWIN, Prof. Larkin; Rector of Laval University, 1972-77; President of the Royal Society of Canada, 1976-77; *b* 22 June 1924; *s* of T. J. Kerwin and Catherine Lonergan-Kerwin; *m* 1950, Maria Guadeloupe Turcot; five *s* three *d. Educ:* St Francis Xavier Univ. (BSc 1944); MIT (MSc 1946); Université Laval (DSc 1949). Laval University: Dir, Dept of Physics, 1961-67; Vice-Dean, Faculty of Sciences, 1967-68; Vice-Rector, Studies and Research, 1969-72. Sec.-Gen., IUPAP, 1972-. Hon. LLD: St Francis Xavier, 1970; Toronto, 1973; Concordia, 1976; Hon. DSc: British Columbia, 1973; McGill, 1974. Médaille du Centenaire, 1967; Médaille de l'Assoc. Canadienne des Physiciens, 1969; Médaille Pariseau, 1965. Kt Comdr with star, Holy Sepulchre of Jerusalem, 1974. *Publications:* Atomic Physics, 1963 (trans. French, 1964, Spanish, 1968); papers in jls. *Recreation:* sailing. *Address:* 2166 Parc Bourbonnière, Sillery, Quebec 6, Canada. *T:* (418) 656-2272. *Club:* Cercle Universitaire (Quebec).

KESSEL, Prof. William Ivor Neil, MD; FRCP, FRCPE, FRCPsych; Professor of Psychiatry, University of Manchester, since 1965; *b* 10 Feb. 1925; *s* of Barney Kessel and Rachel Isabel Kessel; *m* 1958, Pamela Veronica Joyce (*née* Boswell); one *s* one *d. Educ:* Highgate Sch.; Trinity Coll., Cambridge (MA, MD); UCH Med. Sch.; Inst. of Psychiatry. MSc Manchester. FRCP 1967; FRCPE 1968; FRCPsych 1972. Staff, Inst. of Psych., 1960; scientific staff, MRC Unit for Epidemiol. of Psych. Illness, 1961, Asst Dir 1963; Hon. Sen. Lectr, Edinburgh Univ., 1964; Dean, Faculty of Med., Univ. of Manchester, 1974-76. Member: NW RHA, 1974-77; GMC; Adv. Council on Misuse of Drugs, 1972; Chm., Adv. Cttee on Alcoholism, DHSS, 1975-; Cons. Adviser on alcoholism to DHSS. *Publications:* Alcoholism (with Prof. H. J. Walton), 1965, 3rd edn 1977; articles on suicide and self-poisoning, alcoholism, psych. in gen. practice, psychosomatic disorders, psych. epidemiol. *Address:* Department of Psychiatry, University Hospital of South Manchester, West Didsbury, Manchester M20 8LR. *T:* 061-455 8111, ext. 2616.

KESWICK, Henry Neville Lindley; Chairman: Matheson & Co. Ltd, since 1975; Jardine Japan Investment Trust Ltd, since 1977; Proprietor, The Spectator, since 1975; *b* 29 Sept. 1938; *e s* of Sir William Keswick, *qv. Educ:* Eton Coll.; Trinity Coll., Cambridge. BA Hons Econs and Law. Dir, Jardine, Matheson & Co. Ltd, Hong Kong, 1967 (Chairman, 1972-75); Chm., Reunion Properties Co. Ltd; Director: British Bank of the Middle East; MacMillan Bloedel Ltd, Vancouver; Sun Alliance and London Insurance, 1975-; Robert Fleming Holdings Ltd. (Unofficial) JP Hong Kong 1971. *Recreation:* country pursuits. *Address:* 10 Egerton Place, SW3 2EF. *Clubs:* White's, Turf; Third Guards.

KESWICK, Sir John (Henry), KCMG 1972 (CMG 1950); Director: Jardine Matheson & Co. Ltd, Hong Kong (Chm. 1971-72); Matheson & Co. Ltd, London (Chairman, 1966-70); *b* 1906; *s* of late Henry Keswick; *m* 1940, Clare, *d* of late Gervase Elwes and Lady Winefride Elwes; one *d. Educ:* Eton; Trinity Coll., Cambridge. Min. of Economic Warfare, 1940; Political Liaison Officer, SE Asia Comd, 1942; British Chamber of Commerce, Shanghai, 1946. Chm., China Assoc.; Vice-Pres., Sino-British Trade Council; Mem., GB-China Cttee. Hon. Treas., National Association of Youth Clubs, until 1977. *Address:* 5 Chester Place, NW1 4NB; Portrack House, Holywood, Dumfries. *T:* Newbridge 276; Matheson & Co. Ltd, 3 Lombard Street, EC3V 9AQ. *T:* 01-480 6633. *Clubs:* Boodle's, Buck's, White's.
See also Sir W. J. Keswick.

KESWICK, Sir William (Johnston), Kt 1972; Director, Matheson & Co. Ltd, 1943-75 (Chairman, 1949-66); *b* 6 Dec. 1903; *s* of late Major Henry Keswick of Cowhill Tower, Dumfries, Scotland; *m* 1937, Mary, *d* of late Rt Hon. Sir Francis Lindley, PC, GCMG; three *s* one *d. Educ:* Winchester Coll.; Trinity Coll., Cambridge. Director: Hudson's Bay Co., 1943-72 (Governor 1952-65); Bank of England, 1955-73; British Petroleum Co. Ltd, 1950-73; Jardine, Matheson & Co. Ltd (Hong Kong and Far East); Chm. of various public companies in Far East; Chm., Shanghai Municipal Council of late International Settlement; Mem., Royal Commission on Taxation of Profits and Income; Brigadier Staff Duties 21 Army Gp; Mem., Royal Company of Archers. Trustee, National Gallery 1964-71. *Recreations:* shooting, fishing. *Address:* Theydon Priory, Theydon Bois, Essex. *T:* Theydon Bois 2256; Glenkiln, Shawhead, Dumfries, Scotland. *Club:* White's.
See also Sir J. H. Keswick, H. N. L. Keswick.

KETTLEWELL, Dr Henry Bernard Davis; retired; Senior Research Officer, Genetics Unit, Department of Zoology, University of Oxford, 1954-74; Emeritus Fellow of Wolfson College, Oxford; *b* 24 Feb. 1907; *s* of late Henry Kettlewell and late Kate Davis; *m* 1936, Hazel Margaret, *d* of Sir Frank Wiltshire, MC; one *s* one *d. Educ:* Charterhouse; Paris; Caius Coll., Cambridge. MA, MB, BChir Cantab; DSc Oxon, 1975; MRCS, LRCP. Hosp. appts, St Bartholomew's, Miller and Hackney Hosps; subseq. GP, Cranleigh; Anaesthetist, St Luke's Hosp., Guildford; served War of 1939-45, EMS Woking War Hosp.; emigrated to S Africa, 1949-52; research Internat. Locust Control, Cape Town Univ.; undertook several expedns to Kalahari, Belgian Congo, Mozambique, and Knysna Forest; Nuffield Research Fellowship, Dept Genetics, Dept Zoology, Oxford, 1952; lecture tours in USA and Canada; visited Brazil, 1958 on occasion of Darwin Centenary for Life Magazine, and Czechoslovakia, 1965 as Govt guest; co-founder, Rothschild-Cockayne-Kettlewell Collection of British Lepidoptera (now Nat. Collection RCK) in British Museum of Natural History, London; on several cttees for Nature Conservancy. Producer of several films showing basic evolutionary principles. Darwin Medal, USSR, 1959; Mendel Medal, 1965. *Publications:* Butterflies and Moths, 1963; (with Julian Huxley) Darwin and his World, 1965; (contrib.) Ecological Genetics and Evolution, 1971; The Evolution of Melanism, 1973; (contrib.) Evolution: The Modern Synthesis, ed Julian Huxley, 3rd edn, 1974; (contrib.) Encyclopedia Italiana, 1974; numerous papers in Nature, Heredity, Science, Scientific American, and other sci. jls on genetics and ecological subjects, esp. industrial melanism. *Recreations:* shooting, salmon fishing, devising lobster traps, gardening (growing hybrid beans and azaleas). *Address:* Steeple Barton Vicarage, Oxford OX5 3QP. *T:* Steeple Aston 357, Oxford 56789.

KETTLEWELL, Comdt Dame Marion M., DBE 1970 (CBE 1964); General Secretary, Girls' Friendly Society, since 1971; *b* 20 Feb. 1914; *d* of late George Wildman Kettlewell, Bramling, Virginia Water, Surrey, and of Mildred Frances (*née* Atkinson), Belford, Northumberland. *Educ:* Godolphin Sch., Salisbury; St Christopher's Coll., Blackheath. Worked for Fellowship of Maple Leaf, Alta, Canada, 1935-38; worked for Local Council, 1939-41; joined WRNS as MT driver, 1941; commnd as Third Officer WRNS, 1942; Supt WRNS on Staff of Flag Officer Air (Home), 1961-64; Supt WRNS Training and Drafting, 1964-67; Director, WRNS, 1967-70. *Recreations:* needlework, walking, and country life. *Address:* 38 Rochester Row, SW1P 1BT.
See also R. W. Kettlewell.

KETTLEWELL, Richard Wildman, CMG 1955; Colonial Service, retired 1962; Consultant to Hunting Technical Services, since 1963; *b* 12 Feb. 1910; *s* of late George Wildman Kettlewell and of Mildred Frances Atkinson; *m* 1935, Margaret Jessie Palmer; one *s* one *d. Educ:* Clifton Coll.; Reading and Cambridge Univs. BSc 1931; Dip. Agric. Cantab 1932; Associate of Imperial Coll. of Tropical Agriculture (AICTA), 1933. Entered Colonial Agricultural Service, 1934; appointed to Nyasaland. Served War of 1939-45 (despatches) with 2nd Bn King's African Rifles, 1939-43; rank of Major. Recalled to agricultural duties in Nyasaland, 1943; Dir of Agriculture, 1951-59; Sec. for Natural Resources, 1959-61; Minister for Lands and Surveys, 1961-62. *Address:* Orchard Close, Overnorton, Chipping Norton, Oxon. *T:* Chipping Norton 2407. *Club:* MCC.
See also Comdt Dame M. M. Kettlewell.

KEVILL-DAVIES, Christopher Evelyn, CBE 1973; JP; DL; *b* 12 July 1913; 3rd *s* of William A. S. H. Kevill-Davies, JP, Croft Castle, Herefordshire; *m* 1938, Virginia, *d* of Adm. Ronald A. Hopwood, CB; one *s* one *d. Educ:* Radley College. Served with Suffolk Yeomanry, 1939-43 and Grenadier Gds, 1943-45, France, Belgium and Germany. Mem., Gt Yarmouth Borough Council, 1946-53; Chm., Norfolk Mental Deficiency HMC, 1950-69; Mem., East Anglian Regional Hosp. Bd, 1962 (Vice-Chm. 1967); Vice-Chm., E Anglian RHA, 1974-. JP 1954, DL 1974, Norfolk; High Sheriff of Norfolk, 1965. *Recreation:* gardening. *Address:* The Old Hall, Blofield, Norwich. *T:* Norwich 713208; Flat A 15, Sloane Avenue Mansions, Sloane Avenue, SW3. *T:* 01-584 1904. *Clubs:* Cavalry and Guards; Norfolk (Norwich).

KEVILLE, Sir (William) Errington, Kt 1962; CBE 1947; *b* 3 Jan. 1901; *s* of William Edwin Keville; *m* 1928, Ailsa Sherwood, *d* of late Captain John McMillan; three *s* two *d. Educ:* Merchant Taylors'. Pres., Chamber of Shipping, 1961 (Vice-Pres. 1960, Mem. of Council, 1940-); Chairman: Gen. Coun. of British Shipping, 1961; International Chamber of Shipping, 1963-68; Cttee of European Shipowners, 1963-65; Member: Executive Council of Shipping Federation Ltd, 1936-68; Board of PLA, 1943-59; National Maritime Board, 1945-68; Mem. of Cttee of Lloyd's Register of Shipping, 1957-68; Director: Shaw Savill & Albion Co. Ltd, 1941-68 (former Dep. Chm.); National Bank of New Zealand Ltd, 1946-75; Economic Insurance Co. Ltd, 1949-68 (Chm., 1962-68); National Mortgage & Agency Co. of NZ Ltd, 1950-68; British Maritime Trust Ltd, 1959-72 (Chm. 1962-68); Furness Withy & Co. Ltd, 1950-68 (Chm., 1962-68); Chm., Air Holdings Ltd, 1968-69. *Recreations:* walking, golf, history. *Address:* Stroud Close, Grayswood, Haslemere, Surrey GU27 2DJ. *T:* Haslemere 3653. *Club:* Royal Over-Seas League.

KEWISH, John Douglas, CB 1958; TD 1944; DL; Registrar, Westminster County Court, 1971-73; *b* 4 May 1907; *s* of late John James Kewish, Birkenhead; *m* 1934, Marjorie Phyllis, *d* of late Dr Joseph Harvey, Wimbledon; one *s* one *d. Educ:* Birkenhead Sch. Admitted a Solicitor, 1931. Served TA, 1928-45; served 1939-44, with 4th Bn Cheshire Regt (UK, France and Belgium); commanded 4th Bn, 1940-44; commanded depots, The Cheshire Regt and The Manchester Regt and 24 Machine Gun Training Centre, 1944-45. Hon. Col 4th Bn Cheshire Regt, 1947-62. Chm., Cheshire T & AFA, 1951-59. Head of County Courts Branch in Lord Chancellor's Dept, 1960-71; Mem. Civil Judicial Statistics Cttee, 1966-68. Chm., Liverpool Shipwreck and Humane Soc., 1953-60. DL Cheshire, 1952. *Address:* Roughlee, Brockway East, Tattenhall, Chester. *T:* Tattenhall 70669.

KEY, Maj.-Gen. Berthold Wells, CB 1947; DSO; MC; psc; IA (retired); *b* 19 Dec. 1895; *s* of late Dr J. M. Key; *m* 1917, Aileen Leslie (*d* 1951), *d* of late Col E. L. Dunsterville, RE; (one *s* killed in action in Italy) two *d. Educ:* Dulwich Coll. Joined 45th Rattrays Sikhs, IA, 1914; European War, 1914-19. Mesopotamia (wounded, MC); Afghanistan, 1919; NWF of India, 1930 (despatches); NWF Waziristan, 1936-37 (despatches, DSO); SE Asia, 1941-45; Comd, 2nd (Royal) Bn The Sikh Regt; Comd, 8 Ind. Bde, 1940-41; Comd 11 Ind. Div. 1942; ADC to the King, 1945-47; Comd, Rawalpindi Dist, 1946; Comd, Lahore Dist, 1947; Col, The Sikh Regt, 1947-62. *Recreation:* golf. *Address:* Naini, St George's Road, Sandwich, Kent.

KEY, Sir Charles (Edward), KBE 1956 (CBE 1946); CB 1952; *b* 22 March 1900; *s* of late E. T. and late F. M. Key, Tunbridge Wells; *m* 1st, 1935, Doris May Watkins (decd); no *c* ; 2nd, 1953, Annie Elizabeth King. *Educ:* St John's, Tunbridge Wells. War Office, 1915-60: Assistant Secretary, 1942; Director of Finance, 1949-54; Deputy Under-Secretary of State, War Office, 1954-60, retired. Medal of Freedom with bronze palm (USA), 1946; Officer Order of Orange-Nassau (Netherlands), 1947. *Address:* The Cottage, Highfield Road, East Grinstead, West Sussex RH19 2DX. *T:* East Grinstead 25321. *Club:* Reform.

KEY, Maj.-Gen. Clement Denis, MBE 1945; late RAOC; Clerk to the Governors, Tudor Hall School, Banbury, since 1976; *b* 6 June 1915; *s* of late William Clement Key, Harborne, Birmingham; *m* 1941, Molly, *d* of late F. Monk, Kettering, Northants; two *s. Educ:* Seaford Coll. Commnd in RAOC, 1940; served in: England, 1940-44; France, Belgium, Burma, Singapore, 1944-48; Staff Coll., Camberley, 1945; England, 1948-51; USA, 1951-54; England, 1954-59; jssc 1954; Belgium, 1959-61; War Office, 1961-64; Dep. Dir of Ordnance Services, War Office, 1964-67; Dep. Dir of Ordnance Services, Southern Comd, 1967; Comdr, UK Base Organisation, RAOC, 1968-70; retd, 1970. Hon. Col, RAOC (T&AVR), 1968-71; Col Comdt, RAOC, 1972-75. Bursar, Tudor Hall Sch., Banbury, 1971-76. *Recreations:* rowing, gardening, bee-keeping. *Address:* 104 Maidenhead Road, Stratford-upon-Avon, Warwicks. *T:* Stratford-upon-Avon 4345.

KEY, Rt. Rev. John Maurice, DD Lambeth, 1960; MA; an Assistant Bishop, Diocese of Exeter, since 1975; *b* 4 June 1905; *s* of late Preb. Frederick John Key, Lichfield, and Winifred Mary Head, Hexham, Northumberland; *m* 1935, Agnes Joan Dence (JP 1946-), *d* of late Rev. A. T. Dence, Abbotskerswell, Devon; three *s* one *d. Educ:* Rossall Sch.; Pembroke Coll., Cambridge; Westcott House, Cambridge. Assistant Curate, S. Mary's, Portsea, 1928-32; Vicar of Aylesbeare, Exeter, 1932-34; Rector of Highweek with S. Mary's, Newton Abbot, 1934-40; Rector of Stoke Damerel with S. Bartholomew's and S. Luke's. Devonport, 1940-47; Rural Dean of the Three Towns (Plymouth), 1944-47; Bishop Suffragan of Sherborne, 1947-59; Bishop of Truro, 1959-73. *Recreations:* music, gardening and country. *Address:* Donkeys, Stover, Newton Abbot, Devon. *T:* Newton Abbot 3997.

KEY, Sir Neill C.; *see* Cooper-Key.

KEYES, family name of **Baron Keyes.**

KEYES, 2nd Baron, *cr* 1943, of Zeebrugge and of Dover; **Roger George Bowlby Keyes;** Bt, *cr* 1919; RN, retired; *b* 14 March 1919; 2nd *s* of Admiral of the Fleet Baron Keyes, GCB, KCVO, CMG, DSO and Eva Mary Salvin Bowlby (*d* 1973), Red Cross Order of Queen Elisabeth of Belgium, *d* of late Edward Salvin Bowlby, DL, of Gilston Park, Herts, and Knoydart, Inverness-shire; *S* father 1945; *m* 1947, Grizelda Mary, 2nd *d* of late Lieut-Col William Packe, DSO; three *s* two *d. Educ:* King's Mead Sch., Seaford; RNC, Dartmouth. *Heir: s* Hon. Charles William Packe Keyes, *b* 8 Dec. 1951. *Address:* Elmscroft, Charlton Lane, West Farleigh, near Maidstone, Kent. *T:* Maidstone 812477.

KEYNES, Lady; (Lydia Lopokova); *b* Russia, 21 Oct. 1892; *d* of Vassili Lopokoff, Leningrad, and Constanzia Douglas; *m* 1925, 1st and last Baron Keynes, CB, FBA (*d* 1946), Fellow and Bursar of King's Coll., Cambridge. *Educ:* Imperial Ballet Sch., St Petersburgh. First stage appearance, Marinsky Theatre, St Petersburg, 1901; solo parts in Imperial Russian Ballet; Opera, Paris, 1910; Winter Garden Theatre, New York, 1911; as an actress, several parts in New York, 1914-16; subsequently with Diaghileff's Russian Ballet, New York and London; The Lilac Fairy in Diaghileff's revival of The Sleeping Princess, 1921. Created rôle of Mariuccia in Massine's Les Femmes de Bonne Humeur, 1917, and with Leonide Massine, The Can-Can Dancers in La Boutique Fantasque, 1919; Camargo Society, 1930-32; Vic-Wells Ballet, 1932-33; (Lady) Olivia in Twelfth Night, Old Vic, 1933; Nora Helmer in A Doll's House, 1934; Hilda Wangel in The Master Builder, 1936; Celimene in The Misanthrope, 1937; Mem. of Council, Arts Council of GB, Aug. 1946-49. *Address:* Tilton, Firle, Sussex.

KEYNES, Sir Geoffrey (Langdon), Kt 1955; MA, MD Cantab; Hon. LLD Edinburgh; Hon. DLitt: Oxford, Cambridge; Birmingham; Sheffield; Reading; FRCP, FRCS England, FRCS Canada, FRCOG; Hon. Fellow, Pembroke College, Cambridge; Hon. Librarian and late Member of Council Royal College of Surgeons; Hunterian Trustee, 1958; Consulting Surgeon: St Bartholomew's Hospital; New End Endocrine Clinic and City of London Truss Society; a Trustee of the National Portrait Gallery, 1942-66, Chairman, 1958-66; *b* Cambridge, 25 March 1887; 2nd *s* of late John Neville Keynes; *m* 1917, Margaret Elizabeth (*d* 1974), *d* of late Sir George Darwin, KCB; four *s. Educ:* Rugby Sch.; Pembroke Coll., Cambridge (Foundation Scholar); 1st Class Natural Science Tripos, 1909; Entrance Scholar, St Bartholomew's Hospital, 1910; Brackenbury Surgery Scholar and Willett Medal Operative Surgery, 1913; House Surgeon St Bartholomew's Hospital, 1913; Lieut RAMC, 1914; Major RAMC; Surgical Specialist, BEF (despatches); Chief Asst St Bartholomew's Hospital, 1920; Hunterian Prof., RCS, 1923, 1929, 1945; Cecil Joll Prize, RCS, 1953; Harveian Orator, RCP, 1958; Fitzpatrick Lectr, RCP, 1966; Wilkins Lectr, Royal Society, 1967; Osler Orator and Gold Medal, 1968. Actg Air Vice-Marshal, Sen. Cons. Surg., RAF, 1939-45. Sir Arthur Sims Commonwealth Travelling Professor, 1956. Hon. Foreign Corresp. Mem. Grolier Club, New York; Hon. Mem., Mod. Lang. Assoc., 1966; formerly Pres. Bibliographical Soc. of London; Hon. Fellow American Association Surgeons; Hon. Freeman, Soc. of Apothecaries, 1964; Hon. Fellow, Royal Society of Medicine, 1966. Hon. Fellow, Darwin Coll., Cambridge, 1976. Hon. Gold Medal, RCS, 1969. *Publications:* Blood Transfusion, 1922, 1949; many articles in medical journals; Bibliographies of John Donne, 1914, 1932, 1958, and 1972; William Blake, 1921, 1953; Sir Thomas Browne, 1924 and 1968; William Harvey, 1928 and 1953; Jane Austen, 1929; William Hazlitt, 1931; John Evelyn, 1937 and 1968; John Ray, 1950; Rupert Brooke, 1954 and 1959; Robert Hooke, 1960; Siegfried Sassoon, 1962; Sir William Petty, 1971; George Berkeley, Bishop of Cloyne, 1975; edited Writings of William Blake, 1925, 1927, 1957 and 1966; of Sir Thomas Browne, 1928, 1964, 1968, of Izaak Walton, 1929, etc.; Compiled William

Blake's Illustrations to the Bible, 1957; Blake Studies 1949 and 1971; Bibliotheca Bibliographici (cat. of his library), 1964; William Blake, Poet, Printer, Prophet, 1964; Life of William Harvey, 1966 (James Tait Black Memorial Prize); Drawings of William Blake: 92 Pencil Studies, 1971; William Blake's Watercolour Designs for the Poems of Thomas Gray, 1972; William Blake's Laocoön: A Last Testament, 1977. *Address:* Lammas House, Brinkley, Newmarket, Suffolk CB8 0SB. *T:* Stetchworth 268. *Club:* Roxburghe.
See also R. D. Keynes, S. J. Keynes.

KEYNES, Prof. Richard Darwin, MA, PhD, ScD Cantab; FRS 1959; Professor of Physiology, University of Cambridge, since 1973; Fellow of Churchill College, since 1961; Fellow of Eton; *b* 14 Aug. 1919; *e s* of Sir Geoffrey Keynes, *qv; m* 1945, Anne Pinsent Adrian, *e d* of 1st Baron Adrian, OM, FRS, and Dame Hester Agnes Adrian, DBE, *o d* of Hume C. and Dame Ellen Pinsent, DBE; three *s* (and one *s* decd). *Educ:* Oundle Sch. (Scholar); Trinity Coll., Cambridge (Scholar). Temporary experimental officer, HM Anti-Submarine Establishment and Admiralty Signals Establishment, 1940-45. 1st Class, Nat. Sci. Tripos Part II, 1946; Michael Foster and G. H. Lewes Studentships, 1946; Research Fellow of Trinity Coll., 1948-52; Gedge Prize, 1948; Rolleston Memorial Prize, 1950. Demonstrator in Physiology, University of Cambridge, 1949-53; Lecturer, 1953-60; Fellow of Peterhouse, 1952-60; Head of Physiology Dept and Dep. Dir, 1960-64, Dir, 1965-73, ARC Inst. of Animal Physiology. Sec.-Gen., Internat. Union for Pure and Applied Biophysics, 1972-. A Vice-Pres., Royal Society, 1965-68. For. Member: Royal Danish Acad., 1971; American Philosophical Soc., 1977. Dr *hc* Univ. of Brazil, 1968. *Publications:* papers in Journal of Physiology, Proceedings of Royal Soc., etc. *Recreations:* sailing, gardening. *Address:* 3 Herschel Road, Cambridge. *T:* 53107; Primrose Farm, Wiveton, Norfolk. *T:* Cley 317.
See also S. J. Keynes.

KEYNES, Stephen John; Director: Arbuthnot Latham Holdings Ltd; Arbuthnot Latham & Co. Ltd; Sun Life Assurance Society Ltd; Arab Financial Consultants Company (Kuwait); The Anglo-Indonesian Plantations Ltd; Vice Chairman, Oryx Investments Ltd; *b* 19 Oct. 1927; 4th *s* of Sir Geoffrey Keynes, *qv; m* 1955, Mary, *o d* of late Senator the Hon. Adrian Knatchbull-Hugessen, QC (Canada), and of Margaret, *o d* of G. H. Duggan; three *s* two *d . Educ:* Oundle Sch.; King's Coll., Cambridge (Foundn Scholar). MA Cantab. Served with Royal Artillery, 1949-51. Partner, J. F. Thomasson & Co., Private Bankers, 1961-65; Director, Charterhouse Japhet Ltd and Charterhouse Finance Corp., 1956-72. Mem. ITA, later IBA, 1969-74. Mem. Cttee and Treas., Islington and North London Family Service Unit, 1956-68; Mem. Adv. Cttee, Geffrye Museum; Trustee, Centerprise Community Project, 1971-75. *Recreations:* Medieval manuscripts, painting, gardening, travelling. *Address:* 16 Canonbury Park South, Islington, N1. *T:* 01-226 8170; White Hart Cottage, Brinkley, Newmarket, Suffolk. *T:* Stetchworth 223; Pot Ing, Gunnerside, Swaledale, Richmond, Yorks. *Club:* City of London.
See also R. D. Keynes.

KEYS, Prof. Ivor Christopher Banfield, CBE 1976; MA, DMus Oxon; FRCO; Hon. RAM; Professor of Music, University of Birmingham, since 1968; *b* 8 March 1919; *er s* of Christopher Richard Keys, Littlehampton, Sussex; *m* 1944, Margaret Anne Layzell; two *s* two *d. Educ:* Christ's Hospital, Horsham; Christ Church, Oxford. FRCO 1935; music scholar and asst organist, Christ Church Cathedral, Oxford, 1938-40 and 1946-47. Served with Royal Pioneer Corps, 1940-46. Lecturer in Music, Queen's University of Belfast, 1947, Reader, 1950, Sir Hamilton Harty Professor of Music, QUB, 1951-54; Prof. of Music, Nottingham Univ., 1954-68. Pres., RCO, 1968-70. Hon. DMus QUB, 1972. *Publications:* Sonata for Violoncello and Pianoforte; Completion of Schubert's unfinished song Gretchens Bitte; Concerto for Clarinet and Strings; Prayer for Pentecostal Fire (choir and organ); The Road to the Stable (3 Christmas songs with piano); Magnificat and Nunc Dimittis (choir and organ); (Book) The Texture of Music: Purcell to Brahms, 1961; Brahms Chamber Music, 1974. Reviews of Music, in Music and Letters, and of books, in Musical Times. *Recreation:* bridge. *Address:* Barber Institute of Fine Arts (Department of Music), PO Box 363, Birmingham B15 2TS.

KHACHATURYAN, Aram Ilych; Order of Lenin, 1939; Russian composer and conductor; *b* Tiflis, Georgia, 6 June 1903; 3rd *s* of an Armenian bookbinder; *m* 1936, Nina Makarova, composer; one *s* one *d . Educ:* Moscow Univ. Studied biology, but soon accepted for Genesin Music Sch. ('cello, composition; grad. 1929); Moscow Conservatoire, 1929-34 (pupil of Miaskovsky). His First Symphony performed at the Conservatoire, 1934,

Leningrad, 1936, and elsewhere in Russia and abroad during this period. The Piano Concerto in D flat, 1936, introd. at Queen's Hall, London, 1940, later in America and Europe. Teacher, Genesin Musical-Pedagog. Inst., 1950, also Prof. in composition at Moscow Conservatoire, 1950; first trip abroad, Dec. 1950, meeting other composers in Rome; first visit to Britain, 1955, conducting his music in London and Manchester; tour of Latin America, 1957, and elsewhere later; conducted programme of own works with London Symphony Orch., Jan. 1977. Other distinctions and awards include: Merited Artist; Member Supreme Soviet of Armenian Soviet Socialist Republic; People's Artist of USSR, 1954; Lenin Prize, 1959. Particularly interested in folk and national music; widely popular works inc. Spartacus suites (used as incidental music for The Onedin Line, BBC TV), and Sabre Dance. *Works: chamber music:* Dance in B flat for violin and piano, 1926; Song-Poem for violin and piano, 1929; Sonata in D minor for violin and piano, 1932; String Quartet in C major, 1932; Double Fugue for string quartet, 1932; Trio in G minor for clarinet, violin and piano, 1932; *piano music:* First Album of Children's Pieces, 1926-47; Poem in C sharp minor, 1927; Dance, 1927; 7 Recitatives and Fugues, 1928-36; Suite, 1932; Toccato, 1932; 3 Marches, 1939-44; 3 Pieces for two pianos, 1945; 5 Pieces from the music to Othello, 1955; 4 Pieces from the music to Macbeth, 1955; Sonatina in C major, 1958; Sonata, 1961; Second Album of Children's Pieces, 1965; *orchestral:* Dance Suite, 1932-33; Symphony No 1, 1934; The Valencian Widow, Suite, 1939-40; Symphony No 2, 1943-44; Gayaneh, Suites Nos 1-3, 1943; Masquerade, Suite, 1944; Solemn Overture, To the End of War, 1945; Russian Fantasy, 1946; Symphony No 3 (Symphony-Poem), 1947; Symphonic Dithyramb in Memory of Lenin, 1948; The Battle of Stalingrad, Suite, 1949-50; Solemn Poem, 1950-52; Concert Waltz, 1955; Spartacus, Suites Nos 1-3, 1955; Poema Festivo, 1956; Greetings Overture, 1958-59; Lermontov Suite, 1959; Spartacus, Suite No 4, 1966; *concertos , etc:* Piano Concerto in D flat, 1936; Violin Concerto in D minor, 1940 (also for flute and orch.); Cello Concerto in E major, 1946; Concerto-Rhapsody for piano, 1955, rev.; Concerto-Rhapsody for violin, 1961; Concerto-Rhapsody for cello, 1963; *voice and orchestra:* Three Concert Arias (Armenian texts), 1944-46; Ode of Joy, for mezzo-soprano, choir, ten harps, unison violin, band and orch., 1956; Ballade about the Fatherland, for bass and orch., 1961; *ballets:* Happiness, 3 acts, 6 sc., 1939; Gayaneh, 1st version, 4 acts, 5 sc., 1940-42, rev. 1952; 2nd version, 3 acts, 7 sc., 1957; Spartacus, 4 acts, 9 sc., 1950-56, rev. 1957-58; *incidental music:* Macbeth, 1933, 1955; The Velencian Widow, 1940; Masquerade, 1940; The Kremlin Chimes, 1942; Deep Prospecting, 1943; Ilya Golovin, 1949; King Lear, 1955; also music for plays by various Armenian playwrights, etc; *film music:* Pepo, 1934; Zangezur, 1938; The Garden, 1938; Salavat Yulayev, 1939; Prisoner No 217, 1945; The Russian Question, 1948; Vladimir Ilyich Lenin, 1948-49; They Have a Native Country, 1949; The Battle of Stalingrad (two series), 1949; The Secret Mission, 1950; Admiral Ushakov, 1953; Ships storming the Bastions, 1953; Othello, 1955; Saltanat, 1955; The Duel, 1957; *songs , etc; band music:* songs for voice and piano, for mixed choir and piano, marching and working songs, folk song arrangements, etc; music for military and brass bands, and for balalaika; National Anthem of Soviet Armenia, 1944 (adopted 1945). *Address:* c/o Laudan International Promotions, 20 Edith Road, West Kensington, W14 9BA. *T:* 01-603 4736.

KHAMA, Sir Seretse M., KBE 1966 (OBE 1963); first President, Republic of Botswana, since 1966; Prime Minister of Bechuanaland, 1965-66; *b* 1 July 1921; *s* of Sekgoma and Tebogo Khama; *m* 1948, Ruth Williams; three *s* one *d. Educ:* Fort Hare, University of South Africa (BA); Balliol Coll., Oxford; Inner Temple. Bechuanaland: MEC, 1961; Pres., Democratic Party, 1962; MLA, 1965. Chancellor, University of Botswana, Lesotho and Swaziland, 1967-70. Hon. PhD, Fordham, NY, 1967. Hon. LLD, Univ. of Botswana, Lesotho and Swaziland, 1965. Hon. Fellow, Balliol Coll., Oxford, 1969. *Address:* State House, Gaborone, Botswana.

KHAN, Vice-Adm. Afzal Rahman, Sitara-i-Quaid-i-Azam 1958; Hilal-i-Quaid-i-Azam 1961; Hilal-i-Pakistan 1964; Hilal-i-Jurat 1965; Chairman, ARK International, since 1970; *b* 20 March 1921; *s* of late Abdur Rahman Khan, landlord, Gurdaspur District; *m* 1944, Hameeda Khan; one *s* two *d. Educ:* Baring High Sch., Batala; Govt Coll., Lahore. Joined Indian Mercantile Marine Trng Ship Dufferin, 1936; entered Royal Indian Navy, 1938; Actg Sub-Lieut 1940; Lieut 1942; Lieut-Comdr 1947; Comdr 1950; Captain 1953; Cdre 1958; Rear-Adm. 1959; Vice-Adm. 1961. War of 1939-45: active service, HM Ships in Atlantic, Mediterranean and N Sea and in Royal Indian Navy ships in Indian Ocean and Burma Coast. After Independence in 1947, comd various ships and shore estabs of Pakistan Navy and held other sen. appts; Specialist in Gunnery; psc, jssc; C-in-C,

Pakistan Navy, 1959; retd from Navy, 1966. Minister for Defence, Pakistan, 1966-69. Order of Humayun (Iran), 1961; Legion of Merit (US), 1960 and 1964. *Recreations:* shooting, deep-sea fishing, tennis, golf, study of naval history. *Address:* The Anchorage, 27b South Central Avenue, 8th South Street, Defence Housing Society, Karachi, Pakistan. *T:* 541550. *Clubs:* Sind, Rawalpindi; Golf, Gymkhana (Karachi).

KHAN, Sir Muhammad Zafrulla; *see* Zafrulla Khan.

KHAN, Gen. Yahya; *see* Yahya Khan, Gen. Agha Muhammad.

KHORANA, Prof. Har Gobind; Sloan Professor of Chemistry and Biology, Massachusetts Institute of Technology, since 1970; *b* Raipur, India, 9 Jan. 1922; *s* of Shri Ganpat Rai and Shrimata Krishna (Devi); *m* 1952, Esther Elizabeth Sibler; one *s* two *d. Educ:* Punjab Univ. (BSc, MSc); Liverpool Univ. (PhD, Govt of India Student). Post-doctoral Fellow of Govt of India, Federal Inst. of Techn., Zurich, 1948-49; Nuffield Fellow, Cambridge Univ., 1950-52; Head, Organic Chemistry Group, BC Research Council, 1952-60. Univ. of Wisconsin: Co-Dir, Inst. for Enzyme Research, 1960-70; Prof., Dept of Chemistry, 1962-70; Conrad A. Elvehjem Prof. in the Life Sciences, 1964-70. Visiting Professor: Rockefeller Inst., NY, 1958-60; Stanford Univ., 1964; Harvard Med. Sch., 1966. Has given special or memorial lectures in USA, Poland, Canada, Switzerland, UK and Japan. Fellow: Chem. Inst. of Canada; Amer. Assoc. for Advancement of Science; Amer. Acad. of Arts and Sciences; Overseas Fellow, Churchill Coll., Cambridge; Member: Nat. Acad. of Sciences; Deutsche Akademie der Naturforscher Leopoldina. Hon. Dr Science, Chicago, 1967. Merck Award, Chem. Inst. Canada, 1958; Gold Medal for 1960, Professional Inst. of Public Service of Canada; Dannie-Heinneman Preiz, Germany, 1967; Remsen Award, Johns Hopkins Univ., ACS Award for Creative Work in Synthetic Organic Chemistry, Louisa Gross Horwitz Award, Lasker Foundn Award for Basic Med. Research, Nobel Prize for Medicine (jtly), 1968. *Publications:* Some Recent Developments in the Chemistry of Phosphate Esters of Biological Interest, 1961; numerous papers in Biochemistry, Jl Amer. Chem. Soc., etc. *Recreations:* hiking, swimming. *Address:* Department of Biology, Massachusetts Institute of Technology, Cambridge, Mass 02139, USA.

KIBBEY, Sidney Basil; Under-Secretary, Department of Health and Social Security, 1971-76; *b* 3 Dec. 1916; *y s* of late Percy Edwin Kibbey and Winifred Kibbey, Mickleover, Derby; *m* 1939, Violet Gertrude Eyre; (twin) *s* and *d. Educ:* Derby Sch. Executive Officer, Min. of Health, 1936; Principal, Min. of National Insurance, 1951; Sec., Nat. Insurance Adv. Cttee, 1960-62; Asst Sec., Min. of Pensions and Nat. Insurance, 1962. *Address:* 29 Beaulieu Close, Datchet, Berks. *T:* Slough 49101.

KIDD, Dame Margaret (Henderson), (Dame Margaret Macdonald), DBE 1975; QC (Scotland), 1948; Sheriff Principal of Perth and Angus, 1966-74 (of Dumfries and Galloway, 1960-66); *b* 14 March 1900; *e d* of James Kidd, Solicitor, Linlithgow (sometime MP (U) for W Lothian), and late J. G. Kidd (née Turnbull); *m* 1930, Donald Somerled Macdonald (*d* 1958), WS Edinburgh; one *d. Educ:* Linlithgow Acad.; Edinburgh Univ. Admitted to the Scottish Bar, 1923; contested (U) West Lothian, 1928. Keeper of the Advocates' Library, 1956-69; Editor Court of Session Reports in Scots Law Times, 1942-76; Vice-Pres. British Federation of University Women, Ltd. *Address:* 5 India Street, Edinburgh EH3 6HA. *T:* 031-225 3867.

KIDD, Robert Hill, CB 1975; Head of Northern Ireland Civil Service, since 1976; *b* 3 Feb. 1918; *s* of Andrew Kidd and Florence Hill, Belfast; *m* 1942, Harriet Moore Williamson; three *s* two *d. Educ:* Royal Belfast Academical Instn; Trinity Coll., Dublin. BA 1940, BLitt 1941. Army, 1941-46: commnd 1942, Royal Ulster Rifles, later seconded to Intell. Corps. Entered Northern Ireland Civil Service, 1947; Second Sec., Dept of Finance, NI, 1969-76. *Recreations:* gardening, caravanning, photography. *Address:* 24 Massey Court, Belfast BT4 3GJ. *T:* Belfast 768693.

KIDMAN, Thomas Walter, ERD 1954; Regional Administrator, East Anglian Regional Health Authority, 1973-75, retired; *b* 28 Aug. 1915; *s* of Walter James Kidman and late Elizabeth Alice Kidman (née Littlejohns); *m* 1939, Lilian Rose Souton; one *s* two *d . Educ:* Cambridge Central Sch.; Cambs Techn. Coll. FHA. War service, 1939-46: Warrant Officer, RAMC, BEF France, 1940; Major, Suffolk Regt, seconded Corps of Mil. Police, MEF Egypt and Palestine, 1943-46; served in TA/AER, 1939-67. Local Govt Officer, Health and Educn, Cambridgeshire CC, 1930-48; East Anglian Regional Hosp. Bd: Admin. Officer, 1948; Asst Sec., 1952; Dep. Sec., 1957; Sec. of Bd, 1972. Mem., NHS Health Adv. Service, 1976; Chm., Cambs

Mental Welfare Assoc., 1977-. *Recreations:* photography, walking, gardening, golf. *Address:* Alwoodley, 225 Arbury Road, Cambridge CB4 2JJ. *T:* Cambridge 57384. *Club:* Ely City Golf.

KIDRON, Abraham; Ambassador of Israel to the Court of St James's, since 1977; *b* 19 Nov. 1919; *m* 1946, Shoshanna; two *d* . *Educ:* Hebrew Univ. of Jerusalem (BA). Captain, Israel Def. Forces, 1948. Min. of Foreign Affairs, 1949-50; Attaché, Embassy of Israel, Rome, 1950-52; Min. of Foreign Affairs, 1953-54; Consul, Cyprus, 1954-56; First Sec. (Press), Embassy of Israel, London, 1957-59; Head of Res. Dept and Spokesman for Min. of Foreign Affairs, 1959-63; Minister, Israel Legation, Yugoslavia, 1963-65; Ambassador to the Phillipines, 1965-67; Asst Dir Gen., Min. of Foreign Affairs, 1969-71, Dep. Dir Gen., 1972-73, Dir Gen., 1973-76; Ambassador to the Netherlands, 1976-77. *Recreation:* golf. *Address:* c/o Embassy of Israel, 2 Palace Green, W8 4QB. *T:* 01-937 8050.

KIDWELL, Raymond Incledon, QC 1968; a Recorder, since 1972; *b* 8 Aug. 1926; *s* of Montague and Dorothy Kidwell; *m* 1st, 1951, Enid Rowe (marr. diss. 1975); two *s* ; 2nd, 1976, Carol Evelyn Beryl Maddison, *d* of late Warren G. Hopkins, Ontario. *Educ:* Whitgift Sch.; Magdalen Coll., Oxford. RAFVR, 1944-48. BA (Law) 1st cl. 1950; MA 1951; BCL 1st cl. 1951; Vinerian Law Schol., 1951; Eldon Law Schol., 1951; Arden Law Schol., Gray's Inn, 1952; Birkenhead Law Schol., Gray's Inn, 1955. Called to Bar, 1951; Lectr in Law, Oriel Coll., Oxford, 1952-55; Mem., Winn Commn on Personal Injuries, 1966-68; Mem., Bar Council, 1967-71; Chm., Overseas Relations Cttee of Bar Council, 1971. *Address:* Sanderstead House, Rectory Park, Sanderstead, Surrey. *T:* 01-657 4161; Burrows Farm West, Croyde, North Devon. *T:* Croyde 890576; 2 Crown Office Row, Temple, EC4. *T:* 01-353 9337.

KIELY, Dr David George; Under Secretary; Director-General, Electronics Research, Procurement Executive, Ministry of Defence, since 1976; Chairman, R&D Policy Committee of the General Lights Authorities of the UK and Eire, since 1974; *b* 23 July 1925; *o s* of late George Thomas and Susan Kiely, Ballynahinch, Co. Down; *m* 1956, Dr Ann Wilhelmina (*née* Kilpatrick), MB, BCh, BAO, DCH, DPH, MFCM, Hillsborough, Co. Down; one *s* one *d.* *Educ:* Down High Sch., Downpatrick; Queen's Univ., Belfast (BSc, MSc); Sorbonne (DSci). CEng, FIEE, FInstP; psc 1961. Appts in RN Scientific Service from 1944; Head of Electronic Warfare Div., ASWE, 1965-68; Head of Communications and Sensor Dept, ASWE, 1968-72; Dir-Gen., Telecommunications, PE, MoD, 1972-74; Dir-Gen., Strategic Electronic Systems, PE, MoD, 1974-76. Governor, Portsmouth Coll. of Technology, 1965-69. *Publications:* Dielectric Aerials, 1953; chapter: in Progress in Dielectrics, 1961; in Fundamentals of Microwave Electronics, 1963; papers in Proc. IEE and other learned jls, etc. *Recreations:* fly fishing, gardening, World Pheasant Assoc. *Address:* Cranleigh, Havant Road, Emsworth, Hants. *T:* Emsworth 2250. *Club:* Naval and Military.

KIER, Olaf, CBE 1970; Chairman and Managing Director of J. L. Kier & Co. Ltd, 1934-76; President and Director, French Kier Holdings Ltd; *b* Copenhagen, 4 Sept. 1899; *s* of Hector Kier, Cdre Royal Danish Navy; naturalized British subject, 1947; *m* 1st, 1924 (marr. diss.); two *d* (one *s* decd); 2nd, 1963, Bente Gudrun Tummler; one *s.* *Educ:* Copenhagen Univ. MSc Civil Engrg. FICE 1955. Resident in UK from 1922. Founded J. L. Kier & Co. Ltd, Civil Engrg Contractors, 1932 (became a public company, 1963). Underwriting Member of Lloyds, 1948. Comdr, Order of Dannebrog, 1966. *Address:* Abbotsbury Manor, Barley, Royston, Herts. *T:* Barkway 427. *Club:* Carlton.

KIESINGER, Kurt Georg; Member of Bundestag, 1949-58 and since 1969; Chancellor of the Federal Republic of Germany, 1966-69; *b* 6 April 1904; *m* Marie-Luise Schneider; one *s* one *d.* · *Educ:* Tübingen Univ.; Berlin Univ. Lawyer. Minister-Pres., Baden-Württemberg 1958-66; Pres., Bundesrat, 1962-63. Chm., Christian Democratic Group, 1958. Member: Consultative Assembly, Council of Europe, 1958 (Vice-Pres.); WEU Assembly, 1958; Central Cttee, Christian Democratic Party (Chm., 1967-71). DIuris *hc:* Univ. of Cologne, 1965; New Delhi, 1967; Maryland, 1968; Coimbra, 1968. Grand Cross, Order of Merit, German Federal Republic; Grand Cross, Order of Merit, Italian Republic; Grand Officier de la Légion d'Honneur, Palmes Académiques. *Address:* Bundeshaus, 53 Bonn, West Germany.

KIKI, Hon. Sir (Albert) Maori, KBE 1975; MP for Port Moresby, since 1972, and Deputy Prime Minister and Minister for Defence, Foreign Affairs and Trade, Papua New Guinea, since 1975; Chairman of the Constitutional Commission, since 1976; *b*

21 Sept. 1931; *s* of Erevu Kiki and Eau Ulamare; *m* 1957, Elizabeth Hariae Miro; two *s* three *d* . *Educ:* London Missionary Soc. Sch.; Sogeri Central Sch., Papua New Guinea; Fiji Sch. of Med. (Pathology); Papua New Guinea Admin. Coll. Medical Orderly, Kerema, Gulf Province, 1948; Teacher Trng, Sogeri, CP, 1950; Central Med. Sch., Fiji, 1951; Dept of Public Health, Port Moresby, 1954. Formed first trade union in Papua New Guinea and Pres., Council of Trade Unions; Welfare Officer, CP, Land Claims work amongst Koiari people, 1964; studied at Admin. Coll., 1964-65; Foundn Mem. and first Gen. Sec. of Pangu Pati (PNG's 1st Political League); Mem., Port Moresby CC, 1971. Minister for Lands, 1972. *Publications:* Ten Thousand Years in a Lifetime (autobiog.), 1970; (with Ulli Beier) HoHao: art and culture of the Orokolo people, 1972. *Recreations:* care of farm; formerly Rugby (patron and founder of PNG Rugby Union). *Address:* PO Box 1739, Boroko, Papua New Guinea; (private) Granville Farm, 8 Mile, Port Moresby, PNG; Central Government Offices, Waigani, Port Moresby, PNG. *T:* (office) 27 1288.

KILBRACKEN, 3rd Baron, *cr* 1909, of Killegar; **John Raymond Godley;** journalist and author; *b* 17 Oct. 1920; *er s* of 2nd Baron, CB, KC, and Elizabeth Helen Monteith, *d* of Vereker Monteith Hamilton and *widow* of Commander N. F. Usborne, RN; *S* father 1950; *m* 1943, Penelope Anne (marr. diss., 1949), *y d* of Rear-Adm. Sir C. N. Reyne, KBE; one *s* (and one *s* decd). *Educ:* Eton; Balliol Coll., Oxford (MA). Served in RNVR (Fleet Air Arm), as air pilot, 1940-46 (DSC 1945); entered as naval airman, commissioned 1941; Lieut-Comdr 1944; commanded Nos 835 and 714 Naval Air Sqdns. A reporter for many UK, US and foreign journals, 1947-; mainly as foreign corresp., 1960-74; major assignments in Cuba, China, Yemen, Mozambique, Angola, Kurdistan, Aden; cameraman (TV and stills), 1962-. Joined Parly Liberal Party, 1960; transferred to Labour, 1966. Hon. Sec., Connacht Hereford Breeders' Assoc., 1973-76. Pres., British-Kurdish Friendship Soc., 1975-. *Publications:* Even For An Hour (poems), 1940; Tell Me The Next One, 1950; The Master Forger, 1951; Living Like a Lord, 1955; A Peer behind the Curtain, 1959; Shamrocks and Unicorns, 1962; Van Meegeren, 1967; (ed) Letters from Early New Zealand, 1951. TV documentaries: The Yemen, 1964; Morgan's Treasure, 1965; Kurdistan, 1966. *Recreations:* ornithology, bee-keeping. *Heir: s* Hon. Christopher John Godley [*b* 1 Jan. 1945; *m* 1969, Gillian Christine, *yr d* of Lt-Comdr S. W. Birse, RN retd, Alverstoke; one *s* one *d.* *Educ:* Rugby; Reading Univ. (BSc Agric.)]. *Address:* Killegar, Cavan, Ireland. *T:* Cavan 049-34309. *See also Hon. W. A. H. Godley.*

KILBRANDON, Baron *cr* 1971 (Life Peer), of Kilbrandon, Argyll; **Charles James Dalrymple Shaw,** PC 1971; a Lord of Appeal in Ordinary, 1971-76; *b* 15 Aug. 1906; *s* of James Edward Shaw, DL, County Clerk of Ayrshire, and Gladys Elizabeth Lester; *m* 1937, Ruth Caroline Grant; two *s* three *d.* *Educ:* Charterhouse; Balliol Coll., Oxford; Edinburgh Univ. Admitted to Faculty of Advocates, 1932, Dean of Faculty, 1957; KC 1949; Sheriff of Ayr and Bute, 1954-57; Sheriff of Perth and Angus, 1957; Senator of Coll. of Justice in Scotland and Lord of Session, 1959-71. Chairman: Standing Consultative Council on Youth Service in Scotland, 1960-68; Departmental Cttee on Treatment of Children and Young Persons, 1964; Scottish Law Commn, 1965-71; Commn on the Constitution, 1972-73 (Mem., 1969-72); Bd of Management, Royal Infirmary, Edinburgh, 1960-68. Hon. LLD Aberdeen, 1965; Hon. DSc (Soc. Sci.) Edinburgh, 1970. Hon. Fellow, Balliol Coll., Oxford, 1969, Visitor, 1974-; Hon. Bencher, Gray's Inn, 1971. *Address:* Kilbrandon House, Balvicar, by Oban. *T:* Balvicar 239. *Clubs:* New, Royal Highland Yacht (Oban).

KILBURN, Prof. Tom, CBE 1973; FRS 1965; Professor of Computer Science, University of Manchester, since 1964; *b* 11 Aug. 1921; *o s* of John W. and Ivy Kilburn, Dewsbury; *m* 1943, Irene (*née* Marsden); one *s* one *d.* *Educ:* Wheelwright Grammar Sch., Dewsbury; Sidney Sussex Coll., Cambridge; Manchester Univ. MA Cambridge 1944. Telecommunications Research Estab., Malvern, 1942-46. Manchester Univ., 1947-; PhD 1948; Lecturer, 1949; Senior Lecturer, 1951; DSc 1953; Reader in Electronics, 1955; Prof. of Computer Engineering, 1960. FIEE; FBCS 1970. *Publications:* papers in Jl of Instn of Electrical Engineers, etc. *Address:* 11 Carlton Crescent, Urmston, Lancs. *T:* Urmston 3846.

KILDARE, Marquess of; Maurice FitzGerald; landscape and contract gardener; *b* 7 April 1948; *s* and *heir* of 8th Duke of Leinster, *qv* ; *m* 1972, Fiona Mary Francesca, *d* of Harry Hollick; one *s* one *d* . *Educ:* Millfield School. *Heir: s* Earl of Offaly, *qv* . *Address:* 7 Littleworth Hill, Wantage, Oxon.

KILDARE and LEIGHLIN, Bishop of, (RC), since 1967; **Most Rev. Patrick Lennon,** DD; *b* Borris, Co. Carlow, 1914. *Educ:* Rockwell Coll., Cashel; St Patrick's Coll., Maynooth. BSc 1934; DD 1940. Prof. of Moral Theology, St Patrick's Coll., Carlow, 1940; Pres., St Patrick's Coll., 1956-66; Auxiliary Bishop and Parish Priest of Mountmellick, 1966-67. *Address:* Bishop's House, Carlow. *T:* Carlow 41102.

KILÉNYI, Edward A.; Professor of Music, Florida State University; *b* 7 May 1911; *s* of Edward Kilényi and Ethel Frater; *m* 1945, Kathleen Mary Jones; two *d. Educ:* Budapest; since childhood studied piano with Ernö Dohnányi; Theory and conducting Royal Academy of Music. First concert tour with Dohnányi (Schubert Centenary Festivals), 1928; concert tours, recitals, and soloist with Principal Symphony Orchestras, 1930-39, in Holland, Germany, Hungary, Roumania, France, Scandinavia, North Africa, Portugal, Belgium; English debut, 1935, with Sir Thomas Beecham in Liverpool, Manchester, London; tours, 1940-42, and 1946-, US, Canada, Cuba. Columbia and Remington Recordings internationally distributed. Served War of 1939-45, Capt. US Army, European theatre of operations. *Address:* c/o Florida State University, Tallahassee, Fla 32306, USA.

KILFEDDER, James Alexander; MP (UU) North Down since 1970; Barrister-at-Law; *b* 16 July 1928; *yr s* of late Robert and Elizabeth Kilfedder; unmarried. *Educ:* Model Sch. and Portora Royal Sch., Enniskillen, NI; Trinity Coll., Dublin (BA); King's Inn, Dublin. Called to English Bar, Gray's Inn, 1958. MP (UU) Belfast West, 1964-66. Mem. (Official Unionist), N Down, NI Assembly, 1973-75; Mem. (UUUC) N Down, NI Constitutional Convention, 1975-76. Former Chief Whip and Hon. Sec., Ulster Unionist Parly Party; Mem., Trustee Savings Banks Parly Cttee. *Recreation:* walking in the country. *Address:* 7 Gray's Inn Square, WC1. *T:* 01-405 6226; Eastonville, Donaghadee Road, Millisle, NI. *T:* Donaghadee 3222; House of Commons, SW1. *T:* 01-219 3563.

KILGOUR, Dr John Lowell; Under-Secretary, and Chief Medical Adviser, Ministry of Overseas Development, since 1973, also Head of International Health Division, Department of Health and Social Security, since 1971; *b* 26 July 1924; *s* of Ormonde John Lowell Kilgour and Catherine (*née* MacInnes); *m* 1955, Daphne (*née* Tully); two *s. Educ:* St Christopher's Prep. Sch., Hove; Aberdeen Grammar Sch.; Aberdeen Univ. MB, ChB 1947, MRCGP, FFCM. Joined RAMC, 1948; served in: Korea, 1950-52; Cyprus, 1956; Suez, 1956; Singapore, 1961-64 (Brunei, Sarawak); comd 23 Para. Field Amb., 1954-57; psc 1959; ADMS HQ FARELF, 1961-64; jssc 1964. Joined Min. of Health, 1968, Med. Manpower and Postgrad. Educn Divs; UK Deleg. to WHO and to Council of Europe Public Health Cttees; Chm., European Public Health Cttee; Mem. WHO Expert Panel on Communicable Diseases, 1972-; Chm., Cttee for Internat. Surveillance of Communicable Diseases, 1976. Chm., Bureau of Tropical Medicine and Hygiene; Member Management Boards: Liverpool Sch. of Tropical Medicine; London Sch. of Tropical Medicine and Hygiene; RPMS, Hammersmith; British Postgrad. Med. Fedn; an Assessor, Tropical Medicine Res. Bd, MRC; Governor, Inst. of Development Studies. Member: British Nat. Cttee of the Blind; Imperial Cancer Soc.; LEPRA. Mem. Editorial Bd, Tropical Doctor. *Publications:* chapter in, Migration of Medical Manpower, 1971; contrib. Hospital Medicine, Health Trends and other med. jls. *Recreations:* reading, gardening, two dachshunds, travel. *Address:* Poolside, Portesbery, London Road, Camberley, Surrey. *T:* Camberley 23122. *Clubs:* Athenæum; Royal Windsor Racing.

KILLALOE, Bishop of, (RC), since 1967; **Most Rev. Michael Harty;** *b* Feb. 1922; *s* of Patrick Harty, Lismore, Toomevara, Co. Tipperary, Ireland. *Educ:* St Flannan's Coll., Ennis, Ire.; St Patrick's Coll., Maynooth, Ire.; University Coll., Galway. Priest, 1946; Prof., St Flannan's Coll., Ennis, 1948; Dean, St Patrick's Coll., Maynooth, 1949, 1955-67; Asst Priest, dio. Los Angeles, 1954. BA, BD, LCL, DD (Hon.); Hon. Dipl. in Educn. *Address:* Westbourne, Ennis, Co. Clare, Ireland. *T:* Ennis 21638.

KILLALOE, KILFENORA, CLONFERT and KILMACDUAGH, Diocese of; see Limerick and Killaloe.

KILLANIN, 3rd Baron, *cr* 1900; **Michael Morris,** Bt, *cr* 1885; MBE 1945; TD 1945; MA; Author, Film Producer; President, International Olympic Committee, since 1972 (Vice-President 1968-72); *b* 30 July 1914; *o s* of late Lieut-Col Hon. George Henry Morris, Irish Guards, 2nd *s* of 1st Baron, and Dora Maryan [who *m* 2nd, 1918, Lieut-Col Gerard Tharp, Rifle Brigade (*d* 1934)], *d* of late James Wesley Hall, Melbourne, Australia; *S* uncle, 1927; *m* 1945, Mary Sheila Cathcart, MBE 1946, *o d* of Rev. Canon Douglas L. C. Dunlop, MA,

Kilcummin, Galway; three *s* one *d. Educ:* Eton; Sorbonne, Paris; Magdalene Coll., Cambridge. BA 1935; MA 1939; formerly on Editorial Staff, Daily Express; Daily Mail, 1935-39; Special Daily Mail War Correspondent Japanese-Chinese War, 1937-38. Political Columnist Sunday Dispatch, 1938-39. Served War of 1939-45 (MBE, TD), KRRC (Queen's Westminsters); Brigade Maj. 30 Armd Bde, 1943-45. Director: Irish Shell Ltd; Bovril (Ireland) Ltd (Chm.); Chubb's Lock and Safe (Ireland) Ltd (Chm.); Chubb Alarms (Ireland) Ltd (Chm.); Chubb Fire Security Ireland Ltd (Chm.); Ulster Bank Ltd; Ulster Investment Ltd (Chm.); Lombard and Ulster Banking (Ireland) Ltd (Chm.); Northern Telecom (Ireland) Ltd (Chm.); Beamish & Crawford Ltd; Fitzwilton Ltd; Coyle Hamilton Life and Pensions Ltd (Chm.); President: Olympic Council of Ireland, 1950-72; Incorporated Sales Managers' Association (Ireland), 1955-58; Galway Chamber of Commerce, 1952-53; Chm. of the Dublin Theatre Festival, 1958-70. Member: Council Irish Red Cross Soc., 1947-72; Cttee RNLI (a Vice-Pres.); Cultural Adv. Cttee to Minister for External Affairs, 1947-72; Nat. Monuments of Ireland Advisory Council (Chm., 1961-65); Irish Nat. Sports Council, 1970-72; Irish Turf Club (Steward 1972-75); National Hunt Steeplechase Cttee; first President, Irish Club, London, 1947-65; Trustee, Irish Sailors and Soldiers Land Trust; Hon. Consul-General for Monaco, in Ireland 1961-77; Hon. LLD NUI, 1975; Hon. DLitt, New Univ. of Ulster, 1977. Mem., French Acad. of Sport, 1974. Knight of Honour and Devotion of Sovereign Order of Malta, 1948; Finnish Order of Olympic Merit, 1952; Star of Italy, 1958; Comdr Order of The Grimaldi, Monaco, 1961; Comdr Grand Cross, Germany, 1972; Comdr of the Sacred Treasure, Japan, 1972; Order of Merit, Italy, 1973; Cav. Order of Merit of Duarte Sanchez y Mella, Dominican Republic, 1974; Officer, Legion of Honour, France, 1975; Knight Grand Cross of the Order of Civil Merit, Spain, 1976; Comdr Order of Sports Merit, Ivory Coast, 1977; decorations from Austria, Brazil, Columbia, USSR etc. *Films:* (with John Ford) The Rising of the Moon; Gideon's Day; Young Cassidy; Playboy of the Western World; Alfred the Great; Connemara and its Pony. *Publications:* Contributions to British, American and European Press; Four Days; Sir Godfrey Kneller; Shell Guide to Ireland (with Prof. M. V. Duignan); (ed with J. Rodda) The Olympic Games, 1976. *Heir:* s Hon. (George) Redmond (Fitzpatrick) Morris [*b* 26 Jan. 1947; *m* 1972, Pauline, *o d* of Geoffrey Horton, Dublin; one *s* one *d. Educ:* Ampleforth; Trinity Coll., Dublin]. *Address:* 30 Lansdowne Road, Dublin 4. *T:* 763362; St Annins, Spiddal, County Galway. *T:* Galway 83103. *Clubs:* Garrick, Beefsteak; Stephen's Green (Dublin); County (Galway).

KILLEARN, 2nd Baron, *cr* 1943; **Graham Curtis Lampson;** 4th Bt *cr* 1866; *b* 28 Oct. 1919; *er s* of 1st Baron Killearn, PC, GCMG, CB, MVO, and his 1st wife (*née* Rachel Mary Hele Phipps) (*d* 1930), *d* of W. W. Phipps; *S* father as 2nd Baron, 1964, and kinsman as 4th Bt, 1971; *m* 1946, Nadine Marie Cathryn, *o d* of late Vice-Adm. Cecil Horace Pilcher, DSO; two *d. Educ:* Eton Coll.; Magdalen Coll., Oxford (MA). Served war of 1939-45, Scots Guards (Major). US Bronze Star. *Heir:* half-b Hon. Victor Miles George Aldous Lampson, Captain RARO, Scots Guards [*b* 9 Sept. 1941; *m* 1971, Melita Amaryllis Pamela Astrid, *d* of Rear-Adm. M. C. Morgan-Giles, *qv*; two *d*]. *Address:* 6 Trevor Street, SW7. *T:* 01-584 7700. *Club:* MCC. *See also Sir N . C . Bonsor , Bt , Lord Eliot .*

KILLEN, Hon. Denis James, LLB; MP (Lib) for Moreton, Queensland, since 1955; Minister for Defence, Commonwealth of Australia, since Nov. 1975; *b* 23 Nov. 1925; *s* of James W. Killen, Melb.; *m* 1949, Joyce Claire; three *d'. Educ:* Brisbane Grammar Sch.; Univ. of Queensland. Barrister-at-Law. Jackaroo; RAAF (Flight Serjeant); Mem. staff, Rheem (Aust.) Pty Ltd. Minister for the Navy, 1969-71; Opposition Spokesman: on Educn, 1973-74; on Defence, 1975. Foundn Pres., Young Liberals Movement (Qld); Vice-Pres., Lib. Party, Qld Div., 1953-56. *Recreations:* tennis, horseracing. *Address:* Parliament House, Canberra, ACT 2600, Australia. *T:* 733955. *Clubs:* Johnsonian, Tattersall's, Irish Association, QTC (Brisbane), Brisbane Cricket.

KILLIAN, James Rhyne, Jr; Hon. Chairman of Corporation, Massachusetts Institute of Technology, USA, since 1971; *b* 24 July 1904; *s* of James R. and Jeannette R Killian; *m* 1929, Elizabeth Parks; one *s* one *d. Educ:* Trinity Coll. (Duke Univ.), Durham, North Carolina; Mass Institute of Technology, Cambridge, Mass (BS). Asst Managing Editor, The Technology Review, MIT, 1926-27; Managing Editor, 1927-30; Editor, 1930-39; Exec. Asst to Pres., MIT, 1939-43; Exec. Vice-Pres., MIT, 1943-45; Vice-Pres., MIT, 1945-48; 10th Pres. of MIT, 1948-59 (on leave 1957-59); Chm. of the Corporation, 1959-71. Special Asst to Pres. of United States for Science and Technology, 1957-59; Mem., 1957-61, Chm. 1957-59,

Consultant-at-large, 1961-73, President's Science Advisory Cttee; Mem., President's Bd of Consultants on Foreign Intelligence Activities, 1956-59 (Chm., 1956-57); Mem. of President's Commission on National Goals, 1960; Chm., President's Foreign Intelligence Advisory Board, 1961-63. Mem., Bd of Trustees, Mitre Corporation; Pres. Bd of Trustees, Atoms for Peace Awards, Inc., 1959-69; Mem., Bd of Visitors, Tulane Univ., 1960-69; Trustee: Institute for Defense Analyses, Inc., 1959-69 (Chm., 1956-57, 1959-61); Mount Holyoke Coll., 1962-72; Alfred P. Sloan Foundn, 1954-77; Boston Museum of Science; Chairman: Carnegie Commn on Educl TV, 1965-67; Corp. for Public Broadcasting, 1973-74 (Dir, 1968-75); Director: Polaroid Corp.; former Director: Amer. Tel. & Tel. Co.; General Motors Corp.; JBM; Ingersoll-Rand Co.; Fellow Amer. Acad. of Arts and Sciences; Hon. Mem., Amer. Soc. for Engrg Educn; Mem., Nat. Acad. of Engineering; Moderator, Amer. Unitarian Assoc., 1960-61; President's Certificate of Merit, 1948; Certificate of Appreciation, 1953, and Exceptional Civilian Service Award, 1957, Dept of the Army; Public Welfare Medal of the Nat. Acad. of Sciences, 1957; Officier Légion d'Honneur (France), 1957. Gold Medal Award, Nat. Inst. of Social Sciences, 1958; World Brotherhood Award, Nat. Conf. of Christians and Jews, 1958; Award of Merit, Amer. Inst. of Cons. Engineers, 1958; Washington Award, Western Soc. of Engineers, 1959; Distinguished Achievement Award, Holland Soc. of NY, 1959; Gold Medal of Internat. Benjamin Franklin Soc., 1960; Good Govt Award, Crosscup-Pishon Post, American Legion, 1960; Hoover Medal, 1963; George Foster Peabody Award, 1968 and 1976. Hon. degrees: ScD: Middlebury Coll., 1945; Bates Coll., 1950; University of Havana, 1953; University of Notre Dame, Lowell Technological Inst., 1954; Columbia Univ., Coll. of Wooster, Ohio, Oberlin Coll., 1958; University of Akron, 1959; Worcester Polytechnic Inst., 1960; University of Maine, 1963; DEng: Drexel Inst. of Tech., 1948; University of Ill., 1960; University of Mass., 1961; LLD: Union Coll., 1947; Bowdoin Coll., Northeastern Univ., Duke Univ., 1949; Boston Univ., Harvard Univ., 1950; Williams Coll., Lehigh Univ., University of Pa, 1951; University of Chattanooga, 1954; Tufts Univ., 1955; University of Calif. and Amherst Coll., 1956; College of William and Mary, 1957; Brandeis Univ., 1958; Johns Hopkins Univ., New York Univ., 1959; Providence Coll., Temple Univ. 1960; University of S Carolina, 1961; Meadville Theological Sch., 1962; DAppl Sci., University of Montreal, 1958; EdD, Rhode Island Coll., 1962; HHD, Rollins Coll., 1964; DPS, Detroit Inst. of Technology, 1972. Address: 77 Massachusetts Avenue, Cambridge, Mass 02139, USA. Clubs: St Botolph (Boston); The Century, University (New York).

KILLICK, Sir John (Edward), KCMG 1971 (CMG 1966); Ambassador and UK Permanent Representative to NATO, since 1975; b 18 Nov. 1919; s of late Edward William James Killick and Doris Marjorie (née Stokes); m 1949, Lynette du Preez (née Leach); no c. Educ: Latymer Upper Sch.; University Coll., London, Fellow 1973; Bonn Univ. Served with HM Forces, 1939-46: Suffolk Regt, W Africa Force and Airborne Forces. Foreign Office, 1946-48; Control Commn and High Commn for Germany (Berlin, Frankfurt and Bonn), 1948-51; Private Sec. to Parly Under-Sec., Foreign Office, 1951-54; British Embassy, Addis Ababa, 1954-57; Canadian Nat. Def. Coll., 1957-58; Western Dept, Foreign Office, 1958-62; Imp. Def. Coll., 1962; Counsellor and Head of Chancery, British Embassy, Washington, 1963-68; Asst Under-Sec. of State, FCO, 1968-71; Ambassador to USSR, 1971-73; Dep. Under-Sec. of State, FCO and Permanent Rep. on Council of WEU, 1973-75. Recreations: golf, tennis, sailing. Address: UK Delegation to NATO, BFPO 49. Clubs: East India, Devonshire, Sports and Public Schools, Brooks's, Royal Commonwealth Society, Royal African Society.

KILLICK, Paul Victor St John, OBE 1969; HM Diplomatic Service, retired; Ambassador to the Dominican Republic, 1972-75; b 8 Jan. 1916; s of C. St John Killick and Beatrice (née Simpson); m 1947, Sylva Augusta Leva; one s two d. Educ: St Paul's School. Served with Army, N Africa and Italy, 1939-46 (despatches 1944). Diplomatic Service: Singapore, 1946-47; Tokyo, 1947-49; Katmandu, 1950-53; FO, 1953-55; Oslo, 1955-58; San Francisco, 1958-60; Djakarta, 1960-61; Rome, 1962-66; Pretoria/Cape Town, 1966-70; Tangier, 1971-72. Recreation: walking. Address: c/o Barclays Bank Ltd, 1 Brompton Road, SW3 1EB.

KILMAINE, 6th Baron, cr 1789; **John Francis Archibald Browne**, Bt 1636; CBE 1956; a Trustee: the Historic Churches Preservation Trust; the Dulverton Trust (Secretary, 1953-66); High Steward of Harwich, 1966-76; a Governor of the Thomas Wall Trust; b 22 Sept. 1902; e s of 5th Baron and Lady Aline Kennedy (d 1957), d of 3rd Marquess of Ailsa; S father 1946; m

1930, Wilhelmina Phyllis, o d of Scott Arnott, Tanners, Brasted, Kent; one s two d. Educ: Winchester; Magdalen Coll., Oxford, MA. On staff of British Xylonite Co. Ltd, 1925-29; Administrative Sec. to University Coll., Southampton, 1930-33; Sec. of the Oxford Society, 1933-40, Chm., 1949-73; Sec., Pilgrim Trust, 1945-67; Chairman: Charities Investment Managers Ltd, 1965-74; Rochester Diocesan Adv. Cttee for care of Churches, 1970-75. Served War of 1939-45 as Lt-Col RASC and on Staff, 1940-45 (despatches twice). Hon. DCL Oxford, 1973. Heir: s Hon. John David Henry Browne [b 2 April 1948. Educ: Eton. Dir, Fusion (Bickenhill) Ltd]. Address: The Mount House, Brasted, Kent. Club: Travellers'.

KILMANY, Baron, cr 1966 (Life Peer), of Kilmany; **William John St Clair Anstruther-Gray**; 1st Bt, cr 1956; PC 1962; MC 1943; Lord-Lieutenant of Fife, since 1974; b 1905; o s of late Col W. Anstruther-Gray, MP, DL, JP, of Kilmany; m 1934, Monica Helen, OBE 1946, JP, o c of late Geoffrey Lambton, 2nd s of 4th Earl of Durham; two d. Educ: Eton; Christ Church, Oxford, MA (Hons). Lieut, Coldstream Guards, 1926-30; served Shanghai Defence Force, 1927-28; rejoined Sept. 1939 and served N Africa, France, Germany, etc with Coldstream Guards and Lothians and Border Horse; Major, 1942; MP (U) for North Lanark, 1931-45; up to Sept. 1939 Parly Private Sec. to Rt Hon. Sir John Colville, MP, Sec. of State for Scotland, and previously to the Financial Sec. to the Treasury, and to Sec. for Overseas Trade; Asst Postmaster-Gen., May-July 1945; Crown nominee for Scotland on Gen. Medical Council, 1952-65. Contested (U) Berwick and East Lothian, Feb. 1950; MP (U) Berwick and East Lothian, 1951-66. Chm. of Ways and Means and Dep. Speaker, House of Commons, 1962-64 (Dep. Chm., 1959-62); Chm. Conservative Members' 1922 Cttee, 1964-66. Elected Mem. National Hunt Cttee, 1948; Mem., Horserace Betting Levy Bd, 1966-74. DL Fife, 1953. Address: Kilmany, Cupar, Fife. T: Gauldry 247. Clubs: Pratt's, Brooks's, Cavalry and Guards, Turf, Jockey; New (Edinburgh); Royal and Ancient (St Andrews).
See also J. C. Macnab of Macnab.

KILMARNOCK, 7th Baron cr 1831; **Alastair Ivor Gilbert Boyd**; Chief of the Clan Boyd; b 11 May 1927; s of 6th Baron Kilmarnock, MBE, TD, and Hon. Rosemary Guest (d 1971), er d of 1st Viscount Wimborne; S father, 1975; m 1954, Diana Mary (marr. diss. 1970, she d 1975), o d of D. Grant Gibson; m 1977, Hilary Ann, yr d of Leonard Sidney and Margery Bardwell; one s. Educ: Bradfield; King's Coll., Cambridge. Lieutenant, Irish Guards, 1946; served Palestine, 1947-48. Publications: Sabbatical Year, 1958; The Road from Ronda, 1969; The Companion Guide to Madrid and Central Spain, 1974. Heir: b Dr the Hon. Robin Jordan Boyd, MB BS, MRCP, MRCPEd, DCH, b 6 June 1941. Address: Plaza de Mondragón 7, Ronda, Malaga, Spain. Club: Pratt's.

KILMISTER, Prof. Clive William; Professor of Mathematics, King's College, London, since 1966; b 3 Jan. 1924; s of William and Doris Kilmister; m 1955, Peggy Joyce Hutchins; one s two d. Educ: Queen Mary Coll., Univ. of London. BSc 1944, MSc 1948, PhD 1950. King's Coll. London: Asst Lectr, 1950; Lectr, 1953; Reader, 1959. Gresham Prof. of Geometry, 1972-. Pres., British Soc. for History of Mathematics, 1973-76. Publications: Special Relativity for Physicists (with G. Stephenson), 1958; Eddington's Statistical Theory (with B. O. J. Tupper), 1962; Hamiltonian Dynamics, 1964; The Environment in Modern Physics, 1965; Rational Mechanics (with J. E. Reeve), 1966; Men of Physics: Sir Arthur Eddington, 1966; Language, Logic and Mathematics, 1967; Lagrangian Dynamics, 1967; Special Theory of Relativity, 1970; The Nature of the Universe, 1972; General Theory of Relativity, 1973. Recreation: opera going. Address: 11 Vanbrugh Hill, Blackheath, SE3 7UE. T: 01-858 0675.

KILMORE, Bishop of, (RC), since 1972; **Most Rev. Francis J. McKiernan**, DD; b 3 Feb. 1926; s of Joseph McKiernan and Ellen McTague. Educ: Aughawillan National School; St Patrick's Coll., Cavan; University College, Dublin; St Patrick's Coll., Maynooth. BA, BD, HDE. St. Malachy's Coll., Belfast, 1951-52; St Patrick's Coll., Cavan, 1952-53; University Coll., Dublin, 1953-54; St Patrick's Coll., Cavan, 1954-62; Pres., St Felim's Coll., Ballinamore, Co. Leitrim, 1962-72. Editor of Breifne (Journal of Breifne Historical Society), 1958-72. Address: Bishop's House, Cullies, Cavan. T: 049-31496.

KILMORE and ELPHIN and ARDAGH, Bishop of, since 1959; **Rt. Rev. Edward Francis Butler Moore**, DD; b 1906; s of Rev. W. R. R. Moore; m 1932, Frances Olivia Scott; two s two d. Educ: Trinity Coll., Dublin (MA, PhD, DD). Deacon, 1930; Priest, 1931; Curate, Bray, 1930-32; Hon. Clerical Vicar, Christ Church Cathedral, Dublin, 1931-35; Curate, Clontarf, 1932-34;

Incumbent, Castledermot with Kinneagh, 1934-40; Greystones, Diocese of Glendalough, 1940-49; Chaplain to Duke of Leinster, 1934-40; Rural Dean, Delgany 1950-59; Canon of Christ Church, Dublin, 1951-57; Archdeacon of Glendalough, 1957-59. *Recreations:* tennis, golf, fishing. *Address:* See House, Kilmore, Cavan, Ireland. *T:* Cavan 56. *Club:* University (Dublin).

KILMOREY, 6th Earl of; *see* Needham, Richard Francis.

KILMUIR, Countess of; *see* De La Warr, Countess.

KILNER, Cyril; Assistant Editor, Doncaster Gazette, 1952-75, retired; *b* 5 Sept. 1910; *s* of Bernard Kilner and Edith Annie (*née* Booker); *m* 1949, Joan Siddons; one *s* one *d. Educ:* Mexborough Grammar School. Army War Service in Royal Tank Regt, 1940-45. Reporter, Barnsley Independent, 1927-30; Reporter, Sports Editor, Sub-Editor, Barnsley Chronicle, 1931-47; Reporter, Sub-Editor, Yorkshire Evening News (Doncaster edn), 1947-52. Member: The Press Council, 1968-74; Nat. Exec. Council, NUJ, 1958-72 (Pres., 1969, Mem. of Honour, 1976). Hon. Gen. Treasurer, Internat. Fedn. of Journalists, 1972-76. *Recreations:* watching (sports, TV etc.), reading, motoring, travelling. *Address:* Cranford, 159 Boothferry Road, Goole, N Humberside. *T:* Goole 4309.

KILNER BROWN, Hon. Sir Ralph; *see* Brown.

KILPATRICK, Rev. George Dunbar; Dean Ireland's Professor of Exegesis of Holy Scripture, Oxford, 1949-77; Fellow of the Queen's College, Oxford; Fellow of University College, London, since 1967; *b* Coal Creek, Fernie, BC, Canada, 15 Sept. 1910; *o c* of late Wallace Henry and Bessie Kilpatrick; *m* 1943, Marion, *d* of Harold Laver and Dorothy Madeline Woodhouse; one *s* three *d. Educ:* Ellis Sch., BC; St Dunstan's Coll.; University Coll., London; Oriel Coll., Oxford (Scholar); University of London, Granville Scholar, 1931; BA Classics (1st Class), 1932; University of Oxford, BA Lit. Hum. (2nd Class), 1934, Theology (2nd Class), 1936, Junior Greek Testament Prize, 1936, Senior Greek Testament Prize, 1937, Junior Denyer and Johnson Scholarship, 1938, BD 1944; Grinfield Lecturer, 1945-49; DD 1948; Schweich Lecturer, 1951. Deacon 1936; Priest 1937; Asst Curate of Horsell, 1936; Tutor, Queen's Coll., Birmingham, 1939; Asst Curate of Selly Oak, 1940; Acting Warden of Coll. of the Ascension, Birmingham, 1941; Rector of Wishaw, Warwicks, and Lecturer at Lichfield Theological Coll., 1942; Head of Dept of Theology and Reader in Christian Theology, University Coll., Nottingham, 1946. Vice-Pres., British and Foreign Bible Soc., 1958. *Publications:* The Origins of the Gospel according to St Matthew, 1946; The Trial of Jesus, 1953; Remaking the Liturgy, 1967. Editor: The New Testament in Greek, British and Foreign Bible Society's 2nd edn, 1958; contributions to periodicals. *Recreation:* reading. *Address:* The Queen's College, Oxford; 27 Lathbury Road, Oxford. *T:* Oxford 58909.

KILPATRICK, Prof. Robert; Dean, Faculty of Medicine, University of Leicester, since 1975; Professor and Head of Department of Clinical Pharmacology and Therapeutics, University of Leicester; *b* 29 July 1926; *s* of Robert Kilpatrick and Catherine Sharp Glover; *m* 1950, Elizabeth Gibson Page Forbes; two *s* one *d. Educ:* Buckhaven High Sch.; Edinburgh Univ. MB, ChB (Hons) 1949; MD 1960; FRCP(Ed) 1963; FRCP 1975. Med. Registrar, Edinburgh, 1951-54; Lectr, Univ. of Sheffield, 1955-66; Rockefeller Trav. Fellowship, MRC, Harvard Univ., 1961-62; Commonwealth Trav. Fellowship, 1962; Prof. of Clin. Pharmacology and Therapeutics, Univ. of Sheffield, 1966-75; Dean, Faculty of Medicine, Univ. of Sheffield, 1970-73. Chm., Adv. Cttee on Pesticides, 1975; Chm., Soc. of Endocrinology, 1975; Mem., GMC, 1972-. *Publications:* articles in med. and sci. jls. *Recreations:* golf, sailing. *Address:* The Barn, Smeeton Westerby, Leics LE8 0QL. *T:* Kibworth 2202. *Club:* Royal and Ancient (St Andrews).

KILPATRICK, Sir William (John), KBE 1965 (CBE 1958); Chairman: Mulford Holdings Ltd; Kilpatrick Holdings Ltd; Director, Guardian Assurance Group; *b* 27 Dec. 1906; *s* of late James Park Scott Kilpatrick, Scotland; *m* 1932, Alice Margaret Strachan; one *s* three *d. Educ:* Wollongong, NSW. Sqdn Ldr, RAAF, 1942-45. Pastoral interests, Victoria. Mem., Melbourne City Council, 1958-64. Chm. Cancer Service Cttee, Anti-Cancer Coun. of Vic., 1958-; Dep. Nat. Pres., Nat. Heart Foundn of Aust., 1960-64; Chm., Finance Cttee, Nat. Heart Foundn of Aust., 1960-; Pres. Aust. Cancer Soc., 1961-64, 1974-; World Chm., Finance Cttee, Internat. Union Against Cancer, 1961-; Ldr Aust. Delegn to 8th Internat. Cancer Congr, Moscow, 1962. Nat. Chm. Winston Churchill Mem. Trust, 1965; Chm., Drug Educn Sub-Cttee, Commonwealth Govt, 1970; Chm., Plastic

and Reconstructive Surgery Foundn, 1970. *Recreations:* golf, swimming. *Address:* 8 Hopetoun Road, Toorak, Victoria 3142, Australia. *T:* 20 5206. *Clubs:* Naval and Military, Victorian Golf, VRC, VATC (all Melbourne); Commonwealth (Canberra).

KILROY, Dame Alix; *see* Meynell, Dame Alix.

KILROY-SILK, Robert; MP (Lab) Ormskirk since Feb. 1974; *b* 19 May 1942; *m* 1963, Jan Beech; one *s* one *d. Educ:* Saltley Grammar Sch., Birmingham; LSE (BScEcon). Lectr, Dept of Political Theory and Institutions, Liverpool Univ., 1966-74. PPS to Minister for the Arts, 1974-75; Vice-Chm., Merseyside Gp of MPs, 1974-75; Member: Select Cttee on Race Relations and Immigration, 1974; Select Cttee on Public Accounts, 1975. Governor, National Heart and Chest Hospital, 1974-. *Publications:* Socialism since Marx, 1972; (contrib.) The Role of Commissions in Policy Making, 1973; articles in Political Studies, Manchester School of Economic and Social Science, Political Quarterly, Industrial and Labor Relations Review, Parliamentary Affairs, etc. *Recreations:* family, swimming, cinema, reading. *Address:* Trees, Lock Mead, Maidenhead, Berks. *T:* Maidenhead 21401.

KILVINGTON, Frank Ian; Headmaster of St Albans School since 1964; *b* West Hartlepool, 26 June 1924; *e s* of H. H. Kilvington; *m* 1949, Jane Mary, *d* of Very Rev. Michael Clarke, *qv*; one *s* one *d. Educ:* Repton (entrance and foundn scholar); Corpus Christi, Oxford (open class. scholar). 2nd cl. Lit Hum, 1948; MA 1950. Served War of 1939-45: RNVR, 1943-46 (Lt); West Africa Station, 1943-45; RN Intelligence, Germany, 1945-46. Westminster School: Asst Master, 1949-64; Housemaster of Rigaud's House, 1957-64. Chm., St Albans Marriage Guidance Council, 1968-74; Pres., St Albans and Herts Architectural and Archæological Soc., 1974-77. E-SU Page Scholar, 1976-77. *Publication:* A Short History of St Albans School, 1970. *Recreations:* music, local history. *Address:* Abbey Gateway, St Albans, Herts AL3 4HB. *T:* St Albans 55702. *Club:* East India, Devonshire, Sports and Public Schools.

KIMBALL, Marcus Richard; MP (C) Gainsborough Division of Lincolnshire since Feb. 1956; *b* 18 Oct. 1928; *s* of late Major Lawrence Kimball; *m* 1956, June Mary Fenwick; two *d. Educ:* Eton; Trinity Coll., Cambridge. Contested Derby South, Gen. Election, 1955. Privy Council Rep., Council of RCVS, 1969. Jt Master and Huntsman: Fitzwilliam Hounds, 1950-51 and 1951-52; Cottesmore Hounds, 1952-53, 1953-54, 1955-56 (Jt Master, 1956-58). Chm., British Field Sports Soc., 1966. Lt Leics Yeo. (TA), 1947; Capt., 1951. Mem. Rutland CC, 1955. *Address:* Great Easton Manor, Market Harborough, Leics LE16 8TB. *T:* Rockingham 333; Altnaharra, Lairg, Sutherland IV27 4AE. *T:* Altnaharra 224; 70 Cranmer Court, Sloane Avenue, SW3. *T:* 01-536 3257. *Clubs:* White's, Pratt's.

KIMBER, Sir Charles Dixon, 3rd Bt, *cr* 1904; *b* 7 Jan. 1912; *o* surv. *s* of Sir Henry Dixon Kimber, 2nd Bt, and Lucy Ellen, *y d* of late G. W. Crookes; *S* father 1950; *m* 1st, 1933, Ursula (marr. diss., 1949), *er d* of late Ernest Roy Bird, MP; three *s*; 2nd, 1950, Margaret Bonham (marr. diss., 1965), Writer; one *d* (and one *s* decd). *Educ:* Eton; Balliol Coll., Oxford (BA). *Heir:* *s* Timothy Roy Henry Kimber [*b* 3 June 1936; *m* 1960, Antonia Kathleen Brenda (marr. diss. 1974), *d* of Sir Francis Williams, Bt, *qv*; two *s*]. *Address:* No 2 Duxford, Hinton Waldrist, near Faringdon, Oxon. *T:* Longworth 820004.

KIMBER, Derek Barton, OBE 1945; Chairman, Austin & Pickersgill Ltd, since 1973; Director, Equity Capital for Industry Ltd, since 1977; *b* 2 May 1917; *s* of George Kimber and Marion Kimber (*née* Barton); *m* 1943, Gwendoline Margaret Maude Brotherton; two *s* two *d. Educ:* Bedford Sch.; Imperial Coll., London Univ.; Royal Naval Coll., Greenwich. MSc(Eng), FCGI, DIC; FRINA, FIMechE, FIMarE, MNECInst, FWeldI, FRSA. Royal Corps of Naval Constructors, 1939-49; Consultant, Urwick, Orr & Partners Ltd, 1950-54; Fairfield Shipbuilding & Engineering Co. Ltd: Manager, 1954; Dir, 1961; Dep. Man. Dir, 1963-65; Dir, Harland & Wolff Ltd, 1966-69; Dir Gen., Chemical Industries Assoc., 1970-73; Director: A. & P. Appledore International Ltd, 1974-; British Ship Research Assoc. (Trustees) Ltd, 1973-. Dir, Glasgow Chamber of Commerce, 1962-65. Chm., C. & G. Jt Adv. Cttee for Shipbuilding, 1968-70; Pres., Clyde Shipbuilders Assoc., 1964-65; Member: Shipbuilding Industry Trng Bd, 1964-69; Scottish Cttee, Lloyds Register of Shipping, 1964-65, Gen. Cttee, 1973-; Technical Cttee, 1976-; Research Council, British Ship Res. Assoc., 1973-; Brit. Tech. Cttee, Amer. Bureau of Shipping, 1976-; Standing Cttee, Assoc. of W European Shipbuilders, 1976-; Chm., Management Bd, Shipbuilders & Repairers Nat. Assoc., 1974-76, Vice-Pres., 1976-77; Mem., Jt Industry Cons.

Cttee, (SRNA/CSEU), 1966-76. Member: EDC for Chem. Industry, 1970-72; Process Plant Working Party (NEDO), 1970-72; CBI Central Council, 1970-72, 1975-; CBI Northern Reg. Council, 1973- (Chm. 1975-77). Member: Council, RINA, 1961- (Chm., 1973-75, Pres. RINA 1977-); Council, Welding Inst., 1959-74, 1976-; Council, NE Coast Inst. of Engrs and Shipbuilders, 1974-; Bd, CEI, 1977-; C. & G. Insignia Award Cttee, 1970-. Liveryman, Worshipful Co. of Shipwrights, 1967 (Asst to Court 1974-). Governor, Imperial Coll., London Univ., 1967-. Fellow, Fellowship of Engineering, 1976. *Publications:* papers on shipbuilding subjects in learned soc. Trans. *Recreations:* shipbuilding, DIY, golf, rough gardening. *Address:* Broughton, Monk's Road, Virginia Water, Surrey. *T:* Wentworth 4274. *Clubs:* Brooks's, City Livery, MCC, Den Norske Klub.

KIMBER, Gurth, CMG 1952; *b* 19 Jan. 1906; *s* of late R. J. Kimber; *m* 1943, Joan, *d* of late Roy Gibson; two *d. Educ:* Perse; Clare Coll., Cambridge. Appointed Dominions Office, 1928; Asst UK Government Representative, Canberra, 1934-35; Official Sec., United Kingdom High Commissioner's Office, Canberra, 1946-50; Dep. High Commissioner for the UK, Bombay, 1952-54; Counsellor, British Embassy, Dublin, 1956-60; British Dep. High Commissioner, Canberra, 1962-65; retired, 1966. *Recreation:* sailing. *Address:* 32 Bear Street, Nayland, Suffolk.

KIMBER, Herbert Frederick Sidney; Director and General Manager, Southern Newspapers Ltd, since 1975; Chairman, Bird Bros, Basingstoke, since 1976; Member, Press Council, since 1977; *b* 3 April 1917; *s* of H. G. Kimber; *m* Patricia Boulton (*née* Forfar); one *s. Educ:* elementary sch., Southampton. Southern Newspapers Ltd, office boy, 1931. Served War, Royal Navy, 1939-46: commissioned Lieut RNVR, 1941. Manager, Dorset Evening Echo, 1960; Advertisement Manager-in-Chief, Southern Newspapers Ltd, 1961; then Dep. Gen. and Advertisement Manager, 1972; Gen. Manager, 1974. Chm., Bird Bros Ltd, Basingstoke (Associate Co. of Southern Newspapers), 1976. Newspaper Society: Mem. Council, 1974; Industrial Relations Cttee, 1975. *Recreations:* reading, travel, gardening under protest. *Address:* Cree, Holly Hill Lane, Sarisbury Green, Hants SO3 6AD. *T:* Locks Heath 2351. *Clubs:* Royal Naval; Royal Southampton Yacht.

KIMBERLEY, 4th Earl of, *cr* 1866; **John Wodehouse;** Bt, 1611; Baron Wodehouse, 1797; Lt Grenadier Guards; *b* 12 May 1924; *o s* of 3rd Earl and Margaret (*d* 1950), *d* of late Col Leonard Howard Irby; *S* father 1941; *m* 1st, 1945; 2nd, 1949; one *s;* 3rd, 1953; two *s;* 4th, 1961; one *s;* 5th, 1970. *Educ:* Eton; Cambridge. Lieut, Grenadier Guards, 1942-45: Active Service NW Europe. Mem., House of Lords Defence Gp, 1976-; Vice-Pres., Liberal Action Gp for Electoral Reform; Liberal Spokesman on: aviation and aerospace; defence; voluntary community services. Vice-Pres., World Council on Alcoholism; Mem., Nat. Council on Alcoholism. Mem., British Bobsleigh Team, 1949-58. *Recreations:* shooting, big game fishing, all field sports, gardening. *Heir: s* Lord Wodehouse, *qv. Address:* House of Lords, Westminster, SW1; Hailstone House, Cricklade, Swindon, Wilts. *T:* Cricklade 344. *Clubs:* Cavalry and Guards, Bath, Liberal, MCC; Royal Cornwall Yacht, Falmouth Shark Angling (Pres.), Shark Angling of Great Britain.

KIMBERLEY AND KURUMAN, Bishop of, since 1976; **Rt. Rev. Graham Charles Chadwick;** *b* 3 Jan. 1923; *s* of William Henry and Sarah Ann Chadwick; *m* 1955, Jeanne Suzanne Tyrell; one *s. Educ:* Swansea Grammar School; Keble Coll., Oxford (MA); St Michael's Coll., Llandaff. RNVR, 1942-46. Deacon 1950, priest 1951; Curate, Oystermouth, Dio. Swansea and Brecon, 1950-53; Diocese of Lesotho, 1953-63; Chaplain, University Coll., Swansea, 1963-68; Senior Bursar, Queen's Coll., Birmingham, 1968-69; Diocesan Missioner, Lesotho, and Warden of Diocesan Training Centre, 1970-76. *Address:* Bishopsgarth, Bishop's Avenue, Box 921, Kimberley, 8300, S Africa. *T:* Kimberley 28702.

KIMBLE, George (Herbert Tinley), PhD; retired; *b* 2 Aug. 1908; *s* of John H. and Minnie Jane Kimble; *m* 1935, Dorothy Stevens Berry; one *s* one *d. Educ:* Eastbourne Grammar Sch.; King's Coll., London (MA); University of Montreal (PhD). Asst Lecturer in Geography, University of Hull, 1931-36; Lecturer in Geography, University of Reading, 1936-39. Served War as Lt and Lt-Comdr, British Naval Meteorological Service, 1939-44. Prof. of Geography and Chm. Dept of Geography, McGill Univ., 1945-50; Sec.-Treasurer, Internat. Geographical Union, 1949-56; Chm., Commn on Humid Tropics, Internat. Geog. Union, 1956-61. Dir, Amer. Geog. Soc., 1950-53; Dir, Survey of Tropical Africa, Twentieth Century Fund, NY, 1953-60. Chm., Dept of Geography, Indiana Univ., 1957-62; Prof. of Geography, Indiana Univ., 1957-66; Research Dir, US Geography Project, Twentieth Century Fund, 1962-68. Rushton Lecturer, 1952; Borah Lecturer, University of Idaho, 1956; Haynes Foundn Lectr, University of Redlands, 1966; Visiting Prof., University of Calif. (Berkeley), 1948-49; Stanford Univ., 1961; Stockholm Sch. of Economics, 1961. *Publications:* Geography in the Middle Ages, 1938; The World's Open Spaces, 1939; The Shepherd of Banbury, 1941; (co-author) The Weather, 1943 (Eng.), 1946 (Amer.), (author) 2nd (Eng.) edn, 1951; Military Geography of Canada, 1949; The Way of the World, 1953; Our American Weather, 1955; Le Temps, 1957; Tropical Africa (2 vols), 1960; Tropical Africa (abridged edition), 1962; (with Ronald Steel) Tropical Africa Today, 1966; Man and his World, 1972; From the Four Winds, 1974; (ed for Hakluyt Soc.) Esmeraldo de Situ Orbis, 1937; (ed for American Geographical Soc. with Dorothy Good) Geography of the Northlands, 1955; articles in: Geog. Jl, Magazine, Review; Canadian Geog. Jl; Bulletin Amer. Meteorological Soc.; The Reporter; Los Angeles Times; The New York Times Magazine. *Recreations:* music, gardening. *Address:* Summerclose, Stoodleigh, Tiverton, Devon. *T:* Oakford 201.

KIMMINS, Lt-Gen. Sir Brian Charles Hannam, KBE 1956 (CBE 1944); CB 1946; DL; retired; *b* 30 July 1899; *s* of late Dr Charles William Kimmins and Dame Grace Kimmins, DBE; *m* 1929, Marjory, *d* of late Lt-Col W. J. Johnston, CBE, Lesmurdie, Elgin, Scotland; one *s* two *d. Educ:* Harrow; RMA, Woolwich. Commissioned RA 1917; served France and Flanders, 1918; in RHA in India, 1920-26; RHA in Egypt, 1926-28; ADC to Lord Lloyd, High Commissioner for Egypt and the Sudan, 1928-29; Adjutant RMA, Woolwich, 1930-33; Bde Major 147 Inf. Bde (TA), 1935-37; Staff Coll., Minley Manor, 1938-39; GSO 2 HQ, BEF, France, 1939-40: Instructor Staff Coll., 1940-41; GSO 1 ops GHQ Home Forces, 1941; DDMT War Office, 1941-42; BGS Southern Command, 1942; CRA Guards Armoured Div., 1943; Director of Plans, SEAC, 1944; Asst Chief of Staff, HQ, SACSEA, 1945; Chief of Staff HQ Combined Operations, 1946; Dir of Quartering, War Office, 1947-50; GOC, Home Counties District and 44th Div. TA, 1950-52; Dir, Territorial Army and Cadets, 1952-55; GOC Northern Ireland District, 1955-58. Col Comdt, Royal Artillery, 1955-64. DL, Somerset, 1968. Legion of Merit degree of Comdr (USA), 1946. Legion of Honour degree of Officer, Croix de Guerre (France), 1949. OStJ 1959. *Recreations:* fishing, golf. *Address:* Lamb Cottage, South Petherton, Somerset. *Club:* Army and Navy.

KIMMINS, Simon Edward Anthony, VRD 1967; Lt-Comdr RNR; *b* 26 May 1930; *s* of late Captain Anthony Kimmins, OBE, RN, and of Mrs Elizabeth Kimmins; *m* 1976, Jonkvrouwe Irma de Jonge. *Educ:* Horris Hill; Charterhouse. Man. Dir, London American Finance Corpn Ltd (originally BOECC Ltd), 1957-73; Dir (non-exec.), Balfour Williamson, 1971-74; Chief Exec., Thomas Cook Gp, 1973-75; Dir, Debenhams Ltd (non-exec Dir, 1972-75). Vice-Pres., British Export Houses Assoc., 1974- (Chm., 1970-72). Governor, Royal Shakespeare Theatre, 1975-. *Recreations:* cricket (played for Kent), golf, shooting. *Address:* Flat 6, 43 Lennox Gardens, SW1. *T:* 01-584 0520. *Clubs:* Garrick, MCC, The Pilgrims; Haagseclub.

KIMPTON, Lawrence Alpheus; Director, Standard Oil (Indiana), 1958, Executive, 1960, Vice-President, 1963, Assistant to Chairman of the Board, 1969-71, retired; *b* 7 Oct. 1910; *s* of Carl Edward Kimpton and Lynn (*née* Kennedy); *m* 1st, 1943, Marcia Drennon (*d* 1963); 2nd, 1975, Mary Townsend Kimpton. *Educ:* Stanford Univ., Stanford, Calif. (AB, MA); Cornell Univ., Ithaca, NY (PhD). Hon. DSc, Beloit Coll., 1952; Hon. LLD of several univs; 24th Hon. Stanford Fellow, 1959. Deep Springs Coll., Calif: Instructor, 1935-36; Dean and Dir, 1936-41; Dean, College of Liberal Arts, Prof. of Mathematics and Philosophy, University of Kansas City, 1942-43; University of Chicago: Chief Admin. Officer, Atomic Bomb Project, 1943-44; Prof. of Philosophy and Education, 1944-46; Academic Vice-Pres., Prof. of Philosophy and Education, 1946-47; Vice-Pres. in Charge of Development, 1950-51; Chancellor and Prof. of Philosophy, 1951-60; Dean of Students, Prof. of Philosophy, Stanford Univ., 1947-50; Hon. Trustee: Museum of Science and Industry, 1961; Univ. of Chicago; Newberry Library, 1962-. Director: Chessie System; C&O Railroad; B&O Railroad. *Recreations:* boating, reading. *Address:* Box 211, Lakeside, Michigan 49116, USA. *Clubs:* Chicago, Commercial, Tavern, Wayfarers' Chicago Yacht (Chicago); Bohemian (San Francisco).

KINAHAN, Charles Henry Grierson, CBE 1972; JP; Director, Bass Ireland Ltd, Belfast, and subsidiary companies, since 1956; *b* 10 July 1915; *e s* of Henry Kinahan, Belfast, and Ula, *d* of late Rt Rev. C. T. P. Grierson, Bishop of Down and Connor and

Dromore; *m* 1946, Kathleen Blanche McClintock, MB, BS, *e d* of Rev. E. L. L. McClintock; three *s. Educ:* Stowe School. Singapore Volunteer Corps, 1939-45, POW Singapore, 1942-45. Commerce, London, 1933-38 and Malaya, 1938-56. Dir, Dunlop Malayan Estates Ltd, 1952-56; Man. Dir, Lyle and Kinahan Ltd, Belfast, 1956-63. Mem. (Alliance) Antrim S, NI Constitutional Convention, 1975-76. Belfast Harbour Comr, 1966-; Chm., 1969-73, Pres., 1975, NI Marriage Guidance Council; Mem. Senate, QUB, 1968-; Chairman: NI Historic Buildings Council, 1973-; Ulster '71 Exhibn, 1971; NI Mountain Rescue Working Party. JP 1961, High Sheriff 1971, Co. Antrim; Mem., Antrim District Council (Alliance Party), 1976-. *Recreations:* mountain trekking, farming, classical music. *Address:* Carrigeen Lodge, Parkgate, Templepatrick, Co. Antrim. *T:* Templepatrick 32379. *Club:* Royal Over-Seas League.
   See also Sir R. G. C. Kinahan.

KINAHAN, Adm. Sir Harold (Richard George), KBE 1949 (CBE 1942); CB 1945; retired; *b* 4 June 1893; *s* of Vice-Adm. R. G. Kinahan, Belfast; *m* 1919, Mary Kathleen Downes (*d* 1970); two *d. Educ:* RN Colls, Osborne and Dartmouth. Entered RNC, Osborne, 1906; Lt 1914; Comdr 1927; Capt. 1934; Rear-Adm. 1943; Vice-Adm. 1947; Adm. 1950. DPS, Admiralty, 1944-46; Flag Officer Comdg 1st Cruiser Sqdn, Mediterranean Fleet, 1946-47; Vice-Pres., 1947-49, Pres., 1949-50, Ordnance Board; Pres., RNC, Greenwich, 1950-52; retired list, 1952. *Address:* Severnridge, Almondsbury, Bristol.

KINAHAN, Sir Robert (George Caldwell), (Sir Robin Kinahan), Kt 1961; ERD 1946; JP; DL; Chairman: Ulster Bank Ltd; Bass Ireland Ltd; Inglis & Co Ltd; E. T. Green Ltd; Director: National Westminster Bank Ltd; Gallaher Ltd; Eagle Star Insurance Co. Ltd (local); Standard Telephones and Cables (Northern Ireland) Ltd; *b* 24 Sept. 1916; *s* of Henry Kinahan, Lowwood, Belfast; *m* 1950, Coralie I., *d* of late Capt. C. de Burgh, DSO, RN; two *s* three *d. Educ:* Stowe Sch., Buckingham. Vintners' Scholar (London), 1937. Served Royal Artillery, 1939-45, Capt. Councillor, Belfast Corporation, 1948; JP Co. Antrim, 1950, DL 1962; High Sheriff: Belfast, 1956; Co. Antrim, 1969. Mem. N Ireland Adv. Commn, 1972-73. MP (N Ireland), Clifton constituency, 1958-59. Lord Mayor of Belfast, 1959-61. Hon. LLD (Belfast) 1962. *Recreations:* gardening, family life. *Address:* Castle Upton, Templepatrick, Co. Antrim. *T:* Templepatrick 32466. *Clubs:* Ulster (Belfast); Kildare Street and University (Dublin).
   See also C. H. G. Kinahan.

KINCH, Anthony Alec; Head of Division for Food Processing Industries, Commission of the European Communities, since 1973; *b* 13 Dec. 1926; *s* of E. A. Kinch, OBE, retd Polit. Adviser, Iraq Petroleum Co. Ltd, and C. T. Kinch (*née* Cassidy); *m* 1952, Barbara Patricia (*née* Paton Walsh); four *s* two *d. Educ:* Ampleforth; Christ Church, Oxford (MA). Practised at Bar, 1951-57; Contracts Man., Electronics Div., Plessey Co. Ltd, 1957-60; Legal Adviser and Insce Consultant, R. & H. Green and Silley Weir Ltd, 1960-66; Dir, Fedn of Bakers, 1966-73. KHS. *Recreation:* living. *Address:* Commission of the European Communities, 200 Rue de la Loi, 1049 Brussels, Belgium. *T:* 735-00-40, ext. 1531.

KINCHIN SMITH, Michael; Controller, Development, Personnel, BBC, since 1976; *b* 8 May 1921; *s* of Francis John Kinchin Smith, Lectr in Classics, Inst. of Educn, London, and Dione Jean Elizabeth, *d* of Sir Francis Henry May, GCMG, sometime Governor of Hong Kong; *m* 1947, Rachel Frances, *er d* of Rt Hon. Sir Henry Urmston Willink, Bt, MC, QC, Master of Magdalene Coll., Cambridge; four *s* two *d. Educ:* Westminster Sch. (King's Schol.); Christ Church, Oxford (Schol.). 1st cl. hons Mod. History; Pres. Oxford Union, 1944. Served with 2nd and 3rd Bns, Coldstream Guards in Italian Campaign (Captain; despatches). Commercial and Admin. Trainee, ICI Ltd, 1947; joined BBC as Asst, Staff Admin, 1950; Admin Officer, Talks (Sound), 1954; Asst Estabt Officer, TV, 1955; Estabt Officer, Programmes, TV, 1961; Staff Admin Officer, 1962; Asst Controller, Staff Admin, 1964; Controller, Staff Admin, 1967. Chm. Exec. Council, RIPA, 1975-77 (Vice-Chm. 1973-75); FIPM (Mem. Nat. Cttee on Payment and Employment Conditions, 1974-); Lay Selector, ACCM, 1963-73 (Mem. Candidates Cttee, 1966-69); Lay Chm., Richmond and Barnes Deanery Synod, 1970-76; Mem. General Synod, C of E, 1975-; 1st Chm., Mortlake with East Sheen Soc., 1969-71; Chm., Assoc. of Amenity Societies in Richmond-upon-Thames, 1973-77. *Publication:* (jtly) Forward from Victory, 1943. *Recreations:* walking, local history. *Address:* 17 Temple Sheen Road, SW14 7PY. *T:* 01-876 5301.

KINCRAIG, Hon. Lord; Robert Smith Johnston; a Senator of the College of Justice in Scotland, since 1972; *b* 10 Oct. 1918; *s* of W. T. Johnston, iron merchant, Glasgow; *m* 1943, Joan, *d* of late Col A. G. Graham, Glasgow; one *s* one *d. Educ:* Strathallan, Perthshire; St John's Coll., Cambridge; Glasgow Univ. BA (Hons) Cantab, 1939; LLB (with distinction) Glasgow, 1942. Mem. of Faculty of Advocates, 1942; Advocate-Depute, Crown Office, 1953-55; QC (Scotland) 1955; Home Advocate Depute, 1959-62; Sheriff of Roxburgh, Berwick and Selkirk, 1964-70; Dean of the Faculty of Advocates of Scotland, 1970-72. Contested (U) Stirling and Falkirk Burghs General Election, 1959. *Recreation:* golf. *Address:* Westwood, Longniddry, East Lothian. *Club:* Hon. Company of Edinburgh Golfers (Edinburgh).

KINDERSLEY, family name of Baron Kindersley.

KINDERSLEY, 3rd Baron *cr* 1941; **Robert Hugh Molesworth Kindersley;** Director: Lazard Bros & Co. Ltd; Sun Alliance & London Insurance Group; Swedish Match Company; Witan Investment Co. Ltd; *b* 18 Aug. 1929; *s* of 2nd Baron Kindersley, CBE, MC, and Nancy Farnsworth (*d* 1977), *d* of Dr Geoffrey Boyd, Toronto; *S* father, 1976; *m* 1954, Venice Marigold (Rosie), *d* of late Captain Lord (Arthur) Francis Henry Hill; three *s* one *d. Educ:* Eton; Trinity Coll., Oxford; Harvard Business Sch., USA. Lt Scots Guards; served Malaya, 1948-49. *Heir: s* Hon. Rupert John Molesworth Kindersley [*b* 11 March 1955; *m* 1975, Sarah, *d* of late John D. Warde]. *Address:* Ramhurst Manor, near Tonbridge, Kent.

KINDERSLEY, David Guy; stone-carver and designer of alphabets (self-employed); *b* 11 June 1915; *s* of Guy Molesworth Kindersley and Kathleen Elton; *m* 1957, Barbara Pym Eyre Petrie; two *s* one *d. Educ:* St Cyprian's, Eastbourne (prep. sch.); Marlborough Coll., Wilts. Apprenticed to Eric Gill, ARA, 1933-36. Taught at Cambridge Coll. of Arts and Technology, 1946-57; one-time adviser to MoT on street-name alphabets; adviser to Shell Film Unit on design of titles, 1949-58; consultant to Letraset Internat., 1964-; Sen. Research Fellow, William Andrews Clark Memorial Library, Univ. of California, Los Angeles, 1967. Chm., Wynkyn de Worde Soc., 1976. *Publications:* Optical Letter Spacing and its Mechanical Application, 1966 (rev. and repub. by Wynkyn de Worde Soc., 1976); Mr Eric Gill, 1967; contribs to Printing Technology, Penrose Annual, Visible Language. Limited edns: Variations on the Theme of 26 Letters, edn 50, 1969; Graphic Sayings, edn 130, 1973; State Cut, edn 250, 1978. *Recreation:* archaeology. *Address:* 45 Highworth Avenue, Cambridge CB4 2BQ. *T:* Cambridge 57349. *Clubs:* Arts, Double Crown; (Hon. Mem.) Rounce and Coffin (Los Angeles).

KING, family name of Earl of Lovelace.

KING; *see* Maybray-King.

KING, Sir Albert, Kt 1974; OBE 1958; Leader, Labour Group, Leeds Metropolitan District Council, since 1975 (Leader of the Council with one break, 1958-75); *b* 20 Aug. 1905; *s* of George and Ann King; *m* 1928, Pauline Riley; one *d. Educ:* Primrose Hill, Leeds. Full-time officer, engrg, 1942-70, retd. Hon. Freedom of the City of Leeds, 1976. *Recreations:* walking, reading. *Address:* 25 Brook Hill Avenue, Leeds LS17 8QA. *T:* Leeds 684684. *Clubs:* Beeston Working Men's, East Leeds Labour (Leeds).

KING, Albert Leslie, MBE 1945; *b* 28 Aug. 1911; *s* of late William John King and of Elizabeth Mary Amelia King; *m* 1938, Constance Eileen Stroud; two *d. Educ:* University Coll. Sch., Hampstead. Joined Shell-Mex and BP Statistical Dept, 1928. Joined Territorial Army, 1939; Major, RA, 1944. Manager, Secretariat, Petroleum Board, 1947; Manager, Trade Relations Dept, Shell-Mex and BP Ltd, 1948; Gen. Manager: Administration, 1954; Sales, 1957; Operations, 1961; apptd Dir, 1962, Managing Dir, 1963-66. Dep. Dir-Gen., BIM, 1966-68. FCCA 1965. Hon. JDipMA, 1965. *Address:* Highlands, 50 Waggon Road, Hadley Wood, Barnet, Herts. *T:* 01-449 6424. *Clubs:* MCC; Surrey CCC, Saracens.

KING, Alexander, CMG 1975; CBE 1948; Chairman, International Federation of Institutes for Advanced Study, since 1974; *b* Glasgow, 26 Jan. 1909; *s* of J. M. King; *m* 1933, Sarah Maskell Thompson; three *d. Educ:* Highgate Sch.; Royal College of Science, London (DSc); University of Munich. Demonstrator, 1932, and later Senior Lecturer, until 1940, in physical chemistry, Imperial Coll. of Science; Dep. Scientific Adviser, Min. of Production, 1942; Head of UK Scientific Mission, Washington, and Scientific Attaché, British Embassy 1943-47; Head of Lord President's Scientific Secretariat, 1947-50; Chief

Scientific Officer, Dept of Scientific and Industrial Research, 1950-56; Dep. Dir, European Productivity Agency, 1956-61; Dir for Scientific Affairs, OECD, 1961-68, Dir-Gen., 1968-74. Adviser, Govt of Ontario. Assoc. Fellow, Center for the Study of Democratic Institutions, Santa Barbara, Calif. Leader Imperial Coll. Expedition to Jan Mayen, 1938; Harrison Prize of Chemical Soc., 1938; Gill Memorial Prize, Royal Geographical Society, 1938, Mem. Council, 1939-41; Hon. Sec. Chemical Soc., 1948-50; Founder and Exec. Mem., Club of Rome. DSc (hc) Ireland, 1974; Hon. DUniv Open, 1976. *Publications:* various chemistry textbooks, and papers in Journal of The Chemical Soc., Faraday Soc.; numerous articles on education, science policy and management. *Address:* 168 Rue de Grenelle, Paris 75007, France. *Club:* Athenæum.

KING, Alexander Hyatt; musical scholar; a Deputy Keeper, Department of Printed Books, British Museum, 1959-76, retired; *b* 18 July 1911; *s* of Thomas Hyatt King and Mabel Jessie (*née* Brayne); *m* 1943, Evelyn Mary Davies; two *s*. *Educ:* Dulwich Coll.; King's Coll., Cambridge (schol.; MA). Entered Dept of Printed Books, British Museum, 1934; Dep. Keeper, 1959-76; Supt of Music Room, 1944-73; Music Librarian, Ref. Div., British Library, 1973-76. Hon. Sec., British Union Catalogue of Early Music, 1948-57; Mem. Council, Royal Musical Assoc., 1949-, Editor, Proc. of the Assoc., 1952-57, Pres., 1974-; Pres. Internat. Assoc. of Music Libraries, 1955-59 (Hon. Mem., 1968), Pres., UK Br., 1953-68, Vice-Chm. jt cttee, Internat. Musicological Soc. and IAML, for Internat. Inventory of Musical Sources, 1961-76; Chm., exec. cttee, Brit. Inst. of Recorded Sound, 1951-62. Sandars Reader in Bibliography, Univ. of Cambridge, 1962; Vice-Chm., exec. cttee, Grove's Dictionary of Music, 1970-74; Trustee, Hinrichsen Foundn, 1976-; Hon. Librarian, Royal Philharmonic Soc., 1970-. Mem., Zentralinst. für Mozartforschung, 1953. *Publications:* Chamber Music, 1948; (jtly) catalogue: Music in the Hirsch Library, 1951; catalogue: Exhibition of Handel's Messiah, 1951; Mozart in Retrospect, 1955, 3rd edn 1976; Mozart in the British Museum, 1956, repr. 1975; exhibn catalogue: Henry Purcell—G. F. Handel, 1959; Some British Collectors of Music, 1963; 400 Years of Music Printing, 1964, 2nd edn 1968; Handel and his Autographs, 1967; Mozart Chamber Music, 1968, 2nd edn 1970; Mozart String and Wind Concertos, 1977; *edited:* (jtly) Mozart's Duet Sonata in C K19d, 1953; illustr. edn of Alfred Einstein's Short History of Music, 1953; P. K. Hoffmann's Cadenzas and elaborated slow movements to 6 Mozart piano concertos, 1959; (jtly) 2nd edn of Emily Anderson's Letters of Mozart and his Family, 1966; Concert Goer's Companion series, 1970-; Auction catalogues of Music, 1973-; *contribs to:* Year's Work in Music, 1947-51; Schubert, a symposium, 1947; Grove's Dictionary, 5th edn 1954; Music, Libraries and Instruments, 1961; Deutsch Festschrift, 1963; Essays in honour of Victor Scholderer, 1970; Grasberger Festschrift, 1975; Essays in honour of Sir Jack Westrup, 1976; various articles. *Recreations:* watching cricket, opera, exploring Suffolk. *Address:* 29 Lauradale Road, N2 9LT. *T:* 01-883 1623. *Club:* MCC.

KING, Alison; Co-ordinator Properties, since 1974, and Director/Administrator, Premises, since 1969, Women's Royal Voluntary Service. Flight-Capt., Operations, Air Transport Auxiliary, 1940-45. Dir, Women's Junior Air Corps, 1952-58; Gen. Sec., NFWI, 1959-69. Chm., British Women Pilots' Assoc., 1956-64. *Publication:* Golden Wings, 1956 (repr. 1975). *Recreations:* writing, painting in oils. *Address:* 4 Chagford House, Chagford Street, NW1. *T:* 01-262 4631. *Club:* University Women's.

KING, Prof. Anthony Stephen; Professor of Government, University of Essex, since 1969; *b* 17 Nov. 1934; *o s* of late Harold and of Marjorie King; *m* 1965, Vera Korte (*d* 1971). *Educ:* Queen's Univ., Kingston Ont. (1st Cl. Hons, Hist. 1956); Magdalen Coll., Oxford (Rhodes Schol.; 1st Cl. Hons, PPE, 1958). Student, Nuffield Coll., Oxford, 1958-61; DPhil (Oxon) 1962. Fellow of Magdalen Coll., Oxford, 1961-65; Amer. Council of Learned Societies Fellow, Columbia Univ., NY, 1962-63; Vis. Prof., Univ. of Wisconsin, 1967; Fellow, Center for Advanced Study in the Behavioral Scis, Stanford, Calif., 1977-78. Elections Commentator, BBC and Observer; Univ. of Essex: Sen. Lectr, 1966-68; Reader, 1968-69. Editor, British Jl of Political Science, 1972-77. *Publications:* (with D. E. Butler) The British General Election of 1964, 1965; (with D. E. Butler) The British General Election of 1966, 1966; (ed) British Politics: People, Parties and Parliament, 1966; (ed) The British Prime Minister, 1969; (with Anne Sloman) Westminster and Beyond, 1973; British Members of Parliament: a self-portrait, 1974; (ed) Why is Britain becoming Harder to Govern?, 1976; Britain Says Yes: the 1975 referendum on the Common Market, 1977; frequent contributor to British and American jls and periodicals. *Recreations:* music, theatre, holidays, walking. *Address:*

Department of Government, University of Essex, Wivenhoe Park, Colchester, Essex CO4 3SQ. *T:* Colchester 44144; The Mill House, Middle Green, Wakes Colne, Colchester, Essex CO6 2BP. *T:* Earls Colne 2497. *Club:* United Oxford & Cambridge University.

KING, Prof. Basil Charles; Professor of Geology, Bedford College, University of London, 1956-77, now Emeritus; *b* 1 June 1915; *s* of Charles William Argent King; *m* 1939, Dorothy Margaret Wells; two *s* two *d*. *Educ:* King Edward VI Sch., Bury St Edmunds; Durham Univ.; London Univ. Demonstrator, Bedford Coll., London, 1936-38; Chemist and Petrologist, Geological Survey of Uganda, 1938-46; Mineralogist, Geological Survey of Nigeria, 1946-48; Senior Lecturer, University of Glasgow, 1948-56. FRSE 1950. Bigsby Medal, Geological Soc., 1959; André Dumont Medal, Société Géologique de Belgique, 1967; Murchison Medal, Geological Soc., 1971. *Publications:* geological publications on E Africa, Nigeria, Botswana and Scotland. *Address:* 1 Catacol, Lochranza, Isle of Arran, Scotland. *T:* Lochranza 658.

KING, Dr Brian Edmund; Director, since 1967, and Chief Executive, since 1977, Wira (formerly Wool Industries Research Association); *b* 25 May 1928; *s* of Albert Theodore King and Gladys Johnson; *m* 1952 (marr. diss.); two *s*; *m* 1972, Eunice Wolstenholme; one *d*. *Educ:* Pocklington Sch.; Leeds Univ. TMM (Research) Ltd, 1952-57; British Oxygen, 1957-67. *Recreations:* bridge, swimming, tennis. *Address:* 8 Bankfield, Shelley, Huddersfield, W Yorks HD8 8JA. *T:* Kirkburton 4613.

KING, Cecil Edward; *b* 1912; *m* 1944, Isabel Haynes; two *s* one *d*. *Educ:* conventionally, 1917-33. Joined HM Consular Service, 1934; served in Europe, North and South America, W Africa, Middle East; pensioned off 1970. Mem., UN Joint Inspection Unit, Geneva, 1972-77. *Address:* c/o National Westminster Bank Ltd, 208 Piccadilly, W1A 2DG.

KING, Cecil (Harmsworth); *b* 20 Feb. 1901; *e* surv. *s* of Sir Lucas White King, CSI, and Geraldine Adelaide Hamilton, *d* of Alfred Harmsworth, barrister of the Middle Temple; *m* 1st, 1923, Agnes Margaret, *d* of the Rev. Canon G. A. Cooke, DD, Regius Prof. of Hebrew, Oxford, and Canon of Christ Church; two *s* one *d* (and one *s* decd). 2nd, 1962, Dame Ruth Railton, *qv*. *Educ:* Winchester; Christ Church, Oxford (2nd class hons history, MA). Dir, Daily Mirror, 1929; Dep. Chm., Sunday Pictorial, 1942; Chairman: Daily Mirror Newspapers Ltd and Sunday Pictorial Newspapers Ltd, 1951-1963; International Publishing Corp., 1963-68; The Reed Paper Group, 1963-68; Wall Paper Manufacturers, 1965-67; British Film Institute, 1948-52; Newspaper Proprietors' Assoc., 1961-68; Nigerian Printing & Publishing Co., 1948-68; Butterworth & Co. Ltd, 1968. Director: Reuters, 1953-59; Bank of England, 1965-68. Part-time Mem., National Coal Board, 1966-69. Mem., National Parks Commn, later Countryside Commn, 1966-69. Gold Badge for services to City of Warsaw; Gold Medal for services to British paper trade. Hon. DLitt Boston, 1974. *Publications:* The Future of the Press, 1967; Strictly Personal, 1969; With Malice Towards None: a war diary, 1970; Without Fear or Favour, 1971; The Cecil King Diary 1965-70, 1972; On Ireland, 1973; The Cecil King Diary 1970-74, 1975. *Recreation:* reading. *Address:* 23 Greenfield Park, Dublin 4, Ireland. *T:* Dublin 695870.

See also Sir G . V . K . Burton .

KING, Charles Andrew Buchanan, CMG 1961; MBE 1944; HM Diplomatic Service, retired; Chairman, Premier Sauna Ltd; *b* 25 July 1915; *s* of late Major Andrew Buchanan King, 7th Argyll and Sutherland Highlanders and of Evelyn Nina (*née* Sharpe). *Educ:* Wellington Coll.; Magdalene Coll., Cambridge (MA). Vice-Consul: Zürich, 1940, Geneva, 1941; Attaché, HM Legation, Berne, 1942; transf. to FO, 1946; 2nd Sec., Vienna, 1950; transf. to FO 1953; to Hong Kong, 1958; to FO 1961; retired, 1967; Head of W European Div., Overseas Dept, London Chamber of Commerce, 1968-70. *Recreation:* travel. *Address:* 19 Archery Close, W2. *Club:* Bath.

KING, Charles Martin M.; *see* Meade-King.

KING, Colin Sainthill Wallis-; *see* Wallis-King.

KING, Rev. Cuthbert, CIE 1946; MA Oxon; ICS (retired); *b* 27 Jan. 1889; *s* of Rev. E. G. King, DD, and Mary, *d* of Rt Rev. B. F. Westcott, Durham; *m* 1921, Elsie Vivienne (*née* Harris), MBE 1946, K-i-H (1st Cl.) 1936 (*d* 1960). *Educ:* Sherborne Sch.; Christ Church, Oxford; Göttingen; Trinity Coll., Dublin. Indian Civil Service (Punjab), 1913-47; last appointments as Commissioner of Multan, Lahore and Rawalpindi Divs. On Military Service, IARO, 1917-20. Mem. of Order of Cloud and

Banner (Chinese), 1945. Deacon, 1949; Priest, 1950. *Recreations:* golf, literature, languages, art. *Address:* c/o Lloyds Bank, Richmond, Surrey.

KING, Prof. David Anthony, FRIC, MInstP; Brunner Professor of Physical Chemistry, University of Liverpool, since 1974; *b* 12 Aug. 1939; *s* of Arnold King and Patricia (*née* Vardy), Durban; *m* 1971, Anne Julia (*née* Donat); two *s*. *Educ:* St John's Coll., Johannesburg; Univ. of the Witwatersrand, Johannesburg. BSc, PhD (Rand), ScD (E Anglia). Shell Scholar, Imperial Coll., 1963-66; Lectr in Chemical Physics, Univ. of E Anglia, Norwich, 1966-74. Member: Comité de Direction of Centre de Cinétique Physique et Chimique, Nancy, 1974-; Nat. Exec., Assoc. of Univ. Teachers, 1970 (Nat. Pres., 1976-77). Mem. Editorial Bd, Jl of Physics C, 1977-. *Publications:* papers on the physics and chemistry of solid surfaces in: Proc. Royal Soc., Surface Science, Jl Chem. Soc., Jl of Physics, etc. *Recreations:* photography, reading, squash. *Address:* 18 Eaton Road, Liverpool L19 0PW. *T:* (home) 051-427 9498, (office) 051-709 6022 (ext. 2560).

KING, Prof. Edmund James, MA, PhD, DLit; Professor of Education, University of London King's College, since 1975; *b* 19 June 1914; *s* of James and Mary Alice King; *m* 1939, Margaret Mary Breakell; one *s* three *d*. *Educ:* Univ. of Manchester (BA, MA); Univ. of London (PhD, DLit). Taught in grammar schs, 1936-47; Asst, then Sen. Asst to Dir of Extra-Mural Studies, Univ. of London, 1947-53; Lectr, subseq. Reader, Univ. of London King's Coll., 1953-75, also Dir, Comparative Research Unit, King's Coll., 1970-73. Visiting appts at Amer. and Can. univs; also in Melbourne, Tokyo, Tehran, etc; lecturing and adv. assignments in many countries. *Publications:* Other Schools and Ours, 1958, 4th edn 1973; World Perspectives in Education, 1962, 2nd edn 1965; (ed) Communist Education, 1963; Society, Schools and Progress in the USA, 1965; Education and Social Change, 1966; Comparative Studies and Educational Decision, 1968; Education and Development in Western Europe, 1969; (ed) The Teacher and the Needs of Society, 1970; The Education of Teachers: a comparative analysis, 1970; (with W. Boyd) A History of Western Education, 1972; Post-compulsory Education, vol. I: a new analysis in Western Europe, 1974; vol. II: the way ahead, 1975 (both with C. H. Moor and J. A. Mundy); (ed) Reorganizing Education, 1977. *Recreations:* gardening, music, writing. *Address:* 40 Alexandra Road, Epsom, Surrey.

KING, Very Rev. Edward Laurie; Dean of Cape Town since 1958; *b* 30 Jan. 1920; *s* of William Henry and Norah Alice King; *m* 1950, Helen Stuart Mathers, MB, BCh, MMed; two *s* three *d*. *Educ:* King's Coll., Taunton; University of Wales (BA). Deacon, 1945; priest, 1946, Monmouth; Associate in Theology (S Af.). Curate of Risca, 1945-48; Diocese of Johannesburg, 1948-50; Rector of Robertson, Cape, 1950-53; Rector of Stellenbosch, 1953-58. *Recreations:* cricket, reading. *Address:* The Deanery, Upper Orange Street, Cape Town, South Africa. *T:* 45-2609. *Club:* City.

KING, Evelyn Mansfield, MA; MP (C) South Dorset since 1964; *b* 30 May 1907; *s* of Harry Percy King and Winifred Elizabeth Paulet; *m* 1935, Clare Arthur Felton Crutchley, DSO; one *s* two *d*. *Educ:* Cheltenham Coll.; King's Coll., Cambridge; Inner Temple. Cambridge Univ. Correspondent to the Sunday Times, 1928-30; Asst Master Bedford Sch., 1930; Headmaster and Warden, Clayesmore Sch., 1935-50; Gloucestershire Regt 1940; Acting Lt-Col 1941. MP (Lab) Penryn and Falmouth Div. of Cornwall, 1945-50; Parly Sec., Min. of Town and Country Planning, 1947-50. Resigned from Labour Party, 1951, and joined Conservative Party; contested (C) Southampton (Itchen), 1959. Member of Parly delegations: Bermuda and Washington, 1946; Tokyo, 1947; Cairo and ME, 1967; Jordan and Persian Gulf, 1968; Kenya and Seychelles, 1969; Malta, 1970 (leader); Malawi, 1971 (leader); Mem. Select Cttee on Overseas Aid, 1971; Chm. Food Cttee, 1971-73. *Publications:* (with J. C. Trewin) Printer to the House, Biography of Luke Hansard, 1952. *Recreations:* farming, riding. *Address:* Embley Manor, near Romsey, Hants. *T:* Romsey 512342; 11 Barton Street, SW1. *T:* 01-222 4525; Athelhampton, Dorset. *Clubs:* Carlton; Royal Dorset Yacht (Weymouth).
See also R. G. Cooke.

KING, Francis Henry, FRSL; Author; *b* 4 March 1923; *o s* of Eustace Arthur Cecil King and Faith Mina Read. *Educ:* Shrewsbury; Balliol Coll., Oxford. Chm., Soc. of Authors, 1975-77. *Publications:* novels: To the Dark Tower, 1946; Never Again, 1947; An Air That Kills, 1948; The Dividing Stream, 1951 (Somerset Maugham Award, 1952); The Dark Glasses, 1954; The Widow, 1957; The Man on the Rock, 1957; So Hurt

and Humiliated (short stories), 1959; The Custom House, 1961; The Japanese Umbrella (short stories), 1964 (Katherine Mansfield Short Story Prize, 1965); The Last of the Pleasure Gardens, 1965; The Waves Behind the Boat, 1967; The Brighton Belle (short stories), 1968; A Domestic Animal, 1970; Flights (two short novels), 1973; A Game of Patience, 1974; The Needle, 1975; Hard Feelings (short stories), 1976; Danny Hill, 1977; *poetry:* Rod of Incantation, 1952; *general* (ed): Introducing Greece, 1956; Japan, 1970. *Address:* 19 Gordon Place, W8 4JE. *T:* 01-937 5715. *Club:* PEN.

KING, Gen. Sir Frank (Douglas), GCB 1976 [KCB 1972; CB 1971); MBE 1953; Commander, Northern Army Group, and C-in-C BAOR, since 1976; ADC General to the Queen, since 1977; *b* 9 March 1919; *s* of Arthur King, Farmer, and Kate Eliza (*née* Sheard), Brightwell, Berks; *m* 1947, Joy Emily Ellen Taylor-Lane; one *s* two *d*. *Educ:* Wallingford Gram. Sch. Joined Army, 1939; commnd into Royal Fusiliers, 1940; Parachute Regt, 1943; dropped Arnhem, Sept. 1944; Royal Military College of Science (ptsc), 1946; Staff Coll., Camberley (psc), 1950; comd 2 Parachute Bn, Middle East, 1960-62; comd 11 Infantry Bde Gp, Germany, 1963-64; Military Adviser (Overseas Equipment), 1965-66; Dir, Land/Air Warfare, MoD, 1967-68; Dir, Military Assistance Overseas, MoD, 1968-69; Comdt, RMCS, 1969-71; GOC-in-C, Army Strategic Comd, 1971-72; Dep. C-in-C UK Land Forces, 1972-73; GOC and Dir of Ops, N Ireland, 1973-75. Col Comdt, Army Air Corps, 1974-. Kermit Roosevelt Lectr, 1977. *Recreations:* golf, gardening, flying. *Address:* c/o Williams and Glyn's Bank, Columbia House, 69 Aldwych, WC2. *Club:* Berkshire Golf.

KING, Frank Gordon, QC 1970; *b* 10 March 1915; *s* of late Lt-Col Frank King, DSO, OBE; *m* 1937, Monica Beatrice, *d* of late Arthur Collins; two *s* one *d*. *Educ:* Charterhouse, Godalming; Christ's Coll., Cambridge (BA 1936, LLB 1933). Served War of 1939-45; RA 1939-46, Major 1943. Called to the Bar, Gray's Inn, 1946. A Church Commissioner, 1973-. *Address:* 24 Old Buildings, Lincoln's Inn, WC2. *T:* 01-405 1124; Red Chimneys, Warren Drive, Kingswood, Surrey. *Club:* Walton Heath Golf.

KING, Frederick Ernest, FRS 1954; MA, DPhil DSc Oxon; PhD London; Scientific Adviser to British Petroleum Co. Ltd, 1959-71, retired; *er s* of late Frederick and Elizabeth King, Bexhill, Sussex. *Educ:* Bancroft's Sch.; University of London; Oriel Coll., Oxford. Ramsay Memorial Fellow, 1930-31; Demonstrator, Dyson Perrins Laboratory, 1931-34; University Lecturer and Demonstrator in Chemistry, Oxford Univ., 1934-48, and sometime lecturer in Organic Chemistry, Magdalen Coll. and Balliol Coll.; Sir Jesse Boot Prof. of Chemistry, University of Nottingham, 1948-55; Dir in charge of research, British Celanese Ltd, 1955-59. Fellow Queen Mary Coll., 1955. *Publications:* scientific papers mainly in Jl of Chem. Soc. *Recreations:* mountaineering, gardening. *Address:* 360 The Water Gardens, W2; Glyde's Farm, Ashburnham, East Sussex. *Club:* Athenæum.

KING, Sir Geoffrey Stuart, KCB 1953 (CB 1943); KBE 1946; MC 1918; Civil Service, retired. *b* 1894; *s* of late Charles James Stuart King, Chardstock, Devon; *m* 1920, Ethel Eileen May, *y d* of late D. C. M. Tuke, Chiswick House; four *s*. Sec. Assistance Bd, 1944-48; Dep. Sec., Ministry of National Insurance, 1949-51; Permanent Sec., Ministry of Pensions and National Insurance, 1953-55 (Ministry of National Insurance, 1951); retired, 1955. *Address:* Oliver's Farm, Ash, near Sevenoaks, Kent TN15 7HT.

KING, Mrs Grace M. H.; *see* Hamilton-King.

KING, Hilary William, CBE 1964 (MBE 1944); HM Diplomatic Service, retired; *b* 10 March 1919; *s* of Dr W. H. King, Fowey, Cornwall; *m* 1947, Dr Margaret Helen Grierson Borrowman; one *s* three *d*. *Educ:* Sherborne; Corpus Christi Coll. Cambridge. Served War of 1939-45 (MBE). Apptd Mem. Foreign (subseq. Diplomatic) Service, Nov. 1946. A Vice-Consul and Acting Consul in Yugoslavia, 1947-48; apptd 2nd Sec., 1947; transferred to Foreign Office, 1949; promoted 1st Sec., 1950; transf. to Vienna as a Russian Sec., 1951; 1st Sec., Washington, 1953; transf. Foreign Office, 1958; Commercial Counsellor, Moscow, 1959; acted as Chargé d'Affaires, 1960; Ambassador (and Consul-Gen.) to Guinea, 1962-65; St Antony's Coll., Oxford, Oct. 1965-June 1966; Counsellor of Embassy, Warsaw, 1966-67; Head of UN (Economic and Social) Dept, FCO, 1968-71; Consul-Gen., Hamburg, 1971-74. *Recreation:* sailing. *Address:* Fuaim an Sruth, South Cuan, Oban, Argyll PA34 4TU. *Club:* Clyde Cruising.

KING, Ivor Edward, CB 1961; CBE 1943; CEng, FRINA; Royal Corps of Naval Constructors; Director of Dockyards,

Admiralty, 1958-61; b 1899; s of John and Minnie Elizabeth King, Pembroke Dock; m 1923, Doris, d of John and Catherine Hill, Lee, SE; three d. Educ: Royal Naval College, Greenwich. Formerly Manager, HM Dockyards, Portsmouth, Malta, Sheerness and Bermuda. Constructor Capt. to Commander-in-Chief, Mediterranean, 1942-44. Served War, 1942-44 (CBE). Hon. Vice-Pres., Royal Institution of Naval Architects. Recreation: golf. Address: 10 Combe Park, Bath BA1 3NP. T: Bath 23047.

KING, Sir James Granville Le Neve, 3rd Bt, cr 1888; TD; b 17 Sept. 1898; s of Sir John Westall King, 2nd Bt, and Frances Rosa (d 1942), d of John Neve, Oaken, Staffs; S father 1940; m 1928, Penelope Charlotte, a of late Capt. E. Cooper-Key, CB, MVO, RN; one s two d. Educ: Eton; King's Coll., Cambridge. Heir: s John Christopher King [b 31 March 1933; m 1958, Patricia Monica (marr. diss. 1972), o d of late Lt-Col Kingsley Foster and of Mrs Foster, Hampton Court Palace; one s one d]. Address: Church Farm House, Chilbolton, Hants. Club: Brooks's.
See also Sir Neill Cooper-Key.

KING, Prof. James Lawrence; Regius Professor of Engineering, University of Edinburgh, since 1968; b 14 Feb. 1922; s of Lawrence Aubrey King and Wilhelmina Young McLeish; m 1951, Pamela Mary Ward Hitchcock; one s one d. Educ: Latymer Upper Sch.; Jesus Coll., Cambridge; Imperial Coll., London. Min. of Defence (Navy), 1942-68. Recreation: walking. Address: 2 Arboretum Road, Edinburgh EH3 5PD. T: 031-552 3854.

KING, Prof. Jeffrey William Hitchen, MSc, CEng, FICE, FIStructE; Professor of Civil Engineering, Queen Mary College, University of London, 1953-72, now Emeritus Professor; b 28 Sept. 1906; s of George and Edith King, Wigan; m 1930, Phyllis Morfydd Harris, d of Rev. W. Harris; one s one d. Educ: Ashton-in-Makerfield Grammar Sch.; Manchester Univ. Engineer and Agent to Cementation Co. Ltd, British Isles, Spain and Egypt, 1927-36; Research Engineer, Michelin Tyre Co. 1936-37; Lecturer in Civil Engineering, University Coll., Nottingham, 1937-47; Reader in Civil Engineering, Queen Mary Coll., London, 1947-53. Governor, Queen Mary Coll., 1962-65; formerly Mem., Academic Board and Vice-Chm., Civil Engineering Cttee of Regional Advisory Council for Higher Technological Education; formerly mem., Research Cttee, formerly Chm., Concrete Specification Cttee and Cttee on Accelerated Testing of Concrete, Instn of Civil Engineers; formerly Mem. BSI Cttees, CEB/4/4, CEB/21. Publications: papers in Journals of Instn of Civil Engineers, Instn of Structural Engineers, and Inst. of Mine Surveyors, and in various technical periodicals. Recreations: many and varied. Address: The Nook, Crayke Road, Easingwold, York YO6 3PN. T: Easingwold 21151.

KING, John George Maydon, CMG 1959; OBE 1953 (MBE 1945); retired from Colonial Agricultural Service; b 26 Jan. 1908; 2nd s of late Harold Edwin and Elizabeth Lindsay King, Durban, Natal, SA; m 1st, 1938, Françoise Charlotte de Rham (d 1966), Lausanne; two s; 2nd, 1970, Violet, widow of Colin MacPherson, late of Tanganyika Administration Service. Educ: University Coll. Sch. (Preparatory); Oundle Sch.; London Univ. (Wye Coll.); Cambridge Univ. (Colonial Office Schol., Cambridge Univ. and Imperial Coll. of Tropical Agric.). Appointed to Colonial Agricultural Service as Agricultural Officer, Tanganyika, 1932-46; seconded to Cambridge Univ. as Lecturer in Tropical Agric. to Colonial Services Courses, 1946-48; Dir of livestock and Agricultural Services, Basutoland, 1948-54; Dir of Agriculture, Uganda, 1954-60, Swaziland, 1960-63; Regional Manager, Lower Indus Project, Hyderabad-Sind, 1964-66. Recreations: fishing and shooting; photography. Address: c/o Mrs Leigh, 11 King's Close, Henley-on-Thames. Club: Farmers'.

KING, John Leonard; Chairman, Babcock & Wilcox Ltd, since 1972; b Aug. 1918; yr s of Albert John King and Kathleen King; m 1st, 1941, Lorna Kathleen Sykes (d 1969); three s one d; 2nd, 1970, Hon. Isabel Monckton, y d of 8th Viscount Galway. Founded Whitehouse Industries Ltd, 1945 and Ferrybridge Industries Ltd, subseq. Pollard Ball & Roller Bearing Co. Ltd (Man. Dir 1945, Chm. 1961-69). Chairman: Babcock International Inc.; British Nuclear Associates Ltd; SKF (UK) Ltd, 1976-; R. J. Dick Inc. (USA); Dick Corp. (USA); Dick Precismeca Inc. (USA); Vice-Pres., Babcock & Wilcox Española SA (Spain); Director: S. G. Warburg International Holdings Ltd; CIF Babcock Fives (France). Chm., Appeal Cttee, Nat. Soc. for Cancer Relief. Member: NEDC Cttee on Finance for Investment; Review Bd for Govt Contracts; Grand Council, CBI; Financial Policy Cttee, CBI; Chairman: City and

Industrial Liaison Council; British Olympic Appeals Cttee. Mem. Engineering Industries Council, 1975-. MFH Badsworth Foxhounds, 1949-58; MFH Duke of Rutland's Foxhounds (Belvoir), 1958-72. Recreations: hunting, field sports, racing. Address: Cleveland House, St James's Square, SW1Y 4LN. T: 01-930 9766; Wartnaby, Melton Mowbray, Leics LE14 3HY. T: Melton Mowbray 822220. Clubs: White's; Brook (New York).

KING, Dr John William Beaufoy; Chief Scientific Officer, ARC Animal Breeding Research Organisation; b 28 June 1927; s of late John Victor Beaufoy and Gwendoleen Freda King; m 1951, Pauline Margaret Coldicott; four s. Educ: Marling Sch., Stroud; St Catharine's Coll., Cambridge; Edinburgh Univ. BA Cantab 1947, MA Cantab 1952; PhD Edinburgh 1951; FIBiol 1974; FRSE 1975. ARC Animal Breeding Res. Organisation, 1951-. Kellogg Foundn Schol. to USA, 1954; Genetics Cons. to Pig Industry Develt Authority, 1959; David Black Award (services to pig industry), 1966; Nuffield Foundn Fellowship to Canada, 1970; Vis. Lectr, Göttingen Univ., 1973. Publications: papers in scientific jls. Recreations: gardening, shooting, dog training. Address: 15 Merchiston Avenue, Edinburgh EH10 4PJ. T: 031-229 3909. Club: Farmers'.

KING, Joseph, OBE 1971; Industrial Advisor, Advisory, Conciliation and Arbitration Service, North West Region, since 1975; b 28 Nov. 1914; s of John King, coal miner, and Catherine King (née Thompson); m 1939, Lily King (née Pendlebury); one s five d. Educ: St James' RC Sch., Atherton, Lancashire. Left school at age of 14 and commenced work in cotton mill, 1929. Took active part in Union of Textile and Allied Workers from early years in industry. Elected, 1949: Labour Councillor, Tyldesley; Trades Union Organiser; Dist. Sec., NE Lancs. Gen. Sec., Nat. Union of Textile and Allied Workers, 1962-75; Jt Gen. Sec., Amalgamated Textile Workers' Union, 1974; Mem., TUC Gen. Council, 1972-75; Member, many cttees in Textile Industry. Created Accrington Pakistan Friendship Association, 1961 (Pres.). JP Accrington, 1955. Recreations: pleasure is in domestic work in the home and family and in trade union and political field. Address: 14 Coleridge Drive, Baxenden, Accrington, Lancs. T: Accrington 34788.

KING, Laurence (Edward), OBE 1971; FSA; FSA Scot; FRSA; FRIBA; Architect; Senior Partner and Founder of firm of Laurence King and Partners, Chartered Architects; Tutor at Royal College of Art, 1936-39 and 1946-51; Lecturer at Royal College of Art, 1951-58; b 28 June 1907; o s of late Frederick Ernest King and Flora King (née Joyner); unmarried. Educ: Brentwood Sch.; University of London. Architectural Education under late Prof. Sir Albert Richardson at University of London, 1924-29; entered private practice in 1933. Served in the Army during 1939-45 War, principally in Middle East; rank, Major. Commenced Architectural practice again in 1946. Architect for the United Westminster Schools, Grey Coat Hospital, Eastbourne and Framlingham Colleges. Re-built: Grey Coat Hospital, 1955; Wren's Church of St Magnus, London Bridge, 1951; Wren's Church of St Mary-le-Bow (Bow Bells) (completed, 1964); Walsingham Parish Church, rebuilt after destruction by fire in 1961, completed 1964; has designed several churches in New Housing areas. Has undertaken work for the following religious communities: Nashdom Abbey; Malling Abbey; Burnham Abbey; St John's Convent, Clewer; St Saviour's Priory, Haggerston. Architect for St James' Church, Marden Ash, completed 1958; St Mary's Church, South Ruislip, completed 1959; St Nicholas, Fleetwood, 1961; Ascension Church, Chelmsford, 1962; St Mary and St Nicholas, Perivale, 1965; St Mary, Hobs Moat, Solihull, 1967; St Michael, Letchworth, 1967; St John's, North Woolwich, 1968; St James, Leigh-on-Sea, 1969; Architect to Blackburn Cathedral, 1962; Consulting Architect for Exeter Cathedral, 1965, and for Cathedral and Dio. of Gibraltar, 1974; Architect for Worksop Priory (restoration and major extensions completed 1974); for various houses and schools incl. Brentwood Sch., Sutton Valence Sch., Emanuel Sch., Wandsworth, Westminster City Schools, Queen Anne's School, Caversham; architect for the Coopers' Co. and Coborn School, completed 1974; St Davids C of E Comp. Sch., Hornsey (in course of erection); numerous Church interior decoration and furnishing schemes including High Altar and furnishings for Eucharistic Congress, 1958; Architect for restoration of various ancient Churches, particularly in London, Middx, Essex, Suffolk, Norfolk, Herts, Notts, Kent, Devon; Architect in association with late A. B. Knapp-Fisher, FRIBA for extensions to the Queen's Chapel of the Savoy for Royal Victorian Order. Mem. Archbishop's Commn in connection with repair of churches, 1951-52; Hon. Cons. Architect for Historic Churches Preservation Trust; Member: General Synod; Council for Places of Worship; Chm., Worship and Arts Assoc. Freeman, City of London. Liveryman: Worshipful Co. of Barbers; Worshipful Co. of Needlemakers; Chm., Ward of

Cordwainer Club, London, 1972-73; Mem., Worshipful Co. of Parish Clerks. *Publications:* Sanctuaries and Sacristies; Essex section, Collin's Guide to English Parish Churches; and various articles and reviews in magazines and periodicals. *Recreations:* the visual arts, the theatre, travel. *Address:* (Home) The Wayside, Shenfield Common, Brentwood, Essex. *T:* Brentwood 210438; (Office) 5 Bloomsbury Place, WC1A 2QA. *T:* 01-580 6752. *Clubs:* Athenæum, Boodle's, City Livery, Art Workers' Guild.

KING, **Michael Gardner; His Honour Judge King;** a Circuit Judge since 1972; *b* 4 Dec. 1920; *s* of late David Thomson King and late Winifred Mary King, Bournemouth; *m* 1951, Yvonne Mary Lilian, *d* of late Lt-Col M. J. Ambler; two *s* one *d. Educ:* Sherborne Sch.; Wadham Coll., Oxford (MA). Served in RN, Lieut RNVR, 1940-46. Called to Bar, Gray's Inn, 1949. Dep. Chm., IoW QS, 1966-72; Dep. Chm., Hants QS, 1968-72. *Recreations:* sailing, shooting, golf, tennis. *Address:* Oak Cottage, East End, Lymington, Hants. *T:* East End 625. *Clubs:* Hampshire (Winchester); Royal Naval Sailing Association, Royal Lymington Yacht.

KING, **Philip;** playwright and actor; *b* 1904. First play produced, 1940. *Plays include:* Without the Prince, 1940; Come to the Fair, 1940; See How They Run, 1944; (with Falkland L. Cary) Crystal Clear, 1945; On Monday Next..., 1949; (with Anthony Armstrong) Here We Come Gathering, 1951; As Black as She's Painted, 1952; Serious Charge, 1953; (with Falkland L. Cary), Sailor Beware, 1955; Watch It Sailor, 1961; Pools Paradise, 1961; (with Falkland L. Cary), Rock-A-Bye, Sailor, 1962; How Are You, Johnnie, 1963; (with Falkland L. Cary), Big Bad Mouse, 1966; I'll Get My Man, 1966; (with Parnell Bradbury) Dark Lucy, 1970; (with John Boland) Murder in Company, 1972; (with John Boland) Elementary My Dear, 1974; (with John Boland) Who Says Murder?, 1975. *Address:* 3 Woodland Way, Withdean, Brighton BN1 8BA. *T:* Brighton 505675. *Clubs:* Constitutional, Savage.

KING, **Phillip,** CBE 1975; ARA 1977; sculptor; *b* 1 May 1934; *s* of Thomas John King and of Gabrielle (*née* Liautard); *m* 1957, Lilian Odelle; one *s. Educ:* Mill Hill Sch.; Christ's Coll., Cambridge Univ. (languages); St Martin's Sch. of Art (sculpture). Teacher at St Martin's Sch. of Art, 1959-; Asst to Henry Moore, 1959-60; taught for one term at Bennington Coll., Vermont, USA, 1964. Trustee, Tate Gallery, 1967-69; Mem. Art Panel, Arts Council, 1977-. Boise Scholarship, 1960; Peter Stuyvesant Travel Bursary, 1965; First Prize, Socha Piestanskych Parkov, Piestany, Czechoslovakia, 1969. *Address:* c/o Rowan Gallery, 31a Bruton Place, Berkeley Square, W1X 7AB. *T:* 01-493 3727.

KING, **Ralph Malcolm MacDonald,** OBE 1968; Colonial Service, retired; Director, Legislative Drafting Courses, Commonwealth Secretariat, Jamaica, 1974-75, Trinidad, 1976, and Barbados, 1977; *b* 8 Feb. 1911; *s* of Dr James Malcolm King and Mrs Norah King; *m* 1948, Rita Elizabeth Herring; two *s* one *d. Educ:* Tonbridge Sch. Solicitor (Hons) 1934. Asst to Johnson, Stokes and Master, Solicitors, Hong Kong, 1936-41. Commissioned Middx Regt, 1941; prisoner of war, 1941-45; demobilised, 1946. Colonial Legal Service, 1947; Legal Officer, Somaliland, 1947; Crown Counsel, Somaliland, 1950. Called to Bar, Gray's Inn, 1950. Solicitor-General, Nyasaland, 1953; Attorney-General, Nyasaland, 1957-61. Disbarred at his own request and since restored to Roll of Solicitors, in April 1961. Legal Draftsman to Government of Northern Nigeria, 1963-67, and to Northern States of Nigeria, 1967-73. *Recreations:* tennis, walking. *Address:* St John's Lodge, Burgh Hill, Hurst Green, Etchingham, E Sussex. *Club:* Royal Over-Seas League.

KING, **Sir Richard (Brian Meredith),** KCB 1976 (CB 1969); MC 1944; Executive Secretary, IMF/World Bank Development Committee, since 1976; *b* 2 Aug. 1920; *s* of late Bernard and Dorothy King; *m* 1944, Blanche Phyllis Roberts; two *s* one *d. Educ:* King's Coll. Sch., Wimbledon. Air Ministry, 1939; Min. of Aircraft Prod., 1940. Army 1940-46: Major, N Irish Horse; N Af. and Ital. campaigns (MC, Cassino). Min. of Supply, 1946; Asst Principal, Ministry of Works, 1948; Principal, 1949; Asst Regional Dir (Leeds), 1949-52; seconded Treas., 1953-54; Prin. Priv. Sec. to Minister of Works, 1956-57; Asst Sec., 1957; seconded Cabinet Off., 1958 (Sec. of Commonwealth Educn. Conf. (Oxford), 1959; Constitutional Confs: Kenya, 1960; N Rhodesia, Nyasaland and Fed. Review, 1960; WI Fedn, 1961); Dept of Tech. Co-op., on its formation, 1961; Min. of Overseas Develt, on its formation, 1964: Under-Sec., 1964; Dep. Sec., 1968; Permanent Sec., 1973-76. *Publications:* The Planning of the British Aid Programme, 1971; Criteria for Europe's Development Policy to the Third World, 1974. *Recreations:* music, lawn tennis, gardening, doing-it-himself. *Address:* c/o

International Bank for Reconstruction and Development, 1818 H Street NW, Washington, DC 20433, USA.

KING, **Maj.-Gen. Robert Charles Moss,** CB 1955; DSO 1945; OBE 1944; retired; *b* 6 June 1904; *s* of Robert Henry Curzon Moss King, ICS and Mrs King; *m* 1940, Elizabeth Stuart Mackay (*d* 1966); two *d. Educ:* Clifton Coll.; RMC, Camberley. 2nd Lieut, W Yorks Regt, 1924; Capt. 1935. Served War of 1939-45: India, Malaya, Java, Assam and Burma (despatches). Maj.-Gen. 1955. GOC Home Counties District and 44th (HC) Infantry Division TA, Deputy Constable Dover Castle, 1954-56; Dir of Quartering, War Office, 1957-58. *Recreations:* shooting and fishing. *Address:* Church Place, Eversley Cross, Hants.

KING, **Robert Shirley;** Under-Secretary, Department of Health and Social Security, since 1976; *b* 12 July 1920; *s* of Rev. William Henry King, MC, TD, MA, and late Dorothy King (*née* Sharpe); *m* 1st, 1947, Margaret Siddall (*d* 1956); two *d*; 2nd, 1958, Mary Rowell; one *s* two *d. Educ:* Alexandra Road Sch., Oldham; Manchester Grammar Sch.; Trinity Coll., Cambridge (Schol., MA). Served War, RAF, 1940-45. Colonial Service, Tanganyika, 1949-62 (Dist Comr, Geita, 1959-62); Home Office: Principal, 1962-69 (seconded to Civil Service Dept, 1968-69); Asst Sec., 1969-70; transf., with Children's Dept, to DHSS, 1971; DHSS, Asst Sec., 1971-76. *Recreations:* walking, gardening, African affairs. *Address:* 63 Warwick Road, Bishop's Stortford, Herts. *T:* Bishop's Stortford 52009.

KING, **Dame Ruth;** *see* Railton, Dame R.

KING, **Sir Sydney (Percy),** Kt 1975; OBE 1965; JP; District Organiser, National Union of Agricultural and Allied Workers, since 1946; Chairman, Trent Regional Health Authority, since 1973; *b* 20 Sept. 1916; *s* of James Edwin King and Florence Emily King; *m* 1944, Millicent Angela Prendergast; two *d. Educ:* Brockley Central School. Member: N Midland Regional Board for Industry (Vice-Chm. 1949); Sheffield Regional Hosp. Bd, 1963-73 (Chm. 1969-73); E Midland Economic Planning Council, 1965; E Midlands Gas Board, 1970; MAFF E Midland Regional Panel, 1977. JP 1956, Alderman 1967, Kesteven. *Recreations:* reading, music, talking. *Address:* 49 Robertson Drive, Sleaford, Lincs. *T:* Sleaford 2056.

KING, **Thomas Jeremy, (Tom);** MP (C) Bridgwater since March 1970; Opposition Spokesman for Energy, since 1976; *b* 13 June 1933; *s* of late J. H. King, JP; *m* 1960, Jane, *d* of Robert Tilney, *qv*; one *s* one *d. Educ:* Rugby; Emmanuel Coll., Cambridge (MA). National service, 1951-53: commnd Somerset Light Inf., 1952; seconded to KAR; served Tanganyika and Kenya; Actg Captain 1953. Cambridge, 1953-56. Joined E.S. & A. Robinson Ltd, Bristol, 1956; various positions up to Divisional Gen. Man., 1964-69; Chm., Sale, Tilney Co Ltd, 1971- (Dir 1965-). PPS to: Minister for Posts and Telecommunications, 1970-72; Minister for Industrial Develt, 1972-74; Front Bench spokesman for Industry, 1975-76; Vice-Chm., Cons. Parly Industry Cttee, 1974. *Recreations:* cricket, ski-ing. *Address:* House of Commons, SW1.

KING, **Air Vice-Marshal Walter MacIan,** CB 1961; CBE 1957; retired, 1967; *b* 10 March 1910; *s* of Alexander King, MB, ChB, DPH, and Hughberta Blannin King (*née* Pearson); *m* 1946, Anne Clare Hicks; two *s. Educ:* St Mary's Coll., Castries, St Lucia, BWI; Blundell's Sch., Tiverton, Devon. Aircraft Engineering (Messers Westland Aircraft Ltd, Handley-Page Ltd, Saunders-Roe Ltd), 1927-33; joined Royal Air Force, 1934; Overseas Service: No 8 Sqdn, Aden, 1935-37; South-east Asia, 1945-47; Middle East (Egypt and Cyprus), 1955-57. Student: RAF Staff Coll., 1944; Joint Services Staff Coll., 1947; IDC, 1954. Directing Staff, RAF Staff Coll., 1957-58; Comdt, No 16 MU, Stafford, 1958-60; Dir of Equipment (B), Air Ministry, 1961-64; Air Cdre Ops (Supply), HQ's Maintenance Command, during 1964; Senior Air Staff Officer, RAF Maintenance Command, 1964-67. Joined Hooker Craigmyle & Co. Ltd, 1967; Gen. Manager, Hooker Craigmyle (Scotland) Ltd, 1969-72; Dir, Craigmyle & Co. (Scotland) Ltd, 1972-76. *Recreations:* swimming (rep. RAF in inter-services competition, 1934); gardening. *Address:* 24 Arthur's Avenue, Harrogate HG2 0DX.

KING, **Sir Wayne Alexander,** 8th Bt *cr* 1815; *b* 2 Feb. 1962; *s* of Sir Peter Alexander King, 7th Bt, and of Jean Margaret, *d* of Christopher Thomas Cavell, Deal; *S* father, 1973. *Address:* Charlestown, 365 London Road, Upper Deal, Deal, Kent.

KING-HAMILTON, **Myer Alan Barry,** QC 1954; **His Honour Judge King-Hamilton;** a Circuit Judge (formerly an additional Judge of the Central Criminal Court), since 1964; *b* 9 Dec. 1904; *o s* of Alfred King-Hamilton; *m* 1935, Rosalind Irene Ellis; two *d. Educ:* Bishop's Stortford Grammar Sch.; Trinity Hall,

Cambridge (BA 1927, MA 1929; Pres. Cambridge Union Soc., 1927). Called to Bar, Middle Temple, 1929; served War of 1939-45, RAF, finishing with rank of Squadron Leader; served on Finchley Borough Council, 1938-39 and 1945-50. Recorder of Hereford, 1955-56; Recorder of Gloucester, 1956-61; Recorder of Wolverhampton, 1961-64; Dep. Chm. Oxford County Quarter Sessions, 1955-64, 1966-71; Leader of Oxford Circuit, 1961-64. Elected Bencher, Middle Temple, 1961. Elected to General Council of Bar, 1958. Freeman of City of London; Master, Needlemakers Co., 1969. *Recreations:* cricket, gardening, the theatre. *Address:* Central Criminal Court, Old Bailey, EC4. *Clubs:* Royal Air Force, MCC.

KING-HARMAN, Captain (Robert) Douglas, DSO 1941; DSC and Bar; Royal Navy; *b* Barbadoes, BWI, 18 Aug. 1891; 2nd *s* of Sir C. A. King-Harman, KCMG (*d* 1939), and Lady Constance King-Harman (*d* 1961), Ouse Manor, Sharnbrook, Bedfordshire; *m* 1st, 1916, Lily Moffatt (marr. diss., 1926; she *d* 1966); one *s*; 2nd, 1927, Elizabeth Lilian Bull (*d* 1974); 3rd, 1975, Eve Mary Palmer. *Educ:* Royal Naval Coll., Dartmouth. Entered Navy, 1904; served in destroyers, Grand Fleet and Dover Patrol, 1914-18; at Jutland; DSC given for his part in HMS Swift in action between destroyers Swift and Broke and German destroyers, 1917; the bar to DSC was for minesweeping after the Armistice of 1918; retired 1928 and entered Singapore Pilotage; returned to Navy, Sept. 1939 and served until 1946; retired from Singapore Pilotage, 1948. *Address:* Jakins, Great Gransden, Cambs. *T:* Great Gransden 346.

KING-HELE, Desmond George, FRS 1966; Deputy Chief Scientific Officer, Space Department, Royal Aircraft Establishment, Farnborough, since 1968; *b* 3 Nov. 1927; *s* of late S. G. and of B. King-Hele, Seaford, Sussex; *m* 1954, Marie Thérèse Newman; two *d. Educ:* Epsom Coll.; Trinity Coll., Cambridge. BA (1st cl. hons Mathematics) 1948; MA 1952. At RAE, Farnborough, from 1948, working on space research from 1955. Mem., International Academy of Astronautics, 1961; FIMA; FRAS. Eddington Medal, RAS, 1971; Charles Chree Medal, Inst. of Physics, 1971; Lagrange Prize, Acad. Royale de Belgique, 1972. Lectures: Jeffreys, RAS, 1971; Halley, Oxford, 1974; Bakerian, Royal Soc., 1974. *Publications:* Shelley: His Thought and Work, 1960, 2nd edn 1971; Satellites and Scientific Research, 1960; Erasmus Darwin, 1963; Theory of Satellite Orbits in an Atmosphere, 1964; (ed) Space Research V, 1965; Observing Earth Satellites, 1966; (ed) Essential Writings of Erasmus Darwin, 1968; The End of the Twentieth Century?, 1970; Poems and Trixies, 1972; Doctor of Revolution, 1977; numerous papers in Proc. Royal Society, Nature, Keats-Shelley Memor. Bull., New Scientist, Planetary and Space Science, and other scientific and literary jls. *Recreations:* tennis, walking, reading. *Address:* 3 Tor Road, Farnham, Surrey. *T:* Farnham 4755.

KING-MARTIN, Brig. John Douglas, CBE 1966; DSO 1957; MC 1953; Deputy Commander, HQ Eastern District, 1968-70, retired; *b* 9 March 1915; *s* of late Lewis King-Martin, Imperial Forest Service; *m* 1940, Jeannie Jemima Sheffield Hollins, *d* of late S. T. Hollins, CIE; one *s* one *d. Educ:* Allhallows Sch.; RMC Sandhurst. Commnd 1935; 3rd Royal Bn 12 Frontier Force Regt, IA, 1936; Waziristan Ops, 1936-37; Eritrea, Western Desert, 1940-42; Staff Coll., Quetta, 1944; Bde Maj., 1944-46, India, Java; GSO 2, Indian Inf. Div., Malaya, 1946-47; transf. to RA, 1948; Battery Comdr, 1948-50, 1951-54; Korea, 1952-53; CO, 50 Medium Regt, RA, 1956-57; Suez, Cyprus, 1956-57; Coll. Comdr, RMA Sandhurst, 1958-60; Dep. Comdr and CRA, 17 Gurkha Div., 1961-62; Comdr, 17 Gurkha Div., 1962-64; Comdr, Rhine Area, 1964-67. Lieut-Col 1956; Brig. 1961. ADC to The Queen, 1968-70. *Recreations:* golf, painting, photography. *Address:* White House Farm, Polstead, Suffolk. *T:* Boxford 210327. *Clubs:* East India, Devonshire, Sports and Public Schools.

KING MURRAY, Ronald; *see* Murray, Ronald K.

KING-REYNOLDS, Guy Edwin, JP; Head Master, Dauntsey's School, West Lavington, since Sept. 1969; *b* 9 July 1923; *er s* of late Dr H. E. King Reynolds, York; *m* 1st, 1947, Norma Lansdowne Russell (*d* 1949); 2nd, 1950, Jeanne Nancy Perris Rhodes; one *d. Educ:* St Peter's Sch., Yorks; Emmanuel Coll., Cambridge (1944-47). Served RAF, 1942-44. BA 1946, MA 1951. Asst Master, Glenhow Prep. Sch., 1947-48; Head of Geography Dept, Solihull Sch., Warwickshire, 1948-54; family business, 1954-55; Head of Geography, Portsmouth Grammar Sch., 1955-57; Solihull School: Housemaster, 1957-63, Second Master, 1963-69. Part-time Lecturer in International Affairs, Extra-Mural Dept, Birmingham Univ.; Chm., Solihull WEA. LRAM (speech and drama) 1968. JP Solihull, 1965-69, Wiltshire, 1970-. *Recreations:* drama (director and actor);

travel, living in Italy, squash racquets. *Address:* Head Master's House, Dauntsey's School, West Lavington, Wilts SN10 4HE. *T:* Lavington 3382; Sandpipers, 12 Rectory Road, Llangwm, near Haverfordwest, Dyfed.

KING-TENISON, family name of **Earl of Kingston.**

KINGDOM, Thomas Doyle, CB 1959; Controller, Government Social Survey Department, 1967-70, retired; *b* 30 Oct. 1910; *er s* of late Thomas Kingdom; *m* 1937, Elsie Margaret, *d* of late L. C. Scott, MBE, Northwood; two *d. Educ:* Rugby; King's Coll., Cambridge (MA). Entered Civil Service as Asst Principal, Inland Revenue, 1933; transferred to Unemployment Assistance Bd, 1934; seconded to HM Treasury as Dep. Dir, Organisation and Methods, 1945-49; Under Sec., 1955. Chm., Exec. Council, Royal Inst. of Public Administration, 1965-66. Chm. West London Suppl. Benefit Appeal Tribunal, 1971-. *Address:* 2 Grosvenor Road, Northwood, Mddx HA6 3HJ. *T:* Northwood 22006. *Club:* United Oxford & Cambridge University.

KINGHAM, James Frederick; His Honour Judge Kingham; a Circuit Judge, since 1973; *b* 9 Aug. 1925; *s* of Charles William and Eileen Eda Kingham; *m* 1958, Vivienne Valerie Tyrrell Brown; two *s* two *d. Educ:* Wycliffe Coll.; Queens' Coll., Cambridge (MA); Graz Univ., Austria. Served with RN, 1943-47. Called to Bar, Gray's Inn, 1951; Mem. Gen. Council of Bar, 1954-58; Mem. Bar Council Sub-Cttee on Sentencing and Penology. A Recorder, 1972-73. Dep. County Comr, Herts Scouts, 1971-, formerly Asst County Comr for Venture Scouts. *Recreations:* mountain activities, squash, ski-ing, youth work, history, gardening, football. *Address:* Copelands, Blackmore Way, Blackmore End, Wheathampstead, Herts. *T:* Kimpton 832308. *Clubs:* Northampton and County (Northampton); Union (Cambridge).

KINGHORN, Squadron Leader Ernest; *b* 1 Nov. 1907; *s* of A. Kinghorn, Leeds; *m* 1942, Eileen Mary Lambert Russell; one *s* (and one *s* one *d* decd). *Educ:* Leeds, Basel and Lille Universities. Languages Master Ashville Coll., Doncaster Grammar Sch. and Roundhay Sch., Leeds. Served in Intelligence Branch, RAF. British Officer for Control of Manpower, SHAEF, and Staff Officer CCG. MP (Lab) Yarmouth Division of Norfolk, 1950-51, Great Yarmouth, 1945-50. *Address:* 59 Queens Avenue, Hanworth, Middx.

KINGHORN, William Oliver; Chief Agricultural Officer, Department of Agriculture and Fisheries for Scotland, 1971-75; *b* 17 May 1913; *s* of Thomas Kinghorn, Duns, and Elizabeth Oliver; *m* 1943, Edith Johnstone; one *s* two *d. Educ:* Berwickshire High Sch.; Edinburgh Univ. BSc (Agr) Hons, BSc Hons. Senior Inspector, 1946; Technical Develt Officer, 1959; Chief Inspector, 1970. *Publication:* contrib. Annals of Applied Biology, 1936. *Recreation:* golf. *Address:* 23 Cumloden Avenue, Edinburgh EH12 6DR. *T:* 031-357 1435.

KINGMAN, John Frank Charles, FRS 1971; Professor of Mathematics in the University of Oxford, since 1969; *b* 28 Aug. 1939; *er s* of Frank Edwin Thomas Kingman and Maud Elsie Harley; *m* 1964, Valerie Cromwell; one *s* one *d. Educ:* Christ's Coll., Finchley; Pembroke Coll., Cambridge. MA, ScD Cantab; Smith's Prize, 1962. Fellow of Pembroke Coll., Cambridge, 1961-65. Asst Lectr in Mathematics, 1962-64; Lectr, 1964-65, Univ. of Cambridge; Vis. Prof., Univ. of Western Australia, 1963, 1974; Reader in Mathematics and Statistics, 1965-66, Prof. 1966-69, Univ. of Sussex; Vis. Prof., Stanford Univ., USA, 1968. Mem., Brighton Co. Borough Council, 1968-71; Chm., Regency Soc. of Brighton and Hove, 1975-. Mem., Internat. Statistical Inst., 1967; Chm., 1973-76, Vice-Pres., 1976-, Inst. of Statisticians. Fellow, Inst. of Mathematical Statistics (USA), 1968 (Wald Meml Lectr, 1977). Junior Berwick Prize (London Math. Soc.), 1967. *Publications:* Introduction to Measure and Probability (with S. J. Taylor), 1966; The Algebra of Queues, 1966; Regenerative Phenomena, 1972; papers in mathematical and statistical jls. *Address:* Mathematical Institute, 24 St Giles, Oxford OX1 3LB; 8 Montpelier Villas, Brighton, East Sussex BN1 3DH.

KINGS NORTON, Baron *cr* 1965, of Wotton Underwood (Life Peer); **Harold Roxbee Cox,** Kt 1953; PhD, DIC, FIMechE, Hon. FRAeS; Chairman: Landspeed Ltd, since 1975; Berger Jenson & Nicholson Ltd, 1967-75; Metal Box Co., 1961-67 (Director, 1957-67, Deputy Chairman, 1959-60); Director: Dowty Rotol, 1968-75; Ricardo & Co. (Engineers) 1927 Ltd, 1965-77; British Printing Corporation, 1968-77; Hoechst UK, 1970-75; President, Royal Institution, 1969-76; Chancellor, Cranfield Institute of Technology, since 1969; *b* 6 June 1902; *s* of late William John Roxbee Cox, Birmingham; *m* 1927, Marjorie, *e d* of late E. E. Withers, Northwood; two *s. Educ:* Kings Norton

Grammar Sch.; Imperial Coll. of Science and Technology (Schol.). Engineer on construction of Airship R101, 1924-29; Chief Technical Officer, Royal Airship Works, 1931; Investigations in wing flutter and stability of structures, RAE, 1931-35; Lectr in Aircraft Structures, Imperial Coll., 1932-38; Principal Scientific Officer. Aerodynamics Dept, RAE, 1935-36; Head of Air Defence Dept, RAE, 1936-38; Chief Technical Officer, Air Registration Board, 1938-39; Supt of Scientific Research, RAE, 1939-40; Dep. Dir of Scientific Research, Ministry of Aircraft Production, 1940-43; Dir of Special Projects Ministry of Aircraft Production, 1943-44; Chm. and Man. Dir Power Jets (Research and Development) Ltd, 1944-46; Dir National Gas Turbine Establishment, 1946-48; Chief Scientist, Min. of Fuel and Power, 1948-54; Chm. Gas Turbine Collaboration Cttee, 1941-44, 1946-48; Mem. Aeronautical Research Council, 1944-48, 1958-60; Chairman: Coun. for Scientific and Industrial Research, 1961-65; Council for National Academic Awards, 1964-71; Air Registration Bd. 1966-72; Past Pres. Royal Aeronautical Soc. Fellow of Imperial Coll. of Science and Technology, 1960; FCGI 1976. Membre Correspondant, Faculté Polytechnique de Mons, 1946. R38 Memorial Prize, 1928; Busk Memorial Prize, 1934; Wilbur Wright Lecturer, 1940; Wright Brothers Lecturer (USA), 1945; Hawksley Lecturer, 1951; James Clayton Prize, 1952; Thornton Lectr, 1954; Parsons Memorial Lectr, 1955; Handley Page Memorial Lectr, 1969. Hon. DSc: Birmingham, 1954; Cranfield Inst. of Technology, 1970; Hon. DTech Brunel, 1966; Hon. LLD CNAA, 1969. Bronze Medal, Univ. of Louvain, 1946; Medal of Freedom with Silver Palm, USA, 1947. *Publications:* numerous papers on theory of structures, wing flutter, gas turbines, civil aviation and airships. *Address:* Westcote House, Chipping Campden, Glos. *T:* Evesham 840 440. *Clubs:* Athenæum, Royal Automobile.

KINGSALE, 35th Baron *cr* 1223 (by some reckonings 30th Baron); **John de Courcy;** Baron Courcy and Baron of Ringrone; Premier Baron of Ireland; Chairman, Strand Publications Ltd, since 1971; Director, D'Olier, Grantmesnil & Courcy Acquisitions Ltd, since 1970; *b* 27 Jan. 1941; *s* of Lieutenant-Commander the Hon. Michael John Rancé de Courcy, RN (killed on active service, 1940), and Joan (*d* 1967), *d* of Robert Reid; *S* grandfather, 1969. *Educ:* Stowe; Universities of Paris and Salzburg. Short service commission, Irish Guards, 1962-65. At various times before and since: law student, property developer, film extra, white hunter, bingo caller, etc. *Recreations:* shooting, food and drink, palaeontology, self deception. *Heir: cousin* Nevinson Russell de Courcy [*b* 21 July 1920; *m* 1954, Nora Lydia, *yr d* of James Arnold Plint; one *s* one *d*]. *Address:* Grove Farm, Bourton, Gillingham, Dorset. *T:* Bourton 498. *Club:* Cavalry and Guards'.

KINGSBOROUGH, Viscount; Robert Charles Henry King-Tenison; *b* 20 March 1969; *s* and *heir* of 11th Earl of Kingston, *qv.*

KINGSFORD, Reginald John Lethbridge, CBE 1963; MA; Fellow of Clare College, Cambridge, since 1949; *b* 10 Sept. 1900; *o s* of late Rev. R. L. Kingsford and late Gertrude Rodgers; *m* 1927, Ruth (*d* 1971), *o d* of late W. F. A. Fletcher, Biggleswade; one *s*. *Educ:* Sherborne Sch. (scholar); Clare Coll., Cambridge (scholar). General Manager, Cambridge Univ. Press, London, 1936-48; Sec. to the Syndics of the Cambridge University Press, 1948-63. Mem. of Council, Publishers' Association, 1940-53; Pres. of Publishers' Association, 1943-45; Mem. Governing Body of Sherborne Sch., 1945-71. *Publication:* The Publishers' Association, 1896-1946, 1970. *Recreation:* books. *Address:* 2 Barrow Close, Cambridge. *T:* 52963. *Club:* United Oxford & Cambridge University.

KINGSHOTT, (Albert) Leonard; Director, Lloyds Bank International, responsible for Merchant Banking activities, since 1977; *b* 16 Sept. 1930; *s* of A. L. Kingshott and Mrs K. Kingshott; *m* 1958, Valerie Simpson; two *s* one *d*. *Educ:* London Sch. of Economics (BSc); ACIS 1958. Flying Officer, RAF, 1952-55; Economist, British Petroleum, 1955-60; Economist, British Nylon Spinners, 1960-62; Financial Manager, Iraq Petroleum Co., 1963-65; Chief Economist, Ford of Britain, 1965; Treas., Ford of Britain, 1966-67; Treas., Ford of Europe, 1968-70; Finance Dir, Whitbread & Co., 1972; Man. Dir, BSC, 1972-77. *Publication:* Investment Appraisal, 1967. *Recreations:* golf, chess. *Address:* The White House, Great Warley, Brentwood, Essex. *T:* Brentwood 210671.

KINGSHOTT, Air Vice-Marshal Kenneth, CBE 1972; DFC 1953; Deputy Chief of Staff Operations and Intelligence, Headquarters Allied Air Forces Central Europe, since 1977; *b* 8 July 1924; *s* of Walter James Kingshott and Eliza Ann Kingshott; *m* 1948, Dorrie Marie (*née* Dent); two *s*. *Educ:*

Edmonton County Grammar Sch. Joined RAF, 1943; served: Singapore and Korea, 1950; Aden, 1960; Malta, 1965; MoD, London, 1968; OC RAF Cottesmore, 1971; HQ 2 Allied Tactical Air Force, 1973; HQ Strike Command, 1975. *Recreations:* golf, tennis, music. *Address:* c/o Lloyds Bank Ltd, 6 Pall Mall, SW1. *Club:* Royal Air Force.

KINGSLEY, Sir Patrick (Graham Toler), KCVO 1962 (CVO 1950); Secretary and Keeper of the Records of the Duchy of Cornwall, 1954-72 (Assistant Secretary, 1930-54); *b* 1908; *s* of late Gerald Kingsley; *m* 1947, Priscilla Rosemary, *o d* of late Capt. Archibald A. Lovett Cameron, RN; three *s* one *d*. *Educ:* Winchester; New Coll., Oxford. OUCC 1928-30 (Capt. 1930), OUAFC 1927 and 1929. Served War of 1939-45 with Queen's Royal Regt. *Address:* Eastlands House, Cowfold, Sussex.

KINGSLEY, Roger James, CEng, FIChemE; Managing Director, Lankro Chemicals Group Ltd, since 1972; *b* 2 Feb. 1922; *s* of Felix Kingsley and Helene Kingsley; *m* 1949, Valerie Marguerite Mary (*née* Hanna); one *s* two *d*. *Educ:* Manchester Grammar Sch.; Faculty of Technol., Manchester Univ. (BScTech); Harvard Business Sch. (Internat. Sen. Managers Program). Served War, Royal Fusiliers, 1940-46; Commando service, 1942-45; Captain; mentioned in despatches, 1946. Chemical Engr, Petrocarbon Ltd, 1949-51; technical appts, ultimately Tech. Dir, Lankro Chemicals Ltd, 1952-62; gen. management appts, Lankro Chemicals Group Ltd, 1962-. Director: ICI-Lankro Plasticisers Ltd, 1972-; Fallek-Lankro Corp., Tuscaloosa, Ala, 1976-. Pres., IChemE, 1974-75 (Vice-Pres., 1969-71 and 1973-74). Member: Court of Governors, Univ. of Manchester Inst. of Science and Technol., 1969-; Adv. Cttee for Chem. Engrg and Fuel Technol., Univ. of Sheffield, 1977. *Publications:* contrib. Chem. Engr, and Proc. IMechE. *Recreations:* skiing, riding, music. *Address:* Fallows End, Wicker Lane, Hale Barns, Cheshire WA15 0HQ. *T:* 061-980 6253. *Club:* Anglo-Belgian.

KINGSTON, 11th Earl of, *cr* 1768; **Barclay Robert Edwin King-Tenison,** Bt 1682; Baron Kingston, 1764; Viscount Kingsborough, 1766; Baron Erris, 1800; Viscount Lorton, 1806; formerly Lieutenant, Royal Scots Greys; *b* 23 Sept. 1943; *o s* of 10th Earl of Kingston and Gwyneth, *d* of William Howard Evans (who *m* 1951, Brig. E. M. Tyler, DSO, MC, late RA; she *m* 1963, Robert Woodford); *S* father 1948; *m* 1st, 1965, Patricia Mary (marr. diss. 1974), *o d* of E. C. Killip, Llanfairfechan, N Wales; one *s* one *d*; 2nd, 1974, Victoria, *d* of D. C. Edmonds. *Educ:* Winchester. *Heir: s* Viscount Kingsborough, *qv. Address:* c/o Barclays Bank Ltd, 65 High Street, Camberley, Surrey. *Club:* Cavalry and Guards.

KINGSTON (ONTARIO), Archbishop of, (RC), since 1967; **Most Rev. Joseph Lawrence Wilhelm,** DD, JCD; *b* Walkerton, Ontario, 16 Nov. 1909. *Educ:* St Augustine's Seminary, Toronto; Ottawa Univ., Ottawa, Ont. Ordained priest, Toronto, 1934. Mil. Chaplain to Canadian Forces, 1940-46 (MC, Sicily, 1943). Auxiliary Bishop, Calgary, Alberta, 1963-66. Hon. DD Queen's Univ., Kingston, Ont, 1970. *Address:* Archbishop's House, Kingston, Ont, Canada.

KINGSTON-UPON-THAMES, Archdeacon of; *see* Jacob, Ven. B. V.

KININMONTH, Sir William (Hardie), Kt 1972; PPRSA, FRIBA, FRIAS; Architectural Consultant, formerly Senior Partner, Sir Rowand Anderson, Kininmonth and Paul, architects, Edinburgh; *b* 8 Nov. 1904; *s* of John Kininmonth and Isabella McLean Hardie; *m* 1934, Caroline Eleanor Newsam Sutherland; one *d*. *Educ:* George Watson's Coll., Edinburgh. Architectural training in Edinburgh Coll. of Art, and in offices of Sir Edwin Lutyens, Sir Rowand Anderson and Paul, and Wm N. Thomson; entered partnership Rowand Anderson and Paul, 1933; served War of 1939-45: RE 1940, North Africa, Sicily and Italy; resumed architectural practice, 1945; buildings for Edinburgh Univ., Renfrew Air Port and Naval Air Station, Edinburgh Dental Hospital, Town Hall, churches, banks, hospitals, schools, housing, etc. Saltire and Civic Trust Awards. Appointed: 1955, Adviser to City of Edinburgh, for development of Princes Street; 1964, to design new Festival Theatre and Festival Centre. Pres., Royal Scottish Academy, 1969-73 (formerly Treas. and then Sec.); Pres. Edinburgh Architectural Association, 1951-53; Member: Royal Fine Arts Commn for Scotland, 1952-65; Council RIBA, 1951-53; Council Royal Incorp. of Architects in Scot., 1951-53 Board, Edinburgh Coll. of Art, 1951-, Board Merchant Co. of Edinburgh, 1950-52. Edinburgh Dean of Guild Court, 1953-69. Hon. LLD Dundee, 1975; Hon. RA; Hon. RSW. *Address:* 16 Rutland Square, Edinburgh EH1 2BB. *T:* 031-229 5515, 5516, 5517; The Lane House, 46a Dick Place, Edinburgh EH9 2JE. *T:* 031-667 2724. *Clubs:* Scottish Arts, New (Edinburgh).

KINLOCH, Sir Alexander (Davenport), 12th Bt of Gilmerton, cr 1685; Major Special Reserve Grenadier Guards, retired 1952; b 17 Sept. 1902; s of Brig.-Gen. Sir David Kinloch, 11th Bt, and Elinor Lucy (d 1943), d of Col Bromley Davenport of Capesthorne, Cheshire; S father 1944; m 1st, 1929, Alexandra (marr. diss., 1945), d of Frederick Y. Dalziel, New York; two d; 2nd, 1946, Anna (marr. diss., 1965), d of late Thomas Walker, Edinburgh; one s three d; 3rd, 1965, Ann, d of Group Capt. F. L. White and Mrs H. R. White, London; one s. Educ: Eton. Mem. of Queen's Body Guard for Scotland (Royal Company of Archers). Heir: s David Kinloch, b 5 Aug. 1951. Address: Gilmerton House, North Berwick, East Lothian. Clubs: White's; New (Edinburgh).
See also Hon. H. W. Astor, Baron Brownlow, Baron Grantley.

KINLOCH, Sir John, 4th Bt, of Kinloch, cr 1873; b 1 Nov. 1907; e s of Sir George Kinloch, 3rd Bt, OBE, and Ethel May (d 1959), y d of late Major J. Hawkins; S father 1948; m 1934, Doris Ellaline, e d of C. J. Head, London; one s two d. Educ: Charterhouse; Magdalene Coll., Cambridge. Served with British Ministry of War Transport as their repr. at Abadan, Persia, and also in London. Recreations: shooting, golf. Heir: s David Oliphant Kinloch, CA [b 15 Jan. 1942; m 1968, Susan Minette, y d of Maj.-Gen. R. E. Urquhart, qv; three d]. Address: Aldie Cottage, Fossoway, Kinross-shire. T: Fossoway 305. Club: New (Edinburgh).

KINLOSS, Lady (12th in line, of the Lordship cr 1602); Beatrice Mary Grenville Freeman-Grenville (surname changed by Lord Lyon King of Arms, 1950); b 1922; e d of late Rev. Hon. Luis Chandos Francis Temple Morgan-Grenville, Master of Kinloss; S grandmother, 1944; m 1950, Dr Greville Stewart Parker Freeman-Grenville, FSA, FRAS (name changed from Freeman by Lord Lyon King of Arms, 1950), Capt. late Royal Berks Regt, er s of late Rev. E. C. Freeman; one s two d. Heir: s Master of Kinloss, qv. Address: North View House, Sheriff Hutton, Yorks. T: Sheriff Hutton 447. Club: Royal Commonwealth Society.

KINLOSS, Master of; Hon. Bevil David Stewart Chandos Freeman-Grenville; b 20 June 1953; s of Dr Greville Stewart Parker Freeman-Grenville, FSA, Capt. late Royal Berks Regt, and of Lady Kinloss, qv. Educ: Redrice Sch. Address: North View House, Sheriff Hutton, Yorks.

KINMONTH, Prof. John Bernard; Surgeon and Director of Surgical Unit, St Thomas' Hospital, and Professor of Surgery in the University of London, since 1955; Consultant in Vascular Surgery to the RAF, since 1958; b 9 May 1916; s of Dr George Kinmonth; m 1946, Kathleen Margaret, d of late Admiral J. H. Godfrey, CB; two s two d. Educ: Dulwich Coll.; St Thomas's Hosp. Medical Sch. House Surgeon, Resident Asst Surgeon, etc, St Thomas' Hosp., 1938-43. Wing Comdr, Surgical Specialist, RAFVR, 1944-47. Research Asst, St Bartholomew's Hosp., 1947-48; Research Fellow, Harvard Univ., 1948-49; Asst Surgeon, St Bartholomew's Hosp., 1950-54. Arris and Gale Lecturer, 1951, Hunterian Prof., 1954, RCS; Sir Arthur Sim's Commonwealth Travelling Professor, 1962. Past Pres., European Soc. Cardiovascular Surgery; Vice-Pres. and Matas Lectr, Internat. Cardiovascular Soc.; Member: University of London Cttee on Colleges Overseas in Special Relations; Surgical Research Soc.; Physiological Soc.; Vascular Surgical Soc. (Pres. 1973); Council, RCS, 1977-. Consultant Adviser in Surgery to Min. of Health. Hon. Prof. Universidad Peruana Cayetano Heredia, 1968. Hon. Member: Brazilian Soc. Angiology; Internat. Soc. Lymphology (Asellius Medal); Associé Etranger, Académie de Chirurgie; Lombard Soc. Surgery; Soc. for Vascular Surgery, USA, 1975. Mickle Fellow, Univ. of London, 1974. Hon. FRCR, 1975; Hon. FACS, 1976. Publications: Vascular Surgery, 1962; The Lymphatics: Diseases, Lymphography and Surgery, 1972; articles on gen. and cardiovascular surgery and physiology in scientific journals and on cruising in sailing journals. Recreations: sailing, music, ornithology. Address: 70 Ladbroke Road, W11. T: 01-727 6045; St Thomas' Hospital, SE1. T: 01-928 9292. Clubs: Royal Cork Yacht, Royal Cruising, Irish Cruising, Cruising Association.

KINNAIRD, family name of Baron Kinnaird.

KINNAIRD, 13th Baron cr 1682, of Inchture; Graham Charles Kinnaird; Baron Kinnaird of Rossie (UK), 1860; Flying Officer RAFVR; b 15 Sept. 1912; e s of 12th Baron Kinnaird, KT, KBE, and Frances Victoria (d 1960), y d of late T. H. Clifton, Lytham Hall, Lancs; S father, 1972; m 1st, 1938, Nadia (who obtained a decree of divorce, 1940), o c of H. A. Fortington, Isle of Jethou, Channel Islands; 2nd, 1940, Diana, yr d of R. S. Copeman, Roydon Hall, Diss, Norfolk; four d (one s decd). Educ: Eton. Demobilised RAF, 1945. Address: Rossie Priory, Inchture,

Perthshire. T: Inchture 246; Durham House, Durham Place, SW3. Clubs: Brooks's, Carlton, Pratt's; New (Edinburgh).

KINNEAR, Ian Albert Clark, CMG 1974; HM Diplomatic Service; Consul-General, San Francisco, since 1977; b 23 Dec. 1924; s of late George Kinnear, CBE and Georgina Lilian (née Stephenson), Nairobi; m 1966, Rosemary, d of Dr K. W. D. Hartley, Cobham; two d. Educ: Marlborough Coll.; Lincoln Coll., Oxford (MA). HM Forces, 1938-42 (1st E Africa Reconnaissance Regt). Colonial Service (later HMOCS): Malayan Civil Service, 1951-56: District Officer, Bentong, then Alor Gajah, Asst Sec. Econ. Planning Unit; Kenya, 1956-63: Asst Sec., then Sen. Asst Sec., Min. of Commerce and Industry; 1st Sec., CRO, later Commonwealth Office, 1963-66; 1st Sec. (Commercial), British Embassy, Djakarta, 1966-68; 1st Sec. and Head of Chancery, British High Commn, Dar-es-Salaam, 1969-71; Chief Sec., later Dep. Governor, Bermuda, 1971-74; Senior British Trade Comr, Hong Kong, 1974-77. Recreations: painting, golf. Address: c/o Foreign and Commonwealth Office, SW1A 2AH. Club: Royal Commonwealth Society.

KINNEAR, Nigel Alexander, FRCSI; Surgeon to Federated Dublin Voluntary Hospitals until 1974, retired; b 3 April 1907; s of James and Margaret Kinnear; m 1947, Frances Gardner; one d. Educ: Mill Hill Sch.; Trinity Coll., Dublin (MA, MB). Surgeon to Adelaide Hosp., Dublin, 1936; Regius Prof. of Surgery, TCD, 1967-72. President: RCSI, 1961; Royal Academy of Medicine of Ireland, 1968; James IV Surgical Assoc. Hon. FRCSGlas. Publications: articles in surgical jls. Recreations: salmon fishing, gardening. Address: Summerseat Cottage, Clonee, Co. Meath. T: Dunboyne 255353. Clubs: Old Millhillian; Kildare Street and University (Dublin).

KINNOCK, Neil Gordon; MP (Lab) Bedwellty, since 1970; b 28 March 1942; s of Gordon Kinnock, Labourer, and Mary Kinnock (née Howells), Nurse; m 1967, Glenys Elizabeth Parry; one s one d. Educ: Lewis Sch., Pengam; University Coll., Cardiff. BA in Industrial Relations and History, UC, Cardiff (Chm. Socialist Soc., 1962-65; Pres. Students' Union, 1965-66). Tutor Organiser in Industrial and Trade Union Studies, WEA, 1966-70; Mem., Welsh Hosp. Bd, 1969-71. PPS to Sec. of State for Employment, 1974-75. Dir, Tribune Publications, 1974-; Mem., Editorial Bd, Labour Research Dept, 1974-. Publications: Wales and the Common Market, 1971; As Nye Said, 1977; contribs to Tribune, Guardian, New Statesman, etc. Recreations: male voice choral music, reading, walking, children; supporting Cardiff City AFC. Address: House of Commons, SW1.

KINNOULL, 15th Earl of, cr 1633; Arthur William George Patrick Hay; Viscount Dupplin and Lord Hay, 1627, 1633, 1697; Baron Hay (Great Britain), 1711; b 26 March 1935; o surv. s of 14th Earl and Mary Ethel Isobel Meyrick (d 1938); S father 1938; m 1961, Gay Ann, er d of Sir Denys Lowson, 1st Bt; one s three d. Educ: Eton. Chartered Land Agent, 1960; Mem., Agricultural Valuers' Assoc., 1962. Fellow, Chartered Land Agents' Soc., 1964. Mem., National Council on Inland Transport, 1964-76. Mem. of Queen's Body Guard for Scotland (Royal Company of Archers), 1965. Junior Cons. Whip, House of Lords, 1966-68; Cons. Opposition Spokesman on Aviation, House of Lords, 1968-70. Chm., Property Owners' Building Soc., 1976- (Dir, 1971-). Mem., Air League Council, 1972; Council Mem., Deep Sea Fishermen's Mission, 1977. Vice-Pres., Nat. Assoc. of Parish Councils, 1970. FRICS 1970. Heir: s Viscount Dupplin, qv. Address: 15 Carlyle Square, SW3; Pier House, Seaview, Isle of Wight. Clubs: Turf, Pratt's, White's, MCC.

KINROSS, 4th Baron cr 1902; David Andrew Balfour, OBE 1968; TD; DL; Writer to the Signet, practising in Edinburgh, since 1931; b 29 March 1906; second s of 2nd Baron Kinross and Caroline Elsie (d 1969), d of A. H. Johnstone Douglas, DL; S brother, 1976; m 1st, 1936, Araminta Peel (marr. diss. 1941); one d; 2nd, 1948, Helen (d 1969), d of late A. W. Hog, Edinburgh; one s; 3rd, 1972, Ruth Beverley, d of late W. H. Mill and formerly wife of K. W. B. Middleton. Educ: Sherborne; Edinburgh Univ. Qualified Solicitor, 1931; joined WS Society, 1931. Commissioned RA (TA), 1926; served War of 1939-45, Europe and Burma; Lt-Col 78 LAA Regt RA, 1942, 56 Anti-Tank Regt RA, 1944; Hon. Col 278 (Lowland) Field Regt RA (TA), 1964-67. Member Queen's Body Guard for Scotland (Royal Company of Archers). National Chairman, British Legion, Scotland, 1965-68; Chm., Astley Ainslie, Edenhall and Associated Hospitals, Edinburgh, 1957-74. DL Edinburgh, 1966. Recreations: shooting, gardening and travel. Heir: s Hon. Christopher Patrick Balfour [b 1 Oct. 1949; m 1974, Susan, d of I. R. Pitman, WS]. Address: 58 India Street, Edinburgh EH3 6HD. T: 031-225 2651; The Forge Cottage, Humbie, East

Lothian. *T:* Humbie 277. *Clubs:* Army and Navy; New (Edinburgh); Hon. Co. of Edinburgh Golfers.

KINROSS, John Blythe, CBE 1967 (OBE 1958); *b* 31 Jan. 1904; *s* of late John Kinross, RSA, architect, and late Mary Louisa Margaret Hall; *m* 1st, 1930; one *s* two *d*; 2nd, 1943, Mary Elizabeth Connon; one *s* two *d. Educ:* George Watson's Coll., Edinburgh. Manager Issue Dept, Gresham Trust, until 1933 when started business on own account as Cheviot Trust (first Issuing House to undertake small issues). Joined Industrial & Commercial Finance Corp. Ltd at inception, 1945; Gen. Man., 1948; Exec. Dir, 1961; Dep. Chm., 1964-74. Mem. Finance Cttee, Royal College of Surgeons, 1956-; Hon. Financial Adviser to Royal Scottish Academy, 1950-. Founded Mary Kinross Charitable Trust, 1957 (includes Good Companions Workshops Ltd, Student Homes Ltd and various med. res. projects). Chairman: Scottish Industrial Finance Ltd; London Atlantic Investment Trust Ltd; Estate Duties Investment Trust Ltd, 1973-76; Director: Equity Income Trust Ltd; House of Fraser Ltd, 1966-72; Imperial Investments Ltd; Scottish Ontario Investment Co. Ltd; Investment Trust of Guernsey Ltd and other companies. Hon. RSA, 1957; Hon. FFARCS, 1961. *Recreation:* farming. *Address:* 23 Cumberland Terrace, NW1. *T:* 01-935 8979; (office) 01-928 7822. *Club:* Athenæum.

KINSELLA, Thomas; poet; Professor of English, Temple University, Philadelphia, since 1970; *b* 4 May 1928; *m* 1955, Eleanor Walsh; one *s* two *d.* Entered Irish Civil Service, 1946; resigned from Dept of Finance, 1965. Artist-in-residence, 1965-67, Prof. of English, 1967-70, Southern Illinois Univ. Elected to Irish Academy of Letters, 1965. J. S. Guggenheim Meml Fellow, 1968-69, 1971-72. *Publications: poetry:* Poems, 1956; Another September, 1958; Downstream, 1962; Nightwalker and other poems, 1968; Notes from the Land of the Dead, 1972; Butcher's Dozen, 1972; A Selected Life, 1972; Finistère, 1972; New Poems, 1973; Selected Poems 1956 to 1968, 1973; Vertical Man and The Good Fight, 1973; One, 1974; A Technical Supplement, 1976; (trans.) The Táin, 1969; (ed) Selected Poems of Austin Clarke, 1976. *Address:* 47 Percy Place, Dublin, Ireland.

KINSEY, Joseph Ronald, JP; *b* 28 Aug. 1921; *s* of Walter and Florence Annie Kinsey; *m* 1953, Joan Elizabeth Walters; one *d. Educ:* Birmingham elementary and C of E schools. Shop management trng; served RAF ground staff, 1940-47; GPO telephone engr, 1947-57; started own business, florists, horticultural and fruit shop, 1957. MP (C) Birmingham, Perry Barr, 1970-Feb. 1974; contested (C) Birmingham, Perry Barr, Oct. 1974. JP Birmingham, 1962. *Address:* 147 Grange Road, Birmingham B24 0ES. *T:* 021-373 4606.

KINSLEY, Rev. Prof. James, MA, PhD, DLitt; FBA 1971; Professor of English Studies and Head of Department of English Studies, University of Nottingham, since 1961; *b* Borthwick, Midlothian, 17 April 1922; *s* of late Louis Morrison Kinsley, Gorebridge; *m* 1949, Helen, 2nd *d* of late C. C. Dawson, Dewsbury; two *s* one *d. Educ:* Royal High Sch., Edinburgh; Edinburgh Univ.; Oriel Coll., Oxford. MA Edinburgh and James Boswell Scholar, 1943; BA Oxford (1st cl. Hons Sch. of Eng. Lang. and Lit.), 1947; PhD Edinburgh, 1951; MA Oxford, 1952; DLitt Edinburgh, 1959. Served with RA, 1943-45 (Captain). Lectr in English, University Coll. of Wales, 1947-54; Prof. of English Language and Literature in Univ. of Wales (at Swansea), 1954-61; Dean, Faculty of Arts, Univ. of Nottingham, 1967-70. Lectures: William Will Meml, 1960, 1975; Gregynog, Aberystwyth, 1963; Warton, British Acad., 1974. Editor, Renaissance and Modern Studies, Nottingham Miscellany, 1961-68; Gen. Editor: Oxford English Novels, 1967-77; Oxford English Memoirs and Travels, 1969-77. Vice-President: Tennyson Soc., 1963-; Scottish Text Soc., 1971-. Ordained deacon 1962, priest 1963; Public Preacher, Southwell Diocese, 1964; Mem., C of E Liturgical Commn, 1976-. FRSL 1959; FRHistS 1961. *Publications:* (ed) Lindsay, Ane Satyre of the Thrie Estaits, 1954; Scottish Poetry: A Critical Survey, 1955; (ed) W. Dunbar: Poems, 1958; (ed) John Dryden: Poems, 4 vols, 1958; (ed) Lindsay, Squyer Meldrum, 1959; (ed) Robert Burns: Poems and Songs, 1959; (ed) Dryden, The Works of Virgil, 1961; (ed with Helen Kinsley) Dryden, Absalom and Achitophel, 1961; (ed) John Dryden: Poetical Works, 1962; (ed) John Dryden: Selected Poems, 1963; (with J. T. Boulton) English Satiric Poetry: Dryden to Byron, 1966; (ed) J. Galt, Annals of the Parish, 1967; (ed) Robert Burns: Poems and Songs, 3 vols, 1968; (ed) The Oxford Book of Ballads, 1969; (textual editor) The Novels of Jane Austen, 5 vols, 1970-71; (ed with George Parfitt) Dryden's Criticism, 1970; (with Helen Kinsley) Dryden: The Critical Heritage, 1971; (ed) Alexander Carlyle of Inveresk: Anecdotes and Characters, 1973. Contribs to Encyclopædia Britannica, Review of English Studies, Medium Aevum, Modern Language Review, etc. *Recreations:* carpentry,

gardening, folk-song. *Address:* 17 Elm Avenue, Beeston, Nottingham NG9 1BU. *T:* Nottingham 257438.

KINTORE, 12th Earl of, *cr* 1677; **James Ian Keith;** Lord Keith of Inverurie, 1677 (Scot.); Bt 1897; Baron 1925; Viscount Stonehaven 1938; CEng; AIStructE; Major, RM, Royal Marine Engineers; Member Royal Company of Archers; *b* 25 July 1908; *er s* of John Lawrence Baird, 1st Viscount Stonehaven, PC, GCMG, DSO, and Lady Ethel Sydney Keith-Falconer (later Countess of Kintore, 11th in line), *e d* of 9th Earl of Kintore; name changed from Baird to Keith, 1967; *S* to Viscountcy of Stonehaven, 1941, and to Earldom of Kintore, 1974; *m* 1935, Delia Virginia, *d* of William Loyd; two *s* one *d. Educ:* Eton; Royal School of Mines, London. UK Delegate to Council of Europe and Western European Union, 1954-64. Councillor, Grampian Region (Chm., Water Services Cttee). DL Kincardineshire, 1959; Vice-Lieut, 1965-76. *Heir: s* Master of Kintore, Lord Inverurie, *qv. Address:* Keith Hall, Inverurie, Aberdeenshire AB5 0LD. *T:* Inverurie 21564. *Clubs:* Beefsteak; New (Edinburgh); Rand (Johannesburg).

KIPARSKY, Prof. Valentin Julius Alexander, MA, PhD; Finnish writer and Professor, Helsinki, retired 1974; Member of the Finnish Academy, 1977; *b* St Petersburg, 4 July 1904; *s* of Professor René Kiparsky and Hedwig (*née* Sturtzel); *m* 1940, Aina Dagmar, MagPhil, *d* of Rev. Matti Jaatinen and Olga (née Jungmann); one *s. Educ:* St Annen-Schule, St Petersburg; St Alexis Sch., Perkjärvi, Finland; Finnish Commercial Sch., Viipuri, Finland; Helsinki Univ.; Prague Univ.; and research work in different countries. Helsinki University: Junior Lectr, 1933, Sen. Lectr, 1938, actg Prof., 1946, Prof., 1947 and again, 1963. Visiting Prof., Indiana Univ., Bloomington, USA, 1952, Minnesota Univ., USA, 1961-62; Prof. of Russian Language and Literature, University of Birmingham, 1952-55, when he returned to Finland; Prof. of Slavonic Philology, Freie Univ., Berlin, 1958-63. Co-Editor: Slavistische Veröffentlichungen (W Berlin), 1958-; Scando-Slavica (Copenhagen), 1963-. Lt Finnish Army, 1939-40, 1941-42; Translator and Interpreter to Finnish Govt, 1942-44; Director: Finnish Govtl Inst. for studies of USSR, 1948-50; Osteuropa-Institut, W Berlin, 1958-63. Pres., Societas Scientiarum Fennica; Mem., Finn. Acad.; Corresp. Member: Akad. der Wissenschaften und der Literatur, Mainz; Internat. Cttee of Slavists. Dr *hc*: Poznań, 1973; Stockholm 1975. Comdr of the Finnish Lion, 1954; Order Zasługi (Poland, 1974. *Publications:* Die gemeinslavischen Lehnwörter aus dem Germanischen, 1934; Fremdes im Baltendeutsch, 1936; Die Kurenfrage, 1939; Suomi Venäjän Kirjallisuudessa, 1943 and 1945; Venäjän Runotar, 1946; Norden i den Ryska Skönlitteraturen, 1947; Wortakzent der russischen Schriftsprache, 1962; Russische historische Grammatik I, 1963; English and American Characters in Russian Fiction, 1964; Russische historische Grammatik II, 1967, III, 1974; numerous articles in various languages in learned jls. *Recreation:* cycling. *Address:* Maurinkatu 8-12 C 37, Helsinki, Finland.

KIPPING, Sir Norman (Victor), GCMG 1966; KBE 1962; Kt 1946; JP; *b* 11 May 1901; *y s* of P. P. and Rose E. Kipping, London; *m* 1928, Eileen Rose; two *s* one *d. Educ:* University Coll. Sch.; Birkbeck Coll., London. Research Dept, GPO, 1920-21, as jun. engineer; Internat. Western Electric Co., 1921-26; Standard Telephones & Cables Ltd, 1926-42, finally as works manager; Head of Regional Div., Min. of Production, 1942-45; Under-Sec. Bd of Trade, 1945; Dir-Gen., FBI, 1946-65; retired 1965 on formation of Confedn of British Industry. Dir, Brit. Overseas Fairs Ltd from foundation, 1953 (Chm. 1958-66). FIEE, FIPE (Chm. Council, 1940-41). Chm. Coun. University Coll. Sch., 1960-71; President: Consultative Council of Professional Management Orgs, 1966-76; Anglo-Finnish Soc., 1966-74; Past Sec., Anglo-Amer. Coun. on Productivity; past Member: Br. Productivity Coun.; Dollar Exports Coun.; Export Coun. for Europe; Brit. Nat. Export Coun.; Nat. Prod. Advisory Council; BBC Adv. Council; Fulton Cttee on Civil Service. Led missions for FBI to India, Japan, Nigeria and for HM Govt to Zambia. Hon. Fellow, BIM (Elbourne Lectr, 1965). Hon. DSc Loughborough, 1966. Commander: Order of Dannebrog (Denmark), 1948; Order of the Lion (Finland), 1959; Order of Merit of the Italian Republic, 1962; Order of Vasa (Sweden), 1962. *Publication:* The Suez Contractors, 1969; Summing Up (memoirs), 1972. *Recreations:* shooting, gardening. *Address:* 36 Barrydene, Oakleigh Road North, Whetstone, N20 9HG. *T:* 01-445 4054. *Club:* East India, Devonshire, Sports and Public Schools.

KIRALFY, Prof. Albert Kenneth Roland; Professor of Law, King's College, London, since 1964; *b* Toronto, 5 Dec. 1915; *s* of Bolossy Kiralfy, Theatrical Impresario, and Helen Dawnay; *m* 1960, Roberta Ann Routledge. *Educ:* Streatham Grammar Sch.; King's Coll., London Univ. LLB 1935, LLM 1936, PhD 1949,

London. Served War of 1939-45. Called to the Bar, Gray's Inn, 1947. King's Coll., London: Asst Lectr, 1937-39 and 1947-48; Lectr, 1948-51; Reader, 1951-64; Dean of Law Faculty, 1974-77; Fellow of King's College, 1971. Chm., Bd of Studies in Laws, London Univ., 1971-74. Vis. Prof., Osgoode Hall Law Sch., Toronto, 1961-62; Exchange Scholar, Leningrad Law Sch., Spring 1964, Moscow Law Sch., April 1970; Prague Acad. of Sciences, April 1975. Dir, Comparative Law Course, Luxembourg, Aug. 1968. Chm., Council of Hughes Parry Hall, London Univ., 1970-. Mem. Editorial Bd, Internat. and Comparative Law Quarterly, 1956-. *Publications:* The Action on the Case, 1951; The English Legal System, 1954 (and later edns; 5th edn 1973); A Source Book of English Law, 1957; Potter's Historical Introduction to English Law, (4th edn) 1958; (with Dr G. Jones) Guide to Selden Society Publications, 1960; Translation of Russian Civil Codes, 1966; chapter, English Law, in Derrett, Introduction to Legal Systems, 1968; (with Miss R. A. Routledge) Guide to Additional MSS at Gray's Inn Library, 1971; General Editor, Comparative Law of Matrimonial Property, 1972; contributed: Encyclopædia of Soviet Law (Leiden), 1973; Contemporary Soviet Law, 1974; East-West Business Transactions, 1974; Common Law, Encyclopædia Britannica, 1974; Codification in the Communist World, 1975; various legal jls. *Rapporteur*, The Child without Family Ties, Congress of Jean Bodin Soc., Strasbourg, 1972. *Recreations:* travel, reading, languages. *Address:* 25 Woodhayes Road, Wimbledon, SW19 4RF.

KIRBY, Sir Arthur (Frank), GBE 1969 (KBE 1957); CMG 1945; FCIT; *b* Slough, 13 July 1899; *s* of George and Lily Maria Kirby; *m* 1935, Winifred Kate, *d* of Fred Bradley, Waterloo Park, Liverpool; one *d*. *Educ:* Sir William Borlase's Sch., Marlow; London Sch. of Economics. Entered Service GWR 1917; returned 1919 after serving with London Rifle Brigade and 2nd Rifle Brigade; special training for six years with GWR; entered Colonial Service, Asst Sec., Takoradi Harbour, Gold Coast, 1928; Traffic Manager, Gold Coast Railway, 1936; Asst Supt of the Line, Kenya and Uganda Railways and Harbours, 1938; Gen. Man., Palestine Railways and Ports Authority and Dir Gen. Hejaz Railway, 1942-48; Supt of the Line, E African Railways and Harbours, 1949-50; Asst Comr for Transport, E Africa High Commn, 1951-52; Actg Comr for Transport, 1952-53; Gen. Manager, East African Railways and Harbours 1953-57; Commissioner for East Africa, London, 1958-63; Chairman: British Transport Docks Board, 1963-67; Nat. Ports Council, 1967-71; Pres., Shipping and Forwarding Agents Inst., 1966. Vice-Pres., Royal Commonwealth Society (Dep. Chm., 1965-68); Dep. Chm., Gt Ormond Street Children's Hosp., 1963-69; Governor, National Hosp. for Nervous Diseases, 1966-69; Mem. Council, Royal Society of Arts, 1966-71. Chm., Palestine Assoc.; Treasurer, British Inst. in Eastern Africa. OStJ. Liveryman, Worshipful Co. of Barber Surgeons, 1977-. *Address:* 6 Baltimore Court, The Drive, Hove, E Sussex BN3 3PR.

KIRBY, Dennis, MVO 1961; MBE 1955; Directeur Adjoint, European Investment Bank, since 1974; *b* 5 April 1923; *s* of William Ewart Kirby and Hannah Kirby; *m* 1943, Mary Elizabeth Kilby; one *d*. *Educ:* Hull Grammar Sch.; RNC Greenwich; Queen's Coll., Cambridge. Lt (A) RNVR (fighter pilot), 1940-46. Colonial Service, Sierra Leone, 1946-62 (District Comr, 1950; Perm. Sec., 1961-62); 1st Sec., UK Diplomatic Service, 1962; General Manager: East Kilbride Development Corp., 1963-68; Irvine Development Corp., 1967-72; Industrial Dir, Scotland, DTI, 1972-74. MBIM. *Publication:* Careers in New Town Building, 1970. *Recreations:* shooting, fishing, skiing, golf, squash. *Address:* European Investment Bank, 2 place de Metz, Luxembourg; Monkton Hall, Southwood, Troon, Ayrshire. *Club:* Royal Naval Volunteer Reserves (Scotland) (Glasgow).

KIRBY, Prof. Gordon William, ScD, PhD; FRIC; FRSE; Regius Professor of Chemistry, University of Glasgow, since 1972; *b* 20 June 1934; *s* of William Admiral Kirby and Frances Teresa Kirby (*née* Townson); *m* 1964, Audrey Jean Rusbridge, *d* of Col C. E. Rusbridge; two *s*. *Educ:* Liverpool Inst. High Sch.; Gonville and Caius Coll., Cambridge (MA, PhD, ScD); FRIC 1970; FRSE 1975. 1851 Exhbn Senior Student, 1958-60, Asst Lectr, 1960-61, Lectr, 1961-67, Imperial Coll. of Science and Technology; Prof. of Organic Chemistry, Univ. of Technology, Loughborough, 1967-72; Mem., Chem. Cttee, SRC, 1971-75. Corday-Morgan Medal, Chem. Soc., 1969; Tilden Lectr, Chem. Soc., 1974-75. *Publications:* Co-editor: Elucidation of Organic Structures by Physical and Chemical Methods, vol. IV, parts I, II, and III, 1972; Fortschritte der Chemie organischer Naturstoffe, 1971-; contributor to Jl Chem. Soc., etc. *Address:* Chemistry Department, The University, Glasgow G12 8QQ.

KIRBY, Gwendolen Maud, MVO; Matron, The Hospital for Sick Children, Great Ormond Street, 1951-69; *b* 17 Dec. 1911; 3rd *d* of late Frank M. Kirby, Gravesend, Kent. *Educ:* St Mary's Sch., Calne, Wilts. State Registered Nurse: trained at Nightingale Training Sch., St Thomas' Hosp., SE1. 1933-36; The Mothercraft Training Soc., Cromwell House, Highgate, 1936; State Certified Midwife: trained at General Lying-in Hosp., York Road, Lambeth, 1938-39; Registered Sick Children's Nurse: trained at the Hospital for Sick Children, Great Ormond Street, WC1, 1942-44. Awarded Nightingale Fund Travelling Scholarship, 1948-49, and spent 1 year in Canada and United States. Mem. of Gen. Nursing Council, 1955-65. *Address:* Brackenfield, Winsford, Minehead, Som.

KIRBY, Jack Howard, CBE 1972; Chairman, International Tanker Owners Pollution Federation, 1968-73; Chairman, Shell Tankers (UK) Ltd, 1963-72; Managing Director, Shell International Marine Ltd, 1959-72; Director, Shell International Petroleum Co. Ltd, 1969-72; *b* 1 Feb. 1913; *s* of late Group Captain Frank Howard Kirby, VC, CBE and late Kate Kirby; *m* 1940, Emily Colton; one *s*. *Educ:* Sir Roger Manwood's Sch., Sandwich. Joined Shell, 1930, retired 1972; in USA with Shell, 1937-52, incl. secondment to British Shipping Mission and British Petroleum Mission, Washington, DC, 1940-46. Chm., Lights Adv. Cttee, 1958-. Pres., Chamber of Shipping of the UK, 1971-72. Chevalier 1st Class, Order of St Olav, 1968. *Recreations:* golf, fishing, gardening, bridge. *Address:* September Song, West Drive, Sunningdale, Ascot, Berks SL5 0LF. *T:* Wentworth 4154. *Clubs:* Berkshire Golf, Royal and Ancient Golf.

KIRBY, Air Cdre John Lawrance, CB 1946; CBE 1943; JP; DL; RAF; *b* 1899; *s* of Wilson Kirby, York; *m* 1941, Rachel Margaret Cunningham, *y d* of R. G. Smith; two *s* three *d*. *Educ:* Archbishop Holgate's Sch., York. JP Grimsby, 1951; DL Lincs, 1952. *Address:* Utterby Close, Louth, Lincs. *T:* North Thoresby 240.

KIRBY, Louis; Editor, Evening News, since 1974; Vice-Chairman, Evening News Ltd, since 1975; *b* 30 Nov. 1928; 2nd *s* of late William Kirby and Anne Kirby; *m* 1st, 1952, Marcia Teresa Lloyd (marr. diss. 1976); three *s* two *d*; 2nd, 1976, Heather Veronica (*née* Nicholson); one *s*. *Educ:* Our Lady Immaculate, Liverpool; Coalbrookdale High Sch. Daily Mail: Gen. Reporter, subseq. Courts Corresp., and Polit. Corresp., 1953-62; Daily Sketch: Chief Reporter, subseq. Leader Writer and Polit. Editor, Asst Editor, Exec. Editor, and, Actg Editor, 1962-71; Daily Mail (when relaunched): Dep. Editor, 1971-74. Dir, Associated Newspaper Gp, 1977-. *Recreations:* tennis, theatre, birdwatching, Brighton. *Address:* Evening News, Northcliffe House, EC4Y 0JA. *T:* 01-353 6000.

KIRBY, Hon. Sir Richard (Clarence), Kt 1961; Chairman, Advertising Standards Council, since 1973; *b* 22 Sept. 1904; *s* of Samuel Enoch Kirby and Agnes Mary Kirby, N Queensland; *m* 1937, Hilda Marie Ryan; two *d*. *Educ:* The King's Sch., Parramatta; University of Sydney (LLB). Solicitor, NSW, 1928; called to Bar, 1933; served AIF, 1942-44; Mem. Adult Adv. Educl Council to NSW Govt, 1944-46; Judge, Dist Court, NSW, 1944-47; Mem. Austr. War Crimes Commn, 1945, visiting New Guinea, Morotai, Singapore, taking evidence on war crimes; Australia Rep. on War Crimes, Lord Mountbatten's HQ, Ceylon, 1945; Royal Commissioner on various occasions for Federal, NSW and Tasmanian Govts, 1945-47; Acting Judge Supreme Court of NSW, 1947; Chief Judge, Commonwealth Court of Conciliation and Arbitration, 1956-73; Austr. Rep., UN Security Council's Cttee on Good Offices on Indonesian Question, 1947-48, participating in Security Council Debates, Lake Success, USA; Chm. Stevedoring Industry Commn, 1947-49; (first) Pres., Commonwealth Conciliation and Arbitration Commn, 1956-73. Chm., Nat. Stevedoring Conf., 1976-77. *Recreations:* horse racing and breeding. *Address:* The White House, Berrara, NSW 2540, Australia. *T:* Nowra 412171. *Clubs:* Athenæum, Victoria Racing, Victoria Amateur Turf, Moonee Valley Racing and Mornington Racing, Victoria Golf (Melbourne).

KIRBY, Walter, CIE 1945; BSc (Birmingham); retired; *b* 6 Dec. 1891; *m* 1st, 1920, Lily Watkins (*d* 1957); two *d*; 2nd, 1961, Violet Eveline Harris. *Educ:* Birmingham Univ. (BSc 1919). Past Pres. Mining Geological and Metallurgical Institute of India. Joined Dept of Mines in India as Junior Inspector of Mines, 1921; Senior Inspector, 1925-38; Chief Inspector of Mines in India, 1938-46; retired, 1946. *Address:* 4 Haddington Street, The Range, Toowoomba, Queensland 4350, Australia.

KIRCHEIS, John Reinhardt; Regional Executive, Mobil South, since 1976; *b* 4 April 1916; *s* of J. R. Kircheis III and Thelba

Deibeet; *m* 1940, Jean Ohme; two *d. Educ:* Buena Vista College. Teacher and Prin., Bode Public Schools, 1937; Account Analyst, General Motors Corp., 1940; Lt-Comdr, USNR, 1942; various assignments, Mobil Oil Corp., 1946; Vice-Pres. and Area Manager, Mobil Europe Inc., 1966; Man. Dir, Mobil Oil Co. Ltd, 1968; Chm., Mobil Oil Co. Ltd and Mobil Holdings Group, 1969-75. *Recreations:* golf, fishing, music. *Address:* Mobil Oil Corporation, 150 East 42nd Street, New York, NY 10017, USA. *Clubs:* Directors', Royal Automobile, New Century.

KIRCHNER, Bernard Joseph, CBE 1944; *b* 1894; *er s* of Alexander and Teresa Kirchner; *m* 1st, 1924, Vivienne Mary (*d* 1949), *y d* of late Lt-Col T. P. Ffrench, IA, and step-*d* of late Ray Knight, ICS; two *d* ; 2nd, 1957, Margaret Jane, *o d* of late T. M. Upton, and *widow* of G. W. F. Brown. *Educ:* Imperial Coll. of Science, London Univ. European War, 1914-18, France and Flanders, Artists' Rifles, South Staffs Regt and RAF (wounded, 1914 Star, Gen. Service and Victory Medals). Joined The Statesman, Calcutta, 1922; Mgr The Englishman, 1928-30; Man. Editor Delhi office of The Statesman, 1932-41, and 1946-48; Dir, 1940; London Agent, The Statesman, 1948-54; Mem. of Nat. Service Advisory Cttee, Delhi, 1939-41; Chief Press Adviser, Govt of India, 1941-44; Vice-Chm. Ex-Services Assoc., India, 1946; Delhi Corresp., The Times, 1946-47. Mem. Council of Commonwealth Press Union; Pres. London Assoc. of British Empire Newspapers Overseas, 1953-54. Silver Jubilee Medal, 1935. *Address:* 7 Bell Road, East Molesey, Surrey.

KIRK, Alexander Comstock; US Ambassador (retired); *b* 26 Nov. 1888; *s* of James Alexander Kirk and Clara Comstock. *Educ:* Yale; Harvard; Ecole Libre des Sciences Politiques. American Embassy, Berlin, 1915; American Legation, The Hague, 1917. Amer. Commission to negotiate peace, Paris, 1918-19; Asst to Sec. of State, 1919; Amer. Embassy, Tokyo, 1920; Amer. Legation, Peking, 1922; Amer. Embassy, Mexico City, 1924; Dept of State, Washington, DC, 1925; Amer. Embassy, Rome, 1928-38; Chargé d'Affaires, Moscow, 1938, Berlin, 1939; Minister-Counsellor, Rome, 1940; Envoy Extraordinary and Minister Plenipotentiary to Egypt and Saudi Arabia, 1941; Ambassador to Govt of King of Hellenes, 1943; US Rep., Advisory Council for Italy, 1944; US Adviser to Supreme Allied Comdr-in-Chief Mediterranean Theatre; Ambassador to Italy, 1944; retired, 1946. *Address:* 4630 Calle Altivo, Tucson, Arizona 85718, USA.

KIRK, Prof. Geoffrey Stephen, DSC 1945; LittD; FBA 1959; Regius Professor of Greek, University of Cambridge, since 1974; Fellow of Trinity College, Cambridge, since 1974; *b* 3 Dec. 1921; *s* of Frederic Tilzey Kirk, MC, and Enid Hilda (*née* Pentecost); *m* 1st, 1950, Barbara Helen Traill (marr. diss. 1975); one *d* ; 2nd, 1975, Kirsten Jensen. *Educ:* Rossall Sch.; Clare Coll., Cambridge. LittD Cambridge, 1965. Served War in Royal Navy, 1941-45; commissioned 1942; Temp. Lt, RNVR, 1945. Took Degree at Cambridge, 1946; Research Fellow, Trinity Hall, 1946-49; Student, Brit. Sch. at Athens, 1947; Commonwealth Fund Fellow, Harvard Univ., 1949-50; Fellow, Trinity Hall, 1950-70; Cambridge University: Asst Lecturer in Classics, 1951; Lecturer in Classics, 1952-61; Reader in Greek, 1961-65; Prof. of Classics, Yale Univ., 1965-70; Prof. of Classics, Bristol Univ., 1971-73. Visiting Lecturer, Harvard Univ., 1958; Sather Prof. of Classical Literature, University of California, Berkeley, 1968-69. MA (Yale) 1965. *Publications:* Heraclitus, the Cosmic Fragments, 1954; (with J. E. Raven) The Presocratic Philosophers, 1958; The Songs of Homer, 1962 (abbrev., as Homer and the Epic, 1965); Euripides, Bacchae, 1970; Myth, 1970; The Nature of Greek Myths, 1974; Homer and the Oral Tradition, 1977; articles in classical, archæological and philosophical journals. *Recreation:* sailing. *Address:* Trinity College, Cambridge; 136 Castle Street, Woodbridge, Suffolk.

KIRK, Grayson Louis; President Emeritus, Columbia University; *b* 12 Oct. 1903; *s* of Traine Caldwell Kirk and Nora Eichelberger; *m* 1925, Marion Louise Sands; one *s. Educ:* Miami Univ. (AB); Clark Univ. (AM); Ecole Libre des Sciences Politiques, Paris, 1928-29. PhD University of Wisconsin, 1930. Prof. of History, Lamar Coll., Beaumont, Tex, 1925-27; Social Science Research Coun. Fellowship (chiefly spent at London Sch. of Economics), 1936-37; Instructor in Political Science, 1929-30, Asst Prof., 1930-36, Associate Prof., 1936-38, Prof., 1938-40, University of Wisconsin; Associate Prof. of Government, Columbia Univ., 1940-43; Head, Security Section, Div. of Political Studies, US Dept of State, 1942-43; Mem. US Delegn Staff, Dumbarton Oaks, 1944; Exec. Officer, Third Commn, San Francisco Conf., 1945. Research Associate, Yale Inst. of Internat. Studies, 1943-44; Prof. of Government, Columbia Univ., 1943-47; Prof. of Internat Relations, Acting Dir of Sch. of Internat. Affairs, and Dir of European Inst., 1947-49. Appointed Provost in Nov. 1949, and also Vice-Pres in July

1950; became acting head of Columbia in President Eisenhower's absence on leave, March 1951; Pres. and Trustee of Columbia Univ., 1953-68; Bryce Prof. of History of Internat. Relations, Columbia, 1959-72, Emeritus Prof., 1972. Trustee: Greenwich Savings Bank; The Asia Foundation; French Inst.; Lycée Français of NY; Academy of Political Science (Vice-Pres. and Dir); American Philosophical Soc.; Pilgrims of the US (Vice-Pres.); Council on Foreign Relations; Amer. Acad. of Arts and Sciences; Amer. Soc. of French Legion of Honour (Pres.). Director: International Business Machines Corporation; Dividend Shares Inc.; Nation-Wide Securities Co. Inc.; France-America Soc. Hon. LLD: Miami, 1950; Waynesburg Coll., Brown Univ., Union Coll, 1951; Puerto Rico, Clark, Princeton, New York, Wisconsin, Columbia, Jewish Theol. Seminary of America, 1953; Syracuse, Williams Coll., Pennsylvania, Harvard, Washington, St Louis, Central Univ., Caracas, Univ. of the Andes, Merida, Venezuela, Univ. of Zulia, Maracaibo, Venezuela, Univ. of Delhi, India, Thamasset Univ., Bangkok, 1954; Johns Hopkins Univ., Baltimore, Amherst, 1956; Dartmouth Coll., Northwestern Univ., 1958; Tennessee, 1960; St Lawrence, 1963; Denver, Notre Dame, Bates Coll., 1964; Waseda (Japan), Michigan, 1965; Sussex, 1966; Hon. LHD N Dakota, 1958; Hon. PhD Bologna, 1951; Dr of Civil Law King's Coll., Halifax, Nova Scotia, 1958. Associate KStJ 1959. Comdr, Order of Orange-Nassau, 1952; Hon. KBE, 1955; Grand Officer, Order of Merit, of the Republic, Italy, 1956; Grand Officier Légion d'Honneur, France, 1973. Medal of the Order of Taj, Iran, 1961; Grand Cross, Order of George I (Greece), 1965; Order of the Sacred Treasure, 1st Class (Japan), 1965; Comdr, Ordre des Palmes Académiques (France), 1966. *Publications:* Philippine Independence, 1936; Contemporary International Politics (with W. R. Sharp), 1940; (with R. P. Stebbins) War and National Policy, Syllabus, 1941; The Study of International Relations in American Colleges and Universities, 1947. *Address:* Columbia University, 125 Maiden Lane, New York, NY 10038, USA. *T:* 943-8186. *Clubs:* Athenæum; Century, University, (New York).

KIRK, Rt. Hon. Herbert Victor, PC (N Ireland) 1962; Member (U) for South Belfast, Northern Ireland Assembly, 1973-75; *b* 5 June 1912; *s* of Alexander and Mary A. Kirk; *m* 1944, Gladys A. Dunn; three *s. Educ:* Queen's Univ., Belfast (BComSc). MP Windsor Div. of Belfast, NI Parlt, 1956-72; Minister of Labour and Nat. Insce, Govt of N Ireland, 1962-64; Minister of Education, 1964-65; Minister of Finance, 1965-72, Jan.-May 1974, resigned. FCA 1940. JP Co. Borough Belfast. *Recreation:* golf. *Address:* 38 Massey Avenue, Belfast BT4 2JT, Northern Ireland. *Clubs:* Royal Portrush Golf, Belvoir Park Golf (Pres.).

KIRK, James Balfour, CMG 1941; MB, ChB; FRCP; DPH; DTM and H; retired; *b* 7 April 1893; *s* of John A. G. Kirk, Falkirk, and Jessie Y. Rintoul, also of Falkirk; *m* 1917, Jane C., *d* of Hume Purdie, LDS, Edinburgh; three *d. Educ:* Falkirk High Sch.; George Watson's Coll., Edinburgh; Edinburgh Univ. (Vans Dunlop Scholar). Private, 9th Bn Royal Scots, Aug.-Dec. 1914; 2nd Lt, RFA 1914-16; Lt RAMC, 1917-20 (1914-15 Star, Victory and General Service Medals); Medical Officer of Health, Port Louis, Mauritius, 1922-26; Acting Dir, Medical and Health Dept, Mauritius, 1926-27; Dir, Medical and Health Dept, Mauritius, 1927-41; Dir of Medical Services, Gold Coast, 1941-44; Dir, Health Div. Greece Mission, UNRRA, 1945; Chief Medical Officer, Central Headquarters, Displaced Persons Operation UNRRA, Germany, Aug. 1945-Feb. 1946; Temp. MO, Min. of Health, 1946-62. *Publications:* Public Health Practice in the Tropics, 1928; Hints on Equipment and Health for Intending Residents in the Tropics, 1926; Practical Tropical Sanitation, 1936; numerous articles on public health and medical subjects. *Recreations:* gardening, photography. *Address:* 16 Brook Lane, Haywards Heath, West Sussex RH16 1SG. *T:* Lindfield 2185.

KIRK, John Henry, CBE 1957; Emeritus Professor of Marketing (with special reference to horticulture), University of London; *b* 11 April 1907; *s* of William Kirk, solicitor; *m* 1946, Wilfrida Margaret Booth; two *s. Educ:* Durban High Sch., S Africa; Universities of S Africa, Cambridge, North Carolina and Chicago. Ministry of Agriculture (from 1934, as economist and administrator); Under-Sec., 1959-65; Prof. of Marketing, Wye Coll., 1965-72. *Publications:* Economic Aspects of Native Segregation, 1929; Agriculture and the Trade Cycle, 1933. Contributions to Journals of Sociology, Economics and Agricultural Economics. *Recreation:* gardening. *Address:* Burrington, Cherry Gardens, Wye, Ashford, Kent. *T:* Wye 812640.

KIRK, Dame (Lucy) Ruth, DBE 1975; Patron, Society for the Protection of the Unborn Child; *m* 1941, Norman Eric Kirk (later, Rt Hon. Norman Kirk, PC, Prime Minister of New

Zealand; *d* 1974); three *s* two *d*. Awarded title, Dame of the Order of the British Empire, for public services. *Address:* 7 Rimu Vale Street, Rotorua, New Zealand.

KIRK, Dame Ruth; *see* Kirk, Dame L. R.

KIRKALDY, Prof. John Francis, DSc (London); FGS; Emeritus Professor of Geology, University of London, since 1974; *b* 14 May 1908; *o s* of late James and Rose Edith Kirkaldy, Sutton, Surrey; *m* 1935, Dora Muriel, *e d* of late Grimshaw Heyes Berry, Enfield, Middlesex; four *d*. *Educ:* Felsted Sch.; King's Coll., London. 1st Cl. Special Hons BSc (Geol.) 1929; MSc 1932; DSc 1946. Demonstrator in Geology, King's Coll., 1929-33; Asst Lectr in Geology, University Coll., London, 1933-36; Lectr in Geology, King's Coll., London, 1936-47. War Service with Meteorological Branch, RAF, Sqdn Ldr, 1939-45. Reader in Geology and Head of Dept, Queen Mary Coll., 1947-62; Prof. of Geology and Head of Dept, QMC, 1962-74. FKC 1970; Fellow, Queen Mary College, 1976. Daniel Pidgeon Fund, Geol. Soc., 1935; Foulerton Award, Geologists' Assoc., 1947. *Publications:* Outline of Historical Geology (with A. K. Wells), 1948 (and subseq. edns); General Principles of Geology, 1954 (and subseq. edns); Rocks and Minerals in Colour, 1963. Papers in Quart. Jl Geol. Soc.; Proc. Geol. Assoc., Geol. Mag., etc. *Recreations:* gardening, Scottish country dancing. *Address:* Stone House, Byfield Road, Chipping Warden, Banbury, Oxon. *T:* Chipping Warden 689. *Club:* Geological Society's.

KIRKBRIDE, Sir Alec Seath, KCMG 1949 (CMG 1942); Kt 1946; CVO 1954; OBE 1932; MC; Ambassador in Libya, 1954, retired (Minister, 1951-54); Director of the British Bank of the Middle East, 1956-72; *b* 19 Aug. 1897; *m* 1st, 1921, Edith Florence James (*d* 1966); three *s*; 2nd, 1967, Ethel Mary James. Military Service, 1916-21; British Rep., Es Salt, Transjordan, 1921; Junior Asst Sec., Palestine Govt, 1922, Asst Sec., 1926; Asst British Resident, Transjordan, 1927; District Commissioner, Galilee and Acre, 1937; British Resident, in Transjordan, 1939; Minister to the Hashemite Kingdom of the Jordan, 1946; representative of HM Government to Permanent Mandates Commission, Geneva, 1936, 1938, and 1939. *Publications:* A Crackle of Thorns, 1956; An Awakening, 1972; From the Wings, 1976. *Address:* 33 Fernhurst Drive, Goring by Sea, Worthing, West Sussex.

KIRKE, Rear-Adm. David Walter, CB 1967; CBE 1962 (OBE 1945); Director: Brim Exports Ltd, since 1970; Sudan British Development Co. Ltd; Cleveland International Ltd; Mercantile Airship Transportation Ltd; Intercontinental Skyship Ltd; Consultant, Coverdale Training Ltd; *b* 13 March 1915; *s* of late Percy St George Kirke and late Alice Gertrude, *d* of Sir James Gibson Craig, 3rd Bt; *m*. 1st, 1936, Tessa O'Connor (marr. diss., 1950); one *s*; 2nd, 1956, Marion Margaret Gibb; one *s* one *d*. *Educ:* RN Coll., Dartmouth. China Station, 1933-35; Pilot Training, 1937; served War of 1939-45, Russian Convoys, Fighter Sqdns; loaned RAN, 1949-50; Chief of Naval Aviation, Indian Navy, New Delhi, 1959-62. Rear-Adm. 1965; Flag Officer, Naval Flying Training, 1965-68; retired, 1968. MBIM, 1967. *Recreation:* golf. *Address:* Lismore House, Pluckley, Kent. *T:* Pluckley 439. *Clubs:* Naval and Military, Naval.

KIRKHAM, Rt. Rev. John Dudley Galtrey; *see* Sherborne, Bishop Suffragan of.

KIRKHILL, Baron *cr* 1975 (Life Peer), of Kirkhill, Aberdeen; **John Farquharson Smith,** JP; LLD; Minister of State, Scottish Office, since 1975; *b* 7 May 1930; *s* of Alexander F. Smith and Ann T. Farquharson; *m* 1965, Frances Mary Walker Reid; one step-*d*. *Educ:* Robert Gordon's Colleges, Aberdeen. Lord Provost of the City and Royal Burgh of Aberdeen, 1971-75. Hon. LLD Aberdeen, 1974. *Recreation:* golf. *Address:* 3 Rubislaw Den North, Aberdeen. *T:* Aberdeen 34167.

KIRKLEY, Sir (Howard) Leslie, Kt 1977; CBE 1966; Member of Board of Crown Agents, since 1974; Chairman, Disasters Emergency Cttee, since 1977 (Vice-Chairman, 1974-77); *b* Manchester, 1911; *m* 1st, Elsie May, (*née* Rothwell) (*d* 1956); 2nd, Constance Nina Mary, (*née* Bannister-Jones); three *s* two *d*. *Educ:* Manchester Central High Sch. Associate of the Chartered Inst. of Secretaries (ACIS). Worked in local government in Manchester until War of 1939-45 (during which he was engaged in relief work in Europe). Founder and Hon. Sec. of the Leeds and District European Relief Cttee; Gen. Sec., Oxford Cttee for Famine Relief, 1951-61; Dir, Oxfam, 1961-74. Pres., Gen. Conf., Internat. Council of Voluntary Agencies, 1968-71, Chm., Governing Board, 1972-76. Chairman: Standing Conf. on Refugees, 1974- (Vice-Chm., 1969-74); UK Standing Conf. on 2nd UN Develt Decade, 1975-76; Vice-Chm., Voluntary Cttee for Overseas Aid and Develt, 1973-76. Hon.

MA: Oxford, 1969; Leeds, 1970; Bradford, 1974. Fellow, Manchester Polytechnic, 1971. Knight Comdr of the Order of St Sylvester (conferred by HH the Pope), 1963; holds other foreign decorations. *Address:* 25 Capel Close, Oxford. *T:* Oxford 53167.

KIRKMAN, Gen. Sir Sidney Chevalier, GCB 1951 (KCB 1949; CB 1944); KBE 1945 (CBE 1943; OBE 1941); MC; retired; *b* 29 July 1895; *s* of late J. P. Kirkman, Bedford; *m* 1932, Amy Caroline Erskine Clarke; two *s*. *Educ:* Bedford Sch.; RMA, Woolwich. Served European War, 1914-18 (wounded twice, MC, despatches). Staff Coll. Camberley, 1931-32. Served War of 1939-45: Brig. RA, 8th Army, 1942; Comd 50 (N) Div., 1943; Comd British 13th Corps in Italy, 1944; GOC-in-C Southern Comd 1945; Comd 1 Corps BLA, 1945; Dep. Chief of Imperial Gen. Staff, 1945-47; Quartermaster-Gen. to the Forces, 1947-50; Mem. of Army Council, 1945-50; Col Comdt RA, 1947-57; Special Financial Representative in Germany, 1951-52; Dir Gen. of Civil Defence, 1954-60; Chm. Central Fire Brigades Advisory Council for England and Wales, 1957-60. Comdr, Legion of Merit (USA); Officier Légion d'Honneur, Croix de Guerre (France). *Address:* 8 Courtenay Place, Lymington, Hants SO4 9NQ. *Club:* Army and Navy.

KIRKMAN, William Patrick; Secretary, University of Cambridge Appointments Board, since 1968; Fellow, Wolfson College, Cambridge (formerly University College); *b* 23 Oct. 1932; *s* of late Geoffrey Charles Aylward Kirkman and Bertha Winifred Kirkman; *m* 1959, Anne Teasdale Fawcett; two *s* one *d*. *Educ:* Churcher's Coll., Petersfield, Hants; Oriel Coll., Oxford. 2nd cl. hons, mod. langs, 1955; MA 1959; MA (Cantab) by incorporation, 1968. National Service, 1950-52, RASC (L/Cpl). Editorial staff: Express & Star, Wolverhampton, 1955-57; The Times, 1957-64 (Commonwealth staff, 1960-64, Africa Correspondent, 1962-64). Asst Sec., Oxford Univ. Appointments Cttee, 1964-68. Chm., Standing Conf. of University Appointments Services, 1971-73; Mem., Management Cttee, Central Services Unit for Univ. Careers and Appointments Services, 1971-74. Trustee and Hon. Sec., Sir Halley Stewart Trust. *Publications:* Unscrambling an Empire, 1966; contributor to: Commonwealth, International Affairs, Africa Contemporary Record, Financial Times, BBC, etc. *Recreations:* broadcasting, gardening, church activities, writing. *Address:* 19 High Street, Willingham, Cambridge CB4 5ES. *T:* Willingham 60393. *Club:* Royal Commonwealth Society.

KIRKNESS, Donald James; Under-Secretary, Establishment and Finance Division, Ministry of Overseas Development (formerly Overseas Development Administration); *b* 29 Sept 1919; *s* of Charles Stephen and Elsie Winifred Kirkness; *m* 1947, Monica Mary Douch; one *d*. *Educ:* Harvey Grammar Sch., Folkestone. Exchequer and Audit Dept, 1938. Served War: RA and Royal Berkshire Regt, 1939-46. Colonial Office, 1947 (Asst Principal); Financial and Economic Adviser, Windward I, 1955-57; Asst Secretary: Colonial Office, 1962; Dept of Economic Affairs, 1966; Under-Secretary, 1969; Civil Service Dept, 1970-73; DTI, 1973; ODM (Africa Div.), 1973. *Address:* 113 Blackheath Park, SE3.

KIRKPATRICK, Sir Ivone Elliott, 11th Bt, *cr* 1685; *b* 1 Oct. 1942; *s* of Sir James Alexander Kirkpatrick, 10th Bt and Ellen Gertrude, *o d* of Captain R. P. Elliott, late RNR; *S* father 1954. *Educ:* Wellington Coll., Berks; St Mark's Coll., University of Adelaide. Heir: *b* Robin Alexander Kirkpatrick, *b* 19 March 1944. *Address:* c/o ANZ Bank, 32 Grenfell Street, Adelaide, SA 5000, Australia.

KIRKPATRICK, John Lister; Joint Senior Partner, Thomson McLintock & Co, Chartered Accountants, Glasgow and Edinburgh, since 1974; *b* 27 June 1927; *s* of late Henry Joseph Rodway Kirkpatrick and Nora (*née* Lister); *m* 1965, Helen Lindsay (*née* Heap) (marr. diss. 1976); one *s* one *d*; *m* 1977, Gay Elmslie (*née* Goudielock). *Educ:* Inverness Royal Acad. CA. Served RNVR, 1944-47. Thomson McLintock & Co.: apprentice, 1948; qual. CA 1952; Partner, 1958. Partner: Thomson McLintock & Co. (elsewhere in UK); McLintock Main Lafrentz & Co. (internat. firm). Mem., BoT Accountants' Adv. Cttee, 1967-72; Vice-Pres., Inst. of Chartered Accountants of Scotland, 1975-77, Pres., 1977-78. *Publications:* various papers. *Recreations:* fishing, gardening, sailing. *Address:* 40 Lanton Road, Glasgow G43 2SR. *T:* 041-633 1407. *Clubs:* Caledonian; Western (Glasgow); New (Edinburgh); Royal Northern Yacht.

KIRKPATRICK, William Brown; Director and Manager, Finance for Shipping Limited (a subsidiary of Finance for Industry Limited), since 1976; *b* 27 April 1934; *s* of late Joseph Kirkpatrick and Mary Laidlaw Kirkpatrick (*née* Brown), Thornhill, Dumfries-shire. *Educ:* Morton Acad., Thornhill;

George Watson's Coll., Edinburgh; Univ. of Strathclyde (BScEcon); Columbia Business Sch., NY (MS and McKinsey Scholar); Stanford Business Sch. After two years in manufacturing industry in Glasgow, Dundee and London, joined Industrial and Commercial Finance Corp. Ltd (now subsid. of Finance for Industry Ltd), 1960; held various posts in the City, 1960-64 and 1972-74, and in Scotland, 1964-72, inc. Scottish Area Man., 1969-72, and a number of directorships; Industrial Dir, Industrial Develt Divn, Scottish Office, 1974-76 (on secondment). *Recreations:* the countryside, bridge, collecting paintings. *Address:* 20 Abbotsbury House, Abbotsbury Road, W14 8EN. *T:* 01-603 3087; 74 Norwood Park, Bearsden, Glasgow G61 2RZ. *T:* 041-943 0601. *Club:* Caledonian.

KIRKUP, James; travel writer, poet, novelist, playwright, translator, broadcaster; *b* 23 April 1923; *o s* of James Harold Kirkup and Mary Johnston. *Educ:* South Shields High Sch.; Durham Univ. (BA). FRSL 1962. Atlantic Award in Literature (Rockefeller Foundation), 1950; Keats Prize for Poetry, 1974; Gregory Fellow in Poetry, University of Leeds, 1950-52. Visiting Poet and Head of English Dept, Bath Academy of Art, Corsham Court, Wilts, 1953-56; Lectr in English, Swedish Ministry of Education, Stockholm, 1956-57; Prof. of Eng. Lang. and Lit., University of Salamanca, 1957-58, of English, Tohoku Univ., Sendai, Japan, 1958-61; Lecturer in English Literature, University of Malaya in Kuala Lumpur, 1961-62; Literary Editor, Orient/West Magazine, Tokyo, 1963-64; Prof., Japan Women's Univ., 1964-; Poet in Residence and Visiting Prof., Amherst Coll., Mass, 1968-; Prof. of English Literature, Nagoya Univ., 1969-72. Arts Council Fellowship in Creative Writing, Univ. of Sheffield, 1974-75; Morton Vis. Prof. of Internat. Literature, Ohio Univ., 1975-76; Playwright in Residence, Sherman Theatre, University Coll., Cardiff, 1976-77. President: Poets' Soc. of Japan, 1969; Blackmore Soc., 1970; Inst. of Pyschophysical Res., 1970. Mabel Batchelder Award, 1968. *Plays performed:* Upon this Rock (perf. Peterborough Cathedral), 1955; Masque, The Triumph of Harmony (perf. Albert Hall), 1955; The True Mistery of the Nativity, 1957; Dürrenmatt, The Physicists (Eng. trans.), 1963; Dürrenmatt, The Meteor (Eng. trans.); Dürrenmatt, Play Strindberg (Eng. trans.), 1972; The Magic Drum (children's play), 1972; Dürrenmatt, Portrait of a Planet, 1972; Dürrenmatt, The Conformer, 1974; Schiller, Don Carlos, 1975; Cyrano de Bergerac, 1975; *television plays performed:* The Peach Garden, Two Pigeons Flying High, etc. Contributor to BBC, The Listener, The Spectator, Times Literary Supplement, Time and Tide, New Yorker, Botteghe Oscure, London Magazine, Japan Qly, English Teachers' Magazine (Tokyo), etc. *Publications:* The Drowned Sailor, 1948; The Cosmic Shape, 1947; The Creation, 1950; The Submerged Village, 1951; A Correct Compassion, 1952; A Spring Journey, 1954; Upon This Rock, 1955; Camara Laye, The Dark Child (Eng. trans.), 1955; Ancestral Voices (Eng. trans.), 1956; Camara Laye, The Radiance of the King (Eng. trans.), 1956; The True Mistery of the Nativity, 1957; The Descent into the Cave, 1957; The Only Child (autobiog.), 1957; Simone de Beauvoir, Memoirs of a Dutiful Daughter (Eng. trans.), 1958; The Girl from Nowhere (Eng. trans.), 1958; Sorrows, Passions and Alarms, 1959; The Prodigal Son (poems), 1959; It Began in Babel (Eng. trans.), 1961; The Captive (Eng. trans.), 1962; Sins of the Fathers (Eng. trans.), 1962; The Gates of Paradise (Eng. trans.), 1962; These Horned Islands, A Journal of Japan, 1962; frères Gréban, The True Mistery of the Passion, 1962; The Love of Others (novel), 1962; Refusal to Conform, 1963; Tropic Temper: a Memoir of Malaya, 1963; The Heavenly Mandate (Eng. trans.), 1964; Daily Life of the Etruscans (Eng. trans.), 1964; Erich Kästner, The Little Man (Eng. trans.), 1966; Erich Kästner, The Little Man and The Little Miss (Eng. trans.), 1969; Heinrich von Kleist, The Tales of Hoffmann (Eng. trans.), 1966; Michael Kohlhaas (Eng. trans.), 1966; Japan Industrial, 1964-65 (2 vols) Daily Life in the French Revolution, 1964; Tokyo, 1965; England, Now, 1965; Japan, Now, 1966; Camara Laye, A Dream of Africa (Eng. trans.), 1967; Frankly Speaking, I-II, 1968; Paper Windows: Poems from Japan, 1968; Bangkok, 1968; One Man's Russia, 1968; Filipinescas, 1968; Streets of Asia, 1969; Japan Physical, 1969; Aspects of the Short Story, 1969; Shepherding Winds (anthol.), 1969; Songs and Dreams (anthol.), 1970; White Shadows, Black Shadows: Poems of Peace and War, 1970; Hong Kong, 1970; Japan Behind the Fan, 1970; The Eternal Virgin (Eng. trans of Valéry's La Jeune Parque), 1970; The Body Servant; poems of exile, 1971; Insect Summer (novel for children), 1971; A Bewick Bestiary (poems), 1971; (trans., with C. Fry) The Oxford Ibsen, vol III, Brand and Peer Gynt, 1972; (trans.) Selected Poems of Takagi Kyozo, 1973; The Magic Drum (children's novel), 1973; Heaven, Hell and Hara-Kiri, 1974; (with Birgit Skiöld) Zen Gardens, 1974; Scenes from Sesshu, 1977; Anthology of Contemporary Japanese Poetry,

1978. *Recreation:* standing in shafts of sunlight. *Address:* BM-Box 2780, London WC1V 6XX.

KIRKWOOD, family name of **Baron Kirkwood.**

KIRKWOOD, 3rd Baron *cr* 1951, of Bearsden; **David Harvie Kirkwood;** Warden of Stephenson Hall, since 1974, and Senior Lecturer in Metallurgy, since 1976, Sheffield University; *b* 24 Nov. 1931; *s* of 2nd Baron Kirkwood and of Eileen Grace, *d* of Thomas Henry Boalch; *S* father, 1970; *m* 1965, Judith Rosalie, *d* of late John Hunt; three *d. Educ:* Rugby; Trinity Hall, Cambridge (MA, PhD). Lectr in Metallurgy, Sheffield Univ., 1962. *Heir: b* Hon. James Stuart Kirkwood [*b* 19 June 1937; *m* 1965, Alexandra Mary, *d* of late Alec Dyson; two *d*]. *Address:* 56 Endcliffe Hall Avenue, Sheffield S10 3EL. *T:* Sheffield 663107.

KIRKWOOD, Ian Candlish, QC (Scot.) 1970; *b* 8 June 1932; *o s* of late John Brown Kirkwood, OBE, and of Mrs Constance Kirkwood, Edinburgh; *m* 1970, Jill Ingram Scott; two *s. Educ:* George Watson's Boys' Coll., Edinburgh; Edinburgh Univ.; Univ. of Michigan, USA. MA (Edin) 1952; LLB (Edin) 1954; LLM (Mich) 1956. Called to Scottish Bar, 1957; apptd Standing Junior Counsel to Scottish Home and Health Dept, 1963; Mem. Rules Council (Court of Session). Pres., Wireless Telegraphy Appeal Tribunal in Scotland. Contested (C) Dunfermline Burghs, 1964, 1966, 1970. *Recreations:* fishing, golf, chess. *Address:* 58 Murrayfield Avenue, Edinburgh EH12 6AY. *T:* 031-337 3468; Low Kirkland, Kirkcudbright.

KIRKWOOD, Prof. Kenneth, MA; Rhodes Professor of Race Relations, University of Oxford, since 1954; Fellow of St Antony's College, since 1954, and Sub-Warden, 1968-71; *b* Benoni, Transvaal, 1919; *s* of late Thomas Dorman Kirkwood and Lily Kirkwood (*née* Bewley); *m* 1942, Deborah Burton, *d* of late Burton Ireland Collings and Emily Frances Collings (*née* Loram); three *s* three *d.* BA; BSc Rand. Captain, South African Engineer Corps, War of 1939-45; served in East Africa, North Africa and Italy (despatches). Lecturer, University of the Witwatersrand, 1947; Lecturer, University of Natal, 1948-51; Fellowship, University of London (Inst. of Commonwealth Studies, 1952); Carnegie Travelling Fellowship, USA, 1953; Senior Research Officer, Inst. of Colonial Studies, Oxford Univ., 1953; Organiser of Institute for Social Research, University of Natal, 1954. Chm. Regional Cttee, S African Inst. of Race Relations in Natal, 1954; UK Rep. SA Inst. of Race Relations, 1955. Investigation on behalf UNESCO into trends in race relations in British Non-Self-Governing Territories of Africa, 1958; Visiting Prof. of Race Relations (UNESCO), University Coll. of Rhodesia and Nyasaland, 1964; composed memorandum on meaning, and procedure for further study of 'racial discrimination,' for UN Div. of Human Rights, 1966-67; Mem., Africa Educational Trust, Oxfam, etc, 1955-. *Publications:* The Proposed Federation of the Central African Territories, 1952; other booklets and articles on race relations and international affairs; contributions to revision of Lord Hailey's An African Survey, 1957, and 2nd edn, Vol. VIII, Cambridge History of the British Empire, 1963; Britain and Africa, 1965; Editor, St Antony's Papers: African Affairs, number 1, 1961; number 2, 1963; number 3, 1969. *Address:* St Antony's College, Oxford. *T:* Oxford 55867.

KIRKWOOD, Sir Robert (Lucien Morrison), OJ 1974; KCMG 1972; Kt 1959; Chairman, Sugar Manufacturers' Association of Jamaica, 1945-74; Chairman: West Indies Sugar Association, 1946-74; Citrus Growers Association, 1944-60; *b* Yeo, Fairy Cross, N Devon, 9 Jan. 1904; *e s* of late Major John Hendley Morrison Kirkwood, DSO, sometime MP for Southend Div. of Essex, and Gertrude Agnes, *e d* of Sir Robert Park Lyle, 1st and last Bt, Eaton Place, SW1; *m* 1925, Sybil Attenborough (*d* 1977), Hartford House, Nottingham; one *s* two *d. Educ:* Wixenford; Harrow; Le Rosey (Switzerland). Joined Tate & Lyle, 1922; Managing Dir, The United Sugar Company, 1929-36; Dir Yorks Sugar Co., 1928-36 and Central Sugar Co. (Peterborough), 1929-36; joined Board of Tate & Lyle, 1935; Man. Dir, West Indies Sugar Co., Jamaica, 1937; Dir, Caroni Ltd, Trinidad, 1937. MLC Jamaica, 1942-62. Rep. Jamaica on Colonial Sugar Cttee, 1937-. Rep. West Indies at Internat. Sugar Confs, 1953, 1956, 1958, 1961, 1965, 1968, 1973. Pres. Sugar Club of New York, 1965-66; Chm. International Sugar Council, 1966. Mem. various Govt Bds and Cttees in Jamaica. *Recreations:* gardening, golf and good food. *Address:* Haven House, Sandwich. *T:* 3264. *Clubs:* White's, Queen's; St George's (Sandwich); The Brook (New York).

KIRSOP, Arthur Michael Benjamin; Chairman, Tootal Ltd, 1975-76; *b* 28 Jan. 1931; *s* of Arthur Kirsop and Sarah (*née* Cauthery); *m* 1957, Patricia (*née* Cooper); two *s. Educ:* St Paul's

Sch., Brazil; Glasgow Academy; Univ. of Oxford (BA). Joined English Sewing Cotton Co. Ltd, 1955; Area Sales Man., 1957; Export Sales Man., 1961; Man. Dir, Thread Div., 1964; Dir, English Sewing Cotton Co. Ltd, 1967 (later English Calico Ltd, then Tootal Ltd); Jt Man. Dir, 1973-76; Chief Exec., 1974-76. Hon. Consul for the Netherlands, 1971-. *Recreations:* gardening, sport. *Address:* Peel House, 5 Planetree Road, Hale, Cheshire WA15 9JJ. *T:* 061-980 5173. *Club:* St James's (Manchester).

KIRSTEIN, Lincoln Edward; Director: School of American Ballet; New York City Ballet Company; *b* Rochester, NY, 4 May 1907; *s* of Louis E. Kirstein and Rose Stein; *m* 1941, Fidelma Cadmus; no *c. Educ:* Harvard Coll.; BS 1930. Edited Hound & Horn, 1927-34; founded School of American Ballet, 1934; founded and directed American Ballet Caravan, 1936-41; Third US Army (Arts, Monuments and Archives Section), 1943-45. Editor, The Dance Index, 1941-47. *Publications:* Flesh is Heir, 1932, repr. 1975; Dance, A Short History of Theatrical Dancing, 1935; Blast at Ballet, 1938; Ballet Alphabet, 1940; Drawings of Pavel Tchelitchew, 1947; Elie Nadelman Drawings, 1949; The Dry Points of Elie Nadelman, 1952; What Ballet is About, 1959; Three Pamphlets Collected, 1967; The Hampton Institute Album, 1968; Movement and Metaphor: four centuries of ballet, 1970; Lay This Laurel, 1974; Nijinsky, Dancing, 1975; *verse:* Rhymes of a PFC (Private First Class), 1964; *monographs:* Gaston Lachaise, 1935; Walker Evans, 1938; Latin American Art, 1942; American Battle Art, 1945; Henri Cartier-Bresson, 1946; Dr William Rimmer, 1946; Elie Nadelman, 1948; Pavel Tchelitchew, 1964; W. Eugene Smith, 1970; *edited:* The Classic Dance, Technique and Terminology, 1951; William Shakespeare: A Catalogue of the Works of Art in the American Shakespeare Festival Theater, 1964; Elie Nadelman, 1973; New York City Ballet, 1973; Nijinsky Dancing, 1975. *Address:* School of American Ballet, 144 West 66th Street, New York NY 10023, USA. *T:* 877-0600.

KIRTON, Robert James, CBE 1963; MA, FIA; Director, Equity and Law Life Assurance Society, Ltd, 1944-77 (General Manager, 1939-66; Actuary, 1947-66); Chairman, Equity and Law Unit Trust Managers Ltd, 1969-77; *b* 13 July 1901; *er s* of late Albert William Kirton, Ealing, Middlesex; *m* 1931, Isabel Susan, *y d* of late Henry Hosegood, JP, Bristol; two *s* two *d. Educ:* Merchant Taylors' Sch.; Peterhouse, Cambridge. Scottish Widows' Fund and Life Assurance Soc., 1923-32; Scottish Amicable Life Assce Soc., 1932-38; Equity and Law Life Assce, Soc. Ltd, 1938-. Chm., Life Offices' Assoc., 1945-47; Chm. Royal UK Beneficent Assoc., 1958-74; Nat. Council of Social Service: Hon. Treas., 1962-72; Vice-Pres., 1972-; Trustee, Charities Official Investment Fund, 1962-77; Governor, London Sch. of Economics, 1963-; Vice-Chm., St Peter's Hosp., 1967-75; Mem. Council, Bath Univ., 1967-75; Mem., Buitengewoon Lid, Actuarial Genootschap, Holland, 1949. Silver Medal, Institute of Actuaries, 1966. *Publications:* contrib. Jl Inst. Actuaries, Trans. Faculty of Actuaries (with A. T. Haynes). *Recreations:* walking, ski-ing and squash rackets. *Address:* Byron Cottage, North End Avenue, NW3 7HP. *T:* 01-455 0464. *Club:* Athenæum.

KIRWAN, Sir (Archibald) Laurence (Patrick), KCMG 1972 (CMG 1958); TD; BLitt Oxon; Director and Secretary, Royal Geographical Society, 1945-75; *b* 1907; 2nd *s* of Patrick Kirwan, Cregg, County Galway, Ireland, and Mabel Norton; *m* 1st, 1932, Joan Elizabeth Chetwynd; one *d*; 2nd, 1949, Stella Mary Monck. *Educ:* Wimbledon Sch.; Merton Coll., Oxford. Asst Dir of the Archaeological Survey of Nubia, Egyptian Dept of Antiquities, 1929-34; Field Dir, Oxford Univ. Excavations to Sudan, 1934-37; Tweedie Fellowship in Archæology and Anthropology, Edinburgh Univ., 1937-39. Boston and Philadelphia Museums, 1937; Exploratory journeys, Eastern Sudan and Aden Protectorate, 1938-39. TARO Capt., General Staff, 1939; Major, 1941; Lieut-Col 1943; Joint Staffs, Offices of Cabinet and Ministry of Defence, 1942-45; Hon. Lt-Col, 1957. Editor, Geographical Journal, 1945-; Pres., Brit. Inst. in Eastern Africa, 1961-. Pres. (Section E), British Assoc. for the Advancement of Science, 1961-62; Member: Court of Arbitration, Argentine-Chile Frontier Case, 1965-68 (Leader, Field Mission, 1966); Sec. of State for Environment's Adv. Cttee on Landscape Treatment of Trunk Roads, 1968- (Dep. Chm., 1970-); UN Register of fact-finding experts, 1968-; Court, Exeter Univ., 1969-; a Governor, Imperial Coll. of Science and Technology, 1962-; British Academy/Leverhulme Vis. Prof., Cairo, 1976; Mortimer Wheeler Lectr, Brit. Acad., 1977. Fellow, University Coll., London; Hon. Fellow, SOAS. Hon. Member: Geographical Societies of Paris, Vienna, Washington; Royal Inst. of Navigation; Institut d'Egypte; Hon. Fellow, American Geographical Soc. Founder's Medal, RGS, 1975. Knight Cross of the Order of St Olav, Norway. *Publications:* Excavations and Survey between Wadi-es-Sebua and Adindan,

1935 (with W. B. Emery); Oxford University Excavations at Firka, 1938; The White Road (polar exploration), 1959; papers on archæology, historical and political geography, exploration, in scientific and other publications. *Recreation:* travelling. *Address:* Royal Geographical Society, SW7. *T:* 01-589 5466. *Club:* Geographical.

KIRWAN, Sir Laurence; see Kirwan, Sir A. L. P.

KIRWAN-TAYLOR, Harold George, MA, MB, BCh Cantab; FRCS; *b* 14 April 1895; *s* of Alfred George Taylor and Mary Kirwan; *m* 1926, Elizabeth Mary (marriage dissolved, 1946), *d* of late J. R. J. Neild; one *s* three *d. Educ:* Epsom Coll.; Trinity Coll., Cambridge. Hon. Consulting Obstetric and Gynæcological Surgeon: St George's Hospital; War Memorial Hospital, Woolwich; Hon. Consulting Gynæcological Surgeon, Royal National Orthopædic Hospital; Hon. Cons. Surg., The General Lying-in Hospital, Lambeth; late Lectr on Obstetrics and Gynæcology, St George's Hospital; late Obstetric Consultant, Borough of Woolwich and Bexley Heath; late Cons. in Gynaecology, Min. of Pensions. Late Examiner: Univ. of Cambridge; Univ. of Durham; Soc. of Apothecaries; Conjoint Board and Central Midwives Board. Served European War, 1914-18, as Surgeon Probationer RNVR and later as Surgeon Royal Navy. Served 1940-43, MEF (despatches), as Lieut-Col, with short period as Temporary Consulting Surgeon, MEF; 1943-45, service in BNAF and Italy, retiring with rank of Hon. Col AMS. Late Prospective Conservative Candidate E Woolwich and Royal Borough of Kingston. Freeman of City of London. *Publications:* various articles in medical journals. *Recreations:* shooting, fishing, riding, golf, farming. *Address:* Denne, Mersham, near Ashford, Kent. *T:* Aldington 278. *Club:* Boodle's.

KISCH, John Marcus, CMG 1965; Planning Inspector, Department of the Environment, since 1972; *b* 27 May 1916; *s* of late Sir Cecil Kisch, KCIE, CB, and late Myra Kisch; *m* 1951, Gillian Poyser; four *d. Educ:* Rugby Sch.; King's Coll., Cambridge. Asst Principal, Board of Inland Revenue, 1938; Asst Principal, Colonial Office, 1939. Served Royal Corps of Signals, 1939-45. Principal, Colonial Office, 1945; seconded E Africa High Commission, 1951; Kenya Govt 1952; Asst Sec., Colonial Office, 1956; seconded CRO, 1964; transferred Min. of Defence, 1965; Asst Sec., MoD (Navy Dept), 1965-68; Asst Sec., ODM, later ODA, 1968-72. *Recreations:* tennis, croquet. *Address:* Hatchford Corner, Cobham, Surrey. *T:* Cobham 2138; 21 Pembroke Square, W8. *T:* 01-937 8590. *Club:* Reform.

KISCH, Royalton; Artistic Director, Cork Street Art Gallery; Conductor of Symphony Concerts; *b* London, 20 Jan. 1919; *s* of late E. Royalton Kisch, MC and Pamela Kisch; *m* 1940, Aline, *d* of late Bruce Hylton Stewart and M. F. (Molly) Hylton Stewart; one *s* two *d. Educ:* Wellington Coll., Berks; Clare Coll., Cambridge. Has conducted Royal Festival Hall concerts with London Philharmonic Orchestra, London Symphony Orchestra, Philharmonia Orchestra, Royal Philharmonic Orchestra, etc. Guest conductor to Hallé Orchestra, Birmingham Symphony Orchestra, etc. Has also conducted concerts in Europe with Paris Conservatoire Orchestra, Palestine Symphony Orchestra, Florence Philharmonic Orchestra, Athens State Symphony Orchestra, Pasdeloup Orchestra of Paris, Royal Opera House Orchestra of Rome, San Carlo Symphony Orchestra of Naples, Vienna Symphony Orchestra, etc. Has broadcast on BBC with London Symphony Orchestra, Royal Philharmonic Orchestra, and Philharmonia Orchestra. Gramophone recordings for Decca. Specialist in English and French paintings of 20th century. Mem., Friends of Tate Gallery. *Recreations:* good food and wine. *Address:* 2 Edwardes Square, Kensington, W8. *T:* 01-602 6655. *Club:* Hurlingham.

KISSEN, Hon. Lord; Manuel Kissen; a Senator of the College of Justice in Scotland since 1963; *b* 2 May 1912; *er s* of Lewis and Annie Kissen; *m* 1964, Mrs Victoria Solomons (*d* 1976), *widow* of Professor Edward Solomons, New York, USA. *Educ:* Hutchesons' Boys' Grammar Sch., Glasgow; Glasgow Univ. (MA, LLB). Solicitor, 1934. Served with RAF, 1940-45 (despatches). Admitted to Faculty of Advocates, 1946; Standing Junior Counsel in Scotland to Min. of Labour and to Min. of Nat. Insurance, 1948-55. QC (Scotland) 1955. Chm. National Health Service Tribunal (Scotland), 1962-63; Chm. Law Reform Cttee for Scotland, 1964-70, Mem., Restrictive Practices Court, 1966-; Chm. Scottish Valuation Adv. Council, 1967-71. Mem., Parole Bd for Scotland, 1975-. Hon. LLD Glasgow, 1968. *Address:* 22 Braid Avenue, Edinburgh EH10 6EE. *T:* 031-447 3000. *Club:* Scottish Arts (Edinburgh).

KISSEN, Manuel; see Kissen, Hon. Lord.

KISSIN, family name of Baron Kissin.

KISSIN, Baron *cr* 1974 (Life Peer), of Camden in Greater London; **Harry Kissin;** Chairman, Guinness Peat Group, since 1973 (Chairman, Lewis & Peat Ltd, 1961-72); Chairman and Director of other public and private companies in the City of London, since 1934; *b* 23 Aug. 1912; *s* of Israel Kissin and Reusi Kissin (*née* Model), both of Russian nationality; *m* 1935, Ruth Deborah Samuel, London; one *s* one *d*. *Educ:* Danzig and Switzerland. Dr of Law, Basle. Swiss lawyer until 1933. Dir, Royal Opera Hse, Covent Gdn, 1973-; Chm., Royal Opera House Trust, 1974-. Chm. Council, Inst. of Contemporary Art, 1969-76. *Address:* 44 Frognal Lane, Hampstead, NW3. *T:* 01-435 8711. *Clubs:* Reform, East India, Devonshire, Sports and Public Schools.

KISSINGER, Henry Alfred; Bronze Star (US); University Professor of Diplomacy, School of Foreign Service, Georgetown University, since 1977; Counselor to Center for Strategic and International Studies, Georgetown University, since 1977; Special Consultant for World Affairs, NBC, since 1977; Senior Fellow, Aspen Institute, since 1977; *b* 27 May 1923; *s* of Louis Kissinger and Paula (*née* Stern); *m* 1st, 1949, Anne Fleischer (marr. diss. 1964); one *s* one *d* ; 2nd, 1974, Nancy Maginnes. *Educ:* George Washington High Sch., NYC; Harvard Univ., Cambridge, Mass (AB, MA, PhD). Teaching Fellow, Harvard Univ., 1950-54; Study Director: Council on Foreign Relations, 1955-56: Rockefeller Bros Fund, 1956-58; Associate Professor of Govt, Harvard Univ., 1958-62, Prof. of Govt, 1962-71, and Faculty Mem., Center for Internat. Affairs, Harvard; Director: Harvard Internat. Seminar, 1951-71; Harvard Defense Studies Program, 1958-71; Asst to US President for Nat. Security Affairs, 1969-75; Secretary of State, USA, 1973-77. Consultant to various government agencies: (jtly) Nobel Peace Prize, 1973; Presidential Medal of Freedom, 1977. *Publications:* A World Restored: Castlereagh, Metternich and the Restoration of Peace, 1957; Nuclear Weapons and Foreign Policy, 1957 (Woodrow Wilson Prize, 1958; citation, Overseas Press Club, 1958); The Necessity for Choice: Prospects of American Foreign Policy, 1961; The Troubled Partnership: a reappraisal of the Atlantic Alliance, 1965; Problems of National Strategy: A Book of Readings (ed), 1965; American Foreign Policy: three essays, 1969, 3rd edn 1977; articles in Foreign Affairs, Harper's Magazine, The Reporter, New York Times Sunday Magazine, etc. *Address:* Suite 520, 1800 K Street, NW, Washington, DC 20006, USA. *Clubs:* Century, Harvard (New York); Cosmos, Federal City, Metropolitan (Washington); St Botolph (Boston).

KISTIAKOWSKY, Prof. Emeritus George Bogdan; Professor of Chemistry, Harvard University, 1938-71 (Chairman, 1947-50), Emeritus since 1971; Special Assistant to the President of the USA for Science and Technology, 1959-61; Vice-President, National Academy of Sciences, 1965-72; *b* Kiev, Ukraine, 18 Nov. 1900; *s* of Bogdan Kistiakowsky and Mary Berenstam; came to USA, 1926; naturalized citizen, 1933; *m* 1st, 1926, Hildegard Moebius (marr. diss. 1942); one *d* ; 2nd, 1945, Irma E. Shuler (marr. diss. 1962); 3rd, 1962, Elaine Mahoney. *Educ:* University of Berlin (DPhil). Fellow and Staff Mem. Chem. Dept, Princeton, 1926-30; Asst Prof., 1930-33, Associate Prof., 1933-38, Harvard. On leave from Harvard to: Nat. Defense Research Cttee, 1941-43; Los Alamos Lab., 1944-46. Member: President's Science Adv. Cttee, 1957-64; Gen. Adv. Cttee to US Arms Control and Disarmament Agency, 1962-68. Mem. National Acad. of Sciences, etc; Hon. Fellow, Chem. Soc., London; Foreign Mem. Royal Society, London, 1959. Hon. DSc: Harvard Univ., 1955; Williams Coll., 1958; Oxford Univ., 1959; University of Pennsylvania, 1960; University of Rochester, 1960; Carnegie Inst. of Technology, 1961; Princeton Univ., 1962; Case Institute, 1962; Columbia Univ., 1967. Medal for Merit, USA, 1946; King's Medal for Services in the Cause of Freedom, 1948; Willard Gibbs Medal, 1960; Medal of Freedom (awarded by Pres. Eisenhower), 1961; George Ledlie Prize, Harvard Univ., 1961; Nat. Medal of Science (awarded by Pres. Johnson), 1967; Peter Debye Award, 1968; Theodore William Richards, 1968; Priestley Medal, 1972, and several other awards. *Publications:* Photochemical Processes, 1929; A Scientist at the White House, 1976; numerous articles. *Address:* 12 Oxford Street, Cambridge, Mass 02138, USA. T: University 617-495-4083.

KITAJ, R. B.; artist; *b* Ohio, 1932; *m* (wife decd); two *c* . *Educ:* Ruskin Sch. of Art, Oxford; RCA (ARCA). Lives in London. One-man Exhibitions: Marlborough New London Gall., 1963, 1970; Marlborough Gerson Gall., NY, 1965, 1974; Los Angeles County Museum of Art, 1965; Stedelijk Mus., Amsterdam, 1967; Mus. of Art, Cleveland, 1967; Univ. of Calif, Berkeley, 1967; Galerie Mikro, Berlin, 1969; Kestner Gesellschaft, Hanover, 1970; Boymans-van-Beuningen Mus., Rotterdam,

1970; (with Jim Dine) Cincinnati Art Mus., Ohio, 1973; Marlborough Fine Art, 1977. *Address:* c/o Marborough Fine Art (London) Ltd, 39 Old Bond Street, W1.

KITCHEN, Frederick Bruford, CBE 1975; *b* Melbourne, 15 July 1912; *o s* of F. W. Kitchen, Malvern, Vic, Australia; *m* 1936, Una Bernice Sloss; two *s* one *d*. *Educ:* Melbourne Grammar Sch.; Melbourne Univ. (BSc). Joined family firm (in Melb.), J. Kitchen and Sons Pty Ltd, which had become a Unilever soap co., 1934. Sales Dir, Lever Bros Ltd, Canada, 1946. Came to England, 1949, as Chm., Crosfields (CWG) Ltd; Chm., Lever Bros Ltd, 1957; Marketing Dir, Lever Bros & Associates Ltd, 1960; Chm., Van den Berghs & Jurgens Ltd, 1962-74; Mem., Price Commn, 1973-75. Past Pres.: Incorp. Soc. of British Advertisers; Internat. Fedn of Margarine Assocs; Margarine and Shortening Manufacturers' Assoc. Associate, Royal Australian Chemical Inst. *Recreation:* gardening. *Address:* Southdown, Yal Yal Road, Merricks, Victoria 3916, Australia. T: 059-898411. *Club:* Australian (Melbourne).

KITCHEN, Sir Geoffrey, Kt 1963; TD; Chairman: United British Securities Trust Ltd, since 1965; *b* 20 Dec. 1906; *m* 1946, Joan Aistrope. *Educ:* Bradford Grammar Sch.; St John's Coll., Oxford (MA). Served War of 1939-45, RA, with 8th Army in Middle East and Italy (despatches); Lt-Col. Pearl Assurance Co. Ltd, 1934-76: Dir, 1948; Dep. Chm., 1952; Chm., 1956-71; Pres., 1972-76. Director: Estates & General Investments Ltd; Kellock Holdings Ltd; Michael Hooker and Associates Ltd; Schlesinger Ltd; Trident Gen. Insurance Co. Ltd; Trident Life Assurance Co. Ltd; United Kingdom Property Co. Ltd. Chm., London and Holyrood Trust Ltd, 1964-71. Chm., Industrial Life Offices' Assoc., 1958-60. Governor, St Mary's Hosp., 1960-63. Pres. of Appeals, NPFA, 1965-66. Life Associate, British Red Cross Soc. Freeman, City of London; Liveryman and Mem. Court, Worshipful Co. of Gunmakers (Master, 1969); Liveryman, Guild of Air Pilots and Air Navigators. *Recreations:* shooting, golf, tennis. *Address:* Ghyll Manor, Rusper, Horsham, West Sussex. *T:* Rusper 288. *Club:* Carlton.

KITCHEN, Stanley, FCA; Partner, Touche Ross & Co., Chartered Accountants, Birmingham, since 1948; *b* 23 Aug. 1913; *s* of late Percy Inman Kitchen and Elizabeth Kitchen; *m* 1941, Jean Craig; two *d* . *Educ:* Rugby Sch. ACA 1937, FCA 1953. Army, 1939-46: Major, RASC. Sec., British Rollmakers Corp. Ltd, Wolverhampton, 1946-48; Partner, Foster & Stephens, Birmingham, 1948 (merged with Touche Ross & Co., 1965). Birmingham and West Midlands Soc. of Chartered Accountants: Mem. Cttee, 1951-; Sec., 1953-55; Pres., 1957-58; Inst. of Chartered Accountants in England and Wales: Mem. Council, 1966-; Vice-Pres., 1974-75; Dep. Pres., 1975-76; Pres., 1976-77. *Publications:* Learning to Live with Taxes on Capital Gains, 1967; Important Aspects of Professional Partnerships, 1974. *Recreations:* gardening, golf. *Address:* 1194 Warwick Road, Knowle, Solihull, West Midlands B93 9LL. *T:* Knowle 2360. *Clubs:* Birmingham, Chamber of Commerce (Birmingham).

KITCHENER OF KHARTOUM and of Broome; 3rd Earl, *cr* 1914; **Henry Herbert Kitchener,** TD; DL; Viscount, *cr* 1902, of Khartoum; of the Vaal, Transvaal, and Aspall, Suffolk; Viscount Broome, *cr* 1914, of Broome, Kent; Baron Denton, *cr* 1914, of Denton, Kent; late Major, Royal Corps of Signals; *b* 24 Feb. 1919; *er s* of Viscount Broome (*d* 1928) and Adela Mary Evelyn, *e d* of late J. H. Monins, Ringwould House, near Dover; *S* grandfather, 1937. *Educ:* Sandroyd Sch.; Winchester Coll.; Trinity Coll., Cambridge. DL Cheshire 1972. *Heir: b* Hon. Charles Eaton Kitchener [*b* 11 March 1920; *m* 1959, Ursula Hope Luck; one *d*]. *Address:* 56 Elm Park Road, SW3. *T:* 01-352 5468; 435 Chester Road, Hartford, Northwich, Cheshire. *T:* Sandiway 883287. *Club:* Brooks's.

KITCHIN, John Leslie Harlow, DipArch; RIBA; Chief Architect (Under Secretary), Department of Education and Science, since 1975; *b* 11 Oct. 1924; *o s* of late Eric J. H. Kitchin and Muriel Harper; *m* 1956, Madeleine, *d* of late Fernand and Renée Coutant, Reims; two *s* one *d* . *Educ:* Wolverhampton Grammar Sch.; Worcester Coll., Oxford; Birmingham Sch. of Architecture (1947-52). Served with RAF, Bomber Comd, 1943-47. Joined Min. of Educn Develt Gp as Asst Architect, 1952; designed schools and buildings for handicapped children, youth, community; Dept of Educn and Science, 1964-: Head of Building Productivity Gp, 1965; Asst Chief Architect, 1967. *Publications:* various DES building bulletins; articles in architectural and educnl press. *Recreation:* landscape painting. *Address:* 5 Queen's Gardens, W5 1SE. *T:* 01-997 8284.

KITCHING, Maj.-Gen. George, CBE 1945; DSO 1943; Canadian Military Forces, retired; Director: A. Bradshaw & Son; Empire

Club of Canada; Co-ordinator, Duke of Edinburgh's Award in Canada, since 1967; Executive Director, Canadian National Committee, United World Colleges, since 1969; *b* 1910; *m* 1946, Audrey Calhoun; one *s* one *d. Educ:* Cranleigh; Royal Military College. 2nd Lieut Glos Regt, 1930. Served War of 1939-45 with Royal Canadian Regt, in Sicily, Italy and North-West Europe; commanding Canadian Infantry Brigade, 1943; actg Maj.-Gen., 1944 (despatches, DSO, CBE). Subseq. Vice-Chief of General Staff at Army Headquarters, Ottawa; Chairman of the Canadian Joint Staff in London, 1958-62. GOC Central Command, Canada, 1962-65, retd. Commander: Order of Orange Nassau (Netherlands); Military Order of Italy; Order of Merit (US). *Address:* 3 Riverside Crescent, Toronto 3, Ont, Canada. *Clubs:* National (Toronto); Rideau Golf.

KITCHING, John Alwyne, OBE 1947; FRS 1960; ScD (Cambridge); PhD (London); Professor of Biology, University of East Anglia, 1963-74, now Emeritus Professor; Dean of School of Biological Sciences, 1967-70; Leverhulme Fellowship, 1974; *b* 24 Oct. 1908; *s* of John Nainby Kitching; *m* 1933, Evelyn Mary Oliver; one *s* three *d. Educ:* Cheltenham Coll.; Trinity Coll., Cambridge. BA 1930, MA 1934, ScD 1956; PhD London. Lecturer: Birkbeck Coll., London, 1931; Edinburgh Univ., 1936; Bristol Univ., 1937; Rockefeller Fellow, Princeton Univ., 1938; Research in aviation-medical problems under Canadian Nat. Research Council, 1939-45; Reader in Zoology, University of Bristol, 1948-63. *Publications:* contrib. Jl of Experimental Biol., Jl of Ecology, Jl of Animal Ecology, etc. *Recreations:* travel, gardening. *Address:* University of East Anglia, University Plain, Norwich NR4 7TJ; 29 Newfound Drive, Cringleford, Norwich NR4 7RY.

KITCHING, Wilfred, CBE 1964; retired as General of The Salvation Army (1954-63) and from Chairmanship of various Salvation Army Companies, etc; *b* 22 Aug. 1893; *s* of late Commissioner Theodore Kitching, CBE; *m* 1929, Kathleen Bristow. *Educ:* Friern Barnet Grammar Sch. Corps and Divisional Officer, 1915-25, 1929-39; National Sec. for Salvation Army Bands 1925-29, National Young People's Sec. 1939-45; Field Sec., 1945-46; Chief Sec. for Australia, 1946-48. Territorial Leader for Sweden, 1948-51. British Commissioner, Officer responsible for Evangelical and Red Shield Services in Great Britain and Ireland, 1951-54. *Publications:* A Goodly Heritage (autobiography); numerous instrumental and vocal compositions published by The Salvation Army. *Recreation:* music. *Address:* 19 Montserrat, West Parade, Bexhill on Sea, East Sussex.

KITSON, family name of **Baron Airedale**.

KITSON, Alexander Harper, JP; Executive Officer, Transport and General Workers Union; *b* 21 Oct. 1921; *m* 1942, Ann Brown McLeod; two *d. Educ:* Kirknewton Sch., Midlothian, Scotland. Lorry Driver, 1935-45; Trade Union official, 1945-. Mem., Freight Integration Council, 1969-. Mem. Nat. Exec. Cttee of Labour Party, 1968-. *Address:* Transport and General Workers Union, Transport House, Smith Square, SW1P 3JB. *T:* 01-828 7788.

KITSON, Maj.-Gen. Frank Edward, CBE (mil.) 1972 (OBE 1968; MBE 1959); MC 1955 and Bar 1958; Commandant, Staff College, Camberley, since 1978; *b* 15 Dec. 1926; *s* of late Vice-Adm. Sir Henry Kitson, KBE CB and of Lady (Marjorie) Kitson (*née* de Pass); *m* 1962, Elizabeth Janet, *d* of Col C. R. Spencer, OBE; three *d. Educ:* Stowe. 2nd Lt Rifle Bde, 1946; served BAOR, 1946-53; Mil. Intell. Officer, Kenya, 1953-55; Company Comdr, Malaya, 1957; Bn second in command, Cyprus, 1962-64; CO 1st Bn, Royal Green Jackets, 1967-69; Defence Fellow, University Coll., Oxford, 1969-70; Comdr, 39 Inf. Bde, NI, 1970-72 (CBE for gallantry); Comdt, Sch. of Infantry, 1972-74; GOC 2nd Division, later 2nd Armoured Division, 1976-78. *Publications:* Gangs and Counter Gangs, 1960; Low Intensity Operations, 1971; Bunch of Five, 1977. *Recreations:* riding, fishing, shooting. *Address:* c/o Lloyds Bank, Farnham, Surrey. *Club:* Boodle's.

KITSON, Sir George (Vernon), KBE 1957 (CBE 1946); HM Foreign Service; retired 1959; *b* 10 Feb. 1899; *s* of late George and Frances Kitson, Wakefield; *m* 1935, Phoebe, *yr d* of late John Owen George, Hirwaun, Glamorganshire; no *c. Educ:* Queen Elizabeth Grammar Sch., Wakefield; Clare Coll., Cambridge (MA). Served RFC and RAF, 1917-19; entered HM Consular Service in China, 1922; Served at: Peking, Shanghai, Canton, Mukden, Harbin, Chungking, Hankow, Swatow, Chefoo, Nanking; Chinese Sec. at HM Embassy, Chungking, 1942-45; Counsellor, FO, 1945-47; Deputy High Commissioner for the UK at Bombay, 1947-50; Counsellor, Office of Commissioner General for SE Asia, Singapore, 1951-52; HM

Consul-General at Milan, 1952-58. High Sheriff of Breconshire, 1968-69. *Recreations:* gardening, walking. *Address:* Llais-yr-Afon, Crickhowell, Powys. *T:* Crickhowell 810298.

KITSON, Sir Timothy (Peter Geoffrey), Kt 1974; MP (C) Richmond, Yorkshire, since 1959; *b* 28 Jan. 1931; *s* of late Geoffrey H. and of Kathleen Kitson; *m* 1959, Diana Mary Fattorini; one *s* two *d. Educ:* Charterhouse; Royal Agricultural College, Cirencester. Farmed in Australia, 1949-51. Member: Thirsk RDC, 1954-57; N Riding CC, 1957-61. PPS to Parly Sec. to Minister of Agriculture, 1960-64; an Opposition Whip, 1967-70; PPS to the Prime Minister, 1970-74, to Leader of the Opposition, 1974-75. *Recreations:* shooting, hunting, racing. *Address:* Leases Hall, Leeming Bar, Northallerton, North Yorks. *T:* Bedale 2180.

KITTO, Rt. Hon. Sir Frank (Walters), PC 1963; KBE 1955; Chancellor, University of New England, since 1970; Chairman, Australian Press Council, since 1976; *b* 30 July 1903; *s* of late James W. Kitto, OBE, Austinmer, New South Wales; *m* 1928, Eleanor, *d* of late Rev. W. H. Howard; four *d. Educ:* North Sydney High Sch.; Sydney Univ. BA 1924; Wigram Allen Scholar, G. and M. Harris Scholar and Pitt Cobbett Prizes in Faculty of Law, and LLB first class hons, 1927; called to Bar of NSW, 1927. KC (NSW), 1942. Challis Lecturer in Bankruptcy and Probate, Sydney Univ., 1930-33; Justice of the High Court of Australia, 1950-70. Mem. Council, University of New England, 1967-, Deputy Chancellor, 1968-70. *Address:* Jindalee, Biddulph Road, Armidale, NSW 2350, Australia. *T:* Armidale 75.3250. *Club:* Australian (Sydney).

KITTO, H. D. F., FBA, 1955; FRSL 1957; Professor of Greek, University of Bristol, 1944-62, Emeritus since 1962; *b* 1897; *s* of late H. D. Kitto, Stroud, Glos; *m* 1928, Ann Kraft; one *s* one *d. Educ:* Crypt Grammar Sch., Glos; St John's Coll., Cambridge. Asst to Professor of Greek and then Lecturer in Greek, University of Glasgow, 1921-44. Visiting Prof., Cornell Univ., 1954; Brandeis Univ., 1959; Sather Professor, University of California, 1960-61; Ziskind Prof., Brandeis Univ., 1962-63; Regents' Professor, University of California (Santa Barbara), 1963-64. Hon. D-ès-lettres, Aix-Marseille, 1961. *Publications:* In the Mountains of Greece, 1933; Greek Tragedy, 1939, 3rd edn 1961; The Greeks (Pelican), 1951; Form and Meaning in Drama, 1956; Sophocles: Dramatist and Philosopher, 1958; Sophocles' Antigone, Electra and Oedipus Rex (translated into English verse), 1962; Poiesis, 1966; articles and reviews in Classical journals. *Recreations:* music and Greek. *Address:* 9 Southfield Road, Bristol BS6 6AX.

KITTS, Sir Francis (Joseph), Kt 1966; Mayor of Wellington, New Zealand, since 1956; *b* 1914. Elected to: Wellington City Council, 1950; Wellington Harbour Board, 1950; Wellington Hospital Board, 1950. MP for Wellington Central, 1954-60. *Address:* Town Hall, Wellington; 25a Shannon Street, Wellington, New Zealand.

KITZINGER, Uwe; Dean of INSEAD (European Institute of Business Administration) Fontainebleau, since 1976; Emeritus Fellow of Nuffield College, Oxford, since 1976; *b* 12 April 1928; *o s* of late Dr G. Kitzinger and Mrs L. Kitzinger, Abbots Langley, Herts; *m* 1952, Sheila Helena Elizabeth (*née* Webster), Rumwell, Somerset; five *d. Educ:* Watford Grammar Sch.; Balliol Coll. and New Coll. (Foundn Schol.), Oxford. 1st in Philosophy, Politics and Economics, MA, BLitt; Pres., Oxford Union, 1950. Economic Section, Council of Europe, Strasbourg, 1951-58; Nuffield College, Oxford: Research Fellow, 1956-62, Official Fellow, 1962-66; Acting Investment Bursar, 1962-64; Investment Bursar, 1964-76; Ford Fellow in European Politics, 1966-76. Assessor of Oxford University, 1967-68. Visiting Prof.: of Internat. Relations, Univ. of the West Indies, 1964-65; of Government, at Harvard, 1969-70; at Univ. of Paris (VIII), 1970-73. Leave of absence as Adviser to Sir Christopher Soames, Vice-Pres. of the Commn of the European Communities, Brussels, 1973-75. Mem., ODM Cttee for University Secondment, 1966-68; Mem., British Universities Cttee of Encyclopædia Britannica, 1967-73; Chm., Cttee on Atlantic Studies, 1967-70. Directly elected Mem., Nat. Council of European Movement, 1974-76; Mem. Council, RIIA, 1976-. *Publications:* German Electoral Politics, 1960, German edn, 1960; The Challenge of the Common Market, 1961 (Amer. edn, The Politics and Economics of European Integration, 1963, et al); Britain, Europe and Beyond, 1964; The Background to Jamaica's Foreign Policy, 1965; The European Common Market and Community, 1967; Commitment and Identity, 1968; The Second Try, 1968; Diplomacy and Persuasion, 1973, French edn, 1974; Europe's Wider Horizons, 1975; (with D. E. Butler) The 1975 Referendum, 1976. Founding Editor, Jl of Common Market Studies, 1962-77. *Recreations:* sailing, travel, old buildings. *Address:* INSEAD, boulevard de Constance, 77305 Fontainebleau, France. *T:* Paris 422 4827; Standlake Manor, near Witney, Oxon. *T:* Standlake 266. *Clubs:* Reform; Royal Solent (Yarmouth, IoW).

KLARE, Hugh John, CBE 1967; writes regular column in Justice of the Peace on penal and criminological problems; *b* Berndorf, Austria, 22 June 1916; *yr s* of F. A. Klare; *m* 1946, Eveline Alice Maria, *d* of Lieut-Col J. D. Rankin, MBE. *Educ:* privately. Came to England, 1932. Served war in Middle East and Europe; Major. Dep. Dir, Economic Organisation Br., Brit. Control Commn for Germany, 1946-48; Sec., Howard League for Penal Reform, 1950-71; seconded to Coun. of Europe as Dep. Head, Div. of Crime Problems, 1959-61; Head of Div., 1971-72; Member of Council: Internat. Soc. of Criminology, 1960-66; Inst. for Study and Treatment of Delinquency, 1964-66; Nat. Assoc. for Care and Resettlement of Offenders, 1966-71. Chm. Planning Cttee, Brit. Congress on Crime, 1966. Member: Bd of Visitors, Long Lartin Prison, 1972-; Gloucestershire Probation and Aftercare Cttee, 1972-; Parole Board, 1972-74. A Governor, British Inst. of Human Rights, 1974-. *Publications:* Anatomy of Prison, 1960; (ed and introd) Changing Concepts of Crime and its Treatment, 1966; (ed jtly) Frontiers of Criminology, 1967; People in Prison, 1972. *Address:* 28 Pittville Court, Albert Road, Cheltenham GL52 3JA. *T:* Cheltenham 34224.

KLEFFENS, Eelco Nicolaas van; Netherlands Minister of State (life), 1950; *b* Heerenveen (Netherlands), 17 Nov. 1894; *m* 1935, Margaret Helen Horstman. *Educ:* University of Leyden. Adjusted shipping questions arising out of European War for Netherlands, 1919; Mem. Secretariat League of Nations, 1919-21; Sec. to directorate of Royal Dutch Petroleum Co., 1921-23; deputy-chief of legal section, Netherlands Ministry for Foreign Affairs, 1923-27; deputy-chief of diplomatic section, 1927-29; chief of diplomatic section, 1929-39; appointed Minister to Switzerland and Netherlands representative with League of Nations, 1939; Minister for Foreign Affairs of the Netherlands, 1939-46; Minister without portfolio and Netherlands representative on Security Council and Economic and Social Council of UN, 1946-47; Netherlands Ambassador to the United States of America, 1947-50; Minister to Portugal, 1950-56; Permanent Representative of Netherlands on NATO Council and OEEC (Paris), 1956-58; Chief Representative in UK of High Authority of European Coal and Steel Community, 1958-67; Pres., IX Session United Nations General Assembly. Pres., Arbitral Tribunal established under Bonn-Paris Agreements, 1952-54, by France, Germany, UK, USA, 1957-70. Holds several hon. degrees; Corresponding Mem., Netherlands and Portuguese Academy of Sciences; Mem. of Curatorium, Hague Academy of International Law, 1947-68; Hon. Member, Amer. Soc. of Internat. Law. Grand Cross: Orange-Nassau (Netherl.); Legion of Honour (France); St Gregory (Holy See); Christ (Portugal), *et al. Publications:* The Relations between the Netherlands and Japan in the Light of International Law, 1605-1919, 1919; The Rape of the Netherlands, 1940; Sovereignty in International Law, 1953; Hispanic Law until the end of the Middle Ages, 1968; articles in periodicals. *Address:* Casal de Santa Filomena, Almoçagême, Colares, Portugal. *Clubs:* Haagsche (The Hague); Eça de Queiroz (Lisbon); Century (New York).

KLEIN, Bernat, CBE 1973; FSIAD 1974; Chairman and Managing Director, Bernat Klein Design Ltd, since 1966; *b* 6 Nov. 1922; *s* of Lipot Klein and Serena Weiner; *m* 1951, Margaret Soper; one *s* two *d. Educ:* Senta, Yugoslavia; Bezalel Sch. of Arts and Crafts, Jerusalem; Leeds Univ. Designer to: Tootal, Broadhurst, Lee, 1948-49; Munrospun, Edinburgh, 1949-51; Chm. and Man. Dir, Colourcraft, 1952-62; Man. Dir of Bernat Klein Ltd, 1962-66. Exhibitions of paintings: E-SU, 1965; Alwyn Gall., 1967; O'Hana Gall., 1969; Assoc. of Arts Gall., Capetown, Goodman Gall., Johannesburg, and O'Hana Gall., 1972; Laing Art Gall., Newcastle upon Tyne, 1977. *Publications:* Eye for Colour, 1965; Design Matters, 1976. *Recreations:* reading, tennis, walking. *Address:* High Sunderland, Galashiels, Selkirkshire. *T:* Selkirk 20730.

KLEINDIENST, Richard Gordon; Partner, Law firm of Welch, Morgan & Kleindienst, since 1976; *b* 5 Aug. 1923; *s* of Alfred R. Kleindienst and late Gladys Love, Massachusetts; *m* 1948, Margaret Dunbar; two *s* two *d. Educ:* Harvard Coll. (*Phi Beta Kappa, magna cum laude*); Harvard Law Sch. Associate and Partner of Jennings, Strouss, Salmon & Trask, Phoenix, Arizona, 1950-57; Sen. Partner of Shimmel, Hill, Kleindienst & Bishop, 1958-Jan. 1969. Dep. Attorney-Gen. of the US, Jan. 1969-Feb. 1972; Actg Attorney-Gen. of the US, Feb. 1972-June 1972; Attorney-Gen. of the US, 1972-73, resigned 1973; private practice of law, Washington DC, 1973-75. Pres., Federal Bar Assoc., US, 1972- (was Pres. elect, Oct. 1971-72); Mem. Amer.

Bar Assoc., Labor Section; Mem., Bd of Dirs, Washington Nat. Symphony Orch. Hon. Dr of Laws, Susquehanna Univ., 1973. *Recreations:* golf, chess, classical music, art. *Address:* Suite 203, 1101 17th Street NW, Washington, DC 20036, USA; 8464 Portland Place, McLean, Va 22101, USA.

KLEINPOPPEN, Prof. Hans Johann Willi; Professor of Experimental Physics, University of Stirling, since 1968 (Head of Physics Department, 1970-73); Director of Institute of Atomic Physics, University of Stirling, since 1975; *b* Duisburg, Germany, 30 Sept. 1928; *m* 1958, Renate Schröder. *Educ:* Univ. of Giessen (Dipl. Physics); Univ. of Tübingen. Dr re.nat. et habil. 1961. Habilitation, Tübingen, 1966; Vis. Fellow, Univ. Colorado, 1967-68; Vis. Associate Prof., Columbia Univ., 1968; Fellow, Center for Theoretical Studies, Univ. of Miami, 1972-73. Chairman: Internat. Symposium on Physics of One-and Two-Electron Atoms (Arnold Summerfield Centennial Meml Meeting, Munich 1968); Internat. Symposium on Electron and Photon Interactions with Atoms, in honour of Ugo Fano, Stirling, 1975. FInstP 1969; Fellow Amer. Physical Soc. 1969; FRAS 1974. *Publications:* (ed with F. Bopp) Physics of the One-and Two-Electron Atoms, 1969; (ed with M. R. C. McDowell) Electron and Photon Interactions with Atoms, 1976; (with P. G. Burke) series editor, Physics of Atoms and Molecules; papers in Zeitschr. f. Physik, Z. f. Naturf., Physical Review, Jl of Physics, Physics Letters, Internat. Jl of Quantum Chemistry. *Address:* Dunvegan Lodge, 10 Upper Glen Road, Bridge of Allan, Stirlingshire. *T:* Bridge of Allan 2067.

KLEINWORT, Sir Alexander Santiago, 2nd Bt, *cr* 1909; *b* 31 Oct. 1892; *e s* of Sir Alexander D. Kleinwort, 1st Bt; *S* father, 1935; *m* 1938, Yvonne, *d* of late John Bloch. *Educ:* St John's Coll., Oxford. *Heir: b* Ernest Greverus Kleinwort, *qv. Address:* 1 Third Avenue, Hove, East Sussex. *T:* Hove 71752.

KLEINWORT, Sir Cyril (Hugh), Kt 1971; Chairman; Kleinwort, Benson, Lonsdale Ltd, since 1968; Kleinwort, Benson Ltd, 1966-71; Joint Vice-Chairman, Commercial Union Assurance Co., 1959-75; Chairman, Committee on Invisible Exports, 1968-75; *b* 17 Aug. 1905; *s* of Sir Alexander D. Kleinwort, 1st Bt; *m* 1933, Elisabeth Kathleen Forde; three *d. Educ:* privately. Served as Lieut-Commander, RNVR, 1939-45. Member: British Overseas Trade Bd, 1972-75; Adv. Cttee, Queen's Award to Industry, 1971-75. One of HM Lieutenants, City of London, 1976-. Hon. DLitt City, 1973. *Recreations:* hunting, yachting. *Address:* 64 Sussex Square, W2; Eyford House, Upper Slaughter, near Cheltenham. *T:* Stow on the Wold 30380.

KLEINWORT, Ernest Greverus; Director, Kleinwort, Benson, Lonsdale Ltd, 1961-74 (Chairman, 1961-68); *b* 13 Sept. 1901; *s* of late Sir Alexander Drake Kleinwort, 1st Bt, and late Etienette, Lady Kleinwort (*née* Girard); *heir-pres.* to Sir Alexander S. Kleinwort, 2nd Bt, *qv*; *m* 1932, Joan Nightingale, MBE, JP, *d* of late Prof. Arthur William Crossley, CMG, CBE, FRS, LLD, DSc; one *s* one *d. Educ:* Jesus Coll., Cambridge. Partner Kleinwort Sons & Company, 1927-47. RAFVR, 1942-45. Actg Chm. of Kleinwort, Sons & Co. Ltd, 1947-61; Chm. Kleinwort Benson Ltd, 1961-66; Member: Accepting Houses Cttee, 1945-66; Internat. Board of Trustees, World Wildlife Fund, 1967-76 (Mem. of Honour, 1976). Council, Wildfowl Trust, 1967- (Vice-Pres., 1970-). Comdr of Order of Golden Ark, Netherlands, 1974. *Recreations:* landscaping and development of his garden, charitable work, swimming. *Address:* Heaselands, Haywards Heath, West Sussex; 50 South Audley Street, W1.

KLIBANSKY, Raymond, MA, PhD; Frothingham Professor of Logic and Metaphysics, McGill University, Montreal, 1946-75, now Emeritus Professor; General Editor, Corpus Platonicum Medii Aevi, UAI, since 1936; *b* Paris, 15 Oct. 1905; *s* of late Hermann Klibansky. *Educ:* Paris; Odenwald Sch.; Univs of Kiel, Hamburg, Heidelberg. PhD, 1929; MA Oxon by decree, 1936. Asst, Heidelberg Acad., 1927-33; Lecturer in Philosophy: Heidelberg Univ., 1931-33; King's Coll., London, 1934-36; Oriel Coll., Oxford, 1936-48; Dir of Studies, Warburg Inst., Univ. of London, 1947. Forwood Lectr in Philosophy of Religion, Univ. of Liverpool, 1938-39; Cardinal Mercier Prof. of Philosophy, Univ. of Louvain, 1956; Visiting Professor: of History of Philosophy, Université de Montréal, 1947-68; Univ. of Rome, 1961; Univ. of Genoa, 1964. Temp. Civil Servant, FO, 1941-46. President: Inst. Internat. de Philosophie, Paris, 1966-69 (Hon. Pres. 1969-); Société Internationale pour l'étude de la Philos. Médiévale, Louvain, 1968-72 (Hon. Pres., 1972-); Canadian Soc. for History and Philosophy of Science, 1959-72 (Pres. Emeritus, 1972-). Corresp. Mem., Heidelberg Acad., 1964-. FRSC; FRHistS; Fellow: Accademia Nazionale dei Lincei, Rome; Acad. of Athens; Académie Internationale d'Histoire des Sciences, Paris; Imperial Iranian Acad. of Philosophy, Teheran;

Hon. Fellow, Warburg Inst., Univ. of London. DPhil *hc* Ottawa. Joint Editor: Magistri Eckardi Opera Latina, 1933-36; Philosophy and History, 1936; Mediaeval and Renaissance Studies, 1941-68. Editor: Philosophical Texts, 1951-62; Philosophy and World Community, 1957-71; Philosophy in the Mid-Century, 1958-59; Contemporary Philosophy, 1968-71. *Publications:* Ein Proklos-Fund und seine Bedeutung, 1929; Heidelberg Acad. edn of Opera Nicolai Cusani, 1929-33; The Continuity of the Platonic Tradition, 1939; (with E. Panofsky and F. Saxl) Saturn and Melancholy, 1964; articles in Jahresberichte d., Heidelberger Akademie, Proceedings of British Acad., Enciclopedia Italiana, and elsewhere. *Address:* McGill University, Montreal, Canada.

KLIEN, Walter; musician (concert pianist), since 1933; *b* 27 Nov. 1928. *Educ:* Frankfurt-am-Main; Vienna. Concert tours in: Europe, USA, Canada, South America, South Africa, Far East. Many recordings, which include complete solo-works by Mozart and Brahms, also the complete Schubert Sonatas. *Address:* c/o Harold Holt Ltd, 122 Wigmore Street, W1.

KLUG, Aaron, FRS 1969; PhD (Cantab); Member of Scientific Staff of Medical Research Council at MRC Laboratory of Molecular Biology, Cambridge, since 1962; Fellow of Peterhouse, since 1962; *b* 11 Aug. 1926; *s* of Lazar Klug and Bella Silin; *m* 1948, Liebe Bobrow, Cape Town, SA; two *s. Educ:* Durban High Sch.; Univ. of the Witwatersrand (BSc); Univ. of Cape Town (MSc). Junior Lecturer, 1947-48; Research Student, Cavendish Laboratory, Cambridge, 1949-52; Rouse-Ball Research Studentship, Trinity Coll., Cambridge, 1949-52; Colloid Science Dept, Cambridge, 1953; Nuffield Research Fellow, Birkbeck Coll., London, 1954-57; Dir, Virus Structure Research Group, Birkbeck Coll., 1958-61. Leeuwenhoek Lectr, Royal Soc., 1973; Dunham Lectr, Harvard Medical Sch., 1975. Foreign Hon. Mem., Amer. Acad. of Arts and Sciences, 1969. *Publications:* papers in scientific jls. *Recreations:* reading, gardening. *Address:* 70 Cavendish Avenue, Cambridge. *T:* 48959.

KLYNE, Prof. William; MA Oxon, DSc London, PhD Edinburgh; Professor of Chemistry, Westfield College, University of London, 1960-77; *b* 23 March 1913; *s* of late Carl Adolphe Klein and Ivy Adkin, Enfield, Middx; *m* 1949, Dr Barbara Evelyn Claytor; one *s* one *d. Educ:* Highgate Sch.; New Coll., Oxford. Asst in Medical Chemistry, University of Edinburgh, 1936-39; Lecturer, 1939-47; Lecturer in Biochemistry, Postgrad. Med. Sch. of London, 1947-52; Reader in Biochemistry, London, 1952-60; Dean, Fac. of Science, Westfield Coll., 1971-73; Vice-Principal, 1973-76. Mem. Editorial Board, Biochemical Journal, 1949-55. Hon. Sec., Chemical Soc., 1966-72; Vice-Pres., Perkin Div., Chemical Soc., 1972-75. Mem. Jt Commn on Biochemical Nomenclature, IUPAC-IUB, 1977. *Publications:* Practical Chemistry for Medical Students, 1946; Chemistry of Steroids, 1957; (with Dr J. Buckingham) Atlas of Stereochemical Correlations, 1974; (ed 3 vols with Prof. P. B. D. de la Mare) Progress in Stereochemistry, 1954-62; contrib. to chemical and biochemical journals. *Address:* 19 Malcolm Road, SW19. *T:* 01-946 4194; Bay View, Studland, Swanage, Dorset BH19 3AS. *T:* Studland 325. *Club:* Athenæum.

KNAGGS, Kenneth James, CMG 1971; OBE 1959; Consultant, Commonwealth Development Corporation, since 1974; *b* 3 July 1920; *e s* of late James Henry Knaggs and Elsie Knaggs (*née* Walton); *m* 1945, Barbara, *d* of late Ernest James Page; two *s. Educ:* St Paul's Sch., London. Served War, 1939-46 (Major). Northern Rhodesia Civil Service, 1946; Sec. to Govt, Seychelles, 1955; Northern Rhodesia: Asst Sec., 1960; Under Sec., 1961; Permanent Sec., Min. of Finance and subseq. the same in Zambia, 1964; retd 1970. European Rep. and Manager, Zambia Airways, 1970-72. *Recreations:* walking, gardening, languages, cooking. *Address:* High House Farm, Earl Soham, near Framlingham, Suffolk IP13 7SN. *T:* Earl Soham 416.

KNAPP-FISHER, Rt. Rev. and Ven. Edward George; Archdeacon of Westminster, since 1975; a Canon of Westminster Abbey, since 1975; an Assistant Bishop, Diocese of London, since 1976; *b* 8 Jan. 1915; *s* of late Rev. George Edwin Knapp-Fisher and of Agatha Knapp-Fisher; *m* 1965, Joan, *d* of R. V. Bradley, Claremont, CP, SA. *Educ:* King's School, Worcester; Trinity College, Oxford. Assistant Curate of Brighouse, Yorks, 1939; Chaplain, RNVR, 1942; Chaplain of Cuddesdon College, 1946; Chaplain of St John's College, Cambridge, 1949; Vicar of Cuddesdon and Principal of Cuddesdon Theological College, 1952-60; Bishop of Pretoria, 1960-75. Member, Anglican Roman-Catholic Preparatory Commission, 1967-68; Member, Anglican-Roman Catholic Internat. Commn, 1969-. *Publications:* The Churchman's

Heritage, 1952; Belief and Prayer, 1964; To be or not to be, 1968; Where the Truth is Found, 1975. *Recreation:* walking. *Address:* 1 Little Cloister, Westminster Abbey, SW1. *T:* 01-222 4027. *Club:* United Oxford & Cambridge University.

KNARESBOROUGH, Bishop Suffragan of, since 1972; **Rt. Rev. Ralph Emmerson;** *b* 7 June 1913; *s* of Thomas and Alys Mary Emmerson; *m* 1942, Ann Hawthorn Bygate; no *c. Educ:* Leeds Grammar Sch.; King's Coll., London (BD, AKC); Westcott House, Cambridge. Leeds Educn Authority Youth Employment Dept, 1930-35; Curate, St George's, Leeds, 1938-41; Priest-in-Charge, Seacroft Estate, 1941-48; Rector of Methley and Vicar of Mickletown, 1949-56; Vicar of Headingley, 1956-66; Hon. Canon of Ripon Cath., 1964; Residentiary Canon and Canon Missioner for Dio. Ripon, 1966-72. *Address:* 76 Leadhall Lane, Harrogate HG2 9NW. *T:* Harrogate 872111.

KNATCHBULL, family name of **Baron Brabourne.**

KNEALE, (Robert) Bryan (Charles), RA 1974 (ARA 1970); sculptor; *b* 19 June 1930; *m* 1956, Doreen Lister; one *s* one *d. Educ:* Douglas High Sch.; Douglas Sch. of Art, IOM; Royal Academy Schools: Rome prize, 1949-51; RA diploma. Tutor, RCA Sculpture Sch., 1964-; Head of Sculpture Sch., Hornsey, 1967; Assoc. Lectr, Chelsea Sch. of Art, 1970. Exhibitions: at Redfern Gallery, 1954, 1956, 1958, 1960, 1962, 1964, 1967, 1970, 1976; John Moores, 1961; Sixth Congress of Internat. Union of Architects, 1961; Art Aujourd'hui, Paris, 1963; Battersea Park Sculpture, 1963; Profile III Bochum, 1964; British Sculpture in the Sixties, Tate Gall., 1965; Whitechapel Gall. Retrospective, 1966; Battersea Park, 1966; Structure, Cardiff Metamorphis Coventry, 1966; New British Painting and Sculpture, 1967-68; City of London Festival, 1968; Holland Park, Sculpture in the Cities, Southampton, and British Sculptors, RA, 1972; Holland Park, 1973; Royal Exchange Sculpture Exhibition, 1974; New Art, Hayward Gallery, 1975. Arts Council Tours, 1966-71. Collections: Arts Council of Gt Britain; Contemp. Art Soc.; Manx Museum; Leics Educn Authority; Nat. Galls of Victoria, S Australia and New Zealand; City Art Galls, York, Nottingham, Manchester, Bradford and Leicester; Tate Gall.; Beaverbrook Foundn, Fredericton; Museum of Modern Art, Sao Paulo, Brazil; Bahia Museum, Brazil; Oriel Coll., Oxford; Museum of Modern Art, New York; City Galleries, Middlesbrough, Birmingham, Wakefield; Fitzwilliam Museum, Cambridge; W Riding Educn Authority. *Address:* 7 Winthorpe Road, SW15. *T:* 01-788 0869.

KNEALE, Prof. William Calvert, FBA 1950; White's Professor of Moral Philosophy, University of Oxford, and Fellow of Corpus Christi College, 1960-66; *b* 22 June 1906; *s* of late William Kneale; *m* 1938, Martha Hurst, Fellow of Lady Margaret Hall, Oxford; one *s* one *d. Educ:* Liverpool Institute; Brasenose Coll., Oxford (Classical Scholar). Senior Hulme Scholar, Brasenose Coll., 1927, studied in Freiburg and Paris; Asst in Mental Philosophy, University of Aberdeen, 1929; Asst Lecturer in Philosophy, Armstrong Coll., Newcastle upon Tyne, 1931; Lecturer in Philosophy, Exeter Coll., Oxford, 1932; Fellow, 1933-60; Senior Tutor, 1945-50; Emeritus Fellow, 1960. War of 1939-45, temp. Civil Servant, Ministry of Shipping (later War Transport). Vice-Pres., British Acad., 1971-72. Hon. Fellow, Brasenose Coll., Oxford, 1962, and Corpus Christi Coll., Oxford, 1966. Hon. LLD Aberdeen, 1960; Hon. DLitt: Durham, 1966; St Andrews, 1973. *Publications:* Probability and Induction, 1949; (with M. Kneale) The Development of Logic, 1962; On Having a Mind, 1962; articles in Mind, Proceedings of Aristotelian Society, etc. *Address:* 4 Bridge End, Grassington, near Skipton, North Yorks. *T:* Grassington 752710.

KNEBWORTH, Viscount; John Peter Michael Scawen Lytton; *b* 7 June 1950; *s* and *heir* of 4th Earl of Lytton, *qv. Educ:* Downside; Reading Univ. (BSc, Estate Management). ARICS 1976. *Address:* Lillycombe, Porlock, Somerset. *T:* Porlock 862353.

KNELL, Rt. Rev. Eric Henry, MA Oxon; Assistant Bishop, Diocese of Oxford, 1972; *b* 1 April 1903; *s* of Edward Henry and Edith Helen Knell; unmarried. *Educ:* Trinity College, Oxford. Assistant Curate of St Barnabas, Southfields, 1928; Domestic Chaplain to Bishop of Lincoln, 1933; in charge of Trinity College, Oxford, Mission in Stratford, E15, 1936; Vicar of Emmanuel, Forest Gate, 1941; Vicar of Christ Church, Reading, 1945; Archdeacon of Berkshire, 1955-67; Suffragan Bishop of Reading, 1955-72. *Address:* College of St Barnabas, Lingfield, Surrey.

KNIGHT, Most Rev. Alan John; see West Indies, Archbishop of.

KNIGHT, Sir Allan Walton, Kt 1970; CMG 1960; FIE (Aust.); Commissioner, The Hydro-Electric Commission, Tasmania, Australia, since 1946; *b* 26 Feb. 1910; *s* of late Mr and Mrs G. W. Knight, Lindisfarne, Tasmania; *m* 1936, Margaret Janet Buchanan; two *s* one *d*. *Educ:* Hobart Technical Coll.; University of Tasmania. Diploma of Applied Science, 1929; BSc 1932; ME 1935; BCom 1946. Chief Engineer, Public Works Dept, Tasmania, 1937-46. Member: Australian Univs Commn, 1966-74; Council, Tasmanian Coll. of Advanced Education, 1968-75. Peter Nicol Russell Medal, Instn of Engrs of Australia, 1963; William Kernot Medal, Univ. of Melbourne, 1963; Wilfred Chapman Award, Inst. of Welding, Australia, 1974; John Storey Medal, Inst. of Management, Australia, 1975. *Recreation:* royal tennis. *Address:* 64 Waimea Avenue, Hobart, Tasmania 7005, Australia. *T:* Hobart 251498. *Club:* Tasmanian (Hobart).

KNIGHT, Andrew Stephen Bower; Editor, The Economist, since 1974; *b* 1 Nov. 1939; *s* of M. W. B. Knight and S. E. F. Knight; *m* 1st, 1966, Victoria Catherine Brittain (marr. diss.); one *s* (Casimir); 2nd, 1975, Begum Sabiha Rumani Malik; one *d*. *Educ:* Ampleforth Coll.; Balliol Coll., Oxford. Joined J. Henry Schroder Wagg & Co., 1962; Investors Chronicle, 1964; The Economist, 1966. *Address:* 25 St James's Street, SW1. *Club:* Brooks's.

KNIGHT, Sir Arthur (William), Kt 1975; Chairman, Courtaulds Ltd, since 1975; *b* 29 March 1917; *s* of Arthur Frederick Knight and Emily Scott; *m* 1st, 1945, Beatrice Joan Osborne (*née* Oppenheim) (*d* 1968); one *s* three *d*; 2nd, 1972, Sheila Elsie Whiteman. *Educ:* Tottenham County Sch.; London Sch. of Economics (evening student) (BCom). J. Sainsbury, Blackfriars, 1933-38; LSE, Dept of Business Admin (Leverhulme Studentship), 1938-39; Courtaulds, 1939. Served War, Army, 1940-46. Courtaulds, 1946-: apptd Dir, 1958; Finance Dir, 1961. Non-exec. Director: Pye Holdings, 1972-75; Rolls-Royce (1971), 1973-; Richard Thomas & Baldwin, 1966-67. Member: Council of Manchester Business Sch., 1964-71; Cttee for Arts and Social Studies of Council for Nat. Academic Awards, 1965-71; Commn of Enquiry into siting of Third London Airport, 1968-70; Council of Industry for Management Educn, 1970-73; Finance Cttee, RIIA, 1971-75; Council, RIIA, 1975-; Court of Governors, London Sch. of Economics, 1971-; Economic Cttee, CBI, 1965-72; Cairncross (Channel Tunnel) Cttee, 1974-75; NIESR Exec. Cttee, 1976. *Publications:* Private Enterprise and Public Intervention: the Courtauld experience, 1974; various papers. *Recreations:* walking, sailing, music, reading. *Address:* 9 Radnor Place, W2 2TF. *T:* 01-262 7621. *Club:* Reform.

KNIGHT, Prof. Bert Cyril James Gabriel, DSc London; Professor of Microbiology, University of Reading, 1951-69, Emeritus since 1969; *b* 4 Feb. 1904; *s* of late Cyril Fennel Knight and Kate Knight (*née* Gabriel); *m* 1st, 1929, Doris, *d* of late G. D. Kemp; one *d*; 2nd, 1944, Frideswide, *d* of late Dr H. F. Stewart; two *s* two *d* (and one *s* decd). *Educ:* Reigate Grammar Sch.; University Coll., London. BSc (Chemistry), University Coll., London, 1925; MSc 1927; DSc 1938. Worked on problems of bacterial physiology at London Hosp., 1929-34, and at Middlesex Hosp., 1934-38, in Medical Research Council Unit for Bacterial Chemistry. Halley Stewart Research Fellow, 1934-38; Biochemist, Lister Institute of Preventive Medicine, Serum Dept, Elstree, 1939-43; Wellcome Research Laboratories, Beckenham (Depts of Biochemistry and Bacteriology), 1943-50. Joint Editor, Journal of General Microbiology, 1946-70. Visiting Commonwealth Prof., New York Univ. Medical Sch., Nov. 1947-Jan. 1948. *Publications:* Bacterial Nutrition, 1936; Growth Factors in Microbiology, 1945; (trans. with J. Stewart) Stendhal's Life of Henry Brulard, 1959. Papers in: Biochem. Jl, British Journal of Experimental Pathology, Journal Chem. Soc., Jl Gen. Microbiol., Bull. Soc. Chim. biol., etc. Harvey Lecture, NY, 1947; William Henry Welch Lecture, NY, 1948. *Recreations:* 18th-20th century French and English literature, walking. *Address:* 28 Park Parade, Cambridge CB5 8AL.

KNIGHT, Charles, VPRWS 1961 (RWS 1935; ARWS 1933); ROI 1933; Landscape Painter and Designer; Vice-Principal, Brighton College of Art and Crafts, 1959-67, retired; *b* 27 Aug. 1901; *s* of Charles and Evelyn Mary Knight; *m* 1934, Leonora Vasey (*d* 1970); one *s*. Art training, Brighton Coll. of Art; Royal Academy Schools, London (Turner Gold Medal); works in permanent collections, London, British Museum, Victoria and Albert Museum, Sheffield, Leeds, Hull, Oxford, Brighton, Hove, Eastbourne, Preston, etc; regular exhibitor RA, 1924-65. Illustrated monograph by Michael Brockway, 1952. *Address:* Chettles, 34 Beacon Road, Ditchling, Sussex. *T:* Hassocks 3998.

KNIGHT, Edmund Alan; Commissioner of Customs and Excise, 1971-77; *b* 17 June 1919; *s* of Arthur Philip and Charlotte Knight; *m* 1953, Annette Ros Grimmitt; one *d*. *Educ:* Drayton Manor Sch.; London Sch. of Economics. Entered Exchequer and Audit Dept, 1938; HM Customs and Excise, 1948; Asst Sec., 1957; Sec. to Cttee on Turnover Taxation, 1963-64; seconded to Inland Revenue, 1969-71. Member: SITPRO Bd, 1971-76; EDC for Internat. Freight Movement, 1971-76. *Address:* 40 Park Avenue North, Harpenden, Herts.

KNIGHT, Eric John Percy Crawford L.; *see* Lombard Knight.

KNIGHT, Esmond Pennington; actor; *b* 4 May 1906; 3rd *s* of Francis and Bertha Knight; *m* 1st, 1929, Frances Clare (marr. diss.); one *d*; 2nd, 1946, Nora Swinburne, *qv*. *Educ:* Willington Prep. Sch.; Westminster. Made first appearance on stage at Pax Robertson's salon in Ibsen's Wild Duck, 1925; Old Vic., 1925-27; Birmingham Repertory Co., 1927-28; Contraband, Prince's Theatre; To What Red Hell, Wyndham's, 1928; The Children's Theatre; Fashion, Kingsway; Maya, Studio des Théâtres des Champs-Elysées, Paris, 1929; Art and Mrs Bottle, Royalty; Hamlet, Queen's, 1930; Salome, Gate; Waltzes from Vienna, Alhambra, 1931; Wild Violets, Drury Lane, 1932; Three Sisters, Drury Lane; Streamline, Palace, 1934; Wise Tomorrow, Lyric; Van Gogh, Arts Theatre Club; Night Must Fall, Cambridge Theatre, 1936; The Insect Play, Little; The King and Mistress Shore, Little, 1937; Crest of the Wave, Tour; Twelfth Night, Phœnix, 1938; in management with Wilson Barrett, King's, Hammersmith and Edinburgh, 1939; Peaceful Inn, Duke of York's; Midsummer Night's Dream, Open Air, 1940. Joined RNVR (HMS King Alfred, Drake, Excellent, Prince of Wales); discharged from Navy as a result of being blinded in HMS Prince of Wales during action with Bismarck, 1941. Returned to stage in Crisis in Heaven, March 1945; shared lead with Evelyn Laye in The Three Waltzes, Princes. Season of plays with travelling Repertory Theatre, King's, Hammersmith, 1946; The Relapse, 1947; Memorial Theatre, Stratford-on-Avon, 1948-49; Caroline (by Maugham), Arts Theatre Club; Old Vic Co., Edinburgh Festival, 1950, in Bartholomew Fair by Ben Jonson; Who is Sylvia, Criterion, 1950; Sir Laurence Olivier's Festival Season, St James's Theatre, 1951; Heloise, Duke of York's; Montserrat, Lyric; Bermuda Festival (Bermuda); Emperor's Clothes (New York); Age of Consent; Bell, Book and Candle, Phœnix, 1955; The Caine Mutiny, Hippodrome, 1956; The Country Wife, Adelphi, 1957; The Russian, Lyric, Hammersmith, 1958; A Piece of Silver (Cheltenham), 1960; The Lady from the Sea, Queen's, 1961; Becket, Taming of the Shrew, Aldwych, 1961; Two Stars for Comfort, Garrick, 1962; Last Old Vic Season, 1962-63; Season, Mermaid, 1965; Edinburgh Festival: Winter's Tale, and Trojan Women 1966; Getting Married, Strand, 1967; Greenwich Theatre: Martin Luther King, 1969; Spithead, 1969; The Servants and the Snow, 1970; Mister, Duchess, 1971; Family Reunion, '69 Theatre Co., Manchester, 1973; The Cocktail Party, '69 Theatre Co., Manchester, 1975; Loves Old Sweet Song, Greenwich, 1976; Three Sisters, Cambridge, 1976; Henry V and Agincourt, The Archer's Tale, Open Air Theatre, 1976. *Films:* Romany Love, 77 Park Lane, The Ringer, Pagliacci, Waltzes from Vienna, Black Roses (Ufa, Berlin), What Men Live By, The Bermondsey Kid, The Blue Squadron, Girls Will Be Boys, Dandy Dick, Someday, Crime Unlimited, Contraband, The Silver Fleet, Half-Way House, King Henry V, A Canterbury Tale, Black Narcissus, Hamlet, Red Shoes, Gone to Earth, The River, 1950, Helen of Troy (Rome), 1954, The Dark Avenger, Ratcliffe in Olivier's Richard III, The Sleeping Prince, On Secret Service, Battle of the V1; Sink the Bismarck; The Spy Who Came in From the Cold; Anne of the Thousand Days; Where's Jack, 1968; The Boy who turned Yellow; The Yellow Dog; Robin and Marian, 1975. Assisted in making several Natural History films. *Television:* has appeared frequently on BBC and Independent Television, notably in Dickens and Ibsen; Dr Finlay's Casebook; Elizabeth I; The Pallisers; Fall of Eagles; History of the English-speaking Peoples; Shades of Greene; Ballet Shoes; Quiller; I Claudius; 1900: Voices from the Past; Kilvert's Diaries; Supernatural. Also tours with his one man show: Agincourt—The Archer's Tale. *Publications:* Seeking the Bubble (Autobiography), 1943; Story in Blackwood's, Jan. 1942; various articles in daily and weekly Press. *Recreation:* painting. *Address:* c/o Peter Eade Ltd, 9 Cork Street, W1X 1PD. *T:* 01-734 2858. *Club:* Savage.

KNIGHT, Geoffrey Cureton, MB, BS London; FRCS; FRCPsych; Consulting Neurological Surgeon in London, since 1935; Hon. Consultant Neurosurgeon: West End Hospital for Neurology and Neurosurgery; SE Metropolitan Regional Neurosurgical Centre; Royal Postgraduate Medical School of London; Teacher of Surgery, University of London; *b* 4 Oct. 1906; *s* of Cureton Overbeck Knight; *m* 1933, Betty, *d* of Francis Cooper Havell, London; two *s*. *Educ:* Brighton Coll.; St Bartholomew's Hosp. Medical Sch. Brackenbury Surgical Schol.

St Bart's Hosp., 1930. Ho. Surg. and Chief Asst, Surgical Professorial Unit at St Bart's Hosp.; Demonstrator in Physiology, St Bart's Hosp. Medical Sch.; Leverhulme Research Scholar, Royal College of Surgeons, 1933-35; Mackenzie Mackinnon Research Scholar, 1936-38; Bernard Baron Research Scholar, 1938; Hunterian Prof., 1935-36 and 1963. FRSocMed; Fellow Soc. Brit. Neurological Surgeons; Fellow Med. Soc. London; Vice-Pres., Internat. Soc. for Psychosurgery. Neurological Surg. Armed Forces of Czecho-Slovakia, 1941; Hon. Fellow, Czecho-Slovak Med. Soc., Prague, 1946; Officer, Order of the White Lion of Czecho-Slovakia, 1946. *Publications:* contrib. med. jls on aetiology and surgical treatment of diseases of the spine and nervous system and the surgical treatment of mental illness. *Recreations:* gardening, swimming. *Address:* 7 Aubrey Road, Campden Hill, W8. *T:* 01-727 7719 (Sec., 01-935 7549). *Club:* Hurlingham.

KNIGHT, Geoffrey Egerton, CBE 1970; Director: Guinness Peat Group Ltd, since 1976; Guinness Peat Aviation Ltd, since 1977; Executive Vice Chairman, Fenchurch Insurance Holdings Ltd, and Director, a number of subsidiary companies, since 1975; *b* 25 Feb. 1921; *s* of Arthur Egerton Knight and Florence Gladys Knight (*née* Clarke); *m* 1947, Evelyn Bugle; two *d. Educ:* Stubbington House; Brighton Coll. Royal Marines, 1939-46. Joined Bristol Aeroplane Co. Ltd, 1953; Dir, Bristol Aircraft Ltd, 1956; Dir, BAC Ltd, 1964-77, Vice Chm., 1972-76. *Publication:* Concorde: the inside story, 1976. *Address:* 33 Smith Terrace, SW3. *T:* 01-352 5391. *Club:* Boodle's.

KNIGHT, Dr Geoffrey Wilfred; retired; Regional Medical Officer, North West Thames Regional Health Authority, 1973-76; *b* 10 Jan. 1920; *s* of Wilfred Knight and Ida Knight; *m* 1944, Christina Marion Collins Scott; one *s* one *d. Educ:* Leeds Univ. Med. Sch. MB, ChB, MD, DPH (Chadwick Gold Medal). County Med. Officer of Health, Herts, 1962-73. Formerly: Governor, Nat. Inst. of Social Work; Member: Personal Social Services Council; Central Midwives Bd; Exec. Cttee, Child Health Bureau; Adv. Panel, Soc. for Health Educn; formerly Mem., Govt Techn. and Sci. Cttee on Disposal of Toxic Wastes. *Recreations:* painting, golf. *Address:* Orchard Leigh, Hailey Lane, Hailey, Hertford, Herts SG13 7NY. *T:* Hoddesdon 62252.

KNIGHT, Prof. (George Richard) Wilson, CBE 1968; MA Oxon; FRSL; FIAL; Professor of English Literature, Leeds University, 1956-62, now Emeritus (Reader in English Literature, Leeds University, 1946-56); *b* 19 Sept. 1897; *s* of George Knight and Caroline L. Jackson; unmarried. *Educ:* Dulwich Coll.; St Edmund Hall, Oxford. Served European War, Middle East; Master at Seaford House, Littlehampton, 1920, and St Peter's, Seaford, 1921; St Edmund Hall, 1922-23; Honour Sch. of English Language and Literature, 1923; Chess, Oxford *v* Cambridge, 1923; Master at Hawtreys, Westgate-on-Sea, 1923-25, and Dean Close Sch., Cheltenham, 1925-31; Chancellors' Prof. of English, Trinity Coll., University of Toronto, 1931-40; Master at Stowe, Buckingham, 1941-46. Stage: Shakespearian productions at Hart House Theatre, Toronto, 1932-40; produced and acted in: Hamlet, Rudolf Steiner Hall, London, 1935; This Sceptred Isle, Westminster Theatre, London, 1941; productions (Agamemnon, Athalie, Timon of Athens) and performances (Timon, Lear, Othello, Shylock) at Leeds Univ., 1946-60; Shakespeare's Dramatic Challenge (dramatic recital), Northcott Theatre, Exeter, 1975 and 1976, and various other centres, 1976-77, including World Shakespeare Congress, Washington, 1976, Video-tape Yeovil Coll., 1977. Lectures and lecture recitals since 1951: Cambridge (Clark Lectures), London, Nottingham (Byron Foundn Lecture), Canada, S Africa, USA and W Indies. BBC talks and readings on Shakespeare and Byron, 1963-64 and tape recordings (USA); joint-petitioner, Byron Memorial (Westminster Abbey, 1969); shareholder, Byron Soc. Jl, 1972. Sculpted by Robert Russin, USA, and Kenneth Carter, Exeter, 1975. Mem., Internat. Adv. Cttee, World Shakespeare Congress, Vancouver, 1971; Powys Centenary, Cambridge, 1972. Pres., Devonshire Assoc., 1971; Hon. Vice-Pres., Spiritualist Assoc. of Great Britain, 1955; Hon. Life Pres., Dulwich Coll. Literary Soc., 1971. Hon. Fellow St Edmund Hall, Oxford, 1965; Hon. LittD Sheffield, 1966; Hon. DLitt Exon, 1968. Hon. Mem., Mark Twain Soc., 1976. *Publications:* Myth and Miracle, 1929; The Wheel of Fire, 1930; The Imperial Theme, 1931; The Shakespearian Tempest, 1932; The Christian Renaissance, 1933; Principles of Shakespearian Production, 1936; Atlantic Crossing, 1936; The Burning Oracle, 1939; This Sceptred Isle, 1940; The Starlit Dome, 1941; Chariot of Wrath, 1942; The Olive and the Sword, 1944; The Dynasty of Stowe, 1945; Hiroshima, 1946; The Crown of Life, 1947; Christ and Nietzsche, 1948; Lord Byron: Christian Virtues, 1952; Laureate of Peace, 1954; The Last of the Incas, 1954 (play, first prod. Sheffield, 1954; BBC 1974); The Mutual Flame, 1955; Lord Byron's Marriage, 1957; The Sovereign Flower, 1958; The

Golden Labyrinth, 1962; Ibsen, 1962; Shakespearian Production, 1964; The Saturnian Quest, 1965; Byron and Shakespeare, 1966; Shakespeare and Religion, 1967; Poets of Action, 1967; Gold-Dust, 1968; Neglected Powers, 1971; (ed) W. F. Jackson Knight, Elysion, 1970; Jackson Knight: a biography, 1975; Vergil and Shakespeare, 1977; Shakespeare's Dramatic Challenge, 1977; also contribs to: John Masefield, OM, ed G. Handley-Taylor, 1960; Powys to Knight (letters, ed Robert Blackmore), 1977; Times Literary Supplement, The Yorkshire Post, Review of English Studies, Essays in Criticism, Contemporary Review, etc. *Address:* Caroline House, Streatham Rise, Exeter EX4 4PD.

KNIGHT, Gerald Hocken, CBE 1971; MA, MusB Cantab; DMus Lambeth; FRCM; FRCO (Choirmaster's Diploma); FRSCM; ADCM; Director of the Royal School of Church Music, 1952-72 (Associate-Director, 1947-52); Overseas Commissioner of the Royal School of Church Music since 1973; Hon. Organist to Archbishop of Canterbury, since 1953; *b* 27 July 1908; *o s* of Alwyne and Edith Knight, Wyngarvey, Par, Cornwall. *Educ:* Truro Cathedral Sch.; Peterhouse, Cambridge (Choral Exhibitioner); College of St Nicolas, Chislehurst; Royal College of Music. Asst Organist, Truro Cathedral, 1922-26; Peterhouse, Cambridge, 1926-29; John Stewart of Rannoch Scholar in Sacred Music, Cambridge Univ.; Organist and Choirmaster, St Augustine's, Queen's Gate, South Kensington, 1931-37; Tutor, College of St Nicolas, Chislehurst, 1932-38; Organist and Master of the Choristers, Canterbury Cathedral, 1937-52; Warden and Fellow of College of St Nicolas, Canterbury, 1945-52; External Examiner, Yorks Trg Colls Exam. Bd, 1937-41; Airman, RAF, 1942-43; Education Officer, Royal Air Force, 1943-45. Mem., House of Laity, Church Assembly, 1945-55; Mem., Archbishops' Psalter Revision Commission, 1958-63. Hon. Fellow: St Michael's Coll., Tenbury, 1953; Westminster Choir Coll., Princeton, New Jersey, USA, 1965. Hon. RAM; Hon. FTCL. *Publications:* Accompaniments (with J. Eric Hunt) to Merbecke's Communion Service, 1933; Music for Dorothy L. Sayers' plays, The Zeal of Thy House, 1937, and The Devil to Pay, 1939. Jt Musical Editor, Hymns Ancient and Modern, revised 1950; Jt Editor (with Dr William L. Reed), The Treasury of English Church Music, 1965; (ed) The Revised Parish Psalter, 1967; A Manual of Plainsong (Revised Psalter), 1969; Accompaniments for Unison Hymn-Singing, 1971. *Address:* Addington Palace, Croydon CR9 5AD. *T:* 01-654 7677. *Club:* Athenæum.

KNIGHT, Gilfred Norman; President of the Society of Indexers since 1969; *b* 12 Sept. 1891; *y s* of William Frederick Knight, Solicitor; unmarried. *Educ:* Bradfield Coll.; Balliol Coll., Oxford (MA). Tancred Scholar, Lincoln's Inn, 1914; called to Bar, Lincoln's Inn, 1918. Served European War, 1914-18: commnd in E Surrey Regt, 1914; severely wounded at Battle of Loos, 1915; Captain and Adjt, No 16 Officer Cadet Bn, 1917; Staff of Judge Advocate-General, 1918-19. Sec. to West Indian and Atlantic Gp, British Empire Exhibn, 1923, 1924. Asst Sec. to West India Cttee, 1919-26, and 1938-39. Sec. to Co. of London TA&AFA, 1927. Guardian to Heir Apparent of Rampur State, India, 1931-32. Civil Service: Censorship, 1940-42; War Office, 1942-56. Founded Soc. of Indexers, 1957 and first Hon. Sec.; Chm., 1962. Wheatley Gold Medal for outstanding index, 1967; Carey Award, Soc. of Indexers, 1977. Is a Freemason (LGR). *Publications:* Chess Pieces: An Anthology, 1949; (with F. L Pick) The Pocket History of Freemasonry, 1953; The Freemason's Pocket Reference Book, 1955; (ed) Training in Indexing, 1969; (with W. F. Guy) King, Queen and Knight: A Chess Anthology, 1975; Indexing, The Art of, 1977; (with Frederick Smyth) The Pocket Cyclopædia of Freemasonry, 1977; numerous contribs to West Indies Chronicle, Chess, Masonic Record, and The Indexer. *Recreations:* chess, book reviewing. *Address:* Scio House, Roehampton, SW15 3TD. *T:* 01-789 1649. *Clubs:* Civil Service; Hastings Chess; Barnet Chess (Hon. Life Pres., 1972).

KNIGHT, Air Vice-Marshal Glen Albyn Martin, CB 1961; CBE 1956; *b* 10 Sept. 1903; *e s* of Lt-Col G. A. Knight, OBE, VD, Melbourne, Australia; *m* 1933, Janet Elizabeth Warnock, *o d* of Peter Crawford, Dargavel, Dumfriesshire; two *d. Educ:* Scotch Coll., Melbourne, Australia; Melbourne Univ. MB, BS, 1927; Diploma in Laryngology and Otology (RCP & S), 1937. House Surgeon and Physician, Alfred and Children's Hospitals, Melbourne; joined Medical Branch, RAF, 1932. War Service: South Africa, Malta (despatches), Italy; PMO Desert Air Force. Principal Medical Officer, 2nd Tactical Air Force, 1956-57; Dep. Dir-Gen. of Medical Services, Royal Air Force, 1958-61, retired, 1961. QHS 1959-61. *Recreation:* golf. *Address:* Craig Gowan, Laurieston Road, Gatehouse-of-Fleet, Kirkcudbrightshire. *T:* Gatehouse 417.

KNIGHT, Harold Murray, DSC 1945; Governor and Chairman of Board, Reserve Bank of Australia, since 1975; *b* 13 Aug. 1919; *s* of W. H. P. Knight, Melbourne; *m* 1951, Gwenyth Catherine Pennington; four *s* one *d. Educ:* Scotch Coll., Melbourne; Melbourne Univ. Commonwealth Bank of Australia, 1936-40. AIF (Lieut), 1940-43; RANVR (Lieut), 1943-45. Commonwealth Bank of Australia, 1946-55; Asst Chief, Statistics Div., Internat. Monetary Fund, 1957-59; Reserve Bank of Australia: Research Economist, 1960-62; Asst Manager, Investment Dept, 1962-64, Manager, 1964-68; Dep. Governor and Dep. Chm. of Board, 1968-75. *Publication:* Introducción al Analisis Monetario (Spanish), 1959. *Address:* (office) Reserve Bank of Australia, 65 Martin Place, Sydney, NSW 2000, Australia.

KNIGHT, Henry Lougher; HM Lieutenant, Mid-Glamorgan, since 1974; *b* 7 Aug. 1907; *e s* of Robert Lougher Knight; *m* 1932, Pamela, *d* of E. Colville Lyons; three *s. Educ:* Radley; Exeter Coll., Oxford. Regular Army, RA and RHA, invalided 1934. Chartered Land Agent, 1939; Chartered Surveyor, 1970. Pres., Chartered Land Agents Soc., 1964. JP Glam 1946; DL Glam 1957. *Address:* Tythegston Court, Bridgend, Mid-Glamorgan. *T:* Porthcawl 3379. *Clubs:* Bath, Marylebone Cricket; Cardiff and County (Cardiff).

KNIGHT, Joan Christabel, (Mrs Jill Knight), MBE 1964; MP (C) Edgbaston since 1966; *m* 1947, Montague Knight; two *s. Educ:* Fairfield Sch., Bristol; King Edward Grammar Sch., Birmingham. Mem., Northampton County Borough Council, 1956-66. Member: Parly Select Cttee on Race Relations and Immigration, 1969-72; Council of Europe, 1977-. Kentucky Colonel, USA, 1973. *Recreations:* music, reading, tapestry work, theatre-going, antique-hunting. *Address:* House of Commons, SW1. *Club:* Constitutional.

KNIGHT, Very Rev. Marcus; Dean of Exeter, 1960-72; *b* 11 Sept. 1903; *e s* of late Mark Knight, Insurance Manager; *m* 1931, Claire L. Hewett, MA, *o d* of late Charles H. Hewett, Bank Dir; two *s. Educ:* Christ's Hosp.; University of London; Birkbeck Coll. (BA Hons); King's Coll. (BD Hons); Fellow of King's Coll.; Union Theological Seminary, New York; STM 1930. Curacies at Stoke Newington and Ealing; Priest-Vicar of Exeter Cathedral; Vicar of Cockington, 1936-40; Vicar of Nuneaton; RD of Atherstone, 1940-44; Examining Chaplain to Bishop of Coventry, 1944; Canon of St Paul's, 1944-60, Precentor, 1944-54, Chancellor, 1954-60. Hon. Sec. Church of England Council for Education, 1949-58; Chapter Treas., St Paul's, 1950-60; Church Commissioner, 1968-72. Hon. LLD Exeter, 1973. *Publications:* Spiritualism, Reincarnation, and Immortality, 1950; (part author) There's an Answer Somewhere, 1953; many papers and reviews. *Recreations:* reading, TV, bowls. *Address:* 1 Execliff, Trefusis Terrace, Exmouth, Devon. *T:* Exmouth 71153.

KNIGHT, Richard James, MA; JP; Head Master of Monkton Combe School, 1968-July 1978; *b* 19 July 1915; *s* of Richard William Knight; *m* 1953, Hilary Marian, *d* of Rev. F. W. Argyle; two *s* one *d. Educ:* Dulwich Coll. (Scholar); Trinity Coll., Cambridge (Scholar). 1st class Hons Classical Tripos Pt I, 1936, Part II, 1937. Asst Master, Fettes Coll., Edinburgh, 1938-39. Served War of 1939-45 in Gordon Highlanders, Capt. Asst Master and Housemaster, Marlborough Coll., 1945-56; Headmaster of Oundle Sch., 1956-68. JP Bath, 1970, Avon, 1974. *Recreations:* cricket and other games. *Address:* (until July 1978) Head Master's House, Monkton Combe School, Bath; (from July 1978) 123 Midford Road, Bath.

KNIGHT, Warburton Richard; Director of Educational Services, Bradford Metropolitan District Council, since 1974; *b* 2 July 1932; *s* of Warburton Henry Johnston and Alice Gweneth Knight; *m* 1961, Pamela Ann (*née* Hearmon); two *s* one *d. Educ:* Trinity Coll., Cambridge (MA). Teaching in Secondary Modern and Grammar Schs in Middlesex and Huddersfield, 1956-62; joined West Riding in junior capacity, 1962; Asst Dir for Secondary Schs, Leics, 1967; Asst Educn Officer for Sec. Schs and later for Special and Social Educn in WR, 1970. Hon. Treasurer, Soc. of Educn Officers. *Recreations:* general cultural interests, conventional outdoor sports and European interests. *Address:* Westwinds, Spion Kop, Thorner, Leeds LS14 3EB. *T:* Leeds 892356.

KNIGHT, William Arnold, CMG 1966; OBE 1954; Controller and Auditor-General of Uganda, 1962-68, retired; *b* 14 June 1915; *e s* of late William Knight, Llanfairfechan, and of Clara Knight; *m* 1939, Bronwen Parry; one *s* one *d. Educ:* Friars' Sch., Bangor; University Coll. of North Wales (BA Hons). Entered Colonial Audit Dept as an Asst Auditor, 1938; service in Kenya, 1938-46; Mauritius, 1946-49; Sierra Leone, 1949-52; British Guiana, 1952-57; Uganda, 1957-68; Commissioner, inquiry into economy and efficiency, Uganda, 1969-70. *Recreations:* fishing and gardening. *Address:* Neopardy Mills, near Crediton, Devon. *T:* Crediton 2513. *Club:* East India, Devonshire, Sports and Public Schools.

KNIGHT, Wilson; see Knight, G. W.

KNIGHTLEY; see Finch-Knightley.

KNIGHTON, William Myles; Under Secretary, Department of Trade, since 1974; *b* 8 Sept. 1931; *s* of George Harry Knighton, OBE, and Ella Knighton (*née* Stroud); *m* 1957, Brigid Helen Carrothers; one *s* one *d. Educ:* Bedford School; Peterhouse, Cambridge (BA). Asst Principal, Min. of Supply, 1954; Principal, Min. of Aviation, 1959; Cabinet Office, 1962-64; Principal Private Sec. to Minister of Technology, 1966-68; Asst Sec., Min. of Technology, subseq. Dept of Trade and Industry and Dept of Trade, 1967-74. *Recreations:* gardening, hill-walking, painting. *Address:* 115 Dacre Park, SE13 5BZ. *T:* 01-852 8267. *Club:* United Oxford & Cambridge University.

KNIGHTS, Lionel Charles, MA, PhD; King Edward VII Professor of English Literature, University of Cambridge, 1965-73, now Emeritus Professor; Fellow, Queens' College, Cambridge, 1965-73; *b* 15 May 1906; *s* of C. E. and Lois M. Knights; *m* 1936, Elizabeth M. Barnes; one *s* one *d. Educ:* grammar schs; Selwyn Coll. (Hon. Fellow, 1974), and Christ's Coll., Cambridge Univ.; Charles Oldham Shakespeare Scholar, 1928; Members' Prize, 1929. Lecturer in English Literature, Manchester Univ., 1933-34, 1935-47; Prof. of English Lit., Univ. of Sheffield, 1947-52; Winterstoke Prof. of English, Bristol Univ., 1953-64; Andrew Mellon Vis. Prof., Univ. of Pittsburgh, 1961-62 and 1966; Mrs W. Beckman Vis. Prof., Berkeley, 1970. Mem. of editorial board of Scrutiny, a Quarterly Review, 1932-53. Docteur (*hc*) de l'Univ. de Bordeaux, 1964; Hon. DUniv York, 1969; Hon. DLitt Manchester, 1974. *Publications:* Drama and Society in the Age of Jonson, 1937; Explorations: Essays in Literary Criticism, 1946; Shakespeare's Politics, Shakespeare Lecture, British Academy, 1957; Some Shakespearean Themes, 1959; An Approach to Hamlet, 1960; (ed with Basil Cottle), Metaphor and Symbol, 1961; Further Explorations, 1965; Public Voices: literature and politics (Clark Lectures), 1971; Explorations 3, 1976. *Address:* 57 Jesus Lane, Cambridge.

KNIGHTS, Philip Douglas, CBE 1976 (OBE 1971); QPM (Dist. Service) 1964; Chief Constable, West Midlands Police, since 1975; *b* 3 Oct. 1920; *s* of Thomas James Knights and Ethel Knights; *m* 1945, Jean Burman. *Educ:* King's Sch., Grantham. Lincolnshire Constabulary: Police Cadet, 1938-40; Constable, 1940. Served War, RAF, 1943-45. Sergeant, Lincs Constab., 1946; seconded to Home Office, 1946-50; Inspector, Lincs Constab., 1953, Supt 1955, Chief Supt 1957. Asst Chief Constable, Birmingham City Police, 1959; seconded to Home Office, Dep. Comdt, Police Coll., 1962-66; Dep. Chief Constable, Birmingham City Police, 1970; Chief Constable, Sheffield and Rotherham Constab., 1972-74; Chief Constable, South Yorks Police, 1974-75. Winner of Queen's Police Gold Medal Essay Competition, 1965. Mem. Lord Devlin's Cttee on Identification Procedures, 1974-75. FBIM. *Recreations:* sport, gardening. *Address:* West Midlands Police Headquarters, PO Box 52, Lloyd House, Colmore Circus Queensway, Birmingham B4 6NQ. *T:* 021-236 5000.

KNIGHTS, Maj.-Gen. Robert William, CB 1969; CBE 1960; GOC Southern Command, Australia, 1966-69, retired; *b* 24 June 1912; *s* of late William James Knights, Canberra, Australia; *m* 1937, Betty Adrienne, *d* of late George Leonard Davis, Sale, Victoria, Australia; one *s* two *d. Educ:* Telopea Park High Sch., Canberra; Royal Military College, Duntroon, Canberra. Lt, Australian Staff Corps, 1932; Adj., CMF, 1933-39. Served War of 1939-45: Middle East and Australia, Lt-Col, 1943. Staff, RMC, Duntroon, 1945-47; AHQ, 1947-49; Joint Services Staff Coll., UK, 1949; seconded Dept of Defence, 1950-51; Dir of Personnel Administration, AHQ, Melbourne, 1951-54; Brig., 1954; idc, 1957; Maj.-Gen., 1958; Head of Australian Joint Services Staff, London, 1958-59; Extra Gentleman Usher to the Queen, 1958-60; GOC, W Comd, Aust., 1960; Comdt, RMC, Duntroon, 1960-61; Chm., Joint Planning Cttee, Dept of Defence, Australia, 1962-63. QMG, AHQ, Australia, 1964-66. *Address:* 128 Empire Circuit, Yarralumla, ACT 2600, Australia. *Clubs:* Naval and Military (Melbourne); Commonwealth (Canberra).

KNILL, Sir John Kenelm Stuart, 4th Bt *cr* 1893, of The Grove, Blackheath; Civil Servant, Ministry of Defence, 1963-77; *b* 8 April 1913; *s* of Sir John Stuart Knill, 3rd Bt and Lucy Emmeline (*d* 1952), *o d* of Captain Thomas Willis, MN, FRGS; *S* father, 1973; *m* 1950, Violette Maud Florence Martin Barnes;

two s. *Educ:* St Gregory's School, Downside. Gas industry apprenticeship, 1932-39; industrial management trainee, 1945-48; canal transport proprietor, 1948-54; pig farmer, 1954-63. Served as Lieut, RNVR, 1940-45 (Atlantic Star, Italy, France and Germany Stars). *Recreations:* canal and railway restoration (Member of Kennet and Avon Canal Trust, Great Western Soc., Inland Waterways Assoc.); scouting. *Heir: s* Thomas John Pugin Bartholomew Knill, [*b* 24 Aug. 1952; *m* 1977, Kathleen Muszynski]. *Address:* Canal Cottage, Bathampton, Somerset. *T.:* Bath 63603. *Club:* Victory Services.

KNOLLYS, family name of **Viscount Knollys.**

KNOLLYS, 3rd Viscount, of Caversham, *cr* 1911; **David Francis Dudley Knollys;** Baron *cr* 1902; *b* 12 June 1931; *s* of 2nd Viscount Knollys, GCMG, MBE, DFC, and Margaret, *o d* of Sir Stuart Coats, 2nd Bt; *S* father 1966; *m* 1959, Hon. Sheelin Virginia Maxwell (granted, 1959, title, rank and precedence of a baron's *d,* which would have been hers had her father survived to succeed to barony of Farnham), *d* of late Lt-Col Hon. Somerset Maxwell, MP and late Mrs Remington Hobbs; three *s* one *d. Educ:* Eton. Lt, Scots Guards, 1951. *Heir: s* Hon. Patrick Nicholas Mark Knollys, *b* 11 March 1962. *Address:* Bramerton Grange, Norwich NR14 7HF. *T:* Surlingham 266. *Club:* White's.

KNOPF, Alfred A.; publisher; Chairman Alfred A. Knopf, Inc., 1957-72, now Chairman Emeritus; *b* 12 Sept. 1892; *s* of Samuel Knopf and Ida Japhe; *m* 1st, 1916, Blanche Wolf (*d* 1966); one *s*; 2nd, 1967, Helen Norcross Hedrick. *Educ:* Mackenzie Sch.; Columbia Coll. AB (Columbia), 1912; Pres., Alfred A. Knopf, Inc., NYC, 1918-57 (Chm. of the Board, 1957-). Gold Medal, Amer. Inst. of Graphic Arts, 1950; C. A. Pugsley Gold Medal for conservation and preservation, 1960; Alexander Hamilton Medal, Columbia Coll., 1966; Francis Parkman Silver Medal, Soc. of Amer. Historians, 1974; Distinguished Service Award, Assoc. of Amer. Univ. Presses, 1975; Distinguished Achievement Awards: Drexel Univ. Library Sch. Alumni Assoc., 1975; Nat. Book Awards Cttee, 1975. Fellow, Amer. Acad. of Arts and Scis, 1976. Hon. LHD: Yale, 1958; Columbia, 1959; Bucknell, 1959; William and Mary, 1960; Lehigh, 1960; Michigan, 1969; Bates Coll., 1971; Hon. LLD (Brandeis), 1963; Hon. DLitt: Adelphi, 1966; Chattanooga, 1966; C. W. Post Center, Long Island Univ., 1973. Notable Achievement Award, Brandeis Univ., 1977. *Address:* (home) Purchase, NY 10577, USA. *TA:* KSP KNOPF.

KNORPEL, Henry; Under-Secretary (Principal Assistant Solicitor), Department of Health and Social Security, since 1971; *b* 18 Aug. 1924; 2nd *s* of late Hyman Knorpel and Dora Knorpel; *m* 1953, Brenda Sterling; two *d. Educ:* City of London Sch.; Magdalen Coll., Oxford. BA 1945, BCL 1946, MA 1949. Called to Bar, Inner Temple, 1947; practised 1947-52; entered Legal Civil Service as Legal Asst, Min. of Nat. Insce, 1952; Sen. Legal Asst, Min. of Pensions and Nat. Insce, 1958; Law Commn, 1965; Min. of Social Security, 1967; Asst Solicitor, Dept of Health and Social Security, 1968. Vis. Lecturer: Kennington Coll. of Commerce and Law, 1950-58; Holborn Coll. of Law, Languages and Commerce, 1958-70; Polytechnic of Central London, 1970-. *Address:* Conway, 32 Sunnybank, Epsom, Surrey KT18 7DX. *T:* Epsom 21394.

KNOTT, Sir John Laurence, Kt 1971; CBE 1960; Director: Australian Consolidated Industries Ltd; Nicholas International Ltd; Equity Trustees Co. Ltd; Gibbs Bright & Co. (Australian) Pty Ltd; World Airways Inc., California; Jennings Industries Ltd (Australian); Norwich (Australian) Life Insurance; Slough Estates (Australian) Pty Ltd; Chairman: ACTA (Australian) Pty; SAAB/Scania (Australian) Pty Ltd; Pacific Can Ltd; *b* 6 July 1910; *s* of J. Knott, Kyneton, Victoria; *m* 1935, Jean R., *d* of C. W. Milnes; three *s* one *d. Educ:* Cobram State Sch.; Melbourne Univ. (Dip Com). Private Sec. to Minister for Trade Treaties, 1935-38; Sec., Aust. Delegn, Eastern Gp Supply Council, New Delhi, 1940; Exec. Officer, Secondary Industries Commn, 1943-45; Mem. Jt War Production Cttee; Dir, Defence Prod. Planning Br., Dept of Supply, 1950-52; Sec., Dept of Defence Prod., 1957-58; Mem., Aust. Defence Mission to US, 1957; Sec., Dept of Supply, Melb., 1959-65; Leader, Aust. Mission to ELDO Confs: London, 1961; Paris, 1965, 1966; Rome, 1967; Vice-Pres., ELDO Council, 1967-69. Dep. High Comr for Australia, London, 1966-68; Dir-Gen., Australian PO, 1968-72; idc; AASA, FCIS, AFAIM, LCA. Pres., ESU (Victoria). Mem. Council, Melbourne Univ. *Recreations:* bowls (Vice-Pres., Royal Victorian Bowling Assoc., 1957-58), golf, gardening. *Address:* 3 Fenwick Street, Kew, Victoria 3101, Australia. *T:* 86 7777. *Clubs:* East India, Devonshire, Sports and Public Schools (London); Rotary, Melbourne, West Brighton (Melbourne); Union (Sydney); Commonwealth (Canberra).

KNOTT, Air Vice-Marshal Ronald George, CB 1967; DSO 1944; DFC 1943; AFC 1955; retired 1972; *b* 19 Dec. 1917; *s* of late George Knott and of Edith Rose Knott; *m* 1941, Hermione Violet (*née* Phayre); three *s* one *d. Educ:* Borden Grammar Sch., Sittingbourne, Kent. No 20 Sqdn RAF, 1938-40; No 5 Flight IAFVR, 1940-41; HQ Coast Defence Wing, Bombay, 1942; No 179 Sqdn, 1943-44; No 524 Sqdn, 1944-45; RAF, Gatow (Ops), 1949-50; OC, RAF Eindhoven, 1950-51; HQ 2nd TAF, 1951-52; RAF Staff Coll., 1952; Flying Trng Comd, 1953-55; Chief Flying Instructor, Central Flying Sch., 1956-58; Air Plans, Air Min., 1959; OC, RAF Gutersloh, 1959-61; ACOS Plans, 2 ATAF, 1962-63; Defence Res. Policy Staff Min. of Def. 1963; DOR2 (RAF), Min. of Def., 1963-67; SASO, HQ NEAF Cyprus, 1967-70; AOA, HQ Air Support Comd, RAF, 1970-72. *Recreations:* squash, gardening, painting, building. *Address:* Pilgrims Cottage, Charing, Kent. *T:* Charing 2723.

KNOWELDEN, Prof. John, MD, FRCP, FFCM, DPH, JP; Professor of Community Medicine (formerly of Preventive Medicine and Public Health), University of Sheffield, since 1960; Academic Registrar, Faculty of Community Medicine, since 1977; *b* 19 April 1919; *s* of Clarence Arthur Knowelden; *m* 1946, Mary Sweet; two *s. Educ:* Colfe's Grammar Sch., Lewisham; St George's Hosp. Med. Sch.; London Sch. of Hygiene and Trop. Med.; Johns Hopkins Sch. of Public Health, Baltimore. Surg. Lt, RNVR, 1942-46. Rockefeller Fellowship in Preventive Med., 1947-49; Lectr in Med. Statistics and Mem., MRC Statistical Research Unit, 1949-60. Civil Consultant in Community Medicine to Royal Navy, 1977-. Editor, Brit. Jl of Preventive and Social Medicine, 1959-69 and 1973-76. Formerly Hon. Sec., Sect. of Epidemiology, Royal Society Medicine and Chm., Soc. for Social Medicine; Mem., WHO Expert Advisory Panel on Health Statistics. *Publications:* (with Ian Taylor) Principles of Epidemiology, 2nd edn, 1964; papers on clinical and prophylactic trials and epidemiological topics. *Recreations:* photography, gardening. *Address:* 2 St Helen's Croft, Grindleford, Sheffield S30 1JG. *T:* Hope Valley 30014.

KNOWLES, Sir Charles (Francis), 7th Bt *cr* 1765; *b* 20 Dec. 1951; *s* of Sir Francis Gerald William Knowles, 6th Bt, FRS, and of Ruth Jessie, *d* of late Rev. Arthur Brooke-Smith; *S* father, 1974. *Educ:* Marlborough Coll.; Oxford Sch. of Architecture (BA 1974; DipArch 1977). *Recreations:* shooting, travel. *Heir: cousin* Peter Cosby Knowles. *Address:* Merlin Haven House, Wootton Under Edge, Glos.

KNOWLES, Colin George; Head of Public Affairs, Imperial Tobacco Ltd, since 1973; *b* 11 April 1939; *s* of George William Knowles, Tarleton, Lancs; *m* 1st, 1961, Mary B. D. Wickliffe, *e d* of William Wickliffe, Co. Antrim, NI; two *d*; 2nd, 1971, Mrs (Marjorie) Alison Taylor, *y d* of late Major R. Balfour Kerr, TD, DL, JP, Haddington, East Lothian; three step *d. Educ:* King George V Grammar Sch., Southport. MInstM 1966; MIPR 1970; BAIE 1972; MBIM 1972. Joined John Player & Sons, 1960; sales and marketing management appts; Head of Public Relations, 1971-73. Mem. Council, Tobacco Trade Benevolent Assoc., 1975-. Director: Nottingham Festival Assoc. Ltd, 1969-71; English Sinfonia Orchestra, 1972-; Midland Sinfonia Concert Soc. Ltd, 1972-; (also co-Founder) Assoc. for Business Sponsorship of The Arts Ltd, 1977- (Chm. Exec. Cttee, 1975-). Arts sponsorship includes responsibility for: Internat. Cello Competition (with Tortelier), Bristol, 1975 and 1977; Pompeii AD 79 Exhibn, Royal Acad., 1976-77 (Mem., Pompeian Exhibn Policy Cttee, 1975-76); new prodns at Royal Opera House, Covent Garden, at Glyndebourne, and at National Theatre. Governor: Manning Grammar Sch., Nottingham, 1972-73; Claysmore Sch., Dorset, 1975-. Liveryman, Worshipful Co of Tobacco Pipe Makers and Tobacco Blenders; Freeman, City of London. FRSA 1975; FRCSoc 1976. OStJ 1977. *Publications:* papers, articles and documentary film treatments on the arts, sponsorship, and tobacco industry topics. *Recreations:* infrequently—with discretion. *Address:* 1 Grosvenor Place, SW1X 7HB. *T:* 01-235 7010. *Clubs:* Carlton, Junior Carlton, MCC.

KNOWLES, George Peter; Registrar of the Province and Diocese of York, and Archbishop of York's Legal Secretary, since 1968; *b* 30 Dec. 1919; *s* of Geoffrey Knowles and Mabel Bowman; *m* 1948, Elizabeth Margaret Scott; one *s* two *d. Educ:* Clifton Coll., Bristol; Queens' Coll., Cambridge. MA, LLB. Served war, Royal Artillery, 1939-46 (Lieut). Admitted a solicitor, 1948; Chm., York Area Rent Tribunal, 1959; Mem., Mental Health Review Tribunal for Yorkshire Regional Health Authority Area, 1960. *Recreations:* fishing, wildlife. *Address:* The Old Rectory, Skelton, York YO3 6XY. *T:* Beningbrough 301. *Clubs:* RAC; Yorkshire (York).

KNOWLES, Prof. Jeremy Randall, FRS 1977; Professor of Chemistry, Harvard University, since 1974; *b* 28 April 1935; *s* of Kenneth Guy Jack Charles Knowles and Dorothy Helen Swingler; *m* 1960, Jane Sheldon Davis; three *s*. *Educ:* Magdalen College Sch.; Balliol Coll., Merton Coll. and Christ Church, Oxford (MA, DPhil). Sir Louis Stuart Exhibr, Balliol Coll., Oxford, 1955-59; Harmsworth Schol., Merton Coll., Oxford, and Research Lectr, Christ Church, Oxford, 1960-62; Research Associate, Calif. Inst. of Technology, 1961-62; Fellow of Wadham Coll., Oxf., 1962-74; Univ. Lectr, Univ. of Oxford, 1966-74. Visiting Prof., Yale Univ., 1969, 1971; Sloan Vis. Prof., Harvard Univ., 1973. *Publications:* research papers and reviews in learned jls. *Address:* 44 Coolidge Avenue, Cambridge, Mass 02138, USA. *T:* (617) 876-8469.

KNOWLES, Hon. Sir Leonard Joseph, Kt 1974; CBE 1963; **Hon. Chief Justice Knowles;** Chief Justice of the Bahamas since 1973; *b* Nassau, 15 March 1916; *s* of late Samuel Joseph Knowles; *m* 1939, Harriet Hansen, *d* of John Hughes, Liverpool; two *s*. *Educ:* Queen's Coll., Nassau, Bahamas; Faculty of Laws, King's Coll., Univ. of London (LLB); first Bahamian student to take and pass Higher Sch. Certif. in Bahamas, 1934; LLB Hons 1937, Cert. of Honour in Final Bar Examinations. Called to the Bar, Gray's Inn, London, 1939; Lord Justice Holker Scholar, Gray's Inn, 1940; practised law in Liverpool for some years. Served War of 1939-45, Royal Air Force (radar). Returned to Nassau, 1948, and was called to local Bar; Attorney-at-Law and Actg Attorney-Gen. of the Bahamas, 1949; Registrar-Gen., 1949-50. Past Stipendiary and Circuit Magistrate. Chm., Labour Board, Bahamas, 1953-63; MLC (Upper House of Legislature), 1960-63; President, Senate, 1964; re-elected, 1967, 1968, and continued to hold that office until 1972. Has always been an active lay preacher. Chm., Fund-raising Cttee of Persis Rodgers Home for the Aged, Bahamas. *Recreations:* music, motion photography, swimming. *Address:* PO Box N862, Nassau, Bahamas; Supreme Court, Nassau, Bahamas. *Club:* Royal Commonwealth Society.

KNOWLES, Maurice Baxendale, CBE 1952; late Government Actuary's Department; *b* 6 Nov. 1893; *m* 1919, Lilla Shepherdson (decd); one *s* one *d*. *Educ:* Bridlington Sch. Served European War, 1914-18, in 3 London Regt and RFC. *Address:* 164 Foxley Lane, Purley, Surrey.

KNOWLES, Wyn; Editor, Woman's Hour, BBC, since 1971; *b* 30 July 1923; *d* of Frederick Knowles and Dorothy Ellen Knowles (*née* Harrison). *Educ:* St Teresa's Convent, Effingham; Convents of FCJ in Ware and Switzerland; Polytechnic Sch. of Art, London. Cypher Clerk, War Office, 1944-45. Secretarial work, 1948-57; joined BBC, 1951; Asst Producer, Drama Dept, 1957-60; Woman's Hour: Producer, Talks Dept, 1960-65; Asst Editor, 1965-67; Dep. Editor, 1967-71. *Recreations:* travel, cooking, writing, painting, enthusiastic bursts of jewellery designing, patchwork, walking, riding, swimming, sun-soaking. *Address:* 80A Parkway, Regent's Park, NW1 7AN. *T:* 01-485 8258.

KNOX, family name of **Earl of Ranfurly.**

KNOX, Bryce Harry; Commissioner (and Secretary), HM Customs and Excise, since 1975; *b* 21 Feb. 1929; *e s* of Brice Henry Knox and Rose Hetty Knox; *m* 1957, Norma, *d* of late George Thomas and of Rose Thomas; one *s*. *Educ:* Stratford Grammar Sch.; Nottingham Univ. BA(Econ). Asst Principal, HM Customs and Excise, 1953; Principal, 1958; on loan to HM Treasury, 1963-65; Asst Sec., HM Customs and Excise, 1966; seconded to HM Diplomatic Service, Counsellor, Office of UK Perm. Rep. to European Communities, 1972-74; Under-Sec., HM Customs and Excise, 1974. *Address:* 9 Manor Way, Blackheath, SE3 9EF. *T:* 01-852 9404. *Club:* Reform.

KNOX, Col Bryce Muir, MC 1944 and Bar, 1944; TD 1947; Lord-Lieutenant of Ayr and Arran (formerly County of Ayr), since 1974 (Vice-Lieutenant, 1970-74); Director, Lindustries Ltd; *b* 4 April 1916; *s* of late James Knox, Kilbirnie; *m* 1948, Patricia Mary Dunsmuir; one *s* one *d*. *Educ:* Stowe; Trinity Coll., Cambridge. Served with Ayrshire (ECO) Yeomanry, 1939-45, N Africa and Italy; CO, 1953-56; Hon. Col, 1969-71; Hon. Col, The Ayrshire Yeomanry Sqdn, Queen's Own Yeomanry, T&AVR, 1971-77. Member, Queen's Body Guard for Scotland, Royal Company of Archers. CStJ. *Recreation:* foxhunting. *Address:* Martnaham Lodge, By Ayr KA6 6ES. *T:* Dalrymple 204. *Club:* Cavalry and Guards.

KNOX, David Laidlaw; MP (C) Leek Division of Staffordshire since 1970; *b* 30 May 1933; *s* of late J. M. Knox, Lockerbie and Mrs C. H. C. Knox (*née* Laidlaw), Greencroft, Lockerbie, Dumfriesshire. *Educ:* Lockerbie Academy; Dumfries Academy; London Univ. (BSc (Econ) Hons). Management Trainee, 1953-56; Printing Executive, 1956-62; O&M Consultant, 1962-70. Contested (C): Stechford, Birmingham, 1964 and 1966; Nuneaton, March 1967. PPS to Ian Gilmour, Minister of State for Defence, 1973, Sec. of State for Defence, 1974. Secretary: Cons. Finance Cttee, 1972-73; Cons. Trade Cttee, 1974; Cons. Employment Cttee, 1976-77. Chairman: W Midlands Area Young Conservatives, 1963-64; W Midlands Area Cons. Political Centre, 1966-69; a Vice-Chm., Cons. Party Organisation, 1974-75. Editor, Young Conservatives National Policy Group, 1963-64. *Recreations:* watching association football, reading. *Address:* House of Commons, SW1.

KNOX, Prof. Henry Macdonald; Professor of Education, The Queen's University of Belfast, since 1951; *b* 26 Nov. 1916; *e s* of Rev. R. M. Knox, Edinburgh, and J. E. Church; *m* 1945, Marian, *yr d* of N. Starkie, Todmorden; one *s* one *d*. *Educ:* George Watson's Coll., Edinburgh; University of Edinburgh. MA 1938; MEd 1940; PhD 1949. Served as Captain, Intelligence Corps, commanding a wireless intelligence section, Arakan sector of Burma, and as instructor, War Office special wireless training wing, 1940-46. Lecturer in Education, University Coll. of Hull, 1946; Lecturer in Education, University of St Andrews, 1949; Dean of Faculty of Education, QUB. Sometime Examiner in Educn, Universities of Leeds, Sheffield, Aberdeen, Glasgow, Wales and Ireland (National); occasional Examiner, Universities of Edinburgh, Dublin and Bristol. Member: N Ireland Council for Educl Research; Governing Body, Stranmillis and St Joseph's Colls of Educn, Belfast; Adv. Cttee on Supply and Training of Teachers for NI. Formerly Member: Advisory Council on Educn for N Ireland; Senior Certificate Examination Cttee for N Ireland; Adv. Bd for Postgraduate Studentships in Arts Subjects, Ministry of Educn for N Ireland. *Publications:* Two Hundred and Fifty Years of Scottish Education, 1696-1946, 1953; John Dury's Reformed School, 1958; Introduction to Educational Method, 1961; Schools in Europe (ed W. Schultze): Northern Ireland, 1969; numerous articles in educational journals. *Address:* 69 Maryville Park, Belfast BT9 6LQ. *T:* 665588.

KNOX, Henry Murray Owen, OBE 1944; Senior Partner, Oxley, Knox & Co., Stock-jobbers, retired, 1965; *b* 5 March 1909; *yr s* of late Brig.-Gen. and Mrs H. O. Knox; *m* 1932, Violet Isabel (*d* 1962), *yr d* of late Mr and Mrs Frank Weare, The Dell, Tunbridge Wells, Kent; two *s*; *m* 1963, Mrs E. M. Davidson. *Educ:* Charterhouse; Trinity Coll., Oxford (MA Hons Law). Joined Oxley, Knox & Co., 1930; Partner, 1931. Served War of 1939-45, Queen's Own Royal West Kent Regt (despatches, wounded, OBE); various appts. Staff, ending in Col "A" Organisation, HQ 21 Army Group. Master, Skinners' Company, 1951-52 and 1972-73. Stock Exchange Council, 1948-64; Dep. Chm., Stock Exchange, 1958-64. Governor: Tonbridge Sch.; Charterhouse Sch.; Sutton's Hosp. in Charterhouse. *Recreations:* golf, gardening. *Address:* Brooklands, Manwood Road, Sandwich, Kent. *Club:* Boodle's.

KNOX, His Eminence Cardinal James Robert, DD, DCL; Prefect of the Sacred Congregation for the discipline of the Sacraments and of the Sacred Congregation for Divine Worship, since 1974; President, Permanent Committee for International Eucharistic Congresses, since 1973; Member of Sacred Congregation for: Evangelization of Peoples, since 1973; Oriental Churches, since 1974; Catholic Education, since 1974; Bishops, since 1974; Member: Pontifical Commission for Revision of Code of Oriental Canon Law, since 1974; Council for the Public Affairs of the Church, since 1974; Pontifical Commission for the Revision of the Code of Canon Law, since 1974; *b* 2 March 1914; *s* of John Knox and Emily (*née* Walsh). *Educ:* St Ildephonsus Coll., New Norcia, Australia; Pontifical Urban College de Propaganda Fide, Rome. Priest, 1941; Vice-Rector, Pontifical Urban College de Propaganda Fide, Rome, 1945-48; attached to Secretariat of State of HH Pope Pius XII, 1948-50; Sec. of Apostolic Internunciature in Tokyo, Japan, 1950-53; Titular Archbishop of Melitene, 1953; Apostolic Delegate to British East and West Africa, 1953-57; Apostolic Internuncio in India, 1957-67; Archbishop of Melbourne, 1967-74. Cardinal, 1973. *Publication:* De Necessitudine Deiparam Inter et Eucharistiam, 1949. *Address:* Vatican City State, Europe.

KNOX, Mrs Jean M.; *see* Swaythling, Lady.

KNOX, John; Under-Secretary, Department of Trade and Industry, retired, 1974; Head of Research Contractors Division, 1972-74; *b* 11 March 1913; *s* of William Knox and May Ferguson; *m* 1942, Mary Blackwood Johnston; one *s* one *d*. *Educ:* Lenzie Acad.; Glasgow Univ. (Kitchener's Schol.; MA). Business Management Trng, 1935-39; joined RAE, 1939; Op. Research with RAF, 1939-45; Asst Chief Scientific Adviser,

Min. of Works, 1945-50; Dep. Dir and Dir, Intelligence Div., DSIR, 1950-58; Dep. Dir (Industry), DSIR, 1958-64; Min. of Technology, later DTI: Asst Controller, 1964-65; CSO, Head of External Research and Materials Div., 1965-68; Head of Materials Div., 1968-71; Head of Res. Div., 1971-73. *Publications:* occasional articles on management of research, development and industrial innovation. *Recreation:* golf. *Address:* Traquair, 11 Haylings Grove, Leiston, Suffolk IP16 4DU. *T:* Leiston 83111.5.

KNOX, Prof. Joseph Alan Cruden; Professor of Physiology in the University of London, at Queen Elizabeth College, 1954-74, now Emeritus; *b* 23 March 1911; *s* of Dr Joseph Knox; *m* 1945, Elsa Margaret Henry; one *d. Educ:* Aberdeen Grammar Sch.; Glasgow High Sch.; Glasgow Univ. MB, ChB (Glasgow) 1935; MD (Hons) 1948; House Surgeon and Physician, Glasgow Royal Infirmary, 1935-36; Asst to Prof. of Physiology, Glasgow Univ., 1936-40; Lecturer in Physiology: Glasgow Univ., 1940-44; King's Coll., London, 1944-48; Senior Lecturer, King's Coll., 1948-54. Mem. of Physiological Soc., 1941; Mem. of British Biophysical Soc., 1960. *Publications:* papers in Jl of Physiology, British Heart Jl, etc. *Recreations:* reading, gramophone, railways. *Address:* 129 Northumberland Road, North Harrow, Harrow, Middlesex HA2 7RB. *T:* 01-866 6778.

KNOX, Sir Malcolm; *see* Knox, Sir T. M.

KNOX, Robert, MA, MD, FRCP, FRCPath; Emeritus Professor of Bacteriology, University of London (Professor of Bacteriology, Guy's Hospital Medical School, 1949-69); *b* 1904; *s* of Dr Robert Knox, radiologist; *m* 1936, Bessie Lynda Crust; three *d. Educ:* Highgate; Balliol Coll., Oxford (Classical Scholar); St Bartholomew's Hosp. 1st Class Hon. Mods, 1924, 2nd Class Lit Hum, 1926; BA Oxford, 1927; MB, BS London, 1932; MD 1934; MRCS 1932; LRCP 1932, MRCP 1934, FRCP 1953; FCPath, 1964. House Physician and Chief Asst St Bartholomew's Hosp., 1932-35; MA Cambridge 1935; Demonstrator in Pathology, University of Cambridge, 1935-37; Mem. of Scientific Staff, Imperial Cancer Research Fund, 1937-39; Dir of Public Health Laboratories (Med. Research Council) at Stamford, 1939, Leicester 1940, and Oxford, 1945; MA Oxford, 1945. Fellow Royal Society Medicine; Member: Pathological Soc.; Soc. of Gen. Microbiology; Assoc. of Clinical Pathologists. *Publications:* on bacteriological subjects in medical and scientific journals. *Recreation:* coxed Oxford Univ., 1925. *Address:* Oakhurst, Warren Drive, Kingswood, Surrey. *Club:* Athenæum.

KNOX, Sir (Thomas) Malcolm, Kt 1961; Principal, University of St Andrews, 1953-66; Hon. Fellow, Pembroke College, Oxford, 1950; Hon. LLD Edinburgh, Pennsylvania and Dundee; Hon. DLitt Glasgow; *b* Birkenhead, Cheshire, 28 Nov. 1900; *e s* of James Knox, MA, and Isabella Russell Marshall, Tillicoultry, Clackmannan; *m* 1st, Margaret Normana McLeod Smith (*d* 1930), Tarbert, Harris; 2nd, Dorothy Ellen Jolly (*d* 1974), Thornton-le-Fylde, Lancs; 3rd, Joan Mary Winifred Sumner, MA, Marlow. *Educ:* Mostyn House, Parkgate, Cheshire; Bury Grammar Sch.; Liverpool Institute; Pembroke Coll., Oxford. Entered business of Lever Brothers Ltd as Sec. to 1st Lord Leverhulme, 1923; various executive and secretarial positions in firms managing Lever Brothers' West African interests, 1925-31; Lecturer in Philosophy, Jesus Coll., Oxford, 1931-33; Fellow and Tutor, 1933-36; Lecturer in Greek Philosophy, Queen's Coll., Oxford, 1934-36; Prof. of Moral Philosophy, University of St Andrews, 1936-53, Dep. Principal, 1951-52. Acting Principal, 1952-53. Gifford Lecturer, University of Aberdeen, 1965-66 and 1967-68. Chm. Govs of Morrison's Acad., Crieff, 1946-62; Chm. Advisory Council on Education in Scotland, 1957-61; Mem. Catering Wages Commission, 1943-46; Mem. Nat. Reference Tribunal for the Coal Industry of Great Britain, 1943-56; Mem. Review Body on Doctors' and Dentists' Remuneration, 1962-65. *Publications:* Translation, with commentary, of Hegel's Philosophy of Right, 1942, Hegel's Early Theological Writings, 1948; Hegel's Political Writings, 1964; Hegel's Aesthetics, 1975; Hegel's Natural Law, 1975; Action, 1968; A Layman's Quest, 1969; A Heretic's Religion, 1976; articles and reviews in periodicals. *Address:* 19 Victoria Terrace, Crieff, Perthshire. *T:* 2808.

KNOX-JOHNSTON, Robin, (William Robert Patrick Knox-Johnston), CBE 1969; Marina Consultant since 1974; Managing Director, St Katharines Yacht Haven Ltd, since 1975; *b* 17 March 1939; *s* of late David Robert Knox-Johnston and Elizabeth Mary Knox-Johnston (*née* Cree); *m* 1962, Suzanne (*née* Singer); one *d. Educ:* Berkhamsted School. Master Mariner, FRGS, ARINA. Merchant Navy, 1957-67. First person to sail single-handed non-stop Around the World 14 June 1968 to 22 April 1969, in yacht Suhaili; won Sunday Times

Golden Globe, 1969; won Round Britain Race, Ocean Spirit, 1970; won round Britain Race, British Oxygen, 1974. Chm., Troon Marina Ltd, 1976; Director: Mercury Yacht Harbours Ltd, 1970-73; Rank Marine International, 1973-75; Hoo Marina Ltd, 1974-; Hogg Robinson Knox-Johnston (Yacht Brokers), 1976-. Pres., British Olympic Yachting Appeal, 1977-; Mem. Exec. Cttee, RNLI, 1973-. Freeman, Borough of Bromley, Kent, 1969; Younger Brother, Trinity House, 1973. Lt-Comdr RNR 1971. *Publications:* A World of my Own, 1969; Sailing, 1975. *Recreation:* sailing. *Address:* Cherry Trees, School Lane, Hamble, Hants. *T:* Hamble 3366. *Clubs:* Savage, Naval, Royal Ocean Racing.

KNOX-MAWER, Ronald; a Metropolitan Stipendary Magistrate, since 1975; *b* 3 Aug. 1925; *s* of George Robert Knox-Mawer and Clare Roberts; *m* 1951, June Ellis; one *s* one *d. Educ:* Grove Park Sch.; Emmanuel Coll., Cambridge (MA). Royal Artillery, 1943-47. Called to Bar, Middle Temple; Wales and Chester Circuit, 1947-52; Chief Magistrate and Actg Chief Justice, Aden, 1952-58; Chief Magistrate, Puisne Judge and Actg Chief Justice, Fiji, and Chief Justice, Nauru and Tonga, 1958-70; Northern Circuit, 1970-75. *Publications:* ed, Aden and Fiji Law Reports 1937-1966; short stories in Punch, Cornhill, Argosy, Times, etc; various papers in legal jls. *Recreation:* countryside. *Address:* c/o Oriel Chambers, 14 Water Street, Liverpool L2 8TD. *T:* 051-236 7191. *Club:* Royal Commonwealth Society.

KNUDSEN, Semon Emil; Chairman and Chief Executive, White Motor Corporation, since 1971; *b* 2 Oct. 1912; *o s* of William S. and Clara Euler Knudsen; *m* 1938, Florence Anne McConnell; one *s* three *d. Educ:* Dartmouth Coll.; Mass Inst. of Technology. Joined General Motors, 1939; series of supervisory posts; Gen. Man., Detroit Diesel Div., 1955; Gen. Man., Pontiac Motor Div., 1956; Gen. Man., Chevrolet Motor Div., 1961; Dir of General Motors and Gp Vice-Pres. i/c of all Canadian and overseas activities, 1965; Exec. Vice-Pres. with added responsibility for domestic non-automotive divs, 1966, also defense activities, 1967; resigned from Gen. Motors Corp., 1968; Pres., Ford Motor Co., 1968-69. Director: UAL Inc.; United Airlines; Ohio Bell Telephone Co.; Cowles Communications; Michigan Bank; Michigan National Bank; Michigan National Corp.; First National Bank in Palm Beach. Vice Chm., Motor Vehicle Manufrs Assoc. Director: Nat. Multiple Sclerosis Soc.; Greater Cleveland Growth Assoc.; Mem., MIT Corp. *Recreations:* golf, tennis, deepsea fishing, hunting. *Address:* White Motor Corporation, 35129 Curtis Boulevard, Eastlake, Ohio 44094, USA. *Clubs:* Detroit, Detroit Athletic, Yondotega (Detroit); Bloomfield Hills Country (Mich); Pepper Pike (Ohio); Union (Cleveland).

KNUTSFORD, 5th Viscount *cr* 1895; **Julian Thurstan Holland-Hibbert,** CBE 1957; Bt 1853; Baron 1888; JP; *b* 3 May 1920; *o s* of 4th Viscount Knutsford, and Viola Mary (*d* 1964), *d* of Thomas Meadows Clutterbuck; *S* father, 1935. *Educ:* Eton; Trinity Coll., Cambridge. Served War of 1939-45, Coldstream Guards. Mem. National Advisory Council on Employment of the Disabled. JP Herts, 1953. OStJ. *Heir:* cousin Michael Holland-Hibbert [*b* 27 Dec. 1926; *m* 1951, Hon. Sheila Constance, *er d* of 5th Viscount Portman; two *s* one *d*]. *Address:* Munden, Watford, Herts. *T:* Garston 72002.

KNUTTON, Maj.-Gen. Harry, CB 1975; MSc, CEng, FIEE, MBIM; Director-General, City and Guilds of London Institute, since 1976; *b* Rawmarsh, Yorks, 26 April 1921; *m* 1958, Pamela Brackley, E Sheen, London; three *s* one *d. Educ:* Wath-upon-Dearne Grammar Sch.; RMCS. Commnd RA, 1943; served with 15th Scottish and 1st Airborne Divs, NW Europe, 1944-45; India, 1945-47; Instructor in Gunnery, 1946-49; Project Officer, Min. of Supply, 1949-51; served Middle East, 1953-55; Directing Staff, RMCS, 1955-58; jssc 1958; various staff appts, MoD, 1958-60, 1962-64, 1966-67; Comdr Missile Regt, BAOR, 1964-66; Comdr Air Defence Bde, 1967-69; Fellow, Loughborough Univ. of Technology, 1969-70; Dir-Gen. Weapons (Army), 1970-73; Dir, Royal Ordnance Factories and Dep. Master-Gen. of Ordnance, 1973-75; retd. Col Comdt, RA, 1977-. Teacher, Whitgift Foundn, 1975-76. Member: Associated Examining Bd, 1976; Nat. Adv. Council on Education for Industry and Commerce. Governor, Imperial Coll. of Science and Technology, 1976-. *Recreations:* golf, sailing. *Address:* 43 Essendene Road, Caterham, Surrey. *T:* Caterham 47278. *Club:* Army and Navy.

KODICEK, Egon Hynek, CBE 1974; MD Prague, PhD Cantab; FRS 1973; FIBiol; Director of Dunn Nutritional Laboratory, Medical Research Council and University of Cambridge, 1963-73; Fellow, Wolfson College, Cambridge, 1973-75, Emeritus Fellow, 1977; *b* 3 Aug. 1908; *s* of Emma and Samuel Kodicek, MD; *m* 1936, Jindriska E. M. Hradecká, MD, DOMS; two *d.*

Educ: Charles Univ., Medical Sch., Prague; Trinity Coll., Cambridge. MD Prague, 1932; Diploma of Specialist for Internal Diseases and Metabolic Disorders, Prague, 1938; PhD Cantab., 1942. Charles Univ., Prague: clinical and experimental research work in Endocrinology, and Nutrition, 1932-39; Demonstrator, Dept of Internal Medicine, 1932-34; Asst-Physician, 1934-38; Physician-in-Charge, Endocrinological Outpatient Unit, Dept of Internal Medicine, 1938-39. Scholar of Soc. for Protection of Science and Learning, 1939; Mem. Scientific Staff, MRC, 1947-73; Hon. Consultant in Nutrition, United Cambridge Hosps, 1972-. Vis. Lectr, Harvard, Yale, Columbia and University of California, 1952, 1958; Lectr, under Nicolaysen Scheme, University of Oslo, 1964; Sandoz Foundn Lectr in Endocrinology, British Postgrad. Med. Fedn, 1973; Thomas Young Lectr, St George's Hosp., London, 1973. Member: Cttee of Biochemical Soc., 1961-65; Council of Nutrition Soc., 1964-67, 1968-71 (Pres., 1971-74; Hon. Mem., 1974-); Nat. Cttee for Nutritional Sciences, Royal Society, 1967-75; Nat. Cttee for Biochemistry, Royal Society, 1970-75; Chm., Commn V, Internat. Union of Nutritional Sciences, 1973-76. Hon. Mem., Czechoslovakia Med. Soc. of J. E. Purkyné, 1968-; Hon. Mem., Amer. Inst. of Nutrition, 1969-. Gottlieb Duttweiler Prize, 1972; Prix André Lichtwitz, 1972; Brit. Nutrition Foundn Prize, 1973; Sabato Visco Prize, 1973; (with Prof. H. De Luca) Prix Roussel, Paris, 1974; CIBA Medal and Prize, Biochem. Soc., 1974. *Publications:* scientific papers in Biochemical Jl, Jl of General Microbiology, and other British and foreign scientific jls. *Address:* Strangeways Laboratory, Wort's Causeway, Cambridge. *T:* Cambridge 43231. 11 Bulstrode Gardens, Cambridge. *T:* Cambridge 57321.

KOECHLIN, Patricia Rosemary, OBE 1956; Member of British Show Jumping Team, 1947-64; *b* 22 Nov. 1928; *d* of late Capt. Eric Hamilton Smythe, MC, Légion d'Honneur, and late Frances Monica Smythe (*née* Curtoys); *m* 1963, Samuel Koechlin, Switzerland; two *d. Educ:* St Michael's Sch., Cirencester; Talbot Heath, Bournemouth. Show Jumping: first went abroad with British Team, 1947; Leading Show Jumper of the Year, 1949, 1958 (with T. Edgar), and 1962; European Ladies' Championship: Spa, 1957; Deauville, 1961; Madrid, 1962; Hickstead, 1963; Harringay: BSJA Spurs, 1949, 1951, 1952, 1954 (Victor Ludorum Championship), 1953 and 1954; Harringay Spurs, 1953; Grand Prix, Brussels, 1949, 1952 and 1956. Ladies' record for high jump (2 m. 10 cm.) Paris, 1950; won in Madrid, 1951. White City: 1951 (Country Life Cup); 1953 (Selby Cup). Was Leading Rider and won Prix du Champion, Paris, 1952; Leading Rider, etc, Marseilles, 1953; Individual Championship, etc, Harrisburg, Penn, USA, 1953; Pres. of Mexico Championship, New York, 1953; Toronto (in team winning Nations Cup), 1953; Lisbon (won 2 events), Grand Prix, Madrid, and Championship, Vichy, 1954; Grand Prix de Paris and 3 other events, 1954; Bruxelles Puissance and new ladies' record for high jump (2m. 20 cm.), Leading Rider of Show, 1954; BHS Medal of Honour, Algiers Puissance and Grand Prix, 4 events in Paris, 4 events at White City including the Championship, 1955; Grand Prix and Leading Rider of Show and 4 other events, Brussels, 1956; Grand Prix Militaire and Puissance, Lucerne; Mem. British Equestrian Olympic Team, Stockholm (Show Jumping Bronze Medal), 1956; IHS National Championship, White City; Leading Rider and other events, Palermo, 1956; won 2 Puissance events, Paris, 1957; BSJA, 1957; Ladies' National Championship in 1954-59 and 1961 and 1962 (8 times); Daily Mail Cup, White City, 1955, 1957, 1960, 1962; Mem. winning British Team, White City: 1952, 1953, 1956, 1957; Amazon Prize, Aachen, 1958; Queen's Cup, Royal Internat. Horse Show, White City, 1958; Preis von Parsenn, Davos, 1957, 1958, 1959; Championship Cup, Brussels Internat. Horse Show, 1958; Lisbon Grand Prix, 1959; Olympic Trial, British Timken Show, and Prix de la Banque de Bruxelles at Brussels, 1959. Lucerne Grand Prix; Prince Hal Stakes, Country Life and Riding Cup, White City; Pembroke Stakes, Horse Show Cttee Cup, and Leading Rider, Dublin (all in 1960). Mem. British Olympic Team in Rome, 1960. Copenhagen Grand Prix; Amazon Prize, Aachen; John Player Trophy, White City; St Gall Ladies Championship (all in 1961); Saddle of Honour and Loriners' Cup, White City, 1962; British Jumping Derby, Hickstead, 1962. Hon. Freeman, Worshipful Co. of Farriers, 1955; Freeman of the City of London, 1956; Hon. Freeman, Worshipful Company of Loriners, 1962; Yeoman, Worshipful Company of Saddlers, 1963. *Publications:* (as Pat Smythe): Jump for Joy; Pat Smythe's Story, 1954; Pat Smythe's Book of Horses, 1955; One Jump Ahead, 1956; Jacqueline rides for a Fall, 1957; Three Jays against the Clock, 1957; Three Jays on Holiday, 1958; Three Jays go to Town, 1959; Horses and Places, 1959; Three Jays over the Border, 1960; Three Jays go to Rome, 1960; Three Jays Lend a Hand, 1961; Jumping Round the World, 1962; Florian's Farmyard, 1962; Flanagan My Friend, 1963; Bred to Jump, 1965; Show Jumping, 1967; (with

Fiona Hughes) A Pony for Pleasure, 1969; A Swiss Adventure, 1970; (with Fiona Hughes) Pony Problems, 1971; A Spanish Adventure, 1971; A Cotswold Adventure, 1972. *Recreations:* tennis, swimming, music, ski-ing, sailing, all sports, languages. *Address:* Sudgrove House, Miserden, near Stroud, Glos. *T:* Miserden 360; Im Steinacker, 4149 Burg-im-Leimental, BE, Switzerland. *T:* Basle 751411. *Club:* Lansdowne.

KOELLE, Vice-Adm. Sir Harry (Philpot), KCB 1959 (CB 1957); *b* 16 Aug. 1901; *s* of late Rev. C. Philpot Koelle, Rector of Wickford, Essex, and Durley, Hampshire; *m* 1st, 1930, Enid (*d* 1942), *d* of C. F. Corbould Ellis, JP, Reading; one *d* ; 2nd, 1948, Elizabeth Anne, *d* of late Sir Philip Devitt, 1st and last Bt; two *d. Educ:* Rossall; RN Colleges, Osborne and Dartmouth. Joined RN 1915. Served HMS Bellerophon and Renown, 1917-18. Served War of 1939-45: HMS Royal Sovereign and Duke of York; Deputy Dir of Manning, Admiralty, 1945-48. Dir of Welfare and Service Conditions, Admiralty, 1953-55; Command Supply Officer, Plymouth, 1955-57; Dir-General Supply and Secretariat Branch, Admiralty, 1957-60. Comdr 1938; Capt. 1948; Rear-Adm. 1955; retired 1960. *Recreation:* racing. *Address:* Mill House, Thornford, near Sherborne, Dorset. *Club:* Army and Navy.

KOENIGSBERGER, Prof. Franz, DSc; FIMechE; Professor of Machine Tool Engineering, University of Manchester Institute of Science and Technology, 1961-75, now Emeritus; *b* 9 Nov. 1907; *s* of Hans and Margaret Koenigsberger; *m* 1934, Lilli Gertrude Kate (*née* Schlesinger); one *s* one *d. Educ:* Goethe-Schule, Berlin; Technische Hochschule, Berlin-Charlottenburg. Research Asst for Machine Tools, Technische Hochschule, Berlin-Charlottenburg, 1931-32; Draughtsman and Designer of machine tools, 1932-35; Chief Designer and Chief Engr, Machine Tool Dept, Ansaldo SA, Genoa, 1936-38; Chief Mech. Engr, Cooke & Ferguson Ltd, Manchester, 1939-47; Lectr in Mech. Engrg, 1947-54; Sen. Lectr in Prod. Engrg, 1954-57; Reader in Machine Tools and Prod. Processes, The Manchester Coll. of Science and Technology, 1957-61. Managing Editor, Industrial and Production Engineering International (Munich); Jt Editor, Fertigung (Bern, Switzerland). President: Manchester Assoc. of Engineers, 1965-66; Internat. Inst. of Prod. Engrg Research (CIRP), 1965-66; Manchester Technology Assoc., 1971-72. Thomas Lowe Gray Prize, 1944, and Water Arbitration Prize, 1951, of Instn of Mech. Engrs; Constantine Medal, 1956, and Butterworth Medal, 1961, of Manchester Assoc. of Engineers; Inst. Prod. Engrs Medal, 1966. Medaille de Vermeil, Soc. d'Encouragement de la Récherche et l'Invention, 1972. DrIngEh Berlin, 1969; Hon. Dr Ghent, 1970; Hon. DTech Bradford, 1974; Hon. Fellow, Manchester Polytechnic, 1975. *Publications:* Design for Welding, 1948; Welding Technology, 1949 (1953, 1961); Spanende Werkzeugmaschinen, 1961; Design Principles of Metal Cutting Machine Tools, 1964; (with J. Tlusty) Machine Tool Structures, 1970; (with C. Ruiz) Design for Strength and Production, 1970; papers in Proceedings Institution Mechanical Engineers, The Production Engineer, Welding Jl, British Welding Jl. *Recreations:* music, photography. *Address:* 7 Singleton Road, Heaton Moor, Stockport SK4 4PW. *T:* 061-432 4677.

KOENIGSBERGER, Prof. Helmut Georg, MA, PhD; Professor of History, King's College London, since 1973; *b* 24 Oct. 1918; *s* of late Georg Felix Koenigsberger, chief architect, borough of Treptow, Berlin, Germany, and of late Käthe Koenigsberger (*née* Born); *m* 1961, Dorothy M. Romano; two *d* (twins). *Educ:* Adams' Grammar Sch., Newport, Shropshire; Gonville and Caius Coll., Cambridge. Asst Master: Brentwood Sch., Essex, 1941-42; Bedford Sch., 1942-44. Served War of 1939-45, Royal Navy, 1944-45. Lecturer in Economic History, QUB, 1948-51; Senior Lecturer in Economic History, University of Manchester, 1951-60; Prof. of Modern History, University of Nottingham, 1960-66; Prof. of Early Modern European History, Cornell, 1966-73. Visiting Lecturer: Brooklyn Coll., New York, 1957; University of Wisconsin, 1958; Columbia University, 1962; Cambridge Univ., 1963; Washington Univ., St Louis, 1964. Sec., 1955-75, Vice-Pres., 1975-, Internat. Commn for the History of Representative and Parliamentary Institutions. *Publications:* The Government of Sicily under Philip II of Spain, 1951, new edn, as The Practice of Empire, 1969; The Empire of Charles V in Europe (in New Cambridge Modern History II), 1958; Western Europe and the Power of Spain (in New Cambridge Modern History III), 1968; Europe in the Sixteenth Century (with G. L. Mosse), 1968; Estates and Revolutions, 1971; The Habsburgs and Europe, 1516-1660, 1971; (ed) Luther: a profile, 1972; contrib. to historical journals. *Recreations:* playing chamber music, sailing, travel. *Address:* King's College London, Strand, WC2.

KOEPPLER, Sir Henry, (Sir Heinz), Kt 1977; CBE 1967 (OBE 1957); FRHistS; Warden of Wilton Park, 1946-77, and Warden, European Discussion Centre, 1972-77; Assistant Under Secretary of State, Foreign and Commonwealth Office, 1975-77; Provost of the Institute for the Study of Interaction between Foreign and Domestic Policies, and Distinguished Visiting Professor, Baylor University, Waco, Texas, from Aug. 1978; *b* 30 June 1912; *o s* of late Friedrich and Gertrude Koeppler. *Educ:* Univs of Berlin, Heidelberg, Kiel (Christian Albrecht Haus), Magdalen Coll., Oxford. MA, DPhil(Oxon). Sen. Demy, Magdalen Coll., 1937-39; Lectr, Bd of Faculty of Modern History, Oxford, 1937-39. Political Intelligence Dept, FO, 1940-42; Asst Regional Dir, Political Warfare Exec., 1943-45. Visiting Prof. Univ. of Heidelberg, 1960-61; Consultant, Ford Foundation, 1961; Visiting Distinguished Prof., Ohio State Univ., 1966; Vis. Prof. of West-European Studies and Government, Indiana Univ., Bloomington, USA, 1970. President's Medallion for service to internat. educn, Wisconsin Univ., 1974; first Joseph Bech Meml Gold Medal, 1977. *Publications:* A Lasting Peace (with M. Garnett), 1940; articles in: Jl of Theological Studies, English Historical Review, The Round Table; *relevant publication:* A Unique Contribution to International Relations: the story of Wilton Park, by D. M. Keezer, 1973. *Recreation:* diminishing jargon. *Address:* 111 Ashley Gardens, SW1P 1HJ. *T:* 01-828 2828. *Clubs:* Athenæum; Chanctonbury Ring (Wiston); Cornwallis Post (San Francisco).

KOESTLER, Arthur, CBE 1972; CLit 1974; FRSL; FRAS; author; *b* Budapest, Hungary, 5 Sept. 1905; *o s* of Henrik and Adela Koestler; *m* 1935, Dorothy Asher, Zürich; divorced 1950; no *c*; *m* 1950, Mamaine Paget; divorced 1953; no *c*; *m* 1965, Cynthia Jefferies. *Educ:* University of Vienna. Foreign Correspondent in Middle East, Paris, Berlin, 1926-31; Mem. of Graf Zeppelin Arctic Expedition, 1931; travels in Russia and Soviet Central Asia, 1932-33; covering the Spanish Civil War for News Chronicle, London, 1936-37; imprisoned by General Franco; served 1939-40 in French Foreign Legion and 1941-42 in British Pioneer Corps. Fellow, Centre for Advanced Study in the Behavioural Sciences, Stanford, 1964-65. Hon. LLD Queen's Univ., Kingston, Ont, 1968. Sonning Prize, 1968. *Publications:* Spanish Testament, 1938; The Gladiators, 1939; Darkness at Noon, 1940; Scum of the Earth, 1941; Arrival and Departure, 1943; The Yogi and the Commissar, 1945; Twilight Bar, 1945; Thieves in the Night, 1946; Insight and Outlook, 1948; The God that Failed (with others), 1949; Promise and Fulfilment, 1949; The Age of Longing, 1950; Arrow in the Blue, 1952; The Invisible Writing, 1954; The Trail of the Dinosaur, 1955; Reflections on Hanging, 1956; The Sleepwalkers, 1959; The Lotus and the Robot, 1960; Suicide of a Nation? (ed), 1963; The Act of Creation, 1964; The Ghost in the Machine, 1967; Drinkers of Infinity, 1968; The Case of the Midwife Toad, 1971; The Roots of Coincidence, 1972; The Call-Girls, 1972; (with others) The Challenge of Chance, 1973; The Heel of Achilles, Essays 1968-1973, 1974; The Thirteenth Tribe, 1976; (with others) Life After Death, 1976; (ed with J. R. Smythies) Beyond Reductionism—New Perspectives in the Life Sciences: The Alpbach Symposium 1968, 1969; contribs: Encyclopaedia of Philosophy, 1967; Encyclopaedia Britannica, 1974; *relevant publications:* Arthur Koestler, by John Atkins, 1956; Arthur Koestler, Das Literarische Werk, by Peter Alfred Huber, Zürich, 1962; Arthur Koestler, Cahiers de l'Herne, 1975; Astride the Two Cultures: Arthur Koestler at Seventy, ed Harold Harris, 1975. *Recreations:* canoeing, chess, good wine. *Address:* c/o A. D. Peters, 10 Buckingham Street, WC2.

KOGAN, Prof. Maurice; Professor of Government and Social Administration, Brunel University, since 1969; *b* 10 April 1930; *s* of Barnett and Hetty Kogan; *m* 1960, Ulla Svensson; two *s*. *Educ:* Stratford Grammar Sch.; Christ's Coll., Cambridge (MA). Entered Civil Service, admin. cl. (1st in open examinations), 1953. Sec., Secondary Sch. Exams Council, 1961; Sec., Central Advisory Council for Educn (England), 1963-66; Harkness Fellow of Commonwealth Fund, 1960-61. Asst Sec., DES, 1966. Member: Educn Sub-Cttee, Univ. Grants Cttee, 1972-75; SSRC, 1975; Davies Cttee on Hosp. Complaints' Procedure, 1971; Houghton Cttee on Teachers' Pay, 1974; Head of School, Sch. of Social Sciences, Brunel Univ., 1971-74. George A. Miller Vis. Prof., Univ. of Illinois, 1976. *Publications:* The Organisation of a Social Services Department, 1971; Working Relationships within the British Hospital Service, 1971; The Government of Education, 1971; The Politics of Education, 1971; (ed) The Challenge of Change, 1973; County Hall, 1973; Advisory Councils and Committees in Education, 1974; Educational Policy-Making, 1975; contribs to New Society, TES, THES, Jl of Social Policy. *Recreations:* reading, listening to music. *Address:* 48 Duncan Terrace, Islington, N1 8AL. *T:* 01-226 0038.

KOHL, Helmut; Chairman, Christian Democratic Union of Western Germany, since 1973; Leader of the Opposition, Bundestag, since 1976; *b* 3 April 1930; *s* of Hans and Cecilie Kohl; *m* 1960, Hannelore Renner; two *s*. *Educ:* Frankfurt Univ.; Heidelberg Univ. (dr. phil 1958 Heidelberg). Adv. Mem., Management Group for chemical industries, Rheinland-Pfalz, 1959; Dir, ZDF, 1970-. President: Rheinland-Pfalz CDU, 1965; Parly CDU of Landtag, Rheinland-Pfalz, 1959; Mem., Central Cttee, 1964, Vice-Chm., 1970-73, CDU of W Germany; Minister-Pres. for Rheinland-Pfalz, 1969-76; Mem. Bundesrat, 1969-76. *Publications:* Hausputz hinter den Fassaden, 1971; Zwischen Ideologie und Pragmatismus, 1973. *Address:* 6700 Ludwigshafen/Rhein, Marbacher Strasse 11, W Germany. *T:* 680019.

KOHLER, Foy David; Professor, Center for Advanced International Studies, University of Miami, since 1967; *b* 15 Feb. 1908; *s* of Leander David Kohler and Myrtle McClure; *m* 1935, Phyllis Penn. *Educ:* Toledo and Ohio State Univs, Ohio. US Foreign Service: posts include (1932-): Amer. Emb., London, 1944; Adviser to US Mem., 2nd Session of Council of UN Relief and Rehabilitation Admin., Montreal, Can., Sept. 1944; 1st Sec. Amer. Emb., Moscow, 1947; Counselor, 1948; Minister, Oct. 1948; Chief, Internat. Broadcasting Div., Dept of State, 1949; VOA 1949; Asst Administr, Internat. Information Admin, 1952; Policy Planning Staff, Dept of State, 1952; Counselor, Amer. Emb., Ankara, Turkey, 1953-56; detailed ICA, 1956-58; Deputy Asst Sec. of State for European Affairs, 1958-59; Asst Sec. of State, 1959-62; US Ambassador to USSR, 1962-66; Deputy Under-Sec. of State for Political Affairs, United States, 1966-67; Career Ambassador, USA, 1966-67 (Career Minister, Foreign Service of USA, 1959). Holds honorary doctorates. *Publication:* Understanding the Russians: a citizen's primer, 1970. *Recreations:* golf, swimming. *Address:* 215 Golf Club Circle, Village of Tequesta, Jupiter, Fla 33458, USA.

KOHLER, Irene; pianist; Professor, Trinity College of Music, London; *b* London; *m* 1950, Dr Harry Waters, medical practitioner. *Educ:* Royal College of Music. Studied with Arthur Benjamin (Challen Medal, Danreuther Prize, etc); travelling scholarship to Vienna; studied there with Edward Steuermann and Egon Wellesz. BMus; Hon. FTCL, GRSM, LRAM, ARCM. First professional engagement, Bournemouth, 1933, resulting in engagement by BBC; played at first night of 40th Promenade Season, 1934. First foreign tour (recitals and broadcasts), Holland, 1938. During War of 1939-45 gave concerts for the Forces in this country and toured France and Belgium, also India and Burma, under auspices of ENSA; subsequently played in many countries of Europe and made tours. Eugene Goossens selected her for first European performance of his Phantasy Concerto; broadcast 1st performance of Sonata by Gunilla Lowenstein, Stockholm. She gave 3 concerts at the Festival Hall in Festival of Britain Year, 1951. Canadian American Tour, 1953; World Tour, 1955-56; African Tour, 1958; 2nd African Tour, 1959; Bulgarian Tour, 1959; 2nd World Tour, 1962; Czechoslovakian Tour, 1963; Scandinavian Tour, 1970; Far and Middle East Tour, 1972. Film appearances include: Train of Events, Odette, Secret People, Lease of Life, and a documentary for the Ministry of Information. *Address:* 28 Castelnau, SW13. *T:* 01-748 5512.

KOHNSTAMM, Max, Comdr Order of Orange Nassau; Principal, European University Institute of Florence, since 1975; *b* 22 May 1914; *s* of Dr Philip Abraham Kohnstamm and Johanna Hermana Kessler; *m* 1944, Kathleen Sillem; two *s* three *d*. *Educ:* Univ. of Amsterdam (Hist. Drs); American Univ., Washington. Private Sec. to Queen Wilhelmina, 1945-48; subseq. Head of German Bureau, then Dir of European Affairs, Netherlands FO; Sec. of High Authority, 1952-56; 1st Rep. of High Authority, London, 1956; Sec.-Gen. (later Vice-Pres.), Action Cttee for United States of Europe, 1956-75; Pres., European Community Inst. for Univ. Studies, 1958-75. Co-Chm., Cttee on Soc. Develt and Peace, World Council of Churches and Pontifical Commn for Justice and Peace, 1967-75; European Pres., Trilateral Commn, 1973-75. *Publications:* The European Community and its Role in the World, 1963; (ed jtly) A Nation Writ Large?, 1972. *Recreations:* tennis, walking. *Address:* Badia Fiesolana, San Domenico di Fiesole, Florence, Italy. *T:* (55) 477931.

KOHOBAN-WICKREME, Alfred Silva, CVO 1954; Member Ceylon Civil Service; Secretary to the Cabinet, 1968-70; *b* 2 Nov. 1914; *m* 1941, Mona Estelle Kohoban-Wickreme. *Educ:* Trinity Coll., Kandy; University Coll., Colombo. BA (Hons) London, 1935. Cadet, Ceylon Civil Service, 1938; served as Magistrate, District Judge, Asst Govt Agent etc, until 1948; Chief Admin. Officer, Ceylon Govt Rly, 1948; Asst Sec., Min. of Home Affairs, 1951; attached to Ceylon High Commissioner's Office in

UK, May-July, 1953; Dir of Social Services and Commissioner for Workmen's Compensation, Ceylon, 1953; Conservator of Forests, Ceylon, 1958; Port Commissioner, Ceylon, 1959; Postmaster General and Dir of Telecommunications, Dec. 1961; Permanent Sec., Ministry of: Local Govt and Home Affairs, April 1964; Cultural Affairs and Social Services, June 1964; Ministry of Communications, 1965. Organised the Queen's Tour in Ceylon, April 1954 (CVO). *Recreations:* sports activities, particularly Rugby football, tennis and cricket. *Address:* 6 Kalinga Place, Jawatta Road, Colombo 5, Sri Lanka. *T:* (residence) 86385.

KOHT, Paul; Ambassador of Norway to Denmark, since 1975; *b* 7 Dec. 1913; *s* of Dr Halvdan Koht and Karen Elisabeth (*née* Grude); *m* 1938, Grete Sverdrup; two *s* one *d*. *Educ:* University of Oslo. Law degree, 1937. Entered Norwegian Foreign Service, 1938; held posts in: Bucharest, 1938-39; London, 1940-41; Tokyo, 1941-42; New York, 1942-46; Lisbon, 1950-51; Mem. Norwegian Delegn to OEEC and NATO, Paris, and Perm. Rep. to Coun. of Europe, 1951-53; Dir General of Dept for Econ. Affairs, Min. of For. Affairs, Oslo, 1953-56; Chargé d'Affaires, Copenhagen, 1956-58; Ambassador to USA, 1958-63; Ambassador to Fed. Republic of Germany, 1963-68; Ambassador to the Court of St James's, 1968-75. Comdr, Order of St Olav; Comdr 1st Class, Order of Dannebrog; Grand Cross, Order of Merit (Federal Republic of Germany). *Address:* Royal Norwegian Embassy, Trondhjems Plads 4, 2100 København K, Denmark.

KOKOSCHKA, Oskar, CBE 1959; artist and writer; *b* Pöchlarn, Austria, 1 March 1886; *m* Olda (*née* Palkovsky); British subject since 1947. *Educ:* Vienna Sch. of Industrial Art. Worked in Vienna from 1905; in Berlin, 1910, joined group of expressionist painters; first one-man exhibn, Paul Cassirer's Gall., 1910; contrib. to Der Sturm. Served as Cavalry Officer, Russian and Italian fronts, 1915-17 (wounded). Prof. Acad. of Art, Dresden, 1919-24; travelled throughout Europe, North Africa and Near East, painting landscapes and panoramic views of cities, 1924-31; returned to Vienna, 1931; to Prague, 1934, became a Czech citizen; works included in Nazi exhibn of "Degenerate Art", Munich, 1937; to England, 1938; Founder, Internat. Summer Acad. of Fine Arts, Salzburg, and has taught there since 1953. Has held one-man exhibns in Austria, Germany, Italy, Holland, France, Switzerland, USA, etc; in Great Britain: Tate Gallery, 1962; Marlborough Fine Art Galleries, 1967, 1969, 1976. Order of Merit of Federal Republic of Germany, 1956. Winner of the Rome Prize, 1960; Erasmus Prize (jt), 1960; Hon. Academician, Royal Academy, 1970; Hon. DLitt Oxon, 1963. Freedom of Vienna, Salzburg and Pöchlarn. *Works include:* portraits, landscapes, illustrations, compositions (politically symbolic works, etc). *Publications:* A Sea ringed with Visions (short stories), 1962; Mein Leben (autobiography), 1971 (My Life, 1974); London Views, British Landscapes, 1972; Saul and David (lithographs), 1973; *plays:* Mörder, Hoffnung der Frauen, 1907; Der brennende Dornbusch, Hiob, 1911; Orpheus and Eurydice, 1916, etc; *relevant publications:* Kokoschka: The Work of the Painter, by H. M. Wingler, 1958; Oskar Kokoschka: The Artist and his Time, by J. P. Hodin, 1966. *Address:* 1844 Villeneuve, Vaud, Switzerland.

KOLBUSZEWSKI, Prof. Janusz, DSc (Eng), PhD, DIC, Dipl.Ing; FICE; FCIT; Professor of Transportation and Environmental Planning and Head of Department, University of Birmingham, since 1965 (Professor of Highway and Traffic Engineering, 1959-64, of Transportation, 1964-65); *b* 18 Feb. 1915; *s* of Jan Alexander and Bronislawa Kolbuszewski; *m* 1946, Marie-Louise Jasinska; one *s* one *d*. *Educ:* Technical University of Lwow, Poland (Dipl.Ing); Imperial Coll. of Science and Technology, University of London. PhDEng, London, 1948; DIC 1948; DSc(Eng), London, 1968. Lecturer, Technical Univ. of Lwow, Poland, until 1939. Served War of 1939-45: Polish, French and British Armies. Imperial Coll. Science and Technology, London, 1945-48; Prof., Dir of Studies, Polish University Coll., London, 1948-50; Lecturer, Sen. Lecturer, Reader, in charge of Graduate Schs in Foundation Engrg and in Highway and Traffic Engineering, University of Birmingham, 1951-59. Lectr of Honour, Inst. Traffic Sci., Japan, 1972; James Forrest Lectr, ICE, 1972. Member: Civil Engrg and Aero Cttee, SRC, 1967; Research Cttee, ICE, 1966; Transport Bd, CNAA, 1974. Governor, Birmingham Coll. of Arts. Hon. Mem., Midlands Soc. for Soil Mechanics and Foundn Engrg. Lister Prize, Midland Branch of IStructE, 1953; Nusey Prize, Soc. of Engineers, London, 1967; Certificate of Merit, Inst. of Highway Engineers, 1977. *Publications:* various scientific papers on Geometry, Perspective, Soil Mechanics, Foundations and Highway Engineering, Transportation and Planning. *Recreations:* travelling, oil painting. *Address:* Passy, Star Lane, All Stretton, Salop. *T:* Church Stretton 3149.

KOLHAPUR, Maharaja of; Maj.-Gen. HH Sir Shahaji Chhatrapati, (adopted these names in lieu of those of Vikramsinha Rao Puar, on succeeding); GCSI, 1947 (KCSI, 1941); *b* 4 April 1910. Formerly Maharaja of Dewas (Senior Branch); succeeded as Maharaja of Kolhapur, 1947; State merged with Bombay, 1949. Appointed Major and Hon. ADC to HM King Emperor George VI, 1946; Hon. Maj.-Gen. Indian Army, 1962. *Address:* Kolhapur, Maharashtra, India.

KOLLER, Prof. Pius Charles, PhD, DSc; Professor Emeritus, University of London, since 1969 (Professor of Cytogenetics, Institute of Cancer Research, University of London, 1944-69, retired); *b* 3 April 1904; *m* 1946, Anna Edith Olsen, Denmark; three *d*. *Educ:* Universities of Budapest, Cambridge and Edinburgh. PhD Budapest, 1926; DSc Edinburgh, 1934. Rockefeller Fellow, Pasadena, Calif, 1936-37; Lecturer, University of Edinburgh, 1938-44; Research Cytologist, Royal Cancer Hospital, 1944-46, and Chester Beatty Research Inst., 1946-54. Vis. Prof., Harvard Med. Sch., 1970. Consultant, Internat. Atomic Energy Agency, Bandung, Indonesia, 1973. *Publications:* Chromosomes and Genes, 1968; Chromosome Breakage: a chapter in Progress in Biophysics, 1969; The Role of Chromosomes in Cancer Biology, 1972; numerous scientific papers in Jl of Genetics, Heredity, Brit. Jl of Cancer etc, 1936-68. *Recreations:* philosophy, gardening, reading. *Address:* Brushwood, 37 Gaviots Way, Gerrard's Cross, Bucks. *T:* Gerrard's Cross 82057.

KOLO, Sule; Managing Director, Alheri Enterprises; Director of numerous companies; Consultant, Knight Frank & Rutley (Nigeria); High Commissioner for Nigeria in London, 1970-75; *b* 1926; *m* 1957, Helen Patricia Kolo; one *s* three *d*. BSc (Econ); attended Imperial Defence College. Counsellor, Nigerian High Commn in London, 1962; Perm. Sec., Nigerian Min. of Defence, 1963; Perm. Sec., Nigerian Min. of Trade, 1966; Nigeria's Perm. Representative to European Office of UN and Ambassador to Switzerland, 1966; Chm. of GATT, 1969. FREconS; FRSA 1973 (RSA silver medal, 1973). Franklin Peace Medal, 1969. *Recreations:* swimming, tennis. *Address:* PO Box 917, Jos, Nigeria. *Clubs:* Travellers'; Island (Lagos).

KOLTAI, Ralph; freelance stage designer; designer for Drama, Opera and Dance, since 1950; resigned as Head of School of Theatre Design, Central School of Art and Design (1965-73); *b* 31 July 1924; Hungarian-German; *s* of Dr(med) Alfred Koltai and Charlotte Koltai (*née* Weinstein); *m* 1956, Annena Stubbs. *Educ:* Central Sch. of Art and Design (Dip. with Dist.). Early work entirely in field of opera. First production, Angelique, for London Opera Club, Fortune Theatre, 1950. In following years designed for virtually every opera company in Britain, *ie* The Royal Opera House, Sadler's Wells, Scottish Opera, National Welsh Opera, The English Opera Group. First of 7 ballets for Ballet Rambert, Two Brothers, 1958. Apptd Associate Designer for Royal Shakespeare Company, 1963, re-apptd, 1976; *productions:* The Caucasian Chalk Circle, 1962; The Representative, 1963; The Birthday Party; Endgame; The Jew of Malta, 1964; The Merchant of Venice; Timon of Athens, 1965; Little Murders, 1967; Major Barbara, 1970; Too True To Be Good, 1975; Old World, 1976; for National Theatre: an "all male" As You Like It, 1967; Back to Methuselah, 1969; has worked in most countries in Western Europe, also Bulgaria, Argentine, USA, Canada, Australia; *other notable productions include:* for Sadler's Wells: The Rise and Fall of the City of Mahagonny, 1963; From the House of the Dead, 1965; Bluebeard's Castle, 1972; Wagner's (complete) Ring Cycle, 1973; for The Royal Opera House: Taverner, 1972; for Sydney Opera House: Tannhauser, 1973; for Netherlands Opera: Wozzeck, 1973; Billy, Drury Lane, 1974; Fidelio, Munich, 1974; Verdi's Macbeth, Edinburgh Festival, 1976. London Drama Critics Award, Designer of the Year, 1967 (for Little Murders and As You Like It); (jtly) Gold Medal, Internat. Exhibn of Stage Design, Prague Quadriennale, 1975. *Recreation:* photography. *Address:* 30 Chapel Street, Belgrave Square, SW1. *T:* 01-235 0636.

KOMINSKI, Daniel; *see* Kaye, Danny.

KONOVALOV, Sergey, MA Oxon, BLitt Oxon; Professor of Russian in the University of Oxford, 1945-67, now Emeritus; Emeritus Fellow of New College, Oxford; *b* Moscow, 31 Oct. 1899; *s* of Alexander Konovalov, Minister of Trade and Industry in Russian Provisional Government of 1917, and of Nadejda Vtorov; *m* 1949, Janina Ryzowa. *Educ:* Classical Lycée, Moscow; Exeter Coll., Oxford (Diploma in Economics and Political Science 1921, BLitt 1927; MA 1936). Professor of Russian Language and Literature, University of Birmingham, 1929-45; Lecturer in Slavonic Studies, University of Oxford, 1930-45; Hon. Lecturer at University of London (Sch. of

Slavonic Studies), 1931-32, 1940-41. Mem. Internat. Cttee of Slavists, 1958-68. Editor, Birmingham Russian Memoranda, 1931-40; co-editor: Birmingham Polish Monographs, 1936-39; Bibliographies of Research Work in Slavonic Countries, 1932-34; editor and contributor, Blackwell's Russian Texts, and OUP's Russian Readers and Oxford Slavonic Papers, vols I-XIII, 1950-67. *Publications:* Anthology of Contemporary Russian Literature, 1932; Russian Critical Essays, (ed with D. J. Richards), 1971-72; article Soviet Union in Encyclopædia Britannica Year-Book, 1941; Russo-Polish Relations: an Historical Survey (in collaboration), 1945. *Address:* 175 Divinity Road, Oxford.

KONSTANT, Rt. Rev. David Every; Auxiliary Bishop of Westminster (Bishop in Central London) (RC), and Titular Bishop of Betagbara, since 1977; *b* 16 June 1930; *s* of Antoine Konstant and Dulcie Marion Beresford Konstant (*née* Leggatt). *Educ:* St Edmund's College, Old Hall Green, Ware; Christ's College, Cambridge (MA); Univ. of London Inst. of Education (PGCE). Priest, dio. Westminster, 1954; Cardinal Vaughan School, Kensington, 1959; Diocesan Adviser on Religious Education, 1966; St Michael's School, Stevenage, 1968; Director, Westminster Religious Education Centre, 1970. *Publications:* various books on religious education and liturgy. *Recreation:* music. *Address:* 31 Holland Park Gardens, W14 8EA. *T:* 01-603 7409.

KOO, Vi Kyuin Wellington; Judge of International Court of Justice, 1957-67 (Vice-President, 1964-67); *b* 1888. *Educ:* Columbia Univ. (Doctor of Philosophy). Sec. to Pres. of China; Councillor in Foreign Office; Minister to USA, 1915; attended Peace Conference as China's Plenipotentiary, and later as Head of the Chinese Delegation, 1919; Chinese delegate to the Assembly and China's representative on the Council of the League of Nations at Geneva, 1920-22; Chinese Minister to Great Britain, 1921; Plenipotentiary to Washington Conference, 1921-22; Minister of Foreign Affairs, Peking, 1922-24; Finance Minister, 1926; Prime Minister and Minister of Foreign Affairs, 1926-27; Mem. on the International Court of Arbitration at The Hague, 1927-57; Minister of Foreign Affairs, China, 1931; Chinese Assessor to the Commission of Inquiry of the League of Nations, 1932; Chinese Minister to France, 1932-35; Chinese Ambassador to France, 1936-41; Chinese Ambassador in London, 1941-46; Chinese representative on the Council of the League of Nations at Geneva, 1932-34; Delegate 13th and 14th Assemblies of League of Nations and to the Special Assembly of the League of Nations, 1932-33; Delegate to the World Monetary and Economic Conference, London, 1933; Delegate to Conference for Reduction and Limitation of Armaments, at Geneva, 1933; Chief Delegate to Assemblies of League of Nations, 1935-36 and 1938; Special Envoy to Accession of Leopold to throne of Belgium, 1938; Delegate to sessions of League Coun., 1937-39 (Pres. 96th); Chief Deleg. to Brussels Conference, Nov. 1937; Special Envoy to coronation of His Holiness Pius XII; Ambassador Extraordinary to 800th Anniversary of Foundation of Portugal, 1940; Chief Delegate to Dumbarton Oaks Conf.; Rep. on War Crimes Commn, London; Delegate and Actg Chief Delegate to San Francisco Conf. to draft UN charter; Chinese Ambassador in Washington, 1946-56; Delegate to UNRRA and FAO, 1946-49; Mem., Far Eastern Commn, 1946-49; Senior Advisor to General Chiang Kai-Shek, 1956-57, 1967-74; Senior Adviser to Pres. Yen Chia-kan, 1975-. *Publications:* Status of Aliens in China, 1912; Memorandum presented to Lytton Commission (3 volumes), 1932. Hon. degrees: LLD: Columbia, Yale, St John's, Birmingham, Aberdeen, Manchester; LHD, Rollins Coll.; DCL, Miami. *Recreations:* tennis, golf, fishing, skiing. *Address:* 1185 Park Avenue, New York, NY 10028, USA.

KOOPMANS, Prof. Tjalling Charles; Alfred Cowles Professor of Economics, Yale University, USA, since 1967 (Professor of Economics, Yale, since 1955); *b* Holland, 28 Aug. 1910; *m* 1936, Truus Wanningen; one *s* two *d*. *Educ:* Univ. of Utrecht (MA, Phys. and Maths); Univ. of Leiden (PhD, Math. Statistics). Lectr, Netherlands Sch. of Economics, Rotterdam, 1936-38; Economist, Financial Section, League of Nations, Geneva, 1938-40; Special Lectr, Sch. of Business, New York Univ., 1940-41; Research Associate, Princeton Univ., 1940-41; Economist, Penn Mutual Life Ins. Co., 1941-42; Statistician, Combined Shipping Adjustment Bd, Washington, 1942-44; Research Associate, Cowles Commn for Research in Economics, Univ. of Chicago, 1944-54; Associate Prof. of Economics, 1946-48, Prof. of Economics, 1948-55, Univ. of Chicago; Dir of Research, Cowles Commn, 1948-54; Frank W. Taussig Prof. of Economics, Harvard Univ., 1960-61; Dir, Cowles Foundn, 1961-67. Member: Econometric Soc. (Mem. 1934-, Fellow, 1940-, Vice-Pres. 1949, Pres. 1950, Council Mem. 1949-55, 1966-71, 1973-); Amer. Econ. Assoc., 1941-; (Corresp.) Royal Netherlands Acad.

of Arts and Scis, 1950-; ISI, 1952-; Amer. Math. Soc., 1952-; Inst. of Management Scis, 1954-; Ops Research Soc. of Amer., 1954-; Amer. Acad. of Arts and Scis, 1960-; Nat. Acad. of Scis, 1969-. Nobel Prize for Economics (jt), 1975; Honours and Awards from Belgium, Netherlands and USA. *Publications:* Linear Regression Analysis of Economic Time Series (PhD Thesis), 1936; Tanker Freight Rates and Tankship Building, 1939; Three Essays on the State of Economic Science: Allocation of Resources and the Price System, The Construction of Economic Knowledge, The Interaction of Tools and Problems in Economics, 1957; ed and contrib. Cowles Commn Monographs Nos 10 and 13, 1950 and 1951; Co-ed and contrib. No 14, 1953; contrib. Studies in the Economics of Transportation (by Beckmann, McGuire and Winsten), 1956; Selected Scientific Papers, 1937-69, repr. 1970; numerous articles to economic and other professional jls, reveiews, annals, proc. confs and papers. *Address:* (office) Cowles Foundation, Box 2125 Yale Station, New Haven 06520, USA. *T:* (203) 436 2578; (home 459 Ridge Road, Hamden, Connecticut 06517, USA. *T:* (203) 248 5872.

KOOTENAY, Bishop of, since 1971; **Rt. Rev. Robert Edward Fraser Berry;** *b* Ottawa, Ont; *s* of Samuel Berry and Claire Hartley; *m* 1951, Margaret Joan Trevorrow Baillie; one *s* one *d*. *Educ:* Sir George Williams Coll., Montreal; McGill Univ., Montreal; Montreal Diocesan Theological Coll. Assistant, Christ Church Cathedral, Victoria, BC, 1953-55; Rector: St Margaret's, Hamilton, Ont, 1955-61; St Mark's, Orangeville, Ont, 1961-63; St Luke's, Winnipeg, Manitoba, 1963-67; St Michael and All Angels, Kelowna, BC, 1967-71. Hon. DD, Montreal Diocesan Theol Coll., 1973. *Address:* (home) 1857 Maple Street, Kelowna, BC, Canada. *T:* (604) 762-2923; (office) Box 549, Kelowna, BC V1Y 7P2, Canada. *T:* (604) 762-3306.

KOPAL, Prof. Zdeněk; Professor of Astronomy, University of Manchester, since 1951; *b* 4 April 1914; 2nd *s* of Prof. Joseph Kopal, of Charles University, Prague, and Ludmila (*née* Lelek); *m* 1938, Alena, *o d* of late Judge B. Muldner; three *d*. *Educ:* Charles University, Prague; University of Cambridge, England; Harvard Univ., USA. Agassiz Research Fellow, Harvard Observatory, 1938-40; Research Associate in Astronomy, Harvard Univ., 1940-46; Lecturer in Astronomy, Harvard Univ., 1948; Associate Prof., Mass Institute of Technology, 1947-51. Vice-Pres., Foundation Internationale du Pic-du-Midi; Mem. Internat. Acad. of Astronautical Sciences, New York Acad. of Sciences; Chm., Cttee for Lunar and Planetary Exploration, Brit. Nat. Cttee for Space Research; Mem. Lunar-Planetary Cttee, US Nat. Space Bd. Editor-in-Chief, Astrophysics and Space Science, 1968-; Editor: Icarus (internat. jl of solar system); The Moon (internat. jl of lunar studies), 1969-. Pahlavi Lectr, Iran, 1977. Gold Medal, Czechoslovak Acad. of Sciences, 1969; Copernicus Medal, Krakow Univ., 1974. For. Mem., Greek Nat. Acad. of Athens, 1976; DSc (*hc*) Krakow, 1974. *Publications:* An Introduction to the Study of Eclipsing Variables, 1946 (US); The Computation of Elements of Eclipsing Binary Systems, 1950 (US); Tables of Supersonic Flow of Air Around Cones, 3 vols, 1947-49 (US); Numerical Analysis (London), 1955; Astronomical Optics (Amsterdam), 1956; Close Binary Systems, 1959; Figures of Equilibrium of Celestial Bodies, 1960; The Moon, 1960; Physics and Astronomy of the Moon, 1962, 2nd edn 1971; Photographic Atlas of the Moon, 1965; An Introduction to the Study of the Moon, 1966; The Measure of the Moon, 1967; (ed) Advances in Astronomy and Astrophysics, 1968; Telescopes in Space, 1968; Exploration of the Moon by Spacecraft, 1968; Widening Horizons, 1970; A New Photographic Atlas of the Moon, 1971; Man and His Universe, 1972; The Solar System, 1973; Mapping of the Moon, 1974; The Moon in the Post-Apollo Stage, 1974; over 300 original papers on astronomy, aerodynamics, and applied mathematics in publications of Harvard Observatory, Astrophysical Journal, Astronomical Journal, Astronomische Nachrichten, Monthly Notices of Royal Astronomical Society, Proc. Amer. Phil. Soc., Proc. Nat. Acad. Sci. (US), Zeitschrift für Astrophysik, etc. *Recreation:* mountaineering. *Address:* Greenfield, Parkway, Wilmslow, Cheshire. *T:* Wilmslow 22470.

KORNBERG, Prof. Arthur; Professor of Biochemistry, Stanford University, since 1959; *b* Brooklyn, 3 March 1918; *s* of Joseph Kornberg and Lena Katz; *m* 1943, Sylvy R. Levy; three *s*. *Educ:* College of the City of New York (BSc 1937); University of Rochester, NY (MD 1941). Strong Memorial Hospital, Rochester, 1941-42; National Insts of Health, Bethesda, Md, 1942-52; Professor of Microbiology, Washington Univ., and Head of Dept of Microbiology, 1953-59; Head of Dept of Biochemistry, Stanford Univ., 1959-69. Commissioned Officer, US Public Health Service, 1942; Medical Dir, 1951. MNAS; MAAS; Mem. Amer. Phil Soc. Foreign Mem., Royal Soc., 1970. Paul Lewis Award in Enzyme Chemistry, 1951; Nobel Prize (joint) in Medicine, 1959. Hon. LLD City Coll. of New York,

1960; Hon. DSc: University of Rochester, 1962; Univ. of Pennsylvania, 1964; Univ. of Notre Dame, 1965; Washington Univ., St Louis, 1968; Princeton Univ., 1970; Colby Coll., 1970; Hon. LHD, Yeshiva Univ., 1962; MD (*hc*) Univ. of Barcelona, 1970. Hon. Fellow, Weizmann Inst., 1965. *Publications:* Articles in scientific jls. *Address:* 365 Golden Oak Drive, Portola Valley, Calif, USA; Stanford University School of Medicine, Palo Alto, Calif.

KORNBERG, Prof. Hans Leo, MA, DSc Oxon, ScD Cantab, PhD Sheffield; FRS 1965; FIBiol 1965; Sir William Dunn Professor of Biochemistry, University of Cambridge, and Fellow of Christ's College, since 1975; Chairman, Royal Commission on Environmental Pollution, since 1976; *b* 14 Jan. 1928; *o s of* Max Kornberg and Margarete Kornberg (*née* Silberbach); *m* 1956, Monica Mary (*née* King); twin *s* two *d. Educ:* Queen Elizabeth Grammar Sch., Wakefield; University of Sheffield. Commonwealth Fund Fellow of Harkness Foundation, at Yale University and Public Health Research Inst., New York, 1953-55; Mem. of scientific staff, MRC Cell Metabolism Res. Unit, University of Oxford, 1955-60; Lecturer of Worcester Coll., Oxford, 1958-61; Prof. of Biochemistry, Univ. of Leicester, 1960-75; Res. Associate of University of Calif, Berkeley, 1954, of Harvard Med. Sch., Boston, 1958; Visiting Instructor, Marine Biological Lab., Woods Hole, Mass, 1964, 1965, 1966; Visiting Professor: Univ. of Miami, 1970-; Univ. of Cincinnati, 1974; CIBA Lectr, Rutgers, NJ, 1968; Life Sciences Lectr, Univ. of Calif. at Davis, California, 1971; Leeuwenhoek Lectr, Royal Soc., 1972; Guest Lectr, Australian Biochem. Soc., 1973; Weizmann Meml Lectr, Israel, 1975; Fedn European Biochem. Socs Springer Lectr, 1975; Griffith Meml Lectr, Soc. General Microbiology, 1976; Barton Wright Lectr, Inst. Biol., 1977; Leverhulme Meml Lectr, Liverpool, 1977. Member: SRC, 1967-72 (Chm., Science Bd, 1969-72); UGC Biol. Sci. Cttee, 1967-77; NATO Adv. Study Inst. Panel, 1970-76 (Chm., 1974-75). A Managing Trustee, Nuffield Foundn, 1973-; Alternate Governor, Hebrew Univ. of Jerusalem, 1976-. Vice-Pres., Inst. of Biol., 1971-73. FRSA 1972. Hon. Mem., Amer. Soc. Biol Chem., 1972-. Hon. ScD Cincinnati, 1974. Hon. DSc Warwick, 1975. Colworth Medal of Biochemical Soc., 1965; Otto Warburg Medal, Biochem. Soc. of Federal Republic of Germany, 1973. *Publications:* (with Sir Hans Krebs) Energy Transformations in Living Matter, 1957; articles in scientific jls. *Recreations:* cooking and conversation. *Address:* Pine Trees, 111 Glebe Road, Cambridge CB1 4TE; Christ's College, Cambridge CB2 3BU.

KÖRNER, Prof. Stephan, JurDr, PhD; FBA 1967; Professor of Philosophy, Bristol University, since 1952, and Yale University, since 1970; *b* Ostrava, Czechoslovakia, 26 Sept. 1913; *o s of* Emil Körner and Erna (*née* Maier); *m* 1944, Edith Laner, BSc, JP; one *s* one *d. Educ:* Classical Gymnasium; Charles' Univ., Prague; Trinity Hall, Cambridge. Army Service, 1936-39, 1943-46. University of Bristol: Lectr in Philosophy, 1946; Dean, Faculty of Arts, 1965-66; Pro-Vice-Chancellor, 1968-71; Visiting Prof. of Philosophy: Brown Univ., 1957; Yale Univ., 1960; Texas Univ., 1964; Indiana Univ., 1967. President: Brit. Soc. for Philosophy of Science, 1965; Aristotelian Soc., 1967; Internat. Union of History and Philosophy of Science, 1969; Mind Assoc., 1973. Editor, Ratio, 1961-. *Publications:* Kant, 1955; Conceptual Thinking, 1955; The Philosophy of Mathematics, 1960; Experience and Theory, 1966; Kant's Conception of Freedom (British Acad. Lecture), 1967; What is Philosophy?, 1969; Categorical Frameworks, 1970; Abstraction in Science and Morals (Eddington Meml Lecture), 1971; (ed) Practical Reason, 1974; (ed) Observation and Interpretation, 1957; (ed) Explanation, 1976; Experience and Conduct, 1976; contribs to philosophical periodicals. *Recreation:* walking. *Address:* 10 Belgrave Road, Bristol BS8 2AB.

KOSSOFF, David; actor; designer-illustrator; *b* 24 Nov. 1919; *s of* Louis and Anne Kossoff, both Russian; *m* 1947, Margaret (Jennie) Jenkins; two *s. Educ:* elementary sch.; Northern Polytechnic. Commercial Artist, 1937; Draughtsman, 1937-38; Furniture Designer, 1938-39; Technical Illustrator, 1939-45. Began acting, 1943; working as actor and illustrator, 1945-52, as actor and designer, 1952-. BBC Repertory Company, 1945-51. Took over part of Colonel Alexander Ikonenko in the Love of Four Colonels, Wyndham's, 1952; Sam Tager in The Shrike, Prince's, 1953; Morry in The Bespoke Overcoat, and Tobit in Tobias and the Angel, Arts, 1953; Prof. Lodegger in No Sign of the Dove, Savoy, 1953; Nathan in The Boychik, Embassy, 1954 (and again Morry in The Bespoke Overcoat); Mendele in The World of Sholom Aleichem, Embassy, 1955, and Johannesburg, 1957; one-man show, One Eyebrow Up, The Arts, 1957; Man on Trial, Lyric, 1959; Stars in Your Eyes, Palladium, 1960; The Tenth Man, Comedy, 1961; Come Blow Your Horn, Prince of Wales, 1962; one-man show, Kossoff at the Prince Charles,

1963, later called A Funny Kind of Evening (many countries); Enter Solly Gold, Mermaid, 1970; Cinderella, Palladium, 1971; Bunny, Criterion, 1972; own Bible storytelling programmes on radio and TV, as writer and teller, 1964-66; solo performance (stage), 'As According to Kossoff', 1970-. Has appeared in many films. Won British Acad. Award, 1956. Elected MSIA 1958. FRSA 1969. *Play:* Big Night for Shylock, 1968. *Publications:* Bible Stories retold by David Kossoff, 1968; The Book of Witnesses, 1971; The Three Donkeys, 1972; The Voices of Masada, 1973; The Little Book of Sylvanus, 1975; You Have a Minute, Lord?, 1976. *Recreations:* conversation, watching other actors work. *Address:* 45 Roe Green Close, Hatfield, Herts.

KOSTELANETZ, André; orchestra conductor; *b* Leningrad, Russia; *s of* Nachman Kostelanetz and Rosalie Dimscha; *m* 1st, 1938, Lily Pons, soprano (marr. diss. 1958; she *d* 1976); 2nd, 1960, Sara Gene Orcutt (marr. diss., 1969). *Educ:* St Peter's Sch.; St Petersburg Conservatory of Music. Hon. MusD: Albion Coll., Albion, Mich, 1939; Cincinnati Conservatory of Music, 1945. Came to United States 1922, naturalised 1928. For many years conducted own shows over Columbia Broadcasting System; directed music for several motion pictures; selected by radio editors of US and Canada for Fame Award as leading conductor for several years running. Made overseas tours conducting soldier orchestras organized and trained by him, N Africa, Persian Gulf, Italian Theatre, summer 1944; China, Burma, India and European theatres, winter 1944-45. Regular guest conductor with all leading orchestras in US (New York Philharmonic, Boston Symphony, Philadelphia Orchestra, San Francisco Symphony, etc), Canada, S America and Europe. Inaugurated Special Non-Subscription Concerts of New York Philharmonic Orchestra, 1953; Principal Conductor and Artistic Dir, NY Philharmonic Promenades. Records with his own orchestra for Columbia Records. Awarded Asiatic-Pacific ribbon by Army for overseas services. *Address:* 1995 Broadway, New York, NY 10023, USA.

KOSYGIN, Alexei Nikolaevich; Hero of Socialist Labour (twice); Order of Lenin (six times); Order of the Red Banner; Chairman, Council of Ministers of the Union of Soviet Socialist Republics, since 1964; Member, Politburo of the Central Committee of the Communist Party since 1966 (also Member, 1948-52); *b* Petersburg (Leningrad), 1904. *Educ:* Leningrad Co-operative Technical Sch.; Leningrad Textile Inst. Worked in consumer co-op. system in Siberian Territory, 1924-30; Foreman, Shop Superintendent, Zhelyabov Textile Mill, Leningrad, 1935-37; Dir, October Spinning and Weaving Mill, Leningrad, 1937-38; Head of Dept, Leningrad Regional Cttee of CPSU(B), 1938; Chm. Leningrad City Council, 1938-39; People's Commissar for Textile Industry, 1939-40; Dep. Chm. Council of People's Commissars of the USSR, 1940-46; Chm. Council of People's Commissars of RSFSR, 1943-46; Deputy of Supreme Soviet, 1946-; Dep. Chm., Council of Ministers of the USSR, 1946-March 1953, Dec. 1953-1956, 1957-60; Minister: of Finance, 1948; of Light Industry, 1949-53; of Light and Food Industry, 1953; of Consumer Goods Industry, 1953-54; First Dep. Chm. USSR Council of Ministers' State Economic Commn in charge of current economic planning, and Minister of the USSR, 1956-57; Chm., State Planning Cttee, 1959-60 (First Dep. Chm., 1957); First Dep. Chm., 1960-64, Council of Ministers of USSR. Mem. of Communist Party of Soviet Union, 1927-; Mem. Central Cttee, CPSU, 1939-; Alternate Mem., Politburo, CPSU(B), 1946-48; Mem. Politburo, CPSU(B) Central Cttee, 1948-52; Alternate Mem., Presidium, CPSU Central Cttee, 1952-53, 1957-60; Mem. Presidium, CPSU Central Cttee, 1960-66; Mem. Politburo, CPSU Central Cttee, 1966-. *Address:* The Kremlin, Moscow, USSR.

KOTCH, Mrs John Keith; *see* Purden, R. L.

KOTELAWALA, Col Rt. Hon. Sir John (Lionel), PC 1954; CH 1956; KBE 1948; *m*; one *d. Educ:* Christ's Coll., Cambridge; Royal College, Colombo. Mem. State Council, 1931; Minister for Communications and Works, 1935; Minister for Transport and Works, 1947; Prime Minister and Minister of Defence and External Affairs, Ceylon, 1953-56. LLD University of Ceylon. Grand Cross, Legion of Honour (France), 1954; Grand Cross, Order of Merit (Italy), 1954; Grand Cross, Order of Rising Sun (Japan), 1954; Grand Cross, Order of Merit (Germany), 1955; Grand Cross, Order of White Elephant (Thailand), 1955. *Publication:* An Asian Prime Minister's Story, 1956. *Recreations:* polo, tennis, riding. *Address:* Brogues Wood, Biddenden, Kent; Ratmalana, Sri Lanka. *Clubs:* Orient, No 10 (Institute of Directors); Sinhalese Sports; Eighty.

KOTSOKOANE, Hon. Joseph Riffat Larry; Minister of Agriculture, Co-operatives and Marketing, Lesotho, since 1976; Member of Parliament, since 1974; *b* 19 Oct. 1922; *s of* Basotho parents, living in Johannesburg, South Africa; *m* 1947, Elizabeth (*née* Molise); two *s* three *d.* BSc (SA); BSc Hons (Witwatersrand); Cert. Agric. (London). Development Officer, Dept of Agric., Basutoland, 1951-54; Agric. Educn Officer i/c of Agric. Sch. for junior field staff, 1955-62; Agric. Extension Officer i/c of all field staff of Min. of Agric., 1962-63; Prin. Agric. Off. (Dep. Dir), Min. of Agric., 1964-66; High Comr for Lesotho, in London, 1966-69; Ambassador to Germany, Holy See, Rome, France, and Austria, 1968-69; Permanent Sec. and Hd of Diplomatic Service, Lesotho, 1969-70; Permanent Sec. for Health, Educn and Social Welfare, Lesotho, 1970-71; High Comr for Lesotho in East Africa, Nigeria and Ghana, 1972-74; Minister: of Foreign Affairs, Lesotho, 1974-75; of Education, 1975-76. Guest of Min. of Agric., Netherlands, 1955; studied agric. educn, USA (financed by Carnegie Corp. of NY and Ford Foundn), 1960-61; FAO confs in Tunisia, Tanganyika and Uganda, 1962 and 1963; Mem. Lesotho delegn to 24th World Health Assembly, 1971; travelled extensively to study and observe methods of agric. administration, 1964; meetings on nutrition, Berlin and Hamburg, 1966; diplomatic trainee, Brit. Embassy, Bonn, 1966. *Recreations:* swimming, tennis, amateur dramatics, photography, debating, reading, travelling. *Address:* Ministry of Agriculture, PO Box 24, Maseru, Lesotho, Southern Africa.

KOVACEVICH, Stephen B.; *see* Bishop-Kovacevich.

KOZYGIN; *see* Kosygin.

KRABBÉ, Col Clarence Brehmer, OBE 1918; DL; *b* 1886; *s* of Charles Krabbé, Buenos Aires; *m* 1915, Joan Alison (*d* 1968), *d* of Col A. Evans-Gordon, IA; one *s* (killed 1940) one *d. Educ:* Dulwich Coll.; Trinity Coll., Oxford. Served European War, 1914-19, with Berks Yeomanry and RFC, Gallipoli and France (despatches). Col Berks Home Guard, 1943-45. Chm., Royal Berks Hosp., 1942-48; Chm., S Berks Conservative Assoc., 1946-52; Vice-Chm., Berks T & AF Assoc., 1950-54; Mem., Oxford Regional Hosp. Bd, 1947-62 (Vice-Chm. 1951-62). Mem., Board of Governors, Oxford United Hosps, 1953-57; Mem. of Reading and District Hosp. Management Cttee (Chm., 1948-50), 1948-66; Mem. St Birinus Hosp. Management Cttee, 1962-66. DL Berks, 1946. High Sheriff of Berks, 1952-53. *Recreations:* curling, gardening. *Address:* Calcot Green, near Reading, Berks. *T:* Reading 27428.

KRAMER, Prof. Ivor Robert Horton, MDS; FDSRCS, FFDRCSI, FRCPath; Professor of Oral Pathology, Institute of Dental Surgery, University of London, since 1962, and Dean and Director of Studies of the Institute, since 1970; Head of Department of Pathology, Eastman Dental Hospital, since 1950; *b* 20 June 1923; *yr s* of late Alfred Bertie and Agnes Maud Kramer; *m* 1946, Elisabeth Dalley; one *s. Educ:* Royal Dental Hosp. of London Sch. of Dental Surgery; MDS 1955; FDSRCS 1960 (LDSRCS 1944); FRCPath 1970 (MCRPath 1964); FFDRCSI 1973. Asst to Pathologist, Princess Louise (Kensington) Hosp. for Children, 1944-48; Wright Fleming Inst. of Microbiol., 1948-49; Instr in Dental Histology, Royal Dental Hosp. Sch. of Dental Surgery, 1944-50; Asst Pathologist, Royal Dental Hosp., 1950-56; Institute of Dental Surgery: Lectr in Dental Path., 1949-50, Sen. Lectr, 1950-57; Reader in Oral Path., 1957-62; Sub-dean, 1950-70; Civilian Cons. in Dental Path., RN, 1967-. Member: WHO Expert Adv. Panel on Dental Health, 1975-; Bd of Faculty of Dental Surgery, RCS, 1964-, Council, RCS, 1977-; Mem. Council for Postgrad. Med. Educn in Eng. and Wales, 1972- (Chm., Dental Cttee, 1972-); Pres., Odontological Section, RSocMed, 1973-74; Pres., British Div., Internat. Assoc. for Dental Res., 1974-, Hon. Pres. of the Assoc., 1974-75. Editor, Archives of Oral Biology, 1959-69. Lectures: Wilkinson, Manchester, 1962; Charles Tomes, RCS, 1969; Holme, UCH, 1969; Elwood Meml, QUB, 1970; Hutchinson, Edinburgh, 1971. Howard Mummery Prize, BDA, 1966; Maurice Down Award, Brit. Assoc. of Oral Surgeons, 1974. *Publications:* (with R. B. Lucas) Bacteriology for Students of Dental Surgery, 1954, 3rd edn 1966; (with J. J. Pindborg and H. Torloni) World Health Organization International Histological Classification of Tumours: odontogenic tumours, jaw cysts and allied lesions, 1972; (with B. Cohen) Scientific Foundations of Dentistry, 1976; numerous papers in med. and dental jls. *Address:* c/o Institute of Dental Surgery, Gray's Inn Road, WC1X 8LD. *T:* 01-837 7251; 16 College Gardens, SE21 7BE. *T:* 01-693 7076.

KRAMRISCH, Stella, PhD; Professor of Indian Art, Institute of Fine Arts, New York University, since 1964; Curator of Indian Art, Philadelphia Museum of Art, since 1954; *d* of Jacques Kramrisch, scientist, and Berta Kramrisch; *m* 1929, Laszlo Neményi (*d* 1950). *Educ:* Vienna University. Prof. of Indian Art, Univ. of Calcutta, 1923-50; Prof. in the Art of South Asia, Univ.

of Pennsylvania, 1950-69; Lectr on Indian Art, Courtauld Inst. of Art, Univ. of London, 1937-41. Editor: Jl Indian Soc. of Oriental Art, 1932-50; Artibus Asiae, 1959-. Hon. Dr of Literature, Visva Bharati Univ. *Publications:* Principles of Indian Art, 1924; Vishnudharmottara, 1924; History of Indian Art, 1929; Indian Sculpture, 1932; Asian Miniature Painting, 1932; A Survey of Painting in the Deccan, 1937; Indian Terracottas, 1939; Kantha, 1939; The Hindu Temple, 1946; Arts and Crafts of Travancore, 1948; Dravida and Kerala, 1953; Art of India, 1954; Indian Sculpture in the Philadelphia Museum of Art, 1960; The Triple Structure of Creation, 1962; The Art of Nepal, 1964; Unknown India: Ritual Art in Tribe and Village, 1968. *Address:* Philadelphia Museum of Art, PO Box 7646, Philadelphia, Pa 19101, USA; University of New York, Institute of Fine Arts, 1 East 78th Street, New York, NY 10021, USA.

KRAUS, Otakar, OBE 1973; operatic singer; *b* Prague, 1909; *m* Maria Graf; one *s. Educ:* privately; in Prague and in Milan. Engaged as Principal Baritone, National Opera House, Bratislava; subsequently at: Opera House, Brno; State Opera House, Prague; Royal Opera House, Covent Garden. Has also appeared with Carl Rosa Opera, English Opera Group, at Glyndebourne, Bayreuth, Aldeburgh, Vienna State Opera, Munich, Venice, (Scala) Milan, Nederlandsche Opera, Amsterdam. *Address:* 223 Hamlet Gardens, W6. *T:* 01-748 7366.

KREBS, Sir Hans (Adolf), Kt 1958; FRS 1947; FRCP; MD Hamburg, 1925; MA Cantab, 1934; Research Scientist in the Nuffield Department of Clinical Medicine, Radcliffe Infirmary, Oxford, and Supernumerary Fellow of St Cross College, Oxford, since 1967; Visiting Professor of Biochemistry, Royal Free Hospital School of Medicine, since 1967; *b* 25 Aug. 1900; *e s* of late Georg Krebs, MD, and Alma Davidson, Hildesheim, Germany; *m* 1938, Margaret Cicely, *d* of J. L. Fieldhouse, Wickersley, Yorks; two *s* one *d. Educ:* Universities of Göttingen, Freiburg i. B., Munich, Berlin. Asst Kaiser Wilhelm Institut f. Biologie, Dept of Prof. O. H. Warburg, Berlin-Dahlem, 1926-30; Privatdozent f. int. Medizin, Freiburg, 1932; Rockefeller research student, Cambridge, 1933-34; Demonstrator in Biochemistry, Cambridge, 1934-35; Lecturer in Pharmacology, University of Sheffield, 1935-38; Lecturer i/c Dept of Biochemistry, University of Sheffield, 1938-45; Prof., 1945-54. Whitley Prof. of Biochemistry, and Fellow of Trinity Coll., Oxford, 1954-67. Hon. Degrees from Universities of Chicago, Freiburg, Paris, Glasgow, Sheffield, London, Berlin (Humboldt), Jerusalem, Leicester, Leeds, Granada, Pennsylvania, Wales, Bordeaux, Bristol, Hannover and Valencia. Hon. Member: Belgian Royal Academy of Medicine, 1962; Amer. Assoc. of Physicians, 1972; Deutsche Ges. Inn. Med., 1972; Société de Biologie, Paris, 1973. Hon. Fellow, Nat. Inst. of Sciences of India, 1956; Associé étranger, Académie Nationale de Médecine, Paris, 1973; Foreign Hon. Mem., Amer. Acad. of Arts and Sciences, 1957; Mem., Amer. Philosophical Soc., 1960; Foreign Associate, Amer. Nat. Acad. of Science, 1964; Hon. Fellow, Weizmann Inst. Science, 1972. (Jointly) Nobel Prize for Medicine, 1953; Royal Medal, Royal Society, 1954; Gold Medal of Netherlands Soc. for Physics, Medical Science, and Surgery, 1958; Copley Medal of Royal Society, 1961. Gold Medal, RSM, 1965. *Publications:* (with Prof. H. Kornberg) Energy Transformations in Living Matter, 1957; Papers on biochemical subjects in scientific journals. *Address:* Nuffield Department of Clinical Medicine, Radcliffe Infirmary, Oxford; 27 Abberbury Road, Oxford.

KREISEL, Prof. Georg, FRS 1966; Professor of Logic and the Foundations of Mathematics, Stanford University, Stanford, California, USA; *b* 15 Sept. 1923. *Address:* Department of Philosophy, Stanford University, Stanford, California 94305, USA.

KREMER, Michael, MD; FRCP; Emeritus Neurologist, Middlesex Hospital, W1; Honorary Consulting Neurologist, National Hospital, Queen Square, WC1; Hon. Consultant Neurologist to St Dunstan's, since 1966; Hon. Consultant in Neurology to the Army, since 1969; *b* 27 Nov. 1907; *s* of W. and S. Kremer; *m* 1933, Lilian Frances (*née* Washbourn); one *s* two *d. Educ:* Middlesex Hosp. Medical Sch. BSc 1927; MD 1932; FRCP 1943. *Recreations:* music, reading, photography. *Address:* 121 Harley Street, W1. *T:* 01-935 4545. *Club:* Royal Automobile.

KRESTIN, David, MD (London), BS, MRCP; Consulting Physician, London Jewish Hospital; Medical Specialist, Ministries of Pensions and of National Insurance; late Physician with charge of Out-Patients, Dreadnought Hospital; Medical Registrar, Prince of Wales' Hospital; Lecturer in Medicine, N-E London Post-Graduate Medical College; *b* London; *s* of Dr S.

Krestin; *m* Ruth Fisher; one *s*. *Educ:* University of London; London Hosp. Medical Coll.; University of Pennsylvania. Anatomy prize, London Hosp.; MRCS, LRCP 1922; MB, BS London 1923, Hons Medicine and Surgery; MD London 1926, MRCP 1926. Clinical Asst, House Surg., House Physician, Medical Registrar and First Asst, London Hosp.; Rockefeller Medical Fellowship, 1928-29; Fellow in Pathology, Henry Phipps Institute, University Penna; Yarrow Research Fellow, London Hosp. *Publications:* Pulsation in Superficial Veins, Lancet, 1927; The Seborrhœic facies in Post-Encephalitic Parkinsonism, Quart. Jour. Med., 1927; Congenital Dextrocardia and Auric. Fibrillation, Brit. Med. Jour., 1927; Latent Pulmonary Tuberculosis, Quart. Journ. Med., 1929; Glandular Fever, Clinical Journal, 1931 and other medical papers. *Recreation:* fishing. *Address:* 14 Spaniards End, NW3. *T:* 01-455 1500.

KRETZMER, Herbert, lyric writer, feature writer and theatre critic, Daily Express, London, since 1962; *b* Kroonstad, OFS, S Africa, 5 Oct. 1925; *s* of William and Tilly Kretzmer; *m* 1961, Elisabeth Margaret Wilson (marr. diss., 1973); one *s* one *d*. *Educ:* Kroonstad High Sch.; Rhodes Univ., Grahamstown. Entered journalism, 1946, writing weekly cinema newsreel commentaries and documentary films for African Film Productions, Johannesburg. Reporter and entertainment columnist, Sunday Express, Johannesburg, 1951-54; feature writer and columnist, Daily Sketch, London, 1954-59; Columnist, Sunday Dispatch, London, 1959-61. As lyric writer, contributed weekly songs to: That Was The Week.., Not So Much A Programme.., BBC 3, That's Life. Wrote lyrics for Ivor Novello Award song Goodness Gracious Me, 1960, and ASCAP award song Yesterday When I was Young, 1969; Gold record for She, 1974; Our Man Crichton, Shaftesbury Theatre, 1964 (book and lyrics); The Four Musketeers, Drury Lane, 1967 (lyrics); wrote libretto for The Song of Hiawatha (oratorio), 1977; *film:* Can Heironymus Merkin Ever Forget Mercy Humppe And Find True Happiness?, 1969 (lyrics); has also written lyrics for other films, and for TV programmes. *Publications:* Our Man Crichton, 1965; (jointly) Every Home Should Have One, 1970. *Address:* 55 Lincoln House, Basil Street, SW3. *T:* 01-589 2541.

KRIKORIAN, Gregory, CB 1973; Solicitor for the Customs and Excise since 1971; *b* 23 Sept. 1913; *s* of late Kevork and late Christine Krikorian; *m* 1943, Seta Mary, *d* of Souren Djirdjirian; one *d*. *Educ:* Polytechnic Secondary Sch.; Lincoln Coll., Oxford (BA). Called to Bar, Middle Temple, 1939; practised at Bar, 1939; BBC Overseas Intell. Dept, 1940; served in RAF as Intell. Officer, Fighter Comd, 1940-45 (despatches); practised at Bar, 1945-51, Junior Oxford Circuit, 1947; joined Solicitor's Office, HM Customs and Excise, 1951. *Publication:* (jtly) Customs and Excise, in Halsbury's Laws of England, 1975. *Recreations:* gardening, bird-watching. *Address:* The Coach House, Hawkchurch, Axminster, Devon. *T:* Hawkchurch 414. *Clubs:* Reform, Civil Service, MCC.

KRISH, Mrs Felix; *see* Moiseiwitsch, Tanya.

KRISHNA, Sri, CIE 1942; DSc (London), PhD, FRIC, FNA; late Scientific Adviser to High Commission of India and Scientific Liaison Officer, London; Deputy Director, Council of Scientific and Industrial Research, New Delhi, India, 1952; Vice-Pres. and Director of Research, Forest Research Institute, Dehra Dun, UP, India, 1950; Biochemist since 1928; *b* 6 July 1896; *s* of M. Mohan; *m* 1st, 1925, Usha Khanna (*d* 1929); (one *s* decd); 2nd, 1972, Olga Hellerman. *Educ:* Forman Coll., Lahore; Government Coll., Lahore; Queen Mary Coll., London; King's Coll., London. Prof. of Chemistry, University of the Punjab, Lahore, 1925-28. *Publications:* numerous scientific. *Recreations:* tennis, etc. *Address:* 62 Perryn Road, Acton, W3 7LX; 88 Rajpur Road, Dehra Dun, UP, India.

KRISTENSEN, Prof. Thorkil; Director, Institute for Development Research, Copenhagen, 1969-72; Secretary-General, Organisation for Economic Co-operation and Development, 1960-69; *b* Denmark, 9 Oct. 1899; *m* 1931, Ellen Christine Nielsen; one *s* one *d*. *Educ:* School of Commerce; People's Coll., Askov; University of Copenhagen (Cand. polit.). Dipl. Polit. and Econ. Sciences, 1927. Lectr in High Sch. of Commerce, Aarhus, and in University of Copenhagen, 1927-38; Prof. of Commercial and Industrial Economics: University of Aarhus, 1938-47; Sch. of Advanced Commercial Studies, Copenhagen, 1947-60. Mem., Danish Parliament, 1945-60; Minister of Finance, 1945-47 and 1950-53; Mem. Finance Cttee, 1947-49 and 1953-60; Mem. Consultative Assembly of Council of Europe, 1949-50; Mem. Foreign Affairs Cttee, 1953-60; Mem. Nordic Council, 1953-60; Mem. Acad. of Technical Sciences; Pres. Foreign Policy Soc., 1948-60; Pres. Nat. Anti-

Unemployment Fedn, 1956-60; Mem. Assurance Council, 1958-60; Mem. Institute of History and Economics. DrSc Pol *hc* (Ankara), 1962. *Publications:* several, on finance, 1930-39; The Food Problem of Developing Countries, 1968. Editor of: De europaeiske markedsplaner (European Markets-Plans and Prospects), 1958; The Economic World Balance, 1960; Development in Rich and Poor Countries, 1974, etc. *Address:* Odinsvej 18, 3460 Birkerød, Denmark.

KRISTIANSEN, Erling (Engelbrecht), Grand Cross, Order of Dannebrog; Hon. GCVO 1974; Royal Danish Ambassador to the Court of St James's, 1964-77; *b* 31 Dec. 1912; *s* of Kristian Engelbrecht Kristiansen, Chartered Surveyor, and Andrea Kirstine (*née* Madsen); *m* 1938, Annemarie Selinko, novelist. *Educ:* Herning Gymnasium; University of Copenhagen (degree awarded equiv. of MA Econ). Postgraduate Studies, Economics and Internat. Relations, Geneva, Paris, London, 1935-37. Sec.-Gen., 1935, Pres. 1936, of the Fédération Universitaire Internationale pour la Société des Nations. Danish Civil Servant, 1941; served with: Free Danish Missions, Stockholm, 1943; Washington, 1944; London, 1945; joined Danish Diplomatic Service and stayed in London until 1947; Danish Foreign Ministry, 1947-48; Head of Denmark's Mission to OEEC, Paris, 1948-50; Sec. to Economic Cttee of Cabinet, 1950-51; Asst Under-Sec. of State, 1951; Dep. Under-Sec. of State (Economic Affairs), Danish For. Min., 1954-64. Grand Officier, Légion d'Honneur; Kt Comdr: Order of St Olav; Order of White Rose of Finland; Star of Ethiopia; Knight Grand Cross, Icelandic Falcon; Comdr, Order of Northern Star of Sweden. *Publication:* Folkeforbundet (The League of Nations), 1938. *Recreations:* skiing, fishing and other out-door sports, modern languages. *Address:* 4 Granhøjen, Dk-2900, Hellerup, Denmark. *Clubs:* MCC; Special Forces *et al*.

KROHN, Dr Peter Leslie, FRS 1963; Professor of Endocrinology, University of Birmingham, 1962-66; *b* 8 Jan. 1916; *s* of Eric Leslie Krohn and Doris Ellen Krohn (*née* Wade); *m* 1941, Joanna Mary French; two *s*. *Educ:* Sedbergh; Balliol Coll., Oxford. BA 1st Cl. Hons Animal Physiol, 1937; BM, BCh Oxon, 1940. Wartime Research work for Min. of Home Security, 1940-45; Lectr, then Reader in Endocrinology, University of Birmingham, 1946-53; Nuffield Sen. Gerontological Research Fellow and Hon. Prof. in University, 1953-62. *Publications:* contrib. to scientific jls on physiology of reproduction, transplantation immunity and ageing. *Recreations:* ski-ing, mountain walking. *Address:* La Forêt, St Mary, Jersey, Channel Islands. *T:* Jersey Central 62158.

KROLL, Dss Dr Una (Margaret Patricia); Deaconess Doctor; family doctor, since 1960; worker deaconess, since 1970; writer and broadcaster, since 1970; *b* 25 Dec. 1925; *d* of George Hill, CB, DSO, MC, and Hilda Hill; *m* 1957, Leopold Kroll; one *s* three *d*. *Educ:* St Paul's Girls' Sch.; Malvern Girls' Coll.; Girton Coll., Cambridge; The London Hosp. MB, BChir (Cantab) 1951; MA 1969. MRCGP 1967. House Officer, 1951-53; Overseas service (Africa), 1953-60; General Practice, 1960-. Theological trng, 1967-70; political work as a feminist, with particular ref. to status of women in the churches in England and internationally, 1970-. *Publications:* Transcendental Meditation: a signpost to the world, 1974; Flesh of My Flesh: a Christian view on sexism, 1975; Lament for a Lost Enemy: study of reconciliation, 1976; contrib. Cervical Cytology (BMJ), 1969. *Recreations:* preaching, reading, sitting. *Address:* 2 Church Lane, Merton Park, SW19 3NY. *T:* 01-542 1174. *Club:* University Women's.

KRUSIN, Sir Stanley (Marks), Kt 1973; CB 1963; Second Parliamentary Counsel, 1970-73; *b* 8 June 1908; *m* 1st, 1937 (she *d* 1972); one *s* one *d*; 2nd, 1976. *Educ:* St Paul's Sch.; Balliol Coll., Oxford. Called to the Bar, Middle Temple, 1932. Served RAFVR, Wing Comdr, 1944. Dep. Sec., British Tabulating Machine Co. Ltd, 1945-47. Entered Parliamentary Counsel Office, 1947; Parliamentary Counsel, 1953-69. *Address:* 5 Coleridge Walk, NW11. *T:* 01-458 1340. *Club:* Royal Air Force.

KUBELIK, Rafael; conductor and composer; Chief Conductor of Bayerischer Rundfunk, München, since 1961; *b* Bychory, Bohemia, 29 June 1914; *s* of Jan Kubelik, violinist, and Marianne (*née* Szell); *m* 1942, Ludmila Bertlova, (decd), violinist; one *s*; *m* 1963, Elsie Morison, singer. *Educ:* Prague Conservatoire. Conductor, Czech Philharmonic Society, Prague, 1936-39; Musical Director of Opera, Brno, Czechoslovakia, 1939-41; Musical Dir, Czech Philharmonic Orchestra, 1941-48; Musical Dir, Chicago Symphony Orchestra, 1950-53; Musical Dir of the Covent Garden Opera Company, 1955-58; Music Dir, Metropolitan Opera, New York, 1973-74. Compositions include: 5 operas; 2 symphonies with chorus; a third symphony (in one movement); 5 string quartets; 1 violin concerto; 1 cello concerto; 1 cantata; Requiems: Pro Memoria

Uxoris; Libera Nos; Quattro Forme per Archi; songs; piano and violin music. *Address:* Kastanienbaum, Haus im Sand, Switzerland.

KUBRICK, Stanley; producer, director, script writer; *b* 26 July 1928; *s* of Dr Jacques L. Kubrick and Gertrude Kubrick; *m* 1958, Suzanne Christiane Harlan; three *d. Educ:* William Howard Taft High Sch ; City Coll. of City of New York. Joined Look Magazine, 1946. At age of 21 made Documentary, Day of the Fight; made Short for RKO, Flying Padre. *Feature Films:* Fear and Desire, 1953 (at age of 24); Killer's Kiss, 1954; The Killing, 1956; Paths of Glory, 1957; Spartacus, 1960; Lolita, 1962; Dr Strangelove or How I Learned to Stop Worrying and Love the Bomb, 1964; 2001: A Space Odyssey, 1968; A Clockwork Orange, 1971; Barry Lyndon, 1975. *Recreations:* literature, music, public affairs. *Address:* c/o Loeb & Loeb, 10100 Santa Monica Boulevard, Suite 2200, Los Angeles, Calif 90067, USA.

KUENSSBERG, Ekkehard von, CBE 1969; FRCGP; President, Royal College of General Practitioners, since 1976; *b* 1913; *s* of Prof. Eberhard von Kuenssberg; *m* 1941, Dr Constance Ferrar Hardy; two *s* two *d . Educ:* Schloss Schule, Salem; Univs of Innsbruck, Heidelberg and Edinburgh. MB, ChB 1939. Gen. practice throughout (Edin.). RAMC, 1944-46 (Lt-Col, DADMS E Africa Comd). Mem , Safety of Drugs Cttee, 1964-71; Chm., Gen. Med. Services Cttee, Scotland; Mem., GMSC, UK, 1960-68; Assessor, Edin. Univ. Ct. 1971-. RCGP: Chm. Council, 1970-73; Hon. Treas., Research Foundn Bd, 1960-77; Mackenzie Lectr, 1970: Wolfson Travelling Prof., 1974. Mem., Lothian Area Health Bd, 1974-; Mem. Council, Queen's Nursing Inst., 1972-76. Foundation Council Award, RCGP, 1967; Hippocrates Medal, 1974 (SIMG). FRSocMed. *Publications:* The Team in General Practice, 1966; An Opportunity to Learn 1977. *Recreations:* skiing, forestry. *Address:* Little Letham, Haddington, East Lothian. *T:* Haddington 2529.

KUHN, Heinrich Gerhard, FRS 1954; DPhil, MA; Reader in Physics, Oxford University, 1955-71, now Emeritus; Fellow of Balliol College 1950-71. now Emeritus; *b* 10 March 1904; *s* of Wilhelm Felix and Martha Kuhn; *m* 1931, Marie Bertha Nohl; two *s. Educ:* High Sch., Lueben (Silesia); Universities of Greifswald and Goettingen. Lecturer in Physics, Goettingen Univ., 1931; Research at Clarendon Laboratory, Oxford, 1933; Lecturer, University Coll., Oxford, 1938; work for atomic energy project, 1941-45; University Demonstrator, Oxford, 1945-55. Dr *hc* Aix-Marseille, 1958. Holweck Prize, 1967. *Publications:* Atomspektren, 1934 (Akad. Verl. Ges., Leipzig); Atomic Spectra, 1962, 2nd edn 1970; articles on molecular and atomic spectra and on interferometry. *Address:* 25 Victoria Road, Oxford. *T:* 55308.

KUNCEWICZ, Mrs Witold; *see* Herlie, Eileen.

KUNERALP, Zeki, Hon. GCVO 1971; Turkish Ambassador to Spain, since 1972; *b* Istanbul, 5 Oct. 1914; *s* of Ali Kemal and Sabiha, *d* of Mustafa Zeki Pasha; *m* 1943, Necla Ozdilci; two *s. Educ:* Univ. of Berne. DrIuris 1938. Entered Diplomatic Service, 1940: served Bucharest, Prague, Paris, Nato Delegn and at Min. of Foreign Affairs, Ankara; Asst Sec.-Gen. 1957; Sec.-Gen. 1960; Ambassador to Berne, 1960, to Court of St James's, 1964-66; Sec.-Gen. at Min. of Foreign Affairs, Ankara, 1966-69; Ambassador to Court cf St James's, 1969-72. Mem., Hon. Soc. of Knights of the Round Table. Holds German, Greek, Italian, Papal, Jordanian, Iranian and National Chinese orders. *Recreations:* reading, ballet. *Address:* Embajada de Turquia, Calle de Monte Esquinza 48, Madrid, Spain. *Clubs:* National Liberal, Hurlingham, Travellers'.

KÜNG, Prof. Dr Hans; Ordinary Professor of Dogmatic and Ecumenical Theology and Director of Institute for Ecumenical Research, University of Tübingen, since 1963; *b* Sursee, Lucerne, 19 March 1923. *Educ:* schools in Sursee and Lucerne; Papal Gregorian Univ., Rome (LPhil, LTh); Sorbonne; Inst. Catholique, Paris. DTheol 1957. Further studies in Amsterdam, Berlin, Madrid, London. Ordained priest, 1954. Pastoral work, Hofkirche, Lucerne, 1957-59; Asst for dogmatic theol., Univ. of Münster, 1959-60; Ord. Prof. of fundamental theol., Univ. of Tübingen, 1960; official theol. consultant (peritus) to 2nd Vatican Council, 1962; Visiting Professor: Union Theol. Seminary, NYC, 1968; Univ. of Basle, 1969; guest lectures at univs in Europe, America, Asia and Australia. Editor series, Theologische Meditationen; co-Editor series, Okumenische Forschungen; Associate Editor: Tübingen Theologische Quartalschrift; Jl of Ecum. Studies; Mem. Exec. Editorial Cttee, Concilium. Holds hon. doctorates. *Publications:* (first publication in German) The Council and Reunion, 1961; That the World may Believe, 1963; The Living Church, 1963; The Changing Church, 1965; Justification: the doctrine of Karl Barth and a Catholic reflection, 1965; Structures of the Church, 1965; The Church, 1967; Truthfulness: the future of the Church, 1968; Infallible? an inquiry, 1971 (paperback 1972); 20 Thesen zum Christsein, 1975; On Being a Christian, 1976; Was ist Firmung?, 1976; Jesus im Widerstreit: ein jüdisch-christlicher Dialog (with Pinchas Lapide), 1976; Gottesdienst-warum?, 1976; contribs to Theologische Meditationen, and to Christian Revelation and World Religions, ed J. Neuner, 1967. American edns of the above books and also of contribs to Theol. Med., etc, the latter under one title, Freedom Today, 1966. *Address:* D-74 Tübingen, Waldhäuserstrasse 23, SW Germany.

KUROSAWA, Akira; Japanese film director; *b* 1910. *Educ:* Keika Middle School. Assistant Director, Toho Film Co., 1936. Mem. Jury, Internat. Film Fest. of India, 1977. Directed first film, Sugata Sanshiro, 1943. *Films include:* Sugata Sanshiro, Ichiban Utsukushiku, Torano Owofumu Otokotachi, Rashomon (1st Prize, Venice Film Festival), Hakuchi, Ikiru, The Seven Samurai, Living, Kakushi Toride no San Akunin, The Hidden Fortress, Throne of Blood, Yojimbo, The Bad Sleep Well, Tsubaki Sanjuro, Tengoku To Jigoku, Red Beard, 1965; Dodeska-Den, 1970; Dersu Uzala (Oscar Award), 1975.

KURTI, Prof. Nicholas, CBE 1973; FRS 1956; MA Oxon; DrPhil (Berlin); FInstP; Emeritus Professor of Physics, University of Oxford; Vice-President, Royal Society, 1965-67; *b* 14 May 1908; *s* of late Charles Kürti and Margaret Pintér, Budapest; *m* 1946, Georgiana, *d* of late Brig.-Gen. C. T. Shipley and Mrs Shipley, Oxford; two *d. Educ:* Minta-Gymnasium, Budapest; University of Paris (Licence ès sci. phys.); University of Berlin (DrPhil). Asst, Techn Hochschule Breslau, 1931-33; Research Position, Clarendon Laboratory, Oxford, 1933-40; UK Atomic Energy Project, 1940-45; University Demonstrator in Physics, Oxford, 1945-60; Reader in Physics, Oxford, 1960-67; Prof. of Physics, Oxford, 1967-75; Senior Research Fellow, Brasenose Coll., 1947-67; Professorial Fellow, 1967-75. Buell G. Gallagher Visiting Prof., City Coll., New York, 1963; Vis. Prof., University of Calif, Berkeley, 1964. A Governor, College of Aeronautics, Cranfield, 1953-69. Member: Electricity Supply Research Council, 1960-; Advisory Cttee for Scientific and Technical Information, 1966-68; Chm., Adv. Cttee for research on Measurement and Standards, Dept of Trade and Industry, 1969-73. Member: Council, Royal Soc., 1964-67; Council, Soc. Française de Physique, 1957-60, 1970-73; Council, Inst. of Physics and Physical Soc., 1969-73; Treasurer, CODATA (Cttee on data for sci. and technol., ICSU), 1973-; Chm., Cttee of Management, Science Policy Foundn, 1970-75. Foreign Hon. Mem., Amer. Acad. Arts and Sciences, 1968; Foreign Mem., Finnish Acad. of Science and Letters, 1974; Hon. Member: Hungarian Acad. of Sciences, 1970; Société Française de Physique, 1974; Akad. der Wissenschaften der DDR, 1976. Holweck Prize (British and French Physical Socs), 1955; Fritz London Award, 1957; Hughes Medal, Royal Soc., 1969. Chevalier de la Légion d'Honneur, 1976. *Publications:* (jointly) Low Temperature Physics, 1952. Papers in scientific periodicals on cryophysics and magnetism; articles in the New Chambers's Encyclopædia. *Address:* 38 Blandford Avenue, Oxford OX2 8DZ. *T:* 56176; Engineering Laboratory, Parks Road, Oxford OX1 3PJ. *T:* 59988. *Club:* Athenæum.

KUSCH, Prof. Polykarp; Eugene McDermott Professor, Department of Physics, The University of Texas at Dallas, since 1972; *b* Germany, 26 Jan. 1911; *s* of John Matthias Kusch and Henrietta van der Haas; *m* 1935, Edith Starr McRoberts (*d* 1959); three *d*; *m* 1960, Betty Jane Pezzoni; two *d. Educ:* Case Inst. of Technology, Cleveland, O (BS); Univ. of Illinois, Urbana, Ill. (MS, PhD). Asst, Univ. of Illinois, 1931-36; Research Asst, Univ. of Minnesota, 1936-37; Instr in Physics, Columbia Univ., 1937-41; Engr, Westinghouse Electric Corp., 1941-42; Mem. Tech. Staff, Div. of Govt Aided Research, Columbia Univ., 1942-44; Mem. Tech. Staff, Bell Telephone Laboratories, 1944-46; Columbia University: Associate Prof. of Physics, 1946-49; Prof. of Physics, 1949-72; Exec. Officer, Dept of Physics, 1949-52, Chm. 1960-63; Exec. Dir, Columbia Radiation Laboratory, 1952-60; Vice-Pres. and Dean of Faculties, 1969-70; Exec. Vice-Pres. and Provost, 1970-71. Member: Nat. Acad. of Sciences, US; American Philosophical Soc. Hon. DSc: Case Inst. of Technology, 1955; Ohio State Univ., 1959; Colby Coll., 1961; Univ. of Illinois, 1961; Yeshiva Univ., 1976. (Jointly) Nobel Prize in Physics, 1955. *Publications:* technical articles in Physical Review and other jls. *Address:* University of Texas at Dallas, Department of Physics, PO Box 688, Richardson, Texas 75080, USA; 724 Paldao, Dallas, Texas 75240, USA. *T:* (214)661-1247.

KUSTOW, Michael David; Associate Director, National Theatre, since 1973; writer, stage director, exhibition organiser; *b* 18 Nov. 1939; *m* 1973, Orna, *d* of Jacob and Rivka Spector, Haifa, Israel. *Educ:* Haberdashers' Aske's; Wadham Coll., Oxford (BA Hons English). Festivals Organiser, Centre 42, 1962-63; Royal Shakespeare Theatre Company: Dir, RSC Club, Founder of Theatreground, Editor of Flourish, 1963-67; Dir, Inst. of Contemporary Arts, 1967-70. *Productions:* Punch and Judas, Trafalgar Square, 1963; I Wonder, ICA, 1968; Nicholas Tomalin Reporting, 1975; Brecht Poetry and Songs, 1976; *Exhibitions:* Tout Terriblement Guillaume Apollinaire, ICA, 1968; AAARGH! A Celebration of Comics, ICA, 1971; *Publications:* Punch and Judas, 1964; The Book of US, 1968; Tank: an autobiographical fiction, 1975. *Recreations:* painting, jazz. *Address:* c/o A. D. Peters, 10 Buckingham Street, WC2N 6BU. *T:* 01-839 2556.

KUTSCHER, Hans, Dr Jur; President, Court of Justice of the European Communities, since 1976 (Judge of Court, since 1970); *b* Hamburg, 14 Dec. 1911; *m* 1946, Irmgard Schroeder; two step *d*. *Educ:* Univ. of Graz, Austria; Univ. of Freiburg-im-Breisgau, Berlin. Started career as civil servant; Ministry of: Commerce and Industry, Berlin, 1939; Transport, Baden Württemberg, 1946-51; Foreign Affairs, Bonn, 1951; Sec., Legal Cttee and Conf. Cttee of Bundesrat, 1951-55; Judge, Federal Constitutional Court, 1955-70. Hon. Prof., Univ. of Heidelberg, 1965. Hon. Bencher, Middle Temple, 1976. Awarded Grand Cross Bundesverdienstkreuz, with star and sash, of Federal Germany, 1970. *Publications:* Die Enteignung, 1938; Bonner Vertrag mit Zusatzvereinbarungen, 1952; various contribs to professional jls. *Recreations:* literature, history. *Address:* Court of Justice of the European Communities, Kirchberg, PO Box 1406, Luxembourg. *T:* 4303 200; rue Nicolas Petit 4, Luxembourg-Ville, Luxembourg. *T:* 20230; Viertelstrasse 10, 7506 Bad Herrenalb-Neusatz, Federal Republic of Germany. *T:* 07083-2818.

KUZNETS, Prof. Simon, MA, PhD; Economist and Statistician, USA; Professor Emeritus of Economics, Harvard University; *b* Kharkov, Ukraine, 30 April 1901; *s* of Abraham Kuznets and Pauline (*née* Friedman); *m* 1929, Edith Handler; one *s* one *d*. *Educ:* Columbia Univ., USA. BA 1923, MA 1924, PhD 1926. Nat. Bureau of Economic Research, New York, 1927- (Mem. staff); Asst Prof. Economics and Statistics, Univ. of Pennsylvania, 1930-54; Associate Dir, Bureau of Planning and Statistics, WPB, Washington, DC, 1942-44; Economic Adviser, Nat. Resources Commn of China, 1946; Adviser, Nat. Income Cttee of India, 1950-51; Prof. of Political Economy, Johns Hopkins Univ., 1954-60; Prof. of Economics, Harvard Univ., 1960-71. Marshall Lectures, Cambridge Univ., delivered 1969; Nobel Prize in Economics, 1971. Hon. Fellow, Royal Statistical Soc. (England); FAAAS; Fell. Amer. Statistical Assoc.; Member: Internat. Statistical Inst.; Amer. Philosophical Soc.; Econometric Soc.; Royal Acad. of Sciences, Sweden, etc. Hon. ScD: Princeton; Pennsylvania; Harvard; Hon. DHL: Columbia; Brandeis, 1975; PhD Hebrew Univ. of Jerusalem. *Publications:* Cyclical Fluctuations in Retail and Wholesale Trade, 1926; Secular Movements in Production and Prices, 1930; Seasonal Variations in Industry and Trade, 1934; Commodity Flow and Capital Formation, 1938; National Income and its Composition (2 vols, 1919-38), 1941; National Product since 1869, 1946; Upper Income Shares, 1953; Economic Change, 1954; Six Lectures on Economic Growth, 1959; Capital in the American Economy, 1961; Modern Economic Growth, 1966; Economic Growth of Nations: Total Output and Production Structure, 1971; Population, Capital and Growth, 1974. *Address:* Department of Economics, Harvard University, Cambridge, Mass 02138, USA; 67 Francis Avenue, Cambridge, Mass 02138, USA.

KWAKYE, Dr Emmanuel Bamfo; Vice-Chancellor, University of Science and Technology, Kumasi, Ghana, since 1974; *b* 19 March 1933; *s* of Rev. W. H. Kwakye and F. E. A. Kwakye; *m* 1964, Gloria E. (*née* Mensah); two *d*. *Educ:* a Presbyterian sch., Ghana; Achimota Secondary Sch., Ghana; Technical Univ., Stuttgart, West Germany (DipIng, DrIng). Development Engr, Siemens & Halske, Munich, W Germany, 1960-62; Univ. of Science and Technology, Kumasi: Lectr, 1964; Sen. Lectr, 1966; Associate Prof., 1966; Head of Dept, 1970; Dean of Faculty, 1971; Pro Vice-Chancellor, 1971. *Publications:* design and research reports on digital equipment. *Recreations:* tennis, indoor games, opera and operette. *Address:* University of Science and Technology, Kumasi, Ghana. *T:* Kumasi 5351 (ext. 200).

KWAN SAI KHEONG; Vice-Chancellor, University of Singapore, since 1975; *b* 11 Sept. 1920; *s* of F. H. Kwan; *m* 1945, Sim Poh Geok; one *s* one *d*. *Educ:* Raffles Instn, Singapore;

Raffles Coll., Singapore; Royal College of Art, London. BA Hons, ARCA. Teacher, 1946-53; various appts in Min. of Educn; Permanent Sec. and Dir of Educn, Singapore, 1966-75; concurrently Chm., Singapore Nat. Commn for UNESCO, 1968-75. Hon. DLitt, Singapore, 1973; Hon. DEd, Chulalongkorn Univ., Bangkok, 1977. Public Administration Medal (Gold, Singapore Govt award), 1963; Meritorious Service Medal (Singapore Govt), 1968; L'Ordre des Palmes Académiques (French Govt), 1977. *Recreations:* painting, inventing. *Address:* 34-N Mount Elizabeth, Singapore 9. *T:* 2351272. *Clubs:* Pyramid, American, Island Country (all in Singapore).

KWAPONG, Alexander Adum, MA, PhD Cantab; Vice-Chancellor, University of Ghana, 1966-76; *b* Akropong, Akwapim, 8 March 1927; *s* of E. A. Kwapong and Theophilia Kwapong; *m* 1956, Evelyn Teiko Caesar, Ada; five *d*. *Educ:* Presbyterian junior and middle schools, Akropong; Achimota Coll.; King's Coll., Cambridge (Exhibr, Minor Schol. and Foundn Schol.). BA 1951, MA 1954, PhD 1957, Cantab. 1st cl. prelims, Pts I and II, Classical Tripos, 1951; Sandys Res. Student, Cambridge Univ.; Richards Prize, Rann Kennedy Travel Fellowship, King's Coll., Cambridge. Lectr in Classics, UC Gold Coast, 1953, Sen. Lectr in Classics 1960; Vis. Prof., Princeton Univ., 1961-62; Prof. of Classics, Univ. of Ghana, 1962; Dean of Arts, Pro-Vice-Chancellor, Univ. of Ghana, 1963-65. Chairman: Educn Review Cttee, Ghana Govt, 1966-67; Smithsonian Instn 3rd Internat. Symposium, 1969; Assoc. of Commonwealth Univs, 1971. Member: Admin. Bd, Internat. Assoc. Univs, Paris; Exec. Bd, Assoc. African Univs; Bd of Trustees, Internat. Council for Educnl Develt, NY; Aspen Inst. for Humanistic Studies; Bd of Dirs, Internat. Assoc. for Cultural Freedom, Paris. Fellow, Ghana Academy of Arts and Sciences. Hon. DLitt Warwick. *Publications:* contribs to: Grecs et Barbars, 1962; Dawn of African History (ed R. Oliver); Man and Beast: Comparative Social Behaviour (ed J. F. Eisenberg and W. S. Dillon), 1971; various articles in classical jls, especially on Ancient and Greco-Roman Africa; various addresses and lectures. *Recreations:* tennis, billiards, music and piano-playing. *Club:* Athenæum.

KYLE, Elisabeth, (Agnes M. R. Dunlop); novelist and writer of books for children; *d* of late James Dunlop, Ronaldshaw Park, Ayr; unmarried. *Publications:* first novel published 1932; since then she has had about fifty books published, in Britain and America (also in translations); The Begonia Bed, 1934; Orangefield, 1938; The Mirrors of Versailles, 1939; Broken Glass, 1940; The White Lady, 1941; But We Are Exiles, 1942; The Pleasure Dome, 1943; The Skaters' Waltz, 1944; Carp Country, 1946; Mally Lee, 1947; A Man of Talent, 1948; Douce, 1950; The Tontine Belle, 1951; Conor Sands, 1952; Forgotten as a Dream, 1953; The Regent's Candlesticks, 1954; A Stillness in the Air, 1956; The Other Miss Evans, 1958; Oh Say, Can You See?, 1959; Return to the Alcazar, 1962; Mirror Dance, 1970; The Scent of Danger, 1971; The Silver Pineapple, 1972; *children's books:* Visitors from England, 1941; Vanishing Island, 1942; Behind the Waterfall, 1944; The Seven Sapphires, 1944; Holly Hotel, 1945; Lost Karin, 1946; The Mirrors of Castle Doone, 1947; West Wind, 1948; The House on the Hill, 1949; The Provost's Jewel, 1950; The Lintowers, 1951; The Captain's House, 1952; The Reiver's Road, 1953; The House of the Pelican, 1954; Caroline House, 1955; Run to Earth, 1957; Queen of Scots, 1957; Maid of Orleans, 1957; The Money Cat, 1958; The Eagle's Nest, 1961; Girl with a Lantern, 1961; Girl With An Easel, 1963; Girl With A Pen, 1964; Girl With A Song, 1964; Victoria, 1964; Girl with a Destiny, 1965; The Boy who asked for More, 1966; Love is for the Living, 1966; High Season, 1968; Queen's Evidence, 1969; The Song of the Waterfall, 1969; The Stilt Walkers, 1972; The Heron Tree, 1973; Free As Air, 1974; Down the Water, 1975; The Yellow Coach, 1976; All the Nice Girls, 1976; The Key of the Castle, 1976. *Recreations:* music, travel, collecting antiques. *Address:* 10 Carrick Park, Ayr, Scotland. *T:* Ayr 63074.

KYLE, Air Chief Marshal Sir Wallace (Hart), GCB 1966 (KCB 1960; CB 1953); KCVO 1977; CBE 1945; DSO 1944; DFC 1941; Governor of Western Australia, since 1975; *b* 22 Jan. 1910; *s* of A. Kyle, Kalgoorlie, Western Australia; *m* 1941, Molly Rimington (*née* Wilkinson); three *s* one *d*. *Educ:* Guildford Sch., WA; RAF Coll., Cranwell. 17 Sqdn, 1930-31; Fleet Air Arm, 1931-34; Flying Instructor, 1934-39; served War of 1939-45; Bomber Command, 1940-45; Staff Coll., 1945-47; Middle East, 1948-50; ADC to King George VI, 1949; Asst Commandant, RAF Coll., Cranwell, 1950-52; Dir of Operational Requirements, Air Ministry, 1952-54; AOC Malaya, 1955-57; ACAS (Op. Req.), 1957-59. AOC-in-C Technical Training Command, 1959-62; VCAS, 1962-65; AOC-in-C, Bomber Command, 1965-68, Strike Command, 1968; retired. ADC to the Queen, 1952-56. Air Marshal, 1961; Air Chief Marshal, 1964; Air ADC to the Queen, 1966-68. KStJ 1976. *Recreations:* cricket, squash, golf. *Address:* Government House, Perth, WA 6000, Australia. *Club:* Royal Air Force.

KYNASTON, Nicolas; freelance organist, since 1971; *b* 10 Dec. 1941; *s* of Roger Tewkesbury Kynaston and Jessie Dearn Caecilia Kynaston (*née* Parkes); *m* 1961, Judith Felicity Heron; two *s* two *d*. *Educ:* Westminster Cathedral Choir Sch.; Downside; Accademia Musicale Chigiana, Siena; Conservatorio San Cecilia, Rome; Royal Coll. of Music. Organist of Westminster Cathedral, 1961-71; concert career, 1971-, travelling throughout Europe, North America, Asia and Africa. Début recital, Royal Festival Hall, 1966; Recording début, 1968. Jury member: Grand Prix de Chartres, 1971; St Albans Internat. Organ Festival, 1975. Hon. FRCO 1976. Records incl. 5 nominated Critic's Choice; EMI/CFP Sales Award, 1974; MTA nomination Best Solo Instrumental Record of the Year, 1977. *Recreations:* walking, church architecture. *Address:* The Old Vicarage, Wiggenhall Saint Peter, near King's Lynn, Norfolk. *T:* Saint Germans 301.

KYNCH, Prof. George James, ARCS, DIC, PhD (London); FIMA; Professor of Mathematics at the Institute of Science and Technology and in the University of Manchester, since 1957; Dean, Faculty of Technology, 1973-75; *b* 26 Oct. 1915; *s* of Vincent Kynch; *m* 1944, Eve, *d* of Edward A. Robinson; one *s* two *d*. *Educ:* Selhurst Grammar Sch.; Imperial Coll. of Science, London. BSc in physics, 1935, and mathematics, 1936; PhD 1939; Sir John Lubbock Memorial Prize, 1936. Demonstrator at Imperial Coll., 1937; Lecturer at Birmingham Univ., 1942-52; Prof. of Applied Mathematics, University Coll. of Wales, Aberystwyth, 1952-57. Founder Mem., Council of Inst. of Mathematics and its Applications, 1963-66; President: Northenden Civic Soc., 1966-; Manchester Literary and Philosophical Soc., 1971-73. Hon. MScTech Manchester, 1960. *Publications:* Mathematics for the Chemist, 1955; articles in scientific jls. *Recreations:* caravanning, dry stone wall-building, canals, cruising. *Address:* Rectory Cottage, Ford Lane, Northenden, Manchester M22 4NQ; University of Manchester Institute of Science and Technology, PO Box 88, Sackville Street, Manchester M60 1QD. *T:* 061-236 3311.

KYNNAIRD, Viscount; Prince Don Filippo Giambattista Francesco Aldo Maria Rospigliosi; *b* 4 July 1942; *s* and *heir* of 11th Earl of Newburgh, *qv*; *m* 1972, Donna Luisa, *d* of Count Annibale Caccia Dominioni; one *d*.

KYRLE POPE, Rear-Adm. Michael Donald, CB 1969; MBE 1946; *b* 1 Oct. 1916; *e s* of late Comdr R. K. C. Pope, DSO, OBE, RN retd, and of Mrs A. J. Pope (*née* Macdonald); *m* 1947, Angela Suzanne Layton; one *s* one *d*. *Educ:* Wellington Coll., Berks. Joined RN, 1934; Sen. Naval Off., Persian Gulf, 1962-64; MoD (Naval Intell.), 1965-67; Chief of Staff to C-in-C Far East, 1967-69; retd 1970. Comdr 1951; Capt. 1958; Rear-Adm. 1967. Gen. Manager, Middle East Navigation Aids Service, Bahrain, 1971-77. *Recreations:* country pursuits, sailing. *Address:* Hopfields, Westmill, Buntingford, Herts. *T:* Royston 71835. *Club:* Army and Navy.
See also Sir J. E. Pope.

L

LABOUCHERE, Sir George (Peter), GBE 1964; KCMG 1955 (CMG 1951); *b* 2 Dec. 1905; *s* of late F. A. Labouchere; *m* 1943, Rachel Katherine, *d* of Hon. Eustace Hamilton-Russell. *Educ:* Charterhouse Sch.; Sorbonne, Paris. Entered Diplomatic Service, 1929. Served in Madrid, Cairo, Rio de Janeiro, Stockholm, Nanking, Buenos Aires. UK Deputy-Commissioner for Austria, 1951-53; HM Minister, Hungary, 1953-55; Ambassador to Belgium, 1955-60; Ambassador to Spain, 1960-66. Retired, 1966. Member of Council, Friends of the Tate Gallery; Mem., Dilettanti Society; FRSA. *Recreations:* shooting, fishing, Chinese ceramics, contemporary painting and sculpture. *Address:* Dudmaston, Bridgnorth, Salop. *Clubs:* Brooks's, Pratt's, Beefsteak.

LABOUISSE, Henry (Richardson); Executive Director, United Nations Children's Fund (UNICEF), since 1965; lawyer, US; *b* New Orleans, La., 11 Feb. 1904; *s* of Henry Richardson Labouisse; *m* 1935, Elizabeth Scriven Clark (*d* 1945); one *d*; *m* 1954, Eve Curie, *qv*. *Educ:* Princeton Univ. (AB); Harvard

Univ. (LLB). Attorney-at-Law, NYC, 1929-41. Joined US State Dept, 1941; Minister Economic Affairs, US Embassy, Paris, 1945; Chief, Special Mission to France of Economic Co-operation Administration, 1951-54; Director, UN Relief and Works Agency for Palestine Refugees, 1954-58; Consultant, International Bank for Reconstruction and Development, 1959-61 (Head of IBRD Mission to Venezuela, 1959); Director, International Co-operation Admin., 1961-62; US Ambassador to Greece, 1962-65. Hon. LLD: University of Bridgeport, 1961; Princeton Univ., 1965; Lafayette Coll., 1966; Tulane Univ., 1967. *Recreations:* swimming, golf, reading. *Address:* UNICEF, United Nations, New York, NY 10017, USA; 1 Sutton Place South, NY 10022, USA. *Clubs:* Century Association, University (NY); Metropolitan, Chevy Chase (Washington).

LABOUISSE, Mrs H. R.; *see* Curie, Eve.

LACEY, Daniel; *see* Lacey, W. D.

LACEY, George William Brian; Keeper, Department of Transport, Science Museum, London, since 1971; *b* 15 Nov. 1926; *m* 1956, Lynette (*née* Hogg); two *s*. *Educ:* Brighton, Hove and Sussex Grammar Sch., 1938-44; Brighton Technical Coll., 1944-47. BSc(Eng) 2nd Cl. Hons (External, London). National Service, REME, 1947-49. Rolls-Royce Ltd, Derby: Grad. Apprentice, Tech. Asst, Mechanical Develt and Performance Analysis, 1949-54. Asst Keeper, Science Museum, London, SW7, 1954. Chairman: Historical Gp, Royal Aeronautical Soc., 1971-; Assoc. British Transport Museums, 1973-. *Recreation:* golf. *Address:* 7 Wilmington Close, Hassocks, W Sussex BN6 8QB. *T:* Hassocks 3231.

LACEY, Gerald, CIE 1942; BSc; FCGI; FICE; FRSA; Chartered Civil Engineer; Consultant, Sir M. Macdonald and Partners, 1950-75, retired; *b* 26 July 1887; 3rd *s* of late Thomas Stephen Lacey, MInstCE; *m* 1918, Elsie Ann, *d* of Charles Willford, ISO, PWD; two *s*. *Educ:* Westminster City Sch.; City and Guilds Central Tech. Coll., London. Course in civil and mechanical engineering, Central Tech. Coll., 1904-07; Bramwell medallist; BSc Engineering, 1st Class Hons, London Univ.; early training with G. H. Hill and Sons, Consulting Engineers, Westminster, Thames Conservancy and Chiswick Urban District Council; Assistant Engineer, Indian Service of Engineers, 1910; Military Service attached 1st KGO Sappers and Miners, 1917-19; 3rd Afghan War, 1919; Under-Secretary to Government, PWD, 1924-27; Irrigation Research Officer and Prof. Civil Engineering, Roorkee Coll., 1928-32; Superintending Engineer, 1934; Member of Council Inst. of Civil Engineers, 1940; Chief Engineer Eastern Canals. Irrigation Branch PWD, UP, 1941; retired 1942; Lieut-Colonel Corps of Indian Engineers, 1942-44; Prof. Civil Engineering, Roorkee Coll., March 1945; Principal Roorkee Coll., Dec. 1945; retired, Dec. 1946; Member: Colonial Office East Africa Rice Mission, 1948; British Honduras Rice Mission, 1949; Abyan Mission (Aden Protectorate), 1951; British Guiana Mission, 1953; Co-Director FAO, UN Training Centre and Study Tour on Irrigation and Drainage, held in USSR 1956; Aden Protectorate, 1957. Drainage and Irrigation Adviser, part-time, CO, 1950-58. Kennedy Gold Medal of Punjab Engineer Congress, 1930; Awarded Telford Gold Medal of InstCE, 1958. *Publications:* Papers in Procs ICE, 1930, 1934, 1946, 1958, 1972 and 1973. *Address:* Cottage on the Links, Steepways, Hindhead, Surrey GU26 6PG. *T:* Hindhead 5742. *Club:* East India, Devonshire, Sports and Public Schools.

LACEY, Janet, CBE 1960; Consultant to Churches' Council for Health and Healing, since 1973; Director, Family Welfare Association, 1969-73; Director, Christian Aid Department, British Council of Churches, 1952-May 1968, retired; *b* 25 Oct. 1903; *d* of Joseph Lacey, Property Agent, and Elizabeth Lacey. *Educ:* various schools, Sunderland; Drama Sch., Durham. YWCA, Kendal, 1926; General Secretary, YMCA/YWCA Community Centre, Dagenham, 1932; YMCA Education Secretary, BAOR, Germany, 1945; Youth Secretary, British Council of Churches, 1947. Hon. DD Lambeth, 1975. *Publications:* A Cup of Water, 1970; series booklets, Refugees, Aid to Developing Countries, Meeting Human Need with Christian Aid, 1956-64. *Recreations:* theatre, music, reading, crosswords. *Address:* Flat 8, Lesley Court, Strutton Ground, SW1. *T:* 01-222 4573. *Club:* Nikaean.

LACEY, (William) Daniel, CBE 1961; Director-General, Design Office, Department of the Environment, Property Services Agency, since 1975; *b* 8 Jan. 1923; *s* of Ivor Ewart and Mary Lacey; *m* 1946, Julie Ellen (*née* Chandler); no *c*. *Educ:* Bishop Gore's Grammar Sch., Swansea. FRIBA 1967; MRTPI. Assistant Architect, Herts County Council, 1946-55; Assistant County Architect, Notts County Council, 1955-58; County Architect, Notts County Council, 1958-64; Chief Architect,

1964-69, Head of Architects and Building Br., 1969-75, DES. RIBA: Hon. Sec., 1967-69; Vice-Pres., 1971-72. Awarded Gran Premio Con Menzione Speciale at Milan Triennale Exhibition, 1960. *Publications:* various papers in Architectural Journals. *Recreation:* gardening. *Address:* c/o Department of the Environment, 2 Marsham Street, SW1. *Club:* Reform.

LACHMAN, Harry; impressionist painter; film director; *b* La Salle, Illinois, 29 June 1886; *m* 1927 (in France), Quon Tai, Chinese concert singer. *Educ:* La Salle High Sch.; High School at Ann Arbor. Orphan at age of ten. Made his own way by selling newspapers, waiting on table at college; Cover Artist, Saturday Evening Post, Colliers, McCall's Cosmopolitan Magazines; went to France with his savings, 1912, and painted for the first time in his life; three months later had two pictures accepted and hung in the Salon Nationale, Paris; since then has shown in various American Exhibitions, England, Spain, and Paris Salons; four paintings bought by the French Government for the Musée du Luxembourg, the National Museum of France; decorated with the cross of the Legion of Honor for services rendered 1914-20 and for artistic achievements; managed the Metro-Goldwyn Studio in Nice, 1927; directed pictures in England for Paramount, 1929: Under the Greenwood Tree, The Outsider, Aren't We All, Down Our Street; directed pictures in France for Paramount, 1930: La Belle Marinière, La Couturière de Luneville, Mistigri; went to Hollywood to direct for Fox, 1932: Face in the Sky, Paddy the Next Best Thing, Charlie Chan at the Circus, Baby Take a Bow (first Shirley Temple starring picture), The Man Who Lived Twice, The Devil is Driving, It Happened in Hollywood, Our Relations, No Time to Marry, George White Scandals, Charlie Chan in Rio, Murder Over New York, Dead Men Tell; went to England to direct for Fox, 1939: They Came By Night, 1942. Discovered: Rita Hayworth, Merle Oberon, Margot Graham, Binnie Barnes, Phyllis Calvert, Jean Gabin; directed: Spencer Tracy, Gertrude Lawrence, Sir John Gielgud, Cary Grant, Madeline Renaud, Grace Moore, Noël-Noël, Pierre Blanchard. After 30 years returned to painting and exhib. in Hammer Galls, New York; exhib. Los Angeles, 1959. Has been painting in Spain, Morocco, Italy and France. Represented in: Chicago Art Inst.; Luxembourg Museum, Paris; Min. of Beaux Arts, Paris; Museum of Modern Art, Rome, etc. Chevalier de l'Ordre des Arts et des Lettres France,1967; Most Honoured Citizen of Los Angeles; Knight of Mark Twain. *Recreation:* fishing. *Address:* 718 N Beverly Drive, Beverly Hills, Calif 90210, USA.

LACHS, Henry Lazarus; a Recorder of the Crown Court since 1972; *b* 31 Dec. 1927; *s* of Samuel and Mania Lachs; *m* 1959, Edith Bergel; four *d. Educ:* Liverpool Institute High Sch.; Pembroke Coll., Cambridge (MA, LLB). Called to Bar, Middle Temple, 1951. Chm., Merseyside Mental Health Review Tribunal, 1968-; Asst Dep. Coroner of Liverpool, 1969-. Chm. of Governors, King David High Sch., Liverpool, 1971-. *Address:* 41 Menlove Gardens West, Liverpool L18 2ET. *T:* 051-722 5936.

LACHS, Manfred; Judge, International Court of Justice, since 1967 (President, 1973-76); *b* 21 April 1914; *m* Halina Kirst. *Educ:* Univs of Cracow, Vienna, London and Cambridge; Univ. of Cracow, Poland (LLM 1936, Dr jur 1937); Univ. of Nancy, France (Dr); Univ. of Moscow (DSc Law). Legal Adviser, Polish Ministry Internat. Affairs, 1947-66 (Ambassador, 1960-66). Prof., Acad. Polit. Sci., Warsaw, 1949-52; Prof. Internat. Law, Univ. of Warsaw, 1952; Dir, Inst. Legal Scis, Polish Academy of Sciences, 1961-67. Chm., Legal Cttee, UN Gen. Assemblies, 1949-52, 1955; Rep. of Poland, UN Disarmament Cttee, 1962-63. Rapporteur, Gen. Colloque. Internat. Assoc. Juridical Sciences, UNESCO, Rome, 1948; Internat. Law Commn, UN, 1962; Chm., Legal Cttee UN Peaceful Uses of Outer Space, 1962-66; Vice-Pres., UNITAR. Member: Inst. of Internat. Law; Curatorium, Hague Acad. of Internat. Law (Vice-Pres.); Acad. of Bologna; Polish Acad. of Sciences. Hon. Mem., Amer. Soc. Internat. Law; LLD (Hon.), Univs of: Budapest 1967; Algiers 1969; Delhi 1969; Nice 1972; Halifax, 1973; Bruxelles, 1973; Bucarest, 1974; New York, 1974; Southampton, 1975; Howard (Washington), 1975; Sofia, 1975; Vancouver, 1976; London, 1976. Gold medal for outstanding contribs devel. rule of law outer space, 1966; World Jurist Award for enormous contrib. to improvement of justice, Washington, 1975; also other awards. *Publications:* War Crimes, 1945; The Geneva Agreements on Indochina, 1954; Multilateral Treaties, 1958; The Law of Outer Space, 1964; Polish-German Frontier, 1964; The Law of Outer Space—an experience in law making, 1972; numerous essays and articles in eleven languages. *Address:* International Court of Justice, Peace Palace, The Hague, Holland. *T:* 92-44-41.

LACK, Henry Martyn, RE 1948 (ARE 1934); ARCA 1933; Artist; *b* 5 Dec. 1909; *s* of Arthur Henry Lack, Bozeat, Northants, and Laura Sophia Keyston; *m* 1941, Phyllis Mary Hafford, Leicester; no *c. Educ:* Wellingborough Sch.; Leicester College of Art (Royal Exhibition); Royal College of Art. Member of Sakkarah Expedition (Egypt), 1934-36. Master: Christ's Hospital, Horsham, 1937-46; Northampton School of Art, 1947; Tutor, Engraving School, RCA, South Kensington, 1947-53; Senior Master, Hastings School of Art, 1953-68, Acting Principal part 1968; Mem. Epigraphic Survey, Oriental Inst., Univ. of Chicago, at Luxor, Egypt, 1968-76. Served War of 1939-45 (Captain), in North Africa, Sicily, Italy and Middle East, 1942-46. Represented by prints in BM and V&A; Works purchased by Contemporary Art Soc., British Council, Univ. of Reading, S London Art Gallery. Has exhibited widely abroad through the British Council and at home at Royal Academy and Royal Society of Painter-Etchers and Engravers, etc. *Recreations:* travel, gardening. *Address:* 17 White Rock, Hastings, Sussex TN34 1JY.

LACK, Victor John Frederick, FRCP, FRCS; FRCOG; retired. *Educ:* London Hospital. Examiner: Universities of Oxford and Cambridge and Central Midwives' Board; Midwifery and Diseases of Women Conjoint Board, London; late Lectr in Midwifery and Diseases of Women, Birmingham Univ.; Asst Obst. Queen Elizabeth Hosp., Birmingham; Obst. Regist., Ho. Surg. and Ho. Phys. London Hosp. Obstetrical and Gynæcological Surgeon, London Hospital; Cons. Obstetrician Greenwich Borough Council Maternity Home; Gynæcologist King George's Hosp., Ilford; Obst. and Gyn. Surgeon, Royal Bucks Hosp., Aylesbury. FRSM (Mem. Obst. Sect.); a Vice-Pres., RCOG, 1955-. *Publications:* (jointly) Ten Teachers of Midwifery and Diseases of Women. Contrib. to medical jls. *Address:* 82 Bradwell Road, Loughton, Milton Keynes, Bucks MK8 0AL. *T:* Shenley Church End 243.

LACON, Sir George Vere Francis, 7th Bt, *cr* 1818; *b* 25 Feb. 1909; *s* of Sir George Haworth Ussher Lacon, 6th Bt and Vere Valerie Florence Eleanore (*d* 1916), *o d* of late H. S. H. Lacon, Ormesby Hall, Norfolk; *S* father 1950; *m* 1935, Hilary Blanche (marriage dissolved, 1956) *yr d* of C. J. Scott, Adyar, Walberswick; two *s*; *m* 1957, Kathlyn, *d* of late E. Pilbrow, London. *Educ:* Eton. *Heir: s* Edmund Vere Lacon [*b* 3 May 1936; *m* 1963, Gillian, *o d* of J. H. Middleditch, Wrentham, Suffolk; one *s* one *d*]. *Address:* Cliff House, Southwold, Suffolk.

LACOSTE, Paul, DUP; Rector, Université de Montréal, since 1975; *b* 24 April 1923; *s* of Emile Lacoste and Juliette Boucher Lacoste; *m* 1973, Louise Marcil; one *d. Educ:* Univ. de Montréal (BA, MA, LPh, LLL). DUP 1948. Fellow, Univ. of Chicago, 1946-47; Univ. de Montréal: Prof., Faculty of Philosophy, 1948; Full Prof., 1958; Vice-Rector, 1968-75. Practising lawyer, 1964-66. Hon. LLD McGill, 1975. *Publications:* (jtly) Justice et paix scolaire, 1962; A Place of Liberty, 1964; Le Canada au seuil du siècle de l'abondance, 1969; Principes de gestion universitaire, 1970. *Address:* Université de Montréal, PO Box 6128, Montréal H3C 3J7, Canada. *T:* 343-6776; 2900 boulevard Edouard-Montpetit, Montréal. *Club:* St-Denis (Montréal).

LA COUR, Leonard Francis, OBE 1973 (MBE 1952); FRS 1970; Professor, University of East Anglia, since 1973; *b* 28 July 1907; *o c* of Francis La Cour and Maud (*née* Coomber); *m* 1935, Anne Wilkes; no *c. Educ:* Merton Sch., Surrey. John Innes Institute: Sen. Exper. Officer 1948, Chief Exper. Officer 1956, Senior Principal Scientific Officer, 1970, retired 1972. Hon. MSc East Anglia, 1969. *Publications:* (with C. D. Darlington) The Handling of Chromosomes, 6th edn 1976; various research articles in scientific jls. *Recreation:* gardening. *Address:* 24 Cranleigh Rise, Eaton, Norwich NR4 6PQ.

LACRETELLE, J. de; *see* de Lacretelle.

LACY, George Arthur; Managing Director and Chief Executive Officer, Chrysler United Kingdom Ltd, since 1976; *b* 26 Jan. 1921; *s* of William Charles Lacy; *m* 1949, Pauline DeLaurier; one *s* two *d. Educ:* University of Toronto. General Plants Manager, Chrysler Canada Ltd, 1972-73; Vice Pres. Manufacturing, Chrysler Canada Ltd, 1973-76; Dep. Man. Dir, Chrysler UK Ltd, 1976. *Recreation:* golf. *Address:* Chrysler United Kingdom Ltd, Whitley, Coventry CV3 4GB. *T:* Coventry 303505.

LACY, Sir Hugh Maurice Pierce, 3rd Bt, *cr* 1921; *b* 3 Sept 1943; *s* of Sir Maurice John Pierce Lacy, 2nd Bt, and of his 2nd wife, Nansi Jean, *d* of late Myrddin Evans, Bangor, Caernarvonshire; *S* father, 1965; *m* 1968, Deanna, *d* of Howard Bailey. *Educ:* Aiglon Coll., Switzerland. *Heir: b* Patrick Bryan Finucane Lacy [*b* 18 April 1948; *m* 1971, Phyllis Victoria, *d* of E. P. H. James; one *s*].

LADAS, Mrs Diana Margaret; *b* 8 Feb. 1913; *er d* of late Bertram Hambro and late Mrs Charles Boyle; *m* 1945, Alexis Christopher Ladas (marr. diss. 1955); one *s*. *Educ:* Downe House Sch.; Girton Coll., Cambridge. Before the war, Sec. in Geneva, Malta and London. During War of 1939-45, worked as temp. asst Principal in Min. of Economic Warfare, Board of Trade and Political Warfare executive in Cairo. Transferred to UNRRA, worked in Athens, Washington and London; on the staff of British Information Services, in New York, 1948-50. Began teaching at Westminster Tutors, 1955; joined staff of Heathfield Sch., 1958; Dep. Head of Moira House Sch., 1959, Head Mistress, 1960; Vice-Principal of Queen's Gate Sch., 1962-65; Head Mistress, Heathfield Sch., 1965-72. *Recreations:* gardening and travelling. *Address:* Wick Farm, Langport, Somerset. *T:* Langport 250193.

LAFITTE, Prof. François; Professor of Social Policy and Administration, University of Birmingham, since Oct. 1959; *b* 3 Aug. 1913; *s* of Françoise Lafitte and adopted *s* of late Havelock Ellis; *m* 1938, Eileen (*née* Saville). (one *s* decd). *Educ:* Collège Municipal, Maubeuge; George Green's Sch., Poplar; St Olave's Grammar Sch., Southwark; Worcester Coll., Oxford. Research and translating for Miners' Internat. Fed., 1936-37; on research staff, and subseq. Dep. Sec., PEP, 1938-43; on editorial staff of The Times, as special writer on social questions, 1943-59; Chm. of PEP research groups on health services, 1943-46, on housing policy, 1948-51. Dean of Faculty of Commerce and Social Science, Birmingham, Univ., 1965-68. Member: Home Office Advisory Council on the Treatment of Offenders, 1961-64; Adv. Cttees Social Science Research Council, 1966-69; Redditch New Town Corp., 1964-75; Chm., British Pregnancy Adv. Service, 1968-. *Publications:* The Internment of Aliens, 1940; Britain's Way to Social Security, 1945; Family Planning in the Sixties, 1964; (part author) Socially Deprived Families in Britain, 1970; many PEP Planning monographs; many papers on abortion and related issues; contributed to British Journal of Delinquency, Eugenics Review, Chambers's Encyclopædia. etc. *Address:* The University, Birmingham B15 2TT. *T:* 021-472 1301; 77 Oakfield Road, Birmingham B29 7HL. *T:* 021-472 2709. *Clubs:* Royal Society of Medicine (London); University (Birmingham).

LAGDEN, Godfrey William; Director: Elm Park Petrol & Oil Supplies Ltd, since 1958; Preflor Ltd, since 1968; *b* 12 April 1906; *s* of Augustine William and Annie Lagden; *m* 1935, Dorothy Blanche Wheeler. *Educ:* Richmond Hill Sch., Richmond, Surrey. Sun Insurance Office, London, 1931-34; IBM (United Kingdom) Ltd, 1934-. MP (C) Hornchurch, 1955-66. *Recreations:* cricket, water polo, boxing, and dog breeding. *Address:* St Austell, 187 Southend Arterial Road, Hornchurch, Essex. *T:* Ingrebourne 42770. *Clubs:* Constitutional, Wig and Pen, Spanish.

LAGESEN, Air Vice-Marshal Philip Jacobus, CB 1974; DFC 1945; AFC 1959; Air Officer Commanding 1 Group, Bawtry, since 1975; *b* 25 Aug. 1923; *s* of late Philip J. Lagesen, Johannesburg, South Africa; *m* 1944, Dulcie, *d* of late H. McPherson, Amanzimtoti, Natal, S Africa; one *s* one *d*. *Educ:* Jeppe, Johannesburg. Served War, 1939-45, South African Air Force. Joined RAF, 1951; Flying Instructor, Rhodesia Air Trng Gp, 1952-55; Kenya, 1953-55; No 50 Squadron, 1955-57; Staff, RAF Flying Coll., Manby, 1957-59; PSO, C-in-C Middle East, 1959-61; Comdr, No 12 (B) Sqdn, 1961-64; Wing Comdr Ops, No 1 (B) Group 1964-66; CO, RAF Tengah, Singapore, 1966-69; SPSO, Strike Comd, 1969-70; Dir Ops (S), RAF, MoD, 1970-72; SASO, HQ Strike Comd, 1972-73; Dep. Comdr, RAF Germany, 1973-75. *Recreations:* golf, motoring. *Address:* c/o Lloyds Bank, 6 Pall Mall, SW1. *Club:* Royal Air Force.

LAGHZAOUI, Mohammed; Ouissam El Ouala (1st class) and Commander of the Order of the Crown, Morocco; Moroccan Ambassador to France, 1971-72; *b* Fez, Morocco, 27 Sept. 1906; *m* 1940, Kenza Bouayad; three *s* three *d*. *Educ:* Moulay Idriss Coll., Fez. Founded many commercial and industrial companies; Chm., Société marocaine des Transports Laghzaoui. During French Protectorate over Morocco, he was Mem. Government's Council (many times Chm.); one of principal Signatories to Act of Independence, 1944; Dir-Gen. of Nat. Security (apptd by late Mohammed V), 1956-60. Then, as Dir-Gen. of Office chérifien des Phosphates (first nat. mining concern) he promoted production and export; later, he was responsible for Office marocain des Phosphates, and Coordinator of Nat. Mining and Industrial Cos. In charge of four ministries: Industry, Mining, Tourism and Handicraft, and was Pres. of Afro-Asiatic Assoc. for Economic Development, 1966-69; Moroccan Ambassador to UK, 1969-71. Holds foreign

orders. *Recreations:* bridge, football. *Address:* Résidence Laghzaoui, Route de Suissi, Rabat, Morocco.

LAGOS, Archbishop of, (RC), since 1973; **Most Rev. Anthony Olubunmi Okogie,** DD; *b* Lagos, 16 June 1936. *Educ:* St Gregory's Coll., Lagos; St Peter and St Paul's Seminary, Ibadan; Urban Univ., Rome. Priest, 1966; appointments include: Acting Parish Priest, St Patrick's Church, Idumagbo; Asst Priest, Holy Cross Cathedral, Lagos; Religious Instructor, King's Coll., Lagos; Director of Vocations, Archdiocese of Lagos; Manager, Holy Cross Group of Schools, Lagos; Master of Ceremonies, Holy Cross Cathedral; Auxiliary Bishop of Oyo, 1971-72; Auxiliary Bishop to Apostolic Administrator, Archdiocese of Lagos, 1972-73. *Address:* Holy Cross Cathedral, PO Box 8, Lagos, Nigeria.

LAHORE, Bishop of, since 1968; **Rt. Rev. Inayat Masih;** *b* 14 Sept. 1918; *m* 1952, Farkhanda; one *d*. *Educ:* Punjab Univ., Lahore; Bishop's Coll., Calcutta; Serampore Univ. Curate, Holy Trinity cum Lahore Cathedral Parish, 1947-50; Vice-Princ., St John's Divinity Sch., Narowal, Dio. of Lahore, 1950-52; Priest i/c Pattoki District, 1952-53; higher studies in USA, 1953-55; Priest i/c Gojra District, Lahore Dio., 1955-59; Exec. Sec., West Pakistan Christian Coun., 1959-65; Archdeacon of Lahore, 1965-68. Moderator, Church of Pakistan, 1971-74. *Recreations:* reading, badminton. *Address:* Bishopsbourne, Cathedral Close, The Mall, Lahore, Pakistan. *T:* Lahore 53790.

LAIDLAW, Christophor Charles Fraser; a Managing Director, The British Petroleum Co. Ltd, since 1972; Chairman, BP Oil, since 1977; *b* 9 Aug. 1922; *m* 1952, Nina Mary Prichard; one *s* three *d*. *Educ:* Rugby Sch.; St John's Coll., Cambridge (MA). Served War of 1939-45: Europe and Far East, Major on Gen. Staff. Joined British Petroleum, 1948: BP Rep. in Hamburg, 1959-61; Gen. Manager, Marketing Dept, 1963-67; Dir, BP Trading, 1967; Dir (Ops), 1971-72; President, BP: Belgium, 1967-71; Italiana, 1972-73; Germany, 1972. *Recreation:* fishing. *Address:* Britannic House, Moor Lane, EC2Y 9BU. *Clubs:* Bath, Anglo-German.

LAIDLAW, William Allison, MA, LittD; Professor of Classics in the University of London, Queen Mary College, 1949-64, now Emeritus Professor; *b* 15 July 1898; *s* of James and Sarah A. Laidlaw. *Educ:* Wesley Coll., Dublin; Trinity Coll., University of Dublin. Classical Foundation Scholar, Vice-Chancellor's Medallist in Latin, Vice-Chancellor's Prize for Latin Prose; Senior Moderator in Classics and in Mental and Moral Science, 1922; Lecturer in Classics and Philosophy, University of W. Australia, 1923-28; Student of British Sch., Athens, 1929; Asst Lecturer in Classics, University Coll., Southampton, 1929-31; Lecturer in Latin, University of St Andrews, 1931-46; Reader in Classics, University of London, Queen Mary Coll., 1946-49; Ford Visiting Prof. of Classics, University of Ibadan, 1964-65. *Publications:* A History of Delos, 1933; The Prosody of Terence, 1938; Latin Literature, 1951; contribs to: Oxford Classical Dictionary, 1949; Fifty Years of Classical Scholarship, 1954, Chambers's Encyclopædia: articles, notes, reviews in various classical journals. *Recreation:* music. *Address:* Minvale, St Anthony's Road, Blundellsands, Liverpool L23 8TN. *T:* 051-924 1279.

LAILEY, John Raymond N.; *see* Nicholson-Lailey.

LAINE, Cleo, (Mrs Clementina Dinah Dankworth); vocalist; *b* 28 Oct. 1927; British; *m* 1st, 1947, George Langridge (marr. diss. 1957); one *s*; 2nd, 1960, John Philip William Dankworth, *qv*; one *s* one *d*. Joined Dankworth Orchestra, 1953. Melody Maker and New Musical Express Top Girl Singer Award, 1956; Moscow Arts Theatre Award for acting role in Flesh to a Tiger, 1958; Top place in Internat. Critics Poll by Amer. Jazz magazine, Downbeat, 1965. Lead, in Seven Deadly Sins, Edinburgh Festival and Sadler's Wells, 1961; acting roles in Edin. Fest., 1966, 1967. Many appearances with symphony orchestras performing Façade (Walton) and other compositions; played Julie in Show Boat, Adelphi, 1971. Frequent TV appearances. Woman of the Year, 9th annual Golden Feather Awards, 1973; Edison Award, 1974. *Recreation:* painting. *Address:* International Artistes Representation, Regent House, 233 Regent Street, WC1. *T:* 01-439 8401.

LAING, Austen, CBE 1973; Director General, British Fishing Federation Ltd, since 1962; *b* 27 April 1923; *s* of William and Sarah Ann Laing; *m* 1945, Kathleen Pearson; one *s* one *d*. *Educ:* Bede Grammar Sch., Sunderland; Newcastle Univ. BA (Social Studies) and BA (Econs). Lectr, Univ. of Durham, 1950-56; Administrator, Distant Water Vessels Develt Scheme, 1956-61. Mem. Cttee of Inquiry into Veterinary Profession, 1971-75. *Publications:* numerous articles in British and foreign jls on fishing industry. *Address:* Boulder Cottage, Swanland, North Ferriby, North Humberside HU14 3PE. *T:* Hull 631383. *Club:* Army and Navy.

LAING, Hector; Chairman, United Biscuits (Holdings) Ltd, since 1972 (Director, 1953; Managing Director, 1964); Director, Court of the Bank of England; *b* 12 May 1923; *s* of Hector Laing and Margaret Norris Grant; *m* 1950, Marian Clare, *d* of Maj.-Gen. Sir John Laurie, Bt, *qv*; three *s*. *Educ:* Loretto Sch., Musselborough, Scotland; Jesus Coll., Cambridge. Served War, Scots Guards, 1942-47 (American Bronze Star, despatches, 1944); final rank, Captain. McVitie & Price: Dir, 1947; Chm., 1963. Mem. Bd, Royal Insurance Co.; Chm., Food and Drink Industries Council, 1977-. *Recreations:* gardening, flying, fishing, shooting. *Address:* High Meadows, Windsor Road, Gerrards Cross, Bucks. *T:* Gerrards Cross 82437. *Club:* White's.

LAING, Prof. John Archibald, PhD; MRCVS; Courtauld Professor of Animal Husbandry and Hygiene, at Royal Veterinary College, University of London, since 1959; *b* 27 April 1919; *s* of late John and Alexandra Laing; *m* 1946, June Margaret Lindsay Smith, *d* of Hugh Lindsay Smith, Downham Market; one *s* two *d*. *Educ:* Johnston Sch.; Royal (Dick) School of Veterinary Studies, Edinburgh University; Christ's Coll. Cambridge. BSc(Edinburgh); MRCVS; PhD Cantab. FIBiol. Aleen Cust Scholar, Royal Coll. of Veterinary Surgeons. Research Officer, 1943-46, Asst Veterinary Investigation Officer, 1946-49, Ministry of Agriculture; Lecturer in Veterinary Science, 1949-51, Senior Lecturer in Veterinary Medicine, 1951-57, Reader in Veterinary Science, 1957-59, University of Bristol. Anglo-Danish Churchhill Fellowship, University of Copenhagen, 1954; Vis. Prof., Univ. of Queensland and John Thompson Memorial Lectr, 1970. Consultant to FAO, UN, 1955-56; Representative of FAO in Dominican Republic, 1957-58; Consultant to UNESCO in Central America, 1963-65; Mem., British Agricultural Mission to Peru, 1970. Editor, British Veterinary Journal. Sec., Perm. Cttee, Internat. Congress on Animal Reproduction; Member: Governing Body, Houghton Poultry Research Station, 1968-74; Council, Royal Veterinary Coll.; University Fedn for Animal Welfare (Treasurer, 1969-75; Chm., 1975-77). *Publications:* Fertility and Infertility in the Domestic Animals, 1955, 2nd edn 1970; papers on animal breeding and husbandry in various scientific journals. *Address:* Ayot St Lawrence, Herts. *T:* Stevenage 820413. *Clubs:* Athenæum, Farmers'.

LAING, Sir (John) Maurice, Kt 1965; Chairman: John Laing & Son Ltd; John Laing Construction Ltd; Director, Bank of England; *b* 1 Feb. 1918; *s* of Sir John Laing, *qv*; *m* 1940, Hilda Violet Richards; one *s*. *Educ:* St Lawrence Coll., Ramsgate. RAF, 1941-45. Member: UK Trade Missions to Middle East, 1953, and to Egypt, Sudan and Ethiopia, 1955; Economic Planning Bd, 1961; Export Guarantees Adv. Council, 1959-63; Min. of Transport Cttee of Inquiry into Major Ports of Gt Brit. (Rochdale Cttee), 1961-62; Nat. Economic Develt Council, 1962-66. First Pres., CBI, 1965-66; President: British Employers Confederation, 1964-65; Export Group for the Constructional Industries, 1976-; Fedn of Civil Engrg Contractors, 1977. Visiting Fellow, Nuffield Coll., 1965-70; A Governor: Administrative Staff Coll., 1966-72; Nat. Inst. of Economic and Social Research, 1964-. Hon. LLD University of Strathclyde, 1967. Has keen interest in Church activities at home and abroad. *Recreations:* sailing, swimming. *Address:* Reculver, 63 Totteridge Village, N20 8AG. *Clubs:* Royal Yacht Squadron, Royal Ocean Racing (Commodore, 1973-75, Admiral, 1976-), Royal Burnham Yacht (Burnham-on-Crouch), Royal Southern Yacht, etc.

LAING, Sir John (William), Kt 1959; CBE 1951; FIOB; Life President John Laing and Son Ltd, since 1957; *b* 24 Sept. 1879; *s* of John Laing, Sebergham, Cumberland; *m* 1910, Beatrice (*d* 1972), *y d* of William Harland, Chartered Accountant, Stockton on Tees; two *s*. *Educ:* Carlisle Grammar Sch. Past Member: Building Research Cttee (Chm. 1945); Nat. House Builders' (Past Vice-Chm.); Registration Council (Past Chm. Specification Cttee); Inst. of Builders (Past Mem. Council); Fedn of Civil Engrg Contractors (Past Mem. Cttee); British Standards Instn (Past Mem. Standing Cttee). Pres. London Bible Coll. Vice-President: British and Foreign Bible Soc.; Crusaders' Union; Mem. Council, Scripture Gift Mission; Trustee, Inter-Varsity Fellowship Trust Ltd; Vice-Pres. Fact and Faith Films. *Address:* Fair Holme, Marsh Lane, Mill Hill, NW7.

See also Sir John Maurice Laing, Sir W. K. Laing.

LAING, Sir Kirby; *see* Laing, Sir W. K.

LAING, Sir Maurice; *see* Laing, Sir J. M.

LAING, Percy Lyndon, CMG 1970; retired as Commissioner of Works, NZ; Chairman: NZ Natural Gas Corporation; Hume Industries (NZ) Ltd; Director, New Zealand Forest Products Ltd; *b* 12 July 1909; *s* of Percy William and Jessie Laing, Dunedin, NZ; *m* 1937, Mabel Collis Wood; one *s*. *Educ:* Otago Boys' High Sch.; Univ. of Canterbury, NZ. Chief Designing Engineer, NZ Min. of Works, 1951-55; Dir. of Roading (Highways), 1959-62; Comr of Works, 1965-69, retd. Pres. NZ Inst of Engineers, 1962. *Publications:* contribs to engineering jls, etc. *Recreations:* golf, fishing. *Address:* 53 Chesham Avenue, Taupo, New Zealand. *T:* 2115K. *Club:* Wellington (Wellington, NZ).

LAING, Ronald David, MB, ChB, DPM; Chairman, Philadelphia Association Ltd, since 1964; *b* 7 Oct. 1927; *s* of D. P. M. and Amelia Laing. *Educ:* Glasgow Univ. Glasgow and West of Scotland Neurosurgical Unit, 1951; Central Army Psychiatric Unit, Netley, 1951-52; Psychiatric Unit, Mil. Hosp., Catterick, 1952-53; Dept of Psychological Med., Glasgow Univ., 1953-56; Tavistock Clinic, 1956-60; Tavistock Inst. of Human Relations, 1960-; Fellow, Foundns Fund for Research in Psychiatry, 1960-67; Dir, Langham Clinic for Psychotherapy, 1962-65; Fellow, Tavistock Inst. of Med. Psychology, 1963-64; Principal Investigator, Schizophrenia and Family Research Unit, Tavistock Inst. of Human Relations, 1964-67. *Publications:* The Divided Self, 1960 (London and New York) (Pelican edn, 1962, Penguin repr. 1971); The Self and Others, 1961 (London and New York) (rev. edn 1969, Penguin, 1971); (jtly) Reason and Violence (introd. by J. P. Sartre), 1964 (London and New York) (Pantheon, 1971); (jtly) Sanity, Madness and the Family, 1965 (London and New York); The Politics of Experience and the Bird of Paradise (Penguin), 1967 (London, repr. 1971), (Pantheon, 1967, New York); Knots, 1970 (London), (Pantheon, 1970, New York), (Penguin, 1972); The Politics of the Family, 1971 (London); The Facts of Life, 1976 (Pantheon, New York); Do You Love Me, 1977 (London). *Address:* 2 Eton Road, NW3. *T:* 01-722 9448.

LAING, (William James) Scott; international trade and marketing consultant, New York City; *b* 14 April 1914; *er s* of late William Irvine Laing and Jessie C. M. Laing (*née* Scott); one *s*. *Educ:* George Watson's Coll., Edinburgh Univ. Appointed to Dept of Overseas Trade, 1937; Asst to Commercial Counsellor, British Embassy, Buenos Aires, 1938; Second Sec. (Commercial), Buenos Aires, 1944; First Sec. (Commercial), Helsinki, 1947; Consul, New York, 1950; Consul-Gen. (Commercial), New York, 1954; Counsellor (Commercial), Brussels and Luxembourg, 1955; Consultant to UN Secretariat, Financial Policies and Institutions Section, 1958, African Training Programme, 1960; Chief, Sales Section, UN Secretariat, 1962-76, retired. Editor, UN Jl, 1964. *Publications:* reports and articles on international commerce and finance. *Address:* 212 East 48th Street, New York, NY 10017, USA. *Club:* Caledonian.

LAING, Sir (William) Kirby, Kt 1968; JP, MA, FICE, FIOB; Deputy Chairman, The Laing Group of Cos, since 1976; *b* 21 July 1916; *s* of Sir John Laing, *qv*; *m* 1939, Joan Dorothy Bratt; three *s*. *Educ:* St Lawrence Coll., Ramsgate; Emmanuel Coll., Cambridge. Served with Royal Engineers, 1943-45. John Laing & Son Ltd: Pupil, 1937; Joint Man. Dir, 1946; Chm., 1957-76. President: London Master Builders Assoc., 1957; Reinforced Concrete Assoc., 1960; Nat. Fedn of Building Trades Employers, 1965, 1967 (Hon. Mem., 1975); ICE, 1973-74 (a Vice-Pres., 1970-73). Chm., Nat. Jt Council for Building Industry, 1968-74. Chm., Adv. Commn on Fixed Offshore Installations, Dept of Energy, 1975-. Member: DSIR Jt Cttee on Soils, 1958-61; BRS Building Ops and Economics Cttee, 1960-66; MPBW Nat. Consultative Cttee, 1965-67. Member: Board of Govs, St Lawrence Coll (Pres., 1977); St Stephen's Coll., Broadstairs; Court of Governors, The Polytechnic of Central London, 1963-. Trustee, Inter-Varsity Fellowship; Mem. Council, The Covenanter Union. Fellow, Fellowship of Engineering; Hon. Mem., Amer. Assoc. of Civil Engineers. *Publications:* papers in Proc. ICE and other jls concerned with construction. *Address:* John Laing and Son Ltd, NW7 2ER. *Club:* Naval and Military.

LAIRD, Edgar Ord, (Michael Laird), CMG 1969; MBE 1958; HM Diplomatic Service, retired; *b* 16 Nov. 1915; *s* of late Edgar Balfour Laird; *m* 1940, Heather Lonsdale Forrest; four *d*. *Educ:* Rossall; Emmanuel Coll., Camb. Surveyor, Uganda Protectorate, 1939. Served Army, 1939-46 (Major). Appointed to Malayan Civil Service, 1947; Sec. to Government, Federation of Malaya, 1953-55; Sec. for External Defence, Federation of Malaya, 1956; Sec., Federation of Malaya Constitutional

Commission, 1956-57; Dep. Sec., Prime Minister's Dept, Federation of Malaya, 1957. Appointed to Commonwealth Relations Office, 1958; First Sec. (Finance), Office of British High Comr, Ottawa, Canada, 1960-63; High Comr in Brunei, 1963-65; Dep. High Comr, Kaduna, 1965-69; RNC Greenwich, 1969-70; Head of Hong Kong and Indian Ocean Dept, FCO, 1970-72; British Govt Rep., West Indies Associated States, 1972-75. *Recreations:* music, reading. *Address:* Clarendon House, 33 The Strand, Topsham, Exeter. *Club:* Royal Commonwealth Society.

LAIRD, Gavin Harry; Member, Executive Council, Amalgamated Union of Engineering Workers, since 1975; Director, British National Oil Corporation, since 1976; *b* 14 March 1933; *s* of James and Frances Laird; *m* 1957, Catherine Gillies Campbell; one *d*. *Educ:* Clydebank High School. Convener of Shop Stewards, Singer Manufacturing Co. Ltd, UK, 1964-71; full-time Trade Union Official, 1971-. Part-time Dir, Highlands and Islands Develt Bd, 1975-76. Member: Scottish Industrial Develt Adv. Bd, 1975-; Adv. Council for Applied R&D, 1977-. *Recreations:* hill walking, reading, bowls. *Address:* 35 Holmdene Court, Southlands Grove, Bickley BR1 2DA. *T:* 01-464 2376. *Club:* AUEW Social Club (Clydebank).

LAIRD, Hon. Melvin R.; Senior Counsellor for National and International Affairs, Reader's Digest Association, since 1974; *b* 1 Sept. 1922; *s* of Melvin R. Laird and Helen Laird (*née* Connor); *m* 1945, Barbara Masters; two *s* one *d*. *Educ:* Carleton Coll., Northfield, Minn (BA 1944). Enlisted, US Navy, 1942, commissioned, 1944; served in Third Fleet and Task Force 58 (Purple Heart and other decorations). Elected: to Wisconsin State Senate, 1946 (re-elected, 1948); to US Congress, Nov. 1952 (83rd through 90th; Chm., House Republican Conf., 89th and 90th); Sec. of Defense, 1969-72; Counsellor to President of US, 1973-74. Director: Chicago Pneumatic Tool Co.; Metropolitan Life Insurance Co.; Northwest Airlines; Communications Satellite Corp.; Purolator Inc.; Investors Gp of Cos; Phillips Petroleum Co. Member Board of Trustees: George Washington Univ.; Kennedy Center. Various awards from Assocs, etc (for med. research, polit. science, public health, nat. educn); many hon. memberships and hon. degrees. *Publications:* A House Divided: America's Strategy Gap, 1962; Editor: The Conservative Papers, 1964; Republican Papers, 1968. *Recreations:* golf, fishing. *Address:* Suite 212, 1730 Rhode Island Avenue NW Washington, DC 20036, USA. *Club:* Burning Tree (Washington, DC).

LAIRD, Michael; *see* Laird, E. O.

LAITHWAITE, Prof. Eric Roberts; Professor of Heavy Electrical Engineering, Imperial College of Science and Technology, London, since 1964; *b* 14 June 1921; *s* of Herbert Laithwaite; *m* 1951, Sheila Margaret Gooddie; two *s* two *d*. *Educ:* Kirkham Gram. Sch.; Regent Street Polytechnic; Manchester Univ. RAF, 1941-46 (at RAE Farnborough, 1943-46). BSc 1949, MSc 1950. Manchester Univ.: Asst Lectr, 1950-53; Lectr, 1953-57; Sen. Lectr, 1957-64; PhD 1957; DSc 1964. Pres., Assoc. for Science Educn, 1970. S. G. Brown Award and Medal of Royal Society, 1966; Prof. of Royal Instn, 1967-. *Publications:* Propulsion without Wheels, 1966; Induction Machines for Special Purposes, 1966; The Engineer in Wonderland, 1967; Linear Electric Motors, 1971; The Dictionary of Butterflies and Moths, 1975; (with M. W. Thring) How to Invent, 1977; many papers in Proc. IEE (7 premiums) and other learned jls. *Recreations:* entomology, gardening. *Address:* The Circles, Wentworth Close, Ditton Hill, Surbiton, Surrey. *T:* 01-398 3919. *Club:* Athenæum.

LAITHWAITE, John, FIMechE, FInstPet; Vice Chairman, Capper Neill Ltd, since 1972; Chairman, Process Plant Association, since 1975; *b* 29 Nov. 1920; *s* of Tom Prescott Laithwaite and Mary Anne Laithwaite; *m* 1943, Jean Chateris; one *s* two *d*. *Educ:* Manchester Univ. (BSc Hons Mech. Eng). FIMechE 1974; FInstPet 1960; AMInstW 1950. Wm Neill & Son (St Helens) Ltd, 1942-43; Dartford Shipbuilding & Engineering Co., 1943-44; Dir, Wm Neill & Son (St Helens) Ltd, 1955-58, Man. Dir, 1958-64; Dir, Capper Neill Ltd, 1965, Man. Dir, 1968. Member: Council, Engrg Industries Council; NW Regional Management Centre. *Publications:* articles on process plant industry and pressure vessel standardisation. *Recreations:* shooting, golf. *Address:* Lane End, Hatton, Cheshire. *T:* Norcott Brook 446. *Clubs:* Royal Birkdale, Haydock Park.

LAITHWAITE, Sir (John) Gilbert, GCMG 1953 (KCMG 1948); KCB 1956; KCIE 1941 (CIE 1935); CSI 1938; Director, Inchcape Overseas Ltd, since 1969 (Deputy Chairman Inchcape & Co. Ltd, 1960-64; Director 1964-69); former Chairman: Bedford Life Assurance Co. Ltd; Bedford General Insurance Co. Ltd; UK Committee of Federation of Commonwealth Chambers of Commerce; *b* 5 July 1894; *e s* of late J. G. Laithwaite, formerly of the Post Office Survey. *Educ:* Clongowes; Trinity Coll., Oxford (Scholar). Hon. Fellow, Trinity Coll., Oxford, 1955. Served in France with 10th Lancs Fusiliers, 1917-18 (wounded); appointed to India Office, 1919; Principal, 1924; specially attached to Prime Minister (Mr Ramsay MacDonald) for 2nd Indian Round Table Conference, Sept.-Dec. 1931; Secretary, Indian Franchise (Lothian) Committee, Jan.-June 1932; Secretary, Indian Delimitation Cttee, Aug. 1935-Feb. 1936; Private Secretary to the Viceroy of India (Marquess of Linlithgow), 1936-43, and a Secretary to the Governor-General 1937-43; Assistant Under-Secretary of State for India, 1943; an Under-Secretary (Civil) of the War Cabinet, 1944-45; Deputy Under-Secretary of State for Burma, 1945-47, for India, 1947, for Commonwealth Relations, 1948-49; Ambassador, 1950-51 (United Kingdom Representative, 1949-50) to the Republic of Ireland; High Commissioner for the UK in Pakistan, 1951-54; Permanent Under-Secretary of State for Commonwealth Relations, 1955-59. Vice-Chm., Commonwealth Inst., 1963-66; Governor, Queen Mary Coll., Univ. of London, 1959-; Trustee, Hakluyt Soc., 1958- (Pres., 1964-69); Vice-Pres., Royal Central Asian Soc., 1967- (Chm. Council, 1964-67); Vice-Pres., RGS, 1969 (Pres., 1966-69); Mem. Standing Commn on Museums and Galleries, 1959-72. A Freeman of the City of London, 1960. Master, Tallowchandlers' Co., 1972-73. Hon. LLD Dublin, 1957. Kt of Malta, 1960. *Publications:* The Laithwaites, Some Records of a Lancashire Family, 1941, rev. edn 1961; Memories of an Infantry Officer, 1971; etc. *Address:* c/o Grindlay's Bank Ltd, 13 St James's Square, SW1. *Clubs:* Travellers', United Oxford & Cambridge University, City of London.

LAKE, Sir (Attwell) Graham, 10th Bt *cr* 1711; Senior Technical Adviser, Ministry of Defence; *b* 6 Oct. 1923; *s* of Captain Sir Attwell Henry Lake, 9th Bt, CB, OBE, RN, and of Kathleen Marion, *d* of late Alfred Morrison Turner; *S* father, 1972. *Educ:* Eton and Cambridge (2nd Devonshire Course). British High Commission, Wellington, NZ, 1942; Gilbert and Ellice Military Forces, 1944; Colonial Administrative Service, 1945 (Secretary to Govt of Tonga, 1950-53); Norris Oakley Bros, 1957; Min. of Defence, 1959; British High Commission, New Delhi, 1966; attached Foreign and Commonwealth Office, 1969-72. *Recreations:* golf, bridge, chess, skiing. *Heir: b* Willoughby Alfred Lake [*b* 31 Aug. 1925; *m* 1952, Elizabeth Elsie Faith, *d* of Sir Rupert Turner Havelock Clarke, 2nd Bt; two *d*].

LAKEMAN, Miss Enid; Director, Electoral Reform Society, since 1960; *b* 28 Nov. 1903; *d* of Horace B. Lakeman and Evereld Simpson. *Educ:* Tunbridge Wells County Sch.; Bedford Coll., Univ. of London. Posts in chemical industry, 1926-41; WAAF, 1941-45; Electoral Reform Soc., 1945-. Parly candidate (L): St Albans, 1945; Brixton, 1950; Aldershot, 1955 and 1959. *Publications:* When Labour Fails, 1946; (with James D. Lambert) Voting in Democracies, 1955, (2nd edn 1959; 3rd and 4th edns, 1970 and 1974, as sole author, as How Democracies Vote); Nine Democracies, 1973 (2nd edn 1975); pamphlets; articles in polit. jls. *Recreations:* travel, gardening. *Address:* 37 Culverden Avenue, Tunbridge Wells, Kent TN4 9RE. *T:* Tunbridge Wells 21674. *Club:* National Liberal.

LAKER, Frederick Alfred; Chairman and Managing Director, Laker Airways Ltd, since 1966; *b* 6 Aug. 1922; British. *Educ:* Simon Langton Sch., Canterbury. Short Brothers, Rochester, 1938-40; General Aircraft, 1940-41; Air Transport Auxiliary, 1941-46; Aviation Traders, 1946-60; British United Airways, 1960-65; Laker Airways (International) Ltd, 1966-. *Recreations:* horse breeding, racing, sailing. *Address:* c/o Laker Airways, Gatwick Airport, Horley, Surrey. *T:* (office) 01-668 9363, Crawley 31222. *Clubs:* Eccentric, Little Ship.

LAKIN, Sir Henry, 3rd Bt, *cr* 1909; *b* 8 Oct. 1904; *s* of Sir Richard Lakin, 2nd Bt, and Mildred Alice (*d* 1960), *d* of G. J. Shakerley; *S* father, 1955; *m* 1927, Bessie (*d* 1965), *d* of J. D. Anderson, Durban; one *s* (one *d* decd); 2nd, 1965, Grace, *d* of John Kyme, Manchester. *Educ:* Eton; Jesus Coll., Cambridge. BA 1926. *Heir: s* Michael Lakin [*b* 28 Oct. 1934; *m* 1st, 1956, Margaret (marr. diss., 1963), *d* of Robert Wallace, Co. Armagh; 2nd, 1965, Felicity-Ann, *d* of A. D. Murphy, Kenya; one *s* one *d*]. *Address:* Torwood, PO Rosetta, Natal, S Africa.

LAKING, George Robert, CMG 1969; Chief Ombudsman and Privacy Commissioner, New Zealand, since 1977; *b* Auckland, NZ, 15 Oct. 1912; *s* of R. G. Laking; *m* 1940, Patricia, *d* of H. Hogg; one *s* one *d*. *Educ:* Auckland Grammar Sch.; Auckland Univ.; Victoria Univ. of Wellington (LLB). Prime Minister's and Ext. Affairs Depts, 1940-49; New Zealand Embassy, Washington: Counsellor, 1949-54; Minister, 1954-56. Dep. Sec.

of Ext. Affairs, Wellington, NZ, 1956-58; Acting High Comr for NZ, London, 1958-61, and NZ Ambassador to European Economic Community, 1960-61; New Zealand Ambassador, Washington, 1961-67; Sec. of Foreign Affairs and Permanent Head, Prime Minister's Dept, NZ, 1967-72; Ombudsman, 1975-77. *Address:* 3 Wesley Road, Wellington 1, New Zealand. *T:* 728-454.

LAL, Shavax Ardeshir, CIE 1941; Advocate, High Court, Bombay; *b* 12 Nov. 1899; *s* of Ardeshir Edulji Lal, Nasik, Bombay Presidency; *m* 1933, Coomi, *d* of N. N. Master; three *d*. *Educ:* Fergusson College and Law College, Poona. Practised law, 1926-30; joined Bombay Judicial Service, 1930; transferred to Legal Department, Bombay, 1930; Assistant Secretary to Government of Bombay, Legal Department, 1932-36; nominated member and Secretary of Council of State, 1936-46; Secretary to Government of India, Ministry of Law, 1947-48; Secretary to Governor-General of India, 1948-50; Secretary to President of India, 1950-54. *Address:* Windcliffe, Pedder Road, Bombay, India.

LALANDI, Lina, OBE 1975; Artistic Director, English Bach Festival, since 1962; *b* Athens; *d* of late Nikolas Kaloyeropoulos (former Dir of Byzantine Museum, Athens, and Dir of Beaux Arts, Min. of Educn, Athens) and Toula Gelekis. *Educ:* Athens Conservatoire (grad. with Hons in Music); privately, in England (harpsichord and singing studies). First appeared as harpsichord soloist at Royal Festival Hall, 1954; thereafter, international career in Concert, Radio and TV. Founded English Bach Festival Trust, 1962. *Recreations:* cats, cooking, Flamenco. *Address:* 15 South Eaton Place, SW1W 9ER. *T:* 01-730 5925.

LALOUETTE, Marie Joseph Gerard; Attorney, Durban, South Africa; *b* 24 Jan. 1912; 3rd *s* of late Henri Lalouette and Mrs H. Lalouette; *m* 1942, Jeanne Marrier d'Unienville; four *s* two *d*. *Educ:* Royal Coll., Mauritius; Exeter Coll., Oxford; London School of Economics; Middle Temple. District Magistrate, Mauritius, 1944; Electoral Commissioner, 1956; Addl. Subst. Procureur-General, 1956; Master, and Registrar, Supreme Court, 1958; Assistant Attorney-General, 1959; Solicitor-General, 1960; Puisne Judge, 1961; Senior Puisne Judge, Supreme Court, Mauritius, 1967-70. *Publications:* Digest of Decisions of Supreme Court of Mauritius, 1926-43; The Mauritius Digest to 1950; A First Supplement to the Mauritius Digest, 1951-55; A Second Supplement to the Mauritius Digest, 1956-60; contrib. Internat. Encyclopedia of Comparative Law. *Recreations:* music, gardening. *Address:* 56 Grantchester, St Andrews Street, Durban, Republic of South Africa.

LAM, Martin Philip; Under-Secretary, Department of Industry (formerly Trade and Industry), since 1970; *b* 10 March 1920; *m* 1953, Lisa Lorenz; one *s* one *d*. *Educ:* University College Sch.; Gonville and Caius Coll., Cambridge. Served War of 1939-45, Royal Signals. Asst Principal, Board of Trade, 1947; Nuffield Fellowship (Latin America), 1952-53; Asst Sec., 1960; Counsellor, UK Delegn to OECD, 1963-65. *Address:* 22 The Avenue, Wembley, Middlesex. *T:* 01-904 2584.

LAMARQUE, Walter Geoffrey, MBE 1947; *b* 12 Feb. 1913; *s* of late Charles and Elma Lamarque, West Byfleet, Surrey; *m* 1945, Patricia Aikman; two *s* one *d*. *Educ:* Marlborough Coll.; Oriel Coll., Oxford (Scholar). 1st Class Classical Mods, 1934; 2nd Class Lit.Hum., 1936. Indian Civil Service, 1936-47; served in Madras Presidency, and in Government of India at New Delhi and Calcutta. Joined Board of Trade, 1947; UK Trade Commissioner, Melbourne, Australia, 1947-50; Karachi, 1951-55. Joined Commonwealth Relations Office, 1957; First Secretary (Finance), UK High Commission Office, Ottawa, 1957-60; British Deputy Commissioner, Enugu, Nigeria, 1960-63; Africa Economic Department, CRO, 1963-65; Head of E Africa Dept, ODM, 1965-71; Permanent UK Deleg. to FAO, 1971-73. *Recreations:* fox-hunting, golf. *Address:* Elphin House, Coxwold, York YO6 4AD. *T:* Coxwold 452. *Club:* Yorkshire (York).

LAMB, family name of Baron Rochester.

LAMB, Albert, (Larry Lamb); Director, since 1970, Editorial Director, since 1971, News International Ltd; Editor, The Sun, 1969-72 and since 1975; *b* 15 July 1929; *m* Joan Mary Denise Grogan; two *s* one *d*. Editor, (Manchester) Daily Mail, 1968-69. *Recreations:* fell-walking, cricket, fishing. *Address:* 5 Durward House, 31 Kensington Court, W8.

LAMB, Albert Thomas, CMG 1974; MBE 1953; DFC 1945; HM Diplomatic Service; Ambassador to Kuwait, 1974-77; *b* 23 Oct. 1921; *s* of R. S. Lamb and Violet Lamb (*née* Haynes); *m* 1944, Christina Betty Wilkinson; one *s* two *d*. *Educ:* Swansea

Grammar Sch. Served RAF 1941-46. FO 1938-41; Embassy, Rome, 1947-50; Consulate-General, Genoa, 1950; Embassy, Bucharest, 1950-53; FO 1953-55; Middle East Centre for Arabic Studies, 1955-57; Political Residency, Bahrain, 1957-61; FO 1961-65; Embassy, Kuwait, 1965; Political Agent in Abu Dhabi, 1965-68; Inspector, 1968-70, Sen. Inspector, 1970-73, Asst Under-Sec. of State and Chief Inspector, FCO, 1973-74. *Address:* c/o Foreign and Commonwealth Office, SW1; 4 Queen's Court, Queensway, W2. *T:* 01-229 5716. *Club:* Travellers'.

LAMB, Air Vice-Marshal George Colin, CB 1977; CBE 1966; AFC 1947; Chief of Staff, No 18 Group Strike Command, RAF, since 1975; *b* 23 July 1923; *s* of late George and Bessie Lamb, Hornby, Lancaster; *m* 1945, Nancy Mary Godsmark; two *s*. *Educ:* Lancaster Royal Grammar School. War of 1939-45: commissioned, RAF, 1942; flying duties, 1942-53; Staff Coll., 1953; Air Ministry, special duties, 1954-58; OC No 87 Sqdn, 1958-61; Dir Admin. Plans, MoD, 1961-64; Asst Comdt, RAF Coll., 1964-65; Dep. Comdr, Air Forces Borneo, 1965-66; Fighter Command, 1966; MoD (Dep. Command Structure Project Officer), 1967; HQ, Strike Command, 1967-69; OC, RAF Lyneham, 1969-71; RCDS, 1971-72; Dir of Control (Operations), NATS, 1972-74; Comdr, Southern Maritime Air Region, RAF Mount Batten, 1974-75. Mem., RFU, 1973-. MBIM. *Recreation:* international Rugby football referee, cricket (Pres., Adastrian Cricket Club). *Address:* Hill End, Pinner Hill, Pinner, Middlesex HA5 3XT; 15 Rushington Avenue, Maidenhead, Berks. *T:* Maidenhead 22624. *Club:* Royal Air Force.

LAMB, Harold Norman; Regional Administrator, South East Thames Regional Health Authority, since 1973; *b* 21 July 1922; *s* of Harold Alexander and Amelia Lamb; *m* 1946, Joyce Marian Hawkyard; one *s* one *d*. *Educ:* Saltley Grammar School. FHA. House Governor, Birmingham Gen. Hosp., 1958; Dep. Sec., United Birmingham Hosps, and House Governor, Queen Elizabeth Hosp., 1961; Sec., SE Metrop. RHB, 1968. Mem. Exec. Council, Royal Inst. of Public Admin, 1970. *Recreations:* golf, music. *Address:* 114 Carlton Road, Reigate, Surrey. *Club:* Walton Heath Golf.

LAMB, Prof. John; James Watt Professor of Electrical Engineering, University of Glasgow, since Sept. 1961; *b* 26 Sept. 1922; *m* 1947, Margaret May Livesey; two *s* one *d*. *Educ:* Accrington Grammar Sch.; Manchester Univ. BSc (1st class Hons) Manchester Univ. 1943; Fairbairn Prizeman in Engineering; MSc 1944, PhD 1946, DSc 1957, Manchester. Ministry of Supply Extra-Mural Res., 1943-46. Assistant Lecturer, 1946-47, Lecturer, 1947-56, Reader, 1956-61, in Electrical Engineering at Imperial Coll. (London Univ.); Assistant Director, Department of Electrical Engineering, Imperial Coll., 1958-61. Pres., British Soc. of Rheology, 1970-72. Chm., Scottish Industry Univ. Liaison Cttee in Engrg, 1969-71; Member: Nat. Electronics Council, 1963-; CNAA, 1964-70. MIEE 1967; FInstP 1960; Fellow, Acoustical Society of America, 1960; FRSE 1968. *Publications:* numerous in Proc. Royal Society, Trans Faraday Society, Proc. Instn Electrical Engineers, Proc. Physical Society, Journal Acoustical Society of America, Quarterly Reviews of Chem. Society, Nature, Phys. Review, Journal of Polymer Science; contrib.: (The Theory and Practice of Ultrasonic Propagation) to Principles and Practice of Non-destructive Testing (ed) J. H. Lamble), 1962; (Dispersion and Absorption of Sound by Molecular Processes) to Proc. International School of Physics "Enrico Fermi' Course XXVII (ed D. Sette), 1963; (Thermal Relaxation in Liquids) to Physical Acoustics, Vol. II (ed W. P. Mason), 1965; (Theory of Rheology) to Interdisciplinary Approach to Liquid Lubricant Technology (ed P. M. Ku), 1973; (Viscoelastic and Ultrasonic Relaxation Studies) to Molecular Motions in Liquids (ed J. Lascombe), 1974. *Recreations:* walking, wine-making, music. *Address:* Royston, 10 Crown Road North, Glasgow G12 9DH. *T:* 041-339 2101.

LAMB, Hon. Kenneth Henry Lowry; Special Adviser (Broadcasting Research), British Broadcasting Corporation, since 1977; *b* 23 Dec. 1923; *y s* of 1st Baron Rochester, CMG; *m* 1952, Elizabeth Anne Saul; one *s* two *d*. *Educ:* Harrow; Trinity Coll., Oxford (MA). President of the Union, Oxford, 1944. Instructor-Lieut, Royal Navy, 1944-46. Lecturer, then Senior Lecturer in History and English, Royal Naval Coll., Greenwich, 1946-53. Commonwealth Fund Fellow in United States, 1953-55. Joined BBC in 1955 as a Talks Producer (Radio); became a Television Talks Producer, 1957, and then Chief Assistant, Current Affairs, TV talks, 1959-63; Head of Religious Broadcasting, BBC, 1963-66; Secretary to the BBC, 1967-68; Dir, Public Affairs, BBC, 1969-77. *Recreations:* cricket, walking, golf. *Address:* BBC, Broadcasting House, W1A 1AA;

25 South Terrace, Thurloe Square, SW7. *T:* 01-584 7904. *Clubs:* MCC, National Liberal; Royal Fowey Yacht.
See also Baron Rochester.

LAMB, Larry; *see* Lamb, A.

LAMB, Sir Lionel (Henry), KCMG 1953 (CMG 1948); OBE 1944; HM Diplomatic Service, retired; *b* 9 July 1900; *s* of late Sir Harry Lamb, GBE, KCMG; *m* 1927, Jean Fawcett (*née* MacDonald); one *s. Educ:* Winchester; Queen's Coll., Oxford. Appointed HM Consular Service in China, Dec. 1921; Consul (Gr. II), 1935; served Shanghai, 1935-37; Peking, 1937-40; Consul (Gr. I), 1938; Superintending Consul and Assistant Chinese Secretary, Shanghai, 1940; transferred to St Paul-Minneapolis, 1943; Chinese Counsellor, HM Embassy, Chungking, 1945; HM Minister, Nanking, 1947-49; Chargé d'Affaires, Peking, China, 1951-53; Ambassador to Switzerland, 1953-58, retired. *Address:* Roxford Barn, Hertingfordbury, Herts.

LAMB, Captain William John, CVO 1947; OBE 1944; RN retired; *b* 26 Dec. 1906; *s* of late Sir Richard Amphlett Lamb, KCSI,CIE, ICS, and Kathleen Maud Barry; *m* 1948, Bridget, *widow* of Lieut-Commander G. S. Salt, RN; two *d. Educ:* St Anthony's, Eastbourne; RNC Osborne and Dartmouth. Commander, 1941; Staff of C-in-C Mediterranean Fleet, 1940-42; Staff of C-in-C, Eastern Fleet, 1942-44; Executive Officer, HMS Vanguard, 1945-47; Deputy Director of Naval Ordnance, 1948-50; Comd HMS Widemouth Bay and Captain (D) 4th Training Flotilla, Rosyth, 1951-52; Commanding Admiralty Signal and Radar Establishment, 1952-54; Commanding HMS Cumberland, 1955-56. Hon. Life Mem., BIM, 1974. *Recreation:* sailing. *Address:* Westons, Bank, Lyndhurst, Hampshire. *T:* Lyndhurst 2620. *Club:* Royal Cruising.

LAMB, Prof. Willis E(ugene), Jr; Professor of Physics and Optical Sciences, University of Arizona, since 1974; *b* Los Angeles, California, USA, 12 July 1913; *s* of Willis Eugene Lamb and Marie Helen Metcalf; *m* Ursula Schaefer. *Educ:* Los Angeles High Sch.; University of California (BS, PhD). Columbia Univ.: Instructor in Physics, 1938-43, Associate, 1943-45, Assistant Professor, 1945-47, Associate Professor, 1947-48, Professor of Physics 1948-52; Professor of Physics, Stanford Univ., California, 1951-56; Wykeham Prof. of Physics and Fellow of New Coll., University of Oxford, 1956-62; Yale University: Ford Prof. of Physics, 1962-72; Gibbs Prof. of Physics, 1972-74. Morris Loeb Lectr, Harvard Univ., 1953-54; Lectr, University of Colorado, Summer, 1959; Shrum Lectr, Simon Fraser Univ., 1972; Visiting Professor, Tata Institute of Fundamental Research, Bombay, 1960; Guggenheim Fellow, 1960-61; Visiting Professor, Columbia Univ., 1961; Fulbright Lecturer, University of Grenoble, Summer, 1964. MNAS, 1954. Hon. DSc Pennsylvania, 1954; MA (by decree), Oxford, 1956; Hon. MA Yale, 1961; Hon. Fellow, Institute of Physics and Physical Society, 1962; Res. Corp Award, 1954; Rumford Medal, American Academy of Arts and Sciences, 1953; (jointly) Nobel Prize in Physics, 1955; Guthrie Award, The Physical Society, 1958; Yeshiva University Award, 1962; Hon. LHD Yeshiva, 1965. *Publications:* (with M. Sargent and M. O. Scully) Laser Physics, 1974; contributions to The Physical Review, Physica, Science, Journal of Applied Physics, etc. *Address:* Department of Physics, University of Arizona, Tucson, Arizona 85721, USA.

LAMBART, family name of Earl of Cavan.

LAMBART, Julian Harold Legge; *b* 7 May 1893; *s* of late Brig.-General E. A. Lambart, CB, RA, and late Mary Louisa, *d* of Sir James Walker, 2nd Bt, of Sand Hutton; *m* 1948, Margaret, *widow* of Sir Walford Davies. *Educ:* Eton Coll.; King's Coll., Cambridge. Served European War, 1914-18, as Capt. RFA (Croix de Guerre). Assistant Master at Eton, 1919; Lower Master, 1945-59; Vice-Provost, 1959-67. *Recreations:* travel and architecture. *Address:* Whitewell, St Davids, Haverfordwest, Dyfed. *T:* St Davids 383.

LAMBART, Sir Oliver Francis, 2nd Bt *cr* 1911; Lieut late RASC; *b* 6 April 1913; *s* of 1st Bt and Kathleen Moore-Brabazon; *S* father, 1926. *Heir:* none. *Address:* Beau Parc, Co. Meath. *Club:* Turf.

LAMBERT, family name of Viscount Lambert.

LAMBERT, 2nd Viscount, *cr* 1945, of South Molton; **George Lambert,** TD; *b* 27 Nov. 1909; *e s* of 1st Viscount Lambert, PC; *S* father, 1958; *m* 1939, Patricia Mary, *d* of J. F. Quinn; one *d* (one *s* decd). *Educ:* Harrow Sch.; New Coll., Oxford. War of 1939-45: TA, Lieut-Colonel 1942. MP (L-Nat) South Molton Division, Devon, July 1945-Feb. 1950. (Nat. L-C) Torrington Division, Devon, 1950-58. Chm., Devon and Exeter Savings Bank, 1958-70. Formerly Chm. Governors, Seale-Hayne Agricultural Coll., Newton Abbot, Devon. Pres., Young Farmers' Club, 1968-70; Life Vice-Pres., National Federation of Young Farmers' Clubs, 1970. DL Devon, 1969-70. *Recreation:* golf. *Heir presumptive: b* Hon. Michael John Lambert [*b* 29 Sept. 1912; *m* 1939, Florence Dolores, *d* of late N. L. Macaskie, QC; three *d*]. *Address:* Les Fougères, 1806 St-Légier, Switzerland. *T:* (021) 53 10 63. *Clubs:* Carlton, Army and Navy.
See also Hon. Margaret Lambert, P. W. Gibbings.

LAMBERT, Sir Anthony (Edward), KCMG 1964 (CMG 1955); HM Diplomatic Service, retired; *b* 7 March 1911; *o s* of late R. E. Lambert, Pensbury House, Shaftesbury, Dorset; *m* 1948, Ruth Mary, *d* of late Sir Arthur Fleming, CBE; two *d. Educ:* Harrow; Balliol Coll., Oxford (Scholar). Entered HM Foreign (subseq. Diplomatic) Service, 1934, and served in: Brussels, 1937; Ankara, 1940; Beirut and Damascus, 1942; Brussels, 1944; Stockholm, 1949; Athens, 1952; HM Minister to Bulgaria, 1958-60; HM Ambassador to: Tunisia, 1960-63; Finland, 1963-66; Portugal, 1966-70. *Address:* 28 Victoria Road, W8. *Club:* Travellers'.

LAMBERT, Ven. Charles Henry, MA; Archdeacon of Lancaster, 1959-66, Emeritus, 1966; Vicar of St Cuthbert's, Lytham, 1960-66; Senior Examining Chaplain to Bishop of Blackburn; *b* 13 Jan. 1894; *s* of Henry and Frances Ann Lambert; *m* 1920, Dorothy Ellen Birch; three *s* one *d. Educ:* Primary Schools; privately; Leeds Univ.; Cuddesdon Coll. BA 1916; MA 1932; deacon 1917; priest 1918; Curate of Redcar, 1917-20; of Guisborough, 1920-22; Rector of St Denys with St George, York, 1922-24; Vicar of Royston, Yorks, 1924-28; Rector of St Mary Bishophill Senior with St Clement, York, 1928-34; Warden of Whalley Abbey, 1934-45; Director of Religious Education, diocese of Blackburn, 1934-46; Canon, Blackburn, 1934-46; Archdeacon of Blackburn, 1946-59; Proctor, 1929-34, York, 1935-45; Blackburn. OCF 1941-44; Archbishops' Visitor to RAF, 1944-45; Rural Dean of Whalley, 1942-45. *Publications:* Go Ye,.... Teach, 1939; Whalley Abbey, Yesterday and To-Day, 1948. *Recreations:* reading, walking, keenly interested in all outdoor sports. *Address:* 71a Upper Church Road, Weston-super-Mare, Avon. *T:* Weston-super-Mare 27851.

LAMBERT, David Arthur Charles; General Secretary, National Union of Hosiery and Knitwear Workers, since 1975; *b* 2 Sept. 1933; *m;* two *s* one *d. Educ:* Hitchin Boys' Grammar Sch., Herts. Employed as production worker for major hosiery manufr; active as lay official within NUHKW; full-time official, NUHKW, 1964-. *Address:* 55 New Walk, Leicester LE1 7EB.

LAMBERT, Sir Edward (Thomas), KBE 1958 (CBE 1953); CVO 1957; retired from Foreign Service, 1960; *b* 19 June 1901; *s* of late Brig. and Mrs T. S. Lambert; *m* 1936, Rhona Patricia Gilmore; one *s* one *d. Educ:* Charterhouse and Trinity Coll., Cambridge. Member of HM Diplomatic (formerly Foreign) Service. Entered Far Eastern Consular Service, 1926; served at Bangkok, Batavia, Medan, Curaçao, and The Hague. Consul-General, Geneva, 1949-53, Paris, 1953-59. Commandeur, Légion d'Honneur, 1957. *Recreations:* reading and travel. *Address:* Crag House, Aldeburgh, Suffolk. *T:* 2296.

LAMBERT, Eric Thomas Drummond, CMG 1969; OBE 1946; KPM 1943; retd, 1968; *b* 3 Nov. 1909; *s* of late Septimus Drummond Lambert. *Educ:* Royal Sch., Dungannon; Trinity Coll., Dublin. Indian (Imperial) Police, 1929-47: Political Officer for Brahmaputra-Chindwin Survey, 1935-36, and Tirap Frontier Tract, 1942; District Comr, Naga Hills, 1938. Served with Chinese Vth Army, Indo-Burma Front, 1942; Chief Civil Liaison Officer XXXIII Corps, XIVth Army, 1944; FCO, 1947-68, with service in SE Asia, W Africa, S America, Nepal, Afghanistan. Chinese Armed Forces Distinguished Service, 1st Order, 1st class, 1943. Trustee, Nat. Library of Ireland. *Publications:* Assam (jointly with Alban Ali), 1943; Carabobo 1821, 1974; articles in jls of RGS and Royal Siam Soc.; Man in India; The Irish Sword. *Recreations:* golf, historical research, lecturing. *Address:* Drumkeen, Glenamuck, Carrickmines, Co. Dublin. *T:* 893169. *Club:* Stephen's Green (Dublin).

LAMBERT, Sir Greville Foley, 9th Bt, *cr* 1711; *b* 17 Aug. 1900; *s* of late Lionel Foley Lambert, 4th *s* of 6th Bt; *S* cousin (Sir John Foley Grey), 1938; *m* 1932, Edith Roma, *d* of Richard Batson; three *d. Educ:* Rugby Sch. Chartered Accountant. *Heir:* kinsman, John Hugh Lambert [*b* 31 May 1910; *m* 1947, Edith Davies; one *s*]. *Address:* 1 Linden Court, Hampton Lane, Solihull, West Midlands.
[*But his name does not, at the time of going to press, appear on the Official Roll of Baronets*.]

LAMBERT, Guy William, CB 1942; BA; *b* 1 Dec. 1889; 2nd *s* of late Col J. A. Lambert, Brookhill, Claremorris, Co. Mayo, and Grace, *e d* of late W. D. Fane, Fulbeck Hall, Lincs; *m* 1917, Nadine, *y d* of late Wilson Noble, Park Place, Henley-on-Thames; one *s* two *d. Educ:* Cheltenham Coll.; St John's Coll., Oxford. Higher Div. Clerk, War Office, 1913; Private Secretary to Sir C. Harris, KCB, Assistant Financial Secretary, 1915; Private Secretary to H. W. Forster, Financial Secretary, 1916; Chevalier, Légion d'Honneur, 1920; Principal Private Secretary to successive Secretaries of State for War, Rt Hon. Sir L. Worthington-Evans Bt, GBE, and Rt Hon. T. Shaw, CBE, 1926-29; Assistant Under-Secretary of State for War, 1938-51. President Society for Psychical Research, 1955-58. Fellow, Irish Genealogical Research Soc., 1970. Silver Jubilee Medal, 1935; Coronation Medal, 1937. *Address:* Flat 7, 86 Elm Park Gardens, SW10 9PD. *T:* 01-352 3686. *Clubs:* Athenæum, Leander, London Rowing.
See also Sir A. C. W. Drew.

LAMBERT, Harold George; Member, panel of independent inspectors for local inquiries for Department of the Environment, since 1971; Under-Secretary, Ministry of Agriculture, Fisheries and Food, 1964-70; *b* 8 April 1910; *s* of late Rev. David Lambert; *m* 1934, Winifred Marthe, *d* of late Rev. H. E. Anderson, Farnham, Surrey; two *s. Educ:* King Edward's Sch., Birmingham; Corpus Christi Coll., Cambridge (MA); Imperial College of Science, London. Entered Ministry of Agriculture and Fisheries, 1933; Private Secretary to Parliamentary Secretary, 1938-39; Sec., Agricultural Machinery Develt Bd, 1942-45; Assistant Secretary, 1948. *Recreations:* music, art, travel. *Address:* 25 Lenham Avenue, Rottingdean, Sussex. *Club:* Royal Commonwealth Society.

LAMBERT, Maj.-Gen. Harold Roger, CBE 1941; DSC 1916; RM, retired; *b* 26 Jan. 1896; *y s* of late G. B. Lambert, PWD, Madras, India; *m* 1918, Ruth Noel St Clair (*d* 1955), *d* of late Rev. Dr W. St Clair Tisdall, DD; (one *s,* Lieut RN, DSC and bar, missing, presumed killed, 1943); *m* 1955, Elizabeth Lois King-Church. *Educ:* Dulwich Coll. 2nd Lieut RM, 1913; served in European War, 1914-19; Royal Naval Staff Coll., Greenwich, 1924-25; Staff Coll., Camberley, 1927-28; Plans Division of Naval Staff, Admiralty, 1929-32 and 1933-36; Senior Officer RM, on Staff of C-in-C, Portsmouth, 1936-38; commanded RM Field Formations in Orkneys, Norway, Iceland, Middle East and Sicily, 1939-44; Maj.-Gen. 1942; ADC to the King, 1943; Comdt Portsmouth Div. RM, 1944; 1939-43 Star, Africa Star, Italy Star; retired 1944. Chm., St Birinus Gp Hosps Management Cttee, 1951-61; Member: Oxon CC, 1955-61; Rural Dist Council, Henley, 1958-61. *Address:* 27 Victoria Hill, Eye, Suffolk. *T:* Eye 313.

LAMBERT, Henry Uvedale Antrobus; Vice-Chairman, Barclays Bank Limited, since 1973; Deputy Chairman, Agricultural Mortgage Corporation Ltd, since 1977; Director, Sun Alliance and London Insurance Group and other companies; *b* 9 Oct. 1925; *o s* of Roger Uvedale Lambert and Muriel, *d* of Sir Reginald Antrobus, KCMG, CB; *m* 1951, Diana, *y d* of Captain H. E. Dumbell, Royal Fusiliers; two *s* one *d. Educ:* Winchester College (Scholar); New College, Oxford (Exhibitioner). MA. Served War of 1939-45, Royal Navy, in HM Ships Stockham and St Austell Bay in Western Approaches and Mediterranean, subseq. RNR; Lt-Comdr (retired). Entered Barclays Bank 1948; a Local Dir at Lombard Street, 1957, Southampton, 1959, Birmingham, 1969; Vice-Chm., Barclays Bank UK Management Ltd, 1972. *Recreations:* fishing, gardening, golf, naval history. *Clubs:* Brooks's, MCC. *Address:* c/o Barclays Bank Ltd, 54 Lombard Street, EC3P 3AH.

LAMBERT, Jack Walter, CBE 1970; DSC 1944; Associate Editor, The Sunday Times; *b* 21 April 1917; *o s* of Walter and Ethel Lambert; *m* 1940, Catherine Margaret, Hon. ARCM, *e d* of Alfred Read, CBE; one *s* two *d. Educ:* Tonbridge Sch. Served with Royal Navy in Atlantic, Arctic and North Sea (Light Coastal Forces), 1940-46, dispatches 1944 (Ordinary Seaman; Lieut-Commander). Joined Sunday Times as Assistant Literary Editor, 1948; Literary and Arts Editor, 1960-76. Member: Nat. Council, British Drama League; Drama Adv. Cttee, British Council (Chm. 1968-69); Bd of Management, British Theatre Assoc., 1972-; Council, RADA, 1972-; Mem., Arts Council of GB, 1968-76: Mem., Drama Panel, 1965-76 (Chm. 1968-76); Theatre Enquiry, 1967-69; Vice-Chm., New Activities Cttee, 1969-70; Chm., Computer Booking Working Party, 1969-72; Cttee, Royal Literary Fund; Member: Theatres Adv. Cttee, 1973-75; Cttee of Management, Soc. of Authors, Mem. Council, 1975-; Dir, Theatre Investment Fund, 1972-. Governor, British Inst. of Recorded Sound, 1966-69, 1977-; Trustee, Phoenix Trust, 1975. Officier de l'Ordre des arts et des lettres, 1975; Officier de l'Ordre National du Mérite, 1976. *Publications:*

Penguin Guide to Cornwall, 1939; The Bodley Head Saki (ed), 1963; Drama in Britain, 1964-73, 1974; much occasional writing and broadcasting on literature, music and the theatre. *Recreation:* singing lieder. *Address:* 30 Belsize Grove, NW3. *T:* 01-722 1668. *Clubs:* Garrick, Beefsteak.

LAMBERT, John Henry, CMG 1975; HM Diplomatic Service; Ambassador to Tunisia, since 1977; *b* 8 Jan. 1921; *s* of Col R. S. Lambert, MC, and Mrs H. J. F. Mills; *m* 1950, Jennifer Ann (*née* Urquhart); one *s* two *d. Educ:* Eton Coll.; Sorbonne; Trinity Coll., Cambridge. Grenadier Guards, 1940-45 (Captain). Appointed 3rd Secretary, HM Embassy, The Hague, 1945; Member of HM Foreign Service, 1947; FO, 1948; 2nd Secretary, Damascus, 1951; 1st Secretary, 1953; FO, 1954; Dep. to UK Representative on International Commn for Saar Referendum, 1955; Belgrade, 1956; Head of Chancery, Manila, 1958; UK Delegation to Disarmament Conference, Geneva, 1962; FO, 1963; Counsellor, Head of Chancery, Stockholm, 1964-67; Head of UN (Political) Dept, FCO, 1967-70; Commercial Counsellor and Consul-Gen. Vienna, 1971-74; Minister and Dep. Comdt, Berlin, 1974-77. *Recreations:* tennis, golf. *Address:* c/o Foreign and Commonwealth Office, SW1; 16 Woodfall Street, SW3. *T:* 01-730 3222. *Clubs:* MCC; Hurlingham, Royal St George's Golf.

LAMBERT, Hon. Margaret (Barbara), CMG 1965; PhD; British Editor-in-Chief, German Foreign Office Documents, since 1951; *b* 7 Nov. 1906; *yr d* of 1st Viscount Lambert, PC. *Educ:* Lady Margaret Hall, Oxford; London School of Economics. BA 1930, PhD 1936. Served during War of 1939-45 in European Service of BBC. Assistant Editor British Documents on Foreign Policy, 1946-50; Lecturer in Modern History, University College of the South-West, 1950-51; Lecturer in Modern European History, St Andrews University, 1956-60. *Publications:* The Saar, 1934; When Victoria began to Reign, 1937; (with Enid Marx) English Popular and Traditional Art, 1946, and English Popular Art, 1952. *Address:* 39 Thornhill Road, Barnsbury Square, N1. *T:* 01-607 2286; 1 St Germans, Exeter.

LAMBERT, Richard Stanton, MA; Supervisor of Educational Broadcasts, Canadian Broadcasting Corporation, 1943-60; *b* 25 Aug. 1894; *s* of late Richard Cornthwaite Lambert and Lilian Lambert, London; *m* 1918, Kate Elinor, *d* of Sydney T. Klein; one *s* one *d; m* 1944, Joyce, *d* of Edward Morgan. *Educ:* Repton; Wadham Coll., Oxford (classical scholar). Joined staff of The Economist, 1916; served with the Friends' Ambulance Unit, 1916-18; Lecturer to University Tutorial Classes, Sheffield, 1919; Staff Tutor for Tutorial Classes, University of London, 1924; Head of Adult Education Section, BBC, 1927; Editor, The Listener, 1928-39; Member of Commission on Educational and Cultural Films, 1929-33; of Governing Body of British Film Institute, 1933-40; Vice-Chairman, British Institute of Adult Education, 1936-39; Education Adviser to Canadian Broadcasting Corporation, 1940-43, 1960-61. Couns. to UNESCO on media of mass communication, 1946. *Publications:* The Prince of Pickpockets, 1930; A Historian's Scrapbook, 1932; The Railway King, 1934; When Justice Faltered, 1935; (jointly with Harry Price) The Haunting of Cashen's Gap, 1935; The Innocence of Edmund Galley, 1936; The Universal Provider, 1938; Propaganda, 1938; The Cobbett of the West, 1939; Ariel and all his Quality, 1940; Home Front, 1940; Old Country Mail, 1941; For the Time is at Hand, 1946; The Adventure of Canadian Painting, 1947; Franklin of the Arctic, 1949; The Fortunate Traveller, 1950; North for Adventure, 1953; Exploring the Supernatural, 1955; Redcoat Sailor, 1956; Trailmaker, 1957; The Great Heritage, 1958; The Twentieth Century, 1960; School Broadcasting in Canada, 1962; Mutiny in the Bay, 1963; Renewing Nature's Wealth (Ontario Forests), 1967; Greek and Roman Myths and Legends, 1967, 1971; The Gothic Rectory, 1971. Edited (jointly) Memoirs of the Unemployed, 1933; For Filmgoers Only, 1934; Grand Tour, 1935; Art in England, 1938; translated and printed Vida's Game of Chess, 1921; Walafrid Strabo's Hortulus, 1923, and Plays of Roswitha, 1922-23; ed and printed Sir John Davies' Orchestra or a Poeme of Dancing, 1922. *Recreation:* gardening. *Address:* 2713 Seaview Road, Victoria, BC, Canada.

LAMBERT, Dr Royston James; writer; Director of the Reynolds Gallery, Plymouth; *b* 7 Dec. 1932; *s* of Albert Edward Lambert and Edith Alice Tyler; unmarried. *Educ:* Barking Abbey Sch.; Sidney Sussex Coll., Cambridge; Magdalen Coll., Oxford. Open Exhibitioner, Magdalen Coll., Oxford, 1951; Major Scholar, Sidney Sussex Coll., Cambridge, 1954; Hentsch Prize, 1954. 1st class Hist. Tripos Pt I (dist), 1954, 1st class Pt II 1955, MA 1959, PhD 1960, Cantab; BA Oxon, 1955. Bachelor Schol., Sidney Sussex Coll., Cambridge, 1956-58, Research Fellow, 1958-61; Nuffield Senior Sociological Schol., LSE, 1961-64; Ehrman Fellow, King's Coll., Cambridge, 1962-69; Headmaster,

Dartington Hall Sch., 1969-73; Dir, Dartington Res. Unit, 1969-75; Advisor on Educn to Dartington Hall Trust, 1973-75. Founded and directed Research Unit into Boarding Education, 1964-68; directed research for Public Schools Commn, 1966-68; directed research for Home Office into Approved School system, 1968-. Founded Boarding Schools Assoc., 1966. *Publications:* Sir John Simon and English Social Administration, 1963; Nutrition in Britain 1950-1960, 1964; The State and Boarding Education, 1966; The Hothouse Society, 1968; New Wine in Old Bottles?: Studies in integration in the Public Schools, 1968; Manual to the Sociology of the School, 1970; Alternatives to School (W. B. Curry Meml Lecture), 1971; The Chance of a Lifetime?, 1975; contribs in: The Public Schools (G. Kalton, 1966); Religious Education (ed. P. Jebb, 1968); The Progressive School (ed. M. Ash, 1968); Education in the Seventies, 1971; Appendix to the First Report of the Public Schools Commission; pamphlets on education, and articles in learned journals on social and administrative history, art history, sociology and education. *Recreations:* restoring paintings; herbaceous borders; Bavarian Rococo; Victorian Gothic; Irish setters. *Address:* Island House, The Barbican, Plymouth. *T:* Plymouth 63318.

LAMBERT, Prof. Victor Francis, MD, ChM, FRCS, FRCSE; Professor of Oto-laryngology, Manchester University, 1947-64; Professor Emeritus, 1964; Director, English Sewing Cotton Co., 1947-68; *b* Chequerbent, Lancs, 12 Aug. 1899; *s* of James and Ann Lambert; *m* 1st, 1930, Myra (*d* 1950), *d* of William and Eva Farnworth, Bolton, Lancs; one *s* one *d*; 2nd, 1954, Margaret, *d* of John and Beatrice Norris, Whalley Range, Manchester; one *d*. *Educ:* Bolton Sch.; Manchester Univ. Inns of Court OTC, Royal Artillery, 1917-19. Formerly: Director of Department of Oto-laryngology, Manchester Royal Infirmary; Christie Hospital and Holt Radium Inst.; Laryngologist, Christie Hospital and Holt Radium Inst.; Consultant to Department of Education of the Deaf, University of Manchester; Cons. Surgeon, Manchester Victoria Memorial Jewish Hospital. Hon. Laryngologist, Royal Manchester College of Music; Pres. Sect. of Laryngology, RSM, 1954-55; Chairman Richard Arkwright Educ. Scholarship; Governor of Bolton School; President, Old Boltonians Association, 1962; Member Manchester Regional Hosp. Board, 1951-60; former Member Court of Examiners, RCS of England and Edinburgh; Examiner, National University of Ireland; President: N of England Oto-laryngological Soc., 1950 (Hon. Life Mem.); Manchester Surgical Society, 1955-56; British Assoc. Oto-laryngologists, 1960-64; Manchester Medical Soc., 1963-64; Semon Lecture, 1959; Guest Lecturer, Canadian Medical Society, British Columbia Div., 1963; Watson Williams Memorial Lecture, University of Bristol, 1964. MB, ChB (Victoria Univ., Manchester), 1923; FRCSEd 1927; FRCS Eng (*ad eund.*) 1949; ChM (Victoria Univ., Manchester) 1932; MD 1940. Jobson Horne Memorial Prize, 1963. *Publications:* papers and articles in Journal of Laryngology and Otology; Proc. Royal Society Med.; Anatomical Society of Great Britain; Medical Press; Manchester Univ. Med. Sch. Gazette; Clinical Journal; BMJ Journal of Anatomy. *Recreations:* golf and music. *Address:* (home) 45 The Downs, Altrincham, Cheshire. *T:* 061-928 4144.

LAMBERT, Maj.-Gen. William Harold, CB 1954; CBE 1944; *b* 29 May 1905; *s* of late Brig.-General T. S. Lambert, CB, CMG, and late Geraldine Rachel (*née* Foster); *m* 1933, Rachel Nina Maxwell; two *d*. *Educ:* The New Beacon, Sevenoaks; Charterhouse; RMC Sandhurst. Commissioned 1924; Lieut, 1926; ADC to GOC-in-C Western Command, India, 1929-31; Adjut 1st E. Lancs Regt, 1932-35; Adjut Depot, E. Lancs Regt, 1936-37; Captain, 1937; psc 1938; GSO3 War Office, 1939-40; GSO2, 44 Div. 1940-41; GSO1 44 Div. 1941-42; OC4 Royal West Kent Regt, 1942-43; GSO1 Instructor, Staff Coll., Haifa, 1943-44; BGS 13 Corps, Feb.-Nov. 1944; Comdt 13 Inf. Bde, 1944-45; BGS 30 Corps Dist., 1945-46; Assistant Comdt Staff Coll., Camberley, 1946-47; idc 1948; DDSD(A) War Office, 1948-52; Comdt 18 Inf. Bde March-Sept. 1952 and Jan.-Aug. 1953; Comdt 1 Malay Inf. Bde, 1952-53; Comdt 1st Federal Div., Malaya, 1953-55; Director, Personnel Administration, War Office, 1955-58, retired. *Recreation:* sailing. *Address:* Little Redlap, near Dartmouth, Devon. *T:* Dartmouth 2679.

LAMBIE, David; MP (Lab) Ayrshire Central since 1970; *b* 13 July 1925; *m* 1954, Netta May Merrie; one *s* four *d*. *Educ:* Kyleshill Primary Sch.; Ardrossan Academy; Glasgow University; Geneva University. BSc, DipEd. Teacher, Glasgow Corp., 1950-70. Chm., Glasgow Local Assoc., Educnl Inst. for Scotland, 1958-59; Chm., Scottish Labour Party, 1964; Chief Negotiator on behalf of Scottish Teachers in STSC, 1969-70. FEIS, 1970. *Recreation:* football. *Address:* 11 Ivanhoe Drive, Saltcoats, Ayrshire, Scotland. *T:* Saltcoats 64843. *Club:* Bute and North Ayrshire Constituency Labour Social (Saltcoats).

LAMBO, Prof. Thomas Adeoye, OBE 1962; MD, DPM; FRCPE; JP 1968; Deputy Director-General, World Health Organization, since 1973 (Assistant Director-General, 1971-73); *b* 29 March 1923; *s* of Chief D. B. Lambo, The Otunbade of Igbore, Abeokuta, and Madam F. B. Lambo, The Iyalode of Egba Christians; *m* 1945, Dinah Violet Adams; three *s*. *Educ:* Baptist Boys' High Sch., Abeokuta; Univs of Birmingham and London. From 1949, served as House Surg. and House Phys., Birmingham, England; Med. Officer, Lagos, Zaria and Gusau; Specialist, Western Region Min. of Health, 1957-60; Consultant Psychiatrist, UCH Ibadan, 1956-63; Sen. Specialist, Western Region Min. of Health, Neuro-Psychiatric Centre, 1960-63; Prof. of Psychiatry and Head of Dept of Psychiatry and Neurology, Univ. of Ibadan, 1963-74; Dean, Medical Faculty, Univ. of Ibadan, 1966-68; Vice-Chancellor, Univ. of Ibadan, 1968-71. Member: Scientific Council for Africa (Chm., 1965-70); Expert Adv. Panel on Mental Health, WHO, 1959-71; UN Perm. Adv. Cttee on Prevention of Crime and the Treatment of Offenders (Chm. 1968-71); Exec. Cttee, World Fedn for Mental Health, 1964-; Scientific Adv. Panel, Ciba Foundn, 1966-; WHO Adv. Cttee on Med. Research, 1970-71; Scientific Cttee on Advanced Study in Developmental Sciences, 1967-; Vice-Chm., UN Adv. Cttee on Application of Science and Technology to Development, 1970-71; Co-Chm., Internat. Soc. for Study of Human Development, 1968-; Chm., West African Examinations Council, 1969-71, etc. Mem. Pontifical Acad. of Sciences, 1974-. JP Western State, 1968. Hon. DSc Ahmadu Bello, 1967; Hon. LLD: Kent State, 1969; Birmingham 1971; hon. doctorates: Dahomey, 1973; Aix-Marseille, 1974; Long Island, NY, 1975; Louvain, 1976. Haile Sellassie African Res. Award, 1970. *Publications:* (jtly) Psychiatric Disorders Among the Yorubas, 1961; monographs, and contribs to medical and other scientific jls. *Recreation:* tennis. *Address:* World Health Organization, 1211 Geneva 27, Switzerland. *T:* 34 60 61; (home) Chemin des Châtaigniers 27, 1292 Chambésy-Genève, Switzerland. *T:* 58 19 42.

LAMBOLL, Alan Seymour, JP; Underwriting Member of Lloyd's since 1975; company director; *b* 12 Oct. 1923; *s* of late Frederick Seymour Lamboll and Charlotte Emily Lamboll. *Educ:* Ascham St Vincents, Eastbourne (preparatory sch.); Marlborough Coll. BBC Engineering Staff, 1941-43. Served War: Royal Signals, East Africa Command (Captain), 1943-47. Dir, family firm of wine merchants, City of London, Slack & Lamboll, Ltd, 1947-54. Lloyd's Insurance Broker, Alexr Howden, Stewart Smith (Home), 1954-57; Past Director: Anglo-Portuguese Agencies Ltd (Insurance and Reinsurance Agents), 1957-62; Aga Dictating Machine Co. Ltd, 1962-70; Roger Grayson Ltd, Wine Merchants, 1971-74; Director: Catel Trust Ltd; Ellinger Heath Western (Underwriting Agencies) Ltd; BRC High Tower Ltd; JP Inner London, 1965- (Dep. Chm.). Mem. Council: City and Guilds of London Inst., 1965-78; Toynbee Hall, 1958- (Hon. Sec., 1968-); Drama Centre London Ltd, 1974- (Chm. Council, 1975-). Mem., Royal Gen. Theatrical Fund Assoc., 1963- (Vice-Chm., 1967-); Governor, Mermaid Theatre Trust, 1966-77. Master, Worshipful Co. of Distillers, 1972-73; Master, Worshipful Co. of Parish Clerks, 1975-76; Freedom of City of London, 1947; Common Council, Ward of Langbourn, 1949-70; Alderman, Ward of Castle Baynard, 1970-78; Sheriff, City of London, 1976-77. St John Council for London, 1971-; CStJ 1973. FRSA 1970. *Recreations:* theatre, music. *Address:* E4 Albany, Piccadilly, W1V 9RH. *T:* 01-734 0364. *Clubs:* Athenæum, Garrick, Pratt's.

LAMBORN, Harry George; MP (Lab) Southwark, Peckham, since 1974 (Southwark, May 1972-1974); *b* 1 May 1915; *s* of late Cecil Lamborn, Dulwich; *m* 1938, Lilian Ruth Smith; two *s* one *d*. *Educ:* LCC elementary school. Camberwell Borough Council: Mem., 1953-65; Chm. Health Cttee, 1954-63; Mayor of Camberwell, 1963-64. LCC: Mem., 1958-65; Chm. Health Cttee, 1962-65; GLC: Mem., 1964-73; Dep. Chm., 1971-72. PPS to Chancellor of Exchequer, 1974-. Governor: King's Coll. Hosp., 1965-; Bethlem and Maudsley Hosps, 1966-. Dir, Royal Arsenal Co-operative Soc., 1965-72; Member: Labour Party, 1933-; Union of Shop Distributive and Allied Workers, 1933-; Central Health Services Council, 1963-68. MRSH. *Recreations:* walking, cricket. *Address:* 53 Farne Close, Hailsham, Sussex.

LAMBRICK, Hugh Trevor, CIE 1944; DLitt; Fellow of Oriel College, Oxford, 1947-71, Emeritus Fellow since 1971; *b* 20 April 1904; 2nd *s* of late Rev. C. M. Lambrick; *m* 1948; Gabrielle Margaret (*d* 1968), *yr d* of late H. H. Jennings; two *s*. *Educ:* Rossall; Oriel Coll., Oxford (1st Cl. Hons. Mod. Hist. 1926); DLitt Oxon 1971. Entered ICS 1927; Assistant Commissioner in Sind, 1931; Deputy Commissioner, Upper Sind Frontier, 1934; Collector of Sholapur, 1936; Superintendent of Census, Sind, 1939; Secretary to Governor of Sind, 1941; Civil Adviser to Chief Administrator of Martial Law, Sind, 1942;

Special Commissioner for Sind, 1943-46; retired 1947; Spalding Senior Res. Fellow, Oriel Coll., Oxford, 1947, Treasurer, 1951-55, Res. Fellow and Lectr, 1955-71. FSA 1971. *Publications:* Sir Charles Napier and Sind, 1952; John Jacob of Jacobabad, 1960, illustrated edn, 1975; History of Sind, Vol. I, 1964, 2nd edn 1976; The Terrorist, 1972; Sind before the Muslim Conquest, 1973; numerous articles on Historical and Archæological subjects in Journal of Sind Historical Society since 1935 (President, 1940-43); Census of India, 1941, Vol. XII; Sind. *Recreation:* music. *Address:* Pickett's Heath, Boars Hill, Oxford. *Club:* East India, Devonshire, Sports and Public Schools.

LAMBTON, family name of Earldom of Durham.

LAMBTON, Prof. Ann Katharine Swynford, OBE 1942; FBA 1964; BA, PhD; Professor of Persian, University of London, since 1953; *b* 8 Feb. 1912; *d* of late Hon. George Lambton. PhD London, 1939; DLit London, 1953. Press Attaché, British Embassy (formerly Legation), Tehran, 1939-45; Senior Lecturer in Persian, School of Oriental and African Studies, 1945-48; Reader in Persian, University of London, 1948-53. Hon. DLit Durham, 1971; Hon. LittD Cambridge, 1973. *Publications:* Three Persian Dialects, 1938; Landlord and Peasant in Persia, 1953; Persian Grammar, 1953; Persian Vocabulary, 1964; The Persian Land Reform 1962-66, 1969; (ed, with others) The Cambridge History of Islam, vols 1-11, 1971. *Address:* c/o School of Oriental and African Studies, University of London, WC1. *T:* 01-637 2388.

LAMBTON, Antony Claud Frederick, (Viscount Lambton, courtesy title by which he was known when his father was Earl of Durham); *b* 10 July 1922; *s* of 5th Earl of Durham (*d* 1970) (whose title he disclaimed), and Diana (*d* 1924), *o d* of Granville Farquhar; *m* 1942, Belinda, *d* of Major D. H. Blew-Jones, Westward Ho!, North Devonshire; one *s* five *d*. MP (C) Berwick upon Tweed Div. of Northumberland, 1951-73; Parly Under-Sec. of State, MoD, 1970-May 1973; PPS to the Foreign Secretary, 1955-57. Heir to disclaimed peerages: *s* Hon. Edward Richard Lambton (Baron Durham), *b* 19 Oct. 1961. *Address:* Garden House, Lambton Castle, Fence Houses, Co. Durham; Biddick Hall, Chester-le-Street, Co. Durham.

LAMFORD, (Thomas) Gerald; Commandant, The Police College, since 1976; *b* Carmarthen, 3 April 1928; *s* of late Albert Lamford and Sarah Lamford (*née* Cunnick); *m* 1952, Eira Hale; one *s* one *d*. *Educ:* Technical Coll., Swansea; London Univ. (LLB 1969); Police Coll. (Intermed. Comd Course, 1969; Sen. Comd Course, 1973). Radio Officer, Merchant Navy, 1945; Wireless Operator, RAF, 1946-48, Aden. Joined Carmarthen Constab. (now Dyfed Powys Police), 1949; reached rank of Chief Inspector with substantial background of op. experience in CID and Crime Squad; Force Trng Officer, 1965-69; Supt and Dep. Divl Comdr, Haverfordwest, 1970; Chief Supt, Divl Comdr, Llanelli, 1971-74; Asst Chief Constable, Greater Manchester Police, 1974. Vis. Prof. of Police Science, John Jay Coll. of Criminal Justice, City Univ. of New York, 1972; sometime Vis. Lecturer: Southern Police Inst., Univ. of Louisville, Ky; N Eastern Univ., Boston; Centre of Legal Res., NY Univ. Sch. of Law; Rutgers Univ., NJ; Mercy Coll., Detroit. County Comr, St John Amb. Bde, Pembrokeshire, 1970; SBStJ. Org. Secretary, 1975-76: NW England National Amb. Competition for Policemen; N of England and Scotland Amb. Competition for Policewomen and Cadets. Member: Adv. Cttee on Social Effects of Television, BBC, 1975-; Adv. Cttee for Adult Educn, Univ. of Surrey, 1976-; Bd of Governors, Police Coll., 1977-. *Publications:* articles in Police Studies, Internat. Rev. of Police Develt, and Police Rev. *Recreations:* music, photography, Georgian antiques. *Address:* Bramshill Park, near Hartley Wintney, Hants. *T:* Hartley Wintney 2407.

LAMING, Rev. Canon Frank Fairbairn; Priest-in-Charge, St Ninian's, Glenurquhart, and Hon. Canon, Inverness Cathedral, since 1974; *b* 24 Aug. 1908; *s* of William John Laming and Maude Elizabeth (*née* Fairbairn); *m* 1939, Ruth Marion, *d* of Herbert William Pinder and Rose Marion (*née* Price). *Educ:* King Edward VI Sch., Retford; The Theological Coll., Edinburgh. In business, 1925-33; Edinburgh Theological Coll., 1933-36; Luscombe Scholar, 1936; Durham LTh, 1936. Deacon, 1936; Priest, 1937; Assistant Priest, Christ Church, Glasgow, 1936-39; Priest in Charge, St Margaret, Renfrew, 1939-44; Rector, Holy Trinity Church, Motherwell, 1944-53; Rector and Provost of St Mary's Cathedral, Glasgow, 1953-66; Provost of St Andrew's Cathedral, Inverness, 1966-74. Editor, Year Book and Directory of the Episcopal Church in Scotland, 1976-. *Recreations:* woodworking, gardening, fishing. *Address:* St Ninian's, Glenurquhart, Drumnadrochit, Inverness IV3 6TN. *T:* Glenurquhart 264.

LAMOND, James Alexander, JP; MP (Lab) Oldham East, since 1970; *b* Burrelton, Perthshire, 29 Nov. 1928; *s* of Alexander N. G. Lamond and Christina Lamond (*née* Craig); *m* 1954, June Rose Wellburn; three *d*. *Educ:* Burrelton Sch.; Coupar Angus Sch. Draughtsman, 1944-70. PPS to Minister of State: for NI, 1974-75; DHSS, 1975-76. Mem., Aberdeen City Council, 1959-71; Lord Provost of Aberdeen, 1970-71; Lord Lieutenant of the County of the City of Aberdeen, 1970-71. Mem., AUEW (TASS), 1944- (Chm., No 1 Divisional Council of DATA, 1965-70); Pres., Aberdeen Trades Council, 1969. Pres., World Peace Council. JP Aberdeen. *Recreations:* golf, travel, reading, thinking. *Address:* 15 Belvidere Street, Aberdeen AB2 4QS. *T:* Aberdeen 51074. *Clubs:* Labour, Irish (Oldham); Trades Council, Boilermaker's (Aberdeen).

LAMONT, Norman Stewart Hughson; MP (C) Kingston-upon-Thames since May 1972; Opposition Spokesman on Industry, since 1976; Merchant Banker (N. M. Rothschild & Sons); *b* Lerwick, Shetland, 8 May 1942; *s* of late Daniel Lamont and of Helen Irene (*née* Hughson); *m* 1971, Alice Rosemary, *d* of Lt-Col Peter White; one *s*. *Educ:* Loretto Sch. (scholar); Fitzwilliam Coll., Cambridge (BA). Chm., Cambridge Univ. Conservative Assoc., 1963; Pres., Cambridge Union, 1964; Cambridge Union Debating tour of USA, 1965. PA to Rt Hon. Duncan Sandys, MP, 1965; Conservative Research Dept, 1966-68; Mem., Editorial Bd of Crossbow, 1969-72; Chm., Coningsby Club, 1970-71; Chm., Bow Group, 1971-72. Contested (C) East Hull, Gen. Election, 1970. PPS to Minister for the Arts, 1974; an Opposition Spokesman on Prices and Consumer Affairs, 1975-76. Secretary: Cons. Parly Finance Cttee, 1973-74; Treasurer, Cons. Friends of Israel, 1975-; Mem., Select Cttee on Procedure, 1976-. Mem. Political Cttee, Carlton Club, 1974-. *Publications:* newspaper articles and various Bow Group memoranda. *Recreations:* reading, ornithology, following Association football and American politics. *Address:* House of Commons, SW1. *Club:* Carlton.

LAMONT, William Dawson, MA, DPhil; *b* Prince Edward Island, Canada, 3 Feb. 1901; 4th *s* of Rev. Murdoch Lamont, Rothiemurchus, Inverness-shire, and Euphemia Ann Hume; *m* 1930, Ann Fraser, *d* of Dr David Christie, Glasgow; no *c*. *Educ:* Glasgow Univ. (Edward Caird Medallist; First Class in Moral and Mental Philosophy 1924, Euing Fellow and Ferguson Scholar 1924); Balliol Coll., Oxford. Assistant in Moral Philosophy, University of Glasgow, 1926, and Lecturer, 1929; Professor of Philosophy, University of Cairo, 1942. Principal of Makerere Coll., East Africa, 1946-49. Served with Clyde River Patrol and as Naval Intelligence Liaison Officer, West Scotland, 1939-42. Hon. Secretary Anglo-Egyptian Union, 1944; Vice-Chairman Cairo Group of RIIA, 1944. FSA Scot. 1968. HonDLitt, University of East Africa, 1965. *Publications:* Introduction to Green's Moral Philosophy, 1934; Principles of Moral Judgement, 1946; The Value Judgement, 1955; The Early History of Islay, 1966; Ancient and Mediæval Sculptured Stones of Islay, 1968; articles (on philosophical subjects) in Mind, Proceedings of the Aristotelian Society, Philosophy; (on historical subjects) in Scottish Studies, Proceedings of the Royal Irish Academy. *Recreations:* walking, sailing. *Address:* 37 Kirklee Road, Glasgow G12 0SP. *T:* 041-339 5399.

LAMPE, Rev. Prof. Geoffrey William Hugo, MC 1945; DD; FBA 1963; Regius Professor of Divinity, Cambridge University, since 1971; Fellow of Gonville and Caius College, since 1960; Hon. Canon of Ely Cathedral, since 1971 (Canon, 1960-71); *b* 13 Aug. 1912; *s* of late B. M. Lampe and Laura M. Lampe; *m* 1938, Elizabeth Enid Roberts; one *s* one *d*. *Educ:* Blundell's Sch.; Exeter Coll., Oxford (scholar, MA), DD 1953; Queen's Coll., Birmingham. Ordained, 1937; Curate of Okehampton, 1937-38; Assistant Master, King's Sch., Canterbury, 1938-41; Chaplain to the Forces, 1941-45; Fellow and Chaplain of St John's Coll., Oxford, 1943-53, Hon. Fellow, 1976; Professor of Theology, Birmingham Univ., 1953-59; Dean of the Faculty of Arts, 1955-59; Vice-Principal, 1957-60; Ely Prof. of Divinity, Cambridge Univ., 1959-71; Bampton Lectr, Oxford Univ., 1976. Hon. DD, Edinburgh, 1959; Teol. Dr (*hc*) Lund, 1965. Hon. Canon of Birmingham Cathedral, 1957-59. *Publications:* Aspects of the New Testament Ministry, 1948; The Seal of the Spirit, 1951; Reconciliation in Christ, 1956; (ed) Justification by Faith, 1954; I Believe, 1960; (ed) A Patristic Greek Lexicon, vol. 1, 1961-vol. 5, 1969; (ed) The West from the Fathers to the Reformation (Cambridge History of the Bible), 1969; various essays in symposia and articles in theological journals. *Address:* Gonville and Caius College, Cambridge; Prospect Cottage, Warkworth Street, Cambridge CB1 1EG.

LAMPLOUGH, Maj.-Gen. Charles Robert Wharram, CBE 1945; DSC 1918; DL; JP; Royal Marines, retired; *b* 10 June 1896; *s* of late Robert Lamplough and Louisa Lamplough,

Scarborough; *m* 1921, Doris Mary Ford; one *d. Educ:* Warwick Sch. Served European War, 1914-18: joined Royal Marines, 1914, and served in Mediterranean and in Grand Fleet, Dardanelles and Zeebrugge (DSC). Served, 1919-39, in HM ships in various waters and held instructional and staff appointments at home and in Far East. Served War of 1939-45 on Naval Staff, Admiralty, and in 1943 returned to Far East as Maj.-General on staff of Supreme Allied Commander, SEAC (CBE). ADC to King George VI, 1946; Maj.-General Commanding Plymouth Group, Royal Marines, 1946-49; retired, 1949; Hon. Colonel Comdt, Plymouth Group Royal Marines, 1953-57. DL Devonshire, 1966; JP County of Devon, 1954. *Address:* Falklands, 32 Salterton Road, Exmouth, Devon. *T:* Exmouth 3648.

LAMPLUGH, Rt. Rev. Kenneth Edward Norman; Residentiary Canon, 1951-62, Hon. Canon, 1962, Hon. Chaplain, 1972, Winchester Cathedral; Chaplain and Sub-Prelate of the Venerable Order of St John of Jerusalem, since 1962; *b* 9 Nov. 1901; *m* 1928, Naomi Ford (*d* 1973); three *s* one *d. Educ:* King's Coll., Cambridge; Cuddesdon Coll., Oxford. Deacon 1925; Priest 1926; Curate of Lambeth, 1925-28; Curate of Pietermaritzburg Cathedral, Natal, 1928-31; Vicar of St Mary's, Durban, 1931-33; Vicar of Hartley Wintney, 1934; Commiss. to Bishop of Natal, 1937; Vicar of Lymington, 1941; Rural Dean of Lyndhurst, 1942; officiating CF, 1940-46; Archdeacon and Canon Residentiary of Lincoln, 1947-51; Warden of Lincoln Diocesan Association of Lay Readers, 1947; Suffragan Bishop of Southampton, 1951-71. Examining Chaplain to Bishop of Winchester, 1951-71. Chaplain, QEII Premier World Cruise, 1968. Chairman: Wessex Council on Alcoholism, 1969; Atherley School, Southampton, 1952-71; Talbot Heath School, Bournemouth, 1962-71; Council of Southampton University, 1951-71. Fellow, Soc. of St Mary and St Nicholas, Lancing, 1952. Pres., Hants Assoc. for the Blind, 1951-72; Chm., Hants and IoW Assoc. for the Deaf, 1951-72. *Recreation:* travelling. *Address:* Butts Close Cottage, Winchester, Hants. *T:* Winchester 68533.

LAMPLUGH, Maj.-Gen. Stephen, CB 1954; CBE 1943; retired 1955; Past Director of Civil Defence, Northern Region (Newcastle upon Tyne), 1955-64; *b* 25 May 1900; *s* of late George William Lamplugh, FRS, Driffield, Yorks; *m* 1938, Mary Lewis, *d* of A. H. Vesey, Suddon Grange, Wincanton, Somerset; one *s* one *d. Educ:* St Albans; RMA, Woolwich. 2nd Lieut RE, 1919; Major, 1938; Lt-Col (temp.), 1940; Brigadier (temp.), 1942; Maj.-Gen. (temp.), 1945 and 1952; Colonel, 1945; Brigadier, 1947; Maj.-General, 1953. Served Near East, 1922-23; NW Frontier, 1930; France, 1939-40 (despatches) psc 1937. Commander Rhine District, BAOR, 1952-55, retired 1955. Chairman Joint War Office Treasury Cttee, 1955. *Recreations:* normal. *Address:* Quarry Cottage, Charlton Horethorne, Sherborne, Dorset. *T:* Corton Denham 249.

LAMPSON, family name of **Baron Killearn.**

LANCASTER, Bishop Suffragan of, since 1975; **Rt. Rev. Dennis Fountain Page;** *b* 1 Dec. 1919; *s* of Prebendary Martin Fountain Page and Lilla Fountain Page; *m* 1946, Margaret Bettine Clayton; two *s* one *d. Educ:* Shrewsbury Sch.; Gonville and Caius Coll., Cambridge (MA); Lincoln Theological Coll. Curate, Rugby Parish Church, 1943; Priest-in-Charge, St George's Church, Hillmorton, Rugby, 1945; Rector of Hockwold, Vicar of Wilton and Rector of Weeting, Norfolk, 1949; Archdeacon of Huntingdon and Vicar of Yaxley, 1965-75; Hon. Canon of Ely Cathedral, 1968. *Recreations:* music, carpentry, gardening. *Address:* Winmarleigh Vicarage, Preston PR3 0LA.

LANCASTER, Bishop of, (RC), since 1962; **Rt. Rev. Brian Charles Foley;** *b* Ilford, 25 May 1910. *Educ:* St Cuthbert's Coll., Ushaw; Gregorian Univ., Rome. Priest, 1937; Assistant Priest, Shoeburyness; subseq. Assistant Priest, Romford; Parish Priest, Holy Redeemer, Harold Hill, and Holy Cross, Harlow. Canon of Brentwood Diocese, 1959. *Address:* Bishop's House, Cannon Hill, Lancaster.

LANCASTER, Archdeacon of; *see* Gower-Jones, Ven. G.

LANCASTER, Dame Jean, DBE 1963; *b* 11 Aug. 1909; *d* of late Richard C. Davies; *m* 1967, Roy Cavander Lancaster. *Educ:* Merchant Taylors' Sch., Crosby, Lancashire. Director, Women's Royal Naval Service, 1961-64. *Address:* 2 Fair Meadow, Rye Hill, Rye, E Sussex.

LANCASTER, Joan Cadogan; Director, India Office Library and Records, 1972-July 1978; *b* 2 Aug. 1918; *yr d* of Cyril Cadogan Lancaster and Mary Ann Lancaster. *Educ:* Charles Edward

Brooke Sch., London; Westfield Coll., Univ. of London. BA 1940, MA 1943; ALA 1943; FRHistS 1956; FSA 1960. Asst Librarian, University Coll., Leicester, and Asst Archivist, the Museum, Leicester, 1940-43. Served War, ATS, 1943-46. Archivist, City of Coventry, 1946-48; Asst Librarian, Inst. of Historical Research, Univ. of London, 1948-60; Asst Keeper, India Office Records, 1960-67; Dep. Librarian and Dep. Keeper, India Office Library and Records, 1968-72. Reviews Editor, Archives (Jl of British Records Assoc.), 1951-57, Editor, Archives, 1957-63. *Publications:* Guide to St Mary's Hall, Coventry, 1949; Bibliography of historical works issued in the United Kingdom 1946-56 (Inst. of Historical Research), 1957; Guide to lists and catalogues of the India Office Records, 1966; Godiva of Coventry, 1967; India Office Records: Report for the years 1947-67 (FCO), 1970; contribs on Coventry to Victoria County History, 1969, and to Historic Towns, vol. 2, 1974; articles and reviews in Bulletin of Inst. of Historical Research, Archives, etc. *Recreations:* music, photography. *Address:* 43 Craignair Road, Tulse Hill, SW2. *T:* 01-674 3451. *Club:* United Oxford & Cambridge University.

LANCASTER, Vice-Admiral Sir John (Strike), KBE 1961; CB 1958; retired 1962; *b* 26 June 1903; *s* of George Henry Lancaster; *m* 1927, Edith Laurie Jacobs; two *d. Educ:* King Edward VI Sch., Southampton. Joined RN, 1921; Commander, 1940; Captain, 1951; Rear-Admiral, 1956; Vice-Admiral, 1959. Served War of 1939-45: HMS Gloucester; RN Barracks, Portsmouth; Persian Gulf; HMS Ocean. Rear-Admiral Personnel, Home Air Command, Lee-on-the-Solent, 1956; Director-General of Manpower, 1959-62; Chief Naval Supply and Secretariat Officer, 1959-62. *Recreation:* gardening. *Address:* Moorings, Western Way, Alverstoke, Hants. *Club:* Army and Navy. *See also* P. M. Lancaster.

LANCASTER, Sir Osbert, Kt 1975; CBE 1953; Artist and Writer; *b* 4 Aug. 1908; *o s* of late Robert Lancaster and Clare Bracebridge Manger; *m* 1933, Karen (*d* 1964), 2nd *d* of late Sir Austin Harris, KBE; one *s* one *d; m* 1967, Anne Scott-James, *qv. Educ:* Charterhouse; Lincoln Coll., Oxford; Slade Sch. Hon. FRIBA. Cartoonist Daily Express since 1939; Foreign Office (News Dept), 1940; Attached to HM Embassy, Athens, 1944-46; Sydney Jones Lecturer in Art, Liverpool Univ., 1947. Adviser to GLC Historic Buildings Bd, 1969-. Governor King Edward VII Sch., King's Lynn. Hon. DLitt: Birmingham Univ., 1964; Newcastle-upon-Tyne, 1970; St Andrews, 1974; Oxon, 1975. Fellow, University College, London, 1967. Theatre Décors: Pineapple Poll, Sadler's Wells, 1951; Bonne Bouche, Covent Garden, 1952; Love in a Village, English Opera Group, 1952; High Spirits, Hippodrome, 1953; Rake's Progress, Edinburgh (for Glyndebourne), 1953; All's Well That Ends Well, Old Vic, 1953; Don Pasquale, Sadler's Wells, 1954; Coppelia, Covent Garden, 1954; Napoli, Festival Ballet, 1954; Falstaff, Edinburgh (for Glyndebourne), 1955; Hotel Paradiso, Winter Garden, 1956; Zuleika, Saville, 1957; L'Italiana in Algeri, Glyndebourne, 1957; Tiresias, English Opera Group, 1958; Candide, Saville, 1959; La fille mal gardée, Covent Garden, 1960; She Stoops to Conquer, Old Vic, 1960; La Pietra del Paragone, Glyndebourne, 1964; Peter Grimes, Bulgarian National Opera, Sofia, 1964; L'Heure Espagnole, Glyndebourne, 1966; The Rising of the Moon, Glyndebourne, 1970; The Sorcerer, D'Oyly-Carte, 1971. *Publications:* Progress at Pelvis Bay, 1936; Our Sovereigns, 1936; Pillar to Post, 1938; Homes, Sweet Homes, 1939; Classical Landscape with Figures, 1947; The Saracen's Head, 1948; Drayneflete Revealed, 1949; Façades and Faces, 1950; Private Views, 1956; The Year of the Comet, 1957; Etudes, 1958; Here, of All Places, 1959, reissued as A Cartoon History of Architecture, 1964; Signs of the Times, 1961; All Done From Memory (Autobiog.), 1963; With an Eye to the Future (Autobiog.), 1967; Temporary Diversions, 1968; Sailing to Byzantium, 1969; Recorded Live, 1970; Meaningful Confrontations, 1971; Theatre in the Flat, 1972; The Littlehampton Bequest, 1973; (with Anne Scott-James) The Pleasure Garden, 1977. *Recreation:* topography. *Address:* 12 Eaton Square, SW1. *Clubs:* Brooks's, Pratt's, Beefsteak, Garrick.

LANCASTER, Patricia Margaret; Headmistress, Wycombe Abbey School, since 1974; *b* 22 Feb. 1929; *d* of Vice-Adm. Sir John Lancaster, *qv. Educ:* Univs of London (BA) and Southampton (Certif. Educn). English Mistress, St Mary's Sch., Calne, 1951-58; Housemistress, St Swithun's Sch., Winchester, 1958-62; Headmistress, St Michael's, Burton Park, Petworth, 1962-73. *Recreation:* theatre. *Address:* Wycombe Abbey School, High Wycombe, Bucks. *T:* High Wycombe 20381.

LANCE, Rev. Preb. John Du Boulay, MC 1945; MA; Prebendary of Henstridge in Wells Cathedral, since 1974; *b* 14 March 1907; *s* of late Rev. Arthur Porcher Lance and Harriet Agatha Lance,

Buckland St Mary, Somerset; *m* 1936, Lena Winifred Clifford; one *s*. *Educ:* Marlborough; Jesus Coll., Cambridge; Cuddesdon Theological Coll. Assistant Curate, St Peter, Wolverhampton, 1930-34; Missioner, Trinity Coll., Oxford. Mission, Stratford, 1934-36; Vicar of Bishops Lydeard, 1936-47. Chaplain to the Forces, 1941-46 (despatches). Vicar of St Andrew's, Taunton, 1947-57; Preb. of Wells, 1951-63; Rector of Bathwick, Bath, 1957-63; Archdeacon of Wells and Canon of Wells Cathedral, 1963-73; Diocesan Dir of Ordinands, Wells, 1974-76. Proctor in Convocation, 1959-64; Diocesan Adviser in Christian Stewardship, 1961-67; Warden, Abbey Retreat House, Glastonbury, 1965-. *Address:* The Glebe House, Corfe, Taunton, Somerset. *T:* Blagdon Hill 404. *Club:* Hawks (Cambridge).

LANCELYN GREEN, Roger G.; *see* Green, R. G. L.

LANCHBERY, John Arthur, FRAM; Principal Conductor, Royal Ballet, since 1959; Musical Director, Australian Ballet, since 1972; *b* London, 15 May 1923; *s* of William Lanchbery and Violet (*née* Mewett); *m* 1951, Elaine Fifield (divorced 1960); one *d*. *Educ:* Alleyn's Sch., Dulwich; Royal Academy of Music. Henry Smart Composition Scholarship, 1942. Served, Royal Armoured Corps, 1943-45. Royal Academy of Music, 1945-47; Musical Director, Metropolitan Ballet, 1948-50; Sadler's Wells Theatre Ballet, 1951-57; Royal Ballet, 1957-. ARAM 1953; Bolshoi Theatre Medal, Moscow, 1961. *Publications:* Arrangements and Compositions of Ballets include: Pleasuredrome, 1949; Eve of St Agnes (BBC commission), 1950; House of Birds, 1955; La Fille Mal Gardée, 1960; The Dream, 1964; Don Quixote, 1966; Giselle, 1968; La Sylphide, 1970; Tales of Beatrix Potter, 1971; Tales of Hoffman, 1972; Merry Widow, 1975; Month in the Country, 1976. *Recreations:* walking, reading. *Club:* Garrick.

LANCHESTER, Elsa; Actress; *d* of James Sullivan and Edith Lanchester; *m* 1929, Charles Laughton (*d* 1962); became American Citizen, 1950. *Educ:* Privately. Started the Children's Theatre, Charlotte Street, Soho, 1918; first appearance on stage, 1922; afterwards played at Lyric, Hammersmith, in The Way of the World, 1924, in The Duenna, 1924 and in Riverside Nights, 1926; first appearance in New York at Lyceum Theatre, 1931; joined Old Vic-Sadler's Wells company, 1933; was Peter Pan, Palladium, 1936; was in They Walk Alone, New York, 1941; 10 years as star of Turnabout Theatre, Los Angeles, California; Turnabout Theatre, nightly continuously, from 1941. Acted in The Party, London, 1958. Has appeared in films including The Constant Nymph, Potiphar's Wife, The Private Life of Henry VIII, David Copperfield, Bride of Frankenstein, Naughty Marietta, The Ghost Goes West, Rembrandt, Vessel of Wrath, Ladies in Retirement, Son of Fury, Passport to Destiny, Lassie Come Home, Spiral Staircase, Razor's Edge, The Big Clock, The Inspector General, The Secret Garden, Come to the Stable, Buccaneer Girl, The Glass Slipper, Witness for the Prosecution, Bell, Book and Candle, Mary Poppins, That Darn Cat, Blackbeard's Ghost, Me Natalie, Rascal, My Dog, The Thief, Willard, Terror in the Wax Museum, Arnold. Television series, The John Forsythe Show; talk shows: Jack Paar; David Frost; Dick Cavitt; Johnny Carson; Joey Bishop. *Publication:* Charles Laughton and I, 1938. *Recreation:* wild flowers. *Address:* 9405 Brighton Way, Beverly Hills, Calif 90210, USA.

LANCHIN, Gerald; Under Secretary, Shipping Policy Division, Department of Trade, since 1975; *b* 17 Oct. 1922; *o s* of late Samuel Lanchin, Kensington; *m* 1951, Valerie Sonia Lyons; one *s* two *d*. *Educ:* St Marylebone Grammar Sch.; London Sch. of Economics. BCom 1st cl. hons 1951; Leverhulme Schol. 1950-51. Min. of Labour, 1939-51; served with Army, RAOC and REME, 1942-46; Board of Trade (subseq. DTI and Dept of Trade): Asst Principal, 1952; Principal 1953; 1st Sec., UK Delegn to OEEC, Paris, 1955-59; Principal, Estabt and Commercial Relations and Exports Divs, 1959-66; Asst Sec., Finance and Civil Aviation Divs, 1966-71; Under-Sec., Tariff and Commercial Relations and Export Divs, 1971-75. *Recreations:* reading, gardening, music. *Address:* Herrick, Doggetts Wood Close, Chalfont St Giles, Bucks. *T:* 02-404 2822. *Club:* Reform.

LAND, Edwin Herbert; US physicist and inventor; Founder Chairman of Board, Chief Executive Officer, and Director of Research, Polaroid Corporation, Cambridge, Massachusetts (President, 1937-75); Fellow and Visiting Institute Professor, Massachusetts Institute of Technology, since 1956; Member, Board of Trustees, Ford Foundation, since 1967; *b* Bridgeport, Connecticut, 7 May 1909; *s* of Harry M. and Matha G. Land; *m* 1929, Helen Maislen; two *d*. *Educ:* Norwich Acad.; Harvard. Founded Polaroid Corporation, 1937. War of 1941-45, in charge of research into development of weapons and materials, and

cons. on missiles to US Navy. Invented polarizer for light in form of extensive synthetic sheet; also camera which produces complete photograph immediately after exposure, 1947. Member: President's Foreign Intelligence Adv. Bd; Nat. Commn on Technology, Automation, and Economic Progress, 1965-66; Carnegie Commn on Educational TV, 1966-67; William James Lectr on Psychology, Harvard, 1966-67. Awards include: Hood Medal and Progress Medal, RPS; Cresson Medal and Potts Medal, Franklin Inst.; Scott Medal, Philadelphia City Trusts; Rumford Medal, Amer. Acad. of Arts and Sciences, 1945; Holley Medal, Amer. Soc. Mech. Engrs, 1948; Duddell Medal, British Physical Soc., 1949. Presidential Medal of Freedom, 1963; Nat. Medal of Science, 1967. Mem., President's Science Adv. Cttee, USA. Fellow: Photographic Soc. of America; Amer. Acad. of Arts and Sciences (Past Pres.); Royal Photographic Society; Nat. Acad. of Science, etc. Hon. MRI, 1975; Hon. Fellow: Royal Microscopical Society, and many other American and foreign learned bodies. ScD (Hon.) Harvard Univ., 1957, and holds many other hon. doctorates in science and law. *Publications:* contributions Journal Opt. Soc. America, Amer. Scientist, Proceedings of Nat. Acad. of Science. *Recreations:* music, horseback riding. *Address:* 163 Brattle Street, Cambridge, Mass 02108, USA. *T:* Univ. 4-6000; 730 Main Street, Cambridge, Mass 02139. *Clubs:* Harvard (NY and Boston); Century Association (New York); St Botolph, Harvard Faculty (Boston); Cosmos (Washington, DC).

LAND, Prof. Frank William, MSc, PhD London; Professor of Education, University of Hull, 1961-77; *b* 9 Jan. 1911; *s* of Charles and Mary Land; *m* 1937, Nora Beatrice Channon; two *s* one *d*. *Educ:* King's Coll., University of London. Assistant Master, The Grammar School, Hampton-on-Thames, 1933-37; Mathematics Lecturer: College of St Mark and St John, Chelsea, 1937-39; Birkbeck Coll., London, 1939-40. Instructor Lieut, Royal Navy, 1940-46. Vice-Principal, College of St Mark and St John, Chelsea, 1946-49; Senior Lecturer, University of Liverpool, 1950-61. Chairman, Association of Teachers in Colleges and Departments of Education, 1956-57. *Publications:* Recruits to Teaching, 1960; The Language of Mathematics, 1961. *Recreations:* gardening, walking. *Address:* 4 West End Road, Cottingham, North Humberside.

LANDA, Hon. Abram, CMG 1968; LLB; Agent-General for New South Wales in London, 1965-70; *b* 10 Nov. 1902; *s* of late D. Landa, Belfast; *m* 1930, Perla (*d* 1976), *d* of late L. Levy; one *s* one *d*. *Educ:* Christian Brothers' Coll., Waverley, NSW; University of Sydney. Solicitor, 1927-. MLA for Bondi, NSW, 1930-32 and 1941-65; Minister for Labour and Industry, 1953-56; Minister for Housing and Co-operative Societies, 1959-65; Minister for Housing, NSW, 1956-65. Past Member Senate, University of Sydney; Past Trustee, NSW Public Library. *Recreations:* swimming, bowls. *Address:* 22 Coolong Road, Vaucluse, NSW, Australia. *Club:* Tattersall's (Sydney).

LANDALE, Russell Talbot; HM Diplomatic Service, retired 1971; Consul-General, Amsterdam, 1969-71; *b* 25 Oct. 1911; 3rd *s* of late W. H. Landale and Ethel (*née* Talbot); *m* 1938, Margaret Myfanwy George; two *d* (one *s* decd). *Educ:* Berkhamsted Sch.; Wiesbaden Konservatorium; Rackows Kaufmännische Schule, Dresden; Institut de Touraine, Tours. British Tabulating Machine Co. (now ICL), 1933-39; HM Forces, 1940-46; Diplomatic Service, 1946-71. Chevalier de l'Ordre de Méduse, 1974. *Recreations:* viticulture, writing, music (compositions include Song of the Waves, Silver Jubilee Rag, Last Time We Met, Love has almost Gone, Meribel, Tulips of Holland, Let Our People Go, On Poets, Carol's Dance, Petit Nocturne Petite Valse, songs for children). *Address:* Fleur de France, Route de l'Ormée, 06140 Vence, France. *T:* Vence 580369.

LANDAU, Dennis Marcus; Deputy Chief Executive Officer, Co-operative Wholesale Society Ltd, since 1974; *b* 18 June 1927; *s* of late Michael Landau, metallurgist. *Educ:* Haberdashers' Aske's Hampstead Sch. Schweppes Ltd, 1952; Man. Dir, Scweppes (East Africa) Ltd, 1958-62; Chivers-Hartley: Prodn Dir, 1963; Man. Dir, 1966-69; Chm., Schweppes Foods Div., 1969; Dep. Chm. and Man. Dir, Cadbury Schweppes Foods, 1970; Controller, Food Div., Co-operative Wholesale Society Ltd, 1971. Director: C. W. S. Svineslagterier A/s; Co-operative Retail Services Ltd; Sorbie Cheese Ltd; J. W. French (Milling & Baking Holdings) Ltd. Mem., Metrication Bd, 1972-; Mem., Exec. Cttee, Food Manufacturers' Fedn Inc., 1972-. *Recreations:* Rugby, cricket, music. *Address:* 9 Grey Road, Altrincham, Cheshire WA14 4BT. *T:* 061-928 4116. *Club:* Bath; Lancashire CC.

LANDER, Donald Hartley; Vice President, Europe, Chrysler Corporation, and President, Chrysler International SA, since

1976; b 2 Aug. 1925; s of late Ralph Lander and of Ruby Lander; m 1946, Dorothy Marguerite (née Balmer); one s three d. Educ: Whitby High Sch., Ont, Canada; Univ. of BC (extension course). Sales and marketing, General Motors, 1945-59, Chrysler Corp., 1959-67; Vice-Pres., Parts Div., Chrysler Canada Ltd, 1967-68; Gen. Man., Import Vehicle Div., Chrysler Corp., 1968-69; Exec. Vice Pres., Chrysler Canada, 1969-70; Dep. Man. Dir, Chrysler UK Ltd, 1970-73, Man. Dir, 1973-76. Recreations: golf, skiing, water skiing. Address: 9 Phillimore Gardens, W8.

LANDER, Frank Patrick Lee, OBE 1944; MD, FRCP; Principal Medical Officer, Guardian & Royal Exchange Assurance Co.; Member, Lord Chancellor's Pensions Appeals Tribunal; Consulting Physician, Royal Free Hospital, since 1937, Brompton Hospital and Putney Hospital since 1939; b 1906; e s of Edward Lee and Alice Mary Lander, Morecambelake, Dorset; m 1932, Dorothy Briggs; two s. Educ: Dover Coll.; Middlesex Hospital. Medical Registrar: Middlesex Hospital, 1931, Brompton Hospital, 1934. Lt-Col, RAMC, 1941-45: North Africa, Sicily and Italy (despatches). Examiner in Medicine, University of London, University of Cambridge, University Coll., of the West Indies, and Royal College of Physicians. Formerly Censor, and Senior Censor, Royal College of Physicians. Publications: various articles in leading medical journals. Recreation: fishing. Address: 11 Wimpole Street, W1. T: 01-580 2955. Club: Savile.

LANDON, Alfred Mossman; Independent Oil Producer; b 9 Sept. 1887; s of John Manuel Landon and Anne Mossman; m 1915, Margaret Fleming (d 1918); one d; m 1930, Theo Cobb; one s one d. Educ: University of Kansas. Republican State Chm., 1928; Governor of Kansas, 1933-37; Republican nominee for Pres. of United States, 1936; Delegate to Eighth International Conference, Lima, Peru, 1938; Chm. Kansas Delegation Republican Nat. Convention, 1940, 1944, and 1948; Mem. Methodist Church; Member, Kansas Bar; Member, Phi Gamma Delta; Mason, Elks, Odd Fellows. Hon. LHD Kansas State, 1968; Hon. LLD Emporia Coll., 1969. Distinguished Citizenship Award: Washburn Univ., 1967; Baker Univ., 1975. Recreations: horseback riding, fishing, bridge. Address: PO Box 1280, Topeka, Kansas 66601, USA; Prospect Hills, Topeka, Kansas 66606, USA. T: 233-4136.

LANDON, Howard Chandler Robbins; author and music historian; b 6 March 1926; s of William Grinnell Landon and Dorothea LeBaron Robbins. Educ: Aiken Preparatory Sch.; Lenox Sch.; Swarthmore Coll.; Boston Univ., USA (BMus). European rep. of Intercollegiate Broadcasting System, 1947; founded Haydn Soc. (which recorded and printed music of Joseph Haydn), 1949; became a Special Correspondent of The Times, 1957 and contrib. to that newspaper until 1961. Visiting Prof., Queen's Coll., NYC, 1969; Regents Prof. of Music, Univ. of California (Davis), 1970 and 1975; Hon. Professorial Fellow, University Coll., Cardiff, 1971. Hon. DMus: Boston Univ., 1969; Queen's Univ., Belfast, 1974. Verdienstkreuz für Kunst und Wissenschaft from Austrian Govt, 1972. Publications: The Symphonies of Joseph Haydn, 1955 (London); The Mozart Companion (co-ed with Donald Mitchell), 1956 (London); The Collected Correspondence and London Notebooks of Joseph Haydn, 1959 (London); Essays on Eighteenth-Century Music, 1969 (London); Ludwig van Beethoven: a documentary study, 1970 (London); critical edn of the 107 Haydn Symphonies, (completed) 1968; five-vol. biog. of Haydn: vol. 3, Haydn in England, 1976; vol. 4, Haydn: The Years of Creation, 1977; vol. 5, Haydn: The Late Years, 1977; vol. 1, Haydn: The Early Years, and vol. 2, Haydn in Eszterhaza, 1978-79; scholarly edns of eighteenth-century music (various European publishing houses). Recreations: swimming, cooking, walking. Address: Anton Frankgasse 3, Vienna 1180, Austria. T: 314205; Hirschbach 114 (Vitis), 3942 Austria. T: 02854/35518.

LANE, Dr Anthony John, FRCP, FFCM; Regional Medical Officer, North Western Regional Health Authority, since 1974; b 6 Feb. 1926; s of John Gill Lane and Marian (née Brumfield); m 1948, Hannah Holečková; one s two d. Educ: St Christopher's Sch., Letchworth; Emmanuel Coll., Cambridge. MA,MB,BChir. House posts in surgery, medicine, obstetrics and paediatrics, 1949-51; MO with Methodist Missionary Soc., Andhra State, India, 1951-57; Registrar: Tropical Diseases, UCH, 1958; Gen. Med., St James' Hosp., Balham, 1958-61; Infectious Diseases, Western Hosp., Fulham, 1961-63; MO (Trainee), Leeds RHB, 1963-64; Asst Sen. MO, Leeds RHB, 1964-66; Principal Asst Sen. MO, Leeds RHB, 1966-70; Dep. Sen. Admin. MO, SW Metrop. RHB, 1970-71; Sen. Admin. MO, Manchester RHB, 1971-74. Publications: contrib. Positions, Movements and Directions in Health Services Research, 1974; contrib. Proc. Royal Soc. Med. Recreations: music, competitive indoor games, walking, gardening. Address:

4 Queens Road, Wilmslow, Cheshire, SK9 5HS. T: (office) 061-236 9456.

LANE, Dr Anthony Milner, FRS 1975; Deputy Chief Scientific Officer, Atomic Energy Research Establishment, Harwell, since 1976; b 27 July 1928; s of Herbert William Lane and Doris Ruby Lane (née Milner); m 1952, Anne Sophie Zissman; two s one d. Educ: Trowbridge Boys' High Sch.; Selwyn Coll., Cambridge. BA Maths, PhD Theoretical Physics. Joined Harwell, 1953. Publications: Nuclear Theory, 1963; numerous research articles in Review of Modern Physics, Phys. Review, Nuclear Physics, etc. Recreations: gardening, bird-watching. Address: Nayles Bridge Cottage, Church Road, Blewbury, Didcot, Oxon OX11 9PY. T: Blewbury 850416.

LANE, David Neil; HM Diplomatic Service; Counsellor, British Embassy, Ankara, since 1975; b 16 April 1928; er s of late Clive Lane and of Hilda Lane, Bath; m 1968, Sara, d of Cecil Nurcombe, MC; two d. Educ: Abbotsholme Sch.; Merton Coll., Oxford (Cl. I Mod. Hist.). Army, 1946-48; Foreign (later Foreign and Commonwealth) Office: 1951-53, 1955-58, 1963-68, 1972-74; British Embassy, Oslo, 1953-55; Ankara, 1959-61; Conakry, 1961-63; UK Mission to the United Nations, New York, 1968-72; Pres., UN Trusteeship Council, 1971-72; UK Delegate, Internat. Exhibns Bureau, 1973-74. Recreations: music, walking, ski-ing. Address: British Embassy, Ankara, Turkey. T: 27 43 10. Club: Travellers'.

LANE, David William Stennis Stuart; Chairman, Commission for Racial Equality, since 1977; b 24 Sept. 1922; s of Hubert Samuel Lane, MC; m 1955, Lesley Anne Mary Clauson; two s. Educ: Eton; Trinity Coll., Cambridge; Yale Univ. Served War of 1939-45 (Navy). British Iron and Steel Federation, 1948 (Sec., 1956); Shell International Petroleum Co., 1959-67. Called to the Bar, Middle Temple, 1955. Chm., N Kensington Cons. Assoc., 1961-62. Contested (C) Lambeth (Vauxhall), 1964, Cambridge, 1966; MP (C) Cambridge, Sept. 1967-Nov. 1976; PPS to Sec. of State for Employment, 1970-72; Parly Under-Sec. of State, Home Office, 1972-74. Recreations: walking, golf, cricket. Address: 40 Chepstow Place, W2; 5 Spinney Drive, Great Shelford, Cambridge. Club: MCC.

LANE, Hon. Dame Elizabeth (Kathleen), DBE 1965; Hon. Mrs Justice Lane; a Judge of the High Court, Family Division (formerly Probate, Divorce and Admiralty Division), since 1965; b 9 Aug. 1905; o d of late Edward Alexander Coulborn and late Kate May Coulborn (née Wilkinson); m 1926, Henry Jerrold Randall Lane, CBE (d 1975); one s decd. Educ: Malvern Girls Coll. and privately. Barrister, Inner Temple, 1940; Master of the Bench, 1965. Mem. of Home Office Committee on Depositions in Criminal Cases, 1948. An Asst Recorder of Birmingham, 1953-61; Chm. of Birmingham Region Mental Health Review Tribunal, 1960-62; Recorder of Derby, 1961-62; Commissioner of the Crown Court at Manchester, 1961-62; Judge of County Courts, 1962-65; Acting Dep. Chm., London Sessions, 1965. Chm., Cttee on the Working of the Abortion Act, 1971-73. Recreations: travel, needlework. Address: The Royal Courts of Justice, Strand, WC2.

LANE, Frank Laurence, CBE 1961; Chairman: Elder Dempster Lines Ltd, 1963-May 1972; b 1912; s of late Herbert Allardyce Lane, CIE, and late Hilda Gladys Duckle Lane (née Wraith); m 1938, Gwendolin Elizabeth Peterkin; one s. Educ: Wellington Coll., Berks; New Coll., Oxford. Mansfield & Co. Ltd, Singapore and Penang, 1934-42; BOAC, UK and USA, 1942-45; Mansfield & Co. Ltd, Singapore, 1945-61; Elder Dempster Lines Ltd, Liverpool, 1962-72. Recreations: golf, fishing. Address: House in the Trees, Emery Down, Lyndhurst, Hampshire. T: Lyndhurst 2497.

LANE, Rt. Hon. Sir Geoffrey Dawson, PC 1974; Kt 1966; AFC 1943; **Rt. Hon. Lord Justice Geoffrey Lane;** a Lord Justice of Appeal, since 1974; b 17 July 1918; s of late Percy Albert Lane, Lincoln; m 1944, Jan, d of Donald Macdonald; one s. Educ: Shrewsbury; Trinity Coll., Cambridge. Served in RAF, 1939-45; Sqdn-Leader, 1942. Called to Bar, Gray's Inn, 1946; Bencher 1966. QC 1962. Dep. Chm., Beds. QS, 1960-66; Recorder of Bedford, 1963-66; a Judge of the High Court of Justice, Queen's Bench Div., 1966-74. Mem., Parole Board, 1970-72 (Vice-Chm., 1972). Address: Royal Courts of Justice, Strand, WC2.

LANE, Jane, (Mrs Andrew Dakers); author; (Elaine) y d of late Mason Kidner; m 1937, Andrew Dakers; one s. Adopting pseudonym of Jane Lane (maiden name of maternal grandmother), wrote first novel at age of seventeen. Publications: Undaunted, 1934; Be Valiant Still, 1935; King's Critic, 1935; Prelude to Kingship, 1936; Come to the March, 1937; Sir Devil May Care, 1937; You Can't Run Away, 1940;

England for Sale, 1943; He Stooped to Conquer, 1944; Gin and Bitters, 1945; His Fight is Ours, 1946; London Goes to Heaven, 1947; Parcel of Rogues, 1948; Fortress in the Forth, 1950; Dark Conspiracy, 1952; The Sealed Knot, 1952; The Lady of the House, 1953; Thunder on St Paul's Day, 1954; The Phœnix and the Laurel, 1954; Conies in the Hay, 1957; Command Performance, 1957; Queen of the Castle, 1958; Ember In the Ashes, 1960; Sow the Tempest, 1960; Farewell to the White Cockade, 1961; The Crown for a Lie, 1962; A State of Mind, 1964; The Wind through the Heather, 1965; From the Snare of the Hunters, 1968; The Young and Lonely King, 1969; The Questing Beast, 1970; A Call of Trumpets, 1971; The Severed Crown, 1972; Bridge of Sighs, 1973; Heirs of Squire Harry, 1974; A Summer Storm, 1976; A Secret Chronicle, 1977; in addition to these: *books for children:* The Escape of the King, 1950; The Escape of the Prince, 1951; Desperate Battle, 1953; The Escape of the Queen, 1957; The Escape of the Duke, 1960; The Escape of the Princess, 1962; The Trial of the King, 1963; The Return of the King, 1964; The March of the Prince, 1965; The Champion of the King, 1966; *biographies and history:* King James the Last, 1943; Titus Oates, 1949; Puritan, Rake and Squire, 1950; The Reign of King Covenant, 1961; Cat among the Pigeons, 1959. *Recreations:* riding and embroidery. *Address:* Kingsbury, 97 Sea Road, Angmering-on-Sea, Sussex.

LANE, John; Under-Secretary, Department of Transport, since 1976; *b* 23 Oct. 1924; *e s* of R. J. I. and M. E. L. Lane; *m* 1954, Ruth Ann Crocker; one *s. Educ:* John Lyon Sch., Harrow; HMS Conway; Univ. of London (BSc(Econ)). Served Merchant Navy, 1943-47. Joined Ministry of Transport, 1950; Statistician, 1954; Asst Sec. to Council on Prices, Productivity and Incomes, 1959-61; Principal, MoT, 1962; Asst Sec., 1966; Under-Sec., DoE, 1972; Regional Dir, SE Region and Chm., SE Economic Planning Bd, 1973-76. *Address:* Broomfields, Lamberhurst, Kent. *T:* Lamberhurst 427.

LANE, Kenneth Frederick; an Adviser on Civil Service Reform, since 1970; *b* 22 March 1928; British; *m* 1950, Kathleen Richards; one *s* two *d. Educ:* Emanuel Coll., Cambridge. Degree in Maths. Steel Industry in Sheffield, 1951-59; North America, 1959-61; Rio Tinto-Zinc Corp., 1961-65; Man. Dir, RTZ Consultants Ltd, 1965-70; Dir, RTZ Corp., 1970-75. *Recreations:* boat building, sailing. *Address:* 47 Bexley Road, SE9. *T:* 01-850 4367.

LANE, Margaret; novelist, biographer, journalist; *b* 23 June 1907; *o d* of late H. G. Lane; *m* 1st, 1934, Bryan (marr. diss. 1939), *e s* of Edgar Wallace; 2nd, 1944, 15th Earl of Huntingdon, *qv* ; two *d. Educ:* St Stephen's, Folkestone; St Hugh's Coll., Oxford (MA). Reporter, Daily Express, 1928-31; special correspondent: in New York and for International News Service, USA, 1931-32: for Daily Mail, 1932-38. President: Women's Press Club, 1958-60; Dickens Fellowship, 1959-61, 1970; Johnson Soc., 1971; Brontë Soc., 1975. *Publications:* Faith, Hope, No Charity (awarded Prix Femina-Vie Heureuse), 1935; At Last the Island, 1937; Edgar Wallace: The Biography of a Phenomenon, 1938; Walk Into My Parlour, 1941; Where Helen Lies, 1944; The Tale of Beatrix Potter, 1946; The Brontë Story, 1953; A Crown of Convolvulus, 1954; A Calabash of Diamonds, 1961; Life With Ionides, 1963; A Night at Sea, 1964; A Smell of Burning, 1965; Purely for Pleasure, 1966; The Day of the Feast, 1968; Frances Wright and the Great Experiment, 1971; Samuel Johnson and his World, 1975; Flora Thompson, 1976. *Address:* Blackbridge House, Beaulieu, Hants.

LANE, Hon. Mrs Miriam; *see* Rothschild, Hon. Miriam.

LANE, Ronald Anthony Stuart, CMG 1977; MC 1945; Vice Chairman, Standard Chartered Bank Ltd, since 1977; *b* 8 Dec. 1917; 2nd *s* of late Wilmot Ernest Lane and F. E. Lane (*née* Blakey); *m* 1948, Anne Brenda, 2nd *d* of E. Walsh; one *s* one *d. Educ:* Lancing College. FIB. Served War, 1940-45, 7th Light Cavalry, Indian Army, India and Burma (Major). Joined Chartered Bank of India, Australia & China, 1937; served in Far East, 1939-60; Gen. Manager, 1961, Chief Gen. Manager, 1972, Man. Dir, 1973-77, Standard Chartered Bank Ltd. Mem., Export Guarantees Adv. Council, 1973- (Dep. Chm., 1977). *Recreations:* sailing, gardening. *Address:* West Hold, By the Church, West Mersea, Essex CO5 8QD. *T:* West Mersea 2563. *Clubs:* East India, Devonshire, Sports and Public Schools; MCC; West Mersea Yacht.

LANE, Prof. Ronald Epey, CBE 1957; Emeritus Nuffield Professor of Occupational Health, University of Manchester (Professor, 1945-65); *b* 2 July 1897; *s* of E. E. Lane; *m* 1924, Winifred E. Tickner; one *s* one *d. Educ:* Simon Langton Sch. Canterbury; Guy's Hospital. Served European War, RFC, 1915-19. Guy's Hospital, 1919-24, qualified, 1923; General Medical practice, 1925-27; MRCP, 1925. Medical Officer, Chloride Elec. Storage Co. Ltd, 1928; Physician, Salford Roya. Hospital, 1935; FRCP, 1938; Milroy Lecturer (Royal College of Physicians), 1947, McKenzie Lecturer, 1950. Mem. of various Govt Advisory Cttees. *Publications:* original papers on Lead Poisoning, Medical Education, Occupational Health and Universities, in Lancet, BMJ, Brit. Jl of Industrial Med., Jl of Industrial Hygiene and Toxicology, etc. *Recreations:* golf, fishing. *Address:* 3 Daylesford Road, Cheadle, Cheshire. *T:* 061-428 5738. *Club:* Athenæum.

LANE, Rear-Adm. Walter Frederick Boyt, CB 1960; DSC 1941; MIMechE; MIMarE; Director of Marine Engineering, Admiralty, 1958-61; *b* 7 Feb. 1909; *s* of W. H. Lane, Freshwater, IoW; *m* 1931, Anne Littlecott; one *s. Educ:* RN Engineering Coll., Devonport. Eng.-in-Chief, Admiralty, Bath, 1957; Rear-Adm., 1957; retired. Formerly Director, Fairfields (Eng.) Co., Glasgow. *Recreations:* tennis, painting. *Address:* Foxleaze, Limpley Stoke, Wilts. *T:* Limpley Stoke 3225.

LANE FOX, Col Francis Gordon Ward; Vice-Lieutenant of West Riding of Yorkshire, 1968-74; Royal Horse Guards, 1919-46, retired; *b* 14 Oct. 1899; *s* of late C. Ward Jackson; assumed surname of Lane Fox in lieu of that of Jackson, by deed poll, 1937; *m* 1929, Hon. Marcia Agnes Mary, *e d* of 1st and last Baron Bingley, PC (*d* 1947); two *s* one *d. Educ:* Eton; RMC, Sandhurst. West Riding of Yorkshire: JP 1948; DL 1952; CC 1949, CA 1955. KStJ 1965. Officer Order of the Crown, with Palm, and Croix de Guerre, with Palm (Belgium), 1946. *Address:* The Little House, Bramham Park, Wetherby, W Yorks LS23 6LS. *T:* Boston Spa 843220. *Clubs:* Cavalry and Guards; Yorkshire (York).

LANESBOROUGH, 9th Earl of *cr* 1756; **Denis Anthony Brian Butler;** DL; Baron of Newtown-Butler, 1715; Viscount Lanesborough, 1728; Major, Leicestershire Yeomanry (RA); *b* 28 Oct. 1918; *er s* of 8th Earl and Grace Lilian, *d* of late Sir Anthony Abdy, 3rd Bt; *S* father 1950; *m* 1939, Bettyne Ione (marr. diss. 1950), *d* of late Sir Lindsay Everard; one *d* (and one *d* decd). *Educ:* Stowe. Leicestershire Yeomanry; Lieutenant, 1939; Major, RAC, TA (TD), 1945. Member: Nat. Gas Consumers' Council, 1973-; Trent RHA, 1974-. DL 1962, JP 1967, Leicester. *Heir: kinsman,* Comdr Terence Brinsley John Danvers Butler, RN; *b* 7 March 1913. *Address:* Swithland Hall, Loughborough. *T:* Rothley 2001.

LANG, Andrew Richard, FRS 1975; Reader in Physics, University of Bristol, since 1966; *b* 9 Sept. 1924; *s* of late Ernest F. S. Lang and late Susannah (*née* Gueterbock); unmarried. *Educ:* University College of South-West, Exeter, (BSc Lond. 1944; MSc Lond. 1947); Univ. of Cambridge (PhD 1953). Research Dept, Lever Bros, Port Sunlight, 1945-47; Research Asst, Cavendish Laboratory, 1947-48; North American Philips, Irvington-on-Hudson, NY, 1952-53; Instructor, Harvard Univ., 1953-54; Asst Professor, Harvard Univ., 1954-59; Lectr in Physics, Univ. of Bristol, 1960-66. MInstP, Mem. Geol Assoc.; Mem. Soc. Sigma Xi. Charles Vernon Boys Prize, Inst. of Physics, 1964. *Publications:* contribs to learned jls. *Address:* 1B Elton Road, Bristol BS8 1SJ. *T:* Bristol 39784.

LANG, Prof. David Marshall, MA, PhD, DLit, LittD; Professor of Caucasian Studies in the University of London since 1964; Warden of Connaught Hall, University of London, since 1955; *b* 6 May 1924; *s* of Dr David Marshall Lang, Medical Practitioner, Bath, and Mrs May Rena Lang; *m* 1956, Janet, *d* of late George Sugden, Leeds; one *s* two *d* (and one *s* decd). *Educ:* Monkton Combe Sch.; St John's Coll., Cambridge. Actg Vice-Consul, Tabriz, 1944-46; 3rd Sec., British Embassy, Tehran, 1946; Research Fellow, St John's Coll., Cambridge, 1946-52; Lectr in Georgian, School of Oriental and African Studies, University of London, 1949-58; Senior Fellow, Russian Inst., Columbia Univ., 1952-53; Reader in Caucasian Studies, University of London, 1958-64; Vis. Prof. of Caucasian Languages, University of California, Los Angeles, 1964-65. Hon. Sec., Royal Asiatic Society, 1962-64; Vice-Pres., Holborn Soc., 1973-; Pres., Georgian Cultural Circle, 1974-. Hon. Dr Philological Sciences, Tbilisi State Univ.; Prix Brémond, 1971. *Publications:* Studies in the Numismatic History of Georgia in Transcaucasia, 1955; Lives and Legends of the Georgian Saints, 1956; The Wisdom of Balahvar, 1957; The Last Years of the Georgian Monarchy, 1957; The First Russian Radical; Alexander Radishchev, 1959; A Modern History of Georgia, 1962; Catalogue of the Georgian Books in the British Museum, 1962; The Georgians, 1966; The Balavariani, 1966; Armenia, Cradle of Civilization, 1970; (with C. Burney) The Peoples of the Hills, 1971; (ed) Guide to Eastern Literatures, 1971; The Bulgarians, 1976; (with C. Walker) The Armenians, 1976; articles in Bulletin of School of Oriental and African Studies, Encyclopædia Britannica, etc. *Recreations:*

music, foreign travel. *Address:* (office) School of Oriental and African Studies, University of London, WC1. *T:* (home) 01-387 6181. *Club:* Leander.

LANG, Lt.-Gen. Sir Derek (Boileau), KCB 1967 (CB 1964); DSO 1944; MC 1941; Associate Consultant, PA Management Consultants Ltd, since 1975; *b* 7 Oct. 1913; *s* of Lt-Col C. F. G. Lang and Mrs Lumsden Lang (*née* M. J. L. Forbes); *m* 1st, 1942, M. Massy Dawson (*d* 1953); one *s* one *d*; 2nd, 1953, A. L. S. Shields (marr. diss. 1969); 3rd, 1969, Mrs E. H. Balfour. *Educ:* Wellington Coll.; RMC Sandhurst. Commnd, The Queen's Own Cameron Highlanders, 1933; Adjutant, TA, 1938; Chief Instructor, Sch. of Infantry, 1943-44; Comdr, 5th Camerons, 1944-45; Comdt, Sch. of Infantry, BAOR, 1945-46; Directing Staff, Staff Coll., Camberley, 1947-48; Staff, Australia, 1949-51; GSO1, War Office, 1951-53; Chief Instructor, Sch. of Infantry Tactical Wing, 1953-55; AAG, War Office, 1955-57; NDC, 1957-58; Comd Infty Bde (153-TA), 1958-60; Chief of Staff, Scottish Comd, 1960; Gen. Officer Commanding, 51st Highland Div. and District, Perth, 1962-64; Dir of Army Training, 1964-66; GOC-in-C, Scottish Command, 1966-69; Governor of Edinburgh Castle, 1966-69; Sec., Univ. of Stirling, 1970-73; Hon. Col, 153 (Highland) Regt, RCT (Volunteers), T&AVR, 1970-76; Pres., Army Cadet Force Assoc. (Scotland). OStJ. FBIM. *Publication:* Return to St Valéry, 1974. *Recreations:* golf, shooting. *Address:* 4 Belford Place, Edinburgh. *Clubs:* Army and Navy; New (Edinburgh); Senior Golfers' Society; Hon. Co. of Edinburgh Golfers (Muirfield).
See also J. M. Hunt.

LANG, Rev. Gordon; Nonconformist Minister, Pen-y-waun Church, Cwmbran, 1956-77; Member of Board, Cwmbran New Town Corporation, 1955-64; *b* Monmouth, 1893; *e s* of T. W. Lang, JP; *m* 1916, Emilie Anne, *d* of J. W. Evans, Leechpool, Chepstow; one *s* one *d*. *Educ:* Monmouth Grammar Sch.; Cheshunt. MP (Lab) Oldham, 1929-31; Stalybridge and Hyde Div. of Ches., 1945-51. Hon. Chaplain to Showmen's Guild of Great Britain and Ireland, 1930-; Associate Mem., CPA, 1945-; Chairman: Parliamentary Federal Group; Proportional Representation Soc., 1947-51; Hon. Sec. United Europe Movement; Vice-Pres. International Youth Bureau, 1946-56; Mem. Council of Hansard Soc., 1948-54; Exec. Mem. Internat. Union of Parliamentarians, 1946-51. Criminologist. *Publications:* Biography of Mr Justice Avory, 1935; Modern Epistles, 1952; Mind Behind Murder, 1960; fiction and many works and papers on Applied Psychology and Criminology. *Address:* 6 Bigstone Grove, Tutshill, Chepstow, Gwent. *T:* Chepstow 2462. *Club:* Authors'.

LANG, Henry George, CB 1977; company director, since 1977; *b* 3 March 1919; *s* of Robert and Anna Lang; *m* 1942, Octavia Gwendolin (*née* Turton); one *s* four *d*. *Educ:* Victoria Univ., Wellington. DPA, BA, BCom. Private enterprise, 1939-44; RNZAF, 1944-46. NZ government service: various economic appointments, 1946-55; Economic Advisor to High Comr in London, 1955-58; Treasury, 1958-77, Sec. to Treasury, 1968-77. Vis. Prof. of Economics, Victoria Univ. of Wellington, 1977-. *Publications:* (with J. V. T. Baker) Economic Policy and National Income, in, NZ Official Year Book, 1950; articles in learned journals. *Recreations:* skiing, swimming, reading. *Address:* 81 Hatton Street, Wellington, NZ. *T:* 768 788. *Clubs:* Wellington, University (both Wellington, NZ).

LANG, Sir John (Gerald), GCB 1954 (KCB 1947; CB 1946); *b* 20 Dec. 1896; *s* of late George and Rebecca Lang, Woolwich; *m* 1st, 1922, Emilie J. (*d* 1963), *d* of late Henry S. Goddard, Eastbourne; one *d*; 2nd, 1970, Kathleen Winifred, *widow* of C. G. E. Edmeades, and *d* of late Henry S. Goddard. *Educ:* Aske's Haberdashers' Sch., Hatcham. Second Div. Clerk, Admiralty, 1914; Royal Marine Artillery, Lt, 1917-18; Returned to Admiralty: Asst Principal, 1930; Principal, 1935; Asst Sec., 1939; Principal Asst Sec., 1942; Under-Sec., 1946; Sec., Admiralty, SW1, 1947-61. Chm. Bettix Ltd, 1961-70. Principal Adviser on Sport to the Government, 1964-71, and Dep. Chm., Sports Council, 1965-71. Mem. Bd of Govs, Bethlem Royal Hosp. and Maudsley Hosp., 1961-70; Treasurer, 1969-, Hon. Vice Pres., 1977, RINA; Vice-Pres., Royal Naval Assoc. *Recreations:* gardening, motoring. *Address:* 2 Egmont Park House, Walton-on-the-Hill, Tadworth, Surrey. *T:* Tadworth 2200. *Clubs:* Royal Automobile, Samuel Pepys (Pres. 1965).

LANG, Rev. John Harley; Head of Religious Broadcasting, BBC, since 1971; Chaplain to the Queen, since 1976; *b* 27 Oct. 1927; *e s* of Frederick Henry Lang and Eileen Annie Lang (*née* Harley); *m* 1972, Frances Rosemary Widdowson; two *d*. *Educ:* Merchant Taylors' Sch.; King's Coll., London. MA Cantab, BD London, LRAM. Subaltern, XII Royal Lancers, 1951-52; Asst Curate, St Mary's Portsea, 1952-57; Priest Vicar, Southwark Cathedral, 1957-60; Chaplain, Emmanuel Coll., Cambridge, 1960-64; Asst Head of Religious Broadcasting, BBC, 1964-67; Head of Religious Programmes, Radio, 1967-71. *Recreation:* music. *Address:* Applewood, Sacombe Green, Ware, Herts.

LANG, John Russell, CBE 1963; Deputy Chairman, The Weir Group Ltd, 1968-73; *b* 8 Jan. 1902; *s* of Chas Russell Lang, CBE; *m* 1st, 1934, Jenny (*d* 1970), *d* of Sir John Train, MP, of Cathkin, Lanarkshire; four *d* (one *s* decd); 2nd, 1973, Gay Mackie. *Educ:* Loretto Sch., Musselburgh; France and USA. Dir, G. & J. Weir Ltd, 1930-67. Chairman, Weir Housing Corp., 1946-66. President, Scottish Engineering Employers' Association, 1963-64. Mem., Toothill Cttee and EDC for Mec. Eng. Lt-Col 277 Field Regt, RA (TA), 1937. *Recreations:* hunting, shooting, golf. *Address:* The White House of Milliken, Brookfield, Renfrewshire. *T:* Johnstone 20898. *Clubs:* Western (Glasgow); Prestwick Golf.

LANG, William Marshall F.; *see* Farquharson-Lang.

LANGDALE, Simon John Bartholomew; Headmaster, Eastbourne College, since Sept. 1973; *b* 26 Jan. 1937; *s* of G. R. Langdale and H. J. Langdale (*née* Bartholomew); *m* 1962, Diana Marjory Hall; two *s* one *d*. *Educ:* Tonbridge Sch.; St Catharine's Coll., Cambridge. Taught at Radley Coll., 1959-73 (Housemaster, 1968-73). *Recreations:* cricket, Rugby fives, real tennis, china fairings. *Address:* Headmaster's House, Eastbourne College, Sussex BN21 4JX. *T:* Eastbourne 37655. *Clubs:* Hawks (Cambridge); Free Foresters, Jesters.

LANGDON, Alfred Gordon, CMG 1967; CVO 1966; QPM 1961; Managing Director, Security Specialists Ltd, Kingston, Jamaica; *b* 3 July 1915; *s* of Wilfred James Langdon and Norah (*née* Nixon); *m* 1947, Phyllis Elizabeth Pengelley; one *s* two *d*. *Educ:* Munro Coll., Jamaica. Berkhampstead Sch., Herts. Bank of Nova Scotia, Kingston, Jamaica, 1933-37; Jamaica Infantry Volunteers, 1937-39; Jamaica Constabulary Force, 1939-70: Asst Comr of Police, 1954-62; Dep. Comr, 1962-64; Comr, 1964-70, retd. Security Advisor, Min. of Home Affairs, Jamaica, 1970-72. *Recreations:* fishing, tennis, swimming. *Club:* Kingston Cricket.

LANGDON, (Augustus) John; chartered surveyor and land agent; *b* 20 April 1913; *e s* of late Rev. Cecil Langdon, MA and Elizabeth Mercer Langdon, MBE; *m*; two *d*; *m* 1949, Doris Edna Clinkard; one *s*. *Educ:* Berkhamsted Sch.; St John's Coll., Cambridge (Nat. Science Tripos; MA). FRICS (Chartered Land Agent); FRSA. Asst to J. Carter Jonas & Sons, Oxford, 1936-37, Partner 1945-48; Suptg Lands Officer, Admty, 1937-45; Regional Land Comr, Min. of Agriculture, 1948-65; Dep. Dir, Agric. Land Service, Min. of Agriculture, 1965-71; Chief Surveyor, Agricultural Develt and Advisory Service, MAFF, 1971-74; with the National Trust in London, 1974-76. Chm., Statutory Cttee on Agricultural Valuation; RICS: Mem., Gen. Council; Mem., Land Agency and Agricultural Divisional Council, 1971-75. *Publications:* contrib. Rural Estate Management (ed R. C. Walmsley), Fream's Elements of Agriculture, professional and agric. jls. *Recreations:* gardening, walking, collecting. *Address:* Thorn Bank, Long Street, Sherborne, Dorset DT9 3BS. *T:* Sherborne 2910. *Club:* United Oxford & Cambridge University.

LANGDON, David, FRSA, FSIA; Cartoonist and Illustrator; Member of Punch Table; regular contributor to Punch since 1937, to The New Yorker since 1952; Cartoonist to Sunday Mirror, since 1948; *b* 24 Feb. 1914; *er s* of late Bennett and Bess Langdon; *m* 1955, April Sadler-Phillips; two *s* one *d*. *Educ:* Davenant Gram. Sch., London. Architect's Dept, LCC, 1931-39; Executive Officer, London Rescue Service, 1939-41; served in Royal Air Force, 1941-46; Squadron Leader, 1945. Editor, Royal Air Force Jl, 1945-46. Creator of Billy Brown of London Town for LPTB. Official Artist to Centre International Audio-Visuel d'Etudes et de Recherches, St Ghislain, Belgium. Exhibitions: Oxford, New York, London. *Publications:* Home Front Lines, 1941; All Buttoned Up, 1944; Meet Me Inside, 1946; Slipstream (with R. B. Raymond), 1946; The Way I See It, 1947; Hold Tight There!, 1949; Let's Face It, 1951; Wake Up and Die (with David Clayton), 1952; Look at You, 1952; All in Fun, 1953; Laugh with Me, 1954; More in Fun, 1955; Funnier Still, 1956; A Banger for a Monkey, 1957; Langdon At Large, 1958; I'm Only Joking, 1960; Punch with Wings, 1961; How to Play Golf and Stay Happy, 1964; David Langdon's Casebook, 1969; How To Talk Golf, 1975. *Recreations:* golf, non-League soccer. *Address:* South Copse, Nightingales Lane, Chalfont St Giles, Bucks HP8 4SF. *T:* Chalfont St Giles 2935. *Clubs:* RAF, Royal Automobile.

LANGDON, John; see Langdon, A. J.

LANGDON, Michael, CBE 1973; Principal Bass Soloist, Royal Opera House, Covent Garden, since 1951; *b* 12 Nov. 1920; *s of* Henry Langdon, Wednesfield Road, Wolverhampton; *m* 1947, Vera Duffield, Norwich; two *d. Educ:* Bushbury Hill Sch., Wolverhampton. First Principal Contract, Royal Opera House, Covent Garden, 1951; first Gala Performance, before Queen Elizabeth II (Gloriana), 1953; Grand Inquisitor in Visconti Production of Don Carlos, 1958; debut as Baron Ochs (Rosenkavalier), 1960; first International Engagement (Hamburg), 1961; first Glyndebourne Festival, 1961; since then, has appeared in international performances in Paris, Berlin, Aix-en-Provence, San Francisco and Los Angeles, 1962; Lausanne, Geneva, Vienna and Budapest, 1963; Zürich, New York, 1964; Geneva, Marseilles, 1965; Seattle, Buenos Aires; Houston, 1975; Gala Performances, 1967, 1969. *Recreations:* swimming, walking and Association football (now only as spectator). *Address:* 34 Warnham Court, Grand Avenue, Hove, East Sussex. *Club:* Savage.

LANGDON, Richard Norman Darbey, FCA; Managing Partner, Spicer and Pegler, since 1971; *b* 19 June 1919; *s of* Norman Langdon and Dorothy Langdon; *m* 1944; two *s. Educ:* Shrewsbury Sch. Officer, RA, 1939-46. Admitted Mem. Inst. of Chartered Accountants in England and Wales, 1947; joined Spicer and Pegler, 1949, Partner 1953. Dep. Chm., First Nat. Finance Corp. Ltd; Chairman: Finlay Packaging Ltd; Hammond and Champness Ltd. *Recreations:* sailing, gardening, bricklaying. *Address:* Rough Hill House, Munstead, near Godalming, Surrey. *T:* Godalming 21507. *Clubs:* City of London; Old Salopian.

LANGDON-DOWN, Barbara; see Littlewood, Lady (Barbara).

LANGFORD, 9th Baron, *cr* 1800; **Colonel Geoffrey Alexander Rowley-Conwy,** OBE 1943; RA, retired; Constable of Rhuddlan Castle and Lord of the Manor of Rhuddlan; *b* 8 March 1912; *s of* late Major Geoffrey Seymour Rowley-Conwy (killed in action, Gallipoli, 1915), Bodrhyddan, Flints, and of Bertha Gabrielle Rowley-Conwy, JP (now of Bodrhyddan), *d of* late Lieutenant Alexander Cochran, Royal Navy, Ashkirk, Selkirkshire; *S* kinsman 1953; *m* 1st, 1939, Ruth St John (marr. diss. 1956), *d of* late Albert St John Murphy, The Island House, Little Island, County Cork; 2nd, 1957, Grete (*d* 1973), *d of* Col E. T. C. von Freiesleben, formerly Chief of the King's Adjutants Staff to the King of Denmark and now of Snekkersten, Denmark; three *s*; 3rd, 1975, Susan Winifred Denham, *d of* C. C. H. Denham, Chester. *Educ:* Marlborough RMA Woolwich. Served War of 1939-45, with RA; Singapore, (POW escaped) and with Indian Mountain Artillery in Burma, 1941-45 (despatches, OBE); Staff Coll., Quetta, 1945; Berlin Airlift, Fassberg, 1948-49; GSOI 42 Inf. Div., TA, 1949-52; Lt-Col 1945; retired 1957; Colonel (Hon.), 1967. *Heir:* s Hon. Owen Grenville Rowley-Conwy, *b* 27 Dec. 1958. *Address:* Bodrhyddan, Rhuddlan, Clwyd. *Club:* Army and Navy.

LANGFORD-HOLT, Sir John (Anthony), Kt 1962; Lieutenant-Commander RN (Retired); MP (C) Shrewsbury Division of Salop since 1945; *b* 30 June 1916; *s of* late Ernest Langford-Holt; *m* 1953, Flora Evelyn Innes Stuart (marr. diss. 1969); one *s* one *d*; *m* 1971, Maxine, *d of* H. Maxworthy, Bexhill-on-Sea. *Educ:* Shrewsbury Sch. Joined RN and Air Branch (FAA), 1939. Sec. of Conservative Parl. Labour Cttee, 1945-50; Chm., Anglo-Austrian Soc., 1960-63, 1971-; Member: Commonwealth Parliamentary Association; IPU, and other Internat. Bodies; Parliamentary and Scientific Cttee. Director: Authority Investments Ltd; Siebe Gorman Holdings Ltd; Tretol Ltd. Freeman and Liveryman of City of London; Mem. Court, Company of Horners. *Address:* House of Commons, SW1. *Club:* White's.

LANGHAM, Sir James (Michael), 15th Bt *cr* 1660; TD 1965; *b* 24 May 1932; *s of* Sir John Charles Patrick Langham, 14th Bt, and of Rosamond Christabel (MBE 1969), *d of* late Arthur Rashleigh; *S* father, 1972; *m* 1959, Marion Audrey Eleanor, *d of* O. H. Barratt, Gararagua Estate, Tanzania; two *s* one *d. Educ:* Rossall School, Fleetwood. Served as Captain, North Irish Horse, 1953-67. *Recreations:* shooting, skin-diving. *Heir:* s John Stephen Langham, *b* 14 Dec. 1960. *Address:* Claranagh, Tempo, Co. Fermanagh. *T:* Tempo 247.

LANGHORNE, Richard Tristan Bailey; Junior Bursar, Steward and Fellow, St John's College, Cambridge, since 1974; *b* 6 May 1940; *s of* Edward John Bailey Langhorne and Rosemary Scott-Foster; *m* 1971, Helen Logue, *o d of* William Donaldson, CB and Mary Donaldson; one *s* one *d. Educ:* St Edward's Sch., Oxford; St John's Coll., Cambridge (Exhibr). BA Hist. Tripos,

1962; Certif. in Hist. Studies, 1963; MA 1965. Tutor in History, Univ. of Exeter, 1963-64; Research Student, St John's Coll., Cambridge, 1964-66; Supervisor of Clare Coll., Cambridge, 1964-66; Lectr in History, 1966-74 and Master of Rutherford Coll., 1971-74, Univ. of Kent at Canterbury. *Publications:* chapter in The Twentieth Century Mind, 1971; reviews and articles in Historical Jl and History. *Recreations:* music, railways. *Address:* St John's College, Cambridge; 15 Madingley Road, Cambridge. *Club:* Athenæum.

LANGKER, Sir Erik, Kt 1968; OBE 1959; Artist; *b* 3 Nov. 1898; *s of* Christian and Elizabeth Langker; *m* 1929, Alice, *d of* Robert Pollock; one *s* one *d. Educ:* Fort St Boys' High Sch.; Julian Ashton Art Sch.; Royal Art Society Sch.; studied under Sir William Ashton. Exhibited widely throughout Commonwealth and America. Assoc. Mem. 1926, Fellow 1928, Pres. 1946-, Royal Art Soc. NSW; President: Art Gall. of NSW, 1961- (Vice-Pres., 1958, Trustee, 1947-); Sydney Arts Foundation, 1969; Captain Cook Trust; La Perouse Trust; Foundation President: Nat. Opera of Australia; Opera Guild of NSW; North Shore Historical Soc. Chairman: Independent Theatre Ltd, 1946-; North Side Arts Festival; Member: Winston Churchill Meml Trust; State Adv. Council for Technical Educn; Trustee, Children's Library and Craft Movement, etc. *Publication:* Australian Art Illustrated, 1947. *Recreations:* music, hiking. *Address:* Lombardy, 8 Eastview Street, Wollstonecroft, NSW 2065, Australia. *T:* 43-1209. *Club:* Savage (NSW).

LANGLEY, Brig. Charles Ardagh, CB 1962; CBE 1945; MC 1916 (Bar, 1918); *b* 23 Aug. 1897; *s of* late John Langley, CBE, Under Sec. of State, Egyptian Govt, 1922; *m* 1st, 1920, V. V. M. Sharp (*d* 1931); one *s* one *d*; 2nd, 1936, M. J. Scott; two *d. Educ:* Cheltenham Coll.; Royal Military Academy, Woolwich. Served European War: commissioned Royal Engineers, 1915; France, 1916, served in field co. and as Adjutant to divisional engineers (MC and Bar; despatches three times). Subseq. took course of higher military engineer training, including one year at Cambridge Univ.; Railway Training Centre, Longmoor, 1922-27; seconded to Great Indian Peninsular Railway, 1927-33, in connection with electrification of Bombay-Poona main line, including construction of power station at Kalyan; Railway Trg Centre, Longmoor, 1933-38; various appointments, including Chief Instructor of Railways, War Office, 1938-40; War of 1939-45: responsible for initial transportation developments in Middle East; later formed Transportation Trg Centre for raising and training Docks and Inland Water Transport troops of Indian Engineers. Dep. Quartermaster-Gen. (Movements and Transportation), Allied Land Forces, South East Asia Command, 1943-45 (despatches, CBE); Commandant, Transportation Trg Centre, Longmoor, 1946. Inspecting Officer of Railways, 1946-58, Chief Inspecting Officer, 1958-63, Min. of Transport. Consultant: British Railways Bd, 1963-66; Transmark, 1972-73; Kennedy & Donkin, 1974; Projects Manager, UKRAS (Consultants) Ltd, 1966-69, Man. Dir, 1969-72. Pres. Junior Institution of Engineers, 1961-62. FCIT. *Publications:* several military text books on transportation. *Recreation:* gardening. *Address:* Beeches, Little Austins, Farnham, Surrey. *T:* Farnham 5712.

LANGLEY, Noel A.; author-playwright; *b* Durban, SA, 25 Dec. 1911; *m* 1937, Naomi Mary Legate (marriage dissolved, 1954); three *s* two *d*; *m* 1959, Pamela Deeming. *Educ:* Durban High Sch.; University of Natal, SA. Plays produced in London: Queer Cargo; For Ever; Edward My Son (with Robert Morley); Little Lambs Eat Ivy; Cage Me a Peacock; The Burning Bush; The Land of Green Ginger, 1966; The Snow Queen, 1967. Plays produced in New York: Farm of Three Echoes, 1939; The Walrus and the Carpenter, 1941. Films: Maytime, 1936 (USA); The Wizard of Oz, 1938 (USA); They Made Me a Fugitive, 1946; Cardboard Cavalier, Adam and Evalyn, 1948; Trio, Tom Brown's School Days, 1950; Scrooge, 1951; Ivanhoe (USA), Pickwick Papers (adaptation and direction), 1952; Knights of the Round Table (USA), 1953; Our Girl Friday (Adventures of Sadie) (screenplay and direction); Trilby and Svengali (screenplay and direction); Vagabond King (USA), 1954; The Search for Bridey Murphy (screenplay and direction), 1957. *Publications:* Cage Me a Peacock, 1935; There's a Porpoise Close Behind Us, 1936; Hocus Pocus, 1941; Land of Green Ginger, 1937; The Music of the Heart, 1946; The Cabbage Patch, 1947; Nymph in Clover, 1948; The Inconstant Moon, 1949; Tales of Mystery and Revenge, 1950; The Rift in the Lute, 1952; Where Did Everybody Go?, 1960; An Elegance of Rebels, 1960; The Loner, 1967; My Beloved Teck, 1970; A Dream of Dragon Flies, 1972; (jointly) There's a Horse in My Tree, Somebody's Rocking My Dream Boat, Cuckoo in the Dell. *Address:* c/o Eric Glass Ltd, 28 Berkeley Square, W1X 6HD.

LANGLEY MOORE, D.; see Moore, Doris L.

LANGMAN, Sir John Lyell, 3rd Bt, cr 1906; b 9 Sept. 1912; o s of Sir Archibald Langman, 2nd Bt, CMG, North Cadbury Court, Somerset, and late Eleanor Katherine, 2nd d of 1st Baron Lyell; S father 1949; m 1936, Pamela, o d of Capt. Spencer Kennard; two d (one d decd). Educ: Eton; Christ Church, Oxford. Heir: none. Address: Perrotts Brook Farm, near Cirencester, Glos. T: North Cerney 283.

LANGRIDGE, Philip Gordon; concert and opera singer (tenor), since 1964; b 16 Dec. 1939; m 1962, Margaret Hilary Davidson; one s two d. Educ: Maidstone Grammar Sch.; Royal Academy of Music, London. Glyndebourne Festival, 1964; Wexford Festival, 1965; Music Theatre Ensemble, 1967; Handel Opera Soc., 1967; BBC Promenade Concerts, 1970; engaged with Netherlands Opera for l'Incoronazione di Poppea (Monteverdi), 1971, 1973, 1974; Idomeneo (Mozart), 1976; Il Barbier di Siviglia (Rossini), 1976; also with Scottish Opera for The Justified Sinner (Thomas Wilson), 1976. Recordings of works by Arne, Monteverdi, Schutz, Bach, Handel, Dauvergne, Henze, Tippett, Weill, Holliger. Recreation: collecting Edwardian and Victorian postcards. Address: 9 Marsworth Avenue, Pinner, Mddx HA5 4UD. T: 01-428 0061.

LANGRISHE, Sir Hercules (Ralph Hume), 7th Bt cr 1777; b 17 May 1927; s of Sir Terence Hume Langrishe, 6th Bt, and Joan Stuart (d 1976), d of late Major Ralph Stuart Grigg; S father, 1973; m 1955, Hon. Grania Sybil Enid Wingfield, d of 9th Viscount Powerscourt; one s three d. Educ: Summer Fields, St Leonards; Eton. 2nd Lieut, 9th Queen's Royal Lancers, 1947; Lieut, 1948; retd 1953; Recreations: shooting, fishing. Heir: s James Hercules Langrishe, b 3 March 1957. Address: Ringlestown House, Kilmessan, Co. Meath. T: Navan 25243; Knocktopher Abbey, Co. Kilkenny. T: Kilkenny 28618. Clubs: Cavalry and Guards; Kildare Street and University (Dublin).

LANGSTONE, Rt. Rev. John Arthur William; see Edmonton (Alberta), Bishop of.

LANGTON; see Temple-Gore-Langton, family name of Earl Temple of Stowe.

LANGTON, Bernard Sydney, CBE 1966; JP; Greater Manchester County Councillor since 1973; Trustee, since 1967 and Vice-Chairman, since 1974, Young Volunteer Force Foundation (Chairman, Advisory Council, 1967-71); b 1 Aug. 1914; s of Leon and Theresa Langton; m 1st, 1942, Betty Siroto (marr. diss. 1972); two d; 2nd, 1975, Margaret Stephen Tait Davies (née Gatt), BSc, LTI. Educ: Blackpool Grammar Sch.; Manchester Univ. Manchester City Council, 1945-74, Alderman 1963-74 (past Chm., Watch Cttee, Rivers Cttee, Fire Brigade Cttee); Chm. Recreation and Arts Cttee, Greater Manchester CC, 1973-77. Mem., Police Council Great Britain, 1956-67; Governor, Police Coll., 1956-67; Mem., Police Adv. Board, 1957-67; Mem., Race Relations Board, 1966-68; Chm., Manchester Port Health Authority, 1956-74; Nat. Pres., Assoc. of Sea and Air Port Health Authorities of GB, 1972-73; Mem., Gen. Adv. Coun. of ITA, 1969-72; Mem., Countryside Commn, 1975-. Mem., Ct of Governors, Manchester Univ., 1975-. JP Manchester 1961. Recreations: gardening, theatre, music. Address: 17 Alan Road, Manchester M20 9NQ. T: 061-434 4000.

LANGTON, Sir Henry Algernon; see under Calley, Sir H. A.

LANGTON, Thomas Bennett, MC 1942; Chairman, Leslie Langton Holdings Ltd, 1972-77; Underwriting Member of Lloyd's, since 1946; b 6 March 1917; s of Leslie P. Langton and Mildred (née Holmwood); m 1943, Lucy Barbara Ettrick Welford; three d. Educ: Radley; Jesus Coll., Cambridge (MA). Called to Bar, Middle Temple, 1939. Served War of 1939-45: commnd Irish Guards, 1940; No 8 Commando, 1941; Special Boat Section (Middle East), 1942; 1st SAS Regt, 1943-45; Major. Partner, Leslie Langton & Son, Lloyd's Underwriting Agents, 1946-53; Chm., Leslie Langton & Sons Ltd, 1953-; Director: Devitt Langton & Dawnay Day, 1965-; AA Insurance Services, 1967-72. Chm., Lloyd's Underwriting Agents Assoc., 1966-67; Mem. Cttee of Lloyd's, 1968-71, 1973-76; Dep. Chm., of Lloyd's, 1973, 1974. Mem. Council, Radley Coll., 1958-73; Mem. Bd, Royal Merchant Navy Sch., Bearwood, 1975-. Mem. Court of Skinners' Co., 1959-, Master 1964-65. Mem. Indep. Schs Careers Organisation, 1970-; Chm., Project Trust, 1971-. Hon. Corp. 39th (City of London) Signal Regt (V), 1973-. Recreations: sport, especially rowing (Steward, Henley Royal Regatta); antiques. Address: 40 St Cross Road, Winchester, Hants. T: Winchester 65345. Clubs: City of London, London Rowing; Hawks (Cambridge); Leander; Richmond Football.

LA NIECE, Rear-Adm. Peter George, CB 1973; CBE 1967; Director, Astley & Pearce Ltd, since 1976; b 23 July 1920; s of George David Nelson La Niece and Gwynneth Mary (née Morgan); m 1948, Evelyn Mary Wrixon Babington; two s one d. Educ: Whitgift Sch., Croydon. Entered RN, 1937; served War of 1939-45 in battleships, cruisers and destroyers; Gunnery Specialist 1945; Comdr 1953; Captain 1961; comd HMS Rame Head, 1962; Senior UK Polaris Rep., Washington, 1963-66; comd HMS Triumph, 1966-68; Cdre Clyde in Comd Clyde Submarine Base, 1969-71; Rear-Adm. 1971; Flag Officer Spithead and Port Admiral, Portsmouth, 1971-73; retired 1973. Recreation: sailing. Address: Charltons, Yalding, Kent ME18 6DF. T: Hunton 761. Club: Army and Navy.

LANKESTER, Richard Shermer; Clerk of Expenditure Committee, House of Commons, since 1975; Registrar of Members' Interests, since 1976; b 8 Feb. 1922; s of Richard Ward Lankester; m 1950, Dorothy, d of Raymond Jackson, Worsley; three s one d. Educ: Haberdashers' Aske's Hampstead Sch.; Jesus Coll., Oxford (MA). Served Royal Artillery, 1942-45. Entered Dept of Clerk of House of Commons, 1947; Clerk of Standing Cttees, 1973-75. Co-Editor, The Table, 1962-67. Address: Meadow Bank, Beech Way, Gerrards Cross, Bucks. T: Gerrards Cross 84539.

LANSBURY, Angela Brigid; actress; b London, England, 16 Oct. 1925; d of Edgar Lansbury and late Moyna MacGill (who m 1st, Reginald Denham); m 1st, Richard Cromwell; 2nd, 1949, Peter Shaw; one s one d and one step s; naturalized American citizen, 1951. Educ: South Hampstead High Sch. for Girls; Webber Douglas Sch. of Singing and Dramatic Art, Kensington; Feagin Sch. of Drama and Radio, New York. With Metro-Goldwyn-Mayor, 1943-50; films included: Gaslight, 1944; National Velvet, 1944; Dorian Gray, 1944; Harvey Girls, 1946; Till the Clouds Roll By, 1946; If Winter Comes, 1947; State of the Union, 1948; Samson and Delilah, 1949. As free lance, 1950-: films include: Kind Lady, 1951; The Court Jester, 1956; The Long Hot Summer, 1957; The Reluctant Debutante, 1958; Summer of the 17th Doll, 1959; A Breath of Scandal, 1959; Dark at the Top of the Stairs, 1960; Blue Hawaii, 1962; All Fall Down, 1962; The Manchurian Candidate, 1963; In the Cool of the Day, 1963; The World of Henry Orient, 1964; Out of Towners, 1964; Harlow, 1965; Bedknobs and Broomsticks, 1972; Black Flowers for the Bride, 1972; plays: appearances include: Hotel Paradiso (Broadway debut), 1957; Helen, in A Taste of Honey, Lyceum Theatre, New York, 1960; Anyone can Whistle (Broadway musical), 1964; Mame (Tony Award for best actress in a Broadway musical), Winter Garden, NYC, 1966-68; Dear World (Broadway), 1969 (Tony Award); Gypsy (Broadway Musical), Piccadilly, 1973, US tour, 1974 (Tony Award; Chicago, Sarah Siddons Award, 1974); Gertrude, in Hamlet, Nat. Theatre, 1975. Address: Knockmourne, Conna, Co. Cork, Republic of Ireland.

LANSDOWN, Mrs Richard; see Tindall, G. E.

LANSDOWNE, 8th Marquess of (GB), cr 1784; **George John Charles Mercer Nairne Petty-Fitzmaurice,** 29th Baron of Kerry and Lixnaw, 1181; Earl of Kerry, Viscount Clanmaurice, 1723; Viscount FitzMaurice and Baron Dunkeron, 1751; Earl of Shelburne, 1753; Baron Wycombe, 1760; Earl of Wycombe and Viscount Calne, 1784; PC 1964; b 27 Nov. 1912; o s of Major Lord Charles George Francis Mercer Nairne, MVO (killed in action, 1914; 2nd s of 5th Marquess), and Lady Violet Mary Elliot (she m 2nd, 1916, 1st Baron Astor of Hever), d of 4th Earl of Minto; S cousin, 1944; m 1st, 1938, Barbara, (d 1965), d of Harold Stuart Chase, Santa Barbara; two s one d (and one d decd); 2nd, 1969, Mrs Polly Carnegie, d of Viscount Eccles, qv. Educ: Eton; Christ Church, Oxford. Sec. Junior Unionist League for E Scotland, 1939. Served War of 1939-45, Capt. Royal Scots Greys 1940, formerly 2nd Lt Scottish Horse (TA); Major 1944; served with Free French Forces (Croix de Guerre, Légion D'Honneur); Private Sec. to HM Ambassador in Paris (Rt Hon. A. Duff Cooper). 1944-45. Lord-in-Waiting to the Queen, 1957-58; Joint Parliamentary Under-Sec. of State, Foreign Office, 1958-62; Minister of State for Colonial Affairs, 1962-64, and for Commonwealth Relations, 1963-64. Mem. Royal Company of Archers (Queen's Body Guard for Scotland); JP, Perthshire, 1950; DL Wilts, 1952-73. Patron of two livings. Chm., Victoria League in Scotland, 1952-56; Inter-Governmental Cttee on Malaysia, 1962. Chm., Franco-British Soc., 1972-; Pres., Franco-Scottish Soc. Prime Warden, Fishmongers' Company, 1967-68. Heir: s Earl of Shelburne, qv. Address: Meikleour House, Perthshire. Clubs: Turf; New (Edinburgh).
See also Baroness Nairne.

LAPOINTE, Col Hon. Hugues, PC (Canada) 1949; QC; Lieutenant-Governor of Quebec since 1966; *b* Rivière-du-Loup, Quebec, 3 March 1911; *s* of Rt Hon. Ernest Lapointe, PC, QC, Minister of Justice at Ottawa, and Emma Pratte; *m* 1938, Lucette, *d* of Dr and Mrs R. E. Valin, Ottawa. *Educ:* University of Ottawa (BA 1932); Laval Univ., Quebec (LLL 1935). Mem. of Quebec Bar, July 1935; KC 1949. Served War of 1939-45, Overseas, with Regt de la Chaudière. Elected (L) to House of Commons, Lotbinière County Constituency, 1940, 1945, 1949, 1953. Delegate to Gen. Assembly, UN: Paris, Sept. 1948; Lake Success, April 1949; Lake Success, Sept. 1950 (Vice-Chm. Canadian Delegation). Parliamentary Asst to Minister of National Defense, 1945, to Sec. of State for External Affairs, 1949; Solicitor-Gen. of Canada, 1949; Minister of Veterans Affairs, Aug. 1950; Postmaster Gen., 1955; Agent-Gen. for Quebec in the United Kingdom, 1961-66. Hon. Col, Le Régiment de la Chaudière, 1970. Hon. LLD: University of Ottawa, 1954; Royal Military Coll. of Canada, 1967. Croix de Guerre avec palme. KStJ 1966; Kt Grand Cross, Sovereign and Milit. Order of Malta, 1966. Is a Roman Catholic. *Address:* Residence of the Lieutenant-Governor, 1010 St Louis Road, Quebec 6, Canada. *Clubs:* Garrison (Quebec); Royal Quebec Golf (Boischatel).

LAPSLEY, Air Marshal Sir John (Hugh), KBE 1969 (OBE 1944); CB 1966; DFC 1940; AFC 1950; Director-General, Save the Children Fund, 1974-75; *b* 24 Sept. 1916; *s* of late Edward John Lapsley, Bank of Bengal, Dacca, and Norah Gladis Lapsley; *m* 1942, Jean Margaret MacIvor; one *s* one *d*. *Educ:* Wolverhampton Sch.; Royal Air Force Coll., Cranwell. Served in Fighter Squadrons in UK, Egypt and Europe, 1938-45; psc 1946; Air Ministry Directorate of Policy, 1946-48; Commander No 74 Fighter Squadron and Air Fighting Development Squadron, 1949-52; HQ Fighter Command Staff, 1952-54; 2nd TAF Germany, 1954-58; Ministry of Defence Joint Planning Staff, 1958-60; Deputy Chief of Staff Air, 2nd Allied TAF, 1960-62; IDC, 1963; Secretary to Chiefs of Staff Cttee and Director of Defence Operations Staff, Ministry of Defence, 1964-66; No 19 Group, RAF Coastal Comd, 1967-68; AOC-in-C, RAF Coastal Comd, 1968-69; Head of British Defence Staff and Defence Attaché, Washington, 1970-73. Mem. Council, Officers' Pension Soc., 1976- Fellow RSPB. *Recreations:* golf, ornithology. *Address:* c/o Lloyds Bank, 6 Pall Mall, SW1. *Club:* Royal Air Force.

LAPUN, Sir Paul, Kt 1974; Member for South Bougainville, Papua New Guinea House of Assembly, since 1964; *b* 1923; *m* 1951, Lois, two *s* one *d*. *Educ:* Catholic Mission, Vunapope. Teacher, Catholic Mission, 1947-61. Under-Secretary for Forests, Papua and New Guinea, 1964-67. Founder, Pangu Party, 1967 (Leader, 1967-68; Dep. Parly Leader, 1968-); Minister: for Mines and Energy, 1972-75; for Health, 1975-77. Hon. Mem., Ihternat. Mark Twain Soc., USA. *Address:* Box 2352, Konedobu, Papua New Guinea. *T:* 44271.

LAQUEUR, Walter; Director, Institute of Contemporary History and Wiener Library, London, since 1964; *b* 26 May 1921; *s* of late Fritz Laqueur and late Else Laqueur; *m* 1941, Barbara (*née* Koch), *d* of Prof. Richard Koch and Maria Koch (*née* Rosenthal); two *d*. *Educ:* Agricultural labourer during War, 1939-44. Journalist, free lance author, 1944-55; Editor of Survey, 1955-65; Co-editor of Journal of Contemporary History, 1966-. Prof., History of Ideas, Brandeis Univ., 1967-71; Prof. of Contemporary History, Tel Aviv Univ., 1970-; Vis. Prof.: Chicago Univ.; Johns Hopkins Univ.; Harvard Univ. Chm., Res. Council, The Center for Strategic and Internat. Studies, Georgetown Univ., Washington. *Publications:* Communism and Nationalism in the Middle East, 1956; Young Germany, 1961; Russia and Germany, 1965; The Road to War, 1968; Europe Since Hitler, 1970; Out of the Ruins of Europe, 1971; Zionism, a History, 1972; Confrontation: the Middle East War and World Politics, 1974; Weimar: a Cultural History, 1918-33, 1974; Guerrilla, 1976; Terrorism, 1977; (ed jtly) A Reader's Guide to Contemporary History, 1972. *Recreations:* swimming, motorboating. *Address:* 8 Eastville Avenue, NW11. *T:* 01-458 6552; 1800 K Street NW, Washington, DC, USA.

LARCOM, Sir (Charles) Christopher (Royde), 5th Bt, *cr* 1868; Partner in Grieveson, Grant & Co., Stockbrokers, since 1960; *b* 11 Sept. 1926; *s* of Sir Philip Larcom, 4th Bt, and Aileen Monica Royde (*née* Colbeck); *S* father, 1967; *m* 1956, Barbara Elizabeth, *d* of Balfour Bowen; four *d*. *Educ:* Radley; Clare Coll., Cambridge. (Wrangler, 1947; BA, 1947; MA, 1951). Served RN (Lieutenant), 1947-50. Articled to Messrs Spicer and Pegler (Chartered Accountants), 1950-53; ACA 1954; FCA 1965; joined Grieveson, Grant and Co., 1955; Member, The Stock Exchange, London, 1959 (Mem. Council, 1970-). *Recreations:* sailing, music. *Address:* Butlers, Hatfield Peverel, near Chelmsford, Essex. *T:* Chelmsford 380508. *Club:* Bath.

LARDINOIS, Petrus Josephus; President, Cooperative Centrale Rabobank, since 1977; *b* Norbeck, 13 Aug. 1924; *m* Maria Hubertina Gerardine Peeters; two *s* three *d*. *Educ:* Wageningen Agricultural Coll. Various agricultural posts until 1960; entered Ministery of Agriculture and Fisheries, 1960; Agricultural Attaché, Dutch Embassy, London, 1960-63; Mem., Second Chamber, 1963-73 (Catholic People's Party); Mem., European Parliament, 1963-73; Minister of Agriculture and Fisheries, 1967-72; Comr for Agriculture, Commn of the European Communities, 1973-76. Pres., Brabant Farmers' Union, 1965. *Address:* Noorbeek Central Rabobank, Beneluxlaan 33, Utrecht, Netherlands.

LARGE, Prof. John Barry; Professor of Applied Acoustics, Institute of Sound and Vibration Research, University of Southampton, since 1969; *b* 10 Oct. 1930; *s* of Thomas and Ada Large; *m* 1958, Barbara Alicia Nelson; two *s*. *Educ:* Queen Mary Coll., London Univ.; Purdue Univ., USA. BScEng (Hons), MS. Group Engr, EMI Ltd, Feltham, Mddx, 1954-56; Sen. Systems Engr, Link Aviation, Binghampton, NY, USA, 1956-58; Chief Aircraft Noise Unit, Boeing Co., Seattle, USA, 1958-69. Mem., Noise Adv. Council, 1976-. Hon. Dep. Chief Scientific Officer, Royal Aircraft Estabt, 1974-; Adjunct Prof. of Mechanical Engrg, Univ. of Utah, USA, 1974-. *Publications:* contrib. (regarding aircraft noise, etc) to: Commn of European Communities, Eur 5398e, 1975; Agard Lecture Series 77, Adv. Gp for Aerospace Research and Develt, NATO, Agard LS 77, 1975; Proc. 5th Worlds' Airports Conf., Instn of CE, 1976; Internoise 77, Zurich; RSH Conf., Eastbourne, 1977. *Recreations:* skiing, gardening. *Address:* Chinook, Southdown Road, Shawford, Hants. *T:* Twyford 712307.

LARGE, Maj.-Gen. Stanley Eyre, MBE 1945; QHP 1974; Director of Medical Services, United Kingdom Land Forces, 1975-78, retired; *b* 11 Aug. 1917; *s* of Brig. David Torquil Macleod Large and Mrs Constance Lucy Large; *m* 1941, Janet Mary (*née* Brooks); three *s*. *Educ:* Edinburgh; Cheltenham Coll.; Caius Coll., Cambridge (MA,MD); St Thomas' Hosp. FRCP, FRCPE. Commnd in RAMC, 1942; war service in Tunisia, Italy, Austria, Greece, with field ambs and as Regimental MO; psc 1948; spec. medicine; served in hosps at home and overseas as med. specialist, later consultant in medicine, with particular interest in diseases of chest, 1950-65; various sen. admin. appts in Cyprus and BAOR from 1965. *Publications:* contrib. med. literature. *Recreations:* travel, skiing, golf, photography; formerly running (half blue, Cambridge v Oxford, mile, 1937). *Address:* Churt House, Churt, Farnham, Surrey GU10 2PX. *T:* Frensham 2642.

LARKCOM, Eric Herbert Larkcom J.; *see* Jacobs-Larkcom.

LARKIN, Alfred Sloane, CIE 1944; *b* 11 June 1894; *s* of late George Larkin, Ballsbridge, Co. Dublin; *m* 1925, Phyllis (*d* 1974), *d* of late Thomas Hodson, Wainfleet, Lincs; one *s*. *Educ:* High Sch., Dublin; Trent Coll., Derbyshire; Trinity Coll., Dublin. Entered Indian Civil Service, 1921; late Additional Member, Board of Revenue, Government of Bengal. *Address:* 3 Ashburnham Road, Eastbourne, E Sussex BN21 2HU.

LARKIN, John Cuthbert, MA; Headmaster, Wyggeston School, Leicester, 1947-69, retired; *b* 15 Oct. 1906; *s* of J. W. Larkin; *m* 1933, Sylvia Elizabeth Pilsbury; one *s* three *d*. *Educ:* King Edward VI Sch., Nuneaton; Downing Coll., Cambridge. Assistant Master, Shrewsbury Sch., 1928-45; Headmaster, Chesterfield Grammar Sch., 1946-47. *Recreations:* cricket, gardening. *Address:* Groves Cottage, Summers Lane, Totland Bay, Isle of Wight. *T:* Freshwater 2506.

LARKIN, Philip (Arthur), CBE 1975; MA; FRSL; poet and novelist; *b* 9 Aug. 1922; *o s* of Sydney and Eva Emily Larkin. *Educ:* King Henry VIII Sch., Coventry; St John's Coll., Oxford (Hon. Fellow, 1973). Has held posts in different libraries since 1943. Jazz correspondent for the Daily Telegraph, 1961-71. Vis. Fellow, All Souls Coll., Oxford, 1970-71. Foreign Hon. Member, Amer. Acad. of Arts and Sciences, 1975. Hon. DLit Belfast, 1969; Hon. DLitt: Leicester, 1970; Warwick, 1973; St Andrews, 1974; Sussex, 1974. The Queen's Gold Medal for Poetry, 1965; Loines Award for Poetry, 1974; A. C. Benson Silver Medal, RSL, 1975; Shakespeare Prize, FVS Foundation of Hamburg, 1976. *Publications:* The North Ship (poems), 1945; Jill (novel), 1946 (rev. edn 1964); A Girl in Winter (novel), 1947; The Less Deceived (poems), 1955; The Whitsun Weddings (poems), 1964; All What Jazz (essays), 1970; (ed) The Oxford Book of Twentieth Century English Verse, 1973; High Windows (poems), 1974. *Address:* c/o Faber & Faber Ltd, 3 Queen Square, WC1N 3AU.

LARKING, Lt-Col Sir (Charles) Gordon, Kt 1970; CBE 1951; Chartered Accountant; *b* 31 Aug. 1893; *s* of late Charles Larking, Norwich; *m* 1917, Kathleen Ethel Pank (*d* 1970), Norwich; two *s* one *d*. *Educ:* Norwich. Served European War, 1914-19, Royal Fusiliers, Royal Sussex, MGC (Egypt and France); War of 1939-45, commanded 8th Bn E. Surrey Regt, 1939-42; British Legion: National Chairman, 1947-50 (visited Malaya, Burma, Australia, New Zealand, Kenya, Uganda, Tanganyika, S Africa, Canada and US); National Treasurer, 1962-70. Member of Maidstone Borough Council, 1922-74; Mayor, 1931-32, 1944-45, 1950-51; Alderman, 1941-74; Hon. Freeman, 1948. *Recreations:* cricket and football. *Address:* Pear Patch, Loose, Maidstone.

LARMOUR, Sir (Edward) Noel, KCMG 1977 (CMG 1966); HM Diplomatic Service, retired; Member, Price Commission, since 1977; *b* 25 Dec. 1916; *s* of Edward and Maud Larmour, Belfast, N Ireland; *m* 1946, Nancy, 2nd *d* of Thomas Bill; one *s* two *d*. *Educ:* Royal Belfast Academical Institution (Kitchener Scholar); Trinity Coll., Dublin (Scholar) (1st Class Hons and University Studentship in Classics, 1939); Sydney Univ., NSW. Royal Inniskilling Fusiliers, 1940; Burma Civil Service, 1942; 14th Punjab Regt, 1943; Civil Affairs Staff (Burma), 15 Ind. Corps, 1944-45; Major; Dep. Secretary to Governor of Burma, 1947; Commonwealth Relations Office, 1948; served in New Zealand, Singapore, Australia and Nigeria, 1950-68; Asst Under-Secretary of State, 1964; Dep. Chief of Administration, FCO, 1968-70; High Comr, Jamaica, and non-resident Ambassador, Haiti, 1970-73; Asst Under Sec. of State, FCO, 1973-75; High Comr (non-resident) for New Hebrides, 1973-76; Dep. Under Sec. of State, FCO, 1975-76. *Recreations:* cricket, golf, music. *Address:* 68 Wood Vale, N10. *T:* 01-444 9744. *Clubs:* Royal Commonwealth Society; MCC.

LARSEN, Roy Edward; Vice-Chairman of Board, Time Incorporated, since 1969 (Director, 1933, President, 1939-60, Chairman, Executive Committee, 1960-69); *b* 20 April 1899; *s* of Robert Larsen and Stella Belyea; *m* 1927, Margaret Zerbe; three *s* one *d*. *Educ:* Boston Latin Sch.; Harvard Univ. Circulation Manager, Time, 1922; Vice-President, Time Inc., 1927-39; Publisher Life, 1936-46. Overseer Harvard Univ., 1940-46, 1953-59; Chairman National Citizens Commn for Public Schools, 1949-56; Chairman of the Board of the Fund for the Advancement of Education, 1955-67; Member President's Cttee on Education Beyond the High School; Trustee, Ford Foundation, 1957-69; Chm. of Bd, Nantucket Conservation Foundn; Mem. Bd of Governors, Nature Conservancy; Hon. Trustee, New York Public Library. Chevalier, French Legion of Honour, 1950. Hon. LLD: Marietta Coll., 1946; Bucknell Univ., 1950; New York Univ., 1952; Harvard, 1953; Dartmouth Coll., 1954; Boston Univ., 1956; Hon. LHD, Kalamazoo Coll., 1951; Hon. LittD, Oberlin Coll., 1958. Hon. Phi Beta Kappa, 1957. *Address:* Time Inc., Time & Life Building, Rockefeller Center, New York, NY 10020, USA. *T:* Judson 6-1212; 4900 Congress Street, Fairfield, Conn 06431, USA. *Clubs:* Harvard, Century, River, University, Links (New York); Lyford Cay (Bahamas).

LARSON, Frederick H., DFM 1943; General Manager, Business Development, Alberta Opportunity Co., Edmonton, Alberta (Alberta Crown Corporation), since 1974; *b* 24 Nov. 1913; *s* of Herman B. and Martha C. Larson; *m* 1941, Dorothy A. Layng; one *s*. *Educ:* University of Saskatchewan. Observer, RCAF, 1941-43. Member for Kindersley, Parliament of Canada, 1949-53; Delegate to UN, Paris, 1952. Ten years in oil and gas business, production refining and sales, domestic and offshore; eight years in financial trust business, representing financial interests, Canada amd Jamaica; three years in construction and engineering; agricultural interests, Saskatchewan; Agent-Gen. for Province of Saskatchewan in London, 1967-73. *Recreation:* golf. *Address:* c/o Guaranty Trust Company, 10010 Jasper Avenue, Edmonton, Alberta, Canada. *Clubs:* Ranchmen's (Calgary); Mayfair Golf (Edmonton, Alta).

LARTIGUE, Sir Louis C.; *see* Cools-Lartigue.

LASCELLES, family name of Earl of Harewood.

LASCELLES, Viscount; David Henry George Lascelles; *b* 21 Oct. 1950; *s* and *heir* of 7th Earl of Harewood, *qv*. *Educ:* The Hall Sch.; Westminster. *Address:* 2 Orme Square, W2.

LASCELLES, Rt. Hon. Sir Alan Frederick, PC 1943; GCB 1953 (KCB 1944; CB 1937); GCVO 1947 (KCVO 1939; MVO 1926); CMG 1933; MC; MA; Past Director: The Midland Bank; Royal Academy of Music; Private Secretary to the Queen, 1952-53; Keeper of the Queen's Archives, 1952-53 (of the King's Archives, 1943-52); *b* 11 April 1887; *s* of Hon. F. C. Lascelles; *m* 1920, Hon. Joan Thesiger (*d* 1971), *e d* of 1st Viscount

Chelmsford; two *d* (one *s* decd). *Educ:* Marlborough Coll.; Trinity Coll., Oxford (Hon. Fellow, Trinity Coll., Oxford, 1948). Served in France with Bedfordshire Yeomanry, 1914-18; Captain, 1916; ADC to Lord Lloyd, when Governor of Bombay, 1919-20; Assistant Private Secretary to Prince of Wales, 1920-29; Secretary to Governor General of Canada, 1931-35; Assistant Private Secretary to King George V, 1935, and to King George VI, 1936-43, Private Secretary, 1943-52. Chairman, The Pilgrim Trust, 1954-60; Chairman, Historic Buildings Council for England, 1953-63; LLD (Hon.) Bristol and Durham; Hon. DCL (Oxon), FRAM (Hon.). *Address:* Kensington Palace, W8. *See also* Viscount Chandos.

LASCELLES, Daniel Richard, CBE 1962; *b* 18 Sept. 1908; 4th *s* of Councillor A. Lascelles, JP, Darlington; *m* 1941, Mildred Joyce Burr; two *s* one *d*. *Educ:* Durham Sch.; St John's Coll., Cambridge. Called to Bar, Inner Temple, 1930; Sarawak Administrative Service, 1932; Circuit Judge, Sarawak, 1948; Colonial Legal Service, 1951; Acting Puisne Judge, 1951; Puisne Judge of Supreme Court of Sarawak, North Borneo and Brunei, 1952-62. Legal Chairman Pensions Appeal Tribunals, 1964-74; Chairman, Medical Appeal Tribunals, 1967-74; Member, Mental Health Review Tribunal, 1967-74. *Recreations:* shooting, gardening, golf, tennis. *Address:* 39 13th Avenue, Edenvale, Johannesburg, 1610 South Africa.

LASCELLES, Sir Francis (William), KCB 1954 (CB 1937); MC; MA; Clerk of the Parliaments, 1953-58; *b* 23 March 1890; *s* of late Lieut-Colonel H. A. Lascelles, Woolbeding, Midhurst; *m* 1924, Esmée Marion, *d* of late C. A. Bury, Downings, Co. Kildare; two *s*. *Educ:* Winchester; Christ Church, Oxford. Served in European War, 1914-19 with Sussex Yeomanry (wounded, MC). *Address:* Field House, Orford, Suffolk. *T:* Orford 361.

LASCELLES, Maj.-Gen. Henry Anthony, CB 1967; CBE 1962 (OBE 1945); DSO 1944; *b* 10 Jan. 1912; *s* of Edward Lascelles and Leila Kennett-Barrington; *m* 1941, Ethne Hyde Ussher Charles. *Educ:* Winchester; Oriel Coll., Oxford (BA). Served War of 1939-45: Egypt, North Africa, Sicily and Italy, rising to second in command of an armoured brigade. Instructor, Staff Coll., Camberley, 1947-49; GSO 1, HQ 7th Armoured Div., BAOR, 1949-52; Comdg Officer 6th Royal Tank Regt, BAOR, 1952-55; Instructor NATO Defence Coll., 1955-56; Brigadier Royal Armoured Corps HQ 2nd Infantry Div., BAOR, 1956-57; National Defence Coll., Canada, 1958-59; BGS Military Operations, War Office, 1959-62; Chief of Staff, HQ Northern Ireland Command, 1962-63; Maj.-General, General Staff, Far East Land Forces, 1963-66. Director-General, Winston Churchill Memorial Trust, 1967-. *Recreations:* squash, tennis, golf, music, gardening. *Address:* Manor Farm Cottage, Hedgerley Green, Bucks. *T:* Gerrards Cross 83582. *Club:* Naval and Military.

LASCELLES, Mary Madge, FBA 1962; Hon. Fellow, Somerville College, 1967; *b* 7 Feb. 1900; *d* of William Horace and Madeline Lascelles. *Educ:* Sherborne School for Girls; Lady Margaret Hall, Oxford. Research Studentship, Westfield Coll., 1923; Assistant Lecturer, Royal Holloway Coll., 1926; Somerville College: Tutor in English Language and Literature, 1931; Fellow, 1932-67; Vice-Principal, 1947-60; University Lecturer in English Literature, 1960-66; Reader, 1966-67. *Publications:* Jane Austen and her Art, 1939; Shakespeare's Measure for Measure, 1953; (ed) The Works of Samuel Johnson, vol. ix, A Journey to the Western Islands of Scotland, 1971; The Adversaries and Other Poems, 1971; Notions and Facts, 1973; contributions to learned journals, etc. *Address:* 3 Stratfield Road, Oxford OX2 7BG. *T:* Oxford 57817. *Club:* University Women's.

LASDUN, Sir Denys (Louis), Kt 1976; CBE 1965; FRIBA; architect in private practice with Alexander Redhouse and Peter Softley, since 1960; *b* 8 Sept. 1914; *s* of Norman Lasdun and Julie Abrahams; *m* 1954, Susan Bendit; two *s* one *d*. *Educ:* Rugby Sch.; Architectural Assoc. Served with Royal Engineers, 1939-45 (MBE). Practised with Wells Coates, Tecton and Drake. Hoffman Wood Professor of Architecture, University of Leeds, 1962-63. Assessor, Competitions for Belgrade Opera Hse, 1971, and new Parly Bldg, London, 1971-72. Member: Jerusalem Town Planning Sub-Cttee, 1970; Mars Gp. Works include: housing and schools for Bethnal Green and Paddington; new store for Peter Robinson, Strand (now London HQ, NSW Govt, acted as Consultant Architect); flats at 26 St James's Place; Royal College of Physicians; Fitzwilliam College, and Christ's College extension, Cambridge; new University of East Anglia and work for the Universities of London (SOAS, Inst. of Educn, Law Inst.), Leicester and Liverpool; Royal Instn of Chartered Surveyors, Parliament Square; National Theatre, South Bank; new EEC HQ for European Investment Bank,

Luxembourg; Cannock Community Hospital, Staffs; Sotheby & Co. Trustee, BM, 1975-; Member: V & A Adv. Cttee, 1973-; Slade Cttee, 1976-. Hon. Fellow, American Institute of Architects, 1966; Hon. FRCP, 1975. Hon. DLitt E Anglia, 1974. RIBA London Architecture Bronze Medallist, 1960 and 1964; RIBA Gold Medal, 1977; Civic Trust Awards: Class I, 1967; Group A, 1969; Special Award, Sao Paulo Biennale, Brazil, 1969. *Publications:* A Language and a Theme, 1976; contributions to architectural and other papers incl. An Architects Approach to Architecture. Lectures given in UK, USA, Spain, Portugal and Norway. *Address:* 25 Dawson Place, W2.

LASH, Rt. Rev. William Quinlan; *b* 5 Feb. 1905; *s* of Nicholas Alleyne and Violet Maud Lash. *Educ:* Tonbridge Sch., Emmanuel Coll., Cambridge; Westcott House. BA 1927; MA 1932; Deacon, 1928; Priest, 1929; Curate, S Mary's Church, Portsea, 1928-32; Christa Seva Sangha, Poona, 1932; Acharya, Christa Prema Seva Sangha, Poona, 1934-49, 1953-61; Bishop of Bombay, 1947-61; Asst Bishop of Truro, Hon. Canon of St Mary's Cathedral, Truro, 1962-73; Vicar of St Clement, 1963-73. *Publications:* Approach to Christian Mysticism, 1947; The Temple of God's Wounds, 1951. *Address:* The Friary, Hilfield, Dorchester, Dorset. *T:* Cerne Abbas 346.

LASKEY, Sir Denis (Seward), KCMG 1974 (CMG 1957); CVO 1958; HM Diplomatic Service, retired; *b* 18 Jan. 1916; *s* of F. S. Laskey; *m* 1947, Perronnelle Mary Gemma, *d* of late Col Sir Edward Le Breton, MVO; one *s* three *d. Educ:* Marlborough Coll.; Corpus Christi Coll., Oxford. 3rd Secretary, Diplomatic Service, 1939; FO, Sept. 1939-June 1940; served in Army, 1940-41; FO, 1941-46; Berlin, 1946-49; Member UK Delegation to UN, New York, 1949-53; FO, 1953-59; Private Secretary to Secretary of State for Foreign Affairs, 1956-59; Minister, HM Embassy, Rome, 1960-64; Under-Secretary, Cabinet Office, 1964-67; Minister, HM Embassy, Bonn, 1967-68; Ambassador to: Rumania, 1969-71; Austria, 1972-75. *Recreations:* ski-ing, fishing, golf. *Address:* Loders Mill, near Bridport, Dorset. *Club:* Leander (Henley-on-Thames).

LASKI, Marghanita; (Mrs J. E. Howard); *b* 24 Oct. 1915; *d* of late Neville J. Laski, QC; *m* 1937, John Eldred Howard; one *s* one *d. Educ:* Ladybarn House Sch., Manchester; Somerville Coll., Oxford. MA Oxon. Novelist, critic, journalist. Mem., Annan Cttee of Inquiry into Future of Broadcasting, 1974-77. Hon. Fellow, Manchester Polytechnic, 1971. F. D. Maurice Meml Lectures, 1974. *Publications:* Love on the Supertax (novel), 1944; The Patchwork Book (anthology), 1946; To Bed with Grand Music (pseudonymous novel), 1946; Stories of Adventure, 1947; (ed) Victorian Tales, 1948; Tory Heaven (novel), 1948; Little Boy Lost (novel), 1949; Mrs Ewing, Mrs Molesworth, Mrs Hodgson Burnett (criticism), 1950; The Village (novel), 1952; The Victorian Chaise-Longue (novel), 1953; The Offshore Island (play), 1959; Ecstasy: A study of some secular and religious experiences, 1961; Domestic Life in Edwardian England, 1964; (ed, with E.G. Battiscombe) A Chaplet for Charlotte Yonge, 1965; The Secular Responsibility (Conway Memorial Lecture), 1967; Jane Austen and her World, 1969; George Eliot and her World, 1973; Kipling's English History, 1974 (radio programme, 1973). Radio and TV programmes. *Address:* c/o David Higham Associates, 5-8 Lower John Street, W1R 3PE.

LASKIN, Rt. Hon. Bora, PC(Can) 1973; FRSC; Chief Justice of Canada since Dec. 1973; *b* 5 Oct. 1912; *s* of late Max and Bluma Laskin; *m* 1938, Peggy Tenenbaum; one *s* one *d. Educ:* Univ. of Toronto (BA, MA, LLB); Osgoode Hall Law Sch.; Harvard Univ. (LLM). Lectr in Law, Univ. of Toronto, 1940-43; Asst Prof., 1943-45; Lectr, Osgoode Hall Law Sch., 1945-49; Prof. of Law, Univ. of Toronto, 1949-65; apptd: Justice, Ontario Court of Appeal, Aug. 1965; Justice, Supreme Court of Canada, March 1970. Hon. Bencher, Lincoln's Inn, 1974. Hon. LLD: Queen's; Edinburgh; Trent; Toronto; Alberta; Manitoba; York; Dalhousie; Law Soc. of Upper Canada; McGill; Ottawa; Simon Fraser; Ontario Inst. for Studies in Educn; Victoria; Yeshiva; Hon. DCL: New Brunswick; Windsor; W Ontario; Hon. DPhil Hebrew Univ., Jerusalem. *Publications:* Canadian Constitutional Law (3rd edn), 1969; The British Tradition in Canadian Law, 1969. *Address:* 200 Rideau Terrace, Apt 1405, Ottawa, Ontario K1M 0Z3, Canada. *T:* 746-6884. *Club:* Rideau (Ottawa).

LASKO, Prof. Peter Erik, FSA; Professor of the History of Art, Courtauld Institute, University of London, since 1974; Director, Courtauld Institute, since 1974; *b* 5 March 1924; *s* of Leo Lasko and Wally Lasko (*née* Seifert); *m* 1948, Gwendoline Joan Norman; three *d. Educ:* Courtauld Institute, Univ. of London. BA Hons 1949. Asst Keeper at British Museum, 1950-65; Prof. of

the Visual Arts, Univ. of East Anglia, 1965-73. *Publication:* Ars Sacra 800-1200 (Pelican History of Art), 1972. *Address:* Courtauld Institute, University of London, 20 Portman Square, W1. *T:* 01-935 9292. *Club:* Athenæum.

LASKY, Melvin Jonah, MA; Editor, Encounter Magazine, since 1958; *b* New York City, 15 Jan. 1920; *s* of Samuel Lasky and Esther Lasky (*née* Kantrowitz); *m* 1947, Brigitte Newiger; one *s* one *d. Educ:* City Coll. of New York (BSS); Univ. of Michigan (MA); Columbia Univ. Literary Editor, The New Leader (NY), 1942-43; US Combat Historian in France and Germany, 1944-45; Capt., US Army, 1946; Foreign Correspondent, 1946-48; Editor and Publisher, Der Monat (Berlin), 1948-58; Co-Editor, Encounter Magazine (London), 1958-; Editorial Director, Library Press, NY, 1970-; Publisher, Alcove Press, London, 1972-. Univ. of Michigan, Sesquicentennial Award, 1967. *Publications:* Reisenotizen und Tagebücher, 1958; Africa for Beginners, 1962; Utopia and Revolution, 1976; contributor to: America and Europe, 1951; New Paths in American History, 1965; Sprache und Politik, 1969; Festschrift for Raymond Aron, 1971; (ed) The Hungarian Revolution, 1957. *Address:* c/o Encounter, 59 St Martins Lane, WC2N 4JS. *T:* 01-836 4194. *Club:* Garrick.

LAST, Prof. Raymond Jack, FRCS; Professor of Applied Anatomy, and Warden, Royal College of Surgeons, 1949-70; *b* 26 May 1903; English. *Educ:* Adelaide High Sch., Australia. MB, BS (Adelaide), 1924; Medical practice S. Australia, 1927-38; arrived London, 1939; Surgeon, EMS, Northern Hospital, N21, 1939-40. OC Abyssinian Medical Unit, Hon. Surgeon to Emperor Haile Selassie I, also OC Haile Selassie Hospital, Surgeon to British Legation, Addis Ababa, 1941-44; returned to London, Lieut-Colonel, RAMC, 1945; ADMS, British Borneo, 1945-46. Anatomical Curator and Bland Sutton Scholar, RCS, 1946; FRCS 1947; Adviser to Central Government of Pakistan on organization and conduct of primary FRCS instruction, Colombo Plan, 1961. Vis. Prof. of Anatomy: UCLA, 1970-77; Mt Sinai Sch. of Medicine, NY, 1971-72. *Publications:* Anatomy, Regional and Applied, 5th edn, 1972, 6th edn 1977; Wolff's Anatomy of Eye and Orbit, 6th edn, 1968; Aids to Anatomy, 12th edn, 1962; contrib. to Journals of Surgery; various articles. *Address:* 22 Koonga Avenue, Prospect, SA 5082, Australia. *T:* (08) 44 94 15.

LATEY, Hon. Sir John (Brinsmead), Kt 1965; MBE 1943; **Hon. Mr Justice Latey;** Judge of the High Court of Justice, Family Division (formerly Probate, Divorce and Admiralty Division), since 1965; *b* 7 March 1914; *s* of late William Latey, CBE, QC, and of Anne Emily, *d* of late Horace G. Brinsmead; *m* 1938, Betty Margaret (*née* Beresford); one *s* one *d. Educ:* Westminster; Christ Church, Oxford. MA (Hon. Sch. Jurispr.). Called to the Bar, 1936; QC 1957. Served in Army during War, 1939-45, mainly in MEF (Lieut-Colonel, 1944-). General Council of the Bar, 1952-56, 1957-61 and 1964- (Hon. Treasurer, 1959-61). Master of the Bench of the Middle Temple, 1964. Chairman, Lord Chancellor's Cttee on Age of Majority, 1965-67. Dep. Chairman, Oxfordshire QS, 1966. *Publications:* (Asst Ed.) Latey on Divorce, 14th edn, 1952; Halsbury's Laws of England (Conflict of Laws: Husband and Wife), 1956. *Recreations:* golf, bridge, chess. *Address:* 33 Pembroke Gardens, W8. *T:* 01-603 6760. *Club:* United Oxford & Cambridge University.

LATHAM, family name of **Baron Latham.**

LATHAM, 2nd Baron *cr* 1942, of Hendon; **Dominic Charles Latham;** *b* 20 Sept. 1954; *s* of Hon. Francis Charles Allman Latham (*d* 1959) and of Gabrielle, *d* of Dr S. M. O'Riordan; *S* grandfather, 1970. *Heir: yr* twin *b* Anthony Latham, *b* 20 Sept. 1954.

LATHAM, Arthur Charles; MP (Lab) City of Westminster, Paddington, since 1974 (Paddington North, Oct. 1969-1974); *b* Leyton, 14 Aug. 1930; *m* 1951, Margaret Latham; one *s* one *d. Educ:* Romford Royal Liberty Sch.; Garnett Coll. of Educn. Lectr in Further Educn, Southgate Technical Coll., 1967-. Mem., Havering Council (formerly Romford Borough Council) 1952- (Alderman, 1962-); Leader, Lab. Gp, Romford and Havering Councils, 1962-70. Contested (Lab): Woodford, 1959; Rushcliffe, Notts, 1964. Mem., NE Regional Metropolitan Hosp. Bd, 1966-72. Jt Chm., All Party Gp for Pensioners, 1971-; Chairman: Tribune Gp, 1975-76; Greater London Lab. Party, 1977-; Vice-Chm., Nat. Cttee, Labour League of Youth, 1949-53; Vice-President: Labour Action for Peace; AMA; Treasurer, Liberation (Movement for Colonial Freedom); Member: British Campaign for Peace in Vietnam; Campaign for Nuclear Disarmament. *Recreations:* bridge, chess, cricket. *Address:* House of Commons, SW1; 17 Tudor Avenue, Gidea Park, Romford, RM2 5LB.

LATHAM, Cecil Thomas, OBE 1976; Stipendiary Magistrate, Greater Manchester (sitting at Salford), since 1976; *b* 11 March 1924; *s* of Cecil Frederick James Latham and Elsie Winifred Latham; *m* 1945, Ivy Frances (*née* Fowle); one *s* one *d*. *Educ:* Rochester Cathedral Choir Sch.; King's Sch., Rochester. Solicitor. War Service, 1942-45. Asst Clerk, Magistrates' Courts: Chatham, 1939-42; Maidstone, 1945; Leicester, 1948-54; Bromley, 1954-63; Dep. Justices' Clerk, Liverpool, 1963-65; Justices' Clerk, Manchester, 1965-76. *Publications:* (ed) Stone's Justices' Manual, 101st-109th edns; How Much?: determining maintenance in Magistrates' Courts, 1976; contrib. Criminal Law Rev., Justice of Peace, Family Law. *Recreation:* music. *Address:* 19 Southdown Crescent, Cheadle Hulme, Cheshire SK8 6EQ. *T:* 061-485 1185.

LATHAM, Christopher George Arnot; Deputy Chairman, James Latham Ltd, since 1973; Forestry Commissioner, since 1973; Vice-President, Institute of Wood Science; *b* 4 June 1933; *s* of Edward Bryan Latham, *qv*; *m* 1963, Jacqueline Cabourdin; three *s*. *Educ:* Stowe Sch.; Clare Coll., Cambridge (MA). FCA. Articled Fitzpatrick Graham, chartered accountants, 1955; joined James Latham Ltd, timber importers, 1959, Dir 1963. Chairman: Timber Res. and Develt Assoc., 1972-74; Commonwealth Forestry Assoc., 1975-77; Vice-Pres., Inst. of Wood Science, 1973. *Recreations:* riding, sailing, tennis, collecting toby jugs. *Address:* Place Farm, Doddinghurst, Brentwood, Essex. *T:* Coxtie Green 73293.

LATHAM, E(dward) Bryan, CBE 1964; MM 1915; BA 1974; Director, since 1921, President, since 1972, James Latham Ltd, Timber Importers, London (Managing Director, 1939-51, Chairman, 1951-71); *b* 7 May 1895; *s* of late E. Locks Latham, The Towers, Theydon Bois, Essex, and late Emily Latham (*née* Chappell); *m* 1927, Anne Arnot Duncan, Newton of Lathrisk, Fife; two *s*. *Educ:* Felsted, Essex; Open Univ. Served European War, 1914-18 (MM): France, Indian Frontier, Palestine; Lieut, 17th London Regt, later Captain, 19th Punjabi Regt. Governor Metropolitan Hosp., London, 1930-40; Chm., Nat. Sawmilling Assoc., 1942-43; Pres. Timber Trade Fedn of UK, 1945-47; Governing Council, Commonwealth Forestry Association, 1945- (Chm., 1961; Vice-Pres., 1964-); Gen. Council, British Standards Inst., 1946-48; Mem. Education Cttee, FBI, 1956-66; Founder-Pres., Inst. of Wood Science, 1956-58, Mem. Council, 1959-; Mem. Forestry Commn, 1957-63. Mem. British Delegs to Commonwealth Forestry Confs: London, 1947; Ottawa, 1952; to 5th World Forestry Congress, Seattle, 1960; Hon. Pres. Univ. of Edinburgh Forestry Assoc., 1962-63; Pres., Timber Research and Development Assoc. (TRADA), 1973- (Vice-Pres., 1963-69; Chm., 1943-44; Mem. Council, 1943-70); Pres., Timber Trade Benevolent Fund; Member: Business Archives Council, 1962-68; Furniture and Timber Industry Training Board, 1965-71; F.Inst. of Wood Science, London, 1957-72; F.Forest History Foundation, Yale Univ., 1959-70; FRSA 1961. Mem. Royal Horticultural Soc., Surrey; Pres. Launceston Agric. Soc., 1967. *Publications:* Victorian Staffordshire Portrait Figures, 1953; Timber: Its Development and Distribution, 1957; Wood from Forest to Man, 1964; History of the Timber Trade Federation of the UK, 1965; Territorial Soldiers War, 1967; Trebartha, the House by the Stream: a Cornish history, 1970. Contributor to: Encyclopædia Britannica, Empire Forestry Review, Wood, Timber Trades Journal, Unasylva (FAO), etc. *Recreations:* fishing, riding, natural history, gardening; collector of Victorian Staffordshire Portrait figures. *Address:* Trebartha House, near Launceston, Cornwall. *T:* Coad's Green 336. *Club:* Army and Navy.
   See also C . G . A . Latham .

LATHAM, Sir Joseph, Kt 1960; CBE 1950; Chairman: Metal Industries Ltd, 1968-72; Director: Thorn Electrical Industries, Ltd; George Wimpey and Co. Ltd; Director Emeritus, Black & Decker Manufacturing Co., USA; *b* 1 July 1905; *s* of John and Edith Latham, Prestwich, Lancs; *m* 1932, Phyllis Mary Fitton; one *s* one *d*. *Educ:* Stand Grammar Sch. Chartered Accountant, 1926; Liaison Officer, Lancashire Associated Collieries, 1935; Director and Secretary, Manchester Collieries Ltd, 1941; Director-General of Finance, National Coal Board, 1946-55; Finance Member, NCB, 1955-56; Deputy Chairman, NCB, 1956-60. Vice-Chm., AEI, 1964-65, Dep. Chm., 1965-68, Man. Dir, 1967-68. Mem., ECGD, Advisory Council, 1964-69; Chm., Economic Development Cttees, Food Processing and Chocolate & Sugar Confectionery Industries, 1965-66. *Address:* 25 Badingham Drive, Leatherhead, Surrey. *T:* Leatherhead 72433. *Club:* Effingham Golf.

LATHAM, Michael Anthony; MP (C) Melton since Feb. 1974; *b* 20 Nov. 1942; *s* of Wing-Comdr S. H. Latham, RAF and Mrs G. K. Ranoszek; *m* 1969, Caroline Terry; one *s*. *Educ:* Marlborough Coll.; King's Coll., Cambridge; Dept of Educn,

Oxford. BA Cantab 1964, MA Cantab 1968, CertEd Oxon 1965. Housing and Local Govt Officer, Conservative Research Dept, 1965-67; Parly Liaison Officer, Nat. Fedn of Building Trades Employers, 1967-73; Dir, House-builders Fedn, 1971-73. Westminster City Councillor, 1968-71. Contested (C) Liverpool, West Derby, 1970. Vice-Chm., Cons. Parly Housing Cttee, 1974-76; Member: House of Commons Expenditure Cttee, 1974-; Jt Cttee on Statutory Instruments, 1974-75; Jt Ecclesiastical Cttee of both Houses of Parliament, 1974-. Dir, Lovell Homes Ltd, 1975-. Mem. Bd of Management, Shelter, 1976-. CofE Deleg. to BCC, 1977-. *Publications:* articles on housing, land, town planning and building. *Recreations:* gardening, fencing, listening to classical music, cricket. *Address:* House of Commons, SW1A 0AA. *Club:* Carlton.

LATHAM, Sir Richard Thomas Paul, 3rd Bt, *cr* 1919, of Crow Clump; *b* 15 April 1934; *s* of Sir (Herbert) Paul Latham, 2nd Bt, and Lady Patricia Doreen Moore (*d* 1947), *o d* of 10th Earl of Drogheda; *S* father, 1955; *m* 1958, Marie-Louise Patricia, *d* of Frederick H. Russell, Vancouver, BC; two *d*. *Educ:* Eton; Trinity Coll., Cambridge. *Address:* 830 Rockbridge Road, Santa Barbara, Calif 93108, USA.

LATHAM, Robert Clifford, CBE 1973; Fellow and Pepys Librarian, Magdalene College, Cambridge, since 1972; *b* 11 March 1912; *s* of Edwin Latham, and Alice Latham, Audley, Staffs; *m* 1st, 1939, Eileen Frances Redding Ramsay (*d* 1969); one *s* one *d*; 2nd, 1973, Rosalind Frances Birley. *Educ:* Wolstanton County Grammar Sch., Staffs; Queens' Coll., Cambridge (scholar). Hist. Tripos Pt I 1932, Pt II 1933; MA 1938. Asst Lectr in History, King's Coll., London, 1935; Lectr, 1939; University Reader in History, Royal Holloway Coll., London, 1947; Visiting Associate Prof., Univ. of Southern California, Los Angeles, 1955; Prof. of History, Univ. of Toronto, 1968; Research Fellow, Magdalene Coll., Cambridge, 1970. *Publications:* (ed) Bristol Charters, 1509-1899 (Bristol Rec. Soc., vol. xii), 1947; (ed, with Prof. W. Matthews) The Diary of Samuel Pepys (ix vols), 1970-76; articles and reviews in learned and other jls. *Recreations:* music, gossip. *Address:* Magdalene College, Cambridge CB3 0AG. *T:* Cambridge 61545.

LATHBURY, General Sir Gerald (William), GCB 1962 (KCB 1956; CB 1950); DSO 1943; MBE 1940; DSC (USA) 1944; Governor of Gibraltar, 1964-69; *b* 14 July 1906; *m* 1942, Jean Thin; two *d*; *m* 1972, Mrs Mairi Gibbs, *widow* of Patrick Somerset Gibbs. *Educ:* Wellington Coll.; Royal Military Coll., Sandhurst, 1924-25; gazetted to Oxfordshire and Buckinghamshire Light Infantry, 1926; Gold Coast Regt, 1928-33; Staff Coll., 1937-38; served throughout War of 1939-45 in France and Belgium, North Africa, Sicily, Italy and North-West Europe; Palestine, 1945-46; Imperial Defence Coll., 1948; GOC 16 Airborne Division (TA), 1948-51; Commandant, Staff Coll., Camberley, 1951-53; Vice-Adjutant-General, War Office, 1954; Commander-in-Chief, East Africa, 1955-57; Director-General of Military Training, War Office, 1957-60; General Officer Commanding-in-Chief, Eastern Command, 1960-61; Quartermaster-General to the Forces, 1961-65; ADC General to the Queen, 1962-65. Colonel, West India Regt, 1959; Jamaica Regt, 1962-68; Colonel Comdt, 1st Green Jackets, 43rd and 52nd, 1961-65; Colonel Comdt, The Parachute Regt, 1961-65. *Address:* Casa San Pedro, Gata de Gorgos, Prov. Alicante, Spain. *Club:* Army and Navy.

LATHE, Prof. Grant Henry; Professor of Chemical Pathology, University of Leeds, 1957-77, now Emeritus Professor; *b* 27 July 1913; *s* of Frank Eugene and Annie Smith Lathe; *m* 1st, 1938, Margaret Eleanore Brown; one *s*; 2nd, 1950, Joan Frances Hamlin; one *s* two *d*. *Educ:* McGill Univ.; Oxford Univ. ICI Research Fellow: Dept. of Biochemistry, Oxford Univ., 1946; Dept. of Chemical Pathology, Post Graduate Medical School of London, 1948; Lecturer in Chemical Pathology, Guy's Hospital Medical School, 1948; Biochemist, The Bernhard Baron Memorial Research Laboratories, Queen Charlotte's Maternity Hospital, London, 1949. John Scott Award (with C. R. J. Ruthven), 1971, for invention of gel filtration. *Publications:* papers in medical and biochemical journals. *Recreations:* skating, listening to music. *Address:* 14 Lidgett Park Road, Leeds LS8 1JN. *T:* 66-1507.

LATIMER, Sir (Courtenay) Robert, Kt 1966; CBE 1958 (OBE 1948); *b* 13 July 1911; *er s* of late Sir Courtenay Latimer, KCIE, CSI; *m* 1944, Elizabeth Jane Gordon (*née* Smail); one *s* one *d*. *Educ:* Rugby; Christ Church, Oxford. ICS, 1934 (Punjab); IPS, 1939; Vice-Consul, Bushire, 1940-41; Sec. Foreign Publicity Office, Delhi, 1941-42; Sec. Indian Agency Gen., Chungking, 1944; in NW Frontier Prov., as Asst Political Agent N Waziristan, Dir of Civil Supplies, Sec. to Governor and District Comr, Bannu, 1942-43 and 1945-47. HM Overseas Service,

1948; served in Swaziland, 1948-49; Bechuanaland Protectorate, 1951-54; Office of High Comr for Basutoland, the Bechuanaland Protectorate and Swaziland, as Asst Sec., 1949-51; Sec. for Finance, 1954-60; Chief Sec., 1960-64; Minister, British Embassy, Pretoria, 1965-66; Registrar, Kingston Polytechnic, 1967-76. *Recreations:* golf, photography. *Address:* Benedicts, Old Avenue, Weybridge, Surrey.

LATNER, Prof. Albert Louis; Professor of Clinical Biochemistry, University of Newcastle upon Tyne, since 1963, and Director of Cancer Research Unit, since 1967; Consultant Clinical Biochemist, Royal Victoria Infirmary, Newcastle upon Tyne, since 1948; *b* 5 Dec. 1912; *s* of Harry Latner and Miriam Gordon; *m* 1936, Gertrude Franklin. *Educ:* Imperial College of Science and University College, London; University of Liverpool. ARCSc, 1931; MSc (London) 1933; DIC, 1934; MB, ChB (Liverpool) 1939; MD (Liverpool) 1948; FRIC 1953; MRCP 1956; DSc (Liverpool) 1958; FRCPath 1964; FRCP 1964. Lectr in Physiology, Univ. of Liverpool, 1933-36 and 1939-41; Pathologist in RAMC, 1941-46; Sen. Registrar, Postgrad. Medical Sch., 1946-47; Lectr in Chem. Pathol., King's Coll., Univ. of Durham, 1947-55; Reader in Medical Biochemistry, Univ. of Durham, 1955-61; Prof. of Clin. Chem., Univ. of Durham, 1961-63. Vis. Lectr, Amer. Assoc. Clinical Chemists, 1972. Chm. Assoc. of Clinical Biochemists, 1958-61 (Pres., 1961-63); Mem., Editorial Bd of Clinica Chimica Acta, 1960-68; Co-editor, Advances in Clinical Chemistry, 1971-. Titular Member, Section of Clinical Chemistry, International Union of Pure and Applied Chemistry, 1967-73. Wellcome Prize, 1976. *Publications:* (co-author) Isoenzymes in Biology and Medicine, 1968; Cantarow and Trumper Clinical Biochemistry, 7th edn, 1975; Chapter on Metabolic Aspects of Liver Disease in Metabolic Disturbances in Clinical Medicine (ed G. A. Smart), 1958; Chapters on Chemical Pathology and Clinical Biochemistry in British Encyclopædia of Med. Practice, Med. Progress (ed Lord Cohen of Birkenhead), 1961, 1962, 1964, 1966 and 1968; Chapter on Isoenzymes in Recent Advances in Clinical Pathology, Series IV, 1964; Section on Isoenzymes in Advances in Clinical Chemistry (ed C. P. Stewart), 1966; (ed with O. Bodansky and contrib. section on Isoelectric Focusing) Advances in Clinical Chemistry, 1975; contribs to Medical and Scientific Journals dealing with cancer, liver disease, pernicious anæmia, the serum proteins in disease and isoenzymes. *Recreations:* art, photography, gardening. *Address:* Ravenstones, Rectory Road, Gosforth, Newcastle upon Tyne NE3 1XP. *T:* Gosforth 858020. *Clubs:* Athenæum, Savage.

LATOUR-ADRIEN, Hon. Sir (Jean François) Maurice, Kt 1971; Chief Justice of Mauritius, since 1970; *b* 4 March 1915; 2nd *s* of late Louis Constant Emile Adrien and late Maria Ella Latour. *Educ:* Royal Coll., Mauritius; Univ. Coll., London; Middle Temple, London. LLB 1940. Called to the Bar, Middle Temple, 1940. Mauritius: Dist Magistrate, 1947; Crown Counsel, 1950; Additl Subst. Procureur and Advocate-Gen., 1954; Sen. Crown Counsel, 1958; Asst Attorney-Gen., 1960; Solicitor-Gen., 1961; Dir of Public Prosecutions, 1964; Puisne Judge, 1966. Vice-Pres., Inst. Internat. de Droit d'Expression Française (IDEF). KLJ 1969. *Publication:* Editor, Yearly Mauritius Law Reports. *Address:* Vacoas, Mauritius.

LATTER, Leslie William; Director General, Merseyside Passenger Transport Executive, since 1977; *b* 4 Nov. 1921; *s* of William Richard and Clara Maud Latter; *m* 1948, Pamela Jean Marsh; one *s*. *Educ:* Beckenham Grammar Sch., Kent. IPFA, FRVA. Served Royal Air Force, 1940-46. London County Council, 1947-62; Chief Asst, Beckenham Borough Council, 1962-64; Asst Borough Treasurer, Bromley, 1964-68; Dep. Borough Treasurer, Greenwich, 1968-74; Dir of Finance and Administration, Merseyside PTE, 1974-77. *Recreations:* gardening, music. *Address:* Merseyside Passenger Transport Executive, 24 Hatton Garden, Liverpool L3 2AN. *T:* 051-236 7411. *Club:* Skal (Liverpool).

LATTIMORE, Owen; Professor of Chinese Studies, Leeds University, 1963-70, now Professor Emeritus; Director, Page School of International Relations, 1938-50 and Lecturer in History to 1963, Johns Hopkins University, USA; *b* Washington, DC, 29 July 1900; *s* of David Lattimore and Margaret Barnes; *m* 1926, Eleanor, (*d* 1970), *d* of Dr T. F. Holgate, Evanston, Ill.; one *s*. *Educ:* St Bees Sch., Cumberland; Research Student at Harvard Univ., 1929. Early childhood in China; returned to China, 1919; engaged in business in Tientsin and Shanghai, 1920; Journalism in Tientsin, 1921; business in Tientsin and Peking with Arnhold and Co., 1922-25; travelled in Mongolia, 1926; in Chinese Turkestan, 1927; studied in America, 1928, 1929; travelled in Manchuria, as Fellow of Social Science Research Council, 1929-30; Research work in Peking, as

Fellow of Harvard-Yenching Institute, 1930-31; Research Fellow, Guggenheim Foundation, Peking, 1931-33; travelled in Mongolia, 1932-33; editor, Pacific Affairs, 1934-41; research work in China and Mongolia, 1934-35, 1937; Political Adviser to Generalissimo Chiang Kai-Shek, 1941-42; Director, Pacific Operations, Office of War Information, San Francisco, 1943; accompanied Vice-President Wallace in Siberia and China, 1944; economic consultant, American Reparations Mission in Japan, 1945; UN Technical Aid Mission, Afghanistan, 1950; Visiting Lecturer: Ecole Pratique des Hautes Etudes, Sorbonne, 1958-59; University of Copenhagen, 1961. Travelled in Soviet Central Asia, 1960, Mongolia, 1961, 1964, 1966, 1969, 1970, 1971, 1972, 1973, 1974, China, 1972. Chichele Lecturer, Oxford, 1965. Awarded Cuthbert Peek Grant by Royal Geographical Society for travels in Central Asia, 1930; gold medallist, Geographical Society of Philadelphia, 1933; Patron's Medal, Royal Geographical Society, 1942; Univ. of Indiana Medal, Perm. Internat. Altaistic Congress, 1974. FRGS; Fellow, Royal Asiatic Society; Member: Royal Central Asian Society; American Historical Society; American Philosophical Society; For. Member, Academy of Sciences, Mongolian People's Republic; Hon. Member: American Geographical Society, Soc. Csoma Körösi, Hungary. Hon. DLitt Glasgow, 1964; Hon. PhD Copenhagen, 1972. *Publications:* The Desert Road to Turkestan, 1928; High Tartary, 1930; Manchuria: Cradle of Conflict, 1932; The Mongols of Manchuria, 1934; Inner Asian Frontiers of China, 1940; Mongol Journeys, 1941; Solution in Asia, 1945; China, A Short History (with Eleanor Lattimore), 1947; The Situation in Asia, 1949; Sinkiang, Pivot of Asia, 1950; Ordeal by Slander, 1950; Nationalism and Revolution in Mongolia, 1955; Nomads and Commissars, 1962; Studies in Asian Frontier History, 1962; Silks, Spices and Empire (with Eleanor Lattimore), 1968; contributor to periodicals. *Recreation:* cycling. *Address:* 26 rue de Picpus, 75012 Paris, France.

LATTIN, Francis Joseph, CMG 1953; Barrister-at-law; *b* 23 March 1905; *s* of John Lattin, Morland, Westmorland; *m* 1934, May Sadler, Harrogate; one *s* (and one *s* decd). *Educ:* Appleby Grammar Sch.; Durham Univ. (MA); Cambridge Univ.; called to the Bar, Gray's Inn. Assistant District Officer, Colonial Administrative Service, Uganda, 1930; Deputy Controller of Prices and Military Contracts, Kenya, 1942; Development Comr, Uganda, 1949. MLC 1949, MEC 1951, Uganda; Mem. East African Legislative Assembly, 1951; London Representative, Uganda Electricity Board, 1952. Bursar, Grey Coll., Durham, 1963-68. *Publications:* (jointly) Economic Survey of Western Uganda, 1951; articles on various aspects of colonial development. *Recreation:* interest in all outdoor sports. *Address:* The Green, Tirril, Penrith, Cumbria. *T:* Penrith 2960. *Club:* Royal Commonwealth Society.

LATTO, Dr Douglas; private medical practice; Chairman, British Safety Council, since 1971 (Vice-Chairman, 1968-71); *b* Dundee, Scotland, 13 Dec. 1913; *s* of late David Latto, Town Clerk of Dundee, and late Christina Latto; *m* 1945, Dr Edith Monica Druitt; one *s* three *d*. *Educ:* Dundee High Sch.; St Andrews Univ. MB, ChB (St And.) 1939; DObst, RCOG 1944, MRCOG 1949. During War: Ho. Surg., Dundee Royal Infirmary, 1939; Ho. Phys., Cornelia and East Dorset Hosp., Poole, 1940; Resident Obstetrician and Gynaecologist, Derbyshire Hosp. for Women, Derby, 1940; Res. Surgical Officer Hereford Gen. Hosp., 1941; Res. Obst. and Gynaec., East End Maternity Hosp., London, 1942; Res. Obst. and Gynaec. City of London Maternity Hosp., 1943; Res. Surgical Officer, Birmingham Accident Hosp., 1944; Casualty Officer, Paddington Gen. Hosp., London, 1944; Asst Obst. and Gynaec., Mayday Hosp., Croydon, 1945. Res. Obst. and Gynaec., Southlands Hosp., Shoreham-by-Sea, Sussex, 1946-49; Asst, Nuffield Dept of Obstetrics and Gynaecology, Radcliffe Infirmary, Oxford, 1949-51. Member: BMA; Council, Soil Assoc.; Chm., Plantmilk Soc.; Vice-Pres., International Vegetarian Union; Governor, Internat. Inst. of Safety Management. Mem., Order of the Cross. FRSocMed; FRPSL 1975. Silver Jubilee Medal, 1977. *Publications:* Smoking and Lung Cancer: a report to all Members of Parliament for the British Safety Council, May 1969; contribs to BMJ; Proc. Royal Soc. Med.; Philatelic Jl; etc. *Recreations:* squash, travelling, gardening, philately (Internat. Stamp Exhibns: Large Gold Medal, London, 1970; Gold Medal, Brussels, 1972, Munich, 1973, Basle, 1974; Large Gold Medal, Paris 1975; Large Gold Medal and Prix d'Honneur, Copenhagen, 1976). *Address:* Lethnot Lodge, 4 Derby Road, Caversham, Reading, Berks RG4 0EY. *T:* Reading 472282; 59 Harley Street, W1N 1DD. *T:* 01-580 1070.

LATYMER, 7th Baron, *cr* 1431; **Thomas Burdett Money-Coutts;** Member, since 1948, Chairman, 1948-75, London Committee of Ottoman Bank; *b* 6 Aug. 1901; *e s* of 6th Baron and Hester Frances, 4th *d* of late Maj.-Gen. John Cecil Russell, CVO; *S*

father 1949; *m* 1925, Patience, *d* of late W. Courtenay-Thompson and Mrs Herbert Money; one *s* two *d. Educ:* Radley; Trinity Coll., Oxford. Served War of 1939-45. OStJ. *Heir: s* Hon. Hugo Neville Money-Coutts [*b* 1 March 1926; *m* 1st, 1951, Penelope Ann Clare (marr. diss., 1965), *yr d* of late T. A. Emmet and of Baroness Emmet of Amberley; two *s* one *d*; 2nd, 1965, Jinty, *d* of P. G. Calvert, London; one *s* one *d*]. *Address:* San Rebassa, Moscari, Mallorca. *Club:* MCC.

LAUDER, Sir George Andrew Dick-, 12th Bt, *cr* 1688; *b* 17 Nov. 1917; *s* of Lt-Col Sir John North Dalrymple Dick-Lauder, 11th Bt, and Phyllis (*d* 1976), *d* of late Brig.-Gen. H. A. Iggulden, CIE; *S* father 1958; *m* 1945, Hester Marguerite, *y d* of late Lt-Col G. C. M. Sorell-Cameron, CBE, Gorthleck House, Gorthleck, Inverness-shire; two *s* two *d. Educ:* Stowe; RMC. 2nd Lt Black Watch, 1937; served War of 1939-45, Palestine, Somaliland, Middle East (52nd Commandos), Sudan, Crete (POW); Major, 1945. KLJ 1974; Chancellor, Commandery of Lochore, 1974. *Publications:* Let Soldiers Lust, 1963; Our Man for Ganymede, 1969; A Skull and Two Crystals, 1972. *Heir: s* Piers Robert Dick-Lauder, *b* 3 Oct. 1947. *Address:* Firth Mill House, near Roslin, Midlothian EH25 9QQ. *T:* Penicuick 72107. *Club:* Puffins (Edinburgh).

LAUDERDALE, 17th Earl of, *cr* 1624; **Patrick Francis Maitland;** Baron Maitland, 1590; Viscount Lauderdale, 1616; Viscount Maitland, Baron Thirlestane and Boltoun, 1624; Bt of Nova Scotia, 1680; Hereditary Bearer of the National Flag of Scotland, 1790 and 1952; Company Director; Industrial Consultant; Consultant in Economic Geography; *b* 17 March 1911; *s* of Reverend Hon. Sydney G. W. Maitland and Ella Frances (*née* Richards); *S* brother, 1968; *m* 1936, Stanka, *d* of Professor Milivoje Lozanitch, Belgrade Univ.; two *s* two *d. Educ:* Lancing Coll., Sussex; Brasenose Coll., Oxford. BA Hons Oxon, 1933; Journalist 1933-59. Appts include: Balkans and Danubian Corresp., The Times, 1939-41; Special Corresp. Washington, News Chronicle, 1941; War Corresp., Pacific, Australia, New Zealand, News Chronicle, 1941-43. Foreign Office, 1943-45. MP (U) for Lanark Div. of Lanarks, 1951-Sept. 1959 (except for period May-Dec. 1957 when Ind. C). Founder and Chairman, Expanding Commonwealth Group, House of Commons, 1955-59; re-elected Chairman, Nov. 1959. Editor of The Fleet Street Letter Service, and of The Whitehall Letter, 1945-58. Mem., Coll. of Guardians of National Shrine of Our Lady of Walsingham, Norfolk, 1955-. President, The Church Union, 1956-61. FRGS. *Publications:* European Dateline, 1945; Task for Giants, 1957. *Heir: s* The Master of Lauderdale, Viscount Maitland, *qv. Address:* 10 Ovington Square, SW3. *T:* 01-589 7451; 12 St Vincent Street, Edinburgh. *T:* 031-556 5692. *Clubs:* Caledonian, New (Edinburgh); Royal Scottish Automobile (Glasgow).

LAUDERDALE, Master of; *see* Maitland, Viscount.

LAUGHLAND, Graham Franklyn Bruce, QC 1977; a Recorder of the Crown Court, since 1972; *b* 18 Aug. 1931; 3rd *s* of late Andrew and late Constance Laughland; *m* 1969, Victoria Nicola Christina Jarman. *Educ:* King Edward's Sch., Birmingham; Christ Church, Oxford. Called to Bar, Inner Temple, 1958; Mem. Gen. Council of Bar, 1970; Dep. Chm., Bucks QS, 1971. Standing Counsel to the Queen's Proctor, 1968; First Prosecuting Counsel to the Inland Revenue (Midland and Oxford Circuit), 1973-77. *Address:* 4 King's Bench Walk, Temple, EC4 7DL. *T:* 01-353 3581; 20 Bryanston Mews East, W1H 7FH. *T:* 01-262 5713.

LAUGHTON, Prof. Eric; Firth Professor of Latin in the University of Sheffield, 1952-76, now Emeritus; *b* 4 Sept. 1911; 2nd *s* of Rev. G. W. Laughton; *m* 1938, Elizabeth Gibbons; one *s* one *d. Educ:* King Edward VII Sch., Sheffield; St John's Coll., Oxford (open classical scholar). Asst in Humanity Dept, University of Edinburgh, 1934-36; University of Sheffield: Asst Lecturer in Classics, 1936; Lecturer in Classics, 1939; Senior Lecturer, 1946; Public Orator, 1955-68; Pro-Vice-Chancellor, 1968-72. Service in Intelligence Corps, South East Asia, 1943-45. *Publications:* verse translation of Papyrus (17th-century Latin poem by J. Imberdis), 1952; The Participle in Cicero, 1964. Articles and reviews in various classical journals. *Recreations:* walking, music. *Address:* Forelane, Deerhurst, Glos. *T:* Tewkesbury 295437.

LAUGHTON-SCOTT, Edward Hey, QC 1971; **His Honour Judge Laughton-Scott;** a Circuit Judge, since 1976; *b* 18 March 1926; *s* of Dr F. G. Laughton-Scott and Mrs R. Laughton-Scott (*née* Inskip); *m* 1952, Elizabeth Cecilia Macneece Foster; two *s* one *d. Educ:* Sunningdale Sch.; Tonbridge Sch.; Merton Coll., Oxford (MA). Served Life Guards, 1944-47 (Captain); Inns of Court Regt (TA), 1950-58 (Major). Called to Bar, Inner Temple,

1951; Mem. Bar Council, 1959-63 and 1968-72, Treasurer 1971; Mem. Senate, 1969-72; Bencher, Inner Temple, 1966. Dep. Chm., Hants QS, 1967-71; a Recorder of the Crown Court, 1972-76. Mem., Bar Cttee for Royal Commn on Assizes and Quarter Sessions, 1968-69; Chm., Bar Cttee on Rights of Audience in Crown Courts, 1971; Chm., Sub-Cttee of Bar Council on VAT and Fee Collection, 1972-76. Appeal Steward, British Boxing Bd of Control, 1972-; Assessor, GMC and GDC, 1973-76. Renter Warden, Skinners Co., 1973. *Recreations:* golf, sailing, shooting, bridge. *Address:* 4 Hobury Street, Chelsea, SW10. *T:* 01-352 4610. *Clubs:* Garrick; Hampshire (Winchester); Royal London Yacht.

LAURENCE, Peter Harold, CMG 1976; MC 1944; Chief Inspector, HM Diplomatic Service (Assistant Under-Secretary of State), since 1974; *b* 18 Feb. 1923; *s* of late Ven. George Laurence, MA, BD and late Alice (*née* Jackson); *m* 1948, Elizabeth Aïda Way; two *s* one *d. Educ:* Radley Coll.; Christ Church, Oxford. 60th Rifles, 1941-46 (Major). Entered Foreign Service, 1948; Western Dept, FO, 1948-50; Athens, 1950-53; Asst Political Adviser, Trieste, 1953-55; 1st Sec., Levant Dept, FO, 1955-57; Prague, 1957-60; Cairo, 1960-62; North and East African Dept, FO, 1962-65; Personnel Dept, DSAO, 1965-67; Counsellor, 1965; Political Adviser, Berlin, 1967-69; Visiting Fellow, All Souls Coll., 1969-70; Counsellor (Commercial), Paris, 1970-74. *Address:* c/o Foreign and Commonwealth Office, SW1. *T:* 01-233 4776; Ley Marden, Yarnscombe, Barnstable, N Devon. *Club:* United Oxford & Cambridge University.

LAURIE, Lt-Col George H. F. P. V.; *see* Vere-Laurie.

LAURIE, Maj.-Gen. Sir John Emilius, 6th Bt, *cr* 1834; CBE 1940; DSO 1916; *b* 12 Aug. 1892; *S* father 1936; *m* 1922, Evelyn Clare, *o d* of late Lt-Col L. J. Richardson-Gardner, 14th Hussars; one *s* two *d.* Served European War, 1914-18 (despatches 5 times, DSO and bar, Chevalier Légion d'Honneur); commanded 6th (Morayshire) Bn Seaforth Highlanders, 1918-19, and 2nd Bn Seaforth Highlanders, 1934-38; Comdr, Tientsin Area, British Troops in China, 1939-40 (despatches); 157 Inf. Bde., France, 1940 (CBE); 52nd (Lowland) Div., 1941-42; Combined Operations Training Centre, Inveraray; retired 1945; Col, Seaforth Highlanders, 1947-57. *Heir: s* Robert Bayley Emilius Laurie [*b* 8 March 1931; *m* 1968, Laurelie, *er d* of late Sir Reginald Williams, 7th Bt, MBE, ED; two *d*]. *Address:* Crossford, Bulstrode Way, Gerrards Cross, Bucks. *Clubs:* Army and Navy, Caledonian, MCC.

See also H. Laing.

LAURIE, Col Vernon Stewart, CBE 1964 (OBE 1945); TD; DL; *b* 23 Feb. 1896; *o s* of Lt-Col R. M. Laurie, DSO, TD, DL, late of Ford Place, Stifford, Essex; *m* 1922, Mary, 2nd *d* of Selwyn R. Pryor, late of Plaw Hatch, Bishop's Stortford, Herts; one *s* one *d. Educ:* Eton; Christ Church, Oxford. Served European War, 1914-18; Essex RA (TF); 2 Lt 1914, Lt 1915, Capt. 1918, France, Egypt and Palestine (despatches twice). Served War of 1939-45: Lt-Col comdg 147 Essex Yeomanry, RA, 1939-42; 107 LAA Regt RA, 1942-44; 22 LAA Regt RA, 1944-45; N Africa, Malta and Italy. Hon. Col Essex Yeomanry, 1956-60. Actg Master Essex Union Foxhounds, 1946-48, Jt Master, 1956-57. Master Saddlers Co., 1955 and 1958. Mem. London Stock Exchange, 1921-; Dir, Brit. Empire Securities & General Trust, 1929- (Chm., 1947-72). Pres., Chelmsford Conservative Assoc., 1945-49; Chairman: Romford Constituency Assoc., 1952-55; Billericay Constituency Assoc., 1955-56 (Pres., 1956-67). DL 1946, High Sheriff 1950, Essex. *Recreation:* foxhunting. *Address:* The Old Vicarage, South Weald, Brentwood, Essex. *T:* Brentwood 221358. *Clubs:* United Oxford & Cambridge University, MCC.

LAURISTON, Alexander Clifford, QC 1972; **His Honour Judge Lauriston;** a Circuit Judge, since 1976; *b* 2 Oct. 1927; *s* of Alexander Lauriston and Nellie Lauriston (*née* Ainsworth); *m* 1954, Inga Louise Cameron; two *d. Educ:* Coatham Sch., Redcar, Yorks; Trinity Coll., Cambridge (MA). National Service: Army, Green Howards and RAPC, 2nd Lieut, 1948-50. Called to Bar, Inner Temple, 1952. A Recorder of the Crown Court, 1972-76. Mem., Loriners' Co., 1969. *Recreations:* riding, motor sports, tennis, golf, painting, music. *Address:* Lynthorpe, Fireball Hill, Sunningdale, Berks. *T:* Ascot 22400. *Club:* Berkshire Golf.

See also R . B . Lauriston.

LAURISTON, Richard Basil; a Recorder of the Crown Court, since 1974; a Permanent Chairman of Industrial Tribunals, since 1976; formerly Senior Partner, Alex Lauriston & Son, Solicitors, Middlesbrough; *b* 26 Jan. 1917; *s* of Alexander Lauriston, MBE,

and Nellie Lauriston; *m* 1944, Monica, *d* of Wilfred Leslie Deacon, BA, Tonbridge, and Dorothy Louise Deacon; three *s*. *Educ:* Sir William Turner's Sch., Redcar; St John's Coll., Cambridge (MA, LLB). Solicitor, 1948. Commnd and served in War of 1939-45, Royal Corps of Signals. *Recreations:* fishing, travelling. *Address:* 26 Easby Lane, Great Ayton, North Yorks TS9 6JZ. *T:* Great Ayton 2429.
See also A . C . *Lauriston* .

LAUTERPACHT, Elihu, QC 1970; Legal Adviser to the Australian Department of Foreign Affairs, since 1975; Fellow of Trinity College, Cambridge, since 1953; Lecturer in Law, University of Cambridge, since 1958; *b* 13 July 1928; *o s* of late Sir Hersch Lauterpacht, QC and Rachel Steinberg; *m* 1955, Judith Maria (*d* 1970), *er d* of Harold Hettinger; one *s* two *d*; *m* 1973, Catherine Daly. *Educ:* Phillips Acad., Andover, Mass; Harrow; Trinity Coll., Cambridge (Entrance Schol.). 1st cl. Pt II of Law Tripos and LLB; Whewell Schol. in Internat. Law, 1950; Holt Schol. 1948 and Birkenhead Schol. 1950, Gray's Inn; called to Bar, 1950. Joint Sec., Interdepartmental Cttee on State Immunity, 1950-52; Asst Lectr in Law, Univ. of Cambridge, 1953; Sec., Internat. Law Fund, 1955; Dir of Research, Hague Academy of Internat. Law, 1959-60; Vis. Prof. of Internat. Law, Univ. of Delhi, 1960. Chm., East African Common Market Tribunal, 1972-; Consultant to Central Policy Review Staff, 1972-74; mem. arbitration panel, Internat. Centre for Settlement of Investment Disputes; Deputy Leader: Australian Delegn to UN Law of the Sea Conf., 1975-77; Australian Delegn to UN Gen. Assembly, 1975-76. Editor: British Practice in International Law, 1955-; International Law Reports, 1960-. Comdr, Order of Merit, Chile, 1969; awarded Annual Cert. of Merit, Amer. Soc. Internat. Law, 1972. *Publications:* Jerusalem and the Holy Places, 1968; (ed) International Law: the collected papers of Sir Hersch Lauterpacht, vol I, 1970, vol. II, 1975, vol. III, 1977; various articles on international law. *Address:* (1975-77) Department of Foreign Affairs, Canberra, Australia; Trinity College, Cambridge. *T:* Cambridge 58201; 3 Essex Court, Temple, EC4. *T:* 01-353 2624; 7 Herschel Road, Cambridge. *T:* Cambridge 54707. *Club:* Athenæum.

LAUWERYS, Prof. Joseph Albert; Director, Atlantic Institute of Education, Nova Scotia, 1970-76, now Emeritus; Professeur Associé, Sorbonne, 1969-74; Professor of Comparative Education in University of London Institute of Education, 1947-70, now Emeritus Professor; *b* 7 Nov. 1902; *s* of Henry and Louise Lauwerys (*née* Nagels); *m* 1931, Waltraut Dorothy Bauermeister; three *s*. *Educ:* Ratcliffe Coll., Leicester; Bournemouth Sch.; King's Coll., London Univ. BScGen, 1st Cl. Hons 1927; Special BSc 1st Cl., Chemistry, 1928; Associate of Institute of Chemistry, 1928; Fellow, 1942. Special Physics BSc, 1929; Science Master, Stirling House, Bournemouth; Sen. Physics Master, Christ's Hosp., Horsham, 1928-32; Lectr in Methods of Science, Inst. of Educn, 1932-41. Reader in Educn, 1941-46. Joint Editor, World Year Book of Education, 1947-70. Rockefeller Foundation, Consultant in Education, 1937; Visiting Professor: Teachers' Coll., Columbia Univ., 1939 and 1951; University of Indiana, 1952; University of Southern Calif., 1953, 1955, 1957, 1959, 1961; University of Michigan, 1954; Kyushu Univ., Japan, 1956; University of Cape Town and Witwatersrand, 1958; International Christian Univ., Tokyo, 1959; University of Chile, 1962; University of Concepción, 1964 and 1965; University of Bahia, 1966; University of Ankara, 1968. Centennial Prof., American University of Beirut, 1967. Dir Commission of Enquiry, Conference of Allied Ministers of Education, 1945; Consultant to UNESCO, 1946-48. Hon. Prof. Univ. of Ankara. Chm., Internat. New Educn Fellowship; Mem., UNESCO Good Offices and Conciliation Commn, 1971-; Pres., Assoc. Montessori Internationale. DSc (Ghent), 1946; DLitt (London), 1958. Comdr, Ordre des Palmes Académiques, 1961. *Publications:* Education and Biology, 1934; Chemistry, 1938; Film in the School, 1936; Film and Radio as Educational Media, 1939; Educational Problems in the Liberated Countries, 1946; The Roots of Science, 1947; The Enterprise of Education, 1955; Morals, Democracy and Education, 1958; (with H. C. Barnard) Handbook of British Educational Terms, 1963; Essays in Comparative Education (3 vols), 1969; Man's Impact on Nature, 1971; (ed) Education at Home and Abroad, 1973; The Purposes of Canadian Education, 1973; Science, Morals and Moralogy, 1977; numerous textbooks, articles, reviews and papers including contrib. to Chambers's Encyclopædia, Encyclopædia Britannica, etc. *Recreations:* walking, chess. *Address:* Aston House, Chilworth, Surrey. *T:* Bramley 2040.

LAVELLE, Roger Garnett; Under Secretary, HM Treasury, since 1975; *b* 23 Aug. 1932; *s* of Henry Allman Lavelle and Evelyn Alice Garnett; *m* 1956, Elsa Gunilla Odeberg; three *s* one *d*. *Educ:* Leighton Park; Trinity Hall, Cambridge (BA, LLB). Asst Principal, Min. of Health, 1955; Principal, HM Treasury, 1961;

Special Assistant (Common Market) to Lord Privy Seal, 1961-63; Private Sec. to Chancellor of the Exchequer, 1965-68; Asst Secretary, HM Treasury, 1968. *Recreations:* music and gardening. *Address:* 36 Cholmeley Crescent, Highgate, N6. *T:* 01-340 4845.

LAVER, Frederick John Murray, CBE 1971; Member, National Research Development Corporation, since 1974; *b* 11 March 1915; *er s* of late Clifton F. Laver and Elsie Elizabeth Palmer, Bridgwater; *m* 1948, Kathleen Amy Blythe; one *s* two *d*. *Educ:* Plymouth Coll. BSc London. Entered PO Engrg Dept, 1935; PO Research Stn, 1935-51; Radio Planning, 1951-57; Organization and Efficiency, 1957-63; Asst Sec., HM Treasury, 1963-65; Chief Scientific Officer, Min. of Technology, 1965-68; Director, National Data Processing Service, 1968-70; Mem., PO Corp., 1969-73. Vis. Prof., Computing Lab., Univ. of Newcastle upon Tyne, 1975, 1976. Mem. Council: IEE, 1966-69, 1972-73; British Computer Soc., 1969-72; Nat. Computing Centre, 1966-68, 1970-73; IEE Electronic Divl Bd, 1966-69, 1970-73. CEng, FIEE; FBCS. *Publications:* Electric Power, 1957; Electrons at Work, 1957; Waves, 1959; Energy, 1962; Introducing Computers, 1965; Information Engineering and Society (Maurice Lubbock Lecture, Oxford), 1974; Computers, Communications and Society, 1975; An Introduction to the Uses of Computers, 1976; several scientific papers. *Recreations:* reading, writing, and watching the sea. *Address:* Woodrising, Bickwell Valley, Sidmouth, Devon EX10 8RF. *T:* Sidmouth 5005.

LAVER, Patrick Martin; Head of Rhodesia Dept, Foreign and Commonwealth Office, since 1975; *b* 3 Feb. 1932; *s* of late James Laver, CBE, RE, FRSL, and late Veronica Turleigh; *m* 1966, Marianne Ford (marr. diss. 1973); one *d*. *Educ:* Ampleforth Coll., Yorks; New Coll., Oxford. Third Sec., Foreign Office, 1954; Second Sec., Djakarta, 1956; FO, 1957; Paris, 1958; Yaoundé, 1961; UK Delegn to Brussels Conf., 1962; First Sec., FO, 1963; UK Mission to UN, New York, 1964; Diplomatic Service Admin., 1965; Commercial Sec., Nairobi, 1968; FCO, 1970; Counsellor (Economic), Pretoria, 1973; UK Delegn to Conf. on Security and Co-operation in Europe, Geneva, 1974. *Address:* Flat 4, 10 The Glebe, SE3 9TG. *T:* 01-852 3905. *Club:* Athenæum.

LAVER, William Scott, CBE 1962; HM Diplomatic Service, retired; *b* 7 March 1909; *s* of Robert John Laver, Latchingdon, Essex, and Frances Lucy (*née* Pasmore), Windsor; *m* 1969, Marjorie Joan Hall, Chislehurst, Kent. *Educ:* St Dunstan's Coll., Catford; Downing Coll., Cambridge. Dept of Overseas Trade, 1932; Asst to Commercial Counsellor: Brussels, 1934, Rome, 1936; Commercial Sec., Rio de Janeiro, 1940; Commercial Sec., Cairo, 1946; Foreign Office, 1950-51; Financial Sec., Bahrain, 1951; Political Agent, Bahrain, 1951-52; Counsellor (Economic), Belgrade, 1954; Counsellor (Commercial), Oslo, 1958-62; Ambassador to Congo Republic, Gabon, Republic of Chad, and Central African Republic, 1962-66. *Address:* Flat 30, Mapledene, Kemnal Road, Chislehurst, Kent. *Club:* Royal Automobile.

LAVERICK, Elizabeth, PhD, CEng, FIEE, FInstP, FIEEE (US); Deputy Secretary, Institution of Electrical Engineers, since 1971; *b* 25 Nov. 1925; *d* of William Rayner and Alice Garland; *m* 1946 (marr. diss. 1960); no *c*. *Educ:* Dr Challoner's Grammar Sch., Amersham; Durham Univ. Research at Durham Univ., 1946-50; Section Leader at GEC, 1950-53; Microwave Engineer at Elliott Bros, 1954; Head of Radar Research Laboratory of Elliott-Automation Radar Systems Ltd, 1959; Jt Gen. Manager, Elliott-Automation Radar Systems Ltd, 1968-69, Technical Dir, 1969-71. President, Women's Engineering Soc., 1967-69; Governor, Hatfield Polytechnic; Member: IEE Electronics Divisional Bd, 1967-70; Council IEE, 1969-70; Council, Inst. of Physics and Physical Soc., 1970-73; DE Adv. Cttee on Women's Employment, 1970-76; Hon. Fellow, UMIST, 1969. *Publications:* contribs to IEE and IEEE Jls. *Recreations:* music, gardening. *Address:* Arden, Watford Road, Radlett, Herts. *T:* Radlett 4841.

LAVILLA, Teresa; *see* Berganza, Teresa.

LAVIN, Mary, (Mrs M. MacDonald Scott); Writer; *b* East Walpole, Mass, USA, 11 June 1912; *m* 1st, 1942, William Walsh (*d* 1954), MA, NUI; three *d*; 2nd, 1969, Michael MacDonald Scott. *Educ:* National Univ. of Ireland, Dublin (Graduate, MA; Hon DLitt, 1968). Mem. of Irish Academy of Letters, President, 1971. Guggenheim Fellow 1959, 1962 and 1972. Katherine Mansfield Prize, 1961; Ella Lynam Cabot Award, 1971; Eire Soc. Gold Medal, Boston, 1974; Arts Award, Royal Meath Assoc., 1975; Gregory Medal, Dublin, 1975; Personality of the Year, Royal Meath Assoc., 1976. *Publications:* Tales from

Bective Bridge (short stories, awarded James Tait Black Memorial Prize), 1942 (London, 1943); The Long Ago (short stories), 1944; The House in Clewe Street (novel), 1945. At Sally Gap (Boston), 1946; The Becker Wives, 1946; Mary O'Grady (novel), 1950; Patriot Son (short stories), 1956; A Single Lady (short stories); A Likely Story (short novel), 1957; Selected Stories, 1959 (New York); The Great Wave (short stories), 1961; Stories of Mary Lavin, 1964; In the Middle of the Fields (short stories), 1966; Happiness (short stories), 1969; Collected Stories, 1971; A Memory and other Stories, 1972; The Second Best Children in the World, 1972; The Stories of Mary Lavin, vol II, 1973; The Shrine and other stories, 1976; Stories of Mary Lavin, vol. III, 1978. *Address:* The Abbey Farm, Bective, Navan, Co. Meath. *T:* Navan 21243; Mews Eleven, Lad Lane, Rere Fitzwilliam Place, Dublin. *T:* 63031.

LAVINGTON, Cyril Michael, MBE 1946; **His Honour Judge Lavington;** a Circuit Judge (formerly Judge of County Courts), since 1971; *b* 21 June 1912; *s* of Cyril Claude Lavington, MB, BS of Bristol and Nora Vernon Lavington; *m* 1950, Frances Anne (marr. diss. 1968), *d* of Colston Wintle, MD, of Bristol; one *s*. Barrister-at-Law, Middle Temple, 1936; Western Circuit, Wilts QS. Joined Army, 1939; Major, DAA and QMG, 1 GRTD, N Africa, 1943; DAAG 37 Mil. Miss. to Yugoslav Army of Nat. Liberation, 1944; DAAG 3 Corps, Greece, 1945 (despatches twice, MBE). Returned to practice, 1946. Recorder of Barnstaple, 1964-71, Honorary Recorder, 1972-; Dep. Chm., Quarter Sessions: Dorset, 1962-71; Wiltshire, 1970-71; Hampshire, 1971. *Recreations:* sailing, gardening. *Address:* Stockadon Villa, St Mellion, Saltash, Cornwall. *T:* St Dominick 50259. *Clubs:* Royal Yachting Association; Bar Yacht; Royal Western Yacht (Plymouth).

LAVOIPIERRE, Jacques Joseph Maurice; Judge of the Supreme Court, Mauritius, 1956-65; Attorney-General, Mauritius, 1960-64; (after new constitution came into force, reverted to private practice); *b* 4 April 1909; 3rd *s* of Antoine Lavoipierre and Elisa la Hausse de Lalouvière; *m* 1939, Pauline Koenig; two *s* one *d*. *Educ:* Royal Coll., Mauritius; King's Coll., London (LLB); Middle Temple. Magistrate, Mauritius, 1944; Civil Comr, 1946; Magistrate, Industrial Court, 1949; Master and Registrar, Supreme Court, 1952; Substitute Procureur and Advocate-Gen., 1954. QC (Mauritius), 1961. Coronation Medal, 1953. *Address:* Curepipe, Mauritius. *Clubs:* Mauritius Turf, Grand Sable (Mauritius).

LAVRIN, Prof. Janko (John), MA; Professor of Slavonic Languages, University of Nottingham, 1923, Emeritus Professor since 1953; *b* 10 Feb. 1887; *s* of John Lavrin and Gertrude (*née* Golobich), both Slovene; *m* 1928, Nora (*née* Fry); two *s*. *Educ:* Austria, Russia, and partly in Scandinavia. Began as journalist in Russia, 1910; Russian war correspondent, 1915-17. During War of 1939-45, attached to BBC (European service) as broadcaster and language supervisor. Public lecturer. *Publications:* Aspects of Modernism, 1935; An Introduction to the Russian Novel, 1942 (repr. 1974); Dostoevsky, 1943 (repr. 1968); Tolstoy, 1944 (repr. 1968); Pushkin and Russian Literature, 1947 (repr. 1968); Nietzsche, 1948, new edn 1971; From Pushkin to Mayakovsky, 1948; Ibsen, 1950 (repr. 1968); Nikolai Gogol, 1951 (repr. 1968); Goncharov, 1954 (repr. 1968); Russian Writers, 1954; Lermontov, 1959; Tolstoy (in German), 1961; Dostojevsky (in German), 1963; Literature and the Spirit of the Age (in Slovene), 1968; Russia, Slavdom and the Western World, 1969; Nietzsche, 1971; A Panorama of Russian Literature, 1973. *Recreation:* travels. *Address:* 28 Addison Gardens, W14. *T:* 01-603 8347. *Club:* PEN.

LAW, family name of **Barons Coleraine and Ellenborough.**

LAW, Alfred Noel, CMG 1947; MC 1918; retired; *b* 1895; *s* of late Frank Law; *m* 1937, Kathleen, *d* of A. Fishkin, Newcastle upon Tyne; one *d*. *Educ:* Northampton Sch.; Hertford Coll., Oxford. Served European War, 1914-19, with 4th Battalion Northamptonshire Regiment. Entered Colonial Service (Palestine), 1920; District Commissioner, Haifa, Palestine, 1942-48; Chief Sec., British Administration, Somalia, 1948-50; Dep. Dir of Education (Administration), Uganda, 1950-53; Ministry of Education, Labour and Lands, Nairobi, Kenya, 1954-57. *Address:* 23 The Sheraton, Oak Avenue, Kenilworth, 7700 South Africa.

LAW, Eric John Ewan; Hon. Mr Justice Law; Justice of Appeal, since 1965 and Vice-President, since 1975, Court of Appeal for East Africa; *b* 10 June 1913; *er s* of late Sir Charles Ewan Law; *m* 1948, Patricia Constance Elizabeth, *d* of C. W. S. Seed, CBE; two *s* one *d*. *Educ:* Wrekin Coll.; St Catharine's Coll., Cambridge (Exhibitioner), MA (Hons). Called to Bar, Middle Temple, 1936. War Service, 1939-42: E Yorks Regt and KAR,

Capt. Asst Judicial Adviser to Govt of Ethiopia, 1942-44; Crown Counsel, Nyasaland, 1944-53; Resident Magistrate, Tanganyika, 1953-55; Senior Resident Magistrate, 1955-56; Asst Judge, Zanzibar, 1956-58; Judge, Tanganyika, 1958-64. *Recreations:* fishing, sailing. *Address:* c/o Court of Appeal for East Africa, PO Box 30187, Nairobi, Kenya. *Clubs:* Nairobi, Muthaiga (Kenya); Dar es Salaam Yacht (Tanzania).

LAW, Francis Stephen, (Frank Law); Chairman: Varta Group UK, since 1971; IWKA Group UK, since 1971; Director: B. Elliott and Co. Ltd, since 1968; National Freight Corporation, since 1969; *b* 31 Dec. 1916; *s* of Henry and Ann Law-Lowensberg; *m* 1959, Nicole Vigne (*née* Fesch); one *s* (one *d* by previous *m*). *Educ:* on the Continent. War service, 1939-45. Wills Law & Co., 1947; Truvox Engrg, 1960, subseq. Dir of Controls and Communications; Mem., Org. Cttee, NFC, 1968. *Recreations:* music, reading, theatre, skiing, tennis, riding, swimming. *Address:* 61 Cadogan Square, SW1. *T:* 01-235 7879. *Clubs:* Boodle's, Hurlingham; Pilgrims.

LAW, Frank William, MA, MD, BChir Cantab, FRCS, LRCP; KStJ; Consulting Ophthalmic Surgeon, Guy's Hospital; Consulting Surgeon, Moorfields Eye Hospital; Hon. Visiting Ophthalmologist, Johns Hopkins Hospital, Baltimore; Treas. and Past Pres. Ophth. Soc. of UK; Councillor and late Master Oxford Ophth. Congress; Mem., Chapter General and Ophth. Hosp. Cttee, Order of St John; British Mem. Council, European Ophth. Soc.; Life Mem., Irish Ophth. Soc.; Membre d'Honneur, Soc. Belge d'Ophth.; Hon. Mem., Greek Ophth. Soc., Pan-American Medical Assoc. and American Acad. Ophth.; American Medical Assoc.; Canadian Ophth. Soc.; Past Master, Company of Spectacle Makers, and Freeman of the City of London; *b* Isleworth, 1898; *y s* of late Thomas Law and Emma Janet MacRae; *m* 1929, Brenda, *d* of Edwin Thomas; one *s* one *d*. *Educ:* St Paul's Sch.; St John's Coll., Cambridge; Middlesex Hosp. Served European War, France and Flanders, 1917-19, Royal Field Artillery; Capt. Lady Margaret Boat Club, 1922; Spare Man for Varsity Boat and Trial Cap, 1922; rowed 2 for Cambridge, 1923; Late Consultant to the Army in Ophthalmology and Surgeon to Queen Alexandra Military Hosp., Millbank; late Consulting Ophthalmic Surgeon, King Edward VII Hospital for Officers; Past Pres. and Councillor, Faculty of Ophthalmologists; Sec. Gen., International Ophth. Congress, 1950; Past Mem. International Ophthalmological Council. *Publications:* Ultra-Violet Therapy in Eye Disease, 1934; History of Moorfields Eye Hospital, 1975; articles in Brit. Jl of Ophthalmology, Transactions of Ophthalmological Society, and other Med. Jls. *Recreations:* music, fishing, shooting. *Address:* Baldersby Cottage, Chipperfield, Herts WD4 9DB. *T:* Kings Langley 62905; Flat 14, 59 Weymouth Street, W1N 3LH. *T:* 01-935 7328. *Clubs:* Athenæum, MCC, Savage; Leander.

LAW, Harry Davis; Director, Preston Polytechnic, since 1973; *b* 10 Nov. 1930; *s* of Harold and Edna Betina Law; *m* 1956, Hazel M. Harding; one *s* one *d*. *Educ:* King Edward VI Sch., Stafford; Keele Univ. (BA); Manchester Univ. (PhD). FRIC. Demonstrator, Keele Univ., 1957-58; Commonwealth Fund Fellow, Cornell Med. Sch., NY, 1958-59; ICI Research Fellow, Liverpool Univ., 1959-60; Head, Chemistry, Miles Labs, Stoke Poges, subseq. Head, Therapeutic Research Labs, 1960-65; Head Chemistry and Biol., Liverpool Reg. Coll. Technology, 1965-69; Head Chemistry and Chm., Faculty of Science, Liverpool Polytechnic, 1969-71; Dep. Dir, Glasgow Coll. of Technology, 1971-73. Chm., CNAA Bd Instl and Domestic Science, 1975-. *Publications:* The Organic Chemistry of Peptides, 1970; numerous pubns in learned jls. *Recreation:* fishing. *Address:* Westcroft, 40 Clifton Drive, Fairhaven, Lytham St Annes, Lancs FY8 1AX. *T:* Lytham 738055.

LAW, Adm. Sir Horace (Rochfort), GCB 1972 (KCB 1967; CB 1963); OBE 1950; DSC 1941; retired 1972; Chairman, R. & W. Hawthorn Leslie & Co., since 1973; *b* 23 June 1911; *s* of S. Horace Law, MD, FRCSI, and Sybil Mary (*née* Clay); *m* 1941, Heather Valerie Coryton; two *s* two *d*. *Educ:* Sherborne Sch. Entered Royal Navy, 1929; gunnery specialist, 1937. Served War of 1939-45 (DSC): AA Cruisers: Cairo, 1939; Coventry, 1940; Cruiser Nigeria, 1942; Comdr 1946; Capt. 1952; comd HMS Centaur, 1958 and Britannia, RN Coll., 1960; Rear-Adm. 1961; Vice-Adm. 1965; Flag Officer Sea Training, 1961-63; Flag Officer, Submarines, 1963-65; Controller of the Navy, 1965-70; C-in-C, Naval Home Comd, and Flag Officer, Portsmouth Area, 1970-72; First and Principal Naval Aide-de-Camp to the Queen, 1970-72. Mem., Security Commn, 1973-. President: RINA, 1975-77; Officers' Christian Union, 1976-. *Recreations:* sailing, gardening. *Address:* West Harting, Petersfield, Hants. *Club:* Royal Ocean Racing.

LAW, Col Hugh Francis d'Assisi Stuart, DSO 1940; OBE 1956; MC 1917; TD; DL; *b* 29 Jan. 1897; *s* of late Hugh Alexander Law; *m* 1928, Susan Rosemary Dacre, *e d* of Sir George Clerk, 9th Bt of Penicuik; two *s* one *d. Educ:* Shrewsbury; RMC Sandhurst. 2nd Lt Irish Guards, 1915; with Irish Guards, France and Flanders, 1915-18; Acting Capt., 1916; attached General Headquarters, Intelligence, 1916; Capt., 1918 (wounded, MC); with Irish Guards Army of Occupation of Rhineland; ADC to GOC 22nd Army Corps, 1919; ADC Governor and C-in-C, Malta, 1921; with Irish Guards, Turkey, 1922-24; retired, 1931; Brevet Major, Irish Guards, Regular Army Reserve of Officers; Major 5th Bn Border Regt, 1932; Lt-Col, 1938; Col (Temp.) 1941; Commanding 5th Bn Border Regt, 1938-41; served France and Belgium, 1940 (DSO, despatches 1941) and in Middle East, 1943-45. Comdr Sub-District of South-West Scotland, 1941-43; Comdr Sub-Area of the Lebanon, 1943-45; Comdr Cyprus, 1945; Sec., Army Cadet Force in Scotland, 1948-65. DL Co. of Midlothian, 1965. *Recreations:* shooting, fishing, riding, gardening. *Address:* The Barony House, Lasswade, Midlothian. *T:* Lasswade 3217.

LAW, James, QC (Scot.) 1971; *b* 7 June 1926; *s* of late George Law, MA, and of Isabella Rebecca Lamb (or Law), MA; *m* 1956, Kathleen Margaret, *d* of Alexander Gibson; two *s* one *d. Educ:* Kilmarnock Academy; Girvan High Sch.; Univ. of Glasgow (MA 1948, LLB 1950). Admitted to Faculty of Advocates, 1951; Advocate-Depute, 1957-64. Mem., Criminal Injuries Compensation Bd, 1970. *Address:* 7 Gloucester Place, Edinburgh EH3 6EE. *T:* 031-225 2974. *Clubs:* New, Caledonian (Edinburgh).

LAW, Margaret Dorothy, OBE 1951; MA; Consultant Editor, Chambers's Encyclopædia; *d* of Thomas Robert Evans, Shrewsbury, and Dorothy, *d* of late David Davies; *m* 1925, George Edward, *s* of late Rev. William Law, Vicar of Rotherham; two *s. Educ:* St Leonards Sch., St Andrews; Girton Coll., Cambridge. Dir of Encyclopædia Britannica, 1925-43; Managing Editor Chambers's Encyclopædia, 1943-63; Mem. Cambridge Univ. Women's Appts Board, 1959-66. *Recreations:* swimming and reading. *Address:* Courtup Hill, Maplehurst, Sussex. *T:* Cowfold 429.

LAW, Phillip Garth, AO 1975; CBE 1961; MSc, FTS, FAIP; Vice-President, Victoria Institute of Colleges, since 1966; Director of the Antarctic Division, Department of External Affairs, Australia, and Leader of the Australian National Antarctic Research Expeditions (ANARE), 1949-66; *b* 21 April 1912; *s* of Arthur James Law and Lillie Lena Chapman; *m* 1941, Nellie Isabel Allan; no *c. Educ:* Hamilton High Sch.; Ballarat Teachers' Coll.; Melbourne Univ. Science master, State secondary schs, Vic., 1933-38; Tutor in Physics, Newman Coll., Melbourne Univ., 1940-47; Lectr in Physics, 1943-48. Research Physicist and Asst Sec. of Scientific Instrument and Optical Panel of Austr. Min. of Munitions, 1940-45. Sen. Scientific Officer, ANARE, 1947-48; cosmic ray measurements in Antarctica and Japan, 1948; Expedition relief voyages to Heard I. and Macquarie I., 1949, 1951, 1952, 1954. Australian observer with Norwegian-British-Swedish Antarctic Exped., 1950; Leader of expedition: to establish first permanent Australian station in Antarctica at Mawson, MacRobertson Land, 1954; which established second continental station at Davis, Princess Elizabeth Land, 1957; which took over Wilkes station from USA, 1959; to relieve ANARE stations and to explore coast of Australian Antarctic Territory, annually, 1955-66. Chm., Australian Nat. Cttee for Antarctic Research; Member: Council of Melbourne Univ., 1959-; Council, La Trobe Univ., 1964-74; Pres., Royal Soc. of Victoria, 1967, 1968. Trustee, Science Museum of Victoria, Melbourne, 1968-. Pres., Grad. Union, Melbourne Univ., 1972-77. Fellow, Australian Acad. of Technological Sciences. Hon. DAppSc (Melbourne). Founder's Gold Medal, RGS, 1960. *Publications:* (with John Bechervaise) ANARE, 1957; chapters in: It's People that Matter, ed Donald McLean, 1969; Search for Human Understanding, ed M. Merbaum and G. Stricker, 1971; ed series of ANARE scientific reports; numerous papers on Antarctica and education. *Recreations:* tennis, ski-ing, skin diving, music, photography. *Address:* 16 Stanley Grove, Canterbury, Vic 3126, Australia. *Clubs:* University (Sydney); Melbourne, Kelvin, Melbourne Cricket, Royal South Yarra Lawn Tennis (Melbourne).

LAW, Sylvia, OBE 1977; Principal Planner, Greater London Council, since 1972; *b* 29 March 1931; *d* of late Reginald Howard Law and late Dorothy Margaret Law. *Educ:* Lowther Coll.; Girton Coll., Cambridge (MA); Regent Street Polytechnic (DipTP). Teaching, Benenden Sch., 1952-55; market research, Unilever Ltd, 1955-58; town and country planning, Kent CC and GLC, 1959-. Royal Town Planning Institute: Mem. Council, 1965-; Chm. of Educn Cttee, 1970-73; Vice-

Pres., 1972-74; Pres., 1974-75. *Publications:* (contrib.) Recreational Economics and Analysis, 1974; (ed) Planning and the Future, 1976; articles in RTPI Jl, Official Architecture and Planning, Planning Outlook, Town Planning Rev., Greater London Intelligence Qly, etc. *Recreations:* sailing, music, photography. *Address:* My Lady's Cottage, Cranbrook, Kent. *T:* Sissinghurst 307. *Club:* University Women's.

LAWDER, Rear-Adm. Keith Macleod, CB 1948; OBE 1919; Associate of the Chartered Institute of Secretaries; *b* 1893; *s* of F. E. Lawder; *m* 1918; two *d* (one *s* decd). *Educ:* Fettes Coll., Edinburgh. Joined Royal Navy, 1910; served European War, 1914-18 and War of 1939-45; retired, 1949. *Address:* Brook Cottage, South Zeal, Okehampton, Devon EX20 2QB. *T:* Whiddon Down 308. *Club:* Climbers'.

LAWES, Sir John (Claud Bennet), 4th Bt, *cr* 1882; *b* 9 Sept. 1898; *er s* of Sir John Lawes-Wittewronge, 3rd Bt, and Helena Ramsey (*d* 1961), *d* of Henry Ramsey Cox of Folkestone; relinquished surname of Wittewronge by deed poll, 1951; *S* father, 1931; *m* 1st, 1928, Kathleen Marjorie Livingstone (*d* 1938), *er d* of Gerald Tylston Hodgson; one *s*; 2nd, 1938, Naomi Josephine Helen, *y d* of Lancelot Wykeham Badnall; one *d. Educ:* Blundell's Sch., Tiverton. *Heir: s* John Michael Bennet Lawes, *b* 24 Oct. 1932. *Address:* Le Clos du Coudré, St Pierre du Bois, Guernsey, CI.

LAWLEY, Dr Leonard Edward; Director of Kingston Polytechnic since 1969; *b* 13 March 1922; *yr s* of late Albert Lawley; *m* 1944, Dorothy Beryl Round; one *s* two *d. Educ:* King Edward VI Sch., Stourbridge; Univs of Wales and Newcastle upon Tyne. BSc, PhD, FInstP. Served with RAF, 1941-46; Lectr, Univ. of Newcastle upon Tyne, 1947-53; Sen. Lectr, The Polytechnic, Regent Street, 1953-57; Kingston Coll. of Technology: Head of Dept of Physics and Maths, 1957-64; Vice-Principal, 1960-64; Principal, 1964-69. *Publications:* various papers in scientific jls on transmission ultrasonic sound waves through gases and liquids and on acoustic methods for gas analysis. *Address:* 62 Blakes Avenue, New Malden, Surrey. *T:* 01-942 6083.

LAWLOR, Prof. John James, MA, DLitt, FSA; Professor of English Language and Literature, University of Keele, since 1950; *b* 5 Jan. 1918; *o s* of Albert John Lawlor, Chief Armourer, RN, and Teresa Anne Clare Lawlor, Plymouth; *m* 1941, Thelma Joan Weeks, singer; one *s* three *d. Educ:* Ryder's; Magdalen Coll., Oxford. BA Hons English Cl. I, 1939. Service in Devonshire Regt, 1940-45; Asst Chief Instructor, 163 Artists' Rifles OCTU, 1943-44; CMF, 1944-45; AMG Austria. Sen. Mackinnon Scholar, Magdalen Coll., 1946; Sen. Demy, 1947; Lectr in English, Brasenose and Trinity Colls, 1947-50; University Lectr in Eng. Lit., Oxford, 1949-50. Fellow of Folger Shakespeare Library, Washington, DC, 1962. Toured Australian and NZ Univs and visited Japan, 1964. Ziskind Visiting Prof., Brandeis Univ., Mass., 1966; Vis. Prof., Univ. of Hawaii, 1972. Permanent Sec.-Treasurer, Internat. Assoc. of University Profs. of English; Contrib. Mem. Medieval Academy of America; Gov., Oswestry Sch.; Pres., N Staffs Drama Assoc.; Mem. Western Area Cttee, Brit. Drama League; Vice-Pres., The Navy League. *Publications:* The Tragic Sense in Shakespeare, 1960; Piers Plowman, an Essay in Criticism, 1962; The Chester Mystery Plays (with Rosemary Sisson), perf. Chester, 1962; The Vision of Piers Plowman, commnd, Malvern, 1964; (ed) Patterns of Love and Courtesy, 1966; (with W. H. Auden) To Nevill Coghill from Friends, 1966; Chaucer, 1968; (ed) The New University, 1968; (ed) Higher Education: patterns of change in the seventies, 1972; (as James Dundonald): Letters to a Vice-Chancellor, 1962; La Vita Nuova, 1976; articles on medieval and modern literature in various journals and symposia. *Recreations:* travel, book-collecting, any sort of sea-faring. *Address:* 14 Church Plantation, Keele, Staffs. *T:* Keele Park 397; 37 Cumnor Hill, Oxford. *T:* Cumnor 3652; Belle Vue House, Tintern, Gwent. *T:* Tintern 455. *Clubs:* Athenæum; Royal Fleet (Devonport).

LAWRANCE, Mrs June Cynthia; Headmistress of Harrogate College, since 1974; *b* 3 June 1933; *d* of Albert Isherwood and Ida Emmett; *m* 1957, Rev. David Lawrance, MA, BD; three *d. Educ:* St Anne's Coll., Oxford (MA). Teaching appts: Univ. of Paris, 1954-57; Cyprus, 1957-58; Jordan, 1958-61; Oldham, Lancs, 1962-70; Headmistress, Broughton High Sch., Salford, 1971-73. *Recreations:* music, French literature, chess. *Address:* Harrogate College, N Yorks. *T:* Harrogate 504543.

LAWRANCE, Keith Cantwell; Under-Secretary, Civil Service Department, since 1971; *b* 1 Feb. 1923; *s* of P. J. Lawrance; *m* 1952, Margaret Joan (*née* Scott); no *c. Educ:* Latymer Sch., N9. Clerical Officer, Admiralty, 1939. Served War, RNVR, 1942-46;

Sub-Lt (A), 1945. Exec. Officer, Treasury, 1947; Asst Principal, Post Office, 1954; Principal, Post Office, 1959; Asst Sec., Dept of Economic Affairs, Dec. 1966. *Recreations:* model engineering, music, electronics. *Address:* 8 Clement Road, Wimbledon, SW19. *T:* 01-947 1676. *Club:* Reform.

LAWRENCE, family name of **Baron Lawrence** and of **Baron Trevethin and Oaksey.**

LAWRENCE, 5th Baron *cr* 1869; **David John Downer Lawrence;** Bt 1858; *b* 4 Sept. 1937; *s* of 4th Baron Lawrence and of Margaret Jean, *d* of Arthur Downer, Kirdford, Sussex; *S father*, 1968. *Educ:* Bradfield College. *Address:* c/o Bird & Bird, 2 Gray's Inn Square, WC1.

LAWRENCE, Arnold Walter, MA; FSA; Professor of Archæology, University College of Ghana, and Director, National Museum of Ghana, 1951-57; Secretary and Conservator, Monuments and Relics Commission of Ghana, 1952-57; Laurence Professor of Classical Archæology, Cambridge University, 1944-51, and Fellow of Jesus College; *b* 2 May 1900; *s* of T. R. Lawrence; *m* 1925, Barbara Thompson; one *d. Educ:* City of Oxford Sch.; New Coll., Oxford. Student, British Schs of Athens and Rome; Ur excavations, 1923; Craven Fellow, 1924-26; Reader in Classical Archæology, Cambridge Univ., 1930; Corr. Mem., German Archæological Institute; literary executor of T. E. Lawrence, 1935; Military Intelligence, Middle East, 1940; Scientific Officer, Coastal Command, RAF, 1942; Ministry of Economic Warfare, 1943; lectured in Latin America, 1948; Leverhulme Research Fellow, 1951. *Publications:* Later Greek Sculpture and its Influence, 1927; Classical Sculpture, 1929; Herodotus, Rawlinson's translation revised and annotated, 1935; Greek Architecture (Pelican History of Art), 1957, rev. edns 1967, and 1974; Trade Castles and Forts of West Africa, 1963, abr. as Fortified Trade Posts: the English in West Africa, 1968; Greek and Roman Sculpture, 1972; (ed) T. E. Lawrence by his Friends, 1937; (ed) Letters to T. E. Lawrence, 1962, etc. *Recreation:* going to and fro in the earth and walking up and down in it. *Address:* c/o Barclays Bank, 68 Lombard Street, EC3.

LAWRENCE, Bernard Edwin, CBE 1957; Chief Education Officer, County of Essex, 1939-65, retired; Dean of the College of Preceptors, 1958-68, Vice President, since 1969; *b* 3 Jan. 1901; *s* of late Albert Edward and Emma Lawrence; *m* 1925, Dorothy Rosa Collings; two *s* one *d. Educ:* Sir Joseph Williamson's Sch., Rochester; Worcester Coll., Oxford. BA Oxon double first class Hons 1922; MA 1930; PhD, University Coll. London, 1934. Asst Master: George Green's Sch., 1923-25; Skinners' Sch., 1925-28; Lecturer: Goldsmiths' Coll., 1928-35; Birkbeck Coll., 1930-35; Asst Dir of Education, Essex, 1936-39; Chairman: Educational Commission to Uganda and Kenya, 1961; Nat. Inst. of Adult Educn, 1964-69. Pres. Assoc. of Chief Educn. Officers, 1957-58. Chevalier de la Légion d'Honneur, 1958. *Publications:* The Administration of Education in Britain, 1972; occasional contribs to Educational Jls and to Proceedings of London Mathematical Society and Mathematical Gazette. *Recreation:* gardening. *Address:* Chapel House, Ingatestone, Essex.

LAWRENCE, Prof. Clifford Hugh; Professor of Medieval History, Bedford College, University of London, since 1970; *b* 28 Dec. 1921; *s* of Ernest William Lawrence and Dorothy Estelle; *m* 1953, Helen Maud Curran; one *s* five *d. Educ:* Stationers' Co.'s Sch.; Lincoln Coll., Oxford. BA 1st Cl. Hons Mod. Hist. 1948, MA 1953, DPhil 1956; FRHistS. War service in RA and Beds and Herts: 2nd Lieut 1942, Captain 1944, Major 1945. Asst Archivist to Co. of Gloucester, 1949. Bedford Coll., London: Asst Lectr in History, 1951; Lectr, 1953-63; Reader in Med. History, 1963-70. External Examr, Univ. of Newcastle upon Tyne, 1972-74, and Univ. of Bristol, 1975. Mem., Press Council, 1976-. *Publications:* St Edmund of Abingdon, History and Hagiography, 1960; The English Church and the Papacy in the Middle Ages, 1965; (contrib.) Pre-Reformation English Spirituality, 1967; (contrib.) The Christian Community, 1971; articles and reviews in Eng. Hist. Review, History, Jl Eccles. Hist., Encycl. Brit., Lexicon für Theol u Kirche, etc. *Recreations:* gardening, painting. *Address:* 11 Durham Road, SW20 0QH. *T:* 01-946 3820.
See also G . C . Lawrence.

LAWRENCE, Sir David (Roland Walter), 3rd Bt, *cr* 1906; late Captain, Coldstream Guards, 1951; *b* 8 May 1929; *er s* of Sir Roland Lawrence, 2nd Bt, MC, and Susan, 3rd *d* of late Sir Charles Addis, KCMG; *S father* 1950; *m* 1955, Audrey, Duchess of Leeds, *yr d* of Brig. Desmond Young, OBE, MC. *Educ:* Radley; RMC Sandhurst. *Heir: b* Clive Wyndham Lawrence [*b* 6 Oct. 1939; *m* 1966, Sophia Annabel Stuart, *d* of

Hervey Stuart Black, Balfron, Stirlingshire; three *s . Address:* 28 High Town Road, Maidenhead, Berks. *Club:* Cavalry and Guards.

LAWRENCE, Dennis George Charles, OBE 1963; Under-Secretary, Department of Industry, since 1974; *b* 15 Aug. 1918; *s* of late George Herbert and Amy Frances Lawrence; *m* 1946, Alida Jantine, *d* of late Willem van den Berg, The Netherlands. *Educ:* Haberdashers' Aske's Hatcham School. Entered Civil Service as Clerical Officer, Min. of Transport, 1936; served RA, 1939-46; Exec. Officer 1946; Asst Principal, Central Land Board, 1947; Principal, 1949; GPO, 1953; Asst Sec. 1960; Sec., Cttee on Broadcasting, 1960-62; Asst Sec., GPO, 1962; Under-Secretary: GPO, 1969; Min. of Posts and Telecommunications, 1969-74. *Recreation:* walking. *Address:* Monks Ford, Monk Sherborne, Hants. *T:* Basingstoke 850193.

LAWRENCE, Evelyn M., BSc (Econ.) London, PhD; **(Mrs Nathan Isaacs);** *b* 31 Dec. 1892; *d* of Samuel and Mary Lawrence, Walton-on-Thames; *m* 1950, Nathan Isaacs, OBE (*d* 1966). *Educ:* Tiffins Sch., Kingston-on-Thames; Stockwell Training Coll.; London Sch. of Economics, University of London. Teacher in LCC schs, 1913-24; BSc Econ. 1st cl. Hons 1923; Ratan Tata and Metcalfe scholar, London Sch. of Economics, 1924-26; on staff of Malting House Sch., Cambridge, 1926-28; Commonwealth Fund scholar, USA, 1929; Chief Social Worker, London Child Guidance Clinic, 1929-30; Lecturer in Education, National Training Coll. of Domestic Subjects, 1931-43. Dir, National Froebel Foundation, and Editor, Froebel Foundation Bulletin, 1943-63. Hon. Sec. British Psychological Soc., Education Section, 1931-34; Mem. of Council of Eugenics Soc., 1949-59. *Publications:* The Relation between Intelligence and Inheritance, 1931. Editor: Friedrich Froebel and English Education, 1952. *Recreations:* walking, gardening, music. *Address:* Grove Cottage, Owletts Lane, Ashurst Wood, East Grinstead, W Sussex. *T:* Forest Row 2728.

LAWRENCE, Sir Frederick, Kt 1963; OBE 1957; JP; *b* 23 Sept. 1889; *s* of Lawrence Isaacs, London; *m* 1921, Gertrude (*d* 1974), *d* of Asher Simons; one *d. Educ:* LCC Sch. Founder, Chairman and Managing Director of: Fredk Lawrence Ltd, London, W2 (now retired); B. Maggs & Co., Bristol; Maggs Furniture Industries Ltd; formerly Chm., Croydon Estates Ltd. Served in 1914-18 War with RE (Signals). Mem. LCC, 1946-65; Mem., NW Metropolitan Regional Hosp. Bd, 1950-66; Mem. Bd of Govs, St Mary's Hosp., Paddington, 1948; formerly Pres., Paddington (S) Cons. and Unionist Assoc., 1962; Mem., Paddington Borough Council, 1934-65; Alderman, 1942; Dep. Mayor, 1942-44; Mayor, 1944-45; Dep. Leader, 1945-65; Dep. Chm. LCC, 1953-54; Mem., Bow St Magistrates' Panel, 1954-64; Chm. Paddington Gp Hosp. Management Cttee, 1948-60; Member: House Cttee, St Mary's Hosp.; Council, Wright-Fleming Inst. for Microbiology, 1961; British Post-graduate Medical Fedn, 1953-65; Vice-Pres., Anti-Tuberculosis League of Israel. JP, Co. London, 1943. *Recreations:* Association football, golf; dancing. *Address:* 77 Albion Gate, Hyde Park, W2. *T:* 01-723 6964. *Clubs:* Coombe Hill Golf, Potters Bar Golf.

LAWRENCE, Geoffrey Charles, CMG 1963; OBE 1958; *b* 11 Nov. 1915; *s* of Ernest William Lawrence; *m* 1945, Joyce Acland Madge, MBE 1959, *d* of M. H. A. Madge, MC. *Educ:* Stationers' Company's Sch.; Brasenose Coll., Oxford. Served 1939-46, Middlesex Yeo. and Brit. Mil. Administration of Occupied Territories (Major). HM Overseas Civil Service (Colonial Administrative Service). Administrative Officer, Somaliland Protectorate, 1946; Asst Chief Sec., 1955; Financial Sec., 1956; Financial Sec., Zanzibar and Mem. of East African Currency Board, 1960-63; Colonial Office, 1964-66; ODM, later ODA, FCO, 1966-73; ODM, 1973-76. *Address:* c/o Barclays Bank Ltd, 42 Coombe Lane, SW20.
See also C . H . Lawrence.

LAWRENCE, Sir Guy Kempton, Kt 1976; DSO 1943; OBE 1945; DFC 1941; Chairman, Food and Drink Industries Council, 1973-77; *b* 5 Nov. 1914; *s* of Albert Edward and Bianca Lawrence; *m* 1947, Marcia Virginia Powell; two *s* one *d . Educ:* Marlborough Coll. FBIM, FIGD. RAFO, 1934-45; War of 1939-45: Bomber Pilot (48 sorties), Sqdn Comdr, 78 Sqdn, Gp Captain Trng, HQ Bomber Command (DFC DSO, despatches, OBE). Contested (L) Colne Valley, 1945. Man. Dir, Chartair Ltd-Airtech Ltd, 1945-48; Chairman: Glacier Foods Ltd, 1948-75; Findus (UK) Ltd, 1967-75; Dep. Chairman: J. Lyons & Co. Ltd, 1950-75; Spillers French Holdings Ltd, 1972-75; Vice-Chm., DCA Food Industries Inc., 1973-; Dir, Eagle Aircraft Services, 1977-. Member of Stock Exchange, London, 1937-45. British Ski Team, FIS, 1937-38. *Recreations:* farming, carpentry, squash, tennis. *Address:* Courtlands, Kier Park, Ascot, Berks SL5 7DS. *T:* Ascot 21074. *Club:* Royal Air Force.

LAWRENCE, Ivan John; Barrister-at-law; MP (C) Burton, since Feb. 1974; *b* 24 Dec. 1936; *o s* of Leslie Lawrence, Brighton; *m* 1966, Gloria Hélène, *d* of Charles Crankshaw, Newcastle; one *d. Educ:* Brighton, Hove and Sussex Grammar Sch.; Christ Church, Oxford (MA). Nat. Service with RAF, 1955-57. Called to Bar, Inner Temple, 1962; S Eastern Circuit. Contested (C) Peckham (Camberwell), 1966 and 1970. Sec., Cons. Parly Legal Cttee. Pres., Nat. Assoc. of Approved Driving Instructors. *Publications:* pamphlets and newspaper articles on law and related topics. *Address:* 1 Essex Court, Temple, EC4Y 9AR. *T:* 01-353 5776; Dunally Cottage, Lower Halliford Green, Shepperton, Mddx. *T:* Walton-on-Thames 24692; Grove Farm, Drakelow, Burton-on-Trent. *T:* Burton-on-Trent 44360.

LAWRENCE, Air Vice-Marshal John Thornett, CB 1975; CBE (mil.) 1967 (OBE (mil.) 1961); AFC 1945; Rolls Royce Ltd, since 1975; *b* 16 April 1920; *s* of late T. L. Lawrence, JP, and Mrs B. M. Lawrence; *m* 1951, Hilary Jean (*née* Owen); three *s* one *d. Educ:* The Crypt School, Gloucester. RAFVR 1938. Served War of 1939-45 in Coastal Command (235, 202 and 86 Squadrons); Directing staff, RAF Flying Coll., 1949-53; CO 14 Squadron, 1953-55; Group Captain Operations, HQ AFME, 1962-64; CO RAF Wittering, 1964-66; AOC, 3 Group, Bomber Command, 1967; Student, IDC, 1968; Dir of Organisation and Admin Plans (RAF), 1969-71; Dir-Gen. Personnel Management (RAF), 1971-73; Comdr N Maritime Air Region and AOC Scotland and NI, 1973-75, retired 1975. Mem. Council, Cheltenham Ladies' Coll. Order of Leopold II, Belgium, 1945; Croix de Guerre, Belgium, 1945. *Recreations:* golf, tennis, sailing. *Address:* Paul Mead Edge, Stroud, Gloucester. *Club:* Royal Air Force.

LAWRENCE, Sir John (Waldemar), 6th Bt, *cr* 1858; OBE 1945; Editor of Frontier since 1957; *b* 27 May 1907; *s* of Sir Alexander Waldemar Lawrence, 4th Bt, and Anne Elizabeth Le Poer (*née* Wynne); *S* brother, Sir Henry Eustace Waldemar Lawrence, 5th Bt, 1967; *m* 1948, Jacynth Mary (*née* Ellerton); no *c. Educ:* Eton; New Coll., Oxford (MA, Lit. Hum.). Personal Asst to Dir of German Jewish Aid Cttee, 1938-39; with BBC as European Intelligence Officer and European Services Organiser, 1939-42; Press Attaché, HM Embassy, USSR, 1942-45; became freelance writer, 1946. Chairman: Centre for Study of Religion and Communism, 1969; GB USSR Assoc., 1970. Officer, Order of Orange Nassau, 1950. *Publications:* Life in Russia, 1947; Russia in the Making, 1957; A History of Russia, 1960; The Hard Facts of Unity, 1961; Russia (Methuen's Outlines), 1965; Soviet Russia, 1967; Russians Observed, 1969; Take Hold of Change, 1976. *Recreations:* travelling, reading in ten languages. *Heir: b* George Alexander Waldemar Lawrence [*b* 22 Sept. 1910; *m* 1949, Olga, *d* of late Peter Schilovsky; one *s* two *d*]. *Address:* 24 St Leonard's Terrace, SW3. *T:* 01-730 8033. *Club:* Athenæum.

LAWRENCE, Marjorie Florence, CBE 1977; dramatic soprano; Professor of Voice and Director of Opera Workshop, Southern Illinois University, Carbondale, Illinois, 1960-73, retired; Professor Emeritus; Professor of Voice: University of Arkansas at Little Rock, since 1974; Newcomb College, Tulane University, New Orleans, Louisiana, 1956-60; *b* Dean's Marsh, Vic., Australia; *d* of William Lawrence and Elizabeth Smith; *m* 1941, Dr Thomas Michael King, New York. *Educ:* privately. Studied voice with Mme Cécile Gilly, Paris, Louis Bachner, New York. Début with Monte Carlo Opera Co., as Elizabeth in Tannhäuser, 1932; début with Paris Grand Opera Co., as Ortrud in Lohengrin, 1932; début with Metropolitan Opera Co., as Brüennhilde in Die Walküre, 1935. Has appeared with Chicago, St Louis, and San Francisco opera companies, and in the Teatro Colon of Buenos Aires and Palacio de Belles Artes, Mexico City; has sung with leading symphony orchestras of the world. Stricken with infantile paralysis in Mexico City, June 1941; although unable to walk, made "come-back" as Venus in Tannhäuser at Metropolitan Opera, 1942, and as Isolde in Tristan und Isolde at Metropolitan Opera, 1943: in 1944 made a 50,000-mile troop concert tour of Australia and the South West Pacific; 1945, made two troop concert tours of England, Belgium, Germany, and France, and sang at Buckingham Palace for the King and Queen; 1946, returned to the Paris Opera. Marjorie Lawrence Opera Theater, S Illinois Univ., Carbondale, Ill, dedicated 26 Feb. 1971. FRSA 1969. Hon. DHL Ohio, 1969. Légion d'Honneur (France), 1946. *Publication:* Interrupted Melody, The Story of My Life (New York, Australia and New Zealand, London), 1949 (made into film, 1955; repr. 1969). *Address:* Route 5, Box 152, Hot Springs, Arkansas 71901, USA.

LAWRENCE, Michael Hugh, CMG 1972; Head of the Administration Department, House of Commons, since 1972; *b* 9 July 1920; *s* of late Hugh Moxon Lawrence and of Mrs. L. N. Lawrence; *m* 1948, Rachel Mary (BA Cantab), *d* of late Humphrey Gamon, Gt Barrow, Cheshire; one *s* two *d. Educ:*

Highgate (Scholar); St Catharine's Coll., Cambridge (Exhibnr; MA). Served Indian Army, 1940-45. Indian Civil Service, 1945-46; Asst Clerk, House of Commons, 1947; Senior Clerk, 1948; Deputy Principal Clerk, 1962; Clerk of the Overseas Office, 1967-72; Clerk Administrator, House of Commons Services Cttee, 1972-76. Sec., History of Parliament Trust, 1959-66. *Recreations:* beagling, lawn tennis, looking at churches. *Address:* 29 Vine Court Road, Sevenoaks, Kent. *T:* Sevenoaks 54972.

LAWRENCE, Robert Leslie Edward, CBE 1975 (OBE 1944); ERD 1952; FCIT; FRSA; Vice-Chairman, British Railways Board, since 1975 (Member, since 1971); Chairman: BRE Metro Ltd, since 1971; British Rail Property Board, since 1972; Transmark Ltd, since 1976; *b* 29 Oct. 1915; *s* of late Robert Riach Lawrence; *m* 1940, Joyce Marjorie (*née* Ricketts); one *s* one *d. Educ:* Dulwich Coll. Served War of 1939-45 (despatches, 1942, 1945), RE; 2nd Lt; Col 1945; Hon. Col, 73 Movement Control Regt, RE, 1963-65; Col, Engr and Rly Staff Corps RE (TA). Traffic Apprentice, LNER, 1934; Headquarters, LNER, 1938; appts in operating depts, 1946-59; London Midland Region: Divisional Man., 1959; Line Manager, 1961; Asst Gen. Manager, 1963-67; Chm. and Gen. Manager, 1968-71; Gen. Manager, Sundries Div., 1968; Chairman: BR Hovercraft Ltd, 1971-72; British Rail Engineering, 1971-76; Transmark Ltd, 1972. Mem., Nat Freight Corporation, 1969-; Dir, Mersey Docks and Harbour Bd, 1971-72. Mem., Energy Commn, 1977-. Vice-Pres., Inst. of Transport, 1970-72 (Mem., Council, 1959-62). Governor, Dulwich Coll., 1970, Dep. Chm. Bd, 1973-. Past Pres., Rly Students Assoc.; Chm., Movement Control Officers Club. Liveryman, Co. of Loriners. Freeman, City of London. OStJ. Legion of Merit (US), 1945. *Publications:* various papers, Inst. of Transport. *Recreations:* swimming, Rugby football. *Address:* 37 Oakfield Gardens, SE19 1HQ. *T:* 01-670 7649; Clifford Cottage, St Levan, Cornwall. *T:* Sennen 297. *Clubs:* Army and Navy, MCC.

LAWRENCE, Samuel Chave; *b* 9 June 1894; *s* of late John Lawrence, DLit, Prof. of English, Tokyo Univ.; *m* 1st, 1917, Dorothy Austen Storey (*d* 1943); two *d;* 2nd, 1955, Lucia Rosa de Maria. *Educ:* Collège Classique Cantonal, Lausanne; Universities of Tokyo and Berlin. Enlisted Queen's Westminster Rifles, Aug. 1914; 2nd Lt Leicestershire Regt 1915; Lt 1917; Consular Service, 1919; Vice-Consul, Washington, 1920; Cologne, 1924; Acting Consul, Mainz, 1925; Vice-Consul, Naples, 1926; Chicago, 1929; Consul (local rank), Santos, 1931; Acting Consul-Gen., São Paulo, in 1931; Consul at Pará, 1934; Chargé d'Affaires, Tegucigalpa, 1938; Consul, Curacao, 1939; Consul-Gen. (local rank) Duala, 1943; Consul, Turin, 1946-48, retd. *Recreation:* photography.

LAWRENCE, Air Vice-Marshal Thomas Albert, CB 1945; RCAF, retired; *b* 1895; *s* of K. J. Lawrence; *m* 1921, Claudine Audrey Jamieson. AOC, 2 Training Comd, BCATP, 1942-44; AOC, NW Air Comd, Canada, 1944-47, retd. Comdr, Legion of Merit (USA), 1945. *Address:* 581 Avenue Road, Toronto 7, Ont, Canada.

LAWRENCE, Sir William, 4th Bt, *cr* 1867; Sales Consultant, Long and Hambly Ltd; retired as Senior Executive, Wilmot Breeden, Ltd; Major East Surrey Regiment; *b* 14 July 1913; *er s* of Sir William Matthew Trevor Lawrence, 3rd Bt, and Iris Eyre (*d* 1955), *y d* of late Brig.-Gen. E. M. S. Crabbe, CB; *S* father, 1934; *m* 1940, Zoë (marr. diss., 1945), *yr d* of H. S. S. Perther, Stowford, Headington, Oxford; *m* 1945, Pamela, *yr d* of J. E. Gordon, Beechbank, Bromborough, Cheshire; one *s* two *d. Educ:* Bradfield Coll. FRHS. Pres., W Warwickshire Scout Council; Vice-Pres., Stratford on Avon and S Warwickshire Cons. Assoc. *Recreation:* gardening. *Heir: s* William Fettiplace Lawrence, *b* 23 Aug. 1954. *Address:* The Knoll, Walcote, near Alcester, Warwicks. *T:* Great Alne 303. *Club:* Royal Automobile.

LAWRENCE-JONES, Sir Christopher, 6th Bt *cr* 1831; Division Medical Officer, Imperial Chemical Industries Ltd (Paints Division), since 1975; *b* 19 Jan. 1940; *s* of Commander B. E. Jones, RN (*d* 1958) (*yr s* of Sir Lawrence Jones, 4th Bt), and Margaret Louise, *d* of late G. M. Cookson; *S* uncle, Sir Lawrence Jones, 5th Bt, MC, 1969; *m* 1967, Gail, *d* of C. A. Pittar, FRACS, Auckland, NZ; two *s. Educ:* Sherborne; Gonville and Caius Coll., Cambridge; St Thomas' Hospital. MA Cantab 1964; MB, BChir Cantab 1964; DIH Eng. 1968. *Recreation:* sailing. *Heir: s* Mark Christopher Lawrence-Jones, *b* 28 Dec. 1968. *Address:* Silwood House, London Road, Ascot, Berks. *Club:* Royal Society of Medicine.

LAWRENCE-WILSON, Harry Lawrence; Under-Secretary, Procurement Executive, Ministry of Defence, 1971-72; *b* 18

March 1920; *s* of late H. B. Wilson and of Mrs May Wilson, Biddenden, Kent; *m* 1945, Janet Mary Gillespie; two *s* one *d*. *Educ:* Cranbrook Sch.; Worcester Coll., Oxford. Served Indian Army, 1940-46. Colonial Office, 1946-47; MoD, 1947-66; Cabinet Office, 1967-69. Asst Principal, 1947; Principal, 1948; Assistant Secretary, 1956; Under-Secretary, 1961; Under-Secretary: Min. of Technology, 1969-70; DTI, 1970-71; CSD, 1971. *Address:* 22 Marlborough Crescent, Riverhead, Sevenoaks, Kent.

LAWRIE, James Haldane; General Administrator, D'Oyly Carte Opera Trust Ltd; *b* 28 March 1907; *e s* of late Allan James Lawrie, KC, and late Ethel Annette Lawrie, *d* of Judge Richard Adams, QC. *Educ:* Newlands, Seaford, Sussex; Fettes Coll., Edinburgh (Open Schol.); University Coll., Oxford (Open Schol.). Lloyds Bank Ltd, 1930-37; Secretary, 1937-45, London Manager, 1940-45, National Bank of New Zealand Ltd; Chm., British Overseas Banks Assoc., 1944-45; Vice-Pres. British Bankers' Assoc., 1944-45; Council London Chamber of Commerce, 1944-48; Gen. Man., 1945-48, Industrial and Commercial Finance Corp. Ltd; Chm. and Man. Dir, National Film Finance Co. Ltd, 1948-49, when it became National Film Finance Corp.; Man. Dir, National Film Finance Corp., 1949-53; film producer and theatrical manager, including 59 Theatre Company, 1953-65; Chm., Air Transport Licensing Bd, 1971-72 (Mem., 1965, Dep. Chm., 1968); Mem. CAA, 1972-76. Mem., BBC Gen. Advisory Council, 1952-59; Chairman: Nat. Sch. of Opera, 1948-63; English Opera Gp, 1950-60; British Film Academy, 1958-59; Phoenix Opera, 1964-75; Sec., Soc. of Film and Television Arts, 1959-61; Member: Plant Cttee on Distribution and Exhibition of Cinematograph Films, 1949; Hutton Cttee on Purchase Tax, 1952. *Address:* Flat 2, 24 Palace Court, W2. *T:* 01-727 8349. *Club:* Savile.

LAWS, Richard Maitland, PhD; Director, British Antarctic Survey, since 1973; *b* 23 April 1926; *s* of Percy Malcolm Laws and Florence May (*née* Heslop); *m* 1954, Maureen Isobel Winifred (*née* Holmes); three *s*. *Educ:* Dame Allan's Sch., Newcastle-on-Tyne; St Catharine's Coll., Cambridge. BA Cantab 1947, MA 1952, PhD 1953; FInstBiol 1973. Biologist and Base Leader, Falkland Is Dependencies Survey, 1947-53; Biologist and Whaling Inspector, F/F Balaena, 1953-54; Principal Sci. Officer, Nat. Inst. of Oceanography, 1954-61; Dir, Nuffield Unit of Tropical Animal Ecology, Uganda, 1961-67; Dir, Tsavo Research Project, Kenya, 1967-68; Smuts Meml Fund Fellowship, 1968-69; Leverhulme Research Fellowship, 1969; Head, Life Sciences Div., British Antarctic Survey, 1969-73. Bruce Medal, RSE, 1954; Scientific Medal, Zool Soc. London, 1965; Polar Medal, 1977. *Publications:* (with I. S. C. Parker and R. C. B. Johnstone) Elephants and their Habitats, 1975; numerous papers in biol jls. *Recreations:* walking, photography, painting. *Address:* 3 The Footpath, Coton, Cambridge CB3 7PX. *T:* Madingley 567.

LAWSON, family name of **Baron Burnham.**

LAWSON, Charles, QC 1961; **His Honour Judge Lawson;** a Circuit Judge, since 1972; *b* 23 Feb. 1916; 2nd *s* of late Barnet Lawson, London; *m* 1943, Olga Daphne Kay; three *d*. *Educ:* Grocers' Company Sch.; University College, London. LLB 1937. Served War of 1939-45: in Army, 1940-46; Major, Royal Artillery. Recorder: Burton-upon-Trent, 1965-68; Gloucester, 1968-71. Bencher, Inner Temple, 1968. *Recreations:* golf, music. *Address:* Mayes Green Cottage, Ockley, Surrey RH5 5PM. *T:* Forest Green 317.

LAWSON, Prof. Donald Douglas; Professor of Veterinary Surgery, University of Glasgow, since 1974; *b* 25 May 1924; *s* of Alexander Lawson and Jessie Macnaughton; *m* 1949, Barbara Ness; two *s* two *d*. *Educ:* Whitehill Sch., Glasgow; Glasgow Veterinary Coll. MRCVS, BSc, DVR. Asst in Veterinary Practice, 1946-47; Asst, Surgery Dept, Glasgow Vet. Coll., 1947-49; Glasgow Univ.: Lectr, Vet. Surgery, 1949-57; Sen. Lectr, 1957-66; Reader, 1966-71; Titular Prof., 1971-74. *Publications:* many articles in Veterinary Record and Jl of Small Animal Practice. *Recreations:* gardening, motoring. *Address:* Burnbrae, Balfron, Glasgow G63 0NY. *T:* Balfron 232 03604.

LAWSON, Rear-Adm. Frederick Charles William, CB 1971; DSC 1942 and Bar, 1945; Chief Executive, Royal Dockyards, Ministry of Defence, 1972-75; *b* 20 April 1917; *s* of M. L. Lawson, formerly of Public Works Dept, Punjab, India; *m* 1945, Dorothy (*née* Norman), Eastbourne; one *s* three *d*. *Educ:* Eastbourne Coll.; RNEC. Joined RN, 1935; specialised in engrg; Cmdr 1949; Captain 1960; Cdre Supt Singapore, 1965-69; Rear-Adm. 1969; Flag Officer, Medway and Adm. Supt, HM Dockyard, Chatham, 1969-71, retired. *Recreation:* golf. *Address:* Weaverhoult, Woolley Street, Bradford-on-Avon, Wilts. *Club:* Army and Navy.

LAWSON, Frederick Henry, DCL 1947; FBA 1956; Part-time Professor of Law, University of Lancaster, 1964-77; *b* Leeds, 14 July 1897; *s* of Frederick Henry Lawson and Mary Louisa Austerberry; *m* 1933, Elspeth, *yr d* of late Captain Alexander Webster, Kilmarnock; one *s* two *d*. *Educ:* Leeds Grammar Sch. Hastings Exhibitioner in Classics (Hon. Scholar), Queen's Coll., Oxford, 1915; Akroyd Scholar, 1915. Served European War, 1916-18. 1st Class, Final Hon. School of Modern History, 1921; 1st Class, Final Hon. School of Jurisprudence, 1922. Barrister-at-Law, Gray's Inn, 1923; Lecturer in Law, University Coll., Oxford, 1924-25, Christ Church, 1925-26, CCC, 1925-26 and 1927-30; Junior Research Fellow, Merton Coll., Oxford, 1925-30, official Fellow and Tutor in Law, 1930-48. Studied at Göttingen, 1926-27; University Lecturer in Byzantine Law, 1929-31; All Souls Reader in Roman Law, 1931-48; Temp. Principal in Ministry of Supply, 1943-45; Prof. of Comparative Law, and Fellow of Brasenose Coll., Oxford, 1948-64. Visiting Prof., Univ. of California, 1953; Thomas M. Cooley Lectr, Univ. of Michigan Law Sch., 1953; Joint Editor Journal of Comparative Legislation and International Law, 1948-52, of International and Comparative Law Quarterly, 1952-55; Senior Editor, Journal of Society of Public Teachers of Law, 1955-61; Member International Social Science Council, 1952-58; Lecturer in Roman Law, Council of Legal Education, 1954-58 (Reader, 1958-64); Visiting Lecturer, New York University School of Law, 1956, 1959, 1962, 1965; Visiting Professor, University of Pennsylvania Law School, 1959 (Spring Semester); University of Michigan Law School, 1959 (Fall Semester); University of Houston, 1967-68. Mem. Internat. Acad. of Comparative Law, 1958-; Sec.-Gen., Internat. Assoc. of Legal Science, 1964-69. Hon. Doctor: Louvain, 1958; Paris, 1964; Ghent, 1968; Hon. Dr jur. Frankfurt; Hon. LLD: Glasgow, 1960; Lancaster, 1977. *Publications:* (with Sir D. L. Keir) Cases in Constitutional Law, 1st edn 1928, 6th edn (with D. J. Bentley) 1977; Negligence in the Civil Law, 1950; The Rational Strength of English Law (Hamlyn Lectures), 1951; A Common Lawyer looks at the Civil Law (Thomas M. Cooley Lectures), 1955; An Introduction to the Law of Property, 1958; (with D. J. Bentley) Constitutional and Administrative Law, 1961; The Oxford Law School, 1850-1965, 1968; The Roman Law Reader, 1969; The Remedies of English Law, 1972; Selected Essays, 1977; much re-editing, including Buckland and McNair, Roman Law and Common Law, 2nd edn 1952. *Address:* 6 Thirsk Road, Stokesly, N Yorks. *T:* Stokesly 710268.

LAWSON, George McArthur; *b* Edinburgh, 11 July 1906; *s* of Alexander Lawson and Euphemia Gordon McPherson McArthur; *m* 1939, Margaret Robertson Munro; two *s* (and one *s* decd). *Educ:* St Bernard's; North Merchiston elementary schools. Staff tutor with National Council of Labour Colleges, 1937-40; West of Scotland Organiser with NCLC, 1940-50; Secretary, Edinburgh Trades Council, 1950-54. MP (Lab) Lanarkshire, Motherwell, April 1954-Feb. 1974, Motherwell and Wishaw, Feb.-Oct. 1974, retired; an An Opposition Whip, 1959-64; Government Whip, 1964; Dep. Chief Government Whip, 1966-67. Mem., Scottish Adv. Cttee, Nature Conservancy Council; Exec. Mem., Nat. Trust for Scotland. Campaign Dir, Scotland is British Campaign, 1976-. *Address:* Brooklyn, 37 Burnblea Street, Hamilton, Lanarkshire. *T:* Hamilton 21691.

LAWSON, Prof. Gerald Hartley; Professor of Business Finance, Manchester Business School, University of Manchester, since 1969; financial and economic consultant; *b* 6 July 1933; of English parents; *m* 1957, Helga Elisabeth Anna Heine; three *s*. *Educ:* King's Coll., Univ. of Durham. BA (Econ), MA (Econ); MBA Manchester; FCCA. Accountant in industry, 1957-59; Lectr in Accountancy and Applied Economics, Univ. of Sheffield, 1959-66; Prof. of Business Studies, Univ. of Liverpool, 1966-69. Prof., Univ. of Augsburg, Germany, 1971-72. *Publications:* (with D. W. Windle): Tables for Discounted Cash Flow, etc, Calculations, 1965 (repr. 1977); Capital Budgeting in the Corporation Tax Regime, 1967; Enterprise Valuation: a cashflow approach, 1978; many articles and translations. *Recreations:* cricket, skiing. *Address:* Manchester Business School, Booth Street West, Manchester M15 6PB. *T:* 061-273 8228. *Club:* Manchester Business School.

LAWSON, Lt-Col Harold Andrew Balvaird, CVO 1971 (MVO 1963); Rothesay Herald since 1939; Lyon Clerk and Keeper of the Records of the Court of the Lord Lyon, 1929-66; *b* 19 Oct. 1899; 2nd *s* of late Dr Charles Wilfrid Lawson, Edinburgh; *m* 1934, Kathleen Alice, *o d* of Alexander Banks, of Banks & Co., Printers; one *d*. *Educ:* George Watson's Coll.; Edinburgh Univ. Joined RFA, 1916; 2nd Lieut, 1919; RA (TA), 1942; Major, 1936; Lieut-Colonel, 1939; Unicorn Pursuivant, 1929-39. OStJ 1968. *Recreations:* golf, badminton. *Address:* Lyon Office, HM Register House, Edinburgh. *T:* 031-556 7255.

LAWSON, Sir Henry (Brailsford), Kt 1963; MC 1917; retired as Chief Legal Adviser and a Deputy Chief General Manager, Lloyds Bank Ltd, 1963; *b* 19 Feb. 1898; *s* of H. P. Lawson; *m* 1930, Mona Lilian, *e d* of Dr B. Thorne Thorne; three *s* one *d. Educ:* Lancing Coll.; Trinity Coll., Cambridge (BA, LLB). Member Council, 1943, Vice-President, 1961-62, President, 1962-63, of Law Society. *Address:* Churchmead, Pirbright, Surrey. *T:* Brookwood 4133.

LAWSON, Hugh McDowall, BScEng London; CEng, FICE, FIMunE; Director of Leisure Services, Nottingham City Council, 1973-76; *b* Leeds, 13 Feb. 1912; *s* of late John Lawson, Pharmaceutical Chemist; *m* 1937, Dorothy, *d* of late Rev. T. H. Mallinson, BA; two *s. Educ:* Nottingham High Sch.; University Coll., Nottingham. Served in Royal Engineers, 1940-44. MP (Common Wealth) Skipton Div. of Yorks, 1944-45. Contested (Common Wealth) Harrow West Div., 1945; (Lab) Rushcliffe Div., 1950; (Lab) King's Lynn Div., 1955. Dep. City Engr, Nottingham, 1948-73. Mem. Council, ICE, 1972-75. *Address:* 45 Hazel Grove, Mapperley, Nottingham NG3 6DQ. *T:* 605241.

LAWSON, Air Vice-Marshal Ian Douglas Napier, CB 1965; CBE 1961; DFC 1941, Bar 1943; RAF, retired; Director of Marketing, British Aircraft Corporation, since 1974; *b* 11 Nov. 1917; *y s* of late J. L. Lawson and Ethel Mary Lawson (*née* Ludgate); *m* 1945, Dorothy Joyce Graham Nash; one *s* one *d. Educ:* Brondesbury Coll.; Polytechnic, Regent Street. Aircraft Industry, 1934-39. Joined RAFVR 1938. Served War of 1939-45 (despatches thrice): Bomber Comd, 1940-41; Middle East Comd, 1941-45. Permanent Commission, 1945. Bomber Comd, 1945-46; Staff Coll., 1946; Air Ministry, 1946-49; Transport Comd, 1949-50; Middle East Comd, 1950-52; JSSC, 1953; Ministry of Defence, 1953-56; Flying Coll., Manby, 1956-57; Transport Comd, 1957-62; Air Forces Middle East, 1962-64; Commandant, RAF Coll., Cranwell, 1964-67; Asst Chief Adviser (Personnel and Logistics), MoD, 1967-69. Joined BAC, 1969. MBIM. US Legion of Merit. *Recreations:* gardening, motor sport. *Address:* Grove House, Lacock, Wilts. *T:* Lacock 307. *Club:* Royal Air Force.

LAWSON, John Alexander Reid, FRCGP; General Medical Practitioner, since 1948; Regional Adviser in General Practice, Tayside Region, since 1972; *b* 30 Aug. 1920; *s* of Thomas Reid Lawson and Helen Scrimgour Lawson; *m* 1944, Pat Kirk; two *s* two *d. Educ:* High Sch. of Dundee; Univ. of St Andrews (MB, ChB). RAMC, 1944-47 (Major). Surgical Registrar, Royal Infirmary, Dundee, 1947-48. Royal College of General Practitioners: Mem., 1952; Fellow, 1967; Chm. Council, 1973-76. Mem. Cttee of Enquiry into Competence to Practice, 1974-76; Chm., Jt Cttee on Postgraduate Training for General Practice, 1975-. *Recreations:* shooting, fishing, golf, gardening. *Address:* The Ridges, 458 Perth Road, Dundee. *T:* Dundee 67408. *Club:* Royal and Ancient Golf (St Andrews).

LAWSON, Sir John Charles Arthur Digby, 3rd Bt, *cr* 1900; DSO 1943; MC 1940; Lieutenant-Colonel 11th Hussars, retired; Chairman, Fairbairn Lawson Ltd, Leeds, and subsidiary companies; *b* 24 Oct. 1912; *e s* of Sir Digby Lawson, Bt, TD, JP, and late Mrs Gerald Wallis (*née* Iris Mary Fitzgerald); *S* father 1959; *m* 1st, 1945, Rose (marr. diss., 1950), *widow* of Pilot Officer William Fiske, RAF, and *er d* of late D. C. Bingham and late Lady Rosabelle Brand; 2nd, 1954, Tresilla Ann Eleanor (de Pret Roose), *d* of late Major E. Buller Leyborne Popham, MC; one *s. Educ:* Stowe; RMC, Sandhurst. Served War of 1939-45 (despatches twice, MC, DSO). Comd Inns of Court Regt, 1945-47; retired, 1947. Colonel, 11th Hussars (PAO), 1965-69; Hon. Col, The Royal Hussars (PWO), 1969-73. Legion of Merit (US). *Heir: s* Charles John Patrick Lawson, *b* 19 May 1959. *Address:* Abbey Hill, Jervaulx, Ripon, N Yorks. *T:* Jervaulx 209. *Clubs:* Cavalry and Guards, MCC.

LAWSON, Hon. Sir Neil, Kt 1971; Hon. Mr Justice Lawson; Judge of High Court of Justice, Queen's Bench Division, since 1971; *b* 8 April 1908; *s* of late Robb Lawson and Edith Marion Lawson (*née* Usherwood); *m* 1933, Gweneth Clare (*née* Wilby); one *s* one *d.* Called to Bar, Inner Temple, 1929; QC 1955; Recorder of Folkestone, 1962-71; a Law Commissioner, 1965-71. RAFVR, 1940-45. Hon. Fellow, LSE, 1974. Foreign decorations: DK (Dato' Peduka Kerubat), 1959, DSN (Dato' Setia Negara), 1962, PSMB (Dato' Sri Mahota), 1969, Brunei. *Recreations:* literature, music, the country. *Address:* 30a Heath Drive, Hampstead, NW3.

LAWSON, Nigel; MP (C) Blaby, Leicestershire, since Feb. 1974; journalist; *b* 11 March 1932; *s* of Ralph Lawson and Joan Elisabeth Lawson (*née* Davis); *m* 1955, Vanessa Mary Addison, 2nd *d* of late Felix Addison Salmon; one *s* three *d. Educ:* Westminster; Christ Church, Oxford (Scholar). 1st class hons PPE, 1954. Served with Royal Navy (Sub-Lt RNVR), 1954-56. Mem. Editorial Staff, Financial Times, 1956-60; City Editor, Sunday Telegraph, 1961-63; Special Assistant to Prime Minister (Sir Alec Douglas-Home), 1963-64; Financial Times columnist and BBC broadcaster, 1965; Editor of the Spectator, 1966-70; regular contributor to: Sunday Times and Evening Standard, 1970-71; The Times, 1971-72; Fellow, Nuffield Coll., Oxford, 1972-73; Special Pol Advr, Cons. Party HQ, 1973-74. Contested (C), Eton and Slough, 1970. An Opposition Whip, 1976-. Dir, British American and General Trust. Chm., Coningsby Club, 1963-64. Vice-Chm., Cons. Political Centre Nat. Adv. Cttee, 1972-75. *Publication:* The Power Game (with Jock Bruce-Gardyne), 1976. *Address:* The Old Rectory, Stoney Stanton, Leics. *T:* Sapcote 2208; 39 Tedworth Square SW3, *T:* 01-352 2691. *Clubs:* Garrick, Political Economy.

LAWSON, Maj.-Gen. Richard George, DSO 1962; OBE 1968; General Officer Commanding 1st Armoured Division, since Dec. 1977; *b* 24 Nov. 1927; *s* of John Lawson and Florence Rebecca Lawson; *m* 1956, Ingrid Lawson; one *s. Educ:* St Alban's Sch.; Birmingham Univ. CO, Independent Squadron, RTR (Berlin), 1963-64; CofS, South Arabian Army, 1967; CO, 5th RTR, 1968-69; Comdr, 20th Armoured Bde, 1972-73; Asst Military Deputy to Head of Defence Sales, 1975-77. Leopold Cross (Belgium), 1963; Knight Commander, Order of St Sylvester, 1964. *Publications:* Strange Soldiering, 1963; All the Queen's Men, 1967; Strictly Personal, 1972. *Address:* Lombard Cottage, Petworth, Sussex. *T:* Petworth 42397. *Club:* Army and Navy.

LAWSON, Sir William (Howard), 5th Bt *cr* 1841; DL; *b* 15 July 1907; *s* of Sir Henry Joseph Lawson, 3rd Bt, and Ursula Mary (*d* 1960), *o c* of Philip John Canning Howard, Corby Castle, Carlisle; *S* brother, 1975; *m* 1933, Joan Eleanor, *d* of late Arthur Cowie Stamer, CBE; three *s* one *d. Educ:* Ampleforth College. DL Cumberland, 1963. *Recreations:* field sports. *Heir: s* John Philip Howard [*b* 6 June 1934; assumed surname and arms of Howard by Royal Licence, 1962; *m* 1960, Jean Veronica, *d* of late Col John Evelyn Marsh, DSO, OBE; two *s* one *d*]. *Address:* Wood House, Warwick Bridge, Carlisle. *T:* Carlisle 60330.

LAWSON DICK, Clare; OBE 1975; BBC Controller Radio 4, 1975-76; *b* 13 Oct. 1913; *d* of John Lawson Dick, MD, FRCS, and Winifred Lawson Dick (*née* Duke). *Educ:* Channing Sch., Highgate; King's Coll., London (Dip. Journalism). Joined BBC, 1935. *Recreations:* enjoying the amenities of London; escaping from London into the country. *Address:* Flat 8, 92 Elm Park Gardens, SW10. *T:* 01-352 8395.

LAWSON JOHNSTON, family name of **Baron Luke.**

LAWSON JOHNSTON, Hon. Hugh de Beauchamp, TD 1951; DL; *b* 7 April 1914; *yr s* of 1st Baron Luke of Pavenham, KBE, and *b* of 2nd Baron Luke, *qv; m* 1946, Audrey Warren, *d* of late Colonel F. Warren Pearl and late Mrs A. L. Pearl; three *d. Educ:* Eton; Chillon Coll.; Corpus Christi, Cambridge. BA 1934, MA (Cantab), 1938. With Bovril Ltd, 1935-71, finally as Chm. Territorial Service with 5th Bn Beds and Herts Regt, 1935-; Captain, 1939, and throughout War. Director: Tribune Investment Trust Ltd (Chm.); Pitman Ltd (Chm.). Chm. of Cttees, United Soc. for Christian Literature. High Sheriff of Bedfordshire, 1961-62; DL Beds, 1964. *Recreations:* hunting, walking, gardening, photography. *Address:* Flat 1, 28 Lennox Gardens, SW1. *T:* 01-584 1446; Melchbourne Park, Bedfordshire. *T:* Riseley 282.

LAWSON-TANCRED, Sir Henry, 10th Bt, *cr* 1662; JP; *b* 12 Feb. 1924; *e surv. s* of Major Sir Thomas Lawson-Tancred, 9th Bt, and Margery Elinor (*d* 1961), *d* of late A. S. Lawson, Aldborough Manor; *S* father, 1945; *m* 1950, Jean Veronica (*d* 1970), 4th and *y d* of late G. R. Foster, Stockeld Park, Wetherby, Yorks; five *s* one *d. Educ:* Stowe; Jesus Coll., Cambridge. Served as Pilot in RAFVR, 1942-46. JP West Riding, 1967. *Heir: s* Andrew Peter Lawson-Tancred, *b* 18 Feb. 1952. *Address:* Aldborough Manor, Boroughbridge, Yorks. *T:* Boroughbridge 2716.

LAWTON, Frank Dickinson, CB 1972; Solicitor, Department of Employment, 1967-76; *b* 14 July 1915; *o s* of F. W. Lawton, CB, OBE, and Elizabeth Mary (*née* Savage); *m* 1943, Margaret Joan, *o d* of Frederick Norman Reed; one *s* two *d. Educ:* Epsom Coll.; Law Society's Sch. of Law. Solicitor (hors), 1937. Entered Solicitor's Dept, Ministry of Labour, 1939; seconded to Treasury, Solicitor's Dept, 1940; returned to Solicitor's Dept, Ministry of Labour, 1947; Assistant Solicitor, 1959; Solicitor, Min. of Labour (now Dept of Employment), Oct. 1967. Mem. Court of Assts, Scriveners' Co. (Master 1970-71; Mem. Examination Cttee, 1967-76). *Address:* Riversdale, Tarrant

Monkton, Blandford Forum, Dorset. *T:* Tarrant Hinton 203. *Club:* Athenæum.

LAWTON, Rt. Hon. Sir Frederick (Horace), PC 1972; Kt 1961; **Rt. Hon. Lord Justice Lawton;** a Lord Justice of Appeal, since 1972; *b* 21 Dec. 1911; *o s* of William John Lawton; *m* 1937, Doreen (*née* Wilton); two *s*. *Educ:* Battersea Grammar Sch.; Corpus Christi Coll., Cambridge (Hon. Fellow, 1968). Barrister, Inner Temple, 1935; Bencher, 1961. Served with London Irish Rifles, 1939-41; invalided out of Army, 1941, and returned to practice at the Bar. QC 1957; Judge of the High Court of Justice, Queen's Bench Div., 1961-72. Recorder of City of Cambridge, 1957-61; Dep. Chm., Cornwall QS, 1968-71. Member: Bar Council, 1957-61; Departmental Cttee on Proceedings before Examining Justices, 1957-58; Standing Cttee on Criminal Law Revision, 1959- (Chm., 1977-); Inter-departmental Cttee on Court of Criminal Appeal, 1964-65; Chm., Adv. Cttee on Legal Educn, 1976-. Presiding Judge, Western Circuit, 1970-72. President, British Academy of Forensic Sciences, 1964. *Address:* 2 Harcourt Buildings, Temple, EC4Y 9DB. *T:* 01-353 3720; Mordryg, Stoptide, Rock, near Wadebridge, Cornwall. *T:* Trebetherick 3375. *Club:* Garrick.

LAWTON, Harold Walter, MA; Docteur de l'Université de Paris; Officier d'Académie; Emeritus Professor, University of Sheffield, since 1964; *b* Stoke-on-Trent, 27 July 1899; *y s* of late William T. C. and Alice Lawton; *m* 1938, Bessie, *y d* of T. C. Pate; two *s* one *d*. *Educ:* Middle Sch., Newcastle under Lyme; Rhyl Grammar Sch.; Universities of Wales and Paris. BA Hons (Wales) 1921; MA (Wales) 1923; Fellow University of Wales, 1923-26; Docteur de l'Univ. de Paris, 1926. University College, Southampton: Lecturer in French, 1926-37; Professor of French, 1937-50; Dean of Faculty of Arts, 1945-49; University of Sheffield: Professor of French, 1950-64; Warden of Ranmoor House, 1957-63; Deputy Pro-Vice-Chancellor, 1958-61; Pro-Vice-Chancellor, 1961-64. Médaille d'Argent de la Reconnaissance Française, 1946; Officier d'Académie, 1948. *Publications:* Térence en France au XVIe Siècle: éditions et traductions (Paris), 1926; repr. 1970; Handbook of French Renaissance Dramatic Theory, 1950, repr. 1972; J. du Bellay, Poems, selected with introduction and notes, 1961; Térence en France au XVIe Siècle: imitation et influence, 1972; articles and reviews to British and French periodicals. *Recreations:* walking, drawing. *Address:* Ranmoor, 4 Timber Bank, Vigo Village, Meopham, Kent DA13 0RZ. *T:* Fairseat 822712.

LAWTON, Ven. John Arthur; Archdeacon of Warrington since 1970; Rector of Winwick since 1969; *b* 19 Jan. 1913; *s* of Arthur and Jennie Lawton; unmarried. *Educ:* Rugby; Fitzwilliam House, Cambridge (MA); Cuddesdon Theological College, Oxford. Curate, St Dunstan, Edgehill, Liverpool, 1937-40; Vicar of S Anne, Wigan, 1940-56; Vicar of St Luke, Southport, 1956-60; Vicar of Kirkby, Liverpool, 1960-69. *Address:* Winwick Rectory, Golborne Road, Winwick, Warrington WA2 8SZ. *T:* Warrington 32760.

LAWTON, Kenneth Keith Fullerton; His Honour Judge Lawton; a Circuit Judge since 1972; *b* 6 Aug. 1924; *o s* of late John William Lawton, MA, BSc, and Susan Fullerton; *m* 1st, 1959, Muriel Iris (*née* Parry) (*d* 1974); 2nd, 1975, Dorothy, *d* of Harold Rogers, Lancaster. *Educ:* Barrow Grammar Sch.; Trinity Hall, Cambridge (Exhibr, MA). Fleet Air Arm, 1943-45. Called to Bar, Middle Temple, 1947; practised Liverpool Bar, 1948-70; part-time Dep. Chm., Lancs QS, 1969 (full-time 1970); Mem., Lancs SW Probation and After-Care Cttee, 1973-74. Contested (C) Barrow, 1951. JP Lancs, 1969. *Recreations:* gardening, reading. *Address:* 19 St Anne's Road, Liverpool L17 6BN. *T:* 051-427 3339. *Clubs:* Athenæum, Artists (Liverpool).

LAWTON, Louis David, QC 1973; Barrister-at-Law; a Recorder of the Crown Court, since 1972; *b* 15 Oct. 1936; *m* 1959, Helen Margaret (*née* Gair); one *s* two *d*. *Educ:* Repton Sch.; Sidney Sussex Coll., Cambridge (MA). Called to Bar, Lincoln's Inn, 1959. *Address:* (home) Copmanthorpe Manor, Copmanthorpe, York; (chambers) 2 Harcourt Buildings, Temple, EC4. *Club:* United Oxford & Cambridge University.

LAWTON, Philip Charles Fenner, CBE 1967; DFC 1941; Group Director and Chairman, BEA, 1972-73; Member: British Airways Board, 1972-73; Board, BOAC, 1972-73; Director, Stewart Wrightson (Aviation) Ltd, since 1974; *b* Highgate, London, 18 Sept. 1912; *o s* of late Charles Studdert Lawton and late Mabel Harriette Lawton; *m* 1941, Emma Letitia Gertrude, *y d* of late Lieut-Colonel Sir Henry Kenyon Stephenson, 1st Bt, DSO, and Frances, Hassop Hall, Bakewell, Derbyshire; one *s* one *d*. *Educ:* Westminster Sch. Solicitor, 1934-39. Joined AAF, 1935. Served War of 1939-45 (despatches twice, Group Captain): Pilot with 604 Aux. Sqdn (night fighters), 1939-41;

Staff Officer HQ, Fighter Command, 1942; Station Commander, RAF Predannock; RAF Portreath; RAF Cranfield and Special Duties for Inspector-General, RAF, 1943-45. Joined BEA, 1946; Commercial and Sales Dir, 1947-71, Mem. Corporation 1964, Exec. Bd Member 1971; Chm., BEA Airtours, 1969-72. LLB Hons Degree, 1933; FCIT (MInstT 1955). *Address:* Adversane House, Billingshurst, West Sussex. *T:* Billingshurst 2559; 17 Pembroke Walk, W8. *T:* 01-937 3091. *Club:* RAF.

LAXNESS, Halldor Kiljan; Icelandic writer; *b* 23 April 1902; *s* of Gudjon Helgason and Sigridur Halldorsdottir, Iceland; *m* 1st, Ingibjörg Einarsdottir; one *s*; 2nd, Audur Suensdottir; two *d*. Awarded Nobel literary prize, 1955; Sonning Prize, 1969. *Publications:* (many of which have been translated into English): The Great Weaver of Cashmere, 1927; Salka Valka, 1934; Independent People (an epic), 1939; The Atom Station, 1947 (English trans. 1961); Happy Warriors, 1956 (English trans. 1958); World Light, 1969; Paradise Reclaimed; Fish Can Sing; Independent People (play), 1972; Translations into Icelandic: Farewell to Arms by Ernest Hemingway; Candide by Voltaire, etc. *Address:* PO Box 664, Reykjavik, Iceland.

LAYCOCK, Sir Leslie (Ernest), Kt 1974; CBE 1967 (OBE 1960); JP; Company Director; *b* 14 Sept. 1903; *s* of Ernest Bright Laycock and Margaret Ann Laycock; *m* 1931, Hilda Florence, *d* of Christopher Ralph Carr; two *s*. *Educ:* Uppingham Sch.; Leeds Univ. (BCom). President: Leeds and District Woollen Manufacturers Assoc., 1937-39; Leeds & Holbeck Building Soc., 1969-71 (Vice-Pres., 1967-69); Vice-President, Assoc. of British Chambers of Commerce, 1962- (Past Pres., Leeds Chamber; Past Chm, Assoc. of Yorks Chambers); Chm., WR Br., Inst. of Dirs, 1958-72; Chairman: Governors, Leeds Coll. of Commerce, 1948-69; Advisory Cttee to Leeds Prison, 1961-; Harrogate (White Rose) Theatre Trust Ltd, 1961-65 (Pres., 1965-73); Leeds Regional Hosp. Bd, 1963-73; Member Ct, Leeds Univ., 1953-. Civil Defence Director Operations, W Riding, 1958-68. JP Leeds, 1952-. *Recreations:* tennis, badminton, sailing, bridge. *Address:* The Gables, Rayleigh Road, Harrogate. *T:* Harrogate 66219. *Clubs:* Naval and Military; Leeds (Leeds); Club, Sports (Harrogate).

LAYE, Evelyn, CBE 1973; actress; singer; *b* London, 10 July 1900; *o d* of Gilbert Laye and Evelyn Froud; *m* 1st, 1926, Sonnie Hale (from whom she obtained a divorce, 1931); 2nd, 1934, Frank Lawton (*d* 1969). *Educ:* Folkestone; Brighton. Made first appearance on stage, Theatre Royal, Brighton, 1915, as Nang-Ping in Mr Wu. First London appearance in The Beauty Spot, Gaiety, 1918; first big success in title-role of The Merry Widow, Daly's, 1923; subsequently starred in London in Madame Pompadour, Daly's, 1923; The Dollar Princess, Daly's, 1925; Cleopatra, Daly's, 1925; Betty in Mayfair, Adelphi, 1925; Merely Molly, Adelphi, 1926; Princess Charming, Palace, 1927; Lilac Time, Daly's, 1927; Blue Eyes, Piccadilly, 1928; The New Moon, Drury Lane, 1929; Bitter Sweet, His Majesty's, 1930; Helen!, Adelphi, 1932; Give Me A Ring, Hippodrome, 1933; Paganini, Lyceum, 1937; Lights Up, Savoy, 1940; The Belle of New York, Coliseum, 1942; Sunny River, Piccadilly, 1943; Cinderella, His Majesty's, 1943; Three Waltzes, Prince's, 1945; Cinderella, Palladium, 1948; Two Dozen Red Roses, Lyric, 1949; Peter Pan, Scala, 1953; Wedding in Paris, Hippodrome, 1954-56; Silver Wedding, Cambridge, 1957; The Amorous Prawn, Saville/Piccadilly, 1959-62; Never Too Late, Prince of Wales, 1964; The Circle, Savoy, 1965; Strike A Light!, Piccadilly, 1966; Let's All Go Down the Strand, Phoenix, 1967; Charlie Girl, Adelphi, 1969; Phil the Fluter, Palace, 1969; No Sex, Please-We're British, Strand, 1971-73. First New York appearance in Bitter Sweet, Ziegfeld Theatre, 1929; subsequently on Broadway in Sweet Aloes, Booth, 1936; Between the Devil, Majestic, 1937. Film début in silent production, The Luck of the Navy, 1927. Films include: One Heavenly Night (Hollywood), 1932; Waltz Time, 1933; Princess Charming, 1934; Evensong, 1935; The Night is Young (Hollywood), 1936; Make Mine A Million, 1959; Theatre of Death, 1967; Within and Without, 1969; Say Hello to Yesterday, 1971. Numerous broadcasts and television appearances. *Publication:* Boo, to my Friends (autobiography), 1958. *Address:* c/o Film Rights Ltd, Hammer House, 113 Wardour Street, W1V 4EH.

LAYFIELD, Sir Frank Henry Burland Willoughby, Kt 1976; QC 1967; *b* 9 Aug. 1921, Toronto; *s* of late H. D. Layfield; *m* 1965, Irene Patricia, *d* of Captain J. D. Harvey, RN (retired); one *s* one *d*. *Educ:* Sevenoaks Sch. Army, 1940-46. Called to the Bar, Gray's Inn, 1954, Bencher, 1974. Chairman: Inquiry into Greater London Development Plan, 1970-73; Cttee of Inquiry into Local Government Finance, 1974-76. *Publications:* (with A. E. Telling) Planning Applications, Appeals and Inquiries, 1953; (with A. E. Telling) Applications for Planning Payments, 1955; Engineering Contracts, 1956. *Recreations:* walking, tennis.

Address: 2 Mitre Court Buildings, Temple, EC4Y 7BX. *T:* 01-353 2246.

LAYMAN, Captain Herbert Francis Hope, DSO and Bar, 1940; RN; *b* 23 March 1899; *s* of Major F. H. Layman, 11th Hussars; *m* 1934, Elizabeth, *o d* of Rear-Admiral A. P. Hughes; one *s* one *d. Educ:* Haileybury. Grand Fleet, 1918; Fleet Signal Officer, Home Fleet, 1933-36. Director of Radio Equipment, Admiralty, 1949-51; Commanded HMS Hotspur, 1939-41; HMS Rajah, 1945-46; Royal Naval Air Station, Culham, Oxon, 1947-48; Chief of Staff to Commander-in-Chief, The Nore, 1951-53; retired, 1953. Vice-Pres., Tennis and Rackets Association. *Publications:* articles on Rackets. *Address:* Cleve House, Blewbury, Didcot, Oxon.

LAYTON, family name of **Baron Layton.**

LAYTON, 2nd Baron *cr* 1947, of Danehill; **Michael John Layton;** Executive Board Member, British Steel Corporation, 1967-77; Director, Economist Newspaper Ltd, since 1973; *b* 28 Sept. 1912; *s* of Walter Thomas, 1st Baron Layton, and Eleanor Dorothea (*d* 1959), *d* of Francis B. P. Osmaston; *S* father, 1966; *m* 1938, Dorothy, *d* of Albert Luther Cross, Rugby; one *s* one *d. Educ:* St Paul's Sch.; Gonville and Caius Coll., Cambridge. BA Mech. Scis Cantab, 1934; CEng, FIMechE. Student Apprentice, British Thomson Houston Co. Ltd, Rugby (specialised in Industrial Admin), 1934-37; Student Engr, Goss Printing Co., Chicago, 1937-39; Works Man. and Production Engr, Ibbotson Bros & Co. Ltd, Sheffield, Manufacturing 25-pounder armour piercing shot, 1939-43; Gen. Man., two armoured car production plants, Rootes Ltd, Birmingham, 1943-46; Mem. Control Commn for Germany in Metallurgy Br. and latterly in Econ. Sub-Commn, assisting at formation of OEEC, 1946-48; Head of Internat. Relations Dept of British Iron and Steel Fedn, 1948-55; Sales Controller, 1956, Dir, 1960, Asst Man. Dir, 1965-67, Man. Dir, 1967, The Steel Co. of Wales Ltd. *Heir: s* Hon. Geoffrey Michael Layton [*b* 18 July 1947; *m* 1969, Viviane (marr. diss. 1970), *y d* of François Cracco, Belgium]. *Address:* 6 Old Palace Terrace, The Green, Richmond, Surrey.
See also Hon. C. W. Layton.

LAYTON, Dr (Lt-Col) Basil Douglas Bailey, CD 1958; Principal Medical Officer, International Health, Department of National Health and Welfare, Canada, 1956-72; *b* 8 Aug. 1907; *s* of David Bailey Layton and Mary Eliza Merrick; *m* 1938, Marion Marie McDonald; three *s* one *d. Educ:* University of Toronto Medical Sch. (MD); Harvard University School of Public Health (MPH). Postgrad. medical study, 1931-36; medical practice, 1936-42. RCAMC, 1942-46: service in Canada, UK, and NW Europe. Dept of National Health and Welfare, 1946-72. Certified Specialist, Public Health, Royal Coll. of Phys and Surgs, Canada, 1951; postgrad. public health studies, Harvard School of Public Health, 1951-52. Canadian Army (Militia), RCAMC, 1949-58; retired Lt-Col, OC No 10 Medical Co., RCAMC(M). Mem. Canadian Delegn to 11th-24th World Health Assemblies, Head of Delegn to 15th, 16th; Pres., 25th World Health Assembly. Alternate to Canadian Mem., 1957-59, Mem. (Canada) 1962-65, 1968-71, Chm., 1963-64, of Exec. Board, WHO. Vice-President American Public Health Assoc., 1962-63; Vice-President, Harvard Public Health Alumni Assoc., 1961-63; President, 1963-64. Delta Omega (Beta Chapter) Hon. PH Fraternity, 1952. Fellow, American Public Health Assoc., 1957. France-Germany Star, Defence, Canada War Services and Victory Medals, 1946. *Publications:* scientific articles in Canadian Medical Assoc. Journal, Canadian Public Health Assoc. Journal, etc. *Address:* 1411 The Highlands, 515 St Laurent Boulevard, Ottawa, Ontario K1K 3X5. *T:* 749-5886.

LAYTON, Hon. Christopher Walter; Director, Computer Electronics, Telecommunications and Air Transport Equipment Manufacturing, Directorate-General of Internal Market and Industrial Affairs, Commission of the European Communities, since 1973; *b* 31 Dec. 1929; *s* of 1st Baron Layton; *m* 1st, 1952, Anneliese Margaret, *d* of Joachim von Thadden, Hanover (marr. diss. 1957); one *s* one *d*; 2nd, 1961, Margaret Ann, *d* of Leslie Moon, Molesey, Surrey; three *d. Educ:* Oundle; King's Coll., Cambridge. Intelligence Corps, 1948-49; ICI Ltd, 1952; The Economist Intelligence Unit, 1953-62; Economic Adviser to Liberal Party, 1962-69; Dir, Centre for European Industrial Studies, Bath Univ., 1968-71; Chef de Cabinet to Commissioner Spinelli, Commn of European Communities, 1971-73. *Publications:* Transatlantic Investment, 1966; European Advanced Technology, 1968; Cross-frontier Mergers in Europe 1970; (jtly) Industry and Europe, 1971; (jtly) Ten Innovations: International Study on Development Technology and the Use of Qualified Scientists and Engineers in Ten Industries, 1972. *Address:* Directorate-General of Internal Market and Industrial Affairs, Commission of the European Communities, 200 rue de la Loi, 1049 Brussels, Belgium.
See also Baron Layton.

LAYTON, Paul Henry; His Honour Judge Layton; a Circuit Judge (formerly Deputy Chairman, Inner London Quarter Sessions, since 1965); *b* Walsall, 11 July 1905; *s* of Frank George Layton, MRCS, LRCP, and Dorothea Yonge; *m* 1950, Frances Evelyn Weekes, Ottawa; two *s. Educ:* Epsom Coll.; St John's Coll., Cambridge (MA). Called to Bar, Inner Temple, 1929; Joined Oxford Circuit, 1930; Recorder of Smethwick, 1952-64; Dep. Chm., Staffs QS, 1955-65; Chm., Agricultural Land Tribunal, W Midlands, 1955-65; Mem., Mental Health Review Tribunal, Birmingham Region, 1960-65; Recorder of Walsall, 1964-65. Served War of 1939-45, AAF and RAF. *Recreation:* gardening. *Address:* 70A Leopold Road, SW19 7JQ. *T:* 01-946 0865.

LAYTON, Thomas Arthur; writer on wine and food; editor; wine merchant; *b* 31 Dec. 1910; *s* of late T. B. Layton, DSO, FRCS, and Edney Sampson; *m* 1935, Eleanor de P. Marshall; one *s* one *d. Educ:* Bradfield Coll., Berks. Vintners' Co. Travelling Schol., 1929. Public Relations Officer, Wine Trade, 1951. Pres., Circle of Wine Tasters, 1936. *Publications:* Choose Your Wine, 1940 (rewritten, 1959); Table for Two, 1942; Restaurant Roundabout, 1944; Five to a Feast, 1948; Wine's my Line, 1955; Choose Your Cheese, 1957; Winecraft, 1959; Wines and Castles of Spain, 1959; Wines of Italy, 1961; Vignes et Vins de France (trans.), 1962; Choose Your Vegetables, 1963; Modern Wines, 1964; A Year at The Peacock, 1964; Cheese and Cheese Cookery, 1967; Wines and Chateaux of the Loire, 1967; Cognac and Other Brandies, 1968; Wines and People of Alsace, 1969; The Way of St James, 1976. Editor: Wine Magazine, 1958-60; Anglo-Spanish Journal (Quarterly), 1960-. *Recreations:* wine, travelling in Spain. *Address:* Grindfield, Furners Green, Uckfield, Sussex. *T:* Chelwood Gate 244.

LAZARUS, Peter Esmond, CB 1975; a Deputy Secretary, Department of Transport, since 1976; *b* 2 April 1926; *er s* of late Kenneth M. Lazarus and Mary R. Lazarus (*née* Halsted); *m* 1950, Elizabeth Anne Marjorie Atwell, *e d* of late Leslie H. Atwell, OBE; three *s. Educ:* Westminster Sch.; Wadham Coll., Oxford (Open Exhibition). Served RA, 1945-48. Entered Ministry of Transport, 1949: Secretary, London and Home Counties Traffic Advisory Cttee, 1953-57; Private Secretary to Minister, 1961-62; Asst Sec., 1962; Under-Sec., 1968-70; Under-Sec., Treasury, 1970-72; Dep. Sec., DoE, 1973-76. Chm., Assoc. of First Div. Civil Servants, 1969-71. Chm., Council, Liberal Jewish Synagogue, St John's Wood, 1972-75. *Recreations:* music, reading. *Address:* 28 Woodside Avenue, N6 4SS. *T:* 01-883 3186. *Club:* Reform.

LAZARUS, Robert Stephen, QC; National Insurance Commissioner, since 1966; *b* 29 Oct. 1909; *s* of late Solomon and Mabel Lazarus; *m* 1938, Amelia (*née* Isaacs); two *d. Educ:* Marlborough Coll.; Caius Coll., Cambridge. Called to the Bar, at Lincoln's Inn, 1933; QC 1958. Member Legal Aid Cttee, 1961-66. Bencher, 1964. Served with RASC, 1940-46. *Recreations:* music, gardening. *Address:* 41 The Cliff, Roedean, Brighton, E Sussex BN2 5RF. *T:* Brighton 691162.

LAZELL, Henry George Leslie; Hon. President, Beecham Group Ltd (Chairman, 1958-68; President, 1968-70); Chairman, Beecham Incorporated, 1962-72; *b* 23 May 1903; *e s* of late Henry William Lazell and late Ada Louise Pickering; *m* 1928, Doris Beatrice Try; one *s. Educ:* LCC Elementary Sch. Left school at age of 13; various clerical employments until 1930; Accountant, Macleans Ltd, 1930; Secretary, 1930; Director and Secretary, 1936; Secretary, Beecham Group Ltd, 1939; Managing Director, Macleans Ltd, and Director, Beecham Group Ltd, 1940; Managing Director, Beecham Group Ltd, 1951; Director, ICI Ltd, 1966-68. Member of Association of Certified and Corporate Accountants, 1929, Fellow, 1965; Associate, Chartered Institute of Secretaries, 1930, Fellow, 1934. *Publication:* From Pills to Penicillin, 1975. *Recreations:* sailing, theatre-going, reading. *Address:* Tamarisk Cottage, Princess Hotel, PO Box 837, Hamilton, Bermuda. *Clubs:* Thirty, Royal Bermuda Yacht.

LAZENBY, Prof. Alec, FTS; Director, Grassland Research Institute, since 1977; *b* 4 March 1927; *s* of G. and E. Lazenby; *m* 1957, Ann Jennifer, *d* of R. A. Hayward; one *s* two *d. Educ:* Wath on Dearne Grammar Sch.; University Coll. of Wales, Aberystwyth. MSc (Wales), MA, PhD (Cantab). Scientific Officer, Welsh Plant Breeding Station, 1949-53; Demonstr in Agricultural Botany, 1953-58, Lectr in Agricultural Botany, 1958-65, Univ. of Cambridge; Fellow and Asst Tutor, Fitzwilliam Coll., Cambridge, 1962-65; Foundation Prof. of Agronomy, Univ. of New England, NSW, 1965-70, now

Professor Emeritus; Vice-Chancellor, Univ. of New England, Armidale, NSW, 1970-77. *Publications:* (jt Editor) Intensive Pasture Production, 1972; (jt Editor) Australian Field Crops, vol I, 1975; papers on: pasture plant breeding; agronomy; weed ecology, in various scientific jls. *Recreation:* golf. *Address:* Grassland Research Institute, Hurley, near Maidenhead, Berks. *T:* Littlewick Green 3631.

LEA, Christopher Gerald, MC; **His Honour Judge Christopher Lea;** a Circuit Judge, since 1972; *b* 27 Nov. 1917; *y s* of late George Percy Lea, Franche, Kidderminster, Worcs; *m* 1952, Susan Elizabeth Dorrien Smith, *d* of Major Edward Pendarves Dorrien Smith, Greatwood, Restronguet, Falmouth, Cornwall; two *s* one *d* (and one *d* decd). *Educ:* Charterhouse; RMC, Sandhurst. Commissioned into XX The Lancashire Fusiliers, 1937, and served with Regt in UK until 1939. Served War of 1939-45 (despatches, MC): with Lancashire Fusiliers, No 11 Special Air Service Bn, and Parachute Regt in France, Italy and Malaya. Post-war service in Indonesia, Austria and UK; retired, 1948. Called to Bar, Inner Temple, 1948; Oxford Circuit. Mem. Nat. Assistance Bd Appeal Tribunal (Oxford Area), 1961-63; Mem. Mental Health Review Tribunal (Oxford Region), 1962-68. A Metropolitan Magistrate, 1968-72; Dep. Chm., Berks QS, 1968-71. *Address:* Simms Farm House, Mortimer, Berks. *T:* Mortimer 332360. *Club:* English-Speaking Union.
See also Sir G. H. Lea.

LEA, David Edward; an Assistant General Secretary of the TUC, since 1977; *b* 2 Nov. 1937; *s* of Edward Cunliffe Lea and Lilian May Lea. *Educ:* Farnham Grammar Sch.; Christ's Coll., Cambridge (MA Econ). Economist Intelligence Unit, 1961; Economic Dept, TUC, 1964, Asst Sec., 1967, Sec. 1970. Jt Sec., TUC-Labour Party Liaison Cttee, 1972-. Member: Royal Commn on the Distribution of Income and Wealth, 1974-; Adv. Gp on Channel Tunnel and Cross-Channel Services; Cttee of Inquiry on Industrial Democracy, 1975-77; Energy Commn, 1977-; Retail Prices Index Adv. Cttee, 1977-; Expert Adviser, UN Commn on Transnational Corporations, 1977-. *Publications:* Trade Unionism, 1966; contrib. The Multinational Enterprise, 1971; Industrial Democracy (TUC). *Address:* 17 Ormonde Mansions, 106 Southampton Row, WC1B 4BP. *T:* 01-405 6237.

LEA, Sir Frederick (Measham), Kt 1966; CB 1960; CBE 1952 (OBE 1944); DSc; FRIC; Hon. FRIBA; Hon. FIOB; Director of Building Research, Department of Scientific and Industrial Research, 1946-65; *b* 10 Feb. 1900; *s* of late Measham Lea, CIE, OBE; *m* 1938, Eleanor, *d* of Frank James. *Educ:* King Edward VI Sch., Birmingham; Univ. of Birmingham. Admiralty, 1922-25; Building Research Station, 1925-65; Guest Research Associate, Nat. Bureau of Standards, Washington, DC, USA, 1928-29; Mem. of Council, Royal Inst. of Chemistry, 1943-46, 1948-51; Chm., Concrete Cttee, Internat. Commn on Large Dams, 1953-59; Pres. Internat. Council for Building Research, 1955-57, 1959-62; Pres., Internat. Union of Testing and Res. Labs for Materials and Structures, 1957-58. Hon. Mem., Amer. Concrete Inst. Walter C. Voss Award, American Society for Testing and Materials, 1964. *Publications:* Chemistry of Cement and Concrete (3rd edn 1970); Science and Building, 1971; (with J. T. Crennel) Alkaline Accumulators, 1928; many papers in scientific and technical journals. *Address:* Rivergarth, Bar Meadows, Malpas, Truro, Cornwall. *T:* Truro 3791. *Club:* Reform.

LEA, Lt-Gen. Sir George (Harris), KCB 1967 (CB 1964); DSO 1957; MBE 1950; Lieutenant, HM Tower of London, 1972-75; Managing Director, Martin-Scott & Co. Ltd, since 1975, *b* 28 Dec. 1912; *s* of late George Percy Lea, Franche, Kidderminster, Worcs; *m* 1948, Pamela Elizabeth, *d* of Brig. Guy Lovett-Tayleur; one *s* two *d*. *Educ:* Charterhouse; RMC, Sandhurst. Commnd into Lancashire Fusiliers, 1933, and served with Regt in UK, China and India until 1940. Served War of 1939-45 with Lancashire Fusiliers and Parachute Regt in India, N Africa, Italy and NW Europe. Post-war service: Regtl duty and on staff with Parachute Regt, Royal Marine Commando Bde and SAS Regt in UK, China and Malaya. Post-war staff appts in Allied Command Europe (SHAPE) and as Dep. Military Secretary (War Office); Comd 2nd Inf. Bde Group, 1957-60; GOC 42 (Lancs) Div. and North-West District, 1962-63; Comdr Forces, Northern Rhodesia and Nyasaland, 1963-64; Director of Borneo Operations and Commander Land Forces, Borneo, 1965-66; Head, British Defence Staff, Washington, 1967-70, retired. Col, The Lancashire Fusiliers, 1965-68; Col, The Royal Regt of Fusiliers, 1974-77 (Dep. Col for Lancashire, 1968-73). Brandt's Ltd, 1973-75. Dato Seri Setia, Order of Paduka Stia Negara, Brunei, 1965. *Address:* Malmaison, Les Ruisseaux, St Brelade, Jersey, Channel Islands. *Clubs:* Victoria, United (Jersey, CI).
See also C. G. Lea.

LEA, Rear-Adm. John Stuart Crosbie; Director General Naval Manpower and Training, since 1977; *b* 4 June 1923; *m* 1947, Patricia Anne Thoseby; one *s* two *d*. *Educ:* Boxgrove Sch., Guildford; Shrewsbury Sch.; RNEC, Keyham. Entered RN, 1941; Cruisers Sheffield and Glasgow, 1943; RNEC, 1942-45 (at sea, 1943); HMS Birmingham, 1945; entered Submarines, 1946; HMS/Ms Talent, Tireless, Aurochs, Explorer; Sen. Engr, HMS Forth (Depot Ship), 1952-53; on Staff, RNEC; psc 1958; Sqdn Engr Officer, 2nd Destroyer Sqdn and HMS Daring; Staff of CinC Portsmouth; Naval Staff in Ops Div., 1963-65; Engr Officer, HMS Centaur, 1966; Staff of Flag Officer Submarines; 1st Dep. Supt, Clyde Submarine Base, 1967-68; idc 1969; Dir of Naval Admin. Planning, 1970-71; Cdre HMS Nelson, 1972-75; Asst Chief of Fleet Support, 1976-77. Comdr 1957; Captain 1966; Rear-Adm. 1976. *Recreations:* walking, gardening. *Address:* c/o Lloyds Bank, Hayling Island, Hants.

LEA, Sir Thomas Claude Harris, 3rd Bt, *cr* 1892; *b* 13 April 1901; *s* of Sir Sydney Lea, 2nd Bt, and Mary Ophelia, *d* of Robert Woodward, of Arley Castle, Worcs; *S* father, 1946; *m* 1st, 1924, Barbara Katherine (*d* 1945), *d* of Albert Julian Pell, Wilburton Manor, Isle of Ely; one *s* four *d*; 2nd, 1950, Diana, *d* of Howard Thompson, Coton Hall, Bridgnorth, Salop. *Educ:* Lancing Coll.; Clare Coll., Cambridge. Served War of 1939-45: joined RNVR 1940 as Sub-Lieut; Lieut-Commander 1943; Commander, 1945; demobilised, 1946. *Recreations:* fishing, shooting, ornithology. *Heir:* s Thomas Julian Lea, [*b* 18 Nov. 1934; *m* 1970, Gerry Valerie, *d* of late Captain Gibson C. Fahnestock and of Mrs David Knightly, Brockenhurst, Hants; one *s* two *d*]. *Address:* Coneybury, Bayton, near Kidderminster, Worcs. *TA:* Bayton, Worcs. *T:* Clows Top 323.

LEACH, Archibald A.; *see* Grant, Cary.

LEACH, Arthur Gordon, CIE 1933; late Indian Civil Service; *b* 16 March 1885; *s* of A. F. Leach, Charity Commissioner; *m* 1914, Margaret Sydney Woods (*d* 1969); one *d* (one *s* decd). *Educ:* Bradfield Coll.; New Coll., Oxford. Entered Indian Civil Service 1909; served in Madras as Sub-Collector, Special Settlement Officer, Collector and Sec. to Government in the Public Works and Labour Dept; retd 1934; Mem. Legislative Assembly, Delhi, 1933; IARO attached 9th Gurkha Rifles, 1917-19. *Address:* Cuttmill Rise, Puttenham, Guildford. *T:* Elstead 3147.

LEACH, Bernard (Howell), CH 1973; CBE 1962; Founder and Director of The Leach Pottery, St Ives, Cornwall, since 1920; *b* 5 Jan. 1887; *o s* of Andrew John Leach, Puisne Judge, Straits Settlements; *m* 1st, 1909, Edith Muriel, *o d* of Dr William Evans Hoyle, Dir of the Nat. Museum of Wales, Cardiff; two *s* three *d*; 2nd, 1936, Laurie Cookes; one adopted *s*; 3rd, 1955, Janet Darnell, American potter. *Educ:* Beaumont Coll.; Slade Sch. of Art. Studied at Slade Sch. of Art, 1903. Practised etching; went to Japan, 1909, studied pottery under Kenzan VI; returned to England, started The Leach Pottery at St Ives, Cornwall; revisited Japan and Korea, 1934-35; exhibited widely in England and abroad, and taught many students; lectured across USA, sponsored by Inst. of Contemp. Art, 1950, 1953, 1960; revisited Japan as guest of Nat. Craft Soc. Exhibitions: with Shoji Hamada, at Gallerie de France, Paris, 1964; Caracas, 1966; Crane Kalman Gall., London, 1967; Tokyo, Osaka, Okinawa and London, 1969, 1971; London, Tokyo, Okayama, 1973. Visited Venezuela and Columbia on Lectures and Exhibns for Brit. Council, 1966. Retrospective Exhibns: Arts Council, London, 1961; Tokyo, 1961; V&A 1977. Amer. Ceramic Soc., Binns Medal for 1950; Japanese Foundn Award, 1974. Fellow, UCL, 1974. Hon. DLitt Exeter, 1961. Order of the Sacred Treasure (Japan), 2nd Class, 1966. Freedom of the Borough of St Ives, 1968. *Publications:* A Potter's Book, 1940; A Potter's Portfolio, 1951; Japan Diary (in Japanese), 1953-54; (Eng. trans A Potter in Japan, 1960); Kenzan and His Tradition, 1966; (with J. P. Hodin) Bernard Leach: a potter's work, 1967; Drawings, Verse & Belief, 1973; Shoji Hamada, Potter, 1976; Bernard Leach: the potter's challenge, 1976. *Recreations:* cricket, tennis. *Address:* The Leach Pottery, St Ives, Cornwall. *T:* St Ives 6398.

LEACH, Prof. Sir Edmund Ronald, Kt 1975; FBA 1972; MA Cantab, PhD London; Provost of King's College, Cambridge, since 1966; Professor of Social Anthropology, since 1972 (University Reader, 1957-72); *b* 7 Nov. 1910; *s* of late William Edmund Leach; *m* 1940, Celia Joyce, *d* of late Henry Stephen Guy Buckmaster; one *s* one *d*. *Educ:* Marlborough Coll.; Clare Coll., Cambridge (Exhibnr). Served War of 1939-45, Burma Army. Commercial Asst, Butterfield & Swire, Shanghai, 1932-37; Graduate Student, LSE, 1938-39, 1946-47; Lectr, later Reader, in Social Anthrop., LSE, 1947-53 (Hon. Fellow, 1974); Lectr, Cambridge, 1953-57. Anthropological Field Research: Formosa, 1937; Kurdistan, 1938; Burma, 1939-45; Borneo, 1947; Ceylon, 1954, 1956. Fellow of King's Coll., Cambridge,

1960-66; Fellow, Center for Advanced Study in Behavioral Sciences, Stanford, 1961; Sen. Fellow, Eton Coll., 1965-; Hon. Fellow, SOAS, 1974; Hinkley Vis. Prof., Johns Hopkins Univ., 1976. Hon. degrees: Chicago 1976, Brandeis 1976. Mem., Social Science Research Council, 1968-72; Trustee, British Museum, 1975-. Royal Anthrop. Institute: Vice-Pres., 1964-66, 1968-70, Pres., 1971-75 (Curl Essay Prize, 1951, 1957; Rivers Medal, 1958; Henry Myers Lectr, 1966); Chm. Assoc. of Social Anthropologists, 1966-70; Pres. British Humanist Assoc., 1970-72; Malinowski Lectr, 1959; Munro Lectr, 1963, 1977; Myers Lectr, 1966; Reith Lectr, 1967; Morgan Lectr, 1975; Radcliffe-Brown Lectr, 1976; Marett Lectr, 1977. Foreign Hon. Mem., Amer. Acad. of Arts and Sciences, 1968. *Publications:* Social and Economic Organization of the Rowanduz Kurds, 1940; Social Science Research in Sarawak, 1950; Political Systems of Highland Burma, 1954; Pul Eliya: A Village in Ceylon, 1961; Rethinking Anthropology, 1961; A Runaway World?, 1968; Genesis as Myth, 1970; Lévi-Strauss, 1970; Culture and Communication, 1976; Editor and contributor to various anthrop. symposia; numerous papers in Man, Journal of the Royal Anthropological Institute, American Anthropologist, South Western Journal of Anthropology, Daedalus, European Archives of Sociology, New Society, Current Anthropology, etc.; various articles in Encyclop. Britannica, Internat. Encyclop. of the Social Sciences. *Recreations:* ski-ing, travel. *Address:* Provost's Lodge, King's College, Cambridge CB2 1ST. *T:* Cambridge 50411. *Club:* United Oxford & Cambridge University.

LEACH, Adm. Sir Henry (Conyers), KCB 1977; Commander-in-Chief, Fleet, and Allied Commander-in-Chief, Channel and Eastern Atlantic, since 1977; *b* 18 Nov. 1923; 3rd *s* of Captain John Catterall Leach, MVO, DSO, RN and Evelyn Burrell Leach (*née* Lee), Yarner, Bovey Tracey, Devon; *m* 1958, Mary Jean, *yr d* of Adm. Sir Henry McCall, *qv*; two *d. Educ:* St Peter's Court, Broadstairs; RNC Dartmouth. Cadet 1937; served in: cruiser Mauritius, S Atlantic and Indian Ocean, 1941-42; battleship Duke of York, incl. Scharnhorst action, 1943-45; destroyers in Mediterranean, 1945-46; spec. Gunnery, 1947; various gunnery appts, 1948-51; Gunnery Officer, cruiser Newcastle, Far East, 1953-55; staff appts, 1955-59; comd destroyer Dunkirk, 1959-61; comd frigate Galatea as Captain (D) 27th Sqdn and Mediterranean, 1965-67; Dir of Naval Plans, 1968-70; comd Commando Ship Albion, 1970; Asst Chief of Naval Staff (Policy), 1971-73; Flag Officer First Flotilla, 1974-75; Vice-Chief of Defence Staff, 1976-77. Comdr 1955; Captain 1961; Rear-Adm. 1971; Vice-Adm., 1974; Adm., 1977; psc 1952; jssc 1961. *Recreations:* fishing, gardening. *Address:* Admiralty House, Northwood, Mddx HA6 3HP. *T:* Northwood 24604; Wonston Lodge, Wonston, Winchester, Hants. *T:* Sutton Scotney 327.

LEACH, Norman, CMG 1964; Under-Secretary, Foreign and Commonwealth Office (Overseas Development Administration), 1970-72; *b* 8 March 1912; *s* of W. M. Leach. *Educ:* Ermysted's Gram. Sch., Skipton in Craven, Yorks; St Catharine's Coll., Cambridge (Scholar). 1st Class Hons, Pts I and II English Tripos, 1933 and 1934; Charles Oldham Shakespeare Schol., 1933. Asst Principal, Inland Revenue Dept, 1935; Under-Secretary: Ministry of Pensions and National Insurance, 1958-61; Dept of Technical Co-operation, 1961-64; ODM, 1964-70. *Address:* Low Bank, 81 Gargrave Road, Skipton in Craven, North Yorks. *T:* Skipton 3719.

LEACH, Sir Ronald (George), GBE 1976 (CBE 1944); Kt 1970; FCA; Senior Partner in firm of Peat, Marwick, Mitchell & Co., Chartered Accountants, 1966-77; *b* 21 Aug. 1907; *s* of William T. Leach, 14 Furze Croft, Hove; *m* Margaret Alice Binns. *Educ:* Alleyn's. Dep. Financial Sec. to Ministry of Food, Sept. 1939-June 1946. Member: Cttee on Coastal Flooding, 1953; Inquiry into Shipping, 1967-70; National Theatre Board, 1972-; Chairman: Consumer Cttee for GB (Agricultural Marketing Acts, 1931-49), 1958-67; Accounting Standards Steering Cttee, 1970-76. Pres. Inst. of Chartered Accountants in England and Wales, 1969-70. Hon. LLD Lancaster, 1977. *Address:* Waterlane Farm, Headcorn, Kent. *T:* Headcorn 890249; 37 Lowndes Street, W1. *T:* 01-235 8670. *Clubs:* Athenæum, Beefsteak.

LEADBEATER, Howell; Controller of Supplies, 1968-76, and Board Member, Property Services Agency, Department of the Environment, 1972-76, retired 1976; *b* 22 Oct. 1919; *s* of late Thomas and Mary Ann Leadbeater; *m* 1946, Mary Elizabeth Roberts; two *s* one *d. Educ:* Pontardawe Grammar Sch.; University College of Swansea. Army Service, 1940-46: Adjt 11th E African Divl Signals. Min. of Works, later MPBW and Dept of Environment: Asst Principal, 1948; Asst Sec., 1958; Under Sec., 1968; Under/Dep. Sec., 1973. *Address:* Milk Wood, Stokesheath Road, Oxshott, Surrey. *T:* 01-970 2614.

LEADBETTER, David Hulse, CB 1958; Assistant Under-Secretary of State, Department of Education and Science, 1964-68 (Under Secretary, Ministry of Education, 1953-64); *b* 14 Aug. 1908; *s* of late Harold Leadbetter; *m* 1933, Marion, *d* of late Horatio Ballantyne, FRIC, FCS; two *s* two *d* (and one *d* decd.). *Educ:* Whitgift; Merton Coll., Oxford. Entered Board of Education, 1933. *Address:* Old Mill House, Yetminster, Sherborne, Dorset. *T:* Yetminster 872216.

LEADBITTER, Edward; MP (Lab) The Hartlepools, since 1964; *b* 18 June 1919; *s* of Edward Leadbitter, Easington, Durham; *m* 1940, Phyllis Irene Mellin, Bristol; one *s* one *d. Educ:* State Schs; Teachers' Training Coll. Served War, 1939-45, with RA; commissioned 1943; War Office Instructor in Gunnery. Joined Labour Party, 1938; Pres., Hartlepools Labour Party, 1958-62. Became Teacher. Member: West Hartlepool Borough Council; NUPE; Town Planning and Finance Cttees; Estimates Cttee, 1966-69; Select Cttee on Science and Technology, 1970-; Chairman; Industrial Development Cttee; Parly Lab. Party Ports Cttee, 1974. Organizer of Exhibition on History of Labour Movement, 1956. *Address:* 30 Hylton Road, Hartlepool, Cleveland.

LEADBITTER, Jasper Michael, OBE 1960; HM Diplomatic Service, retired 1973; Secretary, Royal Humane Society, since 1974; *b* 25 Sept. 1912; *s* of late Francis John Graham Leadbitter, Warden, Northumberland, and Teresa del Riego Leadbitter; *m* 1942, Anna Lisa Hahne Johansson, Stockholm, Sweden; one *d. Educ:* Shrewsbury and Dresden. Asst Press Attaché, Stockholm, 1938-45, Press Attaché, 1945-47; established in Diplomatic Service, 1947; Foreign Office, 1947; Panama, 1948; Actg Consul-Gen., Detroit, 1952; First Sec. (Information), Buenos Aires, 1953 and Helsinki, 1956; Foreign Office, 1958; HM Consul and, later, 1st Sec. at Léopoldville, Congo, Dec. 1959 and at Brazzaville, 1961; Dep. Permanent UK Representative to Council of Europe and Consul at Strasbourg, March 1962; HM Consul-Gen., Berlin, Nov. 1963-66; Consul, Palermo, 1966-69; Consul-Gen., Hanover, 1969-73. *Recreation:* travel. *Address:* Oak Lodge, Bayhall Road, Tunbridge Wells, Kent. *Clubs:* Hurlingham, East India, Devonshire, Sports and Public Schools.

LEAHY, John Henry Gladstone, CMG 1973; HM Diplomatic Service; Assistant Under Secretary of State, Foreign and Commonwealth Office, since 1977; *b* 7 Feb. 1928; *s* of late William Henry Gladstone and late Ethel Leahy; *m* 1954, Elizabeth Anne Pitchford; two *s* two *d. Educ:* Tonbridge Sch.; Clare Coll., Cambridge; Yale University. RAF, 1950-52; FO, 1952-54 (Asst Private Sec. to Minister of State, 1953-54); 3rd, later 2nd Sec., Singapore, 1955-57; FO, 1957-58; 2nd, later 1st Sec., Paris, 1958-62; FO, 1962-65; Head of Chancery, Tehran, 1965-68; Counsellor, FCO, 1969; Head of Personnel Services Dept, 1969-70; Head of News Dept, FCO, 1971-73; Counsellor and Head of Chancery, Paris, 1973-75; seconded as Under Sec., NI Office, 1975-76. Member of Livery, Skinners' Co., 1954. *Recreations:* golf, tennis, squash. *Address:* c/o Personnel Records Section, Foreign and Commonwealth Office, SW1; 50 Stanford Road, W8 5PZ. *T:* 01-937 6948. *Clubs:* Royal Automobile; Royal Wimbledon Golf.

LEAKE, Prof. Bernard Elgey, PhD, DSc, FGS; Head of Department of Geology, and Keeper of Geological Collections in Hunterian Museum, University of Glasgow, since 1974; *b* 29 July 1932; *s* of late Norman Sidney Leake and Clare Evelyn (*née* Walgate); *m* 1955, Gillian Dorothy Dobinson; five *s. Educ:* Wirral Grammar Sch., Bebington, Cheshire; Liverpool Univ. (1st Cl. Hons BSc, PhD); Bristol Univ. (DSc 1974). Leverhulme post-doctoral Res. Fellow, Liverpool Univ., 1955-57; Asst Lectr, subseq. Lectr in Geology, Bristol Univ., 1957-68, Reader in Geol., 1968-74; Res. Associate, Berkeley, Calif, 1966. Sec., Cttee on amphibole nomenclature, Internat. Mineral Assoc., 1968-; Member: Council, Mineral Soc., 1965-68; Council, Geol Soc., 1971-74 (Lyell Medal, 1977); publication cttees, Mineral and Geol Socs, 1970-. Editor: Mineralogical Magazine, 1970-; Jl of Geol Soc., 1973 and 1974. *Publications:* A catalogue of analysed calciferous and sub-calciferous amphiboles together with their nomenclature and associated minerals, 1968 (Geol Soc. America Special Paper 98); about 60 papers in geol, mineral and geochem. jls on geol. of Connemara, study of amphiboles, X-ray fluorescence anal. of rocks and use of geochem. in identifying origins of highly metamorphosed rocks. *Recreations:* walking, reading, theatre, gardening, museums, genealogy, study of railway and agricultural development. *Address:* Geology Department, The University, Glasgow G12 8QQ. *T:* 041-339 8855, ext. 7435; 2 Garngaber Avenue, Lenzie, Kirkintilloch, Dunbartonshire.

LEAKEY, Maj.-Gen. Arundell Rea, CB 1967; DSO 1945; MC 1941 (Bar 1942); Director and Secretary, Wolfson Foundation, since 1968; *b* 30 Dec. 1915; parents British; *m* 1950, Muriel Irene Le Poer Trench; two *s. Educ:* Weymouth Coll.; Royal Military Coll., Sandhurst. Command of 5th Royal Tank Regt, 1944; Instructor at Staff Coll., Camberley, 1951-52; Comdr, 1st Arab Legion Armoured Car Regt, 1954-56; Instructor (Col), Staff Coll., Camberley, 1958-60; Comdr, 7th Armoured Brigade, 1961-63; Dir-Gen. of Fighting Vehicles, 1964-66; GOC Troops in Malta and Libya, 1967-68; retired 1968. Czechoslovakian Military Cross, 1944. *Recreations:* squash, tennis. *Address:* c/o Williams & Glyn's Bank Ltd, Kirkland House, Whitehall, SW1. *Club:* Naval and Military.

LEAKEY, Prof. Felix William; Professor of French Language and Literature, Bedford College, London, since 1973; *b* 29 June 1922; *s* of Hugh Leakey and Kathleen Leakey (*née* March); *m* 1947, Daphne Joan Sleep (*née* Salter); one *s* two *d. Educ:* St Christopher Sch., Letchworth; Queen Mary Coll., London. BA, PhD (London). Asst Lectr, then Lectr in French, Univ. of Sheffield, 1948-54; Univ. of Glasgow: Lectr in French, 1954-64; Sen. Lectr, 1964-68; Reader, 1968-70; Prof. of French, Univ. of Reading, 1970-73. Carnegie Research Fellow, 1961-62; Leverhulme Research Fellow, 1971-72. Assoc. of University Profs of French: Hon. Sec., 1972-73; Jt Hon. Sec., 1973-75; Vice-Chm., 1975-76; Chm., 1976-77. *Publications:* Baudelaire and Nature, 1969; (ed, jtly) The French Renaissance and its Heritage: essays presented to Alan Boase, 1968; Sound and Sense in French Poetry (Inaugural Lecture, with readings on disc), 1975; (ed jtly) Samuel Beckett, Drunken Boat, 1977; contribs to: French Studies; Rev. d'hist. litt. de la France; Rev. de litt. comparée; Rev. des sciences humaines; Etudes baudelairiennes; etc. *Recreations:* foxhunting, beagling, riding, Association football, music. *Address:* Department of French, Bedford College (University of London), Regent's Park, NW1 4NS. *T:* 01-486 4400.

LEAKEY, Mary Douglas, FBA 1973; Director, Olduvai Gorge Excavations; *b* 6 Feb. 1913; *d* of Erskine Edward Nicol and Cecilia Marion Frere; *m* 1936, Louis Seymour Bazett Leakey, FBA (*d* 1972); three *s. Educ:* privately. Geological Soc. of London, Prestwich Medal and Nat. Geographic Soc. Hubbard Medal (jointly with late L. S. B. Leakey); Hon. DSc Witwatersrand, 1968; Hon DSSc Yale, 1976. *Publications:* Olduvai Gorge, vol. 3, Excavation in Beds I and II, 1971; various papers in Nature and other scientific jls. *Recreations:* reading, game watching. *Address:* c/o National Museum, Box 30239, Nairobi, Kenya.

See also R . E . F . Leakey .

LEAKEY, Richard Erskine Frere; Director, National Museums of Kenya, since 1974 (Administrative Director, 1968-74); *b* 19 Dec. 1944; *s* of late Louis Seymour Bazett Leakey, FBA, and of Mary Leakey, *qv; m* 1970, Dr Meave (*née* Epps); three *d. Educ:* Nairobi Primary Sch.; Lenana (formerly Duke of York) Sch., Nairobi. Self employed tour guide and animal trapper, 1961-65; Dir, Photographic Safaris in E Africa, 1965-68. Co-leader, palaeontol expedn to Lake Natron, Tanzania, 1963-64; expedn to Lake Baringo, Kenya, in search of early man, 1966; Co-leader, Internation Omo River Expedn, Ethiopia, in search of early man, 1967; Leader, E Turkana (formerly E Rudolf) Res. Proj. (multi-nat., interdisciplinary sci. consortium investigation of Plio/Pleistocene, Kenya's northern Rift Valley), 1968–. Chairman: Wildlife Clubs of Kenya Assoc.; Foundn for Res. into Origin of Man (FROM); Trustee, E African Wild Life Soc. *Publications:* (contrib.) General History of Africa, vol. 1, 1976; articles on palaeontol. in Nature, Jl of World Hist., Science, Amer. Jl of Phys. and Anthropol. *Address:* PO Box 40658, Nairobi, Kenya.

LEAN, David, CBE 1953; film director; *b* 25 March 1908; *s* of late Francis William le Blount Lean and Helena Annie Tangye; *m* ; one *s; m* 1949, Ann Todd, *qv* (marr. diss. 1957); *m* 1960, Mrs Leila Matkar. *Educ:* Leighton Park Sch., Reading. Entered film industry as number board boy, 1928; edited and did commentary for Gaumont Sound News and British Movietone News; then edited Escape Me Never, Pygmalion, 49th Parallel, etc. Co-directed, with Noel Coward, In Which We Serve. *Directed:* This Happy Breed, Blithe Spirit, Brief Encounter, Great Expectations, Oliver Twist, The Passionate Friends, Madeleine, The Sound Barrier (British Film Academy Award, 1952), Hobson's Choice, Summer Madness (Amer. title Summertime), The Bridge on the River Kwai, Lawrence of Arabia (US Academy Award, 1963, Italian silver ribbon, 1964), Doctor Zhivago, Ryan's Daughter. Officier de l'Ordre des Arts et des Lettres, France, 1968.

LEAPER, Prof. Robert Anthony Bernard, CBE 1975; Professor of Social Administration, University of Exeter, since 1970; *b* 7 June 1921; *s* of William Bambrick Leaper and Gertrude

Elizabeth (*née* Taylor); *m* 1950, Elizabeth Arno; two *s* one *d. Educ:* Ratcliffe Coll., Leicester; St John's Coll., Cambridge (MA); Balliol Coll., Oxford (MA). Dipl. Public and Social Admin. (Oxon). Coal miner, 1941-44. Warden, St John Bosco Youth Centre, Stepney, 1945-47; Cadet officer, Civil Service, 1949-50; Co-operative Coll., Stanford Hall, 1950-56; Principal, Social Welfare Trng Centre, Zambia, 1956-59; Lectr, then Sen. Lectr, then Acting Dir, Social Admin., UC, Swansea, 1960-70. Exec., later Vice-Chm., Nat. Council of Social Service, 1964-77; Pres., European Region, Internat. Council on Social Welfare, 1971-78; Regional Chm., Job Creation Programme and NHS Staff Appeal Tribunal, 1975-77. Editor, Social and Economic Administration. Médaille de l'Ecole Nationale de Santé, France, 1975. *Publications:* Communities and Social Change, 1966; Community Work, 1969, 2nd edn 1972. *Recreations:* walking, railways, wine. *Address:* Birchcote, New North Road, Exeter. *T:* Exeter 72565. *Club:* University Staff (Exeter).

LEAR, Cyril James; Editorial Manager, News Group Newspapers Ltd, 1974-76 (Editor, News of the World, 1970-73); *b* 9 Sept. 1911; *s* of R. H. Lear, Plymouth; *m* Marie Chatterton; five *s* one *d. Educ:* Hoe Grammar Sch., Plymouth. Served War of 1939-45: Rifleman, Queen's Westminsters; Major, Royal Berks Regt. Western Morning News, 1928-32; Torquay Times, 1932-34; Daily Mail, 1934-38; Daily Telegraph, 1938-39; News of the World, 1946-70: Features Editor, Asst Editor, Dep. Editor. *Address:* c/o News Group Newspapers Ltd, 30 Bouverie Street, EC4. *T:* 01-353 3030.

LEARMONT, Captain Percy Hewitt, CIE 1946; RIN retired; *b* 25 June 1894; *s* of late Capt. J. Learmont, OBE, DL, JP, Penrith and Skinburness, Cumberland; *m* 1926, Doris Orynthia, *e d* of E. G. Hartley, Dunoon, Argyll; one *s* one *d. Educ:* HMS Conway. Served European War, HMS Alsatian, 1914-17; HMS Ceres, 1917-19; joined RIN, 1919; Comdr, 1935; Extended Defence Officer, Calcutta, 1939-41; Capt. Superintendent, HMI Dockyard, Bombay, 1941-42; in command HMIS Bahadur, 1942-43; Capt., 1942; Naval Officer-in-Charge, Calcutta, 1943-45; in command HMIS Akbar, 1945; HMIS Kakauri, 1946; retired, 1946. *Address:* Crofters, Curry Rivel, Langport, Somerset. *T:* Curry Rivel 317. *Club:* Royal Commonwealth Society.

LEAROYD, Wing Comdr Roderick Alastair Brook, VC 1940; RAF; *b* 5 Feb. 1913; *s* of late Major Reginald Brook Learoyd and Marjorie Scott Boadle. *Educ:* Wellington Coll. *Address:* 11 Baronsmere Court, Manor Road, Barnet, Hertfordshire EN5 2JZ.

LEARY, Brian Leonard; Senior Prosecuting Counsel to the Crown at the Central Criminal Court, since 1971; *b* 1 Jan. 1929; *o s* of late A. T. Leary; *m* 1965, Myriam Ann Bannister, *d* of Kenneth Bannister, CBE, Mexico City. *Educ:* King's Sch. Canterbury; Wadham Coll., Oxford. MA Oxon. Called to the Bar, Middle Temple, 1953; Harmsworth Scholar. *Recreations:* travel, sailing, growing herbs. *Address:* The Old Rectory, Ightham, Kent. *T:* Borough Green 882608; 5 Paper Buildings, Temple, EC4. *T:* 01-353 7811.

LEARY, Leonard Poulter, CMG 1973; MC 1917; QC (New Zealand) 1953; retired; *b* 1891; *s* of Richard Leary and Florence Lucy Giesen; *m* ; three *s* two *d* (and one *d* decd). *Educ:* Palmerston North High Sch.; Wellington Coll.; Victoria and Auckland University Colleges (LLB). Called to the Bar, New Zealand, 1920. Served European War, 1914-18: Samoan Exped. Force (NZR), 1914; Special Reserve RFA Egypt and France, 1914-18 (Captain, MC); served War of 1939-45: NZ Home Forces; Lt-Col RNZA, Actg CRA, 1944. Mem., later Chm., Disciplinary Cttee of NZ Law Soc., 1948-74; Chairman: Lake Weed Control Soc.; Okere Ratepayers' Assoc.; Manuperua Baths Cttee. *Publications:* New Zealanders in Samoa, 1918; Tutankhamen (musical play), 1923; Abbess of Whitby (musical play), 1924. *Recreations:* music, gardening, fishing. *Address:* RD4 Otaramarae, Rotorua, New Zealand. *T:* Okere Falls 387. *Clubs:* Northern, Officers' (Auckland).

LEASK, Lt-Gen. Sir Henry (Lowther Ewart Clark), KCB 1970 (CB 1967); DSO 1945; OBE 1957 (MBE 1945); GOC Scotland and Governor of Edinburgh Castle, 1969-72, retired; *b* 30 June 1913; *s* of Rev. James Leask, MA; *m* Zoë de Camborne, *d* of Col W. P. Paynter, DSO, RHA; one *s* two *d* . 2nd Lt Royal Scots Fusiliers, 1936. Served War of 1939-45 in Mediterranean and Italy; GSO 1942; Bde Major Inf. Bde 1943; 2nd in Comd and CO, 8 Bn Argyll and Sutherland Highlanders, 1944-45; Comd 1st Bn London Scottish, 1946-47; Gen. Staff Mil. Ops, WO, 1947-49; Instr Staff Coll., 1949-51; Comd 1st Bn The Parachute Regt, 1952-54; Asst Military Sec. to Sec. of State for War, 1955-57; Comdt, Tactical Wing Sch. of Inf., 1957-58; Comd Infantry

Bde, 1958-61; idc 1961; Dep. Mil. Sec. to Sec. of State for War, 1962-64; GOC 52 Lowland Div., 1964-66; Dir of Army Training, MoD (Army), 1966-69. Brig. 1961, Maj.-Gen. 1964, Lt-Gen. 1969. Col of the Royal Highland Fusiliers, 1964-69; Col Comdt, Scottish Div. of Infantry, 1968-72. *Recreations:* shooting and fishing. *Address:* Duchray House, Aberfoyle, Perthshire. *T:* Aberfoyle 355. *Clubs:* Army and Navy; New (Edinburgh).

LEASOR, (Thomas) James; author; Director: Pagoda Films Ltd, since 1959; Jason Love Ltd, since 1964; Elm Tree Books Ltd, 1970-73; *b* 20 Dec. 1923; *s* of late Richard and Christine Leasor, Erith, Kent; *m* 1951, Joan Margaret Bevan, Barrister-at-law, *o d* of late Roland S. Bevan, Crowcombe, Somerset; three *s. Educ:* City of London Sch.; Oriel Coll., Oxford. Kentish Times, 1941-42. Served in Army in Burma, India, Malaya, 1942-46, Capt. Royal Berks Regt. Oriel Coll., Oxford, 1946-48, BA 1948; MA 1952; edited The Isis. On staff Daily Express, London, 1948-55, as reporter, then columnist (William Hickey), foreign correspondent, feature writer. Contrib. to many American and British magazines, newspapers and periodicals; scriptwriter for TV series The Michaels in Africa. FRSA. OStJ. *Publications: novels:* Not Such a Bad Day, 1946; The Strong Delusion, 1951; NTR-Nothing to Report, 1955; Passport to Oblivion, 1964; Spylight, 1966; Passport in Suspense, 1967; Passport for a Pilgrim, 1968; They Don't Make Them Like That Any More, 1969; A Week of Love, 1969; Never had a Spanner on Her, 1970; Love-all, 1971; Follow the Drum, 1972; Host of Extras, 1973; Mandarin Gold, 1973; The Chinese Widow, 1974; Jade Gate, 1976. *non-fiction:* Author by Profession, The Monday Story, 1951; Wheels to Fortune, The Serjeant Major, 1954; The Red Fort; (with Kendal Burt) The One That Got Away, 1956; The Millionth Chance, 1957; War at the Top, 1959; (with Peter Eton) Conspiracy of Silence, 1959; Bring Out Your Dead, 1961; Rudolf Hess: The Uninvited Envoy, 1961; Singapore: The Battle that changed the World, 1968; Green Beach, 1975; No Medals, 1977. *Recreation:* vintage cars. *Address:* Swallowcliffe Manor, Salisbury, Wilts. *T:* Tisbury 248; Casa do Zimbro, Praia da Luz, Lagos, Algarve, Portugal. *Club:* Garrick.

LEATHAM, Dr Aubrey (Gerald), FRCP; Physician: St George's Hospital since 1954; National Heart Hospital since 1956; Dean, Institute of Cardiology, 1962-69; *b* 23 Aug. 1920; *s* of Dr H. W. Leatham (*d* 1973), Godalming and Kathleen Pelham Burn (*d* 1971), Nosely Hall, Leicester; *m* 1954, Judith Augustine Savile Freer; one *s* three *d. Educ:* Charterhouse; Trinity Hall, Cambridge; St Thomas' Hospital. BA Cambridge 1941; MB, BChir 1944; MRCP 1945; FRCP 1957. House Phys., St Thomas' Hosp., 1944; RMO, Nat. Heart Hosp., 1945; Phys., RAMC, 1946-47; Sherbrook Research Fellow, Cardiac Dept, and Sen. Registrar, London Hosp., 1948-50; Asst Dir, Inst. of Cardiology, 1951-54. Goulstonian Lectr, RCP, 1958. R. T. Hall Travelling Prof., Australia and NZ, 1963. Member: Brit. Cardiac Soc.; Sociedad Peruana de Cardiologia, 1966; Sociedad Colombiana de Cardiologia, 1966. Royal Order of Bhutan, 1966. *Publications:* Auscultation of the Heart and Phonocardiography, 1970; articles in Lancet, British Heart Jl, etc, on auscultation of the heart and phonocardiography, artificial pacemakers, coronary artery disease, etc. *Recreations:* ski-ing and ski-touring, mountain walking, tennis, racquets, gardening, photography. *Address:* 75 Albert Drive, SW19 6LB. *T:* 01-788 5759; 45 Wimpole Street, W1M 7D9. *T:* 01-935 5295; Rookwood Lane House, West Wittering, Sussex.

LEATHART, Air Cdre James Anthony, CB 1960; DSO 1940; Manager, Machinery Division, Cleanacres Ltd; *b* 5 Jan. 1915; *s* of P. W. Leathart, BSc, MD, Ear, Nose and Throat Specialist, Liverpool; *m* 1939, E. L. Radcliffe, Birkenhead; two *s* one *d. Educ:* St Edward's, Oxford; Liverpool Univ. Joined Auxiliary Air Force (610 County of Chester Squadron), 1936; transferred RAF, 1937; Chief of Staff Headquarters, 12 Group, RAF, 1959-61; Dir of Operational Requirements, Air Ministry, 1961-62, retd. Oct. 1962. *Recreations:* fly-fishing, motoring, ornithology, gardening. *Address:* Wortley Farmhouse, Wotton-under-Edge, Glos. *T:* Wotton-under-Edge 2312.

LEATHEM, John Gaston, JP; Headmaster of Taunton School, 1945-66; *b* 14 May 1906; *s* of late J. G. Leathem, MA, ScD, fellow and senior bursar of St John's Coll., Cambridge, and Annie Muir (*née* McMullan), Belfast. *Educ:* Marlborough Coll.; St John's Coll., Cambridge. Pres. Cambridge Union, 1929. Housemaster, St Lawrence Coll., Ramsgate, 1929; Asst Master, Marlborough Coll., 1932; Headmaster, King Edward VII Sch.; King's Lynn, 1939; Marlborough Town Council, 1938; JP King's Lynn, 1941; Somerset Education Cttee, 1946-55; Somerset County Council, 1952-55. JP Somerset 1953; Chm. Juvenile Bench, 1959-68; Chm., Bench, 1968-76. *Recreations:* foreign travel, walking. *Address:* 8 Parkfield Road, Taunton,

Somerset. *T:* Taunton 5385. *Clubs:* Royal Over-Seas League; Somerset County (Taunton); Jesters.

LEATHER, Sir Edwin (Hartley Cameron), KCMG 1974; KCVO 1975; Kt 1962; Governor and C-in-C of Bermuda, 1973-77; author, writer for television and broadcaster; *b* 22 May 1919; *s* of Harold H. Leather, MBE, Hamilton, Canada, and Grace C. Leather (*née* Holmes); *m* 1940, Sheila A. A. (CStJ), *d* of Major A. H. Greenlees, Hamilton; two *d. Educ:* Trinity College Sch., Canada; Royal Military Coll., Kingston, Canada. Served War of 1939-45 with Canadian Army, UK and in Europe, 1940-45. Contested (C) South Bristol, 1945; MP (C) N Somerset, 1950-64. Director: William Baird Ltd, 1966-73; William Baird Textiles, 1969-73; Hill Samuel & Co. Ltd, 1969-73 (W 3d Chm). Exec. Cttee: British Commonwealth Producers Organisation, 1960-63; British Caribbean Assoc.; Chairman: Horder Centres for Arthritics, 1962-65; Nat. Union, Cons and Unionist Assocs, 1969-70 (Chm., 1969-70); Mem., Nat. Executive Cttee, and Central Board of Finance, Conservative Party, 1963-70; Dep. Chm., Yehudi Menuhin Sch. Canadian Legion rep. on Exec. Cttee of Brit. Commonwealth Ex-Servicemen's League, 1954-63; Pres., Institute of Marketing, 1963-67. Chm., Bath Festival Soc., 1960-65. Lay reader, in Church of England. Mem. Council, Imp. Soc. of Knights Bachelor, 1969-. Dep. Chm., English Speaking Union, 1973. FRSA 1969. KStJ 1974. Nat. Inst Social Sciences Gold Medal for 1977, NY. Hon. Citizen, Kansas City, USA. Medal of Merit, Royal Canadian Legion. *Address:* Mangrove View, South Road, Paget, Bermuda. *Clubs:* Carlton; Hamilton (Hamilton); Royal Bermuda Yacht.

LEATHER, Ted; *see* Leather, Sir E. H. C.

LEATHERLAND, Baron, *cr* 1964, of Dunton (Life Peer); **Charles Edward Leatherland,** OBE 1951; Treasurer and Member of Council, University of Essex, from foundation until 1973; *b* 18 April 1898; *e s* of John Edward Leatherland, Churchover, Warwicks; *m* 1922, Mary Elizabeth, *d* of Joseph Henry Morgan, Shareshill, Staffs; one *s* one *d. Educ:* Harborne, Birmingham; University Extension Courses. Asst Editor, Daily Herald, until retirement, 1963. Served European War, 1914-19 (despatches, MSM); enlisted, 1914, aged 16; served in France, Belgium, Germany; Company Sgt Major, Royal Warwicks Regt; Essex TA Assoc., 1946-68, and E Anglian TA Assoc., 1968. Chm., Essex County Council, 1960-61 (Vice-Chm. 1952-55 and 1958-60); CA Essex, 1946-68. Dep. Chm., Epping Magistrates Bench. JP (Essex) 1944-70; DL Essex, 1963-75. Mem. Bd of Basildon Development Corporation, 1967-71. Addtl Mem., Monopolies Commn, to consider newspaper mergers, 1969. Chm., E Counties Regional Council of the Labour Party, 1950-66. DUniv. Essex, 1973. *Publications:* (part author) The Book of the Labour Party, 1925; Labour Party pamphlets; contribs on local govt affairs in Municipal Jl and general press; essays on economic and social subjects (4 Prince of Wales gold medals, 1923 and 1924). *Recreations:* formerly fox hunting, now walking. *Address:* 19 Starling Close, Buckhurst Hill, Essex. *T:* 01-504 3164.

LEATHERS, family name of Viscount Leathers.

LEATHERS, 2nd Viscount, *cr* 1954; **Frederick Alan Leathers;** Baron Leathers, 1941; Director: National Westminster Bank, Outer London Region; *b* 4 April 1908; *er s* of 1st Viscount Leathers, PC, CH, LLD; *S* father, 1965; *m* 1940, Elspeth Graeme, *yr d* of late Sir Thomas (Alexander) Stewart; two *s* two *d. Educ:* Brighton Coll.; Emmanuel Coll., Cambridge (MA (hons) in Economics). Mem. of Baltic Exchange. Director: Wm Cory & Son Ltd, 1929-72 (Chm.); Cory Mann George Ltd, 1941-72 (Chm.); Cory Ship Towage Ltd, 1941-72 (Chm.); Smit & Cory International Port Towage Ltd, 1970-72 (Chm.); Hull Blyth & Co. Ltd, 1949-72 (Chm.); Rea Ltd, 1941-72 (Chm.); St Denis Shipping Co. Ltd, 1957-72 (Chm.); Laporte Industries Ltd, 1959-71; Laporte Industries (Holdings) Ltd, 1959-71; Tunnel Cement Ltd, 1960-74; Guardian Cement Co. Ltd, 1963-71; New Zealand Cement Holdings Ltd, 1963-71. Member: Court of Worshipful Company of Shipwrights; Court of Watermen's and Lightermen's Company; Fellow Institute of Chartered Shipbrokers; FRPSL; FRSA; MInstPet. *Heir: s* Hon. Christopher Graeme Leathers [*b* 31 Aug. 1941; *m* 1964, Maria Philomena, *yr d* of Michael Merriman, Charlestown, Co. Mayo; one *s* one *d*]. *Address:* Hills Green, Kirdford, Sussex. *T:* Kirdford 202. *Club:* Royal Automobile.

LEATHES, Maj.-Gen. Reginald Carteret de Mussenden, CB 1960; MVO 1947; OBE 1952; *b* 19 Sept. 1909; *s* of late Major Carteret de M. Leathes; *m* 1939, Marjorie Mary Elphinston; three *s* one *d. Educ:* Imperial Service Coll. 2nd Lt, Royal Marines, 1928; HMS Resolution, 1931-33; ADC to Governor of Queensland, 1935-37; 1st Bn Royal Marines, 1940-43; 42

Commando RM, 1943-44; GSO1 HQ, SACSEA, 1944-45; GSO1 HQ, Land Forces Hong Kong, 1945-46; HMS Vanguard, 1947; RN Staff Coll., 1947-49; 45 Commando RM, 1950-52; Comdt Amphibious Sch., RM, 1952-55; Col GS Staff Comdt Gen., RM, 1956; idc 1957, ADC to the Queen, 1957-58. Chief of Staff to Comdt Gen., RM, 1958-60; Maj.-Gen. Commanding Royal Marines, Portsmouth, 1961-62. Retired, 1962. Col Comdt, RM, 1971-74. Officer Order of Phoenix (Greece), 1933; Chevalier Legion of Honour and Croix de Guerre (France), 1945; Officer Order of Cloud and Banner (China), 1945. *Recreations:* fishing, ski-ing. *Address:* Highbrook, Ardingly, Sussex RH17 6SS. *T:* Ardingly 892295.

LEAVER, Christopher, JP; Managing Director, Russell & McIver Group of Companies (Wine Merchants); *b* 3 Nov. 1937; *s* of Dr Robert Leaver and Mrs Audrey Kerpen; *m* 1975, Helen Mireille Molyneux Benton. *Educ:* Eastbourne Coll. Commissioned (Army), RAOC, 1956-58. Member, Retail Foods Trades Wages Council, 1963-64. JP Inner London, 1970; Member: Council, Royal Borough of Kensington and Chelsea, 1970-73; Court of Common Council (Ward of Dowgate), City of London, 1973; Alderman (Ward of Dowgate), City of London, 1974. Mem. Ct of Assistants, Carmen's Company, 1973; Mem. Bd of Brixton Prison, 1975; Governor, Christ's Hospital Sch., 1975. *Recreations:* gardening, music, travel, old motor cars. *Address:* 52 Old Church Street, Chelsea, SW3 5DB. *T:* 01-352 2273. *Clubs:* City Livery, Guildhall.

LEAVETT, Alan; Under-Secretary (Countryside, Sport and Recreation), Department of the Environment, since 1977; *b* 4 May 1924; *s* of George Leavett and Mabel Dorothy (*née* Witts); *m* 1948, Jean Mary, *d* of Arthur Wanford, ISO, Harwich; three *d*. *Educ:* Gosport County Sch.; UC, Southampton. BA Hons 1943. MAP (RAE), 1943; HM Customs and Excise, 1947; HM Foreign (subseq. Diplomatic) Service, 1949; 3rd Sec., Rio de Janeiro, 1950-53; 1st Sec., Bangkok, 1955-59; UK Perm. Delegate to ECAFE, 1958; Cabinet Office, 1961; Sec.-Gen., Uganda Constitutional Conf., 1961; Min. of Housing and Local Govt, 1963; Sec., Noise Adv. Council, 1970; Under-Sec., Civil Service Selection Bd, 1973; Under Sec., DoE, 1974-. *Publication:* Historic Sevenoaks, 1969. *Recreation:* book-collecting, music. *Address:* 5 Beechy Lees Road, Otford, Sevenoaks, Kent. *Club:* Athenæum.

LEAVEY, John Anthony, BA; Director: Smith & Nephew Associated Companies Ltd; S.F. Air Treatment Ltd; Chairman, Wilson (Connolly) Holdings Ltd; *b* 3 March 1915; *s* of George Edwin Leavey and Marion Louise Warnock; *m* 1952, Lesley Doreen, *d* of Rt Hon. Sir Benjamin Ormerod. *Educ:* Mill Hill Sch.; Trinity Hall, Cambridge. Served War, 1939-46; 5th Royal Inniskilling Dragoon Guards. MP (C) Heywood and Royton Div. of Lancashire, 1955-64. *Recreation:* fishing. *Address:* c/o 2 Temple Place, Victoria Embankment, WC2R 3BP. *Club:* Carlton.

LEAVIS, Frank Raymond, PhD; Hon. Visiting Professor of English, University of York, 1965; Hon. Fellow of Downing College, Cambridge, 1962-64 (Fellow, 1936-62); University Reader in English, 1959-62; Editor of Scrutiny, a Quarterly Review, 1932-53; *b* 14 July 1895; *s* of Harry Leavis; *m* 1929, Queenie Dorothy Roth; two *s* one *d*. *Educ:* Perse Sch.; Emmanuel Coll., Cambridge (Scholar). Historical Tripos and English Tripos; research and university teaching; one of the founders of Scrutiny, 1932. Cheltenham Lectr, 1968; Vis. Prof., Univ. of Wales, 1969; Churchill Prof. Dept of English, Bristol Univ., 1970. Hon. Mem. Amer. Acad. of Arts and Sciences, 1963. Hon. LittD: Leeds, 1965; York, 1967; QUB, 1973; Delhi, 1973; Hon. LLD Aberdeen, 1970. *Publications:* Mass Civilization and Minority Culture, 1930; D. H. Lawrence, 1930; New Bearings in English Poetry, 1932; For Continuity, 1933; Culture and Environment (with Denys Thompson), 1933; Revaluation: Tradition and Development in English Poetry, 1936; Education and the University, 1943; The Great Tradition: George Eliot, James and Conrad, 1948; The Common Pursuit, 1952; D. H. Lawrence: Novelist, 1955; Two Cultures?: The Significance of C. P. Snow, 1962; Retrospect of Scrutiny, 1963; Anna Karenina and Other Essays, 1967; (comp.) A Selection from Scrutiny, 1968; (with Q. D. Leavis) Lectures in America, 1969; English Literature in Our Time and the University, 1969; (with Q. D. Leavis) Dickens the Novelist, 1970; Nor Shall My Sword, 1972; Letters in Criticism, 1974; The Living Principle: English as a Discipline of Thought, 1975; Thought, Words and Creativity, 1976. Editor, Towards Standards of Criticism, 1933; Determinations, 1934; Mill on Bentham and Coleridge, 1950. *Address:* 12 Bulstrode Gardens, Cambridge.

LE BAILLY, Vice-Adm. Sir Louis (Edward Stewart Holland), KBE 1972 (OBE 1952); CB 1969; Director-General of Intelligence, Ministry of Defence, 1972-75; *b* 18 July 1915; *s* of Robert Francis Le Bailly and Ida Gaskell Le Bailly (*née* Holland); *m* 1946, Pamela Ruth Berthon; three *d*. *Educ:* RNC Dartmouth. HMS Hood, 1932; RNEC, 1933-37; HMS Hood, 1937-40; HMS Naiad, 1940-42; RNEC, 1942-44; HMS Duke of York, 1944-46; Admiralty, 1946-50; HMS Bermuda, 1950-52; RNEC, 1955-58; Admiralty: Staff Officer to Dartmouth Review Cttee, 1958; Asst Engineer-in-Chief, 1958-60; Naval Asst to Controller of the Navy, 1960-63; IDC, 1963; Dep. Dir of Marine Engineering, 1963-67; Naval Attaché, Washington, DC, and Comdr, British Navy Staff, 1967-69; Min. of Defence, 1970-72; Vice-Adm. 1970, retired 1972. Member: Council, Inst. for Study of Conflict; Chairmen's Panel, Civil Service Selection Bd. FIMechE; FInstPet; MIMarE. *Address:* c/o Barclays Bank, Market Square, Chippenham, Wilts. *Club:* Boodle's.

LE BAS, Air Vice-Marshal Michael Henry, CB 1969; CBE 1966; DSO 1944; AFC 1954; retired; *b* 28 Sept. 1916; *s* of late R. W. O. Le Bas and of Florence Marrs; *m* 1945, Moyra Benitz; one *s* one *d*. *Educ:* St George's Coll., Buenos Aires; Malvern Coll. Joined RAF, 1940; served in Fighter Command, Malta, Western Desert, and Italy, 1941-44; RAF Staff Coll., 1948-51; HQ 2 TAF and RAF Wildenrath, 1951-54; Sch. of Land Air Warfare, 1954-56; Suez, 1956; OC, RAF Coningsby, 1959-61; HQ Bomber Comd, 1961-63; SASO, Air Forces Middle East, 1963-66; AOC No. 1 Group, Bomber Command, 1966-68; AOC No. 1 (Bomber) Gp, Strike Comd, 1968; Dir Gen. of Personal Services (RAF), MoD, 1969-71. *Recreations:* golf, shooting, photography. *Address:* c/o Midland Bank, Oakham, Rutland. *Club:* Royal Air Force.

LEBETER, Fred; Keeper, Department of Transport and Mining, Science Museum, 1953-67; *b* 27 Dec. 1903; *e s* of Arthur Lebeter, Mining Engineer, and Lucy Wilson; *m* 1926, Sybil Leah, *o d* of Henry Ward; one *d* decd. *Educ:* Rotherham and Bridgnorth Gram. Schs; Birmingham Univ. BSc 1925; MSc (Research on Classification of British Coals) 1926. Manager, Magnesite Mines and Works, Salem, S India, 1926-31; Lecturer in Mining, Heanor Mining Sch., 1931-33; Sen. Lectr in Mining, Chesterfield Tech. Coll., 1933-37; Asst Keeper, Science Museum, 1937-39; Dep. Chief Mining Supplies Officer, Min. of Fuel and Power, 1939-47; Asst Keeper, Science Museum, 1947-49, Dep. Keeper, 1949-53. Consultant on Mine Ventilation and Underground Transport, 1931-; Mem. Council Nat. Assoc. of Colliery Managers (Midland Br.), 1935-37; Adviser to Coal Commission, Germany, on Mining Supplies, 1944; UK rep. to European Coal Organisation, 1945-47. United Kingdom delegate to European Coal Organisation, Paris, 1946. Mem., Industrial Cttee, National Museum of Wales, 1959-67. Retired 1967. *Publications:* contributor of many technical articles to Colliery Engineering, Mine and Quarry Engineering, historical articles in Zeitschrift für Kunst und Kultur im Bergbau, etc. *Recreations:* sport and gardening. *Address:* The Lodge, 9a Southdown Road, Seaford, E Sussex BN25 4PA. *T:* Seaford 894751.

LEBLANC, Rt. Rev. Camille André; Chaplain at Caraquet Hospital; *b* Barachois, NB, 25 Aug. 1898. *Educ:* Collège Sainte-Anne, Church Point, NS; Grand Séminaire Halifax, NS. Priest, 1924; Subseq. Curé at Shemogue and the Cathedral of Nôtre Dame de l'Assomption, Moncton; Bishop of Bathurst, 1942-69. *Address:* c/o Caraquet Hospital, Caraquet, NB, Canada.

LEBLOND, Prof. C(harles) P(hilippe), MD, PhD, DSc; FRSC 1951; FRS 1965; Professor of Anatomy, McGill University, Canada, since 1948; *b* 5 Feb. 1910; *s* of Oscar Leblond and Jeanne Desmarchelier; *m* 1936, Gertrude Elinor Sternschuss; three *s* one *d*. *Educ:* Sch. St Joseph, Lille, France; Univs. of Lille, Nancy, Paris, Montreal. L-ès-S, Nancy 1932; MD Paris 1934; PhD Montreal 1942; DSc Sorbonne 1945. Asst in Histology, Med. School, Univ. of Paris, 1934-35; Rockefeller Fell., Sch. of Med., Yale Univ., 1936-37; Asst, Laboratoire de Synthése Atomique, Paris, 1938-40; McGill Univ.: Lectr in Histology and Embryology, 1941-42; Asst Prof. of Anatomy, 1942-43; Assoc. Prof. of Anatomy, 1946-48; Prof. of Anatomy, 1948-; Chm. of Dept of Anatomy, 1957-75. Mem. Amer. Assoc. of Anatomists; Fellow, Amer. Acad. of Arts and Scis. Hon. DSc Acadia, 1972. *Publications:* over 300 articles in anatomical journals. *Recreation:* country. *Address:* (home) 68 Chesterfield Avenue, Westmount, PQ H3Y 2M5, Canada. *T:* 514- 486-4837; (office) Department of Anatomy, McGill University, 3640 University Street, Montreal, PQ H3A 2B2, Canada. *T:* 514-392-4931.

LE BRETON, David Francis Battye; HM Commissioner in Anguilla, since 1974; *b* 2 March 1931; *e s* of late Lt-Col F. H. Le Breton, MC, and Elisabeth Le Breton (*née* Trevor-Battye), Endebess, Kenya; *m* 1961, Patricia June Byrne; one *s* two *d*.

Educ: Winchester; New Coll., Oxford. Colonial Administrative Service, Tanganyika, 1954; Private Sec. to Governor, 1959-60; Magistrate, 1962; Principal, CRO, 1963; HM Diplomatic Service, 1965; First Sec., Zanzibar, 1964; Lusaka, 1964-68; FCO, 1968-71; Head of Chancery, Budapest, 1971-74. *Recreations:* travel, flying. *Address:* The Valley, Anguilla; Brackenwood, Frenchstreet, near Westerham, Kent.

le BROCQUY, Louis, FSIA 1960; painter since 1939; *b* Dublin, 10 Nov. 1916; *s* of late Albert le Brocquy, MA, and late Sybil Staunton; *m* 1st, 1938, Jean Stoney (marr. diss., 1948); one *d*; 2nd, 1958, Anne Madden Simpson; two *s*. *Educ:* St Gerard's Sch., Wicklow, Ireland. Self-taught. Founder-mem. of Irish Exhibn of Living Art, 1943; Visiting Instructor, Central Sch. of Arts and Crafts, London, 1947-54; Visiting Tutor, Royal Coll. of Art, London, 1955-58. Member: Irish Council of Design, 1963-65; Council, Soc. of Designers in Ireland, 1974-. Dir, Kilkenny Design Workshops, 1965-. Represented Ireland, Venice Biennale (awarded internat. prize), 1956. Work exhibited in "50 Ans d'Art Moderne", Brussels, 1958; Marzotto, 1962-63, 1968-69; Pittsburgh Internat., 1961-62, 1964-65; Recklinghausen, 1966, 1967; "Art Vivant", Fondation Maeght, 1967, 1968; Rijeka, 1968, 1970, 1972, 1974; Biennale, Tokyo, 1970-71; Biennale, Brno, 1970, 1972, 1974. One Man Shows: Leicester Galleries, London, 1948; Gimpel Fils, London, 1947, 1949, 1951, 1955, 1956, 1957, 1959, 1961, 1966, 1968, 1971, 1974; Waddington Galleries, Dublin, 1951; Robles Gallery, Los Angeles, 1960; Gallery Lienhard, Zürich, 1961; Dawson Gallery, Dublin, 1962, 1966, 1969, 1971, 1973, 1974, 1975; Municipal Gallery of Modern Art, Dublin, 1966 and Ulster Gallery, Belfast (retrospective), 1966-67; Gimpel-Hanover, Zürich, 1969; Gimpel, NY, 1971; Fondation Maeght, 1973; Bussola, Turin, 1974; Arts Council, Belfast, 1975; Musée d'Art Moderne, Paris, 1976. Public Collections possessing work include: Albright Museum, Buffalo; Arts Council, London; Carnegie Inst., Pittsburgh; Centre National d'Art Pompidou, Paris; Chicago Arts Club; Detroit Inst. of Art; Dublin Municipal Gallery; Fort Worth Center, Texas; J. H. Hirshhorn Foundation, Washington; Fondation Maeght, St Paul; Leeds City Art Gallery; Musée d'Art Moderne, Paris; Museo de Arte Moderna, São Paolo; Tate Gallery; Ulster Museum, Belfast; V. & A. Museum. RHA 1950; FRSA 1974. Chevalier de la Légion d'Honneur, 1974. Hon. DLitt Dublin, 1962. Commandeur du Bontemps de Médoc et des Graves, 1969. *Illustrated work:* The Táin, trans. Thomas Kinsella, 1969; The Playboy of the Western World, Synge, 1970. *Address:* c/o Gimpel Fils, 30 Davies Street, W1Y 1LG.

LE CARRÉ, John; *see* Cornwell, David John Moore.

LE CHEMINANT, Peter, CB 1976; Deputy Secretary, Department of Energy, since 1974; *b* 29 April 1926; *s* of William Arthur Le Cheminant; *m* 1959, Suzanne Elisabeth Horny; three *s*. *Educ:* Holloway Sch.; London Sch. of Economics. Sub-Lt, RNVR, 1944-47. Min. of Power, 1949; Cabinet Office, 1950-52 and 1964-65; UK Delegn to ECSC, 1962-63; Private Sec. to Prime Minister, 1965-68; Asst Sec., Min. of Power, later Min. of Technology, 1968-71; Under-Sec., DTI, 1971-74. *Recreation:* water sports. *Address:* 87 Manor Road North, Hinchley Wood, Esher, Surrey.

LE CHEMINANT, Air Chief Marshal Sir Peter (de Lacey), KCB 1972 (CB 1968); DFC 1943, and Bar, 1951; Deputy Commander-in-Chief, Allied Forces, Central Europe, since 1976; *b* 17 June 1920; *s* of Lieut-Colonel Keith Le Cheminant and Blanche Etheldred Wake Le Cheminant (née Clark); *m* 1940, Sylvia, *d* of J. van Bodegom; one *s* two *d*. *Educ:* Elizabeth Coll., Guernsey; RAF Coll., Cranwell. Flying posts in France, UK, N Africa, Malta, Sicily and Italy, 1940-44; comd No 223 Squadron, 1943-44; Staff and Staff Coll. Instructor, 1945-48; Far East, 1949-53; comd No 209 Sqn, 1949-51; Jt Planning Staff, 1953-55; Wing Comdr, Flying, Kuala Lumpur, 1955-57; jssc 1958; Dep. Dir of Air Staff Plans, 1958-61; comd RAF Geilenkirchen, 1961-63; Dir of Air Staff Briefing, 1964-66; SASO, HQ FEAF, 1966-67, C of S, 1967-68; Comdt Joint Warfare Estabt, MoD, 1968-70; Asst Chief of Air Staff (Policy), MoD, 1971-72; UK Mem., Perm. Mil. Deputies Gp, CENTO, Ankara, 1972-73; Vice-Chief of Defence Staff, 1974-76. *Recreations:* golf, swimming, shooting. *Address:* Blossom House, Salford, Chipping Norton, Oxon. *Club:* Royal Air Force.

LECHIN-SUAREZ, Brigadier General Juan, Condor de los Andes, Guerrillero José Miguel Lanza, Mérito Aeronautico, Mérito Naval (Bolivia); Minister for Planning and Coordination, since 1974; *b* 8 March 1921; *s* of Juan Alfredo Lechín and Julia Suárez; *m* 1947, Ruth Varela; one *s* three *d*. *Educ:* Bolivian Military College. Chief of Ops, Bolivian Army HQ, 1960-61; Military and Air Attaché, Bolivian Embassy, Bonn, 1962-63;

Comdr, Bolivian Army Fifth Inf. Div., 1964; Pres., Bolivian State Mining Corp. (with rank of Minister of State), 1964-68; Comdr, Bolivian Army Third Inf. Div., 1969; Bolivian Ambassador to the UK and to the Netherlands, 1970-74. Das Grosse Verdienstkreuz (Fed. Rep. Germany). *Recreations:* tennis, swimming. *Address:* Avenida Busch 2066, La Paz, Bolivia.

LECHMERE, Sir Berwick (Hungerford), 6th Bt, *cr* 1818; JP; DL; Land Agent; *b* 21 Sept. 1917; *s* of Sir Ronald Berwick Hungerford Lechmere, 5th Bt, and of Constance Marguerite (née Long); *S* father, 1965; *m* 1954, Norah Garrett Elkington; no *c*. *Educ:* Charterhouse; Magdalene Coll., Cambridge. High Sheriff of Worcs, 1962, JP, 1966, DL 1972. FRICS. *Heir:* cousin Reginald Anthony Hungerford Lechmere [*b* 24 Dec. 1920; *m* 1956, Anne Jennifer Dind; three *s* one *d*]. *Address:* Severn End, Hanley Castle, Worcester. *T:* Upton-on-Severn 2130.

LECKIE, John, CB 1955; Management Project Co-ordinator, Export Credits Guarantee Department, 1972-74; *b* 2 Sept. 1911; *o s* of late Alexander M. Leckie; *m* 1937, Elizabeth Mary Murray Brown; two *s*. *Educ:* Hamilton Academy; Glasgow Univ. (MA, BSc). Entered Administrative Class, Home Civil Service, by competitive examination, 1934; Customs and Excise Dept, 1934; transferred to Board of Trade, 1940; Head of Board of Trade Delegation, Washington, USA, 1943-45; Adviser on Commercial Policy, 1950; Under-Sec., 1950-60, Second Sec., 1960-64, BoT; Deputy Secretary: Min. of Technology, 1964-70; DTI, 1970-72, retd 1972. *Address:* 1 The Wedges, West Chiltington Lane, Itchingfield, Horsham, Sussex RH13 7TA.

LECKIE, Air Marshal Robert, CB 1943; DSO 1917; DSC 1916; DFC 1918; retired; *o s* of late Samuel Leckie, Glasgow; *m* Bernice, *y d* of Mrs Douglas O'Kane, La Plata, Maryland, USA. *Educ:* Glasgow. Joined RNAS 1915; served in North Sea, European War, 1914-18 (despatches, DSC, DFC, DSO); Lieut-Colonel 1st Central Ontario Regt; commanded No. 1 Canadian Wing, RCAF; Director of Flying Operations, Canadian Air Board, 1920; Member Canadian Air Board, 1921-22; Boys' Training Wing, Halton (RAF), 1922; RN Staff Coll., England, 1922-23; HQ Staff Coastal Comd, 1923-25; commanded: (RAF) HMS Hermes (Aircraft Carrier), 1925-27; (RAF) HMS Courageous (Aircraft Carrier), 1927-29; RAF Station, Bircham Newton, 1929-31; at RAF Marine Experimental Station, Felixstowe, England, 1931; commanded: 210 Flying Boat Squadron, 1931; RAF Station, Pembroke Dock, 1931-33; RAF Station, Hendon, 1933-35; Supt RAF Reserve, i/c Elem. Civil Flying Schools, 1933-35; ADC to the King, 1936; Director of Training, Air Ministry, 1935-38; commanded RAF Medit. (HQ Malta), 1938-39; to Canada as Director of Training, RCAF, 1940; Member Air Council for Training, RCAF, 1940; Acting Chief of Air Staff, RCAF, 1943; Chief of Air Staff, RCAF, 1944; retired, 1947. Order of Polonia Restituta, 1st Class (Poland); US Legion of Merit, Degree of Commander; Order of White Lion, Class II (Czechoslovakia); Commandeur de la Légion d'Honneur (France). *Publications:* various articles, magazines and service journals. *Recreations:* golf, hunting and fishing. *Address:* 303 Acacia Avenue, Rockcliffe Park, Ottawa, Ontario K1M 0M1, Canada. *Clubs:* Royal Air Force; Gatineau Fish and Game.

LECKONBY, William Douglas, CBE 1967; Collector of Customs and Excise, London Port, 1963-67, retired; *b* 23 April 1907; *m* 1933; one *d*. *Educ:* Hymers Coll., Hull. Entered Customs and Excise, 1928; subsequently held various posts in that department. *Address:* Ebor, Withyham Road, Groombridge, Sussex. *T:* Groombridge 481.

LECKY, Arthur Terence, CMG 1968; HM Diplomatic Service, retired; *b* 10 June 1919; *s* of late Lieut-Colonel M. D. Lecky, DSO, late RA, and late Bertha Lecky (née Goss); *m* 1946, Jacqualine (*d* 1974), *d* of late Dr A. G. Element; three *s*. *Educ:* Winchester Coll.; Clare Coll., Cambridge (1938-39). Served RA, 1939-46. FO (Control Commission for Germany), 1946-49; FO, 1950-54; Vice-Consul, Zürich, 1954-56; FO, 1957-61; First Secretary, The Hague, 1962-64, FCO (formerly FO), 1964-70, retired. *Address:* Harthill House, Godshill, Fordingbridge, Hants. *T:* Fordingbridge 52070.

LECKY, Maj.-Gen. Samuel Knox, OBE 1967; BSc(Eng), CEng, FIMechE, MBIM; Minister (Defence Supply), British Embassy, Tehran, since 1977; *b* 10 Feb. 1926; *s* of late J. D. Lecky, Coleraine; *m* 1947, Sheila Jones; one *s* two *d*. *Educ:* Coleraine Acad.; Queen's Univ., Belfast (BSc). Commnd REME, 1946; served Egypt, 1951-52; Kenya, 1953-54; jssc 1964; AA&QMG HQ 1(BR) Corps, 1965-66; CREME 4 Div., 1966-68; Sec., Principal Personnel Officers, MoD, 1968-70; RCDS, 1971; Comdt, SEME, 1972-74; DEME, BAOR, 1975; Dir, Military

Assistance Office, MoD, 1976-77. *Recreations:* fishing, shooting. *Address:* c/o Williams & Glyn's Bank, Victoria Road, Farnborough, Hants GU14 7PA. *Club:* Army and Navy.

LECLERC, Maj.-Gen. Pierre Edouard, CBE 1943; MM; ED; CD; *b* 20 Jan. 1893; *s* of late Pierre Leclerc, Civil Engineer, Montreal; *m* 1st, 1918, Esther (*d* 1956), *d* of Capt. Olsen Norlie, Bergen, and Arundal, Norway; one *d*; 2nd, 1958, Germaine, *d* of late Robert Sarra-Bournet, Montreal. *Educ:* Mont St Louis Coll., Montreal; Methodist Institute, Westmount, PQ. Joined Canadian Expeditionary Force, 1915, as Sapper; commissioned, 1916; qualified Canadian Militia Staff Course, 1935; commanded 5th Canadian Infantry Bde, 1940 (overseas); Maj.-General, 1942; GOC 7th Canadian Div., 1942; GOC Canadian and Newfoundland Army Forces, Newfoundland, Oct. 1943; retired from Canadian Army, 1945. Mem., Sir Arthur Currie Branch, Montreal, Quebec, The Royal Canadian Legion, 1945. Hon. Colonel Le Regt de Joliette, 1955-; Hon. President Canadian Corps Association, 1956. *Address:* 5444, Coolbrook Avenue, Montreal 248, PQ, Canada. *Clubs:* Canadian (Montreal); Royal Commonwealth Society (Montreal Branch).

LECONFIELD, Baron; see Egremont.

LECOURT, Robert; Commandeur, Legion of Honour; Croix de Guerre; Rosette de la Résistance; President, Court of Justice, European Community, 1967-76; *b* 19 Sept. 1908; *s* of Léon Lecourt and Angéle Lépron; *m* 1932, Marguerite Chabrerie; one *d*. *Educ:* Rouen; Univ. de Caen (DenDroit). Advocate, Court of Appeal: Rouen, 1928; Paris, 1932. Served with French Air Force, 1939-40; Mem. Resistance Movt, 1942-44; Deputy for Paris, 1945-58 and for Hautes Alpes, 1958-61, National Assembly; Pres., MRP Party, 1945-48 and 1952-57; Minister of Justice, 1948-49 and 1957-58; Minister of State responsible for co-operation with Africa, 1958-61. Judge, Court of Justice, European Community, 1962. Hon. Bencher, Gray's Inn, 1972; DUniv Exeter, 1975. Holds numerous foreign decorations. *Publications:* Nature juridique de l'action en réintégrande, 1931; Code pratique du travail, Responsabilité des architectes et entrepreneurs, etc, 1932-39; Le Juge devant le marché commun, 1970; L'Europe des juges, 1976; contrib. Le Monde, Figaro, Aurore, and other European jls. *Address:* 11 Boulevard Suchet, 75016 Paris, France. *T:* 504-27-95.

LEDERBERG, Prof. Joshua, PhD; Professor and Executive Head, Department of Genetics, School of Medicine, Stanford University, USA, since 1959; *b* Montclair, NJ, USA, 23 May 1925; *s* of Zwi H. and Esther Lederberg (*née* Goldenbaum); *m* 1968, Marguerite Stein Kirsch, MD; one *d*, one step-*s*. *Educ:* Stuyvesant High Sch., NYC; Columbia Coll. (BA); Yale Univ. (PhD). Assistant Professor of Genetics, University of Wisconsin, 1948; Associate Professor, 1950; Professor, 1954. Shared in discoveries concerning genetic re-combination, and organization of genetic material of bacteria, contributing to cancer research; discovered a method of artificially introducing new genes into bacteria in investigation of hereditary substance. Member: National Academy of Sciences, United States, 1957. ScD (*hc*): Yale Univ.; Columbia Univ.; Univ. of Wisconsin; MD (*hc*), Univ. of Turin. (Jointly) Nobel Prize in Medicine, 1958. *Publications:* contribs to learned journals on genetics, bacteria and general biological problems. *Address:* Department of Genetics, Stanford University, Stanford, California 94305, USA. *T:* 415-4975801.

LEDGER, Sir Frank, (Joseph Francis), Kt 1963; Company Director (engineering etc); *b* 29 Oct. 1899; *s* of Edson and Annie Frances Ledger; *m* 1923, Gladys Muriel Lyons; one *s* two *d*. *Educ:* Perth Boys' Sch., Perth, WA. President: J. E. Ledger Cos; Mitchell Cotts Gp; Dir, Mitchell Cotts Australia; Governing Dir, Ledger Investments; Past Chm. of Dirs, S Australian Insurance Co.; Director: Chamber of Manufrs Insurance Co.; ARC Engineering Co.; Winget Moxey (WA) Pty Ltd; Lake View and Star Ltd; Member, Past Chairman: WA Branch of Inst. of Directors (London); WA Govt Industrial Develt Adv. Cttee; Pres., Royal Commonwealth Society (WA Branch); Past President: WA Chamber of Manufacturers; WA Employers Federation; Ironmasters Assoc. (WA); Metal Industries Assoc. (WA); Inst. of Foundrymen (WA); Past Vice-Pres., Associated Chamber of Manufacturers (Canberra). Pres., WA Trotting Assoc.; Vice-Pres., Australian Trotting Council. *Recreations:* golfing, sailing. *Address:* 2 The Esplanade, Peppermint Grove, Western Australia. *Clubs:* Weld, Perth, Royal Freshwater Bay Yacht, Cottesloe Golf; WA Turf, WA Cricket Association (all in Perth, WA).

LEDGER, Sir Joseph Francis; see Ledger, Sir Frank.

LEDGER, Philip (Stevens); Director of Music and Organist, King's College, Cambridge, since 1974; Conductor, Cambridge University Musical Society, since 1973; *b* 12 Dec. 1937; *s* of Walter Stephen Ledger and Winifred Kathleen (*née* Stevens); *m* 1963, Mary Erryl (*née* Wells); one *s* one *d*. *Educ:* Bexhill Grammar Sch.; King's Coll., Cambridge (Maj. Schol.). John Stewart of Rannoch Schol. in Sacred Music; 1st Cl. Hons in Pt I and Pt II, of Music Tripos; MA, MusB (Cantab). FRCO, Limpus and Read prizes, LRAM, ARCM. Master of the Music, Chelmsford Cathedral, 1962-65; Dir of Music, Univ. of East Anglia, 1965-73 (Dean of Sch. of Fine Arts and Music, 1968-71). An Artistic Dir, Aldeburgh Festival of Music and the Arts, 1968-. *Publications:* (ed) Anthems for Choirs 2 and 3, 1973; other edns of Byrd, Handel and Purcell; carol arrangements. *Recreations:* swimming, theatre, membership of Sette of Odd Volumes. *Address:* 15 Dane Drive, Cambridge CB3 9LP. *T:* Cambridge 68180. *Club:* Athenæum.

LEDGER, Ronald Joseph; Casino Proprietor and Manager; *b* 7 Nov. 1920; *s* of Arthur and Florence Ledger; *m* 1946, Madeleine Odette de Villeneuve; three *s* one *d*. *Educ:* Skinners Grammar Sch., Tunbridge Wells; Nottingham Univ. Toolroom Engineer, 1938-42. Served RAF, 1942-47, fitter, Leading Aircraftsman; India three years. Univ. of Nottingham, 1947-49 (Diploma in Social Science); Staff Training Officer, Enfield Highway Co-op. Society, 1949; Business Partner, 1950, Company Director, 1953, Employment Specialists. Mem. Herts CC, 1952-54. Contested (Lab) Rushcliffe Div. of Nottingham, 1951; MP (Lab and Co-op) Romford, 1955-70. Director: Enfield Electronics (CRT) Ltd, 1958; London Co-operative Society Ltd, 1961. Chairman, Hairdressing Council, 1966-. Proprietor, Halland Hotel, Seaview, Isle of Wight. *Recreations:* tennis, cricket, golf, snooker. *Address:* Elgin House, Ryde Road, Seaview, Isle of Wight. *T:* Seaview 3117. *Clubs:* Sandown and Shanklin Golf, Ryde Golf, Enfield Golf.

LEDINGHAM, Colonel George Alexander, DSO 1940; MC; *b* 8 March 1890; *e s* of late Alexander Ledingham, SSC, Advocate in Aberdeen. Served European War (despatches, MC, wounded); commanded 98th (Surrey and Sussex Yeomanry QMR) Field Regt, RA, 1937-42 (despatches twice, DSO); Colonel, 1942; Commander Military Government, South Brabant, on liberation, 1944; and Province of Westphalia occupation, 1945; Secretary-General United Nations War Crimes Commission, 1945-48. *Recreations:* croquet, handicraft; played Rugby football for Scotland, 1913; captained United Services *v* South Africans, 1917. *Address:* 63 Ridgeway North, PO Box BW 326, Borrowdale, Rhodesia. *T:* 884148.

LEDINGHAM, Prof. John Marshall, MD, FRCP; Consultant Physician, The London Hospital, since 1954; Professor of Medicine, University of London, at London Hospital Medical College, since 1971; *b* 1916; *s* of late Prof. Sir John C. G. Ledingham, CMG, FRS, of The Lister Institute, London, and late Lady Barbara Ledingham; *m* 1950, Josephine, *d* of late Matthew and Jane Metcalf, Temple Sowerby, Westmorland; two *s*. *Educ:* Whitgift Sch.; University College, London; The London Hospital. BSc (London) First Class Hons in Physics, 1936; MRCS, LRCP, 1942; MD (London) Gold Medal, 1951, FRCP, 1957. Service in RAMC as Graded Clinical and Experimental Pathologist, in UK, France, Middle and Far East, 1942-47. Lectr in Medicine, London Hosp. Med. Sch., 1948-53; Univ. Reader in Medicine, 1953-64; Prof. of Experimental Medicine, 1964-71, London Hosp. Med. Coll., London Univ. Editor, Dep. Chm. and Chm. Editorial Bd, Clinical Science, 1965-70. Past Pres., Section of Exptl Med. and Therapeutics, RSM. Bertram Louis Abrahams Lectr, RCP, 1970; Censor, RCP, 1975. *Publications:* numerous scientific, mainly in field of hypertension and renal disease, 1938-. *Address:* 11 Montpelier Walk, SW7. *T:* 01-584 7976.

LEDWIDGE, Sir (William) Bernard (John), KCMG 1974 (CMG 1964); HM Diplomatic Service, retired; Chairman, United Kingdom Committee for UNICEF, since 1976; *b* 9 Nov. 1915; *s* of late Charles Ledwidge and Eileen O'Sullivan; *m* 1st, 1948, Anne Kingsley (marr. diss. 1970); one *s* one *d*; 2nd, 1970, Flora Groult. *Educ:* Cardinal Vaughan Sch.; King's Coll., Cambridge; Princeton Univ., USA. Commonwealth Fund Fellow, 1937-39; served War of 1939-45: RA 1940; Indian Army, 1941-45. Private Secretary to Permanent Under-Secretary, India Office, 1946; Secretary, Frontier Areas Cttee of Enquiry, Burma, 1947; Foreign Office, 1947-49; British Consul, St Louis, USA, 1949-52; First Secretary, British Embassy, Kabul, 1952-56; Political Adviser British Military Govt, Berlin, 1956-61; Foreign Office, 1961-65; Minister, Paris, 1965-69; Ambassador to Finland, 1969-72; Ambassador to Israel, 1972-75. Mem., Police Complaints Bd, 1977-. *Recreations:* golf, bridge, chess. *Address:* 54 rue de Bourgogne, 75007 Paris, France. *T:* 705 8026; 19 Queen's Gate Terrace, SW7. *T:* 01-584 4132. *Club:* Travellers'.

LEE, family name of **Baron Lee of Newton.**

LEE OF ASHERIDGE, Baroness cr 1970 (Life Peer), of the City of Westminster; **Janet Bevan, (Jennie Lee),** PC 1966; Director of Tribune; Member of Central Advisory Committee on Housing; Member, National Executive Committee, Labour Party, 1958-70 (Chairman, 1967-68); b 3 Nov. 1904; d of James Lee, Fifeshire miner; m 1934, Rt Hon. Aneurin Bevan, PC, MP (d 1960). Educ: Edinburgh Univ. MA, LLB. MP (Lab) North Lanark, 1929-31, Cannock, 1945-70. Parly Sec., Ministry of Public Building and Works, 1964-65; Parly Under-Sec. of State, Dept of Education and Science, 1965-67, Minister of State, 1967-70. Hon. LLD Cambridge, 1974. Publications: Tomorrow is a New Day, 1939; Our Ally, Russia, 1941; This Great Journey, 1963. Address: 67 Chester Row, SW1.

LEE OF NEWTON, Baron cr 1974 (Life Peer), of Newton, Merseyside; **Frederick Lee,** PC 1964; b 3 Aug. 1906; s of Joseph Wm and Margaret Lee; m 1938; one d. Educ: Langworthy Road Sch. Engineer. Chairman: Works Cttee, Metro-Vickers Ltd, Trafford Park, Manchester; National Cttee, Amal. Engineering Union, 1944-45; formerly Member Salford City Council. MP (Lab): Hulme, Manchester, 1945-50, Newton, Lancs, 1950-Feb. 1974; PPS to Chancellor of Exchequer, 1948; Parly Sec., Min. of Labour and Nat. Service, 1950-51; Minister of Power, 1964-66; Secretary of State for the Colonies, 1966-67; Chancellor of the Duchy of Lancaster, 1967-69. Address: Sunnyside, 52 Ashton Road, Newton-le-Willows, Merseyside.

LEE, Sir Arthur (James), KBE 1966 (CBE 1959); MC and Bar (1939-45); Company Director; National President, Returned Services League, Australia, 1960-74 (State President, 1954-60); b 30 July 1912; s of Arthur James and Kathleen Maud Lee; m 1945, Valerie Ann Scanlan; three s one d. Educ: Collegiate School of St Peter, Adelaide. Company Director, Lee's Hotels Ltd; Chm., Regional Cttees Services Canteen Fund, S Australia. Recreation: golf. Address: 2 Arthur Street, Toorak Gardens, SA 5065, Australia. T: 35106. Clubs: Adelaide, Naval and Military, Royal Adelaide Golf (Adelaide).

LEE, Arthur James, DSC (and Bar); Controller of Fisheries Research and Development, Ministry of Agriculture, Fisheries and Food, since 1977; b 17 May 1920; s of Arthur Henry and Clara Lee; m 1953, Judith Graham; three d. Educ: City Boys' Sch., Leicester; St Catharine's Coll., Cambridge (MA). Served War of 1939-45 (DSC and Bar). Apptd: Scientific Officer at Fisheries Laboratory, Lowestoft, 1947; Dep. Dir of Fishery Research, 1965, Dir, 1974-77. Publications: contribs to various marine science jls. Recreation: gardening. Address: 191 Normanston Drive, Oulton Broad, Lowestoft, Suffolk. T: Lowestoft 4707.

LEE, His Honour Arthur Michael, DSC 1941; QC 1961; DL; a Circuit Judge (formerly Judge of County Courts), 1962-77; b 22 Aug. 1913; s of Edward Cornwall Lee and Katherine Sybil Lee (née Wilberforce); m 1940, Valerie Burnett Georges Drake-Brockman; two s. Educ: Horris Hill Preparatory Sch.; Winchester Coll. (Scholar); Brasenose Coll. (Heath Harrison Schol.), Oxford. Honours Degree in Philosophy, Politics and Economics, 1935, in Law, 1936. Called to Bar, Middle Temple (Harmsworth Scholar), 1937. Served War of 1939-45, RNVR: served in destroyers, Atlantic convoys; Lieut, 1939; Lieut-Commander, 1943; Acting Commander, 1945. Returned to practice at the Bar, Jan. 1946; Recorder of Penzance, 1960-62; Dep. Chm., Hants QS, 1960-71. Chm., Hants Area Probation and After-Care Cttee, 1969-77. Chairman Governors, Horris Hill Sch., Newbury, 1964-70. DL Hants, 1975. Publications: ed Shawcross on Motor Insurance, 1947; ed Shaw on Evidence in Criminal Cases, 1950. Recreation: fishing. Address: The Manor Farm House, Easton, Winchester, Hants. T: Itchen Abbas 277. Club: Hampshire.

LEE, Christopher Frank Carandini; actor; entered film industry, 1947; b 27 May 1922; s of Geoffrey Trollope Lee (Lt-Col 60th KRRC), and Estelle Marie Carandini; m 1961, Birgit, d of Richard Emil Kroencke; one d. Educ: Wellington Coll. RAFVR, 1941-46 (Flt Lieut; mentioned in despatches, 1944). Films include: Moulin Rouge; Tale of Two Cities; Dracula; Rasputin; The Devil Rides Out; Private Life of Sherlock Holmes; The Wicker Man; The Three Musketeers; The Four Musketeers; The Man with the Golden Gun; To the Devil, a Daughter; Airport '77. Officier des Arts et des Lettres, France, 1973. Publications: Christopher Lee's 'X' Certificate, 1975 (2nd edn 1976); Christopher Lee's Archives of Evil, USA 1975 (2nd edn 1976); (autobiog.) Tall, Dark and Gruesome, 1977. Recreations: travel, opera, golf, cricket. Address: c/o Robert Littman Co., 409 N Camden Drive, Beverly Hills, Calif 90210, USA. Clubs: Buck's, MCC; Honourable Company of Edinburgh Golfers; Travellers' (Paris); Bay Hill and Lodge (Orlando, Fla, USA); Bel-Air Country (Los Angeles, USA).

LEE, Air Chief Marshal Sir David (John Pryer), GBE 1969 (KBE 1965; CBE 1947; OBE 1943); CB 1953; retired, 1971; b 4 Sept. 1912; s of late John Lee, Byron Crescent, Bedford; m 1938, Denise, d of late Louis Hartoch; one s one d. Educ: Bedford Sch.; RAF Coll., Cranwell. NWFP, India, 1933-36; Central Flying Sch., Upavon, 1937; RAF Examining Officer, Supt. of Reserve, 1938-39; Bomber Command, Hemswell, 1939-40; RAF Staff Coll. (student), 1942; Deputy Director Plans, Air Ministry, 1943-44; OC 904 Fighter Wing, Batavia, Java, 1945-46; Directing Staff, RAF Staff Coll., 1948-50; Deputy Director Policy, Air Ministry, 1951-53; OC RAF Scampton, Lincs, 1953-55; Secretary, Chiefs of Staff Cttee, Ministry of Defence, 1956-59; AOC, AFME (Aden), 1959-61; Comdt, RAF Staff Coll., 1962-65; Air Member for Personnel, MoD, 1965-68; UK Military Rep. to NATO, 1968-71. Chairman: Grants Cttee, RAF Benevolent Fund, 1971-; Exec. Cttee, Nuffield Trust for Armed Forces, 1975-. Address: Danemore Cottage, South Godstone, Surrey. Club: Royal Air Force.

LEE, Sir Desmond; see Lee, Sir H. D. P.

LEE, Rev. Donald Rathbone, MBE 1945; Superintendent, Jersey Methodist Circuit, since 1977; President of the Methodist Conference, 1973; Moderator, Free Church Federal Council, 1975-76; b 28 March 1911; s of Thomas and Alice Lee, Stockport, Cheshire; m 1940, Nora Olive Fothergill, Greenock, Renfrewshire; two s three d. Educ: Stockport Grammar School; Handsworth College, Birmingham. BD (London). Methodist Circuit appointments in: Greenock, 1935; Runcorn, 1936; Edinburgh, 1937; Perth, 1940; Stockport, 1947; Upminster, 1951; Oxford, Wesley Memorial, 1952; Worcester, 1957; Sutton Coldfield, 1964-68; Chm., Southampton District, 1968-77. Religious Advr (Free Church), Southern Television, 1972-77. Chm., Adv. Cttee, Inter-Church Travel Ltd, 1976-. Royal Army Chaplains' Dept, 1942-47 (Senior Chaplain, 1st Infantry Div., 1946). Recreations: music, gardening, ecumenical travel. Address: 22 Vauxhall, St Helier, Jersey, CI. T: Jersey Central 22763.

LEE, Edward, MSc, PhD; FInstP; Director, Admiralty Research Laboratory, Teddington, 1971-74, retired; b 2 March 1914; s of Thomas and Florence Lee; m 1942, Joan Pearson; three d. Educ: Consett Grammar Sch.; Manchester Univ.; Pembroke Coll., Cambridge. Admiralty Research Laboratory, 1939-46; Ministry of Defence, 1946-48; Dept of Physical Research, Admiralty, 1948-51; Admiralty Research Laboratory, 1951-55; Dir of Operational Research, Admty, 1955-58; Dep. Dir, Nat. Physical Laboratory, 1958-60; Director, Stations and Industry Div., DSIR, 1960-65; Dep. Controller (R), Min. of Technology, 1965-70; Head of Res. Services, Dept of Trade and Industry, 1970-71. Publications: scientific papers. Recreations: golf, gardening. Address: 8 Courtlands Avenue, Hampton, Mddx. T: 01-979 1081.

LEE, (Edward) Stanley, FRCS; Consulting Surgeon Westminster Hospital; formerly Civilian Consultant in Surgery of Neoplastic Diseases, Queen Alexandra Military Hospital; Surgeon Emeritus, Guildford Radiotherapy Centre; b 1907. Educ: Westminster Hospital. MB, BS 1931; FRCS, 1933; MS London, 1936. Past Member of Court of Examiners, Royal College of Surgeons, England, 1953-59; Past Member: Grand Council British Empire Cancer Campaign; Internat. Union against Cancer; Assoc. of Head and Neck Oncologists of GB. FRSM; Sen. Fellow, Assoc. of Surgeons. Hon. Mem. Royal College of Radiologists. Publications: contributions to medical literature, etc. Address: Westminster Hospital, SW1; Little Gates, Benenden, Kent.

LEE, George Russell, CMG 1970; Acting Assistant Director, Ministry of Defence, since 1967; b 11 Nov. 1912; s of Ernest Harry Lee and Alice Mary Lee (née Russell); m 1947, Annabella Evelyn (née Dargie); one s one d. Educ: Birkenhead Sch., Cheshire. WO and MoD, 1940-. Address: 30 Christ Church Crescent, Radlett, Herts. T: Radlett 5914.

LEE, Sir (George) Wilton, Kt 1964; TD 1940; President of Arthur Lee & Sons Ltd and Group of Companies, since 1976 (Chairman, 1949-76, Managing Director, 1949-68, Joint Managing Director, 1968-72); b 8 April 1904; e s of Percy W. Lee, Tapton Holt, Sheffield; m 1934, Bettina Stanley, e d of Colonel R. B. Haywood, TD; three s. Educ: Uppingham Sch.; Queens' Coll., Cambridge. Member Exec. Cttee, BISF, 1953-67 (Joint Vice-President, 1966-67); Founding Chm., British Independent Steel Producers' Assoc., 1967-69; Chairman: S Yorks Industrialists' Council; S Yorks Board of Eagle Star

Insurance Co. Ltd, 1948-74. Master Cutler, 1950-51. Chm. City of Sheffield Cons. and Nat. Lib. Fedn., 1959-70. Town Trustee of the City of Sheffield; JP, 1950-64. Vice-Consul for Norway, 1950-. *Recreations:* golf, shooting, fishing. *Address:* Thornfield, Lindrick Common, near Worksop, Nottinghamshire. *T:* Dinnington 2810. *Club:* Sheffield (Sheffield).

LEE, Gilbert Henry Clifton; Chairman, European Hotel Corporation NV, 1975-76; *b* 19 April 1911; *s* of Walter Lee and Sybil Townsend; *m* 1938, Kathleen Cooper; two *d. Educ:* Worksop College. FCIT. Joined Imperial Airways, 1931; served overseas India, E Africa, Pakistan; Gen. Man., West African Airways Corp., 1949-52; BOAC: Traffic Manager, 1953; Gen. Sales Man., 1955; Commercial Dir, 1959; Mem. Bd, BOAC, 1961-73; Chm., BOAC Associated Cos Ltd, 1961-75. *Recreation:* golf. *Address:* Dana, Callow Hill, Virginia Water, Surrey. *T:* Wentworth 2195. *Clubs:* Bath; Wentworth (Virginia Water).

LEE, Sir (Henry) Desmond (Pritchard), Kt 1961; MA; President, Hughes Hall, Cambridge, since 1974; *b* 30 Aug. 1908; *s* of Rev. Canon Henry Burgass Lee; *m* 1935, Elizabeth, *d* of late Colonel A. Crookenden, CBE, DSO; one *s* two *d. Educ:* Repton Sch. (George Denman Scholar); Corpus Christi Coll., Cambridge (Entrance Scholar). 1st Class Part 1 Classical Tripos, 1928; Foundation Scholar of the College; 1st Class Part 2 Classical Tripos, 1930; Charles Oldham Scholar; Fellow of Corpus Christi Coll., 1938, Life Fellow, 1948-68; Tutor, 1935-48; University Lecturer in Classics, 1937-48; Headmaster of Clifton Coll., 1948-54; Headmaster of Winchester Coll., 1954-68. Fellow, University Coll., later Wolfson Coll., Cambridge, 1968-73, Hon. Fellow, 1974. Regional Comr's Office, Cambridge, 1941-44; Mem. Council of the Senate, 1944-48. Mem. Anderson Cttee on Grants to Students, 1958-59; Chm., Headmasters' Conference, 1959-60, 1967. Hon. DLitt (Nottingham), 1963. *Publications:* Zeno of Elea: a Text and Notes (in Cambridge Classical Studies), 1935; Aristotle, Meteorologica, 1952; Plato, Republic, 1955, rev. edn 1974; Plato, Timæus and Critias, 1971; Entry and Performance at Oxford and Cambridge, 1966-71, 1972. *Address:* 8 Barton Close, Cambridge.

LEE, Col Tun Sir Henry Hau Shik, SMN 1959 (Federation of Malaya); KBE 1957 (CBE 1948); JP; Chairman: Development & Commercial Bank Ltd; China Press Ltd; The Timber Syndicate; Board of Governors of Lady Templer Hospital; Council of Elders of Malayan Chinese Association; Director: Golden Castle Finance Corporation, Berhad (Chairman) and Singapore; Hong Leong Finance Co Ltd; International Telephone & Telegraph Corporation; Fancy Tile Works, Berhad; President: Royal Commonwealth Society; Selangur Kwang Tung Association; Federation of Kwang Tung Association; All Malaya Kochow Association; Wine and Food Society; Federation of Malaya Golf Association; Golf Association of Malaysia; Vice-President: Malayan Zoological Society; sole Proprietor of H. S. Lee Tin Mines, Malaya; *b* 19 Nov. 1901; *e s* of late K. L. Lee; *m* 1st, 1922 (wife *d* 1926); one *s* ; 2nd, 1929, Choi Lin (*née* Kwan); four *s* two *d* (and one *s* decd). *Educ:* Queen's Coll., Hongkong; Univ. of Cambridge. BA (Cantab) 1923. War of 1939-45; Chief of Passive Defence Forces, Kuala Lumpur, 1941; Col in Allied Armed Forces, 1942-45. Co-founder, Alliance Party, 1952; Minister of Transport, 1953-56; Minister of Finance, 1956-59. Past Chairman: Federal Finance Cttee, and other political cttees. Member: Standing Sub-Cttee of MCA; Supervisory Council of Bernama, 1967-; Past President: Oxford and Cambridge Soc.; Royal Commonwealth Soc.; Selangor Chinese Chamber of Commerce; Kuen Cheng Girls' Sch.; All Malaya Chinese Mining Assoc.; Associated Chinese Chambers of Commerce, Malaya and Singapore; United Lee's Assoc.; Selangor MCA; Sen. Golfers' Soc., Malaya, 1957-58, 1960-63; Fedn Malaya Red Cross Soc.; Fedn Malaya Olympic Council; Past Member: KL Sanitary Board; Council FMS Chamber of Mines; Council of State, Selangor; Malayan Union Advisory Council; Tin Advisory Cttee; Chinese Tin Mines Rehabilitation Loans Board; War Damage Commn; Federal Finance Cttee; Malayan Tin Delegn to all Internat. Tin Meetings; Fed. Leg. Council, 1948-57; Fed. Exec. Council, 1948-57; Dir, Ops. Cttee, 1948-55. Alliance Exec. Cttee and Alliance Nat. Council, 1953-59; Merdeka Mission to London, 1956; Financial Mission to London, 1957; Mem. Cabinet, 1957-59. JP, Kuala Lumpur, 1938. Hon. Mem. clubs: Selangor Chinese Recreation (Hon. Vice-Pres.); Royal Selangor Golf; Lake; Selangor Miners' (Pres., 1938-); Kuala Lumpur Rotary; Selangor Turf. Mem., British Assoc. of Malaysia; Member, Four Hundred Club, London. FREconS (Eng.). *Recreations:* riding, golf, tennis. *Address:* 23 Jalan Langgak Golf, Kuala Lumpur, Malaysia. *Clubs:* Selangor; Singapore Island Country; Royal and Ancient Golf (St Andrews).

LEE, John Michael Hubert; MP (Lab) Birmingham, Handsworth, since Feb. 1974; Barrister-at-Law; *b* 13 Aug. 1927; *s* of Victor Lee, Wentworth, Surrey, and late Renee Lee; *m* 1960, Margaret Ann, *d* of James Russell, ICS, retired, and Kathleen Russell; one *s* one *d. Educ:* Reading Sch.; Christ's Coll., Cambridge (Open Exhibnr Modern Hist.; MA). Colonial Service: Administrative Officer, Ghana, 1951-58; Principal Assistant Secretary, Min. of Communications, Ghana, 1958. On staff of BBC, 1959-65. Called to the Bar, Middle Temple, 1960; practising, Midland and Oxford Circuit, 1966-. MP (Lab) Reading, 1966-70; Chm., W Midland Gp of Labour MPs, 1974-75. Mem., TGWU, 1959-. *Publications:* articles in Fabian Commonwealth magazine Venture and TGWU Jl Record; chapter in the Radical Future (ed Whitaker), 1967. *Recreations:* gardening, tennis, good conversation, walking. *Address:* 2 Dr Johnson's Buildings, EC4. *Club:* Royal Over-Seas League.

LEE, John (Thomas Cyril); His Honour Judge John Lee; Circuit Judge (attached Midland Oxford Circuit), since Sept. 1972; *b* 14 Jan. 1927; *s* of Cyril and Dorothy Lee; *m* 1956, Beryl Lee (*née* Haden); one *s* three *d. Educ:* Holly Lodge Grammar Sch., Staffs; Emmanuel Coll., Cambridge (MA, LLB). Called to Bar, Gray's Inn, 1952. Practised, Oxford Circuit, 1952-72. Chairman various Tribunals. *Recreation:* golf. *Address:* 38 Britannia Square, Worcester WR1 3DN. *T:* Worcester 28838. *Clubs:* Union and County (Worcester); Worcester Golf and Country.

LEE KUAN YEW; Prime Minister, Singapore, since 1959; *b* 16 Sept. 1923; *s* of Lee Chin Koon and Chua Jim Neo; *m* 1950, Kwa Geok Choo; two *s* one *d. Educ:* Raffles Coll., Singapore; Fitzwilliam Coll., Cambridge, Hon Fellow, 1969. Double first Law Tripos, Star for special distinction. Called to Bar, Middle Temple, 1950, Hon. Bencher, 1969. Advocate and Solicitor, Singapore, 1951. Formed People's Action Party, 1954, Sec.-Gen., 1954-. Fellow, Inst. of Politics, Harvard, 1968; Hoyt Fellow, Berkeley Coll., Yale, 1970. Hon. CH 1970; Hon. GCMG 1972. Holds many hon. degrees, hon. fellowships and foreign orders. *Recreations:* reading, walking, golf. *Address:* Prime Minister's Office, Singapore. *T:* 31155.

LEE, Laurie, MBE 1952; poet and author; *m* 1950, Catherine Francesca Polge; one *d. Educ:* Slad Village Sch.; Stroud Central Sch. Travelled Mediterranean, 1935-39; GPO Film Unit, 1939-40; Crown Film Unit, 1941-43; Publications Editor, Ministry of Information, 1944-46; Green Park Film Unit, 1946-47; Caption Writer-in-Chief, Festival of Britain, 1950-51. *Publications:* The Sun My Monument (Poems), 1944; Land at War (HMSO), 1945; (with Ralph Keene) A Film in Cyprus, 1947; The Bloom of Candles (Poems), 1947; The Voyage of Magellan, 1948; My Many-Coated Man (Poems), 1955; A Rose for Winter, 1955; Cider With Rosie (autobiography), 1959; Pocket Poets (Selection), 1960; The Firstborn, 1964; As I Walked Out One Midsummer Morning (autobiography), 1969; I Can't Stay Long, 1976. *Recreations:* indoor sports, music, travel. *Address:* 49 Elm Park Gardens, SW10. *T:* 01-352 2197. *Clubs:* Chelsea Arts, Garrick.

LEE, Rt. Rev. Paul Chun Hwan; see Seoul (Korea), Bishop of.

LEE, Stanley; see Lee, (Edward) S.

LEE, Tsung-Dao; Enrico Fermi Professor of Physics at Columbia University, USA, since 1964; *b* 25 Nov. 1926; 3rd *s* of C. K. and M. C. Lee; *m* 1950, Jeannette H. C. Chin; two *s. Educ:* National Chekiang Univ., Kweichow, China; National Southwest Associated Univ., Kunming, China; University of Chicago, USA. Research Associate: University of Chicago, 1950; University of California, 1950-51; Member, Inst. for Advanced Study, Princeton, 1951-53. Columbia University: Asst Professor, 1953-55; Associate Professor, 1955-56; Professor, 1956-60; Member, Institute for Advanced Study, Princeton, 1960-63; Columbia Univ.: Adjunct Professor, 1960-62; Visiting Professor, 1962-63; Professor, 1963-. Nobel Prize for the non-conservation of parity (with C. N. Yang), 1957; Albert Einstein Award in Science, 1957; Member, National Academy of Sciences, 1964. Hon. Dr Science, Princeton Univ., 1958. *Publications:* mostly in Physical Review. *Address:* Department of Physics, Columbia University, New York, New York 10027, USA.

LEE, Sir William (Allison), Kt 1975; OBE 1945; TD 1948; DL; Chairman, Northern Regional Health Authority, since 1973; *b* 31 May 1907; *s* of Samuel Percy and Florence Ada Lee, Darlington; *m* 1st, 1933, Elsa Norah (*d* 1966), *d* of late Thomas Hanning, Darlington; 2nd, 1967, Mollie Clifford, *d* of late Sir Cuthbert Whiteside, Knysna, S Africa; no *c. Educ:* Queen Elizabeth Grammar Sch., Darlington. Insurance Branch Manager, retd. Served R Signals, 1935-53; Dep. Comdr, 151 Inf. Bde (TA), 1953-58; County Comdt, Durham ACF, 1962-70.

Mem., Darlington RDC, 1949-61, Chm. 1957-60. Chairman: Winterton HMC, 1967-70 (Mem., 1954-70); Newcastle Reg. Hosp. Bd, 1973-74 (Mem., 1956-74). DL County of Durham, 1965. *Recreations:* beagling, fell walking, gardening. *Address:* The Woodlands, Woodland Road, Darlington, Co. Durham. *T:* Darlington 62318. *Clubs:* Army and Navy; Cleveland (Middlesbrough).

LEE, Rev. W(illiam) Walker; Chairman of the Bolton and Rochdale District of the Methodist Church since 1957; President, Conference of the Methodist Church, 1965; Chairman, Leeds District of Methodist Church since Sept. 1966; *b* 1909; *s* of Matthew and Florence Lee; *m* 1935, Laura Annie Linsley; one *d*; *m* 1975, Kathleen Burgess. *Educ:* King James I Grammar Sch., Bishop Auckland; Hartley Victoria Theological Coll., Manchester. Minister: Redditch Methodist Circuit, 1931-35; Birmingham Mission, 1935-40; Leeds Mission, 1940-44; Superintendent: Wednesbury Mission, 1944-49; Bolton Mission, 1949-57. Member of Methodist Delegation in Conversations between Church of England and Methodist Church, 1955-63. Hon. MA (Manchester). *Recreation:* gardening. *Address:* 281 Otley Road, West Park, Leeds LS16 5LN. *T:* Leeds 785546.

LEE, Sir Wilton; *see* Lee, Sir G. W.

LEE YONG LENG, Dr; Professor and Head of Department of Geography, University of Singapore, since 1977; *b* 26 March 1930; *m* Wong Loon Meng; one *d*. *Educ:* Univs of Oxford, Malaya and Singapore. BLitt (Oxon), MA (Malaya), PhD (Singapore). Research Asst, Univ. of Malaya, 1954-56; University Lectr/Sen. Lectr, Univ. of Singapore, 1956-70; Associate Prof., Univ. of Singapore, 1970-71; High Comr for Singapore in London, 1971-75; Ambassador to Denmark, 1974-75, and Ireland, 1975; Min. of Foreign Affairs, Singapore, 1975-76. *Publications:* North Borneo, 1965; Sarawak, 1970; articles in: Population Studies; Geog. Jl; Erdkunde; Jl Trop. Geog., etc. *Recreations:* swimming, tennis, travelling, reading. *Address:* Department of Geography, University of Singapore, Bukit Timah Road, Singapore 10.

LEE-BARBER, Rear-Adm. John, CB 1959; DSO 1940 and Bar 1941; Admiral Superintendent, HM Dockyard, Malta, 1957-59, retired; *b* 16 April 1905; *s* of Richard Lee-Barber, Herringfleet, near Great Yarmouth; *m* 1939, Suzanne (*d* 1976), *d* of Colonel Le Gallais, ADC, MC, La Moye, Jersey, CI; two *d*. *Educ:* Royal Naval Colleges, Osborne and Dartmouth. Service in destroyers and in Yangtze gunboat until 1937; CO Witch, 1937-38; CO Griffin, 1939-40-41; Commander, 1941; CO Opportune, 1942-44; 2nd in Command, HMS King Alfred, 1945; CO, HMS St James, 1946-47; Captain, 1947; Senior Officer Reserve Fleet, Harwich, 1948-49; Naval Attaché, Chile, 1950-52; CO Agincourt and Captain D4, 1952-54; Commodore, Inshore Flotilla, 1954-56; Rear-Admiral, 1957. Polish Cross of Valour, 1940. *Recreation:* sailing. *Address:* The Vines, The Quay, Wivenhoe, Essex. *T:* Wivenhoe 5810. *Club:* Royal Ocean Racing.

LEE HOWARD, Leon Alexander, DFC 1944; writer and journalist; *b* 18 June 1914; *m* 1973, Madelon Dimont. *Educ:* privately. Served War of 1939-45: RAF Coastal Command, 1940-43; RAF Operational Film Production Unit, 1943-45. Editor: Woman's Sunday Mirror, 1955-59; Sunday Pictorial, 1959-61; Daily Mirror, 1961-71. Hon. Knight of Mark Twain, 1977. *Publications:* fiction: as Leigh Howard: Crispin's Day, 1952; Johnny's Sister, 1954; Blind Date, 1955; as Alexander Krislov: No Man Sings, 1956. *Recreations:* writing, journalism. *Address:* 9 Hopefield Avenue, NW6.

LEE POTTER, Air Marshal Sir Patrick (Brunton), KBE 1958 (CBE 1953; OBE 1946); MD (Sheffield) 1936; *b* 15 March 1904; *s* of Samuel Lee Potter and Isabella Henrietta Handyside; *m* 1933, Audrey Mary Pollock; two *s*. *Educ:* Epsom Coll.; Sheffield Univ. MB, ChB 1928. Joined RAF Medical Branch, 1928; DTM & H, 1931; DPH 1934; MD 1936. OC RAF Institute of Pathology, 1939; served War of 1939-45: Middle East and Air Ministry (despatches twice, OBE); OC 21 Mobile Field Hospital, 1940-42; Air Ministry, 1943-45; psa 1947; DMS, RNZAF, 1948-50; Director Hygiene and Research, Air Ministry, 1951-53; PMO, Bomber Command, 1953-55; PMO, MEAF, 1955-57; Director General, RAF Medical Services, 1957-62. Air Vice-Marshal, 1956. QHS 1953-62. KStJ. *Publication:* RAF Handbook of Preventive Medicine, 1947. *Recreation:* golf. *Address:* Barge Cottage, Rolvenden, Kent. *Club:* Royal Air Force.

LEECH, Robert Radcliffe; His Honour Judge Leech; a Circuit Judge (formerly Judge of County Courts), since 1970; *b* 5 Dec. 1919; *s* of late Edwin Radcliffe Leech; *m* 1951, Vivienne Ruth, *d*

of A. J. Rickerby, Carlisle; two *d*. *Educ:* Monmouth Sch.; Worcester Coll., Oxford (Open Classics Exhibnr 1938). Served War, 1940-44, Border Regt (despatches twice). Called to Bar, Middle Temple, 1949 (Harmsworth Law Scholar); Dep. Chm., Cumberland QS, 1966-71. *Recreations:* sailing, golf. *Address:* Goldsmith Building, Temple, EC4; Brackenrigg, Bassenthwaite, Keswick, Cumbria CA12 4PD. *Club:* Cumberland County (Carlisle).

LEECH-PORTER, Maj.-Gen. John Edmund, CB 1950; CBE 1945 (OBE 1944); OStJ; *b* 1896; *s* of Henry Leech-Porter, Winchester. *Educ:* Imperial Service Coll., Windsor. 2nd Lt RMA, 1914; served European War, 1914-19. Major, 1934; Lt-Col, 1941; Actg Brig., 1942-45; served in Sicily, 1943, and NW Europe, 1944-45; comdg Portsmouth Gp, 1949, Plymouth Gp, 1950-51, Royal Marines; retired list, 1951. Comdr Order of Leopold II with Palm; Croix de Guerre with Palm. *Recreations:* fishing, shooting, golf. *Address:* Camplehaye Hotel, Lamerton, Tavistock, Devon.

LEECHMAN, Hon. Lord; James Graham Leechman; a Senator of the College of Justice in Scotland, 1965-76; *b* 6 Oct. 1906; *s* of late Walter Graham Leechman, solicitor, Glasgow, and late Barbara Louisa Leechman (*née* Neilson); *m* 1935, Margaret Helen Edgar; two *d*. *Educ:* High Sch. and Univ., Glasgow. MA 1927; BSc 1928; LLB 1930. Admitted to Membership of Faculty of Advocates, 1932; Advocate-Depute, 1947-49; KC 1949; Clerk of Justiciary, 1949-64; Solicitor-Gen. for Scotland, 1964-65. *Recreation:* golf. *Address:* 626 Queensferry Road, Edinburgh EH4 6AT. *T:* 031-339 6513.

LEECHMAN, Barclay, CMG 1952; OBE 1941; Executive Director, Tanganyika Sisal Growers' Assoc., 1959-66; Chairman, Transport Licensing Authority, Tanganyika, 1956-59; Member for Social Services, Tanganyika, 1948-55; retired from Colonial Service, 1956; *b* Eastbourne, 28 Sept. 1901; *e s* of late Alleyne Leechman, MA, FLS, FCS, Bexhill, and late of Colonial Civil Service and late Jean Macmaster Leechman; *m* 1933, Grace, 4th *d* of late Frederick William Coller, Cape Town, SA; no *c*. *Educ:* Oundle Sch. Cadet, Colonial Administrative Service, Tanganyika, 1925; Asst District Officer, 1928; District Officer, 1937; Dep. Provincial Commissioner, 1944; Labour Commissioner, 1946. Seconded as Sec. of East African Economic Council, Nairobi, 1940-41, and Dir of Economic Control, Aden, 1943-45. Pres. Fedn of Tanganyika Employers, 1964-66 (Vice-Pres., 1959-63). Fellow, Ancient Monuments Soc. *Recreations:* books and music. *Address:* c/o Grindlay's Bank, 13 St James's Square, SW1. *Clubs:* Reform, Farmers'; City (Cape Town).

LEECHMAN, James Graham; *see* Leechman, Hon. Lord.

LEEDALE, Harry Heath, CBE 1972; Controller of Surtax and Inspector of Foreign Dividends, 1968-74; *b* 23 June 1914; *s* of John Leedale and Amy Alice Leedale (*née* Heath), New Malden; *m* 1st, 1940, Audrey Beryl (*née* Platt) (*d* 1970); one *d*; 2nd, 1971, Sheila Tyas Stephen. *Educ:* Henry Thornton Sch., Clapham, London. Served War, RAF, 1941-46. Entered Inland Revenue, 1933; Controller, Assessments Div., 1961; Asst Clerk to Special Commissioners of Income Tax, 1963; Controller, Superannuation Funds Office, 1964. *Recreations:* gardening, foreign travel. *Address:* 22 Leopold Avenue, Wimbledon SW19 7ET. *T:* 01-946 4611; Lavender Cottage, Rotherfield, Sussex. *T:* Rotherfield 2424.

LEEDS, Bishop of, (RC), since 1966; **Rt. Rev. William Gordon Wheeler,** MA Oxon; *b* 5 May 1910; *o s* of late Frederick Wheeler and Marjorie (*née* Upjohn). *Educ:* Manchester Gram. Sch.; University Coll. and St Stephen's House, Oxford; Beda Coll., Rome. Curate, St Bartholomew's, Brighton, 1933; Curate, St Mary and All Saints, Chesterfield, 1934; Asst Chaplain, Lancing Coll., 1935. Received into Roman Catholic Church at Downside, 1936; Beda Coll., Rome, 1936-40; ordained priest, 1940; Asst, St Edmund's, Lower Edmonton, 1940-44; Chaplain of Westminster Cathedral and Editor of Westminster Cathedral Chronicle, 1944-50; Chaplain to the Catholics in the University, London, 1950-54, and Ecclesiastical Adviser to the Union of Catholic Students, 1953-60; Privy Chamberlain to HH The Pope, 1952; Hon. Canon of Westminster, 1954, Administrator of Cathedral, 1954-64; Created Domestic Prelate to HH Pope Pius XII, 1955; Conventual Chaplain to the British Association of the Sovereign and Military Order of Malta, 1958; Coadjutor Bishop of Middlesbrough, 1964-66. *Publications:* Edited and contributed to Homage to Newman, 1945; Richard Challoner, 1947; The English Catholics, etc. Contribs to Dublin Review, The Tablet, etc. *Address:* Bishop's House, Eltofts, Carr Lane, Thorner, Leeds LS14 3HF. *T:* Leeds 892687. *Club:* Athenæum.

LEEDS, Auxiliary Bishop of, (RC); see Moverley, Rt Rev. Gerald.

LEEDS, Archdeacon of; see Page, Ven. A. C.

LEEDS, Sir George (Graham Mortimer), 7th Bt cr 1812; b 21 Aug. 1927; s of Sir Reginald Arthur St John Leeds, 6th Bt, and of Winnaretta, d of late Paris Eugene Singer; S father, 1970; m 1954, Nicola (marr. diss. 1965, she d 1972), d of Douglas Robertson McBean, MC; three d. Educ: Eton. Formerly Captain, Grenadier Guards. Heir: cousin Christopher Anthony Leeds [b 31 Aug. 1935; m 1974, Elaine Joyce, d of late Sqdn Ldr C. H. A. Mullins]. Address: Roche Bois, Mont ès Tours, St Aubin, Jersey.

LEEK, James, CBE 1941; lately Director BSA Co. Ltd, BSA Guns Ltd, BSA Motor Cycles Ltd; Ariel Motors Ltd, Birmingham; Monochrome Ltd; Triumph Engineering Co. Ltd, Coventry; President Birmingham Chamber of Commerce, 1949; b 12 Sept. 1892; s of Richard Harley and Annie Leek; m 1917, Kathleen Louise, d of J. E. Riley, Manufacturer, Bradford; one s. Educ: Newport Grammar School, Newport. Address: Sandown, 19 Banbury Road, Stratford-on-Avon, Warwicks. T: Stratford-on-Avon 3590.

LEEMING, John Coates; a Commissioner of Customs and Excise, since 1975; b 3 May 1927; s of late James Arthur Leeming and Harriet Leeming; m 1949 (marr. diss. 1974); two s. Educ: Chadderton Grammar Sch., Lancs; St John's Coll., Cambridge (Schol.). Teaching, Hyde Grammar Sch., Cheshire, 1948. Asst Principal, HM Customs and Excise, 1950 (Private Sec. to Chm.); Principal: HM Customs and Excise, 1954; HM Treasury, 1956; HM Customs and Excise, 1958; Asst Sec., HM Customs and Excise, 1965; IBRD (World Bank), Washington, DC, 1967; Asst Sec., 1970, Under Sec., 1972, CSD. Recreation: golf. Address: 10 Woodcote Green Road, Epsom, Surrey. T: Epsom 25397. Club: Royal Automobile.

LEEPER, Richard Kevin; Life President of the Lep Group Ltd; b 14 July 1894; s of late William John Leeper of Stranorlar, Co. Donegal; m 1916, Elizabeth Mary Fenton (d 1975); two s. Educ: Sligo Gram. Sch.; London Univ. Served in Army, European War, 1914-18; Dir of Transport, MAP, 1940-45. Engaged in shipping and forwarding in Yugoslavia, 1920-32; Managing Dir of Lep Transport Ltd and Chief Executive of the Lep Group of Companies, 1932; Chm., The Lep Gp Ltd, 1956-72. MCIT; FRSA. Kt Comdr, Order of Holy Sepulchre; Order of St Sava (Yugoslavia), 1930. Address: Sunlight Wharf, Upper Thames Street, EC4. T: 01-236 5050; Holly Wood House, West Byfleet, Surrey. T: Byfleet 42537.

LEES, Prof. Anthony David, FRS 1968; Deputy Chief Scientific Officer, and Professor of Insect Physiology, Agricultural Research Council at Imperial College Field Station, Ascot; b 27 Feb. 1917; s of Alan Henry Lees, MA and Mary Hughes Bomford; m 1943, Annzella Pauline Wilson; one d. Educ: Clifton Coll., Bristol; Trinity Hall, Cambridge (Schol.). BA 1939; PhD (Cantab) 1943; ScD 1966. Mem., ARC Unit of Insect Physiology at Zoology Dept, Cambridge, 1945-67; Lalor Fellow, 1956; Vis. Prof., Adelaide Univ., 1966; Hon. Lectr, London Univ., 1968. Pres., Royal Entomological Soc., 1973-75. Publications: scientific papers. Recreations: gardening, fossicking. Address: Wells Lane Corner, Sunninghill, Ascot, Berks.

LEES, Sir Antony; see Lees, Sir W. A. C.

LEES, C(harles) Norman; a Recorder of the Crown Court, since 1972; b 4 Oct. 1929; s of late Charles Lees, Bramhall, Cheshire; m 1961, Stella, d of Hubert Swann, Stockport; one d. Educ: Stockport Sch.; Univ. of Leeds. LLB 1950. Called to Bar, Lincoln's Inn, 1951. A Legal Chm. of Disciplinary Cttee, Potato Marketing Bd, 1965-; Dep. Chm., Cumberland County QS, 1969-71; Mem., Mental Health Review Tribunal, Manchester Region, 1971-. Recreations: squash rackets, music, history. Address: 102 Heathbank Road, Cheadle Hulme, Cheadle, Cheshire. T: 061-485 3973; 1 Deans Court, Crown Square, Manchester M3 3JL. Clubs: Manchester (Manchester); Northern Lawn Tennis.

LEES, David, CBE 1963; Rector, The High School of Glasgow, 1950-76; b 12 Aug. 1910; s of late David Lees and Margaret W. Lees, Airdrie; m 1935, Olive, d of Arthur and Alice Willington, Montreal; one s two d. Educ: Airdrie Academy; Glasgow, McGill and London Univs. MA (Hons) Glasgow, 1930; MA in Education, McGill, 1932; BA (Hons) London, 1945. Principal Teacher of Classics, Campbeltown Gram. Sch., 1933-46; Rector, Elgin Academy, 1946-49; Dir of Education, Roxburghshire,

1949-50. Hon. LLD Glasgow, 1970. Recreation: bridge. Address: Oaklea, 16 Larch Road, Glasgow G41 5DA. T: 041-427 0322. Clubs: St Andrew Bridge (Glasgow); Campbeltown (Argyll).

LEES, Prof. Dennis Samuel; Professor of Industrial Economics, University of Nottingham, since 1968; b 20 July 1924; s of Samuel Lees and Evelyn Lees (née Withers), Borrowash, Derbyshire; m 1950, Elizabeth Bretisch, London; two s one d. Educ: Derby Technical Coll.; Nottingham Univ. BSc(Econ), PhD. Lecturer and Reader in Economics, Keele Univ., 1951-65; Prof. of Economics, University Coll., Swansea, 1965-67. Visiting Prof. of Economics: Univ. of Chicago, 1963-64; Univ. of California, Berkeley, 1971; Univ. of Sydney, 1975. Mem., Economists' Advisory Gp Ltd, 1966-; Chairman: Nat. Ins. Advisory Committee, 1972-; Industrial Injuries Advisory Council, 1973-; Member: Chief Scientist's Research Cttee, DHSS, 1973-; Freeman, City of London, 1973. Publications: Local Expenditure and Exchequer Grants, 1956; Health Thru Choice, 1961; Economic Consequences of the Professions, 1966; Economics of Advertising, 1967; Financial Facilities for Small Firms, 1971; Impairment, Disability, Handicap, 1974; Economics of Personal Injury, 1976; articles on industrial and social policy in: Economica, Jl of Political Economy, Amer. Econ. Rev., Jl of Law and Econ., Jl Industrial Econ., Jl Public Finance. Recreations: cricket and pottering. Address: 8 Middleton Crescent, Beeston, Nottingham. T: Nottingham 258730. Club: National Liberal.

LEES, Geoffrey William; Headmaster, St Bees School, since 1963; b 1 July 1920; o s of late Mr F. T. Lees and of Mrs Lees, Manchester; m 1949, Joan Needham, yr d of late Mr and Mrs J. Needham, Moseley, Birmingham. Educ: King's Sch., Rochester; Downing Coll., Cambridge. Royal Signals, 1940-46 (despatches): commissioned 1941; served in NW Europe and Middle East, Captain. 2nd Class Hons English Tripos, Pt I, 1947; History Tripos, Part II, 1948; Asst Master, Brighton Coll., 1948-63. Leave of absence in Australia, Asst Master, Melbourne Church of England Gram. Sch., 1961-62. Recreations: reading, games, walking. Address: St Bees School, Cumbria. T: St Bees 263. Clubs: MCC; Hawks', Union (Cambridge).

LEES, Norman; see Lees, C. N.

LEES, Roland James, CB 1977; Director, Royal Signals and Radar Establishment, Malvern, 1976-77; b 3 Dec. 1917; s of late Roland John Lees and late Ada Bell (née Jeavons), Stourbridge, Worcs; m 1948, Esmé Joyce, d of late Alfred Thomas Hill, Malvern Link, Worcs; no c. Educ: King Edward's Sch., Stourbridge; St John's Coll., Cambridge. BA Cantab 1939; BSc London 1939; MA Cantab 1942. Dir, Scientific Research Electronics and Guided Weapons, Min. of Supply, 1955-56; Head of Airborne Radar Dept, RRE, 1957-58; Head of Instruments and Electrical Engrg Dept, RAE, 1959-62; Dir, Signals Research and Development Establishment, 1963-65; Dep. Dir (Equipment), RAE, 1966-72; Dir, RRE, 1972-76. Assessor to Lord Mountbatten, Inquiry into Prison Security, 1966. Address: Fairoaks, 4 Frensham Vale, Lower Bourne, Farnham, Surrey GU10 3HN. T: Frensham 3146.

LEES, Air Marshal Sir Ronald Beresford, KCB 1961 (CB 1946); CBE 1943; DFC; retired as C-in-C, RAF, Germany, 1963-65; b 27 April 1910; s of John Thomas and Elizabeth Jane Lees; m 1931, Rhoda Lillie Pank; one s one d. Educ: St Peter's Coll., Adelaide, Australia. Joined Royal Australian Air Force, 1930; transferred Royal Air Force, 1931. ADC to the Queen, 1952-53 (to King George VI, 1949-52); AOC No 83 Gp, 2nd TAF in Germany, 1952-55; Asst Chief of Air Staff (Operations), 1955-58; SASO, Fighter Command, 1958-60; Dep. Chief of the Air Staff, 1960-63; Air Marshal, 1961. Address: Jelbra, RMB 367, Albury, NSW 2640, Australia. Club: Commercial.

LEES, Stanley Lawrence, MVO 1952; Under-Secretary, Ministry of Transport, 1967-70, retired; b 1911; yr s of Dr Charlie Lees and Eveleen Lees, Tunbridge Wells; m 1938, Audrey, d of A. E. Lynam, Oxford; two s two d. Educ: Rugby Sch.; New Coll., Oxford. Solicitor, 1936; Solicitor's Office, Inland Revenue, 1936; Secretaries' Office, Inland Revenue, 1943; Royal Navy, 1944; HM Treasury, 1946; Under-Sec., 1958; Dir of Organisation and Methods, 1959-66. Address: 3 Malbrook Road, Putney, SW15. T: 01-788 6732.

LEES, Sir Thomas (Edward), 4th Bt, cr 1897; landowner; b 31 Jan. 1925; 2nd s of Sir John Victor Elliott Lees, 3rd Bt, DSO, MC, and Madeline A. P. (d 1967), d of Sir Harold Pelly, 4th Bt; S father 1955; m 1949, Faith Justin, d of G. G. Jessiman, OBE, Great Durnford, Wilts; one s three d. Educ: Eton; Magdalene Coll., Cambridge. Served War in RAF; discharged 1945, after losing eye. Magdalene, Cambridge, 1945-47; BA Cantab 1947 (Agriculture). Since then has farmed at and managed South Lytchett estate. Chairman: Lytchett Minster Gospel Film Assoc. Ltd; Post Green Community Trust Ltd. Mem., General Synod of C of E, 1970-. JP 1951, CC 1952-74, High Sheriff 1960, Dorset. *Recreations:* field sports, sailing. *Heir:* s Christopher James Lees, *b* 4 Nov. 1952. *Address:* Post Green, Lytchett Minster, Poole, Dorset. *T:* Lytchett Minster 2317. *Clubs:* Farmers', Royal Cruising.

LEES, Sir Thomas Harcourt Ivor, 8th Bt *cr* (UK) 1804, of Black Rock, County Dublin; *b* 6 Nov. 1941; *s* of Sir Charles Archibald Edward Ivor Lees, 7th Bt, and of Lily, *d* of Arthur Williams, Manchester; *S* father, 1963. *Heir: kinsman* John Cathcart d'Olier-Lees [*b* 12 Nov. 1927; *m* 1957, Wendy Garrold, *yr d* of late Brian Garrold Groom; two *s*].

LEES, Walter Kinnear P.; *see* Pyke-Lees.

LEES, Sir (William) Antony (Clare), 3rd Bt *cr* 1937; *b* 14 June 1935; *s* of Sir (William) Hereward Clare Lees, 2nd Bt, and of Lady (Dorothy Gertrude) Lees, *d* of F. A. Lauder; *S* father, 1976. *Educ:* Eton; Magdalene Coll., Cambridge (MA). *Heir:* none. *Address:* Waterside Cottage, New Mill, Pewsey, Wilts SN9 5LD.

LEES-MILNE, James; author; *b* 6 Aug. 1908; *er s* of George Crompton Lees-Milne, Crompton Hall, Lancs and Wickhamford Manor, Worcs; *m* 1951, Alvilde, formerly wife of 3rd Viscount Chaplin and *d* of late Lt-Gen. Sir Tom Molesworth Bridges, KCB, KCMG, DSO; no *c. Educ:* Eton Coll.; Magdalen Coll., Oxford. Private Sec. to 1st Baron Lloyd, 1931-35; on staff, Reuters, 1935-36; on staff, National Trust, 1936-66; Adviser on Historic Buildings to National Trust, 1951-66. 2nd Lieut Irish Guards, 1940-41 (invalided). FRSL 1957; FSA 1974; Hon. FTCM, 1948. *Publications:* The National Trust (ed), 1945; The Age of Adam, 1947; National Trust Guide: Buildings, 1948; Tudor Renaissance, 1951; The Age of Inigo Jones, 1953; Roman Mornings, 1956 (Heinemann Award, 1956); Baroque in Italy, 1959; Baroque in Spain and Portugal, 1960; Earls of Creation, 1962; Worcestershire: A Shell Guide, 1964; St Peter's, 1967; English Country Houses: Baroque 1685-1714, 1970; Another Self, 1970; Heretics in Love, 1973; Ancestral Voices, 1975; William Beckford, 1976; Prophesying Peace, 1977. *Recreations:* walking, sightseeing. *Address:* 19 Lansdown Crescent, Bath. *T:* Bath 316182. *Club:* Brooks's.

LEES-SPALDING, Rear-Adm. Ian Jaffery, CB 1973; RN retd; CEng; FIMechE; Administrator, London International Film School, since 1975; *b* London, 16 June 1920; *s* of Frank Souter Lees-Spalding and Joan (*née* Bodily); *m* 1946, June Sandys Lyster Sparkes; two *d. Educ:* Blundells Sch.; RNEC. MBIM, MIMarE. Served War of 1939-45 (King's Commendation for Bravery, 1941; Royal Lifesaving Inst. medal, 1942): Served in HMS Sirius, HM Submarines Trespasser, Teredo, Truculent, Andrew, HMS Duchess, Cleopatra and Tiger. Cadet 1938; Lt-Comdr 1950; Comdr 1952; Captain 1962; Chief of Staff to C-in-C, Naval Home Comd as Commodore, 1969; Chief Staff Officer (Technical) to C-in-C, Western Fleet, as Rear-Adm, 1971, retd 1974. *Recreations:* music, sailing, travelling. *Address:* St Olaf's, Wonston, Sutton Scotney, Hants S021 3LP. *T:* Sutton Scotney 249. *Club:* Army and Navy.

LEESE, Lt-Gen. Sir Oliver William Hargreaves, 3rd Bt, *cr* 1908; KCB 1943 (CB 1942); CBE 1940; DSO 1916; *b* 27 Oct. 1894; *e s* of 2nd Bt and Violet Mary (*d* 1947), 4th *d* of late Albert G. Sandeman; *S* father, 1937; *m* 1933, Margaret Alice (*d* 1964), *o d* of late Cuthbert Leicester-Warren. *Educ:* Ludgrove; Eton. Served European War, 1914-18 (wounded three times, DSO, despatches twice); Adj. 3rd Bn Coldstream Guards, 1920-22; Adj. OTC Eton, 1922-25; Staff Coll., Camberley, 1927-28; Bde Major, 1st Guards Brigade, 1929-32; DAA and QMG London District, 1932-33; Gen. Staff Officer, 2nd Grade, The War Office, 1935-36; commanded 1st Bn Coldstream Guards, 1936-38; Gen. Staff Officer, 1st Grade, Staff Coll., Quetta, 1938-40; Brigadier, 20th Guards Brigade, 1940; Dep. Chief of the Gen. Staff BEF, 1940; Brigadier, 29th Independent Brigade Group, 1940; Comdr West Sussex Div., 1941; Comdr, 15th (Scottish) Div., Comdr Guards Armoured Div., 1941; Commanding 30th Corps, 1942; Comdr, 8th Army, 1944; C-in-C Allied Land Forces South-East Asia, 1944-45; GOC-in-C Eastern Command, 1945-46; retired, 1946. Dep. Lt County of Salop, 1947. Hon. Col Shropshire Yeo., 1947-62; JP 1949-63; High Sheriff of Salop, 1958. Pres. Combined Cadet Force Assoc., 1950-71. Lieut, Tower of London, 1954. Pres. Warwickshire County Cricket Club, 1959-75; Nat. Pres., British Legion, 1962-70; Pres. Shropshire County Cricket Club, 1962-73; Chm., Old Etonian Assoc., 1964-73 (Pres., 1946); Pres. MCC, 1965-66; Pres.

Cricket Soc., 1969-73. *Heir: b* Alexander William Leese, *b* 27 Sept. 1909. *Address:* Dolwen, Cefn Coch, Llanrhaeadr, Oswestry, Salop. *T:* Llanrhaeadr 411.

LE FANU, Mrs W. R.; *see* Maconchy, Elizabeth.

LEFEBVRE, Prof. Arthur Henry; Professor and Head of School of Mechanical Engineering, Purdue University, since 1976; *b* 14 March 1923; *s* of Henri and May Lefebvre; *m* 1952, Elizabeth Marcella Betts; two *s* one *d. Educ:* Long Eaton Grammar Sch; Nottingham Univ.; Imperial Coll., London. DSc (Eng), DIC, PhD, CEng, FIMechE, FRAeS. Ericssons Telephones Ltd: Engrg apprentice, 1938-41; Prodn Engr, 1941-47; res. work on combustion and heat transfer in gas turbines, Rolls Royce, Derby, 1952-61; Prof. of Aircraft Propulsion, Coll. of Aeronautics, 1961-71; Prof. and Hd of Sch of Mechanical Engrg, Cranfield Inst. of Technol., 1971-76. Mem., AGARD Combustion and Propulsion Panel, 1957-61; Mem., AGARD Propulsion and Energetics Panel, 1970; Chm., Combustion Cttee, Aeronautical Res. Council, 1970-74. *Publications:* papers on combustion and heat transfer in Proc. Royal Soc., internat. symposium vols on combustion, combuston and flame, combustion science and technology. *Recreations:* music, reading, golf. *Address:* 1741 Redwood Lane, Lafayette, Indiana 47905, USA. *T:* (317) 447-0117.

LEFEVER, Kenneth Ernest, CB 1974; Official Side Member, Civil Service Appeal Board, since 1976; *b* 22 Feb. 1915; *s* of E. S. Lefever and Mrs E. E. Lefever; *m* 1939, Margaret Ellen Bowley; one *s* one *d. Educ:* County High Sch., Ilford. Board of Customs and Excise: joined Dept as Officer, 1935; War Service, 1942-46 (Captain, RE); Principal Inspector, 1966; Dep. Chief Inspector, 1969; Collector, London Port, 1971; Chief Inspector, 1972; Dir of Organisation and Chief Inspector, 1974. Comr, Bd of Customs and Excise, 1972-75, retd. *Recreations:* gardening, walking, cricket. *Address:* Trebarwith, 37 Surman Crescent, Hutton Burses, Brentwood, Essex. *T:* Brentwood 212110. *Club:* MCC.

LE FÈVRE, Prof. Raymond James Wood, PhD, DSc London; FRS; FRIC; FRACI; FAA; Professor of Chemistry, 1946-71, now Emeritus, and Head of the School of Chemistry, 1948-71, in the University of Sydney; *b* 1 April 1905; *s* of Raymond James and Ethel May Le Fèvre; *m* 1931, Catherine Gunn Tideman; one *s* one *d. Educ:* Isleworth County Sch.; Queen Mary Coll., University of London. Lecturer in Organic Chemistry, University Coll., London, 1928; Reader, 1939; Chemical Adviser to RAF and RAAF in UK, Far East, and Australia, 1939-44; Asst Dir R & D (Armament Chemistry), Ministry of Aircraft Production, London, 1944; Head, Chem. Dept, RAE Farnborough, 1944-46. Hon. Associate, Macquarie Univ., NSW, 1971-. Trustee, Mitchell Library, Sydney, 1947; Mem., Development Council NSW University of Technology, 1948-50; Trustee, Museum of Applied Arts and Science, Sydney, 1947-75. Foundation Fellow, Austr. Acad. of Science, 1953. Liversidge Lecturer, 1960; Masson Lecturer, ANZAAS, 1967; Pres., Royal Society NSW, 1961. Pres. NSW Br., Royal Aust. Chem. Inst. Smith Medal, Royal Aust. Chem. Inst., 1952; Coronation Medal, 1953; Medal of Royal Soc. of NSW, 1969. Fellow, Queen Mary Coll., London, 1962. *Publications:* Dipole Moments, 3rd edn 1953; Molecular Polarizability and Refractivity, 1965; Establishment of Chemistry within Australian Science, 1968; about 450 papers on chemical research topics, mostly in Jl Chem. Soc., Trans. Faraday Soc., Austr. Jl Chem., etc. *Recreation:* pleasant work. *Address:* 6 Aubrey Road, Northbridge, Sydney, NSW 2063, Australia. *T:* 951018.

LEFF, Prof. Gordon; Professor of History, University of York, since 1969; *b* 9 May 1926; *m* 1953, Rosemary Kathleen (*née* Fox); one *s. Educ:* Summerhill Sch.; King's Coll., Cambridge. BA 1st Cl. Hons, PhD, LittD. Fellow, King's Coll., Cambridge, 1955-59; Asst Lectr, Lectr, Sen. Lectr, in History, Manchester Univ., 1956-65; Reader in History, Univ. of York, 1965-69. *Publications:* Bradwardine and the Pelagians, 1957; Medieval Thought, 1958; Gregory of Rimini, 1961; The Tyranny of Concepts, 1961; Richard Fitzralph, 1963; Heresy in the Later Middle Ages, 2 vols, 1967; Paris and Oxford Universities in 13th and 14th Centuries, 1968; History and Social Theory, 1969; William of Ockham: the metamorphosis of scholastic discourse, 1975; The Dissolution of the Medieval Outlook, 1976. *Recreations:* walking, gardening, watching cricket, listening to music. *Address:* The Sycamores, 12 The Village, Strensall, York YO3 8XS. *T:* York 490358.

le FLEMING, Sir William Kelland, 11th Bt *cr* 1705; *b* 27 April 1922; *s* of Sir Frank Thomas le Fleming, 10th Bt, and of Isabel Annie Fraser, *d* of late James Craig, Manaia, NZ; *S* father, 1971; *m* 1948, Noveen Avis, *d* of C. C. Sharpe, Rukuhia, Hamilton,

NZ; three s four d. *Heir:* s Quentin John le Fleming [b 27 June 1949; m 1971, Judith Ann, d of C. J. Peck, JP; one s one d]. *Address:* Kopane RD6, Palmerston North, New Zealand.

LE GALLAIS, Sir Richard (Lyle), Kt 1965; Regional Chairman, Industrial Tribunals (Bristol), since 1972; b 15 Nov. 1916; s of late William Le Gallais and Mrs Cory; m 1947, Juliette Forsythe; two s. *Educ:* Victoria Coll., Jersey; Inns of Court Sch. of Law. Called to Bar, 1939; Dep. Asst JAG (SEAC) 1945. Pres. War Crimes Tribunal, Singapore, 1946 (Lt-Col). Advocate, Royal Court, Jersey, 1947; Resident Magistrate, Kenya, 1949; Sen. Res. Magistrate and Acting Puisne Judge, N Rhodesia, 1958; Chief Justice, Aden, 1960-67. Mem. Panel of Chairmen, Industrial Tribunals for England and Wales, 1968-72. *Recreations:* gastronomy, music. *Address:* Bainly House, Gillingham, Dorset. *T:* Bourton 373. *Club:* Army and Navy.

LE GALLIENNE, Eva; Theatrical Producer, Director and Actress; b London, England, 11 Jan. 1899; d of Richard Le Gallienne and Julie Norregaard. *Educ:* College Sévigné, Paris, France. Début Prince of Wales Theatre, London, in The Laughter of Fools, 1915; New York Début in The Melody of Youth, 1916; appeared in NY and on tour, in Mr Lazarus, season of 1916-17; with Ethel Barrymore in The Off Chance, 1917-18; Not So Long Ago, 1920-21; Liliom, 1921-22; The Swan, 1923; Hannele in The Assumption of Hannele, by Hauptmann, 1923; Jeanne d'Arc, by Mercedes de Acosta, 1925; The Call of Life, by Schnitzler, 1925; The Master Builder, by Henrik Ibsen, 1925-26. Founder and Director Civic Repertory Theatre, NY, 1926; played in Saturday Night, The Three Sisters, Cradle Song, 2x2-5, The First Stone, Improvisations in June, The Would-Be Gentleman, L'Invitation au Voyage, The Cherry Orchard, Peter Pan, On the High Road, The Lady from Alfaqueque, Katerina, The Open Door, A Sunny Morning, The Master Builder, John Gabriel Borkman, La Locandiera, Twelfth Night, Inheritors, The Good Hope, Hedda Gabler, The Sea Gull, Mlle. Bourrat, The Living Corpse, Women Have Their Way, Romeo and Juliet, The Green Cockatoo, Siegfried, Allison's House, Camille, Liliom (revival), Dear Jane, Alice in Wonderland, L'Aiglon, 1934; Rosmersholm, 1935; Uncle Harry, 1942; Cherry Orchard, 1944; Thérèse, 1945; Elizabeth I in Schiller's Mary Stuart, Phœnix Theatre, NYC, 1958; toured in same, 1959-60; Elizabeth the Queen, 1961-62; The Sea Gull, 1963; Ring Round the Moon, 1963; The Mad Woman of Chaillot, 1964; The Trojan Women, 1964; Exit the King, 1967; All's Well That Ends Well, Amer. Shakespeare Theatre, 1970; Mrs Woodfin in The Dream Watcher, 1975; Fanny Cavendish in The Royal Family, NYC, 1976, tour, 1977. Man. Dir of Amer. Repertory Theatre, which did six classic revivals in repertory, NY, 1946 and 1947; Dir The Cherry Orchard, Lyceum Theatre, NY, 1967-68. Hon. MA (Tufts Coll.), 1927, and several honorary doctorates from 1930. Member Actors' Equity Assoc. and Managers' Protective Assoc.; Founder National Woman's Party. Has won various awards; Gold Medal, Soc. Arts and Sciences, 1926; Am. Acad. of Arts and Letters medal for good speech, 1945; Drama League Award, 1976; Handel Medallion, 1976; Anta Award, 1977. Cross of St Olav (Norway), 1961. *Publications:* At 33 (autobiography), 1934; Flossie and Bossy, (NY) 1949, (London) 1950; With A Quiet Heart, 1953; A Preface to Hedda Gabler, 1953; The Master Builder, a new translation with a Prefatory Study, 1955; trans. Six Plays by Henrik Ibsen, 1957 (NYC); trans. The Wild Duck and Other Plays by Henrik Ibsen, 1961 (NYC); The Mystic in the Theatre: Eleonora Duse, 1966 (NYC and London); articles for New York Times, Theatre Arts Monthly, etc. *Recreations:* gardening, painting. *Address:* Weston, Conn 06880, USA.

LEGARD, Capt. Sir Thomas (Digby), 14th Bt, cr 1660; Captain Royal Artillery; b 16 Oct. 1905; e s of Sir D. A. H. Legard, 13th Bt; S father, 1961; m 1935, Mary Helen, e d of late Lt-Col E. G. S. L'Estrange Malone; three s. *Educ:* Lancing; Magdalene Coll., Cambridge. *Heir:* s Charles Thomas Legard [b 26 Oct. 1938; m 1962, Elizabeth, d of John M. Guthrie, High House, East Ayton, Scarborough; two s one d]. *Address:* Scampston Hall, Malton, North Yorks. *T:* Rillington 224. *Club:* MCC.

LEGER, Rt. Hon. Jules, CC (Canada) 1974; CMM; CD; Governor-General and Commander-in-Chief of Canada, since 14 Jan. 1974; Chancellor and Principal Companion, Order of Canada; Chancellor and Commander, Order of Military Merit; b 4 April 1913; s of Ernest Léger and Alda Beauvais; m 1938, Gabrielle Carmel; one d. *Educ:* Coll. of Valleyfield, PQ; Univ. of Montreal; Univ. of Paris (DLitt 1938); McGill Univ. (LLD 1960). Associate Editor, Le Droit, 1938-39; Asst Press Censor, 1939-40; Prof. of Diplomatic History and Current Affairs, Univ. of Ottawa, 1939-42; Dept of External Affairs, Canada: Third Sec., 1940; Santiago, 1943; Second Sec., 1944; First Sec., 1946; London, 1947-48; UN Gen. Assembly, Paris, 1948-49; seconded to Prime Minister's Office, 1949-50; Asst Under-Sec. of State, 1951-53; Ambassador to Mexico, 1953-54; Under-Sec. of State, 1954-58; Perm. Rep. to NATO Council, 1958-62; Ambassador to: Italy, 1962-64; France, 1964-68; Under-Sec. of State, 1968-73; Ambassador to Belgium and Luxembourg, 1973. KStJ 1974. *Address:* Government House, Ottawa, Ontario K1A 0A1, Canada.
See also His Eminence Cardinal P. E. Léger.

LÉGER, His Eminence Cardinal Paul Emile; b Valleyfield, Quebec, Canada, 26 April 1904; s of Ernest Léger and Alda Beauvais. *Educ:* Ste-Thérèse Seminary; Grand Seminary, Montreal. Seminary of Philosophy, Paris, 1930-31; Seminary of Theology, Paris, 1931-32; Asst Master of Novices, Paris, 1932-33; Superior Seminary of Fukuoka, Japan, 1933-39; Prof., Seminary of Philosophy, Montreal, 1939-40; Vicar-Gen., Diocese of Valleyfield, 1940-47; Rector, Canadian Coll., Rome, 1947-50; consecrated bishop in Rome and apptd to See of Montreal, 1950; elevated to Sacred Coll. of Cardinals and given titular Church of St Mary of the Angels, 1953; Archbishop of Montreal, 1950-67; resigned to work as a missionary in Africa; Parish Priest, St Madeleine Sophie Barat parish, Montreal, 1974-75. Variety Club award, 1976. Has several hon. doctorates both from Canada and abroad. Holds foreign decorations. *Address:* 2065 Sherbrooke Street West, Montréal, PQ H3H IG6, Canada.
See also Rt Hon. J. Léger.

LEGG, Allan Aubrey R.; see Rowan-Legg.

LEGG, Keith (Leonard Charles), PhD, MSc, BSc (Eng); CEng, FIMechE, FRAeS, FCIT; Director, Hong Kong Polytechnic, since 1975; b 24 Oct. 1924; s of E. H. J. Legg; m 1947, Joan, d of H. E. Green; two s. *Educ:* London Univ. (External); Cranfield Inst. of Technology. Engineering apprenticeship, 1940-45; Dep. Chief Research and Test Engr, Asst Chief Designer, Chief Project and Structural Engr, Short Bros & Harland Ltd, Belfast, 1942-56; Chief Designer and Prof., Brazilian Aeronautical Centre, São Paulo, 1956-60; Head of Dept and Prof., Loughborough Univ. of Technology, 1960-72 (Sen. Pro Vice-Chancellor, 1967-70); Dir, Lanchester Polytechnic, 1972-75. Chm., Internat. Directing Cttee, CERI/OECD Higher Educn Institutional Management, 1973-75; Member: Road Transport Industrial Trng Bd, 1966-75; Council, Royal Aeronautical Soc.; Hong Kong Management Assoc. Council; Bd of Educn; Environmental and Pollution Council of Hong Kong; Hong Kong Productivity Council. Adviser to OECD in Paris; Mem. various nat. and professional cttees. Fellow, Hong Kong Inst. Engrg. *Publications:* numerous: on aerospace structures and design, transport systems, higher educn and educnl analytical models. *Recreations:* most sports, especially tennis, badminton and squash; aid to the handicapped. *Address:* Hong Kong Polytechnic, Hung Hom, Kowloon. *T:* Kowloon 334358; 11 Upper Cliff Close, Penarth, Glamorgan. *T:* Penarth 702267.

LEGGATE, John Mortimer, MB, ChB, FRCS; Dean of the Faculty of Medicine, University of Liverpool, 1953-69, retired; b 7 April 1904; s of late Dr James Leggate, Liverpool; m 1936, Grace, d of late Rev. John Clark, Newport, Fife; one s. *Educ:* Liverpool Coll.; University of Liverpool. Gladstone Divinity Prize, 1923; Pres., Guild of Undergraduates, University of Liverpool, 1927-28; MB, ChB (Hons) 1929; MRCS, LRCP, 1929; FRCS, 1933; John Rankin Fellow in Anatomy, 1929-30. Resident Surgical Officer and Surgical Tutor, Liverpool Royal Infirmary, 1932; Prof. of Surgery, Moukden Med. Coll. (Manchuria), 1935-41 and 1946-49; Resident Asst Surgeon, David Lewis Northern Hosp., Liverpool, 1941-43. Served War of 1939-45, Major, RAMC, comdg Field Surgical Unit, D Day Landing, 1944 (despatches); OC Surgical Div. of a Gen. Hosp. in India, 1945-46; demobilised, 1946 (Hon. Lt-Col). Sen. Registrar in Neuro-Surgical Unit at Walton Hosp., Liverpool, 1950-51. *Address:* 19 Skipton Avenue, Banks Road, Southport, Merseyside. *T:* Southport 29171.

LEGGATT, Andrew Peter, QC 1972; a Recorder of the Crown Court, since 1972; b 8 Nov. 1930; er s of Captain William Ronald Christopher Leggatt, DSO, RN and Dorothea Joy Leggatt (née Dreyer); m 1953, Gillian Barbara Newton; one s one d. *Educ:* Eton; King's Coll., Cambridge (Exhibr). MA 1957. Nat. service commn in Rifle Bde, 1949-50; TA, 1950-59. Called to Bar, Inner Temple, 1954, Bencher, 1976. Mem., Bar Council, 1971-74, Mem. Senate, 1974-; Hon. Mem., American Bar Assoc., 1975. Inspector (for Dept of Trade), London & Counties Securities Group, 1975. *Recreations:* gardening, listening to music. *Address:* The Old Vicarage, Old Woking, Surrey GU22 9JF. *T:* Woking 63734; 1 Harcourt Buildings, Temple, EC4Y 9DA. *T:* 01-353 9631. *Club:* MCC.

LEGGATT, Hugh Frank John; Senior Partner, Leggatt Brothers (Fine Art Dealers); *b* 27 Feb. 1925; 2nd *s* of late Henry and Beatrice Leggatt; *m* 1953, Jennifer Mary Hepworth; two *s*. *Educ:* Eton; New Coll., Oxford. RAF, 1943-46. Joined Leggatt Bros, 1946; Partner, 1952; Senior Partner, 1962. Pres., Fine Art Trade Provident Instn, 1960-63; Chm., Soc. of London Art Dealers, 1966-70. Hon. Sec., Heritage in Danger, 1974-. *Publications:* contribs to newspapers and jls. *Address:* 3 Albert Place, W8. *T:* 01-937 3797; Broadfield Farm, Eastington, near Northleach, Glos. *T:* Windrush 293. *Club:* White's.

LEGGE, family name of **Earl of Dartmouth.**

LEGGE, Prof. (Mary) Dominica, FBA 1974; Personal Professor of French (Anglo-Norman Studies), University of Edinburgh, 1968-73, Professor Emeritus, 1973; *b* 26 March 1905; 2nd *d* of late James Granville Legge and Josephine (*née* Makins). *Educ:* Liverpool Coll., Huyton; Somerville Coll., Oxford. BA Hon. Mod. Lang, BLitt, MA, DLitt. Editor, Selden Soc., 1928-34; Mary Somerville Res. Fellow, 1935-37; Asst Lectr, Royal Holloway Coll., 1938-42; Voluntary asst, BoT, 1942; Asst, Dundee Univ. Coll., 1942; Lectr, 1943, Reader, 1953, Univ. of Edinburgh. Hon. Fellow, Somerville Coll., 1968. FRHistS, FSAScot; Corresp. Fellow, Mediaeval Acad. of America. Officier des Palmes Académiques. *Publications:* (with Sir William Holdsworth) Year-Book of 10 Edward II, 1934-35; Anglo-Norman Letters and Petitions, 1941; (with E. Vinaver) Le Roman de Balain, 1942; Anglo-Norman in the Cloisters, 1950; Anglo-Norman Literature and its Background, 1963; (with R. J. Dean) The Rule of St Benedict, 1964; contribs to learned jls and volumes, British and foreign. *Recreations:* music, walking. *Address:* 191a Woodstock Road, Oxford OX2 7AB. *T:* Oxford 56455. *Clubs:* Royal Over-Seas League; University of Edinburgh Staff.

LEGGE, Rt. Rev. William Gordon; see Newfoundland, Western, Bishop of.

LEGGETT, Douglas Malcolm Aufrère, MA, PhD, DSc; FRAeS; FIMA; Vice-Chancellor, University of Surrey, 1966-Sept. 1975; *b* 27 May 1912; *s* of George Malcolm Kent Leggett and Winifred Mabel Horsfall; *m* 1943, Enid Vida Southall; one *s* one *d*. *Educ:* Rugby Sch.; Edinburgh Univ.; Trinity Coll., Cambridge. Wrangler, 1934; Fellow of Trinity Coll., Cambridge, 1937; Queen Mary Coll., London, 1937-39; Royal Aircraft Establishment, 1939-45; Royal Aeronautical Society, 1945-50; King's Coll., London, 1950-60; Principal, Battersea Coll. of Technology, 1960-66. FKC 1974; DUniv Surrey 1975. *Publications:* contrib. to scientific and technical jls. *Address:* Southlands, Fairoak Lane, Oxshott, Surrey. *T:* Oxshott 3061.

LEGGETT, Sir Frederick William, KBE 1951; Kt 1941; CB 1933; *b* 23 Dec. 1884; *s* of late F. J. Leggett and Frances Mary, *d* of William Murphy, Huntingdon; *m* 1st, Edith Guinevere (*d* 1949), *d* of Henry Kitson, Woodford; one *s* three *d*; 2nd, Beatrice Melville, *d* of Joseph Roe. *Educ:* City of London and Strand Schs; King's Coll., London. Entered Civil Service, 1904; Private Sec. to Parliamentary Sec., Board of Trade, 1915; to Minister of Labour, 1917; Asst Sec. Ministry of Labour, 1919; Under-Sec., 1939; Chief Industrial Commissioner, 1940-42; Mem. of Government Mission of Inquiry into Industrial Conditions in Canada and United States, 1926. Brit. Govt Member of Governing Body of ILO, 1932-44, Chm., 1937-38; Dep. Sec. Ministry of Labour and National Service, 1942-45. Member: British Reparations Mission, Moscow, 1945; Anglo-American Cttee of Inquiry into Palestine, 1946; Docks Emergency Cttee, 1949; Cttee on London Transport, 1956-57; Chairman: London and S-E Regional Board for Industry, 1947-48; London Docks Disputes Inquiry Cttee, 1950; Building Apprenticeship and Training Council, 1953; Bldg and Civil Engrg Holidays Management Bd, 1946-; Industrial Relations Adviser, Anglo-Iranian Oil Co., 1947-60. Vice-Pres. Royal Coll. of Nursing, 1948-. *Address:* Downside Lodge, West Kingston, Sussex. *T:* Rustington 6074. *Club:* Reform.

LEGH, family name of **Baron Newton.**

LEGH, Charles Legh Shuldham Cornwall-, CBE 1977 (OBE 1971); DL; *b* 10 Feb. 1903; *er s* of late Charles Henry George Cornwall Legh, of High Legh Hall, Cheshire, and late Geraldine Maud, *d* of Lt-Col Arthur James Shuldham, Royal Inniskilling Fusiliers; *m* 1930, Dorothy, *er d* of late J. W. Scott, Seal, Sevenoaks; one *s* two *d*. Served 1939-45 with AAF and RAF. JP Cheshire, 1938-73; High Sheriff, 1939; DL, 1949; CC 1949-77. Chm., Cheshire Police Authority, 1957-74; Chm., New Cheshire CC, 1974-76 (Shadow Chm., 1973). *Address:* High Legh House, Knutsford, Cheshire WA16 0QR. *T:* Lymm 2303. *Clubs:* Carlton, MCC.

LEGH, Major Hon. Sir Francis (Michael), KCVO 1968 (CVO 1967; MVO 1964); Major (retired), Grenadier Guards; Treasurer since 1962 (Private Secretary, 1959-71), to the Princess Margaret; also Equerry to Queen Elizabeth the Queen Mother, since 1956 (Assistant Private Secretary and Equerry, 1956-59); *b* 2 Aug. 1919; 3rd *s* of 3rd Baron Newton and Hon. Helen Winifred Meysey-Thompson (*d* 1958); *m* 1948, Ruadh Daphne (*d* 1973), *o c* of late Alan Holmes Watson; one *s* one *d*. *Educ:* Eton; Royal Military College, Sandhurst. Served War of 1939-45 (despatches); Italy, 1943-45; GSO2, Military Mission to Greece. *Recreations:* shooting, golf. *Address:* Orchard House, Littlestone-on-Sea, New Romney, Kent. *T:* New Romney 3167. *Clubs:* White's, Brooks's, Pratt's, Beefsteak, Cavalry and Guards.

LE GOY, Raymond Edgar Michel, FCIT; Director General for Transport, Commission of the European Communities, since 1973; *b* 1919; *e s* of J. A. S. M. N. and May Le Goy; *m* 1960, Ernestine Burnett, Trelawny, Jamaica; two *s*. *Educ:* William Ellis Sch.; Gonville and Caius Coll., Cambridge (MA). 1st cl. hons Hist. Tripos, 1939, 1940. Sec. Cambridge Union. Served Army, 1940-46: Staff Captain, HQ E Africa, 1944; Actg Major, 1945. LPTB, 1947; Min. of Transport, 1947; UK Shipping Adviser, Japan, 1949-51; Far East and SE Asia, 1951; Asst Secretary: MoT, 1958; Min. of Aviation, 1959; BoT, 1966; Under-Sec., 1968, BoT, later DTI. *Publication:* The Victorian Burletta, 1953. *Recreations:* theatre, music, race relations. *Address:* Directorate General for Transport, Commission of the European Communities, 120 rue de la Loi, Brussels, Belgium; 124 Avenue P. Vanden Thoren, Auderghem, Belgium; 199 Goldhurst Terrace, NW6. *Clubs:* National Liberal, Players'.

LE GRICE, Very Rev. F(rederick) Edwin, MA; Dean of Ripon, since 1968; *b* 14 Dec. 1911; *s* of Frederick and Edith Le Grice; *m* 1940, Joyce Margaret Hildreth; one *s* two *d*. *Educ:* Paston Sch., North Walsham; Queens' Coll., Cambridge; Westcott House, Cambridge. BA (2nd class hons Mathematics, 2nd class hons Theology) 1934; MA 1946. Asst Curate: St Aidan's, Leeds, 1935-38; Paignton, 1938-46; Vicar of Totteridge, N20, 1946-58; Canon Residentiary and Sub-Dean of St Albans Cathedral, 1958-68; Examining Chaplain to the Bishop of St Albans, 1958-68. A Church Comr, 1973-. Mem., Church Commn on Crown Appts, 1977-. *Address:* The Minster House, Ripon, North Yorks HG4 1PE. *T:* Ripon 3615.

LEHANE, Maureen, (Mrs Peter Wishart); concert and opera singer; *d* of Christopher Lehane and Honor Millar; *m* 1966, Peter Wishart, composer. *Educ:* Queen Elizabeth's Girls' Grammar Sch., Barnet; Guildhall Sch. of Music and Drama. Studied under Hermann Weissenborn, Berlin (teacher of Fischer Dieskau); also under John and Aida Dickens (Australian teachers of Joan Sutherland); gained Arts Council award to study in Berlin. Speciality is Handel: has sung numerous leading roles with Handel opera societies of England and America, in London, and in Carnegie Hall, New York; gave a number of master classes on the interpretation of Handel's vocal music (notably at s'Hertogenbosch Festival, Holland, July 1972; invited to repeat them in 1973). Debut at Glyndebourne, 1967. Festival appearances include: Stravinsky Festival, Cologne; City of London; Aldeburgh; Cheltenham; Three Choirs; Bath; Oxford Bach, etc; has toured N America; also 3-month tour of Australia at invitation of ABC and 2-month tour of Far East and ME, 1971. Title rôle in: Handel's Ariodante, Sadler's Wells, 1974; (her husband's 4th opera) Clytemnaestra, London, 1974; Purcell's Dido and Aeneas, Netherlands Opera, 1976. Cyrus in first complete recording of Handel's Belshazzar. Appears regularly on BBC; also in promenade concerts. Has made numerous recordings (Bach, Haydn, Mozart, Handel, etc). *Publication:* Songs of Purcell (ed, Peter Wishart and Maureen Lehane). *Recreations:* cooking, gardening, reading. *Address:* c/o Artists International Management, 3 and 4 Albert Terrace, NW1 7SU. *T:* 01-586 2093/4.

LEHMANN, Andrew George; Managing Director, 1968, and Deputy Chairman, since 1970, Linguaphone Institute Ltd; *b* 1922; British; *m* 1942, Alastine Mary, *d* of late K. N. Bell; two *s* one *d*. *Educ:* Dulwich Coll.; The Queen's Coll., Oxford. MA, DPhil Oxon. Served with RCS and Indian Army, 6th Rajputana Rifles. Fenced for England (Sabre), 1939. Asst lecturer and lecturer, Manchester Univ., 1945-51; Prof. of French Studies, 1951-68, Dean of Faculty of Letters and Soc. Scis, Univ. of Reading, 1960-68. Vis. Prof. of Comparative Literature, Univ. of Mainz, 1956; Hon. Prof., Univ. of Warwick, 1968. Mem., Hale Cttee on University Teaching Methods, 1961; Chm., Industrial Council for Educnl and Trng Technology, 1974-. Mem., Anglo-French Permanent Mixed Cultural Commission, 1963-68. Adviser: Chinese Univ. of Hong Kong, 1964; Haile Selassie I Univ., Ethiopia, 1965. Member: Hong Kong Univ. Grants Cttee,

1966; Academic Planning Board, New Univ. of Ulster, 1966; Court and Council, Bedford Coll., London Univ., 1971; British Library Adv. Cttee (Reference), 1975-; Princeton Univ. Academic Adv. Council, 1975-. Governor, Ealing Tech. Coll., 1974. Dir, DRS Ltd, 1977. *Publications:* The Symbolist Aesthetic in France, 1950 and 1967; Sainte-Beuve, a portrait of the Critic, 1962; articles in various periodicals and learned reviews. *Recreations:* music, travel, gardening. *Address:* 3 Hanover Terrace, NW1. *T:* 01-723 8215. *Club:* Athenæum.

LEHMANN, Beatrix; Actress; *b* 1 July 1903; 3rd *d* of late Rudolph Chambers Lehmann. *Educ:* home; Paris. Trained for stage at Royal Academy of Dramatic Art. First professional engagement, Sidney in The Bill of Divorcement on a tour of South Coast Village Halls. First London appearance, Lyric Theatre, Hammersmith, 1924, as Peggy in The Way of the World; subsequently played numerous West End parts. Appearances include: Lavinia in Mourning Becomes Electra; Abbie in Desire Under the Elms; Mrs Alving in Ghosts; Family Reunion; No Sign of the Dove; Blood Wedding; Waltz of the Toreadors; Garden District; Lady Macbeth in Macbeth, Old Vic; Miss Bordereau in The Aspern Papers; A Cuckoo in the Nest; Marfa Kabanova in The Storm, Old Vic; Hecuba, Mermaid; The Night I Chased the Women with an Eel; Peer Gynt, Chichester, 1970; Reunion in Vienna, Chichester, 1971; Mother Adam, Arts, 1971; Romeo and Juliet, Stratford-on-Avon, 1973. Entered films, 1935, The Cat and the Canary, 1977. TV appearances include series Love for Lydia, 1977. Radio Actress of the Year award, 1976. *Publications:* two novels; a number of short stories. *Recreations:* swimming and history. *Address:* c/o International Creative Management, 22 Grafton Street, W1.

LEHMANN, Prof. Hermann, MD, PhD, ScD, FRCP; FRS 1972, FRIC, FRCPath; Professor of Clinical Biochemistry, Cambridge University, 1967-77, now Emeritus; University Biochemist to Addenbrooke's Hospital, Cambridge, University Department of Clinical Biochemistry (formerly Biochemistry), Cambridge, 1963-77; Fellow of Christ's College, Cambridge, since 1965; *b* 8 July 1910; *s* of Paul Lehmann, Publisher, and Bella Lehmann (*née* Apelt); *m* 1942, Benigna Norman-Butler; one *s* two *d* (and one *s* decd). *Educ:* Kreuzschule, Dresden; Universities of Freiburg-i-B, Frankfurt, Berlin, Heidelberg. MD (Basle) 1934; Research Asst, Heidelberg, 1934-36; Research Student: Sch. of Biochem., also Christ's Coll., Cambridge, 1936-38. PhD (Cambridge), 1938; Beit Memorial Fellow for Med. Res., 1938-42. RAMC 1943-47. Colonial Med. Research Fellow for Malnutrition and Anæmia, Makerere Coll., Uganda, 1947-49; Cons. Pathologist, Pembury Hosp., Kent, 1949-51; Sen. Lectr, (Reader, 1959), Chem. Pathol. St Bart's Hosp., 1951-63. Hon. Dir, MRC Abnormal Haemoglobin Unit (WHO Ref. Centre for Abnormal Haemoglobins), 1963-75. Rockefeller Travelling Fellowship to USA, 1954. Pres., British Soc. for Haematology, 1975-76. Hon. Prof., University of Freiburg-i-B, 1964-; Mem., WHO Expert Adv. Panel on Human Genetics; Chm., WHO Expert Cttee on Haemoglobins and Thalassaemia. Dr med *hc* Johann Wolfgang Goethe Universität, Frankfurt a/M, 1972; Rivers Medal, Royal Anthrop. Inst., 1963; Courtney Evans Prize, RCP and Royal Soc., 1976; other academic honours incl. named lectures, and Hon. Corresp. Memberships. *Publications:* Man's Haemoglobins (with R. G. Huntsman), 1966, 2nd edn 1974; (ed with R. M. Schmidt and T. H. J. Huisman) The Detection of Hemoglobinopathics, 1974; (with P. A. M. Kynoch) Human Haemoglobin variants and their Characteristics, 1976; articles in sci. jls. *Address:* 22 Newton Road, Cambridge CB2 2AL. *Club:* Athenæum.

LEHMANN, John Frederick, CBE 1964; FRSL; Editor of the London Magazine from its foundation to 1961; Managing Director of John Lehmann Ltd from its foundation to 1952; Founder and Editor of New Writing and of Orpheus; *b* 2 June 1907; *s* of late Rudolph (King's Chambers Lehmann and Alice Marie Davis. *Educ:* Eton (King's Scholar); Trinity Coll., Cambridge. Partner and Gen. Manager, The Hogarth Press, 1938-46; Advisory Editor, The Geographical Magazine, 1940-45. Editor, New Soundings (BBC Third Programme), 1952, The London Magazine, 1954. Chm. Editorial Advisory Panel, British Council, 1952-58; Pres., Royal Literary Fund, 1966-76. Vis. Professor: Univ. of Texas, and State Univ. of Calif. at San Diego, 1970-72; Univ. of Calif. at Berkeley, 1974; Emory Univ., Atlanta, 1977. Pres. Alliance Française in Great Britain, 1955-63. Officer, Gold Cross, Order of George I (Greece), 1954, Comdr, 1961; Officier Légion d'Honneur, 1958; Grand Officier, Etoile Noire, 1960; Officier, Ordre des Arts et des Lettres, 1965. Prix du Rayonnement Français, 1961. *Publications:* A Garden Revisited, 1931; The Noise of History, 1934; Prometheus and the Bolsheviks, 1937; Evil Was Abroad, 1938; Down River, 1939; New Writing in Europe, 1940; Forty Poems, 1942; The Sphere of Glass, 1944; Shelley in Italy, 1947; The Age of the Dragon, 1951; The Open Night, 1952; The Whispering Gallery (Autobiography I), 1955; I Am My Brother (Autobiography II), 1960; Ancestors and Friends, 1962; Collected Poems, 1963; Christ the Hunter, 1965; The Ample Proposition (Autobiography III), 1966; A Nest of Tigers, 1968; In My Own Time (condensed one-volume autobiography), 1969 (USA); Holborn, 1970; The Reader at Night and other poems, 1974; Virginia Woolf and Her World, 1975; In the Purely Pagan Sense, 1976; Edward Lear and His World, 1977. *Editor:* Poems from New Writing, 1946, French Stories from New Writing, 1947, The Year's Work in Literature, 1949 and 1950, English Stories from New Writing, 1950, Pleasures of New Writing, 1952; The Chatto Book of Modern Poetry, 1956 (with C. Day Lewis); The Craft of Letters in England, 1956; Modern French Stories, 1956; Coming to London, 1957; Italian Stories of Today, 1959; Selected Poems of Edith Sitwell, 1965; (with Derek Parker) Edith Sitwell: selected letters, 1970. *Recreations:* gardening, swimming, reading. *Address:* 85 Cornwall Gardens, SW7. *Clubs:* Garrick, Bath, Eton Viking.

LEHMANN, Rosamond Nina; 2nd *d* of R. C. Lehmann and Alice Davis; *m* 1928, Hon. Wogan Philipps (*see* 2nd Baron Milford); one *s* (and one *d* decd). *Educ:* privately; Girton Coll., Cambridge (scholar). *Publications:* Dusty Answer, 1927; A Note in Music, 1930; Invitation to the Waltz, 1932; The Weather in the Streets, 1936; No More Music (play), 1939; The Ballad and the Source, 1944; The Gypsy's Baby, 1946, repr. 1973; The Echoing Grove, 1953; The Swan in the Evening, 1967; (with W. Tudor Pole) A Man Seen Afar, 1965; (with Cynthia, Baroness Sandys) Letters From our Daughters, 2 vols, 1971; A Sea-Grape Tree, 1976. *Recreations:* reading, music. *Address:* 70 Eaton Square, SW1.

LEHRER, Thomas Andrew; writer of songs since 1943; *b* 9 April 1928; *s* of James Lehrer and Anna Lehrer (*née* Waller). *Educ:* Harvard Univ. (AB 1946, MA 1947); Columbia Univ.; Harvard Univ. Student (mathematics, especially probability and statistics) till 1953. Part-time teaching at Harvard, 1947-51. Theoretical physicist at Baird-Atomic, Inc., Cambridge, Massachusetts, 1953-54. Entertainer, 1953-55, 1957-60. US Army, 1955-57. Lecturer in Business Administration, Harvard Business Sch., 1961; Lecturer: in Education, Harvard Univ., 1963-66; in Psychology, Wellesley Coll., 1966; in Political Science, MIT, 1962-71; Vis. Lectr, Univ. of Calif, Santa Cruz, 1972-. *Publications:* Tom Lehrer Song Book, 1954; Tom Lehrer's Second Song Book, 1968; contrib. to Annals of Mathematical Statistics, Journal of Soc. of Industrial and Applied Maths. *Recreation:* piano. *Address:* PO Box 121, Cambridge, Massachusetts 02138, USA. *T:* (617) 354-7708.

LEICESTER, 6th Earl of, *cr* 1837; **Anthony Louis Lovel Coke;** Viscount Coke 1837; farmer, since 1976; *b* 11 Sept. 1909; *s* of Hon. Arthur George Coke (killed in action, 1915) (2nd *s* of 3rd Earl) and of Phyllis Hermione (Lady Howard-Vyse), *d* of late Francis Saxham Elwes Drury; *S* cousin, 1976; *m* 1st, 1934, Moyra Joan (marr. diss. 1947), *d* of late Douglas Crossley; two *s* one *d*; 2nd, 1947, Vera Haigh, Salisbury, Rhodesia. *Educ:* Gresham's School, Holt. Served War of 1939-45 in RAF. Career spent ranching. *Recreations:* general. *Heir: s* Viscount Coke, *qv*. *Address:* Mhowani, PO Box 529, Plettenberg Bay, Cape Province, 6600, Republic of S Africa.

LEICESTER, Bishop of, since 1953; **Rt. Rev. Ronald Ralph Williams,** MA, DD; *b* 14 Oct. 1906; *s* of Rev. Ralph Williams and Mary, *d* of Joseph Sayers; *m* 1934, Cicely Maud, *o d* of Edward Glanville Kay, Enfield; no *c*. *Educ:* Judd Sch., Tonbridge; Gonville and Caius Coll., Cambridge; Ridley Hall, Cambridge. 2nd Class, Division I, English Tripos Part I, Cambridge, 1926; 1st Class Theological Tripos, Part I, 1927; 1st Class with distinction, Part II, 1928; Carus Greek Testament Prize, 1927; Scholefield Greek Testament Prize, 1928; Archbishop Cranmer Prize, 1932; Hulsean Preacher, 1934. Tutor, St Aidan's Coll., Birkenhead, 1928-29; Curate, Leyton Parish Church, 1929-31; Chaplain, Ridley Hall, Cambridge, 1931-34; Examining Chaplain to Bishop of Chelmsford, 1931; Home Education Secretary, CMS, 1934-40; Religious Division, Ministry of Information, 1940-45 (Director, 1943-45); Lieut MOI Home Guard; Commissary to Bishop of Tasmania, 1944; Examining Chaplain to Bishop of Durham, 1945; Principal, St John's Coll., Durham, 1945-53; Hon. Canon Durham Cathedral, 1953-54; Proctor in Convocation of York, 1950. President Queen's Coll., Birmingham, 1957-63; Visitor, Ridley Hall, Cambridge, 1957. Trustee, Historic Churches Preservation Trust, 1960. C of E Rep. to Brussels Ecumenical Centre, and Mem., Consultative Cttee of Churches of European Community, 1973-; Chairman: C of E Bd for Social Responsibility, 1961-76; C of E Council for Foreign Relations; Pres., European Christian Industrial Movement, 1975-. Entered House of Lords, 1959.

Hon. Fellow, St Peter's Coll., Oxford, 1961. FRSA 1972. DD Lambeth, 1954; Hon. DD Cantab, 1974; Hon. LLD Leicester, 1976. *Publications:* Religion and the English Vernacular, 1940; The Strife Goes On, 1940; The Christian Religion, 1941; Authority in the Apostolic Age, 1950; The Perfect Law of Liberty, 1952; The Acts of the Apostles, 1953; Reading Through Hebrews, 1960; The Word of Life, 1960; Take thou Authority, 1961; The Bible in Worship and Ministry, 1962; Letters of John and James (Commentary), 1965; What's right with the C of E, 1966; I Believe-and why, 1971; Faith and the Faith, 1973. *Recreations:* golf, walking, climbing. *Address:* Bishop's Lodge, Springfield Road, Leicester LE2 3BD. *T:* Leicester 708985. *Clubs:* Alpine, English-Speaking Union, MCC; Leicestershire (Leicester).

LEICESTER, Archdeacon of; *see* Cole, Ven. Ronald Berkeley.

LEIGH, family name of **Baron Leigh.**

LEIGH, 4th Baron *cr* 1839; **Rupert William Dudley Leigh;** TD; DL; *b* 14 March 1908; *o* s of late Major Hon. Rupert Leigh; *S* uncle, 1938; *m* 1931, Anne (*d* 1977), *d* of Ellis Hicks Beach, Witcombe Park, Glos; four s. *Educ:* Eton; RMC, Sandhurst. 11th Hussars, 1928-36, Royal Gloucestershire Hussars, 1937-44 (Lieut-Colonel, 1st RGH, 1943). Served with Notts (Sherwood Rangers) Yeomanry in NW Europe, 1944-45. CStJ 1969. *Heir: s* Hon. John Piers Leigh [*b* 11 Sept. 1935; *m* 1st, 1957, Cecilia Poppy (marr. diss. 1974), *y d* of late Robert Cecil Jackson, Redlynch, Wilts; one s one *d*; 2nd, Susan, *d* of John Cleave, Whitenash, Leamington Spa]. *Address:* Stoneleigh Abbey, Kenilworth, Warwickshire. *T:* Kenilworth 53981; Adlestrop House, Moreton-in-Marsh, Glos. *T:* Kingham 364. *Club:* Cavalry and Guards.

LEIGH, Archibald Denis, MD, FRCP; Consultant Physician, Bethlem Royal and Maudsley Hospitals since 1949; Secretary-General, World Psychiatric Association, since 1966; Hon. Consultant in Psychiatry to the British Army, since 1969; Lecturer, Institute of Psychiatry; *b* 11 Oct. 1915; *o* s of Archibald Leigh and Rose Rushworth; *m* 1941, Pamela Parish; two s three *d. Educ:* Hulme Grammar Sch.; Manchester Univ.; University of Budapest. Manchester City Schol. in Medicine, 1932; BSc 1936; MB, ChB (1st class hons) 1939; Dauntesey Med. Sen. Schol., Prof. Tom Jones Exhibitioner in Anatomy; Sidney Renshaw Jun. Prize in Physiol.; Turner Med. Prize; John Henry Agnew Prize; Stephen Lewis Prize; Prize in Midwifery; MRCP 1941; MD (Manchester), 1947; FRCP, 1955. RAMC, 1940-45 (Lt-Col); Adviser in Neurology, Eastern Army, India. 1st Assistant, Dept of Neurology, London Hospital; Nuffield Fellow, 1947-48; Clinical Fellow, Harvard Univ., 1948. Recognised Clinical Teacher, London Univ.; Founder European Society of Psychosomatic Research; Editor-in-Chief and Founder, Journal of Psychosomatic Res.; Editorial Bd, Japanese Journal of Psychosomatic Medicine, Medicina Psychosomatica, Psychosomatic Medicine, Behaviour Therapy; Examiner in Psychological Med., Edinburgh Univ., 1958-65; Beattie Smith Lectr, Melbourne Univ., 1967. Governor, Bethlem Royal and Maudsley Hospitals, 1956-62; President Sect. of Psychiatry, Royal Society Med., 1967-68. Hon. Member: Deutschen Gesellschaft für Psychiatrie und Nervenheilkunde; Italian Psychosomatic Soc.; Assoc. Brasileira de Psiquiatria; Sociedad Argentina de Medicina Psicosomática; Polish Psychiatric Assoc.; Corresp. Mem., Pavlovian Soc. of N America; Hon. Corresp. Mem., Austn Acad. of Forensic Scis; Hon Fellow: Swedish Soc. of Med. Scis; Soc. Colombiana de Psiquiatría; Soviet Soc. of Neurologists and Psychiatrists; Czechoslovak Psychiatric Soc. Distinguished Fellow, Amer. Psychiatric Assoc. *Publications:* (trans. from French) Psychosomatic Methods of Painless Childbirth, 1959; The Historical Development of British Psychiatry, Vol. I, 1961; Bronchial Asthma, 1967; chapters in various books; papers on neurology, psychiatry, history of psychiatry and psychosomatic medicine. *Recreations:* fishing, collecting. *Address:* 152 Harley Street, W1. *T:* 01-935 8868; The Grange, Otford, Kent. *T:* Otford 3427.

LEIGH, Sir John, 2nd Bt, *cr* 1918; *b* 24 March 1909; *s* of Sir John Leigh, 1st Bt, and Norah Marjorie, CBE (*d* 1954); *S* father 1959; *m* 1959, Ariane, *d* of late Joseph Wm Allen, Beverly Hills, California, and *widow* of Harold Wallace Ross, NYC. *Educ:* Eton; Balliol Coll., Oxford. *Heir: b* Eric Leigh [*b* 13 April 1913; *m* 1st, 1934, Joan Fitzgerald Lane (marr. diss., 1939); one s; 2nd, 1939, Mary Babette Jaques; one s one *d*]. *Address:* 23 Quai du Mont Blanc, Geneva, Switzerland. *T:* 31 53 63. *Clubs:* Brooks's; Travellers' (Paris).

LEIGH, Neville Egerton, CVO 1967; Clerk of the Privy Council since 1974; *b* 4 June 1922; *s* of late Cecil Egerton Leigh; *m* 1944, Denise Margaret Yvonne, *d* of late Cyril Denzil Branch, MC;

two *s* one *d. Educ:* Charterhouse. RAFVR, 1942-47 (Flt-Lt). Called to Bar, Inner Temple, 1948. Legal Asst, Treasury Solicitors Dept, 1949-51; Senior Clerk, Privy Council Office, 1951-65; Deputy Clerk of Privy Council, 1965-74. *Address:* 11 The Crescent, Barnes, SW13 0NN. *T:* 01-876 4271. *Club:* Army and Navy.

LEIGH, Ralph Alexander, CBE 1977; FBA 1969; LittD; Professor of French, University of Cambridge, since 1973; Professorial Fellow of Trinity College, Cambridge, since 1973 (Fellow, 1952, Prælector, since 1967, Senior Research Fellow, 1969); *b* London, 6 Jan. 1915; *m* 1945, Edith Helen Kern (*d* 1972); one s one *d. Educ:* Raine's Sch. for Boys, London; Queen Mary Coll., Univ. of London; Univ. of Paris (Sorbonne). BA London 1st class hons. 1936; Diplôme de l'Université de Paris, 1938. Served War, 1941-46: RASC and Staff; CCG; Lieut (ERE list) 1942; Major, 1944. Lectr, Dept of French, Univ. of Edinburgh, 1946; Lectr, 1952-69, Reader, 1969-73, Cambridge Univ. Vis. Prof., Sorbonne, 1973. Mem., Inst. for Adv. Studies, Princeton, 1967. Leverhulme Fellow, 1959-60, 1970. LittD (Cambridge) 1968. *Publications:* Correspondance Complète de Jean Jacques Rousseau, vols I-XXXIII, 1965-78 (in progress); contribs to Revue de littérature comparée; Modern Language Review; French Studies; Studies on Voltaire; The Library, etc. *Recreation:* book-collecting. *Address:* Trinity College, Cambridge.

LEIGH-PEMBERTON, John, AFC 1945; artist painter; *b* 18 Oct. 1911; *s* of Cyril Leigh-Pemberton and Mary Evelyn Megaw; *m* 1948, Doreen Beatrice Townshend-Webster. *Educ:* Eton. Studied Art, London, 1928-31. Past Member Royal Institute of Painters in Oils and other Societies. Served 1940-45 with RAF as Flying Instructor. Series of pictures for Coldstream Guards, 1950. Festival Almanack, 1951, for Messrs Whitbread; Royal Progress, 1953, for Shell Mex & BP Ltd. Works in public and private collections, UK and America; decorations for ships: City of York, City of Exeter, Britannic, Caledonia, Corfu, Carthage, Kenya, Uganda. Many series of paintings, chiefly of natural history subjects, for Midland Bank Ltd. *Publications:* A Book of Garden Flowers, 1960; A Book of Butterflies, Moths and other Insects, 1963; British Wildlife, Rarities and Introductions, 1966; Garden Birds, 1967; Sea and Estuary Birds, 1967; Heath and Woodland Birds, 1968; Vanishing Wild Animals of the World, 1968; Pond and River Birds, 1969; African Mammals, 1969; Australian Mammals, 1970; North American Mammals, 1970; Birds of Prey, 1970; European Mammals, 1971; Asian Mammals, 1971; South American Mammals, 1972; Sea and Air Mammals, 1972; Wild Life in Britain, 1972; Disappearing Mammals, 1973; Ducks and Swans, 1973; Lions and Tigers, 1974; Baby Animals, 1974; Song Birds, 1974; Leaves, 1974; Big Animals, 1975; Apes and Monkeys, 1975; Reptiles, 1976; Seals and Whales, 1976. *Address:* 5 Roehampton Gate, Roehampton, SW15. *T:* 01-876 3332.

LEIGH-PEMBERTON, Robert, (Robin Leigh-Pemberton); Vice Lord-Lieutenant of Kent, since 1972; Deputy Pro-Chancellor of University of Kent at Canterbury, since 1970; Chairman, National Westminster Bank Ltd, since 1977 (Director, 1972, Deputy Chairman, 1974); Director: Birmid Qualcast Ltd, since 1966 (Deputy Chairman, 1970; Chairman, 1975-77); University Life Assurance Society, since 1967; Redland Ltd, since 1972; *b* 5 Jan. 1927; *e s* of late Robert Douglas Leigh-Pemberton, MBE, MC, Sittingbourne, Kent; *m* 1953, Rosemary Davina, *d* of late Lt-Col D. W. A. W. Forbes, MC, and the Marchioness of Exeter; five s. *Educ:* St Peter's Court, Broadstairs; Eton; Trinity Coll., Oxford (MA). Grenadier Guards, 1945-48. Called to Bar, Inner Temple, 1954; practised in London and SE Circuit until 1960. County Councillor (Chm. Council, 1972-75), 1961-77, C Ald. 1965, Kent. Member: SE Econ. Planning Council, 1972-74; Medway Ports Authority, 1974-76; Prime Minister's Cttee on Local Govt Rules of Conduct, 1973-74; Cttee of Enquiry into Teachers' Pay, 1974. Vice-Pres., Inst. of Bankers, 1977-. Governor: Wye Coll., 1970-; London Business Sch., 1977-. FRSA 1977; FBIM 1977. JP 1961-75, DL 1970, Kent. *Recreation:* country life. *Address:* Torry Hill, Sittingbourne, Kent ME9 0SP. *T:* Milstead 258; 66 Westminster Gardens, Marsham Street, SW1. *Clubs:* Turf, Brooks's, Cavalry and Guards.

LEIGH-WOOD, Roger, DL; *b* 16 Aug. 1906; *s* of Sir James Leigh-Wood, KBE, CB, CMG, and Joanna Elizabeth Turnbull; *m* 1936, Norah Elizabeth Holroyde; four s. *Educ:* Winchester Coll.; Trinity Coll., Oxford. Lt-Comdr RNVR, 1939-45. Brown Shipley & Co. Ltd, 1930-42; Eastern Bank Ltd, 1945, Chm. 1967-71; Chartered Bank, 1967-72 (Dep. Chm. 1971); Commercial Union Assce Co. Ltd, 1948-71; Dalgety Ltd, 1948-72; Chm., Scott & Bowne Ltd, 1964. High Sheriff of Hampshire, 1964-65; DL Hants, 1970. *Recreations:* yachting, gardening;

formerly athletics (Pres. Oxford Univ. Athletic Club, 1929; British Olympic Team, 1928; Empire Games Team, 1930). *Address:* Summerley, Bentworth, Alton, Hants. *T:* Alton 62077. *Club:* Royal Yacht Squadron.

LEIGHTON OF ST MELLONS, 2nd Baron, *cr* 1962; **John Leighton Seager;** Bt 1952; *b* 11 Jan. 1922; *er s* of 1st Baron Leighton of St Mellons, CBE, JP, and of Marjorie, *d* of William Henry Gimson, Breconshire; *S* father, 1963; *m* 1953, Elizabeth Rosita, *o d* of late Henry Hopgood, Cardiff; two *s* one *d* (and one *d* decd). *Educ:* Caldicott Sch.; The Leys Sch., Cambridge. *Heir: s* Hon. Robert William Henry Leighton Seager, *b* 28 Sept. 1955. *Address:* 185 Lake Road West, Cardiff.

LEIGHTON, Clare, RE 1934; *b* 1899; *d* of late Marie Connor Leighton, and late Robert Leighton. *Educ:* privately; Brighton School of Art; Slade School. Elected Member of Society of Wood Engravers, 1928; First prize International Engraving Exhibition, Art Institute of Chicago, 1930; Fellow National Acad. of Design, New York; Member, Society of American Graphic Arts; Member, National Inst. of Arts and Letters, USA, 1951. Prints purchased for permanent collection of British Museum, Victoria and Albert Museum, National Gallery of Canada, Museums of Boston, Baltimore, New York, etc. Designed: 33 stained glass windows for St Paul's Cathedral, Worcester, Mass; 12 plates for Josiah Wedgwood & Sons Ltd. *Publications:* Illustrated with wood engravings the following books: Thomas Hardy's The Return of the Native, 1929; Thornton Wilder's The Bridge of San Luis Rey, 1930; The Sea and the Jungle, 1930; Wuthering Heights, 1931; E. Madox Roberts's The Time of Man, 1943; North Carolina Folk Lore, 1950; Woodcuts: examples of the Work of Clare Leighton, 1930; The Trumpet in the Dust, 1934; Writer: How to do Wood Engraving and Woodcuts, 1932; Wood Engraving of the 1930's, 1936; Tempestuous Petticoat, 1948; written and illustrated: The Musical Box, 1932; The Farmer's Year, 1933; The Wood That Came Back, 1934; Four Hedges, 1935; Country Matters, 1937; Sometime, Never, 1939; Southern Harvest, 1942; Give us this Day, 1943; Where Land meets Sea, 1954. *Address:* Woodbury, Conn 06798, USA.

LEIGHTON, Prof. Kenneth, MA, DMus; LRAM; composer; pianist; Reid Professor of Music, University of Edinburgh, since 1970; *b* 2 Oct. 1929; *s* of Thomas Leighton; *m* 1953, Lydia Vignapiano; one *s* one *d*. *Educ:* Queen Elizabeth Grammar Sch., Wakefield; Queen's Coll., Oxford (schol.). MA 1955; DMus 1960); Petrassi, Rome. Prof. of Theory, RN Sch. of Music, 1952-53; Gregory Fellow in Music, Leeds Univ., 1953-56; Lectr in Music Composition, Edinburgh Univ., 1956-68; Lectr in Music, Oxford Univ., and Fellow of Worcester Coll., 1968-70. Hon. DMus St Andrews. *Compositions:* Concertos for: piano (3); violin; cello; viola and two pianos; symphony for string orchestra; two string quartets; piano quintet; sonatas for: violin and piano (2); piano (3); partita for cello and piano; orchestral works; Burlesque, Passacaglia, Chorale and Fugue; two symphonies; The Birds (chorus and strings); The Light Invisible (tenor, chorus and orch.), etc; Fantasia Contrappuntistica (piano); incidental music for radio and television drama; church, organ, and piano music. *Recreation:* walking. *Address:* Faculty of Music, University of Edinburgh, Alison House, Nicolson Square, Edinburgh EH8 9BH.

LEIGHTON, Leonard Horace; Under Secretary, Department of Energy, since 1974; *b* 7 Oct. 1920; *e s* of Leonard and Pearl Leighton, Bermuda; *m* 1945, Mary Burrowes; two *s*. *Educ:* Rossall Sch.; Magdalen Coll., Oxford (MA). FInstF. Royal Engrs, 1940-46; Nat. Coal Bd, 1950-62; Min. of Power, 1962-67; Min. of Technology, 1967-70; Dept of Trade and Industry, 1970-74. *Publications:* papers in various technical jls. *Recreation:* gardening. *Address:* 19 McKay Road, Wimbledon, SW20 0HT. *T:* 01-946 4230.

LEIGHTON, Sir Michael (John Bryan), 11th Bt, *cr* 1693; *b* 8 March 1935; *o s* of Colonel Sir Richard Tihel Leighton, 10th Bt, and Kathleen Irene Linda, *o d* of Major A. E. Lees, Rowton Castle, Shrewsbury; *S* father 1957; *m* 1974, Mrs Amber Mary Ritchie. *Educ:* Stowe; Tabley House Agricultural Sch.; Cirencester Coll. *Address:* Loton Park, Shrewsbury, Salop.

LEIGHTON-BOYCE, Guy Gilbert; Accountant and Comptroller General, HM Customs and Excise, since 1973; *b* 23 Oct. 1920; *s* of late Charles Edmund Victor and Eleanor Fannie Leighton-Boyce; *m* 1945, Adrienne Jean Elliott Samms; two *s* two *d*. *Educ:* Dulwich Coll. HM Customs and Excise, 1939. Served War, RAF, 1941-46. Asst Sec., 1960; Under Sec., 1973. *Publications:* Irish Setters, 1973; (with James Iliff) Tephrocactus, 1973; articles in Cactus and Succulent jls. *Recreations:* looking at pictures; dogs, plants. *Address:* 220 Leigham Court Road, Streatham, SW16 2RB. *T:* 01-769 4844. *Club:* Kennel.

LEINSDORF, Erich; orchestral and operatic conductor; *b* Vienna, 4 Feb. 1912; *s* of Ludwig Julius Leinsdorf and Charlotte (*née* Loebl); *m* 1st, 1939, Anne Frohnknecht (marr. diss. 1968); three *s* two *d*; 2nd, 1968, Vera Graf. *Educ:* University of Vienna; State Academy of Music, Vienna (dipl.). Assistant conductor: Salzburg Festival, 1934-37; Metropolitan Opera, NY, 1937-39; Chief Conductor, German operas, 1939-43; Conductor, Rochester Philharmonic, 1947-56; Director, NYC Opera, 1956; Music Cons. Director, Metropolitan Opera, 1957-62; Music Director, Boston Symphony Orchestra, 1962-69. Director, Berkshire Music Center, Berkshire Music Festival, 1963-69; guest appearances with virtually every major orchestra in the USA and Europe, incl. Philadelphia Orchestra, Los Angeles, St Louis, New Orleans, Minneapolis, Cleveland, New York, Concertgebouw Amsterdam, Israel Philharmonic, London Symphony, New Philharmonia, San Francisco Opera, Bayreuth, Holland and Prague Festivals, BBC. Records many symphonies and operas. Former Member Executive Cttee, John F. Kennedy Center for Performing Arts. Fellow, American Academy of Arts and Sciences. Holds hon. degrees. *Publications:* Cadenza (autobiog.), 1976; transcriptions of Brahms Chorale Preludes; contribs. to Atlantic Monthly, Saturday Review, New York Times, High Fidelity. *Address:* 27 Carwall Avenue, Mount Vernon, New York 10552, USA.

LEINSTER, 8th Duke of, *cr* 1766; **Gerald FitzGerald;** Baron of Offaly, 1205; Earl of Kildare, 1316; Viscount Leinster (Great Britain), 1747; Marquess of Kildare, 1761; Earl of Offaly, 1761; Baron Kildare, 1870; Premier Duke, Marquess, and Earl, of Ireland; Major late 5th Royal Inniskilling Dragoon Guards; Chairman, CSE Aviation Group of Cos; *b* 27 May 1914; *o s* of 7th Duke of Leinster and May (*d* 1935), *d* of late Jesse Etheridge; *S* father, 1976; *m* 1st, 1936, Joane (who obtained a divorce, 1946), *e d* of late Major McMorrough Kavanagh, MC, Borris House, Co. Carlow; two *d*; 2nd, 1946, Anne Eustace Smith; two *s*. *Educ:* Eton; Sandhurst. *Heir: s* Marquess of Kildare, *qv*. *Recreations:* flying, fishing, shooting. *Address:* Langston House, Chadlington, Oxford OX7 3LU. *T:* Chadlington 436. *Club:* Cavalry.

LEISHMAN, Frederick John, CVO 1957; MBE 1944; Director: Hill, Samuel & Co. Ltd; The Hill Samuel Group (SA) Ltd; Partner and Chairman, Hill Samuel & Co. oHG; Director, Jonas Woodhead & Sons Ltd; *b* 21 Jan. 1919; *s* of Alexander Leishman and Freda Mabel (*née* Hood); *m* 1945, Frances Webb, Evanston, Illinois, USA; two *d*. *Educ:* Oundle; Corpus Christi, Cambridge. Served RE, 1940-46, and with Military Government, Germany, 1945-46; Regular Commission, 1945; resigned, 1946. Joined Foreign Service, 1946; FO, 1946-48; Copenhagen, 1948-51; Civil Service Selection Board, 1951; Assistant Private Secretary to the Foreign Secretary, 1951-53; First Secretary, Washington, 1953-58; First Secretary and Head of Chancery, Teheran, 1959-61; Counsellor, 1961; HM Consul-General, Hamburg, 1961-62; Foreign Office, 1962-63. FRSA. *Recreations:* golf, fishing. *Address:* 5 Eccleston Square, SW1. *Clubs:* Travellers'; London Scottish Rugby Football; Hawks (Cambridge); Royal Ashdown Forest Golf; Rand (Johannesburg).

LEITCH, Sir George, KCB 1975 (CB 1963); OBE 1945; Chairman, Short Brothers Ltd, since 1976; *b* 5 June 1915; *er s* of late James Simpson and Margaret Leitch; *m* 1942, Edith Marjorie Maughan; one *d*. *Educ:* Wallsend Grammar Sch.; King's Coll., University of Durham. Research and teaching in mathematics, 1937-39. War Service in Army (from TA), 1939-46 (despatches, OBE): Lieut-Colonel in charge of Operational Research in Eastern, then Fourteenth Army, 1943-45; Brigadier (Dep. Scientific Adviser, War Office), 1945-46; entered Civil Service as Principal, 1947; Ministry of Supply, 1947-59 (Under-Secretary, 1959); War Office, 1959-64; Ministry of Defence: Asst Under-Secretary of State, 1964-65; Dep. Under-Sec. of State, 1965-72; Procurement Executive, MoD: Controller (Policy), 1971-72; Secretary, 1972-74; Chief Exec., 1974-75. Commonwealth Fund Fellow, 1953-54. Hon. DSc (Durham), 1946. *Recreations:* swimming, gardening. *Address:* 73 Princes Way, Wimbledon, SW19. *T:* 01-788 4658.

LEITCH, Isabella, OBE 1949; MA, DSc; retired as Director Commonwealth Bureau of Animal Nutrition (1940-60); *b* 13 Feb. 1890; 3rd *d* of John Leitch and Isabella McLennan. *Educ:* Peterhead Academy; Aberdeen Univ. MA (Hons Mathematics and Natural Philosophy), 1911; BSc, 1914; research in Genetics and Physiology at Copenhagen Univ., 1914-19; DSc 1919. Staff of Rowett Research Institute, 1923-29; Staff of Imperial (now Commonwealth) Bureau of Animal Nutrition, 1929. Hon. LLD (Aberdeen), 1965. *Publications:* (with Frank E. Hytten) The Physiology of Human Pregnancy, 1964; (with A. W. Boyne and G. F. Garton) Composition of British Feedingstuffs, 1976; also contributions on genetics, physiology, and nutrition in MRC

Special Report Series and scientific journals, etc. *Recreation:* hill-climbing. *Address:* 30 Ashgrove Road West, Aberdeen. *T:* Aberdeen 43697. *Clubs:* Farmers'; Strathcona (Bucksburn, Aberdeen).

LEITCH, William Andrew, CB 1963; Law Reform Consultant, Government of Northern Ireland, since 1973; Examiner of Statutory Rules, Northern Ireland Assembly, 1974; *b* 16 July 1915; *e s* of Andrew Leitch, MD, DPH, Castlederg, Co. Tyrone, and May, *d* of W. H. Todd, JP, Fyfin, Strabane, Co. Tyrone; *m* 1939, Edna Margaret, *d* of David McIlvennan, Solicitor, Belfast; one *s* two *d. Educ:* Methodist Coll., Belfast; Queen's Univ., Belfast; London Univ. (LLB). Admitted Solicitor, NI, 1937; Asst Solicitors Dept, Ministry of Finance, NI, 1937-43; Asst Parly Draftsman, 1944-56; First Parly Draftsman, 1956-74. Hon. LLM, Queen's Univ., Belfast, 1967. *Publications:* A Handbook on the Administration of Estates Act (NI), 1955, 1957; (jointly) A Commentary on the Interpretation Act (Northern Ireland) 1954, 1955; articles in Northern Ireland Legal Qly, etc. *Recreations:* fishing, golf, reading. *Address:* 53 Kensington Road, Belfast BT5 6NL. *T:* Belfast 654784.

LEITH, family name of **Baron Burgh.**

LEITH, Sir Andrew George F.; *see* Forbes-Leith.

LEITH-BUCHANAN, Sir Charles (Alexander James), 7th Bt *cr* 1775; *b* 1 Sept. 1939; *s* of John Wellesley MacDonald Leith-Buchanan (*g s* of 4th Bt) (*d* 1956) and Jane Elizabeth McNicol (*d* 1955), *d* of Ronald McNicol; *S* cousin, 1941; *m* 1962, Mary Anne Kelly; one *s* one *d. Heir: s* Gordon Leith-Buchanan, *b* 18 Oct. 1974. *Address:* 9814 Barlow Road, Fairfax, Va 22030, USA.

LEITHEAD, James Douglas; *b* 4 Oct. 1911; *s* of late William Leithead, Berwick-on-Tweed; *m* 1936, Alice, *d* of late Thomas Wylie, Stirling, Scotland; one *s. Educ:* Bradford Grammar Sch. Accountant, 1927-32; ACA 1932; FCA 1960; Chartered Accountant, 1932-39. Lecturer Bradford Technical Coll., 1934-39; Secretarial Assistant, Midland (Amalgamated) District (Coal Mines) Scheme, 1939-42; Ministry of Supply, 1942-45; BoT, 1945-64; HM Diplomatic Service, 1965-68; BoT, later DTI, 1968-72, retired. British Trade Commissioner: Australia, 1950-63; New Zealand, 1963-67. Vice-Pres., W Australian Branch of Royal Commonwealth Soc., 1957-63. *Recreation:* golf. *Address:* 48 Eaton Road, Appleton, Oxon.

LEJEUNE, Maj.-Gen. Francis St David Benwell, CB 1949; CBE 1944; *b* 1 March 1899; 2nd *s* of late J. F. P. Lejeune, Bedford; *m* 1927, Joyce Mary, *d* of late Charles E. Davies, Hampton Court; one *s* one *d. Educ:* Bedford; RMA, Woolwich. 2nd Lieut, RA, 1917; served European War, 1914-18, France and Belgium (despatches); seconded RAF, Somaliland and Iraq Operations, 1920-24; GSO 3 War Office, 1929; Asst Military Attaché, Washington, 1932-34; Special Mission in Spain, 1938-39. War of 1939-45 served in Italy and Burma (despatches); Maj.-General, 1944; Chief of Staff AA Command, Comdr AA Group, 1944; Director Technical Training, War Office, 1946; President Ordnance Board, 1947; retired, 1949; International Staff, NATO, 1952-62; psc; pac. *Address:* 68 South Cliff, Bexhill on Sea, East Sussex. *T:* Bexhill 211971.

LELOIR, Luis Federico; Director, Institute of Biochemical Research, Campomar, since 1947; Head of Department of Biochemistry, University of Buenos Aires, since 1962; *b* Paris, 6 Sept. 1906; *m* Amelie Zuherbuhler de Leloir; one *d. Educ:* Univ. of Buenos Aires. Engaged in research in Gt Britain, Argentina and USA; subseq. at Inst. of Biology and Experimental Med., Buenos Aires, 1946. Chm., Argentine Assoc. for Advancement of Science, 1958-59; Mem. Directorate, Nat. Research Council, 1958-64; Mem., Nat. Acad. of Med., 1961; Foreign Mem: Royal Society, 1972; Nat. Acad. of Sciences, USA; Amer. Acad. of Arts and Sciences; Amer. Philosophical Soc. Holds several hon. doctorates and has won numerous prizes, etc, inc. Nobel Prize for Chemistry, 1970. *Address:* Instituto de Investigaciones Bioquímicas, Fundación Campomar, Obligado 2490, Buenos Aires 28, Argentina. *T:* 783-2871.

LEMAN, Paul H.; President, Alcan Aluminium Ltd, since 1972; Chairman, Aluminum Company of Canada, Ltd, since 1975 (President, 1969-75); *b* 6 Aug. 1915; *s* of J. B. Beaudry Leman and Caroline Leman (*née* Beique); *m* 1939, Jeannine F. Prud'homme; two *s* three *d. Educ:* Collège Ste Marie, Montreal (BA); Univ. of Montreal (LL.L). Harvard Graduate School of Business Administration. Admitted to Quebec Bar, 1937; joined Aluminum Co. of Canada, Ltd, 1938: Asst Sec., 1943; Treas., 1949; Vice-Pres., 1952; Dir, 1963; Exec. Vice-Pres., 1964; Treas., Saguenay Power Co. Ltd, 1945; Alcan Aluminium Ltd: Dir,

1968; Exec. Vice-Pres., 1969. *Recreations:* golf, tennis, fishing. *Address:* 43 Maplewood Avenue, Montreal, Quebec H2V 2L9, Canada. *Clubs:* Mount Bruno Country, Kanawaki Golf, Mount Royal, University (Montreal).

LE MARCHANT, Sir Denis, 5th Bt, *cr* 1841; *b* 28 Feb. 1906; *er s* of Brigadier-General Sir Edward Thomas Le Marchant, 4th Bt, KCB, CBE, JP, DL, and Evelyn Brooks (*d* 1957), *er d* of late Robert Millington Knowles, JP, DL, Colston Bassett Hall, Nottinghamshire; *S* father, 1953; *m* 1933, Elizabeth Rowena, *y d* of late Arthur Hovenden Worth; one *s* one *d* (and one *s* decd). *Educ:* Radley. High Sheriff, Lincolnshire, 1958. *Heir: s* Francis Arthur Le Marchant, *b* 6 Oct. 1939. *Address:* Hungerton Hall, Grantham, Lincolnshire. *T:* Knipton 244.

LE MARCHANT, Spencer; MP (C) High Peak Division of Derbyshire since 1970; *b* 15 Jan. 1931; *s* of Alfred Le Marchant and Turdis Le Marchant (*née* Mortensen); *m* 1955, Lucinda Gaye Leveson Gower; two *d. Educ:* Eton. National Service and Territorial Commissions, Sherwood Foresters. Mem., Stock Exchange, 1954-; Partner, L. Messel & Co., 1961-. Mem., Westminster City Council, 1956-71; contested (C) Vauxhall, 1966. PPS to Chief Sec., Financial Sec. and Minister of State, Treasury, 1972-74; PPS Dept of Energy, 1974; an Opposition Whip, 1974-. *Address:* Hillside, Chinley, Derbyshire SK12 6BX; Rivermill, Grosvenor Road, SW1. *Club:* White's.

LE MASURIER, Sir Robert (Hugh), Kt 1966; DSC 1942; Bailiff of Jersey, 1962-74; *b* 29 Dec. 1913; *s* of William Smythe Le Masurier and Mabel Harriet Briard; *m* 1941, Helen Sophia Sheringham; one *s* two *d. Educ:* Victoria Coll., Jersey. MA 1935; BCL 1936. Sub-Lieut RNVR, 1939; Lieut RNVR, 1943; Lieut-Commander RNVR, 1944. Solicitor-General, Jersey, 1955; Attorney-General, Jersey, 1958. *Recreations:* sailing, carpentry. *Address:* La Ville-à-l'Evêque, Trinity, Jersey. *Clubs:* Royal Ocean Racing; St Helier Yacht, United (Jersey).

LE MAY, Group Captain William Kent, CBE 1943 (OBE 1942); RAF; *b* 29 June 1911; *s* of Percy Kent and Kate Le May (decd); *m* 1938, Greta Lettice Violet Blatchley; two *s* two *d. Educ:* Tonbridge Sch.; Agricultural Coll., Wye. Aux. Air Force, 1931-40, No. 500 County of Kent Squadron; permanent commission, 1946; retired, 1961. *Club:* Royal Air Force.

LE MESURIER, Captain Edward Kirby, CBE 1961; MVO 1935; RN; gardener's mate (unskilled); *b* 11 Dec. 1903; *s* of Captain Charles Edward Le Mesurier, CB, RN, and Florence Kirby; *m* 1930, Eleanor, *d* of Lt-Col Norton Churchill; one *s* two *d. Educ:* RN Colleges. Served RN, 1917-53; War of 1939-45 (despatches). Sec., Nat. Rifle Assoc., 1953-68. *Address:* Glentworth, Wotton-under-Edge, Glos. *T:* 3227.

LEMIEUX, Most Rev. (M.) Joseph; Delegate of St Peter's Basilica, Rome, since 1971; *b* Quebec City, 10 May 1902; *s* of Joseph E. Lemieux and Eva (*née* Berlinguet). *Educ:* College of St Anne de la Pocatière; Dominican House of Studies, Ottawa; College of Angelico, Rome; Blackfriars, Oxford. Missionary to Japan, 1930; Parish Priest, Miyamaecho, Hakodate, Japan, 1931-36; First Bishop of Sendai, 1936; resigned, 1941; Administrator of Diocese of Gravelbourg, Sask., 1942; Bishop of Gravelbourg, 1944-53; Archbishop of Ottawa, 1953-66; Apostolic Nuncio to Haiti, 1966-69; Apostolic Pro-Nuncio in India, 1969-71. *Address:* Palazzo San Carlo, Vatican City.

LEMIEUX, Prof. Raymond Urgel, OC (Canada), 1968; FRS 1967; Professor of Organic Chemistry, University of Alberta, since 1961; *b* 16 June 1920; *s* of Octave Lemieux; *m* 1948, Virginia Marie McConaghie; one *s* five *d* (and one *s* decd). *Educ:* Edmonton, Alberta. BSc Hons (Chem.) Alta, 1943; PhD (Chem.) McGill, 1946. Research Fellow, Ohio State Univ., 1947; Asst Professor, Saskatchewan Univ., 1948-49; Senior Research Officer, National Research Council, Canada, 1949-54, Member, 1976-; Professor, Ottawa Univ., 1954-61. FRSC 1955. Chem. Inst. of Canada Medal, 1964; C. S. Hudson Award, American Chem. Society, 1966. Hon. DSc: New Brunswick Univ., 1967; Laval Univ., 1970; Univ. de Provence, 1973; Univ. of Ottawa, 1975. *Publications:* over 150 research papers mainly in area of carbohydrate chemistry in Canadian Journal of Chemistry, etc. *Recreations:* golf, curling, fishing. *Address:* 7602, 119th Street, Edmonton, Alberta, Canada. *T:* 436-5167. *Clubs:* University of Alberta Faculty, Mayfair Golf and Country (Edmonton).

LEMMON, Cyril Whitefield, FRIBA, AIA; Architect, Honolulu, Hawaii (Private Practice), 1946-69; *b* Kent, 27 Oct. 1901; *s* of T. E. Lemmon and Catherine Whitefield; *m* 1st, 1921, Ethel Belinda Peters, artist (marr. diss., 1936); no *c* ; 2nd, 1938, Rebecca Robson Ramsay; two *d. Educ:* University of Pennsylvania, Philadelphia, Pa. Fifth-year Studio Instructor and

Lecturer in the School of Architecture, University of Liverpool, 1933-36; Consulting Architect to Government of India for Rebuilding of Quetta, 1936; Consulting Architect to MES for all military buildings in India, 1938. Lieut-Colonel, Royal Indian Engineers, 1941; Director of Civil Camouflage in India, 1943; GSO 1, GHQ, India and 11th Army Group, 1943-44. President, Hawaii Chapter, AIA, 1950. Exhibited paintings in Salon des Tuileries, Paris, 1933; travel in United States, Mexico, Europe, N Africa and Asia. Public Lectures on Architecture and Painting. *Publications:* contributions to professional journals on Architecture. *Recreations:* golf, swimming, *Address:* 4999 Kahala Avenue, Apartment 302, Honolulu, Hawaii 96816, USA. *Clubs:* Kiwanis, Oahu Country, etc. (Honolulu).

LEMNITZER, General Lyman L., DSM (US Army) (with 3 Oak Leaf Clusters); DSM (US Navy); DSM (US Air Force); Silver Star; Legion of Merit (Officer's Degree); Legion of Merit; Supreme Allied Commander, Europe, 1963-69; Commander-in-Chief, US European Command, 1962-69; *b* Pennsylvania, 29 Aug. 1899; *s* of late William L. Lemnitzer; *m* 1923, Katherine Mead Tryon; one *s* one *d. Educ:* Honesdale High Sch.; US Military Academy. Duty with troops, Instructor at Army Schools, etc., 1920-40; War Plans Division, War Dept General Staff, 1941; Comdg General, 34th Anti-Aircraft Artillery Bde, and Allied Force HQ England, as Asst Chief of Staff for Plans and Ops, 1942 (2nd in Command, Secret Submarine Mission to contact friendly French Officials in N Africa); served in Europe and N Africa, 1942-45; with Joint Chiefs of Staff, 1945-47; Dep. Comdt National War Coll., 1947-49; Asst to Secretary of Defence, 1949-50; Head of US Delegn to Military Cttee of the Five (Brussels Pact) Powers. London; Student, Basic Airborne Course, Fort Benning, 1950; Comdg General 11th Airborne Div., 1951, 7th Infantry Div. (in Korea), 1951-52; DCS (Plans and Research), 1952-55; Comdg General Far East and 8th US Army, 1955; C-in-C, Far East and UN Commands, and Governor of Ryukyu Is, 1955-57; Vice-Chief of Staff, 1957-59, Chief of Staff, 1959-60, US Army; Chairman Joint Chiefs of Staff, 1960-62. Holds several hon. doctorates. Hon. CB and Hon. CBE (Great Britain); Grand Cross, Legion of Honour (France); Grand Cross, Order of Merit (Germany), 1969; and numerous other foreign Orders and decorations. *Recreations:* golf, fishing, photography, interested in baseball, correspondence with his many friends around the world. *Address:* 3286 Worthington Street, NW, Washington, DC 20015, USA.

LEMON, Sir (Richard) Dawnay, Kt 1970; CBE 1958; QPM 1964; Chief Constable of Kent, 1962-74; *b* 1912; *o s* of late Lieut-Colonel F. J. Lemon, CBE, DSO, and of Mrs Laura Lemon; *m* 1939, Sylvia Marie Kentish; one *s* one *d* (and one *d* decd). *Educ:* Uppingham Sch.; RMC, Sandhurst. Joined West Yorks Regt, 1932; retired 1934. Metropolitan Police, 1934-37; Leicestershire Constabulary, 1937-39; Chief Constable of East Riding of Yorkshire, 1939-42; Chief Constable of Hampshire and Isle of Wight, 1942-62. *Recreations:* cricket, golf, shooting. *Address:* West Coggers, St Margaret's Bay, Dover. *T:* Dover 852685. *Clubs:* Naval and Military, MCC; Royal Yacht Squadron, Cowes (hon.).

LENANTON, Lady; see Oman, C. M. A.

LENDRUM, Prof. Alan Chalmers, MA, MD, BSc, ARPS; FRCPath; Professor of Pathology, University of Dundee, 1967-72, Professor Emeritus, 1972; *b* 3 Nov. 1906; *yr s* of late Rev. Dr Robert Alexander Lendrum and Anna, *e d* of late James Guthrie of Pitforthie, Angus; *m* 1934, Elizabeth Bertram, *e d* of late Donald Currie, BA, LLB; two *s* one *d. Educ:* High Sch., Glasgow; Ardrossan Acad.; University of Glasgow. Asst to Sir Robert Muir, MD, FRS, 1933; Lecturer in Pathology, University of Glasgow; Prof. of Pathology, Univ. of St Andrews, 1947-67. Visiting Prof. of Pathology, Yale, 1960. Kettle Meml Lecture, RCPath, 1973. Hon. For. Mem. Argentine Soc. of Normal and Pathological Anatomy; Hon. Member: Pathol Soc. of GB and Ireland; Nederlandse Patholoog Anatomen Vereniging; Dialectic Soc., Glasgow Univ.; Forfarshire Medical Assoc.; Hon. Fellow, and ex-Pres., Inst. Med. Lab. Tech. Dean of Guildry of Brechin, 1971-73. Capt. RAMC (TA) retd. Sims Woodhead Medal, 1971. Chm. of Governors, Duncan of Jordanstone Coll. of Art, Dundee, 1975-. *Publications:* (co-author) Recent Advances in Clinical Pathology, 1948; Trends in Clinical Pathology, 1969; publications in medical journals. *Address:* Invergowrie House, Dundee DD2 1UA. *T:* Dundee 66666.

LENG, Maj-Gen. Peter John Hall, CB 1975; MBE 1962; MC 1945; Commander 1 (British) Corps (designate); *b* 9 May 1925; *s* of J. Leng; *m* Virginia Rosemary Pearson; three *s* two *d. Educ:* Bradfield Coll. Served War of 1939-45: commissioned in Scots Guards, 1944; Guards Armoured Div., Germany (MC). Various

post-war appts; Guards Independent Parachute Company, 1949-51; commanded: 3rd Bn Royal Anglian Regt, in Berlin, United Kingdom and Aden, 1964-66; 24th Airportable Bde, 1968-70; Dep. Military Sec., Min. of Defence, 1971-73; Comdr Land Forces, N Ireland, 1973-75; Dir, Mil. Operations, MoD, 1975-78. Colonel Commandant: RAVC, 1976-; RMP, 1976-. *Recreations:* fishing, shooting, painting. *Address:* Tilshead House, Tilshead, Wilts. *T:* Shrewton 227. *Club:* Cavalry and Guards'.

LENNARD, Sir Richard Barrett-; see Lennard, Sir T. R. F. B.

LENNARD, Lt-Col Sir Stephen Arthur Hallam Farnaby, 3rd Bt, *cr* 1880; late Scots Guards; formerly President, S. H. Lennard and Co. Ltd, Investment Dealers, Vancouver, BC (retired); *b* 31 July 1899; *o s* of Lt-Col Sir Henry Arthur Hallam Farnaby Lennard, 2nd Bt, and Beatrice (*d* 1948), *d* of Albemarle Cator, Woodbastwick Hall, Norfolk; *S* father, 1928; *m* 1st, 1928, Mary Isabel (*d* 1970), *er d* of Lawrence Bruce Latimer, Vancouver, BC; 2nd, 1970, Margaret Jean, *widow* of Group Captain William Neville Cumming, OBE, DFC, RAF, and *o d* of Daniel Hockin, Vancouver, BC. *Educ:* Winchester; RMC, Sandhurst. Lt Scots Guards, 1918-25; residing in Vancouver since 1925. Served War of 1939-45, with BEF, France, 1940; MEF and 8th Army, 1941-42; Persia and Iraq, 1943, and India, 1943-45; latterly on the Staff, retiring with rank of Lt-Col, 1945. 1939-45 Star and N African Star with 8th Army Clasp. *Recreations:* shooting and fishing. *Heir:* none. *Address:* Glenhead, Whonnock, BC. *T:* 462-7277. *Club:* Vancouver (Vancouver).

LENNARD, Sir (Thomas) Richard (Fiennes) Barrett-, 5th Bt, *cr* 1801; OBE 1970; *b* 12 Dec. 1898; *s* of 4th Bt and Lepel Julia (*d* 1959), *d* of late Rev. Henry Thornton Pearse; *S* father, 1934; *m* 1922, Kathleen Finora, *d* of late Hon. John Donohoe FitzGerald; one *d. Educ:* Brighton Coll.; Clare Coll., Cambridge. Norwich Union Insurance Gp: Dir, 1941; Vice-Pres., 1960; Senior Vice-Pres. and Vice-Chm., 1963; retired 1973; East Anglia Trustee Savings Bank: Manager, 1938; Trustee, 1943; Vice-Chm., 1946; Chm., 1957; Vice-Chm., 1971; retired 1974. KStJ. *Heir: cousin* Rev. Hugh Dacre Barrett-Lennard [*b* 27 June 1917. *Educ:* Radley. Served War of 1939-45 (despatches), Capt. Essex Regt. Is a Priest of London Oratory]. *Address:* 31 Swallowfield Park, Reading, Berks. *Clubs:* Royal Automobile; Leander.

LENNIE, Douglas; *b* 30 March 1910; *e s* of Magnus S. Lennie; *m* 1941, Rhona Young Ponsonby; two *s. Educ:* Berkhamsted Sch.; Guy's Hospital, LDS, RCS, 1934; Northwestern University, Chicago, DDS, 1938. Served War of 1939-45, Temporary Surg. Lt-Comdr (D) RNVR; formerly Surgeon Dentist to Queen Mary. *Address:* 72 Chiltley Way, Liphook, Hants.

LENNON, Dennis, CBE 1968; MC 1942; Senior Partner, Dennis Lennon & Partners, since 1950; *b* 23 June 1918; British; *m* 1948, Else Bull-Andersen; three *s. Educ:* Merchant Taylors' Sch.; University Coll., London. Served Royal Engineers, 1939-45 (despatches): 1st, 7th, 6th Armd Divs; captured in France 1940, later escaped; 7th Armd Div., N Africa; 6th Armd Div., Italy. Dir, Rayon Industry Design Centre, 1948-50; private practice, 1950-. Main Work: Jaeger shops; London Steak Houses; co-ordinator of interior, RMS Queen Elizabeth II; Chalcot Housing Estate, Hampstead; approved plans for Criterion site, Piccadilly Circus; Central Dining Room, Harrow Sch.; Arts Club. Work for stage: set for Capriccio, Glyndebourne; 9 state galas, Royal Opera House. FRIBA, FSIA, FRSA. *Recreations:* arts and design. *Address:* Hamper Mill, Watford, Herts. *T:* Watford 34445. *Clubs:* Savile; Royal Thames Yacht.

LENNON, Prof. (George) Gordon; Gynæcologist in private practice; Professor Emeritus, University of Western Australia, Perth, 1974; *b* 7 Oct. 1911; *s* of late J. Lennon; *m* 1940, Barbara Brynhild (*née* Buckle); two *s. Educ:* Aberdeen Academy; Aberdeen Univ. MB, ChB Aberdeen, 1934; served in hospital posts in Aberdeen, Glasgow, London, Birmingham; MRCOG 1939; FRCOG 1952; MMSA 1943; ChM (Hons) Aberdeen, 1945. Served War of 1939-45, Sqdn-Ldr in charge of Surgical Div., RAFVR, 1942-46. First Asst, Nuffield Dept of Obstetrics and Gynæcology, Radcliffe Infirmary (University of Oxford), 1946-51; Prof. of Obstetrics and Gynæcology, Univ. of Bristol, 1951-67; Dean, Faculty of Med., Univ. of WA, Perth, 1967-74. Visiting Professor: Iraq and Turkey, 1956; South Africa and Uganda, 1958; Iran, 1965. *Publications:* Diagnosis in Clinical Obstetrics; articles in British Medical Journal, Proceedings of the Royal Society of Medicine, Journal of Obstetrics and Gynæcology of the British Empire, etc. *Recreation:* golf. *Address:* 8 Linden Gardens, Floreat Park, WA 6014, Australia.

LENNON, Most Rev. Patrick; see Kildare and Leighlin, Bishop of, (RC).

LENNOX; see Gordon-Lennox and Gordon Lennox.

LENNOX, Robert Smith, JP; Lord Provost of Aberdeen, 1967-70 and 1975-77; b 8 June 1909; m 1963, Evelyn Margaret; no c. Educ: St Clement Sch., Aberdeen. Hon. LLD Aberdeen, 1970. JP Aberdeen. Address: 7 Gillespie Crescent, Ashgrove, Aberdeen. T: Aberdeen 43862.

LENNOX-BOYD, family name of **Viscount Boyd of Merton.**

LENNY, Most Rev. Francis; Auxiliary Bishop of Armagh, (RC), and titular Bishop of Rotdon, since 1974; b 27 Sept. 1928; s of Francis Patrick Lenny and Mary Agnes O'Rourke. Educ: St Patrick's Coll., Armagh; St Patrick's Coll., Maynooth (BA, BD, LCL). Secretary to Cardinal D'Alton, 1955-63; Secretary to Cardinal Conway, 1963-72. Address: Parochial House, Mullavilly, Tandragee, Craigavon, Co. Armagh. T: Tandragee 840840.

LEON, Sir John (Ronald), 4th Bt, cr 1911; Actor (stage name, John Standing); b 16 Aug. 1934; er s of 3rd Bt and of Kay Hammond, qv; S father, 1964; m 1961, Jill (marr. diss. 1972), d of Jack Melford; one s. Educ: Eton. Late 2nd Lt, KRRC. Plays include: Darling Buds of May, Saville, 1959; leading man, season, Bristol Old Vic, 1960; The Irregular Verb to Love, Criterion, 1961; Norman, Duchess, 1963; So Much to Remember, Vaudeville, 1963; The Three Sisters, Oxford Playhouse, 1964; See How They Run, Vaudeville, 1964; Seasons at Chichester Theatre, 1966, 1967; The Importance of Being Earnest, Haymarket 1968; Ring Round the Moon, Haymarket, 1968; The Alchemist, and Arms and the Man, Chichester, 1970; Popkiss, Globe, 1972; A Sense of Detachment, Royal Court, 1972; Private Lives, Queen's and Globe, 1973, NY and tour of USA, 1974; Jingo, Aldwych, 1975. Films: The Wild and the Willing, 1962; Iron Maiden, 1962; King Rat, 1964; Walk, Don't Run, 1965; Zee and Co., 1973; Rogue Male, 1976; The Eagle has Landed, 1976. Television appearances incl. Arms and the Man; The First Churchills; Charley's Aunt, etc. Recreation: painting. Heir: s Alexander John Leon, b 3 May 1965. Address: 98 Ebury Street, SW1.

LEON TROUT, Sir H.; see Trout, Sir H. L.

LEONARD, Dick; see Leonard, Richard Lawrence.

LEONARD, Rt. Rev. Graham Douglas; see Truro, Bishop of.

LEONARD, (Hamilton) John, QC 1969; a Recorder, since 1972; b 28 April 1926; s of late Arthur Leonard and Jean Leonard, Poole, Dorset; m 1948, Doreen Enid, yr d of late Lt-Col Sidney James Parker, OBE, and late May Florence Parker, Sanderstead, Surrey; one s one d. Educ: Dean Close Sch., Cheltenham; Brasenose Coll., Oxford (MA). Coldstream Guards (Captain), 1944-47. Called to Bar, Inner Temple, 1951; South-Eastern Circuit. 2nd Junior Prosecuting Counsel to the Crown at Central Criminal Court, 1964-69; Dep. Chm., Surrey QS, 1969-71; Comr, CCC, 1969-71. Member: General Council of the Bar, 1970-74, Senate, 1971-74, Senate of Four Inns and the Bar, 1974-77. Chm., Criminal Bar Assoc., 1975-77. Member: Home Sec.'s Adv. Bd on Restricted Patients, 1973-; Deptl Cttee to Review Laws on Obscenity, Indecency and Censorship, 1977-. Mem. Council, Hurstpierpoint Coll., 1975-. Recreations: books, music, painting. Address: 6 King's Bench Walk, Temple, EC4Y 7DR. T: 01-353 1696; Field End, Harps Oak Lane, Merstham, Surrey RH1 3AN. T: Merstham 4472. Club: Garrick.

LEONARD, Hugh, (John Keyes Byrne); playwright since 1959; Literary Editor, Abbey Theatre, 1976-77; b 9 Nov. 1926; m 1955, Paule Jacquet; one d. Educ: Presentation College, Dun Laoghaire. Stage plays: The Big Birthday, 1956; A Leap in the Dark, 1957; Madigan's Lock, 1958; A Walk on the Water, 1960; The Passion of Peter Ginty, 1961; Stephen D, 1962; The Poker Session, and Dublin 1, 1963; The Saints Go Cycling In, 1965; Mick and Mick, 1966; The Quick and the Dead, 1967; The Au Pair Man, 1968; The Barracks, 1969; The Patrick Pearse Motel, 1971; Da, 1973; Thieves, 1973; Summer, 1974; Times of Wolves and Tigers, 1974; Irishmen, 1975; Time Was, 1976; A Life, 1977. TV play Silent Song (Italia Award, 1967); TV serial Nicholas Nickleby, 1977; London Belongs to Me, 1977. Film: Herself Surprised, 1977. Publication: The Bully and the Chap (autobiog.), 1977. Recreations: chess, travel, living. Address: Killiney Heath, Killiney, Co. Dublin. T: Dublin 853988. Clubs: Dramatists'; PEN (Dublin).

LEONARD, James Charles Beresford Whyte, MA Oxon; **His Honour Judge Leonard;** a Circuit Judge (formerly Deputy Chairman of Quarter Sessions, Inner London and Middlesex), since 1965; Judge of the Mayor's and City of London Court, since 1973; b 1905; s of Hon. J. W. Leonard, KC; m 1939, Barbara Helen, d of late Capt. William Incledon-Webber; two s one d. Educ: Clifton Coll.; Christ Church, Oxford. Called to the Bar, Inner Temple, 1928, Bencher 1961. Served 1940-45, with RAF. Recorder of Walsall, Staffs, 1951-64; Junior Counsel to Ministry of Agriculture, Fisheries and Food, Forestry Commission and Tithe Redemption Commission, 1959-64; Deputy Chairman of QS: Co. of London, 1964-65; Oxfordshire, 1962-71. Chm., Adv. Cttee dealing with internment under Civil Authorities (Special Powers) Act (NI) 1962, April-Nov. 1972; Comr under Terrorism (N Ireland) Order 1972, 1972-74; Dep. Chm., Appeal Tribunal, 1974-75. Address: 1 Paper Buildings, Temple, EC4. T: 01-583 1870; Cross Trees, Sutton Courtenay, Oxon. T: Sutton Courtenay 230.
See also Earl of Westmeath.

LEONARD, John; see Leonard, H. J.

LEONARD, Richard Lawrence, (Dick Leonard); Assistant Editor, The Economist, since 1974; b 12 Dec. 1930; s of Cyril Leonard, Pinner, Mddx, and late Kate Leonard (née Whyte); m 1963, Irène, d of Dr Ernst Heidelberger, Colombes, France, and of Dr Gertrud Heidelberger, Bad Godesberg, Germany; one s one d. Educ: Ealing Grammar Sch.; Inst. of Education, London Univ.; Essex Univ. (MA). School teacher, 1953-55; Dep. Gen. Sec., Fabian Society, 1955-60; journalist and broadcaster, 1960-68; Sen. Research Fellow (Social Science Research Council), Essex Univ., 1968-70. Mem., Exec. Cttee, Fabian Soc., 1972- (Chm., 1977-78). Trustee, Assoc. of London Housing Estates, 1973-. Contested (Lab) Harrow W, 1955; MP (Lab) Romford, 1970-Feb. 1974; PPS to Rt Hon. Anthony Crosland, 1970-74; Mem., Speaker's Conf. on Electoral Law, 1972-74. Introduced Council Housing Bill, 1971; Life Peers Bill, 1973. Publications: Guide to the General Election, 1964; Elections in Britain, 1968; (ed jtly) The Backbencher and Parliament, 1972; Paying for Party Politics, 1975; contrib.: Guardian, Sunday Times, Observer, New Society, Encounter, etc. Recreations: walking, neglecting the garden. Address: 16 Albert Street, NW1.

LEONARD, Sir Walter McEllister, Kt 1977; DFC; Chairman: Ampol Petroleum Ltd, since 1970 (Managing Director, 1963; General Manager, 1949-63; Director, 1958); Ampol Exploration Ltd, since 1970 (Managing Director, 1967); Director, Australian Industry Development Corporation; Member, Sydney Cove Redevelopment Authority; b Grafton, 22 Feb. 1915; s of W. Leonard Grafton; m 1949, Yvonne M., d of J. V. Brady; two s three d. Educ: Cootamundra High Sch. Articled clerk in a chartered accountant's office, 1933-38; joined Ampol Petroleum Ltd, 1938; Chief Accountant, 1940; Sec., 1941. Served War, RAAF, Bomber Command, 1942-45 (DFC). Asst to Managing Dir, Ampol Petroleum Ltd, 1946-49; Dir, Ampol Exploration Ltd, 1954-; Dir Bowling Centres Ltd, 1961-. Address: 51 Cutler Road, Clontarf, NSW 2093, Australia. Clubs: Royal Sydney Yacht Squadron; American National; RAC; Manley Golf; Elanora Country.

LEONARD-WILLIAMS, Air Vice-Marshal Harold Guy, CB 1966; CBE 1946; DL; retired; Member, Somerset County Council, since 1973; b 10 Sept. 1911; s of late Rev. B. G. Leonard-Williams; m 1937, Catherine Estelle, d of late G. A. M. Levett; one d. Educ: Lancing Coll.; RAF Coll., Cranwell. 58 Sqdn, 1932-33; 208 Sqdn, Middle East, 1933-36; No 17 Signals Course, 1936-37; Instructor, RAF Coll., 1937-38; Advanced Air Striking Force, France, 1939-40 (despatches, 1940); Air Min. (Signals), 1940-43; Chm., Brit. It Communications Bd, 1943-46; RAF Staff Coll., 1947; Dep. CSO, RAF Middle East, 1947-50; Jt Services Staff Coll., 1950-51; CO Radio Engrg Unit, 1951-53; Dep. Dir Signals, Air Min., 1953-56; Sen. Techn. Staff Off., 90 Signals Gp, 1956-57; Dir of Signals, Air Min., 1957-59; Comdt No 1 Radio Sch., 1959-61; Comd. Electronics Off., Fighter Comd., 1961-63; AOA, HQ Far East Air Force, and AOC, HQ Gp, 1963-65; Dir-Gen. of Manning (RAF), Air Force Dept, 1966-68. DL Somerset 1975. Officer, Legion of Merit (US), 1945. Recreations: gardening, boating, do-it-yourself. Address: Open-barrow, Barrows Park, Cheddar, Somerset. T: Cheddar 742474. Club: Royal Air Force.

LEONE, Giovanni; President of the Italian Republic since Dec. 1971; b Naples, 3 Nov. 1908; s of Mauro Leone and Maria Gioffrida; m 1946, Vittoria Michitto; three s (and one s. decd). Educ: Naples Univ. Degrees in Law, 1929 and Polit. Science, 1930. Prof. of Law, Comenius Univ., 1933; Univ. of: Messina, 1936; Bari, 1940; Naples, 1948; Deputy, Constituent Assembly, 1946; MP, 1948-71; Chm., Chamber of Deputies, 1955-63;

Prime Minister, 1963 and 1968; nominated Senator for Life, 1967, for special merits to nation. *Publications:* Tattato di diritto processuale penale; Istituzioni di diritto processuale penale; Manuale di diritto processuale penale; Testimonianze; Cinque mesi a Palazzo Chigi. *Address:* Palazzo del Quirinale, Rome, Italy. *T:* 4699.

LEONTIEF, Prof. Wassily; Professor of Economics, New York University, since 1975; *b* Leningrad, Russia, 5 Aug. 1906; *s of* Wassily Leontief and Eugenia Leontief (*née* Bekker); *m* 1932, Estelle Helena Marks; one *d. Educ:* Univ. of Leningrad (Learned Economist, 1925); Univ. of Berlin (PhD 1928). Research Associate, Univ. of Kiel, Germany, 1927-28; Economic Adviser to Chinese Govt, Nanking, 1928-29; Nat. Bureau of Econ. Res., NY, 1931; Instr Economics, Harvard Univ., 1932-33, Asst Prof., 1933-39, Associate Prof., 1939-46, Prof., 1946-75. Dir, Harvard Economic Research Project, 1948-72; Guggenheim Fellow, 1940-50; Chm., 1965-75, and Sen. Fellow, Soc. of Fellows, Harvard Univ. President: Amer. Econ. Assoc., 1970; Sect. F, BAAS, 1976; Mem., Nat. Acad. of Sciences, 1974; Corr. Mem., Institut de France, 1968; Corr. FBA, 1970; Hon. MRIA, 1976. Hon. PhD: Brussels, 1962; York, 1967; Dr *hc* : Louvain, 1971; Paris (Sorbonne), 1972; Pennsylvania, 1976; Lancaster, 1976. Nobel Prize in Economic Science, 1973. Order of the Cherubim, Univ. of Pisa, 1953. Officier, Légion d'Honneur, 1968. *Publications:* Structure of the American Economy 1919-29, 1941, 2nd edn 1953; Studies in the Structure of the American Economy, 1953; Input-Output Economics, 1966; Essays in Economics, 1966; The Future of the World Economy, 1977; contribs to learned jls. *Recreation:* fly fishing. *Address:* Department of Economics, Tisch Hall, New York University, Washington Square, New York, NY 10003, USA. *Club:* Harvard (New York).

LE PATOUREL, Brig. Herbert Wallace, VC 1943; DL; Director, Harveys of Bristol, since 1969; *b* 20 June 1916; *yr s of* late Herbert Augustus Le Patourel (Attorney-General for Guernsey) and Mary Elizabeth Daw; *m* 1949, Babette Theresa Beattie; two *d. Educ:* Elizabeth Coll., Guernsey. Bank Clerk, 1934-37; 2nd Lt Royal Guernsey Militia, 1936; transferred to The Hampshire Regt, 1937; served War of 1939-45 (despatches, VC); Instructor at Staff Coll., Quetta, 1945-47; Instructor, School of Infantry, Warminster, 1948-50; Parachute Regt, 1950-53; CO, 14th Para Bn and 5th Bn The Royal Hampshire Regt TA, 1954-57; GSO1. British Joint Services Mission, Washington, DC, 1958-60; Dep. Comdr, Ghana Army, 1960-61; Dep. Comdr, 43 Div./District, 1961-62; retired 1962. Executive Asst to the Directors of Showerings Vine Products and Whiteways Ltd, 1965-69. DL Avon, 1974. *Recreations:* sailing, gardening. *Address:* Ford Farm, Ford, Chewton Mendip, Bath. *Clubs:* Army and Navy; Royal Channel Islands Yacht.

LE PATOUREL, John Herbert, FBA 1972; MA, DPhil Oxon; Docteur *hc* Caen; Professor Emeritus, University of Leeds; Archivist to Royal Court of Guernsey since 1946; *b* Guernsey, 29 July 1909; *er s of* late H. A. Le Patourel (HM Attorney-Gen. for Guernsey) and Mary Elizabeth Daw; *m* 1939, Hilda Elizabeth Jean Bird, BA, FSA; three *s* one *d. Educ:* Elizabeth Coll., Guernsey; Jesus Coll., Oxford (King Charles I Scholar); Goldsmiths' Company's Senior Student, 1931-33. Asst Lecturer, Dept of History, University Coll., London, 1933; Lecturer, 1936; Reader in Medieval History, University of London, 1943; Prof. of Medieval History, 1945-70, Research Prof., 1970-74, and Dir, Graduate Centre for Medieval Studies, 1967-70, Univ. of Leeds. Leverhulme Research Fellow, 1950-51. Pres., Leeds Philosophical and Literary Soc., 1966-68; Patron, Thoresby Soc. (Pres. 1949-55); Vice-Pres., Royal Historical Soc., 1968-70; Hon. Vice-Pres., Yorkshire Archæological Soc. (Pres., 1965-69). Hon. Mem., Soc. Guernesiaise. *Publications:* The Medieval Administration of the Channel Islands, 1199-1399, 1937; The Building of Castle Cornet, Guernsey, 1958; The Manor and Borough of Leeds, 1066-1400, 1957; The Norman Empire, 1976; articles, etc, in English and French historical periodicals, publications of Channel Island societies, etc. *Address:* Westcote, Hebers Ghyll Drive, Ilkley, West Yorks. *T:* Ilkley 4406.

LE POER TRENCH, family name of **Earl of Clancarty.**

LE POER TRENCH, Brinsley; *see* Clancarty, 8th Earl of.

LEPPARD, Captain Keith André, CBE 1977; RN; Director Public Relations (Royal Navy), 1974-77; *b* 29 July 1924; *s of* Wilfred Ernest Leppard and Dora Gilmore Keith; *m* 1954, Betty Rachel Smith; one *s* one *d. Educ:* Purley Grammar Sch. MRAeS 1973; MBIM 1973. Entered RN, FAA pilot duties, 1943; Opnl Wartime Service, Fighter Pilot, N Atlantic and Indian Oceans, 1944-45; Fighter Pilot/Flying Instr, Aircraft Carriers and Air Stns, 1946-57; CO 807 Naval Air Sqdn (Aerobatic Display Team, Farnborough), 1958-59; Air Org./Flying Trng Staff appts, 1959-63; Comdr (Air), HMS Victorious, 1963-64; Jt Services Staff Coll., 1964-65; Dir, Naval Officer Appts (Air), 1965-67; Chief Staff Officer (Air), Flag Officer Naval Air Comd, 1967-69; Chief Staff Officer (Ops/Trng), Comdr Far East Fleet, 1969-71; CO, Royal Naval Air Stn, Yeovilton, and Flag Captain to Flag Officer Naval Air Comd, 1972-74. Naval ADC to the Queen, 1976-77. *Recreations:* country life, tennis, golf. *Address:* Little Holt, Kingsley Green, Haslemere, Surrey. *T:* Haslemere 2797. *Club:* Royal Commonwealth Society.

LEPPARD, Raymond John; conductor, harpsichordist, composer; Principal Conductor, BBC Northern Symphony Orchestra, since 1972; *b* 11 Aug. 1927; *s of* A. V. Leppard. *Educ:* Trinity Coll., Cambridge. Fellow of Trin. Coll., Cambridge, Univ. Lecturer in Music, 1958-68. Hon. Keeper of the Music, Fitzwilliam Museum, 1963. Conductor: Covent Garden, Sadler's Wells, Glyndebourne, and abroad; Musical Dir, English Chamber Orch., 1960-77. Commendatore al Merito della Repúbblica Italiana, 1974. *Publications:* realisations of Monteverdi: Il Ballo delle Ingrate, 1958; L'Incoronazione di Poppea, 1962; L'Orfeo, 1965; Il Ritorno d'Ulisse, 1972; Realisations of Francesco Cavalli: Messa Concertata, 1966; L'Ormindo, 1967; La Calisto, 1969; Magnificat, 1970; L'Egisto, 1974; British Academy Italian Lecture, 1969, Procs Royal Musical Assoc. *Recreations:* music, theatre, books, friends. *Address:* c/o Colbert Artists Management, 111 West 57th Street, New York, NY 10019, USA.

LE QUESNE, Sir (Charles) Martin, KCMG 1974 (CMG 1963); HM Diplomatic Service; *b* 10 June 1917; *s of* C. T. Le Quesne, QC; *m* 1948; three *s. Educ:* Shrewsbury; Exeter Coll., Oxford. Served in Royal Artillery, 1940-45. Apptd HM Foreign Service, 1946; 2nd Sec. at HM Embassy, Baghdad, 1947-48; 1st Secretary: Foreign Office, 1948-51, HM Political Residency, Bahrain, 1951-54; attended course at NATO Defence Coll., Paris, 1954-55; HM Embassy, Rome, 1955-58; Foreign Office, 1958-60; apptd HM Chargé d'Affaires, Republic of Mali, 1960, subsequently Ambassador there, 1961-64; Foreign Office, 1964-68; Ambassador to Algeria, 1968-71; Dep. Under-Sec. of State, FCO, 1971-74; High Comr in Nigeria, 1974-76. *Recreations:* gardening, bridge. *Address:* Beau Désert, St Saviour's, Jersey, Channel Islands. *T:* Jersey-Central 22076. *Clubs:* Reform (Chairman 1973-74); United (Jersey); Royal Channel Islands Yacht.
See also J. G. Le Quesne, L. P. Le Quesne.

LE QUESNE, John Godfray, QC 1962; Chairman, Monopolies and Mergers Commission, since 1975 (a part-time Member since Oct. 1974); Judge of Courts of Appeal of Jersey and Guernsey, since 1964; a Recorder, since 1972; *b* 1924; 3rd *s of* late C. T. Le Quesne, QC; *m* 1963, Susan Mary Gill; two *s* one *d. Educ:* Shrewsbury Sch.; Exeter Coll., Oxford (MA). Pres. of Oxford Union, 1943. Called to bar, Inner Temple, 1947; Master of the Bench, Inner Temple, 1969; admitted to bar of St Helena, 1959. Dep. Chm., Lincs (Kesteven) QS, 1963-71. Chm. of Council, Regent's Park Coll., Oxford, 1958-. *Recreations:* music, walking. *Address:* 1 Crown Office Row, Temple, EC4. *T:* 01-353 3731. *Club:* Reform.
See also Sir C. M. Le Quesne, L. P. Le Quesne.

LE QUESNE, Prof. Leslie Philip, DM, MCh, FRCS; Professor of Surgery, Middlesex Hospital Medical School and Director, Department of Surgical Studies, Middlesex Hospital, since 1963; *b* 24 Aug. 1919; *s of* late C. T. Le Quesne, QC; *m* 1969, Pamela Margaret, *o d of* Dr A. Fullerton, Batley, Yorks; two *s. Educ:* Rugby; Exeter Coll., Oxford; Middlesex Hosp. Med. Sch. Jun. Demonstrator, Path. and Anat., 1943-45; House Surgeon, Southend Hosp. and St Mark's Hosp., 1945-47; Appointments at Middlesex Hospital: Asst, Surgical Professorial Unit, 1947-52; Asst Dir, Dept of Surgical Studies, 1952-63; Surgeon, 1960-63. Sir Arthur Sims Commonwealth Travelling Prof., 1975. Editor, Post Graduate Med. Jl, 1951-52. Arris and Gale Lectr, RCS, 1952; Baxter Lectr, Amer. Coll. Surgs, 1960. Examr in Surgery, Universities London, Glasgow, Birmingham, Malaya, Khartoum and Bristol; Mem., Ct of Examrs, RCS, 1971-. Formerly Chm., Assoc. of Profs of Surgery; Pres., Surgical Res. Soc. Chm., The British Jl of Surgery. Hon. FRACS, 1975. Moynihan Medal, 1953. *Publications:* medical articles and contribs to text books; Fluid Balance in Surgical Practice, 2nd edn, 1957. *Recreations:* sailing, reading. *Address:* 8 Eton Villas, NW3 4SX.
See also Sir C. M. Le Quesne, J. G. Le Quesne.

LE QUESNE, Sir Martin; *see* Le Quesne, Sir C. M.

LERMON, Norman, QC 1966; **His Honour Judge Lermon;** a Circuit Judge (formerly County Court Judge), since 1971; *b* 12

Dec. 1915; *s* of late Morris and Clara Lermon; *m* 1939, Sheila Veronica Gilks; one *d. Educ:* Clifton Coll.; Trinity Hall, Cambridge. Joined Royal Fusiliers, 1939; commnd into S Wales Borderers, 1940; served in 53 (W) and 11th Armoured Divs; Staff Officer Ops (Air) 8th Corps, France, Holland and Germany; Major, 1945; NW Europe 1946 (despatches). Called to the Bar, 1943. *Recreations:* golf, reading. *Address:* 2 Harcourt Buildings, Temple, EC4.

LERNER, Alan Jay; playwright; lyricist; *b* NYC, 31 Aug. 1918. *Educ:* Bedales Sch., Hants; Choate Sch., Wallingford, USA; Harvard Univ. Pres., Dramatists' Guild of America, 1958-63; Mem., Songwriter's Hall of Fame, 1971; Bd of Governors: Nat. Hosp. for Speech Disorders; NY Osteopathic Hosp. *Musical plays:* with F. Loewe: What's up, 1943; The Day before Spring, 1945; Brigadoon, 1947 (filmed 1954; NY Drama Critics' Circle Award, 1947; Christopher Award, 1954); Paint your Wagon, 1951 (filmed and produced, 1969); My Fair Lady, 1956 (filmed 1964; NY Drama Critics' Circle Award, Donaldson Award, Antoinette Perry Award, 1956); Camelot, 1960 (filmed 1968); with K. Weill, Love Life, 1948; with B. Lane, On a Clear Day you can see Forever, 1965 (filmed 1970; Grammy Award, 1966); with A. Previn, Coco, 1969; Gigi, 1973 (Antoinette Perry Award, 1973-74); with L. Bernstein, 1600 Pennsylvania Avenue, 1976; *films:* Royal Wedding, 1951; An American in Paris, 1951 (Academy Award, Screenwriters' Guild Award, 1951); Gigi, 1958 (two Academy Awards, Screenwriters' Guild Award, 1958); The Little Prince, 1975. *Address:* 10 East 40th Street, NY 10016, USA. *T:* 212-679-2211. *Clubs:* Players, Lambs, Shaw Soc.

LERNER, Max; Author; Syndicated newspaper column appears New York Post, Los Angeles Times and elsewhere; Professor of American Civilization and World Politics, Brandeis University, USA, 1949-73, now Emeritus; Professor of Human Behavior, Graduate School of Human Behavior, US International University, San Diego; *b* 20 Dec. 1902; *s* of Benjamin Lerner and Bessie Podel; *m* 1st; two *d* (and one *d* decd); 2nd, 1941, Edna Albers; three *s. Educ:* Yale Univ. (BA); Washington Univ., St Louis (MA); Robert Brookings Graduate Sch. of Economics and Government (PhD). Encyclopædia of Social Sciences, 1927, managing editor; Sarah Lawrence Coll., 1932-36, Prof. of Social Science; Harvard, 1935-36, Prof. of Government; Prof. of Political Science, Williams Coll., 1938-43; Ford Foundation Prof. of Amer. Civilization, Sch. of Internat. Studies, University of Delhi, 1959-60; Ford Foundn res. project on European unity, 1963-64. Editor of the Nation, 1936-38; Editorial Director PM, 1943-48; Columnist for the New York Star, 1948-49. *Publications:* It is Later Than You Think, 1938, rev. edn, 1943; Ideas are Weapons, 1939; Ideas for the Ice Age, 1941; The Mind and Faith of Justice Holmes, 1943; Public Journal, 1945; The Third Battle for France, 1945; The World of the Great Powers, 1947; The Portable Veblen, 1948; Actions and Passions, 1949; America as a Civilization, 1957; The Unfinished Country, 1959; Education and a Radical Humanism, 1962; The Age of Overkill, 1962; Tocqueville and American Civilization, 1966; (ed) Essential Works of John Stuart Mill, 1961; (ed) Tocqueville, Democracy in America, 1966; Values in Education, 1976. *Address:* 445 E 84th Street, New York, NY 10028, USA; (office) New York Post, 210 South Street, New York, NY 10002, USA.

LeROY-LEWIS, David Henry, FCA; Chairman, Akroyd and Smithers, since 1976; Member, Stock Exchange Council, since 1961 (a Deputy Chairman, 1973-76); *b* 14 June 1918; *er s* of late Stuyvesant Henry LeRoy-Lewis and late Bettye LeRoy-Lewis; *m* 1953, Cynthia Madeleine, *er d* of Comdr John C. Boldero, DSC, RN (Retd), and Marjorie Agnes Boldero; three *d. Educ:* Eton. FCA 1947. Chairman, Continental Union Trust Ltd, 1974-. Director: Continental Union Trust Ltd, 1948; Industrial & General Trust Ltd, 1967; Akroyd & Smithers Ltd, 1970; Trustees Corp. Ltd, 1973; Touche, Remnant & Co., 1974. *Recreations:* shooting, fishing. *Address:* Bramlands, Woodmancote, Henfield, W Sussex BN5 9TQ. *T:* Henfield 3611. *Clubs:* Bath, Gresham, MCC.

LESLIE, family name of **Earl of Rothes.**

LESLIE, Lord; James Malcolm David Leslie; *b* 4 June 1958; *s* and *heir* of 21st Earl of Rothes, *qv. Educ:* Eton. *Address:* Tanglewood, West Tytherley, Salisbury, Wilts.

LESLIE, Prof. David Clement; Professor of Nuclear Engineering, University of London, and Head of Department of Nuclear Engineering, Queen Mary College, since 1968; *b* Melbourne, 18 Dec. 1924; *o s* of Clement and Doris Leslie; *m* 1952, Dorothea Ann Wenborn; three *s* two *d. Educ:* Westminster; Leighton Park; Wadham Coll., Oxford (MA, DPhil). Royal Navy, 1944-47. Postgrad. research in physics, 1948-50; Sir W. G. Armstrong

Whitworth Aircraft, Coventry, 1951-54; Guided Weapons Div., RAE Farnborough, 1954-58; UKAEA Harwell and Winfrith, 1958-68. Mem., Scientific and Technical Cttee, EEC, 1973-. *Publications:* Developments in the Theory of Turbulence, 1973; papers in Proc. Royal Soc., Quarterly Jl of Mechanics and Applied Maths, Nature, Nuclear Science and Engrg, etc. *Recreations:* history, walking, child-watching. *Address:* 22 Piercing Hill, Theydon Bois, Essex. *T:* Theydon Bois 3249.

LESLIE, Doris, (Lady Fergusson Hannay); novelist and historian; *m* Sir Walter Fergusson Hannay (*d* 1961). *Educ:* London; Brussels; studied art in Florence. Served in Civil Defence, 1941-45. Woman of the Year for Literature (Catholic Women's League), 1970. *Publications: novels:* Full Flavour; Fair Company; Concord in Jeopardy; Another Cynthia; House in the Dust; Folly's End; The Peverills; Peridot Flight; As the Tree Falls; Paragon Street; The Marriage of Martha Todd; A Young Wives' Tale; The Dragon's Head; Call Back Yesterday; *biographical studies:* Royal William (Life of William IV); Polonaise (Life of Chopin); Wreath for Arabella (Life of the Lady Arabella Stuart); That Enchantress (Life of Abigail Hill, Lady Masham); The Great Corinthian (Portrait of the Prince Regent); A Toast to Lady Mary (Life of Lady Mary Wortley Montagu); The Perfect Wife (Life of Mary Anne Disraeli, Viscountess Beaconsfield), 1960; I Return (The Story of François Villon), 1962; This for Caroline (Life of Lady Caroline Lamb), 1964; The Sceptre and the Rose (marriage of Charles II and Catherine of Braganza) 1967; The Rebel Princess (Life of Sophia Dorothea, wife of George I), 1970; The Desert Queen (Life of Lady Hester Stanhope), 1972; The Incredible Duchess (Life of Elizabeth Chudleigh, Duchess of Kingston), 1974; Notorious Lady (Life of Margaret Power, Countess of Blessington), 1976; The Warrior King (Reign of Richard Coeur de Lion and his Crusade), 1977. *Address:* c/o A. P. Watt & Son, 26/28 Bedford Row, WC1R 4HL.

LESLIE, Mrs D. G.; *see* Erskine-Lindop, A. B. N.

LESLIE, Rt. Rev. Ernest Kenneth; *see* Bathurst, (NSW), Bishop of.

LESLIE, Rear-Adm. George Cunningham, CB 1970; OBE 1944; MA; Domestic Bursar and Fellow of St Edmund Hall, Oxford, since 1970; *b* 27 Oct. 1920; 4th *s* of Col A. S. Leslie, CMG, WS, and Mrs M. I. Leslie (*née* Horne); *m* 1953, Margaret Rose Leslie; one *s* three *d. Educ:* Uppingham. Entered RN, 1938; War service in HMS York, Harvester, Volunteer and Cassandra, 1939-45; comd HMS: Wrangler, 1950-51; Wilton, 1951; Surprise, 1954-55; Capt. Fishery Protection Sqdn, 1960-62; Cdre HMS Drake, 1964-65; comd HMS Devonshire, 1966-67; Flag Officer, Admiralty Interview Bd, 1967-68; NATO HQ, Brussels, 1968-70. Comdr 1952; Capt. 1958; Rear-Adm. 1967; retired 1970. *Recreations:* sailing, golf, painting, country pursuits. *Address:* St Edmund Hall, Oxford.

LESLIE, Gilbert Frank; His Honour Judge Leslie; a Circuit Judge (formerly Judge of County Courts); *b* 25 Aug. 1909; *e s* of late F. L. J. Leslie, JP and late M. A. Leslie (*née* Gilbert), Harrogate; *m* 1947, Mary Braithwaite, MD, JP, *e d* of late Col W. H. Braithwaite, MC, TD, DL and Mrs E. M. Braithwaite, Harrogate; three *d. Educ:* St Christopher Sch., Letchworth; King's Coll., Cambridge (MA). Called to the Bar, Inner Temple, 1932; joined North-Eastern Circuit. Served War of 1939-45; Private Sherwood Foresters, 1939; commissioned West Yorkshire Regt, 1940; on Judge-Advocate-General's staff from Nov. 1940; finally ADJAG, HQ BAOR; released Nov. 1945 (Hon. Lt-Col). Asst Recorder, Newcastle upon Tyne City Quarter Sessions, 1954-60, Sheffield City Quarter Sessions, 1956-60; Recorder of Pontefract, 1958-60; Recorder of Rotherham, 1960; Dep. Chm., West Riding Quarter Sessions, 1960-63; Judge of County Court Circuit 14, 1960; Circuit 46, 1960-63; Circuit 42, 1963-; actg Dep. Chm., Inner London Area Sessions, 1965-71. A Dep. Chm., Agricultural Lands Tribunal (Yorkshire Area), 1958-60. Manager, 1974-77, Vice-Pres., 1975-77, Royal Instn of GB. Mem. Board of Faculty of Law and Court of Governors, Sheffield Univ., 1958-61; Governor, 1964-, Chm. of Governors, 1974-, Parsons Mead Sch. for Girls. *Recreation:* gardening. *Address:* Ottways, 26 Ottways Lane, Ashtead, Surrey. *T:* Ashtead 74191. *Club:* Reform.

LESLIE, Harald Robert; *see* Birsay, Hon. Lord.

LESLIE, Ian (William) Murray, CBE 1971 (OBE 1954); Editor of Building (formerly The Builder), 1948-70; Vice-Chairman, The Builder Ltd, 1970-75; *b* 13 March 1905; 2nd *s* of John Gordon Leslie, MB, CM, Black Isle, Inverness, and Agnes Macrae, Kintail, Wester Ross; *m* 1st, 1929, Josette (marr. diss. 1974), 2nd *d* of late André Délètraz, actor, Paris; one *s* ; 2nd, 1974, G. M.

Vivian Williams, barrister-at-law, d of Evan Hughes, Tintagel, Cornwall. *Educ:* St Paul's (foundation scholar); Crown and Manor Boys' Club, Hoxton. Joined editorial staff of The Builder, 1926; Associate Editor, 1937. Mem. Council, National Assoc. of Boys' Clubs, 1944-54; Chm. London Federation of Boys' Clubs, 1945-50; Mem. Metropolitan Juvenile Courts panel, 1947-61. Founder-Pres., Internat. Assoc. of the Building and Construction Press (UK section), 1970-; made survey (with John B. Perks) of Canadian construction industry for The Builder, 1950; organized £1000 house, architectural competition for The Builder, 1951; made survey of housing, South Africa and Rhodesia, for The Builder, 1954. Chm., Building Industry Youth Trust, 1975-. Pres., Invalids Cricket Club, 1974-. Associate RICS; Hon. Mem. of Art Workers' Guild. Hon. FRIBA; Hon. FIOB. *Recreations:* watching cricket; sleep. *Address:* 64 Hamilton Terrace, NW8 9UJ. *T:* 01-289 0178. *Clubs:* Savage, Architectural Association (Hon. Mem.), MCC.

LESLIE, Sir John (Norman Ide), 4th Bt *cr* 1876; *b* 6 Dec. 1916; *s* of Sir (John Randolph) Shane Leslie, 3rd Bt and Marjorie (*d* 1951), *y d* of Henry C. Ide, Vermont, USA; *S* father, 1971. *Educ:* Downside; Magdalene College, Cambridge (BA 1938). Captain, Irish Guards; served War of 1939-45 (prisoner-of-war). Kt of Honour and Devotion, SMO Malta, 1947; KCSG 1958. *Recreations:* ornithology, ecology. *Heir: b* Desmond Arthur Peter Leslie [*b* 29 June 1921; *m* 1st, 1945, Agnes Elizabeth, *o d* of late Rudolph Bernauer, Budapest; two *s* one *d*; 2nd, 1970, Helen Jennifer, *d* of late Lt-Col E. I. E. Strong; two *d*]. *Address:* 19 Piazza in Piscinula, Rome, Italy. *Clubs:* Travellers'; Circolo della Caccia (Rome).

LESLIE, Hon. John Wayland; Flight Lieutenant late RAFVR (invalided 1943); *b* 16 Dec. 1909; 2nd *s* of 19th Earl of Rothes; *m* 1932, Coral Angela, *d* of late G. H. Pinckard, JP, Combe Court, Chiddingfold, Surrey, and 9 Chesterfield Street, Mayfair; one *s* one *d. Educ:* Stowe Sch.; Corpus Christi Coll., Cambridge. Mem. of Royal Company of Archers (Queen's Body Guard for Scotland). Mem. Clothworkers' Co. *Recreations:* shooting, fishing, stalking. *Address:* East Kintrockat, Brechin, Angus. *T:* Brechin 2739. *Club:* New (Edinburgh).

LESLIE, Samuel Clement, CBE 1946; Consultant on information policy to industrial and official bodies, since retirement as Head of the Information Division of the Treasury, 1959; Member, Northern Ireland Development Council, 1955-65; *b* Perth, Western Australia, 15 July 1898; *m* 1924, Doris Frances Falk; one *s* two *d. Educ:* Melbourne C of E Gram. Sch.; Melbourne Univ. (MA); Balliol Coll., Oxford (Rhodes Scholar, DPhil). Post-graduate work in philosophy; Lecturer in Philosophy, University Coll. of North Wales, 1922-23; Senior Lecturer in Philosophy, Melbourne Univ., 1924-25; accompanied Mr S. M. Bruce (Australian Prime Minister) to Imperial Conference of 1926; remained in Britain and entered business; Publicity Manager to Gas Light & Coke Co., 1936-40; Director of Public Relations, Ministry of Supply, 1940, Home Office and Ministry of Home Security, 1940-43; Principal Asst Sec., Home Office, etc., 1943-45; Dir, Council of Industrial Design, 1945-47. *Publications:* Front Line 1940-41, 1942 (official publication, anon.); The Rift in Israel, 1971. *Address:* 5a View Road, N6. *Club:* Reform.

LESLIE MELVILLE, family name of **Earl of Leven and Melville.**

LESSER, Most Rev. Norman Alfred, CMG 1971; MA Cantab; ThD 1962; DD Lambeth 1963; *b* 16 March 1902; *s* of Albert Lesser, Liverpool; *m* 1930, Beatrice Barnes, Southport; one *d. Educ:* Liverpool Collegiate Sch.; Fitzwilliam Hall and Ridley Hall, Cambridge. Curate St Simon and St Jude, Anfield, Liverpool, 1925-26; Curate Holy Trinity, Formby, Lancs, 1926-29; Liverpool Cathedral, 1929-31; Vicar St John, Barrow-in-Furness, 1931-39; Rector and Sub-Dean, Nairobi Cathedral, 1939; Provost of Nairobi, 1942; Bishop of Waiapu, 1947-71; Primate and Archbishop of New Zealand, 1961-71. *Recreation:* model-making. *Address:* 4 Sealy Road, Napier, New Zealand. *T:* Napier 53509.

LESSING, Charlotte; Editor of Good Housekeeping since 1973; *b* 14 May; *m* 1948, Walter B. Lessing; three *d. Educ:* Henrietta Barnet Sch.; evening classes. Univ. of London Dipl. Eng. Lit. Journalism and public relations: New Statesman and Nation; Lilliput (Hulton Press); Royal Society of Medicine; Notley Public Relations; Good Housekeeping, 1964-. *Publications:* short stories and feature articles. *Recreations:* travel, wine. *Address:* 809 Howard House, Dolphin Square, SW1.

LESSING, Mrs Doris (May); author; *b* Persia, 22 Oct. 1919; *d* of Captain Alfred Cook Tayler and Emily Maude McVeagh; lived in Southern Rhodesia, 1924-49; *m* 1st, 1939, Frank Charles Wisdom (marr. diss., 1943); one *s* one *d*; 2nd, 1945, Gottfried Anton Nicholas Lessing (marr. diss., 1949); one *s*. Associate Member: AAAL, 1974; Nat. Inst. of Arts and Letters (US), 1974. Hon. Fellow, MLA (Amer.), 1974. *Publications:* The Grass is Singing, 1950; This Was the Old Chief's Country, 1951; Martha Quest, 1952; Five, 1953 (Somerset Maugham Award, Soc. of Authors, 1954); A Proper Marriage, 1954; Retreat to Innocence, 1956; Going Home, 1957; The Habit of Loving, 1957; A Ripple from the Storm, 1958; Fourteen Poems, 1959; In Pursuit of the English, 1960; The Golden Notebook, 1962 (Prix Médicis 1976 for French trans., Carnet d'or); A Man and Two Women (short stories), 1963; African Stories, 1964; Landlocked, 1965; Particularly Cats, 1966; The Four-Gated City, 1969; Briefing for a Descent into Hell, 1971; The Story of a Non-Marrying Man, 1972; The Summer Before the Dark, 1973; The Memoirs of a Survivor, 1975; *play:* Play with a Tiger, 1962. *Address:* c/o Curtis Brown, 1 Craven Hill, W2 3EP.

LESSOF, Prof. Maurice Hart; Professor of Medicine, University of London at Guy's Hospital Medical School, since 1971; *b* 4 June 1924; *s* of Noah and Fanny Lessof; *m* 1960, Leila Liebster; one *s* two *d. Educ:* City of London Sch.; King's Coll., Cambridge. Appts on junior staff of Guy's Hosp., Canadian Red Cross Memorial Hosp., etc; Research Fellow, Johns Hopkins Hosp., Baltimore, 1958-59, Vis. Prof. 1968; Physician, Greenwich District Hosp., 1964; Clinical Immunologist and Physician, Guy's Hosp., 1967. External examr, Univ. of Ibadan, 1976. Pres., Sect. of Medicine, RSocMed, 1977. *Publications:* various papers in med. jls and chapters on allergic and hypersensitive states. *Recreation:* painting. *Address:* 8 John Spencer Square, Canonbury, N1 2LZ. *T:* 01-226 0919. *Club:* Athenæum.

LESTANG, Sir M. C. E. C. N. de; *see* Nageon de Lestang.

LESTER, Anthony Paul, QC 1975; *b* 3 July 1936; *e s* of Harry and Kate Lester; *m* 1971, Catherine Elizabeth Debora Wassey; one *s* one *d. Educ:* City of London Sch.; Trinity Coll., Cambridge (Exhibnr) (BA); Harvard Law Sch. (Harkness Commonwealth Fund Fellowship) (LLM). Called to Bar, Lincoln's Inn, 1963 (Mansfield scholar). Served Royal Artillery, 1955-57. Chm., Fabian Soc., 1973. Special Adviser to: Home Secretary, 1974-76; Standing Adv. Commn on Human Rights, 1975-77. Member: Council of Justice; Court of Governors, London Sch. of Economics; Internat. Law Assoc. Cttees on Water Resources and on Human Rights; Trustee, Runnymede Trust. Governor, British Inst. of Human Rights. *Publications:* Justice in the American South, 1964 (Amnesty Internat.); (co-ed.) Shawcross and Beaumont on Air Law, 3rd edn, 1964; (co-author) Race and Law, 1972; contrib. to British Nationality, Immigration and Race Relations, in Halsbury's Laws of England, 4th edn, 1973; various articles on internat. law, race relations and public affairs. *Address:* 2 Hare Court, Temple, EC4. *T:* 01-353 0076. *Club:* Garrick.

LESTER, James Theodore; MP (C) Beeston, since Feb. 1974; an Opposition Whip, since 1975; *b* 23 May 1932; *s* of Arthur Ernest and Marjorie Lester; *m* 1953, Iris Yvonne Whitby; two *s. Educ:* Nottingham High School. Nat. Service Commn RAOC. Jt Man. Dir, Lester's (Nottm) Ltd, Footwear Distributors. Mem. Bingham RDC, 1964; Mem. Notts CC, 1967 (Chm. Finance Cttee, 1969-74). Contested (C) Bassetlaw, Oct. 1968 and 1970. *Recreations:* reading, music, countryside, travelling. *Address:* The Whinyards, East Bridgford, Notts. *T:* East Bridgford 330. *Club:* Constitutional.

LESTER, Richard; Film Director; *b* 19 Jan. 1932; *s* of Elliott and Ella Young Lester; *m* 1956, Deirdre Vivian Smith; one *s* one *d. Educ:* Wm Penn Charter Sch.; University of Pennsylvania (BSc). Television Director: CBS (USA), 1951-54; AR (Dir TV Goon Shows), 1956. Directed The Running, Jumping and Standing Still Film (Acad. Award nomination; 1st prize San Francisco Festival, 1960). *Feature Films directed:* It's Trad, Dad, 1962; Mouse on the Moon, 1963; A Hard Day's Night, 1964; The Knack, 1964 (Grand Prix, Cannes Film Festival); Help, 1965 (Best Film Award and Best Dir Award, Rio de Janeiro Festival); A Funny Thing Happened on the Way to the Forum, 1966; How I won the War, 1967; Petulia, 1968; The Bed Sitting Room, 1969 (Gandhi Peace Prize, Berlin Film Festival); The Three Musketeers, 1973; Juggernaut, 1974 (Best Dir award, Teheran Film Fest.); The Four Musketeers, 1974; Royal Flash, 1975; Robin and Marian, 1976; The Ritz, 1976. *Recreations:* composing, playing popular music. *Address:* Twickenham Film Studios, St Margaret's, Twickenham, Mddx.

LESTER SMITH, Ernest; *see* Smith, E. L.

LESTOR, Joan; MP (Lab) Eton and Slough since 1966; *b* Vancouver, British Columbia, Canada; one *s* one *d* (both adopted). *Educ:* Blaenavon Secondary Sch., Monmouth; William Morris Secondary Sch., Walthamstow; London Univ. Diploma in Sociology. Nursery Sch. Teacher, 1959-66. Member: Wandsworth Borough Council, 1958-68; LCC, 1962-64; Exec. Cttee of the London Labour Party, 1962-65; Nat. Exec., Labour Party, 1967- (Chm., 1977-). Contested (Lab) Lewisham West, 1964. Parliamentary Under-Secretary: Dept of Educn and Science, Oct. 1969-June 1970; FCO, 1974-75; DES, 1975-76. Chm. Council, Nat. Soc. of Children's Nurseries, 1969-70. *Recreations:* theatre, reading, playing with children, cycling. *Address:* House of Commons, SW1; 59 Magdalen Road, SW18.

L'ESTRANGE, Laurence Percy Farrer, OBE 1958; HM Diplomatic Service; retired; company director and consultant; *b* 10 Sept. 1912; *s* of late S. W. L'Estrange and Louie Knights L'Estrange (*née* Farrer); *m* 1933, Anne Catherine (*née* Whiteside); two *s. Educ:* Shoreham Grammar Sch., Shoreham, Sussex; Univ. of London. Employed at HM Embassy, Caracas, 1939, and Acting Vice-Consul, 1941 and 1942. Resigned and joined RAF, 1943-46. HM Vice-Consul, Malaga, 1946; Second Sec., San Salvador, 1949; Chargé d'Affaires, 1952; Vice-Consul, Chicago, 1953; First Sec. (Commercial): Manila, 1954; Lima, 1958; Chargé d'Affaires, 1961; seconded to Western Hemisphere Exports Council, in charge of Latin American Div., 1962; HM Consul, Denver, 1963; Counsellor (Commercial), Lagos, 1967; Ambassador to Honduras, 1969-72. FRSA 1973. *Recreations:* golf, riding, sailing, fishing and shooting. *Address:* 11 Lauder Place, East Linton, East Lothian. *Clubs:* Royal Automobile, Travellers'.

L'ETANG, Hugh Joseph Charles James; Editor of The Practitioner since 1973; *b* 23 Nov. 1917; *s* of late Dr J. G. L'Etang and Frances L'Etang; *m* 1951, Cecily Margaret Tinker, MD, MRCP; one *s* one *d. Educ:* Haileybury Coll.; St John's Coll., Oxford; St Bartholomew's Hosp.; Harvard Sch. of Public Health. BA 1939, BM, BCh 1942, DIH 1952. War Service, 1943-46, RMO 5th Bn Royal Berks Regt; TA from 1947, RAMC; Lt-Col 1953-56. Medical Adviser: North Thames Gas Bd, 1948-56; British European Airways, 1956-58; John Wyeth & Brother Ltd, 1958-69; Asst and Dep. Editor, The Practitioner, 1969-72. Hira S. Choukè Lectr, Coll. of Physicians of Philadelphia, 1972. Member: RUSI; IISS; Military Commentators' Circle (Hon. Sec.); Amer. Civil War Round Table, London; Sherlock Holmes Soc. *Publications:* The Pathology of Leadership, 1969; articles in Practitioner, Jl RAMC, Army Qtly, Brassey's Annual. *Recreation:* medical aspects of military and foreign affairs. *Address:* 27 Sispara Gardens, SW18 1LG. *T:* 01-870 3836. *Club:* United Oxford & Cambridge University.

LETHBRIDGE, Captain Sir Hector (Wroth), 6th Bt, *cr* 1804; *b* 26 Aug. 1898; *s* of Sir Wroth Periam Christopher Lethbridge, 5th Bart, and Alianore (*y d* of late Edward Chandos Pole, Radbourne Hall, Derby, and Lady Anne Chandos Pole, *d* of 5th Earl of Harrington); *S* father, 1950; *m* 1946, Diana, widow of Major John Vivian Bailey, The Royal Scots Fusiliers, and *er d* of Lt-Col Frank Noel, Hopton Hall, Great Yarmouth; one *s* one *d. Educ:* Radley. Served European War, 1914-18: Officers Cadet Bn, 1916; commissioned, The Rifle Brigade, 1917; France, 1917-18 (POW); India, 1919-20; RARO, 1920; recalled, 1939; served War of 1939-45, in Gold Coast, 1941; invalided home, 1941; demobilized, 1945. *Recreations:* tennis, shooting, golf. *Heir: s* Thomas Periam Hector Noel Lethbridge [*b* 17 July 1950; *m* 1976, Susan Elizabeth Rocke; one *s*]. *Address:* Long Sutton House, Langport, Somerset. *T:* Long Sutton 284. *Clubs:* Junior Carlton; Somerset County (Taunton).

LE TOCQ, Eric George, CMG 1975; HM Diplomatic Service; British Government Representative in the West Indies Associated States, since 1975; *b* 20 April 1918; *s* of Eugene Charles Le Tocq; *m* 1946, Betty Esdaile; two *s* one *d. Educ:* Elizabeth Coll., Guernsey; Exeter Coll., Oxford (MA). Served War of 1939-45: commissioned in Royal Engineers, 1939; North Africa, 1942-43; Italy, 1943; Austria and Greece; major. Taught Modern Languages and Mathematics at Monmouth Sch., 1946-48; Assistant Principal, Commonwealth Relations Office, 1948; Karachi, 1948-50; Principal, 1950; Dublin, 1953-55; Accra, 1957-59; Assistant Secretary, 1962; Adviser on Commonwealth and External Affairs, Entebbe, 1962; Deputy High Commissioner, Uganda, 1962-64; Counsellor, British High Commission, Canberra, 1964-67; Head of E African Dept, FCO, 1968-71; High Comr in Swaziland, 1972-75. *Recreations:* golf and gardening. *Address:* c/o Foreign and Commonwealth Office, SW1. *Club:* Royal Commonwealth Society.

LETSON, Major-General Harry Farnham Germaine, CB 1946; CBE 1944; MC; ED; CD; *b* Vancouver, BC, 26 Sept. 1896; *e s* of late J. M. K. Letson, Vancouver, BC; *m* 1928, Sally Lang Nichol; no *c. Educ:* McGill Univ.; University of British Columbia; University of London. BSc (UBC) 1919; PhD (Eng) London, 1923. Active Service Canadian Army, 1916-19; Associate Professor Mechanical and Electrical Engineering, University of BC, 1923-36; on Active Service Canadian Army, 1939-46; Adjt-General Canadian Army, 1942-44; Commander of Canadian Army Staff in Washington, 1944-46; Secretary to Governor-General of Canada, 1946-52; Adviser on Militia, Canadian Army, 1954-58, retired. Hon. Colonel British Columbia Regt, 1963. LLD (University of BC), 1945. *Recreations:* fishing, shooting. *Address:* 474 Lansdowne Road, Ottawa K1M 0X9, Canada. *Clubs:* Rideau, Country (Ottawa); Vancouver (Vancouver, BC).

LETTS, Charles Trevor; Underwriting Member of Lloyd's, since 1948; Deputy Chairman of Lloyd's, 1966 (entered Lloyd's, 1924; Member, 1941; Committee, 1964-67); *b* 2 July 1905; *o s* of late Charles Hubert and Gertrude Letts; *m* 1942, Mary R. (Judy), *o d* of late Sir Stanley and late Lady (Hilda) Woodwark; two *s* one *d. Educ:* Marlborough Coll. Served RNVR, Lieut-Commander, 1940-45. Member: Cttee, Lloyd's Underwriters' Assoc., 1960-70 (Chairman, 1963-64); Council, Lloyd's Register of Shipping, 1964-77 (Chairman, Yacht Sub-Cttee, 1967-75); Salvage Association, 1963-70. *Recreations:* sailing, golf. *Address:* Bearwood, Holtye, Edenbridge, Kent. *T:* Cowden 472. *Club:* Royal Ocean Racing.

LETWIN, Prof. William; Professor of Political Science, London School of Economics, since 1976; *b* 14 Dec. 1922; *s* of Lazar and Bessie Letwin; *m* 1944, Shirley Robin; one *s* . *Educ:* Univ. of Chicago (BA 1943, PhD 1951); London Sch. of Economics (1948-50). Served US Army, 1943-46. Postdoctoral Fellow, Economics Dept, Univ. of Chicago, 1951-52; Research Associate, Law Sch., Univ. of Chicago, 1953-55; Asst. Prof. of Industrial History, MIT, 1955-60; Associate Prof. of Economic History, MIT, 1960-67; Reader in Political Science, LSE, 1966-76. Chm., Bd of Studies in Economics, Univ. of London, 1971-73. *Publications:* (ed) Frank Knight, on The History and Method of Economics, 1956; Sir Josiah Child, 1959; Documentary History of American Economic Policy, 1961, 2nd edn 1972; Origins of Scientific Economics 1660-1776, 1963; Law and Economic Policy in America, 1965; articles in learned jls. *Address:* 3 Kent Terrace, NW1 4RP. *T:* 01-262 2593.

LEUCHARS, Maj.-Gen. Peter Raymond, CBE 1966; Deputy Commissioner-in-Chief, St John Ambulance Brigade; *b* 29 Oct. 1921; *s* of Raymond Leuchars and Helen Inez Leuchars (*née* Copland-Griffiths); *m* 1953, Hon. Gillian Wightman Nivison, *d* of 2nd Baron Glendyne; one *s. Educ:* Bradfield College. Commnd in Welsh Guards, 1941; served in NW Europe and Italy, 1944-45; Adjt, 1st Bn Welsh Guards, Palestine, 1945-48; Bde Major, 4 Guards Bde, Germany, 1952-54; GSO1 (Instr.), Staff Coll., Camberley, 1956-59; GSO1 HQ 4 Div. BAOR, 1960-63; comd 1st Bn Welsh Guards, 1963-65; Principal Staff Off. to Dir of Ops, Borneo, 1965-66; comd 11 Armd Bde BAOR, 1966-68; comd Jt Operational Computer Projects Team, 1969-71; Dep. Comdt Staff Coll., Camberley, 1972-73; GOC Wales, 1973-76. Col, The Royal Welch Fusiliers, 1974-. Pres., Guards' Golfing Soc., 1977. Order of Istiqlal (Jordan), 1946. *Recreations:* golf, shooting, travel, photography. *Address:* 5 Chelsea Square, SW3 6LF. *T:* 01-352 6187. *Clubs:* Pratt's, Belfry; Royal Mid-Surrey Golf; Sunningdale Golf (Captain 1975).

LEUCKERT, Mrs Harry; see Muir, Jean Elizabeth.

LEVEEN, Jacob; Senior Member, Wolfson College (formerly University College), Cambridge; Keeper of Department of Oriental Printed Books and Manuscripts, British Museum, 1953-56; retired; *b* 24 Dec. 1891; *o* surv. *c* of late David and Rose Leveen; *m* 1928, Violet Egerton (marr. diss. 1963), *yr d* of late Capt. George Egerton Pearch; one *s* decd. *Educ:* Jews' Coll.; University Coll., London (Prizeman in Greek, and Hollier Scholar in Hebrew); School of Oriental and African Studies (BA with First Class Honours in Arabic; Ouseley Scholar in Arabic). Entered British Museum, 1914; Deputy Keeper, Dept of Oriental Printed Books and Manuscripts, 1944. War Service, 1916-20. *Publications:* Part IV of Catalogue of Hebrew and Samaritan Manuscripts in British Museum, 1935; The Hebrew Bible in Art (Schweich Lectures in Biblical Archæology, British Academy), 1944; (ed) A Digest of Commentaries on the Babylonian Talmud, British Museum, 1961; studies in the text of the Psalms (in Journal of Theological Studies and Vetus Testamentum); occasional articles and reviews in learned, art and popular journals. *Recreations:* talking, music, art and literature. *Address:* 5 Brookside, Cambridge. *T:* 50619. *Club:* Athenæum.

LEVEN, 14th Earl of, **and MELVILLE,** 13th Earl of, *cr* 1641; **Alexander Robert Leslie Melville;** Baron Melville, 1616; Baron Balgonie, 1641; Earl of Melville, Viscount Kirkcaldie, 1690; Lord-Lieutenant of Nairn since 1969; *b* 13 May 1924; *e s* of 13th Earl and Lady Rosamond Sylvia Diana Mary Foljambe (*d* 1974), *d* of 1st Earl of Liverpool; *S* father, 1947; *m* 1953, Susan, *er d* of Lieut-Colonel R. Steuart-Menzies of Culdares, Arndilly House, Craigellachie, Banffshire; two *s* one *d. Educ:* Eton. ADC to Governor General of New Zealand, 1951-52. Formerly Capt. Coldstream Guards; retired, 1952. DL, County of Nairn, 1961; Convener, Nairn CC, 1970. *Heir: s* Lord Balgonie, *qv. Address:* Glenferness House, Nairn. *T:* Glenferness 202. *Clubs:* Naval and Military, Pratt's; New (Edinburgh).

LEVENE, Ben, ARA 1975; painter; *b* 23 Dec. 1938; *s* of Mark and Charlotte Levene. *Educ:* Slade School (DFA). Boise Scholarship, 1961; lived in Spain, 1961-62. First one-man show, 1973. *Address:* 26 Netherby Road, SE23. *T:* 01-699 1674.

LEVER, family name of **Viscount Leverhulme.**

LEVER, Sir Christopher; *see* Lever, Sir T. C. A. L.

LEVER, Rt. Hon. Harold, PC 1969; MP (Lab) Manchester Central, since 1974 (Manchester Exchange, 1945-50; Manchester, Cheetham, 1950-74); Chancellor of the Duchy of Lancaster, since 1974; *b* Manchester, 15 Jan. 1914; *s* of late Bernard and Bertha Lever; *m* 1962, Diane, *d* of Saleh Bashi; three *d* (and one *d* from late wife). *Educ:* Manchester Grammar Sch. Called to Bar, Middle Temple, 1935. Promoted Defamation Act, 1952, as a Private Member's Bill. Joint Parliamentary Under-Secretary, Dept of Economic Affairs, 1967; Financial Sec. to Treasury, Sept. 1967-69; Paymaster General, 1969-70. Chm., Public Accounts Cttee, 1970-73. Treasurer, Socialist International, 1971-73. *Address:* House of Commons, SW1.

LEVER, Jeremy Frederick, QC 1972; *b* 23 June 1933; *s* of A. Lever. *Educ:* Bradfield Coll.; University Coll., Oxford; Nuffield Coll., Oxford. Served RA, 1951-53. 1st cl. Jurisprudence, 1956, MA Oxon; Pres., Oxford Union Soc., 1957, Trustee, 1972-. Fellow, All Souls Coll., Oxford, 1957-. Called to Bar, Gray's Inn, 1957. Dir, (non-exec.), Dunlop Holdings Ltd, 1973-. *Publications:* The Law of Restrictive Practices, 1964; other legal works. *Recreations:* walking, music. *Address:* 39 Manor House, Marylebone Road, NW1. *T:* 01-723 4605; 31 Vernon Terrace, Brighton. *T:* Brighton 722645. *Club:* Garrick.

LEVER, John Michael, QC 1977; a Recorder of the Crown Court, since 1972; *b* 12 Aug. 1928; *s* of late John Lever and Ida Donaldson Lever; *m* 1964, Elizabeth Marr; two *s. Educ:* Bolton Sch.; Gonville and Caius Coll., Cambridge (Schol.). 1st cl. hons BA. Flying Officer, RAF, 1950-52. Called to Bar, Middle Temple, 1951 (Blackstone Schol.); practised Northern Circuit from 1952; Asst Recorder, Salford, 1969-71. Governor, Bolton Sch. *Recreations:* theatre, fell-walking. *Address:* Rawlinson House, Heath Charnock, Chorley, Lancs.

LEVER, Rt. Hon. Norman Harold; *see* Lever, Rt. Hon. Harold.

LEVER, Sir (Tresham) Christopher (Arthur Lindsay), 3rd Bt *cr* 1911; *b* 9 Jan. 1932; *s* of Sir Tresham Joseph Philip Lever, 2nd Bt, and Frances Yowart Parker (*d* 1959) *d* of late Lindsay Hamilton Goodwin; *S* father, 1975; *m* 1st, 1970, Susan Mary (marr. diss. 1974), *d* of late John Armytage Nicholson, Enniscoe, Crossmolina, Co. Mayo; 2nd, 1975, Linda Weightman McDowell, *d* of late James Jepson Goulden, Tennessee, USA. *Educ:* Eton; Trinity Coll., Cambridge. BA 1954, MA 1957 (Hist. and Eng. Lang. and Litt.). Lieut, 17th/21st Lancers, 1950. *Publications:* Goldsmiths and Silversmiths of England, 1975; Naturalized Animals of the British Isles, 1977; contribs to The Times, Financial Times, Connoisseur, Apollo, Country Life, Field, Illustrated London News. *Recreations:* golf, fishing, deer-stalking, natural history, antiques. *Heir:* none. *Address:* Rye Mead House, Winkfield, Windsor Forest, Berks. *T:* Winkfield Row 2604. *Club:* Buck's.

LEVERHULME, 3rd Viscount, *cr* 1922, of the Western Isles; **Philip William Bryce Lever,** TD; Baron, *cr* 1917; Bt, *cr* 1911; Knight of Order of St John of Jerusalem; Major, Cheshire Yeomanry; Lord-Lieutenant of City and County of Chester since 1949; Advisory Director of Unilever Ltd; *b* 1 July 1915; *s* of 2nd Viscount and Marion, *d* of late Bryce Smith of Manchester; *S* father, 1949; *m* 1937, Margaret Ann (*d* 1973), *o c* of John Moon, Tiverton; three *d. Educ:* Eton; Trinity Coll., Cambridge. Hon. Air Commodore 663 Air OP Squadron, RAuxAF; Hon. Air Commodore 610 (County of Chester) Squadron, Royal Auxiliary Air Force; Dep. Hon. Col, Cheshire Yeomanry, T&AVR, 1971-72, Hon. Col, 1972-. Pres. Council,

Liverpool Univ., 1957-63, Sen. Pro-Chancellor, 1963-66. Member: National Hunt Cttee, 1961 (Steward, 1965-68); Deputy Senior Steward, Jockey Club, 1970-73, Senior Steward, 1973-76; Council of King George's Jubilee Trust; Chairman, Exec. Cttee Animal Health Trust, 1964. Hon. FRCS 1970; Hon. ARCVS 1975. Hon. LLD Liverpool, 1967. *Recreations:* shooting, hunting. *Heir:* none. *Address:* Thornton Manor, Thornton Hough, Wirral, Merseyside; Badanloch, Kinbrace, Sutherland; 16 Clarendon Road, W11. *Clubs:* Boodle's; Jockey.
See also Col Sir J. G. C. Pole, Bt.

LEVERSEDGE, Leslie Frank, CMG 1955; MA Cantab; Economic Secretary to Northern Rhodesia Government, 1956-60, retired; *b* 29 May 1904; *s* of F. E. Leversedge, UP, India; *m* 1945, Eileen Melegueta Spencer Payne; two *s* three *d. Educ:* St Paul's Sch., Darjeeling, India; St Peter's Sch., York; St John's Coll., Cambridge; Inner Temple, London. Cadet in Colonial Administrative Service, Northern Rhodesia, Dec. 1926; District Officer, Dec. 1928; Provincial Commissioner, Jan. 1947; Senior Provincial Commissioner, Dec. 1948. Development Secretary to Northern Rhodesia Government, 1951-56. MLC 1951; MEC 1951. British Council Local Correspondent for Kent, 1963-75. FRSA 1973. *Recreation:* squash rackets. *Address:* Earley House, Petham, Canterbury, Kent CT4 5RY. *T:* Petham 285.

LEVESON, Lord; Granville George Fergus Leveson Gower; *b* 10 Sept. 1959; *s* and *heir* of 5th Earl Granville, *qv.*

LEVESON GOWER, family name of **Earl Granville.**

LEVESQUE, Most Rev. Louis, ThD; *b* 27 May 1908; *s* of Philippe Levesque and Catherine Levesque (*née* Beaulieu); *Educ:* Laval Univ. Priest, 1932; Bishop of Hearst, Ontario, 1952-64; Archbishop of Rimouski, 1967-73. Chm., Canadian Cath. Conf., 1965-67; Mem. Congregation Bishops, Rome, 1968-73. *Address:* 57 Avenue Hotel-de-Ville, Mont-Joli, PQ, Canada.

LÉVESQUE, Hon. René; Premier of Province of Québec, Canada, since 1976; *b* 24 Aug. 1922; *s* of Dominique Lévesque and Diane Dionne; *m* 1947, Louise L'Heureux; two *s* one *d. Educ:* schs in New Carlisle and Gaspé; Québec Univ. (BA); Law Sch., Laval, Québec. Overseas duty as reporter with US Forces (attached to Office of War Information, Europe), 1944-45; reporter and commentator, Canadian Broadcasting Corp., 1946-59. Mem., Québec Nat. Assembly, 1960-70, 1976-; Minister, Public Works, Natural Resources and Social Welfare, 1960-66; Mem. Opposition, 1966-70; Pres., Parti Québécois, 1966-77. *Publication:* Option—Québec, 1968. *Recreations:* tennis, swimming, skiing, reading, movies. *Address:* Government Buildings, Edifice J, Québec, Canada. *T:* 643-5321. *Club:* Cercle Universitaire (Québec).

LEVEY, Michael Vincent, MVO 1965; MA Oxon and Cantab; Director of the National Gallery, since 1973 (Deputy Director, 1970-73); *b* 8 June 1927; *s* of O. L. H. Levey and Gladys Mary Milestone; *m* 1954, Brigid Brophy, *qv*; one *d. Educ:* Oratory Sch.; Exeter Coll., Oxford, Hon. Fellow, 1973. Served with Army, 1945-48; commissioned, KSLI, 1946, and attached RAEC, Egypt. National Gallery: Asst Keeper, 1951-66, Dep. Keeper, 1966-68, Keeper, 1968-73. Slade Prof. of Fine Art, Cambridge, 1963-64; Supernumerary Fellow, King's Coll., Cambridge, 1963-64. *Publications:* Six Great Painters, 1956; National Gallery Catalogues: 18th Century Italian Schools, 1956; The German School, 1959; Painting in 18th Century Venice, 1959; From Giotto to Cézanne, 1962; Dürer, 1964; The Later Italian Paintings in the Collection of HM The Queen, 1964; Canaletto Paintings in the Royal Collection, 1964; Tiepolo's Banquet of Cleopatra (Charlton Lecture, 1962), 1966; Rococo to Revolution, 1966; Bronzino (The Masters), 1967; Early Renaissance, 1967 (Hawthornden Prize, 1968); Fifty Works of English Literature We Could Do Without (co-author), 1967; Holbein's Christina of Denmark, Duchess of Milan, 1968; A History of Western Art, 1968; Painting at Court (Wrightsman Lectures), 1971; 17th and 18th Century Italian Schools (Nat. Gall. catalogue), 1971; The Life and Death of Mozart, 1971; The Nude: Themes and Painters in the National Gallery, 1972; (co-author) Art and Architecture in 18th Century France, 1972; The Venetian Scene (Themes and Painters Series), 1973; Botticelli (Themes and Painters Series), 1974; High Renaissance, 1975; The World of Ottoman Art, 1976; Jacob van Ruisdael (Themes and Painters Series), 1977; The Case of Walter Pater, 1978; contributions Burlington Magazine, etc. *Address:* 185 Old Brompton Road, SW5. *T:* 01-373 9335.

LEVI, Prof. Edward Hirsch; Glen A. Lloyd Distinguished Service Professor, University of Chicago, since 1977; *b* 26 June 1911; *s* of Gerson B. Levi and Elsa B. Levi (*née* Hirsch); *m* 1946, Kate Sulzberger; three *s. Educ:* Univ. of Chicago; Yale Univ. Law

Sch. Univ. of Chicago: Asst Prof. of Law, 1936-40; Prof. of Law, 1945-75; Dean of the Law School, 1950-62; Provost, 1962-68; President, 1968-75; Pres. emeritus, 1975; Attorney-Gen. of US, 1975-77. Special Asst to Attorney-Gen., Washington, DC, 1940-45; 1st Asst, War Div., Dept of Justice, 1943; 1st Asst, Anti-trust Div., 1944-45; Chm., Interdeptl Cttee on Monopolies and Cartels, 1944; Counsel, Subcttee on Monopoly Power Judiciary Cttee, 81st Congress, 1950; Member: White House Task Force on Educn, 1966-67; President's Task Force on Priorities in Higher Educn, 1969-70; White House Central Gp in Domestic Affairs, 1964; Citizens Commn on Graduate Medical Educn, 1963-66; Sloan Commn on Cable Communications, 1970-71; Nat. Commn on Productivity, 1970-; Commn on Foundations and Private Philanthropy, 1969-70. Mem. Council, American Law Inst., 1965-; American Bar; Illinois Bar; Chicago Bar; Supreme Court, 1945-; Amer. Judicature Soc.; Council on Legal Educn for Profl. Responsibility, 1968-74; Order of Coif; Phi Beta Kappa; res. adv. bd, Commn Econ. Develt, 1951-54; bd Dirs, SSRC, 1959-62; Nat. Commn on Productivity, 1970-75; Nat. Council on the Humanities, 1974-75. Trustee: Urban Inst.; Internat. Legal Center; Museum of Science and Industry; Russell Sage Foundn; Aspen Inst. for Humanist Studies; Univ. Chicago, 1966; Woodrow Wilson Nat. Fellowship Foundn, 1972-75; Inst. Psycho-analysis, Chicago, 1961-75; Hon. Trustee: Inst. of Internat. Educn; Univ. of Chicago, 1975. Benjamin N. Cardozo Lectr, 1969; John Randolph Tucker Lecture, 1973. Fellow: Amer. Bar Foundn; Amer. Acad. Arts and Scis. Hon. degrees: LHD: Hebrew Union Coll.; Loyola Univ.; DePaul Univ.; Kenyon Coll.; Univ. of Chicago; Bard Coll.; LLD: Univ. of Michigan; Univ. of California at Santa Cruz; Univ. of Iowa; Jewish Theological Seminary of America; Brandeis Univ.; Lake Forest Coll.; Univ. of Rochester; Univ. of Toronto; Yale Univ.; Notre Dame; Denison Univ., Nebraska Univ. Law Sch.; Univ. of Miami; Boston Coll.; Ben N. Cardozo Sch. of Law, Yeshiva Univ., NYC; Columbia Univ., Law Sch.; Dropsie Univ., Pa; Univ. of Pa Law Sch. Legion of Honour (France); Distinguished Citizen Award, Ill St. Andrews Soc., 1976; Herbert H. Lehman Ethics Medal, Jewish Theol. Seminary, 1976; Learned Hand Medal, Fedn Bar Council, NYC, 1976; Wallace Award, Amer.-Scottish, Foundn, 1976. *Publications:* Introduction to Legal Reasoning, 1949; Four Talks on Legal Education, 1952; Point of View, 1969; The Crisis in the Nature of Law, 1969; Elements of the Law (ed, with Roscoe Steffen), 1936; Gilbert's Collier on Bankruptcy (ed, with James W. Moore), 1936; Member, editorial board: Jl Legal Educn, 1956-68; Encyclopaedia Britannica, 1968-75; Associate Editor, Natural Law Forum, 1956-68. *Address:* (office) 1116 East 59th Street, Chicago, Illinois 60637, USA. *T:* (312) 753-1234; (home) 4950 Chicago Beach Drive, Chicago, Illinois 60615. *Clubs:* Quadrangle, Columbia Yacht, Mid-America (Chicago); Commercial, Economic, Standard, Century (New York); Chicago, Cosmos (DC).

LÉVI-STRAUSS, Claude; Commandeur de la Légion d'Honneur, 1976; Commandeur, Ordre Nationale du Mérite, 1971; Member of French Academy, since 1973; Professor, Collège de France, since 1959; Director of Studies, Ecole pratique des hautes études, Paris, since 1950; *b* 28 Nov. 1908; *s* of Raymond Lévi-Strauss and Emma Lévy; *m* 1st, 1932, Dina Dreyfus; 2nd, 1946, Rose-Marie Ullmo; one *s*; 3rd, 1954, Monique Roman; one *s*. *Educ:* Lycée Janson-de-Sailly, Paris; Sorbonne. Prof., Univ. of São Paulo, Brazil, 1935-39; Vis. Prof., New School for Social Research, NY, 1941-45; Cultural Counsellor, French Embassy, Washington, 1946-47; Assoc. Curator, Musée de l'Homme, Paris, 1948-49. Corresp. Member: Royal Acad. of Netherlands; Norwegian Acad.; British Acad.; Nat. Acad. of Sciences, USA; Amer. Museum of Natural History; Amer. Philos. Soc.; Royal Anthrop. Inst. of Great Britain; London Sch. of African and Oriental Studies. Hon. Dr: Brussels, 1962; Oxford, 1964; Yale, 1965; Chicago, 1967; Columbia, 1971; Stirling, 1972; Univ. Nat. du Zaïre, 1973. *Publications:* La Vie familiale et sociale des Indiens Nambikwara, 1948; Les Structures élémentaires de la parenté, 1949 (The Elementary Structures of Kinship, 1969); Race et histoire, 1952; Tristes Tropiques, 1955, complete edn, 1973 (A World on the Wane, 1961); Anthropologie structurale, Vol. 1, 1958, Vol. 2, 1973 (Structural Anthropology, Vol. 1, 1964, Vol. 2, 1977); Le Totémisme aujourd'hui, 1962 (Totemism, 1963); La Pensée sauvage, 1962 (The Savage Mind, 1966); Le Cru et le cuit, 1964 (The Raw and the Cooked, 1970); Du Miel aux cendres, 1967 (From Honey to Ashes, 1973); L'Origine des manières de table, 1968; L'Homme nu, 1971; Anthropologie structurale deux, 1973; La Voie des masques, 1975; *relevant publications:* Conversations with Lévi-Strauss (ed G. Charbonnier), 1969; by Octavio Paz: On Lévi-Strauss, 1970; Claude Lévi-Strauss: an introduction, 1972. *Address:* 2 rue des Marronniers, 75016 Paris, France. *T:* 288-34-71.

LEVINE, Sydney; a Recorder, North-Eastern Circuit, since 1975; *b* 4 Sept. 1923; *s* of Rev. Isaac Levine and Mrs Miriam Levine; *m* 1959, Cécile Rona Rubinstein; three *s* one *d*. *Educ:* Bradford Grammar Sch.; Univ. of Leeds (LLB). Called to the Bar, Inner Temple, 1952; Chambers in Bradford, 1953-. *Recreations:* music, gardening. *Address:* 1 Grove Road, Shipley, W Yorks. *T:* Shipley 51581.

LEVINGE, Major Sir Richard Vere Henry, 11th Bt, *cr* 1704; MBE 1941; Chairman, The Salmon and Trout Association; Chairman, Committee of Management, Atlantic Salmon Research Trust; Director, GEI International Ltd; *b* 30 April 1911; *o s* of 10th Bt and Irene Marguerite (who *m* 2nd, 1916, Major R. V. Buxton), *d* of late J. H. C. Pix of Bradford; *S* father, 1914; *m* 1st, 1935, Barbara Mary, 2nd *d* of late George J. Kidston, CMG; two *s* three *d*; 2nd, 1976, Jane Millward. *Educ:* Eton; Balliol Coll., Oxford (Domus Exhibition). Retired, 1976, as Dep. Man. Dir, Arthur Guinness Son & Co. Ltd. Chm. Cttee of Management, Salmon Res. Trust of Ireland, until 1977. War Service, 1939-45: Lovat Scouts and Staff (despatches Burma 1945). *Recreations:* shooting, fishing. *Heir:* s Richard George Robin Levinge [*b* 18 Dec. 1946; *m* 1969, Hilary Jane, *d* of Dr Derek Mark, Co. Wicklow]. *Address:* Spindles, 27 The Grove, Radlett, Herts. *Clubs:* Flyfishers'; Kildare Street and University (Dublin).

LEVIS, Maj.-Gen. Derek George, CB 1972; OBE 1951; DL; Deputy Director of Medical Services, Southern Command, 1970-71; *b* 24 Dec. 1911; *er s* of late Dr George Levis, Lincoln; *m* 1938, Doris Constance Tall; one *d*. *Educ:* Stowe Sch.; Trinity Coll., Cambridge; St Thomas' Hospital, London. BA Cantab 1933; MRCS, LRCP 1936; MB, BChir (Cantab), 1937; DPH 1949. Commnd into RAMC, 1936; house appts, St Thomas' Hospital, 1936-37; served in: China, 1937-39; War of 1939-45 (1939-45 Star, Pacific Star, France and Germany Star, Defence and War Medal): Malaya and Java, 1939-42; Ceylon, 1942-43; NW Europe, 1944-45; qualified as specialist in Army Health, RAM Coll., 1949; Asst Director Army Health, HQ British Troops Egypt, 1949-51; Deputy Asst Dir Army Health, HQ British Commonwealth Forces, Korea, 1952-53 (Korean Co. Medal and UN Medal); Asst Dir Army Health: Malaya Comd, 1953-55 (Gen. Service Medal, Clasp Malaya, despatches); War Office, 1956-58; Deputy Director, Army Health, HQ, BAOR, 1958-62; Comdt Army School of Health, 1962-66; Director of Army Health, Australian Military Forces, Melbourne, 1966-68; Dep. Director Army Health, HQ Army Strategic Comd, 1968; Director of Army Health, MoD (Army), 1968-70. QHP 1969-71. Col Comdt, RAMC, 1973-76. Co. Comr, St John's Ambulance Brigade, Lincs, 1972-. Mem., Faculty of Community Physicians, RCP, 1971. DL Lincs, 1976. OStJ 1968. *Publications:* contribs to Journal RAMC and Proc. Royal Society Med. *Recreations:* fishing, gardening. *Address:* Dial House, Navenby, Lincoln. *T:* Lincoln 810571.

LÉVIS MIREPOIX, Antoine, Duc de; Grand d'Espagne; Commandeur de la Légion d'Honneur, Croix de Guerre, Grand Croix de l'Ordre d'Adolphe de Nassau; author; Member of the French Academy since 1953; Mainteneur de l'Académie des Jeux floraux de Toulouse; Commandeur, Ordre des Palmes Académiques; *b* 1 Aug. 1884; *s* of Henri and Henriette de Chabannes La Palice; *m* 1911, Nicole de Chaponay; one *s*. *Educ:* Lycée de Toulouse; Sorbonne (Licencié en philosophie). Lecturer for the Alliance française; Mission Maria Chapdeleine, Canada; President, Cincinnati de France; President, Institut France-Canada. *Publications:* Le Seigneur Inconnu, 1922; Montségur, 1924; François 1er, 1931; Vieilles races et Temps nouveaux, 1934; Les Campagnes ardentes, 1934; Le Coeur secret de Saint-Simon, 1935; Le Siècle de Philippe le Bel, 1936; La Politesse (with M. de Vogüé), 1937; Sainte-Jeanne de France, fille de Louis XI, 1943; Les Trois Femmes de Philipe-Auguste, 1947; Les Guerres de religion, 1947; La France de la Renaissance (Grand Prix Gobert de l'Académie française), 1948; La Tragédie des Templiers, 1955; Aventure d'une famille française, 1955; Que signifie 'le Parti de Ducs', 1964; Le roi n'est mort qu'une fois, 1965; Le livre d'or des Maréchaux de France, 1970; L'Attentat d'Agnani, 1970; St Louis: Roi de France, 1970; Henri IV, 1971; Grandeur et misère de l'individualisme française, 1973; La France féodale (6 vols). *Heir:* s Charles Henri, Marquis de Lévis Mirepoix [*b* 4 Jan. 1912; *m* 1962, Mme Françoise Foucault; one *s* one *d*]. *Address:* 27 rue Daru, 75008 Paris, France; Léran, 09600 Laroque-d'Olmes, *Clubs:* Jockey (Vice-President), Union, Interallié (Paris).

LEVITT, Walter Montague, MD, FRCP, FRCR; Barrister-at-Law; Hon. Consulting Radiotherapist, St Bartholomew's Hospital, since 1945; *b* 1900; *e s* of Lewis and Caroline Levitt, Rathmines, Co. Dublin; *m* 1929, Sonia Esté Nivinsky (*d* 1977), BSc, MRCS, DPH; no *c*. *Educ:* High Sch., Dublin; University

Coll., Dublin (Med. Schol. and 1st cl. Exhbnr); Cambridge (DMRE); Frankfurt. Called to the Bar, Lincoln's Inn, 1946. Demonstrator of anatomy, 1920-21, of pathology, 1921; formerly: Lectr in X-Ray Therapy, Cambridge Univ.; Dir, Dept of Radiotherapy, London Clinic; Hon. Physician i/c, Dept of Radiotherapy, St George's Hosp.; MO i/c Radiotherapeutic Dept, St Bartholomew's Hosp. Member: Minister of Labour's Adv. Panel in Radiology; Clinical Res. Cttee, British Empire Cancer Campaign; Dep. Comr, 1967-69, Dep. Chm., 1969-73, Metropolitan Traffic Comrs. Hon. Assoc. Editor, British Jl of Radiology. Hon. Secretary: Section of Radiology, Internat. Cancer Conf., London, 1928; Radiology Section, BMA Centenary Meeting, London, 1932; Deleg. to Internat. Cancer Congress, Atlantic City, 1939. Foundn Fellow, Vice-Pres., Chm., Therapeutic Cttee, Faculty of Radiologists, 1940-43; Fellow, Vice-Pres., and Pres., Section of Radiology, RSM, 1945-46; formerly Hon. Med. Sec., BIR. Freeman, City of London; Liveryman, Apothecaries' Co., 1956. Gold Medallist, Mercers Hosp., 1922. *Publications:* Deep X-Ray Therapy in Malignant Disease (with Introduction by Lord Horder), 1930; completed and edited Knox's Text Book of X-Ray Therapeutics, 1932; Handbook of Radiotherapy for Senior and Post-graduate students, 1952; Short Encyclopædia of Medicine for Lawyers, 1966; Section on Diseases of the Blood in Paterson's Treatment of Malignant Disease by X-Rays and Radium, 1948; Section on X-Ray therapy in Bourne and Williams' Recent Advances in Gynæcology, 1952; Chapter on Reticulosis and Reticulosarcoma (with R. Bodley Scott) in British Practice in Radiotherapy, 1955; various articles on medico-legal subjects. *Address:* 19 Sussex Square, W2. *T:* 01-262 3003; Gray's Inn Chambers, Gray's Inn, WC1. *T:* 01-242 5226. *Club:* United Oxford & Cambridge University.

LEVY, Sir (Enoch) Bruce, Kt 1953; OBE 1950; retired, 1951; *b* 19 Feb. 1892; *s* of William and Esther Ann Levy; *m* 1925, Phyllis R., *d* of G. H. Mason; no *c. Educ:* Primary Sch.; Banks Commercial Coll.; Victoria University College (BSc). Brought up on farm to age 18; appointed Dept Agriculture, 1911; agrostologist to 1937; charge seed-testing station. Ecological studies Grasslands and indigenous vegetative cover of NZ; transferred to DSIR, 1937, and appointed Director Grasslands Division; Director Green-keeping Research; Chairman NZ Institute for Turf Culture (Life Mem. 1957); Official Rep. International Grassland Conference, Great Britain, 1937, Netherlands, 1949; Lecture tour, Great Britain, 1949-50; Member: Rotary International; Grassland Assoc. (Life Mem. 1951); NZ Animal Production Society (Life Mem. 1961); Manawatu Catchment Board; Central Standing Cttee, Soil Conservation; Trustee, Grassland Memorial Trust (Chm. 1966-68). Life Member NZ Royal Agric. Society, 1956. Hon. Dr of Science, University of NZ; R. B. Bennett Empire Prize, 1951 (Royal Society of Arts, London). *Publications:* Grasslands of New Zealand, 1943 (revised and enlarged, 1951, 1955 and 1970); Construction, Renovation and Care of the Bowling Green, 1949; Construction, Renovation and Care of the Golf Course, 1950. 150 scientific papers in popular and scientific journals in NZ and overseas. *Recreations:* bowling, gardening. *Address:* 217 Fitzherbert Avenue, Palmerston North, New Zealand. *T:* 80-803 Palmerston North.

LEVY, Sir Ewart Maurice, 2nd Bt *cr* 1913; *b* 10 May 1897; *o s* of Sir Maurice Levy, 1st Bt; *S* father, 1933; *m* 1932, Hylda (*d* 1970), *e d* of late Sir Albert Levy; one *d. Educ:* Harrow. High Sheriff of Leicestershire, 1937; served, 1940-45, Royal Pioneer Corps, Lieut-Colonel, 1944; BLA, 1944-45 (despatches). JP Co. Leicester. *Heir:* none. *Address:* Welland House, Weston-by-Welland, Market Harborough, Leicestershire. *Club:* Reform.

LEVY, George Joseph; Chairman, H. Blairman & Sons Ltd, since 1965; *b* 21 May 1927; *s* of Percy and Maude Levy; *m* 1952, Wendy Yetta Blairman; one *s* three *d . Educ:* Oundle Sch. Joined H. Blairman & Sons Ltd (Antique Dealers), 1950, Dir, 1955. Pres., British Antique Dealers Assoc., 1974-76. Chm., Grosvenor House Antiques Fair, 1978-. Dep. Chm., Friends of Kenwood, 1977-. *Recreations:* tennis, photography. *Address:* 27 Oakhill Avenue, NW3 7RD. *T:* 01-435 9528.

LEWANDO, Sir Jan (Alfred), Kt 1974; CBE 1968; Chairman, Carrington Viyella Ltd, 1970-75; *b* 31 May 1909; *s* of Maurice Lewando and Eugenie Lewando (*née* Goldsmid); *m* 1948, Nora Slavouski; three *d. Educ:* Manchester Grammar Sch.; Manchester University. Served War of 1939-45, British Army: British Army Staff, Washington DC and British Min. of Supply Mission, 1941-45 (Lt-Col, 1943). Marks & Spencer Ltd, 1929-70 (Dir 1954); Chm., Consolidated Textile Mills Ltd, Canada, 1972-75; Pres., Carrington Viyella Inc. (USA), 1971-75; Director: Carrington Tesit (Italy), 1971-75; Heal and Son Holdings, 1975- (Dep. Chm., 1977-); Bunzl Pulp & Paper Ltd,

1976-; W. A. Baxter & Sons Ltd, 1975-; Johnston Industries Inc. (USA), 1976-; Edgars Stores Ltd (South Africa), 1976-; Chm., Gelvenor Textiles Ltd, S Africa, 1973-75. Pres., British Textile Confedn, 1972-73; Member: British Overseas Trade Bd, 1972-77 (Mem., European Trade Cttee, 1973-); BNEC, 1969-71; Export Council for Europe, 1965-69; European Steering Cttee, CBI, 1968-71; Grand Council, CBI, 1971-75. FBIM 1972; FRSA 1973. Companion, Textile Inst., 1972. Legion of Merit (US), 1946. *Address:* Davidge House, Knotty Green, Beaconsfield, Bucks. *T:* Beaconsfield 4987.

LEWEN, John Henry, CMG 1977; Ambassador to the People's Republic of Mozambique, since 1975; *b* 6 July 1920; *s* of Carl Henry Lewen and Alice (*née* Mundy); *m* 1945, Emilienne Alette Julie Alida Galant; three *s. Educ:* Christ's Hospital; King's Coll., Cambridge. Royal Signals, 1940-45. HM Foreign (subseq. Diplomatic) Service, 1946; HM Embassy: Lisbon, 1947-50; Rangoon, 1950-53; FO, 1953-55; HM Embassy: Rio de Janeiro, 1955-59; Warsaw, 1959-61; FO, 1961-63; Head of Chancery, HM Embassy, Rabat, 1963-67; Consul-General, Jerusalem, 1967-70; Inspector of HM Diplomatic Estabts, 1970-73; Dir, Admin and Budget, Secretariat-Gen. of Council of Ministers of European Communities, 1973-75. OStJ 1969. *Recreations:* singing, sailing. *Address:* c/o Foreign and Commonwealth Office, SW1. *Club:* Travellers'.

LEWES, Suffragan Bishop of, since 1977; **Rt. Rev. Peter John Ball**, CGA; *b* 14 Feb. 1932; *s* of Thomas James and Kathleen Obena Bradley Ball. *Educ:* Lancing; Queens' Coll., Cambridge; Wells Theological College. MA (Nat. Sci.). Ordained, 1956; Curate of Rottingdean, 1956-58; Co-founder and Brother of Monastic Community of the Glorious Ascension, 1960 (Prior, 1960-77). Fellow of Woodard Corporation, 1962-71; Member: Archbishops' Council of Evangelism, 1965-68; Midlands Religious Broadcasting Council of the BBC, 1967-69. *Recreations:* squash (Cambridge Blue, 1953) and music. *Address:* c/o Church House, 9 Brunswick Square, Brighton, E Sussex.

LEWES, Archdeaconry; *see* Lewes and Hastings.

LEWES, John Hext, OBE 1944; Lieutenant of Dyfed, since 1974 (Lord Lieutenant of Cardiganshire, 1956-74); *b* 16 June 1903; *s* of late Colonel John Lewes, RA, and of Mrs Lewes (*née* Hext); *m* 1929, Nesta Cecil, *d* of late Captain H. Fitzroy Talbot, DSO, RN; one *s* two *d. Educ:* RN Colleges Osborne and Dartmouth. Sub-Lieut, 1923, Lieut, 1925; specialised in Torpedoes, 1928; Commander, 1939; commanded: HMS Shikari, Intrepid, 1941-42 (despatches); Ameer, 1944-45 (despatches); retired 1947, with war service rank of Captain, RN. Now farming. FRAgSs 1972. KStJ 1964. *Address:* Llanllyr, near Lampeter, Dyfed. *T:* Aeron 323.

LEWES AND HASTINGS, Archdeacon of; *see* Godden, Ven. M. L.

LEWIN, Captain (Edgar) Duncan (Goodenough), CB 1958; CBE 1953; DSO 1941; DSC 1939; Royal Navy, retired; Chairman, Hawker Siddeley Dynamics, since 1977; *b* 9 Aug. 1912; *s* of Captain G. E. Lewin, RN; *m* 1943, Nancy Emily Hallett, Tintinhull, Somerset; one *s* one *d. Educ:* RN Coll., Dartmouth. Cadet, HMS Royal Oak, 1930; specialized in flying, 1935. Served in HMS Ajax, River Plate action, 1939; Comd 808 Squadron in HMS Ark Royal, 1941; served staff of Admiral Vian in Mediterranean and Pacific, 1944-45. Comd HMS Glory, in Korean waters, 1952-53; Director of Air Warfare, Admiralty, 1953-54; Comd HMS Eagle, 1955; Director of Plans, Admiralty, 1956-57; retired from Navy and joined Board of Blackburn's, 1957; Sales Director, Hawker Siddeley Aviation Ltd, 1968-71; Man. Dir, Hawker Siddeley Dynamics, 1971-77. *Recreations:* croquet, gardening. *Address:* Hatching Green Lodge, Harpenden, Herts. *T:* Harpenden 62034.

LEWIN, George Ronald; military historian; *b* 11 Oct. 1914; *s* of late Frank Lewin, Halifax; *m* 1938, Sylvia Lloyd Sturge; two *s* one *d*, (and one *s* decd). *Educ:* Heath Sch., Halifax; The Queen's Coll., Oxford (Hastings Scholar, 1st Class Hon. Mods, 1st Class Lit. Hum., Goldsmiths' Exhibitioner). Editorial Assistant, Jonathan Cape Ltd, Publishers, 1937. Served in Royal Artillery, N Africa and NW Europe (wounded, despatches), 1939-45. Producer, BBC Home Talks Dept, 1946; Chief Asst, Home Service, 1954; Head, 1957; Chief, 1963. Retired 1965. Editor, Hutchinson Publishing Gp, 1966-69. Leverhulme Res. Fellow, 1973. *Publications:* Rommel as Military Commander, 1968; (ed) Freedom's Battle, vol. 3, The War on Land 1939-45, 1969; Montgomery as Military Commander, 1971; Churchill as War Lord, 1973; Man of Armour: Lieut-General Vyvyan Pope and the development of armoured warfare, 1976; Slim the Standard-

Bearer, the biography of Field Marshal the Viscount Slim, 1976; The Life and Death of the Afrika Korps, 1977; numerous articles and reviews on military history. *Address:* Camilla House, Forest Road, East Horsley, Surrey. *T:* East Horsley 3779. *Club:* Army and Navy.

LEWIN, Adm. Sir Terence (Thornton), GCB 1976 (KCB 1973); MVO 1958; DSC 1942; Chief of Naval Staff and First Sea Lord, since 1977; First and Principal Naval ADC to The Queen, since 1977; *b* Dover, 19 Nov. 1920; *m* 1944, Jane Branch-Evans; two *s* one *d. Educ:* The Judd Sch., Tonbridge. Joined RN, 1939; War Service in Home and Mediterranean Fleets in HMS Valiant, HMS Ashanti in Malta Convoys, N Russian Convoys, invasion N Africa and Channel (despatches); comd HMS Corunna, 1955-56; Comdr HM Yacht Britannia, 1957-58; Captain (F) Dartmouth Training Squadron and HM Ships Urchin and Tenby, 1961-63; Director, Naval Tactical and Weapons Policy Division, MoD, 1964-65; comd HMS Hermes, 1966-67; Asst Chief of Naval Staff (Policy), 1968-69; Flag Officer, Second-in-Comd, Far East Fleet, 1969-70; Vice-Chief of the Naval Staff, 1971-73; C-in-C Fleet, 1973-75; C-in-C Naval Home Command, 1975-77. Flag ADC to the Queen, 1975-77. Rear-Adm., 1968; Vice-Adm., 1970; Adm., 1973. FBIM 1973. Elder Brother of Trinity House, 1975; Hon. Freeman of Skinners' Co., 1976. *Recreations:* golf; formerly athletics and Rugby football (rep. RN at both, 1947-48). *Address:* Mall House Flat, Admiralty Arch, SW1.

LEWIN, Walpole Sinclair; Consultant Neurological Surgeon to Addenbrooke's Hospital, Cambridge, since 1955; Associate Lecturer in Medicine, University of Cambridge, since 1976; *b* 20 Aug. 1915; *s* of Eric Sinclair Lewin, London; *m* 1947, Marion Cumming; one *s* one *d. Educ:* University College, and University College Hospital, London. MRCS, LRCP 1939; MB, BS 1939; MS (London) 1942; FRCS 1940; MA (Cantab) 1970. University College First Entrance Exhibn, 1934; Magrath Clin. Schol., and Atkinson Morley Surgical Schol., 1939; Leverhulme Research Grant, RCS, 1947. Sometime House Physician, House Surgeon, Cas., Surgical Officer, Harker Smith Surgical Registrar, UCH; First Asst, Nuffield Dept of Surgery, Oxford; Clinical Lectr in Neurosurgery, Univ. of Oxford; Asst Neurological Surgeon, Radcliffe Infirmary, Oxford, 1949-61; Consultant Neurological Surgeon to Army. Hunterian Professor, RCS, 1948; Erasmus Wilson Demonstrator, RCS, 1965; Mem. Council, RCS, 1970- (Vice Pres., 1976-77). Mem. Scientific Adv. Council, Huntingdon Res. Centre, 1974-. Ruscoe Clarke Lectr, Birmingham, 1967; Victor Horsley Meml Lectr, 1975. Fellow: Assoc. of Surgeons; Royal Soc. Med.; Soc. of British Neurological Surgeons; Cambridge Phil. Soc.; Member: BMA; Internat. Soc. of Surgeons. Chm., Central Cttee, Hosp. Med. Services, 1968-71; Vice-Chm., Jt Consultants Cttee, 1967-71; Member: Central Health Services Council, 1966-76; General Med. Council, 1971; Council, BMA, 1968- (Chm., 1971-76); deleg., Gen. Assembly World Med. Assoc., 1971-, Council Mem., 1974- (Chm., 1977-); Council, World Fedn of Medical Educn; Delegate, Standing Cttee Doctors of EEC, 1971- (Pres., 1974-77); Vice President: Commonwealth Med. Assoc., 1972-; Internat. Soc. Psychiatric Surgery; Corres. Member: Amer. Assoc. of Neurological Surgeons; Amer. Acad. of Neurological Surgery; Deutsche Gesellschaft für Neurochirurgie; Hon. Mem., Brazil Med. Assoc. Served Army, 1942-47; Lieut-Colonel, RAMC; OC Surgical Div., MEF. Fellow: University Coll. London; Darwin Coll., Cambridge. Hon. DSc Hull, 1974. *Publications:* The Management of Head Injuries, 1966. Section, British Surgical Progress, 1958. Papers to Medical Journals on Neurosurgical subjects. *Recreations:* tennis, gardening. *Address:* Martins Lodge, 4 Babraham Road, Cambridge. *T:* Cambridge 48843; (Addenbrooke's Hospital), Cambridge 45151. *Club:* Athenæum.

LEWIS, family name of **Baron Essendon** and **Barony of Merthyr.**

LEWIS, Maj.-Gen. Alfred George, CBE 1969; Managing Director, Alvis Ltd, since 1973; Chairman, Self Changing Gears Ltd, since 1976; *b* 23 July 1920; *s* of Louis Lewis; *m* 1946, Daye Neville, *d* of Neville Greaves Hunt; two *s* two *d. Educ:* St Dunstan's Coll.; King's Coll., London. Served War of 1939-45, India and Burma. Commanded 15th/19th Hussars, 1961-63; Dir, Defence Operational Requirements Staff, MoD, 1967-68; Dep. Comdt, Royal Mil. Coll. of Science, 1968-70; Dir Gen., Fighting Vehicles and Engineer Equipment, 1970-72, retired 1973. Hon. Col, Queen's Own Mercian Yeomanry, 1977-. FIWM 1975. *Recreations:* shooting, golf, sailing. *Address:* c/o National Westminster Bank Ltd, Sydenham, SE26. *Club:* Cavalry and Guards.

LEWIS, Sir Allen (Montgomery), Kt 1968; Governor of St Lucia, since 1974; *b* 26 Oct. 1909; *s* of George Ferdinand Montgomery Lewis and Ida Louisa (*née* Barton); *m* 1936, Edna Leofrida Theobalds; three *s* two *d. Educ:* St Mary's Coll., St Lucia. LLB Hons (external) London, 1941. Admitted to practice at Bar of Royal Court, St Lucia (later Supreme Court of Windward and Leeward Islands), 1931; called to English Bar, Middle Temple, 1946; in private practice, Windward Islands, 1931-59; Acting Magistrate, St Lucia, 1940-41; Acting Puisne Judge, Windward and Leeward Islands, 1955-56; QC 1956; Judge: of Federal Supreme Court, 1959-62; of British Caribbean Court of Appeal, 1962; of Court of Appeal, Jamaica, 1962-67; Acting President, Court of Appeal, Jamaica, 1966; Acting Chief Justice of Jamaica, 1966; Chief Justice, West Indies Associated States Supreme Court, 1967-72; Chm., Nat. Devclt Corp., St Lucia, 1972-74. MLC, St Lucia, 1943-51; Member, Castries Town Council, 1942-56 (Chairman six times); President W Indies Senate, 1958-59. Served on numerous Government and other public cttees; Comr for reform and revision of laws of St Lucia, 1954-58; rep. St Lucia, Windward Islands, and W Indies at various Conferences. Director, St Lucia Branch, British Red Cross Society, 1955-59; President: Grenada Boy Scouts' Assoc., 1967; St John Council for St Lucia. Served as President and/or Cttee Member, cricket, football and athletic associations, St Lucia, 1936-59. Chancellor, Univ. of WI, 1975-; Hon. LLD Univ. of WI, 1974. Chief Scout, St Lucia, 1976-. Coronation Medal, 1953; Silver Jubilee Medal, 1977. KStJ. *Publication:* Revised Edition of Laws of St Lucia, 1957. *Recreations:* gardening, swimming. *Address:* Government House, Castries, St Lucia. *Clubs:* Royal Commonwealth Society, West Indian; St Lucia Golf.

LEWIS, Adm. Sir Andrew Mackenzie, KCB 1971 (CB 1967); DL; Commander-in-Chief, Naval Home Command, and Flag Officer Portsmouth Area, 1972-74; Flag ADC to The Queen, 1972-74; *b* 24 Jan. 1918; *s* of late Rev. Cyril Lewis; *m* 1943, Rachel Elizabeth Leatham; two *s. Educ:* Haileybury. Director of Plans, Admiralty, 1961-63; in command of HMS Kent, 1964-65; Director-General, Weapons (Naval), 1965-68; Flag Officer, Flotillas, Western Fleet, 1968-69; Second Sea Lord and Chief of Naval Personnel, 1970-71. DL Essex 1975. *Address:* Coleman's Farm, Finchingfield, Braintree, Essex. *Club:* Brooks's.

LEWIS, Anthony; see Lewis, J. A.

LEWIS, Sir Anthony Carey, Kt 1972; CBE 1967; Principal of the Royal Academy of Music, since 1968; *b* 1915; *s* of late Colonel Leonard Carey Lewis, OBE, and Katherine Barbara Lewis; *m* 1959, Lesley, *d* of Mr and Mrs Frank Lisle Smith. *Educ:* Wellington; Peterhouse, Cambridge (Organ Schol.). MA, MusB Cantab. Joined music staff of BBC, 1935; director Foundations of Music and similar programmes; responsible many revivals 16th-18th century music; War of 1939-45, served MEF; planned and supervised music in BBC Third Programme, 1946; Peyton-Barber Prof. of Music, Univ. of Birmingham, 1947-68, and Dean of the Faculty of Arts, 1961-64. Pres. RMA, 1963-69; Chairman: Music Adv. Panel, Arts Council of GB, 1954-65; Music Adv. Cttee, British Council, 1967-73; Founder and Gen. Editor, Musica Britannica; Chairman: Purcell Soc.; Purcell-Handel Festival, 1959; Dir, English Nat. Opera, 1974-; Governor, Wellington Coll. Hon. RAM; FRCM; Hon. FRNCM; Hon. FTCL; Hon. GSM. Hon. MusD Birmingham. *Compositions include:* Psalm 86 (Cambridge, 1935); A Choral Overture (Queen's Hall, 1937); City Dances for Orchestra (Jerusalem, 1944); Trumpet Concerto (Albert Hall, 1947); Three Invocations (Birmingham, 1949); A Tribute of Praise (Birmingham, 1951); Horn Concerto (London, 1956); Canzona for Orchestra, Homage to Purcell (Birmingham, 1959). Conductor many recordings, especially Purcell and Handel. *Publications:* research: A Restoration Suite (Purcell and others), 1937; Venus and Adonis (Blow), 1939; Matthew Locke, 1948; Libera me (Arne), 1950; Coronation Anthems (Blow), 1953; Apollo and Daphne (Handel), 1956; Odes and Cantatas (Purcell), 1957; Anthems (3 vols), (Purcell), 1959-62; Fairy Queen (Purcell), 1966; Athalia (Handel), 1967. Editor, English Songs Series; numerous contributions on musical subjects to various periodicals. *Address:* Royal Academy of Music, Marylebone Road, NW1 5HT.

LEWIS, Sir Arthur; see Lewis, Sir W. A.

LEWIS, Arthur William John; MP (Lab) Newham North West, since 1974 (West Ham, Upton, 1945-50; West Ham North, 1950-74); Ex-Trade Union Official (National Union of General and Municipal Workers); *b* 21 Feb. 1917; *s* of late J. Lewis; *m* 1940, Lucy Ethel Clack; one *d. Educ:* Elementary Sch.; Borough Polytechnic. Shop steward of his Dept of City of London Corporation at 17; Vice-Chairman of TU branch (City of London NUGMW) at 18; full-time London district official NUGMW 1938-48; Member of London Trades Council and Holborn City Trades Council, various joint industrial councils,

Government cttees, etc; Member: ASTMS; APEX. Member: Estimates Cttee; Expenditure Cttee. Formerly Member Exec. Cttee, London Labour Party; Chairman Eastern Regional Group of Labour MPs, 1950-; Member Eastern Regional Council of Labour Party and Exec. Cttee of that body, 1950-. Served in the Army. *Recreations:* swimming, motoring, boxing, general athletics. *Address:* 1 Doveridge Gardens, Palmers Green, N13.

LEWIS, Bernard, BA, PhD; FBA 1963; FRHistS; Cleveland E. Dodge Professor of Near Eastern Studies, Princeton University, and Long-term Member of School of Social Science, Institute for Advanced Study, since 1974; *b* London, 31 May 1916; *s* of H. Lewis, London; *m* 1947, Ruth Hélène (marr. diss. 1974), *d* of late Overretsagfører M. Oppenhejm, Copenhagen; one *s* one *d.* *Educ:* Wilson Coll.; The Polytechnic; Universities of London and Paris (Fellow UCL 1976). Derby Student, 1936. Asst Lecturer in Islamic History, Sch. of Oriental Studies, University of London, 1938; Prof. of History of Near and Middle East, SOAS, London Univ., 1949-74. Served RAC and Intelligence Corps, 1940-41; attached to Foreign Office, 1941-45. Visiting Prof. of History, University of Calif, Los Angeles, 1955-56, Columbia Univ., 1960 and Indiana Univ., 1963; Class of 1932 Lectr, Princeton Univ., 1964; Vis. Mem., Inst. for Advanced Study, Princeton, New Jersey, 1969; Gottesman Lectr, Yeshiva Univ., 1974. Membre Associé, Institut d'Egypte, Cairo, 1969; Hon. Fellow, Turkish Historical Soc., Ankara, 1972; Hon. Dr, Hebrew Univ., Jerusalem, 1974; For. Mem., Amer. Philosophical Soc., 1973. Certificate of Merit for services to Turkish Culture, Turkish Govt, 1973. *Publications:* The Origins of Ismā'īlism, 1940; Turkey Today, 1940; British contributions to Arabic Studies, 1941; Handbook of Diplomatic and Political Arabic, 1947, 1956; (ed) Land of Enchanters, 1948; The Arabs in History, 1950 (5th rev. edn, 1970); Notes and Documents from the Turkish Archives, 1952; The Emergence of Modern Turkey, 1961 (rev. edn, 1968); The Kingly Crown (translated from Ibn Gabirol), 1961; co-ed. with P. M. Holt, Historians of the Middle East, 1962; Istanbul and the Civilization of the Ottoman Empire, 1963; The Middle East and the West, 1964; The Assassins, 1967; Race and Colour in Islam, 1971; Islam in History, 1973; Islam to 1453, 1974; co-ed., Encyclopædia of Islam, 1956-; (ed, with others) The Cambridge History of Islam, vols 1-11, 1971; Islam from the Prophet Muhammad to the Capture of Constantinople, 2 vols, 1974; History, Remembered, Recovered, Invented, 1975; (ed) The World of Islam: Faith, People, Culture, 1976; articles in learned journals. *Address:* Near Eastern Studies Department, Jones Hall, Princeton University, Princeton, NJ 08540, USA. *Club:* Athenæum.

LEWIS, Bernard; His Honour Judge Bernard Lewis; a Circuit Judge (formerly a County Court Judge), since 1966; *b* 1906; 3rd *s* of late Solomon and Jeannette Lewis, London; *m* 1934, Harriette, *d* of late I. A. Waine, Dublin, London and Nice; one *s.* *Educ:* Trinity Hall, Cambridge (MA). Called to the Bar, Lincoln's Inn, 1929. Mem. S-E Circuit. Hon. Mem., Central Criminal Court Bar Mess. *Recreations:* revolver shooting, bricklaying. *Address:* Trevelyan House, Arlington Road, St Margaret's, Middx. *Clubs:* Reform; Ham and Petersham Rifle and Pistol.

LEWIS, Cecil Arthur, MC; Author; *b* Birkenhead, 29 March 1898; *m* 1921 (marr. diss. 1940); one *s* one *d* ; *m* 1942 (marr. diss. 1950); no *c* ; *m* 1960. *Educ:* Dulwich Coll.; University Coll. Sch.; Oundle. Royal Flying Corps, 1915 (MC, despatches twice); Manager Civil Aviation, Vickers, Ltd, 1919; Flying Instructor to Chinese Government, Peking, 1920, 1921; one of four founders of BBC, Chm. of Programme Board, 1922-26; Varied Literary Activities: stage, screen (first two adaptations of Bernard Shaw's plays to screen, 1930-32), and television plays (Nativity, Crucifixion and Patience of Job, 1956-59) and production connected therewith. RAF, 1939-45. Sheep farming, South Africa, 1947-50. United Nations Secretariat, New York, radio and television, 1953-55. Commercial television, London, 1955-56. Daily Mail, 1956-66; retd. *Publications:* Broadcasting From Within, 1924; The Unknown Warrior, trans. from French of Paul Raynal, 1928; Sagittarius Rising, 1937; The Trumpet is Mine, 1938; Challenge to the Night, 1938; Self Portrait: Letters and Journals of the late Charles Ricketts, RA (Editor), 1939; Pathfinders, 1943; Yesterday's Evening, 1946; Farewell to Wings, 1964; Turn Right for Corfu, 1972; Never Look Back (autobiog.), 1974; A Way to Be, 1977. *Address:* c/o National Westminster Bank, 97 Strand, WC2.

LEWIS, Brig. Sir Clinton (Gresham), Kt 1941; OBE 1928; *b* 25 Nov. 1885; *s* of J. Hardwicke Lewis, late of Veytaux, Switzerland; *m* 1916, Lilian Eyre (*d* 1962), *d* of late Rev. Walter Wace; one *s* one *d* (and one *s* decd). *Educ:* privately, Montreux, Switzerland. Royal Military Acad., Woolwich, 1903-04 (Sword

of Honour); Commission RE 1904; joined Survey of India, 1907; in charge Miri Mission Survey, NE Frontier, 1911-12; served European War, 1914-18 (despatches, Bt Major); Afghan War, 1919; Indo-Afghan Boundary Commission, 1919; with Turco-Iraq frontier delimitation commission, 1927; Surveyor-Gen. of India, 1937-41; employed with Ord. Survey, 1942-45. Hon. Sec. RGS, 1944-46, Vice-Pres. 1946-50. Founders' Gold Medal RGS 1937. *Publication:* (co-editor) first edition The Oxford Atlas, 1951. *Address:* 10 Gainsborough Gardens, Hampstead, NW3. *T:* 01-435 4478.

See also Lt-Col W. G. Hingston, Maj.-Gen. J. M. H. Lewis.

LEWIS, Prof. Dan, PhD; DSc; FRS 1955; Quain Professor of Botany, London University, since 1957; *b* 30 Dec. 1910; *s* of Ernest Albert and Edith J. Lewis; *m* 1933, Mary Phœbe Eleanor Burry; one *d. Educ:* High Sch., Newcastle-under-Lyme, Staffs; Reading University (BSc); PhD, DSc (London). Research Scholar, Reading Univ., 1935-36; Scientific Officer, Pomology Dept, John Innes Hort. Inst., 1935-48; Head of Genetics Dept, John Innes Horticultural Institution, Bayfordbury, Hertford, Herts, 1948-57. Rockefeller Foundation Special Fellowship, California Inst. of Technology, 1955-56; Visiting Prof. of Genetics, University of Calif, Berkeley, 1961-62; Royal Society Leverhulme Visiting Professor: University of Delhi, 1965-66; Singapore, 1970. Pres., Genetical Soc., 1968-71; Mem., UGC, 1969-74. *Publications:* Editor, Science Progress; scientific papers on Genetics and Plant Physiology. *Address:* 56/57 Myddleton Square, EC1R 1YA. *T:* 01-278 6948.

LEWIS, David Courtenay M.; *see* Mansel Lewis.

LEWIS, David Henry L.; *see* LeRoy-Lewis.

LEWIS, David John, JP; Practising Architect; Lord Mayor of Liverpool, 1962-63; *b* 29 April 1900; Welsh; *m* 1919, Margaret Elizabeth Stubbs; no *c. Educ:* Aberystwyth Univ.; Faculty of Architecture, Liverpool Univ. Liverpool City Council, 1936-74; Alderman, 1952-74; Hon. Alderman, 1974. Chm. Educn Cttee, 1961-62; Past Chm. Royal Liverpool Philharmonic Soc.; Chm. Liverpool Welsh Choral Union; Pres. Liverpool Male Voice Soc.; Chm. Merseyside Youth Orchestra; Acting Chm. British Council, Liverpool. JP Liverpool. *Recreations:* music, county cricket, football (Rugby), reading biography. *Address:* 4 Ivyhurst Close, Aigburth, Liverpool 19. *T:* 051-427 2911. *Clubs:* Lyceum, Masonic, Press (Liverpool).

LEWIS, David Malcolm, MA, PhD; FBA 1973; Tutor in Ancient History, Christ Church, Oxford, since 1955 (Student, 1956); University Lecturer in Greek Epigraphy, Oxford, since 1956; *b* London, 7 June 1928; *s* of William and Milly Lewis; *m* 1958, Barbara, *d* of Prof. Samson Wright, MD, FRCP; four *d. Educ:* City of London Sch.; Corpus Christi Coll., Oxford (MA); Princeton Univ. (PhD). National Service with RAEC, 1949-51. Mem., Inst. for Advanced Study, Princeton, 1951-52, 1964-65. Student, British Sch. at Athens, 1952-54; Junior Research Fellow, Corpus Christi Coll., Oxford, 1954-55. *Publications:* (with John Gould) Pickard-Cambridge: Dramatic Festivals of Athens (2nd edn), 1968; (with Russell Meiggs) Greek Historical Inscriptions, 1969; articles in learned jls. *Recreations:* opera, gardening. *Address:* Christ Church, Oxford. *T:* Oxford 42820.

LEWIS, David Thomas, CB 1963; Hon. Professorial Fellow, Department of Chemistry, University College of Wales, Aberystwyth, since 1970; *b* 27 March 1909; *s* of Emmanuel Lewis and Mary (*née* Thomas), Breconshire, Wales; *m* 1st, 1934, Evelyn (*née* Smetham); one *d* ; 2nd, 1959, Mary (*née* Sadler). *Educ:* Brynmawr County Sch.; University Coll. of Wales, Aberystwyth. BSc (Wales), 1st Class Hons in Chemistry, 1930; PhD (Wales), 1933; DSc (Wales), 1958. Senior Chemistry Master, Quakers' Yard Secondary Sch., 1934-38; Asst Lecturer, University Coll., Cardiff, 1938-40. Various scientific posts finishing as Principal Scientific Officer, Ministry of Supply, Armaments Research Establishment, 1941-47, and as Senior Superintendent of Chemistry Div., Atomic Weapons Research Establishment. Aldermaston, 1947-60; Govt Chemist, 1960-70. FRIC 1940; FRSH 1964. Dawes Memorial Lectr, 1965. Scientific Governor, British Nutrition Foundn, 1967; Member: British National Cttee for Chemistry (Royal Society), 1961-70; British Pharmacopœia Commission, 1963-73. *Publications:* Ultimate Particles of Matter, 1959; Mountain Harvest (Poems), 1964. Analytical Research Investigations in learned Jls; Scientific Articles in Encyclopædias, Scientific Reviews, etc. *Recreations:* writing, fishing, shooting. *Address:* Green Trees, 24 Highdown Hill Road, Emmer Green, Reading, Berks. *T:* Reading 471653.

LEWIS, Sir Edward (Roberts), Kt 1961; Member of London Stock Exchange since 1925; Chairman: Decca Ltd; The Decca

Record Co. Ltd; The Decca Navigator Co. Ltd; Decca Radar Ltd; Decca Survey Ltd; *b* 19 April 1900; *s* of late Sir Alfred Lewis, KBE; *m* 1st, 1923, Mary Margaret Hutton (*d* 1968), *d* of late Rev. George Dickson Hutton; one *s* (and one *s* decd); 2nd, 1973, Jeanie Margaret Smith. *Educ:* Rugby Sch.; Trinity Coll., Cambridge. Gold Albert Medal (RSA) 1967. *Address:* 69A Cadogan Place, SW1; Bridge House Farm, Felsted, Essex. *Club:* United Oxford & Cambridge University.

LEWIS, Eiluned; Writer; 2nd *d* of late Hugh Lewis, MA Cantab, JP, and Eveline Lewis, MA, JP, Glan Hafren, Newtown, Montgomeryshire; *m* 1937, Graeme Hendrey (*d* 1972), MIEE; one *d*. *Educ:* Levana, Wimbledon; Westfield Coll., University of London. Editorial Staff, News-Chronicle; Editor's Asst, Sunday Times, 1931-36. *Publications:* Dew on the Grass (Book Guild gold medal), 1934; (with Peter Lewis) The Land of Wales, 1937; The Captain's Wife, 1943; In Country Places, 1951; The Leaves of the Tree, 1953; Honey Pots and Brandy Bottles, 1954; Selected Letters of Charles Morgan, with Memoir, 1967; and two books of verse; regular contributor to Country Life. *Address:* Rabbits Heath Cottage, Bletchingley, Surrey.

LEWIS, Eric William Charles, CB 1971; Member, Civil Service Appeal Board, since 1975; *b* 13 Oct. 1914; *s* of William and May Frances Lewis; *m* 1939, Jessie Davies; two *d*. *Educ:* Christ's Hospital. LLB London. Joined Estate Duty Office, 1933; Army (Captain, RA), 1942-46; Admin. Staff Coll., 1949; Asst Controller, 1955, Deputy Controller, 1958, Controller, 1964-74, Estate Duty Office, Bd of Inland Revenue. *Publication:* contrib. Capital Taxes Encyclopaedia, 1976. *Address:* 31 Deena Close, Queens Drive, W3 0HR. *T:* 01-992 1752.
See also Sir R. C. G. St L. Ricketts.

LEWIS, Ernest Gordon, (Toby), CMG 1972; OBE 1958; HM Diplomatic Service; Head of Gibraltar and General Department, Foreign and Commonwealth Office, since 1975; *b* New Zealand, 26 Sept. 1918; *s* of George Henry Lewis; *m* 1949, Jean Margaret, *d* of late A. H. Smyth. *Educ:* Otago Boys' High Sch.; Otago Univ., NZ. Served War, Army, with 2nd NZ Div., Middle East, 1939-46 (Lt-Col; despatches, MBE). Joined Colonial Service, Nigeria, 1947; Administrator, Turks and Caicos Is, 1955-59; Permanent Sec., to Federal Govt of Nigeria, 1960-62; First Sec., Pakistan, 1963-66; Foreign and Commonwealth Office, 1966-69; Kuching, Sarawak, 1969-70; Governor and C-in-C, Falkland Islands, and High Comr, British Antarctic Territory, 1971-75. *Recreations:* golf, tennis, fishing. *Address:* 65 Eaton Square, SW1. *Club:* Army and Navy.

LEWIS, Esyr ap Gwilym, QC 1971; a Recorder of the Crown Court, since 1972; *b* 11 Jan. 1926; *s* of late Rev. T. W. Lewis, BA, and Mary Jane May Lewis (*née* Selway); *m* 1957, Elizabeth Anne Vidler Hoffmann, 2nd *d* of O. W. Hoffmann, Bassett, Southampton; four *d*. *Educ:* Salford Grammar Sch.; Mill Hill Sch.; Trinity Hall, Cambridge (MA, LLB). Served War in Intelligence Corps, 1944-47. Exhibitioner, 1944, Scholar, 1948, at Trinity Hall (Dr Cooper's Law Studentship, 1950); 1st cl. hons, Law Tripos II, 1949, 1st cl. LLB, 1950, Cambridge. Holker Sen. Schol., Gray's Inn, 1950; Called to Bar, Gray's Inn, 1951; Law Supervisor, Trinity Hall, 1950-55; Law Lectr, Cambridgeshire Technical Coll., 1949-50. Member: Bar Council, 1965-68; Council of Legal Education, 1967-; Criminal Injuries Compensation Bd, 1977-. Contested (L) Llanelli, 1964. *Publication:* contributor to Newnes Family Lawyer, 1963. *Recreations:* reading, gardening, watching Rugby football. *Address:* 2 South Square, Gray's Inn, WC1. *T:* 01-405 5918; Farrar's Building, Temple, EC4Y 7BD. *T:* 01-583 9241. *Clubs:* Reform; Cardiff and County; Old Millhillians; Bristol Channel Yacht.

LEWIS, Gwynedd Margaret; a Recorder of the Crown Court, since Dec. 1974; barrister-at-law; *b* 9 April 1911; *d* of late Samuel David Lewis and Margaret Emma Lewis. *Educ:* King Edward's High Sch., Birmingham; King's Coll., Univ. of London. BA. Called to Bar, Gray's Inn, 1939; Mem., Midland and Oxford Circuit; Dep. Stipendiary Magistrate for City of Birmingham, 1962-74. Legal Mem., Mental Health Review Tribunal for the W Midlands Region, 1972-. *Recreations:* archaeology, bird-watching, riding, sailing. *Address:* 7 Heaton Drive, Edgbaston, Birmingham B15 3LW. *T:* 021-454 1514; Troutbeck, Leintwardine, Salop.

LEWIS, Captain Henry E., CBE 1942; RN (retired); *b* 24 Sept. 1889; *s* of W. C. Lewis, Plymouth, Devon; *m* 1911, E. E. Rice, Plympton, Devon; one *d*. *Educ:* Plymouth. *Recreations:* tennis, etc. *Address:* 8 Fastnet House, South Parade, Southsea PO5 2JG. *T:* Portsmouth 31768.

LEWIS, Henry Gethin, DL, JP; Chairman and Managing Director of private companies; *b* 31 Oct. 1899; *e s* of late Henry Gethin Lewis, LLD, JP, High Sheriff of Glamorgan, 1920-21, Porthkerry, Glamorgan; *m* 1925, Gwendolen Joan, 5th *d* of T. W. David, JP, Ely Rise, Cardiff; one *s* two *d*. *Educ:* Shrewsbury Sch.; Trinity Coll., Oxford (MA). Served European War 2nd Lt RFC with 48 Sqdn, 1918, BEF France (POW). Called to the Bar, Inner Temple, 1925. RAFVR, 1939-45, Sqdn-Ldr 1943. JP 1957, DL 1961, High Sheriff of Glamorgan, 1958. Chief Comr for Wales, St John Ambulance Bde, 1958-66; KStJ; Mem., Welsh Hosp. Bd, 1958-64, and Mem. Bd of Governors, United Cardiff Hosps, 1958-64. *Address:* Cliffside, Penarth, South Glamorgan. *T:* Penarth 707096. *Clubs:* Royal Air Force; Leander (Henley-on-Thames); Cardiff and County (Cardiff); Penarth Yacht.

LEWIS, Henry Nathan; Joint Managing Director, Marks & Spencer Ltd, since 1973; *b* 29 Jan. 1926; *m* 1953, Jenny Cohen; one *s* two *d*. *Educ:* Stockport Sch.; Manchester Univ. (BA Com); LSE. Served RAF, 1944-48. Marks & Spencer Ltd, 1950; Dir, 1965. Industrial Governor, British Nutrition Foundn. Governor: Jerusalem Inst. of Management; Carmel Coll.; Chm., Yad Vashem Cttee; Mem., Campaign and Finance Cttees, Joint Israel Appeal, Bd of Deputies of British Jews. *Address:* Michael House, Baker Street, W1A 1DN.

LEWIS, H(erbert) J(ohn) Whitfield, CB 1968; Partner, Clifford Culpin & Partners, Architects and Town Planners; *b* 9 April 1911; *s* of Herbert and Mary Lewis; *m* 1963, Pamela (*née* Leaford); one *s* three *d*. *Educ:* Monmouth Sch.; Welsh Sch. of Architecture. Associate with Norman & Dawbarn, Architects and Consulting Engineers; in charge of housing work, 1945-50; Principal Housing Architect, Architects Dept, London County Council, 1950-59; County Architect, Middlesex County Council, 1959-64; Chief Architect, Ministry of Housing and Local Govt, 1964-71. FRIBA; FRTPI, DisTP 1957. *Recreations:* music, electronics. *Address:* 8 St John's Wood Road, NW8. *Club:* Savile.

LEWIS, Rt. Rev. Hurtle John; *see* Queensland, North, Bishop of.

LEWIS, Prof. Hywel David, MA, BLitt; Professor of History and Philosophy of Religion, in the University of London, 1955-77; *b* 21 May 1910; *s* of Rev. David John and Rebecca Lewis, Waenfawr, Cærnarvon; *m* 1943, Megan Elias Jones, MA (*d* 1962), *d* of J. Elias Jones, Bangor; *m* 1965, K. A. Megan Pritchard, *d* of T. O. Pritchard, Pentrefoelas. *Educ:* University Coll., Bangor; Jesus Coll., Oxford. Lecturer in Philosophy, University Coll., Bangor, 1936; Senior Lecturer, 1947; Prof. of Philosophy, 1947-55; President: Mind Association, 1948-49, Aristotelian Soc., 1962-63; Chm. Council, Royal Inst. of Philosophy; Soc. for the Study of Theology, 1964-66; President: Oxford Soc. for Historical Theology, 1970-71; London Soc. for Study of Religion, 1970-72; Inst. of Religion and Theology, 1972-; International Soc. for Metaphysics, 1974-; Editor, Muirhead Library of Philosophy; Editor, Religious Studies; Leverhulme Fellow, 1954-55; Visiting Professor: Brynmawr Coll., Pa, USA, 1958-59; Yale, 1964-65; University of Miami, 1968; Boston Univ., 1969; Emory Univ., 1977-78; Lectures: Robert McCahan, Presbyterian Coll., Belfast, 1960; Wilde, in Natural and Comparative Religion, Oxford, 1960-63; Edward Cadbury, Birmingham, 1962-63; Centre for the Study of World Religions, Harvard, 1963; Ker, McMaster Divinity Coll., Ont, 1964; Owen Evans, University Coll., Aberystwyth, 1964-65; Firth Meml, Nottingham, 1966; Gifford, Edinburgh, 1966-68; L. T. Hobhouse Meml, London, 1966-68; Elton, George Washington Univ., 1969; Otis Meml, Wheaton Coll., 1969; Drew, London, 1973-74. Commemoration Preacher, University of Southampton, 1958; Commemoration Lectr, Cheshunt Coll., Cambridge, 1960, and Westminster Coll., 1964. Fellow of King's Coll., London, 1963; Dean of the Faculty of Theology in the University of London, 1964-68; Dean of the Faculty of Arts, King's Coll., 1966-68, and Faculty of Theology, 1970-72. Warden, Guild of Graduates, University of Wales; Mem., Advisory Council for Education (Wales), 1964-67. Mem., Gorsedd of Bards. Hon. DD St Andrews. *Publications:* Morals and the New Theology, 1947; Morals and Revelation, 1951; (ed) Contemporary British Philosophy, Vol. III, 1956, Vol. IV, 1976; Our Experience of God, 1959; Freedom and History, 1962; (ed) Clarity is not Enough, 1962; Teach yourself the Philosophy of Religion, 1965; World Religions (with R. L. Slater), 1966; Dreaming and Experience, 1968; The Elusive Mind, 1969; The Self and Immortality, 1973; (ed) Philosophy East and West, 1975; (ed with G. R. Damodaran) The Dynamics of Education, 1975; Gwerinaeth, 1940; Y Wladwriaeth a'i Hawdurdod (with Dr J. A. Thomas), 1943; Ebyrth, 1943; Diogelu Diwylliant, 1945; Crist a Heddwch, 1947; Dilyn Crist, 1951; Gwybod am Dduw, 1952; Hen a Newydd, 1972; contributions to Mind, Proc.

of Aristotelian Society, Philosophy, Ethics, Hibbert Jl, Philosophical Quarterly, Analysis, Efrydiau Athronyddol, Llenor, Traethodydd, etc. *Address:* 1 Normandy Park, Normandy, near Guildford, Surrey.

LEWIS, Sir Ian (Malcolm), Kt 1964; QC (Nigeria) 1961; MA Cantab, LLB; **His Honour Judge Sir Ian Lewis;** a Circuit Judge, since 1973; *b* 14 Dec. 1925; *s* of late Prof. Malcolm M. Lewis, MC, MA, LLB, and late Eileen (*née* O'Sullivan); *m* 1955, Marjorie, *d* of late W. G. Carrington; one *s*. *Educ:* Clifton Coll. (Governor, 1972-, Mem. Council, 1975-); Trinity Hall, Cambridge (Scholar, 1st cl. hons Law Tripos Pt 2, and LLB). Served with RAFVR, 1944-47. Called to Bar, Middle Temple, 1951; pupil of R. W. Goff (now Rt Hon. Lord Justice Goff), 1951. Western Circuit, 1951; Crown Counsel, Nigeria, 1953; Northern Nigeria: Solicitor-Gen., 1958; Dir of Public Prosecutions, 1962; Attorney-Gen. and Minister in the Government of Northern Nigeria, 1962-66; Chancellor, Diocese of Northern Nigeria, 1964-66; a Justice, Supreme Court of Nigeria, 1966-72; Justice of Appeal, Anguilla, 1972-73; Comr in NI dealing with detention of terrorists, 1972-75; Mem., Detention Appeal Tribunal for NI, 1974-75; Adviser to Sec. of State for NI on Detention, 1975-; Liaison Judge for Wiltshire, and Hon. Vice-Pres., Magistrates Assoc., Wilts, 1973-. MEC, N Nigeria, 1962-66; Adv. Coun. on the Prerogative of Mercy, House of Assembly, 1962-66. Mem. of Nigerian Bar Council, 1962-66; Mem. of Nigerian Council of Legal Education, 1962-66; Assoc. Mem. Commonwealth Parly Assoc. Hon. LLD, Ahmadu Bello Univ., Nigeria, 1972. *Recreations:* swimming (Capt. Cambridge Univ. Swimming and Water Polo, 1949); bridge; sailing; trying to find chapels in Wales where Grandfather "Elfed" (late Rev. H. Elvet Lewis, CH, DD) had not preached. *Address:* Denehurst, 10 Southfield Road, Westbury-on-Trym, Bristol BS9 3BH. *T:* Bristol 626942. *Clubs:* Royal Commonwealth Society; Hawks (Cambridge); Clifton, Constitutional (Bristol).

LEWIS, Prof. Jack, FRS 1973; FRIC; Professor of Chemistry, and Fellow of Sidney Sussex College, University of Cambridge, since 1970; (first) Warden of Robinson College, Cambridge, since 1975; *b* 13 Feb. 1928; *m* 1951, Elfreida Mabel (*née* Lamb); one *s* one *d*. *Educ:* Barrow Grammar Sch. BSc London 1949; PhD Nottingham 1951; DSc London 1961; MSc Manchester 1964; MA Cantab, 1970; ScD Cantab 1977. Lecturer: Univ. of Sheffield, 1953-56; Imperial Coll., London, 1956-57; Lecturer-Reader, University Coll., London, 1957-62; Prof. of Chemistry: Univ. of Manchester, 1962-67; UCL, 1967-70. Firth Vis. Prof., Univ. of Sheffield, 1969; Lectures: Frontiers of Science, Case/Western Reserve, 1963; Tilden, RIC, 1966; Miller, Univ. of Illinois, 1966; Shell, Stanford Univ., 1968; Venables, Univ. of N Carolina, 1968; A. D. Little, MIT, 1970; Boomer, Univ. of Alberta, 1971; AM, Princeton, 1972; Baker, Cornell, 1974; Nyholm, Chem. Soc., 1974. Member: CNAA Cttee, 1964-70; Exec. Cttee, Standing Cttee on Univ. Entry, 1966-; Schs Council, 1966-; SRC: Polytechnics Cttee, 1973-; Chemistry Cttee (Chm., 1975-); Science Bd, 1975-; UGC (Phy. Sci.), 1975-. American Chem. Soc. Award in Inorganic Chemistry, 1970; Transition Metal Award, Chem. Soc., 1973. *Publications:* papers, mainly in Jl of Chem. Soc. *Address:* Chemistry Department, University Chemical Laboratory, Lensfield Road, Cambridge CB2 1EW. *Club:* Athenæum.

LEWIS, Sir John Duncan; *see* Orr-Lewis.

LEWIS, John Gaywood; Special Commissioner of Income Tax, since 1971; *b* 11 Aug. 1916; *s* of late George Gaywood Lewis and Elizabeth Ann Lewis (*née* Wood); *m* 1944, Mary Critchley Harris; two *s*. *Educ:* Brighton, Hove and Sussex Grammar Sch.; London School of Economics (LLB). Served RNVR (Coastal Forces), 1941-46. Entered Inland Revenue (Estate Duty Office), 1935; Asst Sec., 1959. *Address:* 12 Vine Avenue, Sevenoaks, Kent TN13 3AH. *T:* Sevenoaks 52637. *Club:* Naval.

LEWIS, Maj.-Gen. (Retd) John Michael Hardwicke, CBE 1970 (OBE 1955); *b* 5 April 1919; *s* of Brig. Sir Clinton Lewis, *qv*; *m* 1942, Barbara Dorothy (*née* Wright); three *s*. *Educ:* Oundle; RMA, Woolwich. Commissioned, 2nd Lieut, RE, 1939. Served War: in 18 Div. and Special Force (Chindits), in Far East, 1940-45. Staff Coll., Camberley, 1949; CRE, Gibraltar, 1959-61; Instr, JSSC, 1961-63; IDC, 1966; Asst Chief of Staff (Ops), HQ Northern Army Gp, 1967-69; Brig. GS (Intell.), MoD, 1970-72; ACOS (Intelligence), SHAPE, 1972-75. *Publication:* Michiel Marieschi: Venetian artist, 1967. *Recreation:* English water-colours. *Address:* Bedford's Farm, Frimley Green, Surrey. *T:* Deepcut 5188.

LEWIS, Ven. John Wilfred; *b* 25 Sept. 1909; *e s* of Fritz and Ethel Mary Lewis; *m* 1938, Winifred Mary Griffin; one *s* two *d*. *Educ:*

privately; Gonville and Caius Coll., Cambridge. History Tripos Pt I Cl. II, 1932; BA 1933; MA, 1937; Steel Studentship (University), 1933; Exhibitioner, 1933-34; Westcott House, 1934; Deacon, 1935; Priest, 1936; Asst Dir of London Diocesan Council for Youth, 1935-37; Head of Oxford House, 1937-40; Vicar of Kimbolton, 1940-46; Dir, Hereford Diocesan Council of Educn, 1943-63; Rector of Cradley, 1946-60; Archdeacon of Ludlow, 1960-70; Rector of Wistanstow, 1960-70; Archdeacon of Hereford and Canon Residentiary of Hereford Cathedral, 1970-76; Prebendary of Colwall in Hereford Cathedral, 1948-76; Archdeacon Emeritus, 1977. *Recreations:* walking, sailing. *Address:* 9 Claremont Hill, Shrewsbury. *T:* Shrewsbury 65685.

LEWIS, (Joseph) Anthony; Chief London Correspondent, New York Times, 1965-72, editorial columnist, since 1969; *b* 27 March 1927; *s* of Kassel Lewis and Sylvia Lewis (*née* Surut), NYC; *m* 1951, Linda, *d* of John Rannells, NYC; one *s* two *d*. *Educ:* Horace Mann Sch., NY; Harvard Coll. (BA). Sunday Dept, New York Times, 1948-52; Reporter, Washington Daily News, 1952-55; Legal Corresp., Washington Bureau, NY Times, 1955-64; Nieman Fellow, Harvard Law Sch., 1956-57. Governor, Ditchley Foundation, 1965-72. Pulitzer Prize for Nat. Correspondence, 1955 and 1963; Heywood Broun Award, 1955; Overseas Press Club Award, 1970. Hon. DLitt: Adelphi Univ. (NY), 1964; Rutgers Univ., NJ, 1973. *Publications:* Gideon's Trumpet, 1964; Portrait of a Decade: The Second American Revolution, 1964; articles in American law reviews. *Recreation:* dinghy sailing. *Address:* 84 State Street, Boston, Mass 02109, USA. *Clubs:* Garrick; Tavern (Boston).

LEWIS, Kenneth; DL; MP (C) Rutland and Stamford since 1959; Chairman, Conservative Back Bench Labour Committee, 1963-64; *b* 1 July 1916; *s* of William and Agnes Lewis, Jarrow; *m* 1948, Jane, *d* of Samuel Pearson, of Adderstone Mains, Belford, Northumberland; one *s* one *d*. *Educ:* Jarrow; Edinburgh Univ. Served War of 1939-45. RAF, 1941-46; Flt Lt. Chm. Business and Holiday Travel Ltd. Contested (C) Newton-le-Willows, 1945 and 1950, Ashton-under-Lyne, 1951. CC Middx, 1949-51; Mem. NW Metropolitan Hosp. Management Cttee, 1949-62; Trustee: Uppingham Sch.; Oakham Sch. DL Rutland 1973. *Recreations:* music, painting. *Address:* 96 Green Lane, Northwood, Middx. *T:* Northwood 23354; Dale Cottage, Preston, Rutland. *Clubs:* Junior Carlton, Pathfinder, St Stephen's.

LEWIS, Maj.-Gen. Kenneth Frank Mackay, CB 1951; DSO 1944; MC 1918; retired; *b* 29 Jan. 1897; *s* of Frank Essex Lewis and Anne Florence Mackay; *m* 1930, Pamela Frank Menzies Pyne; two *s*. *Educ:* privately. Commissioned 2nd Lt RH & RFA, 1916; served with 9th Scottish Div., France and Belgium, 1916-18; ADC to GOC Lowland Div., 1921; ADC to GOC. Upper Silesia Force, 1922; Iraq Levies, 1923-25; Adjutant, Portsmouth and IOW, 1926-29; Royal West African Frontier Force, Nigeria Regt, 1929-30; Colchester, 1930-33; India, School of Artillery, 1933-37; Military Coll. of Science, UK, 1938; School of Artillery, Larkhill, 1939-41; CO 7th Survey Regt, 1942; CO 185 Field Regt, 1943; CRA 43 and 49 Divisions, 1944 and 1945 (despatches); CCRA Palestine, 1947 and 1948 (despatches); BRA Western Command, UK, 1948; GOC 4th Anti-Aircraft Group, 1949-50; Dir of Royal Artillery, War Office, Dec. 1950-54; retired, 1954; Col Comdt RA, 1957-62. OStJ 1955. Order of Leopold, Croix de Guerre (Belgium). *Recreations:* books and music. *Address:* 18 Beverley Road, Colchester CO3 3NG. *T:* Colchester 76507. *Club:* Army and Navy.

LEWIS, Leonard, QC 1969; *b* 11 May 1909; *e s* of Barnet Lewis; *m* 1939, Rita Jeanette Stone; two *s* one *d*. *Educ:* Grocer's Company Sch.; St John's Coll., Cambridge (Major Schol.). Wrangler, Wright's Prizeman, MA Cantab; BSc 1st class Hons London. Called to Bar, 1932 and started to practise. Served War of 1939-45, RAF. *Recreation:* tennis. *Address:* East Park House, Newchapel, near Lingfield, Surrey. *T:* Lingfield 114.

LEWIS, Prof. Leonard John, CMG 1969; BSc; DipEd; Professor of Education, with special reference to Education in Tropical Areas, in the University of London, 1958-73, now Emeritus; *b* 28 Aug. 1909; of Welsh-English parentage; *s* of Thomas James Lewis and Rhoda Lewis (*née* Gardiner); *m* 1940, Nora Brisdon (marr. diss. 1976); one *s* (and one *s* decd). *Educ:* Lewis Sch., Pengam; University Coll., of South Wales and Monmouth (BSc); University of London Institute of Education (DipEd). Lecturer, St Andrew's Coll., Oyo, Nigeria, 1935-36; Headmaster, CMS Gram. Sch., Lagos, Nigeria, 1936-41; Education Sec., CMS Yoruba Mission, 1941-44; Lectr, University of London Institute of Education, 1944-48; Editorial staff, Oxford Univ. Press, 1948-49; Prof. of Educn and Dir of Institute of Educn, University Coll. of Ghana, 1949-58. Nuffield Visiting Prof., University of Ibadan, 1966. Hon. Professorial Fellow, University Coll.,

Cardiff, 1973; Hon. Fellow, Coll. of Preceptors, 1974. Coronation Medal, 1953. *Publications:* Equipping Africa, 1948; Henry Carr (Memoir), 1948; Education Policy and Practice in British Tropical Areas, 1954; (ed and contrib.) Perspectives in Mass Education and Community Development, 1957; Days of Learning, 1961; Education and Political Independence in Africa, 1962; Schools, Society and Progress in Nigeria, 1965; The Management of Education (with A. J. Loveridge), 1965. *Recreations:* music, walking. *Address:* Plas Pant-y-Berllan, Capel Isaac, Llandeilo, Dyfed. *T:* Dryslwyn 468.

LEWIS, Michael ap Gwilym, QC 1975; a Recorder of the Crown Court, since 1976; *b* 9 May 1930; *s* of Rev. Thomas William Lewis and Mary Jane May Selway; *m* 1959, Audrey, *yr d* of Charles Leslie Thomas, Neath, Glam; three *s* one *d*. *Educ:* Mill Hill; Jesus Coll., Oxford (Scholar). MA (Mod. History). 2nd Lieut, 2nd Royal Tank Regt, 1952. Called to Bar, Gray's Inn, 1956; South Eastern Circuit. *Address:* Farrar's Building, Temple, EC4Y 7BD. *T:* 01-583 9241.

LEWIS, Norman; author; *s* of Richard and Louise Lewis. *Educ:* Enfield Grammar Sch. Served War of 1939-45, in Intelligence Corps. *Publications:* Sand and Sea in Arabia, 1938; Samara, 1949; Within the Labyrinth, 1950; A Dragon Apparent, 1951; Golden Earth, 1952; A Single Pilgrim, 1953; The Day of the Fox, 1955; The Volcanoes Above Us, 1957; The Changing Sky, 1959; Darkness Visible, 1960; The Tenth Year of the Ship, 1962; The Honoured Society, 1964; A Small War Made to Order, 1966; Every Man's Brother, 1967; Flight from a Dark Equator, 1972; The Sicilian Specialist, 1974; Napoli '44, 1978. *Address:* c/o Wm Collins Sons & Co. Ltd, 14 St James's Place, SW1.

LEWIS, Prof. Norman Bache, MA, PhD; retired; *b* 8 Nov. 1896; *o s* of G. D. and L. A. Lewis, Newcastle-under-Lyme; *m* 1928, Julia, *o d* of John and Catherine Wood, Riddlesden, Keighley; one *d* (one *s* decd). *Educ:* Boys' High Sch., Newcastle-under-Lyme (foundation scholar); University of Manchester (Jones scholar). Served European War in RFA, 1917-19. Manchester University: Hovell and Shuttleworth Prizes in History, 1919; BA in History Hons Cl I and graduate scholarship in History, 1921; Research Fellowship in History, 1922. University of Sheffield: Lecturer in Dept of Modern History, 1924; Senior Lecturer in Mediæval History, 1946; Reader in Mediæval History, 1955; Prof. of Mediæval History in the University of Sheffield, 1959-62, Emeritus Prof., 1962. *Publications:* articles in historical journals. *Recreations:* music and walking. *Address:* 8 Westcombe Park Road, SE3 7RB. *T:* 01-858 1763.

LEWIS, Percival Cecil; QC; President of the Industrial Court, Antigua, since 1976; *b* St Vincent, 14 Aug. 1912; *s* of late Philip Owen Lewis; *m* 1936, Gladys Muriel Pool; one *s* one *d*. *Educ:* St Vincent Intermediate Sch.; St Vincent Gram. Sch. Called to Bar, Middle Temple, 1936. Practised in Uganda and St Vincent, 1936-40; Registrar and Additional Magistrate, St Lucia, 1940-43; Magistrate, Dominica, 1943-45; Crown Attorney, St Vincent, 1945-52; Crown Attorney, St Lucia, 1952-54; Attorney-Gen., Leeward Islands, 1954-56; Puisne Judge of Supreme Court of Windward and Leeward Islands, 1956-76; Justice of Appeal of the WI Assoc. States Supreme Court, 1967-75. *Recreations:* gardening and swimming. *Address:* c/o Industrial Court, PO Box 118, St Johns, Antigua, West Indies.

LEWIS, Peter Tyndale; Chairman, John Lewis Partnership, since 1972; *b* 26 Sept. 1929; *s* of Oswald Lewis and Frances Merriman Lewis (*née* Cooper); *m* 1961, Deborah Anne, *d* of Sir William (Alexander Roy) Collins, CBE and Priscilla Marian, *d* of late S. J. Lloyd; one *s* one *d*. *Educ:* Eton; Christ Church, Oxford. National service, Coldstream Guards, 1948-49; MA (Oxford) 1953; called to Bar (Middle Temple) 1956; joined John Lewis Partnership, 1959. Member: Council, Industrial Soc., 1968-; Design Council, 1971-74; Chm., Retail Distributors' Assoc., 1972. *Address:* John Lewis & Co. Ltd, Oxford Street, W1A 1AX.

LEWIS, Richard, CBE 1963; FRAM, FRMCM, LRAM; Concert and Opera Singer, Tenor; *b* of Welsh parents; *m* 1963, Elizabeth Robertson; one *s* (and one *s* by a previous *m*). *Educ:* Royal Manchester Coll. of Music (schol.; studied with Norman Allin); RAM. As a boy won many singing competitions in N England; Gold Medals of Assoc. Bd exams, 1935, 1937. Served in RCS during war and whilst so doing sang in Brussels and Oslo. English début in leading rôle of Britten's Opera The Rape of Lucretia at Glyndebourne, where he has appeared each season since 1947; several opera, concert, recital appearances, Edinburgh Festival; created parts: Troilus in Sir William Walton's Opera Troilus and Cressida; Mark in The Midsummer Marriage, and Achilles in King Priam, both Operas by Michael Tippett; sang in first perf. of Stravinsky's Canticum Sacrum,

under composer's direction, Venice Festival; sang Aaron in first British performance of Schoenberg's opera Moses and Aaron at Covent Garden. Recitalist and oratorio singer, particularly in name part of Elgar's The Dream of Gerontius. In addition to appearance at Glyndebourne is a guest artist at Covent Garden, San Francisco, Chicago, Vienna State Opera and Berlin State Opera Houses; début Teatro Colon, Buenos Aires, 1963. Sings frequently on the Continent and has made several tours of America; also toured Australia and New Zealand, 1957, 1964. Leading part in first American presentation of Cherubini's Opera, Medea, San Francisco, USA, 1958, where he has now appeared for ten seasons; Has appeared with leading European and American orchestras, etc including the New York Philharmonic, Chicago Symphony, San Francisco Symphony, and Philadelphia Orchestras, etc. Has made numerous recordings and appearances on radio and television. Pres., ISM, 1975-76. *Recreations:* private film making, tennis, golf. *Address:* White Acre, Highgate Road, Forest Row, West Sussex.

LEWIS, Maj.-Gen. (retd) Robert Stedman, CB 1946; OBE 1942; late IA; *b* 20 March 1898; *s* of Sidney Cooke Lewis, MInstCE, and Mary Anne Jane Lewis Lloyd; *m* 1925, Margaret Joan Hart; one *s* one *d*. *Educ:* Amesbury Sch., Bickley Hall, Kent; Bradfield Coll., Berks; Royal Military Academy, Woolwich. 2nd Lt RFA 1915; Seconded to RFC in 1916 and 1917 and served as a pilot in France in 100 Squadron RFC; served in France with RFA, 1918; proceeded to India with RFA, 1919; Seconded to Indian Army Ordnance Corps, 1922, and permanently transferred to Indian Army, 1925, with promotion to Capt.; Major, 1933; Bt Lt-Col 1937; Lt-Col 1940; Col 1944; employed at General Headquarters, India, 1939; Dir of Ordnance Services (India), 1945; retired, 1948. High Sheriff of Radnorshire, 1951. *Address:* Y Neuadd, Rhayader, Powys. *T:* Rhayader 227.

LEWIS, Captain Roger Curzon, DSO 1939; OBE 1944; RN retired; *b* 19 July 1909; *s* of late F. W. and K. M. Lewis; *m* 1944, Marguerite Christiane (*d* 1971), *e d* of late Captain A. D. M. Cherry, RN, retd; two *s*. *Educ:* Royal Naval Coll., Dartmouth. HMS Lowestoft, Africa Station, 1927-29; HMS Vivien and HMS Valentine, 6th Flotilla Home Fleet, 1930-32; Qualifying Lt T 1933; HMS Enterprise, East Indies Station, 1935-37; Staff of HMS Vernon, 1938-39; HMS Florentino, 1939-40; HMS Rodney, 1940-42; Staff of Comdr-in-Chief Mediterranean, 1942-45; Superintendent of Torpedo Experimental Establishment, Greenock, 1950-55; Capt. of the Dockyard and Queen's Harbourmaster, Chatham, 1955-58; retired, 1959. *Address:* 3 Albion Street, Shaldon, Teignmouth, Devon TQ14 0DF.

LEWIS, Roland Swaine, FRCS; Honorary Consultant Surgeon to the ENT Department, King's College Hospital, since 1973 (Consultant Surgeon, 1946-65, Senior Consultant Surgeon, 1965-73); Honorary Consultant ENT Surgeon: to Mount Vernon Hospital and The Radium Institute; to Norwood and District Hospital; *b* 23 Nov. 1908; *s* of Dr William James Lewis, MOH, and Constance Mary Lewis, Tyrwaun, Ystalyfera; *m* 1936, Mary Christianna Milne (Christianna Brand); one adopted *d*. *Educ:* Epsom Coll.; St John's Coll., Cambridge; St George's Hospital. BA Cantab 1929; FRCS 1934; MA Cantab 1945; MB BCh Cantab 1945. Surgical Chief Asst, St George's Hospital, 1935. Major, RAMC (ENT Specialist), 1939-45. *Publications:* papers to medical journals. *Recreations:* ornithology, fishing. *Address:* 88 Maida Vale, W9 1PR. *T:* 01-624 6253.

LEWIS, Ronald Howard; MP (Lab) Carlisle since 1964; *b* 16 July 1909; *s* of Oliver Lewis, coal miner; *m* 1937, Edna Cooke; two *s*. *Educ:* Elementary Sch. and Cliff Methodist Coll. Left school at 14 years of age and worked in coal mines (Somerset; subseq. Derbyshire, 1930-36); then railways (LNER Sheds, Langwith Junction); left that employment on being elected to Parliament. Mem., Blackwell RDC 1940- (twice Chm.); Derbyshire CC, 1949-; Mem. Bd of Directors, Pleasley Co-operative Soc. Ltd, 1948-70 (Pres. 1952). Mem. NUR. Methodist Local Preacher. *Recreations:* walking, football, gardening. *Address:* 22 Alandale Avenue, Langwith Junction, Mansfield, Notts. *T:* Shirebrook 2460.

LEWIS, Saunders, MA; Welsh writer and dramatist; *b* 15 Oct. 1893; *s* of Rev. Lodwig Lewis and Mary Margaret Thomas; *m* 1924, Margaret Gilcriest; one *d*. *Educ:* privately; Liverpool Univ. *Publications:* plays: The Eve of St John, 1921; Gwaed yr Uchelwyr, 1922; Buchedd Garmon, 1937; Amlyn ac Amig, 1940; Blodeuwedd, 1948; Eisteddfod Bodran, 1952; Gan Bwyll, 1952; Siwan a Cherddi Eraill, 1956; Gymerwch Chi Sigaret?, 1956; Brad, 1958; Esther, 1960; Serch Yw'r Doctor (light opera libretto), 1960; Cymru Fydd, 1967; Problemau Prifysgol, 1968; Dwy Briodas Ann, 1973; Dramau'r Parlwr, 1975; *novels:* Monica, 1930; Merch Gwern Hywel, 1964; *poetry:* Mair Fadlen,

1937; Byd a Betws, 1941; *criticism:* A School of Welsh Augustans, 1924; Williams Pantycelyn, 1927; Ceiriog, 1929; Braslun o Hanes Llenyddiaeth Gymraeg Hyd 1535, 1932; Daniel Owen, 1936; Ysgrifau Dydd Mercher, 1945; Meistri'r Canrifoedd, 1973; *political and economic:* Canlyn Arthur, 1938; also many pamphlets in the Welsh language; *translations:* Molière, Doctor er ei Waethaf, 1924; Beckett, With aros Godot, 1970; (ed with introd.) Ievan Glan Geirionydd, 1931; (ed with introd.) Straeon Glasynys, 1943; (ed) Crefft y Stori Fer (radio broadcasts), 1949. Translations of plays have been presented on stage and television in English, German, and Spanish. *Address:* 158 Westbourne Road, Penarth, South Glam.

LEWIS, Thomas Loftus Townshend, FRCS; Consultant Obstetric and Gynæcological Surgeon at Guy's Hospital, Queen Charlotte's Maternity Hospital and Chelsea Hospital for Women, since 1948; Hon. Consultant in Obstetrics and Gynaecology, to the Army, since 1973; *b* 27 May 1918; *e s* of late Neville Lewis and his first wife, Theodosia Townshend; *m* 1946, Kathleen Alexandra Ponsonby Moore; five *s*. *Educ:* Diocesan Coll., Rondebosch, S Africa; St Paul's Sch.; Cambridge Univ.; Guy's Hospital. BA Cantab (hons in Nat. Sci. Tripos), 1939; MB, BChir Cantab, 1942. FRCS 1946; MRCOG 1948; FRCOG 1961. House Appointments Guy's Hospital, 1942-43; Gold Medal and Prize in Obstetrics, Guy's Hospital, 1942. Volunteered to join South African Medical Corps, 1944; seconded to RAMC and served as Capt. in Italy and Greece, 1944-45. Returned to Guy's Hospital; Registrar in Obstetrics and Gynæcology, 1946, Obstetric Surgeon, 1948; Surgeon, Chelsea Hosp. for Women, 1950; Surgeon, Queen Charlotte's Maternity Hosp., 1952. Examiner in Obstetrics and Gynæcology: University of Cambridge, 1950; University of London, 1954; Royal College of Obstetricians and Gynæcologists, 1952; London Soc. of Apothecaries, 1955; University of St Andrews, 1960. Hon. Sec. and Mem. Council, Royal College of Obstetricians and Gynæcologists, 1955-68, 1971-, Vice-Pres., 1976-; Mem. Council Obstetric Section, Royal Society of Med., 1953-. Guest Prof. to Brisbane, Australia, Auckland, New Zealand, 1959, Johns Hopkins Hosp., Baltimore, 1966; Litchfield Lectr, University of Oxford, 1968; Sims-Black Prof. to Australia, NZ and Rhodesia, 1970. *Publications:* Progress in Clinical Obstetrics and Gynæcology, 2nd edn 1964; Obstetrics, 11th edn (jointly), 1966; Queen Charlotte's Textbook of Obstetrics, 12th edn (jointly), 1970; Gynaecology, 12th edn (jointly), 1970; French's Index of Differential Diagnosis, 10th edn (jointly), 1973. Contributions to: Lancet, BMJ, Practitioner, Proc. Roy. Soc. Med., Encyclopædia Britannica Book of the Year (annual contrib.), etc. *Recreations:* ski-ing, sailing, tennis, golf, croquet, water ski-ing, underwater swimming, photography, viniculture on the Isle of Elba. *Address:* 109 Harley Street, W1. *T:* 01-935 5855; (home) 13 Copse Hill, Wimbledon, SW20. *T:* 01-946 5089. *Clubs:* Royal Wimbledon Golf; United Hospitals Rugby Football (ex-Pres.).

LEWIS, Trevor Oswin, JP; Chairman, Countryside Commission's Committee for Wales, since 1973; *b* 29 Nov. 1935; *s* of 3rd Baron Merthyr, PC, KBE, TD, and of Violet, *y d* of Brig.-Gen. Sir Frederick Charlton Meyrick, 2nd Bt, CB, CMG; *S* father, 1977, as 4th Baron Merthyr, but disclaimed his peerage for life; also as 4th Bt (*cr* 1896) but does not use the title; *m* 1964, Susan Jane, *yr d* of A. J. Birt-Llewellin; one *s* three *d*. *Educ:* Downs Sch.; Eton; Magdalen Coll., Oxford; Magdalene Coll., Cambridge. Mem. Countryside Commn, 1973-. JP Dyfed, formerly Pembs, 1969. *Heir (to disclaimed peerage): s* David Trevor Lewis, *b* 21 Feb. 1977. *Address:* Hean Castle, Saundersfoot, Dyfed SA69 9AL. *T:* Saundersfoot 812222.

LEWIS, Dame Vera Margaret; *see* Lynn, Dame Vera.

LEWIS, Wilfrid Bennett, CC (Canada) 1967; CBE 1946; FRS 1945; FRSC 1952; MA; PhD; Senior Vice-President, Science, Atomic Energy of Canada Ltd, 1963-73, retired; Distinguished Professor of Science, Queen's University, since 1973; *b* 24 June 1908; *s* of Arthur Wilfrid Lewis and Isoline Maud Steavenson; unmarried. *Educ:* Haileybury Coll., Herts; Gonville and Caius Coll., Cambridge, Hon. Fellow 1971. Cavendish Laboratory, Cambridge, research in Radio-activity and Nuclear Physics, 1930-39; Research Fellowship, Gonville and Caius Coll., 1934-40; University Demonstrator in Physics, 1934; University Lecturer in Physics, 1937; lent to Air Ministry as Senior Scientific Officer, 1939; Chief Superintendent Telecommunications Research Establishment, Ministry of Aircraft Production, 1945-46; Dir of Division of Atomic Energy Research, National Research Council of Canada, 1946-52; Vice-Pres. Research and Development, Atomic Energy of Canada, Ltd, 1952-63. Canadian Representative United Nations Scientific Advisory Cttee, 1955-. Fellow American Nuclear Soc., 1959 (Pres., 1961); For. Associate, Nat. Acad. of Engineering,

USA, 1976; Hon. Fellow: IEE, 1974; UMIST, 1974. Hon. DSc: Queen's Univ., Kingston, Ontario, 1960; Saskatchewan, 1964; McMaster Univ., Hamilton, Ontario, 1965; Dartmouth Coll., New Hampshire, 1967; McGill Univ., Montreal, 1969; Royal Mil. Coll., Kingston, Ont, 1974; Laurentian, 1977; Birmingham, 1977; Hon. LLD: Dalhousie Univ., Halifax, Nova Scotia, 1960; Carleton Univ., Ottawa, 1962; Trent Univ., Peterborough, Ont, 1969; Toronto, 1972; Victoria, BC, 1975. Amer. Medal of Freedom, with Silver Palms, 1947. First Outstanding Achievement Award, Public Service of Canada, 1966; Atoms for Peace Award (shared), 1967; Can. Assoc. of Physicists 25th anniversary special Gold Medal, 1970; Royal Medal, Royal Soc., 1972. *Publications:* Electrical Counting, 1942; (ed jtly) International Arrangements for Nuclear Fuel Reprocessing, 1977; articles in Wireless Engineer, 1929, 1932 and 1936; papers in Proc. Royal Society A. 1931, 1932, 1933, 1934, 1936, 1940; etc. *Recreation:* walking. *Address:* Box 189, 13 Beach Avenue, Deep River, Ontario K0J 1P0. *T:* 613-584-3561; Physics Department, Queen's University, Kingston, Ontario K7L 3N6. *T:* (office) 613-547-2869, (residence) 613-544-9667.

LEWIS, Sir (William) Arthur, Kt 1963; PhD; BCom (London); MA (Manchester); James Madison Professor of Political Economy, Princeton University, since 1968; *b* 23 Jan. 1915; 4th *s* of George F. and Ida Lewis, Castries, St Lucia; *m* 1947, Gladys Jacobs; two *d*. *Educ:* St Mary's Coll., St Lucia; London Sch. of Economics. Lecturer at London Sch. of Economics, 1938-47; Reader in Colonial Economics, University of London, 1947; Stanley Jevons Prof. of Political Economy, University of Manchester, 1948-58; Principal, University Coll. of the West Indies, 1959-62; Vice-Chancellor, University of the West Indies, 1962-63; Prof. of Public and International Affairs, Princeton Univ., 1963-68; Pres., Caribbean Development Bank, 1970-73. Assigned by United Nations as Economic Adviser to the Prime Minister of Ghana, 1957-58; Dep. Man. Dir, UN Special Fund, 1959-60. Temp. Principal, Board of Trade, 1943, Colonial Office, 1944; Consultant to Caribbean Commn, 1949: Mem. UN Group of Experts on Under-developed Countries, 1951; Part-time Mem. Board of Colonial Development Corporation, 1951-53; Mem. Departmental Cttee on National Fuel Policy, 1951-52; Consultant to UN Economic Commission for Asia and the Far East, 1952; to Gold Coast Govt, 1953: to Govt of Western Nigeria, 1955. Mem. Council, Royal Economic Soc., 1949-58; Pres. Manchester Statistical Soc., 1955-56. Chancellor, Univ. of Guyana, 1966-73. Hon. LHD: Columbia, Boston Coll.; Hon. LLD: Toronto, Wales, Williams, Bristol, Dakar, Leicester, Rutgers, Brussels, Open Univ.; Hon. LittD: West Indies, Lagos; Hon. DSc, Manchester. Corresp. Fellow, British Acad., 1974; Hon. Fellow, LSE; For. Fellow Amer. Acad. of Arts and Sciences; Mem., Amer. Phil. Soc.; Hon. Fellow Weitzmann Inst; Distinguished Fellow, Amer. Economic Assoc., 1970. *Publications:* Economic Survey, 1918-1939, 1949; Overhead Costs, 1949; The Principles of Economic Planning, 1949; The Theory of Economic Growth, 1955; Politics in West Africa, 1965; Development Planning, 1966; Reflections on the Economic Growth of Nigeria, 1968; Some Aspects of Economic Development, 1969; Tropical Development 1880-1913, 1971; Growth and Fluctuations 1870-1913, 1978; articles in technical, economic and law jls. *Address:* Woodrow Wilson School, Princeton University, Princeton, NJ 08540, USA.

LEWIS, William Edmund Ames, OBE 1961; Charity Commissioner, 1962-72; *b* 21 Sept. 1912; *s* of late Ernest W. Lewis, FRCSE, Southport, Lancashire; *m* 1939, Mary Elizabeth, *e d* of late C. R. Ashbee; two *s* one *d*. *Educ:* Merchant Taylors', Great Crosby; Emmanuel Coll., Cambridge. Barrister-at-law, Inner Temple, 1935. Entered Charity Commission, 1939; Asst Commissioner, 1953-61; Sec., 1961-69. Served in RAF, 1941-46. *Recreations:* music, painting. *Address:* Watermans, Ewhurst Green, Robertsbridge, East Sussex. *T:* Staplecross 523. *Club:* United Oxford & Cambridge University.

LEWIS, Wilmarth Sheldon, FSA, FRSA, FRSL; Hon. MA (Yale 1937); Hon. LittD (Brown, 1945, Rochester, 1946, Delaware, 1961, Cambridge 1962); Hon. LHD (Trin. Coll., Hartford, 1950, Bucknell 1958, Melbourne, 1972); Hon. DLitt (NUI, 1957); Hon. LLD (Yale 1965, Hartford 1972); Yale Medal, 1965; Founder and Editor Yale Edn of Horace Walpole's Correspondence since 1933; *b* 14 Nov. 1895; *s* of Azro N. and Miranda Sheldon Lewis; *m* 1928, Annie Burr Auchincloss (*d* 1959). *Educ:* Thacher Sch.; Yale Univ. (BA 1918). Served European War as 2nd Lt 144 Field Artillery, 1917-19; War of 1939-45 as Chief, Central Information Div., Office of Strategic Services, 1941-43; Research Assoc., Yale Univ., 1933-38; Fellow of Yale Univ., 1938-64; Fellow Amer. Acad. of Arts and Sciences; Mem., Amer. Philosoph. Soc. Chairman: Yale Library Assoc., 1933-45; Librarian's Council, Library of Congress, 1941-47; John Carter Brown Library Assoc., 1943-46; Hon. Fellow,

Pierpont Morgan Library, 1970. Trustee: Institute for Advanced Study, Princeton, 1945-; Thacher Sch., 1940-46, 1954-74; Brooks Sch., 1946-49; Miss Porter's Sch., 1941-65; Watkinson Library, 1941-; Redwood Library, 1946-74; Henry Francis duPont (Winterthur) Museum, Delaware, 1954-76; John Carter Brown Library, 1955-75; Heritage Foundn, 1962-76; John F. Kennedy Library, 1964-; Mem. Commission: on National Portrait Gallery (Washington), 1964-76; National Coll. of Fine Arts, 1958-73. FSA 1967. Donald F. Hyde Award (Princeton), 1968; Benjamin Franklin Medal, RSA, 1975. *Publications*: Tutor's Lane, 1922; Three Tours Through London, 1748, 1776, 1797 (Colver Lectures, Brown Univ.); The Yale Collections, 1946: Collector's Progress, 1951; Horace Walpole's Library (Sandars Lectures), 1957; Horace Walpole (A. W. Mellon Lectures), 1960; One Man's Education, 1967; See for Yourself, 1971; Read As You Please, 1977. Editor: A Selection of Letters of Horace Walpole, 1926, 1951, 1973; Horace Walpole's Fugitive Verses, 1931; (with Ralph M. Williams) Private Charity in England, 1747-57, 1938; Yale Edition of Horace Walpole's Correspondence, 39 vols, 1937-74, with completion (50 vols) about 1980. *Address*: Farmington, Conn 06032, USA. *Clubs*: Athenæum (London); Century, Grolier, Yale (New York); Tavern (Boston); Metropolitan (Washington); Pacific Union (San Francisco); Rowfant (Cleveland).

LEWIS-BOWEN, Thomas Edward Ifor; a Recorder of the Crown Court, since Oct. 1974; *b* 20 June 1933; *s* of Lt-Col J. W. Lewis-Bowen and Mrs K. M. Lewis-Bowen (*née* Rice); *m* 1965, Gillian Brett; one *s* two *d*. *Educ*: Ampleforth; St Edmund Hall, Oxford. Called to Bar, Middle Temple, 1958. *Address*: 90 Eaton Crescent, Swansea, West Glamorgan. *T*: Swansea 59736; Clynfiew, Boncath, Dyfed.

LEWIS-JONES, Captain (Robert) Gwilym, CBE 1969; ADC 1976; RN retired; Member (C) for Carshalton, Greater London Council, since 1977; Director, London Centre Housing Association; *b* 22 Feb. 1922; *s* of Captain David Lewis Jones and Olwen Lewis Jones (*née* Evans), Corris and Dolgellau; *m* 1946, Ann Mary, *d* of David and Margaret Owen, Dolgellau; two *s*. *Educ*: Tywyn Grammar Sch.; Gonville and Caius Coll., Cambridge. CEng, AFRAeS, MBIM. FAA Observers Course, 1942-43; 842 Sqdn in HM Ships Indefatigable, Furious and Fencer on Murmansk and Atlantic convoys, 1943-45; Long Air Communications Course, 1945-46; Long Air Electronics/Electrical Course, 1946-47; RRE Malvern, 1947-49; Long Ships Electrical Course, 1950; RAE Farnborough, 1950-53; Sen. Aircraft Engr Off., HMS Albion, 1953-56; Dep. Comd Engr Off., Staff of Flag Officer Naval Air Comd, 1956-58; Head of Air Electrical Comd, RN Air Stn Brawdy, 1958-61; Sqdn Weapons Off., HMS Caesar and 8th Destroyer Sqdn, 1961-63; Exec. Off. and 2nd in Comd, HMS Condor, 1963-65; Gen. Man., RN Aircraft Yard, Belfast, 1965-67; Dir of Aircraft Armament, MoD (N), 1967-68; Jt Services Planning and Co-ordinating Off. responsible for Armed Forces participation in Investiture of Prince of Wales, 1967-69; Sen. Officers War Course, RNC Greenwich, 1969-70; Staff of Dir Gen. Ships (Directorate Naval Ship Production), 1970-72; Dir, Fleet Management Services, 1973-75; Dir, Naval Management and Orgn, 1975-76. Lt-Comdr 1952; Comdr 1958; Captain 1967. Croydon Borough Comr, Scout Assoc. *Recreations*: golf, Association and Rugby football, choral music, and Welsh language. *Address*: Gwynedd, 1 Hadley Wood Rise, Surrey CR2 5LY. *T*: 01-660 9168; Erw Wen, Dolgellau, Gwynedd.

LEWISHAM, Viscount; William Legge; Chartered Accountant; *b* 23 Sept. 1949; *e s* and *heir* of 9th Earl of Dartmouth, *qv*. *Educ*: Eton; Christ Church, Oxford. Secretary, Oxford Union Soc., 1969. Contested (C): Leigh, Lancs, Feb. 1974; Stockport South, Oct. 1974. *Recreations*: squash, watching football. *Address*: The Manor House, Chipperfield, King's Langley, Herts. *Clubs*: Turf, Bath.

LEWISHAM, Archdeacon of; *see* Davies, Ven. Ivor Gordon.

LEWISOHN, Anthony Clive Leopold; His Honour Judge Lewisohn; a Circuit Judge, since 1974; *b* 1 Aug. 1925; *s* of John Lewisohn and Gladys (*née* Solomon); *m* 1957, Lone Ruthwen Jurgensen; two *s*. *Educ*: Stowe; Trinity Coll., Oxford (MA). Royal Marines, 1944-45; Lieut, Oxf. and Bucks LI, 1946-47. Called to Bar, Middle Temple, 1951; S Eastern Circuit. *Recreations*: golf, foreign travel.

LEWISON, Peter George Hornby, CBE 1977; Chairman, National Dock Labour Board, 1969-77; Member, National Ports Council, 1972-77; *b* 5 July 1911; *s* of George and Maud Elizabeth Lewison; *m* 1937, Lyndsay Sutton Rothwell; one *s* one *d*. *Educ*: Dulwich; Magdalen Coll., Oxford. Dunlop Rubber Co., Coventry, 1935-41; Min. of Supply (seconded), 1941-44; RNVR

(Special Br.), 1944-46. Min. of Labour, 1946-47; Personnel Manager, British-American Tobacco Co. Ltd, 1947-68, retd. *Recreations*: music, cricket, golf, bird-watching. *Address*: Court Hill House, East Dean, Chichester, Sussex. *T*: Singleton 200. *Clubs*: MCC; Goodwood Golf.

LE WITT, Jan; painter, poet and designer; *b* 3 April 1907; *s* of Aaron Le Witt and Deborah (*née* Koblenz); *m* 1939, Alina Prusicka; one *s*. *Educ*: Czestochowa. Began artistic career as self-taught designer in Warsaw, 1927; first one-man exhibn of his graphic work, Soc. of Fine Arts, Warsaw, 1930. Co-author and illustrator of children's books, publ. several European langs. Settled in England, 1937; Brit. subject, 1947-; Member of Le Witt-Him partnership, 1933-54. During War of 1939-45 executed (in partnership) a series of murals for war factory canteens, posters for Min. of Inf., Home Office, GPO, etc. Co-designer of murals for Festival of Britain, 1951, and Festival Clock, Battersea Park. First one-man exhibn, Zwemmer Gall., London, 1947; subseq. Hanover Gall. London, 1951; in Rome, 1952; Zwemmer Gall., 1953; New York, 1954; Milan, 1957; Paris, 1960; Grosvenor Gall., London, 1961; Paris, 1963; Musée d'Antibes, 1965; Salon d'Automne, Paris, 1963; Salon de Mai, Paris, 1964; Warsaw (retrosp.), 1967; Venice (retrosp.) (organised by City of Venice), 1970; Paris, 1972. In 1955 when at top of his profession, he gave up graphic design to devote himself entirely to painting. *Works at*: Musée National d'Art Moderne, Paris; Nat. Museum, Jerusalem; Nat. Museum, Warsaw; Musée d'Antibes; Museum and Art Gall., Halifax; City Art Gall., Middlesbrough; British Council; Contemp. Art Soc., London; and in private collections. Represented in collective exhibns in Tate Gall., London, and many foreign galleries. Other artistic activities: décors and costumes for Sadler's Wells Ballet; glass sculptures Venice (Murano); tapestry designs, Aubusson. Gold Medal, Vienna, 1948; Gold Medal Triennale, Milan, 1954; Mem., Alliance Graphique Internationale, 1948-60; Mem., Exec. Council, Société Européenne de Culture, Venice, 1961-. *Publications*: Vegetabull, 1956 (London and New York); A Necklace for Andromeda, 1976; contribs to Poetry Review; Adam; Comprendre, Malahat Review, etc. *Relevant Publication*: Sir Herbert Read, Jean Cassou, Pierre Emmanuel and John Smith (jointly), Jan Le Witt, London 1971, Paris 1972, NY 1973. *Recreations*: music, swimming against the current. *Address*: The Studio, 117 Ladbroke Road, Holland Park, W11 3PR. *T*: 01-229 1570. *Club*: PEN.

LEWITTER, Prof. Lucjan Ryszard; Professor of Slavonic Studies, University of Cambridge, since 1968; *b* 1922; *m*. *Educ*: schools in Poland; Perse Sch., Cambridge; Christ's Coll., Cambridge. PhD 1951. Univ. Asst Lectr in Polish, 1948; Fellow of Christ's Coll., 1951; Dir of Studies in Modern Languages, 1951-64; Tutor, 1960-68; Vice-Master, 1977; Univ. Lectr in Slavonic Studies (Polish), 1953-68. *Publications*: articles in learned jls. *Address*: Department of Slavonic Studies, Sidgwick Avenue, Cambridge CB3 9DA. *T*: Cambridge 56411. *Club*: United Oxford & Cambridge University.

LEWTHWAITE, Brig. Rainald Gilfrid, CVO 1975; OBE 1974; MC 1943; Director of Protocol, Hong Kong, 1969-76; *b* 21 July 1913; 2nd *s* of Sir William Lewthwaite, 2nd Bt of Broadgate, Cumberland, and Beryl Mary Stopford Hickman; *b* of Sir William Anthony Lewthwaite, 3rd Bt, *qv*; *m* 1936, Margaret Elizabeth Edmonds, MBE 1942, 2nd *d* of Harry Edmonds and late Florence Jane Moncrieffe Bolton, High Green, Redding, Conn, USA; two *s* one *d* (and one *d* decd). *Educ*: Rugby Sch.; Trinity Coll., Cambridge. BA (Hons) Law 1934. Joined Scots Guards, 1934. Served War of 1939-45 (MC, despatches twice). Retired as Defence and Military Attaché, British Embassy, Paris, 1968. French Croix-de-Guerre with Palm, 1945. *Recreation*: country life. *Address*: Broadgate, Millom, Cumbria LA18 5JZ. *T*: Broughton-in-Furness 295; 14 Edwardes Square, W8 6HE. *T*: 01-602 6323. *Clubs*: Cavalry and Guards, The Pilgrims.

LEWTHWAITE, Sir William Anthony, 3rd Bt, *cr* 1927; Solicitor of Supreme Court, 1937-75; *b* 26 Feb. 1912; *e s* of Sir William Lewthwaite, 2nd Bt, JP, and Beryl Mary Stopford (*d* 1970), *o c* of late Major Stopford Cosby Hickman, JP, DL, of Fenloe, Co. Clare; *S* father, 1933; *m* 1936, Lois Mairi, *o c* of late Capt. Robertson Kerr Clark and Lady Beatrice Minnie Ponsonby, *d* of 9th Earl of Drogheda (who *m* 2nd, 1941, 1st Baron Rankeillour, PC; she *d* 1966); two *d* (er adopted) (and one *d* decd). *Educ*: Rugby; Trinity Coll., Cambridge, BA. Signalman Royal Corps of Signals, 1942-43; Lt, Grenadier Guards, 1943-46. Mem. Council, Country Landowners Association, 1949-64. Mem. Cttee: Westminster Law Society, 1964-73; Brooks's Club. *Heir*: *b* Brig. Rainald Gilfrid Lewthwaite, *qv*. *Address*: 73 Dovehouse Street, SW3 6JZ. *T*: 01-352 7203.

LEY, Arthur Harris, FRSA; FRIBA, AADip, FIStructE, CompRAeS; Senior Partner, Ley Colbeck & Partners, Architects; *b* 24 Dec. 1903; *s* of late Algernon Sydney Richard Ley, FRIBA, and Esther Eliza Harris; *m* 1935, Ena Constance Riches; one *d. Educ:* Westminster City Sch.; AA Coll. of Architecture. Architect for: Principal London Office Barclays Bank International; Head Office Nat. Mutual Life Assce Soc.; Palmerston Hse, EC2; Baltic Hse, EC3; Bishops House, Bishopsgate; Broad Street House; Hqrs Marine Soc.; Hqrs SBAC; Hqrs RAeS; Hqrs Instn Struct. Engrs; York Hall, Windsor Gt Park; Aircraft Research Assoc. Estab., Bedford. Factories and Office Blocks for: Vickers Ltd, at Barrow, etc.; British Aircraft Corporation at Weybridge and Hurn; Wallpaper Manufrs Ltd; Sir Isaac Pitman & Sons; Decca Radar Ltd; Ever Ready Co.; also numerous office blocks in the City of London, Leeds, Inverness and Vancouver. Banks for: Hambro; Nat. Provincial; Barclays; Bank of Scandinavia; Head London office, Hongkong and Shanghai Bank. Central area develt, Watford and Ashford, Kent. Hospitals: Watford and Harrow. Schools: London, Hertfordshire, Barrow in Furness and Surrey. Mem. Council: Architects Registr. Coun. of UK, 1958-60; Instn Struct. Engrs, 1951-54; London Chamber of Commerce, 1955-; Associated Owners of City Properties (Pres., 1971-77). Hosp. Bd, Ravenscourt Pk, 1972-. Governor, Bishopsgate Foundn; Mem. Court, City Univ.; Liveryman: Worshipful Co. of Paviors (Master, 1962), and of Upholders (Master, 1966); Freeman, City of London; Sheriff 1964-65, and Mem. Court of Common Council, City of London, 1964-; Churchwarden of St Mary-le-Bow. Grand Officer of the Order of Merit (Chile). *Publications:* contributions to journals and technical press. *Address:* Weston House, 77 St John Street, EC1M 4HP. *T:* 01-253 5555; Mixbury, Bridgewater Road, Weybridge, Surrey KT13 0EL. *T:* Weybridge 42701. *Clubs:* City Livery (Pres., 1968-69), Guildhalll, Anglo-Belgian, United Wards (Pres., 1961), Bishopsgate Ward (Pres., 1966).

LEY, Francis Douglas, MBE 1961; TD; DL; JP; Chairman: Ley's Malleable Castings Co. Ltd; Ewart Chainbelt Co. Ltd; Ley's Foundries and Engineering Ltd; W. Shaw & Co. Ltd; *b* 5 April 1907; *yr s* of Major Sir Gordon Ley, 2nd Bt (*d* 1944); *heir-pres.* to brother, Sir Gerald Gordon Ley, 3rd Bt, *qv; m* 1931, Violet Geraldine Johnson; one *s* one *d. Educ:* Eton; Magdalene Coll., Cambridge (MA). JP 1939, DL 1957, Derbyshire. High Sheriff of Derbyshire, 1956. *Address:* Shirley House, Shirley, Derby DE6 3AZ. *T:* Brailsford 327. *Club:* Cavalry and Guards.

LEY, Sir Gerald Gordon, 3rd Bt, *cr* 1905; TD; Captain, 1st Derbyshire Yeomanry; *b* 5 Nov. 1902; *e s* of Major Sir Henry Gordon Ley, 2nd Bt, and late Rhoda Lady Ley, *d* of Herbert Prodgers, Kington St Michael, Chippenham, Wilts; *S* father 1944; *m* 1st, 1936, Rosemary Catherine Cotter (marr. diss. 1956), *d* of late Captain Duncan Macpherson, Royal Navy; three *d*; 2nd, 1958, Grace Foster (marr. diss. 1968). *Educ:* Eton; Oxford Univ., BA Agriculture. Manages estates in Cumberland; High Sheriff of Cumberland, 1937. Lord of the Manors of Lazonby, Kirkoswald, Staffield and Glassonby. Served Duke of Lancaster's Own Yeomanry, 1927-39; War Service, 1939-40; 1st Derbyshire Yeomanry, 1940-45. *Heir: b* Francis Douglas Ley, *qv. Recreations:* fishing, salmon in particular; shooting. *Address:* Lazonby Hall, near Penrith, Cumbria CA10 1AZ. *TA:* Lazonby, Cumbria. *T:* Lazonby 218.
See also Earl of Lonsdale .

LEYLAND, Norman Harrison; Director, National & Commercial Development Capital Ltd, since 1972; Investment Bursar, Brasenose College, Oxford, since 1965; *b* 27 Aug. 1921; *m* 1st, J. I. McKillop; one *s* two *d*; 2nd, 1971, E. C. Wiles. *Educ:* Manchester Grammar Sch.; Brasenose Coll., Oxford. Dir, Oxford Centre for Management Studies, 1965-70. Chm., Consumers' Cttee for Great Britain, 1967-70. Fellow: Brasenose Coll., Oxford, 1948-; Oxford Centre for Management Studies. *Address:* Brasenose College, Oxford. *Club:* Lansdowne.

LEYLAND, Peter; *see* Pyke-Lees, Walter K.

LEYLAND, Sir V. E. N.; *see* Naylor-Leyland.

LEYTON, Dr (Robert) Nevil (Arthur); Consulting Physician, specialising in Migraine, since 1950; *b* 15 June 1910; *s* of Prof. A. S. F. Leyton, MD, DSc, FRCP, and Mrs H. G. Leyton, MD; *m* 1943, Wendy (*d* 1960), *er d* of Tom and Dylis Cooper; one *s. Educ:* private; Gonville and Caius Coll., Cambridge; Westminster Hospital (entrance Schol.). BA (Cantab) Double Hons Natural Sciences Tripos, 1932; MA 1938. Ho. Phys. and Surg., Westminster Hospital, 1937. Served with RAF, 1943-46, and with 601 Squadron RAuxAF, 1947-57; retired rank Squdn Leader. Registrar (Med.), St Stephen's Hospital, 1947-50; Hon. Cons. Physician to Migraine Clinic, Putney Health Centre,

1950-68; Hon. Cons. in migraine to Royal Air Forces Assoc., 1947-; Hon. Cons Physician to Wendy Leyton Memorial Migraine Centre, Harley Street, 1961-; Sen. Medical Adviser, International Migraine Foundn, 1961-; Consulting Physician to Kingdom of Libya, 1968-69; MO, 1971-72, Chief MO, 1972-73, Gath's Mine Hosp., Mashaba, Rhodesia; Specialist Paediatrician, Estate Group Clinics, Lagos, Nigeria, 1975-76; Consultant Physician, County Hosp., Tralee, Eire, 1976-77. President, 601 Squadron RAuxAF Old Comrades Assoc., 1963-. Air Force Efficiency Medal, 1954. *Publications:* Migraine and Periodic Headache, 1952 (USA, 1954); Headaches, The Reason and the Relief, 1955 (USA); Migraine, 1962; Migraine, Modern Concepts and Preventative Treatment, 1964; contrib.: Lancet, British Medical Journal, Medical World and Journal, Lancet (USA), etc. *Recreations:* travel, riding, horse racing, lawn tennis (Cambridge Univ. Blue, 1933), squash racquets. *Address:* 49 Harrington Gardens, SW7. *Club:* Mashaba Lions.

LI, Choh-Ming, Hon. KBE 1973 (Hon. CBE 1967); Vice-Chancellor, The Chinese University of Hong Kong, since 1964; *b* 17 Feb. 1912; *s* of Kanchi Li and Mewching Tsu; *m* 1938, Sylvia Chi-wan Lu; two *s* one *d. Educ:* Univ. of California at Berkeley (MA, PhD). Prof. of Economics, Nankai and Southwest Associated and Central Univs in China, 1937-43; Mem., China's special mission to USA, Canada and UK, 1943-45; Dep. Dir-Gen., Chinese Nat. Relief and Rehabilitation Admin. (CNRRA), 1945-47; China's chief deleg. to UN Relief and Rehabilitation Confs and to UN Econ. Commn for Asia and Far East, 1947-49; Chm., Board of Trustees for Rehabilitation Affairs, Nat. Govt of China, 1949-50; Expert on UN Population Commn and Statistical Commn, 1952-57; Lectr, Assoc. Prof., and Prof. of Business Admin., and sometime Dir of Center for Chinese Studies, Univ. of California (Berkeley), 1951-63. Hon. Dr of Laws: Hong Kong, 1967; Michigan, 1967; Marquette, 1969; Western Ontario, 1970; Hon. Dr Social Science, Pittsburgh, 1969. Hon. Mem., Internat. Mark Twain Soc. Elise and Walter A. Haas Internat. Award, Univ. of California, 1974. *Publications:* Economic Development of Communist China, 1959; Statistical System of Communist China, 1962; (ed) Industrial Development in Communist China, 1964; (ed) Asian Workshop on Higher Education, 1969; The First Six Years, 1963-69, 1971; The Emerging University, 1970-74. *Recreations:* tennis, calligraphy. *Address:* The Vice-Chancellor's Residence, The Chinese University of Hong Kong, Shatin, New Territories, Hong Kong. *Clubs:* American, Country (Hong Kong).

LI, Fook Kow, CMG 1975; JP; Secretary for Home Affairs, Hong Kong, since 1977; *b* 5 June 1922; *s* of Tse Fong Li; *m* 1946, Edith Kwong Li; four *c. Educ:* Massachusetts Inst. of Technology (BSc,MSc). Mem. Hong Kong Admin. Service; Teacher, 1948-54; Resettlement Officer, 1955-58; Labour Officer, 1959-60; various posts in Colonial Secretariat, incl. Asst Sec., Asst Financial Sec., Asst Estabt Officer, Dep. Financial Sec. and Estabt Officer, 1961-69; Dep. Dir of Commerce and Industry, 1970; Dep. Sec. for Home Affairs, 1971-72; Dir of Social Welfare, 1972; Sec. for Social Services, 1973. JP Hong Kong, 1959. *Address:* Colonial Secretariat, Hong Kong. *T:* 5-95550. *Clubs:* Royal Hong Kong Jockey, Hong Kong Country, Chinese, Hong Kong (Hong Kong).

LI, Hon. Simon Fook Sean; Hon. Mr Justice Li; Puisne Judge, Hong Kong, since 1971; *b* 19 April 1922; 2nd *s* of late Koon Chun Li and late Tam Doy Hing Li; *m* Marie Veronica Lillian Yang; four *s* one *d. Educ:* King's Coll., Hong Kong; Hong Kong Univ.; Nat. Kwangsi Univ.; University Coll., London Univ. (LLB 1950). Barrister-at-Law, Lincoln's Inn, 1951. Crown Counsel, Attorney-General's Chambers, Hong Kong, 1953; Senior Crown Counsel, 1962; District Judge, Hong Kong, 1966. *Recreations:* hiking, swimming. *Address:* Puisne Judge's Chambers, Courts of Justice, Hong Kong. *T:* 5-236535. *Clubs:* Royal Commonwealth Society; Hong Kong, Chinese (Hong Kong).

LIARDET, Maj.-Gen. Henry Maughan, CB 1960; CBE 1945 (OBE 1942); DSO 1945; DL; *b* 27 Oct. 1906; *s* of late Maj.-Gen. Sir Claude Liardet, KBE, CB, DSO, TD, DL; *m* 1933, Joan Sefton, *d* of Major G. S. Constable, MC, JP; three *s. Educ:* Bedford School. 1st Commission for Territorial Army, 1924, Royal Artillery; Regular Commission, Royal Tank Corps, 1927; service UK, India, Egypt, 1927-38; Staff Coll., Camberley, 1939; War of 1939-45: War Office, 1939-41; active service in Egypt, N. Africa, Italy, 1941-45; General Staff appointments, command of Regiment and Brigade (despatches twice); idc, 1955; Chief of Staff, British Joint Services Mission (Army Staff), Washington, DC, 1956-58; ADC to the Queen, 1956-58; Director-General of Fighting Vehicles, WO, 1958-61; Deputy Master-General of the Ordnance, War Office, 1961-64, retired. Colonel Comdt, Royal Tank Regt, 1961-67. Dir, British Sailors' Soc., 1961; Chm.,

SS&AFA W Sussex Cttee, 1966-77. DL, Sussex, 1964-74, W Sussex 1974. West Sussex CC, 1964-74; Alderman, 1970-74. Pres. Sussex Council, Royal British Legion, 1975. *Recreations:* shooting, gardening. *Address:* Warningcamp House, Arundel, West Sussex. *T:* Arundel 882533. *Clubs:* Army and Navy; Sussex.

LIBBY, Dr Willard Frank; Professor of Chemistry, University of California, since 1959; Director, Institute of Geophysics, since 1962; *b* Grand Valley, Colorado, 17 Dec. 1908; *s* of Ora Edward Libby and Eva May (*née* Rivers); *m* 1940, Leonor Hickey (marr. diss. 1966); twin *d*; *m* 1966, Dr Leona Marshall. *Educ:* Grammar and High Sch., near Sebastopol, California; Univ. of California, Berkeley. BS, 1931; PhD, 1933. Instr of Chemistry, Univ. of California, 1933-38; Asst Prof., 1938-45; Associate Prof., 1945; Guggenheim Meml Foundn Fellowship, Princeton Univ., 1941; War work in Manhattan District Project Columbia Univ., (on leave from Univ. of Calif), 1941-45; Prof. of Chemistry, Dept of Chemistry, and Inst. for Nuclear Studies, now Enrico Fermi Inst. for Nuclear Studies, Univ. of Chicago, 1945-59; Research Associate, Washington Geophysical Lab., Carnegie Instn, 1954-59; Vis. Professor: Univ. of Colorado, Boulder, 1967-70; Univ. of S. Florida, Tampa, 1972-; Atomic Energy Commission: Mem., 1954-59; Cttee of Sen. Reviewers, 1945-52; Gen. Advisory Cttee, 1950-54, 1960-62; Member: AEC's Plowshare Advisory Cttee, 1959-72; Cttee of Selection, Guggenheim Memorial Foundn, 1959-; Edit. Board, Science, 1962-70. Consultant, Douglas Aircraft Co., 1962-69. Member: Air Resources Bd, Calif, 1967-72; Earthquake Council, Calif, 1972-; President's Task Force on Air Pollution, 1969-70; US-Japan Cttee on Scientific Co-operation, 1970-73; Advisor and Consultant to various cos, commns and univs. Mem., Editorial Bd, Space Life Science, 1970-. Pres. and Dir, Isotope Foundn. Holds hon. doctorates in Science. Nobel Prize for Chemistry, 1960. Has received numerous awards from universities and scientific institutions. Member: National Academy of Science; Royal Swedish Academy of Science, American Phil. Society; American Academy of Arts and Sciences; Heidelberg Academy Science; Amer. Nuclear Soc.; Corres. Fellow, British Acad.; Mem. several professional societies and fraternities. *Publications:* Radiocarbon Dating, 1952 (2nd edn, 1955); author of numerous articles appearing principally in scientific journals (Journal American Chemistry Society, Phys. Review, Proc. National Academy Science, Journal Geophys. Research, Science, etc.). *Recreations:* swimming, golf. *Address:* (office) Department of Chemistry, University of California, 405 Hilgard Avenue, Los Angeles, California 90024, USA. *T:* 825-1968. *Clubs:* Metropolitan, Century Association (New York); Cosmos (Washington, DC); Explorer's (Los Angeles).

LICHFIELD, 5th Earl of, *cr* 1831; **Thomas Patrick John Anson;** Viscount Anson and Baron Soberton, 1806; *b* 25 April 1939; *s* of Viscount Anson (Thomas William Arnold) (*d* 1958) and Princess Georg of Denmark (*née* Anne Fenella Ferelith Bowes-Lyon); *S* grandfather, 1960; *m* 1975, Lady Leonora Grosvenor, *d* of Duke of Westminster, *qv*; one *d*. *Educ:* Harrow Sch.; RMA, Sandhurst. Joined Regular Army, Sept. 1957, as Officer Cadet; Grenadier Guards, 1959-62 (Lieut). Now Photographer. FRPS; FIIP. *Heir: kinsman* Geoffrey Rupert Anson [*b* 28 Jan. 1929; *m* 1957, Verna Grace Hall; three *s* one *d*]. *Address:* 20 Aubrey Walk, W8. *T:* 01-727 4468; (seat) Shugborough Hall, Stafford. *T:* Little Haywood 881454. *Club:* Cavalry and Guards.

LICHFIELD, Bishop of, since 1975; **Rt. Rev. Kenneth John Fraser Skelton,** CBE 1972; *b* 16 May 1918; *s* of Henry Edmund and Kate Elizabeth Skelton; *m* 1945, Phyllis Barbara, *y d* of James Emerton; two *s* one *d*. *Educ:* Dulwich Coll.; Corpus Christi Coll., Cambridge; Wells Theological Coll. 1st Cl. Class. Tripos, Pt 1, 1939; 1st Cl. Theol. Tripos, Pt 1, 1940; BA 1940, MA 1944. Deacon, 1941; Priest, 1942; Curate: Normanton-by-Derby, 1941-43; Bakewell, 1943-45; Bolsover, 1945-46; Tutor, Wells Theol Coll., and Priest-Vicar, Wells Cathedral, 1946-50; Vicar of Howe Bridge, Atherton, 1950-55; Rector, Walton-on-the-Hill, Liverpool, 1955-62; Exam. Chap. to Bp of Liverpool, 1957-62; Bishop of Matabeleland, 1962-70; Asst Bishop, Dio. Durham, Rural Dean of Wearmouth and Rector of Bishopwearmouth, 1970-75. Select Preacher, Cambridge Univ., 1971, 1973. *Recreation:* Music. *Address:* Bishop's House, The Close, Lichfield, Staffs WS13 7LG.

LICHFIELD, Dean of; *see* Holderness, Rt Rev. G. E.

LICHFIELD, Prof. Nathaniel; Professor of Economics of Environmental Planning, University College London, since 1966; Senior Partner, Nathaniel Lichfield & Partners, Planning Development, Transportation and Economic Consultants, since 1962; *b* 29 Feb. 1916; 2nd *s* of Hyman Lichman and Fanny (*née* Grecht); *m* 1st, 1942, Rachel Goulden (*d* 1969); two *d*; 2nd,

1970, Dalia Kadury; one *s* one *d*. *Educ:* Raines Foundn Sch.; University of London. BSc (EstMan), PhD (Econ), PPRTPI, FRICS, CEng, MIMunE. From 1942 has worked continuously in urban and regional planning, specialising in econs of planning from 1950, with particular reference to social cost-benefit in planning and land policy; worked in local and central govt depts and private offices. Consultant commns in UK and abroad, incl. UN. Special Lectr, UCL, 1950. Vis. Prof., Univ. of California, Univ. of Tel Aviv, Hebrew Univ. Jerusalem, and Technion, Haifa. *Publications:* Economics of Planned Development, 1956; Cost Benefit Analysis in Urban Redevelopment, 1962; Cost Benefit Analysis in Town Planning: A Case Study of Cambridge, 1966; Israel's New Towns: A Development Strategy, 1971; (with Prof. A. Proudlove) Conservation and Traffic: a case study of York, 1975; (with Peter Kettle and Michael Whitbread) Evaluation in the Urban and Regional Planning Process, 1975; papers in Urban Studies, Regional Studies, Land Economics, Town Planning Review. *Recreation:* finding out less and less about more and more. *Address:* 13 Chalcot Gardens, Englands Lane, NW3 4YB. *T:* 01-586 0461. *Club:* Reform.

LICHINE, Mme David; *see* Riabouchinska, Tatiana.

LICKLEY, Robert Lang, CBE 1973; BSc; DIC; FRSE; CEng; FIMechE; FRAeS; AFAIAA; Head of Rolls Royce Support Staff, National Enterprise Board, since 1976; *b* Dundee, 19 Jan. 1912. *Educ:* Dundee High Sch.; Edinburgh Univ. (Hon. DSc 1972); Imperial Coll. (Fellow, 1973); FCGI 1976. Formerly: Professor of Aircraft Design, College of Aeronautics, Cranfield; Managing Director, Fairey Aviation Ltd; Hawker Siddeley Aviation Ltd, 1960-76 (Asst Man. Dir, 1965-76). Pres., IMechE, 1971. FRSE 1977. *Recreation:* golf. *Address:* National Enterprise Board, 12/18 Grosvenor Gardens, SW1.

LICKORISH, Leonard John, CBE 1975; Director General, British Tourist Authority, since 1970; *b* 10 Aug. 1921; *s* of Adrian J. and Josephine Lickorish; *m* 1945, Eileen Maris Wright; one *s*. *Educ:* St George's Coll., Weybridge; University Coll., London (BA). Served RAF, 1941-46. British Travel Association: Research Officer, 1946; Asst Dir Gen, 1955; Gen. Man., 1963. Officer of Crown of Belgium, 1967. *Publications:* The Travel Trade, 1955; The Statistics of Tourism, 1975; numerous for nat. and internat. organisations on internat. travel. *Recreations:* sailing, gardening. *Address:* 46 Hillway, Highgate, N6 6EP. *Clubs:* Royal Over-seas League, Royal Automobile.

LIDBURY, Sir Charles, Kt, *cr* 1941; Director of Westminster Bank Ltd, and of Westminster Foreign Bank Ltd, 1935-62; *b* 30 June 1880; *s* of Frank Albert Lidbury; *m* 1909, Mary (*d* 1939), *d* of George Moreton, Kinderton Hall, Middlewich, Cheshire; two *d*. General Manager Westminster Foreign Bank Ltd, 1928-47; General Manager, Westminster Bank Ltd, 1927-30; Chief General Manager Westminster Bank Ltd, 1930-47; President of Institute of Bankers, 1939-46. *Address:* Winter Field, Melbury Abbas, Shaftesbury, Dorset. *T:* Shaftesbury 2274.

LIDBURY, Sir John (Towersey), Kt 1971; FRAeS; Vice-Chairman, since 1974, Deputy Managing Director, since 1970, Hawker Siddeley Group Ltd (Director, 1960); *b* 25 Nov. 1912; *m* 1939, Audrey Joyce (*née* Wigzell); one *s* two *d*. *Educ:* Owen's Sch. Joined Hawker Aircraft Ltd, 1940; Dir, 1951, Gen. Manager, 1953, Man. Dir, 1959, Chm., 1961; Jt Man. Dir, Hawker Siddeley Aviation Ltd, 1959, Dir and Chief Exec., 1961, Dep. Chm. and Man. Dir, 1963-77; Chm., Hawker Siddeley Dynamics Ltd, 1971-77 (Dep. Chm., 1970); Dep. Chm., High Duty Alloys Ltd, 1971-; Dir, Hawker Siddeley International Ltd, 1963-; Pres., 1969-70, Mem. Council, 1959-77, Soc. of British Aerospace Companies Ltd. FBIM. JP Kingston-upon-Thames, 1952-62. *Address:* 18 St James's Square, SW1Y 4LJ. *T:* 01-930 6177.

LIDDELL, family name of **Baron Ravensworth.**

LIDDELL, Dr Donald Woollven; FRCP 1964; FRCPsych; Head of Department of Psychological Medicine, King's College Hospital; *b* 31 Dec. 1917; *m* 1954, Emily (*née* Horsfall); one *s* one *d*. *Educ:* Aldenham Sch.; London Hospital. MRCP 1941; Neurological training as RMO, The National Hospital, Queen Square, 1942-45; Psychiatric training, Edinburgh and Maudsley Hospital. Medical Superintendent, St Francis Hospital, Haywards Heath, 1957-61; retired as Physician to Bethlem and Maudsley Hosps, 1968. Examr to RCP and RCPsych. Founder FRCPsych, 1971. *Publications:* contrib. Journal of Mental Science, Journal of Neurology, Psychiatry and Neuro-surgery, American Journal of Mental Diseases, Journal of Social Psychology. *Address:* 49 Bury Walk, SW3.

LIDDELL, Edward George Tandy, FRS 1939; MD, BCh, MA, Oxon; *b* 25 March 1895; *yr s* of Dr John Liddell, Harrogate, and Annie Louisa (*née* Tandy); *m* 1923, Constance Joan Mitford, *y d* of late Dr B. M. H. Rogers; three *s* one *d. Educ:* Summer Fields; Harrow; Trinity Coll., Oxon; St Thomas' Hospital. 1st class Physiology Finals, Oxford, 1918; Asst Serum Dept, Lister Institute, 1918; Senior Demy, Magdalen Coll., Oxford, 1918; BM Oxon, 1921; Fellow of Trinity Coll., Oxford, 1921-40; University Lecturer in Physiology, Oxford Univ., 1921-40; Waynflete Professor of Physiology, Oxford, 1940-60; Professor Emeritus, 1960; Fellow of Magdalen Coll., 1940-60, Emeritus Fellow, 1970. Formerly: Mem., Hebdomadal Council, Gen. Bd, Bodleian Curators, Oxford Univ.; Chm., Oxford Eye Hosp.; Examr, Oxford, Cambridge, London, Sheffield Univs. Osler Meml Medal, Oxford Univ., 1975. *Publications:* Papers, various since 1923, on physiology of central nervous system, published in Journal Physiol., Brain, Proc. Royal Society, Quarterly Journal of Experimental Physiology; assistant author of Sherrington's Mammalian Physiology, 1929; Reflex Activity of the Spinal Cord, 1932 (jointly); The Discovery of Reflexes, 1960. *Recreation:* FRHS. *Address:* 69 Old High Street, Headington, Oxford OX3 9HT.

LIDDELL, (John) Robert; author; *b* 13 Oct. 1908; *e s* of late Major J. S. Liddell, CMG, DSO, and Anna Gertrude Morgan. *Educ:* Haileybury Coll.; Corpus Christi Coll., Oxford. Lecturer in Universities of Cairo and Alexandria, 1942-51, and assistant professor of English, Cairo Univ., 1951; Head of English Dept, Athens Univ., 1963-68. *Publications:* The Last Enchantments, 1948; The Rivers of Babylon, 1959; An Object for a Walk, 1966; The Deep End, 1968; Stepsons, 1969, and other novels; A Treatise on the Novel, 1947; Aegean Greece, 1954; The Novels of I. Compton-Burnett, 1955; Byzantium and Istanbul, 1956; The Morea, 1958; The Novels of Jane Austen, 1963; Mainland Greece, 1965; Cavafy: a critical biography, 1974; The Novels of George Eliot, 1977. *Address:* c/o Barclays Bank, High Street, Oxford.

LIDDELL, Laurence Ernest, CBE 1976; ERD, TD; Director, Department of Physical Education, University of Edinburgh, since 1959; *b* Co. Durham, 27 Oct. 1916; *m* 1940, Alys Chapman, Askrigg, Yorks; two *s* one *d. Educ:* Yorebridge Grammar Sch.; Leeds Univ. (BA); Carnegie Coll. (DipPE). Schoolmaster, Aysgarth Sch., 1938-39; Reserve and Territorial Officer, The Royal Scots, 1939-59; served in France and Belgium (wounded, despatches), 1939-40; served in E Africa, 1944-45; Lectr in Educn, King's Coll., Durham Univ., 1946-59; Lt-Col comdg Univ. OTC, 1955-59; Chm., Adv. Sports Council for Scotland, 1968-71; Chm., Main Stadium Cttee for 1970 Commonwealth Games in Edinburgh, 1967-70; Mem., UK Sports Councils, 1968-75; Chm., Scottish Sports Council, 1972-75. *Publications:* Batsmanship, 1958; (jtly) Orienteering, 1965. *Recreations:* golf; formerly: cricket (played for Univ., Army, 11 yrs Captain Northumberland, MCC, Captain English Minor Counties XI v NZ, 1958); Association football (played for Univ. and Yorks Amateurs); hockey (played for Northumberland and English Northern Counties). *Address:* 11 Claverhouse Drive, Edinburgh EH16 6BR. *T:* 031-664 2198. *Clubs:* Lord's Taverners; Lowland Brigade (Edinburgh).

LIDDELL, Peter John, DSC 1944; MA; Chairman, North West Water Authority, since 1973; Member, National Water Council, since 1973; *b* 2 June 1921; *s* of Comdr Lancelot Charles Liddell, OBE, RN, and Rosalie Liddell (*née* Ballantyne); *m* 1st, 1948, Dorothy Priscilla Downes; two *s* one *d*; 2nd, 1960, Helen Ann, *d* of Rear-Adm. A. W. Laybourne, CB, CBE, and of Helen (*née* Burnett). *Educ:* Ampleforth; Wadham Coll., Oxford (MA). Served RNVR, 1940-46 (DSC). Member: Cumberland River Board, 1954-65; Cumberland River Authority, 1964-74 (Vice-Chm., 1967-70, Chm., 1970-73); Chm., Assoc. of River Authorities, 1971-74 (Vice-Chm., 1969-71; Chm. Fisheries Cttee, 1966-71); Mem. Internat. Adv. Gp, Internat. Salmon Foundn, NYC, 1970- (Chm., 1970-72); President: Inst. of Fisheries Management, 1972- (Vice-Pres. 1969-72); River Eden and District Fisheries Assoc., 1970- (Chm. 1956-70). Mem. Exec. Cttee: Central Council of Physical Recreation, 1968-73; Salmon and Trout Assoc.; Atlantic Salmon Res. Trust Ltd; Scottish Salmon Angling Fedn; Cumberland and Westmorland Playing Fields Assoc. Mem., The Sports Council, 1969-71; Chm., Northern Sports Council, 1971-74 (Dep. Chm., 1967-71); Vice-Chm., Standing Conf. of Northern Sport and Recreation, 1967-71; Member: Fisheries Adv. Cttee, Water Resources Bd, 1967-71; Inland Waterways Amenity Adv. Council, 1971-74; Water Cttee, Country Landowners Assoc., 1971-75, and 1977-; British Cttee, Internat. Water Supply Assoc., 1971- (Chm., 1974-); Water Space Amenity Commn; Council, Freshwater Biological Assoc. (Hon. Treas., 1975-); Council, Estuarine and Brackish Water Sciences Assoc. Membre d'Honneur, Assoc.

Nat. de Défense des Rivières à Saumons, Paris. Winston Churchill Travelling Fellowship, 1968. FZS, FIFM. Vis. Fellow, Univ. of Salford. Freeman: City of Newcastle upon Tyne, 1953; City of London, 1969. *Publications:* The Salmon Rivers of Eire: a report, 1971; articles in various jls, yearbooks, etc. *Recreations:* fishing, shooting, following all forms of sport and recreation. *Address:* Moorhouse Hall, Warwick-on-Eden, Carlisle CA4 8PA. *T:* Wetheral 60356; 30d Cadogan Square, SW1. *T:* 01-584 4660. *Clubs:* White's, Beefsteak, Flyfishers', MCC; The Brook (NY); Cumberland County (Carlisle).

LIDDELL, Robert; see Liddell, J. R.

LIDDERDALE, Sir David (William Shuckburgh), KCB 1975 (CB 1963); Clerk of the House of Commons, 1974-76; *b* 30 Sept. 1910; *s* of late Edward Wadsworth and Florence Amy Lidderdale; *m* 1943, Lola, *d* of late Rev. Thomas Alexander Beckett, Tubbercurry and Ballinew; one *s. Educ:* Winchester; King's Coll., Cambridge (MA). Assistant Clerk, House of Commons, 1934. Served War of 1939-45, The Rifle Brigade; active service, N Africa and Italy. Senior Clerk, 1946, Fourth Clerk at the Table, 1953, Second Clerk Assistant, 1959, Clerk Assistant, 1962, House of Commons. Joint Secretary, Assoc. of Secretaries-General of Parliaments (Inter-Parliamentary Union), 1946-54, Mem., 1954-76, Vice-Pres., 1973-76, Hon. Vice-Pres., 1976. *Publications:* The Parliament of France, 1951; (with Lord Campion) European Parliamentary Procedure, 1953; (ed) Erskine May's Parliamentary Practice, 19th edn, 1976. *Recreation:* walking. *Address:* 46 Cheyne Walk, SW3. *T:* 01-352 0432. *Clubs:* Travellers', MCC.

LIDDIARD, Richard England; Chairman, Czarnikow Group Ltd, since 1974; *b* 21 Sept. 1917; *s* of late E. S. Liddiard, MBE, and M. A. Brooke; *m* 1943, Constance Lily, *d* of late Sir William J. Rook; one *s* three *d. Educ:* Oundle; Worcester Coll., Oxford (MA). Lt-Col, Royal Signals, 1939-46. Chairman: C. Czarnikow Ltd, 1958-74; Sugar Assoc. of London, 1959-; British Fedn of Commodity Assocs, 1962-70, Vice-Chm., 1970-77; London Commodity Exchange, 1972-76; Mem., Cttee on Invisible Exports, 1966-70. Mem. Ct of Assts, Worshipful Co. of Haberdashers, 1958, Master 1977. FRSA. MC (Poland), 1941. *Recreation:* golf. *Address:* Oxford Lodge, 52 Parkside, Wimbledon, SW19. *T:* 01-946 3434. *Club:* Junior Carlton.

LIDDIARD, Ronald; Director of Social Services, Birmingham, since 1974; *b* 26 July 1932; *s* of Tom and Gladys Liddiard; *m* 1957, June Alexandra (*née* Ford); two *d. Educ:* Canton High Sch., Cardiff; Colleges of Commerce and Technology, Cardiff; Birmingham Univ. Dip. Municipal Admin, Certif. Social Work. Administrator, 1958-60; Social Worker, 1960-64; Sen. Administrator, 1964-70; Dir of Social Services, Bath, 1971-74. *Publications:* articles in social work and health jls. *Address:* Snow Hill House, 10-15 Livery Street, Birmingham B3 2PE. *T:* 021-235 2992.

LIDDLE, Sir Donald (Ross), Kt 1971; JP; DL; Chairman, Cumbernauld Development Corporation, since 1972; *b* 11 Oct. 1906; *s* of Thomas Liddle, Bonnington, Edinburgh; *m* 1933, May, *d* of R. Christie, Dennistoun, Glasgow; one *s* two *d. Educ:* Allen Glen's School, Glasgow. Served War of 1939-45 with RAOC, Burma and India; Major, 1944. DL, County of Glasgow, 1963; JP 1968; Lord Provost of Glasgow, 1969-72. Chm., Scottish Tourist Consultative Council, 1973-. CStJ 1970. Hon. LLD Strathclyde, 1971. *Address:* 15 Riddrie Crescent, Riddrie Knowes, Glasgow G33 2QG. *Clubs:* Army and Navy; Conservative (Glasgow).

LIESNER, Hans Hubertus; Chief Economic Adviser, Departments of Industry, Trade and Prices and Consumer Protection, since 1976; *b* 30 March 1929; *e s* of Curt Liesner, lawyer, and Edith L. (*née* Neumann); *m* 1968, Thelma Seward; one *s* one *d. Educ:* German grammar schs; Bristol Univ. (BA); Nuffield Coll., Oxford; MA Cantab. Asst Lectr, later Lectr, in Economics, London Sch. of Economics, 1955-59; Lectr in Economics, Univ. of Cambridge; Fellow, Dir of Studies in Economics and some time Asst Bursar, Emmanuel Coll., Cambridge, 1959-70; Under-Sec. (Economics), HM Treasury, 1970-76. *Publications:* The Import Dependence of Britain and Western Germany, 1957; Case Studies in European Economic Union: the mechanics of integration (with J. E. Meade and S. J. Wells), 1962; Atlantic Harmonisation: making free trade work, 1968; Britain and the Common Market: the effect of entry on the pattern of manufacturing production (with S. S. Han), 1971; articles in jls, etc. *Recreations:* ski-ing, cine-photography. *Address:* 32 The Grove, Brookmans Park, Herts AL9 7RN. *T:* Potters Bar 53269. *Club:* Reform.

LIFAR, Serge; Dancer, Choreographer, Writer, Painter; Director, Université de Danse, since 1958; Professeur de Chorélogie, Sorbonne; Maître de Ballet, Théâtre National de l'Opéra, Paris, since 1968 (formerly Professeur); *b* Kieff, South Russia, 2 April 1905; *s* of Michel Lifar. Pupil of Bronislava Nijinska, 1921; joined Diaghileff company, Paris, 1923; studied under Cecchetti. Dir, Institut Chorégraphique, 1947-75. First London appearance, in Cimarosiana and Les Fâcheux, Coliseum, 1924. Choreographer (for first time) of Stravinsky's Renard, 1929; produced Prométhée, Opera House, Paris, 1929. Cochran's 1930 Revue, London Pavilion, 1930; returned to Paris, produced and danced in Bacchus and Ariadne, Le Spectre de la Rose, Giselle, and L'Après-midi d'un Faune, 1932; Icare, David Triomphant, Le Roi Nu, 1936; Alexandre le Grand, 1937; arranged season of Ballet at the Cambridge, London, 1946; Choreographer of Noces Fantastiques, Romeo et Juliette (Prokofiev), 1955. Paintings exhibited: Paris, 1972; Cannes, 1974; Monte Carlo, Florence, Venice, London. Prix de l'Académie Française; Corres. Mem., Institut de France. *Publications:* Traditional to Modern Ballet, 1938; Diaghilev, a biography, 1940; A History of Russian Ballet from its Origins to the Present Day (trans. 1954); The Three Graces, 1959; Ma Vie, 1965 (in Eng., 1969). *Address:* Villa les Lauriers, avenue du Commandant-Bret, 06 Cannes, France.

LIFFORD, 8th Viscount *cr* 1781; **Alan William Wingfield Hewitt;** *b* 11 Dec. 1900; 2nd but *o* surv. *s* of Hon. George Wyldbore Hewitt (*d* 1924; 7th *s* of 4th Viscount Lifford) and Elizabeth Mary, *e d* of late Charles Rampini, DL, LLD, Advocate; *S kinsman* 1954; *m* 1935, Alison Mary Patricia, *d* of T. W. Ashton, The Cottage, Hursley, nr Winchester; one *s* three *d*. *Educ:* Winchester; RMC, Sandhurst. Lieut late Hampshire Regt. *Heir: s* Hon. Edward James Wingfield Hewitt [*b* 27 Jan. 1949; *m* 1976, Alison, *d* of Robert Law]. *Address:* Field House, Hursley, Hants. *T:* Hursley 75203.
See also Sir Anthony Swann, Bt.

LIGGINS, Sir Edmund (Naylor), Kt 1976; TD 1947; Solicitor; *b* 21 July 1909; *s* of Arthur William and Hannah Louisa Liggins; *m* 1952, Celia Jean Lawrence, *d* of William Henry and Millicent Lawrence; three *s* one *d*. *Educ:* King Henry VIII Sch., Coventry; Rydal Sch. Joined TA, 1936; commissioned 45th Bn (RWR), RE; served War: comd 399 Battery, RA, subseq. 498 LAA Battery, RA, 1942-45. Subseq. commanded 198 Indep. Battery, RA, 1948-51. Senior Partner, Liggins & Co., Solicitors, Coventry and Leamington Spa. Elected Mem. Council, Law Society, 1963, Vice-Pres., 1974-75, Pres., 1975-76 (Chm., Non-Contentious Business Cttee of Council, 1968-71; Chm., Educn and Trng Cttee, 1973-74); Chm., West Midland Legal Aid Area Cttee, 1963-64; Pres., Warwickshire Law Soc., 1969-70. Mem., Court of Univ. of Warwick. Hon. Mem., Amer. Bar Assoc. *Recreations:* cricket, rugby football, squash rackets; amateur theatre. *Address:* Hareway Cottage, Hareway Lane, Barford, Warwickshire CV35 8DB. *T:* Barford 246. *Clubs:* MCC, Forty, Eccentric; Coventry and North Warwickshire Cricket, Drapers' (Coventry).

LIGHT, (Sidney) David; Under Secretary, Civil Service Department, since 1975; *b* 9 Dec. 1919; *s* of late William Light; *m* Edna Margaret Honey; one *s*. *Educ:* King Edward VI Sch., Southampton. RAF, 1940-46. HM Customs and Excise, 1938; HM Treasury, 1948-68; Asst Sec., CS Commn, 1969-75. *Recreations:* watching cricket, travel. *Address:* The Hill Cottage, Upton Grey, Hants RG25 2RA. *T:* Long Sutton 433. *Clubs:* Royal Commonwealth Society; Hampshire Cricket.

LIGHTBODY, Ian (Macdonald), CMG 1974; Secretary for Administration, Hong Kong Government, since 1977; *b* 19 Aug. 1921; *s* of Thomas Paul Lightbody and Dorothy Marie Louise Lightbody (*née* Cooper); *m* 1954, Noreen, *d* of late Captain T. H. Wallace, Dromore, Co. Down; three *s* one *d*. *Educ:* Queens Park Sch., Glasgow; Glasgow Univ. (MA). War service, Indian Army, India and Far East, 1942-46 (Captain); Colonial Admin. Service, Hong Kong, 1945; various admin. posts; District Comr, New Territories, 1967-68; Defence Sec., 1968-69; Coordinator, Festival of Hong Kong, 1969; Comr for Resettlement, 1971; Sec. for Housing and Chm., Hong Kong Housing Authority, 1973-77. MLC 1971; MEC 1977. *Recreation:* walking. *Address:* 6 Mount Kellett Road, The Peak, Hong Kong. *Clubs:* Hong Kong, Royal Hong Kong Jockey.

LIGHTBOWN, Ronald William, MA, FSA, FRAS; Keeper of the Library, Victoria and Albert Museum, since 1976; *b* Darwen, Lancs, 2 June 1932; *s* of Vincent Lightbown and Helen Anderson Burness; *m* 1962, Mary Dorothy Webster; one *s*. *Educ:* St Catharine's Coll., Cambridge (MA). FSA, FRAS. Victoria and Albert Museum: Asst Keeper, Library, 1958-64; Asst Keeper, Dept of Metalwork, 1964-73; Dep. Keeper,

Library, 1973-76. *Publications'* Catalogue of Italian Sculpture (pt author), V&A Museum, 1964; Catalogue of Scandinavian and Baltic Silver, V&A Museum, 1975; Catalogue of French Silver, V&A Museum, 1977; French Secular Goldsmith's work of the Middle Ages, 1978; Sandro Botticelli, 1978; many articles in learned jls, incl. Burlington Magazine, Warburg Jl and Art Bulletin. *Recreations:* reading, travel, music, conversation. *Address:* Victoria and Albert Museum, Exhibition Road, SW7 2RL. *T:* 01-589 6371.

LIGHTHILL, Sir (Michael) James, Kt 1971; FRS 1953; FRAeS; Lucasian Professor of Mathematics, University of Cambridge, since 1969; *b* 23 Jan. 1924; *s* of E. B. Lighthill; *m* 1945, Nancy Alice Dumaresq; one *s* four *d*. *Educ:* Winchester Coll.; Trinity Coll., Cambridge. Aerodynamics Division, National Physical Laboratory, 1943-45; Fellow, Trinity Coll., Cambridge, 1945-49; Sen. Lectr in Maths, Univ. of Manchester, 1946-50; Beyer Prof. of Applied Mathematics, Univ. of Manchester, 1950-59; Dir, RAE, Farnborough, 1959-64; Royal Soc. Res. Prof., Imperial Coll., 1964-69. Chm., Academic Adv. Cttee, Univ. of Surrey, 1964; Member: Adv. Council on Technology, 1964; NERC, 1965-70; Shipbuilding Inquiry Cttee, 1965; (part-time) Post Office Bd, 1972-74; First Pres., Inst. of Mathematics and its Applications, 1964-66; a Sec. and Vice-Pres., Royal Soc., 1965-69; Pres., Internat. Commn on Mathematical Instruction, 1971-74. FRAeS 1961. Foreign Member: American Academy of Arts and Sciences, 1958; American Philosophical Soc., 1970; US Nat. Acad. of Sciences, 1976; US Nat. Acad. of Engineering, 1977. Associate Mem., French Acad. of Sciences, 1976. Hon. Fellow American Inst. of Aeronautics and Astronautics, 1961. Hon. DSc: Liverpool, 1961; Leicester, 1965; Strathclyde, 1966; Essex, 1967; Princeton, 1967; East Anglia, 1968; Manchester, 1968; Bath, 1969; St Andrews, 1969; Surrey, 1969; Cranfield, 1974; Paris, 1975; Aachen, 1975. Royal Medal, Royal Society, 1964; Gold Medal, Royal Aeronautical Society, 1965, etc. Comdr Order of Léopold, 1963. *Publications:* Introduction to Fourier Analysis and Generalised Functions, 1958; Mathematical Biofluiddynamics, 1975; Newer Uses of Mathematics, 1977; Waves in Fluids, 1978; articles in Royal Soc. Proc. and Trans, Qly Jl of Mechanics and Applied Maths, Philosophical Magazine, Jl of Aeronautical Scis, Qly Jl of Maths, Aeronautical Qly, Communications on Pure and Applied Maths, Proc. Cambridge Philosophical Soc., Jl of Fluid Mechanics, Reports and Memoranda of ARC; contrib. to Modern Developments in Fluid Dynamics: High Speed Flow; High Speed Aerodynamics and Jet Propulsion; Surveys in Mechanics; Laminar Boundary Layers. *Recreations:* music and swimming. *Address:* Department of Applied Mathematics and Theoretical Physics, Silver Street, Cambridge CB3 9EW. *Club:* Athenæum.

LIGHTMAN, Harold, QC 1955; Master of the Bench of Lincoln's Inn; *b* 8 April 1906; *s* of Louis Lightman, Leeds; *m* 1936, Gwendoline Joan, *d* of David Ostrer, London; three *s*. *Educ:* City of Leeds Sch.; privately. Accountant, 1927-29. Barrister, Lincoln's Inn, 1932. Home Guard, 1940-45. Defence Medal, 1946. Liveryman, Company of Glovers, 1960. *Recreations:* cooking, reading. *Address:* Stone Buildings, Lincoln's Inn, WC2. *T:* 01-242 3840; Dial Cottage, Withyham Road, Cooden, Sussex. *Club:* Royal Automobile.

LIGHTMAN, Ivor Harry; Under Secretary, Food Prices and Distribution Division, Department of Prices and Consumer Protection, since 1976; *b* 23 Aug. 1928; *s* of late Abraham Lightman, OBE and Mary (*née* Goldschneider); *m* 1950, Stella Doris Blend; one *s*. *Educ:* Abergele Grammar Sch. Clerical Officer, Min. of Food, 1946; Nat. Service, RAOC (Corp.), 1946-49; Officer of Customs and Excise, 1949-56; Asst Principal, Ministry of Works, 1957; Asst Private Sec. to successive Ministers, 1959-60; Principal, Ministry of Works, 1961-65; Sec., Banwell Cttee on Construction Contracts, 1962-64; Principal, HM Treasury, 1965-67; Asst Sec., MPBW, 1967-70; Asst Sec., CSD, 1970-73; Under Sec., Price Commn, 1973-76. *Recreations:* local amenity preservation society, talking. *Address:* 22 Walkerscroft Mead, West Dulwich, SE21. *T:* 01-670 4743.

LIGHTMAN, Lionel; Under-Secretary, Department of Trade, since 1975; *b* 26 July 1928; *s* of late Abner Lightman and late Gitli Lightman (*née* Szmul); *m* 1952, Helen, *y d* of late Rev. A. Shechter and late Mrs Shechter; two *d*. *Educ:* City of London Sch.; Wadham Coll., Oxford (MA). Nat. Service, RAEC, 1951-53 (Temp. Captain). Asst Principal, BoT, 1953; Private Sec. to Perm. Sec., 1957; Principal 1958; Trade Comr, Ottawa, 1960-64; Asst Sec. 1967; Asst Dir, Office of Fair Trading, 1973-75. *Address:* 55 The Pryors, East Heath Road, NW3 1BP. *T:* 01-435 3427.

LIGHTON, Sir Christopher Robert, 8th Bt, *cr* 1791; MBE 1945; *b* 30 June 1897; *o s* of 7th Bt and Helen (*d* 1927), *d* of late James

Houldsworth, Coltness, Lanarkshire; *S* father, 1929; *m* 1st, 1926, Rachel Gwendoline (marr. diss. 1953), *yr d* of late Rear-Admiral W. S. Goodridge, CIE; two *d*; 2nd, 1953, Horatia Edith, *d* of A. T. Powlett, Godminster Manor, Bruton, Somerset; one *s*. *Educ:* Eton Coll.; RMC. Late The King's Royal Rifle Corps; rejoined the Army in Aug. 1939 and served War of 1939-45. *Heir: s* Thomas Hamilton Lighton, *b* 4 Nov. 1954. *Address:* Elphinstone House, North Berwick, East Lothian.

LIGHTWOOD, Reginald, MD; FRCP; DPH; Consulting Physician to The Hospital for Sick Children, Great Ormond Street, London, and Consulting Paediatrician to St Mary's Hospital, London, since 1963; *b* 1898; *s* of late John M. Lightwood, Barrister-at-Law, and Gertrude (*née* Clench); *m* 1937, Monica Guise Bicknell, *d* of Laurance G. Ray; two *s*. *Educ:* Monkton Combe Sch., Bath. Served European War in Royal Artillery, 1917-19. Jelf Medal and Alfred Hughes Memorial Prize, King's Coll., London, 1919; MD (London), 1924, FRCP 1936. Hon. Medical Staff: Westminster Hospital, 1933-39 (resigned); Hospital for Sick Children, Great Ormond Street, London, 1935-63; St Mary's Hospital, London, 1939-63; Prof. of Pediatrics, American University of Beirut, 1964 and 1965, and Civilian Consultant to Royal Jordanian Army Medical Service; Prof. of Paediatrics and Child Health, University Coll. of Rhodesia, 1966-69. Kenneth Blackfan Memorial Lecturer, Harvard Medical Sch., 1953; Visiting Prof. of Pediatrics: Boston Univ., 1966; Univ. of Calif, Los Angeles, 1969. Cons. Pædiatrician to Internat. Grenfell Assoc., Newfoundland, 1970-71. Pres., British Pædiatric Assoc., 1959-60; FRSM; Hon. Fellow, Amer. Acad. of Pediatrics; Mem., Irish Pædiatric Soc.; Hon. Member: Swedish Pædiatric Soc.; Portuguese Pædiatric Soc.; Mark Twain Soc. of America; corresp. Member: Société de Pédiatrie de Paris; Amer. Pediatric Soc. *Publications:* Textbooks: Pædiatrics for the Practitioner (ed jtly with Prof. W. Gaisford); Sick Children (with Dr F. S. W. Brimblecombe and Dr D. Barltrop); scientific papers and articles on pædiatrics in medical journals, textbooks, etc. *Address:* c/o Paediatric Unit, St Mary's Hospital Medical School, Norfolk Place, Praed Street, W2. *Club:* Bath.

LILEY, Sir (Albert) William, KCMG 1973 (CMG 1967); PhD; FRSNZ; FRCOG; Professor in Perinatal Physiology, New Zealand Medical Research Council Postgraduate School of Obstetrics and Gynæcology, University of Auckland; *b* 12 March 1929; *s* of Albert Harvey Liley; *m* 1953, Helen Margaret Irwin, *d* of William Irwin Hunt; two *s* three *d*, and one adopted *d*. *Educ:* Auckland Grammar Sch.; University of Auckland; University of Otago; Australian National Univ.; Columbia Univ. BMedSc 1952; MB, ChB (UNZ) 1954; PhD (ANU) 1957; Dip. Obst. (UA) 1962; FRSNZ 1964; FRCOG 1971. Research Schol. in Physiology, ANU, 1955-56. Sandoz Research Fellow in Obstetrics, Postgrad. Sch. of Obstetrics and Gynæcology, 1957-58; NZMRC Research Fellow in Obstetrics, 1959-. United States Public Health Service Internat. Research Fellowship, 1964-65. Hon. FACOG, 1975. Hon. DSc Victoria Univ., Wellington, 1971. *Publications:* numerous articles in physiological, obstetric and pædiatric journals. *Recreations:* farming, forestry. *Address:* 19 Pukenui Road, Epsom, Auckland 3, New Zealand. *T:* 656-433.

LILFORD, 7th Baron, *cr* 1797; **George Vernon Powys;** *b* 8 Jan. 1931; *s* of late Robert Horace Powys (*g g grandson* of 2nd Baron) and of Vera Grace Bryant, Rosebank, Cape, SA; *S* kinsman, 1949; *m* 1st, 1954, Mrs Eve Bird (marr. diss.); 2nd, 1957, Anuta Merritt (marr. diss., 1958); 3rd, 1958, Norma Yvonne Shell (marr. diss., 1961); 4th, 1961, Mrs Muriel Spottiswoode (marr. diss., 1969); two *d*; 5th, 1969, Margaret Penman; one *s* two *d*. *Educ:* St Aidan's Coll., Grahamstown, SA; Stonyhurst Coll. *Recreations:* boating, cricket. *Heir: s* Hon. Mark Vernon Powys, *b* 16 Nov. 1975. *Address:* Buitenzorg, Pagasvlei Road, Constantia, 7800 Cape, S Africa.

LILIENTHAL, David Eli; Business Executive; Author; *b* Morton, Ill., 8 July 1899; *s* of Leo Lilienthal and Minna Rosenak; *m* 1923, Helen Marian Lamb; one *s* one *d*. *Educ:* DePauw Univ. (AB, LLD); LLB Harvard, 1923. Admitted Illinois bar, 1923; practised law, Chicago, 1923-31; Wisconsin Public Service Commn, 1931-33; Director, Tennessee Valley Authority, 1933 (Chairman 1941-46); Chairman, State Dept Board of Consultants on international control of atomic energy, 1946; Chairman, US Atomic Energy Commn, 1946-50; Chairman, Development and Resources Corporation, 1955-; Member of: Delta Upsilon, Delta Sigma Rho, Sigma Delta Chi, Phi Beta Kappa, American Academy of Arts and Sciences; Amer. Philosoph. Soc.; Iran Council of Asia Soc., NY; Trustee, The Twentieth Century Fund. Freedom Award, 1949; Public Welfare Medal of National Academy of Science, 1951. Holds Hon. Doctorates from Institutions in USA; also foreign awards;

Commendador de la Orden El Sol del Peru, 1964; Order of Rio Blanco, Brazil, 1972. *Publications:* TVA-Democracy on the March, 1944; This I Do Believe, 1949; Big Business: A New Era, 1953; The Multinational Corporation, 1960; Change, Hope and the Bomb, 1963; The Journals of David E. Lilienthal, Vols I and II, 1964; Vol. III, 1966; Vol. IV, 1969; Vol. V, 1971; Vol. VI, 1976; Management: a Humanist Art, 1967; articles in miscellaneous periodicals. *Recreations:* gardening, small-boat sailing. *Address:* (home) 88 Battle Road, Princeton, NJ 08540, USA; (office) 1271 Avenue of the Americas, New York, NY 10020, USA. *Clubs:* Century Association (New York).

LILL, John Richard; concert pianist; Professor at Royal College of Music; *b* 17 March 1944; *s* of George and Margery Lill. *Educ:* Leyton County High Sch.; Royal College of Music. FRCM; Hon. FTCL; FLCM. Gulbenkian Fellowship, 1967. First concert at age of 9; Royal Festival Hall debut, 1963; Promenade Concert debut, 1969. Numerous broadcasts on radio and TV; has appeared as soloist with all leading British orchestras. Recitals and concertos throughout Great Britain, Europe, USA, Canada, Scandinavia, USSR, Japan and Far East, Australia, New Zealand, etc. Overseas tours as soloist with many orchestras including London Symphony Orchestra and London Philharmonic Orchestra. Complete recordings of Beethoven sonatas and concertos. Chappell Gold Medal; Pauer Prize; 1st Prize, Royal Over-Seas League Music Competition, 1963; Dinu Lipatti Medal in Harriet Cohen Internat. Awards; 1st Prize, Internat. Tchaikovsky Competition, Moscow, 1970. *Recreations:* chess, walking, avoiding news media. *Address:* c/o Harold Holt Ltd, 134 Wigmore Street, W1H 9FF. *T:* 01-935 2331.

LILLEY, Prof. Geoffrey Michael, CEng, FRAeS, MIMechE, FIMA; Head of Department of Aeronautics and Astronautics, University of Southampton, since 1964; *b* Isleworth, Mddx, 16 Nov. 1919; *m* 1948, Leslie Marion Wheeler; one *s* two *d*. *Educ:* Isleworth Grammar Sch.; Battersea and Northampton Polytechnics; Imperial Coll. BSc(Eng) 1944, MSc(Eng) 1945, DIC 1945. Gen. engrg trg, Benham and Kodak, 1936-40; Drawing Office and Wind Tunnel Dept, Vickers Armstrong Ltd, Weybridge, 1940-46; Coll. of Aeronautics: Lectr, 1946-51; Sen. Lectr, 1951-55; Dep. Head of Dept of Aerodynamics, 1955, and Prof. of Experimental Fluid Mechanics, 1962-64. Member: Aeronautical Res. Council (Mem. Applied Aerodynamics, Fluid Motion and Noise Res. Cttees; past Mem. Council and Chm. Aerodynamics, Noise, Fluid Motion and Performance Cttees); Noise Advisory Council (Chm., Noise from Air Traffic Working Group); Past Chm., Aerodynamics Cttee, Engrg Sci. Data Unit. Consultant to Rolls Royce; Past Consultant to AGARD and OECD. *Publications:* articles in reports and memoranda of: Aeronautical Research Council; Royal Aeronautical Soc., and other jls. *Recreations:* music, chess, walking. *Address:* Highbury, Pine Walk, Chilworth, Southampton SO1 7HQ. *T:* Southampton 69109.

LILLICRAP, Harry George, CBE 1976; Director, Telephone Rentals Ltd, since 1976; *b* 29 June 1913; *s* of late Herbert Percy Lillicrap; *m* 1938, Kathleen Mary Charnock; two *s*. *Educ:* Erith County Sch.; University College, London. BSc(Eng) 1934. Post Office Engineering Dept, 1936-50; Principal, Post Office, 1951; Assistant Secretary, 1958; Under-Secretary, 1964; Director of Radio Services, 1964-67; Sen. Dir Planning, Sen. Dir Customer Services, PO, 1967-72; Chm., Cable and Wireless, 1972-76. *Address:* Thornhurst, Felbridge, East Grinstead, West Sussex. *T:* East Grinstead 25811.

LILLIE, Beatrice, (Lady Peel); actress; *b* Toronto, 29 May 1898; *d* of John Lillie, Lisburn, Ireland, and Lucie Shaw; *m* 1920, Sir Robert Peel, 5th Bt (*d* 1934); (one *s* killed on active service 1942). *Educ:* St Agnes' Coll., Belleville, Ontario. First appearance, Alhambra, 1914; at the Vaudeville, Prince of Wales's etc., 1915-22; in The Nine O'Clock Revue, Little Theatre, 1922; first New York appearance, Times Square Theatre, in André Charlot's Revue, 1924; in Charlot's Revue at Prince of Wales's, 1925; in New York, 1925-26; at The Globe and The Palladium, 1928; This Year of Grace, New York, 1928; Charlot's Masquerade, at the Cambridge, London, 1930; New York; 1931-32; at the Savoy and London Palladium, 1933-34; New York, 1935; Queen's, London, 1939; Big Top, Adelphi, 1940; Troops: Africa, Italy, etc., 1942-45; Seven Lively Arts, Ziegfeld, New York, 1945; Better Late, Garrick, London, 1946; appeared in television and radio programmes, England and America, 1946-47; Inside USA, New York, 1948, subs. on tour for one year, USA; returned to London (cabaret), 1950 and June 1951. Solo artiste at several Royal performances; appeared in NY television, 1951-52; produced one-woman show, Summer Theatre, 1952; subs. on tour and produced show in Broadway, Oct. 1952-June 1953. Radio and TV, London, July-Aug. 1953.

Road tour in US of this production, Sept. 1953-June 1954; London, 1954-55. An Evening with Beatrice Lillie, Globe, AEWBL, Florida, Feb and March, 1956; 2nd one-woman show, Beasop's Fables, USA, June-Sept. 1956; Ziegfeld Follies, New York, 1957; Auntie Mame, Adelphi, London, 1958. Appeared in films: Exit Smiling, 1927; Doctor Rhythm, 1938; On Approval, 1944; Around the World in Eighty Days, 1956; Thoroughly Modern Millie, 1967. Free French Liberation Medal, N Africa, 1942, also African Star and George VI Medal, Donaldson Award, USA, 1945, also Antoinette Perry Award, New York, 1953, and many others. *Publication:* (with J. Philip and J. Brough) Every Other Inch a Lady, 1973. *Recreation:* painting. *Address:* c/o J. Elliot Brooks, 4 Little Essex Street, WC2R 3LD.

LILLIE, Very Rev. Henry Alexander, MA; Dean of Armagh, and Keeper of Armagh Public Library, since 1965; *b* 11 May 1911; *s* of David William Lillie and Alicia Lillie (*née* Morris), Carrick-on-Shannon; *m* 1942, Rebecca Isobel, *yr d* of Andrew C. Leitch, Homelea, Omagh, Co. Tyrone; one *d. Educ:* Sligo Grammar Sch.; Trinity Coll., Dublin. BA 1935, MA 1942. Junior Master, Grammar Schools: Elphin, 1932; Sligo, 1932-34. Deacon, 1936; Curate Asst, Portadown, 1936-41; Incumbent of: Milltown, 1941-47; Kilmore, 1947-52; Armagh, 1952-65; Armagh Cathedral: Prebendary of Tynan, 1952-60; Treas., 1960-61; Chancellor, 1961; Precentor, 1961-65. *Recreations:* reading, fishing, gardening. *Address:* The Library, Abbey Street, Armagh BT61 7DY. *T:* Armagh 523142.

LILLIE, John Adam; QC; LLD; *b* 25 July 1884; *e s* of Thomas Lillie and Ellen Harper Tait. *Educ:* Brockley's Acad., Broughty Ferry; Aberdeen Grammar Sch.; University of Aberdeen (MA 1906); University of Edinburgh (LLB 1910). Admitted to Faculty of Advocates, 1912; called to English Bar, 1921; Lecturer on Mercantile Law, University of Edinburgh, 1928-47; KC (Scotland) 1931; Member Royal Commn on Workmen's Compensation, 1938; Sheriff of Fife and Kinross, 1941-71. Chairman for Scotland Board of Referees under Income Tax Acts, 1942-55; Chairman for Scotland and NI of British Motor Trade Assoc. Price Protection Cttee, 1949-52; Legal Commissioner and Dep. Chairman, General Board of Control for Scotland, 1944-62; Convener of the sheriffs, 1960-65; Hon. LLD Aberdeen, 1967. *Publications:* The Mercantile Law of Scotland (6th edn, 1965); Articles in Green's Encyclopædia of the Law of Scotland on Company Law, and Sale of Goods; The Northern Lighthouses Service, 1965; Tradition and Environment in a Time of Change, 1970; An Essay on Speech Literacy, 1974; A Family History, 1976. *Address:* 85 Great King Street, Edinburgh. *T:* 031-556 1862. *Clubs:* Scottish Liberal, Caledonian (Edinburgh).

LILLINGSTON, George David I. I.; *see* Inge-Innes-Lillingston.

LIM, Sir Han-Hoe, Kt, *cr* 1946; CBE 1941; Hon. LLD (Malaya); MB, ChB (Edinburgh); JP; Pro-Chancellor, University of Malaya, 1949-59; *b* 27 April 1894; 2nd *s* of late Lim Cheng Sah, Singapore; *m* 1920, Chua Seng Neo; two *s* two *d. Educ:* St Andrew's Sch. and Raffles Institution; University of Edinburgh. RMO North Devon General Hospital, with charge of Military Auxiliary Hospital, 1919; Municipal Commissioner, Singapore, 1926-31; Member of Legislative Council, Straits Settlements, 1933-42, and its Finance Cttee, 1936-42; Member of Exec. Council, Straits Settlements, 1939-42; Member of Advisory Council, Singapore, 1946-48; Member of Exec. Council, Singapore, 1948-50. Member of Council, King Edward VII College of Medicine, Singapore, 1930-42; Mem. and Chm., Public Services Commission, Singapore, 1952-56. *Recreations:* tennis, chess. *Address:* 758 Mountbatten Road, Singapore 15. *T:* 40655. *Club:* Garden (Singapore).

LIMBU; *see* Rambahadur Limbu.

LIMENTANI, Prof. Uberto; Professor of Italian, University of Cambridge, since 1962; Fellow of Magdalene College, Cambridge, since 1964; *b* Milan, 15 Dec. 1913; *er s* of Prof. Umberto Limentani and Elisa Levi; *m* 1946, Barbara Hoban; three *s. Educ:* University of Milan (Dr in Giurispr., Dr in Lettere); University of London (PhD); University of Cambridge (MA). Commentator and script-writer Italian Section, BBC European Service, 1939-45. Lector 1945, Assistant Lecturer, 1948, Lecturer, 1952, in Italian, University of Cambridge. Corresp. Member Accademia Letteraria Ital. dell'Arcadia, 1964. Commendatore, Ordine al Merito della Repubblica Italiana, 1973. *Publications:* Stilistica e Metrica, 1936; Poesie e Lettere Inedite di Salvator Rosa, 1950; L'Attività Letteraria di Giuseppe Mazzini, 1950; La Satira nel Seicento, 1961; The Fortunes of Dante in Seventeenth Century Italy, 1964; (ed) The Mind of Dante, 1965. Co-editor yearly review, Studi Secenteschi (founded 1960); an ed. of Italian Studies. Trans. E. R. Vincent's

Ugo Foscolo Esule fra gli Inglesi, 1954. Several contrib. on Italian Literature to: Encyclopædia Britannica; Cassell's Encyclopædia of Literature; Italian Studies; La Bibliofilia; Giornale Storico della Letteratura Italiana; Amor di Libro; Studi Secenteschi; Il Pensiero Mazziniano; Bollettino della Domus Mazziniana; Il Ponte; Cambridge Review; Modern Language Review. *Recreation:* walking in the Alps. *Address:* 17 St Barnabas Road, Cambridge. *T:* Cambridge 58198.

LIMERICK, 6th Earl of, *cr* 1803 (Ire.); **Patrick Edmund Pery,** MA, CA; Baron Glentworth, 1790 (Ire.); Viscount Limerick, 1800 (Ire.); Baron Foxford, 1815 (UK); Director: Kleinwort, Benson Ltd; Union Miniere SA; Tanganyika Concessions Ltd and subsidiary cos; Mallinson Denny Ltd; International Investment Trust Ltd; Vice-President, Association of British Chambers of Commerce (President, 1974-77); Member: Council, London Chamber of Commerce; British Overseas Trade Board; Chairman, Committee for Middle East Trade, since 1975 (Vice-Chairman, 1968-72 and 1974-75); *b* 12 April 1930; *e s* of 5th Earl of Limerick, GBE, CH, KCB, DSO, TD, and Angela Olivia (*see* Dowager Countess of Limerick); *S* father, 1967; *m* 1961, Sylvia Rosalind Lush (*see* Countess of Limerick); two *s* one *d. Educ:* Eton; New Coll., Oxford. CA 1957. Commercial Bank of Australia Ltd (London Adv. Bd), 1969-72. Parly Under-Sec. of State for Trade, Dept of Trade and Industry, 1972-74. Pres., Ski Club of Gt Britain; Vice-Pres., Alpine Ski Club. *Recreations:* skiing, mountaineering. *Heir:* *s* Viscount Glentworth, *qv*. *Address:* Chiddinglye, West Hoathly, East Grinstead, West Sussex. *T:* Sharpthorne 810214; 30 Victoria Road, W8 5RG. *T:* 01-937 0573.

LIMERICK, Countess of; Sylvia Rosalind Pery, MA; President: UK Committee for UN Children's Fund, since 1972; National Association for Maternal and Child Welfare, since 1973; Vice-Chairman, Foundation for the Study of Infant Deaths, since 1971; Member, Kensington, Chelsea and Westminster Area Health Authority, since 1977; *b* 7 Dec. 1935; *e d* of Maurice Stanley Lush, *qv*; *m* 1961, Viscount Glentworth (now 6th Earl of Limerick, *qv*); two *s* one *d. Educ:* St Swithun's, Winchester; Lady Margaret Hall, Oxford (MA). Research Asst, Foreign Office, 1959-62. Mem., Bd of Governors, St Bartholomew's Hosp., 1970-74; Vice-Chm., Community Health Council, S District of Kensington, Chelsea, Westminster Area, 1974-77; a Vice-President: London Br. of British Red Cross Soc., 1972- (Nat. HQ Staff, 1962-66; Pres., Kensington and Chelsea Div., 1966-72); Invalid Children's Aid Assoc., 1976-. Member: Cttee of Management, Inst. of Child Health, 1976-; Council and Cttee of Management, King Edward's Hospital Fund, 1977-. *Recreations:* music, mountaineering, ski-ing. *Address:* 30 Victoria Road, W8 5RG. *T:* 01-937 0573.

LIMERICK, Dowager Countess of, GBE 1954 (DBE 1946; CBE 1942); CH 1974; DL; **Angela Olivia Pery;** Vice-President, British Red Cross Society, since 1976; *b* 27 Aug. 1897; *yr d* of late Lt-Col Sir Henry Trotter, KCMG, CB; *m* 1926, Hon. Edmund Colquhoun Pery, later 5th Earl of Limerick, GBE, CH, KCB, DSO, TD (*d* 1967); two *s* one *d. Educ:* North Foreland Lodge, Broadstairs; London Sch. of Economics. Served as VAD at home and overseas, 1915-19; Poor Law Guardian, 1928-30; on Kensington Borough Council, 1929-35, Chm of Maternity and Child Welfare and Public Health Cttees; Mem. for South Kensington on LCC, 1936-46; Privy Council rep. on Gen. Nursing Council for England and Wales, 1933-50; Mem. of Royal Commn on Equal Pay, and of various Govt Cttees; Dep. Chm. of War Organization BRCS and Order of St John, 1941-47; Vice-Chm., League of Red Cross Societies, 1957-73; Chm., Standing Commn, Internat. Red Cross, 1965-73; Chm., Council, British Red Cross Soc., 1974-76. President: Multiple Sclerosis Soc., 1968-76; Hosp. and Homes of St Giles; Vice-President: Internat. Council of Social Service; Family Welfare Assoc.; Family Planning Assoc.; Governor: Star and Garter Home, Richmond, 1948-75 (Vice-Pres., 1975); Queen Alexandra Hosp. Home, Worthing. DL West Sussex, 1977. Hon. LLD Manchester Univ., 1945, Leeds Univ., 1951. DStJ, 1952. Commander's Gold Cross, Order of Merit, Republic of Austria, 1959. Red Cross Decorations and awards from the National Societies of Australia, Austria, Belgium, Canada, Czechoslovakia, Denmark, Ethiopia, Finland, France, Germany, Greece, Iran, Mexico, Netherlands, Philippines, Roumania, South Africa, Sweden, Turkey, USA and Yugoslavia. *Address:* Chiddinglye, West Hoathly, East Grinstead, West Sussex RH19 4QT. *T:* Sharpthorne 810214. See also Earl of Limerick and P. F. Thorne.

LIMERICK and KILLALOE, Bishop of, since 1976; **Rt. Rev. Edwin Owen,** MA; Bishop of Killaloe, Kilfenora, Clonfert and Kilmacduagh, 1972-76 (diocese amalgamated with Limerick, Ardfert and Aghadoe, and Emly, 1976); *b* 3 Nov. 1910; *s* of late

William Rowland Owen; *m* 1940, Margaret Mary Williams, BA; one *s* one *d*. *Educ:* Royal School, Armagh; Trinity College, Dublin (MA). Deacon 1934, priest 1935, Dublin; Curate of Glenageary, 1934-36; Christ Church, Leeson Park, Dublin, 1936-38; Minor Canon of St Patrick's Cathedral, Dublin, 1935-36; Chancellor, 1936-38; Succentor, 1938-42; Incumbent of Birr with Eglish, 1942-57; Canon, Killaloe Cathedral, 1954-57; Rector of Killaloe and Dean of Killaloe Cathedral, 1957-72; Diocesan Secretary of Killaloe and Kilfenora, 1957-72. *Recreation:* classical music. *Address:* Clarisford, Killaloe, Co. Clare, Ireland. *T:* Limerick (061) 76247. *Club:* Friendly Brothers (Dublin).

LINCOLN, Bishop of, since 1974; **Rt. Rev. Simon Wilton Phipps,** MC 1945; *b* 6 July 1921; *s* of late Captain William Duncan Phipps, CVO, RN, and Pamela May Ross; *m* 1953, Mary, *widow* of Rev. Dr James Welch and *d* of late Sir Charles Eric Palmer. *Educ:* Eton; Trinity Coll., Cambridge; Westcott House, Cambridge. Joined Coldstream Guards, 1940; commnd, 1941; Capt., 1944; ADC to GOC-in-C Northern Comd India, Nov. 1945; Mil. Asst to Adjt Gen. to the Forces, War Office, 1946; Major, 1946. BA (History) Cantab, 1948; MA 1953; Pres., Cambridge Univ. Footlights Club, 1949. Ordained 1950. Asst Curate, Huddersfield Parish Church, 1950; Chaplain, Trinity Coll., Cambridge, 1953; Industrial Chaplain, Coventry Dio., 1958; Hon. Canon, Coventry Cath., 1965; Bishop Suffragan of Horsham, 1968-74. Member: Council, Industrial Soc.; Home Sec.'s Cttee of Inquiry into Liquor Licensing Laws, 1971-72. *Publication:* God on Monday, 1966. *Recreations:* walking, painting, cooking. *Address:* The Bishop's House, Eastgate, Lincoln.

LINCOLN, Dean of; *see* Fiennes, Very Rev. Hon. O. W. T.-W.

LINCOLN, Archdeacon of; *see* Adie, Ven. M. E.

LINCOLN, Sir Anthony (Handley), KCMG 1965 (CMG 1958); CVO 1957; Ambassador to Venezuela, 1964-69; *b* 2 Jan. 1911; *s* of late J. B. Lincoln, OBE; *m* 1948, Lisette Marion Summers; no *c*. *Educ:* Mill Hill Sch.; Magdalene Coll., Cambridge (BA). Prince Consort and Gladstone Prizes, 1934. Appointed Asst Principal, Home Civil Service, 1934; subsequently transferred to Foreign Service; served in Foreign Office; on UK Delegation to Paris Peace Conf., 1946, and in Buenos Aires. Counsellor, and Head of a Dept of Foreign Office, 1950. Dept. Sec.-Gen., Council of Europe, Strasbourg, France, 1952-55; Counsellor, British Embassy, Copenhagen, 1955-58; British Ambassador to Laos, 1958-60; HM Minister to Bulgaria, 1960-63; Officer Order of Orange Nassau, 1950; Comdr Order of Dannebrog, 1957. *Publication:* Some Political and Social Ideas of English Dissent, 1937. *Recreations:* country pursuits. *Clubs:* Brooks's, Reform.

LINCOLN, Anthony Leslie Julian, QC 1968; Practising Barrister, Writer and Broadcaster; a Recorder of the Crown Court, since 1974; *b* 7 April 1920; *s* of Samuel and Ruby Lincoln. *Educ:* Highgate; Queen's Coll., Oxford (Schol., MA). Served Somerset Light Inf. and RA, 1941-45. Called to Bar, 1949; Bencher, Lincoln's Inn, 1976. Vice-Princ., Working Men's Coll., 1955-60; Chm. and Trustee, Harrison Homes for the Elderly, 1963-; Chm., Working Men's Coll. Corp., 1969-; Trustee, Fund for Research into Ageing Process. Associate MNI, 1975. *Publications:* Wicked, Wicked Libels, 1972; (ed) Lord Eldon's Anecdote Book, 1960; regular contribs to Observer, Spectator and other jls. *Recreations:* fishing, cricket, walking. *Address:* 9 Paultons Sq., Chelsea, SW3. *T:* 01-352 0519; Heale Park Cottage, Upper Woodford, Salisbury, Wilts; 2 Hare Court, Temple, EC4. *T:* 01-353 0076. *Club:* Beefsteak.

LINCOLN, F(redman) Ashe, QC 1947; MA, BCL; Captain RNVR; a Recorder, since 1972 (Recorder of Gravesend, 1967-71); Master of the Bench, Inner Temple, since 1955; Master of the Moots, 1955-64, and 1968-70; *s* of Reuben and Fanny Lincoln; *m* 1933, Sybil Eileen Cohen; one *s* one *d*. *Educ:* Hoe Gram. Sch., Plymouth; Haberdashers' Aske's Sch.; Exeter Coll., Oxford, 1928; called to Bar, Inner Temple, Nov. 1929; joined RNV(S)R, 1937; served in Royal Navy (RNVR), Sept. 1939-May 1946; Mediterranean, 1943, with commandos in Sicily and Italy at Salerno landings, 1943; assault crossing of Rhine, March 1945 (despatches twice). Dep. World Pres., Internat. Assoc. of Jewish Lawyers and Jurists, 1973-. Renter Warden of Worshipful Company of Plaisterers, 1946-47, Master, 1949-50; Freeman and Liveryman of City of London; fought general election 1945 (C) Harrow East Div. (Middx.); Chm. Administrative Law Cttee of Inns of Court Conservative Association, 1951; Mem. Exec., Gen. Council of the Bar, 1957-61. Chm., Criminal Law Cttee, Assoc. Liberal Lawyers. Associate MNI, 1976. Vice-Pres., RNR Officers' Club; Chm., London Devonian Assoc.; Mem., Exec., London Flotilla.

Publications: The Starra, 1939; Secret Naval Investigator, 1961. *Recreations:* yachting, tennis. *Address:* 2 Harcourt Buildings, Temple, EC4. *T:* 01-353 7202. *Clubs:* Athenæum, Royal Automobile, MCC, Naval; Royal Corinthian Yacht (Burnham-on-Crouch and Cowes); Bar Yacht; Royal Naval and Royal Albert Yacht (Portsmouth).

LINCOLN, Air Cdre Philip Lionel, CB 1945; DSO 1918; MC 1916; late RAF; late Chairman, R. Passmore & Co. Ltd; *b* 20 Jan. 1892; *s* of Philip Passmore Lincoln and Louisa Baxter; *m* 1916, Kathleen Daisy Shepherd (*d* 1965); two *s*. *Educ:* Framlingham Coll. Entered family business R. Passmore & Co., 1910, partner 1913; Pres., Building Industry Distributors, 1948. 2nd Lt Northumberland Fusiliers, 1914; Capt. 1915; Major, 1917; Lt-Col 1918; served France and Italy (wounded twice, despatches, MC, DSO); demobilised 1919. Flying Officer AAF Balloon Branch; Squadron Leader to Command No 902 Squadron, 1938; Wing Comdr 1939; Group Capt. 1940; Air Commodore, 1941. *Address:* 2 Church Lane, Bearsted, Maidstone, Kent. *T:* Maidstone 37106.

LIND-SMITH, His Honour Gerard Gustave; a Circuit Judge (formerly Judge of County Courts), 1959-75; *b* 1903; *o s* of C. F. Lind-Smith, Liverpool; *m* 1928, Alexandra Eva, *e d* of Lt-Col J. C. Kirk, CBE, Monmouthshire; three *d*. *Educ:* Wellington Coll.; University Coll., Oxon. Called to Bar, Inner Temple, 1928. JP and Dep. Chm. Ches. QS, 1957, Chm., 1961-68. Recorder of Birkenhead, 1958-59. *Address:* Pitt House, Wellesbourne, Warwick. *Club:* English-Speaking Union.

LINDBERGH, Anne Spencer Morrow; author, United States; *b* 1906; *d* of Dwight Whitney Morrow and Elizabeth Reeve Morrow (*née* Cutter); *m* 1929, Col Charles Augustus Lindbergh, AFC, DFC (*d* 1974); three *s* two *d* (and one *s* decd). *Educ:* Miss Chapin's Sch., New York City; Smith Coll., Northampton, Mass (two prizes for literature). Received Cross of Honour of United States Flag Association for her part in survey of air route across Atlantic, 1933; received Hubbard Gold Medal of National Geographical Soc. for work as co-pilot and radio operator in flight of 40,000 miles over five continents, 1934. Hon. MA, Smith Coll., Mass., 1935. *Publications:* North to the Orient, 1935; Listen, the Wind, 1938; The Wave of the Future, 1940; The Steep Ascent, 1944; Gift from the Sea, 1955; The Unicorn and other Poems, 1935-55, 1958; Dearly Beloved, 1963; Earth Shine, 1970; Bring Me a Unicorn (autobiog.), 1972; Hour of Gold, Hour of Lead (autobiog.), 1973; Locked Rooms and Open Doors: diaries and letters 1933-35, 1974; The Flower and the Nettle: diaries and letters 1936-39, 1976. *Address:* Scott's Cove, Darien, Conn 06820, USA.

LINDELL, John Henry Stockton, CMG 1973; ED (CMF) 1971; MD, MS; retired as Chairman of Victorian Hospitals and Charities Commission, Australia, 1972; *b* 17 March 1908; *s* of John Lindell and Georgina Stockton; *m* 1941, Margaret Annie Rolland; two *s* two *d*. *Educ:* Melbourne High Sch.; Melbourne Univ. MB, BS 1940; MS 1946, MD 1948. Medical Supt, Royal Melbourne Hosp., 1943-53; Chm., Victorian Hospitals and Charities Commn, 1953-72. FPS 1948; FHA 1954. *Publication:* A Regional Plan for Hospitals, 1953. *Recreations:* reading, woodworking. *Address:* 13 Eaglemont Crescent, Eaglemont, Victoria 3084, Australia. *T:* 45 2039. *Clubs:* Beefsteak (Melbourne); Royal Automobile Club of Victoria.

LINDEN, Anya; Ballerina, Royal Ballet, 1958-64; *b* 3 Jan. 1933; English; *d* of George Charles and Ada Dorothea Eltenton; *m* 1963, Hon. John Sainsbury, *qv*; two *s* one *d*. *Educ:* Berkeley, Calif; Sadler's Wells Sch. Entered Sadler's Wells Sch., 1947; promoted to 1st Company, 1951; became Soloist, 1952. Principal rôles in the ballets: Coppelia; Sylvia; Prince of Pagodas; Sleeping Beauty; Swan Lake; Giselle; Cinderella; Agon; Solitaire; Noctambules; Fête Etrange; Symphonic Variations; Invitation; Firebird; Lady and the Fool; Antigone; Seven Deadly Sins. Mem. Council and Appeal Cttee, Nat. Council for One-Parent Families. Founding Mem., British Theatre Museum (Mem. Adv. Council, 1975-). Director: Ballet Rambert; Royal Ballet Sch., 1977-. *Recreations:* drawing, gardening. *Address:* c/o Royal Opera House, Covent Garden, WC2.

LINDESAY-BETHUNE, family name of **Earl of Lindsay.**

LINDISFARNE, Archdeacon of; *see* Bates, Ven. Mansel Harry.

LINDLEY, Sir Arnold (Lewis George), Kt 1964; DSc; CGIA, FIMechE, FIEE; Deputy-Chairman, Motherwell Bridge (Holdings) Ltd, 1965; *b* 13 Nov. 1902; *s* of George Dilnot Lindley; *m* 1927, Winifred May Cowling (*d* 1962); one *s* one *d*; *m* 1963, Mrs Phyllis Rand. *Educ:* Woolwich Polytechnic. Chief Engineer BGEC, South Africa, 1933; Director: East Rand

Engineering Co., 1943; BGEC, S Africa, 1945; Gen. Manager Erith Works, GEC, 1949; GEC England, 1953; Vice-Chm. 1959, Managing Dir, 1961-62, Chm., 1961-64, of GEC; retd. Chairman: BEAMA, 1963-64; Internat. Electrical Assoc., 1962-64; Engineering Industry Trng Bd, 1964-74. President, Instn of Mechanical Engineers, 1968-69; Chm., Council of Engineering Instns, 1972-73 (Vice-Chm., 1971-72); Member: Council, City Univ., 1969-; Design Council, 1971-. Appointed by Govt to advise on QE2 propulsion turbines, 1969. *Recreations:* sailing and golf. *Address:* The Crest, Raggleswood, Chislehurst, Kent. *T:* 01-467 2159. *Club:* Chislehurst Golf.

LINDLEY, Bryan Charles; Chief Executive and Managing Director, since 1973, Director, 1968-73, Electrical Research Association Ltd; *b* 30 Aug. 1932; *m* 1956, Joan Mary McGill; one *s*. *Educ:* Reading Sch.; University Coll., London. BSc (Eng) 1954; PhD 1960; FIMechE 1968; FIEE 1968; FInstP 1968; FInstD 1968. National Gas Turbine Establishment, Pyestock, 1954-57; Hawker Siddeley Nuclear Power Co. Ltd, 1957-59; C. A. Parsons & Co. Ltd, Nuclear Research Centre, Newcastle upon Tyne, 1959-61; International Research and Development Co. Ltd, Newcastle upon Tyne, 1962-65; Man., R&D Div., C. A. Parsons & Co. Ltd, Newcastle upon Tyne, 1965-68; Dir, ERA Patents Ltd, 1968-; Chm. and Man. Dir, ERA Autotrack Systems Ltd, 1971-. Member: Res. and Technol. Cttee, CBI, 1974-; British Nat. Cttee, CIGRE, 1974-; Engrg Design Adv. Cttee, Design Council, 1975-; Watt Cttee on Energy; Nat. Electronics Council. Chm., Sci. Educn and Management Div., IEE, 1974-75. *Publications:* articles on plasma physics, electrical and mechanical engineering, management science, impact of technological innovation, etc, in learned jls. *Recreations:* literature, ski-ing. *Address:* 9 Mawcroft Court, 19 York Street, W1. *Club:* Number Ten.

LINDLEY, Prof. Dennis Victor; Professor and Head of Department of Statistics and Computer Science (formerly Department of Statistics), University College, London, since 1967; *b* 25 July 1923; *s* of Albert Edward and Florence Louisa Lindley; *m* 1947, Joan Armitage; one *s* two *d*. *Educ:* Tiffin Boys' Sch., Kingston-on-Thames; Trinity Coll., Cambridge. MA Cantab 1948. Min. of Supply, 1943-45; Nat. Physical Lab., 1945-46 and 1947-48; Statistical Lab., Cambridge Univ., 1948-60 (Dir, 1957-60); Prof. and Head of Dept of Statistics, UCW, Aberystwyth, 1960-67. Vis. Professor: Chicago and Stanford Univs, 1954-55; Harvard Business Sch., 1963; Univ. of Iowa, 1974-75. Guy Medal (Silver), Royal Statistical Soc., 1968. Fellow, Inst. Math. Statistics; Fellow, American Statistical Assoc.; Mem., Internat. Statistical Inst. *Publications:* (with J. C. P. Miller) Cambridge Elementary Statistical Tables, 1953; Introduction to Probability and Statistics (2 vols), 1965; Making Decisions, 1971; contribs to Royal Statistical Soc., Biometrika, Annals of Math. Statistics. *Address:* 8 Hill Close, NW11 7JP. *T:* 01-455 4822.

LINDNER, Doris Lexey Margaret; sculptress; *b* 8 July 1896. *Educ:* Norland Place, London; St Martin's Art School; Frank Calendron Animal Sch.; British Academy, Rome. Modelled animals for Royal Worcester Porcelain Co. for over 40 years. Has made bronzes of horses; also carved in stone, wood, concrete etc. *Recreation:* bridge. *Address:* Studio Cottage, Broad Campden, Glos. *T:* Evesham 840608.

LINDO, Sir (Henry) Laurence, OJ 1973; GCVO 1973; Kt 1967; CMG 1957; High Commissioner for Jamaica in London, 1962-73; *b* 13 Aug. 1911; *e s* of Henry Alexander and Ethel Mary Lindo (*née* Gibson); *m* 1943, Holly Robertson Clacken; two *d*. *Educ:* Jamaica Coll., Jamaica; Keble Coll., Oxford. Rhodes Scholar, 1931; OUAC 1934. Inspector of Schools, Jamaica, 1935; Asst Information Officer, 1939-43; Asst Sec., Colonial Secretariat, 1945; Principal Asst Sec., 1950. Administrator, Dominica, Windward Islands, 1952-59; Actg Governor, Windward Islands, 1957 and 1959; Governor's Sec., Jamaica, 1960-62; Ambassador to: France, 1966-72; Federal Republic of Germany, 1967-70. *Address:* c/o Royal Bank of Canada, Cockspur Street, SW1. *Clubs:* Travellers', Royal Commonwealth Society (West Indian), MCC, Royal Over-Seas League.

LINDON, Sir Leonard (Charles Edward), Kt 1964; MS, FRCS, FRCSE, FRACS; Hon. Surgeon and Neuro-Surgeon, Royal Adelaide Hospital; Associate Lecturer in Surgery, University of Adelaide; *b* Adelaide, 8 Feb. 1896; *s* of late J. H. Lindon, Adelaide; *m* 1921, Jean, *d* of late Dr H. Marten; two *s* one *d*. *Educ:* Geelong Gram. Sch.; St Peter's Coll., Adelaide; Universities of Adelaide and Oxford; London and Guy's Hospitals. Rhodes Scholar 1918. MB, BS 1919; MRCS LRCP 1920; FRCSEd 1922; FRCS 1922; MS Adelaide 1923; FRACS 1929. Served European War, 1914-18: Private, AIF, 1914-16;

served War of 1939-45; Lt-Col, Australian Army Medical Corps, AIF, 1939-41 (despatches). Pres., Royal Australasian Coll. of Surgeons, 1959-61 (Vice-Pres., 1957-59); Mem., BMA (Pres. South Australian Branch, 1934-35). *Address:* 178 North Terrace, Adelaide, SA 5000, Australia. *Club:* Adelaide (Adelaide, SA).

LINDOP, Audrey Beatrice Noël E.; *see* Erskine-Lindop, A. B. N.

LINDOP, Sir Norman, Kt 1973; MSc, CChem, FRIC; Director, The Hatfield Polytechnic, since 1969; *b* 9 March 1921; *s* of Thomas Cox Lindop and May Lindop, Stockport, Cheshire; *m* 1974, Jenny C. Quass; one *s*. *Educ:* Northgate Sch., Ipswich; Queen Mary Coll., Univ. of London (BSc, MSc). Various industrial posts, 1942-46; Lectr in Chemistry, Queen Mary Coll., 1946; Asst Dir of Examinations, Civil Service Commn, 1951; Sen. Lectr in Chemistry, Kingston Coll. of Technology, 1953; Head of Dept of Chemistry and Geology, Kingston Coll. of Technology, 1957; Principal: SW Essex Technical Coll. and Sch. of Art, 1963; Hatfield Coll. of Technology, 1966. Chairman: Council for Professions Supplementary to Medicine, 1973; Home Office Data Protection Cttee, 1976-; Member: SRC, 1974-; CNAA, 1974-; US-UK Educnl (Fulbright) Commn, 1971-. Chm., Hatfield Philharmonic Soc., 1970. Fellow, QMC, 1976; FRSA. *Recreations:* mountain walking, music (especially opera). *Address:* Hatfield Polytechnic, PO Box No 109, Hatfield, Herts. *T:* Hatfield 68100.

LINDOP, Prof. Patricia Joyce, (Mrs G. P. R. Esdale); Professor of Radiation Biology, University of London, since 1970; *b* 21 June 1930; 2nd *c* of Elliot D. Lindop and Dorothy Jones; *m* 1957, Gerald Paton Rivett Esdale; one *s* one *d*. *Educ:* Malvern Girls' Coll.; St Bartholomew's Hospital Med. Coll.; BSc (1st cl. Hons), MB, BS, PhD; DSc London 1974; MRCP 1956; FRCP 1977. Skinner Prize (Child Health), 1953. Registered GP, 1954; Ciba Foundation Award for Research on Ageing, 1957; Wm Gibson Research Schol., RSM, 1957-59. Research and teaching in physiology and medical radiobiology at Med. Coll. of St Bartholomew's Hosp., 1955-. Hon. Mem., RCR, 1972. UK Mem., Continuing Cttee of Pugwash Confs on Science and World Affairs (Asst Sec. Gen., 1961-71); Mem., Royal Commn on Environmental Pollution, 1974-; Member Council: Westfield Coll., Univ. of London, 1967-77; St Bartholomew's Hospital Med. Coll., 1977-. Chm. and Trustee, Soc. for Education in the Applications of Science, 1968-. Consultant to Cttee 10 of ICRU, 1972-. Member Council: Science and Society, 1975-; Soc. for Protection of Science and Learning, 1974-; formerly Mem. Council, British Inst. of Radiology. *Publications:* (ed jtly with G. A. Sacher) Radiation and Ageing, 1966; jt contributor with C. Proukakis to Pathology of Irradiation (ed Berdjis, Williams and Wilkins), 1971; papers to relevant jls. *Recreation:* still looking for time. *Address:* 58 Wildwood Road, NW11 6UP. *T:* 01-455 5860. *Club:* Royal Society of Medicine.

LINDSAY, family name of **Earl of Crawford** and **Baron Lindsay of Birker.**

LINDSAY, 14th Earl of, *cr* 1633; **William Tucker Lindesay-Bethune;** Lord Lindsay of The Byres, 1445; Baron Parbroath, 1633; Viscount Garnock; Baron Kilbirny, Kingsburne, and Drumry, 1703; Representative Peer, 1974-59; late Major, Scots Guards; Member of Queen's Body Guard for Scotland, Royal Company of Archers; *b* 28 April 1901; *s* of 13th Earl and Ethel (*d* 1942), *d* of W. Austin Tucker, Boston, USA; assumed addtl surname of Bethune, 1939; *S* father, 1943; *m* 1925, Marjory, DStJ, *d* of late Arthur J. G. Cross and Lady Hawke; two *s* two *d*. Served War of 1939-45 (wounded); retd pay, 1947. Hon. Col, Fife and Forfar Yeomanry/Scottish Horse, 1957-62. Zone Comr for Northern Civil Defence Zone of Scotland, 1963-69. Pres., Shipwrecked Fishermen and Mariners Royal Benevolent Soc., 1966-76. DL Co. of Fife. KStJ. *Heir: s* Viscount Garnock, *qv*. *Address:* Lahill, Upper Largo, Fife KY8 6JE. *T:* Upper Largo 251. *Clubs:* Cavalry and Guards; Leander (Henley).

LINDSAY OF BIRKER, 2nd Baron, *cr* 1945; **Michael Francis Morris Lindsay;** Professor Emeritus in School of International Service, The American University, Washington, DC; *b* 24 Feb. 1909; *e s* of 1st Baron Lindsay of Birker, CBE, LLD, and Erica Violet (*née* Storr) (*d* 1962); *S* father 1952; *m* 1941, Li Hsiao-li, *d* of Col Li Wen-chi of Lishih, Shansi; one *s* two *d*. *Educ:* Gresham's Sch., Holt; Balliol Coll., Oxford. Adult education and economic research work in S Wales, 1935-37; Tutor in Economics, Yenching Univ., Peking, 1938-41; Press Attaché, British Embassy, Chungking, 1940. Served War of 1939-45, with Chinese 18th Group Army, 1942-45. Vis. Lectr at Harvard Univ., 1946-47; Lectr in Econs, University Coll., Hull, 1948-51; Sen. Fellow of the Dept of Internat. Relations, ANU, Canberra, 1951-59 (Reader in Internat. Relations, 1959); Prof. of Far

Eastern Studies, Amer. Univ., Washington, 1959-74, Chm. of E Asia Programme, 1959-71. Visiting Professor: Yale Univ., 1958; Ball State Univ., Indiana, 1971-72. *Publications:* Educational Problems in Communist China, 1950; The New China, three views, 1950; China and the Cold War, 1955; Is Peaceful Co-existence Possible?, 1960; The Unknown War: North China 1937-45, 1975; Kung-ch'an-chu-i Ts' o-wu ts'ai Na-li, 1976; articles in learned journals. *Recreations:* wireless, tennis. *Heir: s* Hon. James Francis Lindsay, *b* 29 Jan. 1945. *Address:* 6812 Delaware Street, Chevy Chase, Md 20015, USA. *T:* (301)-656-4245.

LINDSAY, Maj.-Gen. Courtenay Traice David, CB 1963; Director-General of Artillery, War Office, 1961-64, retired; *b* 28 Sept. 1910; *s* of late Courtenay Traice Lindsay and Charlotte Editha (*née* Wetenhall); *m* 1934, Margaret Elizabeth, *d* of late William Pease Theakston, Huntingdon; two *s. Educ:* Rugby Sch.; RMA Woolwich. 2nd Lt RA, 1930. Mem., Ordnance Board (Col), 1952; Dir of Munitions, British Staff (Brig.), Washington, 1959; Maj.-Gen. 1961. *Address:* Huggits Farm, Stone-in-Oxney, Tenterden, Kent. *Club:* Royal Automobile.

LINDSAY, Donald Dunrod, CBE 1972; *b* 27 Sept. 1910; *s* of Dr Colin Dunrod Lindsay, Pres. BMA 1938, and Mrs Isabel Baynton Lindsay; *m* 1936, Violet Geraldine Fox; one *s* one *d. Educ:* Clifton Coll., Bristol; Trinity Coll., Oxford. Asst Master, Manchester Gram. Sch., 1932; Asst Master, Repton Sch., 1935; temp. seconded to Bristol Univ. Dept of Education as lecturer in History, 1938; Senior History Master, Repton Sch., 1938-42; Headmaster: Portsmouth Gram. Sch., 1942-53; Malvern Coll., 1953-71. Dir, Independent Schs Information Service, 1972-77. Chm., Headmasters' Conference, 1968. Governor, Harrow Sch., 1977-. *Publications:* A Portrait of Britain Between the Exhibitions, 1952; A Portrait of Britain, 1688-1851, 1954; A Portrait of Britain Before 1066, 1962; Authority and Challenge, Europe 1300-1600, 1975. *Recreations:* walking, theatre, music. *Address:* 34 Belgrave Road, Seaford, East Sussex.

LINDSAY, Maj.-Gen. Edward Stewart, CB 1956; CBE 1952 (OBE 1944); DSO 1945; Assistant Master General of Ordnance, 1961-64; Deputy Controller, Ministry of Supply, 1957-61; *b* 11 July 1905; *s* of Col M. E. Lindsay, DSO, DL, Craigfoodie, Dairsie, Fife; *m* 1933, Margaret, *d* of late Gen. Sir Norman Macmullen, GCB, CMG, CIE, DSO; two *d* (one *s* decd). *Educ:* Harrow Sch.; Edinburgh Univ. (BSc). 2nd Lt, RA 1926; served War of 1939-45, NW Europe (OBE, DSO); despatches, 1946; Col 1949; Brig. 1953; Maj.-Gen. 1955; Prin. Staff Officer to High Comr, Malaya, 1954-56; retired. Comdr Legion of Merit, USA, 1947. *Address:* Hill Cottage, Eversley, Hants. *T:* Eversley 3107. *Club:* Army and Navy.

LINDSAY, Rt. Rev. Hugh; *see* Hexham and Newcastle, Bishop of, (RC).

LINDSAY, Jack; author, *b* Melbourne, Australia, 1900; *s* of late Norman Lindsay; *m* 1958, Meta Waterdrinker; one *s* one *d. Educ:* Queensland Univ., BA, DLitt, FRSL. Soviet Badge of Honour, 1968. *Publications:* Fauns and Ladies (Poems); Marino Faliero (Verse Drama); Hereward (Verse drama); Helen Comes of Age (Three verse plays); Passionate Neatherd (Poems); William Blake, Creative Will and the Poetic Image, an Essay; Dionysos; The Romans; The Anatomy of Spirt; Mark Antony; John Bunyan; Short History of Culture; Handbook of Freedom; Song of a Falling World; Byzantium into Europe; Life of Dickens; Meredith; The Romans were Here; Arthur and his Times; A World Ahead; Daily Life in Roman Egypt; Leisure and Pleasure in Roman Egypt; Men and Gods on the Roman Nile; Origins of Alchemy; Origins of Astrology; Cleopatra; The Clashing Rocks; Helen of Troy; The Normans; translations of Lysistrata, Women in Parliament (Aristophanes), complete works of Petronius, Love Poems of Propertius, A Homage to Sappho, Theocritos, Heronadas, Catullus, Ausonius, Latin Medieval Poets, I am a Roman; Golden Ass; Edited Metamorphosis of Aiax (Sir John Harington, 1956;) Loving Mad Tom (Bedlamite Verses); Parlement of Pratlers (J. Eliot, 1593); Blake's Poetical Sketches; Into Action (Dieppe), a poem; Russian Poetry, 1917-55 (selections and translations); Memoirs of J. Priestley; Blast-Power and Ballistics; *novels:* Cressida's First Lover; Rome for Sale; Cæsar is Dead, Storm at Sea; Last Days with Cleopatra; Despoiling Venus; The Wanderings of Wenamen; Come Home at Last; Shadow and Flame; Adam of a New World; Sue Verney; 1649; Lost Birthright; Hannibaal Takes a Hand; Brief Light; Light in Italy; The Stormy Violence; We Shall Return; Beyond Terror; Hullo Stranger; The Barriers are Down; Time to Live; The Subtle Knot; Men of Forty-Eight; Fires in Smithfield; Betrayed Spring; Rising Tide; Moment of Choice; The Great Oak; Arthur and His Times; The Revolt of the Sons; The Way the Ball Bounces; All on the Never-Never

(filmed as Live Now-Pay Later); Masks and Faces; Choice of Times; Thunder Underground; *history:* 1764; The Writing on the Wall; *autobiography:* Life Rarely Tells; The Roaring Twenties; Fanfrolico and After; Meetings with Poets; *art-criticism;* The Death of the Hero; Life of Turner; Cézanne; Courbet; William Morris; The Troubadours. *Recreation:* anthropology. *Address:* Castle Hedingham, Halstead, Essex.

LINDSAY, Sir James Harvey Kincaid Stewart, Kt 1966; Director of International Programmes, Administrative Staff College, Henley-on-Thames, since 1970; *b* 31 May 1915; *s* of Arthur Harvey Lindsay and Doris Kincaid Lindsay; *m* Marguerite Phyllis Boudville (one *s* one *d* by previous marriage). *Educ:* Highgate Sch. Joined Metal Box Co. Ltd, 1934; joined Metal Box Co. of India Ltd, 1937; Man. Dir, 1961; Chm., 1967-69. President: Bengal Chamber of Commerce and Industry; Associated Chambers of Commerce and Industry of India, 1965-66. Director: Indian Oxygen Co., 1966; Westinghouse, Saxby Farmer Ltd, 1966. Pres., Calcutta Management Association, 1964; Pres., All India Management Assoc., 1964-69; Mem. of Governing Body: Indian Inst. of Management, Calcutta, 1964; Administrative Staff Coll. of India, 1965; Indian Institutes of Technology, 1966; National Council of Applied Economic Research, 1966; All-India Board of Management Studies, 1964; Indian Inst. of Foreign Trade, 1965; BoT Central Adv. Council of Industries, Direct Taxes Adv. Cttee, 1966; National Council on Vocational and Allied Trades, 1963. Trustee, Inst. of Family and Environmental Research, 1971-. Dir, Nimbus International Business Development Ltd, 1975-. FInstM 1975; FBIM 1971. *Recreations:* music, golf, riding, table tennis. *Address:* Christmas Cottage, Lower Shiplake, near Henley-on-Thames, Oxon. *T:* Wargrave 2859. *Clubs:* East India, Devonshire, Sports and Public Schools; Delhi Gymkhana (New Delhi).

LINDSAY, Hon. James Louis; *b* 16 Dec. 1906; *yr s* of 27th Earl of Crawford and Balcarres; *m* 1933, Bronwen Mary, *d* of 8th Baron Howard de Walden; three *s* one *d. Educ:* Eton; Magdalen Coll., Oxford. Served 1939-45 war, Major KRRC. Contested (C) Bristol South-East, 1950 and 1951; MP (C) N Devon, 1955-Sept. 1959. *Address:* Cornhill, Rolvenden, Kent. *T:* Rolvenden 330.

LINDSAY, John Vliet; Mayor of New York City, 1965-73 (elected as Republican-Liberal, Nov. 1965, re-elected as Liberal-Independent, Nov. 1969); *b* 24 Nov. 1921; *s* of George Nelson and Eleanor (Vliet) Lindsay; *m* 1949, Mary Harrison; one *s* three *d. Educ:* St Paul's Sch., Concord, NH; Yale Univ. BA 1944; LLB 1948. Lt US Navy, 1943-46. Admitted to: NY Bar, 1949; Fed. Bar, Southern Dist NY, 1950; US Supreme Court, 1955; DC Bar, 1957. Mem., law firm of Webster, Sheffield, NYC, 1949-55, 1957-61, 1974-. Exec. Asst to US Attorney Gen., 1955-56; Mem., 86th-89th Congresses, 17th Dist, NY, 1959-65. Hon. DrLaws Harvard, 1969. *Publications:* Journey into Politics, 1967; The City, 1970; The Edge, 1976. *Address:* 1 West 67th Street, New York, NY 10023, USA.

LINDSAY, Kenneth; *b* 16 Sept. 1897; *s* of George Michael Lindsay and Anne Theresa Parmiter; unmarried. *Educ:* St Olave's; Worcester Coll., Oxford. Served European War, HAC, 1916-18; Pres., Oxford Union, 1922-23; Leader, First Debating Visit to Amer. Univs. Barnett Research Fellow, Toynbee Hall, 1923-26; Councillor and Guardian, Stepney, 1923-26; Dir of Voluntary Migration Societies, Dominions Office, 1929-31; First Gen. Sec. Political and Economic Planning, 1931-35; MP (Ind. Nat.) Kilmarnock Burghs, 1933-45; MP (Ind.) Combined English Universities, 1945-50; Civil Lord of the Admiralty, 1935-37; Parliamentary Sec., Board of Education, 1937-40; Founder of Youth Service, and of CEMA (now Arts Council); Mem. Council, National Book League; a Vice-President: Educational Interchange Council (Ex-Chm.), 1968-73; Anglo-Israel Assoc. (Dir, 1962-73); Vis. Prof. at many Amer. Univs. Contested Oxford, Harrow and Worcester. *Publications:* Social Progress and Educational Waste; English Education; Eldorado-An Agricultural Settlement: Towards a European Parliament; European Assemblies. *Recreations:* Association Football, Oxford University, 1921-22; Corinthians; cricket, Authentics. *Address:* 48 Basildon Court, Devonshire Street, W1. *T:* 01-486 2178. *Club:* Athenæum.

LINDSAY of Dowhill, Sir Martin (Alexander), 1st Bt *cr* 1962, of Dowhill; CBE 1952; DSO 1945; Representer of Baronial House of Dowhill, 22nd in derivation from Sir William Lindsay, 1st of Dowhill, 1398; *b* 22 Aug. 1905; *s* of late Lt-Col A. B. Lindsay, 2nd KEO Gurkhas; *m* 1st, 1932, Joyce (marr. diss., 1967), *d* of late Major Hon. Robert Lindsay, Royal Scots Greys; two *s* one *d*; 2nd, 1969, Lœlia, Duchess of Westminster, *o d* of 1st Baron Sysonby, PC, GCB, GCVO, Treasurer to HM King George V. *Educ:* Wellington Coll.; RMC, Sandhurst. 2nd Lt Royal Scots Fusiliers, 1925. Served Army 1925-36 and 1939-45. Active

service on staff Norway 1940 (despatches), and commanded 1st
Bn The Gordon Highlanders, 51st Highland Div., in 16
operations, July 1944-May 1945 (despatches, wounded, DSO);
Lt-Col; seconded 4th Bn Nigeria Regt, 1927; travelled West to
East Africa through Ituri Forest, Belgian Congo, 1929; Surveyor
to British Arctic Air-Route Expedition to Greenland (King's
Polar Medal), 1930-31; Leader British Trans-Greenland
Expedition, 1934; Prospective National Unionist Candidate,
Brigg Div., 1936-39; MP (C) Solihull Div. of Warwicks, 1945-
64. DL for County of Lincoln, 1938-45; Chm., West Midlands
Area of Conservative and Unionist Associations, 1949-52;
Murchison Grant, Royal Geographical Society; Gold Medallist,
French Geographical Soc.; Medallist Royal Belgian
Geographical Soc.; André Plaque, Royal Swedish Soc. for
Geography and Anthropology; Hon. Member Royal Belgian
Geographical Soc.; a Mem. of the Queen's Body Guard for
Scotland (Royal Company of Archers); Gold Staff Officer,
Coronation, 1953. *Publications:* Those Greenland Days, 1932;
The Epic of Captain Scott, 1933; Sledge, 1935; So Few Got
Through: the Diary of an Infantry Officer, 1946; Three Got
Through: Memoirs of an Arctic Explorer, 1947; The House of
Commons (Britain in Pictures), 1947; Shall We Reform "the
Lords"?, 1948; The Baronetcy, 1977. *Heir:* s Ronald Alexander
Lindsay [b 6 Dec. 1933; m 1968, Nicoletta, yr d of Capt. Edgar
Storich, Italian Navy, retd; three s one d]. *Address:* The Old
Vicarage, Send, near Woking, Surrey. *T:* Guildford 223157.
Club: Boodle's.

LINDSAY, Sir William, Kt 1963; CBE 1956; DL; *b* 22 March
1907; *er s* of late James Robertson Lindsay, Tower of Lethendy,
Meikleour, Perthshire, and late Barbara Coupar, *d* of late Sir
Charles Barrie; *m* 1936, Anne Diana, *d* of late Arthur Morley,
OBE, KC; one s two d. *Educ:* Trinity Coll., Glenalmond; Christ
Church, Oxford. BA 1928, MA 1931; Barrister-at-Law, Inner
Temple, 1931. Dir, Royal Caledonian Schs, 1934-; Admin
Officer, HM Treas., 1940-45. Member: Cuckfield UD Council,
1946-67 (Chm. 1951-54); Mid-Sussex Water Bd, 1946-60 (Chm.
1952-60); E Sussex CC, 1949- (Ald. 1957, Chm. 1961-64); Nat.
Health Exec. Coun. for E Sussex, 1954-66; Hailsham Hospital
Management Cttee, 1956-68; National Parks Commn, 1961-68,
Countryside Commn, 1968-72; Chairman: E Grinstead
Conservative Assoc., 1948-51 and 1957-59; Sussex Co. Cons.
Org., 1951-53 and 1958-59; Vice-Chm., 1951-54 and 1957-60
and Hon. Treas. 1960-69 of SE Area of Nat. Union of Cons. and
Unionist Assocs; Mem. Nat. Exec. Cttee of Conservative Party,
1952-54 and 1957-69. DL West Sussex, 1970-. Dir, Mid Sussex
Water Co., 1961-. *Address:* Wickham Farm, Haywards Heath,
West Sussex. *T:* Haywards Heath 371. *Club:* Bath.

LINDSAY-HOGG, Sir William (Lindsay), 3rd Bt *cr* 1905; *b* 12
Aug. 1930; *s* of Sir Anthony Henry Lindsay-Hogg, 2nd Bt and
Frances (*née* Doble; she *d* 1969); S father, 1968; *m* 1961, Victoria
Pares (marr. diss. 1968); one *d. Educ:* Stowe. Man. Dir, Roebuck
Air Charter Ltd, 1967-70, Chm. 1970-74. Hereditary Cavaliere
d'Italia. *Recreations:* riding, skiing. *Heir:* nephew Edward William
Lindsay-Hogg [b 23 May 1910; m 1st, 1936, Geraldine (marr.
diss. 1946), d of E. M. Fitzgerald; one s; 2nd, 1957, Kathleen
Mary, widow of Captain Maurice Cadell, MC and d of James
Cooney]. *Address:* Underwoods, Edgefield, Melton Constable,
Norfolk NR24 2AR. *T:* Saxthorpe 590.

LINDSAY-SMITH, Iain-Mór; Executive Editor, The Observer,
since 1977; *b* 18 Sept. 1934; *s* of Edward Duncanson Lindsay-
Smith and Margaret Anderson; *m* 1960, Carol Sara (*née*
Paxman); one s. *Educ:* High Sch. of Glasgow. Scottish Daily
Record, 1951-57; Commissioned 1st Bn Cameronians (Scottish
Rifles), 1953-55; Daily Mirror, 1957-60; Foreign Editor, subseq.
Features Editor, Daily Mail, 1960-71; Dep. Editor, Yorkshire
Post, 1971-74; Editor, Glasgow Herald, 1974-77. *Recreations:*
Highland bagpipes, foreign affairs, outdoors, travel. *Address:*
c/o The Observer, 8 St Andrew's Hill, EC4V 5JA. *Clubs:* Press,
Burke.

LINDSEY, 14th Earl of, *cr* 1626, and **ABINGDON,** 9th Earl of,
cr 1682; **Richard Henry Rupert Bertie;** Baron Norreys, of
Rycote, 1572; *b* 28 June 1931; *o s* of Hon. Arthur Michael
Bertie, DSO, MC (*d* 1957) and Aline Rose (*d* 1948), *er d* of
George Arbuthnot-Leslie, Warthill, Co. Aberdeen, and widow
of Hon. Charles Fox Maule Ramsay, MC; S cousin, 1963; *m*
1957, Norah Elizabeth Farquhar-Oliver, *yr d* of Mark Oliver,
OBE, Edgerston, Jedburgh, Roxburghshire; two s one *d. Educ:*
Ampleforth. Lieut, Royal Norfolk Regt (Supplementary
Reserve of Officers), 1951. Underwriting Member of Lloyd's,
1958-; company director; Chm., Anglo-Ivory-Coast Soc., 1974-
77. High Steward of Abingdon, 1963. *Heir:* s Lord Norreys, qv.
Address: Hunsdonbury, Hunsdon, Ware, Hertfordshire. *Clubs:*
Turf, White's.

LINDSEY, Archdeacon of; *see* Dudman, Ven. R. W.

LINDT, Auguste Rudolph, LLD; retired as Swiss Ambassador; *b*
Berne, Switzerland, 5 Aug. 1905. Studied law at Universities of
Geneva and Berne. Special correspondent of several European
newspapers, in Manchuria, Liberia, Palestine, Jordan, the
Persian Gulf, Tunisia, Roumania and Finland, 1932-40. Served
in Swiss Army, 1940-45. Special delegate of International Cttee
of the Red Cross at Berlin, 1945-46. Press Attaché, 1946,
Counsellor, 1949, Swiss Legation in London. Switzerland's
Permanent Observer to the United Nations (appointed 1953)
and subseq. Minister plenipotentiary (1954); appointments
connected with work of the United Nations: Chairman Exec.
Board of UNICEF, 1953 and 1954; President, UN Opium
Conference, 1953; Head of Swiss Delegation to Conference on
Statute of International Atomic Energy Agency, held in New
York, 1956. United Nations High Commissioner for Refugees
(elected by acclamation), Dec. 1956-60; Swiss Ambassador to
USA, 1960-63; Delegate, Swiss Fed. Council for Technical Co-
operation, 1963-66; Swiss Amassador to Soviet Union and
Mongolia, 1966-69, on leave as International Red Cross Comr-
Gen. for Nigeria-Biafra relief operation, 1968-69; Swiss
Ambassador to India and Nepal, 1969-70. Adviser to Pres. of
Republic of Rwanda, 1973-75. Pres., Internat. Union for Child
Welfare, Geneva, 1971-. Hon. DrUniv Geneva, 1960; Hon. Dr,
Coll. of Wilmington, Ohio, 1961. *Publication:* Special
Correspondent with Bandits and Generals in Manchuria, 1933.
Address: c/o Union Bank of Switzerland, 3001 Berne,
Switzerland.

LINE, Maurice Bernard, MA; FLA; Director General, British
Library Lending Division, since 1974 (Deputy Director General,
1973-74); *b* 21 June 1928; *s* of Bernard Cyril and Ruth Florence
Line; *m* 1954, Joyce Gilchrist; one s one d. *Educ:* Bedford Sch.;
Exeter Coll., Oxford (MA). Library Trainee, Bodleian Library,
1950-51; Library Asst, Glasgow Univ., 1951-53; Sub-Librarian,
Southampton Univ., 1954-65; Dep. Librarian, Univ. of
Newcastle upon Tyne, 1965-68; Librarian, Univ. of Bath, 1968-
71; Librarian, Nat. Central Library, 1971-73; Project Head,
DES Nat. Libraries ADP Study, 1970-71. Member: Library
Adv. Council for England, 1972-75; British Library Board,
1974-. AIInfSci. *Publications:* Bibliography of Russian
Literature in English Translation to 1900, 1963; The College
Student and the Library, 1965; Library Surveys, 1967; contribs
to: Jl of Documentation; Aslib Proc.; Jl of Librarianship, etc.
Recreations: music, walking, other people. *Address:* 37 Firs
Crescent, Harrogate, North Yorks. *T:* Harrogate 872984.

LINES, (Walter) Moray, CBE 1969; Chairman, Lines Brothers
Ltd, 1962-71 (Joint Managing Director, 1962-70); *b* 26 Jan.
1922; *er s* of late Walter Lines; *m* 1955, Fiona Margaret Denton;
three s one d. *Educ:* Gresham Sch. Joined Board of Lines Bros
Ltd, 1946; Chm., British Toy Manufacturers Assoc., 1968-70.
Address: The Old Rectory, Shirwell, near Barnstaple, N Devon.
T: Shirwell 265.

LINFOOT, Dr Edward Hubert, MA, DPhil, DSc (Oxon); ScD
(Cantab); John Couch Adams Astronomer in the University of
Cambridge and Assistant Director of the University
Observatory, 1948-70; *b* 8 June 1905; *s* of late George E. Linfoot;
m 1935, Joyce, *o d* of James and Ellen Dancer; one s one d.
Educ: King Edward VII Sch., Sheffield; Balliol Coll., Oxford.
Oxford Junior Mathematical Scholar, 1924; Senior
Mathematical Scholar, 1928; Goldsmiths' Senior Student, 1926;
J. E. Procter Visiting Fellow, Princeton Univ., USA, 1929;
Tutor in Mathematics, Balliol Coll., 1931; Asst Lecturer in
Math., Bristol Univ., 1932, Lecturer, 1935. *Publications:* Recent
Advances in Optics, 1955; Qualitätsbewertung optischer Bilder,
1960; Fourier Methods in Optical Image Evaluation, 1964;
papers in scientific journals. *Recreations:* music, chess,
gardening. *Address:* 7 Sherlock Road, Cambridge. *T:*
Cambridge 56513.
See also L . M . MacDougall .

LINFORD, Alan C.; *see* Carr Linford.

LING, Arthur George, FRIBA; PPRTPI; architect and town
planner in practice with Arthur Ling and Associates; *b* 20 Sept.
1913; *s* of George Frederick Ling and Elsie Emily (*née* Wisbey);
m 1939, Marjorie Tall; one s three *d. Educ:* Christ's Hospital;
University College, London (Bartlett School of Architecture).
BA (Architecture), London. Architect in Office of E. Maxwell
Fry and Walter Gropius, 1937-39; Structural Engineer with
Corporation of City of London (Air raid shelters and War debris
clearance), 1939-41; Member town planning team responsible
for preparation of County of London Plan, 1943, under direction
of J. H. Forshaw and Sir Patrick Abercrombie, 1941-45; Chief
Planning Officer, London County Council, 1945-55; Head of

Department of Town Planning, University College, London Univ., 1947-48; Sen. Lecturer in Town Planning, 1948-55; City Architect and Planning Officer, Coventry, 1955-64; Prof. and Head of Dept of Architecture and Civic Planning, Univ. of Nottingham, 1964-69, Special Prof. of Environmental Design, 1969-72. Visiting Professor: University of Santiago, Chile, 1963; Univ. of NSW, Australia, 1969; Chancellor Lectures, Univ. of Wellington, NZ, 1969. Joint Architect for Development Plan for University of Warwick. Cons. Architect Planner, Runcorn New Town Corporation. Former Chairman, Board of Chief Officers, Midlands Housing Consortium; Past Vice-Pres., RIBA; President: RTPI, 1968-69; Commonwealth Assoc. of Planners, 1968-76. Mem., Sports Council, 1968-71; Vice-Chm., E Midlands Sports Council, 1968-76. Pres., Heckington Village Trust. RIBA Dist. in Town Planning, 1956; Silver Medallist (Essay), 1937; Hunt Bursary, 1939. Fellow University College, London, 1967. *Publications:* Contrib. to professional journals on architecture and town planning. *Address:* The Old Rectory, Howell, Sleaford, Lincolnshire.

LING, Maj.-Gen. (Retd) Fergus Alan Humphrey, CB 1968; CBE 1964; DSO 1944; DL; Vice-Lord-Lieutenant of Surrey, since 1975; Defence Services Consultant, Institute for the Study of Conflict, since 1970; *b* 5 Aug. 1914; 3rd *s* of John Richardson and Mabel Ling; *m* 1940, Sheelah Phyllis Sarel; two *s* three *d*. *Educ:* Stowe Sch.; Royal Military Coll., Sandhurst. Comd 2nd/5th Queen's, 1944; GSO 1 (Ops), GHQ, Middle East, 1945-46; British Liaison Officer, US Infantry Centre, 1948-50; Comd Regt Depot, Queen's Royal Regt, 1951; Directing Staff, Staff Coll., Camberley, 1951-53; comd 5th Queen's, 1954-57; Asst Military Secretary, War Office, 1957-58; comd 148 North Midland Brigade (TA), 1958-61; DAG, HQ, BAOR, 1961-65; GOC: 54 (East Anglian) Division/District, 1965-67; East Anglian District, 1967-68; Eastern District, 1968-69. Col, The Queen's Regt, 1973- (Dep. Col, 1969-73). Chairman, Surrey T&AVR Cttee, 1973-; Vice-Chm., SE T&AVR Assoc. DL Surrey, 1970. *Recreations:* homes and gardens, country pursuits. *Address:* Grove Cottage, Shalford, near Guildford, Surrey. *T:* Guildford 61567. *Club:* Royal Commonwealth Society.

LING, John de Courcy; *see* de Courcy Ling.

LINGARD, Peter Anthony, CBE 1977; TD; Deputy Director General, St John Ambulance Association, since 1977; *b* 29 Feb. 1916; *s* of Herbert Arthur Lingard and Kate Augusta Burdett; *m* 1946, Enid Nora Argile; two *d*. *Educ:* Berkhamsted Sch.; London Univ. (BCom). Served RA, 1939-46; Major, 1943 (despatches twice). Co. of London Electric Supply Gp, 1936; Area Manager Lambeth and Camberwell, County Group, 1947; Commercial Officer, S Western Sub-Area, 1948, Chief Commercial Officer, 1959-62, London Electricity Board; Commercial and Development Adviser, Electricity Council, 1962-65; Mem., Electricity Council, 1965-72; Chm., E Midlands Electricity Bd, 1972-77. Member: CEGB, 1972-75; Directing Cttee, Internat. Union of Producers and Distributors of Electrical Energy, 1973-77. Member: Ct of Governors, Admin. Staff Coll; Council, IEE; Council of Industrial Soc.; E Midlands Econ. Planning Council; Nottingham Univ. Ct. CompIEE 1967. FBIM 1973. *Recreations:* photography, sailing, walking, reading. *Address:* The Dumble, High Street, Orford, Woodbridge, Suffolk IP12 2NW. *T:* Orford 622. *Clubs:* Royal Automobile; Aldeburgh Yacht.

LINGS, Dr Martin; Keeper Emeritus of Oriental Manuscripts and Printed Books, British Library; *b* 24 Jan. 1909; *e s* of late George Herbert Lings and late Gladys Mary Lings (*née* Greenhalgh), Burnage, Lancs; *m* 1944, Lesley, 3rd *d* of late Edgar Smalley. *Educ:* Clifton Coll.; Magdalen Coll., Oxford; Sch. of Oriental and African Studies, Univ. of London. Class. Mods 1930, BA English 1932, MA 1937, Oxon; BA Arabic 1954, PhD 1959, London. Lectr in Anglo-Saxon and Middle English, Univ. of Kaunas, 1935-39; Lectr in English Lit., Univ. of Cairo, 1940-51; Asst Keeper, Dept of Oriental Printed Books and Manuscripts, British Museum, 1955-70; Deputy Keeper, 1970; Keeper, 1971; seconded to the British Library, 1973. FRAS. *Publications:* The Book of Certainty, 1952; (with A. S. Fulton) Second Supplementary Catalogue of Arabic Printed Books in the British Museum, 1959; A Moslem Saint of the Twentieth Century, 1961 (trans. French 1967, Arabic 1972); Ancient Beliefs and Modern Superstitions, 1965; Shakespeare in the Light of Sacred Art, 1966; The Elements and Other Poems, 1967; The Heralds and Other Poems, 1970; A Sufi Saint of the Twentieth Century, 1971; What is Sufism?, 1975 (trans. French, 1977); (with Y. H. Safadi) Third Supplementary Catalogue of Arabic Printed Books in the British Library, 1976; (with Y. H. Safadi) The Qur'ān, Catalogue of an Exhibition at the British Library, 1976; The Quranic Art of Calligraphy and Illumination, 1977; articles in Encycl. Britannica, Encycl. Islam,

Studies in Comparative Religion, etc. *Recreations:* walking, gardening, music. *Address:* 3 French Street, Westerham, Kent. *T:* Westerham 62855.

LINK, Edwin Albert; inventor, airman, ocean engineer; Consultant, The Singer Co.; President, Marine Science Center, Florida; Director and Trustee, Harbor Branch Foundation Inc.; *b* 26 July 1904; *s* of Edwin A. Link and Katherine Link; *m* 1931, Marion Clayton; one *s* (and one *s* decd). *Educ:* Binghamton and Lindsley Schools. Aviator, 1927-; President, founder, Link Aviation Inc., 1935-53; President, General Precision Equipment Corp., 1958-59. Director Emeritus, Allegheny Airlines. Inventor Link Aviation Trainers. Founder, Link Foundation, 1953. Awarded Exceptional Service Medal, USAF; Wakefield Medal, RAeS, 1947; also varied awards from American organisations; holds honorary doctorates from Tufts University, Syracuse Univ. and Hamilton Coll.; Hon. DSc, Florida Inst. of Technology, 1970. *Publications:* Simplified Celestial Navigation (with P. V. H. Weems), 1940; articles on diving development and research in National Geographic magazines. *Address:* 10 Avon Road, Binghamton, NY 13905, USA; RD1, Box 194, Fort Pierce, Fla 33450, USA.

LINKLATER, Nelson Valdemar, CBE 1974 (OBE 1967); Drama Director, Arts Council of Great Britain, 1970-77; *b* 15 Aug. 1918; *s* of Captain Arthur David Linklater and Elsie May Linklater; *m* 1944, Margaret Lilian Boissard; two *s*. *Educ:* Imperial Service Coll.; RADA. RNVR, 1939-46 (final rank Lieut (S)). Professional theatre as actor and business manager, 1937-39. Documentary Films Manager, Army Kinema Corp., 1946-48; Arts Council of Great Britain: Asst Regional Dir (Nottingham), 1948-52; Asst and Dep. Drama Dir (London), 1952-70. Chm., CPRE, Wallingford Area Cttee, 1977-. Mem. Bd, Anvil Productions (Oxford Playhouse), 1977-. *Recreations:* painting, reading, gardening. *Address:* 1 Church Close, East Hagbourne, Oxon OX11 9LP. *T:* Didcot 813340.

LINKS, Mrs J. G.; *see* Lutyens, Mary.

LINLEY, Viscount; David Albert Charles Armstrong-Jones; *b* 3 Nov. 1961; *s* and *heir* of 1st Earl of Snowdon, *qv*, and *s* of HRH the Princess Margaret.
See under Royal Family.

LINLITHGOW, 3rd Marquess of, *cr* 1902; **Charles William Frederick Hope,** MC 1945; TD 1973; Earl of Hopetoun, 1703; Viscount Aithrie, Baron Hope, 1703; Baron Hopetoun (UK) 1809; Baron Niddry (UK), 1814; Bt (Scotland), 1698; Captain (retired), 19th (Lothians and Border Horse) Armoured Car Company, Royal Tank Corps (Territorial Army); Lord-Lieutenant of West Lothian, since 1964; Director, Eagle Star Insurance Co. Ltd; *b* 7 April 1912; *er s* of 2nd Marquess of Linlithgow, KG, KT, PC and Doreen Maud, CI 1936, Kaisar-i-Hind Medal 1st Class (*d* 1965), 2nd *d* of Rt Hon. Sir F. Milner, 7th Bt; *S* father 1952; *m* 1st, 1939, Vivien (*d* 1963), *d* of Capt. R. O. R. Kenyon-Slaney, and of Lady Mary Gilmour; one *s* one *d*; 2nd, 1965, Judith, *widow* of Esmond Baring. *Educ:* Eton; Christ Church, Oxford. Lieut, Scots Guards R of O; served War of 1939-45 (prisoner, MC). *Heir:* *s* Earl of Hopetoun, *qv*. *Address:* Hopetoun House, South Queensferry, West Lothian. *T:* 031-331 1169. *Club:* White's.
See also Baron Glendevon, Countess of Pembroke.

LINNELL, Prof. Wilfred Herbert, MSc, DSc, PhD, FRIC, FPS; retired as Dean of the School of Pharmacy, University of London (1956-62); Professor of Pharmaceutical Chemistry, 1944-62; Professor Emeritus, 1962; Fellow of School of Pharmacy, University of London, 1962; *b* Sandbach, Cheshire, 1894; *s* of John Goodman and Evelyn Pring Linnell; *m* 1927, Margery, *d* of R. H. Hughes, Streetly; one *s*. *Educ:* Stockport Grammar Sch.; University of Durham; Lincoln Coll., Oxford; Armstrong Coll., Durham Univ., 1919-23; awarded the Earl Grey Memorial Fellowship, which was held at Lincoln Coll., Oxford; Governor, Chelsea College of Science and Technology. Research Chemist at HM Fuel Research Station, 1924-26; Examiner to the Pharmaceutical Society for Statutory Examinations since 1917; Corresp. étranger de l'Acad. Royale de Médecine de Belgique; Corresp. étranger de l'Acad. de Pharmacie de France. *Publications:* original contribs to science, published in the Journal of the Chemical Society, Journal of Society of Chemical Industry, and Journal of Pharmacy and Pharmacology. *Recreation:* sailing. *Address:* 103 Park Avenue, Ruislip, Middlesex.

LINSTEAD, Sir Hugh (Nicholas), Kt 1953; OBE 1937; Chairman, Macarthys Pharmaceuticals Ltd, *b* 3 Feb. 1901; *e s* of late Edward Flatman Linstead and Florence Evelyn Hester; *m* 1928, Alice Winifred Freke; two *d*. *Educ:* City of London Sch.;

Pharmaceutical Society's Sch. (Jacob Bell Scholar); Birkbeck Coll. Pharmaceutical chemist; barrister-at-law, Middle Temple, 1929. MP (C) Putney Div. of Wandsworth, 1942-64. Secretary: Pharmaceutical Society of Great Britain, 1926-64; Central Pharmaceutical War Cttee, 1938-46; Pres., Internat. Pharmaceutical Fedn, 1953-65; Member, Medical Research Council, 1956-64; Chairman and Vice-Chairman, Joint Negotiating Cttee (Hospital Staffs), 1946-48; Member Poisons Board (Home Office), 1935-57; Chairman: Wandsworth Group Hospital Cttee, 1948-53; Parliamentary and Scientific Cttee, 1955-57; Library Cttee, House of Commons, 1963-64; Franco-British Parliamentary Relations Cttee, 1955-60. Member: Central Health Services Council (Min. of Health), 1951-66; Departmental Cttee on Homosexual Offences and Prostitution; Departmental Cttee on Experiments on Animals. Parliamentary Charity Comr for England and Wales, 1956-60. First Chm., Farriers' Registration Council, 1976-. Comr for Training Scout Officers, Boy Scouts' Assoc., 1932-41; Hon. LLD: British Columbia, 1956; Toronto, 1963; Hon. Member American and Canadian Pharmaceutical Assocs, British Dental Assoc. and other societies; Corresponding Member Académie de Médecine de France and Académie de Pharmacie de Paris; Mem. Court, Farriers Co. (Master 1971-72). Commandeur de la Légion d'Honneur; Officier de la Santé Publique (France); Kt Comdr Al Merito Sanitario (Spain). *Address:* 15 Somerville House, Manor Fields, SW15 3LX. *Club:* Athenæum.

LINTERN, Bernard Francis; journalist; *b* 26 Nov. 1908; *e s* of late Rev. F. G. Lintern and Beatrice Golding; *m* 1931, Mary, *e d* of late Arthur Watts. *Educ:* Chigwell; University of London. Editor of Discovery, and Associate-editor of Television, 1932-34; Associate-editor of Industria Britanica, 1934; Editorial Director, Lawrence H. Tearle Publications, Cape Town and Johannesburg, 1950-60; Editor of The Stethoscope and Pharmacy News, Director, Marketing Publications Ltd, 1961-63. Seaman, RN, 1940; Lieut, RNVR, 1942; Combined Operations, 1941; attached, Fleet Air Arm, 1942-46. *Address:* 194 Russell Court, Woburn Place, WC1H 0LR. *Clubs:* Naval, Wig and Pen; Southern African Naval Officers' (Johannesburg).

LINTON, Alan Henry Spencer, MVO 1969; HM Diplomatic Service; Consul-General, Detroit, USA, since 1976; *b* Nottingham, 24 July 1919; *s* of Rt Rev. James Henry Linton, DD and Alicia Pears (*née* Aldous); *m* 1959, Kaethe Krebs; four *d*. *Educ:* St Lawrence, Ramsgate; Magdalen Coll., Oxford (MA). Served War, RA, 1940-46. HM Overseas Civil Service, Tanganyika, 1947-62; FO, 1963-65; First Sec. (Inf.), Vienna, 1965-69; Head of Chancery, Lusaka, Zambia, 1970-73; First Sec. (Commercial), Kingston, Jamaica, 1973-75; Dep. High Comr, Kingston, 1975-76. *Recreations:* skiing, sailing, photography. *Address:* c/o Foreign and Commonwealth Office, King Charles Street, SW1A 2AH. *Clubs:* Royal Over-Seas League; Detroit, Detroit Yacht (USA).

LINTOTT, Sir Henry, KCMG 1957 (CMG 1948); Director, Glaxo Holdings Ltd; *b* 23 Sept. 1908; *s* of late Henry John Lintott, RSA, and of Edith Lunn; *m* 1949, Margaret Orpen; one *s* one *d*. *Educ:* Edinburgh Acad.; Edinburgh Univ.; King's Coll., Cambridge. Entered Customs and Excise Dept, 1932; Board of Trade, 1935-48; Dep. Secretary-General, OEEC, 1948-56. Dep. Under-Secretary of State, Commonwealth Relations Office, 1956-63; British High Commissioner in Canada, 1963-68. *Address:* Rest-harrow, Spithurst Road, Barcombe, Lewes, East Sussex BN8 5EF. *T:* Barcombe 400449.

LIPFRIEND, Alan; His Honour Judge Lipfriend; Circuit Judge since 1974; *b* 6 Oct. 1916; 2nd *s* of I. and S. Lipfriend; *m* 1948, Adèle Burke; one *s*. *Educ:* Central Foundation Sch., London; Queen Mary Coll., London. BSc(Eng) (Hons) 1938. Design Staff, Hawker Aircraft Ltd, 1939-48. Called to Bar, Middle Temple, 1948; Pres., Appeal Tribunal, under Wireless and Telegraphy Act, 1949, apptd 1971. *Recreations:* theatre and all sport. *Address:* 10 Woodside Avenue, N6 4SS. *T:* 01-883 4420. *Club:* Royal Automobile.

LIPMAN, Vivian David, DPhil; FRHistS, FSA; Director of Ancient Monuments and Historic Buildings, Department of the Environment, since 1972; *b* 27 Feb. 1921; *s* of late Samuel N. Lipman, MBE, and Cecelia (*née* Moses); *m* 1964, Sonia Lynette Senslive; one *s*. *Educ:* St. Paul's Sch.; Magdalen (Classical Demy) and Nuffield Colls, Oxford (MA). Served War, 1942-45, in Royal Signals and Intelligence Corps. Entered Civil Service as Asst Principal, 1947; Principal, 1950; Asst Sec., 1963; Under-Sec., 1972; Crown Estate Paving Commissioner, 1972. Hon. Research Fellow, University Coll. London, 1971-. Vice-Pres. (Pres., 1965-67), Jewish Historical Soc. of England, 1967-. *Publications:* Local Government Areas, 1949; Social History of the Jews in England, 1954; A Century of Social Service, 1959;

(ed) Three Centuries of Anglo-Jewish History, 1961; The Jews of Medieval Norwich, 1967. *Recreation:* reading detective stories. *Address:* 33 Kensington Court, W8 5BG. *T:* 01-937 8382. *Club:* Athenæum.

LIPMANN, Fritz (Albert), MD, PhD; Professor of Biochemistry, Rockefeller University, since 1965 (Rockefeller Institute, 1957-65); Head of Biochemical Research Laboratory, Mass. General Hospital, 1941-57; Professor of Biological Chemistry, Harvard Medical School, 1949-57; *b* Koenigsberg, Germany, 12 June 1899; *s* of Leopold Lipmann and Gertrud Lachmanski; *m* 1931, Elfreda M. Hall; one *s*. *Educ:* Universities of Koenigsberg, Berlin, Munich. MD Berlin, 1924; PhD Koenigsberg, Berlin, 1927. Research Asst, Kaiser Wilhelm Inst., Berlin and Heidelberg, 1927-31; Research Fellow, Rockefeller Inst. for Medical Research, New York, 1931-32; Research Assoc., Biological Inst. of Carlsberg Foundation, Copenhagen, 1932-39; Res. Assoc., Dept of Biological Chem., Cornell University Med. Sch., NY, 1939-41; Res. Fellow in Surgery, 1941-43, and Associate in Biochemistry, 1943-49, Harvard Medical Sch.; Prof. of Biological Chemistry, Mass. General Hospital, 1949-57. Carl Neuberg Medal, 1948; Mead Johnson and Co. Award, 1948. Hon. MD, Marseilles, 1947; Hon. DSc: Chicago, 1953; Sorbonne, 1966; Harvard, 1967; Rockefeller, 1971; Hon. Doc. Humane Letters: Brandeis, 1959; Albert Einstein College of Medicine of Yeshiva Univ., 1964; Nobel Prize in Medicine and Physiology, 1953; National Medal of Science, 1966. Member: National Academy of Sciences, American Association for Advancement of Science, American Chemical Society, Society of Biological Chemists, Harvey Society, Biochem. Society, Society of American Microbiologists; Fellow Danish Royal Academy of Sciences; Fellow, NY Academy Science; Foreign Member Royal Society, 1962. *Publications:* Wanderings of a Biochemist, 1971; articles in German, American and English journals. *Address:* (office) The Rockefeller University, New York, NY 10021, USA; (home) 201 East 17th Street, New York, NY 10003, USA.

LIPSCOMB, Maj.-Gen. Christopher Godfrey, CB 1961; DSO and Bar 1945; Chief of Joint Services Liaison Organisation, BAOR, Bonn, 1958-61, retired; *b* 22 Dec. 1907; *s* of Godfrey Lipscomb and Mildred Agnes (*née* Leatham); *m* 1937, Ellen Diana Hayward; two *s*. *Educ:* Charterhouse; Sandhurst. Commissioned into Somerset Light Infantry, 1928; seconded Nigerian Regt, Royal West African Frontier Force, 1933-39; Commanded 4th Somerset LI, 1944-46; Staff Coll., 1947; AA&QMG, SW District, 1948-50; Comd 19 Inf. Bde, 1950-53; Commandant Senior Officers' Sch., 1954-56; Comd Hanover District, BAOR, 1957-58. *Address:* Crockerton House, Warminster, Wilts.

LIPSCOMB, Air Vice-Marshal (retired) Frederick Elvy, CB 1958; CBE 1953; *b* 2 Sept. 1902; *s* of late Arthur Bossley Lipscomb, St Albans; *m* 1931, Dorothy May (*d* 1964), *d* of Frederick Foskett, Berkhamsted, Herts; no *c*. *Educ:* Aldenham Sch.; Middlesex Hospital. MRCS LRCP 1927; DTM&H (Eng.), 1933; DPH (London) 1934. Commnd RAF 1927; psa 1946. Served Aden, Malta, Palestine; War of 1939-45, Mediterranean and West Africa (despatches thrice). Director of Hygiene and Research, Air Ministry, 1950; Principal Medical Officer, Far East Air Force, 1951-54; Dep. Director General RAF Medical Services, 1954-55; Principal Medical Officer, Home Command, 1955-57. KHP 1952; QHP 1952-57. CStJ 1952. *Publications:* Tropical Diseases section, Conybeare's Textbook of Medicine, 6th to 9th edns. Contributions to British Medical Journal, RAF Quarterly, etc. *Address:* 79 Perry Street, Wendover, Bucks.

LIPSCOMB, Prof. William Nunn; Abbott and James Lawrence Professor of Chemistry, Harvard University, since 1971; Nobel Laureate in Chemistry, 1976; *b* 9 Dec. 1919; *s* of late William Nunn Lipscomb Sr, and of Edna Patterson Porter; *m* 1947, Mary Adele Sargent; one *s* one *d*. *Educ:* Univ. of Kentucky (BS); California Inst. of Technology (PhD). Univ. of Minnesota, Minneapolis: Asst Prof. of Physical Chem., 1946-50; Associate Prof., 1950-54; Actg Chief, Physical Chem. Div., 1952-54; Prof. and Chief of Physical Chem. Div., 1954-59; Harvard Univ.: Prof. of Chemistry, 1959-71 (Chm., Dept of Chem., 1962-65). MA (hon.) Harvard, 1959; DSc (hon.) Kentucky, 1963; Dr *hc* Munich, 1976. Member: Amer. Acad. of Arts and Sciences, 1959-; Nat. Acad. of Sciences, USA, 1961-; Foreign Mem., Netherlands Acad. of Arts and Sciences, 1976. *Publications:* Boron Hydrides, 1963 (New York); (with G. R. Eaton) Nuclear Magnetic Resonance Studies of Boron and Related Compounds, 1969 (New York); contribs to scientific jls concerning structure and function of enzymes and natural products in inorganic chem. and theoretical chem. *Recreations:* tennis, chamber music. *Address:* Gibbs Chemical Laboratory, Harvard University, 12 Oxford Street, Cambridge, Mass 02138, USA. *T:* 617-495-4098.

LIPSEY, Prof. Richard George; Sir Edward Peacock Professor of Economics, Queen's University, Kingston, Ontario, since 1970; *b* 28 Aug. 1928; *s* of R. A. Lipsey and F. T. Lipsey (*née* Ledingham); *m* 1960, Diana Louise Smart; one *s* two *d. Educ:* Univ. of British Columbia (BA 1st Cl. Hons 1950); Univ. of Toronto (MA 1953); LSE (PhD 1957). Dept of Trade and Industry, British Columbia Provincial Govt, 1950-53; LSE: Asst Lectr, 1955-58; Lectr, 1958-60; Reader, 1960-61; Prof. 1961-63; Univ. of Essex: Prof. of Economics, 1963-70; Dean of School of Social Studies, 1963-67. Vis. Prof., Univ. of California at Berkeley, 1963-64; Simeon Vis. Prof., Univ. of Manchester, 1973. Economic Consultant, NEDC, 1961-63; Member of Council: SSRC, 1966-69; Royal Economic Soc., 1968-71. Fellow, Econometric Soc., 1972. Editor, Review of Economic Studies, 1960-64. *Publications:* An Introduction to Positive Economics, 1963, 4th edn 1975; (with P. O. Steiner) Economics, 1966, 5th edn 1978; (with G. C. Archibald) An Introduction to a Mathematical Treatment of Economics, 1967, 3rd edn 1977; The Theory of Customs Unions: a general equilibrium analysis, 1971; (with G. C. Archibald) An Introduction to Mathematical Economics, 1975; articles in learned jls on many branches of theoretical and applied economics. *Recreations:* skiing, fishing, walking. *Address:* Department of Economics, Queen's University, Kingston, Ontario, Canada.

LIPSON, Prof. Henry Solomon, CBE 1976; FRS 1957; Professor of Physics, University of Manchester Institute of Science and Technology, 1954-77, now Emeritus; *b* 11 March 1910; *s* of Israel Lipson and Sarah (*née* Friedland); *m* 1937, Jane Rosenthal; one *s* two *d. Educ:* Hawarden Grammar Sch.; Liverpool Univ. BSc 1930, MSc 1931, DSc 1939 (Liverpool); MA Cambridge, 1942; MSc Tech., Manchester, 1958; Oliver Lodge Scholar, Liverpool, 1933; Senior DSIR Grant, Manchester, 1936. Junior Scientific Officer, National Physical Lab., 1937; Asst in Crystallography, Cambridge, 1938; Head of Physics Dept, Manchester College of Technology, 1945; Dean, Faculty of Technology, Manchester Univ., 1975. President Manchester Literary and Philosophical Society, 1960-77. Visiting Professor of Physics: University of Calcutta, 1963-64; Technion, Haifa, 1969. *Publications:* The Interpretation of X-ray Diffraction Photographs (with Drs Henry and Wooster), 1951; Determination of Crystal Structures (with Dr Cochran), 1953; Fourier Transforms and X-Ray Diffraction (with Prof. Taylor), 1958; Optical Transforms: Their Preparation and Application to X-ray Diffraction Problems (with Prof. Taylor), 1964; Optical Physics (with Dr Lipson), 1968; The Great Experiments in Physics, 1968; Interpretation of X-ray Powder Diffraction Patterns (with Dr Steeple), 1970; Crystals and X-rays (with R. M. Lee), 1970; (ed) Optical Transforms, 1972; papers in Royal Society Proceedings, Acta Crystallographica, etc. *Recreations:* table-tennis, D-I-Y. *Address:* 22 Cranmer Road, Manchester M20 0AW. *T:* 061-445 4517.

LIPSTEIN, Prof. Kurt; Professor of Comparative Law, Cambridge University, 1973-76; Fellow of Clare College, Cambridge, since 1956; *b* 19 March 1909; *e s* of Alfred Lipstein, MD and Hilda (*née* Sulzbach); *m* 1944, Gwyneth Mary Herford; two *d. Educ:* Goethe Gymnasium, Frankfurt on Main; Univs of Grenoble and Berlin; Trinity Coll., Cambridge. Gerichtsreferendar 1931; PhD Cantab 1936; LLD 1977. Called to Bar, Middle Temple, 1950, Hon. Bencher, 1966. Univ. Lectr, Cambridge, 1946; Reader in Conflict of Laws, Cambridge Univ., 1962-73. Dir of Research, Internat. Assoc. Legal Science, 1954-59. Vis. Professor: Univ. of Pennsylvania, 1962; Northwestern Univ., Chicago, 1966, 1968; Paris I, 1977. *Publications:* The Law of the EEC, 1974; joint editor and contributor: Dicey's Conflict of Laws, 6th edn, 1948-8th edn, 1967; Leske-Loewenfeld, Das Eherecht der europäischen Staaten, 1963; International Encyclopaedia of Comparative Law, vol. Private International Law, 1972; contrib. Annales de la Faculté de droit d'Istamboul, Brit. Jl Internat. Law, Camb. Law Jl, Communicazioni e Studi, Internat. and Comp. Law Qly, Hague Recueil, Jl du droit internat., Jurisclasseur de droit internat., Modern Law Rev., Ottawa Law Rev., Revista de l'Instituto de derecho comparado, Trans of the Grotius Soc., etc. *Address:* Clare College, Cambridge. *T:* Cambridge 58681; 7 Barton Close, Cambridge. *T:* 57048; 13 Old Square, Lincoln's Inn, WC2A 3UA. *T:* 01-405 5441.

LIPTON, Marcus, CBE 1965 (OBE 1949); JP; MP (Lab) Lambeth Central, since 1974 (Lambeth, Brixton, 1945-74); *b* 29 Oct. 1900; *s* of late Benjamin Lipton and of Mary Lipton, Sunderland. *Educ:* Hudson Road Council Sch.; Bede Grammar Sch., Sunderland; Merton Coll., Oxford (Goldsmiths' Company Exhibitioner) MA. Barrister-at-law, Gray's Inn, 1926. Councillor, Stepney Borough Council, 1934-37. Contested (Lab) Brixton, 1935. Alderman, Lambeth Borough Council, 1937-56; Hon. Freeman, London Borough of Lambeth, 1974. JP County

of London, 1939. Private, TA, 1939; Lieut-Colonel, 1944. Councillor, Binfield Parish Council, 1955-59. President: Lambeth Central Labour Party; Brixton Branch, British Legion; Southern Sunday Football League; Chairman, Anglo-Nepalese, Anglo-Bulgarian and Anglo-Haitian Parliamentary Groups. *Recreation:* giving advice. *Address:* 3 Wellington Court, Shelton Street, WC2. *T:* 01-836 7885.

LISBURNE, 8th Earl of, *cr* 1776; **John David Malet Vaughan;** Viscount Lisburne and Lord Vaughan, 1695; barrister-at-law; *b* 1 Sept. 1918; *o s* of 7th Earl of Lisburne; *S* father, 1965; *m* 1943, Shelagh, *er d* of late T. A. Macauley, 1266 Redpath Crescent, Montreal, Canada; three *s. Educ:* Eton; Magdalen Coll., Oxford (BA, MA). Called to Bar, Inner Temple, 1947. Captain, Welsh Guards. Dep. Chm., Westward Television Ltd; Dir, British Home Stores Ltd. *Heir: s* Viscount Vaughan, *qv. Address:* 22 York House, Kensington Church Street, W8. *T:* 01-937 3043; Sloane Square House, Holbein Place, SW1W 8NT; Cruglas, Ystrad Meurig, Dyfed. *T:* Pontrhydfendigaid 230. *Clubs:* Turf, Pratt's.

LISLE, 7th Baron, *cr* 1758; **John Nicholas Horace Lysaght;** *s* of late Hon. Horace G. Lysaght and Alice Elizabeth, *d* of Sir John Wrixon Becher, 3rd Bt; *b* 10 Aug. 1903; *S* grandfather, 1919; *m* 1st, 1928, Vivienne Brew (who obtained a divorce, 1939; she *died* 1948); 2nd, 1939, Mary Helen Purgold, Shropshire. *Heir: b* Horace James William Lysaght [*b* 1908; *m* 1st, 1930, Joanna Mary Nolan (marr. diss., 1951); four *s*; 2nd, 1953; two *d*]. *Address:* 4 Bramerton Street, Chelsea, SW3.

LISLE, Aubrey Edwin O.; *see* Orchard-Lisle.

LISSACK, Victor Jack; a Recorder of the Crown Court, since 1972; solicitor in own practice since 1954; *b* 10 Sept. 1930; *s* of Maurice Solomon Lissack and Anna Lilian Lissack (*née* Falk); *m* 1953, Antoinette Rosalind Mildred Rose; two *s. Educ:* Peterborough Lodge Prep. Sch.; Wyoming High Sch., Ohio; Gresham's Sch., Holt; Law Soc. Sch. of Law. Articled, Hicks Arnold & Co., Solicitors, 1947-52, qual. 1954. Member: Donovan Cttee on Court of Criminal Appeal, 1964-65; James Cttee on Distribution of Criminal Business, 1974-75; Southern Area Council of British Boxing Bd of Control, 1964-; Mem. Exec. Cttee, 1966-75, Chm. 1975-, Prisoners' Wives Service; Trustee and Vice-Chm. Bd of Management, London Centre, 1974-; Sec., London Criminal Courts Solicitors' Assoc., 1970-74, Pres., 1974-76; Mem. Exec., Soc. of Conservative Lawyers, 1971-74; Sec., Gardner Cttee on Penal Reform, 1971-72; Sec., Gardner Cttee on Children and Young Persons Act, 1973-. *Recreations:* sporadic sailing, gentle golf, constant car cleaning. *Address:* 52 Wildwood Road, Hampstead, NW11. *T:* 01-455 8766; 8 Bow Street, Covent Garden, WC2E 7AJ. *T:* 01-240 2010. *Club:* United and Cecil.

LISSMANN, Hans Werner, FRS 1954; Reader, Department of Zoology, Cambridge, 1966-77, and Director, Sub-Department of Animal Behaviour, 1969-77; Fellow of Trinity College, Cambridge, since 1955; *b* 30 April 1909; *s* of Robert and Ebba Lissmann; *m* 1949, Corinne Foster-Barham; one *s. Educ:* Kargala and Hamburg. Dr.rer.nat., Hamburg, 1932; MA, Cantab, 1947. Asst Director of Research, Dept of Zoology, Cambridge, 1947-55; Lecturer, 1955-66. *Address:* 9 Bulstrode Gardens, Cambridge. *T:* 56126.

LISTER; *see* Cunliffe-Lister, family name of Earl of Swinton.

LISTER, Sir (Charles) Percy, Kt 1947; DL; *b* 15 July 1897; 3rd *s* of late Charles Ashton Lister, CBE; *m* 1953, Mrs Geraldine Bigger, Portstewart, Ulster. *Educ:* Mill Hill; RMC, Sandhurst. 18th QMO Royal Hussars. Past Chairman and Managing Director: R. A. Lister and Co. Ltd, Dursley; United Kingdom Commercial Corp., 1940-45; Past Director: Sir W. G. Armstrong Whitworth (Engineers) Ltd; Hawker Siddeley Group Ltd. Member: Capital Issues Cttee, 1946-47; Dollar Exports Councils, 1949-64; Iron and Steel Board, 1953-58. DL County of Gloucester, 1960. *Recreations:* hunting, yachting, golf. *Address:* Stinchcombe Hill House, Dursley, Glos. *TA* and *T:* Dursley 2030. *Club:* Cavalry and Guards.

LISTER, Lt-Col (Bt Col) Harry Laidman, OBE 1946; TD 1943; JP; retired; Vice Lord-Lieutenant, County of Cleveland, since 1974; *b* 25 Oct. 1902; *s* of John James Lister, JP, and Margaret Lister; *m* 1st, 1930, Janet McLaren; two *s*; 2nd, 1971, Elizabeth Emmeline Walmsley. *Educ:* Durham School. Coal exporter and shipbroker, 1927-58; Welfare Officer, South Durham Steel & Iron Co., 1958-69. Joined TA, 1925, 55th Medium Bde; BEF, 1940, France and Belgium with 85th (Tees) HAA Regt RA, TA (despatches 1940); comd 53 City of London HAA Regt, TA, 1940; served in London, 1940-41, and India, 1942-45; comd 85

(City of London) Medium Regt, 1944-45; comd 6th Cadet Bn Durham LI, 1945; raised and comd 654 LAA Regt RA, TA, 1946; comd 427 (M) HAA Regt RA, TA, 1948; Bt Col 1952; RofO 1952; comd 18th Bn Home Guard, 1953-56, when disbanded. Mem., Hartlepool Borough Council, 1945-48; Mem. Management Cttee, Hartlepool Gp of Hosps, 1958-74; Mem. T&AFA, Co. Durham, 1947-52 and 1953-68. DL Co. Durham, 1956; JP Co. Durham and Hartlepool, 1958. *Recreation:* Rugby football (Captain 1926-27, Pres. 1969, Hartlepool Rovers FC; played for Durham County, 1923-28). *Address:* 10 Cliff Terrace, Hartlepool, Cleveland TS24 0PU. *T:* Hartlepool 66042.

LISTER, Very Rev. John Field, MA; Provost of Wakefield, since 1972; Rural Dean of Wakefield, since 1972; *b* 19 Jan. 1916; *s* of Arthur and Florence Lister. *Educ:* King's Sch., Worcester; Keble Coll., Oxford; Cuddesdon Coll., Oxford. Asst Curate, St Nicholas, Radford, Coventry, 1939-44; Asst Curate, St John Baptist, Coventry, 1944-45; Vicar of St John's, Huddersfield, 1945-54; Asst Rural Dean of Halifax, 1955-61; Archdeacon of Halifax, 1961-72; Vicar of Brighouse, 1954-72. Examng Chaplain to Bishop of Wakefield, 1972-. Hon. Canon of Wakefield Cathedral, 1961, Canon, 1968. Chaplain to the Queen, 1966-72. *Address:* The Cathedral Vicarage, Margaret Street, Wakefield WF1 2DQ, West Yorks. *T:* Wakefield 72402. *Club:* National.

LISTER, Laurier, OBE 1976; Theatrical Director and Manager, since 1947; Director and Administrator, Yvonne Arnaud Theatre, Guildford, 1964-June 1975; *b* 22 April 1907; *s* of George Daniel Lister and Susie May Kooy. *Educ:* Dulwich Coll. Trained as actor at Royal Academy of Dramatic Art, 1925-26; appeared in Noël Coward's Easy Virtue, 1926; with Bristol Repertory Company, 1926-27; three seasons with Stratford-upon-Avon Festival Company, and also toured Canada and the USA with them, 1927-29; spent a year in S Africa with Olga Lindo's Company, 1930; Death Takes a Holiday, Savoy, 1931; The Lake, Westminster and Piccadilly, 1933; visited Finland with Sir Nigel Playfair's Company, 1933; Hervey House, His Majesty's, 1934; This Desirable Residence, Criterion, 1935; Parnell, New, 1936; People of our Class, New, 1938; The Flashing Stream, Lyric, 1938; also in New York, Biltmore, 1939. Served in RAF, 1940-45. Wrote, with Dorothy Massingham, The Soldier and the Gentlewoman, Vaudeville, 1933; with Hilda Vaughan, She Too Was Young, Wyndham's and New, 1938. Organized Poetry Recitals at the Lyric, Hammersmith, and Globe, 1946-47. Devised, directed and (except for the first two) presented under his own management, the following intimate revues: Tuppence Coloured, Lyric, Hammersmith, and Globe, 1947-48; Oranges and Lemons, Lyric, Hammersmith, and Globe, 1948-49; Penny Plain, St Martin's, 1951-52; Airs on a Shoestring, Royal Court, 1953-55; Joyce Grenfell Requests the Pleasure, Fortune and St Martin's, 1954-55, later, in New York, Bijou, 1955; Fresh Airs, Comedy, 1956. Directed plays in USA, 1957 and 1958; appointed Artistic Director to Sir Laurence Olivier's Company, 1959; Dear Liar (directed and presented) and The Art of Living (directed), Criterion, 1960; J. B., Phœnix, 1961 (directed and presented); Asst to Sir Laurence Olivier at Chichester Festivals, 1962, 1963. *Publications:* She Too Was Young, 1938; The Apollo Anthology, 1954. *Recreations:* gardening, travelling. *Address:* c/o National Westminster Bank Ltd, 57 Aldwych, WC2.

LISTER, Sir Percy; *see* Lister, Sir C. P.

LISTER, Raymond (George), MA Cantab; President, Royal Society of Miniature Painters, Sculptors and Gravers, since 1970; Chairman, Board of Governors, Federation of British Artists, since 1976 (Governor, since 1972); *b* 28 March 1919; *s* of late Horace Lister and Ellen Maud Mary Lister (*née* Arnold); *m* 1947, Pamela Helen, *d* of late Frank Bishop Brutnell; one *s* one *d. Educ:* St John's Coll. Choir Sch., Cambridge; Cambridge and County High Sch. for Boys. Served apprenticeship in family firm (architectural metalworking), 1934-39; specialised war service (engrg), 1939-45; Dir of family firm, 1941-; Man. Editor, Golden Head Press, 1952-72. Hon. Senior Mem., University Coll., now Wolfson Coll., Cambridge, 1971-75, Sen. Res. Fellow, 1975-. Liveryman, Blacksmiths' Co., 1957. Assoc. Mem. 1946, Mem. 1948, Royal Soc. of Miniature Painters; Pres., Private Libraries Assoc., 1971-74; Vice-Pres., Architectural Metalwork Assoc., 1970-75, Pres., 1975-77. *Publications:* Decorative Wrought Ironwork in Great Britain, 1957; Decorative Cast Ironwork in Great Britain, 1960; Edward Calvert, 1962; Beulah to Byzantium, 1965; Victorian Narrative Paintings, 1966; William Blake, 1968; Hammer and Hand, 1969; Samuel Palmer and his Etchings, 1969; A Title to Phoebe, 1972; British Romantic Art, 1973; Samuel Palmer: a biography, 1974; (ed) The Letters of Samuel Palmer, 1974; Infernal Methods: a Study of William Blake's art techniques, 1975; Apollo's Bird, 1975; For Love of

Leda, 1977; contrib. Climbers' Club Jl, The Irish Book, Blake Studies, Blake Newsletter, Gazette des Beaux-arts, Connoisseur, Studies in Romanticism. *Recreations:* mountaineering in the fens, merels. *Address:* Windmill House, Linton, Cambs CB1 6NS. *T:* Cambridge 891248. *Clubs:* City Livery, Savile, Sette of Odd Volumes (Pres. 1960).

LISTER, Dame Unity (Viola), DBE 1972 (OBE 1958); Member of Executive, European Union of Women, since 1971 (Vice-Chairman, 1963-69); Member: European Movement, since 1970; Conservative Group for Europe, since 1970; *b* 19 June 1913; *d* of Dr A. S. Webley; *m* 1940, Samuel William Lister. *Educ:* St Helen's, Blackheath; Sorbonne Univ. of Paris. Member, London County Council, 1949-65 (Dep.-Chm., 1963-64); Chairman: Women's Nat. Advisory Cttee, 1966-69; Nat. Union of Conservative and Unionist Assocs, 1970-71 (Mem. Exec); Mem., Inner London Adv. Cttee on Appt of Magistrates, 1966-. Vice-Chm., Horniman Museums (Chm., 1967-70); Governor: Royal Marsden Hosp., 1952-; various schools and colleges. *Recreations:* languages, travel, music, gardening, theatre, museums, reading, walking. *Address:* 32 The Court Yard, Eltham, SE9 5QE. *T:* 01-850 7038. *Club:* Europe House (ex-Ladies' Carlton).

LISTER-KAYE, Sir John (Christopher Lister), 7th Bt, *cr* 1812; *b* 13 July 1913; *s* of Sir Lister Lister-Kaye, 6th Bt and Emily Mary Lister-Kaye (*d* 1944); *S* father, 1962; *m* 1942, Audrey Helen Carter; one *s* one *d. Educ:* Oundle; Loughborough Coll. *Heir:* *s* John Phillip Lister Lister-Kaye [*b* 8 May 1946; *m* 1972, Sorrel, *e d* of Count Henry Bentinck; one *s* twin *d*]. *Address:* Briarwood Cottage, East End, Lymington, Hants SO4 8SY. *T:* East End 215.

LISTON, David Joel, OBE 1975 (MBE (mil.) 1944); Pro-Rector, Polytechnic of Central London; Education Adviser to British Overseas Trade Board; *b* 27 March 1914; *s* of Edward Lichtenstein and Hannah Davis, Manchester; *m* Eva Carole Kauffmann; one *s* two *d. Educ:* Manchester Grammar Sch.; Wadham Coll., Oxford (Open and Philip Wright Exhibr). MA (Lit. Hum.). FSS. Joined Metal Box Co. 1937. TA, 1938; active service, 1939-46; 2nd in comd 8 Corps Sigs (Major, MBE, despatches). Rejoined Metal Box as Head, Information and Statistics Div., 1946; Gen. Man., Plastics Group, 1955; Man. Dir, Shorko-Metal Box, 1961; seconded as Asst Dir Manchester Business Sch., 1966. Member: British Nat. Cttee on Distribution, Internat. Chamber of Commerce, 1949-55; Council, British Plastics Fedn, 1956-69; Management Trng and Develt Cttee, Central Trng Council, 1967-69; NW Regional Council, BIM, 1966-69; CNAA, Cttee for Arts and Social Studies (Vice-Chm.), 1964-71; Econ. Devel Cttees for Food Manufrg and for Chemical Industries, 1969-72; Bd of Governors, English-Speaking Union, 1973-, and its Nat. Cttee for England and Wales, 1974-; Council, London Regional Management Centre, 1976-; Consultative Cttee on Adult Educn for Boroughs of Camden and Westminster, 1976-; Chm., Liberal Party Industrial Policy Panel, 1975-. Industrial Adviser to Min. of Technology, 1969-70, to DTI, 1970-72. Vis. Fellow, Admin. Staff Coll., 1972-. *Publications:* (editor) Hutchinson's Practical Business Management series, 1971; The Purpose and Practice of Management, 1971; Education and Training for Overseas Trade, BOTB, 1973. *Recreations:* travel, walking, current affairs. *Address:* Inglewood West, Sheiling Road, Crowborough, E Sussex. *T:* Crowborough 5781; 35 Marylebone Road, NW1. *T:* 01-486 6721. *Club:* National Liberal, English-Speaking Union.

LISTON, James Malcolm, CMG 1958; Chief Medical Adviser, Foreign and Commonwealth Office, Overseas Development Administration, 1970-71; *b* 1909; *m* 1935, Isobel Prentice Meiklem, Edinburgh; one *s* one *d. Educ:* Glasgow High Sch.; Glasgow Univ. MB, ChB, Glasgow, 1932; DTM & H Eng., 1939; DPH University of London, 1947; FRCP Glasgow, 1963. Medical Officer, Kenya, 1935; Director of Medical and Health Services, Sarawak, 1947-52; Deputy Director of Medical Services, Hong Kong, 1952-55; Director of Medical Services, Tanganyika, 1955-59; Permanent Secretary to Ministry of Health, Tanganyika, 1959-60; Deputy Chief Medical Officer: Colonial Office, 1960-61; Dept of Tech. Co-op., 1961-62; Chief Medical Adviser, Dept of Tech. Co-op., 1962-64; Medical Adviser, Min. of Overseas Develt, 1964-70. *Address:* Honeybrae, Nine Mile Burn, Midlothian. *T:* West Linton 253.

LISTON-FOULIS, Sir Ian P., 13th Bt, *cr* 1634; Language Teacher, Madrid, since 1966; *b* 9 Aug. 1937; *s* of Lieut-Colonel James Alistair Liston-Foulis, Royal Artillery (killed on active service, 1942), and of Mrs Kathleen de la Hogue Moran; *S cousin,* Sir Archibald Charles Liston Foulis, 1961. *Educ:* Stonyhurst Coll.; Cannington Farm Inst., Somerset (Dip. Agr.); Madrid (Dip. in Spanish). National Service, 1957-59; Argyll and

Sutherland Highlanders, Cyprus, 1958 (Gen. Service Medal). Language Teacher, Estremadura and Madrid, 1959-61; Trainee, Bank of London and South America, 1962; Trainee, Bank of London and Montreal (in Nassau, 1963, Guatemala City, 1963-64, Managua, Nicaragua, 1964-65); Toronto (Sales), 1965-66. Member: Spanish Soc. of the Friends of Castles; Friends of the St James Way. *Recreations:* long-distance running, swimming, walking, climbing, travelling, foreign languages and customs, reading, history, fishing, outboard motorboating. *Address:* Menéndez Pelayo 13, Piso 7, Izqda, Madrid 9, Spain.

LISTOWEL, 5th Earl of, *cr* 1822; **William Francis Hare,** PC 1946; GCMG 1957; Baron Ennismore, 1800; Viscount Ennismore, 1816; Baron Hare (UK), 1869; Chairman of Committees, House of Lords, 1965-76; *b* 28 Sept. 1906; *e s* of 4th Earl and Hon. Freda Vanden-Bempde-Johnstone (*d* 1968), *y d* of 2nd Baron Derwent; *S* father, 1931; *m* 1st, 1933, Judith (marr. diss., 1945), *o d* of R. de Marffy-Mantuano, Budapest; one *d*; 2nd, 1958, Stephanie Sandra Yvonne Wise (marr. diss., 1963), Toronto; one *d*; 3rd, 1963, Mrs Pamela Read; two *s* one *d. Educ:* Eton; Balliol Coll., Oxford. PhD London Univ. Lieut, Intelligence Corps; Whip of Labour Party in House of Lords, 1941-44; Parliamentary Under-Secretary of State, India Office, and Deputy Leader, House of Lords, 1944-45; Postmaster-General, 1945-47; Secretary of State for India, April-Aug. 1947; for Burma, 1947-Jan. 1948; Minister of State for Colonial Affairs, 1948-50; Joint Parliamentary Secretary, Ministry of Agriculture and Fisheries, 1950-51; Member (Lab) LCC for East Lewisham, 1937-46, for Battersea North, 1952-57. Governor-General of Ghana, 1957-60. Jt Patron, British Tunisian Soc.; President: British-Cameroon Soc.; Voluntary Euthanasia Soc.; Council for Aid to African Students; Jt Pres., Anti-Slavery Soc. for Protection of Human Rights; Vice-Pres., European-Atlantic Gp. *Publications:* The Values of Life, 1931; A Critical History of Modern Æsthetics, 1933 (2nd edn, as Modern Æsthetics: an Historical Introduction, 1967). *Heir: s* Viscount Ennismore, *qv. Address:* 7 Constable Close, Wildwood Road, NW11. *Club:* Athenæum.
See also Viscount Blakenham, Baron Grantley, Hon. A. V. Hare, Earl of Iveagh, Sir Robert Milnes Coates, Bt.

LITCHFIELD, Jack Watson, FRCP; Consulting Physician, St Mary's Hospital, since 1972 (Physician, 1946-72 and Physician i/c Cardiac Department, 1947-72); *b* 7 May 1909; *s* of H. L. Litchfield, Ipswich; *m* 1941, Nan, *d* of A. H. Hatherly, Shanghai; two *s* one *d. Educ:* Ipswich Sch.; Oriel Coll., Oxford (Scholar); St Mary's Hospital. Theodore Williams Schol. in Physiology, 1929, in Pathology, 1931; Radcliffe Schol. in Pharmacology, 1932; BA (2nd class hons) 1930; BM, BCh 1933; University schol. at St Mary's Hospital Medical Sch., 1931; MRCP 1936; FRCP 1947. Medical Registrar: St Mary's Hospital, 1936; Brompton Hospital, 1938; Physician, King Edward Memorial Hosp., W13, 1947-69. Served in RAMC in N Africa, Italy, etc (despatches), Lt-Col i/c Medical Div. Member Assoc. of Physicians of Great Britain and Ireland. *Publications:* papers on various subjects in medical journals. *Recreations:* gardening, walking. *Address:* Elm Green, Bradfield St Clare, Bury St Edmunds, Suffolk. *T:* Cockfield Green 399.

LITCHFIELD, Captain John Shirley Sandys, OBE 1943; RN; *b* 27 Aug. 1903; *e s* of late Rear-Admiral F. S. Litchfield-Speer, CMG, DSO, and late Cecilia Sandys; *m* 1939, Margaret, *d* of late Sir Bertram Portal, KCB, DSO, and late Hon. Lady Portal; one *s* two *d. Educ:* St Aubyns, Rottingdean; RN Colleges Osborne and Dartmouth. Midshipman and Lieut in HMS Renown during Royal Cruise to India and Japan, 1921-22 and to Australia and NZ, 1927; Yangtse river gunboat, 1929-31; RN Staff Coll., 1935; comd naval armoured trains and cars, Palestine, 1936 (despatches); Staff Officer (Ops) to C-in-C Mediterranean, 1936-38; comd HMS Walker, 1939, HMS Norfolk 1943, HMS Tyne, 1946-47 and HMS Vanguard, 1951-53; Naval SO, Supreme War Council, 1939, Joint Planning Staff, 1940; SO (O) Western Approaches, 1941; Russian Convoys and N. Africa landings, 1941-43; planning staff, Normandy ops, 1944; Combined Chiefs of Staff, Washington, 1945; National War College of US, 1947-48; Dep. Director Naval Intelligence, 1949-50; idc 1951; Director of Ops, Admiralty, 1953-54; retired 1955. CC Kent, 1955-58. MP (C) Chelsea, 1959-66. Mem. Lloyd's. Liveryman, Vintner's Company. *Address:* Snowfield, Bearsted, Kent. *Club:* Royal Navy Club of 1765 and 1785.

LITHERLAND, Prof. Albert Edward, FRS 1974; FRSC 1968; Professor of Physics, University of Toronto, since 1966; *b* 12 March 1928; *e s* of Albert Litherland and Ethel Clement; *m* 1956, (Elizabeth) Anne Allen; two *d. Educ:* Wallasey Grammar Sch.; Univ. of Liverpool (BSc, PhD). State Scholar to Liverpool Univ., 1946; Rutherford Memorial Scholar to Atomic Energy of Canada, Chalk River, Canada, 1953; Scientific Officer at Atomic

Energy of Canada, 1955-66. Canadian Assoc. of Physicists Gold Medal for Achievement in Physics, 1971; Rutherford Medal and Prize of Inst. of Physics (London), 1974. *Publications:* numerous, in scientific jls. *Address:* 3 Hawthorn Gardens, Toronto, Ontario M4W 1P4, Canada. *T:* 416-923-5616.

LITHGOW, Sir William (James), 2nd Bt of Ormsary, *cr* 1925; DL; Shipbuilder; Chairman: Lithgows (Holdings) Ltd; Scott Lithgow Drydocks Ltd; Campbeltown Shipyard Ltd; Western Ferries (Argyll) Ltd; Vice-Chairman, Scott Lithgow Ltd; Director, Bank of Scotland; *b* 10 May 1934; *o s* of late Sir James Lithgow, 1st Bt of Ormsary, GBE, CB, MC, TD, DL, JP, LLD, and Gwendolyn Amy, *d* of late John Robinson Harrison of Scalesceugh, Cumberland; *S* father, 1952; *m* 1964, Valerie Helen (*d* 1964) 2nd *d* of late Denis Scott, CBE, and of Mrs Laura Scott; *m* 1967, Mary Claire, *d* of Colonel F. M. Hill, CBE; two *s* one *d. Educ:* Winchester Coll. Member: Board of Nat. Ports Council, 1971-; Exec. Cttee, Scottish Council Develt and Industry, 1969-; Scottish Regional Council of CBI, 1969-76; Board, Clyde Port Authority, 1969-71; West Central Scotland Plan Steering Cttee, 1970-74; General Board, Nat. Physical Lab., 1963-66; Greenock Dist Hosp. Bd, 1961-66. Hon. President Students Assoc. and Member Court, University of Strathclyde, 1963-69. CEng, FRINA; FBIM; MInstPI. Member, Queen's Body Guard for Scotland (Royal Company of Archers). DL Renfrewshire, 1970. *Recreations:* country pursuits, farming, invention, photography. *Heir: s* James Frank Lithgow, *b* 13 June 1970. *Address:* Drums, Langbank, Renfrewshire. *T:* Langbank 606; Ormsary, By Lochgilphead, Argyllshire. *T:* Ormsary 252. *Clubs:* Oriental; Western, Royal Scottish Automobile (Glasgow).

LITTEN, Maurice Sidney, RP 1968; portrait painter; *b* 3 May 1919; *s* of Sidney Mackenzie Litten and Margaret Lawson; *m* 1958, Alma Jean Thomson; one *s. Educ:* Skinners' Company's Sch.; St Martin's Sch. of Art; Goldsmiths' Sch. of Art. Served RAMC, 1939-46; 1st prize All India Services Art Exhbn, 1942. Exhibits at Royal Academy, Royal Soc. of Portrait Painters, Royal Soc. of British Artists. Principal commissions include: HM the Queen and HRH the Duke of Edinburgh for RMCS, 1954; Countess Bathurst; Maharanee of Cooch Behar; Sir Anthony Elkins; Arthur Wontner; Marchioness of Donegal; Lord Shawcross, 1970. *Recreations:* music, theatre, swimming, sailing. *Address:* Studio 6, 49 Roland Gardens, SW7. *T:* 01-373 0653. *Clubs:* Chelsea Arts, Hurlingham.

LITTERICK, Thomas; MP (Lab) Selly Oak, Birmingham, since Oct. 1974; *b* 25 May 1929; *s* of late William Litterick. *Educ:* Dundee Sch. of Economics; Queen's Coll., Dundee; Univ. of Warwick. BSc Econ London; MA Industrial Relations Warwick. Sen. Lectr, Management Studies, Lanchester Coll. of Technology, Coventry, 1961-67; Lectr, Industrial Relations, Univ. of Aston, 1967-74. Chairman: Kenilworth Lab. Party, 1969-70; Warwick and Leamington Constituency Lab. Party, 1970-72 (Political Educn Officer, 1969-70). Mem., Kenilworth UDC, 1970-74. *Address:* House of Commons, SW1A 0AA. *Club:* Stirchley Co-operative Working Men's.

LITTLE, David John; His Honour Judge Little; Recorder of Londonderry and Judge for the County of Londonderry, since 1965; *er s* of late Rev. Dr James Little, MP for County Down (*er s* of Francis and Helen Little, Ouley House, Glascar, Co. Down), and Jeanie Graham Hastings, *d* of Rev. Hugh Hastings and Esther Hastings (*née* Larmor); *m* 1939, Nora Eileen Thomson; two *d. Educ:* Royal Belfast Academical Instn; St Andrew's Coll., Dublin; TCD. MA, LLB. Called to Bar 1938 and Inner Bar 1963, N Ireland. Crown Prosecutor for Co. Down and Belfast. MP (U) West Down, Parlt of NI, 1959-65. *Recreations:* golf, reading, walking. *Address:* Seaforth, Whitehead, Co. Antrim. *T:* Whitehead 3722. *Club:* Royal Co. Down.

LITTLE, Hon. Sir Douglas (Macfarlan), Kt 1973; Justice of Supreme Court of Victoria, Australia, 1959-74; *b* 23 July 1904; *s* of John Little and Agnes Little (*née* Macfarlan); *m* 1931, Ida Margaret Chapple; one *d. Educ:* State Sch.; Scotch Coll.; Ormond Coll., Univ. of Melbourne (MA, LLM). QC (Aust.) 1954. Practised profession of the law in Melbourne since admission in 1929. Served War, with RAAF, 1942-45. *Recreation:* golf. *Address:* 2 Lansell Crescent, Camberwell, Melbourne, Victoria 3124, Australia. *T:* 295361. *Clubs:* Australian (Melbourne); Metropolitan Golf.

LITTLE, Ian Malcolm David, AFC 1943; FBA 1973; Special Adviser, International Bank for Reconstruction and Development, since 1976; *b* 18 Dec. 1918; *s* of Brig.-Gen. M. O. Little, CB, CBE, and Iris Hermione Little (*née* Brassey); *m* 1946, Doreen Hennessey; one *s* one *d. Educ:* Eton; New Coll., Oxford (MA, DPhil). RAF Officer, 1939-46. Fellow: All Souls

Coll., Oxford, 1948-50; Trinity Coll., Oxford, 1950-52; Nuffield Coll., Oxford, 1952-76, Emeritus Fellow, 1976. Dep. Dir, Economic Section, Treasury, 1953-55; Mem., MIT Centre for Internat. Studies, India, 1958-59 and 1965; Vice-Pres., OECD Develt Centre, Paris, 1965-67; Prof. of Economics of Underdeveloped Countries, Oxford Univ., 1971-76. Dir, Investing in Success Ltd, 1960-65; Bd Mem., British Airports Authority, 1969-74. Dir, Gen. Funds Investment Trust, 1974-76. *Publications:* A Critique of Welfare Economics, 1950; The Price of Fuel, 1953; (jtly) Concentration in British Industry, 1960; Aid to Africa, 1964; (jtly) International Aid, 1965; (jtly) Higgledy-Piggledy Growth Again, 1966; (jtly) Manual of Industrial Project Analysis in Developing Countries, 1969; (jtly) Industry and Trade in Some Developing Countries, 1970; Project Analysis and Planning, 1974; many articles in learned jls. *Address:* International Bank for Reconstruction and Development, 1818 H Street NW, Washington, DC 20433, USA; 1603 35th Street, NW, Washington DC 20007, USA. *T:* 202-337-0163.

LITTLE, John Eric Russell, OBE 1961 (MBE 1943); HM Diplomatic Service, retired; *b* 29 Aug. 1913; *s* of William Little and Beatrice Little (*née* Biffen); *m* 1945, Christine Holt; one *s* one *d. Educ:* Strand Sch. Served in FO, 1930-40, and in Army, 1940-41. Transferred to Minister of State's Office, Cairo, 1941, and seconded to Treasury. Returned to FO and appointed to British Middle East Office, 1946. Transferred to FO, 1948; Consul, Milan, 1950 (acting Consul-General, 1951, 1952); Bahrain as Asst Political Agent, 1952 (acting Political Agent, 1953, 1954, 1955); 1st Secretary, Paris, 1956; Asst Finance Officer, Foreign Office, 1958; HM Consul-General: Basra, 1962-65; Salonika, 1965-70; Counsellor, British Embassy, Brussels, 1970-72. *Recreations:* walking, reading, music. *Address:* Golna, Stonestile Lane, Hastings, East Sussex.

LITTLE, John Philip Brooke B.; *see* Brooke-Little.

LITTLE, Prof. Kenneth Lindsay; Professor of African Urban Studies, Edinburgh University, since 1971; *b* 19 Sept. 1908; *e s* of late H. Muir Little, Liverpool; *m* 1st, 1939, Birte Hoeck (marr. diss.); one *s* one *d*; 2nd, 1957, Iris May Cadogan. *Educ:* Liverpool Coll.; Selwyn Coll., Cambridge; Trinity Coll., Cambridge (William Wyse Student). MA Cantab 1944; PhD London 1945. Lectr in Anthropology, LSE, 1946; Reader in Social Anthropology, 1950-65, Professor, 1965-71, Edinburgh Univ. Frazer Lectr, Cambridge Univ., 1965. Leverhulme Res. Fellow, 1974-76. Vis. Prof., 1949-74, at Univs of New York, California, Washington, North Western, Fisk, Ghana and Khartoum. Chm., Adv. Cttee on Race Relations Research (Home Office), 1968-70. Pres., Sociology Section, British Assoc., 1968. *Publications:* Negroes in Britain, 1948 (rev. edn, 1972); The Mende of Sierra Leone, 1951 (rev. edn, 1967); Race and Society, 1952; West African Urbanization, 1967; African Women in Towns, 1973; Urbanization as a Social Process, 1974. *Recreation:* West African drumming and dancing. *Address:* 60 North Castle Street, Edinburgh 2. *T:* 031-226 7127.

LITTLE, Most Rev. Thomas Francis; *see* Melbourne, Archbishop of, (RC).

LITTLE, William Morison, CBE 1972; BSc; MICE, MIEE, FCIT; Deputy Chairman, Scottish Transport Group, 1969-76, Managing Director, 1969-75; *b* Leith, 12 Oct. 1909; *s* of Wm J. S. Little and May Morison; *m* 1940, Constance Herries; one *s* one *d. Educ:* Melville Coll.; Edinburgh Univ. Manager of Corporation Transport at: St Helens, 1941; Reading, 1945; Edinburgh, 1948. Subseq. Chm. of Scottish Bus Gp and subsidiary cos, 1963; part-time Mem., Nat. Bus Co., 1968-75. President: Scottish Road Transport Assoc., 1951; Municipal Passenger Transport Assoc., 1963; CIT, 1974-. Mem. Council, Public Road Transport Assoc. (formerly Public Transport Assoc.; Chm. Council, 1965-66, 1966-67). *Publications:* contribs to technical press and Inst. of Transport (Henry Spurrier Memorial Lecture, 1970). *Recreation:* walking. *Address:* 14 Temple Village, Gorebridge, Midlothian EH23 4SQ. *T:* Temple 283. *Clubs:* National Liberal; Scottish Liberal (Edinburgh).

LITTLECHILD, Prof. Stephen Charles; Professor of Commerce and Head of Department of Industrial Economics and Business Studies, University of Birmingham, since 1975; *b* 27 Aug. 1943; *s* of Sidney F. Littlechild and Joyce M. Littlechild; *m* 1974, Kate Crombie. *Educ:* Wisbech Grammar Sch.; Univ. of Birmingham (BCom); Univ. of Texas (PhD). Temp. Asst Lectr in Ind. Econs, Univ. of Birmingham, 1964-65; Harkness Fellow, Stanford Univ., 1965-66; Northwestern Univ., 1966-68; Univ. of Texas at Austin, 1968-69; ATT Post-doctoral Fellow, UCLA and Northwestern Univ., 1969; Sen. Res. Lectr in Econs, Graduate Centre for Management Studies, Birmingham, 1970-72; Prof. of

Applied Econs and Head of Econs, Econometrics, Statistics and Marketing Subject Gp, Aston Management Centre, 1972-75; Vis. Scholar, Dept of Econs, Univ. of California at Los Angeles, 1975. *Publications:* Operational Research for Managers, 1977; numerous articles in econs and ops res. jls. *Recreations:* football, poker. *Address:* Faculty of Commerce and Social Science, University of Birmingham, Edgbaston, Birmingham B15 2TT. *T:* 021-472 1301.

LITTLEJOHN, William Hunter, RSA 1973 (ARSA 1966); Head of the Drawing and Painting Department, Gray's School of Art, Aberdeen, since 1970; *b* Arbroath, 16 April 1929; *s* of late William Littlejohn and of Alice Morton King. *Educ:* Arbroath High Sch.; Dundee Coll. of Art (DA). National Service, RAF, 1951-53; taught Art at Arbroath High Sch. until 1966, then Lectr, Gray's Sch. of Art, Aberdeen. *One man exhibitions:* The Scottish Gallery, Edinburgh, 1962, 1967, 1972, 1977. Exhibits in RA, RSA, SSA, etc. *Address:* 16 Colville Place, Arbroath, Angus, Scotland. *T:* Arbroath 74402. *Club:* Edinburgh Arts.

LITTLEJOHN COOK, George Steveni; HM Diplomatic Service, retired; *b* 29 Oct. 1919; *s* of late William Littlejohn Cook, OBE, and Xenia Steveni, BEM; *m* 1st, 1949, Marguerite Teresa Bonnaud; one *d*; 2nd, 1964, Thereza Nunes Campos; one *s*. *Educ:* Wellington Coll.; Trinity Hall, Cambridge. Served with 2nd Bn Cameronians (Scottish Rifles), 1939-46, rank of Capt.; POW Germany; Political Intelligence Dept, Foreign Office, 1945-46. Entered Foreign Service, 1946; Third Secretary, Foreign Office, 1946-47; Second Secretary, Stockholm, 1947-49; Santiago, Chile, 1949-52; First Secretary, 1950; Foreign Office, 1952-53; Chargé d'Affaires, Phnom-Penh, 1953-55; Berne, 1956-58; Director of British Information Service in Brazil, 1959-64; Head of Information Depts, FO (and FCO), 1964-69; Counsellor and Consul-General, Bangkok, 1969-71. *Recreations:* painting, sailing, ski-ing. *Address:* Quinta da Madrugada, Lagos, Algarve, Portugal. *Clubs:* Brooks's, Travellers', Royal Automobile.

LITTLER, Sir Emile, Kt 1974; Theatrical Impresario, Producer, Author and Company Director; *b* Ramsgate, Kent, 9 Sept. 1903; *s* of F. R. and Agnes Littler; *m* 1933, Cora Goffin (actress); two *d. Educ:* Stratford-on-Avon. Served apprenticeship working on stage of the Theatre; was Asst Manager of Theatre in Southend, 1922; subsequently worked as Asst Stage Manager, Birmingham Rep. Theatre; in US, 1927-31; became Manager and Licensee of Birmingham Rep. Theatre for Sir Barry Jackson, Sept. 1931. Personally started in Management, Sept. 1934; theatrical productions include: Victoria Regina; 1066 and All That; The Maid of the Mountains, 1942, new production, Palace, 1972; The Night and the Music; Claudia; The Quaker Girl; Lilac Time; Song of Norway; Annie Get Your Gun; Zip Goes a Million; Blue for a Boy; Love from Judy; Affairs of State; Book of the Month; Hot Summer Night; Signpost to Murder; Kill Two Birds; The Right Honourable Gentleman; Latin Quarter; The Impossible Years; 110 in the Shade, Student Prince; Desert Song; Annual Pantomimes in London and big cities of British Isles. Director: Eagle Star Insurance Co.; Chm., London Entertainments Ltd (controlling Palace Theatre); Past Pres., Soc. of West End Theatre Managers, 1964-67, 1969-70; a Governor, Royal Shakespeare Theatre, Stratford-on-Avon. Prominent play-doctor and race-horse owner. *Publications:* (jointly): Cabbages and Kings; Too Young to Marry; Love Isn't Everything; and 100 Christmas Pantomimes. *Recreations:* tennis, swimming, racing. *Address:* Palace Theatre, Shaftesbury Avenue, W1. *T:* 01-734 9691/2; The Trees, 72 Lewes Road, Ditchling, Sussex. *Clubs:* Royal Automobile, Clermont.

LITTLER, (James) Geoffrey; Deputy Secretary, HM Treasury, since 1977; *b* 18 May 1930; *s* of late James Edward Littler and Evelyn Mary Littler (*née* Taylor); *m* 1958, Shirley, *d* of late Sir Percy Marsh, CSI, CIE; one *s. Educ:* Manchester Grammar Sch.; Corpus Christi Coll., Cambridge (MA). Asst Principal, Colonial Office, 1952-54; transf. to Treasury, 1954; Principal 1957; Asst Sec. 1966; Under-Sec. 1972. Chm., EEC Monetary Cttee Deputies, 1974-77. *Recreation:* music. *Address:* 5 Earl's Court Gardens, SW5 0TD. *T:* 01-373 2911. *Club:* Reform.

LITTLER, William Brian, CB 1959; MSc, PhD; *b* 8 May 1908; *s* of William Littler, Tarporley, Ches; *m* 1937, Pearl Davies, Wrexham; three *d. Educ:* Grove Park, Wrexham; Manchester Univ.; BSc (1st Class), Chemistry, 1929; MSc, 1930; PhD, 1932; Beyer Fellow, 1930-31. Joined Res. Dept, Woolwich, 1933; loaned by Min. of Supply to Defence Res. Bd, Canada; Chief Supt, Cdn Armament Research and Devel. Establishment, Valcartier, Quebec, 1947-49; Supt of Propellants Research, Explosives Research and Devel. Estab., Waltham Abbey, 1949-50; in industry (Glaxo Laboratories Ltd, Ulverston), 1950-52; Dir of Ordnance Factories (Explosives), Min. of Supply, 1952-

55; Principal Dir of Scientific Research (Defence), Ministry of Supply, 1955-56; Dir-Gen. of Scientific Research (Munitions), Ministry of Supply, 1956-60; Dep. Chief Scientist, Min. of Defence (Army), 1960-65; Minister, and Head of Defence R&D Staff, British Embassy, Washington, DC, 1965-69; Chemist-in-Charge, Quality Assurance Directorate (Materials), Royal Ordnance Factory, Bridgwater, 1969-72. *Publications:* Papers on Flame and Combustion in Proc. Royal Society and Jour. Chem. Soc. *Recreations:* golf, swimming. *Address:* The Old School House, Catcott, near Bridgwater, Som. *T:* Chilton Polden 722412.

LITTLETON, family name of **Baron Hatherton.**

LITTLEWOOD, Lady (Barbara); Consultant with Barlows, Solicitors, of Guildford; *b* 7 Feb. 1909; *d* of Dr Percival Langdon-Down, Teddington; *m* 1934, Sir Sydney Littlewood (*d* 1967); one *s. Educ:* Summerleigh Sch., Teddington; King's Coll., London, (BSc). Admitted solicitor, 1936. Pres. West Surrey Law Soc., 1952-53; Mem. Home Office Departmental Committees on: the Summary Trial of Minor Offences, 1954-55; Matrimonial Proceedings in Magistrates' Courts, 1958-59; Financial Limits prescribed for Maintenance Orders made in Magistrates' Courts, 1966-68. Pres., Nat. Fedn of Business and Professional Women's Clubs of Gt Brit. and N Ire., 1958-60; Pres. Internat. Fedn of Business and Professional Women, 1965-68; Lay Member, Press Council, 1968-74. JP Middx, 1950-. *Recreation:* occasional golf. *Address:* 26 St Margarets, London Road, Guildford, Surrey. *T:* Guildford 4348.

LITTLEWOOD, Rear-Adm. Charles, CB 1954; OBE 1942; retired; *b* 1 Jan. 1902; *s* of Alfred Littlewood, Croydon, Surrey; *m* 1924, Doris Helen, *d* of William Mackean, London, SW16; no *c. Educ:* Falconbury Sch. (Preparatory), Purley; RN Colls Osborne and Dartmouth. Entered RN 1915; Midshipman, Emperor of India, 1918; Lt (E) RNEC Keyham, 1924; served in Ramillies, Concord, Erebus, Admiralty Experimental Station, 1924-32; Engineer Officer; HMS Ardent, 1932-34; HMS Apollo, 1934-36; Comdr (E) 1936; Flotilla Eng. Officer, HMS Kempenfelt, 1936-38; Manager Engineering Dept, Malta Dockyard, 1938-44; Actg Captain (E) 1942; Captain (E) 1945; Eng. Officer in HMS Howe, Brit. Pacific Fleet, served at Okinawa Operation, 1944-46; Asst Engineer in Chief, 1946-49; Manager Engineering Dept, Rosyth Dockyard, 1949-52; Rear-Admiral, 1952; Asst Dir of Dockyards, 1952-55, retd 1955. *Address:* Saddlers Mead, Sid Road, Sidmouth, Devon. *T:* Sidmouth 5482.

LITTLEWOOD, James, CB 1973; Director, Department for National Savings, since 1972 (Deputy Director, 1967-72); *b* Royton, Lancashire, 21 Oct. 1922; *s* of late Thomas and Sarah Littlewood; *m* 1950, Barbara Shaw; two *s* one *d. Educ:* Manchester Grammar Sch.; St John's Coll., Cambridge (Scholar, MA). Army (Captain), 1942-46. Asst Principal, HM Treasury, 1947; Private Sec. to Financial Sec., 1949-50; Principal, 1950; Civil Service Selection Bd, 1951-52; Sec. to Cttee on Administrative Tribunals and Enquiries, 1955-57; Colombo Plan Conf. Secretariat, 1955 and 1959. Asst Sec., 1962; Under Sec., 1969. *Recreations:* golf, bridge. *Address:* 35 Ridings Avenue, N21. *T:* 01-366 2226. *Club:* United Oxford & Cambridge University.

LITTLEWOOD, Joan (Maud); theatre artist. *Educ:* London. Dir, Theatre of Action, Manchester (street theatre), 1931-37; founder, Theatre Union, Manchester, introducing individual work system, 1937-39; freelance writer, 1939-45 (banned from BBC and ENSA for political opinions); founded Theatre Workshop with Gerry Raffles, 1945; touring in GB, Germany, Norway, Sweden with original works, 1945-53; moved to Theatre Royal, Stratford, London, with classics, 1953; invited to Theatre of the Nations, Paris, 1955, then yearly (Best Production of the Year three times); Centre Culturel, Hammamet, Tunisia, 1965-67; Image India, Calcutta, 1968; creation of Children's Environments, Bubble Cities linked with Music Hall, around Theatre Royal, Stratford, 1968-75. Left England to work in France, 1975; Seminar Relais Culturel, Aix-en-Provence, 1976. Productions include: Lysistrata, 1958 (Gold Medal, East Berlin, 1958; Olympic Award, Taormina, 1959), transferred to London and Broadway from Stratford, 1960-61; Sparrers Can't Sing (film), 1962; O What a Lovely War (with Gerry Raffles and the Company), 1963. Mem., French Academy of Writers, 1964. Dr *hc* , Univ. of the Air, 1977. *Recreation:* theatre. *Address:* 1 Place Louis Revol, 38200 Vienne, France.

LITTMAN, Mark, QC 1961; Deputy Chairman, British Steel Corporation, since 1970; Director: Rio Tinto-Zinc Corporation Ltd, since 1968; Commercial Union Assurance Co. Ltd, since 1970; British Enkalon Ltd, since 1976; Amerada Hess Corp.

(US), since 1973; Envirotech Corp. (US), since 1974; Granada Group, since 1977; *b* 4 Sept. 1920; *s* of Jack and Lilian Littman; *m* 1965, Marguerite Lamkin, USA. *Educ:* Owen's Sch.; London Sch. of Economics; The Queen's Coll., Oxford. BScEcon. (first class hons) 1939; MA Oxon 1941. Served RN, Lieut, 1941-46. Called to Bar, Middle Temple, 1947, Bencher, 1970; practised, as Barrister-at-law, 1947-67; Member: General Council of the Bar, 1968-72; Senate of Inns of Court and the Bar, 1968-. Board Mem., British Nat. Oil Corp., 1976-; Mem. Royal Commn on Legal Services, 1976-. *Address:* 79 Chester Square, SW1. *Clubs:* Garrick, Reform; Century Association (New York).

LIVERMAN, John Gordon, CB 1973; OBE 1956; Deputy Secretary, Department of Energy, since 1974; *b* London, 21 Oct. 1920; *s* of late George Gordon Liverman and of Hadassah Liverman; *m* 1952, Peggy Earl; two *s* one *d. Educ:* St Paul's Sch.; Trinity Coll., Cambridge (BA). Served with RA, 1940-46. Asst Principal, Min. of Power, 1947, Principal, 1948; Volta River Preparatory Commission, Accra, 1953; Treasury, 1956; Asst Sec., Min. of Power, 1957; Office of Minister for Science, 1961; Under-Secretary: Min. of Technology (formerly Min. of Power), 1964-70; DTI, 1970-72; Dep. Sec., DTI, 1972-74. Mem., British Nat. Oil Corp., 1976-. *Address:* 11 Linkfield Lane, Redhill, Surrey. *Club:* Royal Commonwealth Society.

LIVERMORE, Sir Harry, Kt 1973; Lord Mayor of Liverpool, 1958-59; *b* 17 Oct. 1908; *m* 1940, Esther Angelman; one *s* one *d. Educ:* Royal Grammar Sch., Newcastle upon Tyne; Durham Univ. Solicitor; qualified, 1930; practises in Liverpool. Mem., Liverpool City Council (Chm. Libraries and Leisure Activities Cttee); Vice-President: Royal Liverpool Philharmonic Soc.; Liverpool Everyman Theatre, Ltd; Chm., Merseyside Arts Assoc. *Recreations:* music, golf. *Address:* 18 Burnham Road, Liverpool L18 6JU. *T:* 051-724 2144.

LIVERPOOL, 5th Earl of, *cr* 1905 (2nd creation); **Edward Peter Bertram Savile Foljambe;** Baron Hawkesbury, 1893; Viscount Hawkesbury, 1905; *b* posthumously, 14 Nov. 1944; *s* of Captain Peter George William Savile Foljambe (killed in action, 1944) and of Elizabeth Joan (who *m* 1947, Major Andrew Antony Gibbs, MBE, TD), *d* of late Major Eric Charles Montagu Flint, DSO; *S* great uncle, 1969; *m* 1970, Lady Juliana Noel, *e d* of Earl of Gainsborough, *qv* ; two *s. Educ:* Shrewsbury School; Univ. for Foreigners, Perugia. *Heir: s* Viscount Hawkesbury, *qv. Address:* The Grange Farm, Exton, near Oakham, Leics; Flat 4, 27 Holland Park Avenue, W11. *Clubs:* Turf, Pratt's.

LIVERPOOL, Archbishop of, (RC), and Metropolitan of Northern Province with Suffragan Sees, Hexham, Lancaster, Leeds, Middlesbrough and Salford, since 1976; **Most Rev. Derek John Harford Worlock;** *b* 4 Feb. 1920; 2nd *s* of Captain Harford Worlock and Dora (*née* Hoblyn). *Educ:* St Edmund's Coll., Ware, Herts. Ordained RC Priest, 1944. Curate, Our Lady of Victories, Kensington, 1944-45; Private Secretary to Archbishop of Westminster, 1945-64; Rector and Rural Dean, Church of SS Mary and Michael, London, E1, 1964-65; Bishop of Portsmouth, 1965-76. Privy Chamberlain to Pope Pius XII, 1949-53; Domestic Prelate of the Pope, 1953-65; *Peritus* at Vatican Council II, 1963-65; Consultor to Council of Laity, 1967-76; Episcopal Secretary to RC Bishops' Conference, 1967-76. Member: Synod Council, 1976-; Holy See's Laity Council and Cttee for the Family, 1977-; English delegate to Internat. Synod of Bishops, 1974 and 1977. Knight Commander of Holy Sepulchre of Jerusalem, 1966. *Publications:* Seek Ye First (compiler), 1949; Take One at Bedtime (anthology), 1962; English Bishops at the Council, 1965; Turn and Turn Again, 1971; Give Me Your Hand, 1977. *Address:* Archbishop's House, 87 Green Lane, Liverpool L18 2EP. *T:* 051-722 2379.

LIVERPOOL, Bishop of, since 1975; **Rt. Rev. David Stuart Sheppard;** *b* 6 March 1929; *s* of Stuart Morton Winter Sheppard, Solicitor, and Barbara Sheppard; *m* 1957, Grace Isaac; one *d* . *Educ:* Sherborne; Trinity Hall, Cambridge (MA); Ridley Hall Theological Coll. Asst Curate, St Mary's, Islington, 1955-57; Warden, Mayflower Family Centre, Canning Town, E16, 1957-69; Bishop Suffragan of Woolwich, 1969-75. Cricket: Cambridge Univ., 1950-52 (Captain 1952); Sussex, 1947-62 (Captain 1953); England (played 22 times) 1950-63 (Captain 1954). *Publications:* Parson's Pitch, 1964; Built as a City, 1974. *Recreations:* family, reading, music, painting, theatre. *Address:* Bishop's Lodge, Woolton Park, Woolton, Liverpool L25 6DT.

LIVERPOOL, Auxiliary Bishops of, (RC); *see* Gray, Rt Rev. Joseph, Harris, Rt Rev. Augustine.

LIVERPOOL, Dean of; *see* Patey, Very Rev. E. H.

LIVERPOOL, Archdeacon of; see Corbett, Ven. C. E.

LIVINGS, Henry; *b* 20 Sept. 1929; *m* 1957, Judith Francis Carter; one *s* one *d*. *Educ:* Park View Primary Sch.; Stand Grammar Sch.; Liverpool Univ. Served in RAF. Joined Puritex, Leicester. Theatre Royal Leicester, then many Repertories; Theatre Workshop, 1956. 1st TV play, 1961; 1st stage play, 1961. *Publications:* contribs to Penguin New English Dramatists 5 and 6; Kelly's Eye and Other Plays, 1964; Eh?, 1965; Good Griefl, 1968; The Little Mistress Foster Show, 1969; Honour and Offer, 1969; Pongo Plays 1-6, 1971; This Jockey Drives Late Nights, 1972; The Ffinest Ffamily in the Land, 1973; Jonah, 1974; Six More Pongo Plays, 1975; That the Medals and the Baton be Put on View, 1975; Cinderella, 1976. *Recreations:* darts, dominoes, chess, clay pigeon shooting. *Address:* 33 Woods Lane, Dobcross, Oldham, Lancs. *T:* Saddleworth 2965. *Club:* Film Exchange (Manchester).

LIVINGSTON, James Barrett, CBE 1972; DSC 1942; Consultant (formerly Director; retired 1970), Rockware Group Ltd.; Director, Rockware Glass Ltd., since 1947 (Joint Managing Director, 1951-60; Managing Director, 1960-69; Vice-Chairman, 1967-69); *b* 13 Sept. 1906; *yr s* of late Capt. David Liddle Livingston and Ruth Livingston, Bombay and Aberdour; *m* 1933, Joyce Eileen, *fourth d* of late Arthur and Lilian Birkett, Clements Inn and Southwold; one *s* one *d*. *Educ:* HMS Worcester. Served War of 1939-45, RN: Staff Officer (Ops) 10th Cruiser Sqdn, Norwegian Campaign; North Russian and Malta Convoys (despatches 1943); Ops Div. Admiralty, 1943-45 (Comdr). Joined Rockware Group of Cos, 1945; Exec. Director, British Hartford-Fairmont Ltd, 1947-50. Director: Portland Glass Co. Ltd, 1956-69; Jackson Bros (Knottingley) Ltd, 1968-69 (Chm.); Burwell, Reed & Kinghorn Ltd, 1962-71; Blewis & Shaw (Plastics) Ltd, 1960-70; Automotated Inspection Machinery Ltd, 1962-69; Garston Bottle Co. Ltd, 1966-69 (Chm.); Forsters Glass Co. Ltd, 1967-69; also other Glass and Associated Companies. Member: Bd of Govs, Charing Cross Hospital, 1956-73 (Chm., Medical School Council, 1967-73); Council, Glass Manufacturers' Fedn 1967 (Pres. 1970-71); Nat. Cttee, Assoc. of Glass Container Manufacturers, 1959-69 (Vice-Pres.); Nat. Jt Industrial Council 1959-69; Court of Ironmongers' Co., 1946 (Master, 1960-61); Adv. Cttee to Faculty of Materials Technology, Sheffield University, 1969-71; Council CBI, 1970-71; Furniture Develt Council, 1972-; Council, Royal College of Art, 1970-71. *Recreations:* golf, racket re-strings, gardening. *Address:* (home) Ferroners, Beaconsfield, Bucks. *T:* Beaconsfield 3853.

LIVINGSTON, Air Marshal Sir Philip C., KBE 1950 (CBE 1946); CB 1948; AFC 1942; retired; FRCS; FRCSE, LRCP, DPH, DOMS; *b* 2 March 1893; *y s* of Clermont Livingston, Cleveland, Vancouver Island, BC, Canada; *m* 1920, Lorna Muriel, *o d* of C. W. Legassicke Crespin, London, Eng.; one *s* (and one *s* decd). *Educ:* Jesus Coll., Cambridge; London Hosp. Served European War, 1914-17, RNVR 4th Destroyer Flotilla, 1915; 10th Cruiser Sqdn, 1916. Qualified Jan. 1919; joined RAF, 1919, as MO; served India, Iraq, Far East; Consultant in Ophthalmology, 1934-46; Dep. Dir RAF Medical Services, 1947; Dir-Gen., 1948-51. Chadwick Prize and Gold Medal for researches in applied physiology, 1938. CStJ. *Publications:* Montgomery, Moynihan, and Chadwick Lectures, 1942-45; *autobiography:* Fringe of the Clouds, 1962; many papers on subjects connected with vision. *Recreation:* rowing (rowed 3 in winning Cambridge Univ. Crew, March 1914). *Address:* Maple Bay, RR1, Duncan, BC, Canada.

LIVINGSTONE, James, CMG 1968; OBE 1951; *b* 4 April 1912; *e s* of late Angus Cook Livingstone, sometime Provost of Bo'ness, Scotland, and Mrs Jean Fraser Aitken Wilson Livingstone; *m* 1945, Dr Mair Eleri Morgan Thomas, MB, ChB, BSc, DPH, FRCPath, *e d* of late John Thomas, DSc, Harlech and Mrs O. M. Thomas, Llanddewi Brefi and Wilmslow; one *d* (one *s* decd). *Educ:* Bo'ness Acad.; Edinburgh Univ.; Moray House Trng Coll., Edinburgh. Adult Educn and School Posts, Scotland and Egypt, 1936-42; British Coun. Service, Egypt and Iran, 1942-45; Middle East Dept, 1945-46; Asst Rep., Palestine, 1946-48; Dep. Dir, Personnel Dept, 1949; Dir, Personnel Dept, 1956; Controller, Establishments Div., 1962; Controller, Overseas A Div. (Middle East and Africa), 1969-72, retired. *Recreations:* photography, exploring the West Highlands and Islands. *Address:* 21 Park Avenue, NW11 7SL. *T:* 01-455 7600; Tan-yr-allt, Llangeitho, Dyfed. *Clubs:* Royal Commonwealth Society, Travellers'.

LIVINGSTONE, James Livingstone, MD, FRCP; Retired; Consulting Physician: King's College Hospital; Brompton Hospital; St Dunstan's; *b* 8 May 1900; *m* 1935, Janet Muriel Rocke; two *s* one *d*. *Educ:* Worksop Coll., Notts; King's Coll.,

University of London; King's Coll. Hospital. MRCS, LRCP, 1922; MB, BS 1923; MRCP 1925; MD London 1925; FRCP 1933. RAF, 1918-19. Fellow of King's Coll., London. Member: Assoc. of Physicians of Gt Britain; Thoracic Soc. *Publications:* Bronchitis and Broncho-pneumonia in Brit. Encyc. of Med. Practice, 2nd edn; Modern Practice in Tuberculosis, 1952; jt editor contributions to medical journals. *Recreations:* golf, fishing. *Address:* 11 Chyngton Road, Seaford, East Sussex. *Club:* Seaford Golf.

LLANDAFF, Bishop of, since 1976; **Rt. Rev. John Richard Worthington Poole Hughes;** *b* 8 Aug. 1916; *s* of late Canon W. W. Poole Hughes, Warden of Llandovery College and late Bertha Cecil (*née* Rhys). *Educ:* Uppingham School; Hertford College, Oxford; Wells Theological College. BA (Lit. Hum.) 1939, MA 1945. Royal Artillery, 1939-45. Deacon, 1947; Priest, 1948; Curate St Michael and All Angels, Aberystwyth, 1947-50; UMCA Missionary, 1950-57; Staff, St Michael's College, Llandaff, 1957-59; Home Secretary, Universities' Mission to Central Africa, 1959-62; Bishop of South-West Tanganyika, 1962-74; Asst Bishop of Llandaff and Asst Curate, Llantwit Major, 1975. *Publication:* Asomaye na Afahamu (SPCK), 1959. *Recreations:* photography, writing. *Address:* Llys Esgob, The Cathedral Green, Llandaff, Cardiff, S. Glam CF5 2EB.

LLANDAFF, Dean of; see Davies, Very Rev. A. R.

LLEWELLYN, Bryan Henry; Chairman, Thomson Travel Ltd, and Managing Director, Thomson Publications Ltd, since 1977; *b* 1 May 1927; *s* of Nora and Charles Llewellyn; *m* 1965, Pamela (*née* Pugh) (legally separated). *Educ:* Charterhouse; Clare Coll., Cambridge (BA). Commissioned, The Queen's, 1946. Research Asst, Dept of Estate Management, Cambridge, 1954; joined Fisons Ltd, 1955; Marketing Manager, Greaves & Thomas Ltd, 1960; Regional Marketing Controller, Thomson Regional Newspapers Ltd, 1962; Marketing Dir, TRN Ltd, 1966; Managing Director: Thomson Holidays Ltd, 1969; Thomson Travel Ltd, 1972; Exec. Dir, Thomson Organisation Ltd, 1972. Non-Exec. Dir, Orion Insurance Ltd, 1976. *Address:* c/o Thomson Publications Ltd, Elm House, Elm Street, WC1X 0BP.

LLEWELLYN, Sir David (Treharne), Kt 1960; Captain, late Welsh Guards; *b* Aberdare, 17 Jan. 1916; 3rd *s* of Sir David Richard Llewellyn, 1st Bt, LLD, JP, and of Magdalene Anne (*d* 1966), *yr d* of late Rev. Henry Harries, DD, Porthcawl; *m* Joan Anne Williams, OBE, 2nd *d* of R. H. Williams, Bonvilston House, Bonvilston, near Cardiff; two *s* one *d*. *Educ:* Eton; Trinity Coll., Cambridge. BA 1938. Served War of 1939-45; enlisted Royal Fusiliers, serving in ranks; commissioned Welsh Guards; North-West Europe, 1944-45. Contested (Conservative) Aberavon Div. of Glamorgan, 1945. MP (C) Cardiff, North, 1950-Sept. 1959; Parliamentary Under-Sec. of State, Home Office, 1951-52 (resigned, ill-health). Mem. Nat. Union of Journalists. *Publications:* Nye: The Beloved Patrician, 1961; The Adventures of Arthur Artfully, 1974. *Address:* The Old Rectory, Yattendon, Newbury, Berks.

LLEWELLYN, Dr Donald Rees; JP; Vice-Chancellor, University of Waikato, since 1964; *b* 20 Nov. 1919; *s* of late R. G Llewellyn, Dursley; *m* 1943, Ruth Marian, *d* of late G. E. Blandford, Dursley; one *s* one *d*. *Educ:* Dursley Grammar Sch.; Univ. of Birmingham, 1939-41, BSc 1st cl. hons Chem. 1941, DSc 1957; Oxford 1941-44, DPhil 1943. Research Fellow, Cambridge Univ., 1944-46; Lectr in Chemistry, UC of N Wales, 1946-49; ICI Research Fellow, UCL, 1949-52; Lectr in Chemistry, UCL, 1952-57; Prof. of Chemistry and Dir of Labs, Univ. of Auckland, 1957-64; Asst Vice-Chancellor, Univ. of Auckland, 1962-64. Mem., NZ Atomic Energy Cttee, 1958-. Member: Council, Hamilton Teachers Coll., 1965-; Bd of Governors, Waikato Tech. Inst., 1968-; Pres., NZ Nat. Field Days Soc., 1969-. JP Waikato, 1971. FRIC 1952; FNZIC 1957; FRSA 1960. *Publications:* numerous papers on application of stable isotopes in Jl Chem. Soc. and others. *Recreations:* squash, tennis, showjumping (FEI Judge), photography, travel. *Address:* Hamilton RD3, New Zealand. *T:* 69-172. *Club:* Hamilton (NZ).

LLEWELLYN, Sir (Frederick) John, KCMG 1974; Director-General, British Council, since 1972; *b* 29 April 1915; *er s* of late R. G. Llewellyn, Dursley, Glos.; *m* 1939, Joyce, *d* of late Ernest Barrett, Dursley; one *s* one *d*. *Educ:* Dursley Gram. Sch.; University of Birmingham. BSc, 1st Cl. Hons Chemistry, 1935; PhD, 1938; DSc, 1951 (Birmingham); FRIC, 1944, FNZIC, 1948; FRSA, 1952; FRSNZ, 1964. Lecturer in Chemistry, Birkbeck Coll., 1939-45; Dir, Min. of Supply Research Team, 1941-46; ICI Research Fellow, 1946-47; Prof. of Chemistry, Auckland Univ. Coll., 1947-55; Vice-Chancellor and Rector, University of Canterbury, Christchurch, NZ, 1956-61;

Chairman: University Grants Cttee (NZ), 1961-66; N Zealand Broadcasting Corp., 1962-65; Vice-Chancellor, Exeter Univ., 1966-72. Mem. Senate, University of New Zealand, 1956-60; Mem. Council of Scientific and Industrial Research, 1957-61, 1962; Mem. NZ Atomic Energy Cttee, 1958; Mem. NZ Cttee on Technical Education, 1958-66; Chairman: NZ Council of Adult Educn, 1961-66; NZ Commonwealth Scholarships and Fellowships Cttee, 1961-66; Member Council: Royal Society of NZ, 1961-63; Assoc. of Commonwealth Univs, 1967-72; Member: Inter-University Council for Higher Education Overseas, 1967-72; British Council Cttee for Commonwealth Univ. Interchange, 1968-72; Representative of UK Universities on Council of Univ. of Ahmado Bello, Nigeria, 1968-72. Chm., Northcott Theatre Bd of Management, 1966-72. Hon. LLD: Canterbury, 1962; Victoria Univ. of Wellington, 1966; Exeter, 1973; Birmingham, 1975; Hon. DSc Salford, 1975. *Publications:* Crystallographic papers in Jl of Chemical Soc., London, and in Acta Crystallographica. *Recreations:* photography and travel. *Address:* The British Council, 10 Spring Gardens, SW1A 2BN. *T:* 01-930 8466. *Club:* Athenæum.

LLEWELLYN, Col Sir Godfrey; *see* Llewellyn, Col Sir R. G.

LLEWELLYN, Sir Henry Morton, (Sir Harry Llewellyn), Kt 1977; CBE 1953 (OBE 1944); MA; late Warwicks Yeomanry; President, Whitbread Wales Ltd, since 1972; Chairman: Davenco (Engineers) Ltd; Grid Management & Finance Ltd; South Wales Board, Eagle Star Assurance Co., since 1964; Wales Board, Nationwide Building Society, since 1972; Director: Whitbread International Ltd; Cardiff Malting Co. Ltd; Chepstow Racecourse Co. Ltd; Member, South Wales Regional Board, Lloyds Bank, since 1963; Vice-Chairman, Civic Trust for Wales, since 1960; *b* 18 July 1911; 2nd *s* of Sir David Llewellyn, 1st Bt, and *heir-pres.* to Lt-Col Sir Rhys Llewellyn, 2nd Bt, *qv*; *m* 1944, Hon. Christine Saumarez, 2nd *d* of 5th Baron de Saumarez; two *s* one *d. Educ:* Oundle; Trinity Coll., Cambridge (MA). Riding Ego, came 2nd in Grand National 'chase, 1936, 4th, 1937. Nat. Hunt Cttee, 1946-; The Jockey Club, 1969. Jt Master Monmouthshire Hounds, 1952-57, 1963-65; Captain winning Brit. Olympic Show-Jumping Team, Helsinki (riding Foxhunter), 1952; Chm., Brit. Show Jumping Assoc., 1967-69; Pres. and Chm., British Equestrian Fedn, 1976-. Chm., Welsh Sports Council, 1971; Mem., GB Sports Council, 1971-. Pres., Inst. of Directors (Wales), 1963-65. Formerly Director: North's Navigation Colliery Ltd; TWW Ltd. Mem., Wales Tourist Board, 1969-75. DL Monmouthshire, 1952, JP 1954-68, High Sheriff 1966. US Legion of Merit, 1945; Royal Humane Soc. Medal for life-saving, 1956. *Recreations:* hunting, all sports, wild life photography. *Address:* Llanvair Grange, near Abergavenny, Gwent. *T:* Nantyderry 880222. *Club:* Cavalry and Guards.

LLEWELLYN, Rear-Adm. Jack Rowbottom, CB 1974; Assistant Controller of the Navy, 1972-74; retired; *b* 14 Nov. 1919; *s* of Ernest and Harriet Llewellyn, Ashton under Lyne, Lancs; *m* 1944, Joan Isabel, *d* of Charles and Hilda Phillips, Yelverton, Devon; one *s. Educ:* Purley County Sch. Entered RN, 1938; RNEC, Keyham, 1939. Served War of 1939-45: HMS Bermuda, 1942; RNC, Greenwich, 1943; HMS Illustrious, 1945. Engr in Chief's Dept, Admlty, 1947; HMS Sluys, 1949; HMS Thunderer, 1951; HMS Diamond, 1953; Comdr, 1953; Asst Engr in Chief, on loan to Royal Canadian Navy, 1954; in charge Admty Fuel Experimental Station, Haslar, 1958; HMS Victorious, 1960; Asst Dir, Marine Engrg, MoD (N), 1963; Captain, 1963; in command, HMS Fisgard, 1966; Dep. Dir, Warship Design, MoD (N), 1969; Rear-Adm., 1972. *Recreations:* travel, gardening. *Address:* Bell Cottage, Pipehouse, Freshford, near Bath, Avon. *T:* Limpley Stoke 3580.

LLEWELLYN, Sir John; *see* Llewellyn, Sir F. J.

LLEWELLYN, John Charles, JP; His Honour Judge Llewellyn; a Circuit Judge (formerly a Judge of County Courts, and a Deputy Chairman, Inner London Area Sessions), since 1965; *b* 11 Feb. 1908; *o s* of late J. E. Llewellyn, Letchworth, Herts; *m* 1937, Rae Marguerite Cabell Warrens, *d* of Lt-Col E. R. C. Warrens, DSO, Froxfield, Hants; one *s* two *d. Educ:* St Christopher Sch., Letchworth; Emmanuel Coll., Cambridge (MA, LLB). Barrister, Inner Temple, 1931; Master of the Bench, Inner Temple, 1963. Common Law Counsel to PO, 1960-65; Recorder of King's Lynn, 1961-65. Mem. Gen. Council of the Bar, 1956-60, and 1961-65; Chm. JP Advisory Council, Carpet Industry of Gt Brit., 1958-; Dep. Chm. Agric. Land Tribunal (Eastern Region), 1959-65; JP Greater London, 1965-. *Recreation:* riding. *Address:* Bulford Mill, Braintree, Essex. *T:* 20616; 2 Temple Gardens, EC4. *T:* 01-353 7907. *Clubs:* Athenæum, Boodle's.

LLEWELLYN, John Desmond Seys; His Honour Judge Seys Llewellyn; a Circuit Judge, (formerly a County Court Judge), since 1971; *b* 3 May 1912; *s* of Charles Ernest Llewellyn, FAI and Hannah Margretta Llewellyn, of Cardiff; *m* 1939, Elaine, *d* of H. Leonard Porcher, solicitor, and Mrs Hilda Porcher, JP, of Pontypridd; three *s. Educ:* Cardiff High School; Jesus College, Oxford; Exhibitioner, MA. Joined Inner Temple, 1936. War Service, RTR, 1940-46 (Captain). Called to the Bar, Inner Temple, in absentia OAS, 1945; Profumo Prizeman, 1947; practised on Wales and Chester Circuit, 1947-71; Local Insurance Appeal Tribunal, 1958-71; Dep. Chm., Cheshire QS, 1968-71; joined Gray's Inn, *ad eundem*, same day as youngest son, 1967. Contested Chester Constituency (L), 1955 and 1956. *Recreations:* languages, travel, archaeology, art galleries, music, two English Setters. *Address:* Chetwyn House, Gresford, Clwyd. *T:* Gresford 2419; Farrar's Building, Temple. *Club:* Athenæum (Liverpool).

LLEWELLYN, Rev. John Francis Morgan, MA; Chaplain at the Chapel Royal of St Peter ad Vincula within HM Tower of London, since 1974; Chaplain, Order of St John of Jerusalem, since 1974; *b* 4 June 1921; *s* of late Canon D. L. J. Llewellyn; *m* 1955, Audrey Eileen (*née* Binks). *Educ:* King's College Sch., Wimbledon; Pembroke Coll., Cambridge (MA); Ely Theological Coll. Served War, 1941-45, in Royal Welch Fusiliers and in India (Captain). Curate of Eltham, 1949-52; Chaplain and Asst Master, King's College Sch., Wimbledon, 1952-58; Headmaster, Cathedral Choir Sch., and Minor Canon of St Paul's Cathedral, 1958-74; Sacrist and Warden of College of Minor Canons, 1968-74; Dep. Priest-in-Ordinary to the Queen, 1968-70, 1974-, Priest-in-Ordinary, 1970-74. Sub-Chaplain, Order of St John of Jerusalem, 1970-74; Chaplain, City Solicitor's Co., 1975-. *Recreations:* cricket, golf, fishing. *Address:* Chaplain's Residence, HM Tower of London, EC3N 4AB. *T:* 01-709 0765. *Club:* Hawks (Cambridge).

LLEWELLYN, Lt-Col Sir Rhys, 2nd Bt, cr 1922; late Welsh Guards; *b* 9 March 1910; *e s* of Sir David Llewellyn, 1st Bt, LLD, and Magdalene (*d* 1966), *d* of Rev. H. Harries, DD, Porthcawl; *S* father, 1940; unmarried. *Educ:* Oundle; Trinity Coll., Cambridge, MA. Man. Dir, Graigola Merthyr Co. Ltd, Swansea, 1934-47. Master of Talybont Foxhounds, 1936-40; Supplementary Reserve of Officers, Welsh Guards, June 1939; War of 1939-45 (France and Germany, despatches); Regular Army Reserve of Officers, 1945-61. High Sheriff of Glamorgan, 1950-51. Comdr, Order of St John of Jerusalem. *Publication:* Breeding to Race, 1965. *Heir: b* Sir Henry Morton Llewellyn, *qv. Address:* 8C Bedford Towers, Brighton BN1 2JG.

LLEWELLYN, Richard; *see* Lloyd, R. D. V. L.

LLEWELLYN, Col Sir (Robert) Godfrey, 1st Bt cr 1959; Kt 1953; CB 1950; CBE 1942 (OBE 1927); MC 1918; TD; DL; JP; Chairman Welsh Hospital Board, 1959-65; Director of Companies; Chairman of the Wales and Monmouthshire Conservative and Unionist Council, 1949-56, President, 1958, 1962, 1966, 1967, 1968, 1969; President, National Union of Conservative and Unionist Associations, 1962 (Vice-Chairman 1952-53, Chairman 1954-55); Chairman Glamorgan TA and AFA, 1953-58; *b* 13 May 1893; *y s* of Robert William Llewellyn, DL, JP, Cwrt-Colman, Bridgend and Baglan Hall, Briton-Ferry, Glamorgan; *m* 1920, Frances Doris (*d* 1969), *d* of Rowland S. Kennard, JP, Little Harrow, Christchurch, Hants; one *s* one *d. Educ:* Royal Naval Colls, Osborne and Dartmouth. Joined Royal Navy, 1906; Midshipman, 1910; Sub-Lt 1913; resigned, 1914; served European War, with Montgomeryshire Yeomanry Cavalry to 1917 when attached Royal Welch Fusiliers; commanded Brigade Signal Troop 6th Mounted Brigade, 1917-18; Captain 1918; 4th Cavalry Div. Signal Squadron, 1918 (despatches twice, MC); Commanded 53rd Div. Signals (TA), 1920-29; Major, 1920; Bt Lt-Col, 1924; Lt-Col 1925; Bt Col 1928; Dep. Chief Signal Officer, Western Command, 1929-37; retired, 1937; Hon. Col 53rd Div. Signals, Royal Corps Signals, 1929-33. Col i/c Administration, Home Guard and Home Guard Adviser, S Wales District, 1940-44; Hon. Col 38th Div. Royal Corps Signals, 1941-49; Col Commandant Glamorgan Army Cadet Force, 1943-49; formerly Hon. Col 16th (Welsh) Battalion The Parachute Regt, TA. JP Neath Borough, 1925. Pres. of the Bath and West Show, 1956; Chm. of Organising Cttee Empire and Commonwealth Games, 1958. DL Glamorgan, 1936-74, Gwent, 1974-; DL Mon, 1960; JP Glamorgan County, 1934; High Sheriff: of Glamorgan, 1947-48, of Monmouth, 1963-64. KStJ 1969. *Recreations:* yachting, shooting, fishing, racing. *Heir: s* Captain Michael Rowland Godfrey Llewellyn, Grenadier Guards R of O [*b* 15 June 1921; *m* 1st, 1946, Bronwen Mary (marr. diss. 1951), *d* of Sir (Owen) Watkin Williams-Wynn, 8th Bt; 2nd, 1956, Janet Prudence, *y d* of Lt-Col Charles Thomas Edmondes, DL, JP, Ewenny Priory,

Bridgend, Glam; three d. Educ: Harrow; RMC Sandhurst]. Address: Tredilion Park, Abergavenny, Gwent. T: 2178. Clubs: Carlton, Pratt's, Naval and Military; Royal Thames Yacht, Royal Automobile; Cardiff and County (Cardiff).

LLEWELLYN, Rt. Rev. William Somers; Assistant Curate of Tetbury with Beverstow, since 1977; b 16 Aug. 1907; s of Owen John and Elizabeth Llewellyn; m 1947, Innis Mary, d of Major Arthur Dorrien-Smith, Tresco Abbey, Isles of Scilly; three s. Educ: Eton; Balliol and Wycliffe Hall, Oxford. BA 1929; diploma in Theology (with dist.) 1934; MA 1937. Priest, 1936; Curate of Chiswick, 1935-37; Vicar of Badminton, with Acton Turville, 1937-49. CF 1940-46; served with Royal Gloucestershire Hussars in Egypt and Western Desert, and as Senior Chaplain with 8th Army HQ, Canal Area and East Africa; Vicar of Tetbury with Beverston, 1949-61; Rural Dean of Tetbury, 1955-61; Archdeacon of Lynn, 1961-72; first Suffragan Bishop of Lynn, 1963-72; Priest-in-charge of Boxwell with Leighterton, 1973-77. Address: Scrubbetts, Kingscote, Tetbury, Glos. T: Leighterton 236.

LLEWELLYN-JONES, Frank; see Jones, F. Ll.

LLEWELLYN JONES, Ilston Percival; a Recorder of the Crown Court, since 1972; Consultant, Turberville Smith & Co., Uxbridge, since 1967; b 15 June 1916; s of Rev. L. Cyril F. Jones and Gertrude Anne Jones; m 1963, Mary Evelyn; one s (by a former m). Educ: Baswich House and Fonthill prep. schs; St John's Sch., Leatherhead. Admitted Solicitor, Nov. 1938; practised privately until served Sussex Yeomanry RA and 23rd Field Regt RA (commnd), 1939-42; Solicitors Dept, Metropolitan Police, New Scotland Yard, 1942-48; private practice, Torquay, 1948-52; Devon County Prosecuting Solicitor, 1952-56; Clerk to N Devon Justices, 1956-62; private practice, London, 1962-67. Recreations: now mainly golf; formerly Rugby football, tennis, squash, swimming, cross country running. Address: The Willow, Parsonage Lane, Farnham Common, Bucks. T: Farnham Common 2738. Clubs: Harlequin Football; Burnham Beeches Golf.

LLEWELYN, Sir John Michael D. V.; see Venables-Llewelyn.

LLEWELYN-DAVIES, family name of **Baron Llewelyn-Davies** and **Baroness Llewelyn-Davies of Hastoe.**

LLEWELYN-DAVIES, Baron, cr 1963 (Life Peer); **Richard Llewelyn-Davies,** MA, FRIBA; FRTPI; Emeritus Professor of Urban Planning, University College London; in private practice as Senior Partner, Llewelyn-Davies, Weeks, Forestier-Walker & Bor; b 24 Dec. 1912; s of Crompton Llewelyn Davies and Moya Llewelyn Davies (née O'Connor); m 1943, Patricia (see Baroness Llewelyn-Davies of Hastoe); three d. Educ: privately; Trinity Coll., Cambridge; Ecole des Beaux Arts, Paris; Architectural Association. Architect, LMS Railways, 1942-48. Director: Investigation into Functions and Design of Hospitals; Division of Architectural Studies, Nuffield Foundation, London, 1953-60. Prof. of Architecture, University College London, 1960-69, Prof. of Urban Planning 1969-75. First Pres., World Soc. for Ekistics, 1965; Chm., The Centre for Environmental Studies, 1967-; Mem., Royal Fine Art Commn, 1961-72. Consulting Architect: to Times Publishing Co. Ltd for new offices at Printing House Square; for rebuilding of London Stock Exchange; for many hosps in the UK and overseas. Other projects include: Master Planner, Memorial Teaching Hosp., Memorial Univ., Newfoundland, 1967-; Tate Gallery Extensions; new village at Rushbrooke, Suffolk (West Suffolk Award, 1957); Nuffield diagnostic centre and maternity hosp. at Corby, Northants (RIBA Bronze Medal, 1957); Master Plan for Washington New Town, Co. Durham, 1966; Master Plan for new city of Milton Keynes, 1967-. Hon. Fellow, American Institute of Architects, 1970. Publications: (jointly) Studies in the Functions and Design of Hospitals, 1955; (jointly) Building Elements, 1956; (jointly) The Design of Research Laboratories, 1960; contributions to Nature, Journal of RIBA, Architects' Journal, Architectural Review, Architectural Record, Jl Town Planning Inst., Jl Royal Inst. of Chemistry. Address: 36 Parkhill Road, NW3. T: 01-485 6576; 4 Fitzroy Square, W1P 6JA. T: 01-387 0541. Club: Brooks's.

LLEWELYN-DAVIES OF HASTOE, Baroness cr 1967, of Hastoe (Life Peer); **Patricia Llewelyn-Davies,** PC 1975; Captain of the Gentlemen at Arms (Government Chief Whip in House of Lords), since 1974; Chairman, Women's National Cancer Control Campaign, 1972; b 16 July 1915; d of Charles Percy Parry and Sarah Gertrude Parry (née Hamilton); m 1943, Richard Llewelyn-Davies (now Baron Llewelyn-Davies, qv); three d. Educ: Liverpool Coll., Huyton; Girton Coll., Cambridge. Civil Servant, 1940-51 (Min. of War Transp., FO,

Air Min., CRO). Contested (Lab) Wolverhampton S-W, 1951, Wandsworth Cent., 1955, 1959. A Baroness-in-Waiting (Govt Whip), 1969-70; Opposition Chief Whip, House of Lords, 1973-74 (Deputy, 1972-73). Hon. Sec., Lab. Parly Assoc., 1960-69. Member: Bd of Govs, Hosp. for Sick Children, Gt Ormond Street, 1955-67 (Chm. Bd, 1967-69); Court, Univ. of Sussex, 1967-69. Dir, Africa Educnl Trust, 1960-69. Co.-Chm., Women's Nat. Commn, 1976-. Address: 36 Parkhill Road, NW3. T: 01-485 6576.

LLOYD, family name of **Barons Lloyd, Lloyd of Hampstead** and **Lloyd of Kilgerran.**

LLOYD, see Geoffrey-Lloyd.

LLOYD, see Selwyn-Lloyd.

LLOYD, 2nd Baron, cr 1925, of Dolobran; **Alexander David Frederick Lloyd,** MBE 1945; DL; Captain Welsh Guards (Reserve); Director: Lloyds Bank Ltd; Lloyds Bank International; Lloyds Bank Unit Trust Managers; Beehive Life Insurance; Chairman, National Bank of New Zealand, since 1970 (Vice-Chairman, 1969); b 30 Sept. 1912; o s of 1st Baron and Hon. Blanche (d 1969) (late Maid of Honour to Queen Alexandra), d of late Hon. F. C. Lascelles; S father, 1941; m 1942, Lady Victoria Jean Marjorie Mabel Ogilvy, e d of 11th Earl of Airlie; two d (one s decd). Educ: Eton; Cambridge (MA). Served in British Council prior to War of 1939-45; served War of 1939-45 in Palestine, Syria and NW Europe. Pres. Navy League, 1948-51; Mem. LCC, 1949-51. Lord in Waiting to King George VI, Oct. 1951-Feb. 1952, to the Queen until Dec. 1952; Jt Under-Sec. of State for Home Dept with responsibility for Welsh Affairs, Nov. 1952-Oct. 1954; Parliamentary Under-Sec. of State for the Colonies, Oct. 1954-Jan. 1957. Mem., White Fish Authority and Herring Bd, 1963-69. Pres. Commonwealth and British Empire Chambers of Commerce, 1957-61. Board of Governors, London Sch. of Hygiene and Tropical Medicine. DL Herts 1963. Recreations: shooting, fishing. Address: Clouds Hill, Offley, Hitchin, Herts. T: Offley 350. Club: White's.

LLOYD OF HAMPSTEAD, Baron cr 1965 (Life Peer); **Dennis Lloyd,** QC 1975; Quain Professor of Jurisprudence in the University of London (University College), since 1956; b 22 Oct. 1915; 2nd s of Isaac and Betty Lloyd; m 1940, Ruth Emma Cecilia Tulla; two d. Educ: University Coll. Sch.; University Coll., London; Gonville and Caius Coll., Cambridge. LLB (London) 1935; BA 1937, MA 1941, LLD 1956 (Cantab). Called to Bar, 1936; Yorke Prize, 1938; in practice in London, 1937-39 and 1946-. Served War of 1939-45 in RA and RAOC, Liaison Officer (DADOS) with Free French Forces in Syria and Lebanon, 1944-45. Reader in English Law, University Coll., London, 1947-56; Fellow of University Coll., London; Dean of Faculty of Laws, University of London, 1962-64; Head of Dept of Law, University Coll.; Member: Law Reform Cttee; Consolidation Bills Cttee, 1965-77; European Communities Cttee; Joint Cttee on Theatre Censorship; Joint Cttee on Broadcasting; Select Cttee on Bill of Rights; Interim Action Cttee on Film Industry; Conseil de la Fédération Britannique de l'Alliance Française; Chairman: Nat. Film Sch. Cttee; Planning Cttee for Nat. Film Sch.; Mem. Ct, RCA; Chairman: Governors, Nat. Film School, 1970-; British Film Inst., 1973-76 (Governor, 1968-76); Chm. Council, University Coll. Sch. Publications: Unincorporated Associations, 1938; Rent Control, 1st edition, 1949, 2nd edition, 1955; Public Policy: A Comparative Study in English and French Law, 1953; United Kingdom: Development of its Laws and Constitution, 1955; Business Lettings, 1956; Introduction to Jurisprudence, 1st edn, 1959, 3rd edn, 1972; The Idea of Law, 1964, rev. imps, 1968, 1970, 1973, 1976, Japanese trans., 1969; Law (Concept Series), 1968; contrib. to periodicals. Recreations: painting, listening to music. Address: 6 Pump Court, Temple, EC4. T: 01-236 3938; 18 Hampstead Way, NW11. T: 01-455 0954. Clubs: Athenæum, PEN (Hon. Mem.).

LLOYD OF KILGERRAN, Baron cr 1973 (Life Peer), of Llanwenog, Cardigan; **Rhys Gerran Lloyd,** CBE 1953; QC 1961; JP; Barrister-at-law; b 12 Aug. 1907; s of late J. G. Lloyd, Kilgerran, Pembrokeshire; m 1940, Phyllis, d of late Ronald Shepherd, JP, Hants; two d. Educ: Sloane Sch.; Selwyn Coll., Cambridge (science scholar). MA Cantab; BSc London. Wartime service in scientific research Departments of Air Ministry and MAP, 1939-46. Royal Commn on Awards to Inventors, 1946. Contested (L) Anglesey, General Election, 1959. In practice at Patent Bar, 1946-68. Director: Martonair International Ltd; Terrapin International Ltd; Target Unit Trust Managers (Wales) Ltd; Strayfield Ltd; Chairman: Education Trust; Brantwood Trust. Mem., Sainsbury Cttee on NHS, 1965-67. Vice-Chm., Victoria League, 1975. Pres., Welsh Liberal Party, 1971-74; Pres., UK Liberal Party, 1973-74, Jt

Treas., 1977-. Pres., Inst. of Patentees and Inventors, 1975-. Hon. Fellow, Selwyn Coll., Cambridge, 1967-. JP Surrey, 1954. *Publications:* Kerly on Trade Marks, 8th edn, 1960; Halsbury's Trade Marks and Designs, 3rd edn, 1962. *Address:* 15 Haymeads Drive, Esher, Surrey. *Clubs:* Reform, Royal Commonwealth Society, City Livery.

LLOYD, Rev. (Albert) Kingsley; President of the Conference of the Methodist Church, 1964; *b* 1903; *s* of Rev. Albert Lloyd; *m* 1926, Ida Marian (*née* Cartledge) (*d* 1969); one *s* one *d*; 2nd, 1972, Katharine G., *d* of A. G. L. Ives, *qv. Educ:* Kingswood Sch., Bath; Richmond Coll., Surrey (University of London). Methodist Circuit Minister: London, Bedford, Cambridge, 1926-52; Chm., London N Dist, 1951-53. Secretary, Dept of Connexional Funds of the Methodist Church, 1952-69. Chm., Methodist Ministers' Housing Soc. Governor, Kingswood Sch. Wesley Historical Soc. Lectr, 1968. *Recreation:* gardening. *Address:* 13 High Street, Orwell, Royston, Herts.

LLOYD, Anthony (John Leslie), QC 1967; Barrister-at-law; Attorney-General to HRH The Prince of Wales, since 1969; *b* 9 May 1929; *o s* of Edward John Boydell Lloyd and Leslie Johnston Fleming; *m* 1960, Jane Helen Violet, *er d* of C. W. Shelford, Chailey Place, Lewes, Sussex. *Educ:* Eton (Schol.); Trinity Coll., Cambridge (Maj. Schol.). National Service, 1st Bn Coldstream Guards, 1948; Montague Butler Prize, Cambridge, 1950; Sir William Browne Medal, 1951. Choate Fellow, Harvard, 1952; Fellow of Peterhouse, 1953; Fellow of Eton, 1974. Called to Bar, Inner Temple, 1955; Bencher, 1976. Trustee: Crafts Centre of Great Britain, 1967-72; Smiths Charity, 1971; Glyndebourne Arts Trust, 1973 (Chm., 1975); Member: Educn Cttee, ILEA, 1969-70; Top Salaries Review Body, 1971-. Chm., Chichester Diocesan Bd of Finance, and Mem., Bishop's Council, 1972-76; Governor: West London Coll., 1970-74; Polytechnic of the South Bank, 1971-73. *Recreations:* music, carpentry; formerly running (ran for Cambridge in Mile, White City, 1950). *Address:* 68 Strand-on-the-Green, Chiswick, W4. *T:* 01-994 7790; Ludlay, Berwick, East Sussex. *T:* Alfriston 870204. *Club:* Brooks's.

LLOYD, Prof. Antony Charles; Professor of Philosophy, Liverpool University, since 1957; *b* 15 July 1916; *s* of Charles Mostyn Lloyd and Theodosia Harrison-Rowson. *Educ:* Shrewsbury Sch.; Balliol Coll., Oxford. Asst to Prof. of Logic and Metaphysics, Edinburgh Univ., 1938-39 and 1945; served in Army, 1940-45; Lecturer in Philosophy, St Andrews Univ., 1946-57. *Publications:* Chapters in Cambridge History of Later Ancient Philosophy; articles in philosophical journals. *Address:* The University, Liverpool L69 3BX.

LLOYD, Arnold; see Lloyd, W. A. de G.

LLOYD, Dr Brian Beynon; Director, Oxford Polytechnic, since 1970; *b* 23 Sept. 1920; *s* of David John Lloyd, MA Oxon and Olwen (*née* Beynon); *m* 1949, Reinhild Johanna Engeroff; four *s* three *d* (inc. twin *s* and twin *d*). *Educ:* Newport High Sch.; Winchester Coll. (Schol.); Balliol Coll., Oxford (Domus and Frazer Schol.). Special Certif. for BA (War) Degree in Chem., 1940; took degrees BA and MA, 1946; Theodore Williams Schol. and cl. I in Physiology, 1948; DSc 1969. Joined Oxford Nutrition Survey after registration as conscientious objector, 1941; Pres., Jun. Common Room, Balliol, 1941-42; Chm., Undergraduate Rep. Coun., 1942; Biochemist: SHAEF Nutrition Survey Team, Leiden, 1945; Nutrition Survey Group, Düsseldorf, 1946. Fellow of Magdalen by exam. in Physiology, 1948-52, by special election, 1952-70; Senior Tutor, 1963-64; Vice-Pres., 1967 and 1968; Emeritus Fellow, 1970; Senior Research Officer, later Univ. Lectr, Univ. of Oxford, 1948-70; Senior Proctor, 1960-61. Mem., Health Educn Council, 1975-; Chm., CNAA Health and Med. Services Bd, 1975-. Vis. Physiologist, New York, 1963. Pres., Section I, British Assoc. for the Advancement of Science, 1964-65. Chm. of Govs, Oxford Coll. of Technology, 1963-69; Chm. of Dirs, Oxford Gallery, 1967-. *Publications:* Gas Analysis Apparatus, 1960; (jt ed) The Regulation of Human Respiration, 1962; Cerebrospinal Fluid and the Regulation of Respiration, 1965; articles in physiological and biochemical jls. *Recreations:* Klavarskribo, Correggio, haemoglobin, the analysis of running records. *Address:* High Wall, Pullen's Lane, Oxford. *T:* Oxford 63353.
See also Sir J. P. D. Lloyd.

LLOYD, (Charles) Christopher; author, historian; *b* 2 Sept. 1906; *s* of E. S. Lloyd, CSI, and M. Young; *m* 1938, Katharine Brenda Sturge; one *s* one *d. Educ:* Marlborough; Lincoln Coll., Oxford. Lecturer: Bishop's Univ., Quebec, 1930-34; Royal Naval Coll., Dartmouth, 1934-45; Lectr, 1945-66, Prof. of History, 1962-66, Royal Naval College, Greenwich; retired, 1967. Editor, The Mariner's Mirror, 1970-. *Publications:* The Navy and the Slave Trade, 1949; The Nation and the Navy, 1961; Medicine and the Navy, 1961; William Dampier, 1966; The British Seaman, 1968; Mr Barrow of the Admiralty, 1970; The Search for the Niger, 1973; The Nile Campaign: Nelson and Napoleon in Egypt, 1973; Nelson and Sea Power, 1973; Atlas of Maritime History, 1976, etc. *Address:* Lions Wood, Dern Lane, Heathfield, East Sussex. *T:* Horam Road 2702. *Club:* Travellers'.

LLOYD, Charles William, MA; JP; Master, Dulwich College, 1967-75; *b* 23 Sept. 1915; *s* of late Charles Lloyd and late Frances Ellen Lloyd, London; *m* 1939, Doris Ethel, *d* of late David Baker, Eastbourne; one *s* one *d* (and one *d* decd). *Educ:* St Olave's Sch.; Emmanuel Coll., Cambridge. Asst Master Buckhurst Hill Sch., 1938-40. War Service with RA, 1940-46 (despatches). Asst Master Gresham's Sch., Holt, 1946-51; Headmaster, Hutton Gram. Sch., near Preston, 1951-63; Headmaster, Alleyn's Sch., London, 1963-66. Trustee, Nat. Maritime Museum, 1974-. JP Inner London, 1970. *Publication:* contrib. to Domesday Geography of SE England (Surrey) ed by H. C. Darby. *Recreations:* golf, gardening. *Address:* Crowlink, 7 The Broadway, Alfriston, Sussex. *T:* Alfriston 870552.

LLOYD, Christopher; see Lloyd, Charles C.

LLOYD, Christopher, MA, BSc (Hort.); writer on horticulture; regular gardening correspondent, Country Life, since 1963; *b* 2 March 1921; *s* of late Nathaniel Lloyd and Daisy (*née* Field). *Educ:* Wellesley House, Broadstairs, Kent; Rugby Sch.; King's Coll., Cambridge (MA Mod Langs); Wye Coll., Univ of London (BSc Hort.). Asst Lectr in Decorative Horticulture, Wye Coll., 1950-54. Then returned to family home at Great Dixter and started Nursery in clematis and uncommon plants. *Publications:* The Mixed Border, 1957; Clematis, 1965, rev. edn 1977; Shrubs and Trees for Small Gardens, 1965; Hardy Perennials, 1967; Gardening on Chalk and Lime, 1969; The Well-Tempered Garden, 1970; Foliage Plants, 1973; frequent contributor to gardening magazines, also to Jl of Royal Horticultural Soc. *Recreations:* walking, piano playing (mainly Brahms), canvas embroidery. *Address:* Great Dixter, Northiam, Rye, East Sussex TN31 6PH. *T:* Northiam 3107.

LLOYD, Maj.-Gen. Cyril, CB 1948; CBE 1944 (OBE 1943); TD 1945 (2 bars); psc: Director-General, City and Guilds of London Institute, 1949-67, Consultant, since 1968, President, since 1976; Chairman, Associated Examining Board for General Certificate of Education, since 1970; *b* 1906; *s* of late A. H. Lloyd. *Educ:* Brighton Grammar Sch.; London and Cambridge Univs. First Class in Mathematics, Physics, Divinity. Fellow of Institute of Physics; FRGS; MRST; Lecturer and Teacher; Research Worker in Science; Sussex Territorials (RA), 1929-39; Major, 1939; BEF, 1939-40 (despatches); General Staff, Canadian Army, 1940-42 (despatches, OBE); served various overseas theatres; a Dep Chief of Staff, 21 Army Group, 1943-45; Invasion of Europe (despatches, CBE), 1944-45; Dir-Gen. of Army Education and Training, 1945-49; Member: Council of Boy Scouts Assoc., 1950-70; Council Assoc. of Techn. Institutions, 1961-64; Central Adv. Council for Educn (England) and Adv. Cttee on Educn in Colonies, 1949-53; Adv. Council on Sci. Policy (Jt Enquiry on Technicians, 1962-65; Bd, Internat. Centre for Advanced Technical and Vocational Trg (Turin); Council for Tech. Education and Training for Overseas Countries; Regional Adv. Council for Higher Technological Educn (London), 1950-67; Parly and Scientific Cttee; Nat. Adv. Council for Educn in Industry and Commerce, 1945-68; Southern Regional Council for Further Educn; Council, Instn of Environmental Studies; Vice-Pres. Brit. Assoc. for Commercial and Industrial Educn (Chm. 1955-58); Industrial Trg Council, 1958-64; Central Trg Council and its General Policy Cttee, 1964-68; Chm., Governing Body, National Institute of Agricultural Engineering, 1960-70; Schools Broadcasting Council for the UK, 1962-65; W Sussex Educn Cttee; Council Rural Industries Bureau, 1960-67; Pres., SASLIC, 1970; Pres., Soc. for Promotion of Vocational Trng and Educn, 1973; Chm., Ctee on Scientific Library Services; Chm. Governors, Crawley Coll. of Further Educn; Vice-Pres., Crawley Planning Gp; Chief Officer, Commonwealth Tech. Trg Week, 1961; Treas., 1963 Campaign for Educn; Mem. Council for Educl Advance; Trustee: Edward James Foundn; Industrial Trg Foundn; Pres., Roffey Park Management Inst. Governor, Imperial Coll., 1950-70; Mem. Delegacy, City and Guilds Coll., 1950-70; Hon. Exec. Principal, West Dean Coll., 1969-72. Founder Life Mem., Cambridge Soc. Liveryman, Goldsmiths' Co. and Freeman of City of London; FRSA. *Publications:* booklets: British Services Education, 1950; Human Resources and New Systems of Vocational Training and Apprenticeship, 1963; contrib. to jls. *Recreations:* the countryside, sailing, and traditional crafts. *Address:* The Pheasantry, Colgate, Horsham, Sussex RH13 6HU. *Club:* Athenæum.

LLOYD, Air Vice-Marshal Darrell Clive Arthur; Deputy Commander, Royal Air Force Germany, since 1976; *b* 5 Nov. 1928; *s* of Cecil James Lloyd and Doris Frances Lloyd; *m* 1957, Pamela (*née* Woodside); two *s*. *Educ:* Stowe; RAF Coll., Cranwell. Commnd 1950; ADC to C-in-C, ME Air Force, 1955-57; Instr, Central Flying Sch., 1958-60; Personal Air Sec. to Sec. of State for Air, 1961-63; CO, RAF Bruggen, 1968-70; RCDS, 1972; Dir of Defence Policy, UK Strategy Div., 1973-75. *Recreations:* travel, golf, painting. *Address:* c/o Lloyds Bank, 6 Pall Mall, SW1. *Club:* Royal Air Force.

LLOYD, Denis Thelwall; His Honour Judge Denis Lloyd; a Circuit Judge, since 1972; *b* 3 Jan. 1924; *s* of late Col Glyn Lloyd, DSO, FRCVS, Barrister-at-Law; *m* 1950, Margaret Sheila (*d* 1976), *d* of Bernard Bushell, Wirral, Ches; one *s* two *d*. *Educ:* Wellington College. Enlisted KRRC, 1942; commnd KRRC Dec. 1942; Central Mediterranean Force, (Italy, S France, Greece) 1943-45; attached 1st York and Lancaster Regt and then joined Parachute Regt, 1944; Palestine, 1945-46; GSO3 (ops) HQ British Troops Austria, 1946; Staff Captain British Mil. Mission to Czechoslovakia, 1947. Called to the Bar, Gray's Inn, 1949; joined NE Circuit, 1950; an Asst Recorder, Leeds, 1961-67; Recorder of Pontefract, 1971; Dep. Chm., WR Yorks QS, 1968-71. Dep. Chm., Agricultural Land Tribunal, Yorks and Lancs, 1968. Contested (L): York, 1964; Hallam Div. of Sheffield, 1966. Czech War Cross, 1946. *Recreations:* gardening, fishing. *Address:* Bridge End Farm, Brough, Bradwell, Derbyshire. *T:* Hope Valley 20205.

LLOYD, Major Sir (Ernest) Guy (Richard), 1st Bt *cr* 1960; Kt 1953; DSO 1917; DL; late Administrator J. and P. Coats, Ltd, Glasgow (retired 1938); *b* 7 Aug. 1890; *e s* of late Major E. T. Lloyd, late Bengal Civil Service; *m* 1918, Helen Kynaston, *yr d* of late Col E. W. Greg, CB; one *s* three *d* (and one *d* decd). *Educ:* Rossall; Keble Coll., Oxford, MA. Served European War, 1914-18 (despatches, DSO); War of 1939-45, 1940. MP (U) East Renfrewshire, Scotland, 1940-Sept. 1959. DL, Dunbartonshire, 1953. *Recreations:* fishing and gardening. *Heir: s* Richard Ernest Butler Lloyd, *qv*. *Address:* Rhu Cottage, Carrick Castle, Lochgoilhead, Argyll.
See also Sir A. M. A. Denny, Bt, Sir Robert Green-Price, Bt.

LLOYD, Frederick John, CBE 1977; FCIT; Director General, West Midlands Passenger Transport Executive, since 1969; *b* 22 Jan. 1913; *m* 1942, Catherine Johnson (*née* Parker); one *s* one *d*. *Educ:* Ackworth Sch., Yorks; Liverpool Univ. (BSc). FIA 1947; FIS 1949; FSS 1953; FCIT 1968. War Service, Operational Res., Bomber Comd, 1942-45. Royal Insurance Co., 1933-47; London Passenger Transport Bd, 1947; London Transport Board, 1948-69: Staff Admin Officer, 1952; Divl Supt (South), 1957; Chief Operating Manager (Central Buses), 1961; Chief Commercial and Planning Officer, 1965-69. *Publications:* contribs to actuarial and transport jls. *Recreations:* golf, photography and gardening. *Address:* 8 Cliveden Coppice, Sutton Coldfield, West Midlands B74 2RG. *T:* 021-308 5683. *Club:* Whittington Barracks Golf (Lichfield, Staffs).

LLOYD, George Peter, CMG 1965; Deputy Governor, Bermuda, since 1974; *b* 23 Sept. 1926; *er s* of late Sir Thomas Ingram Kynaston Lloyd, GCMG, KCB; *m* 1957, Margaret Harvey; two *s* one *d*. *Educ:* Stowe Sch.; King's Coll., Cambridge. Lieut, KRRC, 1945-48; ADC to Governor of Kenya, 1948; Cambridge, 1948-51 (MA; athletics blue); District Officer, Kenya, 1951-60; Principal, Colonial Office, 1960-61; Colonial Secretary, Seychelles, 1961-66; Chief Sec., Fiji, 1966-70; Defence Sec., Hong Kong, 1971-74. *Address:* Montpelier, Devonshire, Bermuda. *Clubs:* Royal Commonwealth Society; Royal Bermuda Yacht (Bermuda); Hong Kong (Hong Kong); Muthaiga (Nairobi, Kenya).

LLOYD, Major Sir Guy; see Lloyd, Major Sir E. G. R.

LLOYD, Very Rev. Henry Morgan, DSO 1941; OBE 1959; MA; Dean of Truro and Rector of St Mary, Truro, since 1960; *b* 9 June 1911; *y s* of late Rev. David Lloyd, Weston-super-Mare, Somerset; *m* 1962, Rachel Katharine, *d* of late J. R. Wharton, Haffield, nr Ledbury; one *d*. *Educ:* Canford Sch.; Oriel Coll., Oxford; Cuddesdon Theological Coll. Deacon, 1935; priest, 1936; Curate of Hendon Parish Church, Middlesex, 1935-40. Served War as Chaplain RNVR, 1940-45. Principal of Old Rectory Coll., Hawarden, 1946-48; Secretary of Central Advisory Council of Training for the Ministry, 1948-50; Dean of Gibraltar, 1950-60. *Recreations:* walking and archæology. *Address:* The Deanery, Truro. *Club:* Royal Commonwealth Society (Fellow).
See also Brig. T. I. Lloyd.

LLOYD, Dame Hilda Nora, DBE 1951; Emeritus Professor of Obstetrics and Gynæcology at Queen Elizabeth Hospital and University of Birmingham; Senior Surgeon, Women's Hospital and Maternity Hospital, Birmingham; *b* 11 Aug. 1891; *d* of John Shufflebotham and Emma Jenkins; *m* 1930, Bertram A. Lloyd (*d* 1948); no *c*; *m* 1949, Baron Rose, FRCS. *Educ:* King Edward's High School for Girls, Birmingham; University of Birmingham (BSc 1914, MB, ChB 1916); London Hospital. MRCS, LRCP 1918; FRCS 1920; FRCOG 1936; FRSM; President RCOG, 1949-52; Member Med. Women's Federation. retired, 1954. *Recreations:* mountaineering, gardening. *Address:* Baysham Orchard, Ross-on-Wye, Hereford. *Club:* VAD Ladies.

LLOYD, Air Chief Marshal Sir Hugh Pughe, GBE 1953 (KBE 1942; CBE 1941); KCB 1951 (CB 1942); MC; DFC; retired; Hon. LLD (Wales); *b* 12 Dec. 1895; *m* Kathleen (*d* 1976), *d* of late Maj. Robert Thornton Meadows, DSO, MD; one *d*. Served European War, 1914-18, with Army and RAF (DFC, MC); War of 1939-45 (CBE, CB, KBE); Air ADC to the King, 1940-41; AOC Malta, 1941-42; Comdr, Allied Coastal Air Forces, Mediterranean, 1943-44; Comdr, Commonwealth Bomber Force, Okinawa, 1944-45; Senior Instructor Imperial Defence Coll., 1946-47; C-in-C, Air Command Far East, 1947-49; AOC-in-C Bomber Command, 1950-53; retired 1953. Master Peshawar Vale Hounds, 1934-36. Order of Legion of Merit (USA), 1944; Officier Légion d'Honneur, 1944. *Publication:* Briefed to Attack, 1949. *Address:* Peterley Manor Farm, Great Missenden, Bucks. *T:* 2959.

LLOYD, Ian Stewart; MP (C) Havant and Waterloo, since 1974 (Portsmouth, Langstone, 1964-74); Economic Adviser, British and Commonwealth Shipping, since 1956 (Director of Research, 1956-64); *b* 30 May 1921; *s* of Walter John Lloyd and late Euphemia Craig Lloyd; *m* 1951, Frances Dorward Addison, *d* of late Hon. W. Addison, CMG, OBE, MC, DCM; three *s*. *Educ:* Michaelhouse; University of the Witwatersrand; King's Coll., Cambridge. President, Cambridge Union, and Leader, Cambridge tour of USA, 1947; MA 1951; MSc 1952. Econ. Adviser, Central Mining and Investment Corporation, 1949-52; Member, SA Board of Trade and Industries, 1952-55; Director, Acton Soc. Trust, 1956. Chairman, UK Cttee and Vice-Chairman, International Exec., International Cargo Handling Co-ordination Assoc., 1961-64. Chairman: Cons. Parly Shipping and Shipbuilding Cttee, 1974-; Select Cttee on Sci. Sub-Cttee, 1975-. Member, UK Delegation, Council of Europe, Western European Union, 1968-72; UK rep., Internat. Parly Conf., Bucharest, 1975. *Publications:* contribs to SA Journal of Economics and Journal of Industrial Economics. *Recreations:* yachting, ski-ing, good music. *Address:* Bakers House, Priors Dean, Petersfield, Hants. *Clubs:* Brooks's, Army and Navy, Royal Yacht Squadron; Royal Cork Yacht.

LLOYD, His Honour Ifor Bowen, QC; a County Court Judge, later a Circuit Judge, 1959-76 (Judge of Wandsworth County Court, 1964-76); *b* 9 Sept. 1902; *er s* of late Rev. Thomas Davies Lloyd and Mrs Margaret Lloyd; *m* 1938, Naomi, *y d* of late George Pleydell Bancroft; one *s* one *d*. *Educ:* Winchester (Exhibitioner); Exeter Coll., Oxford (Scholar). BA Oxford (Mod. Hist.), 1924; called to Bar, Inner Temple, 1925, KC 1951, Bencher 1959; Yarborough Anderson scholar, 1926; Midland Circuit; President, Hardwicke Society, 1929. Liberal Candidate, Burton Division of Staffordshire, 1929, Chertsey Division of Surrey, 1931. Member General Council of the Bar, 1950, 1957. *Address:* 11 King's Bench Walk, Temple, EC4. *T:* 01-353 1729. *Club:* Reform.

LLOYD, James Monteith, CMG 1961; Deputy Chairman, Industrial Disputes Tribunal, Jamaica, since 1976; *b* 24 Nov. 1911; *s* of late Jethro and Frances Lloyd; *m* 1936, Mavis Anita Frankson; two *s* two *d*. *Educ:* Wolmer's High Sch., Jamaica. Called to Bar, Lincoln's Inn, 1948. Jamaica: entered Public Service as Asst, Registrar-General's Dept; 1931 (2nd Class Clerk, 1939, 1st Class Clerk, 1943, Asst Registrar-General, 1947); Asst Secretary, Secretariat, 1950; Principal Asst Secretary, Secretariat, 1953 (seconded to Grenada on special duty, Dec. 1955-May 1956); Permanent Secretary, Jamaica, 1956; Administrator, Grenada, 1957-62; Permanent Secretary, Jamaica, 1962-72; Chm., Ombudsman Working Party, Jamaica, 1972; retired from Civil Service, 1975. Chief Comr, Scouts, Jamaica, 1973-. Coronation Medal, 1953; Jamaica Independence Medal, 1962. *Recreations:* cricket, tennis, golf. *Address:* (home) 5 Melwood Avenue, Kingston 8, Jamaica; (office) 74 Slipe Road, Kingston 8, Jamaica. *Clubs:* Jamaica; Kingston CC; YMCA.

LLOYD, John Davies Knatchbull, OBE 1957; MA; FSA; DL; JP; *b* 28 April 1900; *e s* of late John Maurice Edward Lloyd, Plas Trefaldwyn, Montgomery, Barrister-at-law, and Alice Norton, *yr d* of late Maj.-Gen. Charles Stirling Dundas (of Dundas),

Bengal Artillery; unmarried. *Educ:* Winchester; Trinity Coll., Oxford. Secretary to the Council for the Preservation of Rural Wales, 1929-46; Secretary to Powysland Club, 1937-67; Mayor of Montgomery, 9 years, 1932-38, 1961, 1962; Commission in RAFVR, 1940; High Sheriff, Montgomeryshire, 1940; Chairman: Montgomeryshire Health Executive Council, 1948-51; Montgomeryshire Joint Planning Cttee, 1953-55; County Library Cttee, 1957-74; Member: Historic Buildings Council for Wales, 1953-75; Ancient Monuments Board for Wales, 1954 (Chairman, 1959-); Council, National Museum of Wales; Royal Commn on Ancient Monuments (Wales), 1967-74; Chairman, St Asaph Diocesan Faculty Advisory Cttee, 1961. JP 1934, DL 1960, Powys (formerly Montgomery). Hon. LLD Wales, 1969. Editor, Archæologia Cambrensis, 1956-69. *Publications:* various articles in Archæologia Cambrensis and in Montgomeryshire Collections (publication of Powysland Club); *A Guide to Montgomery* (published by the Corporation, 1936, 1948 and 1961); (Editor) *Montgomeryshire Handbook* (published by C. Council, 1949, 1958 and 1963); *A Montgomery Notebook* (privately printed), 1971. *Recreations:* music, archæology. *Address:* Bron Hafren, Garthmyl, Montgomery, Powys. *T:* Berriew 261. *Club:* Brooks's.

LLOYD, John Owen, CBE 1965; HM Diplomatic Service, retired; *b* 7 Feb. 1914; *s* of late George Thomas Lloyd, ICS; *m* 1st, 1940, Ellen Marjorie Howard Andrews; one *s* one *d*; 2nd, 1972, Mrs Barbara Diana Clarke. *Educ:* Marlborough; Clare Coll., Cambridge. Probationer Vice-Consul, Tokyo, 1937; Acting Vice-Consul, Hankow, 1940-41; served at Tokyo, 1941; Vice-Consul, 1943; on staff of HM Special Commission, Singapore, 1946; transferred to Foreign Office, 1948; Foreign Office Representative, Canadian National Defence Coll., 1952; First Secretary (Commercial), Paris, 1953-56; First Secretary, Office of Comr-Gen., Singapore, 1957; Counsellor, Office of the Commissioner-General, Singapore, 1958-60; Foreign Service Inspector, 1960-63; Consul-General: Osaka-Kobe, 1963-67; San Francisco, 1967-70; Ambassador to Laos, 1970-73, retired 1974. *Publication:* A Governor's Sermons (trans. of Governor of Osaka Prefecture Gisen Sato's work), 1967. *Address:* 18 Reynolds Close, NW11.

LLOYD, Sir (John) Peter (Daniel), Kt 1971; Chairman, Cadbury Fry Pascall Australia Ltd, 1953-71; *b* 30 Aug. 1915; *s* of late David John Lloyd; *m* 1947, Gwendolen, *d* of late William Nassau Molesworth; two *s* four *d*. *Educ:* Rossall Sch.; Brasenose Coll., Oxford (MA). Royal Artillery, 1940-46 (despatches, Order of Leopold, Belgian Croix de Guerre). Member: Council, Univ. of Tasmania, 1957-; Council, Australian Admin. Staff Coll., 1959-71; Board, Commonwealth Banking Corp., 1967-; Board, Goliath Cement Holdings, 1969-; Board, Australian Mutual Provident Society, 1970; Board, Tasmanian Board Mills, 1974-. *Address:* Stonecrest, Sorell, Tasmania 7172, Australia. *Clubs:* Tasmanian (Hobart); Australian (Sydney).
See also B. B. Lloyd.

LLOYD, Prof. John Raymond; *see under* Lloyd, M. R.

LLOYD, Rev. Kingsley; *see* Lloyd, Rev. A. K.

LLOYD, Leslie; General Manager, Western Region, British Rail, since 1976; *b* 10 April 1924; *s* of Henry Lloyd and Lilian Wright; *m* 1953, Marie Snowden; one *s* two *d*. *Educ:* Hawarden Grammar Sch. RAF, 1943-47. British Rail: Management Trainee, Eastern Reg., 1949-52; Chief Controller, Manchester, 1953-56; Freight Officer, Sheffield, 1956-59; Modernisation Asst, King's Cross, 1959-61; Dist Manager, Marylebone, 1961-63; Movements Supt, Great Northern Line, 1963-64; Ops Officer, Eastern Reg., 1964-67; Man., Sundries Div., 1967; Movements Man., Western Reg., 1967-69; Chief Ops Man., British Rail HQ, 1969-76. *Recreations:* golf, gardening. *Address:* Headquarters, Western Region, British Rail, Paddington Station, W2. *T:* 01-723 7000, ext. 2819.

LLOYD, Martin, MA (Cantab); *b* 1908; 2nd *s* of late Thomas Zachary Lloyd, Edgbaston, Birmingham; *m* 1943, Kathleen Rosslyn, *y d* of late Colonel J. J. Robertson, DSO, Wick, Caithness; two *s* two *d*. *Educ:* Marlborough Coll.; Gonville and Caius Coll., Cambridge (1st Class Parts I and II Mod. Languages Tripos). Asst Master, Rugby Sch., 1930-40; on military service, 1940-44. Headmaster of Uppingham Sch., 1944-65; Warden, Missenden Abbey Adult Educn Coll., 1966-74. *Address:* Norton Cottage, Pitchcombe, Stroud, Glos. *T:* Painswick 812329.

LLOYD, Prof. Michael Raymond; Senior Partner, Sinar Associates, Tunbridge Wells, since 1973; Consultant Head, Hull School of Architecture, 1974-77; *b* 20 Aug. 1927; *s* of W. R. Lloyd; *m* 1957, Berit Hansen; one *s* two *d*. *Educ:* Wellington

Sch., Somerset; AA School of Architecture. AA Dipl. 1953; ARIBA 1954; MNAL 1960. Private practice and Teacher, State School of Arts and Crafts, Oslo, 1955-60 and 1962-63; First Year Master, AA School of Architecture, 1960-62; Dean, Faculty of Arch., and Prof. of Arch., Kumasi Univ. of Science and Technology, 1963-66; Principal, AA Sch. of Architecture, 1966-71; Consultant, Land Use Consultants (Internat.) Lausanne, 1971-72. *Publications:* (as J. R. Lloyd) Tegning og Skissing; ed World Architecture, Vol. I Norway, Vol. III Ghana; Shelter in Society: Norwegian Laftehus. *Recreations:* sailing, ski-ing. *Address:* Studley Cottage, Bishops Down, Park Road, Tunbridge Wells, Kent.

LLOYD, Norman, FRSA, ROI, 1935; Landscape Painter; *b* 16 Oct. 1895; *s* of David Lloyd and Jane Ogilvie; *m* 1923, Edith Eyre-Powell (*d* 1971). *Educ:* Hamilton and Sydney Art School, Australia. Exhibitioner Royal Academy and Royal Institute of Oil Painters; Salon des Artistes Français, Paris; Laureat du Salon Mention Honorable, 1948; Silver Medal, Portrait Salon, Paris, 1956; Palmes, Acad. Française, 1957. Member Société des Artistes Français, Paysagistes; Member Internat. Assoc. of Plastic Arts, 1962. *Recreation:* travel.

LLOYD, Colonel Pen; *see* Lloyd, Colonel Philip H.

LLOYD, Peter, CBE 1957; Director, Booth International Holdings Ltd; *b* 26 June 1907; *s* of late Godfrey I. H. Lloyd and late Constance L. A. Lloyd; *m* 1st, 1932, Nora K. E. Patten; one *s* one *d*; 2nd, 1951, Joyce Evelyn Campbell. *Educ:* Gresham's Sch.; Trinity Coll., Cambridge (MA). Industrial Research in Gas Light and Coke Co., London, 1931-41; Royal Aircraft Establishment, 1941-44; Power Jets (Research and Development), 1944-46. National Gas Turbine Establishment, Pyestock, 1946-60, Deputy Director, 1950; Dir-Gen. Engine R&D, Mins of Aviation and Technology, 1961-69; Head of British Defence Research and Supply Staff, Canberra, 1969-72. Chm., Gas Turbine Collaboration Cttee, 1961-68. FRAeS, FInstF. Pres., Cambridge Univ. Mountaineering Club, 1928-29. Himalayan expeditions: Nanda Devi, 1936; Everest, 1938; Langtang Himal, 1949; Kulu, 1977. *Publications:* various papers in scientific and technical journals. *Recreations:* mountaineering, fishing, gardening. *Address:* Heath Hill, Old Park Lane, Farnham, Surrey. *T:* Farnham 4995. *Clubs:* Athenæum, Alpine (Vice-Pres., 1961-63, Pres., 1977-).

LLOYD, Sir Peter; *see* Lloyd, Sir J. P. D.

LLOYD, Peter Gordon, CBE 1976 (OBE 1965); British Council Representative, Greece, since 1976; *b* 20 Feb. 1920; *s* of Peter Gleave Lloyd and Ellen Swift; *m* 1952, Edith Florence (*née* Flurey); two *s* one *d*. *Educ:* Royal Grammar Sch., Newcastle upon Tyne; Balliol Coll., Oxford (Horsley Exhibnr, 1939; BA, MA 1948). RA (Light Anti-Aircraft), subseq. DLI, 1940-46, Captain. Teacher, 1946-49; British Council, 1949-: Brit. Council, Belgium and Hon. Lector in English, Brussels Univ., 1949-52; Reg. Dir, Mbale, Uganda, 1952-56; Dep. Dir Personnel, 1956-60; Representative: Ethiopia, 1960-68; Poland, 1969-72; Nigeria, 1972-76. *Publications:* (introd) Huysman, A Rebours, 1940; The Story of British Democracy, 1959; critical essays on literature in periodicals. *Recreations:* literature, music, travel. *Address:* 25 Shenley Hill, Radlett, Herts. *T:* Radlett 7310. *Club:* United Oxford & Cambridge University.

LLOYD, Colonel Philip Henry, (Pen), CBE 1968; TD; DL; JP; Farmer, Landowner and Company Director; *b* 7 April 1905; *s* of late Samuel Janson Lloyd, JP; *m* 1943, Monica, *d* of W. C. Beasley-Robinson, and *widow* of H. R. Murray-Philipson, MP; no *c*. *Educ:* Oundle. Chairman: Breedon and Cloud Hill Lime Works Ltd; Breedon General Services Ltd; British Tar Products Ltd; Ironstone Royalty Owners Assoc., 1970-; Director: Cavendish Syndicate; Cocker Chemical Co.; Adv. Dir, Nottingham Local District, Barclays Bank, 1969-; Hon. Mem., Trustee Savings Bank of Leicester and Notts, 1975. Member: County Councils Assoc.; Council for Small Industries in Rural Areas (Chm. for Leics); Local Authorities Mutual Investment Trust (Chm., 1974); Local Authorities Management Services and Computer Cttee (Vice-Chm., 1973-74); Governor: Brooksby Agricultural Coll.; Wyggeston Hospital; Member: East Midlands Economic Planning Council, 1965-72; Inter-Departmental Cttee on Coroners and Death Certification, 1965-71; Library Advisory Council (England), 1965-71; Board of Visitors, Gartree Prison (Chairman), 1966-75; Leicestershire Agricultural Exec. Cttee, 1960-71; Landowners' Standing Conference, Ironstone; Liveryman, Worshipful Company of Farmers. Military Mem., T&AFA, 1950-70. Chm., Leics Police Authority, 1974-; Mem., ACC Police Cttee, 1974-; Vice-Chairman, Leicester and County Mission for the Deaf, 1961-75. DL Leicestershire, 1950; High Sheriff of Leicestershire, 1957;

CA, 1960; Vice-Chm. Leicestershire CC, 1960-61, Chm., 1961-74. Farming approximately 950 acres. FIMinE 1937. FRSA 1970. Hon. MA, Loughborough Univ. of Technology, 1969. *Recreations:* hunting (Joint Master Fernie Fox Hounds, 1946-62), shooting, breeding Springer spaniels, golf, tennis. *Address:* Stone House, Blaston, Market Harborough, Leics. *T:* Hallaton 234. *Club:* Boodle's.

LLOYD, Richard Dafydd Vivian Llewellyn, (Richard Llewellyn); author; *b* Wales; *m* 1st, 1952, Nona Theresa Sonsteby (marr. diss., 1968), Chicago; 2nd, 1974, Susan Frances Heimann, MA, New York. *Educ:* St David's, Cardiff; London. Coalmining; studied hotel management in Italy; film writing and producing; Captain, The Welsh Guards, 1942. *Publications:* (as Richard Llewellyn) How Green Was My Valley, 1939; None but the Lonely Heart, 1943, new completed edn, 1968; A Few Flowers for Shiner, 1950; A Flame for Doubting Thomas, 1954; Sweet Witch, 1955; Mr Hamish Gleave, 1956; The Flame of Hercules, 1957; Warden of the Smoke and Bells, 1958; Chez Pavan, 1959; A Man in a Mirror, 1961; Up, Into the Singing Mountain, 1963; Sweet Morn of Judas' Day, 1964; Down Where the Moon is Small, 1966; The End of the Rug, 1968; But We Didn't Get the Fox, 1970; White Horse to Banbury Cross, 1972; The Night is a Child, 1972; Bride of Israel, My Love, 1973; A Hill of Many Dreams, 1974; Green, Green My Valley Now, 1975; At Sunrise, The Rough Music, 1976; Tell Me Now, and Again, 1977. Has also written for the younger reader. *Plays:* Poison Pen, 1937; Noose, 1947; The Scarlet Suit, 1962; Ecce!, 1974; Hat!, 1974. *Recreations:* economics, anthropology, photography. *Address:* c/o Michael Joseph Ltd, 52 Bedford Square, WC1B 3EF. *Club:* Cavalry and Guards.

LLOYD, Richard Ernest Butler; Chief Executive, Williams & Glyn's Bank Ltd, since 1970; *b* 6 Dec. 1928; *s* and *heir* of Major Sir (Ernest) Guy Richard Lloyd, Bt, *qv*; *m* 1955, Jennifer Susan Margaret, *e d* of Brigadier Ereld Cardiff, *qv*; three *s*. *Educ:* Wellington Coll.; Hertford Coll., Oxford (MA). Nat. Service (Captain, Black Watch), 1947-49. Joined Glyn, Mills & Co., 1952; Exec. Dir, 1964-70. Director: Australia & New Zealand Bank Ltd and Australia & New Zealand Banking Gp Ltd, 1961-75 (Dep. Chm. 1965-71); National and Commercial Banking Group, 1974-; Royal Bank of Scotland Ltd, 1974-; Legal & Gen. Assce Soc., 1966-. Member: SE Regional Council, CBI, 1966-72; Nat. Econ. Develt Council, 1973-; Industrial Develt Adv. Bd, 1972-77; Cttee to Review the Functioning of Financial Institutions, 1977-; Council, Inst. of Bankers, 1970-75; Council of Management, Ditchley Foundn, 1974-; Council, Inst. for Study of Drug Dependence, 1968-75; Council, Marie Curie Meml Foundn, 1964-70. *Recreations:* walking, fishing, gardening. *Address:* Sundridge Place, Sundridge, Sevenoaks, Kent TN14 6DD. *T:* Westerham 63599. *Club:* Boodle's.

LLOYD, Maj.-Gen. Richard Eyre, CB 1959; CBE 1957 (OBE 1944); DSO 1945; late RE, retired, Sept. 1962; Arms Control and Disarmament Research Unit, Foreign and Commonwealth Office, 1966-73; *b* 7 Dec. 1906; *s* of late Lieut-Colonel W. E. Eyre Lloyd; *m* 1939, Gillian, *d* of late Rear-Adm. J. F. C. Patterson, OBE; one *s* two *d*. *Educ:* Eton; Pembroke Coll. (Cambridge). 2nd Lieut in Royal Engineers, 1927. Served War of 1939-45 on Staff, also with RE in North West Europe; Lieut-Colonel 1942; Colonel, 1951; Brigadier, 1955; Maj.-Gen., 1957. Chief of Staff, Middle East Land Forces, 1957-59; Director of Military Intelligence, 1959-62. Colonel Comdt, Intelligence Corps, 1964-69. *Recreation:* sailing. *Address:* Snooks Farm House, Walhampton, Lymington, Hants. *T:* Lymington 73569.

LLOYD, Richard Hey; Organist and Master of the Choristers, Durham Cathedral, since 1974; *b* 25 June 1933; *s* of Charles Yates Lloyd and Ann Lloyd; *m* 1962, Teresa Morwenna Willmott; four *d*. *Educ:* Lichfield Cathedral Choir Sch.; Rugby Sch. (Music Scholar); Jesus Coll., Cambridge (Organ Scholar). MA, FRCO, ARCM. Asst Organist, Salisbury Cath., 1957-66; Organist and Master of the Choristers, Hereford Cath., 1966-74; Conductor, Three Choirs Festival, 1966-74 (Chief Conductor 1967, 1970, 1973). Examiner, Associated Bd of Royal Schs of Music, 1967-. Member Council: Friends of Cathedral Music, 1968-; RCO, 1974-. Special Comr, RSCM, 1972-. *Publications:* church music. *Recreations:* cricket, theatre, travel, reading. *Address:* 6 The College, Durham. *T:* Durham 64766.

LLOYD, Prof. Seton Howard Frederick, CBE 1958 (OBE 1949); FBA 1955; Archæologist; Professor of Western Asiatic Archæology, University of London, 1962-69, now Emeritus; *b* 30 May 1902; *s* of John Eliot Howard Lloyd and Florence Louise Lloyd (*née* Armstrong); *m* 1944, Margery Ulrica Fitzwilliams Hyde; one *s* one *d*. *Educ:* Uppingham; Architectural Assoc. ARIBA 1926; Asst to Sir Edwin Lutyens, PRA, 1926-28; excavated with Egypt Exploration Society, 1928-

30; excavated in Iraq for University of Chicago Oriental Institute, 1930-37; excavated in Turkey for University of Liverpool, 1937-39; FSA 1938; Technical Adviser, Government of Iraq; Directorate-General of Antiquities, 1939-49; Director British Institute of Archæology, Ankara, Turkey, 1949-61. Hon. MA (Edinburgh), 1953. FSA 1939 (Vice-Pres., 1965-69). Lawrence of Arabia Meml Medal, RCAS, 1971. *Publications:* Mesopotamia (London), 1936; Sennacherib's Aqueduct at Jerwan, (Chicago), 1935; The Gimilsin Temple (Chicago), 1940; Presargonid Temples (Chicago), 1942; Ruined Cities of Iraq (Oxford), 1942; Twin Rivers, (Oxford), 1942; Foundations in the Dust (London), 1947; Early Anatolia (Pelican), 1956; Art of the Ancient Near East (London), 1961; Mounds of the Ancient Near East (Edinburgh), 1963; Highland Peoples of Anatolia (London), 1967; Excavation Reports and many articles in journals. *Recreation:* travel. *Address:* Woolstone Lodge, Faringdon, Oxon. *T:* Uffington 248. *Club:* Chelsea Arts.

LLOYD, Brigadier Thomas Ifan, CBE 1957; DSO 1944; MC 1940; retired; *b* 20 March 1903; *s* of late Rev. David Lloyd, Vicar of St Paul's, Weston-super-Mare, Somerset; *m* 1927, Irene Mary, *d* of Andrew Fullerton, CB, CMG, FRCS, of Belfast, N. Ireland; one *s* one *d*. *Educ:* Westminster Sch.; RMA, Woolwich. Commissioned into the Corps of Royal Engineers as Second Lieut, 1923; concluded military career as Dep. Engineer-in-Chief (Brigadier), War Office, 1955-57. Founder, Railway Conversion League, 1958. *Publications:* Twilight of the Railways—What Roads they'll Make!, 1957; Paper, Instn Civil Engineers, 1955. *Recreations:* golf, bridge. *Address:* 24 Grove Road, Merrow, Guildford, Surrey GU1 2HP. *T:* Guildford 75428. *Club:* Royal Commonwealth Society.
See also Very Rev. H. M. Lloyd.

LLOYD, Prof. (William) Arnold de Gorges; Professor of Education in the University of Cambridge 1959-71; Fellow of Trinity College, since 1961; Chairman, Cambridge Schools Classics Project, Nuffield Foundation, 1965-71; *b* 20 May 1904; *s* of Dr Jonathan Lloyd, OBE, and Mary Gorges Lloyd; *m* 1st, 1929, Margaret Elizabeth Manley; three *d*; 2nd, 1952, Daphne Stella Harris; two *s* one *d*. *Educ:* Sidcot Sch., Somerset; Birmingham Univ. (Flounders Scholar); Institut J. J. Rousseau, Geneva; Sorbonne. MA Birmingham 1936; PhD Cambridge, 1946. Schoolmaster in primary, technical and grammar schools, 1926-32 and 1938-44; director of adult education, 1934-38; Lecturer in Education, Selly Oak Colleges, 1933-34; University of Nottingham, 1946-52; Prof. of Education, Dean of the Faculty and Dep. Chairman of the Institute of Social Research, University of Natal, 1952-56; Senior Prof. of Education, University of the Witwatersrand, 1956-59. Travelling fellowship for Universities of Italy, Switzerland and France, 1956; Carnegie fellowship for Universities of USA, 1957; British Council travel grant to visit English universities, 1958; Commissioner to report on technical education in France, 1959. Fellow of Haverford Coll., Pennsylvania, 1959. Consultant, curricula in Education, European University, Council of Europe, 1966-68. Associate editor, Journal of Conflict Resolution, Chicago, 1956-. Editor, Pædagogica Europaea, 1964-. *Publications:* God in the experience of men, 1938; God in the experience of youth, 1940; Quaker Social History, 1950; Creative Learning, 1953; Education and Human Relations, 1957; The Old and the New Schoolmaster, 1959; The Principles and Practice of Education, 1964; (ed) International Dictionary of Educational Terms, vol I, England and Wales, 1970. *Recreations:* Quaker and family history; cabinet-making; book-binding. *Address:* Trinity College, Cambridge; Withersfield House, Withersfield, West Suffolk.

LLOYD DAVIES, John Robert; *see* Davies.

LLOYD-DAVIES, Oswald Vaughan; Surgeon: Middlesex Hospital since 1950; St Mark's Hospital for diseases of the Colon and Rectum since 1935; Consulting Surgeon, Connaught Hospital; formerly Surgeon, Hampstead General Hospital; *s* of late Rev. Samuel Lloyd-Davies, BA; *m* 1st, 1939, Menna (*d* 1968), *d* of late Canon D. J. Morgan, MA; one *s* one *d*; 2nd, 1970, Rosamund Mary Ovens, *d* of late Rev. E. V. Bond, MA. *Educ:* Caterham Sch.; Middlesex Hospital Medical Sch., London Univ. MRCS, LRCP, 1929; MB, BS (London) 1930; FRCS 1932; MS (London) 1932. Fellow Royal Society of Med. (Past Pres. sect. of proctology); Fellow Assoc. of Surgeons of Great Britain and Ireland; Member, Harveian Society. *Publications:* various chapters in British Surgical Practice; articles on colon, rectal and liver surgery. *Recreations:* gardening, fishing. *Address:* 16 Devonshire Place, W1. *T:* 01-935 2825; Townsend Close, Ashwell, Herts. *T:* Ashwell 2386.

LLOYD DAVIES, Trevor Arthur, MD; FRCP; *b* 8 April 1909; *s* of Arthur Lloyd Davies and Grace Margret (*née* Bull); *m* 1936,

Joan (*d* 1972), *d* of John Keily, Co. Dublin; one *d*; *m* 1975, Margaret, *d* of Halliday Gracey. *Educ:* Woking Grammar Sch.; St Thomas' Hospital, SE1. MRCS, LRCP 1932; MB, BS London (gold medal and hons in surgery, forensic med., obst. and gynæc.); MRCP 1933; MD London 1934; FRCP 1952. Resident Asst Physician, St Thomas' Hospital, 1934-36; Prof. of Social Medicine, University of Malaya, 1953-61; Senior Medical Inspector of Factories, Min. of Labour and Dept of Employment and Productivity, 1961-70; Chief Med. Adviser, Dept of Employment, 1970-73. QHP 1968-71. *Publications:* The Practice of Industrial Medicine, 2nd edn, 1957; Respiratory Diseases in Foundrymen, 1971; numerous papers on industrial and social medicine, in Lancet and Medical Journal of Malaya. *Recreations:* gardening, carpentry and bricklaying. *Address:* The Old Bakery, High Street, Elmdon, near Saffron Walden, Essex CB11 4NL. *Club:* Athenæum.

LLOYD-ELEY, John, QC 1970; a Recorder of the Crown Court, since 1972; *b* 23 April 1923; *s* of Edward John Eley; *m* 1946, Una Fraser Smith; two *s*. *Educ:* Xaverian Coll., Brighton; Exeter Coll., Oxford (MA). Barrister, Middle Temple, 1951; South-Eastern Circuit; Mem., Bar Council, 1969. *Recreations:* farming, travel. *Address:* 1 Hare Court, Temple, EC4Y 7BE. *T:* 01-353 5324; Luxfords Farm, East Grinstead. *T:* East Grinstead 21583.

LLOYD GEORGE, family name of **Earl Lloyd George of Dwyfor** and **Viscount Tenby.**

LLOYD GEORGE OF DWYFOR, 3rd Earl, *cr* 1945; **Owen Lloyd George;** Viscount Gwynedd, 1945; *b* 28 April 1924; *s* of 2nd Earl Lloyd George of Dwyfor, and Roberta Ida Freeman, 5th *d* of Sir Robert McAlpine, 1st Bt; *S* father, 1968; *m* 1949, Ruth Margaret, *o d* of Richard Coit; two *s* one *d*. *Educ:* Oundle. Welsh Guards, 1942-47. European War, 1944-45. Formerly Captain Welsh Guards. Director: Bland Payne Ltd; Marchwiel Holdings Ltd; Sir Alfred McAlpine & Son (International) Ltd. An Underwriting Member of Lloyd's. Carried the Sword at Investiture of HRH the Prince of Wales, Caernarvon Castle, 1969. Mem., Historic Buildings Council for Wales, 1971. *Heir: s* Viscount Gwynedd, *qv*. *Recreation:* shooting. *Address:* 43 Cadogan Square, SW1; Brimpton Mill, near Reading, Berks. *Clubs:* White's, City of London, Pratt's.

LLOYD-HUGHES, Sir Trevor Denby, Kt 1970; Chairman, Lloyd-Hughes Associates Ltd, Government and Parliamentary Consultants; *b* 31 March 1922; *er s* of late Elwyn and Lucy Lloyd-Hughes, Bradford, Yorks; *m* 1st, 1950, Ethel Marguerite Durward (marr. diss., 1971), *o d* of late J. Ritchie, Dundee and Bradford; one *s* one *d*; 2nd, 1971, Marie-Jeanne, *d* of Marcel and Helene Moreillon, Geneva; one *d* (and one adopted *d*—a Thai girl). *Educ:* Woodhouse Grove Sch., Yorks; Jesus Coll., Oxford (MA). Commissioned RA, 1941; served with 75th (Shropshire Yeomanry) Medium Regt, RA, in Western Desert, Sicily and Italy, 1941-45. Asst Inspector of Taxes, 1948; freelance journalist, 1949; joined staff of Liverpool Daily Post, 1949; Political Corresp., Liverpool Echo, 1950, Liverpool Daily Post, 1951. Press Secretary to the Prime Minister, 1964-69; Chief Information Adviser to Govt, 1969-70. Member of Circle of Wine Writers, 1961, Chm., 1972. *Recreations:* yoga, playing the Spanish guitar, golf, walking, travel. *Address:* 14 Westminster Gardens, Marsham Street, SW1P 4JG. *T:* 01-821 1833. *Clubs:* Reform, Belfry; Liver (Liverpool).

LLOYD-JOHNES, Herbert Johnes, OBE 1973; TD 1950; FSA; *b* 9 Dec. 1900; *e s* of Herbert Thomas Lloyd-Johnes, MC, and Georgina Mary Lloyd-Johnes, Dolaucothy, Co. Carmarthen; *m* 1942, Margaret Ruth Edgar (Lieut, FANY, War of 1939-45); two *d*. *Educ:* St Andrews; Malvern. Spent much of his time in Poland, 1931-39; Member British Military Mission to Poland, 1939; a Senior British Liaison Officer to Polish Forces, 1940-46. Chairman: Historic Buildings Council for Wales, 1967-77 (Mem. 1955-); Welsh Folk Museum Cttee, 1953-55; Rural Industries Cttee for Monmouth, Glamorgan and Radnor, 1955-66; Mem. Council, Nat. Trust of GB, 1967-74; Member Ct and Council: Nat. Library of Wales, 1948; Nat. Museum of Wales, 1949; Member Court of Governors of University of Wales, 1952; Governor University College of S Wales and Monmouth, Cardiff. Major RA, TA, Pembroke and Cardigan. Hon. LLD Wales, 1973. Cross For Valour (Poland), 1939. *Publications:* (with Sir Leonard Twiston-Davies) Welsh Furniture, 1950, repr. 1971; contributor to several learned journals. *Recreation:* reading. *Address:* Fosse Hill, Coates, near Cirencester, Glos. *T:* Kemble 279. *Club:* Boodle's.

LLOYD JONES, Cyril Walter, CIE 1925; FCGI; FICE; *b* 6 March 1881; *e s* of late Richard Lloyd Jones; *m* 1907, Edith Kathleen, *d* of Frederick Penty; two *s* two *d*. *Educ:* Aske's Sch.;

Imperial College of Science. Chief Engineer, HEH Nizam's State Railway Board, 1913; Agent, 1919; Managing Director, 1930; English Agent, 1941; retired. *Address:* Roundhay, Pit Farm Road, Guildford, Surrey.
See also C.P. Scott.

LLOYD JONES, David Elwyn, MC 1946; Under-Secretary, Department of Education and Science, since 1969; *b* 20 Oct. 1920; *s* of late Daniel and Blodwen Lloyd Jones; *m* 1955, Mrs E. W. Gallie (*widow* of Ian Gallie), *d* of late Prof. Robert Peers, CBE, MC and late Mrs F. D. G. Peers; no *c* (one step *s*). *Educ:* Ardwyn Grammar Sch., Aberystwyth; University College of Wales, Aberystwyth. War of 1939-45: British Army, 1941; Indian Army, 1942-46; served 1st Bn, The Assam Regt, in Burma Campaign (Major, MC). Entered Ministry of Education, 1947. Principal Private Sec. to Chancellor of the Duchy of Lancaster, 1960-61; Asst Sec., Min. (later Dept) of Educn and Science, 1961-69. Hon. Sec., Assam Regt Assoc., 1948-. *Address:* 5 Playfair Mansions, Queen's Club Gardens, W14. *T:* 01-385 0586. *Clubs:* MCC, Roehampton.

LLOYD-JONES, David Trevor, VRD 1958; **His Honour Judge Lloyd-Jones;** a Circuit Judge, since 1972; *b* 6 March 1917; *s* of Trevor and Anne Lloyd-Jones, Holywell, Flints; *m* 1st, 1942, Mary Violet, *d* of Frederick Barnardo, MB, London; one *d*; 2nd, 1958, Anstice Elizabeth, MB, BChir, *d* of William Henry Perkins, Whitchurch; one *s* one *d*. *Educ:* Holywell Grammar School. Banking, 1934-39 and 1946-50. Called to the Bar, Gray's Inn, 1951; practised Wales and Chester Circuit, 1952-71; Prosecuting Counsel to Post Office (Wales and Chester Circuit), 1961-66; Dep. Chm., Caerns QS, 1966-70, Chm, 1970-71; Legal Mem., Mental Health Appeal Tribunal (Wales Area), 1960-72; Dep. Chm., Agricultural Land Tribunal (Wales Area), 1968-72. Served War of 1939-45, RNVR and RNR, Atlantic, Mediterranean and Pacific; Lt-Comdr, RNR, retd. *Recreations:* golf, music. *Address:* 29 Curzon Park North, Chester. *T:* Chester 20965. *Club:* Army and Navy.

LLOYD-JONES, Sir (Harry) Vincent, Kt 1960; a Judge of the High Court of Justice, Family Division (formerly Probate, Divorce and Admiralty Division), 1960-72; *b* 16 Oct. 1901; 3rd *s* of late Henry Lloyd-Jones; *m* 1933, Margaret Alwena, *d* of late G. H. Mathias; one *s* one *d*. *Educ:* St Marylebone Grammar Sch. (Old Philological); University Coll., London; Jesus Coll., Oxford. Exhibitioner English Language and Literature, Jesus Coll., Oxford, 1921; BA (Eng. Lang. and Lit.) 1923; BA (Jurisprudence) 1924; MA 1927. President Oxford Union Society, (Summer Term) 1925. Member Oxford Union Debating Team in USA, 1925. Called to Bar by Inner Temple, 1926, Master of the Bench, 1958; practised Common Law Bar; Wales and Chester Circuit; QC 1949. Recorder of Chester, 1952-58; Recorder of Cardiff, 1958-60. Hon. Fellow: Jesus Coll., Oxford, 1960; University Coll., London, 1962. *Recreations:* reading, walking. *Address:* 24 Vincent Square, SW1P 2NJ. *T:* 01-834 5109.

LLOYD-JONES, Prof. (Peter) Hugh (Jefferd); FBA 1966; Regius Professor of Greek in the University of Oxford and Student of Christ Church since 1960; *b* 21 Sept. 1922; *s* of Major W. Lloyd-Jones, DSO, and Norah Leila, *d* of F. H. Jefferd, Brent, Devon; *m* 1953, Frances Elisabeth Hedley; two *s* one *d*. *Educ:* Lycée Français du Royaume Uni, S. Kensington; Westminster Sch.; Christ Church, Oxford. Served War of 1939-45, 2nd Lieut, Intelligence Corps, India, 1942; Temp. Captain, 1944. 1st Cl. Classics (Mods), 1941; MA 1947; 1st Cl., LitHum, 1948; Chancellor's Prize for Latin Prose, 1947; Ireland and Craven Schol., 1947; Fellow of Jesus Coll., Cambridge, 1948-54; Asst Lecturer in Classics, University of Cambridge, 1950-52, Lecturer, 1952-54; Fellow and E. P. Warren Praelector in Classics, Corpus Christi Coll., Oxford, 1954-60; J. H. Gray Lecturer, University of Cambridge, 1961; Visiting Prof., Yale Univ., 1964-65, 1967-68; Sather Prof. of Classical Literature, Univ. of California at Berkeley, 1969-70; Alexander White Vis. Prof., Chicago, 1972; Vis. Prof., Harvard Univ., 1976-77. Fellow, Morse Coll., Yale Univ. Hon. Mem., Greek Humanistic Soc., 1968. Hon. DHL Chicago, 1970. *Publications:* Appendix to Loeb Classical Library edn of Aeschylus, 1957; Menandri Dyscolus (Oxford Classical Text), 1960; Greek Studies in Modern Oxford, 1961; (trans.) Paul Maas, Greek Metre, 1962; (ed) The Greeks, 1962; Tacitus (in series The Great Historians), 1964; (trans.) Aeschylus: Agamemnon, The Libation-Bearers, and The Eumenides, 1970; The Justice of Zeus, 1971; (ed) Maurice Bowra, 1974; Females of the Species: Semonides of Amorgos on Women, 1975; Myths of the Zodiac, 1978; contributions to periodicals. *Recreations:* cats, watching cricket. *Address:* Christ Church, Oxford. *T:* Oxford 48737; Gateways, Harberton Mead, Oxford. *T:* Oxford 62393.

LLOYD JONES, Richard Anthony; Under-Secretary, Welsh Office, since 1974; *b* 1 Aug. 1933; *s* of Robert and Anne Lloyd Jones; *m* 1955, Patricia Avril Mary Richmond; two *d*. *Educ:* Long Dene Sch., Edenbridge; Nottingham High Sch.; Balliol Coll., Oxford (MA). Entered Admiralty, 1957; Asst Private Sec. to First Lord of the Admiralty, 1959-62; Private Sec. to Secretary of the Cabinet, 1969-70; Asst Sec., Min. of Defence, 1970-74. *Recreations:* music, walking. *Address:* Penlan, 141 Heol Isaf, Radyr, Cardiff. *Club:* United Oxford & Cambridge University.

LLOYD-JONES, Sir Vincent; *see* Lloyd-Jones, Sir H. V.

LLOYD MEAD, William Howard; *see* Mead.

LLOYD-MOSTYN, family name of Baron Mostyn.

LLOYD OWEN, Maj.-Gen. David Lanyon, CB 1971; DSO 1945; OBE 1954; MC 1942; Membership Secretary, Wildfowlers' Association of Great Britain & Ireland for Shooting and Conservation, since 1976; *b* 10 Oct. 1917; *s* of late Capt. Reginald Charles Lloyd Owen, OBE, RN; *m* 1947, Ursula Evelyn, *d* of late Evelyn Hugh Barclay, and of Hon. Mrs Barclay, MBE; three *s*. *Educ:* Winchester; RMC, Sandhurst. 2nd Lieut, The Queen's Royal Regt, 1938. Comdr, Long Range Desert Group, 1943-45. Military Asst to High Commissioner in Malaya, 1951-53; Comdg 1st Queen's, 1957-59; Comdr 24 Infantry Bde Group, 1962-64; GOC Cyprus District, 1966-68; GOC Near East Land Forces, 1968-69. Pres., Regular Commns Bd, 1969-72, retd. Knight of Malta, 1946. *Publication:* The Desert My Dwelling Place, 1957. *Address:* The Old Rectory, Newton Flotman, Norwich NR15 1QB. *T:* Swainsthorpe 470468. *Club:* Naval and Military.

LLOYD PHILLIPS, Ivan, CBE 1963 (OBE 1959); DPhil Oxon; *b* Cambridge, June 1910; *er s* of late Rev. A. Lloyd Phillips, formerly Vicar of Ware, Herts; *m* 1941, Faith Macleay, *o c* of late Brig.-Gen. G. M. Macarthur Onslow, CMG, DSO, Camden, New South Wales; one *s*. *Educ:* Worksop Coll.; Selwyn Coll., Cambridge; Balliol Coll., Oxford. Appointed Colonial Administrative Service, 1934; served in: Gold Coast, 1934-38; Palestine, 1938-47; District Commissioner, Gaza-Beersheba, 1946-47; Colonial Office, 1947-48; Cyprus, 1948-51; Commissioner, Nicosia-Kyrenia, 1950-51; Singapore, 1951-53; Commissioner-General's Office, 1951-52; Dep. Secretary for Defence, 1952-53; Malaya, 1953-62; Secretary to Chief Minister and Minister for Home Affairs, 1955-57; Secretary, Ministry of the Interior, 1957-62. Secretary, Oxford Preservation Trust, 1962-65; Inst. of Commonwealth Studies, Oxford Univ., 1965-70. Chairman, Oxfordshire Playing Fields Assoc., 1966-77, Pres., 1977-. Duke of Edinburgh's award for service to Nat. Playing Fields Movement, 1974. Commander, Order of Defender of the Realm (Malaysia), 1958. *Address:* Cranmer Cottage, Dorchester-on-Thames, Oxfordshire. *T:* Oxford 340026. *Clubs:* Travellers', MCC.

LLOYD-ROBERTS, George Charles, MChir; FRCS; Consultant Orthopædic Surgeon, St George's Hospital, since 1957; Consultant Orthopædic Surgeon, The Hospital for Sick Children, Great Ormond Street, since 1955; Consultant in Paediatric Orthopaedics to the RAF, since 1970 and RN, since 1972; *b* 23 Nov. 1918; *e s* of Griffith and Gwendoline Lloyd-Roberts; *m* 1947, Catherine Lansing Ray (marr. diss. 1967), *widow* of Edward Lansing Ray, St Louis, Missouri; one *s* two *d*. *Educ:* Eton Coll.; Magdalene Coll., Cambridge. BA, MB, BChir (Cantab), 1943, MChir (Cantab), 1966; FRCS, 1949. Graded Surgical Specialist, RAMC, 1944, Surgeon, Yugoslav and Italian Partisan Forces. Late 1st Assistant, Orthopædic Dept, St George's Hospital, 1954; Clinical Research Assistant, Royal National Orthopædic Hospital, 1952; Nuffield Fellow in Orthopædic Surgery, 1952. Mem. Council, RCS, 1976-; President: British Orthopædic Assoc., 1977-78; Orthopædic Section, RSM, 1976-77. Mem. Council, Game Conservancy, 1977-. Robert Jones Gold Medal of British Orthopædic Assoc., 1953. *Publications:* Orthopædics in Infancy and Childhood, 1972; The Hip Joint in Childhood, 1977; (ed) Orthopædic Surgery, 1968; articles on orthopædic subjects in medical journals. *Recreations:* fishing, shooting. *Address:* 9 Cheyne Place, SW3. *T:* 01-352 5622; (Private Consulting Room), Hospital for Sick Children, Great Ormond Street, WC1. *Club:* Boodle's.

LLOYD WEBBER, Andrew; composer; *b* 22 March 1948; *s* of William Southcombe Lloyd Webber, *qv*; *m* 1971, Sarah Jane Tudor (*née* Hugill); one *d*. *Educ:* Westminster Sch. Composer of musicals (with lyrics by Timothy Rice): Joseph and the Amazing Technicolour Dreamcoat, 1968 (rev. 1973); Jesus Christ Superstar, 1970; Jeeves, 1975; Evita, 1976. Film scores:

Gumshoe, 1971; The Odessa File, 1974. Composed Variations on a theme of Paganini, 1977. *Publication:* (with Timothy Rice) Evita, 1978. *Recreation:* architecture. *Club:* Savile.

LLOYD WEBBER, William Southcombe, DMus (London) 1938; FRCM 1963; FRCO 1933; FLCM 1963; Hon. RAM 1966; Director, London College of Music, since 1964; Professor of Theory and Composition, Royal College of Musice, since 1946; Musical Director, Central Hall, Westminster, since 1958; *b* 11 March 1914; *m* 1942, Jean Hermione Johnstone; two *s*. *Educ:* Mercers' School; Royal College of Music. Organist: Christ Church, Newgate Street, 1929-32; St Cyprian's, Clarence Gate, 1932-39; All Saints, Margaret Street, 1939-48. Examiner to Associated Board of Royal Schools of Music, 1946-64; Vice-Pres., Incorporated Assoc. of Organists; Past Pres. and Hon. Mem., London Assoc. of Organists; Mem. Council, Royal College of Organists, 1946- (Hon Treas., 1953-64); Mem. Senate, London Univ., 1964-67. Master, Worshipful Co. of Musicians, 1973-74; Guild Master, Civic Guild of Old Mercers, 1977. *Publications:* many instrumental, choral and educational works; contrib. to Musical Times, Musical Opinion. *Recreations:* chess, bridge. *Address:* 13A Sussex Mansions, Old Brompton Road, SW7. *T:* 01-589 8614. *Club:* Chelsea Arts.
See also A . Lloyd Webber .

LOACH, Kenneth; television and film director; *b* 17 June 1936. *Educ:* King Edward VI School, Nuneaton; St Peter's Hall, Oxford. BBC Trainee, Drama Dept, 1963. Television: Diary of a Young Man, 1964; 3 Clear Sundays, 1965; The End of Arthur's Marriage, 1965; Up The Junction, 1965; Coming Out Party, 1965; Cathy Come Home, 1966; In Two Minds, 1966; The Golden Vision, 1969; The Big Flame, 1969; After A Lifetime, 1971; The Rank and File, 1972; Days of Hope, 1975; The Price of Coal, 1977. Films: Poor Cow, 1968; Kes, 1970; In Black and White, 1970; Family Life, 1972. *Address:* c/o BBC TV Centre, Wood Lane, W12.

LOANE, Most Rev. Marcus Lawrence; *see* Sydney, Archbishop of.

LOBB, Howard Leslie Vicars, CBE 1952; FRIBA, MRAIC, AIStructE, FRSA; Consultant to Howard, Lobb, Ratcliff, Leather and Partners, Architects and Planners; *b* 9 March 1909; *e s* of late Hedley Vicars Lobb and Mary Blanche (*née* Luscombe); *m* 1949, Charmian Isobel (*née* Reilly); three *s*. *Educ:* privately; Regent Street Polytechnic School of Architecture. During War of 1939-45, Architect to various ministries: subseq. built numerous schools for County Authorities; HQ of City and Guilds of London Inst., W1; British Pavilion Brussels International Exhibition, 1958; Cons. Architect for Hunterston Nuclear Power Station, Ayrshire; Dungeness Nuclear Power Station; Newcastle Racecourse; Newmarket Rowley Mile, for Jockey Club; Car park, Savile Row, for City of Westminster; HQ for British Council, SW1; Nat. Yacht Racing Centre, Weymouth; Calgary Exhbn and Stampede, Upper Alberta, Canada. Chairman Architectural Council, Festival of Britain, and later Controller (Constr.) South Bank Exhibition. Member RIBA Council and Executive, 1953-56; Life Vice-Pres. (formerly Chm.), London Group of Building Centres; Chm., Architects' Registr. Council, UK, 1957-60; Hon. Secretary, Architects' Benevolent Society. Freeman of City of London; Master, Worshipful Co. of Masons, 1974-75. *Publications:* contrib. various Arch. Journals, Reviews, etc. *Recreations:* sailing, gardening, colour photography, model railways. *Address:* 180 Tottenham Court Road, W1P 9LE. *T:* 01-636 8575; Blackhill, Esher, Surrey. *T:* Esher 63092; 2 Admiral's Wharf, Cowes, Isle of Wight. *T:* Cowes 2414. *Clubs:* Athenæum, Arts; Royal Corinthian Yacht (Vice-Cdre 1960-63); Royal London Yacht; Island Sailing (Cowes); Tamesis (Teddington) (Cdre, 1954-57).

LOCH, family name of Baron Loch.

LOCH, 3rd Baron *cr* 1895, of Drylaw; **George Henry Compton Loch;** Major late 11th Hussars; *b* 3 Feb. 1916; *s* of 2nd Baron and Lady Margaret Compton (*d* 1970), *o d* of 5th Marquess of Northampton; *S* father 1942; *m* 1st, 1942, Leila Mary Grace Isabel Hill Mackenzie (marr. diss., 1946); one *d*; 2nd, 1946, Mrs Betty Castillon du Perron (marr. diss., 1952); 3rd, 1952, Joan Dorothy Hawthorn Binns (marr. diss.); 4th, 1975, Sylvia Barbara Beauchamp-Wilson, *o d* of A. G. Beauchamp Cameron. *Educ:* Eton; RMC, Sandhurst. *Heir:* *b* Hon. Spencer Douglas Loch, MC 1945 [*b* 1920; *m* 1948, Hon. Rachel (*d* 1976), *yr d* of Group Captain H. L. Cooper, AFC, and of Baroness Lucas and Dingwall (Nan Ino Herbert-Cooper who *d* 1958); two *s* one *d*. *Educ:* Wellington Coll.; Trinity Coll., Cambridge. Major Grenadier Guards; called to Bar, 1948]. *Address:* Quinta das Esporas, Vale Telheiro, Loulé, Algarve, Portugal; Stoke College, Stoke-by-Clare, Suffolk.

LOCK, Air Vice-Marshal Basil Goodhand, CBE 1969; AFC 1954; Director General of Security (RAF), and Commandant-General RAF Regiment, since 1977; *b* 25 June 1923; *s* of J. S. Lock; *m* 1944, Mona Rita; one *s*. Entered RAF from Durham Univ. Air Sqdn; commnd RAF, 1943; various operational sqdns, 1944-47; Exchange Sqdn posts, USA, 1947-48; Flying Instructor, RAF Coll., Cranwell, 1950-51; OC, HC Exam. Unit, 1951-54; HQ MEAF, 1954-57; Ops (O), Air Min., 1958-61; OC Flying, RAF Leeming, 1961-63; Plans (Cento), 1964-66; OC, RAF West Raynham, 1967-69; SDS (Air), JSSC, 1969-71; Dir of Ops (AS), MoD, 1971-73; Dir of Personal Services, MoD, 1974-75; Air Vice-Marshal 1975; Comdr Northern Maritime Air Region and Air Officer Scotland and NI, 1975-77. MBIM. *Recreations:* golf, music, motor sport. *Address:* (home) Hereford House, Village Way, Little Chalfont, Bucks. *T:* Little Chalfont 2746. *Club:* Royal Air Force.

LOCK, (Cecil) Max, FRIBA (Dist. TP), AADip, FRTPI; Head of Max Lock Group; *b* 29 June 1909; *s* of Cecil William Best Lock and Vivian Cecil Hassell. *Educ:* Berkhamsted Sch.; Architectural Assoc., London. Entered private practice, 1933; (firm established as Max Lock 1933, Max Lock Group 1944, Max Lock & Associates 1950, Max Lock & Partners 1954); retired 1972; now practising as Max Lock Group of Planning and Development Consultants, in partnership with Michael Theis; currently Max Lock Group Nigeria, as consultants to Govt of NE State Nigeria, engaged on surveys and master plans for Maiduguri, Nguru, Potiskum, Bauchi, Gombe, Yola-Jimeta and Mubi; retired 1975 to live mainly in Cornwall. Member Watford Borough Council, 1936-40; on staff of AA School of Architecture, 1937-39; Head of Hull School of Architecture, 1939; Leverhulme Research Schol. (carried out a Civic Diagnosis of Hull). Surveys and plans by Max Lock Group for: Middlesbrough, 1946; The Hartlepools, 1948; Portsmouth District, 1949; Bedford, 1951; by Max Lock and Partners, Surveys and Plans for Amman, Aqaba (Jordan), 1954-55; Town Plans for development of Iraq at Um Qasr, Margil and Basrah, 1954-56; New Towns at El Beida, Libya, 1956, and Sheikh Othman, Aden, 1960. Survey and plan for the Capital City and Territory of Kaduna for Government of Northern Nigeria, 1965-66. British Town Centre redevelopment plans, 1957-71, include: Sevenoaks; Thetford; Sutton Coldfield; Salisbury; Brentford; redevelopment of new central housing communities at Oldham; development of Woodley Airfield, Reading; a plan for Central Area of Beverley, Yorks. Visiting Professor: Dept of City Planning, Harvard Univ., 1957; University of Rio de Janeiro, 1960, 1968; Guest Chairman, 5th Australian National Planning Congress, 1960. Member Council, TPI, 1946-50 and 1961-63. *Publications:* The Middlesbrough Survey and Plan, 1946; The Hartlepools Survey and Plan, 1948; The Portsmouth and District Survey and Plan, 1949; Bedford by the River, 1952; The New Basrah, 1956; Kaduna, 1917-1967-2017: A Survey and Plan of the Capital Territory for the Government of Northern Nigeria, 1967; contribs to RIBA Journal, TPI Journal, Town Planning Review, etc. *Recreations:* music, pianist. *Address:* 7 Victoria Square, SW1. *T:* 01-834 7071; Old Corn Mill, Addicraft, Linkinhorne, Liskeard, Cornwall. *T:* Liskeard 62510. *Club:* Reform.

LOCK, George David; Managing Director, Private Patients Plan, since 1975; *b* 24 Sept. 1929; *s* of George Wilfred Lock and Phyllis Nita (*née* Hollingworth); *m* 1965, Ann Elizabeth Biggs; four *s* one *d*. *Educ:* Haileybury and ISC; Queens' Coll., Cambridge (MA). British Tabulating Machine Co. Ltd (now ICL), 1954-59; Save & Prosper Group Ltd, 1959-69; American Express, 1969-74; Private Patients Plan, 1974-. Non-exec. Dir, Cavendish Medical Centre, 1975-. *Recreations:* bridge, music, family activities, entertaining. *Address:* (home) Buckhurst Place, Horsted Keynes, Sussex RH17 7AH. *T:* Danehill 599; (business) Private Patients Plan, Eynsham House, Crescent Road, Tunbridge Wells, Kent TN1 2PL. *T:* Tunbridge Wells 26255. *Club:* Institute of Directors.

LOCK, Mrs John; see Gérin, Winifred.

LOCK, John Arthur, QPM 1975; Deputy Assistant Commissioner, Metropolitan Police, and National Co-ordinator, Regional Crime Squads of England and Wales, since 1976; *b* 20 Oct. 1922; *s* of Sidney George Lock and Minnie Louise Lock; *m* 1950, Patricia Joyce Lambert; two *d*. *Educ:* George Palmer Central School, Reading. Royal Air Force, 1941-46; Wireless Operator/Air Gunner; Flying Officer. Joined Metropolitan Police, 1946. *Recreations:* Association football (Vice-Chm., Met. Police FC), tennis, sailing. *Address:* 11 Garden Way, Loughton, Essex. *Club:* Royal Air Force.

LOCK, Lt-Comdr John Duncan, RN; Chairman, Association of District Councils of England and Wales, since 1974; *b* 5 Feb.

1918; *s* of Brig. Gen. F. R. E. Lock, DSO, and Mary Elizabeth Lock; *m* 1947, Alice Aileen Smith; three *d*. *Educ:* Royal Naval Coll., Dartmouth. Served as regular officer in Royal Navy (retiring at his own request), 1931-58: specialised in navigation and navigated Battleships HMS King George V and Howe, the Cruiser Superb, destroyers and minesweepers. Served War of 1939-45: took part in Battle of Atlantic, Norwegian and N African campaigns, Pacific War and Normandy and Anzio landings. Farmed family estate in Somerset, 1958-61. Admty Compass Observatory as specialist in magnetic compasses, 1962-. Eton RDC, 1967-74; Chm., Bucks Br., RDC Assoc., 1969-74; Mem., Beaconsfield Dist Council, 1973-; Chairman: Assoc. of Dist Councils of England and Wales, 1974- (Chm. Assoc.'s Council and Policy Cttee, and Chm. Bucks Br., 1974-). Chm., Beaconsfield Constituency Conservative Assoc., 1972-75. *Recreations:* gardening, shooting, bee-keeping. *Address:* Fen Court, Oval Way, Gerrards Cross, Bucks SL9 8QD. *T:* Gerrards Cross 82467.

LOCK, Max; see Lock, C. M.

LOCK, Stephen Penford, FRCP; MA; Editor, British Medical Journal, since 1975; *b* 8 April 1929; *er s* of Wallace Henry Lock, Romford, Essex; *m* 1955, Shirley Gillian Walker, *d* of E. W. Walker, Bridlington, Yorks; one *s* one *d*. *Educ:* City of London Sch.; Queens' Coll., Cambridge; St Bartholomew's Hosp., London. MA 1953; MB 1954; MRCP 1963; FRCP 1974. Ho. Phys., Bart's, Brompton, and Central Middlesex Hosps, and Med. Officer, RAF Bomber Comd, 1954-57; Jun. Registrar, London Hosp., London, 1958; Jun. Asst Editor, The Lancet, 1959; Registrar in Pathology, Hosp. for Sick Children, Gt Ormond St., London, 1959-61, and at Bart's, 1961-62; Sen. Registrar in Pathology, Lewisham Hosp., London, 1962-64; Asst Editor, British Med. Jl, 1964-69, Sen. Asst Editor, 1969-74, Dep. Editor, 1974-75. Med. Corresp., BBC Overseas Service, 1966-74. Organiser of Finnish Postgrad. Courses in Med. Writing at Univs of Helsinki, Turku, Oulu, Tampere and Kuopio, 1971-73; organiser of Iraq Postgrad. courses in med. writing, Univs of Bagdhad and Mosul, 1975; organiser of Postgrad. courses in med. writing, London, 1975 and Kuwait, Shiraz, Edinburgh, Dublin, Birmingham, 1976. Member: Council, Res. Defence Soc., 1976; Med. Adv. Cttee, British Council, 1976; Publications Cttee, King's Fund, 1977. Vice-Pres., Internat. Union of the Medical Press, 1976. *Publications:* An Introduction to Clinical Pathology, 1965; Health Centres and Group Practices, 1966; The Enemies of Man, 1968; Better Medical Writing, 1970; Family Health Guide, 1972; Medical Risks of Life, 1976; Thorne's Better Medical Writing, 2nd edn 1977; (ed) Adverse Drug Reactions, 1977; (ed) Remembering Henry, 1977; articles on haematology and medical writing in British, American, Swiss and Finnish jls. *Recreations:* as much opera as possible, hill walking, gardening. *Address:* 115 Dulwich Village, SE21 7BJ. *T:* 01-693 6317. *Club:* Athenæum.

LOCKE, Arthur D'Arcy, (Bobby Locke); professional golfer; Playing Professional at Observatory Golf Club, Johannesburg; *b* Germiston, Transvaal, 20 Nov. 1917; *s* of Charles James Locke; *m* 1943; one *d*; *m* 1958, Mary Fenten, USA. *Educ:* Benoni High Sch. Won Open and Amateur South African Championships, 1935; won Irish, Dutch and New Zealand Open Championships, 1938; French Open Championship, 1952-53; British Open Championship, 1949, 1950, 1952, 1957; Canadian Open, 1947; Mexican Open, 1952; Egyptian Open, 1954; German Open, 1954; Swiss Open, 1954; Australian Open, 1955; Member Professional Golfers' Association (London). Served War of 1939-45, Middle East and Italy as Pilot, South African Air Force. *Publication:* Bobby Locke on Golf, 1953.

LOCKE, Bobby; see Locke, A. D'A.

LOCKE, Hon. Charles Holland, CC (Canada) 1971; MC, QC; Judge, Supreme Court of Canada, 1947-62, retired; *b* Morden, Manitoba, 16 Sept. 1887; *s* of Judge Corbet Locke, QC, and Esther Alice Locke (*née* Holland), both of Morden, Manitoba; *m* 1916, Marie Amelie, *d* of late Clayton M. Weiss; one *s* two *d*. *Educ:* Morden Public Sch.; read Law with Arnold W. Bowen, Morden, and A. B. Hudson, KC, Winnipeg. Called to Bar of Manitoba, 1910; British Columbia, 1928; Ontario, 1962; KC Manitoba, 1923, in BC 1936; QC Ontario, 1962. Served in France with 61st Battery, Canadian Field Artillery (MC). *Address:* (office) 116 Albert Street, Ottawa, Ontario, Canada.

LOCKE, John Howard; Director, Health and Safety Executive, since 1975; *b* 26 Dec. 1923; *s* of Percy Locke and Josephine Locke (*née* Marshfield); *m* 1948, Eirene Sylvia Sykes; two *d*. *Educ:* Hymers Coll., Hull; Queen's Coll., Oxford. Ministry of Agriculture, Fisheries and Food, 1945-65; Under-Secretary: Cabinet Office, 1965-66; MoT, 1966-68; Dept of Employment and Productivity, 1968-71; Dep. Sec., Dept of Employment, 1971-74. *Address:* 4 Old Palace Terrace, The Green, Richmond-on-Thames, Surrey. *T:* 01-940 1830; Old Box Trees, East Preston, Sussex.

LOCKETT, Richard Jeffery, CBE 1949; *b* 16 Sept. 1907; *s of* Richard Cyril Lockett and Beatrice (*née* Bell); *m* 1939, Mary Edna Crist, Oakland, California; one *s* one *d. Educ:* Winchester Coll.; Christ Church, Oxford. Sugar Planter and Cotton Merchant, Peru, 1928-50; responsible for procurement Peruvian Cotton for Ministry of Supply, 1941-45; Chairman, British Chamber of Commerce, Peru, 1943-44. Director: Cunard Steam Ship Co. Ltd, 1952-68; Royal Insurance Co. Ltd, 1954-74; Combined English Mills (Spinners) Ltd, 1961-64; Matthew Clark & Sons (Holdings) Ltd, 1962-72. Permanent Delegate of Peru to International Sugar Council, 1960-70. High Sheriff of Cheshire, 1967-68. *Recreations:* shooting, fishing, gardening. *Address:* Glassburn, by Beauly, Inverness-shire. *T:* Cannich 203.

LOCKHART; *see* Bruce Lockhart.

LOCKHART, Sir Muir Edward S.; *see* Sinclair-Lockhart.

LOCKHART, Gen. Sir Rob (McGregor Macdonald), KCB 1946 (CB 1944); CIE, 1942; MC; Indian Army (retired); *b* 1893; 3rd *s* of late R. Bruce Lockhart, formerly of Eagle House, Sandhurst, Berks; *m* 1918, Margaret Amy, *yr d* of late Col Sir R. Neil Campbell, KCMG, IMS; one *s* three *d. Educ:* Marlborough Coll.; RMC, Sandhurst; Staff Coll., Camberley. Commissioned ULIA, 1913; joined 51st Sikhs FF, March 1914. Acting governor, NWFP (India) Jan.-Aug. 1947. C-in-C IA, Aug.-Dec. 1947; retired 1948. Dir of Ops, Malaya, Dec. 1951-Feb. 1952; Dep. Dir, Feb. 1952-March 1953. Dep. Chief Scout, Boy Scouts' Association, 1951-61; President: Greater London Central Scout County (Scout Assoc.), 1965-72; Assoc. of British Officers of Indian Army, 1969-75. Order of Star of Nepal (2nd Class), 1946. *Address:* c/o Lloyds Bank Ltd, Cox's & King's Branch, 6 Pall Mall, SW1.

LOCKHART, Robert Douglas, MD, ChM; LLD; FSAScot, FRSE; Hon. Curator, Anthropology Museum (Cultural), University of Aberdeen; Regius Professor of Anatomy, University of Aberdeen, 1938-Sept. 1965; Dean of the Faculty of Medicine, 1959-62; *b* 7 Jan. 1894; *s* of William Lockhart and Elizabeth Bogie. *Educ:* Robert Gordon's Coll., Aberdeen; University, Aberdeen (MB, ChB 1918). Ho. Surg. Aberdeen Royal Infirmary; Surgeon-Probationer, RNVR, 1916; Surgeon-Lt, RN 1918; Lecturer in Anatomy, Aberdeen Univ., 1919; Prof. of Anat., Birmingham Univ. 1931; Past Pres., Anatomical Soc. of Great Britain and Ireland. *Publications:* Chapter, Ways of Living, in Man and Nature, 1926; Myology Section in Cunningham's Anatomy, 1964; Living Anatomy—photographic atlas, 1963, 7th edn 1974; Anatomy of the Human Body, 1969; contributor to Kodak Med. Film Library, 1933; Structure and Function of Muscle, 1960 (2nd rev. edn, vol. 1, ed Bourne, 1972). *Recreations:* roses and rhododendrons. *Address:* 25 Rubislaw Den North, Aberdeen AB2 4AL. *T:* Aberdeen 37833.

LOCKHART, Stephen Alexander, CMG 1960; OBE 1949; *b* 19 March 1905; *o s* of late Captain Murray Lockhart, RN, Milton Lockhart, and of Leonora Rynd; *m* 1944, Angela Watson; two *s* two *d. Educ:* Harrow; Jesus Coll., Cambridge. Served Lisbon, 1940-43; Ministry of Information, 1943; Press Attaché, Lisbon, 1944, Brussels, 1945; First Sec. (Information), Brussels, 1946-51; Foreign Office, 1951; First Sec., Buenos Aires, 1952-55; UK Rep., Trieste, 1955-57; HM Consul-Gen., Leopoldville, and in French Equatorial Africa, 1957-60; HM Consul-Gen., Zürich, 1960-62; HM Ambassador to Dominican Republic, 1962-65, retired; re-employed in FCO, 1965-70; Hon. Consul, Oporto, 1970-75. *Recreations:* swimming, bridge. *Address:* 10 Shelley Court, Tite Street, SW3. *Club:* United Oxford & Cambridge University.

LOCKHART-MUMMERY, Hugh Evelyn, MD, MChir; FRCS; Serjeant-Surgeon to the Queen, since 1975 (Surgeon to HM Household, 1969-75, to the Queen, 1974-75); Consultant Surgeon: St Mark's Hospital since 1951; St Thomas' Hospital since 1960; King Edward VII's Hospital for Officers since 1968; RAF since 1975; *b* 28 April 1918; *s* of John Percy Lockhart-Mummery, FRCS; *m* 1946, Elizabeth Jean Crerar, *d* of Sir James Crerar, KCSI, CIE; one *s. Educ:* Stowe Sch.; Trinity Coll., Cambridge; Westminster Hosp. Med. Sch. MB, BCh 1942; FRCS 1943; MChir 1950; MD 1956. Served RAF, 1943-46. Examr in Surgery, Univ. of London, 1965; Pres., Sect. of Proctology, RSM, 1966. Hon. Fellow, (French) Académie de Proctologie, 1961; Hon. Fellow, Amer. Soc. of Colon and Rectal Surgeons, 1974. *Publications:* chapters in surgical textbooks; articles on surgery of the colon and rectum in Brit. jls.

Recreations: golf, fishing. *Address:* 5 Hereford Square, SW7 4TT. *T:* 01-373 3630; 149 Harley Street, W1N 2DE. *T:* 01-935 4444. *Club:* Royal Air Force.

LOCKLEY, Ven. Harold; Archdeacon of Loughborough and Vicar of All Saints, Leicester, since 1963; Senior Examining Chaplain to Bishop of Leicester since 1951; Part-time Lecturer in Divinity, University of Leicester; *b* 16 July 1916; *s* of Harry and Sarah Elizabeth Lockley; *m* 1947, Ursula Margaret, JP, *d* of Rev. Dr H. Wedell and Mrs G. Wedell (*née* Bonhoeffer); three *s. Educ:* Loughborough Coll. (Hons Dip. Physical Education); London University; Westcott House, Cambridge. BA Hons 1937, BD Hons 1943, MTh 1949, London Univ.; PhD 1955, Nottingham Univ. Chaplain and Tutor, Loughborough Coll., 1946-51; Vicar of Glen Parva and South Wigston, 1951-58. OCF Royal Leics Regt, 1951-58; Chaplain, Leicester Royal Infirmary Maternity Hospital, 1967-74; Proctor in Convocation of Canterbury, 1960-; Canon Chancellor of Leicester Cathedral, 1958-63. *Publications:* Editor, Leicester Cathedral Quarterly, 1960-63. *Recreations:* walking and foreign travel. *Address:* 1 Knighton Grange Road, Leicester. *T:* Leicester 707328. *Clubs:* English-Speaking Union, National Liberal.

LOCKLEY, Ronald Mathias; author and naturalist; *b* 8 Nov. 1903. Hon. MSc Wales, 1977. *Publications:* Dream Island, 1930; The Island Dwellers, 1932; Island Days, 1934; The Sea's a Thief, 1936; Birds of the Green Belt, 1936; I Know an Island, 1938; Early Morning Island, 1939; A Pot of Smoke, 1940; The Way to an Island, 1941; Shearwaters, 1942; Dream Island Days, 1943; Inland Farm, 1943; Islands Round Britain, 1945; Birds of the Sea, 1946; The Island Farmers, 1947; Letters from Skokholm, 1947; The Golden Year, 1948; The Cinnamon Bird, 1948; Birds of Pembrokeshire, 1949; The Charm of the Channel Islands, 1950; (with John Buxton) Island of Skomer, 1951; Travels with a Tent in Western Europe, 1953; Puffins, 1953; (with Rosemary Russell) Bird Ringing, 1953; The Seals and the Curragh, 1954; Gilbert White, 1954; (with James Fisher) Sea-Birds, 1954; Pembrokeshire, 1957; The Pan Book of Cage Birds, 1961; Britain in Colour, 1964; The Private Life of the Rabbit, 1964; Wales, 1966; Grey Seal, Common Seal, 1966; Animal Navigation, 1967; The Book of Bird-Watching, 1968; The Channel Islands, 1968, rev. edn, A Traveller's Guide to the Channel Islands, 1971; The Island, 1969; The Naturalist in Wales, 1970; Man Against Nature, 1970; Seal Woman, 1974; Ocean Wanderers, 1974; Orielton, 1977; *edited:* Natural History of Selborne, by G. White, 1949, rev. edn 1976; Nature Lover's Anthology, 1951; The Bird-Lover's Bedside Book, 1958; *compiled:* In Praise of Islands, 1957. *Address:* c/o André Deutsch, 105 Great Russell Street, WC1B 3LJ.

LOCKSPEISER, Sir Ben, KCB 1950; Kt 1946; FRS 1949; FIMechE, FRAeS; *b* 9 March 1891; *s* of late Leon and Rose Lockspeiser, London; *m* 1920, Elsie Shuttleworth (*d* 1964); one *s* two *d*; *m* 1966, Mary Alice Heywood. *Educ:* Grocers' Sch.; Sidney Sussex Coll., Cambridge (Hon. Fellow); Royal School of Mines. MA; Hon. DSc Oxford; Hon. DEng Witwatersrand; Hon. DTech, Haifa; Aeronautical Research at Royal Aircraft Establishment, Farnborough, 1920-37; Head of Air Defence Dept, RAE, Farnborough, 1937-39; Asst Dir of Scientific Research, Air Ministry, 1939; Dep. Dir of Scientific Res., Armaments, Min. of Aircraft Production, 1941; Dir of Scientific Research, Ministry of Aircraft Production, 1943; Dir-Gen. of Scientific Research, Ministry of Aircraft Production, 1945; Chief Scientist to Ministry of Supply, 1946-49; Sec. to Cttee of Privy Council for Scientific and Industrial Research, 1949-56; retired 1956. President: Engineering Section of British Association, 1952; Johnson Soc., 1953-54; Council European Organization for Nuclear Research, 1955-57; Medal of Freedom (Silver Palms), 1946. *Recreations:* music, gardening. *Address:* Birchway, 15 Waverley Road, Farnborough, Hants. *T:* Farnborough, Hants, 43021. *Club:* Athenæum.

LOCKWOOD, Betty; Chairman, Equal Opportunities Commission, since 1975; *b* 22 Jan. 1924; *d* of Arthur Lockwood and Edith Alice Lockwood. *Educ:* Eastborough Girls' Sch., Dewsbury; Ruskin Coll., Oxford. Asst Agent, Reading Labour Party, 1948-50; Sec./Agent, Gillingham Constituency Labour Party, 1950-52; Yorkshire Regional Women's Officer of Labour Party, 1952-67; Chief Woman Officer and Asst Nat. Agent of Labour Party, 1967-75. Secretary: Nat. Labour Women's Adv. Cttee, 1967-75; Nat. Jt Cttee, Working Women's Organisations, 1967-75; Vice-Chm., Internat. Council of Social Democratic Women, 1969-75; Chairman: Mary Macarthur Educnl Trust, 1971-; Mary Macarthur Holiday Homes, 1971-. Editor, Labour Woman, 1967-71. *Recreations:* walking and country pursuits, music. *Address:* 18 Winchester Court, Vicarage Gate, W8 7AB. *T:* 01-937 5269. *Club:* Soroptimist.

LOCKWOOD, Prof. David, FBA 1976; Professor of Sociology, University of Essex, since 1968; *b* 9 April 1929; *s* of Herbert Lockwood and Edith A. (*née* Lockwood); *m* 1954, Leonore Davidoff; three *s. Educ:* Honley Grammar Sch.; London Sch. of Economics. BSc(Econ) London, 1st Cl. Hons 1952; PhD London, 1957. Trainee, textile industry, 1944-47; Cpl, Intell. Corps, Austria, 1947-49. Asst Lectr and Lectr, London Sch. of Economics, 1953-60; Rockefeller Fellow, Univ. of California, Berkeley, 1958-59; Univ. Lectr, Faculty of Economics, and Fellow, St John's Coll., Cambridge, 1960-68. Visiting Professor: Dept of Sociology, Columbia Univ., 1966-67; Delhi Univ., 1975. Mem., SSRC (Chm., Sociol. and Soc. Admin Cttee), 1973-76. *Publications:* The Blackcoated Worker, 1958; The Affluent Worker in the Class Structure, 3 vols (with John H. Goldthorpe), 1968-69; numerous articles in learned jls and symposia. *Recreation:* walking. *Address:* 82 High Street, Wivenhoe, Essex. *T:* Wivenhoe 3530.

LOCKWOOD, Lt-Col John Cutts, CBE 1960; TD; JP; *s* of late Colonel John Lockwood and Mrs Lockwood, Kingham, Oxon. Served European War, 1914-18, in Essex Regt and Coldstream Guards; War of 1939-45, with Essex Territorials; Staff Captain in JAG Dept; later Legal Officer to SHAEF Mission to Denmark, and with them in Copenhagen, 1945. MP (C) Central Hackney, 1931-35; Romford, 1950-55. Barrister, Middle Temple; Mem. of Hon. Co. of Basket-makers and Freeman of the City of London. Order of Dannebrog (Denmark). *Recreation:* gardening. *Address:* Bishops Hall, Lambourne End, Essex. *T:* 01-500 2016. *Club:* Royal Automobile.

LOCKWOOD, Sir Joseph (Flawith), Kt 1960; Director, since 1954, and Chairman, 1954-74, EMI Limited and subsidiaries; Director: The Beecham Group, 1966-75; Smiths Industries Ltd (previously S. Smith & Sons (England) Ltd), since 1959; Hawker Siddeley Group, since 1963; Laird Group Ltd, since 1970; *b* 14 Nov. 1904. Manager of flour mills in Chile, 1924-28; Technical Manager of Etablissements, Henry Simon Ltd, in Paris and Brussels, 1928-33; Director, 1933; Dir Henry Simon Ltd, Buenos Aires, Chm. Henry Simon (Australia) Ltd, Dir Henry Simon (Engineering Works) Ltd, etc, 1945, Chm. and Managing Dir, Henry Simon Ltd, 1950; Dir, NRDC, 1951-67; Chm., IRC, 1969-71 (Mem., 1966-71); Dir, British Domestic Appliances Ltd, 1966-71 (Chm., 1966-70); Member: Engineering Advisory Council, Board of Trade, 1959; Export Council for Europe, 1961-63; Export Credits Guarantee Adv. Council, 1963-67; Council Imperial Soc. of Knights Bach. Director: Sandown Park Ltd, 1969; Epsom Grandstand Assoc. Ltd, 1969; United Racecourses Ltd, 1969. Hon. Treasurer British Empire Cancer Campaign, 1962-67; Chairman: Royal Ballet Sch. Endowment Fund, 1960-; Governors, Royal Ballet Sch.; Royal Ballet, 1971-; Young Vic Theatre Company, 1974-75; Vice-Pres., Central Sch. of Speech and Drama (Chm., Governors, 1965-68); Member: Arts Council, 1967-70; South Bank Theatre Board, 1968-. CompIEE. *Publications:* Provender Milling-the Manufacture of Feeding Stuffs for Livestock, 1939; Flour Milling (trans. into various languages), 1945. *Address:* 33 Grosvenor Square, W1X 9LL. *Club:* Carlton.

LOCKWOOD, Margaret Mary; Actress; *b* Karachi, India, 15 Sept. 1916; (*née* Margaret Lockwood); *m* Rupert W. Leon (marr. diss.); one *d. Educ:* Sydenham Girls' High Sch. Studied for Stage under Italia Conti and at Royal Academy of Dramatic Art. Appeared in films: Lorna Doone; Case of Gabriel Perry, 1934; Midshipman Easy; Jury's Evidence; Amateur Gentleman, 1935; Irish for Luck; Beloved Vagabond; Street Singer, 1936; Who's Your Lady Friend; Owd Bob; Bank Holiday, 1937; The Lady Vanishes; A Girl Must Live; Stars Look Down; Night Train to Munich, 1939; Quiet Wedding, 1940; Alibi; Man in Grey, 1942; Dear Octopus; Give Us The Moon; Love Story, 1943; Place of One's Own; I'll Be Your Sweetheart, 1944; Wicked Lady; Bedelia, 1945; Hungry Hill; Jassy, 1946; The White Unicorn, 1947; Look Before You Love, 1948; Cardboard Cavalier; Madness of the Heart, 1949; Highly Dangerous, 1950; Laughing Anne, 1952; Trent's Last Case, 1952; Trouble in the Glen, 1954; Cast A Dark Shadow, 1955; The Slipper and the Rose, 1976. Named top money-making Star in Britain by motion Picture Poll; Motion Picture Herald Fame Poll, 1945 and 1946; Winner Daily Mail Film Award, 1945-46, 1946-47 and 1947-48. Stage tour in Private Lives, 1949; Peter Pan, 1949-50, 1950-51 and 1957-58; Pygmalion, 1951; Spider's Web, Savoy, 1954-56; Subway in the Sky, Savoy, 1957; And Suddenly It's Spring, Duke of York's, 1959-60; Signpost to Murder, Cambridge Theatre, 1962-63; Every Other Evening, Phœnix, 1964-65; An Ideal Husband, Strand, 1965 and Garrick, 1966; The Others, Strand, 1967; On a Foggy Day, St Martin's, 1969; Lady Frederick, Vaudeville, 1970; Relative Values (nat. tour), 1972, Westminster, 1973; Double Edge, Vaudeville, 1975-76; Quadrille (nat. tour), 1977. BBC (TV) series (with daughter Julia) The Flying Swan, March-Sept. 1965; Yorkshire TV series, Justice, 1971, 1972-73, 1974. *Recreations:* crossword puzzles and swimming. *Address:* c/o Herbert de Leon, Fielding House, 13 Bruton Street, W1.

LOCKWOOD, Robert; Chairman, General Motors European Advisory Council, since 1977; *b* 14 April 1920; *s* of Joseph A. Lockwood and Sylvia Lockwood; *m* 1947, Phyllis M. Laing; one *s* one *d. Educ:* Columbia Univ. (AB); Columbia Law Sch. (LLB). Attorney, Bar of New York, 1941; US Dist of New York and US Supreme Court, 1952. Pilot, USAAF (8th Air Force), 1944-45. Attorney: Ehrich, Royall, Wheeler & Holland, New York, 1941 and 1946-47; Sullivan & Cromwell, New York, 1947-54; Sec. and Counsel, Cluett, Peabody & Co., Inc., New York, 1955-57; Man. Dir, Cluett, Peabody & Co., Ltd, London, 1957-59; General Motors: Overseas Ops, Planning and Develt, 1960-61; Asst to Man. Dir, GM Argentina, Buenos Aires, 1962; Asst to Man. Dir, and Manager, Parts, Power and Appliances, GM Continental, Antwerp, 1964-66; Branch Man., Netherlands Br., GM Continental, Rotterdam, 1967-68; Man., Planning and Develt, GM Overseas Ops, New York, 1969-73; Vice Pres., GM Overseas Corp., and Gen. Man., Japan Br., 1974-76; Exec. Vice Pres., Isuzu Motors Ltd, Tokyo, 1976. *Recreations:* tennis, chess, reading, ballet. *Address:* Flat J, Upper Feilde, 71 Park Street, W1Y 3HB. *T:* 01-499 2160. *Clubs:* Port Washington Yacht (New York); Tokyo Lawn Tennis (Tokyo).

LOCKWOOD, Walter Sydney Douglas, CBE 1962 (OBE 1948); CEng; FRAeS; FInstProdE; *b* 4 Jan. 1895; *s* of Walter Lockwood, Thetford, Norfolk; *m* 1924, Constance Rose, *d* of T. F. Bayliss, Norwich. *Educ:* Thetford Sch.; Bristol Univ. Served European War, 1914-18: Gloucester Regt, France and Belgium (Belgian Croix de Guerre; despatches; wounded). Joined design staff of Sir W. G. Armstrong Whitworth Aircraft Ltd, 1921; became Works Man., 1944. Armstrong Whitworth Aircraft: Works Dir, 1950; Dir and Gen. Man., 1955; Man. Dir, 1960; Man. Dir, Whitworth Gloster Aircraft Ltd (when Armstrong Whitworth Aircraft and Gloster Aircraft Companies merged), 1961-63 (when Co. dissolved); Dir, Hawker Siddeley Aviation Ltd, 1961-64, retired. Mem. Coun., SBAC, 1960. *Address:* Wayside, Abbey Road, Leiston, Suffolk.

LODER, family name of **Baron Wakehurst.**

LODER, Sir Giles Rolls, 3rd Bt, *cr* 1887; DL; *b* 10 Nov. 1914; *o s* of late Capt. Robert Egerton Loder, *s* of 2nd Bt, and late Muriel Rolls, *d* of J. Rolls-Hoare; *S* grandfather, 1920; *m* 1939, Marie, *o d* of late Captain Symons-Jeune, Runnymede House, Old Windsor; two *s. Educ:* Eton; Trinity Coll., Cambridge (MA). High Sheriff of Sussex, 1948-49; DL West Sussex, 1977. FLS. VMH. *Recreations:* sailing, horticulture. *Heir: s* Edmund Jeune Loder [*b* 26 June 1941; *m* 1966, Penelope Jane (marr, diss. 1971), *d* of Ivo Forde; one *d*]. *Address:* Leonardslee, Horsham, West Sussex. *T:* Lower Beeding 305. *Club:* Royal Yacht Squadron.

LODGE, Henry Cabot; Politician, US; President's Special Representative to the Vatican, 1970; *b* 5 July 1902; *s* of George Cabot Lodge and Mathilda Elizabeth Frelinghuysen Davis; *g s* of late Henry Cabot Lodge, Senator (US); *m* 1926, Emily Sears; two *s. Educ:* Middx Sch., Concord, Mass.; Harvard (AB *cum laude*; LLD). Boston Transcript, New York Herald Tribune, 1923-32. Thrice elected US Senator from Massachusetts. Harvard Overseer. Senate author of the Lodge-Brown Act which created Hoover Commission; Chm., resolutions cttee, Republican National Convention, 1948; US Senate Foreign Relations Cttee. Campaign Manager of effort to win Republican nomination for Gen. Eisenhower, 1951-52; Mem. President's Cabinet and US Rep. to UN, 1953-60. Republican nominee for Vice-Pres., USA, 1960. Dir-Gen., Atlantic Inst., Paris, 1961-63; Ambassador to Vietnam, 1963-64, 1965-67, to Federal Republic of Germany, 1968-69. US Representative at Vietnam Peace Talks, Paris, Jan.-Nov. 1969. Had reached grade of reserve Captain when US entered war; served as Major United States Army, with first American tank detachment in Brit. 8th Army, Libya, 1942 (citation); resigned from Senate for further Army service (first Senator to do so since the Civil War); Italy, 1944; Lt-Col S France, Rhine and S Germany, 1944-45 (Bronze Star, US, 1944, Legion of Merit, 1945, Légion d'Honneur and Croix de Guerre with palm, France, 1945). Maj.-Gen., US Army Reserve. Has been awarded numerous Hon. Degrees; Sylvanus Thayer Medal, West Point; Theodore Roosevelt Assoc. Medal; Gold Medal from Pres. Eisenhower, 'for selfless and invaluable service to our nation'. Order of Polonia Restituta; Order of African Redemption, Liberia; Grand Cross of Merit, Order of Malta; National Order, Republic of Viet Nam. *Publications:* The Storm Has Many Eyes, 1973; As It Was, 1976; articles for Atlantic Monthly, Collier's, Life, Reader's Digest, Saturday

Evening Post. *Address:* 275 Hale Street, Beverly, Mass 01915, USA.

LODGE, Sir Thomas, Kt 1974; Consultant Radiologist, United Sheffield Hospitals, 1946-74, retired; Clinical Lecturer, Sheffield University, 1960-74; *b* 25 Nov. 1909; *s* of James Lodge and Margaret (*née* Lowery); *m* 1940, Aileen Corduff; one *s* one *d*. *Educ:* Univ. of Sheffield. MB, ChB 1934, FFR 1945, FRCP 1967, FRCS 1967. Asst Radiologist: Sheffield Radium Centre, 1936; Manchester Royal Infirmary, 1937-38; 1st Asst in Radiology, United Sheffield Hosps, 1938-46. FRSocMed. Hon. FFR RCSI; Hon. FRACR 1963; Hon. FACR 1975; Hon. MSR 1975. *Publications:* Recent Advances in Radiology, 3rd edn 1955, 4th edn 1964 and 5th edn 1975; articles in Brit. Jl Radiology, Clinical Radiology, etc. *Recreation:* gardening. *Address:* 44 Sussex Square, Brighton, East Sussex BN2 1GE.

LODGE, Thomas C. S.; *see* Skeffington-Lodge.

LODGE, Tom Stewart, CBE 1967; Chairman, Criminological Scientific Council, Council of Europe, since 1975 (Member, since 1970); Director of Research and Statistics, Home Office, 1969-73; *b* 15 Dec. 1909; *s* of George Arthur and Emma Eliza Lodge, Batley, Yorks; *m* 1936, Joan McFadyean (*d* 1961); one *d*. *Educ:* Batley Grammar Sch.; Merton Coll., Oxford. BA Hons Maths 1931, MA 1934; FIA 1939. Prudential Assurance Co., 1931-43; Min. of Aircraft Production, 1943-46; Admty as Superintending Actuary, 1946-50; Statistical Adviser, Home Office, 1950; Statistical Adviser and Dir of Research, Home Office, 1957. *Publications:* articles in British and French jls. *Address:* Chaddesley, Slines Oak Road, Woldingham, Caterham, Surrey CR3 7HL. *T:* Woldingham 3003. *Club:* Civil Service.

LOEHNIS, Sir Clive, KCMG 1962 (CMG 1950); Commander RN (retired); *b* 24 Aug. 1902; *s* of H. W. Loehnis, Barrister-at-Law, Inner Temple; *m* 1929, Rosemary Beryl, *d* of late Major Hon. R. N. Dudley Ryder, 8th Hussars; one *s* one *d*. *Educ:* Royal Naval Colls, Osborne, Dartmouth and Greenwich. Midshipman, 1920; Lt, 1924; qualified in signal duties, 1928; Lt-Comdr, 1932; retired, 1935; AMIEE 1935. Re-employed in Signal Div. Admiralty, 1938; Comdr on retd List, 1942; Naval Intelligence Div., 1942; demobilised and entered Foreign Office, 1945; Dep. Dir, Government Communications Headquarters, 1952-60; Dir, Government Communications HQ, 1960-64. Dep. Chm., Civil Service Selection Bd, 1967-70. *Address:* 12 Eaton Place, SW1. *T:* 01-235 6803. *Clubs:* White's, MCC. *See also Baron Remnant.*

LOEWE, Frederick; composer; concert pianist; *b* Vienna, 10 June 1901; *s* of Edmund Loewe, actor. Began career as concert pianist playing with leading European orchestras; went to US, 1924; first musical, Salute to Spring, produced in St Louis, 1937; first Broadway production, Great Lady, 1938; began collaboration with Alan Jay Lerner, *qv*, in 1942, since when has written music for: Day Before Spring, 1945; Brigadoon, 1947 (1st musical to win Drama Critics' Award); Paint Your Wagon, 1951 (best score of year); My Fair Lady, 1956 (many awards); Gigi (film), 1958 (Oscar), (stage) 1974; Camelot, 1960; The Little Prince, 1975 (film). DMus *hc* Univ. of Redlands, Calif; Dr of Fine Arts *hc* Univ. of NYC. *Address:* c/o ASCAP, 575 Madison Avenue, New York, NY 10022, USA. *Clubs:* Players', Lambs (New York); Palm Springs Racquet.

LOEWEN, Gen. Sir Charles (Falkland), GCB 1957 (KCB 1954; CB 1945); KBE 1951 (CBE 1944); DSO 1945; late RA; *b* 17 Sept. 1900; *s* of late Charles J. Loewen, MA, Vancouver, Canada, and Edith Loewen; *m* 1928, Kathleen, *d* of late Maj.-Gen. J. M. Ross; two *s*. *Educ:* Haileybury Coll.; Royal Military College, Kingston, Canada. 2nd Lt RFA 1918; Capt. 1931; Bt Major, 1937; Major, 1938; Bt Lt-Col 1939; Col 1942; Maj.-Gen. 1944; Lt-Gen. 1950; Gen. 1954. Served War of 1939-45, in Norway (despatches) and in Italy (despatches); comd: 1st Inf. Div., 1944-45; 6th Armd Div., 1946; 1st Armd Div., 1947; Northumb. Dist and 50th (Inf.) Div. (TA), 1948-49; GOC-in-C Anti-Aircraft Command, 1950-53; GOC-in-C, Western Command, April-Sept. 1953; C-in-C Far East Land Forces, 1953-56; Adjutant-Gen. to the Forces, 1956-59; ADC Gen. to the Queen, 1956-59. Col Comdt, RA, 1953-63. Hon. DSc Mil., Roy. Mil. Coll. Canada, 1966. Comdr Legion of Merit (US), 1945. *Recreations:* fishing, gardening. *Address:* 13969 Trites Road, Surrey, BC, Canada. *Clubs:* Army and Navy; Vancouver (Vancouver).

LOEWENSTEIN-WERTHEIM-FREUDENBERG, Hubertus Friedrich, Prince of, Dr iur, LittD (*hc*); Commander's Cross of German Order of Merit, 1968; Special Adviser, German Government, Press and Information Office, 1960-71; Member of Parliament, 1953-57; *b* Schoenwoerth Castle, near Kufstein, Tirol, 14 Oct. 1906; *y s* of Prince Maximilian Loewenstein-Wertheim-Freudenberg and Constance, *y d* of 1st Baron Pirbright, PC; *m* 1929, Helga Maria Mathilde v. d. Schuylenburg; three *d*. *Educ:* Gymnasium at Gmunden and Klagenfurt, Austria; Universities at Munich, Hamburg, Geneva, and Berlin. Referendar Berlin Kammergericht, 1928, Doctor iuris utriusque, Hamburg, 1931; member of Catholic Centre Party, 1930; leader of Republican Students, and Republican Youth, Berlin, 1930; Prussian delegate to Munich, 1932; left Germany, 1933; returned 1946; Visiting Prof. of Hist. and Gov. to USA and Canada of the Carnegie Endowment for International Peace, 1937-46; Lecturer in History, University of Heidelberg, during 1947. Publisher and editor, Das Reich, Saarbrücken, 1934-35; Founder of American Guild for German Cultural Freedom, 1936; Founder and leader, German Action movement, 1949-. Southern German Editor, Die Zeit, 1952-53; Pres., Free German Authors' Assoc., 1973 and 1977. Hon. DLitt Hamline Univ., 1943. Grand Cross of Athos, 1966; Commendatore, Order of Merit (Italy), 1970. *Publications:* The Tragedy of a Nation, 1934; After Hitler's Fall, Germany's Coming Reich, 1934; A Catholic in Republican Spain, 1937; Conquest of the Past, autobiography (till 1933), 1938; On Borrowed Peace, autobiography (1933 to 1942), 1942; The Germans in History, 1945; The Child and the Emperor: a Legend, 1945; The Lance of Longinus, 1946; The Eagle and the Cross, 1947; Deutsche Geschichte, 1950 5th rev. edn, 1976; Stresemann, biography, 1953; Die römischen Tagebücher des Dr von Molitor, 1956; (co-author Volkmar von Zuehlsdorff) Das deutsche Schicksal 1945-1957, 1957; (same co-author) NATO, The Defence of the West, 1963; Towards The Further Shore (autobiography), 1968; Botschafter ohne Auftrag, 1972; Seneca: Kaiser ohne Purpur, 1975; Tiberius Imperator, 1977; Invitation to Capri, 1978; Apulia: Land of Destiny, 1978; contributions to (previous to 1933) Berliner Tageblatt, Vossische Zeitung, etc; (after 1933) Spectator, Nineteenth Century Review, Contemporary Review, American Mercury, Atlantic Monthly, New York Herald Tribune, Commonweal, American Scholar, Social Science, Die Tat, Die Zeit, etc. *Recreations:* swimming, riding. *Address:* c/o Mrs Milburne, Weeks Farm, Egerton, Kent; Lahnstrasse 50, 53 Bonn-Bad Godesberg, Federal Republic of Germany.

LOEWY, Raymond; Industrial Designer; Founder: Raymond Loewy International Inc., consultant designers to US and foreign corporations; Compagnie de l'Esthétique Industrielle, Paris; Raymond Loewy International Ltd, London; Raymond Loewy Co., Lausanne; Lecturer: Massachusetts Institute of Technology; Harvard Graduate School of Business Administration; Institute of Design Technology, Moscow; *b* Paris, 5 Nov. 1893; *s* of Maximillian Loewy and Marie Labalme; naturalized citizen of US 1938; *m* 1948, Viola Erickson; one *d*. *Educ:* Chaptal Coll., Paris; Paris Univ.; Ecole de Lanneau (grad. eng.). Art Director, Westinghouse Electric Co. 1929; started private organization of Industrial Design, 1929. Served as Capt. Corps of Engineers attached to Gen. Staff, 5th Army, France, 1914-18; Liaison Officer, AEF (Officer Legion of Honour, Croix de Guerre, with 4 citations; Interallied Medal); Comdr, Fr. Legion of Honour, 1959. Hon. RDI 1937; FRSA 1942; Fellow (Past Pres.), American Soc. of Industrial Designers; Lectr, Coll. of Arch., University of Calif; American Design Award, 1938; Hon. Doctor of Fine Arts, University of Cincinnati, 1956; Dr, Calif Coll. of Design, LA. Member: Society of Automotive Engineers; Amer. Soc. Mech. Engrs; Adv. Board on Vocational Educn, Bd of Educn, NYC; Assoc. Mem. Soc. of Naval Arch. and Marine Engrs; Soc. of Space Medicine; Vice-Pres. French Chamber of Commerce of the US, 1958. Inc. in Thousand Makers of Twentieth Century, Sunday Times, 1969; Fellow, Amer. Acad. of Achievement, 1970. Mem., President's Cttee on Employment of the Handicapped, 1965-; Habitability Consultant to NASA Apollo Saturn Application program, 1967-; Skylab and Space Shuttle Orbiter; Design Consultant to Soviet Union State Cttee for Science and Technology, 1973-. Knight of Mark Twain. *Publications:* The Locomotive-its Esthetics, 1937; Never Leave Well Enough Alone (autobiography), 1951 (trans. various langs). *Address:* (office) 39 Avenue d'Iéna, Paris, France; 25 Bruton Street, W1; 600 Panorama Road, Palm Springs, Calif, USA; 2 Chemin des Trois Rois, Lausanne, Switzerland; (home) Manoir de la Cense, Rochefort-en-Yvelines; 20 rue Boissiere, Paris XVI, France; Tierra Caliente, Palm Springs, Calif. *Clubs:* Racquet, Tennis (Palm Springs, Calif), NY Athletic.

LOFTHOUSE, Reginald George Alfred, FRICS; Chief Surveyor, Ministry of Agriculture, Fisheries and Food, 1973-76; *b* Workington, 30 Dec. 1916; *m* 1939, Ann Bernardine Bannan; three *d*. *Educ:* Workington Secondary Sch.; with private land agent, Cockermouth. Chartered Surveyor and Land Agent

(Talbot-Ponsonby Prizeman). Asst District Officer, Penrith, 1941-42; District Officer, Carlisle, for Cumberland War Agric. Exec. Cttee, 1942-43; Asst Land Comr (WR), 1943-46; Land Commissioner: N and E Ridings, 1946-48; Derbs, Leics, Rutland, Northants, 1948-50; Somerset and Dorset, 1950-52; Regional Land Comr, Hdqtrs, 1952-59, and SE Region, 1959-71; Regional Officer, SE Region, Agric., Develt and Adv. Service, 1971-73. Vis. Lectr in Rural Estate Management and Forestry, Regent Street Polytechnic, 1954-62. Member: Bd of Governors, Coll. of Estate Management, 1963- (Chm. 1972-); Court and Council, Reading Univ., 1973-; Delegacy for Nat. Inst. for Res. in Dairying, Shinfield, 1974-; Gen. Council, RICS, 1974-76; RICS Land Agency and Agric. Div. Council, 1974-; Hon. Life Mem., Cambridge Univ. Land Soc.; Chm. Farm Bldgs Cttee 1973-, Mem. Engrg and Bldgs Res. Bd 1973-, Jt Consultative Organisation. Liveryman, Loriners' Co., 1976; Freeman, City of London, 1976. *Publications:* contrib. professional, techn. and countryside jls. *Address:* Ministry of Agriculture, Fisheries and Food, Great Westminster House, Horseferry Road, SW1P 2AE. *Clubs:* Athenæum, City Livery, MCC.

LOFTS, Norah, (Mrs Robert Jorisch); *b* 27 Aug. 1904; *d* of Isaac Robinson and Ethel (*née* Garner); *m* 1st, 1931, Geoffrey Lofts (decd); one *s*; 2nd, 1949, Dr Robert Jorisch. *Educ:* West Suffolk County Sch. *Publications:* I Met a Gypsy, 1935; White Hell of Pity, 1937; Out of This Nettle, 1939; Road to Revelation, 1941; Jassy, 1944; Silver Nutmeg, 1947; Women of the Old Testament, 1949; A Calf for Venus, 1949; The Luteplayer, 1951; Bless This House, 1954; Queen in Waiting, 1955; Afternoon of An Autocrat, 1956; Scent of Cloves, 1958; Heaven In Your Hand, 1959; The Town House, 1959; The House at Old Vine, 1961; The House at Sunset, 1963; The Concubine, 1964; How Far to Bethlehem?, 1965; (with M. Weiner) Eternal France, 1969; The Lost Ones, 1969; The King's Pleasure, 1970; Lovers All Untrue, 1970; A Rose For Virtue, 1971; Charlotte, 1972; Nethergate, 1973; Crown of Aloes, 1974; Knights Acre, 1974; The Homecoming, 1975; The Lonely Furrow, 1976; Domestic Life in England, 1976; Queens of Britain, 1977. *As Peter Curtis:* You're Best Alone, 1939; Dead March in Three Keys, 1940; Lady Living Alone, 1944; The Devil's Own, 1959. *Address:* Northgate House, Bury St Edmunds, Suffolk. *T:* Bury St Edmunds 2680.

LOFTUS, Viscount; Charles John Tottenham; Instructor of French, Strathcona-Tweedsmuir School, Calgary; *b* 2 Feb. 1943; *e s* and *heir* of 8th Marquess of Ely, *qv*; *m* 1969, Judith Marvelle, *d* of Dr J. J. Porter, FRS, Calgary, Alberta; one *s* one *d*. *Educ:* Trinity Coll. Sch., Port Hope, Ont; Ecole Internationale de Genève; Univ. of Toronto (MA). *Heir:* s Hon. Andrew John Tottenham, *b* 26 Feb. 1973. *Address:* 1424 Springfield Place SW, Calgary, Alberta T2W 0Y1, Canada.

LOFTUS, Col Ernest Achey, CBE 1975 (OBE (mil.) 1928); TD 1929; MA (TCD), BSc Econ. (London), LCP, FRGS, FRSA, MRST; Member RSL; DL; a pedagogue for 74 years and retired 1975 as the oldest civil servant in the World (see Guinness Book of Records); in service of Zambian Government 1963-75; *b* 11 Jan. 1884; *s* of Capt. William Loftus, Master Mariner, Kingston-upon-Hull; *m* 1916, Elsie, *er d* of Allen Charles Cole, West Tilbury, Essex; two *s*. *Educ:* Archbishop Holgate's Gram. Sch., York; Trinity Coll., Dublin. Senior Geography Master, Palmer's Sch., Grays, Essex, 1906-19; Head of Junior Sch., Southend on Sea High Sch. for Boys, 1919-20; Asst Dir of Educn, Southend-on-Sea, 1920-22; Headmaster, Barking Abbey Sch., 1922-49; a select speaker, Conf. of Educn Cttees, Oxford, 1936; coined term 'Health Science' and drew up first syllabus of work (London Univ.) in that subject, 1937; an Educn Officer in Kenya, 1953-60, in Nyasaland, 1960-63, in Zambia, 1963-75; formed two Cadet Corps and raised four Territl Units in Co. Essex; served with The Essex Regt 1910-29; European War in Gallipoli 1915, Egypt 1916, France 1918; Staff Officer for Educn 67th Div., Independent Force and Kent Force, 1917; a pioneer officer in what became RAEC; Lt-Col Commanding 6th Essex Regt, 1925-29; Mem. Essex Territorial Army Association 1925-29; Brevet Col, 1929; served in War of 1939—Pioneer Corps, 1939-42, commanding No 13 (Italian) Group in France and No 31 Group in London, etc.; Founder Hon. Sec. Essex County Playing Fields Association, 1925-29; Hon. Organiser or Sec. various Appeals, in Essex. Mem. Standing Cttee Convocation, London Univ., 1944-53, and Bedell of Convocation, 1946-53. A chm. Nat. Assistance Board, 1949-53; Mem. Exec. Cttee Essex Playing Fields Assoc., 1925-53; Mem. Thurrock UDC 1946-53, Vice-Chm. 1951-52; Controller, Civil Defence, Thurrock area, 1951-53. Freeman, City of Kingston-upon-Hull, 1968. For some years a Governor, The Strand Sch. (Brixton), Palmer's Sch. (Grays), etc. A Selborne Lectr. DL Essex 1929-75, now inactive. Mason, 1915-; Rotarian (Pres., Barking, 1935), 1930-. *Publications:* Education and the Citizen; History of a Branch of the Cole Family; Growls and Grumbles; A History of Barking

Abbey (with H. F. Chettle); A Visual History of Africa, 1953, 16 reprints, 2nd edn 1974; A Visual History of East Africa; and brochures for the East African Literature Bureau. Contributor of feature articles in London Daily and Weekly Press, etc. on Education; author of 8 scenes of Barking Pageant, 1931, and of Elizabethan scene in Ilford Pageant of Essex, 1932. *Recreations:* historical and genealogical research. *Address:* c/o Kingscote, Furze Hill, Kingswood, Surrey. *Club:* Royal Commonwealth Society.

LOGAN, Sir Donald (Arthur), KCMG 1977 (CMG 1965); HM Diplomatic Service, retired; *b* 25 Aug. 1917; *s* of late Arthur Alfred Logan and Louise Anne Bradley; *m* 1957, Irène Jocelyne Angèle, *d* of Robert Everts (Belgian Ambassador at Madrid, 1932-39) and Alexandra Comnène; one *s* two *d*. *Educ:* Solihull. Fellow, Chartered Insurance Institute, 1939. War of 1939-45: commissioned, RA, Sept. 1939; Major, 1942; British Army Staff, Washington, 1942-43; Germany, 1945. Joined HM Foreign (subseq. Diplomatic) Service, Dec. 1945; Foreign Office, 1945-47; HM Embassy, Tehran, 1947-51, as First Sec. (Commercial); Foreign Office, 1951-53; Asst Political Agent, Kuwait, 1953-55; Asst Private Sec. to Sec. of State for Foreign Affairs, 1956-58; HM Embassy, Washington, 1958-60; HM Ambassador to Guinea, 1960-62; Foreign Office, 1962-64; Information Counsellor, British Embassy, Paris, 1964-70; Ambassador to Bulgaria, 1970-73; Dep. Permanent UK Rep. to NATO, 1973-75; Ambassador and Permanent Leader, UK Delegn to UN Conf. on Law of the Sea, 1976-77. Vice-Pres., Internat. Exhibitions Bureau, Paris, 1963-67. *Address:* 6 Thurloe Street, SW7 2ST. *T:* 01-589 4010. *Clubs:* Brooks's, Royal Automobile.

LOGAN, Sir Douglas (William), Kt 1959; DPhil, MA, BCL; Principal of the University of London, 1948-75; President, British Universities Sports Board and Federation, 1953-75; Chairman, British Student Sports Federation, 1971-77; Deputy Chairman, Universities Superannuation Scheme Ltd (Chairman, 1974-77); *b* Liverpool, 27 March 1910; *yr s* of Robert Logan and Euphemia Taylor Stevenson, Edinburgh; *m* 1st, 1940, Vaire Olive Wollaston (from whom he obtained a divorce); two *s*; 2nd, 1947, Christine Peggy Walker; one *s* one *d*. *Educ:* Liverpool Collegiate Sch.; University Coll., Oxford (Open Classical Scholar). First Classes: Hon. Mods 1930, Lit. Hum. 1932, Jurisprudence, 1933; Oxford Univ. Senior Studentship, 1933; Harmsworth Scholar, Middle Temple, 1933 (Hon. Bencher, 1965); Henry Fellowship Harvard Law Sch., 1935-36; Asst Lecturer, LSE, 1936-37; Barstow Scholarship, 1937; called to Bar, Middle Temple, 1937; Fellow of Trinity Coll., Cambridge, 1937-43; Principal, Ministry of Supply, 1940-44; Clerk of the Court, University of London, 1944-47. Rede Lecturer, 1963. Fellow: Wye Coll., 1970; Imperial Coll., 1974; School of Pharmacy, 1975. Vice-Chm., Association of Commonwealth Univs, 1961-67 (Chm. 1962-63; Hon. Treasurer, 1967-74; Dep. Hon. Treasurer, 1974-); Vice-Chm., Athlone Fellowship Cttee, 1959-71; Dep. Chm., Commonwealth Scholarships Commn; Member: Marshall Scholarships Commn, 1961-67; Nat. Theatre Bd, 1962-68; a Governor, Old Vic (Vice-Chm., 1972-), and Bristol Old Vic; a Trustee, City Parochial Foundation, 1953-67; Member: Anderson Cttee on Grants to Students, 1958-60; Hale Cttee on Superannuation of Univ. Teachers, 1958-60; Northumberland Cttee on Recruitment to the Veterinary Profession, 1962-64; Maddex Working Party on the Superannuation of Univ. Teachers, 1965-68. Mem. British Delegation to 1st, 2nd, 3rd, and 4th Commonwealth Educn Confs, Oxford, 1959, Delhi, 1962, Ottawa, 1964, and Lagos, 1968; Commonwealth Medical Conf. Edinburgh, 1965. Hon. Mem., Pharmaceutical Soc. Hon. Fellow: LSE, 1962; University Coll., Oxford, 1973; University Coll. London, 1975. Hon. DCL Western Ontario; Hon. DLitt Rhodesia; Hon. LLD: Melbourne, Madras, British Columbia, Hong Kong, Liverpool, McGill, CNAA, London; Hon. FDSRCS; Hon. FRIBA. Chevalier de l'Ordre de la Légion d'Honneur. *Address:* Restalrig, Mountain Street, Chilham, Kent CT4 8DQ. *T:* Chilham 640. *Club:* Athenæum.

LOGAN, Lt-Col John, TD 1945; Vice-Lieutenant, Stirlingshire, since 1965; *b* 25 May 1907; *s* of Crawford William Logan and Ada Kathleen Logan (*née* Kidston); *m* 1937, Rosaleen Muriel O'Hara (*d* 1967); one *s* one *d*. *Educ:* Eton Coll., Windsor. British American Tobacco Co. Ltd (China), 1928-32; Imperial Tobacco Co. (of Great Britain and Ireland) Ltd, 1932-39. POW in Germany, 1940-45 (Captain, 7th Argyll and Sutherland Hdrs; Co, 1949-50). Imperial Tobacco Co. (of Great Britain and Ireland) Ltd, 1946-67. DL Stirlingshire, 1956. *Recreations:* shooting, fishing. *Address:* Wester Craigend, Stirling. *T:* Stirling 5025. *Club:* Western (Glasgow).

LOGAN, Thomas Moffat, CBE 1963; retired as Under-Secretary, National Assistance Board, 1966; *b* 21 June 1904; *s* of late John

Logan, builder and contractor, Carluke, Lanarkshire; *m* 1947, Freda Evelyn Andrew; no *c*. *Educ:* Hamilton Academy. Carluke Parish Council 1922; Relieving Officer, Lanark County Council, 1929; National Assistance Board: Area Officer, 1934; Asst Principal, 1942, Principal, 1945; Asst Sec., (Head of Organization and Methods), 1955; Under-Sec., 1964. *Recreations:* gardening, do-it-yourself, dancing. *Address:* Wayside, 52 Seafield Road, Bournemouth BH6 3JF. *T:* Bournemouth 49931.

LOGAN, William Philip Dowie, MD, PhD, BSc, DPH, FRCP; Director, Division of Health Statistics, WHO, 1961-74; *b* 2 Nov. 1914; *s* of late Frederick William Alexander Logan and late Elizabeth Jane Dowie; *m* Barbara (*née* Huneke); four *s* two *d* (and one *s* decd). *Educ:* Queen's Park Sch., Glasgow; Universities of Glasgow and London. RAF Med. Branch, 1940-46 (Squadron Leader). Hospital appointments in Glasgow, 1939-40 and 1946. Gen. practice in Barking, Essex, 1947-48; General Register Office, 1948-60 (Chief Medical Statistician, Adviser on Statistics to Ministry of Health, Head of WHO Centre for Classification of Diseases, and Member, WHO panel of experts on Health Statistics). *Publications:* contribs on epidemiology, vital and health statistics in official reports and medical jls. *Address:* 10 chemin de la Tourelle, 1209 Geneva, Switzerland.

LOGSDON, Geoffrey Edward, CBE 1962; TD 1950; Clerk to Worshipful Company of Mercers, 1952-74; *b* 24 July 1910; *o s* of late Edward Charles Logsdon; *m* 1st, 1943, Marie Carolinne Dumas (*d* 1957); one *s* one *d*; 2nd, 1958, Barbara Joyce Bird. *Educ:* City of London Sch. Admitted Solicitor, 1937; Legal Asst, Mercers' Company, 1945-52; Commissioned RA (TA), 1938. Served War of 1939-45: Malta, Middle East and UK. Lt-Col Comd 458 (M) HAA Regt (Kent) RA, TA, 1949-52. Formerly Clerk to: Jt Grand Gresham Cttee; The City and Metropolitan Welfare Charity; Mem. City of London Savings Cttee; Chm., Governors, Nat. Corp. for Care of Old People, 1973-; Governor, Dauntsey's School, 1974-. FRSA 1972. *Address:* Sandford Way, Pound Lane, Burley, Ringwood, Hants BH24 4EF. *T:* Burley 3335.

LOGUE, Christopher; *b* 23 Nov. 1926; *s* of John Logue and Molly Logue (*née* Chapman); unmarried. *Educ:* Prior Park Coll., Bath; Portsmouth Grammar Sch. Private in Black Watch, two years in Army prison, discharged with ignominy, 1948. Member: Equity; Assoc. of Cinematograph, Television and Allied Technicians. *Publications:* verse: Wand & Quadrant, 1953; First Testament, 1955; Weekdream Sonnets, 1955; Devil, Maggot & Son, 1956; The Man Who Told His Love, 1958; Songs, 1959; Songs from The Lilywhite Boys, 1960; Patrocleia, 1962; The Arrival of the Poet in the City, 1963; ABC, 1966; The Words of The Establishment Songs, 1966; Pax, 1967; New Numbers, 1969; The Girls, 1969; Twelve Cards, 1972; twenty Verse Posters between 1958 and 1971; The Crocodile (illus. Binette Schroeder), 1976; plays: The Trial of Cob & Leach, 1959; (with Harry Cookson) The Lilywhite Boys, 1959; Antigone (a version), 1961; (with Hugo Claus) Friday, 1971; (with Donald Frazer) War Music, 1977; prose: True Stories, 1966; True Stories (2) (illus. Bert Kitchen), 1973; Ratsmagic (illus. Wayne Anderson), 1976; contrib. Private Eye, The Times, The Sunday Times, Arion, Vogue, The Statesman, etc; as Count Palmiro Vicarion: Lust, a pornographic novel, 1957; (ed) Count Palmiro Vicarion's Book of Limericks, 1957; (ed) Count Palmiro Vicarion's Book of Bawdy Ballads, 1957. *Screen plays:* The End of Arthur's Marriage (dir Ken Loach), 1963; Savage Messiah (dir Ken Russell), 1972. *Play:* The Story of Mary Frazer, 1962. *Recordings:* Red Bird (with Tony Kinsey and Bill Le Sage), 1960; Songs from The Establishment (singer Annie Ross), 1962; The Death of Patroclus (with Vanessa Redgrave, Alan Dobie and others), 1963. *Film roles:* Swinburne, in Ken Russell's Dante's Inferno, 1966; John Ball, in John Irvin's The Peasants' Revolt, 1969; Cardinal Richelieu, in Ken Russell's The Devils, 1970. *Address:* 18 Denbigh Close, W11.

LOKOLOKO, Sir Tore, GCMG 1977; OBE; Governor-General of Papua New Guinea, since 1977; *b* 21 Sept. 1930; *s* of Loko Loko Tore and Kevau Sarufa; *m* 1950, Lalahaia Meakoro; four *s* six *d*. *Educ:* Sogeri High Sch., PNG. Dip. in Cooperative, India. Chm., PNG Cooperative Fedn, 1965-68; MP, 1968-77 (two terms); Minister for Health, and Dep. Chm. of National Exec. Council, 1968-72. Rep. PNG: Co-op. Conf., Australia, 1951; S Pacific Conf., Lae, 1964; attended UN Gen. Assembly, 1969, and Trusteeship Council, 1971. *Address:* Government House, Port Moresby, Papua New Guinea. *T:* 25 9366.

LOMAS, Harry, CBE 1972; QFSM 1970; Chief Fire Officer, Manchester Fire Brigade, 1968-74; *b* 9 June 1916; *s* of Harry Lomas, market gardener, Ashton-under-Lyne; *m* 1940, Ivy Mona Snelgrove; one *s* two *d*. *Educ:* Heginbotham Sch., Ashton-

under-Lyne. Mem. Instn Fire Engrs. Manchester City Police Fire Bde, 1939; HM Royal Marines, 1942-46; Nat. Fire Service, 1946-48; Manchester City Fire Bde, 1948: Stn Officer, 1950; Asst Divisional Officer, 1955; Divisional Officer, 1957; Dep. Chief Officer, 1966. OStJ 1970. *Recreations:* cine photography, gardening. *Address:* 25 St Andrews Road, Heaton Moor, Stockport, Cheshire. *T:* 061-432 7279.

LOMAS, Kenneth, JP; MP (Lab) Huddersfield West, since 1964; *b* 16 Nov. 1922; *s* of George Lomas and Rhoda Clayton; *m* 1945, Helen Wilson; two *s* one *d*. *Educ:* Ashton-under-Lyne Elementary and Central Schs. Served with Royal Marines and RM Commando Group, 1942-46 (Sergeant). Central Office, Union of Shop, Distributive and Allied Workers, 1937-55; Asst Regional Organiser Blood Transfusion Service, 1955-64. Contested (Lab) Blackpool South, 1951 and Macclesfield, 1955. PPS to Minister of Technology, 1969-70. Mem., Cttees for Econ., Military, Educn, Inf. and Cultural Affairs, N Atlantic Assembly. JP Cheshire, 1961; Upper Agbrigg Co. Sessions, 1972-. *Recreations:* arguing, watching football, reading. *Address:* House of Commons, SW1.

LOMAX, Sir John Garnett, KBE 1953 (MBE 1928); CMG 1944; MC 1917; HM Diplomatic Service, retired; *b* Liverpool, 27 Aug. 1896; *s* of Rev. Canon Edward Lomax and Bessie Garnett; *m* 1922, Feridah Yvette Krajewski; two *s*. *Educ:* Liverpool Coll.; Liverpool Univ. Served European War, France, Belgium, India, and Egypt; Driver, RFA (West Lancs), 1915, Lt 1916. HM Vice-Consul, New Orleans, 1920, Chicago, 1921; Vice-Consul and 2nd Sec. HM Legation, Bogota, 1926-30; 2nd Commercial Sec. HM Embassy, Rio de Janeiro, 1930; transferred to HM Embassy, Rome, 1935; HM Commercial Agent, Jerusalem, 1938; Commercial Counsellor, HM Embassy, Madrid, 1940; HM Legation, Berne, 1941; Commercial Counsellor at Angora, 1943; Minister (commercial), British Embassy, Buenos Aires, 1946-49; Ambassador to Bolivia, 1949-56. *Publication:* The Diplomatic Smuggler, 1965. *Recreations:* golf, sailing, riding, shooting. *Address:* Tanterfyn, Llaneilian, Anglesey, Gwynedd; 803 Nelson House, Dolphin Square, SW1. *Clubs:* Reform, Royal Automobile.

LOMBARD KNIGHT, Eric John Percy Crawford; Chairman, English Transcontinental Ltd, Bankers, since 1977; Deputy Chairman, Lombard North Central Ltd, 1971-76 (Joint Chairman, 1965-71, and Managing Director, 1947-71, Lombard Banking Ltd); Chairman and Director of companies; *b* 17 Aug. 1907; *yr s* of late Herbert John Charles and Mary Henrietta Knight; *m* 1933, Peggy Julia (*née* Carter); one *s* one *d*. *Educ:* Ashford Grammar Sch. Served War of 1939-45, RAF. British Mercedes Benz; Bowmaker Ltd; established Lombard Banking, 1947; Chm. Lombank Ltd, 1951-71 (Man. Dir, 1951-68). *Recreation:* Association football. *Address:* The White House, Sanderstead Village, Surrey. *T:* 01-657 2021. *Clubs:* Caledonian; Addington Golf.

LOMER, Dennis Roy; Member, Central Electricity Generating Board, since 1977; *b* 5 Oct. 1923; *s* of Bertie Cecil Lomer and Agnes Ellen Coward; *m* 1949, Audrey May Bick; one *s* one *d*. With Consulting Engineers, 1948-50; joined Electricity Supply Industry, 1952; Project Engr, Transmission Div., 1961; Asst Chief Transmission Engr, 1965; Generation Construction Div. (secondment at Dir level), 1972; Dep. Dir-Gen. (Projects), 1973; Dir-Gen., Transmission Div., 1975. MIEE. *Recreations:* golf, sailing. *Address:* Henley House, Heathfield Close, Woking, Surrey GU22 7JQ. *T:* Woking 64656. *Club:* West Hill Golf (Surrey).

LONDESBOROUGH, 9th Baron, *cr* 1850; **Richard John Denison;** *b* 2 July 1959; *s* of John Albert Lister, 8th Baron Londesborough, TD, AMICE, and of Elizabeth Ann, *d* of late Edward Little Sale, ICS; *S* father, 1968. *Educ:* Wellington College. *Address:* Dragon House, Edgioak, Redditch, Worcs.

LONDON, Bishop of, since 1973; **Rt. Rev. and Rt. Hon. Gerald Alexander Ellison,** PC 1973; Dean of the Chapels Royal, since 1973; Prelate of the Order of the British Empire, and of the Imperial Society of Knights Bachelor, since 1973; *b* 19 Aug. 1910; *s* of late Preb. John Henry Joshua Ellison, CVO, Chaplain in Ordinary to the King, Rector of St Michael's, Cornhill, and of Sara Dorothy Graham Ellison (*née* Crum); *m* 1947, Jane Elizabeth, *d* of late Brig. John Houghton Gibbon, DSO; one *s* two *d*. *Educ:* St George's, Windsor; Westminster Sch.; New Coll., Oxford (Hon. Fellow, 1974); Westcott House, Cambridge. Curate, Sherborne Abbey, 1935-37; Domestic Chaplain to the Bishop of Winchester, 1937-39; Chaplain RNVR, 1940-43 (despatches); Domestic Chaplain to Archbishop of York, 1943-46; Vicar, St Mark's Portsea, 1946-50; Hon. Chaplain to Archbishop of York, 1946-50; Canon of Portsmouth, 1950;

Examining Chaplain to Bishop of Portsmouth, 1949-50; Bishop Suffragan of Willesden, 1950-55; Bishop of Chester, 1955-73. Select Preacher: Oxford Univ., 1940, 1961, 1972; Cambridge Univ., 1957. Chaplain, Master Mariners' Company, 1946-73; Chaplain, Glass Sellers' Company, 1951-73; Chaplain and Sub-Prelate, Order of St John. Mem. Wolfenden Cttee on Sport, 1960; Chairman: Bd of Governors, Westfield Coll., Univ. of London, 1953-67; Council of King's Coll., London, 1973 (FKC, 1968); Archbishop's Commn on Women and Holy Orders, 1963-66; Mem., Archbishop's Commn on Church and State, 1967; President: Actors Church Union; Pedestrians Assoc. for Road Safety, 1964-75. Hon. Bencher Middle Temple, 1976. Chm., Oxford Soc. A Steward of Henley Regatta. *Publications:* The Churchman's Duty, 1957; The Anglican Communion, 1960. *Recreations:* oarsmanship, walking. *Address:* London House, 8 Barton Street, Westminster, SW1P 3RX. *Clubs:* Grillions; Leander.

LONDON, Archdeacon of; *see* Woodhouse, Ven. S. M. F.

LONDON, CENTRAL, Bishop in, (RC); *see* Konstant, Rt Rev. David.

LONDON, EAST, Bishop in, (RC); *see* Guazzelli, Rt Rev. Victor.

LONDON, NORTH, Bishop in, (RC); *see* Harvey, Rt Rev. Philip.

LONDON, WEST, Bishop in, (RC); *see* Mahon, Rt Rev. Gerald Thomas.

LONDONDERRY, 9th Marquess of, *cr* 1816; **Alexander Charles Robert Vane-Tempest-Stewart;** Baron Londonderry, 1789; Viscount Castlereagh, 1795; Earl of Londonderry, 1796; Baron Stewart, 1814; Earl Vane, Viscount Seaham, 1823; *b* 7 Sept. 1937; *s* of 8th Marquess of Londonderry and Romaine (*d* 1951), *er d* of Major Boyce Combe, Great Holt, Dockenfield, Surrey; *S* father 1955; *m* 1st, 1958, Nicolette (marr. diss. 1971), *d* of Michael Harrison, Netherhampton, near Salisbury, Wilts; two *d*; 2nd, 1972, Doreen Patricia Wells, *qv*; two *s*. *Educ:* Eton. *Heir: s* Viscount Castlereagh, *qv*. *Address:* Wynyard Park, Billingham, Cleveland TS22 5NF. *T:* Wolviston 317.

LONDONDERRY, Marchioness of; *see* Wells, Doreen P.

LONG, family name of Viscount Long.

LONG, 4th Viscount, *cr* 1921, of Wraxall; **Richard Gerard Long;** *b* 30 Jan. 1929; *s* of 3rd Viscount and Gwendolyn (*d* 1959), *d* of Thomas Reginald Hague Cook; *S* father, 1967; *m* 1957, Margaret Frances, *d* of Ninian B. Frazer; one *s* two *d*. *Educ:* Harrow. Wilts Regt, 1947-49. Vice-Pres. and formerly Vice-Chm., Wilts Royal British Legion; President: Wessex Fuchsia Gp; Bath Gliding Club. Vice-Pres., Bath Light Operatic Soc. *Heir: s* Hon. James Richard Long, *b* 31 Dec. 1960. *Address:* The Lodge, Coppice Hill, Bradford on Avon, Wilts. *Club:* Royal Over-Seas League.

LONG, Athelstan Charles Ethelwulf, CMG 1968; CBE 1964 (MBE 1959); Managing Director, Anegada Corporation Ltd, British Virgin Islands, since 1973; President, British Virgin Islands Conagada Hotels Ltd, since 1974; *b* 2 Jan. 1919; *s* of Arthur Leonard Long and Gabrielle Margaret Campbell (historical writer and novelist as Marjorie Bowen); *m* 1948, Edit Mäjken Zadie Harriet Krantz, *d* of late Erik Krantz, Stockholm; two *s*. *Educ:* Westminster Sch.; Brasenose Coll., Oxford. Served War of 1939-45: commnd into RA, 1940; seconded 7th (Bengal) Battery, 22nd Mountain Regt, IA, 1940; served Malaya; POW as Capt., 1942-45. Cadet, Burma Civil Service, 1946-48; Colonial Admin. Service (N Nigeria), 1948; Sen. District Officer, 1958; Resident, Zaria Province, 1959; Perm. Sec., Min. of Animal Health and Forestry, 1959; started new Min. of Information as Perm. Sec., 1960; Swaziland: appointed Govt Sec., 1961; Chief Sec., 1964; Leader of Govt business in Legislative Council and MEC, 1964-67; HM Dep. Comr, 1967-68; Administrator, later Governor, of the Cayman Is, 1968-71; Temp. Comr of Anguilla, March-July 1972; Admin. Sec., Inter-University Council, 1972-73. FRGS; FRAS. Chm. Governing Council, Waterford Sch., 1963-68. *Recreations:* travel, golf, reading. *Address:* Anegada Corporation Ltd, Box 437, Tortola, British Virgin Islands.

LONG, Ernest, CBE 1962; Member of Central Electricity Generating Board and of Electricity Council, 1957-62; *b* 15 Aug. 1898; *er s* of late John H. Long, Carlisle; *m* 1st, 1923, Dorothy Phœbe (*d* 1973), *y d* of late John Nichol, Carlisle; one *s*; 2nd, 1975, Cicely, *widow* of A. G. Buck. *Educ:* Carlisle Grammar Sch. Town Clerk's Dept and City Treasurer's Dept, Carlisle Corporation, 1915-25; articled to City Treasurer, Carlisle.

Served RFC and RAF, 1917-19. Chief Audit Asst, Croydon Corporation, 1928-30; Dep. City Treasurer, Coventry, 1930-35; Borough Treasurer: Luton, 1935-36, Finchley, 1936-42; City Treasurer, Newcastle upon Tyne, 1942-44; Secretary, Institute of Municipal Treasurers and Accountants, 1944-48 (Hon. Fellow, and Collins Gold Medallist, 1927); Dep. Chief Accountant, British Electricity Authority, 1948-51; Secretary, British (later Central) Electricity Authority, 1951-57. Fellow, Member of Council (1947-75), President 1960, Inst. of Chartered Secretaries and Administrators (formerly Chartered Inst. of Secretaries). Member: Colonial Local Government Advisory Panel, 1948-53; Departmental Cttee on Legal Aid in Criminal Proceedings, 1964-66; Chartered Accountant (Society Gold Medallist, 1924). *Publications:* various articles and lectures on accountancy and public administration. *Recreations:* golf, crosswords. *Address:* 2 Strawberry Bank, Scotby, Carlisle, Cumbria CA4 8BP. *T:* Scotby 267. *Club:* Border (Carlisle).

LONG, Air Vice-Marshal Francis William, CB 1946; DL; *b* 1899; *s* of Rev. F. P. Long, Oxford; *m* 1921, Doreen Langley, *d* of Rev. F. L. Appleford; one *d*. *Educ:* Lancing Coll. Joined RAF 1918; member Schneider Trophy Team, 1931. AOC No 23 Gp, Flying Training Command, 1952-53; retd, 1953. DL Herts, 1963. *Address:* 19 Marina Court, Douglas Avenue, Exmouth, Devon. *T:* Exmouth 6320.

LONG, Gerald; Chief Executive, Reuters, since 1963 (General Manager, 1963-73; Managing Director, since 1973); Chairman, Visnews Ltd, since 1968; Chairman of Executive Committee, International Institute of Communications Ltd, since 1973; *b* 22 Aug. 1923; *o s* of Fred Harold Long and Sabina Long (*née* Walsh); *m* 1951, Anne Hamilton Walker; two *s* three *d*. *Educ:* St Peter's Sch., York; Emmanuel Coll., Cambridge. Army Service, 1943-47. Joined Reuters, 1948; served as Reuter correspondent in Germany, France and Turkey, 1950-60; Asst General Manager, 1960. *Recreation:* cooking. *Address:* 37 Wood Lane, Highgate, N6 5UD. *T:* 01-340 4543.

LONG, Hubert Arthur, CBE 1970; Deputy Secretary, Exchequer and Audit Department, 1963-73; *b* 21 Jan. 1912; *s* of Arthur Albert Long; *m* 1937, Mary Louise Parker; three *s*. *Educ:* Taunton's Sch., Southampton. Entered Exchequer and Audit Department, 1930. *Address:* 48 Hayes Lane, Bromley, Kent. *T:* 01-460 4251.

LONG, Ven. John Sanderson, MA; Archdeacon of Ely, Hon. Canon of Ely and Rector of St Botolph's, Cambridge, since 1970; *b* 21 July 1913; *s* of late Rev. Guy Stephenson Long and Ivy Marion Long; *m* 1948, Rosamond Mary, *d* of Arthur Temple Forman; one *s* three *d*. *Educ:* St Edmund's Sch., Canterbury; Queens' Coll., Cambridge; Cuddesdon Theological Coll. Deacon, 1936; Priest, 1937; Curate, St Mary and St Eanswythe, Folkestone, 1936-41. Chaplain, RNVR, 1941-46. Curate, St Peter-in-Thanet, 1946; Domestic Chaplain to the Archbishop of Canterbury, 1946-53; Vicar of: Bearsted, 1953-59; Petersfield with Sheet, 1959-70; Rural Dean of Petersfield, 1962-70. *Recreations:* walking, gardening. *Address:* St Botolph's Rectory, Summerfield, Cambridge CB3 9HE. *T:* Cambridge 50684.

LONG, Olivier; Ambassador; Director-General, GATT, since 1968; *b* 1915; *s* of Dr Edouard Long and Dr Marie Landry; *m* 1946, Francine Roels; one *s* two *d*. *Educ:* Univ. de Paris, Faculté de Droit et Ecole des Sciences Politiques; Univ. de Genève. PhD Law, 1938; Rockefeller Foundn Fellow, 1938-39; PhD Pol. Sc., 1943. Swiss Armed Forces, 1939-43; International Red Cross, 1943-46; Swiss Foreign Affairs Dept, Berne, 1946-49; Washington Embassy, 1949-54; Govt Delegate for Trade Agreements, 1955-66; Head of Swiss Delegn to EFTA, 1960-66; Ambassador to UK and Malta, 1967-68. Prof., Graduate Inst. of Internat. Studies, Geneva, 1962-. *Publications:* several on political sciences and trade policies. *Address:* General Agreement on Tariffs and Trade, Villa le Bocage, Palais des Nations, CH-1211 Geneva 10, Switzerland. *T:* (022) 34-60-11.

LONG, Sir Ronald, Kt 1964; Solicitor; *b* 5 Sept. 1902; *s* of Sydney Richard and Kate Long; *m* 1931, Muriel Annie Harper; one *s* two *d*. *Educ:* Earls Colne Grammar Sch.; The School, Stamford, Lincs. President, The Law Society, 1963-64. Chm., Stansted Airport Consultative Cttee. *Recreations:* fishing, gardening. *Address:* Ayletts Farm, Halstead, Essex. *T:* Halstead 2072.

LONG, Captain Rt. Hon. William Joseph, PC (N Ireland) 1966; JP; Minister of Education, Northern Ireland, 1969-72; MP (Unionist) Ards, Parliament of Northern Ireland, 1962-72; *b* 23 April 1922; *s* of James William Long and Frederica (Walker); *m* 1942, Dr Elizabeth Doreen Mercer; one *s*. *Educ:* Friends' Sch., Great Ayton, Yorks; Edinburgh Univ.; RMC, Sandhurst.

Served Royal Inniskilling Fusiliers, 1940-48. Secretary: NI Marriage Guidance Council, 1948-51; NI Chest and Heart Assoc., 1951-62. Parliamentary Secretary, Min. of Agriculture, NI, 1964-66; Sen. Parliamentary Secretary, Min. of Development, NI, Jan.-Oct. 1966; Minister of Educn, 1966-68; Minister of Home Affairs, Dec. 1968-March 1969; Minister of Develt, March 1969-May 1969. *Recreations:* cricket, horticulture, angling, sailing, model engineering, aviation. *Address:* Lisvarna, Warren Road, Donaghadee, Co. Down. *T:* Donaghadee 2538.

LONGBOTHAM, Samuel; Lord-Lieutenant of the Western Isles, since 1975; *b* Elgin, Morayshire, 19 March 1908; *s* of George Longbotham and Elizabeth Longbotham (*née* Monks); *m* 1941, Elizabeth Rae, *d* of Donald Davidson, Glasgow; two *s* one *d*. *Educ:* Elgin. Served War, 1940-46: with RA and Intelligence Corps: commissioned, 1944. Major, Lovat Scouts TA (RA), 1952-60; Major, North Highland ACF, 1968-75. Man. Dir, Stornoway Gazette, Stornoway, Isle of Lewis. DL Ross and Cromarty, 1964. *Recreations:* angling, gardening, walking, reading, family life. *Address:* 25 Lewis Street, Stornoway, Isle of Lewis, Scotland. *T:* Stornoway 2519.

LONGBOTTOM, Charles Brooke; *b* 22 July 1930; *s* of late William Ewart Longbottom, Forest Hill, Worksop; *m* 1962, Anita, *d* of G. Trapani, Sorrento, Italy, and Mrs Basil Mavroleon, 49 Grosvenor Square, W1; two *d*. *Educ:* Uppingham. Contested (C) Stockton-on-Tees, 1955; MP (C) York, 1959-66; Parly Private Secretary to Mr Iain Macleod, Leader of the House, 1961-63. Barrister, Inner Temple, 1958; Chairman: Austin & Pickersgill, Shipbuilders, Sunderland, 1966-72; A&P Appledore International Ltd; Seascope Holdings Ltd; Seascope Shipbrokeers Ltd; Director: Seascope Ltd; Seascope Insurance Services Ltd.; Seascope Underwriting Agencies Ltd; Chairman, Ariel Foundation, 1960-. Member: General Advisory Council, BBC, 1965-75; Community Relations Commn, 1968-70. Member of Lloyds. *Recreations:* shooting, golf and racing. *Address:* 66 Kingston House North, SW7. *Clubs:* White's, Carlton; Yorkshire (York).

LONGDEN, Sir Gilbert (James Morley), Kt 1972; MBE 1944; MA (Cantab), LLB; *b* 16 April 1902; *e s* of late Lieut-Colonel James Morley Longden, Castle Eden, Co. Durham, and of late Kathleen, *d* of George Blacker Morgan, JP; unmarried. *Educ:* Haileybury; Emmanuel Coll., Cambridge. Secretary ICI (India) Ltd, 1930-36; travelled throughout Asia (Middle and Far East) and in North and South America. Student at University of Paris, 1937. Called up from AOER into DLI, 1940; served with 2nd and 36th Divisions in Burma campaigns (MBE (mil.)). Adopted Parliamentary Candidate for Morpeth, 1938; contested (C) Morpeth, 1945; MP (C) SW Herts, 1950-Feb. 1974. UK Representative to Council of Europe, 1953-54; United Kingdom Delegate to 12th and 13th Sessions of United Nations; Past Chairman: Conservative Gp for Europe; Great Britain-East Europe Centre. Vice-Chm., British Council. *Publications:* A Conservative Philosophy, 1947; and (jointly): One Nation, 1950; Change is our Ally, 1954; A Responsible Society, 1959; One Europe, 1969. *Recreations:* reading, writing, gardening. *Address:* 89 Cornwall Gardens, SW7 4AX. *T:* 01-584 5666. *Clubs:* Travellers', Hurlingham.

LONGDEN, Maj.-General Harry Leicester, CB 1947; CBE 1944 (OBE 1940); late The Dorsetshire Regt; psc; *b* 12 Dec. 1900. 2nd Lieut Dorset Regt, 1919; Major, 1938. Served War of 1939-45, France and North-West Europe (despatches, OBE, CBE, CB). Temp. Maj.-Gen., 1946; retired pay, 1948.

LONGDEN, Henry Alfred, CEng, FICE, FIMinE, MIMM; FGS; Director, Trafalgar House Investments Ltd, 1970-76; *b* 8 Sept. 1909; *s* of late Geoffrey Appleby Longden and late Marjorie Mullins; *m* 1935, Ruth, *d* of Arthur Gilliat, Leeds; one *s* four *d*. *Educ:* Oundle; Birmingham Univ. (BSc Hons). Served in Glass Houghton and Pontefract Collieries, 1930; Asst Gen. Manager, Stanton Ironworks Co., 1935; Gen. Manager, Briggs Colliers Ltd, 1940; Director: Blackwell Colliery Co., 1940; Briggs Collieries Co., 1941; New Hucknall Colliery Co., 1941; Area Gen. Manager, 1947, and Production Dir, 1948, NE Div., NCB; Dir-Gen., Production, NCB, 1955; Chm., W Midlands Div., NCB, 1960; Chm. and Chief Exec., Cementation Co. Ltd, 1963-70 (Dep. Chm. and Chief Exec, 1961-63). President: Instn of Mining Engineers, 1958; Engineering Industries Assoc., 1965-71; Member: Engineering Industry Trg Bd, 1967-70; Confedn of British Industry, 1968. Fellow, Fellowship of Engineering, 1977. *Publication:* Cadman Memorial Lecture, 1958. *Recreations:* Rugby football, cricket, tennis, shooting, fishing, sailing. *Address:* Raeburn, Northdown Road, Woldingham, Surrey. *T:* Woldingham 2245. *Club:* Brooks's.

LONGE, Desmond Evelyn, MC 1944; DL; President and Chairman, Norwich Union Insurance Group, 1964 (Vice-President, 1963); Chairman: Norwich Union Life Insurance Society, 1964; Norwich Union Fire Insurance Society Ltd, 1964; Maritime Insurance Co. Ltd, 1968; Scottish Union and National Insurance Co., 1968; East Coast Grain Ltd, 1962; Napak Ltd, 1969; D. E. Longe & Co. Ltd, 1962; Norwich Winterthur Holdings Ltd, 1976; *b* 8 Aug. 1914; *y s* of late Rev. John Charles Longe, MA, Spixworth Park, Norfolk; *m* 1944, Isla (*née* Bell); one *s* one *d*. *Educ:* Woodbridge Sch., Suffolk. Director: Eastern Counties Newspapers Ltd; Anglia TV Ltd. Member: BR Eastern Region Bd, 1969-70; BR London Midland Region Bd, 1971-74; (and Dep. Chm.) BR London and SE Region Bd, 1975-77. Mem., E Anglia Econ. Planning Council, 1965-68. A Church Commissioner, 1970-76. DL Norfolk, 1971; High Sheriff, Norfolk, 1975. Croix de Guerre avec Palme (French), 1944. *Recreations:* travel, hunting, fishing. *Address:* Woodton Grange, Bungay, Suffolk. *T:* Woodton 260. *Clubs:* Special Forces, MCC; Norfolk County (Norwich).

LONGFORD, 7th Earl of, *cr* 1785, **Francis Aungier Pakenham,** KG 1971; PC 1948; Baron Longford, 1759; Baron Silchester (UK), 1821; Baron Pakenham (UK), 1945; Leader of the House of Lords, 1964-68; Lord Privy Seal, 1966-68; *b* 5 Dec. 1905; 2nd *s* of 5th Earl of Longford, KP, MVO; *S* brother (6th Earl) 1961; *m* 1931, Elizabeth (*see* Countess of Longford); four *s* three *d* (and one *d* decd). *Educ:* Eton; New Coll., Oxford, MA. 1st Class in Modern Greats, 1927. Tutor, University Tutorial Courses, Stoke-on-Trent, 1929-31; Cons. Party Economic Res. Dept, 1930-32. Christ Church, Oxford: Lecturer in Politics, 1932; Student in Politics, 1934-46, and 1952-64. Prospective Parliamentary Labour Candidate for Oxford City, 1938. Enlisted Oxford and Bucks LI (TA), May 1939; resigned commission on account of ill-health, 1940. Personal assistant to Sir William Beveridge, 1941-44; a Lord-in-Waiting to the King, 1945-46; Parliamentary Under-Secretary of State, War Office, 1946-47; Chancellor of the Duchy of Lancaster, 1947-48; Minister of Civil Aviation, 1948-51; First Lord of the Admiralty, May-Oct. 1951; Lord Privy Seal, 1964-65; Secretary of State for the Colonies, 1965-66. Chairman: The National Bank Ltd, 1955-63; Sidgwick and Jackson, 1970-. Chm., Nat. Youth Employment Council, 1968-71; Joint Founder: New Horizon Youth Centre, 1964; New Bridge for Ex-Prisoners, 1956. *Publications:* Peace by Ordeal (The Anglo-Irish Treaty of 1921), 1935 (repr. 1972); (autobiog.) Born to Believe, 1953; (with Roger Opie), Causes of Crime, 1958; The Idea of Punishment, 1961; (autobiog.) Five Lives, 1964; Humility, 1969; (with Thomas P. O'Neill) Eamon De Valera, 1970; (autobiog.) The Grain of Wheat, 1974; Abraham Lincoln, 1974; Jesus Christ, 1974; Kennedy, 1976. *Heir:* *s* Hon. Thomas Frank Dermot Pakenham (does not use title, Lord Silchester) [*b* 14 Aug. 1933; *m* 1964, Valerie, *y d* of McNair Scott, Huish House, Old Basing, Hants; two *s* two *d*. *Educ:* Ampleforth; Magdalen Coll., Oxford]. *Address:* Bernhurst, Hurst Green, East Sussex. *T:* Hurst Green 248; 18 Chesil Court, Chelsea Manor Street, SW3. *T:* 01-352 7794. *Club:* Garrick.
See also Lady Antonia Fraser, A. D. Powell.

LONGFORD, Countess of; Elizabeth Pakenham, CBE 1974; *b* 30 Aug. 1906; *d* of late N. B. Harman, FRCS, 108 Harley Street, W1, and of Katherine (*née* Chamberlain); *m* 1931, Hon. F. A. Pakenham (*see* 7th Earl of Longford); four *s* three *d* (and one *d* decd). *Educ:* Headington Sch., Oxford; Lady Margaret Hall, Oxford (MA). Lectr for WEA and Univ. Extension Lectr, 1929-35. Contested (Lab) Cheltenham, 1935, Oxford, 1950; candidate for King's Norton, Birmingham, 1933-43. Mem., Rent Tribunal, Paddington and St Pancras, 1947-54; Trustee, National Portrait Gall., 1968-; Mem. Adv. Council, V&A Museum, 1969-75. Hon. DLitt Sussex 1970. *Publications:* (as Elizabeth Pakenham): Points for Parents, 1956; Catholic Approaches (ed), 1959; Jameson's Raid, 1960; weekly articles for Daily Express, 1954-56; (as Elizabeth Longford) Victoria RI, 1964 (James Tait Black Memorial Prize for Non-Fiction, 1964); Wellington: Years of the Sword, 1969 (Yorkshire Post Prize); Wellington: Pillar of State, 1972; The Royal House of Windsor, 1974; Churchill, 1974; Byron's Greece, 1975; Life of Byron, 1976; contrib. Burke's Guide to the Royal Family, 1973; weekly articles for Sunday Times, 1961-63. *Recreations:* gardening, reading. *Address:* Bernhurst, Hurst Green, East Sussex. *T:* Hurst Green 248; 18 Chesil Court, Chelsea Manor Street, SW3. *T:* 01-352 7794.
See also Lady Antonia Fraser.

LONGFORD, Elizabeth; *see* Longford, Countess of.

LONGHURST, Henry Carpenter, CBE 1972; journalist, author, broadcaster, etc; *b* 18 March 1909; *s* of Henry William Longhurst, JP, and Mrs Constance Longhurst, Bedford; *m* 1938,

Claudine Marie Sier; one *s* one *d. Educ:* Charterhouse (scholar); Clare Coll., Cambridge (BA Econ). Captain Cambridge Univ. Golf team, 1930 (and in USA 1931). Journalist: Sunday Times, etc since 1932. MP (Nat. C) Acton Division of Middlesex, 1943-45. Journalist of the Year Special Award, 1969; Walter Hagen Award for contrib. to Anglo-American golf relations, 1973. *Publications:* Candid Caddies, 1936; Golf, 1937; It Was Good While it Lasted, 1941; I Wouldn't Have Missed It, 1946; You Never Know Till You Get There, 1950; Golf Mixture, 1952; Round in Sixty-Eight, 1953; The Borneo Story, 1957; Adventure in Oil, 1959; Spice of Life, 1963; Only on Sundays, 1964; Never on Weekdays, 1968; My Life and Soft Times (autobiog.), 1971. *Recreations:* fishing, travel. *Address:* Clayton Windmills, Hassocks, Sussex. *Clubs:* Bath, Garrick; (Hon. Life Mem.) Royal and Ancient (St Andrews).

LONGLAND, Cedric James, MVO 1949; Surgeon, Glasgow Royal Infirmary, 1954-77; *b* 30 Sept. 1914; *s* of Frank Longland; *m* 1945, Helen Mary Cripps; three *d. Educ:* Monkton Combe Sch. MB, BS (Hons in Medicine) London, 1937; House Surgeon and Demonstrator of Pathology, St Bartholomew's Hosp.; FRCS, 1939; MS London, 1949. 1 Airborne Division; Lieut RAMC 1942, Temp. Major, RAMC, 1943; SMO Bermuda Command, 1945; First Assistant, Surgical Professorial Unit, St Bartholomew's Hospital, 1947; Assistant Surgical Professorial Unit, University College Hospital, 1951. Bronze Cross (Holland), 1945. *Publications:* articles in Lancet and British Journal of Surgery. *Address:* 11 Campbell Drive, Bearsden, Dunbartonshire. *T:* 041-942 0798.

LONGLAND, Sir David Walter, Kt 1977; CMG 1973; Parliamentary Commissioner for Administrative Investigations, Queensland, since 1974; *b* 1 June 1909; 2nd *s* of David Longland and Mary McGriskin; *m* 1935, Ada Elizabeth Bowness; one *s* one *d. Educ:* Queensland Govt Primary and Secondary Schs. Queensland Educn Dept, High Sch. teaching, 1926. Appointed: to State Treasury Dept, 1938; Premier's Dept, 1939; (re-apptd) Treasury Dept, 1940; (re-apptd) Premier's Dept, 1942; Officer in Charge of Migration for Qld, 1946; Under-Sec., Dept of Works and Housing, 1957; Chm., Public Service Bd, Qld, 1969. FASA, FAIM, FRIPA. *Recreations:* tennis, surfing, reading, gardening. *Address:* 88 Lloyd Street, Camp Hill, Queensland 4152, Australia. *T:* 398-1152. *Club:* Rotary (Brisbane).

LONGLAND, Sir Jack, (Sir John Laurence), Kt 1970; Director of Education, Derbyshire, 1949-70; *b* 26 June 1905; *e s* of late Rev. E. H. Longland and late Emily, *e d* of Sir James Crockett; *m* 1934, Margaret Lowrey, *y d* of late Arthur Harrison, Elvet Garth, Durham; two *s* two *d. Educ:* King's Sch., Worcester; Jesus Coll., Cambridge (Rustat Exhibitioner and Scholar). 2nd Class, 1st Part Classical Tripos, 1925; 1st Class, 1st Division, Historical Tripos, Part II, 1926; 1st Class with special distinction, English Tripos, 1927; Charles Kingsley Bye-Fellow at Magdalene Coll., Cambridge, 1927-29; Austausch-student, Königsberg Univ., 1929-30; Lectr in English at Durham Univ., 1930-36; Dir Community Service Council for Durham County, 1937-40; Regional Officer of Nat. Council of Social Service, 1939-40; Dep. Educn Officer, Herts, 1940-42; County Educn Officer, Dorset CC, 1942-49. Athletic Blue; Pres., Cambridge Univ. Mountaineering Club, 1926-27; Member: Mount Everest Expedn, 1933; British East Greenland Expedn, 1935; Pres., Climbers' Club, 1945-48 and Hon. Mem., 1964; Pres., Alpine Club, 1973-76 (Vice-Pres., 1960-61); Member: Colonial Office Social Welfare Adv. Cttee, 1942-48; Develt Commn, 1948-; Adv. Cttee for Educn in RAF, 1950-57; Adv. Cttee for Educn in Germany, 1950-57; Central Adv. Council for Educn in England and Wales, 1948-51; Nat. Adv. Council on the Training and Supply of Teachers, 1951-; Children's Adv. Cttee of the ITA, 1956-60; Wolfenden Cttee on Sport, 1958-60; Outward Bound Trust Council, 1962-73; Central Council of Physical Recreation Council and Exec., 1961-72; Electricity Supply Industry Training Bd, 1965-66; Royal Commn on Local Govt, 1966-69; The Sports Council, 1966-74 (Vice-Chm. 1971-74); Countryside Commn, 1969-74; Commn on Mining and the Environment, 1971-72; Water Space Amenity Commn, 1973-76; President: Assoc. of Educn Officers, 1960-61; British Mountaineering Council, 1962-65; Chairman: Mountain Leadership Training Bd, 1965-; Council for Environmental Educn, 1968-75. *Publications:* literary and mountaineering articles in various books and journals. *Recreations:* mountain climbing and walking. *Address:* Bridgeway, Bakewell, Derbyshire. *T:* Bakewell 2252. *Clubs:* Savile, Alpine, Achilles.

LONGLAND, Sir John Laurence; see Longland, Sir Jack.

LONGLEY, Sir Norman, Kt 1966; CBE; DL; retired as Chairman, James Longley (Holdings) Ltd, Building and Civil Engineering Contractors, Crawley, Sussex; *b* 14 Oct. 1900; *s* of Charles John Longley and Anna Gibson Marchant; *m* 1925, Dorothy Lilian Baker; two *s* one *d. Educ:* Clifton. West Sussex County Council, 1945-61, Alderman 1957-61. President: National Federation of Building Trades Employers, 1950; International Federation of Building and Public Works Contractors, 1955-57. Hon. Fellow, Institute of Builders. DL West Sussex, 1975. Hon. DSc Heriot-Watt, 1968. Coronation Medal, 1953. *Recreation:* horticulture. *Address:* The Beeches, Crawley, Sussex. *T:* Crawley 20253. *Club:* Royal Automobile.

LONGLEY-COOK, Vice-Adm. Eric William, CB 1950; CBE 1943; DSO 1945; *b* 6 Oct. 1898; *s* of late Herbert William Cook and late Alice Longley; *m* 1st, 1920, Helga Mayre Lowles (*d* 1962); one *d*; 2nd, 1965, Elizabeth, *widow* of Sir Ulick Temple Blake, 16th Baronet. *Educ:* Osborne and Dartmouth. Served at sea European War, 1914-18 and War of 1939-45 (despatches thrice). Rear-Adm., 1948; Vice-Adm., 1951; Dir of Naval Intelligence, 1948-51; retired, 1951. Formerly: Man. Dir, Fairfield Shipbuilding & Engineering Co., London; Dir, Lithgow Group; Member: Cttee, Lloyd's Register; Amer. Bureau of Ships; a Gen. Comr of Income Tax. Légion d'Honneur and Croix de Guerre, 1943. *Recreations:* golf, gardening. *Address:* Fletcher's, West Lavant, near Chichester, West Sussex. *Club:* Naval and Military.

LONGMORE, William James Maitland, CBE 1972; Director: Lloyds Bank International Ltd, 1971-75; Bank of London & South America Ltd, 1960-75; *b* 6 May 1919; 2nd *s* of late Air Chief Marshal Sir Arthur Murray Longmore, GCB, DSO; *m* 1941, Jean, *d* of 2nd Baron Forres of Glenogil; three *d. Educ:* Eton Coll. Royal Air Force, 1938-46 (Wing Comdr). Balfour, Williamson & Co. Ltd, 1946-75 (Chm., 1967-75). Vice-Chm., 1966-70, Chm., 1970-71, BNEC for Latin America. *Recreations:* shooting, sailing. *Address:* Strete End House, Bishop's Waltham, Hants SO3 1FS. *T:* Bishop's Waltham 2794. *Club:* Royal Yacht Squadron.

LONGRIGG, John Stephen, CMG 1973; OBE 1964; HM Diplomatic Service; Counsellor, Foreign and Commonwealth Office, since 1976; *b* 1 Oct. 1923; *s* of Brig. Stephen Hemsley Longrigg, *qv*; *m* 1st, 1953, Lydia Meynell (marr. diss. 1965); one *s* one *d*; 2nd, 1966, Ann O'Reilly; one *s. Educ:* Rugby Sch.; Magdalen Coll., Oxford (BA). War Service, Rifle Bde, 1942-45 (despatches). FO, 1948; Paris, 1948; Baghdad, 1951; FO, 1953; Berlin, 1955; Cabinet Office, 1957; FO, 1958; Dakar, 1960; Johannesburg, 1962; Pretoria, 1962; Washington, 1964; FO, 1965-67; Bahrain, 1967-69; FCO, 1969-73; seconded to HQ British Forces, Hong Kong, 1974-76. *Recreation:* golf. *Address:* 2 The Cedars, 3 Westcombe Park Road, Blackheath, SE3. *T:* 01-692 0694. *Clubs:* Reform; Royal Blackheath Golf.
See also R . E . Longrigg .

LONGRIGG, Roger Erskine; author; *b* 1 May 1929; *s* of Brig. S. H. Longrigg, *qv*; *m* 1957, Jane Chichester; three *d . Educ:* Bryanston Sch.; Magdalen Coll., Oxford (BA Hons Mod. Hist.). *Publications:* A High Pitched Buzz, 1956; Switchboard, 1957; Wrong Number, 1959; Daughters of Mulberry, 1961; The Paper Boats, 1963; The Artless Gambler, 1964; Love among the Bottles, 1967; The Sun on the Water, 1969; The Desperate Criminals, 1971; The History of Horse Racing, 1972; The Jevington System, 1973; Their Pleasing Sport, 1975; The Turf, 1975; The History of Foxhunting, 1975; The Babe in the Wood, 1976; The English Squire and his Sport, 1977. *Recreations:* most rural diversions; a few urban ones. *Address:* Orchard House, Crookham, Hants. *T:* Aldershot 850333. *Clubs:* Brooks's, Pratt's.

LONGRIGG, Brigadier Stephen Hemsley, OBE 1927; DLitt (Oxon); *b* 7 Aug. 1893; *s* of W. G. Hemsley Longrigg; *m* 1922, Florence (*d* 1976), *d* of Henry Aitken Anderson, CSI, CIE; two *s* one *d. Educ:* Highgate Sch.; Oriel Coll., Oxford. Served Royal Warwickshire Regt, European War and after, 1914-21; Major 1918 (despatches twice). Govt of Iraq, 1918-31; Inspector-Gen. of Revenue, 1927-31; Iraq Petroleum Co., 1931-51; War of 1939-45: Gen. Staff, GHQ, Cairo, 1940-41; Chief Administrator of Eritrea, 1942-44, Brigadier, 1940-45 (despatches). Governor of Highgate Sch., 1946, Chairman of Governors, 1954-65. Chairman, British Petroleum Employers' Cttee for International Labour Affairs, 1946-51. Vice-President, Royal Central Asian Society; Member Council, Royal Institute of International Affairs, 1956-64; Lecture tours: Scandinavia, 1952; Germany, 1954; US and Canada, 1956 and annually, 1959-66. Visiting Professor: Columbia Univ., Summer, 1966; University of Colorado, 1967. Order of the Rafidain (Iraq), 1931; Lawrence of Arabia Medallist, 1962; Sir Richard Burton Memorial Medallist, 1969. *Publications:* Four Centuries of Modern Iraq, 1925; Short History of Eritrea, 1945 (repr. USA, 1975); Iraq, 1900 to 1950, 1953; Oil in the Middle East, 1954 (3rd edn 1968);

Syria and Lebanon under French Mandate, 1958; (in collaboration) Iraq, 1958; The Middle East, a Social Geography, 1963 (2nd edn 1970). *Address:* 34 Albury Park, Albury, near Guildford, Surrey. *T:* Guildford 6413298. *Clubs:* Athenæum, East India, Sports and Public Schools.
See also J. S. Longrigg, R . E . Longrigg .

LONGSTRETH THOMPSON, Francis Michael; *see* Thompson, F. M. L.

LONGUET-HIGGINS, Prof. Hugh Christopher, FRS 1958; DPhil (Oxon); Royal Society Research Professor, University of Sussex, since 1974; *b* 11 April 1923; *e s* of late Rev. H. H. L. Longuet-Higgins. *Educ:* Winchester (schol.); Balliol Coll., Oxford (schol., MA). Research Fellow of Balliol Coll., 1946-48; Lecturer and Reader in Theoretical Chemistry, University of Manchester, 1949-52; Prof. of Theoretical Physics, King's Coll., University of London, 1952-54; FRSE; John Humphrey Plummer Professor of Theoretical Chemistry, University of Cambridge, 1954-67; Royal Soc. Res. Prof., Univ. of Edinburgh, 1968-74; Fellow of Corpus Christi Coll., 1954-67, Life Fellow 1968; Hon. Fellow: Balliol Coll., Oxford, 1969; Wolfson Coll., Cambridge, 1977. Warden, Leckhampton House, 1961-67; Harrison Memorial Prizeman (Chemical Society), 1950. Editor of Molecular Physics, 1958-61. Foreign Associate, US National Academy of Sciences, 1968. *Publications:* co-author, The Nature of Mind (Gifford Lectures), 1972; papers on theoretical physics, chemistry and biology in scientific journals. *Recreations:* music and arguing. *Address:* Centre for Research on Perception and Cognition, Laboratory of Experimental Psychology, University of Sussex, Falmer, Brighton BN1 9QY.

LONGUET-HIGGINS, Michael Selwyn, FRS 1963; Royal Society Research Professor, University of Cambridge, since 1969; *b* 8 Dec. 1925; *s* of late Henry Hugh Longuet and Albinia Cecil Longuet-Higgins; *m* 1958, Joan Redmayne Tattersall; two *s* two *d. Educ:* Winchester Coll. (Schol.); Trinity Coll., Cambridge (Schol.). (BA). Admiralty Research Lab., Teddington, 1945-48; Res. Student, Cambridge, 1948-51; PhD Cambridge, 1951; Rayleigh Prize, 1951; Commonwealth Fund Fellowship, 1951-52; Res. Fellow, Trinity Coll., Cambridge, 1951-55. Nat. Inst. of Oceanography, 1954-69. Visiting Professor: MIT, 1958; Institute of Geophysics, University of California, 1961-62; Univ. of Adelaide, 1964. Prof. of Oceanography, Oregon State Univ., 1967-69. *Publications:* papers in applied mathematics, esp. seismology and physical oceanography, dynamics of sea waves and currents, etc. *Recreations:* music, gardening, mathematical toys. *Address:* Gage Farm, Comberton, Cambridge CB3 7DH.

LONGWORTH, Sir Fred, Kt 1966; DL; retired Trade Union Secretary; Vice-Chairman, Lancashire County Council, 1967-73 (Chairman, 1964-67); *b* 15 Feb. 1890; *s* of James and Cresina Longworth; *m* 1916, Mary Smith. *Educ:* Tyldesley Upper George Street County Sch. Mem., Tyldesley UDC, 1940-70 (Chm., 1948-49, 1961-62); Mem., Lancs CC, 1946-73; CA, 1952; Mem., Educn Cttee, County Councils Assoc.; Mem., Council and Court, Lancaster Univ. DL Lancs 1968. *Recreations:* reading, music, politics, education. *Address:* 30 Crawford Avenue, Tyldesley, near Manchester. *T:* Atherton 2906.

LONGWORTH, Ian Heaps, PhD; FSA; Keeper of Prehistoric and Romano-British Antiquities, British Museum, since 1973; *b* 29 Sept. 1935; *yr s* of late Joseph Longworth and Alice (*née* Heaps); *m* 1967, Clare Marian Titford; one *s. Educ:* King Edward VII, Lytham; Peterhouse, Cambridge. Open and Sen. Scholar, Matthew Wren Student, 1957, MA, PhD, Cantab. Temp. Asst Keeper, Nat. Museum of Antiquities of Scotland, 1962-63; Asst Keeper, Dept of British and Medieval Antiquities, Brit. Mus., 1963-69; Asst Keeper, Dept of Prehistoric and Romano-British Antiquities, Brit. Mus., 1969-73. Mem., Ancient Monuments Bd for England, 1977-. Hon. Sec., Prehistoric Soc., 1966-74, Vice-Pres., 1976-; Sec., Soc. of Antiquaries of London, 1974-. *Publications:* Yorkshire (Regional Archaeologies Series), 1965; (with G. J. Wainwright) Durrington Walls—excavations 1966-68, 1971; articles in various learned jls on topics of prehistory. *Address:* 2 Hurst View Road, South Croydon, Surrey CR2 7AG. *T:* 01-688 4960. *Club:* MCC.

LONSDALE, 7th Earl of (UK), *cr* 1807; **James Hugh William Lowther,** Viscount and Baron Lowther, 1797; Bt 1764; *b* 3 Nov. 1922; *er s* of Anthony Edward, Viscount Lowther (*d* 1949), and Muriel Frances, Viscountess Lowther (*d* 1968), 2nd *d* of late Sir George Farrar, Bt, DSO, and Lady Farrar; *S* grandfather, 1953; *m* 1975, Caroline, *y d* of Sir Gerald Ley, Bt, *qv* ; one *d* (and three *s* three *d* of previous marriages). *Educ:* Eton. Armed Forces, 1941-46; RAC and East Riding Yeo. (despatches, Capt.).

Structural engineering, 1947-50. Farmer, forester, and director of associated and local companies in Cumbria; Chairman: Lakeland Investments Ltd and of nine subsid. or associated cos; Plan Invest Gp Ltd; Director: Cannon Assurance Ltd; Border TV; North Housing Group Ltd, and of subsid. and associated concerns. Chm., Northern Adv. Council for Sport and Recreation, 1966-71; Member: Northern Region Economic Planning Council, 1964-72; Court of Newcastle Univ.; Sports Council, 1971-74; English Tourist Bd, 1971-75; TGO (Pres., 1971-73); Forestry Cttee for GB (Chm., 1974-76); President: NW Area British Legion, 1961-73; NW Div. YMCA, 1962-72; Cumberland and Westmorland NPFA; British Deer Soc., 1963-70; Lake District Naturalists' Trust, 1963-73; local agricultural societies, etc. *Heir: s* Viscount Lowther, *qv. Address:* Askham Hall, Penrith, Cumbria. *T:* Hackthorpe 208. *Clubs:* Carlton, Brooks's, National Sporting; Northern Counties (Newcastle upon Tyne).

LONSDALE, Maj.-Gen. Errol Henry Gerrard, CB 1969; MBE 1942; Transport Officer-in-Chief (Army) 1966-69; *b* 26 Feb. 1913; 2nd *s* of Rev. W. H. M. Lonsdale, Arlaw Banks, Barnard Castle; *m* 1944, Muriel Allison, *d* of E. R. Payne, Mugswell, Chipstead; one *s* one *d. Educ:* Westminster Sch.; St Catharine's Coll., Cambridge (MA). 2nd Lt, RASC, 1934; Bt Lt-Col 1952; Col 1957; Brig. 1961; Maj.-Gen. 1966. Sudan Defence Force, 1938-43 (despatches); CRASC, 16 Airborne Div., 1947-48; AA & QMG, War Office, 1951-53; CRASC, 1st Commonwealth Div. Korea, 1953-54; 1st Federal Div., Malaya, 1954-56 (despatches); Asst Chief of Staff Logistics, Northern Army Group, 1957-60; DDST, 1st Corps, 1960-62; Comdr, RASC Training Centre, 1962-64; Inspector, RASC, 1964-65; ADC to the Queen, 1964-66; Inspector, RCT, 1965-66; psc; jssc. Col Comdt, RCT, 1969-. Hon. Colonel: 160 Regt RCT(V), 1969-74; 562 Para Sqdn RCT(V), 1969-. FCIT (MInstT) 1966. Vice-President: Transport Trust, 1969; Internat. Union for Modern Pentathlon and Biathlon, 1976-. Chairman: Modern Pentathlon Assoc. of Great Britain, 1967; Inst. of Advanced Motorists, 1971. *Recreations:* modern pentathlon, golf, photography, driving. *Address:* Stoke House, Stogursey, near Bridgwater, Somerset TA5 1TA. *T:* Nether Stowey 763. *Clubs:* East India, Devonshire, Sports and Public Schools, MCC.

LOOKER, Sir Cecil (Thomas), Kt 1969; Chairman, Australian United Corporation Ltd; Principal Partner, Ian Potter & Co., Sharebrokers, 1967-76 (Partner, 1953); Director of various other companies; *b* 11 April 1913; *s* of Edward William and Martha Looker; *m* 1941, Jean Leslyn Withington; one *s* two *d. Educ:* Fort Street Boys' High Sch., Sydney; Sydney Univ. (BA). Apptd to Commonwealth Public Service, 1937; Private Sec. to Prime Minister (Rt Hon. now Sir Robert Menzies), 1939-41. War of 1939-45: RANVR, 1942-45. Resigned Commonwealth Public Service, 1946, and joined Ian Potter & Co. Chm., Stock Exchange of Melbourne, 1966-72 (Mem. 1962-); Pres., Australian Associated Stock Exchanges, 1968-71. Apptd by Dept of Territories as Dir of Papua and New Guinea Development Bank, 1966; Chm., Exec. Cttee, Duke of Edinburgh's Third Commonwealth Study Conf., Aust., 1966-68. *Recreation:* farming. *Address:* 26 Tormey Street, North Balwyn, Victoria 3104, Australia. *T:* 857-9316. *Clubs:* Australian, Royal Automobile Club of Victoria (Melbourne) (President).

LOOMBE, Claude Evan, CMG 1961; *b* 9 Aug. 1905; *yr s* of late Arthur Thomas Loombe and Catherine Jane Jermy; *m* 1936, Zoë Isabella, *o d* of late R. D. Hotchkis, MD, and Penelope, *d* of late Alexander Ionides; three *d.* Entered Chartered Bank, 1925; service in Ceylon, China and India; seconded to Min. of Finance, Iraq Govt, 1941-45. Entered service of Bank of England as an Adviser, 1945; Adviser to the Governors, 1964-65; retired 1965; Dir, British Bank of the Middle East, 1965-77 (Chm., 1967-74); Member: Kuwait Currency Bd, 1960-69; Jordan Currency Bd, 1948-65; Sudan Currency Bd, 1956-60; Libyan Currency Commn, 1952-56. Vice-Pres., Middle East Assoc. Iraqi Order of Al-Rafidain, 4th Class, 1946; Jordan Independence Order, 2nd Class, 1961; Order of Jordanian Star (1st Class), 1965. *Address:* 64 Shepherd's Way, Liphook, Hants. *T:* Liphook 722060. *Club:* Oriental.

LOOSLEY, Stanley George Henry, MC 1944; MA Cantab; JP Glos; Headmaster of Wycliffe College, 1947-67; *b* 18 July 1910; *s* of Harold D. and Edith M. Loosley; *m* 1938, Margaret Luker; two *s* one *d. Educ:* Wycliffe Coll.; St John's Coll., Cambridge. Asst Master, Wycliffe Coll., 1934-39; War of 1939-45, RA, Sept. 1939-Oct. 1945; Major OC 220 Field Battery, 1941 (despatches, MC); NW Europe Campaign, 1944; sc; Bde Major RA 43 Div., 1945; Senior Asst Master, Wycliffe Coll., 1945-47. *Recreations:* travel, educational design. *Address:* Brillings Cottage, Chalford Hill, Stroud, Glos. *T:* Brimscombe 3505. *Club:* Royal Over-Seas League.

LOPES, family name of **Baron Roborough.**

LOPOKOVA, Lydia; see Keynes, Lady.

LORAINE, Dr John Alexander, FRCPEd; Medical Research Council External Scientific Staff, Department of Community Medicine, University of Edinburgh, since 1972; *b* 14 May 1924; *s* of Lachlan Dempster Loraine and Ruth (*née* Jack); *m* 1974, Alison Blair. *Educ:* George Watson's Boys' Coll., Edinburgh; Univ. of Edinburgh. MB ChB (Hons) 1946, PhD 1949, DSc 1959; FRCPEd 1960. House Phys., Royal Infirmary, Edinburgh, under Prof. Sir Stanley Davidson, 1946; Mem., Scientific Staff, MRC Clinical Endocrinology Unit, Edinburgh, 1947-61; Dir of the Unit, 1961-72. Visiting Prof. of Endocrinology, Donner Laboratory and Donner Pavilion, Univ. of Calif., Berkeley, USA, 1964. Hon. Senior Lecturer: Dept of Pharmacology, 1965-72, Dept of Community Medicine, 1972-, Univ. of Edinburgh. Founder Chm., Doctors and Overpopulation Gp, 1972-; Vice-Chm., Conservation Soc., 1974-. Mem., Internat. Union for Scientific Study of Population. *Publications:* (co-author) Hormone Assays and their Clinical Application, 1958, 4th edn 1976; (co-author) Recent Research on Gonadotrophic Hormones, 1967; (co-author) Fertility and Contraception in the Human Female, 1968; Sex and the Population Crisis, 1970; The Death of Tomorrow, 1972; (ed) Reproductive Endocrinology and World Population, 1973; (ed) Environmental Medicine, 1974; (ed) Understanding Homosexuality: its biological and psychological bases, 1974; Syndromes of the 'Seventies, 1977; author and co-author of numerous scientific and popular pubns dealing with sex hormones, fertility, contraception, population and related issues, incl. women's rights, mineral resources and environmental pollution. *Recreations:* reading modern history and political biography, music, bridge, golf. *Address:* 20 Buckingham Terrace, Edinburgh EH4 3AD. *T:* 031-332 3698. *Club:* University of Edinburgh Staff.

LORAM, Vice-Adm. David Anning, MVO 1957; Deputy Supreme Allied Commander Atlantic, since 1977; *b* 24 July 1924; *o* surv. *s* of late Mr and Mrs John A. Loram; *m* 1958, Fiona, *o d* of late Vice-Adm. Sir William Beloe, KBE, CB, DSC; three *s. Educ:* Royal Naval Coll., Dartmouth (1938-41). Served War: HMS Sheffield, Foresight, Anson, Zealous, 1941-45. ADC to Governor-Gen. of New Zealand, 1946-48; specialised in Signal Communications, 1949; served in HMS Chequers, 1951; Equerry to the Queen, 1954-57; qualified helicopter pilot, 1955; commanded HMS Loch Fada, 1957; Directing Staff, JSSC, 1959-60; served in HMS Belfast, 1961; Naval Attaché, Paris, 1964-67; commanded HMS Arethusa, 1967; Dir, Naval Ops and Trade, 1970-71; commanded HMS Antrim, 1971; Comdr British Forces, FO Malta, and NATO Comdr SE Mediterranean, 1973-75; Comdt, Nat. Defence Coll., 1975-77. Mem., RN Cresta Team, 1954-59. *Recreations:* golf, squash, walking. *Address:* Box C-01, Naval Party 1964 (Saclant), BFPO Ships.

LORANT, Stefan; *b* 22 Feb. 1901; *m* 1963, Laurie Robertson; two *s. Educ:* Evangelical Gymnasium, Budapest; Academy of Economics, Budapest; Harvard University (MA 1961). Editor: Das Magazin, Leipzig, 1925; Bilder Courier, Berlin, 1926; Muenchner Illustrierte Presse, 1927-33; Weekly Illustrated, Picture Post, 1938-40; Founder of Lilliput, Editor, 1937-40. Hon. LLD, Knox Coll., Galesburg, Ill., 1958. *Publications:* I Was Hitler's Prisoner, 1935; Lincoln, His Life in Photographs, 1941; The New World, 1946; F.D.R., a pictorial biography, 1950; The Presidency, a pictorial history of presidential elections from Washington to Truman, 1951; Lincoln: a picture story of his life, 1952, rev. and enl. edns 1957, 1969; The Life of Abraham Lincoln, 1954; The Life and Times of Theodore Roosevelt, 1959; Pittsburgh, the story of an American city, 1964, rev. and enl. edn 1975; The Glorious Burden: the American Presidency, 1968, rev. and enl. edn, 1976; Sieg Heil: an illustrated history of Germany from Bismarck to Hitler, 1974; Chronicles of My Time, 1978. *Address:* Farview, Lenox, Mass 01240, USA. *T:* Lenox 637-0666.

LORD, Sir Ackland (Archibald), Kt 1971; OBE 1970; Director of companies, Australia; Founder and Donor of A. A. Lord Homes for the Aged Inc., Hobart, Tasmania; Past Chairman (Founder): (A.A.) Lords Ltd, Wholesale Hardware and Steel Merchants, 1949-59 (Director to 1969); Lords Holdings Ltd, 1952-59 (Director, 1959-69); Director: Melbourne Builders Lime & Cement Co.; Big Ben Scaffolds Pty Ltd; U-Hire Pty Ltd; Melcann Holdings Ltd; *b* 11 June 1901; *s* of late J. Lord, Tasmania; *m* Ethel Dalton, MBE, *d* of late C. Dalton, Hobart. *Educ:* St Virgil's Coll., Hobart. Has given distinguished services to the community in Victoria and Tasmania. Past Chm. Galvanised Iron Merchants Assoc.; Council Mem., Ryder Cheshire Foundn (Vic.) for Internat. Centre, Dehra Dun, India;

Past Member: Trotting Control Bd; Melbourne & Metropolitan Trotting Assoc. (Chm.); Life Governor: various Melb. Hosps; Royal Victoria Inst. for the Blind, etc. *Address:* Lawrenny, 3 Teringa Place, Toorak, Victoria 3142, Australia. *T:* 24-5283. *Clubs:* Hardware (Melbourne); Victoria Racing; Moonee Valley Racing.

LORD, Alan, CB 1972; Director of Planning and Corporate Development, Dunlop, since 1977; *b* 12 April 1929; *er s* of Frederick Lord and Anne Lord (*née* Whitworth), Rochdale; *m* 1953, Joan Ogden; two *d. Educ:* Rochdale; St John's Coll., Cambridge. Entered Inland Revenue, 1950; Private Sec. to Dep. Chm. and to Chm. of the Board, 1952-54; HM Treasury, 1959-62; Principal Private Sec. to First Secretary of State (then Rt Hon. R. A Butler), 1962-63; Comr of Inland Revenue, 1969-73, Dep. Chm. Bd, 1971-73; Principal Finance Officer to DTI, subseq. to Depts of Industry, Trade, and Prices and Consumer Protection, 1973-75; Second Permanent Sec. (Domestic Econ.), HM Treasury, 1975-77. *Address:* 22 Greystone Park, Sundridge, Sevenoaks, Kent. *T:* Westerham 63657. *Club:* Reform.

LORD, Cyril, LLD (Hon.); Chairman and Managing Director, Cyril Lord Ltd, 1945-68; Director, numerous Companies in Great Britain, Northern Ireland, and South Africa, 1945-68; *b* 12 July 1911; *m* 1936, Bessie Greenwood (marr. diss. 1959); two *s* two *d*; *m* 1974, Aileen Parnell, widow. *Educ:* Central Sch., Manchester; Manchester Coll. of Technology (Associate), and University. Dir of Hodkin & Lord Ltd, 1939; Technical Adviser to the Cotton Board, England, 1941. Hon. LLD Florida Southern Coll., 1951. *Recreations:* yachting, tennis. *Clubs:* Royal Automobile, Naval and Military; Royal Corinthian (Cowes); Ballyholme Yacht (N Ire.).

LORD, Geoffrey; Secretary and Treasurer, Carnegie United Kingdom Trust, since 1977; *b* 24 Feb. 1928; *s* of Frank Lord and Edith Lord; *m* 1955, Jean; one *s* one *d. Educ:* Rochdale Grammar Sch.; Univ. of Bradford (MA Applied Social Studies). AIB. Midland Bank Ltd, 1946-58; Probation and After-Care Service, 1958-76: Dep. Chief Probation Officer, Greater Manchester, 1974-76. *Recreations:* philately, walking, gardening. *Address:* 9 Craigleith View, Ravelston, Edinburgh EH4 3JZ. *T:* 031-337 7623.

LORD, John Herent; a Recorder of the Crown Court, since 1972; *b* 5 Nov. 1928; *s* of Sir Frank Lord, KBE; *m* 1959, June Ann, *d* of George Caladine, Rochdale; three *s. Educ:* Manchester Grammar Sch.; Merton Coll., Oxford (BA (Jurisprudence), MA). Half Blue, Oxford Univ. lacrosse XII, 1948 and 1949; represented Oxfordshire (Southern Counties Champions), 1949, and Middlesex 1950. Called to Bar, Inner Temple, 1951; The Junior of Northern Circuit, 1952; Asst Recorder of Burnley, 1971. *Recreations:* photography, shooting. *Address:* Three Lanes, Greenfield, Oldham, Lancs. *T:* Saddleworth 2198. *Clubs:* St James (Manchester); Leander.

LORD, Maj.-Gen. Wilfrid Austin, CB 1954; CBE 1952; MEng, CEng; FIMechE; FIEE; REME, retired; *b* 20 Sept. 1902; *s* of late S. Lord, Rochdale and Liverpool; *m* 1937, Mabel (*d* 1973), *d* of late T. Lamb, York and Carlisle; one *s. Educ:* Birkenhead Institute; Liverpool Univ. Formerly RAOC, Lt 1927; Capt. 1933; Major 1935; Local Lt-Col 1940, Col 1947; Temp. Brig. 1949; Temp. Maj.-Gen. 1950; Maj.-Gen. 1950; Dir Mechanical Engineers, GHQ, ME Land Forces, 1950-53; Dir, Mechanical Engineering, War Office, 1954-57; retired, 1957. Col Comdt REME, 1957-63. *Address:* Old School House, Upper Farringdon, Alton, Hants GU34 3DT.

LORD, William Burton Housley; Director, Royal Armament Research and Development Establishment, since 1976; *b* 22 March 1919; *s* of Arthur James Lord and Elsie Lord (*née* Housley); *m* 1942, Helena Headon Jaques; two *d. Educ:* King George V Sch., Southport; Manchester Univ.; London Univ. (External MSc); Trinity Coll., Cambridge (MA). Enlisted Royal Fusiliers, wartime commn S Lancs Regt, 1941-46. Cambridge Univ., 1946. Entered Civil Service, 1949; joined Atomic Weapons Res. Estab., 1952; Head of Metallurgy Div., AWRE, 1958; moved to MoD, 1964; Asst Chief Scientific Adviser (Research), 1965; Dep. Chief Scientist (Army), 1968-71; Dir Gen., Establishments, Resources and Programmes (B), MoD, 1971-76. *Publications:* papers on metallurgy in learned jls. *Recreations:* amateur radio, walking, orienteering, water sports. *Address:* Fort Halstead, Sevenoaks, Kent TN14 7BP.

LOREN, Sophia; film actress; *b* 20 Sept. 1934; *d* of Ricardo Scicolone and Romilda Villani; *m* 1957, Carlo Ponti, film producer (marriage annulled in Juarez, Mexico, Sept. 1962; marriage in Paris, France, April 1966); two *s. Educ:* parochial sch. and Teachers' Institute, Naples. First leading role in, Africa sotto i Mari, 1952; acted in many Italian films, 1952-55; subsequent films include: The Pride and the Passion; Boy on a Dolphin; Legend of the Lost; The Key; Desire under the Elms; Houseboat; The Black Orchid (Venice Film Festival Award, 1958); That Kind of Woman; It Started in Naples; Heller in Pink Tights; The Millionairess; Two Women (Cannes Film Festival Award, 1961); A Breath of Scandal; Madame sans Gêne; La Ciociara; El Cid; Boccaccio 70; Five Miles to Midnight; Yesterday, Today and Tomorrow; The Fall of the Roman Empire; Marriage, Italian Style; Operation Crossbow; Lady L; Judith; A Countess from Hong Kong; Arabesque; Sunflower; The Priest's Wife; The Man of La Mancha; The Verdict; The Voyage; Una Gionnata Particolare. *Publication:* Eat with Me, 1972. *Address:* Chalet Daniel Burgenstock, Luzern, Switzerland.

LORENZ, Prof. Dr Konrad, MD, DPhil; Director, Department for Animal Sociology, Institute for Comparative Ethology, Austrian Academy of Sciences, since 1973; Director of Max-Planck-Institut für Verhaltenphysiologie, 1961-73 (Vice-Director, 1954); *b* 7 Nov. 1903; *s* of Prof. Dr Adolf Lorenz and Emma Lorenz (*née* Lecher); *m* 1927, Dr Margarethe Lorenz (*née* Gebhardt); one *s* two *d*. *Educ:* High Sch., Vienna; Columbia Univ., New York; Univ. of Vienna. Univ. Asst at Anatomical Inst. of University of Vienna (Prof. Hochstetter), 1928-35; Lectr in Comparative Anat. and Animal Psychol., University of Vienna, 1937-40; University Lectr, Vienna, 1940; Prof. of Psychol. and Head of Dept, University of Königsberg, 1940; Head of Research Station for Physiology of Behaviour of the Max-Planck-Inst. for Marine Biol., 1951. Hon. Prof., University of Münster, 1953 and München, 1957. Nobel Prize for Physiology or Medicine (jtly), 1973. Mem., Pour le Mérite for Arts and Science; Hon. Member: Assoc. for Study of Animal Behaviour, 1950; Amer. Ornithol. Union, 1951, etc; For. Mem., Royal Society, 1964. For. Assoc. Nat. Acad. of Sciences, USA, 1966. Hon. degrees: Leeds, 1962; Basel, 1966; Yale, 1967; Oxford, 1968; Chicago, 1970; Durham, 1972; Birmingham, 1974. Gold Medal, Zoological Soc., New York, 1955; City Prize, Vienna, 1959; Gold Boelsche Medal, 1962; Austrian Distinction for Science and Art, 1964; Prix Mondial, Cino del Duca, 1969. Grosse Verdienstkreuz, 1974; Bayerische Verdienstorden, 1974. *Publications:* King Solomon's Ring, 1952; Man Meets Dog, 1954; Evolution and Modification of Behaviour, 1965; On Aggression, 1966; Studies in Animal and Human Behaviour, 1970; (jtly) Man and Animal, 1972; Civilized Man's Eight Deadly Sins, 1974; Behind the Mirror, 1977; articles in Tierpsychologie, Behaviour, etc. *Address:* Institut für Vergleichende Verhaltensforschung, Abt. 4, Tiersoziologie, Adolf-Lorenzgasse 2, A-3422 Altenberg, Austria.

LORIMER, Hew Martin, RSA; FRBS; Sculptor; Representative in Fife of National Trust for Scotland; *b* 22 May 1907; 2nd *s* of late Sir Robert Stodart Lorimer, KBE, Hon. LLD, ARA, RSA, architect, and of Violet Alicia (*née* Wyld); *m* 1936, Mary McLeod Wylie (*d* 1970), 2nd *d* of H. M. Wylie, Edinburgh; two *s* one *d*. *Educ:* Loretto; Edinburgh Coll. of Art, Andrew Grant Scholarship, 1933 and Fellowship, 1934-35. National Library of Scotland, Edinburgh, sculptor of the 7 allegorical figures, 1952-55; Our Lady of the Isles, South Uist, 1955-57; St Francis, Dundee, 1957-59. *Recreations:* music, travel, home. *Address:* Kellie Castle, Pittenweem, Fife. *T:* Arncroach 271. *Club:* Scottish Arts (Edinburgh).

LORIMER, Sir (Thomas) Desmond, Kt 1976; *b* 20 Oct. 1925; *s* of Thomas Berry Lorimer and Sarah Ann Lorimer; *m* 1957, Patricia Doris Samways; two *d*. *Educ:* Belfast Technical High Sch. Chartered Accountant, 1948; Fellow, Inst. of Chartered Accountants in Ireland, 1957. Practised as chartered accountant, 1952-74; Sen. Partner, Harmood, Banner, Smylie & Co., Belfast, Chartered Accountants, 1960; Chairman: McCleery L'Amie Gp Ltd, 1970; Lamont Holdings Ltd, 1973; Dir, Ruberoid Ltd, 1972. Pres., Inst. of Chartered Accountants in Ireland, 1968-69; Chairman: Ulster Soc. of Chartered Accountants, 1960; NI Housing Exec., 1971-75 (resp. for unification of public authority housing within single authority); Mem., Rev. Body on Local Govt in NI, 1970. *Recreations:* gardening and golf. *Address:* Windwhistle House, 6 Circular Road West, Cultra, Holywood, Co. Down BT18 0AT. *T:* Holywood 3323. *Clubs:* Junior Carlton; Royal Belfast Golf (Co. Down).

LÖRINCZ-NAGY, János, Golden Grade of Order of Merit for Labour; Hungarian Ambassador to the Court of St James's, since 1976; *b* 19 Dec. 1931; *m* Ida Lörincz-Nagy; one *d*. *Educ:* Foreign Affairs Acad., Budapest; Coll. of Polit. Sciences, Budapest. Entered Diplomatic Service, 1953; Press Attaché, Peking, 1953-55; 2nd Sec., Djakarta, 1957-61; Dep. Head of

Personnel Dept, 1964-68; Ambassador to Ghana, 1968-72; Head of Press Dept, 1972-74; Ambassador, Head of Hungarian Delegn to Internat. Commn of Control and Supervision in Saigon, 1974; Ambassador to Sweden, 1975-76. *Recreations:* reading and walking. *Address:* 35 Eaton Place, SW1X 8YB. *T:* 01-235 4048.

LORING, Sir (John) Nigel, KCVO 1964 (CVO 1953); MRCS, LRCP; Apothecary to the Household of Queen Elizabeth the Queen Mother, 1953, and to the Household of the Duke of Gloucester, 1959-66 (to the Household of King George VI and to that of The Princess Elizabeth and The Duke of Edinburgh, 1949-52; to that of Queen Mary, 1949-53; to HM Household, 1952-64); now in private practice only; *b* 31 Aug. 1896; *s* of late Nele Loring, Market Drayton, Salop; *m* 1932, Sylvia, 2nd *d* of late Col Blakeney-Booth, Billingham Manor, IoW; one *d* (and one *d* decd). *Educ:* RNC Osborne; Tonbridge Sch.; St Thomas's Hospital. Served European War 1914-19, RNR (Dover Patrol); War of 1939-45, Flight Lt 1941, Sqdn Ldr 1942 (despatches). Past Pres. of the Chelsea Clinical Soc.; Freeman, Worshipful Society of Apothecaries, London. *Recreations:* eighteenth century furniture, music. *Address:* 4 Woden House, Goring-on-Thames, Oxon. *T:* Goring-on-Thames 2922.

LORNE, Marquess of; Torquhil Ian Campbell; *b* 29 May 1968; *s* and *heir* of 12th Duke of Argyll, qv.

LOSEY, Joseph; Film Director; *b* 14 Jan. 1909; *s* of Joseph Walton Losey and Ina Higbee; *m*; two *s*. *Educ:* Dartmouth Coll., New Hampshire; Harvard Univ. Resident in England from 1952. Directed first Broadway play, 1932; subseq. productions include: (with Charles Laughton) Galileo Galilei, by Bertholt Brecht, NY and Hollywood, 1947; (with Wilfrid Lawson) The Wooden Dish, London, 1954; short films from 1938; radio from 1942; first feature film, The Boy with Green Hair, 1948; Hollywood films include: The Dividing Line; The Prowler; films since 1952 include: Time Without Pity; Blind Date; The Criminal; The Damned; Eve; The Servant; King and Country; Modesty Blaise; Accident; Boom; Secret Ceremony; Figures in a Landscape; The Go-Between (Golden Palm, Cannes Film Festival, 1971); The Assassination of Trotsky; A Doll's House; Galileo; The Romantic Englishwoman; Mr Klein. Guest Prof., 1970, DLitHon, 1973, Dartmouth Coll., NH. Chevalier de l'Ordre des Arts et des Lettres. *Recreation:* work. *Address:* c/o Georges Beaume, 5 quai Malaguais, 75006 Paris. *T:* 325-2759.

LOSS, Joshua Alexander, (Joe Loss); band-leader; *b* 22 June 1909; *s* of Israel and Ada Loss; *m* 1938, Mildred Blanch Rose; one *s* one *d*. *Educ:* Jewish Free Sch., Spitalfields; Trinity Coll. of Music; London Coll. of Music. Played as silent film accompanist, Coliseum, Ilford and at Tower Ballroom, Blackpool, 1926; formed own orchestra at Astoria Ballroom, Charing Cross Road, 1930; first broadcast, 1934, then broadcast every week. Joined Regal Zonophone record co.; hit record, 1936, with Begin the Beguine (gold disc for sales of a million over 25 years); is now joint longest serving artiste on EMI label, has 50-year contract. First record with EMI I Only Have Eyes For You; hit singles inc. Wheels Cha Cha, The Maigret Theme, The Steptoe Theme; gold discs for long-playing albums inc. Joe Loss Plays Glenn Miller and All Time Party Hits. Was one of first West End bands to play in provinces in ballrooms and to top bill in variety theatres; toured all through war inc. overseas. After war TV included: Come Dancing, Bid for Fame, Home Town Saturday Night, and Holiday Parade; was featured in This Is Your Life; panel member, New Faces. Joined Mecca, 1959, became resident at Hammersmith Palais; won 14 Carl Alan Awards; Musical Express Top Big Band Award, 1963, 1964; Weekend Magazine Top Musical Personality Award, 1964; and Music Publishers' Assoc. Award as outstanding personality of 1976. Has played for dancing on QE2 world cruises, at Buckingham Palace and Windsor Castle on numerous occasions, and at pre-wedding balls for Princess Margaret, Princess Alexandra and Princess Anne and for Queen's 50th birthday celebrations. *Recreations:* motoring, watching television, collecting watches, playing with grandchildren. *Address:* Morley House, Regent Street, W1. *T:* 01-580 1212. *Club:* Middlesex County Cricket (Life Member).

LOTEN, Harold Ivens, MBE 1950; JP; Member of Council, 1945-76, Chairman of Council and Pro-Chancellor, 1950-71, University of Hull; *b* 28 June 1887; *s* of Arthur Richard and Caroline Loten; *m* 1914, Hilda Mary, *d* of John S. Kemp; two *d* (one *s* killed on active service, RNVR). *Educ:* St Bede's Sch., Hornsea. Served 1st Bn HAC Infantry, 1917-18. Sheriff of City and County of Kingston upon Hull, 1943-44, JP East Riding of Yorks, 1945; Pres. Hull Incorp. Chamber of Commerce and Shipping, 1946 and 1947. Manager, Midland Bank Ltd, Silver

Street, Hull, 1937-49. Life Mem. Ct, Univ. of Hull. Fellow, Institute of Bankers; Pres., Rotary Club of Hull, 1943-44. Lay Preacher, 1905-. Hon. LLD Hull, 1956. *Recreations:* gardening and reading. *Address:* Briar Garth, Atwick Road, Hornsea, North Humberside. *T:* Hornsea 3138.

LOTH, David; Editor and Author; *b* St Louis, Missouri, 7 Dec. 1899; *s* of Albert Loth and Fanny Sunshine. *Educ:* University of Missouri. Staff of New York World, 1920-30; Editor and Publisher The Majorca Sun, 1931-34; NY Times, 1934-41; US Govt Information Services, 1941-45; Information Dir, Planned Parenthood Federation of America, 1946-51; Acting Nat. Dir, 1951; Information Dir, Columbia Univ. Bicentennial, 1953-54; Assoc. Nieman Fellow, Harvard Univ., 1957-58; Lecturer, Finch Coll., 1961-65. Senior Editor-Writer, High Sch. Geog. Project of Assoc. of Amer. Geographers, 1967-68. Consultant, Psychological Corp., 1969-76. Contributor to various English, American, and Australian publications. *Publications:* The Brownings; Lorenzo the Magnificent; Charles II; Philip II; Public Plunder; Alexander Hamilton; Lafayette; Woodrow Wilson; Chief Justice; A Long Way Forward; Swope of GE; The Erotic in Literature; Pencoyd and the Roberts Family; Crime Lab.: How High is Up; The City Within a City; Crime in Suburbia; The Marriage Counselor; Gold Brick Cassie; Economic Miracle in Israel; Co-author: American Sexual Behaviour and the Kinsey Report; Report on the American Communist; For Better or Worse; Peter Freuchen's Book of the Seven Seas; The Frigid Wife; The Emotional Sex; Ivan Sanderson's Book of Great Jungles; The Taming of Technology. *Address:* 2227 Canyon Boulevard, Boulder, Colo 80302, USA.

LOTHIAN, 12th Marquess of *cr* 1701; **Peter Francis Walter Kerr;** Lord Newbattle, 1591; Earl of Lothian, 1606; Baron Jedburgh, 1622; Earl of Ancram, Baron Kerr of Nisbet, Baron Long-Newton and Dolphingston, 1633; Viscount of Brien, Baron Kerr of Newbattle, 1701; Baron Ker (UK), 1821; DL; Lord Warden of the Stannaries and Keeper of the Privy Seal of the Duke of Cornwall, since 1977; *b* 8 Sept. 1922; *s* of late Captain Andrew William Kerr, RN, and Marie Constance Annabel, *d* of Capt. William Walter Raleigh Kerr; *S* cousin, 1940; *m* 1943, Antonella, *d* of late Maj.-Gen. Sir Foster Newland, KCMG, CB, and Mrs William Carr, Ditchingham Hall, Norfolk; two *s* four *d. Educ:* Ampleforth; Christ Church, Oxford. Lieut, Scots Guards, 1943. Mem. Brit. Delegation: UN Gen. Assembly, 1956-57; European Parliament, 1973; UK Delegate, Council of Europe and WEU, 1959. PPS to Foreign Sec., 1960-63; a Lord in Waiting (Govt Whip, House of Lords), 1962-63, 1972-73; Joint Parliamentary Sec., Min. of Health, April-Oct. 1964; Parly Under-Sec. of State, FCO, 1970-72. Chm., Scottish Council, British Red Cross Soc., 1976-. Mem., Queen's Body Guard for Scotland (Royal Company of Archers). Mem., Prince of Wales Council, 1976-. DL, Roxburgh, 1962. Kt, SMO Malta. *Heir:* s Earl of Ancram, *qv. Address:* Melbourne Hall, Derby. *T:* Melbourne 2163; Monteviot, Jedburgh, Roxburghshire. *T:* Ancrum 288; 54 Upper Cheyne Row, SW3. *Clubs:* Boodle's, Beefsteak; New (Edinburgh).
See also Col Sir D. H. Cameron of Lochiel, Earl of Euston.

LOTT, Dr Bernard Maurice, OBE 1966; English Language Teaching Development Adviser, British Council; *b* 13 Aug. 1922; *s* of late William Lott and of Margaret Lott (*née* Smith); *m* 1949, Helena, *d* of late Clarence Winkup; two *s* one *d. Educ:* Bancroft's Sch.; Keble Coll., Oxford (MA); Univ. of London (MA Distinction, PhD); Univ. of Edinburgh (Dip. in Applied Linguistics, Dist.). RN, 1942-46. Brit. Council Lectr in English, Ankara Univ. and Gazi Inst. of Educn, Turkey, 1949-55; Brit. Council Asst Rep., Finland, 1955-57; Prof. of Eng. and Head of Dept, Univ. of Indonesia, 1958-61; Dir of Studies, Indian Central Inst. of Eng., 1961-66; Dep. Controller, Educn Div., Brit. Council, 1966-72; Controller, Eng. Teaching Div., Brit. Council, 1972-75; Brit. Council Representative, Poland, 1975-77. *Publications:* Gen. Editor, New Swan Shakespeare series, and edited: Macbeth, 1958, Twelfth Night, 1959, Merchant of Venice, 1962, Hamlet, 1968 (also Open Univ. edn 1970), King Lear, 1974; Much Ado About Nothing, 1977; contribs on teaching of English as foreign lang. to Times Educnl Supp. and Eng. Lang. Teaching Jl. *Recreations:* local studies, music. *Address:* 8 Meadway, NW11 7JT. *T:* 01-455 0918.

LOTT, Air Vice-Marshal Charles George, CB 1955; CBE 1944; DSO 1940; DFC 1940; Royal Air Force, retired; *b* 28 Oct. 1906; *s* of late Charles Lott, Sandown; *m* 1936, Evelyn Muriel Little; two *s* one *d. Educ:* Portsmouth Junior Technical Sch. Joined Royal Air Force as Aircraft Apprentice, 1922; learned to fly at Duxford in No 19 Squadron, 1927-28; Sergeant, 1928; Commissioned 1933 and posted to No 41 Squadron; Iraq, 1935-38; HQ No 11 Gp, 1938-39; Commanded No 43 Squadron, 1939-40 (DFC, wounded, DSO); Temp. Wing Comdr, 1941; HQ

13 Group, 1940-42; Sector Comdr, Fighter Command, 1952; Acting Group Capt. 1942; Temp. Group Captain 1944; RAF Delegation (USA), 1944-45; Group Captain 1947; Air Commodore, 1954; Air Vice-Marshal, 1956; Dir Air Defence, SHAPE, 1955-57; Commandant, Sch. of Land/Air Warfare, Old Sarum, Wilts, 1957-59. Retd 1959. *Club:* Royal Air Force.

LOTT, Frank Melville, CBE 1945; DDS, MScD, PhD; retired; formerly Professor and Chairman of the Prosthodontics Department, University of Southern California, USA; *b* 9 Nov. 1896; *s* of Charles Lott, Uxbridge, Ont.; *m* 1933, Mabel Maunder Martin; one *s* one *d. Educ:* Toronto, Ont. Prof., Prosthetic Dentistry, University of Toronto. Dir-Gen. Dental Services, Canadian Forces, 1939-46; Col Comdt Royal Canadian Dental Corps. *Publications:* Bulletins of Canadian Dental Research Foundation and papers to dental congresses and journals. *Recreations:* photography, fishing, hunting. *Address:* 1445 Oakdale, Pasadena, Calif 91106, USA.

LOTZ, Dr Kurt; German business executive; *b* 18 Sept. 1912; *m* Elizabeth Lony; two *s* one *d. Educ:* August-Vilmar-Schule, Homberg. Joined Police Service, 1932; Lieut 1934. Served Luftwaffe (Gen. Staff; Major), 1942-45. Employed by Brown Boveri & Cie, Dortmund, 1946; Head of Business Div., Mannheim, 1954; Dir 1957; Chm. 1958-67; Mem. Board of Directors in parent company, Baden, Switzerland, 1961; Managing Director, 1963-67. Dep. Chm., 1967-68, Chm., 1968-71, Volkswagenwerk AG. Member: Deutscher Rat für Landespflege; Beratender Ausschuss für Forschung und Technologie des Bundesministers für Forschung u. Technologie; Board, Deutsch-Indische Gesellschaft e.V. Mem., Rotary Internat. Hon. Senator, Heidelberg Univ., 1963; Hon. Prof., Technische Universität Carolo Wilhelmina, Brunswick, 1970. Dr rer. pol. *hc* Wirtschaftshochschule (Inst. of Economics) Mannheim, 1963. *Recreations:* hiking, hunting. *Address:* 69 Heidelberg, Ludolf-Krehl-Strasse 35, Germany.

LOUDON, John Hugo; Jonkheer (Netherlands title); Knight in the Order of the Netherlands Lion, 1953; Grand Officer, Order of Orange-Nassau, 1965; KBE (Hon.) (Gt Brit.), 1960; Officer, Légion d'Honneur, 1963; holds other decorations; Chairman: International Advisory Committee for Chase Manhattan Bank, since 1965; Board, Atlantic Institute, since 1969; European Advisory Committee, Ford Motor Company, since 1976; *b* 27 June 1905; *s* of Jonkheer Hugo Loudon and Anna Petronella Alida Loudon (*née* van Marken); *m* 1931, Baroness Marie Cornelie van Tuyll van Serooskerken; three *s* (and one *s* decd). *Educ:* Netherlands Lyceum, The Hague; Utrecht Univ., Holland. Doctor of Law, 1929. Joined Royal Dutch/Shell Group of Cos, 1930; served in USA, 1932-38; Venezuela, 1938-47 (Gen. Man., 1944-47); Man. Dir, 1947-52, Pres., 1952-65, Chm., 1965-76, Royal Dutch Petroleum Co.; Principal Dir, Bataafse Petroleum Maatschappij NV, and Man. Dir the Shell Petroleum Co. Ltd, 1947-65 (Dir, 1965-76); Senior Man. Dir, Royal Dutch Shell Gp, 1957-65, retired; former Chm. and Man. Dir, Shell Internat. Petroleum Co. Ltd; former Chairman: Shell Oil Co. (New York); Shell Caribbean Petroleum Co. (New York); Shell Petroleum NV, The Hague, 1966-76; Bataafse Internationale Petroleum Maatschappij NV; former Director: Cia Shell de Venezuela Ltd; Shell Western Holdings Ltd; Bataafse Internationale Chemie Mij. NV; Shell Internat. Chemical Co. Ltd.; Vice-Chm. Bd, Royal Netherlands Blast-furnaces & Steelworks, NV, 1971-76; Director: Orion Bank Ltd, 1971-; Chase Manhattan Corp., 1971-76; Estel NV Hoesch-Hoogovens, 1972-76. Chm., INSEAD, 1971-. Mem. Bd Trustees, Ford Foundation, 1966-75. Internat. Pres., World Wildlife Fund, 1977-. *Recreations:* golf, yachting. *Address:* 48 lange Voorhout, The Hague, Holland; Koekoeksduin, Aerdenhout, Holland. *T:* Haarlem 245924. *Clubs:* White's; Royal Yacht Squadron.

LOUDOUN, Countess of (13th in line) *cr* 1633; **Barbara Huddleston Abney-Hastings;** Lady Campbell Baroness of Loudoun, 1601; Lady Tarrinzean and Mauchline, 1638; the 3 English baronies of Botreaux 1368, Stanley 1456, and Hastings 1461, which were held by the late Countess, are abeyant, the Countess and her sisters being *co-heiresses*; *b* 3 July 1919; assumed by deed poll, 1955, the surname of Abney-Hastings in lieu of that of Griffiths; *S* mother, 1960; *m* 1st, 1939 (marr. diss., 1945), Capt. Walter Strickland Lord; one *s*; 2nd, 1945, Capt. Gilbert Frederick Greenwood (*d* 1951); one *s* one *d*; 3rd, 1954, Peter Griffiths (who assumed by deed poll the surname of Abney-Hastings in lieu of his patronymic, 1958); three *d. Heir: s* Lord Mauchline, *qv. Address:* Harpsichord House, Cobourg Place, Hastings, E Sussex.

LOUDOUN, Donaldson; Metropolitan Magistrate, 1961-76; Barrister-at-law; *b* 30 Jan. 1909; *m* 1st, 1933, Irene Charpentier;

one *s* two *d*; 2nd, 1949, Clare Dorothy Biggie. Called to the Bar, Gray's Inn, 1934. Served War of 1939-45: BEF, 1939-40; Captain, Intelligence Corps (Parachute Section), 1944; Major, 1945; served in France, 1944; Belgium, 1945. *Recreation:* golf. *Address:* 2 Clifton Road, Wimbledon, SW19.

LOUDOUN, Maj.-Gen. Robert Beverley, CB 1973; OBE 1965; Director, Mental Health Foundation, since 1977; Chairman, National Small Bore Rifle Association, since 1975; *b* 8 July 1922; *s* of Robert and Margaret Loudoun; *m* 1950, Audrey Stevens; two *s*. *Educ:* University College Sch., Hampstead. Served War of 1939-45 (despatches): enlisted Royal Marines, 1940; commissioned, 1941; 43 Commando, Central Mediterranean, 1943-45; 45 Commando, Hong Kong, Malta and Palestine, 1945-48. Instructor, RNC Greenwich, 1950-52; Staff of C-in-C America and West Indies, 1953-55; RN Staff Coll., 1956; Adjt, 40 Commando, Malta and Cyprus, 1958-59; USMC Sch., Quantico, Virginia, 1959-60; MoD, 1960-62; Second-in-Command, 42 Commando, Singapore and Borneo, 1963-64; CO, 40 Commando, Far East, 1967-69; Brig., UK Commandos, Plymouth, 1969-71; Maj.-Gen. RM Training Gp, Portsmouth, 1971-75, retired 1975. *Recreations:* sport as a spectator, painting. *Address:* 2 Warwick Drive, Putney, SW15 6LB. *Club:* Army and Navy.

LOUGH, Prof. John, FBA 1975; Professor of French, University of Durham (late Durham Colleges), 1952-Sept. 1978; *b* 19 Feb. 1913; *s* of Wilfrid Gordon and Mary Turnbull Lough, Newcastle upon Tyne; *m* 1939, Muriel Barker; one *d*. *Educ:* Newcastle upon Tyne Royal Grammar Sch.; St John's Coll., Cambridge; Sorbonne. Major Schol., St John's Coll., 1931; BA, First Cl. Hons Parts I and II Mod. and Medieval Langs Tripos, 1934; Esmond Schol. at British Inst. in Paris, 1935; Jebb Studentship, Cambridge, 1936; PhD 1937, MA 1938, Cambridge. Asst (later Lectr), Univ. of Aberdeen, 1937; Lectr in French, Cambridge, 1946. Leverhulme Res. Fellow, 1973. Hon. Dr, Univ. of Clermont, 1967; Hon. DLitt Newcastle, 1972. Officier de l'Ordre National du Mérite, 1973. *Publications:* Locke's Travels in France, 1953; (ed) selected Philosophical Writings of Diderot, 1953; (ed) The Encyclopédie of Diderot and d'Alembert: selected articles, 1954; An Introduction to Seventeenth Century France, 1954; Paris Theatre Audiences in the 17th and 18th centuries, 1957; An Introduction to Eighteenth Century France, 1960; Essays on the Encyclopédie of Diderot and D'Alembert, 1968; The Encyclopédie in 18th Century England and other studies, 1970; The Encyclopédie, 1971; The Contributors to the Encyclopédie, 1973; (ed with J. Proust) Diderot: Œuvres complètes, vols V-VIII, 1977; (with M. Lough) An Introduction to Nineteenth Century France, 1978; Writer and Public in France, 1978; articles on French literature and ideas in 17th and 18th centuries in French and English learned jls. *Address:* 1 St Hild's Lane, Gilesgate, Durham DH1 1QL. *T:* Durham 3034.

LOUGHBOROUGH, Lord; Peter St Clair-Erskine; *b* 31 March 1958; *s* and *heir* of 6th Earl of Rosslyn, *qv*. *Educ:* Ludgrove Sch.; Eton Coll. *Recreations:* church music, piano. *Address:* Cedar House, Shurlock Row, Berks. *Clubs:* MCC; Old Etonian Golfing Assoc.

LOUGHBOROUGH, Archdeacon of; *see* Lockley, Ven. Harold.

LOUGHEED, Hon. (Edgar) Peter, QC (Can.); Premier of Alberta, Canada, since 1971; *b* Calgary, 26 July 1928; *s* of late Edgar Donald Lougheed and Edna Bauld; *m* 1952, Jeanne Estelle Rogers, Edmonton; two *s* two *d*. *Educ:* public and secondary schs, Calgary; Univ. of Alberta (BA, LLB); Harvard Grad. Sch. of Business (MBA). Read law with Calgary firm of lawyers; called to Bar of Alberta, 1955, and practised law with same firm, 1955-56. Joined Mannix Co. Ltd, as Sec., 1956 (Gen. Counsel, 1958, Vice-Pres., 1959, Dir, 1960). Entered private legal practice, 1962. Elected: Provincial Leader of Progressive Conservative Party of Alberta, also Member for Calgary West, 1965, and became Leader of the Official Opposition; Conservatives won Provincial Election, 1971, when he became Premier of Alberta (Conservatives re-elected 1975). *Recreations:* all team sports (formerly football with Edmonton Eskimos). *Address:* (office) Legislative Buildings, Edmonton, Alberta, Canada.

LOUGHLIN, Dame Anne, DBE 1943 (OBE 1935); General Secretary, Tailors and Garment Workers Trade Union, 1948-53; *b* 28 June 1894; *d* of Thomas Loughlin, Leeds. *Educ:* Leeds. General organiser, 1916-48; General Council, Trades Union Congress, 1929 (Pres. 1943). Retired.

LOUGHLIN, Charles William; trade union official; retired 1974; *b* 16 Feb. 1914; *s* of late Charles Loughlin, Grimsby; *m* 1945, May, *d* of David Arthur Dunderdale, Leeds; one *s* (one *d* decd).

Educ: St Mary's Sch., Grimsby; National Council of Labour Colls. Area Organiser, Union of Shop, Distributive and Allied Workers, 1945-74. MP (Lab) Gloucestershire West, 1959-Sept. 1974; Parly Sec., Min. of Health, 1965-67; Jt Parly Sec., Min. of Social Security, then Dept of Health and Social Security, 1967-68; Parly Sec., Min. of Public Building and Works, 1968-70. *Address:* 22 Templenewsam View, Leeds 15. *T:* Leeds 476354.

LOUGHRAN, James; Principal Conductor and Musical Adviser, Hallé Orchestra, since 1971; *b* 30 June 1931; *s* of James and Agnes Loughran; *m* 1961, Nancy (*née* Coggon); two *s*. *Educ:* St Aloysius' Coll., Glasgow; Bonn, Amsterdam and Milan. 1st Prize, Philharmonia Conducting Competition, 1961. Asst Conductor, Bournemouth Symphony Orchestra, 1962; Associate Conductor, Bournemouth Symphony Orchestra, 1964; Principal Conductor, BBC Scottish Symphony Orchestra, 1965-71. *Address:* Hallé Concerts Society, 30 Cross Street, Manchester M2 7BA.

LOUSADA, Sir Anthony (Baruh), Kt 1975; Consultant with Stephenson Harwood, Solicitors (Partner, 1935-73); *b* 4 Nov. 1907; *s* of Julian George Lousada and Maude Reignier Conder; *m* 1st, 1937, Jocelyn (marr. diss. 1960), *d* of late Sir Alan Herbert, CH; one *s* three *d*; 2nd, 1961, Patricia, *d* of C. J. McBride, USA; one *s* one *d*. *Educ:* Westminster; New Coll., Oxford. Admitted Solicitor, 1933. Min. of Economic Warfare, 1939-44; Min. of Production and War Cabinet Office, 1944-45. Member: Coun., Royal College of Art, 1952- (Hon. Fellow, 1957; Sen. Fellow., 1967; Vice-Chm., 1960-72; Treasurer, 1967-72; Chm., 1972-); Cttee, Contemp. Art Soc., 1955-71 (Vice-Chm., 1961-71); Fine Arts Cttee, British Council (visited Japan on behalf of Council, 1970, to set up exhibn of sculpture by Barbara Hepworth); GPO Adv. Cttee on Stamp Design, 1968; Council, Friends of Tate Gallery, 1958- (Hon. Treasurer, 1960-65, Chm., 1971-); Chm., Works of Art Cttee, DoE, 1977; Trustee, Tate Gallery, 1962-69 (Vice-Chm., 1965-67; Chm., 1967-69). Officer, Order of Belgian Crown, 1945. *Recreations:* painting, sailing. *Address:* The Tides, Chiswick Mall, W4. *T:* 01-994 2257. *Clubs:* Garrick; London Corinthian Sailing.

LOUTH, 16th Baron, *cr* 1541, **Otway Michael James Oliver Plunkett;** *b* 19 Aug. 1929; *o s* of Otway Randal Percy Oliver Plunkett, 15th Baron, and Ethel Molly, *d* of Walter John Gallichen, Jersey, Channel Islands; *S* father, 1950; *m* 1951, Angela Patricia Culinane, Jersey; three *s* two *d*. *Heir:* s Hon. Jonathan Oliver Plunkett, BSc, *b* 4 Nov. 1952. *Address:* Gardone, Holmfield Drive, St Brelade, Jersey, Channel Islands.

LOUTIT, John Freeman, CBE 1957; FRS 1963; MA, DM, FRCP; External Scientific Staff Medical Research Council, 1969-75, Visitor at Radiobiology Unit since 1975; *b* 19 Feb. 1910; *s* of John Freeman Loutit, Perth, WA; *m* 1941, Thelma Salusbury; one *s* two *d*. *Educ:* C of E Grammar Sch., Guildford, W Australia; Univs of W Australia, Melbourne, Oxford, London. Rhodes Scholar (W Australia), 1930; BA Oxon 1933, BM, BCh Oxon 1935. Various appointments, London Hosp., 1935-39; MA (Oxon) 1938; Director, South London Blood Supply Depot, 1940-47; DM Oxon, 1946; Dir, Radiobiological Research Unit, AERE Harwell, 1947-69. FRCP 1955. VMD (*hc*) Stockholm, 1965. Officer, Order of Orange-Nassau (Netherlands) 1951. *Publications:* Irradiation of Mice and Men, 1962; Tissue Grafting and Radiation (jointly), 1966; articles in scientific journals. *Recreations:* cooking, gardening. *Address:* Green Farm, Milton Lane, Steventon, Oxon. *T:* Steventon 279.

LOVAT, 17th Baron *cr* before 1440 (*de facto* 15th Baron, 17th but for the Attainder); **Simon Christopher Joseph Fraser,** DSO 1942; MC; TD; JP; DL; 24th Chief of Clan Fraser; *b* 9 July 1911; *s* of 16th Baron and Hon. Laura Lister (*d* 1965), 2nd *d* of 4th Baron Ribblesdale; *S* father, 1933; *m* 1938, Rosamond, *o d* of Sir Delves Broughton, 11th Bt; four *s* two *d*. *Educ:* Ampleforth; Magdalen Coll., Oxford, BA. Lt, Scots Guards, 1932-37, retd. Served War of 1939-45: Capt. Lovat Scouts, 1939; Lt-Col 1942; Brig. Commandos, 1943 (wounded, MC, DSO, Order of Suvarov, Légion d'Honneur, Croix de Guerre avec palme; Norway Liberation Cross). Under-Sec. of State for Foreign Affairs, 1945. DL 1942, JP 1944, Inverness. Awarded LLD (Hon.) by Canadian universities. Owns about 190,000 acres. Order of St John of Jerusalem; Knight of Malta. *Heir:* s Master of Lovat, *qv*. *Address:* Balblair, Beauly, Inverness-shire. *Club:* Cavalry and Guards.

See also Earl of Eldon, Rt Hon. Hugh Fraser, Sir Fitzroy Maclean, Bt, Lord Reay.

LOVAT, Master of; Hon. **Simon Augustine Fraser;** *b* 28 Aug. 1939; *s* of 17th Baron Lovat, *qv*; *m* 1972, Virginia, *d* of David Grose; one *d*. *Educ:* Ampleforth Coll. Lieut Scots Guards, 1960. *Address:* Beaufort Castle, Beauly, Inverness-shire.

LOVE, Enid Rosamond, (Mrs G. C. F. Whitaker), OBE 1973; Educational Consultant to Yorkshire Television Ltd, 1973-74 (Head of Educational Programmes, 1968-73); *b* 15 May 1911; *d* of late Cyril Maurice Love and late Louise Gaston (*née* Harrison), Reading, Berks; *m* 1965, Geoffrey Charles Francis Whitaker. *Educ:* Royal Masonic Sch. for Girls; University of London (Bedford Coll. and Institute of Historical Research). Teaching in various public and grammar schs, 1934-44; Head Mistress, County Grammar Sch. for Girls, Wokingham, Berks, 1944-49. Joined BBC, 1949, as Regional Education Officer for School Broadcasting Council; Asst Head of Sch. Broadcasting (Sound), 1951-56. Asst Head of School Broadcasting (Television), BBC, 1956-59; Head of School Broadcasting, Associated-Rediffusion Ltd, 1959-63; Head Mistress, Sydenham Sch., 1963-68. *Publications:* occasional contributions to educational journals. *Recreations:* reading, walking, foreign travel. *Address:* Welburn House, 6 Lock Mead, Maidenhead, Berks.

LOVEDAY, Alan (Raymond); Solo Violinist; *b* 29 Feb. 1928; *s* of Leslie and Margaret Loveday; *m* 1952, Ruth Stanfield; one *s* one *d. Educ:* privately; Royal College of Music (prizewinner). Made debut at age of 4; debut in England, 1946; has given many concerts, broadcasts, and made TV appearances, in this country and abroad, playing with all leading conductors and orchestras; repertoire ranges from Bach (which he likes to play on an un-modernised violin), to contemporary music. Professor at RCM, 1955-72. Hon. ARCM 1961. *Recreations:* tennis, golf, chess, bridge. *Address:* c/o Royal College of Music, Prince Consort Road, SW7.

LOVEDAY, Rt. Rev. David Goodwin, MA; Assistant Bishop, Diocese of Oxford, since 1971; *b* 13 April 1896; 6th *s* of late J. E. T. Loveday, JP, of Williamscote, near Banbury, Oxon; unmarried. *Educ:* Shrewsbury Sch. (Careswell Exhibitioner); Magdalene Coll., Cambridge (Sizar), 2nd cl. Class. Tripos, Part I, 2nd cl. Theol. Tripos, Part I. Deacon, 1923; Priest, 1924; Asst Master, Malvern Coll., 1917-19; Asst Master and Chaplain, Aldenham Sch.; 1922-25; Clifton Coll., 1925-31; Headmaster of Cranleigh Sch., 1931-54; Archdeacon of Dorking and Examining Chaplain, Guildford, 1954-57; Suffragan Bishop of Dorchester, 1957-71. Select Preacher: Cambridge 1933 and 1954, Dublin, 1951, Oxford, 1955 and 1957. *Address:* Wardington, Banbury, Oxon. *T:* Cropredy 219.

LOVEDAY, George Arthur, TD; Partner in Read Hurst-Brown & Co., subsequently Rowe & Pitman, Hurst-Brown, 1948-75, retired; Chairman, The Stock Exchange, 1973-75; *b* 13 May 1909; *s* of late A. F. Loveday, OBE; *m* 1st, 1935, Sylvia Mary Gibbs (*d* 1967); two *s*; 2nd, 1967, Penelope Elton Dugdale (*née* Cunard), widow of Brig. N. Dugdale. *Educ:* Winchester Coll.; Magdalen Coll., Oxford. Hons Mod. Langs, MA. Stock Exchange, 1937-39; served RA, 1939-45, Major 1941; Lt-Col comdg Herts Yeomanry, 1954. Mem., Stock Exchange, 1946, Mem. Council, 1961, Dep. Chm., 1971. Mem. Council, Bath Univ., 1975. *Recreation:* golf. *Address:* Bushton Manor, Bushton, Swindon, Wilts. *Club:* Boodle's.

LOVEGROVE, Geoffrey David, QC 1969; **His Honour Judge Lovegrove;** a Circuit Judge (formerly County Court Judge), since 1971; *b* 22 Dec. 1919; *s* of late Gilbert Henry Lovegrove; *m* 1959, Janet, *d* of John Bourne; one *s* two *d. Educ:* Haileybury; New College, Oxford (MA). Army, 1940-46. Called to the Bar, Inner Temple, 1947; Dep. Chairman, W Sussex Quarter Sessions, 1965-71. Innholders' Company: Liveryman, 1945; Mem., Court of Assistants, 1973. *Address:* 1 King's Bench Walk, Temple, EC4.

LOVELACE, 5th Earl of, *cr* 1838; **Peter Axel William Locke King;** Baron King and Ockham, 1725; Viscount Ockham, 1838; *b* 26 Nov. 1951; *s* of 4th Earl and of Manon Lis, *d* of Axel Sigurd Transo, Copenhagen, Denmark; *S* father, 1964. *Address:* Torridon House, Torridon, Ross-shire.

LOVELACE, Lt-Col Alec, CMG 1958; MBE 1941; MC; *b* 1907; *m* 1948, Eleanor, *d* of W. E. Platt. *Educ:* Dorchester Grammar Sch.; University College of the South-West, Exeter; Birkbeck Coll., University of London. Served War of 1939-45 in Army (Lt-Col), Education Officer, Mauritius, 1946; Civil Commissioner, 1949; Administrator, Antigua, 1954; Defence Officer, The West Indies, 1958; Administrator of Dominica, Windward Islands, 1960-64, retired. CStJ. *Address:* North Lane, Guestling Thorn, near Hastings, East Sussex.

LOVELL, Sir (Alfred Charles) Bernard, Kt 1961; OBE 1946; FRS 1955; Professor of Radio Astronomy, University of Manchester, and Director of Jodrell Bank Experimental Station, Cheshire, now Nuffield Radio Astronomy Laboratories, since 1951; *b* 31 Aug. 1913; *s* of G. Lovell, Oldland Common, Gloucestershire; *m* 1937, Mary Joyce Chesterman; two *s* three *d. Educ:* Kingswood Grammar Sch., Bristol; University of Bristol. Asst Lectr in Physics, Univ. of Manchester, 1936-39; Telecommunication Res. Establishment, 1939-45; Physical Laboratories, Univ. of Manchester and Jodrell Bank Experimental Station, Cheshire; Lectr, 1945, Sen. Lectr, 1947, Reader, 1949, in Physics. Reith Lectr, 1958; Lectures: Condon, 1962; Guthrie, 1962; Halley, 1964; Queen's, Berlin, 1970; Brockington, Kingston, Ont, 1970; Bickley, Oxford, 1977; Crookshank, RCR, 1977. Vis. Montague Burton Prof. of Internat. Relations, Univ. of Edinburgh, 1973. Member: ARC, 1955-58; SRC, 1965-70; Amer. Philosophical Soc., 1974-. Pres., RAS, 1969-71; Vice-Pres., Internat. Astronomical Union, 1970-76; Pres., British Assocn, 1975-76. Pres., Inc. Guild of Church Musicians, 1976-. Hon. Fellow, Society of Engineers, 1964; Hon. Foreign Member American Academy of Arts and Sciences, 1955; Hon. Life Member, New York Academy, 1960; Hon. Member, Royal Swedish Academy, 1962. Hon. LLD: Edinburgh, 1961; Calgary, 1966; Hon. DSc: Leicester, 1961; Leeds, 1966; London, 1967; Bath, 1967; Bristol, 1970; DUniv Stirling, 1974; DUniv Surrey, 1975; Hon. FIEE, 1967; Hon. FInstP, 1976. Duddell Medal, 1954; Royal Medal, 1960; Daniel and Florence Guggenheim International Astronautics Award, 1961; Ordre du Mérite pour la Recherche et l'Invention, 1962; Churchill Gold Medal, 1964; Maitland Lecturer and Silver Medallist, Institution of Structural Engineers, 1964. Commander's Order of Merit, Polish People's Republic, 1975. *Publications:* Science and Civilisation, 1939; World Power Resources and Social Development, 1945; Radio Astronomy, 1951; Meteor Astronomy, 1954; The Exploration of Space by Radio, 1957; The Individual and The Universe, (BBC Reith Lectures, 1958); The Exploration of Outer Space (Gregynog Lectures, 1961); Discovering the Universe, 1963; Our Present Knowledge of the Universe, 1967; (ed with T. Margerison) The Explosion of Science: The Physical Universe, 1967; The Story of Jodrell Bank, 1968; The Origins and International Economics of Space Exploration, 1973; Out of the Zenith, 1973; Man's Relation to the Universe, 1975; P. M. S. Blackett: a biographical memoir, 1976; In the Centre of Immensities, 1978; many publications in Physical and Astronomical journals. *Recreations:* cricket, gardening, music. *Address:* The Quinta, Swettenham, Cheshire. *T:* Lower Withington 254. *Club:* Athenæum.

LOVELL, Arnold Henry; Under-Secretary, HM Treasury, since 1975; *b* 5 Aug. 1926; *s* of Alexander and Anita Lovell; *m* 1950, Joyce Harmer; one *s* one *d. Educ:* Hemsworth Grammar Sch., Yorks; London School of Economics (BScEcon, 1st Cl. Hons). HM Treasury: Asst Principal, 1952; Principal, 1956; Asst Financial Adviser to UK High Commn, New Delhi, India, 1962-65; re-joined HM Treasury, Monetary Policy Div., 1965-70; Asst Sec., 1967; Balance of Payments Div., 1970-75; Under-Sec., Fiscal Policy Div., 1975-. *Recreations:* walking, Stafford bull terriers. *Address:* 15 Clifford Avenue, Chislehurst, Kent BR7 5DY. *T:* 01-467 1116.

LOVELL, Stanley Hains, CMG 1972; ED; consultant surgeon; *b* 22 Sept. 1906; *er s* of late John Hains Lovell; *m* 1935, Eleanor, *o d* of late Dr Edgar Harold Young; three *d. Educ:* Fort Street Boys' High Sch.; St Andrew's Coll., Univ. of Sydney. MB, BS, MS Sydney; FRACS. Served War of 1939-45, Middle East and Pacific (despatches); Col, RAAMC. Hon. Consultant Surgeon, Royal Prince Alfred, Rachel Forster, Prince Henry, Prince of Wales and Eastern Suburbs Hosps. Fellow, Australian Medical Assoc.; Pres., NSW Medical Defence Union, 1958-. Formerly: Mem. Court of Examrs, and Chm., NSW State Cttee, RACS; Lectr in Clinical Surgery, Sydney Univ.; Examr in Surgery, Sydney Univ.; External Examr, Univ. of Queensland. *Publications:* contrib. various surgical jls. *Recreation:* gardening. *Address:* 229 Macquarie Street, Sydney, NSW 2000, Australia. *T:* 2321060. *Club:* Australian (Sydney).

LOVELL-DAVIS, family name of **Baron Lovell-Davis.**

LOVELL-DAVIS, Baron *cr* 1974 (Life Peer), of Highgate; **Peter Lovell Lovell-Davis;** *b* 8 July 1924; *s* of late William Lovell Davis and late Winifred Mary Davis; *m* 1950, Jean Graham; one *s* one *d. Educ:* Christ's Coll., Finchley; King Edward VI Sch., Stratford-on-Avon; Jesus Coll., Oxford. BA Hons English, MA. Served War, RAF (Pilot), to Flt-Lt, 1943-47. Oxford, 1947-50. Managing Dir, Central Press Features Ltd, 1952-70; Dir, various newspaper and printing cos. Chm., Colour Features Ltd; Chairman: Davis & Harrison Ltd, 1970-73; Features Syndicate, 1971-74. A Lord in Waiting (Govt Whip), 1974-75; Parly Under-Sec. of State, Dept of Energy, 1975-76. Adviser to various Govt Cttees, Health Educn Council, Labour Party and Govt, on media. *Recreations:* industrial archaeology, inland waterways, bird-watching, walking, sketching—and flying kites. *Address:* 80 North Road, Highgate, N6 4AA. *T:* 01-348 3919.

LOVELOCK, Douglas Arthur, CB 1974; Chairman, Board of Customs and Excise, since 1977; *b* 7 Sept. 1923; *s* of late Walter and Irene Lovelock; *m* 1961, Valerie Margaret (*née* Lane); one *s* one *d. Educ:* Bec Sch., London. Entered Treasury, 1949; Min. of Supply, 1952; Private Sec. to Permanent Sec., 1953-54; Principal, 1954; Private Sec. to successive Ministers of Aviation (Rt Hon. Peter Thorneycroft and Rt Hon. Julian Amery), 1961-63; Asst Sec., 1963; Under-Sec. (Contracts), Min. of Technology, subseq. Min. of Aviation Supply, 1968-71; Asst Under-Sec. of State (Personnel), MoD, 1971-72; Dep. Sec., DTI, 1972-74, Depts of Trade, Industry, Prices and Consumer Protection, 1974-77. *Recreations:* walking, gardening, outdoor activities generally. *Address:* The Old House, 91 Coulsdon Road, Old Coulsdon, Surrey. *T:* Downland 55211.

LOVELOCK, Prof. James Ephraim, FRS 1974; Independent Consultant since 1964; Visiting Professor, University of Reading, since 1967; *b* 26 July 1919; *s* of Tom Arthur Lovelock and Nellie Ann Elizabeth (*née* March); *m* 1942, Helen Mary Hyslop; two *s* two *d. Educ:* Strand Sch., London; Manchester and London Univs. BSc, PhD, DSc, ARIC. Staff Scientist, Nat. Inst. for Med. Research, 1941-61; Rockefeller Fellow, Harvard Univ., 1954-55; Yale Univ., 1958-59; Prof. of Chemistry, Baylor Univ. Coll. of Medicine, Texas, 1961-64. Mem. Sigma Xi, Yale Chapter, 1959. *Publications:* numerous papers and patents. *Recreations:* walking, painting, computer programming, reading. *Address:* Bowerchalke, Salisbury, Wilts. *T:* Salisbury 78387.

LOVEMORE, Wing Comdr Robert Baillie, DSO 1919; RAFVR; late 3rd Battalion London Regiment (Royal Fusiliers), RFC and RAF; *e s* of late W. B. Lovemore, JP, of Swaziland; *m* Gwendolen Amy, *o d* of late H. C. Edwards, England; one *s. Educ:* Michaelhouse, Natal. Served European War, 1914-18 (despatches twice, DSO). Served as pilot Air Mail Lines, Union Airways, South African Airways and Wilson Airways (Kenya). Established and commanded E. African flying training scheme, 1939-40; 117 Squadron, Middle East Command, 1940-41; No 7, and subs. No 6, Air Schools in Training Command, Union of South Africa, 1942-46. *Address:* Blythe Glade, PO Emerald Hill, Port Elizabeth, South Africa.

LOVERIDGE, Joan Mary, OBE 1968; Matron and Superintendent of Nursing, St Bartholomew's Hospital, 1949-67; *b* 14 Aug. 1912; *d* of William Ernest Loveridge. *Educ:* Maidenhead, Berkshire. Commenced training, 1930, Royal National Orthopædic Hospital, W1; St Bartholomew's Hospital, 1933-37; Radcliffe Infirmary, Oxford, Midwifery Training, 1937-38; Night Sister, Ward Sister, Matron's Office Sister, Assistant Matron, St Bartholomew's Hospital. *Address:* Third Acre, 3 Wisborough Gardens, Wisborough Green, Sussex.

LOVERIDGE, Sir John (Henry), Kt 1975; CBE 1964 (MBE 1945); Bailiff of Guernsey, since 1973; Barrister-at-Law; Judge of Appeal for Jersey, since 1974; *b* 2 Aug. 1912; *e s* of late Henry Thomas and Vera Lilian Loveridge; *m* 1946, Madeleine Melanie, *o d* of late Eugene Joseph C. M. Tanguy; one *s* one *d. Educ:* Elizabeth Coll., Guernsey; Univ. of Caen. Called to Bar, Middle Temple, 1950. Advocate of Royal Court of Guernsey, 1951; HM Solicitor-General, Guernsey, 1954-60; HM Attorney-General, Guernsey, 1960-69; Deputy Bailiff of Guernsey, 1969-73. RAFVR, 1954-59. CStJ 1975. *Recreations:* reading, swimming, sport. *Address:* Kinmount, Sausmarez Road, St Martin's, Guernsey. *T:* Guernsey 38038. *Club:* Royal Guernsey Golf.

LOVERIDGE, John Warren, JP; MP (C) Havering, Upminster, since 1974 (Hornchurch, 1970-74); Principal of St Godric's College since 1954; farmer; *b* 9 Sept. 1925; *s* of C. W. Loveridge and Emily (Mickie), *d* of John Malone; *m* 1954, Jean Marguerite (JP, S Westminster), *d* of E. J. Chivers; three *s* two *d. Educ:* St John's Coll., Cambridge (MA). Contested (C) Aberavon, 1951, Brixton (LCC), 1952; Hampstead Borough Council, 1953-59. Mem., Parly Select Cttee on Expenditure (Mem. General Purposes Sub-Cttee); former Mem., Procedure Cttee; Vice-Chm., Cons. Smaller Business Cttee. Treasurer/Trustee, Hampstead Conservative Assoc., 1959-74. Pres., Axe Cliff Golf Club. JP West Central Division, 1963. FRAS; MRIIA. Liveryman, Girdlers' Co. *Recreations:* painting, historic houses and early furniture, shooting. *Address:* House of Commons, SW1A 0AA. *Clubs:* Carlton, Hurlingham.

LOVETT, Maj.-Gen. Osmond de Turville, CB 1947; CBE 1945; DSO 1943, and Bar 1944; late 2nd Gurkha Rifles; retired; *b* 1898; *s* of William Edward Turville Lovett, Tamworth, Dunster; *m* 1940, Eleanor Barbara, *d* of late Albert Leslie Wright, late of

Butterley Hall, Derbyshire; no *c. Educ:* Blundells, Tiverton; Cadet Coll., Wellington, India. 2nd Lieut, Indian Army, 1917; served European War, 1914-18, India, Mesopotamia; NW Persia, 1919-21 (wounded); transferred 2nd Gurkhas, 1919; Major, 1936; War of 1939-45, 10th Army, transferred to 8th Army, Middle East Forces (wounded); Central Mediterranean Force; Brigadier, 1943; temp. Maj.-General, 1945; retired, 1948. Farming. *Recreations:* polo, tennis, fishing. *Address:* c/o Standard Bank of South Africa, Mooi River, Natal, South Africa; c/o Lloyds Bank (Cox's and King's Branch), 6 Pall Mall, SW1. *Club:* Naval and Military.

LOVETT, Robert Abercrombie; Banker, United States; *b* 14 Sept. 1895; *s* of Robert Scott Lovett and Lavinia Chilton (*née* Abercrombie); *m* 1919, Adèle Quartley Brown; one *s* (one *d* decd). *Educ:* Yale Univ. (BA), 1918; law study, Harvard, 1919-20; course in business administration, Harvard Grad. Schools, 1920-21. Clerk, National Bank of Commerce, NY City, 1921-23; employee, Brown Brothers & Co., 1923; partner, 1926; continued in successor firm, Brown Brothers Harriman & Co. until 1940. Served as Special Asst to Secretary of War, and as Asst Secretary of War for Air in charge of Army Air Program, 1940-45. Under-Secretary of State, 1947-49; Deputy Secretary of Defence, 1950-51; Secretary of Defence, 1951-Jan. 1953. Readmitted Brown Brothers Harriman & Co., March 1953. Director: Union Pacific Railroad Co.; Union Pacific Corp. Life Member Emeritus, Corp. of MIT. Holds hon. degrees. Served (pilot to Lieut-Commander) US Naval Air Service, March 1917-Dec. 1918 (Navy Cross, DSM). Grand Cross of the Order of Leopold II (Belgium), 1950; Presidential Medal of Freedom, USA, 1963. *Address:* Locust Valley, Long Island, NY 11560, USA. *Clubs:* Century, Yale, Links (New York); Creek (Locust Valley); Metropolitan (Washington, DC).

LOVICK, Albert Ernest Fred; Chairman, 1964-68, Director, 1950-68 and since 1969, Co-operative Insurance Society Ltd; Director: CWS Ltd since 1949; Shoefayre Ltd, since 1975; *b* 19 Feb. 1912; *s* of late Arthur Alfred Lovick and late Mary Lovick (*née* Sharland); *m* 1934, Florence Ena Jewell; no *c. Educ:* Elementary Sch., Eastleigh, Hants; Peter Symonds, Winchester. Hearne & Partner, rating surveyors, 1928; Eastleigh Co-operative Society, 1929-33; Harwich, Dovercourt and Parkeston CS, 1933-35; Managing Secretary, Basingstoke CS, 1935-49. During War of 1939-45, government cttees. Member, Basingstoke Borough Council, 1946-49. Chairman: Centratours Ltd; Cumbrian Co-op. Society Ltd, Carlisle. Member: Export Credits Guarantees Advisory Council, 1968-73; Bristol Rent Assessment Cttee, 1973-; Bristol Rent Tribunal, 1973-. Fellow, Co-operative Secretaries Assoc.; FCIS; FIArb. *Recreations:* golf, gardening. *Address:* 1 Miller Street, Manchester, 4; Coedway, Bristol Road, Stonehouse, Glos GL10 2BQ. *T:* Stonehouse 3167. *Club:* Royal Commonwealth Society.

LOW, family name of **Baron Aldington.**

LOW, Sir Alan (Roberts), Kt 1977; Governor, Reserve Bank of New Zealand, 1967-77; *b* 11 Jan. 1916; 4th *s* of Benjamin H. Low and Sarah Low; *m* 1940, Kathleen Mary Harrow; one *s* two *d. Educ:* Timaru Main Sch.; Timaru Boys' High Sch.; Canterbury University College. MA 1937. Joined Reserve Bank of New Zealand, 1938; Economic Adviser, 1951; Asst Governor, 1960; Deputy Governor, 1962; Governor, 1967. Army Service, 1942-44; on loan to Economic Stabilisation Commission, 1944-46. *Publications:* contributions to Economic Record. *Recreations:* gardening, music, reading. *Address:* 83 Penrose Street, Lower Hutt, New Zealand. *T:* 699-526. *Club:* Wellington (NZ).

LOW, Prof. Donald Anthony, DPhil; Vice-Chancellor, Australian National University, since 1975; *b* 22 June 1927; *o s* of late Canon Donald Low and Winifred (*née* Edmunds); *m* 1952, Isobel Smails; one *s* two *d. Educ:* Univ. of Oxford (MA, DPhil). Open Scholar in Modern History, 1944 and Amelia Jackson Sen. Student, 1948, Exeter Coll., Oxford; Lectr, subseq. Sen. Lectr, Makerere Coll., University Coll. of E. Africa, 1951-58; Uganda corresp., The Times, 1952-58; Fellow, subseq. Sen. Fellow in History, Res. Sch. of Social Sciences, ANU, 1959-64; Founding Dean of Sch. of African and Asian Studies, and Prof. of Hist., Univ. of Sussex, 1964-72 (Dir, Graduates in Arts and Social Studies, 1970-71); Dir, Res. Sch. of Pacific Studies, and Prof. of Hist., ANU, 1973-75. Sen. Visitor, Nuffield Coll., Oxford, 1956-57; Vis. Prof., Univ. of Calif, Berkeley, and Chicago Univ., 1967. FAHA 1973; FASSA 1975; Hon. Fellow, Inst of Develt Studies, UK, 1972. *Publications:* Buganda and British Overrule, 1900-1955 (with R. C. Pratt), 1960; (ed) Soundings in Modern South Asian History, 1968; (with J. C. Iltis and M. D. Wainwright) Government Archives in South Asia: a guide to national and state archives in Ceylon, India and Pakistan, 1969; Buganda in

Modern History, 1971; The Mind of Buganda, 1971; Lion Rampant: essays in the study of British imperialism, 1973; Congress and the Raj, facets of the Indian struggle, 1917-1947, 1977; Oxford History of East Africa: (contrib.) Vol. I, 1963 and Vol. II, 1965; (contrib. and ed jtly) Vol. III, 1976; articles on internat. history in jls. *Address:* 21 Balmain Crescent, Acton, Canberra, ACT 2600, Australia.

LOW, Sir James (Richard) Morrison-, 3rd Bt, *cr* 1908; DFH, CEng, MIEE; Director, Osborne & Hunter Ltd, Glasgow and Kirkcaldy, since 1956 (Electrical Engineer with firm, 1952-); *b* 3 Aug. 1925; *s* of Sir Walter John Morrison-Low, 2nd Bt and Dorothy Ruth de Quincey Quincey (*d* 1946); *S* father 1955; *m* 1953, Ann Rawson Gordon; one *s* three *d. Educ:* Ardvreck; Harrow; Merchiston. Served Royal Corps of Signals, 1943-47; demobilised with rank of Captain. Faraday House Engineering Coll., 1948-52. *Recreations:* shooting, piping. *Heir: s* Richard Walter Morrison-Low, *b* 4 Aug. 1959. *Address:* Kilmaron Castle, Cupar, Fife. *T:* Cupar 2248. *Clubs:* Royal and Ancient Golf (St Andrews); New, Royal Scottish Pipers Society (Edinburgh).

LOWE, Arthur, actor since 1945; *b* 22 Sept. 1915; *s* of Arthur Lowe and Mary Annie Lowe (*née* Ford); *m* 1948, Joan Cooper, actress; one *s. Educ:* Manchester. Various repertory companies, 1945-52; Larger than Life, Duke of York's, 1950; Hassan, Cambridge, 1951; Call Me Madam, Coliseum, 1952-53; Pal Joey, Princes, 1954; The Pajama Game, Coliseum, 1955-57; A Dead Secret, Piccadilly, 1957; The Ring of Truth, Savoy, 1959; Stop It, Whoever You Are, Arts, 1961; various plays, Royal Court, 1963-67; Home and Beauty, Old Vic, 1968; Ann Veronica, Cambridge, 1969; The Tempest, Old Vic, 1974; Bingo, Royal Court, 1974; Dad's Army, Shaftesbury, 1975. Films: London Belongs to Me, Floodtide, 1948; Kind Hearts and Coronets, Stop Press Girl, Poet's Pub, Spider and the Fly, 1949; Cage of Gold, 1950; The Woman for Joe, Who Done It, 1955; Green Man, 1956; Boy and the Bridge, 1958; Follow that Horse, The Day they Robbed the Bank of England, 1959; Go to Blazes, 1961; This Sporting Life, 1962; You're Joking, of course, The White Bus, 1965; If, Bed Sitting Room, 1968; Spring and Port Wine, Fragment of Fear, Rise and Rise of Michael Rimmer, 1969; Dad's Army, 1970; Ruling Class, 1971; O Lucky Man, Theatre of Blood, Adolf Hitler, my Part in his Downfall, 1972; No Sex Please, We're British, 1973; Man about the House, 1974; Royal Flash, Adventures of Tom Jones, 1975. Numerous TV plays, series etc, inc. Dad's Army, also much radio work. Various nominations and awards. *Address:* Flat C, 2 Maida Avenue, Little Venice, W2 1TF. *T:* 01-262 1782. *Clubs:* BAFTA, BBC.

LOWE, Group Captain Cyril Nelson, MC, DFC; BA Cambridge; late OC, RAF Station, Amman, Trans Jordan; *b* 7 Oct. 1891; *s* of Rev. C. W. Nelson Lowe, MA; *m* Ethel Mary Watson; one *s* two *d. Educ:* Dulwich Coll.; Pembroke Coll., Cambridge. Rugby Blue at Cambridge, 1911-12-13; first played for England v S. Africa in 1913, and subsequently gained 25 International Caps; Commission Aug. 1914 in ASC, and qualified for 1914 Star; seconded to Royal Flying Corps, 1916; No. 11 Squadron RFC France, 1916-17; 24 Squadron RFC, France, 1918 (MC, DFC). *Address:* Little Brook, Burrow Hill, Chobham, Surrey.

LOWE, Sir David, Kt 1962; CBE 1950; DL; Chairman: Elvingston Estates Ltd, since 1962; British Society for the Promotion of Vegetable Research; *b* 12 May 1899; *s* of late Provost David Lowe, Musselburgh; *m* 1932, Katherine Cecile Jane, *d* of late Roderick Ross, CVO, CBE, Edinburgh; three *d. Educ:* Musselburgh Grammar Sch. President, National Farmers' Union of Scotland, 1948-49; President, Edinburgh Chamber of Commerce and Manufactures, 1958-60 and 1962-63; Governor, Edinburgh and East of Scotland College of Agriculture. Chairman: David Lowe & Sons Ltd, 1943-63; Thomson & Mathieson Ltd, 1959-65; Livingston Development Corporation (New Town), 1962-65; Scottish Horticultural Advisory Cttee, 1961-69. Director, National Seed Development Organisation Ltd. Member: Agricultural Research Council, 1954-64 (Dep. Chairman, 1958-64); Agricultural Marketing Development Exec. Cttee, 1962-68; Cinematograph Films Council, 1958-63. Chairman, Scottish Agric. & Horti. Apprenticeship Scheme, 1949-74. Vice-President, Scottish Council Development & Industry, 1963-68. Trustee, Scottish Country Industries Development Trust, 1960-66. VMH 1972. DL East Lothian, 1975. Hon. DSc Edinburgh, 1966. FRSE 1961; FRAgSs, 1970. *Recreation:* plant breeding. *Address:* Elvingston, Gladsmuir, East Lothian. *T:* Longniddry 52128. *Club:* Naval and Military.

LOWE, David Nicoll, OBE 1946; MA, BSc; FRSE; Secretary, Carnegie United Kingdom Trust, 1954-70; *b* 9 Sept. 1909; *s* of George Black Lowe and Jane Nicoll, Arbroath, Angus; *m* 1939, Muriel Enid Bryer, CSP; one *s* three *d. Educ:* Arbroath High Sch.; St Andrews Univ. (Kitchener Scholar). MA 1931; BSc (1st Class Hons Botany) 1934; President Union, 1933-34; President Students' Representative Council, 1934-35; Founder President, University Mountaineering Club; Asst Secretary British Assoc. for the Advancement of Science, 1935-40, Secretary 1946-54. War Cabinet Secretariat, 1940-42 and 1945-46; Ministry of Production, 1942-45. Joint Hon. Secretary, Society of Visiting Scientists, 1952-54; Member Executive Cttee: Scottish Council of Social Service, 1953-71; Nat. Trust for Scotland, 1971-; Member, Countryside Commn for Scotland, 1968-. Chairman: Scottish Congregational Coll., 1961-68; Pollock Meml Missionary Trust, 1973-; Governor, Scottish Nat. Meml to David Livingstone, 1974-. Contributor to Annual Register, 1947-59. Queen's Silver Jubilee Medal, 1977. *Recreations:* those of his family and gardening. *Address:* Caddam, Perth Road, Crieff, Perthshire. *Club:* Royal Over-Seas League.

LOWE, Air Chief Marshal Sir Douglas (Charles), GCB 1977 (KCB 1974; CB 1971); DFC 1943; AFC 1946; Controller, Aircraft, Ministry of Defence Procurement Executive, since 1975; *b* 14 March 1922; *s* of John William Lowe; *m* 1944, Doreen Elizabeth (*née* Nichols); one *s* one *d. Educ:* Reading School. Joined RAF, 1940; No 75 (NZ) Sqdn, 1943; Bomber Comd Instructors' Sch., 1945; RAF Coll., Cranwell, 1947; Exam. Wing CFS, 1950; Air Min. Operational Requirements, 1955; OC No 148 Sqdn, 1959; Exchange Officer, HQ SAC, USAF, 1961; Stn Comdr Cranwell, 1963; idc 1966; DOR 2 (RAF), MoD (Air), 1967; SASO, NEAF, 1969-71; ACAS (Operational Requirements), 1971-73; AOC No 18 Group, RAF, 1973-75. *Recreations:* gardening, domestic odd-jobbing, photography, theatre, music. *Address:* c/o Lloyds Bank Ltd, Byfleet, Surrey. *Club:* Royal Air Force.
See also Baron Glanusk.

LOWE, Douglas Gordon Arthur, QC 1964; Barrister-at-Law; a Recorder of the Crown Court, 1972-75 (Recorder of Lincoln, 1964-71); *b* 7 Aug. 1902; *o s* of Arthur John Lowe; *m* 1930, Karen, *e d* of Surgeon Einar Thamsen; one *s. Educ:* Highgate Sch.; Pembroke Coll., Cambridge (Exhibitioner, MA). Called to the Bar, Inner Temple, 1928; Bencher, Inner Temple, 1957. Dep. Chm., Warwicks QS, 1965-71. Councillor, Hampstead Borough Council, 1940-44; Governor, Highgate Sch., 1939-76 (Chairman, 1965-76); Chairman, Oxford Mental Health Tribunal, 1962-64. Member, Criminal Injuries Compensation Board, 1965-77. *Publication:* (with Arthur Porritt, now Lord Porritt) Athletics, 1929. *Recreations:* walking, gardening; formerly athletics, cricket, Association football, Eton fives, lawn tennis and golf. (President Cambridge Univ. Athletic Club; Assoc. Football and Athletics Blue; winner Olympic 800 meters, 1924 and 1928; Hon. Secretary Amateur Athletic Assoc., 1931-38). *Address:* Yeomans, Lake Road, Virginia Water, Surrey; 12 King's Bench Walk, Temple, EC4. *T:* 01-353 5892. *Clubs:* Carlton; Achilles; Hawks (Cambridge).

LOWE, Air Vice-Marshal Sir Edgar (Noel), KBE 1962 (CBE 1945); CB 1947; Director General of Supply Co-ordination, Ministry of Defence, 1966-70, retired (Inspector General of Codification and Standardisation, 1964); *b* 1905; *s* of late Albert Henry Lowe, Church Stretton, Shropshire; *m* 1948, Mary McIlwraith, *o d* of George M. Lockhart, Stair House, Stair, Ayrshire; one *s* one *d.* Served India, 1934-38; psa 1939; served in France 1939-40 (despatches); Air Commodore, Director of Organisation (Forecasting and Planning), Air Ministry, 1945-47; idc 1949; ADC to the King, 1949-52, to the Queen, 1952-57; Directing Staff, RAF Staff Coll., Bracknell, 1950-51; Director of Organisation, Air Ministry, 1951-53; Deputy Asst Chief of Staff (Logistics), SHAPE, 1953-56; Senior Air Staff Officer, HQ No 41 Group, RAF, 1956-58; AOC No 40 Group, RAF, 1958-61; Director-General of Equipment, Air Ministry, 1961-64. *Address:* Wyndford, 97 Harestone Hill, Caterham, Surrey. *T:* Caterham 45757. *Club:* Royal Air Force.

LOWE, Sir Francis (Reginald Gordon), 3rd Bt *cr* 1918; *b* 8 Feb. 1931; *s* of Sir Francis Gordon Lowe, 2nd Bt, and Dorothy Honor, *d* of late Lt-Col H. S. Woolrych; *S* father, 1972; *m* 1st, 1961, Franziska Cornelia Steinkopf (marr. diss. 1971); two *s*; 2nd, 1971, Helen Suzanne, *y d* of late Sandys Stuart Macaskie; one *s. Educ:* Stowe; Clare College, Cambridge (BA, LLB). Called to the Bar, Middle Temple, 1959; South Eastern Circuit. *Recreation:* market gardening. *Heir: s* Thomas William Gordon Lowe, *b* 14 Aug. 1963. *Address:* 6 Parkfields, Putney, SW15 6NH. *T:* 01-789 5765; Bagwich, Godshill, Isle of Wight. *T:* Godshill 252; 4 New Square, Lincoln's Inn, WC2A 3RJ. *T:* 01-242 8508.

LOWE, Geoffrey Colin; Under Secretary (Management Services and Manpower), Departments of Industry, Trade, and Prices and Consumer Protection, since 1974; *b* 7 Sept. 1920; *s* of late Colin Roderick and late Elsie Lowe; *m* 1948, Joan Stephen; one *d. Educ:* Reigate Grammar Sch. GPO, 1937; Exchequer and Audit Dept, 1939. Served War, RAFVR, 1941-46 (Flt-Lt). Asst Principal, Min. of Civil Aviation, 1947; Private Sec. to Permanent Sec., MCA, 1950; Principal, 1950; Colonial Office, 1954-57; Min. of Transport and Civil Aviation, 1957-61; Civil Air Attaché, SE Asia, 1961-64; Asst Sec., Overseas Policy Div., Min. of Aviation, 1964-68; Investment Grants Div., Bd of Trade, 1968-71; Counsellor (Civil Aviation), British Embassy, Washington, 1971-73, Counsellor (Civil Aviation and Shipping), Washington, 1973-74. *Recreations:* theatre, crossword puzzles. *Address:* Starlings, 36a Monkhams Avenue, Woodford Green, Essex IG8 0EY. *T:* 01-504 7035.

LOWE, Dr John; Head, County Educational Policy Reviews, Education and Training Division, OECD, since 1973; *b* 3 Aug. 1922; *s* of John Lowe and Ellen (*née* Webb); *m* 1949, Margaret James; two *s* one *d. Educ:* Univ. of Liverpool (BA Hons 1950); Univ. of London (CertEd 1951, PhD 1960). Lectr, subseq. Sen. Lectr, Univ. of Liverpool, 1955-63; Dir, Extra-Mural Studies, Univ. of Singapore, 1963-64; Dir, Dept of Adult Educn and Extra-Mural Studies, subsequently Head, Dept of Educnl Studies, Univ. of Edinburgh, 1964-72; OECD: Consultant in field, 1964-; Principal Administrator, 1973-. Sec./Treas., Internat. Congress of Univ. Adult Educn, 1972-76. *Publications:* Adult Education in England and Wales, 1970; (ed) Adult Education and Nation-Building, 1970; (ed) Education and Nation-Building in the Third World, 1971; The Education of Adults: a world perspective, 1975; articles in educnl and hist. jls. *Recreations:* reading, music, theatre, swimming. *Address:* 3 Rue Ribera, 75016 Paris, France. *T:* 306 3799. *Club:* National Liberal.

LOWE, John Eric Charles, MVO 1965; MBE 1937; *b* 11 Aug. 1907; 6th *s* of late John Frederick Lowe; *m* 1935, Trudy (*née* Maybury); one *s* two *d. Educ:* Burghley Road Sch., Highgate. Vice-Consul, Jibuti, 1930-37, Harar, 1940; Political Officer, Aden Protectorate, 1940; served in HM Forces, Somaliland and Ethiopia, 1941-46; Senior Asst, Foreign Office, 1947-49; Acting Consul, Suez, 1949; Vice-Consul, Beira, 1950; Vice-Consul, Hamburg, 1951 and Frankfurt, 1953; 2nd Secretary, Helsinki, 1953; Political Agent's Representative, Mina-Al-Ahmadi (Kuwait), 1956; Vice-Consul, Leopoldville, 1959; Consul, Khartoum, 1962; Consul-General, Basra, 1965-67; retired, Sept. 1967. Order of the Two Niles (Sudan), 1965. *Recreations:* gardening, golf, sailing. *Address:* 16 Deepdene, Wadhurst, Sussex. *T:* Wadhurst 3301.

LOWE, John Evelyn, MA, FSA, FRSA; Principal, West Dean College, Chichester, West Sussex, since 1972; consultant to: The Weald and Downland Open Air Museum, Singleton, Sussex, since 1974 (Director, 1969-74); Seibu Ltd, Tokyo; foreign travel consultant, journalist and photographer; *b* 23 April 1928; *s* of late Arthur Holden Lowe; *m* 1956, Susan Helen Sanderson; two *s* one *d. Educ:* Wellington Coll., Berks; New Coll., Oxford. Served in RAEC, 1947-49 (Sgt Instructor). Victoria and Albert Museum, Dept of Woodwork, 1953-56; Deputy Story Editor, Pinewood Studios, 1956-57; Victoria and Albert Museum: Dept of Ceramics, 1957-61; Assistant to the Director, 1961-64; Dir, City Museum and Art Gall., Birmingham, 1964-69. Member: Council of the British School at Rome, 1968-70; Crafts Adv. Cttee, 1973-. *Publications:* books and articles on the applied arts and foreign travel. *Recreations:* Japan, music, reading, travel. *Address:* Duffryn, Liphook, Hants. *T:* Liphook 723104.

LOWE, Prof. Kenneth Gordon, MD; FRCP, FRCPE, FRCPGlas; Physician to the Queen in Scotland, since 1971; Consultant Physician, Dundee Royal Infirmary, since 1952; Hon. Professor of Medicine, Dundee University, since 1969; *b* 29 May 1917; *s* of Thomas J. Lowe, MA, BSc, Arbroath, and Flora MacDonald Gordon, Arbroath; *m* 1942, Nancy Young, MB, ChB, twin *d* of Stephen Young, Logie, Fife; two *s* one *d. Educ:* Arbroath High Sch.; St Andrews Univ. (MD Hons). Served with RAMC, 1942-46; Registrar, Hammersmith Hosp., Royal Postgrad. Med. Sch., 1947-52; Sen. Lectr in Medicine, St Andrews Univ., 1952-61. *Publications:* contribs to med. and scientific jls, mainly on renal, metabolic and cardiac disorders. *Recreations:* reading, fishing. *Address:* 36 Dundee Road, West Ferry, Dundee. *T:* Dundee 78787. *Club:* Flyfishers.

LOWE, Dr Robert David; Dean, St George's Hospital Medical School, since 1971; Hon. Consultant to St George's Hospital; *b* 23 Feb. 1930; *s* of John Lowe and Hilda Althea Mead; *m* 1952, Betty Irene Wheeler; one *s* three *d. Educ:* Leighton Park Sch.; Emmanuel Coll., Cambridge; UCH Medical School. BCh, MB,

MA, MD, PhD Cantab; FRCP, LMSSA. Medical Specialist, RAMC, 1955-59; Research Asst, UCH Med. Sch., 1959-61; St George's Hosp. Med. Sch.: MRC Res. Fellow, 1961-62; Wellcome Sen. Res. Fellow in Clinical Science, 1963-64; Sen. Lectr in Medicine, St Thomas' Hosp. Med. Sch., 1964-70; Hon. Consultant to St Thomas' Hosp., 1966-70. AUCAS: Exec. Mem., 1967-; Chm., 1972-. *Publications:* (with B. F. Robinson) A Physiological Approach to Clinical Methods, 1970; papers on peripheral circulation, hypertension, adrenergic mechanisms, central action of angiotensin, control of cardiovascular system. *Recreations:* bridge, squash, hill-walking. *Address:* Brockhurst, 17 Melrose Road, Southfields, SW18 1ND. *T:* 01-874 5806.

LOWENSTEIN, Prof. Otto Egon, FRS 1955; FRSE; DSc (Glasgow); PhD (Birmingham); DrPhil (Munich);Honorary Senior Research Fellow, Neurocommunications Research Unit, Birmingham University Medical School, since 1976 (Leverhulme Emeritus Research Fellow, 1974-76); *b* 24 Oct. 1906; *s* of Julius Lowenstein and Mathilde Heusinger; *m* 1st, Elsa Barbara, *d* of R. Ritter; two *s*; 2nd, Gunilla Marika, *d* of Prof. Gösta Dohlman; one step *s. Educ:* Neues Realgymnasium, Munich; Munich Univ. Asst, Munich Univ., 1931-33; Research Scholar, Birmingham Univ., 1933-37; Asst Lecturer, University College, Exeter, 1937-38; Senior Lecturer, Glasgow Univ., 1938-52; Mason Prof. of Zoology and Comparative Physiology, Birmingham Univ., 1952-74. President: Assoc. for the Study of Animal Behaviour, 1961-64; Section D, British Assoc., 1962; Institute of Biology, 1965-67; Member Council, Royal Society, 1968-69. *Publications:* Revision of 6th edn of A Textbook of Zoology (Parker and Haswell), Vol. I; The Senses, 1966; papers in various learned journals on Electrophysiology and Ultrastructure of Sense Organs, esp. inner ear of vertebrates. *Recreations:* music, golf, painting. *Address:* 22 Estria Road, Birmingham B15 2LQ. *T:* 021-440 2526.

LOWNDES, Alan; artist (painter); *b* 23 Feb. 1921; *s* of Samuel and Jenny Lowndes; *m* 1959, Valerie (*née* Holmes); one *s* two *d. Educ:* Christ Church C of E Sch., Stockport. Left school at 14; apprenticed to a house decorator. Served War of 1939-45: joined Cheshire Regt TA as Private, 1st Sept. 1939 (Africa Star, 8th Army Clasp, etc); demobilised (still a Private) at end of War after serving in the Desert and Italy. Attended life drawing and painting evening classes at Stockport Coll.; worked as a textile designer; painted in spare time; finally gave up job to paint full time, 1949; lived in Cornwall up to 1970. First exhibited at Crane Kalman Gallery, Manchester, 1950. *Exhibitions:* England, America, Germany, Belgium, Italy; regular exhibitions at Crane Kalman Gall., London. Paintings in the following collections (amongst others): Arts Council; Nuffield Foundation; Walker Art Gall., Liverpool; City Art Gall., Manchester; Coventry Art Gall.; Plymouth Art Gall.; Balliol Coll. *Recreations:* observing the public in public places and public houses. *Address:* 13 St George's Close, Upper Cam, Dursley, Glos. *T:* Dursley 2014. *Club:* Chelsea Arts.

LOWNIE, Ralph Hamilton; A Metropolitan Stipendiary Magistrate, since 1974; *b* 27 Sept. 1924; *yr s* of James H. W. Lownie and Jesse H. Aitken; *m* 1960, Claudine Therese, *o d* of Pierre Lecrocq, Reims; one *s* one *d. Educ:* George Watson's Coll.; Edinburgh Univ. (MA,LLB). Royal Engineers, 1943-47, NW Europe. WS 1952; Mem. Faculty of Advocates 1959; called to Bar, Inner Temple, 1962. Judicial Dept, Kenya, 1954-63; Min. of Legal Affairs, Kenya, 1963-65; Admin of Justice Dept, Bermuda, 1965-72. *Recreations:* hill-walking, military heraldry. *Address:* Camberwell Magistrates Court, SE5. *Club:* Nairobi (Kenya).

LOWREY, Air Comdt Dame Alice, DBE 1960; RRC 1954; Matron-in-Chief, Princess Mary's Royal Air Force Nursing Service, 1959-63 (retired); *b* 8 April 1905; *d* of William John Lowrey and Agnes Lowrey (formerly Walters). *Educ:* Yorkshire; Training Sch., Sheffield Royal Hospital. Joined PMRAFNS, 1932; served in Iraq and Aden. Principal Matron: HQ, MEAF and FEAF, 1956-58; HQ, Home Command and Technical Training Command, 1958-59. Air Commandant, 1959. Officer Sister Order of St John, 1959. *Address:* c/o Midland Bank, St Nicholas Street, Scarborough, N Yorkshire YO11 2HN; Flat 4, The Homestead, South Green, Southwold, E Suffolk.

LOWRY, Hugh Avant, CB 1974; retired 1974; Comptroller and Auditor-General for Northern Ireland, 1971-74; *b* 23 May 1913; *s* of late Hugh George Lowry, HM Inspector of Taxes, and late Ellen Louisa Lowry (*née* Avant); *m* 1939, Marjorie Phyllis Mary (*née* Hale); two *d. Educ:* Watford Grammar Sch.; Gonville and Caius Coll., Cambridge. 1st Cl. Hons, both parts, Classical Tripos, 1932-35; MA; Apptd Asst Principal, Ministry of Labour for Northern Ireland, 1936. Served War, as Observer in Fleet

Air Arm, RNVR, 1943-46. Served in various Ministries of Govt of N Ireland in various grades. Sec. to Nat. Assistance Bd for N Ireland, 1956-57; Second Sec. and Dir of Establishments, Min. of Finance for Northern Ireland, July 1970-June 1971. *Recreations:* bridge, bowls, golf; watching games he used to play-Rugby football, cricket, tennis. *Address:* Woodridings, 7A Greenway Park, Chippenham, Wilts. *T:* Chippenham 3260. *Club:* Civil Service.

LOWRY, John Patrick; Director of Personnel, British Leyland Ltd, since 1975; *b* 31 March 1920; *s* of John McArdle and Edith Mary Lowry; *m* 1952, Sheilagh Mary Davies; one *s* one *d* . *Educ:* Wyggeston Grammar Sch., Leicester; London Sch. of Economics (evening student). BCom London; FIPM, FBIM. Statistical Clerk, Engineering Employers' Fedn, 1938; served Army, 1939-46; various posts in EEF, 1946-70, Dir 1965-70; Dir of Industrial Relations, British Leyland Motor Corp., 1970, Board Dir 1972. Member: UK Employers' Delegn, ILO, 1962, 1963, 1967; Court of Inquiry, Barbican and Horseferry Road Building Disputes, 1967; Court of Inquiry, Grunwick Dispute, 1977; Chm., CBI Industrial Relations and Wages and Conditions Cttee; Member: CBI Employment Policy Cttee; EEF Policy Cttee; EEF Management Bd. Pres., Inst. of Supervisory Management, 1972-74. *Recreations:* British Leyland, theatre, gardening, fishing, and British Leyland! *Address:* The Old Forge, Bramley, Guildford, Surrey. *T:* Bramley 2397.

LOWRY, Mrs Noreen Margaret (Nina); Her Honour Judge Lowry; a Circuit Judge, since 1976; *b* 6 Sept. 1925; *er d* of late John Collins, MC, and of Hilda Collins, Ham, Richmond, Surrey; *m* 1st, 1950, Edward Lucas Gardner, QC (marr. diss., 1962); one *s* one *d* ; 2nd, 1963, Richard John Lowry, *qv* ; one *d.* *Educ:* Bedford High Sch.; Birmingham Univ. LLB Birmingham, 1947. Called to the Bar, Gray's Inn, 1948. Criminal practice on S Eastern Circuit, Central Criminal Court, Inner London Sessions, etc., practising as Miss Nina Collins; Metropolitan Stipendiary Magistrate, 1967-76. Mem. Criminal Law Revision Cttee, 1975-. *Recreations:* theatre, travel. *Address:* 3 Temple Gardens, EC4. *T:* 01-353 1662.

LOWRY, Mrs Richard; *see* Lowry, Mrs N. M.

LOWRY, Richard John, QC 1968; His Honour Judge Richard Lowry; *b* 23 June 1924; *s* of late Geoffrey Charles Lowry, OBE, TD, and late Margaret Spencer Lowry; *m* 1963, Noreen Margaret Lowry, *qv* ; one *d.* *Educ:* St Edward's Sch.; University College, Oxford. RAF, 1943; qualified as pilot and commnd, 1944; No 228 Group Staff Officer, India, 1945; Flt-Lieut, 1946. University College, Oxford, 1942-43 and 1946-48; BA, 1948, MA 1949. Called to Bar, Inner Temple, 1949; Bencher 1977; Member, General Council of Bar, 1965-69. Dep. Chm., Herts QS, 1968; a Recorder, 1972-77. Mem., Home Office Adv. Council on Penal System, 1972-. *Recreations:* theatre, swimming, fossicking; formerly rowing (Oxford Univ. wartime VIII, 1943). *Address:* 3 Temple Gardens, Temple, EC4. *T:* 01-353 1662. *Clubs:* Garrick; Leander (Henley-on-Thames).

LOWRY, Rt. Hon. Sir Robert Lynd Erskine, PC 1974; PC (NI) 1971; Kt 1971; Lord Chief Justice of Northern Ireland, since 1971; *b* 30 Jan. 1919; *o s* of late William Lowry (Rt Hon. Mr Justice Lowry) and Catherine Hughes Lowry, 3rd *d* of Rev. R. J. Lynd, DD; *m* 1945, Mary Audrey, *o d* of John Martin, 43 Myrtlefield Park, Belfast; three *d.* *Educ:* Royal Belfast Academical Institution; Jesus Coll., Cambridge (Hon. Fellow 1977). Entrance Exhibn. (Classics); Scholar, 1939; 1st Class Classical Tripos, Part I, 1939, Part II 1940; MA 1944. Served HM Forces, 1940-46; Tunisia, 1942-43 with 38 Irish Inf. Bde; commissioned Royal Irish Fusiliers, 1941; Major, 1945; Hon. Colonel: 7th Bn Royal Irish Fusiliers, 1969-71 (5th Bn, 1967-68); 5th Bn Royal Irish Rangers, 1971-76. Called to the Bar of N Ireland, 1947; Bencher of the Inn of Court, 1955-; Hon. Bencher, Middle Temple, 1973; Hon. Bencher, King's Inns, Dublin, 1973; QC (N Ireland), 1956. Counsel to HM Attorney-General, 1948-56; Judge of the High Court of Justice (NI), 1964-71. Member Departmental Cttees on Charities, Legal Aid and Registration of Title; Dep. Chm., Boundaries Commn (NI) 1964-71; Chairman: Interim Boundary Commn (NI Constituencies), 1967; Permanent Boundary Commn, 1969-71; Dep. Chm., Lord Chancellor's Cttee on NI Supreme Court; Member, Jt Law Enforcement Commn, 1974; Chairman: N Ireland Constitutional Convention, 1975; Council of Legal Educn (NI), 1976-. Governor, Royal Belfast Academical Instn, 1956-71, Chm., Richmond Lodge Sch., 1956-77; Chm. Governing Bodies Assoc. (NI), 1965. *Recreations:* golf (Pres., Royal Portrush GC, 1974-); showjumping (Chm., SJAI Exec., 1970-72; Mem. Nat. Equestrian Fedn, 1969-; Internat. Showjumping Judge, 1973-). *Address:* White Hill, Crossgar, Co. Down. *T:* Crossgar 397. *Clubs:* Army and Navy, MCC.

LOWRY-CORRY, family name of **Earl of Belmore.**

LOWSON, Sir Ian (Patrick), 2nd Bt *cr* 1951; *b* 4 Sept. 1944; *s* of Sir Denys Colquhoun Flowerdew Lowson, 1st Bt and of Patricia, OStJ, *yr d* of 1st Baron Strathcarron, PC, KC; *S* father, 1975. *Educ:* Eton; Duke Univ., USA. OStJ. *Address:* Bandirran, Balbeggie, Perthshire.

LOWTHER, family name of **Earl of Lonsdale** and **Viscount Ullswater.**

LOWTHER, Viscount; Hugh Clayton Lowther, *b* 27 May 1949; *s* and *heir* of 7th Earl of Lonsdale, *qv* , and of Tuppina Cecily, *d* of late Captain G. H. Bennet; *m* 1971, Pamela Middleton.

LOWTHER, Captain Hon. Anthony George, MBE 1954; DL; *b* 23 Sept. 1925; *yr s* of Viscount Lowther (*d* 1949); granted 1954, title, rank and precedence of an earl's son which would have been his had his father survived to succeed to earldom of Lonsdale; *m* 1958, Lavinia, *o c* of late Thomas H. Joyce, San Francisco, California; one *s* three *d.* *Educ:* Eton; RMA, Sandhurst. Joined Army, 1943; 2nd Lieut, 12th Royal Lancers, 1946; served in Egypt, 1946; Palestine, 1946-47; Malaya, 1951-54; Captain, 1952; retired 1954. Director: Lakeland Investments Ltd; Carlisle (New) Racecourse Co. Ltd. Chm., Cumbria Police Cttee; CC Westmorland, 1960-74, CC Cumbria 1973-; Member: NW Regional Water Authority, 1973- (of Cumberland River Authy until 1974); NW Regional Land Drainage Cttee, 1974-; High Sheriff of Westmorland, 1964; DL Westmorland, 1964-74; DL Cumbria 1974. Dep. Master 1956, Master 1974, Ullswater Foxhounds. *Address:* Whitbysteads, Askham, Penrith, Cumbria. *T:* Hackthorp 284. *Clubs:* White's, National Sporting, Naval and Military; Cumberland County (Carlisle).

LOWTHER, Lt-Col Sir William (Guy), 5th Bt, *cr* 1824; OBE 1952; DL; retired; one of HM Body Guard of the Honourable Corps of Gentlemen-at-Arms since 1962; *b* 9 Oct. 1912; *o s* of Lieut-Colonel Sir Charles Bingham Lowther, 4th Bt, CB, DSO, and Marjorie Noel (*d* 1925), *d* of Thomas Fielden, MP, of Grimston, Yorks; *S* father, 1949; *m* 1939, Grania Suzanne Douglas Campbell, OStJ, *y d* of late Major A. J. H. Douglas Campbell, OBE, of Blythswood, and the Hon. Mrs Douglas Campbell; one *s* one *d.* *Educ:* Winchester; RMC, Sandhurst. 2nd Lieut, 8th Hussars, 1932; served Palestine, 1936 (despatches); War of 1939-45, in W. Desert (prisoner); Captain, 1941; Major, 1945; Lieut-Colonel, 1951; Staff Coll., 1947; Staff appointment, 1948 and 1949. Served Korea, 1950-51, Lieut-Colonel comd 8th Hussars (despatches); commanding BAOR, 1952-53; retired Jan. 1954. Comr, St John Ambulance Bde for Clwyd (formerly Denbighshire), 1966; Dep. Chief Comr for N Wales. High Sheriff 1959, DL 1969, Clwyd. KStJ. *Heir: s* Major Charles Douglas Lowther, Queen's Royal Irish Hussars [*b* 22 Jan. 1946; *m* 1st, 1969, Melanie Musgrave (marr. diss. 1975), *d* of late R. C. Musgrave and of Mrs J. S. H. Douglas, Ravensheugh, Selkirk; 2nd, 1975, Florence Rose, *y d* of Col A. J. H. Cramsie]. *Address:* Erbistock Hall, near Wrexham. *T:* Overton 244. *Club:* Cavalry and Guards.

LOWTHIAN, George Henry, CBE 1963 (MBE 1949); General Secretary, Amalgamated Union of Building Trade Workers, 1951-73, retired; Part-time Member, British Transport Docks Board, since 1963; *b* 30 Jan. 1908; *s* of Ernest and Margaret Lowthian; *m* 1933, Florence Hartley; one *s* one *d.* *Educ:* Creighton Sch., Carlisle. Branch Secretary, 1930-45; District Secretary, 1934-45; Exec. Council, 1940-45; Divisional Secretary, 1945-50; TUC General Council, 1951-73, Chairman, 1963-64; Chairman, Industrial Training Council, 1960-62; Chairman, Board of Directors, Industrial Training Service, 1965-. Mem., Workmen's Compensation and Pneumoconiosis, Byssinosis and Miscellaneous Diseases Benefit Bds, 1975-. *Recreations:* photography, motoring. *Address:* 17 Holly Way, Mitcham, Surrey. *T:* 01-764 2200.

LOY, Francis David Lindley; Stipendiary Magistrate at Leeds since 1974; *b* 7 Oct. 1927; *s* of late Archibald Loy and late Sarah Eleanor Loy; *m* 1954, Brenda Elizabeth Walker; three *d.* *Educ:* Repton Sch.; Corpus Christi Coll., Cambridge. BA Hons (Law) 1950. Royal Navy, 1946-48. Called to the Bar, Middle Temple, 1952; practised North-Eastern Circuit, 1952-72; Recorder (Northern Circuit), 1972; Stipendiary Magistrate of Leeds, 1972-74. Hon. Sec., Soc. of Provincial Stipendiary Magistrates. *Recreations:* golf, reading, English History, walking. *Address:* 4 Wedgewood Drive, Roundhay, Leeds LS8 1EF; The Red House, The Turning, Sheringham, Norfolk. *T:* Sheringham 2356. *Club:* Leeds (Leeds).

LOYD, Christopher Lewis, MC 1943; Landowner; *b* 1 June 1923; 3rd and *o* surv. *s* of late Arthur Thomas Loyd, OBE, JP,

Lockinge, Wantage, Berks, and Dorothy, *d* of late Paul Ferdinand Willert, Headington, Oxford; *m* 1957, Joanna, *d* of Captain Arthur Turberville Smith-Bingham, Evans Close, Malmesbury, Wilts; two *s* one *d*. *Educ:* Eton; King's Coll., Cambridge (MA). Served 1942-46, with Coldstream Guards, Captain. ARICS 1952, FRICS 1955. Mem., Jockey Club. Trustee, Wallace Collection, 1973-. JP 1950, DL 1954, Oxfordshire (formerly Berks); High Sheriff of Berkshire, 1961. *Address:* Lockinge, Wantage, Oxfordshire. *T:* East Hendred 265. *Clubs:* Boodle's, Buck's.

LOYD, Sir Francis Alfred, KCMG 1965 (CMG 1961); OBE 1954 (MBE 1951); Director, London House for Overseas Graduates; *b* 5 Sept. 1916; *s* of Major A. W. K. Loyd, Royal Sussex Regt; *m* 1946, Katharine Layzell Layzell; two *d*. *Educ:* Eton; Trinity Coll., Oxford (MA). District Officer, Kenya, 1939; Mil. Service, E Africa, 1940-42; Private Secretary to Governor of Kenya, 1942-45; HM Consul, Mega, Ethiopia, 1945; District Comdr, Kenya, 1947-55; Commonwealth Fund Fellowship to USA, 1953-54; Provincial Commissioner, 1956; Permanent Secretary, Governor's Office, 1962-63; HM Commissioner for Swaziland, 1964-68. *Recreations:* golf, gardening. *Address:* London House, Mecklenburgh Square, WC1. *T:* 01-837 8888; 53 Park Road, Aldeburgh, Suffolk. *Clubs:* Royal Commonwealth Society; Vincent's (Oxford).

LOYDEN, Edward; MP (Lab) Liverpool Garston since Feb. 1974; *b* 3 May 1923; *s* of Patrick and Mary Loyden; *m* 1944, Rose Ann; one *s* two *d* (and one *d* decd). *Educ:* Friary RC Elem. School. Shop boy, margarine factory, 1937; Able-Seaman, MN, 1938-46; Seaman Port Worker, Mersey Docks & Harbour Co., 1946-74. Member: Liverpool City Council, 1960; Liverpool District Council, 1973; Merseyside Met. CC, 1973. Shop Steward, TGWU, 1954, Branch Chm. 1959; Mem. District Cttee, Docks and Waterways, 1967; Mem. Nat. Cttee, TGWU, 1968; Pres., Liverpool Trades Council, 1967; Pres., Merseyside Trades Council, 1974. *Recreations:* full-time political. *Address:* House of Commons, SW1; 456 Queens Drive, Liverpool L4 8UA. *T:* 051-226 4478. *Clubs:* Gillmoss Labour, Woolton Labour.

LOYN, Prof. Henry Royston, DLitt; FSA, FRHistS; Professor of History, Westfield College, University of London, since 1977; *b* 16 June 1922; *s* of late Henry George Loyn and Violet Monica Loyn; *m* 1950, Patricia Beatrice, *d* of late R. S. Haskew; three *s*. *Educ:* Cardiff High Sch.; University Coll., Cardiff (MA 1949, DLitt 1968). FRHistS 1958; FSA 1968. Dept of History, University Coll., Cardiff: Asst Lectr, 1946; Lectr, 1949; Sen. Lectr, 1961; Reader, 1966; Prof. of Medieval Hist., 1969-77; Dean of Students, 1968-70 and 1975-76. President: Historical Assoc., 1976-79; Glam Hist. Soc., 1975-; Cardiff Naturalists Soc., 1975-76. Vice-Pres., Soc. for Medieval Archaeol., 1971-74. *Publications:* Anglo-Saxon England and the Norman Conquest, 1962; Norman Conquest, 1965; Norman Britain, 1966; Alfred The Great, 1967; A Wulfstan MS, Cotton, Nero Ai, 1971; (ed with H. Hearder) British Government and Administration, 1974; (with J. Percival) The Reign of Charlemagne, 1975; The Scandinavians in Britain, 1977; contribs to Eng. Hist. Rev., History, Antiquaries Jl, and Med. Archaeol. *Recreations:* natural history, gardening. *Address:* Westfield College, Kiddepore Avenue, NW3. *Club:* Athenæum.

LUARD, (David) Evan (Trant); MP (Lab) Oxford, 1966-70 and since Oct. 1974; Parliamentary Under-Secretary of State, Foreign and Commonwealth Office, 1969-70 and since 1976; Fellow of St Antony's College, Oxford, since 1957; *b* 31 Oct. 1926; *s* of Colonel T. B. Luard, DSO, RM, Blackheath. *Educ:* Felsted; King's Coll., Cambridge (Maj. Schol.). Factory worker, 1949-50; HM Foreign Service, 1950-56; served in Hong Kong, Peking, London; resigned, 1956. Oxford City Councillor, 1958-61. Delegate, UN General Assembly, 1967-68. Contested (Lab) Oxford, Feb. 1974. *Publications:* (part author) The Economic Development of Communist China, 1959 (2nd edn 1961); Britain and China, 1962; Nationality and Wealth, 1964; (ed) The Cold War, 1965; (ed) First Steps to Disarmament, 1966; (ed) The Evolution of International Organisations, 1967; Conflict and Peace in the Modern International System, 1968; (ed) The International Regulation of Frontier Disputes, 1970; (ed) The International Regulations of Civil Wars, 1972; The Control of the Sea-bed, 1974; Types of International Society, 1976; International Agencies: the Emerging Framework of Interdependence, 1977; articles in International Affairs, The China Quarterly, World Politics, World Today, The Annals. *Recreations:* music, painting. *Address:* House of Commons, SW1A 0AA; St Antony's College, Oxford. *T:* 59651.

LUARD, Evan; see Luard, D. E. T.

LUARD, Commander William Blaine, OBE 1945; FRIN; RN (retired); Naval Officer, Author and Inventor; *b* 2 Jan. 1897; *e s* of late Major William Du Cane Luard, RE, and late Maud, *d* of Sir Robert Blaine; *m* 1929, May Gladys Hayes. *Educ:* Mowden Sch., Brighton; RN Colleges, Osborne and Dartmouth. Invalided, 1917, as a Sub-Lieut. Contributor to numerous publications. Co-inventor, Addison-Luard Course and Distance Calculator; Sestral-Luard Navigator, and other navigational devices. Rejoined 1940; special duties (OBE, Croix de Guerre and palm). Co-inventor four devices in production during war. President Little Ship Club, 1944-54; Chairman, Cornwall Sea Fisheries Cttee, 1947-67. Special Study of French and English Fisheries. *Publications:* A Celtic Hurly-Burly, 1931; All Hands, 1933; Yachtsman's Modern Navigation and Practical Pilotage, 1933; Conquering Seas, 1935; Wild Goose Chase, 1936; ABC of Blue Water Navigation, 1936; Northern Deeps, 1937; Changing Horizons, 1946; Where the Tides Meet, 1948; The Little Ship Navigator, 1950. *Recreations:* yachting, cruising. *Address:* Trelour, Mawnan Smith, near Falmouth, Cornwall TR11 5LE. *T:* Mawnan Smith 250328. *Clubs:* Royal Cruising, Little Ship (Hon. Life Mem.); Royal Fowey Yacht (Fowey); Royal Cornwall Yacht (Falmouth); Ocean Cruising.

LUBBOCK, family name of **Baron Avebury.**

LUBBOCK, Sir Alan, Kt 1963; MA, FSA; *b* 13 Jan. 1897; 6th *s* of Frederic Lubbock, Ide Hill, Kent; *m* 1918, Helen Mary, *d* of late John Bonham-Carter, Adhurst St Mary, Petersfield; two *s*. *Educ:* Eton; King's Coll., Cambridge. Served in Royal Artillery, 1915-19 and 1939-45. Fellow of King's, 1922-28. Hants County Council, 1932-74 (Alderman 1939, Vice-Chairman 1948, Chairman 1955-67); JP (Hants) 1935; DL; High Sheriff of Hants, 1949-; Member: National Parks Commission, 1954-61; Royal Commission on Common Land, 1955; War Works Commission, 1959-64. Chairman: Council, Southampton Univ., 1957-69 (Pro-Chancellor, 1967); County Councils Assoc., 1965-69 (Vice-Chairman 1963); Nat. Foundn for Educnl Research, 1967-73. Hon. LLD Southampton, 1969. *Publication:* The Character of John Dryden, 1925. *Address:* Adhurst St Mary, Petersfield, Hants. *T:* Petersfield 3043. *Clubs:* United Oxford & Cambridge University; Leander.

LUBBOCK, Christopher William Stuart; a Master of the Supreme Court (Queen's Bench Division), since 1970; *b* 4 Jan. 1920; 2nd *s* of late Captain Rupert Egerton Lubbock, Royal Navy; *m* 1947, Hazel Gordon, *d* of late Gordon Chapman; one *s* one *d*. *Educ:* Charterhouse; Brasenose Coll., Oxford. Served 1939-46, RNVR. Called to Bar, Inner Temple, 1947. *Recreation:* chatting to music publishers. *Address:* Great Horkesley, Essex. *Club:* Pratt's.

LUBBOCK, Roy; *b* 1 Oct. 1892; *s* of Frederic Lubbock and Catherine Gurney; *m* 1919, Yvonne Vernham; two *s*. *Educ:* Eton (Scholar); King's Coll., Cambridge (Exhibitioner, scholar); Fellow of Peterhouse, Cambridge and University Lecturer in Engineering, 1919-60; Bursar of Peterhouse, 1929-31 and 1940-45, Tutor, 1934-40. *Address:* Riding Oaks, Hildenborough, Tonbridge, Kent.

LUCAN, 7th Earl of, *cr* 1795; **Richard John Bingham;** Bt 1632; Baron Lucan, 1776; Baron Bingham (UK), 1934; *b* 18 Dec. 1934; *e s* of 6th Earl of Lucan, MC; *S* father, 1964; *m* 1963, Veronica, *d* of late Major C. M. Duncan, MC, and of Mrs J. D. Margrie; one *s* two *d*. *Educ:* Eton. Lieut (Res. of Officers) Coldstream Guards. *Heir:* *s* Lord Bingham, *qv*.

LUCAS, family name of **Baron Lucas of Chilworth.**

LUCAS; see Keith-Lucas.

LUCAS OF CHILWORTH, 2nd Baron *cr* 1946, of Chilworth; **Michael William George Lucas;** *b* 26 April 1926; *er s* of 1st Baron and Sonia, *d* of Marcus Finkelstein, Libau, Latvia; *S* father, 1967; *m* 1955, Ann-Marie, *o d* of Ronald Buck, Southampton; two *s* one *d*. *Educ:* Peter Symond's Sch., Winchester. Served with Royal Tank Regt. TEng(CEI); FIMI (Mem. Council, 1972-76); AMBIM. President: Inst. HGV Instrs, 1972-; League of Safe Drivers, 1976-. *Heir:* *s* Hon. Simon William Lucas, *b* 6 Feb. 1957. *Address:* Connaught Lodge, Brownhill Road, Chandlers Ford, Hants.
   See also Hon. I. T. M. Lucas.

LUCAS OF CRUDWELL, Baroness (10th in line) *cr* 1663 and **DINGWALL, Lady** (6th in line) *cr* 1609; **Anne Rosemary Palmer;** *b* 28 April 1919; *er d* of Group Captain Howard Lister Cooper, AFC, and Baroness Lucas and Dingwall; *S* mother, 1958; is a *co-heir* to Barony of Butler; *m* 1950, Major the Hon. Robert Jocelyn Palmer, MC, JP, late Coldstream Guards, 3rd and e surv. s of 3rd Earl of Selborne, PC, CH; two s one d. Heir: er s Hon. Ralph Matthew Palmer, b 7 June 1951. Address: The Old House, Wonston, Winchester, Hampshire.

LUCAS, Charles Vivian; Chief Executive, Devon County Council, since 1974; solicitor; b 31 May 1914; s of Frank and Mary Renshaw Lucas, Malvern, Worcs; m 1941, Oonah Holderness; two s two d. Educ: Malvern Coll.; abroad; London Univ. (LLB). Clerk, Devon County Council, 1972-74; Clerk to the Lieutenancy of Devon, 1972-. Recreations: sport, bridge. Address: Highfield Lodge, 7 Salterton Road, Exmouth EX8 2BR. Club: Golf and Country (Exeter).

LUCAS, Christopher Charles; Under Secretary, Home Oil Policy Division, Department of Energy, since 1976; b 5 June 1920; s of Charles Edwin Lucas and Mabel Beatrice Read; m 1945, Beryl June Vincent; two d. Educ: Devonport High Sch.; Balliol Coll., Oxford (Newman Exhibnr). Min. of Fuel, 1946; Central Econ. Planning Staff, 1948; HM Treasury, 1950-70; Cabinet Office, 1970-72; Sec., NEDC, 1973-76. Recreation: riding. Address: 34 Essendene Road, Caterham, Surrey. T: Caterham 44031.

LUCAS, Colin Anderson, OBE 1972; BA Cantab; FRIBA; Architect; b London, 1906; 2nd s of late Ralph Lucas, Engineer, and late Mary Anderson Juler; m 1930, Dione Narona Margaris (marr. diss.), d of Henry Wilson; two s; m 1952, Pamela Margaret, e d of late Sir Gerald Campbell, GCMG; Educ: Cheltenham Coll.; Trinity Coll., Cambridge; Cambridge Univ. Sch. of Architecture. In practice in London, 1928-; Founder Mem. of Mars (Modern Architectural Research Group). Publications: works published in England, America and Continent. Recreations: sailing, ski-ing, travel. Address: 2 Queen's Grove Studios, Queen's Grove, NW8 6EP.

LUCAS, Sir Cyril (Edward), Kt 1976; CMG 1956; FRS 1966; Director of Fisheries Research, Scotland (Department of Agriculture and Fisheries for Scotland) and Director Marine Laboratory Aberdeen, 1948-70; b Hull, Yorks, 30 July 1909; o s of late Archibald and Edith Lucas, Hull; m 1934, Sarah Agnes (d 1974), o d of late Henry Alfred and Amy Rose; two s one d. Educ: Grammar Sch., Hull; University Coll., Hull. BSc (London) 1931, DSc (London) 1942. FRSE 1939; Vice-Pres., 1962-64; Neill Prize, 1960. Research Biologist, University Coll., Hull, 1931; Head of Dept of Oceanography, University Coll., Hull, 1942. UK Expert or Delegate to various internat. confs on Marine Fisheries and Conservation, 1948-, and Chm. of research cttees in connexion with these; Chm., Consultative and Liaison Cttees, Internat. Council for Exploration of Sea, 1962-67; Member: Adv. Cttee on Marine Resources Research, FAO, 1964-72 (Chm. 1966-71); Council for Scientific Policy, 1968-70; Nat. Environmental Res. Council, 1970-. Hon. DSc Hull, 1975; Hon. LLD Aberdeen, 1977. Publications: various scientific, particularly on marine plankton and fisheries research in Bulletins of Marine Ecology (Joint Editor), Jl of Marine Biological Assoc., etc and various international jls. Address: 16 Albert Terrace, Aberdeen AB1 1XY. T: Aberdeen 25568.

LUCAS, Donald William; Fellow of King's College, Cambridge, 1929, and Director of Studies in Classics, 1935-65; University Lecturer in Classics, 1933-69; P. M. Laurence Reader in Classics, 1952-69; b 12 May 1905; s of Frank William Lucas and Ada Ruth Blackmur; m 1933, Mary Irene Cohen; one s one d. Educ: Colfe's Gram. Sch.; Rugby; King's Coll., Cambridge. War of 1939-45: FO, 1940-44. Publications: The Greek Tragic Poets, 1950; Aristotle Poetics, 1968; translations (from Euripides): Bacchae, 1930; Medea, 1949; Ion, 1949; Alcestis, 1951; Electra, 1951; Joint Editor, Classical Quarterly, 1953-59; articles and reviews in classical journals and Encyclopædia Britannica. Recreations: travel and reading. Address: 39 Bridle Way, Grantchester, Cambs. T: Trumpington 3108; Pwllymarch, Llanbedr, Gwynedd. T: Llanbedr 208.

LUCAS, Maj.-Gen. Geoffrey, CB 1957; CBE 1944; b 19 Oct. 1904; s of Henry Lucas, Mossley Hill, Liverpool; m 1927, Mabel Ellen, d of Dr George Henry Herald, Leeds; one s one d. Educ: Liverpool Institute; RMC, Sandhurst. Commissioned, 1925, in Royal Tank Corps; Staff Coll., Camberley, 1938; served War of 1939-45 in Italy and Greece; DQMG, BAOR, 1947-50; Dep. Dir Personnel Admin, War Office, 1950-53; Dep. Fortress Comd, Gibraltar, 1953-56; Chief Administrative Officer, Suez Operations, 1956; Maj.-Gen. i/c Admin, FARELF, 1957; retired, 1958. Address: Newbold House, Linkway, Camberley, Surrey. T: Camberley 65544.

LUCAS, Ian Albert McKenzie, CBE 1977; Principal of Wye College, University of London, since 1977; b 10 July 1926; s of Percy John Lucas and Janie Inglis (née Hamilton); m 1950, Helen Louise Langerman; one s two d. Educ: Clayesmore Sch.;

Reading Univ.; McGill Univ. BSc, MSc; FRAgS. Lectr, Harper Adams Agricl Coll., 1949-50; Pig. Res. Worker, Rowett Res. Inst., Aberdeen, 1950-57 and 1958-61; Res. Fellow, Ruakura Res. Station, New Zealand, 1957-58; Prof. of Agriculture, UCNW, Bangor, 1961-77. Publications: scientific papers in Jl Agricl Science, Animal Production, Brit. Jl Nutrition and others. Recreation: sailing. Address: Court Lodge, Brook, Ashford, Kent TN25 5PF. T: Wye 812341. Club: Farmers'.

LUCAS, Hon. Ivor Thomas Mark; HM Diplomatic Service; Head of Middle East Department, Foreign and Commonwealth Office, since 1975; b 25 July 1927; 2nd s of George William Lucas, 1st Baron Lucas of Chilworth, and Sonia (née Finkelstein); m 1954, Christine Mallorie Coleman; three s. Educ: St Edward's Sch., Oxford; Trinity Coll., Oxford (MA). Served in Royal Artillery, 1945-48 (Captain). BA Oxon 1951. Entered Diplomatic Service, 1951; Middle East Centre for Arabic Studies, Lebanon, 1952; 3rd, later 2nd Sec., Bahrain, Sharjah and Dubai, 1952-56; FO, 1956-59; 1st Sec., British High Commn, Karachi, 1959-62; 1st Sec. and Head of Chancery, British Embassy, Tripoli, 1962-66; FO, 1966-68; Counsellor, British Embassy, Aden, 1968-69 (Chargé d'Affaires, Aug. 1968-Feb. 1969); Dep. High Comr, Kaduna, Nigeria, 1969-71; Counsellor, Copenhagen, 1972-75. Recreations: music, cricket, tennis. Address: 65 Newstead Way, SW19. Club: Royal Commonwealth Society.

LUCAS, Major Sir Jocelyn (Morton), 4th Bt cr 1887; KBE 1959; MC; late 4th Battalion Royal Warwickshire Regt; b 27 Aug. 1889; 2nd s of Sir Edward Lingard Lucas, 3rd Bt and Mary Helen (d 1915), d of Henry Chance, Sherborne, Warwick; S father, 1936; m 1st, 1933, Edith (d 1956), d of late Very Rev. David Barry Cameron, DD, JP, Dundee, and widow of Sir Trehawke Herbert Kekewich, Bt, Peamore, Devon; 2nd, 1960, Mrs Thelma Grace de Chair (d 1974), d of Harold Dennison Arbuthnot, Field Place, Compton, Surrey. Educ: Eton; Royal Military Coll., Sandhurst. Joined 4th (Special Reserve Bn) Royal Warwicks Regt, 1909; served European War, 1914-19 (wounded, prisoner, MC) Oct. 1914, subseq. ADC to Gen. Sir Sydney Lawford, Army of Occupation, Cologne; Vice-Pres., Royal Over-Seas League and Chm. of the Hospitality Cttee, 1938-; welfare liaison officer for Dominion troops, London District, 1940-48; founder and Chm. Allies Welcome Cttee, 1940-50; also of Returned Prisoners of War Advice Cttee, 1944-48. MP (C) Portsmouth, South, 1939-66; Member: Parly delegn to France, 1946 and 1957; Commonwealth Conf., Ottawa, 1952; led delegn to Denmark, 1955, to Sweden, 1962, and to France for 50th Anniversary of Anglo-French Condominion of the New Hebrides. Has hunted several packs of hounds; served as part-time auxiliary fireman, 1938-42 (Section Leader); broken back and other injuries while fire fighting; Chm. Empire War Memorial Fund (St Paul's); a Governor and Mem. Council of Royal Veterinary Coll.; a Vice-Pres., Kennel Club; Pres. Pitt Street Settlement; Chm. British Sportsman's Club, 1957-68; was responsible for legalisation of fishing on Serpentine, 1942 and holds Fishing Licence No. 1 for the Royal Parks; holds RAC Pilot's Certificate 893. Comdr, Order of Orange-Nassau. Czechoslovak Military Medal of Merit, 1st Class. Publications: Hunt and Working Terriers; Pedigree Dog Breeding; The Sealyham Terrier; the New Book of the Sealyham; Simple Doggie Remedies, etc. Recreations: travel, all equestrian and field sports, breeding pedigree dogs. Heir: cousin Thomas Edward Lucas [b 16 Sept. 1930; m 1958, Charmian (d 1970), d of Col J. S. Powell; one s]. Address: Michelmersh Court, Romsey, Hants SO5 0NS. T: Braishfield 68270. Clubs: Carlton, Kennel, MCC.

LUCAS, Ven. John Michael; Archdeacon of Totnes and Vicar of Chudleigh Knighton, since 1976; b 13 June 1921; s of Rev. Stainforth John Chadwick Lucas and Dorothy Wybray Mary Lucas; m 1952, Catharina Madeleine Bartlett; three s (one d decd). Educ: Kelly Coll., Tavistock; Lichfield Theological Coll. Deacon 1944, priest 1945, dio. Exeter; Asst Curate: Parish of Wolborough, 1944; Parish of Ashburton, 1950; Rector of Weare Giffard with Landcross and Vicar of Monkleigh, 1952; Vicar of Northam, 1962. Recreations: family recreations, garden. Address: The Vicarage, Chudleigh Knighton, Newton Abbot, Devon. T: Chudleigh 853030.

LUCAS, Keith Stephen; Director, British Film Institute, since Sept. 1972; b 28 Aug. 1924; m 1969, Rona Stephanie Lucas (née Levy); two s one d (and two step s). Educ: Royal Coll. of Art (ARCA). London Press Exchange, 1956-64; Prof. of Film and Television, Royal Coll. of Art, 1964-72 (first holder of Chair). Member: Nat. Panel for Film Festivals; Council, Children's Film Foundn; Governor: North East London Poly., 1971-72; Canterbury Sch. of Art, 1971-74; Vice-Pres., Centre Internat. de Liaison des Ecoles de Cinéma et de Télévision, 1970-72; Hon.

Fellow, Royal Coll. of Art. *Recreations:* writing, painting. *Address:* British Film Institute, 81 Dean Street, W1V 6AA. *T:* 01-437 4355.

LUCAS, Percy Belgrave, DSO 1943 and Bar 1945; DFC 1942; Chairman, GRA Property Trust Ltd, 1965-75 (Vice-Chairman, 1975-76; Managing Director, 1957-65); Director, Stowe School Ltd; *b* Sandwich Bay, Kent, 2 Sept. 1915; *y s* of late Percy Montagu Lucas, Prince's, Sandwich, form. of Filby House, Filby, Norfolk; *m* 1946, Jill Doreen, *d* of Lt-Col A. M. Addison, Ascot; two *s* (and one *s* decd). *Educ:* Stowe; Pembroke Coll., Cambridge. Editorial Staff, Sunday Express, 1937-40. Joined RAFVR, 1939; Commanded: 249 (Fighter) Sqdn, Battle of Malta, 1942; 616 (Fighter) Sqdn, 1943; Coltishall Wing, Fighter Command, 1943; 613 Sqdn, North-West Europe, 1944-45; Fighter Command, HQ Staff, 1942; Air Defence of Great Britain HQ Staff, 1944; demobilised with rank of Wing Comdr, 1946. Contested (C) West Fulham, 1945; MP (C) Brentford and Chiswick, 1950-59. Capt. Cambridge Univ. Golf team, 1937; Pres. Hawks Club, Cambridge, 1937; English International Golf team, 1936, 1948, 1949 (Capt. 1949); British Walker Cup team, 1936, 1947, 1949 (Capt. 1949). President: Golf Foundation Ltd, 1963-66; Nat. Golf Clubs Advisory Assoc., 1963-69; Assoc. of Golf Club Secretaries, 1968-74. Member: General Advisory Council, BBC, 1962-67; Council, National Greyhound Racing Soc. of Great Britain, 1957-72; Policy Cttee, Nat. Greyhound Racing Club Ltd, 1972-77; AAA Cttee of Inquiry, 1967; Exec. Cttee, General Purposes and Finance Cttee; Central Council of Physical Recreation; Management Cttee, Crystal Palace Nat. Sports Centre, 1961-73; Sports Council, 1971-; Vice-Patron, Amateur Athletic Assoc.; British Olympic Assoc. Gov., Stowe Sch. Croix de Guerre avec Palmes, 1945. *Recreations:* golf, photography. *Address:* 38 Onslow Square, SW7 3NS. *T:* 01-584 8373. *Clubs:* Bath; Sandy Lodge Golf; Walton Health Golf; Prince's Golf; Royal West Norfolk Golf.

LUCAS, Prof. Raleigh Barclay; Professor of Oral Pathology, University of London, since 1954; Consultant Pathologist, Royal Dental Hospital of London, since 1950; *b* 3 June 1914; *s* of H. Lucas; *m* 1942, Violet Sorrell; one *d* (one *s* decd). *Educ:* George Watson's Coll.; Univ. of Edinburgh. MB, ChB (Edinburgh) 1937; DPH 1939; MD 1945; MRCP 1946; FRCPath 1963; FRCP 1974; FDS RCS 1974. Asst Bacteriologist, Edinburgh Royal Infirmary, 1939-40; Pathologist, Stoke Mandeville Hosp. and Royal Buckinghamshire Hospital, 1947-49; Reader in Pathology, University of London, 1950-54; Dean, Sch. of Dental Surgery, Royal Dental Hospital of London, 1958-73. Examiner in Pathology and Bacteriology for dental degrees, Univs of London, Birmingham, Sheffield, Liverpool and Wales. Served War of 1939-45, Major RAMC; FRSocMed; Fellow and Past Pres., Royal Medical Society; Mem. Pathological Soc. of Great Britain and Ireland; Mem. BMA. *Publications:* Bacteriology for Students of Dental Surgery (jointly), 1954; Pathology of Tumours of the Oral Tissues, 1964; various articles in medical and scientific journals. *Address:* Department of Pathology, Royal Dental Hospital of London, WC2. *T:* 01-930 8831.

LUCAS-TOOTH, Sir Hugh; see Munro-Lucas-Tooth.

LUCE, Mrs Henry Robinson, (Clare Boothe); playwright and author since 1933; *d* of William F. and Ann Snyder Boothe; *m* 1st, 1923, George Tuttle Brokaw; 2nd, 1935, Henry Robinson Luce (*d* 1967). *Educ:* St Mary's Sch., Garden City, Long Island; The Castle, Tarrytown, New York. Associate Editor Vogue, 1930; Associate Editor Vanity Fair, 1931-32; Managing Editor Vanity Fair, 1933-34. Mem. of Congress from 4th District of Connecticut, 1943-47. United States Ambassador to Italy, 1953-57. Mem. Edit. Bd, Encyclopaedia Britannica, 1974-. Holds hon. doctorates. Dame of Magistral Grace, SMO Malta; Kt Gr. Cross, Order of Merit, Italy. *Publications:* Stuffed Shirts, 1933; Europe in the Spring (English Title-European Spring), 1940; (ed) Saints For Now, 1952; *plays:* Abide with Me, 1935; The Women, 1936; Kiss the Boys Goodbye, 1938; Margin for Error, 1939; Child of the Morning, 1952; articles to magazines. *Address:* Honolulu, Hawaii, USA.

LUCE, Richard Napier; MP (C) Shoreham, since 1974 (Arundel and Shoreham, Apr. 1971-1974); *b* 14 Oct. 1936; *s* of Sir William Luce, GBE, KCMG, and of Margaret, *d* of late Adm. Sir Trevylyan Napier, KCB; *m* 1961, Rose, *d* of Sir Godfrey Nicholson, Bt; two *s*. *Educ:* Wellington Coll.; Christ's Coll., Cambridge. 2nd cl. History. Nat. Service officer, 1955-57, served in Cyprus. Overseas Civil Service, served as District Officer, Kenya, 1960-62; Brand Manager, Gallaher Ltd, 1963-65; Marketing Manager, Spirella Co. of GB; Dir, National Innovations Centre, 1968-71; Chairman: IFA Consultants Ltd, 1972-; Selanex Ltd, 1973-; Courtenay Stewart International Ltd,

1975-; Mem. European Adv. Bd, Corning Glass International, 1975-. Contested (C) Hitchin, 1970. PPS to Minister for Trade and Consumer Affairs, 1972-74; an Opposition Whip, 1974-75. Secretary: Cons. Parly Foreign Affairs Cttee, 1975-; Cons. Parly Fisheries Cttee, 1975-. *Recreations:* sailing, walking, reading, etc. *Address:* House of Commons, Westminster, SW1.

LUCET, Charles (Ernest); French Ambassador, retired; *b* Paris, 16 April 1910; *s* of Louis Lucet and Madeleine Lucet (*née* Zoegger); *m* 1931, Jacqueline Bardoux; one *s* one *d*. *Educ:* University of Paris. Degree in law, also degree of Ecole Libre des Sciences Politiques. French Embassy, Washington, 1935-Nov. 1942; then joined Free French movement and was apptd to its mission in Washington; attached to Foreign affairs Commissariat in Algiers, 1943; First Sec., Ankara, 1943-45; Asst Dir for Middle Eastern Affairs, Foreign Affairs Min., Paris, 1945-46; First Counsellor: Beirut, 1946; Cairo, 1949; Dept Head of Cultural Relations Div. of Foreign Affairs Min., Paris, 1950-53; rank of Minister Plenipotentiary, 1952; Mem. French Delegn to UN, serving as Dep. Permanent Rep. to UN and to Security Council, 1953-55; Minister Counsellor, French Embassy, Washington, 1955-59; Dir of Political Affairs, Foreign Affairs Min., Paris, 1959-65; Ambassador to USA, 1965-72; Ambassador to Italy, 1972-75. Commandeur de la Légion d'Honneur; Commandeur de l'Ordre National du Mérite; holds foreign decorations. *Address:* 9 rue de Thann, 75017 Paris, France. *T:* 622-5676.

LUCEY, Most Rev. Cornelius; see Cork, Bishop of, (RC).

LUCEY, Rear-Adm. Martin Noel, CB 1973; DSC 1944; RN retired; Director General, National Association of British and Irish Millers, since 1975; *b* 21 Jan. 1920; *s* of A. N. Lucey; *m* 1947, Barbara Mary Key; two *s* one *d*. *Educ:* Gresham's Sch., Holt. Entered RN, 1938. Served War of 1939-45: qualif. in navigation, 1944; "N" 10th Destroyer Sqdn, 1944. Comdr, 1953; Mem. NATO Defence Coll., 1954; Captain, 1961; Captain "F7" HMS Puma, 1964; Cdre, Sen. Naval Officer, West Indies, 1968; Rear-Adm., 1970; Adm. President, RNC Greenwich, 1970-72; Flag Officer, Scotland and NI, 1972-74. *Recreation:* painting. *Address:* Oldways, Houghton, Arundel, West Sussex.

LUCIE-SMITH, Edward; see Lucie-Smith, J. E. M.

LUCIE-SMITH, (John) Edward (McKenzie); poet and art critic; *b* Kingston, Jamaica, 27 Feb. 1933; *s* of John Dudley Lucie-Smith and Mary (*née* Lushington); unmarried. *Educ:* King's Sch., Canterbury; Merton Coll., Oxford (MA). Settled in England, 1946. Education Officer, RAF, 1954-56; subseq. worked in advertising and as free-lance journalist and broadcaster. FRSL. *Publications:* A Tropical Childhood and other poems, 1961 (jt winner, John Llewellyn Rhys Mem. Prize; winner, Arts Coun. Triennial Award); (ed, with Philip Hobsbaum) A Group Anthology, 1963; Confessions and Histories, 1964; (with Jack Clemo, George MacBeth) Penguin Modern Poets 6, 1964; (ed) Penguin Book of Elizabethan Verse, 1965; What is a Painting?, 1966; (ed) The Liverpool Scene, 1967; (ed) A Choice of Browning's Verse, 1967; (ed) Penguin Book of Satirical Verse, 1967; Thinking about Art, 1968; Towards Silence, 1968; Movements in Art since 1945, 1969; (ed) British Poetry Since 1945, 1970; (with Patricia White) Art in Britain 69-70, 1970; (ed) A Primer of Experimental Verse, 1971; (ed with S. W. Taylor) French Poetry: the last fifteen years, 1971; A Concise History of French Painting, 1971; Symbolist Art, 1972; Eroticism in Western Art, 1972; The First London Catalogue, 1974; The Well Wishers, 1974; The Burnt Child (autobiog.), 1975; The Invented Eye (early photography), 1975; World of the Makers, 1975; (with Celeste Dars) How the Rich Lived, 1976; Joan of Arc, 1976; (with Celestine Dars) Work and Struggle, 1977; contribs to Times, Sunday Times, Listener, Spectator, New Statesman, Evening Standard, Encounter, London Magazine, etc. *Recreations:* walking the dog, malice. *Address:* c/o Deborah Rogers Ltd, 29 Goodge Street, W1.

LUCKHOO, Hon. Sir Edward Victor, Kt 1970; QC (Guyana); Hon. Mr Justice Luckhoo; Chancellor and President of Court of Appeal, Guyana, since 1969; *b* Guyana (when Br. Guiana), 24 May 1912; *s* of late E. A. Luckhoo, OBE. *Educ:* New Amsterdam Scots Sch.; Queen's Coll., Guyana; St Catherine's Coll., Oxford (BA). Called to Bar, Middle Temple, 1936; QC Guyana 1965. Began career in magistracy as acting Magistrate, Essequibo District, 1943. *Address:* Court of Appeal, Georgetown, Guyana; 17 Lamaha Street, Georgetown, Guyana.

LUCKHOO, Hon. Sir Joseph (Alexander), Kt 1963; Judge, Court of Appeal, Jamaica, since 1967; Chairman, Law Reform Committee, Jamaica, since 1973; *b* 8 June 1917; *e s* of late Joseph Alexander Luckhoo, KC and Irene Luckhoo; *m* 1964, Leila

Patricia Singh; three *s* one *d*. *Educ:* Queen's Coll., British Guiana; University Coll., London; Middle Temple. BSc London, 1939. Barrister, Middle Temple, 1944; practised at Bar, British Guiana. Crown Counsel, British Guiana, 1949; Legal Draftsman, 1953; acted as Solicitor Gen., British Guiana, 1952, 1954 and 1955; Puisne Judge, British Guiana, 1956; Acting Chief Justice, 1959; Chief Justice, 1960-66; Chief Justice Guyana, 1966; Acting Pres., Court of Appeal, Jamaica, 1972, 1973, and 1974-76. Chm. Judicial Service Commission, 1961-66. *Publications:* Editor: Law Reports of British Guiana, 1956-58; British Guiana section of West Indian Reports, 1958-61, Jamaica section, 1970-72. *Recreations:* watching cricket and tennis; table tennis. *Address:* Judges' Chambers, Court of Appeal, Kingston, Jamaica. *Club:* Royal Commonwealth Society (West Indian).

LUCKHOO, Sir Lionel (Alfred), KCMG 1969; Kt 1966; CBE 1962; QC (Guyana) 1954; *b* 2 March 1914; 2nd *s* of late Edward Alfred Luckhoo, OBE, Solicitor, and Evelyn Luckhoo; *m* Sheila Chamberlin; two *s* three *d*. *Educ:* Queen's Coll., Georgetown, Brit. Guiana; Middle Temple, London. MLC, 1949-51; Mem. State Coun., 1952-53; Minister without Portfolio, 1954-57; Mem. Georgetown Town Council, 1950-64; Mayor, City of Georgetown, 1954, 1955, 1960, 1961 (Dep. Mayor three times); High Comr in UK, for Guyana, May 1966-70; for Barbados, Nov. 1966-70; Ambassador of Guyana and Barbados, to Paris, Bonn and The Hague, 1967-70. Pres., MPCA Trade Union, Brit. Guiana, 1949-52; Pres. of several Unions; has served on Commns of Enquiry, Public Cttees, Statutory Bodies, Legal Cttees, Drafting Cttees, Disciplinary Cttees, etc. Head of Luckhoo & Luckhoo, Legal Practitioners. Mem. of the Magic Circle. Listed in the Guinness Book of Records as the World's most successful advocate with 200 successful defences in murder cases. *Publications:* (jtly) The Fitzluck Theory of Breeding Racehorses, 1952; I Believe; God is Love; Life After Death; The Xmas Story; Sense of Values; Dear Atheist. *Recreations:* cricket, horse-racing. *Address:* Lot 1, Croal Street, Georgetown, Guyana. *Clubs:* Royal Commonwealth Society (West Indian), Crockford's, Twenty-one.

LUCRAFT, Frederick Hickman, CBE 1952; *b* 10 May 1894; *s* of late Frederick Thomas Lucraft, Customs and Excise Dept; *m* 1927, June, *d* of John Freeman Wright, Dover; one *s* one *d*. *Educ:* Grocers' Company's Sch. Entered Inland Revenue, 1913. Served European War, King's Own Royal Lancaster Regt, 1914-17. Railway Traffic Establishment, 1917-19; Inter-allied Railway Commn, Cologne SubCommn, 1919-22; demobilised with rank of Capt., 1922. Regional Services Dir, Min. of Fuel and Power, North-Western Region, 1942-45; Dep. Accountant and Comptroller Gen., Inland Revenue, 1945-47; Special Comr of Income Tax, Clerk to the Special Commissioners and Inspector of Foreign Dividends, Inland Revenue, 1947-59; HM Treasury, 1959-60. *Address:* 100 Dean Court Road, Rottingdean, Brighton BN2 7DJ. *T:* Brighton 34195.

LUCY, Sir Edmund J. W. H. C. R. F.; see Fairfax-Lucy.

LUDDINGTON, Sir Donald (Collin Cumyn), KBE 1976; CMG 1973; CVO 1974; Chairman, Public Service Commission, Hong Kong, since 1977; *b* 18 Aug. 1920; *s* of late F. Norman John Luddington, Ceylon Civil Service, and late M. Myrtle Amethyst Payne; *m* 1945, Garry Brodie Johnston; one *s* one *d*. *Educ:* Dover Coll.; St Andrews Univ. (MA). Served War, Army, 1940-46, KOYLI and RAC, Captain. Hong Kong Govt, 1949-73; Sec. for Home Affairs, 1971-73; Governor, Solomon Islands, 1974-76. *Recreations:* walking, hockey, squash. *Address:* Flat 9A, 3 Cox's Road, Kowloon, Hong Kong. *Clubs:* Royal Commonwealth Society; Hong Kong (Hong Kong); Kowloon Cricket.

LUDLOW, Archdeacon of; see Woodhouse, Ven. Andrew Henry.

LUDLOW, (Ernest John) Robin; Head of Publicity, Strutt and Parker; *b* 2 May 1931; *s* of late Donald Ernest Ludlow and of Marcia Dorothea Marsden-Jacobs, Buxted, Sussex; *m* 1970, Sonia Louise Hatfeild; one *s* one *d*. *Educ:* Framlingham Coll., Suffolk; RMA, Sandhurst. Regular Army: RMA Sandhurst, 1949-52; commissioned RASC, 1952; Staff, RMA Sandhurst, 1954-57; retd 1957. TA: Kent and County of London Yeomanry (Sharpshooters), 1959-68; The Queen's Regt, Major, 1971-. J. Lyons & Co. Ltd (Sales Management), 1957-60; The Economist (Sales Management and Marketing Promotion), 1960-72; Press Sec. to the Queen, 1972-73; Dep. Dir, Aims of Industry, 1973-77. *Recreations:* shooting, gardening, Territorial Army. *Address:* Grove Farm, Wingmore, Elham, near Canterbury, Kent. *T:* Elham 553. *Club:* Cavalry and Guards.

LUDWIG, Christa; singer; *b* Berlin, 16 March; *d* of Anton Ludwig, singer, stage director and opera general manager and Eugenie (*née* Besalla), singer; *m* 1st, 1957, Walter Berry (marr. diss. 1970), baritone; one *s*; 2nd, 1972, Paul-Emile Deiber, actor and stage-director. *Educ:* Matura. Staedtische Buehnen, Frankfurt; Landestheater Darmstadt; Landestheater, Hannover; Vienna State Opera; guest appearances in New York, Chicago, London, Berlin, Munich, Tokyo, Milan, Rome, Lucerne, Salzburg, Epidauros, Zürich, Holland, Los Angeles, Cleveland, Saratoga, Bayreuth, Copenhagen, Gent, Montreal, Prague, Budapest and others. Kammersängerin, Austria, 1962; First Class Art and Science, Austria, 1969; Mozart Medaille, Austria, 1969. *Recreations:* listening to music, theatre, concerts, reading. *Address:* c/o Music and Arts SA, Tobelhofstrasse 2, CH-8044 Zurich, Switzerland; Fridolin-Hoferstrasse 17, CH-6045 Meggen, Switzerland.

LUFF, Richard William Peter, FRICS; City Surveyor, Corporation of London, since 1975; *b* 11 June 1927; *s* of Victor and Clare Luff; *m* 1950, Betty Chamberlain; no *c*. *Educ:* Hurstpierpoint Coll., Sussex; Coll. of Estate Management. Service in RA, India and UK, 1945-48. Estates and Valuation Dept, MCC, 1949-65; Asst Valuer, GLC, 1968-75. Royal Institution of Chartered Surveyors: Mem., Gen. Practice Divl Council, 1973-; Chm., Valuation and Rating Cttee, 1974-; Mem., Gen. Council, 1975-; Dep. Chm., Public Affairs Cttee, 1975-. Mem., Furniture History Soc. Mem. Ct of Assts, Chartered Surveyors' Co., 1977-. *Publications:* Furniture in England—the age of the joiner (with S. W. Wolsey), 1968; articles and papers on compensation and allied property matters; nearly 50 articles on furniture history in Antique Collector, Country Life, and Connoisseur, 1961-73. *Recreations:* collecting antiquarian objects, writing and lecturing on English furniture. *Address:* Blossoms, Bloomfield Park, Sunningdale, Ascot, Berks SL5 0JT. *T:* Ascot 23806. *Club:* Surrey County Cricket.

LUFT, Arthur Christian; His Honour Deemster Luft; HM Second Deemster, Isle of Man, since 1974; *b* 21 July 1915; *e s* of late Ernest Christian Luft and late Phoebe Luft; *m* 1950, Dorothy, *yr d* of late Francis Manley; two *s*. *Educ:* Bradbury Sch., Cheshire. Served Army, 1940-46. Admitted to Manx Bar, 1940; Attorney-Gen., IOM, 1972-74. Chairman: IOM Criminal Injuries Compensation Tribunal, 1974-; Prevention of Fraud (Unit Trust) Tribunal, 1974-; IOM Licensing Appeal Court, 1974-. Pres., Manx Deaf Soc., 1975-. *Recreations:* theatre, watching cricket, reading. *Address:* Leyton, Victoria Road, Douglas, Isle of Man. *T:* Douglas 21048. *Clubs:* Ellan Vannin, Manx Automobile (Douglas).

LUFT, Rev. Hyam Mark, MA, MLitt; FRHistS; JP; Headmaster, Merchant Taylors' School, Crosby, since April 1964; *b* 1913; *s* of I. M. Luft, Liverpool; *m* 1943, Frances, *er d* of F. Pilling, CBE; two *s* one *d*. *Educ:* Liverpool Institute; St John's Coll., University of Durham (Foundation Scholar). BA (1st Cl. Classics) 1934; Dip. TPT 1935; MA 1937; MLitt 1953. Deacon, 1937; Priest, 1938. Asst Priest, Liverpool Diocese, 1937-56; Asst Master, Merchant Taylors' Sch., Crosby, 1941-56; Headmaster, Blackpool Grammar Sch., 1956-64. Pres., Literary and Philosophical Soc. of Liverpool, 1953-54; Mem., Religious Education Commn, 1967-. Fellow-Commoner, Emmanuel Coll., Cambridge, 1968. JP Lancs, 1968-. *Publication:* History of Merchant Taylors' School, Crosby, 1620-1970, 1970. *Recreations:* lakeland walking, foreign travel and lecturing. *Address:* 44 St Michael's Road, Liverpool 23. *T:* 051-924 6034. *Club:* East India, Devonshire, Sports and Public Schools.

LUKAKAMWA, Lt-Col Samuel Eli, psc; Minister of Works and Housing, Uganda, since 1973; *b* 14 Jan. 1941; *m* 1968, Angella Lukakamwa; one *s* three *d*. *Educ:* Busoga Coll., Mwiri, Uganda (Cambridge Sch. Cert. level). Mons Officer Cadet Sch., Surrey, UK, 1963; Uganda Army: Platoon Comdr, 1963-65; Company Comdr, 1965-66; Gen. HQ, Uganda Armed Forces: Actg Camp Comdt, 1966-67; Camp Comdt, 1967-68; Staff College (Army) UK, 1969 (psc); DAA&QMG, 1970 (Principal Asst Sec., Min. of Educn (for one month), 1970); Asst Adjt and Quartermaster Gen., at Gen. HQ, Uganda Armed Forces, 1971; High Comr for Uganda in London, 1971-72. President's Commendation, 1973; Efficiency Medal, 1973; Republic Medal, 1974. *Recreations:* plays cricket, tennis and football. *Address:* Ministry of Works and Housing, PO Box 10, Entebbe, Uganda.

LUKE, 2nd Baron *cr* 1929, of Pavenham; **Ian St John Lawson Johnston,** KCVO 1976; TD; DL; JP; *b* 7 June 1905; *e s* of 1st Baron and Hon. Edith Laura (*d* 1941), *d* of 16th Baron St John of Bletsoe; *S* father, 1943; *m* 1932, Barbara, *d* of Sir FitzRoy Hamilton Anstruther-Gough-Calthorpe, 1st Bt; four *s* one *d*. *Educ:* Eton; Trinity Coll., Cambridge, MA. Chairman, Electrolux Ltd; Director: Ashanti Goldfields Corporation Ltd;

Gateway Building Society and other companies; Chm., Bovril Ltd, 1943-70. One of HM Lieutenants, City of London, 1953-. Hon. Col 5th Bn Beds Regt, 1947-62; OC 9th Bn Beds and Herts Regt, 1940-43; Chairman: Area Cttee for National Fitness in Herts and Beds, 1937-39; London Hospitals Street Collections Cen. Cttee, 1943-45; Beds TAA, 1943-46; Duke of Gloucester's Red Cross and St John Fund, 1943-46; Nat. Vice-Pres., Royal British Legion; Chm., National Playing Fields Assoc., 1950-76; an Hon. Sec., Assoc. of British Chambers of Commerce, 1944-52; Mem. of Church Assembly (House of Laity), 1935; Lay Reader, St Alban's dio., 1933-; Mem., International Olympic Cttee, 1952-; President: Incorporated Sales Managers Assoc., 1953-56; Advertising Assoc., 1955-58; Outdoor Advertising Council, 1957; Operation Britain Organisation, 1957-62; London Chamber of Commerce, 1952-55; Inst. of Export, 1973-; Chm. Governors, Queen Mary Coll., Univ. of London, 1963-. MFH Oakley Hunt, 1947-49. CC, DL, JP, Bedfordshire. *Heir: s* Hon. Arthur Charles St John Lawson Johnston [*b* 13 Jan. 1933; *m* 1st, 1959, Silvia Maria (marr. diss. 1971), *yr d* of Don Honorio Roigt and Doña Dorothy Goodall de Roigt; one *s* two *d*; 2nd, 1971, Sarah, *d* of Richard Hearne; one *s*]. *Address:* Odell Castle, Odell, Beds MK43 7BB. *T:* Bedford 720240. *Club:* Carlton.

See also Hon. H. de B. Lawson Johnston, Sir I. J. Pitman.

LUKE, Hon. Sir Emile Fashole, KBE 1969 (CBE 1959); Speaker of the House of Representatives, Sierra Leone, 1968-73; *b* 19 Oct. 1895; *s* of late Josiah Thomas Steven Luke and late Dorcas Evangeline Luke; *m* 1929, Sarah Christina Jones-Luke (decd); two *s* one *d. Educ:* Wesleyan Methodist High Sch.; Fourah Bay Coll.; Lincoln's Inn. Civil Servant, 1913-19; practised Law, 1926-44; City Councillor, Freetown, 1940-44; Asst Police Magistrate, 1944-45; Police Magistrate, 1945-51; Senior Police Magistrate, 1951; Actg Judge, Bathurst, Gambia, 1953; Actg Puisne Judge, 1951-54; Puisne Judge, Sierra Leone, 1954-59, retired; Acting Chief Justice, in Sierra Leone and Gambia, on various occasions between 1956 and 1968, and Appeal Court Justice on several occasions, 1960-68. Chief Scout, Scouts Assoc., Sierra Leone, 1969 (awarded the Silver Wolf); Bronze Wolf, World Bureau, 1971. DCL (hc) Univ. of Sierra Leone, 1976. Grand Cordon, Order of Cedar of Lebanon, 1971; Grand Cordon, Order of Menelik II, Ethiopia, 1972. *Recreations:* tennis and walking. *Address:* 85 Motor Road, Wilberforce, PO Box 228, Freetown, Sierra Leone. *T:* Freetown 30602. *Clubs:* Royal Commonwealth Society; Freetown Dinner (Freetown).

LUKE, Eric Howard Manley, CMG 1950; FRCSE 1922; FRACS 1932; retired; *b* 18 Aug. 1894; *s* of Sir Charles Luke; *m* 1923, Gladys Anne, *d* of Col J. J. Esson, CMG; one *s* two *d. Educ:* Wellington Coll.; Otago Univ.; Edinburgh Univ. MB, ChB, Otago Univ., NZ, 1920; senior surgeon, Wellington Hospital, NZ, 1925-50; Thoracic Surgeon, East Coast Hospitals, 1942-54; Chm. of Council, British Medical Association, NZ Branch, 1944-49; President BMA, NZ Branch, 1950. Has a citrus orchard. *Recreations:* formerly Rugby; now bowls and gardening. *Address:* Keri Keri, Bay of Islands, NZ. *Club:* Wellington (Wellington, NZ).

LUKE, Peter (Ambrose Cyprian), MC 1944; playwright and short story writer, freelance since 1967; *b* 12 Aug. 1919, *e s* of late Sir Harry Luke, KCMG, DLitt Oxon and Joyce Fremlin; *m* 1st, Carola Peyton-Jones (decd); 2nd, Lettice Crawshaw (marr. diss.); one *s* one *d*; 3rd, June Tobin; two *s* three *d. Educ:* Eton; Byam Shaw Sch. of Art; Atelier André Lhote, Paris. Served War, 1939-46 with Rifle Bde in ME, Italy and NW Europe. Sub-Editor, Reuters News Desk, 1946-47; wine trade, 1947-57; Story Editor, ABC TV, 1958-62; Editor, The Bookman (ABC TV), 1962-63; Editor, Tempo (ABC TV Arts Programme), 1963-64; Drama Producer, BBC TV, 1963-67. Dir, Edwards-Mac Liammoir Dublin Gate Theatre Co., 1977-. Author TV plays: Small Fish are Sweet, 1958; Pigs Ear with Flowers, 1960; Roll on Bloomin' Death, 1961; (with William Sansom) A Man on Her Back, 1965; Devil a Monk Wou'd Be, 1966. Produced, Silent Song, BBC TV (Prix Italia, 1967). Wrote and directed films: Anach Cuan (about Sean O Riada), BBC TV, 1967; Black Sound--Deep Song (about Federico Garcia Lorca), BBC TV, 1968; wrote stage plays: Hadrian the Seventh, prod. Birmingham Rep. 1967, Mermaid 1968, Theatre Royal, Haymarket and Broadway, 1969 (Antoinette Perry Award nomination, 1968-69); Bloomsbury, Phoenix, 1974. OStJ 1940. *Publications:* The Play of Hadrian VII, 1968; Sisyphus and Reilly, an autobiography, 1972; translations from the Spanish: Yerma, by Frederico Garcia Lorca, 1972; Rings for a Spanish Lady (Anillos para Una Dama) by Antonio Gala, 1974; short stories in: Envoy, Cornhill, Pick of Today's Short Stories, Winter's Tales, Era, New Irish Writing, etc. *Recreations:* literature, agriculture, tauromachia. *Address:* La Almona, El Chorro, Prov. de Málaga, Spain; The Dower House, Emo Court, Co. Laois, Ireland. *Club:* Kildare Street and University.

LUKE, Sir Stephen (Elliot Vyvyan), KCMG 1953 (CMG 1946); *b* 26 Sept. 1905; *o c* of late Brigadier-General Thomas Mawe Luke, CBE, DSO; *m* 1st, 1929, Helen Margaret Reinold; two *s*; 2nd, 1948, Margaret Stych; one *d. Educ:* St George's Sch., Harpenden; Wadham Coll., Oxford. Asst Clerk, House of Commons, 1930; Asst Principal, Colonial Office, 1930; Asst Private Sec. to successive Secs of State, 1933-35; seconded to Palestine Administration, 1936-37; Sec., Palestine Partition Commission, 1938; Under-Sec., Cabinet Office, 1947-50; Asst Under-Sec. of State, Colonial Office, 1950-53; Comptroller for Development and Welfare in the West Indies, and British Co-Chm. of Caribbean Commn, 1953-58; Comr for preparation of WI Federal Organisation, 1956-58; Senior Crown Agent for Oversea Governments and Administrations, 1959-68; Interim Comr for the West Indies, May 1962-68; Mem. Exec. Cttee, W India Cttee, 1969-72. Chm., Board of Governors, St George's Sch., Harpenden, 1963-68. Dir, Pirelli Ltd and other companies, 1968-76. First Class Order of Laila Jasa (PSLJ) (Brunei), 1966. *Recreation:* gardening. *Address:* Merryfields, Breamore, Fordingbridge, Hants. *T:* Breamore 389. *Club:* United Oxford & Cambridge University.

LUKE, William Edgell; Chairman, since 1959 (Managing Director, 1949-73), Lindustries Ltd (formerly the Linen Thread Co. Ltd) and associated companies at home and abroad; Director: Powell Duffryn Ltd, since 1966; Bankers Trust (Holdings) Ltd, since 1975; *b* 9 June 1909; *s* of George Bingley Luke and Violet Edgell; *m* 1st, Muriel Aske Haley (marr. diss.); one *s* one *d*; 2nd, Constance Anne Reid; two *d. Educ:* Old Hall, Wellington; Kelvinside Academy, Glasgow. Served War of 1939-45: Major, Intelligence Corps, S Africa and Central America. Mem. Grand Coun., FBI, 1947-73 (Chm. Scottish Council, 1957) (FBI is now CBI); Mem. Coun. of Aims of Industry, 1958-; Chm. Industrial Advisers to the Blind Ltd, 1963-67; Chm., UK-S Africa Trade Assoc., 1963-; Mem., Brit. Nat. Export Council, and Chm., BNEC Southern Africa Cttee for Exports to Southern Africa, 1965-68; Mem., BOTB Adv. Council, 1975-; Trustee, South Africa Foundation. FBIM. Master, Worshipful Company of Makers of Playing Cards, 1958. Royal Order, Crown of Yugoslavia, 1944. *Recreations:* golf, water ski-ing, music and travel. *Address:* Minster House, Priorsfield Road, Hurtmore, Godalming, Surrey GU7 2RG; Trevor House, 100 Brompton Road, SW3. *T:* 01-584 6161. *Clubs:* Royal Thames Yacht, Travellers'; Western Province (Cape Town).

LUMBY, Sir Henry, Kt 1973; CBE 1957; DL, JP; Chairman of Lancashire County Council, 1967-73; Chairman, Liverpool Diocesan Board of Finance, since 1977; *b* 9 Jan. 1909; *m* 1936, Dorothy Pearl Watts; two *s. Educ:* Merchant Taylors' Sch., Crosby. Served War of 1939-45 (POW, 1942-45). Mem., The Stock Exchange. Mem., Lancs CC, 1946; Alderman, 1956-74; Leader of Conservative Gp, Lancs CC, 1965-73; DL 1965, JP 1951, High Sheriff 1973, Lancashire. *Recreation:* gardening. *Address:* The Dawn, Dark Lane, Ormskirk, Lancs. *T:* Ormskirk 72030.

LUMET, Sidney; film director; *b* Philadelphia, 25 June 1924; *o s* of Baruch and Eugenia Lumet; *m* Rita Gam (marr. diss.); *m* 1956, Gloria Vanderbilt (marr. diss. 1963); *m* 1963, Gail Jones; one *d. Educ:* Professional Children's Sch., NY; Columbia Univ. Served US Army, SE Asia, 1942-46. Appeared as child actor: Dead End; The Eternal Road; Sunup to Sunday; Schoolhouse on the Lot; My Heart's in the Highlands; Dir, Summer Stock, 1947-49; taught acting, High Sch. of Professional Arts; Associate Dir, CBS, 1950, Dir, 1951-. TV shows include: Danger; Your Are There; Alcoa: The Sacco and Vanzetti Story; Goodyear Playhouse; Best of Broadway; Omnibus. Films directed include: Twelve Angry Men, 1957; Stage Struck, 1958; That Kind of Woman, 1959; The Fugitive Kind, 1960; A View from the Bridge, Long Day's Journey into Night, 1962; Fail Safe, 1964; The Pawnbroker, The Hill, 1965; The Group, 1966; The Deadly Affair, 1967; Bye Bye Braverman, Last of the Mobile Hot Shots, Child's Play, The Seagull, 1969; The Anderson Tapes, 1971; The Offence, 1973; Serpico, Murder on the Orient Express, 1974; Dog Day Afternoon, 1975; Network, 1977; Equus, 1977; *Play:* Caligula, 1960. *Address:* c/o CBS Inc., 6121 Sunset Boulevard, Hollywood, Calif. 90028, USA.

LUMLEY, family name of **Earl of Scarbrough.**

LUMLEY, Viscount; Richard Osbert Lumley; *b* 18 May 1973; *s* and *heir* of 12th Earl of Scarbrough, *qv.*

LUMLEY, Air Cdre Eric Alfred, CBE 1948; MC 1918; MD, BCh, DPH, DTM&H; RAF retired; lately Medical Officer to RAF Recruiting Centre, Birmingham; *b* 7 Dec. 1891; *s* of Joseph Alfred Lumley and Henrietta Lumley (*née* Barnes), Tullamore,

King's County, Ireland; *m* 1920, Elsie Clift (*d* 1969), Redcar, Yorks; one *s* two *d. Educ:* Wesley Coll., Dublin; Dublin Univ. MB, BCh, BAO (Univ. of Dublin), 1914; LM Rotunda, 1914; DPH (London), 1930; DTM&H (London), 1946; MD (Dublin), 1948; Capt. RAMC, 1914-18 (MC); service with 8/10 Gordon Highlanders, No. 138 Field Amb., 36th (Ulster) Divisonal Artillery, etc. Joined RAF, 1919; Group Capt. 1928; Air Cdre 1946; served in Egypt, Iraq (2 tours), Aden (2 tours), as well as home appts, 1919-38; War of 1939-45; PMO British Forces in Aden, 1938-40; OC, RAF Hosp., Ely, 1940-42; SMO Nos 27 & 28 Groups RAF, 1942-44; PMO Fighter Comd, 1944-46; PMO, RAF in India and Royal Indian Air Force, 1946-47; RAF Rep. on Govt of India Cttee (Roy. Cttee) on Integration of Medical Services of Indian Armed Forces, 1947; retd from RAF, 1950. Public Health Service MO, 1950-52; Civilian MO employed by Air Ministry, 1952-65. *Publications:* Army and Air Force Doctor, 1971; various, in BMJ, Jl Indian Med. Assoc. and Sports India. *Recreations:* cricket, golf, billiards, trout and salmon fishing. *Address:* Gindle's Cottage, Walmersley, Bury, Lancs. *T:* 061-764 2529.

LUMLEY-SAVILE, family name of **Baron Savile**.

LUMSDEN, Dr David James; Principal, Royal Scottish Academy of Music and Drama, Glasgow, since 1976; *b* Newcastle upon Tyne, 19 March 1928; *m* 1951, Sheila Daniels; two *s* two *d. Educ:* Dame Allan's Sch., Newcastle upon Tyne; Selwyn Coll., Cambridge. Organ scholar, Selwyn Coll., Cambridge, 1948-51; BA Class I, 1950; MusB (Barclay Squire Prize) 1951; MA 1955; DPhil 1957. Asst Organist, St John's Coll., Cambridge, 1951-53; Res. Student, 1951-54; Organist and Choirmaster, St Mary's, Nottingham, 1954-56; Founder/Conductor, Nottingham Bach Soc., 1954-59; Rector Chori, Southwell Minster, 1956-59; Dir of Music, Keele, 1958-59; Prof. of Harmony, Royal Academy of Music, 1959-61; Fellow and Organist, New Coll., Oxford, and Lectr in the Faculty of Music, Oxford Univ., 1959-76. Conductor, Oxford Harmonic Soc., 1961-63; Organist, Sheldonian Theatre, 1964-76; Harpsichordist to London Virtuosi, 1972-75. Pres., Inc. Assoc. of Organists, 1966-68; Hugh Porter Lectr, Union Theological Seminary, NY, 1967; Vis. Prof., Yale Univ., 1974-75; Conductor, Oxford Sinfonia, 1967-70; Choragus, Oxford Univ., 1968-72. Hon. Editor, Church Music Soc., 1970-73. *Publications:* An Anthology of English Lute Music, 1954; Thomas Robinson's Schoole of Musicke, 1603, 1971; Articles in: The Listener; The Score; Music and Letters: Galpin Soc. Jl; La Luth et sa Musique; La Musique de la Renaissance, etc. *Recreations:* reading, theatre, camping, photography, travel, etc. *Address:* 353 Albert Drive, Pollokshields, Glasgow. *Club:* Glasgow Art.

LUMSDEN, James Alexander, MBE 1945; TD 1962; DL; Partner, Maclay, Murray & Spens, Solicitors, Glasgow, since 1947; *b* 24 Jan. 1915; *s* of late Sir James Robert Lumsden and Lady (Henrietta) Lumsden (*née* Macfarlane Reid); *m* 1947, Sheila, *d* of late Malcolm Cross and Evelyn Cross (*née* Newlands); three *s. Educ:* Rugby Sch.; Corpus Christi Coll., Cambridge. BA Cantab, LLB. Director: Bank of Scotland, 1958; Weir Group Ltd, 1957; William Baird & Co. Ltd, 1959; Scottish Western Investment Co. Ltd and other companies in Murray Johnstone Group, 1967- (Chm., 1971-); Scottish Provident Instn, 1968- (Chm., 1977-); and other companies; Dir, Burmah Oil Co. Ltd, 1957-76 (Chm., 1971-75). Mem. Jenkins Cttee on Company Law. DL Dunbartonshire, 1966. *Recreations:* shooting and other country pursuits. *Address:* Bannachra, Helensburgh, Dunbartonshire. *T:* Arden 653. *Clubs:* Naval and Military, Caledonian; New (Edinburgh); Western (Glasgow).

LUNCH, John, CBE 1975; VRD 1965; FCA, FCIT; Director-General of the Port of London Authority, and Board Member, 1971-76; Chairman: Comprehensive Shipping Group, 1973-75; Transcontinental Air Ltd, 1973-75; *b* 11 Nov. 1919; *s* of late Percy Valentine Lunch and late Amy Lunch (*née* Somerville); *m* 1943, Joyce Barbara Clerke; two *s. Educ:* Roborough Sch., Eastbourne. Served Navy, Lt RNVR, Medit. and Home Fleets, 1939-46, subseq. Permanent RNVR, later RNR; Lt-Comdr RNR, retd list, 1969; Lt-Col RE (T&AVR), Engrg and Railway Staff Corps, 1971, Col, 1976. In business in City, 1946-48: Asst Man. Dir, Tokenhouse Securities Corp. Ltd, 1947, and dir several cos; British Transport Commn, 1948-61: road and rail transport, passenger and goods, and ancillary businesses; Joined PLA as Chief Accountant, 1961; Dir of Finance, 1965; also Dir of Commerce, 1966; Asst Dir-Gen., responsible docks and harbour, 1969; Chairman: (and founder) PLA Port Users Consultative Cttee, 1966-71; Internat. Port Develt Cttee, Internat. Assoc. of Ports and Harbors, 1972-76; Member Council: Inst. of Chartered Accountants, 1970-77; Chartered Inst. of Transport, 1973-76; Solent Protection Soc., 1976-; Chm.

(and founder), RNLI Manhood Br., 1976-. Hon. Mem. Internat. Assoc. of Airport and Seaport Police. FBIM 1971; FInstM 1973; FRSA (Council nominee) 1976. Freeman, Watermen & Lightermen's Co. of River Thames, 1970, Court Mem., 1976-. *Publications:* The Chartered Accountant in Top Management, 1965; A Plan for Britain's Ports, 1975. *Recreations:* sailing, gardening, fishing, golf, art. *Address:* Twittens, Itchenor, Chichester, West Sussex PO20 7AN. *T:* Birdham 512105. *Clubs:* Army and Navy, Press; Royal Wimbledon Golf; Itchenor Sailing (West Sussex).

LUND, John Walter Guerrier, CBE 1975; FRS 1963; DSc, PhD; Botanist, at Windermere Laboratory of Freshwater Biological Association, since 1945; Deputy Chief Scientific Officer; *b* 27 Nov. 1912; *s* of George E. Lund and Kate Lund (*née* Hardwick); *m* 1949, Hilda M. Canter; one *s* one *d. Educ:* Sedbergh Sch.; Univs of Manchester and London. Demonstrator in Botany, Univ. of Manchester, also Queen Mary Coll. and Chelsea Polytechnic, Univ. of London, 1935-38; Temp. Lectr in Botany, Univ. of Sheffield, 1936; PhD (London) 1939; Staff Biologist, W Midland Forensic Science Laboratory, Birmingham, 1938-45; DSc (London) 1951. *Publications:* papers and articles in scientific jls, symposium vols, etc. *Recreation:* gardening. *Address:* Ellerbeck, Ellerigg Road, Ambleside, Cumbria LA22 9EU. *T:* Ambleside 2369.

LUND, Sir Thomas (George), Kt 1958; CBE 1948; Director-General, International Bar Association, since 1969; Secretary-General, International Legal Aid Association, since 1963; *b* 6 Jan. 1906; *s* of late Kenneth Fraser Lund, MA, MB, Cowper Cottage, Mundesley, Norfolk; *m* 1931, Catherine Stirling, *d* of late Arthur John Audsley; one *d. Educ:* Westminster Sch. Admitted a Solicitor, 1929; Asst Solicitor, The Law Soc., 1930; Asst Sec., 1937; Secretary-General, 1939-69; Treas., Internat. Bar Assoc., 1950-69; Chm. Board of Management, College of Law, 1962-69; Dir, Solicitors' Benevolent Assoc., 1949-69; Past Master, Worshipful Co. of Solicitors of the City of London; Liveryman, Worshipful Co. of Cordwainers. Past Pres., British Academy of Forensic Sciences. Local Dir, Sun Alliance London Gp. *Publications:* The Solicitors Act, 1941, 1943; ed a section of Halsbury's Laws of England; contributed many articles to English and American legal jls. *Recreations:* foreign travel, motoring, gardening. *Address:* International Bar Association, Byron House, 7-9 St James's Street, SW1A 1EE; Bryanston Court, George Street, W1. *Club:* Athenæum.

LUNKOV, Nikolai Mitrofanovich; Soviet Ambassador to the Court of St James's, since 1973; also to Malta; *b* Pavlovka, Ryazan Region, 7 Jan. 1919; *Educ:* Lomonosov Technical Inst., Moscow. Diplomatic Service, 1943-; Asst Minister of Foreign Affairs, 1951-52; Dep. Political Counsellor, Soviet Control Commn in Germany, 1952-54; Counsellor, Stockholm, 1954-57; Dep. Head, Dept of Internat. Organizations, Ministry of Foreign Affairs, 1957; 3rd European Dept, 1957-69; Head of Scandinavian Dept, Min. of Foreign Affairs, 1959-62; Ambassador to Norway, 1962-68; Head of Dept of Cultural Relations with Foreign Countries, 1968-71; Head of 2nd European Dept, 1971-73. Mem. of Collegium of Min. of Foreign Affairs, 1968-73. Awarded orders and medals. *Address:* Embassy of the USSR, 13 Kensington Palace Gardens, W8.

LUNN, Peter Northcote, CMG 1957; OBE 1951; HM Diplomatic Service; retired 1972; *b* 15 Nov. 1914; *e s* of late Sir Arnold Lunn; *m* 1939, Hon. (Eileen) Antoinette (*d* 1976), *d* of 15th Visc. Gormanston; three *s* three *d. Educ:* Eton. Joined RA, 1940; served 1940-46 (Malta, Italy and BAOR); entered FO, 1947; Vienna, 1948-50; Berne, 1950-53; Germany, 1953-56; London, 1956-57; Bonn, 1957-62; Beirut, 1962-67; FCO, 1967-72. Mem., Brit. International Ski team, 1931-37, Capt. 1934-37; Capt. British Olympic Ski team, 1936. *Publications:* High-Speed Skiing, 1935; Evil in High Places, 1947; A Skiing Primer, 1948, rev. edn 1951. *Club:* Ski Club of Great Britain.

LUNS, Dr Joseph Marie Antoine Hubert; Officer, Order of Orange-Nassau, 1947; Knight Grand Cross, Order of the Netherlands Lion, 1971; Hon. GCMG; Hon. CH 1971; Secretary-General of NATO, since 1971; *b* 28 Aug. 1911; *m* Baroness E. C. van Heemstra; one *s* one *d. Educ:* sec. schs, Amsterdam and Brussels; universities of Leyden, Amsterdam, London and Berlin. Attaché of Legation, 1938; 2nd Sec., 1942; 1st Sec., 1945; Counsellor, 1949. Served in: Min. for For. Affairs, 1938-40; Berne, 1940-41; Lisbon, 1941-43; London, at Netherlands Min. for For. Affairs, 1943-44, and at Netherlands Embassy, 1944-49; Netherlands Delegn to UN, NY, 1942-52; Minister of Foreign Affairs, The Netherlands, 1952-71. MP (Second Chamber, Netherlands), July-Oct. 1956 and March-June 1959. Hon. Fellow, London Sch. of Economics, 1969. Prix Charlemagne, Aachen, 1967; Gustav Stresemann Medal, 1968.

Hon. DCL: Harvard, 1970; Oxon, 1972; Exeter, 1974; Dr Humanities, Hope Coll., USA, 1974. Holds numerous foreign orders. *Publications:* The Epic of The Royal Netherlands Navy; articles on Royal Netherlands Navy in Dutch and foreign jls, and articles on international affairs in International Affairs, La Revue Politique, and others. *Recreation:* swimming. *Address:* c/o North Atlantic Treaty Organisation, Brussels 39, Belgium. *Clubs:* Reform (Hon. Mem.); Haagsche, De Witte (Netherlands).

LUNT, Rt. Rev. Francis Evered; *b* 15 Oct. 1900; *e s* of late Francis Bryan Lunt; *m* 1938, Helen Patricia, *y d* of late Alfred Bolton; three *d. Educ:* University Coll., Durham (LTh 1923); London Coll. of Divinity. Deacon, 1925; Priest, 1927; Curate of St Andrew and St Mary, Maidenhead, 1925-31; St Barnabas, Cambridge, 1931-34; licensed to officiate, Diocese of Ely, 1933-43; Chaplain, Downing Coll., Cambridge and Cambridge Pastorate, 1934-43; Hon. Fellow, Downing Coll., 1966-; MA Cambridge, 1939; Senior Chaplain to Oxford Undergraduates and Rector of St Aldate, Oxford, 1943-51; Dean of Bristol, 1951-57; Bishop Suffragan of Stepney, 1957-68. MA Oxford (Oriel Coll.), 1945. Select Preacher, Univ. of Cambridge, 1943 and 1962; Surrogate, 1943; Examining Chaplain to Bishop of Oxford, 1946-51, to Bishop of Portsmouth, 1949-51. Mem. Council, Ridley Hall, Cambridge, 1950-71. *Address:* Ridgeway House, Felpham, Sussex.

LUNT, Maj.-Gen. James Doiran, CBE 1964 (OBE 1958); MA (Oxon); FRGS; Domestic Bursar, and Fellow, Wadham College, Oxford, since Jan. 1973; *b* 13 Nov. 1917; *s* of late Brig. W. T. Lunt, MBE, Camberley, Surrey; *m* 1940, Muriel, *d* of late A. H. Byrt, CBE, Bournemouth; one *s* one *d. Educ:* King William's Coll., IOM; RMC, Sandhurst. 2nd Lieut, Duke of Wellington's Regt, 1937; served with 4th Bn Burma Rifles, 1939-41; Burma Campaign, 1942; transf. to 16/5th Queen's Royal Lancers, 1949; served with Arab Legion, 1952-55; comd 16/5th Queen's Royal Lancers, 1957-59; comd Fed. Regular Army, Aden, 1961-64; Dir of Admin. Planning (Army), MoD, 1964-66; Defence Adviser to British High Commissioner, India, 1966-68; Chief of Staff, Contingencies Planning, SHAPE, 1969-70; Vice-Adjt-Gen., MoD, 1970-72; Col, 16th/5th The Queen's Royal Lancers, 1975-. Order of Independence (Jordan), 1956; Commander, Order of South Arabia, 1964. *Publications:* Charge to Glory, 1961; Scarlet Lancer, 1964; The Barren Rocks of Aden, 1966; Bokhara Burnes, 1969; From Sepoy to Subedar, 1970; The Duke of Wellington's Regiment, 1971; 16th/5th The Queen's Royal Lancers, 1973; John Burgoyne of Saratoga, 1975. *Recreations:* golf, fishing, writing. *Address:* Hilltop House, Little Milton, Oxon. *T:* Great Milton 242. *Clubs:* Cavalry and Guards, Flyfishers'.

LUNT, Rev. Canon Ronald Geoffrey, MC 1943; MA, BD; Vicar of Martley, since 1974; Chief Master, King Edward's School, Birmingham, 1952-74; *b* 25 June 1913; *s* of late Rt Rev. G. C. L. Lunt, DD, Bishop of Salisbury; *m* 1945, Veslemoy Sopp Foss, Oslo, Norway; one *s* two *d. Educ:* Eton (King's Scholar); The Queen's Coll., Oxford (Scholar, 1st class Lit. Hum.); Westcott House, Cambridge. Assistant Master, St George's Sch., Harpenden, 1935; Haberdashers' Sch., Hampstead, 1936-37; Deacon, 1938; Priest, 1939; Master in Orders at Radley Coll., Abingdon, 1938-40; CF 1940-45; Middle East, 1941-44 (MC); CF 3rd class, SCF 1 Airborne Division, 1945; Headmaster, Liverpool Coll., 1945-52. Won Cromer Greek Prize, 1937; Page Scholar to USA, 1959; Select Preacher: University of Cambridge, 1948, 1960, Oxford, 1951-53. Chm., Birmingham Council of Churches, 1957-60; Hon. Canon, Birmingham Cathedral, 1969. Mem., Birmingham Educn Cttee, 1952-74. Life Governor, Queen's Coll., Birmingham, 1957; Trustee, 1954, Chm., 1971-74, E. W. Vincent Trust; Governor, 1952, Sen. Vice-Pres., 1971-72, Pres., 1973, Birmingham and Midland Inst. Pres., Incorporated Assoc. of Head Masters, 1962. Mem., Press Council, 1964-69. BD (Oxon), 1967. *Publications:* Edition of Marlowe's Dr Faustus, 1937, Edward II, 1938; contrib. to Arts v. Science, 1967; articles in Theology, Hibbert Journal, and other journals. *Recreations:* travel, gardening. *Address:* The Station House, Ledbury, Herefordshire. *T:* Ledbury 3174; Wichenford 577.

LUPTON, Prof. Thomas; Professor of Organisational Behaviour and Deputy Director, Manchester Business School, since 1966; *b* 4 Nov. 1918; *s* of Thomas Lupton, blacksmith, and Jane Lupton (*née* Vowell); *m* 1st, 1942, Thelma Chesney; one *d*; 2nd, 1963, Dr Constance Shirley Wilson; one *s* one *d. Educ:* Elem. and Central Sch.; Technical Coll.; Ruskin Coll.; Oriel Coll., Oxford; Univ. of Manchester. DipEconPolSci (Oxon), MA (Oxon), PhD (Manch.). Served War, HM Forces, 1939-41 and 1944-46; Marine Engr: 1932-39, 1941-44. Research Posts: Liverpool Univ., 1951-54; Manchester Univ., 1954-57; Lectr in Sociology,

Manchester Univ., 1957-59; Head of Dept of Industrial Admin, Coll. of Advanced Techn., Birmingham, 1959-64; Montague Burton Prof. of Ind. Rel., Univ. of Leeds, 1964-66. Gen. Editor, Jl of Management Studies, 1966-76; Dir, Pirelli General Cables Ltd, 1970-; Member: Civil Service Arbitration Tribunal, 1967-70; Arbitration Panel, Dept of Employment, 1969-; various official commns and tribunals, 1960-. *Publications:* On the Shop Floor, 1963; Industrial Behaviour and Personnel Management, 1964; Management and the Social Sciences, 1966 (rev. for Penguin, 1972); Selecting a Wage Payment System (with D. Gowler), 1969; Job and Pay Comparisons (with A. M. Bowey), 1973; Wages and Salaries (with A. M. Bowey), 1974; articles in Jl of Management Studies, Manchester Sch., Production Engineer, etc. *Recreations:* camping, fell walking, Association football. *Address:* 8 Old Broadway, Manchester M20 9DF. *T:* 061-445 3309.

LUPU, Radu; pianist; *b* 30 Nov. 1945; *s* of Mayer Lupu, lawyer, and Ana Gabor, teacher of languages; *m* 1971, Elizabeth Wilson. *Educ:* Moscow Conservatoire. 1st prize: Van Cliburn Competition, 1966; Enescu Internat. Competition, 1967; Leeds Internat. Pianoforte Competition, 1969. *Recreations:* history, art, sport. *Address:* c/o Harrison/Parrott Ltd, 22 Hillgate Street, W8 7SR. *T:* 01-229 9166.

LURGAN, 4th Baron *cr* 1839; **William George Edward Brownlow;** *b* 22 Feb. 1902; *o s* of 3rd Baron and Lady Emily Julia Cadogan (*d* 1909), *d* of 5th Earl Cadogan, KG; *S* father, 1937. *Educ:* Eton; Oxford. *Heir:* cousin John Desmond Cavendish Brownlow, OBE, *b* 29 June 1911. *Address:* c/o Messrs Lee & Pembertons, 45 Pont Street, SW1X 0BX. *Clubs:* Turf; Ulster (Belfast).

LURIA, Prof. Salvador Edward; Sedgwick Professor of Biology, Massachusetts Institute of Technology, since 1964; *b* 13 Aug. 1912; *s* of David Luria and Ester Sacerdote; *m* 1945, Zella Hurwitz; one *s. Educ:* Turin Univ. (MD 1935). Res. Fellow, Inst. of Radium, Paris, 1938-40; Res. Asst, Columbia Univ. Medical School, NY, 1940-42; Guggenheim Fellow, Vanderbilt and Princeton Univs, 1942-43; Instructor in Bacteriology, Indiana Univ., 1943-45, Asst Prof., 1944-47, Associate Prof. 1947-50; Prof. of Bacteriology, Illinois Univ., 1950-59; Prof. and Chm. of Dept of Microbiology, MIT, 1959-64. Fellow of Salk Inst. for Biol Studies, 1965-. Associate Editor, Jl Bacteriology, 1950-55; Editor: Virology, 1955-; Biological Abstracts, 1958-62; Member: Editorial Bd, Exptl Cell Res. Jl, 1948-; Advisory Bd, Jl Molecular Biology, 1958-64; Hon. Editorial Advisory Bd, Jl Photochemistry and Photobiology, 1961-. Lecturer: Univ. of Colorado, 1950; Jesup, Notre Dame, 1950; Nieuwand, Notre Dame 1959; Dyer, Nat. Insts of Health, 1963. Member: Amer. Phil Soc.; Amer. Soc. for Microbiology (Pres. 1967-68); Nat. Acad. of Scis; Amer. Acad. of Arts and Scis; AAAS; Soc. Genetic Microbiology; Genetics Soc. of America; Amer Assoc. Univ. Profs; Sigma Xi. Prizes: Lepetit, 1935; Lenghi, 1965; Louisa Gross Horowitz of Columbia University; Nobel Prize for Physiology or Medicine (jtly), 1969. Hon. ScD: Chicago, 1967; Rutgers, 1970; Indiana, 1970. *Recreation:* sculpting. *Address:* 48 Peacock Farm Road, Lexington, Mass 02173, USA.

LUSAKA, Archbishop of, (RC), since 1969; **Most Rev. Emanuel Milingo;** *b* 13 June 1930; *s* of Yakobe Milingo Chilumbu and Tomaide Lumbiwe Miti. *Educ:* Kachebere Seminary, Malawi; Pastoral Inst., Rome; University Coll., Dublin. Curate: Minga Parish, Chipata Dio., 1958-60; St Mary's Parish, 1960-61; Chipata Cathedral, 1963-64; Parish Priest, Chipata Cathedral, 1964-65; Sec. for Communications at Catholic Secretariat, Lusaka, 1966-69. Founder, The Daughters of the Redeemer, Congregation for young ladies, 1971. *Publications:* A make-Joni, 1972; To die to give life, 1975; Summer lectures for the Daughters of the Redeemer, 1976; Lukango, 1977. *Recreation:* music. *Address:* PO Box RW3, Lusaka, Zambia. *T:* Lusaka 81607.

LUSCOMBE, Rt. Rev. Lawrence Edward; *see* Brechin, Bishop of.

LUSH, Christopher Duncan; HM Diplomatic Service; Counsellor, British Embassy, Paris, since 1974; *b* 4 June 1928; *s* of Eric Duncan Thomas Lush and Iris Leonora (*née* Greenfield); *m* 1967, Marguerite Lilian, *d* of Frederick Albert Bolden; one *s. Educ:* Sedbergh; Magdalen Coll., Oxford. Called to Bar, Gray's Inn, 1953. Asst Legal Adviser, FO, 1959-62; Legal Adviser, Berlin, 1962-65, Dep. Political Adviser, Berlin, 1965-66; FO (later FCO), 1966-69; Head of Chancery, Amman, 1969-71; Head of Aviation and Telecommunications Dept, FCO, 1971-73; Canadian Nat. Defence Coll., 1973-74. *Publications:* articles in Internat. and Compar. Law Qly, Connoisseur. *Address:* British Embassy, 35 rue du Faubourg St Honoré, 75008 Paris; Greywings, Fairlight, Sussex. *Club:* Travellers'.

LUSH, Maurice Stanley, CB 1944; CBE 1942; MC 1916; *b* 23 Nov. 1896; *s* of late Hubert Stanley Lush; *m* 1930, Diana Ruth, *d* of late Charles Alexander Hill; one *s* two *d*. *Educ:* Tonbridge Sch.; RMA, Woolwich. European War, RA, 1915-19 (MC and Bar); Egyptian Army, 1919-22; Sudan Political Service from 1919; Secretary HM Legation, Addis Ababa, 1919-22; District Commissioner, Sudan, 1922-26; Assistant Civil Secretary Sudan Government, 1926-29; Private Secretary to Governor-General of Sudan, 1929-30; Dep. Governor, Sudan, 1930-35; Sudan Agent, Cairo, 1935-38; Governor, Northern Province, Sudan, 1938-41. War of 1939-45 recalled from RARO as Brig.; Deputy Chief Political Officer, Ethiopia, 1941-42; Military Administrator, Madagascar, 1942; Deputy Chief Civil Affairs Officer British Military Administration, Tripolitania, 1942-43; Executive Commissioner and Vice-President, Allied Commission, Italy, 1943-46; Resident representative for Germany and Austria of Intergovernmental Cttee on Refugees, 1946-47; Chief of Mission in Middle East, IRO, 1947-49; Special Representative for Middle East of IRO, 1949-51; Rep. Anglo-Saxon Petroleum Co., Libya, 1952-56; Man. Dir, Pakistan Shell Oil Co. Ltd, 1956-59. Vice-Pres., British and Foreign Bible Soc. FRGS. Order of the Nile, 3rd Class; Officer, Legion of Merit US, 1945; Comdr Order of Knights of Malta, 1945. *Recreation:* walking. *Address:* 3 Carlton Mansions, Holland Park Gardens, W14 8DW. *T:* 01-603 4425. *Club:* Athenæum.
See also Countess of Limerick.

LUSHINGTON, Sir Henry Edmund Castleman, 7th Bt *cr* 1791; *b* 2 May 1909; *s* of Sir Herbert Castleman Lushington, 6th Bt and Barbara Henrietta (*d* 1927), *d* of late Rev. William Greville Hazlerigg; *S* father, 1968; *m* 1937, Pamela Elizabeth Daphne, *er d* of Major Archer R. Hunter, Wokingham, Berks; one *s* two *d*. *Educ:* Dauntsey's Sch. Served War of 1939-45, Flt-Lieut, RAFVR. Metropolitan Police, 1935-58; retired as Superintendent. *Recreations:* gardening, golf. *Heir: s* John Richard Castleman Lushington [*b* 28 Aug. 1938; *m* 1966, Bridget Gillian Margaret, *d* of Colonel John Foster Longfield, Saunton, Devon; three *s*]. *Address:* Carfax, Crowthorne, Berkshire. *T:* Crowthorne 2819. *Clubs:* Royal Air Force; East Berks Golf.

LUSTGARTEN, Edgar; author, journalist, broadcaster; *b* 3 May 1907; *s* of Joseph and Sara Lustgarten; *m* 1932, Joyce (*née* Goldstone) (*d* 1972); no *c*. *Educ:* Manchester Grammar Sch.; St John's Coll., Oxford. Pres., Oxford Union, 1930. Practising Barrister, 1930-40; Radio Counter-Propaganda, 1940-45; BBC Staff Producer, 1945-48; Organiser: BBC Television Programme, In The News, 1950-54; ATV Television Prog., Free Speech, 1955-61; Chm., ATV Television Prog., Fair Play, 1962-65; Narrator, BBC Focus Prog., 1965-68. Solo Broadcaster in many BBC series of Famous Trials, 1952-. *Publications:* novels: A Case to Answer, 1947; Blondie Iscariot, 1948; Game for Three Losers, 1952; I'll never leave you, 1971; *studies in true crime:* Verdict in Dispute, 1949; Defender's Triumph, 1951; The Woman in the Case, 1955; The Business of Murder, 1968; The Chalk Pit Murder, 1975; A Century of Murderers, 1975; The Illustrated Story of Crime, 1976. *Address:* c/o Curtis Brown Ltd, 1 Craven Hill, W2.

LUSTY, Sir Robert (Frith), Kt 1969; *b* 7 June 1909; *o s* of late Frith Lusty; *m* 1st, 1939, Joan Christie (*d* 1962), *y d* of late Archibald Brownlie, Glasgow; 2nd, 1963, Eileen, *widow* of Dr Denis Carroll. *Educ:* Society of Friends' Co-educational Sch., Sidcot. Joined editorial staff The Kent Messenger, 1927; abandoned journalism for publishing and entered production and editorial departments Messrs Hutchinson and Company, 1928; appointed manager associated company, Messrs Selwyn & Blount, 1933; left in 1935 to join Michael Joseph Ltd, on its formation, resigned as Deputy Chairman, 1956, to become Man. Dir, Hutchinson Publishing Gp, until retirement in 1973; a Governor of the BBC, 1960-68 (Vice-Chairman, 1966-68); Member Council of Publishers' Assoc., 1955-61; Chairman: National Book League, 1949-51 and of its 1951 Festival Cttee; Soc. of Bookmen, 1962-65; Publication Panel, King Edward's Hosp. Fund for London. Liveryman Stationers' Co., 1945; Freeman of City of London. A Governor and Councillor, Bedford Coll., 1965-71. Hon. Mem., Eygalières Football Club. FRSA 1969. *Publication:* Bound to be Read (autobiog.), 1975. *Address:* B5 (Upper) Albany, Piccadilly, W1. *T:* 01-734 0668; The Old Silk Mill, Blockley, Moreton-in-Marsh, Glos. *T:* Blockley 335. *Club:* Garrick.

LUTHER, Rt. Rev. Arthur William; Bishop, Church of North India, and Regional Secretary of the Leprosy Mission, since 1973; *b* 21 March 1919; *s* of William and Monica Luther; *m* 1946, Dr Kamal Luther; one *s* two *d*. *Educ:* Nagpur University; India (MA, BT); General Theological Seminary, New York (STD 1957). Deacon, 1943; Priest, 1944; in USA and Scotland for study and parish work, 1952-54; Chaplain to Bishop of Nagpur, 1954; Head Master, Bishop Cotton School, Nagpur, 1954-57; Bishop of Nasik, 1957-70; Bishop of Bombay, 1970-73; held charge of Kolhapur Diocese concurrently with Bombay Diocese, Dec. 1970-Feb. 1972. *Address:* Smellie Bungalow, Nelson Square, Nagpur, Maharashtra, India. *T:* Nagpur 25856.

LUTTRELL, Lt-Col Geoffrey Walter Fownes, MC 1945; JP; Vice Lord-Lieutenant of Somerset, since 1968; *b* 2 Oct. 1919; *s* of late Geoffrey Fownes Luttrell of Dunster Castle, Somerset; *m* 1942, Hermione Hamilton, *er d* of late Capt. Cecil Gunston, MC, and of Lady Doris Gunston. *Educ:* Eton; Exeter Coll., Oxford. Served War of 1939-45, with 15th/19th King's Royal Hussars, 1940-46; North Somerset Yeomanry, 1952-57; Lt-Col 1955; Hon. Col, 6th Bn LI, TAVR, 1977-. Liaison Officer, Ministry of Agriculture, 1965-71. Regional Dir, Lloyds Bank, 1972-. Member: National Parks Commn, 1962-66; Wessex Regional Cttee, Nat. Trust, 1970-; SW Electricity Bd, 1969-. DL Somerset, 1958-68; High Sheriff of Somerset, 1960; JP 1961. *Address:* Court House, East Quantoxhead, Bridgwater, Somerset. *T:* Holford 242. *Club:* Cavalry and Guards.

LUTYENS, (Agnes) Elisabeth, (Mrs Edward Clark), CBE 1969; musician, composer; *b* London, 1906; 3rd *d* of late Sir Edwin Landseer Lutyens, OM, KCIE, PRA, LLD and of late Lady Emily Lutyens; *m* 1st, 1933, Ian Herbert Campbell Glennie (marr. diss.); one *s* twin *d* ; 2nd, 1942, Edward Clark (*d* 1962); one *s*. *Compositions include:* The Pit, a dramatic scene (for tenor, bass, women's chorus, and orchestra); 3 Symphonic Preludes for orchestra; String Quartet No. 6; O Saisons, O Châteaux (Rimbaud) (for soprano and strings); String Trio; Viola Concerto; Six Chamber Concertos; Valediction for clarinet and piano, 1954; Infidelio, 1954; Four Nocturnes, 1954; 6 Tempi for 10 Instruments, 1957; Music for Orchestra, I, II, III; Quincunx for Orchestra, 1959; Wind Quintet, 1961; Symphonies for Solo Piano, Wind, Harps and Percussion, 1961; The Country of the Stars (cantata), 1963; Hymn of Man, 1965; The Valley of Hatsu-se, 1966; Akapotik Rose, 1966; And Suddenly It's Evening, 1967; The Numbered, opera, 1966; Time Off? Not a ghost of a chance, charade in 4 scenes and 3 interruptions, 1968; Isis and Osiris, lyric drama, 1969; Novenaria (for orchestra), 1969; The Tides of Time, 1969; Essence of our Happinesses (cantata), 1970; Oda a la tormenta (Neruda), 1971; The Tears of Night, 1972; Vision of Youth, 1972; Rape of the Moone, 1973; De Amore (cantata), 1973; The Waiting Game (music-theatre), 1973; Plenum III for string quartet, 1974; Winter of the World (for orchestras), commissioned by English Bach Festival, 1974; also music for numerous films and radio features. City of London Midsummer Prize, 1969. Hon. DMus York, 1977. *Publication:* A Goldfish Bowl (autobiography), 1972. *Address:* 13 King Henry's Road, NW3. *T:* 01-722 8505.
See also Mary Lutyens.

LUTYENS, Mary, (Mrs J. G. Links), FRSL; writer since 1929; *b* 31 July 1908; *y d* of late Sir Edwin Lutyens, OM, KCIE, PRA, and late Lady Emily Lutyens; *m* 1st, 1930, Anthony Sewell (marr. diss. 1945; decd); one *d* ; 2nd, 1945, J. G. Links, OBE. *Educ:* Queen's Coll., London; Sydney, Australia. FRSL 1976. *Publications:* fiction: Forthcoming Marriages, 1933; Perchance to Dream, 1935; Rose and Thorn, 1936; Spider's Silk, 1939; Family Colouring, 1940; A Path of Gold, 1941; Together and Alone, 1942; So Near to Heaven, 1943; And Now There is You, 1953; Week-End at Hurtmore, 1954; The Lucian Legend, 1955; Meeting in Venice, 1956; Cleo, 1973; *for children:* Julie and the Narrow Valley, 1944; *autobiography:* To Be Young, 1959; *edited:* Lady Lytton's Court Diary, 1961; (for Krishnamurti) Freedom from the Known, 1969; The Only Revolution, 1970; The Penguin Krishnamurti Reader, 1970; The Urgency of Change, 1971; *biography:* Effie in Venice, 1965; Millais and the Ruskins, 1967; The Ruskins and the Grays, 1972; Krishnamurti: the years of awakening, 1975; also numerous serials, afterwards published, under pseudonym of Esther Wyndham; contribs to Apollo, The Cornhill, The Walpole Soc. Jl. *Recreations:* reading, cinema-going. *Address:* 2 Hyde Park Street, W2. *T:* 01-262 0455.
See also Elisabeth Lutyens.

LUTZ, Marianne Christine; Headmistress, Sheffield High School for Girls (Girls' Public Day School Trust), since 1959; *b* 9 Dec. 1922; *d* of Dr H. Lutz. *Educ:* Wimbledon High Sch., GPDST; Girton Coll., Cambridge (Schol.); University of London. Asst Mistress (History) at: Clergy Daughters' Sch., Bristol, 1946-47; South Hampstead High Sch., GPDST, 1947-59. Former Member: History Textbooks Panel for W Germany (under auspices of FO and Unesco); Diocesan Educn Council and other educational advisory bodies; Professional Cttee, Univ. of Sheffield; Member: Ct, Univ. of Sheffield; Historical Assoc.; Headmistresses' Assoc.; Schnauzer Club of Great Britain. *Publications:* several in connection with Unesco work and

Historical Assoc. *Recreations:* travel, crosswords, books, opera, art and theatre. *Address:* 34 The Glen, Endcliffe Vale Road, Sheffield S10 3FN.

LUXON, Benjamin, FGSM; baritone; *b* Camborne, Cornwall, 1937; *m* 1969, Sheila Amit; two *s* one *d. Educ:* Truro Sch.; Westminster Trng Coll.; Guildhall Sch. of Music. Teacher of Physical Education until becoming professional singer, 1963. Repertoire includes lieder, folk music, oratorio (Russian, French and English song), and operatic rôles including: Aldeburgh: Tarquinius, The Rape of Lucretia, 1969; King Arthur, 1971; BBC TV, Owen Wingrave, 1970; Covent Garden: Owen Wingrave, 1972; Death, Taverner, 1972; Marcello, La Bohème, 1974; Wolfram, Tannhäuser, 1975; Diomede, Troilus and Cressida, 1976; Glyndebourne: (tour) Eugène Onegin, 1971, 1975; Ulisse, Il ritorno d'Ulisse, 1972, 1973; Count, Le Nozze di Figaro, 1973; Gamekeeper, The Cunning Little Vixen, 1975; Ford, Falstaff, 1976, 1977; Don Giovanni, 1977; English National Opera: Posa, Don Carlos, 1974. Recorded Hugo Wolf Mörike Lieder, 1974. Appointed Bard of the Cornish Gorsedd, 1974. Third prize, Munich Internat. Festival, 1961; Gold Medal GSM, 1963. FGSM 1970. *Recreations:* collecting English watercolours and drawings; tennis, swimming. *Address:* 4 Prospect Road, New Barnet, Herts.

LUXTON, William John, CBE 1962; Director, London Chamber of Commerce and Industry, 1964-74 (Secretary, 1958-74); *b* 18 March 1909; *s* of late John Luxton; *m* 1942, Megan, *d* of late John M. Harries; one *s* one *d. Educ:* Shebbear Coll., N Devon; London Univ. Wallace Brothers & Co. Ltd (merchant bankers), 1926-38. Called to the Bar, Lincoln's Inn, 1938; Chancery Bar, 1938-40. Served with Royal Armoured Corps, 1940-45. Legal Parliamentary Secretary, Association of British Chambers of Commerce, 1947-53 (Vice-Pres., 1974); Secretary Birmingham Chamber of Commerce, 1953-58; Dir, Fedn of Commonwealth Chambers of Commerce, 1958-74. *Address:* Abbots Lodge, Abbotswood, Guildford, Surrey. *T:* Guildford 63439.

LUYT, Sir Richard (Edmonds), GCMG 1966 (KCMG 1964; CMG 1960); KCVO 1966; DCM 1942; Vice-Chancellor and Principal, University of Cape Town, since 1968; *b* 8 Nov. 1915; *m* 1st, 1948, Jean Mary Wilder (*d* 1951); one *d;* 2nd, 1956, Eileen Betty Reid; two *s. Educ:* Diocesan Coll., Rondebosch, Cape, SA; Univ. of Cape Town (BA); Trinity Coll., Oxford (MA). Rhodes Scholar from S Africa, 1937. Entered Colonial Service and posted to N Rhodesia, 1940; War Service, 1940-45: with Mission 101, in Ethiopia, 1941; remained in Ethiopia with British Military Mission, for remainder of War. Returned to N Rhodesia, Colonial Service, 1945; transferred to Kenya, 1953; Labour Commissioner, Kenya, 1954-57; Permanent Secretary to various Ministries of the Kenya Government, 1957-60; Secretary to the Cabinet, 1960-61; Chief Secretary, Northern Rhodesia, 1962-64; Governor and C-in-C, British Guiana, 1964-66, until Guyana Independence; Governor-General of Guyana, May-Oct. 1966. Hon. LLD Natal, 1972. *Recreations:* gardening, sport, particularly Rugby (Oxford Blue, 1938) and cricket (Oxford Captain 1940) (also played for Kenya at cricket). *Address:* University of Cape Town, Rondesbosch 7700, South Africa. *Clubs:* Royal Commonwealth Society; Nairobi (Kenya); Civil Service (Cape Town).

LWOFF, Prof. André; Commandeur de la Légion d'Honneur, 1966 (Officier, 1960; Chevalier, 1947); Médaille de la Résistance, 1946; Directeur de l'Institut de Recherches Scientifiques sur le Cancer, 1968-72; Professor of Microbiology, Faculté des Sciences, Paris, 1959-68, and Head of Department of Microbial Physiology, Pasteur Institute, since 1938; *b* Ainay-le-Château, Allier, France, 8 May 1902. *Educ:* (Fac. des Sciences et de Méd.) Univ. of Paris. MD (Paris) 1927; DSc (Paris) 1932. With the Pasteur Institute, 1921-. Foreign Member of the Royal Society (London), 1958; also Hon. or Foreign Member of American Academies, etc; Pres., Internat. Assoc. of Societies of Microbiology, 1962. Vis. Prof., Albert Einstein Coll. of Medicine, New York, 1964. Holds hon. doctorates in science and law at British and other foreign univs. Awarded several prizes and medals from 1928 onwards, both French and foreign, for his work; Nobel Prize for Medicine (jointly), 1965; Einstein Award, 1967. *Publications:* L'Evolution physiologique, Collection de microbiologie, Hermann éd., 1944 (Paris); Problems of Morphogenesis in Ciliates, The Kinetosomes in Development, Reproduction and Evolution, 1950 (New York); Biological Order, 1962, MIT. *Recreation:* painting. *Address:* 69 avenue de Suffren, 75007 Paris, France. *T:* Suffren 27-82.

LYALL, Andrew Gardiner, CMG 1976; Assistant Secretary, Department of the Environment, since 1970; *b* 21 Dec. 1929; *s* of late William Lyall and of Helen (*née* Gardiner); *m* 1953, Olive Leslie Gennoe White; one *s* one *d. Educ:* Kirkcaldy High Sch.

Joined MoT, 1951; Asst Shipping Attaché, British Embassy, Washington, DC, 1961-64; Principal, Nationalised Industry Finance and Urban Transport Planning, 1965-70; Asst Sec., Railways Div., 1970-72; seconded to FCO as Counsellor, UK Representation to European Communities, 1972-75. *Recreations:* walking, reading. *Address:* 5 Barrowfield, Cuckfield, Haywards Heath, West Sussex. *T:* Haywards Heath 54606. *Club:* Reform.

LYALL, Gavin Tudor; author; *b* 9 May 1932; *s* of J. T. and A. A. Lyall; *m* 1958, Katharine E. Whitehorn, *qv* ; two *s. Educ:* King Edward VI Sch., Birmingham; Pembroke Coll., Cambridge (BA). RAF, 1951-53 (Pilot Officer, 1952). Journalist with: Picture Post, 1956-57; BBC, 1958-59; Sunday Times, 1959-63. *Publications:* The Wrong Side of the Sky, 1961; The Most Dangerous Game, 1964; Midnight Plus One, 1965; Shooting Script, 1966; Venus with Pistol, 1969; Blame the Dead, 1972; Judas Country, 1975; Operation Warboard, 1976. (As Editor) Freedom's Battle: The RAF in World War II, 1968. *Recreations:* real beer, cooking, military history, model making. *Address:* 14 Provost Road, NW3 4ST. *T:* 01-722 2308.

LYALL, Katharine Elizabeth; *see* Whitehorn, K.

LYALL, William Chalmers, MBE 1952; HM Diplomatic Service; Counsellor (Administration), British Embassy, Bonn, since 1974; *b* 6 Aug. 1921; *s* of John Brown Lyall and Margaret Angus Leighton Stevenson Lyall; *m* 1948, Janet Lawson McKechnie; two *s* one *d. Educ:* Kelty Public and Beath Secondary schools. Min. of Labour, 1940-48; HM Forces, 1941-47; FO, 1948; Hankow, 1948-51; São Paulo, 1952-53; Manila, 1953-55; FO, 1955-57; Caracas, 1957-60; Bahrain, 1960-64; FO, 1964-65; DSAO, 1965-68; FCO, 1968-69; Consul-General, Genoa, 1969-73; FCO, 1973. *Recreations:* music, photography. *Address:* British Embassy, Bonn, BFPO 19.

LYALL GRANT, Maj.-Gen. Ian Hallam, MC 1944; Director General, Supply Co-ordination, Ministry of Defence, 1970-75; retired; *b* 4 June 1915; *s* of Col H. F. Lyall Grant, DSO; *m* 1951, Mary Jennifer Moore; one *s* two *d. Educ:* Cheltenham Coll.; RMA, Woolwich; Cambridge Univ. (MA). Regular Commission, RE, 1935; service in: India, Burma and Japan, 1938-46 (MC; twice mentioned in despatches); Cyprus and Egypt, 1951-52; Imperial Defence Coll., 1961; Aden, 1962-63; Comdt, Royal School of Mil. Engineering, 1965-67; Maj.-Gen. 1966; Dep. QMG, 1967-70, retired 1970. Col Comdt, RE, 1972-. *Recreations:* sailing, fishing, paintings. *Address:* Kingswear House, Kingswear, S Devon. *T:* Kingswear 359. *Club:* Naval and Military.

LYCETT, Brigadier Cyril Vernon Lechmere, OBE 1921; BA; *b* 14 May 1894; *s* of A. E. Lechmere and J. M. Lycett; *m* 1921, Alexandra Sandika Camarioto (*d* 1970); two *d. Educ:* King Edward VI Sch., Birmingham; Trinity Coll., Cambridge (Scholar). Entered army, Royal Engineers (SR) 1914; served European War, 1914-18 (despatches twice, OBE). Transferred Royal Corps of Signals, 1922; Chairman Wireless Telegraphy Board, 1938-42; served War of 1939-45; DD 'Y' War Office, 1943-44; Director of Signal Intelligence, India and SEAC, 1945-46, retired 1946. Sec. Royal Horticultural Soc., 1946-56. *Address:* 504 Plantation Place, Anaheim, Calif 92806, USA.

LYDDON, William Derek Collier; Chief Planning Officer, Scottish Development Department, since 1967; *b* 17 Nov. 1925; *s* of late A. J. Lyddon, CBE, and E. E. Lyddon; *m* 1949, Marian Louise Kaye Charlesworth, *d* of late Prof. J. K. Charlesworth, CBE; two *d. Educ:* Wrekin Coll.; University Coll., London. BA (Arch.) 1952; ARIBA 1953; DipTP 1954; AMTPI 1963; FRTPI 1973. Depute Chief Architect and Planning Officer, Cumbernauld Development Corp., 1962; Chief Architect and Planning Officer, Skelmersdale Development Corp., 1963-67. Vice-Pres., Internat. Soc. of City and Regional Planners, 1973. *Recreations:* walking, reading. *Address:* 38 Dick Place, Edinburgh EH9 2JB. *T:* 031-667 2266.

LYDFORD, Air Marshal Sir Harold Thomas, KBE 1954 (CBE 1945); CB 1948; AFC; Commander of Legion of Merit, USA; *b* 1898; *m* Isabel Broughton Smart. *Educ:* privately. Wing Comdr 1937; Group Capt. 1942; Air Cdre 1946; Air Vice-Marshal 1947; Air Marshal 1953; Dir of Organisation, Air Min., 1941; Mem. RAF delegn, Washington, DC, 1942-44; AOC No 28 Group, 1944; AOC British Forces, Aden, 1945-48; Comdt-General RAF Regiment, 1948-50; AOC No 18 Group, Coastal Command, and Senior Air Force Officer in Scotland, 1950-52; AOC-in-C Home Comd, 1952-March 1956, retd. *Address:* Merchiston, Hare Hatch, Twyford, Berks. *Clubs:* Naval and Military, Royal Air Force.

LYELL, family name of **Baron Lyell**.

LYELL, 3rd Baron cr 1914, of Kinnordy; **Charles Lyell**; Bt; 1894; b 27 March 1939; s of 2nd Baron, VC (killed in action, 1943), and Sophie, d of Major S. W. and Lady Betty Trafford; S father, 1943. Educ: Eton; Christ Church, Oxford. 2nd Lieut Scots Guards, 1957-59. CA Scotland. Heir: none. Address: 20 Petersham Mews, SW7. T: 01-584 9419; Kinnordy House, Kirriemuir, Angus. T: Kirriemuir 2848. Club: Turf.

LYGO, Adm. Sir Raymond Derek, KCB 1977; FIBM; Vice Chief of Naval Staff, since 1975; b 15 March 1924; s of late Edwin T. Lygo and of Ada E. Lygo; m 1950, Pepper Van Osten, USA; two s one d. Educ: Valentine's Sch., Ilford; Ilford County High Sch.; Clarke Coll., Bromley. The Times, 1940; Naval Airman, RN, 1942; Sub-Lt (A) RNVR, 1943; flew Seafires from Indefatigable and Implacable; transf. to RN, 1945; CFS 1946; jet fighters, USN, 1949-51; USS Roosevelt, Coral Sea, Philippine Sea; CO, 759 Sqdn, 1951; Veryan Bay, 1953; CO, 800 Sqdn, Ark Royal, 1954-56; CO, HMS Lowestoft, 1961-63; Dep. Dir Naval Air Warfare, 1964-66; CO, HMS Juno, 1967-69; CO, HMS Ark Royal, 1969-71; Flag Officer Carriers and Amphibious Ships, 1972-74; Dir Gen., Naval Manpower and Training, 1974-75. Recreations: building, gardening, joinery. Address: Mereworth Lawn, Borough Green, Kent. T: Borough Green 2802. Club: Royal Naval and Royal Albert Yacht (Portsmouth).

LYGON, family name of **Earl Beauchamp**.

LYLE, Sir Gavin Archibald, 3rd Bt cr 1929; estate manager, farmer; company director; b 14 Oct. 1941; s of late Ian Archibald de Hoghton Lyle and of Hon. Lydia Yarde-Buller (who m 1947, as his 2nd wife, 13th Duke of Bedford; marr. diss. 1960; now Lydia Duchess of Bedford), d of 3rd Baron Churston; S grandfather, 1946; m 1967, Suzy Cooper; three s one d. Heir: s Ian Abram Lyle, b 25 Sept. 1968. Address: Glendelvine, Caputh, Perthshire PH1 4JN. T: Caputh 225.

LYLE, Sir Ian D., Kt 1959; DSC; President of Tate & Lyle Ltd (Chairman 1954-64); b 1907; s of late Colonel Arthur Lyle, OBE, TD, Barrington Court, Ilminster, Somerset; m 1935, Julia Margaret (d 1962), d of David McWhirter McKechnie, South Africa; one s two d. Educ: Shrewsbury Sch.; St John's Coll., Oxford. Address: Tate & Lyle Ltd, 21 Mincing Lane, EC3; Barrington Court, Ilminster, Somerset. T: South Petherton 243. Clubs: White's; Royal Thames Yacht.

LYLE, John Oliver; Chairman, Tate & Lyle Ltd since 1964; b 26 April 1918; o s of late Sir Oliver Lyle and of Lilian Isobel, Lady Lyle (née Spicer); m 1944; one d; m 1960, Jill Margaret Pilkington (née Skinner); one s one d. Educ: Uppingham; Clare Coll., Cambridge. Joined HAC 1939; Lieut, RA; transferred RAF for flying duties, 1942, 26 and 234 Squadrons. Joined Tate & Lyle Ltd, 1945; appointed to Board, 1951. Mem., Aims of Industry Council. Address: 21 Mincing Lane, EC3. T: 01-626 6525. Clubs: White's, MCC.

LYLE, Thomas Keith, CBE 1949; MA, MD, MChir (Cantab); FRCP, FRCS; Consulting Ophthalmic Surgeon: King's College Hospital (Ophthalmic Surgeon, 1938-69); Moorfields Eye Hospital (Ophthalmic Surgeon, 1936-69); National Hospital, Queen Square (Ophthalmic Surgeon, 1936-69); Director, Orthoptic Department, Moorfields Eye Hospital, 1947-69; Dean of Institute of Ophthalmology, British Post-graduate Medical Federation of University of London, 1959-67; Teacher of Ophthalmology, University of London; b 26 Dec. 1903; s of late Herbert Willoughby Lyle, MD, FRCS, Fircliff, Portishead, Somerset; m 1949, Jane Bouverie, e d of late Major Nigel Maxwell, RA, and Mrs Maxwell, Great Davids, Kingwood, Henley-on-Thames; one s three d. Educ: Dulwich Coll.; Sidney Sussex Coll., Cambridge (Exhib.); King's College Hospital (Burney Yeo Schol.). Todd medal for Clinical Medicine; House Physician, House Surg., Sen. Surg. Registrar; First Asst Neurol. Dept, King's Coll. Hosp., 1929-33; House Surgeon, Royal Westminster Ophth. Hosp., 1934. Civilian Consultant in Ophth., RAF, 1948-; Consultant in Ophth. Dept of Civil Aviation, Board of Trade; Hon. Consultant in Ophth., BALPA. Examiner in Ophthalmology: Bristol Univ., 1947-50; RCS, 1949-55; FRCS (Ophthalmology), 1958-66; FRCSE (Ophthalmology), 1960; Mem. Council, Faculty of Ophthalmologists, 1946-69, Pres., 1965-68, and Rep. on Council of RCS, 1958-63; Chm., Specialist Adv. Cttee in Ophthalmology, RCS; Past Mem., International Council of Ophthalmology; Mem. Court of Assts, Soc. of Apothecaries, Master, 1962-63. Order of St John: Deputy Hospitaller, 1960-69; Hospitaller, 1969-; Chm., Hosp. Cttee; Member Council: Med. Protection Soc.; Royal London Soc. for the Blind; Past Pres., Internat. Strabismological Assoc.; Member: Cttee of Management, Inst of Opthalmology; Ophth.

Soc. UK, Pres. 1968-70; Orthoptists Bd, Council for Professions Supplementary to Medicine; Soc. Franc. d'Opthalmologie; FRSocMed (Vice-Pres. Ophth. Section, Pres. United Services Section, 1964-66); Hon. Mem. Ophth. Socs of Australia, New Zealand and Greece. Chas H. May Memorial Lectr, New York, 1952; Doyne Memorial Lectr, Oxford, 1953; Alexander Welch Lectr, Edinburgh, 1965; Vis. Lectr, Blindness Res. Foundn, Univ. of the Witwatersrand, SA, 1974. Nettleship Medal, 1959; Richardson Cross Medal, 1972. Served RAFVR, 1939-46, Temp. Air Cdre Cons. in Ophth. RAF overseas (despatches). KStJ 1960 (CStJ 1956); Kt, Order of Holy Sepulchre, 1970. Publications: (co-ed with Sylvia Jackson) Practical Orthoptics in the Treatment of Squints, 1937, 5th edn (co-ed with K. C. Wybar) 1967; (co-ed with Hon. G. J. O. Bridgeman) Worth's Squint by F. B. Chavasse, 9th edn 1959; (co-ed with A. G. Cross) May and Worth's Diseases of the Eye, 13th edn 1968; (co-ed with late H. Willoughby Lyle) Applied Physiology of the Eye, 1958; articles in British Jl Ophth., Lancet, BMJ, Med. Press and Circular, etc, chapters in Sorsby's Modern Trends in Ophthalmology, 1948, in Stallard's Modern Practice in Ophthalmology, 1949 and in Rob and Rodney Smith's Operative Surgery, 1958. Recreations: lawn tennis, riding, ski-ing. Address: 23 Harley House, Marylebone Road, NW1. T: 01-935 5213; Cherrycroft House, Kingwood, near Henley-on-Thames, Oxon. T: Rotherfield Greys 234. Clubs: Bath, Royal Air Force, Royal Automobile.

LYMBERY, Robert Davison, QC 1967; **His Honour Judge Lymbery**; a Circuit Judge (formerly Judge of County Courts), since 1971; b 14 Nov. 1920; s of Robert Smith Lymbery and late Louise Lymbery; m 1952, Pauline Anne, d of John Reginald and Kathleen Tuckett; three d. Educ: Gresham's Sch.; Pembroke Coll., Cambridge. Served Army, 1940-46; commissioned 17/21 Lancers, 1941; Middle East, Italy, Greece (Royal Tank Regt), 1942-46, Major. Pembroke Coll., 1939-40, 1946-48 (MA, LLB 1st class hons). Foundation Exhibn. 1948; called to Bar, Middle Temple, 1949; Harmsworth Law Scholar, 1949; practice on Midland Circuit, 1949-71. Recorder of Grantham, 1965-71, now Honorary Recorder; Chairman: Rutland QS, 1966-71 (Dep. Chm., 1962-66); Bedfordshire QS, 1969-71 (Dep. Chm., 1961-69); Commissioner of Assize, 1971; Chm. Stevenage New Town Licensed Premises Cttee, 1966-. Recreations: golf, cricket, motoring, gardening. Address: Park Lodge, Knebworth, Herts. T: Stevenage 813308; 2 Crown Office Row, Temple, EC4. T: 01-353 1365. Club: Hawks (Cambridge).

LYMINGTON, Viscount; **Oliver Kintzing Wallop**; Lieut RNVR (retired); b 14 Jan. 1923; s and heir of 9th Earl of Portsmouth, qv; m 1st, 1952, Maureen (marr. diss. 1954), o d of Lt-Col Kenneth B. Stanley; 2nd, 1954, Ruth Violet (marr. diss. 1974), yr d of late Brig.-General G. C. Sladen, CB, CMG, DSO, MC; one s two d; 3rd, 1974, Julia Kirwan-Taylor (née Ogden), d of Graeme Ogden, DSO. Educ: Eton. Address: The Old Rectory, Aldon Lane, Offham, near Maidstone, Kent. Clubs: Buck's, Royal Automobile.

LYMPANY, Miss Moura, FRAM 1948; concert pianist; b Saltash, Cornwall, 18 Aug. 1916; British; d of John and Beatrice Johnstone; m 1944, Lt-Col Colin Defries (marr. diss. 1950); m 1951, Bennet H. Korn, American Television Executive (marr. diss. 1961); one s decd. Educ: Belgium, Austria, England. First public performance at age of 12, 1929, at Harrogate, playing Mendelssohn G Minor Concerto. Won second prize out of 79 competitors at Ysaye International Pianoforte Competition at Brussels, 1938. Has played in USA, Canada, South America, Australia, New Zealand, India, and all principal European countries. Records for HMV and Decca. Recreations: gardening, tapestry, reading. Address: c/o Ibbs & Tillett, 124 Wigmore Street, W1.

LYNAM, Jocelyn Humphrey Rickman, MA (Oxon); Headmaster Dragon School, Oxford, 1933-65; b 27 June 1902; s of Alfred Edmund and Mabel Agnes Lynam; m 1965, Barbara Frearson. Educ: The Dragon School, Oxford; Rugby (Scholar); Hertford Coll. (Exhibitioner), Oxford. Asst master at The Dragon School, 1925; Joint Headmaster, 1933. Served on Council of Incorporated Association of Preparatory Schools, 1936-38, 1940-42, 1944-46, 1949-51, 1953-55, 1958-. Chairman of Council of IAPS, 1941 and 1942. Recreations: gardening; formerly cricket (Rugby School XI) and hockey (Oxford Univ., 1925). Address: 6 Chadlington Road, Oxford. Club: Vincent's (Oxford).

LYNCH, Rev. Prebendary Donald MacLeod, CBE 1972; MA; Chief Secretary of the Church Army, 1960-76; Prebendary of Twiford in St Paul's Cathedral, 1964-76, now Prebendary Emeritus; Chaplain to the Queen, since 1969; Priest-in-Charge of Seal, St Lawrence, in the diocese of Rochester, since 1974; b 2

July 1911; *s* of Herbert and Margaret Lynch; *m* 1st, 1941, Ailsa Leslie Leask; three *s* one *d*; 2nd, 1963, Jean Wileman. *Educ:* City of London Sch.; Pembroke Coll., Cambridge; Wycliffe Hall, Oxford. Curate, Christ Church, Chelsea, 1935; Tutor, Oak Hill Theological Coll., 1938; Curate, St Michael's, Stonebridge Park, 1940; Minister, All Saints, Queensbury, 1942; Vicar, St Luke's, Tunbridge Wells, 1950; Principal, Church Army Training Coll., 1953. *Recreations:* reading and gardening. *Address:* St Lawrence Vicarage, Stone Street, near Sevenoaks, Kent TN15 0LQ. *T:* Sevenoaks 61766.

LYNCH, Francis Joseph, JP; Member, Industrial Tribunal, since 1975; *b* 15 March 1909; *s* of William Patrick and Agnes Mary Lynch; *m* 1952, Florence Petrie; one *s* one *d*. *Educ:* St John's Cathedral Sch., Salford, Lancs. Political Agent, Labour Party, 1933-55; Salford City Council, 1935-49; JP, Salford, 1949-60, Surrey (now SW London), 1961-74, Derbyshire, 1974-. Served War, RA, (Sgt), Italy, 1940-45. Confederation of Health Service Employees: Organiser, 1945; Regional Sec., 1948; Nat. Officer, 1954; Asst Gen. Sec., 1967; Gen. Sec., 1969-74. *Recreation:* walking. *Address:* 1 Low Meadow, Whaley Bridge, Derbyshire. *T:* Whaley Bridge 2708.

LYNCH, John; Teachta Dala (TD) for Cork, Parliament of Ireland, since 1948; Taoiseach (Head of Government of Ireland), 1966-73 and since 1977; Leader of Fianna Fail, since 1966; *b* 15 Aug. 1917; *y s* of Daniel Lynch and Norah O'Donoghue; *m* 1946, Mairin O'Connor. *Educ:* Christian Brothers' Schools, N Monastery, Cork; University College, Cork; King's Inns, Dublin. Entered Civil Service (Dept of Justice), 1936; called to Bar, 1945; resigned from Civil Service, became Mem. Munster Bar and commenced practice in Cork Circuit, 1945. Parly Sec. to Govt and to Minister for Lands, 1951-54; Minister for: Education, 1957-59; Industry and Commerce, 1959-65; Finance, 1965-66. Alderman, Co. Borough of Cork, 1950-57; Mem. Cork Sanatoria Board and Cttee of Management, N Infirmary, Cork, 1950-51 and 1955-57; Mem. Cork Harbour Comrs, 1956-57; Vice-Pres., Consultative Assembly of Council of Europe, 1958; Pres., Internat. Labour Conf., 1962. Hon. LLD: Dublin, 1967; Nat. Univ. of Ireland, 1969; Hon. DCL N Carolina, 1971. Grand Cross, Order of the Crown (Belgium), 1968. Robert Schumann Gold Medal, 1973. *Address:* 21 Garville Avenue, Rathgar, Dublin 6, Ireland.

LYNCH, Prof. John; Director of Institute of Latin American Studies since 1974 and Professor of Latin American History since 1970, University of London; *b* 11 Jan. 1927; *s* of late John P. Lynch and of Teresa M. Lynch, Boldon Colliery, Co. Durham; *m* 1960, Wendy Kathleen, *d* of late Frederick and Kathleen Norman; two *s* three *d*. *Educ:* Corby Sch. Sunderland; Univ. of Edinburgh; University College, London. MA Edinburgh 1952; PhD London 1955. Army, 1945-48. Asst Lectr and Lectr in Modern History, Univ. of Liverpool, 1954-61; Lectr in Hispanic and Latin American History, University Coll., London, Reader 1964. Corresp. Mem., Academia Nacional de la Historia, Argentina, 1963. *Publications:* Spanish Colonial Administration 1782-1810, 1958; Spain under the Habsburgs, vol. 1 1964, vol. 2 1969; (with R. A. Humphreys) The Origins of the Latin American Revolutions, 1808-1826, 1965; The Spanish American Revolutions 1808-1826, 1973. *Address:* 8 Templars Crescent, N3 3QS. *T:* 01-346 1089.

LYNCH, Martin Patrick James; Under Secretary, Ministry of Overseas Development, since 1975; *b* 4 June 1924; 2nd *s* of late Frederick Lynch, DSM, and late Elizabeth Yeatman; *m* 1959, Anne, *d* of late Major Gerald McGorty, MC, MB, RAMC; two *s* one *d* (and one *s* decd). *Educ:* London Oratory School. RAF, 1942-49; Exec. Officer, HM Treasury, 1950; Asst Private Sec. to Financial Sec., 1953-54; Private Sec. to Minister Without Portfolio, 1954-55; Principal, 1958; Asst Sec., Min. of Overseas Develt, 1966 and 1971-75; Counsellor, UK Treasury and Supply Delegn, Washington, and UK Alternate Dir, World Bank, 1967-71. FRSA 1973; Chm., Assoc. for Latin Liturgy, 1976- (Mem. Council, 1973-76). Kentucky Colonel, 1970. *Recreation:* painting. *Address:* 29 Boileau Road, W5 3AP. *T:* 01-997 4004. *Club:* Reform.

LYNCH, Patrick, MA; MRIA 1962; Professor of Political Economy (Applied Economics), University College, Dublin, since 1975; *b* 5 May 1918; *s* of Daniel and Brigid Lynch, Co. Tipperary and Dublin; *m* Mary Crotty (*née* Campbell), MA. *Educ:* Univ. Coll., Dublin. Fellow Commoner, Peterhouse, Cambridge, 1956. Entered Irish Civil Service, 1941; Asst Sec. to Govt, 1950; Univ. Lectr in Econs, UC Dublin, 1952, Associate Prof., 1966. Chm., Aer Lingus, 1954-75. Has acted as economic consultant to OECD, Council of Europe, Dept of Finance, Dublin, Gulbenkian Inst., Lisbon. Directed surveys sponsored by Irish Govt with OECD into long-term Irish educnl needs,

1965, and into requirements of Irish economy in respect of scientific res., develt and technology, 1966; estab. Science Policy Res. Centre in Dept of Applied Econs, UC Dublin, 1969. Mem. Bd, Allied Irish Banks, 1971- (Dep. Chm., 1976-). Mem., various Irish Govt Commns and Cttees, 1952-; Member: Club of Rome, 1973; EEC Economic and Monetary Union 1980 Group, 1974; Nat. Science Council, 1968-; Exec. Cttee, Economic and Social Research Inst.; Nat. Economic and Social Council, 1973-76; European Science Foundn, 1971-; Chairman: Medico-Social Research Board, 1966-72; Public Service Adv. Council, 1973-77; Mem., Higher Educn Authority, 1968-72; Mem. Ed. Board: Economic and Social Review; University Review; European Teacher; Chm., Nat. Library of Ireland Soc., 1969-72; Chm., Irish Anti-Apartheid Movement, 1972; Member: Irish Assoc. for Civil Liberty; Movement for Peace in Ireland. Chm., Inst. of Public Administration, 1973-77; Member: Governing Body UC Dublin, 1963-75; Senate NUI, 1972-; Treasurer, RIA, 1972-. Hon. DUniv Brunel, 1976. *Publications:* Planning for Economic Development in Ireland, 1959; (with J. Vaizey) Guinness's Brewery in the Irish Economy, 1960; (jtly) Economics of Educational Costing, 1969; (with Brian Hillery) Ireland in the International Labour Organisation, 1969; (with B. Chubb) Economic Development Planning, 1969; essays in various symposia, etc; articles in Administration, The Bell, Encycl. Britannica, Econ. History Review, Irish Hist. Studies, Irish Jl of Educn, Statist. Studies, University Review, etc. *Address:* University College, Dublin 4, Ireland. *T:* Dublin 693244.

LYNCH, Rt. Hon. Phillip Reginald, PC 1977; Treasurer of Australia, since 1975, and Minister responsible for the Department of Finance, since 1976; Deputy Leader, Federal Parliamentary Liberal Party, since 1973; MHR since 1966; *b* 27 July 1933; *m* 1958, Leah; three *s*. *Educ:* Xavier Coll., Melbourne; Melbourne Univ. (BA, DipEd). Management consultant; co. dir. Victorian State Pres., Young Liberal Movement; Nat. Pres., Aust. Jaycees, 1966. Minister for the Army, 1968-69; Minister for Immigration and Minister assisting the Treasurer, 1969-71; Minister for Labor, 1971-72; Dep. Opposition Leader, 1972-75. Vice-Pres., Exec. Cttee of Commonwealth Parly Assoc., 1972-75; represented Australia at confs in Geneva, Hong Kong, Jakarta, Manila, Paris and Teheran. Certificate of Merit, Royal Humane Soc., 1953. *Publications:* essays on Australian economy in jls and periodicals throughout Australia over past ten years. *Recreations:* sailing, swimming, reading. *Address:* Parliament House, Canberra, ACT, Australia. *T:* Canberra 732134. *Clubs:* Naval & Military (Melbourne); Davey's Bay Yacht (Victoria).

LYNCH-BLOSSE, Sir Richard Hely, 17th Bt *cr* 1622; 2nd Lt, RAMC; *b* 26 Aug. 1953; *s* of Sir David Edward Lynch-Blosse, 16th Bt, and of Elizabeth, *er d* of Thomas Harold Payne, Welwyn Garden City; *S* father, 1971; *m* 1976, Cara, *o d* of George Sutherland, Welwyn Garden City. *Educ:* Royal Free Hosp. Sch. of Medicine. Medical student, 1971; commnd RAMC, July 1975. *Heir: cousin* (Eric) Hugh Lynch-Blosse, OBE [*b* 30 July 1917; *m* 1946, Jean Evelyn, *d* of Commander Andrew Robertson Hair, RD, RNR; one *s* one *d* (and one *d* decd)]. *Address:* c/o National Westminster Bank, 13 Stonehills, Welwyn Garden City, Herts.

LYNCH-ROBINSON, Sir Niall (Bryan), 3rd Bt *cr* 1920; DSC 1941; late Lieut RNVR; Chairman, Leo Burnett Ltd; *b* 24 Feb. 1918; *s* of Sir Christopher Henry Lynch-Robinson, 2nd Bt and Dorothy (*d* 1970), *d* of Henry Warren, Carrickmines, Co. Dublin; *S* father 1958; *m* 1940, Rosemary Seaton, *e d* of Mrs M. Seaton Eller; one *s* one (adopted) *d*. *Educ:* Stowe. Sub-Lieut 1939, Lieut 1940, RNVR; served War of 1939-45 (DSC, Croix de Guerre). *Recreations:* fishing, gardening. *Heir: s* Dominick Christopher Lynch-Robinson, *b* 30 July 1948. *Address:* The Old Parsonage, East Clandon, Surrey.

LYNDEN-BELL, Prof. Donald; Professor of Astrophysics, University of Cambridge, since 1972; *b* 5 April 1935; *s* of Lt-Col L. A. Lynden-Bell, MC and M. R. Lynden-Bell (*née* Thring); *m* 1961, Ruth Marion Truscott, MA, PhD; one *s* one *d*. *Educ:* Marlborough; Clare Coll., Cambridge (MA, PhD). Harkness Fellow of the Commonwealth Fund, NY, at the California Inst. of Technology and Hale Observatories, 1960-62; Research Fellow and then Fellow and Dir of studies in mathematics, Clare Coll., Cambridge, 1960-65; Asst Lectr in applied mathematics, Univ. of Cambridge, 1962-65; Principal Scientific officer and later SPSO, Royal Greenwich Observatory, Herstmonceux, 1965-72; Dir, Inst. of Astronomy, Cambridge, 1972-77. Visiting Associate, Calif. Inst. of Technology and Hale Observatories, 1969-70. *Publications:* contrib. to Monthly Notices of Royal Astronomical Soc. *Recreations:* hill walking, golf, squash racquets. *Address:* Institute of Astronomy, The Observatories, Madingley Road, Cambridge CB3 0HA. *T:* Cambridge 62204.

LYNE, Air Vice-Marshal Michael Dillon, CB 1968; AFC (two Bars); MBIM; DL; b 23 March 1919; s of late Robert John Lyne, Winchester; m 1943, Avril Joy Buckley, d of late Lieut-Colonel Albert Buckley, CBE, DSO; two s two d. Educ: Imperial Service Coll.; RAF Coll., Cranwell. Commissioned and joined No 19 Fighter Squadron, July 1939; Merchant Ship Fighter Unit, 1941; Comdg No 54 Fighter Squadron, 1946-48; Comdg RAF Wildenrath, 1958-60; Air Attaché, Moscow, 1961-63; Commandant, Royal Air Force Coll., Cranwell, 1963-64; Air Officer Commanding No 23 Group, RAF Flying Training Command, 1965-67; Senior RAF Instructor, Imperial Defence Coll., 1968-69; Dir-Gen. Training, RAF, 1970-71; retired. Sec., Diocese of Lincoln, 1971-76. Vice-Chm. (Air), TAVR Assoc. for East Midlands, 1977-. Vice Chm., Governing Body, Bishop Grosseteste Coll., 1976-. Vice-President: RAF Gliding and Soaring Assoc.; RAF Motor Sport Assoc. DL Lincs, 1973. Recreations: sailing, gardening. Address: Far End, Far Lane, Coleby, Lincoln LN5 0AH. T: Lincoln 810468. Clubs: Royal Air Force; Royal Air Force Yacht, Royal Mersey Yacht.

LYNEN, Prof. Feodor, Dr phil; Pour le mérite, 1971; Director, Max-Planck-Institut für Biochemie, since 1972; Professor of Biochemistry, University of Munich, since 1953; b 6 April 1911; s of Wilhelm and Frieda Lynen; m 1937, Eva (née Wieland); two s three d. Educ: Univ. of Munich (Dr phil). Extraordinary Prof., Univ. of Munich, 1947-53; Dir, Max-Planck-Institut für Zellchemie, 1954-72. Foreign Member, Royal Society, 1975. Dr med hc Freiburg, 1960; Dr rer nat hc Seoul, 1968; DSc hc Miami, 1968. Nobel Prize for Medicine, 1964. Publications: articles in Biochim. Biophys. Acta, Eur. J. Biochem., Hoppe-Seyler's Z. Physiologie. Recreations: skilaufen, wandern, schwimmen, radfahren. Address: Max-Planck-Institut für Biochemie, D-8033 Martinsried, Bundesrepublik Deutschland. T: 85 85 323.

LYNN, Bishop Suffragan of, since 1973; **Rt. Rev. William Aubrey Aitken;** Archdeacon of Lynn since 1973; b 2 Aug. 1911; s of late Canon R. A. Aitken, Great Yarmouth; m 1937, Margaret Cunningham; three s two d. Educ: Norwich Grammar School; Trinity College, Oxford (MA Modern History, 2nd class Hons). Curate of: Tynemouth, 1934-37; Kingston, Jamaica, 1937-40; Rector of Kessingland, 1940-43; Vicar of Sprowston, 1943-53; St Margaret's, King's Lynn, 1953-61; Archdeacon of Norwich, 1961-73. Proctor in Convocation, 1944-; Hon. Canon of Norwich, 1958. Recreations: football, cricket, sailing. Address: Elsing, Dereham, Norfolk. T: Swanton Morley 455.

LYNN, Archdeacon of; see under Lynn, Suffragan Bishop of.

LYNN, Prof. Richard; Professor of Psychology, New University of Ulster, since 1972; b 20 Feb. 1930; s of Richard and Ann Lynn; m 1956, Susan Maher; one s two d. Educ: Bristol Grammar Sch.; King's Coll., Cambridge. Lectr in Psychology, Univ. of Exeter, 1956-67; Prof. of Psychology, Dublin Economic and Social Research Inst., 1967-71. Publications: Attention, Arousal and the Orientation Reaction, 1966; The Irish Braindrain, 1969; The Universities and the Business Community, 1969; Personality and National Character, 1971; An Introduction to the Study of Personality, 1972; (ed) The Entrepreneur, 1974; articles on personality and social psychology. Recreation: do-it-yourself house renovation. Address: Dundery House, Coleraine, Co. Londonderry; 60 Geraldine Road, SW18. Club: Arts (Dublin).

LYNN, Stanley B.; see Balfour-Lynn.

LYNN, Dame Vera, (Dame Vera Margaret Lewis), DBE 1975 (OBE 1969); singer; b 20 March 1917; d of Bertram Samuel Welch and Annie Welch; m 1941, Harry Lewis; one d. Educ: Brampton Rd Sch., East Ham. First public appearance as singer, 1924; joined juvenile troupe, 1928; ran own dancing school, 1932; broadcast with Joe Loss and joined Charlie Kunz 1935; singer with Ambrose Orch., 1937-40, then went solo; voted most popular singer, Daily Express comp., 1939, and named Forces Sweetheart; own radio show, Sincerely Yours, 1941-47; starred in Applesauce, London Palladium, 1941; sang to troops in Burma, etc, 1944; subseq. Big Show (radio), USA; London Laughs, Adelphi; appeared at Flamingo Hotel, Las Vegas, and many TV shows, USA and Britain; also appearances in Holland, Denmark, Sweden, Norway, Germany, Canada, NZ and Australia; in seven Command Performances, also films and own shows on radio. Records include Auf Wiederseh'n (over 12 million copies sold), became first British artiste to top American Hit Parade. Hon. Citizen Winnipeg, 1974. FInstD. Publication: Vocal Refrain (autobiog.), 1975. Recreations: gardening, painting, sewing, swimming.

LYNN, Wilfred; Director: National Westminster Bank Ltd (Outer London Board), 1969-73; b 19 May 1905; s of late Wilfred Crosland Lynn and Alice Lynn; m 1936, Valerie, e d of late B. M. A. Critchley; one s one d (twins). Educ: Hull Grammar School. Entered National Provincial Bank Ltd, 1921; Joint General Manager, 1953; Chief General Manager, 1961; Director, 1965-69. Recreation: golf. Address: c/o National Westminster Bank Ltd, 15 Bishopsgate, EC2.

LYNNE, Gillian; director, choreographer, dancer, actress; d of late Leslie Pyrke and late Barbara Pyrke (née Hart); m 1948, Patrick St John Back (marr. diss., but close friends). Educ: Baston-Bromley, Kent; Arts Educnl School. Leading soloist, Sadlers Wells Ballet, 1944-51; star dancer, London Palladium, 1951, 1952, 1953; film, Master of Ballantrae, 1952; lead in Can-Can, London Coliseum, 1954-55; Becky Sharp in Vanity Fair, Windsor, 1956; guest principal dancer, Covent Garden, Sadlers Wells Aida, Samson and Delilah, 1957; Tannhauser, Covent Garden; ballerina in Chelsea at Nine, 1958; title role in Puss in Boots, Frou Frou in The Merry Widow, 1959; lead in New Cranks, 1959; Wanda, Rose Marie, Cinderella, Out of My Mind, lead in revue, 1960-61; staged revue England Our England, Princes, 1961; leading lady, 5 Past Eight Show, Edinburgh, 1962; choreographed first ballet Owl and the Pussycat, Western Theatre Ballet, 1962; Queen of the Cats, London Palladium, 1962-63; directed revue Round Leicester Square, 1963; conceived, directed, choreographed and starred in modern dance revue Collages, Edinburgh Fest., 1963, transf. to Savoy; chor. 1st film Wonderful Life, 1963-64; chor. musical films Every Day's a Holiday and Three Hats for Lisa, 1964; chor. musicals The Roar of the Greasepaint and Pickwick, Broadway, 1965; directed, chor. The Match Girls, Globe, 1966; chor. Flying Dutchman, Covent Garden, 1966; dir., chor. Bluebeard, Sadlers Wells Opera, 1966; chor. and staged musical nos in Half a Sixpence (film), 1966-67; How Now Dow Jones, Broadway, 1967; chor. Midsummer Marriage, 1968 and The Trojans, 1969, Covent Garden; chor. new ballet Breakaway, Scottish Theatre Ballet, 1969; Phil the Fluter, Palace, 1969; dir. new prod. Bluebeard, Sadlers Wells Opera, London Coliseum, 1969; dir. and chor. musical Love on the Dole, Nottingham Playhouse, 1970; dir. Tonight at Eight, Hampstead, 1970, and Fortune, 1971; staged 200 Motels (pop-opera film), 1971; dir. Lillywhite Lies, Nottingham, 1971; chor. Ambassador, Her Majesty's, 1971; chor. Man of La Mancha (film), 1972; dir and chor. Liberty Ranch, Greenwich, 1972; dir. and chor., Once Upon a Time, 1972; chor. The Card, Queen's, 1973; staged musical nos in Quilp (film), 1974; chor. Hans Andersen, 1975; staged A Comedy of Errors, Stratford, 1976 (TV musical, ATV, 1977); co-dir, A Midsummer Night's Dream, Stratford, 1977; has also appeared in or choreographed TV shows inc. Peter and the Wolf, 1958 (narr. and mimed all 9 parts); Puck, Midsummer Night's Dream, 1958; Val Doonican Shows, 1970; Mary Hopkin Series, 1970; Perry Como Special, 1971; Marty Feldman Show, 1971; At the Hawk's Well (ballet), 1975; There was a Girl, 1976; Nana Mouskouri Series, 1976; prod and devised TV Noël Coward and Cleo Laine Specials, 1968; four BBC TV Specials, 1975; Petula Clark Special, 1975; first colour special for ABC, with Australian Ballet and Sydney Symphony Orch., and stage prod. Sydney Opera House, The Fool on the Hill, 1975; Muppet Show Series, ATV, 1976-77. Publications: articles in Dancing Times. Address: 25 The Avenue, Bedford Park, Chiswick, W4. Club: Pickwick.

LYNTON, Norbert Caspar; Professor of the History of Art, University of Sussex, since 1975; b 22 Sept. 1927; s of Paul and Amalie Christiane Lynton; m 1st, 1949, Janet Irving; two s; 2nd, 1969, Sylvia Anne Towning; two s. Educ: Douai Sch.; Birkbeck Coll., Univ. of London (BA Gen.); Courtauld Inst., Univ. of London (BA Hons). Lectr in History of Art and Architecture, Leeds Coll. of Art, 1950-61; Sen. Lectr, then Head of Dept of Art History and Gen. Studies, Chelsea Sch. of Art, 1961-70. London Corresp. of Art International, 1961-66; Art Critic, The Guardian, 1965-70; Dir of Exhibitions, Arts Council of GB, 1970-75; Vis. Prof. of History of Art, Open Univ., 1975. Publications: (jtly) Simpson's History of Architectural Development, vol. 4 (Renaissance), 1962; Kenneth Armitage, 1962; Paul Klee, 1964; The Modern World, 1968; articles in Burlington Mag., Times Lt. Sup., Studio International, Architectural Design, Art in America, Smithsonian, Leonardo, etc. Recreations: art, people, music, travel. Address: Haydon Lodge, 22 East Drive, Brighton BN2 2BQ. T: Brighton 680315.

LYON; see Bowes Lyon and Bowes-Lyon.

LYON, Alexander Ward; MP (Lab) York since 1966; b 15 Oct. 1931. Contested (Lab) York, 1964. Addtl PPS to the Treasury Ministers, 1969; PPS to Paymaster General, 1969; Opposition Spokesman: on African Affairs, 1970; on Home Affairs, 1971;

Min. of State, Home Office, 1974-76. Mem., Younger Cttee on Intrusions into Privacy. *Address:* House of Commons, SW1. *T:* 01-219 3589.

LYON, Mary Frances, ScD; FRS 1973; Head of Genetics Section, Medical Research Council Radiobiology Unit, Harwell, since 1962; *e d* of Clifford James Lyon and Louise Frances Lyon (*née* Kirby). *Educ:* King Edward's Sch., Birmingham; Woking Grammar Sch.; Girton Coll., Cambridge, ScD 1968; FIBiol. MRC Scientific Staff, Inst. of Animal Genetics, Edinburgh, 1950-55; MRC Radiobiology Unit, Harwell, 1955-. Clothworkers Visiting Research Fellow, Girton Coll., Cambridge, 1970-71. *Publications:* papers on genetics in scientific jls. *Address:* MRC Radiobiology Unit, Harwell, Berks OX11 0RD. *T:* Rowstock 393.

LYON, (Percy) Hugh (Beverley), MC, MA; *b* 14 Oct. 1893; *s* of late P. C. Lyon, CSI; *m* 1920, Nancy Elinor (*d* 1970), 3rd *d* of William Richardson, Guisborough and Sandsend; three *d*; *m* 1973, Elizabeth Knight (*née* Beater). *Educ:* Rugby Sch.; Oriel Coll., Oxford. Served with 6th Bn the Durham Light Infantry, 1914-19; Captain, 1917; MC 1917; wounded, 1918; prisoner of war, May 1918. Newdigate Prize Poem, 1919; BA and MA 1919; 1st class Final School Lit. Hum., 1921. Asst Master, Cheltenham Coll., 1921-26; Rector of the Edinburgh Academy, 1926-31; Headmaster of Rugby Sch., 1931-48; Director, Public Schools Appointments Bureau, 1950-61. *Publications:* Songs of Youth and War, 1917; Turn Fortune, 1923; The Discovery of Poetry, 1930. *Address:* Springhill, Amberley, Stroud, Glos. *T:* Amberley 2275.

LYON, Robert, MA (Dunelm); RBA; RP; retired as Principal, Edinburgh College of Art (1942-60); *b* 18 Aug. 1894; 3rd *s* of Charles Lyon, Elgin, and Grace Mortimer Wood, Yorkshire; *m* 1924, Mabel Sansome Morrison, Blundellsands; one *s*. *Educ:* Royal College of Art, London; British School at Rome. Served with King's Liverpool Regt, 1914-19; Lecturer in Fine Art and Master of Painting, King's Coll., Newcastle upon Tyne (Univ. of Durham), 1932; Mem. Soc. Mural Painters; professional practice includes Mural Painting. Exhibitor: Royal Society of Portrait Painters; Royal Academy and New English Art Club. *Recent work includes:* murals for Western General Hosp., Edinburgh, and King's College Hosp. Dental Dept. *Recreation:* fishing. *Address:* Little Alliss, Rushlake Green, East Sussex. *T:* Rushlake Green 323.

LYON, Maj.-Gen. Robert, CB 1976; OBE 1964 (MBE 1960); General Officer Commanding South West District, since 1975; *b* Ayr, 24 Oct. 1923; *s* of David Murray Lyon and Bridget Lyon (*née* Smith); *m* 1951, Constance Margaret Gordon; one *s* one *d*. *Educ:* Ayr Academy. Commissioned, Aug. 1943, Argyll and Sutherland Highlanders. Served Italy, Germany, Palestine, Greece; transf. to Regular Commn in RA, 1947; Regtl Service, 3 RHA in Libya and 19 Field in BAOR, 1948-56; Instr, Mons Officer Cadet Sch., 1953-55; Staff Coll., 1957; DAQMG, 3 Div., 1958-60; jssc, 1960; BC F (Sphinx) Bty 7 PARA, RHA, 1961-62 (Bt Lt-Col); GSO1, ASD2, MoD, 1962-65 (Lt-Col); CO 4 Lt Regt, RA, 1965-67, Borneo (despatches), UK and BAOR (Lt-Col); as Brig.: CRA 1 Div., 1967-69, BAOR; IDC, 1970; Dir Operational Requirements, MoD, 1971-73; DRA (Maj.-Gen.), 1973-75. Col Comdt RA, 1976-. *Recreations:* golf, fishing, skiing. *Address:* HQ South West District, Bulford Camp, Wilts; Woodside, Braemar, Aberdeenshire, Scotland. *Club:* Army and Navy.

LYON, Stanley Douglas; Deputy Chairman, Imperial Chemical Industries Ltd, 1972-77 (Director, 1968-77); *b* 22 June 1917; *s* of Ernest Hutcheon Lyon and late Helen Wilson Lyon; *m* 1941, May Alexandra Jack; three *s*. *Educ:* George Heriot's Sch., Edinburgh; Edinburgh Univ. (BSc Hons Engrg). AMICE, FBIM. Major, Royal Engrs, 1939-46. ICI Ltd: Engr, Dyestuffs Div., 1946; Engrg Dir, Wilton Works, 1957; Prodn Dir, Agricl Div., 1962; Dep. Chm. 1964, Chm. 1966, Agric. Div. *Recreations:* golf, tennis, gardening, sculpture. *Address:* Bramble Carr, Danby, Whitby, N Yorks.

LYON-DALBERG-ACTON, family name of **Baron Acton.**

LYONS, family name of **Baron Lyons of Brighton.**

LYONS OF BRIGHTON, Baron *cr* 1974 (Life Peer), of Brighton, E Sussex; **Braham Jack Dennis Lyons;** Independent Public Relations Consultant, since 1976; *b* 11 Sept. 1918; *s* of late Ralph and Dena Lyons; *m* 1st, 1940, Laurie Adele Lion (marr. diss. 1957); two *s*; 2nd, 1961, Mary Priscilla Woolley (decd); one *d*. *Educ:* St Paul's School. Features Editor, Everybody's Weekly, 1946; Man. Director, Modern Features Ltd, 1951; Gen. Manager of Public Relations Div., Pritchard

Wood & Partners (now part of Wasey Quadrant), 1952-63; Man. Director of Infoplan Ltd, 1963-68; Partner, Traverse-Healy Lyons & Partners, 1968-75; Dir, London Communications Consortium, 1976-. *Address:* 2 Clifton Terrace, Brighton BN1 3HA. *T:* Brighton 202346. *Club:* Reform.

LYONS, Bernard, CBE 1964; JP; DL; Chairman and Managing Director of UDS Group Ltd; *b* 30 March 1913; *m* 1938, Lucy Hurst; three *s* one *d*. *Educ:* Leeds Grammar Sch. Chm., Yorkshire and NE Conciliation Cttee, Race Relations Bd, 1968-70; Member: Leeds City Council, 1951-65; Community Relations Commn, 1970-72. Life Pres., Leeds Jewish Representative Council. JP Leeds, 1960; DL West Riding, Yorks, 1971. Hon. LLD Leeds, 1973. *Recreation:* farming. *Address:* Upton Wood, Fulmer, Bucks. *T:* Fulmer 2404.

LYONS, Dennis John, CB 1972; CEng, FRAeS; Director General of Research, Department of the Environment, 1971-76; *b* 26 Aug. 1916; *s* of late John Sylvester Lyons and of Adela Maud Lyons; *m* 1939, Elisabeth, *d* of Arnold and Maria Friederika Müller Haefliger, Weggis, Switzerland; five *s* two *d*. *Educ:* Grocers' Company School; Queen Mary Coll., London Univ. (Fellow, 1969). Aerodynamics Dept, Royal Aircraft Estabt, 1937; RAFVR, 1935-41; Aerodynamics Flight Aero Dept, RAE, 1941-51; Head of Experimental Projects Div., Guided Missiles Dept, RAE, 1951; Head of Ballistic Missile Group, GW Dept, 1956; Head of Weapons Dept, RAE, 1962; Dir., Road Research Laboratory, 1965-72. Member: Adv. Board for Res. Councils, 1973-76; SRC, 1973-76; Engineering Bd, SRC, 1970-76; Natural Environment Res. Council, 1973-76. Pres. OECD Road Research Unit, 1968-72. Hon. Mem., Instn Highway Engineers. *Publications:* papers in scientific jls. *Recreations:* skiing, pottery-making, philately. *Address:* Summerhaven, Gough Road, Fleet, Hants. *T:* 4773.

LYONS, Edward, LLB, QC 1974; MP (Lab) Bradford West, since 1974 (Bradford East, 1966-74); a Recorder of the Crown Court, since 1972; *b* 17 May 1926; *s* of late A. Lyons and of Mrs S. Taylor; *m* 1955, Barbara, *d* of Alfred Katz; one *s* one *d*. *Educ:* Roundhay High Sch.; Leeds Univ. LLB (Hons) 1951. Served Royal Artillery, 1944-48; Combined Services Russian Course, Cambridge Univ., 1946; Interpreter in Russian, Brit. CCG, 1946-48. Called to Bar, Lincoln's Inn, 1952. Contested (Lab) Harrogate, 1964. PPS at Treasury, 1969-70; Chairman: Lab. Party Parly Legal and Judicial Gp, 1974-77; Lab. Party Parly Home Office Gp, 1974-77 (Dep. Chm., 1970-74); Member: Lab. Party Nat. Exec. Council Sub Cttee on Human Rights, 1975-; House of Commons Select Cttee on European Secondary Legislation; Jt Lords/Commons Select Cttee on Consolidation of Statute Law. Special Emissary of Internat. Commn of Jurists to S African Govt, 1969; Mem., Exec. of Justice, 1974-; Member: Soc. of Labour Lawyers; Fabian Soc.; Anti-Slavery Soc.; Amnesty. *Recreations:* history, opera. *Address:* House of Commons, SW1; 38 Park Square, Leeds. *T:* 39422; 15 Old Square, Lincoln's Inn, WC2. *T:* 01-831 7517; 4 Primley Park Lane, Leeds LS17 7JR. *T:* 685351.

LYONS, Sir Edward Houghton, Kt 1977; Chairman, Katies Ltd (numerous subsidiaries); wholesaler and retailer of women's clothing, Australia. *Address:* Katies Ltd, Box 4259, GPO, Sydney 2001, NSW, Australia; 47 Kneale Street, Holland Park Heights, Brisbane, Queensland, Australia. *T:* 49 6461.

LYONS, Hon. Dame Enid Muriel, GBE 1937; retired 1962; Member Board of Control, Australian Broadcasting Commission, 1951-62; Hon. Fellow College of Nursing, Australia (FCNA), 1951; an original Vice-President, Australian Elizabethan National Theatre Trust, 1954; *b* Leesville (formerly Duck River), Tasmania, 9 July 1897; *d* of William Charles Burnell; *m* 1915, Rt Hon. Joseph Aloysius Lyons, PC, CH (*d* 1939); five *s* six *d*. *Educ:* State Sch.; Teachers' Training Coll., Hobart. Vice-Pres. of Executive Council, Australia, 1949-51; first woman member of Federal Cabinet; MHR for Darwin, Tasmania, 1943-51; first woman MHR; re-elected at general elections, 1946, 1949. Newspaper columnist, 1951-54. *Publications:* So We Take Comfort (autobiog.), 1965; The Old Haggis (collection), 1970; Among the Carrion Crows (autobiog.), 1973. *Address:* Home Hill, Middle Road, Devonport, Tasmania.

LYONS, Eric (Alfred), OBE 1959; PPRIBA; DistTP; FSIA; architect in private practice since 1945; *b* 2 Oct. 1912; *s* of Benjamin and Caroline Lyons; *m* 1944, Catherine Joyce Townsend; two *s* two *d*. *Educ:* The Polytechnic Sch. of Architecture. DistTP, RIBA, 1961; Architecture Award, RIBA, 1966; Mem. RIBA Coun., 1960-63, 1964-; Vice-Pres., RIBA, 1967, 1968, Senior Vice-Pres. 1974, Pres., 1975-77. Eleven awards for Good Design in Housing by Min. of Housing and

Local Govt; six awards by Civic Trust. In partnership with G. Paulson Townsend, 1945-50; Partner, Eric Lyons Cunningham Partnership, 1963-. Hon. Fellow, Amer. Inst. of Architects. *Principal works:* housing at Blackheath, Ham, Cambridge, Weybridge, etc; Architect to the Worlds End Chelsea Redevelopment Scheme; other work includes housing and schools for various local authorities. *Recreations:* music, drama. *Address:* Mill House, Bridge Road, Hampton Court, Surrey. *T:* 01-979 6656.

LYONS, Prof. Francis Stewart Leland, MA, PhD, LittD Dublin; FRHistS; FBA 1974; MRIA; Provost of Trinity College, Dublin, since 1974; *b* 11 Nov. 1923; *e s* of Stewart Lyons and Florence May Leland; *m* 1954, Jennifer Ann Stuart McAlister; two *s. Educ:* Dover Coll.; Trinity Coll., Dublin. Lecturer in History, University Coll., Hull, 1947-51; Fellow of Trinity Coll., Dublin, 1951-64; Prof. of Modern History, Univ. of Kent, 1964-74. Master of Eliot Coll., Univ. of Kent, 1969-72. Hon. Fellow, Oriel Coll., Oxford, 1975. Hon. DLitt Pennsylvania, 1975. *Publications:* The Irish Parliamentary Party, 1951; The Fall of Parnell, 1960; Internationalism in Europe, 1815-1914, 1963; John Dillon: a biography, 1968; Ireland since the Famine, 1971; Charles Stewart Parnell, 1977; articles and reviews in various historical jls. *Recreations:* walking, squash rackets. *Address:* Provost's House, Trinity College, Dublin. *T:* Dublin 772941. *Club:* Kildare Street and University (Dublin).

LYONS, Hamilton; Sheriff of North Strathclyde (formerly Renfrew and Argyll, and Ayr and Bute), since 1968; *b* 3 Aug. 1918; *s* of Richard Lyons and Annie Cathro Thomson; *m* 1943, Jean Cathro Blair; two *s. Educ:* Gourock High Sch.; Greenock High Sch.; Glasgow Univ. BL (Glasgow) 1940. Practised as Solicitor, Greenock, until 1966; Sheriff Substitute of Inverness, Moray, Nairn and Ross and Cromarty at Stornoway and Lochmaddy, 1966-68. Member: Coun. of Law Soc. of Scotland, 1950-66 (Vice-Pres., 1962-63); Law Reform Cttee for Scotland, 1954-64; Cttee of Inquiry on Children and Young Persons, 1961-64; Cttee of Inquiry on Sheriff Courts, 1963-67; Sheriff Court Rules Coun., 1952-66; Scottish Probation Adv. and Trng Coun., 1959-69. *Recreation:* sailing. *Address:* 14 Cloch Road, Gourock, Inverclyde PA19 1AB. *T:* Gourock 32566. *Club:* Royal Gourock Yacht.

LYONS, Sir (Isidore) Jack, Kt 1973; CBE 1967; Chairman and Managing Director, Glanfield Securities Ltd; Deputy Chairman: Alexandre Ltd; Managing Director, Bridge End Properties Ltd; Director: UDS Group Ltd; John Collier Ltd, and other companies; *b* 1 Feb. 1916; *s* of Samuel H. Lyons and Sophia Niman; *m* 1943, Roslyn Marion Rosenbaum; two *s* two *d. Educ:* Leeds Grammar Sch. Chm., Leeds Musical Festival, 1955-72, Vice-Pres., 1973; Chm., London Symphony Orchestra Trust, 1974 (Jt Chm., 1963-70), Trustee, 1970- (Hon. Mem., LSO, 1973); Chm., Shakespeare Exhibn (quater-centenary celebrations Stratford-upon-Avon), 1964; Mem. Exec. Cttee, Royal Acad. of Dancing, 1964; Life Trustee, Shakespeare Birthplace Trust, 1967; Mem., Culture Adv. Cttee, UNESCO, 1973-, Dep. Chm., Fanfare for Europe, 1972-73; Chm., FCO US Bicentennial Cttee for the Arts, 1973-. Vice-Pres., Jt Palestine Appeal, 1972 (Dep. Chm. 1957); Chm., Fedn of Jewish Relief Organisations, 1958. Member: Canadian Veterans' Assoc., 1964; Pilgrims, 1965. Dep. Chm., Governors of Carmel Coll., 1961-69; Mem. Ct, York Univ., 1965. Hon. FRAM, 1973. DUniv York, 1975. *Recreations:* music, the arts and swimming. *Address:* Blundell House, 2 Campden Hill, W8. *T:* 01-727 2750. *Club:* Carlton.

LYONS, James, OBE 1964; FDSRCSE; FFDRCSIre; retired as dental surgeon, 1974; Hon. Consultant Dental Surgeon to Northern Ireland Hospitals Authority, 1952; *b* 4 June 1887; *s* of Richard Lyons, Sligo; *m* 1916, Kathleen Arnold, *d* of George Myles, Crieff, Scotland; two *s* one *d. Educ:* Clevedon Sch., Somerset; Royal Coll. of Surgeons, Edinburgh. LDS 1912; FDS 1951, RCS Edinburgh; FFD 1963, RCS, Ireland. Hon. Dental Surgeon to Royal Victoria Hospital, Belfast, 1927-51; Lectr on Dental Materia Medica, at Dental Sch. of Queen's Univ., Belfast, 1935-52. Member: Dental Bd of UK, 1939-56; British Dental Assoc. (Pres. N Ireland Branch, 1939-41); N Ireland Health Services Bd, 1948-66; General Dental Council, 1956-61. Hon MDS QUB, 1971. *Recreations:* photography, motoring. *Address:* High Trees, 4 Kincraig Park, Newtownalley, Co. Antrim, NI.

LYONS, Sir James (Reginald); JP; Airport Manager, Cardiff Airport, since 1955; *b* 15 March 1910; *s* of James Lyons; *m* 1937, Doreen Mary Fogg; one *s. Educ:* Howard Gardens High Sch.; Cardiff Technical Coll. Served War of 1939-45: Royal Tank Regt, 1940-46 (1939-45 Star, Africa Star, Italy Star, Defence Medal, War Medal of 1939-45). Civil Service, 1929-65: Post Office, Min. of Supply, Min. of Aviation. Mem., Wales Tourist Bd. Glamorgan CC, 1965-; Cardiff City Council: Councillor, 1949-58; Alderman, 1958-; Lord Mayor of Cardiff, 1968-69. Mem., BBC Broadcasting Council. JP Cardiff, 1966-. OStJ; KCSG. *Recreations:* Rugby football, swimming, tennis. *Address:* 101 Minehead Avenue, Sully, S Glam. *T:* Sully 530403. *Club:* Civil Service.

LYONS, Prof. John, FBA 1973; Professor of Linguistics, University of Sussex, since 1976; *b* 23 May 1932; *s* of Michael A. Lyons and Mary B. Lyons (*née* Sullivan); *m* 1959, Danielle J. Simonet; two *d. Educ:* St Bede's Coll., Manchester; Christ's Coll., Cambridge. MA; PhD 1961. Lecturer: in Comparative Linguistics, SOAS, 1957-61; in General Linguistics, Univ. of Cambridge, 1961-64; Prof. of General Linguistics, Edinburgh Univ., 1964-76. *Publications:* Structural Semantics, 1964; Introduction to Theoretical Linguistics, 1968; New Horizons in Linguistics, 1970; Chomsky, 1970, 2nd edn 1977; Semantics, vols 1 and 2, 1977; articles and reviews in learned journals. *Address:* School of Social Sciences, University of Sussex, Falmer, Brighton BN1 9QN.

LYONS, John; General Secretary, Electrical Power Engineers' Association, since 1973; Engineers' and Managers' Association, since formation by EPEA, 1977; *b* 19 May 1926; *s* of Joseph and Hetty Lyons; *m* 1954, Molly McCall; two *s* two *d. Educ:* St Pauls Sch.; Polytechnic, Regent Street; Cambridge Univ. (BA Econ). RN 1944-46. Asst. to Manager of Market Research Dept, Vacuum Oil Co., 1950; Research Officer: Bureau of Current Affairs, 1951; Post Office Engineering Union, 1952-57; Asst. Sec., Instn of Professional Civil Servants 1957-66, Dep. Gen. Sec. 1966-72. Member: Nat. Enterprise Bd, 1975-; Exec. Cttee PEP, 1975-; Exec. Cttee, IPA, 1976; Sec., Employees Nat. Cttee in Electricity Supply Industry, 1976-; Chm., NEDO Working Party on Industrial Trucks, 1977-. Governor, Kingsbury High School, 1974-. *Publications:* various papers and articles, incl. British Assoc. paper. *Recreations:* family first, music, reading and gardening. *Address:* Engineers' and Managers' Association, Station House, Fox Lane North, Chertsey, Surrey. *T:* Chertsey 64131.

LYONS, Brig. Richard Clarke, CIE 1946; MC; *b* 4 June 1893; *m* 1920, Francis Emily Gavin (*d* 1969), *d* of late Col A. L. Lindesay; two *s* one *d. Educ:* Rugby; RMA Woolwich. Royal Artillery, 1914-27; Indian Army, 1927; Chief Inspector of Armaments, India, 1942; Ordnance Consulting Officer for India (India Office), 1945; retired, 1948. Served European War, 1914-18 (wounded, MC, despatches). *Address:* 32 Apsley Road, Clifton, Bristol BS8 2SS. *T:* Bristol 36909. *Club:* Army and Navy.

LYONS, Sir Rudolph, Kt 1976; QC 1953; His Honour Judge Lyons; a Circuit Judge (and Honorary Recorder of Liverpool), since 1972; *b* 5 Jan. 1912; *er s* of late G. Lyons; *m* 1936, Jeannette, *yr d* of late Philip Dante; one *s* two *d. Educ:* Leeds Grammar Sch.; Leeds Univ. (LLB). Called to Bar, Gray's Inn, 1934; Mem., Gen. Council of the Bar, 1958-70; Master of the Bench, Gray's Inn, 1961-. Recorder of: Sunderland, 1955-56; Newcastle upon Tyne, 1956-61; Sheffield, 1961-65; Leeds, 1965-70; Recorder and Judge of the Crown Ct of Liverpool, 1970-71. Comr, Central Criminal Court, 1962-70; Comr of Assize, 1969; Leader of N Eastern Circuit, 1961-70; Solicitor-Gen., 1961-65, Attorney-Gen., 1965-70, County Palatine of Durham. Jt Pres., Council, HM Circuit Judges, 1974. *Recreation:* gardening. *Address:* (home) 8 Brookside, Alwoodley, Leeds LS17 8TD. *T:* Leeds 683274; St George's Hall, Liverpool L1 1JJ. *Club:* Racquet (Liverpool).

LYONS, Terence Patrick; Executive Director (Personnel), Williams & Glyn's Bank Ltd, since 1969; Member, Monopolies and Mergers Commission, since 1975; *b* 2 Sept. 1919; *s* of Maurice Peter Lyons and Maude Mary Elizabeth Lyons (*née* O'Farrell); *m* 1945, Winifred Mary Normile; two *d. Educ:* Wimbledon Coll.; King's College, London; London Sch. of Economics. CompIPM, FIB. Indian Armd Corps, 1940-46. Unilever Ltd, 1948-54; Philips Electrical Industries Ltd, 1954-60; Ilford Ltd, 1960-66; Staveley Industries Ltd, 1966-69. Pres., Inst. of Personnel Management, 1971-73; Mem. Council, Inst. Bankers, 1975-; Chairman: Manpower Services Adv. Panel, CBI, 1975-; Educn and Trng Cttee, CBI, 1976-77 (Vice-Chm., 1977-); Council, Fedn of London Clearing Bank Employers, 1976-78 (Mem., 1971-). *Publications:* The Personnel Function in a Changing Environment, 1971; contrib. personnel management and banking jls. *Recreations:* sailing, golf, tennis, music. *Address:* Winter Ride, 2 Rosefield, Kippington Road, Sevenoaks, Kent. *T:* Sevenoaks 56989. *Clubs:* Royal Automobile; Tandridge Golf, Chipstead Sailing.

LYONS, Thomas; MP (N Ireland) North Tyrone 1943-69, retired; farmer; *b* 18 Feb. 1896; *s* of late J. J. Lyons, JP, farmer, Newtownstewart, Co. Tyrone, and Elizabeth McFarland, Ballinamallaght, Donemana, Co. Tyrone; *m* 1927, Clarice E. Kiss, Croydon, Sydney, Australia; two *s* one *d. Educ:* Albert Agricultural Coll., Glasnevin, Dublin. Enlisted 1915, in N Irish Horse, served European War, France, with that Regt until transferred, 1917, to Royal Irish Fus. (wounded). Went to Australia, 1922; returned N Ireland, 1939; entered politics as result of by-election, Aug. 1943; Dep. Speaker and Chm. of Ways and Means, House of Commons, N Ireland, 1955-69. JP 1944, High Sheriff 1961, Co. Tyrone. *Address:* Riversdale, Newtownstewart, Co. Tyrone. *T:* Newtownstewart 253. *Club:* Tyrone County (Omagh).

LYONS, Sir William, Kt 1956; President, Jaguar Cars Co. Ltd, since 1972; *b* 4th Sept. 1901, Blackpool; *s* of William Lyons; *m* 1924, Greta, *d* of Alfred Jenour Brown; two *d* (one *s* decd). *Educ:* Arnold Hse, Blackpool. Founded in partnership, Swallow Sidecar Co., 1922, which, after several changes in name, became Jaguar Cars Ltd (Chm. and Chief Exec., until 1972); formerly: Dep. Chm., British Leyland Motor Corp.; Chm. and Chief Exec., Daimler Co. Ltd; Chm., Coventry Climax Engines; Chm., Lanchester Motor Co. Ltd and other subsid. cos; retired 1972. Past President: Soc. of Motor Manufrs and Traders, 1950-51; Motor Industry Research Assoc., 1954; Motor Trades Benevolent Fund, 1954; Fellowship of the Motor Industry (FMI). RDI 1954; FRSA 1964; Hon. AMIAE. Hon. DTech Loughborough, 1969. Coventry Award of Merit Gold Medal, 1970; Gold Medal, AA, 1972. *Recreation:* golf. *Address:* Wappenbury Hall, Wappenbury, near Leamington Spa, Warwickshire. *T:* Marton 632209.

LYSAGHT, family name of **Baron Lisle.**

LYTHALL, Basil Wilfrid, CB 1966; MA; a Member of Admiralty Board of Defence Council; Chief Scientist (Royal Navy), since 1964, also Deputy Controller, Research and Development Establishment, Procurement Executive, since 1971; *b* 15 May 1919; *s* of Frank Herbert Lythall and Winifred Mary (*née* Carver); *m* 1942, Mary Olwen Dando; one *s. Educ:* King Edward's Sch., Stourbridge; Christ Church, Oxford. Joined Royal Naval Scientific Service, 1940; Admiralty Signal and Radar Establishment, 1940-53; Admiralty Research Laboratory, 1954-57; Asst Dir of Physical Research, Admty, 1957-58; a Dep. Chief Scientist, Admty Signal and Radar Estabt (later Admty Surface Weapons Estabt), 1958-60; first Chief Scientist of Admty Underwater Weapons Estabt, Portland, 1960-64. Trustee, National Martime Museum, 1974-. *Publications:* occasional articles in learned jls. *Recreations:* walking, music. *Address:* 48 Grove Way, Esher, Surrey. *T:* 01-398 2958. *Club:* Athenæum.

LYTHGO, Wilbur Reginald, OBE 1964; HM Diplomatic Service, retired; *b* 7 June 1920; *yr s* of late Alfred and Marion Lythgo, Monkton, Ayrshire; *m* 1943, Patricia Frances Sylvia Smith; two *s. Educ:* Palmer's Sch., Grays, Essex. Joined Home Office, 1937. Served in RASC, 1939-41 and Indian Army, 1941-46. Rejoined Home Office, 1946; British Information Services, New Delhi, 1948-54; UK High Commn, New Delhi, 1956-59; British High Commn, Ottawa, 1962-66; Head of Office Services and Supply Dept, DSAO, 1966-68; Counsellor, British Embassy, and Consul-Gen., Washington DC, 1968-71; Consul-Gen., Cleveland, Ohio, 1971-73. Hon. Kentucky Col, 1971. *Recreations:* reading, gardening. *Address:* 10125 Kenswood Drive, Chilliwack, BC V2P 6H4, Canada. *T:* (604) 792 6126.

LYTHGOE, Prof. Basil, FRS 1958; Professor of Organic Chemistry, Leeds University, 1953-Sept. 1978; *b* 18 Aug. 1913; 2nd *s* of Peter Whitaker and Agnes Lythgoe; *m* 1946, Kathleen Cameron, *er d* of H. J. Hallum, St Andrews; two *s. Educ:* Leigh Grammar Sch.; Manchester Univ. Asst Lectr, Manchester Univ., 1938; Univ. Lectr, Cambridge Univ., 1946. Fellow of King's Coll., Cambridge, 1950. *Publications:* papers on chemistry of natural products, in Jl of Chem. Soc. *Recreation:* mountaineering. *Address:* 113 Cookridge Lane, Leeds LS16 0JJ. *T:* Leeds 678837.

LYTHGOE, Ian Gordon, CB 1975; retired; *b* 30 Dec. 1914; *s* of John and Susan Lythgoe; *m* 1st, 1939, Marjory Elsie Fleming; three *s*; 2nd, 1971, Mary Margaret Pickard. *Educ:* Southland Boys' High Sch., Invercargill; Victoria UC, Wellington. MComm (Hons); FCA(NZ). Private Sec., Ministers of Finance, 1944-53; Asst Sec., Treasury, 1962; State Services Commission: Mem., 1964-66; Dep. Chm., 1967-70; Chm., 1971-74. NZ Soc. of Accountants: Mem. Council, 1966-76; Vice-Pres., 1973-74; Pres., 1974-75. Director: Challenge Corporation Ltd; Philips Electrical Industries of NZ Ltd. *Recreations:* gardening,

reading. *Address:* Winara Avenue, Waikanae, New Zealand. *T:* 5113. *Club:* Wellington (Wellington, NZ).

LYTTELTON, family name of **Viscount Chandos** and of **Viscount Cobham.**

LYTTELTON, Humphrey Richard Adeane; musician; band-leader (specializing in Jazz); journalist; *b* Eton, Bucks, 23 May 1921; *s* of late Hon. George William Lyttelton; *m* 1st, 1948, Patricia Mary Braithwaite (marr. diss. 1952); one *d*; 2nd, 1952, Elizabeth Jill, *d* of Albert E. Richardson; two *s* one *d. Educ:* Sunningdale Sch.; Eton Coll.; self-taught as regards musical educn. Served War of 1939-45: Grenadier Guards, 1941-46. Camberwell Art Sch., 1947-48; Cartoonist, Daily Mail, 1949-53. Formed his own band, 1948; leader of Humphrey Lyttelton's Band, and free-lance journalist, 1953-. Numerous recordings and television appearances; recent jazz festival appearances, Bracknell, Zürich, Camden, Montreux, Newcastle, Warsaw, 1976. Compère, BBC Jazz programmes: Jazz Scene, Jazz Club, etc. *Publications:* I Play as I Please, 1954; Second Chorus, 1958; Take It from the Top (autobiog.), 1975; contributor: Melody Maker, 1954-; Reynolds News, 1955-62; Sunday Citizen, 1962-67; Harper's & Queen's; Punch. *Address:* BBC Light Music Department, Broadcasting House, Portland Place, W1A 4WW. *T:* 01-580 4468; (home) Alyn Close, Barnet Road, Arkley, Herts.

LYTTLETON, Prof. Raymond Arthur, FRS; MA, PhD; Professor of Theoretical Astronomy and Fellow of St John's College, University of Cambridge; Member, Institute of Astronomy (formerly Institute of Theoretical Astronomy), University of Cambridge, since 1967; *o s* of William John Lyttleton and Agnes (*d* of Patrick Joseph Kelly), Warley Woods, near Birmingham, formerly of Ireland; *m* Meave Marguerite, *o d* of F. Hobden, Parkstone, formerly of Shanghai; no *c. Educ:* King Edward's Grammar Sch., Five Ways; King Edward's Sch., Birmingham; Clare Coll., Cambridge. Wrangler; Tyson Medal for Astronomy. Procter Visiting Fellowship, Princeton Univ., USA; Exptl Officer, Min. of Supply, 1940-42; Technical Asst to Scientific Adviser to the Army Council, War Office, 1943-45. Lectr in Mathematics, 1937-59, Stokes Lectr, 1954-59, Reader in Theoretical Astronomy, 1959-69 (resigned), Univ. of Cambridge. Jacob Siskind Vis. Prof., Brandeis Univ., USA, 1965-66; Vis. Prof., Brown Univ., USA, 1967-68; Halley Lectr, Oxford Univ., 1970. Mem. of Council, Royal Society, 1959-61; Geophysical Sec. of Royal Astronomical Soc., 1949-60 and Mem. of Council, 1950-61, 1969-72; Fellow, 1934-. Hopkins Prize (for 1951) of Cambridge Philosophical Soc.; Gold Medallist of Royal Astronomical Soc., 1959; Royal Medallist of Royal Society, 1965. *Publications:* The Comets and their Origin, 1953; The Stability of Rotating Liquid Masses, 1953; The Modern Universe, 1956; Rival Theories of Cosmology, 1960; Man's View of the Universe, 1961; Mysteries of the Solar System, 1968; (Play) A Matter of Gravity (produced by BBC, 1968); papers on astrophysics, cosmogony, cosmology, physics, dynamics, and geophysics in Proc. Royal Soc., Monthly Notices of Royal Astron. Soc., Proc. Camb. Phil Soc., etc. *Recreations:* golf, motoring, music; wondering about it all. *Address:* 165 Huntingdon Road, Cambridge. *T:* 54910; St John's College, Cambridge. *T:* 61621; Institute of Astronomy, Madingley Road, Cambridge. *T:* Cambridge 62204.

LYTTON, family name of **Earl of Lytton.**

LYTTON, 4th Earl of, *cr* 1880; **Noel Anthony Scawen Lytton,** OBE 1945; Viscount Knebworth, 1880; Baron Lytton, 1866; Baron Wentworth, 1529; Bt 1838; *b* 7 April 1900; *s* of 3rd Earl of Lytton, OBE, and 16th Baroness Wentworth (*d* 1957); *S* father, 1951; *m* 1946, Clarissa Mary, *er d* of late Brig.-Gen C. E. Palmer, CB, CMG, DSO, RA, and of Mrs Palmer, Christchurch, Hants; two *s* three *d. Educ:* Downside; RMC Sandhurst. Lieut, Rifle Bde, 1921, attached King's African Rifles, 1922-27; Administrator, Samburu and Turkhana District, Kenya, 1924-25; Instructor (Economics), Sandhurst, 1931-35; Captain Rifle Bde, 1936; Staff Capt., War Office, 1937; Major, 1938; served War of 1939-45 (temp. Lt-Col) in N Africa, Italy, Greece and Austria; Administrator, Patras District, Greece, 1944; Chief Staff Officer, Mil. Government of Vienna, 1945-46; retd, 1946. Leader, Working Boys' Club, Bermondsey, 1937-39; formerly Member: Youth Adv. Council; Central Adv. Council for Educn (England). Farmer, 1959-; author; a crossbencher, House of Lords. Freeman: Missolonghi, Greece; Kismayu, Somalia. *Publications:* The Desert and the Green (autobiography), 1957; Wilfrid Scawen Blunt (biog.), 1961; Mickla Bendore (novel), 1962; Lucia in Taormina (novel), 1963; The Stolen Desert (history), 1966. *Heir: s* Viscount Knebworth, *qv. Address:* House of Lords, SW1A 0PW.

See also Baron Cobbold, Hon. C. M. Woodhouse.

LYTTON SELLS, Arthur Lytton, MA (Cambridge), Docteur de l'Université de Paris, Lauréat de l'Académie française; Officier d'Académie; *b* Edgbaston, Birmingham, England, 28 May 1895; *s* of Arthur Sells and Elizabeth Whittaker; *m* 1929, Iris Esther, MA, *d* of F. T. Robertson, JP, formerly editor of Adelaide Advertiser, Adelaide, South Australia; one *s. Educ:* King Edward VII School, Sheffield; Univs of Cambridge and Paris. Scholar of Sidney Sussex Coll., Cambridge, 1914-15, 1919-21; served HAC, 1918-19; Lectr, Cambridge, 1923-29; Univ. Lectr in French, 1929; Prof. of French, Durham Univ., 1930-51; Prof. of English Literature, Padua Univ., 1946; Prof. of French and Italian at Indiana Univ., 1951; Research Prof. Emer., 1965. Visiting Professor: Harvard, 1953, New York Univ., 1954, Assumption Coll., Worcester, Mass, 1967, Wake Forest Univ., N Carolina, 1970-. *Publications:* Les Sources françaises de Goldsmith, 1924, awarded Prix Bordin of the French Academy; The Early Life of J. J. Rousseau, 1929; Molière and La Mothe le Vayer, 1933; The History of Francis Wills, 1935; (with I. E. Sells) Key to Manual of French Translation and Composition, 1937; contrib. France, ed by R. L. G. Ritchie, 1937; Earth of the Tarentines, 1940; Heredia's Hellenism, 1942; The Italian Influence in English Poetry, 1954; Animal Poetry in French and English Literature, 1955; (ed) The Military Memoirs of James II, 1962; The Paradise of Travellers, 1964; (trans.) Mollat and Wolff: The Popular Revolutions of the Late Middle Ages, 1974; Oliver Goldsmith: his life and works, 1975; (with I. Lytton Sells) Thomas Gray: his life and works, 1977. *Recreations:* reading, photography. *Address:* Dunster House, The Avenue, Durham. *T:* 2525. *Club:* Athenæum.

LYVEDEN, 6th Baron *cr* 1859; **Ronald Cecil Vernon;** retired; *b* 10 April 1915; *s* of 5th Baron Lyveden and Ruby (*née* Shanley) (*d* 1932); *S* father, 1973; *m* 1938, Queenie Constance, *d* of Howard Ardern; three *s. Educ:* Te Aroha College. *Heir: e s* Hon. Jack Leslie Vernon [*b* 10 Nov. 1938; *m* 1961, Lynette June, *d* of William Herbert Lilley; one *s* two *d*]. *Address:* 20 Farmer Street, Te Aroha, New Zealand. *T:* 410. *Club:* RSA (Te Aroha).

M

MAAN, Bashir Ahmed, JP; Councillor, City of Glasgow District, since 1974; President, Standing Conference of Pakistani Organisations in UK, since 1974; a Deputy Chairman, Commission for Racial Equality, since 1977; Judge, City of Glasgow District Courts, since 1975; *b* Maan, Gujranwala, Pakistan, 22 Oct. 1926; *s* of Choudhry Sardar Khan Maan and late Mrs Hayat Begum Maan; *m* 1st, 1948 (marr. diss. 1974); one *s* one *d* ; 2nd, 1975, Margaret Ruth, *d* of Maurice W. Herbert and Mrs M. Herbert, Monifieth, Dundee; one *d. Educ:* D. B. High Sch., Qila Didar Singh; Panjab Univ. Involved in struggle for creation of Pakistan, 1943-47; organised rehabilitation of refugees from India in Maan and surrounding areas, 1947-48; emigrated to UK and settled in Glasgow, 1953; Glasgow Sec., Pakistan Social and Cultural Soc., 1955-65, Pres., 1966-69; Vice-Chm., Glasgow Community Relations Council, 1970-75. Councillor, Glasgow Corp., 1970-75; Magistrate, City of Glasgow, 1971-74; Vice-Chm. 1971-74, Chm. 1974-75, Police Cttee, Glasgow Corp.; Police Judge, City of Glasgow, 1974-75; Mem. Exec. Cttee, Glasgow City Labour Party, 1969-70. Contested (Lab) East Fife, Feb. 1974. Mem., BBC Immigrants Programme Adv. Cttee, 1972-; Convener, Pakistan Bill Action Cttee, 1973; Member: Nat. Road Safety Cttee, 1971-75; Scottish Accident Prevention Cttee, 1971-75. Dir, AA Brothers, Glasgow. JP Glasgow, 1968. *Publications:* articles, contrib. to press. *Recreations:* golf, reading. *Address:* 20 Sherbrooke Avenue, Glasgow G41 4PE. *T:* 041-427 4057. *Club:* St Andrews Golf.

MAAZEL, Lorin; symphony conductor; *b* 6 March 1930; *s* of Lincoln Maazel and Marie Varencove; *m* 1st, 1952, Miriam Sandbank; two *d* ; 2nd, 1969, Israela Margalit; one *s* one *d. Educ:* Pittsburgh University. Début as a conductor at age of 9, as violinist a few years later; by 1941 had conducted foremost US Orchestras, including Toscanini's NBC; since 1952, over 500 concerts in Europe and performances at major festivals, including Edinburgh, Bayreuth, Salzburg and Lucerne; in USA: conducted Boston Symphony, New York Philharmonic, Philadelphia Orchestra, and at Metropolitan, 1960 and 1962. Several world tours, including Latin America, Australia, USSR and Japan. Artistic Director of Deutsche Oper Berlin, 1965-71; Music Director, Radio Symphony Orchestra, 1965-75; Associate Principal Conductor, Philharmonia (formerly New Philharmonia) Orchestra, 1970-72, Principal Guest Conductor, 1976-; Music Director, Cleveland Orchestra, 1972-; Principal Guest Conductor, Orchestre National, 1977-. Has made numerous recordings. Hon. Dr of Music Pittsburgh Univ., 1968; Hon. Dr of Humanities Beaver Coll., 1973. Commander's Cross of Order of Merit, Federal Republic of Germany, 1977. *Address:* c/o Cleveland Orchestra, Severance Hall, Cleveland, Ohio, USA.

MABBOTT, John David, CMG 1946; President of St John's College, Oxford, 1963-69; *b* 18 Nov. 1898; *s* of late Walter John and Elizabeth Mabbott; *m* 1934, Doreen Roach (*d* 1975). *Educ:* Berwickshire High Sch.; Edinburgh Univ.; St John's Coll., Oxford. Asst Lectr in Classics, Reading Univ., 1922; Asst Lectr in Philosophy, Univ. Coll. of North Wales, 1923; John Locke Scholar, Univ. of Oxford, 1923; Fellow of St John's Coll., Oxford, 1924-63, Tutor, 1930-63, and Hon. Fellow, 1969. *Publications:* The State and the Citizen, 1948; An Introduction to Ethics, 1966; John Locke, 1973; contribs to Philosophy, Proc. Aristotelian Soc., Classical Quarterly, Mind. *Address:* Wing Cottage, Mill Lane, Islip, Oxon. *T:* Kidlington 2360.

MABBS, Alfred Walter; Deputy Keeper of Public Records, since 1973; *b* 12 April 1921; *e s* of James and Amelia Mabbs; *m* 1942, Dorothy Lowley; one *s. Educ:* Hackney Downs Sch. Served War, RAF, 1941-46. Asst Keeper, Public Record Office, 1950-66; Principal Asst Keeper, 1967-69; Records Admin. Officer, 1970-73. FRHistS, 1954. *Publications:* Guild Stewards Book of the Borough of Calne (vol. vii, Wilts Arch. and Record Soc.), 1953; The Records of the Cabinet Office to 1922, 1966; Guide to the Contents of the Public Record Office, vol. iii (main contributor), 1968; Exchequer of the Jews, vol. iv (jt contrib.), 1972; The Organisation of Intermediate Records Storage (with Guy Duboscq), 1974; (jt contributor) Establishing a Legislative Framework for the Implementation of NATIS, 1977. *Recreations:* golf, reading. *Address:* 14 Acorn Lane, Cuffley, Herts EN6 4DZ. *T:* Cuffley 3660. *Club:* Royal Commonwealth Society.

MABON, Rt. Hon. (Jesse) Dickson, PC 1977; MP (Lab and Co-op) Greenock and Port Glasgow, since 1974 (Greenock, Dec. 1955-1974); Minister of State, Department of Energy, since 1976; *b* 1 Nov. 1925; *s* of Jesse Dickson Mabon and Isabel Simpson Montgomery; *m* 1970, Elizabeth, *o d* of William Zinn, *qv*; one *s. Educ:* Possilpark, Cumbrae, North Kelvinside Schools. Worked in coalmining industry before Army service, 1944-48. MB, ChB (Glasgow); DHMSA; Visiting Physician, Manor House Hospital, London, 1958-64. President: Glasgow University Union, 1951-52; Scottish Union of Students, 1954-55; Chairman: Glasgow Univ. Labour Club, 1948-50; National Assoc. of Labour Students, 1949-50; contested (Lab) Bute and N Ayrshire, Gen. Election, Oct. 1951; (Lab and Co-op) W Renfrewshire, Gen. Election, May 1955. Political columnist, Scottish Daily Record, 1955-64. Joint Parly Under-Sec. of State for Scotland, 1964-67; Minister of State, Scottish Office, 1967-70; Dep. Opposition Spokesman on Scotland, 1970-72 (resigned over Common Mkt). Chairman: UK Labour Cttee for Europe, 1974-76; Scottish Parly Labour Party, 1972-73, 1975-76; Member: Council of Europe, 1970-72 and 1974-76; Assembly, WEU, 1970-72 and 1974-76; Pres., European Movement, 1975-76. Founder Chm., Manifesto Gp, Parly Lab. Party, 1974-76. Chm., Young Volunteer Force Foundn, 1974-76. FInstPet; Fellow: Faculty of History of Medicine; Soc. of Apothecaries. Freeman of City of London. *Recreations:* golf, theatre. *Address:* House of Commons, SW1.

MABY, (Alfred) Cedric, CBE 1962; HM Diplomatic Service, retired; *b* 6 April 1915; 4th *s* of late Joseph Maby, Penrose, Monmouthshire; *m* 1944, Anne-Charlotte, *d* of Envoyén Elnar Modig, Stockholm; one *s* two *d. Educ:* Cheltenham; Keble Coll., Oxford. Joined HM Consular Service, 1939. Served at Peking, 1939, Chungking, 1940, Tsingtao, 1941, Istanbul, 1943, Angora, 1944, Buenos Aires, 1946, Caracas, 1949, Singapore, 1954; Counsellor and Consul-General, Peking, 1957-59 (Chargé d'Affaires, 1957 and 1958); Deputy Consul-General, New York, 1959-62; Counsellor (Commercial) at Vienna, 1962-64; Asst Sec., Min. of Overseas Development, 1964-67; Consul-General, Zürich, 1968-71; Dir, Trade Promotion for Switzerland, 1970-71. Mem. Governing Body, Church in Wales. High Sheriff Gwynedd, 1976. *Address:* Cae Canol, Penrhyn-Deudraeth, Gwynedd.

McADAM, Sir Ian (William James), Kt 1966; OBE 1957; FRCS, FRCSE; *b* 15 Feb. 1917; *s* of W. J. McAdam and Alice Culverwell; *m* 1st, 1939, Hrothgarde Gibson (marr. diss. 1961); one *s* two *d* ; 2nd, 1967, Lady (Pamela) Hunt, *née* Medawar. *Educ:* Plumtree Sch., S Rhodesia; Edinburgh Univ. MB, ChB. Cambridge Anatomy Sch., 1940; Dept of Surgery, Edinburgh,

1942; Wilkie Surgical Research Fellow, 1942; Clinical Tutor, Royal Infirmary, Edinburgh, 1942; Surgical Specialist, Uganda, 1946; Senior Consultant, Uganda, 1957; Prof. of Surgery, Makerere Univ., Univ. of E Africa, 1957-72, also Consultant Surgeon Uganda Govt and Kenyatta Hosp., Kenya; Consultant to Nat. Insts of Health, Bethesda, Md, 1973-74. *Publications:* various papers in medical jls. *Recreations:* golf, gardening. *Address:* Box 166, Plettenberg Bay, Cape Province, South Africa.
See also Sir Peter Medawar.

MACADAM, Peter; Chairman, BAT Industries Ltd, since 1976; *b* 9 Sept. 1921; *s* of Francis Macadam and Marjorie Mary Browne; *m* 1949, Ann Musson; three *d*. *Educ:* Buenos Aires, Argentina; Stonyhurst Coll., Lancs. Served as Officer in Queen's Bays, 1941-46. Joined BAT Gp tobacco co., Argentina, 1946; Chm. and Gen. Man., gp co., Argentina, 1955-58; PA in London to Dir resp. for Africa, 1959-60 (travelled widely in Africa); Chm., BAT Hong Kong, 1960-62; BAT Main Bd, 1963 (resp. at times for interest in S and Central Africa, S and Central America and Caribbean); Mem., Chm.'s Policy Cttee with overall resp. for tobacco interests and special interest, USA, Canada and Mexico, 1970; Chm., Tobacco Div. Bd and Dir, Gp HQ Bd, 1973; Vice-Chm., 1975. Hon. FBIM; FRSA 1975. *Recreations:* golf, shooting. *Address:* 34 Campden Hill Court, Campden Hill Road, W8 7HS. *T:* 01-937 1389. *Clubs:* Naval and Military, Hurlingham.

McADAM, Prof. Robert, BSc, PhD, CEng, FIMinE, FRSE; Hood Professor of Mining Engineering, Heriot-Watt University, Edinburgh, 1967-75, now Emeritus; *b* 15 March 1906; *y s* of William McAdam, Broomieknowe, Midlothian; *m* 1933, Winifred Julia, *o d* of T. W. Dixon, Edinburgh; one *s*. *Educ:* Lasswade Secondary Sch.; Univ. of Edinburgh. Practical experience in coal mines in Scotland and gold mines in India; Tait research worker on Mine Ventilation, 1930. Sen. Lectr in Mining, Heriot-Watt Coll., Edinburgh, 1931-48; Hood Prof. of Mining, Univ. of Edinburgh and Heriot-Watt Coll., Edinburgh, 1948-67. Heriot-Watt Univ., Edinburgh: Dean of Faculty of Engineering, 1967-69; Vice-Principal, 1970-74. Carried out research work on errors affecting mine surveying operations, production of oil from coal, geophysical prospecting, and mine rescue work. *Publications:* Colliery Surveying, 1953, 1963; Mine Rescue Work, 1955; Mining Explosives, 1958; numerous papers on mining and scientific subjects in Trans of IMinE, Inst. Mining Surveyors, and in technical press. *Address:* Allermuir, Captains Road, Edinburgh EH17 8DT. *T:* 031-664 2770.

McADAM CLARK, James; *see* Clark, James McAdam.

McADDEN, Sir Stephen (James), Kt 1962; CBE 1959; MP (C) Southend East since 1950; Director: Butlins Construction Co. Ltd; Four Circle Development Co. Ltd; *b* 3 Nov. 1907; *s* of William John McAdden and Elizabeth (*née* Mulhern); *m* 1951, Doris Hearle, *d* of Walter and Ethel Gillies, Leytonstone, and *widow* of Captain William Hearle, RAC. *Educ:* Salesian Sch., Battersea. Comd Hackney Bn, Home Guard, Lt.-Col. Councillor: Hackney Borough Council, 1937-45; Woodford Borough Council, 1945-48; Essex County Council, 1947-48. Chairman: West Toxteth (Liverpool) Junior Imperial League, 1929-31, Hackney Branch, 1932-35; Grand Prior, Primrose League, 1955-58. Trustee Liverpool Victoria Friendly Society; National Pres. and Chm., Music Users Assoc.; Vice-Pres., National Chamber of Trade. Mem., Speaker's Panel of Chairman of Cttees, 1966-. Freeman of City of London, 1974. *Recreations:* tennis, cricket, debating. *Address:* 552 Woodgrange Drive, Thorpe Bay, Essex. *T:* Southend-on-Sea 588421; House of Commons, SW1. *Clubs:* St Stephen's; Alexandra Yacht (Southend), Thorpe Bay Yacht.

McADOO, Most Rev. Henry Robert; *see* Dublin, Archbishop of.

MACAFEE, Prof. Charles Horner Greer, CBE 1961; DL; Emeritus Professor of Midwifery and Gynæcology, The Queen's University, Belfast, since 1963 (Professor, Oct. 1945-Oct. 1963, retired); Member of Senate; *b* 23 July 1898; *s* of Rev. Andrew Macafee, BA, and A. H. Macafee, MBE, JP; *m* 1930, Margaret Crymble (*d* 1968), *d* of Prof. C. G. Lowry; two *s* one *d*. *Educ:* Omagh Academy; Foyle Coll., Londonderry. MB, BCh, BAO, First Class Hons, 1921; FRCS 1927; FRCSI 1927; Foundation Fellow, 1929, and Mem. Council, RCOG; Past Pres., Ulster Obstetrical and Gynæcological Soc.; Chm. Adv. Cttee on the Maternity Services in Northern Ireland; Past Pres., Ulster Medical Soc.; Vice-Pres., RCOG, 1961-64; formerly Mem. Northern Ireland Hospitals Authority; formerly External Examiner: Oxford, Dublin, Glasgow and Leeds; Lichfield Lectr, Oxford, 1955; Sims-Black Travelling Prof. to Rhodesia and S Africa, RCOG, 1956; William Meredith Fletcher Shaw

Memorial Lectr, London, 1961. DL, County Down, 1969. Hon. Fellow: Edinburgh Obstetrical Soc., 1972; Ulster Medical Soc., 1977. Hon. DSc Leeds, 1961; Hon. LLD Belfast, 1974. Blair Bell Memorial Medal, RSM, 1965; Eardley Holland Medal, RCOG, 1965. *Publications:* contributed to: Modern Trends in Obstetrics and Gynæcology; Modern Trends in British Surgery; many contribs to Jl of Obstetrics and Gynæcology, British Empire; Proc. RSocMed; Ulster Medical Jl. *Recreations:* reading, writing, gardening. *Address:* The Cottage Stramore Lodge, 142 Warren Road, Ballywilliam, Donaghadee, Co. Down, Northern Ireland.

McALISKEY, (Josephine) Bernadette, (Mrs Michael McAliskey); Founder Member and Member Executive, Irish Republican Socialist Party, 1975; *b* 23 April 1947; *d* of late John James Devlin and Elizabeth Devlin; *m* 1973, Michael McAliskey; two *d*. *Educ:* St Patrick's Girls' Acad., Dungannon; psychology student at Queen's Univ., Belfast, 1966-69. Youngest MP in House of Commons when elected at age of 21; MP (Ind. Unity) Mid Ulster, Apr. 1969-Feb. 1974. *Publication:* The Price of my Soul (autobiog.), 1969. *Recreations:* walking, folk music, doing nothing, swimming.

McALISTER, Michael Ian, FCA; President, Australian Associated Stock Exchanges, since 1972; *b* Leeds, Yorkshire, 23 Aug. 1930; *s* of S. McAlister, CBE, and J. A. McAlister, (*née* Smith); *m* 1953, Patricia (*née* Evans); four *s* three *d*. *Educ:* Brazil; France; St John's Coll., Oxford (MA). Articled Clerk, Price Waterhouse, London, 1954-58; Private Sec. to the Duke of Windsor, 1959-61; Investment Manager, Ionian Bank Ltd, London, 1961-67; Managing Dir, Ionian Bank Trustee Co, London, 1967-68; Slater Walker Securities (Australia): Dep. Chm., 1969-70, Chm., 1970-72. *Recreations:* game fishing, archery, swimming. *Address:* 631 Old Northern Road, Dural, NSW 2158, Australia. *T:* Sydney 651-1795.

McALISTER, Maj.-Gen. Ronald William Lorne, CB 1977; OBE 1968 (MBE 1959); retired 1977; *b* 26 May 1923; 2nd *s* of late Col R. J. F. McAlister, OBE and Mrs T. M. Collins, Bath; *m* 1964, Sally Ewart Marshall; two *d*. *Educ:* Dreghorn Castle Sch., Edinburgh; Sedbergh School. Commnd 3rd QAO Gurkha Rifles, 1942; Adjt 1/3 GR Burma, 1945 (despatches); Adjt 2/10 GR Malaya, 1950-52 (despatches); Instructor, Sch. of Infantry, 1953-55; psc 1956; Bde Major 99 Gurkha Bde, Malaya, 1957-59 (MBE); jssc 1961-62; Asst Sec., Chiefs of Staff Cttee, 1962-64; 2nd in comd and CO 10th PMO Gurkha Rifles, Borneo, 1964-66 (despatches); Internal Security Duties, Hong Kong, 1967-68 (OBE); Instructor, Jt Services Staff Coll., 1968; comd Berlin Inf. Bde, 1968-71; ndc, Canada, 1971-72; Exercise Controller UK Cs-in-C Cttee, 1972-75; Dep. Commander Land Forces Hong Kong and Maj.-Gen. Brigade of Gurkhas, 1975-77. Col, 10th Princess Mary's Own Gurkha Rifles, 1977-. *Recreations:* golf, sailing. *Address:* The Chalet, 41 Callis Court Road, Broadstairs, Kent. *T:* Thanet 62351. *Club:* Army and Navy.

McALLISTER, Sir Reginald (Basil), Kt 1973; CMG 1966; CVO 1963; JP; retired; Trustee: National Party of Australia, Queensland, since 1966; *b* 8 May 1900; *s* of Basil William and Beatrice Maud McAllister; *m* 1951, Joyce Isabel Roper; no *c*. *Educ:* Brisbane Primary and Secondary State Schools. Clerk, Railway Dept, Brisbane, 1916; secretarial duties, Parlt House, Brisbane, and Sec. to Speaker, 1924-26; reporter, State Reporting Bureau, Parlt House, 1926-33; Sec. to Premier of Queensland, 1933-37 (accompanied Premier on missions to: UK AND Canada, 1934; UK and Europe, 1936; UK Internat. Sugar Conf., 1937); Asst Under-Sec., Premier and Chief Secretary's Dept, 1938; Official Sec., Qld Govt Offices, London, 1943-48 (actg Agent-Gen. on many occasions); resumed former duties in Brisbane, 1948; Clerk of Exec. Council of Qld, 1941-43, 1951-66; Under-Sec., Premier's Dept, and Chm., State Stores Board, 1962-66; acted as Sec. to Cabinet on many occasions; retd 1966; Executive Officer of five Premiers and four Governors, 1933-66. State Director, Royal Visits: HM Queen Elizabeth II and Prince Philip, 1963; TRH Duke and Duchess of Gloucester, 1965; HM King and Queen of Thailand, 1962; assisted with Royal Visits: HRH Duke of Gloucester, 1934; HM the Queen and Prince Philip, 1954; HM Queen Elizabeth the Queen Mother, 1958; HRH Princess Alexandra, 1959. Pres., Qld Br., Royal Commonwealth Soc.; Australian-Asian Soc.; Pres., Australia-Japan Soc., 1972; Exec. Cttee, Australian Red Cross Soc; Pres. Council, RGS; Mem. State Council and Executive, Scout Assoc. of Australia. Dep. Chm., Bd of Dirs, Warana Spring Festival, 1965-. Liveryman, Farriers' Co.; Freeman, City of London; JP 1933. *Recreations:* golf, fishing, gardening, politics. *Address:* 34 Scott Road, Herston, Brisbane, Queensland 4006, Australia. *T:* 356 5361. *Clubs:* Queensland Turf, Masonic, Tattersall's, Queensland Lawn Tennis, Royal Autobomile, Brisbane Cricket (all Queensland).

McALPINE, Douglas, MD, FRCP; Emeritus Consultant Physician to the Middlesex Hospital; *b* 19 Aug. 1890; *s* of late Sir Robert McAlpine, 1st Bt, and late Florence Palmer; *m* 1917, Elizabeth Meg Sidebottom (*d* 1941); one *s* one *d*; *m* 1945, Diana, *d* of late Bertram Plummer; one *s*. *Educ*: Cheltenham; Glasgow Univ.; Paris. MB, ChB, Glasgow, 1913; joined RAMC, Aug. 1914; served France till 1915; Aug. 1915, joined Navy as Surgeon Lt, RN; served afloat until 1918 (despatches); elected to staff of several London Hospitals; became Neurologist to Middlesex Hospital, 1924; FRCP 1933. Late Brig. RAMC; Cons. Neurol. MEF, India Comd and SEAC, 1941-45 (despatches). *Publications*: Multiple Sclerosis: a Reappraisal (jointly), 1965, 2nd edn 1972; various papers in medical jls. *Recreations*: fishing, golf. *Address*: Lovells Mill, Marnhull, Dorset.
See also R. D. C. McAlpine.

McALPINE, Sir Edwin; see McAlpine, Sir R. E.

McALPINE, Hon. Sir John (Kenneth), KCMG 1977 (CMG 1970); Chairman, New Zealand Ports Authority, since 1968; *b* 21 July 1906; *s* of Walter Kenneth and Gwendolin Marion McAlpine; *m* 1934, Lesley Ruth Hay; one *s* two *d*. *Educ*: Christ's Coll., Christchurch, New Zealand. MP Selwyn, NZ, 1946-66. Mem. Tawera CC, 1927-63; Pres., Canterbury Federated Farmers, 1945-47. Mem. Bd: Arthur's Pass National Park, 1942-; Lyttleton Harbour, 1937-54 (Chm., 1942-45); Canterbury Univ., 1950-60; Canterbury Agricultural Univ., 1959- (Chm., 1967-). Minister: Railways, Marine, and Printing, 1954-66; Transport and Civil Aviation, 1957-66; Labour, 1956-58. Mem., Exec., NZ Holiday Travel, etc, 1966-; Chairman: South Island, NZ, Promotion Bd, 1937-; Canterbury Progress League, 1937-. *Recreations*: Rugby football, long distance running, gardening, skiing. *Address*: 50 McDougall Avenue, Christchurch 1, New Zealand. *Club*: Christchurch (NZ).

McALPINE, Robert Douglas Christopher, CMG 1967; HM Diplomatic Service, retired; Director, Baring Brothers, since 1969; *b* 14 June 1919; *s* of Dr Douglas McAlpine, *qv*; *m* 1943, Helen Margery Frances Cannan; two *s* one *d* (and one *d* decd). *Educ*: Winchester; New Coll., Oxford. RNVR, 1939-46. Entered Foreign Service, 1946. FO, 1946-47; Asst Private Sec. to Sec. of State, 1947-49; 2nd Sec. and later 1st Sec., UK High Commn at Bonn, 1949-52; FO, 1952-54; Lima, 1954-56; Moscow, 1956-59; FO, 1959-62; Dep. Consul-Gen. and Counsellor, New York, 1962-65; Counsellor, Mexico City, 1965-69. *Recreations*: sailing, tennis, shooting, fishing. *Address*: 81 Dovehouse Street, SW3.

McALPINE, Sir (Robert) Edwin, Kt 1963; Partner, Sir Robert McAlpine & Sons, since 1928; Vice-Chairman, British Nuclear Associates; *b* 23 April 1907; *s* of William Hepburn McAlpine and Margaret Donnison; *m* 1930, Ella Mary Gardner Garnett; three *s* one *d*. *Educ*: Oundle. Joined Sir Robert McAlpine & Sons, 1925. Dep. Chm., British Nuclear Associates, 1973-. *Recreations*: breeding race horses, farming, travel, golf, theatre. *Address*: Benhams, Fawley Green, Henley-on-Thames, Oxon. *T*: Hambleden 246. *Clubs*: Garrick, Caledonian, Jockey.
See also Sir T. G. B. McAlpine, Bt.

McALPINE, Sir Robin, Kt 1969; CBE 1957; Chairman: Sir Robert McAlpine & Sons Ltd, since 1967; Newarthill Ltd, 1972-77; *b* 18 March 1906; *s* of late Sir (Thomas) Malcolm McAlpine, KBE, and late Lady (Maud) McAlpine; *m* 1st, 1939, Nora Constance (*d* 1966), *d* of F. H. Perse; 2nd, 1970, Mrs Philippa Nicolson, *d* of Sir Gervais Tennyson D'Eyncourt, 2nd Bt. *Educ*: Charterhouse. Pres., Federation of Civil Engineering Contractors, 1966-71. *Recreation*: owner and breeder of racehorses. *Address*: Aylesfield, Alton, Hants. *Club*: Jockey.

McALPINE, Sir Thomas (George Bishop), 4th Bt *cr* 1918; Director of Sir Robert McAlpine & Sons; *b* 23 Oct. 1901; *s* of William Hepburn McAlpine (2nd *s* of 1st Bt) and Margaret Donnison, *d* of T. G. Bishop; *S* kinsman, Sir (Alfred) Robert McAlpine, 3rd Bt, 1968; *m* 1st, 1934, Doris Frew (*d* 1964), *d* of late D. C. Campbell and widow of W. E. Woodeson; 2nd, 1965, Kathleen Mary, *d* of late Frederick Best and widow of Charles Bantock Blackshaw; no *c*. *Educ*: Warriston; Rossall Sch. Joined firm of Sir Robert McAlpine on leaving school; eventually became a partner and director; retired from the partnership, 1966. *Recreations*: farming, photography, travel. *Heir*: *b* Sir (Robert) Edwin McAlpine, *qv*. *Address*: The Manor House, Stanford-in-the-Vale, Faringdon, Oxon. *Club*: Royal Automobile.
See also W. S. Blackshaw.

MacANDREW, family name of Baron MacAndrew.

MacANDREW, 1st Baron *cr* 1959; **Charles Glen MacAndrew**; PC 1952; Kt 1935; TD; DL; JP; Hon. LLD (St Andrews); *b* 13 Jan. 1888; *s* of F. G. MacAndrew; *m* 1918, Lilian Cathleen Curran (from whom he obtained a divorce 1938); one *s* one *d*; *m* 1941, Mona, *d* of J. A. Ralston Mitchell, Perceton House, by Irvine; one *d*. *Educ*: Uppingham; Trinity Coll., Cambridge. MP (U) Ayr and Bute, Kilmarnock Div., 1924-29; MP (U) Partick Div., Glasgow, 1931-35; Dep. Chm. of Ways and Means, House of Commons, May-July 1945 and March 1950-Oct. 1951; MP (U) Bute and Northern div. of Ayr and Bute, 1935-59; Dep. Speaker of the House of Commons, 1951-59; Chm. of Ways and Means, 1951-59. Commanded Ayrshire Yeomanry, 1932-36; Hon. Col, 1951-55; DL, JP, Ayrshire. OStJ. *Heir*: *s* Hon. Colin Nevil Glen MacAndrew [*b* 1 Aug. 1919; *m* 1943, Ursula, *yr d* of Capt. Joseph Steel, Lockerbie, Dumfriesshire; two *s* one *d*. *Educ*: Eton; Trinity Coll., Cambridge]. *Address*: The White House, Monkton, Ayrshire. *T*: Prestwick 77872. *Clubs*: Carlton; Royal and Ancient Golf (St Andrews).

MacANDREW, Lt-Col James Orr, TD; DL; Ayrshire Yeomanry; *b* 22 June 1899; *s* of F. G. MacAndrew, Knock Castle, Largs; *m* 1944, Eileen, *o d* of Robin Butterfield; one *d*. *Educ*: Trinity Coll., Glenalmond; Trinity Hall, Cambridge. Served European War, 1914-18, joined RFC 1917; War of 1939-45. Hon. Col Ayrshire Yeomanry, 1955-60. MP (U) Ayr and Bute South Ayrshire Div., 1931-35. Jt Master, Eglinton foxhounds, 1939-40. DL Ayrshire, 1966. *Address*: South Park, Ayr. *T*: Ayr 64783. *Club*: Cavalry and Guards.

MACARA, Sir (Charles) Douglas, 3rd Bt *cr* 1911; *b* 19 April 1904; *s* of 2nd Bt and Lillian Mary (*d* 1971), *d* of John Chapman, Boyton Court, East Sutton, Kent; *S* father, 1931; *m* 1926, Quenilda (marr. diss. 1945), *d* of late Herbert Whitworth, St Anne's-on-Sea; two *d* (one *s* decd). *Heir*: *b* John Keith Macara [*b* 29 Oct. 1905; *m* 1948, Joan Florence Mary Bennett (*née* Stonor) (*d* 1956)].

McARDLE, Michael John Francis, MB, BS (Hons, London), FRCP; Consulting Physician Emeritus for Nervous Diseases, Guy's Hospital; Consulting Physician Emeritus, The National Hospital, Queen Square, WC1; Hon. Consulting Neurologist, Kingston Hospital and St Teresa's Maternity Hospital, Wimbledon, SW19; *b* 1909; *s* of Andrew McArdle; *m* 1955, Maureen MacClancy. *Educ*: Wimbledon Coll.; Guy's Hospital; Paris. Entrance Scholarship, Arts, Guy's Hospital. Medical Registrar, Guy's Hospital; Asst Medical Officer, Maudsley Hospital. Rockefeller Travelling Fellow in Neurology, 1938. War of 1939-45, Temp. Lt-Col, RAMC and Adviser in Neurology, 21st Army Group. *Publications*: papers on neurological subjects in medical journals. *Recreation*: golf. *Address*: 121 Harley Street, W1N 1DH. *T*: 01-935 0244; 35 Marryat Road, Wimbledon, SW19 5BE. *T*: 01-946 4149.

McARDLE, Rear-Adm. Stanley Lawrence, CB 1975; MVO 1952; GM 1953; Flag Officer, Portsmouth, and Port Admiral, Portsmouth, 1973-75; retired; *b* 1922; *s* of Theodore McArdle, Lochmaben, Dumfriesshire; *m* 1st, 1955, (Helen) Joyce, *d* of Owen Cummins, Wickham, Hants; one *d*; 2nd, 1962, Jennifer, *d* of Walter Talbot Goddard, Salisbury, Wilts; one *d*. *Educ*: Royal Hospital Sch., Holbrook, Suffolk. Joined RN, 1938; served War, 1939-45. Lieut 1945; Comdr 1956; Captain 1963. Directorate of Naval Operations and Trade, 1969; Comd HMS Glamorgan, 1970; Dir Naval Trng, Directorage General, Personal Services and Trng (Naval), 1971-73; Rear Admiral 1972. *Address*: Barn Ridge Cottage, Farley, Salisbury, Wilts.

MACARTHUR, Rev. Arthur Leitch, MA, MLitt; General Secretary, United Reformed Church, since 1975; *b* 9 Dec. 1913; *s* of Edwin Macarthur and Mary Macarthur (*née* Leitch); *m* 1950, Doreen Esmé Muir; three *s* one *d*. *Educ*: Rutherford Coll.; Armstrong Coll., Durham Univ. (MA, MLitt Dunelm); Westminster Coll., Cambridge. Ordained, 1937; inducted, Clayport, Alnwick, 1937; served with YMCA in France, 1940. Inducted: St Augustine's, New Barnet, 1944; St Columba's, North Shields, 1950. Gen. Sec., Presbyterian Church of England, 1960-72; Moderator, Presbyterian Church of England, 1971-72; Jt Gen.-Sec., URC, 1972-74; Moderator, URC, 1974-75. Vice-Pres., BCC, 1974-77 (Chm., Admin. Cttee, 1969-74). Director: FCFC and Tavistock Court Ltd; URC Insurance Co., etc. *Recreations*: gardening, golf, walking. *Address*: 7 Selvage Lane, Mill Hill, NW7 3SS. *T*: 01-959 2856.

MacARTHUR, Mrs Charles; see Hayes, Helen.

MACARTHUR, Charles Ramsay, QC (Scot.) 1970; Sheriff of the Lothians and Borders, 1974-76; *s* of late Alastair and late Joan Macarthur; *m* 1973, Rosemary Valda Morgan, Edinburgh. *Educ*: Glasgow Univ. (MA, LLB). Served War of 1939-45:

joined Royal Navy, 1942; demobilised as Lieut, RNVR, 1946. Solicitor, 1952-59; admitted Scottish Bar, 1960; Standing Junior Counsel, Highlands and Islands Development Board, 1968-70. *Recreations:* travel, talking. *Address:* 4 Wardie Road, Edinburgh EH5 3QD. *Clubs:* New (Edinburgh); RNVR (Scotland).

MacARTHUR, (David) Wilson, MA; author and freelance journalist; *b* 29 Aug. 1903; *s* of Dr Alex. MacArthur, MB, CM; *m* 1956, Patricia Knox Saunders; two *s. Educ:* The Academy, Ayr; Glasgow Univ. (MA Hons Eng. Lang. and Lit.). Fiction Editor, Daily Mail and Evening News, London, 1935. Travelled widely in Europe, America and Africa, 1929-39 (over 500 short stories and innumerable articles). Served War of 1939-45, RNVR. Overland by car London to S Africa, 1947, and again 1949-50. Settled in S Rhodesia, 1947; engaged in tree-farming as well as writing, broadcasting, etc. Publisher and Editor, the RTA Jl. *Publications:* Yellow Stockings, 1925; Lola of the Isles, 1926; Mystery of the "David M", 1929; Landfall, 1932; Quest of the Stormalong, 1934; Carlyle in Old Age, 1934; They Sailed for Senegal, 1938; Convict Captain, 1939; The Royal Navy, 1940; The North Patrol, 1941; The Road to the Nile, 1941; East India Adventure, 1945; The Young Chevalier, 1947; The River Windrush, 1946; The River Fowey, 1948; The River Conway, 1952; The River Doon, 1952; Auto Nomad in Sweden, 1948; Traders North, 1951; Auto Nomad in Barbary, 1950; Auto Nomad Through Africa, 1951; Auto Nomad in Spain, 1953; The Desert Watches, 1954; Simba Bwana, 1956; The Road from Chilanga, 1957; Zambesi Adventure, 1960; Harry Hogbin, 1961; Death at Slack Water, 1962; The Valley of Hidden Gold, 1962; Guns for the Congo, 1963; A Rhino in the Kitchen, 1964; The Past Dies Hard, 1965; under pseudonym of David Wilson, The Search for Geoffrey Goring, 1962; Murder in Mozambique, 1963. *Address:* PO Box 411, Marandellas, Rhodesia. *T:* Marandellas 3560.

MacARTHUR, Ian; Director, British Textile Confederation, since 1977; *b* 17 May 1925; *yr s* of late Lt-Gen. Sir William MacArthur, KCB, DSO, MD, DSc, FRCP; *m* 1957, Judith Mary, (RGN 1976), *d* of late Francis Gavin Douglas Miller; three *s* three *d. Educ:* Cheltenham Coll.; The Queen's Coll., Oxford (Scholar, MA). Contested (U), Greenock Gen. Election, May 1955, also by-election, Dec. 1955; MP (C) Perth and E Perthshire, 1959-Sept. 1974; Chm., Scottish Cons. Mems' Cttee, 1972-73. Introduced, as Private Member's Bills: Law Reform (Damages and Solatium) (Scotland) Act, 1962; Interest on Damages (Scotland) Act, 1971; Social Work (Scotland) Act, 1972; Domicile and Matrimonial Proceedings Act, 1973. An Asst Government Whip (unpaid), 1962-63; a Lord Comr of the Treasury and Govt Scottish Whip, 1963-64; Opposition Scottish Whip, 1964-65; an Opposition Spokesman on Scottish Affairs, 1965-70. Personal Asst to the Prime Minister, Rt Hon. Sir Alec Douglas-Home, Kinross and W Perthshire By-Election, Nov. 1963. Hon. Pres., Scottish Young Unionists, 1962-65; Vice-Chm., Cons. Party in Scotland, 1972-75. Formerly Dir of Administration, J. Walter Thompson Co. Ltd. Served War of 1939-45, with RN and RNVR, 1943-46 (Flag Lieut to C-in-C Portsmouth, 1946). *Address:* 42 Roehampton Gate, SW15. *Clubs:* Naval; New (Edinburgh); Puffin's (Edinburgh); Royal County (Perth).

MacARTHUR, Wilson; see MacArthur, D. W.

MACARTHUR-ONSLOW, Maj.-Gen. Sir Denzil, Kt 1964; CBE 1951; DSO 1941; ED; *b* 5 March 1904; *s* of late F. A. Macarthur-Onslow; *m* 1st, 1927, Elinor Margaret (marr. diss. 1950), *d* of late Gordon Caldwell; three *s* one *d*; 2nd, 1950, Dorothy, *d* of W. D. Scott; one *s* one *d. Educ:* Tudor House Sch., Moss Vale; King's Sch., Parramatta, NSW. Commissioned Australian Field Artillery, 1924. Served War of 1939-45 in Middle East and New Guinea (despatches thrice, DSO). GOC 2nd Div. AMF, 1954-58; Citizen Forces Mem. of Australian Mil. Board, 1958-60. *Address:* Mount Gilead, Campbelltown, New South Wales; Camden Park, Menangle, NSW 2568, Australia. *Clubs:* Australian, Royal Sydney Golf, Australasian Pioneers (Sydney, NSW).

MACARTNEY, Carlile Aylmer; FBA 1965; MA, DLitt, Oxon; *b* 1895; *s* of late Carlile Henry Hayes Macartney; *m* Nedella, *d* of late Col Dimitri Mamarchev, Bulgarian Army; no *c. Educ:* Winchester (scholar, Pitt Exhibitioner); Trinity Coll., Cambridge (scholar). Served European War, 1914-18; HBM Vice-Consul (acting), Vienna, 1921-25; with Encyclopædia Britannica, 1926-28; Intelligence Dept, League of Nations Union, 1928-36; Research Dept, Foreign Office, 1939-46; Montagu Burton Prof. of International Relations, Edinburgh Univ., 1951-57; Research Fellow, All Souls Coll., Oxford, 1936-65, Fellow Emeritus, 1976. Former Mem., Sch. of Slavonic

Studies; Foreign Mem., Hungarian Acad., 1947-49; Corresp. Mem., Austrian Acad. of Sciences, 1974. Hon. DLitt Lancaster, 1977. Freeman, City of Cleveland, USA. Grand Decoration of Honour in Gold (Austria), 1974. *Publications:* The Social Revolution in Austria, 1926; Survey of International Affairs for 1925, Part II (with other authors) 1927; The Magyars in the Ninth Century, 1930 (2nd edn 1968); National States and National Minorities, 1934 (2nd edn 1968); Hungary (Modern World Series), 1934 (Hungarian edn, revised, 1936); Hungary and her Successors, 1937 (2nd edn 1965); Studies in the Earliest Hungarian Historical Sources, I-VIII, 1938-52; Problems of the Danube Basin, 1942 (Hungarian translation, 1943); The Mediæval Hungarian Historians, 1953; Oct. 15th, 1957 (2nd edn rev. 1961); (with A. W. Palmer) Independent Eastern Europe, 1961; Hungary: A Short History, 1962; The Habsburg Empire 1790-1918, 1969, 2nd edn 1971; Maria Theresa and the House of Austria, 1969; The Habsburg and Hohenzollern Dynasties in the Seventeenth and Eighteenth Centuries, 1970; contribs to Encyclopædia Britannica, 13th and 14th edns, Chambers's Encyclopædia, and to British and Central European Reviews; translations. *Recreation:* travel. *Address:* Hornbeams, Boars Hill, near Oxford. *T:* Oxford 735224.

MACARTNEY, Sir John Barrington, 6th Bt *cr* 1799, of Lish, Co. Armagh; dairy farmer; *b* 21 Jan. 1917; *s* of John Barrington Macartney (3rd *s* of Sir John Macartney, 3rd Bt; he *d* 1951) and Selina Koch, Hampton, Mackay, Qld, Australia; *S* uncle, Sir Alexander Miller Macartney, 5th Bt, 1960; *m* 1944, Amy Isobel Reinke; one *s. Heir: s* John Ralph Macartney [*b* 24 July 1945; *m* 1966, Suzanne Marle Fowler; one *d*]. *Address:* 37 Meadow Street, North Mackay, Qld 4740, Australia.

MACAULAY, Lt-Col Archibald Duncan Campbell, OBE 1961; Secretary, All England Lawn Tennis Club, Wimbledon, 1946-63; *b* 27 Sept. 1897; *o s* of late Major and Mrs A. Macaulay; unmarried. *Educ:* King's Sch., Canterbury. Served with The Buffs European War, 1914-18 in France, afterwards transferring to Indian Army, 7th Bn Gurkha Rifles, retiring in 1924. Referee and manager of many lawn tennis tournaments in United Kingdom, 1923-39; served with Royal Army Service Corps, 1939-45. *Publication:* Behind the Scenes at Wimbledon, 1965. *Address:* 804 Frobisher House, Dolphin Square, SW1V 3LX. *T:* 01-828 6657. *Clubs:* Naval and Military; All England Lawn Tennis (Wimbledon).

MACAULAY, Sir Hamilton, Kt 1960; CBE 1956; *b* 1901; *s* of late Hugh Stevenson Macaulay, Glasgow; *m* 1930, Marjorie Slinger, *d* of late Francis Gill, Litton, Yorks. *Educ:* Calder HG Sch., Glasgow. Served War of 1939-45 (despatches), Lt.-Col. Pres., Chittagong Chamber of Commerce, 1953-54, 1956-57 and 1959-60; Dep. Pres., Assoc. Chambers of Commerce of Pakistan, 1953-54. Chm., Chittagong Branch UK Assoc. of Pakistan, 1955-56 and 1959-60. Director, Rivers Steam Navigation Co. (Holdings) Ltd, London. *Recreation:* golf. *Address:* The Cottage, Harpers Road, Ash, Surrey. *Club:* Oriental.

MACAULAY, Janet Stewart Alison, MA; Headmistress of St Leonards and St Katharines Schools, St Andrews, 1956-70; *b* 20 Dec. 1909; 3rd *d* of late Rev. Prof. A. B. Macaulay, DD, of Trinity Coll., Glasgow. *Educ:* Laurel Bank Sch., Glasgow; Glasgow Univ.; Somerville Coll., Oxford. BA Oxon 1932; BLitt Oxon 1934; MA Oxon 1936. Asst Mistress, Wycombe Abbey Sch., Bucks, 1933-36; Sutton High Sch. (GPDST), Sutton, Surrey, 1937-45; Headmistress, Blackheath High Sch. (GPDST), 1945-Dec. 1955. Hon. LLD St Andrews, 1977. *Address:* 3 Drummond Place, Edinburgh 3; Grampian Cottage, Kincraig, Inverness-shire.

McAULY, John Roy Vincent; a Recorder of the Crown Court, since 1975; Barrister-at-law, practising in London and on Midland and Oxford Circuit; *b* 9 Sept. 1933; *er s* of Dr John McAulay and Mrs Marty McAulay (née Hüni), West Wickham, Kent; *m* 1970, Ruth Hamilton Smith, Sundridge, Kent; one *s* one *d. Educ:* Whitgift Sch. (Victoria Scholar); Queens' Coll., Cambridge (MA Hons). National Service, Intelligence Corps, 1951-53. Called to Bar, Gray's Inn, 1957 (Lord Justice Holker Scholar); Recorder, Midland Circuit, 1965-67; Mem., Gen. Council of Bar, 1967-71. *Publications:* contrib. Halsbury's Laws of England, 3rd and 4th edns, and other legal pubns. *Recreations:* walking, swimming. *Address:* 1 Harcourt Buildings, Temple, EC4. *T:* 01-353 0375; Highcote House, Bromley Road, Shortlands, Kent. *T:* 01-464 9877. *Clubs:* United Services (Nottingham); Northampton and County (Northampton).

MACAULAY, Hon. Leopold, QC (Canada); BA, LLB, DLS; Barrister, retired; Vice-President, Canadian Red Cross Society; *b* Peterboro, Ont., 25 Nov. 1887; *s* of Robert Macaulay and

Agnes Giroux, Canadians; *m* ; two *s* one *d* ; *m* 1963, Kathleen H. Sherk, Midland, Mich., USA. *Educ:* Lindsay Public Sch.; Harbord Collegiate, Toronto; Univ. of Toronto; Osgoode Hall, Toronto. Provincial Sec. and Registrar of the Province of Ontario, Canada, 1930-31; Minister of Highways, Ontario, 1931-34, and Minister of Public Works, 1934; Pres. Univ. of Toronto Alumni Fedn, 1937-38; Conservative Mem. for South York Riding, Ont., 1926-43; retired 1943; Chm., National Council, Red Cross, Canada, 1951-52; Chm. Board of Regents, Victoria Univ., Toronto, 1951-58. *Recreation:* golf. *Address:* 95 River View Drive, Toronto, Ontario, Canada M4N 3C6. *Clubs:* Rosedale Golf, National.

McAVOY, Sir (Francis) Joseph, Kt 1976; CBE 1969; Chairman: Queensland Canegrowers Council, since 1963 (Member since 1952); Australian Canegrowers Council, since 1952; *b* 26 Feb. 1910; *s* of William Henry McAvoy and Hanorah Catherine McAvoy; *m* 1936, Mary Irene Doolan; four *s* (one *d* decd). *Educ:* Nudgee Coll., Brisbane; Sacred Heart Convent, Innisfail, Qld. Member: Goondi Mill Suppliers Cttee, 1946-79; Innisfail Canegrowers Exec., 1949-79; Metric Conversion Bd (Aust.), 1970-78; Exec. Council of Agriculture, 1963-79; Exec., Aust. Farmers Fedn, 1969-77. *Recreation:* lawn bowls. *Address:* Avoca, Daradgee, Qld 4860, Australia. *T:* 633224. *Clubs:* Rotary (Innisfail, Qld); United Services (Brisbane).

MACBEATH, Prof. Alexander Murray, PhD (Princeton, NJ); MA (Cantab); FRSE; Mason Professor of Pure Mathematics, University of Birmingham, since 1962; *b* 30 June 1923; *s* of late Prof. Alexander Macbeath, CBE; *m* 1951, Julie Ormrod, Lytham St Anne's; two *s. Educ:* Royal Belfast Academical Inst.; Queen's Univ., Belfast; Clare Coll., Cambridge. Entrance Schol., Dixon Prize in Maths, Purser Studentship, 1st class hons in Maths, BA, QUB. Temp. post with Foreign Office, 1943-45. Cambridge, 1945-48; Maj. Entrance Schol., Wrangler Math. Tripos, Part II, dist. Part III, BA, Owst Prize. Commonwealth Fund Fellowship, Princeton, NJ, 1948-50; Smith's Prize, 1949; PhD Princeton, 1950. Research Fellow, Clare Coll., Cambridge, 1950-51; MA Cambridge, 1951. Lectr in Maths, Univ. Coll. of North Staffordshire, 1951-53; Prof. of Maths, Queen's Coll., Dundee, 1953-62. Visiting Professor: California Inst. of Technology, 1966-67; Univ. of Pittsburgh, 1974-75. *Publications:* Elementary Vector Algebra, 1964; papers in: Jl London Mathematical Soc.; Proc. London Math. Soc.; Proc. Cambridge Philosophical Soc.; Quarterly Jl of Mathematics; Annals of Mathematics; Canadian Jl of Mathematics. *Recreation:* swimming. *Address:* 51 Shakespeare Drive, Shirley, Solihull, West Midlands.

McBEATH, Rear-Admiral John (Edwin Home), CB 1957; DSO 1940; DSC 1941; DL; retired, 1958; *b* 27 Sept. 1907; *er s* of late Mr and Mrs J. H. McBeath, Natal, S Africa; *m* 1952, Hon. Janet Mary Blades, *y d* of 1st Baron Ebbisham, GBE; one *s* one *d. Educ:* Massachusetts, USA; Hilton Coll., Natal, S Africa. Entered Royal Navy, 1923; Comdr 1941; Captain, 1945; Rear-Admiral, 1955. During War of 1939-45 commanded destroyers in North Sea, Atlantic, Arctic, Mediterranean (despatches). HM Naval Base, Singapore, 1945-48; Comd First Destroyer Flotilla, Mediterranean Fleet, 1948-50; Chief of Staff to Flag Officer Commanding Reserve Fleet, 1950-52; Commodore, Royal Naval Barracks, Devonport, 1953-55; lent to RNZN, 1955; Chief of Naval Staff and First Member Naval Board, RNZN, 1955-58. ADC to the Queen, 1955. Hon. Commodore, Sea Cadet Corps, 1958-75. DL Surrey, 1968, High Sheriff, 1973-74. Chevalier, Order of Merit (France), 1939. *Address:* Woodbury House, Churt, Surrey. *T:* Headley Down 2275. *Club:* Army and Navy.

MacBETH, George Mann; writer; *b* Scotland, 1932; *s* of George MacBeth and Amelia Morton Mary Mann; *m* 1955, Elizabeth Browell Robson. *Educ:* New Coll., Oxford (read Classics and Philosophy). BBC, 1955-76: Producer, Overseas Talks Dept, 1957; Producer, Talks Dept, 1958; Editor: Poet's Voice, 1958-65; New Comment, 1959-64; Poetry Now, 1965-76. Sir Geoffrey Faber Memorial Award (jointly), 1964; (jtly) Cholmondeley Award, 1977. *Publications: poems:* A Form of Words, 1954; The Broken Places, 1963; A Doomsday Book, 1965; The Colour of Blood, 1967; The Night of Stones, 1968; A War Quartet, 1969; The Burning Cone, 1970; Collected Poems 1958-1970, 1971; The Orlando Poems, 1971; Shrapnel, 1973; A Poet's Year, 1973; In The Hours Waiting For The Blood To Come, 1975; Buying a Heart, 1977; *prose poems:* My Scotland, 1973; *prose:* The Transformation, 1975; The Samurai, 1975; The Survivor, 1977; *anthologies:* The Penguin Book of Sick Verse, 1963; (with J. Clemo and E. Lucie-Smith) Penguin Modern Poets VI, 1964; The Penguin Book of Animal Verse, 1965; (with notes) Poetry, 1900-1965, 1967; The Penguin Book of Victorian Verse, 1968; The Falling Splendour, 1970; The Book of Cats, 1976; *children's*

book: Johah and the Lord, 1969. *Recreation:* motoring. *Address:* 44 Sheen Road, Richmond, Surrey.

McBRIDE, Rt. Hon. Sir Philip Albert Martin, PC 1959; KCMG 1953; *b* 18 June 1892; *s* of late Albert J. McBride, Adelaide; *m* 1914, Rita I., *d* of late E. W. Crews, Kooringa, South Australia; two *s* (and one *s* decd). *Educ:* Burra Public Sch., South Australia; Prince Alfred Coll. MHR for Grey, South Australia, 1931-34; for Wakefield, S Australia, 1946-; Member of Senate for S Australia, 1937-43; Minister without Portfolio assisting Minister for Commerce, March-Aug. 1940; Minister: for the Army and for Repatriation, Aug.-Oct. 1940; for Supply and Development, Oct. 1940-June 1941; for Munitions, 1940-41; Mem. Australian Advisory War Council, Aug.-Oct. 1941; Mem. Economic Cabinet, 1939-40, and War Cabinet, 1940-41; Dep. Leader of Opposition in Senate, 1941-43; Minister for the Interior, 1949-50; Acting Minister for Defence, April-Oct. 1950; Minister: for Defence, 1950-58; for the Navy and for Air, May-July 1951; Leader of Australian Govt Delegn to Defence Conf., London, 1951. *Recreation:* tennis. *Address:* 30 Briar Avenue, Medindie, SA 5081, Australia. *Clubs:* Adelaide (Adelaide); Australian (Melbourne).

McBRIDE, Commandant (Sara) Vonla (Adair); Hon. ADC; Director, Women's Royal Naval Service, since 1976; *b* 20 Jan. 1921; *d* of late Andrew Stewart McBride and Agnes McBride. *Educ:* Ballymena Acad., NI; TCD (Moderatorship in Mod. Lit; BA Hons). MBIM. Teacher of English and French, Ballymena Acad., 1942-45; Housemistress, Gardenhurst Sch., Burnham-on-Sea, Somerset, 1945-49. Joined WRNS, 1949; Hon. ADC to the Queen, 1976. *Publication:* Never at Sea (autobiog.), 1966. *Recreations:* golf, amateur dramatics, entertaining, continental travel. *Address:* Flat 11, 8 The Paragon, Blackheath, SE3. *T:* 01-852 8673.

McBRIDE, Seán; Senior Counsel, Irish Bar; Assistant Secretary-General, United Nations, and United Nations Commissioner for Namibia, 1973-77; *b* 27 Jan. 1904; *s* of late Major John MacBride and late Maud Gonne; *m* 1926, Catalina Bulfin; one *s* one *d. Educ:* St Louis de Ganzague, Paris, Mount St Benedict, Gorey, Co. Wexford, Ireland. Was active in movement for Irish independence and suffered imprisonment in 1918, 1922 and 1930; was Sec. to Mr de Valera; decorated by Irish Govt for Military services in Ireland, 1938. Was a journalist for a number of years before being called to Irish Bar, 1937; Irish correspondent for Havas and some American and South African papers before War of 1939-45. Called to Bar, 1937; called to Inner Bar, 1943; holds record of having become a Senior Counsel in a shorter period of time than any other living member of the Bar; defended many sensational capital cases and had an extensive practice in High Court and Supreme Court. Founder, 1946, and Leader of political party, Clann na Poblachta (Republican Party). Member of Dail Eireann, 1947-58; Minister for External Affairs, Eire, 1948-51. Pres., Council of Foreign Ministers of Council of Europe, 1950; Vice-Pres., OEEC, 1948-51; declined ministerial portfolio, June 1954, on ground of inadequate parliamentary representation; delegate to Council of Europe from Ireland, 1954. Trustee, Internat. Prisoners of Conscience Fund; Mem. Exec., Pan-European Union; Consultant to late President K. N'Krumah in relation to forming OAU; Mem., European Round Table; Mem., Ghana Bar; International Congress of Jurists, New Delhi, 1958 and Rio de Janeiro, 1962; Chm., Irish Assoc. of Jurists; one of the founders of Amnesty International and Chm. Internat. Exec., 1961-75; President: Internat. Commn of Jurists (Sec.-Gen. of the Commn, 1963-70, Mem., 1971-); Internat. Peace Bureau, Geneva, 1972-. Elected to Internat. Gaelic Hall of Fame, 1974; Man of the Year, Irish United Socs, 1975. Nobel Peace Prize (jtly), 1974; Lenin Internat. Prize for Peace, 1977. LLD (hc): Coll. of St Thomas, Minnesota, 1975; Guelph Univ., Canada, 1977; DLitt (*hc*), Bradford Univ., 1977. *Publications:* Civil Liberty, 1948 (pamphlet); Our People—Our Money, 1951. *Recreation:* sailing. *Address:* Roebuck House, Clonskea, Dublin 14. *T:* Dublin 694225; United Nations, New York, NY 10017, USA; PO Box 3550, Lusaka, Zambia.

McBRIDE, Vonla; see McBride, S. V. A.

McBRIDE, William Griffith, AO 1977; CBE 1969; MD, FRCOG; Consultant Obstetrician and Gynaecologist: The Women's Hospital, Sydney, since 1966; St George Hospital, Sydney, since 1957; *b* 25 May 1927; *s* of late John McBride, Sydney; *m* 1957, Patricia Mary, *d* of Robert Louis Glover; two *s* two *d. Educ:* Canterbury High Sch., Sydney; Univ. of Sydney; Univ. of London. MB, BS Sydney 1950; MRCOG 1954; MD Sydney 1962; FRCOG 1968; FAGO 1972. Resident: St George Hosp., Sydney, 1950; Launceston Hosp., 1951; Med. Supt, Women's Hosp., Sydney, 1955-57; Cons. Gynaecologist,

Bankstown Hosp., Sydney, 1957-66. Lectr in Obstetrics and Gynaecology, Univ. of Sydney, 1957-; Examr in Obstetrics and Gynaecology, Univ. of Sydney, 1960-; Medical Dir, Foundation 41 for the study of congenital abnormalities and mental retardation, 1972-. Vis. Prof. of Gynaecology, Univ. of Bangkok, 1968. Mem., WHO Sub-Cttee on safety of oral contraceptives, 1971-. Pres. Sect. of Obstetrics and Gynæcology, AMA, 1966-73. Fellow, Senate of Univ. of Sydney. Member: Faculty of Medicine, Univ. of NSW; Soc. of Reproductive Biology; Endocrine Soc.; Teratology Soc. BP Prize of Institut de la Vie, 1971 (for Discovery of the Teratogenic effects of the Drug Thalidomide; first person to alert the world to the dangers of this drug and possibly other drugs). *Publications:* Drugs, 1960-70; contrib. (on Teratogenic Effect of the Drug Thalidomide), Lancet 1961 (London); numerous papers in Internat. Med. Jls. *Recreations:* tennis, swimming, riding. *Address:* 183 Macquarie Street, Sydney, NSW 2000, Australia. *T:* 221-3898. *Clubs:* Union, Australian Jockey, American National, Royal Sydney Golf (all in Sydney).

McBURNEY, Prof. Charles Brian Montagu, FBA 1966; FSA, MA, PhD, ScD; Professor of Quaternary Prehistory, University of Cambridge, since 1977; Fellow and Director of Studies in Archæology and Anthropology, Corpus Christi College, Cambridge, since 1962; *b* 18 June 1914; *s* of Henry McBurney and Dorothy Lilian (*née* Rundall); *m* 1953, Anne Frances Edmonstone Charles; two *s* one *d*. *Educ:* privately; King's Coll., Cambridge (BA 1937). Research Fellow, King's Coll., Cambridge, 1940-53; Univ. Lectr in Archæology, 1953-67, Reader 1967-77, Prof. (personal chair), 1977-. Membre d'honneur, Soc. Jersiaise. Hon. Corresp. Mem. Istituto Italiano di Paleontologia Umana, Rome. Knight of Order of the Dannebrog (First Class), 1961. *Publications:* (with R. W. Hey) Prehistory and Pleistocene Geology of Cyrenaican Libya, 1955; The Stone Age of Northern Africa, 1960; The Haua Fteah (Cyrenaica) and the Stone Age of the SE Mediterranean, 1967; (ed jtly) France before the Romans, 1974; articles on early prehistory of Iran, Libya, Central and SW Europe, and Britain in Proc. Brit. Acad., Proc. Prehistoric Soc., Jl of Royal Anthropological Inst., L'Anthropologie, Encyclopædia Britannica, etc. *Recreations:* trout fishing, walking, travelling. *Address:* 5 Grange Road, Cambridge. *T:* Cambridge 51385. *Club:* United Oxford & Cambridge University.

McBURNEY, Air Vice-Marshal Ralph Edward, CBE 1945; CD; RCAF, retired; *b* Montreal, Quebec, 17 Aug. 1906; *s* of Irville Albert and Lilian McBurney, Saskatoon, Sask.; *m* 1931, Gertrude Elizabeth Bate, Saskatoon; two *s* one *d*. *Educ:* Univs of Saskatchewan and Manitoba. BSc (EE); Commenced flying training as a cadet in RCAF, 1924; Pilot Officer, 1926; employed on Forest Fire Patrols and photographic mapping; Course in RAF School of Army Co-operation and tour as Instructor in RCAF School of Army Co-operation, 1931; Course at RAF Wireless School, Cranwell, and tour as Signals Adviser at Air Force HQ, Ottawa, 1935-36; RAF Staff Coll., Andover, 1939; Dir of Signals, AFHQ, Ottawa, 1939-42; CO, RCAF Station, Trenton, Ont., 1943; CO, RCAF Station, Dishforth, Yorks, 1943; Air Cdre 1944; Base Comdr of 61 Training Base, and later, 64 Operational Base in No 6 (RCAF) Bomber Group of Bomber Comd; SASO of the Group, Dec. 1944; AOC RCAF Maintenance Comd, 1945-46; Senior Canadian Air Force Liaison Officer, London, 1946-48; AOC Air Materiel Comd, RCAF, Ottawa, 1948-52. Business Consultant, 1952-60; Chief, Technical Information Service, Nat. Research Council, Ottawa, 1960-72. Pres., Internat. Fedn for Documentation, 1968-72. *Address:* 2022 Sharon Avenue, Ottawa, Ontario K2A 1L8, Canada.

MacCABE, Brian Farmer, MC and Bar, 1942; Chairman, Foote, Cone & Belding Ltd (London), since 1948; Director and Senior Vice-President, Foote, Cone & Belding Communications Inc. (New York), since 1953; *b* 9 Jan. 1914; *s* of late James MacCabe and Katherine MacCabe (*née* Harwood); *m* 1940, Eileen Elizabeth Noel Hunter; one *s*. *Educ:* Christ's Coll., London. Executive, C. R. Casson Ltd, 1934-40. Major, RTR (Sqdn Comd, Alamein; Instructor Turkish Staff Coll., Ankara), 1940-45. World-wide Advertising Manager, BOAC, 1945-47; Chm., FCB International Inc. (NY), 1967-74. Mem. Council: Inst. of Practitioners in Advertising, 1951- (Pres., 1963-65); Advertising Assoc., 1952-69 (Mem. Exec. Cttee, 1975-); Internat. Marketing Programme, 1965-. Mem., Reith Commn on Advertising, 1962-66; Dir, American Chamber of Commerce, 1971-; Member: Promotion Cttee, BNEC, 1965-68; Marketing Cttee, Ashridge Management Coll., 1965-; Advertising Standards Authority, 1969-72; Appeals Cttee, Olympic and Commonwealth Games, 1952-; Management Cttee, British Sports Assoc. for the Disabled, 1962-65; Nat. Council, Brit. Polio Fellowship, 1959-65. Royal Humane Soc. Medal for saving life at sea, 1934;

awards for services to advertising, 1957-. *Recreations:* finalist: (800 metres) Olympic Games, Berlin, 1936; (880 yards) British Commonwealth Games, Sydney, 1938; golf, fishing, sailing. *Address:* Somerford, Penn Road, Beaconsfield, Bucks. *T:* Beaconsfield 3365. *Clubs:* Boodle's, Garrick; Wasps RFC; LAC (Vice-Pres.), Bucks AA (Vice-Pres.), Beaconsfield Golf, Denham Golf; Royal Malta Yacht.

McCABE, John; professional musician; composer and pianist; *b* 21 April 1939; *s* of Frank and Elisabeth McCabe; *m* 1974, Monica Christine Smith. *Educ:* Liverpool Institute High Sch. for Boys; Manchester Univ. (MusBac); Royal Manchester Coll. of Music (ARMCM); Hochschule für Musik, Munich. Pianist-in-residence, University Coll., Cardiff, 1965-68; freelance musical criticism, 1966-71. Career as composer and pianist: many broadcasts and recordings as well as concert appearances in various countries. Prizewinner in Gaudeamus Competition for Interpreters of Contemporary Music, Holland, 1969. First European concert tour, 1971; first tour in USA and Canada, 1973. Recordings incl. 16-record set of complete piano music by Haydn; complete piano music of Nielsen (2 records). Awarded Special Citation by Koussevitsky Internat. Recording Foundn of USA, for recording of Symph. No 2 and Notturni ed Alba, 1974; Special Award by Composers' Guild of Gt Brit. (services to Brit. music), 1975; Ivor Novello Award (TV theme tune, Sam), 1977. Hon. FRMCM. *Publications:* many compositions, incl. two operas, ballets, symphonies, concerti, orchestral works incl. The Chagall Windows and Hartmann Variations, Notturni ed Alba, for soprano and orch., chamber music, keyboard works, and vocal compositions. Rachmaninov (short biog.), 1974; Bartok's Orchestral Music (BBC Music Guide), 1974; reviews in Guardian, New Statesman, Records and Recordings, etc. *Recreations:* cricket, books, films. *Address:* 49 Burns Avenue, Southall, Mddx. *T:* 01-574 5039.

McCABE, Most Rev. Thomas, DD; *b* 30 June 1902; *s* of John Patrick and Elizabeth McCabe. *Educ:* St Augustine's School, Coffs Harbour, NSW; St Columba's College, Springwood, NSW; St Patrick's College, Manly, NSW; Propaganda College, Rome. Ordained Priest in Rome, 1925; Administrator of St Carthage's Cathedral, Lismore, NSW, 1931-39; Bishop of Port Augusta, 1939-52; Bishop of Wollongong, 1952-74; retired 1974. *Address:* St Scholastica's Convent, 2 Avenue Road, Glebe Point, NSW 2037, Australia.

McCAFFREY, Thos Daniel; Chief Press Secretary to the Prime Minister, since 1976; *b* 20 Feb. 1922; *s* of William P. and B. McCaffrey; *m* 1949, Agnes Campbell Douglas; two *s* four *d*. *Educ:* Hyndland Secondary Sch. and St Aloysius Coll., Glasgow. Served War, RAF, 1940-46. Scottish Office, 1948-61; Chief Information Officer, Home Office, 1966-71; Press Secretary, 10 Downing Street, 1971-72; Dir of Information Services, Home Office, 1972-74; Head of News Dept, FCO, 1974-76. *Address:* Balmaha, The Park, Great Bookham, Surrey. *T:* Bookham 54171.

MacCAIG, Norman (Alexander); *b* 14 Nov. 1910; *s* of Robert McCaig and Joan MacLeod; *m* 1940, Isabel Munro; one *s* one *d*. *Educ:* Edinburgh University. MA Hons Classics. Schoolteacher, 1932-67 and 1969-70; Fellow in Creative Writing, Univ. of Edinburgh, 1967-69; Lectr in English Studies, Univ. of Stirling, 1970-72, Reader in Poetry, 1972-77. Cholmondeley Award, 1975. *Publications:* poetry: Far Cry, 1943; The Inward Eye, 1946; Riding Lights, 1955; The Sinai Sort, 1957; A Common Grace, 1960; A Round of Applause, 1962; Measures, 1965; Surroundings, 1966; Rings on a Tree, 1968; A Man in My Position, 1969; The White Bird, 1973; The World's Room, 1974; Tree of Strings, 1977; (ed anthology) Honour'd Shade; (with Alexander Scott, ed anthology) Contemporary Scottish Verse. *Recreations:* fishing, music. *Address:* 7 Leamington Terrace, Edinburgh EH10 4JW. *T:* 031-229 1809. *Club:* Scottish Arts (Edinburgh).

McCALL, Charles James, ROI 1949; DA (Edinburgh); artist-painter; *b* 24 Feb. 1907; *s* of late William McCall, Edinburgh; *m* 1945, Eloise Jerwood, *d* of late F. Ward, Bickley, Kent. *Educ:* Edinburgh Univ.; Edinburgh College of Art. RSA Travelling Schol., 1933; Edinburgh College of Art: Travelling Schol., 1936 (Fellow, 1938). Studied in many art galleries in Europe; also in studios in Paris. Returned to London in 1938, exhibiting RA, NEAC, London Group, etc. Commissioned, RE 1940; at end of war taught drawing and painting at Formation College. Has exhibited regularly in London; one-man shows held at: Leicester Galleries, 1950 and 1953; Victor Waddington Galleries, Dublin, 1951; Duveen Graham Galleries, New York, 1955 and 1957; Crane Galleries, Manchester, 1955; Klinkhoff Gallery, Montreal, 1958 and 1960; Whibley Gallery, London, 1963; Federation of British Artists, 1965; Ash Barn Gallery, Stroud,

1965, 1969, 1973; Eaton's Gallery, Winnipeg, Canada, 1966; Nevill Gallery, Canterbury, 1972; Belgrave Gallery, 1975, 1977. BBC TV Programme on his life and work, 1975. Painter of portraits, landscapes, interiors with figures, and of contemporary life. NEAC 1957. Lord Mayor's Art Award, 1963, 1973, 1977. *Recreations:* music, literature, travel. *Address:* 1a Caroline Terrace, SW1W 8JS. *T:* 01-730 8737.

McCALL, Sir (Charles) Patrick (Home), Kt 1971; MBE 1944; TD 1946; solicitor; Clerk of the County Council, 1960-72, Clerk of the Peace, 1960-71, and Clerk of the Lieutenancy, Lancashire, 1960-74; *b* 22 Nov. 1910; *s* of late Charles and Dorothy McCall; *m* 1934, Anne, *d* of late Samuel Brown, Sedlescombe, Sussex; two *s* one *d. Educ:* St Edward's Sch., Oxford. Served 1939-45; Substantive Major TA. Hon. Lt-Col. Mem., Economic and Social Cttee, Commn of European Communities, Brussels. *Recreations:* travel, walking, swimming, gardening. *Address:* Auchenhay Lodge, Corsock, by Castle Douglas, Kirkcudbrightshire. *T:* Corsock 651. *Club:* Royal Automobile. See also R. H. McCall.

McCALL, Adm. Sir Henry (William Urquhart), KCVO 1953; KBE 1951; CB 1949; DSO 1942; retired; *b* 11 June 1895; *s* of Henry John McCall, Largs, Ayrshire, and Isobel Alston McCall (née Dykes); *m* 1926, Helen Mary Leycester; two *d. Educ:* RN Colleges, Osborne and Dartmouth. Entered RNC Osborne, 1908; Lieut 1917; Comdr 1931; Capt. 1937; Naval Attaché, Buenos Aires, 1938-40; comd HMS Dido, 1940-42; Chief of Staff to Head of British Admiralty Delegn, Washington, 1943; comd HMS Howe, 1944-46; Rear-Adm. 1946; Senior British Naval Officer, Middle East, 1946-48; Flag Officer Destroyers, Mediterranean Fleet, 1949-50; Vice-Adm. 1950; Vice-Adm. Commanding Reserve Fleet, 1950-53; Adm. 1953; Retd Sept. 1953. *Address:* Wonston Lee, Wonston, near Winchester, Hants. *T:* Sutton Scotney 344. *Club:* Naval and Military. See also Sir H. C. Leach.

McCALL, John Armstrong Grice, CMG 1964; Assistant Chief Administrative Officer, East Kilbride Development Corporation, 1967-76; *b* 7 Jan. 1913; 2nd *s* of Rev. Canon J. G. McCall; *m* 1951, Kathleen Mary Clarke; no *c. Educ:* Glasgow Academy; Trinity Coll., Glenalmond; St Andrews Univ.; St John's Coll., Cambridge. MA 1st class hons Hist. St Andrews, 1935. Colonial Administrative Service (HMOCS), Nigeria, 1935-67; Cadet, 1936; Class I, 1956; Staff Grade, 1958. Chm., Mid-Western Nigeria Development Corp., Benin City, 1966-67, retired 1967. Scottish Rep., Organizing Cttee, Nigeria-British Chamber of Commerce, 1977-. Mem. 1969, Vice-Chm. 1971, S Lanarkshire Local Employment Cttee; Mem. Panel, Industrial Tribunals (Scotland), 1972-74. *Recreations:* golf, walking. *Address:* Burnside, West Linton, Peeblesshire. *T:* West Linton 488. *Clubs:* Caledonian; Royal and Ancient (St Andrews).

McCALL, John Donald; Director, Consolidated Gold Fields Ltd (Chairman, 1969-76); *b* 1 Feb. 1911; *s* of late Gilbert Kerr McCall; *m* 1942, Vere Stewart Gardner; one *s* one *d. Educ:* Clifton Coll.; Edinburgh Univ. Gold Mining industry, S Africa, 1930-39. Served War of 1939-45: commissioned, Gordon Highlanders. Joined Consolidated Gold Fields Ltd, London, 1946 (Dir, 1959; Jt Dep. Chm., 1968). *Recreations:* gardening, golf. *Address:* 49 Moorgate, EC2R 6BQ. *T:* 01-606 1020. *Club:* Caledonian.

McCALL, Kenneth Murray, DL; Lord Lieutenant of Dumfriesshire, 1970-72; *b* 21 Dec. 1912; *s* of late Major William McCall, DL; *m* 1938, Christina Eve Laurie; two *s* two *d. Educ:* Merchiston Castle School. DL Dumfriesshire, 1973. *Recreations:* shooting, golf. *Address:* Caitloch, Moniaive, Thornhill, Dumfriesshire. *T:* Moniaive 211.

McCALL, Sir Patrick; see McCall, Sir C. P. H.

McCALL, Robin Home, CBE 1976 (OBE 1969); retired 1976; *b* 21 March 1912; *s* of late Charles and Dorothy McCall; *m* 1937, Joan Elizabeth Kingdon; two *s* one *d. Educ:* St Edward's Sch., Oxford. Solicitors Final (Hons), 1935. Served War, RAFVR Night Fighter Controller (Sqdn Ldr); D Day landing Normandy, in command of 15083 GCI, 1944. Asst Solicitor: Bexhill Corp., 1935-39; Hastings Corp., 1939-46; Bristol Corp., 1946-47; Dep. Town Clerk, Hastings, 1947-48; Town Clerk and Clerk of the Peace, Winchester, 1948-72; Sec., Assoc. of Municipal Corporations, later Assoc. of Metropolitan Authorities, 1973-76. Hon. Sec., Non-County Boroughs Cttee for England and Wales, 1958-69; Member: Reading Cttee (Highway Law Consolidation); Morris Cttee (Jury Service); Kennett Preservation Gp (Historic Towns Conservation); Exec. Cttee, European Architectural Heritage Year, 1972-; UK delegn to ECLA (Council of Europe); North Hampshire Hosp. Cttee,

1969-72. *Publications:* various articles and reviews on local govt. *Recreations:* gardening, mountains. *Address:* The Hospice, St Giles Hill, Winchester. *T:* Winchester 4101. *Clubs:* Reform, Alpine.

McCALL, William; General Secretary, Institution of Professional Civil Servants, since 1963; *b* 6 July 1929; *s* of Alexander McCall and Jean Corbet Cunningham; *m* 1955, Olga Helen Brunton; one *s* one *d. Educ:* Dumfries Academy; Ruskin College, Oxford. Civil Service, 1946-52; Social Insurance Dept, TUC, 1954-58; Asst Sec., Instn of Professional Civil Servants, 1958-63; Mem., Civil Service Nat. Whitley Council (Staff Side), 1963-, Chm. 1969-71. Mem., Management Cttee, Social Policy Research Ltd, 1976-; Hon. Treasurer, Parly Scientific Cttee, 1976-; Part-time Mem., Eastern Electricity Board, 1977-. *Recreations:* reading, walking, talking. *Address:* Bayston, Cross Oak Road, Berkhamsted, Herts. *T:* Berkhamsted 4974.

McCALLUM, Archibald Duncan Dugald, TD 1950; MA; Headmaster, Strathallan School, 1970-75; *b* 26 Nov. 1914; *s* of late Dr A. D. McCallum and Mrs A. D. McCallum; *m* 1950, Rosemary Constance, widow of Sqdn Ldr John Rhind, RAF, and *d* of William C. Thorne, OBE, Edinburgh; two *s* (one step *s*). *Educ:* Fettes Coll., Edinburgh; St John's Coll., Cambridge (Classical Sizar). Asst Master and Housemaster, Fettes Coll., 1937-39, 1945-51. Served War of 1939-45 (despatches): Home Forces, India, and Burma. Second Master, Strathallan Sch., 1951-56; Headmaster: Christ Coll., Brecon, 1956-62; Epsom Coll., 1962-70. FRSA 1969-75. *Recreations:* Rugby football, golf, reading. *Address:* 1 Church Row Cottages, Burnham Market, King's Lynn, Norfolk.

McCALLUM, Brig. Frank, CIE 1947; OBE 1936; MC 1923; DL; *b* 11 March 1900; *s* of late Lt-Col D. McCallum, RASC, Edinburgh; *m* 1932, Sybilla Mary de Symons (OBE 1977; County Councillor for Kesteven, Lincs, 1974-76), *d* of late Gen. Sir George Barrow, GCB, KCMG; one *s* (and one *s* decd). *Educ:* George Watson's Coll.; RMC. Commissioned 1918; Brig. 1943. ADC to GOC-in-C Eastern Comd, India, 1928-29; Staff Coll., Quetta, 1934-35; Bde Major, Razmak, 1936-39; GSO2 Meerut Dist, 1940-41; served in Iraq, Persia, Western Desert, and Syria, 1941-46; GSO1, 8 Indian Div., 1941-43; Bde Comd, 1943-46; BGS Northern Comd, India, 1946-47; Dir Staff Duties, Army HQ, Pakistan, 1947. Served 3rd Afghan War, 1919; NWF, 1920-21 and 1923 (MC); NWF, 1936 (OBE) and 1937-39; despatches 7 times, 1936-46; retd 30 May 1948. Asst Regional Food Officer, North Midland Region, 1948-51; Regional Sec. Country Landowners Assoc. for Lincs, Notts, and Derbs, 1951-65; CC Kesteven, Lincolnshire, 1952-74, Alderman, 1964-74. DL Lincolnshire, 1965. Syrian Order of Merit, 1st Class, 1945-46. *Address:* Westborough Grange, near Newark, Notts NG23 5HH. *T:* Long Bennington 285.

McCALLUM, Googie; see Withers, Googie.

McCALLUM, John Neil, CBE 1971; Chairman and Executive Producer, Fauna Films, Australia, since 1967, and John McCallum Productions, since 1976; actor and producer; *b* 14 March 1918; *s* of John Neil McCallum and Lilian Elsie (née Dyson); *m* 1948, Georgette Lizette Withers (see Googie Withers); one *s* two *d. Educ:* Oatlands Prep. Sch., Harrogate; Knox Grammar Sch., Sydney; C of E Grammar Sch., Brisbane; RADA. Served War, 2/5 Field Regt, AIF, 1941-45. Actor, English rep. theatres, 1937-39; Stratford-on-Avon Festival Theatre, 1939; Old Vic Theatre, 1940; British films and theatre, 1946-58; films include: It Always Rains On Sunday; Valley of Eagles; Miranda; London stage plays include: Roar Like a Dove; Janus; Waiting for Gillian; J. C. Williamson Theatres Ltd, Australia: Asst Man. Dir, 1958; Jt. Man. Dir, 1959-65; Man. Dir, 1966. Appeared in: (with Ingrid Bergman) The Constant Wife, London, 1973-74; (with Googie Withers) The Circle, London, 1976-77. Author of play, As It's Played Today, produced Melbourne, 1974. Produced television series, 1967-72: Boney; Barrier Reef; Skippy. Pres., Aust. Film Council, 1971-72. *Recreation:* golf. *Address:* 1740 Pittwater Road, Bayview, NSW 2104, Australia. *T:* Sydney 9976879. *Clubs:* Garrick; Melbourne (Melbourne); Australian, Elanora Country (Sydney).

McCANCE, Sir Andrew, Kt 1947; DSc; LLD; FRS 1943; DL; Chairman, Colville Clugston Shanks Ltd; *b* 30 March 1889; *yr s* of John McCance; *m* 1936, Joya Harriett Gladys Burford (*d* 1969); two *d. Educ:* Morrison's Academy, Crieff; Allan Glen's Sch., Glasgow; Royal School of Mines, London. DSc London, 1916. Asst Armour Manager, W. Beardmore & Co., 1910-19; Founder and Man. Dir, Clyde Alloy Steel Co. Ltd, 1919-30, Pres. 1965-71; Formerly: Chm. and Man. Dir, later Hon. Pres., Colvilles Ltd. Past President: Iron and Steel Inst.; Glasgow and West of Scotland Iron and Steel Inst.; Inst. of Engineers and

Shipbuilders in Scotland: President: British Iron and Steel Federation, 1957, 1958; Instn of Works Managers, 1964-67. Chm., Mechanical Engineering Research Board, DSIR, 1952-58. DL Lanarkshire. Hon. DSc Strathclyde, 1965. Bessemer Medallist, 1940. *Publications:* several papers in Technical Society jls. *Address:* 27 Broom Cliff, Newton Mearns, Glasgow G77 5LG. *T:* 041-639 5115. *Clubs:* Athenæum; Scottish Automobile (Glasgow).

McCANCE, Robert Alexander, CBE 1953; FRS 1948; Professor of Experimental Medicine, Medical Research Council and University of Cambridge, 1945-66, now Emeritus; Director, MRC Infantile Malnutrition Research Unit, Mulago Hospital, Kampala, 1966-68; Fellow of Sidney Sussex College; *b* near Belfast, Northern Ireland, 9 Dec. 1898; *s* of Mary L. Bristow and J. S. F. McCance, linen merchant, Belfast; *m* 1922, Mary L. MacGregor (*d* 1965); one *s* one *d. Educ:* St Bees Sch., Cumberland; Sidney Sussex Coll., Cambridge. RN Air Service and RAF, 1917-18; BA (Cambridge), 1922; Biochemical Research, Cambridge, 1922-25; qualified in medicine King's Coll. Hosp., London, 1927; MD (Cambridge), 1929; Asst Physician i/c biochemical research, King's Coll. Hosp., London; FRCP 1935; Goulstonian Lectr, RCP, 1936; Humphrey Rolleston Lectr, RCP, 1953; Groningen Univ. Lectr, 1958; Leonard Parsons Lectr, Birmingham Univ., 1959; Lumleian Lectr, RCP, 1962. Reader in Medicine, Cambridge Univ., 1938; War of 1939-45, worked on medical problems of national importance; visited Spain and Portugal on behalf of British Council, 1943, South Africa, 1965; i/c Medical Research Council Unit, Germany, 1946-49. Hon. FRCOG; Hon. Member: Assoc. of American Physicians; American Pediatric Soc.; Swiss Nutrition Soc.; Brit. Pædiatric Assoc.; Nutrition Soc. Gold Medal, West London Medico-Chirurgical Soc., 1949. Conway Evans Prize, RCP and Royal Society, 1960; James Spence Medal, Brit. Pæd. Assoc., 1961. Hon. DSc Belfast, 1964. *Publications:* Medical Problems in Mineral Metabolism (Goulstonian Lectures), 1936; (jointly) The Chemical Composition of Foods; An Experimental Study of Rationing; (jointly) Breads White and Brown; numerous papers on the physiology of the newborn animal. *Recreations:* mountaineering, cycling, photography. *Address:* 4 Kent House, Sussex Street, Cambridge CB1 1PH.

McCANN, Hugh James; Irish Ambassador to France, Permanent Representative to OECD and to UNESCO, since 1974 and concurrently Ambassador to Morocco, since 1975; *b* 8 Feb. 1916; *e s* of late District Justice Hugh Joseph McCann, BL, and late Sophie McCann, Dublin; *m* 1950, Mary Virginia Larkin, Washington, DC, USA; four *s* one *d. Educ:* Belvedere Coll., Dublin; London Sch. of Economics, Univ. of London. Served in Dept of Lands, Dublin, and in Dept of Industry and Commerce, Dublin; Commercial Sec., London, 1944-46; First Sec., Dept of External Affairs, Dublin, 1946-48; Counsellor, Irish Embassy, Washington, DC, 1948-54; Irish Minister to Switzerland and Austria, 1954-56; Asst Sec., Dept of External Affairs, Dublin, 1956-58; Irish Ambassador at the Court of St James's, 1958-62; Sec., Dept of Foreign Affairs, Dublin, 1963-74. *Recreations:* golf, tennis, swimming, winter sports and photography. *Address:* 12 avenue Foch, Paris 16e; Frankfield, Mart Lane, Foxrock, Co. Dublin. *Clubs:* Royal Dublin Society, Stephen's Green (Dublin), Woodbrook Golf.

McCANN, Most Rev. James, MA; PhD; DD; LLD; *b* Grantham, Lincs, 31 Oct. 1897; *s* of James W. and Agnes McCann; *m* 1924, Violet, *d* of James and Mary Henderson, Ballymena, Ireland; no *c. Educ:* Royal Belfast Academical Institution; Queen's University, Belfast (BA; Hon. LLD 1966); Trinity College, Dublin (MA, PhD, DD). Ecclesiastical History Prizeman (1st), 1917; Elrington Theological Prizeman (1st), 1930; ordained 1920; held curacies at Ballymena, Ballyclare, Cavan, Oldcastle; Rector of Donaghpatrick, 1930-36; St Mary's, Drogheda, 1936-45; Canon of St Patrick's Cathedral, Dublin, 1944-45; Bishop of Meath, 1945-59; Archbishop of Armagh and Primate of All Ireland, 1959-69. *Publication:* Asceticism: an historical study, 1944. *Recreations:* music, reading. *Address:* c/o Rev. H. A. McCann, The Rectory, Begbroke, Oxford. *T:* Kidlington 3253. *Club:* Kildare Street and University (Dublin).

McCANN, His Eminence Cardinal Owen; *see* Cape Town, Cardinal Archbishop of.

McCANN, Peter Toland McAree, CBE 1977; JP; Lord Provost of the City of Glasgow and Lord-Lieutenant of the City of Glasgow, 1975-77; *b* 2 Aug. 1924; *s* of Peter McCann and Agnes (*née* Waddell); *m* 1958, Maura Eleanor (*née* Ferris); one *s. Educ:* St Mungo's Academy; Glasgow Univ. (BL). Solicitor and Notary Public. Pres., Glasgow Univ. Law Soc., 1946; Pres., St Thomas More Soc., 1959. Mem. Glasgow Corp., 1961. Chm.,

McCann Cttee (Secondary Educn for Physically Handicapped Children), 1971. OStJ 1977. *Recreations:* music, history, model aeroplane making. *Address:* 31 Queen Mary Avenue, Glasgow G42 8DS.

McCARTHY, family name of **Baron McCarthy.**

McCARTHY, Baron *cr* 1975 (Life Peer), of Headington; **William Edward John McCarthy,** DPhil; Fellow of Nuffield College and Oxford Management Centre; University Lecturer in Industrial Relations; engaged in Industrial Arbitration and Chairman of Committees of Inquiry and Investigation, since 1968; *b* 30 July 1925; *s* of E. and H. McCarthy; *m* Margaret McCarthy. *Educ:* Holloway County; Ruskin Coll.; Merton Coll.; Nuffield Coll. MA (Oxon), DPhil (Oxon). Trade Union Scholarship to Ruskin Coll., 1953; Research Fellow of Nuffield Coll., 1959; Research Dir, Royal Commn on Trade Unions and Employers' Assocs, 1965-68; Sen. Economic Adviser, Dept of Employment, 1968-71. Chm., Railway Staff Tribunal, 1973; Special Advisor on Industrial Relations to Sec. of State for Social Services, 1975; Member: Houghton Cttee on Aid to Political Parties, 1975-76; TUC Independent Review Cttee, 1976; Pres., British Univ. Industrial Relations Assoc., 1975; Special Comr, Equal Opportunities Commn, 1977. *Publications:* The Closed Shop in Britain, 1964; The Role of Shop Stewards in British Industrial Relations, 1966; (with V. L. Munns) Employers' Associations, 1967; (with A. I. Marsh) Disputes Procedures in Britain, 1968; The Reform of Collective Bargaining at Plant and Company Level, 1971; ed, Trade Unions, 1972; (with A. I. Collier) Coming to Terms with Trade Unions, 1973; (with N. D. Ellis) Management by Agreement, 1973; (with J. F. O'Brien and V. E. Dowd) Wage Inflation and Wage Leadership, 1975; Making Whitley Work, 1977; articles in: Brit. Jl of Industrial Relns; Industrial Relns Jl. *Recreations:* gardening, theatre. *Address:* 4 William Orchard Close, Old Headington, Oxford. *T:* Oxford 62016. *Club:* Reform.

McCARTHY, Donal John, CMG 1969; HM Diplomatic Service; *b* 31 March 1922; *s* of Daniel and Kathleen McCarthy; *m* 1951, Rosanna Parbury; three *s. Educ:* Holloway Sch.; London Univ. Served Royal Navy, 1942-46. Foreign Office, 1946; Middle East Centre for Arab Studies, 1947-48; 3rd and 2nd Sec., Brit. Embassy, Jedda, 1948-51; 2nd Sec., Political Div., Brit. Middle East Office, 1951-55; 1st Sec., FO, 1955-58; Asst Polit. Agent, Kuwait, 1958-60; Brit. High Commn, Ottawa, 1960-63; FO, 1963-64; Counsellor, Brit. High Commn, Aden, and Polit. Adviser to C-in-C Middle East, 1964-67; Head of Aden Dept, FO, 1967-68, of Arabian Dept, FCO, 1968-70; IDC, 1970-71; Minister (Economic and Social Affairs), UK Mission to UN, 1971-73; Ambassador to United Arab Emirates, 1973-77. *Recreations:* music, skiing, being idle. *Address:* 29a Frognal, NW3. *T:* 01-794 5600; Glenculloo Lodge, Killoscully, Newport, Tipperary, Ireland. *T:* Silvermines 21. *Clubs:* Travellers', Royal Automobile, Ski Club of Great Britain.

McCARTHY, Sir Edwin, Kt 1955; CBE 1952; Chairman, Commonwealth Economic Committee, 1964-67; *b* 30 March 1896; *s* of late Daniel and Catherine McCarthy, Melbourne, Australia; *m* 1938, Marjorie Mary, *d* of George and Alice Graham, Sydney; one *s* one *d. Educ:* Christian Brothers' Coll., Melbourne; Melbourne Univ. Joined Australian Commonwealth Govt Service; Sec., Dept of Commerce, 1945-50. Austr. Shipping representative in USA, 1941-44; also during this period engaged in other work associated with war activities in USA and UK; Australian Comptroller-Gen. of Food, 1945-46. Dep. High Comr for Australia in the United Kingdom, 1950-58; Australian Ambassador to the Netherlands, 1958-62 and to Belgium, 1959-62; Australian Ambassador to the European Economic Community, 1960-64. *Recreation:* golf. *Address:* c/o University Club, Phillip Street, Sydney, NSW 2000, Australia. *Club:* University (Sydney).

McCARTHY, Eugene Joseph; Writer, since 1971; *b* 29 March 1916; *s* of Michael J. and Anna Baden McCarthy; *m* 1945, Abigail Quigley McCarthy; one *s* three *d. Educ:* St John's Univ., Collegeville (BA); Univ. of Minnesota (MA). Teacher in public schools, 1935-40; Coll. Prof. of Econs and Sociology, and civilian techn. Asst in Mil. Intell. for War Dept, 1940-48; US Representative in Congress of 4th District, Minnesota, 1949-58; US Senator from Minnesota, 1959-70. Independent. Holds hon. degrees. *Publications:* Frontiers in American Democracy, 1960; Dictionary of American Politics, 1962; A Liberal Answer to the Conservative Challenge, 1964; The Limits of Power, 1967; The Year of the People, 1969; Other Things and the Aardvark (poetry), 1970; The Hard Years, 1975; contribs to Saturday Review, Commonweal, Harper's. *Address:* 1420 N Street NW, Washington, DC, USA.

McCARTHY, John Haydon, CB 1963; Controller, Central Office, Department of Health and Social Security, Newcastle upon Tyne, 1956-74; *b* 1914; 3rd *s* of late Lt-Comdr Jeremiah and Mrs Margaret McCarthy, Walton-on-Thames; *m* 1947, Mary, *e d* of Ebenezer Barclay, Lanark; three *s. Educ:* St Joseph's (de la Salle) Coll., London. Entered GPO, 1931; transferred Home Office, 1936; Min. of Nat. Insce, 1945; Under-Sec., 1956. *Recreation:* sea fishing. *Address:* 3 Front Street, Whitley Bay, Tyne and Wear. *T:* 20206.

McCARTHY, Mary, (Mrs James West); writer; *b* 21 June 1912; *m* 1933, Harold Johnsrud; *m* 1938, Edmund Wilson; one *s*; *m* 1946, Bowden Broadwater; *m* 1961, James Raymond West. *Educ:* Annie Wright Seminary; Vassar Coll. Theatre critic, Partisan Review, 1937-57, Editor, Covici Friede, 1937-38; Instructor, Bard Coll., 1945-46; Instructor, Sarah Lawrence Coll., 1948. Lectures and broadcasts, 1952-65. Horizon award, 1948; Guggenheim Fellow, 1949-50, 1959-60; National Academy of Arts and Letters award, 1957. Hon. Dr Letters, Syracuse Univ., 1973; Hon. DLitt Hull, 1974. *Publications:* The Company She Keeps, 1942; The Oasis, 1949; Cast a Cold Eye, 1950; The Groves of Academe, 1952; A Charmed Life, 1955; Venice Observed, 1956; Sights and Spectacles, 1956; Memories of a Catholic Girlhood, 1957; The Stones of Florence, 1959; On the Contrary, 1962; The Group, 1963 (filmed 1966); Vietnam, 1967; Hanoi, 1968; The Writing on the Wall and Other Literary Essays, 1970; Birds of America, 1971; Medina, 1972; The Seventeenth Degree, 1974; The Mask of State: a gallery of Watergate portraits, 1974; essays, journalism, short stories and reviews in the New Yorker, Partisan Review, Horizon, The New York Review of Books, The Observer, etc. *Address:* 141 Rue de Rennes, Paris, France.

McCARTHY, Rt. Hon. Sir Thaddeus (Pearcey), PC 1968; KBE 1974; Kt 1964; Judge of the Court of Appeal of New Zealand, 1963-76, President, 1973-76; *b* 24 Aug. 1907; *s* of Walter McCarthy, Napier, merchant; *m* 1938, Joan Margaret Miller; one *s* two *d* (and one *d* decd). *Educ:* St Bede's Coll., Christchurch, New Zealand; Victoria Univ. Coll., Wellington. Master of Laws (1st Class Hons) 1931. Served War of 1939-45 in MEF with 22 Bn 2 NZEF, later as DJAG, 2 NZEF. Practised as Barrister and Solicitor until 1957 when appointed to Supreme Court. Chairman: Royal Commn on State Services, 1961-62; Winston Churchill Memorial Trust, 1966-76; Royal Commissions: on Salary and Wage Fixing Procedures in the State Services, 1968; on Social Security, 1969; on Horse Racing, Trotting and Dog Racing, 1969; on Salaries and Wages in the State Services, 1972; Chm., Royal Commn on Nuclear Power Generation, 1976-; Vice-Pres., NZ Sect., Internat. Commn of Jurists. Hon. Bencher, Middle Temple, 1974. *Recreations:* golf (Captain, Wellington Golf Club, 1952, Pres., 1973-77), fishing, sailing. *Address:* 100 Donald Street, Karori, Wellington 5, New Zealand. *T:* 768-282. *Club:* Wellington (Wellington, NZ) (Pres.).

McCARTIE, Rt. Rev. Patrick Leo; Auxiliary Bishop of Birmingham, (RC), and Titular Bishop of Elmham, since 1977; *b* 5 Sept. 1925; *s* of Patrick Leo and Hannah McCartie. *Educ:* Cotton College; Oscott College. Priest, 1949; on staff of Cotton College, 1950-55; parish work, 1955-63; Director of Religious Education, 1963-68; Administrator of St Chad's Cathedral, Birmingham, 1968-77. *Recreations:* music, walking. *Address:* 84 St Bernard's Road, Olton, Solihull, W Midlands. *T:* 021-706 9721.

McCARTNEY, Hugh; MP (Lab) Dunbartonshire Central, since 1974 (Dunbartonshire East, 1970-74); *b* 3 Jan. 1920; *s* of John McCartney and Mary Wilson; *m* 1949, Margaret; one *s* two *d. Educ:* Royal Technical Coll., Glasgow; John Street Senior Secondary School. Apprentice in textile industry, 1934-39; entered aircraft engrg industry, Coventry, 1939; joined Rolls Royce, Glasgow, 1941; joined RAF as aero-engine fitter, 1942 and resumed employment with Rolls Royce, 1947; representative with company (now one of GKN group) specialising in manufacture of safety footwear, 1951. Joined Ind. Labour Party, 1934; joined Labour Party, 1936. Town Councillor, 1955-70 and Magistrate, 1965-70, Kirkintilloch; Mem., Dunbarton CC, 1965-70. *Recreation:* spectating at football matches and athletic meetings (political activities permitting). *Address:* 63g Townhead, Kirkintilloch, Glasgow G66 1NN.

McCAULEY, Air Marshal Sir John Patrick Joseph, KBE 1955 (CBE 1943); CB 1951; *b* 18 March 1899; *s* of late John and Sophia McCauley; *m* 1926, Murielle Mary, *d* of late John Burke, and of Maude Burke; one *s* two *d. Educ:* St Joseph's Coll., Sydney; RMC, Duntroon; Melbourne Univ. (BCom 1936). Grad. RMC 1919; Aust. Staff Corps, 1919-23; RAAF, 1924-;

passed RAF Staff Coll., 1933; Flying Instructor's Course, Central Flying Sch., RAF, 1934; Dir Trg, RAAF HQ Melbourne, 1937-38; CO 1 Flying Trg Sch. 1939; CO 1 Eng. Sch., 1940; CO RAAF Stn Sembawang, Malaya, 1941-42; CO RAAF Stn, Palembang 11, Sumatra, 1942; SASO RAAF Darwin, 1942; DCAS, 1942-43; Air Cdre Ops, 2nd TAF France and Germany, 1944; DCAS, 1946-47; Chief of Staff, BCOF, Japan, 1947-49; AOC E Area, 1949-53; CAS, RAAF, 1954-57, retd. *Recreations:* tennis, golf. *Address:* 10 Onslow Gardens, Greenknowe Avenue, Potts Point, Sydney, Australia.

McCAUSLAND, Lucius Perronet T.; *see* Thompson-McCausland.

McCAW, Hon. Sir Kenneth (Malcolm), Kt 1975; QC (Australia) 1972; Attorney-General of New South Wales, 1965-75, retired; *b* 8 Oct. 1907; *s* of Mark Malcolm and Jessie Alice McCaw; *m* 1968, Valma Marjorie Cherlin (*née* Stackpool); two *s* one *d. Educ:* matriculated evening college. Left school, 1919; farm and saw-mill hand; clerk, commercial offices and law office, 1922-28; articled law clerk, 1928-33; admitted Solicitor and founded city law firm, 1933; Attorney, Solicitor and Proctor, NSW Supreme Court, until 1965; admitted to NSW Bar, 1965. Councillor, NSW Law Soc., 1945-48. MLA (L) for Lane Cove, NSW, 1947-75. *Recreations:* swimming, walking, Braille reading, music, elocution. *Address:* Woodrow House, Charlish Lane, Lane Cove, NSW 2066, Australia. *T:* 42-1900. *Clubs:* Sydney, Lane Cove Businessmen's, Longueville-Northwood Bowling, (Hon.) Royal Automobile, (Hon.) City Tattersall's, (Charter Mem.) Lane Cove Lions (all Sydney/Metropolitan).

McCLEAN, Prof. (John) David; Professor of Law, University o Sheffield, since 1973; *b* 4 July 1939; *s* of Major Harold McClean and Mrs Mabel McClean; *m* 1966, Pamela Ann Loader; one *s* one *d. Educ:* Queen Elizabeth's Grammar Sch., Blackburn; Magdalen Coll., Oxford (BCL, MA). Called to the Bar, Grays Inn, 1963. Asst Lectr 1961, Lectr 1963, Sen. Lectr 1968, Univ. of Sheffield. Vis. Lectr in Law, Monash Univ., Melbourne, 1968 Vice-Chm., C of E Bd for Social Responsibility, 1977-. Member Gen. Synod of C of E, 1970-; Crown Appts Commn, 1977-. *Publications:* Criminal Justice and the Treatment of Offenders (jtly), 1969; (contrib.) Halsbury's Laws of England, 4th edn 1974; The Legal Context of Social Work, 1975; (jtly) Defendant in the Criminal Process, 1976; (ed jtly) Shawcross and Beaumont, Air Law, 4th edn 1977; (jtly) Recognition and Enforcement of Judgments, etc, within the Commonwealth, 1977; articles in legal periodicals. *Recreation:* detective fiction. *Address:* 6 Burnt Stones Close, Sheffield S10 5TS. *T:* Sheffield 305794. *Club:* Royal Commonwealth Society.

McCLEAN, Rt. Rev. (John) Gerard; *see* Middlesbrough, Bishop of, (RC).

McCLEAN, Kathleen; *see* Hale, Kathleen.

McCLELLAND, William Grigor; Chairman, Laws Stores Ltd, since 1966; Visiting Professor, Durham University Business School, since 1977; Chairman, Washington Development Corporation, since 1977; *b* 2 Jan. 1922; *o c* of Arthur and Jean McClelland, Gosforth, Newcastle upon Tyne; *m* 1946, Diana Avery, *y d* of William Harold and Etha Close; two *s* two *d. Educ:* Leighton Park; Balliol Coll., Oxford. First Class PPE, 1948. Friends' Ambulance Unit, 1941-46. Man. Dir, Laws Stores Ltd, 1949-65; Sen. Res. Fellow in Management Studies, Balliol Coll., 1962-65; Dir, Manchester Business Sch., 1965-77, and Prof. of Business Administration, 1967-77, Univ. of Manchester; Dep. Chm., Nat. Computing Centre, 1966-68; Member: The Consumer Council, 1963-66; Economic Planning Council, Northern Region, 1965-66; IRC, 1966-71; NEDC, 1969-71; SSRC, 1971-74; Economic Development Cttee for the Distributive Trades, 1965-70; Northern Industrial Develt Bd, 1977-; Trustee, Anglo-German Foundn for the Study of Industrial Soc., 1973-; Governor: Nat. Inst. of Econ. and Social Research; Leighton Park Sch., 1952-60 and 1962-66; Treas., International Fellowship of Reconciliation, 1954-65; Trustee, 1956-, and Chm., 1965-, Joseph Rowntree Charitable Trust; Elder, Soc. of Friends, 1958-62. FBIM. *Publications:* Studies in Retailing, 1963; Costs and Competition in Retailing, 1966; And a New Earth, 1976; (ed) Quakers Visit China, 1957; Editor, Jl of Management Studies, 1963-65. *Recreation:* tennis. *Address:* 66 Elmfield Road, Gosforth, Newcastle upon Tyne NE3 4BD.

MACCLESFIELD, 8th Earl of *cr* 1721; **George Roger Alexander Thomas Parker;** Baron Parker, 1716; Viscount Parker, 1721; DL; *b* 6 May 1914; *e s* of 7th Earl of Macclesfield and Lilian Joanna Vere (*d* 1974), *d* of Major Charles Boyle; *S* father, 1975; *m* 1938, Hon. Valerie Mansfield, *o d* of 4th Baron Sandhurst, OBE; two *s*. DL Oxfordshire, 1965. *Heir: s* Viscount Parker, *qv. Address:* Shirburn, Watlington, Oxon.

MACCLESFIELD, Archdeacon of; *see* House, Ven. F. H.

McCLINTOCK, Surg. Rear-Adm. Cyril Lawson Tait, CB 1974; OBE 1964; Medical Officer in Charge, Royal Naval Hospital, Haslar and Command Medical Adviser on staff of Commander-in-Chief Naval Home Command, 1972-75; retired 1975; *b* 2 Aug. 1916; 2nd surv. *s* of late Lawson Tait McClintock, MB, ChB, Loddon, Norfolk; *m* 1966, Freda Margaret, *o d* of late Robert Jones, Caergwle, Denbighshire; two step *s*. *Educ*: St Michael's, Uckfield; Epsom; Guy's Hospital. MRCS, LRCP 1940; DLO 1955. Joined RN Medical Service, 1940; served War of 1939-45 in Western Approaches, N Africa, Eritrea, India and Singapore; Korea, 1950-51; ENT Specialist, RN Hosps, Port Edgar, Chatham, Hong Kong, Portland, Haslar, Malta and Russell Eve Building, Hamilton, Bermuda; MO i/c RN Hosp. Bighi, Malta, 1969; David Bruce RN Hosp. Mtarfa, Malta, 1970-71; Comd Med. Adviser to C-in-C Naval Forces Southern Europe, 1969-71. QHS 1971-75. FRSocMed 1948; MFCM 1974. CStJ 1973. *Recreations*: cricket, tennis, Rugby refereeing, history. *Address*: 5 Ambleside Court, Crescent Road, Alverstoke, Hants. *Clubs*: Army and Navy, MCC.

McCLINTOCK-BUNBURY, family name of **Baron Rathdonnell.**

McCLOSKEY, Bernard Mary; Deputy Director of Public Prosecutions for Northern Ireland, since 1972; *b* 7 Aug. 1924; *s* of Felix and Josephine McCloskey; *m* 1952, Rosalie Donaghy; three *s* two *d*. *Educ*: St Malachy's Coll., Belfast; Queen's Univ., Belfast (LLB (Hons)). Admitted solicitor (Northern Ireland), 1947; private practice, 1947-72. Joint Solicitor to Scarman Tribunal of Enquiry, 1969-71. *Recreations*: swimming, golf. *Address*: 14 Downview Avenue, Belfast 15, Northern Ireland. *T*: (business) 35111. *Club*: Fortwilliam Golf (Hon. Mem.).

McCLOY, John Jay, DSM, MF (US); Partner, Milbank Tweed, Hadley & McCloy, since 1963; Director and Chairman Executive Committee, Squibb Corporation; Hon. Chairman, Board of the Council on Foreign Relations, Inc.; *b* 31 March 1895; *s* of John Jay McCloy and Anna May Snader; *m* 1930, Ellen Zinsser; one *s* one *d*. *Educ*: Amherst Coll. (AB); Harvard Univ. (LLB). Admitted to New York Bar, 1921; mem. of law firm of Cravath, de Gersdorff Swaine & Wood, New York City, 1929-40; expert cons. to Sec. of War, 1940; The Asst Sec. of War, 1941-45; Chm. of The Combined Civil Affairs Cttee of Combined Chiefs of Staff; Mem. of law firm of Milbank, Tweed, Hope, Hadley & McCloy, NY City, 1945-47; Pres. International Bank for Reconstruction and Development, Washington, DC, 1947-49; US Military Governor and US High Comr for Germany, Frankfurt, Germany, 1949-52; Mem. State Dept Cttee on Atomic Energy, 1946-47; Counsel, Milbank, Tweed, Hope & Hadley, 1961; Adviser to President Kennedy on Disarmament, 1961; Chairman: Co-ordinating Cttee of the US on Cuban Crisis, 1962-63; Past Chm., Gen. Adv. Cttee on Arms Control and Disarmament; Mem. Exec. Cttee, The Salk Inst., La Jolla, Calif; Hon. Chairman: Atlantic Institute, 1966-68; Chm., Amer. Council on Germany Inc. Mem., President's Commn on the Assassination of President Kennedy; Mem., American and NY Bar Assocs; Mem., Bar Assoc. of City of New York. Past Chm. and Trustee, Ford Foundation. Retired Director: The Chase Manhattan Bank (Chm. 1953-60); Dreyfus Corp., NYC; Mercedes-Benz of N America, Inc.; Olinkraft Inc.; Metropolitan Life Insurance Co.; Westinghouse Electric Corp.; American Telephone & Telegraph Co; Allied Chemical Corp. Trustee, John M. Olin Foundn. Hon. Trustee: Bd of Trustees, Amherst Coll., Mass (Chm.); Lenox Hill Hosp.; Johns Hopkins Univ.; Treasurer, Amer. Sch. of Classical Studies, Athens; Mem., Bd of Overseers to visit Center for Internat. Studies, Harvard Univ. Capt. FA, AEF. Holds numerous hon. degrees both in US and abroad, also Civic Hons. US Presidential Medal of Freedom and Distinguished Service Medal; Grand Officer of Legion of Honour (France); Grand Officer of Order of Merit of the Republic (Italy); Grand Cross of Order of Merit (Federal Republic of Germany). *Publication*: The Challenge to American Foreign Policy, 1953. *Recreations*: tennis and fishing. *Address*: 1 Chase Manhattan Plaza, New York, NY 10005, USA. *Clubs*: Brook, Links, University, Century, Anglers, Recess, Ausable, Clove Valley Rod and Gun (NY); Metropolitan (Washington).

McCLUNE, Rear-Adm. (William) James; Chief Staff Officer (Engineering) to the Commander-in-Chief, Fleet, since 1976; *b* Londonderry, 20 Nov. 1921; *s* of James McClune, MBE, Carrickmacross, Co. Monaghan, and Matilda (*née* Burns); *m* 1953, Elizabeth, *yr d* of A. E. D. Prideaux, LDS, Weymouth; one *s* one *d*. *Educ*: Model Sch. and Foyle Coll., Derry; QUB (BSc 1st Cl. Hons Elec. Eng, 1941); RN Staff Coll., Greenwich (1961); Univ. of Birmingham (Ratcliff Prizeman, MSc 1970); RN War Coll. (1971). Bronze Medal, CGLI, 1940; Belfast Assoc. of Engrs' Prize, 1940, 1941. CEng, MIEE; MBIM. Radar

Officer, RNVR, 1941-47: HMS Howe and HMS Cleopatra; Staff of Vice-Adm. (Destroyers), Home Fleet; HMS Vanguard; Eng Dept, GPO, 1947-49; RN, 1949-; HMS Euryalus and HMS Mermaid; Weapon Elec. Sch.; HMS Collingwood, HMS Barfleur, HMS Albion; ASRE; HMS Eastbourne; Exec. Officer, RNEC, Manadon; Weapons Dept; Weapon Elec. Officer, HMS London; Ship Dept; Defence Fellowship; Admiralty Interview Bd; Captain, HMS Collingwood; Dir, Naval Manning and Trng (Eng). Captain 1966; Rear-Adm. 1976. Governor, Monkton Combe Sch.; Pres., Royal Naval Amateur Rowing Assoc. Other interests are sailing, flying, amateur radio, education, some Christian causes. *Address*: Trinity House, HM Naval Base, Portsmouth, Hants; 7 Theed Street, SE1. *Clubs*: Royal Commonwealth Society; Royal Naval and Royal Albert Yacht (Portsmouth).

McCLURE, David, RSA 1971 (ARSA 1963); RSW 1965; SSA 1951; Senior Lecturer in Drawing and Painting, Duncan of Jordanstone College of Art, Dundee, since 1971 (Lecturer, 1957); *b* 20 Feb. 1926; *s* of Robert McClure, MM, and Margaret Helena McClure (*née* Evans); *m* 1950, Joyce Dixon Flanigan; two *s* one *d*. *Educ*: Queen's Park Sch., Glasgow; Glasgow Univ., 1943-44; (coal-miner, 1944-47); Edinburgh Univ., 1947-49; Edinburgh Coll. of Art, 1947-52 (DA). Travelled in Spain and Italy, 1952-53; on staff of Edinburgh Coll. of Art, 1953-55; one year painting in Italy and Sicily, 1956-57. *One man exhibitions*: Palermo, 1957; Edinburgh, 1957, 1961, 1962, 1966, 1969; 14 Scottish Painters, London, 1964; Univ. of Birmingham, 1965. *Work in public and private collections*: UK, USA, Canada, Italy. *Publication*: John Maxwell (monograph), 1976. *Recreation*: collecting Victorian china. *Address*: 16 Strawberry Bank, Dundee, Scotland. *T*: Dundee 66959. *Club*: Scottish Arts (Edinburgh).

McCLURE, Ivor Herbert, DSO 1918; 2nd *s* of late Rev. Canon Edmund McClure; *m* 1925, Beatrice Eliott-Drake, *e d* of late Rev. H. M. Eliott-Drake Briscoe, MA, formerly Rector of Burnham Thorpe and Rural Dean of Burnham; one *s* one *d*; *m* 1950, Mabel James Orr, Bow Cottage, Charmouth, Dorset, *y d* of late James Angus, Ochiltree House, Ayrshire. *Educ*: Eton; Harrow; Clare Coll., Cambridge (BA). Served European War, 1914-19 (despatches five times, DSO, 1914 Star). Asst Dir, Cardiff Station, BBC, 1926, Head of Aviation Dept, Automobile Assoc., 1929; Chm., Aviation Section, London Chamber of Commerce, 1934; Operational Adviser, Dir of Civil Aviation, Air Min., 1935; Dir of Operational Services and Intelligence, Dept of Civil Aviation, Air Min., 1937; Asst Sec. Gen. for Air Navigation, Provisional Internat. Civil Aviation Organization (later ICAO), 1945; retd, 1949. *Address*: Sutton, County Brome, Quebec, Canada. *Club*: Royal Automobile.

McCLUSKEY, family name of **Baron McCluskey.**

McCLUSKEY, Baron *cr* 1976 (Life Peer), of Churchhill in the District of the City of Edinburgh; **John Herbert McCluskey,** QC (Scotland) 1967; Solicitor General for Scotland, since 1974; *b* 12 June 1929; *s* of Francis John McCluskey, Solicitor, and Margaret McCluskey (*née* Doonan); *m* 1956, Ruth Friedland; two *s* one *d*. *Educ*: St Bede's Grammar Sch., Manchester; Holy Cross Acad., Edinburgh; Edinburgh Univ. Harry Dalgety Bursary, 1948; Vans Dunlop Schol., 1949; Muirhead Prize, 1949; MA 1950; LLB 1952. Sword of Honour, RAF Spitalgate, 1953. Admitted Faculty of Advocates, 1955; Standing Jun. Counsel to Min. of Power (Scotland), 1963; Advocate-Depute, 1964-71; Sheriff Principal of Dumfries and Galloway, 1973-74. Chm., Medical Appeal Tribunals for Scotland, 1972-74. *Recreations*: golf, tennis. *Address*: 11 Cluny Avenue, Edinburgh EH10 4RN. *T*: 031-447 3880.

McCOLL, Ian; Chairman, Scottish Express Newspapers Ltd, since 1975; *b* 22 Feb. 1915; *e s* of late John and Morag McColl, Glasgow and Bunessan, Isle of Mull; *m* 1968, Brenda, *e d* of late Thomas and of Mrs Mary McKean, Glasgow; one *d*. *Educ*: Hillhead High Sch., Glasgow. Served in RAF, 1940-46 (despatches, 1945): Air Crew, Coastal Comd 202 Sqdn. Joined Scottish Daily Express as cub reporter, 1933; held various editorial executive posts; Editor, Scottish Daily Express, 1961-71; Dir, Beaverbrook Newspapers Ltd, 1971-. Contested (L): Dumfriesshire, 1945; Greenock, 1950. Mem., Presbytery of Glasgow and Synod of Clydesdale, 1953-71; Mem., General Assembly Publications Cttee, until 1971; Session Clerk, Sandyford-Henderson Memorial Church of Scotland, Glasgow, 1953-71; Editor, Daily Express, 1971-74. Mem., Press Council, 1975-. Mem., Inst. of Journalists; Sec., Glasgow branch Nat. Union of Journalists, 1947-48. *Address*: Scottish Express Newspapers Ltd, Park House, Park Circus Place, Glasgow G3 6AF.

McCOLL, Prof. Ian, MS, FRCS, FACS, FRCSE; Professor of Surgery, University of London; Director of the Surgical Unit and Consultant Surgeon to Guy's Hospital; Hon. Consultant Surgeon, King's College Hospital; *b* 6 Jan. 1933; *s* of Frederick George McColl, Kingston Vale; *m* 1960, Dr Jean Lennox, 2nd *d* of Arthur James McNair, FRCS, FRCOG; one *s* two *d. Educ:* Hutchesons' Grammar Sch., Glasgow; St Paul's Sch., London; Guy's Hosp., London. MB, BS 1957; FRCS 1962; FRCSE 1962; MS 1966; FACS 1975. Junior staff appts at St Bartholomew's, Putney, St Mark's, St Peter's, Great Ormond Street, Barnet, St Olave's and Guy's Hosps, 1957-67; Arris and Gale Lectr, RCS, 1964 and 1965; Research Fellow, Harvard Med. Sch., and Moynihan Fellowship, Assoc. of Surgeons, 1967; Reader in Surgery, St Bartholomew's Hosp. Med. Coll., 1967 (Sub dean, 1969). Visiting Professor: Univ. of South Carolina, 1974; Johns Hopkins Hosp., 1976. Examiner: RCS, 1970; Queen's Univ. Belfast, 1972; Univ. of Newcastle, 1974; Univ. of London, 1976. Medical Advisor, BBC Television. Member: Central Health Services Council, 1972-74; Standing Medical Adv. Cttee, 1972-; Standing Nursing Adv. Cttee, 1972-74; Jt Cttee on Higher Surgical Trng, 1972-; Management Cttee, King Edward VII Hospital Fund; Cttee, King's Fund Centre Cttee. Hon. Sec., British Soc. of Gastroenterology, 1970-74. *Publications:* (ed jtly) Intestinal Absorption in Man, 1975; med. articles, mainly on gastroenterology. *Recreation:* squash. *Address:* 10 Gilkes Crescent, Dulwich Village, SE21 7BS. *T:* 01-693 3084. *Club:* Athenæum.

McCOLOUGH, Charles Peter; Chairman and Chief Executive Officer, Xerox Corporation, since 1971; *b* 1 Aug. 1922; *s* of Reginald W. McColough and Barbara Martin McColough; *m* 1953, Mary Virginia White. *Educ:* Dalhousie Univ. (LLB); Harvard Grad. Sch. of Business Administration (MBA). Lehigh Coal & Navigation Co., Philadelphia, 1951-54; Xerox Corp.: Gen. Man., Reproduction Service Centers, 1954-56; Man. Marketing, 1957-59; Gen. Sales Man., 1959-60; Vice-Pres. Sales, 1960-63; Exec. Vice-Pres., Ops, 1963-66; Pres., 1966-68; Pres. and Chief Exec. Officer, 1968-71. Director: Citibank, NA; Citicorp; Fuji Xerox Co., Ltd; Internat. Executive Service Corps (Chm. Exec. Cttee); Rehabilitation International USA; Council for Financial Aid to Educn; Jt Pres., Rank Xerox Ltd; Chm., Listed Company Adv. Cttee, NY Stock Exchange; Trustee: Eisenhower Exchange Fellowship; Univ. of Rochester; US Council of Internat. Chamber of Commerce; Cttee for Economic Develt; Member: Corp. of Greenwich Hospital Assoc. Inc.; Bd Governors, Fairfield Foundn of Diocese of Bridgeport; Develt Council; Harvard Overseers' Cttee to visit the Graduate Sch. of Business Administration; Industries Adv. Cttee of Advertising Council Inc.; Nat. Acad. of Engineering's Nat. Adv. Council on Minorities in Engrg; The Business Council; The Business Redoubtable; Econ. Club of NY; Council on Foreign Relations; Steering Cttee of Nat. Cttee for Full Employment; Adv. Council of Industrial Estates Ltd, Nova Scotia; Adv. Bd, Yale Univ. Sch. of Organization and Management. *Address:* Xerox Corporation, Stamford, Conn 06904, USA. *Clubs:* Harvard, River (New York); Country, Genesee Valley (Rochester); Stanwich, Belle Haven, Greenwich Country (Connecticut).

McCOMB, James Ellis, CBE 1964; DFC 1940; DL; General Manager, Cwmbran New Town Development Corporation, 1962-74; *b* 19 April 1909; *er s* of late D. K. McComb, TD, JP; *m* 1939, Sonia, *d* of late Col H. J. Decker, TD; one *d. Educ:* Stowe Sch. Served War of 1939-45: comd 611 Fighter Sqdn AAF, 1939-40; RAF Staff Coll., 1942; 8th USAF Liaison, 1942; COSSAC Cover Plan, Invasion Europe, 1943; Air Liaison, C-in-C Allied Navies, 1944; SHAEF, 1944-45. Solicitor, 1932; Allen & Overy, City of London, 1933-36; Lancs CC, 1936-48; Dep. Clerk of Peace, Lancs, 1946-48; Gen. Man., Welwyn Garden City and Hatfield New Towns, 1949-62. DL Gwent, 1975. OStJ 1976. *Recreations:* gardening, painting. *Address:* Wye Cottage, Dixton Road, Monmouth. *Club:* RAF Reserves.

McCOMBS, Hon. Sir Terence (Henderson), Kt 1975; OBE 1971; ED 1943; *b* 5 Sept. 1905. *Educ:* Christchurch and Waitaki Boys' High Schs, NZ; University of Canterbury, NZ (MSc(Hons)). CChem, MRIC; Hon. FNZIC. Teaching, 1931-35. MP (NZ), 1935-51; Parly Under-Sec. to Minister of Finance, 1945-47; Minister of Education and Sci. and Ind. Research, 1947-49. Teacher, 1951-55; Headmaster, Cashmere High Sch., Christchurch, 1956-72; High Commissioner for NZ in the UK and Ambassador for NZ in Ireland, 1973-75. Member: Christchurch City Council (Chm., Finance Cttee, 1951-57); Lyttelton Harbour Bd; Bd of Governors, Canterbury Agric. Coll.; Chm., Christchurch Milk Co. Chancellor, Univ. of Canterbury, NZ, 1969-73. Chm., Cttee on Secondary Educn, 1975-76. Freeman, City of London, 1973. *Publications:* scientific papers in: Jl of Chem. Soc.; Science and Technology (NZ). *Recreations:* hockey, rowing. *Address:* 7 Freeman Street,

Christchurch 8, New Zealand. *Clubs:* Reform; University of Canterbury.

McCONE, John A.; US business executive, retired; Chairman, Hendy International Co., 1969-75; *b* 4 Jan. 1902; *s* of Alexander J. McCone and Margaret McCone (*née* Enright); *m* 1938, Rosemary Cooper (*d* 1961); no *c*; *m* 1962, Mrs Theiline McGee Pigott (widow). *Educ:* Univ. of California, Coll. of Engineering. Began as construction engineer, Llewellyn Iron Works; supt Consolidated Steel Corp., 1929; Exec. Vice-Pres. and Dir, 1933-37; Pres. of Bechtel-McCone Corp., Los Angeles, 1937-45; Pres. and Dir, California Shipbuilding Corp., 1941-46; Joshua Hendy Corp., Joshua Hendy Iron Works, 1945-69; Mem. President's Air Policy Commn, 1947-48; Dep. to Sec. of Defense, March-Nov. 1948; Under Sec. of US Air Force, 1950-51. Chm., US Atomic Energy Commn, 1958-61; Dir, Central Intelligence Agency, 1961-65. Chm., Joshua Hendy Corp., 1961-69; holds hon. degrees from Univs and colls in the US. *Recreation:* golf. *Address:* (home) 1100 Oak Grove Avenue, San Marino, Calif 91108, USA; Norcliffe, The Highlands, Seattle, Washington; (office) 612 South Flower Street, Los Angeles, Calif 90017. *T:* Madison 9-3631. *Clubs:* California (Los Angeles); Valley Club of Montecito, Los Angeles Country (Los Angeles); Pacific Union, Bohemian (San Francisco); Burning Tree, Metropolitan, F Street, Chevy Chase (Washington, DC); The Links, Blind Brook (NYC); Cypress Point (Pebble Beach, Calif); Seattle Golf, Ranier (Seattle).

McCONNELL, Albert Joseph, MA, ScD, Hon. DSc: Belfast; Ulster; Hon. ScD Columbia; Hon. LLD NUI; Hon. Fellow of Oriel College, Oxford; Provost of Trinity College, Dublin, 1952-74; Member of Council of State, Ireland, since 1973; *b* 19 Nov. 1903; *s* of Joseph McConnell; *m* 1934, Hilda (*d* 1966), *d* of late Francis McGuire. *Educ:* Ballymena Acad.; Trinity Coll., Dublin (Scholar, First Math. Moderator and Univ. Student); Univ. of Rome. Dr of Univ. of Rome, 1928; Mem. of Royal Irish Academy, 1929; ScD (Dublin), 1929; Fellow of Trinity Coll., Dublin, 1930-52; Chm., Governing Board of Sch. of Theoretical Physics, and Mem. Council of Dublin Inst. for Advanced Studies; Lectr in Maths, Trinity Coll., Dublin, 1927-30; Prof. of Natural Philosophy, Univ. of Dublin, 1930-57; Special Univ. Lectr, Univ. of London, 1949; Vis. Professor: Univ. of Alexandria, 1946-47; Univ. of Kuwait, 1970. *Publications:* Applications of the Absolute Differential Calculus, 1931; Applications of Tensor Analysis, 1957; papers on relativity, geometry and dynamics in various mathematical jls; Joint-editor of the Mathematical Papers of Sir W. R. Hamilton. *Address:* Seafield Lodge, Seafield Road, Killiney, Dublin. *Clubs:* Athenæum, East India, Sports and Public Schools; Dublin University (Dublin).

McCONNELL, Gerard Hamilton, CB 1967; Assistant Under-Secretary of State, Home Office, 1957-74; Principal Finance Officer, 1967-74; *b* 22 Jan. 1913; *s* of late Mr and Mrs J. McConnell; *m* 1939, Dorothy Margaret Drummond Wilson; two *d. Educ:* Manchester Grammar Sch.; St John's Coll., Cambridge, Scottish Home Dept, 1936-46 (Royal Air Force, 1942-44); Home Office, 1946; Asst Sec., 1948. *Address:* 2 The Slade, Clophill, Beds. *T:* Silsoe 60392.

McCONNELL, Comdr Sir Robert Melville Terence, 3rd Bt, *cr* 1900; VRD; RNVR (retired); *b* 7 Feb. 1902; *s* of Sir Joseph McConnell, 2nd Bt, and Lisa (*d* 1956), *d* of late Jackson McGown; *S* father, 1942; *m* 1st, 1928, Rosamond Mary Elizabeth (marr. diss., 1954), *d* of James Stewart Reade, Clonmore, Lisburn, Co. Antrim; three *s* one *d*; 2nd, 1967, Mrs Alice A. M. Hills. *Educ:* Glenalmond; St John's Coll., Cambridge; College of Estate Management, London. Consultant with R. J. McConnell and Co., estate agents, Belfast. *Heir: s* Robert Shean McConnell, *b* 23 Nov. 1930. *Address:* Pigeon Hill, Island Road, Killyleagh, Co. Down, N Ireland.

McCONNELL, Rt. Hon. Robert William Brian, PC (N Ireland) 1964; President of the Industrial Court of Northern Ireland, since 1968; National Insurance Commissioner, Northern Ireland, since 1968; *b* 25 Nov. 1922; *s* of late Alfred E. McConnell, Belfast; *m* 1951, Sylvia Elizabeth Joyce Agnew; two *s* one *d. Educ:* Sedbergh Sch.; Queen's Univ., Belfast (BA, LLB). Called to Bar of Northern Ireland, 1948. MP (U) for South Antrim, NI Parlt, 1951-68; Dep. Chm. of Ways and Means, NI Parlt, 1962; Parly Sec. to Min. of Health and Local Govt for N Ireland, 1963; Minister of Home Affairs for Northern Ireland, 1964-66; Minister of State, Min. of Develt, 1966-67; Leader of the House of Commons, NI, 1967-68. *Recreation:* cattle breeding. *Address:* 50 Glenavy Road, Knocknadona, Lisburn, Co. Antrim, Northern Ireland. *T:* Lisburn 3432.

McCONNELL, William Samuel, DA (RCS); FFARCS; RCS; Consultant Anaesthetist Emeritus, Guy's Hospital; *b* 22 April 1904; *s* of late James McConnell, BA, MB, BCh; *m* 1932, Olive, *d* of late Capt. L. E. Stannard; two *s*. *Educ:* Emanuel Sch., London; Univ. of London. Guy's Hospital Medical Sch.: MRCS, LRCP, 1927; MB, BS (London), 1929; DA (RCS), 1935; FFA, RCS, 1948. Anaesthetist to Guy's Hospital, 1935. Temp. Lt-Col RAMC: Adviser in Anaesthetics, Southern Army, India Comd, 1942-45. Hon. Visiting Anaesthetist, Johns Hopkins Hosp., Baltimore, Md, 1955. Pres., Section of Anaesthetics, RSM, 1969-70. *Publications:* articles on anaesthesia in professional jls. *Address:* 55 Chartfield Avenue, SW15.

MacCONOCHIE, John Angus, MBE 1943; FCIT; Chairman: Furness Withy & Co. Ltd, 1968-72 (Director, 1964-73); Shaw Savill & Albion Co. Ltd, 1968-73 (Director, 1957-73); *b* 12 April 1908; *m* 1938, Peggy, *d* of late Robert Gunson Martindale, MA, Worthing, Sussex; one *s* one *d*. *Educ:* Royal Caledonian Schools, Bushey, Herts. Joined Shaw Savill Line, 1927. Seconded to Min. of War Transport, 1942; served on Staff of Resident Minister for W Africa, Accra; Min. of War Transport Rep. in Gold Coast (MBE); London, 1944; Min. HQ with 21 Army Group; subseq. Paris, Marseilles, Naples. Returned to Shaw Savill Line, 1945: New Zealand, 1949; subseq. Manager for Australia; Gen. Manager for New Zealand, 1953; returned to Britain, 1958; Dir, 1957. Chm., Royal Mail Lines, 1968-73; Director: Economic Insurance, 1967 (Chm. 1969-73); British Maritime Trust, 1966-73; Pacific Steam Navigation Co. Ltd, 1967-73; Pacific Maritime Services, 1967-73; Houlder Bros & Co. Ltd, 1967-73; Whitehall Insurance Co. Ltd, 1967-73; Manchester Liners Ltd, 1968-73; National Bank of New Zealand, 1970 (NZ Bd, 1973-). Member: Council, Chamber of Shipping; Council of Management, Ocean Travel Development (past Chm.); Cttee, NZ Society (PP); Council Fedn of Commonwealth Chambers of Commerce (a NZ Rep.); British Ship Adoption Soc. (past Chm.); Pres., UK Chamber of Shipping, 1972-73 (Pres.-designate 1971); BIM; Inst. of Directors. Patron, Auckland Maritime Soc. *Address:* 8 Killarney Street, Takapuna, Auckland 9, New Zealand. *T:* Auckland 499.667. *Club:* Northern (Auckland).

McCONVILLE, Michael Anthony, MBE 1958; HM Diplomatic Service; *b* 3 Jan. 1925; *s* of late Lt-Col James McConville, MC and late Winifred (*née* Hanley); *m* 1952, Beryl Anne (*née* Jerrett); two *s* four *d*. *Educ:* Mayfield Coll.; Trinity Coll., Dublin. Royal Marines, 1943-46. Malayan Civil Service, 1950-61: served in Perak, Johore, Trengganu, Negri Sembilan, Pahang and Kedah; retd as Chm., Border War Exec. Cttee. CRO (later HM Diplomatic Service), 1961: Colombo, 1963-64; Kingston, Jamaica, 1966-67; Ottawa, 1967-71; Consul-Gen., Zagreb, 1974-77. Kesatria Mankgu Negara (Malaya), 1962. *Publications:* (pseudonym Patrick Plum): articles and short stories in Blackwoods, etc. *Recreations:* walking, gardening, watching Rugby. *Address:* c/o Foreign and Commonwealth Office, SW1A 2AL. *Clubs:* Royal Commonwealth Society; University (Dublin).

McCORKELL, Col Michael William, OBE 1964; TD 1954; Lord-Lieutenant, County Londonderry, since 1975; *b* 3 May 1925; *s* of late Captain B. F. McCorkell, Templeard, Culmore, Co. Londonderry and of Mrs E. M. McCorkell; *m* 1950, Aileen Allen, OBE 1975, 2nd *d* of late Lt-Col E. B. Booth, DSO, Darver Castle, Dundalk, Co. Louth, Eire; three *s* one *d*. *Educ:* Aldenham. Served with 16/5 Lancers, 1943-47; Major (TA) North Irish Horse, 1951; Lt-Col 1961; comd North Irish Horse (TA); retd, 1964. T&AVR Col, NI, 1971-74; Brevet Col, 1974; Pres., T&AVR, NI, 1977-; ADC to the Queen, 1972. Co. Londonderry: High Sheriff 1961, DL 1962. *Recreations:* fishing, shooting. *Address:* Ballyarnett, Londonderry, Northern Ireland. *T:* 51239. *Club:* Cavalry and Guards.

McCORMACK, Most Rev. John; *see* Meath, Bishop of, (RC).

McCORMACK, John P(atrick); General Director, European Operations, General Motors Overseas Corporation, since 1976; *b* New York, 23 Nov. 1923; *s* of John McCormack and Margaret (*née* Bannon); *m* 1952, Marian Martha Luhrs; two *s*. *Educ:* St John's Univ., Jamaica, NY (Bachelor of Business Admin); NY Univ., NYC (LLB). Joined General Motors, 1949; Gen. Clerk, Accounting Dept, NY, 1949, Sen. Clerk 1950, Sen. Accountant 1952; Asst to Treas., Djakarta Br., 1953; Asst Treas., Karachi Br., 1956; Asst Treas., Gen. Motors South African (Pty) Ltd, Port Elizabeth, 1958, Treas. 1961; Asst Finance Man., Overseas Div., NY, 1966; Treas., subseq. Man. Dir, Gen. Motors Continental, Antwerp, 1968; Finance Man., Adam Opel, 1970, Man. Dir and Chm. Bd, 1974. *Recreations:* golf, photography. *Address:* General Motors Overseas Corporation, Stag Lane, Kingsbury, NW9 0EH. *T:* 01-205 1212. *Clubs:* Harpenden Golf, Woburn Golf and Country; Apawamis (Rye, NY).

McCORMACK, John William; Member US House of Representatives 1927-70; House Majority Leader (Democrat) 1955-70 (with exception 4 years Democrat Whip); Speaker, 1962-70; lawyer; *b* Boston, Mass., 21 Dec. 1891; *s* of Joseph H. McCormack and Mary E. O'Brien; *m* 1920, M. Harriet Joyce (*d* 1971). *Educ:* public schools. Admitted Massachusetts Bar, 1913, practised law, Boston, firm of McCormack & Hardy; Mem. Mass Const. Conv., 1917-18, House of Representatives, 1920-22, State Senate, 1923-26. Holds hon. degrees. Kt of Malta, 1st class; Kt Comdr, with star, St Gregory the Great. *Address:* 111 Perkins Street, Jamaica Plain, Mass 02130, USA.

McCORMACK, Mark Hume; President and Chief Executive Officer, International Management Group; *b* 6 Nov. 1930; *s* of Ned Hume McCormack and Grace Wolfe McCormack; *m* 1954, Nancy Breckenridge McCormack; two *s* one *d*. *Educ:* Princeton Univ.; William and Mary Coll. (BA); Yale Univ. (LLB). Admitted to Ohio Bar, 1957; Associate in Arter, Hadden, Wykoff & Van Duzer, 1957-63; Partner, 1964-; started Internat. Management Gp, 1962. *Publications:* The World of Professional Golf, 1967, 9th edn 1975; Arnie: the evolution of a legend, 1967; The Wonderful World of Professional Golf, 1973. Publisher of Golf International (British golf paper), and of Tennis World (British tennis magazine). *Recreation:* golf. *Address:* No 1300, One Erieview Plaza, Cleveland, Ohio 44114, USA. *T:* 216/522-1200. *Clubs:* Sunningdale Golf (Berkshire, England); Country Club of Cleveland (Ohio).

McCORMACK, Percy Hicks, FIA; General Manager and Actuary, Provident Mutual Life Assurance Association, 1938-51, Director, 1951-66; *b* 23 Aug. 1890; *s* of late Martin McCormack, formerly of Knutsford, Cheshire, and Elizabeth Ann, *d* of Edmund Hicks; *m* 1926, Marjorie Vera Stewart, *d* of Charles A. Norris, Frittenden; two *s*. *Educ:* Bickerton, Birkdale; Liverpool Univ. Joint Asst Actuary, Provident Mutual Life Assurance Assoc., 1920; Joint Actuary, 1928; Consulting Actuary, London, Midland & Scottish Railway Co. and British Railways (Midland Region), 1938-55; Dir, London & Lomond Investment Trust Ltd, 1938-68. *Publications:* contribs to jls on actuarial and other subjects. *Address:* 12B Bedford Towers, Brighton, East Sussex. *Club:* Athenæum.

MacCORMICK, Prof. Donald Neil; Regius Professor of Public Law, University of Edinburgh, since 1972, Dean of Faculty of Law, 1973-76; *b* 27 May 1941; *yr s* of J. M. MacCormick, MA, LLD (Glasgow) and Margaret I. Miller, MA, BSc (Glasgow); *m* 1965, Caroline Rona Barr, MA (Glasgow); three *d*. *Educ:* High School, Glasgow; Univ. of Glasgow (MA, 1st cl. Philos. and Eng. Lit.); Balliol Coll., Oxford (BA, 1st cl. Jurisprudence; MA). Called to the Bar, Inner Temple, 1971. Lecturer, St Andrew's Univ. (Queen's Coll., Dundee), 1965-67; Fellow and Tutor in Jurisprudence, Balliol Coll., Oxford, 1967-72, and CUF Lectr in Law, Oxford Univ., 1968-72; Pro-Proctor, Oxford Univ., 1971-72. Prospective Parly Cand. (SNP), Edinburgh North, 1975-. Pres., Assoc. for Legal and Social Philosophy, 1974-76. Mem., Houghton Cttee on Financial Aid to Political Parties, 1975-76. *Publications:* (ed) The Scottish Debate: Essays on Scottish Nationalism, 1970; (ed) Lawyers in their Social Setting, 1976; contribs to various symposia, jls on law, philosophy and politics. *Recreations:* hill walking, bagpiping, sailing. *Address:* The Old College, Edinburgh EH8 9YL.
See also I. S. MacD. MacCormick.

MacCORMICK, Iain Somerled MacDonald; MP (SNP) Argyll since 1974; *b* 28 Sept. 1939; *er s* of John MacDonald MacCormick, MA, LLB, LLD and Margaret Isobel MacCormick, MA, BSc; *m* 1964, Micky Trefusis Elsom; two *s* three *d*. *Educ:* Glasgow High Sch.; Glasgow Univ. (MA). Queen's Own Lowland Yeomanry, 1957-67 (Captain). *Recreations:* Rugby football, Scottish history. *Address:* Airidh Uaine, Lower Soroba, Oban, Argyll. *T:* Oban 2301; House of Commons, SW1. *T:* 01-219 3473.
See also Prof. D. N. MacCormick.

McCORMICK, John Ormsby, CMG 1965; MC 1943; HM Diplomatic Service, retired; *b* Dublin, 7 Feb. 1916; *s* of Albert Victor McCormick and Sarah Beatty de Courcy; *m* 1955, Francine Guieu (*née* Pâris); one *d*, one step *s*. *Educ:* The Leys Sch., Cambridge; New Coll., Oxford. BA Hon. Mods and Greats (Oxford), 1938. Passed Competitive Exam. for Consular Service, 1939, and appointed Asst Officer, Dept of Overseas Trade. Served War of 1939-45, in Royal Corps of Signals, Africa, Sicily, Germany, 1940-45. 2nd Sec. (Commercial), British Embassy, Athens, 1945-47; FO, London, 1948-50; 1st Sec., UK High Commn, Karachi, 1950-52; Consul, New York, 1952-54; transferred to Washington, 1954-55; NATO Defence Coll., 1955; Asst Head, SE Asia Dept, FO, 1956-59; Foreign Service Officer, Grade 6, 1959; Counsellor (Commercial), British

Embassy, Djakarta, 1959-62; Corps of Inspectors, FO, 1962-64; Counsellor (Commercial), British Embassy, Ankara, 1965-67; Consul-General, Lyons, 1967-72. *Recreations:* golf, sailing, philosophy. *Address:* Oldfort, Newcastle, Co. Wicklow, Ireland.

McCORQUODALE, Mrs Barbara; *see* Cartland, Barbara H.

McCOWAN, Anthony James Denys, QC 1972; a Recorder of the Crown Court, since 1972; Barrister-at-Law; *b* 12 Jan. 1928; *yr s* of John Haines Smith McCowan, MBE, and Marguerite McCowan, Georgetown, British Guiana; *m* 1961, Sue Hazel Anne, *d* of Reginald Harvey, Braiseworth Hall, Tannington, Suffolk; two *s* one *d. Educ:* Epsom Coll.; (Open Hist. schol.) Brasenose Coll., Oxford (MA, BCL). Called to Bar, Gray's Inn, 1951, Atkin Scholar. Dep. Chm., E Sussex QS, 1969-71. *Recreations:* tennis, squash, history, travel. *Address:* 48 Sussex Street, SW1. *T:* 01-834 1626; Southernwood, Crendell, Cranborne, Dorset. *T:* Cranborne 393. *Club:* Hurlingham. *See also J . M . Archer.*

McCOWAN, Sir Hew Cargill, 3rd Bt, *cr* 1934; *b* 26 July 1930; *s* of Sir David James Cargill McCowan, 2nd Bt and Muriel Emma Annie, *d* of W. C. Willmott; *S* father, 1965. *Heir:* *b* David William Cargill McCowan, *b* 28 Feb. 1934. *Address:* Vivenda Marbelo, Estrada da Lagoa Azul, Malveira da Serra, Cascais, Portugal.

McCOWEN, Alec, (Alexander Duncan McCowen), OBE 1972; actor; *b* 26 May 1925; *s* of Duncan McCowen and Hon. Mrs McCowen. *Educ:* Skinners' Sch., Tunbridge Wells; RADA, 1941. Repertory: York, Birmingham, etc, 1943-50; Escapade, St James's, 1952; The Matchmaker, Haymarket, 1954; The Count of Clérambard, Garrick, 1955; The Caine Mutiny Court Martial, Hippodrome, 1956; Look Back in Anger, Royal Court, 1956; The Elder Statesman, Cambridge, 1958; Old Vic Seasons, 1959-61: Touchstone, Ford, Richard II, Mercutio, Oberon, Malvolio; Dauphin in St Joan; Algy in The Importance of Being Earnest; Royal Shakespeare Company, 1962-63: Antipholus of Syracuse in The Comedy of Errors; Fool, in King Lear; Father Fontana in The Representative, Aldwych, 1963; Thark, Garrick, 1965; The Cavern, Strand, 1965; After the Rain, Duchess, 1967, Golden Theatre, NY, 1967; Hadrian VII, Birmingham, 1967, Mermaid, 1968, New York, 1969; Hamlet, Birmingham, 1970; The Philanthropist, Royal Court, 1970, NY, 1971; Butley, Criterion, 1972; The Misanthrope, National Theatre, 1973, 1975, NY 1975; Equus, National Theatre, 1973; Pygmalion, Albery, 1974; The Family Dance, Criterion, 1976; Antony and Cleopatra, Prospect Co., 1977. Films include: Frenzy, 1971; Travels with My Aunt, 1972. Evening Standard Drama Award, 1968, 1973; Stage Actor of the Year, Variety Club, 1970. *Recreations:* music, gardening. *Address:* Flat 4, 2 Cresswell Gardens, SW5.

McCRAE, Alister Geddes, CBE 1973; Director, Clyde Port Authority (Chairman, 1966-77); *b* 7 Aug. 1909; *s* of Alexander McCrae and Grace Flora Murdoch; *m* 1938, Margaret Montgomery Reid (*d* 1977); one *s. Educ:* Kelvinside Academy; High School of Glasgow. Joined: P. Henderson & Co., Shipowners, Glasgow, 1927; Irrawaddy Flotilla Co. Ltd (in Burma), 1933; Served War: Middle East and Burma, 1941-45; Lt-Col, Royal Indian Engrs (despatches). Irrawaddy Flotilla Co. Ltd, 1946-48 (Dep. Gen. Manager, in Burma); re-joined P. Henderson & Co., as Partner, 1948; Sen. Partner, 1963; retd 1972. Member: Nat. Dock Labour Bd, 1953-57; British Transport Docks Bd, 1963-65; Nat. Ports Council, 1967-71; Clyde Navigation Trust, 1962-65; Chm., British Ports Assoc., 1972-74. Chm., Glasgow Old People's Welfare Assoc. (Age Concern), 1969-. Freeman, City of London; Liveryman, Worshipful Co. of Shipwrights, 1959. *Recreations:* the arts, the garden, fishing. *Address:* Belwood, Killearn, Stirlingshire G63 9LG. *T:* Killearn 50437. *Club:* Oriental.

McCRAITH, Col Patrick James Danvers, MC 1943; TD; DL; Solicitor and Notary Public; *b* 21 June 1916; *s* of late Sir Douglas McCraith; *m* 1946, Hon. Philippa Mary Ellis, *yr d* of 1st and last Baron Robins, KBE, DSO, of Rhodesia and Chelsea; one *s* one *d. Educ:* Harrow. Served 1939-45 with Sherwood Rangers Yeomanry, N Africa and NW Europe (three times wounded); raised and commanded Yeomanry Patrol of Long Range Desert Group, 1940-41; commanded Sherwood Rangers Yeomanry, 1953-57; Bt Colonel, 1958. Hon. Colonel: B (Sherwood Rangers Yeomanry) Squadron, The Royal Yeomanry, 1968. High Sheriff of Nottinghamshire, 1963; DL Notts, 1965. *Address:* Cranfield House, Southwell, Notts. *T:* Southwell 812129. *Clubs:* Special Forces; Nottingham, Notts United Services (Nottingham).

McCREA, William Hunter, FRS 1952; MA; PhD, ScD (Cambridge); BSc (London); FRSE, FRAS, MRIA; Research Professor of Theoretical Astronomy, University of Sussex, 1966-

72, now Emeritus; *b* Dublin, 13 Dec. 1904; *er s* of late Robert Hunter McCrea; *m* 1933, Marian Nicol Core, 2nd *d* of late Thomas Webster, JP, Burdiehouse, Edinburgh; one *s* two *d. Educ:* Chesterfield Grammar Sch.; Trinity Coll., Cambridge (Scholar); University of Göttingen. Wrangler, Rayleigh Prizeman, Sheepshanks Exhibitioner, and Isaac Newton Student, of Cambridge Univ.; Rouse Ball Travelling Student, and Rouse Ball Senior Student, of Trinity Coll.; Comyns Berkeley Bye-Fellow, Gonville and Caius Coll., Cambridge, 1952-53. Lecturer in Mathematics, Univ. of Edinburgh, 1930-32; Reader in Mathematics, Univ. of London, and Assistant Prof., Imperial Coll. of Science, 1932-36; Prof. of Mathematics: Queen's Univ., Belfast, 1936-44; Univ. of London (Royal Holloway Coll.), 1944-66. Visiting Prof. of Astronomy: Univ. of California, 1956; Case Inst. of Technology, 1964; Univ. of BC, Vancouver, 1975-76; Consulting Astronomer, Kitt Peak National Observatory, Arizona, 1965, 1975; Royal Society Exchange Visitor: to USSR, 1960, 1968; to Mexico, 1971; to Argentina, 1971; to India, 1976; For. Visiting Prof. of American Astronomical Soc. and Vis. Prof., Berkeley Astronomy Dept, 1967; first occupant, Chaire Georges Lemaître, Louvain Univ., 1969; Royal Soc. Leverhulme Vis. Prof. of Astronomy, Cairo Univ., 1973. Visiting Lecturer: Univ. of Liège, 1960; Technische Hochschule, Aachen, 1962; various universities in Greece and Turkey (British Council), 1971; York Univ., 1965; Lectures: Harland, Univ. of Exeter, 1970; Larmor, QUB, 1970; Halley, Oxford, 1975. Temp. Princ. Experimental Officer, Admty, 1943-45; Commnd RAFVR (Training Branch), 1941-45. Mem., Governing Board of School of Theoretical Physics, Dublin Institute for Advanced Studies, 1940-50; Governor: Royal Holloway Coll., 1946-49; Ottershaw Sch., 1947-52; Barclay Sch. for Partially Sighted Girls, 1949-66; Mem. Adv. Council, Chelsea Coll. of Aeronautical and Automobile Engineering, 1958-. Secretary of Section A of British Assoc., 1935-39, Pres. 1966; Pres., Mathematical Assoc., 1973-74. Joint Editor of The Observatory, 1935-37. Pres., Royal Astronomical Soc., 1961-63 (Sec., 1940-49; Foreign Correspondent, 1968-71; Treasurer, 1976-). Fellow, Imperial Coll., 1967-; Leverhulme Emeritus Fellow, 1973-75. Mem., Akademie Leopoldina, 1972-. Keith Prize, RSE, 1939-41; Gold Medal, RAS, 1976. Hon. DSc: National Univ., Ireland, 1954; QUB, 1970. Dr *hc* National Univ., Cordoba, Argentina, 1971; Hon. ScD Dublin, 1972. *Publications:* Relativity Physics, 1935; Analytical Geometry of Three Dimensions, 1942; Physics of the Sun and Stars, 1950; trans. A. Unsöld's The New Cosmos, 1969; Royal Greenwich Observatory, 1975; various papers and reviews in mathematical and astronomical journals. *Address:* 87 Houndean Rise, Lewes, East Sussex. *Club:* Athenæum.

McCREERY, Henry Edwin Lewis, QC 1965; **His Honour Judge McCreery;** a Circuit Judge (formerly Judge of County Courts), since 1971; *b* 26 July 1920; *s* of late Rev. William John McCreery, BD, and late Anne Cullen McCreery; *m* 1945, Margaret Elizabeth Booth; two *d. Educ:* St Andrew's Coll., Dublin; Trinity Coll., Dublin. RAF, 1942-47. Called: Irish Bar King's Inns, 1943; English Bar, Middle Temple, 1946 (Bencher, 1971). Dep. Chm., Quarter Sessions: Cornwall, 1966-71; Devon, 1967-71; Recorder of Salisbury, 1969-71. *Recreation:* gardening. *Clubs:* Royal Air Force; Hampshire (Winchester).

MacCRINDLE, Robert Alexander, QC 1963; commercial lawyer with Shearman and Sterling; Member, Royal Commission on Civil Liability and Compensation for Personal Injury, since 1973; *b* 27 Jan. 1928; *s* of F. R. MacCrindle; *m* 1959, Pauline Dilys, *d* of Mark S. Morgan; one *s* one *d. Educ:* Girvan High Sch.; King's Coll., London; Gonville and Caius Coll., Cambridge. LLB London, 1948. Served RAF, 1948-50, Flt-Lt. LLB Cantab, Chancellor's Medal, 1951. Called to Bar, Gray's Inn, 1952 (Bencher, 1969); Junior Counsel to Board of Trade (Export Credits), 1961-63. Hon. Fellow, American Coll. of Trial Lawyers, 1974. *Publication:* McNair's Law of the Air, 1953. *Recreation:* golf. *Address:* 4 Essex Court, Temple, EC4. *T:* 01-353 6771; 88 avenue de Breteuil, 75015 Paris, France. *T:* 567-1193.

McCRINDLE, Robert Arthur; MP (C) Brentwood and Ongar, since 1974 (Billericay, 1970-74); *b* 19 Sept. 1929; *o s* of Thomas Arthur and Isabella McCrindle; *m* 1953, Myra Anderson; two *s. Educ:* Allen Glen's Coll., Glasgow. Vice-Chm., Sausmarez, Carey & Harris, Financial Consultants, 1972-75; Dir, Langham Life Assurance Co. Ltd, 1972-76; Chm., Cometco Ltd, Commodity Brokers. Contested: Dundee (East), 1959; Thurrock, 1964. Chm., Cons. Pensions Cttee; PPS to Min. of State, Home Office, 1974; Sec., Cons. Health and Social Security Cttee, 1974-; Parliamentary Consultant: British Transport Police Fedn; British Insurance Brokers' Council; Guild of Business Travel Agents. Nat. Vice-Pres., Corp. of Mortgage Brokers, 1970-76. Fellow, Corp. of Insurance Brokers; ACII.

Address: 26 Ashburnham Gardens, Upminster, Essex. *T:* Upminster 27152.

McCRONE, Robert Gavin Loudon; Under-Secretary for Regional Development and Chief Economic Adviser at the Scottish Office, since 1972; Chairman, Scottish Economic Planning Board; *b* 2 Feb. 1933; *s* of Robert Osborne Orr McCrone and Laura Margaret McCrone; *m* 1959, Alexandra Bruce Waddell; two *s* one *d. Educ:* Stowe Sch.; St Catharine's Coll., Cambridge (Economics Tripos); University Coll. of Wales, Aberystwyth (Milk Marketing Bd Research Schol. in agricl economics); Univ. of Glasgow. Economist to Fisons Ltd, 1959-60; Lectr in Applied Economics, Glasgow Univ., 1960-65; Economic Consultant to UNESCO and Mem. Educl Planning Mission to Libya, 1964; Fellow of Brasenose Coll., Oxford, 1965-72 and CUF Lectr in Economics, Oxford Univ., 1966-70; Chm., Oxford Univ. Economics Subfaculty, 1968-70; Mem. NEDC Working Party on Agricl Policy, 1967-68; Economic Adviser to House of Commons Select Cttee on Scottish Affairs, 1969-70; Special Economic Adviser to Sec. of State for Local Govt and Regional Planning, 1970; Sen. Economic Adviser and Head of Economics and Statistics Unit, Scottish Office, 1970-72. *Publications:* The Economics of Subsidising Agriculture, 1962; Agricultural Integration in Western Europe, 1963; Scotland's Economic Progress 1951-60, 1963; Regional Policy in Britain, 1969; Scotland's Future, 1969; contribs to various economic jls. *Recreations:* walking, music. *Address:* 28 Mansionhouse Road, Edinburgh EH9 2JD. *T:* 031-667 6687. *Clubs:* United Oxford & Cambridge University, Royal Commonwealth Society.

McCRONE, Robert Watson, MC 1916; BSc, MICE; ARCST; *b* 6 Feb. 1893; *s* of Edward McCrone, Craigallion, Kilmacolm, Renfrewshire; *m* 1934, Enid Marie, OBE, *d* of B. W. Just, Bristol; three *d. Educ:* Merchiston Castle Sch., Edinburgh; Royal College of Science and Technology, Glasgow; Glasgow Univ. Served European War, 1914-18, in Royal Engineers, 51st Highland Div. (despatches, MC); Croix de Guerre, France, 1918. Founder in 1923 of Metal Industries Group of Companies; Man. Dir and then Chm. until 1955; Dir, British Oxygen Co. Ltd, 1933-63; Chm. or Dir of many other industrial concerns until 1963. Past Mem. East of Scotland Electricity Board. Formerly Governor Royal College of Science and Technology, Glasgow; formerly member of Lloyd's. *Recreations:* farming, yachting. *Address:* Pitliver, by Dunfermline, Fife. *T:* Limekilns 232.

McCRUM, Michael William, MA; Head Master of Eton, since 1970; *b* 23 May 1924; 3rd *s* of Captain C. R. McCrum, RN (retired) and of Ivy Hilda Constance (*née* Nicholson); *m* 1952, Christine Mary Kathleen, *d* of Sir Arthur fforde, *qv*; three *s* one *d. Educ:* Horris Hill, Newbury; Sherborne Sch.; Corpus Christi Coll., Cambridge. Entrance Scholar to CCC, Dec. 1942. Served RN, 1943-45 (Sub-Lt RNVR, Dec. 1943). CCC, Cambridge, 1946-48; Part I, Class. Tripos, First Class, 1947; Part II, First Class, with distinction, 1948. Asst Master, Rugby School, Sept. 1948-July 1950 (Lower Bench Master, 1949-50); Fellow CCC, Cambridge, 1949; Second Tutor, 1950-51; Tutor, 1951-62; Member, Council of the Senate, University of Cambridge, 1955-58, General Board of Faculties, 1957-62; Headmaster, Tonbridge School, 1962-70. Chm., HMC, 1974. *Publication:* (with A. G. Woodhead) Select Documents of the Principates of the Flavian Emperors AD 68-96, 1961. *Address:* The Cloisters, Eton College, Windsor, Berks. *Clubs:* Athenæum, East India, Devonshire, Sports and Public Schools; Hawks (Cambridge).

McCULLOUGH, Charles; see McCullough, I. C. R.

McCULLOUGH, Donald; see McCullough, W. D. H.

McCULLOUGH, (Iain) Charles (Robert), QC 1971; a Recorder of the Crown Court, since 1972; *b* 31 July 1931; *o s* of Thomas W. McCullough, *qv*; *m* 1965, Margaret Joyce, JP Rutland 1973, *o d* of late David H. Patey, MS, FRCS, and of Gladys Joyce (*née* Summers); one *s* one *d. Educ:* Taunton Sch.; Trinity Hall, Cambridge. BA 1955; MA 1960. National Service, 1950-52, commnd Royal Artillery; RA (TA), 1952-54. Barrister, Middle Temple, 1956; Midland and Oxford Circuit (formerly Midland Circuit); Dep. Chm., Notts QS, 1969-71. Mem., General Council of the Bar, 1966-70; Mem., Criminal Law Revision Cttee, 1973-. *Address:* 2 Crown Office Row, Temple, EC4. *T:* 01-353 1365. *Club:* Garrick.

McCULLOUGH, Thomas Warburton, CB 1962; OBE 1954; HM Chief Inspector of Factories, Ministry of Labour, 1958-63; *b* 13 March 1901; *o s* of late Robert McCullough and Emma Warburton, *d* of Thomas Rigby; *m* 1928, Lisette Hunter, *d* of late Henry George Gannaway; one *s. Educ:* Ballymena Academy; Glasgow Univ.; Middle Temple. BSc 1925.

Engineering training, Glasgow, 1917-25; Valuation Dept, Ministry of Finance, Belfast, 1925; joined Factory Dept, Home Office, 1926. Member Joint Advisory Cttee on Conditions in Iron Foundries, 1947; Hon. Adviser Scottish Industrial Groups Advisory Council, 1951-53; Chairman of numerous Joint Standing Cttees, 1950-56. Member: Home Office Inter-Departmental Cttee on Accidents in the Home, 1954-57; National Industrial Safety Cttee, 1954-57, Executive Cttee, 1958-63, Royal Society for Prevention of Accidents; Industrial Grants Cttee, Dept of Scientific and Industrial Research, 1958-63; Nuclear Safety Advisory Cttee, 1960-63; Technical Adviser (Safety), The United Steel Companies Ltd, 1963-67. Hon. Life Member, Royal Society for Prevention of Accidents, 1963; Hon. Fellow, Institution of Industrial Safety Officers, 1964; Hon. Adviser (Safety) British Steel Corp. (formerly British Iron and Steel Fedn), 1964-74; Pres., London Construction Safety Group, 1963-74. Silver Medal, L'Institut National de Sécurité, Paris, 1961; Industrial Safety Award, RoSPA, 1970. *Publications:* sundry contribs to literature of accident prevention in industry. *Recreation:* fly-fishing. *Address:* 69 Walsingham Road, Hove, East Sussex. *Club:* Flyfishers'.

See also I. C. R. McCullough.

McCULLOUGH, (William) Donald (Hamilton), MA; advertising and public relations consultant, writer and broadcaster; *s* of late Rev. W. C. McCullough, BA, LLB, St Margaret's Manse, Hawick; *m* Nan, *yr d* of late Captain H. L. Watts-Jones, RN; three *s* two *d. Educ:* Watson's Coll.; Edinburgh Univ. RAFVR, 1939-40. National Trust: Mem., Exec. and Neptune Cttees, 1950-69; Chm., Publicity Cttee; Mem., CPRE; Mem., Cttee, Norfolk Soc. *Publications:* How to Run a Brains Trust, 1947; with Fougasse: Aces Made Easy, 1934; You Have Been Warned, 1935; Many Happy Returns, 1936; Fancy Meeting You, 1947; Question Mark, 1949; with Ernest Clegg: Countryman County Maps, 1946. *Recreations:* golf, sailing. *Address:* Flagstaff House, Burnham Overy Staithe, Norfolk. *TA* and *T:* Burnham Market 248. *Clubs:* Bath; Brancaster; Pilgrims.

McCUNN, Peter Alexander; Director, since 1969, Executive Deputy Chairman, since 1977, Cable & Wireless Ltd; *b* 11 Nov. 1922; *m* 1943, Margaret Prescott; three *s. Educ:* Mexborough Grammar Sch.; Edinburgh University. Commnd W Yorks Regt, 1942; served in Normandy, Malta, Italy; left Army, Nov. 1946 (Captain). Joined Cable & Wireless, 1947; Director: Cable & Wireless/Western Union International Inc. of Puerto Rico, 1968-70; Cable & Wireless, 1969; Nigerian External Telecommunications Ltd, 1969-72; Sierra Leone External Telecommunications Ltd, 1969-72; Trinidad and Tobago External Telecommunications Ltd, 1972; Jamaica International Telecommunications Ltd, 1972. *Recreations:* music, gardening, swimming, cricket, Association football (now non-active). *Address:* Wychelms, 14 Lime Walk, Pinkneys Green, Maidenhead, Berks. *T:* Maidenhead 24308, (office) 01-242 4433. *Clubs:* Royal Commonwealth Society; Exiles (Twickenham).

McCUSKER, (James) Harold; MP (UU) Armagh since 1974; *b* 7 Feb. 1940; *s* of James Harold McCusker and Lily McCusker; *m* 1965, Jennifer Leslie Mills; three *s. Educ:* Lurgan Coll.; Stranmillis Coll., Belfast. Teacher, 1961-68; Trng Officer, 1968-73; Production Man., 1973-74. Sec. and Whip, Ulster Unionist Party, Westminster, 1975-76. *Address:* 33 Seagoe Road, Portadown, Craigavon BT63 5HW. *T:* Portadown 33876.

McCUTCHEON, Sir (Walter) Osborn, Kt 1966; LFRAIA; Consultant (Partner, 1926-77), Bates, Smart & McCutcheon, Melbourne (Architects, Engineers and Town Planners); *b* 8 April 1899; *s* of W. B. McCutcheon, Solicitor, Melbourne; *m* 1928, Mary, *d* of A. A. Buley; two *s* one *d. Educ:* Wesley Coll., Melbourne; Univ. of Melbourne. Mem. Faculty, Melbourne Univ. School of Architecture; Director, Arch., Melbourne Technical Sch., 1930-39; Member Council, Royal Victoria Inst. of Architecture, 1930-45 (Pres., 1940-42; Mem. Board of Arch. Educn, 1933-39, 1940-42, 1953-57); Pres., Building Indust. Congr. of Victoria, 1934-36; Member Council, RAIA, 1941-42; Chief Architect, Engineers HQ, US Army, SW Pacific Area, 1942-44; Controller of Planning etc to Australian Commonwealth Govt, 1944-46; resumed private practice, 1946. Mem. various cttees; assessor of sundry competitions. Mem., National Capital Planning Cttee, Nat. Capital Develt Commn, 1967-73. Gold Medal, RAIA, 1965. Hon. LLD, Monash Univ., 1968. *Publications:* articles in Architecture in Australia, etc. *Recreations:* sailing, reading. *Address:* (office) 366 St Kilda Road, Melbourne, Vic 3004, Australia. *T:* Melbourne 699-6255; (home) Unit 4, 76 Molesworth Street, Kew, Vic 3101, Australia. *T:* Melbourne 861-7683. *Clubs:* Melbourne, Savage (Melbourne); Peninsula Country Golf, Davey's Bay Yacht, Mornington Yacht.

McDAVID, Sir Edwin Frank, Kt 1953; CMG 1948; CBE 1942 (MBE 1933); retired; *b* 26 Oct. 1895; *s* of late E. N. McDavid, Company Secretary, and Elizabeth McDavid; *m* 1920, Elma Hildred Delph; no *c. Educ:* Queen's Coll., British Guiana. Served with Fitzpatrick, Graham and Co., Chartered Accountants, 1914-20; Secretary, Excess Profits Tax Board of Assessment, British Guiana, 1920; Chief Accountant, British Guiana Govt Railway and Steamer Services, 1923; acted as Man. Dir of above Services, 1928; Deputy Colonial Treas., British Guiana, 1929; Commissioner of Income Tax, 1929-53; Financial Secretary (formerly Colonial Treasurer) and Member of Executive and Legislative Councils, 1935-53; Chairman: British Guiana Rice Marketing Board, 1939-46; British Guiana Rice Development Co., 1952-60; President, State Council, 1953; MEC, MLC, Minister of Lands and Agriculture, 1954-57. Managing Director, Demerara Mutual Life Assurance Society Ltd, 1960-62 (Chairman, 1957-59). Chairman, British Guiana Public Library, 1941-61; Hon. Colonel British Guiana Volunteer Force, 1954-62. *Address:* c/o Barclays Bank Ltd, 8 George Street, Richmond, Surrey.

MacDERMOT, The, (Charles J.), styled Prince of Coolavin; *b* 20 Feb. 1899; 2nd and *e surv. s* of late Charles E., The MacDermot, and Caroline MacDermot; *m* 1954, Felicity, *d* of Edward T. MacDermot, MA, JP, Lillycombe, Porlock, Somerset. *Educ:* Stonyhurst Coll.; Trinity Coll., Dublin. *Heir: b* Sir Dermot F. MacDermot, *qv. Address:* Coolavin, Ballaghaderreen, Co. Roscommon.

MacDERMOT, Brian (Charles), CBE 1966; MVO 1961; HM Diplomatic Service, retired; *b* 29 Jan. 1914; *m* 1949, Mary Arden Hunter; seven *s* two *d* . Probationer Vice-Consul, Peking, China, 1936; served at: Hankow, China, 1939-40; Kobe, Japan, 1940-41; Kunming, South China, 1942; Vice-Consul, Shiraz, Persia, 1943; Paris, 1944, promoted Consul, 1945; Foreign Office, 1946; Consul, Beirut, 1948; First Secretary, Belgrade, 1950; First Secretary, Berne, 1951, acted as Charge d'Affaires, 1951, 1952, 1953; transferred to Foreign Office, 1954; transferred to Holy See, 1955, acted as Chargé d'Affaires, 1958, 1959, 1960 and 1961; HM Consul-General, Oporto, 1962-68; Ambassador and Consul-Gen., Paraguay, 1968-72. *Address:* The Old Rectory, St James, Shaftesbury, Dorset SP7 8HG.

MacDERMOT, Sir Dermot (Francis), KCMG 1962 (CMG 1954); CBE 1947; *b* 14 June 1906; 2nd surv. *s* of late Charles Edward, The MacDermot, Prince of Coolavin; *m* 1934, Betty Steel; three *s. Educ:* Stonyhurst Coll.; Trinity Coll., Dublin, LLD *jure dignitatis*, 1964. Joined HM Consular Service in 1929 and served in Tokyo, Yokohama, Kobe and Osaka in Japan, Manila (Philippines), Tamsui (Formosa), New Orleans, and in the Foreign Office. Appointed a Counsellor in the Foreign Office, 1947; Inspector, HM Foreign Service, 1951; HM Minister to Roumania, 1954-56; HM Ambassador to Indonesia, 1956-59; Assistant Under-Secretary, Foreign Office, 1959-61; HM Ambassador to Thailand, 1961-65. *Recreation:* golf. *Address:* Oughterard, Co. Galway, Eire. *Club:* University (Dublin).
See also The MacDermot.

MACDERMOT, Niall, OBE 1944; QC 1963; barrister-at-law; Secretary-General, International Commission of Jurists, since Dec. 1970; *b* 10 Sept. 1916; *s* of late Henry MacDermot, KC, Dublin; *m* 1940, Violet Denise Maxwell (marr. diss.); one *s* ; *m* 1966, Ludmila Benvenuto. *Educ:* Rugby Sch.; Corpus Christi Coll., Cambridge; Balliol Coll., Oxford. Served in Intelligence Corps, 1939-46; GSO1 HQ 21 Army Group, 1944-45. MP (Lab) Lewisham North, Feb. 1957-59, Derby North, April 1962-1970; Mem. Exec., London Labour Party, 1958-62. Dep. Chm., Beds QS, 1961-64, 1969-72; Recorder of Newark-on-Trent, 1963-64; a Recorder of the Crown Court, 1972-74. Master of the Bench, Inner Temple, 1970-. Financial Sec., Treasury, 1964-67; Minister of State, Min. of Housing and Local Govt, 1967-68. Hon. Treasurer, Justice, 1968-70. Chm., Special NGO Cttee on Human Rights, Geneva, 1973-. Trustee of Tate Gall., 1969-76. *Address:* PO Box 120, 109 route de Chêne, 1224 Geneva, Switzerland. *T:* Geneva 49.35.45.

MacDERMOTT, Baron (Life Peer), *cr* 1947, of Belmont; **John Clarke MacDermott,** PC 1947, PC (Northern Ireland), 1940; MC; LLD; Lord Chief Justice of Northern Ireland, 1951-71; *b* 12 April 1896; *s* of late Rev. John and Lydia Allen MacDermott, Belmont, Belfast; *m* 1926, Louise Palmer, *o d* of Rev. J. C. Johnston, MA, DD; two *s* two *d. Educ:* Campbell Coll., Belfast; Queen's Univ. of Belfast. Foundation Scholar, 1914. Served European War in France: Lieut, 51st Bn MGC (MC). LLB First Class Honours, 1921; Victoria Prizeman and Exhibitioner, King's Inns, Dublin; called to Irish Bar, 1921; Lecturer in Jurisprudence, Queen's Univ. of Belfast, 1931-35; appointed to determine Industrial Assurance Disputes in Northern Ireland, 1929-38; KC (Northern Ireland), 1936; MP (U) Queen's University of Belfast, Parliament of Northern Ireland, 1938-44; Governor, Campbell Coll., 1934-59; Chairman Joint Select Cttee on Road and Rail Transport in Northern Ireland, 1939; Sept. 1939, Major RA; Minister of Public Security for Northern Ireland, June 1940-Nov. 1941; Attorney-General, 1941-44; Judge, High Court of Justice, Northern Ireland, 1944-47; a Lord of Appeal in Ordinary, 1947-51; Chairman, National Arbitration Tribunal, Northern Ireland, 1944-46; Bencher Inn of Court of Northern Ireland; Hon. Bencher Gray's Inn, 1947. Hamlyn Lectures on Protection from Power, 1957; Chairman Commission on Isle of Man Constitution, 1958. Pro-Chancellor, Queen's Univ. of Belfast, 1951-69. Hon. LLD: QUB, 1951; Edinburgh, 1958; Cambridge, 1968. *Address:* Glenburn, 8 Cairnburn Road, Belfast 4. *T:* Belfast 63361. *Clubs:* Athenæum; Ulster (Belfast).
See also Hon. J. C. MacDermott.

MacDERMOTT, Edmond Geoffrey; Metropolitan Stipendiary Magistrate since 1972. Called to Bar, Gray's Inn, 1935; practised NE Circuit; Army, 1939-45; Dept of Dir of Public Prosecutions, 1946-72; Asst Dir of Public Prosecutions, 1968-72. Dep. Circuit Judge, Inner London. *Address:* Horseferry Road Magistrates Court, 70 Horseferry Road, SW1P 2AX.

McDERMOTT, Sir Emmet; *see* McDermott, Sir L. E.

McDERMOTT, Geoffrey Lyster, CMG 1957; diplomat, author and journalist; retired from Foreign Service, 1962; *b* 7 Oct. 1912; *o s* of late Captain J. W. McDermott, CIE, and Mrs G. E. McDermott; *m* 1st, 1937, Ruth Mary, *d* of late Sir Arthur Fleming, CBE; one *s* one *d* ; 2nd, 1947, Elizabeth Marion Robertson; two *s* (and one step *s*). *Educ:* Marlborough Coll. (scholar); King's Coll., Cambridge. Scholar in Mod. Langs at King's, 1930; 1st class hons both parts of Mod. Langs tripos, 1931 and 1933. Entered Diplomatic Service, 1935; 3rd Sec., FO, 1935; Sofia, 1938; 2nd Sec., Ankara, 1941; FO, 1943; 1st Sec., FO, 1944; Cairo, 1946; Santiago, 1948; Chargé d'Affaires there, 1949, 1950, 1951; Counsellor and Head of Permanent Under-Secretary's Dept in the Foreign Office, 1953-56; Minister HM Foreign Service, employed in Foreign Office, 1956-58; ambassadorial rank as Political Representative with Middle East Forces, Cyprus, 1958-61, and as HM Minister in Berlin, 1961-62. Chm., Cttee for the Recognition of German Democratic Republic, 1971-73. FRSA 1958. *Publications:* Berlin: Success of a Mission?, 1963; The Eden Legacy and the Decline of British Diplomacy, 1969; Leader Lost: a biography of Hugh Gaitskell, 1972; The New Diplomacy, 1973; numerous articles. *Recreations:* walking, motoring, and the arts. *Address:* 22 Queen Street, W1X 7PJ. *T:* 01-499 1466; The Old Rectory, Ripple, near Tewkesbury, Glos. *T:* Upton-upon-Severn 2444. *Clubs:* Boodle's, Garrick.

MacDERMOTT, Hon. John Clarke; Hon. Mr Justice MacDermott; Judge of the High Court of Northern Ireland, since 1973; *b* 1927; *s* of Baron MacDermott, *qv* ; *m* 1953, Margaret Helen, *d* of late Hugh Dales, Belfast; four *d. Educ:* Campbell Coll., Belfast; Trinity Hall, Cambridge (BA); QUB. Called to Bar, Inner Temple and Northern Ireland; 1949; QC (NI) 1964. *Address:* Royal Courts of Justice, Belfast, Northern Ireland; Stanley House, Church Road, Holywood, Co. Down.

McDERMOTT, Sir (Lawrence) Emmet, KBE 1972; Lord Mayor of Sydney, 1969-72; Alderman, Sydney, 1962-77; Dental Surgeon; *b* 6 Sept. 1911; *s* of O. J. McDermott; *m* 1939, Arline Beatrice Olga; one *s* one *d. Educ:* St Ignatius Coll., Sydney; Univ. of Sydney; Northwestern Univ., Chicago. MDS Sydney; DDS Northwestern; FICD, FRACDS. Hon. Consultant Dental Surgeon: Royal Prince Alfred Hosp., 1942-; Eastern Suburbs Hosp., 1945-; Pres., Bd of Control, United Dental Hosp., Sydney, 1967-; Mem., NSW Dental Bd, 1967-; Pres., Australian Dental Assoc. (NSW Br.), 1960-61; Councillor, Australian Dental Assoc., 1962-66. Mem., Liberal Party State Council, 1969; Councillor, Sydney County Council, 1973-, Dep. Chm., 1975-. Dir, City Mutual Life Assce Soc. Ltd, 1970-, Dep. Chm., 1976; Member: Sydney Cove Redevelopment Authority 1971-76; Convocation, Macquarie Univ., 1966-; Australia-Britain Soc. (NSW Br.), Vice-Pres., 1972-77. *Recreations:* golf, swimming (Sydney Univ. Blue), bowls. *Address:* T&G Tower, Hyde Park Square, Park & Elizabeth Streets, Sydney, NSW 2000, Australia. *T:* 26-3660; 20 Carnarvon Road, Roseville, NSW 2069. *T:* 46-2086. *Clubs:* Australian Jockey, Royal Sydney Golf, Elanora Country, Tattersall's, American National, Chatswood Bowling, City Bowling (all Sydney).

McDIARMID, Hugh; *see* Grieve, C. M.

MACDIARMID, Niall Campbell; Chairman: Sanderson Kayser Ltd, since 1974; CompAir Ltd, since 1974; Director: Sketchley Ltd (Chairman, 1975-77); Provincial Insurance Co. Ltd; Baker Perkins Holdings Ltd; Unicorn Industries Ltd; *b* 7 June 1919; *y s* of Sir Allan Campbell Macdiarmid, and Grace Buchanan (*née* McClure); *m* 1946, Patricia Isobel Mackie-Campbell, *yr d* of Geordie Osmonde Lorne Campbell and Jessie Isobel (*née* Mackie); two *d* (and one *d* decd). *Educ:* Uppingham Sch.; Magdalen Coll., Oxford. Served War of 1939-45 with The Argyll and Sutherland Highlanders (despatches three times). Man. Dir, The Stanton Ironworks Co. Ltd (later Stanton and Staveley Ltd), 1957-62, Chm., 1962-64; Chm., Stewarts and Lloyds Ltd, 1964-69; Dir, The United Steel Companies Ltd, 1964-67; Man. Dir, Northern and Tubes Group, BSC, 1967-69; Dep. Chm., Vickers Ltd, 1970-71. Member: Iron and Steel Board, 1961-67; BSC, 1967-69; E Midlands Gas Board, 1962-67; Pres., Iron and Steel Inst., 1969-70. Trustee of Uppingham School (Chairman, 1967-77); Trustee, Duke of Edinburgh's Award, 1963-71. *Address:* Hillside House, Tinwell Road, Stamford, Lincs. *T:* Stamford 3075. *Club:* Lansdowne.

MACDONALD, family name of **Barons Macdonald** and **Macdonald of Gwaenysgor.**

MACDONALD, 8th Baron *cr* 1776; **Godfrey James Macdonald of Macdonald;** Chief of the Name and Arms of Macdonald; *b* 28 Nov. 1947; *s* of 7th Baron Macdonald, MBE, TD, and of Anne, *o d* of late Alfred Whitaker; *S* father, 1970; *m* 1969, Claire, *e d* of Captain T. N. Catlow, CBE, RN, Gabriel Cottage, Tunstall, Lancs; two *d. Heir: b* Hon. Alexander Donald Archibald Macdonald, *b* 3 Sept. 1953. *Address:* Ostaig House, Isle of Skye. *T:* Ardvasar 226. *Clubs:* Turf; New (Edinburgh).

McDONALD, Hon. Lord; Robert Howat McDonald, MC 1944; a Senator of the College of Justice in Scotland, since 1973; *b* 15 May 1916; *s* of Robert Glassford McDonald, and Roberta May Howat, Paisley, Renfrewshire; *m* 1949, Barbara Mackenzie, *d* of John Mackenzie, Badcaul, Ross-shire; no *c. Educ:* John Neilson Institution, Paisley. MA (Glasgow) 1935; LLB (Glasgow) 1937; admitted Faculty of Advocates, 1946; QC (Scot.) 1957. Served with KOSB, 1939-46 (despatches, 1945). Sheriff Principal of Ayr and Bute, 1966-71. Mem., Criminal Injuries Compensation Board, 1964-71; Pres., Industrial Tribunals for Scotland, 1972-73; Chm., Gen. Nursing Council for Scotland, 1970-73; Chm., Mental Welfare Commn for Scotland, 1965-; Mem., Employment Appeal Tribunal, 1976-. *Recreations:* golf, fishing. *Address:* Parliament House, Edinburgh. *Club:* New (Edinburgh).

MACDONALD OF GWAENYSGOR, 2nd Baron *cr* 1949, of Gwaenysgor, Flint; **Gordon Ramsay Macdonald;** Chairman and Chief Executive in UK of Hayek Consultancy Group; Chairman and Chief Executive: Ferro Metal and Chemical Corporation, since 1977; Satra Consultants (UK) Ltd, since 1977; *b* 16 Oct. 1915; *er s* of 1st Baron Macdonald of Gwaenysgor, PC, KCMG; *S* father, 1966; *m* 1941, Leslie Margaret Taylor; three *d. Educ:* Manchester Univ. MA, Economics and Commerce. Served War, 1940-46; Army, Major, Artillery; GSO2 Operations and Intelligence (despatches, Burma). Board of Trade, 1946-53: Principal, 1946-47; UK Trade Comr, Canberra, ACT, 1947-53. With Tube Investments Ltd, and Man. Dir TI (Export) Ltd, 1953-64; Chief Exec., Telecommunications Group, Plessey Co., 1964-67. *Recreations:* golf, chess. *Heir: b* Hon. Kenneth Lewis Macdonald [*b* 3 Feb. 1921; m 1952, Maureen Margaret Watson-Allan; two *d*].

MACDONALD of Sleat (Btcy); *see under* Bosville Macdonald.

MACDONALD, Adam Davidson, MA, MSc, MD; retired as Leech Professor of Pharmacology in the University of Manchester, Sept. 1964; *b* Perth, Scotland, 17 Oct. 1895; *s* of Robert Macdonald, schoolmaster; *m* 1927, Helen Muriel Anderson, Edinburgh; one *s* two *d. Educ:* High School of Dundee; Univ. of Edinburgh (Neill Arnott Scholar and Goodsir Fellow). Demonstrator in Physiology, Univ. of Edinburgh; Lectr in Experimental Physiology and Reader in Pharmacology, Univ. of Manchester. *Publications:* various papers in physiological and pharmacological journals. *Recreations:* golf, gardening. *Address:* 2 Broadway Avenue, Cheadle, Cheshire. *T:* 061-428 2435.

McDONALD, Alex Gordon; Chief Scientific Officer, Department of Health and Social Security, since 1975; *b* 29 Jan. 1921; *m* 1st, 1942, P. Thomas; 2nd, 1950, J. James; two *d. Educ:* Tiffin Sch., Kingston upon Thames; Royal Coll. of Science (BSc, ARCS). Served RNVR, Lieut (A), Fleet Air Arm, 1939-46. Home Office, 1949; Chief of Staffs, MoD, 1956; Police Research and Develt Br., 1963; DHSS, 1970. Sometime Lectr at: Inst. of Criminology,

Inst. of Advanced Legal Study, London Hosp. Sch. of Forensic Pathology, London Sch. of Hygiene and Trop. Med., and Univ. of Warwick Sch. of Business Studies. Member, Bd of Studies in Community Med., London. Hon. Prof. in Industrial and Business Studies, Univ. of Warwick. *Publications:* contrib. learned jls on OR and Systems Analysis. *Recreations:* Basset Hounds, Blood Hounds, needlework, reading. *Address:* 40 Wolsey Road, East Molesey, Surrey KT8 9EN. *Club:* Kennel.

McDONALD, Sir Alexander Forbes, Kt 1972; *b* 14 Aug. 1911; *s* of late Angus McDonald and late Christina Jane Forbes; *m* 1937, Ethel Marjorie, *d* of late Theodore Crawford, MC, and late Sarah Anne Mansfield; two *s* two *d. Educ:* Hillhead Sch.; Glasgow Univ. BL Glasgow 1933. Chartered Accountant, 1934. Chairman: The Distillers Company, 1967-76; Council, Scotch Whisky Assoc., 1967-76. DL, County of City of Edinburgh, 1963. *Address:* 6 Oswald Road, Edinburgh EH9 2HF. *T:* 031-667 4246.

McDONALD, Alexander Gordon; *see* McDonald, Alex G.

McDONALD, Alexander Hugh, FBA 1967; MA, PhD; LittD; Life Fellow of Clare College, Cambridge, 1973; Honorary Research Fellow, University of Western Australia, since 1975; *b* 19 May 1908; *s* of Rev. William and Mary McDonald; *m* 1941, Joan Urey, *d* of Sir Martin and Ada McIlrath. *Educ:* Auckland Grammar Sch.; Auckland Univ. Coll., NZ; Clare Coll., Cambridge. Univ. of NZ: BA, Sen. Schol. in Greek, 1928; MA, Double First in Latin and Greek, Travelling Scholarship in Arts, 1929; Clare Coll., Cambridge: Exhibitioner, First in Classical Tripos, Part II, 1932; Research at Göttingen Univ., 1933; Senior Research Student, Clare Coll., 1934; PhD (Cambridge) 1936. Lecturer in Ancient History, Nottingham University Coll., 1934-38; Sydney Univ., Australia: Reader in Ancient History, 1939-44; Acting Prof. of Latin, 1945, Prof. of Ancient World History, 1945-51; Lectr in Ancient Hist., Univ. of Cambridge, 1952-73; Fellow, 1952-73, Sen. Tutor, 1954-57, and Steward, 1963-65, Clare Coll., Cambridge. Editor, Current Affairs Bulletin, Australian Army, 1943-46; News Commentator, ABC, 1943-51; Liaison Officer (NSW) for Colonial Service appointments, 1946-51. Acting Prof. of Ancient History, Chicago Univ., 1954. Mem. Inst. Advanced Study, Princeton, NJ, 1966; Chairman Archæol. Faculty, British School at Rome, 1967-70; President: Cambridge Philological Soc., 1968-70; Roman Soc., 1971-74. Hon. LLD Glasgow, 1948; Hon. LittD Auckland, 1967. Hon. FAHA 1975. *Publications:* Japanese Imperialism, 1944; (ed) Trusteeship in the Pacific, 1948; (ed) Oxford Text of Livy, 1937, Vol. V, 1965; Republican Rome, 1966; papers and reviews in Jl of Roman Studies; reviews in Classical Review. *Recreations:* golf, theatre. *Address:* 13A Strathearn, 16 Kings Park Avenue, Crawley, WA 6009, Australia. *T:* Perth (WA) 86.3391. *Club:* University (Sydney).

McDONALD, Prof. Alexander John, MA (Cantab), LLB, WS; Professor of Conveyancing, University of Dundee (formerly Queen's College), since 1955 (Dean of the Faculty of Law, 1958-62, 1965); *b* 15 March 1919; *o s* of late John McDonald, and Agnes Mary Stewart McDonald; *m* 1951, Doreen Mary, *o d* of late Frank Cook, OBE; two *s* two *d. Educ:* Cargilfield Sch.; Fettes Coll. (open scholar); Christ's Coll., Cambridge (Classical Exhibn, BA 1942); Edinburgh Univ. (Thow Schol. and John Robertson Prize in Conveyancing; LLB with dist., 1949). Admitted as Solicitor and Writer to the Signet, 1950; Lectr in Conveyancing, Edinburgh Univ., 1952-55; Registrar of the Diocese of Brechin, 1963-74. Member firm of Thorntons & Dickies, WS, Dundee DD2 1HY. *Address:* 4 Middlebank Crescent, Dundee. *T:* Dundee 66049.

MACDONALD, Alistair; *b* 23 July 1912; 2nd *s* of late Reginald James Macdonald and Dorothy Bolden; *m* 1941, Myra Jones; one *s* six *d. Educ:* King's Sch., Bruton. Called to the Bar, Inner Temple, 1935. Worked with mentally handicapped children, Sunfield Childrens' Homes, Clent, 1936-40; served in RAF, 1940-45; Air Staff (Intelligence), 1943-45 (despatches). Legal Assistant, Law Officers Dept, 1948; Legal Sec. to Law Officers of the Crown, 1950-58; Secretary, The Council on Tribunals, 1958-70; Mem., Lord Chancellor's Dept: Consultant to: Royal Inst. of Public Admin, 1970-72; Emerson Coll., Forest Row, Sussex, 1973-. *Publication:* (with R. E. Wraith and P. G. Hutchesson) Administrative Tribunals, 1973. *Address:* Luxford's, Lewes Road, East Grinstead, W Sussex. *T:* East Grinstead 23365.

MacDONALD, Alistair Archibald, MA, LLB; Sheriff of Grampian, Highland and Islands; at Lerwick and Kirkwall, since 1975; *b* 8 May 1927; *s* of James and Margaret MacDonald; *m* 1950, Jill Russell; one *s* one *d. Educ:* Broughton Sch.; Edinburgh Univ. Called to Scottish Bar, 1954. Formerly Sheriff

Substitute, Caithness, Sutherland, Orkney and Zetland at Lerwick, 1961 and at Kirkwall, 1968. Served in Army, 1945-48. *Address:* West Hall, Shetland Islands; Hall Cottage, Burray, Orkney. *Club:* Aberdeen University.

MACDONALD, Alistair H.; *b* 18 May 1925. *Educ:* Dulwich Coll.; Enfield Technical Coll.; Corpus Christi Coll., Cambridge. MP (Lab) Chislehurst, 1966-70. Councillor, Chislehurst and Sidcup UDC, 1958-62; Alderman, 1964-68, Councillor, 1971-, London Borough of Bromley. *Address:* 79 Oakdene Avenue, Chislehurst, Kent BR7 6DZ. *T:* 01-857 8219.

MACDONALD, Allan Ronald, CMG 1953; *b* 21 Dec. 1906; *s* of Major Ronald Macdonald and Elizabeth Blair Macdonald (*née* Coats); *m* 1st, 1937, Katherine May Hodson; two *s* ; 2nd, 1954, Dr Mary Shaw (*d* 1956). *Educ:* Fettes Coll., Edinburgh; St John's Coll., Cambridge. Ceylon Civil Service, 1929-48; Establishment Sec., Uganda, 1948-51; Colonial Sec., Sierra Leone, 1951-56; Mem. of Lidbury Commn on Gold Coast Public Service, 1951; Chm., Public Service Commn: Kenya, 1956-64; Fedn of South Arabia, 1965-67. *Address:* c/o British Bank of the Middle East, PO Box 199, 99 Bishopsgate, EC2P 2LA. *Club:* United Oxford & Cambridge University.

McDONALD, Allan Stuart; Headmaster, George Heriot's School, Edinburgh, since 1970; *b* 20 Aug. 1922; *s* of Allan McDonald and Clementina Peebles (*née* Stuart), both of Edinburgh; *m* 1948, Margaret Wilson, *d* of late James Adams, Paisley and Stranraer, and of Margaret Wilson (*née* Ferguson); one *s* two *d*. *Educ:* Royal High Sch., Edinburgh; Giffnock and Eastwood Schs, Renfrewshire; Glasgow Univ.; Sorbonne. MA Hons 1944; DipEd 1948. Commnd, Royal Corps of Signals (21st Army Group Signals), 1943-43. Asst Master: Johnstone High Sch., 1948-50; Eastwood Sch., 1950-54; Principal Teacher: Modern Languages, Fortrose Acad., 1954-59; German, George Heriot's Sch., 1959-70; Depute Headmaster, George Heriot's Sch., 1967-70. *Recreations:* formerly Rugby, cricket; now gardening, photography. *Address:* 34 Grange Road, Edinburgh, EH9 1UL. *T:* 031-667 6373.

MACDONALD, Angus Cameron; a Recorder of the Crown Court, since 1974; *b* 26 Aug. 1931; *o s* of Hugh Macdonald, OBE, and Margaret Cameron Macdonald (*née* Westley); *m* 1956, Deborah Anne, *d* of John Denny Inglis, DSO, MC, JP, and Deborah Margery Meiklem Inglis (*née* Thomson); three *d* . *Educ:* Bedford Sch.; Trinity Hall, Cambridge (BA 1954, MA 1960). Nat. service, 1950-51, Commissioned TA, 1951-57. Called to Bar, Gray's Inn, 1955; Resident Magistrate, then Crown Counsel, Nyasaland Govt, 1957-65; Sen. State Counsel, Malawi Govt, 1965-67; practised, NE Circuit, 1967-. *Recreations:* singing, swimming, fishing. *Address:* 21 Lindisfarne Road, Newcastle upon Tyne NE2 2HE. *T:* Newcastle upon Tyne 811695; Blaren, Kilninver, by Oban, Argyll. *T:* Kilmelford 246.

MACDONALD, Archibald J. F., JP; *s* of late Dr G. B. D. Macdonald, MB, ChM, and late Beatrice B. Macdonald; *m* 1945, Hon. Elspeth Ruth Shaw, *y d* of 2nd Baron Craigmyle; two *s*. *Educ:* Chatswood Grammar Sch., Australia; Royal Australian Naval Coll. Joint Chief Executive, Management Research Groups, London, 1937-40; Secretary, Paint Industry Export Group, 1940-49; Dir and Sec., Wartime Paint Manufacturers' Assoc., 1943-45; Dir, Robert Bowran & Co. Ltd, 1949-53; Vice-Chm., Joseph Freeman Sons & Co. Ltd, 1954-66. MP (L) Roxburgh and Selkirk, 1950-51. Member Bd of Visitors, Wormwood Scrubs and Pentonville Prisons. Councillor: Hampstead Borough Council, 1962-65; Camden Borough Council, 1971-76. JP County of London. *Recreations:* travel, people. *Address:* 22 Heath Drive, Hampstead, NW3. *T:* 01-435 2317. *Clubs:* Reform, Garrick.

MacDONALD, Gen. Arthur Leslie, CB 1969; OBE 1953; Chief of Defence Force Staff, Australia, since 1977; *b* 30 Jan. 1919; *s* of late Arthur Leslie MacDonald, Yaamba, Queensland; *m* 1940, Joan Bevington, *d* of late Sidney Brady, Brisbane, Queensland; one *d*. *Educ:* The Southport School, Southport, Queensland; Royal Military College, Duntroon, ACT. Regtl and Staff appts, Aust., ME and New Guinea, 1940-44; Instructor, Staff Coll., Camberley, 1944-45; CO 3rd Bn, The Royal Australian Regt, Korea, 1953-54; Dir of Mil. Ops, AHQ, 1955-56; Senior Aust. Planner, SEATO, Bangkok, 1957-58; Commandant, Jungle Training Centre, Canungra, 1959-60; Dir of Staff Duties, AHQ, 1960-61; Imperial Defence Coll., 1962; Dep. Commander, 1st Div., 1963-64; Commander, Papua and New Guinea Comd, 1965-66; Dep. Chief of the General Staff, 1966-67; Commander Australian Force, Viet Nam, 1968-69; Adjutant-Gen. and 2nd Mil. Mem. of Mil. Board, AMF, 1969-70; GOC Northern Comd, 1970-73; Chief of Operations and Mil. Mem. of Mil.

Board, AMF, 1973; Vice Chief of Gen. Staff, 1973-75; CGS, 1975-77. *Address:* Department of Defence, Canberra, ACT 2600, Australia. *Clubs:* Imperial Service (Sydney); Commonwealth (Canberra); Papua (Port Moresby); Queensland (Brisbane).

McDONALD, Air Marshal Sir Arthur (William Baynes), KCB 1958 (CB 1949); AFC 1935; CEng, FRAeS 1959; DL; retired; *b* 14 June 1903; *s* of late Dr Will McDonald, OBE, Antigua, BWI; *m* 1928, Mary Julia Gray, Hindhead, Surrey; two *s* two *d*. *Educ:* Epsom Coll.; Peterhouse, Cambridge (MA). Joined RAF, 1924; served in Singapore, 1933-35; in Air Ministry, 1939-40; Fighter Command, 1941. Appointed Air Defence Commander, Ceylon, 1942; Air Officer Training, Air HQ, India, 1943-44; Air Officer Commanding No. 106 Group, 1945-46; Comdt RAF Staff Coll., Bulstrode and later Andover, 1947-48; Student Imperial Defence Coll., 1949; OC Aeroplane and Armament Experimental Establishment, under the Ministry of Supply, 1950-52; Director-General of Manning, Air Ministry, 1952-55; Commander-in-Chief, Royal Pakistan Air Force, 1955-57; AOC-in-C, RAF Technical Training Comd, 1958-59; Air Mem. for Personnel, Air Council, 1959-61, retired 1962. DL Hampshire, 1965. *Recreations:* sailing (rep. Great Britain in Olympic Games, 1948), ski-ing. *Address:* Five Oaks, Woodside, Lymington, Hants. *Clubs:* Royal Air Force; Royal Lymington Yacht; RAF Sailing Association (Adm.).

MACDONALD, Coll; Headmaster of Uppingham School, since 1975; *b* 21 Jan. 1924; *s* of Coll Macdonald and Elizabeth (*née* Murray); *m* 1955, Hilary Constance Mowle; two *s*. *Educ:* Rugby Sch.; Christ's Coll., Cambridge (MA). Pilot, RAFVR, 1943-46. Lectr in Greek, Univ. of Sydney, 1949; Lectr in Classics, Univ. of Otago, 1950-51; Asst Master, Bradfield Coll., 1952-55; Asst Master, Sherborne Sch., 1955-60; Head Master: Maidenhead Grammar Sch., 1960-65; Portsmouth Grammar Sch., 1965-75. Research Fellow in Classical Philology, Harvard Univ., 1972-73. *Publications:* (jtly) From Pericles to Cleophon, 1954; (jtly) Roman Politics 80-44 BC, 1960, 2nd edn 1965; (ed) Cicero: De Imperio Cn, Pompei, 1966, 2nd edn 1971; (ed) Cicero: Pro Murena, 1969; (ed) Cicero: De Provinciis Consularibus, 1971; (ed) Cicero: In Catilinam I-IV, Pro Murena, Pro Sulla, Pro Flacco (Loeb Classical Library), 1977; contrib. Greece and Rome, Classical Review. *Recreations:* walking, swimming. *Address:* Uppingham School, Rutland LE15 9QU. *T:* Uppingham 2216.

MACDONALD, David Cameron; Director General, Panel on Takeovers and Mergers, since 1977; *b* 5 July 1936; *s* of James Fraser Macdonald and Anne Sylvia Macdonald (*née* Hutcheson); *m* 1968, Melody Jane Coles; two *d* . *Educ:* St George's Sch., Harpenden; Newport Grammar Sch. Admitted a solicitor with Slaughter and May, 1962; joined Philip Hill Higginson Erlangers (now Hill Samuel & Co. Ltd), 1964; Dir, 1968. Adviser to Govt on Upper Clyde Shipbuilders crisis, 1971. Chm., Issuing Houses Assoc., 1975-77. Mem., BTA, 1971-. *Recreations:* music, fishing. *Address:* 8 Kensington Gate, W8 5NA. *T:* 01-589 2171.

MACDONALD, Prof. Donald Farquhar; Professor of Modern Social and Economic History, University of Dundee, 1967-76 (University of St Andrews, 1955-67); *b* 3 June 1906; 3rd *s* of Donald Macdonald and Annabella Mackenzie; *m* Jeannette Eileen Bickle; one *s*. *Educ:* Dingwall Academy; Aberdeen Univ.; Balliol Coll., Oxford. University Lecturer, Aberdeeen Univ. and University Coll., Exeter, 1934-41; Ministry of Supply and Ministry of Labour and National Service, 1941-43; Secretary (later General Manager), National Assoc. of Port Employers, 1943-55. *Publications:* Scotland's Shifting Population, 1770-1850, 1937; The State and the Trade Unions, 1960, revised edn 1976; The Age of Transition, 1967, etc. *Address:* 11 Arnhall Drive, Dundee. *Club:* United Oxford & Cambridge University.

MACDONALD, Rev. Donald Farquhar Macleod; Principal Clerk of General Assembly of the Church of Scotland, since 1972; *b* 1 May 1915; *s* of John Murchison Macdonald and Margaret Macleod; *m* 1948, Anne Jane Vance Sinclair; one *s* two *d*. *Educ:* North Kelvinside Secondary Sch.; Glasgow Univ. (MA, LLB). Ordained to Glasford Parish, 1948; Clerk to Presbytery of Hamilton, 1952-72; Dep. Clerk of General Assembly, 1955-71. *Recreations:* chess, swimming, gardening. *Address:* 121 George Street, Edinburgh. *T:* 031-225 5722; 29 Auchingramont Road, Hamilton, Lanarkshire. *T:* Hamilton 21386; 1 Forth Crescent, Stirling. *Club:* Caledonian (Edinburgh).

MACDONALD, Donald Hardman, CMG 1974; Advisor, Asian Development Bank, since 1974; *b* 16 May 1908; *s* of Archibald J. H. and Elizabeth Macdonald; *m* 1930, Simone Dumortier; one *s* one *d*. *Educ:* City of London Sch. Partner, Charles Fulton &

Co., London, 1935-39; Bank of England, 1939-49; Chief, Allied Bank Commn, Frankfort, 1949-52; Adviser, Bank of England, 1953-54; Bank for International Settlements, Basle, 1954-73 (Head of Banking Dept, 1972-73). *Recreations:* reading, travel, gardening. *Address:* La Grange, Grand'rue, 1297 Founex, Switzerland. *T:* (022) 76.10.64.

MACDONALD, Air Vice-Marshal Donald Malcolm Thomas, CB 1952; RAF retired; *b* 15 Aug. 1909; *s* of late D. P. Macdonald, Tormore, Isle of Skye; *m* 1938, Kathleen Mary de Vere, *d* of late J. T. Hunt, Oxford; one *s* four *d. Educ:* Westminster School. Joined Royal Air Force, 1930. Dir-Gen. of Personal Services, Air Min., 1957-58; Dir-Gen. of Manning, Air Min., 1958-61, retd 1961. Mem. Crofters Commn, 1962-65. *Address:* Torbeag, Clachan Seil, by Oban, Argyll. *T:* Balvicar 311. *Club:* Highland (Inverness).

MacDONALD, Hon. Donald (Stovel), PC (Canada) 1968; MP Rosedale, since 1962; *b* 1 March 1932; *s* of Donald Angus Macdonald and Marjorie Stovel Macdonald; *m* 1961, Ruth Hutchison, Ottawa; four *d. Educ:* Univ. of Toronto (BA 1951); Osgoode Hall Law Sch. (1955); Harvard Law Sch. (LLM 1956); Cambridge Univ. (Dip. in Internat. Law, 1957). Called to Ont Bar, 1955; Prize in Insurance Law, Law Soc. of Upper Canada, 1955; Rowell Fellow, Canadian Inst. of Internat. Affairs, 1956; McCarthy & McCarthy, law firm, Toronto, 1957-62. Parly Sec. to Ministers of Justice, Finance, Ext. Affairs, Industry, 1963-68; Minister without Portfolio, 1968; Pres., Queen's Privy Council, and Govt House Leader, 1968-70; Minister of National Defence, 1970-72; Minister of Energy, Mines and Resources, 1972-75; Minister of Finance, 1975-77. LLD *(hc)* St Lawrence Univ., 1974; Hon. DEng Colorado Sch. of Mines, 1976. *Recreations:* squash, cross-country skiing, tennis. *Address:* 15 Westward Way, Ottawa, Ont K1L 5A8, Canada. *T:* 996-7861. *Clubs:* University (Toronto); Toronto Cricket, Skating and Curling.

MacDONALD, Douglas George; Managing Director, John Menzies (Holdings) Ltd, since 1971; *b* 5 Aug. 1930; *s* of Colin Douglas MacDonald and Jane Grant Stewart; *m* Alexandra von Tschirschky und Boegendorf; one *s. Educ:* Morgan Acad., Dundee; Univ. of St Andrews (BSc). Queen's Own Cameron Highlanders, 1951-57. Potash Ltd, 1957-66;Man. Dir, Wyman Marshall Ltd, 1966-68. Member: National Freight Corp., 1973-; Scottish Telecommunications Bd, 1973-76; Chm., East Lothian Conservative and Unionist Assoc., 1970-73; Director: Radio Forth, 1974-; Scottish Investment Trust Ltd, 1977-. *Recreations:* golf, squash, politics. *Address:* Belton, Gullane, East Lothian EH31 2BE. *T:* Gullane 843189. *Clubs:* Royal Automobile; New (Edinburgh).

McDONALD, Duncan, CBE 1976; BSc, FH-WC, CEng, FIEE, FBIM, SMIEE, FRSE; Director and Chief Executive, Reyrolle Parsons Ltd, Newcastle upon Tyne, since 1976 (Director, 1973); *b* 20 Sept. 1921; *s* of Robert McDonald and Helen Orrick; *m* 1955, Jane Anne Guckian; three *s* one *d. Educ:* Inverkeithing Public Sch.; Dunfermline High Sch.; Edinburgh Univ. (BSc). Grad. App., BTH, Rugby, 1942-45; Transformer Design, Research and Develt, BTH, 1945-54. Bruce Peebles Industries Ltd: Chief Transformer Designer, 1954-59; Chief Engr, 1959; Dir and Chief Engr, 1960; Managing Dir, 1962; Chm. and Chief Exec. (and of A. Reyrolle & Co. Ltd), 1974. Chief Executive, Reyrolle Parsons Ltd, 1976. Member: Scottish Council Develt and Industry, 1967-76; Scottish Economic Council, 1975-. FH-WC 1962. *Publications:* various papers to learned socs, nat. and internat. *Recreation:* fishing. *Address:* 19 North Park Terrace, Edinburgh EH4 1DP. *T:* (home) 031-332 5301; Reyrolle Parsons Ltd, PO Box 1NS, Cuthbert House, All Saints, Newcastle upon Tyne. *T:* (office) Newcastle upon Tyne 24013.

McDONALD, (Edward) Lawson, MA, MD Cantab; FRCP; FACC; Physician, and Physician to the Cardiac Department, London Hospital, since 1960, to National Heart Hospital, since 1961; Cardiologist, to King Edward VII's Hospital for Officers, London, since 1968, to King Edward VII Hospital, Midhurst, since 1970; Lecturer to the Institute of Cardiology, since 1961; Hon. Consultant Cardiologist, Canadian Red Cross Memorial Hospital, Taplow, since 1960; *b* 1918; *s* of Charles Seaver McDonald, Belfast, NI; *m* 1953, Ellen Greig Rattray (marr. diss. 1972); one *s. Educ:* Felsted Sch.; Clare Coll., Cambridge; Middlesex Hospital; Harvard Univ. House appointments Middlesex Hospital, 1942-43. Temp. Surgeon-Lt, RNVR, 1943-46; served War of 1939-45, in N Atlantic and Normandy Campaigns. RMO, Nat. Heart Hosp., 1946-47; Asst Registrar, Inst. of Cardiology, 1947-48; Med. Registrar, Middlesex Hosp., 1948-49; studied in Stockholm, 1949; Asst to Prof. of Medicine, Middlesex Hosp., 1949-52; Rockefeller Travelling Fellow in Medicine, 1952-53; Asst in Medicine, Med. Dept, Peter Bent Brigham Hosp., Boston, Mass. and Research Fellow in

Medicine, Harvard Univ., 1952-53; Clinical and Research Asst, Dept of Cardiology, Middlesex Hosp., 1953-55; Asst Dir, Inst. of Cardiology and Hon. Asst Physician, Nat. Heart Hosp., 1955-61. Visiting Lecturer: American Coll. of Cardiology; Univ. of Toronto, Queen's Univ., Kingston, Ont; Univ. of Bombay; University of Barcelona, Eliseo Migoya Inst. of Cardiology, Bilbao, Spain; Istanbul Univ., Turkey; Univs of Chicago, Cincinnati and Kansas; Harvard Univ.; Mayo Foundation, USA; Univs of Belgrade, Ljubljana and Zagreb, Yugoslavia; Nat. Univ. of Cordoba, Argentine; Univ. of Chile, and Catholic Univ., Santiago; Nat. Univ. of Colombia; Nat. Inst. of Cardiology, Mexico; Nat. Univ. of Mexico; University of San Marcos and University of Cayetano Heredia, Peru; Nat. Univ. of Venezuela. From 1961, has addressed numerous heart societies in Europe, Canada, USA, and South America; St Cyres Lecturer, 1966; First Charles A. Berns Meml Lectr, Albert Einstein Coll. of Medicine, NY, 1973. Advisor to the Malaysian Govt on Cardiac Services. Member: British Cardiac Soc.; Assoc. of Physicians of Great Britain and Ireland, and other societies; FACC; Corresp. Mem. or Hon. Mem. of various socs of Cardiology or Angiology in S America. Hon. Fellow, Turkish Med. Soc.; Mem., Italian Soc. of Cardiology. Editorial Bd, New Istanbul Contribution to Clinical Science. *Publications:* (ed) Pathogenesis and Treatment of Occlusive Arterial Disease, 1960; Medical and Surgical Cardiology, 1969; numerous contribs to learned jls; also papers and addresses. *Recreations:* ski-ing and sailing. *Address:* 9 Upper Wimpole Street, W1M 7TD. *T:* 01-935 7101; 9 Bentinck Mansions, Bentinck Street, W1M 5RJ. *T:* 01-935 0868; The Trippet, Old Bosham, near Chichester, West Sussex. *T:* Bosham 572373.

MacDONALD, George Alan; a Recorder of the Crown Court, since 1972; *b* 21 April 1909; *s* of George John MacDonald, FIEE and Mabel Elizabeth Miriam (*née* Davies); *m* 1937, Frances Marguerite Davies; two *s* one *d. Educ:* St Joseph's, Totland Bay; Manor House, Havant; Hartley Univ. Coll., Southampton. Solicitor, 1931. RNVSR, 1938; Temp. Lt-Comdr RNVR, 1944. Pres., Hampshire Law Soc., 1959; Chairman: Southern Rent Tribunal, 1962-74; Mental Health Review Tribunal for Oxford and Wessex, 1968; Misuse of Drugs Act Tribunal, 1974; Isle of Wight Rent Tribunal, 1974; Mem. Council, Law Soc., 1970; Clerk of the Peace, Portsmouth, 1971. President: Portsmouth Harbour Racing and Sailing Assoc., 1954-64; Havant Hockey Club, 1973-77. *Publications:* occasional contrib. Law Society's Gazette. *Recreations:* hockey (Hampshire 1947-49), gardening, moorland walking, canal cruising, sound radio, cricket. *Address:* 8 King Street, Emsworth PO10 7AZ. *T:* Emsworth 4459; Whitehall House, Bideford, Devon EX39 5HF. *T:* Bideford 2532. *Clubs:* Royal Naval and Royal Albert Yacht (Portsmouth); Royal North Devon Golf.

MACDONALD, George Grant; His Honour Judge Macdonald; a Circuit Judge, since 1972; *b* 5 March 1921; *s* of late Patrick Macdonald, MA, Aberdeen, MB, ChB, Edinburgh, and Charlotte Primrose (*née* Rintoul); *m* 1967, Mary Dolores (*née* Gerrish), *widow* of G. G. Taylor; no *c. Educ:* Kelly Coll., Tavistock; Bristol Univ. (LLB (Hons)). Served War of 1939-45: in Royal Navy, Aug. 1941-July 1946, in Western Approaches, and Mine Sweeping, RNVR. Called to Bar, Gray's Inn, 1947; practised on Western Circuit, from Albion Chambers, Bristol; Dep.-Chm., Dorset QS, apptd 1969; Temp. Recorder of Barnstaple, Dec. 1971. *Recreations:* sailing, bridge, chess. *Address:* Hartfield, Wood Green, Fordingbridge, Hants. *T:* Breamore 248. *Clubs:* Naval; Clifton (Bristol); Royal Motor Yacht (Poole).

MACDONALD, Sir Herbert (George deLorme), KBE 1967 (OBE 1948); JP (Jamaica); retired government officer (Jamaica); company director; sportsman; President Organising Committee, IX Central American and Caribbean Games, 1962, and 8th British Empire and Commonwealth Games, 1966 (compiled and edited history); Chairman, National Sports Ltd (a Government body owning and operating National Stadium and Sports Centre), 1960-67, now President (specially created post); Director: Prospect Beach Ltd; Macdonald Ltd; *b* Kingston, 23 May 1902; *s* of late Ronald Macdonald, JP, planter, and late Louise (*née* Alexander). *Educ:* Wolmer's Boys' Sch., Jamaica; Northeast High Sch., Philadelphia, USA. Clerical and planting activities, 1919-43. Published Sportsman Magazine (with late Sir Arthur Thelwell). Accompanied Jamaica's team to World Olympics, London, 1948, and (as Manager) to Helsinki, 1952, Melbourne, 1956; Chef de Mission, WI Olympic Team to Rome, 1960; Deleg., Tokyo, 1964. Chief Liaison Officer, BWI Central Lab. Org. (USA), 1943-55; Pres., Jamaica Olympic Assoc., 1940-44 and 1956-58; Pres., WI Olympic Assoc. (from inception), 1958-61 (when Polit. Fedn was broken up). Past Pres. etc, various Jamaican sporting assocs and boards; Mem. Exec. Cttee Pan American Sports Organisation which controls

Pan American Games; Exec. Sec., Jamaica Tercentenary Celebrations Cttee, 1955. Mem. Bd of Trustees, Wolmer's Sch. Diploma of Merit, 1966 Internat. Olympic Cttee, 1968. Is an Anglican. *Recreations:* all sports; stamp collecting (athletic stamps); represented Jamaica in football and tennis *v* foreign teams, 1925-32. *Address:* (home) 206 Mountain View Avenue, Kingston 6, Jamaica. *T:* 78213. *Clubs:* (Life Mem., past Hon. Sec.) Kingston Cricket (Kingston, Jamaica); Constant Spring Golf.

MACDONALD, Prof. Hugh Ian; Canada Centennial Medal, 1967; President, York University, Toronto, Ont., since 1974; Professor, Department of Economics and Faculty of Administrative Studies, since 1974; *b* Toronto, 27 June 1929; *s* of Hugh and Winnifred Macdonald; *m* 1960, Dorothy Marion Vernon; two *s* three *d*. *Educ:* public schs, Toronto; Univ. of Toronto; Oxford Univ. BCom (Toronto), MA (Oxon), BPhil (Oxon). Univ. of Toronto: Lectr in Economics, 1955; Dean of Men, 1956; Asst Prof., Economics, 1961. Govt of Ontario: Chief Economist, 1965; Dep. Provincial Treas., 1967; Dep. Treas. and Dep. Minister of Economics, 1968; Dep. Treas. and Dep. Minister of Economics and Intergovernmental Affairs, 1972. Chairman: Bd of Dirs, London House Assoc. of Canada; Adv. Cttee on Confederation to Govt of Ontario; Dir, Ontario Educnl Communications Authority; Special Adviser to Royal Commn on Financial Management and Accountability, Govt of Canada; Member: Nat. Council of CIIA; Bd of Advisors, Internat. Assoc. for Students of Economics and Commerce; Canadian Economics Assoc.; Amer. Economics Assoc.; Royal Economic Soc. (London); Canadian Assoc. for Club of Rome; Inst. of Public Admin of Canada; Lambda Alpha Fraternity (Land Economics); Amer. Soc. for Public Admin; Trustee: Niagara Inst.; Intermet. Past Pres.: Empire Club of Canada; Ticker Club; Canadian Inst. Public Affairs; Past Chm., Toronto Men's Br. of CIIA; Past Mem., Attorney General's Cttee on Securities Legislation. Hon. LLD Toronto, 1974. *Recreations:* hockey, tennis; public service in various organizations. *Address:* 7 Whitney Avenue, Toronto, Ont. M4W 2A7, Canada. *T:* 921-2908; York University, 4700 Keele Street, Downsview, Ont. M3J 1P3, Canada. *T:* 667-2454.

MACDONALD, Iain Smith, MD; Deputy Chief Medical Officer, Scottish Home and Health Department, since 1974; *b* 14 July 1927; *s* of Angus Macdonald, MA and Jabina Urie Smith; *m* 1958, Sheila Foster; one *s* one *d*. *Educ:* Univ. of Glasgow (MD, DPH). Lectr, Univ. of Glasgow, 1955; Deputy Medical Officer of Health: Bury, 1957; Bolton, 1959; joined Scottish Home and Health Dept, 1964. *Address:* 36 Dumyat Drive, Falkirk FK1 5PA. *T:* Falkirk 25100.

MacDONALD, Ian, MC 1945; QC (Scot.) 1964; President, Industrial Tribunals for Scotland, since Dec. 1973; *b* 26 May 1921; *s* of H. J. and J. M. MacDonald; *m* 1946, Elizabeth de Vessey Lawson; one *s* one *d*. *Educ:* Colston's Sch., Bristol; Edinburgh Univ. (MA, LLB). Served 1939-46: Royal Tank Regt (Capt.). TA Lothians and Border Horse, later Queen's Own Lowland Yeomanry, 1948-62. Called to Bar, 1952. Mem., Criminal Injuries Compensation Board, 1972-74. Sheriff Principal of Dumfries and Galloway, Feb.-Dec. 1973. *Recreation:* sport. *Address:* 16 Mayfield Terrace, Edinburgh EH9 1SA. *T:* 031-667 5542. *Club:* Caledonian.

MACDONALD, Ian Wilson, MA; DLitt; CA; Deputy Chairman National and Commercial Banking Group Ltd; Director: Lloyds Bank Ltd; Lloyds and Scottish Ltd (formerly Chairman); Royal Bank of Scotland Ltd (formerly Chairman, and Chairman National Commercial Bank of Scotland Ltd); Chairman, Scottish Hospitals Endowments Research Trust; Review Body on Pay of Doctors and Dentists, since 1971; *b* Old Cumnock, Ayrshire, 28 May 1907; *s* of late Rev. Alexander B. Macdonald, BD, PhD, Dron, Perthshire, and late Dr Mary B. W. Macdonald; *m* 1933, Helen Nicolson, MA; one *s* two *d*. *Educ:* Perth Academy; Edinburgh Academy; Glasgow Univ. Prof. of Accountancy, Univ. of Glasgow, 1938-50. Partner in Kerr Macleod and Macfarlan, CA, Glasgow, 1933-53. Member: Cttee of Investigation into Port Transport Industry, 1945; Court of Inquiry into Omnibus Industry, 1946, Shipbuilding Industry, 1947, Railwaymen's Wages and Hours of Work, 1947; Arbitrator, Nigerian Railways Labour dispute, 1948; Mem. Gen. Claims Tribunal, 1943-58. Member: Cttee of Inquiry: Fishing Industry, 1957-60; Ports and Harbours, 1961-62; Member: S Scotland Electricity Board, 1956-61; National Ports Council, 1963-67; NRDC, 1959-73; CAA, 1972-75. *Recreations:* shooting, fishing *Address:* Seton Court, Gullane, East Lothian EH31 2BD. *Clubs:* Caledonian; New (Edinburgh).

MACDONALD, Ishbel A.; *see* Peterkin, I. A.

McDONALD, Iverach; Associate Editor, The Times, 1967-73; Director, The Times Ltd, 1968-73; *b* 23 Oct. 1908; *s* of Benjamin McDonald, Strathcool, Caithness, and Janet Seel; *m* 1935, Gwendoline, *o d* of late Captain Thomas R. Brown; one *s* one *d*. *Educ:* Leeds Gram. Sch. Asst Editor, Yorkshire Post, 1933; sub-editor, The Times, 1935; correspondent in Berlin, 1937; diplomatic correspondent 1938; Asst Editor, 1948; Foreign Editor, 1952; Managing Editor, 1965. War of 1939-45: Capt., Gen. Staff, 1939-40; travelled extensively in Soviet Union, Far East and America; reported all allied conferences after the war, including San Francisco, 1945, Paris, 1946 and 1947, Moscow, 1947, Colombo, 1950, and Bermuda, 1953. *Publication:* A Man of The Times, 1976. *Address:* Whistlers, Beckley Common, Oxford. *T:* Stanton St John 226. *Club:* Garrick.

McDONALD, Sir James, KBE 1967 (CBE 1956; OBE 1948); British Consul (Hon.), Portland, Oregon USA, since 1938; President, McDonald Dock Co.; Managing Partner: Macdon & Co.; Kermac Investment Co.; Director: Western Transportation Co.; Waterway Terminals Co.; Chairman, Benjamin D. Dagwell Foundation; *b* 23 July 1899; *s* of late James McDonald, Renfrew, Scotland; *m* 1933, Anne, *d* of late Peter Kerr, Portland, Ore, USA; one *s* two *d*. *Educ:* Allen Glen's Sch., Glasgow. Lt, RFC (later RAF), 1917-19. Partner McDonald Gattie & Co., 1927-67; Pres., Norpac Shipping Co., 1940-67. Trustee, Oregon Historical Soc. *Recreations:* walking, farming. *Address:* 11626 SW Military Lane, Portland, Ore, USA. *T:* 636-4775; Inchinnan Farm, Rt 1, Box 1405, Wilsonville, Ore, USA. *T:* 625-6914. *Clubs:* Boodle's; Arlington, University, Racquet (Portland, Ore.).

MacDONALD, Mrs J. G.; *see* Sinclair, I. L.

MACDONALD, Prof. James Alexander, BSc (Agric.), PhD (Edinburgh), DSc (St Andrews); Professor of Botany, University of St Andrews, 1961-77, retired; *b* 17 June 1908; *s* of late James Alexander and Jessie Mary Macdonald; *m* 1935, Constance Mary Simmie; one *d*. *Educ:* Inverness Royal Academy; Edinburgh Univ.; Steven Scholarship in Agriculture, 1930; DSc with Sykes Gold Medal, 1947. Asst Lecturer in Botany, East of Scot. Coll. of Agriculture, 1932-35; St Andrews University: Lecturer in Botany, 1935-52; Senior Lecturer, 1952-60; Dean, Faculty of Science, 1967-69. Pres., Botanical Soc. of Edinburgh, 1955-57; FRSE 1940 (Council Mem., 1956-59); Vice-Pres. RSE, 1961-64. Fellow, Inst. Biology. *Publications:* Introduction to Mycology, 1951; scientific papers in Trans Brit. Mycol. Soc., Annals Applied Biol., Mycologia, Proc. and Trans Bot. Soc. Edinburgh, Proc. and Trans Royal Soc. Edinburgh. *Recreations:* golf, fishing, philately. *Address:* The Cottage, Boarhills, St Andrews, Fife. *T:* Boarhills 272. *Club:* Royal and Ancient (St Andrews).

MACDONALD, John B(arfoot), DDS, MS, PhD; President and Chief Executive Officer, Addiction Research Foundation, since 1976; Executive Director, Council of Ontario Universities, since 1968; Professor of Higher Education, University of Toronto, since 1968; *b* 23 Feb. 1918; *s* of Arthur A. Macdonald and Gladys L. Barfoot; *m* ; two *s* one *d* ; *m* 1967, Liba Kucera; two *d*. *Educ:* Univ. of Toronto, University of Illinois, Columbia Univ. DDS (with hons) Toronto, 1942; MS (Bact) Ill, 1948; PhD (Bact) Columbia, 1953. Lectr, Prev. Dentistry, University of Toronto, and private practice, 1942-44. Canadian Dental Corps, 1944-46 (Capt.) Instr, Bacteriol, University of Toronto, and private practice, 1946-47; Res. Asst, Univ. of Illinois, 1947-48; Kellogg Fellow and Canadian Dental Assoc. Res. Student, Columbia Univ., 1948-49; University of Toronto: Asst Prof. of Bacteriol., 1949-53; Assoc. Prof. of Bacteriol., 1953-56; Chm., Div. of Dental Res., 1953-56; Prof. of Bacteriol., 1956; Cons. in Dental Educn, University of BC, 1955-56; Dir, Forsyth Dental Infirmary, 1956-62 (Cons. in Bacteriol., 1962); Prof. of Microbiol., Harvard Sch., of Dental Med., 1956-62 (Dir of Postdoctoral Studies, 1960-62); President, Univ. of British Columbia, 1962-67. Consultant: Dental Med. Section of Corporate Research Div. of Colgate-Palmolive Co., 1958-62; Donwood Foundn, Toronto, 1967- (Chm. of Bd, 1972-); Science Council of Canada, 1967-69; Addiction Research Foundn of Ontario, 1968- (Mem., 1974-). Chm., Commn on Pharmaceutical Services of the Canadian Pharmaceutical Assoc., 1967-; Consultant, Nat. Inst. of Health, 1968-; Mem., Dental Study Sect., Nat. Inst. of Health, 1961-65; Councillor-at-Large, Internat. Assoc. for Dental Research, 1963-, Pres. 1968-69. Fellow, Mem. or Chm. of numerous assocs. etc, both Canadian and international. FACD 1955; Hon. FICD 1965. Hon. AM, Harvard Univ., 1956; Hon. LLD: Univ. of Manitoba, 1962; Simon Fraser Univ., 1965; Hon DSc Univ. of British Columbia, 1967. *Publications:* Higher Education in British Columbia and a Plan for the Future, 1962, etc.; numerous contribs to learned jls. *Recreations:* golf, tennis. *Address:*

Addiction Research Foundation, 33 Russell Street, Toronto, Ontario. *T:* 595-6000. *Clubs:* University, University of BC Faculty, Vancouver (Vancouver); Canadian, Faculty, University of Toronto (Toronto).

MACDONALD, Air Commodore John Charles, CB 1964; CBE 1957; DFC 1940 (Bar 1942); AFC 1941; Aviation Consultant; *b* 25 Dec. 1910; *s* of late Robert Macdonald; *m* 1952, Gladys Joan, *d* of John Hine, Beaminster, Dorset; two *s*. *Educ:* Berkhamsted Sch.; RAF Cadet Coll., Cranwell. Commissioned RAF, 1930. Served War of 1939-45 in Bomber Command; POW Stalag Luft III, 1942-45, escaped April 1945. Commanded RAF Akrotiri during Suez campaign; UK National Military Representative, SHAPE, 1959-61; Comdr RAF East Africa, 1961-64; Min. of Defence, 1964; retd, 1964. Chevalier, Légion d'Honneur, 1958; Croix de Guerre, 1958. *Recreations:* golf, sailing, shooting. *Address:* Woodbine Cottage, Osmington, Dorset. *T:* Preston 833259. *Club:* Royal Automobile.

MACDONALD, Maj.-Gen. John Frederick Matheson, CB 1959; DSO 1951; OBE 1945; *b* 7 Nov. 1907; *e s* of late Major Eric William Macdonald, Ringmer, Sussex; *m* 1st, 1933, Joan Drayson (*d* 1961), *d* of late Norval H. Prentis, East Bergholt, Suffolk; one *s*; 2nd, 1964, Kathleen Flora, *widow* of Lieut-Col D. W. Mac L. Prinsep, Skinner's Horse. *Educ:* Marlborough Coll.; Royal Military Coll., Sandhurst. 2nd Lt KOSB 1927; Lt (Adjt) 1 KOSB 1935-37; Lt-Col 1 KOSB, 1944; Lt-Col (GSO1) HQ 3 Brit. Inf. Div., 1944-45, France, Belgium, Germany. Lt-Col (AQMG) West Africa Comd, 1948-49; Lt-Col 1 KOSB, Hong Kong and Korea, 1949-51; Lt-Col 1949; Brig. 28 British Commonwealth Brigade, Korea, 1951-52; Brig. 31 Lorried Inf. Brigade, Germany, 1952-54; Imperial Defence Coll., 1955; Brig. 1956; Maj.-Gen., Chief of Staff Scottish Command, 1957-1958; Maj.-Gen. 1957; GOC 52 (Lowland) Division/District, 1958-61; retired, 1961. Hon. Col 4/5 Bn KOSB, TA, 1962-67. County Comr, Boy Scouts, Suffolk, 1962-67. Chevalier, Order of Leopold, with Palm, and Croix de Guerre, 1940, with Palm, Belgium, 1947; Officer, Legion of Merit, USA, 1953. *Address:* The Grange, Elmswell, Bury St Edmunds, Suffolk. *T:* Elmswell 40270.

MACDONALD, John Reginald, QC 1976; barrister-at-law; *b* 26 Sept. 1931; *s* of Ranald Macdonald and Marion Olive (*née* Kirkby); *m* 1958; one *s* one *d*. *Educ:* St Edward's Sch., Oxford; Queen's Coll., Cambridge. Called to Bar, Lincoln's Inn, 1955. Contested (L) Wimbledon, 1966 and 1970 General Elections. Chm., Assoc. of Liberal Lawyers, 1973-. *Recreation:* the theatre. *Address:* 12 New Square, Lincoln's Inn, WC2. *T:* 01-405 3808.

MACDONALD, Kenneth Carmichael; Assistant Under-Secretary of State, Ministry of Defence, since 1975; *b* 25 July 1930; *s* of William Thomas and Janet Millar Macdonald; *m* 1960, Ann Elisabeth (*née* Pauer); one *s* two *d*. *Educ:* Hutchesons' Grammar Sch.; Glasgow Univ. MA (Hons Classics). RAF, 1952-54. Asst Principal, Air Ministry, 1954; Asst Private Sec. to Sec. of State, 1956-57; Private Sec. to Permanent Sec., 1958-61; HM Treasury, 1962-65; MoD, 1965; Asst Sec., 1968; Counsellor (Defence), UK Delegn to NATO, 1973-75. *Recreation:* golf. *Address:* 61 Park Avenue, Bromley, Kent BR1 4EG. *T:* 01-460 6262.

McDONALD, Lawson; *see* McDonald, E. L.

MacDONALD, Rt. Hon. Malcolm John, OM 1969; PC 1935; Chancellor of the University of Durham, since 1970; *b* Lossiemouth, Morayshire, 1901; *s* of late J. Ramsay and Margaret MacDonald; *m* 1946, Mrs Audrey Fellowes Rowley; one *d*. *Educ:* Bedales Sch., Petersfield; Queen's Coll., Oxford, MA. Mem. of LCC, 1927-30. Contested (Lab) Bassetlaw Div., 1923, 1924; MP (Lab) Bassetlaw Div. of Notts, 1929-31 (National Labour), 1931-35; MP (National Government) Ross and Cromarty, 1936-45; Parliamentary Under-Sec., Dominions Office, 1931-35; Sec. of State for Dominion Affairs, 1935-38 and 1938-39; Sec. of State for Colonies, 1935 and 1938-40; Minister of Health, 1940-41; United Kingdom High Comr in Canada, 1941-46; Gov.-Gen. of the Malayan Union and Singapore, May-July 1946; Gov.-Gen. of Malaya, Singapore and British Borneo, 1946-48; Special Ambassador at inauguration of Indonesian Republic, 1949; Comr-Gen. for the UK in South-East Asia, 1948-55; UK Representative on SE Asia Defence Treaty Council, 1955; High Commissioner for the UK in India, 1955-60. Chief of British Delegation and Co-Chm., Internat. Conf. on Laos, 1961-62. Governor and C-in-C, Kenya, 1963; Governor-Gen. Kenya, 1963-64; British High Comr in Kenya, 1964-65; British Special Representative in East and Central Africa, 1965-66; Special Representative of HM Govt in Africa, 1966-69; Special Envoy to Sudan, Nov. 1967, and to Somalia, Dec. 1967. Rhodes Trustee, 1948-57; Chancellor of the

University of Malaya, 1949-61; Visitor, University Coll., Kenya, 1963-64; Senior Research Fellow, Univ. of Sussex, 1971-73. President: Royal Commonwealth Soc., 1971-; Great Britain-China Centre, 1972-; Fedn of Commonwealth Chambers of Commerce, 1971-; VSO, 1975-; Caribbean Youth Develt Trust. Hon. Fellow, Queen's Coll., Oxford. Doctor of Laws and Doctor of Letters, *hc*, Durham; various North American Univs and Univs of Hanoi, Hong Kong, Singapore and Malaya. Freeman of City of Singapore, 1955; Freeman, Burgh of Lossiemouth, 1969. *Publications:* Down North, 1945; The Birds of Brewery Creek, 1947; Borneo People, 1956; Angkor, 1958; Birds in my Indian Garden, 1961; Birds in the Sun, 1962; Treasure of Kenya, 1965; People and Places, 1969; Titans and Others, 1972. *Recreations:* ornithology, collecting, ski-ing. *Address:* Raspit Hill, Ivy Hatch, Sevenoaks, Kent.
See also I. A. Peterkin.

MACDONALD, Dame Margaret; *see* Kidd, Dame Margaret Henderson.

McDONALD, Mrs Margo; Vice-Chairman, Scottish National Party, since 1972; *b* 19 April 1944; *d* of Robert and Jean Aitken; *m* 1965, Peter MacDonald; two *d*. *Educ:* Hamilton Academy; Dunfermline Coll. (Diploma of Physical Educn). Contested (SNP) Paisley, Gen. Elec., 1970; MP (SNP) Glasgow (Govan), Nov. 1973-Feb. 1974; contested (SNP) Glasgow (Govan), Gen. Elec., Feb. 1974 and Oct. 1974. *Recreations:* family life, folk music, theatre, swimming, lazing. *Address:* 115 Bardykes Road, High Blantyre, Glasgow G72 9UH. *T:* Blantyre 823157.

McDONALD, Dr Oonagh; MP (Lab) Thurrock, since July 1976; *b* Stockton-on-Tees, Co. Durham, 21 Feb. 1938; *d* of Dr H. D. McDonald; *m* 1965, Richard. *Educ:* Roan Sch. for Girls, Greenwich; East Barnet Grammar Sch.; Univ. of London (BD Hons 1959; MTh 1962, PhD 1974, King's Coll.). Teacher, St Barnabas Sch., S Woodford, 1959-62; Lectr for Dip. in Sociology, Toynbee Hall, 1964-65; Teacher, Hornsey Grammar Sch. and Boreham Wood Sch., 1964-65; Lectr in Philosophy, Bristol Univ., 1965-76. Mem. Univ. Senate and Court, 1975-76. Member: ASTMS, 1972-; Aircraft Workers' Study Group, 1972-74; Industrial Policy sub-cttee, Labour Party NEC, 1976. Contested (Lab.), S Glos. Feb. and Oct. 1974. Governor: St Mary's and St Paul's Colls of Education, Cheltenham, 1969-75; The Ridings Sch., Winterbourne, 1974-76. *Publications:* (ed) Index of Community Action, 1973; (jtly) A New Approach to Public Ownership, 1974. *Address:* House of Commons, Westminster, SW1A 0AA. *T:* 01-940 5563.

MACDONALD, Patrick Donald, CMG 1953; CVO 1963; *b* 21 July 1909; *s* of late Major E. W. Macdonald and Amy Beatrice Cavalier; *m* 1937, Delia Edith (marr. diss.), 5th *d* of Capt. R. W. Travers, RN (retired); one *s* twin *d*. *Educ:* Marlborough Coll.; St John's Coll., Cambridge. BA 1931. Cadet officer, Gilbert and Ellice Islands Colony, 1932; Administrative Officer, 1936; Sec. to Government, 1935-36 and 1938-39; Asst Sec., Western Pacific High Commission, 1940-42; Asst Colonial Sec., Trinidad and Tobago, 1942-45. Fiji: Administrative Officer, Grade II, 1946, Grade I, 1947; Asst Colonial Sec., 1946-49; Colonial Secretary, Governor's Deputy and Acting Governor: Leeward Islands, 1950-57; Colonial Sec. and Acting Governor, Fiji, 1957-66; Chm., Public and Police Service Commns, 1966-71. *Recreations:* swimming and deep-sea fishing. *Address:* PO Box 1404, Suva, Fiji.

MACDONALD, Sir Peter (George), Kt 1963; DL; Hon. Life President, United Biscuits Ltd (Chairman, 1948-67) and McVitie & Price Ltd (Chairman, 1947-64); former Director: Guardian Assurance Co. Ltd, London; Caledonian Insurance Co. and other companies; Senior Partner, W. & J. Burness, retired 1976, now Consultant; *b* 20 Feb. 1898; *s* of William Macdonald, Darnaway, Forres, and Annie Cameron; *m* 1929, Rachel Irene, *d* of Rev. Dr Robert Forgan; one *s* two *d*. *Educ:* Forres Academy; Edinburgh Univ. Served European War, 1914-18, with Scottish Horse, Black Watch, RGA, and Lovat Scouts. Served with Home Guard, 1940-45; Regional Deferment Officer, Bd of Trade, Edinburgh and SE Scotland; Mem., Edinburgh and dist local Emergency Reconstruction Panel (chm. Food Section); Staff Officer on Scottish Regional Comr's Staff: former Mem. London Council, Inst. of Directors (formerly Chm., Scottish Br.); WS 1927. JP Edinburgh, 1935. DL Edinburgh, 1966. *Recreations:* fishing, shooting, golf. *Address:* 18 Hermitage Drive, Edinburgh EH10 6BZ. *T:* 031-447 1256. *Clubs:* Caledonian (London); Conservative (Edinburgh).

MACDONALD of Clanranald, Ranald Alexander; 24th Chief and Captain of Clanranald; Chairman and Managing Director, Fairfix Contracts Ltd; *b* 27 March 1934; *s* of Captain Kenneth

Macdonald of Inchkenneth, DSO, and Marjory Broad Smith, Basingstoke; *S* kinsman as Chief of Clanranald, 1944; *m* 1961, Jane Campbell-Davys, *d* of I. E. Campbell-Davys, Llandovey, Carms; two *s* one *d. Educ:* Christ's Hospital. Founded: Fairfix Contracts Ltd, 1959; Tektura Wallcoverings, 1970. Chm., British Contract Furnishing Assoc., 1975-76. Lieut (TA) Cameron Highlanders, 1958-68. Mem., Standing Council of Scottish Chiefs, 1957-; Director, Highland Soc. of London; Vice Pres., Caledonian Catholic Assoc. of London. *Recreations:* sailing, fishing. *Heir: s* Ranald Og Angus Macdonald, younger of Clanranald, *b* 17 Sept. 1963. *Address:* 74 Upper Street, N1. *T:* 01-226 3034. *Clubs:* Turf; Puffin's (Edinburgh).

McDONALD, Robert Howat; *see* McDonald, Hon. Lord.

MACDONALD, Vice-Adm. Roderick Douglas, CBE 1966; Chief of Staff to Commander, Allied Naval Forces Southern Europe, since 1976; *b* Java, 25 Feb. 1921; *s* of Douglas and Marjorie Macdonald; *m* 1943, Joan Willis; two *s* (and one *s* decd). *Educ:* Fettes. Entered Royal Navy, 1939. Served War: Fleet and Convoy ops throughout 1939-45 (Atlantic, Norway, Eastern Fleet, East Coast and Normandy). Commanded: HMS Leeds Castle, 1953, also HMS Essington; Sen. Officer, 104th Mine-Sweeping Sqdn and HMS Walkerton, 1957 (despatches, Cyprus); HMS Falmouth, 1961; Naval Forces, Borneo, 1965 (CBE); HMS Galatea; Captain (D): Londonderry Sqdn, 1968; First Frigate Sqdn, Far East, 1969; Captain of the Fleet, 1970; HMS Bristol, 1972; COS to C-in-C, Naval Home Command, 1973-76. Younger Brother of Trinity House; Vice-Pres. and Fellow, Nautical Inst. *Recreation:* painting. *Address: c/o* Lloyds Bank Ltd, 6 Pall Mall, SW1Y 5NH. Braes, Isle of Skye. *Club:* Caledonian.

MACDONALD, Maj.-Gen. Ronald Clarence, CB 1965; DSO 1944 and Bar, 1945; OBE 1953; Director, Griffin Farms Ltd, Wilts; *b* 1 Aug. 1911; 2nd *s* of late Col C. R. Macdonald, CMG; *m* 1939, Jessie Ross Anderson; one *s* one *d. Educ:* Rugby; RMC, Sandhurst. Royal Warwicks Regt: Commissioned, 1931; Comdr 2nd Bn, 1945-46; Comdr 1st Bn, 1953-55; Bn Comdr, France, Germany Campaign, 1944-45; Mil. Asst to CIGS, 1946-49; GSO1, HQ, West Africa Comd, 1950-53; Col Gen. Staff, SHAPE, 1955-56; Comdr 10th Inf. Bde Gp, 1956-59; DDI, War Office, 1959-60; Chief of Staff, HQ Middle East Comd, 1960-62; Dep. Chief of Staff, Headquarters, Allied Land Forces, Central Europe, 1962-65; retired, 1965. Col Royal Warwicks Fusiliers, 1963-68; Dep. Col (Warwicks), The Royal Regt of Fusiliers, 1968-74. *Recreation:* golf. *Address:* Grassmead, Beanacre, near Melksham, Wilts. *Club:* Army and Navy.

MACDONALD, Ronald John, CEng, MIMechE; Director-General, Ordnance Factories/Production, since 1974; *b* 2 Nov. 1919; *s* of Ronald Macdonald and Sarah Jane Macdonald; *m* 1944, Joan Margaret Crew; two *s . Educ:* Enfield Grammar Sch.; Enfield Technical Coll. Engrg apprenticeship at Royal Small Arms Factory, Enfield, 1936-40. Army service, REME, in India, China and Hong Kong, 1943-47 (Major). Established Civil Servant, Royal Small Arms Factory, 1948; Royal Ordnance Factory, Radway Green, 1949; ROF Headquarters, Mottingham, 1953; ROF, Blackburn, 1960; Director: ROF, Birtley, Co. Durham, 1964; Ordnance Factories/Ammunition, 1972. *Address:* 72 Lincoln Park, Amersham, Bucks HP7 0DQ. *T:* Amersham 7402. *Club:* Army and Navy.

MacDONALD, Prof. Simon Gavin George, FRSE; Professor of Physics, University of Dundee, since 1973; Vice-Principal, since 1974; *b* 5 Sept. 1923; *s* of Simon MacDonald and Jean H. Thomson; *m* 1948, Eva Leonie Austerlitz; one *s* one *d . Educ:* George Heriot's Sch., Edinburgh; Edinburgh Univ. (MA (1st Cl. Hons) Maths and Nat. Phil); PhD (St Andrews). FIP 1958, FRSE 1972. Jun. Scientific Officer, RAE, Farnborough, 1943-46; Lectr, Univ. of St Andrews, 1948-57; Senior Lecturer: University Coll. of the West Indies, 1957-62; Univ. of St Andrews, 1962-67; Visiting Prof., Ohio Univ., 1963; University of Dundee: Sen. Lectr, then Prof., 1967-; Dean of Science, 1970-73. Convener, Scottish Univs Council on Entrance, 1977- (Dep. Convener, 1973-77). Chm., Bd of Dirs, Dundee Rep. Th., 1975-; Dir, Fedn of Scottish Theatres, 1976-. *Publications:* Problems and Solutions in General Physics, 1967; Physics for Biology and Premedical Students, 1970, 2nd edn 1975; Physics for the Life and Health Sciences, 1975; articles in physics jls. *Recreations:* bridge, golf, fiction writing. *Address:* 10 Westerton Avenue, Dundee DD5 3NJ. *T:* Dundee 78692. *Club:* Royal Commonwealth Society.

MACDONALD, Air Vice-Marshal Somerled Douglas, CB 1951; CBE 1945; DFC 1920; retired; *b* 1899; *s* of late Dr D. Macdonald, of Glen Urquhart, Inverness-shire; *m* 1949, Hon. Margaret Anne, *d* of 2nd Baron Trent, KBE. *Educ:* George

Watson's Coll., Edinburgh. Served European War, 1914-19: joined RFC, 1917, transferred to RAF, 1918; served in Mesopotamia and Persia; served in Iraq and ME (Egypt), 1924-27, and 1936-37; attached HQ Sudan Defence Force, 1937-39; served War of 1939-45: commanded 3 Wing (Sudan), 263 Wing (Palestine), 213 Wing (Lebanon), 217 Wing (Persia), and Bomber detachment in Iraq during rebellion, 1941; SASO No 9 (Fighter) Group, Fighter Comd, 1944; SASO No 12 (Fighter) Group, 1945; AOC No 11 (Fighter) Group, 1946-48; Assistant Chief of Air Staff (Training), 1948; Inspector-Gen. of Air Training, Western Union, 1950. Head of Air Training Advisory Group, NATO, 1952-54, retired. *Address:* Inglewood Lodge, Kintbury, Berks. *T:* Kintbury 446. *Clubs:* Royal Air Force; Royal Perth.

MACDONALD, Rt. Rev. Thomas Brian, OBE 1970; Coadjutor Bishop of Perth, Western Australia, since 1964; *b* 25 Jan. 1911; *s* of Thomas Joseph Macdonald, MD, and Alice Daisy Macdonald; *m* 1936, Audrey May Collins; three *d. Educ:* Mercers' Sch., Holborn, EC. Licentiate of Theology 1932, Aust. Coll. of Theol. Deacon 1934, priest 1935, Diocese of Ballarat, Vic.; Deacon in charge of All Saints, Ballarat, 1934; Priest in charge of Landsborough, 1935; Rector of Williams, Dio. of Bunbury, 1935-39; Rector of Manjimup, WA, 1939-40. Chaplain, Australian Imperial Forces, 1940-44 (despatches). Rector of Christ Church, Claremont, Dio. of Perth, 1944-50; Chaplain of Collegiate Sch. of St Peter, Adelaide, S Australia, 1950-58; Dean of Perth, Western Australia, 1959-61; Archdeacon of Perth, 1961-63. Administrator, Diocese of Perth during 1963 and 1969. *Address:* 33 Thomas Street, Nedlands, WA 6009, Australia. *Club:* Weld (Perth).

MACDONALD, Air Vice-Marshal Thomas Conchar, CB 1962; AFC 1942; MD (retired); *b* 6 Aug. 1909; *s* of John Macdonald, MA, BSc, and Mary Jane Conchar; *m* 1937, Katharine Cairns Frew. *Educ:* Hermitage Sch.; Glasgow High Sch.; University of Glasgow; MB, ChB 1932; MD 1940; DPH (London) 1949. Joined RAF Medical Br., 1933; served in Iraq, Egypt and England, before 1939. War service included RAF Inst. of Aviation Med., Farnborough, as Asst to Consultant in Applied Physiology, 1939-41; USA and Canada, 1941-42; DPMO (Flying) Fighter Command, 1942-45; Far East, 1945-46 (despatches, AFC). Post-war appts include: PMO 2nd TAF (Germany), 1951-53; Dir of Hygiene and Research, Air Min., 1953-56 (Chm. Aero-Medical Panel of Advisory Gp for Research and Develt (AGARD) of NATO); PMO, Bomber Command, 1956-58; PMO Middle East Air Force, 1958-61; PMO Technical Training Command, RAF, 1961-66. Air Vice-Marshal, 1961. QHP 1961-66; CStJ 1961. *Publications:* contributions to various med. jls. *Recreations:* sailing, fishing. *Address:* Wakeners Wood, Midhurst Road, Haslemere, Surrey. *T:* Haslemere 3685. *Club:* Royal Air Force.

MACDONALD, Hon. Sir Thomas (Lachlan), KCMG 1963; High Commissioner for New Zealand in London, 1961-68; New Zealand Ambassador to the European Economic Community, 1961-67; New Zealand Ambassador to Ireland, 1966-68; *b* 14 Dec. 1898; *s* of Thomas Forsaith and Margaret Ann Macdonald; *m* 1925, Elsie Ann Stuart; one *d. Educ:* South Sch. and Southland Boys' High Sch., Invercargill, NZ. Union Steamship Co. of New Zealand Ltd, 1915-18. Served NZ Mounted Rifles, Egypt and Palestine, 1918-19. Farming in New Zealand, 1919-37 and 1945-55. MP for Mataura, NZ, 1938-46; MP for Wallace, NZ, 1946-57. Min. of Defence, 1949-57, and of External Affairs, 1954-57. Served overseas, North Africa, 2nd NZEF, 1940-43. *Recreations:* tramping, photography, swimming, gardening. *Address:* 1 Camellia Grove, Parklands, Waikanae, New Zealand.

McDONALD, Hon. Sir William (John Farquhar), Kt 1958; *b* 3 Oct. 1911; *s* of John Nicholson McDonald and Sarah McDonald (*née* McInnes); *m* 1935, Evelyn Margaret Koch; two *d. Educ:* Scotch Coll., Adelaide, South Australia. Served AIF, 1939-45, Capt. Councillor, Shire of Kowree, 1946-70. MLA, electorate of Dundas, Victoria, 1947-52, 1955-70; Speaker, Legislative Assembly, Victoria, 1955-67; Minister of Lands, Soldier Settlement, and for Conservation, 1967-70. Mem., Exec. Council, Victoria. Trustee, Shrine of Remembrance, 1955-70. Victoria State Pres., Poll Shorthorn Soc. of Aust., 1962-72; Trustee, Royal Agricultural Soc. of Victoria, 1968-. Trustee, Victoria Amateur Turf Club, 1969. *Address:* Brippick, Neuarpurr, Vic., Australia. *T:* Neuarpurr 5. *Clubs:* Hamilton (Hamilton, Victoria); Australian, Naval and Military (Melbourne).

MACDONALD, Air Chief Marshal Sir William (Laurence Mary), GCB 1965 (KCB 1959; CB 1956); CBE 1946; DFC 1940; *b* 10 Aug. 1908; *s* of William Stephen Macdonald, Co. Cork; *m*

1939, Diana (*d* 1964), *d* of late Nicholas Challacombe; one *s* one *d*. *Educ*: Castleknock Coll., Eire. Joined RAF 1929; Group Capt., 1942; Air Commodore, 1944; Air Vice-Marshal, 1954; Air Marshal, 1960; Air Chief Marshal, 1963. Served War of 1939-45, France, Belgium, Holland, Germany (despatches twice, DFC, CBE). Comdt, Central Flying Sch., 1946-48; Exchange Officer with USAF, USA, 1948-50; Dep. Dir of Plans (Jt Planning), Air Min., 1952; AOC, RAF, Singapore, 1952-54; Asst Chief of Air Staff (Intelligence), 1954-58; Comdr-in-Chief, Middle East, Air Force, 1958-62, and Administrator of the Sovereign Base Areas of Akrotiri and Dhekelia, Cyprus, 1960-62; Air Sec., Ministry of Defence (formerly Air Ministry), 1962-66. Air ADC to the Queen, 1965-66. Governor, Oratory Sch. Chevalier, Legion of Honour; Croix de Guerre; Star of Jordan 1st Class. *Address*: Quarry House, Yateley, Hants. *T*: 873283. *Club*: East India, Sports and Public Schools.

MACDONALD-BUCHANAN, Major Sir Reginald (Narcissus), KCVO 1964 (CVO 1952); MBE 1942; MC 1917; *b* May 1898; *m* 1922, Hon. Catherine Buchanan, *o c* of 1st Baron Woolavington, GCVO; two *s* two *d*. Joined Scots Guards from RMC, Sandhurst, 1916. Served European War (MC); retired, 1926. Chairman: James Buchanan & Co. Ltd; W. P. Lowrie & Co. Ltd, 1939-70; Director: Buchanan-Dewar Ltd, 1939-69; Distillers Co. Ltd, 1930-69. Mem. Council, King Edward VII's Hosp. for Officers (Chm., House and Finance Cttee 1947-69, Vice-Pres. and Treasurer, 1969). Mem. Racecourse Betting Control Bd, 1949-59; Steward of Jockey Club, 1950-51-52; Pres. Hunter's Improvement and Nat. Light Horse Breeding Soc., 1950-51, 1951-52, 1965-66. Master, Worshipful Co. of Distillers, 1952. DL Northamptonshire; High Sheriff, Northamptonshire, 1939; Pres. Northamptonshire County Agricultural Soc., 1951. Joint Master, Pytchley Hounds, 1934-39 and 1946-49; Rejoined Scots Guards, 1939; ADC to Field-Marshal Sir John Dill, 1940-43; served BEF, France, 1940; War Office, 1940-41; British Joint Staff Mission, Washington, 1941-43 (MBE); France and Belgium, 1944-45 when demobilised (despatches, US Bronze Star Medal). *Address*: Cottesbrooke Hall, Northampton. *T*: Creaton 232; 5 Kingston House South, Ennismore Gardens, SW7 1NS. *T*: 01-589 1042; Scatwell, Muir of Ord, Ross-shire. *T*: Scatwell 244; Egerton House, Newmarket. *T*: Newmarket 2151. *Clubs*: Turf, Cavalry and Guards; Royal Yacht Squadron (Cowes); Muthaiga (Nairobi).

MacDONALD SCOTT, Mrs Michael; *see* Lavin, Mary.

MACDONALD-SMITH, Maj.-Gen. Hugh, CB 1977; Director General (formerly Director) of Electrical and Mechanical Engineering (Army), 1975-78; *b* 8 Jan. 1923; *s* of Alexander and Ada Macdonald-Smith; *m* 1947, Désirée Violet (*née* Williamson); one *s* one *d* (and one *d* decd). *Educ*: Llanelli Grammar Sch.; Llandovery Coll.; Birmingham Univ. BSc. CEng, FIMechE, FIEE. Commissioned REME, 1944; served: India, 1945-47; Singapore, 1956-58; BAOR, 1961-63; Technical Staff Course, 1949-51; Staff Coll., Camberley, 1953; Lt-Col, 1963; Asst Dir, Electrical and Mechanical Engineering, HQ Western Comd, 1963-65; Asst Mil. Sec., MoD, 1965-66; Comd REME, 1 (BR) Corps Troops, 1966-67; Technical Gp, REME, 1967-72; Col, 1967; Brig. 1970; Dep. Dir, Electrical and Mechanical Engineering (Eng. Pol.), (Army), 1972-75. Mem. Council, IMechE, 1975-76. *Recreations*: golf, gardening, photography. *Address*: c/o Lloyds Bank Ltd, Llanelli. *Club*: Army and Navy.

MACDONALD-SMITH, Sydney, CMG 1956; retired; *b* 9 July 1908; *s* of late John Alfred Macdonald-Smith, MB, ChB, FRCSE; *m* 1st, 1935, Joyce (*d* 1966), *d* of Austen Whetham, Bridport, Dorset; one *s* one *d*; 2nd, 1968, Winifred Mary Atkinson, JP, *widow* of Captain T. K. W. Atkinson, RN. *Educ*: Nottingham High Sch.; New Coll., Oxford. Entered Colonial Administrative Service, Nigeria, 1931; Controller of Imports, 1945; Director of Supplies, 1947; Under-Sec., Gold Coast, 1949; Permanent Sec. Ministry of Communications and Works, 1950; Chief Regional Officer, Northern Territories, 1954-57; retired Nov. 1957. *Recreation*: gardening. *Address*: Woodman's, Westbourne, Emsworth, Hants. *T*: Emsworth 2943.

McDONAUGH, James, CBE 1970 (OBE 1965); retired 1973; reappointed 1973-75, Director North Europe Department, British Council; *b* 26 July 1912; *s* of late Edward McDonaugh and late Christina, *d* of William Bissell; *m* 1944, Mary-Eithné Mitchell, *d* of James Vyvyan Mitchell; three *s* two *d*. *Educ*: Royal Grammar Sch., Worcester; St Edmund Hall, Oxford (Exhibitioner, MA). Asst Master, Ampleforth Coll., 1935-40; War Service, 1940-45; Lecturer, Graz and Innsbruck Univs, 1947-50; Asst Rep., British Council, Austria, 1950-54; Representative, Malta, 1954-58; Dep. Counsellor (Cultural), Bonn, 1958-59; Dep. Rep., Germany, 1958-61; Dir Specialist

Tours Dept, 1961-65; Asst Controller, Education Div., 1965; Rep., Germany, 1966-73. *Address*: Old Rectory Cottage, Whitestaunton, Chard, Somerset.

MacDONELL of Glengarry, Air Cdre Aeneas Ranald Donald, CB 1964; DFC 1940; Hereditary 22nd Chief of Glengarry; consultant with John Courtis and Partners; *b* 15 Nov. 1913; *e s* of late Ranald MacDonell of Glengarry, CBE; *m* 1st, Diana Dorothy, *yr d* of late Henry Keane, CBE; two *s* one *d*; 2nd, Lois Eirene Frances, *d* of Rev. Gerald Champion Streatfeild; one *s* one *d*. *Educ*: Hurstpierpoint Coll.; Royal Air Force Coll., Cranwell. No. 54 Fighter Sqdn, 1934; Fleet Air Arm, 1935-37; Flying Instructor, 1938-39; Air Ministry, 1939-40; No. 64 Fighter Sqdn, 1940-41; POW, 1941-45; Ministry of Defence, 1946-47; HQ Flying Training Command, 1947-49; Chief Flying Instructor, RAF Coll., Cranwell, 1949-51; Ministry of Defence, 1952-54; Senior RAF Instructor, Joint Services Staff Coll., 1954-56; Air Attaché, Moscow, 1956-58; Dir of Management and Work Study, Ministry of Defence, Air Force Dept, 1960-64, retd. *Recreations*: ciné photography, art, travel. *Address*: 70 Burbage Road, SE24 9HE. *T*: 01-733 1863. *Club*: Royal Air Force.

McDONNELL, family name of Earl of Antrim.

McDONNELL, Christopher Thomas; Assistant Under-Secretary of State, Ministry of Defence, since 1976; *b* 3 Sept. 1931; *s* of Christopher Patrick McDonnell and Jane McDonnell; *m* 1955, Patricia Anne (*née* Harvey) (*d* 1967); three *s* one *d*. *Educ*: St Francis Xavier's Coll., Liverpool; Corpus Christi Coll., Oxford (MA). WO, 1954; HM Treasury, 1966-68; RCDS, 1973. *Address*: 37 Dale Road, Purley, Surrey. *T*: 01-660 5040.

McDONNELL, Denis Lane, OBE 1945; His Honour Judge McDonnell; a Circuit Judge (formerly a County Court Judge), since 1967; *b* 2 March 1914; *o c* of late David McDonnell, LLD and Mary Nora (*née* Lane), Riversdale, Sundays Well, Cork and Fairy Hill, Monkstown, Co. Cork and *gs* of Denny Lane, poet and Young Irelander; *m* 1940, Florence Nina (Micky), *d* of late Lt-Col Hugh T. Ryan, DSO and Clare Emily (*née* Conry), Castle View, Ballincollig, Co. Cork; three *d* (and one *s* one *d* decd). *Educ*: Christian Brothers' Coll., Cork; Ampleforth Coll.; Sidney Sussex Coll., Cambridge (MA). Served in RAFVR, Equipment and Admin. and Special Duties Branches, 1940-45 in UK and with No. 84 Gp in NW Europe (Wing Comdr). Called to Bar, Middle Temple, 1936; Bencher, 1965. Practised at Bar, 1938-40 and 1946-67. *Publications*: Kerr on Fraud and Mistake (7th edn, with J. G. Monroe), 1952; titles on carriage in: Encyclopædias of Forms and Precedents and Court Forms and Precedents; Halsbury's Laws of England; articles in British Tax Review. *Recreations*: family life, listening to music, golf, gardening, pottering. *Address*: Stanmore House, Silverdale Road, Burgess Hill, W Sussex. *T*: Burgess Hill 2158. *Clubs*: Piltdown Golf, Rye Golf, Woking Golf, Royal Cinque Ports Golf.

McDOUALL, John Crichton, CMG 1966; HM Overseas Civil Service, retired; *b* 26 April 1912; *s* of late Rev. Crichton Willoughby McDouall; *m* 1946, Kathleen Glover Moir, *d* of late A. B. Moir, Taikoo, Hong Kong; one *s* two *d*. *Educ*: Monkton Combe Sch.; Jesus Coll., Cambridge; Birmingham Univ. Colonial Administrative Service, Hong Kong, 1934-39; served War of 1939-45, Hong Kong RNVR and POW; Brit. Mil. Administration, Hong Kong, 1945-46; Administrative Service, Hong Kong, 1946-52; Chief Social Welfare Officer, Fedn of Malaya, 1952-57; Sec. for Chinese Affairs, Hong Kong, 1957-67; retired, 1967. Coronation Medal, 1953. *Address*: The Old School, Souldern, Bicester, Oxfordshire. *T*: Fritwell 217.

McDOUGALL, Archibald, MA, BCL; Attorney at Law and pastoralist, USA; *b* Hobart, 5 Aug. 1903; 2nd *s* of late Emeritus Prof. Dugald Gordon McDougall and Helen Ione Atkinson; *m* 1932, Corinne Margaret Cunningham Collins, Mobile, Alabama, and Washington, DC, USA. *Educ*: Hutchins Sch., Hobart; University of Tasmania; Balliol Coll., Oxford; Columbia Univ., New York. BA Tasmania, and Rhodes Scholar, 1924; 1st Class Final Honour Sch. of Jurisprudence, 1926; Proxime Accessit Vinerian Law Scholarship, 1927; 2nd Class Examination for BCL 1927; Commonwealth Fund Fellowship, 1927-29; US Senate Legislative Counsel's Office, Washington, DC 1928; Harmsworth Law Scholarship, 1929; Lecturer in Law, Victoria Univ. of Manchester, 1931-35; called to Bar, Middle Temple, 1932; Mem. of Northern Circuit; practised in Chancery Div. of High Court and in Chancery of County Palatine of Lancaster, 1932-35; Examiner in Law, London Univ., 1934-35; 1936-40 Legal Adviser to Iraqi Ministry for Foreign Affairs, Baghdad, and Prof. of Int. Law at Iraqi Law Sch.; Delegate of Iraq at 17th Assembly of League of Nations,

1936; 1940 travelled extensively through India, Burma, Malaya, NEI, and Australia; Counsel, British Purchasing Commission, New York, 1940-41; Head, Non-Ferrous Metals Div., British Raw Materials Mission, Washington, DC, and UK Staff of Combined Raw Materials Board, 1941-43; Combined Production and Resources Board (UK Staff), Washington, DC, 1944-45; Head of UK Economic Group, US Dept of Commerce and British Embassy, Washington, DC, to Aug. 1946; Legal Counsellor, British Embassy, Cairo, 1946-49; Asst Legal Adviser, Foreign Office, 1949-50. Dep. Comr of Forfeited and Delinquent Lands, 1964-. Pres., Berkeley County Bar Assoc., 1964-65; Member: American Bar Assoc.; W Virginia State Bar; W Virginia Bar Assoc.; Sustaining Mem., Assoc., of Trial Lawyers, USA; admitted US Supreme Court Bar and Fourth Circuit Court of Appeals, 1973. Mem., Amer. Soc. Internat. Law, 1929-. *Publications:* Modern Conveyancing, 1936; and articles in British Year book of International Law. *Recreation:* motoring. *Address:* Oban Hall, Gerrardstown, West Virginia 25420, USA. *T:* Area Code 304,229-5400.

MacDOUGALL of MacDougall, Madam; (Coline Helen Elizabeth); 30th Chief of Clan MacDougall, 1953; *b* 17 Aug. 1904; *e d* of Col Alexander J. MacDougall of MacDougall, 29th Chief, and Mrs Colina Edith MacDougall of MacDougall; *m* 1949, Leslie Grahame-Thomson (who assumed the surname of MacDougall, 1953), RSA, FRIBA, PPRIAS, FSAScot (*d* 1974); resumed surname of MacDougall of MacDougall on succession to Chiefship, 1953. *Educ:* St James's, West Malvern. Served WRNS (Second Officer), 1941-46. *Address:* Dunollie Castle, Oban, Argyll. *T:* Oban 2012.

MacDOUGALL, Brig. David Mercer, CMG 1946; MA; *b* 1904; *m* 1st, 1929, Catherine Crowther; one *d* ; 2nd, 1951, Inez Weir, *o d* of late James Hislop Thompson; two *d* . *Educ:* St Andrews Univ. Cadet Hong Kong Administrative Service, 1928; seconded to Colonial Office as asst principal, Feb. 1937-March 1939; seconded Hong Kong Dept of Information and Sec. Far Eastern Bureau of British Ministry of Information, Oct. 1939; Colonial Office, 1942; British Embassy, Washington, DC, 1943; Dir British Political Warfare Mission, San Francisco, Dec. 1943; Colonial Office, 1944; Brig. Chief Civil Affairs Officer, Hong Kong, 1945; Colonial Sec., Hong Kong, 1946-49; retired, 1949; Order of the Brilliant Star (China), 1946. *Address:* Mercers, Finchingfield, Essex; Blackhill, By Aberfield, Perthshire.

MacDOUGALL, Sir (George) Donald (Alastair), Kt 1953; CBE 1945 (OBE 1942); FBA 1966; Chief Economic Adviser, Confederation of British Industry, since 1973; *b* 26 Oct. 1912; *s* of late Daniel Douglas MacDougall, Glasgow, and late Beatrice Amy Miller; *m* 1st, 1937, Bridget Christabel Bartrum (marr. diss. 1977); one *s* one *d* ; 2nd, 1977, Margaret Hall (*see* L. M. MacDougall). *Educ:* Kelvinside Acad., Glasgow; Shrewsbury Sch.; Balliol Coll., Oxford. George Webb Medley Junior (1934) and Senior (1935) Scholarships in Political Economy; Asst Lecturer (later Lecturer) in Economics, University of Leeds, 1936-39; First Lord of the Admiralty's Statistical Branch, 1939-40; Prime Minister's Statistical Branch, 1940-45 (Chief Asst, 1942-45). Work on Reparations and German Industry, Moscow and Berlin, 1945; Mem. of Heavy Clothing Industry Working Party, 1946; Official Fellow of Wadham Coll., Oxford, 1945-50, Domestic Bursar, 1946-48, Hon. Fellow, 1964-; Econ. Dir, OEEC, Paris, 1948-49; Faculty Fellow, Nuffield Coll., 1947-50, Professorial Fellow, 1951-52, Official Fellow, 1952-64, First Bursar, 1958-64, Hon. Fellow, 1967-; Nuffield Reader in Internat. Economics, Oxford Univ., 1951-52; Chief Adviser, Prime Minister's Statistical Branch, 1951-53; Visiting Prof., Australian Nat. Univ., 1959; MIT Center for Internat. Studies, New Delhi, 1961; Dir, Investing in Success Equities, Ltd, 1959-62; Economic Dir, NEDC, 1962-64; Mem. Turnover Tax Cttee, 1963-64; Dir-Gen., Dept of Economic Affairs, 1964-68; Head of Govt Economic Service, and Chief Economic Adviser to the Treasury, 1969-73. Mem. Council, Royal Econ. Soc., 1950-(Hon. Sec., 1958-70; Vice-Pres., 1970-72, 1974-; Pres., 1972-74); Pres., Soc. for Long Range Planning, 1977, Vice-Pres., 1968-77; Chm., Exec. Cttee NIESR, 1974-; Mem., EEC Study Gp on Economic and Monetary Union, 1974-75; Chm., EEC Study Gp on Role of Public Finance in European Economic Integration, 1975-77. Hon. LLD Strathclyde, 1968; Hon. LittD Leeds, 1971. *Publications:* (part author) Measures for International Economic Stability, UN, 1951; The World Dollar Problem, 1957; (part author) The Fiscal System of Venezuela, 1959; The Dollar Problem: A Reappraisal, 1960; Studies in Political Economy (2 vols), 1975; contrib. to Britain in Recovery, 1938, Lessons of the British War Economy, 1951, and to various economic and statistical jls. *Address:* 86A Denbigh Street, SW1. *T:* 01-821 1998. *Club:* Reform.

MacDOUGALL, Air Cdre Ian Neil, CBE 1964; DFC 1942; Military Liaison, Bristol Composite Materials Ltd, since 1970; *b* 11 June 1920; *s* of late Archibald MacDougall, Colonial Service, and Helen Grace (*née* Simpson); *m* 1944, Dorothy Eleanor, *d* of late John Frankland; one *s* one *d*. *Educ:* Morrison's Academy, Crieff; RAF Coll., Cranwell. Commnd Sept. 1939; served in Fighter Sqdns in Battle of Britain, Syrian and Western Desert Campaigns, Malta and in invasions of Sicily and Normandy; War Studies Lectr at RAF Coll., 1948-50 and USAF Academy, Colorado, 1956-58; Asst Air Attaché, Paris, 1950-53; Chief Flying Instructor, RAF Coll., 1953-56; Supt of Flying, Boscome Down, 1959-62; comd RAF Fighter Stn, Binbrook, 1962-64; SASO 38 Gp, 1964-67; comd Zambian Expedn and Zambian Oil Lift, 1965-66; Air Attaché, Paris, 1967-69; jssc, psc, pfc, cfs; retd Dec. 1969. *Recreation:* fishing. *Address:* Ringtail Cottage, Lower Morton, Thornbury, Glos. *T:* Thornbury 412037. *Club:* Royal Air Force.

MacDOUGALL, Laura Margaret, (Lady MacDougall); Hon. Fellow of Somerville College, Oxford, since 1975; Consultant to National Economic Development Office; *d* of George E. Linfoot and Laura Edith Clayton; *m* 1932, Robert L. Hall (now Lord Roberthall) (marr. diss. 1968); two *d*; *m* 1977, Sir Donald MacDougall, *qv*. *Educ:* Sheffield Girls' High Sch. and High Storrs Grammar Sch.; Somerville Coll., Oxford. Hon. Scholar, 1st Cl. Hons Philosophy, Politics and Economics; Jun. George Webb Medley Scholar. US Govt Office of Price Admin, 1941-44; UNNRA Planning Div., Washington, DC, Sydney and London, 1944-45; Lectr, Lincoln Coll., Oxford, 1944-47; Lectr, 1947-49, and Fellow and Tutor, 1949-75, Somerville Coll., Oxford; University Lectr in Economics, 1949-75. Member: Treasury Purchase Tax Cttee, 1954; Interdeptal Cttee on Economic and Social Research, 1957-58; Gaitskell Co-operative Indep. Commn, 1958; Min. of Ag. Cttee on the Remuneration of Milk Distributors in the UK, 1962; Reith Indep. Commn on Advertising, 1964; Covent Garden Market Authority Adv. Cttee, 1972; Distributive Trades Industrial Trng Bd's Research Cttee, 1972; EDC for Distributive Trades, 1963-75; Monopolies and Mergers Commn, 1973-76; Past Member: Retail Furnishing and Allied Trades Wages Council; Retail Newsagency, Confectioner and Tobacconist Wages Council. Visiting Prof. MIT, USA, 1961-62. *Publications:* US Senate Cttee Print, Effect of War on British Retail Trade, 1943; Distributive Trading: an economic analysis, 1954; Distribution in Great Britain and North America (with Knapp and Winsten), 1961; contribs to: The British Economy, 1945-50, 1962; The British Economy in the 1950s, 1962; (Bolton Cttee, Research Report No 8) The Small Unit in Retail Trade, 1972; numerous contribs to various economic and statistical jls. *Address:* 86A Denbigh Street, Westminster, SW1V 2EX. *T:* 01-821 1998.
See also Dr E . H . Linfoot .

McDOUGALL, Richard Sedgwick, CBE 1957; FCA; Chairman, Building Research Station Steering Committee, 1967-70; *b* 29 May 1904; *o s* of late R. E. C. McDougall and Evelyn Mary, *d* of Richard Sedgwick; *m* 1929, Margaret Sylvia (*d* 1976), *d* of late John Charles Denmead; two *d*. *Educ:* Haileybury Coll. County Treasurer, Hertfordshire County Council, 1939-57; General Manager, Stevenage Development Corporation, 1957-67. Member: Weeks Cttee on Army Works Services, 1956-57; Colonial Secretary's Advisory Cttee on Local Govt, 1950-; North West Metropolitan Regional Hosp. Bd, 1963-68. For British Govt, visited Sierra Leone, 1950, Nyasaland, 1954, Fiji Islands, 1957, and Kenya, 1967. *Recreations:* painting, golf. *Address:* 56 The Shimmings, Boxgrove Road, Guildford, Surrey. *T:* Guildford 69702.

MacDOWALL, Dr David William; Master of University College, Durham, since 1973; *b* 2 April 1930; *o s* of late William MacDowall and late Lilian May MacDowall (*née* Clarkson); *m* 1962, Mione Beryl, *yr d* of late Ernest Harold Lashmar and Dora Lashmar; two *d*. *Educ:* Liverpool Inst.; Corpus Christi Coll., Oxford; British Sch. at Rome. MA, DPhil; FSA, FRAS. Hugh Oldham Scholar 1947, Pelham Student in Roman History 1951; Barclay Head Prize for Ancient Numismatics, 1953 and 1956. 2nd Lieut Royal Signals, 1952. Asst Principal, Min. of Works, 1955; Asst Keeper, Dept of Coins and Medals, British Museum, 1956; Principal, Min. of Educn, 1960; Principal, Univ. Grants Cttee, 1965; Asst Sec. 1970. Hon. Treas., Royal Numismatic Soc., 1966-73; Hon. Sec., Soc. for Afghan Studies, 1972-. *Publications:* The Western Coinages of Nero, 1977; articles in Numismatic Chron., Jl Numismatic Soc. India, Schweizer Münzblätter, Acta Numismatica, S Asian Archaeology, etc. *Recreations:* travel, antiquities, photography, gardening. *Address:* The Master's House, The Castle, Durham. *T:* Durham 65481; Admont, Gravel Path, Berkhamsted, Herts.

McDOWALL, Robert John Stewart, DSc, MD, MRCP; FRCPE; Professor Emeritus in the University of London since 1959; Professor of Physiology, 1923-59, and Dean of Faculty of Medicine and Fellow of King's College, London; Vice-Chairman Medical Advisory Committee and Founder Member, Asthma Research Council; Formerly Examiner for Universities of London, Leeds, Durham, Manchester, Aberdeen, St Andrews, Edinburgh, Sheffield, Bristol, West Indies, Nigeria, RCP, RCS, in India, Egypt, Australasia, and Eire; *b* 1892; *s* of Robert McDowall, Auchengaillie, Wigtonshire, and Fanny Grace Stewart; *m* 1st, 1921, Jessie (*d* 1963), *yr d* of Alexander Macbeth, JP, Pitlochry, Perthshire; two *d*; 2nd, 1964, Dr Jean Rotherham, *d* of Col Ewan Rotherham, TD, DL (Warwickshire). *Educ:* Watson's Coll., Edinburgh; University of Edinburgh (Gold Medal for MD thesis). Assistant and Lecturer in Physiology, University of Edinburgh, 1919-21; Lectr, Experimental Physiology and Experimental Pharmacology, Univ. of Leeds, 1921-23; Lectr in Applied Physiology, London Sch. of Hygiene, 1927-29. Ellis prizeman, 1920; Parkin prizeman, RCP, Edinburgh, 1930; Gunning Victoria Jubilee Cullen Prize, RCP, Edinburgh, 1938; Arris and Gale Lectr, RCS, 1933; Oliver Sharpey Lectr, RCP, 1941; medal of honour, Univ. of Ghent, 1951; has given 3 lecture tours of America. Hon. Fellow: Amer. Acad. of Allergy, 1953; Soc. Française d'Allergie, 1957; European Acad. of Allergy; Finnish Acad. of Allergy. Pres., 4th European Congress of Allergy, 1959; Hon. Mem., British Soc. of Allergy; Extraordinary Mem., British Cardiac Soc. Has been Resident House Physician, Edinburgh Royal Infirmary, and Clinical Tutor in Medicine, Univ. of Edinburgh; served with RAMC, European War, 1914-18, also 1940-41; became DADMS for British Forces in Palestine, Syria, and Cilicia; President, Physiology Sect. British Assoc., 1936; Chairman Board of Intermediate Medical Studies and of Physiology, University of London. *Publications:* Clinical Physiology; The Science of Signs and Symptoms in relation to Modern Diagnosis and Treatment, 4 editions; Handbook of Physiology, 13 editions; The Control of the Circulation of the Blood, 1938, 1957; The Whiskies of Scotland, 1967, 2nd edn 1971 (Swedish, German, Spanish and American edns); Editor, The Mind, by various authors; Sane Psychology, 6 reprints; Anatomy and Physiology for students of Physiotherapy (with Smout) and numerous scientific papers. *Recreations:* chess, curling (1st President, Hampstead Curling Club; 1st President, London Watsonian Curling Club; former Pres. and Hon. Mem., Province of London; skipped England against Scotland, 1966 and 1969); golf (Ex-Captain, Life Mem. and Director, Hampstead Golf Club). *Address:* 34 Park Drive, NW11. *T:* 01-455 2858.
See also J. K. Rotherham.

McDOWALL, Robert William, CBE 1977 (OBE 1966); FSA (Lond.); Secretary, Royal Commission on Historical Monuments (England), since 1973; *b* 13 May 1914; *yr s* of Rev. C. R. L. McDowall; *m* 1939, Avril Betty Everard Hannaford; three *s* one *d. Educ:* Eton; Magdalene Coll., Cambridge (MA). Investigator, Royal Commission on Historical Monuments (England), 1936. Served War, with Royal Engineers, 1939-45. Member: Ancient Monuments Bd for England; Internat. Cttee for Architectural Photogrammetry; UK Cttee of Internat. Council for Monuments and Sites; (Pres.) Surrey Archaeological Soc. *Publications:* contributor to: Monuments Threatened or Destroyed, 1963; Peterborough New Town, 1969; Shielings and Bastles, 1970; County Inventories of RCHM; Archaeologia, Antiquaries Jl (and local archaeological jls). *Address:* Chandlers, Ballsdown, Chiddingfold, Surrey. *T:* Wormley 2995. *Club:* Athenæum.

McDOWELL, Sir Frank (Schofield), Kt 1967; President, McDowells Holdings Ltd, 1971-72 (Chairman and Managing Director, McDowells Ltd, 1935-67, Chairman 1967); *b* 8 Aug. 1889; *s* of John McDowell; *m* 1912, Ethel Sophia Perrott; six *s* one *d. Educ:* Petersham Public School. Grand Master: United Grand Lodge of NSW Freemasons, 1947-49; Mark Master Masons NSW, 1946-48; Inspector General, 33rd Rose Croix SE Central District NSW, 1967-72. *Recreations:* bowls, garden, swimming. *Address:* Melrose, 157 Ewos Parade, Cronulla, Sydney, NSW, Australia. *T:* 5235115. *Clubs:* (Hon. Mem.) All Nations, (Patron) Retailers, (Past Pres.) Sydney Rotary (Sydney); (Patron) South Cronulla Bowling.

McDOWELL, Sir Henry (McLorinan), KBE 1964 (CBE 1959); Chairman, Rhodesian Board, Barclays Bank International, since 1969; Chancellor, University of Rhodesia, since 1971; *b* Johannesburg, S. Africa, 10 Dec. 1910; *s* of John McDowell and Margaret Elizabeth Bingham; *m* 1939, Norah, *d* of Walter Slade Douthwaite; one *s* one *d. Educ:* Witwatersrand Univ.; Queen's Coll., Oxford; Yale Univ. Served War of 1939-45, 1 Bn Northern Rhodesia Regt, East Africa and South-East Asia, 1940-44.

Entered HM Colonial Service (Cadet, Northern Rhodesia), 1938; Clerk, Legislative and Executive Councils, 1945; Assistant Secretary, 1950; Deputy Financial Secretary, 1952. Imperial Defence Coll., 1948; seconded Colonial Office, 1949. Economic and Financial Working Party, in preparation for federation of Rhodesias and Nyasaland, 1953; Federal Treasury, 1954; Secretary, Ministry of Transport, 1955; Secretary, Federal Treasury, 1959-63. Chairman: Exec Cttee, Univ. Coll. of Rhodesia and Nyasaland, 1964; Council of the University of Rhodesia, 1971; Mem., governing bodies, educational institutions, Rhodesia. Director of Companies. Hon. LLD Witwatersrand, 1971; Hon. DLitt Rhodesia, 1975. *Recreations:* walking, reading. *Address:* 6 Malcolm House, Blakiston Street, Salisbury, Rhodesia. *Club:* Salisbury.

MACDUFF, Earl of; David Charles Carnegie; *b* 3 March 1961; *s* and *heir* of 3rd Duke of Fife, *qv.*

MacEACHEN, Hon. Allan Joseph, PC (Canada); MP (L) Cape Breton Highlands-Canso, Nova Scotia, since 1953; President, Privy Council and Government Leader in the House of Commons, Canada, 1970-74 and since 1976; *b* Inverness, Nova Scotia, 6 July 1921; *s* of Angus and Annie MacEachen. *Educ:* St Francis Xavier Univ. (BA 1944); Univ. of Toronto (MA 1946); Univ. of Chicago; MIT. Prof. of Economics, St Francis Xavier Univ., 1946-48; Head of Dept of Economics and Social Sciences; Special Asst and Consultant on Econ. Affairs to Hon. Lester Pearson, 1958; Minister: of Labour, 1963-65; of Nat. Health and Welfare, 1965-68; of Manpower and Immigration, 1968-70; of External Affairs, 1974-76. Hon. Degrees: St Francis Xavier Univ.; Acadia Univ.; Loyola Coll; St Mary's Univ.; Dalhousie Univ.; Wilfrid Laurier Univ. *Address:* Parliament Buildings, Ottawa, Ont, Canada.

McELDERRY, Samuel Burnside Boyd, CMG 1935; *b* 7 Oct. 1885; *s* of late Thomas McElderry and late Alice Knox of Ballymoney, Co. Antrim; *m* 1913, Mildred Mary Orme (*d* 1974); three *d. Educ:* Campbell Coll., Belfast; Trinity Coll., Dublin. Eastern Cadet, 1909; Hong Kong Administrative Service, 1909-28; Deputy Chief Secretary, Tanganyika, 1929-33; Chief Secretary, Zanzibar, 1933-40; retired 1940; attached to office of High Commissioner for Basutoland, Bechuanaland Protectorate and Swaziland (Pretoria and Cape Town), 1940-45; temporarily employed Colonial Office, 1945-46. Member of Council, Royal Commonwealth Society for Blind, 1951-70; Royal National Institute for Blind, 1958-70. *Address:* Fircroft, 19 Kivernell Road, Milford-on-Sea, Lymington, Hants.
See also W. Wenban-Smith.

McELENEY, Most Rev. John, SJ, DD; PhD, MA; Archbishop of Kingston (Jamaica), 1967-70; *b* 13 Nov. 1895; *s* of Charles McEleney and Bridget McEleney (*née* McGaffigan). *Educ:* Woburn Public Sch.; Weston Coll.; Boston Coll. Entered Soc. of Jesus at Yonkers, New York; classical studies at St Andrew on Hudson, 1920-21; Philosophy, Weston Coll. (MA), 1921-23. Teacher, Ateneo de Manila, 1923-27; Theology, 1927-31; formerly: Rector, Shadowbrook Jesuit Novitiate, Lenox, Mass; Rector, Prep. Sch., Fairfield, Conn; Tutor Ateneo de Manila Jesuit Coll., Manila; Provincial, New England Province Soc. of Jesus, 1944-50. Consecrated Bishop, 1950; Vicar Apostolic of Jamaica, 1950; Bishop of Kingston (Jamaica), 1956-67. Hon. Dr of Laws: Fairfield Univ., 1951; Boston Coll., 1968. *Address:* Boston College, Newton, Massachusetts 02167, USA. *T:* (617) 969-0100.

McELHONE, Francis; JP; MP (Lab) Glasgow, Queen's Park, since 1974 (Glasgow, Gorbals, Oct. 1969-1974); Parliamentary Under Secretary of State, Scottish Office, since 1975; *b* Glasgow, 5 April 1929; *m* 1958, Helen Brown; two *s* two *d. Educ:* St Bonaventure's Secondary Sch., Glasgow. Member, Glasgow CC, for Hutchesontown Ward, 1963-; JP Glasgow 1966, Senior Magistrate 1968, Police Judge 1969. PPS to Sec. of State for Industry, 1974-75. *Address:* House of Commons, SW1; 22 Windlaw Road, Carmunnock, Glasgow.

McELLIGOTT, Neil Martin; Metropolitan Magistrate at Great Marlborough Street Magistrates' Court, since 1972 (at Old Street Magistrates' Court, 1961-72); *b* 21 March 1915; *s* of Judge E. J. McElligott, KC, Limerick; *m* 1939, Suzanne, *d* of late Air Chief Marshal Sir Arthur Barratt, KCB, CMG, MC, DL; one *d. Educ:* Ampleforth. Served in Royal Air Force, 1935-45. Called to Bar, Inner Temple, 1945, South Eastern Circuit, Recorder of King's Lynn, 1961. *Recreations:* hunting, racing, fishing, gardening. *Address:* Stone Cottage, Abthorpe, near Towcester, Northants. *T:* Silverstone 310.

McELROY, Roy Granville, CMG 1972; LLD, PhD; Pro-Chancellor of the University of Auckland, since 1968; *b* 2 April

1907; *s* of H. T. G. McElroy and Frances C. Hampton; *m* Joan H., *d* of R. O. H. Biss; two *d. Educ:* Auckland Univ.; Clare Coll., Cambridge. LLM NZ 1929; PhD Cantab 1934; LLD NZ 1936. Barrister and Solicitor. Lectr in Law, Auckland Univ., 1936-37. Mem., Auckland City Council, 1938-53; Dep. Mayor of Auckland, 1953, Mayor, 1965-68; Chm., Auckland Metro Planning Cttee, 1953; Mem., Auckland Regional Planning Authority, 1954-66; Chairman: Auckland Old People's Welfare Cttee, 1950-65; NZ Welfare of Aged Persons Distribution Cttee, 1962-75; Sunset Home Inc., 1972-75; Member: Bd of Trustees, NZ Retirement Life Care, 1972-75; Council, Dr Barnardo's in NZ; Auckland Medico-Legal Soc. Consular Agent of France in Auckland, 1948-72; Dean, Auckland Consular Corps, 1965 and 1971. Chm., NZ Section Internat. Commn of Jurists, 1965-72. Chm. Legal Research Foundn, Auckland Univ., 1968-72; Mem., Auckland Univ. Council, 1939-54 and 1960-75; Chm., Auckland Br., NZ Inst. of Internat. Affairs, 1970. FRSA 1971. Hon. DLitt Auckland Univ., 1976. Chévalier de l'Ordre National de la Légion d'Honneur, 1954. *Publications:* Law Reform Act 1936 NZ, 1937; Impossibility of Performance of Contracts, 1942; articles in Modern Law Review, NZ Law Jl, NZ Financial Times. *Recreation:* reading. *Address:* Highpoint, 119 St Stephens Avenue, Parnell, Auckland, New Zealand. *T:* 30-645. *Club:* Northern (Auckland).

McENERY, John Hartnett; Under Secretary, Concorde and Nationalised Industries Policy Division, Department of Industry, since 1977; *b* 5 Sept. 1925; *y s* of late Maurice Joseph and Elizabeth Margaret McEnery. *Educ:* St Augustine's Sch., Coatbridge; St Aloysius Coll., Glasgow; Glasgow Univ. (MA(Hons)). Served War of 1939-45: RA, 1943-47; Staff Captain, Burma Command, 1946-47. Glasgow Univ., 1947-49. Asst Principal, Scottish Educn Dept, 1949; Principal, 1954; Cabinet Office, 1957; HM Treasury, 1959; Min. of Aviation, 1962; UK Delegn to NATO, 1964; Counsellor (Defence Supply), British Embassy, Bonn, 1966; Asst Sec., Min. of Technology, 1970; Dept of Trade and Industry, 1970-74; Under-Sec. and Regional Dir for Yorks and Humberside, DTI, 1972, Dept of Industry, 1974-77. *Recreations:* various games and sports, chess, travel. *Address:* 56 Lillian Road, SW13 9JF. *Clubs:* Hurlingham; Leeds (Leeds).

McENTEE, Peter Donovan, OBE 1963; HM Diplomatic Service; Governor and Commander-in-Chief of Belize, since 1976; *b* 27 June 1920; *s* of Ewen Brooke McEntee and Caroline Laura Clare (*née* Bayley); *m* 1945, Mary Elisabeth Sherwood; two *d. Educ:* Haileybury Coll., Herts. Served War, HM Forces, 1939-45, KAR (Major). HM Overseas Civil Service, 1946-63: Dist Commissioner; retired as Principal of Kenya Inst. of Administration; First Secretary: Commonwealth Relations Office, 1963; Lagos, 1964-67; Commonwealth Office (later Foreign and Commonwealth Office), 1967-72; Consul-Gen., Karachi, 1972-75. *Recreations:* music, natural history, golf. *Address:* Belize House, Belmopan, Belize. *T:* Belmopan 2146. *Clubs:* Royal Commonwealth Society; Nairobi (Kenya); Sind (Karachi).

MacENTEE, Seán; Member, Dáil Eireann for Dublin South (East), retired May 1969; Member, Council of State; Tánaiste (Deputy Prime Minister), 1959-65; Minister for Health, 1957-65 (of Social Welfare, 1958-61); a consulting electrical engineer, registered patent agent, company director, etc.; *b* 1889; *e s* of James MacEntee, TC, Belfast; *m* Margaret, *d* of late Maurice Browne, of Grange-Mockler, Co. Tipperary; one *s* two *d. Educ:* St Malachy's Coll., Belfast; Belfast College of Technology. Participated in Irish insurrection, 1916; tried by General Court-Martial, May 1916, and sentenced to death (sentence afterwards commuted to penal servitude for life); imprisoned in Dartmoor, Lewes and Portland prisons and released under General Amnesty, June 1917; MP (SF) South Monaghan, Dec. 1918; Member of National Executive Cttee of Irish Volunteers and Irish Republican Army, 1917-21; served with Irish Republican Army, 1916-21; contested County Dublin, Aug. 1923, Dec. 1924; TD (Representative Fianna Fail) Co. Dublin, June 1927; re-elected Sept. 1927, 1932, and 1933; TD Dublin Townships, 1937-48, and Dublin SE, 1948-69; Minister for Finance, Irish Free State, 1932-37, and Eire, 1937-39; Minister for Industry and Commerce, Eire, 1939-41; Minister for Local Government and Public Health, Eire, 1941-46; for Local Government, 1946-48; Minister for Finance, Republic of Ireland, 1951-54. LLD (*hc*) NUI. Kt Grand Cross, Pian Order. *Publications:* Poems (1918); Episode at Easter, 1966. *Address:* Montrose, Trimleston Avenue, Booterstown, Co. Dublin. *T:* 692441.

McEVOY, Air Chief Marshal Sir Theodore Newman, KCB 1956 (CB 1951); CBE 1945 (OBE 1941); *b* 21 Nov. 1904; *s* of late Rev. C. McEvoy, MA, Watford; *m* 1935, Marian, *d* of late W. A. E. Coxon, Cairo; one *s* one *d. Educ:* Haberdashers' School; RAF

Coll., Cranwell. Served with Fighter Squadrons and in Iraq, 1925-36; psa 1937; Air Ministry, 1938-41; commanded Northolt, 1941; Group Captain Operations, HQ Fighter Command, 1942-43; SASO No 11 Group, 1943; SASO No 84 Group, 1944 (despatches); Air Ministry (DST), 1945-47; idc 1948; AOC No 61 Group, 1949-50; Assistant Chief of Air Staff (Training), 1950-53; RAF Instructor, Imperial Defence Coll., 1954-56; Chief of Staff, Allied Air Forces, Central Europe, 1956-59; Air Secretary, Air Ministry, 1959-62; Air ADC to the Queen, 1959-62; retired, 1962. Vice-President, British Gliding Assoc. Commander Order of Polonia Restituta (Poland), 1942. *Recreations:* gliding, golf. *Address:* 75A Boundstone Road, Rowledge, Farnham, Surrey GU10 4AT. *Club:* Royal Air Force.

McEWAN, Geraldine, (Mrs Hugh Cruttwell); actress; *b* 9 May 1932; *d* of Donald and Norah McKeown; *m* 1953, Hugh Cruttwell, *qv*; one *s* one *d. Educ:* Windsor County Girls' School. Acted with Theatre Royal, Windsor, 1949-51; Who Goes There, 1951; Sweet Madness, 1952; For Better For Worse, 1953; Summertime, 1955; Love's Labour's Lost, Stratford-on-Avon, 1956; The Member of the Wedding, Royal Court Theatre, 1957; The Entertainer, Palace, 1957-58; Stratford-on-Avon, 1958: Pericles; Twelfth Night; Much Ado About Nothing; 1961: Much Ado About Nothing; Hamlet; Everything in the Garden, Arts and Duke of York's, 1962; School for Scandal, Haymarket, and USA, 1962; The Private Ear, and The Public Eye, USA, 1963; Loot, 1965; National Theatre, 1965-72: Armstrong's Last Goodnight; Love For Love; A Flea in Her Ear; The Dance of Death; Edward II; Home and Beauty; Rites; The Way of the World; The White Devil; Amphitryon 38; Dear Love, Comedy, 1973; Chez Nous, Globe, 1974; The Little Hut, Duke of York's, 1974; Oh Coward!, Criterion, 1975; On Approval, Haymarket, 1975. *Address:* c/o Larry Dalzell Associates, 3 Goodwin's Court, WC2.

MacEWEN, Ann Maitland, RIBA (DisTP), MRTPI; Planning Consultant; *b* 15 Aug. 1918; *d* of Dr Maitland Radford, MD, DPH, MOH St Pancras, and Dr Muriel Radford; *m* 1st, 1940, John Wheeler, ARIBA, AADip (Hons), Flt-Lt, RAF (killed on active service, 1945); two *d*; 2nd, 1947, Malcolm MacEwen, *qv*; one *d. Educ:* Howell's Sch., Denbigh, N Wales; Architectural Assoc. Sch. of Architecture (AA Dip., RIBA); Assoc. for Planning and Regional Reconstruction Sch. of Planning (SP Dip., MRTPI). Architectural Asst, 1945-46; Planning Asst, Hemel Hempstead New Town Master Plan, 1946-47; Architect-Planner with LCC, 1949-61; Mem., Colin Buchanan's Gp, Min. of Transport, which produced official report, Traffic in Towns, 1961-63; res. work, Transport Section, Civil Engineering Dept, Imperial Coll., 1963-64; Partner, Colin Buchanan and Partners, 1964-73, Consultant, 1973-. Consultant i/c of studies of: Cirencester, 1964; Bath, 1965; regional planning in Ireland and Galway City, for UN, 1968; Canterbury, 1970; Greenwich/Blackheath, for GLC, 1971; Edinburgh, 1972; Senior Lectr, Bristol Univ. Sch. of Advanced Urban Studies, 1974-77. Mem., Noise Adv. Council, 1971-73. RIBA Distinction in Town Planning, 1967. *Recreations:* riding, swimming, cooking and entertaining. *Address:* 10 Vyvyan Terrace, Clifton, Bristol BS8 3DF; Manor House, Wootton Courtenay, Minehead, Somerset. *T:* Timberscombe 325. *Club:* Architectural Association.

M'EWEN, Ewen, CBE 1975; MScEng; FRSE; CEng, FIMechE; FASME; Vice-Chairman (Engineering), Joseph Lucas Ltd, since 1967; *b* 13 Jan. 1916; *e s* of Clement M'Ewen and Doris Margaret Pierce-Hope; *m* 1938, Barbara Dorrien, *d* of W. F. Medhurst; two *s* one *d. Educ:* Merchiston; University Coll., London. BSc (Eng) 1st class Hons, 1935; MSc (Eng) 1948; Head Memorial Medallist and Prizeman, 1935; Graduate Apprentice David Brown & Sons (Huddersfield) Ltd, 1935-37, Research Engineer, 1937-40, Asst Works Manager, 1940-42; served War of 1939-45, 1942-46: Lt-Col 1943; Lt-Col (Hon. Col) REME (TA retd); Asst Dir, Dept of Tank Design, 1943-46; Asst Chief Engineer, Fighting Vehicles Design Dept, 1946-47; Prof. of Agricultural Engineering, King's Coll., Univ. of Durham, Newcastle upon Tyne, 1947-54, and Reader in Applied Mechanics, 1952-54; Dir Armament R and D Establishment, Fort Halstead, 1955-58; Dir of Engineering, Massey Ferguson Ltd, 1958-63; Dep. Man. Dir, 1963, Man. Dir, 1965-67, Hobourn Group Ltd. Commanded REME 50 (N) Infantry Div. (TA), 1949-52. Hon. Col Durham Univ. OTC, 1955-60. Member: Council, Instn of Mech. Engs, 1961- (Vice-Pres., 1970-76; Pres., 1976-77); Design Council, 1971-; Armed Forces Pay Review Body, 1971-; Chm., Metrology and Standards Requirements Bd, 1973-77. Chm., Lanchester Polytechnic, Coventry, 1970-73. Fellow, UCL, 1965; Vis. Prof., Imperial Coll., London, 1971-. Hon. DSc Heriot-Watt 1976; Newcastle, 1977. Liveryman, Glaziers Company; Hammerman, Glasgow.

Publications: papers and articles in Technical Press. *Recreation:* sailing. *Address:* 45 Pearce Avenue, Poole, Dorset BH14 8EG. *T:* Parkstone 742067; Joseph Lucas Ltd, Great King Street, Birmingham B19 2XF. *T:* 021-554 5252. *Clubs:* Army and Navy; Royal Thames Yacht; Parkstone Yacht.

McEWEN, Rev. Prof. James Stevenson, DD; Professor of Church History, University of Aberdeen, 1958-77; Master of Christ's College, Aberdeen, since 1971; *b* 18 Feb. 1910; *s* of Rev. Thomas McEwen and Marjorie Bissett; *m* 1945, Martha M. Hunter, Auchendrane, Alexandria; two *s*. *Educ:* George Watson's Coll., Edinburgh Univ. Ordained Church of Scotland, 1940; held parishes at Rathen, Hawick and Invergowrie; Lecturer in Church History at University of Edinburgh, 1953. *Publication:* The Faith of John Knox, 1961. *Address:* 8 Westfield Terrace, Aberdeen AB2 4RU. *T:* Aberdeen 25413.

McEWEN, Rt. Hon. Sir John, PC 1953; GCMG 1971; CH 1969; Australian former politician and farmer; *b* Chiltern, Victoria, 29 March 1900; *s* of David James McEwen and Amy Ellen (Porter) McEwen; *m* 1st, 1921, Annie McLeod, DBE 1966 (*d* 1967), *d* of John McLeod, Tongala, Victoria; 2nd, 1968, Mary Eileen, *d* of Patrick Aloysius Byrne, Adelaide. Enlisted Australian Imperial Forces, 1918; farmer at Stanhope, Victoria, 1919-76; MHR Echuca, 1934-37, Indi, 1937-49, Murray, 1949-71 (retd); Minister for: the Interior, Australia, 1937-39; External Affairs, 1940; Air and Civil Aviation, 1940-41; Member War Cabinet, 1940-41; Member War Advisory Council, Australia, 1941-45; Member Australian Delegation, UNCIO, San Francisco, 1945; Minister for: Commerce and Agriculture, Australia, 1949-56; Trade, 1956-63; Trade and Industry, 1963-71; led numerous delegns to GATT talks, Geneva; Dep. Leader, Australian Country Party, 1943-58, Leader, 1958-71; Deputy Prime Minister, 1958-71; Prime Minister, Dec. 1967-Jan. 1968. Order of the Rising Sun, 1st Class (Japan), 1973. *Recreations:* farming, reading. *Address:* (office) AMP Tower, 535 Bourke Street, Melbourne, Vic. 3000, Australia. *T:* Melbourne 62-1734. *Club:* Melbourne (Melbourne).

MacEWEN, Malcolm; journalist; *b* 24 Dec. 1911; *s* of late Sir Alexander MacEwen and of Lady (Mary Beatrice) MacEwen; *m* 1st, 1937, Barbara Mary Stebbing, BSc (*d* 1944); one *d*; 2nd, 1947, Mrs Ann Maitland Wheeler (*see* Ann Maitland MacEwen); one *d* (and two step *d*). *Educ:* St Salvator's Sch., St Andrews; Rossall Sch.; Aberdeen Univ.; Edinburgh Univ. (MA, LLB; Editor, The Student). Lost leg in motor cycle accident, 1933. Practised as Solicitor, Inverness, 1937-41; Member (Lab) Ross and Cromarty CC, 1938-40; became journalist, 1941; wrote for Daily Worker, mainly as Parliamentary Correspondent, 1944-56; Asst Editor, Architects' Jl, 1956-60; Editor, RIBA Jl, 1964-71; RIBA: Head of Information Services, 1960-66; Publishing Services, 1966-70; Dir, Public Affairs, 1971-72. Leverhulme Res. Fellow, 1972-73. Mem., Exmoor Nat. Park Cttee, 1973-. Broadcaster and writer on town planning and architectural subjects. Hon. Fellow, RIBA, 1974. *Publications:* Crisis in Architecture, 1974; (ed) Future Landscapes, 1976 *Recreations:* walking, riding. *Address:* Manor House, Wootton Courtenay, Somerset. *T:* Timberscombe 325.

McEWEN, Sir Robert (Lindley), 3rd Bt *cr* 1953; *b* 23 June 1926; 2nd *s* of Sir John McEwen, 1st Bt, of Marchmont and Bardrochat, and of Bridget Mary, *e d* of late Rt Hon. Sir Francis Lindley, GCMG, CB, CBE; *S* brother, 1971; *m* 1954, Brigid Cecilia, *o d* of late James Laver, CBE; two *s* four *d*. *Educ:* Eton (scholar); Trinity College, Cambridge (scholar). Starred 1st Cl. Law Trip. Part II, 1950 (Senior Scholar). Served Grenadier Guards, 1944-47 (Lieut). Barrister, Inner Temple, 1951. Sublector, Trinity College, Cambridge, 1953-55. Contested (C): East Edinburgh, 1964; Roxburgh, Selkirk and Peebles, 1965. Hon. Sheriff, Roxburgh, Berwick and Selkirk, 1971. Chm., Berwickshire Civic Soc., 1973-75. *Publications:* The Law of Monopolies, Restrictive Practices, and Resale Price Maintenance (with Lord Hailsham), 1956; Gatley on Libel and Slander, 7th edn 1973; contrib. to Halsbury's Laws of England; Listener, Spectator, etc.; illustrations in: Iris Origo, Giovanna and Jane; Gavin Maxwell, Ring of Bright Water, and Raven Seek Thy Brother. *Heir: s* James Francis Lindley McEwen, *b* 24 Aug. 1960. *Address:* Marchmont, Berwickshire. *T:* Duns 2321. *Clubs:* Brooks's, Beefsteak; Puffins (Edinburgh).

McEWIN, Hon. Sir (Alexander) Lyell, KBE 1954; President, Legislative Council, South Australia, 1967-75; *b* 29 May 1897; *s* of late A. L. McEwin; *m* 1921, Dora Winifred, *d* of late Mark Williams, Blyth; four *s* one *d*. *Educ:* State Sch.; Prince Alfred Coll., Adelaide. Engaged in farming at Hart, near Blyth, since 1912; Sec., Blyth Agric. Bureau, 1920-26, Pres., 1927-36; Life Mem. State Advisory Bd of Agric., 1930, Chm., 1935-37; Mem. Agric. Settlement Cttee, 1931; Mem. Debt Adjustment Cttee,

1933; Producers' representative for SA on Federal Advisory Cttee for Export Mutton and Beef, prior to appt of Australian Meat Bd, 1934. Entered Legislative Council of South Australian Parliament as Member for Northern District, 1934; Chief Secretary, Minister of Health, and Minister of Mines, 1939-65; Leader of Opposition in Legislative Council, 1965-67. Councillor, Hart Ward of Hutt and Hill Rivers' District Council, 1932-35; transferred to Blyth Dist Council, 1935-53; retired. Member South Australian Rifle Assoc., 1925 (Chairman, 1948-). Chief, Royal Caledonian Society (SA), 1959-68. *Recreation:* bowls. *Address:* 93 First Avenue, St Peters, SA 5069. *T:* 423698.

MACEY, John Percival, CBE 1969; FRICS, FIHM; Vice-President, Surrey and Sussex Rent Assessment Panel, since 1971; *b* 3 Dec. 1906; *s* of Edward Macey; *m* 1931, Jill, *d* of Joseph Gyngell; one *s* one *d*. *Educ:* Varndean Grammar Sch., Brighton. Entered LCC service, 1926; Principal Asst, Housing Dept, 1948-51; Dep. Housing Manager, City of Birmingham, 1951-54; Housing Manager, City of Birmingham, 1954-63; Director of Housing to LCC, later GLC, 1964-71. President: Inst. of Housing, 1957 and 1963; Inst. of Housing Managers, 1969. Served with Royal Engineers, 1939-45 (despatches); retired with rank of Major. *Publications:* Macey on the Housing Finance Act, 1972; The Housing Act, 1974; The Housing Rents and Subsidies Act, 1975; (joint author) Housing Management, 1965, 2nd edn 1973; papers to professional bodies on housing and allied subjects. *Recreations:* motoring, walking, gardening. *Address:* Beke Rew, Marringdean Road, Billingshurst, West Sussex. *T:* 2465.

McFADZEAN, family name of **Baron McFadzean.**

McFADZEAN, Baron, *cr* 1966 (Life Peer); **William Hunter McFadzean,** Kt 1976; Kt 1960; Director, Midland Bank, since 1959 (Deputy Chairman, 1968-77); Hon. President, BICC Ltd, 1973 (Managing Director, 1954-61; Chairman, 1954-73); *b* Stranraer, 17 Dec. 1903; *s* of late Henry and of Agnes McFadzean, Stranraer; *m* 1933, Eileen, *e d* of Arthur Gordon, Blundellsands, Lancs.; one *s* one *d,* one adopted *d. Educ:* Stranraer Academy and High Sch.; Glasgow Univ. Served articles with McLay, McAllister & McGibbon, Chartered Accountants, Glasgow, 1922-27; qualified as Chartered Accountant, 1927; with Chalmers Wade & Co., 1927-32; joined British Insulated Cables Ltd, as Accountant, 1932 (Financial Secretary, 1937; Exec. Manager, 1942); on amalgamation of British Insulated Cables Ltd and Callender's Cable & Construction Co. Ltd, in 1945, appointed to Board of British Insulated Callender's Cables Ltd as Exec. Director (Dep. Chairman, 1947; Chief Exec. Director, 1950), retd 1973; Chairman: Canada Life Unit Trust Managers Ltd, 1971-; Standard Broadcasting Corp. (UK) Ltd, 1972-; Home Oil (UK) Ltd, 1972-; Scurry-Rainbow (UK) Ltd, 1974; Deputy Chairman: RTZ/BICC Aluminium Holdings Ltd, 1967-73; Canada Life Assurance Co. of GB, 1971-; National Nuclear Corp., 1973-; Director: Anglesey Aluminium Ltd, 1968-73; Midland Bank Executor and Trustee Co., 1959-67; English Electric Co., 1966-68; Steel Co. of Wales Ltd, 1966-67; Canadian Imperial Bank of Commerce, 1967-74; Canada Life Assurance Co., 1969-; Home Oil Co. Ltd, 1972-77; Standard Broadcasting Corp. Ltd, 1976-. Pres. FBI, 1959-61. Chairman: Council of Industrial Fedns of EFTA, 1960-63; Export Council for Europe, 1960-64 (Hon. Pres. 1964-71); Commonwealth Export Council, 1964-66; British Nat. Export Council, 1964-66 (Pres. 1966-68); President: Brit. Electrical Power Convention, 1961-62; Brit. Nuclear Forum, 1964-66; Coal Trade Benevolent Assoc., 1967-68; Electrical and Electronics Industries Benevolent Assoc., 1968-69. Vice-President: Middle East Assoc., 1965; City of London Soc., 1965-72; British/Swedish Chamber of Commerce, 1963-74. Member: Inst. of Directors, 1954-76 (Council, 1954-74); Min. of Labour Adv. Bd on Resettlement of Ex-Regulars, 1957-60; Bd of Trade Adv. Council on ME Trade, 1958-60; MoT Shipping Adv. Panel, 1962-64; Ct of British Shippers' Council, 1964-74 (Pres., 1968-71); Council, Foreign Bondholders, 1968-74; Anglo-Danish Soc., 1965-75 (Chm., 1969-75; Hon. Pres., 1975); Adv. Cttee, Queen's Award for Industry, 1965-67 (Chm., Review Cttee, 1970). CompIEE 1956. JDipMA 1965. Commander Order of Dannebrog (Denmark), 1964, Grand Commander, 1974; Grande Oficial da Ordem do Infante Dom Henrique, Portugal, 1972. *Address:* 146 Whitehall Court, SW1A 2EL. *T:* 01-930 3160; Garthland, Woldingham, Surrey CR3 7DH. *T:* Woldingham 3222. *Clubs:* Carlton, MCC.

McFADZEAN, Sir Francis Scott, (Sir Frank), Kt 1975; Director: Shell Transport and Trading Co. Ltd, since 1964; Shell Petroleum Co. Ltd; Chairman, since 1976, and Chief Executive, since 1977, British Airways (Director since 1975); *b* 26 Nov. 1915; *m* 1938, Isabel McKenzie Beattie; one *d. Educ:* Glasgow

Univ.; London Sch. of Economics (Hon. Fellow, 1974). MA. BoT, 1938; Treasury, 1939; War Service, 1940-45; Malayan Govt, 1945; Colonial Develt Corp., 1949; Shell Petroleum Co. Ltd, 1952; Man. Dir, Royal Dutch/Shell Group of Companies, 1964-76; Man. Dir 1971, Chm., 1972-76, "Shell" Transport and Trading Co. Ltd; Chairman: Shell International Marine Ltd, 1966-76; Shell Canada Ltd, 1970-76; Shell Petroleum Co. Ltd, 1972-76; Director: Shell Oil Co., 1972-76; Beecham Group Ltd, 1974. Chairman: Trade Policy Research Centre, 1971; Steering Bd, Strathclyde Div., Scottish Business Sch., 1970-76; Vis. Prof. of Economics, Strathclyde Univ., 1967-76. Hon. LLD Strathclyde, 1970. Comdt, Order of Oranje Nassau. *Publications:* Galoraith and the Planners, 1968; Energy in the Seventies, 1971; The Operation of a Multi-National Enterprise, 1971; The Economics of John Kenneth Galbraith: a study in fantasy, 1977. *Address:* Speedbird House, Heathrow Airport, PO Box 10, Hounslow TW6 2JA.

McFALL, David (Bernard), RA 1963 (ARA 1955); Sculptor; Master of Sculpture, City and Guilds of London Art School, Lambeth, 1956-75; *b* 21 Dec. 1919; *s* of David McFall and Elizabeth McEvoy; *m* 1972, Alexandra Dane, actress; one *d*. *Educ:* Art Schools, Birmingham, Lambeth and Royal College of Art. Official Commissions: Unicorns (pair, 12 ft, gilt-bronze) mounted on roof of Bristol New Council House, known as The Bristol Unicorns, 1950; Finials (pair, carved, Portland stone, 10 ft), Zodiac Clock (8 ft, carved stone and cast aluminium), Bronze Portrait Bust (Alderman Frank Sheppard), 1955, same building; Festival of Britain, Boy and Foal (carved stone 5 ft), 1951, now at Missenden Abbey, Bucks. Pocahontas (bronze), 1956; Bust (bronze, Lord Methuen), 1956; Head of Ralph Vaughan Williams, OM (bronze) in Royal Festival Hall, 1957; 8 ft Statues of St Bride and St Paul in St Bride's Church, Fleet Street; Bronze Head of Sir Winston Churchill, in Grocers Hall, 1958; 8 ft 6 ins Bronze Figure of Sir Winston Churchill, 1959 (Woodford Green); Lord Balfour, House of Commons, 1962; Bust (bronze) Lord Brabazon of Tara (Royal Institution); Memorial to Sir Albert Richardson, PPRA, for Crypt of St Paul's Cathedral; Crucifixion (Portland stone), Church of Our Lady of Lourdes, Thames-Ditton; bust (bronze, Lord Ridley) for Univ., Newcastle upon Tyne; The Golden Gazelle, Abu Dhabi, Trucial States; bronze figure of Sir Winston Churchill, trophy for Dame Felicity Peake Essay Prize; The Black Horse for LTB Victoria Line, 1968; stone frieze on Wm Whitfield's extension to Inst. of Chartered Accountants, London, 1969; bust of Sir Thomas Holmes Sellors, Pres., RCS, 1971; Meml to Sir Gerald Kelly, St Paul's Cathedral Crypt, 1973; busts of: Sir George Godber, for RCP; Prof. George Grenfell Baines, for Building Design Partnership, Preston; late Hugh Stenhouse, Glasgow, 1973-74; Oedipus and Jocasta (stone group), W Norwood Library, 1974; posthumous bust of Josiah Wedgwood, Barlaston, Stoke-on-Trent, 1974-75; portrait head of HRH Prince Charles, Duke of Cornwall, 1974-75; Meml to Lord Fraser of Lonsdale, Westminster Abbey, 1976; Official purchase: The Bullcalf (Chantrey Bequest), 1943. Has exhibited at Royal Academy yearly since 1943. *Recreations:* swimming, cycling. *Address:* 10 Fulham Park Gardens, SW6 4JX. *T:* 01-736 6532; Natura, Fairlight Cove, Sussex TN35 4DJ.

McFALL, Richard Graham; Vice-Chairman, Gill & Duffus Group Ltd, since 1976 (Chairman, 1970-76); *b* 31 Jan. 1920; 3rd *s* of Henry Joseph Marshall and Sarah Gertrude McFall; *m* 1945, Clara Louise Debonnaire Mitford; one *s* one *d*. *Educ:* Holmwood Prep. Sch., Lancs; Clifton Coll., Bristol. Joined Pacol Ltd, 1938; Mil. Service, HAC, 1939-40; Colonial Office, 1941-45 (Asst Sec., then Sec., W African Produce Control Bd); Motor & Air Products Ltd, 1946-48; re-joined Pacol Ltd, 1949, Dir 1951; Chm., London Cocoa Terminal Market Assoc., 1954-55; Chm., Cocoa Assoc. of London, 1958-59; Dir 1962, Man. Dir 1965-74, Gill & Duffus Group Ltd. *Recreations:* golf, travel. *Address:* Beconridge, Beech Avenue, Effingham, Surrey. *T:* Bookham 52772. *Club:* Effingham Golf.

McFARLAND, Sir Basil (Alexander Talbot), 2nd Bt, *cr* 1914; CBE 1954; ERD 1954; HM Lieutenant for the City of Londonderry, 1939-75; *b* 18 Feb. 1898; *o c* of Sir John McFarland, 1st Bt, and Annie, 2nd *d* of late John Talbot, Terryglass, County Tipperary; *S* father, 1926; *m* 1st, 1924, Annie Kathleen (*d* 1952), 2nd *d* of late Andrew Henderson, JP, of Parkville, Whiteabbey, Belfast; one *s* (one *d* decd); 2nd, 1955, Mary Eleanor (*d* 1973), 2nd *d* of late William Dougan, Londonderry. *Educ:* Neuwied-on-Rhine, Germany; Brussels; Bedford Sch. High Sheriff, Londonderry, 1930, 1931, 1932, 1933, 1934, 1935, 1936, 1937, 1938 and 1952; Mayor of Londonderry, 1939, 1945, 1946, 1947, 1948, 1949, 1950. Formerly ADC (Additional) to The Queen. Member: Northern Ireland Air Advisory Council, 1946-65; Londonderry Port & Harbour Commissioners (Chairman, 1952-67); London Midland

Area Board, British Transport Commission, 1955-61; Director: Belfast Banking Co. Ltd, 1930-70; Belfast Bank Executors Trustee Co.; Donegal Railways Co.; Local Dir Commercial Union Assurance Co.; Londonderry Gaslight Co.; Chairman: Sir Alfred McAlpine & Son (Northern Ireland) Ltd; Londonderry & Lough Swilly Railway Co.; Lanes (Derry), Ltd; J. W. Corbett & Sons; A. Thompson & Co. Ltd; Lanes (Fuel Oils) Ltd; Lanes (Business Equipment) Ltd; Lanes (Patent Fuels) Ltd; J. & R. Waterson Ltd; R. C. Malseed & Co. Ltd; Holmes Coal Ltd; Trustee of Magee University College, 1962-65; Comr of Irish Lights. Original Member, NI Unemployment Assistance Board, to 1939. Served War of 1914-18, Artists Rifles, 1918; War of 1939-45, Overseas with 9th Londonderry HAA Regt (despatches); Chm., T&AFA (Co. Londonderry), 1947-62; Hon. Col, 9th Londonderry HAA Regt RA (TA); Pres., NI TA&VR Assoc., 1968-71. Irish Rugby International, 1920-22. Hon. Freeman of City of Londonderry since 1944. CStJ. *Heir: s* John Talbot McFarland [*b* 3 Oct. 1927; *m* 1957, Mary Scott, *er d* of late Dr W. Scott Watson, Londonderry; two *s* two *d*]. *Address:* Aberfoyle, Londonderry. *T:* 62881. *Clubs:* Bath; Ulster (Belfast), Kildare Street (Dublin), Northern Counties (Londonderry).

MacFARLANE, Prof. Alistair George James; Professor of Engineering, University of Cambridge, and Fellow of Selwyn College, Cambridge, since 1974; *b* 9 May 1931; *s* of George R. MacFarlane; *m* 1954, Nora Williams; one *s*. *Educ:* Hamilton Academy; Univ. of Glasgow. BSc 1953, DSc 1969, Glasgow; PhD London 1964; MSc Manchester 1973; MA Cambridge 1974. Metropolitan-Vickers, Manchester, 1953-58; Lectr, Queen Mary Coll., Univ. of London, 1959-65, Reader 1965-66; Reader in Control Engrg, Univ. of Manchester Inst. of Sci. and Technology, 1966-69, Prof. 1969-74. *Publications:* Engineering Systems Analysis, 1964; Dynamical System Models, 1970. *Recreations:* hill walking, photography. *Address:* 9 Dane Drive, Newnham, Cambridge CB3 9LP.

MACFARLANE, (David) Neil; MP (C) Sutton and Cheam, since Feb. 1974; company director; *b* 7 May 1936; *yr s* of Robert and Dulcie Macfarlane; *m* 1961, June Osmond King, Somerset; two *s* one *d*. *Educ:* St Aubyn's Prep. Sch.; Bancroft's, Woodford Green. Short Service Commission, Essex Regt, 1955-58; served TA, 265 LAA, RA, 1961-66. Joined Shell Mex and BP, 1959; contested (C): East Ham (North), 1970; Sutton and Cheam, by-election, 1972. Mem., All Party Select Cttee on Science and Technology; Secretary: Cons. Greater London Mems; Cons. Sports Cttee; Cons. Energy Cttee. Mem., National Trust. *Recreations:* golf, swimming, cricket, cricket-watching. *Address:* Woodford, Lees Gardens, Maidenhead, Berks SL6 4NT. *T:* Maidenhead 26945; 84B Worcester Road, Sutton, Surrey. *Clubs:* Caledonian, MCC; Surrey County Cricket; Huntercombe Golf.

MacFARLANE, Donald, CBE 1963; HM Diplomatic Service, retired; *b* 26 Oct. 1910; *s* of late Donald MacFarlane, CIE; *m* 1933, Jean Carmen, *d* of late Charles Young, Pitt Manor, Winchester; one *s* decd. *Educ:* Stowe; Queens' Coll., Cambridge. Lamson Paragon Supply Co. Ltd, 1932-39. Served in RA and Intelligence Corps, 1939-46 (despatches); North Africa, Sicily, Italy and France; Colonel, head of Anglo-Greek Information Services, Athens, 1945-46. First Secretary, Foreign Service, 1946; British Embassy, China, 1946-49; Foreign Office, 1949-52; British Embassy: Rio de Janeiro, 1952-55; Counsellor (Commercial), Washington, 1955-58; Lisbon, 1958-60; HM Consul-General, Frankfurt-am-Main, 1960-64; Naples, 1964-67; Head of Nationality and Treaty Dept, FCO, 1967-70. *Recreations:* fishing, ski-ing. *Address:* 27 Lennox Gardens, SW1. *Club:* Flyfishers'.

MACFARLANE, Sir George (Gray), Kt 1971; CB 1965; BSc; Dr Ing (Dresden); *b* 8 Jan. 1916; *s* of late John Macfarlane, Airdrie, Lanarks; *m* 1941, Barbara Grant, *d* of Thomas Thomson, Airdrie, Lanarks; one *s* one *d*. *Educ:* Airdrie Academy; Glasgow Univ.; Technische Hochschule, Dresden, Germany. On scientific staff, Air Ministry Research Establishment, Dundee and Swanage, 1939-41; Telecommunications Research Establishment (TRE), Malvern, 1941-60; Deputy Chief Scientific Officer (Individual Merit Post), 1954-60; Deputy Director, National Physical Laboratory, 1960-62; Director, Royal Radar Establishment, 1962-67; Controller (Research), Min. of Technology and Min. of Aviation Supply, 1967-71; Controller, Research and Develt Establishments and Research, MoD, 1971-75. Mem., PO Review Cttee, 1976-77. Deputy-Pres., IEE, 1976- (Vice-Pres., 1972-74); Hunter Meml Lecturer, IEE, 1966. Hon. LLD Glasgow. *Publications:* papers in IEE, Proc. Phys. Society, Phys. Review. *Recreations:* walking, gardening. *Address:* Red Tiles, Orchard Way, Esher, Surrey. *T:* Esher 63778. *Club:* Athenæum.

McFARLANE, Prof. Ian Dalrymple, MBE 1946; Professor of French Literature, Oxford, since 1971; *b* 7 Nov. 1915; *s* of James Blair McFarlane and Valérie Edith Liston Dalrymple; *m* 1939, Marjory Nan Hamilton; one *s* one *d*. *Educ:* Lycée St-Charles, Marseilles; Tormore Sch., Upper Deal, Kent; Westminster Sch.; St Andrews Univ. MA 1st class Hons, 1938; Carnegie Research Scholar, 1938-39. Served 1st Bn Black Watch, RHR, 1940-45. Apptd Lectr in French, Cambridge Univ., 1945; Gonville and Caius Coll.: elected Fellow, 1947; appointed Senior Tutor, 1956; Prof. of French Language and Literature, St Andrews, 1961-70. Member, Scottish Cert. of Educn Examination Board, 1964; Member Academic Planning Board, University of Stirling, 1964-67; Mem. Cttee on Research and Develt in Modern Languages, 1966. Doctor of Univ. of Paris, 1950. *Publications:* Critical edn of M Scève's Délie, 1966; Renaissance France 1470-1589, 1974; various, in learned periodicals. *Recreations:* cricket, music. *Address:* Wadham College, Oxford.

McFARLANE, Prof. James Walter; Professor of European Literature, University of East Anglia, since 1964; *b* 12 Dec. 1920; *s* of James and Florence McFarlane; *m* 1944, Lillie Kathleen Crouch; two *s* one *d*. *Educ:* Bede Grammar Sch., Sunderland; St Catherine's Society, Univ. of Oxford. MA, BLitt 1948. War service, Intell. Corps, 1941-46 (Major); Oxford Soccer blue, 1947; Lectr and Sen. Lectr, Dept of German and Scandinavian Studies, King's Coll., Univ. of Durham, later Univ. of Newcastle upon Tyne, 1947-63; Dean of European Studies, Univ. of East Anglia, 1964-68; Public Orator, 1964-68 and 1974-75; Pro-Vice-Chancellor, 1968-71. Vis. Prof., Univ. of Auckland, NZ, 1967. Mem., BBC Gen. Adv. Council, 1970-75; Chm., East Anglia Regional Adv. Council, 1970-75; Chm., Hunworth Crafts Trust, 1973-; Mem. Exec., Eastern Arts Assoc., 1977-; Editor, Scandinavica: an International Journal of Scandinavian Studies, 1975-. Leverhulme Faculty Fellow in European Studies, 1971-72; Brit. Acad. Wolfson Fellow. Fellow, Det Norske Videnskaps-Akademie, Oslo, 1977; Corresp. Mem., Svenska Litteratursällskapet i Finland, Helsinki, 1977. Commander's Cross, Royal Norwegian Order of St Olav, 1975. *Publications:* (editor and translator) The Oxford Ibsen, 1960-77; vol. 1, Early Plays, 1970; vol. 2, The Vikings at Helgeland, Love's Comedy, The Pretenders, 1962; vol. 3, Brand, Peer Gynt, 1972; vol. 4, The League of Youth, Emperor and Galilean, 1963; vol. 5, Pillars of Society, A Doll's House, Ghosts, 1961; vol. 6, An Enemy of the People, The Wild Duck, Rosmersholm, 1960; vol. 7, The Lady from the Sea, Hedda Gabler, The Master Builder, 1966; vol. 8, Little Eyolf, John Gabriel Borkman, When We Dead Awaken, 1977; Ibsen and the Temper of Norwegian Literature, 1960; Discussions of Ibsen, 1962; Henrik Ibsen, 1970; Modernism: European Literature 1890-1930, 1976. *Recreation:* domestic odd-jobbery. *Address:* The Croft, Stody, Melton Constable, Norfolk. *T:* Melton Constable 505. *Club:* Athenæum.

MACFARLANE, Sir James (Wright), Kt 1973; PhD; FRSE; CEng, FIEE, FIMechE; JP; DL; Managing Director, Cathcart Investment Co. Ltd, since 1964; *b* 2 Oct. 1908; *s* of late James C. Macfarlane, OBE, MIEE, WhSch; *m* 1937, Claire Ross. *Educ:* Allan Glen's Sch.; Royal Technical Coll. (DRTC); Glasgow Univ. (PhD); London Univ. WhSch and WhSen.Sch. FIFire E. War of 1939-45: Home Guard (Major); Intell.; Lt-Col (TA) Comdg Renfrewshire Bn, Army Cadet Force. Apprentice, Engineer and Director, Macfarlane Engrg Co Ltd, 1926-; Chm., Macfarlane Engrg Co Ltd, Cathcart, 1967-69. Dir, National Building Agency, etc. Past Pres., Assoc. of County Councils in Scotland; Past Mem. various instns; Member: Royal Commn on the Police, 1960-62; Departmental Cttee on the Fire Service, 1968-70. JP 1940; entered local govt, 1944; DL 1962, Renfrewshire; Convener, County of Renfrew, 1967-73. Chm. of Governors, Paisley Coll. of Technology. *Publications:* numerous papers in IEE and IMechE Jls. *Recreations:* motor cycles and cars (vintage), sailing. *Address:* Cartbank, 45 Netherlee Road, Glasgow G44 3YU. *T:* 041-637 6135. *Clubs:* RNVR (Scotland); Conservative (Glasgow); Royal Gourock Yacht (Gourock).

MACFARLANE, Janet Alston, MA, LLD (St Andrews); Headmistress of St Leonards and St Katharines Schools, St Andrews, Fife, 1938-55; *e c* of late Charles Macfarlane, JP, Hutton Avenue, West Hartlepool, Co. Durham. *Educ:* Dundee High Sch.; St Andrews Univ. Senior French Mistress, Cheltenham Ladies' Coll., 1927; Vice-Principal, 1931-38; Acting Principal, May-Dec. 1936. *Address:* 33 Town Wall, Hartlepool, Cleveland. *T:* Hartlepool 4304.

McFARLANE, Prof. Jean Kennedy; Professor and Head of Department of Nursing, University of Manchester, since 1974; *b* 1 April 1926; *d* of James and Elvina Alice McFarlane. *Educ:* Howell's Sch., Llandaff; Bedford and Birkbeck Colls, Univ. of London. MA, BSc(Soc), SRN, SCM, HV Tutor's Cert. FRCN

1976. Staff Nurse, St Bartholomew's Hosp., 1950-51; Health Visitor, Cardiff CC, 1953-59; Royal Coll. of Nursing: Organising Tutor, Integrated Cse, Educn Div., London, 1960-62; Educn Officer, Birmingham, 1962-66; Res. Project Ldr (DHSS sponsored), London, 1967-69; Dir of Educn, Inst. of Advanced Nursing Educn, London, 1969-71; Univ. of Manchester: Sen. Lectr in Nursing, Dept of Social and Preventive Medicine, 1971-73; Sen. Lectr and Head of Dept of Nursing, 1973-74. Mem., Royal Commn on NHS, 1976-. *Publications:* The Problems of Developing Criteria of Quality for Nursing Care (thesis), 1969; The Proper Study of the Nurse, 1970. *Recreations:* music, walking, travelling, photography. *Address:* Department of Nursing, University of Manchester, Stopford Building, Oxford Road, Manchester M13 9PT. *T:* 061-273 8241, ext. 182.

MACFARLANE, Neil; *see* Macfarlane, D. N.

MacFARLANE, Maj.-Gen. Robert Goudie, MBE 1952; FRCPE; Deputy Secretary, Scottish Council for Postgraduate Medical Education, since 1975; *b* 1 March 1917; *s* of late Archibald Forsyth MacFarlane and Jessie Robertson Goudie; *m* 1945, Mary Campbell Martin; three *s*. *Educ:* Hillhead High Sch., Glasgow; Glasgow Univ. MB, ChB, 1940; MD 1955; FRCPE 1964; MRCP 1970. Served War: commissioned RAMC, 1941; in Madagascar, India, Burma, 1941-45. Specialist in Medicine and Consultant Physician, 1948-; CO, British Mil. Hosp., Iserlohn, 1968-70; Prof. of Mil. Med., Royal Army Medical Coll., 1970-71; Consulting Physician, BAOR, 1971-73. Dir. of Army Medicine and Consulting Physician to the Army, 1973-74. QHP 1973. *Recreation:* sailing. *Address:* 6 Redholm, Greenheads Road, North Berwick, East Lothian.

MACFARLANE, Robert Gwyn, CBE 1964; FRS 1956; MD; FRCP; retired; *b* 26 June 1907; *o c* of Robert Gray and Eileen Macfarlane; *m* 1936, Hilary, *o c* of H. A. H. and Maude Carson; four *s* one *d*. *Educ:* Highfield Sch., Liphook, Hants; Cheltenham Coll.; St Bartholomew's Hospital, London. MRCS, LRCP, 1933; MB, BS (London), 1933; MD (London), Gold Medal, 1938; MA (Oxford), 1948; FRCP 1960. Sir Halley Stewart Research Fellow, 1935; Asst Clinical Pathologist, Postgrad. Medical School, London, 1936; Asst Bacteriologist, Wellcome Physiological Research Lab., 1939. Major, RAMC, 1944, attached Mobile Bacteriological Research Unit, Normandy and NW Europe. Director, Medical Research Council Blood Coagulation Research Unit, Churchill Hospital, Oxford, 1959-67; Professor of Clinical Pathology, Oxford Univ., 1964-67, now Emeritus (Reader in Haematology, 1957-64); Fellow, All Souls Coll., Oxford, 1963-70, now Quondam Fellow; Clinical Pathologist, Radcliffe Infirmary, Oxford, 1941-67. Vice-President, Haemophilia Society, 1955. *Publications:* (with R. Biggs) Human Blood Coagulation and its Disorders (3rd edn, 1962); papers, chapters in books and encyclopædias on haematological and pathological subjects. *Address:* Mallie's Cottage, Opinan, Laide, Ross-shire.

MACFARLANE, Hon. Sir Robert Mafeking, KCMG 1974 (CMG 1954); Speaker, New Zealand Parliament, 1957-60; *b* Christchurch, NZ, 17 May 1901; *m* 1932, Louisa E., *d* of T. F. Jacobs, Woolston. *Educ:* Christchurch, NZ. Secretary, Christchurch Labour Representation Cttee, 1929; MP (L) (NZ) for Christchurch S, 1936-46, for Christchurch Central, 1946-69; formerly Sen. Opposition Whip. Member Christchurch City Council for many years (Mayor, 1938-41). Chairman Metropolitan Transport Licensing Authority. Served War of 1939-45 with Second New Zealand Expeditionary Force. *Address:* 71 Greenpark Street, Christchurch 2, New Zealand.

MACFARLANE, Maj.-Gen. William Thomson; Chief of Staff, United Kingdom Land Forces, 1976-78; *b* Bath, 2 Dec. 1925; *s* of late James and Agnes Macfarlane; *m* 1955, Dr Helen D. Meredith; one *d*. Commissioned Royal Signals, 1947. Served Egypt, Germany, Singapore. Commanded 16th Parachute Bde Signal Squadron, 1961-63; jssc; Military Asst, Commander FARELF, 1964-66; Comd 1st Div. HQ and Signal Regt, BAOR, 1967-70; Services Mem., Cabinet Office Secretariat, 1970-72; Comd, Corps of Royal Signals, 1972-73; Dir of Public Relations (Army), MoD, 1973-75. *Recreations:* golf, private flying. *Address:* Aveley Lane, Farnham, Surrey. *Club:* Naval and Military.

MacFARQUHAR, Sir Alexander, KBE 1952; CIE 1945; Director of Personnel, United Nations, 1962-67; *b* 6 Nov. 1903; *s* of Roderick MacFarquhar; *m* 1929, Berenice Whitburn; one *s*. *Educ:* Aberdeen Univ. (MA 1st class Hons Classics); Emmanuel Coll., Cambridge. Entered ICS 1926; Deputy Commissioner, Ferozepore, 1930; Deputy Commissioner, Amritsar, 1933; Settlement Officer, Amritsar, 1936; Deputy Secretary, Government of India, 1941; Deputy Director-General,

Directorate-General of Supply, Government of India, 1943; Dir-Gen. Disposals, India, 1946; Commerce and Education Sec. Govt of Pakistan, 1947-51. Resident Rep. to Pakistan of UN Technical Assistance Board, 1952; Regional Rep. to Far East, of UN Technical Assistance Board, Bangkok, 1955; UN Secretary General's Special Adviser for Civilian Affairs in the Congo, 1960. Chm., Pakistan Soc., 1970-. *Address:* Ottershaw, Beverley Lane, Coombe Hill, Kingston-upon-Thames, Surrey.
See also R. L. MacFarquhar.

MacFARQUHAR, Roderick Lemonde; MP (Lab) Belper, since Feb. 1974; *b* 2 Dec. 1930; *s* of Sir Alexander MacFarquhar, *qv*; *m* 1964, Emily Jane Cohen; one *s* one *d*. *Educ:* Fettes Coll.; Oxford Univ. (BA); Harvard Univ. (AM). Specialist on China, Daily Telegraph (and later Sunday Telegraph), 1955-61; Founding Editor, China Quarterly, 1959-68; Rockefeller Grantee, 1962; Reporter, BBC TV programme Panorama, 1963-64; Co-presenter, BBC General Overseas Services '24 Hours' programme, 1972-74. Associate Fellow, St Antony's Coll., Oxford, 1965-68. Mem., Editorial Bd, New Statesman, 1965-69; Ford Foundation Grant, 1968; Senior Research Fellow, Columbia Univ., 1969; Senior Research Fellow, RIIA, 1971-74. Contested (Lab): Ealing South, 1966; Meriden, March 1968. PPS to Minister of State, FCO, March 1974; resignation accepted, April 1975; reappointed June 1975; PPS to Sec. of State, DHSS, 1976-. Member: N Atlantic Assembly, 1974-; Select Cttee for Sci. and Technology, 1976-; Exec. Cttee, Trilateral Commn, 1976-. *Publications:* The Hundred Flowers, 1960; The Sino-Soviet Dispute, 1961; Chinese Ambitions and British Policy (Fabian Pamphlet), 1966; Sino-American Relations, 1949-71, 1972; The Forbidden City, 1972; The Origins of the Cultural Revolution: Vol. 1, Contradictions among the People 1956-1957, 1974; (ed) China under Mao, 1966; articles in Foreign Affairs, The World Today, Atlantic Monthly, Pacific Affairs, Commentary, etc. *Recreations:* reading, listening to music, travel. *Address:* House of Commons, SW1A 0AA. *Clubs:* Newhall and Belper Labour; Kilburn Miners' Welfare.

MacFEELY, Most Rev. Anthony; *see* Raphoe, Bishop of, (RC).

McFETRICH, Cecil, OBE 1949; Director, Ward & Davidson Ltd; Chairman, Sunderland Structural Steel Ltd; Director, Sunderland and Shields Building Soc., etc; *b* 17 Jan. 1911; *y s* of Archibald B. and Hannah B. McFetrich; *m* 1937, Kathleen M. Proom; four *s*. *Educ:* Cowan Terrace Sch., Sunderland; Skerry's Coll., Newcastle upon Tyne. Qual. Chartered Accountant, 1933. After varied industrial and professional experience, joined Bartram & Sons Ltd, South Dock, Sunderland, as Sec., 1936; apptd a Dir, 1939; responsible for sales and marketing, 1945, Man. Dir, 1964-72; Jt Man. Dir, Austin & Pickersgill Ltd, 1968-69, Man. Dir 1969-72, Dep. Chm. and Chm., 1972-75. Mem., Sunderland Town Council, 1942-51 (Chm. Finance Cttee, 1943-44); served on various Nat. Savings Cttees, 1940-63; Chairman: Sunderland Savings Cttee, 1947-63; N Regional Industrial Savings Cttee, 1956-62. Life Governor, Nat. Children's Homes. Liveryman, Worshipful Co. of Shipwrights. Freeman by redemption, City of London. Lord Mayor of London's Gold Medal for Export Achievement, 1963. *Recreations:* snooker, champagne. *Address:* 8 Belle Vue Drive, Sunderland, Tyne and Wear. *T:* Sunderland 226449. *Clubs:* MCC; Sunderland (Sunderland).

MACFIE, Prof. Alec Lawrence, MA, LLB, DLitt (Glasgow); Hon. LLD (Glasgow); Professor of Political Economy, University of Glasgow, 1946-58, retired; *b* 29 May 1898; *s* of Rev. W. G. Macfie, Mowbray, Cape Town; unmarried. *Educ:* High School of Glasgow; University of Glasgow. Served European War, 1917-18, The 2nd Bn The Gordon Highlanders. Lecturer in Political Economy, Glasgow Univ., 1930-45. *Publications:* Theories of the Trade Cycle, 1934; An Essay on Economy and Value, 1936; Economic Efficiency and Social Welfare, 1943; The Individual in Society: Papers on Adam Smith, 1967. *Address:* 21 Tannoch Drive, Milngavie, Glasgow. *Club:* Art (Glasgow).

MACFIE, Maj.-Gen. John Mandeville, CB 1951; CBE 1946; MC 1917; OStJ 1945; *b* 13 Dec. 1891; *s* of Rev. W. G. Macfie, Mowbray, Cape Town; unmarried. *Educ:* S African College School; Glasgow High Sch.; Glasgow Univ. MB, ChB (with honours) Glasgow, 1915. FRCP Glasgow, 1964. Lieut, RAMC, 1915: Dep. Assistant Director of Pathology, India, 1926-29; Dep. Assistant Director-General of Army Medical Services, War Office, 1932-36; Dep. DGAMS War Office, 1943-46; DDMS, East Africa Command, 1946-48; DDMS, Scottish Command, 1949; Commandant RAM Coll., 1949-50; KHS 1950; Dep. Director of Medical Services, Western Command, UK, 1950-51; retired pay, Jan. 1952; Colonel Commandant

RAMC, 1951-56. Commander Order Leopold II of Belgium, 1949. *Recreations:* golf, fishing. *Address:* 21 Tannoch Drive, Milngavie, Glasgow. *Clubs:* Royal Scottish Automobile; Glasgow Art.

McGAHERN, John; author; *b* 12 Nov. 1934; *s* of Francis McGahern and Susan McManus; *m* 1973, Madeline Green. Research Fellow, Univ. of Reading, 1968-71; O'Connor Prof., Colgate Univ., 1969, 1972 and 1977; British Northern Arts Fellow, 1974-76. AE Meml Award, 1962; McCauley Fellowship, 1964; British Arts Council Award, 1967; Soc. of Authors Award, 1975. *Publications:* The Barracks, 1963; The Dark, 1965; Nightlines, 1970; The Leavetaking, 1975; Getting Through, 1978. *Address:* c/o Faber & Faber, 3 Queen Square, WC1N 3AU.

McGARRITY, J(ames) Forsyth, MA, MEd, BSc; HM Senior Chief Inspector of Schools (Scotland), since 1973; *b* 16 April 1921; *s* of late James McGarrity and Margaret Davidson; *m* 1951, Violet S. G. Philp; one *s* one *d*. *Educ:* Bathgate Academy; Glasgow Univ. Schoolmaster, 1949-57; HM Inspector of Schools, 1957-68; HM Chief Inspector of Schools, 1968-73. *Recreations:* golf, gardening. *Address:* 30 Oatlands Park, Linlithgow, Scotland EH49 6AS. *T:* Linlithgow 3258.

McGEE, Prof. James Dwyer, OBE 1952; FRS 1966; MSc Sydney; PhD, ScD, Cantab; CEng; FIEE; FInstP; FRAS; Hon. ARCS; Professor of Applied Physics, 1954-71, now Emeritus, and Senior Research Fellow, since 1971, Fellow, 1977, Imperial College of Science and Technology, University of London; *b* Canberra, ACT, 17 Dec. 1903; *s* of Francis and Mary McGee; *m* 1944, Hilda Mary, *d* of George Winstone, Takapuna, Auckland, NZ; no *c*. *Educ:* St Patrick's Coll., Goulburn, NSW; St John's Coll., Sydney Univ. (MSc); Clare Coll., Cambridge (PhD). 1851 Exhibition Scholar from Sydney Univ. to Cambridge. Nuclear physics research, Cavendish Laboratory, Cambridge, 1928-31; Research physicist, Electric and Musical Industries Research Laboratories, Hayes, Middx. Engaged on research on photo-electricity and electronic problems of Television, 1932-39; research on electronic problems in connection with military operations, in particular the use of infra-red light, 1939-45; returned to work on photo-electronic devices for television and other scientific purposes, 1945-54. Awarded Research Fellowship, Carnegie Inst., Washington, 1960; Hon. Research Associate, Carnegie Inst., 1960, 1962, 1966. Hon. Life Mem. IREE(Aust.), 1939. Hon. DSc Salford, 1972. Awarded prize of Worshipful Company of Instrument Makers, 1968; Callendar Medal, Inst. of Measurement and Control, for contribs to opto-electronics, 1975. *Publications:* chap. on Electronic Generation of Television Signals in Electronics (ed B. Lovell), 1947; ed Vols XII, XVI, XXII, XXVIII, XXXIII, Advances in Electronics: Symposia on Photoelectronic Devices, 1960, 1962, 1966, 1969, 1972; technical papers in Engineering, Physical and Technical Jls. *Recreations:* gardening, music. *Address:* 56 Corringway, W5. *T:* 01-997 7160. *Club:* Athenæum.

McGEE, Prof. James O'Donnell; Professor of Morbid Anatomy, University of Oxford, Fellow of Linacre College, Oxford, since Oct. 1975; *b* 27 July 1939; *s* of Michael and Bridget McGee; *m* 1961, Anne Lee; one *s* two *d*. *Educ:* Univ. of Glasgow. MB, ChB, PhD, MD, MRCPath; MA (Oxon). Various appts in Univ. Dept of Pathology, Royal Infirmary, Glasgow, 1962-69; Roche Inst. of Molecular Biology, Nutley, NJ: MRC Fellow 1969-70; Vis. Scientist 1970-71; Dept of Pathology, Royal Infirmary, Glasgow: Lectr 1971-74; Sen. Lectr, 1974-75. *Publications:* Liver Biopsy Review, 1977; papers on collagen metabolism and liver disease in Proc. Nat. Acad. Sci., Gut, etc. *Recreations:* squash, swimming. *Address:* Linacre College, Oxford. *T:* Oxford 49891.

McGEE, Rt. Rev. Joseph; *see* Galloway, Bishop of, (RC).

McGEOCH, Vice-Adm. Sir Ian (Lachlan Mackay), KCB 1969 (CB 1966); DSO 1943; DSC 1943; *b* 26 March 1914; 3rd *s* of L. A. McGeoch of Dalmuir; *m* 1937, Eleanor Somers, *d* of Rev. Hugh Farrie; two *s* two *d*. *Educ:* The Nautical Coll., Pangbourne. Joined RN, 1932. Comd HM Submarine Splendid, 1942-43; Staff Officer (Ops) 4th Cruiser Sqdn, 1944-45; Comd: HMS Fernie, 1946-47; 4th Submarine Squadron, 1949-51; 3rd Submarine Squadron, 1956-57; Dir of Undersurface Warfare, Admiralty, 1959; IDC 1961; Comd HMS Lion 1962-64; Admiral Pres., RNC, Greenwich, 1964-65; Flag Officer Submarines, 1966-67; Flag Officer, Scotland and Northern Ireland, 1968-70. Trustee, Imperial War Museum, 1977-. Mem., The Queen's Body Guard for Scotland, Royal Co. of Archers, 1969-. Editor, The Naval Review. MPhil Edinburgh, 1975. *Recreations:* sailing, music. *Address:* Southerns, Castle Hedingham, Essex. *Clubs:* Army and Navy; Royal Yacht

Squadron, Royal Naval Sailing Association, Royal Cruising, Royal Northern.

McGHEE, George Crews, Legion of Merit; businessman; former diplomat; Director: Mobil Oil Co., since 1969; Procter and Gamble Co., since 1969; American Security & Trust Co., since 1969; Trans World Airlines, since 1976; *b* Waco, Texas, 10 March 1912; *s* of George Summers McGhee and Magnolia (*née* Spruce); *m* 1938, Cecilia Jeanne DeGolyer; two *s* four *d. Educ:* Southern Methodist Univ., Dallas; Univ. of Oklahoma; Oxford Univ. (Rhodes Schol.); Univ. of London. BS (Oklahoma) 1933; DPhil (Oxon) 1937. Served with US Navy, 1943-45 (Asiatic ribbon with three battle stars). Geologist and geophysicist, 1930-40; Oil producer, sole owner, McGhee Production Co., 1940-. Special Asst to Under-Sec of State for Economic Affairs, 1946; Coordinator for Aid to Greece and Turkey, 1947; Asst Sec. of State for Near Eastern, South Asian and African Affairs, 1949; US Ambassador to Turkey, 1951; Consultant, Nat. Security Council, 1958; Mem. President's Cttee to Study Mil. Asst Program, 1958; Counselor of Dept of State and Chm. of State Dept Policy Planning Council, 1961; Under-Sec. of State for Political Affairs, 1961; US Ambassador to the Federal Republic of Germany, 1963-68; Ambassador-at-Large, 1968-69. Chairman: English Speaking Union of US, 1969-74; Business Council for Internat. Understanding, 1969-73; Trustee: Salzburg Seminar, 1969-; Nat. Civil Service League, 1969-; Population Crisis Cttee, 1969-; Population Crisis Foundn of Texas, 1969-. Trustee: Duke Univ.; Cttee for Economic Development, 1957-; Aspen Institute for Humanistic Studies, 1958-. Chm., Saturday Review World, 1974-77. Hon. Fellow, Queen's Coll., Oxford, 1969. Distinguished Service Citation, Univ. of Oklahoma, 1952; Hon. DCL, Southern Methodist Univ., 1953; Hon. LLD: Tulane Univ., 1957; Univ. of Maryland, 1965; Hon. DSc, Univ. of Tampa, 1969. Ouissam Alaouite Cherifian, Govt Morocco, 1950; Hon. Citizen, Ankara, Turkey, 1954. *Publications:* contribs to Foreign Affairs, Gewerkschaftliche Rundschau, Werk und Wir, Europa Archiv, Universitas, Ruperto-Carola Weltraumfahrt-Raketentechnik, Europa. *Recreations:* hunting, tennis, photography. *Address:* 2808 N Street, NW, Washington, DC 20007, USA; Farmers' Delight, Middleburg, Va, USA. *Clubs:* Metropolitan (Washington, DC); Brook, Century Association (New York); City Tavern Association (Georgetown, DC).

McGHIE, James Ironside, CMG 1973; Special Adviser on Japanese market to British Overseas Trade Board, since 1975; UK Co-Chairman, Japan Task Force, since 1977; *b* 12 Oct. 1915; *s* of William I. McGhie and Annie E. Ratcliffe; *m* 1946, Ellen-Johanne Gran; two *s* one *d. Educ:* King Henry VIII Sch., Coventry. Journalist, 1933-39. Army, 1940-46. Entered Foreign Service, 1946; Stockholm, 1946-49; Helsinki, 1949-52; Foreign Office, 1952-54; Tokyo, 1954-57; Singapore, 1957-58; First Sec., Saigon, 1958-60; Foreign Office, 1960-62; Bucharest, 1962-64 (acted Chargé d'affaires, 1962 and 1963); First Sec., DSAO, 1964-67; Consul-General, Seattle, 1967-70; Counsellor, Stockholm, 1970-72 (acting Chargé d'Affaires, 1971-72); Minister (Commercial and Econ.), Tokyo, 1973-75; retired from HM Diplomatic Service, 1975. Order of the Rising Sun (Japan) 3rd class, 1975. *Recreations:* walking, languages. *Address:* 10 Tylney Avenue, SE19 1LN. *Club:* Travellers'.

McGHIE, Maj.-Gen. (retd) John, CB 1976; MD; FRCPsych; DPM; consultant psychiatrist to GLC and ILEA; Director of Army Psychiatry and Consultant in Psychiatry to the Army, 1970-June 1976; *b* Larkhall, Scotland; *s* of Henry and Agnes McGhie; *m* 1940, Hilda Lilian Owen; two *s. Educ:* Hamilton Academy; Glasgow University. Medical Officer: Glasgow Western Infirmary, 1936-37; Bellshill Maternity Hosp., 1937; Captain, RAMC, 1938; MO, British Mil. Hosp. Rawalpindi, 1939; Major, 2nd in Comd Field Ambulance, 1939-43; Lt-Col, OC Field Amb., 1943-45; Comd Psychiatrist: Scottish Comd, 1948; Far East, 1949-52; OC, Royal Victoria Hosp., Netley, 1956-61; Dir of Army Psychiatry, 1961-67; DDMS, Malaya and Western Comd, 1967-70. *Recreations:* golf, motoring. *Address:* Mandavara, 9 Ross Road, South Norwood, SE25. *T:* 01-653 7488.

McGILL, Maj.-Gen. Allan, CB 1969; CBE 1964 (OBE 1945; MBE 1943); Director of Electrical and Mechanical Engineering (Army), 1966-69; *b* 1914; *s* of William McGill; *m* 1945, Kathleen German. *Educ:* George Heriot's, Edinburgh; Heriot-Watt Coll. (now Heriot-Watt Univ.). Served War of 1939-45 (despatches, 1943). Dir, Electrical and Mechanical Engineering, British Army of the Rhine, 1965-66. Brig., 1961; Maj.-Gen., 1966. Col Comdt, REME, 1969-74. CEng, MIMechE. *Recreations:* motor rallying, ski-ing. *Address:* Tudor House, Vicarage Gardens, Bray, Berks SL6 2AE. *Club:* Army and Navy.

McGILL, Air Vice-Marshal Frank Scholes, CB 1945; FCIS; RCAF, retired; *b* Montreal, 1894; *m* 1924, Margaret, *d* of Thomas Williamson, Montreal; one *s* two *d. Educ:* Montreal High Sch.; McGill Univ., Montreal. Entered service of Dominion Oilcloth and Linoleum Co., 1913; Advertising Manager to this firm, 1924; Dir and Sec., 1930-62, Vice-Pres. (Sales), 1954-62, retired 1962. Dir, Canadair Ltd, 1947-75. Hon. Pres., RCAF Benevolent Fund; Hon. Life Governor, formerly Pres., Montreal Gen. Hos. *Address:* 1700 McGregor Avenue, Montreal, Quebec H3H 1B4, Canada. *Clubs:* University, Montreal Racket, United Services (Hon. Pres.), Mount Bruno Country, St James's, Montreal AAA (Montreal).

MacGILL, George Roy Buchanan, CBE 1965; General Manager, Cumbernauld Development Corporation, 1956-70; Deputy Chairman, Scottish Special Housing Association, 1971-76; *b* 20 Dec. 1905; *s* of George Buchanan MacGill; *m* 1934, Jean Ferguson Anderson; two *d. Educ:* Glasgow High Sch. Chartered Accountant, 1928. FIMTA 1938. Town Chamberlain, Airdrie, 1932; Burgh Chamberlain, Dunfermline, 1947. *Recreations:* golf, music. *Address:* 6 Collylinn Road, Bearsden, Glasgow.

McGILL, Maj.-Gen. Nigel Harry Duncan, CB 1966; Chief of Staff to Commandant-General, Royal Marines, 1967-68, retired, 1968; *b* 15 Oct. 1916; *s* of Lt-Col H. R. McGill; *m* 1944, Margaret Constance Killen; two *s* one *d. Educ:* Victoria Coll., Jersey. Commissioned 2nd Lt RM 1934; Maj.-Gen. 1964; Comdr, Portsmouth Group, RM, 1964-67. Representative Col Comdt RM, 1977-78. *Recreations:* cricket, golf. *Address:* Bryn House, Atlow, Ashbourne, Derbyshire. *Club:* Army and Navy.

McGILL, Rt. Rev. Stephen; *see* Paisley, Bishop of, (RC).

McGILLIGAN, Denis Brian; Assistant Solicitor, Legal Division D, Ministry of Agriculture, Fisheries and Food, since 1973; *b* 26 June 1921; *s* of Michael McGilligan, SC, and Mary Georgina McGilligan (*née* Musgrave); *m* 1952, Hazel Patricia Pakenham Keady; one *s* two *d. Educ:* St Gerard's, Bray, Co. Wicklow; Trinity Coll., Dublin (BA). Practised at Irish Bar, 1945-52; Crown Counsel, Sarawak, and Dep. Legal Adviser, Brunei, 1952-58; Senior Magistrate, Sarawak, 1958-59; Acting Puisne Judge, Combined Judiciary, 1959-60; Senior Magistrate, Sarawak, 1960-63; Puisne Judge, Combined Judiciary of Sarawak, North Borneo and Brunei, March, 1963; Judge of the High Court in Borneo, Malaysia, 1963-66. Called to the Bar, Gray's Inn, 1966. *Recreations:* hockey, swimming, walking, reading. *Address:* Lulworth Cottage, Tubs Hill, Sevenoaks, Kent. *T:* Sevenoaks 53622.

MacGILLIVRAY, Barron Bruce, FRCP; Consultant in Clinical Neurophysiology and Neurology, since 1964, and Dean, School of Medicine, since 1975, Royal Free Hospital; Consultant in Clinical Neurophysiology, National Hospital for Nervous Diseases, since 1971; *b* 21 Aug. 1927; *s* of late John MacGillivray and of Doreene (*née* Eastwood), S Africa; *m* 1955, Ruth Valentine; two *s* one *d. Educ:* King Edward VII Sch., Johannesburg; Univ. of Witwatersrand (BSc Hons 1949); Univ. of Manchester; Univ. of London (MB, BS 1962). FRCP 1973. House Surg., House Phys., Manchester Royal Infirm., 1955-56; RMO, Stockport and Stepping Hill Hosp., 1957-59; Registrar, subseq. Sen. Registrar, Nat. Hosp. for Nervous Diseases, Queen Sq., London, 1959-64; Res. Fellow, UCLA, 1964-65; Cons., Clin. Neurophysiol., Nat. Hosp. for Nervous Diseases, 1971. Pres., Electrophys. Technicians Assoc., 1976. FRSocMed. *Publications:* papers in sci. jls on cerebral electrophysiol., epilepsy, computing and cerebral death. *Recreations:* photography, D-I-Y. *Address:* Rosslyn Tower, 18 St John's Avenue, Putney, SW15 2AA. *T:* 01-788 5213.

MacGILLIVRAY, Prof. Ian, MD, FRCP; FRCOG; Regius Professor of Obstetrics and Gynæcology, University of Aberdeen, since 1965; *b* 25 Oct. 1920; *yr s* of W. and A. MacGillivray; *m* 1950, Edith Mary Margaret Cook; one *s* twin *d. Educ:* Vale of Leven Academy, Alexandria; University of Glasgow. Gardiner Research Schol., 1949-51; Lecturer in Midwifery, 1951-53; University of Glasgow; Senior Lecturer: in Obstetrics and Gynæcology, Univ. of Bristol, 1953-55; in Midwifery and Gynæcology, Univ. of Aberdeen, 1955-61; Prof. of Obstetrics and Gynæcology, University of London, at St Mary's Hospital Medical Sch., 1961-65. MB, ChB 1944, FRCOG 1959 (MRCOG 1949), MD 1953, University of Glasgow; FRCPGlas 1973. *Publications:* Outline of Human Reproduction, 1963; Combined Textbook of Obstetrics and Gynaecology, 1976; Human Multile Reproduction, 1976; contrib. to: British Medical Journal, Lancet, Journal of Obstetrics and Gynæcology of the British Empire; Clinical Science. *Address:* 45 Woodburn Avenue, Aberdeen. *T:* Aberdeen 34681.

McGILLIVRAY, Hon. William Alexander; Chief Justice of Alberta, Canada, since Dec. 1974; *b* 14 Oct. 1918; *s* of Alexander A. and Margaret L. G. McGillivray; *m* 1950, Kathleen A. Bell; two *s* two *d*. *Educ:* Univ. of Alberta, Edmonton, Alta (BA,LLB). Graduated in Law, 1941; admitted to practice, 1942. Bencher, 1958-69, Pres., 1969-70, Law Society of Alberta. *Recreations:* shooting, fishing, golf, bridge. *Address:* The Court House, 611-4th Street, SW, Calgary, Alberta, T2P 1T5, Canada. *T:* 261-7434. *Clubs:* Ranchmen's, Calgary Golf and Country, Glencoe (Calgary).

MacGINNIS, Francis Robert; HM Diplomatic Service; Minister and Deputy Commandant, British Military Government, Berlin, since 1977; *b* 6 March 1924; *s* of late Dr Patrick MacGinnis, Murray House, Chesterfield; *m* 1955, Carolyn, *d* of late Col D. W. McEnery, USA; three *s* two *d*. *Educ:* Stonyhurst; Merton Coll., Oxford (MA). Served with Rifle Bde, 1942-47 (Temp. Captain). Joined HM Foreign (subseq. Diplomatic) Service, 1949; served in London, Washington, Paris and Warsaw; Dir-Gen., British Information Services, New York, 1968-72; Counsellor, Bonn, 1972-76; RCDS, 1976. *Address:* c/o Foreign and Commonwealth Office, SW1. *Club:* Travellers'.

McGIRR, Prof. Edward McCombie, BSc, MD Glasgow; FRCP, FRCPE, FRCPGlas; FACP (Hon.); FFCM; FRSE; Muirhead Professor of Medicine, since Oct. 1961 and Dean of Faculty of Medicine, since 1974, University of Glasgow; Physician, Glasgow Royal Infirmary; Honorary Consultant Physician to the Army in Scotland, since 1975; *b* 15 June 1916; *yr s* of William and Ann McGirr, Hamilton, Lanarkshire; *m* 1949, Diane Curzon, *y c* of Alexander Woods, MBE, TD, DL, and Edith E. C. Woods, Birmingham and London; one *s* three *d*. *Educ:* Hamilton Academy; Glasgow Univ. BSc 1937; MB, ChB (Hons) Glasgow, 1940; MD (Hons) and Bellahouston Medal, 1960. Served RAMC, 1941-46, in UK, India, Burma, Siam, Indo-China; Medical Specialist; demobilized with hon. rank of Major. External Examiner in Medicine for BDS Edinburgh Univ., 1957-60, MB ChB, Edinburgh Univ. 1962-65, Birmingham Univ., 1966-69, Aberdeen Univ., 1967-69, Hong Kong Univ., 1968, Univ. of W Indies, 1972; Examiner for MRCP Edinburgh, Glasgow and London. Visitor, Royal Coll. of Physicians and Surgeons of Glasgow, 1968-70, President 1970-72. Member: Medical Appeals Tribunals, 1961-; Medical Adv. Cttee, Greater Glasgow Health Bd, 1974-; West of Scotland Cttee for Postgrad. Med. Educn; Scottish Cttee for Hosp. Med. Services; West of Scotland Cttee for Hosp. Med. Services; Specialty sub-cttee for medicine, Nat. Medical Consultative Cttee, 1975-. Member: Assoc. of Physicians of Gt Britain and Ireland (mem. of editorial panel, quarterly journal of Medicine, 1968-76; Mem. Council, 1972-76); Scottish Soc. of Physicians; Scottish Soc. for Experimental Med. (Treas., 1960-66); European Thyroid Assoc.; Corresp. Member: Amer. Thyroid Assoc.; Medical Research Soc. (mem. of council, 1967-69); Royal Medico-Chirurgical Soc. of Glasgow (Pres., 1965-66); Internat. Soc. for Internal Medicine; European Assoc. for Internal Medicine. *Publications:* chiefly in relation to thyroid gland dysfunction. *Recreations:* family life, medical work, detective fiction, curling. *Address:* Anchorage House, Bothwell, by Glasgow G71 8NF. *T:* Bothwell 852194; University Department of Medicine, Royal Infirmary, 86 Castle Street, Glasgow G4 0SF. *T:* 041-552 3535, extension 370. *Clubs:* Royal Scottish Automobile, Western (Glasgow).

McGLASHAN, Archibald A., RSA 1939 (ARSA 1935); Artist Painter; *b* 16 March 1888; *s* of John Crooks McGlashan and Agnes Thomson; *m* 1922, Teresa Giuliani (*d* 1971); one *s* two *d*. *Educ:* Paisley; Glasgow. Trained at Glasgow Sch. of Art; travelled extensively on the Continent, visiting chief Art centres. Pictures purchased by:-Scottish Modern Art Assoc.; Glasgow, Belfast, Newcastle, Aberdeen, Paisley, Perth, Dundee, and Edinburgh Corporations; Glasgow Univ., Arts Council of Great Britain. Has exhibited pictures at Royal Scottish Acad., Royal Acad., The Royal Glasgow Institute of the Fine Arts, The Paisley Art Institute, Walker Art Gallery, Liverpool and in America and Canada. *Address:* 35 Roddinghead Road, Whitecraigs, Glasgow G46 6TN. *T:* 041-639 4684. *Club:* Art (Glasgow).

McGLASHAN, John Reid Curtis, CBE 1974; HM Diplomatic Service; Counsellor, Foreign and Commonwealth Office, since 1970; *b* 12 Dec. 1921; *s* of John Adamson McGlashan and Emma Rose May McGlashan; *m* 1947, Dilys Bagnall (*née* Buxton Knight); one *s* two *d*. *Educ:* Fettes; Christ Church, Oxford. RAF (Bomber Command), 1940-45. Entered Foreign Service, 1953; Baghdad, 1955; Tripoli, 1963; Madrid, 1968. *Recreations:* gardening, golf, reading, tennis. *Address:* The Bakehouse, Kingsley Green, Haslemere, Surrey GU27 3LH. *Club:* Vincent's (Oxford).

McGLASHAN, Prof. Maxwell Len, FRIC; Professor of Chemistry and Head of the Department of Chemistry, University College London, since 1974; *b* 1 April 1924; *s* of late Leonard Day and Margaret Cordelia McGlashan; *m* 1947, Susan Jane, *d* of late Col H. E. Crosse, MC, OBE, and late Mrs D. Crosse, Patoka Station, Hawkes Bay, NZ. *Educ:* Greymouth, NZ; Canterbury Univ. Coll., Christchurch, NZ; Univ. of Reading. MSc (NZ) 1946, PhD (Reading) 1951, DSc (Reading) 1962. Asst Lectr, 1946-48, Lectr, 1948-53, Sen. Lectr, 1953, in Chemistry, at Canterbury Univ. Coll., Christchurch, NZ. Sims Empire Scholar, 1949-52; Lectr in Chem., Univ. of Reading, 1954-61; Reader in Chem., Univ. of Reading, 1962-64; Prof. of Physical Chem., Univ. of Exeter, 1964-74. Mem., 1963-65, Vice-Chm., 1965-67, Chm., 1967-71, Commn on Physicochemical Symbols, Terminology, and Units. Chm., Interdivl Cttee on Nomenclature and Symbols, Internat. Union of Pure and Applied Chem., 1971-76; Member: Royal Society Symbols Cttee, 1963-; Council, Faraday Soc., 1965-67; Metrication Bd, 1969-. Mem., Comité Consultatif des Unités (Metre Convention), 1969-; Mem. Council, Chem. Soc., 1970-73; Dean of Faculty of Science, Univ. of Exeter, 1973-74; Mem., Science Research Council Chem. Cttee, 1974-76; Data Compilation Cttee, 1974-; Chm., Ramsay Fellowships Adv. Council, 1975-. Editor, Jl of Chemical Thermodynamics, 1969-. *Publications:* Physicochemical Quantities and Units, 1968 (Royal Inst. of Chem.), 2nd edn, 1971; papers on chemical thermodynamics and statistical mechanics in Proc. Roy. Soc., Trans Faraday Soc., Jl Chem. Thermodynamics, etc. *Recreations:* climbing in the Alps, the theatre. *Address:* 9 Camden Square, NW1 9UY. *T:* 01-267 1583; Department of Chemistry, University College London, 20 Gordon Street, WC1H 0AJ. *T:* 01-387 7050. *Club:* Athenæum.

McGONAGLE, Stephen; Northern Ireland Parliamentary Commissioner for Administration and Commissioner for Complaints, since 1974; *b* 17 Nov. 1914; *m*; five *s* one *d*. *Educ:* Christian Brothers', Derry. Chairman, NI Cttee, Irish Congress of Trade Unions, 1959; Vice-Chm., Derry Develt Commn, 1969-71; Pres., Irish Congress of Trade Unions, 1972-73; Mem., NI Economic Council, Indust. Tribunal, Indust. Ct, until 1973; Dist Sec., Irish Transport and General Workers' Union, Dec. 1973. Chm., NI Police Complaints Bd, 1977-. *Recreations:* fishing, boating, reading. *Address:* (office) 48 High Street, Belfast, Northern Ireland. *T:* Belfast 33821; (home) 10 Kingsfort Park, Derry.

McGONIGAL, Rt. Hon. Sir Ambrose Joseph, PC 1975; Kt 1975; MC 1943 and bar 1944; **Rt. Hon. Lord Justice McGonigal;** Lord Justice of Appeal, Supreme Court of Judicature, Northern Ireland, since 1975 (Judge of High Court of Justice, N Ireland, 1968-75); *b* 22 Nov. 1917; 2nd *s* of Judge John McGonigal, KC and Margaret McGonigal; *m* 1941, Patricia, *o d* of Robert Taylor; two *s* two *d*. *Educ:* Clongowes Wood Coll.; Queen's Univ., Belfast. Served HM Forces, 1939-46; commnd RUR, 1940; 12th Commando, 1943-44 (wounded); Special Boat Service, 1944-45 (despatches). Called to Bar, N Ireland, 1948; to Inner Bar of N Ireland, 1956; Bencher, The Inn of Court of N Ireland, 1964. Member: Cttee on Public Library Service in N Ire.; Cttee on Adult Education in N Ire.; N Ire. Charities Central Investment Fund Advisory Cttee, 1966-74; Senate, QUB, 1969-74. Governor: Armagh Observatory, 1968-; St Joseph's Coll. of Education, 1969-74. *Recreations:* various. *Address:* Bishops Court House, Bishops Court, Co. Down BT30 7EY. *Club:* Special Forces.

MacGONIGAL, Maurice, PRHA; Hon. RA; Hon. RSA; Professor of Painting, Royal Hibernian Academy; Member of Board of Governors, National Gallery of Ireland; Member of Advisory Committees: of Municipal Gallery of Modern Art; for Wolfe Tone Memorial; Coun. of Industrial Design, Ireland; Currency Design Council; *b* Dublin, Jan. 1900; *s* of Frank MacGonigal and Caroline Lane; *m*; two *s*. Studied at Dublin Metropolitan Sch. of Art; Taylor Scholarship in Painting, 1924; interested in Irish Landscape and Genre Painting; exhibited London, America, etc.; is represented by pictures: Municipal Gallery of Modern Art, Dublin, Cork, Belfast and Limerick Galleries; Senate Chambers, Leinster House, Dublin RCP, Nat. Mus. of Ireland. LLD *hc* NUI, 1970. *Address:* 2 Templemore Avenue, Rathgar, Dublin 6, Ireland. *T:* 01-973504.

MACGOUGAN, John; General Secretary, National Union of Tailors and Garment Workers; Member: TUC General Council, since 1970; Manpower Services Commission, since 1977; *b* 21 Aug. 1913; *m* 1941, Lizzie Faulkner; three *s* one *d*. *Educ:* various Northern Ireland Schs; Technical Sch.; Correspondence courses. Accountancy profession, 1930-45. Irish Officer, NUTGW, in charge of all Irish affairs, 1945-69. Contested (Irish Labour) N Ireland Parly Elections, Oldpark 1938, Falls Div. 1951;

Westminster Parly Election, South Down 1950; Member: Belfast Corporation, 1949-58; Executive, Irish TUC, 1950-69 (Pres. 1957-58 and 1963-64). *Recreations:* proletarian pastimes, greyhound racing (owner). *Address:* 45A West Hill, Aspley Guise, Milton Keynes, Bucks. *T:* Milton Keynes 582976.

McGOVERN, George Stanley; US Senator from South Dakota, since 1963; *b* Avon, S Dakota, 19 July 1922; *s* of Rev. Joseph C. McGovern and Francis (*née* McLean); *m* 1943, Eleanor Faye Stegeberg; one *s* four *d. Educ:* Dakota Wesleyan Univ. (BA); Northwestern Univ. (MA, PhD). Served World War II, USAAF (DFC). Teacher, Northwestern Univ., 1948-50; Prof. of History and Govt, Dakota Wesleyan Univ., 1950-53. Exec. Sec., S Dakota Democratic Party, 1953-56; Mem., 1st Dist, S Dakota, US House of Reps, 1957-61; Dir, Food for Peace Programme, 1961-62. Democratic Candidate for US Presidential nomination, 1972. Mem., Amer. Hist. Assoc. *Publications:* The Colorado Coal Strike, 1913-14, 1953; War Against Want, 1964; Agricultural Thought in the Twentieth Century, 1967; A Time of War, A Time of Peace, 1968; (with Leonard F. Guttridge) The Great Coalfield War, 1972; An American Journey, 1974. *Address:* US Senate, Washington, DC 20510, USA; Mitchell, S Dakota, USA.

McGOWAN, family name of **Baron McGowan.**

McGOWAN, 3rd Baron, *cr* 1937; **Harry Duncan Cory McGowan;** Partner, Panmure, Gordon & Co., since 1971; *b* 20 July 1938; *e s* of Harry Wilson McGowan, 2nd Baron McGowan, and Carmen, *d* of Sir (James) Herbert Cory, 1st Bt; *S* father, 1966; *m* 1962, Lady Gillian Angela Pepys, *d* of 7th Earl of Cottenham; one *s* two *d. Educ:* Eton. *Heir: s* Hon. Harry John Charles McGowan, *b* 23 June 1971. *Address:* House of Lords, Westminster, SW1; Highway House, Lower Froyle, Alton, Hants. *T:* Bentley 2104; 33 Thurloe Street, SW7. *T:* 01-584 9986. *Club:* Boodle's.

McGOWAN, Bruce Henry, MA; FRSA; Headmaster, Haberdashers' Aske's School, since 1973; *b* 27 June 1924; *er s* of late Rt Rev. Henry McGowan, sometime Bishop of Wakefield, and Nora Heath McGowan (*née* Godwin); *m* 1947, Beryl McKenzie (*née* Liggitt); one *s* three *d. Educ:* King Edward's Sch., Birmingham; Jesus Coll., Cambridge. War service, Royal Artillery, 1943-46. Asst Master, King's Sch., Rochester, 1949-53; Senior History Master, Wallasey Gram. Sch., 1953-57; Headmaster: De Aston Sch., Market Rasen, Lincs, 1957-64; Solihull Sch., 1964-73. Page Scholar of the English-Speaking Union, 1961. Member: Church Assembly, 1963-70; Public Schools Commn, 1968-70; Chairman: Boarding Schools Assoc., 1967-69; London Division of HMC. *Recreations:* camping, mountain-walking, music, the theatre, rugby refereeing. *Address:* Haberdashers' Aske's School, Elstree, Herts.

McGRADY, Edward Kevin; Member (SDLP) for South Down, Northern Ireland Constitutional Convention, 1975-76; Partner, M. B. McGrady & Co., chartered accountants and insurance brokers; *b* 3 June 1935; *y s* of late Michael McGrady and late Lilian Leatham; *m* 1959, Patricia, *d* of Wm Swail and Margaret Breen; two *s* one *d. Educ:* St Patrick's High Sch., Downpatrick. ACA 1957, FCA 1962. Councillor, Downpatrick UDC, 1961; Chm. of UDC, 1964-73; Vice-Chm., Down District Council, 1973 and 1975-76, Chm. 1974, 1976. 1st Chm. of SDLP, 1971-73; 1st Chm. of SDLP Assembly Party. Mem. (SDLP), S Down, NI Assembly, 1973-75; Head of Office of Executive Planning and Co-ordination (Minister for Co-ordination, Jan.-May 1974). *Recreation:* passive interest in badminton. *Address:* Aileach, Rathkeltair Road, Downpatrick, Co. Down BT30 6NL. *T:* Downpatrick 2307.

McGRATH, Sir Charles (Gullan), Kt 1968; OBE 1964; Chairman: Repco Ltd, since 1957; Nylex Corp. Ltd; Petersville Aust. Ltd; *b* Ballarat, 22 Nov. 1910; *s* of David Charles McGrath and Elizabeth McGrath; *m* 1934, Madge Louise, *d* of Andrew McLaren; one *s* four *d. Educ:* Ballarat High Sch. Gen. Man., Replacement Parts Pty Ltd, 1946-53; Repco Ltd: Dir, 1948; Man. Dir, 1953-67, retd; Chm. of Dirs, 1957. Vice-President, Australian Industries Development Assoc.; Director: Australian Industry Development Corp.; Capel Court Corp.; Ensign Holdings Ltd; Union Fidelity Trustee Co. of Australia Ltd; Vice-Chm., Defence Industrial Cttee; Mem. Bd of Management, Alfred Hosp.; Mem. Council, Australian Administrative Staff Coll. *Recreation:* farming. *Address:* 46 Lansell Road, Toorak, Vic. 3142, Australia. *Clubs:* Australian, Athenæum, Kelvin, Melbourne (Melbourne); Commonwealth (Canberra).

McGRATH, John Cornelius, CBE 1971; FCA; FCIT 1970; Financial Adviser to British Airports Authority; full-time Board

Member and Founder Financial Controller of British Airports Authority, 1966-71; *s* of Patrick and Johanna McGrath; bachelor. *Educ:* St Ignatius Coll. (then Univ. of London). Schoolmaster, 1925-27; Asst to Public Auditor, 1927-34; Lectr in Accountancy and Finance, 1928-39; appointed Public Auditor by HM Treasury, 1934; qual. as Chartered Accountant, 1938; Dep. Man. of Audit Dept, CWS, 1938-66; Chief Accountant and Financial Adviser to LCS, 1947-66. Bd Mem. for Finance of Post Office, 1968-69. Mem., Worshipful Co. of Inn-holders, 1951; Freeman, City of London, 1951. *Recreations:* music, motor racing, travel, swimming. *Address:* 8 River Court, Surbiton, Surrey. *T:* 01-546 3833. *Clubs:* Reform, Royal Automobile, MCC.

McGRATH, Dr Patrick Gerard, CBE 1971; Senior Consulting Psychiatrist and Physician Superintendent, Broadmoor Hospital, since 1956; *b* 10 June 1916; *s* of late Patrick McGrath and Mary (*née* Murray), Glasgow; *m* 1949, Helen Patricia O'Brien; three *s* one *d. Educ:* St Aloysius Coll., Glasgow; Glasgow and Edinburgh Univs. MB, ChB Glasgow 1939; DipPsych Edinburgh 1955; FRCPsych; FRSocMed. RAMC, 1939-46 (Hon. Lt-Col); various trng posts in psychiatry, Glasgow, London and Colchester, 1946-51; Psychiatrist, Ayrshire, 1951-56. *Publications:* chapter in Psychopathic Disorder, 1966; Mentally Abnormal Offender, 1968; contrib. Jl of RSH, Cropwood publications, etc. *Address:* 18 Heathermount Drive, Crowthorne, Berks.

McGRATH, Raymond, BArch (Sydney); FRIBA; FRIAI; RHA; FSIA; architect; Professor of Architecture, Royal Hibernian Academy, 1968; *b* Sydney, NSW, 7 March 1903; *s* of Herbert Edgar McGrath, NZ, and Edith Sorrell, NSW; *m* 1930, Mary Catherine Crozier, Dallas, Texas; one *s* one *d. Educ:* Fort Street Boys Schs; Univ. Sydney (University Medal for English Verse. BArch with first class hons and University Medal, 1926, Wentworth Travelling Fellowship, 1926); Clare Coll., Cambridge (Research Student of Architecture, 1927-29). Australian Medallion of Board of Architects of NSW, 1928; Consultant to the British Broadcasting Corporation, 1930-35; in private practice in London, 1930-39; Principal Architect, Office of Public Works, Dublin, 1948-68; in private practice in Dublin, 1968-. Pres., Soc. of Designers in Ireland, 1972. *Architectural works:* Finella, Cambridge, 1928; studios, furniture and equipment for BBC, 1930-34; interiors of Aircraft for Imperial Airways, 1932; various restaurants, showrooms and exhibitions; The Cenotaph, Leinster Lawn, Dublin, 1950. Appointed architect for The Kennedy Memorial Concert Hall, Dublin, 1964, and Royal Hibernian Acad. of Arts new galleries, Dublin, 1970. Domestic work: Frognal House, Hampstead, St Ann's Hill, Chertsey; various commercial buildings; official works: remodelling of President's House, Dublin; adaptation of Irish Embassies in London and Paris, etc. *Drawings and paintings:* Wood engravings for illustrations; various topographical drawings; paintings in water-colour, gouache and oil. Commissioned as official War Artist, Feb. 1940, to make drawings of Aircraft Production. *Industrial Design:* Furniture, glassware, carpets. *Publications:* Twentieth Century Houses (in Basic English), 1934; Glass in Architecture and Decoration (with A. C. Frost), 1937 (new edn 1961). *Address:* Somerton Lodge, Rochestown Avenue, Co. Dublin. *T:* 854032.

MacGREGOR, Air Vice-Marshal Andrew, CB 1949; CBE 1945; DFC 1918; retired; *b* 25 Oct. 1897; *s* of late Andrew MacGregor, Glen Gyle, Crieff; *m* 1939, Isobel Jane, *d* of Gordon Eadie, Crieff; three *d. Educ:* Morrison's Acad., Crieff. Commissioned Argyll and Sutherland Highlanders and attached RFC, 1917. Served in Egypt and Iraq, 1919-27; graduated RAF Staff Coll., 1928; served in Sudan and Palestine, 1932-37; Dep. Directorate Organisation, Air Ministry, 1940; Senior Air Staff Officer, HQ, No. 4 Group, 1940-42; Air Officer Administrative, N Africa, 1942-44; Asst Commandant, Staff Coll., 1944; Air Officer comdg No. 28 Group, 1945-46; Air Officer Administrative, HQ Fighter Command, 1946-49. Comdr Legion of Honour, 1944; Comdr Order of Crown of Belgium, 1948; Officer of Legion of Merit (USA), 1944; Croix de Guerre. *Address:* Glen Gyle, Crieff, Perthshire, Scotland. *T:* Crieff 2583, *Club:* Caledonian United Services (Edinburgh).

MacGREGOR, Sir Colin (Malcolm), Kt 1959; Chief Justice of Jamaica, 1957-62, retired; *b* 10 April 1901; *s* of John Malcolm MacGregor, Solicitor, Mandeville, Jamaica, and Ann Katherine (*née* Muirhead); *m* 1926, Dorothy Constance Scarlett; one *s* one *d. Educ:* Munro Coll., Jamaica; Denstone Coll., England. Called to Bar, 1922; Clerk, Resident Magistrates' Court, Jamaica, 1925; Resident Magistrate, Jamaica, 1934; Puisne Judge, Jamaica, 1947; Sen. Puisne Judge, Jamaica, 1954-57. Acted as Chief Justice, Jamaica, May-Nov. 1955. *Publications:* (ed) 5 and 6 Jamaica Law Reports. *Recreations:* golf, bridge, philately.

Address: Garth, Knockpatrick, Jamaica. *Club:* Manchester (Mandeville, Jamaica).

MacGREGOR, Duncan; Convenor of the Council of Fellows in Dental Surgery, Royal College of Surgeons of Edinburgh, 1965-67; President Odonto-Chirurgical Society of Scotland, 1956-57; President, British Dental Association, 1960-61 (now Vice-President); *b* 17 Feb. 1892; *s* of A. D. MacGregor and Jessie Steel Proudfoot; *m* 1921, Elizabeth Ruth Doig; one *s* one *d*. *Educ:* George Heriot's Sch.; Royal Coll. of Surgeons and Edinburgh Dental Hospital and Sch. LDS, RCS Edinburgh 1916; Surgeon Probationer, RNVR 1915-17; Surg. Lt (D) RNVR 1917-19; Surg. Lt-Comdr (D) RNVR, retd 1937. Hon. Dental Surg., Edinburgh Dental Hosp. and Sch., 1921-48; Consultant Dental Surg., Edinburgh Dental Hosp., 1948-61; Member: Dental Board of the UK 1946-56; Gen. Dental Council, 1956-66. Fellowship in Dental Surgery, Royal Coll. of Surgeons, Edinburgh, 1951. *Publications:* contributions to dental journals. *Recreations:* sketching, gardening. *Address:* 8 Seton Place, Edinburgh EH9 2JT. *T:* 031-667 5071. *Club:* Caledonian (Edinburgh).

MacGREGOR, Edward Ian Roy, CMG 1966; HM Diplomatic Service, retired; *b* 4 March 1911; *s* of late John MacGregor and late Georgina Agnes MacGregor (*née* Barbor); *m* 1944, Lilianne, *d* of William Swindlehurst, Washington, DC, USA; one *s* one *d*. *Educ:* Methodist Coll., Belfast; Queen's Univ., Belfast (MSc). Wing Comdr RAF, 1936-47. Asst Civil Air Attaché, Washington, 1948-52; Ministry of Transport and Civil Aviation, 1952-59; Civil Air Attaché, Washington, 1959-65; Asst Sec., BoT, 1965-67; Counsellor, FO, 1967-68; Consul-Gen., Detroit, 1968-71. *Address:* Spinneys, Brock Way, Virginia Water, Surrey.

MACGREGOR, Sir Edwin (Robert), 7th Bt *cr* 1828; Assistant Deputy Minister, Ministry of Mines and Petroleum Resources, Province of British Columbia, Victoria, BC; *b* 4 Dec. 1931; *e s* of Sir Robert McConnell Macgregor, 6th Bt, and of Annie Mary Lane; *S* father, 1963; *m* 1952, (Margaret Alice) Jean Peake; one *s* two *d* (and one *s* decd). *Educ:* University of British Columbia. BASc 1955, MASc 1957, Metallurgical Engineering. Member: Assoc. of Professional Engrs, Province of British Columbia; Assoc. of Professional Engrs, Province of Ontario. *Publications:* contribs. to Trans Amer. Inst. of Mining, Metallurgical and Petroleum Engrg, Jl Amer. Chem. Soc. *Recreations:* reading; participation in several outdoor sports such as golf, swimming, fishing, etc.; music. *Heir: s* Ian Grant Macgregor, *b* 22 Feb. 1959. *Address:* 3189 Anders Place, Victoria, BC V9B 4C5, Canada. *T:* (604) 478-1824.

MacGREGOR, Geddes; see MacGregor, J. G.

McGREGOR, Gordon Peter; Principal, Bishop Otter College, Chichester, since 1970; *b* Aldershot, Hants, 13 June 1932; 2nd *s* of William A. K. McGregor and Mary A. McGregor (*née* O'Brien); *m* 1957, Jean Olga Lewis; three *d*. *Educ:* St Brendan's Coll., Bristol; Univ. of Bristol. BA Hons (Bristol) 1953; Dip. (Coll. of Teachers of the Blind), 1958; MEd (E Africa), 1965. Educn Officer, RAF, 1953-56; Asst Master, Worcester Coll. for the Blind, 1956-59; Asst Master, King's Coll., Budo, Uganda, 1959-62; Lecturer in Language Method, Makerere Univ. Coll., Uganda 1963-66; Univ. of Zambia: Sen Lecturer in Educn, 1966; Head of Dept of Education, 1967; Reader and Head of Dept, 1968; Prof. of Educn, 1970. FRSA (invited) 1976. *Publications:* King's College, Budo, The First Sixty Years, 1967; Educating the Handicapped, 1967; English for Education?, 1968; Teaching English as a Second Language, 1970; English in Africa, (UNESCO), 1971; contrib. Univs Qly, Times Higher Educn Supplement. *Recreations:* music, literature, cricket, swimming. *Address:* Bishop Otter College, Chichester, West Sussex. *T:* Chichester 87911.

MacGREGOR of MacGregor, Brig. Sir Gregor, 6th Bt, *cr* 1795; Scots Guards; 23rd Chief of Clan Gregor; Defence and Military Attaché, British Embassy, Athens, since 1975; *b* 22 Dec. 1925; *o s* of Capt. Sir Malcolm MacGregor of MacGregor, 5th Bt, CB, CMG, and Hon. Gylla Lady MacGregor of MacGregor, *qv*; *S* father 1958; *m* 1958, Fanny, *o d* of C. H. A. Butler, Shortgrove, Newport, Essex; two *s*. *Educ:* Eton. Commissioned Scots Guards, 1944; served War of 1939-45. Served in Palestine, 1947-48; Malaya, 1950-51; Borneo, 1965. Staff Coll. Course, 1960; Brigade Major, 16th Parachute Bde Gp, 1961-63; Joint Services Staff Coll., 1965; commanding 1st Bn Scots Guards, 1966-69; GSO1 (BLO) Fort Benning, USA, 1969-71; Col Recruiting, HQ Scotland, 1971; Lt-Col commanding Scots Guards, 1971-74. Mem. of the Royal Company of Archers (Queen's Body Guard for Scotland). *Heir: s* Malcolm Gregor Charles MacGregor of MacGregor, *b* 23 March 1959. *Address:* Edinchip,

Lochearnhead, Perthshire. *T:* Lochearnhead 204. *Clubs:* Buck's, Pratt's.

MacGREGOR of MacGregor, Hon. Lady; (Gylla Constance Susan), OBE 1948; *y d* of late Hon. Eric Norman Rollo; *m* 1925, Capt. Sir Malcolm MacGregor of MacGregor, 5th Bt, CB, CMG (*d* 1958); one *s* (*see* Sir Gregor MacGregor, 6th Bt) one *d*. *Educ:* privately. Three months' training in theatres at Guy's Hospital; in charge of Plaster Dept, Edmonton Special Military Hospital, 1917-19; private sec. to late Ian Colvin, Morning Post, 1921-24; Chm. National Exhibition of Needlework, Edinburgh, 1934; Mem. of Council of Management Empire Exhibition, Glasgow, 1938; Mem. Executive of Scottish Development Council, 1934-46; Vice-Chm. Scottish Cttee of Council for Art and Industry, 1934; Mem. Scottish Housing Advisory Cttee, 1939-42; Mem. of Council of National Trust for Scotland, 1937-46; Chairman of Women's Land Army Cttee Perth West; Mem. of Scottish Tourist Cttee; Mem. of Executive Cttee of Enterprise Scotland, 1947; Chairman Amenity Cttees: North of Scotland Hydro-Electric Board and S of Scotland Electricity Bd, 1964-71; Member: Scottish Cttee of Council of Industrial Design, 1941-49; Royal Fine Art Commission for Scotland, 1943-63. Order of the Vasa, 1st Cl., 1954. *Address:* Craggan House, Lochearnhead, Perthshire. *T:* Lochearnhead 250.

McGREGOR, Ian Alexander, CBE 1968 (OBE 1959); Head of Laboratory of Tropical Community Studies, National Institute for Medical Research, Mill Hill, since 1974; *b* 26 Aug. 1922; *s* of John McGregor and Isabella (*née* Taylor), Cambuslang, Lanarks; *m* 1954, Nancy Joan, *d* of Frederick Small, Mapledurham, Oxon; one *s* one *d*. *Educ:* Rutherglen Academy; St Mungo Coll., Glasgow. LRCPE, LRCSE, LRFPS(G) 1945; DTM&H 1949; MRCP 1962; FRCP 1967; FFCM 1972. Mil. Service, 1946-48 (despatches). Mem. Scientific Staff, Human Nutrition Research Unit, MRC, 1949-53; Dir, MRC Laboratory, The Gambia, 1954-74; Mem. WHO Adv. Panel on Malaria, 1961-; Mem. Malaria Cttee, MRC, 1962-71; Mem. Cttee on Nutrition Surveys, Internat. Union of Nutrition Sciences, 1971-; Mem., Tropical Medicine Res. Bd, MRC, 1974-. Chalmers Medal, Royal Soc. Trop. Med. and Hygiene, 1963; Stewart Prize, BMA, 1970; Darling Foundn Medal, WHO, 1974. *Publications:* scientific papers on infections, nutrition, immunity, child health and community medicine in tropical environments. *Recreations:* ornithology, golf, fishing. *Address:* 210 Hyde End Road, Spencers Wood, near Reading, Berks. *T:* Reading 883417. *Club:* Fajara (The Gambia).

McGREGOR, James Reid, CB 1948; CBE 1945; MC 1916; *m* 1933, Dorothy Janet, *d* of Mr and Mrs Comrie, Ayr; one *s* one *d*. *Educ:* Edinburgh Academy, RMC Sandhurst. Served European War, 1914-18, Gordon Highlanders, 1915-19 (despatches, wounded, MC); War of 1939-45, Director of Army contracts, 1940-44; Private Secretary to Sir James Grigg, Secretary of State for War, 1944-45; Director of Finance, War Office, 1945-59. Member, Public Health Laboratory Service Board, 1961-69. *Address:* Torphins, Burntwood Road, Sevenoaks, Kent.

MacGREGOR, Prof. (John) Geddes, DèsL (Sorbonne), DPhil, DD Oxon, BD Edinburgh et Oxon, LLB Edinburgh; Distinguished Professor of Philosophy, University of Southern California, 1966-75, now Emeritus; Dean of Graduate School of Religion, 1960-66; first holder of Rufus Jones Chair of Philosophy and Religion, Bryn Mawr, USA, 1949-60; Canon Theologian of St Paul's Cathedral, Los Angeles, 1968-74; *b* 13 Nov. 1909; *o s* of late Thomas and Blanche Geddes McGregor, Angus; *m* 1941, Elizabeth, *e d* of late Archibald McAllister, Edinburgh; one *s* one *d*. *Educ:* Universities of Edinburgh, Paris, Heidelberg; The Queen's Coll., Oxford. Senior Assistant to Dean of Chapel Royal in Scotland, at St Giles' Cathedral, Edinburgh, 1939-41; served in Civil Defence, War of 1939-45; Minister, Trinity Church, Glasgow, S1, 1941-49; Assistant to Prof. of Logic and Metaphysics, Edinburgh Univ., 1947-49; Examiner: Swarthmore Coll., USA, 1950, 1953, 1955-57; Hebrew Union Coll., USA, 1959, 1961; Occasional Lectr, Columbia Univ., Amherst Coll., Swarthmore Coll., Princeton Univ., Rutgers Univ., Toronto Univ., Loyola Univ., Villanova Univ.; Visiting Prof., 1958-59, and Graduate Sch. Research Lecturer, 1963, University of Southern California. Visiting Prof.: Univ. of British Columbia, 1963, 1966, 1973; Hebrew Union Coll., 1964-65; Univ. of Santa Clara, 1968; World Campus Afloat (Orient, 1974; Mediterranean, 1975); McGill Univ., Montreal, 1976; Visiting Fellow, Dept of Religious Studies, Yale Univ., 1967-68; Vis. Prof., Inst. for Shipboard Educn (round-the-world-voyage), 1977. Special Preacher: St Paul's Cathedral, London, 1969; Westminster Abbey, 1970. Regent, American-Scottish Foundation, Inc., NY. FRSL 1948. Hon. Phi Kappa Phi, 1972. California Literature Award (Gold Medal, non fiction), 1964. *Publications:* Aesthetic Experience in Religion, 1947; Christian

Doubt, 1951; Les Frontières de la Morale et de la Religion, 1952; From a Christian Ghetto, 1954; The Vatican Revolution, 1957; The Tichborne Impostor, 1957; The Thundering Scot, 1957; Corpus Christi, 1959; Introduction to Religious Philosophy, 1959; The Bible in the Making, 1959; The Coming Reformation, 1960; The Hemlock and the Cross, 1963; God Beyond Doubt, 1966; A Literary History of the Bible, 1968; The Sense of Absence, 1968; So Help Me God, 1970; Philosophical Issues in Religious Thought, 1973; The Rhythm of God, 1974; He Who Lets Us Be: a theology of love, 1975; articles, recordings, reviews. *Recreation:* manual labour. *Address:* 876 Victoria Avenue, Los Angeles, California 90005, USA. *T:* 213-938-4826. *Clubs:* Athenæum, English-Speaking Union, Royal Commonwealth Society; Caledonian (Edinburgh); Union Society (Oxford).

MacGREGOR, John Roddick Russell, OBE 1971; MP (C) South Norfolk, since Feb. 1974; Director: Hill Samuel & Co. Ltd, since 1973; Hill Samuel Registrars Ltd, since 1972; *b* 14 Feb. 1937; *s* of Dr. N. S. R. MacGregor; *m* 1962, Jean Mary Elizabeth Dungey; one *s* two *d. Educ:* Merchiston Castle Sch., Edinburgh; St Andrews Univ. (MA, 1st cl. Hons); King's Coll., London (LLB). Univ. Administrator, 1961-62; Editorial Staff, New Society, 1962-63; Special Asst to Prime Minister, Sir Alec Douglas-Home, 1963-64; Conservative Research Dept, 1964-65; Head of Private Office of Rt Hon. Edward Heath, Leader of Opposition, 1965-68. Hill Samuel & Co. Ltd, 1968-. Chairman: Fedn of University Cons. and Unionist Assocs, 1959; Bow Group, 1963-64; 1st Pres., Conservative and Christian Democratic Youth Community, 1963-65; Treasurer, Federal Trust for Educn and Research; Trustee, European Educnl Research Trust; Govenor, Langley Sch., Norfolk, 1976. *Publications:* contrib. The Conservative Opportunity; also pamphlets. *Recreations:* theatre, opera, reading, travelling, gardening. *Address:* House of Commons, SW1A 0AA.

MACGREGOR, John Roy; His Honour Judge Macgregor; a Circuit Judge, since 1974; Honorary Recorder of Margate, since 1972; *b* Brooklyn, NY, 9 Sept. 1913; 4th *s* of Charles George McGregor, of Jamaica and New York. *Educ:* Bedford School. Called to the Bar, Gray's Inn, 1939; Inner Temple (*ad eundem*), 1968. Served in Royal Artillery, 1939-46; RA (TA) and Special Air Service (TA), 1950-61. Dep. Chm., Cambridgeshire and Isle of Ely QS, 1967-71; a Recorder, 1972-74. Legal Assessor to Gen. Optical Council, 1972-74. *Address:* Nether Gaulrig, Yardley Hastings, Northampton NN7 1HD. *T:* Yardley Hastings 861. *Club:* Special Forces.

McGREGOR, Kenneth, CB 1963; CMG 1951; *b* 11 Feb. 1903; *o c* of late James McGregor and Eugénie Lydia Johnson; *m* 1930, Dorothy Laura Roope, *o d* of late Judge R. Roope Reeve, QC; two *s. Educ:* Westminster (King's Scholar); New Coll., Oxford (Scholar). 1st class Hons; MA. Called to the Bar (Lincoln's Inn). Ministries of Health, Supply and Production; Board of Trade (Under-Secretary); the Senior British Trade Commissioner in Canada, 1958-62, retired. Dir and Consultant, Companies and Trade Assocs, 1963-73. London Borough Councillor, 1968-71. Mem., Performing Right Tribunal, 1966-74. *Address:* Kings Rythe, Emsworth, Hants PO10 7HW. *T:* Emsworth 2014. *Club:* United Oxford & Cambridge University.

McGREGOR, Prof. Oliver Ross; Professor of Social Institutions in the University of London, and Head of Department of Sociology, at Bedford College, since 1964; Joint Director, Rowntree Legal Research Unit, since 1966; *b* 25 Aug. 1921; *s* of late William McGregor and late Anne Olivia Ross; *m* 1944, Nellie Weate; three *s. Educ:* Worksop Coll.; University of Aberdeen; London School of Economics. Temp. civil servant, War Office and Ministry of Agriculture, 1940-44. Asst Lecturer and Lecturer in Economic History, University of Hull, 1945-47; Lecturer, Bedford Coll., 1947-60, Reader in University of London, 1960-64; Simon Senior Research Fellow, University of Manchester, 1959-60. Fellow of Wolfson Coll., Oxford, 1972-75; Dir, Centre for Socio-Legal Studies, Univ. of Oxford, 1972-75. Member: Cttee on Enforcement of Judgment Debts, 1965; Cttee on Statutory Maintenance Limits, 1966; Cttee on Land Use (Recreation and Leisure), 1967; National Parks Commission, 1966-68; Independent Television Authority's General Advisory Council, 1967-73; Countryside Commission, 1968-; Legal Aid Adv. Cttee, 1969-; Cttee on One-Parent Families, 1969-74; Chm., Royal Commn on Press, 1975-77 (Mem., 1974). Pres., Nat. Council for One Parent Families, 1975-. Lectures: Fawcett Meml, 1966; James Seth Meml, 1968; Hobhouse Meml, 1971; Maccabaean in Jurisprudence, 1973. *Publications:* Divorce in England, 1957; ed, Lord Ernle, English Farming Past and Present, 6th edn, 1960; Bibliography of the National Association for the Promotion of Social Science, 1969; (jtly) Separated Spouses, 1970; various papers in British Journal of Sociology

and other journals. *Address:* Far End, Wyldes Close, NW11 7JB. *T:* 01-458 2856. *Club:* Reform.

MacGREGOR, Robert Barr, CMG 1946; MB, ChB, FRCPEd; *b* 14 July 1896; *s* of Patrick MacGregor; *m* 1st, 1921, Helen May Harper (*d* 1964); one *s*; 2nd, 1970, Edith Rushbrooke, *e d* of Thomas Crook, OBE. *Educ:* Dunbar Sch.; Edinburgh University. Served in RAMC, 1918-20; joined Straits Settlements Medical Service, 1920; Director, Medical Services, Straits Settlements and Adviser, Medical Services, Malay Straits, 1940; Director, Medical Services, Federation of Malaya, retired 1951; SMO, Malacca Agricultural Medical Board, 1951-58; RMO, Wooley Hosp., 1965-67; Ship's Surgeon, Royal Fleet Auxiliary, 1967-75. CStJ. *Address:* Oakmead, Bashley Cross Road, New Milton, Hants.

McGRIGOR, Captain Sir Charles Edward, 5th Bt, *cr* 1831; Rifle Brigade, retired; Member Royal Company of Archers (HM Body Guard for Scotland); Exon, Queen's Bodyguard, Yeoman of the Guard, since 1970; *b* 5 Oct. 1922; *s* of Lieut-Colonel Sir Charles McGrigor, 4th Bt, OBE, and of Lady McGrigor; *S* father, 1946; *m* 1948, Mary Bettine, *e d* of Sir Archibald Charles Edmonstone, 6th Bt; two *s* two *d. Educ:* Eton. War of 1939-45 (despatches); joined Army, 1941, from Eton; served with Rifle Bde, N. Africa, Italy, Austria. ADC to Duke of Gloucester, 1945-47, in Australia and England. Mem. Cttee of Management, RNLI and Convenor, Scottish Lifeboat Council. *Recreations:* fishing, gardening. *Heir:* s James Angus Rhoderick Neil McGrigor, *b* 19 Oct. 1949. *Address:* Upper Sonachan, Dalmally, Argyll. *Club:* Boodle's.

McGUINNESS, James Henry, CB 1964; Chairman, Scottish Philharmonic Society Ltd, since 1974; *b* 29 Sept. 1912; *s* of James Henry McGuinness, Scotstoun; *m* 1939, Annie Eveline Fordyce, Ayr; one *s* two *d. Educ:* St Aloysius Coll.; Univ. of Glasgow, 1st Cl. Hons Classics 1932, George Clark Fellow; Trinity Coll., Oxford (schol.), 1st cl. Hons Mods, 1934, 1st cl. Lit. Hum. Under-Secretary, Dept of Health for Scotland, 1959-62; Scottish Development Department, 1962-64; Asst Under-Sec. of State, Scottish Office and Chm., Scottish Economic Planning Bd, 1965-72; Sen. Res. Fellow in Politics, Univ. of Glasgow, 1973-74. Mem., Oil Develt Council for Scotland, 1973-75. Chm., Scottish Baroque Ensemble, 1973-74. *Address:* 10 Greenhill Terrace, Edinburgh EH10 4BS; Kendoon, Dalry, Kirkcudbrightshire. *Club:* Scottish Arts.

McGUINNESS, Rt. Rev. James Joseph; *see* Nottingham, Bishop of, (RC).

McGUINNESS, Norah Allison; artist; *b* Londonderry; *e d* of late Joseph Allison and Jessie McGuinness; *m* 1925, Geoffrey Phibbs, *e s* of Basil Phibbs, Lisheen, Sligo (marr. diss., 1931). *Educ:* Londonderry High Sch. Studied painting at College of Art, Dublin, Chelsea Polytechnical, London and with André Lhote, Paris; Illustrated: Sentimental Journey; Stories from Red Hanorhan (W. B. Yeats), etc. Designed for the Abbey Theatre, Dublin; held Exhibitions in London, Dublin, New York, Paris, Holland and Canada, and represented Ireland at Biennial Exhibition, Venice, 1950. Pictures in private collections in many countries. Hon. LittD TCD, 1973. *Recreations:* gardening and bird watching. *Address:* 53 York Road, Dun Laoghaire, Dublin.

McGUIRE, (Dominic) Paul, CBE 1951; HM Australian Diplomatic Service, retired; *b* 3 April 1903; *s* of James and Mary McGuire; *m* 1927, Frances Margaret Cheadle. *Educ:* Christian Brothers' Coll., Adelaide; University of Adelaide (Tinline Scholar in Australian History). WEA and University Extension Lecturer at University of Adelaide for several years; lectured extensively in USA, 1936-40 and 1946; served with Royal Australian Naval Volunteer Reserve in War of 1939-45. Australian Delegate to United Nations Assembly, 1953; Australian Minister to Italy, 1954-58, Ambassador to Italy, 1958-59; Envoy Extraordinary to Holy See on occasion of Coronation of HH Pope John XXIII, 1958. Commendatore, Order of Merit, Italy, 1967. Knight Grand Cross of St Sylvester, 1959. *Publications: verse:* The Two Men, 1932; *literary criticism:* The Poetry of Gerard Manley Hopkins, 1935; *novels:* 7.30 Victoria, 1935; Prologue to the Gallows, 1935; Cry Aloud for Murder, 1936; Born to be Hanged, 1936; Burial Service, 1937 (reissued in US as Funeral in Eden, 1976); W1, 1937; Spanish Steps, 1940; Price of Admiralty (with F. M. McGuire), 1945; *general:* Restoring All Things (with J. Fitzsimons), 1938; Australian Journey, 1939; Westward the Course, 1942; The Three Corners of the World; Experiment in World Order, 1948; The Australian Theatre (with B. P. Arnott and F. M. McGuire), 1948; Freedom for the Brave, 1949, etc. *Address:* 136 Mills Terrace, North Adelaide, South Australia 5006, Australia. *Clubs:* Athenæum (London); Naval and Military (Adelaide).

McGUIRE, Michael Thomas Francis; MP (Lab) Ince since 1964; *b* 3 May 1926; *m* 1954, Marie T. Murphy; three *s* two *d. Educ:* Elementary Schools. Coal mining: Face-worker; Whole-time Union Branch Secretary, NUM, 1957-64; Mem, local Hosp. Cttee. Joined Lab. Party, 1951; Mem., St Helens Co-op Soc., 1954-. *Recreations:* most out-door sports, especially Rugby League football; traditional music, especially Irish traditional ballads and ceili and pipe band music. *Address:* House of Commons, SW1.

McGUIRE, Robert Ely, CMG 1948; OBE 1943; Indian Civil Service (retired); *b* 22 Aug. 1901; *s* of late Major E. C. McGuire, 2nd Bn York and Lancaster Regt; *m* 1930, Barbara, *d* of late Sir Benjamin Heald, ICS, Judge of the High Court of Judicature, Rangoon; one *s* one *d. Educ:* High Sch., Dublin; Trinity Coll., Dublin. MA (Hons). Entered ICS, 1926; Warden, Burma Oilfields, 1932 and 1940-42; Dep. Commissioner, 1932-42. Secretary to Government of Burma (temp. in India), 1942-45. Dep. Director of Civil Affairs, with rank of Brigadier, British Military Administration in Burma, 1945. Divisional Comr, Burma, 1946-47; Secretary to Governor of Burma, 1947 to 4 Jan. 1948 (date of Independence of Burma). Secretary Cement Makers Federation, 1949-64. *Address:* Corofin, Rookery Way, Haywards Heath, West Sussex RH16 4RE. *T:* Haywards Heath 53692. *Clubs:* East India, Devonshire, Sports and Public Schools; Kildare Street and University (Dublin).

McGURK, Colin Thomas, OBE 1971 (MBE 1963); HM Diplomatic Service; Counsellor (Economic and Commercial), British High Commission, Canberra, since 1977; *b* 9 July 1922; *m* 1946, Ella Taylor; one *s. Educ:* St Mary's Coll., Middlesbrough. Served in Army, 1942-45. HM Foreign (subseq. Diplomatic) Service; served in British Embassies, Cairo, Addis Ababa, Ankara; 3rd Sec., HM Legation, Sofia, 1953-55; 2nd Sec. (Commercial), Athens, 1956-58; FO, 1958-62; HM Consul, Stanleyville, 1962; 1st Sec., Yaoundé, Brussels and Kuwait, 1962-70; Commercial Counsellor, Kuwait, 1971-72; Commercial Inspector, FCO, 1972-75; Counsellor (Economic and Commercial), New Delhi, 1975-77. *Recreations:* painting, sailing. *Address:* c/o Foreign and Commonwealth Office, King Charles Street, SW1A 2AH; 113 High Street, Burnham-on-Crouch, Essex CM0 8AH. *T:* Maldon 782467. *Club:* Royal Burnham Yacht.

McGUSTY, Victor William Tighe, CMG 1942; OBE 1937; OStJ; MB; DTM; *b* 20 June 1887; *m* 1st, 1912, Annie Bayliss; one *s* one *d*; 2nd, 1971, Joyce E. Johnston, Auckland, NZ. *Educ:* Coleraine (Ireland) Academical Institution; Trinity Coll., Dublin. Entered Colonial Medical Service, Fiji, 1912; retired, 1945; Director of Medical Services Colony of Fiji; also Director of Civil Defence and Secretary for Indian Affairs; held various other administrative posts as well as medical in the Colony. After retirement from Colonial Service, N London Postgrad. Med. Sch., 1945-46; GP in North Auckland, 1946-58. *Address:* 32 Hororata Road, Takapuna N2, New Zealand.
    See also Sir R . H . Garvey.

McHARDY, Prof. William Duff; Regius Professor of Hebrew, Oxford University, and Student of Christ Church, since 1960; *b* 26 May 1911; *o s* of late W. D. McHardy, Cullen, Banffshire; *m* 1941, Vera, *y d* of late T. Kemp, York; one *d. Educ:* Fordyce Academy; Universities of Aberdeen, Edinburgh, and Oxford (St John's College). MA, BD (Aberdeen), MA (Edinburgh), DPhil (Oxford). Research Fellow in Syriac, Selly Oak Colleges, Birmingham, 1942; Lecturer in Aramaic and Syriac, University of Oxford, 1945; Samuel Davidson Professor of Old Testament Studies in the University of London, 1948-60. Examiner, Universities of Aberdeen, Cambridge, Durham, Edinburgh, Leeds, London, Oxford and University Colleges of the Gold Coast/Ghana and Ibadan. Hon. Curator of Mingana Collection of Oriental Manuscripts, 1947. Grinfield Lecturer on the Septuagint, Oxford, 1959-61. Dir, New English Bible. Burgess, Royal Burgh of Cullen, 1975. Hon. DD Aberdeen, 1958. *Publications:* articles in journals. *Address:* Christ Church, Oxford; 44 Davenant Road, Oxford. *T:* Oxford 55432.

MACHIN, Arnold, OBE 1965; RA 1956 (ARA 1947); sculptor, FRBS 1955; Master of Sculpture, Royal Academy School, 1958-67; Tutor, Royal College of Art, 1951-58; *b* 1911; *s* of William James Machin, Stoke-on-Trent; *m* 1949, Patricia, *d* of late Lt-Col Henry Newton; one *s. Educ:* Stoke School of Art; Derby School of Art; Royal College of Art. Silver Medal and Travelling Scholarship for Sculpture, 1940; two works in terracotta: St John the Baptist and The Annunciation, purchased by Tate Gallery, 1943; Spring terracotta purchased by President and Council of Royal Academy under terms of Chantrey Bequest, 1947; designed: new coin effigy, 1964, 1967 (decimal coinage); definitive issue of postage stamp, 1967; Silver Wedding

commemorative crown, 1972; commemorative Silver Jubilee crown, 1977. *Recreation:* music. *Address:* 4 Sydney Close, SW3; Offley Rock, Bishop's Offley, Staffordshire.

MACHIN, Edward Anthony, QC 1973; a Recorder of the Crown Court, since 1976; *b* 28 June 1925; *s* of Edward Arthur Machin and Olive Muriel Smith; *m* 1953, Jean Margaret McKanna; two *s* one *d. Educ:* Christ's Coll., Finchley; New Coll., Oxford. MA 1950; BCL 1950; Vinerian Law Scholar, 1950; Tancred Student, 1950; Cassel Scholar, 1951. Called to Bar, Lincoln's Inn, 1951. *Publications:* Redgrave's Factories Acts, 1962, 1966, 1972; Redgrave's Offices and Shops, 1965 and 1973; Redgrave's Health and Safety in Factories, 1976. *Recreations:* music, sailing, languages. *Address:* 11 Bedford Road, Moor Park, Herts. *T:* Northwood 24869. *Club:* Bar Yacht.

MACHIN, George; *b* 30 Dec. 1922; *s* of Edwin and Ada Machin, Sheffield; *m* 1949, Margaret Ena (*née* Heard); one *s. Educ:* Marlcliffe Sch., Sheffield. Served RAF, 1943-47. Engineering Inspector. Shop Steward, and Mem., Sheffield District Cttee, AUEW. Sec., Sheffield Heeley Constituency Lab. Party, 1966-73. Mem., Sheffield City Council, 1967-74. MP (Lab) Dundee E, March 1973-Feb. 1974; contested (Lab) Dundee E, Oct. 1974. Governor, Granville Coll. of Further Educn, Sheffield. *Recreations:* swimming, walking. *Address:* 1 Rattray Street, Dundee. *T:* Dundee 24628.

MACHIN, Kenneth Arthur, QC 1977; *b* 13 July 1936; *o s* of Thomas Arthur Machin and Edith May Machin. *Educ:* St Albans School. Called to the Bar, Middle Temple, 1960; South Eastern Circuit. *Address:* 3 Hare Court, Temple, EC4. *T:* 01-353 7741.

McHUGH, Dr Mary Patricia; Coroner for Southern District of London, since 1965; *b* 5 June 1915; *d* of J. C. McHugh, MB, BS, BAO, Royal Univ., Dublin, and Madeleine Jeffroy Leblan, Brittany, France; *m* 1943, E. G. Murphy, FRCS (marr. diss., 1952); one *s* two *d. Educ:* Nymphenburg, Munich, Bavaria; Notre Dame, Clapham; Birmingham Univ. MB, ChB, 1942; PhD Fac. of Laws, London 1976. Birmingham House Physician and Anæsthetist, St Chad's Hospital, Birmingham, 1942-43; General Practice, London, 1944-65. Called to the Bar, Inner Temple, 1959. Past Chm., Whole Time Coroner's Assoc.; Mem., British Academy of Forensic Sciences, 1963; Founder Mem., RCGP. *Publication:* Treasure Trove and the Law (Med. Sci. Law vol. 16 no 2). *Recreations:* cooking, languages. *Address:* 8 Hitherwood Drive, College Road, Dulwich, SE19. *T:* 01-681 2533, ext. 24, (home) 01-670 8400.

McILVEEN, Brig. Sir Arthur William, Kt 1970; MBE 1961; Brigadier, Salvation Army, New South Wales. Career of service to Servicemen and ex-Servicemen; Padre, Rats of Tobruk Assoc. *Address:* 23 Eddystone Road, Bexley, NSW 2207, Australia.

McILWAIN, Prof. Henry, DSc, PhD; Professor of Biochemistry in the University of London at Institute of Psychiatry, British Postgraduate Medical Federation, since 1954; Hon. Biochemist, Bethlem Royal Hospital and Maudsley Hospital, since 1948; *b* Newcastle upon Tyne, 20 Dec. 1912; *e s* of John McIlwain, Glasgow, and Louisa (*née* Widdowson), Old Whittington; *m* 1941, Valerie, *d* of K. Durston, Bude, Cornwall; two *d. Educ:* King's Coll., Newcastle upon Tyne (University of Durham); The Queen's Coll., Oxford. Leverhulme Research Fellow and later Mem. of Scientific Staff, Medical Research Council, in Council's Dept of Bacterial Chemistry (Middlesex Hosp., London) and Unit for Research in Cell Metabolism (Univ. of Sheffield), 1937-47; Lectr in Biochemistry, Univ. of Sheffield, 1944-47; Senior Lectr (later Reader) in Biochemistry, Inst. of Psychiatry (British Postgraduate Medical Fedn), Univ. of London, 1948-54; Mem. Editorial Bd, Biochemical Jl, 1947-50; Research Associate, Univ. of Chicago, 1951; Visiting Lectr, Univ. of Otago, New Zealand, 1954; Lectr and Medallist, Univ. of Helsinki, 1973; Thudichum Lectr and Medallist, Biochemical Soc., 1975; Dr *hc* Univ. d'Aix-Marseille, 1974. *Publications:* Biochemistry and the Central Nervous System, 1955, 4th edn (with H. S. Bachelard), 1971; Chemotherapy and the Central Nervous System, 1957; (with R. Rodnight) Practical Neurochemistry, 1962; Chemical Exploration of the Brain, 1963; (ed) Practical Neurochemistry, 1975; 250 papers in the Biochemical Journal and other scientific and medical publications. *Address:* 73 Court Lane, SE21 7EF. *T:* 01-693 5334.

McILWRAITH, Arthur Renwick; Sheriff of South Strathclyde, Dumfries and Galloway (formerly Lanark) at Airdrie since 1972; *b* 8 April 1914; *s* of Nicholas Renwick McIlwraith and Adaline Gowans McIlwraith; *m* 1950, Thelma Preston or Sargent; one *s* one *d. Educ:* High Sch. of Glasgow; Univ. of Glasgow (MA, LLB). Grad. 1938. Served War: Highland Light

Infantry, 1939-45. Solicitor, 1945-72. *Recreation:* fishing. *Address:* 17 Bellshaugh Road, Glasgow G12 0SF. *T:* 041-339 6751. *Club:* Nomads.

McINDOE, William Ian; Deputy Secretary, Cabinet Office, since 1976; *b* 11 March 1929; *s* of John McIndoe, Leven, Fife and Agnes Scott; *m* 1st, 1954, Irene Armour Mudie (*d* 1966); one *s* two *d*; 2nd, 1971, Jamesanna Smart (*née* MacGregor). *Educ:* Sedbergh; Corpus Christi Coll., Oxford (MA). 2nd Lieut 2 RHA, 1951-53; entered Commonwealth Relations Office as Asst Principal, 1953; served: Canberra, 1956-58; 1st Sec., Salisbury, 1958-62; Private Sec. to Commonwealth Sec., 1962-63; Private Sec. to Sec. of Cabinet, 1963-65; Asst Sec., Cabinet Office, 1965-66; Scottish Educn Dept, 1966-69; Scottish Develt Dept, 1969-71; Under-Sec., Dept of Agriculture and Fisheries for Scotland, 1971-75; Under Sec., Scottish Economic Planning Dept, 1975-76. *Recreations:* ski-ing, golf. *Address:* 35 Fitzgerald Avenue, SW14 8SZ. *T:* 01-878 2626. *Club:* Royal Commonwealth Society.

MacINNES, Archibald, CVO 1977; Director, London Region, Property Services Agency, Department of the Environment, since 1972; *b* 10 April 1919; *s* of Duncan and Catherine MacInnes; *m* 1950, Nancey Elisabeth Blyth (*d* 1976); one *s* two *d*. *Educ:* Kirkcudbright Academy; Royal Technical Coll., Glasgow. FIMechE. Scott's Shipbuilding and Engineering Co., Greenock, 1937-44; Colonial Service, Nigeria, 1945-59; War Office Works Organisation: Gibraltar, 1959-63; Southern Comd, Salisbury, Wilts, 1963-64; MPBW, Bristol, 1964-68; DoE, Germany, 1968-72. Coronation Medal. *Recreations:* golf, shooting, fishing, gardening. *Address:* (office) St Christopher House, Southwark Street, SE1 0TE. *T:* 01-928 7999, ext. 4569; (home) Lower Road, Homington, Salisbury, Wilts. *T:* Combe Bissett 336.

MacINNES, Helen Clark; novelist; *b* 7 Oct. 1907; *d* of Donald McInnes and Jessica Cecilia Sutherland McDiarmid; *m* 1932, Gilbert Highet, *qv*; one *s*. *Educ:* The Hermitage Sch., Helensburgh; The High School for Girls, Glasgow; Glasgow Univ. (MA); University College, London. *Publications:* Above Suspicion, 1941; Assignment in Brittany, 1942; The Unconquerable, 1944; Horizon, 1945; Friends and Lovers, 1947; Rest and Be Thankful, 1949; Neither Five Nor Three, 1951; I and My True Love, 1953; Pray for a Brave Heart, 1955; North from Rome, 1958; Decision at Delphi, 1961; The Venetian Affair, 1963; Home is the Hunter (play), 1964; The Double Image, 1966; The Salzburg Connection, 1968; Message from Málaga, 1972; The Snare of the Hunter, 1974; Agent in Place, 1976. *Recreations:* two-piano duets; the American West. *Address:* 15 Jefferys Lane, East Hampton, NY 11937, USA.

McINNES, John Colin; Sheriff of Tayside Central and Fife at Cupar and Kirkcaldy, since 1974; *b* 21 Nov. 1938; *s* of late Mr I. W. McInnes, WS, and of Mrs Lucy McInnes, Cupar, Fife; *m* 1966, Elisabeth Mabel Neilson; one *s* one *d*. *Educ:* Cargilfield Sch., Edinburgh; Merchiston Castle Sch., Edinburgh; Brasenose Coll., Oxford (BA); Edinburgh Univ. (LLB). 2nd Lieut 8th Royal Tank Regt, 1957-58; Lieut Fife and Forfar Yeomanry/Scottish Horse (TA), 1958-64. Advocate, 1963. In practice at Scottish Bar, 1963-73; Tutor, Faculty of Law, Edinburgh Univ., 1965-73; Sherfiff of the Lothians and Peebles, 1973-74. Contested (C) Aberdeen North, 1964. *Recreations:* shooting, fishing, gardening, photography. *Address:* Parkneuk, Blebo Craigs, Cupar, Fife KY15 5UG. *T:* Strathkinness 366.

MacINNES, Keith Gordon; HM Diplomatic Service; Counsellor and Head of Chancery, UK Mission, Geneva, since 1977; *b* 17 July 1935; *s* of Kenneth MacInnes and Helen MacInnes (*née* Gordon); *m* 1966, Jennifer Anne Fennell; one *s* one *d*. *Educ:* Rugby; Trinity Coll., Cambridge (MA). HM Forces, 1953-55. FO, 1960; Third, later Second Secretary, Buenos Aires, 1961-64; FO, 1964 (First Sec., 1965); Private Sec. to Permanent Under-Sec., Commonwealth Office, 1965-68; First Sec. (Information), Madrid, 1968-70; FCO, 1970-74; Counsellor and Head of Chancery, Prague, 1974-77. *Recreations:* chess, bridge. *Address:* c/o Foreign and Commonwealth Office, SW1A 2AH.

McINTOSH, Sir Alister (Donald), KCMG 1973 (CMG 1957); Chairman of Trustees, National Library of New Zealand, since 1970; Chairman, New Zealand Historic Places Trust, since 1973; *b* Picton, NZ, 29 Nov. 1906; *e s* of Harry Hobson and Caroline McIntosh; *m* 1934, Doris Hutchinson Pow; one *s*. *Educ:* Marlborough Coll., Blenheim; Victoria University, Wellington, NZ (MA); University of Michigan, Ann Arbor, USA. Labour Dept, 1925; Parliamentary Library, 1926-34; Carnegie Travelling Fellowship, 1932-33; Prime Minister's Dept, New Zealand, 1935-66; Secretary of War Cabinet, 1943-45; Sec. of External Affairs, NZ, 1943-66; Permanent Head, Prime Minister's Dept, 1945-66; New Zealand Ambassador to Italy, 1966-70; Chm., Broadcasting Council of NZ, 1973-76. Attended many Commonwealth Prime Ministers' conferences and United Nations Assemblies as adviser or delegate, 1944-66. Chm., NZ Historic Places Trust, 1973-. Hon. LLD, Univ. of Canterbury, NZ, 1965. *Publication:* Marlborough Provincial History, 1939. *Address:* 11 Wesley Road, Wellington, New Zealand. *Club:* Wellington.

McINTOSH, Prof. Angus; Forbes Professor of English Language, University of Edinburgh, since 1964; *b* 10 Jan. 1914; *s* of late Kenneth and Mary McIntosh (*née* Thompson), Cleadon, Sunderland, Co. Durham; *m* 1939, Barbara, *d* of late Dr William Seaman and Mrs Bainbridge (*née* June Wheeler), New York City; two *s* one *d*. *Educ:* Ryhope Grammar Sch., Co. Durham; Oriel Coll., Oxford (BA, 1st Class Hons, English Lang., and Lit., 1934); Merton Coll., Oxford (Harmsworth Scholar); (Dip. of Comparative Philology, University of Oxford, 1936); Harvard Univ. (Commonwealth Fund Fellow, AM, 1937). MA (Oxford) 1938. Lecturer, Dept of English, University College, Swansea, 1938-46. Served War of 1939-45, beginning as trooper in Tank Corps, finishing as Major in Intelligence Corps. University Lecturer in Mediæval English, Oxford, 1946-48; Lecturer in English, Christ Church, Oxford, 1946-47; Student of Christ Church, 1947-48; Prof. of English Language and General Linguistics, Univ. of Edinburgh, 1948-64; Rockefeller Foundation Fellowship, US, June-Sept. 1949. For. Mem., Finnish Acad. of Science and Letters, 1976. Hon. DPhil Poznan Univ., 1972. *Publications:* books, articles and reviews on subject of English language and related topics. *Recreations:* tennis, squash, fishing, gardening, painting. *Address:* 32 Blacket Place, Edinburgh EH9 1RL. *T:* 031-667 5791. *Club:* Savile.

MacINTOSH, Prof. Frank Campbell; FRS 1954; FRSC 1956; J. M. Drake Professor of Physiology, McGill University, Montreal, Canada, since 1949; *b* 24 Dec. 1909; *s* of Rev. C. C. MacIntosh, DD, and Beenie MacIntosh (*née* Matheson); *m* 1938, Mary M. MacKay; two *s* three *d*. *Educ:* Dalhousie Univ., Halifax, NS (MA); McGill Univ. (PhD). Member of research staff, Medical Research Council of Great Britain, 1938. Hon. LLD: Alberta, 1964; Queen's, 1965; Dalhousie, 1976; Hon. MD Ottawa, 1974. *Publications:* papers in physiological journals. *Address:* Department of Physiology, McGill University, Montreal H3G 1Y6, Canada; 145 Wolseley Avenue, Montreal West, H4X 1V8, Canada. *T:* 481-7939.

McINTOSH, Rev. Canon Hugh; Rector of Christ Church, Lanark, since 1970; *b* 5 June 1914; *s* of Hugh Burns McIntosh and Mary (*née* Winter); *m* 1951, Ruth Georgina, *er d* of late Rev. William Skinner Wilson and Enid (*née* Sanders); two *s* one *d*. *Educ:* Hatfield Coll., Durham (Exhibr); Edinburgh Theological Coll. (Luscombe Schol.). LTh, 1941; BA (dist.), 1942; MA 1945. Deacon and Priest, 1942. Precentor and Senior Chaplain, St Paul's Cathedral, Dundee, 1942-46; Senior Chaplain, St Mary's Cathedral, Edinburgh, 1946-49; Curate, St Salvador's, Edinburgh, 1949-51; Rector, St Adrian's, Gullane, 1951-54; Rector, St John's, Dumfries, 1954; Canon of St Mary's Cathedral, Glasgow, and Synod Clerk of Glasgow and Galloway, 1959; Provost of St Mary's Cathedral, Glasgow, 1966-70. *Recreations:* reading, writing, and (a little) arithmetic. *Address:* The Rectory, Lanark, Scotland. *T:* Lanark 3065.

McINTOSH, Vice-Admiral Sir Ian (Stewart), KBE 1973 (MBE 1941); CB 1970; DSO 1944; DSC 1942; Management Selection Consultant, since 1973; *b* 11 Oct. 1919; *s* of late A. J. McIntosh, Melbourne, Australia; *m* 1943, Elizabeth Rosemary Rasmussen; three *s* (one *d* decd). *Educ:* Geelong Grammar Sch. Entered RN, 1938; comd HM Submarine: H44, 1942; Sceptre, 1943-44; Alderney, 1946-48; Aeneas, 1950-51; Exec. Officer, HMS Ark Royal, 1956-58; comd 2nd Submarine Sqn, 1961-63; comd HMS Victorious, 1966-68; Dir-Gen., Weapons (Naval), 1968-70; Dep. Chief of Defence Staff (Op. Req.), 1971-73, retd 1973. Captain, 1959; Rear-Adm., 1968; Vice-Adm., 1971. Chairman: Sea Cadet Assoc.; HMS Cavalier Trust. *Recreations:* friends, reading, music. *Address:* 19 The Crescent, Alverstoke, Hants. *T:* Gosport 80510. *Club:* Royal Over-Seas League.

MACINTOSH, Sir Robert (Reynolds), Kt 1955; MA, DM, FRCSE, DA; FFARCS; Hon. Fellow: Faculties of Anæsthetists of Australasia, 1950, of Ireland, 1964, of England, 1968; Royal Society of Medicine, 1966; Pembroke College, Oxford, 1965; Nuffield Professor of Anæsthetics, Oxford University, 1937-65; former Hon. Consultant in Anæsthetics, Royal Air Force; *b* Timaru, New Zealand, 17 Oct. 1897; *s* of C. N. Macintosh. *Educ:* Waitaki, New Zealand; Guy's Hospital. Served European War (despatches), Spanish Civil War (Order of Military Merit); War of 1939-45 (Order of Liberty, Norway). Hon. FRCOG. Dr hc Univs of Buenos Aires, Aix-Marseilles and Poznan; Hon.

DSc: Univ. of Wales; Med. Coll. of Ohio. *Publications:* Textbooks, Essentials of General Anæsthesia, Physics for the Anæsthetist, Lumbar Puncture and Spinal Analgesia, Local Anæsthesia, Brachial Plexus; various articles on anæsthesia in medical and dental journals. *Recreations:* golf, tennis. *Address:* 326 Woodstock Road, Oxford. *Clubs:* Bath, Royal Air Force.

McINTOSH, Sir Ronald (Robert Duncan), KCB 1975 (CB 1968); a Director, S. G. Warburg & Co. Ltd, since 1978; *b* 26 Sept. 1919; *s* of late Thomas Steven McIntosh, MD, FRCP, FRCS, and late Christina Jane McIntosh; *m* 1951, Doreen Frances, *o d* of late Commander Andrew MacGinnity, Frinton-on-Sea. *Educ:* Charterhouse (Scholar); Balliol Coll., Oxford. Served in Merchant Navy, 1939-45; Second Mate, 1943-45. Assistant Principal, Board of Trade, 1947; seconded to Dollar Exports Board as General Manager, 1949-51; Trade Commissioner, New Delhi, 1957-61; attached to Lord President's office for work on problems of North East England, April-Oct. 1963; Under-Secretary: Board of Trade, 1963-64; Dept of Economic Affairs, 1964-66; Dep. Under-Sec. of State, 1966-68; Dep. Secretary, Cabinet Office, 1968-70; Dep. Under-Sec. of State, Dept of Employment, 1970-72; Dep. Sec., HM Treasury, 1972-73; Dir-Gen. Nat. Economic Development Office, and Mem. NEDC, 1973-77. Mem., British Overseas Trade Adv. Cttee, 1975-. Chm., King's Coll. Hosp. Medical Sch. Council, 1975-77. Lubbock Meml Lectr, 1974; Mercantile Credit Lect., 1976. Governor, NIESR, 1974-; Mem. Exec. Cttee, PEP. FBIM; FRSA. Hon. DSc Aston, 1977. *Recreations:* sailing, travel. *Address:* 30 Gresham Street, EC2. *Club:* Royal Thames Yacht.

MacINTYRE, Prof. Alasdair Chalmers; University Professor in Philosophy and Political Science, Boston University, since 1972; *b* 12 Jan. 1929; *o s* of Eneas John MacIntyre, MD (Glasgow), and Margaret Emily Chalmers, MB, ChB (Glasgow); *m* 1st, 1953, Ann Peri (marr. diss. 1963); two *d*; 2nd, 1963, Susan Margery Willans; one *s* one *d*. *Educ:* Epsom Coll. and privately; Queen Mary Coll., Univ. of London; Manchester Univ. BA (London); MA (Manchester); MA (Oxon). Lectr in Philosophy of Religion, Manchester Univ., 1951-55; Lectr in Philosophy, Leeds Univ., 1957-61; Research Fellow, Nuffield Coll., Oxford, 1961-62; Sen. Fellow, Council of Humanities, Princeton Univ., 1962-63; Fellow and Preceptor in Philosophy, University Coll., Oxford, 1963-66; Prof. of Sociology, Univ. of Essex, 1966-70; Prof. of History of Ideas, Brandeis Univ., 1970-72. Riddell Lectr, Univ. of Newcastle upon Tyne, 1964; Bampton Lectr, Columbia Univ., USA, 1966. Mem. Nat. Coun. for Diplomas in Art and Design, 1969-70. Hon. Mem., Phi Beta Kappa, 1973; Metcalfe Prize, 1974. *Publications:* Marxism and Christianity, 1954 (revised, 1968); New Essays in Philosophical Theology (ed, with A. G. N. Flew), 1955; Metaphysical Beliefs (ed), 1956; The Unconscious: a conceptual analysis, 1958; A Short History of Ethics, 1965; Secularisation and Moral Change, 1967; Marcuse: an exposition and a polemic, 1970; Sociological Theory and Philosophical Analysis (ed with D. M. Emmet), 1971; Against the Self-Images of the Age, 1971; contributor to: Mind, Philosophy, Philosophical Review, Jl of Philosophy, Amer. Jl of Sociology, Brit. Jl of Sociology, Encounter, New York Review of Books. *Recreations:* walking, reading trash, cooking, sleeping. *Address:* 621 Hale Street, Beverly Farms, Mass 01915, USA. *T:* 617-927-3107.

MACINTYRE, Hon. Sir Donald, Kt 1961; CBE 1947; MP Bulawayo, Federation of Rhodesia and Nyasaland, 1954-63 (MP Bulawayo Central, Southern Rhodesia, 1934-53); *b* Glasgow, 9 Sept. 1891; *s* of Peter Macintyre; *m* 1st, 1912, Gertrude Gill (*d* 1976), Redruth, Cornwall, England; 2nd, 1976, Blanche Gwendoline Fikuart (*née* Horn). *Educ:* Dowanhill Sch., Glasgow. Councillor of Bulawayo (Mayor, various periods). Chairman: Osborn's Bakeries Ltd (also Managing Director); Rhodesian Investment Trust Co. Ltd; Founder and Director McIntyre & Son; Director of other companies. Minister of Finance, Federation of Rhodesia amd Nyasaland, 1953-62. JP Southern Rhodesia, 1935; 1st Alderman, City of Bulawayo, 1950; Freedom of City of Bulawayo, 1955. *Address:* 12 Hall Road, Kumalo, Bulawayo, Rhodesia.

McINTYRE, Donald Conroy; opera singer, free-lance; *b* 22 Oct. 1934; *s* of George Douglas McIntyre and Mrs Hermyn McIntyre; *m*; three *d*. *Educ:* Mount Albert Grammar Sch.; Auckland Teachers' Trng Coll.; Guildhall Sch. of Music. Debut in Britain, Welsh National Opera, 1959; Sadler's Wells Opera, many roles, 1960-67; Royal Opera, Covent Garden, from 1967; also Vienna, Bayreuth, La Scala, Milan and Metropolitan, NY. Principal roles: Barak, in Die Frau Ohne Schatten, Strauss; Wotan and Wanderer, in The Ring, Wagner; Hollander, Wagner; Heyst, in Victory, Richard Rodney Bennet; Bayreuth: Wotan, Wanderer, Hollander, Telramund, in Lohengrin, Klingsor and Amfortas in Parsifal. *Recreations:* gardening,

swimming, tennis. *Address:* 2 Roseneath Close, Orpington, Kent. *T:* Farnborough (Kent) 55368.

McINTYRE, His Honour F(rederick) Donald (Livingstone), QC 1955; a Circuit Judge (formerly Judge of County Courts), 1962-77; *b* 8 July 1905; 2nd *s* of William and Marjorie McIntyre; *m* 1972, Mrs Marjorie Joyce Bowman. *Educ:* Cardiff High Sch.; St Olave's; St John's Coll., Cambridge (History Scholar and MacMahon Law Student; BA, LLB). Called to Bar, Gray's Inn, 1928; joined Inner Temple, 1936. Served War, 1941-46; Officer Royal Air Force (POW, Far East, 1942-45). Dep. Chairman Inner London Sessions, 1965-71; JP Surrey, 1960. *Recreations:* cricket and chess. *Address:* 14 Northwick Terrace, NW8. *T:* 01-289 0897. *Clubs:* Royal Automobile; Union Society (Cambridge).

MacINTYRE, Prof. Iain; Professor of Endocrine Chemistry, University of London, and Director, Endocrine Unit, Royal Postgraduate Medical School, since 1974 (Joint Director, 1967-74); Chairman, Division of Biological Chemistry, since 1974; Hon. Consultant Pathologist, Hammersmith Hospital, since 1960; *b* 30 Aug. 1924; *s* of John MacIntyre, Tobermory, and Margaret Fraser Shaw, Stratherick, Inverness-shire; *m* 1947, Mabel Wilson Jamieson, MA, *y d* of George Jamieson, Largs, Ayrshire; one *d*. *Educ:* Jordanhill Coll. Sch., Glasgow; Univ. of Glasgow. MB, ChB Glasgow 1947; PhD London 1960; MRCPath 1963 (Founder Mem.), FRCPath 1971; FRCP 1977 (MRCP 1969); DSc London 1970. Asst Clinical Pathologist, United Sheffield Hosps, and Hon. Demonstrator in Biochem., Sheffield Univ., 1948-52; Registrar in Chemical Pathology, 1952-54; Sir Jack Drummond Meml Fellow, 1954-56; Asst Lectr in Chem. Path., 1956-59; Reader in Chem. Path., Royal Postgrad. Med. Sch., 1963-67. Vis. Scientist, Nat. Insts of Health, Bethesda, 1960-61; Vis. Prof. of Med., San Francisco Medical Center, 1964. Chm. Organizing Cttee, Hammersmith Internat. Symposium on Endocrinology, 1967-77; Cttee Mem., Soc. for Endocrinology. Member Editorial Board: Clinical Endocrinology; Molecular and Cellular Endocrinology; Jl of Endocrinological Investigation; Jl of Mineral and Electrolyte Metabolism. Gairdner Internat. Award, Toronto, 1967. *Publications:* numerous articles on endocrinology and mineral metabolism. *Recreations:* squash, tennis, chess, music. *Address:* 76 Waterford Road, SW6 2DR. *T:* 01-731 2429. *Club:* Hurlingham.

McINTYRE, Ian James; Controller, BBC Radio 4, since 1976; *b* Banchory, Kincardineshire, 9 Dec. 1931; *y s* of Hector Harold McIntyre, Inverness, and Annie Mary Michie, Ballater; *m* 1954, Leik Sommerfelt, 2nd *d* of late Benjamin Vogt, Kragerø, Norway; two *s* two *d*. *Educ:* Prescot Grammar Sch.; St John's Coll., Cambridge (Scholar; Med. and Mod. Langs Tripos, Pts I and II; BA 1953); Coll. of Europe, Bruges. Pres., Cambridge Union, 1953. Commnd, Intelligence Corps, 1955-57. Current affairs talks producer, BBC, 1957; Editor, At Home and Abroad, 1959; Man. Trng Organiser, BBC Staff Trng Dept, 1960; Programme Services Officer, ITA, 1961; staff of Chm., Cons. Party in Scotland, 1962; Dir of Inf. and Res., Scottish Cons. Central Office, 1965; contested (C) Roxburgh, Selkirk and Peebles, 1966; long-term contract, writer and broadcaster, BBC, 1970-76; presenter and interviewer, Analysis, and other programmes on politics, for. affairs and the arts; travelled widely in Europe, N America, Africa, Asia and ME. *Publications:* The Proud Doers: Israel after twenty years, 1968; (ed and contrib.) Words: reflections on the uses of language, 1975; articles in The Listener. *Recreation:* family life. *Address:* BBC, Broadcasting House, W1A 1AA. *T:* 01-580 4468. *Clubs:* Constitutional; Union (Cambridge).

McINTYRE, Rev. Canon James; Canon Emeritus of Gloucester Cathedral, since 1968; Fellow, University College, Durham, since 1950; working in Trinity College, Toronto, since 1968; *e s* of late Robert and Matilda Anne McIntyre, Auchterarder, Scotland; *m* 1st, 1915, Sybil Mary (*d* 1960), *d* of late Sir H. F. Norbury, KCB, KHS, RN; one *d*; 2nd, 1961, Isolde Meinhardt, *d* of late Gustav Adolf Meinhardt and Marie Dorothea Meinhardt. *Educ:* Merchant Taylors' Sch.; University College, Durham (BA, MLitt); Ely Theological Coll.; S John's Coll., University of Manitoba (BD 1st class); Trinity Coll., University of Toronto (DD). Deacon, 1913; Priest, 1914; Curate of Holy Trinity, Eltham, 1913-15; Incumbent of S Mary, Edmonton, Canada, 1915-16; Minister of S Barnabas, Epsom, 1916-18; Rector of Washford Pyne, 1918-21; Curate in charge of S Paul's, Newton Abbot, 1922-25; Vicar of Bishop's Teignton, 1925-30; Rector of Holy Trinity, Bath, 1930-32; of Lympstone, 1932-46. Chapter Librarian, Gloucester Cathedral, 1946-52; Receiver, 1955-68. Proctor in Convocation (Diocese of Exeter), 1929-31 and 1936-45. Canon Residentiary of Gloucester Cathedral, 1946-68, Canon Emeritus, 1968-. JP for City of Gloucester,

1950-68. Examining Chaplain to Bishop of Worcester, 1953-68; Chaplain to City High Sheriff, Gloucester, 1953. *Recreations:* sea lore and life.

McINTYRE, Cardinal, His Eminence James Francis Aloysius; Archbishop of Los Angeles, California, 1948-70; *b* New York, 25 June 1886; *s* of late James F. McIntyre and Mary (*née* Pelley). *Educ:* Public Sch. 70; Cathedral Coll. and St Joseph's Seminary, New York. Began work as runner at New York Curb Exchange, 1899; with H. L. Horton Co., Wall Street, 1902-15, rising to Office Manager; studied at evening schs and left business world, 1915. Graduated from Cathedral Coll., 1916; Priest, 1921; Curate of St Gabriel's Church, 1921-23; Asst Chancellor and Asst Diocesan Sec., New York, 1923; Chancellor, 1934; Papal Chamberlain, 1934; Domestic Prelate, 1936; Mem. Diocesan Board of Consultors, 1939; Titular Bishop of Cyrene and Auxiliary Bishop of New York, 1941; a Vicar-Gen., Diocese of New York, 1945; Coadjutor Archbishop and Titular Archbishop of Paltus, 1946; Cardinal, 1953. Knight Grand Cross of the Holy Sepulchre, 1946. *Address:* 637 South Kingsley Drive, Los Angeles, Calif 90005, USA.

McINTYRE, James Gordon; *see* Sorn, Hon. Lord.

McINTYRE, Very Rev. Prof. John, DD, DLitt; FRSE; Professor of Divinity, University of Edinburgh, since 1956; Dean of the Order of the Thistle, since 1974; Chaplain to the Queen in Scotland, since 1975 (Extra Chaplain, 1974-75); *b* 20 May 1916; *s* of late John C. McIntyre, Bathgate, Scotland, and Annie McIntyre; *m* 1945, Jessie B., *d* of late William Buick, Coupar Angus; two *s* one *d*. *Educ:* Bathgate Academy; University of Edinburgh; MA (1938); BD (1941); DLitt (1953). Ordained, 1941; Locum Tenens, Parish of Glenorchy and Inishail, 1941-43; Minister of Parish of Fenwick, Ayrshire, 1943-45; Hunter Baillie Prof. of Theology, St Andrew's Coll., University of Sydney, 1946-56; Principal of St Andrew's Coll., 1950-56; Principal Warden, Pollock Halls of Residence, Univ. of Edinburgh, 1960-71; actg Principal and Vice-Chancellor, Edinburgh Univ., 1973-74; Principal, New Coll., and Dean of Faculty of Divinity, 1968-74. FRSE 1977. DD *hc* Glasgow, 1961. *Publications:* St Anselm and His Critics, 1954; The Christian Doctrine of History, 1957; On the Love of God, 1962; The Shape of Christology, 1966; articles and reviews in various learned jls of Theology. *Address:* 11 Minto Street, Edinburgh EH9 1RG. *T:* 031-667 1203.

McINTYRE, Air Commodore Kenneth John, CB 1958; CBE 1951; JP; RAF retired; *b* 23 July 1908; *s* of late William Seymour McIntyre and Winifred May McIntyre, Clevedon, Somerset; *m* 1936, Betty Aveley, *o d* of late Lt-Col Percie C. Cooper, Dulwich. *Educ:* Blundell's Sch.; RMC Sandhurst. Commissioned Royal Tank Regt, 1928; served UK and India; seconded to RAF 1934; permanent commission RAF, 1945. Served War of 1939-45 in UK, France and Belgium. Dep. Dir of Organisation, Air Ministry, 1945-47; Joint Services Staff Coll., 1947-48; Group Capt. 1947; Group Capt. Operations, HQ MEAF, 1948-50; idc 1951; SHAPE (Paris), 1952-54; Air Commodore, 1955; Dir of Policy (Air Staff), Air Ministry, 1955-58. Mem., Dorset CC, 1967; JP Poole, 1967. *Recreation:* gardening. *Address:* The East Penthouse, 57 Branksome Court, Canford Cliffs, Poole, Dorset BH13 7BD. *T:* Canford Cliffs 708250. *Club:* Royal Air Force.

McINTYRE, Sir Laurence Rupert, Kt 1963; CBE 1960 (OBE 1953); Australian diplomat, retired; Director, Australian Institute of International Affairs; *b* Hobart, Tasmania, 22 June 1912; *s* of late L. T. and Hilda McIntyre; *m* 1938, Judith Mary, *d* of John H. Gould; two *s*. *Educ:* Launceston Grammar Sch.; Tasmania Univ.; Exeter Coll., Oxford (Rhodes Scholar). Served Aust. High Commissioner's Office, London, 1936-40; Dept of External Affairs, Canberra, 1940-42; Aust. Embassy, Washington, 1942-47; Counsellor, Dept of External Affairs, Canberra, 1947-50; Actg Commissioner to Malaya, 1950-51; Asst Sec., Dept of External Affairs, Canberra, 1951-52; Commissioner to Malaya, 1952-54; Sen. External Affairs Officer (Minister), London, 1954-57; Aust. Ambassador to Indonesia, 1957-60, to Japan, 1960-65; Deputy Secretary, Australian Dept of External Affairs, 1965-70; Australian Permanent Rep. to the UN, 1970-75. Hon. LLD Tasmania 1975. *Publication:* contrib. to Some Australians Take Stock, 1938. *Address:* 44 Dominion Circuit, Forrest, Canberra, ACT, Australia. *Clubs:* University (Sydney); Commonwealth (Canberra).

McINTYRE, Robert Douglas, MB, ChB (Edinburgh), DPH (Glasgow); JP; Consultant Chest Physician; *b* Dec. 1913; 3rd *s* of Rev. John E. McIntyre and Catherine, *d* of Rev. William Morison, DD; *m* 1954, Letitia, *d* of Alexander Macleod; one *s*. *Educ:* Hamilton Acad.; Daniel Stewart's Coll.; University of Edinburgh. MP (Scottish Nationalist), Motherwell and Wishaw,

April-July 1945. Contested (SNP): Motherwell, 1950; Perth and E Perthshire, 1951, 1955, 1959, 1964; W Stirlingshire, 1966, 1970; Stirling, Falkirk and Grangemouth, by-election 1971, Feb. and Oct. 1974. Pres., Scottish National Party; Mem., Stirling Town Council (Hon. Treas., 1958-64, Provost, 1967-75). DUniv Stirling 1976. JP Co. Stirling. *Publications:* numerous articles on Scottish, political and medical subjects, including regular contribs to the Scots Independent. *Recreation:* yachting. *Address:* 8 Gladstone Place, Stirling. *T:* Stirling 3456. *Clubs:* Scottish Arts; Royal Northern Yacht.

McINTYRE, Stuart Charles, MBE; FCIS; President, Pearl Assurance Company Ltd, since 1977 (Chairman, 1972-77); *b* 6 Feb. 1912; *s* of James and Eleanor McIntyre; *m* 1938, Edith Irene Walton; two *d*. *Educ:* Dulwich Coll. Joined Pearl Assurance Co. Ltd, 1930; Director, 1952. Served War, RAF, Wing Comdr, 1940-46. Director: Arsenal Football Club Ltd, 1962-; The Charter Trust & Agency Ltd, 1962-; The Cross Investment Trust Ltd, 1962-; Property Holding & Investment Trust Ltd, 1965-; Hanover Gate Property & Investment Co. Ltd, 1965-; Property Selection & Investment Trust Ltd, 1966-; Property Selection Finance Ltd, 1966-. Freeman, City of London; Past Master, Glass Sellers' Company. *Recreation:* Association football. *Address:* Barton, East Close, Middleton-on-Sea, Sussex. *T:* Middleton-on-Sea 3746. *Clubs:* Devonshire, Royal Air Force.

McINTYRE, Prof. William Ian Mackay, PhD; MRCVS; Professor of Veterinary Medicine, since 1961, Dean of the Faculty of Veterinary Medicine, since Jan. 1974, University of Glasgow; *b* 7 July 1919; *s* of George John and Jane McIntyre; *m* 1948, Ruth Dick Galbraith; three *s*. *Educ:* Altnaharra Primary and Golspie Secondary Sch., Sutherland; Royal (Dick) Veterinary Coll. (MRCVS); University of Edinburgh (PhD). Clinical Asst, Royal (Dick) Veterinary Coll., 1944-48; Lectr, Vet. Med., Royal (Dick) Vet. Coll., 1948-51; Sen. Lectr, Vet. Med., University of Glasgow, 1951-61. Seconded to University of East Africa, University Coll., Nairobi, as Dean, Faculty of Veterinary Science, and Prof., Clinical Studies, 1963-67. *Publications:* various, on canine nephritis, parasitic diseases and vaccines and clinical communications. *Address:* University of Glasgow Veterinary Faculty, Bearsden Road, Bearsden, Glasgow G61 1QH. *T:* 041-942 2301.

McINTYRE, Surgeon Rear-Adm. William Percival Edwin, CB 1961; RN retired; *b* 21 Aug. 1903; *s* of George McIntyre, Rathgar, Dublin; *m* 1964, Mrs Eve Robertson-Rodger (*d* 1971), widow of P. J. Robertson-Rodger. *Educ:* St Andrews Coll.; Trinity Coll., Dublin. MB, BCh, BAO 1925; MA, MD 1929. Joined RN as Surg. Lt 1925; Surg.-Comdr 1937; Surg.-Captain 1949. Senior Medical Officer (Medical Sect.), RN Hospital, Chatham, 1950-52 and RN Hospital, Plymouth, 1956-58; Fleet Medical Officer, Home Fleet, 1952-54; Surgeon Rear-Adm. 1958; Dep. Medical Dir-Gen., RN, 1958-62. QHP 1958-62. OStJ 1950; CStJ 1960. *Recreations:* golf, tennis. *Address:* Chasmoor, 68 Terenure Road West, Dublin 6.

McIVOR, Rt. Hon. (William) Basil, PC (NI) 1971; *b* 17 June 1928; 2nd *s* of Rev. Frederick McIvor, Methodist clergyman and Lilly McIvor; *m* 1953, Frances Jill Anderson; two *s* one *d*. *Educ:* Methodist Coll., Belfast; Queen's Univ., Belfast. LLB 1948. Called to NI Bar, 1950; Jun. Crown Counsel, Co. Down, Sept. 1974, Resident Magistrate, Dec. 1974. MP (UU) Larkfield, NI Parlt, 1969; Minister of Community Relations, NI, 1971-72; Member (UU) for S Belfast, NI Assembly, 1973-75; Minister of Education, NI, 1974. Governor, Campbell Coll., 1975-. *Recreations:* golf, music, tennis, gardening. *Address:* Larkfield, River Road, Lambeg, Co. Antrim. *T:* Belfast 619672.

MACK, Prof. Alan Osborne, MDS; FDS RCS; Professor of Dental Prosthetics, Institute of Dental Surgery, University of London, since 1967; Consultant Dental Surgeon, Eastman Dental Hospital; Civilian Consultant in Dental Prosthetics to the Royal Air Force since 1976; *b* 24 July 1918; *s* of Arthur Joseph Mack, Glos, and Florence Emily Mack (*née* Norris); *m* 1943, Marjorie Elizabeth (*née* Westacott); two *s* one *d*. *Educ:* Westbourne Park Sch.; London Univ. LDS RCS 1942; MDS Durham, 1958; FDS RCS 1971. House Surgeon, Royal Dental Hosp., Sch. of Dental Surgery, University of London, 1942-43; served in RAF Dental Branch, 1943-47; Demonstrator, Prosthetics Dept Royal Dental Hosp., 1948; successively Asst Dir, Prosthetics Dept, and Senior Lecturer, London Univ., Royal Dental Hosp., 1949-56; Prof. of Dental Prosthetics, Univ. of Newcastle upon Tyne (formerly King's Coll., Univ. of Durham), 1956-67; Examiner in Dental Prosthetics, Royal Coll. of Surgeons of England, 1956; Examiner, University of Manchester, 1959, Leeds, 1961, Glasgow, 1961, Liverpool, 1965, London, 1965, Edinburgh, 1968, Lagos, 1970, Singapore,

Khartoum, 1977; Examination Visitor, GDC; Advisor, Univ. of Malaya. Mem. Board of Faculty, Royal College of Surgeons, 1959. Pres. British Soc. for Study of Prosthetic Dentistry (BSSPD), 1963. Hon. Consultant, Stoke Mandeville Hosp., 1976. Hon. Mem., Amer. Acad. of Implant Dentures, 1966. *Publications:* Full Dentures, 1971; articles in British Dental Jls. *Recreations:* gardening, horse riding. *Address:* Institute of Dental Surgery, Eastman Dental Hospital, Gray's Inn Road, WC1. *T:* 01-837 7251.

MACK, Hon. Sir William (George), KBE 1967; Chief Justice of the Supreme Court of Queensland, Australia, 1966-71; President: Medical Assessment Tribunal, 1964-71; Land Appeal Court, 1963-71; *b* 2 Nov. 1904; *s* of late A. G. Mack; *m* 1937, Ida, *d* of H. W. Mocatta; one *s* one *d*. *Educ:* Maryborough Grammar Sch., Australia. Called to the Bar, Queensland, 1930; associate to Mr Justice Henchman; served War of 1939-45 (Major), New Guinea and Pacific Islands: Lecturer in Probate, Divorce and Admiralty Law, University of Queensland; Judge of the Supreme Court of Queensland, 1950-66, Actg Chief Justice, 1965. Chm., Central Sugar Cane Prices Board, 1957. *Recreations:* blood horse breeding and racing. *Address:* 64 Neville Road, Bald Hills, Qld 4036, Australia; Wetheron, M/S 472 Gayndah, Qld 4625. *Clubs:* Queensland, Queensland Turf (life member) (Brisbane).

MACK SMITH, Denis, FBA 1976; Senior Research Fellow of All Souls College, Oxford, since 1962; *b* 3 March 1920; *s* of Wilfrid Mack Smith and Altiora Gauntlett; *m* 1963, Catharine Stevenson; two *d*. *Educ:* St Paul's Cathedral Choir Sch.; Haileybury Coll.; Peterhouse, Cambridge Univ. (organ and history schols). MA Cantab, MA Oxon. Asst Master, Clifton Coll., 1941-42; Cabinet Offices, 1942-46; Fellow of Peterhouse, Cambridge, 1947-62 (now Emeritus Fellow); Tutor of Peterhouse, 1948-58; Univ. Lectr, Cambridge, 1952-62. Jt Editor, Nelson History of England. For. Hon. Mem., Amer. Acad. of Arts and Sciences. Awards: Thirlwall, 1949; Serena, 1960; Alba, 1972; Villa di Chiesa, 1973; Mondello, 1975; Nove Muse, Duff Cooper Meml., 1977; Commendatore dell' Ordine al Merito della Reppublica Italiana. *Publications:* Cavour and Garibaldi 1860, 1954; Garibaldi, 1957; (jtly) British Interests in the Mediterranean and Middle East, 1958; Italy, a Modern History, 1959 (enlarged edn 1969); Medieval Sicily, 1968; Modern Sicily, 1968; Da Cavour a Mussolini, 1968; (ed) The Making of Italy 1796-1870, 1968; (ed) Garibaldi, 1969; (ed) E. Quinet, Le Rivoluzioni d'Italia, 1970; Victor Emanuel, Cavour and the Risorgimento, 1971; (ed) G. La Farina, Scritti Politici, 1972; Mussolini's Roman Empire: un monumento al duce, 1976. *Address:* All Souls College, Oxford. *T:* Oxford 722251; White Lodge, Osler Road, Headington, Oxford. *T:* Oxford 62878.

McKAIG, Adm. Sir (John) Rae, KCB 1973; CBE 1966; *b* 24 April 1922; *s* of late Sir John McKaig, KCB, DSO, and Lady (Annie Wright) McKaig (*née* Lee); *m* 1945, Barbara Dawn, *d* of Dr F. K. Marriott, MC, Yoxford, Suffolk; two *s* one *d*. *Educ:* Loretto Sch. Joined RN as Special Entry Cadet, 1939; served in cruisers and destroyers in Home and Mediterranean Waters, 1940-43; in Amphibious Force S at invasion of Normandy, 1944; in coastal forces until 1945; qual. in Communications, 1945; Commander, 1952; Captain, 1959; served as Dep. to Chief Polaris Exec., 1963-66; comd HM Signal Sch., 1966-68; Rear-Adm., 1968; Asst Chief of Naval Staff (Operational Requirements), 1968-70; Vice-Adm., 1970; Flag Officer, Plymouth, and Port Admiral, Devonport, Comdr Central Sub Area, E Atlantic, and Comdr Plymouth Sub Area, Channel, 1970-73; Adm., 1973; UK Mil. Rep. to NATO, 1973-75. *Recreations:* offshore sailing, shooting, fishing. *Address:* Hill House, Hambledon, Hants. *Clubs:* Army and Navy; Royal Ocean Racing.

MACKANESS, George Bellamy, MB, BS, DPhil; FRS 1976; President, Squibb Institute for Medical Research and Development, since 1976; *b* Sydney, Australia, 20 Aug. 1922; *s* of James V. Mackaness and Eleanor F. Mackaness; *m* 1945, Gwynneth Patterson; one *s*. *Educ:* Sydney Univ. (MB, BS Hons 1945); London Univ. (DCP 1948); Univ. of Oxford (Hon. MA 1949, DPhil 1953). Resident MO, Sydney Hosp., 1945-46; Resident Pathologist, Kanematsu Inst. of Pathology, Sydney Hosp., 1946-47; Dept of Path., Brit. Postgrad. Med. Sch., London Univ., 1947-48 (DCP); ANU Trav. Scholarship, Univ. of Oxford, 1948-51; Demonstrator and Tutor in Path., Sir William Dunn Sch. of Path., Oxford, 1949-53; Dept of Experimental Pathology, Australian National University: Sen. Fellow, 1954-58; Associate Prof. of Exp. Path., 1958-60; Professorial Fellow, 1960-63; Vis. Investigator, Rockefeller Univ., NY, 1959-60; Prof. of Microbiology, Univ. of Adelaide, 1963-65; Dir, Trudeau Inst. for Med. Res., NY, 1965-76; Adjunct Prof. of Path., NY Univ. Med. Center, 1969-. Member: Allergy and Immunol. Study Sect., Nat. Insts of Health, 1967-71; Bd of Sci. Counsellors, Nat. Inst. of Allergy and Infect. Diseases, 1971-75; Armed Forces Epidemicol Bd, 1967-73; Bd of Governors, W. Alton Jones Cell Science Center, 1970-72; Council, Tissue Culture Assoc., 1973-. Member: Amer. Assoc. of Immunologists; Amer. Assoc. for Advancement of Science; Reticuloendothelial Soc.; Lung Assoc.; Internat. Union Against Tuberculosis; Amer. Soc. of Microbiologists. Mem. Editorial Boards: Jl of Immunol.; Cellular Immunol.; Infection and Immunity; Jl Reticuloend. System; Revue d'Immunol.; Amer. Rev. of Resp. Diseases. Paul Ehrlich-Ludwig Darmstaedter Prize, 1975. *Address:* 313 Cherry Valley Road, Princeton, NJ 08540, USA. *T:* (609) 921-3495.

MACKAY, family name of **Earl of Inchcape, Lord Reay** and **Baron Tanlaw.**

MACKAY, Alastair, CMG 1966; *b* 27 Sept. 1911; *s* of late Alexander Mackay; *m* 1st, 1939, Janetta Brown Ramsay (*d* 1973); one *s* one *d*; 2nd, 1975, Edith Whicher. *Educ:* George Heriot's Sch.; Edinburgh Univ.; Berlin Univ. Entered HM Treasury, 1940. Member UK Treasury and Supply Delegation, Washington, 1951-54; seconded to Foreign Service Inspectorate, 1957-59; Financial Adviser to the British High Commissioner in India, 1963-66; Under-Sec., HM Treasury, 1967-71; Financial and Develt Sec., Gibraltar, 1971-75. *Recreations:* golf, gardening. *Address:* 26 Arnhem Way, Woodhall Spa, Lincolnshire.

McKAY, Sir Alex, (Sir Alick Benson McKay), KBE 1977 (CBE 1965); Director, News International Ltd (Deputy Chairman, 1969-78, Group Managing Director 1976-77); *b* Adelaide, S Australia, 9 Aug. 1909; *s* of George Hugh McKay, Master Mariner; *m* 1st, 1935, Muriel Frieda Searcy (decd); one *s* two *d*; 2nd, 1973, Beverley Hylton, *widow* of Jack Hylton. Joined News Ltd, Adelaide, 1933; Manager, News Ltd, Melbourne, 1939; Manager, News Ltd, Sydney, 1941; Dir and Gen. Man., Argus & Australasian Ltd, 1952; joined Daily Mirror Group, London, 1957, Dir, 1958. Dir, Internat. Publishing Corporation, 1963-69. Trustee, Reuters Ltd, 1975-. Chm. in London, Victoria Promotion Cttee, Australia. *Address:* c/o News International Ltd, 30 Bouverie Street, EC4. *Clubs:* Hurlingham, Garrick.

McKAY, Maj.-Gen. Alexander Matthew, CB 1975; Secretary, Institution of Mechanical Engineers, since 1976; *b* 14 Feb. 1921; *s* of Colin and Anne McKay; *m* 1949, Betty Margaret Lee; one *s* one *d* (and one *d* decd). *Educ:* Esplanade House Sch.; RN Dockyard Sch.; Portsmouth Polytechnic. CEng, FIEE, FIMechE, FBIM, psc, sm. 2nd Lieut REME, 1943; Lieut 1944; Captain 1944; Major 1947; Lt-Col 1960; Col 1966; Brigadier 1968; Maj.-Gen. 1972. Served with 6th Airborne Div.; Staff Coll., Quetta, 1954; staff appts include GSO2, DAA&QMG, DAQMG, AQMG; Dir, Elect. and Mech. Engrg, Army, 1972-75; Col Comdt, REME, 1974-. Gen. Sec., IChemE, 1975-76. Mem. Council, IEE, 1973-. *Recreations:* fly fishing, restoring antique furniture, outdoor sports. *Address:* North West Lodge, Bishop's Sutton, Alresford, Hants. *Club:* Caledonian.

McKAY, Sir Alick Benson; see McKay, Sir Alex.

McKAY, Andrew Foggo; Director-General, Greater Glasgow Passenger Transport Executive, since 1976; *b* 13 March 1923; *s* of William McKay and Janet Foggo McKay; *m* 1945, Elise Katherine Love; one *s* one *d*. *Educ:* Kirkcaldy High Sch. Joined salaried staff, LNER, 1939. Served war in Royal Navy, 1942-46. Returned to salaried staff, LNER, 1946. British Rail: Traffic Apprentice, 1952; Asst to Traffic Manager, 1956; Asst Dist Passenger Manager, 1960; Asst Dist Goods Manager, 1962; Divl Officer (Finance), 1964; Divl Manager, Glasgow, 1966; Passenger Manager, 1968, Asst to Gen. Manager, 1970, and Passenger Manager, 1972, Scottish Region. Director of Planning, GGPTE, 1973. *Recreations:* golf, walking, gardening. *Address:* 9 Brandon Drive, Bearsden, Glasgow G61 3LN. *T:* (home) 041-942 7310; (office) 041-248 5971.

MacKAY, Andrew James; MP (C) Birmingham Stechford, since March 1977; Partner, Jones MacKay & Croxford, Estate Agents, since 1974; *b* 27 Aug. 1949; *s* of Robert James MacKay and Olive Margaret MacKay; *m* 1975, Diana Joy (*née* Kinchin); one *s*. *Educ:* Solihull. Consultant, Birmingham Housing Industries Ltd, 1973-. *Recreations:* golf, squash, good food. *Address:* (office) 83 Edmund Street, Birmingham B3 2ET. *T:* 021-236 8600. *Clubs:* Birmingham (Birmingham); Olton Golf (Solihull); Aberdovey Golf (Wales); Washwood Heath Conservative (Birmingham).

MACKAY, A(rthur) Stewart, ROI 1949; formerly Lecturer, Hammersmith College of Art; *b* 25 Feb. 1909; British. *Educ:* Wilson's Grammar Sch.; Regent Street Polytechnic School of

Art. Art Master, Regent Street Polytechnic School of Art, 1936, Assistant Lecturer, 1936-60. Served War of 1939-45: enlisted Army, Jan. 1942; released with rank of Captain, 1946. Exhibitor: RA (30 pictures), Paris Salon, ROI, RBA, Leicester Galleries, Imperial War Museum; Royal Scottish Academy; New York. *Publication:* How to Make Lino Cuts, 1935; articles for Artist and Kent Life, 1953, 1963. *Recreation:* reading. *Address:* 4 Dog Kennel Hill, East Dulwich, SE22.

MACKAY, Charles; Chief Agricultural Officer, Department of Agriculture and Fisheries for Scotland, since 1975; *b* 12 Jan. 1927; *s* of Hugh and Eliza MacKay; *m* 1956, Marie A. K. MacKay (*née* Mitchell); one *s* one *d*. *Educ:* Strathmore Sch., Sutherland; Lairg Higher Grade Sch., Sutherland; Univ. of Aberdeen (BScAgric); Univ. of Kentucky (MSc). Department of Agriculture and Fisheries for Scotland: Temporary Inspector, 1947-48; Asst Inspector, 1948-54; Inspector, 1954-64; Sen. Inspector, 1964-70; Technical Develt Officer, 1970-73; Dep. Chief Agricl Officer, 1973-75. Hon. Order of Kentucky Colonels, 1960. *Recreations:* fishing, golf. *Address:* Dun Dornaig, 35 Boswall Road, Edinburgh EH5 3RP. *T:* 031-552 6063.

MacKAY, Prof. Donald Iain; Professor of Economics, Heriot-Watt University, Edinburgh, since 1976; Consultant to Secretary of State for Scotland, since 1971; *b* 27 Feb. 1937; *s* of William and Rhona MacKay; *m* 1961, Diana Marjory (*née* Raffan); one *s* two *d*. *Educ:* Dollar Academy; Univ. of Aberdeen (MA). English Electric Co., 1959-62; Lectr in Political Economy, Univ. of Aberdeen, 1962-65; Lectr in Applied Economics, Univ. of Glasgow, 1965-68, Sen. Lectr, 1968-71; Prof. of Political Economy, Univ. of Aberdeen, 1971-76. Lister Lectr, British Assoc. for the Advancement of Science, 1974; Editor, Scottish Jl of Political Economy, 1971-; Sen. Partner, Planning, Economic and Industrial Development Advisors, 1975-. Member: Council, Royal Economic Soc., 1975-; BBC Gen. Adv. Council, 1976-. *Publications:* Geographical Mobility and the Brain Drain, 1969; Local Labour Markets and Wage Structures, 1970; Labour Markets under Different Employment Conditions, 1971; The Political Economy of North Sea Oil, 1975; (ed) Scotland 1980: the economics of self-government, 1977; articles in Econ. Jl, Oxford Econ. Papers, Manch. Sch., Scottish Jl Polit. Econ., Jl Royal Stat. Soc. *Recreations:* chess, golf. *Address:* Newfield, 14 Gamekeeper's Road, Edinburgh EH4 6LU.

MacKAY, Prof. Donald MacCrimmon, BSc, PhD, FInstP; Granada Research Professor of Communication, University of Keele, since 1960; Joint Editor, Experimental Brain Research; *b* 9 Aug. 1922; *o s* of Dr Henry MacKay; *m* 1955, Valerie Wood; two *s* three *d*. *Educ:* Wick High Sch.; St Andrews Univ. BSc (St Andrews) 1943; PhD (London) 1951. Radar research, Admiralty, 1943-46; Assistant Lecturer in Physics, 1946-48, Lecturer, 1948-59, Reader, 1959-60, King's Coll., London. Rockefeller Fellow in USA, 1951. Vis. Prof., Univ. of California, 1969; Lectures: Eddington, 1967; Herter, Johns Hopkins Univ., 1971; Foerster, Univ. of California, 1973; Drummond, Univ. of Stirling, 1975; Fremantle, Balliol Coll. Oxford, 1975; Riddell, Univ. of Newcastle, 1977. *Publications:* (with M. E. Fisher) Analogue Computing at Ultra-High Speed, 1962; (ed) Christianity in a Mechanistic Universe, 1965; Freedom of Action in a Mechanistic Universe, 1967; Information, Mechanism and Meaning, 1969; The Clockwork Image, 1974; Science, Chance and Providence, 1978; Chapters in: Communication Theory, 1953; Information Theory, 1956, 1961; Sensory Communication, 1961; Man and his Future, 1963; Science in its Context, 1964; Information Processing in the Nervous System, 1964; Brain and Conscious Experience, 1966; Structure and Function of Inhibitory Neuronal Mechanisms, 1968; Evoked Brain Potentials, 1969; The Neurosciences, 1971; Non-Verbal Communication, 1972; Handbook of Sensory Physiology, 1973; Cybernetics and Bionics, 1974, etc.; scientific papers on electronic computing, information theory, experimental psychology, neurophysiology. *Recreation:* photography. *Address:* The Croft, Keele, Staffs ST5 5AN. *T:* Newcastle (Staffs) 627300.

MACKAY, Eric Beattie; Editor of The Scotsman since 1972; *b* 31 Dec. 1922; *s* of Lewis Mackay and Agnes Johnstone; *m* 1954, Moya Margaret Myles Connolly; three *s* one *d*. *Educ:* Aberdeen Grammar Sch.; Aberdeen Univ. (MA). Aberdeen Bon-Accord, 1948; Elgin Courant, 1949; The Scotsman, 1950; Daily Telegraph, 1952; The Scotsman, 1953: London Editor, 1957; Dep. Editor, 1961. *Recreations:* travel, golf, theatre. *Address:* 5 Strathearn Place, Edinburgh EH9 2AL. *T:* 031-447 7737. *Club:* Caledonian.

MACKAY, Maj.-Gen. Eric MacLachlan, CBE 1971 (MBE 1944); Managing Director, Cementation Sico Oman Ltd, since 1977; *b*

26 Dec. 1921; *s* of Ian MacLachlan Mackay and Violet Aimée Scott-Smith; *m* 1954, Ruth Thérèse Roth; one *s*. *Educ:* Fettes Coll., Edinburgh. Served War: enlisted Royal Scots Fusiliers, 1940; commissioned Oct. 1941, Royal Engineers; 2/Lieut-Major, 1st Parachute Sqdn, RE, 1941-45, N Africa, Sicily, Italy, Arnhem, PoW (escaped) Norway. OC, Field Company, 20 Indian Div., French Indo-China, 1945-46; 2 i/c 23 Indian Div. Engrs, Java, 1946; OC, 35 Indian Field Company, Malaya, 1947; Supplementary Engrg Course, SME, 1948; GSO 2 Intell., Jt Intell. Bureau, 1949-50; Staff Coll., 1951; GSO 2, Org. and Equipment, HQ, ALFCE, 1952-53; Sen. Instructor Tactics, SME, 1954-55; OC, 33 Field Sqdn, RE, Cyprus, Suez, 1956-58; GSO 2, Wpns, MoD, 1958-60; JSSC, 1960; 2 i/c 2 Div. Engrs, 1961-62; Chief Engr, Malaysian Army, Borneo/Malaya, 1963-65; GSO 1, Co-ord., Master-Gen. of the Ordnance, 1966-67; Col, GS, RSME, 1968-69; Chief Engr (Brig.): Army Strategic Command, 1970-71; UK Land Forces, 1972; Maj.-Gen. 1973; Chief Engr, BAOR, 1973-76, retired. CEng 1976; MICE 1976. DSC (USA), 1944; Pingat Peringatan Malaysia (PPM), 1965. *Recreations:* motoring, skiing, photography. *Address:* c/o Cementation International Ltd, PO Box 4035, Ruwi, Muscat, Sultanate of Oman.

McKAY, Frederick; see McKay, J. F.

MACKAY, Sir (George Patrick) Gordon, Kt 1966; CBE 1962; Director, World Bank since 1975; *b* 12 Nov. 1914; *s* of Rev. Adam Mackay and Katie Forrest (*née* Lawrence); *m* 1954, Margaret Esmé Martin; one *s* two *d*. *Educ:* Gordon Sch., Huntly; Aberdeen Univ. Joined Kenya and Uganda Railways and Harbours (later East African Railways and Harbours), 1938; Chief Asst to Gen. Manager, 1948; Chief Operating Supt, 1954; Dep. General Manager, 1960, General Manager, 1961-64; with World Bank, 1965-. FCIT (MInstT 1961). OStJ 1964. *Recreations:* golf and gardening. *Address:* Cintra, Marley Lane, Haslemere, Surrey. *T:* Haslemere 2451. *Club:* Nairobi (Kenya).

MACKAY, Gillian Helen, (Mrs Walter Tallis); Public Relations Consultant; private pilot; *b* 20 Sept. 1923; *er d* of Stuart Mackay; *m* 1971, Walter John Tallis. *Educ:* Hunmanby Hall. WRNS, 1942-46. Dep. Press Officer, Conservative Central Office, 1947-52; BOAC, 1952-56. Executive Secretary, Guild of Air Pilots and Air Navigators, 1956-68 (Freeman; Liveryman, 1968); Press Officer to Liberal Party Leader, 1968-69; Campaign Manager, Health Education Council, 1969-71; Exec. Dir, Fluoridation Soc., 1971-74. Chm., British Women Pilots' Assoc., 1964-69, 1974-76; Gen. Sec., PR Consultants Assoc., 1974; Sec., Internat. Inst. of Human Nutrition, 1975-76; Member Council, Air League, 1966-71, 1972-76; Membership Sec., The Air League, 1976-. Hon. Advr, Air Safety Gp, 1968-. Companion, RAeS, 1960. Tissandier Diploma, Fédération Aéronautique Internat., 1966. MIPR. *Recreations:* flying, ski-ing, sailing, gardening. *Address:* The Stable House, Burcot, near Abingdon OX14 3DP. *Clubs:* Steering Wheel, Ski Club of Great Britain, Eagle Ski Club.

MACKAY, Sir Gordon; see Mackay, Sir G. P. G.

MACKAY, Ian Keith, CMG 1963; Consultant, since 1976; Assistant to Chairman, Papua New Guinea Broadcasting Commission, 1973-75; *b* 19 Oct. 1909; *s* of David and Margaret Mackay; *m* 1960, Lilian Adele Beatty; one *d*. *Educ:* Nelson Coll., New Zealand. New Zealand Broadcasting Service: Announcer, 1935-36; Sports Announcer, 1937; Station Manager, 1938-43; Senior Executive, Commercial Network, 1943-50; Australia: Asst Manager, Station 2GB, 1950-51; Production Manager, Macquarie Network, 1951-61; Director-General, Nigerian Broadcasting Corporation, 1961-64; Advisor on Mass Media to Minister and NBC Board of Governors, 1964-65; PRO, Papua and New Guinea Administration, 1966-68; Sen. Broadcast Officer, 1969-72, seconded Special Administrative duties in setting up the single broadcasting authority for Papua New Guinea, 1972-73. Member, Royal Society of Literature; Member, Society of Authors. *Publications:* Broadcasting in New Zealand, 1953; Broadcasting in Australia, 1957; Macquarie: The Story of a Network, 1960; Broadcasting in Nigeria, 1964; Presenting Papua and New Guinea, 1967; Broadcasting in Papua New Guinea, 1976; articles on social and historical aspects of broadcasting and articles on broadcasting in developing countries in numerous jls; also papers for UN agencies. *Recreations:* conchology, philately. *Address:* 405A Karori Road, Wellington 5, New Zealand.

McKAY, Very Rev. (James) Frederick, CMG 1972; OBE 1964 (MBE 1953); Superintendent, Australian Inland Mission, 1951-74; Archivist, Australian Inland Mission, 1974-75; Moderator-General, Presbyterian Church of Australia, 1970-73; *b* 15 April 1907; father, Northern Ireland; mother, Australian; *m* 1938,

Margaret Mary Robertson; one *s* three *d. Educ:* Thornburgh Coll., Charters Towers, Qld; Emmanuel Coll., Brisbane, Qld; University of Queensland. MA; BD. Ordained Minister, Presbyterian Church of Australia, 1935; Patrol Padre, Australian Inland Mission (working with Flynn of the Inland), 1935-41; Chaplain, RAAF, 1941-46; Command Chaplain, Middle East, 1943-45; Minister, Toowong Parish, Qld, 1946-50; succeeded Flynn of the Inland, as Superintendent, Aust. Inland Mission, 1951. Moderator, Presbyterian Church of NSW, 1965. Editor, Frontier News, 1951-74. Vocational Award, Sydney Rotary, 1972. *Address:* 65 Baroona Road, Northbridge, NSW 2063, Australia. *T:* Sydney 952757; c/o Australian Inland Mission, 44 Margaret Street, Sydney, NSW 2000, Australia. *T:* Sydney 291735. *Club:* Air Force (Sydney).

MACKAY, Sir James (Mackerron), KBE 1966; CB 1964; *b* 9 Aug. 1907; *o s* of Alexander and Annie Mackay; *m* 1938, Katherine, *d* of R. C. Hamilton; two *s*. *Educ:* Forres and Hamilton Academies; Glasgow and Oxford Universities. Glasgow Univ.: MA, 1929; Assistant in Greek, 1929-30. Balliol Coll., Oxford, 1930-34; Exhibitioner; Mods. and Greats. Lecturer in Humanity, Glasgow Univ., 1934-40. Entered Secretariat, Admiralty, 1940; Assistant Secretary, 1945; Under-Secretary, 1958; Deputy Secretary, 1961; Deputy Under Sec. of State, Min. of Defence, April 1964; Deputy Sec., Min. of Aviation, 1964-66; Deputy Under-Sec. of State, Home Office, 1966-67. Member: Scottish Tourist Bd, 1967-72; Highlands and Islands Develt Bd, 1967-72 (Dep. Chm., 1970-72); Countryside Commn for Scotland, 1967-72; Cttee of Enquiry into Future of Broadcasting, 1974-77. *Recreation:* fly-fishing. *Address:* Cluny, Drumnadrochit, Inverness. *T:* Drumnadrochit 268.

MACKAY, James Peter Hymers, QC (Scotland) 1965; Dean, Faculty of Advocates, since 1976; *b* 2 July 1927; *s* of James Mackay and Janet Hymers; *m* 1958, Elizabeth Gunn Hymers; one *s* two *d. Educ:* George Heriot's Sch., Edinburgh. MA Hons Maths and Nat. Philosophy, Edinburgh Univ., 1948; Lectr in Mathematics, Univ. of St Andrews, 1948-50; Major Schol., Trinity Coll., Cambridge, in Mathematics, 1947, taken up 1950; Senior Schol. 1951; BA (Cantab) 1952; LLB Edinburgh (with Distinction) 1955. Admitted to Faculty of Advocates, 1955; Standing Junior Counsel to: Queen's and Lord Treasurer's Remembrancer; Scottish Home and Health Dept; Commissioners of Inland Revenue in Scotland; Sheriff Principal, Renfrew and Argyll, 1972-74; Vice-Dean, Faculty of Advocates, 1973-76. Part-time Mem., Scottish Law Commn, 1976-. Dir, Stenhouse Holdings Ltd, 1976-. A Comr of Northern Lighthouses, 1975-. *Publication:* Armour on Valuation for Rating, 4th edn (with J. J. Clyde and J. A. D. Hope), 1971. *Recreation:* walking. *Address:* 34 Dick Place, Edinburgh. *T:* 031-667 5995. *Club:* New (Edinburgh).

McKAY, Sir James (Wilson), Kt 1971; DL; former Lord Provost of Edinburgh, and Lord Lieutenant of the County of the City of Edinburgh, 1969-72; *b* 12 March 1912; *s* of John McKay; *m* 1942, Janette Urquhart; three *d. Educ:* Dunfermline High Sch.; Portobello Secondary Sch., Edinburgh. Insurance Broker; Man. Dir, John McKay (Insurance) Ltd, Edinburgh; Director: George S. Murdoch & Partners Ltd, Aberdeen; Church of Scotland, Fire Insurance Trust; Chm., Radio Forth Ltd. Served with RN, 1941-46 (Lieut, RNVR). Hon. DLitt Heriot-Watt, 1972. JP Edinburgh, 1972; DL County and City of Edinburgh, 1972. Order of Cross of St Mark (Greek Orthodox Church), 1970; Knight, Order of Orange-Nassau, 1972. *Recreations:* walking, gardening, reading. *Address:* T'Windward, 11 Cammo Gardens, Edinburgh EH4 8EJ. *T:* 031-336 3615. *Clubs:* Caledonian (Edinburgh); University (Aberdeen); RNVR (Glasgow); Caledonian (Hon Mem.) (San Francisco).

MACKAY, John; Headmaster, Bristol Grammar School, 1960-75; *b* 23 June 1914; *s* of William Mackay, Nottingham, and Eliza Mackay; *m* 1952, Margaret Ogilvie; two *s* two *d. Educ:* Mundella Grammar Sch., Nottingham; University of Nottingham; Merton Coll., Oxford. BA London (External) 1st Class Hons (English), 1935; Cambridge Teacher's Certificate, 1936. On staff of SCM, 1936-38; English Lecturer, St John's Coll., York, 1938-40. Served War of 1939-45, in Royal Navy, 1940-46. Merton Coll., Oxford, 1946-48; DPhil (Oxon) 1953. English Master, Merchant Taylors' School, Crosby, Liverpool, 1948-54; Second Master, Cheltenham Coll., 1954-60. Chm., HMC, 1970, Treasurer, 1974-75. *Recreations:* literature, gardening, cricket, arguing. *Address:* The Old Post Office, Tormarton, Badminton, Glos GL9 1HU. *T:* Badminton 243. *Club:* Constitutional (Bristol).

MACKAY, John Alexander, MA, LittD, DD, LLD, LHD; President of Princeton Theological Seminary, 1936-59, President Emeritus, 1959; *b* Inverness, Scotland, 17 May 1889; *s* of Duncan Mackay and Isabella Macdonald; *m* 1916, Jane Logan Wells; one *s* three *d. Educ:* University of Aberdeen (MA 1912, 1st Cl. Hons in Philosophy); Princeton Theological Seminary (BD 1915). Studied at the University of Madrid, 1915-16, and University of Bonn, 1930. LittD, University of San Marcos, Lima, 1918; DD Princeton Univ., 1937, Aberdeen Univ., 1939, University of Debrecen, Hungary, 1939; LLD Ohio-Wesleyan, 1937, Lincoln Univ., 1953; LHD Boston, 1939; and Hon. Degrees from several colleges; Hon. Fellow, Leland Stanford Univ., 1941. Principal, Anglo-Peruvian Coll., Lima, Peru, 1916-25; Prof. Philosophy, Univ. of San Marcos, Peru, 1925; Writer and Lecturer, South American Fedn YMCA, 1926-32; Pres. Bd Foreign Missions of Presbyterian Church, USA, 1945-51; Pres., World Presbyterian Alliance, 1954-59; Member: Central Cttee World Council of Churches, 1948-54 (Provl Cttee, 1946-48); Council on Theological Education, Presbyterian Church, USA, 1944-46 (Chairman); International Missionary Council, 1948-58 (Chairman); Joint Cttee World Council of Churches and International Missionary Council, 1949- (Chairman, 1949-54); Advisory Council, Dept of Philosophy, Princeton Univ., 1941-62; American Theological Soc.; Hon. For. Mem., British and Foreign Bible Soc.; Trustee of Mackenzie Univ., São Paulo, Brazil (Pres. Bd of Trustees, 1948). Special Lectr at many Univs and Colleges since 1932. Pres., American Assoc. of Theological Schs, 1948; Moderator, General Assembly of the Presbyterian Church in USA, 1953. Comendador, Palmas Magistrales (Peru), 1964. *Publications:* Mas Yo Os Digo, 1927; El Sentido de la Vida, 1931; The Other Spanish Christ, 1932; That Other America, 1935; A Preface to Christian Theology, 1941; Heritage and Destiny, 1943; Christianity on the Frontier, 1950; God's Order, 1953; The Presbyterian Way of Life, 1960; His Life and our Life, 1964; Ecumenics: The Science of the Church Universal, 1964; Christian Reality and Appearance, 1969; Realidad e Idolatria, 1970. Editor, Theology Today, 1944-51 (Chairman Editorial Council, Theology Today, 1951-59). *Recreations:* walking and motoring. *Address:* Meadow Lakes, Apartment 39-09, Hightstown, NJ 08520, USA. *Clubs:* Cosmos (Washington); Nassau (Princeton).

McKAY, Sir John (Andrew), Kt 1972; CBE 1966; QPM 1968; HM Chief Inspector of Constabulary for England and Wales, 1970-72; *b* 28 Nov. 1912; *s* of late Denis McKay, Blantyre, Lanarkshire; *m* 1st, 1947, Gertrude Gillespie Deighan (*d* 1971); two *d*; 2nd, 1976, Mildred Grace Kilday, *d* of Dr Emil Stern and late Grace Mildred Pleasants, San Francisco. *Educ:* Glasgow Univ. MA Glasgow, 1934. Joined Metropolitan Police, 1935; seconded to Army for service with Military Govt in Italy and Austria, 1943-47 (Lt-Col); Asst Chief Constable, then Deputy Chief Constable, Birmingham, 1953-58; Chief Constable of Manchester, 1959-66; HM Inspector of Constabulary, 1966-70. Mem., Panel of Chairmen, CS Selection Bd. Dir, Securicor Ltd; Chm., Cancer Res. Campaign, Tunbridge Wells. Freeman of City of London, 1972. OStJ 1963. Hon. MA, Manchester, 1966; Hon. Fellow, Manchester Polytechnic, 1971. *Address:* 1 Long Slip, Langton Green, Tunbridge Wells, Kent. *Club:* Royal Commonwealth Society.

MACKAY, Maj.-Gen. Kenneth, CB 1969; MBE 1943; idc, psc; GOC, Field Force Command Australia, Nov. 1973-Feb. 1974, retired; *b* 17 Feb. 1917; *m* 1943, Judith, *d* of F. Littler; two *s* one *d. Educ:* University High Sch., Melbourne; RMC Duntroon. Served War of 1939-45: Artillery, and Liaison Officer HQ 9th Australian Division, Middle East, 1940-41; ME Staff Sch., 1942; Bde Maj. 26 Bde, 1942-44; MO 12, War Office, 1944-45; Joint Sec., JCOSA, 1945-48; CO, 67 Inf. Bn, 1948; CO, 3 Bn Royal Aust. Regt, 1949; AHQ, 1949-52; Chief Instructor, Sch. of Tactics and Admin. 1952-55; Asst Aust. Defence Rep. UK, 1955-57; successively Dir of Maintenance, Personnel Admin., Quartering and Military Training, 1957-61; IDC, 1962; Dir Military Operations and Plans, Army HQ, Canberra, 1962-66; Comdr Aust. Force Vietnam, 1966; Commander 1st Division Australian Army, 1967-68; QMG AHQ, 1968-71; GOC Eastern Comd, 1971-73. *Recreations:* fishing, golf. *Address:* 3 Beauchamp Street, Deakin, ACT 2600, Australia. *Clubs:* Australian, Royal Canberra; New South Wales Golf.

McKAY, Mrs Margaret; Public Relations Consultant; *b* Jan. 1911. *Educ:* Elementary. Joined Labour Party 1932. Chief woman officer, TUC, 1951-62; Member of Co-operative Society, 1928-. Held administrative posts with Civil Service Clerical Association and Transport and General Workers' Union. MP (Lab) Clapham, 1964-70. Commander, Order of the Cedar of Lebanon. *Publications:* Generation in Revolt (pen name Margaret McCarthy), 1953; Women in Trade Union History (TUC), 1954; Arab Voices from the Past; Electronic Arabia, 1974; The Chainless Mind, 1974. *Address:* PO Box 668, Abu Dhabi, Union of Arab Emirates.

McKAY, Rev. Roy; Hon. Canon, Chichester Cathedral, since 1957; *b* 4 Nov. 1900; *s* of William McKay and Sarah Evelyn (*née* Littlewood); *m* 1927, Mary Oldham Fraser; one *s* one *d. Educ:* Marlborough Coll.; Magdalen Coll., Oxford. Curate, S Paul's, Kingston Hill, 1926; Curate-in-charge and Vicar of St Mark's Londonderry, Smethwick, 1928; Vicar of Mountfield, Sussex, 1932; Chaplain of Christ's Chapel of Alleyn's College of God's Gift, Dulwich, 1937; Vicar of Goring-by-Sea, Sussex, 1943; Chaplain of Canford Sch., 1948; Head of Religious Broadcasting, 1955-63; Preacher to Lincoln's Inn, 1958-59; Rector of St James, Garlickhythe, EC4, 1965-70. *Publications:* Tell John (with Bishop G. F. Allen), 1932; The Pillar of Fire, 1933; Take Care of the Sense, 1964; John Leonard Wilson: Confessor for the Faith, 1973. *Address:* 64 Thomas More House, Barbican, EC2.

MACKAY, Sir William (Calder), Kt 1968; OBE 1957; MC 1918; JP; *b* 5 Aug. 1896; *s* of William Scoular Mackay and Anne Armstrong Henderson; *m* 1920, Constance May Harris; one *s. Educ:* Hillhead High Sch., Glasgow. Served European War, 1914-18, NZEF (Adjt), France; served War of 1939-45 as Hon. YMCA Comr i/c welfare work in military camps, Air Force stations and naval establishments, Auckland Province. Past Member Board, Auckland Provincial Patriotic Fund; Director, Christchurch YMCA, 1929-33; Director, Auckland YMCA, 1934-45; President, YMCA, 1939-45; Chairman, Campaign Cttee for new Auckland YMCA, 1954; Life Member, YMCA, 1966. Past Member: Council, Auckland Chamber of Commerce; Exec. Cttee, Auckland Provincial Retailers' Assoc.; Auckland City Council, 1948-54; Auckland Harbour Bridge Authority; Council, Auckland, War Memorial Museum (Hon. Life Member, 1962). President, Rotary Club of Auckland, 1944-45; District Gov., Rotary, 1948-49; Member Aims and Objects Cttee, Rotary International, 1949-50. Provincial Comr, Boy Scouts, 1958; Organising Comr for Pan-Pacific Boy Scouts Jamboree, 1959 (Medal of Merit). Patron, Crippled Children Soc. (Mem. Exec., 1935-66, past Vice-Pres., and Pres., 1958-66, Life Mem. 1974, Auckland Branch); Vice-President: NZ Crippled Children Soc., 1964; St John Amb. Assoc. Auckland Centre Trust Bd, 1970; Pres., Nat. Children's Med. Res. Foundn, 1974; Past Area Co-ordinator, Duke of Edinburgh Award for Auckland Province and Mem. NZ Council, 1963. Foundn Mem. Bd, St Andrews Presbyterian Hospital and Hostel for Aged. JP 1940. *Recreations:* fishing, outdoor bowls. *Address:* 416 Remuera Road, Auckland 5, New Zealand. *T:* 502 495. *Club:* Northern (Auckland).

MACKAY-TALLACK, Sir Hugh, Kt 1963; Director, Inchcape & Co. Ltd (Deputy Chairman, 1964-77); Chairman, Capital and National Trust Ltd; Deputy Chairman, The Standard & Chartered Banking Group Ltd; Director: Gray Dawes & Co. Ltd; Gray Dawes Westray (Holdings) Ltd; Bain Dawes Group; The London & Holyrood Trust Ltd; London & Provincial Trust Ltd; Assam & African Investments Ltd (formerly Chairman); *s* of E. H. Tallack and Deborah Lyle Mackay; unmarried. *Educ:* Kelly Coll., Devon; Heidelberg Univ. Served War of 1939-45, with 17th Dogra Regt, in Middle East and Burma; Private Sec. to C-in-C ALFSEA, and Mil. Sec. (Col) to Admiral Mountbatten, Supreme Allied Comdr, SEAC. Formerly: Chm., Macneill & Barry Ltd (Inchcape Gp) Calcutta; Governor of State Bank of India; Director numerous other cos in India; Chm., Indian Tea Assoc., 1954-55; Vice-Chairman, Tea Board of India, 1954-55; Member Government of India Tea Auction Cttee, 1954-55; Chairman, Ross Inst. of India, 1951-64; Pres., Bengal Chamber of Commerce and Industry and Associated Chambers of Commerce of India, 1962-63. Mem., Fedn, Commonwealth Chambers of Commerce. Governor, Nehru Meml Trust. *Recreation:* riding. *Address:* Bicknor Park, near Hollingbourne, Kent; 24 Barrie House, Lancaster Gate, Hyde Park, W2. *T:* 01-262 5877. *Clubs:* White's, Boodle's, Oriental, City of London; Bengal, Tollygunge, Turf (all in Calcutta).

McKEAN, Douglas, CB 1977; Under-Secretary, HM Treasury; *b* 2 April 1917; *s* of late Alexander McKean, Enfield, Mddx; *m* 1942, Anne, *d* of late Roger Clayton, Riding Mill, Northumberland; two *s. Educ:* Merchant Taylors' Sch.; St John's Coll., Oxford. War Office, 1940; transferred to HM Treasury, 1949; Asst Sec., 1956; Under-Sec., 1962; on loan to Dept of the Environment, 1970-72. *Recreations:* walking, travel. *Address:* The Dower House, Forty Hill, Enfield, Middlesex EN2 9EJ. *T:* 01-363 2365. *Club:* United Oxford & Cambridge University.

McKEARNEY, Philip; HM Diplomatic Service; Consul-General, Zagreb, since 1977; *b* 15 Nov. 1926; *s* of Philip McKearney, OBE; *m* 1950, Jean Pamela Walker; two *s. Educ:* City of London Sch.; Hertford Coll., Oxford. 4/7th Dragoon Guards, 1946-53; joined HM Diplomatic Service, 1953; 3rd Sec., British Embassy, Damascus, 1955-56; 1st Sec., British Legation, Bucharest, 1959-62; British Political Agent, Qatar, 1962-65; Counsellor and Consul-Gen., Baghdad, 1968-70; Counsellor, Belgrade, 1970-74; Inspector, FCO, 1975-77. *Address:* c/o Foreign and Commonwealth Office, SW1.

McKEE, Air Marshal Sir Andrew, KCB 1957 (CB 1951); CBE 1944; DSO 1942; DFC 1941; AFC 1938; *b* 1901; *s* of Samuel Hugh McKee, Eyredale, Oxford, Canterbury, NZ; *m* 1949, Cecelia Tarcille, *er d* of Michael Keating, NZ; two *d. Educ:* Christchurch Boys' High Sch., NZ. Joined RAF, 1927. AOC No 205 Group Mediterranean Allied Air Force, 1945-46; Senior Air Staff Officer, MEAF, 1946-47; Comdt OATS, 1947-49; First Comdt, RAF Flying Coll., 1949-51; Air Vice-Marshal, 1952; AOC No 21 Group, 1952-53; Senior Air Staff Officer, Bomber Command, 1953-54; Air Marshal, 1957; Air Officer Commanding-in-Chief, Transport Command, 1955-59, retired. *Address:* 20 Matatua Road, Raumati Beach, Paraparaumu, New Zealand. *Club:* Royal Air Force.

McKEE, Major Sir Cecil; see McKee, Major Sir William Cecil.

McKEE, His Honour Sir Dermot St Oswald, Kt 1974; a Circuit Judge (formerly Judge of County Courts), 1952-74; *b* 22 Sept. 1904; *o s* of Rev. W. S. McKee, Bradford; *m* 1st, 1928, Violet, *d* of late Eli Dalton, Leeds; no *c* ; 2nd, 1970, Mary K. Wallace, *d* of late Eli Dalton. *Educ:* privately; Leeds Univ. (LLB). Called to Bar, Gray's Inn, 1926. Practice, NE Circuit. Served War of 1939-45; Sqdn Leader, RAF, 1940-45. West Riding Quarter Sessions: Deputy Chairman, 1952; Chairman, 1957; Chairman: Cttee Reorganisation of Parishes Measure for Northern Province, 1957; Conscientious Objectors Tribunal, NE Area, 1958; County Court Rules Cttee, 1969-74 (Mem. 1956-). *Recreations:* fly-fishing and shooting. *Address:* Thatched Cottage, Tockwith, York. *T:* Tockwith 281. *Club:* Leeds.

McKEE, Major Sir (William) Cecil, Kt 1959; ERD; JP; Estate Agent; *b* 13 April 1905; *s* of late W. B. McKee and M. G. B. Bulloch; *m* 1932, Florence Ethel Irene Gill; one *d. Educ:* Methodist Coll., Belfast; Queen's Univ., Belfast. Alderman, Belfast Corporation, 1934; High Sheriff, Belfast, 1946; Deputy Lord Mayor, 1947, Lord Mayor of Belfast, 1957-59. JP Belfast, 1957. Pres., NI Br., Inst. of Dirs, 1957-59. Served with Royal Artillery in War of 1939-45. CStJ 1969. Hon. LLD Queen's Univ., Belfast, 1960. *Recreation:* golf. *Address:* 250 Malone Road, Belfast. *T:* Belfast 666979. *Clubs:* Ulster Reform (Belfast); Royal County Down Golf.

McKEE, Dr William James Ernest, MA, MD, FFCM; Regional Medical Officer, Wessex Regional Health Authority, since 1976; *b* 20 Feb. 1929; *s* of John Sloan McKee, MA, and Mrs Annie Emily McKee (*née* McKinley); *m* Josée Tucker; three *d. Educ:* Queen Elizabeth's, Wakefield; Trinity Coll., Cambridge; Queen's Coll., Oxford. MA, MD, BChir (Cantab); LRCP, MRCS, FFCM. Clinical trng and postgrad. clinical posts at Radcliffe Infirmary, Oxford, 1952-57; med. res., financed by Nuffield Provincial Hosps Trust, 1958-61; successive posts in community medicine with Metrop. Regional Hosp. Bds, 1961-69; Sen. Admin. Med. Officer, Liverpool Regional Hosp. Bd, 1970-74; Regional Med. Officer, Mersey RHA, 1974-76. *Publications:* papers on tonsillectomy and adenoidectomy in learned jls. *Address:* 22a Bereweeke Avenue, Winchester SO22 6BH. *T:* Winchester 61369.

McKEEVER, Ronald Fraser, CBE 1975; HM Diplomatic Service, retired; *b* 20 Aug. 1914; *yr s* of late Frederick Leonard McKeever and of late Elizabeth Moore McKeever (*née* Bucher); *m* 1944, Margaret Lilian (*née* Sabine); one *s. Educ:* George Watson's Coll., Edinburgh; Edinburgh Univ. Served in Indian Police, 1935-47. Joined Foreign Service, 1948; Vice-Consul: Dakar, 1948; Chicago, 1950; Consul, Kansas City, 1953; British Embassy, Bonn, 1954; Consul, Gdynia, 1957; Brazzaville, 1959 (Chargé d'Affaires, 1960); Foreign Office, 1961; Consul, Tamsui (Formosa), 1962-66; Ambassador to Togo and Dahomey, 1967-70; Consul-Gen., Naples, 1971-74. *Recreations:* fishing, bird-watching. *Address:* Bowmillholm, St Mungo, by Lockerbie, Dumfriesshire.

MacKEIGAN, Hon. Ian Malcolm; Chief Justice of Nova Scotia and Chief Justice of Appeal Division of Supreme Court of Nova Scotia, since 1973; *b* 11 April 1915; *s* of Rev. Dr J. A. MacKeigan and Mabel (*née* McAvity); *m* 1942, Jean Catherine Geddes; two *s* one *d. Educ:* Univs of Saskatchewan, Dalhousie and Toronto. BA (Great Distinction) 1934, MA 1935, LLB 1938, Dalhousie; MA Toronto 1939. Member of Nova Scotia and Prince Edward Island Bars; QC (Nova Scotia) 1954. Dep. Enforcement Administrator, Wartime Prices and Trade Bd, Ottawa, 1942-46; Dep. Comr, Combines Investigation Commn,

Ottawa, 1946-50; Partner, MacKeigan, Cox, Downie & Mitchell and predecessor firms, Halifax, NS, 1950-73; Chm., Atlantic Develt Bd, 1963-69; Dir, Gulf Oil (Canada) Ltd, 1968-73; Dir, John Labatt Ltd, 1971-73 and other companies. Hon. LLD Dalhousie, 1975. Centennial Medal, 1967. *Publications:* articles in Can. Bar Review and Can. Jl Polit. Sci. and Econs. *Recreations:* fishing, golf. *Address:* 833 Marlborough Avenue, Halifax, NS B3H 3G7, Canada. *T:* 429-2291. *Clubs:* Halifax, Saraguay, Ashburn Golf (Halifax); Royal NS Yacht Squadron, etc.

McKELL, Rt. Hon. Sir William John, GCMG, *cr* 1951; PC 1948; *b* Pambula, NSW, 26 Sept. 1891; *m* 1920; one *s* two *d. Educ:* Public Sch., Surry Hills, Sydney. Served apprenticeship as boiler-maker, Morts' Dock and Engineering Co., Sydney; elected Financial Secretary, Boilermakers' Union; elected Member Legislative Assembly, NSW, at 25 years of age; Member, 1917-47; Minister of Justice (1920-22) at age of 28 years; Minister of Justice and Assistant Colonial Treasurer, 1925-27; visited London and New York on financial mission for State of New South Wales, 1927; Minister for Local Government, 1930; Minister of Justice, 1931-32; Leader of the Opposition, 1939-41; Premier and Colonial Treasurer of New South Wales, 1941-47; official visit to United States and Great Britain, 1945; Governor-General of Australia, 1947-53. Member Malayan Constitutional Commission, 1956-57. Barrister of Supreme Court of New South Wales, 1925; QC 1945. Chairman of Sydney Cricket Ground Trust, 1938. Hon. LLD, Sydney. *Recreations:* always active in football and boxing circles; played first-grade football and boxed in amateur championships. *Address:* 42/14 Leura Road, Double Bay, NSW 2028, Australia.

McKELLEN, Ian (Murray); actor and director since 1961; *b* 25 May; *s* of Denis Murray McKellen and Margery (*née* Sutcliffe). *Educ:* Wigan Grammar Sch.; Bolton Sch.; St Catharine's Coll., Cambridge (BA). Pres., Marlowe Soc., 1960-61. Elected to Council of Equity, 1971-72. 1st appearance (stage): Belgrade Theatre, Coventry, in A Man for all Seasons, Sept. 1961. Arts Theatre, Ipswich, 1962-63; Nottingham Playhouse, 1963-64. 1st London appearance: A Scent of Flowers, 1964 (Clarence Derwent Award). National Theatre Co., 1965, Old Vic and Chichester Festival; A Lily in Little India; Man of Destiny/O'Flaherty VC, Mermaid Theatre, EC4; Their Very Own and Golden City, Royal Court, 1966; The Promise, Fortune and Broadway, 1967; White Lies/Black Comedy; Richard II, Prospect Theatre Co., 1968; Recruiting Officer, Chips with Everything, Cambridge Theatre Co., 1968; revived Richard II with Edward II, Edinburgh Festival; British and European Tour; Mermaid and Piccadilly Theatres, 1969-70; Hamlet, British and European Tours and Cambridge Theatre, WC2, 1971. Founder Mem., Actors' Company: Ruling the Roost, 'Tis Pity She's a Whore, Edin. Fest., 1972; Knots, Wood-Demon, Edin. Fest., 1973, and with King Lear, Brooklyn Acad. of Music, Wimbledon Theatre season, 1974; Royal Shakespeare Co.: Dr Faustus, Edin. Fest., 1974; Marquis of Keith, Aldwych, 1974-75; King John, Aldwych, 1975; Ashes, Young Vic, 1975; Too True to Be Good, Aldwych and Globe, 1975; Romeo and Juliet, The Winter's Tale, Macbeth, Stratford, 1976-77; Romeo and Juliet, Macbeth, The Winter's Tale, Pillars of the Community, Days of the Commune, The Alchemist, Aldwych and RSC Warehouse, 1977-78; solo recitals: Words, Words, Words, Edin. Fest., and Belfast Fest., 1976; repeated with a Shakespeare Anthology, Edin. and Belfast, 1977; Every Good Boy Deserves Favour (music and theatre), RFH, 1977. Directed: Liverpool Playhouse, 1969; Watford and Leicester, 1972; A Private Matter, Vaudeville, 1973; The Clandestine Marriage, Savoy 1975. Films, 1968-: A Touch of Love, The Promise, Alfred the Great. Has appeared on television, 1966-. *Address:* c/o Fraser and Dunlop Ltd, 91 Regent's Street, W1R 8RU. *T:* 01-734 7311.

McKELVEY, Air Cdre John Wesley, CB 1969; MBE 1944; CEng, MRAeS; RAF, retired; Secretary (Appeals), Royal Air Force Benevolent Fund, since 1971; *b* 25 June 1914; *s* of late Captain John Wesley McKelvey, Enfield, Mddx; *m* 1938, Eileen Amy Carter, *d* of John Charles Carter, Enfield; two *s. Educ:* George Spicer Sch., Enfield. RAF Aircraft Apprentice, 1929; commnd 1941 (Eng Branch); served 1939-45, Egypt, Syria, Iraq and Bomber Comd (despatches, 1943); Group Captain 1960; Dep. Dir Intelligence (Tech.), 1962-64; Dir of Aircraft and Asst Attaché, Defence Research and Development, British Embassy, Washington, 1964-66; Air Officer Wales and CO, RAF St Athan, 1966-69; retd Aug. 1969. *Recreations:* photography, gardening. *Address:* Inchmerle, 29 Manorway, Bush Hill Park, Enfield, Mddx EN1 2JD. *T:* 01-360 4054. *Club:* Royal Air Force.

MACKEN, Frederic Raymond, CMG 1964; *b* 23 Sept. 1903; *s* of Charles Alfred Macken and Ella (*née* Steadman); *m* 1929, Alma Doris (*née* Keesing); one *d. Educ:* Whangarei High Sch.; Auckland Univ., New Zealand. LLM (with Hons), 1927. Retired as Commissioner of Inland Revenue for New Zealand, 1964. *Recreations:* bowls, golf. *Address:* 9 Harley Grove, Lower Hutt, Wellington, New Zealand. *T:* 695205. *Club:* Civil Service (Wellington, NZ).

MacKENNA, Hon. Sir Bernard Joseph Maxwell, (Hon. Sir Brian MacKenna), Kt 1961; Judge of the High Court of Justice (Queen's Bench Division), 1961-77; *b* 12 Sept. 1905; unmarried. Called to the Bar, Inner Temple, Jan. 1932; Western Circuit; QC 1950; Master of the Bench of the Inner Temple, 1958. *Address:* 2 Paper Buildings, Temple, EC4. *T:* 01-353 2123. *Clubs:* Athenæum, Beefsteak.

MacKENNA, Sir Brian; *see* MacKenna, Sir Bernard Joseph Maxwell.

McKENNA, David, CBE 1967 (OBE 1946; MBE 1943); FCIT; Member, British Railways Board, 1968-76 (part-time Member, 1976-78); *b* 16 Feb. 1911; *s* of late Rt Hon. Reginald McKenna and Pamela Margaret McKenna (*née* Jekyll); *m* 1934, Lady Cecilia Elizabeth Keppel, *d* of 9th Earl of Albemarle, *qv* ; three *d. Educ:* Eton; Trinity Coll., Cambridge. London Passenger Transport Board, 1934-39, and 1946-55; Asst General Manager, Southern Region of BR, 1955-61; Chief Commercial Officer, HQ, BR, 1962; General Manager, Southern Region of BR, and Chairman Southern Railway Board, 1963-68; Chairman, British Transport Advertising, 1968-. Dir, Isles of Scilly Steamship Co. War Service with Transportation Service of Royal Engineers, 1939-45; Iraq, Turkey, India and Burma; Lieut-Colonel. Pres., Chartered Inst. of Transport, 1972. Chairman of Governors, Sadler's Wells, 1962-76. Hon. Secretary, Royal College of Music; Chairman of Bach Choir, 1964-76. FRCM. Commandeur de l'Ordre National du Mérite, 1974. *Publications:* various papers on transport subjects. *Recreations:* music, sailing. *Address:* Rosteague, Portscatho, Truro, Cornwall. *Clubs:* Brooks's; Royal Cornwall Yacht (Falmouth).

MacKENNA, Robert Merttins Bird, MA, MD, FRCP; Hon. Colonel RAMC, 1954; Dermatologist, King Edward VII's Hospital for Officers, 1946-72, now Consulting Dermatologist; Hon. Consultant in Dermatology to the British Army, 1946-64; Councillor Royal College of Physicians, 1956-59; President: Dermatological Section, Royal Society of Medicine, 1966-67; British Association of Dermatology, 1966-67; Physician in charge of the Department for Diseases of the Skin, St Bartholomew's Hospital, 1946-68, now Hon. Consultant in Dermatology; Emeritus Member, British Association of Dermatologists, 1976; *b* 16 Nov. 1903; *s* of late R. W. MacKenna and Harriet A. S. Bird; *m* 1st, 1927, Helen, *e d* of Thomas Todrick; two *d* ; 2nd, 1943, Margaret, *d* of Rev. Christmas Hopkins and Eleanor Hopkins; two *s. Educ:* RN Colleges, Osborne and Dartmouth; Clare Coll., Cambridge Univ.; St Thomas' Hospital. Resigned from the Navy, 1919; studied at Liverpool Univ., 1920-21; Cambridge, 1921-24; BA (Nat. Sci. Tripos), 1924; MRCS, LRCP, 1926; MA, MB, BCh Cambridge, 1928; MRCP, 1928; MD Cambridge 1931; FRCP, 1941. Junior Asst MO Venereal Diseases Dept, and Clinical Asst, Dermatological Dept, St Thomas' Hosp., 1927-28; Clinical Asst, St John's Hosp., for Diseases of the Skin, 1928; Hon. Asst Dermatologist Liverpool Radium Inst., 1929; Hon. Dermatologist, Liverpool Stanley Hosp., 1929-34; Hon. Dermatologist, Royal Liverpool United Hosp., (Royal Southern Hosp.), 1934-46; Dermatologist, Catterick Military Hosp., Oct. 1939; Comd Specialist in Dermatology, Northern Comd, 1940-41; Adviser in Dermatology and Asst Dir, Hygiene (c), War Office, 1941-43; Cons. Dermatologist to British Army, 1943-45. Malcolm Morris Meml Lectr, 1955; Watson Smith Lectr, 1957; Prosser White Orator, 1968. Hon. Fellow, Amer. Med. Assoc. Hon. Member: Dermatological Section, RSM; Dermatological Assoc. of Australia; Soc. for Investigative Dermatology; Canadian Dermatological Assoc.; NY Dermatolog. Soc.; Deutsche Dermatologische Gesellschaft; Sociedad Venezolana de Dermatologia; Alpha Omega Alpha Honor Med. Soc.; Corresp. Member: Amer. Dermatological Assoc.; Nederlandse Vereniging van Dermatologen; Societas Dermatologica Danica; Societas Dermatologica Austriaca; Societas Dermatologica Svecica; La Société Française de Dermatologie et de Syphiligraphie; Israeli Dermatological Soc. OStJ 1954. *Publications:* Aids to Dermatology, 1929, 1939, 1946, 1954, 1956; Diseases of the Skin, 1932, 1937, 1949 and 1952; Dermatology (jointly with E. L. Cohen), 1964. Joint Editor of The Medical History of Liverpool, 1936; Sections on Dermatology in Medical Annual, 1944-63; editor, Modern Trends in Dermatology, Series I, 1948, Series II, 1953, Series III,

1966; Associate Editor for Dermatological subjects British Encyclopædia of Medical Practice, 2nd Edition, 1950; various papers on dermatological subjects in medical journals. *Address:* 29 Duchess of Bedford House, Campden Hill, W8 7QN.

MacKENNA, Robert Ogilvie, MA, ALA; University Librarian and Keeper of the Hunterian Books and MSS, Glasgow, since 1951; *b* 21 March 1913; *s* of late Dr John G. MacKenna and Katherine Ogilvie; *m* 1942, Ray, *o d* of late Samuel Mullin, Glasgow. *Educ:* Paisley Grammar Sch.; Glasgow Univ. Assistant Librarian, Glasgow Univ., 1936; Sub-Librarian, Leeds Univ., 1946; Librarian, King's Coll., Newcastle upon Tyne (University of Durham), 1947. Served War as officer, RNVR, 1939-45. Trustee, National Library of Scotland, 1953-. President, Scottish Library Association, 1966; Chairman, Standing Conference of National and University Libraries, 1967-69. President Scottish Cricket Union, 1968. Editor, The Philosophical Journal, 1976-. *Recreations:* cricket (played for Scotland, 1935-39 and 1946); hill-walking. *Address:* Glasgow University Library, Glasgow, G12 8QE. *T:* 041-334 2122; 2 Turnberry Avenue, Glasgow, G11 5AQ. *Clubs:* Authors'; College (Glasgow).

McKENNA, Siobhán, (Mrs Denis O'Dea); actress; *b* Belfast, 24 May 1923; *d* of Prof. Owen McKenna and Margaret O'Reilly; *m* 1946, Denis O'Dea; one *s. Educ:* St Louis Convent, Monaghan; Galway Univ. (BA). Semi-professional stage appearances in An Taibhdhearc Theatre, Galway, 1940-43. Joined Abbey Theatre, Dublin, 1944-47. First London appearance in The White Steed, Embassy, 1947. *Films:* Hungry Hill, Daughter of Darkness, The Lost People, The Adventurers, King of Kings, Playboy of the Western World, The Cavern, Dr Zhivago. *Plays:* Fading Mansions, Duchess, 1949; Ghosts, Embassy; Héloise, Duke of York's; Stratford Festival, 1952; Playboy of the Western World, Edinburgh and Paris Festivals; Saint Joan, Arts, 1954, St Martin's, 1955; The Chalk Garden, NY, 1955; Saint Joan, NY, 1956; The Rope-Dancers, NY, 1957; Shakespearian seasons at Stratford, Ontario and Cambridge Drama Festival. (Again in) Playboy of the Western World, Gaiety, Dublin, and Piccadilly, London, 1960; Captain Brassbound's Conversion, Philadelphia, 1961; Saint Joan of the Stockyards, Dublin Festival, 1961, Queen's, London, 1964; Play with a Tiger, London, 1962; Laurette, Dublin Festival, 1964; Juno and the Paycock, Gaiety, Dublin, 1966, Mermaid, 1973 (also directed); On a Foggy Day, St Martin's, 1969; Best of Friends, Strand, 1970; Here are Ladies, Criterion, 1970. Also television for BBC, and New York and Los Angeles. *Publications:* trans. into Gaelic: Mary Rose; Saint Joan. *Recreations:* reading poetry and talking. *Address:* 23 Highfield Road, Rathgar, Dublin, Eire.

MACKENZIE, family name of **Baron Amulree** and **Earl of Cromartie.**

MACKENZIE; *see* Montagu-Stuart-Wortley-Mackenzie, family name of Earl of Wharncliffe.

MACKENZIE of Gairloch; *see under* Inglis of Glencorse.

MACKENZIE, Dr Alastair Stewart, (Sandy); Regional Medical Officer, North West Thames Regional Health Authority, since 1977; *b* 28 April 1930; *s* of late James S. Mackenzie, JP and Anne (*née* Evans). *Educ:* Gyfarthfa Castle Sch., Merthyr Tydfil; Bromsgrove Sch., Worcs; Jesus Coll., Cambridge (MA); University Coll. Hospital. MB, BChir; DMRT, FFCM. Captain and Specialist, RAMC, 1959. Sen. Admin. MO, NE Metrop. Regional Hosp. Bd, 1972; Regional MO, NE Thames RHA, 1974-77. Mem. Council (Section of Epidemiology), RSocMed, 1972; Mem. Council, British Cancer Council, 1972; a British Rep., Hosp. Cttee of EEC, 1974; Mem. Council, Queen's Nursing Inst., 1974; Mem. Bd of Governors, St John's Hosp. for Diseases of Skin, 1974; Mem. Ct of Governors, and Mem. Bd of Management, London Sch. of Hygiene and Trop. Medicine, 1975; Mem. Laboratory Develt Adv. Gp, 1975; Mem. Cttee of Management, Inst. of Child Health, 1976. FRSocMed. *Publications:* various articles on epidemiology and med. care in med. jls. *Recreations:* music, gardening, Egyptology. *Address:* 22A Bolton Gardens, SW5 0AQ. *T:* 01-370 2480; The Old Bakery, Maltings Lane, Great Chishill, Cambs. *T:* Chrishall 559.

McKENZIE, Sir Alexander, KBE 1962; Past Dominion President, New Zealand National Party (1951-62); *b* Invercargill, New Zealand, 1896; *m* 1935, Constance Mary Howard; two *s* two *d. Educ:* Isla Bank Primary Sch.; Southland Technical Coll.; Southland Boys' High Sch. Chm., Ponsonby Electorate, NZ Nat. Party, 1938-41; Chm., Auckland Div., NZ Nat. Party, 1941-51. Overseas Rep. for NZ Forest Products Ltd, 1925-29; engaged in Stock and Share Broking, 1929-; Mem. Auckland Stock Exchange; Dir, of companies covering finance,

merchandising, manufacturing, etc. Mem. Anglican Church. *Recreations:* trout fishing, surfing, bowling, gardening. *Address:* 54 Wallace Street, Herne Bay, New Zealand. *Club:* Auckland (Auckland, NZ).

MACKENZIE, Alexander, OBE 1964; JP; DL; Lord Provost of Dundee and Lord Lieutenant of the County of the City of Dundee, 1967-70; *b* 12 Dec. 1915; *o s* of Alex. and Elizabeth Mackenzie; *m* 1940, Edna Margaret, *d* of Fred Holder; one *d. Educ:* Morgan Academy, Dundee. Secretary (Dundee Branch), League of Nations, 1935-38; Secretary (Dundee Branch), UNA, 1946-49. Member, Dundee Town Council, 1947-; Chairman, Tay Road Bridge Joint Board, 1967-70; Chairman, Dundee High Sch. Directors, 1967-70; Vice-Chairman: Governors, Dundee Coll. of Art and Technology, 1967-70; Tayside Economic Planning Consultative Group, 1969 (Chm. Publicity Cttee, 1969-70); Member: Univ. Court of Dundee, 1967-70; Dundee Harbour Trust, 1967-70. Pres., Dundee Brotherhood, 1948. Assessor, Dundee Repertory Theatre, 1964-70. JP, 1951, DL, 1971, County of the City of Dundee. *Publication:* And Nothing But the Truth, 1976. *Recreation:* reading. *Address:* 18 Whitehall Crescent, Dundee. *T:* 25774.

MACKENZIE, Sir Alexander Alwyne H. C. B. M.; *see* Muir Mackenzie.

MACKENZIE, Sir (Alexander George Anthony) Allan, 4th Bt, of Glen-Muick, *cr* 1890; CD 1957; retired; *b* 4 Jan. 1913; *s* of late Capt. Allan Keith Mackenzie (3rd *s* of 2nd Bt) and Hon. Louvima, *o d* of 1st Viscount Knollys (she *m* 2nd, 1922, Richard Henry Spencer Checkley); *S* uncle, 1944; *m* 1937, Marjorie McGuire, Vancouver, BC; four *d. Educ:* Stowe School. Page of Honour to King George V; Member Royal Canadian Mounted Police, 1932-37; served War of 1939-45, with Seaforth Highlanders of Canada (Captain), in Italy and in NW Europe. Subsequently Black Watch (RHR) of Canada (Regular Army). Canada Centennial Medal, 1967. *Heir:* cousin (James William) Guy Mackenzie [*b* 6 Oct. 1946; *m* 1972, Paulene Patricia Simpson; one *d*]. *Address:* RR1, Cobble Hill, Vancouver Island, British Columbia, Canada.

MACKENZIE, Sir Allan; *see* Mackenzie, Sir (Alexander George Anthony) Allan.

MACKENZIE, Archibald Robert Kerr, CBE 1967; HM Diplomatic Service, retired; *b* 22 Oct. 1915; *s* of James and Alexandrina Mackenzie; *m* 1963, Virginia Ruth Hutchison. *Educ:* Glasgow, Oxford, Chicago and Harvard Universities. Diplomatic Service, with duty at Washington, 1943-45; United Nations, 1946-49; Foreign Office, 1949-51; Bangkok, 1951-54; Cyprus, 1954; Foreign Office, 1955-57; OEEC, Paris, 1957-61; Commercial Counsellor, HM Embassy, Rangoon, 1961-65; Consul-General, Zagreb 1965-69; Ambassador, Tunisia, 1970-73; Minister (Econ. and Social Affairs), UK Mission to UN, 1973-75. *Recreation:* golf. *Address:* Strathcashel Cottage, Rowardennan, near Glasgow G63 0AW. *T:* Balmaha 262. *Clubs:* Royal Commonwealth Society; Royal Scottish Automobile (Glasgow).

MACKENZIE, Chalmers Jack, CC (Canada) 1967; CMG 1943; MC 1918; FRS 1946; FRSC; MEIC; Chancellor, Carleton University, 1954-68; Member Atomic Energy Control Board, 1946-61, and President, 1948-61; President, National Research Council of Canada, 1939-52; Member Defence Research Board, 1946-52; President Atomic Energy of Canada, Limited, 1952-53; Director: Canadian Patents and Development Ltd, 1947-61; Chemcell Ltd and Columbia Cellulose Co., 1954-68; Member, Army Technical Development Board, 1942; Chairman War Technical and Scientific Development Cttee, 1940; Inventions Board, 1940-46; *b* 10 July 1888; *s* of late James Mackenzie, St Stephen, NB; *m* 1st, 1916, Claire Rees (*d* 1922); one *s*; 2nd, 1924, Geraldine Gallon (*d* 1976); two *d. Educ:* St Stephen, NB; Dalhousie Univ. (BE 1909); Harvard Univ. (MCE 1915). Engineering Firm, Maxwell & Mackenzie, 1912-16; Overseas 54th Canadian Infantry Bn, 1916-18 (MC); Prof. Civil Engineering, 1918-39, Dean of College of Engineering, 1921-39, University of Sask., President, Engineering Institute of Canada, 1941; Chairman Saskatoon City Planning Commission, 1928-39; Chairman Saskatoon City Hospital Board, 1937-39. Dir Canadian Geographical Soc., 1937-60. Mem., Canada Council, 1963-69. Hon. LLD: Dalhousie, 1941, Western Ontario, 1943, Queen's, 1944, Saskatchewan, 1945; Carleton, 1969; DEng: Toronto, 1944; Nova Scotia Tech. Coll., 1950; Hon. DSc: McGill, 1941; Laval and Cambridge, 1946; UBC, 1947; Princeton, 1949; McMaster Univ., 1951; Univs of New Brunswick, Montreal, Manitoba, 1953; Ottawa, 1958; RMC, 1964; Hon. DCL Bishop's Univ., 1952. Hon. FRCP(C), 1947; Hon. Mem., Amer. Soc. Civil Engrs, 1952; Hon. FICE, 1968.

US Medal for Merit, 1947; Chevalier de la Légion d'Honneur, 1947; Kelvin Medal, InstMechE, 1954; R. B. Bennett Empire Prize, RSA, 1954; Royal Bank Award, 1968. *Publications:* in scientific and technical press. *Recreations:* golf, curling. *Address:* 210 Buena Vista Road, Rockcliffe Park, Ottawa, Ontario K1M 0V7, Canada. *Clubs:* Rideau, Royal Ottawa Golf (Ottawa).

MACKENZIE, Colin Hercules, CMG 1946; *b* 5 Oct. 1898; *o s* of late Maj.-Gen. Sir Colin Mackenzie, KCB, and Ethel, *er d* of Hercules Ross, ICS; *m* 1940, Evelyn Clodagh, 2nd *d* of Charles and Lady Aileen Meade; one *d. Educ:* Summerfields; Eton (Schol.); King's Coll., Cambridge (1st Class Hons in Economics. Exhibitioner and Senior Scholar, also Chancellor's Medal for English Verse). Served France with 1st Bn Scots Guards in 1918 (wounded). Served in India and with South-East Asia Command, 1941-45, comd Force 136 (CMG, Officier de la Légion d'Honneur). British Economic Mission to Greece, 1946. Dir, J. and P. Coats Ltd, 1928-65. Chairman: Scottish Council, FBI, 1957-59; Scottish Cttee on Electricity, 1961-62; Scottish Arts Council, 1962-70; Inverness Conservative and Unionist Assoc., 1967-70. Hon. Sheriff Inverness-shire. Hon. LLD St Andrews, 1970. *Address:* Kyle House, Kyleakin, Isle of Skye. *T:* Kyleakin 217. *Club:* Special Forces.

McKENZIE, Dan Peter, FRS 1976; PhD; Assistant Director of Research, Department of Geodesy and Geophysics Cambridge University, since 1975; Fellow of King's College, Cambridge, 1965-73 and since 1977; *b* 21 Feb. 1942; *s* of William Stewart McKenzie and Nancy Mary McKenzie; *m* 1971, Indira Margaret (Misra); one *s. Educ:* Westminster Sch.; King's Coll., Cambridge (BA 1963, PhD 1966). Senior Assistant in Research, Cambridge Univ., 1969-75. Hon. MA Cambridge, 1966. *Publications:* papers in learned jls. *Recreation:* gardening. *Address:* 14 Humberstone Road, Cambridge CB4 1JE. *T:* Cambridge 59790.

MacKENZIE, David Alexander; General Secretary, Transport Salaried Staffs' Association, 1973-76; *b* 22 March 1922; *s* of David MacKenzie and Jeannie Ross; *m* 1945, Doreen Joyce Lucas; two *s* one *d. Educ:* Merkinch Public Sch.; Inverness High Sch. Entered London Midland Railway Service, 1936. Served in Royal Navy, 1941-45. Transport Salaried Staffs Assoc.: Divisional Sec., 1952-66; Sen. Asst Sec., 1966-68; Asst Gen. Sec., 1968. Mem., TUC Non-Manual Workers' Cttee; Mem., Air Transport and Travel Industry Trng Bd; Mem., Hotel and Catering Industry Trng Bd. *Recreations:* golf, reading. *Address:* 85 Pendennis Road, Streatham, SW16 2SR. *T:* 01-769 0711.

MACKENZIE, David James Masterton, CMG 1957; OBE 1947 (MBE 1944); FRCP; Hon. Research Associate, Department of Bacteriology, Medical School, University of Cape Town; Visiting Scientist, Malaria Eradication Program, Communicable Disease Center, Atlanta, Georgia, 1965-69; Director of Medical and Health Services in Hong Kong, 1958-64; Colonial Medical Service, retired; *b* 23 July 1905; *s* of John Henderson Mackenzie and Agnes Masterton; two *d. Educ:* Rutherford College School; Edinburgh Univ. MB, ChB, Edinburgh, 1929; DPH (Edinburgh), 1948; MRCPE 1956, FRCPE 1959. Edinburgh Royal Infirmary, 1930-31. Joined Colonial Medical Service, 1934: DDMS Bechuanaland Protectorate, 1944, DMS 1946; DMS Nyasaland, 1949-55; DMS Northern Nigeria, 1955-57. *Recreations:* golf, fishing. *Address:* c/o Royal Bank of Scotland Ltd, 36 St Andrew Square, Edinburgh EH2 2YB; 8 Avondrust Avenue, Bergvliet, Cape, S Africa. *T:* 72-4541. *Clubs:* Royal Cape Golf; Zomba Gymkhana (Malaŵi).

MacKENZIE, Prof. Fraser; Professor of French Language and Literature, University of Birmingham, 1946-73; *b* Wellington, NZ, 3 Nov. 1905; *s* of late Hugh MacKenzie, CMG, Prof. of English Language and Literature, Victoria UC, Wellington, NZ, and late Annie Catherine Watson Stewart. *Educ:* Wellington Coll., NZ (Bristol Pianoforte Scholarship, 1923); Victoria University Coll., NZ; Sorbonne, Paris. Asst Lecturer in French, University of St Andrews, 1934-39; Sen. Lecturer in French, University of Aberdeen, 1939-46. Exchange Prof. of French, University of Montpellier, France, March 1948, 1950, 1952, 1954; Guest Prof. of English, Univ. of Toulouse, 1954; Guest Prof. of Mod. Langs, Victoria University Coll., Wellington, NZ, 1955. Hon. Life Mem., Académie des Jeux Floraux, Toulouse, 1954. Hon. President: Birmingham Univ. Mathematical Soc., 1961-62; Birmingham Univ. Electrical Engineers Soc., 1962-63; Hon. Vice-Pres., Salford Univ. Chem. Soc., 1972-73. DèsL (Paris), 1946; Doctorate (*hc*): University of Montpellier, 1952; University Laval, Quebec, 1967. Chevalier de la Légion d'honneur, 1954. *Publications:* Les Emprunts réciproques de l'anglais et du français, 2 vols (Paris), 1946; (ed) Studies in

French Language, Literature and History offered to Prof. R. L. Graeme Ritchie, 1950. *Recreations:* swimming, travel. *Address:* 3 Braithwaite Street, Karori, Wellington 5, New Zealand.

MacKENZIE, Rt. Hon. Gregor; *see* MacKenzie, Rt Hon. J. G.

MACKENZIE, Vice-Adm. Sir Hugh (Stirling), KCB 1966 (CB 1963); DSO 1942 and Bar 1943; DSC 1945; *b* 3 July 1913; 3rd *s* of Dr and Mrs T. C. Mackenzie, Inverness; *m* 1946, Helen Maureen, *er d* of Major J. E. M. Bradish-Ellames; one *s* two *d. Educ:* Cargilfield Sch.; Royal Naval Coll., Dartmouth. Joined Royal Naval Coll., 1927; qualified in Submarines, 1935. Served throughout War of 1939-45 in Submarines, comdg HMS Thrasher, 1941-43; HMS Tantalus, 1943-45; Comdr 1946; Capt. 1951; Rear-Adm. 1961; Flag Officer, Submarines, 1961-63; Chief Polaris Executive, 1963-68; Vice-Adm. 1964; retired 1968. Chm., Navy League, 1969-74; Dir, Atlantic Salmon Research Trust Ltd, 1969. Hon. Freeman, Borough of Shoreditch, 1942. FBIM. *Recreation:* the country. *Address:* Sylvan Lodge, Puttenham, near Guildford, Surrey. *Club:* Naval and Military.

MACKENZIE, Ian Clayton, CBE 1962; HM Diplomatic Service, retired; Ambassador to Korea, 1967-69; *b* 13 Jan. 1909; *m* 1948, Anne Helena Tylor; one *s* one *d. Educ:* Bedford Sch.; King's Coll., Cambridge. China Consular Service, 1932-41; Consul, Brazzaville, 1942-45, Foreign Office, 1945; 1st Sec., Commercial, Shanghai, 1946-69; Santiago, 1949-53; Commercial Counsellor: Oslo, 1953-58; Caracas, 1958-63; Stockholm, 1963-66. *Address:* Koryo, Armstrong Road, Brockenhurst, Hants. *T:* Brockenhurst 3453.

MACKENZIE, James, FIM, FICeram; Managing Director (Technical), British Steel Corporation, since 1976; *b* 2 Nov. 1924; *s* of James Mackenzie and Isobel Mary Chalmers; *m* 1950, Elizabeth Mary Ruttle; one *s* one *d. Educ:* Queen's Park Sch., Glasgow; Royal Technical Coll., Glasgow (BSc). The United Steel Companies Ltd, Research and Develt Dept, 1944-67; British Steel Corporation, 1967-. Pres., Inst. of Ceramics, 1965-67. *Recreations:* the countryside, golf. *Address:* Cranimoor, Kirby-in-Cleveland, North Yorkshire TS9 7AN. *T:* Wainstones 373. *Club:* Ganton Golf (Yorkshire).

MacKENZIE, James Alexander Mackintosh; Chief Road Engineer, Scottish Development Department, since 1976; *b* Inverness, 6 May 1928; *s* of late James MacKenzie and Jane Ann Mackintosh; *m* 1970, Pamela Dorothy Nixon; one *s* one *d. Educ:* Inverness Royal Acad. FICE, FIMuneE, FIHE. Miscellaneous local govt appts, 1950-63; Chief Resident Engr, Durham County Council, 1963-67; Dep. Dir, 1967-71, Dir, 1971-76, North Eastern Road Construction Unit, MoT, later DoE. *Recreations:* golf, fishing. *Address:* Scottish Development Department, New St Andrew's House, Edinburgh EH1 3SZ. *T:* 031-556 8400, ext. 4288. *Clubs:* Royal Automobile; Royal Scottish Automobile (Glasgow).

MacKENZIE, Rt. Hon. (James) Gregor, PC 1977; MP (Lab) Rutherglen since May 1964; Minister of State, Scottish Office, since 1976; *b* 15 Nov. 1927; *o s* of James and Mary MacKenzie; *m* 1958, Joan Swan Provan; one *s* one *d. Educ:* Queen's Park Sch.; Royal Technical College; Glasgow Univ. (School of Social Studies). Joined Labour Party, 1944. Contested (Lab): East Aberdeenshire, 1950; Kinross and West Perthshire, 1959. Chm., Scottish Labour League, 1948; Mem. and Magistrate, Glasgow Corporation, 1952-55, 1956-64; PPS to Rt Hon. James Callaghan, MP, Oppositon spokesman on Posts and Telecommunications, 1970-74; Parly Under-Sec. of State for Industry, 1975, Min. of State, 1975-76, DoI. Mem., Energy Commn, 1977-. JP Glasgow, 1962. *Address:* 19 Stewarton Drive, Cambuslang, Glasgow G72 8DE. *T:* 041-641 3646; 7 Carrick Court, Kennington Park Road, SE11 4EE. *T:* 01-735 2957.

MacKENZIE, James Sargent Porteous, OBE 1963; *b* 18 June 1916; *s* of late Roderick and Daisy W. MacKenzie; *m* 1944, Flora Paterson; three *s. Educ:* Portree High Sch.; Edinburgh Univ. (MA Hons 1939); Glasgow Univ. (Dip. Social Studies 1947). War Service, 1939-45: Captain RA (Combined Ops, Burma and Normandy). Scottish HQ, Min. of Labour, 1947-56; Labour Advr, UK High Commn, New Delhi, 1959-62 (First Sec., 1956, Counsellor, 1959); Ministry of Labour: Asst Controller, Scottish HQ, 1962-65; Dep. Controller, Yorks and Humberside Regional Office, 1965-67; Principal Dep. Controller, Scottish HQ, Dept of Employment, 1967-72; Asst Sec., 1970; Counsellor (Labour) British Embassy, Bonn, 1972-77, retired 1977. *Address:* 11 Baberton Park, Juniper Green, Edinburgh. *Club:* Royal Commonwealth Society.

McKENZIE, John, CMG 1970; MBE 1947; PhD; HM Diplomatic Service, retired; *b* 30 April 1915; *m* 1943, Sigridur Olafsdóttir; two *s* one *d. Educ:* Archbishop Holgate's Grammar Sch., York; Leeds Univ. Lectr, Univ. of Iceland, 1938-40; Second Sec. and Vice-Consul, Reykjavik, 1945; Consul, Helsinki, 1948; First Sec., 1949; Foreign Office, 1950; Sofia, 1953 (Chargé d'Affaires, 1954, 1955, 1956); Baghdad, 1956; Foreign Office, 1958; Counsellor, seconded to Cabinet Office, 1962; Helsinki, 1964 (Chargé d'Affaires, 1965, 1966); Dep. High Comr Calcutta, 1967-70; Ambassador to Iceland, 1970-75. *Address:* 60 Dome Hill, Caterham, Surrey CR3 6EB. *T:* Caterham 42546.

MACKENZIE, Brig. John Alexander, CBE 1955; DSO 1944 and Bar, 1944; MC 1940 and Bar, 1940; retired; *b* 9 March 1915; *s* of late Louis Robert Wilson Mackenzie; *m* 1952, Beryl Cathreen Culver; one *s. Educ:* Nautical Coll., Pangbourne; RMC, Sandhurst. 2nd Bn Gloucestershire Regt, 1935-43; Bn Comd, 2nd Bn Lancs Fusiliers, Tunisia, Sicily and Italy Campaigns, 1943-44 (despatches, 1944); Bde Comd: 11 Inf. Bde, Italy, 1944; 10 Inf. Bde, Greece, 1945-46; psc 1947; GSO1 HQ British Troops, Berlin, 1948-49; AAG (Organisation), HQ, BAOR, 1950; jssc 1951; GSO1 HQ Western Comd, 1951-54; Comd: Britcom Sub-area, N Korea, 1955; Inf. Trng Team, HQ Jordan Arab Army, 1956; Jt Concealment Centre, 1957-58; Small Arms Sch., Hythe, 1958-59; idc 1960; Comd: 1 Bde, Nigeria, 1961-63; 3 Bde, Congo, 1962; Actg GOC, Royal Nigerian Army, 1963; BGS Army Trng, MoD, 1964-67; ADC to the Queen, 1967-70; Comdt and Inspector of Intelligence, 1967-70; retired 1970. *Recreations:* swimming, sailing, touring Europe. *Address:* Eastling Manor, Eastling, Faversham, Kent.

McKENZIE, Rear-Adm. John Foster, CB 1977; CBE 1974 (OBE 1962); Chief of Naval Staff and Member of Defence Council, New Zealand, since 1975; *b* Waiuku, 24 June 1923; *s* of Dr J. C. McKenzie; *m* 1945, Doreen Elizabeth, *d* of Dr E. T. McElligott; one *s* one *d. Educ:* Timaru Boys' High Sch.; St Andrews Coll., Christchurch, NZ. Served War of 1939-45: Royal Navy; transferred to Royal New Zealand Navy, 1947; Head of Defence Liaison Staff, Singapore, 1959-61; CO, HMNZS Otago, 1962-1963; CO, HMNZS Philomel, 1965; Head, Defence Liaison Staff, London, 1966-68; Imperial Defence Coll., 1969; RNZN, Asst Chief of Defence Staff (Policy), Defence HQ, NZ, 1970-71; Deputy Chief of Naval Staff, 1972; Commodore, Auckland, 1973-75; Rear-Adm., Dec. 1975. ADC 1972-75. *Recreations:* gardening, fishing. *Address:* Chief of Naval Staff, Ministry of Defence, Wellington, New Zealand.

MACKENZIE, John Moncrieff Ord; Vice-Lord-Lieutenant of Peeblesshire, since 1956; *b* 1911; *s* of Kenneth Mackenzie, Dolphinton; *m* 1936, Delia Alice, *d* of late Wyndham Damer Clark, DL, JP, London, SW3; one *s* four *d. Educ:* Rugby; Corpus Christi Coll., Cambridge. WS, 1936. Captain, Lanarkshire Yeomanry (TA); served War of 1939-45 (despatches, Bronze Star Medal, US): GHQ, Liaison Regt. JP 1947, DL 1953, Peeblesshire. *Address:* Dolphinton House, Dolphinton, Peeblesshire. *T:* Dolphinton 286. *Club:* New (Edinburgh).

MACKENZIE, Keith Roderick Turing, MC; Secretary, Royal and Ancient Golf Club of St Andrews, Fife, Scotland, since 1967; *b* 19 Jan. 1921; *s* of Henry Roderick Turing Mackenzie and Betty Dalzell Mackenzie; *m* 1949, Barbara Kershaw Miles; two *s* two *d. Educ:* Uppingham Sch.; RMC, Sandhurst. Served War: Indian Army, 2/6th Gurkha Rifles, 1940-47 (MC, Italy, 1944). Burmah-Shell Oil Storage and Distributing Co. of India, 1947-65; Shell Company of Rhodesia, 1965-66. *Recreations:* gardening, golf. *Address:* Eden Hill, Kennedy Gardens, St Andrews, Fife KY16 9DJ. *T:* St Andrews 3581. *Clubs:* Royal Cinque Ports Golf (Deal); Royal Calcutta Golf (Calcutta); Royal Salisbury Golf (Rhodesia).

MACKENZIE, Kenneth Edward, CMG 1970; HM Diplomatic Service, retired; *b* 28 April 1910; *s* of late A. E. Mackenzie, Dundee, and late K. M. Mackenzie (*née* Foley); *m* 1935, Phyllis Edith Fawkes; one *s. Educ:* schools in India, Australia and in the UK; University Coll., London. Engineering industry, 1926-29; University Coll., London, 1929-32, BSc (Hons) in civil and mechanical engineering. Inst. of Civil Engineers, 1932-34; Dept of Overseas Trade, 1934-36; HM Embassy, Brussels, 1936-40; interned in Germany, 1940-41; HM Embassy, Tehran, 1942-45. Trade Commissioner: in India, 1945-48; in Malaya, 1949-54; Asst Sec., Bd of Trade, 1954-66; Counsellor (Commercial), HM Embassy, Stockholm, and Chargé d'Affaires *ad interim*, 1966-70; Counsellor (Investment), 1973; Counsellor (Investment), HM Embassy, Copenhagen, 1974-75. *Address:* Prestbury, Middle Hill, Englefield Green, Surrey TW2O OJP. *T:* Egham 7877. *Club:* Royal Commonwealth Society.

MACKENZIE, Kenneth Roderick, CB 1965; Clerk of Public Bills, House of Commons, 1959-73; *b* 19 April 1908; *s* of late Walter Mackenzie; *m* 1935, Mary Howard, *e d* of late Lt-Col C. H. Coode, RM; three *s* one *d. Educ:* Dulwich Coll.; New Coll., Oxford (scholar). 1st class Classical Moderations; 2nd class Literæ Humaniores. Asst clerk, House of Commons, 1930; Clerk of Standing Cttees, 1953. *Publications:* The English Parliament, 1950; Parliament, 1959; editions of Sir Bryan Fell's Guide to the Palace of Westminster, 1944-72; verse translations of: Słowacki's In Switzerland, 1953; Mickiewicz's Pan Tadeusz, 1964; Virgil's Georgics, 1969. *Recreations:* riding, gardening. *Address:* Woodnorton, Mayfield, East Sussex. *T:* Mayfield 2317. *Club:* Polish Hearth.

MacKENZIE, Kenneth William Stewart, CMG 1958; CVO 1975; FRAI; a Director of Studies, Royal Institute of Public Administration (Overseas Unit), since 1976; *b* 30 July 1915; *s* of late W. S. MacKenzie and E. MacKenzie (*née* Johnson); *m* 1939, Kathleen Joyce Ingram; one *s* one *d. Educ:* Whitcliffe Mount Gram. Sch., Cleckheaton; Downing Coll., Cambridge. 1st Cl. Hist. Tripos, Part I, 1935; Class II, Div. I, 1936; 1st Cl. Arch. and Anthrop. Tripos, Section A, 1937, BA 1936, MA 1962. Cadet, Colonial Administrative Service, Basutoland, 1938; Asst Sec., Mauritius, 1944; Administrative Officer, Kenya, 1948; Asst Financial Sec., Kenya, 1950; HM Treasury, 1951-53; Dep. Sec., 1954 and Permanent Sec., 1955, Treasury, Kenya; Minister for Finance and Development and Financial Sec., Kenya, 1959-62. MLC Kenya, 1955-62. Retired, 1963 to facilitate constitutional change. Re-employed as Principal, Colonial Office, 1963; Principal, HM Treasury, 1966-70; Asst Sec., DoE, 1970-75. *Publication:* pamphlet, How Basutoland is Governed, 1944. *Recreations:* reading, gardening. *Address:* Beaumont, 28 Greenhurst Lane, Oxted, Surrey RH8 0LB. *T:* Oxted 3848. *Clubs:* Royal Over-Seas League; Achilles; Nairobi (Nairobi).

McKENZIE, Malcolm George, MBE (mil.) 1944; solicitor; Secretary, Commission for the New Towns, since 1974; *b* 11 July 1917; *s* of Captain Simon McKenzie and Hilda Warner; *m* 1945, Flora, *d* of T. Harris, S Shields; one *s* two *d. Educ:* Ealing Grammar Sch.; Coll. of Law. 26th (LEE) RE, TA, 1938; served War, incl. Europe, 1939-46 (MBE); 124th LAA Regt, RA (Major). Administrator, Mddx CC, 1935-59; Under-Sec., County Councils Assoc., 1959-62; Chief Admin. Officer, Commn for the New Towns, 1962-73 (Advisory Tour, Venezuela, 1969). *Recreations:* Welcare (Christian Housing Assoc.), travel. *Address:* 16 Heronsforde, Ealing W13 8JE. *T:* 01-997 6957.

MACKENZIE, Maxwell Weir, OC 1972; CMG 1946; Director: Canadian Imperial Bank of Commerce, since 1955; Canron Ltd, since 1961; International Multifoods Corp., since 1964; *b* 30 June 1907; *s* of late Hugh Blair Mackenzie, Gen. Man., Bank of Montreal, Montreal, and Maude Marion Weir; *m* 1931, Jean Roger Fairbairn; two *s* two *d. Educ:* Lakefield Preparatory Sch., Lakefield, Ont.; Trinity Coll. School, Port Hope, Ont.; McGill Univ., Montreal (BCom 1928). Joined McDonald, Currie & Co., Chartered Accountants of Montreal, 1928; Mem. Soc. of Chartered Accountants of the Province of Quebec, 1929; Jr Partner, McDonald, Currie & Co., Montreal, 1935; on loan to Foreign Exchange Control Board, Ottawa, 1939-42; to Wartime Prices and Trade Board, Ottawa, 1942-44 (Dep. Chm. 1943-44); Mem., Royal Commission on Taxation of Annuities and Family Corporation, 1944; Dep. Minister of Trade and Commerce, 1945-51; Dep. Minister of Defence Production, Canada, 1951-52; Pres., Canadian Chemical & Cellulose Company, Ltd, 1954-59 (Exec. Vice-Pres., 1952-54). Mem., Economic Council of Canada, 1963-71. Dir, Internat. Multifoods Corp., 1964-77. Chairman: Royal Commission on Security, 1966; Federal Inquiry into Beef Marketing, 1975. Hon. LLD McGill, 1973. *Recreation:* ski-ing. *Address:* 383 Maple Lane, Rockcliffe Park, Ottawa K1M 1H7, Canada. *Clubs:* Rideau (Ottawa); Mount Royal (Montreal).

MacKENZIE, Norman Archibald MacRae, CC (Canada) 1969; CMG 1946; MM and Bar, 1918; CD 1968; QC; BA, LLB (Dalhousie); LLM (Harvard); FRSC 1943; Hon. LLD (Mount Allison, New Brunswick, Toronto, Dalhousie, Ottawa, Bristol, Alberta, Glasgow, St Francis Xavier, McGill, Sydney, Rochester, Alaska, California, British Columbia, RMC (Cambridge); DCL (Saskatchewan, Whitman College); DSc Social, Laval; DLitt, Memorial University of Newfoundland; President Emeritus, Hon. Professor of International Law, University of British Columbia, Vancouver, since 1962; President of the University, 1944-62; appointed to The Senate of Canada, 1966, retired 1969; *b* Pugwash, Nova Scotia, Canada, 5 Jan. 1894; *s* of Rev. James A. MacKenzie and Elizabeth MacRae; *m* 1928, Margaret, *d* of A. W. and Helen Thomas; one *s* two *d. Educ:* Pictou Acad.; Dalhousie Univ. (BA 1921, LLB

1923); Harvard (LLM 1924); St John's Coll., Cambridge (Postgrad. Dipl., 1925); Grays' Inn, London. Read Law with McInnes, Jenks and Lovitt; called to Bar of Nova Scotia, 1926; KC 1942; Legal Adviser, ILO, Geneva, 1925-27; Assoc. Prof. of Law, 1927-33, Prof. of International and Canadian Constitutional Law, 1933-40, Toronto Univ.; Pres., University of New Brunswick, 1940-44; Pres., Nat. Conf. of Canadian Universities, 1946-48; Pres., Canadian Club of Toronto, 1939-40; Chm., Research Commission, Canadian Inst. of Internat. Affairs, 1929-40; Founding Mem. and Hon. Chm., National Council CIIA; Chm., Wartime Information Board, Canada, 1943-45; Chm., Reconstruction Commn, Province of New Brunswick, 1941-44; Pres., Toronto Branch, League of Nations Soc., 1932-36; Delegate to Institute of Pacific Relations Conferences, Shanghai 1931, Banff 1933, Yosemite 1936, Virginia Beach 1939, Mont Tremblant 1942; Delegate to British Commonwealth Conferences, Toronto, 1933, Sydney, Australia, 1938; Delegate to 7th Congress on Laws of Aviation, Lyons, France, 1925; War Record: Canadian Inf., 1914-19; 6th Canadian Mounted Rifles' 85th Bn, Nova Scotia Highlanders (MM and Bar); Vice-Pres., National Council of Canadian YMCA's; Chm. Victory Loan Executive Cttee, Fredericton and York, New Brunswick, 1941-44; Mem., University Advisory Board, Dept of Labour; Mem., Advisory Cttee on University Training for Veterans, Dept of Veterans Affairs; Hon. Pres. Save the Children Fund, Canada; Mem., Legal Survey Cttee (Survey of Legal Profession of Canada), 1949-57; Chm., Consultative Cttee on Doukhobor Problems; Mem., Royal Commission on National Development in the Arts, Letters and Sciences, 1949-51; Dir, Bank of Nova Scotia, 1960-69; Mem. Vancouver Advisory Board, Canada Permanent Trust Company, 1962-; East African Commission on University Educn, 1962. Trustee: Teachers Insurance and Annuity Association of America, 1948-; Carnegie Foundation for the Advancement of Teaching, 1951-(Chm. Bd Trustees, 1959); Pres. Canadian Assoc. for Adult Education, 1957-59; Chm., University Grants Cttee, Prov. of NS, 1963-69; Mem. Royal Commission on Higher Educn, Prov. of PEI; Pres., Canadian Centenary Council; Dir, Centennial Commn (Canada); Dir, Fathers of Confedn Memorial Foundn; Pres., Nat. Assoc. of Canadian Clubs. Hon. Fellow, St John's Coll., Cambridge, 1964. John E. Read Medal for contributions to International Law, 1975. *Publications:* Legal Status of Aliens in Pacific Countries, 1937; Canada and Law of Nations (with L. H. Laing), 1938; Canada in World Affairs (with F. H. Soward, J. F. Parkinson, T. W. L. MacDermot), 1941; The Challenge to Education, 1953; First Principles, 1954; (with Jacob Austin) A Canadian View of Territorial Seas and Fisheries, 1956, etc. Contributor to: Canadian Bar Review, Law Journals, etc. *Recreations:* fishing, hunting, golf, tennis, badminton, ski-ing. *Address:* 4509 West 4th Avenue, Vancouver, BC, Canada. *Clubs:* Vancouver, University, Faculty (Vancouver).

MACKENZIE, Sir Robert Evelyn, 12th Bt, *cr* 1673; *b* 15 Feb. 1906; *s* of 11th Bt and Evelyn Mary Montgomery (*d* 1908), *d* of Major-Gen. Sir Edward W. Ward; *S* father, 1935; *m* 1st, 1940, Mrs Jane Adams-Beck (*d* 1953); 2nd, 1963, Mrs Elizabeth Campbell. *Educ:* Eton; Trinity Coll., Cambridge. Mem. of Lloyd's, 1932-71. Intelligence Corps, 1939; British Embassy, Paris, 1944; Foreign Office, 1947; Washington, 1948; Foreign Office, 1951. *Heir: kinsman* Rev. Ramsay Malcolm Bolton Mackenzie [*b* Aug. 1893; *m* 1920, Margaret Cecilia (*d* 1965), *o d* of Rev. G. A. S. Metford; *m* 1971, Joan Mary Davey]. *Address:* 18 Melton Court, Old Brompton Road, SW7 3JQ.

McKENZIE, Prof. Robert Trelford; Professor of Sociology (with special reference to Politics), London School of Economics and Political Science, since 1964; *b* 11 Sept. 1917; *s* of William Meldrum McKenzie and Frances (*née* Chapman). *Educ:* King Edward High Sch., Vancouver; University of British Columbia (BA); University of London (PhD). Taught at University of British Columbia, 1937-42. Served with Canadian Army, 1943-46. Has taught at London Sch. of Economics and Political Science since 1949. Visiting Lectr on Politics at Harvard and Yale Univs, Sept. 1958-Jan. 1959. Hon. LLD Simon Fraser Univ., 1969. *Publications:* British Political Parties: The Distribution of Power within the Conservative and Labour Parties, 1955, 2nd rev. edn, 1964 (translated into Spanish, German and Japanese); (with Allan Silver) Angels in Marble: Working Class Conservatism in Urban England, 1968 (trans, into Japanese). *Recreation:* broadcasting. *Address:* London School of Economics and Political Science, Houghton Street, Aldwych, WC2. *T:* 01-405 7686.

MACKENZIE, Sir Roderick (Campbell), 10th Bt *cr* 1703 (Nova Scotia); student in foreign languages, University of Virginia, Charlottesville, Va; *b* 15 Nov. 1954; *s* of Kenneth Roderick Mackenzie (*d* 1960) and of Elizabeth Carrington, *d* of late William Barbee Settle; *S* kinsman, Sir (Lewis) Roderick

Kenneth Mackenzie, 9th Bt, 1972. *Educ:* Univ. of Virginia. *Heir: cousin* Roderick Edward François McQuhae Mackenzie, CBE, DSC, Captain RN, retired [*b* 11 Dec. 1894; *m* 1938, Marie Evelyn Campbell, *o d* of late W. E. Parkinson; one *s* two *d*]. *Address:* 120 Church Street, Clifton Forge, Virginia 24422, USA. *T:* (703) 862-1203.

MACKENZIE, Sandy; *see* Mackenzie, Dr A. S.

MacKENZIE, William Forbes, CMG 1955; CBE 1951 (OBE 1946); *b* 5 June 1907; *e s* of late Dr A. J. MacKenzie, Salisbury, S Rhodesia; *m* 1934, Marion Elizabeth, *d* of late F. H. Glenton, Johannesburg, S Africa; no *c. Educ:* Merchiston Castle Sch.; Caius Coll., Cambridge. Native Affairs Dept, S Rhodesia, 1927-36; District Officer, Bechuanaland Protectorate, 1937-48; Asst Administrative Sec. to High Comr for Basutoland, Bechuanaland Protectorate and Swaziland, 1948-49; Dep. Resident Comr and Govt Sec., Swaziland, 1949-51; Dep. Res. Comr and Govt Sec., Bechuanaland Protectorate, 1951-53. Res. Comr, Bechuanaland Protectorate 1953-56, retired. *Recreations:* fishing, shooting and golf. *Address:* 9 Kevin Avenue, Chisipite, Salisbury, Rhodesia. *Clubs:* Country (Johannesburg); Bulawayo, Salisbury (Rhodesia).

MACKENZIE, Prof. William James Millar, CBE 1963; FBA 1968; Professor of Politics, Glasgow University, 1966-74, now Emeritus; *b* 8 April 1909; *s* of Laurence Millar Mackenzie, WS, Edinburgh; *m* 1943, Pamela Muriel Malyon; one *s* four *d. Educ:* Edinburgh Academy; Balliol Coll., Oxford (MA) (Ireland Schol. 1929); Edinburgh Univ. (LLB); Fellow of Magdalen Coll., Oxford, 1933-48; Temp. Civil Servant, Air Ministry, 1939-44; Official War Historian, SOE, 1945-48. Faculty Fellow, Nuffield Coll., 1948; Lecturer in Politics, Oxford Univ., 1948; Prof. of Government, Manchester Univ., 1949-66, Glasgow Univ., 1966-74; Special Comr for Constitutional Development, Tanganyika, 1952; Co-opted Mem., Manchester City Educn Cttee, 1953-64; apptd Mem., British Wool Marketing Board, 1954-66; Mem. Royal Commn on Local Govt in Greater London, 1957; Constitutional Adviser, Kenya, 1959; Vice-Chm., Bridges Cttee on Training in Public Administration for Overseas Countries, 1962; Member: Maud Cttee on Management in Local Govt, 1964-66; Cttee on Remuneration of Ministers and Members of Parliament, 1963-64; North-West Regional Economic Planning Council, 1965-66; SSRC, 1965-69; Parry Cttee on University Libraries, 1964-67; Chm., Children's Panel Adv. Cttee, Glasgow City, 1973-75. Hon. LLD: Dundee, 1968; Lancaster, 1970; Manchester, 1975; Hon. DLitt Warwick, 1972. *Publications:* (in part) British Government since 1918, 1950; (jtly) Central Administration in Great Britain, 1957; Free Elections, 1958; (ed with Prof. K. Robinson) Five Elections in Africa, 1959; Politics and Social Science, 1967; (jtly) Social Work in Scotland, 1969; Power, Violence, Decision, 1975; Explorations in Government, 1975; Political Identity, 1977; Biological Ideas in Politics, 1978. *Address:* 5 Kirklee Circus, Glasgow G12 0TW.

MACKENZIE CROOKS, Air Vice-Marshal Lewis, CBE 1963 (OBE 1950); Consultant Adviser in Orthopaedic Surgery, RAF, 1966-70, retired; *b* 20 Jan. 1909; *s* of David Mackenzie Crooks and Mary (*née* McKechnie); *m* 1936, Mildred, *d* of A. J. Gwyther; two *s* one *d. Educ:* Epworth Coll.; Liverpool Univ. MB, ChB 1931; FRCS 1937; ChM (Liverpool) 1945. House Surgeon: Northern Hosp., Liverpool, 1931-32; Shropshire Orthop. Hosp., Oswestry, 1932-33; Sen. House Surgeon: Selly Oak Hosp., Birmingham, 1933-34; All Saints Hosp., London, 1934-35; commnd RAF, 1935; surgical hosp. appts in RAF, 1936-52; overseas service: Palestine, 1937-39; Iraq, 1939-42 (despatches 1941); Egypt, 1950-51. Clinical Tutor, Edinburgh Royal Infirmary, 1947; Cons. in Orthop. Surgery, 1952; Sen. Cons. in Orthop. Surgery, 1955. QHS, 1966-70. *Publication:* article on chondromalaca patellae in Jl of Bone and Joint Surgery. *Recreations:* golf, gardening. *Address:* Trelawny, Harlyn Bay, Padstow, Cornwall PL28 8SF. *T:* St Merryn 520 631. *Clubs:* Royal Air Force; Trevose Golf, Country (Constantine Bay, Cornwall).

McKENZIE JOHNSTON, Henry Butler; Deputy Parliamentary Commissioner for Administration, since 1974; *b* 10 July 1921; *pr s* of Colin McKenzie Johnston and Bernardine (*née* Fawcett Butler); *m* 1949, Marian Allardyce Middleton, *e d* of late Brig. A. A. Middleton and Winifred (*née* Salvesen); one *s* two *d. Educ:* Rugby. Served with Black Watch (RHR), 1940-46; Adjt 6th Bn, 1944-45; Temp. Major 1945. Staff of HM Embassy, Athens, 1946-47; entered Foreign (subseq. Diplomatic) Service, 1947; Paris, 1948-51; British High Commn, Germany, 1951-54; FO, 1954-56; 1st Sec. (Commercial), Montevideo, 1956-60; FO, 1960-63; Counsellor (Information), Mexico City, 1963-66; Dep. High Comr, Port of Spain, 1966-67; seconded to Min. of Overseas Develt, 1968-70; Consul-Gen., Munich, 1971-73;

seconded to Office of Parly Comr, 1973-. *Address:* 6 Pembroke Gardens, W8 6HS. *Club:* Hurlingham.

MACKENZIE-KENNEDY, Brig. Archibald Gordon, CBE 1952 (OBE 1949); DSO 1945; Brigadier late Royal Scots; *b* 1904; *s* of late Maj.-Gen. Sir Edward Charles William Mackenzie-Kennedy, KBE, CB; *m* 1937, Jean Katherine, *d* of H. A. Law, Marble Hill, Ballymore, Co. Donegal. *Educ:* Marlborough; Royal Military College, Sandhurst. 2nd Lt Royal Scots, 1924. Served War of 1939-45: Burma, 1941-45 (DSO); Lt-Col, 1943; Brig., 1947; Comdr Eritrea District, 1950-52; retd 1955. County Comdt, Ulster Special Constabulary, 1955. *Address:* Tarff Old Manse, Kirkcudbright. *T:* Ringford 219.

MACKENZIE STUART, Hon. Lord; Alexander John Mackenzie Stuart; Judge of the Court of Justice, European Communities at Luxembourg, since 1973; a Senator of the College of Justice in Scotland, 1972-73; *b* 18 Nov. 1924; *s* of late Prof. A. Mackenzie Stuart, KC, and Amy Margaret Dean, Aberdeen; *m* 1952, Anne Burtholme Millar, *d* of late J. S. L. Millar, ws, Edinburgh; four *d. Educ:* Fettes Coll., Edinburgh (open Schol.); Sidney Sussex Coll., Cambridge (schol. 1949, 1st cl. Pt II Law Tripos, BA 1949); Edinburgh Univ. (LLB (dist.) 1951). Royal Engineers (Temp. Capt. 1946), 1942-47. Admitted Faculty of Advocates, 1951; QC (Scot.) 1963; Keeper of the Advocates Library, 1970-72. Standing Junior Counsel: to Scottish Home Dept, 1956-57; to Inland Revenue in Scotland, 1957-63. Sheriff-Principal of Aberdeen, Kincardine and Banff, 1971-72. Governor, Fettes College, 1962-72. Hon. Prof., Collège d'Europe, Bruges, 1974-77; DUniv. Stirling, 1973. *Publications:* Hamlyn Lectures: The European Communities and the Rule of Law, 1977; articles in legal publications. *Recreation:* collecting. *Address:* 24 rue de Wormeldange, Rodenbourg, Luxembourg. *T:* 77276; c/o Bank of Scotland, 64 George Street, Edinburgh. *Club:* New (Edinburgh).

MACKEOWN, John Ainslie, CIE 1942; Secretary, Arthur Guinness Son & Co. (Dublin) Ltd, 1952-67; retired; *b* 27 Oct. 1902; *s* of late Rev. William Mackeown; *m* 1935, Vivienne (marr. diss.), *d* of J. L. Musgrave, Hayfield House, Cork; two *s. Educ:* Radley; Worcester Coll., Oxford. Joined ICS, 1925; left India, 1947, after holding posts, Jt Sec. to Govt of India and Comr, Ambala Div. *Recreations:* golf, music, reading, bridge, sailing. *Address:* 57 Leeson Park, Dublin. *T:* Dublin 67964.

McKEOWN, Prof. Thomas, BA British Columbia, PhD McGill, DPhil Oxon, MB, BS London, MD Birmingham, FRCP; Professor of Social Medicine, 1945-77, and Pro-Vice-Chancellor, 1974-77, University of Birmingham; *b* 2 Nov. 1912; *s* of William McKeown; *m* 1940, Esmé Joan Bryan Widdowson; one *s* one *d. Educ:* Universities: British Columbia; McGill (National Research Council Schol.); Trinity Coll., Oxford (Rhodes Scholar); London (Guy's Hospital: Poulton Research Scholar). Demonstrator in biochemistry, McGill; demonstrator in physiology, Guy's Hosp. Lectures: Cutter, Harvard Sch. of Public Health, 1960; Lowell, Mass. General Hosp., 1963; British Council, Australia, 1963; De Frees, Univ. of Pennsylvania, 1969; Teale, RCP, 1969; BMA Winchester, 1970; Cecil and Ida Green, Univ. of BC, 1975. Rock Carling Fellow, Nuffield Provincial Hosps Trust, 1976. Jt Editor, Brit. Jl of Preventive and Social Medicine, 1950-58. *Publications:* A Balanced Teaching Hospital (jointly), 1965; Medicine in Modern Society, 1965; Introduction to Social Medicine (jt) 1966; Screening in Medical Care (jointly), 1968; Medical History and Medical Care (jt Ed.), 1971; The Modern Rise of Population, 1976; The Role of Medicine, 1976; contributions to scientific journals. *Address:* 23 Hintlesham Avenue, Edgbaston, Birmingham B15 2PH. *T:* 021-454 2810.

MACKEOWN, Thomas Frederick William; Administrator and Secretary, University College Hospital, London, 1946-63; *b* 3 Jan. 1904; *s* of Rev. William Mackeown, Rushbrooke, Co. Cork; *m* 1936, Lorraine, *d* of Major R. Hayes, Sherburh-in-Elmet, Yorks; one *d. Educ:* Felsted; Worcester Coll., Oxford (MA). Qualified as Chartered Accountant, 1927. Hospital Administrator: Liverpool Stanley Hospital, 1934-37; Clayton Hospital, Wakefield, 1937-45; Royal Infirmary, Sunderland, 1945-46; Hill Homes, Highgate (actg), 1966; King Edward VII Memorial Hospital, Bermuda, 1967; Vice-Chm., Management Cttee, Harefield and Northwoods Hosps, 1960-74; undertook Hosp. Domestic Staff Survey under aegis of King Edward's Hosp. Fund for London, 1968. Lay FRSocMed, 1974. *Address:* 4 Westhill Court, Millfield Lane, N6. *T:* 01-348 1952.

McKERN, Leo (Reginald McKern); actor; *b* 16 March 1920; *s* of Norman Walton McKern and Vera (née Martin); *m* 1946, Joan Alice Southall, (Jane Holland); two *d. Educ:* Sydney Techn. High Sch. Engrg apprentice, 1935-37; artist, 1937-40; AIF

(Corp., Engrs), 1940-42; actor, 1944; arrived England, 1946; CSEU tour, Germany; Arts Council tours, 1947; Old Vic, 1949-52; Shakespeare Meml Theatre, 1952-54; Old Vic last season, 1962-63; New Nottingham Playhouse, 1963-64; international films and television. *Recreations:* sailing, swimming, photography, painting, ecology, environment preservation. *Address:* Old Barn Cottage, Lower Heyford, Oxford OX5 3PD. *T:* Steeple Aston 47227.

MACKERRAS, (Alan) Charles, CBE 1974; Musical Director, English National Opera, formerly Sadler's Wells Opera, since 1970; Conductor, Hamburg State Opera, since 1966; Chief Guest Conductor, BBC Symphony Orchestra, since 1977; *b* 17 Nov. 1925; *s* of late Alan Patrick and Catherine Mackerras, Sydney, Australia; *m* 1947, Helena Judith (née Wilkins); two *d. Educ:* Sydney Grammar Sch. Principal Oboist, Sydney Symphony Orchestra, 1943-46; Staff Conductor, Sadlers Wells Opera, 1949-53; Principal Conductor BBC Concert Orchestra, 1954-56; freelance conductor with most British orchestras, 1957-66; frequent tours of opera and concerts in Scandinavia, Germany, Italy, Czechoslovakia, Hungary, Rumania, USSR, Belgium, Holland, Australia, S Africa, Canada. Frequent broadcasts BBC; TV programmes of opera and ballet; commercial recordings; appearances at many internat. festivals and opera houses. *Publications:* ballet arrangements of Pineapple Poll and of Lady and the Fool; articles in Opera Magazine, Music and Musicians and other musical jls. *Recreations:* languages, yachting. *Address:* 10 Hamilton Terrace, NW8. *T:* 01-286 4047.

MACKESON, Sir Rupert (Henry), 2nd Bt *cr* 1954; General Manager, Master Classes; *b* 16 Nov. 1941; *s* of Brig. Sir Harry Ripley Mackeson, 1st Bt, and Alethea, Lady Mackeson, *d* of late Comdr R. Talbot, RN; *S* father, 1964. *Educ:* Harrow; Trinity Coll., Dublin (MA). Captain, Royal Horse Guards, 1967, retd 1968. *Recreations:* art, racing. *Heir:* none. *Address:* 2 Orchard Court, Portman Square, W1. *T:* 01-492 1705. *Club:* White's.

MACKESSACK, Lt-Col Kenneth; Vice-Lieutenant, Moray, since 1964; *b* 1902; *s* of late George Ross Mackessack; *m* 1st, 1929, Rose Elizabeth (marr. diss., 1947), *d* of late Sir Henry D. Craik, 3rd Bt, GCIE, KCSI; one *s* one *d*; 2nd, 1947, Nora Joyce, *d* of late Maj.-Gen. C. E. Edward-Collins; one *d. Educ:* Rugby; RMC, Sandhurst. Commissioned Seaforth Highlanders, 1923; Adjt 1935. NW Frontier Ops, 1931; served in Middle East and N Africa, 1940-43 (wounded, despatches); on Gen. Staff and with 51st Highland and 4th Indian Divs; Military Attaché, Washington, 1943-46; retd 1947. Convenor, Moray County Council, 1958-67. Chm. TA Assoc. of Moray, 1954-62. DL Moray, 1954. *Recreations:* shooting, fishing. *Address:* Ardgye, Elgin, Morayshire. *T:* Alves 250.

MACKEY, Most Rev. John; *see* Auckland (NZ), Bishop of, (RC).

MACKEY, Prof. William Arthur, TD; St Mungo Professor of Surgery, University of Glasgow, 1953-72; *b* 1 Oct. 1906; *s* of Arthur Edward Mackey, Schoolmaster, and Elizabeth Annie (née Carr); *m* 1939, Joan Margaret Sykes; two *s* two *d. Educ:* Ardrossan Academy; Univ. of Glasgow. MB, ChB (hons). Asst to Prof. of Pathology, Univ. of Glasgow, 1928; Asst to Regius Prof. of Surgery, University of Glasgow, 1931. Hon. FACS. *Recreations:* golf, gardening, repenting plans and pottering around bohemia. *Address:* 4 West Abercromby Street, Helensburgh, Dunbartonshire G84 9LJ. *T:* Helensburgh 3659. *Clubs:* Royal Commonwealth Society; Royal Scottish Automobile (Glasgow), Glasgow Golf.

MACKIE, family name of **Baron Mackie of Benshie.**

MACKIE OF BENSHIE, Baron *cr* 1974 (Life Peer), of Kirriemuir; **George Yull Mackie,** CBE 1971; DSO 1944; DFC 1944; Chairman: Caithness Glass Ltd, since 1966; Caithness Pottery Co. Ltd; The Benshie Cattle Co. Ltd; *b* 10 July 1919; *s* of late Maitland Mackie, OBE, Hon. LLD; *m* 1944, Lindsay Lyall Sharp, *y d* of Mrs Isabella Sharp, OBE, Aberdeen; three *d* (one *s* decd). *Educ:* Aberdeen Grammar Sch.; Aberdeen Univ. Served War of 1939-45, RAF; Bomber Command, (DSO, DFC); Air Staff, 1944. Farming at Ballinshoe, Kirriemuir, from 1945. Contested (L) South Angus, 1959; MP (L) Caithness and Sutherland, 1964-66. Chm. Scottish Liberal Party, 1965-70. Mem., EEC Scrutiny Cttee (D), House of Lords; Mem., Liberal Shadow Admin; Liberal Spokesman, House of Lords: Devolution, Agriculture, Scotland, Industry. *Publication:* Policy for Scottish Agriculture, 1963. *Address:* Ballinshoe, Kirriemuir, Angus. *T:* Kirriemuir 2270. *Clubs:* Garrick, Farmers', Royal Air Force.

See also John Mackie, Maitland Mackie.

MACKIE, Air Cdre (Retd) Alastair Cavendish Lindsay, CBE 1966; DFC 1943 and Bar 1944; Director General, Health Education Council, since 1972; *b* 3 Aug. 1922; *s* of George Mackie, DSO, OBE, MD, Malvern, Worcs and May (*née* Cavendish); *m* 1944, Rachel Goodson; two *s. Educ:* Charterhouse. Royal Air Force, 1940-68; Under Treas., Middle Temple, 1968; Registrar, Architects' Registration Council, 1970; Sec., British Dental Assoc., 1971. *Recreation:* squash. *Address:* 4 Warwick Drive, SW15 6LB. *T:* 01-789 4544. *Club:* Royal Air Force.

MACKIE, Edwin Gordon; Hon. Ophthalmic Surgeon, United Sheffield Hospitals; Ophthalmic Medical Referee to County Courts; *b* 1896; *e s* of late David Cable Mackie, FSA (Scotland), and Charlotte Fyffe McDonald; *m* 1st, 1931, Mary Owen (*d* 1968), *y d* of F. P. Stokes, Melbourne, Australia; one *s* two *d*; 2nd, 1970, Peggy Lever Brundell Bovill, *o d* of Basil Pickering, MC, JP, East Markham. Educ: Madras Coll.; St Andrews Univ.; Birmingham. Served European War: MEF, BEF, Lt The Royal Scots. MA 1919; MB, ChB, 1924 (Medal Ophthalmology). Resident Posts: Dundee Royal Infirm.; Birmingham and Midland Eye Hospital; DOMS (England), FRCSGlas. Temp. Tutor, Edinburgh, 1927; Asst Surgeon, Royal Hosp., Sheffield, 1927, Surg. 1935. Formerly: Surg., Beckett Hosp., Barnsley; visiting oculist, State Instn, Rampton, etc; Clin. Lectr in Ophthalmology; Lectr in Applied Anat., University of Sheffield; Ext. Examr Queen's Univ., Belfast, and Examr for Dipl. in Ophthalmology, Examining Bd in England; Mem. Council, Sheffield Univ., 1949-51; Mem. Bd of Govs, United Sheffield Hosps, 1954-57. Served War of 1939-45: RAMC; France, Comd Ophthalmologist UK, Lt-Col OC Hosp. MEF. President: N of England Ophthalmological Soc., 1947; Sheffield Medico Chirurgical Soc., 1957. Member: Oxford Ophthalmological Congress; Ophthal. Soc. of UK; Ophthal. Gp Cttee, BMA, 1945-65; Council, Faculty of Ophthalmologists, 1946-66 (Pres., 1959-61, Hon. Mem., 1971); Court, University of Sheffield, 1963-75. Life Trustee, Zachary Merton Charity for Convalescents (Chm., 1966-76). Ophthalmic Lecture Tour, Australia and India, 1955. Middlemore Memorial Lectr, 1955. Convenor, Ophth. Adv. Cttee, Sheffield Region, 1948-63; Visitor, Educational Establishments and Examinations, General Optical Council, UK. *Publications:* articles and papers to: Brit. Jl of Ophthalmology; Trans. Ophthalmolog. Soc. of UK, etc. *Recreations:* heraldry, fishing. *Address:* 357 Fulwood Road, Sheffield S10 3BQ. *T:* Sheffield 662206. *Club:* Sheffield (Sheffield).
See also A. H. M. Evans.

MACKIE, James Richard, CMG 1941; BSc (Agric); *b* 1896; *s* of J. H. Mackie, JP, Castle Cary, Somerset; *m* 1929, Sylvia M. Miller; one *s. Educ:* Sexey's Sch., Bruton; University Coll., Reading. Army, 1914-18 (despatches, Belgian Croix de Guerre). Superintendent in Agricultural Dept, Nigeria, 1921; Dept. Asst Dir of Agriculture, 1928; Asst Dir of Agriculture, 1929; Dir of Agriculture, Nigeria, 1936-45. Mem. Executive Council of Nigeria, 1942-45. Member: Colonial Adv. Cttee for Agriculture, Forestry and Animal Health, 1946-49; Scientific Adv. Cttee, Empire Cotton Growing Corp.; Soulbury Commission (investigating sugar industry in West Indies), 1948-49; Governing Body of Imperial Coll. of Tropical Agriculture, Trinidad, 1949-56; SW Regional Hospital Board: Mem., 1954-63, Chm., Mental Health Cttee, 1957-63; General Comr of Income Tax, 1962-67. *Address:* 3 Bec-en-Hent, Bickwell Valley, Sidmouth, Devon. *T:* Sidmouth 2707.

MACKIE, John; Chairman, Forestry Commission, since 1976; *b* 24 Nov. 1909; *s* of late Maitland Mackie, OBE, Farmer, and Mary Ann Mackie (*née* Yull); *m* 1934, Jeannie Inglis Milne; three *s* two *d. Educ:* Aberdeen Gram. Sch.; North of Scotland Coll. of Agriculture. Managing director of family farming company at Bent, Laurencekirk, Kincardineshire, 1930-; Harold's Park Farm, Nazeing, Waltham Abbey, Essex, 1953-; Vicarage and Plumridge Farms, Hadley Wood, Enfield, 1968-. MP (Lab) Enfield East, 1959-Feb. 1974; Jt Parly Sec., Min. of Agriculture, 1964-70. *Publication:* (for Fabian Soc.) Land Nationalisation. *Recreations:* golf and tennis. *Address:* Harold's Park, Nazeing, Waltham Abbey, Essex. *T:* Nazeing 2202. *Club:* Farmers'.
See also Baron Mackie of Benshie, Maitland Mackie:

McKIE, Rt. Rev. John David; Assistant Bishop of Coventry since 1960; Vicar of Great and Little Packington since 1966; *b* 14 May 1909; *s* of Rev. W. McKie, Melbourne, Vic; *m* 1952, Mary Lesley, *d* of late Brig. S. T. W. Goodwin, DSO and of Mrs Goodwin, Melbourne, Vic; four *d. Educ:* Melbourne Church of England Grammar Sch.; Trinity Coll., Melbourne Univ.; New Coll., Oxford. BA (Trinity Coll., Melbourne Univ.). 1931; MA (New Coll., Oxford), 1945; Deacon, 1932; Priest, 1934; Asst

Chap. Melbourne Church of England Grammar Sch., 1932-33; Chap. and lecturer, Trinity Coll., Melbourne, 1936-39; served War of 1939-45 (despatches): AIF, 1939-44; Asst CG; Vicar Christ Church, South Yarra, 1944-46; Coadjutor, Bishop of Melbourne (with title of Bishop of Geelong) and Archdeacon of Melbourne, 1946-60, Chaplain and Sub-Prelate, Order of St John of Jerusalem, 1949. *Address:* Little Packington Rectory, Meriden, Coventry.
See also Sir W. N. McKie.

MACKIE, John Duncan, CBE 1944; MC, MA, Hon. LLD St Andrews and Glasgow; HM Historiographer in Scotland since 1958; Professor of Scottish History and Literature in the University of Glasgow, 1930-57, retired; Dean of Faculties (Deputy-Principal), 1940-45; visiting Canadian and S African Universities on British Council travel grants; Member Scottish Records Advisory Council and Chairman, Scottish National Register of Archives; a Vice-President, of Society of Antiquaries of Scotland, 1949-53; President of Scottish History Society; President of Historical Association of Scotland, 1949-53; Member, Scottish National Portrait Gallery Advisory Committee; President of Glasgow Archæological Society, 1936-39; *b* 1887; *e s* of late John Beveridge Mackie of the Dunfermline Journal and Lilias Agnes, *d* of James Robb; *m* 1917, Cicely Jean (*d* 1976), *e d* of Alexander Stephen Paterson, Advocate, Edinburgh; two *s* one *d. Educ:* Middlesbrough High Sch.; Jesus Coll., Oxford. 2nd Cl. Classical Mods; 1st Cl. History Finals; Lothian Essay Prize; Hon. LLD (St Andrews), 1950; Hon. LLD (Glasgow). 1959. Lecturer in Modern History, and head of the Dept of Modern History in the University of St Andrews, 1908-26; Prof. of Modern History in the University of London (Bedford Coll.), 1926-30. Served European War, 1914-19, with 14th Battalion Argyll and Sutherland Highlanders, Capt. (Acting Major, twice wounded); Chm. of Glasgow Joint Recruiting Board, 1939-46. Chevalier de la Légion d'Honneur, 1946; KStJ 1955 (CStJ 1948). *Publications:* essays and reviews in the Scottish Historical Review, English Historical Review, History, Encyclopædia Britannica, etc; The Sixteenth Century, in Cassell's History of the British People (1925); Negotiations between James VI and I and Ferdinand I of Tuscany (1927); The Estate of the Burgesses in the Scots Parliament (1923) (with Dr G. S. Pryde); Cavalier and Puritan, 1930; Andrew Lang and House of Stuart, 1935; Thomas Thomson's Memorial on Old Extent (Stair Soc.), 1946; The Earlier Tudors, 1485-1558, 1952; The University of Glasgow, 1451-1951: A Short History, 1954; Scottish History (Readers' Guide), 1956; A History of the Scottish Reformation, 1960; Introd. to Polwarth Papers, V, 1962; A History of Scotland (Pelican), 1964; (ed) Calendar of State Papers relating to Scotland and Mary Queen of Scots, Vol. XIII, 1597-1603, 1969. *Address:* Marley Manor Nursing Home, near Haslemere, Surrey.

MACKIE, John Leslie, FBA 1974; Fellow and Praelector in Philosophy, University College, Oxford, since 1967; *b* 25 Aug. 1917; *s* of late Alexander Mackie and Annie Burnett Mackie (*née* Duncan); *m* 1947, Joan Armiger Meredith; two *s* three *d. Educ:* Knox Grammar Sch., Sydney; Sydney Univ. (BA); Oriel Coll., Oxford (MA). Served War of 1939-45, RAOC, REME, Captain. Lectr in Moral and Political Philosophy, Sydney Univ., 1946; Prof. of Philosophy, Univ. of Otago, 1955; Challis Prof. of Philosophy, Sydney Univ., 1959; Prof. of Philosophy, Univ. of York, 1963. *Publications:* Truth, Probability, and Paradox, 1973; The Cement of the Universe, 1974; Problems from Locke, 1976; Ethics: inventing right and wrong, 1977; articles in philosophical jls, etc. *Address:* University College, Oxford OX1 4BH. *T:* Oxford 41661; 178 Banbury Road, Oxford OX2 7BT. *T:* Oxford 57858.

MACKIE, Lily Edna Minerva; Head Mistress, City of London School for Girls, since 1972; *b* 14 April 1926; *d* of late Robert Wood Mackie and late Lilian Amelia Mackie (*née* Dennis). *Educ:* Plaistow Grammar Sch.; University Coll., London (BA); Lycée de Jeunes Filles, Limoges; Université de Poitiers. Asst Mistress: Ilford County High Sch. for Girls, 1950-59; City of London Sch. for Girls, 1960-64; Head Mistress: Wimbledon County Sch., 1964-69; Ricards Lodge High Sch., Wimbledon, 1969-72. FRSA. *Recreations:* theatre, music, gardening, travel, boating. *Address:* City of London School for Girls, Barbican, EC2Y 8BB. *T:* 01-628 0841. *Club:* Soroptimist International.

MACKIE, Maitland, CBE 1965; Lord-Lieutenant of Aberdeenshire, since 1975; farmer since 1932; *b* 16 Feb. 1912; *s* of late Dr Maitland Mackie and Mary (*née* Yull); *m* 1st, 1935, Isobel Ross (*d* 1960); two *s* four *d*; 2nd, 1963, Martha Pauline Turner. *Educ:* Aberdeen Grammar Sch.; Aberdeen Univ. (BSCAgric). FEIS 1972, FRAgSs 1974. County Councillor, Aberdeenshire, 1951-75 (Convener 1967-75); Chm., NE Develt Authority, 1969-75; Chm., Aberdeen Milk Marketing Bd, 1965-;

Chm., Peterhead Bay Management Co., 1975; Mem., Agric. Sub-Cttee, Univ. Grants Cttee, 1965-75; Mem., Clayson Cttee on Drink Laws in Scotland. KStJ 1977. *Recreation:* travel. *Address:* Cramond House, 17 Rubislaw Den North, Aberdeen AB2 4AL. *T:* Aberdeen 33587. *Clubs:* Farmers'; University (Aberdeen).
See also Baron Mackie of Benshie, John Mackie.

McKIE, Sir William Neil, Kt 1953; MVO 1948; MA, Hon. DMus Oxon, Melbourne; FRSCM, FRCM, FRCO, FTCL, Hon. RAM; Hon. Secretary, Royal College of Organists, 1963-67; Hon. Fellow, Worcester College, Oxford, 1954; Organist and Master of the Choristers, Westminster Abbey, 1941-63 (on leave of absence, 1941-45, during war service, RAF, Volunteer Reserve); *b* Melbourne, Australia, 22 May 1901; *s* of Rev. William McKie; *m* 1956, Phyllis Ross, *widow* of Gerald Walker Birks, OBE, and *d* of John Wardrope Ross, Montreal. *Educ:* Melbourne Grammar Sch.; Royal Coll. of Music; Worcester Coll., Oxford. Organist St Agnes, Kennington Park, 1920-21; organ scholar, Worcester Coll., Oxford, 1921-24; asst music master, Radley Coll., 1923-26; Dir of Music, Clifton Coll., 1926-30; City Organist, Melbourne, 1931-38; Dir of Music, Geelong Grammar Sch., 1934-38; Organist and Instructor in Music, Magdalen Coll., Oxford, 1938-41; Organist at Sheldonian Theatre, 1939-41; Organ prof., Royal Acad. of Music, 1946-62; Hon. Associate Dir, Royal School of Church Music, 1947-52; Dir of Music, Coronation Service, 1953; President: Incorporated Association of Organists, 1950-52; Royal College of Organists, 1956-58; London Soc. of Organists, 1958-59; Incorporated Soc. of Musicians, 1959. Hon. Mem., American Guild of Organists; Hon. Fellow: Westminster Choir Coll., Princeton, NJ, 1965; Royal Canadian Coll. of Organists, 1965. Comdr with Star, Order of St Olav, Norway, 1964. *Address:* 10 Driveway, Ottawa, Ontario K2P 1C7, Canada. *Clubs:* Athenæum, Garrick; Rideau (Ottawa).
See also Rt Rev. J. D. McKie.

McKIERNAN, Most Rev. Francis J.; *see* Kilmore, Bishop of, (RC).

McKILLOP, Edgar Ravenswood, CMG 1952; OBE 1942; Company Director; Commissioner of Works and Permanent Head, Ministry of Works, NZ, 1944-55, retired; *b* 26 July 1895; *s* of Alexander McKillop and Jean Cameron; *m* 1930, Marguerita Anne Mary Dennis. *Educ:* Canterbury Univ. Coll., New Zealand. Civil engineer, New Zealand Government engaged on developmental works; railway construction, irrigation and hydro-electric projects. Served 1914-18 with 1st NZEF overseas (twice wounded). Lt-Col NZ Eng. 2nd NZ Exp. Force, in Pacific, 1939-42; Dep. Comr Def. Constr., 1942-44, in NZ and South Pacific. Past mem. Scientific and Industrial Research Council; FICE and past mem. of Council; FNZ Inst. of Engineers and past mem. of Council. *Recreation:* golf. *Address:* PO Box 3009, Raumati South, Paraparaumu, New Zealand.

McKINLEY, Air Vice-Marshal David Cecil, CB 1966; CBE 1957; DFC 1940; AFC 1944, Bar 1945; RAF; *b* 18 Sept. 1913; *s* of David McKinley, Civil Engineer, and May McKinley (*née* Ward); *m* 1940, Brenda Alice (*née* Ridgway); three *s. Educ:* Bishop Foy Sch., Waterford; Trinity Coll., Dublin. Radio Engineering, Ferranti Ltd, 1935. Entered (regular) Royal Air Force, 1935; served continuously since that date; AOC Malta and Dep. C-in-C (Air), Allied Forces, Mediterranean, 1963-65; SASO, Transport Command, 1966, Air Support Command, 1967-68; retired 1968. Freeman, The Guild of Air Pilots and Air Navigators, 1959. FIN 1949. *Recreations:* sailing, fishing, water ski-ing, gardening. *Address:* Sundial Cottage, Fawley, Hants. *T:* Fawley 891031; Midland Bank, Bushey, Herts. *Club:* Royal Air Force.

McKINNEY, Mrs J. P.; *see* Wright, Judith.

McKINNEY, Sir William, Kt 1964; CBE 1956; *b* 14 Nov. 1897; *s* of James and Edith McKinney; *m* 1st, 1925, Lisla Chesney, *d* of Robert Clyde; one *s*; 2nd 1936, Mary E., *d* of William T. Unsworth. *Educ:* Belfast Royal Academy. Joined Board of Management of Royal Victoria Hospital, Belfast, 1931; subsequently Hon. Sec. First Vice-Chm., Northern Ireland Hospitals Authority, 1948-50 and 1953-55. Custodian Trustee, Belfast Savings Bank (Chm., 1946 and 1967). Chm., Northern Ireland Hospitals Authority, 1956-65. Hon. Treasurer, Queen's Univ., 1966. Hon. LLD Queen's Univ., 1966. *Address:* 5 Deramore Park South, Belfast BT9 5JY. *T:* Belfast 666396.

MacKINNON, Prof. Donald MacKenzie, MA; Norris-Hulse Professor of Divinity, Cambridge University, since 1960; Fellow of Corpus Christi College, Cambridge, since 1960; *b* Oban, 27 Aug. 1913; *o s* of late D. M. MacKinnon, Procurator Fiscal, and late Grace Isabella Rhind; *m* 1939, Lois, *e d* of late Rev. Oliver Dryer; no *c. Educ:* Cargilfield Sch., Edinburgh; Winchester Coll. (scholar); New Coll., Oxford (scholar). Asst in Moral Philosophy (to late Prof. A. E. Taylor) at Edinburgh, 1936-37; Fellow and Tutor in Philosophy at Keble Coll., Oxford, 1937-47; Dir of Course for special courses in Philosophy for RN and RAF cadets at Oxford, 1942-45; Lectr in Philosophy at Balliol Coll., 1945-47; Wilde Lectr in Natural and Comparative Religion at Oxford, 1945-47; Regius Prof. of Moral Philosophy at Aberdeen, 1947-60. Lectures: Scott Holland, 1952; Hobhouse, 1953; Stanton, in the Philosophy of Religion, Cambridge, 1956-59; Gifford, Edinburgh, 1965-66; Prideaux, Exeter, 1966; Coffin, London, 1968; Riddell, Newcastle-upon-Tyne, 1970; D. Owen Evans, Aberystwyth, 1973; Drummond, Stirling, 1977. Pres., Aristotelian Soc., 1976-77. Hon. DD Aberdeen, 1961. Mem. Labour Party. *Publications:* (ed) Christian Faith and Communist Faith, 1953; The Notion of a Philosophy of History, 1954; A Study in Ethical Theory, 1957; (with Prof. G. W. H. Lampe) The Resurrection, 1966; Borderlands of Theology and other papers, 1968; The Stripping of the Altars, 1969; The Problem of Metaphysics, 1974; Some Reflections on the Problem of Evil, 1977; articles, reviews, etc in periodicals and symposia in UK, France and Germany. *Recreations:* walking, cats, the cinema. *Address:* 9 Parker Street, Cambridge; Tigh Grianach, North Connel, Argyll.

MACKINNON, Duncan; *b* 18 Sept. 1909; *e s* of late Capt. William Mackinnon, Loup, Clachan, Argyll; *m* 1932, Pamela Rachel, 2nd *d* of late Capt. R. B. Brassey; one *s* one *d. Educ:* Eton; Magdalen, Oxford. Served War of 1939-45, Argyll and Sutherland Highlanders. Dep. Chm. Eagle Star Assurance Co. Ltd; Director: The Ashdown Investment Trust Ltd; Hambros Investment Trust Ltd; Chm., Discount & General Securities Ltd. Chm. London Discount Market Assoc., 1959-61. JP Oxfordshire, 1945-56; High Sheriff of Oxfordshire, 1949-50. *Recreations:* fishing, shooting. *Address:* 100 Lancaster Gate, W2 3NY; Swinbrook House, Burford, Oxfordshire. *T:* Burford 2216. *Club:* White's.

McKINNON, Hector Brown, CC (Canada) 1968; CMG 1944; retired as Chairman, Tariff Board, Canada; *b* Priceville, Grey Co., Ont, 6 Dec. 1890; *s* of Neil McKinnon and Elizabeth Brown; *m* 1929, Phyllis, *d* of Aldham Wilson, Brandon, Man.; two *s. Educ:* Jarvis Coll. Inst., Toronto; Coll. Inst., Owen Sound, Ont; Normal Sch., Toronto. Past Commissioner of Tariff; Chm. Wartime Prices and Trade Board, 1940-41; Pres., Commodity Prices Stabilization Corporation, 1941-46; Mem., Economic Advisory Cttee; Dir, Canadian Commercial Corporation. Prior to 1926, was engaged in newspaper work in various capacities on staff of The Globe; served as agric. editor, western corresp., city editor, Parly corresp. and editorial writer; served in European War, 1914-18, as Adjt 110th Inf. Bn. Seconded in Eng. to RFC (despatches). Presbyterian. *Address:* 146 Roger Road, Ottawa, Ont, Canada.

McKINNON, Neil Nairn, QC 1957; **His Honour Judge McKinnon;** an Additional Judge, Central Criminal Court, since 1968; *b* 19 Aug. 1909; *s* of late Neil Somerville and Christina McKinnon, Melbourne; *m* 1937, Janet, *d* of late Michael Lilley, Osterley; three *s* four *d. Educ:* Geelong Coll.; Trinity Hall, Cambridge (MA). Squadron Leader, RAFVR, Feb. 1940-Dec. 1945. Called to the Bar, Lincoln's Inn, 1937; Bencher, 1964. Recorder of Maidstone, 1961-68. *Recreation:* cricket. *Address:* Central Criminal Court, Old Bailey, EC4. *Club:* Hawks (Cambridge).

MACKINNON, Dame Patricia; *see* Mackinnon, Dame U. P.

MacKINNON, Peter Ralph, DSC 1942; Underwriting Member of Lloyd's; *b* 6 May 1911; *s* of Norman MacKinnon; *m* 1934, Jean Mary, *d* of G. N. Ogilvie; one *s* two *d. Educ:* Wellington Coll.; Jesus Coll., Cambridge. Entered Lloyd's, 1931; Underwriting Mem., 1932; Dep. Chm., 1964; Member: Cttee, Lloyd's Underwriters Assoc., 1958-73; Cttee of Lloyd's, 1961-64; Cttee Lloyd's Register of Shipping, 1958. Served War of 1939-45: RNVR, 1940; Combined Ops, Europe, N Africa, India, Malaya, Pacific (DSC, despatches twice); retd as Comdr RNVR, 1945. *Recreations:* golf, tennis. *Address:* Gorse Heath, Gerrards Cross, Bucks. *T:* Gerrards Cross 83451. *Clubs:* City University; All England Lawn Tennis; Denham Golf.

MACKINNON, Dame (Una) Patricia, DBE 1977 (CBE 1972); *b* Brisbane, 24 July 1911; *d* of Ernest T. and Pauline Bell; *m* 1936, Alistair Scobie Mackinnon; one *s* one *d. Educ:* Glennie School and St Margaret's School, Queensland. Member Cttee of Management, Royal Children's Hospital, Melbourne, 1948; Vice-President, 1958; President, 1965-. *Recreations:* gardening, reading history and biographies. *Address:* 5 Moralla Road,

Kooyong, Victoria, Australia 3144. *T:* 20-2733. *Club:* Alexandra (Melbourne).

McKINNON, Maj.-Gen. Walter Sneddon, CB 1966; CBE 1961 (OBE 1947); *b* 8 July 1910; *s* of Charles McKinnon and Janet Robertson McKinnon (*née* Sneddon); *m* 1937, Anna Bloomfield Plimmer; four *s* one *d. Educ:* Otago Boys High Sch., Dunedin, NZ; Otago Univ. (BSc); commissioned in NZ Army, 1935; various military courses, including Staff Coll., Camberley, England. Served War of 1939-45: Pacific, Italy (Lt-Col); despatches), Japan (occupation) (OBE); Brigadier, 1953; subsequent appointments: Comdr, Southern Mil. Dist (NZ), 1953; Head, NZ Joint Mil. Mission, Washington, DC, 1954-57; Comdr, Northern Military District, 1957-58; Adjutant-General, 1958-62; Quartermaster-General, 1963-64, Maj.-General, 1965; Chief of the General Staff, NZ Army, 1965-67; retired, 1967. Chm., NZ Broadcasting Corp., 1969-74. Pres., Taupo Regional Museum and Art Centre, 1975-; Mem., Social Develt Council, New Zealand, 1976-. *Recreations:* golf, fishing and gardening. *Address:* 43 Birch Street, Taupo, New Zealand. *Clubs:* Wellesley (Wellington); Taupo Golf.

MACKINTOSH, family name of Viscount Mackintosh of Halifax.

MACKINTOSH OF HALIFAX, 2nd Viscount, *cr* 1957; Baron, *cr* 1948; Bt, *cr* 1935; **John Mackintosh,** OBE 1976; BEM 1946; FInstM 1968; Director, John Mackintosh & Sons Ltd, 1950-76; *b* 7 Oct. 1921; *s* of Harold Vincent Mackintosh (1st Viscount, Baron and Bt) and Constance (*née* Stoneham) (*d* 1975); *S* father, 1964; *m* 1st, 1946 (marr. diss., 1956); two *d*; 2nd, 1956, Gwynneth, *yr d* of Charles H. Gledhill, Halifax, Yorkshire; two *s. Educ:* Bedales Sch.; Trinity Coll., USA. RAOC, 1942-47. Director: Tom Smith & Co. Ltd, 1956; Tudor Auto Services, 1961-72; Thickthorn Farm Ltd, 1955-. President: Confectioners' Benevolent Fund, 1959-60 (Vice-Chm., 1964-67, Chm., 1967-76); Leeds Inst. of Marketing, 1966-68; Chairman: Norfolk Savings Cttee, 1975-; Norwich Savings Cttee, 1966-75; Inst. of Directors (Norfolk and Suffolk Branch), 1968-; Governor, Town Close Preparatory Sch., Norwich; Vice-Chairman: Eastern Region Nat. Savings Cttee; Industrial Savings Cttee, Eastern Region. Hon. Treasurer: London Cttee, World Council Christian Education, 1965-72; Nat. Christian Educn Council, 1972-. *Recreations:* cricket, football. *Heir:* s Hon. (John) Clive Mackintosh, *b* 9 Sept. 1958. *Address:* The Old Hall, Barford, Norwich, Norwich NR9 4AY. *T:* Barnham Broom 271. *Clubs:* Royal Automobile, MCC.

MACKINTOSH, Hon. Lord; Charles Mackintosh, MC; Hon. LLD (Edinburgh); Hon. Fellow, Wadham College, Oxford; one of the Senators of the College of Justice in Scotland, 1944-64; *b* 28 May 1888; *s* of Hugh and Henrietta I. Mackintosh; *m* 1921, Mary Lawrie Prosser; four *d. Educ:* Edinburgh Academy; Wadham Coll., Oxford; Edinburgh Univ. Called to Scots Bar, 1914; served European War, Gallipoli, Palestine, France, 1914-19; KC 1935; Sheriff of Argyll, 1937-42; Sheriff of Inverness, Elgin and Nairn, 1942-44. *Recreation:* golf. *Address:* 55 Northumberland Street, Edinburgh. *T:* 031-556 3681. *Club:* New (Edinburgh).

MacKINTOSH, Sir Angus (MacKay), KCVO 1972; CMG 1958; HM Diplomatic Service, retired; British High Commissioner in Sri Lanka and Ambassador to the Republic of Maldives, 1969-73; *b* 23 July 1915; *s* of Angus MacKintosh, JP, Inverness; *m* 1947, Robina Marigold, *d* of J. A. Cochrane, MC; one *s* three *d. Educ:* Fettes Coll., Edinburgh; University College, Oxford (MA, BLitt). Agricultural Economics Research Institute, Oxford, 1938-41; Nuffield Colonial Research, Oxford, 1941-42. Served Army, 1942-46: Adjutant, 2nd Bn Queen's Own Cameron Highlanders; Major; despatches. Entered Colonial Office as Principal, 1946; Principal Private Secretary to Secretary of State, 1950; Assistant Secretary, 1952; seconded to Foreign Service as Dep. Commissioner-General for the UK in SE Asia, 1956-60; seconded to Cabinet Office, 1961-63; HM High Comr for Brunei, 1963-64; Asst Sec., Min. of Defence, 1964-65; Asst Under-Sec. of State, 1965-66; Senior Civilian Instructor, Imperial Defence Coll., 1966-68; Asst Under-Sec. of State, FCO, 1968-69. DK (Brunei), 1963; NSAIV (Maldives), 1972. *Address:* 9 Leven Terrace, Edinburgh EH3 9LW. *T:* 031-229 1091; Fenecreich, Gorthleck, Inverness IV1 2YS. *T:* Gorthleck 652. *Club:* Royal Commonwealth Society.

MACKINTOSH, Charles; see Mackintosh, Hon. Lord.

MACKINTOSH, David Forbes; Headmaster of Loretto, 1945-60; retired; *b* 7 May 1900; *s* of late Very Rev. Professor H. R. Mackintosh, DD; *m* 1930, Caroline Elisabeth, *o d* of Cyril Meade-King, Clifton, Bristol; three *s* one *d. Educ:* Merchiston;

Oriel Coll., Oxford (MA); Princeton Univ., NJ (AM). Assistant Master at Clifton Coll., 1924-45; Housemaster, 1930-45. Conroy Fellow, St Paul's Sch., USA, 1960. Chm., Scottish Assoc. of Boys' Clubs, 1962-69. *Recreations:* gardening, bowls. *Address:* Bowling Green Cottage, Broadwell, by Lechlade, Glos GL7 3QS. *T:* Filkins 336.

MACKINTOSH, Duncan Robert, CBE 1969 (OBE 1948); *b* 4 Oct. 1902; *s* of Duncan H. Mackintosh; *m* 1937, Mary Isa Grant; one *s* three *d. Educ:* RN Colleges Osborne and Dartmouth; University Coll., London. Joined Royal Dutch Shell Group of Oil Cos, 1923: served in China, Middle East and London; Head of Personnel Admin., Shell Internat. Petroleum, 1952-58. Mem. British Council. Chm. Exec. Cttee, Voluntary Service Overseas, (VSO), 1962-70. *Publications:* (with Alan Ayling): A Collection of Chinese Lyrics, 1965; A Further Collection of Chinese Lyrics, 1969; A Folding Screen, 1974. *Recreations:* bird-watching, gardening. *Address:* Woodfolds, Oaksey, Malmesbury, Wilts. *T:* Crudwell 431. *Club:* Athenæum.

MACKINTOSH, Eric Donald, CBE 1949; JP; DL; Trustee: East Anglian Trustee Savings Bank, since 1942; Trustee Savings Bank of Eastern England, since 1976 (Chairman, 1976-77); *b* 1906; *s* of late John Mackintosh, JP, Halifax; *m* 1928, Gwendolyn, *d* of H. L. France, Halifax; two *s* one *d. Educ:* Halifax New Sch.; Manchester Univ. Director, Cocoa Chocolate and Confectionery Division, Ministry of Food, 1942-45; President, Cocoa, Chocolate and Confectionery Alliance Ltd, 1946-48 (Vice-Pres., 1949-51; Treas., 1957-72). Formerly Director: Norwich Union Fire Insurance Soc.; Norwich Union Life Insurance Soc.; Scottish Union & National Insurance Co. Ltd; Maritime Insurance Co. Ltd; Tom Smith & Co. Ltd (Chm., 1951-71). JP, 1949, DL 1974, High Sheriff, Norfolk, 1971-72. *Recreations:* music, fishing. *Address:* Brooke House, Brooke, Norwich NR15 1JN. *Clubs:* Royal Automobile; Norfolk (Norwich).

MACKINTOSH, (Hugh) Stewart, CBE 1956; Chairman, Scottish Sports Council, 1966-68; Chief Education Officer, Glasgow, 1944-68; *b* 1903; *s* of William Mackintosh, Helmsdale, Sutherland; *m* 1933, Mary, *d* of James Wilson. *Educ:* Helmsdale, Sutherland; Glasgow Univ. (MA, BSc, MEd); Aberdeen Univ. (PhD). Director of Education: Wigtownshire, 1931-37; Aberdeen, 1937-44; Glasgow, 1944. FEIS 1958; Hon. LLD Glasgow, 1969. *Address:* 12 Merrylee Road, Glasgow G43 2SH; Bayview, Helmsdale, Sutherland.

MACKINTOSH, (John) Malcolm, CMG 1975; Assistant Secretary, Cabinet Office, since 1968; *b* 25 Dec. 1921; *s* of late James M. Mackintosh, MD, and Marjorie Mackintosh; *m* 1946, Elena Grafova; two *s* one *d. Educ:* Mill Hill; Edinburgh Academy; Glasgow Univ. MA (Hons) 1948. Served War, Middle East, Italy and Balkans, 1942-46; Allied Control Commn, Bulgaria, 1945-46. Glasgow Univ., 1946-48. Programme Organiser, BBC Overseas Service, 1948-60. Foreign Office, engaged on research, 1960-68. *Publications:* Strategy and Tactics of Soviet Foreign Policy, 1962, 2nd edn 1963; Juggernaut: a history of the Soviet armed forces, 1967. *Recreations:* walking, climbing. *Address:* 21 Ravensdale Avenue, N12 9HP. *T:* 01-445 9714. *Club:* Garrick.

MACKINTOSH, John Pitcairn; MP (Lab) Berwick and East Lothian, 1966-Feb. 1974 and since Oct. 1974; part-time Professor of Politics Edinburgh University, since 1977; freelance writer; television commentator; *b* 24 Aug. 1929; *s* of Colin M. Mackintosh and Mary Victoria (*née* Pitcairn); *m* 1957, Janette M. Robertson (marr. diss. 1963); one *s* one *d* ; *m* 1963, Catherine Margaret Una Maclean; one *s* one *d. Educ:* Melville Coll., Edinburgh; Edinburgh, Oxford and Princeton Univs. DLitt Edinburgh, 1967. Asst Lectr, Glasgow Univ., 1953-54; Lectr in History, Edinburgh Univ., 1954-61; Sen. Lectr in Government, University of Ibadan, Nigeria, 1961-63; Senior Lecturer in Politics, Glasgow Univ., 1963-65; Professor of Politics, Univ. of Strathclyde, 1965-66. Vis. Prof., Birkbeck Coll., London, 1972-. Member, Select Cttees on Agriculture, 1967-69, Scottish Affairs, 1968-70, Procedure, 1966-72, Scrutiny of European Secondary Legislation, 1974-; Vice-Chm., GB/East Europe Centre; Mem., Exec. Cttee, British Council, 1968-73. Chm., Hansard Soc., 1974-. Joint Editor, The Political Quarterly, 1975-. *Publications:* The British Cabinet, 1962; Nigerian Politics and Government, 1966; The Devolution of Power, 1968; British Government and Politics, 1970; (ed) British Prime Ministers in the Twentieth Century, vol. I: Balfour to Chamberlain, 1977. *Recreation:* gardening. *Address:* Nether Liberton House, Gilmerton Road, Edinburgh. *T:* 031-664 3911. *Clubs:* Reform; Edinburgh University.

MACKINTOSH, Captain Sir Kenneth Lachlan, KCVO 1966; Royal Navy (retired); Serjeant at Arms, House of Lords, 1962-71; Yeoman Usher of the Black Rod, 1953-71; Secretary to the Lord Great Chamberlain, 1953-71; *b* 6 July 1902; *s* of Stewart Mackintosh and Alice Ballard; *m* 1st, 1929, Elizabeth (*d* 1960), *d* of Captain Bertram Fawcett; one *s* one *d* (and two *s* decd); 2nd, 1962, Yolande, *d* of Leonard Bickford-Smith. *Educ:* RN Colleges, Osborne and Dartmouth. Directing Staff of RN Staff Coll., 1938; served in: French Fleet, 1939; HMS Duke of York, 1940; HMS Fencer (comd), 1945; HMS Liverpool (comd), and as Chief of Staff to Earl Mountbatten, 1948; Naval Attaché, Paris, 1950; retired, 1953. *Address:* Windalls, Slinfold, Sussex. *T:* Slinfold 242.

MACKINTOSH of Mackintosh, Lt-Comdr Lachlan Ronald Duncan, OBE 1972; 30th Chief of Clan Mackintosh; Vice-Lieutenant of Inverness-shire since 1971; Chairman, Highland Exhibitions Ltd, since 1964; *b* 27 June 1928; *o s* of Vice-Adm. Lachlan Donald Mackintosh of Mackintosh, CB, DSO, DSC (*d* 1957); *m* 1962, Mabel Cecilia Helen (Celia), *yr d* of Captain Hon. John Bernard Bruce, RN; one *s* two *d* (and one *d* decd). *Educ:* Elstree; RNC Dartmouth. Flag Lieut to First Sea Lord, 1951; spec. communications, 1954; served in HM Yacht Britannia, 1957; retd 1963. Vice-Pres., Scottish Conservative and Unionist Assoc., 1969-71. DL 1965, CC 1970-75, Inverness-shire; Regional Cllr, Highland Region, 1974-. *Heir: s* John Lachlan Mackintosh, younger of Mackintosh, *b* 2 Oct. 1969. *Address:* Moy Hall, Moy, Inverness-shire. *T:* Tomatin 211. *Clubs:* Naval and Military; Highland (Inverness).

MACKINTOSH, Malcolm; *see* Mackintosh, J. M.

MACKINTOSH, Stewart; *see* Mackintosh, H. S.

McKISACK, Prof. May; Emeritus Professor of History, University of London, since 1967; *b* 30 March 1900; *o d* of Audley John McKisack, solicitor, Belfast, and Elizabeth (*née* McCullough). *Educ:* Bedford High Sch.; Somerville Coll., Oxford. Mary Somerville Research Fellow, Somerville Coll., Oxford, 1925-28; Lecturer in Mediæval History, University of Liverpool, 1927-35. Fellow and Tutor, Somerville Coll., 1936-55; University Lecturer, 1945-55; Professor of History, University of London (Westfield Coll.), 1955-67; Hon. Fellow, Somerville Coll., 1956; James Bryce Memorial Lecturer, Somerville Coll., 1959; Member of UGC Cttee on Teaching Methods in Universities, 1961. Visiting Professor, Vassar Coll., USA, 1967-68. FRHistS 1928; FSA 1952. *Publications:* The Parliamentary Representation of the English Boroughs in the Middle Ages, 1932; The Fourteenth Century, 1959; Medieval History in the Tudor Age, 1971; articles, reviews in English Historical Review, Review of English Studies, Medium Aevum, etc. *Address:* 59 Park Town, Oxford. *T:* Oxford 57027.

McKISSOCK, Sir Wylie, Kt 1971; OBE 1946; MS (London), FRCS; Consulting Neurological Surgeon in London, 1936-71, now retired; Neurological Surgeon, National Hospital for Nervous Diseases, Queen Square and Metropolitan Ear, Nose and Throat Hospital; Neurological Surgeon, Hospital for Sick Children, Great Ormond Street; Neurological Surgeon, St Andrew's Hospital, Northampton; Visiting Neurological Surgeon, Graylingwell Hospital, Chichester, St James's Hospital, Portsmouth, Belmont Hospital, Sutton, and Park Prewett Hospital, Basingstoke; Associate Neurological Surgeon, Royal Marsden Hospital; Director of Institute of Neurology, Queen Square; Surgeon in Charge, Department of Neuro-Surgery, Atkinson Morley Hospital branch of St George's Hospital; Hon. Civil Consultant in Neuro-Surgery to RAF; Hon. Neurological Surgeon, Welsh Regional Hospital Board; Teacher of Surgery, St George's Hospital Medical School (University of London); Member, Panel of Consultants, Royal Navy, British European Airways, British Overseas Airways Corporation; *b* 27 Oct. 1906; *s* of late Alexander Cathie McKissock; *m* 1934, Rachel, *d* of Leonard Marcus Jones, Beckenham, Kent; one *s* two *d*. *Educ:* King's Coll. and St George's Hospital, University of London. Junior University Schol., St George's Hospital, 1928; Laking Memorial Prize, 1932-33 and 1933-34; Rockefeller Schol. in Neuro-Surgery, 1937-38; Casualty Officer, House Surgeon, House Physician, House Surgeon to Ear, Nose, Throat and Eye Depts, Assistant Curator of Museum, Surgical Registrar, Surgical Chief Asst, St George's Hosp.; Surgical Registrar, Maida Vale Hosp. for Nervous Diseases, Hosp. for Sick Children, Great Ormond St, and Victoria Hospital for Children, Tite St. FRSM; Fellow, Society of British Neurological Surgeons (President, 1966); FRCR (Hon.) 1962; Corresponding Member, American Association of Neurological Surgeons, 1968. Hon. DSc, Newcastle upon Tyne, 1966. *Publications:* contributions to medical journals. *Recreations:* wine, food, gardening,

ornithology, antagonism to Bureaucracy and the enjoyment of retirement. *Address:* Camus na Harry, Lechnaside, Gairloch, West Ross. *T:* Badachro 224.

MACKLEN, Victor Harry Burton, CB 1975; Deputy Chief Scientific Adviser (Projects and Nuclear), Ministry of Defence, since 1969; *b* 13 July 1919; *s* of H. Macklen and A. C. Macklen, Brighton, Sussex; *m* 1950, Ursula Irene Fellows; one *d*. *Educ:* Varndean Sch., Brighton; King's Coll., London. Air Defence Experimental Establishment, 1941; Operational Research Group, 1942; served Army, 1943-49; WO Scientific Staff, 1949-51; Head, Operational Research Section, BAOR, 1951-54; MoD Scientific Staff, 1954-60; Head, Technical Secretariat Reactor Group, UKAEA, 1960-64; Dep. Director, Technical Operations Reactor Group, UKAEA, 1966-67; Asst Chief Scientific Adviser (Studies and Nuclear), MoD, 1967-69. FRSA 1975. *Address:* Stepp House, Hartlip, near Sittingbourne, Kent. *T:* Newington 842591; The Thatch, Burton, near Christchurch, Hants. *T:* Christchurch 3424. *Club:* Army and Navy.

MACKLEY, Garnet Hercules, CMG 1938; *b* Port Chalmers, 9 Dec. 1883; *s* of John Charles Mackley and Esther Styles; *m* 1914, Isabel Robertson; one *s*. *Educ:* Grammar Sch., Invercargill. Cadet in clerical division, Traffic Branch, NZ. Government Railways Department, 1900; had varied experience in railway work in all parts of Dominion in executive capacity; promoted through various ranks of District Office and Head Office; Chief Clerk, Railways Head Office, Wellington, 1928; Assistant General Manager, 1931; General Manager, 1933-40. MP for Masterton, 1943-46; for Wairarapa, 1946-49; MLC, 1950. *Recreations:* fishing, racing, golf, swimming, field athletics. *Address:* Hillview Rest Home, Hospital Road, Tekuiti, King Country, New Zealand.

MACKLEY, George, Hon. Retired RE 1972 (RE 1961; ARE 1950); *b* 13 May 1900; *m* 1927, Caroline Toller, Hemingford Grey; no *c. Educ:* Judd Sch., Tonbridge. Art master, various schools in Kent and Surrey, 1921-45; Headmaster, Thames Ditton Primary Sch., 1945-53; Headmaster, Sutton East Secondary Sch. and Art Department, 1953-60. Hon. Mem., Soc. of Wood Engravers (Associate, 1946). Mem., 1948; Mem., Art Workers' Guild, 1959. Works in permanent collections: Victoria and Albert Museum; Ashmolean Museum; Fitzwilliam Museum; South London Art Gallery; Nat. Museum of Art, Stockholm; Hunt Botanical Library, Pittsburgh. *Publication:* Wood Engraving, 1948. *Recreations:* lurking by, and drawing, waterways and canal and river craft. *Address:* 7 Higham Lane, Tonbridge, Kent. *T:* Tonbridge 3968.

MACKNIGHT, Dame Ella (Annie Noble), DBE 1969; Consultant Emeritus (Obstetrician and Gynaecologist), Queen Victoria Hospital, Melbourne, since 1964; *b* 7 Aug. 1904; 4th *d* of Dr Conway Macknight. *Educ:* Toorak Coll., Melbourne; Univ. of Melbourne, resident student, Janet Clarke Hall. MB, BS 1928; MD Melbourne 1931; DGO Melbourne 1936; MRCOG 1951; FRCOG 1958; FRACS 1971. Hon. Obstetrician and Gynaecologist, Queen Victoria Hosp., Melbourne, 1935-64; Pres., Queen Victoria Hosp., Melbourne, 1971-77 (Vice-Pres., 1965-71); Hon. Sec., 1963-67, Vice-Pres., 1967-70, Pres., 1970-72, Australian Council, RCOG. Hon. MD Monash, 1972. *Recreation:* golf. *Address:* 692 Toorak Road, Malvern, Victoria 3144, Australia. *Clubs:* Lyceum (Melbourne); Royal Melbourne Golf.

McKUEN, Rod; writer, singer and composer; *b* Oakland, Calif, 29 April 1933. Has appeared in numerous films, TV, concerts. President: Stanyan Records; Discus Records; New Gramophone Soc.; Mr Kelly Prodns; Montcalm Prodns; Stanyan Books; Cheval Books; Biplane Books; Rod McKuen Enterprises; Vice-Pres., Tamarack Books; Director: Animal Concern; Rod McKuen Foundn. Mem. Bd of Governors, Nat. Acad. of Recording Arts and Scis; Mem. Bd of Dirs, Amer. Nat. Theatre of Ballet; Mem., Adv. Bd, Internat. Educn; Vice-Pres., Adv. Bd, Fund for Animals; ASCAP; Writers' Guild; AFTRA; MPA; NARAS; AGVA. Has won numerous awards, including Grammy for best spoken word album, Lonesome Cities; nominated Pulitzer Prize in classical music for The City, 1973. *Publications:* And Autumn Came, 1954; Stanyan Street and Other Sorrows, 1966; Listen to the Warm, 1967; Twelve Years of Christmas, 1968; In Someone's Shadow, 1969; With Love, 1970; Caught in the Quiet, 1970; Fields of Wonder, 1971; The Carols of Christmas, 1971; And to Each Season, 1972; Beyond the Boardwalk, 1972; Come to Me in Silence, 1973; America: an Affirmation, 1974; Seasons in the Sun, 1974; Alone, Moment to Moment, 1974; The McKuen Omnibus, 1975; Celebrations of the Heart, 1975; The Sea Around Me, the Hills Above, 1976; Finding my Father: one man's search for identity, 1977; Coming Close to the Earth, 1977; Hand in Hand, 1977; *major classical* *works:* Symphony No One; Concerto for Guitar and Orchestra; Concerto for Four Harpsichords; Concerto for Cello and Orch.; Concerto for Bassoon and Orch.; Seascapes for Piano and Orchestra; Adagio for Harp and Strings; Piano Variations; various other classical commns; numerous lyrics; *film scores:* Joanna, 1968; The Prime of Miss Jean Brodie, 1969; Me, Natalie, 1969; A Boy Named Charlie Brown, 1970; Come to your Senses, 1971; Scandalous John, 1971; Wildflowers, 1971; The Borrowers, 1973; Lisa Bright and Dark, 1973; Emily, 1976; Flying Free, 1976. *Address:* PO Box G, Beverly Hills, Calif 90213, USA; (business) 8440 Santa Monica Blvd, Los Angeles, Calif 90069.

MACKWORTH, Commander Sir David Arthur Geoffrey, 9th Bt, *cr* 1776; RN retired; Managing Director, South Coast Rod Rigging Company Ltd; *b* 13 July 1912; *o s* of late Vice-Admiral Geoffrey Mackworth, CMG, DSO, and Noel Mabel, *d* of late William I. Langford; *S* uncle, 1952; *m* 1st, 1941, Mary Alice (marr. diss. 1972), *d* of Thomas Henry Grylls; one *s*; 2nd, 1973, Beryl Joan, formerly wife of late Ernest Henry Sparkes, and 3rd *d* of late Pembroke Henry Cockayn Cross and of Jeanie Cross. *Educ:* Farnborough Sch., Hants; RNC Dartmouth. Joined RN 1926; served HMS Eagle, HMS Suffolk, 1939-45; Commander, 1948; Naval Adviser to Director of Guided Weapon Research and Development, Ministry of Supply, 1945-49; retired, 1956. MRIN. *Recreations:* sailing, cruising. *Heir: s* Digby John Mackworth [*b* 2 Nov. 1945; *m* 1971, Antoinette Francesca, *d* of Henry James McKenna, Ilford, Essex; one *d*. *Educ:* Wellington Coll. Served Australian Army Aviation Corps, Malaysia and Vietnam (Lieut). With Iranian Helicopters Ltd]. *Address:* 36 Wittering Road, Hayling Island, Hants. *Clubs:* Royal Ocean Racing; Royal Naval and Royal Albert Yacht (Portsmouth); Royal Corinthian Yacht; Royal Naval Sailing Association.

MACKWORTH-YOUNG, Gerard William; Deputy Chairman and Chief Executive, Morgan Grenfell & Co. Ltd, since 1975 (Director since 1974); *b* 10 Oct. 1926; *s* of Gerard Mackworth-Young, CIE and Natalie Hely-Hutchinson; *m* 1949, Lady Evelyn Leslie, *d* of 20th Earl of Rothes; four *d*. *Educ:* Eton College. Served Welsh Guards, 1945-48 (Lieut, RARO). Partner, Rowe & Pitman, stockbrokers, 1953-73; Vice-Chm., Morgan Grenfell Holdings Ltd; Dir, Union Discount Co. of London Ltd; Dir, Willis Faber Ltd. *Recreation:* deerstalking. *Address:* 21 St Petersburgh Place, W2 4LA. *T:* 01-229 4270. *Clubs:* Boodle's, Pratt's; Union (Sydney).
See also Sir *R . C . Mackworth -Young .*

MACKWORTH-YOUNG, Sir Robert Christopher, (Sir Robin Mackworth-Young), KCVO 1975 (CVO 1968; MVO 1961); Librarian, Windsor Castle, and Assistant Keeper of The Queen's Archives, since 1958; *b* 12 Feb. 1920; *s* of late Gerard Mackworth-Young, CIE; *m* 1953, Rosemarie, *d* of W. C. R. Aue, Menton, France; one *s*. *Educ:* Eton; King's Coll., Cambridge. Pres., Cambridge Union Soc., 1948. Served in RAF, 1939-46. HM Foreign Service, 1948-55; Deputy Librarian, Windsor Castle, 1955-58. FSA. *Recreations:* music, electronics, ski-ing. *Address:* Garden House, Windsor Castle. *Club:* Roxburghe.
See also G *. W . Mackworth -Young .*

McLACHLAN, Angus Henry; Director, John Fairfax Ltd, Publishers of Sydney Morning Herald, Australian Financial Review, National Times, Sun, Sun-Herald, etc (Managing Director, 1965-69); *b* 29 March 1908; *s* of James H. and Mabel McLachlan; unmarried. *Educ:* Scotch Coll., Melbourne; University of Melbourne. Melbourne Herald, 1928-36; joined Sydney Morning Herald, 1936; News Editor, 1937-49; General Manager, John Fairfax & Sons Ltd, 1949-64. Jt Man. Dir, Australian Associated Press Pty Ltd, 1965- (Chairman, 1958-59, 1964-65, 1975-); Director: Reuters Ltd, London, 1966-71; Amalgamated Television Services Pty Ltd, 1955-; Macquarie Broadcasting Holdings Ltd, 1966-; David Syme & Co. Ltd, Publishers of The Age, 1970-; Federal Capital Press Ltd, Publishers of Canberra Times, 1970-; Mem. Council, Library of NSW, 1966-75 (Dep. Pres., 1974-75); Mem., Library Council of NSW, 1975-; Member, Sydney University Extension Board, 1960-. *Address:* Box 5303, GPO, Sydney, NSW 2001, Australia. *T:* 233-1550. *Clubs:* London Press; Australian, University, Union (Sydney); Royal Sydney Yacht Squadron.

McLACHLAN, Gordon, CBE 1967; BCom; FCA; Secretary, Nuffield Provincial Hospitals Trust, since 1956; *b* 12 June 1918; *s* of late Gordon and Mary McLachlan; *m* 1951, Monica Mary Griffin; two *d*. *Educ:* Leith Academy; Edinburgh Univ. Served with RNVR, 1939-46; Gunnery Specialist, 1943-46. Accountant, Edinburgh Corp., 1946-48; Dep. Treas., NW Met. Regional Hosps Bd, 1948-53; Accountant Nuffield Foundn, Nuffield Provincial Hosps Trust, Nat. Corp. for Care of Old

People, 1953-56. Asst Dir, Nuffield Foundn, 1955-56. Henry Cohen Lectr, Univ. of Jerusalem, 1969. Consultant, American Hospitals Assoc. and American Hospitals Research and Educational Trust, 1964-65; Member Council, American Hospitals Research and Educational Trust, 1965-74 (citation for meritorious service, AHA, 1976); Mem., Inst. of Medicine, Nat. Acad. of Sciences, Washington DC, 1974. Parker B. Francis Foundn Distinguished Lectr, Amer. Coll. of Hosp. Admin, 1976. General Editor, Nuffield Provincial Hospitals Trust publications; Consulting Editor, Health Services Research Journal (US), 1966-74. Hon. LLD Birmingham, 1977. *Publications:* editor of many publications on Nuffield Provincial Hospitals Trust list; contrib. to Lancet, Practitioner, Times, Twentieth Century, etc. *Recreations:* reading, watching ballet, theatre, Rugby football. *Address:* 3 Prince Albert Road, NW1. *T:* 01-485 6632. *Club:* Caledonian.

McLACHLAN, Air Vice-Marshal Ian Dougald, CB 1966; CBE 1954; DFC 1940; Consultant, Northrop Corporation; Director, Reef Oil NL; *b* Melbourne, 23 July 1911; *s* of Dougald McLachlan, author and teacher, and Bertha Frances (*née* Gilliam); *m* 1946, Margaret Helen Chrystal (marr. diss. 1968); one *d*. *Educ:* Melbourne High Sch.; Royal Military Coll., Duntroon. Imperial Defence Coll., 1954; Dir, Flying Trng, Air Min., London 1955-56; Dep. Chief of Air Staff, Australia, 1959-61; Australian Defence Adviser, Washington, 1962-63; Air Mem. for Supply and Equipment, Australian Air Bd, 1964-68. *Recreations:* tennis, squash, golf. *Address:* 2 Eastbourne Road, Darling Point, NSW 2027, Australia. *T:* 328-7997. *Clubs:* Australian (Sydney); Naval and Military (Melbourne); Melbourne Cricket, Royal Sydney Golf, Royal Canberra Golf.

MACLAGAN, Noel Francis, DSc, MD, FRCP, FRIC; retired; formerly Professor of Chemical Pathology in University of London at Westminster Medical School; Chemical Pathologist, Westminster Hospital, 1947-70; *b* 1904; *y s* of late Oscar Frederick and Ada Maclagan, Newcastle and London; *m* 1933, Annemarie, *d* of Curt and Marie Herzog, London; one *s* one *d*. *Educ:* University Coll. Sch.; University Coll., London (First Cl. Hons BSc Chemistry, 1925); Middlesex Hosp. Medical School (MSc London in Biochemistry, 1933). DSc London, 1946; MD London, 1935; MRCP, 1933; FRIC 1946; FRCP 1952. Asst in Courtauld Inst. of Biochemistry, Middlesex Hosp., 1926-33; House Physician Middlesex Hosp., 1932; whole-time worker for Medical Research Council, 1933-34; Biochemist, Westminster Hosp., 1935-46; Pathologist, EMS, 1939-45; Chemical Pathologist at Westminster Hosp. Medical Sch., 1946-47. Editor, Annals of Clinical Biochemistry, 1974-76. *Publications:* contributions to medical textbooks on various biochemical subjects and articles in scientific journals on thymol turbidity test, thyroid function, lipid metabolism, etc. *Recreations:* music and chess. *Address:* 40 Temple Fortune Lane, NW11. *Clubs:* Athenæum, Savage.

McLAREN, family name of **Baron Aberconway.**

McLAREN, Dr Anne Laura, FRS 1975; Director, Medical Research Council's Mammalian Development Unit, since 1974; *b* 26 April 1927; *d* of 2nd Baron Aberconway; *m* 1952, Donald Michie (marr. diss.); one *s* two *d*. *Educ:* Univ. of Oxford (MA, DPhil). Post-doctoral research, UCL, 1952-55 and Royal Vet. Coll., London, 1955-59; joined staff of ARC Unit of Animal Genetics at Edinburgh Univ., 1959. Mem., Cttee of Managers, Royal Instn, 1976-. Scientific Medal, Zool Soc. London, 1967. *Publications:* Mammalian Chimaeras, 1976; papers on reproductive biology, embryology, genetics and immunology in sci. jls. *Address:* 9 Steele's Road, NW3 4SG.

MacLAREN, Sir Hamish (Duncan), KBE 1951; CB 1946; DFC; Director of Electrical Engineering, Admiralty, 1945-60; *b* 7 April 1898; *s* of Rev. Peter MacLaren, MA, and Constance Hamilton Simpson; *m* 1927, Lorna Cicely, *d* of late Dr R. P. N. B. Bluett, MC, Harrow; one *s* one *d*. *Educ:* Fordyce Academy, Banffshire; Edinburgh Univ. (BSc 1921). Served European war, 1914-18, in RNVR, RNAS and RAF (DFC and Bar, French Croix de Guerre with Palm). After completing degree at Edinburgh Univ. in 1921 joined British Thomson Houston Co., Rugby, as student apprentice. Awarded Bursary by Commission for Exhibition of 1851 for 1921-23; British Thomson Houston Fellowship to spend one year with the GE Co. of Schenectady, USA, 1923-24; on staff of British Thomson Houston, Rugby, 1924-26; joined Admiralty Service as Asst Electrical Engineer, 1926. In Admiralty Service at HM Dockyards, Chatham, Devonport, at Dir of Dockyards Dept, Admiralty, 1933-37, and in Ceylon, 1931-33; Superintending Electrical Engineer, HM Naval Base, Singapore, 1937-40; Asst Dir, Electrical Engineering Dept, Admiralty, 1940-45. Pres. Instn of Electrical Engineers, 1960-61. Hon. LLD St Andrews, 1954; Hon. DSc

Bath, 1970. *Address:* 104 Heath Road, Petersfield, Hants. *T:* Petersfield 4562.

McLAREN, Prof. Hugh Cameron; Professor of Obstetrics and Gynæcology, University of Birmingham, since 1951; *b* 25 April 1913; *s* of John and Flora McLaren, Glasgow; *m* 1939, Lois Muirhead, Bridge of Weir, Scotland; one *s* six *d. Educ:* High Sch. of Glasgow; Univ. of Glasgow; postgraduate studies Glasgow and Aberdeen. MB, ChB Glasgow 1936; MD (Glasgow). Served RAMC, 1941-46; Surgical Specialist (Lt-Col). Univ. of Birmingham, 1946, Reader, 1949. FRCPGlas; FRCSE; FRCOG. Hon. Mem., Amer. Medical Assoc., 1969. Officer, Legion of Merit (Rhodesia), 1977. *Publications:* The Prevention of Cervical Cancer, 1963; contribs to Journal of Obstetrics and Gynæcology, Lancet, Brit. Med. Jl, etc. *Recreations:* golf, gardening. *Address:* 26 Ampton Road, Birmingham B15 2UP. *T:* 021-440 3223.

McLAREN, John Watt, MA, FRCP, FRCR; Physician in charge of X-Ray Department, St Thomas' Hospital, 1946-73; *b* 26 Nov. 1906; *s* of John McLaren and Florence Mary Atkinson. *Educ:* Cheltenham Coll.; Univ. of Cambridge and St Thomas' Hospital, London. MA (Cantab); FFR 1951; FRCP 1963; FRCPE 1972. Junior appointments at St Thomas' Hosp., 1932-35; Chief Asst, X-Ray Dept, 1935-39. Radiologist, Queen Mary's Hosp., East End, 1935-38. Cons. Radiologist, Metropolitan Police, 1946-; Examiner in Radiology, Univs of London and Edinburgh and Faculty of Radiologists; Underwriter at Lloyd's, 1948. *Publications:* (ed) Modern Trends in Diagnostic Radiology, Series 1, 2, 3, 4, 1948, 1953, 1960, 1970; various papers in radiological journals. *Recreations:* motoring, travelling, sailing. *Address:* 118 Castelnau, Barnes, SW13. *T:* 01-748 6101. *Club:* Royal Automobile.

McLAREN, Martin; Director: English China Clays Ltd, since 1973; Archway Unit Trust Managers Ltd, since 1973; *b* 11 Jan. 1914; *s* of late Hon. Francis McLaren; *m* 1943, Nancy Ralston; two *s . Educ:* Eton Coll. (Scholar); New Coll., Oxford; Harvard Univ. (Henry Fellow). Asst Principal, Home Office, 1938. Served War of 1939-45, Grenadier Guards, Major. Principal, Home Office, 1946-47. Barrister, Middle Temple, 1948. MP (C) Bristol North-West, 1959-66, 1970-Sept. 1974; an Asst Govt Whip, 1961-63; a Lord Comr of the Treasury, 1963-64; an Opposition Whip, 1964-66; PPS to Sec. of State for Foreign and Commonwealth Affairs, 1970-74. *Recreations:* squash rackets (half-blue), looking at pictures and buildings. *Address:* 30 Smith Square, SW1. *T:* 01-222 6626. *Club:* Brooks's.

McLAREN, Robin John Taylor; HM Diplomatic Service; Counsellor and Head of Chancery, Copenhagen, since 1975; *b* 14 Aug. 1934; *s* of Robert Taylor McLaren and Marie Rose McLaren (*née* Simond); *m* 1964, Susan Ellen Hatherly; one *s* two *d . Educ:* Richmond and East Sheen County Grammar Sch. for Boys; Ardingly Coll.; St John's Coll., Cambridge (Schol.; MA). Royal Navy, 1953-55. Entered Foreign Service, 1958; language student, Hong Kong, 1959-60; Third Sec., Peking, 1960-61; FO, 1961-64; Asst Private Sec. to Lord Privy Seal (Mr Edward Heath), 1963-64; Second, later First Sec., Rome, 1964-68; seconded to Hong Kong Govt as Asst Political Adviser, 1968-69; First Sec., FCO, 1970-73; Dep. Head of Western Organisations Dept, 1974-75. *Recreations:* music, China, hill-walking. *Address:* c/o Foreign and Commonwealth Office, SW1A 2AH. *Clubs:* United Oxford & Cambridge University, Le Petit Club Français; Hong Kong (Hong Kong).

McLAUCHLAN, Madeline Margaret Nicholls; Head Mistress, North London Collegiate School, since 1965; *b* 4 June 1922; *o c* of late Robert and Gertrude McLauchlan, Birmingham. *Educ:* King Edward VI Grammar Sch. for Girls, Camp Hill, Birmingham; Royal Holloway College, University of London. Asst Mistress: Shrewsbury High Sch., GPDST, 1944; Manchester High Sch., 1952. Senior Walter Hines Page Scholar, English-Speaking Union, 1955. Head Mistress, Henrietta Barnett Sch., 1958. Member: Exec. Cttee, Assoc. of Head Mistresses, 1966, Chm., 1974; Education Cttee, English Speaking Union, 1966; Exec. Cttee, Universities' Central Council on Admissions, 1968; Direct Grant Cttee, GBGSA, 1972-; Council, Westfield Coll., Univ. of London; Council, Nat. Youth Orchestra, 1975. Governor of Imperial Coll., 1968. *Recreations:* music, mountain walking, housekeeping. *Address:* North London Collegiate School, Canons, Edgware, Mddx. *T:* 01-952 0912. *Club:* English-Speaking Union.

McLAUCHLAN, Thomas Joseph, JP; Stipendiary Magistrate, since 1966; *b* 15 May 1917; *s* of Alexander and Helen McLauchlan; *m* 1945, Rose Catherine Gray, MA. *Educ:* St Aloysius Coll., Glasgow; Univ. of Glasgow (BL). Law apprentice, 1936-39 and 1946-47. War service, Merchant Navy

and RAF Y Section, Signals Intell., Wireless Officer, 1940-46. Legal Asst to Manager of large industrial insurance co., 1947-49; Clerk to Glasgow Police Courts, 1949-66. JP Scotland. *Recreations:* golf, bridge, travel. *Address:* Central District Court Chambers, Turnbull Street, Glasgow G1 5PR. *T:* 041-552 7731, ext. 18. *Club:* Centenary (Glasgow).

McLAUGHLAN, Rear-Adm. Ian David, CB 1970; DSC 1941 and Bar, 1953; Admiral Commanding Reserves and Director General, Naval Recruiting, 1970-72, retired; *b* 2 May 1919; *s* of Richard John and Margaret McLaughlan; *m* 1942, Charity Pomeroy Simonds; two *d. Educ:* St Paul's Sch. Entered Navy, 1937; served in destroyers, 1940-45 (despatches three times); comd HMS: Flint Castle, 1948-50; Concord, 1950-52; jssc 1952; Armed Forces Staff Coll., Norfolk, Va, 1953; HMS Jupiter, 1953-55; comd HMS: Chieftain, 1955; Chevron, 1955-56 (despatches); Staff of C-in-C, Portsmouth, 1957-59; Asst Dir of Plans, Admty, 1959-61; Capt. (F), 2nd Frigate Sqdn, 1961-62; idc 1963; Dir, Naval Ops and Trade, 1964-66; comd HMS Hampshire, 1966-67; Chief of Staff to Comdr Far East Fleet, 1967-70. Comdr 1951; Capt. 1958; Rear-Adm. 1968. Commendador d'Aviz, 1956. *Recreations:* gardening, house husbandry. *Address:* The Five Gables, Mayfield, East Sussex. *T:* Mayfield 2218.

McLAUGHLAN, Roy James Philip, CMG 1955; CVO 1956; Inspector-General of Police, Nigeria, retired 1956; *b* 25 July 1898; *s* of late Henry Peter Marius McLaughlan and late Elfrida Greenwood; *m* 1931, Catherine Elizabeth Plaisted, *d* of late Lt-Col Thomas Valentine Plaisted McCammon and Charlotte Amelia Garratt. *Educ:* The English Sch., Cyprus; Stonyhurst Coll., Lancs. Gen. Staff Intelligence, Macedonia, Greece and Turkey, 1917-23. Inspector and Surveyor of Roads, Cyprus, 1925; Nigeria: Asst Supt Police, 1927; Supt, 1944; Asst Comr, 1949; Comr, 1951; Inspector-Gen., 1952. Colonial Police Medal, 1942; King's Police Medal, 1950. OStJ 1955. *Recreations:* shooting and bridge. *Address:* 7 Rosemary Park, Belfast, N Ireland. *T:* Belfast 665755.

McLAUGHLIN, Charles Redmond, MA, MB, ChB, BChir, FRCSE; Consultant Plastic Surgeon: Queen Victoria Hospital, East Grinstead, 1948-69; Kent and Canterbury Hospital, Canterbury, 1953-69; St Bartholomew's Hospital, Rochester, 1962-69; *b* 1 Oct. 1909; *s* of late W. H. McLaughlin, JP, DL and Emma Margaret Brough (*née* Warren); *m* 1936, Rosemary Macdonald; one *s* one *d* (and one *s* decd). *Educ:* Rugby Sch.; Emmanuel Coll., Cambridge; University of Edinburgh. House Phys, Royal Infirmary, Edinburgh; House Surg., Royal Hants County Hosp., Winchester, 1935; Hon. Surg. to Out-patients, Royal Surrey County Hosp., Guildford, 1937-38. Served with RAFVR, Medical Br., 1940-45; Wing Comdr i/c surgical div., 1945. EMS Surg., Queen Victoria Hosp., E Grinstead, 1946-48; Cons. Surg. to SE Metrop. Regional Hosp. Bd, 1948-69. Founder Mem. Brit. Assoc. of Plastic Surgeons, 1948 (Hon. Sec., 1957-59; Mem. Coun., 1960-62); Mem. Ed. Bd, Brit. Jl of Plastic Surgery, 1950-69; Chm. of Adv. Cttee on Plastic Surgery to Regional Bd, 1964-69. *Publications:* Plastic Surgery, 1951; The Royal Army Medical Corps, 1971; The Escape of the Goeben, 1974; chapters in several surgical textbooks; articles in British, American and French jls; editorials in Lancet. *Recreations:* music; writing and reading naval and military history. *Address:* The Oast, Mayfield, East Sussex. *T:* Mayfield 3064.

McLAUGHLIN, Mrs (Florence) Patricia (Alice), OBE 1975; *b* 23 June 1916; *o d* of late Canon F. B. Aldwell; *m* 1937, Henry, *o s* of late Major W. McLaughlin, of McLaughlin & Harvey Ltd, London, Belfast and Dublin; one *s* two *d. Educ:* Ashleigh House, Belfast; Trinity Coll., Dublin. MP (UU) Belfast West, 1955-64; Past Chm., Unionist Soc.; Past Vice-Chm., Women's National Advisory Cttee of Cons. Party; Former Nat. Advisor on Women's Affairs to European Movement. Has been active in voluntary and consumer work for many years; Chairman: Steering Gp on Food Freshness, 1973-75; Housewife's Trust; Mem., Exec. Cttee, BSI. Vice-Pres., Royal Society for Prevention of Accidents. *Recreations:* talking and travelling. *Address:* 92 Iverna Court, W8; The Grey House, Craigavad, Co. Down. *T:* Holywood 2885. *Club:* Constitutional.

MacLAURIN, Ian Charter; Managing Director, TESCO Stores Holdings Ltd, since 1973 (Director, 1970); *b* 30 March 1937; *m* 1961, Ann Margaret (*née* Collar); one *s* two *d. Educ:* Malvern Coll., Worcs. Joined TESCO as trainee, 1960; Supermarket Manager, 1963; Exec. Dir, Supermarket Co., 1965; Managing Dir, TESCO Supermarkets, 1969. *Recreations:* golf, cricket. *Address:* Longdene, Old Lane, Knebworth, Herts SG3 6EP. *T:* Stevenage 812119. *Clubs:* MCC; Lord's Taverners; Band of Brothers.

MACLAY, family name of **Baron Maclay** and **Viscount Muirshiel.**

MACLAY, 3rd Baron *cr* 1922, of Glasgow; **Joseph Paton Maclay;** Bt 1914; Managing Director: Denholm Maclay Co. Ltd; Triport Ferries (Management) Ltd; Director, Milton Shipping Co. Ltd; *b* 11 April 1942; *s* of 2nd Baron Maclay, KBE, and of Nancy Margaret, *d* of R. C. Greig, Hall of Caldwell, Uplawmoor, Renfrewshire; *S* father, 1969; *m* 1976, Elizabeth Anne, *o d* of G. M. Buchanan, Delamere, Pokataroo, NSW; one *s. Educ:* Winchester. *Heir: s* Hon. Joseph Paton Maclay, *b* 6 March 1977. *Address:* Duchal, Kilmacolm, Renfrewshire.

MACLEAN, family name of **Baron Maclean.**

MACLEAN, Baron *cr* 1971 (Life Peer), of Duart and Morvern in the County of Argyll; **Charles Hector Fitzroy Maclean;** Bt 1631; KT 1969; PC 1971; GCVO 1971; KBE 1967; JP; 27th Chief of Clan Maclean; Lord Chamberlain of HM Household since 1971; Chancellor, Royal Victorian Order, since 1971; Scots Guards, Major, retired; Lord Lieutenant of Argyll since 1954; Ensign, Royal Company of Archers (Queen's Body Guard for Scotland); President, Argyll T&AFA; *b* 5 May 1916; *e* surv. *s* of late Hector F. Maclean and Winifred Joan, *y d* of late J. H. Wilding; *S* grandfather, 1936; *m* 1941, Elizabeth, *er d* of late Frank Mann, Upper Farm House, Milton Lilbourne, Wilts; one *s* one *d. Educ:* Canford Sch., Wimborne. Served War of 1939-45 (despatches). Chief Commissioner for Scotland, Boy Scouts Assoc., 1954-59; Chief Scout of the UK and Overseas Branches, 1959-71; Chief Scout of the Commonwealth, 1959-75. Patron: Coombe Trust Fund; Roland House; Argyll Div., Scottish Br., British Red Cross Soc.; Hon. Patron, Friends of World Scouting; Vice Patron: Argyll & Sutherland Highlanders Regimental Assoc.; President: T&AFA of Argyll; Argyll Br., Forces Help Soc. and Lord Robert's Workshops; Convenor, Standing Council of Scottish Chiefs; Hon. President: Argyll Co. Scout Council; Toc H; Scouts Friendly Soc.; Vice President: Highland Cattle Soc.; Scottish Br., Nat. Playing Fields Assoc.; (ex officio) Nat. Small-Bore Rifle Assoc.; Camping Club of GB; Trefoil Residential Sch. for Physically Handicapped Children; Casualties Union; Member of Council: Earl Haig Officers Meml Fund; Scottish Naval, Military and Air Forces Veteran Residences; Royal Zoological Soc.; Outward Bound Trust; Life Member: Highland and Agricultural Soc. of Scotland; Highland Cattle Soc.; Scottish Nat. Fatstock Club; Royal Agricultural Soc. of England. JP Argyll, 1955. *Recreation:* travelling. *Heir* (to Baronetcy only): *s* Hon. Lachlan Hector Charles Maclean, Major, Scots Guards [*b* 25 Aug. 1942; *m* 1966, Mary Helen, *e d* of W. G. Gordon; one *s* one *d* (and one *d* decd)]. *Address:* St James's Palace, SW1. *T:* 01-930 4010; Duart Castle, Isle of Mull. *T:* Craignure 309. *Clubs:* Cavalry and Guards, Pratt's, Royal Commonwealth Society (Mem. Council); Royal Highland Yacht (Oban).
See also D. J. Graham-Campbell.

MACLEAN, Alistair; author; *b* Scotland, 1922. *Educ:* Glasgow Univ. *Publications:* HMS Ulysses, 1955; The Guns of Navarone (filmed 1959), 1957; South by Java Head (filmed 1959), 1958; The Last Frontier (filmed 1960), 1959; (as The Secret Ways, 1961); Night Without End, 1960; Fear Is the Key, 1961 (filmed 1972); The Golden Rendezvous, 1962; (for children) All About Lawrence of Arabia, 1962; Ice Station Zebra (filmed 1968), 1963; When Eight Bells Toll (filmed 1970), 1966; Where Eagles Dare (filmed 1968), 1967; Force 10 From Navarone, 1968; Puppet on a Chain (filmed 1970), 1969; Bear Island, 1971; Captain Cook, 1972; The Way to Dusty Death, 1973; (introd.) Alistair Maclean Introduces Scotland, ed, A. M. Dunnett, 1972; Breakheart Pass, 1974 (filmed 1975); Circus, 1975; The Golden Gate, 1976; Sea Witch, 1977; Goodbye California, 1977; *as Ian Stuart:* The Dark Crusader, 1961; The Satan Bug, 1962. *Screen plays:* Where Eagles Dare, Deakin, Caravan to Vaccares, Puppet on a Chain. *Address:* c/o Wm Collins Sons & Co. Ltd, 14 St James's Place, SW1.

McLEAN, Dr Andrew Sinclair, CBE 1975; FRCP; Director, National Radiological Protection Board, since 1971; *b* 26 March 1919; *s* of Andrew McLean and Janet Forret; *m* 1943, Christine, *d* of Col J. A. Mackintosh; two *d. Educ:* Forres Acad.; Edinburgh Univ. (MB, ChB). DIH. FRCP 1975. House Surg., Royal Northern Infirmary, Inverness, 1943; Captain RAMC, 1943-46; gen. practice, 1946-47; MO, Dept of Atomic Energy, Min. of Supply, Springfields, 1948; SMO, Dept of Atomic Energy, Windscale, 1949-52; UK Atomic Energy Authority: PMO, Industrial Gp, 1952-57; Dir, Health and Safety Br., Industrial Gp, 1957-59; Dir of Health and Safety, 1959-71. Member: Internat. Commn on Radiol Protection, 1969-77; WHO Expert Adv. Panel on Radiation, 1963-; Euratom Gp of Experts resp. for advising on Basic Safety Standards, 1973-;

Nuclear Safety Adv. Cttee, 1960-. *Publications:* papers on radiological health and safety. *Recreations:* cooking, roses, golf. *Address:* Peterhill, Monument Lane, Chalfont St Peter, Bucks. *T:* Chalfont St Giles 3794. *Clubs:* Athenæum; Beaconsfield Golf.

MacLEAN, Col Charles Allan, CBE 1941 (MBE 1918); MC; *b* 22 May 1892; *s* of John MacLean, Tobermory, Isle of Mull, Scotland; *m* 1920, Mabel Elsie (*d* 1976), *y d* of Alfred Matthews, Sherborne St John, Hants; three *s* one *d. Educ:* Tobermory and Kingussie Sch.; Edinburgh Univ. MA 1914; BSc (Agric) 1920; in France with 11th Argyll and Sutherland Highlanders, 1915-19 (MBE, MC, Croix de Guerre, despatches). Joined Indian Agricultural Service, 1920; Cane Commissioner, Bihar, 1939-43; Dir of Agriculture, 1943-46; Commissioner of Agriculture, Baroda, 1946-49; Field Agricultural Officer, Jordan, with UN Relief and Work Agency, 1951-55. Commanded Chota Nagpur Regt AF(I), 1934-38, and Bihar Light Horse AF(I), 1939-41. Mem., Tobermory Town Council, 1958-62; Provost of Tobermory, 1959-62. Pres. Mull and Iona Council of Social Service, 1959-66. Freeman, Burgh of Tobermory, 1975. *Address:* Ulva Cottage, Tobermory, Scotland. *T:* Tobermory 2044.

McLEAN, Colin, CMG 1977; MBE 1964; HM Diplomatic Service; Counsellor, British Embassy, Oslo, since 1977; *b* 10 Aug. 1930; *s* of late Dr L. G. McLean and of H. I. McLean; *m* 1953, Huguette Marie Suzette Leclerc; one *s* one *d. Educ:* Fettes; St Catharine's Coll., Cambridge (MA). 2RHA, 1953-54. District Officer, Kenya, 1955-63; Vice-Principal, Kenya Inst. of Administration, 1963-64; HM Diplomatic Service, 1964-. *Recreations:* climbing, sailing. *Address:* British Embassy, Thomas Heftyesgate 8, Oslo 2, Norway. *T:* 56.38.90/7.

McLEAN, Denis Bazeley Gordon; Deputy Secretary of Defence, New Zealand, since 1977; *b* Napier, NZ, 18 Aug. 1930; *s* of John Gordon McLean and Renée Maitland Smith; *m* 1958, Anne Davidson, Venado Tuerto, Argentina; two *s* one *d. Educ:* Nelson Coll., NZ; Victoria Univ. Coll., NZ (MSc); Rhodes Schol. 1954; University Coll., Oxford (BA). Jun. Lectr in Geology, Victoria UC, 1953-54; joined Dept of External Affairs of NZ Govt, London, 1957; served in: Wellington 1958-60; Washington, 1960-63; Paris, 1963-66; Dep. High Comr, Kuala Lumpur, 1966-68; Asst Sec. (Policy), MoD, Wellington, 1969-72; RCDS, 1972; Dep. High Comr, London, 1973-77. *Recreations:* walking, modest mountaineering, geology. *Address:* 11 Dekka Street, Wellington, New Zealand. *Club:* Travellers'.

MacLEAN, Captain Donald Murdo, DSC 1944; RD 1940; RNR; Retired from Cunard Line, 1962; Commodore Captain Cunard Fleet and commanding RMS Queen Elizabeth, 1960-62; *b* 9 June, 1899; *s* of William MacLean and Isobel (*née* Graham); *m* 1929, Bernice Isobel Wellington; one *s* one *d. Educ:* The Nicholson Sch., Lewis Island. Apprenticed to Cunard Line, 1917-21; served, as Officer, 1921-39. Served War of 1939-45 (despatches): RNR, 1939-46; Trg Comdr RNC, Greenwich, 1941-43; Sen. Officer, 7th Escort Gp, Murmansk and Atlantic and Mediterranean Convoys; Staff Officer C-in-C Mediterranean, 1944-45. Returned to Cunard Line, 1946. ADC to Lord High Comr for Scotland, 1946. *Publications:* Queens' Company, 1965; Cachalots and Messmates, 1973. *Recreations:* golf, fishing, reading and travel. *Address:* Landfall, 99 Newtown Road, Warsash, Southampton. *T:* Locks Heath 3951. *Club:* Master Mariners (Southampton).

MACLEAN, Sir Fitzroy Hew, 1st Bt, *cr* 1957; CBE 1944; *b* 11 March 1911; *s* of Major Charles Maclean, DSO; *m* 1946, Hon. Mrs Alan Phipps, 2nd *d* of 16th Baron Lovat, KT; two *s. Educ:* Eton; Cambridge. 3rd Sec., Foreign Office, 1933; transferred to Paris, 1934, and to Moscow, 1937; 2nd Sec., 1938; transferred to Foreign Office, 1939; resigned from Diplomatic Service, and enlisted as private in Cameron Highlanders; 2nd Lt Aug. 1941; joined 1st Special Air Service Regt Jan. 1942; Capt. Sept. 1942; Lt-Col 1943; Brig. Comdg British Military Mission to Jugoslav partisans, 1943-45. Lees Knowles Lecturer, Cambridge, 1953. MP (C) Lancaster, 1941-59, Bute and N Ayrshire, 1959-Feb. 1974; Parly Under-Sec. of State for War and Financial Sec. War Office, Oct. 1954-Jan. 1957. Member: UK Delegn to North Atlantic Assembly, 1962-74; Council of Europe and WEU, 1972-74. Hon. LLD: Glasgow 1969; Dalhousie 1971; Hon. DLitt Acadia, 1970. French Croix de Guerre, 1943; Order of Kutusov, 1944; Partisan Star (First Class), 1945. *Publications:* Eastern Approaches, 1949; Disputed Barricade, 1957; A Person from England, 1958; Back to Bokhara, 1959; Jugoslavia, 1969; A Concise History of Scotland, 1970; The Battle of Neretva, 1970; To the Back of Beyond, 1974; To Caucasus, 1976. *Heir: s* Charles Maclean, *b* 31 Oct. 1946. *Address:* Strachur House, Argyll. *T:* Strachur 242. *Clubs:* White's, Pratt's; Puffin's (Edinburgh).

McLEAN, Sir Francis (Charles), Kt 1967; CBE 1953 (MBE 1945); *b* 6 Nov. 1904; *s* of Michael McLean; *m* 1930, Dorothy Mabel Blackstaffe; one *s* one *d. Educ:* University of Birmingham (BSc). Chief Engineer, Psychological Warfare Division, SHAEF, 1943-45. Dep. Chief Engineer, BBC, 1952-60; Dep. Dir of Engineering, BBC, 1960-63; Director, Engineering, BBC, 1963-68. Dir, Oxley Developments Ltd, 1961-76. Chm., BSI Telecommunications Industry Standards Cttee. FIEE. *Publications:* contrib. Journal of IEE. *Address:* Clent Cottage, Thornford Road, Crookham Common, near Newbury, Berks. *T:* Headley 319.

MACLEAN, Brig. Gordon Forbes, CBE 1943; MC; DL; *b* 29 May 1897; *s* of George Buchanan Maclean, Pentreheylin, Maesbrook, Shropshire; *m* 1926, Claire, *d* of John Lehane, Melbourne, Australia; one *s. Educ:* Shrewsbury School, Sandhurst, 1914-15; Argyll and Sutherland Highlanders, 1915; Staff Coll., Camberley, 1930-31; Colonel, 1945; retired pay, 1946, with hon. rank of Brigadier. High Sheriff of Shropshire, 1965. DL Shropshire, 1966. *Address:* Pentreheylin, Maesbrook, Salop. *Club:* Army and Navy.

MACLEAN, Vice-Adm. Sir Hector Charles Donald, KBE 1962; CB 1960; DSC 1941; JP; DL; *b* 7 Aug. 1908; *s* of late Captain D. C. H. Maclean, DSO, The Royal Scots; *m* 1933, Opre, *d* of late Captain Geoffrey Vyvyan, Royal Welch Fusiliers; one *s* two *d. Educ:* Wellington. Special Entry into Navy, 1926; Captain 1948; idc 1951; Comd HMS Saintes and 3rd Destroyer Sqdn, 1952-53; Dir of Plans, Admiralty, 1953-56; Comd HMS Eagle, 1956-57; Chief of Staff, Home Fleet, 1958-59; Chief of Allied Staff, Mediterranean, 1959-62; Vice-Adm. 1960; retired 1962. JP Norfolk, 1963; DL Norfolk, 1977. *Address:* Deepdale Old Rectory, Brancaster Staithe, King's Lynn, Norfolk. *T:* Brancaster 281. *Club:* Norfolk (Norwich).

MACLEAN, Hector Ronald; Sheriff of North Strathclyde (formerly Renfrew and Argyll) since 1968; *b* 6 Dec. 1931; *s* of Donald Beaton Maclean and Lucy McAlister; *m* 1967, Hilary Elizabeth Jenkins; three *d. Educ:* High Sch. of Glasgow; Glasgow Univ. Admitted to Faculty of Advocates, 1959. *Recreations:* golf, shooting. *Address:* Barrfield, Houston, Renfrewshire. *T:* Bridge of Weir 612449.

MACLEAN of Pennycross, Rear-Admiral Iain Gilleasbuig, CB 1954; OBE 1944; retired; *b* 25 Nov. 1902; *s* of late Norman H. Maclean; *m* 1st, 1931, Evelyn Marjorie, *d* of late R. A. and Mrs Winton Reid; one step *d*; 2nd, 1973, Nancy Margaret *widow* of E. A. Barnard. *Educ:* Cargilfield; RN Colleges, Osborne and Dartmouth. Joined RN, 1916; Captain, 1945; Rear-Admiral, 1952; Served War of 1939-45: in Combined Operations, HMS Renown and Admiralty. Imperial Defence Coll., 1951; Dep. Engineer in Chief of the Fleet, 1952-55; retired, Nov. 1955. Director, Marine Development, Brush Group, 1956-60. Research Survey for National Ports Council, 1963-64. *Recreations:* fishing, gardening. *Address:* Pear Tree Cottage, Moorlands Drive, Pinkney's Green, Maidenhead, Berks. *T:* Maidenhead 30287. *Club:* Number Ten.

MACLEAN, Ian Albert Druce; Director, Halifax Building Society, 1953-76 (Chairman, 1961-74); Chairman, John Smedley Ltd; Director, Fanhams Hall Services (Ware) Ltd; *b* 23 June 1902; *s* of Alick and Nina Maclean; *m* 1937, Diana, *d* of John and Gertrude Marsden-Smedley; twin *s. Educ:* Marlborough; Pembroke Coll., Cambridge. Tobacco Industry, 1924; Cotton Industry, 1926; Carpet Industry, 1937; Halifax Building Society, 1953. Dir, Building Socs Training Coll. Ltd; Vice-Pres., Building Socs Assoc. Former Dir, Carpets International Ltd. *Recreations:* anything in the open air. *Address:* Ashday Hall, Southowram, Halifax, West Yorks. *T:* Halifax 54441. *Club:* Royal Windermere Yacht.

McLEAN, Ian Graeme; Metropolitan Stipendiary Magistrate since 1970; *b* Edinburgh, 7 Sept. 1928; *s* of Lt-Gen. Sir Kenneth McLean, *qv*; *m* 1957, Eleonore Maria Gmeiner, Bregenz, Austria; two *d. Educ:* Aldenham Sch.; Christ's Coll., Cambridge. BA Hons Law 1950; MA 1955. Intell. Corps, 1946-48. Called to Bar, Middle Temple, Nov. 1951; practised London and on Western Circuit, 1951-55; Crown Counsel, Northern Nigeria, 1955-59; Sen. Lectr and Head of Legal Dept of Inst. of Administration, Northern Nigeria, 1959-62; Native Courts Adviser, 1959-62; returned to English Bar, 1962; practised London and South Eastern Circuit, 1962-70; occasional Dep. Chm., Inner, NE, SW and Mddx Areas, London QS, 1968-70; occasional Dep. Recorder, Oxford, 1969-70; Adjudicator under Immigration Acts, 1969-70. *Publications:* Cumulative Index West African Court of Appeal Reports, 1958; (with Abubakar Sadiq) The Maliki Law of Homicide, 1959; (with Sir Lionel Brett) Criminal Law Procedure and Evidence of Lagos, Eastern

and Western Nigeria, 1963; (with Cyprian Okonkwo) Cases on the Criminal Law, Procedure and Evidence of Nigeria, 1966; (with Peter Morrish) A Practical Guide to Appeals in Criminal Courts, 1970; (with Peter Morrish) The Crown Court, an index of common penalties, etc, 1972; (ed, with Peter Morrish) Harris's Criminal Law, 22nd edn, 1972; (with Peter Morrish) The Magistrates' Court, an index of common penalties, 1973; (with Peter Morrish) The Trial of Breathalyser Offences, 1975; contrib. Archbold's Criminal Pleadings, 38th edn, and Halsbury's Laws of England, 4th edn, title Criminal Law. *Recreations:* family, gardening, writing, languages. *Address:* Highbury Corner Magistrates' Court, 51 Holloway Road, N7.

McLEAN, John, CBE 1947; Member, Council of Foreign Bondholders, 1948-74; a UK Representative on Commonwealth Economic Committee, 1950-62; a General Commissioner of Income Tax for City of London, 1956-68; *b* 19 April 1893; *s* of late Thomas Crawford McLean; *m* 1915, Catherine Kydd Strachan; one *s* two *d. Educ:* Hyndland Sch., Glasgow. Company Director; Chm., George Wills & Sons Ltd, Exporters and Importers, 1949-59, retired. Vice-Pres., London Chamber of Commerce, 1946 (Chm. 1944-46); Vice-Pres., Fedn of Commonwealth Chambers of Commerce, 1951 (Chm. 1948-51); Pres. Assoc. of British Chambers of Commerce, 1948-50; Member: Export Credits Guarantee Advisory Council, 1952-63; Port of London Authority, 1955-64. *Recreation:* golf. *Address:* Glenesk, 57 Brookmans Avenue, Brookmans Park, Hatfield, Herts. *T:* Potters Bar 53336. *Club:* East India, Devonshire, Sports and Public Schools.

MacLEAN, Dr John Alexander, CBE 1968; Chairman, Northern Regional Hospital Board (Scotland), since 1971; *b* 12 Oct. 1903; *s* of Donald MacLean, Achiltibuie, Ross-shire; *m* 1935, Hilda M. L. Munro, BSc, Aberdeen; one *s* one *d. Educ:* Dingwall Academy; Aberdeen Univ. MA, LLB, PhD; FEIS. Aberdeen Educn Authority: Teacher, 1926-39; Asst Dir of Educn, 1939-43; Dir of Educn, Inverness-shire Educn Authority, 1943-68, retd. Member: Exec. Cttee, National Trust for Scotland, 1967-; Scottish Council, Royal Over-Seas League, 1969-; Scottish Arts Council, 1964-68; Sec. of State's Council for Care of Children; Council on School Broadcasting. *Publication:* Sources for History of the Highlands in the Seventeenth Century, 1939. *Recreation:* sport. *Address:* 12 Eriskay Road, Inverness IV2 3LX. *T:* Inverness 31566. *Club:* Royal Over-Seas House (Edinburgh).

McLEAN, John Alexander Lowry, QC 1974; Permanent Secretary, Supreme Court of Northern Ireland, and Clerk of the Crown for Northern Ireland, since 1966; *b* 21 Feb. 1921; *o s* of John McLean and Phoebe Jane (*née* Bowditch); *m* 1950, Diana Elisabeth Campbell, *e d* of S. B. Boyd Campbell, MC, MD, FRCP, and Mary Isabella Ayre, St John's, Newfoundland; one *s* two *d. Educ:* Methodist Coll., Belfast; Queen's University Belfast. Served Intell. Corps, 1943-47. Called to Bar of Northern Ireland, 1949. Asst Sec., NI Supreme Court, and Private Sec. to Lord Chief Justice of NI 1956; Under Treas., Hon. Soc. of Inn of Court of NI, 1966; Clerk of Restrictive Practices Court in NI, 1957. Member: Jt Working Party on Enforcement of Judgments of NI Courts, 1963; Lord Chancellor's Cttee on NI Supreme Court, 1966; Lord Chancellor's Foreign Judgments Working Party, 1974-. *Publications:* contrib. legal periodicals. *Recreations:* not golf. *Address:* 24 Marlborough Park South, Belfast BT9 6HR. *T:* Belfast 667330; Lifeboat Cottage, Cloughey, Co. Down BT22 1HS. *T:* Portavogie 313. *Club:* Royal Commonwealth Society.

McLEAN, (John David) Ruari (McDowall Hardie), CBE 1973; DSC 1943; Senior Partner, Ruari McLean Associates (Design Consultants) (Founder Partner with Fianach Jardine, 1965); *b* 10 June 1917; *s* of late John Thomson McLean and late Isabel Mary McLean (*née* Ireland); *m* 1945, Antonia Maxwell Carlisle; two *s* one *d. Educ:* Dragon Sch., Oxford; Eastbourne Coll. First studied printing under B. H. Newdigate at Shakespeare Head Press, Oxford, 1936. Industrial printing experience in Germany and England, 1936-38; with The Studio, 1938; Percy Lund Humphries, Bradford, 1939. Served Royal Navy, 1940-45. Penguin Books, 1945-46; Book Designer (freelance), 1946-53; Tutor in Typography, Royal College of Art, 1948-51; Typographic Adviser to Hulton Press, 1953; Founder Partner, Rainbird, McLean Ltd, 1951-58; Founder Editor, and Designer, Motif, 1958-67. Typographic Consultant to The Observer, 1960-64; Hon. Typographic Adviser to HM Stationery Office, 1966. Mem., Nat. Council for Diplomas in Art and Design, 1971. Croix de Guerre (French), 1942. *Publications:* George Cruikshank, 1948; Modern Book Design, 1958; Wood Engravings of Joan Hassall, 1960; Victorian Book Design, 1963, rev. edn 1972; Tschichold's Typographische Gestaltung (Trans.), 1967; (ed) The Reminiscences of Edmund Evans, 1967;

Magazine Design, 1969; Victorian Publishers' Book-bindings in Cloth and Leather, 1973; Jan Tschichold, Typographer, 1975; Joseph Cundall, 1976. *Recreations:* sailing, reading, acquiring books. *Address:* Broomrigg, Dollar, Clackmannanshire FK14 7PT. *Clubs:* Double Crown; New (Edinburgh).

MACLEAN, Colonel John Francis, JP; Lord-Lieutenant of Hereford and Worcester, 1974-76 (Lord Lieutenant of Herefordshire, 1960-74); *b* 1 March 1901; *s* of late Montague Francis and Florence Maclean; *m* 1925, Vivienne A. M. Miesegaes (*d* 1969); two *s*. *Educ:* Eton Coll. Started in coal trade with Cannop Coal Co. Ltd, Forest of Dean, 1921; became a Director and Commercial Manager, in 1927, after being employed with United Collieries Ltd, Glasgow. Commnd Herefordshire Regt (TA), 1919-23. Coal Supplies Officer for Forest of Dean, 1939-40; commnd in Grenadier Guards, Sept. 1940, reaching rank of Major. Hon. Colonel, Herefordshire Light Infantry (TA), 1963-67; Pres., West Midland TAVR Assoc., 1970-76. Herefordshire: JP 1946, High Sheriff 1951, DL 1953-60. KStJ 1960. *Recreations:* golf, shooting; formerly lawn tennis and cricket (kept wicket for Worcestershire, 1922-24, and occasionally for Gloucestershire, 1929-30; toured Australia and New Zealand with MCC team, 1922-23). *Address:* Bromsash House, Ross-on-Wye, Herefordshire. *T:* Lea 243.

McLEAN, Lieut-General Sir Kenneth Graeme, KCB, *cr* 1954 (CB 1944); KBE, *cr* 1951; US Legion of Merit, 1945; Officer, Legion of Honour (France); Croix de Guerre (France); *b* 11 Dec. 1896; *s* of late Arthur H. McLean, WS; *m* 1926, Daphne Winifred Ashburner Steele; two *s*. *Educ:* Edinburgh Academy; RMA Woolwich. Commissioned RE 1918; served, in Ireland, 1919-20, and with KGO Bengal Sappers and Miners in India, 1923-29; Staff Coll., Quetta, 1930-31; on General Staff, AHQ, India, 1932-36; Assistant Secretary Cttee of Imperial Defence, 1938; Student at Imperial Defence Coll., 1939. Served France and Germany, 1944-45; Deputy Adjutant-General, GHQ, Far East, 1945-46; Dep. Adjutant-General, GHQ, Middle East, 1946; Vice-Adjutant-General, War Office, 1947-49; Chief of Staff, CCG, and Deputy Military Governor, British Zone in Germany, 1949; Military Secretary to the Secretary of State for War, 1949-51; Chief Staff Officer, Ministry of Defence, 1951-52; Special Duty, War Office, 1952-54. Retired, 1954. Colonel Comdt RE, 1956-61. *Address:* Greenways, Melrose, Roxburghshire.

See also I. G. McLean.

MacLEAN, Kenneth Smedley, MD, FRCP; Consultant Physician to Guy's Hospital, since 1950; *b* 22 Nov. 1914; *s* of Hugh MacLean and Ida Smedley; *m* 1939, Joan Hardaker; one *s* one *d* (and one *s* decd). *Educ:* Westminster; Clare Coll., Cambridge. MRCS, LRCP, 1939; House appts at Guy's, 1939; MB, BChir 1939. RNVR, 1939-46, Surg.-Lt and Surg.-Lt-Comdr. MRCP 1946; House Officer and Medical Registrar, Guy's Hosp., 1946-48; MD Cantab 1948; FRCP 1954; elected to Assoc. of Physicians of Great Britain and Ireland, 1956. Assistant Director, Dept of Medicine, Guy's Hospital Medical Sch., 1949, Director, 1961-63. Chm., University Hosps Assoc., 1975-Aug. 1977. *Publication:* Medical Treatment, 1957. *Recreation:* golf. *Address:* Heathdown, The Ridge, Woldingham, Surrey. *T:* Woldingham 2260.

McLEAN, Lt-Col Neil Loudon Desmond, DSO 1943; *b* 28 Nov. 1918; *s* of Neil McLean; *m* 1949, Daška Kennedy (*née* Ivanović-Banac), Dubrovnik, Jugoslavia. *Educ:* Eton; RMC, Sandhurst. Gazetted Royal Scots Greys, 1938; Palestine Campaign, 1939; served War of 1939-45, Middle East and Far East: Ethiopia under 101 Mission, 1941; Head of First Military Mission to Albania, 1942 and 1943; Lieut-Colonel, 1943; Far East, 1944-45. Contested (C) Preston South, 1950 and 1951; MP (C) Inverness, Dec. 1954-Sept. 1964. Member Highland and Islands Advisory Panel, 1955. Member of Queen's Body Guard for Scotland, Royal Company of Archers. Distinguished Military Medal of Haile Selassie I, 1941. *Publications:* contributions to Chatham House, Royal Central Asian Society Reviews. *Recreations:* travel, riding, shooting, under-water fishing. *Address:* 17 Eaton Square, SW1. *Clubs:* White's, Buck's, Cavalry and Guards, Pratt's; Highland (Inverness).

MACLEAN, Sir Robert (Alexander), KBE 1973; Kt 1955; DL; Chartered Accountant; Chairman, Stoddard Holdings Ltd; a Vice-President, Scottish Council (Development and Industry); Member, Norwich Union Insurance Group (Scottish Advisory Board); *b* 11 April 1908; *s* of Andrew Johnston Maclean, JP, Cambuslang, Lanarkshire, and Mary Jane Cameron; *m* 1938, Vivienne Neville Bourke, *d* of Captain Bertram Walter Bourke, JP, Heathfield, Co. Mayo; two *s* two *d*. *Educ:* Glasgow High Sch. JDipMA. President: Glasgow Chamber of Commerce, 1956-58; Association British Chambers of Commerce, 1966-68;

Chairman: Council of Scottish Chambers of Commerce, 1960-62; Scottish Cttee, Council of Industrial Design, 1949-58 (Mem., CoID, 1948-58); Council of Management, Scottish Industries Exhibns, 1949, 1954 and 1959; Scottish Exports Cttee, 1966-70; Scottish Industrial Estates Corp., 1955-72 (Mem., 1946-72); Pres., British Industrial Exhibn, Moscow, 1966; Vice-Chm., Scottish Bd for Industry, 1952-60; Member: Pigs and Bacon Marketing Commn, 1955-56; BNEC, 1966-70; Scottish Aerodromes Bd, 1950-61; Export Council for Europe, 1960-64; BoT Trade Exhbns Adv. Cttee, 1961-65; Nat. Freight Corp., 1969-72; Regional Controller (Scotland): Board of Trade, 1944-46; Factory and Storage Premises, 1941-44. DL Renfrewshire, 1970. CStJ 1975. FRSA; FBIM. Hon. LLD Glasgow, 1970. *Recreations:* golf, fishing. *Address:* Woodend, Houston, Renfrewshire. *Clubs:* Junior Carlton; Western (Glasgow).

McLEAN, Robert Colquhoun, MA, DSc, FLS; Professor of Botany, University College of South Wales and Monmouthshire, Cardiff, 1919-55; retired Dec. 1955; *b* Kilcreggan, Dunbartonshire, 18 July 1890; *s* of Rev. Robert McLean, MA, Kilcreggan, Dunbartonshire; *m* 1914, Freda Marguerite (*d* 1955), *d* of George Washington Kilner, MA; three *s*. *Educ:* The Leys School, Cambridge; University College, London; St John's Coll., Cambridge. Lecturer in Botany at University Coll., Reading, 1913; has travelled in many parts of the world for botanical purposes and for comparative study of University Systems; General Secretary of International University Conference, founded 1934; President Assoc. of University Teachers, 1940-41; President, International Assoc. of University Professors, 1950; Member: Nature Conservancy, 1949-56; National Parks Commission, 1949-56; Universities Advisory Cttee, British Council, 1953. *Publications:* Plant Science Formulæ, Textbook of Theoretical Botany, Text Book of Practical Botany, and Practical Field Ecology (with W. R. I. Cook); numerous articles in scientific periodicals, etc. *Recreation:* sleep. *Address:* Hickley Lodge, Old Cogan, Penarth, S Glam.

McLEAN, Ruari; *see* McLean, J. D. R. McD. H.

MacLEARY, Donald Whyte; principal male dancer with the Royal Ballet since 1959; Ballet Master to the Royal Ballet, since 1975; *b* Glasgow, 22 Aug. 1937; *s* of Donald Herbert MacLeary, MPS, and Jean Spiers (*née* Leslie). *Educ:* Inverness Royal Academy; The Royal Ballet School. *Classical Ballets:* (full length) Swan Lake, Giselle, 1958; Sleeping Beauty, Cinderella, Sylvia, 1959; Ondine, La Fille Mal Gardée, 1960; (centre male rôle) in Ashton's Symphonic Variations, 1962; Sonnet Pas de Trois, 1964; Romeo and Juliet, 1965; Eugene Onegin, Stuttgart, 1966; Apollo, 1966; Nutcracker, 1968; Swan Lake with N. Makarova, 1972. *Creations:* (1954-74): Solitaire, The Burrow, Danse Concertante, Antigone, Diversions, Le Baiser de la Fée, Jabez and the Devil, Raymonda Pas de Deux (for Frederick Ashton), two episodes in Images of Love; Song of the Earth; Lilac Garden (revival); Jazz Calendar; Raymonda (for Nureyeff); The Man in Kenneth MacMillan's Checkpoint; leading role in Concerto no 2 (Balanchine's Ballet Imperial, renamed); Elite Syncopations, 1974; Kenneth MacMillan's Four Seasons Symphony. Toured Brazil with Royal Ballet, Spring 1973. *Recreations:* reading, theatre, records (all types); riding, fox hunting, swimming. *Address:* 41 Kensington Park Gardens, W11. *T:* 01-727 7202; Bunyan Cottage, Wainwood, Preston, Herts. *Club:* Queen's.

McLEAY, Hon. Sir John, KCMG 1962; MM; retired as Speaker of the House of Representatives, Canberra, Australia (1956-66); Federal Member for Boothby, South Australia, 1949-66; *b* 19 Nov. 1893; *m* 1921, Eileen H. (*d* 1971), *d* of late H. Elden, Geelong; two *s* one *d*. Stretcher Bearer, 13 Field Ambulance, 1st AIF (awarded Military Medal); Life Member, Hindmarsh Ambulance. Formerly: Mayor of City of Unley; Lord Mayor of Adelaide; Member for Unley, House of Assembly, SA; Member Council of Governors, Adelaide Univ. and Scotch Coll., Adelaide. President or Past President various organisations; Hon. Member Town Planning Institute, SA, etc. *Address:* 7 Brae Road, St Georges, SA 5061, Australia.

MacLEAY, His Honour Oswell Searight, JP; a Circuit Judge (formerly Deputy-Chairman, Inner Division Greater London Sessions), 1965-75; Barrister-at-law; *b* 11 Dec. 1905; *o s* of late Oswell Sullivan MacLeay and Ida Marion MacLeay, 29 Draycott Place, SW1; *m* 1930, Viola Elizabeth Mary French, *o d* of late Frank Austen French, MRCS, LRCP, and Dora Emmeline French, Hollamby House, Herne Bay; two *s*. *Educ:* RN College, Osborne; RN College, Dartmouth; Charterhouse; Magdalen Coll., Oxford. Called to the Bar, Inner Temple, 1932; South Eastern Circuit. Recorder of Maidstone, 1959-61. Dep. Chairman, West Kent Quarter Sessions, 1954-62; Asst

Chairman of County of Middlesex Sessions, 1959-60; Dep. Chairman, 1960-61; Dep. Chairman County of London Sessions, 1961-65; Member Mental Health Review Tribunal, 1960-61. Served War, RNVR, 1939-45; Sub-Lieut, 1939; Lieut, 1939; Lieut-Commander, 1941. JP Kent. Member Kent Standing Joint Cttee and Police Authority, 1956-64; Member Malling Rural District Council, 1949-55 (Chairman, 1951-55); Member Visiting Cttee, Maidstone Prison, 1954-58. President Sevenoaks Conservative and Unionist Assoc., 1959-61. *Recreations:* watching and umpiring cricket; naval and military history; travel (particularly by rail). *Address:* The Old Farm House, Wrotham, Kent. *T:* Borough Green 884138. *Clubs:* Naval and Military, MCC; Band of Brothers (Kent).

MACLEHOSE, Sir (Crawford) Murray, GBE 1976 (MBE 1946); KCMG 1971 (CMG 1964); KCVO 1975; HM Diplomatic Service; Governor and Commander-in-Chief, Hong Kong, since 1971; *b* 16 Oct. 1917; *s* of Hamish A. MacLehose and Margaret Bruce Black; *m* 1947, Margaret Noël Dunlop; two *d. Educ:* Rugby; Balliol Coll., Oxford. Served War of 1939-45, Lieut, RNVR. Joined Foreign Service, 1947; Acting Consul, 1947, Acting Consul-General, 1948, Hankow; promoted First Secretary, 1949; transferred to Foreign Office, 1950; First Secretary (Commercial), and Consul, Prague, 1951; seconded to Commonwealth Relations Office, for service at Wellington, 1954; returned to Foreign Office and transferred to Paris, 1956; promoted Counsellor, 1959; seconded to Colonial Office and transferred to Hong Kong as Political Adviser; Counsellor, Foreign Office, 1963; Principal Private Secretary to Secretary of State, 1965-67; Ambassador: to Vietnam, 1967-69; to Denmark, 1969-71. KStJ 1972. *Recreations:* sailing, fishing. *Address:* Government House, Hong Kong; Beoch, Maybole, Ayrshire. *Clubs:* Athenæum, Travellers'.

MacLEISH, Archibald; *b* 7 May 1892; *s* of Andrew MacLeish and Martha Hillard; *m* 1916, Ada Hitchcock; two *s* one *d* (and one *s* decd). *Educ:* The Hotchkiss Sch., Lakeville, Connecticut; Yale Univ. (AB); Harvard Univ. (LLB). Hon. MA Tufts, 1932; Hon. LittD, Wesleyan, 1938; Colby, 1938; Yale, 1939; Pennsylvania, 1941; Illinois, 1947; Rockford Coll., 1952; Columbia, 1954; Harvard, 1955; Princetown, 1965; Massachusetts, 1969; York Univ., Toronto, 1971; Hon. LLD: Dartmouth, 1940; Johns Hopkins Univ., 1941; University of California, 1943; Queen's Coll., Canada, 1948; University of Puerto Rico, 1953; Amherst Coll., 1963; Hon. DCL. Union Coll., 1941; Hon. LHD: Williams Coll., 1942; Washington Univ., 1948. Enlisted as private, United States Army, 1917; discharged with rank of Captain, 1919; spent 12 months in American Expeditionary Force, France. An instructor in government at Harvard, 1919-21; practised law in Boston offices of Choate, Hall and Stewart, 1920-23; devoted his time to travel and literature, 1923-30; Editor of Fortune, 1929-38; Librarian of Congress, 1939-44; Director Office of Facts and Figures, 1941-42; Asst Director of Office of War Information, 1942-43; Asst Secretary of State, 1944-45. Chairman, American Delegation to London Conference, UN, to establish a Cultural and Educational Organisation, 1945; American Member Exec. Board of UNESCO, 1946. Boylston Professor, Harvard Univ., 1949-62. Simpson Lecturer, Amherst Coll., 1963, 1964, 1965, 1966. President American Academy of Arts and Letters, 1953-56. US Medal of Freedom, 1977. Commander, Légion d'Honneur (France); Commander, El Sol del Peru. *Publications:* The Happy Marriage (verse), 1924; The Pot of Earth (verse), 1925; Nobodaddy (verse play), 1925; Streets in the Moon (verse), 1926; The Hamlet of A. MacLeish (verse), 1928; New Found Land, 1930; Conquistador (Pulitzer poetry prize), 1932; Frescoes for Mr Rockefeller's City (verse), 1933; Union Pacific-a Ballet, 1934; Panic (verse play), 1935; Public Speech (verse), 1936; The Fall of the City (verse play for radio), 1937; Land of the Free (verse), 1938; Air Raid (verse play for radio), 1938; America was Promises (verse), 1939; The Irresponsibles (prose), 1940; The American Cause (prose), 1941; A Time to Speak (prose), 1941; American Opinion and the War (Rede Lecture at Cambridge Univ., 1942), 1943; A Time to Act (prose), 1943; The American Story (radio broadcasts), 1944; Actfive and Other Poems, 1948; Poetry and Opinion (prose), 1950; Freedom Is The Right To Choose (prose), 1951; Collected Poems, 1952 (Bollingen Prize, National Book Award, Pulitzer poetry prize); This Music Crept By Me Upon The Waters (verse play), 1953; Songs For Eve (verse), 1954; J.B. (verse play), 1958 (produced NY, Dec. 1958; Pulitzer Prize for Drama, 1959); Poetry and Experience (prose), 1961; The Eleanor Roosevelt Story, 1965 (filmed, 1965, Academy Award, 1966); Herakles (verse play), 1967; A Continuing Journey (prose), 1968; The Wild Old Wicked Man and other poems, 1968; Scratch (prose play), 1971; The Human Season (selected poems), 1972; The Great American Fourth of July Parade (verse play for radio), 1975; New and Collected Poems, 1917-1976, 1976. *Address:* Conway,

Mass 01341, USA. *Clubs:* Century Association (NY); Tavern (Boston).

McLELLAN, David, CMG 1957; ED 1951; Education Consultant, International Bank for Reconstruction and Development, 1965-69; *b* 23 Dec. 1904; *e s* of David McLellan; *m* 1934, Winifred (*née* Henderson); three *s. Educ:* King Edward VII Sch., Lytham; Queen's Coll., Cambridge. Colonial Education Service: Hong Kong, 1931, Chief Inspector of Schools, 1951; Singapore, Dep. Director of Education, and Mem., Legislative Council, 1953; Director of Education and Permanent Secretary to Min. of Education, 1955; Regional Education Adviser to Comr General for UK in SE Asia, 1959-62; Director, Cultural Relations, SEATO, Bangkok, 1963-65. *Recreation:* golf. *Address:* The Alders, 179 Cooden Drive, Bexhill-on-Sea, East Sussex. *T:* Cooden 2650.

McLELLAN, Prof. David; DPhil; Professor of Political Theory, University of Kent, since 1975; *b* 10 Feb. 1940; *s* of Robert Douglas McLellan and Olive May Bush; *m* 1967, Annie Brassart; two *d. Educ:* Merchant Taylors' Sch.; St John's Coll., Oxford (MA, DPhil). Lectr in Politics, Univ. of Kent, 1966-71; Vis. Prof., State Univ. of New York, 1969; Guest Fellow in Politics, Indian Inst. of Advanced Studies, Simla, 1970; Sen. Lectr in Politics, Univ. of Kent, 1972, Reader in Political Theory 1973. *Publications:* The Young Hegelians and Karl Marx, 1969 (French, German, Italian, Spanish and Japanese edns); Marx beforeMarxism, 1970, 2nd edn 1972; Karl Marx: The Early Texts, 1971; Marx's Grundrisse, 1971, 2nd edn 1973; The Thought of Karl Marx, 1971 (Portuguese and Italian edns); Karl Marx: His Life and Thought, 1973, 22nd edn 1976 (German, Italian, Spanish, Japanese, Swedish and Dutch edns); Marx (Fontana Modern Masters), 1975; Engels, 1977. *Recreations:* chess, Raymond Chandler, hill walking. *Address:* Eliot College, University of Kent, Canterbury, Kent CT2 7NS. *T:* Canterbury 63579.

McLELLAN, Eric Burns; His Honour Judge McLellan; a Circuit Judge (formerly County Court Judge), since 1970; Circuit no 51, since 1972; *b* 9 April 1918; *s* of late Stanley Morgan McLellan, Christchurch, Newport, Mon; *m* 1949, Elsa Sarah, *d* of late Gustave Mustaki, Alexandria; one *s* one *d. Educ:* Newport High Sch.; New Coll., Oxford. BA 1939; MA 1967. Served RAF, 1940-46, N Africa, Italy, Egypt, 205 Group; Flt-Lt. Called to Bar, Inner Temple, 1947. Dep. Chm., IoW QS, 1967. Official Principal, Archdeaconry of Hackney, 1967-72; Dep. Chm., Workmen's Compensation Supplementation Bd and Pneumoconiosis, Byssinosis and Miscellaneous Diseases Benefit Bd, 1969-70; Mem., Dept of Health and Social Security Adv. Group on Use of Fetuses and Fetal Material for Research, 1970. *Publications:* contribs to medico-legal jls. *Recreations:* heraldry and genealogy. *Address:* Lone Barn, Catherington, Hants PO8 0SF. *T:* Hambledon 436. *Clubs:* United Oxford & Cambridge University, Royal Air Force; Hampshire (Winchester).

MacLELLAN, Prof. George Douglas Stephen, MA, PhD (Cantab); CEng; FIMechE, FIEE; Professor and Head of Department of Engineering, University of Leicester, since 1965; *b* Glasgow, 1 Nov. 1922; *e s* of late Alexander Stephen MacLellan. *Educ:* Rugby Sch.; Pembroke Coll., Cambridge; Massachusetts Institute of Technology. Mech. Sci. Tripos, 1942. Dept of Colloid Science, Cambridge, and Callenders Cable and Construction Co. Ltd, 1942-44; Fellow, Pembroke Coll., 1944-59; Vickers-Armstrong Ltd, Elswick Works, Newcastle upon Tyne, 1944-46; University Demonstrator and Lecturer in Engineering, Cambridge, 1947-59; Rankine Professor of Mechanical Engineering (Mechanics and Mechanism), University of Glasgow, 1959-65. Commonwealth Fund Fellow, MIT, 1948-49; Visiting Professor, Michigan State University, 1958; MIT, 1962. Pres. of the Soc. of Instrument Technology, 1964-65. Vice-Chm., United Kingdom Automation Council, 1961-64; Member: CNAA, 1970-; Engrg Bd, SRC, 1971-74; Council, IMechE, 1974-76. *Publications:* contribs to mech. and elec. jls. *Address:* Department of Engineering, The University, Leicester LE1 7RH. *T:* Leicester 50000. *Clubs:* Athenæum, Leander.

MacLELLAN, (George) Robin (Perronet), CBE 1969; JP; Chairman, Scottish Tourist Board, since 1974; Director: Scottish National Trust Co. Ltd, since 1970; Nationwide Building Society, since 1972; British Tourist Authority, since 1974; Scottish Industrial and Trade Exhibitions Ltd, since 1975; *b* 14 Nov. 1915; *e s* of George Aikman MacLellan, Glasgow, and Irene Dorothy Perronet Miller, Liverpool; *m* 1941, Margaret, *er d* of Dr Berkeley Robertson, Glasgow; one *s. Educ:* Ardvreck Sch., Crieff; Clifton Coll.; Ecole de Commerce, Lausanne. Chm., George MacLellan Hldgs Ltd, 1965-76; Dep. Chm., British Airports Authority, 1965-75; Pres., Glasgow Chamber of

Commerce, 1970-71; Dir, Govan Shipbuilders Ltd, 1972-74; Mem., Scottish Industrial Develt Bd, 1972-74. Dir, Ardvreck Sch. Ltd, 1970-; Governor, Clifton Coll.; Mem. Council, Scottish Business Sch., 1972-75; Mem. Court, Strathclyde Univ., 1972-76. Member: West Central Scotland Plan Steering Cttee, 1970-75; Scottish Econ. Council, 1968-75; BNEC's Cttee for Exports to Canada, 1964-69; Nat. Trust for Scotland, 1974-; Gen. Adv. Council, IBA, 1976-; BRAdv. Bd (Scottish), 1977-. A Vice-Pres., Assoc. British Chambers of Commerce, 1975-. JP Dunbartonshire, 1973. OStJ 1972. *Publications:* articles on travel, tourism, business matters and Scottish affairs. *Recreations:* swimming, angling, travelling, reading. *Address:* 11 Beechwood Court, Bearsden, Glasgow. *T:* 041-942 3876. *Clubs:* Caledonian; Western (Glasgow); RNVR (Scotland).

McLELLAN, James Kidd, CBE 1974; QPM 1966; Senior Assistant Chief Constable, Strathclyde Police, 1975-76; retired; *b* 16 Oct. 1914; *s* of John Young McLellan, MPS, FBOA, Chemist and Optician, and Robina (*née* Kidd); *m* 1942, Margaret A. G. F. Selby; two *s* one *d*. *Educ:* Lenzie Academy; Glasgow Univ.; Royal Technical Coll. (now Strathclyde Univ.). MA Hons, BSc; ARIC 1948, FRIC 1965. City of Glasgow Police, 1936-65: i/c Police Laboratory, attached to Identification Bureau, 1946-60; Det. Supt (ii) in Ident. Bureau and Scottish Criminal Record Office, 1960; Det. Supt (i) i/c SCRO and IB, 1962; Chief Constable: Motherwell and Wishaw Burgh, 1965; Lanarkshire, 1967. Past Chm. (Scottish Section), Soc. for Analytical Chemistry. *Publications:* articles in Police Jl, Fire Service Jl. *Recreation:* youth work. *Address:* 181 Manse Road, Motherwell, Lanarkshire. *T:* Motherwell 62812.

MacLELLAN, Robin; *see* MacLellan, G. R. P.

McLELLAND, Charles James; Controller, BBC Radio 1 and 2, since 1976; *b* 19 Nov. 1930; *s* of Charles John McLelland and Jessie Steele Barbour; *m* 1961, Philippa Mary Murphy; one *s* three *d*. *Educ:* Kilmarnock Acad.; Glasgow Acad.; Glasgow Univ. MA (Hons). Commissioned Royal Artillery, 1952-54. Sub-Editor, Leader Writer, Glasgow Herald, 1954-58; Scriptwriter, European Productions, BBC, 1958-61; Head of Programmes, Radio Sarawak, 1962-64; Indian Programme Organiser, BBC, 1964-67; Asst Head, Arabic Service, BBC, 1967-71; Head of Arabic Service, 1971-75. *Recreations:* gardening, reading, flying. *Address:* c/o Broadcasting House, W1A 1AA. *Club:* Travellers'.

MacLENNAN, Maj.-Gen. Alastair, OBE 1945; Curator, Royal Army Medical Corps Historical Museum, Mytchett, Hants, 1969-Feb. 1977; *b* 16 Feb. 1912; *s* of Col. Farquhar MacLennan, DSO; *m* 1940, Constance Anne Cook; two *s* one *d*. *Educ:* Aberdeen Grammar Sch.; University of Aberdeen (MB, ChB). Commissioned Lieut, RAMC, 1934; Captain, 1935; Major, 1942; Lieut-Colonel, 1942; Colonel, 1952; Brigadier, 1964; Maj.-General, 1967; retired 1969. Appointments held include regimental, staff and Ministry of Defence in UK, Malta, NW Europe, India, Malaya, Korea, Egypt and Germany; ADGMS (Army), Min. of Defence, 1957-61; DDMS, HQ, BAOR, 1961-64; Inspector Army Medical Services, 1964-66; DDMS: 1 (Br) Corps, 1966-67; HQ Eastern Command, 1967-68; Dep. Dir-Gen., Army Med. Services, MoD, 1968-69; Col Comdt, RAMC, 1971-76. US Bronze Star Medal, 1952. OStJ, 1966. QHP, 1968-69. *Publications:* papers on history of military firearms and on Highland Regts in North America 1756-1783. *Recreations:* bird-watching, military history, collecting antique military firearms and swords, vintage motor-cars. *Address:* 56 Reigate Road, Ewell, Epsom, Surrey. *T:* 01-393 2132.

McLENNAN, Gordon; General Secretary, Communist Party of Great Britain, since 1975; *b* Glasgow, 12 May 1924; *s* of a shipyard worker; *m*; four *c*. *Educ:* Hamilton Crescent Sch., Partick, Glasgow. Engineering apprentice, Albion Motors Ltd, Scotstoun, 1939, later engineering draughtsman. Elected Glasgow Organiser, Communist Party, 1949; Sec., Communist Party in Scotland, 1957; Nat. Organiser, Communist Party of GB, 1966. *Recreations:* golf and other sports; cultural interests. *Address:* Communist Party of Great Britain, 16 King Street, WC2E 8HY. *T:* 01-836 2151.

MacLENNAN, Sir Hector, Kt 1965; MD, FRCP, FRCPGlas, FRCOG; Chairman, Advisory Committee on Distinction Awards, since 1971; Director, Inveresk Research International; *b* 1 Nov. 1905; *s* of Robert Jackson MacLennan and Amy Florence Ross; *m* 1st, 1933, Isabel Margaret Adam (*d* 1973); three *s* one *d*; 2nd, 1976, Jean Elspeth Duncan Lackie. *Educ:* Glasgow High Sch.; University of Glasgow. President Glasgow Univ. Union, 1927. Cons. Surgeon, Glasgow Royal Maternity and Women's Hospital, 1934-71; Senior Cons. Gynæcologist, Victoria Infirmary, Glasgow, 1948; Mem. W Regional Hosp.

Bd, 1950-56. Mem. GMC, 1965-69. Lately External Examr in Obst. and Gynæc., Univs of Birmingham, Newcastle, Aberdeen, Edinburgh, Oxford, Dundee and Cambridge, and, at present, Dublin. Blair-Bell Lectr, 1944; Lloyd-Roberts Lectr, 1964; Osler Lectr, 1966; Arthur Wilson Oration, 1966; Joseph Price Oration, 1966; Harveian Oration, Edinburgh, 1970. President: RCOG, 1963-66; RSM, 1967-69; Chairman: Medico-Pharmaceutical Forum, 1968-70; Scottish Tourist Bd, 1969-74. Lord High Comr to General Assembly of Church of Scotland, 1975 and 1976. Hon. FACOG, 1964; Hon. FCSOG 1965; Hon. FRCSE, 1967; Hon. Fellow, American Assoc. of Obsts and Gynæcs, 1967. Hon. Alumnus: Sloane Hosp. for Women, NY; Nat. Maternity Hosp., Dublin; Master of Midwifery, Royal Society of Apothecaries, 1968. Hon. FRCPGlas 1971; FRCP 1973; Hon. Member: Royal Medico-Chirurgical Soc., Glasgow, 1971; Section of Medical Educn, RSM, 1971. Hon. LLD Glasgow, 1974. *Publications:* contribs to Combined Textbook of Obstetrics and Gynæcology and British Practice of Obstetrics and Gynæcology (1st edn), and sundry others. *Recreations:* fishing, shooting. *Address:* Invercorry, Rogart, Sutherland. *T:* Rogart 344.

See also R. A. R. MacLennan.

MacLENNAN, Hugh; CC (Canada) 1967; Professor, English Literature, McGill University, since 1967 (Associate Professor, 1951-67); *b* 20 March 1907; *s* of Dr Samuel John MacLennan and Katherine MacQuarrie; *m* 1st, 1936, Dorothy Duncan (*d* 1957); 2nd, 1959, Frances Aline, *d* of late Frank Earle Walker and Isabella Scott Benson. *Educ:* Dalhousie Univ.; Oriel Coll., Oxford; Graduate Coll., Princeton. Rhodes Schol. (Canada at large), 1928; PhD (Princeton) 1935. Classics Master, Lower Canada Coll., Montreal, 1935-45; writing, 1945-51. FRS Canada, 1953 (Gold Medal, 1951); FRSL, 1959. Governor-General's Award for Fiction, 1945, 1948, 1959; Governor-General's Award for non-fiction, 1949, 1954. Hon. DLitt: Waterloo Lutheran, 1961; Carleton Univ., 1967; Western Ontario, 1953, Manitoba, 1955; Hon. LLD: Dalhousie, 1956, Saskatchewan, 1959; McMaster, 1965; Toronto, 1966; Laurentian, 1966; Sherbrooke, 1967; British Columbia, 1968; St Mary's, 1968; Hon. DCL Bishop's, 1965. *Publications:* Oxyrhynchus: An Economic and Social Study, 1935; Barometer Rising, 1941; Two Solitudes, 1945; The Precipice, 1948; Cross Country (essays), 1949; Each Man's Son, 1951; Thirty and Three (essays), 1954; The Watch That Ends The Night, 1959; Scotchman's Return (essays), 1960; Return of the Sphinx, 1967; Rivers of Canada, 1974. *Recreations:* walking, gardening. *Address:* 1535 Summerhill Avenue, Montreal, PQ, Canada. *T:* We. 2-8566. *Clubs:* Montreal Amateur Athletic Association, McGill Faculty (Montreal).

MACLENNAN, Sir Ian (Morrison Ross), KCMG 1957 (CMG 1951); HM Diplomatic Service, retired; *b* 30 Oct. 1909; *s* of late W. Maclennan, Glasgow; *m* 1936, Margherita Lucas, *d* of late F. Lucas Jarratt, Bedford; one *s* one *d*. *Educ:* Hymers Coll., Hull; Worcester Coll., Oxford. Appointed Colonial Office, 1933; Dominions Office, 1937; UK High Commissioner's Office, Ottawa, 1938; Pretoria, 1945; UK High Commissioner S Rhodesia, 1951-53; Federation of Rhodesia and Nyasaland, 1953-55; Assistant Under-Secretary of State, CRO, 1955-57; UK High Commissioner in Ghana, 1957-59; Ambassador to the Republic of Ireland, 1960-63; High Commissioner in New Zealand, 1964-69. Mem., Gen. Adv. Council, IBA. *Address:* 26 Ham Street, Richmond, Surrey. *Club:* Travellers'.

McLENNAN, Sir Ian (Munro), KBE 1963 (CBE 1956); Chairman: Australia and New Zealand Banking Group Ltd, and Australia and New Zealand Group Holdings, since 1977; BHP-GKN Holdings Ltd, since 1970; Tubemakers of Australia Ltd, since 1973; Director, ICI Australia Ltd, since 1976; President, Australian Academy of Technological Sciences, since 1976; *b* 30 Nov. 1909; *s* of R. B. and C. O. McLennan; *m* 1937, Dora H., *d* of J. H. Robertson; two *s* two *d*. *Educ:* Scotch Coll., Melbourne; Melbourne Univ. Broken Hill Pty Co. Ltd: Cadet engineer, 1933; Asst Manager, Newcastle Steelworks of BHP Co. Ltd, 1943; Asst Gen. Man., BHP Co. Ltd, 1947; Gen. Man., 1950; Sen. Gen. Man., 1956; Chief Gen. Man., 1959; Man. Dir, 1967-71; Chm., 1971-77. Chairman: Defence (Industrial) Cttee; Ian Clunies Ross Meml Foundn; Australian Mineral Development Laboratories, 1959-67, remaining as Mem. Council; Dep. Chm., Immigration Planning Council, 1949-67. Dir, International Iron and Steel Inst.; Member: Internat. Council, Morgan Guaranty Trust Co. of NY; Australian Mining Industry Council; Australasian Inst. of Mining and Metallurgy (Pres., 1951, 1957 and 1972); Australian Mineral Industries Research Assoc. Ltd. *Recreations:* golf, gardening. *Address:* Apt 3, 112-120 Walsh Street, South Yarra, Victoria 3141, Australia. *Clubs:* Melbourne, Athenæum, Australian (all Melbourne); Union (Sydney); Newcastle (Newcastle); Commonwealth (Canberra); Royal Melbourne Golf; Melbourne Cricket.

MACLENNAN, Robert Adam Ross; MP (Lab) Caithness and Sutherland since 1966; Parliamentary Under-Secretary of State, Department of Prices and Consumer Protection, since 1974; Barrister-at-law; *b* 26 June 1936; *e s* of Sir Hector MacLennan, *qv*; *m* 1968, Mrs Helen Noyes, *d* of Judge Ammi Cutter, Cambridge, Mass, and *widow* of Paul H. Noyes; one *s* one *d*, and one step *s*. *Educ*: Glasgow Academy; Balliol Coll., Oxford; Trinity Coll., Cambridge; Columbia Univ., New York City. Called to the Bar, Gray's Inn, 1962. Parliamentary Private Secretary: to Secretary of State for Commonwealth Affairs, 1967-69; to Minister without Portfolio, 1969-70; Additional Opposition Spokesman: on Scottish Affairs, 1970-71; on Defence, 1971-72; Member: House of Commons Estimates Cttee, 1967-69; House of Commons Select Cttee on Scottish Affairs, 1969-70; Latey Cttee on Age of Majority, 1968. *Recreations*: theatre, music. *Address*: 74 Abingdon Villas, W8; Hollandmake, Barrock, Caithness.

MacLEOD, family name of Baron MacLeod of Fuinary.

MACLEOD, family name of Baroness Macleod of Borve.

MACLEOD OF BORVE, Baroness *cr* 1971 (Life Peer), of Borve, Isle of Lewis; Evelyn Hester Macleod, JP; DL; *b* 19 Feb. 1915; *d* of Rev. Gervase Vanneck Blois (*d* 1961), and Hon. Hester Murray Pakington (*d* 1973), *y d* of 3rd Baron Hampton; *m* 1st, 1937, Mervyn Charles Mason (killed by enemy action, 1940); 2nd, 1941, Rt Hon. Iain Norman Macleod, MP (Minister of Health, 1952-55; Minister of Labour and Nat. Service, 1955-59; Secretary of State for the Colonies, 1959-61; Chancellor of the Duchy of Lancaster and Leader of the House of Commons, 1961-63; Chancellor of the Exchequer, June 1970) (*d* 1970), *e s* of late Norman A. Macleod, MD, Scaliscro, Isle of Lewis; one *s* one *d*. Chairman, Nat. Association of the Leagues of Hospital Friends; first Chm., Nat. Gas Consumers' Council, 1972-; Member: IBA (formerly ITA), 1972-75; Energy Commn, 1977-. JP Middlesex, 1955; DL Greater London, 1977. *Recreation*: my family. *Address*: House of Lords, SW1; 16 Morven Close, Potters Bar, Herts. *Club*: Constitutional.

MacLEOD OF FUINARY, Baron, *cr* 1967 (Life Peer), of Fuinary in Morven; Very Rev. George Fielden MacLeod, Bt, 1924; MC; BA Oxford; DD (Glasgow); Moderator of the General Assembly of the Church of Scotland, May 1957-May 1958 (designation, Very Rev.); Founder of the Iona Community (Leader, 1938-67); Chairman of Scottish Central After Care Council (for ex-prisoners and Borstal inmates); one of Her Majesty's Chaplains in Scotland; *b* 17 June 1895; 2nd *s* of Sir John MacLeod, 1st Bt; *S* nephew, 1944; *m* 1948, Lorna Helen Janet, *er d* of late Rev. Donald Macleod, Balvonie of Inshes, Inverness; two *s* one *d*. *Educ*: Winchester; Oriel Coll., Oxford (Hon. Fellow 1969); Edinburgh Univ. Post Graduate Fellow, Union Theological Coll., New York, 1921; Missioner, British Columbia Lumber Camps, 1922; Collegiate Minister, St Cuthbert's Parish Church, Edinburgh, 1926-30; Minister of Govan Parish Church, Glasgow, 1930-38; Hon. Chaplain Toc H in Scotland; served European War, 1914-18; Captain Argyll and Sutherland Highlanders (MC and Croix de Guerre); Warrack Lecturer on Preaching at Edinburgh and St Andrews Universities, 1936; Select Preacher, Cambridge Univ., 1943 and 1963; Cunningham Lecturer on Evangelism, 1954; first holder of Fosdick Professorship (Rockefeller Foundation), Union Theological Seminary, New York, 1954-55; Danforth Lecturer, USA Universities, 1960 and 1964. Rector of Glasgow Univ., 1968-71. Pres. and Chm. of Council of International Fellowship of Reconciliation, 1963. DLitt Muskingum Univ., USA; Dr of Laws, Iona Coll., New Rochelle, USA. *Publications*: Govan Calling: a book of Broadcast Sermons and Addresses, 1934; contributor to Way to God Series for the BBC; Speaking the Truth in Love: a book on Preaching, 1936; We Shall Rebuild (the principles of the Iona Community), 1944; Only One Way Left, 1956. *Heir* (to Baronetcy only): *s* Hon. John Maxwell Norman MacLeod, *b* 23 Feb. 1952. *Address*: (summer) Iona, by Oban, Argyll; (winter) 23 Learmonth Terrace, Edinburgh EH4 1PG. *T*: 031-332 3262.

McLEOD, Sir Alan Cumbrae Rose, KCVO 1966 (CVO 1955); Surgeon Dentist to The Queen, 1952-75 (to King George VI, 1946-52); *b* Brisbane, Queensland, 9 Dec. 1904; *yr s* of late Frederick Rose McLeod and of Mrs Ellen McLeod; *m* 1939, Noreen Egremont King; one *s* two *d*. *Educ*: Toowoomba Grammar Sch., Queensland. Matric. University of Queensland; DDS University of Pennsylvania, USA, 1928; BSc (Dent) Univ. of Toronto, Canada, 1929; LDS RCS 1948; FDS RCS 1948; Undergraduate and Postgraduate Teaching, 1932-46. East Grinstead Maxillo-Facial Unit, 1939-45. FACD 1959. *Publications*: contributions to dental literature. *Recreation*: woodwork. *Address*: Westbrook, The Batch, Wincanton, Somerset. *T*: Wincanton 32012.

MacLEOD, Angus, CBE 1967; Hon. Sheriff of Lothians and Peebles, since 1972; Procurator Fiscal of Edinburgh and Midlothian, 1955-71; *b* 2 April 1906; *s* of late Alexander MacLeod, Glendale, Skye; *m* 1936, Jane Winifred (*d* 1977), *d* of late Sir Robert Bryce Walker, CBE, LLD; three *s*. *Educ*: Hutchesons Grammar Sch.; Glasgow Univ. (MA, LLB). Solicitor, 1929; general practice, 1929-34; Depute Procurator Fiscal, Glasgow and Edinburgh, 1934-42; Procurator Fiscal of Dumfriesshire, 1942-52, of Aberdeenshire, 1952-55; Temp. Sheriff, Scotland, 1973. Part-time Chm., VAT Appeal Tribunals, 1973. *Recreations*: reading, walking, interested in sport. *Address*: 7 Oxford Terrace, Edinburgh EH4 1PX. *T*: 031-332 5466.

MacLEOD, Aubrey Seymour H.; *see* Halford-MacLeod.

MacLEOD, Sir Charles Henry, 3rd Bt, *cr* 1925; *b* 7 Nov. 1924; *o surv. s* of Sir Murdoch Campbell McLeod, 2nd Bt, and Annette Susan Mary (*d* 1964), *d* of Henry Whitehead, JP, 26 Pelham Crescent, SW7; *S* father 1950; *m* 1957, Gillian, *d* of Henry Bowlby, London; one *s* two *d*. *Educ*: Winchester. *Heir*: *s* James Roderick Charles McLeod, *b* 26 Sept. 1960. *Club*: Brooks's.

MacLEOD, Air Vice-Marshal Donald Francis Graham, CB 1977; of Royal Air Force Dental Services, 1973-77; *b* Stornoway, Isle of Lewis, Scotland, 26 Aug. 1917; *s* of Alexander MacLeod; both parents from Isle of Lewis; *m* 1941, Marjorie Eileen (*née* Gracie); one *s* one *d*. *Educ*: Nicolson Inst., Stornoway, Isle of Lewis; St Andrews Univ.; Royal Coll. of Surgeons, Edinburgh. LDS St And. 1940; FDS RCSEd 1955. Qualif. in Dental Surgery, 1940; two years in private practice. Joined Royal Air Force Dental Branch, 1942; served in various parts of the world, mainly in hospitals doing oral surgery. QHDS, 1972. Royal Humane Society Resuscitation Certificate for life saving from the sea in the Western Isles, 1937. *Recreations*: golf, gardening; Captain of Soccer, St Andrews Univ., 1938 (full blue), Captain of Badminton, 1939 (half blue). *Address*: 20 Witchford Road, Ely, Cambs. *T*: Ely 3164. *Club*: Royal Air Force.

McLEOD, (James) Walter, OBE; FRS 1933; FRSE 1957; Hon. ScD (Dublin), 1946; Hon. LLD (Glasgow), 1961; Emeritus Professor, University of Leeds, since 1952; *b* 2 Jan. 1887; *s* of John McLeod and Lilias Symington McClymont; *m* 1st, 1914, Jane Christina Garvie, MA (Glasgow) (*d* 1953); one *s* five *d*; 2nd, 1956, Joyce Anita Shannon, MB ChB (St Andrews). *Educ*: George Watson's Coll., Edinburgh; Collège Cantonal, Lausanne; Mill Hill Sch.; Glasgow Univ., Coates Scholar, 1909-10, Carnegie Scholar, 1910-11. Research work in Bacteriology, Glasgow Univ. Assistant Lecturer in Pathology, Charing Cross Hospital, London, 1912-14; Temp. Lieut and Captain, RAMC, 1914-19 (despatches four times, OBE); Leeds University: Lecturer in Bacteriology, 1919, Dean of Medical Faculty, 1948-52, Brotherton Prof. of Bacteriology, 1922-52; research work under Scottish Hospital Endowments Research Trust, in the Dept of Surgery, Edinburgh Univ., 1954-63; research work, Central Microbiological Laboratories, Western General Hospital, Edinburgh, 1963-73; President of the Society for General Microbiology, 1949-52. Hon. FRCPath, 1970. Corresponding member of the Société de Biologie, Paris, 1928; Hon. Mem. Scottish Soc. for Experimental Medicine, 1957; Hon. Mem., Pathological Soc. of Great Britain and Ireland, 1961. Worked with Boys Brigade in Leeds, 1919-52, and later in Edinburgh. *Publications*: papers on Bacteriology, etc, in Journal of Pathology, Biochemical Journal, Journal of Hygiene, and Lancet; chapter on bacterial oxidations and reductions in Newer Knowledge of Bacteriology, 1928; chapters on bacterial oxidations, etc, System of Bacteriology, MRC, 1931; Section on Diphtheria, Encyclopædia Britannica, 1961. *Recreations*: golf, fishing. *Address*: 30 Ravelston Gardens, Edinburgh EH4 3LE. *T*: 031-337 1524.
See also Earl of Cromartie.

MacLEOD, Sir John, Kt 1963; TD; *b* 23 Feb. 1913; *y s* of late Duncan MacLeod, CBE, Skeabost, Isle of Skye; *m* 1938, Rosemary Theodora Hamilton, *d* of late Frederick Noel Hamilton Wills, Miserden Park, Stroud, Glos; two *s* three *d*. *Educ*: Fettes Coll., Edinburgh. TA 1935. Served War of 1939-45, 51st Highland Division; France, 1940. MP (Nat. Liberal) Ross and Cromarty Div., 1945-64. *Address*: Turkdean Manor, near Northleach, Glos. *T*: Northleach 410. *Club*: Highland (Inverness).

MACLEOD, Joseph Todd Gordon; author and play producer; *b* 24 April 1903; *o surv. s* of late James Gordon Macleod; *m* 1st, 1928, Kate Macgregor (*d* 1953), *d* of late Robert Davis, Uddingston; 2nd, Maria Teresa, *d* of late Ing. Alfredo Foschini, Rome; one *s* one *d*. *Educ*: Rugby Sch.; Balliol Coll., Oxford. BA 1925; MA 1945; called to Bar, Inner Temple, 1928. Was book-reviewer, private tutor, actor, producer, lecturer on theatre-history. Directed the Festival Theatre, Cambridge, 1933-36; visited theatres in USSR, 1937; Secretary of Huntingdonshire Divisional Labour Party, 1937-38, also Parliamentary Candidate; announcer BBC, 1938-45. Managing Director, Scottish National Film Studios, Glasgow, 1946-47; Convener, Drama, Gœthe Festival Society, 1948-49; produced The Lady from the Sea, Festival of Britain, Aberdeen, 1951; Scottish Episcopal Church chronicle play St Mary's Cathedral, Edinburgh, 1952; toured Holland as guest of Dutch Ministry of Fine Arts, 1946; visited Soviet Union as guest of Moscow and Kiev Cultural Relations Societies, 1947; Silver Medal, Royal Society of Arts for paper on the Theatre in Soviet Culture, 1944. Hon. Member, British Actors' Equity. *Plays performed:* The Suppliants of Aeschylus translated with a verse sequel, 1933; A Woman Turned to Stone, 1934; Overture to Cambridge, 1934; A Miracle for St George, 1935; Leap in September (Arts Council Prize), 1952. *Publications:* Beauty and the Beast, 1927; The Ecliptic (poem), 1930; Foray of Centaurs (poem), 1931; Overture to Cambridge (novel), 1936; The New Soviet Theatre, 1943; Actors Cross the Volga, 1946; A Job at the BBC, 1947; A Soviet Theatre Sketchbook, 1951; The Passage of the Torch (poem), 1951; A Short History of the British Theatre (Italian edn), 1958; Abstractions, 1967; People of Florence, 1968; The Sisters D'Aranyi, 1969; An Old Olive Tree, 1971 (Arts Council Award); poetry under *non-de-plume* Adam Drinan: The Cove, 1940; The Men of the Rocks, 1942; The Ghosts of the Strath, 1943; Women of the Happy Island, 1944; Script from Norway, 1953; contribution on Theatre history to Chambers's Encyclopædia. *Music:* The Kid from the City, 1941. *Recreations:* painting, music, bird-watching. *Address:* Via delle Ballodole 9/7, Trespiano, 50139 Firenze, Italy. *T:* Firenze 417056.

McLEOD, Keith Morrison, CBE 1975; Financial Controller, British Airports Authority, 1971-75; *b* 26 May 1920; *yr s* of John and Mary McLeod; *m* 1943, Patricia Carter; two *s* one *d. Educ:* Bancroft's School. FCIT. Asst Auditor, Exchequer and Audit Dept, 1939; served RAF, 1941-46; Asst Principal, Min. of Supply, 1948; Principal, 1950; BJSM, Washington, 1955-57; Asst Sec., Min. of Supply, 1957; Cabinet Office, 1962; Finance Dir, British Airports Authority, 1966. *Address:* 161 Banstead Road, Banstead, Surrey. *T:* 01-393 9005. *Club:* Reform.

McLEOD, Malcolm Donald; Keeper of Ethnography, British Museum, since 1974; *b* 19 May 1941; *s* of Donald McLeod and Ellen (*née* Fairclough); *m* 1965, Jacqueline Wynborne; two *s* one *d. Educ:* Birkenhead Sch.; Hertford and Exeter Colls, Oxford. MA, BLitt. Lectr, Dept of Sociology, Univ. of Ghana, 1967-69; Asst Curator, Museum of Archaeology and Ethnology, Cambridge, 1969-74; Lectr, Girton Coll., Cambridge, 1969-74; Fellow, Magdalene Coll., Cambridge, 1972-74. *Publications:* articles and reviews in learned jls. *Address:* 6 Burlington Gardens, W1X 2EX.

MacLEOD, Maj.-Gen. Minden Whyte-Melville, CB 1945; CBE 1943; DSO 1918; Commander, US Legion of Merit, 1946; late Royal Artillery; British Advisory Staff, Polish Resettlement Corps, 1946-49; Colonel Commandant Royal Artillery, 1952-61; *b* 1896; *y s* of late M. N. MacLeod, Behar, India; *m* 1926, Violet, *o d* of late Major J. Elsdale Molson and Mrs Molson, of the Pound House, Angmering, Sussex; two *d. Educ:* Rugby; Woolwich; graduated Staff Coll., Dec. 1932; served European War, 1914-18 (DSO, despatches); Iraq, 1920 (medal and clasp); Waziristan, 1921-24 (medal and clasp); North West Frontier of India, 1930 (clasp); War of 1939-45 (despatches, CBE, CB); retired pay, 1949. *Address:* 12 Lower Sloane Street, SW1. *T:* 01-730 2358. *Club:* Naval and Military.

MACLEOD, Norman Donald, MA, LLB; Advocate; Sheriff of Glasgow and Strathkelvin (formerly Lanarkshire at Glasgow), since 1967; *b* 6 March 1932; *s* of Rev. John MacLeod, Loch Carron, and late Catherine MacRitchie; *m* 1957, Ursula Jane, *y d* of George H. Bromley, Inveresk; two *s* two *d. Educ:* Mill Hill Sch.; George Watson's Boys' Coll., Edinburgh; Edinburgh Univ.; Hertford Coll., Oxford. Passed Advocate, 1956. Colonial Administrative Service, Tanganyika: Dist. Officer, 1957-59; Crown Counsel, 1959-64; practised at Scots Bar, 1964-67. *Recreations:* playing with water, in it, on it, and around it. *Address:* 27 Cleveden Drive, Glasgow G12 0SD. *T:* 339-1607. *Club:* Edinburgh Sports.

McLEOD, Gen. Sir Roderick (William), GBE 1964 (CBE 1945); KCB 1958 (CB 1952); DL; *b* 15 Jan. 1905; *s* of Col Reginald George McQueen McLeod, DSO, late RA, and Cicely Knightley (*née* Boyd); *m* 1st, 1933, Camilla Rachel Hunter (*d* 1942), *d* of late Sir Godfrey Fell, KCIE, CSI, OBE; one *d*; 2nd, 1946 Mary Vavasour Lloyd Thomas, MBE (*née* Driver), widow of Major R.

J. H. Thomas, MVO, RHA. *Educ:* Wellington Coll., Berks; RMA, Woolwich. Commissioned 1925, operations, NW Frontier, India, 1931-32; Staff Coll., 1938. Comdr SAS Troops, 1944-45; Dir Military Operations, India, 1945-46; idc 1947; Asst Comdt, Staff Coll., 1948-49; CRA 7th Armoured Div., 1950; Dir of Military Operations, War Office, 1951-54; GOC 6th Armoured Div., 1955-56; Chief Army Instructor, Imperial Defence Coll., Jan.-Dec. 1957; Dep. Chief of Defence Staff, 1957-60; Comdr British Forces, Hong Kong, 1960-61; Gen. 1961; GOC-in-C, Eastern Comd, 1962-65; ADC (Gen.) to the Queen, 1963-65. DL Surrey, 1967. Comdr Order of Leopold II, 1946; Chevalier Legion of Honour, 1945; Croix de Guerre avec Palme, 1945. *Recreations:* ski-ing, sailing. *Address:* Fairhill, The Hockering, Woking, Surrey. *T:* Woking 61477. *Clubs:* Army and Navy, Ski Club of Great Britain, Eagle Ski Club.

MacLEOD, Walter; see MacLeod, J. W.

MACLEOD-SMITH, Alastair Macleod, CMG 1956; *b* 30 June 1916; *s* of late R. A. Smith, MIEE, and Mrs I. Macleod-Smith (*née* Kellner); *m* 1945, Ann (*née* Circuitt); one *s* one *d. Educ:* The Wells House, Malvern Wells, Worcs; Ellesmere Coll., Salop; The Queen's Coll., Oxford. BA Oxon 1938. Entered HM Oversea Service as administrative cadet, Nigeria, 1939; Asst Dist Officer, 1942, Dist Officer, Nigeria, 1949; seconded to Windward Islands as Financial and Economic Adviser, 1949-52; Financial Sec., Western Pacific High Commission, 1952-57; Financial Sec., Sierra Leone, 1957-61; since when with Selection Trust Ltd (Dir, 1967). *Recreations:* golf, sailing. *Address:* Roughetts Lodge, Coldharbour Lane, Hildenborough, Kent. *Club:* United Oxford & Cambridge University.

Mac LIAMMÓIR, Micheál; actor, designer, playwright; Director of Dublin Gate Theatre Productions since 1928; *b* Cork, Ireland, 25 Oct. 1899; *s* of Alfred Antony Mac Liammóir and Mary Elizabeth (*née* Lawler Lee). *Educ:* privately. First appearance on stage (as child) at Little Theatre, London, in The Goldfish, 1911; West End parts, 1911-15; studied painting at Slade Sch., 1915-16. Painted and designed for Irish Theatre and Dublin Drama League; lived abroad studying painting till 1927; returned to Ireland and joined Anew McMaster's Shakespearean Co. With Hilton Edwards: opened Galway Gaelic Theatre; they also estab. Dublin Gate Theatre, 1928; has since acted in, and designed for, over 300 prodns there; apptd Dir of Govt subsidized Dublin Gaelic Theatre, 1928; with Dublin Gate Theatre Co., London, 1934; toured in Egypt, 1936-38, Balkan States, 1939. With Hilton Edwards and Gate Co. he played in (his own) Ill Met by Moonlight, Vaudeville, London, 1947; season, Embassy, 1947. First appearance on New York Stage as Larry Doyle in John Bull's Other Island, Mansfield, 1948. Iago in film Othello, 1949; in (his own) Home for Christmas, Gate, 1950; Hedda Gabler, Lyric, Hammersmith, 1954; in revue Gateway to Gaiety (setting, costumes, and contrib. material), Gaiety, Dublin, 1956; The Hidden King, Edinburgh Fest., 1957. The Key of the Door, The Heart's a Wonder (setting and costumes), Lyric, Hammersmith, 1958; appeared in The Informer (adaptation and décor), Dublin, 1958; Much Ado About Nothing, NY, 1959. One-man entertainment, The Importance of Being Oscar, Dublin, 1960, London, 1960 (1966), since 1960 in this programme in Europe, USA, S America, Australia, New Zealand, etc.; One-Man programmes: I Must be Talking to my Friends and Talking about Yeats, in Dublin, subseq. London; film: What's the Matter with Helen, 1971. Various Irish awards for plays, etc. Kronborg Gold Medal, Elsinore, 1952. Hon. LLD, TCD, 1962. Freeman, City of Dublin, 1973. *Publications:* in Irish: Oícheanna Sidhe (faery tales), 1922; Oíche Bhealtaine (play), 1933; Lá agus Oíche (short stories), 1934; Diarmuid agus Gráinne (play), 1935; Ceo Meala Lá Seaca (essays), 1952; Aisteoirí faoi dhá Sholas (memoirs), 1956; Bláth agus Taibhse (poems), 1964; *in English:* All for Hecuba (autobiography), 1946; Put Money in thy Purse (diary), 1954; Ill Met by Moonlight (play), 1957; Each Actor on his Ass (memoirs), 1960; Where Stars Walk (play), 1961; The Importance of Being Oscar, 1963; Ireland (a study of the country and its people), 1966; An Oscar of No Importance (autobiography and study of Wilde), 1968; (with Eavan Boland) W. B. Yeats and His World, 1971; Prelude in Kazbek Street (play), 1973; Enter, a Goldfish: memoirs of an Irish actor, young and old, 1977. *Recreations:* travel, balletomania. *Address:* 4 Harcourt Terrace, Dublin, Ireland. *T:* Dublin 6.7609. *Club:* Arts (Dublin).

McLINTOCK, Sir William Traven, 3rd Bt, *cr* 1934; *b* 4 Jan. 1931; *s* of Sir Thomas McLintock, 2nd Bt and Jean, *d* of R. T. D. Aitken, New Brunswick; *S* father 1953; *m* 1952, André (marr. diss.), *d* of Richard Lonsdale-Hands; three *s*; *m* Heather, *d* of Philip Homfray-Davies; one step *s* one step *d. Educ:* Harrow. *Heir: s* Michael William McLintock, *b* 13 Aug. 1958.

McLUHAN, Prof. (Herbert) Marshall, CC (Canada) 1970; PhD, LLD; FRSC 1964; Professor of English, St Michael's College, University of Toronto, since 1952, Director, Centre for Culture and Technology, since 1963; *b* Edmonton, Alberta, 21 July 1911; *s* of Herbert Ernest and Elsie Naomi McLuhan; *m* 1939, Corinne Keller Lewis, Fort Worth, Texas; two *s* four *d. Educ:* Univ. of Manitoba (BA 1932, MA 1934); Trinity Hall, Cambridge (BA 1936, MA 1939, PhD 1942). Teacher: Univ. of Wisconsin, 1936-37; Univ. of St Louis, 1937-44; Assumption Univ., Ontario, 1944-46; St Michael's Coll., Toronto, 1946-. Albert Schweitzer Prof. in Humanities, Fordham Univ., New York, 1967-68. Jt Editor, Explorations Magazine, 1954-59. Dir, media project for US Office of Educn and Nat. Assoc. of Educnl Broadcasters, 1959-60; Consultor to the Vatican Pontifical Commn for Social Communications, 1973. Many hon. degrees and awards from univs and colleges. Carl Einstein Prize, Young German Art Critics of W Germany, 1967; Molson Award, Canada Council, 1967; IPR President's Award (GB), 1970; Christian Culture Award, Assumption Univ., 1971. Gold Medal of Italian Republic, 1971. *Publications:* The Mechanical Bride: folklore of industrial man, 1951; (ed with E. S. Carpenter) Explorations in Communications, 1960; The Gutenberg Galaxy: the making of typographic man, 1962 (Governor-Gen.'s Award for critical prose, 1963); Understanding Media: the extensions of man, 1964; (with R. J. Schoeck) Voices of Literature, vols I-III, 1964, 1965, 1970; The Medium is the Massage: an inventory of effects, 1967; War and Peace in the Global Village, 1968; (with H. Parker) Through the Vanishing Point: space in poetry and painting, 1968; Counterblast, 1969; The Interior Landscape: selected literary criticism (ed E. McNamara), 1969; Culture is our Business, 1970; From Cliché to Archetype, 1970; Take Today: the executive as drop-out, 1972; (jtly) The City as Classroom, 1977. *Recreation:* media study. *Address:* Centre for Culture and Technology, University of Toronto, Toronto 5, Ontario, Canada. *T:* 416-928-3328; 3 Wychwood Park, Toronto, Ontario M6G 2V5, Canada.

MACLURE, (John) Stuart; Editor, Times Educational Supplement, since 1969; *b* 8 Aug. 1926; *s* of Hugh and Bertha Maclure, Highgate, N6; *m* 1951, Constance Mary Butler; one *s* two *d. Educ:* Highgate Sch.; Christ's Coll., Cambridge. MA. Joined The Times, 1950; The Times Educational Supplement, 1951; Editor, Education, 1954-69. Hon. Fellow, City of Sheffield Polytechnic, 1976. *Publications:* Joint Editor (with T. E. Utley) Documents on Modern Political Thought, 1956; Editor, Educational Documents, 1816-1963, 1965; A Hundred Years of London Education, 1970. *Address:* 109 College Road, Dulwich, SE21. *Club:* MCC.

MACLURE, Lt-Col Sir John William Spencer, 3rd Bt, *cr* 1898; OBE 1945; *b* 4 Feb. 1899; *er s* of Col Sir John Maclure, 2nd Bt, and Ruth Ina Muriel (*d* 1951), *e d* of late W. B. McHardy, Comdr, RN, and Chief Constable of Lanarkshire; *S* father, 1938; *m* 1929, Elspeth King, *er d* of late Alexander King Clark, Wykeham Hatch, West Byfleet; two *s* one *d. Educ:* Wellington Coll.; Royal Military College, Sandhurst. Joined KRRC 1917; Lt-Col 1939; served in France and Flanders, 1918; North Russia, 1919; India, 1920-22 and 1925-28; Burma, 1936-38; commanded Rifle Depôt, 1939-40 and 1941-44; commanded 37 Reinforcement Holding Unit, BWEF, 1944 (OBE); commanded 113 Transit Camp, BLA; at Osnabruck; Comdr British Troops Holland, and 41 (Hook) Garrison, Holland, 1946; RARO 1949-54. *Heir: s* John Robert Spencer Maclure [*b* 25 March 1934; *m* 1964, Jane Monica, *d* of Rt Rev. T. J. Savage, MA; four *s*]. *Address:* Flat 2, 25 Christchurch Road, Winchester, Hants SO23 9SU. *T:* Winchester 4147. *Clubs:* MCC, British Automobile Racing.

McLUSKEY, Rev. J(ames) Fraser, MC; MA, BD, DD; Minister at St Columba's Church of Scotland, Pont Street, London, since 1960; *b* 1914; *s* of James Fraser McLuskey and Margaret Keltie; *m* 1st, 1939, Irene (*d* 1959), *d* of Pastor Calaminus, Wuppertal; two *s*; 2nd, 1966, Ruth Quartermaine (*née* Hunter), *widow* of Lt-Col Keith Briant. *Educ:* Aberdeen Grammar Sch.; Edinburgh Univ. Ordained Minister of Church of Scotland, 1938; Chaplain to Univ. of Glasgow, 1939-47. Service as Army Chaplain, 1943-46 (1st Special Air Service Regt, 1944-46); Sub Warden Royal Army Chaplains' Training Centre, 1947-50; Minister at Broughty Ferry East, 1950-55; Minister at New Kilpatrick, Bearsden, 1955-60. *Publication:* Parachute Padre, 1951. *Recreations:* walking, music, reading. *Address:* St Columba's Church of Scotland, Pont Street, SW1X 0BD. *T:* 01-584 2321. *Clubs:* Caledonian, Special Forces.

MacLYSAGHT, Edward Anthony, LLD, DLitt, MRIA; Member, Irish Manuscripts Commission, 1949-73 (Inspector, 1939-43; Chairman, 1956-73); Chief Herald and Genealogical Officer, Office of Arms, Dublin Castle, 1943-49; Keeper of Manuscripts, National Library of Ireland, 1949-55; *b* at sea, 1887 (bapt. Co. Clare); *m* 1st, 1915, Maureen Pattison; one *s* one *d*; 2nd, 1936, Mary Frances Cunneen; three *s. Educ:* abroad; Nat. Univ. of Ireland (MA). Engaged in cattle-breeding and forestry since 1910; mem. of Irish Convention, 1917-18, Irish Senate, 1922-25; working in South Africa, 1929-30, 1936-38. Mem. Gov. Body, Sch. of Celtic Studies, Dublin Inst for Advanced Studies, 1942-76. *Publications:* The Gael, 1919; Cúrsaí Thomáis, 1927, new edn 1969; Toil Dé 1933; Short Study of a Transplanted Family, 1935; Irish Life in the Seventeenth Century, 1939, 3rd edn 1969; (ed) The Kenmare Manuscripts, 1942; (ed) Analecta Hibernica (14 and 15), 1944; An Aifric Theas, 1947, East Clare (1916-21), 1954; Irish Families: Their Names, Arms and Origins, 1957, 3rd edn 1972; More Irish Families, 1960; Supplement to Irish Families, 1964; The Surnames of Ireland, 1969, enl. edn 1973; (ed) Forth the Banners Go, reminiscences of William O'Brien, 1969; Leathanaigh óm' Dhialann, 1977, etc. *Address:* Raheen, Tuamgraney, Co. Clare. *Club:* United Arts (Dublin).

McMAHON, Sir Brian (Patrick), 8th Bt *cr* 1817; engineer; *b* 9 June 1942; *s* of Sir (William) Patrick McMahon, 7th Bt, and of Ruth Stella, *yr d* of late Percy Robert Kenyon-Slaney; *S* father, 1977. *Educ:* Wellington. BSc, AIM. *Heir: brother* Shaun Desmond McMahon [*b* 29 Oct. 1945; *m* 1971, Antonia Noel Adie]. *Address:* 1 Draycot Road, Chiseldon, Wiltshire.

McMAHON, Christopher William; Executive Director, Bank of England, since 1970; *b* Melbourne, 10 July 1927; *s* of late Dr John Joseph McMahon and late Margaret Kate (*née* Brown); *m* 1956, Marion Elizabeth, *d* of late A. E. Kelso; two *s. Educ:* Melbourne Grammar Sch.; Univ. of Melbourne; Magdalen Coll., Oxford. 1st cl. hons PPE, 1953. Tutor in English Lit., Univ. of Melbourne, 1950; Econ. Asst, HM Treasury, 1953-57; Econ. Adviser, British Embassy, Washington, 1957-60; Fellow and Tutor in Econs, Magdalen Coll., Oxford, 1960-64 (Sen. Tutor, 1961-63); Tutor in Econs, Treasury Centre for Admin. Studies, 1963-64; Mem., Plowden Cttee on Aircraft Industry, 1964-65; entered Bank of England as Adviser, 1964; Adviser to the Governors, 1966-70. Mem., Council of Foreign Bondholders, 1972-. *Publications:* Sterling in the Sixties, 1964; (ed) Techniques of Economic Forecasting, 1965. *Address:* 12 Lyndhurst Road, NW3. *T:* 01-435 1458.

MacMAHON, Gerald John, CB 1962; CMG 1955; *b* 26 Sept. 1909; 2nd *s* of late Jeremiah MacMahon and Kathleen MacMahon (*née* Dodd); unmarried. *Educ:* Clongowes Wood Coll., Co. Kildare, Ireland; Emmanuel Coll., Cambridge (BA). Entered Board of Trade, 1933; Asst Sec., 1942. Imperial Defence Coll., 1949. Senior UK Trade Commissioner in India, 1952-58; Under-Sec., Board of Trade 1958-62 and 1964-70; Admiralty, Nov. 1962-64. *Recreation:* golf. *Address:* 19 Lower Park, Putney Hill, SW15. *Club:* Reform.

McMAHON, Rt. Hon. Sir William, PC 1966; GCMG 1977; CH 1972; MP for Lowe (NSW); Prime Minister of Australia, 1971-72; *b* 23 Feb. 1908; *s* of William Daniel McMahon; *m* 1965, Sonia R. Hopkins; one *s* two *d. Educ:* Sydney Grammar Sch.; St Paul's Coll., Univ. of Sydney (LLB, BEc). Practised as solicitor until 1939. Australian Army, 1940-45, Major. Elected to House of Representatives for Lowe, NSW, in gen. elections, 1949, 1951, 1954, 1955, 1958, 1961, 1963, 1966, 1969, 1972, 1974, 1975. Minister: for Navy, and for Air, 1951-54 (visited Korea and Japan in that capacity, 1952); for Social Services, 1954-56; for Primary Industry, 1956-58; for Labour and National Service, 1958-66; Treasurer, Commonwealth of Australia, 1966-69; Minister for External Affairs, later Foreign Affairs, 1969-71. Vice-Pres., Executive Council, 1964-66; Dep. Leader of Liberal Party, 1966-71, Leader, 1971-72; Acting Minister for Trade, Acting Minister for Labour and Nat. Service, Acting Minister in Charge, CSIRO, Acting Minister for National Development, Acting Minister for Territories, and Acting Attorney-Gen., for short periods, 1956-69; Leader of Aust. Delegation to Commonwealth Parliamentary Conf., New Delhi, Nov. 1957-Jan. 1958; Visiting Minister to ILO Conf., Geneva, June 1960 and June 1964; Pres., ILO Asian Regional Conf., Melbourne, Nov.-Dec., 1962; Mem., Bd of Governors, IMF and World Bank, 1966-69. Chm., Bd of Governors, Asian Development Bank, 1968-69. Led Australian delegns to Bangkok, Djakarta, Wellington, Tokyo, Manila and Saigon, 1970. As Prime Minister officially visited: USA, GB, 1971; Indonesia, Malaysia, Singapore, 1972. *Recreations:* golf, squash, farming. *Address:* Parliament House, Canberra, ACT 2600, Australia; 100 William Street, Sydney, NSW 2011, Australia. *Clubs:* Union, Royal Sydney, Australian, Australian Jockey (Sydney); Melbourne (Melbourne).

McMANNERS, Rev. Prof. John; Canon of Christ Church and Regius Professor of Ecclesiastical History, Oxford University, since 1972; *b* 25 Dec. 1916; *s* of Rev. Canon Joseph McManners and Mrs Ann McManners; *m* 1951, Sarah Carruthers Errington; two *s* two *d. Educ:* St Edmund Hall, Oxford; Durham Univ. BA 1st cl. hons Mod. History Oxon, 1939; DipTheol Dunelm, 1947. Military Service, 1939-45 in Royal Northumberland Fusiliers (Major). Priest, 1948; St Edmund Hall, Oxford: Chaplain, 1948; Fellow, 1949; Dean, 1951; Prof., Univ. of Tasmania, 1956-59; Prof., Sydney Univ., 1959-66; Vis. Fellow, All Souls Coll., Oxford, 1965-66; Prof. of History, Univ. of Leicester, 1967-72. Birkbeck Lectr, Cambridge, 1976. Trustee, Nat. Portrait Gallery, 1970-; Mem. Council, RHistS, 1971; Pres., Ecclesiastical Hist. Soc., 1977-78. FAHA 1970. Officer, Order of King George I of the Hellenes, 1945. *Publications:* French Ecclesiastical Society under the Ancien Régime: a study of Angers in the 18th Century, 1960; (ed) France, Government and Society, 1965, 2nd edn 1971; Lectures on European History 1789-1914: Men, Machines and Freedom, 1966; The French Revolution and the Church, 1969; Church and State in France 1870-1914, 1972; contrib. New Cambridge Modern History vols VI and VIII. *Recreations:* tennis, squash. *Address:* Christ Church, Oxford. *T:* Oxford 47047.

MacMANUS, Emily Elvira Primrose, CBE 1947 (OBE 1930); SRN, SCM, retired; *b* 18 April 1886; *d* of Leonard Strong McManus, MD, of Battersea, London, and Killeaden House, Kiltimagh, Co. Mayo, Eire, and Julia Emily Boyd, Howth, Co. Dublin. *Educ:* Governess and private schs. Gen. Nursing Training, Guy's Hosp., 1908; Midwifery Training, East End Mothers' Home, 1912; Sister, Kasr en Aini Hospital, Cairo, and Private Nursing, Egypt; Sister, King's Lynn; Sister, Guy's Hospital; Sister, QAIMNSR, France, 1915-18 (despatches twice); Asst Matron, Guy's Hosp., 1919; Asst Medical Research Council, Food Experiment, Dr Barnardo's Boys' Garden City, 1922; Matron, Bristol Royal Infirmary, 1923; Matron, Guy's Hosp., 1927-46; Sector Matron, Sector 10, EMS, 1939-46; Principal Matron, TANS, 1923-46; late Mem. Gen. Nursing Council; Chm., Voluntary Advisory Nursing Board for HM Prisons, 1936-46; Mem. Council Queen's Dist Nursing Assoc., Eire; late Mem. Council Queen's Dist Nursing Assoc., and Overseas Nursing Assoc.; Pres. Royal College of Nursing, 1942-44; Nursing Missions: British West Indies, 1946-47; Persia 1948, Turkey, 1949, Holland 1952. Broadcast series, BBC, Mary and her Furry Friends, 1964; Broadcasts, BBC: Silver Lining in series Home this afternoon, 1965; Desert Island Discs, 1966. *Publications:* Hospital Administration for Women, 1934; Nursing in Time of War (Jt), 1939; Matron of Guy's 1956. *Recreations:* fishing, gardening, literature. *Address:* Terry Lodge, Terrybawn, Bofeenaun, Ballina, Co. Mayo, Eire. *T:* Foxford 104. *Club:* Royal Irish Automobile (Dublin).

McMANUS, Francis Joseph; *b* 16 Aug. 1942; *s* of Patrick and Celia McManus; *m* 1971, Carmel V. Doherty, Lisnaskea, Co. Fermanagh; one *d. Educ:* St Michael's Enniskillen; Queen's University, Belfast. BA 1965; Diploma in Education, 1966. Subsequently a Teacher. MP (Unity) Fermanagh and S Tyrone, 1970-Feb. 1974. *Address:* Carrigans, Sligo Road, Enniskillen, Co. Fermanagh, N Ireland. *T:* Enniskillen 3401.

MacMANUS, John Leslie Edward, TD 1945; QC 1970; **His Honour Judge MacManus;** a Circuit Judge (formerly a Judge of County Courts), since 1971; *b* 7 April 1920; *o s* of E. H. MacManus and H. S. MacManus (*née* Colton); *m* 1942, Gertrude (Trudy) Mary Frances Koppenhagen; two *d. Educ:* Eastbourne College. Served 1939-45 with RA: Middle East, Italy, Crete, Yugoslavia; Captain 1942; Major 1945. Called to Bar, Middle Temple, 1947. Dep. Chm., East Sussex QS, 1964-71. *Recreations:* gardening, odd-jobbing, travel. *Address:* The Old Rectory, Twineham, Haywards Heath, West Sussex. *T:* Bolney 221; 1 Crown Office Row, Temple, EC4. *T:* 01-353 1801. *Club:* Sussex Martlets.

McMANUS, Maurice, CBE 1966; JP; DL; Lord Provost of Dundee and Lord Lieutenant of the County of the City of Dundee, 1960-67; *b* 17 Jan. 1906; *s* of Patrick and Ann McManus; *m* 1931, Lillian, *d* of James and Isobel Lindsay; three *s* two *d. Educ:* West Calder. Tutor at National Council of Labour Coll., 1945-. Chm. Dundee City Labour Party, 1950-56; Councillor, Tayside Region, 1974-. Member: Exec. Cttee, Scottish Council for Development and Industry; Scottish Advisory Cttee for Civil Aviation; Court of St Andrews Univ.; Council of Queen's Coll., Dundee; Dundee Univ., 1967; Chairman: Tayside Region Manpower Cttee, 1975-; Tay Road Bridge Jt Bd; Dundee Coll. of Art and Technology; Dundee & N Fife Local Employment Cttee, 1969. JP 1958, DL 1967, Dundee. Hon. LLD Dundee, 1969. *Recreation:* gardening. *Address:* 20 Merton Avenue, Dundee.

McMASTER, Ian, OBE 1960; *b* 28 Jan. 1898; *s* of Rev. Kenneth McMaster and Gertrude Lucy Strachan; *m* 1924, Jane Harvey, MA, FRHistS (*d* 1958); one *d*; *m* 1963, Mary Isabella Blewitt Neville, Warden, St Luke's Home, Oxford. *Educ:* King's Sch., Canterbury; University Coll. Sch., London; Queen's Coll., Oxford (Scholar); Grenoble Univ. Chief History Master, King Edward VI Sch., Birmingham, 1922-35; History Master, Eton Coll., 1935-40; Consul in Florence and Consul-Gen. to Republic of San Marino, 1952-60; HM Foreign Service, retd 1960. Warden, Sheffield Diocesan Conference House, 1960-64. Formerly Mem. Archbishop's Council for Inter-Church Relations; Diocesan Lay Reader. *Recreation:* human problems. *Address:* 3 Garford Road, Oxford. *T:* Oxford 58017.

McMASTER, Stanley Raymond; *b* 23 Sept. 1926; *o s* of F. R. McMaster, Nottinghill, Belfast, N Ireland; *m* 1959, Verda Ruth Tynan, SRN, Comber, Co Down, Northern Ireland; two *s* two *d* (and one *d* decd). *Educ:* Campbell Coll., Belfast; Trinity Coll., Dublin (MA, BComm). Called to the Bar, Lincoln's Inn, 1953. Lectr in Company Law, Polytechnic, Regent Street, 1954-59. Parliamentary and Legal Sec., to Finance and Taxation Cttee, Association of British Chambers of Commerce, 1958-59. MP (UU) Belfast E, March 1959-Feb. 1974; contested (UU) Belfast S, Oct. 1974. *Publications:* various articles in legal and commercial journals. *Recreations:* golf, rowing and shooting. *Address:* Nottinghill, Malone Road, Belfast; 31 Embercourt Road, Thames Ditton, Surrey. *Clubs:* Knock Golf, etc.

McMEEKAN, Brig. Gilbert Reader, CB 1955; DSO 1942; OBE 1942; JP, 1956; retired, Regular Army, 1955; *b* 22 June 1900; *s* of late Major F. H. F. R. McMeekan, RA; *m* 1932, Marion Janet, *d* of late Sir John Percival, KBE; one *s* two *d. Educ:* Wellington Coll.; RMA Woolwich. Commissioned RE 1919; BAOR 1922-24; Sudan Defence Force, 1924-31; Aldershot, 1931-37; Malta, 1938-42; o/c Fortress, RE Malta, 1940-42; CRE 10 Armoured Div. (Alamein), 1942-43; Liaison Staff, USA, 1944-45; Chief Superintendent, Military Engineering Experimental Establishment, Christchurch, 1946-50; Comdr, 25 Eng. Group TA, 1950-52; Comdr, RE Ripon, 1952-55. Officer, American Legion of Merit, 1946. *Address:* Greenacres, Painswick, Glos. *T:* Painswick 812395.
See also Baron Dickinson.

McMEEKIN, Lt-Gen. Sir Terence (Douglas Herbert), KCB 1973 (CB 1972); OBE 1960; Area Appeals Secretary (Avon, Gloucestershire and Wiltshire), Cancer Research Campaign, since 1976; *b* 27 Sept. 1918; *s* of late Herbert William Porter McMeekin, Cogry, Co. Antrim, and Mrs J. K. McMeekin; *m* 1947, Averil Anne Spence Longstaff, 7th *d* of late Dr T. G. Longstaff and Mrs D. H. Longstaff, Fritham, Hants; one *s* two *d. Educ:* King William's Coll., IOM; RMA Woolwich. 2nd Lt RA, 1938; served War of 1939-45 (despatches); GSO2 (L) HQ 8th Army, 1943; Staff Coll., Haifa, 1943; GSO2 (Ops), HQ 3 Corps, 1944; Bde Major RA, 1 Airborne Div., 1945; Battery Comdr, 6 Airborne Div., Palestine, 1945-46; Instructor in Gunnery, 1947-48; GSO2 (Tactics), School of Artillery, Manorbier, 1949-50; DAQMG, HQ 1 (British) Corps, 1952-54; jssc 1955; Battery Comdr, 5 RHA, 1955-57; Bt Lt-Col, 1957; AA & QMG, HQ Land Forces, Hong Kong, 1958-60; comd 29 Field Regt, RA, 1960-62; converted Regt to Commando role, 1962; Col 1962; Chief Instructor (Tactics), School of Artillery, Larkhill, 1962-64; comd 28 Commonwealth Inf. Bde Gp, Malaya, 1964-66; Dir of Public Relations (Army), 1967-68; GOC 3rd Div., 1968-70; Comdt, Nat. Defence Coll. (formerly Jt Services Staff Coll.), 1970-72; GOC SE District, 1972-74, retd 1975. Col Comdt, RA, 1972-. President: Army Cricket Assoc., 1969-72; Combined Services Cricket Assoc., 1971-72. *Recreations:* cricket, most field sports. *Address:* The Old Rectory, Beverston, near Tetbury, Glos. *T:* Tetbury 52735. *Clubs:* Army and Navy, MCC, Stragglers of Asia.

McMENEMEY, William Henry, MA, DM, FRCP, FRCPath, FRCPsych; Emeritus Professor of Pathology, Institute of Neurology, University of London, and Hon. Consulting Pathologist, National Hospitals for Nervous Diseases; *b* 16 May 1905; *s* of William Henry McMenemey and Frances Annie (*née* Rankin); *m* Robina Inkster, MD (Aberdeen); one *s* one *d. Educ:* Birkenhead Sch.; Merton Coll., Oxford; St Bartholomew's Hospital. Formerly: House Physician and Junior Demonstrator in Pathology, St Bart's Hosp.; Registrar in Neurology, Maida Vale Hosp.; Pathologist, Napsbury and Shenley Hosps and Asst Pathologist, West End Hosp. for Nervous Diseases, 1934-37; Asst Pathologist, Radcliffe Infirmary, Oxford, 1937-40; Pathologist, Royal Infirmary, Worcester, 1940-49; Pathologist, Maida Vale Hosp., 1949-70; Prof. of Pathology, Inst of Neurology, 1965-70. Savill Prize, 1932; Charles Hastings Memorial Lectr, 1951; Pres., International Soc. of Clinical Pathology, 1966-69; Sec., Internat. Soc. of Neuropathology,

1967-70; President: Assoc. of Clinical Pathologists, 1958 (Sec. 1943-57); Brit. Neuropathological Soc., 1957-60; Sect. of Neurology, 1960-61 and Sect. of History of Medicine, 1962-64, Royal Soc. Med.; Hon. FRCPath (Australia); Hon. Member: Amer. Soc. of Clinical Pathology; Amer. Assoc. of Neuropathologists; Soc. Française de Biologie Medicale; Romanian Soc. of Medical Sciences; Assoc. Españ. Biopatolog. Clin.; John Shaw Billings Hist. of Medicine Soc.; Corresp. Member: Vereinigung Deutsch. Neuropathologen u. Neuroanat.; Soc. Française de Neurologie. *Publications:* History of Worcester Royal Infirmary, 1947; James Parkinson, 1955; The Life and Times of Sir Charles Hastings, 1959; various writings on neuropathology, clinical pathology and medical history. *Recreations:* music, gardening. *Address:* Manor House, London Road, Morden, Surrey. *Club:* Athenæum.

McMICHAEL, Sir John, Kt 1965; MD, FRCP, FRCPE; FRS 1957; FACP (Hon.); Hon. LLD (Edinburgh); MD (Melbourne); Hon. DSc (Newcastle, Sheffield, Birmingham, Ohio, McGill); Hon. ScD (Dublin); Director, British Post-graduate Medical Federation, 1966-71; Emeritus Professor of Medicine, University of London; *b* 25 July 1904; *s* of James McMichael and Margaret Sproat; *m* 1942, Sybil E. Blake (*d* 1965); four *s* ; *m* 1965, Sheila M. Howarth. *Educ:* Kirkcudbright Acad.; Edinburgh Univ. Ettles Scholar, 1927; Beit Memorial Fellow, 1930-34; Johnston and Lawrence Fellow., Royal Society, 1937-39; Univ. teaching appointments in Aberdeen, Edinburgh and London. Dir, Dept of Medicine, Post-grad. Med. Sch. of London, 1946-66; Mem. Medical Research Council, 1949-53. A Vice-Pres., Royal Soc., 1968-70. Pres., World Congress of Cardiology, 1970. Hon. Member: American Medical Association, 1947; Medical Soc., Copenhagen, 1953; Norwegian Medical Soc., 1954; Assoc. Amer. Physicians, 1959. For. Mem. Finnish Acad. of Science and Letters, 1963; For. Corresp., Acad. Roy. de Med. Belgique, 1971; For. Associate, Nat. Acad. Sci., Washington, 1974. Thayer Lectr, Johns Hopkins Hosp., 1948; Oliver Sharpey Lectr, 1952; Croonian Lectr, 1961, RCP; Watson Smith Lectr RCPEd, 1958. Cullen Prize, RCPEd, 1953. Jacobs Award, Dallas, 1958; Morgan Prof., Nashville, Tenn, 1964. Fellow, Royal Postgrad. Med. Sch., 1972. Moxon Medal, RCP, 1960; Gairdner Award, Toronto, 1960; Wihuri Internat. Prize, Finland, 1968. Harveian Orator, RCP, 1975. Trustee, Wellcome Trust, 1960-77. *Publications:* Pharmacology of the Failing Human Heart, 1951. Numerous papers on: Splenic Anaemia, 1931-35; Cardiac Output in Health and Disease, 1938-47; Lung Capacity in Man, 1938-39; Liver Circulation and Liver Disease, 1932-43. *Recreation:* gardening. *Address:* 2 North Square, NW11. *T:* 01-455 8731. *Club:* Athenæum.

MacMICHAEL, Nicholas Hugh, FSA; Keeper of the Muniments of Westminster Abbey since 1967; *b* 2 Feb. 1933; *o s* of late Canon Arthur William MacMichael and of Elizabeth Helen Royale, *o d* of late Rev. Arthur William Newboult; unmarried. *Educ:* Eastbourne Coll.; Magdalene Coll., Cambridge. Asst Librarian and Asst Keeper of the Muniments of Westminster Abbey, 1956-66; Hon. Sec., 1961-64, Hon. Editor, 1964-70, Harleian Soc.; Member: Exec. Cttee, Soc. of Genealogists, 1963-67; Council: British Archaeological Assoc., 1960-62; Monumental Brass Soc., 1960-66; Kent Archaeological Soc., 1973-. FSA 1962; FRHistS 1972; Fellow, Soc. of Genealogists, 1969. *Publications:* articles in learned jls. *Recreations:* genealogical and heraldic research; ecclesiology; watching cricket. *Address:* 2b Little Cloister, Westminster Abbey, SW1. *T:* 01-799 6893. *Club:* United Oxford & Cambridge University.

McMILLAN, Col Donald, CB 1959; OBE 1945; Chairman, Cable & Wireless Ltd, and associated companies, 1967-72; *b* 22 Dec. 1906; *s* of Neil Munro McMillan and Isabella Jamieson; *m* 1946, Kathleen Ivy Bingham; one *s*. *Educ:* Sloane Sch., Chelsea; Battersea Polytechnic. Post Office Engineering Dept, 1925-54; Director External Telecommunications, Post Office External Telecommunications Executive, 1954-67. BSc Eng (London); FIEE. *Publications:* contribs to Institution Engineers Journal, Post Office Institution Engineers Journal. *Recreations:* golf and gardening. *Address:* 46 Gatehill Road, Northwood, Mddx. *T:* Northwood 22682. *Club:* Grim's Dyke Golf.

McMILLAN, Rt. Rev. Monsignor Donald Neil; Principal RC Chaplain and Vicar General (Army), since 1977; *b* 21 May 1925; *s* of Daniel McMillan and Mary Cameron McMillan (*née* Farrell). *Educ:* St Brendan's Coll., Bristol; Prior Park Coll., Bath; Oscott Coll., Sutton Coldfield. Ordained Priest, Dio. Clifton, 1948; Curate: Bath, 1948-49; Gloucester, 1949-51; Taunton, 1951. Commissioned Army Chaplain, 1951. Served: BAOR, 1961-63, 1966-68, 1975-77; Middle East, 1956-59, 1970-72; Far East, 1952-55. *Recreations:* reading, walking. *Address:* 54 Ennismore Gardens, SW7 1AJ. *T:* 01-584 4685. *Clubs:* Army and Navy, Challoner.

McMILLAN, Prof. Duncan; John Orr Professor of French Language and Romance Linguistics, University of Edinburgh, since 1955; *b* London, 1914; *o s* of late Duncan McMillan and Martha (*née* Hastings); *m* 1945, Geneviève, *er d* of late M and Mme Robert Busse, Paris; one *s*. *Educ:* St Dunstan's Coll.; University Coll., London; Sorbonne, Paris. BA, PhD (London); Diplôme de l'Ecole des Hautes Etudes, Paris. Lecteur d'anglais, Univ. of Paris, 1938-40; Lectr in French and Romance Philology, Univ. of Aberdeen, 1946-50, Univ. of Edinburgh, 1950-55. Served in the Army, 1940-46. Chevalier de la Légion d'Honneur, 1958. *Publications:* La Chanson de Guillaume (Société des anciens textes français), 2 vols, 1949-50; (in collaboration with Madame G. McMillan) An Anthology of the Contemporary French Novel, 1950; Le Charroi de Nîmes, 1972; articles in Romania and other learned journals. *Address:* 4 Clarendon Crescent, Edinburgh. *T:* 031-332 1943. *Club:* Scottish Arts (Edinburgh).

McMILLAN, Prof. Edwin Mattison; Professor of Physics, University of California, 1946-73, now Professor Emeritus; *b* Redondo Beach, Calif, 18 Sept. 1907; *s* of Edwin Harbaugh McMillan and Anna Marie (*née* Mattison); *m* 1941, Elsie Walford Blumer; two *s* one *d*. *Educ:* Calif Institute of Technology (MS); Princeton Univ. (PhD). Univ. of California: National Research Fellow, 1932-34; Research Assoc., 1934-35; Instructor, 1935-36; Asst Prof., 1936-41; Assoc. Prof., 1941-46. Leave of absence for war research, 1940-45. Mem. of staff of Radiation Laboratory, Univ. of Calif., 1934-; Assoc. Dir, 1954-58; Dir, 1958-71; Dir, Lawrence Berkeley Laboratory, 1971-73; Mem. General Advisory Cttee to Atomic Energy Commission, 1954-58. Member: Commission on High Energy Physics of International Union for Pure and Applied Physics (IUPAP), 1960-66; Scientific Policy Cttee of Stanford Linear Accelerator Center (SLAC), 1962-66; Physics Adv. Cttee, Nat. Accelerator Lab. (NAL), 1967-; Trustee, Univs Research Assoc., 1969-; Chm., Cl. I, Nat. Acad. of Sciences, 1968-71. Fellow Amer. Physical Soc. Member: Nat. Acad. of Sciences (USA); American Philosophical Soc.; Fellow, Amer. Acad. of Arts and Sciences. Research Corp. 1950 Scientific Award, 1951; (jtly) Nobel Prize in Chemistry, 1951; (jtly) Atoms for Peace Award, 1963; Alumni Dist. Service Award, Calif. Inst. of Tech., 1966; Centennial Citation, Univ. of California, Berkeley, 1968. Hon. DSc, Rensselaer Polytechnic Institute; Hon. DSc, Gustavus Adolphus Coll. *Address:* University of California, Berkeley, Calif 94720, USA.

MACMILLAN, Rev. Gilleasbuig Iain; Minister of St Giles', The High Kirk of Edinburgh, since 1973; *b* 21 Dec. 1942; *s* of Rev. Kenneth M. Macmillan and Mrs Mary Macmillan; *m* 1965, Maureen Stewart Thomson; one *d*. *Educ:* Oban High School; Univ. of Edinburgh. MA, BD. Asst Minister, St Michael's Parish, Linlithgow, 1967-69; Minister of Portree Parish, Isle of Skye, 1969-73. Hon. Chaplain: Royal Scottish Academy; Royal Coll. of Surgeons of Edinburgh; Soc. of High Constables of City of Edinburgh. *Recreations:* reading, friends, the country, America. *Address:* St Giles' Cathedral, Edinburgh EH1 1RE. *T:* 031-225 4363. *Club:* New (Edinburgh).

MacMILLAN of MacMILLAN, Gen. Sir Gordon Holmes Alexander, of Knap, KCB, 1949 (CB 1945); KCVO, 1954; CBE 1943; DSO 1943; MC (two bars); Hereditary Chief of the Clan MacMillan; Colonel The Argyll and Sutherland Highlanders, 1945-58; Hon. Colonel The Argyll and Sutherland Highlanders of Canada, 1948-72; 402 (A. and S. H.) Lt Regt RA (TA), 1956-61; Vice-Lieutenant Co. of Renfrew, 1955-72; *b* 7 Jan. 1897; *s* of D. A. MacMillan and L. W. Allardice; *m* 1929, Marian Blakiston-Houston, OBE, CStJ, four *s* one *d*. *Educ:* St Edmund's Sch., Canterbury. RMC, Sandhurst, 1915; commissioned in Argyll and Sutherland Highdrs, 1915; served European War in 2nd Bn Argyll and Sutherland Highdrs, France, 1916-18 (MC and two bars): Adjutant, 1917-20; Staff Coll., Camberley, 1928-29; Staff Capt., War Office, 1930-32; GSO3, 1932-34; GSO2 RMC, Kingston, Ont., 1935-37; GSO2 WO and Eastern Command, 1937-40; GSO1, 1940-41; commanding Infantry Brigade, 1941; BGS UK and N Africa, 1941-43 (CBE); commanding Infantry Brigade, Sicily, 1943 (DSO); commanding 15th Scottish, 49 (WR) and 51st Highland Divs, 1943-45, UK, Normandy, Holland and Germany (CB); DWD War Office, 1945-46; GOC Palestine, 1947-48; Gen. Officer, C-in-C, Scottish Command, and Gov. of Edinburgh Castle, 1949-52; Gov. and C-in-C of Gibraltar, 1952-55, retd 1955. Chairman: Cumbernauld New Town Corporation, 1956-65; Greenock Harbour Trust, 1955-65; Erskine Hospital, 1955; Firth of Clyde Dry Dock, 1960-67. DL Renfrewshire, 1950, Vice-Lieutenant, 1955-72. Kt Grand Cross Order of Orange Nassau; KStJ. Mem. of The Queen's Body Guard for Scotland. Hon. LLD (Glasgow), 1964. *Address:* Finlaystone, Langbank, Renfrewshire PA14 6TJ. *T:* Langbank 235. *Club:* Caledonian.

MACMILLAN, Rt. Hon. Harold; see Macmillan, Rt Hon. M. H.

MACMILLAN, Iain Alexander, LLD; Member, Council of Law Society of Scotland, since 1964 (President, 1976-77; Vice-President, 1973); Senior Partner, J. & J. Sturrock & Co., Kilmarnock, since 1952; *b* 14 Nov. 1923; *s* of John and Eva Macmillan; *m* 1954, Edith Janet (*née* MacAulay); two *s* one *d*. *Educ:* Oban High Sch.; Glasgow Univ. (BL). Sec. to Dr O. H. Mavor (James Bridie), 1943. Served war, RAF, France, Germany, India, 1944-47. Glasgow Univ., 1947-50. Subseq. law practice. Hon. LLD Aberdeen, 1975. *Publications:* contribs Jl Law Soc. of Scotland. *Recreations:* golf, sailing. *Address:* 2 Castle Drive, Kilmarnock. *T:* Kilmarnock 25864. *Club:* Western (Glasgow).

MacMILLAN, His Honour James; Judge of County Courts, 1950-65, retired; *b* Schoolhouse, Fisherton, Ayrshire, 18 April 1898; *s* of George Arthur MacMillan, MA, and Catherine, *d* of Alexander McQuiston; *m* 1931, Marjorie J. Triffitt, DSc (*d* 1957); one *d*. *Educ:* Troon Sch.; Ayr Acad.; Glasgow Univ. (MA, LLB). Royal Artillery, 1917-19, Lt. Called to Bar, Middle Temple, 1925, Midland Circuit; Legal Adviser, Ministry of Pensions, 1939-44. Mem. Bar Council, 1947-50; Mem. Supreme Court Rule Cttee, 1948-50; Dep. Chm. Beds Quarter Sessions, 1949-50; County Court Judge, Circuit 37, April-June 1950, Circuit 38, 1950-55, Circuit 39, 1955-65. *Recreation:* walking. *Address:* 28 Battlefield Road, St Albans, Herts. *T:* St Albans 56152. *Club:* Reform.

MACMILLAN, Sir (James) Wilson, KBE 1976 (CBE 1962, OBE 1951); Governing Director, Macmillan Brothers Ltd; President, British Red Cross and Scout Association; *b* 1906; *m* Beatrice Woods. Served in Legislature for many years; formerly Minister of Education, Health and Housing. British Red Cross Badge of Honour, Class I, 1964. *Address:* 3 St Edward Street, Belize City, Belize.

McMILLAN, John, CBE 1969; Chairman, Sportsdata Ltd, since 1976; *b* 29 Jan. 1915; *s* of late William McArthur McMillan, Sydney, NSW; *m* 1958, Lucy Mary, *d* of late Edward Moore, DSO; three *s* two *d*. *Educ:* Scots Coll., Sydney. Programme Dir, Internat. Broadcasting Co., 1934-39. Served War: joined horsed cavalry as trooper, 1939; commissioned, S Wales Borderers, 1940; OC No 1 Field Broadcasting Unit, British Forces Network, 1945-46. Asst, and later Chief Asst, to Controller, BBC Light Programme, 1946-52; Controller of Programmes, Gen. Man. and Dir Rediffusion Television Ltd, 1955-68; Dir of Sport, Indep. Television and rep. of ITV cos at European Broadcasting Union, 1968-71. Dir Theatre Royal Windsor Co., 1964-. *Recreations:* swimming, gardening, study of 1919-39 European history. *Address:* 17 Greville House, Kinnerton Street, SW1X 8EA. *T:* 01-235 7161; Residence Moderne, 83 Bormes, France. *T:* 94-71 04 12. *Club:* Savile.

MacMILLAN, Kenneth; Principal Choreographer to the Royal Ballet, Covent Garden, since 1977; *b* 11 Dec. 1929; *m* 1974, Deborah Williams. *Educ:* Great Yarmouth Gram. Sch. Started as Dancer, Royal Ballet; became Choreographer, 1953; Dir of Ballet, Deutsche Oper, Berlin, 1966-69; Resident Choreographer, and Dir, Royal Ballet, 1970-77. First professional ballet, Danses Concertantes (Stravinsky-Georgiades). Principal ballets: The Burrow; Solitaire; Agon; The Invitation; Romeo and Juliet; Diversions; La Création du Monde; Images of Love; The Song of the Earth; Concerto; Anastasia; Cain and Abel; Olympiad; Triad; Ballade; The Poltroon; Manon; Pavanne; Elite Syncopations; The Four Seasons; Rituals; Requiem. Has devised ballets for: Ballet Rambert, American Ballet, Royal Ballet Sch., theatre, television, cinema, musical shows. *Recreation:* cinema. *Address:* c/o Royal Opera House, Covent Garden, WC2.

MACMILLAN, Malcolm K.; journalist; *b* 21 Aug. 1913; *s* of Kenneth Macmillan and Mary Macaulay; is married. *Educ:* Edinburgh Univ. Served as Private, Infantry, 1939-40. MP (Lab) Western Isles, 1935-70; Chm., Scottish Parliamentary Labour Party, 1945-51; Chm., Govt Advisory Panel on Highlands and Islands, 1947-54; Mem. Post Office Advisory Council, 1946-51; Mem. Scottish Advisory Council on Civil Aviation, 1947-53; Mem. Scottish Economic Conf., 1949-. Chm., Parly Cttee for East West Trade, 1965-70. Contested (United Lab Party) Western Isles, 1974. *Address:* 11 Cross Street, Coulregrein, Stornoway, Isle of Lewis; 69 St Vincent Crescent, Glasgow G3 8NQ.

MACMILLAN, Rt. Hon. (Maurice) Harold, PC 1942; OM 1976; FRS 1962; Chancellor, University of Oxford, since 1960; President, Macmillan Ltd, since 1974 (Chairman, 1963-74; Chairman Macmillan & Co. and Macmillan (Journals), 1963-

67). Prime Minister and First Lord of The Treasury, Jan. 1957-Oct. 1963; MP (C) Bromley, Nov. 1945-Sept. 1964; *b* 10 Feb. 1894; *s* of late Maurice Crawford Macmillan; *m* 1920, Lady Dorothy Evelyn Cavendish, GBE 1964 (*d* 1966), *d* of 9th Duke of Devonshire; one *s* two *d* (and one *d* decd). *Educ:* Eton (Scholar); Balliol Coll., Oxford (Exhibitioner). 1st Class Hon. Moderations, 1919; served during war, 1914-18, in Special Reserve Grenadier Guards (wounded 3 times); ADC to Gov.-Gen. of Canada, 1919-20; retired, 1920; MP (U) Stockton-on-Tees, 1924-29 and 1931-45; contested Stockton-on-Tees, 1923 and 1945; Parliamentary Sec., Ministry of Supply, 1940-42; Parliamentary Under-Sec. of State, Colonies, 1942; Minister Resident at Allied HQ in North-West Africa, 1942-45; Sec. for Air, 1945; Minister of Housing and Local Government, 1951-54; Minister of Defence, Oct. 1954-April 1955; Sec. of State for Foreign Affairs, April-Dec. 1955; Chancellor of the Exchequer, Dec. 1955-Jan. 1957. First Pres., Game Research Assoc., 1960-65. A Vice-Pres., Franco-British Soc., 1955; a Trustee, Historic Churches Preservation Fund, 1957-. Freeman of: City of London (Stationers' and Newspaper Makers' Company, 1957), 1957; Bromley, Kent, 1957; Hon. Freedom of City of London, 1961; Toronto, 1962; Stockton-on-Tees, 1968. Hon. Fellow Balliol Coll., Oxford, 1957. Hon. DCL Oxford, 1958; DCL Oxford (by diploma), 1960; LLD Cambridge, 1961, Sussex, 1963. Benjamin Franklin Medal, RSA, 1976. *Publications:* Industry and the State (jointly), 1927; Reconstruction: A Plea for a National Policy, 1933; Planning for Employment, 1935; The Next Five Years, 1935; The Middle Way, 1938 (re-issued 1966); Economic Aspects of Defence, 1939; Memoirs: Vol. I, Winds of Change, 1966; Vol. II, The Blast of War, 1967; Vol. III, Tides of Fortune, 1969; Vol. IV, Riding the Storm 1956-1959, 1971; Vol. V, Pointing the Way 1959-61, 1972; Vol. VI, At the end of the Day 1961-63, 1973; Past Masters, 1975. *Address:* Macmillan & Co. Ltd, 4 Little Essex Street, WC2; Birch Grove House, Chelwood Gate, Haywards Heath, West Sussex. *Clubs:* Carlton, Beefsteak, Buck's.
See also Rt Hon. Julian Amery, J. T. Faber, Rt Hon. M. V. Macmillan.

MACMILLAN, Rt. Hon. Maurice (Victor), PC 1972; MP (C) Farnham, since 1966; *b* 27 Jan. 1921; *s* of Rt Hon. Harold Macmillan, *qv*; *m* 1942, Hon. Katharine Margaret Alice Ormsby-Gore, DBE 1974; 2nd *d* of 4th Baron Harlech, KG, PC, GCMG; three *s* one *d* (and one *s* decd). *Educ:* Eton; Balliol Coll., Oxford. Served War of 1939-45 with Sussex Yeomanry. Mem. of Kensington Borough Council, 1949-53. Contested (C) Seaham Harbour, 1945, Lincoln, 1951, Wakefield, by-election, 1954; MP (C) Halifax, 1955-64; Economic Sec. to the Treasury, Oct. 1963-64; Chief Sec. to the Treasury, 1970-72; Sec. of State for Employment, 1972-73; Paymaster-General, 1973-74. Chairman: Macmillan & Co. Ltd, 1967-70; Macmillan Journals Ltd, 1967-70; Macmillan & Cleaver Ltd, 1967-70; Dep. Chm., Macmillan (Holdings) Ltd, 1966-70; formerly also Director: Monotype Corporation Ltd; Yorkshire Television Ltd; and Exec. Chm., Wider Share Ownership Council. *Address:* 12 Catherine Place, SW1; Highgrove, Doughton, near Tetbury, Glos. *Clubs:* Turf, Beefsteak, Pratt's, Garrick, Carlton.
See also Rt Hon. Julian Amery, J. T. Faber.

MACMILLAN, Prof. Robert Hugh; Head of School of Automotive Studies, Cranfield Institute of Technology, since 1977; *b* 27 June 1921; *s* of H. R. M. Macmillan and E. G. Macmillan (*née* Webb); *m* 1950, Anna Christina Roding, Amsterdam; one *s* two *d*. *Educ:* Felsted Sch.; Emmanuel Coll., Cambridge. Technical Branch, RAFVR, 1941; Dept of Engrg, Cambridge Univ., 1947; Prof. of Mech. Engrg, Swansea, 1956; Dir, Motor Industry Res. Assoc., 1964-77. Assoc. Prof., Warwick Univ., 1965. Mem. Council, Loughborough Univ., 1966-; Chm. Council, Automobile Div., IMechE, 1976-77; Mem., Noise Adv. Council, 1970-. FRSA; FRPSL. *Publications:* Theory of Control, 1951; Automation, 1956. *Recreations:* music, philately. *Address:* 25 Church Lane, Lillington, Leamington Spa, Warwicks. *T:* Leamington Spa 25558. *Club:* Royal Automobile.

McMILLAN, Thomas McLellan; MP (Lab) Glasgow Central since 1966; *b* 12 Feb. 1919; *s* of James and Isabella McMillan; *m* 1946, Mary Elizabeth Conway; one *s* one *d*. *Educ:* secondary sch. Glasgow City Councillor, 1962; Magistrate and Bailie of Burgh, 1964. *Address:* House of Commons, SW1. *T:* 01-219 3000.

MACMILLAN, Wallace, CMG 1956; Director, Management Selection Ltd; *b* 16 Oct. 1913; *s* of late David Hutchen Macmillan and late Jean Wallace, Newburgh, Fife; *m* 1947, Betty Bryce, *d* of late G. R. Watson and of Mrs M. Y. Watson; three *s*. *Educ:* Bell-Baxter Sch.; University of St Andrews; Kiel Univ.; Corpus Christi Coll., Oxford. Administrative Officer,

Tanganyika, 1937; District Officer, 1947; Administrator of Grenada, BWI, 1951-57. Acted as Governor, Windward Is, periods 1955. Federal Establishment Sec. (subsequently Permanent Sec., Min. of Estabts and Service Matters), Federation of Nigeria, 1957-61. Mem., Victoria League. *Recreations:* bridge, chess, tennis, golf. *Address:* The Willows, Blueberry Road, Bowdon, Cheshire.

MACMILLAN, Sir Wilson; *see* Macmillan, Sir. J. W.

McMINN, Prof. Robert Matthew Hay; Sir William Collins Professor of Human and Comparative Anatomy, Royal College of Surgeons of England, Professor of Anatomy, Institute of Basic Medical Sciences, University of London, and Conservator of the Hunterian Museum, since 1970; *b* 20 Sept. 1923; *o s* of late Robert Martin McMinn, MB, ChB, Auchinleck and Brighton, and Elsie Selene Kent; *m* 1948, Margaret Grieve Kirkwood, MB, ChB, DA; one *s* one *d*. *Educ:* Brighton Coll. (Schol.); Univ. of Glasgow. MB, ChB 1947, MD (commendation) 1958, Glasgow; PhD Sheffield 1956. Hosp. posts and RAF Med. Service, 1947-50; Demonstrator in Anatomy, Glasgow Univ., 1950-52; Lectr in Anatomy, Sheffield Univ., 1952-60; Reader 1960-66, Prof. of Anatomy 1966-70, King's Coll., London Univ. Late Examnr to RCS and Univs of London, Cambridge, Singapore and Makerere. Arris and Gale Lectr, RCS, 1960; Arnott Demonstrator, RCS, 1970. Former Treas., Anatomical Soc. of Gt Britain and Ireland; Sec., Assoc. of Clinical Anatomists; FRSocMed; Member: Amer. Assoc. of Anatomists; British Soc. of Gastroenterology; BMA; Trustee, Skin Res. Foundn. *Publications:* Tissue Repair, 1969; The Digestive System, 1974; The Human Gut, 1974; Colour Atlas of Human Anatomy, 1977; articles in various med. and sci. jls. *Recreations:* motoring, photography, archaeology, short-wave radio. *Address:* 74 Dorling Drive, Ewell, Epsom, Surrey. *T:* 01-393 6839.

McMINNIES, John Gordon, OBE 1965; HM Diplomatic Service, retired 1977; *b* 1 Oct. 1919; *s* of William Gordon McMinnies and Joyce Millicent McMinnies; *m* 1947, Mary (*née* Jackson), novelist. *Educ:* Bilton Grange; Rugby Sch.; Austria (language trng). Reporter: Western Mail, 1938; Reuters, 1939. Served War, Army, 1940-46: comd R Troop, RHA; retd, Major. HM Diplomatic Service (Athens, Warsaw, Bologna, Malaysia, Cyprus, Nairobi, Lusaka, New Delhi), 1946-77; retd, Counsellor. *Recreations:* crazy paving, crosswords, cricketology, the sea. *Address:* Villa Woodland, Avenue de Verdun, Ajaccio, Corsica.

McMORRAN, Helen Isabella, MA; Life Fellow, Girton College, Cambridge; *b* 26 July 1898; *d* of late Thomas McMorran and late Louise Maud White. *Educ:* Sutton High Sch., GPDST; Girton Coll., Cambridge. Assistant Librarian, Bedford Coll., London, 1921-28; Girton Coll., Cambridge: Librarian, 1930-62; Vice-Mistress, 1946-62; Registrar of the Roll, 1947-69. Member of Council, Girls' Public Day School Trust, 1952-69; Trustee, Homerton Coll., Cambridge, 1954-67. *Publications:* Editor, Girton Review, 1932-62; Joint Editor (with K. T. Butler) of Girton College Register, 1869-1946, 1948. *Address:* 41 Sherlock Close, Cambridge. *T:* Cambridge 51359. *Club:* University Women's.

McMULLAN, Henry Wallace, OBE 1967; Member of Independent Broadcasting Authority (formerly Independent Television Authority), 1971-74; *b* 20 Feb. 1909; *s* of William Muir McMullan and Euphemia McMullan; *m* 1934, Roberta Tener Gardiner; three *s*. *Educ:* King William's Coll., IOM. Worked on Belfast Telegraph and Belfast Newsletter; Producer and Commentator, BBC NI, 1930; Lt-Comdr RNVR, Map Room, Admty, 1939; Head of Programmes, BBC NI, 1945-69. *Recreations:* gardening, watching and listening to people, television and radio. *Address:* 119 Garner Crescent, Nanaimo, British Columbia, Canada. *Club:* Naval.

McMULLEN, Rear-Admiral Morrice Alexander, CB 1964; OBE 1944; Flag Officer, Admiralty Interview Board, HMS Sultan, Gosport, 1961-64, retired; Director, Civil Defence for London, 1965-68; *b* Hertford, 16 Feb. 1909; *m* 1st, 1946, Pamela (*née* May) (marr. diss. 1967), widow of Lt-Comdr J. Buckley, DSC, RN; two step *s*; 2nd, 1972, Peggy, *widow* of Comdr Richard Dakeyne, RN. *Educ:* Oakley Hall, Cirencester; Cheltenham Coll. Entered Royal Navy, as Paymaster Cadet, HMS Erebus. Appts prewar included: S Africa Station, 1929-32; China Station, 1933-36; Asst Sec. to Lord Chatfield, First Sea Lord, 1936-38; Served War of 1939-45 (despatches, OBE); Atlantic, North Sea, Norwegian waters; served in HMS Prince of Wales (battle with Bismarck, and Atlantic Charter Meeting, working for Sir Winston Churchill, then Prime Minister); HQ, Western Approaches as Secretary to Chief of Staff, 1941-43; Member

Allied Anti-Submarine Survey Board, 1943; served Mediterranean, 1944-45 (Anzio Landing, re-entry into Greece, invasion of S. France). Post-war appointments at home included Dep. Dir Manning (Suez operation), 1956-58, and Captain of Fleet to C-in-C Far East Station, Singapore, 1959-61. Chairman Royal Naval Ski Club, 1955-58. *Recreations:* fishing, sailing, skiing, shooting. *Address:* 3 The Crescent, Alverstoke, Hants. *T:* Gosport 82974. *Clubs:* Naval and Military, Royal Cruising, Royal Naval Sailing Association.

McMULLIN, Hon. Sir Alister (Maxwell), KCMG 1957; Chancellor, University of Newcastle, NSW, since 1966; President of the Australian Senate, 1953-71; *b* Scone, NSW, Australia, 14 July 1900; *s* of W. G. McMullin, Aberdeen, NSW; *m* 1945, Thelma Louise (*née* Smith); one *d*. *Educ:* Public Sch., Australia. Elected to the Australian Senate, 1951, Senator to New South Wales. Chm., Gen. Council, Commonwealth Parly Assoc., 1959-60, 1969-70. Chm., Scott Memorial Hospital, Scone, NSW, 1934-40. Hon. DLitt Newcastle, NSW, 1966. *Address:* St Aubins, Scone, NSW 2337, Australia.

McMURRAY, David Bruce, MA; Headmaster, Loretto School, since 1976; *b* 15 Dec. 1937; *s* of late James McMurray, CBE, and of Kathleen McMurray (*née* Goodwin); *m* 1962, Antonia Murray; three *d*. *Educ:* Loretto Sch.; Pembroke Coll., Cambridge (BA, MA). National service, Royal Scots, 1956-58, 2nd Lieut. Pembroke Coll., Cambridge, 1958-61; Asst Master, Stowe Sch., 1961-64; Fettes College: Asst Master, 1964-72; Housemaster, 1972-76. CCF Medal, 1976. *Recreations:* cricket, golf, sub-aqua diving, poetry, lecturing. *Address:* Pinkie House, Loretto School, Musselburgh, East Lothian, Scotland. *T:* 031-665 3108. *Clubs:* Free Foresters; Edinburgh Sports (Edinburgh).

McMURTRIE, Group Captain Richard Angus, DSO 1940; DFC 1940; Royal Air Force, retired; *b* 14 Feb. 1909; *s* of Radburn Angus and Ethel Maud McMurtrie; *m* 1st, 1931, Gwenyth Mary (*d* 1958), 3rd *d* of Rev. (Lt-Col) H. J. Philpott; no *c*; 2nd, 1963, Laura, 4th *d* of Wm H. Gerhardi. *Educ:* Royal Grammar Sch., Newcastle on Tyne. First commissioned in Territorial Army (72nd Brigade, RA), 1927; transferred to Royal Air Force, 1929, as Pilot Officer; served in No 2 (AC) Squadron, 1931-32, and Fleet Air Arm (442 Flight, and 822 Squadron in HMS Furious), 1932-33; Cranwell, 1934-35; Flt-Lieut, 1935; Calshot and No. 201 (Flying Boat) Squadron, 1935-38; Squadron Leader, 1938, and commanded Recruits Sub-Depot, RAF, Linton-on-Ouse; served War of 1939-45 (despatches thrice, DFC, DSO); No 269 GR Squadron, 1939-41; Wing Commander, 1940; HQ No 18 Group RAF, 1941; Group Captain, commanding RAF Station, Sumburgh (Shetlands), 1942-43; HQ Coastal Command, 1943; RAF Staff Coll., Air Ministry, Whitehall, and HQ Transport Command, 1944; commanded RAF Station, Stoney Cross, Hants, 1945; and formed and commanded No. 61 Group (Reserve Command), 1946; Joint Services Mission, Washington, DC, 1946-49; commanded RAF Station, Cardington, 1949-52; HQ No 1 Group, RAF, 1952-54; Royal Naval College, Greenwich, 1954; HQ, Supreme Allied Commander, Atlantic (NATO), Norfolk, Virginia, USA, 1954-56; HQ, Coastal Command, RAF, Northwood, Mddx, 1957-59, now farming. *Recreations:* sailing, photography. *Address:* Rose in Vale Farm, Constantine, Falmouth, Cornwall. *TA* and *T:* Constantine 338. *Club:* RAF Yacht (Hon. Life Mem.), Royal Cornwall Yacht.

MACNAB, Brigadier Sir Geoffrey (Alex Colin), KCMG 1962 (CMG 1955); CB 1951; retired; *b* 23 Dec. 1899; *s* of Brig.-General Colin Macnab, CMG; *m* 1930, Norah Cramer-Roberts. *Educ:* Wellington Coll.; RMC Sandhurst. 1st Commission, 1919, Royal Sussex Regt; Captain, Argyll and Sutherland Highlanders, 1931; Staff Coll., Camberley, 1930-31; Military Attaché, Prague and Bucharest, 1938-40; served War of 1939-45, campaigns Western Desert, Greece, Crete; Brigadier, 1944; Military Mission, Hungary, 1945; DMI, Middle East, 1945-47; Military Attaché, Rome, 1947-49; Military Attaché, Paris, 1949-54; retired 1954. Service in Ireland, Germany, Far East, India, Middle East. Secretary, Government Hospitality Fund, 1957-68. *Address:* Stanford House, Stanford, Ashford, Kent. *T:* Sellindge 2118. *Clubs:* Army and Navy, MCC.

MACNAB of Macnab, James Charles; The Macnab; 23rd Chief of Clan Macnab; landowner and farmer since 1957; *b* 14 April 1926; *e s* of Lt-Col James Alexander Macnabb, MBE, TD (*de jure* 21st of Macnab), London, SW3, and of Mrs G. H. Walford, Wokingham, Berks; *S gt uncle,* Archibald Corrie Macnab, 22nd Chief, 1970; *m* 1959, Hon. Diana Mary, *er d* of Rt Hon. Lord Kilmany, *qv*; two *s* two *d*. *Educ:* Cothill House; Radley Coll.; Ashbury Coll., Ottawa. Served in RAF and Scots Guards, 1944-45; Lieut, Seaforth Highldrs, 1945-48. Asst Supt, Fedn of Malaya Police Force, 1948; retd, 1957. CC, Perth and Kinross Jt County Council, 1964-75; Dist Councillor, 1961-64. Member,

Royal Company of Archers, Queen's Body Guard in Scotland. JP 1968. *Recreations:* shooting, travel. *Heir: s* James William Archibald Macnab, younger of Macnab, *b* 22 March 1963. *Address:* Kinnell House, Killin, Perthshire FK21 8SR. *T:* Killin 212. *Clubs:* Brooks's; New, Puffins (Edin.).

MACNAB, Brigadier John Francis, CBE 1957 (OBE 1943); DSO 1945; *b* 15 Sept. 1906; *o surv. s* of late Colonel Allan James Macnab, CB, CMG, FRCS, IMS, and Nora, *d* of Lieut-General Sir Lewis Dening, KCB, DSO; *m* 1938, Margaret, *d* of C. M. Treadwell; one *s* one *d. Educ:* Wellington Coll., Berks; RMC Sandhurst. Joined Queen's Own Cameron Highlanders, 1926; Lieut, 1929; seconded for service with KAR, 1929-35 and 1937; served with Cameron Highlanders, Catterick, and Regimental Depôt, Inverness, 1935-37; served War of 1939-45, Italian Somaliland, Abyssinia, Madagascar, Burma (despatches twice); Comd 1st Nyasaland Bn, KAR, 1941-43; Commander: 30th E African Inf. Bde, 1943; 21 (E African) Inf. Bde. Monsoon Campaign, Burma, 1944. Dep. President Regular Commissions Board, 1946; Comd 2nd Bn The Seaforth Highlanders, 1947; Colonel, Vice-President Sandhurst Selection Board, 1948; Comd: 6th Highland Bde, 2nd Div. BAOR, 1949-51; 153 Highland Bde, Highland Div., 1951-54; GHQ Troops, E Africa, 1954-57; Dep. Commander East Anglian District, Nov. 1957-Dec. 1959, retired. Late Hon. Colonel, Tanganyika Rifles and late Hon. Colonel, 6th and 2/6th Bn, KAR. Representer of House of Barravorich in Clan Macnab. *Recreations:* fishing and piping. *Address:* c/o Williams & Glyn's Bank Ltd, (Holt's Branch), Kirkland House, Whitehall, SW1; 45/4 Marina Street, Pieta, Malta, GC. *Club:* Army and Navy.

McNAB JONES, Robin Francis, FRCS; Surgeon: ENT Department, St Bartholomew's Hospital, since 1961; Royal National Throat, Nose and Ear Hospital, since 1962; *b* 22 Oct. 1922; *s* of E. C. H. Jones, CBE, and M. E. Jones, MBE; *m* 1950, Mary Garrett; one *s* three *d. Educ:* Manchester Grammar Sch.; Dulwich Coll.; Med. Coll., St Bartholomew's Hosp. (MB BS 1945); FRCS 1952. Ho. Surg., St Bart's, 1946-47; MO, RAF, 1947-50; Demonstrator of Anatomy, St Bart's, 1950-52; Registrar, Royal Nat. Throat, Nose and Ear Hosp., 1952-54; Sen. Registrar, ENT Dept, St Bart's, 1954-59; Lectr, Dept of Otolaryngology, Univ. of Manchester, 1959-61; Dean, Inst. of Laryngology and Otology, Univ. of London, 1971-76. Mem., Court of Examiners, RCS, 1972-; External Examiner, Univ. of Riyadh, Saudi Arabia; Hon. Sec., Sect. of Otology, RSocMed, 1964-66; Vice-Pres., Sect. of Laryngology, RSocMed, 1975-. *Publications:* various chapters in standard med. textbooks; contribs to med. jls. *Recreations:* tennis, golf, fishing, gardening. *Address:* 108 Harley Street, W1N 1AF. *T:* 01-935 7811; 52 Oakwood Avenue, Beckenham, Kent BR3 2PJ. *T:* 01-650 0217.

MACNAGHTEN, Sir Patrick (Alexander), 11th Bt *cr* 1836; Project Manager, Cadbury Schweppes Foods Ltd; *b* 24 Jan. 1927; *s* of Sir Antony Macnaghten, 10th Bt, and of Magdalene, *e d* of late Edmund Fisher; *S* father, 1972; *m* 1955, Marianne, *yr d* of Dr Erich Schaefer and Alice Schaefer, Cambridge; three *s. Educ:* Eton; Trinity Coll., Cambridge (BA Mechanical Sciences). Army (RE), 1945-48. Project Engineer, Cadbury Bros (later Cadbury Schweppes), 1950-69; in General Management, Cadbury-Schweppes Foods Ltd, 1969-. *Recreations:* dinghy sailing, farming. *Heir: s* Malcolm Francis Macnaghten, *b* 21 Sept. 1956. *Address:* Cofton Crest, Cherry Hill Drive, Barnt Green, Birmingham B45 8JY. *T:* 021-445 2341; Dundarave, Bushmills, Co. Antrim, Northern Ireland. *T:* Bushmills 215. *Club:* Barnt Green Sailing.

MACNAGHTEN, Robin Donnelly, MA; Headmaster of Sherborne, since 1974; *b* 3 Aug. 1927; 2nd *s* of late Sir Henry P. W. Macnaghten and of Lady Macnaghten; *m* 1961, Petronella, *er d* of Lt-Col A. T. T. Card and late Mrs Card; two *s* one *d. Educ:* Eton (Schol.); King's Coll., Cambridge (Schol.). 1st cl. Class. Tripos Pt I, 1947; 1st cl. with dist. Pt II, 1948; Browne Medallist; MA 1954. Travelled in Italy and Turkey, 1949. Asst, Mackinnon Mackenzie & Co., Bombay, 1949-54. Asst Master, Eton Coll., 1954, and Housemaster, 1965. *Publication:* trans. Vita Romana (by U. E. Paoli), 1963. *Recreations:* numismatics (FRNS), walking, gardening. *Address:* Abbey Grange, Sherborne, Dorset DT9 3AP. *T:* Sherborne 2025. *Clubs:* Royal Automobile; Western India Turf (Bombay).

McNAIR, family name of Baron McNair.

McNAIR, 2nd Baron *cr* 1955, of Gleniffer; **Clement John McNair;** *b* 11 Jan. 1915; *s* of 1st Baron McNair, CBE, QC, and Marjorie (*d* 1971), *yr d* of late Sir Clement Meacher Bailhache; *S* father, 1975; *m* 1941, Vera, *d* of Theodore James Faithfull; two *s* one *d. Educ:* Shrewsbury; Balliol Coll., Oxford. Served War of 1939-45, Major, RA. *Publications:* Wagonload, 1971; A Place

Called Marathon, 1976. *Heir: s* Hon. Duncan James McNair, *b* 26 June 1947. *Address:* House of Lords, SW1.

McNAIR, Air Vice-Marshal James Jamieson; Principal Medical Officer, Headquarters Support Command, Royal Air Force, 1974-77; *b* 15 June 1917; *s* of Gordon McNair and Barbara MacNaughton; *m* 1945, Zobell Pyper (*d* 1977). *Educ:* Kirkcudbright Academy; Huntly Gordon Sch.; Aberdeen Univ.; London Sch. of Hygiene and Tropical Medicine; Liverpool Sch. of Tropical Medicine. MB, ChB; FFCM; DPH; DTM&H. Sqdn Med. Officer, UK, N Africa, Sicily, Italy, 1942-45; OC, RAF Sch. of Hygiene at Home and Egypt, 1946-51; SMO, 66, 21 and 25 Gp HQ at Home, 1951-57; SMO Air HQ and OC RAF Hosp. Ceylon, 1957-59; OC RAF Inst. of Hygiene, 1959-62; DGMS Staff, Air Min., 1962-65; OC RAF Hosp. Changi, Singapore, 1965-67; PMO HQ's Fighter Comd, 1967-68; OC Jt Service Med. Rehabilitation Unit, 1968-71; Dir of Health and Research, MoD (Air), 1971-74; Dep. Dir GMS RAF, 1974; QHP 1974-77. CStJ. *Recreations:* golf, gardening, travel. *Address:* Wakenills Cottage, Hedgehog Lane, Haslemere, Surrey GU27 2PJ. *T:* Haslemere 51389. *Clubs:* Royal Air Force; Hankley Common Golf.

MACNAIR, Maurice John Peter; His Honour Judge Macnair; a Circuit Judge since 1972; *b* 27 Feb. 1919; *s* of late Brig. J. L. P. Macnair and Hon. Mrs J. L. P. Macnair; *m* 1952, Vickie Reynolds; one *s* two *d. Educ:* Bembridge Sch.; St Paul's Sch.; St Edmund Hall, Oxford. BA 1947. Served War of 1939-45, Captain, RA, 1944. Called to Bar, Gray's Inn, 1948. Dep. Chm., W Sussex QS, 1968-72. *Address:* 28 Rawlings Street, SW3 2LS.

McNAIR, Sir William Lennox, Kt, *cr* 1946; Judge of the Queen's Bench Division, High Court of Justice, 1950-66; *b* 18 March 1892; *s* of late John McNair of Lloyds; unmarried. *Educ:* Aldenham (Schol.); Gonville and Caius Coll., Cambridge (Classical Schol.). First Class Law Tripos, Part I, 1913; Part II, 1914; LLM, 1919; Whewell Exhibitioner in International Law, 1919. Called to Bar, Gray's Inn, 1917; Bencher, 1938; KC 1944; Treasurer, 1951; Vice-Treasurer, 1952. Served with Royal Warwicks. Regt, 1914-18, Captain (despatches). Legal Adviser, Ministry of War Transport, 1941-45. Hon. Fellow Gonville and Caius College, Cambridge, 1951. *Publications:* Joint Editor of Temperley's Merchant Shipping Acts, 1925-72; Joint Editor of Scrutton on Charterparties and Bills of Lading. *Address:* 130 Court Lane, Dulwich, SE21.

McNAIR-WILSON, Michael; *see* McNair-Wilson, R. M. C.

McNAIR-WILSON, Patrick Michael Ernest David; MP (C) New Forest, since 1968 (Lewisham West, 1964-66); Company Director and Consultant; *b* 28 May 1929; *s* of Dr Robert McNair-Wilson; *m* 1953, Diana Evelyn Kitty Campbell Methuen-Campbell, *d* of Hon. Laurence Methuen-Campbell; one *s* four *d. Educ:* Eton. Regular Commission Coldstream Guards, 1947-51; Exec. in French Shipping Co., 1951-53; various appointments at Conservative Central Office, 1954-58; Staff of Conservative Political Centre, 1958-61; Director, London Municipal Society, 1961-63; Public Relations Executive with The British Iron and Steel Federation, 1963-64. Opposition Front Bench Spokesman on fuel and power, 1965-66; Vice-Chm., Conservative Parly Power Cttee, 1969-70; PPS to Minister for Transport Industries, DoE, 1970-74; Opposition Front Bench Spokesman on Energy, 1974-76. Editor of The Londoner, 1961-63. *Recreations:* sailing, pottery. *Address:* 5 Kelso Place, W8. *T:* 01-937 3564; Godfreys Farm, Beaulieu, Hampshire. *T:* Beaulieu 612300.
See also R. M. C. McNair-Wilson.

McNAIR-WILSON, (Robert) Michael (Conal); MP (C) Newbury, since 1974 (Walthamstow East, 1969-74); *b* 12 Oct. 1930; *y s* of late Dr Robert McNair-Wilson and of Mrs Doris McNair-Wilson; *m* 1974, Mrs Deidree Granville. *Educ:* Eton College. During national service, 1948-50, was commissioned in Royal Irish Fusiliers. Farmed in Hampshire, 1950-53. Journalist on various provincial newspapers, and did freelance work for BBC in Northern Ireland, 1953-55. Joined Sidney-Barton Ltd, internat. public relations consultants (Dir 1961-). Contested (C) Lincoln, Gen. Elec., 1964; Mem. Council, Bow Group, 1965-66; Jt Secretary: UN Parly Gp, 1969-70; Cons. Greater London Members Gp, 1970-72; Cons. Aviation Cttee: Sec., 1969-70; Vice-Chm., 1970-72; Chm., 1972-74; Mem., Select Cttee on Nationalised Industries; Mem. Council, Air League, 1972-76. *Publications:* Blackshirt, a biography of Mussolini (jointly), 1959; No Tame or Minor Role, (Bow Group pamphlet on the Common Market) (jointly), 1963. *Recreations:* golf, sailing, skiing, riding. *Address:* 29 St Luke Street, SW3. *Club:* Royal Lymington Yacht.
See also P. M. E. D. McNair-Wilson.

McNALLY, Tom; Political Adviser: to the Prime Minister, since 1976; to the Foreign and Commonwealth Secretary, 1974-76; *b* 20 Feb. 1943; *s* of John P. McNally and Elizabeth May (*née* McCarthy); *m* 1970, Eileen Powell. *Educ:* College of St Joseph, Blackpool; University Coll., London (BScEcon). President of Students' Union, UCL, 1965-66; Vice-Pres., Nat. Union of Students, 1966-67; Asst Gen. Sec. of Fabian Society, 1966-67; Labour Party researcher, 1967-68; Internat. Sec. of Labour Party, 1969-74. *Recreations:* playing and watching sport, reading political biographies. *Address:* 5 Amroth Close, SE23. *T:* 01-699 3333.

McNAMARA, (Joseph) Kevin; MP (Lab) Kingston-upon-Hull Central, since 1974 (Kingston-upon-Hull North, Jan. 1966-1974); *b* 5 Sept. 1934; *s* of late Patrick and Agnes McNamara; *m* 1960, Nora (*née* Jones), Warrington; four *s* one *d. Educ:* various primary schools; St Mary's Coll., Crosby; Hull Univ. (LLB). Head of Dept of History, St Mary's Grammar Sch., Hull, 1958-64; Lecturer in Law, Hull Coll. of Commerce, 1964-66. Sec., Parly Gp, TGWU; Chm., Parly Lab Party NI Group. Commendatore, Order Al Merito della Repubblica Italiana, 1977. *Recreations:* family and outdoor activities. *Address:* House of Commons, SW1; 128/130 Cranbrook Avenue, Hull HU6 7ST.

McNAMARA, Robert Strange; Medal of Freedom with Distinction; President, International Bank for Reconstruction and Development, International Development Association, and International Finance Corporation, since 1968; *b* San Francisco, 9 June 1916; *s* of Robert James McNamara and Clara Nell (*née* Strange); *m* 1940, Margaret McKinstry Craig; one *s* two *d. Educ:* University of California (AB); Harvard Univ. (Master of Business Administration); Asst Professor of Business Administration, Harvard, 1940-43. Served in USAAF, England, India, China, Pacific, 1943-46 (Legion of Merit); released as Lieut-Colonel. Joined Ford Motor Co., 1946; Executive, 1946-61; Controller, 1949-53; Asst General Manager, Ford Div., 1953-55; Vice-President, and General Manager, Ford Div., 1955-57; Director, and Group Vice-President of Car Divisions, 1957-61, President, 1960-61; Secretary of Defense, United States of America, 1961-68. Trustee: Ford Foundn; Brookings Instn. Holds several hon. doctorates; Phi Beta Kappa. *Publication:* The Essence of Security, 1968; One Hundred Countries, Two Billion People: the dimensions of development, 1975. *Address:* 1818 H Street, NW, Washington, DC 20433, USA; 2412 Tracy Place, NW, Washington, DC 20008, USA.

McNAMARA RYAN, Patrick John; *see* Ryan.

McNAUGHTON, Lt-Col Ian Kenneth Arnold; Chief Inspecting Officer of Railways, Department of the Environment, since 1974; *b* 30 June 1920; *er s* of late Brig. F. L. McNaughton, CBE, DSO and Betty, *d* of late Rev. Arnold Pinchard, OBE; *m* 1946, Arthea, *d* of late Carel Begeer, Voorschoten, Holland; two *d. Educ:* Loretto Sch.; RMA Woolwich; RMCS Shrivenham. BScEng, CEng, MIMechE, FCIT, FIRSE. 2nd Lieut RE, 1939; served War of 1939-45, NW Europe (Captain) (despatches); GHQ MELF, 1949 (Major); Cyprus, 1955; OC 8 Rly Sqdn, 1958; Port Comdt Southampton, 1959 (Lt-Col); SIT Transportation HQ BAOR, 1960; retd 1963. Inspecting Officer of Rlys, Min. of Transport, 1963. *Recreations:* gardening, foreign travel. *Address:* Chawton Glebe, Alton, Hants. *T:* Alton 83395.

McNEE, David Blackstock, QPM 1975; Commissioner, Metropolitan Police, since 1977; *b* 23 March 1925; *s* of John McNee, Glasgow, Lanarkshire; *m* 1952, Isabella Clayton Hopkins; one *d. Educ:* Woodside Senior Secondary Sch., Glasgow. Joined City of Glasgow Police, 1946. Apptd Dep. Chief Constable, Dunbartonshire Constabulary, 1968; Chief Constable: City of Glasgow Police, 1971-75; Strathclyde Police, 1975-77. Freeman of the City of London, 1977. FBIM 1977. OStJ 1974. *Recreations:* fishing, golf, music. *Address:* New Scotland Yard, Broadway, SW1H 0BG. *T:* 01-230 1212. *Club:* Royal Commonwealth Society.

McNEE, Sir John (William), Kt 1951; DSO 1918; MD; DSc, FRCP (London, Edinburgh and Glasgow); FRS(E); Regius Professor of Practice of Medicine, Glasgow University, 1936-53; Professor Emeritus, 1953; Physician to the Queen in Scotland, 1952-54 (and to King George VI, 1937-52); Consulting Physician to Royal Navy, 1935-55; Consulting Physician to University College Hospital, London, and to the Western Infirmary, Glasgow; *b* 17 Dec. 1887; *o s* of late John McNee, Glasgow and Newcastle upon Tyne; *m* 1923, Geraldine Z. L., MSc (London) (*d* 1975), *o d* of late Cecil H. A. Le Bas, The Charterhouse, London. *Educ:* Royal Grammar Sch., Newcastle upon Tyne; Glasgow, Freiburg, and Johns Hopkins, USA,

Universities. MB (Hons), 1909; MD (Hons) and Bellahouston Gold Medal, 1914; DSc 1920. Asst Professor of Medicine and Lecturer in Pathology, Glasgow University; Asst Professor of Medicine, and Associate Physician, Johns Hopkins Univ., USA; Consulting Physician UCH, London, and formerly Holme Lecturer in Clinical Medicine, UCH Medical Sch.; Rockefeller Fellow in Medicine, 1923; Lettsomian Lecturer, Medical Society of London, 1931; Croonian Lecturer, RCP, 1932; Harveian Lecturer, Harveian Society, London, 1952; Vicary Lecturer, RCS, 1958. Examiner in Medicine, Universities of Cambridge, St Andrews, Sheffield, Glasgow, Aberdeen, Edinburgh, Leeds, National University of Ireland, and Conjoint Board; Inspector for GMC of all Univs in Gt Britain and Ireland and of Final Examinations in Medicine, 1954-56. Visiting Prof., Harvard Univ., USA (Brigham Hospital), 1949. President: Royal Medico-Chirurgical Society of Glasgow, 1950-51; Gastro-Enterological Society of Great Britain, 1950-51; Assoc. of Physicians, Great Britain and Ireland, 1951-52; BMA 1954-55. Editor, Quarterly Journal of Medicine, 1929-48. Master of the Barber-Surgeons' Company of London, 1957-58; Served European War, Major, RAMC, 1914-19 (despatches, DSO, Comm. Military Order Avis). Served War of 1939-45, Surgeon Rear-Admiral RN, and Consulting Physician to the Navy in Scotland and Western Approaches, 1939-45. Hon. MD (NUI); LLD (Glasgow), LLD (Toronto). *Publications:* Diseases of the Liver-Gall-Bladder and Bile-Ducts (3rd edn, 1929, with Sir Humphrey Rolleston); Text-book of Medical Treatment (with Dunlop and Davidson), 1st edn, and 6th edn 1955; numerous medical papers, especially on diseases of liver and spleen and various war diseases (Trench Fever, Gas Gangrene, War Nephritis, Immersion Foot (RN)), Rescue Ships (RN), New Internat. Med. Code for Ships. *Recreations:* country sports. *Address:* Barton Edge, Worthy Road, Winchester, Hants. *T:* Winchester 65444. *Clubs:* Athenæum, Fly-fishers'.

MacNEECE, W. F.; *see* Foster, Air Vice-Marshal W. F. MacN.

McNEICE, Sir (Thomas) Percy (Fergus), Kt 1956; CMG 1953; OBE 1947; *b* 16 Aug. 1901; *s* of late Canon W. G. McNeice, MA, and Mary Masterson; *m* 1947, Yuen Peng Loke, *d* of late Dr Loke Yew, CMG, LLD; one *s* one *d. Educ:* Bradford Grammar Sch.; Keble Coll., Oxford (MA). Malayan Civil Service, 1925; Captain, Straits Settlements Volunteer Force (Prisoner of War, 1942-45). MLC, Singapore, 1949; MEC 1949; President of the City Council, Singapore, 1949-56, retired. FZS. *Recreations:* bird watching, walking and swimming. *Address:* 1102 Cathay Apartments, Singapore 9. *Club:* Royal Commonwealth Society.

McNEIL, Anne, CBE 1950 (OBE 1946); Secretary, Service Women's Club, 52 Lower Sloane Street, London, 1950-64, retired; *d* of Archibald and Elizabeth McNeil, Thorganby, York. *Educ:* privately. Served WRNS, 1940-50; last appointment, Superintendent (training). *Address:* Birkwood, Thorganby, York YO4 6DH.

McNEIL, Sir Hector, Kt 1969; CBE 1966; President, Babcock & Wilcox Ltd, 1972-73 (Chairman, 1968-71, Managing Director, 1958-68); *b* 20 July 1904; *s* of late Angus McNeil, New Zealand, and late Mary McNeil; *m* 1939, Barbara J. Turner, *d* of late P. S. Turner; one *s* one *d. Educ:* Christchurch, NZ. University of New Zealand (BE). Public Works Dept, New Zealand, 1927-29; State Electricity Commission of Victoria, Australia, 1929-31; joined Babcock & Wilcox Ltd, 1931; General Manager, 1947; Director, 1950; Dep. Managing Director, 1953; Director, National Bank of New Zealand, 1959-. Chm., Export Council for Europe, 1966-69; Member: Export Guarantees Advisory Council, 1968-73; Council BIM, 1971-. President of Inst. of Fuel, 1957-58; FIEE; FIMechE; CIMarE. *Recreations:* shooting, golf. *Address:* Bramber, St George's Hill, Weybridge, Surrey. *T:* Weybridge 48484.

MACNEIL of Barra, Prof. Ian Roderick; The Macneil of Barra; 46th Chief of Clan Macneil and of that Ilk; Ingersoll Professor of Law, Cornell University, since 1976; *b* 20 June 1929; *s* of Robert Lister Macneil of Barra, 45th Chief, and Kathleen, *d* of Orlando Paul Metcalf, NYC, USA; *m* 1952, Nancy, *e d* of James Tilton Wilson, Ottawa, Canada; two *s* one *d* (and one *s* decd). *Educ:* Univ. of Vermont (BA 1950); Harvard Univ. (JD 1955). Lieut, Infty, Army of US, 1951-53 (US Army Reserve, 1950-69, discharged honorably, rank of Major). Clerk, US Court of Appeals, 1955-56; Associate, law firm Sulloway Hollis Godfrey & Soden, Concord, NH, USA, 1956-59. Cornell Univ., USA: Asst Prof. of Law, 1959-62; Associate Prof., 1962-63; Prof. of Law, 1962-72 and 1974-76; Prof. of Law, and Mem., Center for Advanced Studies, Univ. of Virginia, 1972-74. Fulbright Vis. Prof. of Law, University Coll., Univ. of East Africa, Dar es Salaam, Tanzania, 1965-67. Mem. Exec. Cttee, Assoc. of

American Law Schools, 1970-72. Member: American Law Inst.; Standing Council of Scottish Chiefs. *Publications:* Bankruptcy Law in East Africa, 1966; (with R. B. Schlesinger, *et al*) Formation of Contracts: A Study of the Common Core of Legal Systems, 1968; Contracts: Instruments of Social Co-operation-East Africa, 1968; (with R. S. Morison) Students and Decision Making, 1970; Contracts: Exchange Transactions and Relationships, 1971; contrib. US and African law jls. *Recreations:* tennis, gardening. *Heir: s* Roderick Wilson Macneil, Younger of Barra, *b* 22 Oct. 1954. *Address:* 105 Devon Road, Ithaca, NY 14850, USA; Kisimul Castle, Isle of Barra, Scotland. *T:* Castlebay 300. *Club:* Puffin's (Edinburgh).

McNEIL, John Struthers, CBE 1967; Chief Road Engineer, Scottish Development Department, 1963-69; *b* 4 March 1907; *s* of R. H. McNeil, Troon; *m* 1931, Dorothea Yuille; two *s. Educ:* Ayr Academy; Glasgow Univ. BSc Hons, Civil Engineering, 1929; FICE 1955. Contracting and local government experience, 1929-35; joined Ministry of Transport as Asst Engineer, 1935; Divisional Road Engineer, NW Div. of England, 1952-55; Asst Chief Engineer, 1955-57; Dep. Chief Engineer, 1957-63. Telford Gold Medal, ICE. *Publications:* contribs. to technical journals. *Recreations:* fishing, gardening. *Address:* 306-250 Douglas Street, Victoria, BC V8V 2P4, Canada.

McNEILE, Robert Arbuthnot, MBE 1943; Co-Chairman, Arthur Guinness Son & Co. Ltd, since 1975, Managing Director, 1968-75; *b* 14 March 1913; *s* of A. M. McNeile, Housemaster at Eton College; *m* 1944, Pamela Rachel Paton (*née* Pollock); three *s* one *d. Educ:* Eton Coll.; King's Coll., Cambridge. Asst Master, Eton Coll., 1935; joined Arthur Guinness Son & Co. Ltd, 1936. Served War of 1939-45 in Royal Engineers, First Airborne Div., HQ 21st Army Group, Control Commn for Germany; Lt-Col. Chm., Brewers' Society, 1975- (Vice-Chm., 1974-75). *Recreations:* archaeology, ornithology, Tennis, ski-ing, shooting. *Address:* Broad Lane House, Brancaster, Norfolk. *T:* Brancaster 227.

McNEILL, David Bruce, QC 1966; a Recorder of the Crown Court, since 1972 (Recorder of Blackburn, 1969-71); *b* 6 June 1922; *s* of late Ferguson and Elizabeth Bruce McNeill; *m* 1949, Margaret Lewis; one *s* three *d. Educ:* Rydal Sch.; Merton Coll., Oxford. BCL, MA Oxon, 1947. Called to Bar, Lincoln's Inn, 1947 (Cassel Schol.); Bencher, 1974; Northern Circuit, Leader, 1974-. Lecturer in Law, Liverpool Univ., 1948-58. Member: Bar Council, 1968-72; Senate of the Inns of Court and the Bar, 1975- (Vice-Chm., 1976-77; Chm., 1977-78). Commissioned into Reconnaissance Corps, 1943; served in N Africa, Sicily, Italy, Germany. *Address:* Ravelstone, Manley, Cheshire. *T:* Manley 379; 5 Essex Court, Temple, EC4. *T:* 01-353 4365. *Club:* Athenæum (Liverpool).

McNEILL, Maj.-Gen. John Malcolm, CB 1963; CBE 1959 (MBE 1942); *b* 22 Feb. 1909; *s* of Brig.-General Angus McNeill, CB, CBE, DSO, DL, Seaforth Highlanders, and Lilian, *d* of Maj.-General Sir Harry Barron, KCVO; *m* 1939, Barbara, *d* of Colonel C. H. Marsh, DSO, Spilsby, Lincs; two *d. Educ:* Imperial Service Coll., Windsor; RMA, Woolwich. 2nd Lieut, RA, 1929. Served Western Desert, Sicily, Italy, N.W. Europe and Burma, 1939-45; Commanded 1st Regt RHA, 1948-51; Student Imperial Defence Coll., 1952; Dep. Secretary, Chiefs of Staff Cttee, Ministry of Defence, 1953-55; Comdr RA 2nd Div. 1955-58; Comdt School of Artillery, 1959-60; Commander, British Army Staff, and Military Attaché, Washington, DC, 1960-63; Col Comdt RA, 1964-74. Principal Staff Officer to Sec. of State for Commonwealth Relations, 1964-69. ADC to the Queen, 1958-60. *Recreations:* riding, sailing, shooting. *Address:* Beales House, Pilton, Shepton Mallet, Som. *T:* Pilton 212. *Clubs:* Army and Navy, English-Speaking Union.

McNEILL, Peter Grant Brass, PhD; Sheriff of Glasgow and Strathkelvin (formerly Lanarkshire) at Glasgow, since 1965; *b* 3 March 1929; *s* of late William Arnot McNeill and Lillias Philips Scrimgeour; *m* 1959, Matilda Farquhar Rose, *d* of Mrs Christina Rose; one *s* three *d. Educ:* Hillhead High Sch., Glasgow; Morrison's Academy, Crieff; Glasgow Univ. MA (Hons Hist.) 1951; LLB 1954; Law apprentice, Biggart Lumsden & Co., Glasgow, 1952-55; Carnegie Fellowship, 1955; Faulds Fellowship, 1956-59; Scottish Bar, 1956; PhD, 1961. Hon. Sheriff Substitute of Lanarkshire, and of Stirling, Clackmannan and Dumbarton, 1962; Standing Junior Counsel to Scottish Development Dept (Highways), 1964; Advocate Depute, 1964. *Publications:* (ed) Balfour's *Practicks* (Stair Society), 1962-63; (ed jtly) An Historical Atlas of Scotland *c* 400-*c* 1600, 1975; legal and historical articles in Juridical Review, Scots Law Times, Glasgow Herald, etc. *Recreations:* legal history, gardening, bookbinding. *Address:* Sheriffs' Library, County Buildings, PO Box 23, Glasgow G1 1SY. *T:* 041-552 3434.

McNICOL, David Williamson, CBE 1966; Australian Ambassador to South Africa, since 1975; *b* 20 June 1913; *s* of late Donald McNicol, Adelaide; *m* 1947, Elsa Margaret, *d* of N. J. Hargrave, Adelaide; one *s. Educ:* Carey Grammar Sch., Melbourne; Kings Coll., Adelaide; Adelaide Univ. (BA). RAAF, 1940-45. Australian Minister to Cambodia, Laos and Vietnam, 1955-56; idc 1957; Australian Comr to Singapore, 1958-60; Asst Sec., Dept of External Affairs, Australia, 1960-62; Australian High Comr to Pakistan, 1962-65 and to New Zealand, 1965-68; Australian Ambassador to Thailand, 1968-69; Australian High Comr to Canada, 1969-73; Dep. High Comr for Australia in London, 1973-75. *Recreations:* golf, gardening. *Address:* Australian Embassy, PO Box 4749, Cape Town 8000, South Africa. *Clubs:* Naval and Military (Melbourne); Royal Canberra Golf.

McNICOL, Prof. George Paul; Professor of Medicine, and Honororary Consultant Physician, Leeds General Infirmary, since 1971; *b* 24 Sept. 1929; *s* of Martin and Elizabeth McNicol; *m* 1959, Susan Ritchie; one *s* two *d. Educ:* Hillhead High Sch., Glasgow; Univ. of Glasgow. MD, PhD, FRCP, FRCPG, FRCPE, FRCPath. House Surg., Western Infirmary, Glasgow, 1952; House Phys., Stobhill Gen. Hosp., Glasgow, 1953; Regimental MO, RAMC, 1953-55; Asst, Dept Materia Medica and Therapeutics, Registrar, Univ. Med. Unit, Stobhill Gen. Hosp., 1955-57; Univ. Dept of Medicine, Royal Infirmary, Glasgow: Registrar, 1957-59; Hon. Sen. Registrar, 1961-65; Lectr in Medicine, 1963-65; Hon. Cons. Phys., 1966-71; Sen. Lectr in Medicine, 1966-70; Reader in Medicine, 1970-71; Harkness Fellow, Commonwealth Fund, Dept of Internal Medicine, Washington Univ., 1959-61; Hon. Clinical Lectr and Hon. Cons. Phys., Makerere UC Med. Sch. Extension, Kenyatta Nat. Hosp., Nairobi (on secondment from Glasgow Univ.), 1965-66. Hon. FACP. *Publications:* papers in sci. and med. jls on thrombosis and bleeding disorders. *Recreations:* gardening, reading. *Address:* University Department of Medicine, The General Infirmary, Leeds. *T:* Leeds 32799; 3 Creskeld Crescent, Bramhope, Leeds. *T:* Leeds 673906. *Club:* Caledonian.
See also A. H. Smallwood.

McNICOLL, Vice-Adm. Sir Alan (Wedel Ramsay), KBE 1966 (CBE 1954); CB 1965; GM 1941; Australian Ambassador to Turkey, 1968-73; *b* 3 April 1908; 2nd *s* of late Brig.-Gen. Sir Walter McNicoll and Lady McNicoll; *m* 1st, 1937; two *s* one *d*; 2nd, 1957, Frances, *d* of late J. Chadwick. *Educ:* Scotch Coll., Melbourne; Royal Australian Naval Coll. Joined Navy, 1922; Lieut, 1930; Captain, 1949; Rear-Admiral, 1958; Dep. Chief of Naval Staff, 1951-52; Commanded 10th Destroyer Flotilla, 1950; HMAS Australia, 1953-54; IDC, 1955; 2nd Naval Member, Commonwealth Naval Board, 1960-61; Commanded Australian Fleet, 1962-64; Vice-Admiral, 1965; Chief of Naval Staff, Australia, 1965-68. Comdr of Order of Orange Nassau, 1955. *Recreations:* music, painting, fly-fishing. *Address:* 6 Hutt Street, Yarralumla, ACT 2600, Australia.
See also H. Chadwick, Sir J. E. Chadwick, W. O. Chadwick.

MACNIE, William Alexander, CMG 1949; OBE 1941; *b* 1899. *Educ:* High Sch. and University, Glasgow. Served European War, 1914-18, Lieut, 1917-20. Sub-Inspector, Police, British Guiana, 1921; District Inspector, 1925; seconded as additional Assistant Colonial Secretary, 1931; District Commissioner, 1932; Senior District Commissioner, 1936; Principal Assistant Colonial Secretary, 1945; seconded as Competent Authority and Controller of Supplies and Prices, British Guiana, 1939-45; Colonial Secretary, Leeward Islands, 1945-49. MLC, British Guiana, 1951.

McNISH, Althea Marjorie, (Althea McNish Weiss), CMT 1976; freelance textile designer, since 1957; Member, Design Council, since 1974; *b* Trinidad; *d* of late J. Claude McNish, educnl reformer, and of Margaret (*née* Bourne); *m* 1969, John Weiss. *Educ:* Port-of-Spain, by her father and others; London Coll. of Printing; Central School of Art and Crafts; Royal Coll. of Art. NDD, DesRCA; FSIAD (FSIA 1968, MSIA 1960). Painted throughout childhood; after design educn in London, freelance practice, with commns from Ascher and Liberty's, 1957; new techniques for laminate murals, for SS Oriana and hosp. and coll. in Trinidad; Govt of Trinidad and Tobago travelling schol., 1962; interior design (for Govt of Trinidad and Tobago) in NY, Washington and London, 1962. Cotton Bd trav. schol. to report on export potential for British printed cotton goods in Europe, 1963; textile designs in exhibn, Inprint, Manch. and London, 1964-71; collection of dress fabric designs for ICI and Tootal Thomson for promotion of Terylene Toile, 1966; special features for Daily Mail Ideal Home Exhibn, 1966-; interior design for Sec.-Gen. of Commonwealth, 1975; selection panels for Design Council Awards and Design Index, 1968-; Mem. Design Council's Jubilee Souvenir Selection Panel, 1976; textile designs in exhibns of Design Council and BoT: USA, 1969; Sweden, 1969; London, 1970; London and USA, 1972; paintings and hangings in one-man and gp exhibns, London, 1954-, Jamaica, 1975. Research tours; Czechoslovakia, 1968; Yugoslavia, 1972; Tunisia, 1974; Caribbean and North America, 1976; (with John Weiss) exhibited: textile designs, Amsterdam, 1972-74, Design Council, London, 1975, 1977; etched silver dishes, London, 1973. Vis. Lectr, Central Sch. of Art and Crafts and other colls and polytechnics, 1960-; Associate Lectr in Furnishing and Surface Design, London Coll. of Furniture, 1972-. External assessor for educnl and professional bodies, incl. SIAD and NCDAD/CNAA, 1966-; Mem. jury for Leverhulme schols, 1968; Judge: Portuguese textile design comp., Lisbon, 1973; 'Living' Design Awards, 1974. Mem., Fashion and Textiles Design Bd, CNAA, 1975-; Mem. Gov. Body, Portsmouth Coll. of Art, 1972-. *BBC-TV:* studio setting for Caribbean edn of Full House, 1973. Has also appeared, with work, in films for COI and Gas Council. Chaconia Medal (Gold) (Trinidad and Tobago), 1976, for service to art and design. *Publications:* textile designs prod. in many countries, and published in Designers in Britain and design jls. *Recreations:* ski-ing, travelling, music, gardening. *Address:* 142 West Green Road, N15 5AD. *T:* 01-800 1686. *Club:* Soroptimist.

MACONCHY, Elizabeth, (Mrs W. R. Le Fanu), CBE 1977; ARCM; Hon. RAM; composer of serious music; *b* 19 March 1907; of Irish parentage; *d* of Gerald E. C. Maconchy, Lawyer, and Violet M. Poë; *m* 1930, William Richard Le Fanu (author of Bibliography of Edward Jenner, 1951, Betsy Sheridan's Journal, 1960, etc); two *d. Educ:* privately; Royal College of Music, London. Held Blumenthal Scholarship and won Sullivan Prize, Foli and other exhibitions, at RCM; pupil of Vaughan-Williams; travelled with Octavia Scholarship, 1929-30. First public performance: Piano Concerto with Prague Philharmonic Orchestra, 1930. Sir Henry Wood introduced "The Land", Promenade Concerts, 1930. Has had works performed at 3 Festivals of International Society for Contemporary Music (Prague, 1935; Paris, 1937; Copenhagen, 1947). Largest output has been in Chamber Music; String Quartets played as a series in BBC Third Programme, 1955, 1975. Chairman: Composers Guild of Great Britain, 1960; Soc. for Promotion of New Music, 1972-75 (Pres., 1977-). *Publications:* Suite for Orchestra, The Land; Nocturne, Overture, Proud Thames (LCC Coronation Prize, 1953); Dialogue for piano and orchestra; Serenata Concertante for violin and orchestra, 1963; Symphony for double string orchestra; Concertino for: bassoon and string orchestra; clarinet and string orchestra; Piano and chamber orchestra; Concerto for oboe, bassoon and string orchestra; Variazioni Concertanti for oboe, clarinet, bassoon, horn and strings, 1965; Variations for String Orchestra; ten String Quartets (No 5, Edwin Evans Prize; No 9, Radcliffe Award, 1969); Oboe Quintet (Daily Telegraph Prize); Violin Sonata; Cello Divertimento; Duo for 2 Violins; Duo for Violin and Cello; Variations for solo cello; Reflections, for oboe, clarinet, viola and harp (Gedok International Prize, 1961); Clarinet Quintet; Carol Cantata, A Christmas Morning; Samson and the Gates of Gaza for chorus and orchestra, 1964; 3 settings of Gerard Manley Hopkins for soprano and chamber orchestra; Sonatina for harpsichord and Notebook for harpsichord, 1965; Three Donne settings, 1965; Nocturnal for unaccompanied chorus, 1965; Music for brass and woodwind, 1966; An Essex Overture, 1966; 6 Miniatures for solo violin, 1966; Duo for piano duet, 1967; Extravaganza, The Birds, after Aristophanes, 1968; Three Cloudscapes for orchestra, 1968; And Death shall have no Dominion for chorus and brass, 3 Choirs Festival, 1969; Sonata for clarinet and viola, 1969; The Jesse Tree, masque for Dorchester Abbey, 1970; Music for double-bass and piano, 1971; Ariadne (C. Day Lewis), for soprano and orch., King's Lynn Festival, 1971; Faustus, scena for tenor and piano, 1971; Prayer Before Birth, for women's voices, 1971; 3 Bagatelles for oboe and harpsichord, 1972; oboe quartet, 1972; songs for voice and harp, 1974; The King of the Golden River, opera for children, 1975; Epyllion, for solo cello and strings, Cheltenham Festival, 1975; Touchstone, for oboe and chamber organ, 1975; Sinfonietta, for Essex Youth Orch., 1976; Pied Beauty, and Heaven Haven (G. M. Hopkins), for choir and brass, Southern Cathedrals Fest., 1976; Morning, Noon and Night, for harp, Aldeburgh Fest., 1977; Sun, Moon and Stars (Traherne), song cycle for soprano and piano, 1977; Heloise and Abelard, for 3 soloists, chorus and orch., 1977-78. Songs, Piano Pieces, etc. Three One-Act Operas (The Sofa, The Three Strangers, The Departure). *Address:* Shottesbrook, Boreham, Chelmsford, Essex. *T:* Chelmsford 467 286.

MACOUN, Michael John, CMG 1964; OBE 1961; QPM 1954; Overseas Police Adviser, and Inspector-General of Police, Dependent Territories, Foreign and Commonwealth Office, since 1967; Police Training Adviser, Ministry of Overseas Development, since 1967; *b* 27 Nov. 1914; *o s* of late John Horatio Macoun, Comr of Chinese Maritime Customs; *m* 1940, Geraldine Mabel, *o d* of late Brig.-Gen. G. C. Sladen, CB, CMG, DSO, MC; two *s. Educ:* Stowe Sch., Buckingham; Univ. of Oxford (MA). At Metropolitan Police Coll., 1938; Tanganyika Police, 1939-42, 1945-58; Inspector-Gen. of Police, Uganda, 1959-64; Directing Staff, Police Coll., Bramshill, 1965; Commonwealth Office, 1966. War Service, 1943-44. FRGS. Colonial Police Medal, 1951; OStJ 1959. *Recreations:* tennis, ski-bobbing, walking. *Address:* Furzedown, Rowledge, near Farnham, Surrey. *T:* Frensham 3196. *Clubs:* Royal Commonwealth Society; Bourne (Farnham).

MacOWAN, Michael Charles Henry, CBE 1976; Artistic Director, London Academy of Music and Dramatic Art, 1972-73 (Principal, 1954-66); *b* 18 April 1906; *s* of Norman MacOwan and Violet (*née* Stephenson); *m* 1932, Alexis McFarlane (Alexis France); one *d. Educ:* Haileybury Coll. Started as an actor, in 1925; abandoned acting for production; apptd producer Hull Repertory, 1931; Asst Producer and Master of Students, Old Vic, 1933-35; Producer, Westminster Theatre, 1936-39; A Month in the Country, Mourning Becomes Electra, Troilus and Cressida (in modern dress), etc. War service, 1939-45. Apptd Drama Dir Arts Council of Great Britain, 1945; produced Macbeth, Stratford-on-Avon, 1946. London productions include: The Linden Tree, 1947; Cockpit, 1948; A Sleep of Prisoners, 1951; The River Line, 1952; The Applecart, 1953; The Burning Glass, 1954; The Seagull, 1956; The Potting Shed, 1958. Has also undertaken radio and television productions and extensive lecturing and teaching, at home and abroad. *Recreations:* gardening, photography and country pursuits. *Address:* 3 Blake Gardens, SW6 4QA. *T:* 01-736 3520.

McPETRIE, Sir James (Carnegie), KCMG 1966 (CMG 1961); OBE 1953; Chairman, UNESCO Appeals Board; Research Fellow, Department of Public Law, Dundee University; *b* 29 June 1911; *er s* of late James Duncan McPetrie and late Elizabeth Mary Carnegie; *m* 1941, Elizabeth, *e d* of late John Howie; one *d. Educ:* Madras Coll., St Andrews; Univ. of St Andrews; Jesus Coll., Oxford (Scholar), MA (St Andrews) 1933; BA Oxon 1937, MA 1972; Harmsworth Schol., Middle Temple, 1937; Barrister, Middle Temple, 1938. Served War of 1939-45, Royal Artillery and staff of JAG (India); commissioned, 1940; Major, 1944. Legal Asst, Commonwealth Relations Office and Colonial Office, 1946, Sen. Legal Asst, 1947, Asst Legal Adviser, 1952; Legal Adviser, Colonial Office, 1960, Commonwealth Office, 1966, FCO, 1968-71; retired from HM Diplomatic Service, 1971; temporary mem. Legal Staff, DoE, 1972-75. *Address:* Nelson Cottage, Strathkinness, St Andrews, Fife KY16 9SA. *T:* Strathkinness 235. *Club:* United Oxford & Cambridge University.

McPETRIE, James Stuart, CB 1960; *b* 13 June 1902; *s* of John McPetrie and Mary (*née* Simpson); *m* 1st, 1931, Helen Noreen McGregor (*d* 1974); one *s*; 2nd, 1975, Myra, *widow* of John F. Pullen. *Educ:* Robert Gordon's Coll., Aberdeen; Aberdeen Univ. National Physical Laboratory, 1925-43; Radio Physicist, British Supply Mission, Washington, DC, 1943-44; Research Superintendent, Signals Research and Development Establishment, Ministry of Supply, 1944-50; Head of Radio Dept, Royal Aircraft Establishment, 1950-58; Dir-Gen. of Electronics Research and Development at Ministry of Aviation, 1958-62; Consulting Electronic Engineer, 1962-; Dir, Racal Electronics, 1965-69. *Publications:* series of papers on various aspects of radio research to learned societies. *Address:* 8 Edenhurst Court, Torquay, Devon.

MACPHAIL, Sheriff Iain Duncan; Sheriff of Glasgow and Strathkelvin (formerly Lanarkshire) since 1973; *b* 24 Jan. 1938; *o s* of Malcolm John Macphail and late Mary Corbett Duncan; *m* 1970, Rosslyn Graham Lillias, *o d* of E. J. C. Hewitt, MD, TD, Edinburgh; one *s* one *d. Educ:* George Watson's Coll., Edinburgh and Glasgow Univs. MA Hons History Edinburgh 1959, LLB Glasgow 1962. Admitted to Faculty of Advocates, 1963; in practice at Scottish Bar, 1963-73; Faulds Fellow in Law, Glasgow Univ., 1963-65; Lectr in Evidence and Procedure, Strathclyde Univ., 1968-69 and Edinburgh Univ., 1969-72; Standing Jun. Counsel to Scottish Home and Health Dept and to Dept of Health and Social Security, 1971-73; Extra Advocate-Depute, 1973. *Publications:* articles and reviews in legal jls. *Recreations:* music, theatre, reading and writing. *Address:* County Buildings, 149 Ingram Street, Glasgow G1 1SY. *T:* 041-552 3434. *Club:* Western (Glasgow).

MACPHERSON, family name of **Barons Drumalbyn, Macpherson of Drumochter** and **Strathcarron.**

MACPHERSON OF DRUMOCHTER, 2nd Baron, *cr* 1951, of Great Warley, Essex; **(James) Gordon Macpherson;** Chairman and Managing Director of Macpherson, Train & Co. Ltd, and Subsidiary and Associated Companies, since 1964; Chairman, A. J. Macpherson & Co. Ltd (Bankers), since 1973; *b* 22 Jan. 1924; *s* of 1st Baron (*d* 1965) and Lucy Lady Macpherson of Drumochter; *S* father, 1965; *m* 1st, 1947, Dorothy Ruth Coulter (*d* 1974); one *s* two *d*; 2nd, 1975, Catherine, *d* of Dr C. D. MacCarthy; two *d*. *Educ:* Loretto; Wells House, Malvern. Served War of 1939-45, with RAF; 1939-45 Campaign medal, Burma Star, Pacific Star, Defence Medal, Victory Medal. Founder Chm. and Pres., British Importers Confedn, 1972-. Member: Council, London Chamber of Commerce, 1958-73; (Gen. Purposes Cttee, 1959-72); East European Trade Council, 1969-71; PLA, 1973-76; Exec. Cttee, W India Cttee, 1959- (Dep. Chm. and Treasurer, 1971, Chm. 1973-75). Freeman of City of London, 1969; Mem., Butchers' Co., 1969. Governor, Brentwood Sch. JP Essex, 1961-76; Dep. Chm., Brentwood Bench, 1972-76; Mem. Essex Magistrates Court Cttee, 1974-76. Hon. Game Warden for Sudan, 1974; Chief of Scottish Clans Assoc. of London, 1972-74. FRSA 1971; FRES 1940; FZS. *Recreations:* shooting, fishing, golf. *Heir: s* Hon. Thomas Ian Macpherson, *b* 25 July 1948. *Address:* Kyllachy, Tomatin, Invernessshire. *T:* Tomatin 212. *Clubs:* Boodle's; Thorndon Park, House of Lords Yacht; Royal and Ancient (St Andrews).

McPHERSON, Brig. Alan Bruce, CBE 1944; MVO 1933; MC 1915; Indian Army, retired; *b* 6 Jan. 1887; *s* of late Donald William McPherson, Dunvegan, Isle of Skye; *m* 1915, Gladys Lawrie (*decd* 1972), *d* of late Col W. H. Riddell, Bedfordshire Regt; one *d*. *Educ:* Bedford Sch.; RMC Sandhurst. 2nd Lt IA 1906; Lt, 1909; Captain 1915; Major, 1921; Brevet Lt-Col, 1930; Substantive Lt-Col, 1931; Col, 1933; Served European war in France, 1914-15; Egypt, 1915; Mesopotamia, 1915-16 (wounded, despatches twice, MC); DAAG (Demobilization) Bombay 1918-19; Staff Coll. 1920-21; GSOII (Intelligence) 1922; DAAG 1922-26 and 1928-30; Officer in Command Indian War Memorial contingent, Neuve Chapelle, France, 1927; Commandant, 2/9th Jat Regt, 1931-34; Officer in charge the King's Indian Orderly Officers, 1933; AAG Northern Command, India, 1935-37; Operations NWF India, 1936-37; Comdr 11th (Ahmednagar) Infantry Brigade, India and Egypt, 1937-40; Dep. Dir of Mobilization, War Office, 1940-46; retired 1947; re-employed War Office 1947-49, 1950-57. *Publications:* Official Historical Monographs (2nd World War), on Mobilization and Discipline. *Address:* c/o Lt-Col D. J. Cable, OBE, MC, 6 Lammas Park Road, Ealing, W5. *Club:* Naval and Military.

MACPHERSON, Rt. Rev. Colin; *see* Argyll and the Isles, Bishop of, (RC).

MACPHERSON, Colin, MA; CA; Senior Partner, Smith & Williamson, Chartered Accountants, since 1973 (Partner, since 1959); Deputy Chairman, Commission for New Towns, since 1976; *b* 17 Feb. 1927; *s* of Ian Macpherson and Anna Elizabeth McLean; *m* 1951, Christian Elizabeth Randolph; two *s* one *d*. *Educ:* Eton; Trinity Coll., Cambridge (MA). Director: Sun Life Assce, 1968-; Keystone Investment, 1975-. Mem., Pilcher Cttee on Commercial Property Develt, 1975; Vice-Chm., Guide Dogs for the Blind, 1976-. *Recreations:* skiing, shooting. *Address:* Eastbridge, Crondall, near Farnham, Surrey GU10 5RH. *Clubs:* Bath, City of London.

MacPHERSON, Donald, CIE 1946; *b* 22 March 1894; *s* of D. MacPherson, Edinburgh; *m* 1931, Marie Elizabeth, *d* of John Nicholson, Sydney, NSW; two *d*. *Educ:* Royal High Sch. and Univ., Edinburgh. Indian Civil Service; District Magistrate, Bengal, 1928; Commissioner of Excise, 1935; Commissioner of Division, 1944. Retired, 1948. *Address:* 11 Melville Place, Edinburgh EH3 7PR. *T:* 031-225 5716.

MACPHERSON, George Philip Stewart, CBE 1976 (OBE 1943); TD 1945; Director, Kleinwort Benson Lonsdale, 1960-74; *b* 14 Dec. 1903; *s* of late Sir T. Stewart Macpherson, CIE, LLD, ICS, and Lady (Helen) Macpherson, K.-I.-H. (*née* Cameron); *m* 1939, Elizabeth Margaret Cameron, *d* of late James Cameron Smail, OBE, LLD; three *s*. *Educ:* Edinburgh Acad.; Fettes Coll. (Schol.); Oriel Coll., Oxford (Field Schol.; 1st class Classical Mods, 1st class Lit. Hum.; MA 1944), Hon. Fellow, 1973; Yale Univ., USA (Schol.); Edinburgh Univ.; Chartered Accountant (Edinburgh), 1930; partner in Layton-Bennett, Chiene and Tait, CA, 1930-36; Man. Dir, Robert Benson and Co. Ltd, Merchant Bankers, 1936; Chm., Robert Benson Lonsdale & Co. Ltd, 1958-60; Dir, Kleinwort Benson Ltd, 1960-69 (Vice-Chm., 1960-66); Dir Standard Life Assurance Co. Ltd, 1934-76 and of several industrial companies and investment trusts, until 1976 and 1977. Chm., Issuing Houses Association, 1955, 1956; Mem. Exec.

Cttee, Investment Trust Assoc., 1955-68. Chairman: Esmée Fairbairn Charitable Trust, 1969-; English-Speaking Union Finance Cttee, 1969-74; Royal Caledonian Schs Finance Cttee, 1952-73; Mem., Greenwich Hosp. Adv. Panel on financial matters, 1960-76. Governor, Fettes Coll., 1957-76. Hon. DLitt, Heriot Watt, 1971. 7/9 Battalion The Royal Scots, 1927-36; 1st Bn London Scottish, 1939, sc; Brig. 1945, Dir Finance Div. (Brit. Element) Allied Control Commn to Austria, 1945-46. *Publications:* contrib. to Accountants' Magazine. *Recreations:* active outdoor occupations and gardening. Formerly Rugby football and athletics (Oxford XV, 1922-24; Edinburgh Univ. Athletic Blue; Rep. Scotland Long Jump and Hurdles, 1929, and Rugby football, 1922-32; Scottish Rugby Union Cttee, 1934-36). *Address:* The Old Rectory, Aston Sandford, near Aylesbury, Bucks. *T:* Haddenham 291335. *Clubs:* Caledonian, English-Speaking Union; New (Edinburgh).

MACPHERSON, James; Administrative Adviser, Scottish Office, 1970-75, retired; *b* 16 Dec. 1911; *s* of late John Campbell Macpherson and Agnes Arkley Mitchell, Auchterarder, Perthshire; *m* 1939, Marion Cooper Cochrane Allison; two *s* one *d*. *Educ:* George Heriot's Sch. Asst Preventive Officer, subseq. Officer, Customs and Excise, 1932-39; Gunner, TA, 1939; 54th Light AA Regt, RA; service in France, Belgium, Italy, Austria, 1939-46; Brig. 1946; Dir Finance Div. (Br Element), Allied Control Commn to Austria; Princ., Min. of Civil Aviation, 1946-48; Treasury, 1949-53; Asst Sec., Treasury, 1953-63; Scottish Home and Health Dept, 1963-66; Scottish Development Dept, 1966-67; Under-Sec., Scottish Develt Dept, 1967-70. *Recreations:* reading, golf. *Address:* 92 Ravelston Dykes, Edinburgh EH12 6HB. *T:* 031-337 6560. *Clubs:* New (Edinburgh); Hon. Company of Edinburgh Golfers.

MACPHERSON, Roderick Ewen; Registrary, University of Cambridge, since 1969; *b* 17 July 1916; *s* of Ewen Macpherson, Chief Charity Commissioner, and Dorothy Mildred Hensley; *m* 1941, Sheila Joan Hooper, *d* of H. P. Hooper; two *s* two *d*. *Educ:* Eton College; King's College, Cambridge. Math. Tripos, Part II, Wrangler; Math. Tripos, Part III, Distinction; Smith's Prizeman, 1940. Served RAFVR, 1940-46, Navigator (Radio). Fellow, King's Coll., Cambridge, 1942-; Third Bursar, King's College, 1947-50, Second Bursar, 1950-51, First Bursar, 1951-62; University Treasurer, Univ. of Cambridge, 1962-69; Member: Council of the Senate, 1957-62; Financial Board, 1955-62. *Recreations:* gardening, hill-walking. *Address:* Orion, Coton Road, Grantchester, Cambridge CB3 9NX. *T:* Trumpington 2266.

MacPHERSON, Stewart Myles; Radio Commentator; Journalist; Variety Artist; Director of Programs, C-Jay Television, Winnipeg, since 1960; *b* Winnipeg, Canada, 29 Oct. 1908; *m* 1937, Emily Comfort; one *s* one *d*. *Educ:* Canada. Started broadcasting, 1937, on ice hockey; War Correspondent. Commentator on national events and world championships. Question Master, Twenty Questions and Ignorance is Bliss. Compère, Royal Command Variety Performance, 1948. *Publication:* The Mike and I, 1948. *Recreations:* golf, bridge, poker. *Address:* Winnipeg Enterprises Corporation, Winnipeg, Canada; c/o Canadian Broadcasting Corporation, Ottawa, Ontario, Canada.

MACPHERSON of Cluny and Blairgowrie, William Alan, TD 1966; QC 1971; Cluny Macpherson; 27th Chief of Clan Macpherson; a Recorder of the Crown Court, since 1972; *b* 1 April 1926; *s* of Brig. Alan David Macpherson, DSO, MC, RA (*d* 1969) and late Catherine Richardson Macpherson; *m* 1962, Sheila McDonald Brodie; two *s* one *d*. *Educ:* Wellington Coll., Berkshire; Trinity Coll., Oxford (MA). Called to Bar, Inner Temple, 1952. Served, 1944-47, in Scots Guards (Capt.). Commanded (Lt-Col) 21st Special Air Service Regt (TA), 1962-65; now Lt-Col, TARO. Mem., Queen's Body Guard for Scotland, Royal Co. of Archers, 1977-. *Recreations:* golf, fishing; Pres., London Scottish FC. *Heir: s* Alan Thomas Macpherson yr of Cluny and Blairgowrie. *Address:* Newton of Blairgowrie, Perthshire; 2 Garden Court, Temple, EC4. *Club:* Caledonian.

MACPHERSON, Very Rev. William Stuart, MA Cantab; Dean of Lichfield, 1954-69, Dean Emeritus, 1969; Hon. Canon, Ripon Cathedral, 1953-54; *b* 30 Sept. 1901; *s* of late Henry Macpherson, Headingley Hall, Leeds; *m* 1937, Peggy Josephine Wilton; two *s* one *d*. *Educ:* Sedbergh Sch.; Pembroke Coll., Cambridge. BA Cambridge, 1923. Priest, 1932; Curate of Richmond, Yorks, 1932-37; Minor Canon, Ripon Cathedral, 1937-39; Chaplain RNVR, 1939-45; Archdeacon of Richmond, 1951-54, Rector of Richmond, 1945-54. Proctor in Convocation, 1949. *Address:* Yew Tree Cottage, Hawkchurch, Axminster, Devon. *T:* Hawkchurch 485.

MACPHERSON-GRANT, Sir Ewan (George), 6th Bt, *cr* 1838; TD; DL; Member Scottish Faculty of Advocates; Hon. Sheriff Substitute, Counties of Perth and Angus; *b* 29 Sept. 1907; *s* of late George Bertram Macpherson-Grant, OBE (2nd *s* of 3rd Bt) and of Dorothy Eleanor Kellie-MacCallum (*d* 1952); *S* cousin, 1951; *m* 1937, Evelyn Nancy Stopford, *yr d* of late Major Edward Spencer Dickin, Spenford House, Loppington, Salop; one *d. Educ:* Winchester; Christ Church, Oxford. DL, Co. Banff, 1952. Mem. of Royal Company of Archers. *Heir:* none. *Address:* Ballindalloch Castle, Ballindalloch, Banffshire. *T:* Ballindalloch 206; Craigo, by Montrose, Angus. *T:* Hillside 205. *Club:* Army and Navy.

McQUAIL, Paul Christopher; Under Secretary, Department of the Environment, since 1977; *b* 22 April 1934; *s* of Christopher McQuail and Anne (*née* Mullan); *m* 1964, Susan Adler; one *s* one *d. Educ:* St Anselm's, Birkenhead; Sidney Sussex Coll., Cambridge. Min. of Housing and Local Govt, 1957; Principal, 1962; Asst Sec., 1969; DoE, 1970; Special Asst to Permanent Sec. and Sec. of State, 1972-73; Sec., Royal Commn on the Press, 1974-77. *Address:* 158 Peckham Rye, SE22. *T:* 01-693 2865.

MACQUARRIE, Rev. Prof. John, TD 1962; Lady Margaret Professor of Divinity, University of Oxford, and Canon of Christ Church, since 1970; *b* 27 June, 1919; *s* of John Macquarrie and Robina Macquarrie (*née* McInnes); *m* 1949, Jenny Fallow (*née* Welsh); two *s* one *d. Educ:* Paisley Grammar Sch.; Univ. of Glasgow. MA 1940; BD 1943; PhD 1954; DLitt 1964. Royal Army Chaplains Dept, 1945-48; St Ninian's Church, Brechin, 1948-53; Lecturer, Univ. of Glasgow, 1953-62; Prof. of Systematic Theology, Union Theological Seminary, NY, 1962-70, and Chm., Theological Field, 1968-70. Mem., Church Unity Commn, 1974-. Dir, SCM Press, 1970-. Consultant, Lambeth Conf., 1968 and 1978. Governor: St Stephen's Hse, Oxford, 1970-; Pusey House, Oxford, 1975-. Hon. degrees: STD: Univ. of the South, USA, 1967; General Theological Seminary, New York, 1968; DD, Univ. of Glasgow, 1969. *Publications:* An Existentialist Theology, 1955; The Scope of Demythologising, 1960; Twentieth Century Religious Thought, 1963; Studies in Christian Existentialism, 1965; Principles of Christian Theology, 1966; God-Talk, 1967; God and Secularity, 1967; Martin Heidegger, 1968; Three Issues in Ethics, 1970; Existentialism, 1972; Paths in Spirituality, 1972; The Faith of the People of God, 1972; The Concept of Peace, 1973; Thinking about God, 1975; Christian Unity and Christian Diversity, 1975. *Recreation:* numismatics. *Address:* Christ Church, Oxford OX1 1DP. *T:* Oxford 43588.

MACQUEEN, Angus, CMG 1977; Chairman, The British Bank of the Middle East, since 1975 (Director, 1970); Member, London Advisory Committee, The Hongkong and Shanghai Banking Corporation, since 1975; Chairman, Incotes Ltd, since 1975; *b* 7 April 1910; *s* of Donald Macqueen and Catherine Thomson; *m* 1st, 1940, Erica A. L. Sutherland (marr. diss.); one *d*; 2nd, 1950, Elizabeth Mary Barber; one *s* one *d. Educ:* Campbeltown Grammar Sch. Joined Union Bank of Scotland, 1927; Imperial Bank of Persia (now The British Bank of the Middle East), 1930; overseas service in Iraq, Iran, Kuwait, Aden, Lebanon, Morocco; Gen. Manager, 1965-70. Director: The British Bank of the Middle East (Morocco), 1961-70; The Bank of Iran and the Middle East, 1965-74; Bank of North Africa, 1965-70. Member: London Chamber of Commerce (Middle East Section), 1962-66; Council, Anglo-Arab Assoc., 1968-75; Corona (Overseas Students) Housing Assoc., 1969-. AIB (Scot.). National Cedar Medal, Lebanon, 1960. *Recreations:* golf, walking, foreign travel. *Address:* 18 Montagu Square, W1H 1RD. *T:* 01-935 9015. *Clubs:* Oriental, Roehampton.

MacQUEEN, Prof. John; Professor of Scottish Literature and Oral Tradition, since 1972, and Director, School of Scottish Studies, since 1969, University of Edinburgh; *b* 13 Feb. 1929; *s* of William L. and Grace P. MacQueen; *m* 1953, Winifred W. McWalter; three *s. Educ:* Glasgow Univ.; Cambridge Univ. MA English Lang. and Lit., Greek, Glasgow; BA, MA Archaeology and Anthropology, Section B, Cambridge. RAF, 1954-56 (Flying Officer). Asst Prof. of English, Washington Univ. MA Missouri, 1956-59; Lectr in Medieval English and Scottish Literature, 1959-63, Masson Prof. of Medieval and Renaissance Literature, 1963-72, Univ. of Edinburgh. Barclay Acheson Vis. Prof. of Internat. Relations, Macalester Coll., Minnesota, 1967; Vis. Prof. in Medieval Studies, Australian Nat. Univ., 1971. *Publications:* St Nynia, 1961; (with T. Scott) The Oxford Book of Scottish Verse, 1966; Robert Henryson, 1967; Ballattis of Luve, 1970; Allegory, 1970; (ed with Winifred MacQueen) A Choice of Scottish Verse, 1470-1570, 1972; articles and reviews in learned jls. *Recreations:* music, walking, golf, archaeology. *Address:* 9 Learmonth Gardens, Edinburgh EH4 1HD. *T:* 031-

332 1488; Slewdonan, Damnaglaur, Drummore, Stranraer DG9 9QN. *Club:* University Staff (Edinburgh).

MacQUEEN, Maj.-Gen. John Henry, CBE 1943; CD; retired; *b* Canada, 19 Sept. 1893; *s* of John T. and Emma Olding MacQueen; *m* 1917, Aimee Olive Miller Roy; no *c. Educ:* New Glasgow High Sch.; Royal Military College of Canada; Military Coll. of Science, England. Commissioned RCOC 1914; European War, 1914-19, Canada and England; District Ordnance Officer, Military District No. 10, Winnipeg, Manitoba, 1929-38; Dir of Ordnance Services, Canada, 1938-39; Senior Ordnance Officer, 1939, and Asst Quartermaster-Gen. (Ordnance Services), 1940, Dep. Quartermaster Gen., Canadian Military Headquarters, London, England, 1941-45; Master Gen. of the Ordnance, 1945. Pres. Canadian Arsenals Ltd, 1947-61. Served War of 1939-45, Canada, England, France, Italy. Legion of Merit, USA, 1948. Coronation Medal, 1937. *Recreations:* shooting, fishing, golf, bridge. *Address:* 33 Loch Isle Road, Ottawa, Ont K2H 8G5, Canada. *Clubs:* Rideau (Ottawa); Royal Ottawa Golf (Hull, PQ).

McQUIGGAN, John, MBE 1955; Director, United Kingdom-South Africa Trade Association, since 1978; retired at own request from HM Diplomatic Service; *b* 24 Nov. 1922; *s* of John and Sarah Elizabeth McQuiggan; *m* 1950, Doris Elsie Hadler; three *s* one *d. Educ:* St Edwards Coll., Liverpool. Served War, in RAF, 1942-47 (W Africa, Europe and Malta). Joined Dominions Office, 1940; Administration Officer, British High Commission, Canberra, Australia, 1950-54; Second Sec., Pakistan, Lahore and Dacca, 1954-57; First Sec. (Inf.), Lahore, 1957-58; Dep. Dir, UK Inf. Services, Australia (Canberra and Sydney), 1958-61; Dir, Brit. Inf. Services, Eastern Nigeria (Enugu), 1961-64; Dir, Brit. Inf. Services in Uganda, and concurrently First Sec., HM Embassy, Kigali, Rwanda, 1964-69; W African Dept, FCO, 1969-73; HM Consul, Chad, 1970-73 (London based); Dep. High Comr and Counsellor (Econ. and Commercial), Lusaka, Zambia, 1973-76. MIPR 1964; Mem., Internat. Public Relations Assoc., 1975. *Recreations:* tennis, carpentry, craftwork. *Address:* 7 Meadowcroft, Bickley, Kent BR1 2JD. *T:* 01-467 0075; 21 Tothill Street, SW1. *T:* 01-930 6711. *Club:* Royal Commonwealth Society.

MacQUITTY, James Lloyd, QC (N Ire.) 1960; Underwriting Member of Lloyds; Chairman, Ulster Television Ltd, since 1977; *b* 2 Nov. 1912; *s* of James MacQuitty and Henrietta Jane (*née* Little); *m* 1941, Irene Frances McDowell. *Educ:* Campbell Coll. and Methodist Coll., Belfast; St Catherine's Coll., Oxford (MA); Trinity Hall, Cambridge (MA, LLB). Vice-Pres., Cambridge Univ. Conservative Assoc., 1936. Called to English Bar, 1938, to NI Bar, 1941. Chairman: Compensation Appeals Tribunal; Compensation Tribunal for Loss of Employment through Civil Unrest; Transferred Officers' Tribunal; NI Housing Exec. Appeals Bd, and eight Wages Councils in NI; Arbitrator under the Industrial Courts Act 1919; Mem., Industrial Injuries Adv. Council. Before reorganisation in 1973 of Local Govt in NI, was Chm. of former Jt Adv. Bds for Local Authorities' Services, Municipal Clerks, Rural Dist Clerks and County Chief Educn Officers and County Surveyors. Vice-Chm., Management Cttee, Glenlola Collegiate Sch., 1964-75; Chm., Trustees of Ulster Folk and Transport Museum, 1976 (Vice-Chm., 1969-76). Chevalier de l'Ordre de St Lazare, 1962. *Recreations:* swimming, sailing. *Address:* 10 Braemar Park, Bangor, Co. Down, Northern Ireland. *T:* Bangor 4420. *Clubs:* Junior Carlton; Royal Ulster Yacht, Royal Belfast Golf.

MACRAE, Christopher, CBE 1956; MA, DPhil; Vice-President, Ashridge Management College, since 1969 (Principal, 1962-69); *b* 6 Jan. 1910; *s* of John Tait Macrae and Mary (*née* Mackenzie), Kintail, Ross-shire; *m* 1939, Mary Margaret Campbell Greig, *er d* of Robert Elliott, Glasgow; two *s* one *d* (*er d* decd in infancy). *Educ:* Dingwall Acad.; Glasgow Univ. (MA); New Coll., Oxford (DPhil). Civil Servant, 1937-46; Chief Exec. Scottish Counc. (Devel. and Industry), 1946-56; Prof. of Industrial Admin., The Royal Coll. of Science and Technology, Glasgow, and Head of Chesters Residential Management Educn Centre, 1956-62. *Publications:* various articles and papers. *Recreations:* reading, music, walking, climbing, sailing. *Address:* Cluain, Tomnacroich, by Aberfeldy, Perthshire PH15 2LJ. *T:* Kenmore 298.

MacRAE, Prof. Donald Gunn; Professor of Sociology, in the University of London, at the London School of Economics and Political Science, since 1961; *b* 20 April 1921; *o s* of Donald MacRae and Elizabeth Maud Gunn; *m* 1948, Helen Grace McHardy; two *d. Educ:* various schools in Scotland; Glasgow High Sch.; Glasgow Univ.; Balliol Coll., Oxford. MA Glasgow 1942; BA 1945, MA 1949, Oxon. Asst Lectr, LSE, 1945; Univ. Lectr in Sociology, Oxford, 1949; Reader in Sociology, London

Univ., 1954; Prof. of Sociology: UC Gold Coast, 1956; Univ. of California, Berkeley, 1959; Fellow, Center for Advanced Studies in Behavioral Sciences, Stanford, 1967. Vis. Prof., Univ. of the Witwatersrand, 1975. Member: Council, CNAA (Chm. Cttee for Arts and Social Studies); Archbp of Canterbury's Gp on Divorce Law, 1964-66; Gaitskell Commn of Inquiry into Advertising, 1962-66; Internat. Council on the Future of the University, 1973-. *Publications:* Ideology and Society, 1960; Ages and Stages, 1973; Max Weber, 1974; Editor, British Jl of Sociology, until 1965 (from formation). *Recreations:* talking, music, walking. *Address:* 17 Fitzwarren Gardens, N19. *T:* 01-272 4976. *Club:* Athenæum.

MACRAE, **John Esmond Campbell**, DPhil; HM Diplomatic Service, Counsellor (Science and Technology), British Embassy, Paris, since 1975; *b* 8 Dec. 1932; *s* of Col Archibald Campbell Macrae, IMS, and Euretta Margaret Skelton; *m* 1962, Anne Catherine Sarah Strain; four *s*. *Educ:* Sheikh Bagh Sch., Kashmir; Fettes Coll., Edinburgh; Christ Church Oxford (Open Scholar); Princeton, USA. DPhil, MA. Atomic Energy and Disarmament Dept, Foreign Office, 1959-60; 2nd Sec., British Embassy, Tel Aviv, 1961-64; 1st Secretary: Djakarta, 1964; Vientiane, 1964-66; FO, NE African Dept, 1966; Central Dept, 1967-69; Southern African Dept, 1970-72; UK Mission to the UN, New York (dealing with social affairs, population and outer space), 1972-75. *Recreations:* swimming, travel, music. *Address:* c/o Foreign and Commonwealth Office, SW1; 11 rue Stanislas, 75006 Paris. *Club:* United Oxford & Cambridge University.

MACRAE, **Col Robert Andrew Alexander Scarth**, MBE 1953; JP; Lord-Lieutenant of Orkney, since 1972 (Vice-Lieutenant, 1967-72); Farmer; *b* 14 April 1915; *s* of late Robert Scarth Farquhar Macrae, Grindelay House, Orphir, Orkney; *m* 1945, Violet Maud, *d* of late Walter Scott MacLellan; two *s*. *Educ:* Lancing; RMC Sandhurst. 2nd Lt Seaforth Highlanders, 1935; Captain 1939; Major 1948; Lt-Col 1958; Col 1963; retd 1968. Active Service: NW Europe, 1940-45 (despatches, 1945); Korea, 1952-53; E Africa, 1953-54. Hon. Sheriff-Substitute, Orkney, 1974. DL, Co. of Orkney, 1946; JP Orkney, 1975. *Recreations:* sailing, fishing. *Address:* Grindelay House, Orkney. *T:* Orphir 228. *Clubs:* Army and Navy; New, Puffin's (Edinburgh).

MACREADY, **Sir Nevil (John Wilfrid)**, 3rd Bt *cr* 1923; Managing Director, Mobil Oil, since 1975; *b* 7 Sept. 1921; *s* of Lt-Gen. Sir Gordon (Nevil) Macready, 2nd Bt, KBE, CB, CMG, DSO, MC, and Elisabeth (*d* 1969), *d* of Duc de Noailles; *S* father 1956; *m* 1949, Mary, *d* of late Sir Donald Fergusson, GCB; one *s* three *d*. *Educ:* Cheltenham; St John's Coll., Oxford. Served in RA (Field), 1942-47 (despatches); Staff Captain, 1945. BBC European Service, 1947-50. Vice-Pres. and Gen. Manager, Mobil Oil Française, 1972-75. *Recreations:* racing, fishing, theatre. *Heir: s* Charles Nevil Macready, *b* 19 May 1955. *Address:* Langley House, Pirbright, Surrey. *T:* Brookwood 2172. *Clubs:* Boodle's, Naval and Military; Jockey (Paris).

MacRITCHIE, **Prof. Farquhar**, CBE 1968; MA, LLB (Aberdeen); Professor of Conveyancing at Aberdeen University, 1946-74; *b* 1 Nov. 1902; *s* of Donald MacRitchie, Isle of Lewis; *m* 1941, Isobel, *d* of William Ross, Aberdeen; one *s*. *Educ:* Aberdeen Univ. Asst Lecturer in Law, Aberdeen Univ., 1940-45; Lecturer in Mercantile Law, Aberdeen Univ., 1945-46. Hon. Sheriff Substitute in Aberdeen. Convener, Legal Education Cttee, Law Soc. of Scotland, 1955-70; Vice-Pres., Law Soc. of Scotland, 1963. Mem. of firm of Morice & Wilson, Advocates, Aberdeen. Hon. LLD Edinburgh, 1965. *Recreation:* golf. *Address:* 60 Rubislaw Den North, Aberdeen. *T:* 35458. *Club:* University (Aberdeen).

McROBERT, **Brig. Leslie Harrison**, CBE 1943 (OBE 1937); TD 1937; DL; Chartered Accountant; Executive Director, 1945-64, Deputy Chairman, 1951-61, Chairman, 1961-64, Cerebos Ltd and associated cos; Member, North Eastern Railway Board, 1956-64; Member, Local Employment Act, 1960, etc, Advisory Committee, Ministry of Technology (formerly Treasury, later Board of Trade), 1945-70; *b* 22 Aug. 1898; *s* of late James William McRobert, Hartlepool; *m* 1st, 1929, May (*d* 1962), *d* of late W. G. Smith, Alston, Cumberland; two *d*; 2nd, 1963, Dorothy, *widow* of Lt-Col F. Ruddy, MC, DCM. *Educ:* Royal Gram. Sch., Newcastle upon Tyne. European War 1914-18, France and Belgium, RFC and RAF; commanded 55th (Northumbrian) Medium Bde RA and 63rd (Northumbrian) HAA Regt RA and 30, 59 and 28 AA Brigades during 1939-45 War. Chm. TA & AF Assoc., Co. of Durham, 1958-63. Chm. Hartlepools Hosp. Management Cttee, 1950-58; Chm., Friends of the Penrith Hosps, 1971-74. Hon. Colonel: 377 Corps Locating Regt RA (TA), 1955-56; 274 N Field Regt RA (TA), 1956-60; Durham Univ. (now Northumbrian Univs) OTC, 1960-68. DL Durham, 1941; Vice-Lieutenant, 1959-69; High

Sheriff of Co. Durham, 1954-55. *Recreations:* fishing, etc. *Address:* 14 Glyn Garth Court, Glyn Garth, Anglesey, Gwynedd LL59 5BP.

McROBERT, **Rosemary Dawn Teresa**; Director, Retail Trading-Standards Association, since 1974; *b* Maymyo, Burma, 29 Aug. 1927; *e d* of late Lt-Col Ronald McRobert, IMS, and Julie Rees. *Educ:* privately and at Gloucestershire College of Educn. Journalist and broadcaster on consumer subjects, 1957-63; Founder editor, Home Economics, 1954-63; Chief Information Officer, Consumer Council, 1965-70; Consumer Representation Officer, Consumers' Assoc., 1971-73; Adviser on consumer affairs in DTI and Dept of Prices and Consumer Protection, 1973-74. Member Council: Inst. of Consumer Ergonomics, 1974-; Consumers' Assoc., 1974-; Member: Adv. Council on Energy Conservation, 1974-; Design Council, 1975-; Post Office Review Cttee, 1976-; Policyholders' Protection Bd, 1976-. *Recreations:* reading, music, photography, wine, odd jobs in the house. *Address:* 57 Lawford Road, NW5 2LG.

MACRORY, **Sir Patrick (Arthur)**, Kt 1972; Director: Bank of Ireland Group since 1971; Rothman Carreras Ltd since 1971; Barrister-at-Law; *b* 21 March 1911; *s* of late Lt-Col F. S. N. Macrory, DSO, DL, and Rosie, *d* of Gen. Brabazon Pottinger; *m* 1939, Elisabeth, *d* of late Rev. J. F. O. Lewis and of Mrs Lewis; three *s* (one *d* decd). *Educ:* Cheltenham Coll.; Trinity Coll., Oxford (MA). Called to the Bar, Middle Temple, 1937. Served War, 1939-45, Army. Unilever Ltd: joined 1947; Secretary, 1956; Director, 1968-71, retd. Mem., Northern Ireland Development Council, 1956-64; Gen. Treasurer, British Assoc. for Advancement of Science, 1960-65; Chairman: Review Body on Local Govt in N Ireland, 1970; Confedn of Ulster Socs, 1974-; Member: Commn of Inquiry into Industrial Representation, 1971-72; Cttee on the Preparation of Legislation, 1973. Mem. Council, Cheltenham Coll. *Publications:* Borderline, 1937; Signal Catastrophe—the retreat from Kabul, 1842, 1966; Lady Sale's Journal, 1969. *Recreations:* golf, military history. *Address:* Amberdene, Walton-on-the-Hill, Tadworth, Surrey. *T:* Tadworth 3086; Ardmore Lodge, Limavady, Co. Londonderry, N Ireland. *T:* Limavady 2666. *Clubs:* Athenæum, Army and Navy; Walton Heath Golf; Castlerock Golf (Co Londonderry).

McSHINE, **Hon. Sir Arthur Hugh**, TC; Kt 1969; Chief Justice of Trinidad and Tobago, 1968-71; Acting Governor-General, Trinidad and Tobago, 1972; *b* 11 May 1906; *m* Dorothy Mary Vanier; one *s* one *d*. *Educ:* Queen's Royal Coll., Trinidad. Called to Bar, Middle Temple, 1931. Practised at Trinidad Bar for eleven years; Magistrate, 1942; Senior Magistrate, 1950; Puisne Judge, 1953; Justice of Appeal, 1962. Acting Governor-Gen., Trinidad and Tobago, 1970. *Recreations:* music and chess (Pres., Caribbean Chess Fedn and Trinidad Chess Assoc.); flying (holder of private pilot's licence). *Address:* 6 River Road, Maraval, Port-of-Spain, Trinidad. *Clubs:* Trinidad and Tobago Turf, Trinidad and Tobago Yacht.

MacTAGGART, **Sir Andrew (McCormick)**, Kt 1951; Civil Engineer; Company Director, 1928-66; *b* 13 July 1888; *s* of Matthew MacTaggart, Waterside House, Fenwick, Ayrshire; *m* 1st, 1919, Marie Louise (marr. diss. 1961), *d* of Gaston Petit, France; 2nd, 1961, Irene Countess of Craven. *Educ:* Kilmarnock; Glasgow. Completed a 4-year pupilage with Warren & Stewart, Glasgow, 1904-8; Asst Engineer on Nigerian Railways, 1912-16, promoted to permanent staff, resigned, 1916. Served European War, 1914-18, joined Royal Engineers with commission in France, 1917. Rejoined Balfour, Beatty & Co. Ltd in 1919. Responsible for the design and construction of Grampian Company's hydro-electric development in Scotland; in charge of construction of Lochaber Hydro-Electric Scheme in Scotland; responsible for construction of hydro-electric developments in Italy, India, and E Africa, and construction of large irrigation and railway works in Iraq. Pres., Power Securities Corp.; Pres. Fedn of Civil Engineering Contractors, 1948-49, 1949-50, 1950-51; Mem. of Council, British Employers' Confederation, 1940-62. *Recreations:* shooting and fishing. *Address:* Clatfields, Marsh Green, Edenbridge, Kent. *T:* Edenbridge 2819. *Club:* Caledonian.

MACTAGGART, **Sir Ian (Auld)**, 3rd Bt *cr* 1938; Managing Director The Western Heritable Investment Company and Director of several Property and other Companies; *b* Glasgow, 19 April 1923; *e s* of Sir John (Jack) Mactaggart, 2nd Bt, Nassau, Bahamas; *S* father 1960; *m* 1946, Rosemary (marr. diss. 1969), *d* of Sir Herbert Williams, 1st Bt, MP; two *s* two *d*. *Educ:* Oundle; Clare Coll., Cambridge. Served with Royal Engineers in India, 1942-45. Contested (U) Gorbals div. of Glasgow, 1945; contested (C) Fulham, 1970. Mem. (C) London County Council, for Fulham, 1949-51. Chm., Soc. for Individual Freedom. *Heir:*

s John Auld Mactaggart [*b* 21 Jan. 1951; *m* 1977, Patricia, *y d* of late Major Harry Alstair Gordon]. *Address:* 2A Westmoreland Terrace, SW1. *T:* 01-834 8062. *Clubs:* English-Speaking Union; Royal Thames Yacht.

MacTAGGART, Sir William, Kt 1962; PPRSA; RA 1973 (ARA 1968); FRSE 1967; RSA 1948 (ARSA 1937); President, Royal Scottish Academy, 1959-69; *b* Loanhead, 15 May 1903; *er s* of late Hugh Holmes MacTaggart, Engineer and Managing Dir of MacTaggart, Scott & Co. Ltd, Loanhead, and *g s* of late William McTaggart, RSA; *m* 1937, Fanny Margaretha Basilier, Kt 1st Cl. Order of St Olav, Norway, *er d* of late Gen. Ivar Aavatsmark, Oslo, Norway. *Educ:* privately; Edinburgh Coll. of Art; abroad. Elected professional mem. Soc. of Scottish Artists, 1922 (Pres., 1934-36); Mem. Soc. of Eight. Has held one-man exhibitions at home and abroad. Works purchased by Tate Gallery, Contemporary Art Soc. and the Arts Council; also represented in public galleries in Glasgow, Edinburgh, Aberdeen and Bradford, and in USA and Australia. Hon. RA 1959; Hon. RSW; Hon. FRIAS 1968. Hon. Burgess of Loanhead, 1965. Hon. LLD Edinburgh, 1961. Chevalier de la Légion d'Honneur, 1968. *Relevant publication:* Sir William MacTaggart, by H. Harvey Wood, 1974. *Address:* 4 Drummond Place, Edinburgh. *T:* 031-556 1657. *Club:* Scottish Arts (Edinburgh).

MACTAGGART, William Alexander, CBE 1964; JP; Chairman, 1960-70, and Managing Director, 1945-68, Pringle of Scotland Ltd, Knitwear Manufacturers, Hawick; *b* 17 Aug. 1906; *o s* of late William Alexander and Margaret Mactaggart, Woodgate, Hawick; *m* 1932, Marjorie Laing Innes; two *s* one *d. Educ:* Sedbergh Sch., Yorks. Joined Robert Pringle & Son Ltd (later Pringle of Scotland Ltd), 1925; Dir, 1932; Joint Managing Dir, 1933. Served War of 1939-45: Captain, RASC, Holland, Belgium, France, 1942-45. Elder of Lilliesleaf Parish Church. Pres. of Vertish Hill Sports; Chairman: Duke of Buccleuch's Hunt; Hawick Youth Centre. *Recreation:* hunting. *Address:* Bewlie House, Lilliesleaf, Melrose, Roxburghshire. *T:* Lilliesleaf 267.

MacTHOMAS OF FINEGAND, Andrew Patrick Clayhills; 19th Chief of Clan MacThomas (Mac Thomaidh Mhor); *b* 28 Aug. 1942; *o s* of late Captain Patrick Watt MacThomas of Finegand and of Elizabeth, *d* of late Becket Clayhills-Henderson, Invergowrie, Angus; *S* father 1970. *Educ:* St Edward's, Oxford. Manager, Barclaycard, Scotland, 1973-. FSA (Scot.) 1973. Pres., Clan MacThomas Soc., 1970-; Hon. Vice-Pres., Clan Chattan Assoc., 1970-. *Heir: sister* Elizabeth Gillian MacThomas, *b* 15 Feb. 1949. *Address:* 22 India Street, Edinburgh EH3 6HB. *T:* 031-225 3962. *Clubs:* New, Puffin's (Edinburgh).

MacTIER, Sir (Reginald) Stewart, Kt 1961; CBE 1946; Director: The Ocean Steam Ship Co. Ltd, 1955-67; Glen Line Ltd, London, 1939-67; *b* 9 Dec. 1905; *s* of late Major H. C. MacTier, Newton St Loe, Somerset, and of Mary Fitzroy MacTier, *d* of Sir Charles Hobhouse, 3rd Bt; *m* 1941, Mary, *d* of Brig. C. G. Ling, CB, DSO, MC; two *s* one *d. Educ:* Eton; Magdalene Coll., Cambridge. Mansfield & Co. Ltd, Singapore, Shipping Agents, 1928-37; Dep. Dir and subseq. Dir of Port and Transit Control, Min. of War Transport, 1940-45. Chm. Liverpool Steam Ship Owners' Assoc. and Gen. Council of British Shipping, 1960-61; Pres., Inst. Marine Engineers, 1966-67. Comdr Order of Maritime Merit (French); Medal of Victory with silver palm (US). *Address:* Scotnish, Tayvallich, Lochgilphead, Argyll PA31 8PR. *T:* Tayvallich 284.

McTIERNAN, Rt. Hon. Sir Edward (Aloysius), PC 1963; KBE 1951; Justice of the High Court of Australia, 1930-76; *b* 16 Feb. 1892; *s* of Patrick and Isabella McTiernan; *m* 1948, Kathleen, *d* of Sidney and Ann Lloyd, Melbourne. *Educ:* Marist Brothers' High Sch., Sydney; Sydney Univ. (BA, LLB, 1st cl. Hons). Admitted to Bar, NSW, 1917; Lecturer in Law, Sydney Univ.; NSW Parliament, 1920-27; Attorney-Gen., 1920-22 and 1925-27; NSW Govt Representative in London, 1926; MHR for Parkes, Commonwealth Parl., 1928, Papal Chamberlain, 1927. *Address:* 36 Chilton Parade, Warrawee, Sydney, NSW 2074, Australia. *Club:* Australian (Sydney).

MacVICAR, Rev. Kenneth, MBE (mil.) 1968; DFC 1944; Chaplain in ordinary to the Queen in Scotland, since 1974; Minister of Kenmore and Lawers, Perthshire, since 1950; *b* 25 Aug. 1921; *s* of Rev. Angus John MacVicar, Southend, Kintyre; *m* 1946, Isobel Guild McKay; three *s* one *d. Educ:* Campbeltown Grammar Sch.; Edinburgh Univ.; St Andrews Univ. (MA); St Mary's Coll., St Andrews. Mem., Edinburgh Univ. Air Squadron, 1941; joined RAF, 1941: Pilot, 28 Sqdn, RAF, 1942-45, Flt Comdr, 1944-45 (despatches, 1945). Chaplain, Scottish Horse and Fife and Forfar Yeomanry/Scottish Horse, TA, 1953-65. Convener, Church of Scotland Cttee on Chaplains to

HM Forces, 1968-73. Clerk to Presbytery of Dunkeld, 1955-. District Councillor, 1951-74. *Recreation:* golf. *Address:* Manse of Kenmore, Aberfeldy, Perthshire PH15 2HE. *T:* Kenmore 218. *Club:* Overseas (Edinburgh).

MACVICAR, Neil, QC (Scotland) 1960; MA, LLB; Sheriff of Lothian and Borders (formerly the Lothians and Peebles), at Edinburgh, since 1968; *b* 16 May 1920; *s* of late Neil Macvicar, WS; *m* 1949, Maria, *d* of Count Spiridon Bulgari, Corfu; one *s* two *d. Educ:* Loretto Sch.; Oriel Coll., Oxford; Edinburgh Univ. Served RA, 1940-45. Called to Scottish Bar, 1948. Chancellor, Dio. of Edinburgh, 1961-74. *Address:* 39 Dick Place, Edinburgh EH9 2JA. *T:* 031-667 4793. *Club:* New (Edinburgh).

McVITTIE, Maj.-Gen. Charles Harold, CB 1962; CBE 1953; *b* 6 Aug. 1908; *s* of Col R. H. McVittie, CB, CMG, CBE; *m* 1939, Margaret Wark, *d* of Dr T. Divine, Huddersfield; two *s. Educ:* Haileybury; Brighton Coll.; Sandhurst. 2nd Lt Queen's Own Royal West Kent Regt, 1928; transferred to RAOC, 1935; Served War of 1939-45, ADOS Singapore Fortress, 1941-42; POW, 1942-45; comd Vehicle Organization, 1948-50; DOS, GHQ Farelf, 1951-53; comd Technical Stores Organization, 1953-56; comd RAOC Trg Centre, 1956-60; Comdr Stores Organization, RAOC, 1960-63. Hon. Col AER Units RAOC, 1961-64. Col Commandant, RAOC, 1965-69. *Recreation:* fencing (Blue, Sandhurst, 1928). *Address:* Clovers, Garelochhead, Dunbartonshire. *T:* Garelochhead 810266.

McVITTIE, George Cunliffe, OBE 1946; MA Edinburgh, PhD Cantab; Professor of Astronomy, University of Illinois, 1952-72, Emeritus Professor, 1972; Hon. Professor of Theoretical Astronomy, University of Kent at Canterbury, since 1972; *b* 5 June 1904; *e s* of Frank S. McVittie; *m* 1934, Mildred Bond, *d* of Prof. John Strong, CBE; no *c. Educ:* Edinburgh Univ.; Christ's Coll., Cambridge. Asst Lecturer, Leeds Univ., 1930-34; Lecturer in Applied Mathematics, Liverpool Univ., 1934-36; Reader in Mathematics, King's Coll., London, 1936-48; Prof. of Mathematics, Queen Mary Coll., London, 1948-52. War service with Meteorological Office, Air Ministry, and a Dept of the Foreign Office, 1939-45. FRS (Edinburgh), 1943. Mem. Sub-Cttee of Meteorological Research Cttee, 1948-52. Jt Editor of The Observatory, 1938-48. Jt Exec. Editor of Quarterly Journal of Mechanics and Applied Mathematics, 1947-51; Pres., Commn on Galaxies, Internat. Astronomical Union, 1967-70; Sec., American Astronomical Soc., 1961-69. *Publications:* Cosmological Theory, 1937; General Relativity and Cosmology, 1956, 2nd edn, 1965; Fact and Theory in Cosmology, 1961; (ed) Problems of Extra-galactic Research, 1962; papers on Relativity and its astronomical applications, classical mechanics, etc., Proc. Royal Soc. and other journals. *Address:* 74 Old Dover Road, Canterbury, Kent. *Club:* Athenæum.

McVITTIE, Wilfrid Wolters, CMG 1958; *b* 24 May 1906; *s* of Francis McVittie and Emily McVittie (*née* Weber); *m* 1938, Harriett Morna Wilson, *d* of Dr G. Wilson, Toronto; one *s* two *d. Educ:* abroad; King's Coll., Univ. of London. Entered Japan Consular Service, 1930; Consul at Yokohama, 1938; 1st Sec. (Commercial), Buenos Aires, 1946; Counsellor (Commercial), British Embassy, Mexico City, 1948; Counsellor (Commercial) and Consul-Gen., British Embassy, Lisbon, 1952; HM Ambassador to the Dominican Republic, 1958-62. Comendador, Military Order of Christ (Portugal), 1957. *Recreations:* travel, shooting. *Address:* White House, Itchenor, Sussex.

McWATTERS, George Edward; Chairman, Ward White Group Ltd (Chairman of its predecessor, John White Footwear Holdings Ltd, from 1967); Vice-Chairman (Harlech Television), HTV Ltd, since 1970; Local Advisory Director (Peterborough), Barclays Bank Ltd, since 1970; Local Director (Northampton), Commercial Union Assurance Co. Ltd, since 1969; *b* India, 17 March 1922; *s* of Lt-Col George Alfred McWatters and Ellen Mary Christina McWatters (*née* Harvey); *m* 1st, 1946, Margery Robertson (*d* 1959); 2nd, 1960, Joyce Anne Matthews; one *s. Educ:* Clifton Coll., Bristol. Vintners' Scholar, 1947. Served War of 1939-45: enlisted ranks Royal Scots, 1940; commissioned 14th Punjab Regt, Indian Army, 1941-46. John Harvey & Sons (family wine co.): joined, 1947; Dir, 1951; Chm., 1956-66. Estab. a holding co. (Harveys of Bristol Ltd), 1962, but Showerings took over, 1966, and he remained Chm. until resignation, Aug. 1966. Dir, Martins Bank, 1960-70. Mem., CBI Grand Council, 1970-. Governor: Clifton Coll., 1958-; Kimbolton Sch., 1970-. City Councillor, Bristol, 1950-53; contested (C) Bristol South, elecs 1955 and 1959. JP, Bristol, 1960-67; JP, Marylebone, 1969-71. Mem. Cttee, Automobile Assoc., 1962. *Recreations:* tennis, swimming, walking. *Address:* The Cottage, Stonely, Huntingdon PE18 0EH. *T:* Kimbolton 206; 17 Chester Terrace, Regent's Park, NW1 4NG. *T:* 01-935 5305. *Club:* Buck's.

McWATTERS, Stephen John; Headmaster, The Pilgrims' School, since 1976; *b* 24 April 1921; *er s* of late Sir Arthur Cecil McWatters, CIE; *m* 1957, Mary Gillian, *o d* of late D. C. Wilkinson and Mrs G. A. Wilkinson; one *s* two *d. Educ:* Eton (Scholar); Trinity Coll., Oxford (Scholar, MA). 1st Cl. Class. Mods, 1941. Served in The King's Royal Rifle Corps, 1941-45. Distinction in Philosophy section of Litterae Humaniores, Oxford, 1946. Asst Master, Eton Coll., 1947-63 (Master in Coll., 1949-57, Housemaster, 1961-63); Headmaster, Clifton Coll., 1963-75. *Recreations:* music, bird-watching. *Address:* The Pilgrims' School, Winchester SO23 9LT. *T:* Winchester 4189.

McWEENY, Prof. Roy; Professor of Theoretical Chemistry, University of Sheffield, since 1966; *b* 19 May 1924; *o s* of late Maurice and Vera McWeeny; *m* 1947, Patricia M. Healey; one *s* one *d. Educ:* Univ. of Leeds; University Coll., Oxford. BSc (Physics) Leeds 1945; DPhil Oxon. 1949. Lectr in Physical Chemistry, King's Coll., Univ. of Durham, 1948-57; Vis. Scientist, Physics Dept, MIT, USA, 1953-54; Lectr in Theoretical Chemistry, Univ. Coll. of N Staffs, 1957-62; Associate Dir, Quantum Chemistry Gp, Uppsala Univ., Sweden, 1960-61; Reader in Quantum Theory, Univ. of Keele, 1962-64; Prof. of Theoretical Chemistry, 1964-66. Vis. Prof., America, Japan, Europe. *Publications:* Symmetry, an Introduction to Group Theory and its Applications, 1963; (with B. T. Sutcliffe) Methods of Molecular Quantum Mechanics, 1969; Spins in Chemistry, 1970; Quantum Mechanics: principles and formalism, 1972; Quantum Mechanics: methods and basic applications, 1973; contrib. sections in other books and encyclopædias; many research papers on quantum theory of atomic and molecular structure in Proc. Royal Soc., Proc. Phys. Soc., Phys. Rev., Revs. Mod. Phys., Jl Chem. Phys., etc. *Recreations:* drawing, sculpture, travel. *Address:* 12 Eden Court, Clarkehouse Road, Sheffield S10 2LG.

McWHINNIE, Donald; Freelance Director, Stage and Television, since 1960; *b* 16 Oct. 1920; *s* of Herbert McWhinnie and Margaret Elizabeth (*née* Holland). *Educ:* Rotherham Gram. Sch.; Gonville and Caius Coll., Cambridge. MA Cantab 1941. Served War of 1939-45: RAF, 1941-46. Joined BBC, 1947; Asst Head of Drama (Sound), 1953-60, resigned. Theatrical productions include: Krapp's Last Tape, Royal Court, 1958; The Caretaker, Arts and Duchess, 1960, Lyceum, NY, 1961; The Duchess of Malfi, Aldwych, 1960; Three, Arts and Criterion, 1961; The Tenth Man, Comedy, 1961; A Passage to India, Ambassador, NY, 1962; Everything in the Garden, Arts and Duke of York's, 1962; Macbeth, Royal Shakespeare, 1962; Rattle of a Simple Man, Garrick, 1962, Booth, NY, 1963; Doctors of Philosophy, Arts, 1962; The Doctor's Dilemma, Haymarket, 1963; Alfie, Mermaid and Duchess, 1963; Out of the Crocodile, Phœnix, 1963; The Fourth of June, St Martin's, 1964; End Game, Aldwych, 1964; The Creeper, St Martin's, 1965; All in Good Time, Royale, NY, 1965; The Cavern, Strand, 1965; This Winter's Hobby, US Tour, 1966; The Astrakhan Coat, Helen Hayes, NY, 1967; Happy Family, St Martin's, 1967; Tinker's Curse, Nottingham Playhouse, 1968; Vacant Possession, Nottingham Playhouse, 1968; Hamlet, Covent Garden, 1969; No Quarter, Hampstead, 1969; There'll be Some Changes Made, Fortune, 1969; The Apple Cart, Mermaid, 1970; A Hearts and Minds Job, Hampstead, 1971; Meeting at Night, Duke of York's, 1971; Endgame, and Play and Other Plays, Royal Court, 1976; also numerous television productions for BBC and ITV. *Publication:* The Art of Radio, 1959. *Address:* 16 Chepstow Place, W2. *T:* 01-229 2120.

McWHIRTER, Norris Dewar; author, publisher, broadcaster; Director, Guinness Superlatives Ltd, since 1954 (Managing Director, 1954-76); *b* 12 Aug. 1925; *er (twin) s* of William Allan McWhirter, Managing Director of Associated Newspapers and Northcliffe Newspapers Group, and Margaret Williamson; *m* 1957, Carole, *d* of George H. Eckert; one *s* one *d. Educ:* Marlborough; Trinity Coll., Oxford. BA (Internat. Rel. and Econs), MA (Contract Law). Served RN, 1943-46: Sub-Lt RNVR, 2nd Escort Gp, Atlantic; minesweeping Pacific. Dir, McWhirter Twins Ltd, 1950; Chm., Wm McWhirter & Sons, 1955-; co-founder, Redwood Press (Chm., 1966-72); Dir, Gieves Ltd, 1972-. Editor and compiler, Guinness Book of Records, with late Ross McWhirter, 1955-75, 95 edns in 16 languages; 31 million sales. Athletics Correspondent: Observer, 1951-67; Star, 1951-60; BBC TV Commentator, Olympic Games, 1960-72; What's In the Picture, 1957; The Record Breakers, 1972-77. Mem., Sports Council, 1970-73. Mem. Council, Nat. Assoc. for Freedom. Contested (C) Orpington, 1964, 1966. *Publications:* Get To Your Marks, 1951; (ed 1952-56) Athletics World; Dunlop Book of Facts, 1964, 2nd edn, 1966; Guinness Book of Answers, 1976, 1978; Ross: story of a shared life, 1976. *Recreations:* ski-ing (water and snow), athletics (Oxford 100 yds, Scotland 1950-52, GB in Norway 1951); Rugby football (Mddx XV, 1950). *Address:* c/o 2 Cecil Court, London Road, Enfield EN2 6DJ. *T:* 01-366 4551. *Clubs:* Caledonian; Vincent's (Oxford); Achilles.

McWHIRTER, Prof. Robert, CBE 1963; FRCSEd; FRCPEd; FFR; FRSE; Professor of Medical Radiology, Edinburgh University, 1946-70; Director of Radiotherapy, Royal Infirmary, Edinburgh, 1935-70; President, Medical and Dental Defence Union of Scotland, since 1959; *b* 8 Nov. 1904; *s* of Robert McWhirter and Janet Ramsay Gairdner; *m* 1937, Dr Susan Muir MacMurray; one *s. Educ:* Girvan Academy; Glasgow and Cambridge Universities. MB, ChB (High Commendn), Glasgow, 1927; FRCS Edinburgh 1932; DMRE Cambridge, 1933; FFR 1939. Formerly: Student, Mayo Clinic; British Empire Cancer Campaign Research Student, Holt Radium Institute, Manchester; Chief Assistant, X-Ray Dept, St Bartholomew's Hospital, London. Member, British Institute of Radiology; Pres., Sect. of Radiology, RSM, 1956; Fellow Royal College of Radiologists (Twining Memorial Medal, 1943; Skinner Memorial Lecturer, 1956; Warden, 1961-66; Knox Memorial Lecturer, 1963; Pres. 1966-69); Past Pres., Internat. Radio Therapists Visiting Club; Hon. Member, American Radium Society; Membre Corresp. Etranger, Société Française d'Electro-Radiologie Médicale, 1967; Membro d'onore, Società Italiana della Radiologia Medica e Medicine Nucleare, 1968; Hon. Member: Sociedade Brasileira de Patologia Mamária, 1969; Nippon Societas Radiologica, 1970; Groupe Européen des Radiotherapeutes, 1971. Caldwell Memorial Lecturer, American Roentgen Ray Society, 1963; Hon. Fellow: Australasian College of Radiologists, 1954; American College of Radiology, 1965; Faculty of Radiologists, RCSI, 1967. *Publications:* contribs to medical journals. *Recreation:* golf. *Address:* 2 Orchard Brae, Edinburgh EH4 1NY. *T:* 031-332 5800. *Club:* University (Edinburgh).

McWIGGAN, Thomas Johnstone, CBE 1976; Director General Telecommunications, National Air Traffic Services, since 1969 (Civil Aviation Authority, since 1972); *b* 26 May 1918; *s* of late Thomas and of Esther McWiggan; *m* 1947, Eileen Joyce Moughton; two *d. Educ:* UC Nottingham. Pharmaceutical Chemist. FIEE, FRAeS, SMIEEE. Signals Officer (Radar), RAFVR, 1941-46. Civil Air Attaché (Telecommunications) Washington, 1962-65; Dir of Telecommunications (Plans), Min. of Aviation, 1965; Dir of Telecommunications (Air Traffic Services), BoT, 1967. *Publications:* various technical papers. *Recreations:* photography, cabinet-making, gardening. *Address:* The Squirrels, Liberty Lane, Addlestone, Weybridge, Surrey. *T:* Weybridge 43068. *Club:* St George's Hill Tennis.

McWILLIAM, Frederick Edward, CBE 1966; Sculptor; *b* 30 April 1909; *yr s* of Dr William Nicholson McWilliam, Banbridge, County Down, Ireland; *m* 1932, Elizabeth Marion Crowther; two *d. Educ:* Campbell Coll., Belfast; Slade School of Fine Art; Paris. Served War of 1939-45, RAF, UK and Far East. Member of Staff, Slade Sch. of Fine Art, London Univ., 1947-66. Mem. Art Panel, Arts Council, 1960-68. First one-man exhib., sculpture, London Gall., 1939; subsequently Hanover Gallery, 1949, 1952, 1956; Waddington Galleries, 1961, 1963, 1966, 1968, 1971, 1973, 1976; Felix Landau Gallery, Los Angeles; has exhibited in International Open-Air Exhibitions, London, Antwerp, Arnheim, Paris. Work included in British Council touring exhibitions USA, Canada, Germany, South America. Works acquired by: Tate Gallery; Victoria and Albert Museum; Museum Modern Art, New York; National Gallery, S Australia; Art Inst., Chicago; Open-Air Museum, Middleheim, Antwerp; Art Galls, Belfast, Leeds, Coventry, Oldham, New Zealand, Toronto, etc. Fellow, UCL, 1972. Hon. DLit Belfast, 1964. *Relevant Publication:* McWilliam, Sculptor, by Roland Penrose, 1964. *Address:* 8A Holland Villas Road, W14. *T:* 01-603 4859.

McWILLIAM, William Nicholson, CB 1960; *b* 26 Nov. 1897; *er s* of W. N. McWilliam, MD, Banbridge, Co. Down; *m* 1927, V. Maureen, *er d* of H. H. Mussen, Asst Chief Crown Solicitor; one *s* two *d. Educ:* Excelsior Academy, Banbridge; Campbell Coll., Belfast; Trinity Coll., Dublin. Served European War, 1916-18, Lieut, RGA, 1916-18. BA, BAI, 1921. Entered NI Civil Service, 1922; Asst Sec. to Cabinet, NI, 1945-57; Dep. Clerk of the Privy Council, NI, 1945-57; Permanent Sec., Min. of Labour and National Insurance, NI, 1957-62 (retired). Member Boundary Commn for NI, 1963-69. *Address:* Garryard, 34 Massey Avenue, Belfast BT4 2JT. *T:* Belfast 63179.

MADANG, Archbishop of, (RC), since 1976; Most Rev. Leo Arkfeld, CBE (Hon.) 1976; *b* 4 Feb. 1912; *s* of George Arkfeld and Mary Siemer. *Educ:* St Mary's Seminary, Techny, Ill., USA (BA). Bishop of Wewak, Papua New Guinea, 1948-76. *Address:* Box 750, Madang, Papua New Guinea. *T:* 82-2707.

MADARIAGA, Don Salvador de, MA; Honorary President, International Liberal Union and Congress for Freedom of Culture; Founder President, College of Europe (Bruges); Hon. Fellow of Exeter College, Oxford; Member: Spanish Academy of Letters and of Moral and Political Sciences; French Academy of Moral and Political Sciences; Academy of History of Caracas and many other Spanish-American Institutions of Learning; *b* Corunna, Spain, 23 July 1886; *s* of Don Jose de Madariaga, Colonel, Spanish Army, and Dona Ascension Rojo de Madariaga; *m* Constance Archibald, MA Hons (Glasgow) (*d* 1970); two *d*; *m* 1970, Emilia Szekely-Rauman (*b* Budapest). *Educ:* Institute del Cardenal Cisneros, Madrid; Collège Chaptal, Paris; Ecole Polytechnique, Paris; Ecole Nationale Supérieure des Mines, Paris. Technical Adviser to Superintendent of Line, Spanish Northern Railway, 1911-16; Journalist, Publicist and Literary Critic, London, 1916-21; Member of Press Section League of Nations Secretariat, Geneva, 1921-22; Director of Disarmament Section of League of Nations Secretariat, 1922-27; King Alphonso XIII Prof. of Spanish Studies, Oxford, 1928-31; Secretary of the Temporary Mixed Commission for Disarmament, then of the Preparatory Commission for a Disarmament Conference; Secretary of the Third (Disarmament) Commission of the Assembly of the League of Nations, 1922-27; Secretary General of the International Conference for the Supervision of the Trade in Arms, Geneva, April-May 1925; Spanish Ambassador to USA, 1931, to France, 1932-34; Spanish Permanent Delegate to the League of Nations, 1931-36; Visiting Prof. of Spanish, Princeton Univ., 1954. Hans Deutsch European Prize, 1963; Hanseatic Goethe Prize, 1967. MA by Decree of University of Oxford, 1928; Hon. Doctor Universities of Arequipa, Lima, Oxford, Poitiers, Princeton, Liége, Lille; Matricula d'Onore, University of Pavia, 1966. Charlemagne Prize, 1973. Knight Grand Cross of Orders of the Spanish Republic, Légion d'Honneur (France), Jade-in-Gold of China, White Lion of Tchecoslovakia, Aztec Eagle of Mexico, Boyacá of Colombia, Merit of Chile, Sun of Peru, Grand Cross of Order of Merit of Federal Republic of Germany, etc. *Publications:* apart from several publications in Spanish and French, has published: Shelley and Calderon and other Essays on Spanish and English Poetry, 1920; Spanish Folksongs, 1922; The Genius of Spain, 1923; The Sacred Giraffe, 1926; Englishmen, Frenchmen, Spaniards, 1928, 2nd edn 1970; Disarmament, 1929; Sir Bob, 1930; I, Americans, 1930; Don Quixote, 1934; Anarchy or Hierarchy, 1937; Theory and Practice in International Relations, 1938; The World's Design, 1938; Christopher Columbus, 1939; Hernán Cortés, 1941; Spain, 1942; The Heart of Jade, 1944, new edn 1956; Victors, Beware, 1946; The Rise of the Spanish American Empire, 1947; The Fall of the Spanish American Empire, 1947; On Hamlet, 1948; Bolivar, 1952; Portrait of Europe, 1952; Essays with a Purpose, 1953; A Bunch of Errors, 1953; War in the Blood, 1957; Democracy versus Liberty?, 1958; Latin-America between the Eagle and the Bear, 1962; Portrait of a Man Standing, 1967; Morning Without Noon (autobiog.), 1973; frequent contributions to the English, American, Spanish, and Spanish-American press. *Recreation:* a change of work. *Address:* La Palma, CH 6000, Locarno, Switzerland. *Clubs:* Reform (London); Ateneo (Madrid).
See also Prof. L. B. Schapiro.

MADDEN, (Albert) Frederick (McCulloch), DPhil; Reader in Commonwealth Government, Oxford, since 1957; Fellow (and Dean) of Nuffield College since 1958; *b* 27 Feb. 1917; *e s* of A. E. and G. McC. Madden; *m* 1941, Margaret, *d* of Dr R. D. Gifford; one *s* one *d*. *Educ:* privately, by mother; Bishop Vesey's Grammar Sch.; Christ Church, Oxford. Boulter and Gladstone exhibns; BA 1938, BLitt 1939, DPhil 1950. Dep. Sup., Rhodes House Library, 1946-48; Beit Lectr, 1947-57; Sen. Tutor to Overseas Service Courses, 1950-; Dir, Inst. of Commonwealth Studies, 1961-68; Vice-Chm., History Bd, 1968-73. Canadian Vis. Fellow, 1970; Vis. Prof., Cape Town, 1973; Vis. Fellow, Res. Sch., ANU, 1974. Dir, Hong Kong admin. course, 1975-. Dir, Prospect Theatre, 1963-66. FRHistS 1952. *Publications:* (with V. Harlow) British Colonial Developments, 1774-1834, 1953; (with K. Robinson) Essays in Imperial Government, 1963; chapter in Cambridge History of British Empire III, 1959; Imperial Constitutional Documents, 1765-1965, 1966; reviews in English Historical Review, etc. *Recreations:* acting; photographing islands and highlands, hill towns, country houses, churches; Renaissance art; writing music and listening. *Address:* Oak Apples, Shotover Hill, Oxford. *T:* Oxford 62972.

MADDEN, Admiral Sir Charles (Edward), 2nd Bt, *cr* 1919; GCB 1965 (KCB 1961; CB 1955); Vice Lord-Lieutenant of Greater London since 1969; *b* 15 June 1906; *s* of Admiral of the Fleet Sir Charles E. Madden, 1st Bart, GCB, OM, and Constance Winifred (*d* 1964), 3rd *d* of Sir Charles Cayzer, 1st Bart; *S* father, 1935; *m* 1942, Olive, *d* of late G. W. Robins, Caldy,

Cheshire; one *d*. *Educ:* Royal Naval Coll., Osborne. ADC to the Queen, 1955. Commander, 1939; Captain, 1946; Rear-Admiral, 1955; Vice-Admiral, 1958; Admiral, 1961. Chief of Naval Staff, NZ, 1953-55; Dep. Chief of Naval Personnel, 1955-57; Flag Officer, Malta, 1957-59; Flag Officer, Flotillas, Home Fleet, 1959-60; C-in-C Plymouth, 1960-62; C-in-C Home Fleet and NATO C-in-C Eastern Atlantic Command, 1963-65; retired, 1965. Chairman, Royal National Mission to Deep Sea Fishermen, 1971- (Dep. Chm., 1966-71); Vice-Chairman, Sail Training Assoc., 1968-70. Trustee: National Maritime Museum, 1968- (Chm., 1972-77); Portsmouth Royal Naval Museum, 1973-. DL Greater London, 1969. Grand Cross of Prince Henry the Navigator, Portugal, 1960. *Recreation:* painting. *Heir:* *b* Lieut-Colonel John Wilmot Madden, MC, 1944, RA [*b* 1916; *m* 1941, Beatrice Catherine Sievewright; two *s* one *d*]. *Address:* 21 Eldon Road, W8. *Club:* Arts.

MADDEN, Rear-Admiral Colin Duncan, CB 1966; CBE 1964; MVO 1954; DSC 1940 and Bar, 1944; Director General, The Brewers' Society, since 1969; Gentleman Usher of the Scarlet Rod to the Order of the Bath, since 1968; *b* 19 Aug. 1915; *s* of late Archibald Maclean Madden, CMG, and Cecilia Catherine Moor; *m* 1943, Agnes Margaret, *d* of late H. K. Newcombe, OBE, Canada and London, and Eleanor Clare; two *d*. *Educ:* RN Coll., Dartmouth. During War of 1939-45, took part in blocking Ijmuiden harbour and Dutch evacuation; Navigating Officer of 7th Mine Sweeping Flotilla; HMS Arethusa; Assault Group J1 for invasion of Europe, and HMS Norfolk. Thence HMS Triumph. Commander, 1950; Comd HMS Crossbow, 1952; staff of Flag Officer Royal Yachts, SS Gothic and Comdr (N) HM Yacht Britannia, for Royal Commonwealth Tour, 1953-54; Captain, Naval Attaché, Rome; Captain D 7 in HMS Trafalgar; IDC. Comd HMS Albion, 1962; Rear-Admiral, 1965; Senior Naval Member Directing Staff, Imperial Defence Coll., 1965-67; retired, 1967. Dir, Nat. Trade Develt Assoc., 1967-69. *Recreations:* sailing, gardening, tapestry. *Address:* c/o Coutts & Co., 440 Strand, WC2. *Clubs:* Army and Navy; Royal Cruising, Royal Ocean Racing.

MADDEN, Frederick; see Madden, A. F. McC.

MADDEN, Max; MP (Lab) Sowerby, since Feb. 1974; *b* 29 Oct. 1941; *s* of George Francis Leonard Madden and Rene Frances Madden; *m* 1972, Sheelagh Teresa Catherine Howard. *Educ:* Lascelles Secondary Modern Sch.; Pinner Grammar Sch. Journalist: East Essex Gazette; Tribune (political weekly); Sun, London; Scotsman, London; subseq. Press and Information Officer, British Gas Corp., London. Member: Trade and Industry Sub-Cttee, Select Cttee on Public Expenditure; Select Cttee on Conduct of Members; Chm., Parly Lab. Party Employment Gp. *Recreation:* fishing. *Address:* House of Commons, SW1A 0AA. *Club:* Luddendenfoot Working Men's.

MADDEX, Sir George (Henry), KBE 1948; Government Actuary, 1946-58, retired; *b* 1895; *m* 1921, Emily Macdonald Jeffrey (one *s* killed on active service, 1943). *Educ:* Owen's Sch. Pres., Inst. of Actuaries, 1948-50. Dep. Govt Actuary, 1944-46. Fellow, Society of Actuaries (US), 1949; Hon. Fellow, Faculty of Actuaries in Scotland, 1956. *Address:* 1 Clairville Court, Reigate, Surrey. *Clubs:* Naval and Military, St Stephen's.

MADDISON, Vincent Albert, CMG 1961; TD 1953; *b* 10 Aug. 1915; *s* of late Vincent Maddison; *m* 1954, Jennifer Christian Bernard; two *s* one *d*. *Educ:* Wellingborough Sch.; Downing Coll., Cambridge (MA). Colonial Administrative Service, 1939. Served War of 1939-45: Ethiopian and Burma Campaigns. District Officer, Kenya, 1947; seconded to Secretariat, 1948; Director, Trade and Supplies, 1953; Secretary, 1954, Perm. Secretary, 1957-63, Min. of Commerce and Industry; retired from Kenya Government, 1963; Chairman: East African Powers and Lighting Co. Ltd, 1965-70; Tana River Development Co. Ltd, 1965-70; The Kenya Power Co. Ltd 1965-70; Director: Nyali Ltd, 1966-70; Kisauni Ltd, 1966-70; East African Trust and Investment Co. Ltd, 1966-70; East African Engineering Consultants, 1966-70. *Recreations:* riding, gardening, sailing. *Address:* c/o Williams and Glyn's Bank Ltd, 14 Mulcaster Street, St Helier, Jersey, CI. *Clubs:* East India, Devonshire, Sports and Public Schools; Muthaiga Country (Kenya).

MADDOCK, Rt. Rev. David Rokeby; Provost of Bury St Edmunds, since 1976; *b* 30 May 1915; *s* of Walter Rokeby Maddock; *m* 1943, Mary Jesse Hoernle, widow of Edward Selwyn Hoernle, ICS and *d* of Rev. Selwyn Charles Freer; one *s* one *d*. *Educ:* Clifton Coll.; Bristol Univ.; St Catherine's, Oxford; Wycliffe Hall, Oxford. Curate, Chard, Somerset, 1939-43; Vicar, Wilton, Taunton, 1943-47; Rector, Wareham, 1947-61; Rector of Bradford Peverell and Stratton, 1961-66; Rector of West Stafford with Frome Billet, 1966-67. Rural Dean of Purbeck,

1948-61; Canon of Salisbury, 1956-67; Archdeacon of Sherborne, 1961-67; Bishop Suffragan of Dunwich, 1967-76; Archdeacon of Sudbury, 1968-70. Hon. Chaplain Dorset Constabulary, 1964-67. *Recreation:* rough gardening. *Address:* Provost's House, Bury St Edmunds, Suffolk.

MADDOCK, Sir Ieuan, Kt 1975; CB 1968; OBE 1953; FRS 1967; Secretary, British Association for the Advancement of Science, since 1977; Chief Scientist, Department of Industry, 1974-77; Director, National Physical Laboratory, 1976-77; *b* 29 March 1917; British; *m* 1943, Eurfron May Davies; one *s. Educ:* Gowerton Grammar Sch., Glamorgan; University of Wales, Swansea. Entered Government service, Explosives Res. and Devełt, 1940; Principal Scientific Officer, Armament Res. Dept, Fort Halstead, 1949; Head of Field Experiments Div., Atomic Weapons Research Establishment, 1960; Asst Director, AWRE, 1965; Dep. Controller B, 1965-67, Controller (Industrial Technology) 1967-71, Min. of Technology; Chief Scientist, DTI, 1971-74. Member: SRC, 1973-; NERC, 1973-; Science Cons. Cttee to BBC, 1969- (Chm., 1977-); ABRC, 1973-; Adv. Council for Applied R&D, 1977-; Ct, Cranfield Coll. of Technology; Court of Surrey Univ. President: IERE, 1973-75; IMGTechE, 1976; Dep. Chm., Nat. Electronics Council, 1977; Vice-Pres., ASLIB, 1977. Hon. DSc Wales, 1970. *Publications:* in various scientific and technical jls. *Address:* 13 Darell Road, Caversham, Reading, Berks. *T:* Reading 474096.

MADDOCKS, Arthur Frederick, CMG 1974; HM Diplomatic Service; Ambassador and UK Permanent Representative to OECD, Paris, since 1977; *b* 20 May 1922; *s* of late Frederick William Maddocks and Celia Elizabeth Maddocks (*née* Beardwell); *m* 1945, Margaret Jean Crawford Holt; two *s* one *d. Educ:* Manchester Grammar Sch.; Corpus Christi Coll., Oxford. Army, 1942-46; Foreign (later Diplomatic) Service, 1946-: Washington, 1946-48; FO, 1949-51; Bonn, 1951-55; Bangkok, 1955-58; UK Delegn to OEEC, 1958-60; FO, 1960-64; UK Delegn to European Communities, Brussels, 1964-68; Political Adviser, Hong Kong, 1968-72; Dep. High Comr and Minister (Commercial), Ottawa, 1972-76. *Address:* Foreign and Commonwealth Office, SW1. *Clubs:* Athenæum; Hong Kong (Hong Kong).

MADDOCKS, His Honour George; County Court Judge, retired; *b* 5 April 1896; *s* of William and Sarah Alice Maddocks; Southport; *m* 1928, Harriet Mary Louisa Day; two *s* one *d. Educ:* Christ Church Hall, Southport; Manchester Univ. Called to Bar, Middle Temple, 1923. *Address:* 104 Roe Lane, Southport, Lancs.

MADDOCKS, Sir Kenneth (Phipson), KCMG 1958 (CMG 1956); KCVO 1963; *b* 8 Feb. 1907; *s* of Arthur P. Maddocks, Haywards Heath, Sussex; *m* 1951, Elnor Radcliffe, CStJ (*d* 1976), *d* of late Sir E. John Russell, OBE, FRS; no *c. Educ:* Bromsgrove Sch.; Wadham Coll., Oxford. Colonial Administrative Service, Nigeria, 1929; Civil Secretary, Northern Region, Nigeria, 1955-57; Dep. Governor, 1957-58. Acting Governor, Northern Region, Nigeria, 1956 and 1957. Governor and Commander-in-Chief of Fiji, 1958-63; Dir and Secretary, E Africa and Mauritius Assoc., 1964-69. KStJ. *Recreations:* fishing, gardening. *Address:* Abbey House, Sutton Montis, near Yeovil, Som. *T:* Corton Denham 268. *Club:* Athenæum.

MADDOCKS, Rt. Rev. Morris Henry St John; *see* Selby, Bishop Suffragan of.

MADDOX, Sir (John) Kempson, Kt 1964; VRD 1948; Hon. Consulting Physician: Royal Prince Alfred Hospital, Sydney; Royal Hospital for Women, Sydney; *b* Dunedin, NZ, 20 Sept. 1901; *s* of Sidney Harold Maddox and Mabel Kempson; *m* 1940, Madeleine Scott; one *s* one *d. Educ:* N Sydney Boys' High Sch.; Univ. of Sydney. MD, ChM (Sydney) 1924; MRCP 1928; FRACP 1935; FRCP 1958. Served War of 1939-45, Surgeon Comdr, RANR. President: BMA (NSW), 1950; Cardiac Soc. of Australia and NZ, 1958; Asian-Pacific Soc. of Cardiology, 1960-64; Internat. Soc. of Cardiology, 1966-70; Vice-Pres., Nat. Heart Foundation of Australia, 1960-64 (Pres. NSW Div.); FACC 1965; FACP 1968; Hon. Pres., Internat. Soc. of Cardiology, 1970-. Hon. AM (Singapore) 1963. Chevalier de l'Ordre de la Santé Publique, France, 1961; Comendador, Orden Hispolito Unanue (Peru), 1968. *Recreations:* golf, fishing, tennis. *Address:* 8 Annandale Street, Darling Point, Sydney, NSW 2027, Australia. *T:* 32-1707. *Clubs:* Australian (Sydney); Royal Sydney Golf.

MADDOX, John (Royden); writer and broadcaster; Director, Nuffield Foundation, since 1975; *b* 27 Nov. 1925; *s* of A. J. and M. E. Maddox, Swansea; *m* 1st, 1949, Nancy Fanning (*d* 1960); one *s* one *d*; 2nd, 1960, Brenda Power Murphy; one *s* one *d.*

Educ: Gowerton Boys' County Sch.; Christ Church, Oxford; King's Coll., London. Asst Lecturer, then Lecturer, Theoretical Physics, Manchester Univ., 1949-55; Science Correspondent, Guardian, 1955-64; Affiliate, Rockefeller Institute, New York, 1962-63; Asst Director, Nuffield Foundation, and Co-ordinator, Nuffield Foundation Science Teaching Project, 1964-66; Editor, Nature, 1966-73; Man. Dir, Macmillan Journals Ltd, 1970-72; Dir, Macmillan & Co. Ltd, 1968-73; Chm., Maddox Editorial Ltd, 1972-74. Member: Royal Commn on Environmental Pollution, 1976-; Genetic Manipulation Adv. Gp, 1976-; British Library Adv. Council, 1976-; Council on Internat. Develt, 1977-. *Publications:* (with Leonard Beaton) The Spread of Nuclear Weapons, 1962; Revolution in Biology, 1964; The Doomsday Syndrome, 1972; Beyond the Energy Crisis, 1975. *Address:* Nuffield Lodge, Regent's Park, NW1. *T:* 01-722 8871; 5 Ponsonby Road, SW15. *T:* 01-788 0548.

MADEL, William David; MP (C) South Bedfordshire since 1970; *b* 6 Aug. 1938; *s* of late William R. Madel and of Eileen Madel (*née* Nicholls); *m* 1971, Susan Catherine, *d* of Lt-Comdr Hon. Peter Carew; one *d. Educ:* Uppingham Sch.; Keble Coll., Oxford. MA Oxon 1965. Graduate Management Trainee, 1963-64; Advertising Exec., Thomson Organisation, 1964-70. PPS to Parly Under-Sec. of State for Defence, 1973-74, to Minister of State for Defence, 1974. Vice-Chm., Cons. Backbench Employment Cttee, 1974-. *Recreations:* cricket, tennis, travel, reading. *Address:* 120 Pickford Road, Markyate, Herts. *Clubs:* Junior Carlton, Coningsby; Mid-Cheshire Pitt (Chester).

MADGE, Charles Henry; *b* 10 Oct. 1912; *s* of Lieut-Colonel C. A. Madge and Barbara (*née* Hylton Foster); *m* 1st, Kathleen Raine (marr. diss.); one *s* one *d*; 2nd, Inez Pearn (*d* 1976); one *s* one *d. Educ:* Winchester Coll. (Scholar); Magdalene Coll., Cambridge (Scholar). Reporter on Daily Mirror, 1935-36; founded Mass-Observation, 1937; directed survey of working-class saving and spending for National Institute of Economic and Social Research, 1940-42; Research staff of PEP, 1943; Director, Pilot Press, 1944; Social Development Officer, New Town of Stevenage, 1947; Prof. of Sociology, Univ. of Birmingham, 1950-70. Mission to Thailand on UN Technical Assistance, 1953-54. UNESCO Missions to India, 1957-58, to South-East Asia, 1959 and 1960 and Leader of Mission to Ghana for UN Economic Commission for Africa, 1963. *Publications:* The Disappearing Castle (poems), 1937; The Father Found (poems), 1941; part-author of Britain by Mass-Observation, 1938, and other books connected with this organisation; War-time Pattern of Saving and Spending, 1943; (ed) Pilot Papers: Social Essays and Documents, 1945-47; Society in the Mind, 1964; (with Barbara Weinberger) Art Students Observed, 1973; contributions to Economic Journal, Town Planning Review, Human Relations, etc. *Address:* 28 Lynmouth Road, N2.

MADGE, James Richard, CB 1976; Deputy Secretary, Department of the Environment, on secondment as Chief Executive, Housing Corporation, since 1973; *b* 18 June 1924; *s* of James Henry Madge and Elisabeth May Madge; *m* 1955, Alice June Annette (*d* 1975), *d* of late Major Horace Reid, Jamaica; two *d. Educ:* Bexhill Co. Sch.; New Coll., Oxford. Pilot in RAFVR, 1942-46. Joined Min. of Civil Aviation, 1947; Principal Private Secretary: to Paymaster-General, 1950-51; to Minister of Transport, 1960-61; Asst Secretary, Min. of Transport, 1961-66; Under-Sec., Road Safety Gp, 1966-69; Head of Policy Planning, 1969-70; Under-Sec., Housing Directorate, DoE, 1971-73. *Recreations:* lawn tennis, swimming, furniture-making. *Address:* 56 Gordon Place, Kensington, W8. *T:* 01-937 1927.

MADGWICK, Sir Robert Bowden, Kt 1966; OBE 1962; Chairman, Australian Broadcasting Commission, 1967-73; Vice-Chancellor, University of New England, New South Wales, 1954-66; *b* 10 May 1905; *s* of R. C. Madgwick, N Sydney; *m* 1st, 1937, Ailsa Margaret (*d* 1967), *d* of H. J. Aspinall, Sydney; three *d*; 2nd, 1971, Mrs Nance McGrath. *Educ:* North Sydney High Sch.; University of Sydney; Balliol Coll., Oxford. MEc (Sydney); DPhil (Oxon). Lecturer in Economics, University of Sydney, 1929-33; Senior Lecturer in Economic History, University of Sydney, 1936-46; Director, Army Education, Australia, 1941-46; Warden, New England Univ. Coll., 1947-54. Hon. DLitt: Univ. of Sydney, 1961; Univ. of Newcastle, NSW, 1966; Univ. of New England, 1969; Hon. LLD, Univ. of Queensland, 1961. *Publications:* (with E. R. Walker) An Outline of Australian Economics, 1932; Immigration into Eastern Australia, 1788-1851, 1937. *Recreations:* fishing, bowls. *Address:* 3 Collins Road, St Ives, NSW 2075, Australia. *Club:* Killara Golf (Sydney).

MADOC, Maj.-Gen. Reginald William, CB 1959; DSO 1957; OBE 1951; Royal Marines, retired; *b* 15 Aug. 1907; *s* of late

Lieut-Colonel H. W. Madoc, CBE, MVO, Garwick, Isle of Man; *m* 1938, Rosemary, *d* of late Dr Cyril Shepherd, Sydney, Australia; one *d. Educ:* King William's Coll., Isle of Man. 2nd Lieut, RM, 1926; HMS Rodney, 1929-31; HMS Royal Oak, 1932-34; ADC to Governor of Madras, 1934-38; HMS Furious, 1938-39; RM Mobile Naval Base Defence Org., UK, Egypt, Crete, 1940-41 (despatches twice, POW, 1941-45). Instructor, Officers' Sch., RM, 1946; Staff Coll., Camberley, 1947; Instructor, School of Combined Ops, 1948; HMS Vanguard, 1948-49; CO, 42 Commando, RM, Malaya, 1950-51 (despatches); CO Commando Sch., RM, 1952-53; Chief Instructor, School of Amphibious Warfare, 1953-55; Commanded 3rd Commando Bde, RM, Malta, Cyprus, Port Said, 1955-57; ADC to the Queen, 1955-57; Maj.-Gen., Plymouth Gp, RM, 1957-59; Maj.-Gen., Portsmouth Gp, RM, 1959-61; retired 1961. Col Comdt, RM, 1967-68; Rep. Col Comdt, RM, 1969-70. *Address:* The Malthouse, Meonstoke, by Southampton, SO3 1NH. *T:* Droxford 323. *Club:* Army and Navy.

MAEGRAITH, Brian Gilmore, CMG 1968; TD 1975; MA, MB, BSc, DPhil; FRCP, FRCPE, FRACP; Alfred Jones and Warrington Yorke Professor of Tropical Medicine, School of Tropical Medicine, Liverpool University, 1944-72, now Professor Emeritus; Dean of Liverpool School of Tropical Medicine, 1946-75, Vice-President, since 1975; *b* 26 Aug. 1907; *s* of late A. E. R. Maegraith, Adelaide, S Australia; *m* 1934, Lorna Langley, St Peters, Adelaide; one *s. Educ:* St Peter's and St Mark's Colleges, Adelaide University (MB 1930); Magdalen and Exeter Colleges, Oxford (Rhodes Scholar, Rolleston Memorial Prize). Beit Memorial Fellow, 1932-34; Medical Fellow, Exeter Coll., Oxford, 1934-40; Hon. Fellow, St Marks Coll., 1956. University Lecturer and Demonstrator in Pathology, Dean of Faculty of Medicine, Oxford Univ., 1938-44; War of 1939-45, OC Army Malaria Research Unit. Med. Advisory Cttee ODM, 1963-72. Tropical Med. Research Board, MRC, 1960-65, 1966-69; Cttees on Malaria and Abnormal Haemoglobins, 1960-69; Hon. Consulting Physician, Liverpool Royal Infirmary; Consultant in Trop. Med., RAF, 1964-76; Hon. Malariologist, Army, 1967-73; Adviser: Council for Health in Socio-economic Developments, Thailand, 1964-; Faculty Tropical Medicine, Bangkok, 1959-; International Centre for Tropical Medicine, SE Asia; Sec.-Gen., Council of Institutes of Tropical Medicine, Europe and USSR, 1969-72; Hon. Mem., Council of Schs of Tropical Medicine of Europe, 1975-; Pres., Royal Society Tropical Medicine, 1969-71 (Vice-Pres., 1949-51 and 1957-59; Chalmers Gold Medal, 1951); Vis. Prof., Univ. of Alexandria, 1956; Lectures: Lichfield, Oxford, 1955; Maurice Bloch, Glasgow, 1969; Heath Clark, London, 1970; Craig, US Soc. Trop. Med., 1976. Membre d'Honneur: de Soc. Belg. de Méd. Tropicale; Soc. de Pathologie Exotique, Paris; Hon. Member American, Canadian and German Socs of Tropical Medicine and Hygiene, 1961 (Le Prince Award and Medal, 1954); Bernhard Nocht Medal (Hamburg), 1957; Mary Kingsley Medal, Liverpool Sch. of Trop. Med., 1973. DSc (*hc*), Bangkok; MD (Emeritus) Athens, 1972. *Publications:* Pathological Processes in Malaria and Blackwater Fever, 1948; (with A. R. D. Adams) Clinical Tropical Diseases, 5th edn, 1970, 6th edn 1976; Tropical Medicine for Nurses (with A. R. D. Adams), 1956, 4th edn (ed H. M. Gilles), 1975; (with C. S. Leithead) Clinical Methods in Tropical Medicine, 1962; Exotic Diseases in Practice, 1965; (with H. M. Gilles) Management and Treatment of Diseases in the Tropics, 1970. Papers and articles in technical and scientific journals on various subjects. *Address:* 23 Eaton Road, Cressington Park, Liverpool L19 0PN. *T:* 051-427 1133. *Clubs:* Athenæum; Liver, Athenæum (Liverpool).

MAELOR, Baron, *cr* 1966 (Life Peer), of Rhosllanerchrugog; **Thomas William Jones;** JP (Chairman Ruabon Bench); *b* 10 Feb. 1898; *s* of James Jones, Wrexham; *m* 1928, Flossy, *d* of Jonathan Thomas, Birkenhead; one *s* one *d. Educ:* Poncian Boys' Sch.; Bangor Normal Coll. Began working life as a miner; became pupil teacher and went to Bangor Coll. Welfare Officer and Education Officer for Merseyside and North Wales Electricity Board in North Wales. MP (Lab) Merioneth, 1951-66; Formerly: Chairman North Wales Labour Federation; Chairman Wrexham Trades Council. *Address:* Ger-y-Llyn, Poncian, Wrexham, Clwyd.

MAFFEY, family name of **Baron Rugby.**

MAGEE, Bryan; MP (Lab) Leyton, since Feb. 1974; *b* 12 April 1930; *s* of Frederick Magee and Sheila (*née* Lynch); *m* 1954, Ingrid Söderlund (marr. diss.); one *d. Educ:* Christ's Hospital; Lycée Hôche, Versailles; Keble Coll., Oxford (Open Scholar). Pres., Oxford Union, 1953; Final Honour Sch., Mod. Hist., 1952; PPE 1953; MA 1956. Nat. Mil. Service in Austria, 1948-49. English Lectr, Lund, Sweden, 1953-54; Visitors' Officer,

British Council, Oxford, 1954-55; Henry Fellow in Philosophy, Yale, 1955-56. Brewer with Arthur Guinness, Son & Co., 1956-57. Current Affairs Reporter on TV; Critic of the Arts on BBC Radio 3; Regular columnist, The Times, 1974-76; Contributor, numerous pubns. Contested (Lab): Mid-Bedfordshire, Gen. Elec., 1959; By-Elec., 1960. Theatre Critic of The Listener, 1966-67; elected to Critics' Circle (Drama and Music sections) 1970, Council Mem., 1975-. Judge for Evening Standard annual Opera Award, 1973-. Lectr in Philosophy, Balliol Coll., Oxford, 1970-71; Visiting Fellow of All Souls Coll., Oxford, 1973-74. *Publications:* Crucifixion and Other Poems, 1951; Go West Young Man, 1958; To Live in Danger, 1960; The New Radicalism, 1962; The Democratic Revolution, 1964; Towards 2000, 1965; One in Twenty, 1966; The Television Interviewer, 1966; Aspects of Wagner, 1968; Modern British Philosophy, 1971; Popper, 1973; Facing Death, 1977. *Recreations:* music, theatre, travel. *Address:* 12 Falkland House, Marloes Road, W8 5LF. *T:* 01-937 1210. *Clubs:* Garrick, Reform, Savile.

MAGGS, Air Vice-Marshal William Jack, CB 1967; OBE 1943; Fellow and Domestic Bursar, Keble College, Oxford, 1969-77; *b* 2 Feb. 1914; *s* of late Frederick Wilfrid Maggs, Bristol; *m* 1940, Margaret Grace, *d* of late Thomas Liddell Hetherington, West Hartlepool; one *s* one *d. Educ:* Bristol Grammar Sch.; St John's Coll., Oxford (MA). Management Trainee, 1936-38. Joined RAF, 1939; Unit and Training duties, 1939-42; Student, Staff Coll., 1942; Planning Staffs, and participated in, Algerian, Sicilian and Italian landings, 1942-44; SESO Desert Air Force, 1944; Jt Admin. Plans Staff, Cabinet Offices, Whitehall, 1945-48; Instructor, RAF Coll., Cranwell, 1948-50; comd No 9 Maintenance Unit, 1950-52; exchange officer at HQ, USAF Washington, 1952-54; Student Jt Services Staff Coll., 1954-55; No 3 Maintenance Unit, 1955-57; Dep. Director of Equipment, Air Ministry, 1958-59; SESO, HQ, NEAF, Cyprus, 1959-61; Student, Imperial Defence Coll., 1962; Director of Mech. Transport and Marine Craft, Air Ministry, 1963-64; Director of Equipment, Ministry of Defence (Air), 1964-67; SASO, RAF Maintenance Comd, 1967-69. Group Captain, 1958; Air Commodore, 1963; Air Vice-Marshal, 1967. *Recreations:* golf, gardening, cabinet-making. *Address:* Hillside, Noke, near Oxford, OX3 9TT. *T:* Kidlington 3139. *Club:* Royal Air Force.

MAGILL, Air Vice-Marshal Graham Reese, CB 1966; CBE 1962 (OBE 1945); DFC 1941 and Bar, 1943; retired Jan. 1970; *b* 23 Jan. 1915; *s* of late Robert Wilson Magill and late Frances Elizabeth Magill, Te Aroha, NZ; *m* 1942, Blanche Marie Colson; two *s. Educ:* Te Aroha High Sch.; Hamilton Technical Coll., NZ. Joined Royal Air Force, 1936. Served War of 1939-45, Sudan, Egypt, UK, NW Europe; subsequently, UK, Egypt, France. Director of Operations (Bomber and Reconnaissance), Air Ministry, 1959-62; Commandant, RAF College of Air Warfare, Manby, Lincs, 1963-64; Director-General of Organisation (RAF), Ministry of Defence, 1964-67; AOC, 25 Group, RAF, 1967-68; AOC 22 Group, RAF, 1968-69. *Recreations:* generally interested in sport, water sports and motoring. *Address:* Apartado De Correos 32, Puerto de Pollensa, Majorca. *Club:* Royal Air Force.

MAGILL, Sir Ivan Whiteside, KCVO 1960 (CVO 1946); FRCS 1951; FFARCS; MB, BCh, Belfast, 1913; DA 1935; formerly Hon. Consulting Anæsthetist, Westminster, Brompton and St Andrew's, Dollis Hill, Hospitals; *b* Larne, 1888; *s* of Samuel Magill; *m* 1916, Edith (*d* 1973, *d* of Thomas Robinson Banbridge. *Educ:* Larne Grammar Sch.; Queen's Univ., Belfast. Formerly: Consultant Army, Navy, EMS; Senior Anæsthetist, Queen's Hospital, Sidcup; Anæsthetist, Seamens Hospital, Greenwich; Res. MO, Stanley Hospital, Liverpool; Examiner, DA; Robert Campbell Memorial Orator, Belfast, 1939; Bengué Memorial Lecturer, Royal Institute of Public Health, 1950; Hon. Member: Liverpool Medical Institution; American Society of Anæsthesiologists; New York State Society of Anæsthesiologists; British Assoc. of Plastic Surgeons; Canadian Society of Anæsthetists; Hon. Fellow: Royal Society of Medicine, 1956; Faculty of Anæsthetists, Royal College of Surgeons, 1958; Assoc. of Anæsthetists of Great Britain and Ireland, 1958; Hon. FFARCSI, 1961. Henry Hill Hickman Medal, 1938; John Snow Medal, 1958; Canadian Anæsthetists Society Medal, 1963; Medal, American Assoc. of Plastic Surgeons, 1965; Gillies Mem. Lecturer, British Assoc. of Plastic Surgeons, 1965; Ralph M. Waters Prize, Chicago, 1966. Hon. DSc, Belfast, 1945. Frederic Hewitt Lecturer for 1965. *Publications:* contributions and chapters in various medical journals. *Recreation:* trout fishing. *Address:* c/o Williams & Glyn's Bank, Holts Branch, Kirkland House, Whitehall, SW1.

MAGINNIS, John Edward, JP; *b* 7 March 1919; *s* of late Edward Maginnis, Mandeville Hall, Mullahead, Tanderagee; *m* 1944, Dorothy, *d* of late R. J. Rusk, JP, of Cavanaleck, Fivemiletown,

Co. Tyrone; one *s* four *d. Educ:* Moyallon Sch., Co. Down; Portadown Technical Coll. Served War of 1939-45, Royal Ulster Constabulary. MP (UU) Armagh, Oct. 1959-Feb. 1974. JP, Co. Armagh, 1956. Group Secretary, North Armagh Group, Ulster Farmers' Union, 1956-59; Member, Co. Armagh Agricultural Society. *Recreations:* football, hunting, shooting. *Address:* Mandeville Hall, 68 Mullahead Road, Tandragee, Craigavon, Co. Armagh, N Ireland. *T:* Tandragee 260. *Club:* Ulster.

MAGNIAC, Rear-Admiral Vernon St Clair Lane, CB 1961; *b* 21 Dec. 1908; *s* of late Major Francis Arthur Magniac and of Mrs Beatrice Caroline Magniac (*née* Davison); *m* 1947, Eileen Eleanor (*née* Witney); one *s* one *d* (and one *d* decd). *Educ:* Clifton Coll. Cadet, RN, 1926; Served in HM Ships Courageous, Effingham, Resolution and Diamond, 1931-37; RN Engineering Coll., 1937-39; HMS Renown, 1940-43; Combined Ops, India, 1943-45; HM Ships Fisgard, Gambia, and Nigeria, 1945-50; HM Dockyards Chatham, Malta and Devonport, 1950-62. *Recreations:* golf, fishing. *Address:* Cumerew House, Yelverton, Devon.

MAGNUS, Hilary Barrow, TD; QC 1957; National Insurance Commissioner, since Oct. 1964; *b* 3 March 1909; *yr s* of late Laurie Magnus, 34 Cambridge Square, W2; *b* and *heir-pres.* to Sir Philip Magnus-Allcroft, *qv; m* 1950, Rosemary, *d* of G. H. Masefield and *widow* of Quentin Hurst; one *s* one *d* and one step *s. Educ:* Westminster; Christ Church, Oxford. Barrister, Lincoln's Inn, 1933. Bencher, 1963. Served War of 1939-45, Rifle Brigade TA (Lieut-Colonel). JP (Kent) 1948. *Recreation:* gardening. *Address:* The Gate House, Leigh, near Tonbridge, Kent. *T:* Hildenborough 832157; 3 Temple Gardens, EC4. *T:* 01-353 7884. *Clubs:* Garrick, Beefsteak.

MAGNUS, Philip; see Magnus-Allcroft, Sir Philip.

MAGNUS, Samuel Woolf; Justice of Appeal, Court of Appeal for Zambia, 1971; Commissioner, Foreign Compensation Commission, since 977; *b* 10 Sept. 1910; *s* of late Samuel Woolf Magnus; *m* 1938, Anna Gertrude, *o d* of Adolph Shane, Cardiff; one *d. Educ:* University Coll., London. BA Hons, 1931. Called to Bar, Gray's Inn, 1937. Served War of 1939-45, Army. Practised in London, 1937-59. Treas., Assoc. of Liberal Lawyers, Mem. Council, London Liberal Party and Pres., N Hendon Liberal Assoc., until 1959. Contested (L) Central Hackney, 1945. Partner in legal firm, Northern Rhodesia, 1959-63; subseq. legal consultant. QC 1964, MLC 1962, MP Jan.-Oct. 1964, Northern Rhodesia; MP, Zambia, 1964-68. Puisne Judge, High Court for Zambia, 1968. *Publications:* (with M. Estrin) Companies Act 1947, 1947; Companies: Law and Practice, 1948 (4th edn 1968); (with A. M. Lyons) Advertisement Control, 1949; Magnus on Leasehold Property (Temporary Provisions) Act 1951, 1951; Magnus on Landlord and Tenant Act 1954, 1954; Magnus on Housing Repairs and Rents Act 1954, 1954; Magnus on the Rent Act 1957, 1957; (with F. E. Price) Knight's Annotated Housing Acts, 1958; (with Tovell) Magnus on Housing Finance, 1960; Companies Act 1967, 1967; Magnus on the Rent Act 1968, 1969; Magnus on Business Tenancies, 1970; contributor: Law Jl; Halsbury's Laws of England; Encycl. of Forms and Precedents; Atkin's Court Forms and Precedents. *Recreations:* writing, photography, enthusiastic spectator at all games, preferably on TV. *Address:* 2 Harcourt Buildings, Temple, EC4. *T:* 01-353 7202; 33 Apsley House, Finchley Road, St John's Wood, NW8. *T:* 01-586 1679. *Clubs:* National Liberal, No 10.

MAGNUS-ALLCROFT, Sir Philip, 2nd Bt, *cr* 1917; CBE 1971; MA; FRSL; FRHistS; author; *b* 8 Feb. 1906; *er s* of late Laurie Magnus and Dora, *e d* of late Sir I. Spielman, CMG; *S* grandfather, 1933; *m* 1943, Jewell Allcroft, Stokesay Court, Onibury, Shropshire, *d* of late Herbert Allcroft and of Mrs John Rotton. Formally assumed surname of Allcroft (in addition to that of Magnus), 1951. *Educ:* Westminster Sch.; Wadham Coll., Oxford. Civil Service, 1928-32 and 1946-50. Served War of 1939-45 in Royal Artillery and Intelligence Corps (Iceland and Italy); Major. CC 1952, CA 1968-74, Salop (Chairman, Planning Cttee, 1962-74; formerly: Chm., Records Cttee; Vice-Chm., Educn Cttee); Chairman of Governors, Attingham Coll.; JP Salop, 1953-71 (Chm., Juvenile Ct). Trustee, National Portrait Gall., 1970-77. Mem., W Midlands Regional Cttee, Nat. Trust, 1973-. Governor, Ludlow Grammar Sch., 1952-77. *Publications:* (as Philip Magnus): Life of Edmund Burke, 1939; Selected Prose of Edmund Burke (with Introduction), 1948; Sir Walter Raleigh, 1951 (revised edns, 1956, 1968); Gladstone—A Biography, 1954; Kitchener—Portrait of an Imperialist, 1958 (revised edn, 1968); King Edward the Seventh, 1964. *Heir: b* Hilary Barrow Magnus, *qv. Address:* Stokesay Court, Craven Arms, Salop SY7 9BD. *T:* Bromfield 372. *Clubs:* Athenæum, Beefsteak, Brooks's, Pratt's.

MAGNUSSON, Magnus; writer and broadcaster; *b* 12 Oct. 1929; *s* of Sigursteinn Magnusson, Icelandic Consul-Gen. for Scotland, and Ingibjorg Sigurdardottir; *m* 1954, Mamie Baird; one *s* three *d* (and one *s* decd). *Educ:* Edinburgh Academy; Jesus Coll., Oxford (BA). Subseq. Asst Editor, Scottish Daily Express and Asst Editor, The Scotsman. Presenter, various television and radio programmes; Scottish Television Personality of the Year, 1974. Editor, The Bodley Head Archaeologies. Chairman: Stewards, York Archaeol Trust; Scottish Historic Churches Heritage Council; Scottish Youth Theatre; Hon. Vice-Pres., Age Concern Scotland. Rector, Edinburgh Univ., 1975-. FSAScot 1974. Knight of the Order of the Falcon (Iceland), 1975; Silver Jubilee Medal, 1977. *Publications:* Introducing Archaeology, 1972; Viking Expansion Westwards, 1973; The Clacken and the Slate (Edinburgh Academy, 1824-1974), 1974; Hammer of the North (Norse mythology), 1976; BC, The Archaeology of the Bible Lands, 1977; translations (all with Hermann Pálsson): Njal's Saga, 1960; The Vinland Sagas, 1965; King Harald's Saga, 1966; Laxdaela Saga, 1969; (all by Halldor Laxness): The Atom Station, 1961; Paradise Reclaimed, 1962; The Fish Can Sing, 1966; World Light, 1969; Christianity Under Glacier, 1973; (by Samivel) Golden Iceland, 1967; contributor: The Glorious Privilege, 1967; The Future of the Highlands, 1968; Strange Stories, Amazing Facts, 1975; The National Trust for Scotland Guide, 1976. *Recreations:* digging and delving. *Address:* Blairskaith House, Balmore-Torrance, Glasgow G64 4AX. *T:* Balmore 226.

MAGOR, Major (Edward) Walter (Moyle), CMG 1960; OBE 1956 (MBE 1947); DL; *b* 1 June 1911; *e s* of late Edward John Penberthy Magor, JP, Lamellen, St Tudy, Cornwall, and Gilian Sarah Magor, JP; *m* 1939, Daphne Davis (*d* 1972), *d* of late Hector Robert Lushington Graham, Summerhill, Thomastown, Co. Kilkenny; two *d. Educ:* Marlborough; Magdalen, Oxford; Magdalene, Cambridge. MA. Indian Army, 1934-47; RARO, 10th Hussars, 1949-61; Indian Political Service, 1937-39 and 1943-47; Colonial Administrative Service, 1947-61; Kenya: Asst Chief Secretary, 1953; Permanent Secretary, Ministry of Defence, 1954; Acting Minister for Defence, 1956; Secretary to the Cabinet, 1958. Home Civil Service, DTI, formerly BoT, 1961-71; Asst Secretary, 1964; retired 1971. Chm., St John Council for Cornwall, 1973. DL Cornwall, 1974. OStJ 1975. Médaille de La Belgique Reconnaissante, 1961. Lord of the Manor of Kellygreen. *Recreation:* gardening (Mem., Garden Soc.). *Address:* Lamellen, St Tudy, Cornwall. *T:* St Tudy 207. *Club:* Army and Navy.

MAGUINNESS, Prof. William Stuart; Professor of Latin Language and Literature, University of London, King's College, 1946-71; Senior Research Fellow, 1971-72; Head of Department of Classics, 1952-72; General Editor, Methuen's Classical Texts; Vice-President, Classical Association, Orbilian Society, Virgil Society and London Classical Society; *b* 12 Oct. 1903; *s* of George J. Maguinness, Belfast; *m* 1933, Olive D., *d* of George T. Y. Dickinson, Sheffield; one *d. Educ:* Royal Belfast Academical Institution; Trinity Coll., Dublin (Classical Sizarship, Classical Foundation Scholarship; Sen. Moderatorships with Gold Medals in Classics and Modern Literature (French and Italian) and Univ. Studentship in Classics 1926; MA 1929). FKC 1966. Asst Lecturer in Classics, University of Manchester, 1927-30; Lecturer in Classics, University of Sheffield, 1930-46; Administrative Officer, Admiralty, 1941-43; Visiting Lecturer in various Universities in France, Holland, Italy, Brazil, Poland and Greece. *Publications:* contributions on Classical subjects to the Oxford Classical Dictionary, Encyclopædia Britannica, Proc. Leeds Philosophical Society, Classical Review, Classical Quarterly, Revue de la Franco-ancienne, Wiener humanistische Blätter, Rivista di Cultura classica e medioevale, Phoenix, Aevum, Antiquité classique, Estudios Clásicos, Notes and Queries, Vita Latina, various Actes de Congrès and other journals, 1928-; Edition: of Racine's Bérénice, 1929 (2nd edn, 1956); of Virgil's Aeneid, Book XII, 1953 (3rd edn, 1973); 4th (revised) edn of Stobart's Grandeur that was Rome (in collaboration with H. H. Scullard), 1961; Index to the Speeches of Isaeus (in collaboration with the late W. A. Goligher), 1964; English translation of P. Grimal's La Civilisation romaine, 1963, and F. Chamoux' La Civilisation grecque, 1965; Chapter in volume on Lucretius, 1965. *Address:* 25 Hillway, Highgate, N6. *T:* 01-340 3064.

MAGUIRE, (Albert) Michael, MC 1945, MM 1943; QC 1967; *b* 30 Dec. 1922; *s* of late Richard Maguire and Ruth Maguire. *Educ:* Hutton Grammar Sch.; Trinity Hall, Cambridge (BA 1948). Served War of 1939-45, North Irish Horse (Captain), in Africa (MM) and Italy (MC). Inns of Court Regt, 1946. War Crimes Investigation Unit, 1946. Called to the Bar, Middle Temple, 1949 (Harmsworth Scholar); Bencher, 1973. Last Recorder of Carlisle (1970-71). *Address:* Chestnuts, Lower

Bank Road, Fulwood, Preston, Lancs. *T:* Preston 719291. *Clubs:* United Oxford & Cambridge University; Racquet (Liverpool).

MAGUIRE, (Benjamin) Waldo, OBE 1973; *b* 31 May 1920; *s* of Benjamin Maguire and Elizabeth Ann Eldon; *m* 1944, Lilian Joan Martin; four *s. Educ:* Portadown Coll.; Trinity Coll., Dublin. BA 1st cl. hons Philosophy. Intell. Service, WO and FO, 1942-45; BBC Latin American Service, 1945; BBC Radio News, 1946-55; BBC TV News, 1955; Editor, BBC TV News, 1962-64; Controller, News and Public Affairs, NZ Broadcasting Corp., 1965-66; BBC Controller, NI, 1966-72; Head of Information Programmes, NZ TV2, 1975-76. *Recreations:* conversation, angling. *Address:* 116 Park Avenue, Ruislip, Mddx. *T:* Ruislip 35981.

MAGUIRE, Conor A.; Member, European Court of Human Rights, 1965-71; Chief Justice of Eire, 1946-61; *b* 16 Dec. 1889; *s* of C. J. O'L. Maguire, MD, and Florence O'Neill; *m* 1921, Nora Whelan; three *s. Educ:* Clongowes Wood Coll.; Univ. Coll., Dublin. MA, LLB National University of Ireland; Solicitor, 1914; Judge and Land Settlement Commissioner Dail, 1920-22; Called to Bar of Ireland, 1922; Inner Bar, 1932; prominent in the Sinn Fein movement; Member of Dail Eireann for National University of Ireland; Attorney-General, Irish Free State, 1932-36; Judge of the High Court and Judicial Commissioner, 1936; President of the High Court, 1937-46; Chairman Central Council, Irish Red Cross Society, 1940-46; President International Celtic Congress, 1957-61; Irish Representative European Commission of Human Rights, Strasbourg, 1963-65. Commandeur Légion d'Honneur; Order of St Raimon de Penafort (Spain); Grosse Verdienstkreuz (Federal Republic of Germany). LLD (*hc*): NUI; Dublin University. *Recreations:* fishing and shooting. *Address:* St Alban's, Albany Avenue, Monkstown, Co. Dublin.

MAGUIRE, Frank; *see* Maguire, M. F.

MAGUIRE, Air Marshal Sir Harold John, KCB 1966 (CB 1958); DSO 1946; OBE 1949; Political and Economic Adviser to Commercial Union Assurance Co., since 1972, Director, since 1975; *b* 12 April 1912; *s* of Michael Maguire, Maynooth, Ireland, and Harriett (*née* Warren), Kilkishen, Co. Clare, Ireland; *m* 1940, Mary Elisabeth Wild, Dublin; one *s* one *d. Educ:* Wesley Coll., Dublin; Dublin Univ. Royal Air Force Commn, 1933; service in flying boats, 230 Sqdn, Egypt and Far East, 1935-38; commanded night fighter sqdn, UK, 1939-40 and day fighter sqdn, 1940; OC 266 (Fighter) Wing, Dutch E Indies, 1942; POW, Java, 1942; Staff Coll., 1947; Fighter Command Staff Duties, 1948-50; OC, RAF, Odiham, 1950-52; Senior Air Staff Officer, Malta, 1952-55; staff of CAS, Air Ministry, 1955-58; Senior Air Staff Officer, HQ No 11 Group, RAF, 1958-59; AOC No 13 Group, RAF, 1959-61; AOC No 11 Group, Fighter Command, 1961-62; SASO Far East Air Force, 1962-64; ACAS (Intelligence), 1964-65; Dep. Chief of Defence Staff (Intelligence), 1965-68; retired, 1968; Dir-Gen. of Intelligence, MoD, 1968-72. *Address:* c/o Lloyds Bank, 6 Pall Mall, SW1. *Club:* Royal Air Force.

MAGUIRE, Hugh, FRAM; violinist and conductor; Leader, Melos Ensemble; Professor of Violin, Royal Academy of Music; *b* 2 Aug. 1927; *m* 1953, Suzanne Lewis, of International Ballet; two *s* three *d. Educ:* Belvedere Coll., SJ, Dublin; Royal Academy of Music, London (David Martin); Paris (Georges Enesco). Leader: Bournemouth Symphony Orchestra, 1952-56; London Symphony Orchestra, 1956-62; BBC Symphony Orchestra, 1962-67; formerly Leader: Cremona String Quartet, 1966-68; Allegri String Quartet. Artistic Dir, Irish Youth Orch. Violin Tutor, Nat. Youth Orch. of GB. Mem., Irish Arts Council. Hon. MMus Hull, 1975. Harriet Cohen Internat. Award; Councils Gold Medal (Ireland), 1963. *Address:* 1 Alverstone Road, NW2. *T:* 01-459 4787.

MAGUIRE, Meredith Francis (Frank Maguire); MP (Ind) Fermanagh and South Tyrone, since Oct. 1974; publican, Frank's Bar, Lisnaskea; *b* 1929; *m*; three *s* one *d. Educ:* St Mary's Marist Brothers Sch., Athlone. Joined uncle in business in Lisnaskea, later forming own company. *Address:* House of Commons, SW1A 0AA.

MAGUIRE, Michael; *see* Maguire, A. M.

MAGUIRE, Rt. Rev. Robert Kenneth, MA, DD; Co-ordinator, Canadian Conference, Theology '76, 1975-76; *b* 31 March 1923; *s* of late Robert Maguire and late Anne Crozier; unmarried. *Educ:* Trinity Coll., Dublin. BA 1945; Divinity Testimonium, 1947. Deacon, 1947; Priest, 1948. Curate of St Mark, Armagh, 1947-49; St James the Apostle, Montreal, 1949-52; Dean of Residence, Trinity Coll., Dublin, 1952-60; Curate-in-charge of

St Andrew's, Dublin, 1954-57; Minor Canon of St Patrick's Cathedral, Dublin, 1955-58; Dean and Rector of Christ Church Cathedral, Montreal, 1961-62; Bishop of Montreal, 1963-75. DD (*jure dig*.): Dublin Univ., 1963; Montreal Diocesan Theolog. Coll., 1963; DCL (*hc*), Bishop's Univ., Lennoxville, Qué., 1963. *Address:* Box 117, Dunham, Québec J0E 1M0, Canada.

MAGUIRE, Waldo; *see* Maguire, B. W.

MAHER, Very Rev. William Francis, SJ; Provincial Superior of the English Province of the Society of Jesus, since 1976; *b* 20 June 1916. *Educ:* St Ignatius' College, Stamford Hill; Heythrop College, Oxon. STL. Entered the Society of Jesus, 1935; ordained priest, 1948; Principal, Heythrop College, 1974-76. *Address:* 114 Mount Street, W1Y 6AH. *T:* 01-499 5361.

MAHLER, Dr Halfdan; Director-General, World Health Organization, since July 1973; *b* 21 April 1923; *m* 1957, Dr Ebba Fischer-Simonsen; two *s. Educ:* Univ. of Copenhagen (MD, EOPH). Planning Officer, Internat. Tuberculosis Campaign, Ecuador, 1950-51; Sen. WHO Med. Officer, Nat. TB Programme, India, 1951-61; Chief MO, Tuberculosis Unit, WHO/HQ, Geneva, 1961-69; Dir, Project Systems Analysis, WHO/HQ, Geneva, 1969-70; Asst Dir-Gen., WHO, 1970-73. Hon. FRSM 1976; Hon. Fellow: Indian Soc. for Malaria and other Communicable Diseases, Delhi; Faculty of Community Med., RCP, 1975; Hon. Member: Soc. médicale de Genève; Union internat. contre la Tuberculose; Hon. Life Mem., Uganda Medical Assoc., 1976; Assoc. Mem., Belgian Soc. of Trop. Med. Hon. LLD Nottingham, 1975; Hon. MD Karolinska Inst., 1977; Hon. Dr de l'Univ. Toulouse (Sciences Sociales), 1977. Jana Evangelisty Purkyne Medal, Prague, 1974; Charles Univ. Medal, Prague, 1974; Comenius Univ. Gold Medal, Bratislava, 1974; Carlo Forlanini Gold Medal, 1975. *Publications:* papers etc on the epidemiology and control of tuberculosis, the political, social, economic and technological priority setting in the health sector, and the application of systems analysis to health care problems. *Recreations:* sailing, skiing. *Address:* (home) 12 chemin du Pont-Ceard, 1290 Versoix, Switzerland; (office) World Health Organization, Avenue Appia 1211 Geneva 27, Switzerland.

MAHLER, Kurt, FAA 1965; FRS 1948; PhD, DSc; Professor Emeritus, Australian National University, since 1975; *b* 1903. *Educ:* Univs of Frankfurt and Göttingen. Research work at Univs of Göttingen, Groningen, and Manchester. Asst Lecturer at Manchester Univ., 1937-39, 1941-44; Lecturer, 1944-47; Senior Lecturer, 1948-49; Reader, 1949-52; Prof. of Mathematical Analysis, 1952-63; Prof. of Mathematics, Institute of Advanced Studies, ANU, 1963-68; Prof. of Mathematics, Ohio State Univ., USA, 1968-72. De Morgan Medal, 1971; Thomas Ranken Lyle Medal, 1977. *Publications:* Lectures on Diophantine Approximations, 1961; Introduction to p-adic Numbers and their Functions, 1973; Lectures on Transcendental Numbers, 1976; papers on different subjects in pure mathematics (Theory and Geometry of Numbers) in various journals, from 1928. *Recreations:* Chinese, photography. *Address:* Mathematics Department, Institute of Advanced Studies, Australian National University, Canberra, ACT 2600, Australia.

MAHLER, Prof. Robert Frederick, FRCP, FRCPE; Professor of Medicine, University of Wales, since 1970; *b* 31 Oct. 1924; *s* of Felix Mahler and Olga Lowy; *m* 1951, Maureen Calvert; two *s. Educ:* Edinburgh Academy; Edinburgh Univ. BSc; MB, ChB. Research fellowships and univ. posts in medicine, biochemistry and clinical pharmacology at various med. schs and univs: in Gt Britain: Royal Postgrad. Med. Sch., Guy's Hosp., Manchester, Dundee, Cardiff; in USA: Harvard Univ., Univ. of Indiana; in Sweden: Karolinska Inst., Stockholm. *Publications:* contribs to British and Amer. med. and scientific jls. *Recreations:* moving to new places, winter sports, watching Rugby and rowing, music, theatre. *Address:* 4 Brynteg Close, Dyncoed, Cardiff CF2 6AS. *T:* Cardiff 759666. *Club:* Royal Society of Medicine.

MAHON, Denis; *see* Mahon, J. D.

MAHON, Sir George Edward John, 6th Bt, *cr* 1819; *b* 22 June 1911; *s* of 5th Bt and late Hon. Edith Dillon, 2nd *d* of 4th Lord Clonbrock; *S* father, 1926; *m* 1st, 1938, Audrey Evelyn (*d* 1957), *o c* of late Dr Walter Jagger and late Mrs Maxwell Coote; two *s* one *d*; 2nd, 1958, Suzanne, *d* of late Thomas Donnellan, Pirbright, Surrey, and late Mrs Donnellan; one *d. Heir: s* Major William Walter Mahon, Irish Guards [*b* 4 Dec. 1940; *m* 1968, Rosemary Jane, *yr d* of Lt-Col M. E. Melvill, Symington, Lanarkshire; one *s* two *d*]. *Address:* Castlegar, Ahascragh, Co. Galway; Greeninch, Enniskerry, Co. Wicklow.

MAHON, Sir Gerald MacMahon, Kt 1962; Chairman, Medical Appeal Tribunals under Industrial Injuries Acts, 1964-76; *b* 24 July 1904; *o surv. s* of late Foster MacMahon Mahon, and of Mrs Lilian Frances Mahon, OBE (*née* Moore), Sheringham, Norfolk; *m* 1938, Roma Irene Maxtone Mailer; two *s. Educ:* Alleyn Court Preparatory Sch., Dulwich Coll.; Brasenose Coll., Oxford (BA). Called to the Bar (Inner Temple), 1928. Resident Magistrate, Tanganyika, 1936; Judge, HM High Court of Tanganyika Territory, 1949-59; Chief Justice of Zanzibar, 1959-64, retired. *Address:* Moat Cottage, Stratton Audley, Bicester, Oxon. *Club:* Vincent's (Oxford).

MAHON, Rt. Rev. Gerald Thomas; Auxiliary Bishop of Westminster (Bishop in West London) (RC) and Titular Bishop of Eanach Duin since 1970; *b* 4 May 1922; *s* of George Elborne Mahon and Mary Elizabeth (*née* Dooley). *Educ:* Cardinal Vaughan Sch., Kensington; Christ's Coll., Cambridge. Priest, 1946. Teaching, St Peter's Coll., Freshfield, 1950-55; missionary work in Dio. of Kisumu, Kenya, 1955-63; Superior General of St Joseph's Missionary Society of Mill Hill, 1963-70. *Address:* 7 Dukes Avenue, Chiswick, W4 2AA.

MAHON, (John) Denis, CBE 1967; MA Oxon; FBA 1964; Art Historian; Trustee of the National Gallery, 1957-64 and 1966-73; *b* 8 Nov. 1910; *s* of late John FitzGerald Mahon (4th *s* of Sir W. Mahon, 4th Bt) and Lady Alice Evelyn Browne (*d* 1970), *d* of 5th Marquess of Sligo. *Educ:* Eton; Christ Church, Oxford. Has specialised in the study of 17th-Century painting in Italy and has formed a collection of pictures of the period; is a member of the Cttee of the Biennial Exhibitions at Bologna, Italy; was awarded, 1957, Medal for Benemeriti della Cultura by Pres. of Italy for services to criticism and history of Italian art; Accademico d'Onore, Clementine Acad., Bologna, 1964; Serena Medal for Italian Studies, British Acad., 1972. Corresp. Fellow: Accad. Raffaello, Urbino, 1968; Deputazione di Storia Patria per le provincie di Romagna, 1969. Hon. DLitt, Newcastle, 1969. *Publications:* Studies in Seicento Art and Theory, 1947; Mostra dei Carracci, Catalogo critico dei Disegni, 1956 (1963); Poussiniana, 1962; Catalogues of the Mostra del Guercino (Dipinti, 1968; Disegni, 1969); contributed to: Actes of Colloque Poussin, 1960; Friedlaender Festschrift, 1965; Problemi Guardeschi, 1967; articles, including a number on Caravaggio and Poussin, in art-historical periodicals, *eg,* The Burlington Magazine, Apollo, The Art Bulletin, Journal of the Warburg and Courtauld Institutes, Bulletin of the Metropolitan Museum of New York, Gazette des Beaux-Arts, Art de France, Paragone, Commentari, Zeitschrift für Kunstwissenschaft; has collaborated in the compilation of catalogues raisonnés of exhibitions, *eg,* Artists in 17th Century Rome (London, 1955), Italian Art and Britain (Royal Academy, 1960), L'Ideale Classico del Seicento in Italia (Bologna, 1962), Omaggio al Guercino (Cento, 1967). *Address:* 33 Cadogan Square, SW1. *T:* 01-235 7311, 01-235 2530.

MAHON, Peter, JP; Member (L), Liverpool District Council, Old Swan Ward, since 1973; *b* 4 May 1909; *s* of late Alderman Simon Mahon, OBE, JP, Bootle, Liverpool; *m* 1935, Margaret Mahon (*née* Hannon). *Educ:* St James Elementary Sch.; St Edward's Coll. (Irish Christian Brothers). Local Govt Service, 1933-; Bootle: Council, 1933; Mayor, 1954-55; Chm. or Dep. Chm. numerous cttees; Mem. Nat. Cttee of TGWU. Contested (Lab) Blackburn, 1952-54, Preston, 1962-64; MP (Lab) Preston South, 1964-70; contested Liverpool Scotland, April 1971, as first Against Abortion candidate in UK; expelled from Labour Party. Talked out first Abortion Bill, House of Commons, 1966. *Recreations:* football and swimming enthusiast; fond of music. *Address:* Seahaven, Burbo Bank Road, Blundellsands, Liverpool L23 8TA.

MAHON, Simon; MP (Lab) Bootle, since 1955; *b* 1914; *s* of late Alderman Simon Mahon, OBE, JP, Bootle, Liverpool; *m* 1941, Veronica Robertshaw. *Educ:* St James Elementary Sch.; St Joseph's Coll. Served War of 1939-45; commissioned Royal Engineers. Alderman of Bootle Borough Council; Mayor, 1962. Opposition Whip, 1959-61. Trustee, Far Eastern Prisoners of War Fund. KCSG 1968. *Address:* House of Commons, SW1.

MAHONY, Lt-Col John Keefer, VC 1944; *b* 30 June 1911; *s* of Joseph Jackson and Louise Mary Mahony; *m* 1950, Bonnie Johnston, Ottawa; two *d. Educ:* Duke of Connaught Sch., New Westminster, BC, Canada. On editorial staff of Vancouver Daily Province (newspaper) until outbreak of war of 1939-45; mem. Canadian Militia (equivalent of British Territorials) from 1936 until going on active service in Sept. 1939. Served War of 1939-45 (VC): (Canada, UK, Africa, Italy) Westminster Regt, Canadian Army; Major, 1943. Liaison Officer, US Dept of the Army, Washington, DC, 1954; retd as AA and QMG, Alberta Area, 1963. Exec. Dir, Junior Achievement of London, Inc.

Recreations: swimming, lacrosse, baseball. *Address:* 657 Santa Monica Road, London, Ontario, Canada.

MAHTAB, Maharajadhiraja Bahadur Sir Uday Chand, of Burdwan, KCIE, 1945; *b* 1905; *s* of late Maharajadhiraja Bahadur Sir Bijay Chand Mahtab of Burdwan, GCIE, KCSI, IOM; *m* 1929, Radharani Devi, Amritsar, Punjab; three *s* three *d. Educ:* Presidency Coll., Calcutta; Calcutta Univ. (BA 1926). Pres. Non-Muslim block of Bengal Partition meeting, June 1947; Mem., Constituent Assembly. MLA Bengal, 1937-52; is a Zemindar; a Mem. of Damodar Canal Enquiry Cttee, 1938, and of Select Cttee on Calcutta Municipal (amendment) Bill, 1940; Chm. of Burdwan District Flood Relief and Bengal Central Flood Relief Cttees, 1943-44, of Indian Red Cross Appeal (Bengal), 1943-46, of Calcutta War Cttee, 1943-46, and of Damodar Flood Control Enquiry Cttee, 1944; a Mem. of Bengal Tanks Improvement Bill Select Cttee, 1944, of Advisory Cttee to examine cases of Terrorist Convicts in Bengal, 1944, of W Bengal Forest Denudation Enquiry Cttee, 1944, and of Select Cttee on Bengal Agricultural Income Tax Bill, 1944; Pres., British Indian Association; Mem., Central Jute Board, 1951-52; Dir of over 30 business firms and Chm. of several Boards. Mem. of Managing Body of several Government Organisations. Silver Jubilee (1935) and Coronation (1937) medals. *Address:* The Palace, Burdwan, India; Bijay Manzil, Alipore, Calcutta. *Clubs:* Calcutta (Calcutta); Aftab (Burdwan); Gymkhana (Darjeeling).

MAIDEN, Colin James, ME, DPhil; Vice-Chancellor, University of Auckland, New Zealand, since 1971; *b* 5 May 1933; *s* of Henry A. Maiden; *m* 1957, Jenefor Mary Rowe; one *s* three *d. Educ:* Auckland Grammar Sch.; Univ. of Auckland, NZ; Oxford Univ. ME(NZ), DPhil (Oxon). Post-doctorate research, Oxford Univ., Oxford, Eng. (supported by AERE, Harwell), 1957-58; Head of Hypersonic Physics Section, Canadian Armament Research and Develt Estabt, Quebec City, Canada, 1958-60; Sen. Lectr in Mechanical Engrg, Univ. of Auckland, 1960-61; Head of Material Sciences Laboratory, Gen. Motors Corp., Defense Research Laboratories, Santa Barbara, Calif, USA, 1961-66; Manager of Process Engineering, Gen. Motors Corp., Technl Centre, Warren, Michigan, USA, 1966-70. Director: Mason Industries Ltd, 1972-; Farmers Trading Co. Ltd, 1973-. Mem., Metric Adv. Bd, 1972-; Chm., NZ Energy R&D Cttee, 1974-. *Publications:* numerous scientific and technical papers. *Recreations:* tennis, golf, squash. *Address:* 1 Fern Avenue, Auckland, New Zealand. *T:* 685600. *Clubs:* Vincent's (Oxford); Northern, Rotary (Auckland); Remuera Racquets, Eden Epsom Tennis, Auckland Golf.

MAIDMENT, Kenneth John, MA; *b* 29 Oct. 1910; *s* of Francis George Maidment and Jessie Louisa Taylor; *m* 1937, Isobel Felicity, *d* of Archibald Leitch; one *s* three *d. Educ:* Bristol Gram. Sch.; Merton Coll., Oxford. Hertford Scholar, 1929; First Class Classical Hon. Mods, 1930; Craven Scholar, 1930; First Class Litt. Hum., 1932; Junior Research Fellow, Merton Coll., 1932-34; Fellow and Classical Tutor, Jesus Coll. (Oxford), 1934-38; Fellow and Classical Tutor, Merton Coll., 1938-49; Oxford and Bucks Lt Infantry, 1940; seconded War Office, 1941; liaison duties in US, 1942-45, Lt-Col; University Lecturer in Greek Literature, 1947-49; Principal, Auckland Univ. Coll., 1950-57; Vice-Chancellor, Univ. of Auckland, 1957-71. Hon. LLD Auckland, 1970. *Publications:* Critical edition and translation of Antiphon and Andocides (Loeb Library), 1940; contribs to classical journals. *Address:* 9 Highfield Avenue, Headington, Oxford.

MAIDSTONE, Viscount; Daniel James Hatfield Finch Hatton; *b* 7 Oct. 1967; *s* and *heir* of 16th Earl of Winchilsea, *qv.*

MAIDSTONE, Bishop Suffragan of, since 1976; Rt. Rev. Richard Henry McPhail Third; *b* 29 Sept. 1927; *s* of Henry McPhail and Marjorie Caroline Third; *m* 1966, Helen Illingworth; two *d. Educ:* Alleyn's Sch.; Reigate Grammar Sch.; Emmanuel Coll., Cambridge (BA 1950, MA 1955); Lincoln Theological Coll. Deacon 1952, priest 1953; Southwark; Curate: S Andrew, Mottingham, 1952-55; Sanderstead (in charge of St Edmund, Riddlesdown), 1955-59; Vicar of Sheerness, 1959-67; Vicar of Orpington, 1967-76; RD of Orpington, 1973-76; Hon. Canon of Rochester, 1974-76; Proctor in Convocation, 1975-76. *Recreations:* music, walking. *Address:* The Bishop's House, Egerton, Ashford, Kent TN27 9DJ. *T:* Egerton 431.

MAIDSTONE, Archdeacon of; *see* Nye, Ven. N. K.

MAILER, Norman; *b* 31 Jan. 1923; *s* of Isaac Barnett Mailer and Fanny Schneider; *m* 1st, 1944, Beatrice Silverman (marr. diss., 1951); one *d*; 2nd, 1954, Adèle Morales (marr. diss., 1962); two *d*; 3rd, 1962, Lady Jeanne Campbell (marr. diss., 1963); one *d*; 4th, 1963, Beverly Bentley; two *s*; 5th, Carol Stevens; one *d*.

Educ: Harvard. Infantryman, US Army, 1944-46. Co-founder of Village Voice, 1955; An Editor of Dissent, 1953-63. Democratic Candidate, Mayoral Primaries, New York City, 1969. Directed films: Wild 90, 1967; Beyond the Law, 1967; Maidstone, 1968. *Publications:* (American): The Naked and the Dead, 1948; Barbary Shore, 1951; The Deer Park, 1955 (dramatized, 1967); Advertisements for Myself, 1959; Deaths For The Ladies, 1962; The Presidential Papers, 1963; An American Dream, 1964; Cannibals and Christians, 1966; Why Are We In Vietnam?, 1967 (a novel); The Armies of the Night, 1968 (Pulitzer Prize, 1969); Miami and the Siege of Chicago, 1968 (National Book Award, 1969); Of a Fire on the Moon, 1970; The Prisoner of Sex, 1971; Existential Errands, 1972; St George and the Godfather, 1972; Marilyn, 1973; The Faith of Graffiti, 1974; The Fight, 1975; Some Honorable Men, 1976; Genius and Lust, 1976. *Address:* c/o Molly Malone Cook, PO Box 338, Provincetown, Mass 02657, USA.

MAILLART, Ella (Kini); Explorer; *b* 20 Feb. 1903; Swiss father and Danish mother; unmarried. *Educ:* Geneva; and also while teaching French at two schools in England. Took to the seas at 20, cruising with 3 ton Perlette, 10 ton Bonita, 45 ton Atalante-all these manned by girls; then 120 ton Volunteer, 125 ton Insoumise; in Mediterranean, Biscay, Channel; sailed for Switzerland Olympic Games, Paris, 1924 single-handed competition; Hockey for Switzerland as captain in 1931; Ski-ed for Switzerland in the FIS races in 1931-34; went to Russia for 6 months, 1930; travelled in Russian Turkestan for 6 months 1932; went to Manchoukuo for Petit Parisien, 1934; returned overland accompanied by Peter Fleming, via Koko Nor; travelled overland to Iran and Afghanistan in 1937 and 1939, in South India, 1940-45, Nepal, 1951, Everest Base Camp, 1965. Fellow RGS, London; Member; Royal Soc. for Asian Affairs; Club des Explorateurs, Paris. Sir Percy Sykes Medal. *Publications:* Parmi la Jeunesse Russe, 1932; Des Monts Célestes aux Sables Rouges, 1934 (in English as Turkestan Solo, 1934); Oasis Interdites, 1937, reprinted 1971 (in English as Forbidden Journey, 1937); Gipsy Afloat, 1942; Cruises and Caravans, 1942; The Cruel Way, 1947; Ti-Puss, 1952; The Land of the Sherpas, 1955. *Recreations:* ski-ing, gardening. *Address:* c/o David Higham Associates Ltd, 5-8 Lower John Street, W1; 10 Avenue G. Vallette, Geneva, Switzerland. *T:* Geneva 46.46.57; Atchala, Chandolin sur Sierre, Switzerland. *Clubs:* Kandahar; (hon.) Ski Club de Dames Suisse; (hon.) Ski Club of Great Britain; (hon.) Alpine.

MAIN, Frank Fiddes, CB 1965; FRCPEd; Chief Medical Officer, Ministry of Health and Social Services, Northern Ireland, 1954-68, retired; *b* 9 June 1905; *s* of Frank and Mary Main, Edinburgh; *m* 1931, Minnie Roberta Paton; two *s* two *d. Educ:* Daniel Stewart's Coll., Edinburgh; Edinburgh Univ. MB, ChB 1927; DPH 1931; MRCPEd 1954; FRCPEd 1956. Medical Officer of Health, Perth, 1937-48; Senior Administrative Medical Officer, Eastern Regional Hosp. Bd (Scotland), 1948-54. Crown Mem., Gen. Med. Council, 1956-69. QHP 1956-59. *Recreation:* golf. *Address:* Bruce's Cottage, Kilconquhar, Elie, Fife KY9 1LG. *T:* Colinsburgh 312.

MAIN, John Roy, QC 1974; **His Honour Judge Main;** a Circuit Judge, since 1976; *b* 21 June 1930; *yr s* of late A. C. Main, MIMechE; *m* 1955, Angela de la Condamine Davies, *er d* of late R. W. H. Davies, ICS; two *s* one *d. Educ:* Portsmouth Grammar Sch.; Hotchkiss Sch., USA; Brasenose Coll., Oxford (MA). Called to Bar, Inner Temple, 1954; a Recorder of Crown Court, 1972-76. Mem. Special Panel, Transport Tribunal, 1970-76; Dep. Chm., IoW QS, 1971. *Recreations:* boating, gardening, music. *Address:* 8 Oaken Lane, Claygate, Surrey. *T:* Esher 65503.

MAIN, Dr Peter Tester, ERD 1964; FRSM; Director since 1973, and Chief Executive Officer since 1977, Industrial Division, The Boots Company Ltd; *b* 21 March 1925; *s* of Peter Tester Main and late Esther Paterson (*née* Lawson); *m* 1952, Dr Margaret Fimister (*née* Tweddle); two *s* one *d. Educ:* Robert Gordon's Coll., Aberdeen; Univ. of Aberdeen (MB, ChB 1948, MD 1963). FRSM 1957. Captain, RAMC, 1949-51; Lt-Col RAMC (AER), retd 1964. House Surg., Aberdeen Royal Infirmary, 1948; House Physician, Woodend Hosp., Aberdeen, 1949; Demonstrator, Univ. of Durham, 1952; gen. practice, 1953-57; joined Res. Dept, Boots, 1957; Dir of Res., 1968. Vice Pres., Assoc. of British Pharmaceutical Industry, 1977-. *Publications:* contribs on therapeutics to learned jls. *Recreations:* fly fishing, shooting, Scottish music. *Address:* Limehurst, Halam Road, Southwell, Notts. *T:* Southwell 813374. *Club:* Naval and Military.

MAINGOT, Rodney, TC 1976; FRCS; Surgeon and writer; Consulting Surgeon: Royal Free Hospital, Royal Waterloo Hospital, Southend General Hospital, Royal Prince Alfred

Hospital, Sydney; late Regional Consultant in Surgery, Emergency Medical Service; Fellow, Surgical Section, RSM (late President); Fellow, Association of Surgeons of Great Britain and Ireland; Editor-in-Chief, British Journal of Clinical Practice; *b* Trinidad, BWI; *m* Rosalind Smeaton (*d* 1957), Brisbane, Australia; *m* 1965, Evelyn Plesch, London. *Educ:* Ushaw Coll., Durham. House Surg. (twice), Surgical Receiving Officer and Chief Asst to a Surgical Unit, St Bartholomew's Hospital; Surgical Registrar, West London Hospital. Visiting Professor in Surgery: Ohio State Univ. Hosp., 1960; Mount Sinai Hosp., Miami, 1963; Maadi Hosp., Cairo, 1967-68. Served War of 1914-18 (Captain RAMC) in Egypt and Palestine (despatches twice). Editor-in-Chief, Brit. Jl of Clinical Practice. Sydney Body Gold Medallist, 1958. *Publications:* Post Graduate Surgery, 1936; Technique of Gastric Operations, 1941; The Surgical Treatment of Gastric and Duodenal Ulcer, 1945; Techniques in British Surgery, 1950; The Management of Abdominal Operations, 2nd edn 1957; Abdominal Operations, 6th edn 1974; The Relationship of Art and Medicine, 1974; contributor to Surgery of the Gallbladder and Bile Ducts, ed Smith and Sherlock, 1964, also in Operative Surgery, 2nd ed Rob and Smith, 1969; Dr Frank H. Lahey Memorial Lecture in Boston, 1963. *Recreations:* painting, art, travelling, writing. *Address:* 8 Ashley Court, Grand Avenue, Hove, Sussex BN3 2NP.

MAINI, Sir Amar (Nath), Kt 1957; CBE 1953 (OBE 1948); *b* Nairobi, 31 July 1911; *e s* of late Nauhria Ram Maini, Nairobi, Kenya, and Ludhiana, Punjab, India; *m* 1935, Ram Saheli Mehra, Ludhiana; two *s. Educ:* Govt Indian Sch., Nairobi; London Sch. of Economics (BCom, Hons 1932). Barrister-at-law, Middle Temple, London, 1933. Advocate of High Court of Kenya, and of High Court of Uganda. Sometime an actg MLC, Kenya, and Mem., Nairobi Municipal Council. From 1939 onwards, in Uganda; associated with family cotton business of Nauhria Ram & Sons (Uganda) Ltd. Formerly: Mem., Kampala Township Authority, Chm., Kampala Municipal Council, 1st Mayor of Kampala (1950-55); Dep. Chm., Uganda Electricity Board; Member: Uganda Development Corporation; Lint Marketing Board; Civil Defence Bd; Asian Manpower Cttee; Transport Bd; Supplies Bd; Immigration Advisory Bd; Advisory Bd of Health; Railway Advisory Council; Advisory Bd of Commerce; Rent Restriction Bd; Makerere Coll. Assembly, etc. Past Pres. Central Council of Indian Assocs in Uganda; Indian Assoc., Kampala; served on Cttees of Cotton Association. Formerly: Mem. Uganda Legislative and Exec. Councils; Development Council, Uganda; EA Legislative Assembly; EA Postal Advisory Bd; EA Transport Adv. Council; EA Air Adv Council, etc. Minister for Corporations and Regional Communications in the Government of Uganda, 1955-58; Minister of Commerce and Industry in Uganda, 1958-61; Speaker, E African Central Legislative Assembly, 1961-67; Mem., E African Common Market Tribunal, 1967-69. Dep. Chm. Kenya Broadcasting Corp., 1961-63. *Recreations:* walking, reading, golf. *Address:* 55 Vicarage Road, East Sheen, SW14 8RY. *T:* 01-878 1497. *Clubs:* Reform; Nairobi.

MAINLAND, Prof. William Faulkner, MA; Professor of German, University of Sheffield, 1953-70; *b* 31 May 1905; *s* of late George Mainland and of Ada (*née* Froggatt); *m* 1930, Clarice Vowles, *d* of late A. E. Brewer; no *c. Educ:* George Heriot's Sch.; Univ. of Edinburgh. 1st Class Hons. Vans Dunlop Schol. in German; Postgrad. studies in London under late Prof. J. G. Robertson, and in Germany. Asst for French and German at London Sch. of Economics, 1929-30; thereafter attached to German Depts of Univs of: Manitoba, 1930; Manchester, 1935; London (UC, 1937, King's Coll., 1938, Birkbeck Coll., 1938); Sheffield, 1946; Leeds, 1947. Public Orator, Univ. of Sheffield, 1968-70. *Publications:* German for Students of Medicine, 1938; German Lyrics of the Seventeenth Century (with Prof. August Closs), 1941; E. T. A. Hoffmann, Der goldene Topf (Editor), 1942, 2nd edn, 1945; Schiller, Uber naive und sentimentalische Dichtung (Editor), 1951; Schiller and the Changing Past, 1957; Wilhelm Tell in metrical translation with commentary, 1972; chapters on Th. Storm, H. Sudermann, Fr. v. Unruh, H. Kasack, in German Men of Letters, 1961-66; Schiller, Jungfrau v. Orleans (Editor with Prof. E. J. Engel), 1963; Schiller, Wilhelm Tell (Editor), 1968. Reviews and articles on German and Dutch literature. *Recreations:* drawing, painting; Baltic language studies. *Address:* 2 Severn Road, Tree Root Walk, Sheffield S10 2SU. *Club:* University Staff (Sheffield).

MAINWARING, Captain Maurice K. C.; *see* Cavenagh-Mainwaring.

MAIR, Prof. Alexander; Professor of Community and Occupational Medicine (formerly of Public Health and Social Medicine), University of Dundee, since 1954; *m* 1945, Nancy

Waddington; two s one d. *Educ:* Aberdeen Univ. MB, ChB, 1942, DPH, 1948, MD (Hons), 1952 (Aberdeen); DIH (London) 1955; FRCP (Edinburgh) 1966. RAMC 1942-46. Lecturer, Univ. of Aberdeen, 1948-52; Senior Lecturer, Univ. of St Andrews, at Dundee, 1952-54. Medical Dir, Scottish Occupational Health Laboratory Service, Ltd; Member: Steering Cttee and Founder Mem., Dundee and District Occupational Health Service Ltd; Nat. Adv. Cttee for Employment of Disabled; Asbestos Adv. Cttee, 1976-; Adv. Cttee, Health and Safety Exec., 1976-; Health Services Res. Cttee, Chief Scientist for Scotland, 1976-; Industrial Injuries Adv. Council, 1977-; Chm., Scottish Cttee for Welfare of Disabled and Sub-Cttee on Rehabilitation; Consultant, Occupational Health, to RN in Scotland. First Chm., British Soc. for Agriculture Labour Science. Occasional consultant to WHO, Geneva. *Publications:* Student Health Services in Great Britain and Northern Ireland, 1966; (jointly) Custom and Practice in Medical Care, 1968; Sir James Mackenzie, MD, 1973 (Abercrombie Award); contrib.: Cerebral Palsy in Childhood and Adolescence, 1961; Further Studies in Hospital and Community, 1962; numerous publications on Researches into Occupational Diseases, especially Silicosis, Byssinosis, etc. *Address:* Tree Tops, Castle Roy, Broughty Ferry, Angus. *T:* 78727. *Club:* Caledonian.

MAIR, Alexander, MBE 1967; Chief Executive and Director, Grampian Television Ltd, since 1970; *b* 5 Nov. 1922; *s* of Charles Mair and Helen Dickie; *m* 1953, Margaret Isobel Gowans Rennie. *Educ:* Skene, Aberdeenshire; Webster's Business Coll., Aberdeen; Sch. of Accountancy, Glasgow. Associate, ICMA, 1953. Chief Accountant, Bydand Holdings Ltd, 1957-60; Company Sec., Grampian Television, 1961-70; apptd Dir, 1967. Pres., Aberdeen Junior Chamber of Commerce, 1960-61; Hon. Manager, Aberdeen Savings Bank, 1973-; Chm., British Regional Television Assoc., 1973-75; Mem. Council, Aberdeen Chamber of Commerce, 1973. FRSA 1973. *Recreations:* golf, ski-ing, gardening. *Address:* Ravenswood, 66 Rubislaw Den South, Aberdeen AB2 6AX. *T:* Aberdeen 37619. *Clubs:* Caledonian; Royal Northern (Aberdeen).

MAIR, John Magnus; Director of Social Work, Edinburgh, 1969-75; Lecturer in Social Medicine, University of Edinburgh; *b* 29 Dec. 1912; *s* of Joseph Alexander Mair and Jane Anderson; *m* 1940, Isobelle Margaret Williamson (*d* 1969); three s. *Educ:* Anderson Inst., Lerwick; Univs of Aberdeen (MB, ChB) and Edinburgh (DPH). MFCM. Asst GP, Highlands and Islands Medical Service, 1937-40; RAMC, 1940-45; Edinburgh Public Health Dept (latterly Sen. Depute Medical Officer of Health), 1945-69. *Recreation:* golf. *Address:* 35 Charlton Grove, Roslin, Midlothian EH25 9NY. *T:* 031-440 2747. *Club:* Royal Commonwealth Society.

MAIR, Prof. Lucy Philip; Professor of Applied Anthropology, London School of Economics, 1963-68; *b* 28 Jan. 1901; *d* of David Beveridge Mair and Jessy Philip. *Educ:* St Paul's Girls' Sch.; Newnham Coll., Cambridge. London Sch. of Economics: Asst Lectr, 1927; Lectr, 1932; Reader, 1946; Prof., 1963; Hon. Fellow 1975. Australian Land Headquarters Civil Affairs Sch., 1945-46; Lugard Memorial Lectr, Internat. African Inst., 1958; Gildersleeve Visiting Prof. Barnard Coll., Columbia Univ., 1965; Frazer Lecture, Cambridge, 1967; Hon. Prof. of Social Anthropology, Univ. of Kent, 1974-. Hon. Sec. Royal Anthropological Inst., 1974- (Wellcome Medal 1936). Hon. DLitt Durham, 1972. *Publications:* An African People in the Twentieth Century, 1934; Native Policies in Africa, 1936; Australia in New Guinea, 1948, 2nd edn 1971; Primitive Government, 1962; New Nations, 1963; An Introduction to Social Anthropology, 1966, 2nd edn 1972; The New Africa, 1967; Witchcraft, 1969; Marriage, 1971; African Societies, 1974; African Kingdoms, 1977; contribs to Africa, Cahiers d'Etudes Africaines, etc. *Recreations:* music, cooking. *Address:* 19 Hallgate, Blackheath Park, SE3. *T:* 01-852 8531.

MAIR, Prof. William Austyn, CBE 1969; Francis Mond Professor of Aeronautical Engineering, University of Cambridge, since 1952; Head of Engineering Department, since 1973; Fellow of Downing College, Cambridge; *b* 24 Feb. 1917; *s* of William Mair, MD; *m* 1944, Mary Woodhouse Crofts; two s. *Educ:* Highgate Sch.; Clare Coll., Cambridge. Aerodynamics Dept, Royal Aircraft Establishment, Farnborough, 1940-46; Dir, Fluid Motion Laboratory, Univ. of Manchester, 1946-52. Mem. various cttees, Aeronautical Research Council, 1946-. Dir, Hovercraft Development Ltd, 1961-. Chm., Editorial Bd, Aeronautical Qly, 1975-. Silver Medal, RAeS, 1975. *Publications:* papers on aerodynamics. *Address:* 74 Barton Road, Cambridge. *T:* Cambridge 50137. *Club:* United Oxford & Cambridge University.

MAIS, family name of **Baron Mais.**

MAIS, Baron, *cr* 1967 (Life Peer); **Alan Raymond Mais,** GBE 1973 (OBE (mil.) 1944); TD 1944; ERD 1958; DL; JP; Colonel; Director: Royal Bank of Scotland, since 1969; Slag Reduction Co. Ltd; William Sindalls Ltd, since 1969; Chairman: City of London Insurance Co. Ltd, since 1970; Peachey Property Corporation, since 1977; *b* July 1911; *s* of late Capt. E. Mais, Mornington Court, Kensington; *m* 1936, Lorna Aline, *d* of late Stanley Aspinall Boardman, Addiscombe, Surrey; two s one d. *Educ:* Banister Court, Hants; Coll. of Estate Management, London Univ. Commissioned RARO, Royal West Kent Regt, 1929; transf. RE 1931; Major 1939, Lt-Col 1941, Col 1944; served War of 1939-45; France, BEF 1939-40 (despatches); Special Forces, MEF, Iraq and Persia, 1941-43 (despatches); Normandy and NW Europe, 1944-46 (OBE, despatches), wounded; CRE 56 Armd Div., TA, 1947-50; Comd Eng Gp, AER, 1951-54; DDES, AER, 1954-58. Worked for Richard Costain and other cos on Civil Engrg. Works at home and abroad, 1931-38; Private Practice, A. R. Mais & Partners, Structural Engineers & Surveyors, 1938-39 and 1946-48. Dir Trollope & Colls Ltd, Bldg and Civil Engrg contractors and subsid. cos, 1948 (Asst Man. Dir, 1953; Man. Dir 1957; Dep.-Chm. 1961; Chm. and Man. Dir 1963; retired, 1968); Chm., Hay-MSL Consultants, 1971-78. Dir, Nat. Commercial Bank of Scotland, 1966-69. Pres., London Chamber of Commerce and Industry, 1975-78; Past Pres., London Master Builders' Assoc.; Member: Land Commn, 1967-69; House of Lords Select Cttee on EEC, 1974. Lord Mayor of London, 1972-73. Chancellor, City Univ., 1972-73. Served on Corp. of City of London Cttees for Police, City of London Schs, Rates Finance, Billingsgate and Leadenhall Markets, Policy and Parliamentary, Establishments, and Gen. Purposes. Master: Worshipful Company of Paviors, 1975-76; Worshipful Company of Cutlers, 1968-69. Member: EDC Cttee for Constructional Industry, 1964-68; BNEC Cttee for Canada; Marshall Aid Commemoration Commn, 1964-74; Court and Council, City Univ. Comr of Income Tax, 1972-. Treasurer, Royal Masonic Hosp., 1973-. Governor: Ewell Technical Coll., 1954-66; London Univ. Board of Studies; Royal Alexandra and Albert Sch.; Hurstpierpoint Coll.; Birkbeck Coll., London Univ., 1973-. JP; DL Co. London (later Greater London), 1951-76; Lieut, City of London, 1963; Alderman, Ward of Walbrook, 1963; Sheriff, 1969-70; DL Kent, 1976. Vice-Pres. Emeritus, Inst. Quantity Surveyors; Treasurer, Fellowship of Engineering, 1977. FICE, FIStructE, MSocCE (France), FIArb, FRICS, KStJ 1973. Hon. BSc; Hon. DSc City, 1972. Hon. FICE 1975. Order of Patriotic War (1st class), USSR, 1942; Order of Aztec Eagle, Mexico, 1973; Order of Merit, Mexico, 1973. *Publication:* Yerbury Foundation Lecture, RIBA, 1960; Bossom Foundation Lecture, 1971. *Recreations:* family, Territorial Army. *Address:* Chesham House, Wilderness Road, Chislehurst, Kent. *T:* 01-467 0735; 10 St James's Street, SW1. *T:* 01-930 1986. *Clubs:* City Livery, Army and Navy, Special Forces, London Welsh.

MAIS, Francis Thomas; Deputy Secretary, Department of Commerce, Northern Ireland, since 1973; *b* 27 June 1927; *s* of Charles Edward Mais and Emma (*née* McLoughlin); *m* 1973, Margaret Edythe Whitehead (*née* Evans); one d. *Educ:* Barnsley Grammar Sch.; Christ's Coll., Cambridge. Joined Ministry of Commerce, NI, 1951. *Address:* 7 Cross Avenue, Marlborough Park, Belfast BT9 6HO. *T:* Belfast 667666.

MAIS, Hon. Sir (Robert) Hugh, Kt 1971; **Hon. Mr Justice Mais;** Judge of the High Court of Justice, Queen's Bench Division, since 1971; *b* 14 Sept. 1907; *s* of late Robert Stanley Oliver Mais, Chobham, Surrey; *m* 1938, Catherine, *d* of J. P. Pattinson; one s. *Educ:* Shrewsbury Sch.; Wadham Coll., Oxford (MA, 1948, Hon. Fellow, 1971). Called to the Bar, 1930, Bencher, Inner Temple, 1971; Mem. of Northern Circuit. Chancellor of the Diocese of: Manchester, 1948-71; Carlisle, 1950-71; Sheffield, 1950-71. Judge of County Courts: Circuit No 37 (West London), 1958-60; Circuit No 42 (Marylebone), 1960-71. Dep. Chm., Berkshire QS, 1964-71; Commissioner of Assize: SE Circuit, 1964, 1967; Oxford Circuit, 1968, 1969; NE Circuit, 1971. Mem., Winn Cttee on Personal Injuries Litigation. Served as Wing Comdr, RAF, 1940-44. *Recreations:* fishing, golf, lawn tennis. *Address:* Ripton, Streatley-on-Thames, Berks. *T:* Goring 2397. *Club:* Athenæum.

MAISNER, Air Vice-Marshal Aleksander, CB 1977; CBE 1968; AFC 1955; Personnel Executive, Reed International Ltd, since 1977; *b* 26 July 1921; *s* of Henryk Maisner and Helene Anne (*née* Brosin); *m* 1946, Mary (*née* Coverley); one s one d. *Educ:* High Sch. and Lyceum, Czestochowa, Poland; Warsaw Univ. Labour Camps, USSR, 1940-41; Polish Artillery, 1941-42; Polish Air Force, 1943-46; joined RAF, 1946; Flying Trng Comd, 1946-49; No 70 Sqdn Suez Canal Zone, 1950-52; No 50 Sqdn RAF

Binbrook, 1953-55; No 230 (Vulcan) OCU, RAF Waddington, 1955-59; psa 1960; OC Flying Wing, RNZAF Ohakea, 1961-62; Dirg Staff, RAF Staff Coll., Andover, 1963-65; DD Air Plans, MoD, 1965-68; CO, RAF Seletar, Singapore, 1969-70; Asst Comdt, RAF Coll., Cranwell, 1971-73; Dir, Personnel (Policy and Plans), MoD, 1973-75; Asst Air Sec., 1975; Dir-Gen. of Personnel Management, RAF, 1976, retired 1977. *Recreations:* tennis, gardening, golf. *Address:* 14 Orchard Close, Shiplake, Henley-on-Thames, Oxon RG9 4BU. *T:* Wargrave 2671. *Club:* Royal Air Force.

MAISONROUGE, Jacques Gaston; Chairman and Chief Executive, IBM Europe/Middle East/Africa Corporation, since 1974; Director, IBM United Kingdom Holdings Limited, since 1971 (Chairman, 1971-74); Administrator, Compagnie IBM France, since 1965; President, IBM Europe SA, since 1974; Administrator, L'Air Liquide, since 1971; *b* Cachan, Seine, 20 Sept. 1924; *s* of Paul Maisonrouge and Suzanne (*née* Cazas); *m* 1948, Françoise Andrée Féron; one *s* four *d. Educ:* Lycées Voltaire and Saint Louis, Paris. Studied engineering; gained dip. of Ecole Centrale des Arts et Manufactures. Engineer, 1948; various subseq. appts in IBM Corp., France. Philip Morris Inc. Councillor, French Chamber of Commerce, USA, 1964-. Chevalier, Ordre de la Légion d'Honneur; Officier Ordre National du Mérite; Officier des Palmes Académiques; Commander, Order of Merit of the Italian Republic; Commander, Order of Saint Sylvester; Kt of Malta. *Recreations:* interested in sport (tennis, equitation, etc). *Address:* 8 Cité du Retiro, 75008 Paris, France. *Club:* Automobile of France.

MAITLAND, family name of **Earl of Lauderdale.**

MAITLAND, Viscount; Master of Lauderdale; **Ian Maitland;** International Banking Division, National Westminster Bank Ltd, since 1975; *b* 4 Nov. 1937; *s* and *heir* of Earl of Lauderdale, *qv*; *m* 1963, Ann Paule, *d* of Geoffrey Clark; one *s* one *d. Educ:* Radley Coll., Abingdon; Brasenose Coll., Oxford (MA Modern History). Various appointments since 1960; with Hedderwick Borthwick & Co., 1970-75. Royal Naval Reserve (Lieutenant), 1963-73. Lay Reader, Church of England. *Recreations:* photography, sailing. *Heir: s* Master of Maitland, *qv*. *Address:* 150 Tachbrook Street, SW1.

MAITLAND, Master of; Hon. John Douglas Maitland; *b* 29 May 1965; *s* and *heir* of Viscount Maitland, *qv*.

MAITLAND, Alastair George, CBE 1966; Consul-General, Boston, 1971-75, retired; Paris correspondent, Berkshire Eagle, Pittsfield, Mass; *b* 30 Jan. 1916; *s* of late Thomas Douglas Maitland, MBE, and Wilhelmina Sarah Dundas; *m* 1943, Betty Hamilton; two *s* one *d. Educ:* George Watson's Coll., Edinburgh; Universities of Edinburgh (MA First Class Hons), Grenoble and Paris, Ecole des Sciences Politiques. Vice-Consul: New York, 1938; Chicago, 1939; New York, 1939; Los Angeles, 1940; apptd to staff of UK High Commissioner at Ottawa, 1942; apptd to Foreign Office, 1945; Brit. Middle East Office, Cairo, 1948; Foreign Office, 1952; UK Delegation to OEEC, Paris, 1954; Consul-General: at New Orleans, 1958-62; at Jerusalem, 1962-64; at Cleveland, 1964-68; Dir-Gen., British Trade Develt Office, NY, 1968-71. Hon. LLD Lake Erie Coll., Ohio, 1971. CStJ. *Recreations:* music, golf, gardening, reading. *Address:* Heath, Mass, USA; 18 Villa Seurat, Paris 14e, France.

MAITLAND, Sir Donald (James Dundas), GCMG 1977 (CMG 1967); Kt 1973; OBE 1960; HM Diplomatic Service; Ambassador and UK Permanent Representative to the European Communities, since 1975; *b* 16 Aug. 1922; *s* of Thomas Douglas Maitland and Wilhelmina Sarah Dundas; *m* 1950, Jean Marie Young, *d* of Gordon Young; one *s* one *d. Educ:* George Watson's Coll.; Edinburgh Univ. Served India, Middle East, and SE Asia, 1941-47 (Royal Scots; Rajputana Rifles). Joined Foreign Service, 1947; Consul, Amara, 1950; British Embassy, Baghdad, 1950-53; Private Sec. to Minister of State, Foreign Office, 1954-56; Director, Middle East Centre for Arab Studies, Lebanon, 1956-60; Foreign Office, 1960-63; Counsellor, British Embassy, Cairo, 1963-65; Head of News Dept, Foreign Office, 1965-67; Principal Private Sec. to Foreign and Commonwealth Secretary, 1967-69; Ambassador to Libya, 1969-70; Chief Press Sec., 10 Downing St, 1970-73; UK Permanent Rep. to UN, 1973-74; Dep. Under-Sec. of State, FCO, 1974-75. UK Mem., Commonwealth Group on Trade, Aid and Develt, 1975. *Recreations:* flying, hill-walking, music. *Address:* c/o Foreign and Commonwealth Office, SW1. *Club:* Travellers'.

MAITLAND, Comdr Sir John (Francis Whitaker), Kt 1960; *b* 1903; *o s* of late William Whitaker Maitland, CVO, OBE, Loughton Hall, Essex; *m* 1930, Bridget, *er d* of E. H. M. Denny,

Staplefield Place, Sussex; four *s* one *d. Educ:* Osborne, Dartmouth. Royal Navy: retired 1934, rejoined 1939-45; Comdr, 1943. MP (C) Horncastle Div. of Lincolnshire, 1945-66. Pres. Institute of Patentees and Inventors, 1966-75. DL Essex, 1934; JP Essex, 1935; DL Lincolnshire, 1957. Mem. Lindsey CC, 1967. Chm. Council of St John for Lincolnshire, 1966-71; OStJ. FRSA. *Address:* Harrington Hall, near Spilsby, Lincs. *T:* Spilsby 2281.

See also John Bruce-Gardyne.

MAITLAND, Air Vice-Marshal Percy Eric, CB 1945; CBE 1951; MVO 1935; AFC 1918; *b* 26 Oct. 1895; *s* of Surgeon-Captain P. E. Maitland, Royal Navy; *m* 1927, Alison Mary Kettlewell; six *s. Educ:* RN Coll., Osborne and Dartmouth. Royal Navy, 1908-18, attached RNAS 1915 for Airships (AFC); transferred to Royal Air Force 1918 as Captain; specialised in Navigation. Served in Egypt and Iraq; Navigator in Far East Flight to Australia, 1928-29; Staff Officer for Royal Review, 1935 (MVO); Singapore, 1937-39, promoted Group Captain; Flying Training Command, 1939-40; Bomber Command, 1940-43; Air Ministry, Director of Operational Training, 1943; AOC No 2 Group, BAOR, 1945; AOC, No 84 Group, BAOR, 1945-47; AOC No 22 Group; Technical Training Command, 1948-50; retired, 1950. JP Somerset, 1952. *Recreation:* fishing. *Address:* 60 Station Road, Wallingford OX10 0JZ. *T:* Wallingford 38921.

MAITLAND, Sir Richard John, 9th Bt, *cr* 1818; *b* 24 Nov. 1952; *s* of Sir Alexander Keith Maitland, 8th Bt, and of Lavender Mary Jex, *y d* of late Francis William Jex Jackson, Kirkbuddo, Forfar; *S* father, 1963. *Educ:* Rugby; Exeter Univ. BA Hons 1975. *Heir: b* Robert Ramsay Maitland, *b* 14 July 1956. *Address:* Burnside, Forfar, Angus.

MAITLAND-MAKGILL-CRICHTON; see Crichton.

MAJITHIA, Dr Sir Surendra Singh, Kt 1946; Landlord and Industrialist; *b* 4 March 1895; *s* of Hon. Sardar Bahadur Dr Sir Sunder Singh Majithia, CIE, DOL; *m* 1921, Lady Balbir Kaur (*d* 1977), *d* of General Hazura Singh, of Patiala. *Educ:* Khalsa Collegiate High Sch.; Khalsa Coll., Amritsar. Chairman: Saraya Sugar Mills Private Ltd; Sardarnagar Block Development Cttee; Senior Managing Partner, Saraya Surkhi Mill; Director: Punjab & Sindh Bank Ltd, New Delhi; Member: Khalsa College Council, Amritsar; Akal College Council, Gursagar, etc.; UP Tuberculosis Assoc., Lucknow; UP Fruit Development Board, Lucknow. President, Chairman, etc., of many educational foundations and social activities. Past Member various Advisory and Consultative Cttees. Chairman, Lady Parsan Kaur Charitable Trust. Patron: Wrestling Federation of India; UP Badminton Assoc.; Member, Garden Advisory Cttee, Gorakhpur. Hon. DLitt Gorakhpur, 1970. *Address:* PO Sardarnagar, Dist Gorakhpur, Uttar Pradesh, India. *Clubs:* Gorakhpur, Nipal (both in Gorakhpur).

MAJOR; see Henniker-Major.

MAJOR, Kathleen, FBA 1977; Professor (part-time) of History, University of Nottingham, 1966-71; Principal of St Hilda's College, Oxford, 1955-65; Hon. Fellow, St Hilda's College, 1965; *b* 10 April 1906; *er d* of late George Major and Gertrude Blow. *Educ:* various private schools; St Hilda's College, Oxford. Honour School of Modern History, 1928; BLitt 1931. Librarian, St Hilda's College, 1931. Archivist to the Bishop of Lincoln, 1936; Lecturer, 1945, subsequently Reader in Diplomatic in the University of Oxford, until July 1955. Hon. Secretary, Lincoln Record Society, 1935-56 and 1965-74, Hon. Gen. Editor, 1935-75. Hon. DLitt Nottingham, 1961. Member Academic Planning Board for the University of Lancaster, 1962, and of Academic Advisory Cttee, 1964-70. Trustee of the Oxford Preservation Trust, 1961-65; a Vice-President, Royal Historical Society, 1967-71. *Publications:* (joint editor with late Canon Foster) Registrum Antiquissimum of the Cathedral Church of Lincoln, vol. IV, 1938, (sole editor) vols V-X, 1940-73; *Acta Stephani Langton,* 1950; articles in English Hist. Review, Journal of Ecclesiastical Hist., etc. *Recreation:* reading. *Address:* 21 Queensway, Lincoln. *Club:* English-Speaking Union.

MAJURY, Maj.-Gen. James Herbert Samuel, CB 1974; MBE 1961; *b* 26 June 1921; *s* of Rev. Dr M. Majury, BA, DD, and Florence (*née* Stuart), Antrim, N Ireland; *m* 1948, Jeanetta Ann (*née* Le Fleming); two *s. Educ:* Royal Academical Institution, Belfast; Trinity College, Dublin. Royal Ulster Rifles, 1940; attached 15 Punjab Regt, 1942; seconded South Waziristan Scouts, 1943-47; Korean War, 1949 (Royal Ulster Rifles); Prisoner of War, Korea, 1950-53 (despatches 1954); Parachute Regiment, 1957-61; Comd Royal Irish Fusiliers, 1961-62; Comd 2nd Infantry Bde, 1965-67; GOC West Midland District, 1970-73. idc 1968. Col. Comdt, The King's Division, 1971-75, Col

The Royal Irish Rangers, 1972-; Hon. Col, 2nd Bn Mercian Volunteers, 1975-. *Recreations:* golf, coursing. *Address:* Nine Mile Water House, Nether Wallop, Stockbridge, Hants SO20 8DR. *T:* Broughton, Hants, 279. *Clubs:* Naval and Military, XL.

MAKGILL, family name of **Viscount of Oxfuird.**

MAKGILL CRICHTON MAITLAND, Major John David; Vice-Lieutenant of Renfrewshire, since 1972; *b* 10 Sept. 1925; *e s* of late Col Mark Edward Makgill Crichton Maitland, CVO, DSO, DL, JP, The Island House, Wilton, Salisbury, Wilts, and late Patience Irene Fleetwood Makgill Crichton Maitland (*née* Fuller); *m* 1954, Jean Patricia, *d* of late Maj.-Gen. Sir Michael Creagh, KBE, MC, Pigeon Hill, Homington, Salisbury; one *s* one *d*. *Educ:* Eton. Served War, 1944-45, Grenadier Guards. Continued serving until 1957 (temp. Major, 1952; retd 1957), rank Captain (Hon. Major). Governor, West of Scotland Agricl Coll.; Renfrew CC, 1961-75. DL Renfrewshire 1962. *Address:* Houston House, Houston, by Johnstone, Renfrewshire. *T:* Bridge of Weir 612545.

MAKIN, Frank; Chief Inspector, Department of Education and Science, since 1976; *b* 29 Oct. 1918; *s* of Tom Kay Makin and Phyllis H. Makin (*née* Taylor); *m* 1949, Marjorie Elizabeth Thomasson; three *d*. *Educ:* Bolton Municipal Secondary Sch.; Corpus Christi Coll., Cambridge (MA). Asst Master, Cheadle Hulme Sch., Burnley Grammar Sch., and Stretford Grammar Sch., 1941-56; Headmaster, South Hunsley Co. Secondary Sch., Yorks, 1956-62; HM Inspector of Schools, 1962-; Divisional Inspector, 1970-76. *Recreations:* languages, gardening. *Address:* 127 Hookfield, Epsom KT19 8JH. *T:* Epsom 40872.

MAKIN, Hon. Norman John Oswald; *b* Petersham, NSW, Australia, 31 March 1889; *s* of John Hulme Makin and Elizabeth Makin; *m* 1932, Ruby Florence Jennings; two *s*. *Educ:* Superior Public Sch., Broken Hill. Member Commonwealth Parliament for Hindmarsh, 1919-46; Member Joint Cttee Public Accounts, 1922-26; Member Select Cttee case ex-Gunner Yates; Temp. Chairman of Cttees, 1923-29; Speaker House of Representatives, Commonwealth of Australia, 1929-32; Member Advisory War Council, 1940; Ministry for Navy and Munitions, Australia, 1941-46; Minister for Aircraft Production, 1945-46. Australian Ambassador to United States, 1946-51. MP for Sturt, 1954-Nov. 1955, for Bonython Division, Dec. 1955-Nov. 1963, Commonwealth Parliament; retired. President Labour Party, 1936; Secretary Federal Parliamentary Labour Party, 1931; Member of Delegation to United Kingdom, King George V Jubilee in 1935 and to King George VI Coronation in 1937; 1st President of Security Council, Jan. 1946, and President, 1947; Leader, Australian Delegation to United Nations; Leader, Australian Delegation to ILO Conference, San Francisco. Alternate Governor, International Bank and International Monetary Fund; Member, Far Eastern Commn, 1947-48. Hon. Doctor of Laws, Univ. of Syracuse. *Publications:* A Progressive Democracy; Federal Labour Leaders, 1961. *Address:* Flat 219, 7 Raymond Grove, Glenelg, SA 5045, Australia.

MAKINS, family name of **Baron Sherfield.**

MAKINS, Sir Paul (Vivian), 4th Bt *cr* 1903; Company Director, 1962-73; *b* 12 Nov. 1913; *yr s* of Sir Paul Makins, 2nd Bt, and Gladys Marie (*d* 1919), *d* of William Vivian, Queen's Gate, London; *S* brother, 1969; *m* 1945, Maisie, *d* of Major Oswald Pedley and widow of Major C. L. J. Bowen, Irish Guards; no *c*. *Educ:* Eton Coll.; Trinity Coll. Cambridge (MA). Commissioned in Welsh Guards, 1935. Served War of 1939-45: France, 1940; Italy, 1944-45. Dir and Sec. Vitalba Co. Ltd (Gibraltar), 1962-73; Dir, Compañia Rentistica SA (Tangier), 1967-73. Kt of Magistral Grace, SMO Malta, 1955; JP Gibraltar, 1964-70. *Heir:* none. *Address:* c/o Barclays Bank International Ltd, 84-90 Main Street, Gibraltar. *Clubs:* Cavalry and Guards, Pratt's.
See also Archbishop of Southwark.

MAKINSON, William, CBE 1977; Managing Director, since 1974, Member, since 1967, National Research Development Corporation (Chief Executive, Engineering Department, 1965-74); *b* 11 May 1915; *s* of Joshua Makinson and Martha (*née* Cunliffe); *m* 1952, Helen Elizabeth Parker; one *s* three *d*. *Educ:* Ashton-in-Makerfield Grammar Sch.; Manchester Univ. Asst Lecturer, Electronics, Manchester Univ., 1935-36; Education Officer, RAF Cranwell, 1936-39; RAE Farnborough, 1939-52; Hon. Squadron-Ldr, RAF, 1943-45; Superintendent, Blind Landing Experimental Unit, 1952-55; Defence Research Policy Staff, 1955-56; Managing Director, General Precision Systems Ltd, 1956-64; Group Jt Managing Director, Pullin, 1964-65. *Publications:* papers to Royal Aeronautical Society. *Recreation:* golf. *Address:* Tiffany, East Drive, Virginia Water, Surrey. *T:* Wentworth 3490.

MALAMUD, Bernard; Writer; Member, Division of Literature, Bennington College, since 1961; *b* 26 April 1914; *s* of Max and Bertha Malamud; *m* 1945, Ann de Chiara; one *s* one *d*. *Educ:* The City Coll., New York; Columbia Univ. Taught at Oregon State Coll., 1949-61, while writing first four books. Visiting Lecturer, Harvard Univ., 1966-68. Partisan Review Fiction Fellowship, 1956; Ford Foundation Fellowship, Humanities and Arts Program, 1959-60; Member: Amer. Institute of Arts and Letters, 1964; American Academy of Arts and Sciences, 1967. *Publications:* The Natural, 1952; The Assistant, 1957 (Rosenthal Prize, Daroff Memorial Award, 1958); The Magic Barrel (short stories), 1958 (National Book Award, 1959); A New Life, 1961; Idiots First (short stories), 1963; The Fixer, 1966 (National Book Award and Pulitzer Prize for Fiction, 1967); Pictures of Fidelman, 1969; The Tenants, 1971; Rembrandt's Hat (short stories), 1973. *Recreations:* reading, music, poker, art galleries. *Address:* c/o Russell and Volkening, 551 Fifth Avenue, NY 10017, USA.

MALAND, David; Headmaster, Denstone College, since 1969; *b* 6 Oct. 1929; *s* of Rev. Gordon Albert Maland and Florence Maud Maland (*née* Bosence); *m* 1953, Edna Foulsham; two *s*. *Educ:* Kingswood Sch.; Wadham Coll., Oxford. BA 2nd class Mod. Hist., 1951; MA 1957; Robert Herbert Mem. Prize Essay, 1959. Nat. service commn RAF, 1951-53; Asst Master, Brighton Grammar Sch., 1953-56; Senior History Master, Stamford Sch., 1957-66; Headmaster, Cardiff High Sch., 1966-68. *Publications:* Europe in the Seventeenth Century, 1966; Culture and Society in Seventeenth Century France, 1970; (trans.) La Guerre de Trente Ans, by Pagès, 1971; Europe in the Sixteenth Century, 1973; articles and reviews in History. *Address:* Denstone College, Uttoxeter, Staffs. *T:* Rocester 590484. *Club:* East India, Devonshire, Sports and Public Schools.

MALAŴI, SOUTHERN, Bishop of; see Central Africa, Archbishop of.

MALCOLM, Lt-Col Arthur William Alexander, CVO 1954 (MVO 1949); *b* 31 May 1903; *s* of Major Charles Edward Malcolm, London; *m* 1928, Hester Mary, *d* of S. F. Mann, Lawrenny-Caramut, Victoria, Australia; two *s*. *Educ:* Repton. 2nd Lieut, Welsh Guards, 1924; psc 1938; served War of 1939-45 (POW); Lieut-Colonel, 1945; comd 3rd, 2nd and 1st Bn, Welsh Guards, 1945-49. ADC to Governor of Victoria, Australia, 1926-28. Asst Military Attaché, British Embassy, Paris, 1950-52; retired from Army, 1952. Private Secretary to Governor of South Australia, 1953-55; Queen's Foreign Service Messenger, 1955-68. *Recreations:* golf, shooting, fishing. *Address:* Faraway, Sandwich Bay, Kent. *T:* Sandwich 2054. *Clubs:* Army and Navy; Royal St George's Golf, Prince's Golf (Sandwich).

MALCOLM, Sir David (Peter Michael), 11th Bt *cr* 1665; Director, James Capel & Co.; *b* 7 July 1919; *s* of Sir Michael Albert James Malcolm, 10th Bt, and Hon. Geraldine Margot (*d* 1965), *d* of 10th Baron Digby; *S* father, 1976; *m* 1959, Hermione, *d* of Sir David Home, Bt, *qv*; one *d*. *Educ:* Eton; Magdalene Coll., Cambridge (BA). Served with Scots Guards, 1939-46 (Major). Mem., Inst. of Chartered Accountants of Scotland, 1949. Member: Stock Exchange, 1956-; Stock Exchange Council, 1971-. *Recreations:* shooting, golf. *Heir:* cousin Lt-Col Arthur William Alexander Malcolm, *qv*. *Address:* 15 Cromwell Crescent, SW5 9QW. *Clubs:* Pratt's, City of London; New (Edinburgh).

MALCOLM, Dugald, CMG 1966; CVO 1964; TD 1945; HM Diplomatic Service, retired; Minister to the Holy See, 1975-77; *b* 22 Dec. 1917; 2nd *s* of late Maj.-Gen. Sir Neill Malcolm, KCB, DSO, and Lady (Angela) Malcolm; *m* 1957, Patricia Anne Gilbert-Lodge (*d* 1976), *widow* of Captain Peter Atkinson-Clark; one *d* one *step d*. *Educ:* Eton; New Coll., Oxford. Served Argyll and Sutherland Highlanders, 1939-45; discharged wounded. Appointed Foreign Office, Oct. 1945; Served Lima, Bonn, Seoul; HM Vice-Marshal of the Diplomatic Corps, 1957-65; Ambassador: to Luxembourg, 1966-70; to Panama, 1970-74. Member Queen's Body Guard for Scotland (Royal Company of Archers). *Address:* White Court, Alfriston, near Polegate, East Sussex. *T:* Alfriston 870 404. *Club:* Travellers'.

MALCOLM, Ellen, RSA 1976 (ARSA 1968); *b* 28 Sept. 1923; *d* of John and Ellen Malcolm; *m* 1962, Gordon Stewart Cameron, *qv*. *Educ:* Aberdeen Acad.; Gray's Sch. of Art, Aberdeen. DA (Aberdeen) 1944. Teacher of Art, Aberdeen Grammar Sch. and Aberdeen Acad., 1945-62. Paintings in public galleries in Southend, Aberdeen, Perth, Milngavie, Edinburgh, and in private collections in Scotland, England, Wales, America, Switzerland, Sweden and Australia. Chalmers-Jervise Prize, 1946; Guthrie Award, Royal Scottish Acad., 1952; David

Cargill Award, Royal Glasgow Inst., 1973. *Recreation:* reading. *Address:* 7 Auburn Terrace, Invergowrie, Dundee DD2 5AB. *T:* Invergowrie 318.

MALCOLM, George (John), CBE 1965; musician; *b* London, 28 Feb. 1917; *o s* of George Hope Malcolm, Edinburgh, and Johanna Malcolm. *Educ:* Wimbledon Coll.; Balliol Coll., Oxford (Scholar); Royal College of Music (Scholar). MA, BMus (Oxon). Served in RAFVR, 1940-46. Master of the Cathedral Music, Westminster Cathedral, 1947-59, training unique boys' choir for which Benjamin Britten wrote Missa Brevis, Op. 63. Now mainly known as harpsichordist (making frequent concert tours), pianist and conductor. Cobbett Medal, Worshipful Company of Musicians, 1960; Hon. RAM, 1961; Hon. Fellow, Balliol Coll., Oxford, 1966; FRCM 1974. Papal Knight of the Order of St Gregory the Great, 1970. *Address:* 38 Cheyne Walk, SW3. *T:* 01-352 5381.

MALCOLM, Gerald; see Malcolm, W. G.

MALCOLM, Prof. John Laurence; Regius Professor of Physiology, University of Aberdeen, 1959-75, retired; *b* 28 Aug. 1913; *s* of late Professor J. Malcolm, Dunedin, New Zealand; *m* 1st, 1940, Sylvia Bramston (*d* 1958), *d* of late Basil B. Hooper, Auckland, New Zealand; one *s* one *d*; 2nd, 1961, Margaret Irvine Simpson (*d* 1967), *d* of late Colonel J. C. Simpson, Skene, Aberdeenshire. *Publications:* contributions to the Proceedings of Royal Society, Journal of Physiology, Journal of Neurophysiology. *Address:* Heath Cottage, Crathie, Aberdeenshire AB3 5UP.

MALCOLM, Kenneth Robert, CBE 1964; *b* 17 Dec. 1908; 2nd *s* of Ronald Malcolm, Walton Manor, Walton-on-the Hill, Surrey; *m* 1950, Iris Lilian Knowles; two *s* one *d*. *Educ:* Eton; New College, Oxford. Indian Civil Service, 1932-47; Home Civil Service (Ministry of National Insurance, subseq. Dept of Health and Social Security), 1947-73; Under-Sec., 1969, retd 1973. *Address:* Ferndale, Dry Arch Road, Sunningdale, Ascot, Berks. *T:* Ascot 22946. *Club:* Travellers'.

MALCOLM, (William) Gerald, CB 1976; MBE 1943; Permanent Secretary, Department of the Environment for Northern Ireland, 1974-76; *b* Stirling, 19 Dec. 1916; *s* of late John and Jane M. Malcolm; *m* 1949, Margaret Cashel. *Educ:* High Sch. of Stirling; Glasgow Univ. (MA) (Hons French and German, 1945); London Univ. (BA 1945). Served War, Army, 1939-46: RASC and Intelligence Corps; Major, 1944; Africa and Italy Stars, 1939-45. Min. of Home Affairs for NI, Asst Principal, 1948; Min. of Agriculture for NI: Principal, 1956; Asst Sec., 1962; Sen. Asst Sec., 1966; Dep. Sec., 1970. *Recreations:* angling, swimming, ornithology, nature. *Address:* 4 Bryansglen Park, Bangor, Co. Down, Northern Ireland BT20 3RS. *T:* Bangor 69424.

MALCOLMSON, Kenneth Forbes, MA, BMus (Oxon), FRCO; Precentor and Director of Music, Eton College, 1956-71; *b* 29 April, 1911; *m* 1972, Mrs B. Dunhill. Organ Scholar, Exeter Coll., Oxford, 1931-35; Commissioner, Royal School of Church Music, 1935-36; Temporary Organist, St Alban's Cathedral, 1936-37; Organist, Halifax Parish Church, 1937-38; Organist and Master of the Music, Newcastle Cathedral, 1938-55. *Recreations:* gardening, swimming, walking. *Address:* Court Farm, Dingestow, Monmouth, Gwent. *T:* Dingestow 648.

MALDEN; see Scott-Malden.

MALE, Peter John Ellison, CMG 1967; MC 1945; HM Diplomatic Service; Ambassador to Czechoslovakia, since 1977; *b* 22 Aug. 1920; *s* of late H. J. G. Male and late Mrs E. A. Male; *m* 1947, Patricia Janet Payne; five *s* two *d*. *Educ:* Merchant Taylors' Sch.; Emmanuel Coll., Cambridge. HM Forces, 1940-45. HM Foreign Service (now HM Diplomatic Service), 1946; served in: Damascus, 1947-49; Wahnerheide, 1949-53; London, 1953-55; Guatemala City, 1955-57; Washington, 1957-60; London, 1960-62; Oslo, 1962-66; Bonn, 1966-70; New Delhi, 1970-74; Asst Under-Sec. of State, FCO, 1974-77. *Recreations:* gadgets, gardening. *Address:* c/o Foreign and Commonwealth Office, SW1; Swinley Edge, South Ascot, Berks. *Club:* United Oxford & Cambridge University.

MALENKOV, Georgi Maximilianovich; Manager of Ust-Kamenogorsk Hydro-Electric Station, 1957-63, retired; *b* Orenburg, 1901; *m* 1st (marr. diss.); 2nd, Elena Khrushcheva. *Educ:* Moscow Higher Technical Coll. Member of the Communist Party, 1920-; Member of Organisation Bureau of Central Cttee of the Communist Party, 1934; Member Cttee for State Defence, 1941; Member Cttee for Economic Rehabilitation of Liberated Districts, 1943; Dep.-Chairman, Council of

Ministers, 1946; Dep.-Chairman, Council of Ministers of the Soviet Union, 1955-57 (Dep.-Chairman, 1946, Chairman, 1953-55); Minister of Electric Power Stations, 1955-57. Holds title Hero of Socialist Labour, Hammer and Sickle Gold Medal, Order of Lenin (twice).

MALET, Colonel Sir Edward William St Lo, 8th Bt, *cr* 1791; OBE 1953; 8th King's Royal Irish Hussars; retired; *b* 27 Nov. 1908; *o s* of Sir Harry Charles Malet, DSO, OBE, 7th Bt and Mildred Laura (*d* 1951), *d* of Captain H. S. Swiney, Gensing House, St Leonards; *S* father, 1931; *m* 1935, Baroness Benedicta Maasburg, *e d* of Baron William von Maasburg; one *s* two *d*. *Educ:* Dover Coll.; Christ Church, Oxford. BA. Dep.-Chief Civil Affairs Officer, HQ, British Troops, Egypt, 1953-55. President Bridgwater Division, Conservative Assoc., 1959. High Sheriff of Somerset, 1966. *Heir: s* Harry Douglas St Lo Malet, late Lieut, The Queen's Royal Irish Hussars, now Special Reserve [*b* 26 Oct. 1936; *m* 1967, Julia Harper, Perth, WA; one *s*. *Educ:* Downside; Trinity Coll., Oxford]. *Address:* Chargot, Washford, Somerset. *Club:* Cavalry and Guards.

MALHERBE, Ernst G., MA, PhD; Hon. LLD Universities of: Cambridge, Queen's (Kingston, Ont), Melbourne, McGill, Capetown, Rhodes, Natal, Witwatersrand, St Andrews; Principal and Vice-Chancellor, University of Natal, Pietermaritzburg and Durban, 1945-65; *b* OFS, 8 Nov. 1895; *s* of late Rev. E. G. Malherbe, Villiersdorp, Cape Province, French Huguenot descent; *m* Janie A., *d* of Rev. Paul Nel, Moderator of Dutch Reformed Church, Transvaal; three *s* one *d*. *Educ:* Stellenbosch Univ., Stellenbosch, CP (BA, Hons, MA in Philosophy); Columbia Univ., New York (MA and PhD in Education). Union Government Scholarship for 2 years to study Education overseas; Oxford, The Hague, Amsterdam, Germany, etc.; 3 years in succession H. B. Webb Research Scholar for overseas Research in Educational Administration; Fellow of Teachers Coll., Columbia Univ., 1923-34; Chalmers Memorial Prize for Essay on Educational Administration, 1923; invited as special SA representative to Centenary meeting of British Assoc., London, 1931; teacher at Cape Town Training Coll.; Lecturer in Educational Psychology, University of Stellenbosch; Senior Lecturer in Education, University of Cape Town, 5 years; Chief Investigator Education Section Carnegie Poor White Commission of Research, 1928-32; Member of Government Commission to investigate Native Education in South Africa, 1935; Director, National Bureau of Educational and Social Research for SA, 1929-39; Sec. Government Commission on Medical Training in S Africa, 1938. Director of Census and Statistics for Union of South Africa, 1939-40; (Lieut-Col) Director of Military Intelligence, S African Army and Director Army Education Services, 1940-45. Member of Social and Economic Planning Council, 1946-50; of National Council for Social Research, 1945-50; Chairman National War Histories Cttee, 1945-49; President SA Assoc. for the Advancement of Science, 1950-51; President SA Institute of Race Relations, 1966-67; Mem., Govt Commn on Financial Relations between Central Govt and Provinces, 1960-64. Simon Biesheuvel Medal for Study of Man, 1969. *Publications:* Education in S Africa, 1652-1922, 1925; Chapters on S Africa in Year-books of Education, 1932-56; Education and the Poor White, 1929; articles in Chambers's Encyclopœdia, Standard Encyclopaedia for Southern Africa; numerous articles in Educational and Scientific Journals; Carnegie Commmission's Poor White Report on Education, 1932; Education in a Changing Empire, 1932, Educational Adaptations in a Changing Society (Editor), 1937; Entrance Age of University Students in Relation to Success, 1938; Whither Matric?, 1938; Educational and Social Research in SA, 1939; The Bilingual School, 1943; Race Attitudes and Education, 1946; Our Universities and the Advancement of Science, 1951; The Autonomy of our Universities and Apartheid, 1957; Education for Leadership in Africa, 1960; Problems of School Medium in a Bilingual Country, 1962; Into the 70's: Education and the Development of South Africa's Human Resources, 1966; The Need for Dialogue, 1967; The Nemesis of Docility, 1968; Bantu Manpower and Education, 1969; Differing Values, 1973; Education in South Africa, 1923-1973, 1976. *Recreations:* golf, swimming; Full Blue, Stellenbosch University; Half Blue, Capetown University; captained Hockey Team representing CP at inter-provincial tournament. *Address:* By-die-See, Salt Rock, Umhlali, Natal, South Africa. *Club:* Durban (Durban).

MALIK, Bidhubhusan; *b* 11 Jan. 1895; *s* of Raibahadur Chandrasekhar Malik, Chief Judge, Benares State; *m* 1916, Leelabati, *d* of Saratkumar Mitra, Calcutta; two *s*. *Educ:* Central Hindu Coll., Benares (graduated, 1917); Ewing Christian Coll. (MA in Economics, 1919); Allahabad Univ. (LLB 1919); LLD (*hc*), Saugur Univ. Vakil, Allahabad High Court, 1919; started practice in the civil courts in Benares; left for England in Sept.

1922; called to Bar, Lincoln's Inn, 1923; joined Allahabad High Court Bar, 1924; Member of Judicial Cttee of Benares State, 1941; Special Counsel for Income Tax Dept, 1943; Judge, Allahabad High Court, 1944; Chief Justice, High Court, Allahabad, Dec. 1947; thereafter Chief Justice, UP, from 26 July 1948-55, excepting 3 March-1 May 1949, when acted as Governor, Uttar Pradesh. Commissioner for Linguistic Minorities in India, 1957-62. Member: Constitutional Commission for the Federation of Malaya, 1956-57; Air Transport Council of India, 1955-62; National Integration Commn, India. Constitutional Adviser to Mr Jomo Kenyatta and the Kenya African National Union, Lancaster House Conference, London, 1961-62; Constitutional Expert for Republic of Congo appointed by UNO, Aug.-Oct. 1962; Constitutional Adviser to Kenya Government, Kenya Independence Conference, Lancaster House, Sept.-Oct. 1963; Adviser, Mauritius Constitutional Conference, London, Sept.-Nov. 1965. Vice-Chancellor, Calcutta Univ., 1962-68 (Life-Mem. Senate); Mem., Exec. Council, Allahabad Univ., 1971-73. President: Jagat Taran Educn Soc., 1924-; Jagat Taran Degree Coll., 1924-; Jagat Taran Inter Coll., 1924-; Jagat Taran Golden Jubilee Eng. Med. Sch. and Hindi Med. Primary Sch., 1924-; Harijan Ashram Degree Coll., Allahabad, 1968-. Former Mem. Council, Ewing Christian Coll., Pres., Old Boys' Assoc., 1976-. Founder Mem., Lions Club, Allahabad, 1959-60; Rotary Club: Pres., Allahabad; Mem., Allahabad and Calcutta. Founder President: Golf Club, Allahabad, 1949-55; Allahabad Badminton Assoc., 1949-55. *Address:* 23 Muir Road, Allahabad, India.

MALIK, Sardar Hardit Singh, CIE 1941; OBE 1938; Indian Diplomat, retired, 1957; *b* 23 Nov. 1894; *s* of Malik Mohan Singh and Lajanwanti; *m* 1919, Prakash; one *s* two *d. Educ:* Eastbourne Coll.; Balliol Coll., Oxford, England. BA Hons in Mod. Hist., 1915. Served with French Army on Western Front, 1916. Fighter Pilot in RFC, 1917-18 (wounded in air combat over France, 1917); served in RAF, France, Italy and in home defence of UK. Entered ICS; Asst Commissioner, Punjab, 1922-23; Deputy Commissioner, Punjab, 1924-30; Dep. Trade Commissioner, London and Hamburg, 1931-34; Dep. Secretary Government of India, Commerce Dept, 1934-36; Joint Secretary, Government of India, Commerce Dept, 1937; Indian Government Trade Commissioner, New York, 1938; Delegate to International Cotton Conf., Washington, 1939, International Labour Office Conf., New York, 1940, UN Food Conf., Hotsprings, Virginia, 1943, and UN Relief Conf., Atlantic City, USA, 1943. Prime Minister, Patiala, 1944-47. Leader Indian States Industrial Delegation to UK and USA, 1945-46; represented Government of India at First and Second Sessions of Prep. Cttee of UN Conf. on Trade and Employment in London, Nov. 1946, and Geneva, April 1947, respectively. Leader Indian Delegation to UN Conf. on Trade and Employment, Havana, Nov. 1947; High Commissioner for India in Canada, 1947-49; Indian Ambassador to France, 1949-56, also Indian Minister to Norway, 1950-56. President, 3rd General Assembly of International Civil Aviation Organisation, Montreal, 1949; Leader of Indian Delegation to UN General Assembly, Paris, 1952. Grand Officier, Légion d'Honneur, 1954. *Recreations:* golf, cricket and tennis. *Address:* 7 Palam Marg Vasant Vihar, New Delhi. *Clubs:* Gulmarg (Kashmir); Imperial Gymkhana (New Delhi); Delhi Golf; Pine Valley Golf (USA).

MALIK, Yakov Alexandrovich; Order of Lenin, 1944 and 1945; Deputy Foreign Minister of the USSR, since 1960; Permanent Representative of the USSR at the United Nations, 1968-76; *b* in Ukraine, 6 Dec. 1906; *m* ; one *s* one *d* (and one *s* decd). *Educ:* Kharkov Inst. of Economics; Inst. for Diplomatic and Consular Staffs, Moscow. Dep. Chief, Press Dept, Ministry of Foreign Affairs, 1937; Counsellor, 1939, Ambassador, 1942-45, at Tokyo; Political Adviser, Allied Council for Japan, 1946; Deputy Foreign Minister, 1946-53, and Permanent Representative of USSR to United Nations, 1948-52; Soviet Ambassador to the Court of St James's, 1953-60. *Address:* Ministry of Foreign Affairs, Smolenskaya Ploshchad, Moscow, USSR.

MALIM, Comdr David Wentworth, RN, retd; Chairman, Marconi Space & Defence Systems Ltd, since 1970; *b* 28 April 1914; *s* of Frederick Blagden Malim and Amy Gertrude Malim; *m* 1939, Theodora Katharine Thackwell Lewis; one *s* two *d*. *Educ:* RNC, Dartmouth; RNEC, Keyham. Engineer Officer: HMS Cumberland, 1936-38; HMS Edinburgh, 1939-40; RNATE Torpoint, 1940-42; Ordnance Engineer Officer: HMS Warspite, 1943-44; HMS Excellent, 1944-46; Staff, BJSM, Washington, 1947-49; Naval Ordnance Dept, Admiralty, 1949-54; retd as Comdr (E) at own request. Laurence Scott & Electromotors Ltd, 1954-59; Manager, Lancashire Dynamo Co., 1959-61; Jt Man. Dir, Elliot Space & Weapon Automation Ltd,

1962-70. Pres., Electronic Engrg Assoc., 1975-76. *Recreations:* lawn tennis, shooting. *Address:* Warren House, Brocket Park, Lemsford, Herts AL8 7XF. *T:* Welwyn Garden City 23175. *Club:* Army and Navy.

MALIM, Rear-Adm. Nigel Hugh, CB 1971; MVO 1960; FIMechE; FIMarE; Managing Director, Humber Graving Dock & Engineering Co. Ltd, since 1972; Chairman, HGD Steel Stockholders, since 1974; *b* 5 April 1919; *s* of late John Malim, Pebmarsh, and Brenda Malim; *m* 1944, Moonyeen, *d* of late William and Winefride Maynard; two *s* one *d. Educ:* Weymouth Coll.; RNEC Keyham. Cadet, RN, 1936; HMS Manchester, 1940-41; HMS Nofolk, 1942; RNC Greenwich, 1943-45; HMS Jamaica, 1945-47; Staff of RNEC, 1948-50; Admty, 1951-54; HMS Triumph, 1954-56; Admty, 1956-58; HM Yacht Britannia, 1958-60; District Overseer, Scotland, 1960-62; Asst, and later Dep., Dir Marine Engrg, 1962-65; idc 1966; Captain, RNEC Manadon, 1967-69; Chief Staff Officer Technical to C-in-C, W Fleet, 1969-71, retd. *Recreations:* offshore racing and cruising. *Address:* The Old Vicarage, Caistor, Lincoln LN7 6UG. *Clubs:* Royal Ocean Racing, Royal Naval Sailing Association.

MALIN, Peter; see Conner, Rearden.

MALKIN, H(arold) Jordan, CBE 1964; Director of Postgraduate Studies, Royal College of Obstetricians and Gynæcologists, 1967-75, retired; *b* 27 April 1898; *s* of late Sydney and Edith Jordan Malkin (*née* Stormer); *m* 1932, Theresa Joyce Ferris Bearder, *d* of late Cyril Horner Bearder and Mrs Dora Christiana Bearder, Abingdon, Berks; two *d. Educ:* Epworth Coll.; University Coll. and Hospital, London. Royal Field Artillery, 1916-19. University Coll., University Coll. Hospital, 1916 and 1919-24. Consultant Obstetrician and Gynæcologist, Nottingham, 1928-67. Rockefeller Travelling Fellowship, 1926. MD London, 1926; FRCSEd 1925; FRCOG 1938; Hon. LLD Nottingham, 1970. *Address:* 19 Cavendish Crescent South, The Park, Nottingham. *T:* Nottingham 47015; Ivy Cottage, Wargrave Road, Henley-on-Thames, Oxon. *T:* Wargrave 2453. *Club:* Oriental.

MALLABAR, Sir John (Frederick), Kt 1969; FCA; Senior Partner, J. F. Mallabar & Co., Chartered Accountants, since 1929; *b* 19 July 1900; *e s* of Herbert John Mallabar and Gertrude Mallabar, *d* of Hugh Jones, Barrow; *m* 1st, 1931, Henrietta, *d* of George Goodwin-Norris; 2nd, 1949, Annie Emily (Pat), *d* of Charles Mealing, Princes Risborough, and *widow* of Richard Howard Ford, Bodweni, Merionethshire; no *c. Educ:* Sunbury House Sch.; King's Coll., London. Served European War, 1914-18: Inns of Court Regt and 5th KRRC, 1918-19. An Underwriting Member of Lloyds. Chairman: Ruston & Hornby, 1964-66; Harland and Wolff Ltd, 1966-70. Chm., Cttee on Govt Industrial Establishments, 1968-70. *Recreations:* stalking, salmon fishing. *Address:* 39 Arlington House, St James's, SW1; (office) 15 King Street, St James's, SW1. *Club:* Flyfishers'.

MALLABY, Christopher Leslie George; HM Diplomatic Service; Counsellor and Head of Arms Control and Disarmament Department, Foreign and Commonwealth Office, since 1977; *b* 7 July 1936; *s* of late Brig. A. W. S. Mallaby, CIE, OBE, and Margaret Catherine Mallaby (*née* Jones); *m* 1961, Pascale Françoise Thierry-Mieg; one *s* three *d. Educ:* Eton Coll.; King's Coll., Cambridge. British Delegn to UN Gen. Assembly, 1960; 3rd Sec., British Embassy, Moscow, 1961-63; 2nd Sec., FO, 1963-66; 1st Sec., Berlin, 1966-69; 1st Sec., FCO, 1969-71; Harvard Business Sch., 1971; Dep. Dir, British Trade Develt Office, NY, 1971-74; Counsellor and Head of Chancery, Moscow, 1975-77. *Recreations:* fishing, reading, travel. *Address:* 3 Clarence Place, Hampton Court, East Molesey, Surrey KT8 9AU. *T:* 01-977 2133.

MALLABY, Sir (Howard) George (Charles), KCMG 1958 (CMG 1953); OBE 1945; *b* 17 Feb. 1902; *s* of William Calthorpe Mallaby and Katharine Mary Frances Miller; *m* 1955, Elizabeth Greenwood Locker (*née* Brooke), one *step s* two *step d. Educ:* Radley Coll.; Merton Coll., Oxford. BA 1923; MA 1935; MA (Cantab) 1965; Asst Master Clifton Coll., 1923-24; Diocesan Coll., Rondebosch, S Africa, 1926; Assistant Master and House Master, S Edward's Sch., Oxford, 1924-26 and 1927-35; Headmaster, St Bees Sch., Cumberland, 1935-38; District Commissioner for the Special Area of West Cumberland, 1938-39; Dep. Regional Transport Commissioner for North Western Region, 1939-40; Captain, Gen. List, 1940; Major, 1941; Lieut-Col, 1943; Colonel, 1945; served in Military Secretariat of War Cabinet, 1942-45; US Legion of Merit (Degree of Officer), 1946. Secretary, National Trust, 1945-46; Asst Secretary, Ministry of Defence, 1946-48; Secretary-General Brussels Treaty Defence Organisation, 1948-50; Under Secretary, Cabinet Office, 1950-54; Secretary, War Council and Council of Ministers, Kenya,

1954; Dep. Secretary, University Grants Cttee, 1955-57; High Commissioner for the United Kingdom in New Zealand, 1957-59; First Civil Service Commissioner, 1959-64, retired. Chairman of Council of Radley Coll., 1952-57. Governor: St Edward's Sch.; Bedford Coll., London Univ.; Chairman: Cttee on the Staffing of Local Government, 1967; Hong Kong Govt Salaries Commn, 1971; Special Ctte on Structure of Rugby Football Union, 1972-73. Extraordinary Fellow, Churchill Coll., Cambridge, 1964-69. *Publications:* Wordsworth (Extracts from the Prelude with other Poems), 1932; Wordsworth: A Tribute, 1950; From My Level, 1965; Each in his Office, 1972; (ed) Poems by William Wordsworth, 1970. *Address:* Down The Lane, Chevington, W Suffolk. *T:* Chevington 308. *Club:* Army and Navy.

MALLALIEU, Sir Edward Lancelot, (Sir Lance), Kt 1974; QC 1951; Barrister-at-law; Governor Royal Agricultural Society of England; *b* 14 March 1905; *s* of County Alderman F. W. Mallalieu, MP, JP; *m* 1934, Betty Margaret Oxley, *d* of Dr Pride, late of Bridlington, *g d* of late J. W. Oxley of Leeds; one *s* two *d. Educ:* Dragon Sch., Oxford; Cheltenham Coll.; Trinity Coll., Oxford. MA 1930. Called Bar, Inner Temple, 1928; NE Circuit. Sometime farmer in Co. Wicklow, and Dir of Farming Coll. of St Columba. MP (L) Colne Valley, Yorks, 1931-35; PPS to Rt Hon. Sir Donald Maclean, President Board of Education, 1931-32; MP (Lab) Brigg, Lincs, 1948-Feb. 1974; Senior Member, Speaker's Panel of Chairmen, 1964-71; Second Dep. Chm., 1971-73, First Dep. Chm., 1973-74, of Ways and Means. Member Exec., Inter-Parliamentary Union (Geneva), Chairman British Group; Secretary-General, World Assoc. of World Federalists, The Hague (Parliamentary Adviser, 1966); Hon. Vice-Pres., Franco-British Parly Relations Cttee. Hon. Vice-President, Parly Group for World Government. A Director of the French Hospital, Rochester. Second Church Estates Comr, 1965-70. Chevalier, Legion of Honour, 1957. *Address:* 40 Westminster Gardens, Marsham Street, SW1. *Club:* Royal Cruising.
See also J. P. W. Mallalieu.

MALLALIEU, Joseph Percival William; MP (Lab) Huddersfield, 1945-50, East Division of Huddersfield, since 1950; *b* 18 June 1908; 3rd *s* of late County Alderman F. W. Mallalieu, MP; *m* 1945, Harriet Rita Riddle Tinn; one *s* one *d. Educ:* Dragon Sch., Oxford; Cheltenham; Trinity Coll., Oxford; University of Chicago. Oxford Rugger Blue, 1927; President Oxford Union, 1930; Commonwealth Fellow, University of Chicago, 1930-32; Col, Governor of Kentucky's Bodyguard, 1933; worked on London newspapers, 1933-41; served in Royal Navy, 1942-45. PPS to Under-Sec. of State for Air, 1945-46, to Minister of Food, 1946-49; Under-Secretary of State for Defence (Royal Navy), 1964-66; Minister: of Defence (Royal Navy), 1966-67; of State, Board of Trade, 1967-68, Min. of Technology, 1968-69. Member, Management Committee: RNLI, 1959-63; Royal Hosp. Sch., Holbrook, 1947-66. Life Mem., NUJ, 1973. *Publications:* Rats, 1941; Passed to You, Please!, 1942; Very Ordinary Seaman, 1944; Sporting Days, 1955; Extraordinary Seaman, 1957; Very Ordinary Sportsman, 1957. *Recreations:* walking, gardening; watching Huddersfield Town. *Address:* Village Farm, Boarstall, Aylesbury, Bucks. *T:* Brill 454. *Club:* Press.
See also Sir E. L. Mallalieu.

MALLALIEU, Sir Lance; *see* Mallalieu, Sir E. L.

MALLAM, Lieut-Colonel Rev. George Leslie, CSI 1947; CIE 1943; *b* 13 Dec. 1895; *o s* of late George Mallam, Parkstone, Dorset; *m* 1st, 1934, Constance Marie (KIH, silver) (*d* 1944), *d* of late Dr E. J. W. Carruthers; two *s*; 2nd, 1950, Mary Sophronia, *o d* of Canon Cory, St Audrey's, Wilden; one *d. Educ:* Malvern. Commissioned IA, 1916; joined Political Dept, 1921; Counsellor British Legation, Kabul, Afghanistan, 1932. Financial Secretary to Government North-West Frontier Province, 1939; then Chief Secretary, Planning and Development Comr and Revenue and Divisional Comr. Called to Bar, Gray's Inn, 1926. Deacon, 1949; Priest, 1950; Vicar of Eckington, near Pershore, Worcs, 1952-65, retired 1965. *Address:* Abbey Place, Defford Road, Pershore, Worcs. *T:* Pershore 2223.

MALLE, Louis; Film Director; *b* 30 Oct. 1932; *s* of Pierre Malle and Françoise Béghin; one *s. Educ:* Paris Univ.; Institut d'Etudes Politiques. Television, 1953; Asst to Comdt Cousteau on the Calypso, 1953-55. Films: Co-prod. Le Monde du Silence, 1955; Collab. techn of Robert Bresson for Un Condamné a mort s'est echappé, 1956; Author and Producer of: Ascenseur pour l'échafaud, 1957 (Prix Louis-Delluc, 1958); Les Amants, 1958 (Prix spécial du Jury du Festival de Venise, 1958); Zazie dans le métro, 1960; Vie privée, 1962; Le Feu Follet (again, Prix spécial,

Venise, 1963); Viva Maria, 1965 (Grand Prix du Cinema français); Le Voleur, 1966; Histoires extraordinaires (sketch), 1968; Inde 68, 1968; Calcutta, 1969 (prix de la Fraternité; Phantom India, 1969; Le Souffle au Coeur, 1971; Humain, trop Humain, 1972; Place de la République, 1973; Lacombe Lucien, 1974; Black Moon, 1975. *Address:* c/o NEF, 92 Champs Elysées, 75008 Paris, France.

MALLEN, Sir Leonard (Ross), Kt 1967; OBE 1958; JP (S Australia); Medical Practitioner; *b* 18 Dec. 1902; *m* 1926, Eunice M. Pitcher; one *d. Educ:* St Peter's Coll., Adelaide; University of Adelaide. MB, BS, 1925. Member Fed. Council, BMA in Australia, 1948-62; Member Fed. Council AMA, 1962-67; Chairman Fed. Assembly, AMA, 1962-67; Chairman, Pharmaceutical Benefits Advisory Cttee (Australia), 1957-73; President, World Medical Assoc., 1968-69 (Member Council, 1951-61; Chairman Council, 1958-60); Fellow, AMA, 1964; FRACGP, 1963; FRCGP 1972. *Recreations:* golf, tennis. *Address:* 1 Greenwood Grove, Urrbrae Park, SA 5064, Australia. *T:* 79-8603. *Clubs:* Naval, Military and Air Force of S Australia, Adelaide (both Adelaide).

MALLET, Hooper Pelgué; Commodore P&OSN Company, 1960-61, retired; *b* 4 June 1901; *s* of Wesley John Mallet and Harriet Anley; *m* 1932, Ethel Margaret Stewart (*d* 1972), Launceston, Tasmania; no *c. Educ:* Oxenford House Sch., Jersey; HMS Worcester. Royal Naval Reserve, 1918-19; joined P&OSN Co., 1919. *Recreations:* chess, bowls. *Address:* 9 Selworthy Avenue, Melbourne, Vic 3167, Australia.

MALLET, Sir Ivo; *see* Mallet, Sir W. I.

MALLET, John Valentine Granville; Keeper, Department of Ceramics, Victoria and Albert Museum, since 1976; *b* 15 Sept. 1930; *s* of Sir Victor Mallet, GCMG, CVO, and Lady Mallet (*née* Andreae); *m* 1958, Felicity Ann Basset; one *s. Educ:* Winchester Coll.; Balliol Coll., Oxford (BA Modern History). Mil. service in Army: commnd; held temp. rank of full Lieut in Intell. Corps, 1949-50. Messrs Sotherby & Co., London, 1955-62; Victoria and Albert Museum: Asst Keeper, Dept of Ceramics, 1962; Sec. to Adv. Council, 1967-73. Mem., Court of Assistants, Fishmongers' Co., 1970. FRSA. *Publications:* articles on ceramics in Burlington Magazine, Apollo, Connoisseur, Trans English Ceramic Circle, and Faenza. *Recreation:* tennis. *Address:* Victoria and Albert Museum, South Kensington, SW7 2RL. *T:* 01-589 6371.
See also P. L. V. Mallet.

MALLET, Philip Louis Victor; HM Diplomatic Service; Head of Republic of Ireland Department, Foreign and Commonwealth Office, since 1977; *b* 3 Feb. 1926; *e s* of late Sir Victor Mallet, GCMG, CVO and of Christiana Jean, *d* of Herman A. Andreae; *m* 1953, Mary Moyle Grenfell Borlase; three *s. Educ:* Winchester; Balliol Coll., Oxford. Army Service, 1944-47. Entered HM Foreign (subseq. Diplomatic) Service, 1949; served in: FO, 1949; Baghdad, 1950-53; FO, 1953-56; Cyprus, 1956-58; Aden, 1958; Bonn, 1958-62; FO, 1962-64; Tunis, 1964-66; FCO, 1967-69; Khartoum, 1969-73; Stockholm, 1973-76. *Address:* c/o Foreign and Commonwealth Office, SW1. *Club:* Brooks's.
See also J. V. G. Mallet.

MALLET, Roger; Chairman, North Western Electricity Board, 1972-76; *b* 7 June 1912; British; *m* 1942, Kathleen Els Walker; two *s* two *d. Educ:* Eastbourne Coll.; Trinity Hall, Cambridge. BA Mech. Sci. Tripos; CEng, FIEE. West Cambrian Power Co., S Wales, 1937-40; Buckrose Light & Power Co., Yorks, 1940-45; Shropshire, Worcestershire and Staffordshire Electric Power Co., 1945-47; Midlands Electricity Board, 1948-72. *Recreation:* golf. *Address:* 75 Carrwood, Hale Barns, Cheshire, WA15 0ER. *T:* 061-980 3214.

MALLET, Sir (William) Ivo, GBE 1960; KCMG 1951 (CMG 1945); retired as Ambassador to Spain (1954-60); *b* 7 April 1900; *yr s* of late Sir Charles Mallet; *m* 1929, Marie-Angèle, *d* of Joseph Wierusz-Kowalski; two *s* one *d. Educ:* Harrow; Balliol Coll., Oxford. Entered Diplomatic Service, 1925. Served in Constantinople. Angora, London, Berlin, Rome; Asst Private Secretary to Secretary of State for Foreign Affairs, 1938-41; Acting Counsellor in FO, 1941; Counsellor, 1943; Consul-General, Tangier, 1946; Asst Under-Secretary, Foreign Office, 1949; HM Ambassador, Belgrade, 1951. *Address:* Chalet La Combe, Rossinière, Vaud, Switzerland.
See also R. A. Farquharson.

MALLETT, Francis Anthony; Chief Executive, South Yorkshire County Council, since 1973; Clerk of the Lieutenancy, South Yorkshire, since 1974; solicitor; *b* 13 March 1924; *s* of Francis Sidney and Marion Mallett; *m* 1956, Alison Shirley Melville,

MA; two s one *d. Educ:* Mill Hill; London Univ. (LLB). Army, 1943-47: commissioned, Royal Hampshire Regt, 1944; served in Middle East, Italy and Germany. Staff Captain, 160 (South Wales) Infty Bde, 4th (Infty) Bde and 4th (Guards) Bde, successively, 1946 and 1947. Second Dep. Clerk, Hertfordshire CC, 1966-69; Dep. Clerk, West Riding CC, 1969-74. *Recreations:* gardening, fishing, tennis. *Address:* Aketon Springs, Follifoot, Harrogate, N Yorks. *T:* Spofforth 395. *Club:* Lansdowne.

MALLETT, Ven. Archdeacon Peter, QHC 1973; AKC; Chaplain-General to the Forces since July 1974; *b* 1925; *s* of Edwin and Beatrice Mallett; *m* 1958, Margaret Bremer; one *s* two *d. Educ:* King's Coll., London; St Boniface Coll., Warminster, Wilts. Deacon, 1951, priest, 1952. Curate, St Oswald's, Norbury, S London, 1951-54. Joined Royal Army Chaplains' Dept (CF), 1954, and has served overseas in Far East, Aden, Germany (despatches, Malaya, 1957). Has been Senior Chaplain of Aden Brigade, and at RMA, Sandhurst; Dep. Asst Chaplain-General, Berlin, 1968, in N Ireland, 1972; Asst Chaplain-General, BAOR, 1973. OStJ 1976. *Address:* c/o Ministry of Defence (Army), Chaplains Department, Bagshot Park, Bagshot, Surrey GU19 5PL. *Clubs:* Army and Navy, Naval and Military (Hon.).

MALLEY, Cecil Patrick; late Aural Surgeon St Mary's Hospital for Women and Children, Plaistow, Acton Hospital and Hounslow Hospital; Surgeon Metropolitan Ear, Nose and Throat Hospital, Fitzroy Square; *b* Castlebar, Co. Mayo, 5 April 1902; *s* of Luke Malley and Marrion Kearney; *m* ; two *s* one *d. Educ:* O'Connell's Schools; University College, Dublin. MB, BCh, BAO, 1925; FRCS 1933; FICS. Late Resident Surgical Officer St Mary's Hospital, Plaistow; House Surgeon All Saints Hosp.; Aural Registrar Charing Cross Hosp.; Registrar Golden Square Hosp.; Senior Clinical Asst Metropolitan Ear, Nose and Throat Hospital; late Clinical Assistant Ear, Nose and Throat Dept, West London Hospital. *Publications:* Acute Mastoiditis, Otalgia Charing Cross Journal, Section on Larynx in Pye's Surgical Handicraft. *Recreations:* golf, yachting. *Address:* Celymar, Guadalmina Urbanisation, San Pedro, Malaga, Spain. *Clubs:* Royal Thames Yacht, National University.

MALLINSON, Dennis Hainsworth; Director, National Engineering Laboratory, East Kilbride, Department of Industry, since 1974; *b* 22 Aug. 1921; *s* of David and Anne Mallinson; *m* 1945, Rowena Mary Brooke; one *s* two *d. Educ:* Leeds Univ. (BSc). RAE, 1942, early jet engines; Power Jets (R&D) Ltd, later Nat. Gas Turbine Estabt, 1944-63; Min. of Aviation and successors: Asst Dir, 1963; Dir, 1964; Dir-Gen., Engines, Procurement Exec., MoD, 1972-74. Vis. Prof., Strathclyde Univ., 1976-. Member Council: Instn Engrs and Shipbuilders in Scotland, 1977; Scottish Assoc. of Metals, 1976-. *Address:* 9 Blackwood Avenue, Newton Mearns, Glasgow G77 5JY.

MALLINSON, Sir Paul; *see* Mallinson, Sir W. P.

MALLINSON, Col Sir Stuart Sidney, Kt 1954; CBE 1938; DSO 1918; MC; DL; Hon. President, William Mallinson & Sons, Ltd, London (Director, 1912-44, Chairman and Managing Director, 1944-62); Hon. President, William Mallinson & Denny Mott Ltd; President, Timber Research and Development Association, 1963-73; Director, Eastern Electricity Board, 1954; *b* 1888; *s* of Sir Wm Mallinson, 1st Bt; *m* 1916, Marjorie Gray, CBE 1960 (*d* 1969), *d* of late Rev. Alfred Soothill; two *s* (and one *s* killed in action, 1944, one *d* decd). *Educ:* Ashville Coll., Harrogate; Leys Sch., Cambridge. Entered the firm of Wm Mallinson & Sons, Ltd, 1907; joined HAC Aug. 1914; France, Sept. 1914; commissioned April 1915; MC June 1916; transferred to RE as Captain, Sept. 1916; Major, Dec. 1916; Lt-Col, March 1917; (DSO; despatches three times); Officier du Mérite Agricole, 1918; Hon. Colonel 28th Essex AA, 1937-45; Hon. Colonel 563 Regt (Essex) TA, RA, 1947-55; Hon. Colonel 717 Regt (5th Essex) RA, TA, 1955-57. Governor Leys Sch., 1920; Governor: St Felix Sch., Southwold; Chigwell Sch.; Ashville Coll., Harrogate; President, National Sunday School Union, 1923-24; Vice-Pres., English-Speaking Union of the Commonwealth; Pres., Commonwealth Forestry Soc. JP Essex; DL, Essex, 1937; High Sheriff of Essex, 1939; Chairman, Leyton Employment Exchange, 1931-38, 1951-63; DL Greater London, 1966-76; Sector Commander HG; Chairman Essex National Fitness Cttee; County War Welfare Officer; Chairman Essex Playing Fields Assoc., 1945; President Essex County Football Assoc., 1954. OStJ 1951. *Recreations:* fishing, travel. *Address:* The White House, Woodford Green, Essex. *T:* 01-504 1234. *Clubs:* British Sportsman's, Royal Commonwealth Society, English-Speaking Union.

MALLINSON, Sir (William) Paul, 3rd Bt, *cr* 1935; MA, BM, BCh, FRCP; FRCPsych; Hon. Consulting Psychiatrist to St George's Hospital, SW1; Civilian Consultant in Psychiatry to Royal Navy; Chairman, Wm Mallinson & Denny Mott Ltd, 1962-73; *b* 6 July 1909; *s* of Sir William Mallinson, 2nd Bt, and Mabel (*d* 1948), *d* of J. W. Rush, Tunbridge Wells; *S* father, 1944; *m* 1st, 1940, Eila Mary (marr. diss. 1968), *d* of Roland Graeme Guy, Hastings, NZ; one *s* two *d* ; 2nd, 1968, Margaret Cooper, BA, MB, BS, *d* of S. A. Bowden, Barnstaple, Devon. *Educ:* Westminster; Christ Church, Oxford; St Thomas's Hospital. Late Surgeon Lieut-Commander, RNVR. First class Order of the Family, Brunei, 1973. *Heir:* s William John Mallinson [*b* 8 Oct. 1942; *m* 1968, Rosalind Angela, *o d* of Rollo Hoare, Dogmersfield, Hampshire; one *s* one *d*]. *Address:* 25 Wimpole Street, W1. *T:* 01-580 7919; Farm Lane House, Bembridge, Isle of Wight. *T:* 2239. *Clubs:* Athenæum; Royal Thames Yacht; MCC.

MALLORIE, Air Vice-Marshal Paul Richard, AFC 1947; Assistant Chief of Staff (Information Systems), SHAPE, since 1976; *b* 8 March 1923; *s* of late Rev. W. T. Mallorie and Margaret Mallorie; *m* 1951, Ursula Joyce Greig; three *s* one *d* . *Educ:* King's Sch., Canterbury. Flying Instructor, 1945; India and Middle East, 1946-49; Air Ministry, 1951-53; Staff Coll., 1954; No 139 Sqdn, 1955-57; JSSC, 1960; UK Mil. Advisers' Rep., SEATO, Bangkok, 1963-66; OC RAF Wittering, 1967-68; IDC, 1969; Min. of Defence, 1974-76. *Recreations:* gardening, fishing. *Address:* Manor Steps, London Road, Ascot, Berks SL5 7EG. *Club:* Royal Air Force.

MALLOWAN, Sir Max (Edgar Lucien), Kt 1968; CBE 1960; MA, DLit; FBA 1954; FSA; Fellow of All Souls College, Oxford, 1962-71, Emeritus Fellow, 1976; Professor of Western Asiatic Archæology, University of London, 1947-62, now Emeritus Professor; a Trustee of the British Museum; *b* London, 6 May, 1904; *s* of Frederick Mallowan, London; *m* 1930, Agatha Mary Clarissa Miller (Dame Agatha Christie, DBE) (*d* 1976); *m* 1977, Barbara Parker. *Educ:* Lancing; New Coll., Oxford (Hon. Fellow, 1973). Archæologist. Assistant on staff of British Museum and of Museum of University of Pennsylvania Expedition to Ur of the Chaldees, 1925-30 and on staff of British Museum Expedition to Nineveh, 1931-32. Subsequently directed excavations on behalf of British Museum and British School of Archæology in Iraq, at Arpachiyah, 1933; in Syria, at Chagar Bazar, 1934-36, at Brak and at various sites in the Balikh valley, 1937-38. During War of 1939-45 served in RAFVR with rank of Wing Commander; posted for duty with British Military Administration in Tripolitania 1943-44 and served as Adviser on Arab Affairs and subsequently as GSO 1, Deputy Chief Secretary. Director, British School of Archæology in Iraq, 1947-61 (Chairman, 1966-70, Pres., 1970-); President British Institute of Persian Studies, 1961-; Vice-President: British Academy, 1961-62; Egypt Exploration Soc., 1968-. Excavated in Zab valley, 1948, 1955, at Nimrud, 1949-58. Mem. Governing Body, SOAS, 1967-75. Schweich Lectr, 1955, Albert Reckitt Archaeological Lectr, 1969, British Academy. FBA, and corresp. Member: Arab Acad., Baghdad, 1954; German Archæological Inst., 1962; Foreign Member: Académie des Inscriptions et Belles-Lettres, Paris, 1964; Royal Danish Acad. of Letters and Scis, 1974. Museum of Univ. of Pennsylvania, Lucy Wharton Drexel Gold Medal, 1957; Hon. Fellow Metropolitan Museum of Art, New York, 1958. Lawrence of Arabia Meml Medal, RCAS, 1969. Editor: Near Eastern and Western Asiatic series of Penguin books, 1948-65; Iraq, 1948-71. *Publications:* Prehistoric Assyria; Excavations at Chagar Bazar; Excavations in the Balikh Valley; Excavations at Brak: archæological articles in Iraq, Antiquity, The Times, Illustrated London News, etc; Twenty-five Years of Mesopotamian Discovery, 1932-56; (with Sir Leonard Woolley) Ur Excavations, The Neo-Babylonian and Persian Periods, 1962; Early Mesopotamia and Iran, 1965; Nimrud and its Remains, 2 Vols, 1966; contrib. chapters to Cambridge Ancient History, 1967; Elamite Problems, 1969; (with L. G. Davies) Ivories in Assyrian Style, 1970; (with G. Herrmann) Ivories from Nimrud Fascicule III Furniture from SW7 Fort Shalmaneser, 1974; Mallowan's Memoirs, 1977. *Recreations:* trees, travel. *Address:* Winterbrook House, Wallingford, Oxon. *Clubs:* Athenæum, Boodle's.

MALLOWS, Surg. Rear-Adm. Harry Russell; Senior Medical Officer, Shell Centre, since 1977; *b* 1 July 1920; *s* of Harry Mallows and Amy Mallows (*née* Law); *m* 1942, Rhona Frances Wyndham-Smith; one *s* two *d* . *Educ:* Wrekin Coll.; Christ's Coll., Cambridge (MA, MD); UCH, London. FFCM, DPH, DIH. SMO, HM Dockyards at Hong Kong, Sheerness, Gibraltar and Singapore, 1951-67; Naval MO of Health, Scotland and NI Comd, and Far East Stn, 1964-68; Dir of Environmental Medicine, Inst. of Naval Medicine, 1970-73;

Comd MO, Naval Home Comd, 1973-75; QHP, 1974-77; Surgeon Rear-Adm. (Ships and Estabts), 1975-77; retd 1977. *Publications:* articles in BMJ, Royal Naval Med. Service Jl, Proc. RSM. *Recreations:* music, travel. *Address:* c/o National Westminster Bank Ltd, 76 St Thomas Street, Weymouth, Dorset. *Club:* Naval.

MALMESBURY, 6th Earl of *cr* 1800; **William James Harris;** TD 1944 (2 Clasps); JP; Baron Malmesbury, 1788; Viscount FitzHarris, 1800; Official Verderer of the New Forest, 1966-74; Lord-Lieutenant and Custos Rotulorum of Hampshire, since 1973; served Royal Hampshire Regt, TA; *b* 18 Nov. 1907; *o s* of 5th Earl and Hon. Dorothy Gough-Calthorpe (*d* 1972), CBE (Lady of Grace, Order of St John of Jerusalem, Order of Mercy, with bar), *y d* of 6th Lord Calthorpe; *S* father 1950; *m* 1932, Hon. Diana Carleton, *e d* of 6th Baron Dorchester, OBE; one *s* two *d. Educ:* Eton; Trinity Coll., Cambridge (BA). Vice-Pres. of the Cambridge Univ. Conservative Association, 1930; Professional Associate of Surveyors Institution, 1937. Personal Liaison Officer to Min. of Agric., SE Region, 1958-64; Mem., Agric. and Forestry Cttee, RICS, 1953-69; Chm., Hants Agric. Exec. Cttee, 1959-67; Cttee which produced White Paper on the Growing Demand for Water, 1961. Dir, Mid-Southern Water Co., 1961-. Chairman: Hants Br., Country Landowners Assoc., 1954-56; T&AFA, Hants and IoW, 1960-68; Eastern Wessex TA&VRA, 1968-70 (Vice-Pres., 1973-); Hon. Col, 65th (M) Signal Regt, R Sigs (TA), 1959-66; Hon. Col, 2nd Bn The Wessex Regt (V), 1970-73. Mem. Basingstoke RDC, 1946-52; County Councillor, Hants CC, 1952; Vice-Lt, Co. Southampton, 1960-73. Master, Worshipful Co. of Skinners, 1952-53. KStJ 1973. Coronation Medal, 1937, 1953; Silver Jubilee Medal, 1977. *Heir: s* Viscount FitzHarris, *qv. Address:* Greywell Hill, Basingstoke, Hants RG25 1DB. *T:* Odiham 2033. *Club:* Royal Yacht Squadron (Vice-Cdre, 1971-).

MALMESBURY, Bishop Suffragan of, since 1973; **Rt. Rev. Frederick Stephen Temple;** *b* 24 Nov. 1916; *s* of Frederick Charles and Frances Temple; *m* 1947, Joan Catharine Webb; one *s* one *d* (and one *s* decd). *Educ:* Rugby; Balliol Coll., Oxford; Trinity Hall, Cambridge; Westcott House, Cambridge. Deacon, 1947, Priest, 1948; Curate, St Mary's, Arnold, Notts, 1947-49; Curate, Newark Parish Church, 1949-51; Rector, St Agnes, Birch, Manchester, 1951-53; Dean of Hong Kong, 1953-59; Senior Chaplain to the Archbishop of Canterbury, 1959-61; Vicar of St Mary's, Portsea, 1961-70; Archdeacon of Swindon, 1970-73. Proctor, Canterbury Convocation, 1964; Hon. Canon, Portsmouth Cathedral, 1965. *Publication:* (ed) William Temple, Some Lambeth Letters, 1942-44, 1963. *Recreations:* tennis, bathing, reading. *Address:* Morwena, Mill Lane, Swindon, Wilts SN1 4HQ. *T:* Swindon 35798.

MALONE, Sir Denis (Eustace Gilbert), Kt 1977; **Hon. Mr Justice Malone;** Chief Justice of Belize, since 1974; *b* 24 Nov. 1922; *s* of Sir Clement Malone, OBE, QC, and Lady Malone; *m* 1963, Diana Malone (*née* Traynor). *Educ:* St Kitts-Nevis Grammar Sch.; Wycliffe Coll., Stonehouse, Glos; Lincoln Coll., Oxford (BA). Called to Bar, Middle Temple, 1950. Royal Air Force, Bomber Comd, 1942-46. Attorney General's Chambers, Barbados, WI, 1953-61, Solicitor-Gen., 1958-61; Puisne Judge: Belize, 1961-65; Trinidad and Tobago, 1966-74. *Recreations:* tennis, swimming, walking, bridge, reading. *Address:* 18 North Park Street, Belize City Belize. *T:* Belize City 2256.

MALONE, Denis George Withers, OBE 1967; retired as Governor, HM Prison, Dartmoor, (1960-66); lately, HM Prison Service; *b* 12 July 1906; *s* of Col William George Malone and Ida Katharine Withers; *m* 1935, Anita Cecilie Sophie Wolfermann. *Educ:* Douai Sch., Woolhampton, Berks. Asst Housemaster, Housemaster, Dep. Gov. (Gov. Cl. IV) and Gov. (Cl. III, II, I) Borstal and Prison Service of England and Wales, 1931-67; Seconded Foreign Office (German Section), Control Officer I and Sen. Control Officer, CCG Legal Div., Penal Branch, 1947-49; Seconded Colonial Office; Asst Commissioner, Prisons Dept, Kenya, 1950-54; Director of Prisons, Prisons Dept, Cyprus, 1958-60 (despatches). Vice-Pres., Kerikeri and Dist Beautifying Soc. *Recreations:* foreign travel and outdoor activities. *Address:* Kerikeri, Bay of Islands, Northland, New Zealand.

MALONEY, Michael John, MA; JP; Headmaster, Welbeck College, since 1972; *b* 26 July 1932; *s* of John William Maloney and Olive Lois Maloney; *m* 1960, Jancis Ann (*née* Ewing); one *s* one *d . Educ:* St Alban's Sch.; Trinity Coll., Oxford (MA). Nat. Service, 2nd Lieut RA, served with RWAFF, 1955-57. May & Baker Ltd, 1957-58; Asst Master, Shrewsbury Sch., 1958-66; Sen. Science Master, Housemaster, Dep. Headmaster, Eastbourne Coll., 1966-72. JP Worksop, 1975. *Publication:* (with D. E. P. Hughes) Advanced Theoretical Chemistry, 1964. *Recreations:* Rugby football, ornithology, cryptography.

Address: Headmaster's House, Welbeck College, Worksop, Notts. *T:* Worksop 6581. *Club:* East India, Devonshire, Sports and Public Schools.

MALOTT, Deane Waldo; President Cornell University, Ithaca, NY, 1951-63, President Emeritus, 1963; Consultant, Association of American Colleges, 1963-70; *b* 10 July 1898; *s* of Michael Harvey Malott and Edith Gray Johnson; *m* 1925, Eleanor Sisson Thrum; one *s* two *d. Educ:* Univ. of Kansas (AB); Harvard Univ. (MBA). Asst Dean, Harvard Business Sch., 1923-29; Assoc. Prof. of Business, 1933-39; Vice-Pres., Hawaiian Pineapple Co., Honolulu, 1929-33; Chancellor, Univ. of Kansas, 1939-51. Educational Advisor, Ops Analysis Div., US Army Air Corps, 1943-45; Mem., Business Council, Washington, DC, 1944-; Trustee: Corning Museum of Glass, 1952-73; Teagle Foundation, 1952-; William Allen White Foundation, 1952-; Kansas Univ. Endowment Assoc., 1962-; Pacific Tropical Botanical Garden, 1964-; Mem. Bd, Univ. of Kansas Alumni Assoc., 1974-; Director: General Mills, Inc., 1948-70; Citizens Bank, Abilene, Kans, 1944-73; Pitney-Bowes, Inc., 1951-71; First Nat. Bank, Ithaca, NY, 1951-69; Owens-Corning Fiberglas Corp., 1951-72; Lane Bryant, Inc., 1963-77; Servomation Corp., 1963-74; Hon. LLD: Washburn Univ., 1941; Bryant Coll., 1951; Hamilton Coll., 1951; Univ. of California 1954; Univ. of Liberia, 1962; Univ. of New Hampshire, 1963; Emory Univ., 1963; Juniata Coll., 1965; DCS, Univ. of Pittsburgh, 1957; Hon. DHL, Long Island Univ., 1967. Holds foreign Orders. *Publications:* Problems in Agricultural Marketing, 1938; (with Philip Cabot) Problems in Public Utility Management, 1927; (with J. C. Baker) Introduction to Corporate Finance, 1936; (with J. C. Baker and W. D. Kennedy) On Going into Business, 1936; (with B. F. Martin) The Agricultural Industries, 1939; Agriculture-the Great Dilemma (an essay in Business and Modern Society), 1951. *Address:* 322 Wait Avenue, Cornell University, Ithaca, NY 14853, USA. *Clubs:* University, Cornell (New York); Bohemian (San Francisco).

MALPAS, Dr James Spencer, FRCP; Consultant Physician, St Bartholomew's Hospital, since 1973; Director, Imperial Cancer Research Fund Medical Oncology Unit, St Bartholomew's Hospital, since 1976; *b* 15 Sept. 1931; *s* of Tom Spencer Malpas, BSc, MICE and Hilda Chalstrey; *m* 1957, Joyce May Cathcart; two *s. Educ:* Sutton County Grammar Sch.; St Bartholomew's Hosp., London Univ. Schol. in Sci., 1951; BSc Hons, 1952; MB BS, 1955; DPhil, 1965; FRCP 1971. Junior appts in medicine, St Bartholomew's Hosp. and Royal Post-Grad. Med. Sch.; Nat. Service in RAF, 1955-61; Aylwen Bursar, St Bartholomew's Hosp., 1961; Lectr in Medicine, Oxford Univ., 1962-65; St Bartholomew's Hospital: Sen. Registrar in Medicine, 1966-68; Sen. Lectr in Medicine, 1968-72; Dean of Medical Coll., 1969-72. Cooper Res. Schol. in Med., 1966, 1967, 1968. Examr in Medicine, Univ. of Oxford, 1974. Asst Registrar, RCP, 1975-. Jt Editor, Excerpta Medica Review of Leukaemia and Lymphoma. *Publications:* contrib. five medical textbooks; papers in BMJ, Brit. Jl Haematology, Jl Clinical Pathology, etc. *Recreations:* travel, history, painting. *Address:* 64 Belmont Hill, Lewisham, SE13 5DN. *T:* 01-852 1162.

MALPAS, Robert, CBE 1975; Technical, Eastern Europe, Organics Products Director, Imperial Chemical Industries Ltd, since 1975; *b* 9 Aug. 1927; *s* of late Cheshyre Malpas and Louise Marie Marcelle Malpas; *m* 1956, Josephine Dickenson. *Educ:* Taunton Sch.; St George's Coll., Buenos Aires; Durham Univ. BScMechEng (1st Cl. Hons); AMIMechE. Joined ICI Ltd, 1948; moved to Alcudia SA (48.5 per cent ICI), Spain, 1963; ICI Europa Ltd, Brussels, 1965; Chm., ICI Europa Ltd, 1973; ICI Main Board Dir, 1975. Order of Civil Merit, Spain, 1967. *Recreation:* sport. *Address:* 8a Inverness Gardens, Vicarage Gate, W8 4RN. *T:* 01-221 6195. *Club:* Real Automovil Club de España (Madrid).

MALTBY, Antony John, MA; Headmaster of Trent College since 1968; *b* 15 May 1928; *s* of late G. C. Maltby and Mrs Maltby (*née* Kingsnorth); *m* 1959, Jillian Winifred (*née* Burt); four *d. Educ:* Claysmore Sch., Dorset; St John's Coll., Cambridge. BA Hons (History) 1950. Schoolmaster: Dover Coll., 1951-58; Pocklington Sch., 1958-68. *Recreations:* squash, tennis, travel. *Address:* School House, Trent College, Long Eaton, Nottingham NG10 4AD. *T:* Long Eaton 2737. *Clubs:* East India, Devonshire, Sports and Public Schools; Hawks (Cambridge).

MALTBY, Maj.-Gen. (Christopher) Michael, CB 1946; MC; DL; retired pay; *b* 13 Jan. 1891; *er s* of late Christopher James Maltby, Felmersham, Beds; *m* 1927, Hélène Margaret Napier-Clavering (*d* 1974); two *d. Educ:* King's Sch., Canterbury; Bedford Sch.; RMA, Woolwich. Commissioned 1910; joined

Indian Army, 1911; Capt., 1915; Bt Major, 1919; Major, 1927; Bt Lt-Col 1933; Lt-Col 1935; Col 1938; Brig. 1939; Maj.-Gen. 1941. Passed Staff Coll., Quetta, 1923-24; passed RAF Staff Coll., Andover, 1927-28; GSO2 and DAAG AHQ India; GSO1, Quetta Staff Coll. and Baluchistan Dist; Comdr 3rd Jhelum Bde, Calcutta Bde, 19th Indian Inf. Bde, Deccan Dist and British Troops in China. Served Persian Gulf, 1913-14. European War, 1914-18 (wounded, despatches thrice, MC, Bt Maj.); NWF India, 1923-24, 1937 (despatches); commanded in Hong Kong, 1941. DL Somerset, 1953. *Recreation:* shooting. *Address:* c/o Nynehead Court, Wellington, Somerset. *Club:* Naval and Military.

MALVERN, 2nd Viscount *cr* 1955, of Rhodesia and of Bexley; **John Godfrey Huggins**; *b* 26 Oct. 1922; *s* of 1st Viscount Malvern, PC, CH, KCMG and Blanche Elizabeth (*d* 1976), *d* of late James Slatter, Pietermaritzburg, S Africa; *S* father, 1971; *m* 1949, Patricia Marjorie, *d* of Frank Renwick-Bower, Durban, S Africa; two *s* one *d. Educ:* Winchester. Joined RAF 1940; Flight Lt 1944; retd 1945; re-joined RAF, 1952. *Address:* PO Box AP50, Salisbury Airport, Rhodesia.

MALVERN, Harry Ladyman, CBE 1970; Managing Director of Remploy Ltd, 1964-73; *b* 4 June 1908; *s* of late Harry Arthur Malvern, Wirral, Cheshire; *m* 1935, Doreen, *d* of late John James Peters; one *s* one *d. Educ:* Birkenhead Sch., Cheshire. FCA; FInstD. Joint Man. Dir, Spratts Patent Ltd, 1961-64. Pres., Cookham Soc., 1970-; Mem. Exec. Cttee, Royal Assoc. for Disability and Rehabilitation, 1977-. *Recreations:* gardening, reading, archaelogy. *Address:* Meadow Cottage, Hockett Lane, Cookham Dean, Berks SL6 9UF. *T:* Marlow 2043.

MAMO, Sir Anthony (Joseph) Kt 1960; OBE 1955; President of the Republic of Malta, 1974-76; *b* 9 Jan. 1909; *s* of late Joseph Mamo and late Carola (*née* Brincat); *m* 1939, Margaret Agius; one *s* two *d. Educ:* Royal Univ. of Malta. BA 1931; LLD 1934. Mem. Statute Law Revision Commn, 1936-42; Crown Counsel, 1942-51; Prof., Criminal Law, Malta Univ., 1943-57; Dep. Attorney-Gen., 1952-54, Attorney-Gen., 1955, Malta; Chief Justice and President, HM Court of Appeal, Malta, 1957-71; President, HM Constitutional Court, Malta, 1964-71; Governor-General, Malta, 1971-74. QC (Malta) 1957. Hon. DLitt Malta, 1969; Hon. LLD Libya, 1971. KStJ 1969. *Publications:* Lectures on Criminal Law and Criminal Procedure delivered at the University of Malta. *Address:* 49 Stella Maris Street, Sliema, Malta. *T:* 30708. *Clubs:* Casino Maltese, Malta Sports (Malta).

MAMOULIAN, Rouben; stage and screen director; producer; author; *b* 8 Oct. 1897; *s* of Zachary Mamoulian and Virginia Kalantarian; *m* Azadia Newman, Washington, DC. *Educ:* Lycée Montaigne, Paris; Gymnasium, Tiflis; Univ., Moscow. First English production, Beating on the Door, at St James's Theatre, London, Nov. 1922; arrived in Rochester, New York, Aug. 1923; from that date to summer of 1926 was Director of Production at the Eastman Theatre, producing Grand Operas, Operettas, Dramas, and stage presentations, among which were the following: Carmen, Faust, Boris Godounoff, Shanewis, Gilbert and Sullivan Operettas, Sister Beatrice, etc; also organised and was Director of the Eastman Theatre Sch.; came to New York at the end of 1926; started there as a Director of the Theatre Guild Sch.; first production of a play on Broadway, 10 Oct. 1927, Porgy, for the Theatre Guild; Porgy was followed by direction of the following plays on Broadway: Marco Millions, Congai, Wings over Europe, These Modern Women, RUR, The Game of Love and Death, A Month in the Country, A Farewell to Arms, and Solid South; also an opera at the Metropolitan Opera House, Hand of Fate, with L. Stokowski and the Philadelphia Orchestra; Opera Porgy and Bess (music by George Gershwin) for Theatre Guild, New York, 1935; in Los Angeles and San Francisco, 1938. Directed following motion pictures: Applause in 1928; City Streets and Dr Jekyll and Mr Hyde, in 1932; Love Me Tonight, in 1933, and Song of Songs, in 1933; Queen Christina in 1933 and We Live Again in 1934; Becky Sharp (Technicolor) in 1935; The Gay Desperado in 1936; High, Wide and Handsome in 1937; Golden Boy in 1939; The Mark of Zorro in 1940; Blood and Sand (Technicolor) in 1941; Rings on Her Fingers in 1942; Summer Holiday (technicolor musical, based on Eugene O'Neill's Ah Wilderness) in 1947; Silk Stockings (musical film, cinemascope, color) 1957. *Stage productions:* Oklahoma!, 1943; Sadie Thompson, 1944, and Carousel, 1945, St Louis Woman, 1946, musical dramas in New York; Lost In The Stars (musical tragedy), 1949; Arms And The Girl (musical play), 1950, New York; Oklahoma! (for Berlin Arts Festival), 1951; Adolph Zukor's Golden Jubilee Celebration, Hollywood, 1953; Carousel (New Prod.), Los Angeles and San Francisco, 1953; Oklahoma!, new production for Paris, Rome, Milan, Naples and Venice, 1955. Co-Author (with Maxwell Anderson) of musical play The Devil's Hornpipe

(made musical film Never Steal Anything Small), 1959. World Première Perf. of Shakespeare's Hamlet, A New Version, Lexington, Ky, 1966. Tributes and retrospective showings: NY, 1967, 1970, 1971; London, 1968; Montreal, Beverly Hills and Washington, 1970; Amer. Inst. for Advanced Studies, San Francisco, Toronto and Univs of Calif. at LA, S Florida and Yale, 1971; Hollywood, 1972; UCLA, Hollywood, Paris, San Sebastian, 1973; Washington DC, 1974; Univ. of California, Univ. of S California, 1975; Calif State Coll., 1976; Amer. Film Inst., 1976, 1977; Hollywood, N Carolina State Univ., 1977. Guest of Honour: Republics of Armenia and Georgia, 1971; Internat. Film Festivals, Moscow 1971, Iran 1974, Australia 1974, San Sebastian 1974, Boston 1976. Lectures, and appears on TV. Award of Excellence, Armenian Amer. Bicentennial Commemoration Cttee Inc., 1976. *Publications:* Abigayil, 1964; Hamlet Revised and Interpreted, 1965; contrib. Scoundrels and Scalawags, 1968; Ararat, 1969; Foreword to Chevalier, 1973. *Recreations:* swimming, horseback riding, and reading detective stories. *Address:* 1112 Schuyler Road, Beverly Hills, Calif 90210, USA.

MAN, Archdeacon of; *see* Glass, Ven. E. B.

MAN, Maj.-Gen. Christopher Mark Morrice, CB 1968; OBE 1958; MC 1945; retired; *b* 20 July 1914; *s* of late Rev. M. L. Man, MA, and Evelyn Dora Man, Tenterden, Kent; *m* 1940, Georgina, *d* of late James Marr, Edinburgh; no *c. Educ:* Eastbourne Coll.; Emmanuel Coll., Cambridge. (MA). Lieut, Middlesex Regt, 1936; 1st Bn, The Middlesex Regt, 1937-45. Commanded Army Air Transport Training and Development Centre, 1953-55; GSO 1, WO, 1955-57; comdg Infantry Junior Leaders Battalion, 1957-59; comdg 125 Infantry Bde (TA), 1959-62; Head of Commonwealth Liaison Mission, UN Command, Korea and British Military Attaché, Seoul, 1962-64; GOC 49th Infantry Div. TA and N Midland District, 1964-67; Colonel, The Middlesex Regt, 1965-66; Pres., Regular Army Commn, 1967-69; Dep. Colonel The Queen's Regt, 1967-69, Hon. Colonel, 1970-71. Private, Atholl Highlanders, 1969. *Address:* The Old Schoolhouse, Calvine, Pitlochry, Perthshire PH18 5UD. *T:* Calvine 224. *Clubs:* Army and Navy, MCC.

MAN, Morgan Charles Garnet, CMG 1961; Director: Metallurgical Plantmakers' Federation; British Metalworking Plantmakers' Association; Ironmaking and Steelmaking Plant Contractors' Association; *b* 6 Aug. 1915; *s* of Henry Morgan Stoe Man and Nora Loeck; *m* 1st, 1941, Moira Farquharson Main (marr. diss. 1956); two *d*; 2nd, 1956, Patricia Mary (*née* Talbot). *Educ:* Cheltenham Coll.; Queen's Coll., Oxford. Joined HM Consular Service, 1937; Vice-Consul, Beirut, 1937-39; Assistant Oriental Secretary, HM Embassy, Bagdad, 1939; 2nd Secretary, HM Embassy, Jedda, 1943; Consul, Atlanta, Ga, USA, 1946; Consul, Kirkuk, 1948; First Secretary, HM Legation, Damascus, 1949; Oriental Secretary, HM Embassy, Bagdad, 1951; Assistant in American Dept, Foreign Office, Sept. 1953; Head of American Dept, 1954; Counsellor at HM Embassy, Oslo, Nov. 1956; Deputy Political Resident, Bahrain, 1959-62; Minister, HM Embassy, Ankara, 1962-64; HM Ambassador to Saudi Arabia, 1964-68; Senior Civilian Instructor, Imperial Defence Coll., 1968-69; retired, 1970. DL Greater London, 1977. *Address:* c/o Metallurgical Plantmakers' Federation, 7 Ludgate Broadway, EC4V 6DX.

MAN, Maj.-Gen. Patrick Holberton, CB 1966; CBE 1962 (OBE 1946); DSO 1956; MC 1940; *b* 17 March 1913; *s* of Colonel Hubert William Man, CBE, DSO, and Mrs Beryl Man (*née* Holberton); *m* 1938, Barbara Joan Marion Marsh; two *d. Educ:* Rugby Sch.; RMC, Sandhurst. Commissioned into The Hampshire Regt, 1933. Served France and Belgium, 1939-40; Staff Coll., Camberley, 1941; served South-East Asia, 1943-45. RAF Staff Coll., 1946-47; served Middle East, 1950-52; Imperial Defence Coll., 1953; served Malaya, 1954-56, and BAOR, 1959-63; GOC Aldershot District, 1963-66; Dir of Personal Services (Army), 1966-68, retd. Colonel Comdt, Military Provost Staff Corps, 1967-72. MBIM. Bronze Star, 1945; Selangor Meritorious Service, 1956. *Recreation:* ski-ing. *Address:* Quill Farm, Campsea Ashe, near Woodbridge, Suffolk.

MANASSEH, Leonard Sulla, ARA 1976; FRIBA; Partner, Leonard Manasseh & Partners, since 1950; *b* 21 May 1916; *s* of Alan Manasseh and Esther (*née* Elias); *m* 1st, 1947, Karin Williger (marr. diss. 1956); two *s*; 2nd, 1957, Sarah Delaforce; two *s* one *d. Educ:* Cheltenham College; The Architectural Assoc. Sch. of Architecture (AA Dip.). ARIBA 1941, FRIBA 1964; FSIA 1965; RWA 1972. Asst Architect, CRE N London and Guy Morgan & Partners; teaching staff, AA and Kingston Sch. of Art, 1941-43; Fleet Air Arm, 1943-46; Asst Architect, Herts CC, 1946-48; Senior Architect, Stevenage New Town Develt Corp., 1948-50; private practice, 1950; teaching staff, AA

Sch. of Architecture, 1951-59; opened office in Singapore and Malaysia with James Cubitt & Partners (Cubitt Manasseh & Partners), 1953-54. Mem. Council, Architectural Assoc., 1959-66 (Pres., 1964-65); Mem., Council of Industrial Design, 1965-68; Mem. Council, RIBA 1968-70, 1976-. FRSA 1967. Won Festival of Britain restaurant competition, 1950. *Work includes:* houses, housing and schools for GLC and other local authorities; industrial work; conservation plan for Beaulieu Estate; Nat. Motor Museum, Beaulieu; Wellington Country Park, Stratfield Saye. *Publications:* Office Buildings (with 3rd Baron Cunliffe), 1962, Japanese edn 1964; Snowdon Summit Report (Countryside Commission), 1974; (jtly) planning reports and studies. *Recreations:* photography, travel, sketching, watching aeroplanes, being optimistic. *Address:* 6 Bacon's Lane, Highgate, N6 6BL. *T:* 01-340 5528.

MANBY, Mervyn Colet, CMG 1964; special consultant, UN Fund for Drug Abuse Control, since 1975; *b* 20 Feb. 1915; *s* of late Harold B. and Mary Manby (*née* Mills), late of Petistree, Suffolk; *m* 1949, Peggy Aronson, Eastern Cape, South Africa; one *s* one *d. Educ:* Bedford Sch., Bedford; Pembroke Coll., Oxford. Colonial Police Service, 1937; Malaya, 1938-47; Basutoland, 1947-54; Kenya, 1954-64. Dep. Inspector General, Kenya Police, 1961-64; retired, 1964. United Nations Technical Assistance Adviser to Government of Iran, 1965; UN Div. of Narcotic Drugs, 1971-75. Mem. Council, Inst. for Study of Drug Dependence, 1975-. *Address:* Old Well Cottage, Barham, Canterbury, Kent. *T:* Barham 369.

MANCE, Sir Henry (Stenhouse), Kt 1971; Chairman of Lloyd's, 1969, 1970, 1971, 1972 (Deputy Chairman, 1967, 1968); *b* 5 Feb. 1913; *e s* of late Brig.-Gen. Sir H. O. Mance, KBE, CB, CMG, DSO; *m* 1940, Joan Erica Robertson Baker; one *s* three *d. Educ:* Charterhouse; St John's Coll., Cambridge (MA). Entered Lloyd's, 1935; Underwriting Member of Lloyd's, 1940; elected to Cttee of Lloyd's, 1966. Chairman, Lloyd's Underwriters' Assoc., 1965 and 1966; Member, Cttee of Lloyd's Register, 1966-. Min. of War Transport, 1941-46. Chairman: Lloyds Life Assurance Ltd, 1971-; Willis Faber (Underwriting Management), 1973-77; Willis, Faber & Dumas (Agencies), 1973-; Dir for life, Willis, Faber Ltd, 1973-; Dir, Craigmyle & Co. Ltd, 1973-. President: Insurance Inst. of London, 1975-76; Chartered Insurance Institute, 1977-. Treasurer, Church Missionary Soc., 1972-; Trustee of Ridley and Wycliffe Halls. Lloyd's Gold Medal, 1973. *Recreations:* gardening, carpentry, fishing. *Address:* Gatefield Cottage, Okehurst, Billingshurst, W Sussex. *T:* Billingshurst 2155; 9 Pensioners Court, The Charterhouse, EC1. *T:* 01-253 5362. *Club:* National Liberal.

MANCHAM, Hon. James Richard Marie; President, Republic of the Seychelles, 1976-77 (Prime Minister of Seychelles, 1975-76; Chief Minister, 1970-75); *b* 11 Aug. 1939; *e s* of late Richard Mancham and Evelyne Mancham (*née* Tirant); *m* 1963, Heather Jean Evans (marr. diss. 1974); one *s* one *d. Educ:* Seychelles College. Called to Bar, Middle Temple, 1961. Legal practice, Supreme Court of Seychelles. Seychelles Democratic Party (SDP), Pres. 1964; Mem. Seychelles Governing Council, 1967; Leader of Majority Party (SDP), 1967; Mem., Seychelles Legislative Assembly, 1970-76; led SDP to Seychelles Constitutional Conf., London, 1970. Hon. Citizen of New Orleans, 1965. FRSA 1968. Founder, Seychelles Weekly, 1962. *Publication:* Reflections and Echoes from Seychelles, 1972 (poetry). *Recreations:* travel, water sports, writing poetry. *Clubs:* Annabel's; Seychelles, Seychelles Yacht (Seychelles); El Morocco (NY); Régime (Paris); Griffin (Geneva).

MANCHESTER, 10th Duke of, *cr* 1719; **Alexander George Francis Drogo Montagu**, OBE 1940; Earl of Manchester, 1626; Viscount Mandeville, Baron Montagu of Kimbolton, 1620; Commander, Royal Navy, retired; *b* 2 Oct. 1902; *er s* of 9th Duke of Manchester and late Helena (who obtained a divorce, 1931 and *m* 1937, 11th Earl of Kintore), *d* of late Eugene Zimmerman, USA; *S* father, 1947; *m* 1st, 1927, Nell Vere Stead (*d* 1966), Melbourne; two *s*; 2nd, 1969, Mrs Elizabeth Crocker, Pebble Beach, Calif. *Educ:* Osborne; Dartmouth. Entered Royal Navy, 1930. *Recreations:* shooting, etc. Heir: *s* Viscount Mandeville, *qv. Address:* Kapsirowa, Hoey's Bridge PO, Kenya. *Club:* Junior Naval and Military.

MANCHESTER, Bishop of, since 1970; **Rt. Rev. Patrick Campbell Rodger**; *b* 28 Nov. 1920; *s* of Patrick Wylie and Edith Ann Rodger; *m* 1952, Margaret Menzies Menzies, MBE; two *s. Educ:* Cargilfield; Rugby; Christ Church, Oxford; Theological College, Westcott House, Cambridge, Deacon, 1949; Priest, 1950. Asst Curate, St John's Church, Edinburgh, 1949-51, and Chaplain to Anglican Students in Edinburgh, 1951-54. Study Secretary, SCM of Gt Brit. and Ire., 1955-58; Rector, St Fillan's, Kilmacolm, with St Mary's Bridge of Weir, 1958-61; Exec. Sec.

for Faith and Order, World Council of Churches, 1961-66; Vice-Provost, St Mary's Cathedral, Edinburgh, 1966-67; Provost, 1967-70. Chm., Churches' Unity Commn, 1974-; Pres., Conf. of European Churches, 1974-. *Publications:* The Fourth World Conference on Faith and Order, Montreal (ed), 1964; contrib., Theological jls in English and French. *Recreations:* music and walking. *Address:* Bishopscourt, Bury New Road, Manchester M7 0LE. *T:* 061-792 2096. *Clubs:* Royal Commonwealth Society; Manchester (Manchester).

MANCHESTER, Dean of; *see* Jowett, Very Rev. Alfred.

MANCHESTER, Archdeacon of; *see* Ballard, Ven. A. H.

MANCHESTER, William; author; Purple Heart (US) 1945; Fellow, East College, since 1968, writer in residence since 1974, Wesleyan University; *b* 1 April 1922; *s* of William Raymond Manchester and Sallie E. R. (*née* Thompson); *m* 1948, Julia Brown Marshall; one *s* two *d. Educ:* Springfield Classical High School; Univ. of Massachusetts; Dartmouth Coll., NH; Univ. of Missouri. Served US Marine Corps, 1942-45 (Presidential Unit Citation). Reporter, Daily Oklahoman, 1945-46; Reporter, foreign corresp., war corresp., Baltimore Sun, 1947-55; Man. editor, Wesleyan Univ. Publications, 1955-65; Fellow, Center for Advanced Studies, 1959-60, Lectr in English, 1968-69, Wesleyan Univ. Trustee, Friends of Univ. of Massachusetts Library, 1970-76, Pres., 1970-72. Guggenheim Fellow, 1959; Dr of Humane Letters, Univ. of Mass, 1965; Dag Hammarskjold Internat. Prize in Literature, 1967; Overseas Press Club (New York) Award for Best Book of the Year on Foreign Affairs, 1968; Univ. of Missouri Medal, 1969; Connecticut Book Award, 1974. *Publications:* Disturber of the Peace, 1951 (publ. UK as The Sage of Baltimore, 1952); The City of Anger, 1953; Shadow of the Monsoon, 1956; Beard the Lion, 1958; A Rockefeller Family Portrait, 1959; The Long Gainer, 1961; Portrait of a President, 1962; The Death of a President, 1967; The Arms of Krupp, 1968; The Glory and the Dream, 1974; Controversy and other Essays in Journalism, 1976; contrib. to Encyclopedia Britannica and to periodicals. *Recreation:* photography. *Address:* Wesleyan University, Middletown, Conn 06457, USA. *T:* 203-346-4789. *Club:* Authors' Guild (New York).

MANCROFT, family name of **Baron Mancroft**.

MANCROFT, 2nd Baron, *cr* 1937, of Mancroft in the City of Norwich; Bt, *cr* 1932; **Stormont Mancroft Samuel Mancroft;** KBE 1959 (MBE 1945); TD 1950; MA; Chairman, British Greyhound Racing Federation, since 1977; *b* 27 July 1914; *s* of 1st Baron and Phœbe (*d* 1969), 2nd *d* of Alfred Chune Fletcher, MRCS; *S* father, 1942; *m* 1951, Mrs Diana Elizabeth Quarry, *o d* of Lieut-Colonel Horace Lloyd; one *s* two *d. Educ:* Winchester; Christ Church, Oxford. Called to Bar, Inner Temple, 1938; Member of Bar Council, 1947-51; Member St Marylebone Borough Council, 1947-53; a Lord in Waiting to the Queen, 1952-54; Parliamentary Under-Secretary for Home Dept, Oct. 1954-Jan. 1957; Parliamentary Secretary, Min. of Defence, Jan.-June 1957; Minister without Portfolio, June 1957-Oct. 1958, resigned. Dir, GUS, 1958-66; Dep. Chm., Cunard Line Ltd, 1966-71; Mem., Council of Industrial Design, 1960-63; Chm., Horserace Totalisator Bd, 1972-76; Mem., Council on Tribunals, 1972-; President: Inst. of Travel Managers, 1972-; The Institute of Marketing, 1959-63; St Marylebone Conservative Assoc., 1961-67; London Tourist Board, 1963-73. Served RA (TA), 1939-46; Lieut-Colonel (despatches twice, MBE); commissioned TA, 1938; rejoined TA 1947-55. Hon. Col Comdt, RA, 1970. Croix de Guerre. *Publications:* Booking the Cooks (essays from Punch), 1969; A Chinaman in My Bath, 1974. Heir: *s* Hon. Benjamin Lloyd Stormont Mancroft, *b* 16 May 1957. *Address:* 29 Margaretta Terrace, SW3 5NU. *T:* 01-352 7674. *Clubs:* Pratt's; West Ham Boys.

MANDELSTAM, Prof. Joel; FRS 1971; Iveagh Professor of Microbiology, University of Oxford, since 1966; *b* S Africa, 13 Nov. 1919; *s* of Leo and Fanny Mandelstam; *m* 1954, Dorothy Hillier; one *s* one *d; m* 1975, Mary Maureen Dale. *Educ:* Jeppe High Sch., Johannesburg; University of Witwatersrand; Queen Elizabeth Coll., London. Lecturer, Medical Sch., Johannesburg, 1947; Scientific Staff, Nat. Institute for Med. Research, London, 1952-66. Fulbright Fellow, US, 1958-59; Vis. Prof., Univ. of Adelaide, 1971. Mem., ARC, 1973-. Leewenhoek Lectr, Royal Soc., 1975. Editorial Board, Biochemical Journal, 1960-66. *Publications:* Biochemistry of Bacterial Growth (with K. McQuillen), 1968; articles in journals and books on microbial biochemistry. *Address:* Microbiology Unit, Department of Biochemistry, South Parks Road, Oxford. *T:* Oxford 511261.

MANDELSTAM, Prof. Stanley, FRS 1962; Professor of Physics, University of California. *Educ:* University of the Witwatersrand,

Johannesburg, Transvaal, South Africa (BSc); Trinity Coll., Cambridge (BA). PhD, Birmingham. Formerly Professor of Math. Physics, University of Birmingham. *Publications:* (with W. Yourgrau) Variational Principles in Dynamics and Quantum Theory, 1955 (revised edn, 1956); papers in learned journals. *Address:* Department of Physics, University of California, Berkeley, California 94720, USA.

MANDER, Sir Charles (Marcus), 3rd Bt, *cr* 1911; Underwriting Member of Lloyd's; Director: Manders (Holdings) Ltd, Mander Brothers Ltd, until 1958; Arlington Securities Ltd; *b* 22 Sept. 1921; *o s* of Sir Charles Arthur Mander, 2nd Bart, and late Monica Claire Cotterill, *d* of G. H. Neame; *S* father, 1951; *m* 1945, Maria Dolores Beatrice, *d* of late Alfred Brodermann, Hamburg; two *s* one *d*. *Educ:* Eton Coll., Windsor; Trinity Coll., Cambridge. Commissioned Coldstream Guards, 1942; served War of 1939-45, Canal Zone, 1943; Italy, 1943, Germany, 1944; War Office (ADC to Lieut-General R. G. Stone, CB), 1945. High Sheriff of Staffordshire, 1962-63. *Recreations:* shooting, music. *Heir: s* Charles Nicholas Mander, [*b* 23 March 1950; *m* 1972, Karin Margareta, *d* of Arne Norin; two *s* one *d*]. *Address:* Little Barrow, Moreton-in-Marsh, Glos. *T:* Stow-on-the-Wold 30265; Greville House, Kinnerton Street, SW1. *T:* 01-235 1669. *Clubs:* Boodle's; Ski Club of Great Britain; Royal Thames Yacht.

MANDER, Noel Percy; Managing Director, N. P. Mander Ltd, since 1946; *b* 19 May 1912; *s* of late Percy Mander and Emily Pike, Hoxne, Suffolk; *m* 1948, Enid Watson; three *s* two *d*. *Educ:* Haberdashers Aske's Sch., Hatcham. Organ building from 1930, interrupted by war service with RA (Hampshire Bde) in N Africa, Italy and Syria, 1940-46. FSA 1974. Liveryman, Musicians' Co.; Past Master, Parish Clerks' Co. of City of London; Mem., Art Workers' Guild. Builder of Winston Churchill Meml Organ, Fulton, Missouri, and organs in many parts of world; organ builder to St Paul's Cath., London. *Publications:* St Lawrence Jewry, A History of the Organs from the Earliest Times to the Present Day, 1956; St Vedast, Foster Lane, A History of the Organs from Earliest Times to the Present Day, 1961; St Vedast Foster Lane, in the City of London: a history of the 13 United Parishes, 1973; (with C. M. Houghton) St Botolph Aldgate: a history of the organs from the Restoration to the Twentieth Century, 1973. *Recreations:* archaeology, horology. *Address:* St Peter's Organ Works, E2. *T:* 01-739 4747; Earl Soham, Woodbridge, Suffolk. *Club:* Savage.

MANDER, Raymond Josiah Gale; Joint Founder and Director, The Raymond Mander and Joe Mitchenson Theatre Collection, since 1939 (Theatre Collection Trust, since 1977); *b* 15 July; *s* of Albert Edwin Mander, MSA, LRIBA, FIAAS, and Edith Christina Gale. *Educ:* Battersea Grammar Sch. 1st professional appearance on stage, Bedford, 1934; acted in repertory, on tour and in London, until 1946. With Joe Mitchenson, founded Theatre Collection, 1939; during the War, resp. together for many BBC theatre gramophone progs; toured together in ENSA and in jt management, 1943; management of Collection became full-time occupation as authors and theatrical consultants; Collection subject of Aquarius programme, 1971; many TV appearances on theatrical subjects. *Publications:* with Joe Mitchenson: Hamlet Through the Ages, 1952 (2nd rev. edn 1955); Theatrical Companion to Shaw, 1954; Theatrical Companion to Maugham, 1955; The Artist and the Theatre, 1955; Theatrical Companion to Coward, 1957; A Picture History of British Theatre, 1957; (with J. C. Trewin) The Gay Twenties, 1958; (with Philip Hope-Wallace) A Picture History of Opera, 1959; (with J. C. Trewin) The Turbulent Thirties, 1960; The Theatre of London, 1961, illus. by Timothy Birdsall (2nd rev. edn, paperback, 1963; 3rd rev. edn 1975); A Picture History of Gilbert and Sullivan, 1962; British Music Hall: A Story in Pictures, 1965 (rev. and enlarged edn 1974); Lost Theatres of London, 1968 (2nd edn, rev. and enlarged, 1976); Musical Comedy: A Story in Pictures, 1969; Revue: A Story in Pictures, 1971; Pantomime: A Story in Pictures, 1973; The Wagner Companion, 1977; Victorian and Edwardian Entertainments from Old Photographs, 1978; contribs to and revs in Encyc. Britannica, Theatre Notebook, and Books and Bookmen. *Recreations:* going to the theatre, gardening. *Address:* 5 Venner Road, Sydenham, SE26 5EQ. *T:* 01-778 6730.

MANDER, Lady (Rosalie), (R. Glynn Grylls), MA Oxon; Biographer; Lecturer; Cornish ancestry; *m* 1930, Sir Geoffrey Mander (*d* 1962), sometime MP for East Wolverhampton; one *s* one *d*. *Educ:* Queen's Coll., Harley Street, London; Lady Margaret Hall, Oxford. Lectures frequently in USA. *Publications:* Mary Shelley, 1936; Trelawny, 1950; Portrait of Rossetti, 1965. *Address:* Wightwick Manor, Wolverhampton, Staffs; 35 Buckingham Gate, SW1.

MANDEVILLE, Viscount; Sidney Arthur Robin George Drogo Montagu; *b* 5 Feb. 1929; *er s* and *heir* of 10th Duke of Manchester, *qv*; *m* 1955, Adrienne Valerie (marr. diss. 1977), *d* of J. K. Christie. *Address:* Ol Goroshe Farm, PO Subukia, Kenya. *Club:* Muthaiga (Nairobi, Kenya).

MANDI, Lt-Col Raja (Sir) Joginder Sen Bahadur of; KCSI 1931; *b* 20 Aug. 1904; *s* of late Mian Kishan Singh; *m* 1930, *d* of late Kanwar Prithiraj Sinhji, Rajpipla; two *s* two *d*. *Educ:* Queen Mary's Coll. and Aitchison Coll., Lahore. Ascended Gadi, 1913; full ruler, 1925. Visited various countries. Ambassador of Republic of India to Brazil, 1952-56; Member of Lok Sabha, 1957-62. Hon. Lt-Col 3rd/17th Dogra Regt and Bengal Sappers and Miners. *Address:* Bejai Palace, Mandi, Mandi District (HP), India.

MANDUELL, John, FRAM, FRNCM; Principal, Royal Northern College of Music, since 1971; *b* 2 March 1928; *s* of Matthewman Donald Maunduell, MC, MA, and Theodora (*née* Tharp); *m* 1955, Renna Kellaway; three *s* one *d*. *Educ:* Haileybury Coll.; Jesus Coll., Cambridge; Royal Acad. of Music. FRAM 1964; FRNCM 1974; Hon. FTCL 1973. BBC: music producer, 1956-61; Head of Music, Midlands and E Anglia, 1961-64; Chief Planner, The Music Programme, 1964-68; Univ. of Lancaster: Dir of Music, 1968-71; Mem. Court and Council, 1972-. Prog. Dir, Cheltenham Festival, 1969-. Pres., Lakeland Sinfonia. Chm., Music Adv. Cttee, British Council, 1973-. Director: London Opera Centre; Northern Ballet Theatre. Member: Arts Council of GB, 1976- (Chm., Touring Cttee; Dep. Chm., Music Panel); Gulbenkian Foundn Enquiry into Trng Musicians; Governing Bodies, Cheltham's Sch., and National Youth Orch. Engagements and tours as composer, conductor and lectr in Europe, S Africa and USA. Chm. or mem., national and internat. music competition juries. *Publications:* (contrib.) The Symphony, ed Simpson, 1966; *compositions:* Overture, Sunderland Point, 1969; Diversions for Orchestra, 1970; String Quartet, 1976. *Recreations:* cricket; travel; French life, language and literature. *Address:* Royal Northern College of Music, Oxford Road, Manchester M13 9RD. *T:* 061-273 6283.

MANGHAM, Maj.-Gen. William Desmond; Vice Quarter Master General, Ministry of Defence, since 1976; *b* 29 Aug. 1924; *s* of late Lt-Col William Patrick Mangham and Margaret Mary Mangham (*née* Donnachie); *m* 1960, Susan, *d* of late Col Henry Brabazon Humfrey; two *s* two *d*. *Educ:* Ampleforth College. 2nd Lieut RA, 1943; served India, Malaya, 1945-48; BMRA 1st Div. Egypt, 1955; Staff, HQ Middle East, Cyprus, 1956-58; Instructor, Staff Coll., Camberley and Canada, 1962-65; OC 3rd Regt Royal Horse Artillery, 1966-68; Comdr RA 2nd Div., 1969-70; Royal Coll. of Defence Studies, 1971; Chief of Staff, 1st British Corps, 1972-74; GOC 2nd Div., 1974-75. *Recreations:* polo, shooting, golf, tennis. *Address:* c/o Lloyds Bank Ltd, Cox's & King's Branch, 6 Pall Mall, SW1. *Club:* Army and Navy.

MANGO, Prof. Cyril Alexander, FBA 1976; Bywater and Sotheby Professor of Byzantine and Modern Greek, Oxford University, since 1973; *b* 14 April 1928; *s* of Alexander A. Mango and Adelaide Damonov; *m* 1st, 1953, Mabel Grover; one *d*; 2nd, 1964, Susan A. Gerstel; one *d*; 3rd, 1976, Maria C. Mundell. *Educ:* Univ. of St Andrews (MA); Univ. of Paris (Dr Univ Paris). From Jun. Fellow to Lectr in Byzantine Archaeology, Dumbarton Oaks Byzantine Center, Harvard Univ., 1951-63; Lectr in Fine Arts, Harvard Univ., 1957-58; Visiting Associate Prof. of Byzantine History, Univ. of California, Berkeley, 1960-61; Koraës Prof. of Modern Greek and of Byzantine History, Language and Literature, King's Coll., Univ. of London, 1963-68; Prof. of Byzantine Archaeology, Dumbarton Oaks Byzantine Center, 1968-73. FSA. *Publications:* The Homilies of Photius, 1958; The Brazen House, 1959; The Mosaics of St Sophia at Istanbul, 1962; The Art of the Byzantine Empire, Sources and Documents, 1972; Architettura bizantina, 1974. *Address:* Exeter College, Oxford.

MANGWAZU, Timon Sam, MA Oxon; Ambassador of the Republic of Malaŵi to the EEC, Belgium and the Netherlands, since 1973; *b* 12 Oct. 1933; *s* of Sam Isaac Mangwazu, Farmer; *m* 1958, Nelly Kathewera; three *s* three *d*. *Educ:* Ruskin Coll., Oxford; Brasenose Coll., Oxford (BA; MA 1976). Teacher at Methodist Sch., Hartley, S Rhodesia, 1955; Clerical Officer, Government Print, Agricultural Dept and Accountant General's Dept, 1956-62; Asst Registrar of Trade Unions, Ministry of Labour, 1962-63; Malaŵi Ambassador, West Germany, Norway, Sweden, Denmark, Netherlands, Belgium, Switzerland and Austria, 1964-67; High Comr in London for Republic of Malaŵi, and Ambassador to Belgium, Portugal, Netherlands and Holy See, 1967-69; Brasenose Coll., Oxford, 1969-72. *Recreation:* fishing. *Address:* Malaŵi Embassy, 13-17 rue de la Charité, 1040 Brussels, Belgium.

MANHOOD, Harold Alfred; Writer; *b* 6 May 1904; *m* 1937. *Educ:* Elementary Schooling. *Publications:* Nightseed, 1928; Apples by Night, 1932; Crack of Whips, 1934; Fierce and Gentle, 1935; Sunday Bugles, 1939; Lunatic Broth, 1944 (collections of short stories); Gay Agony (novel), 1930; Selected Stories, 1947; A Long View of Nothing (short stories), 1953. *Address:* Holmbush, nr Henfield, W Sussex.

MANIFOLD, Hon. Sir (Thomas) Chester, KBE 1965; Kt 1953; Grazier, Australia; *b* 1897; *s* of Hon. J. Chester and Lilian E. Manifold; *m* 1923, Gwenda, *d* of Maj.-Gen. H. W. and Winifred Grimwade; three *d. Educ:* Geelong Grammar Sch., Victoria; Jesus Coll., Cambridge. Served European War, RFA, 1916-19; War of 1939-45: 2nd AIF, 1940-43 (despatches); VDC, 1943-45. Councillor, Shire of Hampden, 1926-41; Member for Hampden, State Parliament, 1929-35; Hon. Minister, Argyle Government, 1932-33. Chairman, Totalizator Agency Bd of Victoria, 1960-68. Chairman, Victoria Racing Club, 1952-62, Vice-Chairman, 1943-52 and 1962. *Recreations:* racing, golf, tennis. *Address:* Talindert, Camperdown, Victoria 3260, Australia. *T:* Camperdown 31004. *Clubs:* Melbourne, Athenæum, Naval and Military (Melbourne, Victoria).

MANKIEWICZ, Joseph Leo; American writer and film director (independent, no contractual affiliations); *b* 11 Feb. 1909; *s* of Frank Mankiewicz and Johanna (*née* Blumenau); *m* 1939, Rosa Stradner (*d* 1958); two *s* (and one *s* by previous marriage); *m* 1962, Rosemary Matthews; one *d. Educ:* Columbia Univ. (AB 1928). Has written, directed and produced for the screen, 1929-. Received Screen Directors' Guild Award, 1949 and 1950; Screen Writers' Guild Award for best American comedy, 1949 and 1950; First Awards for direction and screen play, Motion Picture Academy, 1950, 1951. President, Screen Directors' Guild of America, 1950. Formed own company, Figaro Inc., 1953, dissolved, 1961. Order of Merit, Italy, 1965. Films include: Manhattan Melodrama, Fury, Three Comrades, Philadelphia Story, Woman of the Year, Keys of the Kingdom, A Letter to Three Wives, No Way Out, All About Eve, People Will Talk, Five Fingers, Julius Caesar, The Barefoot Contessa, Guys and Dolls; The Quiet American; Suddenly Last Summer; The Honey Pot; There Was a Crooked Man; Sleuth. Directed La Bohème for Metropolitan Opera, 1952. *Address:* Long Ridge Road, Bedford, NY 10506, USA.

MANKOWITZ, Wolf; author; Honorary Consul to the Republic of Panama in Dublin, 1971; *b* 7 Nov. 1924; *s* of Solomon and Rebecca Mankowitz; *m* 1944, Ann Margaret Seligmann; four *s. Educ:* East Ham Grammar Sch.; Downing Coll., Cambridge (MA, English Tripos). *Publications:* novels: Make Me An Offer, 1952; A Kid for Two Farthings, 1953; Laugh Till You Cry, 1955 (USA); My Old Man's a Dustman, 1956; Cockatrice, 1963; The Biggest Pig in Barbados, 1965; Penguin Wolf Mankowitz, 1967; *short stories:* The Mendelman Fire, 1957; The Blue Arabian Nights, 1973; The Day of the Women and The Night of the Men (fables), 1977; *histories:* Wedgwood, 1953; The Portland Vase, 1953; An Encyclopedia of English Pottery and Porcelain, 1957; *poetry:* 12 Poems, 1971; *plays:* The Bespoke Overcoat and Other Plays, 1955; Expresso Bongo (musical), 1958-59; Make Me An Offer (musical), 1959; Belle, 1961 (musical); Pickwick, 1963 (musical); Passion Flower Hotel (musical), 1965; The Samson Riddle, 1972; Stand and Deliver! (musical), 1972; *films:* Make Me An Offer, 1954; A Kid for Two Farthings, 1954; The Bespoke Overcoat, 1955; Expresso Bongo, 1960; The Millionairess, 1960; The Long and The Short and The Tall, 1961; The Day the Earth Caught Fire, 1961; The Waltz of the Toreadors, 1962; Where The Spies Are, 1965; Casino Royale, 1967; The Assassination Bureau, 1969; Bloomfield, 1970; Black Beauty, 1971; Treasure Island, 1972; The Hebrew Lesson (wrote and dir.), 1972; The Hireling, 1973; *television:* Dickens of London, 1976; The Extraordinary Mr Poe, 1978. *Recreation:* sleeping. *Address:* The Bridge House, Ahakista, Co. Cork. *T:* Kilcrohane II. *Club:* Savile.

MANKTELOW, Rt. Rev. Michael Richard John; *see* Basingstoke, Bishop Suffragan of.

MANLEY, Prof. Gordon; Emeritus Professor and Research Associate since 1968, University of Lancaster, (Professor of Environmental Sciences, 1964-68); *b* 3 Jan. 1902; *s* of Valentine Manley, Chartered Accountant; *m* 1930, Audrey Fairfax, *d* of late Professor Arthur Robinson, MA, DCL, Master of Hatfield Coll., Durham; no *c. Educ:* Queen Elizabeth's, Blackburn; Manchester Univ.; Caius Coll., Cambridge; MA (Cantab), DSc (Manchester). Meteorological Office, 1925; Greenland Expedition, 1926; Asst Lectr, Birmingham, 1926; Lectr and Head of Dept, Durham, 1928; Univ. Demonstrator and Lectr, Cambridge, 1939-48; Prof. of Geography, Univ. of London (Bedford Coll.), 1948-64. President, Royal Meteorological

Society, 1945-46 (Hon. FRMetS, 1976). Leverhulme Award for work on Pennines, 1937; Buchan Prize (Royal Met. Society), 1943; Symons Lecturer, 1944; Murchison Grant (RGS), 1947; Vis. Lectr, Univ. of Oslo, 1957; Vis. Prof., Texas A&M Univ., 1969. Flt-Lieut, Cambridge University Air Squadron, 1942-45. Correspondent for glaciology, British National Cttee for the International Geophysical Year, 1955-61. Air Ministry, Sub-Cttee for Meteorological Research, 1958-62. Ministry of Technology Visitor, 1964-69. External Examiner, Universities of Bristol, St Andrews, and others. *Publications:* Climate and the British Scene, (5th imp. 1972); papers, chiefly on British and Polar climatology, also on history of cartography, etc, in scientific journals. *Recreation:* travel among mountains. *Address:* 3 Whitwell Way, Coton, Cambridge.

MANLEY, Ivor Thomas; Under-Secretary, Principal Establishment Officer, Department of Energy, since 1974; *b* 4 March 1931; *s* of Frederick Stone and Louisa Manley; *m* 1952, Joan Waite; one *s* one *d. Educ:* Sutton High Sch., Plymouth. Entered Civil Service, 1951; Principal: Min. of Aviation, 1964-66; Min. of Technology, 1966-68; Private Secretary: to Rt Hon. Anthony Wedgwood Benn, 1968-70; to Rt Hon. Geoffrey Rippon, 1970; Principal Private Sec. to Rt Hon. John Davies, 1970-71; Asst Sec., DTI, 1971-74. *Recreations:* walking, badminton, Russian literature. *Address:* 34 Rowhill Avenue, Aldershot, Hants GU11 3LS. *T:* Aldershot 22707.

MANLEY, Hon. Michael Norman; Prime Minister of Jamaica, since 1972; President, People's National Party, Jamaica since 1969 (Member, Executive, since 1952); MP for Central Kingston, Jamaica, since 1967; *b* St Andrew, Jamaica, 10 Dec. 1924; *s* of late Rt Excellent Norman W. Manley, QC, and of Edna Manley (*née* Swithenbank); *m* 1972, Beverly Anderson; one *s* two *d* by previous marriages; one *d* by present marriage. *Educ:* Jamaica Coll.; London Sch. of Economics (BSc Econ Hons). Began as freelance journalist, working with BBC, 1950-51; returned to Jamaica, Dec. 1951, as Associate Editor of Public Opinion, 1952-53; Sugar Supervisor, Nat. Workers' Union, 1953-54; Island Supervisor and First Vice-Pres., 1955-72; Mem. Senate, 1962-67. Leader of the Opposition, Jamaican Parliament, 1969-72. Has held various posts in Labour cttees and in Trade Union affairs; organised strike in sugar industry, 1959, which led to Goldenberg Commn of Inquiry. Hon. Doctor of Laws Morehouse Coll., Atlanta, 1973. Order of the Liberator, Venezuela, 1973; Order of Mexican Eagle, 1975; Order of Jose Marti, Cuba, 1975. *Publications:* The Politics of Change, 1974; A Voice at the Workplace, 1976; The Search for Solutions, 1977. *Recreations:* sports, music, gardening, reading. *Address:* Prime Minister's Office, 1 Devon Road, Kingston 6, Jamaica; (home) Jamaica House, Hope Road, Kingston 6, Jamaica.

MANN, Bruce Leslie Home D.; *see* Douglas-Mann.

MANN, Dr Felix Bernard; medical practitioner; *b* 10 April 1931; *s* of Leo and Caroline Mann. *Educ:* Shrewsbury House; Malvern Coll.; Christ's Coll., Cambridge; Westminster Hosp. MB, BChir, LMCC. Practised medicine or studied acupuncture in England, Canada, Switzerland, France, Germany, Austria and China. *Publications:* Acupuncture; the ancient Chinese art of healing, 1962, 2nd edn 1971; The Treatment of Disease by Acupuncture, 1963; The Meridians of Acupuncture, 1964; Atlas of Acupuncture, 1966; Acupuncture: cure of many diseases, 1971; also edns in Italian, Spanish, Dutch, Finnish and Portuguese; contrib. various jls on acupuncture. *Recreations:* walking in the country and mountains. *Address:* 15 Devonshire Place, W1N 1PB. *T:* 01-935 7575. *Club:* Royal Society of Medicine.

MANN, Frederick (Francis) Alexander, FBA 1974; LLD, DrJur; Solicitor of the Supreme Court, since 1946; Hon. Professor of Law in the University of Bonn, since 1960; *b* 11 Aug. 1907; *s* of Richard Mann and Ida (*née* Oppenheim); *m* 1933, Eleonore (*née* Ehrlich); one *s* two *d. Educ:* Univs of Geneva, Munich, Berlin (DrJur) and London (LLD). Asst, Faculty of Law, Univ. of Berlin, 1929-33; German lawyer, 1933; Internat. Law Consultant, London, 1933-46. Solicitor, 1946; Partner, Herbert Smith & Co, 1957-. Member: Lord Chancellor's Standing Cttee for Reform of Private Internat. Law, 1952-64; numerous Working Parties of Law Commn. Member: Council, British Inst. of Internat. and Comparative Law; Rapporteur, 1952-73, Monetary Law Cttee, Internat. Law Assoc. Mem., Editorial Cttee, British Year Book of International Law. Associate Mem., Institut de Droit International. Lectures at Acad. of Internat. Law at The Hague, 1959, 1964 and 1971, and at numerous Univs in England, Austria, Belgium, Germany, Switzerland and USA. Grand Cross of Merit, Federal Republic of Germany, 1977. *Publications:* The Legal Aspect of Money, 1938 (3rd edn 1971); Studies in International Law, 1973; numerous articles on international law, the conflict of laws, and monetary law in

English and foreign legal pubns and periodicals. *Recreations:* music, walking. *Address:* 28 Addison Avenue, W11 4QR. *T:* 01-603 4912. *Club:* Athenæum.

MANN, Frederick George, FRS 1947; ScD (Cantab), DSc (London), FRIC; Reader Emeritus in Organic Chemistry, Cambridge University, 1964; Fellow of Trinity College, Cambridge; *b* 29 June 1897; *s* of William Clarence Herbert and Elizabeth Ann Mann; *m* 1st, 1930, Margaret Reid (*d* 1950), *d* of William Shackleton, FRAS; two *d*; 2nd, 1951, Barbara, *d* of Percy Thornber; one *d. Educ:* London Univ., 1914-17, 1919 (BSc 1919). Served European War, finally as 2nd Lieut Special Bde, RE, BEF, France, 1917-19. Research student, Downing Coll., Cambridge, 1920-23; PhD (Cantab) 1923; Assistant to Professor of Chemistry (Sir William Pope), 1922; DSc (London), 1929; ScD (Cantab) 1932; FRIC 1929. Lecturer in Chemistry, Cambridge Univ., 1930; Reader in Organic Chemistry, Cambridge Univ., 1946; Fellow and Lecturer, Trinity Coll., Cambridge, 1930, Praelector in Chemistry, 1960. Member Council of Chemical Society, 1935-38, 1940-43, 1946-49, Vice-President, 1958-61; Tilden Lecturer, 1944; Member Council of Royal Institute of Chemistry, 1942-45, 1948-51, Examnr, 1955-60; Visiting Senior Prof. of Chemistry, University of Hawaii, 1946-47. *Publications:* Practical Organic Chemistry, 1936, 4th edn, 1960; Introduction to Practical Organic Chemistry, 1939, 2nd edn, 1964 (both with Dr B. C. Saunders). The Heterocyclic Derivatives of Phosphorus, Arsenic, Antimony, Bismuth, and Silicon, 1950 (2nd edn, 1970); Lord Rutherford on the Golf Course, 1976; numerous papers in Proceedings of the Royal Society, Journal of the Chemical Society, Journal of Society of Chemical Industry, etc. *Recreation:* ornithology. *Address:* 24 Porson Road, Cambridge CB2 2EU. *T:* Cambridge 52704; Trinity College, Cambridge CB2 1TQ. *T:* Cambridge 58201; University Chemical Laboratory, Lensfield Road, Cambridge CB2 1EW. *T:* Cambridge 66499.

MANN, Rev. George Albert Douglas; General Secretary, Free Church Federal Council, since 1970; *b* 17 April 1914; *er s* of George and Alice Mann; *m* 1940, Mabel Harwood; no *c. Educ:* Clifford Road Sch., Ipswich; Manchester Baptist Coll.; Manchester Univ. Minister, Mount Pleasant Baptist Church, Burnley, 1940-42. Chaplain to HM Forces, 1942-45 (now Hon. CF); Sen. Staff Chaplain, ALFSEA, 1945-46. Minister: Park Tabernacle Baptist Church, Great Yarmouth, 1947-52; Union Baptist Church, High Wycombe, 1952-58. Mem. Baptist Union Council, 1948-; Asst Sec., and Sec. of Hosp. Chaplaincy Bd, Free Church Federal Council, 1958-69. *Recreations:* cricket, football, gardening, philately. *Address:* c/o Free Church Federal Council, 27 Tavistock Square, WC1H 9HH. *T:* 01-387 8413.

MANN, Ida, CBE 1950; MA Oxon, DSc London; MB, BS London; FRCS; FRACS; Cons. Surgeon, Royal London Ophthalmic (Moorfields) Hospital; late Member Expert Committee, WHO; late Cons. Ophthalmologist to Government of Western Australia; *b* London, 1893; *d* of F. W. Mann, MBE, and Ellen Packham; *m* 1944, William Ewart Gye, FRS, MD, FRCP (*d* 1952). *Educ:* University of London. Ophthalmic surgeon and research worker; late Research Student, Institute of Pathology, St Mary's Hospital; Henry George Plimmer Fellow of the Imperial College of Science and Technology; Assistant Surgeon, Central London Ophthalmic Hospital; Ophthalmic Surgeon, Royal Free Hospital and Elizabeth Garrett Anderson Hospital; Pathologist, Central London Ophthalmic Hospital; Senior Surgeon Oxford Eye Hospital; Margaret Ogilvie Reader, University of Oxford, 1941, Professor 1945-47; War Service as Head of Research Team for Ministry of Supply. Fellow of St Hugh's College; Gifford Edmonds Prize in Ophthalmology, 1926; Arris and Gale Lecturer, 1928; Doyne Memorial Lecturer, 1929; Montgomery Lecturer, 1935; Nettleship Prize, 1930; Mackenzie Memorial Medal, 1935; Howe Memorial Medal, 1958; Bowman Medal, 1961. Member: Ophthalmological Society of UK and other societies. *Publications:* The Development of the Human Eye; Developmental Abnormalities of the Eye; Culture, Race, Climate and Eye Disease; and numerous papers in medical journals. *Recreation:* travel. *Address:* 56 Hobbs Avenue, Nedlands, Western Australia 6009, Australia.

MANN, Julia de Lacy, MA; Principal, St Hilda's College, Oxford, 1928-July 1955; *o d* of James Saumarez Mann, MA, sometime Fellow of Trinity College, Oxford; *b* Aug. 1891. *Educ:* Bromley High Sch.; Somerville Coll., Oxford. Classical Hon. Mods. 1912; Lit. Hum. 1914. Secretarial work, Admiralty and Foreign Office, 1915-19; Vice-Principal, St Hilda's Coll., 1923-28. Hon. DLitt Oxon, 1973. *Publications:* (with A. P. Wadsworth), The Cotton Trade and Industrial Lancashire, 1600-1780, 1931, Ed. Documents illustrating the Wiltshire Textile Trades in the 18th Century (Wilts Arch. Society,

Records Branch, Vol. XIX), 1964; The Cloth Industry in the West of England, 1640-1880, 1971. *Address:* The Cottage, Bower Hill, Melksham, Wilts. *Club:* University Women's.

MANN, Michael, QC 1972; *b* 9 Dec. 1930; *s* of Adrian Bernard Mann, CBE and Mary Louise (*née* Keen); *m* 1957, Jean Marjorie (*née* Bennett), MRCVS; two *s. Educ:* Whitgift Sch.; King's Coll., London (LLB, PhD). Called to Bar, Gray's Inn, 1953; practised from 1955; Junior Counsel to the Land Commn (Common Law), 1967-71. Asst Lectr 1954-57, Lectr 1957-64, in Law, LSE; part-time Legal Asst, FO, 1954-56. *Publications:* (ed jtly) Dicey, Conflict of Laws, 7th edn, 1957; Dicey and Morris, Conflict of Laws, 8th edn 1967, 9th edn, 1973; articles in Modern Law Review, Internat. and Compar. Law Quarterly. *Recreation:* making model aircraft. *Address:* Netherstone, Promenade de Verdun, Purley, Surrey.

MANN, Rt. Rev. Michael Ashley; Dean of Windsor, since 1976; Chairman, St George's House; Register, Order of the Garter, since 1976; Domestic Chaplain to the Queen, since 1976; *b* 25 May 1924; *s* of late H. G. Mann and F. M. Mann, Harrow; *m* 1949, Jill Joan Jacques; one *d* (and one *s* decd). *Educ:* Harrow Sch.; RMC Sandhurst; Wells Theological Coll.; Graduate School of Business Admin., Harvard Univ. Served War of 1939-45: RMC, Sandhurst, 1942-43; 1st King's Dragoon Guards, 1943-46 (Middle East, Italy, Palestine). Colonial Admin. Service, Nigeria, 1946-55. Wells Theological Coll., 1955-57; Asst Curate, Wolborough, Newton Abbot, 1957-59; Vicar: Sparkwell, Plymouth, 1959-62; Christ Church, Port Harcourt, Nigeria, 1962-67; Dean, Port Harcourt Social and Industrial Mission; Home Secretary, The Missions to Seamen, 1967-69; Residentiary Canon, 1969-74, Vice-Dean, 1972-74, Norwich Cathedral; Adviser to Bp of Norwich on Industry, 1969-74; Bishop Suffragan of Dudley, 1974-76. Governor: Harrow Sch.; The Abbey Girls' Sch., Malvern. MBIM. *Recreations:* military history, philately, ornithology. *Address:* The Deanery, Windsor Castle, Berks SL4 1NJ. *T:* Windsor 65561. *Club:* Cavalry and Guards.

MANN, Murray G.; *see* Gell-Mann.

MANN, Rt. Rev. Peter Woodley; *see* Dunedin, Bishop of.

MANN, Ronald; Deputy Chairman, Grindlays Bank Ltd, 1964-77; Director, Grindlays Holdings Ltd; *b* 22 April 1908; *s* of Harry Ainsley Mann and Millicent (*née* Copplestone); *m* 1935, Beatrice Elinor Crüwell Wright; one *s* three *d. Educ:* Cranleigh Sch., Surrey. The Eastern Produce and Estates Co. Ltd: Asst, Ceylon, 1930-35; Man., Ceylon, 1935-46; Man. Dir, London, 1947-; Chm., Eastern Produce Holdings Ltd, 1957-71. *Recreations:* golf, gardening. *Address:* Fernhurst Place, Fernhurst, near Haslemere, Surrey. *T:* Haslemere 52220. *Club:* Oriental.

MANN, Sir Rupert (Edward), 3rd Bt *cr* 1905; *b* 11 Nov. 1946; *s* of Major Edward Charles Mann, DSO, MC (*g s* of 1st Bt) (*d* 1959), and of Pamela Margaret, *o d* of late Major Frank Haultain Hornsby; *S* great uncle, 1971; *m* 1974, Mary Rose, *d* of Geoffrey Butler, Saffron Walden. *Educ:* Malvern. *Heir:* b Andrew William Mann, *b* 22 Oct. 1947. *Address:* Billingford Hall, Diss, Norfolk. *Clubs:* MCC; Norfolk.

MANN, Thaddeus Robert Rudolph, CBE 1962; FRS 1951; Biochemist; Professor of the Physiology of Reproduction, University of Cambridge, 1967-76, now Emeritus (Reader in Physiology of Animal Reproduction, 1953-67); Fellow of Trinity Hall, Cambridge, since 1961; Member of the Staff of Agricultural Research Council, 1944-76; *b* 1908; *s* of late William Mann and Emilia (*née* Quest); *m* 1934, Dr Cecilia Lutwak-Mann. *Educ:* Trin. Hall, Cambridge; MD Lwòw 1935, PhD Cantab 1937, ScD Cantab 1950; Rockefeller Research Fellow, 1935-37; Beit Mem. Research Fellow, 1937-44. Dir, ARC Unit of Reproductive Physiology and Biochemistry, Cambridge, 1954-76. Awarded Amory Prize of Amer. Academy of Arts and Sciences, 1955; Senior Lalor Fellow at Woods Hole, 1960; Vis. Prof. in Biology at Florida State Univ., 1962; Vis. Prof. in Biological Structure and Zoology, Univ. of Washington, 1968; Vis. Scientist, Reproduction Res. Br., Nat. Insts of Health, USA, 1978. Gregory Pincus Meml Lectr, 1969; Albert Tyler Meml Lectr, 1970. For. Mem., Royal Belgian Acad. of Medicine, 1970. Hon. doctorate: of Veterinary Medicine, Ghent, 1970; of Natural Scis, Cracow, 1973. Cavaliere Ufficiale, Order of Merit (Italy), 1966. *Publications:* The Biochemistry of Semen, 1954; The Biochemistry of Semen and of the Male Reproductive Tract, 1964; papers on Carbohydrate Metabolism of Muscle, Yeast and Moulds, on Metaloprotein Enzymes, and on Biochemistry of Reproduction. *Address:* Trinity Hall, Cambridge; 1 Courtney Way, Cambridge CB4 2EE.

MANN, William Neville, MD, FRCP; Consultant Physician Emeritus, Guy's Hospital, 1976; Physician, King Edward VII's Hospital for Officers, since 1965; b 4 April 1911; s of William Frank Mann and Clara, d of John Chadwick; m Pamela, yr d of late H. E. Chasteney; two s four d. Educ: Alleyn's Sch.; Guy's Hospital. MB, BS (London), 1935; MRCP 1937; MD (London), 1937; FRCP, 1947. House Physician, Demonstrator of Pathology and Medical Registrar, Guy's Hospital, 1935-39. Served, 1940-45, in RAMC in Middle East and Indian Ocean (Temp. Lt-Col). Physician, Guy's Hosp., 1946-76. Hon. Visiting Physician to Johns Hopkins Hosp., Baltimore, USA. Physician: to HM Household, 1954-64; to HM the Queen, 1964-70. Sen. Censor and Sen. Vice-Pres., RCP, 1969-70. Publications: Clinical Examination of Patients (jointly), 1950; The Medical Works of Hippocrates (jointly), 1950. Editor, Conybeare's Textbook of Medicine, 16th edn, 1975. Address: Keats' House, Guy's Hospital, SE1 9RT. T: 01-407 7600. Club: Garrick.

MANN, William Somervell; Music Critic, The Times, since 1960; Radio Broadcaster on music since 1949; Associate Editor, Opera, since 1954; President, The Critics' Circle, 1963-64; b 14 Feb. 1924; s of late Gerald and Joyce Mann; m 1948, Erika Charlotte Emilie Sohler; four d. Educ: Winchester Coll.; Magdalene Coll., Cambridge (BA, MusB). Music Critic, Cambridge Review, 1946-48; Asst Music Critic, The Times, 1948-60. Member: ISM; CAMRA; Royal Musical Assoc.; The Critics' Circle. Publications: Introduction to the Music of J. S. Bach, 1950; (contrib. to symposium) Benjamin Britten, 1952; (contrib. to): The Concerto, 1952; The Record Guide, 1955; Chamber Music, 1957; The Analytical Concert Guide (English Editor), 1957; (contrib.) Music and Western Man, 1958; Let's Fake an Opera (with F. Reizenstein), 1958; Richard Strauss's Operas, 1964; (contrib. to symposium) Michael Tippett, 1965; Wagner's Tristan, Introduction and Translation, 1968; The Operas of Mozart, 1977; contributor: Musical Times, Opera, The Gramophone. Recreations: camping, winemaking, destructive gardening, phillumenism, interior decoration, food and drink, foreign languages, darts, making music. Address: 14 Belvedere Drive, SW19. T: 01-946 0773.

MANNERS, family name of **Baron Manners,** and **Duke of Rutland.**

MANNERS, 5th Baron cr 1807; **John Robert Cecil Manners;** Partner, Osborne, Clarke & Co., Solicitors, Bristol; b 13 Feb. 1923; s of 4th Baron Manners, MC, and of Mary Edith, d of late Rt Rev. Lord William Cecil; S father, 1972; m 1949, Jennifer Selena, d of Ian Fairbairn; one s two d. Educ: Eton; Trinity College, Oxford. Served as Flt-Lieut, RAFVR, 1941-46. Solicitor to the Supreme Court, 1949. Recreations: hunting and shooting. Heir: s Hon. John Hugh Robert Manners, b 5 May 1956. Address: Wortley House, Wotton-under-Edge, Glos. T: Wotton-under-Edge 3174. Clubs: Brooks's; Constitutional (Bristol).

MANNERS, Elizabeth Maude, TD 1962; MA; Headmistress of Felixstowe College, Suffolk, since Sept. 1967; b 20 July 1917; d of William George Manners and Anne Mary Manners (née Sced). Educ: Stockton-on-Tees Sec. Sch.; St Hild's Coll., Durham Univ. BA (Dunelm) 1938; MA 1941. Teacher of French at: Marton Grove Sch., Middlesbrough, 1939-40; Ramsey Gram. Sch., IOM, 1940-42; Consett Sec. Sch., Durham, 1942-44; Yarm Gram. Sch., Yorks, 1944-54; Deputy Head, Mexborough Gram. Sch., Yorks, 1954-59; Head Mistress, Central Gram. Sch. for Girls, Manchester, 1959-67. Vice-President: Girl Guides Assoc., Co. Manchester, 1959-67; Suffolk Agric. Assoc., 1967-. Member: Educn Cttee, Brit. Fedn of Univ. Women, 1966-68; Council, Bible Reading Fellowship, 1973-; Cttee, E Br., RSA, 1974-; Cttee, ISIS East, 1974-. Mem., Suffolk CC and Educn Cttee, 1977-. Enlisted ATS (TA), 1947; commissioned, 1949. FRSA 1972. Coronation Medal, 1953. Publication: The Vulnerable Generation, 1971. Recreations: foreign travel, theatre, motoring, good food and wine. Address: Muirfield, Foxgrove Lane, Felixstowe, Suffolk. T: Felixstowe 3325/4269. Club: East India, Devonshire, Sports and Public Schools.

MANNIN, Ethel, author; e d of Robert Mannin and Edith Gray; b London, 1900; m 1920, J. A. Porteous (d 1954); one d; m 1938, Reginald Reynolds (d 1958). Educ: Local Council Sch. Associate-Editor, theatrical paper, The Pelican, 1918; joined ILP 1932. Publications: Martha, 1923; Hunger of the Sea, 1924; Sounding Brass, 1925; Pilgrims, 1927; Green Willow, 1928; Crescendo, 1929; Children of the Earth, 1930; Confessions and Impressions, 1930; Ragged Banners, 1931; Commonsense and the Child, 1931; Green Figs (stories), 1931; Linda Shawn, 1932; All Experience (travel sketches), 1932; Venetian Blinds, 1933;

Dryad (stories), 1933; Men are Unwise, 1934; Forever Wandering (travel sketches), 1934; Cactus, 1935; The Falconer's Voice (stories), 1935; The Pure Flame, 1936; South to Samarkand (travel), 1936; Women also Dream, 1937; Commonsense and the Adolescent, 1938; Women and the Revolution, 1938; Rose and Sylvie, 1938; Darkness my Bride, 1939; Privileged Spectator (sequel to Confessions), 1939; Julie, 1940; Rolling in the Dew, 1940; Christianity or Chaos: a Re-Statement of Religion, 1940; Red Rose: a Novel based on the Life of Emma Goldman, 1941; Commonsense and Morality, 1942; Captain Moonlight, 1942; The Blossoming Bough, 1943; No More Mimosa (stories), 1943; Proud Heaven, 1944; Bread and Roses, A Survey of and a Blue-Print for Utopia, 1944; Lucifer and the Child, 1945; The Dark Forest, 1946; Comrade, O Comrade, 1947; Late Have I Loved Thee, 1948; Connemara Journal (memoirs), 1948; German Journey (travel), 1948; Every Man a Stranger, 1949; Jungle Journey (travel), 1950; Bavarian Story, 1950; At Sundown, the Tiger..., 1951; The Fields at Evening, 1952; The Wild Swans (Tales from the Ancient Irish), 1952; This Was a Man (biography), 1952; Moroccan Mosaic (travel), 1953; Lover Under Another Name, 1953; Two Studies in Integrity (biography), 1954; So Tiberius (novella), 1954; Land of the Crested Lion (travel), 1955; The Living Lotus, 1956; Pity the Innocent, 1957; Country of the Sea (travel), 1957; A Scent of Hyacinths, 1958; Ann and Peter in Sweden (Children's book), 1958; Ann and Peter in Japan, 1960; Ann and Peter in Austria, 1961; The Blue-eyed Boy, 1959; Brief Voices (autobiography) 1959; The Flowery Sword (travel), 1960; Sabishisa, 1961; Curfew at Dawn, 1962; With Will Adams through Japan, 1962; A Lance for the Arabs (Travels in the Middle East), 1963; The Road to Beersheba (novel), 1963; Rebels' Ride, the Revolt of the Individual, 1964; Aspects of Egypt, some Travels in the United Arab Republic, 1964; The Burning Bush, 1965; The Lovely Land: the Hashemite Kingdom of Jordan, 1965; The Night and its Homing, 1966; Loneliness, A Study of the Human Condition, 1966; An American Journey, 1967; The Lady and the Mystic, 1967; England for a Change (travel), 1968; Bitter Babylon, 1968; The Saga of Sammy-Cat (children's story), 1969; The Midnight Street (novel), 1969; Practitioners of Love, Some Aspects of the Human Phenomenon, 1969; England at Large (travel), 1970; Free Pass to Nowhere (novel), 1970; Young in the Twenties (autobiography), 1971; My Cat Sammy, 1971; The Curious Adventure of Major Fosdick (novel), 1972; England My Adventure (travel), 1972; Mission to Beirut (novel), 1973; Stories from My Life (autobiog.), 1973; Kildoon (novel), 1974; An Italian Journey (travel), 1974; The Late Miss Guthrie (novel), 1976; Sunset over Dartmoor (autobiog.), 1977. Recreation: gardening. Address: Overhill, Shaldon, Teignmouth, Devon.

MANNING, Cecil Aubrey Gwynne; b 1892; s of Charles Walter Manning; m 1915, d of William Twitchett; two s two d; m 1940, d of William Green; one s. Rifleman, 1914-18, Queen's Westminsters and The Rangers (wounded in France, amputation of right arm); ARP and Civil Defence, and Invasion Defence Controller (Camberwell), 1939-44 (Defence Medal). Mem. LCC 1922-32 and 1937-49. Leader of Opposition, 1929-30, Dep. Chm., 1930-31; Member Metropolitan Borough Councils: Wandsworth, 1919-22; Camberwell, 1931-53 (Mayor, 1951-53); Mem., Shepton Mallet UDC, 1954-68 (Chm., 1967-68). MP (Lab) N Camberwell, 1944-50. JP 1927, DL 1931, Co. London. Coronation Medal 1953. Address: Woodstock, Norville Lane, Cheddar, Somerset.

MANNING, Prof. Charles Anthony Woodward; Montague Burton (formerly Cassel) Professor of International Relations, London School of Economics, University of London, 1930-62, now emeritus; b 18 Nov. 1894; s of Dumaresq Williamson Manning and Helena Isabella Bell; m 1939, Marion Somerville (Maisie) Johnston (d 1977). Educ: Diocesan Coll (Bishops), Rondebosch; South African Coll., Cape Town; Brasenose Coll., Oxford. Bishops Rhodes Schol., 1914. Enlisted 18th Royal Fusiliers, 1914; commissioned 7th Oxford and Bucks Lt Inf., 1915; active service France and Salonika, 1915-17 (wounded, despatches twice); Instr 11th Officer Cadet Bn (Actg Capt.), 1917-18; BA Oxon Greats (distinction), 1920; BA Oxon Jurisprudence (1st Cl.), 1921; BCL (1st Cl.), 1922; Sen. Hulme Schol., 1921; Barr., Middle Temple, 1922; ILO (Diplomatic Div.), 1922; League of Nations (Personal Asst to Sec.-Gen.), 1922; Fellow, New Coll., and Law Lecturer, New and Pembroke Colls, Oxford, 1923; Laura Spellman Rockefeller Fellow (Harvard), 1925-26; Dep. Prof. of Internat. Law and Diplomacy, Oxford, 1927; Examiner in Roman Law to Council of Legal Education, 1927-32. Tutor, Zimmern Sch. of International Studies, Geneva, 1925 and subs. summers. Sen. Specialist, Wartime Chatham House, 1939-43. Chm., South Africa Soc., 1964-. Hon. DPhil Pretoria, 1971. Publications: The Policies of the British Dominions in the League of Nations,

1932; (trans.) Völkerrecht im Grundriss by Hatschek, 1930; (editor) Salmond's Jurisprudence, 8th edn, 1930; (edited and contrib. to) Peaceful Change, 1937; University Teaching of Social Sciences, International Relations (Unesco), 1952; The Nature of International Society, 1962; Empire into Commonwealth (in Promise of Greatness), 1968; Austin To-day (in Modern Theories of Law), 1933, and other articles. *Recreations:* watercolour, gardening, music. *Address:* Westcliff, Spaanschemat River Road, Constantia, Cape, 7800, South Africa.

MANNING, Frederick Allan, CVO 1954; ISO 1971; JP; Commissioner for Transport, Queensland, 1967-70, retired (Deputy Commissioner, 1960-67); *b* Gladstone, Qld, Australia, 27 Aug. 1904; British parentage; *m* 1934, Phyllis Maud Fullerton; no *c. Educ:* Central Boys' State Sch. and Boys' Gram. Sch., Rockhampton, Qld. Entered Qld State Public Service as Clerk in Petty Sessions Office, Rockhampton, 1920; Clerk of Petty Sessions and Mining Registrar, 1923; Stipendiary Magistrate and Mining Warden, 1934; Petty Sessions Office, Brisbane, 1926; Relieving Clerk of Petty Sessions and Mining Registrar, 1931 (all parts of State); seconded to Commonwealth Govt for service in Qld Directorate of Rationing Commission, 1942; Asst Dep. Dir of Rationing, 1943. Dep. Dir, 1944, for Qld; returned to Qld Public Service, 1947; Sec., Dept of Transport, 1947-60; JP, Qld, 1925-. Coronation Medal, 1953; State Dir, Royal Visit to Queensland, 1954 (CVO). Exec. Vice-Chm, Qld Road Safety Coun., and Qld Rep. Aust. Road Safety Coun. 1962. Mem., Greyhound Racing Control Bd of Queensland, 1971-77. *Recreation:* bowls. *Address:* 126 Indooroopilly Road, Taringa, Brisbane, Qld 4068, Australia. *T:* 370-1936. *Club:* Tattersalls (Brisbane).

MANNING, Frederick Edwin Alfred, CBE 1954; MC 1919; TD 1937; BSc (Eng.); Hon. MA London; Hon. DEng NSTC; Hon. LLD RMC of Canada; CEng; FIMechE; FIEE; FINucE; DPA (London); retired; *b* 6 April 1897; *s* of late Francis Alfred Manning and late Ellen Lavinia Manning; *m* 1927, Alice Beatrice Wistow, BSc; one *s* one *d* (and one *s* decd.). *Educ:* Christ's Hospital; St Olave's; Univ. of London. Academic Diploma of Mil. Studies, Univ. of London; Certificate in Statistics, Univ. of Vienna. War Service, 1915-20 (Order of St Stanislas, 2nd Class; Order of St Vladimir, 4th Class); RE (TA) 1920-38; Royal Signals (TA), 1938-52. Hon. Col, Univ. of London OTC, 1958-68, retired 1968, retaining rank of Col. Entered GPO 1925; idc 1937; Home Office and Min. of Home Security, 1938-41; GPO, 1941; SHAEF, 1943-45; Asst Sec., Foreign Office (Allied Commission for Austria), 1945-47; GPO, 1947; Dir of the Post Office in Wales and Border Counties, 1950-59; Adviser on Athlone Fellowship Scheme, 1961-72; Chm. Boards for the CS Commn, 1961-68; Hon. Sen. Treas., Univ. of London Union, 1928-52, Chm. of Union Court, 1952-69, Chm., Sports Finance Cttee, 1969-74; Mem. of Senate, Univ. of London, 1952-74 (Chm. Military Educ. Cttee, 1952-55); First Chm. of Convocation, The City Univ., 1967-70; Vice-Pres., Univs in London Catholic Chaplaincy Assoc., 1970-. Metrop. Special Constabulary (Comdt, GPO Div.), 1931-41. KSG 1972. *Recreations:* gardening, Rotary (Pres. Shepperton, 1964-65). *Address:* 1 Range Way, Shepperton, TW17 9NW. *T:* Walton-on-Thames 23400. *Club:* Royal Commonwealth Society.

MANNING, Air Cdre Frederick John, CB 1954; CBE 1948; retired, 1967; *b* 5 May 1912; *s* of Frederick Manning; *m* 1937, Elizabeth Anwyl, *er d* of late Rev. Æ. C. Ruthven-Murray, BA, Bishop Burton, Beverley; four *d* (and one *s* decd). Cadet, P&OSN Co., 1928; Midshipman, RNR, 1929; Actg Sub-Lt, RNR, 1933; Pilot Officer, RAF, 1934; Flt Lt, 269 Squadron, 1938; Actg Group Capt., 1942; Dir of Organisation (Establishments), Air Ministry, 1944-45 (actg Air Commodore); commanding RAF Station Shaibah, Abu Sueir Shallufa, 1945-47 (acting Group Capt.); Group Capt., Organisation, HQ, RAF, Mediterranean and Middle East, 1947-48; Senior Air Adviser, and Dep. Head of Mission, British Services Mission, Burma, 1949-52; Senior Officer i/c Administration HQ Transport Command, 1952; Dep. Dir of Work Study, Air Ministry, 1956-59; Dir of Manning (2) Air Ministry, 1960-63; Air Officer Administration: HQ Near East Air Force, 1963-65; HQ Fighter Comd, 1965-67. *Address:* Myrtle Cottage, Eynsham, Oxford. *Club:* Royal Air Force.

MANNING, Sir George, Kt 1967; CMG 1960; MA; DipSocSci; Mayor of Christchurch, NZ, 1958-68; *b* 11 Feb. 1887; *s* of Richard Manning; *m* 1923, S. E. Willmore; one *s. Educ:* Gowerton Gram. Sch., Wales; Canterbury Univ., NZ. Steelworker, 1906-10; emigrated to NZ, 1910; Secretary: Canterbury WEA, 1921-48; New Zealand WEA, 1923; Dominion Pres., WEA, 1946-49; Adult Education and WEA Lecturer, 1948-58. Councillor, Christchurch City Council, 1927-

29 and 1936-58. Member: Christchurch Tramway Board, 1933-50; Lyttelton Harbour Bd, 1939-40, 1946-71; Council, Univ. of Canterbury, 1958-68. Hon. DCL Canterbury, 1972. *Recreations:* bowls, gardening. *Address:* 7 Bletsoe Avenue, Christchurch 2, New Zealand.

MANNING, Olivia, (Mrs R. D. Smith), CBE 1976; author; *o d* of late Oliver Manning, Commander, RN, and Olivia, *e d* of late David Morrow, Down, Ireland; *m* 1939, Prof. Reginald Donald Smith, New Univ. of Ulster. *Publications: novels:* The Wind Changes, 1938; Artist Among the Missing, 1949; School for Love, 1951; A Different Face, 1953; The Doves of Venus, 1955; The Balkan Trilogy (The Great Fortune, 1960; The Spoilt City, 1962; Friends and Heroes, 1965); The Play Room, 1969; The Rain Forest, 1974; The Danger Tree, 1977; *short stories:* Growing Up, 1948; A Romantic Hero, 1966; *history:* The Remarkable Expedition, 1947; *travel:* The Dreaming Shore, 1950; *humour:* My Husband Cartwright, 1956; *general:* Extraordinary Cats, 1967. Contributed to Horizon, Windmill, Spectator, New Statesman, Punch, The Observer, Sunday Times, The Times, Times Literary Supplement, Vogue, Harper's, The Queen, Saturday Book, Best Short Stories, Winter's Tales, Transatlantic Review, Encounter, Adam. *Recreation:* cats. *Address:* 3/71 Marlborough Place, NW8. *T:* 01-624 1025.

MANNING, Richard Joseph; *b* 28 March 1883; *s* of Richard Manning; *m* 1912, Ada Agnes Baird, 2nd *d* of Capt. James Brown; two *s* (and one *s* lost in the War of 1939-45) three *d*; *m* 1939, Margaret Asher, *o d* of John Wilson, Blundellsands. *Educ:* Clongowes Wood Coll.; University Coll., Blackrock. Inspector of Police, British Guiana, 1909-20; Resident Magistrate, Tanganyika, 1920-25; Resident Magistrate, Jamaica, 1925-27; Police Magistrate, Gold Coast, 1927-32; Puisne Judge, Trinidad and Tobago, 1932-36; Senior Puisne Judge, Palestine, 1936-39; Puisne Judge, SS, 1939; seconded as Puisne Judge, Uganda, 1942-46; retired, 1946. Chm. Advisory Cttee on Detainees, Palestine, 1947 and 1948; Additional Judge, British Guiana, 1948-50. Commissioner, Caura Inquiry, Trinidad, 1950. Acting Judge, Windward and Leeward Islands, 1950-54, 1959, 1960; Chm. Public Utilities Bd, Barbados, 1955-58. Jubilee Medal, 1935; Coronation Medals, 1937 and 1953; Palestine Gen. Service Medal, 1939. *Publication:* British Guiana Police Manual. *Address:* Red Rocks Private Home, Hoylake, Cheshire.

MANNING, Thomas Henry, OC 1974; zoologist; *b* 22 Dec. 1911; *s* of Thomas E. and Dorothy (née Randall) Manning, Shrublands, Dallington, Northampton; *m* 1938, Ella Wallace Jackson. *Educ:* Harrow; Cambridge. Winter journey across Lapland, 1932-33; Survey and Zoological work on Southampton Island, 1933-35; Leader, Brit. Canadian-Arctic Exped., 1936-41; Royal Canadian Navy, 1941-45; Geodetic Service of Canada, 1945-47; Leader Geographical Bureau Expedition to Prince Charles I. (Foxe Basin), 1949; Zoological and Geographical work in James Bay, 1950; Leader Defence Research Board Expeditions: Beaufort Sea, 1951; Banks Island, 1952, 1953; Nat. Mus. Canadian Expedition; King William Island, Adelaide Peninsula, 1957, Prince of Wales Island, 1958. FRGS (Patron's Gold Medal, 1948); Bruce Memorial Prize (Royal Society of Edinburgh, RPS, RSGS), 1944; Massey Medal, Royal Canadian Geographical Soc., 1977. Guggenheim Fellow, 1959. *Publications:* The Birds of North Western Ungava, 1949; Birds of the West James Bay and Southern Hudson Bay Coasts, 1952; Birds of Banks Island, 1956; Mammals of Banks Island, 1958; A Biological Investigation of Prince of Wales Island, 1961; articles in The Auk, Journal Mamm. and Geog. Journal, Canadian Geog. Jl., Canadian Field-Naturalist, Arctic, Nat. Mus. Can. Bull. *Recreations:* shooting, book-binding, cabinet-making, farming. *Address:* RR4, Merrickville, Ont., Canada. *T:* 269-4940.

MANNINGHAM-BULLER, family name of Viscount Dilhorne.

MANS, Maj.-Gen. Rowland Spencer Noel, CBE 1971 (OBE 1966, MBE 1956); Director, Military Assistance Office, 1973-76, retired; *b* 16 Jan. 1921; *s* of Thomas Frederick Mans and May Seigenberg; *m* 1945, Veeo Ellen Sutton; three *s. Educ:* Surbiton Grammar Sch.; RMC, Sandhurst; jssc, psc. Served War, Queen's Royal Regt and King's African Rifles, 1940-45. Regtl and Staff Duty, 1945-59; Instr, Staff Colleges, Camberley and Canada, 1959-63; Comd, 1st Tanganyika Rifles, 1963-64; Staff Duty, Far East and UK, 1964-68; Comd, Aldershot, 1969-72; DDPS (Army), 1967-73. Dep. Col, Queen's Regt (Surrey), 1973-. *Publication:* contributor to: The Guerilla and How to Fight Him, 1963. *Recreations:* writing, reading, gardening. *Address:* Kirke House, Sway Road, Brockenhurst, Hants. *T:* Brockenhurst 2291. *Club:* Army and Navy.

MANSAGER, Felix Norman, KBE (Hon.) 1976 (Hon. CBE 1973); Director and Member of Executive Committee, Hoover Co. USA (President-Chairman, Hoover Co. and Hoover World-wide Corporation, 1966-75); Director, Hoover Ltd UK (Chairman, 1966-75); *b* 30 Jan. 1911; *s* of Hoff Mansager and Alice (*née* Qualseth); *m* Geraldine (*née* Larson); one *s* two *d. Educ:* South Dakota High Sch., Colton. Joined Hoover Co. as Salesman, 1929; Vice-Pres., Sales, 1959; Exec. Vice-Pres. and Dir, 1961. Dir, Harter Bank & Trust Co. Trustee, Indep. Coll. Funds of America; Mem., Bd of Trustees, Ohio Foundn of Independent Colls; Member: Council on Foreign Relations; Newcomen Soc. in N America; Trustee, Graduate Theological Union (Calif); The Pilgrims of the US; Assoc. of Ohio Commodores; Rotary International; Masonic Shrine (32nd degree Mason); Mem. and Governor, Ditchley Foundn; Member Board of Trustees: Gustavus Adolphus Coll.; Augustana Coll. Hon. Mem., World League of Norsemen. Marketing Award, British Inst. of Marketing, 1971. Hon. Mem., Beta Sigma Gamma, Akron Univ., 1974. Hon. Fellow, UC Cardiff, 1973. Hon. Dr of Laws Capital Univ., 1967; Hon. LLD Strathclyde, 1970; Hon. DHL Malone Coll., Canton, Ohio, 1972; Hon. PdD Walsh Coll., Canton, 1974; Hon. Dr Humanities Wartburg Coll., Waverly, Iowa, 1976; Medal of Honor, Vassa Univ., Finland, 1973. Grand Officer, Dukes of Burgundy, 1968; Chevalier: Order of Leopold, 1969; Order of St Olav, Norway, 1971; Legion of Honour, France, 1973; Grande Officiale, Order Al Merito della Republica Italiana, 1975. *Recreation:* golf. *Address:* 3421 Lindel Court NW, Canton, Ohio 44718, USA. *Clubs:* Metropolitan (NYC); Washington; Congress Lake Country; Canton; Torske (Hon.).

MANSBRIDGE, Very Rev. Harold Chad; Provost of St Mary's Cathedral, Glasgow, since 1970; Priest-in-charge, St George's, Maryhill, Glasgow, since 1976; *b* 4 March 1917; *s* of Tom Standish and Lotty Mansbridge; *m* 1945, Margaret Edythe Clark; one *s* one *d. Educ:* Price's School, Fareham, Hants; Kelham Theological College. Deacon 1941, priest 1942, Southwell; Curate of St George, Nottingham, 1941-44; Cullercoats, 1944-45; Stratfield Mortimer, 1945-48; Rector of Shellingford, 1948-60; Priest-in-charge, Fernham, 1948-58, and of Longcot with Fernham, 1958-60; Rector of St Devenick's, Bieldside, Aberdeen, 1960-70; Canon, St Andrew's Cathedral, Aberdeen, 1970. *Recreation:* cooking, and in particular cake making. *Address:* Cathedral House, 39 Kirklee Road, Glasgow G12 0SP.

MANSEL, Rev. Canon James Seymour Denis, MVO 1972; JP; Sub-Dean of HM Chapels Royal, Deputy Clerk of the Closet, Sub-Almoner and Domestic Chaplain to the Queen, since 1965; Canon and Prebendary of Chichester Cathedral, since 1971; *b* 18 June 1907; *e s* of Edward Mansel, FRIBA, Leamington, and Muriel Louisa (*née* Denis Browne); *m* 1942, Ann Monica (*d* 1974), *e d* of Amyas Waterhouse, MD, Boars Hill, Oxford, and Ruth (*née* Gamlen); one *d. Educ:* Brighton Coll.; Exeter Coll., Oxford (MA); Westcott House. Asst Master, Dulwich Coll., 1934-39; Asst Master, Chaplain and House Master, Winchester Coll., 1939-65. Mem., Winchester City Coun., 1950-56. JP: City of Winchester, 1964; Inner London Commn, 1972. FSA. ChStJ. *Address:* Marlborough Gate, St James's Palace, SW1. *T:* 01-930 6609; Field House, Pitt, Winchester. *T:* Winchester 4812. *Club:* Athenæum.

MANSEL, Sir Philip, 15th Bt, *cr* 1621; *b* 3 March 1943; *s* of Sir John Mansel, 14th Bt and Hannah, *d* of Ben Rees; *S* father, 1947; *m* 1968, Margaret, *o d* of Arthur Docker. *Heir:* u Regnier Ranulf Dabridgecourt Mansel [*b* 6 July 1919; *m* 1941, Mary Germaine, *d* of Wing Comdr W. St J. Littlewood, OBE; three *s* two *d*]. *Address:* 123 Chadderton Drive, Chapel House, Newburn, Newcastle upon Tyne.

MANSEL-JONES, David; Vice-Chairman, Huntingdon Research Centre, since 1974; *b* 8 Sept. 1926; *o s* of Rees Thomas Jones and Ceinwen Jones; *m* 1952, Mair Aeronwen Davies; one *s. Educ:* St Michael's Sch., Bryn; London Hospital. MB, BS 1950; MRCP 1973. Jun. Surgical Specialist, RAMC; Dep. Med. Dir, Wm R. Warner & Co. Ltd, 1957-59; Med. Dir, Richardson-Merrell Ltd, 1959-65; formerly PMO, SMO and MO, Cttee on Safety of Drugs; Med. Assessor, Cttee on Safety of Medicines, 1970-; Consultant to WHO; Senior PMO, Medicines Div., DHSS, 1971-74. *Publications:* papers related to safety of medicines. *Recreations:* music, painting. *Address:* 10 Pakenham Close, Cambridge CB4 1PW. *T:* Cambridge 58121; 9 Aldeburgh Lodge Gardens, Aldeburgh, Suffolk.

MANSEL LEWIS, David Courtenay; Lieutenant of Dyfed, since 1974 (HM Lieutenant for Carmarthenshire, 1973-74); JP; *b* 25 Oct. 1927; *s* of late Charlie Ronald Mansel Lewis and Lillian Georgina Warner, *d* of Col Sir Courtenay Warner, 1st Bt, CB; *m* 1953, Lady Mary Rosemary Marie-Gabrielle Montagu-Stuart-Wortley, 4th *d* of 3rd Earl of Wharncliffe; one *s* two *d. Educ:* Eton; Keble Coll., Oxford (BA). Served in Welsh Guards, 1946-49; Lieut 1946, RARO. High Sheriff, Carmarthenshire, 1965; JP 1969; DL 1971. *Recreations:* music, sailing. *Address:* Stradey Castle, Llanelli, Dyfed. *T:* Llanelli 4626. *Clubs:* Cavalry and Guards, Lansdowne; Cruising Association.

MANSELL, Lt-Col George William, CBE 1959; DL; RA, retired; Chairman, new Dorset County Council, 1973-77; *b* 25 Dec. 1904; *s* of late Lt-Col Sir John H. Mansell, KBE, DL, RA (retd); *m* 1st, 1934, Joan (*d* 1940), *d* of late Spencer Dawson, Stratton Hall, Levington, Ipswich; one *s* one *d*; 2nd, 1941, Mary Elizabeth, *d* of late Major C. L. Blew, Hafod, Trefnant, Denbigh. *Educ:* Wellington Coll., Berks; RMA Woolwich. Commnd into RA, 1924; wounded N Africa, 1942; invalided as a result, 1947. Dorset CC, 1950-77: Alderman, 1955-74; Vice-Chm., 1966; Chm., 1967-74; Hon. Alderman, 1977. DL Dorset, 1968. *Recreation:* fishing. *Address:* Kit Robins, Lytchett Matravers, Poole, Dorset. *T:* Morden (Dorset) 240.

MANSELL, Gerard Evelyn Herbert, CBE 1977; Managing Director, External Broadcasting, BBC, since 1972; Deputy Director-General, BBC, since 1977; *b* 16 Feb. 1921; 2nd *s* of late Herbert and of Anne Mansell, Paris; *m* 1956, Diana Marion Sherar; two *s. Educ:* Lycée Hoche, Versailles; Lycée Buffon, Paris; Ecole des Sciences Politiques, Paris; Chelsea Sch. of Art. Joined HM Forces, 1940; served in Western Desert, Sicily and NW Europe, 1942-45; Brigade IO 151 (Durham) Bde, 1942-44; GSO3 (I) 50th (N) Div., 1944; GSO2 (I) 8th Corps, 1944-45 (despatches); GSO2 (I) MI4 (a) War Office, 1946. Joined BBC European Service, 1951; Asst Head, Overseas Talks and Features Dept, 1958, Head, 1961; Controller, BBC Radio 4 (formerly Home Service), and Music Programme, 1965-69; Dir of Programmes, BBC, Radio, 1970. French Croix de Guerre, 1945. *Publication:* Tragedy in Algeria, 1961. *Address:* Bush House, Aldwych, WC2B 4PH.

MANSERGH, Vice-Adm. Sir (Cecil) Aubrey (Lawson), KBE 1953; CB 1950; DSC 1915; retired; *b* 7 Oct. 1898; *s* of Ernest Lawson Mansergh and Emma Cecilia Fisher Hogg; *m* 1st, 1928, Helen Raynor Scott (*d* 1967); one *s* (and one *s* decd); 2nd, 1969, Dora, *widow* of Comdr L. H. L. Clarke, RN. *Educ:* RN Colleges Osborne and Dartmouth. Served European War, 1914-18; Comdr, 1932; Captain, 1938; Commanded HMNZS Achilles, 1942 and HMNZS Leander, 1943, in Pacific; Commodore 1st Cl., Admiralty, 1944-46; Commanded HMS Implacable, 1946-47; Rear-Adm. 1948; Vice-Controller of Navy and Dir of Naval Equipment, 1948-50; Commanded 2nd Cruiser Squadron, 1950-52; Vice-Adm., 1951. Pres., Royal Naval Coll., Greenwich, 1952-54, retired Dec. 1954. *Address:* Hillside, The Green, Rottingdean, Sussex. *T:* Brighton 32213.

MANSERGH, Prof. Philip Nicholas Seton, OBE 1945; DPhil 1936; DLitt Oxon 1960; LittD Cantab 1970; FBA 1973; Master of St John's College, Cambridge, since 1969 (Fellow, 1955-69); Editor-in-chief, India Office Records on the Transfer of Power, since 1967; Hon. Fellow: Pembroke College, Oxford, 1954; Trinity College, Dublin, 1971; *b* 27 June 1910; *yr s* of late Philip St George Mansergh and late Mrs E. M. Mansergh, Grenane House, Tipperary; *m* 1939, Diana Mary, *d* of late G. H. Keeton, Headmaster's Lodge, Reading; three *s* two *d. Educ:* Abbey Sch., Tipperary; College of St Columba, Dublin; Pembroke Coll., Oxford. Sec. OU Politics Research Cttee and Tutor in Politics, 1937-40; Empire Div., Ministry of Information, 1941-46; Dir, 1944-46; Asst Sec., Dominions Office, 1946-47; Abe Bailey Research Prof. of British Commonwealth Relations, RIIA, 1947-53; Smuts Prof. of History of British Commonwealth, Univ. of Cambridge, 1953-April 1970. Visiting Professor: Nat. Univ. of Australia, 1951; Univ. of Toronto, 1953; Duke Univ., NC, 1957 and 1965 (W. K. Boyd Prof. of History); Indian Sch. of International Studies, New Delhi, 1958 and 1966; Reid Lecturer, Acadia Univ., 1960; Smuts Meml Lectr, Cambridge Univ., 1976. Member: Editorial Board, Annual Register, 1947-73; Gen. Advisory Council, BBC, 1956-62; Adv. Council on Public Records, 1966-76; Councillor, RIIA, 1953-57; Chm. Faculty Board of History, 1960-62, Bd of Graduate Studies, 1970-73, Cambridge Univ. *Publications:* The Irish Free State: Its Government and Politics, 1934; The Government of Northern Ireland, 1936; Ireland in the Age of Reform and Revolution, 1940; Advisory Bodies (Jt Editor), 1941; Britain and Ireland, 1942, 2nd edn 1946; The Commonwealth and the Nations, 1948; The Coming of the First World War; Survey of British Commonwealth Affairs (2 vols), 1931-39, 1952 and 1939-52, 1958; Documents and Speeches on Commonwealth Affairs, 1931-62 (3 vols), 1953-63; The Multi-Racial Commonwealth, 1955; (jointly) Commonwealth Perspectives, 1958; South Africa, 1906-1961, 1962; The Irish Question, 1840-1921, 1965, 3rd edn

1975; The Commonwealth Experience, 1969. *Recreation:* lawn tennis. *Address:* The Master's Lodge, St John's College, Cambridge. *T:* Cambridge 55075. *Clubs:* Royal Commonwealth Society; Kildare Street and University (Dublin).

MANSFIELD, family name of **Baron Sandhurst.**

MANSFIELD AND MANSFIELD, 8th Earl of, *cr* 1776 and 1792 (GB); **William David Mungo James Murray;** JP; Baron Scone, 1605; Viscount Stormont, 1621; Baron Balvaird, 1641; (Earl of Dunbar, Viscount Drumcairn, and Baron Halldykes in the Jacobite Peerage); Hereditary Keeper of Bruce's Castle of Lochmaben; Lieutenant The Scots Guards (RARO); an opposition spokesman in the House of Lords, since 1975; *b* 7 July 1930; *o s* of 7th Earl of Mansfield and Mansfield, and of Dorothea Helena, *y d* of late Rt Hon. Sir Lancelot Carnegie, GCVO, KCMG; *S* father, 1971; *m* 1955, Pamela Joan, *o d* of W. N. Foster, CBE; two *s* one *d. Educ:* Eton; Christ Church, Oxford. Malayan campaign, 1949-50. Called to Bar, Inner Temple, 1958; Barrister, 1958-71. Mem., British Delegn to European Parlt, 1973-75. Mem., Tay Salmon Fisheries Bd, 1971-. Dir, General Accident, Fire and Life Assurance Corp. Ltd, 1972-. Ordinary Dir, Royal Highland and Agricl Soc., 1976. President: Scottish Assoc. for Care and Resettlement of Offenders, 1974; Scottish Assoc. of Boys Clubs, 1976; Chm., Scottish Branch, Historic House Assoc., 1976. Mem., Perth CC, 1971-75; Hon. Sheriff for Perthshire, 1974; JP Perth and Kinross District, 1975. *Heir: s* Viscount Stormont, *qv. Address:* Scone Palace, Perthshire; 16 Thorburn House, Kinnerton Street, SW1. *Clubs:* Turf, Pratt's, Garrick, MCC.

MANSFIELD, Hon. Sir Alan (James), KCMG 1958; KCVO 1970; Governor of Queensland, 1966-72; *b* 30 Sept. 1902; 3rd *s* of Judge Edward Mansfield, Brisbane, Qld; *m* 1933, Beryl Susan, *d* of C. G. Barnes; one *s* one *d. Educ:* Sydney Church of England Gram. Sch.; St Paul's Coll., Sydney Univ. (LLB Hons). Admitted to Bars of New South Wales and Queensland, 1924; Lecturer in Law, Univ. of Queensland, 1938-39; Judge of Supreme Court of Queensland, 1940; Chm. Aliens Tribunal, 1942-45; Chm. Land Appeal Court (Qld), 1942-45; Chm. Royal Commns on Sugar Industry, 1942 and 1950; Acting Pres., Industrial Court (Qld), 1945; Mem. Bd of Inquiry into War Atrocities, 1945; Australian Rep., UN War Crimes Commn, London, 1945; Chief Aust. Prosecutor, Internat. Military Tribunal for the Far East, Tokyo, 1946; Senior Puisne Judge, 1947; Actg Chief Justice of Queensland, 1950, Chief Justice, 1956-66. Chm., Central Sugar Cane Prices Bd, 1955-56; Warden of Univ. of Qld, 1956-65; Chancellor of Univ. of Queensland, 1966-76. Administrator of Govt of Qld, Jan. 1957-March 1958, 1963, 1965. Hon. Col, 2/14 Queensland Mounted Inf., 1966-72; Hon. Air Cdre, 23 Sqdn, Citizen Air Force, 1966-72. Hon LLD Queensland, 1970. KStJ 1966. *Recreation:* fishing. *Address:* 81 Monaco Street, Florida Gardens, Surfers' Paradise, Qld 4217, Australia. *Clubs:* Queensland, Johnsonian (Brisbane).

MANSFIELD, Rear-Adm. David Parks, CB 1964; *b* 26 July 1912; *s* of Comdr D. Mansfield, RD, RNR; *m* 1939, Jean Craig Alexander; one *s* one *d. Educ:* RN Coll., Dartmouth; RN Engineering Coll., Keyham. Lt (E) 1934; HMS Nelson, 1934-36; Staff of C-in-C Med., 1936-39; HMS Mauritius, 1939-42; Lt-Comdr (E) 1942; HMS Kelvin, 1942-43; Chatham Dockyard, 1943-46; Comdr (E) 1945; Admty (Aircraft Maintenance Dept) 1946-49; Staff of FO Air (Home), 1949-51; HMS Kenya, 1951-53; RN Engrg Coll., 1953-55; Captain 1954; RNAS Anthorn (in command), 1955-57; RN Aircraft Yard, Fleetlands (Supt.), 1957-60; Admty Dir of Fleet Maintenance, 1960-62; Rear-Adm. 1963; Rear-Adm. Aircraft, on Staff of Flag Officer Naval Air Command, 1963-65. *Recreations:* reading, gardening. *Address:* The Outlook, St Margaret's at Cliffe, near Dover, Kent. *T:* Dover 852237. *Club:* Army and Navy.

MANSFIELD, Vice-Adm. Sir (Edward) Gerard (Napier), KBE 1974; retired 1975; *b* 13 July 1921; *s* of late Vice-Adm. Sir John Mansfield, KCB, DSO, DSC, and of Alice Talbot Mansfield; *m* 1943, Joan Worship Byron, *d* of late Comdr John Byron DSC and late Frances Byron; two *d. Educ:* RNC, Dartmouth. Entered Royal Navy, 1935. Served War of 1939-45 in destroyers and Combined Ops (despatches), taking part in landings in N Africa and Sicily. Comdr, 1953; comd HMS Mounts Bay, 1956-58; Captain 1959; SHAPE, 1960-62; Captain (F) 20th Frigate Sqdn, 1963-64; Dir of Defence Plans (Navy), 1965-67; Cdre Amphibious Forces, 1967-68; Senior Naval Member, Directing Staff, IDC, 1969-70; Flag Officer Sea Training, 1971-72; Dep. Supreme Allied Comdr, Atlantic, 1973-75. *Recreations:* tennis, golf, gardening. *Address:* White Gate House, Ewshott, Farnham, Surrey GU10 5AH. *T:* Aldershot 850325. *Club:* Army and Navy.

MANSFIELD, Eric Harold, ScD; FRS 1971; Deputy Chief Scientific Officer (individual merit), Royal Aircraft Establishment, since 1967; *b* 24 May 1923; *s* of Harold Goldsmith Mansfield and Grace Phundt; *m* 1st, 1947, Mary Ola Purves Douglas (marr. diss. 1973); two *s* one *d*; 2nd, 1974, Eunice Lily Kathleen Shuttleworth-Parker. *Educ:* St Lawrence Coll., Ramsgate; Trinity Hall, Cambridge. MA, ScD, CEng, FRS, FRAeS, FIMA. Research in Structures Department, Royal Aircraft Establishment, Farnborough, Hants: Jun. Scientific Officer, 1943; Scientific Officer, 1948; Sen. Scientific Officer, 1950; Principal Scientific Officer, 1954; Sen. Principal Scientific Officer, 1959. *Publications:* The Bending and Stretching of Plates, 1964; contribs to: Proc. Roy. Soc., Phil. Trans., Quarterly Jl Mech. Applied Math., Aero Quarterly, Aero Research Coun. reports and memos, and to technical press. *Recreations:* bridge, philately, palaeontology, snorkling. *Address:* Evergreens, Tudor Way, Church Crookham, Aldershot, Hampshire. *T:* Fleet 28438.

MANSFIELD, Sir Gerard; *see* Mansfield, Sir E. G. N.

MANSFIELD, Henry, OBE 1976; IPFA, FBCS, DPA; Chief Executive, Cardiff City Council, since 1974; *b* 8 June 1914; *m* 1944, Laura Evelynne (*née* Dykes); three *s* two *d. Educ:* Canton High Sch., Cardiff. Served Cardiff CC, 1930-; City Treasurer and Controller, 1966-74. Pioneered develt of computers in Welsh local govt; Chm., Welsh Local Govt Computer Steering Cttee; represents Assoc. of Dist Councils on LAMSAC (Mem., LAMSAC Computer Adv. Panel), Local Govt Operational Research Cttee, Royal Inst. of Public Admin and Jt Cttee on Use of Computers in Bldg Industry. Mem. (of former) IMTA, 1938 (past Chm., Associates Section and Students' Soc.); Course Pres. for some years at IMTA/IPFA Nat. Residential Courses, Cardiff. Many lectures to student socs and professional bodies, etc. Chm., Wales Local and Public Authorities Savings Cttee; Member: Nat. Local and Public Authorities Savings Cttee; Wales Savings Cttee; Cardiff Savings Cttee. Hon. FBCS, 1975. *Publications:* articles in local govt press. *Recreation:* church work. *Address:* Briarwood, Pwllmelin Lane, Llandaff, Cardiff CF5 2NQ. *T:* Cardiff 562521.

MANSFIELD, Philip (Robert Aked), CMG 1973; HM Diplomatic Service; Commissioner for British Indian Ocean Territory, and Assistant Under-Secretary of State, Foreign and Commonwealth Office, since 1976; *b* 9 May 1926; *s* of Philip Theodore Mansfield, CSI, CIE; *m* 1953, Elinor Russell MacHatton; two *s. Educ:* Winchester; Pembroke Coll., Cambridge. Grenadier Guards, 1944-47. Sudan Political Service, 1950-54. Entered HM Diplomatic Service, 1955; served in: Addis Ababa, Singapore, Paris, Buenos Aires; Counsellor and Head of Rhodesia Dept, FCO, 1969-72; RCDS, 1973; Counsellor and Head of Chancery, 1974-75, Dep. High Comr, 1976, Nairobi. *Recreations:* sailing, bird watching, gardening. *Address:* c/o Foreign and Commonwealth Office, SW1; Gill Mill, Stanton Harcourt, Oxford. *T:* Witney 2554. *Clubs:* Cavalry and Guards; Aberdare Country (Kenya).

MANSFIELD COOPER, Prof. Sir William, Kt 1963; LLM; Professor of Industrial Law, University of Manchester, 1949-70, now Professor Emeritus; Vice-Chancellor of the University, 1956-70; *b* Newton Heath, Manchester, 20 Feb. 1903; *s* of William and Georgina C. Cooper; *m* 1936, Edna Mabel, *o c* of Herbert and Elizabeth Baker; one *s. Educ:* Elementary Sch.; Ruskin Coll., 1931-33; Manchester Univ., 1933-36 (LLB, Dauntesey Jun. Law Schol., Dauntesey Special Prizeman in International Law). Grad. Res. Schol., 1936-37; Lecturer WEA (LLM 1938). University of Manchester: Asst Lecturer, 1938; Lecturer, 1942; Asst to Vice-Chancellor, 1944; Registrar and Senior Lecturer in Law, 1945; Professor of Industrial and Commercial Law, 1949, continuing as Joint Registrar until 1952; Acting Vice-Chancellor, Nov. 1953-May 1954 and July 1954-Oct. 1954. Called to the Bar (Gray's Inn), 1940. Chairman John Rylands Library, 1956-70; Chairman Cttee of Vice-Chancellors and Principals, 1961-64; President, Council of Europe Cttee on Higher Education and Research, 1966-67; Vice-President, Standing Conference of European Rectors and Vice-Chancellors, 1964-69. Dep. Chm., Cttee of Inquiry into London Univ., 1970-72. Hon. Mem., Manchester Royal Coll. Music, 1971. Hon. LLD: Manitoba, 1964; Liverpool, 1970; Manchester, 1970; Hon. DLitt Keele, 1967; Hon. DSc Kharkov, 1970; Hon. DHL Rochester, 1970. Hon. Fellow, Manchester Inst. Science and Technology, 1972. *Publications:* Outlines of Industrial Law, 1947, 6th ed by John C. Wood, 1972; papers and reviews in learned journals. *Recreations:* gardening, bird-watching. *Address:* Fieldgate Cottage, Meldreth, Royston, Herts. *Club:* Athenæum.

MANT, Prof. Arthur Keith, MD; FRCPath; Professor of Forensic Medicine, since 1974, and Head of Department since 1972, Guy's Hospital, University of London; Hon. Consultant in Forensic Medicine, King's College Hospital, since 1967; *b* 11 Sept. 1919; *s* of George Arthur Mant and Elsie Muriel (*née* Slark); *m* 1947, Heather Smith, BA; two *s* one *d* . *Educ:* Denstone Coll., Staffs; St Mary's Hosp., Paddington. MB BS 1949, MD 1950; MRCS, LRCP 1943; FRCPath 1967; MRCP 1977. Dept Obst. and Gynæc., St Mary's Hosp., 1943; RAMC, i/c Path. Section, War Crimes Gp, 1945-48 (Major); Registrar (ex-service), Med. Unit, St Mary's Hosp., 1948-49; Research Fellow, 1949-55, Lectr, 1955-66, Dept of Forensic Med., Guy's Hosp.; Sen. Lectr in Forensic Med., KCH, 1965; Reader in Forensic Med., Guy's Hosp., 1966-74. Visiting Lectr in Med. Jurisprudence and Toxicology, St Mary's Hosp., 1955-. Examiner in Forensic Medicine: NUI, 1960; St Andrews Univ., 1967; Dundee Univ., 1968; RCPath, 1971; Soc. of Apothecaries, 1971; Univ. of Riyadh, Saudi Arabia, 1976; Univ. of Garyounis-Libya, 1976. A. D. Williams Distinguished Scholar Fellowship, Univ. Med. Coll. of Virginia, 1963 and 1968. President: Internat. Assoc. in Accident and Traffic Med., 1972-; British Acad. of Forensic Sci., 1975-76; Past Pres., Forensic Sci. Soc., British Assoc. in Forensic Med.; Vice-Pres., Medico-Legal Soc. Nat. correspondent for GB, Internat. Acad. of Legal and Social Med.; Corresp. Mem., Amer. Acad. of Forensic Sci.; Corresp. For. Mem., Soc. de Méd. Légale; Hon. Member: Brazilian Assoc. for Traffic Med.; Soc. de Méd. Légale, Belgium; Mem., Editorial Bd, Internat. Reference Org. in Forensic Med. (INFORM); English Editor, Zeitschrift für Rechtsmedizin; Internat. Editorial Bd, Excerpta Medica (Forensic Sci. abstracts). Fellow: Indian Acad. of Forensic Sci.; Swedish Soc. of Med. Scis. *Publications:* Forensic Medicine: observation and interpretation, 1960; Modern Trends in Forensic Medicine, Series 3, 1973; contribs to med. and sci. literature. *Recreations:* fishing, orchid culture. *Address:* Department of Forensic Medicine, Guy's Hospital, SE1 9RT. *T:* 01-407 0378; 29 Ashley Drive, Walton-on-Thames, Surrey KT12 1JT. *T:* Walton-on-Thames 25005. *Club:* Athenæum.

MANT, Sir Cecil (George), Kt 1964; CBE 1955; consultant and company director; Consultant to Corporation of London, and Project Co-ordinator for Barbican Arts Centre, since 1972; *b* 24 May 1906; *o s* of late George Frederick Mant and Beatrice May Mant; *m* 1940, Hilda Florence (*née* Knowles); three *d*. *Educ:* Trinity County Sch.; Hornsey School of Art; Northern Polytechnic School of Architecture. ARIBA 1929, FRIBA 1944, resigned 1970. Entered HM Office of Works, 1928. Visiting Lecturer in Architecture and Building to Northern Polytechnic, 1930-39; Departmental Liaison Officer to Works and Buildings Priority Cttee, 1939-40. Ministry of Public Building and Works: Deputy Director-General of Works, 1950-60; Director-General of Works, 1960-63; Controller-Gen. of Works, 1963-67. Served as member and chairman of various cttees, to British Standards Institution and Codes of Practice; Departmental Working Parties and Investigating Boards, Civil Service Commission Selection Boards, Joint Min. of Works and P.O. Study Group on P.O. Buildings Costs and Procedure, etc. Assessor to Advisory Cttee on Building Research, 1958-67; Member, Architecture Consultative Cttee, Hammersmith College of Art and Building, 1966-75. Mem., Guild of Freemen of City of London. *Address:* 44 Hamilton Court, Maida Vale, W9 1QR. *T:* 01-286 8719. *Clubs:* City Livery, Arts.

MANTLE, Philip Jaques, CMG 1952; *b* 7 Aug. 1901; 2nd *s* of late Paul Mantle; *m* 1930, Gwendolen, *d* of late John Webb, CMG, CBE, MC; one *s* one *d*. *Educ:* Bancroft's Sch., Woodford; St John's Coll., Oxford (Scholar, Goldsmiths' exhibitioner, 1st class Mod. Hist. Finals). Entered Inland Revenue Dept, 1923 (Taxes); Secretaries' office, 1928; Asst Secretary Min. of Supply, 1940, Board of Trade, 1942; Deputy Head, Administration of Enemy Property Dept, 1949; Controller-General, 1955-57; Companies Dept, 1957-61; with Charity Commission, 1962; retired 1966. *Address:* 27 Kensington Mansions, Trebovir Road, SW5 9TQ. *T:* 01-370 3683.

MANTON, 3rd Baron, *cr* 1922, of Compton Verney; **Joseph Rupert Eric Robert Watson;** Landowner and Farmer; *b* 22 Jan. 1924; *s* of 2nd Baron Manton and of Alethea, 2nd *d* of late Colonel Philip Langdale, OBE; *S* father, 1968; *m* 1951, Mary Elizabeth, twin *d* of Major T. D. Hallinan, Ashbourne, Glounthaune, Co. Cork; two *s* three *d*. *Educ:* Eton. Joined Army, 1942; commissioned Life Guards, 1943; Captain, 1946; retired, 1947; rejoined 7th (QO) Hussars, 1951-56. *Recreations:* hunting, shooting, racing. *Heir:* *s* Hon. Miles Ronald Marcus Watson, *b* 7 May 1958. *Address:* Houghton Hall, Sancton, York. *T:* Market Weighton 3234. *Clubs:* White's, Jockey.

MANTON, Prof. Irene, BA, ScD, PhD; FRS 1961; Emeritus Professor of Botany, University of Leeds; retired 1969. *Educ:* Girton Coll., Cambridge. BA 1927, PhD 1930, ScD 1940, Cambridge. Has made studies with the light and electron microscope on the ultramicroscopic structure of plants, and studies on the cytology and evolution of ferns. Hon. Member: Danish Acad. of Sciences and Letters, 1953; Deutsche Akad. Leopoldina, 1967; Amer. Acad. of Arts and Sciences, 1969. Hon. DSc: McGill Univ., Canada; Durham Univ., 1966; Hon. Doctorate, Oslo Univ., 1961. *Publications:* Problems of Cytology and Evolution in the Pteridophy Pteridophyta, 1950; papers in scientific journals. *Address:* 15 Harrowby Crescent, West Park, Leeds LS16 5HP.

MANTON, Sidnie M., FRS 1948; MA, PhD, ScD (Cantab); (**Mrs J. P. Harding**); retired as Research Fellow, Queen Mary College, London, 1967; Hon. Research Associate, British Museum (Natural History), since 1977; *b* 4 May 1902; *d* of George S. F. Manton, LDS, RCS, and Milana Manton, London; *m* 1937, J. P. Harding, *qv*; one *s* one *d*. *Educ:* St Paul's Girls' Sch., Hammersmith; Girton Coll., Cambridge. Scholar, 1921-25; Research Student, 1925-28; Fellow, 1928-48; Director of Studies in Natural Sciences, Girton Coll., 1935-42; Demonstrator in Comparative Anatomy, University of Cambridge, 1927-35; Visiting Lecturer, King's Coll., London, 1943-46, Asst Lecturer, 1946-49; Reader in Zoology, University of London, 1949-60. Hon. Dr, Lund, Sweden, 1968. Linnean Gold Medal, 1963. *Publications:* Colourpoint, Longhair and Himalayan Cats, 1971; The Arthropoda: habits, functional morphology and evolution, 1977; papers in scientific journals on zoological subjects. *Recreation:* cat breeding (new varieties). *Address:* 88 Ennerdale Road, Richmond, Surrey. *T:* 2908.

MANUEL, Joseph Thomas, CBE 1970; QPM 1967; one of HM's Inspectors of Constabulary, 1963-74; *b* 10 June 1909; *s* of George and Lucy Manuel; *m* 1933, Millicent Eveline Baker; one *s*. *Educ:* Dorchester Boys' Sch., Dorchester, Dorset. Joined Metropolitan Police, 1929. Served in Allied Military Government, Italy (rank of Captain and Major), 1943-46. Returned Metropolitan Police and promoted: Superintendent, 1954; Chief Superintendent, 1957; Dep. Commander, 1958; Commander 1959. *Recreations:* golf, walking, motoring. *Address:* Cranbrook, Pyrford Road, West Byfleet, Weybridge, Surrey KT14 6RE. *T:* Byfleet 46360.

MANVELL, (Arnold) Roger, PhD (London), DLitt (Sussex); film historian, biographer; scriptwriter and lecturer; Director, British Film Academy, 1947-59; Consultant to the British Academy of Film and Television Arts and Editor of its Journal, 1959-76; Associate Editor, New Humanist (formerly Humanist), 1967-75; Director: Rationalist Press Association Ltd; Pemberton Publishing Co. Ltd, etc; *b* 10 Oct. 1909; *s* of Canon A. E. W. Manvell; *m* 1956, Louise, *d* of Charles Luson Cribb, London. *Educ:* King's Sch., Peterborough; University College, Leicester. Schoolmaster and Lecturer in adult education, 1931-37; Lecturer in Literature and Drama, Dept Extramural Studies, University of Bristol, 1937-40; Ministry of Information, specialising in film work, 1940-45; Research Officer, British Film Institute, 1945-47. Has lectured on film subjects for British Film Institute, British Council and other authorities in Great Britain, US, Canada, Far East, India, Caribbean, W Africa and most European countries; regular broadcaster, 1946-, including BBC's long-established programme The Critics. Visiting Fellow, Sussex Univ.; Bingham Prof. of Humanities, Louisville Univ., 1973; Vis. Prof. of Film, Boston Univ., 1975-77. Governor, London Film School, 1966-74; Vice-Chm., Nat. Panel for Film Festivals, 1974-; Hon. Dir, Sound and Vision Library for World Centre for Shakespeare Studies, Globe Playhouse Trust, 1975-; Member Cttee of Management, Society of Authors, 1954-57, 1965-68; Chairman: Society of Lecturers, 1959-61; Radiowriters' Assoc., 1962-64; Authors' Club, 1972-75. Hon. DFA New England Coll., USA, 1972; Hon. DLitt Leicester, 1974. Commander of the Order of Merit of the Italian Republic, 1970; Order of Merit (First Class) of German Federal Republic, 1971. *Publications:* Film, 1944, revised 1946 and 1950; A Seat at the Cinema, 1951; On the Air (a study of broadcasting in sound and vision), 1953; The Animated Film, 1954; The Film and the Public, 1955; The Dreamers (novel), 1958; The Passion (novel), 1960; The Living Screen (a study of film and TV), 1961; What is a Film?, 1965; This Age of Communication, 1967; New Cinema in Europe, 1966; The July Plot (television play), 1966; New Cinema in the USA, 1968; Ellen Terry, 1968; New Cinema in Britain, 1969; SS and Gestapo, 1969; Sarah Siddons, 1970; Shakespeare and the Film, 1971; The Conspirators: 20 July 1944, 1971; Goering, 1972; Films and the Second World War, 1974; Charles Chaplin, 1974; Love Goddesses of the Movies, 1975; The Trial of Annie Besant, 1976; (ed and contributed) Experiment in the Film, 1949; (contributed) Twenty Years of

British Film, 1947; collaborated: with Rachel Low in The History of the British Film 1896-1906, 1948; with Paul Rotha in revised edn of Movie Parade, 1950; with John Huntley in The Technique of Film Music, 1957; with John Halas in The Technique of Film Animation, 1959, Design in Motion, 1962, and Art in Movement, 1970; with Heinrich Fraenkel in: Dr Goebbels, 1959, Hermann Goering, 1962, The July Plot, 1964, Heinrich Himmler, 1965, The Incomparable Crime, 1967, The Canaris Conspiracy, 1969, History of the German Cinema, 1971, Hess, 1971, Inside Adolf Hitler, 1973, The Hundred Days to Hitler, 1974; Editor: Three British Screenplays, 1950; Penguin Film Review, 1946-49; The Cinema, 1950-52; The Year's Work in the Film (for British Council), 1949 and 1950; International Encyclopedia of Film, 1972; contributed to Encyclopædia Britannica, journals at home and overseas concerned with history and art of the film and history of the Nazi régime. *Recreation:* travel abroad. *Address:* c/o The Rationalist Press, 88 Islington High Street, N1.

MANWARING, Randle (Gilbert), FCIB, FSS; Cirector: Midland Bank Insurance Services, since 1977 (Vice-Chairman, 1974-77); Excess Insurance Group Ltd, since 1975; *b* 3 May 1912; *s* of late George Ernest and Lilian Manwaring; *m* 1941, Betty Violet, *d* of H. P. Rout, Norwich; three *s* one *d*. *Educ:* private schools. Joined Clerical, Medical and Gen. Life Assce Soc., 1929. War service, RAF, 1940-46, W/Cdr; comd RAF Regt in Burma, 1945. Clerical, Medical & Gen. Pensions Rep., 1950; joined C. E. Heath & Co. Ltd, 1956: Asst Dir, 1960, Dir, 1964, Man. Dir. 1969; Founder Dir (Man.), C. E. Heath Urquhart (Life and Pensions), 1966-71, and a Founder Dir, Excess Life Assce Co., 1967-75; Insurance Adviser, Midland Bank, 1971; first Man. Dir, Midland Bank Ins. Services, 1972-74. Chm., Life Soc., Corp. of Insce Brokers, 1965-66; Dep. Chm., Corp. of Insce Brokers, 1970-71; Pres., Soc. of Pensions Consultants, 1968-70. Chairman of Governors: Luckley-Oakfield Sch., 1972-; Northease Manor Sch., 1972-. Diocesan Reader (Chichester), 1968-; Dir, Vine Books Ltd and Crusaders Union Ltd, 1960-. *Publications:* Posies Once Mine (poems), 1951; The Heart of this People, 1954; Satires and Salvation (poems), 1960; A Christian Guide to Daily Work, 1963; Under the Magnolia Tree (poems), 1965; Slave to No Sect (poems), 1966; Crossroads of the Year (poems), 1975; From the Four Winds (poems), 1976; Thornhill Guide to Insurance, 1976; In a Time of Unbelief (poems), 1977; contrib. poems and articles to learned jls in GB and Canada. *Recreations:* music, reading, following cricket. *Address:* High Paddock, Rodmell, Lewes, Sussex BN7 3HU. *T:* Lewes 5646. *Clubs:* Royal Air Force, MCC.

MANZIE, Andrew Gordon; Under-Secretary, Scottish Economic Planning Department, since 1975; *b* 3 April 1930; *s* of late John Mair Manzie and of Catherine Manzie; *m* 1955, Rosalind Clay; one *s* one *d*. *Educ:* Royal High Sch. of Edinburgh; London Sch. of Economics and Political Science (BScEcon). Joined Civil Service as Clerical Officer, Scottish Home Dept, 1947. National Service, RAF, 1949. Min. of Supply: Exec. Officer (Higher Exec. Officer, 1957). Private Sec. to Perm. Sec., Min. of Aviation, 1962; Sen. Exec. Officer, 1963; Principal, 1964; Sec. to Cttee of Inquiry into Civil Air Transport (Edwards Cttee), 1967; Asst Sec., Dept of Trade and Industry, on loan to Min. of Posts and Telecommunications, 1971; Dept of Industry, 1974; Under-Sec., Dir, Office for Scotland, Depts of Trade and Industry, 1975. *Recreations:* golf, reading. *Address:* 20 Avon Road, Barnton, Edinburgh EH4 6RD. *Club:* Royal Commonwealth Society.

MANZINI, Raimondo; Cavaliere di Gran Croce all'Ordine della Repubblica Italiana; GCVO (Hon.) 1969; Secretary-General at Italian Foreign Ministry, since 1975; *b* 25 Nov. 1913. *Educ:* Bologna Univ.; Clark Univ., Mass; Univ. of California. Entered Diplomatic Service, 1940; Sec. to Italian Legation, Lisbon, 1941-43; Ministry of Foreign Affairs in Brindisi (1943) and Salerno (1944); Sec. to Italian Embassy, London, 1944-47; Consul General for Congo, Nigeria and Gold Coast, 1947-50; Consul General, Baden Baden, 1951-52; Head of Information Service, CED, Paris, 1952-53; Ministry of Foreign Affairs, 1953-55; Adviser to the Minister of Foreign Trade, 1955-58; Chef de Cabinet of Minister for Foreign Affairs, 1958; Diplomatic Adviser to the Prime Minister, 1958-59; Adviser to the Minister of Industry, 1959-64; Italian Ambassador to: OECD in Paris, 1965-68; UK, 1968-75. *Address:* Ministero degli Affari Esteri, Palazzo Farnesina, Rome, Italy.

MANZÙ, Giacomo; sculptor; *b* 22 Dec. 1908; *s* of Angelo and Maria Manzù; *m*; three *s* decd. *Educ:* Milan. Professor of Sculpture, Brera Accad., Milan, 1941-54; International Summer Acad., Salzburg, 1954-60. Sculpture Prize, Venice Biennale, 1948; Society of Portrait Sculptors' International Award (Jean Masson Davidson Medal), 1965. Works include: Cathedral main door, Salzburg, and re-designing of bronze doors of St Peter's,

Rome, 1963 (commission won in open international competition); The Door of Peace and War, St Laurenz Church, Rotterdam, 1968. Exhibition of Paintings and Drawings: Haus der Kunst, Munich, 1959; Tate Gall., 1960, Hanover Gall., London, 1965; Moscow, Leningrad, and Kiev, 1966; Bordeaux, 1969. Established permanent collection of his most important works at Ardea, near Rome, 1969. Hon. Member: American Academy of Arts and Letters; National Academies of Argentina and Belgium; Accademia di Belle Arti Sovietica. Hon. Dr RCA 1971. Premio Internazionale Lenin per la pace, 1966. *Publication:* La Porta di S Pietro, 1965. *Relevant publications:* J. Rewald, Giacomo Manzù, 1966; B. Heynold von Graefe, The Doors of Rotterdam, 1969. *Address:* 00040 Ardea, Rome, Italy.

MAPLES, Ven. Jeffrey Stanley; Archdeacon of Swindon and Hon. Canon Diocesan, Bristol Cathedral, since 1974; *b* 8 Aug. 1916; *o s* of Arthur Stanley and Henrietta Georgina Maples; *m* 1945, Isobel Eileen Mabel Wren; four *s* (and one *s* decd). *Educ:* Downing Coll., Cambridge; Chichester Theological Coll. Asst Curate St James, Milton, Portsmouth, 1940-46; Asst Curate, Watlington, Diocese of Oxford, 1946-48. Vicar of Swinderby, Dio. Lincoln, and Diocesan Youth Chaplain, 1948-50; Vicar of St Michael-on-the-Mount, Lincoln, and Director of Religious Education: for Lincoln Dio., 1950-56; for Salisbury Dio., 1956-63; Canon of Lincoln, 1954-56; Chancellor of Salisbury Cathedral, 1960-67; Director of the Bible Reading Fellowship, 1963-67; Proctor in Convocation for Salisbury Diocese, 1957-70; Canon Emeritus of Salisbury Cathedral, 1967-; Vicar of St James, Milton, Portsmouth, 1967-74; Rural Dean of Portsmouth, 1968-73; Hon. Canon, Portsmouth Cathedral, 1972-74. *Address:* 25 Rowden Hill, Chippenham, Wilts SN15 2AQ. *T:* Chippenham 3599.

MAPLES EARLE, Ven. E. E.; *see* Earle.

MAPP, Charles; JP; *b* 1903. *Educ:* elementary and grammar schools. Railway goods agent (retired). Member, Sale Borough Council, 1932-35, 1945-46. Contested: Northwich, 1950; Stretford, 1951; Oldham East, 1955; MP (Lab) Oldham East, Oct. 1959-70, retired. JP 1949-. *Address:* 21 Fairhaven Road, Southport, Merseyside.

MAR, Countess of (*suo jure*, 31st in line from Ruadri, 1st Earl of Mar, 1115); Premier Earldom of Scotland by descent; Lady Garioch, *c* 1320; **Margaret of Mar;** Telecommunications Sales Representative; *b* 19 Sept. 1940; *er d* of 30th Earl of Mar, and Millicent Mary Salton; *S* father, 1975; recognised in surname "of Mar" by warrant of Court of Lord Lyon, 1967, when she abandoned her second forename; *m* 1st, 1959, Edwin Noel Artiss (marr. diss. 1976); one *d*; 2nd, 1976, (cousin) John Salton, recognised in surname "of Mar" by warrant of Lord Lyon, 1976. *Heir: d* Mistress of Mar, *qv*. *Address:* 10 Cranberry Drive, Stourport-on-Severn, Worcestershire DY13 8TH.

MAR, Mistress of; Lady Susan Helen of Mar; *b* 31 May 1963; *d* and *heiress* of Countess of Mar, *qv*.

MAR, 13th Earl of, *cr* 1565, and KELLIE, 15th Earl of, *cr* 1619; John Francis Hervey Erskine; Baron Erskine, 1429; Viscount Fentoun, 1606; Baron Dirleton, 1603; Premier Viscount of Scotland; Hereditary Keeper of Stirling Castle; Representative Peer for Scotland, 1959-63; Major Scots Guards; retired 1954; Major, Argyll and Sutherland Highlanders (TA) retired 1959; Lord Lieutenant of Clackmannan, since 1966; *b* 15 Feb. 1921; *e s* of late Lord Erskine (John Francis Ashley Erskine), GCSI, GCIE; *S* grandfather, 1955; *m* 1948, Pansy Constance (Pres., Scottish Marriage Guidance Council; Jt-Pres., Enterprise Youth; Jt Vice-Chm., Scottish Standing Conf. Voluntary Youth Organisations; Pres., Scottish Assoc. of Youth Clubs; Chm., Youth-at-Risk Adv. Gp; Chm., Scottish Adv. Gp, UNICEF. Elder of Church of Scotland. JP 1971; OStJ 1977), *y d* of late General Sir Andrew Thorne, KCB; three *s* one *d*. *Educ:* Eton; Trinity Coll., Cambridge. 2nd Lieut, Scots Guards, 1941; served in Egypt, N. Africa, Italy and Germany with 2nd Bn Scots Guards and HQ 201 Guards' Brigade, 1942-45 (wounded, despatches). Staff Coll., Camberley, 1950; DAAG, HQ, 3rd Infantry Div., 1951-52. DL Clackmannanshire, 1954, Vice-Lieutenant, 1957, JP 1962; County Councillor for Clackmannanshire, 1955-75 (Vice-Convener, 1961-64); Chairman: Forth Conservancy Board, 1957-68; Clackmannanshire T&AFA, 1961-68. An Elder of the Church of Scotland. Member of the Queen's Body Guard for Scotland (Royal Company of Archers). KStJ 1966. *Heir: s* Lord Erskine, *qv*. *Address:* Claremont House, Alloa, Clackmannanshire. *T:* Alloa 212020. *Club:* New (Edinburgh).

MARA, Rt. Hon. Ratu Sir Kamisese Kapaiwai Tuimacilai, PC 1973; KBE 1969 (OBE 1961); Tui Nayau; Tui Lau; Prime

Minister of Fiji, since 1970; Hereditary High Chief of the Lau Islands; *b* 13 May 1920; *s* of late Ratu Tevita Uluilakeba, Tui Nayau; *m* 1951, Adi Lady Lala Mara (Roko Tui Dreketi); three *s* five *d. Educ:* Fiji; Sacred Heart Coll., NZ; Otago Univ., NZ; Wadham Coll., Oxford (MA), Hon. Fellow, 1971; London Sch. of Economics (Dip. Econ. & Social Admin.). Administrative Officer, Colonial Service, Fiji, Oct. 1950; Fijian MLC, 1953-, and MEC, 1959-61 (elected MLC and MEC, 1959). Member for Natural Resources and Leader of Govt Business; Alliance Party, 1964-66 (Founder of Party); Chief Minister and Mem., Council of Ministers, Fiji, 1967. Hon. Dr of Laws Univ. of Guam, 1969; Hon. LLD: Univ. of Otago, 1973; New Delhi, 1975. Grand Cross, Order of Lion, Senegal, 1975. *Recreations:* athletics, cricket, Rugby football, golf, fishing. *Address:* 11 Battery Road, Suva, Fiji. *T:* 311629. *Clubs:* United Oxford & Cambridge University, Achilles (London); Defence (Suva, Fiji).

MARAJ, Dr James Ajodhya; Vice-Chancellor, University of the South Pacific, since 1975; *b* 28 Sept. 1930; *s* of Ramgoolam Maraj and Popo Maraj; *m* 1951, Etress (*née* Ouditt); two *s* two *d. Educ:* St Mary's Coll. and Govt Teachers' Coll., Trinidad; Univ. of Birmingham (BA, PhD). Teacher, Lectr, 1947-60; Sen. Lectr, Univ. of West Indies, 1965-70; Head, Inst. of Educn, UWI, 1968-70; Dir, Educn Div., Commonwealth Secretariat, 1970-72; Commonwealth Asst Sec.-Gen., 1973-75. External Examr, Educn Adviser and Consultant, etc, to several countries. Medal of Merit, Trinidad and Tobago, 1974. *Publications:* miscellaneous research papers. *Recreations:* sport: cricket, squash, horse-racing; poetry, music. *Address:* University of the South Pacific, Suva, Fiji. *Clubs:* Athenæum, Royal Commonwealth Society, Royal Over-Seas League.

MARCEAU, Marcel; Chevalier de la Légion d'Honneur; Commandeur des Arts et Lettres de la République Française; mime; Founder and Director, Compagnie de Mimes Marcel Marceau, since 1949; *b* Strasbourg, 22 March 1923; *s* of Charles and Anne Mangel; two *s* one *d. Educ:* Ecole des Beaux Arts; Ecole Etienne Decroux; Ecole Charles Dullin. First stage appearance, in Paris, 1946; founded his company, 1949; since then has toured constantly, playing in 65 countries. Created pantomimes and mime dramas, and in particular the character 'Bip' (1947). Has made frequent TV appearances and many short films, as well as a full-length film, Shanks, US 1973. Member: Acad. of Arts and Letters (GDR); Akad. der schönen Künste, Munich. TV Oscar (US), 1955, 1968. Hon. Dr, Univ. of Oregon. Gold Medal of Czechoslovak Republic (for contribution to cultural relations). *Publications:* Les 7 Péchés Capitaux (lithographs); Les Rêveries de Bip (lithographs); La Ballade de Paris et du Monde (text, lithographs, water-colours, drawings in ink and pencil); Alphabet Book; Counting Book; L'Histoire de Bip. *Recreation:* painting. *Address:* Théâtre des Champs-Elysées, 75008 Paris, France. *T:* 256 23 10.

MARCH and KINRARA, Earl of; Charles Henry Gordon-Lennox; *b* 19 Sept. 1929; *s* and *heir* of 9th Duke of Richmond and Gordon, *qv*; *m* 1951, Susan Monica, *o d* of late Colonel C. E. Grenville-Grey, CBE, Hall Barn, Blewbury, Berks; one *s* two *d. Educ:* Eton; William Temple Coll. 2nd Lieut, 60th Rifles, 1949-50. Chartered Accountant, 1956. Church Commissioner, 1963-76; Mem. Gen. Synod of Church of England, formerly Church Assembly, 1960- (Chm., Bd for Mission and Unity, 1967-77); Mem., Central and Exec. Cttees, World Council of Churches, 1968-75. President: Sussex Rural Community Council, 1973-; BHS, 1976-; Vice-Pres., SE England Tourist Bd, 1974-; Dir, Country Gentlemen's Assoc. Ltd, 1975-. *Heir: s* Lord Settrington, *qv. Address:* Goodwood House, Chichester, W Sussex. *T:* (office) Chichester 527107; (home) Chichester 527312.
See also Lord N. C. Gordon Lennox.

MARCH, George Frederick, CMG 1946; MC 1917; *b* 6 July 1893; *o s* of late Frederick J. March, Ockbrook Grange, Derbyshire; *m* 1935, Myrtle Lloyd, Carmarthen; two *s. Educ:* Rugby Sch.; Wye Agricultural Coll. (dip. Agric. 1914). Commissioned in Sherwood Foresters, Aug. 1914; France, 1915-19 (wounded thrice); Egypt (Alexandria), 1919-21; demobilised, 1921; Inspector of Agriculture, Sudan Government, 1921; Senior Inspector of Agriculture, 1928; Asst Director, Agriculture and Forests, 1935; Dep. Director, 1942; Director, 1944-47. Chairman, Rural Water Supplies and Soil Conservation Board. Member Governor-General's Council (Sudan). Agricultural Consultant on mission to Swaziland by Colonial Development Corporation, Jan.-April, 1950; Manager and Secretary, Flishinghurst Farms Ltd, 1950-52; now farming on own (hops, fruit, etc.), in Kent. *Recreations:* fishing, shooting, tennis, golf. *Address:* The Well House, Limes Grove Farm, Hawkhurst, Kent. *TA:* Hawkhurst. *T:* Hawkhurst 2398.

MARCH, Henry Arthur, MA (Oxon); *b* 14 March 1905; *s* of late Edward Gerald March, MD, Reading; *m* 1943, Mary (*d* 1968), *d* of late Rev. P. P. W. Gendall, Launceston; two *s* one *d. Educ:* Leighton Park Sch.; St John's Coll., Oxford. Asst Master, Merchant Taylors' Sch., 1929-39; Head of Modern Language side, 1940-54, and Housemaster, 1945-54, Charterhouse; Headmaster, Cranleigh Sch., 1954-59; Temp. Asst Master, Marlborough Coll., 1959-61; Asst Master, 1961-65. Acting Headmaster, Charterhouse, 1964. *Address:* Horsna Parc, St Tudy, Bodmin, Cornwall.

MARCH, Prof. Norman Henry; Coulson Professor of Theoretical Chemistry, University of Oxford, since 1977; Fellow of University College, Oxford, since 1977; *b* 9 July 1927; *s* of William and Elsie March; *m* 1949, Margaret Joan Hoyle; two *s. Educ:* King's Coll., London Univ. University of Sheffield: Lecturer in Physics, 1953-57; Reader in Theoretical Physics, 1957-61; Prof. of Physics, 1961-72; Prof. of Theoretical Solid State Physics, Imperial Coll., Univ. of London, 1973-77. *Publications:* The Many-Body Problem in Quantum Mechanics (with W. H. Young and S. Sampanthar), 1967; Liquid Metals, 1968; Theoretical Solid State Physics (with W. Jones), 1973; Self-Consistent Fields in Atoms, 1974; Orbital Theories of Molecules and Solids, 1974; Atomic Dynamics in Liquids (with M. P. Tosi), 1976; many scientific papers on quantum mechanics and statistical mechanics in Proceedings Royal Society, Phil. Magazine, etc. *Recreations:* music, chess, cricket. *Address:* Elmstead, 6 Northcroft Road, Englefield Green, Egham, Surrey. *T:* Egham 3078.

MARCHAMLEY, 3rd Baron, *cr* 1908, of Hawkstone; **John William Tattersall Whiteley;** late Lieutenant, Royal Armoured Corps; *b* 24 April 1922; *s* of 2nd Baron and Margaret Clara (*d* 1974), *d* of Thomas Scott Johnstone of Glenmark, Waipara, New Zealand; *S* father, 1949; *m* 1967, Sonia Kathleen Pedrick; one *s.* Served War of 1939-45, Captain, 19th King George V Own Lancers. *Heir: s* Hon. William Francis Whiteley, *b* 27 July 1968. *Address:* Whetcombe, North Huish, South Brent, Devon.

MARCHANT, Edgar Vernon; Member, Civil Service Appeal Board; Director, Paddington Building Society; *b* 7 Dec. 1915; *s* of E. C. Marchant; *m* 1945, Joyce Allen Storey; one *s* two *d. Educ:* Marlborough Coll.; Lincoln Coll., Oxford. Engr, Bahrain Petroleum Co., 1938; various technical and scientific posts in Min. of Aircraft Production, Min. of Supply and RAE, 1940-51; Principal, Min. of Supply, 1951; Principal, BoT, 1955; Asst Sec., BoT, 1959; Asst Registrar of Restrictive Trading Agreements, 1964; Asst Sec., Dept of Economic Affairs, 1966; Nat. Board for Prices and Incomes: Asst Sec., 1967-68; Under-Sec., 1968-71; Under-Sec., DTI, later Dept of Industry, 1971-75. *Recreations:* gardening, messing about in boats. *Address:* 17 Devonshire Gardens, Chiswick, W4 3TN. *Club:* United Oxford & Cambridge University.

MARCHANT, Ernest Cecil, CIE 1946; *b* 27 Sept. 1902; *s* of E. J. Marchant, Cambridge; *m* 1933, Margaret Glen, *d* of Major George Lamb, IMS; two *d. Educ:* Perse Sch.; St John's Coll., Cambridge (Scholar). Asst Master, Oakham Sch., 1925-28; Mem., Royal Soc. Expedn to Great Barrier Reef, 1928-29; Asst Master, Geelong Sch., Australia, 1929-30; Asst Master, Marlborough Coll., 1931-38; Principal, The Daly Coll., India, 1939-46; HM Inspector of Schools, 1947-66, Staff Inspector, 1952-66. *Address:* Burford House, The Common, Chipperfield, Herts WD4 9BY. *T:* Kings Langley 62549.

MARCHANT, Ven. George John Charles; Archdeacon of Auckland and Canon Residentiary, Durham Cathedral, since 1974; *b* 3 Jan. 1916; *s* of late T. Marchant, Little Stanmore, Mddx; *m* 1944, Eileen Lillian Kathleen, *d* of late F. J. Smith, FCIS; one *s* three *d. Educ:* St John's Coll., Durham (MA, BD); Tyndale Hall, Bristol. Deacon 1939, priest 1940, London; Curate of St Andrew's, Whitehall Park, N19, 1939-41; Licence to officiate, London dio., 1941-44 (in charge of Young Churchmen's Movement); Curate of St Andrew-the-Less, Cambridge (in charge of St Stephen's), 1944-48; Vicar of Holy Trinity, Skirbeck, Boston, 1948-54; Vicar of St Nicholas, Durham, 1954-74; Rural Dean of Durham, 1964-74; Hon. Canon of Durham Cathedral, 1972-74. Member of General Synod, 1970- (Proctor in Convocation for Dio. Durham). *Publications:* contribs to The Churchman. *Recreations:* record-music, bird watching. *Address:* 15 The College, Durham. *T:* Durham 2534.

MARCHANT, Sir Herbert (Stanley), KCMG 1963 (CMG 1957); OBE 1946; MA Cantab; *b* 18 May 1906; *s* of E. J. Marchant; *m* 1937, Diana Selway, *d* of C. J. Selway, CVO, CBE; one *s. Educ:* Perse Sch.; St John's Coll., Cambridge (MA 1929). Asst Master, Harrow Sch., 1928-39; Foreign Office, 1940-46; Consul, Denver,

Colorado, USA, 1946-48; First Secretary, British Legation, Bucharest, 1948-49; Counsellor, British Embassy, Paris, 1950-52; Consul-General, Zagreb, 1952-54; Land Commissioner and Consul-General for North Rhine/Westphalia, 1954-55; Consul-General, Düsseldorf, 1954-57; Consul-General, San Francisco, 1957-60; Ambassador to Cuba, 1960-63; Ambassador to Tunisia, 1963-66. Asst Dir, Inst. of Race Relations, 1966-68; UK Representative, UN Cttee for Elimination of Racial Discrimination, 1969-73. Chm., British-Tunisian Soc., 1970-74. *Publication:* Scratch a Russian, 1936. *Recreations:* mountains, spear fishing, theatre. *Club:* Travellers'.

MARCHWOOD, 2nd Viscount, *cr* 1945, of Penang and of Marchwood, Southampton; **Peter George Penny,** Baron *cr* 1937; Bt, *cr* 1933; MBE (mil.) 1944; *b* 7 Nov. 1912; *s* of 1st Viscount Marchwood, KCVO; *S* father, 1955; *m* 1935, Pamela, *o d* of John Staveley Colton-Fox, JP, Todwick Grange, nr Sheffield; two *s* one *d. Educ:* Winchester. Editorial Staff, Sheffield Daily Telegraph and Daily Telegraph and Morning Post, 1929-35; Financial Advertising Staff, Daily Telegraph and Morning Post, 1935-47. Served War of 1939-45, Major, RA. Joined Vine Products Ltd, as General Manager, 1947; Dep. Managing Director, 1951; Chairman and Managing Director, 1955-59; Exec. Dir, Geo. Wimpey & Co (Contractors), 1960-71. *Recreations:* racing, shooting. *Heir:* s Hon. David George Staveley Penny [*b* 22 May 1936; *m* 1964, Tessa Jane, *d* of W. F. Norris; three *s*]. *Address:* Manor House, Cholderton, near Salisbury, Wilts. *T:* Cholderton 200. *Club:* White's.

MARCUS, Frank Ulrich; playwright; Theatre Critic for The Sunday Telegraph, since 1968; *b* Breslau, Germany, 30 June 1928; *s* of late Frederick Marcus and of Gertie Marcus; *m* 1951, Jacqueline (*née* Sylvester); one *s* two *d. Educ:* Bunce Court Sch., Kent (evac. to Shropshire during war); St Martin's Sch. of Art, London. Actor, Dir, Scenic Designer, Unity Theatre, Kensington (later Internat. Theatre Gp). *Stage plays:* Minuet for Stuffed Birds, 1950; The Man Who Bought a Battlefield, 1963; The Formation Dancers, 1964; The Killing of Sister George, 1965 (3 'Best Play of the Year' Awards: Evening Standard, Plays and Players, Variety); Cleo, 1965; Studies of the Nude, 1967; Mrs Mouse, Are You Within?, 1968; The Window, 1969; Notes on a Love Affair, 1972; Blank Pages, 1972; Carol's Christmas, 1973; Beauty and the Beast, 1975; Portrait of the Artist (mime scenario), 1977; Blind Date, 1977; The Ballad of Wilfred the Second, 1977-78; *television plays:* A Temporary Typist, 1966; The Glove Puppet, 1968; *translations:* Schnitzler's Reigen, 1952; Liebelei (TV), 1954; Anatol, 1976; (Molnar's) The Guardsman, 1969; (Kaiser's) From Morning Till Midnight, 1977. *Publications:* The Formation Dancers, 1964; The Killing of Sister George, 1965; The Window, 1968; Mrs Mouse, Are You Within?, 1969; Notes on a Love Affair, 1972; Blank Pages, 1973; Beauty and the Beast, 1977; Blind Date, 1977; contribs to: Behind the Scenes, 1972; Those Germans, 1973; On Theater, 1974 (US), etc, also to London Magazine, Plays and Players, Dramatists' Quarterly (US), New York Times, etc. *Recreation:* observing. *Address:* 42 Cumberland Mansions, Nutford Place, W1H 5ZB. *T:* 01-262 9824; c/o Margaret Ramsay Ltd, 14a Goodwin's Court, St Martin's Lane, WC2.

MARCUSE, Herbert, PhD; Professor of Philosophy, University of California at San Diego, since 1965; *b* Berlin, 19 July 1898; *m* Sophie (*d* 1951); one *s*; *m* 1955, Inge Werner; two step-*s*; American nationality, 1940. *Educ:* Univs of Berlin and Freiberg. Went to USA, 1934; Inst. of Social Research, Columbia Univ., 1934-40; served with Office of Strategic Services and State Dept, 1941-50; Russian Inst., Columbia and Harvard Univs, 1951-53; Prof. of Politics and Philosophy, Brandeis Univ., 1954-65. *Publications:* Reason and Revolution, 1941; Eros and Civilization, 1954; Soviet Marxism, 1958; One-Dimensional Man, 1965; The Ethics of Revolution, 1966; Negations, 1968; An Essay on Liberation, 1969; Counterrevolution and Revolt, 1972; Studies in Critical Philosophy, 1972. *Address:* University of California, San Diego, Calif 92038, USA.

MARDELL, Peggy Joyce; Regional Nursing Officer, North West Thames Regional Health Authority, since 1974; *b* 8 July 1927; *d* of Alfred Edward and Edith Mary Mardell. *Educ:* George Spicer Sch., Enfield; Highlands Hosp., London (RFN); E Suffolk Hosp., Ipswich (Medallist, SRN); Queen Charlotte's Hosp. Battersea Coll. of Further Educn (Hons Dip., RNT). Queens Inst. of District Nursing, Guildford, 1951-52 (SCM); Ward Sister, Night Sister, Bethnal Green Hosp., 1953-55; Sister Tutor, Royal Surrey County Hosp., 1957-64; Asst Regional Nursing Officer, NE Metrop. Regional Hosp. Bd, 1964-70; Chief Regional Nursing Officer, NW Metrop. Regional Hosp. Bd, 1970-74. Lectr, British Red Cross, 1958-60; Examr, Gen. Nursing Council, 1962-70; Member: Royal Coll. of Nursing; Assoc. of Nurse Administrators; Regional Nurse Trng Cttee;

Assessor for Nat. Nursing Staff Cttee. *Recreations:* renovating old furniture, gardening, reading. *Address:* 19 East Meads, Guildford, Surrey. *T:* Guildford 79506.

MARDEN, John Louis, CBE 1976; JP; Chairman, Wheelock, Marden and Co. Ltd; Director, Hong Kong & Shanghai Banking Corporation; *b* Woodford, Essex, 12 Feb. 1919; *s* of late George Ernest Marden; *m* 1947, Anne Harris; one *s* three *d. Educ:* Gresham Sch., Norfolk; Trinity Hall, Cambridge (MA). Served War, as Captain 4th Regt RHA, in N Africa, France and Germany, 1940-46. Joined Wheelock, Marden & Co. Ltd, as trainee (secretarial and shipping, then insurance side of business), 1946; Dir of company, 1952, Chm., 1959. JP Hong Kong, 1964. *Recreations:* golf, water ski-ing, ski-ing. *Address:* PO Box 85, Hong Kong; c/o Wheelock Marden (UK) Ltd, 16 Finsbury Circus, EC2.

MARDER, Prof. Arthur (Jacob), CBE (Hon.) 1971; Professor of History, University of California at Irvine, 1964-77; *b* 8 March 1910; *s* of Maxwell J. Marder and Ida (*née* Greenstein); *m* 1955, Jan North; two *s* one *d. Educ:* Harvard Univ. BA 1931; MA 1934; PhD 1936. MA Oxon, 1969; Hon. DLitt Oxon, 1971. Asst Professor of History, University of Oregon, 1936-38; Research Assoc., Bureau of International Research, Harvard Univ., 1939-41; Research Analyst, Office of Strategic Services, 1941-42; Assoc. Professor, Hamilton Coll., 1943-44; Assoc. Professor, University of Hawaii, 1944-51; Professor, 1951-58; Sen. Professor, 1958-64. Visiting Prof., Harvard Univ., 1949-50; Eastman Prof., Oxford, and Fellow of Balliol Coll., 1969-70. FRHistS 1966; Fellow, J. S. Guggenheim Foundation, 1939, 1945-46, 1958; grantee, American Philosophical Society, 1956, 1958, 1963, 1966, Rockefeller Foundation, 1943; UK Fulbright Fellow Alt., 1954. Corresp. FBA, 1970. Member: American Philosophical Soc., 1972; Council, Amer. Hist. Assoc., 1972-75 (Pres., Pacific Coast Br., 1971-72); Phi Beta Kappa (Foundn Mem., Univ. of Calif, Irvine), 1974. Fellow: American Acad. of Arts and Sciences, 1972; Japan Foundn, 1976. Chesney Memorial Gold Medal of RUSI, 1968; Admiralty Board citation, 1970. *Publications:* The Anatomy of British Sea Power, 1940 (G. L. Beer Prize, Amer. Hist. Assoc., 1941); Portrait of an Admiral, 1952; Fear God and Dread Nought, 3 vols, 1952, 1956, 1959; From the Dreadnought to Scapa Flow, 5 vols, 1961, 1965, 1966, 1969, 1970; From the Dardanelles to Oran, 1974; Operation Menace, 1976; contributions to American Hist. Review, Journal of Modern History, English Hist. Review, etc. *Recreations:* golf, hiking, Chinese cooking. *Address:* c/o Department of History, University of California at Irvine, Irvine, Calif 92717, USA.

MARDER, Bernard Arthur, QC 1977; *b* 25 Sept. 1928; *er s* of late Samuel Marder and Marie Marder; *m* 1953, Sylvia Levy; one *s* on *d. Educ:* Bury Grammar Sch.; Manchester Univ. (LLB 1951). Called to the Bar, Gray's Inn, 1952. Asst Comr, Local Govt and Parly Boundary Commns. Former Mem. Council, National Assoc. for Gifted Children; Trustee, Messenger House Trust. *Address:* Gray's Inn Chambers, Gray's Inn, WC1R 5JA.

MARDON, Lt-Col John Kenric La Touche, DSO 1945; TD 1943; DL; MA; JP; Vice Lord-Lieutenant, Avon, since 1974; Chairman, Mardon, Son & Hall, Ltd, Bristol, 1962-69; Director, Bristol & West Building Society; *b* 29 June 1905; *e s* of late Evelyn John Mardon, Halsway Manor, Crowcombe and late Maud Mary (*née* Rothwell); *m* 1933, Dulcie Joan, 3rd *d* of late Maj.-Gen. K. M. Body, CB, CMG, OBE; two *s* one *d. Educ:* Clifton; Christ's Coll., Cambridge. Commissioned in Royal Devon Yeomanry, 1925; Major, 1938; Lieut-Colonel, RA, 1942; served War of 1939-45, in N.W. Europe, 1944-45 (despatches). JP Somerset, 1948; High Sheriff of Somerset, 1956-57; DL 1962. Master, Society of Merchant Venturers, Bristol, 1959-60; Governor, Clifton Coll., 1957. Pres., Bristol YMCA. *Recreations:* shooting, lawn tennis, squash rackets (rep. Cambridge v. Oxford, 1925). *Address:* Hemington House, Hemington, Bath BA3 5XX. *T:* Faulkland 592.

MARENGO, Kimon Evan; *see* Kem.

MARETT, Sir Robert (Hugh Kirk), KCMG 1964 (CMG 1955); OBE 1942; FRAI; Seigneur de Franc Fief, in Jersey; Director, Royal Trust Co. of Canada (CI) Ltd; Deputy, States of Jersey; *b* 20 April 1907; *s* of late Dr Robert Ranulph Marett, one-time Rector of Exeter Coll., Oxford, and Nora Kirk; *m* 1934, Piedad, *d* of late Vicente Sanchez Gavito, Mexico City; one *d. Educ:* Dragon Sch., Oxford; Winchester Coll. Entered business: Norton, Megaw & Co. Ltd, 1926-30; Mexican Railway Co. Ltd, 1931-36; Shell Petroleum Co., 1937-39; Times Correspondent in Mexico, 1932-38; Ministry of Information, London, Mexico, Washington and Ottawa, 1939-46; First Secretary, HM Foreign Service, 1946; New York, 1946-48; Lima, 1948-52; Foreign

Office, 1952-55; Secretary, Drogheda Cttee, 1952-53; Counsellor (Head of Information Policy Dept, of FO), 1953-55; HM Consul-General, Boston, 1955-58; Asst Under-Secretary of State, Foreign Office, 1959-63; British Ambassador to Peru, 1963-67; special Ambassador for inauguration of President Allende of Chile, 1970. *Publications:* Archæological Tours from Mexico City, 1932; An Eye-Witness of Mexico, 1939; Through the Back Door, An Inside View of Britain's Overseas Information Services, 1968; Peru, 1969; Mexico, 1971; Latin America: British trade and investment, 1973. *Address:* Mon Plaisir, St Aubin, Jersey, CI. *Club:* Travellers'.

MARGADALE, 1st Baron, cr 1964; **John Granville Morrison,** TD; JP; Lord-Lieutenant of Wiltshire, since 1969; Member Royal Company of Archers (Queen's Body Guard for Scotland); *b* 16 Dec. 1906; *s* of late Hugh Morrison; *m* 1928, Hon. Margaret Esther Lucie Smith, 2nd *d* of 2nd Viscount Hambleden; three *s* one *d. Educ:* Eton; Magdalene Coll., Cambridge. Served 1939-45: recruited with Royal Wilts Yeomanry; in MEF, 1939-42. MP (C) Salisbury Division of Wilts, 1942-64; Chairman, Conservative Members' (1922) Cttee, 1955-64. Yeomanry Comdt and Chm., Yeomanry Assoc., 1965-71; Hon. Col, The Royal Wiltshire Yeomanry Sqdn, 1965-71; Hon. Col, The Royal Yeomanry, 1965-71; Dep. Hon. Col, The Wessex Yeomanry, 1971-. DL 1950, JP 1936, High Sheriff, 1938, Wilts. MFH S and W Wilts Foxhounds, 1932-66. KstJ 1972. *Heir:* s Major Hon. James Ian Morrison, TD, late Royal Wiltshire Yeomanry [*b* 17 July 1930; *m* 1952, Clare, *d* of Anthony Lister Barclay, Broad Oak End, Hertford; three *s* one *d*]. *Address:* Fonthill House, Tisbury, Wilts. *T:* Tisbury 202; Islay House, Bridgend, Argyll. *Clubs:* Turf, Jockey, White's.
See also Hon. C. A. Morrison, Hon. M. A. Morrison, Hon. P. H. Morrison.

MARGAI, Sir Albert (Michael), Kt 1965; Lawyer and Politician, Sierra Leone; *b* 10 Oct. 1910; 6th *s* of late M. E. S. Margai and Ndaneh Margai, Gbangbatoke and Bonthe; *m* 1949, Esther; ten *c. Educ:* St Patrick's Roman Catholic Sch., Bonthe; St Edward's Secondary Sch., Freetown; Middle Temple, London. Male Nurse and Dispenser, 1932-44. Practising Barrister, 1948; Sierra Leone Government: MLC and Minister of Education and Local Government and Welfare, 1950-57; MP 1957; Min. of Natural Resources, 1960; Minister of Finance, 1962; Prime Minister of Sierra Leone and Minister of Defence, 1964-67. Founder Member, People's National Party, 1958-. Knight Grand Cross of St Gregory (Vatican), 1962. *Recreation:* tennis.

MARGÁIN, Hugo B.; GCVO; Ambassador of Mexico to the United States, 1965-70 and since 1977; *b* 13 Feb. 1913; *s* of Cesar R. Margáin and Maria Teresa Gleason de Margáin; *m* 1941, Margarita Charles de Margáin; three *s* three *d. Educ:* National Univ. of Mexico (UNAM); National Sch. of Jurisprudence (LLB). Prof. of Constitutional Law, 1947, of Constitutional Writs, 1951-56, and of Fiscal Law, 1952-56, Univ. of Mexico. Govt posts include: Dir-Gen., Mercantile Transactions Tax, 1951-52, and Dir-Gen., Income Tax, 1952-59, Min. for Finance. Official Mayor, Min. for Industry and Commerce, 1959-61; Dep. Minister of Finance, Sept. 1961-Dec. 1964; Sec. of Finance, Aug. 1970-May 1973; Ambassador to the UK, 1973-77. Chm., Nat. Commn on Corporate Profit-Sharing (ie labour participation), 1963-64; Govt Rep. on Bd of Nat. Inst. for Scientific Res., 1962-63 (Chm. of Bd, 1963-64). Holds hon. degrees from univs in USA. Hon. GCVO 1975. *Publications:* Avoidance of Double Taxation Based on the Theory of the Source of Taxable Income, 1956; Preliminary Study on Tax Codification, 1957; (with H. L. Gumpel) Taxation in Mexico, 1957; Civil Rights and the Writ of Amparo in Administrative Law, 1958; The Role of Fiscal Law in Economic Development, 1960; Profit Sharing Plan, 1964; Housing Projects for Workers (Infonavit), 1971. *Recreations:* riding, swimming. *Address:* Embassy of Mexico, 2829 16th Street, NW, Washington, DC 20009, USA.

MARGERISON, Thomas Alan; Chairman, Computer Technology Ltd, since 1971 (Director, since 1966); *b* 13 Nov. 1923; *s* of Ernest Alan Margerison and Isabel McKenzie; *m* 1950, Pamela Alice Tilbrook; two *s. Educ:* Huntingdon Grammar Sch.; Hymers Coll., Hull; King's Sch., Macclesfield; Sheffield University. Research Physicist, 1949; film script writer, Film Producers Guild, 1950; Scientific Editor, Butterworths sci. pubns, Ed. Research, 1951-56; Man. Editor, Heywood Pubns and National Trade Press, 1956. First Scientific Editor, The New Scientist, 1956-61; Science Corresp., Sunday Times, 1961; Dep. Editor, Sunday Times Magazine, 1962; Man. Dir, Thomson Technical Developments Ltd, 1964; Dep. Man. Dir, 1967-69, Chief Exec., 1969-71, London Weekend Television. Scientific broadcaster and journalist, worked for many years with Tonight team on BBC. Responsible for

applying computers to evening newspapers in Reading and Hemel Hempstead. *Publications:* articles and television scripts, indifferent scientific papers; (ed) popular science books. *Recreation:* sailing. *Address:* 63 Dulwich Village, SE21. *T:* 01-693 6627. *Club:* Savile.

MARGESSON, family name of Viscount Margesson.

MARGESSON, 2nd Viscount *cr* 1942, of Rugby; **Francis Vere Hampden Margesson;** *b* 17 April 1922; *o s* of 1st Viscount Margesson, PC, MC, and Frances H. Leggett (*d* 1977), New York; *S* father, 1965; *m* 1958, Helena, *d* of late Heikki Backstrom, Finland; one *s* three *d. Educ:* Eton; Trinity Coll., Oxford. Served War of 1939-45, as Sub-Lt, RNVR. A Director of Thames & Hudson Publications, Inc., New York, 1949-53. ADC to Governor of the Bahamas, 1956; Information Officer, British Consulate-General, NY, 1964-70. *Heir:* s Hon. Richard Francis David Margesson, *b* 25 Dec. 1960. *Address:* Stone Ridge, New York, NY 12484, USA. *Club:* Coffee House (New York).

MARGETSON, John William Denys; Head of Chancery, UK Delegation to NATO, since 1974; *b* 9 Oct. 1927; *yr s* of Very Rev. W. J. Margetson and Marion Constance Lillian (*née* Jenoure); *m* 1963, Miranda, *d* of Sir William Menzies Coldstream, *qv* and Mrs Nancy Spender; one *s* one *d. Educ:* Blundell's; St John's Coll., Cambridge. Lieut, Life Guards, 1947-49. Colonial Service, District Officer, Tanganyika, 1951-60 (Private Sec. to Governor, 1956-57); entered Foreign (subseq. Diplomatic) Service, 1960; The Hague, 1962-63; speech writer to Foreign Sec., 1966-68; Head of Chancery, Saigon, 1968-70; Counsellor 1971, seconded to Cabinet Secretariat, 1971-74. *Recreation:* music. *Address:* UK Delegation to NATO, 1110 Brussels, Belgium; The Agent's House, Easton, Suffolk. *T:* Wickham Market 746348. *Club:* Brooks's.

MARGETSON, Major Sir Philip (Reginald), KCVO 1953 (CVO 1948); MC 1916; QPM 1956; Assistant Commissioner of Police of the Metropolis, 1946-57, retired; *b* 2 Jan. 1894; *s* of late William Parker Margetson and Ellen Maria Snell; *m* 1918, Diana, *er d* of late Sir John Edward Thornycroft, KBE; one *s* (and *er s* killed on active service in N. Africa, 1943). *Educ:* Marlborough; RMC, Sandhurst. Gazetted to RSF, 1915; European War, 1914-18, served 1914-19 (MC); Adjutant 1st Bn 1923; Captain, 1923; Bt Major, 1933; Staff Captain 54th East Anglian Div. (TA) and East Anglian Area, 1928-32; retired and joined Metropolitan Police, 1933; Chief Constable No. 2 District, 1936, No. 1 District, Feb.-Nov. 1938, No. 3 District, Nov. 1938-Feb. 1940; Dep. Asst Commissioner A Dept, New Scotland Yard, Feb.-Aug. 1940; Dep. Asst Commissioner No. 1 District, Aug. 1940-June 1946; Asst Commissioner i/c D Dept, New Scotland Yard, June-Oct. 1946, transferred to A Dept, Oct. 1946. Chairman: Securicor Ltd, 1960-73 (Hon. Pres., 1973); British Security Industry Assoc., 1966-73. CStJ. Officer of the Legion of Honour; Officer of Orange Nassau (Netherlands); Commander Order of the Dannebrog (Denmark); Commander Order of St Olaf (Norway). *Recreation:* gardening. *Address:* 16 Tufton Court, SW1. *T:* 01-222 5544; Steyne Wood Battery, Bembridge, IoW. *T:* Bembridge 2424. *Clubs:* Naval and Military, MCC; Bembridge Sailing (Bembridge).

MARGETTS, Frederick Chilton, CBE 1966 (MBE 1943); Consultant, Containerisation; *b* 2 Nov. 1905; *m* 1929, Dorothy Walls; one *d. Educ:* Driffield Grammar Sch.; St Martin's Grammar Sch., Scarborough. Asst Operating Supt, LNER Scotland, 1946; BR Scotland, 1949; Chief Operating Supt, BR Scotland, 1955; Chief Traffic Manager, 1958, Asst General Manager, 1959, General Manager, 1961, BR York; Member BR Cttee, 1962; Operating Mem., BR Board, 1962-67. *Recreation:* œnology. *Address:* 9 Riseborough House, York YO3 6NQ. *T:* York 26207.

MARION, Dr Léo Edmond, CC (Canada) 1967; MBE 1946; FRSC 1942; FRS (London), 1961; Hon. Professor of Biochemistry; Dean, Faculty of Pure and Applied Science, University of Ottawa, 1965-69, retired; *b* 22 March 1899; *s* of Joseph Marion and Emma Vezina; *m* 1933, Paule Lefort; no *c. Educ:* Queen's (BSc 1926, MSc 1927); McGill (PhD 1929); University of Vienna. Research chemist, National Research Council, 1929-42; Head, Organic Chemistry Section, 1943; Editor in Chief of all Canadian Journals of Research, 1947-65; Vice-President (scientific), National Research Council, Ottawa, 1960-65, Dir, Div. of Chemistry, 1952-63. Hon. Member: Société Chimique de France, 1957; Royal Canadian Inst., Toronto, 1971; President, Chemical Institute of Canada, 1961. President Royal Society of Canada, 1964. Hon. degrees: DSc: Laval, 1954; Ottawa, 1958; Queen's, 1961; British Columbia, 1963; Royal Military Coll., 1965; Carleton, 1965; McGill, 1966;

Poznan, 1967; D. de l'U: Montreal, 1961; Paris, 1962; LLD: Toronto, 1962; Saskatchewan, 1968; DCL, Bishop's, 1966. Member American Chemical Society; Association Canadienne-Française pour l'Avancement des Sciences Medal, 1948; Chem. Inst. of Canada Medal, 1956; City of Paris Medal, 1957; Professional Institute of Canada Medal, 1959; Chem. Inst. of Canada Montreal Medal, 1969. *Publications:* chapters in: The Alkaloids; 195 papers on chemistry of alkaloids. *Address:* 211 Wurtemburg Street, Apartment 1413, Ottawa K1N 8R4, Canada.

MARJOLIN, Robert E.; Officier de la Légion d'Honneur, 1956; Officier du Mérite Agricole, 1958; economist; *b* 27 July 1911; *s* of Ernest Marjolin and Elise Vacher; *m* 1944, Dorothy Smith (*d* 1971); one *s* one *d. Educ:* Sorbonne and Law Sch., Paris; Yale Univ., New Haven, Conn. Asst to Professor Charles Rist at Institut Scientifique de Recherches Economiques et Sociales, 1934-37; Chief Asst, 1938-39. Joined General de Gaulle in London, 1941; Head of French Supply Mission in USA, 1944; Directeur des Relations Economiques Extérieures, Ministère de l'Economie Nationale, 1945; Commissaire Général Adjoint du Plan de Modernisation et d'Equipement, 1946-48; Secretary General, Organisation for European Economic Co-operation, 1948-55; Professor of Economics, University of Nancy, 1955-58; Vice-President, Commission of European Economic Community (Common Market), 1958-67; Prof. of Economics, Univ. of Paris, 1967-69. Member: Internat. Adv. Cttee, Chase Manhattan Bank, 1970-; Gen. Motors European Adv. Council, 1974-; Adviser: American Express Co., 1972-; IBM, 1970-; Director: Royal Dutch; Robeco; Shell Française. Foreign Hon. Member American Academy of Arts and Sciences, 1963. Hon. LLD: Yale, 1965; Harvard, 1967; University of East Anglia, 1967. American Medal of Freedom, 1947; King's Medal, 1947; Grand-Croix de l'Ordre d'Orange-Nassau (Holland), Cavaliere di Gran Croce nell' Ordine al Merito della Repubblica (Italy). Grand-Croix du Mérite de la République Fédérale d'Allemagne, Grand-Croix de l'Ordre Royal du Phœnix (Greece), 1955, Commandeur de l'Ordre du Drapeau (Yugoslavia), 1956. Grand-Officier de l'Ordre de la Couronne (Belgique); Hon. CBE (Great Britain), 1957; Grand Croix de l'Ordre du Dannebrog (Denmark), 1958; Grand Croix de l'Ordre de Leopold II (Belgique), 1967. *Publications:* L'Evolution du Syndicalisme aux Etats-Unis, de Washington à Roosevelt, 1936; Prix, monnaie, production: Essai sur les mouvements économiques de longue durée, 1945; Europe and the United States in the World Economy, 1953. *Address:* 9 rue de Valois, 75001 Paris, France. *T:* 261.3758.

MARJORIBANKS, Edyth Leslia, MA; JP; Headmistress, The Henrietta Barnett School, London, since 1973; *b* 17 Feb. 1927; *d* of Stewart Dudley Marjoribanks and Nancye (*née* Lee). *Educ:* Cheltenham Ladies' Coll.; Girton Coll., Cambridge (BA Hons Hist. 1951, MA 1955); Hughes Hall, Cambridge (Certif. Educn 1952). Talbot Heath, Bournemouth: Asst History Mistress, 1952-57; Head of History Dept, 1957-68; Headmistress, Holly Lodge High Sch., Liverpool, 1969-73. Mem. Governing Council, Examinations Cttee and Curriculum Sub-Cttee of North-West Sec. Schs Exam. Board, 1969-73. JP City of Liverpool, 1971-73, Inner London, 1976. *Address:* 29 Park Farm Close, N2 0PU. *T:* 01-883 6609.

MARJORIBANKS, Sir James Alexander Milne, KCMG 1965 (CMG 1954); Director, Scottish Council (Development and Industry), and Chairman, EEC Committee, since 1971; *b* 29 May 1911; *y s* of Rev. Thomas Marjoribanks, DD, and Mary Ord, *d* of William Logan, Madras CS; *m* 1936, Sonya Patricia, *d* of David Stanley-Alder, Alderford Grange, Sible Hedingham, Essex, and Sylvia Marie Stanley; one *d. Educ:* Merchiston; Edinburgh Academy; Edinburgh Univ. (MA, 1st class hons). Entered Foreign Service, Nov. 1934; HM Embassy, Peking, 1935-38; Consulate-General, Hankow, 1938; Marseilles, 1939-40; Consul, Jacksonville, 1940-42; Vice-Consul, New York, 1942-44; Asst to UK Political Rep., Bucharest, 1944-45; Foreign Office, 1945-49; Dep. to Secretary of State for Foreign Affairs in Austrian Treaty negotiations, 1947-49; Official Secretary, UK High Commn, Canberra, 1950-52; Dep. Head of UK Delegation to High Authority of European Coal and Steel Community, 1952-55; Cabinet Office, 1955-57; HM Minister (Economic), Bonn, 1957-62; Asst Under-Secretary of State, Foreign Office, 1962-65; Ambassador and Head of UK Delegn to European Economic Community, European Atomic Energy Community and ECSC, 1965-71. Dir, The Distillers Co. Ltd, 1971-76. Gen. Council Assessor, Edinburgh Univ. Ct, 1975-. *Recreations:* mountaineering, golf. *Address:* 13 Regent Terrace, Edinburgh EH7 5BN; Lintonrig, Kirk Yetholm, Roxburghshire TD5 8PH. *Club:* New (Edinburgh).

MARK, James, MBE 1943; Under-Secretary, Ministry of Overseas Development, 1965-74, retired; *b* 12 June 1914; *s* of late John Mark and Louisa Mary (*née* Hobson); *m* 1941, Mary Trewent Rowland; three *s* two *d. Educ:* William Hulme's Grammar Sch., Manchester; Trinity Coll., Cambridge; Universities of Munich and Münster. MA 1939. PhD 1939, Cambridge. Intelligence Corps, 1940-46. Principal, Control Office for Germany and Austria, 1946-48; HM Treasury, 1948-64; Asst Secretary, 1950; Economic Counsellor, Washington, 1951-53. Jt Editor, Theology, 1976-. *Publications:* The Question of Christian Stewardship, 1964; articles and reviews on theological and related subjects. *Recreations:* reading, music, gardening. *Address:* 6 Manorbrook, SE3. *T:* 01-852 9289.
See also Sir Robert Mark.

MARK, Sir Robert, GBE 1977; Kt 1973; QPM 1965; Commissioner, Metropolitan Police, 1972-77 (Deputy Commissioner, 1968-72); Director, Phoenix Assurance Co. Ltd, since 1977; *b* Manchester, 13 March 1917; *y s* of late John Mark and Louisa Mark (*née* Hobson); *m* 1941, Kathleen Mary Leahy; one *s* one *d. Educ:* William Hulme's Grammar Sch., Manchester. Constable to Chief Superintendent, Manchester City Police, 1937-42, 1947-56; Chief Constable of Leicester, 1957-67; Assistant Commissioner, Metropolitan Police, 1967-68. Vis. Fellow, Nuffield Coll., Oxford, 1970- (MA Oxon 1971). Member: Standing Advisory Council of Penal System, 1966; Adv. Cttee on Police in Northern Ireland, 1969; Assessor to Lord Mountbatten during his Inquiry into Prison Security, 1966. Royal Armoured Corps, 1942-47: Lieut, Phantom (GHQ Liaison Regt), North-West Europe, 1944-45; Major, Control Commission for Germany, 1945-47. Lecture tour of N America for World Affairs Council and FCO, Oct. 1971; Edwin Stevens Lecture to the Laity, RCM, 1972; Dimbleby Meml Lecture (BBC TV), 1973. Mem. Council, AA, 1977-; Hon. Freeman, City of Westminster, 1977. Hon. LLM Leicester Univ., 1967; Hon. DLitt Loughborough, 1976. *Publication:* Policing a Perplexed Society, 1977. *Address:* Esher, Surrey KT10 8LU.
See also James Mark.

MARKALL, Most Rev. Francis, SJ; *b* 24 Sept. 1905; *e s* of late Walter James Markall and Alice Mary Gray, London. *Educ:* St Ignatius' College, London. Entered Society of Jesus, 1924; continued classical and philosophical studies, 1926-31; Assistant Master, Stonyhurst College, 1931-34; theological studies, 1934-38; Missionary in Rhodesia, 1939-56; Titular Archbishop of Cotieo and Coadjutor with right of succession to Archbishop of Salisbury, April 1956; Archbishop of Salisbury and Metropolitan of Province of Rhodesia, Nov. 1956; retired, 1976. *Address:* c/o PO Box 8060, Causeway, Rhodesia. *Club:* Salisbury (Salisbury).

MARKHAM, Rt. Rev. Bernard; Assistant Bishop, Diocese of Southwark, since 1977; *b* 26 Feb. 1907. *Educ:* Bingley Grammar School; Leeds University (BA Hons History, 1928); College of the Resurrection. Deacon, 1930; Priest 1931. Curate of: Lidget Green, 1930-35; S Francis, N Kensington, 1935-37; Stoke-on-Trent, 1937-39; Vicar of Bierley, 1939-46; Rector of St Benedict, Ardwick, 1946-59; Vicar of St Margaret's, Liverpool, 1959-62; Bishop of Nassau and the Bahamas, 1962-72; Asst Bishop, Dio. of Southwell and Rector of E Bridgford, 1972-77. *Address:* 41 Elm Bank Gardens, Barnes, SW13 0NX.

MARKHAM, Sir Charles (John); 3rd Bt, *cr* 1911; *b* 2 July 1924; *s* of Sir Charles Markham, 2nd Bt, and Gwladys, *e d* of late Hon. Rupert Beckett; *S* father 1952; *m* 1949, Valerie, *o d* of Lt-Col E. Barry-Johnston, Makuyu, Kenya; two *s* one *d. Educ:* Eton. Served War of 1939-45, Lieut in 11th Hussars (despatches). Vice-Chm., Nairobi Co. Council, 1953-55; MLC Kenya, 1955-60. Pres., Royal Agricultural Soc., Kenya, 1958. KStJ 1973. *Heir: s* Arthur David Markham, *b* 6 Dec. 1950. *Address:* PO Box 42263, Nairobi, Kenya, East Africa. *Club:* Cavalry and Guards.

MARKHAM, Roy, FRS 1956; MA, PhD; John Innes Professor of Cell Biology and Director, John Innes Institute, University of East Anglia, Norwich, since 1967; Director, Agricultural Research Council Virus Research Unit, 1960-67 (Hon. Director, 1967-68); *b* 29 Jan. 1916; *m* 1940, Margaret Mullen. *Educ:* St Paul's; Christ's Coll., Cambridge. Fellow of Christ's Coll., Cambridge, 1965-67. Mem. of Council, John Innes Inst., 1964-67. Hon. Mem., Amer. Soc. of Biological Chemists. *Publications:* various. *Address:* John Innes Institute, Colney Lane, Norwich NR4 7UH. *T:* Norwich 52571; 10 Daniels Road, Norwich NR4 6Q2. *T:* Norwich 53429.

MARKING, Henry Ernest, CBE 1969; MC 1944; CompRAeS 1953; FCIT; Chairman, British Tourist Authority, since 1977 (Member, 1969-77); Member, British Airways, since 1971; *b* 11

March 1920; *s* of late Isaac and Hilda Jane Marking. *Educ:* Saffron Walden Gram. Sch.; University Coll., London. Served War of 1939-45: 2nd Bn The Sherwood Foresters, 1941-45; North Africa, Italy and Middle East; Adjutant, 1944-45. Middle East Centre of Arab Studies, Jerusalem, 1945-46. Admitted solicitor, 1948. Asst Solicitor, Cripps, Harries, Hall & Co., Tunbridge Wells, 1948-49; Asst Solicitor, 1949, Sec., 1950, Chief Exec., 1964-72, Chm., 1971-72, BEA; Mem. Bd, BOAC, 1971-72; British Airways Board: Man. Dir, 1972-76; Dep. Chm., 1972-77; Mem., 1977-. Dir, Barclays Bank Internat. Ltd, 1977-. Trustee and Vice-Chm., Leonard Cheshire Foundn, 1962-. FBIM 1971. *Club:* Reform.

MARKOVA, Dame Alicia, DBE 1963 (CBE 1958); **(Dame Lilian Alicia Marks);** Prima Ballerina Assoluta; Professor of Ballet and Performing Arts, College-Conservatory of Music, University of Cincinnati, since 1970; *b* London 1910; *d* of Arthur Tristman Marks and Eileen Barry. With Diaghilev's Russian Ballet Co., 1925-29; Rambert Ballet Club, 1931-33; Vic-Wells Ballet Co., 1933-35; Markova-Dolin Ballet Co., 1935-37; Ballet Russe de Monte Carlo, 1938-41; Ballet Theatre, USA, 1941-46. Appeared with Anton Dolin, guest and concert performances, 1948-50. Co-Founder and Prima Ballerina, Festival Ballet, 1950-51; Guest Prima Ballerina: Buenos Aires, 1952; Royal Ballet, 1953 and 1957; Royal Danish Ballet, 1955; Scala, Milan, 1956; Teatro Municipal, Rio de Janeiro, 1956; Festival Ballet, 1958 and 1959; Guest appearances at Metropolitan Opera House, New York, 1952, 1953-54, 1955, 1957, 1958; Dir, Metropolitan Opera Ballet, 1963-69; produced Les Sylphides for Festival Ballet and Aust. Ballet, 1976. Guest Professor: Royal Ballet Sch., 1973-; Paris Opera Ballet, 1975; Australian Ballet Sch., 1976. Vice-Pres., Royal Acad. of Dancing, 1958-; Governor, Royal Ballet, 1973-. Concert, television and guest appearances (general), 1952-61. BBC series, Markova's Ballet Call, 1960. Queen Elizabeth II Coronation Award, Royal Acad. of Dancing, 1963. Hon. DMus Leicester, 1966. *Publication:* Giselle and I, 1960. *Address:* c/o Barclays Bank Ltd, 451 Oxford Street, W1.

MARKS, family name of **Baron Marks of Broughton.**

MARKS OF BROUGHTON, 2nd Baron, *cr* 1961; **Michael Marks;** *b* 27 Aug. 1920; *o s* of 1st Baron and Miriam (*d* 1971), *d* of Ephraim Sieff; *S* father 1964; *m*; one *s* two *d*. *Heir:* son.

MARKS, Bernard Montague; Chairman and Managing Director, Alfred Marks Bureau Limited, since 1958; Chairman, Federation of Personnel Services of Great Britain, since 1974; Member of Lloyd's, since 1973; *b* 11 Oct. 1923; *s* of Alfred and Elizabeth Marks; *m* 1956, Norma Renton; two *s*. *Educ:* Highgate Public Sch.; Royal Coll. of Science. *Publication:* Once Upon A Typewriter, 1977. *Recreations:* bridge, golf, tennis, skiing. *Address:* Charters, South Ridge, St George's Hill, Weybridge, Surrey. *Clubs:* St George's Hill Golf, St George's Hill Tennis.

MARKS, John Emile, CBE 1970; President of DV Group Ltd since 1958; *s* of late Hyam and Miriam Marks; *m*; two *s* two *d*. *Educ:* Eton College. Served War of 1939-45 (despatches 1944; 1939-45 Star, France and Germany Star, Defence and Victory Medals). Emigrated to Canada, 1951; estab. John Marks Ltd, importers and distributors of sporting goods, 1952; Pres., Douglas Engineering Co. Ltd, Toronto, 1956; estab. Canair Ltd, Windsor, England, 1962 (Chm. and majority shareholder); bought controlling interest in DV Group Ltd, 1963 (inc. Douglas Engrg, Engmark Western Ltd and EngMark Ltd). Pres., British Canadian Trade Assoc., 1966-67, 1969-70; returned to England, 1972; Pres., Canada UK Chamber of Commerce, 1975-76; Vice-Chm., Westminster Chamber of Commerce. *Recreations:* tennis, golf, squash. *Address:* 25 Montrose Court, Princes Gate, SW7 2QQ; DV Group Ltd, PO Box 5500, Don Mills, Ont, Canada. *Clubs:* Bath, Queen's, Royal Automobile; Toronto Cricket, Skating and Curling, Queen's (Toronto).

MARKS, Sir John (Hedley Douglas), Kt 1972; CBE 1966; FCA; Chairman, Development Finance Corporation Ltd, since inception, 1955 (Managing Director, 1955-75); Commissioner, Electricity Commission of NSW; Chairman: Acmil Ltd; Development Holdings Ltd; Garratt's Ltd; Reinsurance Co. of Australasia Ltd; Directorships include: Brambles Industries Ltd (Deputy Chairman); CHEP International Finance SA; CHEP International Investments SA; West Lakes Ltd; Borg-Warner (Aust.) Ltd; Canada Aust. Invest Co. Ltd; DevWest Ltd; Japan Aust. Invest Co. Ltd; R. D. C. Holdings Ltd; Alcan Australia Ltd; Dickson Primer (Consolidated) Ltd; First New Zealand International Ltd; *b* 8 May 1916; *s* of late Frederick William Marks, CBE, and late Viva Bessie Meurant Stinson; *m* 1941, Judith Norma Glenwright; two *d*. *Educ:* St Peter's Prep. Sch.;

Sydney Church of England Sch. Qualified as Chartered Accountant and Secretary, and commenced practice on own behalf, 1937. Served War of 1939-45: enlisted in 2nd AIF, 1939; commissioned, 1941, and rose to rank of Lt-Col. Founded Development Finance Corp. Ltd, Investment Bankers, 1955. Mem., Cttee on Community Health Services (Starr Report), 1968-69; Chm., Cttee of Inquiry into State Taxation (NSW), 1975-76. Chairman Emeritus: The Prince Henry Hosp.; The Prince of Wales Hosp.; Eastern Suburbs Hosp. *Recreations:* yachting, golf, tennis. *Address:* 6b Raglan Street, Mosman, NSW 2088, Australia. *T:* 960 2221. *Clubs:* Australian, Royal Sydney Yacht, Elanora Country, American National, Manly Golf (all in NSW).

MARKS, Kenneth; MP (Lab) Gorton since Nov. 1967; Parliamentary Under-Secretary of State, Department of the Environment, since 1975; *b* 15 June 1920; *s* of Robert P. Marks, Electrician and Edith Collins, Cotton Weaver; *m* 1944, Kathleen Lynch; one *s* one *d*. *Educ:* Peacock Street Sch., Gorton; Central High Sch., Manchester; Didsbury Coll. of Education. Worked in offices of LNER, 1936-40. Joined ranks, Grenadier Guards, 1940-42; commnd into Cheshire Regt, 1942-46 (Capt.); served in Middle East, Malta, Italy, NW Europe and Germany as Infantry Platoon and Company Comdr. Taught in Manchester schs, 1946-67; Headmaster, Clough Top Sec. Sch. for Boys, 1964-67. Parliamentary Private Secretary: to Rt Hon. Anthony Crosland, 1969-70; to Roy Hattersley, 1974-75; to Rt Hon. Harold Wilson, 1975. Member: House of Commons Select Cttee for Educn and Science, 1968-70; Exec. Cttee, Commonwealth Parly Assoc., 1972-75; Select Cttee on Expenditure, 1974-75; Opposition Whip, 1971-72; Chm., Parly Labour Party Educn Gp, 1972-75, NW Reg. Gp, 1974-; Mem., N Atlantic Assembly, 1974-75. *Address:* 1 Epping Road, Denton, Manchester M34 2GB. *T:* 061-336 4147.

MARLAND, Michael, CBE 1977; Headmaster, Woodberry Down School, since 1971; *b* 28 Dec. 1934; *m* 1st, 1955, Eileen (*d* 1968); four *s* one *d*; 2nd, 1971, Rose. *Educ:* Christ's Hospital Sch.; Sidney Sussex Coll., Cambridge (BA). Head of English, Abbey Wood Sch., 1961-64; Head of English and subseq. Dir of Studies, Crown Woods Sch., 1964-71. Member of many educn cttees, incl. Bullock Cttee, Schools Council English Cttee (Chm.). *Publications:* Towards The New Fifth, 1969; The Practice of English Teaching, 1970; Peter Grimes, 1971; Head of Department, 1971; Pastoral Care, 1974; The Craft of the Classroom, 1975; Language Across the Curriculum, 1977; General Editor of: Blackie's Student Drama Series; Longman Imprint Books; The Times Authors; Heinemann Organisation in Schools Series; contrib. Times Educnl Supplement. *Recreations:* music, literature. *Address:* 22 Compton Terrace, N1 2UN. *T:* 01-226 0648; The Green Farmhouse, Cranmer Green, Walshamle-Willows, Bury St Edmunds, Suffolk. *T:* 483.

MARLAR, Edward Alfred Geoffrey, MBE 1944; MA, LLB Cantab; retired as Headmaster of Whitgift School, Croydon (1946-July 1961); *b* 2 Jan. 1901; *s* of J. F. Marlar; *m* 1924, Winifred Stevens; one *s* one *d*. *Educ:* Brighton Coll.; Selwyn Coll., Cambridge (Hons History and Law). Senior History Master, Dunstable Gram. Sch., 1922-27; Senior History and VIth Form Master, Worksop Coll., 1927-34; Headmaster, Moulton Gram. Sch., 1934-37; Headmaster, King Edward VI Sch., Lichfield, 1937-46. *Address:* Warren Edge, Salisbury Road, Eastbourne, E Sussex.

MARLBOROUGH, 11th Duke of, *cr* 1702; **John George Vanderbilt Henry Spencer-Churchill;** DL; Baron Spencer, 1603; Earl of Sunderland, 1643; Baron Churchill, 1685; Earl of Marlborough, 1689; Marquis of Blandford, 1702; Prince of the Holy Roman Empire; Prince of Mindelheim in Suabia; late Captain Life Guards; *b* 13 April 1926; *s* of 10th Duke of Marlborough and Hon. Alexandra Mary Hilda Cadogan, CBE (*d* 1961), *d* of late Henry Arthur, Viscount Chelsea; *S* father, 1972; *m* 1st, 1951, Susan Mary (marr. diss., 1960; she *m* 1962, Alan Cyril Heber-Percy), *d* of Michael Hornby, *qv*; one *s* one *d* (and one *s* decd); 2nd, 1961, Mrs Athina Livanos (marr. diss. 1971; she *d* 1974), *d* of late Stavros G. Livanos, Paris; 3rd, 1972, Rosita Douglas; one *s* one *d* (and one *s* decd). *Educ:* Eton. Lieut Life Guards, 1946; Captain, 1953; resigned commission, 1953. CC 1961, Oxfordshire; JP 1962; DL 1974. *Heir: s* Marquess of Blandford, *qv*. *Address:* Blenheim Palace, Woodstock, Oxon. *Clubs:* Portland, White's.

MARLER, Leslie Sydney, OBE 1957; TD 1946; Hon. President, Capital & Counties Property Co. Ltd, 1971-73 (Chairman, 1950-71); Director, Norwich Union Insurance Societies, 1972-75, Chairman, London Board, 1974-75 (Deputy Chairman, 1972-73); Chairman, Marler Estates Ltd, since 1972; *b* 7 July 1900; *e s* of L. T. Marler, Birdham, Sussex; *m* 1926, Doris Marguerite (JP

Bucks, 1946), 3rd *d* of late H. E. Swaffer, Brighton; one *s* one *d* (and one *s* decd). *Educ:* St Paul's Sch. Served European War, 1914-18, with HAC, 1917-19; re-employed, 1939, as Captain RA; Major 1941; retd 1945. Chm. Buckingham Div., Conservative Assoc., 1946-56, Pres., 1955-77. Master, Worshipful Co. of Merchant Taylors, 1960. Life Mem., Court of The City University, 1970. High Sheriff, Bucks, 1971-72. *Recreations:* fox-hunting, bloodstock breeding, golf, collecting first editions, travel. *Address:* Bolebec House, Whitchurch, Bucks. *T:* Whitchurch 231. *Club:* Junior Carlton.

MARLEY, 2nd Baron *cr* 1930, of Marley in the County of Sussex; **Godfrey Pelham Leigh Aman;** Film Producer; *b* 6 Sept. 1913; *s* of 1st Baron and Octable Turquet (*d* 1969), *d* of late Sir Hugh Gilzean-Reid, DL, LLD, formerly MP for Aston Manor; *S* father 1952; *m* 1956, Catherine Doone Beal. *Educ:* Bedales Sch. Royal Marines, 1939-45. *Heir:* none. *Address:* 104 Ebury Mews, SW1. *T:* 01-730 4844.

MARLING, Sir Charles (William Somerset), 5th Bt *cr* 1882; *b* 2 June 1951; *s* of Sir John Stanley Vincent Marling, 4th Bt, OBE, and Georgina Brenda (Betty) (*d* 1961), *o d* of late Henry Edward FitzRoy Somerset; *S* father, 1977. *Address:* Woodcray Manor Farm, Wokingham, Berks RG11 3HG.

MARLOW, Roger Douglas Frederick, DSC 1943; JP; Deputy Director-General, Institute of Directors, 1975-77; *b* 21 Aug. 1912; *s* of Frederick George Marlow and Mabel Marlow(e), authoress; *m* 1st 1951, Mary (Bernadette Teresa) Savage, actress (*d* 1972); two *s* one *d*; 2nd, 1977, Jean Marian White (*née* Watts). *Educ:* Christ's Hospital; London School of Economics and Political Science. BScEcon (Hons). Initial trng in merchant banking, 1934-35; Executive, Overseas Sections, London Chamber of Commerce, 1935-39. War service, 1939-46, Lt-Comdr RNVR (Commendation (Naval) 1941, DSC). Dep. Asst Sec., London Chamber of Commerce, 1946-60; concurrently, Chief Executive and Secretary: London Building Acts Cttee; Mica Trade Assoc.; Horological Trade Pool Ltd (incl. import Licence admin for BoT); British Essence Mfrs Assoc.; British Aromatic Compound Mfrs Assoc.; Asst Dir-Gen. and Educn Dir, Inst. of Dirs, 1960-75. Member: Essential Oils Adv. Cttee (Govt and Industry), 1946-51; Adv. Panel, PER, Dept of Employment, 1972-; Co-ordinating Sec., Sino-British Trade Council, 1954-60; Mem., Negotiating Mission to USSR for Estabt of Reciprocal Trade Fairs, 1959. Mem. Council, Nat. Inst. of Industrial Psychology, 1960-74; Mem. Court and Council, Univ. of Sussex, 1970-. JP E Sussex, Brighton Div., 1965-. *Publications:* Selling to Finland, 1959; Trading with the Soviet Union, 1959; various articles in trade and professional jls. *Recreations:* tennis, swimming, music, painting, bridge. *Address:* 5 Surrenden Crescent, Brighton, Sussex BN1 6WE. *T:* Brighton 503072.

MARMION, Prof. Barrie P.; Professor of Bacteriology, University of Edinburgh, since 1968; *b* 19 May 1920; *s* of J. P. and M. H. Marmion, Alverstoke, Hants; *m* 1953, Diana Ray Newling, *d* of Dr P. Ray Newling, Adelaide, SA; one *d*. *Educ:* University Coll. and University Coll. Hosp., London. MD London 1947, MRCPA 1963, DSc London 1963, FRCPath 1962, FRCPE 1970. House Surg., UCH, 1942; Bacteriologist, Public Health Laboratory Service, 1943-62; Rockefeller Trav. Fellow, at Walter and Eliza Hall Inst., Melbourne, 1951-52; Foundation Prof., Microbiology, Monash Univ., Melbourne, Australia, 1962-68. *Publications:* (ed) Cruickshank's Medical Microbiology, 12th edn 1973; numerous papers on bacteriology and virology. *Recreations:* tennis, squash, music. *Address:* Flat 1, Ravelston Heights, Ravelston House Park, Edinburgh EH4 3LX. *T:* 031-332 8185.

MARNAN, John Fitzgerald, MBE 1944; QC 1954; **His Honour Judge Marnan;** a Circuit Judge, sitting at Central Criminal Court, since 1972; *b* 23 Jan. 1908; *s* of late T. G. Marnan, Irish Bar; *m* 1st, 1934, Morwenna (marr. diss., 1953), *d* of late Sir Keith Price; one *s* (and one *s* decd); 2nd, 1958, Mrs Diana Back (marr. diss., 1963), *o d* of late Comdr Charles Crawshay, RN (retd), and late Mrs M. L. Greville; 3rd, 1966, Joanna, *o d* of late Maj.-Gen. W. N. Herbert, CB, CMG, DSO. *Educ:* Ampleforth; Trinity Coll., Oxford. Commnd TA (Oxford Univ. OTC), 1929. Called to Bar, 1931; joined Chester and N Wales Circuit; joined Supplementary Reserve, Irish Guards, 1936; served War of 1939-45 (MBE, despatches); Western Europe with Irish Guards, and on staff of 15th (Scottish) Div.; Major (GSO2), 1944. A Metropolitan Magistrate, 1956-58, resigned. Crown Counsel in the Ministry of Legal Affairs, Kenya Government, 1958-59; Federal Justice of the Federal Supreme Court, the West Indies, 1959-62; subseq. Justice of Appeal of the British Caribbean Court of Appeal. Sat as Commissioner at Crown Courts, at Manchester, 1962-63, at Liverpool, 1963, and at Central

Criminal Court, 1964-66; a Dep. Chm., Greater London Sessions, 1966-68; Chm., NE London QS, 1968-71. *Recreation:* field sports. *Address:* 166 Cranmer Court, SW3. *T:* 01-589 5629. *Clubs:* Cavalry and Guards, Pratt's.

MARNHAM, Harold, MBE 1945; QC 1965; Barrister-at-Law; Leader of Parliamentary Bar, 1967-74; *b* 14 July 1911; *y s* of late Arthur Henry Marnham and late Janet Elizabeth Marnham; *m* 1947, Hilary, *y d* of late Ernest Jukes; two *s*. *Educ:* Stellenbosch Boys' High Sch.; Stellenbosch Univ.; Jesus Coll., Cambridge. Called to Bar, Gray's Inn, 1935; Bencher, 1969. Served War 1939-45; BEF, 1939-40; BLA, 1944-45 (despatches); 2nd Lt RA (TA); Capt. 1940; Major 1942; Lt-Col 1945. Dep. Chm., Oxfordshire QS, 1966-71. Chm., Industrial Tribunals, 1975-. *Address:* 1 Raymond Buildings, Gray's Inn, WC1R 5BH. *T:* 01-242 2615. *Clubs:* Hawks (Cambridge); Leander (Henley-on-Thames).

MARNHAM, John Ewart, CMG 1955; MC 1944; TD 1949; HM Diplomatic Service, retired; *b* Hampstead, 24 Jan. 1916; *er s* of late Col Arthur Ewart Marnham, MC, TD, DL, JP, Foxley Grove, Holyport, Berks, and late Dorothy Clare Morgan; *m* 1944, Susan, *er d* of late Walter Foster (formerly Friedenstein), Vienna and London; two *s*. *Educ:* Mill Hill; Jesus Coll., Cambridge. Asst Principal, Colonial Office, 1938. Served War, 1939-45: BEF 1939-40; BLA 1944-45 (despatches); 2nd Lt RA (TA) 1938; Major, 1942; Lt-Col, Commanding 353 (London) Medium Regt RA (TA), 1954-57; Brevet Col, 1958. Principal, Colonial Office, 1946; Asst Sec. 1948; Imperial Defence Coll., 1961; Asst Under-Sec. of State: CO, 1964; Foreign Office, 1966-67; Consul-Gen., Johannesburg, 1967-70; British Govt Rep., WI Associated States, 1970-73; Ambassador to Tunisia, 1973-75. Clerk in Cttee Office, House of Commons, 1977-. *Recreations:* reading, gardening, riding. *Address:* Glebe House, Blake's Lane, Hare Hatch, Berks RG10 9TD. *T:* Wargrave 3469. *Club:* United Oxford & Cambridge University.

MARNHAM, Sir Ralph, KCVO 1957; MChir, FRCS; Serjeant Surgeon to the Queen, 1967-71; Consulting Surgeon to: St George's Hospital; King Edward VII's Hospital for Officers; Fellow: Medical Society of London; Association of Surgeons of Great Britain and Ireland; *b* 7 June 1901; *e s* of Arthur Henry Marnham and late Janet Elizabeth Micklem; *m* 1st, 1927, Muriel, *y d* of Herbert Marnham; one *d*; 2nd, 1942, Helena Mary, *e d* of Patrick Daly; two *s*. *Educ:* Diocesan Coll., Rondebosch, South Africa; Gonville and Caius Coll., Cambridge; St George's Hospital. Allingham Scholarship Surgery; Sir Francis Laking Research Scholarship; Moynihan Fellow Assoc. of Surgeons of Great Britain and Ireland. War of 1939-45: Officer in Charge Surgical Divs of No. 62 and 6 Gen. Hospitals. Cons. Surgeon, 9th Army, East Africa and Southern Command (despatches twice). Usual House Appointments St George's Hospital; also Asst Curator of Museum, Surgical Registrar, and Resident Asst Surgeon. *Publications:* various in medical journals. *Recreation:* golf. *Address:* 74 Eyre Court, Finchley Road, NW8 9TX. *T:* 01-586 3001. *Clubs:* Buck's, Pratt's.

MAROWITZ, Charles; Artistic Director, The Open Space Theatre, since 1968; *b* 26 Jan. 1934; Austrian mother, Russian father. *Educ:* Seward Park High Sch.; University Coll. London. Dir, In-Stage Experimental Theatre, 1958; Asst Dir, Royal Shakespeare Co., 1963-65; Artistic Dir, Traverse Theatre, 1963-64. Drama Critic: Encore Magazine, 1956-63; Plays and Players, 1958-74; The Village Voice, 1955-; The NY Times, 1966-. West End Director: Loot, Criterion, 1967; The Bellow Plays, Fortune, 1966; Fortune and Men's Eyes, Comedy, 1969, etc. Order of the Purple Sash, 1969. *Publications:* The Method as Means, 1960; The Marowitz Hamlet, 1967; A Macbeth, 1970; Confessions of a Counterfeit Critic, 1973; Open Space Plays, 1974; Measure for Measure, 1975; The Shrew, 1975; Artaud at Rodez, 1976; The Act of Being, 1977. *Recreation:* balling. *Address:* The Open Space Theatre, 303 Euston Road, NW1.

MARPLES, family name of **Baron Marples.**

MARPLES, Baron *cr* 1974 (Life Peer), of Wallasey; **Alfred Ernest Marples,** PC 1957; FCA; FRSA; *b* 9 Dec. 1907; *s* of late Alfred Ernest Marples and late Mary Marples; *m* 1956, Mrs Ruth Dobson. *Educ:* Stretford Gram. Sch. Chartered Accountant, 1928; joined London Scottish, July 1939; 2nd Lt Royal Artillery, Jan. 1941; Captain, 1941. MP (C) Wallasey, 1945-Feb. 1974; Parly Sec., Ministry of Housing and Local Government, 1951-54; Joint Parliamentary Sec., Ministry of Pensions and National Insurance, Oct. 1954-Dec. 1955; Postmaster-Gen., 1957-59; Minister of Transport, Oct 1959-64, and Chm., Nationalized Transport Advisory Council, 1963-64; Shadow Minister of Technology, 1964-66; Sponsor,

Conservative Party Public Sector Research Unit, 1967-70. Internat. Dir, Purolator Services Inc. (USA), 1970-; Dir, Purolator Services Ltd (UK), 1970-. Hon. Freeman, Borough of Wallasey, 1970. *Publication:* The Road to Prosperity, 1947. *Recreations:* tennis, mountaineering. *Address:* Les Laverts, Fleurie 69820, France.

MARPLES, Brian John; Emeritus Professor of Zoology, University of Otago, NZ; *b* 31 March 1907; 2nd *s* of George and Anne Marples; *m* 1931, Mary Joyce Ransford; two *s. Educ:* St Bees Sch.; Exeter Coll., Oxford. Lecturer in Zoology, Univ. of Manchester, 1929-35; Lecturer in Zoology, Univ. of Bristol, 1935-37; Prof. of Zoology, Univ. of Otago, NZ, 1937-67. *Publications:* Freshwater Life in New Zealand, 1962; various technical zoological and archaeological papers. *Address:* 1 Vanbrugh Close, Old Woodstock, Oxon.

MARQUAND, David (Ian); Chief Adviser, Secretariat-General, Commission of the European Communities, since 1977; *b* 20 Sept. 1934; *s* of Rt Hon. Hilary Marquand, PC; *m* 1959, Judith Mary (*née* Reed); one *s* one *d. Educ:* Emanuel Sch.; Magdalen Coll., Oxford; St Antony's Coll., Oxford (Sen. Schol.). 1st cl. hons Mod. Hist., 1957. Teaching Asst, Univ. of Calif., 1958-59; Leader Writer, The Guardian, 1959-62; Research Fellow, St Antony's Coll., Oxford, 1962-64; Lectr in Politics, Univ. of Sussex, 1964-66. Contested (Lab) Barry, 1964; MP (Lab) Ashfield, 1966-77; PPS to Minister of Overseas Develt, 1967-69; Jun. Opposition Front-Bench Spokesman on econ. affairs, 1971-72; Member: Select Cttee on Estimates, 1966-68; Select Cttee on Procedure, 1968-73; Select Cttee on Corp. Tax, 1971; British Deleg. to Council of Europe, 1970-73. *Publications:* Ramsay MacDonald, 1977; articles and reviews in Guardian, The Times, The Sunday Times, New Statesman, Encounter, Commentary, etc. *Recreation:* walking. *Address:* Commission of the European Communities, 200 Rue de la Loi, 1049 Brussels, Belgium; 9 Highgate Avenue, N6.

MARQUIS, family name of **Earl of Woolton.**

MARQUIS, James Douglas, DFC 1945; Managing Director, Irvine Development Corporation, since 1972; *b* 16 Oct. 1921; *s* of James Charles Marquis and Jessica Amy (*née* Huggett); *m* 1945, Brenda Eleanor, *d* of Robert Rayner Davey; two *s. Educ:* Shooters Hill Sch., Woolwich. Local Govt, 1938-41. Served War: RAF: Navigation Officer, 1941-46 (RAF 1st cl. Air Navigation Warrant, 1945), 177 Sqdn, 224 Gp, and AHQ Malaya (Sqdn Ldr 1945). Local Govt, 1946-56; Harlow Develt Corp., 1956-68; Irvine Develt Corp.: Chief Finance Officer, 1968-72; Dir of Finance and Admin., 1972. FRMetS 1945; IPFA 1950; FCIS 1953. *Recreations:* sketching and painting (two one-man exhibns; works in collections: Rhodesia, Japan, Denmark, USA, Canada); angling, gardening, ornithology, golf. *Address:* 3 Knoll Park, Ayr KA7 4RH. *T:* Alloway 42212.

MARR, Allan James, CBE 1965; Director and Chairman, EGS Co. Ltd; *b* 6 May 1907; *s* of late William Bell Marr and Hilda May Marr; *cousin* and *heir pres.* to Sir Leslie Lynn Marr, 2nd Bt, *qv*; *m* 1935, Joan de Wolf Ranken; one *s* two *d. Educ:* Oundle; Durham Univ. Apprenticeship, Joseph L. Thompson & Sons Ltd, 1926-31; joined Sir James Laing & Sons Ltd, 1932. Dir, Doxford and Sunderland Shipbuilding and Eng. Co. Ltd; retd from all shipbldg activities, 1973. Pres. Shipbuilding Conf., 1963-65; Fellow of North-East Coast Inst. of Engineers and Shipbuilders (Pres., 1966-68); Mem., RINA. Chm., Research Council of British Ship Research Assoc., 1965-73. *Recreations:* photography, fishing, shooting. *Address:* Dalesford, Thropton, Morpeth, Northumberland. *Club:* Royal Thames Yacht.

MARR, (Sir) Leslie Lynn, (2nd Bt, *cr* 1919, but does not use the title); MA Cambridge; late Flight Lieutenant RAF; *b* 14 Aug. 1922; *o s* of late Col John Lynn Marr, OBE, TD, (and *g s* of 1st Bt,) and Amelia Rachel, *d* of late Robert Thompson, Overdinsdale Hall, Darlington; *S* grandfather 1932; *m* 1st, 1948, Dinora Delores Mendelson (marr. diss. 1956); one *d*; 2nd, 1962, Lynn Heneage; two *d. Educ:* Shrewsbury; Pembroke Coll., Cambridge. *Heir:* cousin Allan James Marr, *qv. Address:* c/o Lloyds Bank, Holt, Norfolk.

MARRACK, Rear-Adm. Philip Reginald, CEng, FIMechE, FIMarE; AMBIM; Director of Dockyard Production and Support, since 1977; *b* 16 Nov. 1922; *s* of Captain Philip Marrack, RN and Annie Kathleen Marrack (*née* Proud); *m* 1954, Pauline Mary (*née* Haag); two *d. Educ:* Eltham Coll.; Plymouth Coll.; RNC Dartmouth; RN Engineering Coll., Manadon. War service at sea, HM Ships Orion and Argus, 1944-45; Advanced Engineering Course, RNC Greenwich, 1945-47; HM Submarines Templar and Token, 1947-50; served in Frigate Torquay, Aircraft Carriers Glory and Hermes, and MoD;

Captain 1965; Commanded Admiralty Reactor Test Estab., Dounreay, 1967-70; CSO (Mat.) on Staff of Flag Officer Submarines, and Asst Dir (Nuclear), Dockyard Dept, 1970-74; Rear-Adm. 1974; Dir, Naval Ship Production, 1974-77. *Recreations:* fly fishing, gardening, viticulture, wine making. *Address:* 26 Crowe Lane, Freshford, Bath BA3 6EB. *T:* Limpley Stoke 2267.

MARRE, Sir Alan (Samuel), KCB 1970 (CB 1955); Parliamentary Commissioner for Administration, 1971-76; ex officio Member, Council on Tribunals, 1971-76; *b* 25 Feb. 1914; *s* of late Joseph and late Rebecca Marre; *m* 1943, Romola Mary (*see* Lady Marre); one *s* one *d. Educ:* St Olave's and St Saviour's Grammar Sch., Southwark; Trinity Hall, Cambridge (Major open Schol.) John Stewart of Rannoch Schol. and 1st cl. hons Class. Trip. Parts I and II. Ministry of Health: Asst Principal, 1936; Principal, 1941; Asst Sec., 1946; Under-Sec., 1952-63; Under-Sec., Ministry of Labour, 1963-64; Dep. Sec.: Ministry of Health, 1964-66; Min. of Labour (later Dept of Employment and Productivity), 1966-68; Second Perm. Under-Sec. of State, Dept of Health and Social Security, 1968-71. Health Service Comr for England, Wales and Scotland, 1973-76; ex officio Mem. Commns for Local Admin., 1974-76. *Recreations:* reading, walking, travel. *Address:* 44 The Vale, NW11 8SG. *T:* 01-458 1787. *Clubs:* Athenæum, MCC.

MARRE, Romola Mary, (Lady Marre); Chairman, London Council of Social Service, since 1974; *b* 25 April 1920; *d* of late Aubrey John Gilling and Romola Marjorie Angier; *m* 1943, Sir Alan Samuel Marre, *qv*; one *s* one *d. Educ:* Chelmsford County High Sch. for Girls; Bedford Coll., Univ. of London. BA Hons Philosophy. Asst Principal (Temp.), Min. of Health, 1941-42; Sgt, subseq. Jun. Comdr, ATS Officer Selection Bd, 1942-45. Organiser, West Hampstead Citizen's Advice Bureau, 1962-65; Dep. Gen. Sec., Camden Council of Social Service, 1965-73; Adviser on Community Health Councils to DHSS, 1974-75. Member: Lord Chancellor's Adv. Cttee on Legal Aid, 1975-; Milk Marketing Bd, 1973-; Steering Cttee for Consumer and Retail Interests, Metrication Bd, 1971-; Chairman: Volunteer Centre, 1973-; Steering Cttee, Nat. Council for Community Health Councils, 1975-76. *Recreations:* cooking, gardening, walking, talking. *Address:* 44 The Vale, NW11 8SG. *T:* 01-458 1787.

MARRIAGE, John Goodbody, QC 1971; a Recorder of the Crown Court, since 1972; *b* 17 Aug. 1929; *s* of late Llewellyn Marriage and late Norah (*née* Goodbody); *m* 1955, Caroline June Swainson; two *s* four *d. Educ:* Downs Sch., Colwall; Leighton Park Sch., Reading; Trinity Hall, Cambridge (BA). Royal Marines, 1947-49. Called to Bar, Inner Temple, 1953. Dep. Chm., W Suffolk QS, 1965-71. Part-time Mem., Horserace Betting Levy Bd, 1976-77. Vice-Chm., Criminal Bar Assoc., 1977. *Recreation:* horses (for pleasure not profit). *Address:* South End House, Bassingbourn, Cambs. *T:* Royston 42327. *Clubs:* Norfolk (Norwich); Lough Derg Yacht.

MARRIAN, Guy Frederic, CBE 1969; FRS 1944; Fellow of University College, London, 1946; Director of Research, Imperial Cancer Research Fund, 1959-68; Professor of Chemistry in Relation to Medicine in the University of Edinburgh, 1939-Sept. 1959; *b* 3 March 1904; *s* of late Frederick York Marrian, AMICE, and of late Mary Eddington Currie; *m* 1928, Phyllis May Lewis; two *d. Educ:* Tollington Sch., London N; University Coll., London. BSc (Hons), 1925; DSc (London), 1930; FRIC 1931; Meldola Medallist, Institute of Chemistry, 1931; William Julius Mickle Fellowship, University of London, 1932; Francis Amory Prize, Amer. Acad. Arts and Sciences, 1948; Beit Memorial Fellowship for Medical Research, 1927-30; Sir Henry Dale Medallist of the Society for Endocrinology, 1966. Lecturer in Dept of Biochemistry, University Coll., London, 1930-33; Assoc. Prof. of Biochemistry, University of Toronto, 1933-36; Prof. of Biochemistry, Univ. of Toronto, 1936-38. Hon. MD Edinburgh, 1975. *Publications:* papers in Biochemical Journal, Journal of Biological Chemistry, etc, mainly on the chemistry of the sex-hormones. *Address:* School Cottage, Ickham, Canterbury, Kent. *T:* Littlebourne 317. *Club:* Athenæum.

MARRINER, Neville; conductor; Founder and Director, Academy of St Martin in the Fields, since 1956; Los Angeles Chamber Orchestra, since 1968; *b* 15 April 1924; *s* of Herbert Henry Marriner and Ethel May Roberts; *m* 1955, Elizabeth Mary Sims; one *s* one *d. Educ:* Lincoln Sch.; Royal College of Music (ARCM). Taught music at Eton Coll., 1948; Prof., Royal Coll. of Music, 1950. Martin String Quartet, 1949; Jacobean Ensemble, 1951; London Symphony Orchestra, 1954. Hon. RAM. *Address:* 67 Cornwall Gardens, SW7 4BA. *Club:* Garrick.

MARRIOTT, Hugh Leslie, CBE 1946; MD London; FRCP; formerly: Consulting Physician; Physician Middlesex Hospital; Lecturer in Middlesex Hospital Medical School; Hon. Consulting Physician to the Army; Examiner to the Conjoint Board of the Royal Colleges of Physicians and Surgeons and to Oxford, London and Glasgow Universities; Croonian Lecturer, Royal College of Physicians; Editor Quarterly Journal of Medicine; Member Association of Physicians of Great Britain; Fellow and ex-Member of Council Royal Society of Medicine; Fellow Royal Society of Tropical Medicine and Hygiene; b Nov. 1900; s of Samuel Augustus Marriott; m 1930, Vida Cureton; no c. Served RAMC 1939-45; Brig. 1942-45; Mission to Middle East for War Office and Medical Research Council, 1941; Consulting Physician to Army and Hon. Consultant to Royal Air Force, India Command, 1942-44; Consulting Physician to Allied Land Forces and Hon. Consultant to Royal Air Force, South-East Asia Command, 1944-45; Burma campaign (CBE). *Publications:* various papers in medical journals and articles in medical text-books. *Address:* Shepherd's Down, Ridgeway, Friston, Eastbourne. *T:* East Dean 3123.

MARRIOTT, Maj.-Gen. Sir John (Charles Oakes), KCVO 1950 (CVO 1937; MVO 1935); CB 1947; DSO 1917; MC; b 1895; s of late Charles Marriott of Stowmarket, Suffolk; m 1920, Maud (d 1960), d of Otto Kahn, New York; one s. *Educ:* Repton. Entered Northants Regt, 1914; served European War, 1915-18 (wounded, despatches, MC, DSO, Croix de Guerre); Military Attaché's Staff, Washington, 1919-20; transferred to Scots Guards, 1920; DAA & QMG London District, 1933-37; commanded 2nd Bn Scots Guards, 1938; served Middle East, 1940-42 (Bar to DSO); commanded 29 Indian Inf. Bde and 201 Guards Bde. Commander Guards Div. 1945-47; GOC London District, 1947-50; retd pay, 1950. *Address:* 7 Pelham Crescent, SW7. *Clubs:* Cavalry and Guards, Turf.

MARRIOTT, John Hayes, CB 1965; OBE 1953; b 14 June 1909; s of late Sir Hayes Marriott, KBE, CMG, and late Alice (née Smith), Malayan Civil Service; m 1936, Barbara Rosemary (née Salmon); two s two d. *Educ:* Uppingham Sch.; King's Coll., Cambridge (MA). Admitted solicitor, 1934; Partner in Deacon & Co., solicitors, 149 Leadenhall Street, EC3, 1936-45. Royal Artillery (HAC), 1939-40; attached MoD, formerly War Office, 1940-69; retd 1969. Royal Order of the Crown, Yugoslavia, 1945. *Address:* 7 Martin's Close, Tenterden, Kent TN30 7AJ. *T:* Tenterden 2497. *Club:* Rye Golf.
See also R. D'A. Marriott.

MARRIOTT, Marjorie Jane; see Speed, M. J.

MARRIOTT, Patrick Arthur; retired as Governor, HM Prison, Parkhurst, Isle of Wight (1951-59); b 20 July 1899; s of late Canon P. A. R. Marriott, St George's Coll., Jerusalem, and late Gertrude E. Marriott; m 1929, Honor Chalfont, d of late Major W. W. Blackden, Royal Munster Fusiliers, and Mrs Blackden, Byways, Yateley, Hants; two s. *Educ:* Christ's Hospital. Sub. Lieut RNAS and Lieut RAF, 1917-21; Lieut British North Borneo Armed Constabulary, 1924-29; joined HM Prison Service as Governor, Class IV, 1929, and has been Governor of Nottingham, Lincoln, Brixton, Pentonville and Parkhurst Prisons. Captain, Hampshire Yeomanry, 1929-35; Major, Royal Artillery, 1939-45. *Address:* Old Court Cottage, Cowbeech, Hailsham, East Sussex RN27 4JA.

MARRIOTT, Sir Ralph G. C. S.; see Smith-Marriott.

MARRIOTT, Richard D'Arcy, CBE 1965; DFC 1944; Assistant Director of Radio (formerly of Sound Broadcasting), BBC, 1957-69; b 9 June 1911; s of late Sir Hayes Marriott, KBE, CMG, Malayan Civil Service; m 1951, Dawn Kingdon; two d. *Educ:* Uppingham; Corpus Christi Coll., Cambridge. Joined BBC, 1933; Foreign Liaison Officer, BBC, 1936; started BBC Monitoring Unit, at outbreak of war, 1939; served as navigator in Fighter Command, RAF, 1942-45 (DFC and Bar); attached as Wing Commander to Control Commission for Germany, in charge of German Broadcasting Service in British Zone, 1945-46. Re-joined BBC as Head of European Liaison, 1946; Head of Transcription Service, BBC, 1951-52; Head of Monitoring Service, BBC, 1952-53; Controller, BBC, Northern Ireland, 1953-56. *Address:* 6 Windmill Hill, Hampstead, NW3. *T:* 01-435 4648.
See also J. H. Marriott.

MARRIOTT, Brig. Sir Robert Ecklin, Kt 1943; VD; FInstCE; BSc; with Sir Owen Williams and Partners, on M1 Construction, 1953-68; retired, 1968; b 15 Oct. 1887; m 1920, Valerie Hoch; four d. m 1953, Mary Bauer; no c. Joined Indian State Railways, 1910; Indian Sappers and Miners (East Africa), 1915-1920; Chief Engineer, 1937, Gen. Man., EI Rly, 1939; Dir Gen. Rlys

Calcutta Area, 1944; Dir General Rlys, Control Commission Germany, 1945; Royal Engineers, 1945-47; Col Commandant, East Indian Rly Regt, Aux. Force, India; ADC to the Viceroy. Bursar, Administrative Staff Coll., Henley-on-Thames, 1948; Air Ministry Works Department, 1951. *Address:* Hartfield, Crick, near Rugby.

MARRIS, Adam Denzil, CMG 1944; b 11 June 1906; o s of late Sir William Marris, KCSI, KCIE; m 1934, B. Waterfield; one s two d. *Educ:* Winchester; Trinity Coll., Oxford. With Lazard Bros & Co. Ltd, 11 Old Broad Street, London, 1929-39; Ministry of Economic Warfare, London, 1939-40; First Sec., HM Embassy, Washington, 1940-41; Counsellor, British Embassy, Washington, 1941; Secretary-General Emergency Economic Cttee for Europe, Aug. 1945-Feb. 1946, with temp. rank of Principal Asst Sec., Foreign Office; Deputy Leader of United Kingdom Delegation to Marshall Plan Conference, July-Sept. 1947, and to Washington Conf. of Cttee for European Economic Co-operation, Nov.-Dec. 1947. Director: Lazard Bros & Co. Ltd, 1947-73 (Man. Dir, 1947-71); Commercial Union Assce Co. Ltd (Vice-Chm.); Barclays Bank Ltd; Australia and New Zealand Banking Group Ltd; P&O Steam Navigation Co. *Address:* Hampen House, Andoversford, Glos. *T:* 279; 36 King's Court North, SW3. *T:* 01-352 8656; 01-588 2721. *Clubs:* Boodle's; Melbourne (Vic).
See also R. L. Wade-Gery.

MARRIS, Dr Robin Lapthorn; Chairman, Department of Economics, University of Maryland, since 1976; b 31 March 1924; s of Eric Denyer Marris, CB, and late Phyllis, d of T. H. F. Lapthorn, JP; m 1st, 1949, Marion Ellinger; 2nd, 1954, Jane Evelina Burney Ayres; one s two d; 3rd, 1972, Anne Fairclough Mansfield; one d. *Educ:* Bedales Sch.; King's Coll., Cambridge. BA 1946, ScD 1968, Cantab. Asst Principal, HM Treasury, 1947-50; UN, Geneva, 1950-52; Fellow of King's Coll., Cambridge, 1951-76; Lectr, 1951-72, Reader, 1972-76, in Econs, Univ. of Cambridge. Vis. Prof., Univ. California, Berkeley, 1961, and Harvard, 1967; Dir, World Economy Div., Min. of Overseas Develt, 1964-66. *Publications:* Economic Arithmetic, 1958; The Economic Theory of Managerial Capitalism, 1964; The Economics of Capital Utilisation, 1964; (with Adrian Wood) The Corporate Economy, 1971; The Corporate Society, 1974; contrib. Econ. Jl, Rev. Econ. Studies, Economica, Jl Manchester Stat. Soc., Jl Royal Stat. Soc., Amer. Econ. Rev., Qly Jl of Econs, Economie Appliquée, etc. *Recreations:* cooking, ski-ing, sailing. *Address:* Department of Economics, University of Maryland, College Park Campus, Md 20742, USA.

MARRISON, Dr Geoffrey Edward; Director and Keeper, Department of Oriental Manuscripts and Printed Books, British Library, London, since 1974; b 11 Jan. 1923; s of John and Rose Marrison; m 1958, Margaret Marian Millburn; one s three d. *Educ:* SOAS, Univ. of London; Bishops' Coll. Cheshunt; Kirchliche Hochschule, Berlin. BA Malay 1948, PhD Linguistics 1967, London. Indian Army, 1942-46. SOAS, 1941-42 and 1946-49; ordained Priest, Singapore, 1952; in Malaya with USPG, 1952-56; Vicar of St Timothy, Crookes, Sheffield, 1958-61; Linguistics Adviser British and Foreign Bible Soc., 1962-67, incl. service in Assam, 1962-64. Asst. Keeper, British Museum, 1967-71, Dep. Keeper 1971-74. Hon. Canon of All Saints Pro-Cathedral, Shillong, 1963. FRAS. *Publications:* The Christian Approach to the Muslim, 1958; articles in Jl Malayan Branch Royal Asiatic Soc., Bible Translator. *Recreation:* ethno-linguistics of South and South East Asia. *Address:* 85 Warwick Road, Thornton Heath, Surrey CR4 7NN. *T:* 01-684 2806.

MARS-JONES, Hon. Sir William (Lloyd), Kt 1969; MBE 1945; Hon. Mr Justice Mars-Jones; a Judge of the High Court of Justice, Queen's Bench Division, since 1969; b 4 Sept. 1915; s of Henry and Jane Mars Jones, Llansannan, Denbighshire; m 1947, Sheila Mary Felicity Cobon; three s. *Educ:* Denbigh County Sch.; UCW, Aberystwyth (LLB Hons); St John's Coll., Cambridge (BA). Entrance Schol., Gray's Inn, 1936; Pres. Students' Rep. Counc. and Central Students' Rep. Counc., UCW, 1936-37; MacMahon Studentship, 1939; Barrister-at-Law, 1941, QC 1957. War of 1939-45, RNVR (MBE); Lt-Comdr RNVR 1945. Contested W Denbigh Parly Div., 1945. Joined Wales and Chester Circuit, 1947, Presiding Judge, 1971-75. Recorder of: Birkenhead, 1959-65; Swansea, 1965-68; Cardiff, 1968-69; Dep. Chm., Denbighshire Quarter Sessions, 1962-68. Bencher, Gray's Inn, 1964. Comr of Assize, Denbigh and Mold Summer Assize, 1965. Member: Bar Council, 1962; Home Office Inquiry into allegations against Metropolitan Police Officers, 1964; Home Secretary's Adv. Council on Penal System, 1966-68. Hon. LLD UCW, Aberystwyth, 1973. *Publications:* contrib. Atkins' Encycl. of Court Forms and Precedents. *Address:* 3 Gray's Inn Square, WC1. *T:* 01-405 3632; The White House, Rhosneigr, Anglesey. *T:* Rhosneigr 293. *Club:* Garrick.

MARSABIT, Bishop of, (RC), since 1964; **Rt. Rev. Charles Cavallera;** *b* Centallo, Cuneo, Italy, 1909. *Educ:* International Missionary College of the Consolata of Turin; Pontifical Univ. of Propaganda Fide of Rome (degree in Missionology). Sec. to Delegate Apostolic of British Africa, 1936-40; Vice-Rector, then Rector, of Urban Coll. of Propaganda Fide of Rome, 1941-47; formerly Titular Bishop of Sufes; Vicar-Apostolic of Nyeri (Kenya), 1947-53; Bishop of Nyeri, 1953-64. *Address:* PO Box 281, Nanyuki, Kenya. *TA:* Bishop Cavallera, Marsabit (Kenya).

MARSDEN, Allen Gatenby, CBE 1945; FCIT; Hon. President of International Transport-Users Commission, Paris; *b* 13 Sept. 1893; *s* of late William Allen Marsden, OBE, and Marianne Turvey; *m* 1st, 1918, Mabel Kathleen Buckley (*decd*); one *s* two *d*; 2nd, 1933, Janet Helen Williamson; one *s*. *Educ:* Adwalm House, Hale; Bedford Grammar Sch. Joined staff of London & North-Western Railway as a probationer, 1909; served European War with commission in 8th Bn Manchester Regt, TF, 1914-16, in Egypt, Cyprus and Gallipoli, invalided home with rank of Capt.; under Dir-Gen. of Transportation, France, 1917; Transport and Storage Div., Min. of Food, 1917-18; Traffic Asst, Ministry of Transport, 1920; transport manager of Cadbury Bros Ltd, Bournville, 1921; subsequently transport Supervisor, Cadbury-Fry Joint Transport until 1940; Dir of Transport, Ministry of Food, Aug. 1940-May 1946; Transport Adviser to Bd of Unilever Ltd, 1946-58. Chm. Transport Cttee, CBI, 1946-58; Vice-Pres., Internat. Container Bureau, Paris, 1948-58; Pres., Internat. Transport Users Commn, Paris, 1948-58. *Recreations:* golf, fishing. *Address:* 64 Heathfield Road, Audlem, near Crewe, Cheshire. *T:* Audley 811555.

MARSDEN, Arthur Whitecombe, MSc, DIC, ARCS, FRIC; Education Officer/Technical Editor, Animal Production and Health Division, FAO, Rome, 1964-73; *b* Buxton, Derbyshire, 14 June 1911; *o s* of late Hubert Marsden and Margaret Augusta Bidwell; *m* 1940, Ailsa Anderson, *yr d* of late William Anderson McKellar, physician, and Jessie Reid Macfarlane, of Glasgow and Chester-le-Street, Co. Durham; one *s* two *d*. *Educ:* St Paul's; Imperial Coll. (Royal College of Science), London. BSc Special and ARCS, 1933; research in agricultural chemistry at Imperial Coll., 1933-36; research asst, 1936; demonstrator, 1937; asst lecturer, 1939; MSc and DIC, 1940. Temp. Instr Lieut RN, 1942; HMS Diomede, 1943; HMS King Alfred, 1944; RN Coll., Greenwich, and HMS Superb, 1945. Lecturer, Imperial Coll., London, 1946; Dept Head, Seale-Hayne Agricultural Coll., Newton Abbot, 1946-48; dir of research to grain companies in Aberdeen, 1948-49. Dir of Commonwealth Bureau of Dairy Science and Technology, Shinfield, Reading, 1950-57; Organising Secretary: 15th International Dairy Congress, London, 1957-60; 2nd World Congress of Man-made Fibres, 1960-63. Hon. Sec., Agriculture Group, Soc. of Chem. Industry, 1947-52, Chm., 1954-56; Organising Cttee of 2nd International Congress of Crop Protection, London, 1949; delegate on OEEC Technical Assistance Mission in USA and Canada, 1951; toured research centres in Pakistan, India, Australia, NZ and USA, Oct. 1954-Feb. 1955. *Publications:* papers in scientific journals. *Recreations:* travel, music, meeting and talking to people, especially from developing countries. *Address:* 109 Willingdon Road, Eastbourne, East Sussex BN21 1TX. *T:* Eastbourne 33602. *Club:* Naval.

MARSDEN, Frank; JP; *b* Everton, Liverpool, 15 Oct. 1923; *s* of Sidney Marsden and Harriet Marsden (*née* Needham); *m* 1943, Muriel Lightfoot; three *s*. *Educ:* Abbotsford Road Sec. Mod. Sch., Liverpool. Served War, with RAF Bomber Command, 115 Sqdn (Warrant Officer), 1941-46. Joined Lab. Party and Co-op. Movement, 1948. MP (Lab) Liverpool, Scotland, Apr. 1971-Feb. 1974. Local Councillor: Liverpool St Domingo Ward, May 1964-67; Liverpool Vauxhall Ward, 1969-71; Knowsley DC, 1976-. Chm. Liverpool Markets, 1965-67; Past Mem. Exec. Cttee: Liverpool Trades Council; Liverpool Lab. Party. JP (City of Liverpool), 1969. *Recreations:* jazz music, gardening. *Address:* 2 Thunderbolt Cottage, 6 Alder Lane, Knowsley, Prescot, Merseyside. *T:* 051-546 5167.

MARSDEN, Sir John Denton, 2nd Bt, *cr* 1924; JP; *b* 25 Aug. 1913; *s* of Sir John Marsden, 1st Bt, and Agnes Mary (*d* 1951), *d* of Thomas Robert Ronald of Little Danson, Welling, Kent; *S* father, 1944; *m* 1939, Hope, *yr d* of late G. E. Llewelyn; two *s* two *d*. *Educ:* Downside, St John's Coll., Cambridge (BA). Served European War of 1939-45 (prisoner); Lt RA. JP; High Sheriff of Lincs, 1955-56. *Recreations:* shooting, fishing. *Heir: s* Nigel John Denton Marsden [*b* 26 May 1940; *m* 1961, Diana Jean Dunn, *er d* of Air Marshal Sir Patrick H. Dunn, *qv*; three *d*]. *Address:* White Abbey, Linton-in-Craven, Skipton, N Yorks.

MARSDEN, Leslie Alfred, CMG 1966; *b* 25 Sept. 1921; *s* of late William Marsden, Stanmore, Middx, and of Kitty Marsden; *m* 1947, Doris Winifred, *d* of late Walter Richard Grant and of Winifred Grant; two *d*. *Educ:* Kingsbury County Sch. Served War: The Queen's Own Royal West Kent Regt, 1940-42; 14th Punjab Regt, Indian Army, 1942-46; serving in India, Burma and Thailand; retd as Hon. Major. Joined Nigeria Police Force, 1946; Commissioner of Police, 1964; Asst Inspector-General, 1966-68. Associate Director, Sierra Leone Selection Trust, 1969; Security Adviser, Standard Telephones and Cables Ltd, 1970. Nigeria Police Medal, 1964; Queen's Police Medal, 1964; Colonial Police Medal, 1958. *Recreations:* golf, swimming, walking, reading. *Address:* Ashbank, 14 Orchard Rise, Groombridge, Sussex. *T:* Groombridge 486. *Club:* Royal Over-Seas League.

MARSDEN, Dr Terence Barclay, FIM; Registrar-Secretary, Institution of Metallurgists, since 1976; *b* 31 March 1932; *s* of late Henry Arthur Marsden and Edith Maud Marsden; *m* 1954, Margaret Jean, *o d* of Percival Charles Davies and late Edith Davies; two *s*. *Educ:* Swansea Grammar Sch.; University Coll. of Swansea (BSc Hons I Metallurgy, Wales, 1952; PhD Wales, 1955). FIM 1970. Technical Officer, ICI Metals Ltd, 1955-60, Develt Officer, 1960-64; Asst Commercial Manager, Imperial Metal Industries Ltd, 1964-67; Tech. Man., CIDEC-Internat. Copper Develt Council, 1967-76. Chm., London Metallurgical Soc., 1974-75. *Publications:* papers in tech. and learned soc. jls on properties and applications of metals and alloys. *Recreations:* bridge, music, swimming, watching cricket. *Address:* Fairmead, 20 Dove Park, Chorleywood, Herts WD3 5NY. *T:* Chorleywood 2229. *Club:* Anglo-Belgian.

MARSDEN-SMEDLEY, Susan; Executive Director, Legal Action Group, and Editor, LAG Bulletin, since 1972; Member, Royal Commission on Legal Services, since 1976; *b* 6 Dec. 1931; *d* of John Marsden-Smedley and Agatha (*née* Bethell). *Educ:* Downe House Sch.; Girton Coll., Cambridge (MA). Called to the Bar, Middle Temple, 1957. Worked in consumer organisations in Britain and US, 1957-65; Senior Research Officer, Consumer Council, 1966-70; Legal Officer, Nuffield Foundation Legal Advice Research Unit, 1970-72. *Publication:* Justice Out of Reach, a case for Small Claims Courts, 1969. *Recreations:* tree planting and preservation, gardening, looking at modern buildings. *Address:* 15 Woodsome Road, NW5 1RX. *T:* 01-485 4938.

MARSH, Ven. Bazil Roland, BA; Archdeacon of Northampton, Non-Residentiary Canon of Peterborough, and Rector of St Peter's, Northampton, since 1964; *b* Three Hills, Alta, Canada, 11 Aug. 1921; *s* of late Ven. Wilfred Carter Marsh and late Mary Jean (*née* Stott), Devil's Lake, North Dakota, USA; *m* 1946, Audrey Joan, *d* of Owen George Oyler, farmer, of Brookmans Park, Hatfield, and Alma Lillian Oyler; three *s* one *d*. *Educ:* State schs in USA and Swindon, Wilts; Leeds Univ.; Coll. of the Resurrection, Mirfield, Yorks. Curate of: St Mary the Virgin, Cheshunt, Herts, 1944-46; St John Baptist, Coventry, 1946-47; St Giles-in-Reading, Berks, 1947-51; Rector of St Peter's, Townsville, Qld, Australia, 1951-56; Vicar of St Mary the Virgin, Far Cotton, Northampton, 1956-64. *Address:* 11 The Drive, Northampton NN1 4RZ. *T:* Northampton 714015. *Club:* Royal Commonwealth Society.

MARSH, Prof. David Charles; Professor of Applied Social Science, University of Nottingham, since 1954; *b* 9 Jan. 1917; *s* of F. C. Marsh, Aberdare, Glam., S Wales; *m* 1941, Maisie Done; one *s*. *Educ:* University of Birmingham. Research Scholar University of Birmingham, 1938-39. Military Service, 1940-46, Royal Artillery. Lecturer, University Coll. of Swansea, 1947-49; Professor of Social Science, Victoria Univ. Coll., Wellington, NZ, 1949-54. *Publications:* National Insurance and Assistance in Great Britain, 1949; The Changing Social Structure of England and Wales, 1958; The Future of the Welfare State, 1964, new edn, 1967; The Welfare State, 1970. *Recreations:* tennis, badminton. *Address:* 239 Chilwell Lane, Bramcote, Notts. *T:* 25-7567.

MARSH, Dame Edith Ngaio; see Marsh, Dame Ngaio.

MARSH, George Fletcher Riley, CB 1951; *b* 16 Oct. 1895; *s* of late Richard Howard Heywood Marsh, director of Geo. Fletcher & Co. Ltd, Derby; *m* 1927, Phyllis Henderson (*d* 1973), *d* of late Frank Barton, Brasted, Kent; one *s* one *d*. *Educ:* Bedford Sch. Entered Civil Service (Naval Store Dept, Admiralty), 1914; Deputy Dir of Stores, 1942; Dir of Stores, 1949-55; retired, 1955. *Address:* 14 Willian Way, Letchworth, Herts.

MARSH, Rt. Rev. Henry Hooper, MA, DD; *b* 6 Oct. 1898; *s* of Rev. Canon Charles H. Marsh, DD; *m* Margaret D. Heakes; one *s* one *d. Educ:* University College, Toronto, BA 1921; Wycliffe College, Toronto, 1924, MA 1925; DD 1962. Deacon, 1924; Priest, 1925; Curate of St Anne, Toronto, 1924-25; Curate of St Paul, Toronto, 1925-30; Priest-in-charge of St Timothy's Mission, City and Diocese of Toronto, 1930-36; Rector, Church of St Timothy, 1936-62; Canon of Toronto, 1956-62; Bishop of Yukon, 1962-67. Canadian Centennial Medal, 1967. *Recreation:* bird watching. *Address:* Hedgerows, RR6, Cobourg, Ont K9A 4J9, Canada.

MARSH, (Henry) John, CBE 1967; international management consultant and lecturer; UK Chairman, W. D. Scott & Co., since 1976; director of companies; *b* 1913; *s* of late Jasper W. P. Marsh and Gladys M. Carruthers; *m* 1950, Mary Costerton; two *s* two *d. Educ:* Chefoo Sch., China; Queen Elizabeth's Grammar Sch., Wimborne. Commerce, China, 1930-32; Shanghai Volunteer Force, 1930-32; engineering apprenticeship and apprentice supervisor, Austin Motor Co., 1932-39. Served War of 1939-45, Royal Army Service Corps TA, 48th and 56th Divisions; Singapore Fortress; BEF France, 1940; Malaya, 1941-42 (despatches twice); Prisoner of War, 1942-45; released with rank of Major, 1946. Personnel Officer, BOAC, 1946-47; Dir of Personnel Advisory Services, Institute of Personnel Management, 1947-49; Dir, Industrial (Welfare) Soc., 1950-61; British Institute of Management: Dir, later Dir-Gen., 1961-73; Asst Chm. and Counsellor, 1973-75. Mem., Nat. Coal Board, 1968-74. Hon. Administrator, Duke of Edinburgh's Study Conference, 1954-56; Chm. Brit. Nat. Conference on Social Work, 1957-60; Member: Youth Service Cttee, 1958-59; BBC General Advisory Council, 1959-64; Advisory Cttee on Employment of Prisoners, 1960-63; Council for Technical Educn and Training for Overseas Countries, 1961-74; UK Advisory Council on Education for Management, 1962-66; Russell Cttee on Adult Educn, 1969-72; Court, Univ. of Cranfield, 1962-69; Court, Univ. of Surrey, 1969-; Food Manufacturing EDC, 1967-69; Adv. Council, Civil Service College, 1970-; UK Mem., Commonwealth Team of Industrial Specialists, 1976-. Governor, King's Coll. Hosp., 1971-74. British Information Service Lecture Tours: India and Pakistan, 1959 and 1963; Nigeria, 1964; Malaysia, 1965; Australia, 1967; Latin America, 1971, 1973; Malaysia, NZ, 1974. FIAM 1969; Hon. Fellow, Canadian Inst. of Management, 1973; Hon. FBIM, 1976. Hon. DSc Bradford, 1968. Verulam Medal, 1976. *Publications:* Ardeshir Dalal Memorial Lecture, India, 1953; The Clarke Hall Lecture, 1957; E. W. Hancock Lecture, 1960; MacLaren Memorial Lecture, 1962; People at Work; Work and Leisure Digest; Partners in Work Relations; Tullis Russell Lecture, 1967; Ethics in Business, 1970; RSA Foster Lecture, 1973. *Recreation:* gardening. *Address:* 13 Frank Dixon Way, Dulwich, SE21. *Club:* Reform.

MARSH, Prof. the Rev. John, CBE 1964; MA (Edinburgh et Oxon), DPhil (Oxon); DD (Hon.) Edinburgh; Moderator, Free Church Federal Council, 1970-71; Principal, Mansfield College, Oxford, 1953-70; *b* 5 Nov. 1904; *s* of George Maurice and Florence Elizabeth Ann Marsh, East Grinstead, Sussex; *m* 1934, Gladys Walker, *y d* of George Benson and Mary Walker, Cockermouth, Cumberland; two *s* one *d. Educ:* The Skinners Company Sch., Tunbridge Wells; Yorkshire United Coll., Bradford; Edinburgh Univ.; Mansfield Coll. and St Catherine's Soc., Oxford; Marburg Univ. Lecturer, Westhill Training Coll., 1932; Minister, Congregational Church, Otley, Yorks, 1934; Tutor and Chaplain, Mansfield Coll., Oxford, 1938; Prof. of Christian Theology, The University, Nottingham, 1949-53. Gray Lectr, Duke Univ., NC; Reinecke Lectr, Prot. Episc. Semin., Alexandria, Va, 1958. Delegate: First Assembly, World Council of Churches, Amsterdam, 1948; Second Assembly, Evanston, Ill., 1954; Third Assembly, New Delhi, 1961; Fourth Assembly, Uppsala, 1968. Sec. World Conference on Faith and Order's Commn on "Intercommunion"; Chm., Section 2 of British Council of Churches Commn on Broadcasting, 1949; Mem., Working Cttee, Faith and Order Dept, World Council of Churches, 1953; Sec., European Commission on Christ and the Church, World Council of Churches, 1955; Mem. Central Religious Advisory Cttee to BBC, 1955-60; Mem. Sub-Cttee of CRAC acting as Religious Advisory Panel to ITA, 1955-65; Chm. British Council of Churches Commn of Faith and Order, 1960-62. Mem. Central Cttee, World Council of Churches, 1961-68; Chm. Division of Studies, World Council of Churches, 1961-68; Select Preacher, University of Oxford, 1962; Chm. Congregational Union of England and Wales, 1962-63; Chairman: Inter-Church Relationships Cttee, Congregational Church in England and Wales, 1964-67; Board of Faculty of Theology, Oxford Univ., 1966-; Exec. Cttee, Congregational Church in England and Wales, 1966-72; Joint Chm. Joint Cttee for Conversations between Congregationalists and

Presbyterians, 1965-72. Chm., Buttermere Parish Council, 1973-. Governor, Westminster Coll., Oxford, 1967-70. *Publications:* The Living God, 1942; Congregationalism Today, 1943; (jtly) A Book of Congregational Worship, 1948; (Jt Ed.) Intercommunion, 1952; contrib. Biblical Authority Today, 1951; and Ways of Worship, 1951; The Fulness of Time, 1952; The Significance of Evanston, 1954; trans. Stauffer, Theology of the New Testament, 1955; A Year with the Bible, 1957; contributed to Essays in Christology for Karl Barth, 1957; Amos and Micah, 1959; trans. Bultmann, The History of the Synoptic Tradition, 1963; Pelican Commentary on St John's Gospel, 1968. *Recreations:* water colour painting, wood turning. *Address:* Rannerdale Close, Buttermere, Cumbria CA13 9UY. *T:* Buttermere 232.

MARSH, John; *see* Marsh, H. J.

MARSH, Leonard George, MEd; Principal, Bishop Grosseteste College, since 1974; *b* 23 Oct. 1930; third *c* of late Ernest Arthur Marsh and Anne Eliza (*née* Bean); *m* 1953, Ann Margaret Gilbert; one *s* one *d. Educ:* Ashford (Kent) Grammar Sch.; Borough Road Coll., London Inst. of Educn; Leicester Univ. Teachers' Certif., Academic Dip. Lectr in Educn and Mathematics, St Paul's Coll., Cheltenham, 1959-61; Lectr, 1961-63, Sen. Lectr, 1963-65, Principal Lectr and Head of Dept, 1965-74, Goldsmiths' Coll., London; Visiting Lectr, Bank Street Coll., New York, and Virginia Commonwealth Univ.; Consultant, OECD, Portugal; Specialist tour to India for British Council. Mem. Gen. Adv. Council, IBA, 1977-. *Publications:* Let's Explore Mathematics, Books 1-4, 1964-67; Children Explore Mathematics, 1967, 3rd edn 1969; Exploring Shapes and Numbers, 1968, 2nd edn 1970; Exploring the Metric System, 1969, 2nd edn 1969; Exploring the Metric World, 1970; Approach to Mathematics, 1970; Alongside the Child in the Primary School, 1970; Let's Discover Mathematics, Books 1-5, 1971-72; Being A Teacher, 1973. *Recreations:* observing the passing countryside from a railway carriage window, keeping up with son's hobbies, photography, theatre going, films, observing the development of one's students. *Address:* The Principal's House, Bishop Grosseteste College, Lincoln LN1 3DY. *T:* Lincoln 28241; Broomfields, The Meadow, Chislehurst, Kent BR7 6AA. *T:* 01-467 6311.

MARSH, Michael John Waller, MC 1942; TD 1954; a Recorder of the Crown Court, since 1974; *b* 12 April 1921; *s* of Arthur Percival Marsh and Gladys Adine Marsh; *m* 1948, Kathleen Harrison; one *s. Educ:* Uppingham; Pembroke Coll., Cambridge (BA). 9th Queen's Royal Lancers, 1942-46; Prince Albert's Own Leics Yeo., 1947-54, retd (Major). Admitted Solicitor, 1949. *Recreations:* shooting; playing around with small boats. *Address:* Park House, Burton Lazars, Melton Mowbray, Leics. *T:* Melton Mowbray 66730.

MARSH, Nevill Francis, CBE 1969; Director-General, St John Ambulance, 1972-76; *b* 13 Aug. 1907; *m* 1935, Betty (*née* Hide); one *s* one *d. Educ:* Oundle Sch., Northants; Clare Coll., Cambridge (MA). Traction Motor Design Staff, Metropolitan-Vickers Electrical Co. Ltd, 1930-32; Mid-Lincolnshire Electric Supply Co. Ltd: Dist Engineer, 1932-38; Engineer and Manager, 1938-48; Chief Commercial Officer, E Midlands Electricity Board, 1948-55; Dep.-Chm., N Eastern Electricity Board, 1955-57; Dep.-Chm., E Midlands Electricity Board, 1957-59; Chm., East Midlands Electricity Board, 1959-61; a Dep. Chm., Electricity Council, 1962-71; Chm., British Electrotechnical Cttee, 1970-72. Dir for Gtr London, St John Ambulance Assoc., 1971-72. Also formerly: Dir, Altrincham Electric Supply Ltd, and Public Utilities (Elec.) Ltd, and Supervising Engineer, Campbeltown & Mid-Argyll Elec. Supply Co. Ltd, and Thurso & District Elec. Supply Co. Ltd. FIEE; Pres. of Assoc. of Supervising Electrical Engineers, 1966-68. KStJ 1973. *Publications:* jt contrib. Jl Inst. Electrical Engineers, 1955. *Address:* Stocksfield, First Avenue, Frinton-on-Sea, Essex CO13 9EZ. *T:* Frinton 2995. *Club:* Royal Air Force.

MARSH, Dame Ngaio, DBE 1966 (OBE 1948); FRSA; Novelist and Theatrical Producer, NZ; *b* 23 April 1899; *d* of Henry Edmond and Rose Elizabeth (Seager) Marsh. *Educ:* St Margaret's Coll., NZ; Canterbury Univ. Coll. Sch. of Art, Christchurch, NZ. On stage for two years; to England in 1928; in partnership with Hon. Mrs Tahu Rhodes as house decorator; first novel published in 1934; travelled in Europe, 1937-38; in New Zealand at outbreak of war and joined Red Cross Transport unit. Producer D. D. O'Connor Theatre Management, 1944-; Hon. Lecturer in Drama, Canterbury Univ., 1948. Hon. DLit Canterbury, NZ. *Publications:* A Man Lay Dead, 1934; Enter a Murderer, 1935; Nursing Home Murder (with Henry Jellett), 1936; Death in Ecstasy, 1937; Vintage Murder, 1937; Artists in Crime, 1938; Death in a White

Tie, 1938; Overture to Death, 1939; Death at the Bar, 1940; Surfeit of Lampreys, 1941; Death and the Dancing Footman, 1942; Colour Scheme, 1943; Died in the Wool, 1945; Final Curtain, 1947; Swing, Brother, Swing, 1948; Opening Night, 1951; Spinsters in Jeopardy, 1953; Scales of Justice, 1954; Off With His Head, 1957; Singing in the Shrouds, 1959; False Scent, 1960; Hand in Glove, 1962; Dead Water, 1964; Black Beech and Honeydew, 1966; Death at the Dolphin, 1967; Clutch of Constables, 1968; When in Rome, 1970; Tied up in Tinsel, 1972; Black As He's Painted, 1974; Last Ditch, 1977. *Plays:* A Unicorn for Christmas, 1962 (Libretto to David Farquhar's Opera from this play); Murder Sails at Midnight, 1973 (adapted from Singing in the Shrouds). *Recreations:* Theatre production, painting, books, travel, gardening. *Address:* c/o Hughes Massie, 69 Great Russell Street, WC1; (Residence) 37 Valley Road, Cashmere, Christchurch, New Zealand. *Club:* PEN.

MARSH, **Norman Stayner**, CBE 1977; QC 1967; Law Commissioner, since 1965; Member, Royal Commission on Civil Liability and Compensation for Personal Injury, since 1973; *b* 26 July 1913; *o s* of Horace Henry and Lucy Ann Marsh, Bath, Som; *m* 1939, Christiane Christinnecke, 2nd *d* of Professor Johannes and Käthe Christinnecke, Magdeburg, Germany; two *s* two *d. Educ:* Monkton Combe Sch.; Pembroke Coll., Oxford. 2nd Class Hons, Final Honour Sch. of Jurisprudence, 1935; 1st Cl. Hons BCL. Vinerian Scholar of Oxford Univ., Harmsworth Scholar of Middle Temple, called to Bar, 1937; practice in London and on Western Circuit, 1937-39; Lieut-Col Intelligence Corps and Control Commission for Germany, 1939-46. Stowell Civil Law Fellow, University Coll., Oxford, 1946-60; University Lecturer in Law, 1947-60; Estates Bursar, University Coll., 1948-56; Secretary-General, International Commission of Jurists, The Hague, Netherlands, 1956-58. Member: Bureau of Conference of Non-Governmental Organisations with Consultative Status with the United Nations, 1957-58; Internat. Cttee of Legal Science (Unesco), 1960-63. Dir of British Institute of International and Comparative Law, 1960-65. Mem., Younger Cttee on Privacy, 1970-72. Hon. Vis. Prof. in Law, KCL, 1972-77. General editor, International and Comparative Law Quarterly, 1961-65; Mem., Editorial Board, 1965-. *Publications:* The Rule of Law as a supra-national concept, in Oxford Essays in Jurisprudence, 1960; The Rule of Law in a Free Society, 1960; Interpretation in a National and International Context, 1974; articles on common law and comparative law in English, American, French and German law jls. *Address:* Law Commission, Conquest House, 37/38 John Street, Theobalds Road, WC1. *T:* 01-242 0861; (private) Wren House, 13 North Side, Clapham Common, SW4. *T:* 01-622 2865.

MARSH, **Rt. Hon. Sir Richard (William)**, PC 1966; Kt 1976; FCIT; Chairman: Newspaper Publishers' Association, since 1976; British Iron and Steel Consumers' Council, since 1977; *b* 14 March 1928; *s* of William Marsh, Belvedere, Kent; *m* 1st, 1950, Evelyn Mary (marr. diss. 1973), *d* of Frederick Andrews, Southampton; two *s*; 2nd, 1973, Caroline Dutton (*d* 1975). *Educ:* Jennings Sch., Swindon; Woolwich Polytechnic; Ruskin Coll., Oxford. Contested Hertford, 1951; Health Services Officer, National Union of Public Employees, 1951-59; Mem., Clerical and Administrative Whitley Council for Health Service, 1953-59; co-opted mem. LCC Children's Cttee, 1959; MP (Lab) Greenwich, Oct. 1959-April 1971; Promoted Offices Act 1961; Member: Select Cttee Estimates, 1961; Chm. Interdepartmental Cttee to Co-ordinate Govt Policy on Industrial Training, 1964; Parly Sec., Min. of Labour, 1964-65; Joint Parly Sec., Min. of Technology, 1965-66; Minister of Power, 1966-68; Minister of Transport, 1968-69. Chm., British Railways Bd, 1971-76; Member: NEDC, 1971-; Freight Integration Council, 1971-. Chairman: Michael Saunders Management Services, 1970-71; Allied Investments Ltd, 1977-; Director: National Carbonising Co. Ltd (Chm., NCC Plant and Transport), 1970-71; Concord Rotoflex International Ltd, 1970-71; Pres., Council ECSC, 1968. Governor: British Transport Staff Coll. (Chm.); London Business Sch. *Address:* c/o 6 Bouverie Street, EC4Y 8AY. *Club:* Reform.

MARSH, **William Thomas**, OBE 1944; MA; Headmaster, St Albans School, 1931-64, retd; Commander RNVR (Sp); *b* Birmingham, 18 March 1897; *o s* of W. T. Marsh; *m* 1923, Olive Constance Nightingale; three *s. Educ:* Northampton Sch.; Queens' Coll., Cambridge (Open Classical Scholar). RNVR, 1916-19; First-class Hons Classical Tripos, 1922; VIth Form Classical Master, Brighton Coll., 1923-27; Headmaster Hertford Grammar Sch., 1927-31. Blue for Athletics and Cross Country. *Recreations:* archæology, music. *Address:* Priory Close, Bishops Cleeve, Cheltenham, Glos. *T:* Bishops Cleeve 3171.

MARSHALL; *see* Johnson-Marshall.

MARSHALL, **Mrs Alan R.;** *see* Marshall, V. M.

MARSHALL, **Alexander Badenoch;** Managing Director, The Peninsular and Oriental Steam Navigation Co., since 1972 (Director, 1968-72); Director: Commercial Union Assurance Ltd; Tube Investments Ltd; *b* 31 Dec. 1924; *m* 1961, Mona Kurina Douglas Kirk; two *s* one *d. Educ:* Trinity Coll., Glenalmond; Worcester Coll., Oxford (MA). Served War, Sub-Lieut RNVR, 1943-46. P&O Group of Companies: Mackinnon Mackenzie & Co., Calcutta, 1947-59; Gen. Manager, British India Steam Navigation Co., 1959-62; Managing Dir, Trident Tankers Ltd, 1962-68. *Recreations:* family, gardening. *Address:* Crest House, Park View Road, Woldingham, Surrey. *T:* Woldingham 2299. *Clubs:* Oriental; Tollygunge (Calcutta).

MARSHALL, **Arthur C.;** *see* Calder-Marshall.

MARSHALL, **Sir Arthur Gregory George**, Kt 1974; OBE 1948; DL; Chairman and Managing Director, Marshall of Cambridge (Engineering) Ltd, since 1942; *b* 4 Dec. 1903; *s* of David Gregory Marshall, MBE, and Maude Edmunds Wing; *m* 1931, Rosemary Wynford Dimsdale, *d* of Marcus Southwell Dimsdale; two *s* one *d. Educ:* Tonbridge Sch.; Jesus Coll., Cambridge. Engrg, MA. Joined Garage Company of Marshall (Cambridge) Ltd, 1926, which resulted in estabt of Aircraft Company, now Marshall of Cambridge (Engineering) Ltd, 1929. Chm., Aerodrome Owners Assoc., 1964-65; Member: Air Cadet Council, 1951-59 and 1965-76; Adv. Council on Technology, 1967-70. DL 1968, High Sheriff of Cambridgeshire and Isle of Ely, 1969-70. *Recreations:* Cambridge Athletics Blue, Olympic Team Reserve, 1924; flying (pilot's licence) since 1928. *Address:* Horseheath Lodge, Linton, Cambridge CB1 6PT. *T:* Cambridge 891318. *Clubs:* Royal Air Force; Hawks (Cambridge).

MARSHALL, **Arthur Hedley**, CBE 1956; MA; BSc (Econ); PhD; City Treasurer, Coventry, 1944-64, retired; Senior Research Fellow in Public Administration, Birmingham University, 1964-74; *b* 6 July 1904; *s* of Rev. Arthur Marshall; *m* 1933, Margaret L. Longhurst; one *s. Educ:* Wolverhampton Grammar Sch.; London Sch. of Economics. Incorporated Accountant (Hons), 1934; Fellow Institute Municipal Treasurers and Accountants and Collins gold medal, 1930 (Pres. 1953-54); DPA (London) 1932. Chm. Royal Institute of Public Administration, 1952-53; Adviser in Local Govt to Sudan Govt, 1948-49; and to Govt of British Guiana, 1955. Chm., Cttee on Highway Maintenance, 1967-70; Member: Colonial Office Local Government Advisory Panel, 1950-; Central Housing Adv. Cttee, 1957-65; Cttee for Training Public Administration in Overseas Countries, 1961-62; Arts Council Drama Panel, 1965-76; Arts Council, 1973-76; Uganda Commission, 1961; Kenya Commission, 1962; Royal Commission on Local Government in England, 1966-69. Hon. LLD Nottingham, 1972. *Publications:* Local Authorities: Internal Financial Control, 1936; Consolidated Loans Funds of Local Authorities (with J. M. Drummond), 1936; Report on Local Government in the Sudan, 1949, and on British Guiana, 1955; Financial Administration in Local Government, 1960; Financial Management in Local Government, 1974; Local Authorities and the Arts, 1974; various contribs to learned jls on Local Government and Accountancy. *Recreation:* music. *Address:* 39 Armorial Road, Coventry CV3 6GH. *T:* Coventry 414652. *Club:* Reform.
See also N. H. Marshall.

MARSHALL, **Bruce;** novelist; *b* 24 June 1899; *s* of Claude Niven Marshall, Edinburgh; *m* 1928, Phyllis, *d* of late William Glen Clark, Edinburgh; one *d. Educ:* Edinburgh Acad.; Trinity Coll., Glenalmond; St Andrews and Edinburgh Univs. Served in Royal Irish Fusiliers, 1914-18 War and in Royal Army Pay Corps and Intelligence in War of 1939-45; MA Edinburgh, 1924; B Com. Edinburgh, 1925; admitted a mem. of the Soc of Accountants in Edinburgh, 1926. *Publications:* Father Malachy's Miracle, 1931; Prayer for the Living, 1934; The Uncertain Glory, 1935; Yellow Tapers for Paris, 1943; All Glorious Within, 1944; George Brown's Schooldays, 1946; The Red Danube, 1947; Every Man a Penny, 1950; The White Rabbit, 1952; The Fair Bride, 1953; Only Fade Away; Thoughts of my Cats, 1954; Girl in May, 1956; The Bank Audit, 1958; A Thread of Scarlet, 1959; The Divided Lady, 1960; A Girl from Lübeck, 1962; The Month of the Falling Leaves, 1963; Father Hilary's Holiday, 1965; The Bishop, 1970; The Black Oxen, 1972; Urban the Ninth, 1973; Operation Iscariot, 1974; Marx the First, 1975; Peter the Second, 1976; The Yellow Streak, 1977; Prayer for a Concubine, 1978. *Address:* c/o Lloyds Bank, 6 Pall Mall, SW1.

MARSHALL, **Dr Edmund Ian;** MP (Lab) Goole since May 1971; *b* 31 May 1940; *s* of Harry and Koorali Marshall; *m* 1969, Margaret Pamela, *d* of John and Maud Antill, New Southgate, N11; one *d. Educ:* Magdalen Coll., Oxford (Mackinnon Schol.);

Liverpool Univ. Double 1st cl. hons Maths, and Junior Mathematical Prize, Oxon, 1961; PhD Liverpool, 1965. Various univ. appts in Pure Maths, 1962-66; mathematician in industry, 1967-71. Mem., Wallasey County Borough Council, 1963-65. Contested (L) Louth Div. of Lincs, 1964 and 1966; joined Labour Party, 1967. PPS to Sec. of State for NI, 1974-76, to Home Sec., 1976-; Chm., Trade and Industry sub-cttee of House of Commons Expenditure Cttee, 1976-. Chm., Mitcham Constituency Labour Party, 1970-71. Member: British Methodist Conf., 1969-72; World Methodist Conf., 1971. British Council of Churches, 1972-. *Publications:* (jtly) Europe: What Next? (Fabian pamphlet), 1969; various papers on pure maths in Jl of London Math. Society. *Recreations:* genealogy, music. *Address:* House of Commons, SW1A 0AA. *Club:* Reform.

MARSHALL, Sir Frank (Shaw), Kt 1971; Solicitor (in private practice); Special Adviser to Government on Third London Airport Project, 1972; Director: Leeds & Holbeck Building Society (President, 1967-69 and since 1977, Vice-President, 1975-77); Barr & Wallace Arnold Trust Ltd and 20 other companies; *b* Wakefield, 26 Sept. 1915; 4th *s* of Charles William and Edith Marshall and *g g s* of Charles Marshall (*b* Wakefield, 1827), of NY, Philadelphia,and Columbia, Miss, who fought in American Civil War; *m* 1941, Mary, *e c* of Robert and Edith Barr, Shadwell House Leeds; two *d*. *Educ:* Queen Elizabeth's Sch., Wakefield; Downing Coll., Cambridge (Scholar). MA, LLB. Served 1940-46, Captain Royal Tank Regt and Staff Officer JAG's Dept, WO. Managing Trustee and Dep. Chm., Municipal Mutual Insurance Co. Ltd. Leeds CC: Leader, and Chm. Finance Cttee, 1967-72; Alderman, 1967-73. Pres., Leeds Law Soc., 1975-76; Chairman: Leeds and Bradford Airport, 1968-69; Local Govt Information Office of England and Wales, 1968-73; Assoc. of Municipal Corps of England, Wales and NI, 1968-73; Jt Negotiating Cttee for Town Clerks and District Council Clerks, 1968-73; Jt Negotiating Cttee for Chief Officers of Local Authorities, 1968-73; Public Administration Adv. Bd, Sheffield Polytechnic, 1969-; Maplin Develt Authority, 1973-74; Leeds Council of Christians and Jews, 1960-; NE Leeds Conservative Assoc., 1962-65; City of Leeds Conservative Assoc., 1967-; Yorks Provincial Area Nat. Union of Cons. and Unionist Assocs, 1976-; Local Authorities Conditions of Service Adv. Bd, 1971-73; Steering Cttee on Local Authority Management Structures; Leeds Grand Theatre and Opera House Ltd, 1969-72; Yorks Reg. Cttee, RSA; The Marshall Enquiry on Greater London, 1977; Vice-Chm., Bd of Governors, Centre for Environmental Studies, 1971-; Member: Yorks and Humberside Economic Planning Council, 1971-74; Uganda Resettlement Bd, 1972-73; Court, Leeds Univ., 1965- (Council, 1965-72 and 1975-); Court, Bradford Univ., 1967-; Council of Management, University Coll. at Buckingham, 1975-; BBC North Regional Council; Leeds Radio Council, BBC, 1969-; Nat. Exec. Cons. and Unionist Party, 1968- (Mem., Gen. Purposes Cttee, 1969, 1976-); Exec. Council (British Section) of Internat. Union of Local Authorities; European Conference of Local Authorities; Council, Leeds Philosophical and Literary Soc. (Vice-Pres.); Exec. Cttee, AA. FRSA. Freeman, City of Leeds, 1976. *Publications:* contribs to Local Govt and other jls, and press articles. *Recreations:* theatre, reading, racing. *Address:* Holtby, North Yorks. *Clubs:* Carlton; Leeds (Leeds).

MARSHALL, Sir Geoffrey, KCVO 1951; CBE 1951 (OBE 1917); MD, FRCP; retired as Consulting Physician to: Guy's Hospital; King Edward VII Hospital, Midhurst, and Brompton Hospital for Diseases of Chest; Hon. Consulting Physician to Ministry of Pensions; Medical Referee to the Civil Service Commission; Chairman Chemotherapy of Tuberculosis Trials Committee of Medical Research Council; Censor and Harveian Orator, Royal College of Physicians; *b* 1887; *s* of Henry Marshall, Bognor, Sussex; *m* 1918, Belle (*d* 1974), *d* of George Philip, Dundee; (one *s* died on active service, MEF, 1941). *Educ:* St Paul's Sch. Demonstrator of Physiology and Medical Registrar, Guy's Hospital; Gold Medal, London MD; Major RAMC, SR, served with Brit. Exp. Force (despatches twice, OBE); Med. Officer i/c Tuberculosis Dept, Sub-dean of Medical Sch. (Guy's Hospital); Pres. Royal Society of Medicine, 1958-60 (late Pres., Section of Medicine, RSM); Hon. Mem. (Past Pres.) Thoracic Soc.; Hon. FRCPI; Hon. FRSocMed. *Publications:* Papers on Medical Subjects, *eg* Surgical Shock in Wounded Soldiers; and many on Respiratory Disease; (ed) Diseases of the Chest, 1952. *Address:* 28 Netherhall Gardens, NW8. *T:* 01-435 6640. *Club:* Royal Automobile.

MARSHALL, Geoffrey, MA, PhD; FBA 1971; Fellow and Tutor in Politics, The Queen's College, Oxford, since 1957; *b* 22 April 1929; *s* of Leonard William and Kate Marshall; *m* 1957, Patricia Ann Christine Woodcock; two *s*. *Educ:* Arnold Sch., Blackpool, Lancs; Manchester Univ. MA Manchester, MA Oxon, PhD Glasgow. Research Fellow, Nuffield Coll., 1955-57. Mem.

Oxford City Council, 1965-74; Sheriff of Oxford, 1970-71. *Publications:* Parliamentary Sovereignty and the Commonwealth, 1957; Some Problems of the Constitution (with G. C. Moodie), 1959; Police and Government, 1965; Constitutional Theory, 1971. *Recreation:* middle-aged squash. *Address:* The Queen's College, Oxford. *T:* Oxford 48411.

MARSHALL, George Wicks, CMG 1974; MBE 1955; BEM 1946; Assistant General Secretary, Association of First Division Civil Servants, since 1976; *b* 6 March 1916; *e s* of G. L. Marshall, Highbury, London, N5; *m* 1946, Mary Cook Kirkland. General Post Office, 1930-48. Served War, Royal Artillery (HAA), 1940-46. Board of Trade, 1948-56; Trade Commn Service, 1956-65; Asst Trade Comr, Nairobi, 1956; Trade Comr: Accra, 1958, Colombo, 1961; Principal Trade Comr, Hong Kong, 1963; Dep. Controller, BoT office for Scotland, 1965; Dep. Dir, Export Services Br., 1967; seconded to HM Diplomatic Service as Counsellor (Commercial) HM Embassy, Copenhagen, 1969-76. *Recreations:* theatre, television, working. *Address:* 22 Woodclyffe Drive, Summer Hill, Chislehurst, Kent BR7 5NT. *T:* 01-467 6607. *Clubs:* Royal Commonwealth Society; Hong Kong (Hong Kong).

MARSHALL, Rt. Rev. Guy, MBE 1943; Vicar of Blakesley with Adstone and Hon. Assistant Bishop, Diocese of Peterborough, since 1974; *b* 5 Nov. 1909; *s* of Edgar Breedon Marshall and Marion (*née* Worsley); *m* 1936, Dorothy Gladys Whiting (*d* 1975); three *s* one *d*; *m* 1977, Harriet Ethel, *d* of Rev. J. J. Moore. *Educ:* Prince Henry's Grammar Sch., Otley; University Coll., Durham; King's Coll., London. AKC 1936. Deacon 1936, Priest 1937. Curate, St Andrew's, Stoke Newington, 1936-38; Chaplain, Missions to Seamen in Southampton, Buenos Aires and Rosario, 1938-42; Chaplain, St Andrew's Seafarers' Chapel, Rosario, 1942-44; Rector, Canon and Sub-Dean, St John's Cath., Buenos Aires, 1944-52; Rector, Stoke Bruerne with Grafton Regis and Alderton, 1953-56; Chaplain, Missions to Seamen, Toronto, 1956-67 and Rector, St Stephen's, Toronto, 1958-67; Bishop Suffragan of Trinidad and Tobago for work in Venezuela, 1967; Bishop in Venezuela, 1972, resigned 1974. *Recreations:* reading, bridge, Rugby Union football, cricket. *Address:* The Vicarage, Blakesley, Towcester, Northants. *T:* Blakesley 507.

MARSHALL, Hedley Herbert, CMG 1959; QC (Nigeria) 1955; LLB (London); FRGS; Deputy Director, British Institute of International and Comparative Law, since 1968; Director, Commonwealth Legal Adv. Service, since 1963; *b* 28 March 1909; *s* of late Herbert Marshall, Sydenham, and Elizabeth, *d* of late Edwin Smith Adams; *m* 1952, Faith, *widow* of Wing-Comdr John Collins Mayhew, RAF; one step-*d*. *Educ:* Dulwich Coll. Prep. Sch.; Dulwich Coll.; London Univ. Admitted Solicitor of Supreme Court, England, 1931; joined Army, 1940; 2nd Lieut 1941; Captain, 1942; Major, 1945; after service at home and overseas, released 1946 and joined Colonial Service; Asst Administrator-Gen., Nigeria, 1946; Magistrate Grade I, 1946; called to Bar, Gray's Inn, 1949; Crown Counsel, Nigeria, 1950; Senior Crown Counsel, 1951; Legal Sec., Northern Region of Nigeria, 1952; Chancellor of Diocese of Northern Nigeria, 1953; Attorney-Gen., and Minister in Govt, Northern Nigeria, 1954-62; Dir of Public Prosecutions, Northern Nigeria, 1959-62; Member: House of Assembly, House of Chiefs and Executive Council, Northern Nigeria, 1951-62; Privy Council, Northern Nigeria, 1954-59; Advisory Cttee on the Prerogative of Mercy, Northern Nigeria, 1959-62. Adviser to Government of Northern Nigeria at Nigerian Constitutional Conferences, 1957 and 1958; Mem. Provisional Council of Ahmadu Bello Univ., 1961. Commissioner for Revision of Laws of Northern Nigeria, 1962-63. Asst Dir (Commonwealth), Brit. Inst. Internat. and Comparative Law, 1963-68. Founder Mem. and Mem. Council, Statute Law Soc. *Publications:* Natural Justice, 1959; rev. edn of The Laws of Northern Nigeria, 1963, in 5 Vols (Vols I to III with F. A. O. Schwarz Jr); contrib to International Encyclopaedia of Comparative Law; contribs to legal and other periodicals. *Recreations:* tennis, swimming, photography. *Address:* The Red House, Bassingbourn, Royston, Herts. *Club:* Royal Commonwealth Society.

MARSHALL, Herbert Percival James; film, theatre and TV producer, director, scriptwriter, author and translator; *b* London, 20 Jan. 1906; *s* of Percival Charles Marshall and Anne Marshall (*née* Organ); *m* 1935, Fredda Brilliant, sculptress, actress. *Educ:* Elementary Sch., Ilford; evening classes, LCC; Higher Inst. of Cinematography, Moscow, USSR. Began as Asst Film Editor, Empire Marketing Bd Film Unit, 1929-30; Asst Dir various Moscow theatres; Drama Dir, Moscow Radio (English), 1933-35; Founder, Dir, Unity Theatre; prod. documentary films, Spanish Civil War; Principal, Unity Theatre Trng Sch.; Lectr, LCC Evening Insts, 1935-39; Founder and Artistic Dir,

Neighbourhood Theatre, S Kensington; Script-writer (with Fredda Brilliant) and Associate Producer (Ealing Studios), 1939-40; apptd Dir, Old Vic (theatre bombed); toured England; Dir for Sadler's Wells Opera Co.; Lectr, RADA, 1940-41; i/c of production, Russian, Czech, Polish and Yugoslav films for Europe (8 langs); broadcasts, BBC, in Russian, 1942-45; Lectr on film art, Amer. Univ., Biarritz, 1945-46; Indep. Film Producer: prod. for J. Arthur Rank, Min. of Educn, NCB, etc; prod., scripted and dir. (with Fredda Brilliant), Tinker (Edinburgh Festival Award), 1946-50; dir. Man and Superman, Arena Theatre (Fest. of Brit.), 1951; prod. official Mahatma Gandhi Biog. Documentary, etc, India, 1951-55; Exec. Producer, TV closed circuit and films for Advision Ltd, London, 1955-56; Film Producer for Govt of India; Principal, Natya Acad. of Dramatic Art, Bombay; Producer, Natya Nat. Theatre Company, 1957-60; Dir, Centre for Soviet and E European Studies, Southern Illinois Univ., apptd Prof., Academic Affairs, 1970. Theatre Architecture Consultant to various projects: Indian Nat. Theatres, 1955-59; Centre 42, London, 1962; Morrison Civic Arts Centre, Lambeth, 1965; Samuel Beckett Theatre, Oxford Univ., 1968-. Lecturer: RCA and NY Univ., 1964; Univ. of Illinois, and Oxford Univ., 1968; Himahcal Pradesh Univ., Hong Kong Univ., La Troge Univ., Monash Univ., Univ. of Melbourne, 1972. Distinguished Visiting Prof., Sch. of Communications, Southern Illinois Univ., Carbondale, 1965, 1968. Many well-known actors and actresses have been produced or directed by him. FRSA 1967. Mather Schol. of the Year, Case Western Reserve, Ohio, 1972. *Publications:* Mayakovsky and His Poetry, 1964 (London); Hamlet Through the Ages (jointly), 1953 (London); Ira Aldridge, The Negro Tragedian (with Mildred Stock), 1953 (London, New York); Poetry of Voznesensky (London and New York) and Yevtushenko (London and New York), 1965; Stanislavsky Method of Direction (London and New York), 1969; Anthology of Soviet Poetry, 1970; (jtly) Collected Works of Eisenstein (London and USA), 1973; (ed) Internat. Library of Cinema and Theatre (20 vols); (ed) Pictorial History of the Russian Theatre, 1974; (ed and introd) Battle Ship Potemkin, 1974. Scores: English Text and Lyrics, Ivan the Terrible (Oratorio by S. Prokoviev and S. M. Eisenstein), 1962 (Moscow); English Texts: 13th and 14th Symphonies, and Execution of Stepan Razin, by D. Shostakovich; Mayakovsky Oratorio Pathetique, by G. Sviridov, 1974, etc. *Recreations:* reading and TV. *Address:* 1204 Chautauqua Street, Carbondale, Ill 62901, USA; Southern Illinois University, Carbondale, Ill 62901, USA.

MARSHALL, Howard Wright; Regional Director, Eastern Region, Departments of Environment and Transport, since 1976; Chairman, East Anglia Regional Economic Planning Board, since 1976; *b* 11 June 1923; *s* of Philip Marshall, MBE, and Mary Marshall; *m* 1st (marr. diss.); two *s*; 2nd, 1963, Carol Yvonne (*née* Oddy); one *d*. *Educ:* Prudhoe West Elementary, Northumberland; Queen Elizabeth Grammar Sch., Hexham. Served War, RAF, 1941-46; POW, 1943-45. Min. of Health, Newcastle upon Tyne, 1940; Regional Offices, Ministries of Health, Local Govt and Planning, Housing and Local Govt, 1948-55; HQ, Min. of Housing and Local Govt, 1955-59; National Parks Commn, 1959-62; Min. of Housing and Local Govt, later DoE, 1962; Asst Sec., 1968; Under Sec., 1976. *Recreations:* gardening, sport. *Address:* Brackenwood, Farthing Green Lane, Stoke Poges, Bucks. *T:* Fulmer 2974. *Club:* Caterpillar.

MARSHALL, Sir Hugo Frank, KBE 1953; CMG 1950; JP; retired; *b* 1905; *s* of late Henry Mieres Marshall and Cecil Mabel Balfour; *m* 1931, Christine Phyllida, *d* of late Major R. Brinckman, OBE; two *s* one *d*. *Educ:* Malvern Coll.; Exeter Coll., Oxford. Colonial Service, Nigeria, 1928; Administrative Officer, Class I, 1946; Staff Grade, 1947; Administrative Sec., Nigeria, 1947-52; Lt-Governor, Western Region, Nigeria, 1952-54; Chief Sec., Federation of Nigeria, 1954-55. JP Wilts 1958. *Recreation:* ornithology. *Address:* Murrell House, Limpley Stoke, near Bath. *T:* Limpley Stoke 2162.

MARSHALL, Sir James, Kt 1953; DL; JP; *b* 23 Oct. 1894; *s* of James and Julia Harriet Marshall, Hounslow, Middlesex; *m* 1939, May Florence Kent (*d* 1972); two *s* two *d*. *Educ:* Whitgift, Croydon. Croydon Borough: Councillor, 1928; Alderman, 1936-68; Mayor, 1945-46. Chm., Croydon Food Control Cttee, 1939-53; Mem. Crawley Development Corporation, 1945-61; Chm. Whitgift Governors, 1944-69. JP 1937; DL Surrey, 1952; DL Greater London, 1966. FRPSL. *Recreations:* lawn tennis, horticulture, philately. *Address:* Bramleys, Kingswood Lane, Selsdon, Surrey. *T:* 01-657 7981. *Club:* Royal Automobile.

MARSHALL, James; MP (Lab) Leicester South, since Oct. 1974; *b* 13 March 1941; *m* 1962, Shirley, *d* of W. Ellis, Sheffield; one *s* one *d*. *Educ:* City Grammar Sch., Sheffield; Leeds Univ. BSc,

PhD. Joined Lab Party, 1960. Mem., Leeds City Council, 1965-68; Leicester City Council: Mem., 1971-76; Chm., Finance Cttee, 1972-74; Leader, 1974. Contested (Lab): Harborough, 1970; Leicester South, Feb. 1974. *Address:* House of Commons, SW1A 0AA; 48 Chiltern Avenue, Cosby, Leicester LE9 5UF. *T:* Leicester 21285.

MARSHALL, John, MA; JP; Headmaster, Robert Gordon's College, Aberdeen, 1960-77; *b* 1 July 1915; *s* of Alexander Marshall and Margaret Nimmo Carmichael; *m* 1940, May Robinson Williamson; two *d*. *Educ:* Airdrie Acad.; Glasgow Univ. MA (1st cl. hons Classics), 1935; Medley Memorial Prizeman, History 1934; John Clark Schol., Classics, 1935. Asst Master: Bluevale Sch., 1937-39; Coatbridge Sec. Sch., 1939-41; Principal Teacher of Classics, North Berwick High Sch., 1941-50; Rector, North Berwick High Sch., 1950-60. Mem., Adv. Coun. on Educn for Scotland, 1955-57; Trustee, Scottish Sec. Schools Travel Trust, 1960- (Chm., 1971-); Pres., Headmasters' Assoc. of Scotland, 1962-64; Mem. Gen. Teaching Coun. for Scotland, 1966-70. JP City of Aberdeen, 1967. *Publications:* numerous articles on educational subjects. *Recreations:* fishing, photography, writing, language studies. *Address:* 11 Hazledene Road, Aberdeen AB1 8LB. *T:* Aberdeen 38003. *Club:* Royal Northern.

MARSHALL, John Alexander; Under Secretary, Northern Ireland Office, since 1977; *b* 2 Sept. 1922; *s* of James Alexander Marshall and Mina Dorothy Marshall; *m* 1947, Pauline Mary (*née* Taylor); six *s*. *Educ:* LCC elem. sch.; Hackney Downs School. Paymaster General's Office, 1939; FO, 1943; HM Treasury, 1947: Principal, 1953; Asst Sec., 1963; Under-Sec., 1972; Cabinet Office, 1974-77. *Recreations:* reading, music. *Address:* 48 Long Lane, Ickenham, Mddx. *T:* Ruislip 72020.

MARSHALL, Rt. Hon. Sir John (Ross), PC 1966; GBE 1974; CH 1973; BA, LLM; Prime Minister of New Zealand, Feb.-Nov. 1972; Leader of the Opposition, 1972-74; Consultant Partner, Buddle Anderson Kent & Co.; Chairman of Directors, National Bank of New Zealand; *b* Wellington, 5 March 1912; *s* of Allan Marshall; *m* 1944, Margaret Livingston; two *s* two *d*. *Educ:* Whangarei High Sch.; Otago Boys' High Sch.; Victoria Univ. Coll. Barrister and Solicitor, 1936; served War, with 2nd NZEF, Pacific Is and Italy, 1941-46 (Inf. Major); MP (Nat.) for Mount Victoria, 1946-54, for Karori, 1954-75; Lectr in Law, Victoria Univ. Coll., 1948-51, Vis. Fellow, 1975-; Minister, Asst to Prime Minister, in charge of State Advances Corp., Public Trust Office and Census and Statistics Dept, 1949-54; Minister of Health, 1951-54, and Information and Publicity, 1951-57; Attorney-Gen. and Minister of Justice, 1954-57; Dep. Prime Minister, 1957; Dep. Leader of the Opposition, 1957-60; Minister of Customs, 1960-61; Minister of Industries and Commerce, 1960-69; Attorney-General, 1969-71; Dep. Prime Minister, and Minister of Overseas Trade, 1960-72; Minister of Labour and Immigration, 1969-72. NZ Rep. at Colombo Plan Conf., New Delhi, 1953; visited US on Foreign Leader Grant, April 1958; NZ Representative: GATT, 1961, 1963, 1966, and ECAFE, 1962, 1964, 1966, 1968, 1970; Commonwealth Prime Ministers' Conf., 1962; Commonwealth Trade Ministers' Conf., 1963, 1966; Commonwealth Parly Conf., 1965; UN 25th Annual Session, NY, 1970; ILO Conf., Geneva, 1971; EEC Negotiations, 1961-71. Mem., Adv. Council, World Peace through Law. Chairman: NZ Commn for Expo 70; Nat. Develt Council, 1969-72; Cttee of Registration of Teachers, 1976-77. Chairman: Philips Electrical Industries; Contractors Bonding Corp.; Norwich Winterthur Insurance (NZ) Ltd; Director: Norwich Union Insurance Soc.; DRG (NZ) Ltd; Hallenstein Bros Ltd; Fletcher Holdings Ltd. Hon. Bencher, Gray's Inn. Hon. LLD Wellington, 1975. *Publication:* The Law of Watercourses, 1957. *Recreations:* fishing, golf. *Address:* 22 Fitzroy Street, Wellington, NZ. *T:* 736.631.

MARSHALL, Martin John, CMG 1967; Director, Finance/Administration, Royal Association for Disability and Rehabilitation, since 1977; lately HM Diplomatic Service; *b* 21 March 1914; *s* of late Harry Edmund Marshall and late Kate Ann (*née* Bishop); *m* 1938, Olive Emily Alice, *d* of Thomas and Olive King; two *d*. *Educ:* Westminster City Sch.; London Sch. of Economics, University of London. Customs and Excise Officer, 1935-39; Technical Officer, Min. of Aircraft Prod., 1940-46; Principal, Min. of Supply, 1947-50. Called to Bar, Gray's Inn, 1947. Trade Commissioner: Montreal, 1950-52; Atlantic Provinces, 1953; Alberta, 1954-57; Principal Trade Commissioner: Montreal, 1957-60; Calcutta (for Eastern India), 1961-63; Dep. High Comr, Sydney, 1963-67; Consul-General, Cleveland, Ohio, 1968-71; Dep. High Comr, Bombay, 1971-74. *Recreations:* ski-ing, golf. *Address:* 8 Sunnyside Place, SW19 4SJ. *T:* 01-946 5570. *Clubs:* Brooks's; Royal Wimbledon Golf.

MARSHALL, Michael; see Marshall, R. M.

MARSHALL, Rt. Rev. Michael Eric; see Woolwich, Bishop Suffragan of.

MARSHALL, Noël Hedley; Counsellor, HM Diplomatic Service, since 1976; NATO Defence College, Rome, 1977-78; b 26 Nov. 1934; s of Arthur Hedley Marshall, qv. Educ: Leighton Park Sch.; Lawrenceville Sch., NJ (E-SU Exchange Scholar, 1953-54); St John's Coll., Cambridge (BA 1957; Sir Joseph Larmor Award, 1957). Pres., Cambridge Union Soc., 1957. Entered Foreign (later Diplomatic) Service; FO, 1957-59; Third Sec., Prague, 1959-61; FO, 1961-63; Second (later First) Sec., Moscow, 1963-65; CRO, 1965-66; First Sec. (Economic): Karachi, 1966-67; Rawalpindi, 1967-70; Chargé d'affaires ai, Ulan Bator, 1967; FCO, 1970-74; First Sec. (later Counsellor) Press, Office of UK Permanent Rep. to European Communities, Brussels, 1974-77. Recreations: sailing, the theatre. Address: c/o Foreign and Commonwealth Office, King Charles Street, SW1. Clubs: Royal Ocean Racing; Europe House.

MARSHALL, Norman, CBE 1975; play producer; b 16 Nov. 1901; s of Lt-Col D. G. Marshall, IMS, and Elizabeth Mackie. Educ: Edinburgh Academy; Worcester Coll., Oxford. Producer, Cambridge Festival Theatre, 1926-33; directed Gate Theatre, 1934-40. Produced many plays in West End, including Parnell, 1936, Victoria Regina, 1937, Of Mice and Men, 1939, The Petrified Forest, 1942, Uncle Vanya, 1943, The First Gentleman, 1946, The Indifferent Shepherd, 1948. Later did a series of productions in countries abroad, including France, Germany, Italy, Israel, India and Pakistan. Shute Lecturer on the Art of the Theatre, Liverpool Univ., 1951. Head of Drama for Associated-Rediffusion Television, 1955-59. Chairman: British Council's Adv. Cttee on Drama, 1961-68; British Theatre Assoc., 1965-76; Joint Chm., National Theatre Building Cttee; Vice-Chm., Theatre's Advisory Council, 1963-74; Pres., Assoc. of British Theatre Technicians (Chm., 1961-73). Governor, Old Vic. Lectures: tours of Canada and Australia, 1961 and 1962; Univs of Cape Town and Natal, 1964; tour of Norway, Sweden, Denmark and Finland, 1973. Directed Romeo and Juliet, and Hamlet, South Africa; Directed: at Chichester Theatre Festival, 1966; at Canterbury Festival, 1970. Midsummer Prize, Corp. of London, 1971. Publications: The Other Theatre, 1948; The Producer and the Play, 1957, 3rd edn 1975. Address: 9 Arundel Court, Jubilee Place, SW3. T: 01-352 0456. Club: Garrick.

MARSHALL, Norman Bertram, MA, ScD; FRS 1970; Professor and Head of Department of Zoology and Comparative Physiology, Queen Mary College, University of London, 1972-77, now Professor Emeritus; b 5 Feb. 1915; s of Arthur Harold and Ruby Eva Marshall; m 1944, Olga Stonehouse; one s three d. Educ: Cambridgeshire High Sch.; Downing Coll., Cambridge. Plankton Biologist, Dept of Oceanography, UC Hull, 1937-41; Army (mostly involved in operational research), 1941-44; seconded from Army for Service in Operation Tabarin to Antarctic, 1944-46; British Museum (Natural History): Marine fishes, 1947-72; Sen. Principal Scientific Officer, 1962-72. In charge of Marine Expedn to Red Sea, 1948-50; Senior Biologist, Te Vega Expedn, 1966-67; Ray Lankester Fellowship, 1977-78. Polar Medal (Silver), 1948; Rosenstiel Gold Medal for distinguished services to marine science. Publications: Aspects of Deep Sea Biology, 1954; The Life of Fishes, 1965; Explorations in the Life of Fishes, 1970; Ocean Life, 1971; various papers in learned jls. Recreations: music, fishing, golf. Address: 6 Park Lane, Saffron Walden, Essex. T: Saffron Walden 22528.

MARSHALL, Prof. Sir (Oshley) Roy, Kt 1974; CBE 1968; Secretary-General, Committee of Vice-Chancellors and Principals, since 1974; b 21 Oct. 1920; s of Fitz Roy and Corene Carmelita Marshall; m 1945, Eirwen Lloyd; one s three d. Educ: Harrison Coll., Barbados, WI; Pembroke Coll., Cambridge; University Coll., London. Barbados Scholar, 1938; BA 1945, MA 1948 Cantab; PhD London 1948. Barrister-at-Law, Inner Temple, 1947. University Coll., London: Asst Lecturer, 1946-48; Lecturer, 1948-56; Sub-Dean, Faculty of Law, 1949-56; Prof. of Law and Head of Dept of Law, Univ. of Sheffield, 1956-69, Vis. Prof. in Faculty of Law, 1969-; on secondment to University of Ife, Ibadan, Nigeria, as Prof. of Law and Dean of the Faculty of Law, 1963-65; Vice-Chancellor, Univ. of West Indies, 1969-74. Chm., Commonwealth Educn Liaison Cttee, 1974-; Mem., Police Complaints Bd, 1977-. Hon. LLD Sheffield, 1972. Publications: The Assignment of Choses in Action, 1950; A Casebook on Trusts (with J. A. Nathan), 1967; Theobald on Wills, 12th edn, 1963. Recreations: racing and cricket. Address: c/o Committee of Vice-Chancellors and Principals, 29 Tavistock Square, WC1H 9EZ.

MARSHALL, Peter Harold Reginald, CMG 1974; United Kingdom Representative on the Economic and Social Council of the United Nations, since Nov. 1975; b 30 July 1924; 3rd s of late R. H. Marshall; m 1957, Patricia Rendell Stoddart; one s one d. Educ: Tonbridge; Corpus Christi Coll., Cambridge. RAFVR, 1943-46. Entered Foreign Service, 1949; FO, 1949-52; 2nd Sec. and Private Sec. to Ambassador, Washington, 1952-56; FO, 1956-60; on staff of Civil Service Selection Board, 1960; 1st Sec. and Head of Chancery, Baghdad, 1961, and Bangkok, 1962-64; Asst Dir of Treasury Centre for Administrative Studies, 1965-66; Counsellor, UK Mission, Geneva, 1966-69, Counsellor and Head of Chancery, Paris, 1969-71; Head of Financial Policy and Aid Dept, FCO, 1971-73; Asst Under-Sec. of State, FCO, 1973-75. Recreations: music, golf. Address: United Kingdom Mission to the United Nations, 845 Third Avenue, New York, NY 10022, USA. Club: Travellers'.

MARSHALL, Air Cdre Philippa Frances, CB 1971; OBE 1956; Director of the Women's Royal Air Force, 1969-73; b 4 Nov. 1920; d of late Horace Plant Marshall, Stoke-on-Trent. Educ: St Dominic's High Sch., Stoke-on-Trent. Joined WAAF, 1941; Comd WRAF Admin. Officer, Strike Comd, 1968-69, Air Cdre 1969; ADC, 1969-73. Recreations: music, cookery. Address: 41 Moorton Avenue, Burnage, Manchester M19 2NG. Club: Royal Air Force.

MARSHALL, Sir Robert (Braithwaite), KCB 1971 (CB 1968); MBE 1945; Second Permanent Secretary, Department of the Environment, since 1973; b 10 Jan. 1920; s of Alexander Halford Marshall and Edith Mary Marshall (née Lockyer); m 1945, Diana Elizabeth Westlake; one s three d. Educ: Sherborne Sch.; Corpus Christi Coll., Cambridge. Mod. Langs, Pt I, 1938-39; Economics Pts I and II, 1945-47. BA Cambridge. Foreign Office temp. appointment, 1939-45. Entered Home Civil Service, 1947; Ministry of Works, 1947-50; Private Sec. to Sec., Cabinet Office, 1950-53; Min. of Works, 1953-62; Min. of Aviation, 1962-66; Min. of Power, 1966-69; Min. of Technology, 1969-70; Under-Sec., 1964; Dep. Sec. 1966; Second Perm. Sec., 1970; Secretary (Industry), DTI, 1970-73. Mem. Council, Surrey Univ. Coronation Medal, 1953. Recreations: travel, gardening, music and arts. Address: Brooklands, Lower Bourne, Farnham, Surrey. T: Frensham 2879.

MARSHALL, Robert Leckie, OBE 1945; Principal, Co-operative College, and Chief Education Officer, Co-operative Union Ltd, 1946-77; b 27 Aug. 1913; s of Robert Marshall and Mary Marshall; m 1944, Beryl Broad; one s. Educ: Univ. of St Andrews (MA Mediaeval and Modern History; MA 1st Cl. Hons English Lit.); Commonwealth Fellow, Yale Univ. (MA Polit. Theory and Govt). Scottish Office, 1937-39. Served War, 1939-46: RASC and AEC; finally Comdt, Army Sch. of Educn. Pres., Co-op. Congress, 1976. Missions on co-op. develt to Tanganyika, Nigeria, India, Kenya and S Yemen. Member: Gen. Adv. Council and Complaints Rev. Bd, IBA, 1973-77; Monopolies and Mergers Commn, 1976-; Distributive Studies Bd, Business Educn Council, 1976-. Hon. MA Open Univ., 1977; Hon. DLitt Loughborough Univ. of Technol., 1977. Publications: contribs to educnl and co-op jls. Recreations: walking, reading, swimming, church architecture, golf. Address: Holly Cottage, 15 Beacon Road, Woodhouse Eaves, Loughborough, Leics LE12 8RN. T: Woodhouse Eaves 890612.

MARSHALL, (Robert) Michael; MP (C) Arundel since Feb. 1974; b 21 June 1930; s of Robert Ernest and Margaret Mary Marshall, The Mount, Hathersage; m 1972, Caroline Victoria Oliphant Hutchison; two step d. Educ: Bradfield Coll.; Harvard and Stanford Univs. MBA Harvard 1960. Joined United Steel Cos Ltd, 1951; Branch Man., Calcutta, 1954-58; Man. Dir, Bombay, 1960-64; Commercial Dir, Workington, 1964-66; Man. Dir, Head Wrightson Export Co. Ltd, 1967-69; Management Consultant, Urwick Orr & Partners Ltd, 1969-74. Vice-Chm., Cons. Party Parly Industry Cttee; Jt Chm., All Party British/Burmese Parly Gp; Sec., British American Univ. Gp; Vice-Chm., All Party Parly Cttee on Management; Mem., Adv. Cttee of Business Graduates Assoc.; liaison MP for W Sussex CC. FRSA. Recreations: cricket commentating, golf, theatre, ballet, travel. Address: Old Inn House, Slindon, Arundel, W Sussex. Clubs: Garrick, MCC; Lords Taverners; Goodwood Golf.

MARSHALL, Maj.-Gen. Roger Sydenham, CB 1974; TD 1948; Director of Army Legal Services, Ministry of Defence, 1971-73, retired; b 15 July 1913; 2nd s of Robert Sydenham Cole Marshall and Enid Edith Langton Cole; m 1940, Beryl Marie, d of William Vaughan Rayner; one d. Solicitor, Supreme Court, 1938. Commnd N Staffs Regt, TA, 1933; mobilised TA, 1939; comd 365 Batt. 65th Searchlight Regt, RA, 1942-44; Trans. Army Legal Services, 1948; DADALS: HQ MELF, 1948-49;

HQ E Africa, 1949-52; GHQ MELF, 1952-53; WO, 1953-55; ADALS: WO, 1955-56; HQ BAOR, 1956-58; WO, 1960-61; HQ E Africa Comd, 1961-62; DDALS, GHQ FARELF, 1962-63; Col Legal Staff, WO, 1964-69; Brig. Legal Staff, 1969-71; Maj.-Gen. 1971. *Recreations:* hunting; reading history. *Address:* Higher Campscott Farm, Lee, N Devon. *T:* Ilfracombe 62885. *Club:* Naval and Military.

MARSHALL, Sir Roy; *see* Marshall, Sir O. R.

MARSHALL, Maj.-Gen. Roy Stuart, CB 1970; OBE 1960; MC 1945; MM 1940; Deputy Sales and Marketing Director, Guided Weapons Division, British Aircraft Corporation; *b* 28 Oct. 1917; *s* of Andrew Adamson Marshall and Bessie Marshall, Whitley Bay, Northumberland; *m* 1946, Phyllis Mary Rawlings; two *s*. *Educ:* Whitley Bay and Monkseaton High Sch. Joined TA 88 (West Lancs) Field Regt, 1939; commd into RA, 1942; War Service in Europe and Middle East, 1939-45; Staff Coll., Camberley, 1947; GSO 2, 2 Inf. Div., 1948-50; DAA & QMG, 6 Inf. Bde, 1950-51; jssc 1952-53; AA & QMG, 1 (BR) Corps, 1958-60; CO 12th Regt RA, 1960-62; Comdr 7th Artillery Bde, 1962-64; Indian Nat. Def. Coll., 1965; Maj.-Gen. RA, BAOR, 1966-69; Dep. Master-General of the Ordnance, 1969-70, retired; Col Comdt, RA, 1972-77. *Recreations:* fishing, golf, bridge. *Address:* 2 Newhayes, Kilmington, Axminster, Devon. *T:* Axminster 32361. *Club:* Army and Navy.

MARSHALL, Thomas Humphrey, CMG 1947; MA; Professor Emeritus, University of London; *b* London, 19 Dec. 1893; *s* of William C. Marshall, architect, and Margaret, *d* of Archdeacon Lloyd, sometime Archdeacon of Waitemata, New Zealand; *m* 1st, 1925, Marjorie Tomson (*d* 1931); 2nd, 1934, Nadine, *d* of late Mark Hambourg; one *s*. *Educ:* Rugby; Trinity Coll., Cambridge. Civilian prisoner in Germany, 1914-18; Fellow of Trinity Coll., Cambridge, 1919-25; Lecturer LSE, 1925; Reader in Sociology, London, 1930; Research Dept of FO, Head of German Section and Dep. Dir, 1939-44; Head of the Social Science Dept, London Sch. of Economics and Political Science, 1944-50; Mem. of Lord Chancellor's Cttee on Practice and Procedure of Supreme Court, 1947-53; Educational Adviser in the British Zone of Germany, 1949-50; Member: UK Cttee for Unesco; UK Delegation to Unesco General Conference, 1952. Martin White Prof. of Sociology, London Sch. of Economics, London Univ., 1954-56; Dir of the Social Sciences Dept, Unesco, 1956-60; Pres., Internat. Sociological Assoc., 1959-62. Hon. DSc Southampton 1969; Hon. DLitt Leicester, 1970; DUniv York, 1971. *Publications:* James Watt, 1925; Class Conflict and Social Stratification (ed), 1938; The Population Problem (ed), 1938; Citizenship and Social Class, 1950; Sociology at the Crossroads and other Essays, 1963; Social Policy, 1965; numerous articles in Economic Journal, Economic History Review, Sociological Review, etc. *Recreation:* music. *Address:* 6 Drosier Road, Cambridge.

MARSHALL, Thurgood; Associate Justice of US Supreme Court, since 1967; *b* 2 July 1908; *s* of William C. and Norma A. Marshall; *m* 1st, 1929, Vivian Burey (*d* 1955); 2nd, 1955, Cecilia A. Suyat; two *s*. *Educ:* Lincoln Univ. (AB 1930); Howard Univ. Law Sch. Admitted Maryland Bar, 1933. Special Counsel, NAACP, 1938-50 (Asst, 1936-38); Dir, NAACP Legal Defense and Educ. Fund, 1940-61. Judge, 2nd Circuit Court of Appeals, 1961-65; Solicitor-Gen. of USA, 1965-67. Holds hon. doctorates at many US Univs. Spingarn Medal, 1946.

MARSHALL, Valerie Margaret, (Mrs A. R. Marshall); Financial Controller, Industrial and Commercial Finance Corporation, since 1969; *b* 30 March 1945; *d* of Ernest Knagg and Marion Knagg; *m* 1972, Alan Roger Marshall; one *s*. *Educ:* Brighton and Hove High Sch.; Girton Coll., Cambridge (MA); London Graduate Sch. of Business Studies (MSc). LRAM. Member: Scottish Cttee, Design Council, 1975-; Monopolies and Mergers Commn, 1976-. *Recreations:* music, ballet, collecting antiquarian books, walking, entertaining. *Address:* Kilmore, 16 Dalkeith Avenue, Dumbreck, Glasgow G41 5BJ. *T:* 041-427 0096. *Club:* Royal Scottish Automobile (Glasgow).

MARSHALL, Dr Walter Charles, CBE 1973; FRS 1971; Member, since 1972, Deputy Chairman, since 1975, UKAEA; *b* 5 March 1932; *s* of late Frank Marshall and Amy (*née* Pearson); *m* 1955, Ann Vivienne Sheppard; one *s* one *d*. *Educ:* Birmingham Univ. Scientific Officer, AERE, Harwell, 1954-57; Research Physicist: University of California, 1957-58; Harvard Univ., 1958-59; AERE, Harwell: Group Leader, Solid State Theory, 1959-60; Head of Theoretical Physics Div., 1960-66; Dep. Dir, 1966-68; Dir, 1968-75; Dir, Research Gp, UKAEA, 1969-75; Chief Scientist, Dept of Energy, 1974-77. Mem., NRDC, 1969-75; Chairman: Adv. Council on R&D for Fuel and Power, 1974-77; Offshore Energy Technology Bd, 1975-77.

Fellow, Royal Swedish Acad. of Engrg Scis, 1977. Hon. DSc Salford, 1977. Editor, Oxford Internat. Series of Monographs on Physics, 1966-. Maxwell Medal, 1964; Glazebrook Medal, 1975. *Publications:* Thermal Neutron Scattering, 1971; research papers on magnetism, neutron scattering and solid state theory. *Recreations:* croquet, chess, gardening, origami. *Address:* Bridleway House, Goring-on-Thames, Oxon. *T:* Goring-on-Thames 2890.

MARSHALL, William; Assistant Under-Secretary of State, Ministry of Defence (Navy), 1968-72, retired; *b* 30 Sept. 1912; *e s* of late Allan and Julia Marshall, Whitecraigs, Renfrewshire; *m* 1st, 1940, Jessie Gardner Miller (*d* 1962); one *s*; 2nd, 1963, Doreen Margaret Read. *Educ:* Allan Glen's Sch., Glasgow; Glasgow Univ. MA Glasgow 1932, LLB (*cum laude*) Glasgow 1935. War of 1939-45: Temp. Asst Principal, Air Ministry, 1940; Service with Royal Navy (Ord. Seaman), and Admin. Staff, Admty, 1941. Private Sec. to Permanent Sec. of Admty (Sir J. G. Lang), 1947-48; Principal Private Sec. to successive First Lords of Admty (Lord Hall, Lord Packenham and Rt Hon. J. P. L. Thomas, later Lord Cilcennin), 1951-54; Gold Staff Officer at Coronation, 1953; Asst Sec. in Admty, 1954; on loan to HM Treasury, 1958-61; returned to Admiralty, 1961. *Recreations:* golf, travel, gardening. *Address:* 37 West Drive, Cheam, Surrey. *T:* 01-642 3399. *Club:* Kingswood Golf (Tadworth).

MARSHALL-CORNWALL, Gen. Sir James (Handyside), KCB 1940 (CB 1936); CBE 1919; DSO 1917; MC 1916; *b* 27 May 1887; *o s* of late Jas Cornwall, Postmaster-Gen. UP, India; *m* 1921, Marjorie (*d* 1976), *d* of late W. Scott Owen, OBE, JP of Cefngwifed, Newtown, Montgomeryshire; one *d* (and one *s* killed on active service, 1944). *Educ:* Cargilfield; Rugby; RMA, Woolwich. Commissioned in Royal Artillery, 1907; served European War in France and Flanders, 1914-18, as Intelligence Officer and Gen. Staff Officer (despatches 5 times, DSO, MC, Bt Major 1916; Bt Lt-Col 1918; Legion of Honour, Belgian Ordre de la Couronne (Croix d'Officier), Belgian Croix de Guerre, American Distinguished Service Medal, Order of the Nile); served on Gen. Staff at War Office, 1918; attended Peace Conference at Paris as mem. of British Delegation, 1919 (CBE); passed Staff Coll., 1919; served in Army of the Black Sea, 1920-23; acted as British Delegate, Thracian Boundary Commission, 1924-25; served in Shanghai Defence Force, 1927; Military Attaché, Berlin, Stockholm, Oslo and Copenhagen, 1928-32; Comdr RA 51st (Highland) Div. TA, 1932-34; Chief of British Military Mission to Egyptian Army, 1937-38; Dir-Gen. Air and Coast Defence, War Office, 1938-39; Special Employment, War Office, 1939-40; III Corps, Comdr, 1940; GOC British Troops in Egypt, 1941; GOC-in-C Western Command, 1941-42 (despatches twice); retd pay, 1943; Amer. Legion of Merit (Comdr), 1946. Editor-in-Chief of Captured German Archives, attached Foreign Office, 1948-51. Pres., Royal Geographical Society, 1954-58 (Hon. Vice-Pres.; Hon. Mem., 1975). *Publications:* Geographic Disarmament, 1935; Marshal Massena, 1965; Napoleon, 1967; Grant, 1970; Foch, 1972; Haig, 1973. *Recreation:* historical research. *Address:* Birdsall House, Malton, N Yorks YO17 9NR. *T:* North Grimston 202. *Clubs:* Brooks's, Beefsteak, Geographical.
See also Baron Middleton.

MARSHAM, family name of **Earl of Romney.**

MARSLAND, Prof. Edward Abson; Professor of Oral Pathology, University of Birmingham, since 1964; *b* Coventry, 18 May 1923; *s* of T. Marsland; *m* 1957, Jose, *d* of J. H. Evans; one *s* two *d*. *Educ:* King Edward's Sch. and Univ. of Birmingham. BDS (1st cl. hons), PhD, FDSRCS, FRCPath. House Surgeon, Gen. and Dental Hosps, Birmingham, 1946; Birmingham University: Research Fellow, 1948-50; Lectr in Dental Pathology, 1950-58; Sen. Lectr, 1958-64; Dir, Birmingham Dental Sch., 1969-74. *Publications:* An Atlas of Dental Histology, 1957; A Colour Atlas of Oral Histopathology, 1975; scientific papers in various jls. *Recreations:* gardening, music, motoring. *Address:* 9 Bryony Road, Selly Oak, Birmingham B29 4BY. *T:* 021-475 4365.

MARSON, Air Vice-Marshal John, CB 1953; CBE 1950; CEng; RAF (retired); *b* 24 Aug. 1906; *s* of late Wing Comdr T. B. Marson, MBE, and late Mrs E. G. Marson, (*née* Atkins); *m* 1935, Louise Joy Stephen Paterson; two *s*. *Educ:* Oakham Sch. RAF Coll., Cranwell, 1924-26. STSO, HQ, Coastal Command, 1949-50; AOC 42 Group, 1951-54; Pres., Ordnance Board, 1956-57 (Vice-Pres., 1954-56); Dir-Gen. of Technical Services, 1957-58; AOC 24 Group, 1959-61. *Recreations:* sailing, golf. *Address:* Marygold, Aldeburgh, Suffolk IP15 5AF. *Clubs:* Royal Air Force; Royal Cruising; Cruising Association; Aldeburgh Golf.

MARTELL, Edward Drewett; Chairman of The Freedom Group; *b* 2 March 1909; *e s* of E. E. Martell and Ethel Horwood; *m* 1932, Ethel Maud Beverley; one *s. Educ:* St George's Sch., Harpenden. In Coal trade, 1926-28, then entered journalism. Past: News Editor, World's Press News; Gen. Manager, The Saturday Review; Managing Editor, Burke's Peerage and Burke Publishing Co.; Sports staff of The Star. Served War of 1939-45, with RAC (Capt.). On demobilisation established own bookselling and publishing company. Mem. LCC, 1946-49; contested (L) Rotherhithe, 1946, and N. Hendon, 1950; East Ham (Ind.), 1957; SE Bristol (Nat. Fellowship C), 1963; Dep. Chm., Liberal Central Assoc., 1950-51; Trustee, Winston Churchill Birthday Trust, 1954. Founded: Free Press Soc., 1955; People's League for the Defence of Freedom, 1956 (first Chm.); Anti-Socialist Front, 1958; National Fellowship (co-founder), 1962; New Daily (also Editor), 1960. *Publications:* (with R. G. Burnett) The Devil's Camera, 1932; (with R. G. Burnett) The Smith Slayer, 1940; The Menace of Nationalisation, 1952; The Menace of the Trade Unions, 1957; Need the Bell Toll?, 1958; (with Ewan Butler) Murder of the News-Chronicle and the Star, 1960; Wit and Wisdom-Old and New, 1961; A Book of Solutions, 1962. *Recreations:* lawn tennis; Sherlock Holmes and Father Brown. *Address:* 43 Gloucester Place, W1.

MARTELL, Vice-Adm. Sir Hugh (Colenso), KBE 1966 (CBE 1957); CB 1963; *b* 6 May 1912; *s* of late Engineer Capt. A. A. G. Martell, DSO, RN (Retd) and of Mrs S. Martell; *m* 1941, Marguerite Isabelle, *d* of late Sir Dymoke White, 2nd Bt; five *s* one *d. Educ:* Edinburgh Academy; RNC Dartmouth. Royal Navy, 1926-67, retired; served War, 1940-45 (despatches): Gunnery Officer in HMS Berwick and HMS Illustrious. Naval Adviser to Dir Air Armament Research and Development, Min. of Supply, 1952-54; Capt. (F) 7 and in Comd HMS Bigbury Bay, 1954-55; Overall Operational Comdr, Nuclear Tests, in Monte Bello Is as Cdre, 1956; IDC, 1957; Capt., HMS Excellent, 1958; Dir of Tactical and Weapons Policy, Admiralty and Naval Mem. Defence Research Policy Staff, Min. of Defence, 1959-62; Admiral Commanding Reserves and Dir-Gen. of Naval Recruiting, 1962-65; Chief of Allied Staff, Mediterranean, Aegean and Black Sea, 1965-67. Director: City and Military Personnel Consultants Ltd; Directors Secretaries Ltd; Secretarial Selection Ltd; HJM Dynamics Ltd; Chairman, Bury Manor Schools Trust Ltd. *Recreation:* sailing. *Club:* Naval.

MARTEN, Francis William, CMG 1967; MC 1943; formerly Counsellor, Foreign and Commonwealth Office; *b* 8 Nov. 1916; *er s* of late Vice-Adm. Sir Francis Arthur Marten and late Lady Marten (*née* Phyllis Raby Morgan); *m* 1940, Hon. Avice Irene Vernon (*d* 1964); one *s* one *d* ; 2nd, 1967, Miss Anne Tan; one *s* . *Educ:* Winchester Coll.; Christ Church, Oxford. Served HM Forces, 1939-46. Entered HM Foreign Service, 1946; served FO, 1946-48; Washington, 1948-52; FO, 1952-54; Teheran, 1954-57; NATO Defence Coll., Paris, 1957-58; Bonn, 1958-62; Leopoldville, 1962-64; Imperial Defence Coll., 1964-65; Dep. High Comr, Eastern Malaysia, 1965-67; ODM, 1967-69. *Recreation:* ski-ing. *Address:* 113 Pepys Road, SE14. *T:* 01-639 1060.

MARTEN, H. N.; see Marten, Neil.

MARTEN, Neil; MP (C) Banbury Division of Oxon, since 1959; *b* 3 Dec. 1916; 3rd *s* of F. W. Marten; *m* 1944, Joan Olive, *d* of Vice-Adm. W. J. C. Lake, CBE; one *s* two *d. Educ:* Rossall Sch.; Law Soc. Solicitor, 1939. Served War of 1939-45 (despatches); Army, 1940-45, Northants Yeomanry, Special Forces, French Resistance, Norwegian Resistance. Foreign Office, 1947-57, Egypt, Turkey, Germany. Croix de Guerre; Norwegian War Medal. PPS to Pres. of Board of Trade, 1960-62; Parliamentary Sec., Ministry of Aviation, 1962-64. Chm., Anglo-Norwegian Parly Group; Member: Exec., 1922 Cttee; Select Cttee European Legislation; CPA; British-Amer. Gp; Franco-British Gp. Vice-President: Disabled Drivers Assoc.; Council, Voluntary Service Overseas. *Recreations:* tennis, ski-ing. *Address:* Swalcliffe House, near Banbury, Oxon. *Club:* Special Forces.

MARTIN, Andrew, QC 1965; PhD (London); Professor of International and Comparative Law, University of Southampton, since 1963; Member: Law Commission, 1965-70; Law Reform Committee, since 1970; *b* 21 April 1906; *m* 1932, Anna Szekely; one *s. Educ:* Lutheran Coll., Budapest; Universities of Budapest, Paris, Vienna, Berlin and London. Barrister-at-Law, Middle Temple, 1940, Bencher, 1976. *Publications:* A Commentary on the Charter of the United Nations (with Norman Bentwich), 1950; Collective Security, 1952; The Changing Charter (with J. B. S. Edwards), 1955; Restrictive Trade Practices and Monopolies, 1957; Law Reform Now (jt ed. and part-author), 1963; Legal Aspects of Disarmament, 1963; numerous papers and articles published by

learned socs and jls. *Recreations:* chamber music and alpine driving. *Address:* 4 Pump Court, Temple, EC4. *T:* 01-353 9178. *Clubs:* Reform, Hurlingham.

MARTIN, Archer John Porter, CBE 1960; FRS 1950; MA, PhD; Consultant to Wellcome Research Laboratories, 1970-73; *b* 1 March 1910; *s* of Dr W. A. P. and Mrs L. K. Martin; *m* 1943, Judith Bagenal; two *s* three *d. Educ:* Bedford Sch.; Peterhouse, Cambridge, Hon. Fellow, 1974. Nutritional Lab., Cambridge, 1933-38; Chemist, Wool Industries Research Assoc., Leeds, 1938-46; Research Dept, Boots Pure Drug Co., Nottingham, 1946-48; staff, Medical Research Council, 1948-52; Head of Phys. Chem. Div., National Inst. of Medical Research, 1952-56; Chemical Consultant, 1956-59; Director, Abbotsbury Laboratories Ltd, 1959-70. Extraordinary Prof., Technological Univ. of Eindhoven, 1965-73; Professorial Fellow, Univ. of Sussex, 1973-. Berzelius Gold Medal, Swedish Medical Soc., 1951; (jointly) Nobel Prize for Chemistry, 1952; John Scott Award, 1958; John Price Wetherill Medal, 1959; Franklin Institute Medal, 1959; Leverhulme Medal, Royal Society, 1963; Koltoff Medal, Acad. of Pharmaceutical Science, 1969; Callendar Medal, Inst. of Measurement and Control, 1971. Hon. DSc, Leeds, 1968; Hon. LLD Glasgow, 1973. *Address:* Abbotsbury, Barnet Lane, Elstree, Herts. *T:* 01-953 1031. *Club:* Chemists' (New York).

MARTIN, Charles Emanuel; Professor of International Law and Political Science, University of Washington, Seattle, Washington, 1925-62; Director University of Washington Institute International Affairs, 1935-62; Emeritus Professor of International Law and Political Science since 1962; *b* Corsicana, Texas, 11 Sept. 1891; *s* of Emanuel Cobb Martin and Roxie Annie Moon; *m* 1921, Jewell Boone; no *c. Educ:* University of California, Berkeley (BA 1914, MA 1915); Columbia Univ. (PhD 1918); Hon. LLD University S Cal. 1942; Columbia Univ, Fellow Int. Law, 1916-17; War Trade Bd and Food Adm. US Govt 1917-18; Coast Artillery Corps, US Army, 1918; Carnegie Endowment Fellow Int. Law, 1918-19; Lecturer on Int. Law and Politics and Sec. Bureau Int. Relations, University Calif., Berkeley, 1919-20; Head Dept Pol Science, University Cal. at Los Angeles, 1920-25; Dean Faculty Social Science, University of Washington, 1926-29 and Head Political Science Dept, 1925-52; mem. Carnegie Endowment European Int. Law Conference, 1926; visiting Prof. Int. Relations, University of Hawaii, 1929; Carnegie Endowment Prof. Int. Relations accredited to universities in Orient and Antipodes, 1929-30; Dir Sch. Pacific and Oriental Affairs, University of Hawaii, 1932; Mem. Govt Bd on Immigration and Naturalization Service, US Dept Labor, 1933; Exchange Prof. Int. Law and Adm., American Univ., Washington, DC, 1942-43; Ednl consultant, Nat. Inst. Public Affairs, Washington, DC, 1942-43; Special Expert to Sec. of US Army and Chm. Bd of Consultants of US Cultural and Social Science Mission to Japan, Sept. 1948-Jan. 1949. Deleg. Inst. Pacific Relations Confs, 1929, 1936, 1950, 1954; in Japan, US, and India. University of Washington and Rockefeller Foundation Research professorship, East and SE Asia, 1954-55; Lectr, Inter-Amer. Acad. of Comparative and Internat. Law, Havana, Cuba, Feb. 1957; Prof. of Amer. Studies, University Philippines, 1962-63; Haynes Prof. Internat. Law, Whittier Coll., Calif., 1964. United States-Mexican pre-recognition Conference, Mexico City, 1923; Summer Sessions at California, Harvard, Texas, Michigan, George Washington, Stanford, Southern California, Hawaii Univs; Special Lecturer at Miss., Emory, La, and NC Univs; Lecturer Canadian Inst. Int. Affairs, 1933, 1943, 1951, 1953; Trustee Am. Inst. Pacific Relations; Dir and Ex Comm., Inst. World Affairs; Ex Comm., Council For. Relations (Seattle Comm.); Am. Commission on Org. of Peace; Pres. World Affairs Symposium (Seattle). Late Pres. and Chm. Board Trustees Seattle World Affairs Council; Trustee Seattle Art Museum, 1940-52. Pres., American Soc. of International Law, 1960-61; Member: Amer., Western, and Pacific NW Political Science Assocs; American Section, Internat. Law Assoc.; Asiatic Soc. of Japan. *Publications:* Policy of the US as Regards Intervention, 1921; An Introduction to the Study of American Constitution, 1926; American Government and Citizenship (with W. H. George), 1927; Politics of Peace, 1929; Permanent Court of International Justice and Question of American Adherence, 1932; various articles on civic, political, public and international affairs; Report of US Cultural and Social Science Mission to Japan (in collaboration), 1949; South and South-east Asia, 1951; Rebirth of a Nation (Japan), 1953; Universalism and Regionalism in International Law and Organization, 1959. Edited: The Pacific Area, 1929; Pacific Problems, 1932; War and Society, 1941; Problems of the Peace, 1945; San Francisco Conference and the UN Organization, 1946; The World in Crisis, 1948; Prospects for World Stability, 1950; New Weapons for the New Diplomacy, 1953. *Recreations:* foreign travel, teaching assignments abroad; organizing internat.

relations institutes as an avocation. *Address:* 3828 48th Avenue NE, Seattle, Washington 98105, USA; Dept Political Science, University of Washington, Seattle, Washington 98105. *T:* Lakeview 4-1117, (office) 543-2780. *Clubs:* Rainier, Monday, Faculty, China (Seattle); Cosmos (Washington, DC); Army and Navy (Manila, RP).

MARTIN, Brig. Cyril Gordon, VC 1915; CBE 1938; DSO 1914; *b* 19 Dec. 1891; *s* of late Rev. John Martin, Foochow, China; *m* 1917, Mab (*d* 1973), *o d* of late Major E. Hingston, RE; one *s* (and one killed in action 1944) one *d. Educ:* Bath Coll.; Clifton Coll. Entered army, 1911; Major, 1928; Lt-Col, 1936; Col, 1939; served European War, 1914-15 (despatches, VC, DSO); EEF Palestine, 1918; NW Frontier of India, 1930-31 (despatches, Bt Lt-Col); Waziristan, 1937 (CBE); Dep. Chief Engineer, Northern Command, India, 1939; Chief Engineer British Troops in Iraq, 1941 (despatches); Chief Engineer NW Army, India; ADC to the King, 1945-47; retired pay, 1947. *Address:* 3 Pinelands Close, St John's Park, Blackheath, SE3 7TF. *T:* 01-858 6620.

MARTIN, Prof. Derek H.; Professor of Physics, Queen Mary College, University of London, since 1967; *b* 18 May 1929; *s* of Alec Gooch Martin and Winifred Martin; *m* 1951, Joyce Sheila Leaper; one *s* one *d. Educ:* Hitchin Boys' Grammar Sch.; Eastbourne Grammar Sch.; Univ. of Nottingham. BSc; PhD; FInstP. Lectr, Queen Mary Coll., London, 1954-58, 1962-63; DSIR Research Fellow, 1959-62; Reader in Experimental Physics, 1963-67; Vis. Prof., Univ. of California, Berkeley, 1965-66; Dean, Faculty of Science, Queen Mary Coll., 1968-70. Mem. Adv. Board for Mathematical and Physical Sciences, Univ. of London, 1969-73; Head of Dept of Physics, QMC, 1970-75; Dir, QMC Industrial Research Ltd, 1973-; Member: Astronomy, Space and Radio Bd, SRC, 1975-; Bd, Athlone Press, 1973-; Adv. Bd, S African Astron. Observatory, 1977-; Royal Greenwich Observatory Commn, 1977-. FRSA; FOSA. Editor, Advances in Physics, 1974-. *Publications:* Magnetism in Solids, 1967; Spectroscopic Techniques, 1967; numerous articles and papers in Proc. Royal Soc., Jl of Physics, etc. *Address:* Hermanus, Hillwood Grove, Brentwood, Essex. *T:* Brentwood 210546.

MARTIN, Douglas Whitwell; Chairman, Gill & Duffus Ltd, 1964-70; President, Gill & Duffus Group Ltd, 1973; *b* 17 Feb. 1906; *s* of Rev. T. H. Martin, MA, and Lily Janet Vaughan Martin; *m* 1st, 1931, Jessie Milroy Lawrie (*d* 1965); three *s*; 2nd, 1967, Margaret Helen Simms, FCIS. *Educ:* Rossall Sch.; Lausanne University. Member of staff, Export Dept of Lever Brothers Ltd, 1923-27; joined Gill & Duffus Ltd, 1929. Underwriting Member of Lloyd's, 1950-69. *Recreations:* reading, theatre. *Address:* 74 Fort George, St Peter Port, Guernsey, CI. *T:* Guernsey 25381. *Club:* Boodle's.

MARTIN, Edward H.; see Holland-Martin.

MARTIN, Edward Kenneth; Consulting Surgeon, University College Hospital; Fellow of University College, London; *s* of Dr Edward Fuller Martin, Weston-super-Mare; *m* 1923, Philippa Parry Pughe (*see* Philippa P. Martin); three *d. Educ:* Charterhouse; University Coll., London. MS, FRCS (Mem. of Court of Examiners); BEF, 1914-18; Temp. Major RAMC. *Publications:* various contributions to medical journals. *Recreation:* travelling. *Address:* 97 Dorset House, Gloucester Place, NW1 5AF. *T:* 01-935 6322.

MARTIN, Frank Vernon, RE 1961 (ARE 1955); MA; MSIA; Wood Engraver; Etcher; Book Illustrator; Head of Department of Graphic Arts, Camberwell School of Art, since 1976, Senior Lecturer since 1965 and Teacher of Etching and Engraving since 1953; *b* 14 Jan. 1921; *er s* of late Thomas Martin; *m* 1942, Mary Irene Goodwin; three *d. Educ:* Uppingham Sch.; Hertford Coll., Oxford; St Martin's Sch. of Art. History Schol., Hertford Coll., Oxford. Served War of 1939-45, Army, 1941-46. Book illustrations for Folio Society, Hutchinson, Geoffrey Bles, Burns Oates, Vine Press and other publishers. One-man exhibitions of prints and drawings, London, 1956, 1961 and 1968; works represented in: Victoria and Albert Museum; Manchester City Art Gallery; Whitworth Art Gallery, Manchester; Fitzwilliam, Cambridge; other public collections at home and abroad. Sec., Royal Society of Painter-Etchers and Engravers, 1956-57. Hon. Academician, Accademia delle Arti del Disegno, Florence, 1962. *Publications:* articles, book reviews, etc, on Engraving and the Graphic Arts. *Recreation:* photography. *Address:* Studio L, 416 Fulham Road, SW6. *T:* 01-385 1089; 2 Ranelagh Avenue, SW6. *T:* 01-736 8896.

MARTIN, The Hon. Fred Russell Beauchamp, MC; Justice of the Supreme Court of Victoria, 1934-57; *b* 28 May 1887; *s* of

Frederick Martin and Alice Maud Evelyn Wood; *m* 1915, Ethel Muriel Swinburne; three *s. Educ:* Wesley Coll., Melbourne; Melbourne Univ. (Queen's Coll.). Called to Victoria Bar, 1911; served in 38th Bn AIF 1915-19 (MC). *Recreations:* golf, bowls. *Address:* Berkeley Street, Hawthorn, Victoria 3122, Australia. *Clubs:* Royal Automobile (Victoria); Peninsula Country Golf.

MARTIN, Frederick George Stephen, CIE 1941; MC; MIME; *b* 26 Aug. 1890; *s* of Frederick Martin, Newcastle-under-Lyme; *m* 1939, Mrs Herta Portzeba, *d* of Fritz Loose, Berlin; no *c.* Served European War, 1914-18 (despatches, MC, wounded twice); entered Indian State Rlys, 1923; Dep. Chief Mechanical Engineer, EI Rly, 1928; Controller of Stores, EI Rly, 1930; Dep. Dir-Gen., Engineering and Civil Production, Dept of Supply, Govt of India, 1939-42; Addl Dir, Gen. Supply Dept, India, 1942-43; Dir in charge, Tata Aircraft Ltd, 1943-46; Tech. Adviser, Tata Industries and Tata Ltd, 1946-59, retired. *Address:* Golmuri, Cranham, Gloucester GL4 8HB. *T:* Painswick 2061.

MARTIN, Frederick Royal, BSc, CEng, FICE, FIStructE; Under-Secretary, Department of the Environment, since 1973; Director, Defence Services II, Property Services Agency, since 1975; *b* 10 Oct. 1919; *s* of late Frederick Martin and Lois Martin (*née* Royal); *m* 1946, Elsie Winifred Parkes; one *s* three *d. Educ:* Dudley Grammar Sch.; Univ. of Birmingham (BSc (Hons)). Asst Engr, Birmingham, Tame and Rea Dist Drainage Bd, 1940; entered Air Min. Directorate-Gen. of Works, as Engrg Asst, 1941; Asst Civil Engr: Heathrow, Cardington, London, 1944-48; Civil Engr: Cambridge, Iraq, Jordan, Persian Gulf, London, 1948-54; Sqdn Leader, RAF (CC), 1949-52; Sen. CE, London, 1954-58; Suptg CE, London, also Chief Engr, Aden, Aden Protectorate, Persian Gulf and E Africa, 1958-62; Suptg CE, Exeter, 1962-64; Min. of Public Bdg and Works, Area Officer, Bournemouth, 1964-66; Suptg CE, Directorate of Civil Engrg Develt, 1966-70; Asst Dir (DCED), 1970-72; Dir of Directorate of Social and Research Services (DSRS), Property Services Agency, 1972; Chief Engineer, Maplin Develt Authority, 1973-74. *Publications:* various papers and articles to Instn Civil Engrs, etc, on airfield pavements. *Recreations:* looking at medieval building, rugby and Assocation football; listening to music; taking photographs; reading; gardening. *Address:* 25 East Avenue, Bournemouth, Dorset BH3 7BS. *T:* Bournemouth 25858.

MARTIN, Air Marshal Sir Harold Brownlow Morgan, KCB 1971 (CB 1968); DSO 1943 (Bar 1944); DFC 1942 (Bar 1943, 1944); AFC 1948; Middle East Future Markets Adviser, Hawker Siddeley International, since 1974; resident in Beirut; *b* Edgecliffe, 27 Feb. 1918; *s* of the late J. H. O. M. Martin, MD, and of Colina Elizabeth Dixon; *m* 1944, Wendy Lawrence, *d* of late Grenville Outhwaite, Melbourne; two *d. Educ:* Bloomfields; Sydney; Randwick. Served war, 1939-45, Bomber Comd; took part in raid on Möhne dam, 1943. psa 1945; won Britannia Flying Trophy, 1947; Air Attaché, British Embassy, Israel, 1952-55; jssc, 1958; idc, 1965. SASO, Near East Air Force and Jt Services Chief of Staff, 1966-67; Air Vice-Marshal 1967; AOC No 38 Gp, Air Support Command, 1967-70; Air Marshal 1970; C-in-C, RAF Germany, and Commander, NATO 2nd Tactical Air Force, 1970-73; Air Member for Personnel, MoD, 1973-74, retired. ADC to HM the Queen, 1963. Oswald Watt Memorial Medal. *Recreations:* flying, horse racing, tennis, travel. *Clubs:* Royal Air Force, Hurlingham, Chelsea Arts.

MARTIN, Lt-Gen. Henry James, CBE 1943; DFC; Chief of Defence Staff, South African Defence Force, retired; *b* 10 June 1910; *s* of Stanley Charles Martin and Susan C. Fourie; *m* 1940, Renée Viljoen; three *s* two *d. Educ:* Grey Coll. Sch., Bloemfontein; Grey Univ. Coll., Bloemfontein. Joined S African Air Force, 1936, and played important rôle in British Empire Training Scheme in South Africa; commanded No 12 Sqdn in Western Desert (DFC, Croix Militaire de première classe Belgique); commanded No 3 Wing (a unit of Desert Air Force) and campaigned from El Alamein to Tunis; returned to Union, 1943. *Recreations:* rugger (represented Orange Free State, 1931-34, Transvaal, 1935-37, South Africa, 1937), golf, tennis. *Address:* 10 Crescent Road, Waterkloof Ridge, Pretoria, S Africa. *Clubs:* Rand (Johannesburg); Pretoria (Pretoria).

MARTIN, Sir James, Kt 1965; CBE 1957 (OBE 1950); DSc; CEng; FIMechE; Managing Director and Chief Designer, Martin-Baker Aircraft Co. Ltd, since formation of Company, 1934; *m*; two *s* two *d.* Founder, Martin Aircraft Co., 1929. Designed: Martin patent balloon barrage cable cutter; 12 gun nose for Havoc night fighter; Spitfire jettison hood; flat feed for 20 mm Hispano gun; M-B1, 2, 3, and 5 prototype aeroplanes; started work on aircraft ejector seats, 1945; explosive hood jettison gear; rocket ejection seats. Hon. FRAeS; RAeS

Wakefield Gold Medal, 1952; Barbour Air Safety Award, 1958; Cumberbatch Air Safety Trophy, 1959; Royal Aero Club Gold Medal. Hon. Fellow, Manchester Inst. of Science and Technology, 1968. Pioneer and authority on aircraft seat ejection. *Publications:* numerous papers on air-survival (read by learned socs in UK and USA). *Recreation:* design work. *Address:* Southlands Manor, Denham, Bucks. *T:* Denham 2214. *Club:* Naval and Military.

MARTIN, James Arthur, CMG 1970; FASA; company director; *b* 1903; *s* of late Arthur Higgins Martin and Gertrude, *d* of George Tippins; unmarried. *Educ:* Stawell and Essendon High Schools, Victoria. FASA 1924. Joined The Myer Emporium Ltd, Melbourne, 1918; The Myer Emporium (SA) Ltd, Adelaide, 1928, Man. Dir 1936, Chm. and Man. Dir, 1956-68, retd; Dir, Myer (Melbourne) Ltd, department store, 1936-68, retd. *Recreations:* horse riding, tennis. *Address:* 17 Hawkers Road, Medindie, SA 5081, Australia. *Clubs:* South Australian Cricket, South Australian Jockey (Adelaide).

MARTIN, Maj.-Gen. James Mansergh Wentworth, CB 1953; CBE 1944; late 8th King George V's Own Light Cavalry; *b* 5 Aug. 1902; *er s* of late James Wentworth Martin, Castle Jane, Glanmire, Co. Cork, Ireland, and late Mrs J. Wentworth Martin, Great Meadow, Hambledon, Surrey; *m* 1944, Mrs Jean Lindsay Barnes, *d* of late Sir Henry Cowan, MP. *Educ:* Charterhouse; Royal Military Academy, Woolwich. Joined RFA 1922; with Royal West African Frontier Force, 1925-27; Private Sec. to Governor of Assam, 1928-29; transferred to Indian Army, 1930. During War of 1939-45, Persia and Iraq, Syria, Tunisia, Sicily, Italy and Burma; Brig., Gen. Staff, 1943-44. Comd 1st Indian Armoured Bde, 1945-47; transferred to Royal Scots Greys, Jan. 1948; Chief of Staff, British Forces in Trieste, 1948-49; Comd 9th Armoured Brigade, 1949-51; Dep. Chief of Staff Allied Land Forces Central Europe, Fontainebleau, 1951-53; GOC Salisbury Plain District, 1953-56; retired Sept. 1956. Vice-Pres. Army Ski Assoc.; Hon. Vice-Pres. Army Football Assoc.; Liveryman of the Merchant Taylors' Company. *Address:* Great Meadow, Hambledon, Godalming, Surrey. *T:* Wormley 2665. *Club:* Cavalry and Guards.

MARTIN, James Purdon, MA, MD, BCh (Belfast), FRCP; Consulting Physician to the National Hospital for Nervous Diseases, Queen Square, WC1; *b* Jordanstown, County Antrim, 1893; *s* of late Samuel Martin, Garmoyle, Bangor, Co. Down; *m* 1st, Majorie, MB, BS (*d* 1937), *d* of Richard Blandy, Madeira; two *s*; 2nd, Janet Smiles Ferguson, MA. *Educ:* Royal Academical Institution and Queen's Univ., Belfast; (Medical Schs: Belfast, St Bart's, St Mary's) BA (first class hons in Mathematical subjects), 1915; Purser Studentship; MB, BCh, BAO, 1920; MRCP, 1922; FRCP 1930; Neurologist to British Post-Graduate Medical Sch., 1935-57. Examnr, London Univ. and Conjoint Bd, 1940-49. Dean: Nat. Hosp. Med. Sch., 1944-48; Inst. Neurology, 1948-49. Mem. of the Senate of Queen's Univ. (representative for Students), 1916-17. Neurologist Eastern Command, Home Forces, 1940-44. Vis. Prof. of Neurology, University of Colorado, 1959. Lumleian Lecturer, RCP, 1947; Arris and Gale Lecturer, RCS, 1963. Hon. Member: Assoc. of British Neurologists; Soc. of Brit. Neuropathologists; Neurolog. Sect., RSM; Soc. Française de Neurologie; Amer. Neurolog. Assoc., etc. FRSocMed (Pres. Neurolog. Sect., 1945-46). *Publications:* The Basal Ganglia and Posture, 1967; many papers on neurological subjects in Brain, The Lancet, etc. *Address:* Craignish, Turner Drive, NW11. *T:* 01-455 5856.

MARTIN, Janet (Mrs K. P. Martin); Houseparent (Children with Special Needs) Hampshire Social Services, since 1976; Member, Press Council, since 1973; *b* Dorchester, Dorset, 8 Sept. 1927; *d* of James Wilkinson; *m* 1951, Peter Martin (SPAA Southampton Health Dist); one *s* one *d. Educ:* Dorchester Grammar Sch., Dorset, and variety of further education/training courses. Formerly: secretary, lecturer, freelance social res. interviewer, etc. Interviewer, MRC Health/Development Study, 1970-. *Address:* 69 Hiltingbury Road, Chandlers Ford, Hants. *T:* Chandlers Ford 5857.

MARTIN, Brig. John Douglas K.; *see* King-Martin.

MARTIN, Vice-Adm. Sir John (Edward Ludgate), KCB 1972 (CB 1968); DSC 1943; FNI; Lieutenant-Governor and Commander-in-Chief of Guernsey, since 1974; *b* 10 May 1918; *s* of late Surgeon Rear-Admiral W. L. Martin, OBE, FRCS and Elsie Mary Martin (*née* Catford); *m* 1942, Rosemary Ann Deck; two *s* two *d. Educ:* RNC, Dartmouth. Sub Lt and Lt, HMS Pelican, 1938-41; 1st Lt, HMS Antelope, 1942; navigation course, 1942; Navigation Officer, 13th Minesweeping Flotilla, Mediterranean, 1943-44, including invasions N Africa, Sicily, Pantelleria, Salerno; RNAS Yeovilton, 1944; Navigation

Officer: HMS Manxman and HMS Bermuda, 1944-46; HMS Nelson, 1947; HMS Victorious, 1948; Staff Coll., 1949; Navigation Officer, HMS Devonshire, 1950-51; Dirg Staff, Staff Coll., 1952-54; Jt Services Planning Staff, Far East, 1954-55; Exec. Off., HMS Superb, 1956-57; Jt Services Staff Coll., 1958; Dep. Dir Manpower Planning and Complementing Div., Admty, 1959-61; Sen. Naval Off., W Indies, 1961-62; Comdr Brit. Forces Caribbean Area, 1962-63; Capt. Britannia Royal Naval Coll., Dartmouth, 1963-66; Flag Officer, Middle East, 1966-67; Comdr, British Forces Gulf, 1967-68 (despatches); Dir-Gen., Naval Personal Services and Training, 1968-70; Dep. Supreme Allied Comdr, Atlantic, 1970-72, retd 1973. Comdr 1951; Captain 1957; Rear-Adm. 1966. Pres., Nautical Inst. *Recreations:* fishing, shooting, beagling (Jt Master Britannia Beagles, 1963-66), sailing. *Address:* Government House, Guernsey, CI; Carr House, Soberton, near Southampton. *T:* Droxford 454. *Clubs:* Army and Navy; Royal Naval Sailing Association; Royal Yacht Squadron.

MARTIN, John Hanbury; *b* 4 April 1892; *s* of W. A. H. Martin, DL, JP, and Frances Hanbury-Williams; *m* 1st, 1934, Avice Blaneid (marr. diss. 1938), *d* of Herbert Trench; 2nd, 1950, Dorothy Helen, *d* of E. Lloyd-Jones, Plas Mancott, Flints. *Educ:* Wellington; Brasenose Coll., Oxford. Served War of 1914-18; Captain, Queen's Westminster Rifles, 1915-19 (wounded). Labour candidate for Great Yarmouth, 1931; MP (Lab) Central Southwark, 1939-48. Co-founder and Chm., Southwark Housing Assoc., 1930-. Mem., London Insurance Cttee, 1936-45; Sec. Franco-British Parly Assoc., 1943-48. *Publications:* Corner of England; Peace Adventure; contrib. to New Survey of London Life and Labour; numerous articles and reviews. *Address:* c/o Barclays Bank Ltd, 68 Lombard Street, EC3. *Club:* Brooks's.

MARTIN, Sir (John) Leslie, Kt 1957; MA, PhD Manchester; MA Cantab; MA Oxon; Hon. LLD Leicester, Hull, Manchester; DUniv Essex; FRIBA; Professor of Architecture, University of Cambridge, 1956-72; Emeritus Professor, 1973; Fellow, Jesus College, Cambridge, 1956-73, Hon. Fellow 1973, Emeritus Fellow, 1976; *b* 17 Aug. 1908; *s* of late Robert Martin, FRIBA; *m*, Sadie Speight, MA, ARIBA; one *s* one *d. Educ:* Manchester Univ. Sch. of Architecture. Asst Lectr, Manchester Univ. Sch. of Architecture, 1930-34; Head of Sch. of Architecture, Hull, 1934-39; Principal Asst Architect, LMS Railway, 1939-48; Dep. Architect, LCC, 1948-53; Architect to the LCC, 1953-56. Slade Prof. of Fine Art, Oxford, 1965-66; Ferens Prof. of Fine Art, Hull, 1967-68; William Henry Bishop Vis. Prof. of Architecture, Univ. of Yale, 1973-74. Lectures: Gropius, Harvard, 1966; Cordingley, Manchester, 1968; Kenneth Kassler, Princeton, 1974; annual, Soc. Arch. Historians, 1976; Townsend, UCL, 1976. Consultant to Gulbenkian Foundn, Lisbon, 1959-69. Buildings include work in Cambridge and for Univs of Cambridge, Oxford, Leicester and Hull. Mem. Council, RIBA, 1952-58 (Vice-Pres., 1955-57); Mem. Royal Fine Art Commn, 1958-72. RIBA Recognised Schs Silver Medallist, 1929; Soane Medallist, 1930; London Architecture Bronze Medallist, 1954; RIBA Distinction in Town Planning, 1956; Civic Trust Award, Oxford, 1957; Commend. Cambridge, 1972; Concrete Soc. Award, Oxford, 1972; Royal Gold Medal for Architecture, RIBA, 1973. Hon. Mem. Assoc. of Finnish Architects, Accademico corrispondente National Acad. of S Luca, Rome. Comdr, Order of Santiago da Espada, Portugal. *Publications:* Jt Editor, Circle, 1937, repr. 1971; The Flat Book, 1939 (in collab. with wife); Whitehall: a Plan for a National and Government Centre, 1965; The Framework of Planning (Inaugural Lecture) Hull, 1967; Jt Editor, Cambridge Urban and Architectural Studies, Vol. I: Urban Space and Structure, 1972; contrib. various jls; papers include: An Architect's Approach to Architecture; Education Without Walls; Education Around Architecture, etc. *Address:* The King's Mill, Great Shelford, Cambridge. *T:* Shelford 2399. *Club:* Athenæum.

MARTIN, Sir John (Miller), KCMG 1952; CB 1945; CVO 1943; British High Commissioner in Malta, 1965-67; *b* 15 Oct. 1904; *s* of late Rev. John Martin; *m* 1943, Rosalind Julia, 3rd *d* of late Sir David Ross, KBE; one *s. Educ:* The Edinburgh Acad.; Corpus Christi Coll., Oxford (Scholar, MA). Entered Civil Service (Dominions Office), 1927; seconded to Malayan Civil Service, 1931-34; Sec. of Palestine Royal Commission, 1936; Private Sec. to the Prime Minister (Rt Hon. Winston Churchill), 1940-45 (Principal Private Sec. from 1941); Asst Under-Sec. of State, 1945-56, Dep. Under-Sec. of State, 1956-65, Colonial Office. KStJ 1966. *Publication:* contrib. to Action This Day-Working with Churchill, 1968. *Address:* The Barn House, Watlington, Oxford. *T:* Watlington 2487. *Club:* Athenæum.

MARTIN, Prof. John Powell; Professor of Sociology and Social Administration, University of Southampton, since 1967; *b* 22

Dec. 1925; s of Bernard and Grace Martin; m 1951, Sheila Feather; three s. *Educ:* Leighton Park Sch., Reading; Univ. of Reading (BA); London Sch. of Economics and Political Science (Certif. in Social Admin., PhD); Univ. of Cambridge (MA). Lectr, London Sch. of Economics, 1953-59; Asst Dir of Research, Inst. of Criminology, Univ. of Cambridge, 1960-66; Fellow, King's Coll., Cambridge, 1964-67. Hill Foundn Vis. Prof., Univ. of Minnesota, 1973; Vis. Fellow, Yale Law Sch., 1974. Mem., Jellicoe Cttee on Boards of Visitors of Penal Instns, 1974-75. *Publications:* Social Aspects of Prescribing, 1957; Offenders as Employees, 1962; The Police: a study in manpower (with Gail Wilson), 1969; The Social Consequences of Conviction (with Douglas Webster), 1971; (ed) Violence and the Family, 1978; articles in: Lancet, British Jl of Criminology, British Jl of Sociology, International Review of Criminal Policy, etc. *Recreations:* sailing, photography, do-it-yourself. *Address:* Department of Sociology and Social Administration, The University, Southampton SO9 5NH. *T:* Southampton 559122. *Club:* Island Sailing (Cowes).

MARTIN, John Sinclair, CBE 1977; farmer; Member, Agricultural Research Council, 1968-78; b 18 Sept. 1931; s of Joseph Martin and Claire Martin, Littleport, Ely; m 1960, Katharine Elisabeth Barclay, MB, BS; three s one d. *Educ:* The Leys Sch., Cambridge; St John's Coll., Cambridge (MA, Dip. in Agriculture). Chairman: Ely Br., NFU, 1963; Littleport and Downham IDB, 1971-; JCO Arable Crops and Forage Bd, 1973-76. Vice-Chm., Great Ouse Local Land Drainage Cttee, AWA, 1974-. Member: Eastern Counties Farmers' Management Cttee, 1960-72; Great Ouse River Authority, 1970-74; Eastern Regional Panel, MAFF, 1972-. *Address:* Denny Abbey, Waterbeach, Cambridge CB5 9PQ. *T:* Cambridge 860282. *Club:* Farmers'.

MARTIN, Mrs Kenneth Peter; see Martin, Janet.

MARTIN, Prof. Laurence Woodward; Vice-Chancellor, University of Newcastle upon Tyne, since 1978; b 30 July 1928; s of Leonard and Florence Mary Martin; m 1951, Betty Parnall; one s one d. *Educ:* St Austell Grammar Sch.; Christ's Coll., Cambridge (MA); Yale Univ. (MA, PhD). Flying Officer, RAF, 1948-50; Instr, Yale Univ., 1955-56; Asst Prof., Mass Inst. of Technology, 1956-61; Rockefeller Fellow for Advanced Study, 1958-59; Associate Prof., Sch. of Advanced Internat. Studies, The Johns Hopkins Univ., 1961-64; Wilson Prof. of Internat. Politics, Univ. of Wales, 1964-68; Prof. of War Studies, King's Coll., Univ. of London, 1968-77; Research Associate, Washington Center of Foreign Policy Research, 1964-. Member: Social Science Research Council, 1969-76 (Chm. Res. Grants Bd); Research Council, Georgetown Univ. Center of Internat. Studies; Consultant, Univ. of California, Los Alamos Scientific Laboratory. *Publications:* The Anglo-American Tradition in Foreign Affairs (with Arnold Wolfers), 1956; Peace without Victory, 1958; Neutralism and Non-Alignment, 1962; The Sea in Modern Strategy, 1967; (jtly) America in World Affairs, 1970; Arms and Strategy, 1973; (jtly) Retreat from Empire?, 1973. *Address:* University of Newcastle upon Tyne, Newcastle upon Tyne NE1 7RU.

MARTIN, Leonard Charles James; Under-Secretary, Ministry of Overseas Development, since 1968; b 26 June 1920; s of Leonard Howard Martin and Esther Martin (née Avis); m 1945, Althea Lilian Charles; three d. *Educ:* Brighton, Hove and Sussex Grammar Sch.; London Sch. of Economics. Served RAFVR, 1941-45. Min. of Educn, and Dept of Educn and Science, 1946-64; ODM, 1965-. UK Permanent Delegate to UNESCO, 1965-68; Mem. Exec. Bd, UNESCO, 1974- (Chm., 1976-). *Address:* Ministry of Overseas Development, Eland House, Stag Place, SW1.

MARTIN, Sir Leslie; see Martin, Sir J. L.

MARTIN, Sir Leslie Harold, Kt 1957; CBE 1954; FRS 1957; FAA; PhD (Cantab); DSc (Australian National University, Melbourne, Qld, NSW, Adelaide); LLD (WA); DLitt (Sydney); Dean of Military Studies, and Professor of Physics, Royal Military College, Duntroon, Canberra, 1967-70; b 21 Dec. 1900; s of Richard Martin, Melbourne; m 1923, Gladys Maude Elaine, d of H. J. Bull; one s (and one s decd). *Educ:* Melbourne High Sch.; Melbourne Univ.; Trinity Coll., Cambridge. Scholar of Exhibn of 1851, 1923; apptd to Natural Philosophy Dept of Melbourne Univ., 1927; Rockefeller Fellow, 1927; Syme Prize, 1934; Associate Professor of Natural Philosophy, University of Melbourne, 1937-45; Professor of Physics, 1945-59; Emeritus Prof., 1960. Defence Scientific Adviser to Aust. Govt, and Chm., Defence Res. and Develt Policy, 1948-67; Comr, Atomic Energy Commn of Aust, 1958-68; Chm., Aust. Univ. Commn, 1959-66. *Address:* 11 Wedge Court, Glen Waverley, Victoria

3150, Australia. *T:* 2321125.
See also R . L . Martin .

MARTIN, Leslie Vaughan; Directing Actuary, Government Actuary's Department (Superannuation and Research), since 1974; b 20 March 1919; s of late Hubert Charles Martin and late Rose Martin (née Skelton); m 1949, Winifred Dorothy Hopkins; one s one d. *Educ:* Price's Sch., Fareham. FIA 1947. Served with RAMC and REME, 1940-46. Deptl Clerical Officer, Customs and Excise, 1936-38; joined Govt Actuary's Dept, 1938; Asst Actuary, 1949; Actuary, 1954; Principal Actuary, 1962. Mem. Council, Inst. of Actuaries, 1971-76; Vice-Chm., CS Medical Aid Assoc., 1976-. Churchwarden, St Barnabas, Dulwich, 1965-70, 1977-, Vice-Chm. of Parish Council, 1970-. *Recreations:* crosswords, travel. *Address:* 35 Pickwick Road, Dulwich Village, SE21 7JN. *T:* 01-733 1864.

MARTIN, Louis Claude, ARCS, DIC, DSc (London); b 16 June 1891; s of late Alfred Harry Martin and Eleanor Gertrude Martin, Norwich; m 1916, Elsie Maud Lock; one s (one d decd). *Educ:* King Edward VI Middle Sch., Norwich; Royal College of Science. Lecturer, West Ham Municipal Technical Coll., 1913-14; served European War, Royal Naval Divisional Engineers, 1914-16; Lecturer and Asst Prof. in Technical Optics, Imperial College, 1917-43, Professor of Technical Optics, 1943-51. Visiting Prof., University of Rochester, NY, USA, 1936-37; Chm. Lens Research Sub-Cttee, Min. of Aircraft Prod., 1941-45; Manager Royal Institution, 1947-49 and 1951-52; Chm. of Optical Group, Physical Soc., 1947-50; Vice-Pres., International Optic Commission, 1950-53; Hon. Fellow, Royal Microscopical Soc., 1967. Deacons' Sec., Beckenham Congregational Church, 1947-49. Reader: Diocese of Norwich, 1958, 1969-71; Diocese of Winchester, 1960. Liveryman, Worshipful Company of Spectacle Makers. *Publications:* (with W. Gamble) Colour and Methods of Colour Reproduction, 1923; Optical Measuring Instruments, 1924; Introduction to Applied Optics, 1930; (with B. K. Johnson) Practical Microscopy, 1931; Technical Optics, 1949; Geometrical Optics, 1955 (with W. T. Welford) Technical Optics, 2nd edn, 1966; Theory of the Microscope, 1966. About forty papers mainly on optical subjects, especially the theory of the microscope. *Recreations:* poetry, sketching. *Address:* Golden Goose Cottage, Wiveton, Holt, Norfolk.

MARTIN, Prof. Nicholas Henry, TD 1947; FRCP, FRIC, FRCPath; Professor of Chemical Pathology, University of London, 1952-70, now Emeritus; Hon. Consultant to St George's Hospital (Consultant from 1947); Advisor, Wessex Regional Health Authority, since 1969; Member Lister Institute since 1954; b 26 Oct. 1906; s of late William and Ellen Renfree Martin, Crellow, Cornwall, and Newcastle; m 1948, Ursula, 2nd d of William Brodie and widow of T. H. Worth, Lincs; two s. *Educ:* Sedbergh Sch.; Durham, Oxford and Munich Univs. Buckle Travelling Fellow, 1929; Oxford Univ. Scholar, Middlesex Hosp., 1932. Served War of 1939-45: Asst Dir of Pathology, 21st Army Group (despatches twice); Consultant to UNRRA, 1945-46; Fellow, Harvard Univ., 1946-47. Hon. Consultant in Chemical Pathology to the Army, 1963-69. Chm., Association of Clinical Pathologists, 1963-68, Pres., 1969-70; Vice-Pres., College of Pathologists, 1966-69. Mem., Governing Body, Lord Mayor Treloar Homes, 1977-. *Publications:* numerous medical and scientific publications in internat. literature. *Recreations:* sailing, gardening, reading. *Address:* Woottons, Woolhampton, Berks. *T:* Woolhampton 3351. *Clubs:* Athenæum, Bath.

MARTIN, Hon. Sir Norman (Angus), Kt 1949; Resident Director in Australasia for Thomas Cook and Son, since 1950; Director several cos; Chairman: Victorian Inland Meat Authority, 1958-73; Australia Day Council; b 24 April 1893; s of Angus Martin, Portland, Vic; m 1919, Gladys, d of Captain Barrett, MC; one s one d. *Educ:* Werribee. Minister of Agriculture, Victoria. A Vice-Pres. of Land and Works, 1943-; MLA for Gunbower, 1934-. Served European War, AIF, 1914-18. Councillor of Cohuna Shire since inauguration of Shire, Pres. 1930-31 and 1939-40; Agent-General for Victoria in the UK, 1945-50. Pres. Leitchville Branch United Country Party, Vic, for fifteen years. *Recreations:* golf, tennis, shooting. *Address:* Longleat, 133 Alexandra Avenue, South Yarra, Victoria 3141, Australia; c/o Thomas Cook and Son, 267 Collins Street, Melbourne, Victoria 3000, Australia. *Clubs:* Royal Automobile; Australian, Savage, VRC (Melbourne).

MARTIN, Olaus Macleod, CIE 1937; b Stornoway, 1 Feb. 1890; s of Rev. Donald John Martin; m 1919, Helen Frances Steele (Kaisar-i-Hind Gold Medal, 1943) (d 1971); four s one d. *Educ:* Edinburgh and Oxford Univs. MA (1st Class Hons Classics and Mental Philosophy) 1911; Indian Civil Service, 1913; Magistrate-Collector, 1921; Divisional Commissioner, 1940;

Development Commissioner, Bengal, 1945; retired from ICS, 1948. British Administration, Eritrea, 1947-51. *Recreations:* riding, tennis, shooting, fishing. *Address:* 32 Drummond Road, Inverness. *T:* Inverness 36035.

MARTIN, Oliver Samuel, QC 1970; **His Honour Judge Martin;** a Circuit Judge, since 1975; *b* 26 Nov. 1919; *s* of Sidney Edward Martin and Nita Martin; *m* 1954, Marion Eve; two *s. Educ:* King's College Sch., Wimbledon; London University. Served RNVR, 1939-46. Called to Bar, Gray's Inn, 1951. Dep. Chm. E Sussex QS, 1970-71; a Recorder of the Crown Court, 1972-75. *Recreations:* golf, music, reading. *Address:* 8 New Square, Lincoln's Inn, WC2. *T:* 01-242 4986.

MARTIN, Patrick William, TD; MA; JP; Headmaster of Warwick School, 1962-77; *b* 20 June 1916; *e s* of Alan Pattinson Martin, Bowness-on-Windermere, Westmorland; *m* 1939, Gwendoline Elsie Helme, MA, St Hilda's Coll., Oxford; two *d. Educ:* Windermere Grammar Sch.; Balliol Coll., Oxford. 2nd cl. hons in Modern History, Balliol Coll., 1937. Asst Master, Abingdon Sch., Berks, 1938-40. Commissioned in TA, 1938; served War of 1939-45, on active service with Royal Artillery, 1940-46; Battery Capt., 1940-42; Comdt Sch. of Artillery, S India; Staff College, Quetta; GSO 2, and 1 HQRA 14th Army in Burma (despatches); British Mil. Mission to Belgium, 1946. Schoolmaster, 1946-49; Asst Dir of Educn, Brighton, 1950-52; Headmaster: Chipping Norton Grammar Sch., 1952-57; Lincoln Sch., 1958-62. Chm., Midland Div., Headmasters' Conf., 1972-; Pres., Headmasters' Assoc., 1976. Chm., Martin Working Party, Royal Agric. Soc. CC Warwickshire, 1977-. JP Warwicks 1966, Dep. Chm., Warwick Petty Sessions. *Publications:* articles in educational and other periodicals. *Recreations:* books, music, foreign countries and people; being alone in the countryside. *Address:* 80 High Street, Kenilwroth, Warwicks. *T:* Kenilworth 54140.

MARTIN, Hon. Paul Joseph James, PC (Canada) 1945; CC (Canada) 1976; QC (Canada); High Commissioner for Canada in the United Kingdom, since 1974; *b* Ottawa, 23 June 1903; *s* of Philip Ernest Martin and Lumina Marie Chouinard; *m* 1936, Alice Eleanor Adams; one *s* one *d. Educ:* Pembroke Separate Schs; St Alexandre Coll.; St Michael's Coll.; University of Toronto (MA); Osgoode Hall Law Sch., Toronto; Harvard Univ. (LLM); Trinity Coll., Cambridge; Geneva Sch. of Internat. Studies. Wilder Fellow, 1928; Alfred Zimmern Schol., 1930; Barrister-at-Law; Partner, Martin, Laird & Cowan, Windsor, Ont, 1934-63; QC 1937. Lectr, Assumption Coll., 1931-34. Can. Govt Deleg. 19th Ass. League of Nations, Geneva, 1938; Parl. Asst to Minister of Labour, 1943; Deleg. to ILO Confs, Phila, 1944, London, 1945. Apptd Sec. of State, 1945. Deleg. to 1st, 4th, 7th, 9th, 10th General Assembly, UN (Chm. Can. Del., 9th, 18th, 19th, 20th, 21st). Deleg. 1st, 3rd, 5th sessions, Economic and Social Council, 1946-47. Minister of National Health and Welfare, Dec. 1946-June 1957; Sec. of State for External Affairs, 1963-68; Pres., N Atlantic Council, 1965-66; Govt Leader in Senate, Canada, 1968-74. First elected to Canadian House of Commons, Gen. Elec., 1935; Rep. Essex East until 1968; apptd to Senate, 1968. Chancellor, Wilfrid Laurier Univ., 1972-. Holds several hon. doctorates. Hon. Life Mem., Canadian Legion. Christian Culture Award, 1956. *Address:* Canadian High Commission, Trafalgar Square, SW1. *T:* 01-930 9741. *Clubs:* Rideau (Ottawa); Beach Grove Golf and Country (Windsor, Ont).

MARTIN, Maj.-Gen. Peter Lawrence de Carteret, CBE 1968 (OBE 1964); Chairman, Lady Grover's Hospital Fund for Officers Families, since 1975; Member, National Executive Committee, Forces Help Society, since 1975; *b* 15 Feb. 1920; *s* of late Col Charles de Carteret Martin, MD, ChD, IMS and of Helen Margaret Hardinge Grover; *m* 1st, 1949, Elizabeth Felicia (marr. diss. 1967), *d* of late Col C. M. Keble; one *s* one *d*; 2nd, 1973, Mrs Valerie Singer. *Educ:* Wellington Coll.; RMC Sandhurst. MBIM 1970. Commnd Cheshire Regt, 1939; BEF (Dunkirk), 1940; Middle East, 1941; N Africa 8th Army, 1942-43 (despatches); invasion of Sicily, 1943; Normandy landings and NW Europe, 1944 (despatches); Palestine, 1945-47; GSO2 (Int.), HQ British Troops Egypt, 1947; Instructor, RMA Sandhurst, 1948-50; psc 1951; Bde Major 126 Inf. Bde (TA), 1952-53; Chief Instructor MMG Div. Support Weapons Wing, Sch. of Infantry, 1954-56; Malayan Ops, 1957-58 (despatches); DAAG GHQ FARELF, 1958-60; CO 1 Cheshire, N Ireland and BAOR, 1961-63; AA&QMG Cyprus District, 1963-65; comd 48 Gurkha Inf. Bde, Hong Kong, 1966-68; Brig. AQ HQ Army Strategic Comd, 1968-71; Dir, Personal Services (Army), 1971-74. Col The 22nd (Cheshire) Regt, 1971; Col Comdt, Mil. Provost Staff Corps, 1972-74. Services Advr, Variety Club of GB, 1976-. *Recreations:* golf, tennis, reading and watching 1 Cheshire winning Athletics championships. *Address:* Lloyds Bank Ltd, Cox's & King's Branch, 6 Pall Mall, SW1.

MARTIN, Rev. Canon Philip Montague; Canon Residentiary and Chancellor of Wells Cathedral, since 1971; *b* 8 Aug. 1913; *o s* of Montague Egerton and Ada Martin; *m* 1940, Mollie Elizabeth, *d* of John Mitchell Ainsworth; one *s* one *d. Educ:* Whitgift Sch.; Exeter Coll., Oxford. Hasker Scholar and Squire Scholar, Oxford; BA 1936, MA 1939; Teachers' Diploma (London) 1945. Deacon, 1937; Priest, 1938, Southwark. Curate of Limpsfield, 1937-40; Curate of Minehead, 1940-44; Asst Master, Clifton Coll., 1944; Chaplain and Lecturer, St Luke's Coll., Exeter, 1945-48; Canon Residentiary of Newcastle Cathedral and Diocesan Dir of Religious Education, 1948-61; Vicar of St Mary the Virgin (University Church), Oxford, 1961-71, with St Cross (Holywell), 1966-71; Chaplain, Nuffield Coll., Oxford, 1969-71; Fellow, St Cross Coll., Oxford, 1970. Examining Chaplain to • Bishop of Newcastle, 1952-73; Rural Dean of Oxford, 1965-68. *Publications:* Mastery and Mercy: a study of two religious poems, 1957; None but He and I and other poems, 1966; Earnest-pennies, 1973. *Address:* 8 The Liberty, Wells.

MARTIN, Philippa Parry; Consulting Surgeon: Western Ophthalmic Hospital; St Mary's Hospital Group; Fellow of University College, London; Hunterian Professor, The Royal College of Surgeons of England; *d* of late Canon T. St J. P. Pughe, Penn, Bucks; *m* 1923, Edward Kenneth Martin, *qv*; three *d. Educ:* Switzerland; St Felix Sch., Southwold; University Coll., and University Coll. Hospital, London. MS, FRCS. Formerly Chm. Editorial Cttee, Med. Women's Fedn. *Publications:* articles in medical journals. *Recreation:* travelling. *Address:* 97 Dorset House, NW1 5AF. *T:* 01-935 6322; Goose Neck, Chinnor Hill, Oxon. *T:* Kingston Blount 51242.

MARTIN, Most Rev. Pierre, Officer, Legion of Honour, 1967; President, Episcopal Conference of The Pacific, since 1971; Former Archbishop of Noumea (1966-71); *b* 22 Feb. 1910. *Educ:* Univ. de Lyon; Lyon Séminaire and in Belgium. Priest, 1939. POW, Buchenwald and Dachau Camps, until 1945. Séminaire de Missions d'Océanie, Lyon: Professor, 1945-47; Supérieure, 1947-53; Provincial, Sté de Marie, Paris, 1953-56; Bishop of New Caledonia, 1956. *Address:* CEPAC, PO Box 1200, Suva, Fiji.

MARTIN, Prof. Raymond Leslie, MSc, PhD, ScD; FRACI, FRIC, FAA; Vice-Chancellor, Monash University, Melbourne, since 1977; *b* 3 Feb. 1926; *s* of Sir Leslie Harold Martin, *qv*; *m* 1954, Rena Lillian Laman; three *s* one *d. Educ:* Scotch Coll., Melbourne; Univ. of Melb. (BSc, MSc); Sidney Sussex Coll., Cambridge (PhD, ScD). FRACI 1956; FRIC 1974; FAA 1971. Resident Tutor in Chemistry, Queen's Coll., Melb., 1947-49; Sidney Sussex Coll., Cambridge: 1851 Exhibn Overseas Scholar, 1949-51; Sen. Scholar, 1952-54; Res. Fellow, 1951-54; Sen. Lectr, Univ. of NSW, 1954-59; Section Leader, 1959-60, and Associate Res. Manager, 1960-62, ICIANZ; Prof. of Inorganic Chem., 1962-72, and Dean of Faculty of Science, 1971, Univ. of Melb.; Australian National University, Canberra: Prof. of Inorganic Chem., Inst. of Advanced Studies, 1972-77, Prof. Emeritus 1977; Dean, Res. Sch. of Chem., 1976-77. Vis. Scientist: Technische Hochschule, Stuttgart, 1953-54; Bell Telephone Labs, NJ, 1967; Vis. Prof., Columbia Univ., NY, 1972. Royal Aust. Chemical Institute: Smith Medal, 1968; Olle Prize, 1974; Fed. Pres., 1968-69. *Publications:* papers and revs on physical and inorganic chem. mainly in jls of London, Amer. and Aust. Chem. Socs. *Recreations:* golf; lawn tennis (Cambridge Univ. team *v* Oxford, Full Blue; Cambs County Colours). *Address:* Vice-Chancellor's Residence, Monash University, Clayton, Vic 3168, Australia. *Clubs:* Melbourne, Melbourne Beefsteak (Melbourne); Hawks (Cambridge).

MARTIN, Col Robert Andrew St George, OBE 1959 (MBE 1949); JP; Lord-Lieutenant of Leicestershire since 1965; *b* 23 April 1914; *o s* of late Major W. F. Martin, Leics Yeo., and late Violet Anne Philippa (née Wynter); *m* 1950, Margaret Grace (JP Leics 1967); *e d* of late J. V. Buchanan, MB, ChB; one *s. Educ:* Eton Coll.; RMC Sandhurst. Commissioned Oxf. and Bucks Lt Inf., 1934; ADC to Gov.-Gen. of S Africa, 1938-40; war service 4 Oxf. and Bucks, 1940-42; 2/7 R Warwick Regt, 1942-44; 5 DCLI, 1944-45 in NW Europe (despatches); DAMS, HQ ALFSEA, 1946; Mil. Asst to C of S, GHQ, SEALF, 1946-49 (MBE); Chief Instr, School of Mil. Admin., 1949-50; 1 Som. LI, 1950-52; AMS, HQ BAOR, 1952-54; 1 Oxf. and Bucks, 1954-55; Military Sec. to Gov.-Gen. of Australia, 1955-57; Comd 1 Oxf. and Bucks Lt Inf. and 1 Green Jackets, 1957-59; Bde Col Green Jackets Bde, 1959-62; Comd Recruiting and Liaison Staff, HQ Western Command, 1962-65. JP Leics, 1965. KStJ 1966. Order of Orange Nassau, 1950. *Recreations:* hunting, shooting, cricket, gardening. *Address:* The Brand, Woodhouse Eaves, Loughborough, Leics LE12 8SS. *T:* Woodhouse Eaves 890269. *Clubs:* Army and Navy, MCC.

MARTIN, Robert Bruce, QC 1977; *b* 2 Nov. 1938; *s* of Robert Martin and Fay Martin; *m* 1967, Elizabeth Georgina (*née* Kiddie); one *s* one *d. Educ:* Shrewsbury Sch.; Liverpool Univ. (LLB Hons 1959). Called to the Bar, Middle Temple, 1960. *Recreations:* music, golf, fishing. *Address:* 5 Essex Court, Temple, EC4 9AH. *T:* 01-353 4265; 39 Waterloo Road, Birkdale, Southport, Merseyside. *T:* Southport 68382. *Clubs:* Royal Automobile; Royal Birkdale Golf.

MARTIN, Robin Geoffrey; Chairman and Chief Executive, Tarmac Ltd, since 1971; *b* 9 March 1921; *s* of Cecil Martin and Isabel Katherine Martin (*née* Hickman); *m* 1946, Margery Chester Yates; two *s* one *d. Educ:* Cheltenham Coll.; Jesus Coll., Cambridge (MA). MIQ. Tarmac Ltd: Dir 1955; Gp Man. Dir 1963; Dep. Chm. 1967; Dir, Serck Ltd, 1971, Dep. Chm., 1974, Chm., 1976; Director: Burmah Oil Co. Ltd, 1975; Ductile Steels Ltd, 1977. Mem., Midlands Adv. Bd, Legal and General Assurance Soc. Ltd, 1977; Chm., Ironbridge Gorge Develt Trust, 1976. Life Governor, Birmingham Univ., 1970. *Recreations:* golf, sailing, ski-ing. *Address:* The Field, The Wergs, Wolverhampton, West Midlands. *T:* Wolverhampton 751719. *Club:* East India, Sports and Public Schools.

MARTIN, Ronald, MBE 1945; Senior Director, Customer Services, Post Office, since 1975; *b* 7 Nov. 1919; *o s* of late Albert and Clara Martin; *m* 1943, Bettina, *o d* of late H. E. M. Billing; one *d. Educ:* St Olave's Grammar Sch. Asst Traffic Superintendent, GPO, 1939. Served War of 1939-45, Royal Signals, NW Europe. GPO: Asst Princ., 1948; Princ., 1950; Treasury, 1954; Princ. Private Sec. to PMG, 1955; Staff Controller, GPO, London, 1956; Asst Sec., 1957; Dir Establishments and Organisation, GPO, 1966; Dir Telecommunications Personnel, 1967; Dir of Marketing, Telecommunications HQ, 1968-75. *Recreations:* music, motoring, amateur mechanics. *Address:* 50 Parkhill Road, Bexley, Kent. *T:* Crayford 523080.

MARTIN, Rupert Claude, MA; JP; *b* 2 July 1905; *s* of late Col C. B. Martin, CMG; *m* 1931, Ellen (*d* 1966), *d* of Henry Wood, Guernsey, CI; one *s* two *d. Educ:* Shrewsbury Sch.; Queen's Coll., Oxford (Classical Scholar), 2nd Class in Greats, 1927; Asst Master at St Paul's Sch., 1927-37; House Master, 1930-37; Headmaster of King's Sch., Bruton, Som., 1937-46, Governor, 1949-; representative of British Council in Switzerland, 1946-48; Headmaster, St Dunstan's, Burnham-on-Sea, 1948-66. Vice-Chm., Incorporated Assoc. of Preparatory Schs, 1957. *Publications:* (Lands and Peoples Series) Switzerland; Italy; Spain; Morocco; Looking at Italy; Looking at Spain. *Recreations:* mountaineering, travel. *Address:* Quantocks, Burnham on Sea, Som. *Clubs:* MCC, I Zingari, Free Foresters, Alpine; Vincent's, Authentics (Oxford).

MARTIN, Samuel Frederick Radcliffe; First Legislative Draftsman to Government of Northern Ireland since 1973; *b* 2 May 1918; 2nd *s* of late William Martin and of Margaret Martin; *m* 1947, Sarah, *y d* of late Rev. Joseph and Margaret McKane; three *s. Educ:* Royal Belfast Academical Instn; Queen's Univ., Belfast (LLB). Called to Bar, Gray's Inn, 1950. Examr, Estate Duty Office, NI, 1939; Professional Asst, Office of Parly Draftsmen, 1956. Mem. Incorp. Council of Law Reporting and of Statute Law Cttee, NI. Formerly Northern Editor, Current Law. *Publications:* articles in NI Legal Qly and Gazette of Incorp. Law Soc. *Recreation:* golf. *Address:* Brynburn, 114 Upper Road, Greenisland, Co. Antrim. *T:* Whiteabbey 62417.

MARTIN, Thomas Ballantyne; *b* 1901; *s* of late Angus Martin, FRCSE, Newcastle upon Tyne, and Robina, *d* of Thomas Pringle, Middleton Hall, Wooler, Northumberland; *m* 1953, Jean Elisabeth, *e d* of Lt-Col O. D. Bennett and Audrey, *d* of Sir Hamilton Grant, 12th Bt of Dalvey; two *d.* BA Cambridge 1923. MP (C) Blaydon Div. of Co. Durham, 1931-35. Political Correspondent of Daily Telegraph, 1937-40. RAFVR; Squadron Leader, Middle East Intelligence Centre, 1940-43; Adviser on Public Relations to UK High Comr in Australia, 1943-45; Sec. of United Europe Movement, 1947-48; Sec. to British all-party delegn to Congress of Europe at The Hague. Mem., London Stock Exchange, 1949-74, retired. *Address:* Dacre Castle, Penrith, Cumbria CA11 0HL. *T:* Pooley Bridge 375. *Clubs:* Army and Navy, Pratt's.

MARTIN, Victor Cecil, OBE; HM Diplomatic Service, retired; *b* 12 Oct. 1915; *s* of Cecil Martin and late Isabel Katherine Martin (*née* Hickman). *Educ:* Cheltenham Coll.; Jesus Coll., Cambridge (Scholar; Classical Tripos Parts 1 and 2; MA). Asst Principal, Board of Education, 1939. Served Intelligence Corps, 1940-45; Major 1944, Persia and Iraq Force. Principal, Min. of Education, 1946; transferred to CRO, 1948; British High Commn, New Delhi, 1951-54, 1956-60; Asst Sec., CRO, 1962;

Head of West Africa Dept, 1961-64; Head of S Asia Dept, 1964-66; Head of Cultural Relations Dept, 1966-68; Dep. High Comr, Madras, 1968-71; Special Adviser to High Comr, British High Commn, New Delhi, 1972-75. *Recreations:* ornithology, travel. *Address:* 76 Swan Court, Flood Street, SW3. *Clubs:* United Oxford & Cambridge University, Royal Commonwealth Society.

MARTIN, William McChesney, Jun.; Counselor, Riggs National Bank, Washington, DC, since 1970; *b* St Louis, Mo, 17 Dec. 1906; *s* of William McChesney Martin and Rebecca (*née* Woods); *m* 1942, Cynthia Davis; one *s* two *d. Educ:* Yale Univ. (BA 1928); Benton Coll. of Law, St Louis, 1931. Graduate student (part time), Columbia Univ., 1931-37. Served in bank examination dept of Federal Reserve Bank of St Louis, 1928-29; Head of statistics dept, A. G. Edwards & Sons, St Louis, 1929-31; partner, May 1931-July 1938. Mem., New York Stock Exch., June 1931-July 1938; Gov., 1935-38; Chm. Cttee on Constitution, 1937-38; Sec. Conway Cttee to reorganize the Exchange, 1937-38; Chm. Bd and Pres. pro. tem. May-June 1938; Pres. July 1938-April 1941. Asst Exec. President's Soviet Protocol Cttee and Munitions Assignments Board, Wash., DC, 1942; appointed Mem. Export-Import Bank, Nov. 1945; Chm. and Pres., 1946-49 (as Chm. of Federal Reserve Board, serves on National Advisory Council on Internat. Monetary and Financial Problems). Asst Sec. of the Treasury, Feb. 1949-April 1951; Chm., Bd of Governors, Fed. Reserve System, 1951-70; US Exec. Dir, IBRD, 1949-52. Dir of several corporations. Trustee: Berry Schs, Atlanta, Ga; Johns Hopkins Univ., Baltimore; Yale Univ.; Nat. Geographic Soc. Holds numerous Hon. Degrees from Univs in USA and Canada. Drafted, Selective Service Act, private, US Army, 1941, Sergeant, GHQ Army War Coll., 1941; Commnd 1st Lt, Inf., Feb. 1942; Captain Aug. 1942; Major, 1943; Lt-Col 1944; Col 1945. Legion of Merit, 1945. *Recreations:* tennis, squash. *Address:* 2801 Woodland Drive, NW, Washington, DC 20008, USA; (office) 800 17th Street, NW, Washington, DC 20006, USA. *Clubs:* West Side Tennis, Yale; Metropolitan, Jefferson Island, Alibi (Washington); Chevy Chase (Md).

MARTIN-BATES, James Patrick, MA; JP; FCIS; FBIM; Director: W. S. Atkins Group Ltd; Avery's Ltd; Charringtons Industrial Holdings Ltd; Hutchinson Ltd; Dormobile Ltd; *b* 17 April 1912; *er s* of late R. Martin-Bates, JP, Perth, Scotland; *m* 1939, Clare, *d* of late Prof. James Miller, MD, DSc; one *s* two *d. Educ:* Perth Academy; Glenalmond; Worcester Coll., Oxford. BA 1933; MA 1944. Lamson Industries, 1933-36; Dorman Long & Co. Ltd, 1936-38; PE Group, 1938-61: Man. Dir, Production Engineering Ltd, 1953-59; Vice-Chm., PE Holdings, 1959-61. Principal, Administrative Staff Coll., Henley-on-Thames, 1961-72. Chm., Management Consultants Association, 1960; Member: Council, British Institute of Management, 1961-66; UK Advisory Council on Education for Management, 1961-66; Council, Glenalmond, 1963-; Bd of Visitors, HM Borstal, Huntercombe, 1964-67; The Council for Technical Education and Training for Overseas Countries, 1962-73; Council, University Coll., Nairobi, 1965-68; Council Chartered Institute of Secretaries, 1965-74; EDC for Rubber Industry, 1965-69. High Sheriff of Buckinghamshire, 1974. Fellow Internat. Acad. of Management, 1964. FCIS 1961; FBIM 1960. *Publications:* various articles in Management Journals. *Recreations:* golf, fishing. *Address:* Ivy Cottage, Fingest, near Henley-on-Thames, Oxon RG9 6QD. *T:* Turville Heath 202. *Clubs:* Caledonian; Leander; Royal and Ancient (St Andrews).

MARTIN-BIRD, Col Sir Richard Dawnay, Kt 1975; CBE 1971 (OBE (mil.) 1953); TD 1950; DL; Chairman and Joint Managing Director, Yates Brothers Wine Lodges Ltd, Manchester; *b* 19 July 1910; *s* of late Richard Martin Bird and Mildred, 2nd *d* of late Peter Peel Yates; *m* 1935, Katharine Blanche, *d* of Sir Arthur Selborne Jelf, CMG; one *s* three *d* (and one *s* decd). *Educ:* Charterhouse. Served with 8th (Ardwick) Bn, The Manchester Regt (TA), 1936-53; war service 1939-45; Lt-Col comdg, 1947-53; Hon. Col, 1953-67; Hon. Col, The Manchester Regt (Ardwick and Ashton) Territorials, 1967-71; Dep. Comdr, 127 Inf. Bde (TA), 1953-57 and 1959-63; Regtl Councillor, The King's Regt, 1967-; ADC (TA) to the Queen, 1961-65; Chairman: E Lancs TA&VRA, 1963-68; TA&VRA for Lancs, Cheshire and IoM, later TA&VRA for NW England and IoM, 1968-75; Vice-Chm., Council, TA&VR Assocs, 1973-75; Mem., TAVR Adv. Cttee, 1973-75. DL Lancs 1964-74, Cheshire 1974; High Sheriff Greater Manchester, 1976. *Address:* Stockinwood, Chelford, Cheshire SK11 9BE. *T:* Chelford 523. *Clubs:* Army and Navy; St James's (Manchester); Winckley (Preston).

MARTIN-JENKINS, Dennis Frederick, TD 1945; Chairman, Ellerman Lines Ltd, since 1967 (Managing Director, 1967-76);

chairman or director of many other companies; *b* 7 Jan. 1911; 2nd *s* of late Frederick Martin-Jenkins, CA and late Martha Magdalene Martin-Jenkins (*née* Almeida); *m* 1937, Rosemary Clare Walker, MRCS, LRCP; three *s*. *Educ:* St Bede's Sch., Eastbourne; Marlborough College. FCIT. Served RA, 1939-45 (Lt-Col). Insce, 1930-35; joined Montgomerie & Workman Ltd, 1935; transf. City Line Ltd, 1938; transf. Hall Line Ltd, 1947 (Dir 1949); Dir, Ellerman Lines Ltd and associated cos, 1950. Chamber of Shipping of UK: Mem. 1956-; Vice-Pres. 1964; Pres. 1965; Chm., Deep Sea Liner Section, 1969. Past Chm., London Gen. Shipowners' Soc.; formerly: Mem. Mersey Docks and Harbour Bd; Mem. Bd, Port of London Authority; Mem., Nat. Dock Labour Bd, 1953-60. Mem. Exec. Cttee, Nat. Assoc. of Port Employers; Chm., Gen. Council of British Shipping for UK, 1963; Mem., British Transport Docks Bd, 1968-; Chm., Internat. Chamber of Shipping, 1971-77. *Recreations:* golf, gardening. *Address:* Oriel Cottage, Shamley Green, Surrey. *T:* Bramley 3558; Flat 36, 105 Hallam Street, W1N 5LU. *T:* 01-580 8764. *Clubs:* United Oxford & Cambridge University; Woking Golf, Royal Cinque Ports Golf, Surrey County Cricket.

MARTINEAU, Charles Herman; Chairman, Electricity Consultative Council for South of Scotland, 1972-76; *b* 3 Sept. 1908; *s* of Prof. Charles E. Martineau, Birmingham; *m* 1939, Margaret Shirley Dolphin; two *s* one *d*. *Educ:* King Edward's Sch., Birmingham. Jas Williamson & Son Ltd, Lancaster and Nairn-Williamson Ltd, Kirkcaldy: Man. Dir, 1952-66. Part-time Mem., S of Scotland Electricity Bd, 1971-76. Mem., Fife CC (Vice-Convener, 1970-73). *Recreations:* chess, golf. *Address:* The Park, Elie, Fife. *T:* Elie 294. *Club:* Royal and Ancient (St Andrews).

See also Bishop of Blackburn.

MARTINEAU, Rt. Rev. Robert Arnold Schürhoff; see Blackburn, Bishop of.

MARTINEZ ZUVIRIA, Gen. Gustavo; Argentine Ambassador to the Court of St James's, 1970-74; *b* 28 Dec. 1915; *s* of Dr Gustavo Martinez Zuviria and Matilde de Iriondo de Martinez Zuviria; *m* 1940, Maria Eugenia Ferrer Deheza; four *s* four *d* (and one *s* decd). *Educ:* Col. El Salvador, Buenos Aires; Mount St Mary's Coll. (Nr Sheffield); San Martin Mil. Academy. Promoted to 2nd Lt, 1938; Capt. 1951. He participated in attempt to overthrow the Peron regime; imprisoned, but when Peron was overthrown, he continued career in Army; among other posts he served in: Cavalry Regt No 12, 1940; Granaderos a Caballo, 1944; Cavalry Regt No 7, 1945; Military Sch.: Instr of cadets, 1944; Asst Dir and Dir of Sch., 1958. Mil. Attaché to Peru, 1955; Chief of 3rd Regt of Cavalry, 1957; Chief of Staff, Argentine Cav. Corps, 1961; Dir, in Superior War Staff Coll., 1962; Dir, Sch. of Cav. and Cav. Inspector, 1963; Comdr, 2nd Cav. Div., 1964; 2nd Comdr, 3rd Army Corps, 1965; Comdr, 1st Army Corps, 1966; Comdr, Southern Joint Forces, 1969; retd from Army and was designated Sec. of State in Intelligence (Secretario de Informaciones de Estado), in 1970. Member: Genealogical Studies Centre, 1962; Nat. Sanmartinian Historical Academy, 1966. Holds several foreign orders. *Publications:* numerous (related to professional and historical subjects); notably Los tiempos de Mariano Necochea, 1961 (2nd edn, 1969) (1st award mil. lit. and award Fundación Eguiguren); Retreta del Desierto, 1956 (8 edns); José Pidsudski; San Martin y O'Brien, 1963; Historia de Angel Pacheco, 1969. *Recreations:* riding, shooting. *Address:* Avenida del Libertador 15249, Acassuso, Buenos Aires, Argentina. *Clubs:* Naval and Military, Travellers', Hurlingham, Turf (all in London); Cowdray Park Polo (Sussex); Circulo Militar, Jockey (Buenos Aires); Club Social de Paraná (Entre Rios).

MARTINS, (Virgilio) Armando; Portuguese Ambassador to the Court of St James's, since 1977; *b* 1 Sept. 1914; *s* of José Júlio Martins and Elvira Janeiro; *m* 1959, Ingrid Bloser; one *s* one *d*. *Educ:* Coimbra and Lisbon Univs. Degree in Law. Entered Foreign Service, 1939; Attaché, Foreign Min., Lisbon, 1941; Consul: Leopoldville, 1943; Liverpool, 1947; Sydney, 1949; special mission, NZ, 1951; First Sec., Tokyo, 1952; Brussels, 1955; Substitute of Permanent Rep. to NATO, 1956; Minister, 2nd Cl., Foreign Min., Lisbon, 1959; NATO, 1961; Ambassador to: Tokyo, 1964; Rome, 1971. *Publications:* books on internat. law, social questions, literary criticism, history, poetry, and the theatre. *Recreations:* oriental studies (Japan), reading, writing. *Address:* 12 Belgrave Square, SW1X 8PP. *T:* 01-235 3688.

MARTINSON, Harry E.; Swedish author and poet; *b* Jämshog, Sweden, 6 May 1904; *s* of Sea Captain Martin Olofsson and Betty Olofsson; *m* 1st, 1929, Moa Martinson (*née* Swartz); 2nd, 1942, Ingrid Lindcrantz. Member, Swedish Academy. Spent early life at sea; many of his subsequent prose and verse compositions deal with nomadic existence. Nobel Prize for Literature (jtly), 1974. Autobiographical work: Flowering Nettles; Cape Farewell; The Road; Aniara (later set to music as opera by Karl-Birger Blondahl). *Publications:* Spökskepp, 1929; Nomad, 1931; Resor utan mål, 1932; Kap Farväl, 1933; Nässlorna blomma, 1935; Vägen ut, 1936; Svärmare o harkrank, 1937; Midsommeardalen, 1938; Det enkla o det svära, 1939; Verklighet till döds, 1940; Den förlorade jaguaren, 1941; Passad, 1945; Vägen till Klockrike, 1948; Cikada, 1953; Aniara, 1956; Gräsen i Thule, 1958; Vagnen, 1960; Utsikt frän en grästuva, 1963; Tre Knivar frän Wei, 1964; Dikter om ljus o mörker, 1971; Tuvor, 1973.

MARTONMERE, 1st Baron, *cr* 1964; **John Roland Robinson,** PC 1962; GBE 1973; KCMG 1966; Kt 1954; MA, LLB; Governor and C-in-C of Bermuda, 1964-72; *b* 22 Feb. 1907; *e s* of Roland Walkden Robinson, Solicitor, Blackpool; *m* 1930, Maysie, *d* of late Clarence Warren Gasque; one *s* one *d*. *Educ:* Trinity Hall, Cambridge. Barrister-at-law, 1929 (Certificate of Honour and Buchanan Prize Lincoln's Inn, 1928); MP (U) Widnes Division of Lancs, 1931-35, Blackpool, 1935-45, S Blackpool, 1945-64. W/Cdr RAFVR, 1940-45. Pres. Royal Lancs Agricultural Society, 1936; Past Pres. Assoc. of Health and Pleasure Resorts; Past Pres. Residential Hotels Assoc. of Great Britain. Past Chm. Conservative Party Commonwealth Affairs Cttee; Chm. Gen. Council, Commonwealth Parliamentary Assoc., 1961-62. Past Dep. Chm. United Kingdom Branch, Commonwealth Parliamentary Association. Hon. Freeman, Town of St George and City of Hamilton (Bermuda). Officer, Legion of Merit (USA). *Heir:* *s* Hon. Richard Anthony Gasque Robinson [*b* 11 March 1935; *m* 1959, Wendy Patricia, *d* of James Blagden; two *s* one *d*]. *Address:* Romay House, Tuckers Town, Bermuda; El Mirador, Lyford Cay, PO Box 7776, Nassau, Bahamas. *Clubs:* Carlton, Junior Carlton; Royal Lytham and St Annes Golf (St Annes); Royal Yacht Squadron (Cowes); Lyford Cay (Bahamas); Hon. Life Member: Royal Bermuda Yacht, Mid-Ocean (Bermuda).

MARTY, Cardinal François, Chevalier de la Légion d'honneur; Archbishop of Paris, since 1968, and Cardinal since 1969; *b* Pachins, Aveyron, 18 May 1904; *s* of François Marty, cultivateur, and Zoé (*née* Gineste). *Educ:* Collège de Graves et Villefranche-de-Rouergue; Séminaire de Rodez; Institut Catholique de Toulouse. Dr en Th. Priest, 1930. Vicaire: Villefranche-de-Rouergue, 1932; Rodez, 1933; Parish Priest: Bournazel, 1940; Rieupeyroux, 1943; Archpriest, Millau, 1949; Vicar-General, Rodez, 1951; Bishop of Saint Flour, 1952; Coadjutor Archbishop, 1959, and Archbishop of Reims, 1960. Pres., Comité Episcopal of Mission de France, 1965; Mem. Bureau, then Vice-Pres., Perm. Council of French Episcopate, 1966, and Pres., French Episcopal Conf., 1969-; responsable des Catholiques orientaux. Mem. Rome Commissions: for Revision of Canon Law; on culte divin du Clergé. *Address:* Maison diocésaine, 8 rue de la Ville l'Evêque, 75008 Paris, France.

MARTYN, Charles Roger Nicholas; Master of the Supreme Court, since 1973; *b* 10 Dec. 1925; *s* of Rev. Charles Martyn; *m* 1960, Helen, *d* of Frank Everson; two *s* one *d*. *Educ:* Charterhouse, 1939-44; Merton Coll., Oxford, 1947-49. MA (Hons) Mod. Hist. Joined Regular Army, 1944; commissioned 60th Rifles (KRRC), 1945; CMF, 1946-47; special release, 1947. Articles, 1950-52, and admitted as solicitor, 1952. Sherwood & Co., Parly Agents (Partner), 1952-59; Lee, Bolton & Lee, Westminster (Partner), 1961-73. Mem. and Dep. Chm., No 14 Legal Aid Area Cttee, 1967-73; Hon. Legal Adviser to The Samaritans (Inc), 1955-73. Chm., Family Welfare Assoc., 1973-78; Member: Gtr London Citizens' Advice Bureaux Management Cttee, 1974-; Council, St Gabriel's Coll. (Further Education), Camberwell, 1973-77 (Vice-Chm); Goldsmiths' Coll. Delegacy, 1977-. *Recreations:* walking, sailing (Vice-Cdre, Thames Barge Sailing Club, 1962-65), observing people, do-it-yourself, nigrology. *Address:* 29 St Albans Road, NW5 1RG. *T:* 01-267 1076.

MARTYN, Joan, OBE 1962; Governor Class II, HM Prison Commission; Governor, Bullwood Hall, 1962-64, retired; *b* 9 Aug. 1899; 3rd *d* of George Harold and Eve Martyn. *Educ:* Municipal Coll., Grimsby; Queenwood, Eastbourne; Bedford Physical Training Coll. (diploma). Staff of St Mary's Coll., Lancaster Gate, London, W2, 1919-36; staff of HM Borstal Institution, Aylesbury, 1937 (Governor 1946-59); Governor, HM Borstal, Cardiff, 1959-62. *Address:* 57 Bargate, Grimsby, S Humberside.

MARTYN-HEMPHILL, family name of **Baron Hemphill.**

MARWICK, Sir Brian (Allan), KBE 1963 (CBE 1954; OBE 1946); CMG 1958; *b* 18 June 1908; *s* of James Walter Marwick and Elizabeth Jane Flett; *m* 1934, Riva Lee, *d* of Major H. C.

Cooper; two *d. Educ:* University of Cape Town; CCC, Cambridge. Administrative Officer: Swaziland, 1925-36; Nigeria, 1937-40; Swaziland, 1941-46; First Asst Sec.: Swaziland, 1947-48; Basutoland, 1949-52; Dep. Resident Comr and Govt Sec., Basutoland, 1952-55; Administrative Sec. to High Comr for Basutoland, the Bechuanaland Protectorate and Swaziland, 1956; Resident Comr, Swaziland, 1957-63; HM Comr, Swaziland, 1963-64; Permanent Secretary: Min. of Works and Town Planning Dept, Nassau, Bahamas, 1965-68; Min. of Educn, Bahamas, 1968-71. *Publication:* The Swazi, 1940. *Recreations:* polo, tennis, golf. *Address:* Hazelwood, Ballaugh, Isle of Man. *Club:* Royal Commonwealth Society.

MARWOOD, Sidney Lionel, CIE 1941; *b* 8 April 1891; *s* of John Marwood, Shipbroker, Liverpool; *m* 1924, Agnes (*d* 1952), *e d* of Adam Rolland Rainy, MP; two *s* one *d*; *m* 1953, Mary, *d* of William Logsdail. *Educ:* St Paul's Sch.; Hertford Coll., Oxford, MA. Commissioned in West Lancs Divisional Engineers, RE (TF), in 1914; saw service in India and Mesopotamia, 1914-19; reverted to Indian Civil Service, 1920, posted to Bihar Province. Collector, 1924, Commissioner, 1939, Revenue Commissioner, Orissa, 1943; retired 1947. Kaisar-i-Hind Gold Medal (I Class) in 1934 after Bihar earthquake. *Address:* 4 Eastergate Green, Rustington, West Sussex.

MARX, Enid Crystal Dorothy, RDI 1944; Painter and Designer; *b* London, 20 Oct. 1902; *y d* of Robert J. Marx. *Educ:* Roedean Sch.; Central Sch. of Arts and Crafts; Royal College of Art Painting Sch. Designing and printing handblock printed textiles, 1925-39. Exhibited in USA and Europe; various works purchased by Victoria and Albert Museum, Musée des Arts Décoratifs, Boston Museum, Scottish Arts Council, Sheffield Art Gall., etc. Mem. Society of Wood Engravers. Wood engraving and autolithography for pattern papers, book jackets, book illustration and decorations, trademarks, etc.; designed moquettes and posters for LPTB. Industrial designing for printed and woven furnishing fabrics, wallpapers, ceramics, plastics; FRSA, FSIA; original mem. National Register of Industrial Designers of Central Institute of Art and Design. Mem. of Bd of Trade design panel on utility furniture. Designed postage stamps: ½d-2d for first issue Elizabeth II; Christmas 1976 issue. Lectures on textiles and folk art. *Publications:* (jointly) English Popular and Traditional Art, 1947; (with Margaret Lambert), English Popular Art, 1951; articles and broadcasts on aspects of industrial design in various countries; author and illustrator of eleven books for children. *Recreations:* study of popular art in different countries; gardening. *Address:* The Studio, 39 Thornhill Road, Barnsbury Square, N1. *T:* 01-607 2286.

MARY LEO, Sister; *see* Niccol, Dame Sister Mary Leo.

MARY REGIS, Sister; *see* Morant, Dame Mary Maud.

MARYON-WILSON, Sir Hubert (Guy Maryon), 13th Bt *cr* 1661; *b* 27 July 1888; *s* of Rev. George Maryon Wilson (*d* 1906), 5th *s* of 9th Bt, and Albinia Frances Short (*d* 1920); assumed surname of Maryon by deed poll; *S* kinsman 1965; *m* 1923, Janet Mary, *d* of late Rev. Ernest Arthur Moxon, Lincs. *Educ:* Radley. *Heir:* none. *Address:* The Grange, Great Canfield, Dunmow, Essex.

MASCALL, Rev. Canon Eric Lionel, DD Oxon, DD Cantab, BSc London; FBA 1974; an Hon. Canon of Truro Cathedral, with duties of Canon Theologian, since 1973; Professor of Historical Theology, London University, at King's College, 1962-73, now Professor Emeritus; Dean, Faculty of Theology, London University, 1968-72; *b* 12 Dec. 1905; *s* of John R. S. Mascall and S. Lilian Mascall, *née* Grundy; unmarried. *Educ:* Latymer Upper Sch., Hammersmith; Pembroke Coll., Cambridge (Scholar); Theological Coll., Ely. BSc (London) 1926; BA (Wrangler) 1927, MA 1931, BD 1943, DD 1958 Cantab; DD Oxon, 1948. Sen. Maths Master, Bablake Sch., Coventry, 1928-31; ordained, 1932; Asst Curate, St Andrew's, Stockwell Green, 1932-35; St Matthew's, Westminster, 1935-37; Sub-warden, Scholae Cancellarii, Lincoln, 1937-45; Lecturer in Theology, Christ Ch., Oxford, 1945-46; Student and Tutor of Christ Ch., Oxford, 1946-62, Emeritus Student, 1962-; University Lectr in Philosophy of Religion, 1947-62; Chaplain at Oxford to Bishop of Derby, 1947-48; Commissary to Archbishop of Cape Town, 1964-73; Examining Chaplain to: Bishop of Willesden, 1970-73; Bishop of Truro, 1973-. Visiting Professor: Gregorian Univ., Rome, 1976; Pontifical Coll. Josephinum, Columbus, Ohio, 1977; Lectures: Bampton, Oxford, 1956; Bampton, Columbia, 1958; Boyle, 1965-66; Charles A. Hart Memorial, Cath. Univ. of America, Washington, DC, 1968; Gifford, Univ. of Edinburgh, 1970-71. FKC, 1968-. Hon. DD St Andrews, 1967. *Publications:* Death or Dogma, 1937; A Guide to Mount Carmel, 1939; Man,

his Origin and Destiny, 1940; The God-Man, 1940; He Who Is, 1943 (rev. edn 1966); Christ, the Christian and the Church, 1946; Existence and Analogy, 1949; Corpus Christi, 1953 (rev. edn 1965). Christian Theology and Natural Science, 1956; Via Media, 1956; Words and Images, 1957; The Recovery of Unity, 1958; The Importance of Being Human, 1958; Pi in the High, 1959; Grace and Glory, 1961; Theology and History (Inaugural Lecture), 1962; Theology and Images, 1963; Up and Down in Adria, 1963; The Secularisation of Christianity, 1965; The Christian Universe, 1966; Theology and The Future, 1968; (jt author) Growing into Union, 1970; The Openness of Being, 1971; Nature and Supernature, 1976; Editor: The Church of God, 1934; The Mother of God, 1949; The Angels of Light and the Powers of Darkness, 1954; The Blessed Virgin Mary, 1963; Theology and the Gospel of Christ, 1977. *Address:* 30 Bourne Street, SW1. *T:* 01-730 2423. *Clubs:* Athenæum, National Liberal.

MASCHLER, Thomas Michael; Chairman of Jonathan Cape Ltd, since 1970; *b* 16 Aug. 1933; *s* of Kurt Leo Maschler and of Rita Masseron (*née* Lechner); *m* 1970, Fay Coventry; one *s* two *d*. *Educ:* Leighton Park School. Production Asst, Andre Deutsch, 1955; Editor, MacGibbon & Kee, 1956-58; Fiction Editor, Penguin Books, 1958-60; Jonathan Cape: Editorial Dir, 1960; Man. Dir, 1966. *Publications:* (ed) Declarations, 1957; (ed) New English Dramatists Series, 1959-63. *Address:* 15 Chalcot Gardens, NW3.

MASEFIELD, Sir Peter (Gordon), Kt 1972; MA Cantab; CEng; FRAeS; FCIT; CIMechE; Chairman, Project Management Ltd, since 1972; Director, Worldwide Estates Ltd, since 1972; Member (part-time), London Transport Executive, since 1973; Director: Nationwide Building Society, since 1973; Worldwide Estates Ltd; Worldwide Properties Ltd; Caledonian Airways, since 1975; *b* Trentham, Staffs, 19 March 1914; *e s* of late Dr W. Gordon Masefield, CBE, MRCS, and Marian A. Masefield (*née* Lloyd-Owen); *m* 1936, Patricia Doreen, 3rd *d* of late Percy H. Rooney, Wallington, Surrey; three *s* one *d*. *Educ:* Westminster Sch.; Chillon Coll., Switzerland; Jesus Coll., Cambridge (BA (Eng) 1935). On Design Staff, The Fairey Aviation Co. Ltd, 1935-37; Pilot's licence, 1937-70; joined The Aeroplane newspaper, 1937, Technical Editor, 1939-43; Air Correspondent Sunday Times, 1940-43; War Corresp. with RAF and US Army Eighth Air Force on active service, 1939-43; Editor, The Aeroplane Spotter, 1941-43; Chm. Editorial Cttee, The Inter-Services Journal on Aircraft Recognition, MAP, 1942-45; Personal Adviser to the Lord Privy Seal (Lord Beaverbrook) and Sec. of War Cabinet Cttee on Post War Civil Air Transport, 1943-45; first British Civil Air Attaché, British Embassy, Washington, DC, 1945-46 (Signator to Anglo-American Bermuda Air Agreement, 1946); Dir-Gen. of Long Term Planning and Projects, Ministry of Civil Aviation, 1946-48; Chief Executive and Mem. of Board of BEA, 1949-55; Managing Dir, Bristol Aircraft Ltd, 1956-60; Man. Dir, Beagle Aircraft Ltd, 1960-67, Chm., 1968-70; Dir, Beagle Aviation Finance Ltd, 1962-71. Chm., British Airports Authority, 1965-71. Chm., Nat. Jt Council for Civil Air Transport, 1950-51; Member: Cairns Cttee on Aircraft Accident Investigation, 1960; Min. of Aviation Advisory Cttees on Civil Aircraft Control and on Private and Club Flying and Gliding; Aeronautical Research Council, 1958-61. Mem., Cambridge Univ. Appointments Bd, 1956-69. Director, Pressed Steel Co. Ltd, 1960-68. RAeS: Chm., Graduates and Students Sect., 1937-39; Mem. Council, 1945-65; Pres., 1959-60; British Commonwealth and Empire Lectr, 1948; RAeS/AFITA Bleriot Meml Lectr, 1966; Pres., Inst. Transport, 1955-56 (Brancker Meml Lectr, 1951, 1967); President: Inst. of Travel Managers, 1967-70; Assoc. of British Aviation Consultants; Chm., Bd of Trustees, Imperial War Museum, 1977-78; Littlewood Meml Lectr, Soc. of Automotive Engrs (USA), 1971. Mem. Council, Royal Aero Club (Chm., Aviation Cttee, 1960-65; Chm., 1968-70). Mem., HMS Belfast Trust. FRSA (Chm.); FBIM. Hon. FAIAA; Hon. FCASI; Hon. DSc Cranfield; Hon DTech Loughborough, 1977. Liveryman, Guild of Air Pilots and Air Navigators. *Publications:* articles on aviation, transport, management, and First World War. *Recreations:* reading, writing, gardening. *Address:* Rosehill, Doods Way, Reigate, Surrey RH2 0JT. *T:* Reigate 42396. *Clubs:* Athenæum, Royal Aero, Steering Wheel; National Aviation (Washington).

MASHAM OF ILTON, Baroness *cr* 1970 (Life Peer); **Susan Lilian Primrose Cunliffe-Lister (Countess of Swinton);** *b* 14 April 1935; *d* of Sir Ronald Sinclair, 8th Bt and of Reba Blair (who *m* 2nd, 1957, Lt-Col H. R. Hildreth, MBE), *d* of Anthony Inglis, MD; *m* 1959, Lord Masham (now Earl of Swinton, *qv*); one *s* one *d* (both adopted). *Educ:* Heathfield School, Ascot; London Polytechnic. Has made career in voluntary social work. *Recreations:* breeding highland ponies, swimming, table tennis,

fishing. *Address:* Dykes Hill House, Masham, near Ripon, N Yorks. *T:* Masham 241.
See also Sir J. R. N. B. Sinclair, Bt.

MASHONALAND, Bishop of, since 1968; **Rt. Rev. John Paul Burrough,** MBE 1946; MA Oxon; *b* 5 May 1916; *s* of Canon E. G. Burrough; *m* 1962, Elizabeth (Bess), *widow* of Stephen John White; one step-*d*. *Educ:* St Edward's Sch.; St Edmund Hall, Oxford; Ely Theol. College. Coach, Tigre Boat Club, Buenos Aires, 1938-39. Captain, Royal Signals, Malaya Campaign (POW), 1940-45. Asst, Aldershot Parish Church, 1946-51; Mission Priest, Dio. of Korea, 1951-59; Anglican Chaplain to Overseas Peoples in Birmingham, 1959-68; Canon Residentiary of Birmingham, 1967-68. Chaplain and Sub-Prelate, Order of St John of Jerusalem, 1969-. *Publication:* Lodeleigh, 1946. *Recreation:* rowing (Oxford crews, 1937 and 1938). *Address:* Bishop's Mount, PO Box UA7, Salisbury, Rhodesia. *Clubs:* Leander (Henley); Vincent's (Oxford); Salisbury (Salisbury).

MASIH, Rt. Rev. Inayat; *see* Lahore, Bishop of.

MASON, family name of **Baron Blackford.**

MASON, Ailsa Mary; *see* Garland, A. M.

MASON, Alan Kenneth; HM Diplomatic Service; HM Consul-General, Hanover, since 1975; *b* 18 May 1920; *s* of Richard Mason and Mary Mason (*née* Williams); *m* 1948, Kathleen Mary Redman; two *s*. *Educ:* Westcliff High School. Served with British and Indian Army, India, Burma, 1940-46. Customs and Excise, 1946-48; Min. of Works, 1949-65 (Sec., Ancient Monuments Bds, 1958-63); Diplomatic Service, 1965: Head of Chancery, Jakarta, 1967-70; Dep. Defence Sec., Hong Kong, 1972-75. *Recreations:* archæology, bird watching, Chinese porcelain, walking, bridge. *Address:* c/o Foreign and Commonwealth Office, SW1A 2AL. *Clubs:* Royal Commonwealth Society; Hong Kong (Hong Kong).

MASON, Hon. Sir Anthony (Frank), KBE 1972 (CBE 1969); Justice, High Court of Australia, since 1972; *b* Sydney, 21 April 1925; *s* of F. M. Mason, Sydney; *m* 1950, Patricia Mary, *d* of Dr E. N. McQueen; two *s*. *Educ:* Sydney Grammar Sch.; Univ. of Sydney. BA, LLB. RAAF Flying Officer, 1944-45. Admitted to NSW Bar, 1951; QC 1964. Commonwealth Solicitor-General, 1964-69; Judge, Court of Appeal, Supreme Court of NSW, 1969-72. Vice-Chm., UN Commn on Internat. Trade Law, 1968. Mem. Council, ANU, 1969-72; Pro-Chancellor, ANU, 1972-75. *Recreations:* gardening, tennis. *Address:* Judges' Chambers, High Court of Australia, Taylor Square, Darlinghurst, Sydney, NSW 2010, Australia; 9 Oswald Street, Cremorne, Sydney, NSW 2090.

MASON, Arthur Malcolm; Director, Reckitt & Colman Ltd (Chairman, 1970-77); *b* 19 Dec. 1915; British parents; *m* 1938, Mary Hall; one *s* (one *d* decd). *Educ:* Linton House, London; Blundells School. Trainee, Unilever Ltd, 1934-38; Chiswick Products Ltd: Asst Sales Man., 1938; Sales and Advertising Man., 1939; Dir, 1943; Chm., 1957; Reckitt & Colman Holdings Ltd: Assoc. Dir, 1957; Dir, 1958; Vice-Chm., 1965-70. FInstD. OStJ 1975. *Recreations:* sailing, sea fishing, gardening. *Address:* Flat 7, Pinecroft, St George's Road, Weybridge KT13 0EN. *T:* Weybridge 48690. *Clubs:* Seaview Yacht, Brading Haven Yacht.

MASON, Prof. Basil John, CB 1973; FRS 1965; DSc (London); Director-General of the Meteorological Office since 1965; *b* 18 Aug. 1923; *s* of late John Robert and Olive Mason, Docking, Norfolk; *m* 1948, Doreen Sheila Jones; two *s*. *Educ:* Fakenham Grammar Sch.; University Coll., Nottingham. Commissioned, Radar Branch RAF, 1944-46. BSc 1st Cl. Hons Physics (London), 1947, MSc 1948; DSc (London) 1956. Shirley Res. Fellow, Univ. of Nottingham, 1947; Asst Lectr in Meteorology, 1948, Lectr, 1949, Imperial Coll.; Warren Res. Fellow, Royal Society, 1957; Vis. Prof. of Meteorology, Univ. of Calif, 1959-60; Prof. of Cloud Physics, Imperial Coll. of Science and Technology (Univ. of London), 1961-65. Hon. Gen. Sec. British Assoc., 1965-70; President: Physics Section, British Assoc., 1965; Royal Meteorol. Soc., 1968-70; Inst. of Physics, 1976-; a Vice-Pres., and Treasurer, Royal Soc., 1976-. UK Perm. Rep., World Meteorological Orgn, 1965- (Mem. Exec. Cttee, 1966-75). Chm. Council, Surrey Univ., 1970-75. Lectures: James Forrest, ICE, 1967; Kelvin, IEE, 1968; Dalton, RIC, 1968; Bakerian, Royal Soc., 1971; Hugh MacMillan, IES, 1975; Symons, Royal Meteorol. Soc., 1976; Halley, Oxford, 1977. Hon Fellow, Imperial Coll. of Science and Technology, 1974. Hon. DSc: Nottingham, 1966; Durham, 1970; Strathclyde, 1975. Hugh Robert Mill Medal, Royal Meterorol. Soc., 1959; Charles Chree Medal and Prize, Inst. Physics and Phys. Soc., 1965; Rumford Medal, Royal Soc., 1972; Glazebrook Medal, Inst.

Physics, 1974; Symons Meml Gold Medal, Royal Meteorol. Soc., 1975. *Publications:* The Physics of Clouds, 1957, 2nd edn 1971; Clouds, Rain and Rain-Making, 1962, 2nd edn 1975; papers in physics and meteorological journals. *Recreations:* foreign travel, music. *Address:* 64 Christchurch Road, East Sheen, SW14. *T:* 01-876 2557. *Club:* Athenæum.

MASON, Brewster; actor; Associate Artist, Royal Shakespeare Company, since 1965; lectures on Drama and Acting at the University of California (Irvine); *b* Kidsgrove, Staffs, 30 Aug. 1922; *s* of Jesse Mason and Constance May Kemp; *m* 1st, 1948, Lorna Whittaker (marr. diss.); one *d*; 2nd, 1966, Kate Meredith. *Educ:* privately; Royal Naval Colls; RADA (Bancroft Gold Medal); Guildhall Sch. of Music and Drama (Hons. Grad.). First appeared as a professional actor at Lyric, Hammersmith, as Flt/Sgt John Nabb in An English Summer, Sept. 1948, followed by London appearances to 1960; took over part of Gen. Allenby in Ross, Haymarket, 1960. First appearance in New York, at Henry Miller Theatre, Sept. 1962, as Sir Lewis Eliot in The Affair. Joined RSC, Aldwych, London, Feb. 1963, to play Kent in King Lear, subseq. appearing at Royal Shakespeare, Stratford, July 1963, as Earl of Warwick in trilogy The Wars of the Roses; since 1963 has appeared in repertory at Stratford and Aldwych, in productions including The Birthday Party, 1964; Hamlet, 1965; Macbeth, All's Well that Ends Well, 1967; Julius Caesar, Merry Wives of Windsor, 1968; Major Barbara, King Henry VIII, 1970; Othello in Othello, 1972; Falstaff in Henry IV and Merry Wives of Windsor, 1975. Director, Shakespeare Festivals in New England. Films include: The Dam Busters, Private Potter, etc. *TV:* first appeared on television, 1953, subseq. playing leading parts, incl. Abel Wharton in The Pallisers, 1974. FGSM 1976. *Recreations:* golf, painting. *Address:* The White House, Tredington, Shipston-on-Stour, Warwicks. *T:* Shipston-on-Stour 61280. *Clubs:* Garrick, Naval; Stage Golfing; Players (New York).

MASON, Sir Dan (Hurdis), Kt 1961; OBE 1940; ERD 1956; *b* 24 July 1911; *e s* of late Charles Mason; *m* 1933, Joyce Louise, *d* of late Horace Young Nutt, Radlett, Herts; three *s* one *d*. *Educ:* Blundell's; Germany. Chm., West London Hospital, 1947-48; Governor, West London Hosp. Med. Sch., 1947-62; Chm., West London Hosp. Med. Trust, 1962-; Chm., Horsham Conservative Assoc., 1951-58; Sussex Conservative Council, 1955-58; Chm., SE Area of Conservative Nat. Union, 1957-62; Chm., Nat. Union of Conservative Assocs, 1966; Mem., Nat. Exec. Cttee of Conservative Party, 1956-; Hon. Treas., Nat. Florence Nightingale Meml Cttee, 1956-66; Dep. Pres. 1966-. Served War of 1939-45, Royal Engineers (Supplementary Reserve) (OBE). *Recreations:* gardening, do-it-yourself, crosswords. *Address:* Chatley House, Norton St Philip, Somerset. *T:* Beckington 325. *Club:* Naval and Military.

MASON, Vice-Adm. Dennis Howard, CB 1967; Warden, St George's House, Windsor Castle, 1972-77; *b* 7 Feb. 1916; *s* of Wilfred Howard Mason, Broadwater, Ipswich, and Gladys (Mouse) Mason (*née* Teague), Trevenson, Cornwall; *m* 1940, Patricia D. M. (*née* Hood); three *d*. *Educ:* Royal Naval Coll., Dartmouth. Served War of 1939-45, Coastal Forces, Frigates and Destroyers; Comdr 1951; Captain 1956; Senior Naval Officer, Northern Ireland, 1961-63; Dir RN Tactical Sch., 1964-65; Rear-Adm. 1965; Chief of Staff to Commander, Far East Fleet, 1965-67; Vice-Adm. 1968; Comdt, Jt Services Staff Coll., 1968-70, retired. ADC 1964. With Paper and Paper Products Industry Training Bd, 1971-72. *Recreations:* shooting, fishing, gardening. *Address:* Church Cottage, East Meon, Hants.

MASON, Vice-Adm. Sir Frank (Trowbridge), KCB 1955 (CB 1953); Hon. FIMechE; FIMarE; retired; Member of Council for Scientific and Industrial Research, 1958-63 (Vice-Chairman, 1962); *b* 25 April 1900; *s* of late F. J. Mason, MBE, JP; *m* 1924, Dora Margaret Brand; one *s* two *d*. *Educ:* Ipswich Sch. RNC, Keyham, 1918; RN Coll., Greenwich, 1921-22; RN Engineering Coll., Keyham, 1922-23; Fleet Gunnery Engineer Officer, Home Fleet, 1943-44; Chief Gunnery Engineer Officer and Dep. Dir of Naval Ordnance, 1947-48; idc 1949. Deputy Engineer-in-Chief of The Fleet, 1950-52; Staff of C-in-C The Nore, 1952-53; Commander, 1934; Captain, 1943; Rear-Adm., 1950; Vice-Adm., 1953; Engineer-in-Chief of the Fleet, 1953-57, retired. Parsons Memorial Lectr, 1956. Chm. Steering Cttee, Nat. Engineering Laboratory, 1958-69, Chm. Adv. Board, 1969, Chm. Adv. Cttee, 1973-75; Mem. Steering Cttee, Nat. Physical Laboratory, 1966-68; Chm., Froude Cttee, 1966. Mem. Council, Institution of Mechanical Engineers, 1953-57, and 1961 (Vice-Pres., 1962, Pres., 1964); Institute of Marine Engineers, 1958 (Chm. of Council, 1962, Vice-Pres. 1963, Pres. 1967); Dep. Chm., Schools Science and Technology Cttee, 1968; Mem. Governing Body: National Council for Technological Awards, 1960-64; Royal Naval Sch., Haslemere, 1953; Ipswich Sch.,

1961-72; Further Education Staff Coll., 1964-74; Navy League, 1967-75; Hurstpierpoint Coll., 1967; Brighton Polytechnic, 1969-73; Mem. Council and Exec. Cttee, City and Guilds of London Inst., 1968-77, Vice Chm., 1970-77, Hon. FCGI 1977. Chm., Standing Conf. on Schools Science and Technology, 1971-75, Vice-Pres., 1975. Founder Fellow, Fellowship of Engineering, 1976. Asst to Court, Worshipful Co. of Shipwrights. Mem. Smeatonian Soc. of Civil Engineers (Pres., 1977). High Steward of Ipswich, 1967. *Address:* Townfield House, 114 High Street, Hurstpierpoint, Sussex. *T:* Hurstpierpoint 833375.
See also Ven. R. J. Mason.

MASON, Sir Frederick (Cecil), KCVO 1968; CMG 1960; HM Diplomatic Service, retired; Director, New Court Natural Resources Ltd, since 1973; *b* 15 May 1913; *s* of late Ernest Mason and Sophia Charlotte Mason (*née* Dodson); *m* 1941, Karen Rørholm; two *s* one *d* (and two *d* decd). *Educ:* City of London Sch.; St Catharine's Coll., Cambridge. Vice-Consul: Antwerp, 1935-36; Paris, 1936-37; Leopoldville, 1937-39; Elisabethville, 1939-40; Consul at Thorshavn during British occupation of Faroes, 1940-42; Consul, Colon, Panama, 1943-45; First Sec., British Embassy, Santiago, Chile, 1946-48; First Sec. (Information), Oslo, 1948-50; Asst Labour Adviser, FO, 1950-53; First Sec. (Commercial), UK High Commission, Bonn, 1954-55; Counsellor (Commercial), HM Embassy, Athens, 1955-56; Counsellor (Economic), HM Embassy, Tehran, 1957-60; Head of Economic Relations Dept, Foreign Office, 1960-64; Under-Sec., Ministry of Overseas Development, 1965, and CRO, 1966; Ambassador to Chile, 1966-70; Under-Sec. of State, FCO, Oct. 1970-Apr. 1971; Ambassador and Perm. UK Rep. to UN and other Internat. Orgns, Geneva, 1971-73. British Mem., Internat. Narcotics Control Bd, Geneva, 1974-77. Grand Cross, Chilean Order of Merit Bernardo O'Higgins, 1968. *Recreations:* ball games, walking, painting. *Address:* The Forge, Ropley, Hants. *T:* Ropley 2285. *Club:* Canning.

MASON, (George Frederick) Peter, QC 1963; **His Honour Judge Mason;** a Circuit Judge; *b* 11 Dec. 1921; *s* of George Samuel and Florence May Mason, Keighley, Yorks; *m* 1950, Faith Maud Bacon (separated 1976); two *s* two *d* (and one *d* decd). *Educ:* Lancaster Royal Grammar Sch.; St Catharine's Coll., Cambridge. Open Exhibnr St Catharine's Coll., 1940. Served with 78th Medium Regt RA (Duke of Lancaster's Own Yeo.) in Middle East and Italy, 1941-45, latterly as Staff Capt. RA, HQ 13 Corps. History Tripos Pt 1, 1st cl. hons with distinction, 1946; called to Bar, Lincoln's Inn, 1947; MA 1948; Cholmeley Schol., 1949. Asst Recorder of Huddersfield, 1961; Dep. Chairman: Agricultural Land Tribunal, W Yorks and Lancs, 1962; West Riding of Yorks Quarter Sessions, 1965-67; Recorder of York, 1965-67; Dep. Chm., NE London QS, 1970-71. *Recreations:* fell walking, carpentry. *Address:* Central Criminal Court, EC4. *T:* 01-248 3277. *Club:* Hawks.

MASON, James; actor; *b* 15 May 1909; *s* of late John Mason and Mabel Gaunt; *m* 1st, 1941, Pamela Kellino (marr. diss., 1965); one *s* one *d*; 2nd, 1971, Clarissa Kaye. *Educ:* Marlborough Coll.; Peterhouse, Cambridge. Début on professional stage in The Rascal, Hippodrome, Aldershot, 1931; Old Vic, 1933-34; Gate Theatre, Dublin, 1934-35. Début in Films, Late Extra, 1935. *Films include:* I Met a Murderer; Thunder Rock; The Man in Grey; Fanny by Gaslight; A Place of One's Own; They were Sisters; The Seventh Veil; The Wicked Lady; Odd Man Out; The Upturned Glass; Caught; The Reckless Moment; Pandora and the Flying Dutchman; Rommel-Desert Fox; Five Fingers; Julius Caesar; The Man Between; A Star is Born; Bigger than Life; North by North-West; Twenty Thousand Leagues under the Sea; Journey to the Center of the Earth; Touch of Larceny; Lolita; Heroes' Island; Tiara Tahiti; The Fall of the Roman Empire; The Pumpkin Eater; Lord Jim; Les Pianos Mécaniques; The Blue Max; Georgy Girl; The Deadly Affair; Duffy; Mayerling; Age of Consent; The Seagull; Spring and Port Wine; Child's Play; Last of Sheila; The Mackintosh Man; Dr Frankenstein; Cold Sweat; 11 Harrowhouse; What Are Friends For; Mandingo; Left Hand of the Law; The Deal; The Schoolteacher and the Devil; Inside Out; Autobiography of a Princess; The Voyage of the Damned; Jesus of Nazareth; The Iron Cross; Fear in the City. *Publication:* (with Pamela Kellino) The Cats in Our Lives, 1949 (US). *Recreation:* painting. *Address:* c/o Al Parker, Ltd, 50 Mount Street, W1.

MASON, James Stephen; Deputy Parliamentary Counsel, since 1975; *b* 6 Feb. 1935; *s* of Albert Wesley Mason and Mabel (*née* Topham); *m* 1961, Tania Jane Moeran; one *s* two *d*. *Educ:* Windsor County Grammar Sch.; Univ. of Oxford (MA, BCL). Called to the Bar, Middle Temple, 1958; in practice, 1961-67; Office of Parly Counsel, 1967-. *Recreations:* reading, walking and playing the piano. *Address:* Cannon Cottage, Well Road, Hampstead, NW3. *T:* 01-435 2917.

MASON, John Charles Moir, CMG 1976; HM Diplomatic Service; Ambassador to Israel, since 1976; *b* 13 May 1927; *o s* of late Charles Moir Mason, CBE and late Madeline Mason; *m* 1954, Margaret Newton; one *s* one *d*. *Educ:* Manchester Grammar Sch.; Peterhouse, Cambridge. Lieut, XX Lancs Fusiliers, 1946-48; BA 1950, MA 1955, Cantab; Captain, Royal Ulster Rifles, 1950-51 (Korea); HM Foreign Service, 1952; 3rd Sec., FO, 1952-54; 2nd Sec. and Private Sec. to Ambassador, British Embassy, Rome, 1954-56; 2nd Sec., Warsaw, 1956-59; 1st Sec., FO, 1959-61; 1st Sec. (Commercial), Damascus, 1961-65; 1st Sec. and Asst Head of Dept, FO, 1965-68; Dir of Trade Develt and Dep. Consul-Gen., NY, 1968-71; Head of European Integration Dept, FCO, 1971-72; seconded as Under-Sec., ECGD, 1972-75; Asst Under-Sec. of State (Economic), FCO, 1975-76. *Address:* c/o Foreign and Commonwealth Office, SW1. *Club:* Athenæum.

MASON, Prof. John Kenyon French, CBE 1973; Regius Professor of Forensic Medicine, University of Edinburgh, since 1973; *b* 19 Dec. 1919; *s* of late Air Cdre J.M. Mason, CBE, DSC, DFC and Alma French; *m* 1943, Elizabeth Latham; two *s*. *Educ:* Downside Sch.; Cambridge Univ.; St Bartholomew's Hosp. MD, FRCPath, DCP, DMJ, DTM&H. Joined RAF, 1943; Dir of RAF Dept of Aviation and Forensic Pathology, 1956; retd as Group Captain, Consultant in Pathology, 1973. L. G. Groves Prize for Aircraft Safety, 1957; R. F. Linton Meml Prize, 1958; James Martin Award for Flight Safety, 1972; Douglas Weightman Safety Award, 1973. *Publications:* Aviation Accident Pathology, 1962; (ed) Aerospace Pathology, 1973; Forensic Medicine for Lawyers, 1977; (ed) The Pathology of Violence, 1977; papers in medical jls. *Address:* Department of Forensic Medicine, Edinburgh University Medical School, Teviot Place, Edinburgh EH8 9AG. *Club:* Royal Air Force.

MASON, Rt. Rev. Kenneth Bruce; *see* Northern Territory, Australia, Bishop of the.

MASON, Ven. Lancelot, MA; Archdeacon of Chichester, 1946-73; Canon Residentiary of Chichester Cathedral, 1949-73, now Canon Emeritus; *b* 22 July 1905; *s* of late Canon A. J. Mason, DD; unmarried. *Educ:* RN Colls Osborne and Dartmouth; Trinity Coll., Cambridge. Deacon, 1928; Priest, 1929; Rector of Plumpton, 1938; Chaplain RNVR, 1939-46 (despatches). *Address:* The Stables, Morton Hall, Retford, Notts.

MASON, Michael Henry, DL; Lieutenant-Commander RNVR, retired; *b* 3 Oct. 1900; *s* of late James Francis and Lady Evelyn Mason, Eynsham Hall, Witney, Oxon.; *m* 1st, 1925, Hon. Annette Sydney Baird (*d* 1950), *e d* of 1st Visc. Stonehaven, PC, GCMG, DSO; no *c*; 2nd, 1951, Dorothy Margaret Sturdee, Thames Ditton, Surrey; two *s* one *d*. *Educ:* Eton; Sandhurst. Has travelled extensively, mostly in wild places, 1939-45. Served in the Royal Navy throughout the war; Atlantic, Mediterranean and Far East. DL 1949, High Sheriff 1951, Oxon. Hon. Director: Royal Agricultural Society of England, 1950-52, and of Oxon Agricultural Soc., 1947-70. CC 1947-61. OStJ 1952. *Publications:* The Arctic Forests, 1924; Deserts Idle, 1928; Trivial Adventures in the Spanish Highlands, 1931; Where Tempests Blow, 1933; Where the River Runs Dry, 1934; The Paradise of Fools, 1936; Spain Untroubled, 1936; The Golden Evening, 1957; The Wild Ass Free, 1959; One Man's War (privately), 1966; In Pursuit of Big Fish, 1968; Willoughby the Immortal, 1969. *Recreations:* wild beasts and birds, sailing. *Address:* Scott's House, Eynsham Park, Witney, Oxon OX8 6PP. *T:* Freeland 881283. *Clubs:* Beefsteak, White's, Turf, Royal Ocean Racing (Cdre, 1937-47), Special Forces; Royal Yacht Squadron (Cowes); Cruising of America (Hon. Life Mem.); Zerzura; Cabo Blanco Fishing (Peru).

MASON, Sir Paul, KCMG 1954 (CMG 1947); KCVO 1958; HM Diplomatic Service, retired; *b* 11 June 1904; *m* 1938, Roberta, *d* of late J. Lorn McDougall, KC, Ottawa; one *s* one *d*. *Educ:* Eton; King's Coll., Cambridge. 1st Cl. Hons Modern History, 1926. Entered Foreign Service, 1928; has served at Brussels, Prague, Ottawa, Lisbon and in Foreign Office; Asst Private Sec. to Sec. of State, 1934-36; Private Sec. to Parliamentary Under Sec. of State, 1936-37; Acting Counsellor, 1945; Minister at Sofia, 1949-51; Asst Under Sec. of State, Foreign Office, 1951-54; Ambassador to The Netherlands, 1954-60; UK Permanent Rep. on N Atlantic Council, 1960-62; Alternate Delegate to Minister of State in Geneva Delegation on Disarmament and Nuclear Tests, 1962-64. Treas., Univ. of Nottingham, 1970-. High Sheriff of Notts, 1970. Chev. Order of Leopold; Gd Cr., Order of House of Orange, 1958. *Recreations:* various. *Address:* Morton Hall, Retford, Notts. *Club:* Lansdowne.

MASON, Peter; *see* Mason, G. F. P.

MASON, Peter Geoffrey, MBE 1946; High Master, Manchester Grammar School, 1962-Aug. 1978; *b* 22 Feb. 1914; *o s* of Harry Mason, Handsworth, Birmingham; *m* 1939, Mary Evelyn Davison; three *d. Educ:* King Edward's Sch., Birmingham; Christ's Coll., Cambridge (Scholar). Goldsmith Exhibitioner, 1935; Porson Scholar, 1936; 1st Class, Classical Tripos, Pts 1 and 2, 1935, 1936. Sixth Form Classical Master, Cheltenham Coll., 1936-40, Rugby Sch., 1946-49; Headmaster, Aldenham Sch., 1949-61. War Service, 1940-46: commissioned into Intelligence Corps, 1940; various staff appointments including HQ 21 Army Group; later attached to a dept of the Foreign Office. Member: Advisory Cttee on Education in the Colonies, 1956; ITA Educnl Adv. Council, 1964-69; Council, University of Salford; Court, Univ. of Manchester; Court of Governors, UMIST; Council, British Volunteer Programme (Chm., 1966-74); Chairman: Council of Educn for World Citizenship; Reg. Conf. on IVS; Court, Sheffield Indep. Grammar Sch. for Boys. *Publications:* articles and reviews in classical journals. *Recreations:* travel, fly-fishing, squash, tennis. *Address:* 143 Old Hall Lane, Fallowfield, Manchester M14 6HL. *T:* 061-224 3929. *Club:* Athenæum.

MASON, Philip, CIE 1946; OBE 1942; writer; *b* 19 March 1906; *s* of Dr H. A. Mason, Duffield, Derbs; *m* 1935, Eileen Mary, *d* of Courtenay Hayes, Charmouth, Dorset; two *s* two *d. Educ:* Sedbergh; Balliol. 1st Cl. Hons Philosophy, Politics and Economics, Oxford, 1927; MA 1952; DLitt 1972. ICS: Asst Magistrate United Provinces, 1928-33; Under-Sec., Government of India, War Dept, 1933-36; Dep. Commissioner Garhwal, 1936-39; Dep. Sec. Govt of India, Defence Co-ordination and War Depts, 1939-42; Sec. Chiefs of Staff Cttee, India, and Head of Conf. Secretariat, SE Asia Command, 1942-44; represented War Dept in Central Assembly, 1946; Joint Sec. to Government of India, War Dept, 1944-47; Tutor and Governor to the Princes, Hyderabad, 1947; retd from ICS, 1947. Mem. Commn of Enquiry to examine problems of Minorities in Nigeria, 1957. Dir of Studies in Race Relations, Chatham House, 1952-58; Dir, Inst. of Race Relations, 1958-69. Chairman: National Cttee for Commonwealth Immigrants, 1964-65; Exec. Cttee, UK Council for Overseas Student Affairs, 1969-75; Trustees, S African Church Develt Trust, 1976-. Hon. Fellow, Sch. of Oriental and African Studies, 1970; Hon. DSc Bristol, 1971. *Publications:* (as Philip Woodruff) Call the Next Witness, 1945; The Wild Sweet Witch, 1947; Whatever Dies, 1948; The Sword of Northumbria, 1948; The Island of Chamba, 1950; Hernshaw Castle, 1950; Colonel of Dragoons, 1951; The Founders, 1953; The Guardians, 1954; (as Philip Mason) Racial Tension, 1954; Christianity and Race, 1956; The Birth of a Dilemma, 1958; Year of Decision, 1960; (ed) Man, Race and Darwin, 1960; Common Sense about Race, 1961; Prospero's Magic, 1962; (ed) India and Ceylon: Unity and Diversity, 1967; Patterns of Dominance, 1970; Race Relations, 1970; How People Differ, 1971; A Matter of Honour, 1974; Kipling: The Glass The Shadow and The Fire, 1975; The Dove in Harness, 1976; A Shaft of Sunlight, 1978. *Recreation:* living in the country. *Address:* Hither Daggons, Cripplestyle, Alderholt, near Fordingbridge, Hants. *T:* Cranborne 318. *Club:* Travellers'.

MASON, Richard; author; *b* 16 May 1919. *Educ:* Bryanston School. *Publications:* novels: The Wind Cannot Read, 1947; The Shadow and the Peak, 1949; The World of Suzie Wong, 1957; The Fever Tree, 1962. *Address:* c/o A. M. Heath & Co. Ltd, 40-42 William IV Street, WC2N 4DD.

MASON, Ven. Richard John; Archdeacon of Tonbridge, since 1977; Vicar of Edenbridge, since 1973; *b* 26 April 1929; *s* of Vice-Adm. Sir Frank Mason, *qv; m* 1972, Susan Eileen Nunnerley. *Educ:* Shrewsbury School. Newspaper journalist, 1949-55; Lincoln Theological College, 1955-58; Asst Curate, Bishop's Hatfield, Herts, 1958-64; Domestic Chaplain to Bishop of London, 1964-69; Vicar of Riverhead with Dunton Green, Kent, 1969-73. *Address:* The Vicarage, Edenbridge, Kent TN8 5DA. *T:* Edenbridge 862258.

MASON, Robert Whyte, CMG 1956; *b* Glasgow, 1905; *s* of William Whyte Mason and Jane Miller MacKellar Watt; *m* 1952, Monica (*d* 1975), *d* of late George H. Powell, Truro. *Educ:* Glasgow Academy; Morrison's Academy, Crieff. Served War of 1939-45, in Army, 1940-45; Lt-Col Gen. Staff, Gen. Headquarters, Middle East; seconded to Ministry of Information as Dir of Policy, Middle East Services, 1943. 1st Sec., British Embassy, Baghdad, 1945; Foreign Office, 1947-48; Political Adviser in Eritrea and Somalia, 1948; 1st Sec. and Consul, British Legation, Amman, 1949; Consul-Gen., Brazzaville, 1951, Chicago, 1954-59; Dir of Research, Librarian and Keeper of the Papers at the Foreign Office, 1960-65. *Publications:* Murder to Measure, 1934; The Slaying Squad, 1934; Courage for Sale, 1939; And the Shouting Dies, 1940;

Three Cheers for Treason, 1940; Cairo Communiqué, 1942; More News from the Middle East, 1943; Arab Agent, 1944; Tandra, 1945; There is a Green Hill, 1946; Tender Leaves, 1950; No Easy Way Out, 1952; (ed) Anthony Trollope's North America, 1968. *Recreations:* golf, opera; writing thrillers. *Address:* 44 Sussex Square, Brighton BN2 1GE. *T:* 685093. *Club:* Travellers'.

MASON, Prof. Ronald, FRS 1975; Professor of Chemistry, University of Sussex, since 1971; *b* 22 July 1930; *o s* of David John Mason and Olwen Mason (*née* James); *m* 1952, E. Pauline Pattinson; three *d. Educ:* Univs of Wales and London. Research Assoc., British Empire Cancer Campaign, 1953-61; Lectr, Imperial Coll., 1961-63; Prof. of Inorganic Chemistry, Univ. of Sheffield, 1963-71. Vis. Prof., Univs in Australia, Canada, France, Israel, NZ and US, inc. A. D. Little Prof., MIT, 1970; Univ. of California, Berkeley, 1975; Ohio State Univ., 1976; North Western Univ., 1977; Prof. associé, Univ. de Strasbourg, 1976; Erskine Vis. Prof., Christchurch, NZ, 1977. SRC: Mem., 1971-75; Chm. Chemistry Cttee, 1969-72; Chm. Science Bd, 1972-75; Data Cttee, 1975-; Mem., Chief Scientist's Requirement Bd, DTI later Dept of Industry, 1973-. Corday-Morgan Medallist, 1965, and Tilden Lectr, 1970, Chemical Society; Medal and Prize for Structural Chem., Chem. Soc., 1973. Schmidt Meml Lectr, Israel, 1977. *Publications:* (ed) Advances in Radiation Biology, 1964 (3rd edn 1969); (ed) Advances in Structure Analysis by Diffraction Methods, 1968 (5th edn 1974); (ed) Physical Processes in Radiation Biology, 1964; many papers in Jl Chem. Soc., etc. *Address:* 14 Roedean Crescent, Brighton, East Sussex. *T:* Brighton 682077. *Club:* Athenæum.

MASON, Rt. Hon. Roy, PC 1968; MP (Lab) Barnsley since March 1953; Secretary of State for Northern Ireland, since 1976; *b* 18 April 1924; *s* of Joseph and Mary Mason; *m* 1945, Marjorie *d* of Ernest Sowden; two *d. Educ:* Carlton Junior Sch.; Royston Senior Sch.; London Sch. of Economics (TUC Scholarship). Went underground at 14 years of age, 1938-53; NUM branch official, 1947-53; mem. Yorks Miners' Council, 1949. Labour party spokesman on Defence and Post Office affairs, 1960-64; Minister of State (Shipping), Bd of Trade, 1964-67; Minister of Defence (Equipment), 1967-April 1968; Postmaster-Gen., April-June 1968; Minister of Power, 1968-69; President, Bd of Trade, 1969-70; Labour party spokesman on Civil Aviation, Shipping, Tourism, Films and Trade matters, 1970-74; Sec. of State for Defence, 1974-76. Mem., Council of Europe and WEU, 1973-. Chm., Yorkshire Gp of Labour MPs; Chm., Miners Gp of MPs. Consultant: Amalgamated Distilled Products, 1971-74; H. P. Bulmer, 1971-74. *Recreation:* work, provided one stays on top of it. *Address:* 12 Victoria Avenue, Barnsley, S Yorks.

MASON, Stewart Carlton, CBE 1968; Curator, Institute of Contemporary Prints, 1972-76; *b* 28 Feb. 1906; *s* of Carlton Willicomb Mason and Alys Kastor; *m* 1941, Ruth Elizabeth Wise; three *s* (and one *s* decd). *Educ:* Uppingham Sch.; Worcester Coll., Oxford (Exhibr, MA). Asst Master: Berkhamsted Sch., 1930-31; Harrow Sch., 1931-37; HM Inspector of Schools, 1937-39 and 1944-47; seconded to Admty, 1939-44; Dir of Educn for Leics, 1947-71. Mem., Nat. Adv. Council on Art Educn, 1957-71; Chairman: Nat. Council for Diplomas in Art and Design, 1970-74 (Vice-Chm., 1961-70); Art and Design Main Cttee, CNAA, 1974-75; Trustee: Tate Gallery, 1966-73; Nat. Gallery, 1971-73; Mem. Adv. Council, Victoria and Albert Museum, 1961-73; Mem., Standing Commn on Museums and Galleries, 1973-76; Chm. of Visual Arts Panel, E Mids Arts Assoc., 1971-75 and Eastern Arts Assoc., 1972-; Chm. Management Cttee, The Minories, Colchester, 1976-; Mem. over many years of Councils of Univs of Leicester, Nottingham, Loughborough and RCA. Hon. DSc Loughborough, 1966; Senior Fellow, RCA (Hon. ARCA 1965). *Publication:* (ed) In Our Experience, 1970. *Address:* The Orangery, Ufford Place, Woodbridge, Suffolk. *T:* Eyke 322.

MASON, Walter W.; *see* Wynne Mason.

MASON, William Ernest; Under-Secretary, Ministry of Agriculture, Fisheries and Food, since 1975; *b* 12 Jan. 1929; *s* of Ernest George and Agnes Margaret Mason; *m* 1959, Jean (*née* Bossley); one *s* one *d. Educ:* Brockley Grammar Sch.; London Sch. of Economics (BScEcon). RAF, 1947-49; Min. of Food, 1949-54; MAFF, 1954; Principal 1963; Asst Sec. 1970. Member: Econ. Develt Cttee for Distrib. Trades, 1975-; Econ. Develt Cttee for Food and Drink Manufg Inds, 1976-. *Recreations:* music, reading, gardening. *Address:* The Haven, Fairlie Gardens, SE23 3TE. *T:* 01-699 5821. *Club:* Reform.

MASSEREENE and FERRARD, 13th Viscount, *cr* 1660; **John Clotworthy Talbot Foster Whyte-Melville Skeffington;** Baron of Loughneagh, 1660; Baron Oriel, 1790; Viscount Ferrard, 1797; Baron Oriel (UK), 1821; DL; *b* 23 Oct. 1914; *s* of 12th Viscount (*d* 1956) and Jean Barbara (*d* 1937), *e d* of Sir John Stirling Ainsworth, MP, JP, 1st Bt, of Ardanaiseig, Argyllshire; *S* father 1956; *m* 1939, Annabelle Kathleen, *er d* of late Henry D. Lewis and of Mrs Henry D. Lewis, Combwell Priory, Hawkhurst, Kent; one *s* one *d. Educ:* Eton. Lt, Black Watch SR, 1933-36, re-employed, 1939-40 (invalided); retired; served in Small Vessels Pool, Royal Navy, 1944. Mem. IPU Delegation to Spain, 1960; Whip, Conservative Peers Cttee (IUP), House of Lords, 1958-65, Jt Dep. Chm., 1965-70; introduced in House of Lords: Deer Act, 1963; Riding Establishments Act, 1964; Export of Animals for Research Bill, 1968; Riding Establishments Act, 1970; moved debates on Overseas Information Services and other matters. Member: CPA delegn to Malaŵi, 1976; Select Cttee on Anglian Water Authority Bill, 1976. Posts in Cons. Constituency organisations incl. Pres., Brighton, Kemp Town Div., Vice-Pres. and former Treasurer, Ashford Div. Chm. and Dir of companies. Driver of leading British car, Le Mans Grand Prix, 1937. One of original pioneers in commercial develt of Cape Canaveral, Florida; promoted first scheduled air service Glasgow-Oban-Isle of Mull, 1968; presented operetta Countess Maritza at Palace Theatre, London. Comr, Hunterston Ore Terminal Hearing, Glasgow, 1973. Pres., of Charitable and other organisations incl.: Ponies of Britain; Kent Hotels and Restaurants Assoc. Pres., Canterbury Br., RNLI. Chief, Scottish Clans Assoc. of London, 1974-76. Chm. Kent Branch Victoria League. Treas., Kent Assoc. of Boys' Clubs. Master, Ashford Valley Foxhounds, 1953-54. Commodore, House of Lords Yacht Club. Freeman, City of London, and Mem. Worshipful Company of Shipwrights. Gold Staff Officer, Coronation, 1953. FZS. DL Antrim, 1957. *Publications:* The Lords, 1973; contributes articles to newspapers, chiefly sporting and natural history. *Recreations:* all field sports; farming; forestry; racing. *Heir:* *s* Hon. John David Clotworthy Whyte-Melville Foster Skeffington [*b* 3 June 1940; *m* 1970, Ann Denise, *er d* of late Norman Rowlandson; one *s* one d]. *Address:* Knock, Isle of Mull, Argyll. *T:* Aros 56; (Seat) Chilham Castle, Kent. *T:* Chilham 319. *Clubs:* Carlton, Turf, Pratt's, Royal Yacht Squadron.

MASSEVITCH, Prof. Alla; Vice-President of the Astronomical Council of the USSR Academy of Sciences since 1952; Professor of Astrophysics, Moscow University, since 1946; *b* Tbilisi, Georgia, USSR, 9 Oct. 1918; *m* 1942; one *d. Educ:* Moscow Univ. Lectured at the Royal Festival Hall, London, and at the Free Trade Hall, Manchester, etc., on The Conquest of Space, 1960; she is in charge of network of stations for tracking Sputniks, in Russia. Pres. Working Group 1 (Tracking and Telemetring) of COSPAR (Internat. Cttee for Space Research) 1961-66. Pres., Commission 35 (Internal Structure of Stars) of the Internat. Astronom. Union, 1967-70. Foreign Mem. Royal Astronomical Society, 1963. Internat. Award for Astronautics (Prix Galabert), 1963; Mem. Internat. Acad. Astronautics, 1964. Vice-Pres., Inst. for Soviet-American Relations, 1967; Mem. Board, Soviet Peace Cttee, and Internat. Peace Cttee, 1965. USSR State Prize, 1975. Govt decorations, USSR, 1963, 1975. *Publications:* 86 scientific papers on the internal structure of the stars, stellar evolution, and optical tracking of artificial satellites, in Russian and foreign astronomical and geophysical journals. *Address:* 48 Pjatnitskaja Street, Moscow, USSR. *T:* 2315461; 1 Vostania Square 403, Moscow. *Club:* Club for Scientists (Moscow).

MASSEY, Anna (Raymond); actress; *b* 11 Aug. 1937; *d* of Raymond Massey, *qv*, and of Adrianne Allen; *m* 1958, Jeremy Huggins (marr. diss., 1963); one *s. Educ:* London; New York; Switzerland; Paris; Rome. *Plays:* The Reluctant Debutante, 1955; Dear Delinquent, 1957; The Elder Statesman, 1958; Double Yolk, 1959; The Last Joke, 1960; The Miracle Worker, 1961; The School for Scandal, 1962; The Doctor's Dilemma, 1963; The Right Honourable Gentleman, 1964; The Glass Menagerie, 1965; The Prime of Miss Jean Brodie, 1966; The Flip Side, 1967; First Day of a New Season, 1967; This Space is Mine, 1969; Hamlet, 1970; Spoiled, 1971; Slag, 1971; Heartbreak House, National Theatre, 1975; Jingo, 1975; Play, Royal Court, 1976. *Films:* Gideon's Day, 1957; Peeping Tom, 1960; Bunny Lake is Missing, 1965; The Looking Glass War, 1969; David Copperfield, 1969; De Sade, 1971; Frenzy, 1972; A Doll's House, 1973. Numerous appearances in TV plays. *Address:* c/o Larry Dalzell Associates, 3 Goodwin's Court, St Martin's Lane, WC2.

MASSEY, Sir Arthur, Kt 1956; CBE 1941; Chief Medical Officer, Ministry of Pensions and National Insurance, 1947-59, retired; *b* 1894; *s* of late Albert Massey, Keighley, Yorks; *m* 1924, Dorothy Blanche Ince, *d* of late Rev. H. H. T. Cleife, MA Cantab; one *d. Educ:* University of Leeds, MD, etc; Hon.

Fellow, American Public Health Assoc.; Vice-President: Royal Society Health; Vocational Guidance Assoc.; KHP, 1950-52; QHP, 1952-53; Examiner in Public Health, Universities of London and Bristol, 1947-50, and Birmingham, 1952-55; MOH, City of Coventry, 1930-47. Chairman: Chadwick Trust, 1969-; Central Council for Health Educn, 1944-46. Lecturer in USA 1944, Yale Univ. 1954. Served 1915-18 in RFA (Lt), and 1943-45 in HG (Lt-Col, Zone Medical Adviser). *Publications:* Epidemiology and Air Travel, 1933; (ed) Modern Trends in Public Health, 1949; various contributions to the medical literature on hospital policy, public health and social insurance. *Recreations:* bridge, gardening, watching cricket. *Address:* 93 Bedford Gardens, W8 7EQ. *T:* 01-727 6951. *Club:* Athenæum. *See also* Sir C. R. Rowley, Bt.

MASSEY, Sir Harrie Stewart Wilson, Kt 1960; PhD Cantab; LLD Melbourne; FRS 1940; Quain Professor of Physics, University College, London, 1950-75, now Emeritus; *b* 1908; *s* of Harrie and Eleanor Massey, Melbourne, Australia; *m* Jessica, *d* of Alex and Alice Mary Barton Bruce, Western Australia; one *d. Educ:* University High Sch., Melbourne; Melbourne Univ. (BA, MSc, Hon. LLD, Hon. DSc); Trinity Coll., Cambridge (PhD); Aitchison Travelling Scholar, Melbourne Univ., 1929-31; Research at Cavendish Laboratory, Cambridge, 1929-33; Exhibition of 1851 Senior Research Student, 1931-33; Independent Lecturer in Mathematical Physics, Queen's Univ., Belfast, 1933-38; Goldsmid Prof. of Mathematics, University of London, University Coll., 1938-50. Rutherford Memorial Lectr, 1967. Temp. Senior Experimental Officer, Admiralty Research Laboratory, 1940; Dep. Chief Scientist, 1941-43, Chief Scientist, 1943, Mine Design Dept, Admiralty; Technical Officer, DSIR Mission to Berkeley, Calif, 1943-45. Vice-President: Atomic Scientists Assoc., 1949-53 (Pres. 1953-57), Royal Astronomical Society, 1950-53; Council Member: Royal Society, 1949-51, 1959-60 (Physical Sec., and a Vice-Pres., 1970-); Physical Soc., 1949- (Pres. 1954-56; Hon. Fellow, 1976). Mem., Governing Board of National Institute for Research in Nuclear Science, 1957-65. Governor: Rugby Sch., 1955-59; Chelsea Polytechnic, 1956-59; Chm. Brit. Nat. Cttee for Space Research, 1959-; Mem. Bureau of Cttee on Space Research, 1959-; Mem. Advisory Council of the Science Museum, 1959-61; Pres. European Prep. Commn for Space Research, 1960-64; Pres. Council ESRO, 1964; Chm. Council for Scientific Policy, 1965-69; Mem., Central Advisory Council for Science and Technology, 1967-69. Vice-Provost, UCL, 1969-73. Assessor, SRC, 1972-; Member: Royal Commn for Exhbn of 1851, 1972-; Prov. Space Science Adv. Bd for Europe, 1974- (Chm.); Anglo-Australian Telescope Bd, 1975-. Corr. Mem., Acad. of Sci., Liège, 1974; Aust. Acad. of Sci, 1976; Mem., Amer. Philosoph. Soc., 1975; Hon. Mem., Royal Met. Soc., 1967-. Hon. DSc: QUB, 1960; Leicester, 1964; Hull, 1968; Adelaide, 1974; Heriot-Watt, 1975; Liverpool, 1975; Hon. LLD Glasgow, 1962; Hon. Fellow, UCL 1976. Hughes Medal, Royal Society, 1955; Royal Medal, Royal Society, 1958. *Publications:* Theory of Atomic Collisions (with N. F. Mott), 1933, 3rd ed., 1965; Negative Ions, 1938, 3rd edn, 1976; Electronic and Ionic Impact Phenomena (with E. H. S. Burhop), 1952, 2nd edn 1969; Atoms and Energy, 1953; The Upper Atmosphere (with R. L. F. Boyd), 1958; Ancillary Mathematics (with H. Kestelman), 1958; New Age in Physics, 1960; Space Physics, 1964; various publications on atomic physics in Proc. of Royal Society and other scientific jls. *Recreations:* cricket, tennis, billiards and snooker, badminton, travel, study of other sciences. *Address:* Kalamunda, 29 Pelhams Walk, Esher, Surrey. *Clubs:* MCC; Melbourne Cricket.

MASSEY, Raymond; Actor and Producer; *b* Toronto, Canada, 30 Aug. 1896; *s* of Chester D. Massey and Anna Vincent; *m* 1st, Margery Fremantle (marr. diss.); one *s*; 2nd, Adrianne Allen (marr. diss.); one *s* one *d*; 3rd, 1939, Dorothy (Ludington) Whitney. *Educ:* Appleby Sch., Ontario; Toronto Univ.; Balliol Coll., Oxford. Hon. DLitt Lafayette Univ. 1939; Hon. LLD Queen's Univ., Kingston, Ontario, 1949; Hon. LittD Hobart Coll., NY, 1953; Hon. Dr Fine Arts: Northwestern Univ., 1959, Ripon Coll., 1962, Wooster Coll., 1966; Hon. Dr Hum., American International Coll., 1960. Served European War, 1915-19 as Lt in Canadian Field Artillery; in France, 1916 (wounded), in USA as Instructor in Field Artillery at Yale and Princeton Univs, 1917 and in Siberia, 1918; staff of Adj.-Gen. Canadian Army, rank of Major, 1942-43; naturalized US Citizen, March 1944. First appearance on professional stage at Everyman Theatre, 1922, in In the Zone, Jonty in The Round Table, played Captain La Hire and Canon D'Estivet in Saint Joan; in 1926 with Allan Wade and George Carr, entered on management of the Everyman Theatre, producing a number of plays and taking a variety of parts; played James Bebb in At Mrs Beam's, the Khan Aghaba in The Transit of Venus, the Rev. MacMillan in An American Tragedy, Robert in Beyond the Horizon, 1926, and Reuben Manassa in the Golden Calf,

1927; Austin Lowe in The Second Man, Joe Cobb in Spread Eagle, and Lewis Dodd in The Constant Nymph, 1928; Randolph Calthorpe in The Black Ace, 1929; Raymond Dabney in The Man in Possession, 1930; Topaze in Topaze, 1930; Randall in Late Night Final, 1931; Hamlet in the Norman Bel Geddes production at Broadhurst Theatre, New York, 1931; Smith in Never Come Back, 1932; Hugh Sebastian in The Rats of Norway; Von Hagen in the Ace, 1933; David Linden in the Shining Hour: At Booth Theatre, New York, 1934, and at St James' Theatre, 1935; Ethan in Ethan Frome, at the National Theatre, New York, 1936; at Apollo Theatre 1938, presented with Henry Sherek, Idiot's Delight, playing the part of Harry Van; Abraham Lincoln in Abe Lincoln in Illinois, Plymouth Theatre, New York, 1938-39; toured the US in this play, 1939-40; in The Doctor's Dilemma, Candida, Pygmalion, Lovers and Friends, The Father, John Brown's Body, The Rivalry, J. B.; I Never Sang for my Father, Duke of York's, 1970. Productions include: The White Chateau, The Crooked Billet, Spread Eagle, The Sacred Flame, The Stag, The Silver Tassie, Symphony in Two Flats, The Man in Possession, Lean Harvest, Late Night Final, Grand Hotel, The Rats of Norway, The Shining Hour, Idiot's Delight. *Films played-in include:* The Scarlet Pimpernel, The Old Dark House, Things to Come, Fire Over England, Under the Red Robe, The Prisoner of Zenda, The Hurricane, The Drum, Abe Lincoln in Illinois, Santa Fé Trail, Reap the Wild Wind, Arsenic and Old Lace, Invaders (49th Parallel), Action in the North Atlantic, The Woman in the Window, God is my Co-Pilot, Hotel Berlin, A Matter of Life and Death, Possessed, Mourning Becomes Electra, Fountainhead, David and Bathsheba, Come Fill the Cup, East of Eden, The Naked and the Dead, The Queen's Guards. Co-star, as "Dr Gillespie" in Television series Dr Kildare. Author of play, The Hanging Judge, produced New Theatre, London, 1952. *Publication:* When I was Young, 1976. *Recreations:* golf, carpentry. *Address:* 913 Beverly Drive, Beverly Hills, California 90210, USA. *Clubs:* Garrick, Century (New York.)
See also Anna Massey.

MASSEY, Roy Cyril; Organist and Master of the Choristers, Hereford Cathedral, since 1974; *b* 9 May 1934; *s* of late Cyril Charles Massey and of Beatrice May Massey; *m* 1975, Ruth Carol Craddock Grove. *Educ:* Univ. of Birmingham (BMus); privately with David Willcocks. FRCO (CHM); ADCM; ARCM; FRSCM (for distinguished services to church music) 1972. Organist: St Alban's, Conybere Street, Birmingham, 1953-60; St Augustine's, Edgbaston, 1960-65; Croydon Parish Church, 1965-68; Warden, RSCM, 1965-68; Conductor, Croydon Bach Soc., 1966-68; Special Comr of RSCM, 1964-; Organist to City of Birmingham Choir, 1954-; Organist and Master of Choristers, Birmingham Cath., 1968-74; Dir of Music, King Edward's Sch., Birmingham, 1968-74. Mem. Council and Examiner, RCO, 1970-; Mem., RCSM Adv. Council, 1976-; Advisor on organs to dioceses of Birmingham and Hereford, 1974-. Pres., Birmingham Organists' Assoc., 1970-75. Fellow, St Michael's Coll., Tenbury, 1976. *Recreations:* motoring, old buildings, Dutch organs. *Address:* 14 College Cloisters, Hereford HR1 2NG. *T:* Hereford 2011. *Club:* Conservative (Hereford).

MASSEY, Prof. Vincent, PhD; FRS 1977; Professor of Biological Chemistry, University of Michigan, since 1963; *b* 28 Nov. 1926; *s* of Walter Massey and Mary Ann Massey; *m* 1950, Margot Eva Ruth Grünewald; one *s* two *d*. *Educ:* Univ. of Sydney (BSc Hons 1947); Univ. of Cambridge (PhD 1953). Scientific Officer, CSIRO, Australia, 1947-50; Ian McMaster Scholar, Cambridge, 1950-53, ICI Fellow, 1953-55; Researcher, Henry Ford Hosp., Detroit, 1955-57; Lectr, then Sen. Lectr, Univ. of Sheffield, 1957-63. Vis. Prof., Univ. of Ill, 1960; Vis. Prof., Univ. of Konstanz, Germany, 1973-74, Permanent Guest Prof., 1975-. *Publications:* over 200 articles in scholarly jls and books. *Recreations:* walking, sailing, gardening. *Address:* Department of Biological Chemistry, University of Michigan, Ann Arbor, Mich 48109, USA. *T:* (313) 7647196.

MASSEY, William Edmund Devereux, CBE 1961; retired from HM Diplomatic Service; *b* 1901; *m* 1942, Ingrid Glad-Block, Oslo; one *d*. Entered Foreign Office, 1922; served in diplomatic and consular posts in Poland, France, Japan, Brazil, Roumania, Sweden, Luxembourg, Germany; Ambassador and Consul-General to Nicaragua, 1959-61. Hon. Consul for Nicaragua in London, 1969-. Freeman of City of London. Representative in Sweden of Order of St John of Jerusalem, 1945-47. Chm., UK Permanent Cttee on Geographical Names for Official Use; UK Deleg., 2nd UN Conf. on Geographical Names, 1972. FRGS. Grand Ducal Commemorative Medal, Luxembourg, 1953. *Address:* 59 Redcliffe Gardens, SW10. *T:* 01-370 2552.

MASSIGLI, René, (Hon.) GCVO 1950; (Hon.) KBE 1938; (Hon.) CH 1954; Grand Cross, Legion of Honour, 1954; *b* 22 March 1888; *s* of late Charles Massigli and late Marguerite Michel; *m* 1932, Odette Boissier; one *d*. *Educ:* Ecole normale supérieure. Mem. of the Ecole Française de Rome, 1910-13; Chargé de cours at the University of Lille, 1913-14; Gen. Sec. at the Conference of Ambassadors, 1920; Maître des Requêtes at the Conseil d'Etat, 1924-28; Ministre plénipotentiaire, Head of the League of Nations' Section at the Ministry of Foreign Affairs, 1928-33; Asst Dir of Political Section at the Ministry of Foreign Affairs, 1933-37, Dir, 1937-38; Ambassador to Turkey, 1939-40; escaped from France, 1943; Commissioner for Foreign Affairs, French Cttee of National Liberation, 1943-44; French Ambassador to Great Britain, Sept. 1944-Jan. 1955; Sec.-Gen. at the Quai d'Orsay, Jan. 1955-June 1956; retired 1956. French Pres., Channel Tunnel Study Gp, 1958-69. *Publications:* Quelques Maladies de l'Etat, 1958; La Turquie devant la guerre, 1964. *Address:* 3 Avenue Robert Schuman, 75007 Paris, France.

MASSINE, Léonide; Choreographer; *b* Moscow, 9 Aug. 1896; *s* of Teodor Affanasievitch and Eugenia Nikolaevna; *m* 1939, Tatiana Vladimirovna Milisnikova; one *s* one *d*. *Educ:* Imperial Ballet Sch., Moscow; pupil of Domashoff, Enrico Cecchetti and Nicolas Legat. Choreographer and principal dancer, Diaghilev Ballet Russe, 1914-20; choreographer, dancer, and artistic dir, Ballet de Monte Carlo, 1932-41; National Ballet Theatre, NY, 1941-44; organized Ballet Russe Highlights, 1945-46; guest artiste and choreographer: Sadler's Wells Ballet, Covent Garden, Royal Opera House, Copenhagen, Teatro Alla Scala, Milan, Opéra-Comique, Paris, 1947-51. Edinburgh Festival 1960; Ballets Européens de Nervi. *Ballets:* Soleil de Nuit, 1915; Las Meninas, 1916; Good Humoured Ladies, Contes Russes, Parade, 1917; La Boutique Fantasque, Le Tricorne, 1919; Le Sacre du Printemps, Le Astuzie Feminili, Pulcinella, Le Rossignol, 1920; Salade, Gigue, Le Beau Danube, Les Facheux, 1924; Les Matelots, Zephire et Flore, 1925; Cimarosiana, 1926; Le Pas d'Acier, Ode, Mercure, 1927; Les Enchantements d'Alcine, Le Roi David, Amphion, 1929-30; Le Beau Danube (2nd version), Belkis, Vecchia Milano, La Belle Hélène, 1932; Les Présages, Les Jeux d'Enfants, The Miracle, 1933; Choreartium, Scuola di Ballo, 1933-34; Le Bal, Union Pacific, Jardin Public, 1935; Symphonie Fantastique, 1936; Gaité Parisienne, Seventh Symphony, St Francis (Nobilissima Visione), 1938; Capriccio Espagnol, Rouge et Noir, Bogatyri, Bacchanal, 1939; Wien 1814, The New Yorker, 1940; Labyrinth, Saratoga, 1941; Aleko, Don Domingo, 1942; Mlle Angot, 1943; Antar, Daphnis et Chloe, Unfortunate Painter, Rêverie Classique, Moonlight Sonata, Mad Tristan, 1944; Bullet in the Ballet, Les Arabesques (revived), Les Matelots (rev.), 1945-46; Boutique Fantasque, Tricorne (rev.), 1946; Mam'selle Angot (2nd version), 1947; Capriccio (de Stravinsky), Episode de la Vie d'un Artiste, Clock Symphony, Sacre du Printemps (rev.), 1948; Quattro Stagioni, Mad Tristan (rev.), Good Humoured Ladies (rev.), Suite Bergamasque, Le Peintre et son Modèle, 1949; La Valse (de Ravel), 1950; Le Bal du Pont du Nord, Symphonie Allégorique (Les Saisons), Donald of the Burthens, Capriccio Espagnol (rev.), 1951; (created) Laudes Evangelli, M'selle Angot (rev.), dances for: Wilhelm Tell, Armida, Didone, Gioconda, 1952; Rezurrezione e Vita, 1954, Arianna, 1954; Commedia Umana, 1960; Le Bal des Voleurs, 1960; The Three Cornered Hat (rev.), 1973; *Staged:* for Royal Ballet, 1968: Boutique Fantasque; Mam'selle Angot. *Films:* (prod. dances and appeared) Carnival in Costa Rica, 1945; (comp. and danced his part): Red Shoes, 1948; Tales of Hoffmann, 1951; Carosello Napoletano, 1953. *Publications:* My Life in Ballet, 1968; Massine on Choreography, 1974.

MASSY, family name of **Baron Massy.**

MASSY, 9th Baron *cr* 1776; **Hugh Hamon John Somerset Massy;** *b* 11 June 1921; *o s* of 8th Baron, and Margaret, 2nd *d* of late Richard Leonard, Meadsbrook, Ashbourne, Co. Limerick, and widow of Dr Moran, Tara, Co. Meath; *S* father 1958; *m* 1943, Margaret, *d* of late John Flower, Barry, Co. Meath; four *s* one *d*. *Educ:* Clongowes Wood Coll.; Clayesmore Sch. Served War, 1940-45, Private, RAOC. *Heir:* *s* Hon. David Hamon Somerset Massy, *b* 4 March 1947.

MASSY-GREENE, Sir (John) Brian, Kt 1972; Chairman, Consolidated Gold Fields Australia Limited, 1966-77 (General Manager and Managing Director, 1962-66, Managing Director, 1966-76); *b* Tenterfield, NSW, 20 April 1916; *s* of late Sir Walter Massy-Greene, KCMG, and Lula May Lomax; *m* 1942, Margaret Elizabeth Ritchie Sharp, *d* of late Dr Walter Alexander Ramsay Sharp, OBE; two *s* two *d*. *Educ:* Sydney C of E Grammar Sch.; Geelong Grammar Sch.; Clare Coll., Cambridge (MA). Served War 1939-45: New Guinea, AIF, as Lieut, 1942-45. Joined Metal Manufacturers Ltd, as Staff Cadet,

1959; later transferred to their wholly-owned subsid. Austral Bronze Co. Pty Ltd; Gen. Manager, 1953-62. Chairman: The Bellambi Coal Co. Ltd, 1964-72; Goldsworthy Mining Ltd, 1965-76; The Mount Lyell Mining & Railway Co. Ltd, 1964-76; Lawrenson Alumasc Holdings Ltd, 1964-73 (Dir, 1962-73); Director: Associated Minerals Consolidated Ltd, 1962-76; Commonwealth Banking Corporation, 1968- (Dep. Chm., 1975-); Commonwealth Mining Investments (Australia) Ltd, 1962-72; Consolidated Gold Fields Ltd, London, 1968-76; Dalgety Australia Ltd, 1967- (Dep. Chm., 1975-); Dunlop Australia Ltd, 1968-; Zip Holdings Ltd, 1964-73. Member: Exec. Cttee, Australian Mining Industry Council, 1967- (Pres. 1971); Manuf. Industries Adv. Council, 1968-77; NSW Adv. Cttee, CSIRO, 1968-75. MInstMet; Member: Aust. Inst. Metals; Aust. Inst. Mining and Metallurgy. FAIM. Recreations: farming, fishing, flying. Address: 38 Roslyndale Avenue, Woollahra, NSW 2025, Australia. T: 36-7213. Club: Australian.

MASTEL, Royston John, CVO 1977; CBE 1969; Assistant Commissioner (Administration and Operations), Metropolitan Police, 1972-76; b 30 May 1917; s of late John Mastel and late Rose Mastel (née Gorton); m 1940, Anne Kathleen Johnson; two s. Educ: Tottenham Grammar School. Joined Metropolitan Police as Constable, 1937; Pilot, RAF, 1941-45; Metro. Police: Sergeant 1946; Inspector 1951; Supt 1955; Comdr, No 2 District, 1966; subseq. Dep. Asst Comr, Head of Management Services Dept and D Dept (Personnel) and Asst Comr (Personnel and Training), 1972. OStJ 1976. Recreations: Rugby football, boxing, riding, golf. Address: c/o National Westminster Bank, Caxton House Branch, 29 Queen Anne's Gate, Westminster, SW1. Club: Royal Air Force.

MASTER, Alfred, CIE 1931; DPhil; ICS (retired); Assistant Keeper, India Office Library, 1951-57; b 12 Feb. 1883; s of George Reginald Master, MRCS, late of Sheringham; m 1909, Dorothy Amy (d 1952), d of Rev. H. A. Thorne; three d. Educ: King Edward VI Sch., Norwich; Epsom Coll.; BNC, Oxford (MA; DPhil 1962). Entered ICS, 1906; Municipal Commissioner, Ahmadabad, 1917; Temp. Major, GSO2; Military Mission to Turkestan, Persia, 1918; officiating Sec. to Government of Bombay, General Dept, 1925; Collector of Bombay City and Suburbs, 1932-34; Lecturer: in Marathi, 1937-38; in Gujarati, 1938-39, in Indian Philology, 1944-50, at the School of Oriental and African Studies, London Univ.; Asst Keeper, India Office Lib., 1951-57; Member Governing Body, School of Oriental and African Studies, 1952-60. Publications: Introduction to Telugu Grammar, 1947; Catalogue of the Gujarati & Rajasthani Manuscripts in the India Office Library by J. F. Blumhardt, revised and enlarged, 1954; A Grammar of Old Marathi, 1964; English edn of L'Indo-Aryen, by Jules Bloch, 1965; articles in journals on Local Government, Linguistics, and Numismatics. Address: Woodchurch, Burleigh Road, Ascot, Berks. T: 22897.

MASTERMAN, Sir Christopher Hughes, Kt 1947; CSI 1944; CIE 1939; ICS (retired); b 7 Oct. 1889; s of late Captain J. Masterman, RN; m 1921, Hope Gladys (d 1972), d of late Henry Gearing; two s. Educ: Winchester; Trinity Coll., Oxford, MA. Entered Indian Civil Service, 1914; Sec. to Govt Education and Public Health Depts, Madras, 1936-39; Collector and District Magistrate, Vizagapatam, 1939-42; Mem. Board of Revenue, Madras, 1943; Chief Sec. and Adviser to the Governor of Madras, 1946; Deputy High Commissioner for UK, Madras, 1947. Address: 1 Derwentwater Road, Wimborne, Dorset. T: Wimborne 6534.

MASTERS, John, DSO 1944; OBE 1945; Author; b 26 Oct. 1914; s of late John Masters, 16th Rajputs, and Ada (née Coulthard; m Barbara Allcard; one s one d (one d decd). Educ: Wellington; RMC, Sandhurst. Commissioned 2nd Lieut, Indian Army, 1934; 2nd Bn, 4th PWO Gurkha Rifles, 1935; Adjutant, 1939; Comdt 3rd Bn, 1944; Bde Major, 114 Ind. Inf. Bde, 1942; 111 Ind. Inf. Bde, 1943; GSO1 19 Ind. Div., 1945; GSO1, MO1, GHQ (I), 1946; GSO2 Staff Coll., Camberley, 1947; retired 1948. Active service: NW Frontier, 1936-37; Iraq, Syria, Persia, 1941; Burma, 1944-45. Publications: Nightrunners of Bengal, 1951; The Deceivers, 1952, repr. 1966; The Lotus and the Wind, 1953; Bhowani Junction, 1954; Coromandel, 1955; Far, Far the Mountain Peak, 1957; Fandango Rock, 1959; The Venus of Konpara, 1960; To the Coral Strand, 1962; Trial at Monomoy, 1964; Fourteen Eighteen, 1965; The Breaking Strain, 1967; The Rock, 1969; The Ravi Lancers, 1972; Thunder at Sunset, 1974; The Field-Marshal's Memoirs, 1975; The Himalayan Concerto, 1976; autobiography: Bugles and a Tiger, 1956; The Road Past Mandalay, 1961; Pilgrim Son, 1971. Recreations: mountains, railways. Address: c/o Brandt, 1101 Park Avenue, New York, NY 10017, USA.

MASTON, Charles James, CB 1965; CBE 1954; b 15 May 1912; s of James and Amelia Maston; m 1940, Eileen Sybil Stopher; no c. Educ: Yeadon and Guiseley Secondary Sch.; Bradford Gram. Sch.; St John's Coll., Cambridge. Asst Principal, Min. of Labour, 1934; Asst Private Sec. to Minister, 1937-39; Principal, 1939. Served HM Forces, 1942-44. Asst Sec., Min. of Labour (later Dept of Employment), 1944; Industrial Relations Dept, 1953-56; Under Secretary: Military Recruitment Dept, 1957-60; Employment Dept, 1960-64; Industrial Relations Dept, 1964-65; Safety, Health and Welfare Dept, 1965-68; Employment Services Div., 1968-72. Recreations: hill walking, philately. Address: Flaska, Doggetts Wood Lane, Chalfont St Giles, Bucks. T: Little Chalfont 2033.

MATABELELAND, Bishop of, since 1977; **Rt. Rev. Robert William Stanley Mercer;** b 10 Jan. 1935; s of Harold Windrum Mercer and Kathleen Frampton. Educ: Grey School, Port Elizabeth, S Africa; St Paul's Theological Coll., Grahamstown, SA (LTh). Deacon 1959, priest 1960, Matabeleland; Asst Curate, Hillside, Bulawayo, 1959-63; Novice, CR, 1963; professed, 1965; at Mirfield, 1963-66; at St Teilo's Priory, Cardiff, 1966-68; Prior and Rector of Stellenbosch, S Africa, 1968-70; deported from SA, 1970; Chaplain, St Augustine's School, Penhalonga, Rhodesia, 1971-72; Rector of Borrowdale, Salisbury, Rhodesia, 1972-77. Address: Box 2422, Bulawayo, Rhodesia. T: 61370.

MATACA, Most Rev. Petero; see Suva, Archbishop of, (RC).

MATCHAN, Leonard Joseph; Chairman, New Guarantee Trust of Jersey Ltd; Hon. Life President, Cope Allman International Ltd; b 26 March 1911; s of late George Matchan and Elsie Harriet Greenleaf; m 1933, Kathleen Artis; one s one d. Educ: Trinity, Croydon. FACCA; JDipMA; Certified Accountant. Vice President and European General Manager, Max Factor, Hollywood, 1936-49. Practice as accountant, 1950-55. President, Toilet Preparations Assoc., 1940-48. Recreation: work. Address: Island of Brecqhou, Channel Islands. T: Brecqhou 33 and Guernsey 25000.

MATES, Lt-Col Michael John; MP (C) Petersfield, since Oct. 1974; b 9 June 1934; s of Claude John Mates; m 1959, Mary Rosamund Paton; two s two d. Educ: Salisbury Cathedral Sch.; Blundell's Sch.; King's Coll., Cambridge (choral schol.). Joined Army, 1954; 2nd Lieut, RUR, 1955; Queen's Dragoon Guards, RAC, 1961; Major, 1967; Lt-Col, 1973; resigned commn 1974. Sec., Cons. NI Cttee, 1974-; introduced Farriers Registration Bill, 1975. Liveryman, Farriers' Co., 1975. Address: House of Commons, SW1A 0AA.

MATHER, Carol; see Mather, David Carol MacDonell.

MATHER, (David) Carol (MacDonell), MC 1944; MP (C) Esher since 1970; an Opposition Whip, since 1975; b 3 Jan. 1919; s of late Loris Emerson Mather, CBE; m 1951, Hon. Philippa Selina Bewicke-Copley, o d of 5th Baron Cromwell, DSO; one s three d. Educ: Harrow; Trinity Coll., Cambridge. War of 1939-45: commissioned Welsh Guards, 1940; served with Commandos, Special Air Service; Western Desert Campaigns, 1941-42; PoW, 1942; escaped, 1943; NW Europe, 1944-45; wounded, 1945; Palestine Campaign, 1946-48. Asst Mil. Attaché, British Embassy, Athens, 1953-56; GSO 1, MI Directorate, War Office, 1957-61; Mil. Sec. to GOC-in-C, Eastern Command, 1961-62; retd as Lt-Col., 1962. Conservative Research Dept, 1962-70. Councillor, Eton Rural Dist., 1965; contested (C) Leicester (NW), 1966. FRGS. Address: Brookfield, Horton, near Slough, Berks. Club: Brooks's.
See also Sir W. L. Mather.

MATHER, Prof. Kenneth, CBE 1956; FRS 1949; DSc (London), 1940; Hon. Professor of Genetics, University of Birmingham, since 1971; b 22 June 1911; e c and o s of R. W. Mather; m 1937, Mona Rhodes; one s. Educ: Nantwich and Acton Grammar Sch.; University of Manchester (BSc 1931). Ministry of Agriculture and Fisheries Research Scholar, 1931-34; Lecturer in Galton Laboratory, University Coll., London, 1934-37; Rockefeller Research Fellow, at California Institute of Technology and Harvard University, 1937-38; Head of Genetics Dept, John Innes Horticultural Institution, 1938-48; Professor of Genetics, University of Birmingham, 1948-65; Vice-Chancellor, Univ. of Southampton, 1965-71, now Emeritus Prof. Member: Agricultural Research Council, 1949-54, 1955-60, and 1969-; Science Research Council, 1965-69; Academic Adv. Cttee of Bath Univ. of Technology, 1967-71; DHSS Cttee on the Irradiation of Food, 1967-74; Cttee on Medical Aspects of Chemicals in Food and the Environment, 1972-74; Wessex Regional Hosp. Bd, 1968-71. Hon. LLD Southampton, 1972; Hon. DSc Bath, 1975. Publications: The Measurement of

Linkage in Heredity, 1938; Statistical Analysis in Biology, 1943; Biometrical Genetics, 1950, 2nd edn 1971; Human Diversity, 1964; The Elements of Biometry, 1967; Genetical Structure of Populations, 1973; (jointly): The Elements of Genetics, 1950; Genes, Plants and People, 1950; Introduction to Biometrical Genetics, 1977; many papers on Genetics, Cytology, and Statistics. *Address:* Department of Genetics, University of Birmingham, B15 2TT. *T:* 021-472 1301; The White House, 296 Bristol Road, Edgbaston, Birmingham B5 7SN. *T:* 021-472 2093. *Club:* Athenæum.

MATHER, Leonard Charles; Chairman, United Dominions Trust, since 1974; Director, Midland Bank Ltd, since 1968; a life Vice-President, Institute of Bankers, since 1970; *b* 10 Oct. 1909; *s* of Richard and Elizabeth Mather; *m* 1937, Muriel Armor Morris. *Educ:* Oldershaw Sch., Wallasey. BCom. (London). Entered Midland Bank, Dale Street, Liverpool, 1926; transf. to London, 1937; served in Gen. Managers' Dept at Head Office, 1937-45; Man., Bolton, 1945-48; Princ., Legal Dept, 1948-50; Asst Gen. Man., 1950-56; Gen. Man., Midland Bank Executor & Trustee Co. Ltd, 1956-58; Jt Gen. Man., Midland Bank Ltd, 1958-63; Asst Chief Gen. Man., 1964-66; Dep. Chief Gen. Man., 1966-68; Chief Gen. Man., 1968-72; Vice-Chm., 1972-74; Director: Midland Bank Trust Co. Ltd, 1968-74; Midland & International Banks Ltd, 1969-74; Montagu Trust, 1969-74; Chm., European Banks' International Co. SA, 1972-74 (Dir, 1970); Dep. Chm., Euro-Pacific Finance Corp. Ltd, 1970-74. FCIS; FIB (Dep. Chm., 1967-69; Pres., 1969-70); Hon. FIB 1974. *Publications:* The Lending Banker, 1955; Banker and Customer Relationship and the Accounts of Personal Customers, 1956; The Accounts of Limited Company Customers, 1958; Securities Acceptable to the Lending Banker, 1960. *Recreations:* golf, bridge. *Address:* Rochester House, Parkfield, Seal, Sevenoaks, Kent. *T:* Sevenoaks 61007. *Club:* East India, Sports and Public Schools.

MATHER, Sir William (Loris), Kt 1968; OBE 1957; MC 1945; TD and 2 clasps 1949; MA, CEng, FIMechE; Chairman, Mather & Platt Ltd, Manchester, since 1960; Vice Lord-Lieutenant of Cheshire, since 1975; *b* 17 Aug. 1913; *s* of Loris Emerson Mather, CBE; *m* 1937, Eleanor, *d* of Prof. R. H. George, Providence, RI, USA; two *s* two *d*. *Educ:* Oundle; Trinity Coll., Cambridge (MA Engrg and Law, 1939). Commissioned Cheshire Yeomanry, 1935; served War of 1939-45: Palestine, Syria, Iraq, Iran, Western Desert, Italy, Belgium, Holland, Germany (wounded twice, MC); Instructor, Staff Coll., Camberley, and GSO1, 1944-45. Director: National Westminster Bank Ltd (Chm., N Regional Bd, 1972-); CompAir Ltd, 1973-; Mather & Platt subsidiary cos; Manchester Ship Canal Co.; Divisional Dir, BSC, 1968-73. Chairman: NW Regional Economic Planning Council, 1968-75; Civic Trust for the NW; Manchester Inst. of Dirs, 1967-72; British Pump Manufrs Assoc., 1970-73; past Pres., Manchester Chamber of Commerce; President: Manchester Guardian Soc. for Protection of Trade, 1971-; British Mech. Engrg Confedn, 1975-; Vice-Pres., Assoc. of British Chambers of Commerce; Pres., Mech. Engrg Council; Member: Council of Industrial Design, 1960-71; Engineering Industries Council, 1976-. Member Court: Manchester Univ.; Salford Univ.; Royal College of Art; Mem. Council, Manchester Business Sch.; Governor: Manchester University Inst. of Science and Technology (Pres., 1976); Manchester Grammar Sch.; Feoffee, Chetham's Hosp. Sch.; Chm., Manchester YMCA. Hon. Fellow, Manchester Coll. of Art and Design, 1967. Comdr, Cheshire Yeomanry, 1954-57; Col and Dep. Comdr, 23 Armoured Bde, TA, 1957-60; ADC to the Queen, 1961-66. FBIM; FRSA. DL City and County of Chester, 1963; High Sheriff of Cheshire, 1969-70. *Recreations:* field sports, ski-ing, swimming. *Address:* Whirley Hall, Macclesfield, Cheshire SK10 4RN. *T:* Macclesfield 2077. *Clubs:* Bath; Leander; St James's (Manchester).
See also D. C. M. Mather.

MATHER-JACKSON, Sir Anthony (Henry Mather), 6th Bt *cr* 1869; retired Mining Engineer; *b* 9 Nov. 1899; *y s* of William Birkenhead Mather Jackson (*d* 1934) (2nd *s* of 2nd Bt) and Georgiana Catherine (*d* 1932), *d* of Rev. Brabazon Hallowes, Glapwell Hall, Chesterfield; *S* brother, 1976; *m* 1923, Evelyn Mary, *d* of Sir Henry Kenyon Stephenson, 1st Bt, DSO; three *d*. *Educ:* Harrow. Commission, Grenadier Guards, 1918-20; coal industry, 1921-47; company director, 1947-71. *Recreations:* formerly shooting, golf, hunting, racing. *Heir:* cousin William Jackson [*b* 18 Sept. 1902; *m* 1st, 1927, Lady Ankaret Howard (*d* 1945), 2nd *d* of 10th Earl of Carlisle; one *s* one *d*; 2nd, 1966, Ina, *d* of late James Leonard Joyce, FRCS]. *Address:* Archway House, Kirklington, Newark, Notts. *Club:* White's.

MATHESON, Arthur Alexander, QC Scotland 1956; MA, LLB; Professor of Scots Law at the University of Dundee (formerly

Queen's College in the University of St Andrews), since 1949; *b* 17 June 1919; *o s* of Charles Matheson, MA, FRSGS, and Edith Margaret Matheson, MA; unmarried. *Educ:* Daniel Stewart's Coll., Edinburgh; Balliol Coll., Oxford (Classical Exhibnr); University of Edinburgh (MA, 1st Cl. Hons in Classics; LLB with distinction; 1st entrance Bursar, 1936; Butcher Meml Prize in Greek; Soc. of Writers to the Signet Prize in Latin; 1st Hardie Prize in Latin Prose; Guthrie Fellowship in Classics; C. B. Black Scholarship in NT Greek; Vans Dunlop Scholarship in Public Law). Admitted to Faculty of Advocates, 1944; in practice at Scottish Bar, 1944-49; Jun. Counsel in Scotland, MoT, 1947-49; Queen's College, Dundee: Lectr in Public Internat. Law, 1950-60; Dean of Faculty of Law, 1955-58 and 1963-64; Master, 1958-66; Mem. Court, Univ. of St Andrews, 1954-66. Hon. Sheriff of Tayside Central, and Fife (formerly Perth and Angus) at Dundee, 1950-. Chancellor, Dio. Brechin, 1958-. A Pres., Speculative Soc., 1948-49; Chm., Robert Louis Stevenson Club, Edinburgh, 1953-56. *Address:* 43 Sutherland Place, Dundee DD2 2HJ. *T:* Dundee 642677. *Club:* New (Edinburgh).

MATHESON, Donald Macleod, CBE 1945; Director, John Smedley Ltd, retired, 1967; *b* 20 June 1896; *o s* of Rev. Donald Matheson; *m* 1931, Enid Futvoye, *e d* of John Marsden-Smedley, Lea Green, near Matlock; no *c*. *Educ:* St George's, Harpenden; Balliol Coll., Oxford. RGA, 1915-18; BEF France, Captain (Acting) Major. Trustee Ernest Cook Trust, 1952-65. Treasurer, Peabody Fund, 1952-62. USA 1919-20; Gas Light & Coke Co., 1921-34, Asst Sec., etc. Sec. National Trust, 1934-45, mem. Cttees, 1945-62. Mem., War Works Commn, 1945-64. *Publications:* translations from French published in UK, India, and Pakistan, 1959-69. *Address:* Grimsbury Bank, Hermitage, Berks.

MATHESON, Sir (James Adam) Louis, KBE 1976 (MBE 1944); CMG 1972; Vice-Chancellor, Monash University, Melbourne, 1959-76; Chancellor, Papua New Guinea University of Technology, 1973-75; Chairman, Australian Science and Technology Council, 1975-77; *b* 11 Feb. 1912; *s* of William and Lily Edith Matheson; *m* 1937, Audrey Elizabeth Wood; three *s*. *Educ:* Bootham Sch., York; Manchester Univ. (MSc 1933). Lectr, Birmingham Univ., 1938-46 (PhD 1946); Prof. of Civil Engineering, Univ. of Melbourne, Australia, 1946-50; Beyer Prof. of Engineering, Univ. of Manchester, 1951-59. FICE (Mem. Council, 1965-); FIStructE (Vice-Pres., 1967-68); FIEAust (Mem. Council, 1961-, Vice-Pres., 1970-74, Pres., 1975-76); Member: Mission on Technical Educn in W Indies, 1957; Royal Commn into failure of King's Bridge, 1963; Ramsay Cttee on Tertiary Educn in Victoria, 1961-63; CSIRO Adv. Council, 1962-67; Exec., Aust. Council for Educational Research, 1964-69; Interim Council, Univ. of Papua and New Guinea, 1965-68; Enquiry into Post-Secondary Educn in Victoria, 1976-; Chairman: Council, Papua New Guinea Inst. of Technology, 1966-73; Aust. Vice-Chancellors' Cttee, 1967-68; Assoc. of Commonwealth Univs, 1967-69; Newport Power Stn Review Panel, 1977; Trustee, Inst. of Applied Science (now Science Mus. of Victoria), 1963- (Pres., 1969-73). Hon. DSc Hong Kong, 1969; Hon. LLD: Manchester, 1972; Monash, 1975; Melbourne, 1975. *Publications:* Hyperstatic Structures; various articles on engineering and education. *Recreation:* music. *Address:* 9/158 West Toorak Road, South Yarra, Victoria 3141, Australia. *Club:* Melbourne.

MATHESON, Very Rev. James Gunn; Moderator of General Assembly of Church of Scotland, May 1975-76; Parish Minister, Portree, Isle of Skye, since 1973; *b* 1 March 1912; *s* of Norman Matheson and Henrietta Gunn; *m* 1937, Janet Elizabeth Clarkson; three *s* one *d* (and one *d* decd). *Educ:* Inverness Royal Academy; Edinburgh Univ. (MA, BD). Free Church of Olrig, Caithness, 1936-39; Chaplain to HM Forces, 1939-45 (POW Italy, 1941-43); St Columba's Church, Blackhall, Edinburgh, 1946-51; Knox Church, Dunedin, NZ, 1951-61; Sec. of Stewardship and Budget Cttee of Church of Scotland, 1961-73. Hon. DD Edinburgh, 1975. *Publications:* Do You Believe This?, 1960; Saints and Sinners, 1975; contrib. theol jls. *Recreations:* gardening, golf, fishing. *Address:* The Manse, Portree, Isle of Skye, Scotland. *T:* Portree 2019. *Club:* Caledonian.

MATHESON, Maj.-Gen. John Mackenzie, OBE 1950; TD 1969; Postgraduate Dean, Faculty of Medicine, University of Edinburgh, since 1971; *b* Gibraltar, 6 Aug. 1912; *s* of late John Matheson and late Nina Short, Cape Town; *m* 1942, Agnes, *d* of Henderson Purves, Dunfermline; one *d*. *Educ:* George Watson's Coll., Edinburgh; Edinburgh Univ. (Vans Dunlop Schol.). MB, ChB 1936; MRCP 1939; MD 1945; FRCSEd 1946; FRCS 1962; FRCP 1972. Royal Victoria Hosp. Tuberculosis Trust Research Fellow, 1936-37; Lieut, RAMC (TA), 1936. Served War of 1939-45: Middle East, N Africa and Italy; Regular RAMC Commn, 1944 (despatches). Clinical Tutor, Surgical Professorial

Unit, Edinburgh Univ., 1947-48; Med. Liaison Officer to Surgeon-Gen. US Army, Washington, DC, 1948-50; Asst Chief, Section Gen. Surgery, Walter Reed Army Hosp., Washington, DC, 1950-51; Cons. Surgeon: MELF, 1963-64; BAOR, 1967; Far East, 1967-69; Jt Prof. Mil. Surg., RAM Coll. and RCS of Eng., 1964-67; Brig. 1967; Comdt and Dir of Studies, Royal Army Med. Coll., 1969-71. QHS 1969-71. Alexander Medal, 1961; Simpson-Smith Memorial Lectr, 1967; Gordon-Watson Lectr, RCS of Eng., 1967. Senior Fellow, Assoc. of Surgeons of GB and Ireland; Vice-Pres., Lothian Div., BMA, 1976. FRSocMed. *Publications:* papers (on gun-shot wounds, gas-gangrene and sterilisation) to medical jls. *Recreation:* travel. *Address:* Pfizer Foundation, Hill Square, Edinburgh EH8 9DR.

MATHESON, Sir Louis; see Matheson, Sir J. A. L.

MATHESON of Matheson, Sir Torquhil (Alexander), 6th Bt *cr* 1882; Chief of Clan Matheson; one of HM Body Guard of the Honourable Corps of Gentlemen at Arms, since 1977; *b* 15 Aug. 1925; *s* of General Sir Torquhil George Matheson, 5th Bt, KCB, CMG; *S* father, 1963, *S* kinsman as Chief of Clan Matheson, 1975; *m* 1954, Serena Mary Francesca, *o d* of late Lt-Col Sir Michael Peto, 2nd Bt; two *d*. *Educ:* Eton. Served War of 1939-45; joined Coldstream Guards, July 1943; commnd, March 1944; 5th Bn Coldstream Guards, NW Europe, Dec. 1944-May 1945 (wounded). Served with 3rd Bn Coldstream Guards: Palestine, 1945-48 (despatches); Tripoli and Egypt, 1950-53; seconded King's African Rifles, 1961-64. Captain, 1952; Major, 1959; retd 1964. 4th Bn, Wilts Regt, TA, 1965-67; Royal Wilts Territorials (T&AVR III), 1967-69. *Heir* (to Baronetcy and Chiefship): *b* Major Fergus John Matheson [*b* 22 Feb. 1927; *m* 1952, Hon. Jean Elizabeth Mary Willoughby, *yr d* of 11th Baron Middleton, KG, MC, TD; one *s* two *d*]. *Address:* Standerwick Court, Frome, Som. *Club:* Leander (Henley-on-Thames).

MATHEW, John Charles, QC 1977; First Senior Prosecuting Counsel to the Crown 1974-77; *b* 3 May 1927; *s* of late Sir Theobald Mathew, KBE, MC, and of Lady Mathew; *m* 1952, Jennifer Jane Mathew (*née* Lagden); two *d*. *Educ:* Beaumont Coll. Served, Royal Navy, 1945-47. Called to Bar, Lincoln's Inn, 1949; apptd Junior Prosecuting Counsel to the Crown, 1959. Elected a Bencher of Lincoln's Inn, 1970. *Recreations:* golf, backgammon, cinema. *Address:* 47 Abingdon Villas, W8. *T:* 01-937 7535. *Club:* Garrick.

MATHEWS, Rev. Arthur Kenneth, OBE 1942; DSC 1944; Vicar of Thursley, 1968-76; Rural Dean of Godalming, 1969-74; *b* 11 May 1906; *s* of late Reverend Canon A. A. and Mrs Mathews; *m* 1936, Elisabeth, *d* of late E. M. Butler and Mrs Butler; no *c*. *Educ:* Monkton Combe Sch.; Balliol Coll., Oxford (Exhibitioner); Cuddesdon Theol. Coll. Deacon 1932, priest 1933, at Wakefield; Asst Curate of Penistone; Padre of the Tanker Fleet of Anglo-Saxon Petroleum Co. Ltd; licensed to officiate, Diocese of Wakefield, 1935-38; Vicar of Forest Row, 1938-44; Temp. Chaplain, RNVR, 1939-44 (Chaplain HMS Norfolk, 1940-44); on staff of Christian Frontier Council, 1944-46; Vicar of Rogate and Sequestrator of Terwick, 1946-54; Rural Dean of Midhurst, 1950-54; Hon. Chaplain to Bishop of Portsmouth, 1950-55; Commissary to: Bishop of Singapore, 1949-64; Bishop of Wellington, 1962-72; Student of Central Coll. of Anglican Communion at St Augustine's Coll., Canterbury, 1954-55; Dean and Rector of St Albans, 1955-63; Rector of St Peter's, Peebles, 1963-68. Hon. Chaplain to Bishop of Norwich, 1969-71. Mem. Governing Body, Monkton Combe Sch. *Recreations:* walking and gardening. *Address:* The Tallet, Westwell, Oxon.

See also Baroness Brooke of Ystradfellte.

MATHEWS, Denis Owen, CMG 1965; OBE 1959; *b* 21 Feb. 1901; *s* of Albert Edward Mathews and Edith (*née* Benton); *m* Violet Morgan; one *s*. *Educ:* Latymer Sch., London; Varndean, Brighton. Served with RAF, 1918; Royal Engineers, 1940-43. Uganda Survey Dept, 1921-46; East Africa Tourist Travel Assoc., 1948-65; UN Tourist Expert, 1965; Dir of Tourism, Information and Broadcasting, Seychelles, 1965-66. Hon. Pres., E African Prof. Hunters' Assoc.; Founder Mem., E African Wildlife Soc. *Publications:* technical papers on tourism and wild-life. *Address:* Bungalow 2, Manor House, Hingham, Norfolk NR9 2HP. *T:* Hingham 507. *Clubs:* Kiambu (Kenya), Mount Kenya Safari (Nanyuki).

MATHEWS, Henry Mends, CIE 1944; CEng, FIEE; *b* 16 Feb. 1903; *s* of late Henry Montague Segundo Mathews, CSI, JP, Northam, Devon; *m* 1st, 1928, Dorothy Bertha Gubbins (*d* 1941); one *s*; 2nd, 1943, Christina Adam (*née* Nemchinovich; marr. diss., 1960); one *d*; 3rd, 1971, Margaret Patricia Humphreys, Condobolin, NSW. *Educ:* The Wells House Sch., Malvern Wells, Worcs; Cheltenham Coll. Asst Engineer, City of

Winnipeg Hydro-Electric System, 1924-26; on staff of Merz & McLellan, consulting engineers, 1927-41; Electrical Commissioner to Govt of India, 1941-48; Chm., Central Technical Power Board, India, 1945-48; joined English Electric Co. Ltd, London, 1948; Dir of Engineering, 1954-68; Dir, Nuclear Design & Construction Ltd, 1966-68; retd, 1968. *Address:* 4 Tower Court, Dunchideock, Exeter EX6 7YD. *Club:* Junior Carlton.

MATHIAS, Lionel Armine, CMG 1953; *b* 23 Jan. 1907; *s* of Hugh Henry Mathias and Amy Duncan Mathias (*née* Mathias); *m* 1935, Rebecca Gordon Rogers; three *d*. *Educ:* Christs Coll., New Zealand; St Paul's Sch.; Keble Coll., Oxford. Appointed Asst District Commissioner, Uganda, 1929; Labour Commissioner, 1949-53; Member: Uganda Exec. Council, 1948, Legislative Council, 1949-53; Kampala Municipal Council, 1952-53; Uganda Students Adviser, 1953-62; Chm., Uganda Britain Soc., 1964-65. *Address:* Little Copt Farm, Shoreham, Sevenoaks, Kent. *T:* Otford 2040.

MATHIAS, Prof. Peter, MA; FBA 1977; Chichele Professor of Economic History, University of Oxford, and Fellow of All Souls College, Oxford, since 1969; *b* 10 Jan. 1928; *o c* of John Samuel and Marion Helen Mathias; *m* 1958, Elizabeth Ann, *d* of Robert Blackmore, JP, Bath; two *s* one *d*. *Educ:* Colston's Sch., Bristol; Jesus Coll., Cambridge (Schol.). 1st cl. (dist) Hist. Tripos, 1950, 1951. Research Fellow, Jesus Coll., Cambridge, 1952-55; Asst Lectr and Lectr, Faculty of History, Cambridge, 1955-68; Dir of Studies in History and Fellow, Queen's Coll., Cambridge, 1955-68. Tutor, 1957-68; Senior Proctor, Cambridge Univ., 1965-66. Asst Ed., Econ. History Rev., 1955-57; Treas., Econ. History Soc., 1968-; Sec., Internat. Econ. History Assoc., 1959-62. Vis. Professor: Univ. of Toronto, 1961; School of Economics, Delhi, 1967; Univ. of California, Berkeley, 1967; Univ. of Pa, 1972; Virginia Gildersteeve, Barnard Coll., Columbia Univ., 1972. Governor, Milton Abbey Sch., 1969-. Chm., Business Archives Council, 1968-72. Pres., Internat. Econ. History Assoc., 1974-; Chm., Econ. and Social History Cttee, SSRC, 1975-; Mem., Exec. Cttee, Internat. Inst. of Economic History Francesco Datini, Prato, 1972-. FRHistS (Vice-Pres., 1976-). *Publications:* The Brewing Industry in England 1700-1830, 1959; English Trade Tokens, 1962; Retailing Revolution, 1967; The First Industrial Nation, 1969; (ed) Science and Society 1600-1900, 1972; General Editor: Cambridge Economic History of Europe, 1968-; Debates in Economic History, 1967-. *Recreation:* travel. *Address:* All Souls College, Oxford. *T:* Oxford 722251.

MATHIAS, Sir Richard Hughes, 2nd Bt, *cr* 1917; Member London Stock Exchange; *b* 6 April 1905; *s* of Sir Richard Mathias, 1st Bt, and Annie, *y d* of Evan Hughes, Cardiff; *S* father 1942; *m* 1st, 1937, Gladys Cecilia Turton (marr. diss., 1960), *o d* of late Edwin Hart, New Hextalls, Bletchingley, Surrey; two *d*; 2nd, 1960, Mrs Elizabeth Baird Murray (*d* 1972), *er d* of late Dr and Mrs Miles of Hendrescythan, Creigiau, Glamorgan; 3rd, 1973, Mrs Hilary Vines (*d* 1975), Malaga, Spain. *Educ:* Eton; Balliol Coll., Oxford. RAF 1940-46 (Staff appt Air Ministry, 1942-46). Mem. Council Royal Nat. Mission to Deep Sea Fishermen, 1953-54. Fellow Corp. of S Mary and S Nicolas (Woodard Schs), 1965; Mem. Council, Hurstpierpoint Coll., 1965- (Chm., 1967-74). *Address:* 8 Oakwood Court, Abbotsbury Road, W14 8JU. *T:* 01-602 2635. *Club:* Reform.

MATHIAS, Winifred Rachel, CBE 1974; Lord Mayor of City of Cardiff, May 1972-May 1973; Member, Local Government Boundary Commission for Wales, since 1974; *b* 11 Feb. 1902; *d* of Charles and Selina Vodden; *m* 1923, William John Mathias (*d* 1949). *Educ:* Howard Gardens High Sch. Sec., ship-owning co., 1919-23. Member, Cardiff City Council, 1954-74; Alderman, 1967-74; formerly Mem., Estates, Public Works, Civic Buildings and Children's Cttees; Deputy Chairman: Health Cttee, 1961-64, 1967-74; Welfare Cttee, 1961-64 (Mem., 1954-70; Chm., 1967-70); Mem., Educn Cttee, 1956-74; Chairman: Social Services, 1970-74; all Primary Schs, 1965-70; Primary Schs Gp 3, 1970-74. Governor, Coll. of Food Technology and Commerce, 1957- (Dep. Chm., 1960-63, Chm., 1963-74). Life Mem., Blind Council (rep. of City Council); Mem., Management Cttee, "The Rest", Porthcawl, 1954-; Past Mem., Whitchurch Hosp. Gp; Founder Mem., Danybryn Cheshire Home, 1961-; Mem., Cardiff Council for the Elderly (Cartref Cttee). *Recreations:* reading, music, needlework, travel. *Address:* 19 Timbers Square, Cardiff CF2 3SH. *T:* Cardiff 28853. *Club:* Roath Conservative (Life Vice-Pres.) (Cardiff).

MATHIESON, William Allan Cunningham, CB 1970; CMG 1955; MBE 1945; Consultant, United Nations Development Programme, since 1976; *b* 22 Feb. 1916; *e s* of Rev. William Miller Mathieson, BD, and Elizabeth Cunningham Mathieson (*née* Reid); *m* 1946, Elizabeth Frances, *y d* of late Henry Marvell Carr, RA; two *s*. *Educ:* High Sch. of Dundee; Edinburgh and Cambridge Univs. Joined Colonial Office, 1939; served War, 1940-45; Royal Artillery in UK, France and Germany (Major, despatches). Rejoined Colonial Office, 1945; Middle East Dept, 1945-48; Private Sec. to Minister of State, 1948-49; Asst Sec., Colonial Office, 1949; Counsellor (Colonial Affairs) UK Delegn to UN, New York, 1951-54; Head of East African Department, CO, 1955-58; Minister of Education, Labour and Lands, Kenya, 1958-60; Under-Sec., Dept of Technical Co-operation, 1963-64; Under-Sec., 1964-68, Dep. Sec., 1968-75, Min. of Overseas Development. Chm., Executive Council, Commonwealth Agricultural Bureaux, 1963; Mem. Exec. Bd, Unesco, 1968-74. *Recreations:* photography, travel. *Address:* 13 Sydney House, Woodstock Road, W4.

MATHIESON, William Gordon, CMG 1963; BEc; FASA; *b* 5 July 1902; *s* of James L. Mathieson; *m* 1934, Margery Macdonald; two *d* (and two *d* decd). *Educ:* Fort Street High Sch.; University of Sydney. Permanent Head, NSW State Treasury, 1959-63; Vice-Pres., Sydney Water Board, 1960-63; Mem., Sydney Harbour Transport Board, 1959-63; Chm., Companies Auditors Board, 1963-67; Auditor General of New South Wales, 1963-67. *Address:* 25 Bell Street, Gordon, NSW 2072, Australia. *T:* 498-1444.

MATILAL, Prof. Bimal Krishna, PhD; Spalding Professor of Eastern Religions and Ethics, University of Oxford, since 1977; Fellow, All Souls College; *b* 1 June 1935; *s* of Hare Krishna Matilal and Parimal Matilal; *m* 1958, Karabi Matilal; one *s* one *d*. *Educ:* Univ. of Calcutta (BA Hons 1954, MA 1956); Harvard Univ. (AM 1963, PhD 1965). Lectr, Sanskrit Coll., Calcutta Univ., 1957-65; Asst Prof., Univ. of Toronto, 1965-67, Associate Prof., 1967-71; Associate Prof., Univ. of Pennsylvania, 1969-70; Vis. Sen. Fellow, SOAS, Univ. of London, 1971-72; Prof., Univ. of Toronto, 1971-77. Founder-Editor, Jl of Indian Philosophy, 1971-. *Publications:* The Navya-nyāya Doctrine of Negation, 1968; Epistemology, Logic and Grammar in Indian Philosophical Analysis, 1971; contrib. Nyāya-Vaiśesika Literature. *Recreation:* gardening. *Address:* Oriental Institute, University of Oxford, Oxford.

MATOKA, Hon. Peter Wilfred, MP; Minister of Local Government and Housing, Republic of Zambia, since 1972; MP for Mwinilunga in Parliament of Zambia; *b* 8 April 1930; member of Lunda Royal Family; *m* 1957, Grace Joyce; two *s* one *d*. *Educ:* Mwinilunga Sch.; Munali Secondary Sch.; University Coll. of Fort Hare (BA Rhodes); American Univ., Washington (Dipl. Internat. Relations). Minister: of Information and Postal Services, 1964-65; of Health, 1965-66; of Works, 1967; of Power, Transport and Works, 1968; of Luapula Province, 1969; High Comr for Zambia in UK and Ambassador to the Holy See, 1970-71; Minister of Health, 1971-72. Mem. Central Cttee, United National Independence Party, 1971-. Pres., AA of Zambia, 1969-70 (Vice-Pres. 1970-71). Kt of St Gregory the Great, 1964; Kt, UAR, 1964; Kt, Ethiopia, 1965. *Recreations:* fishing, shooting, discussion, photography. *Address:* Ministry of Local Government and Housing, PO Box 205, Lusaka, Zambia. *T:* Lusaka 72755; 19 Chisiza Crescent, Lusaka, Zambia. *Club:* Royal Automobile.

MATTHEW, Chessor Lillie, FRIBA, FRIAS, MRTPI; Principal, Duncan of Jordanstone College of Art, Dundee, since 1964; *b* 22 Jan. 1913; *s* of William Matthew and Helen Chessor Matthew (*née* Milne); *m* 1939, Margarita Ellis; one *s*. *Educ:* Gray's School of Art; Robert Gordon's Coll., Aberdeen. Diploma in Architecture; ASIA. Lectr, Welsh Sch. of Architecture, Cardiff, 1936-40. Served RAF, 1940-46, Flt-Lt. Sen. Lectr, Welsh Sch. of Architecture, Cardiff, 1946-57; Head of Sch. of Architecture, Duncan of Jordanstone Coll. of Art, Dundee, 1958-64. *Recreations:* hill walking, foreign travel. *Address:* Craigmhor, 36 Albany Road, West Ferry, Dundee DD1 1AA. *T:* Dundee 78364.

MATTHEWS, Sir Bryan Harold Cabot, Kt 1952; CBE 1944; FRS 1940; MA, ScD; Professor of Physiology, University of Cambridge, 1952-73, Professor Emeritus, 1973; Life Fellow of King's College, 1973 (Fellow, 1929-73); *b* 14 June 1906; *s* of Harold Evan Matthews and Ruby Sarah Harrison; *m* 1926; one *s* two *d*; *m* 1970, Audrey, *widow* of Air Vice-Marshal W. K. Stewart. *Educ:* Clifton Coll.; King's Coll., Cambridge. BA Hons, 1st Class Part II Physiology, 1927; Beit Memorial Fellow for Med. Res., 1928-32; Corresponding Mem. Société Philomatique de Paris; British Mem. of the 1935 International High Altitude Expedition for Physiological Research; Chm. of Flying Personnel Research Cttee, RAF; Consultant to RAF in Applied Physiology; Head of RAF Physiological Research Unit, 1940; Head of RAF Institute of Aviation Medicine, 1944-46.

Asst Dir of Physiological Research, Cambridge, 1932-48, Reader, 1948-52. Dir of Studies, King's Coll., 1932-52. Royal Soc. Leverhulme Vis. Prof. to African med. schs, 1973. Oliver-Sharpey Lecturer, RCP, 1945; Kelvin Lecturer, Instn of Electrical Engineers, 1948. Pres. Section I British Association, 1961; Vice-Pres., Royal Society, 1957 and 1958. *Publications:* Electricity in our Bodies; Essay on Physiological Research in Cambridge University Studies, 1933; Papers on Electrical Instruments and electrical phenomena in the nervous system, etc. in the Journal of Physiology, Proceedings of the Royal Society, etc. *Recreations:* ski-ing, sailing. *Address:* King's College, Cambridge.
See also Dr P. B. C. Matthews.

MATTHEWS, David Napier, CBE 1976 (OBE 1945); MA, MD, MCh (Cambridge); FRCS; Consulting Plastic Surgeon, University College Hospital and Hospital for Sick Children; Plastic Surgeon, King Edward's Hospital for Officers, since 1972; Civilian Consultant in Plastic Surgery to the Royal Navy since 1954; Adviser in Plastic Surgery, Ministry of Health; *b* 7 July 1911; *m* 1940, Betty Eileen Bailey Davies; two *s* one *d*. *Educ:* Leys Sch., Cambridge; Queens' Coll., Cambridge; Charing Cross Hosp. Qualified as doctor, 1935. Surgical Registrar, Westminster Hospital, until 1940; Surgeon Plastic Unit, East Grinstead, 1939-41; Surgical Specialist, RAFVR, 1941-46; Plastic Surgeon: UCH and Hosp. for Sick Children, 1946-77. Royal Nat. Orthopædic Hosp., 1947-54. Consulting Practice as Surgeon 1946-; Hunterian Professor, RCS, 1941, 1944, 1976; President: British Assoc. of Plastic Surgeons, 1954 and 1971; Plastic Section, RSM, 1970-71; Sec., Harveian Soc. of London, 1951, Vice-Pres., 1954, Pres., 1962; Gen. Sec. Internat. Confederation for Plastic Surgery, 1959; Pres., Chelsea Clinical Soc., 1962. Hon. FDSRCS. *Publications:* Surgery of Repair, 1943, 2nd edn, 1946; (Ed.) Recent Advances in the Surgery of Trauma, 1963; chapters in surgical books; contrib. to Lancet, BMJ and Post Graduate Jl etc. *Recreations:* golf, painting. *Address:* 152 Harley Street, W1. *T:* 01-935 2714; (home) 18 Bell Moor, East Heath Road, Hampstead, NW3. *T:* 01-435 7910. *Clubs:* Royal Automobile, Oriental.

MATTHEWS, Prof. Denis (James), CBE 1975; Concert Pianist; (first) Professor of Music, University of Newcastle upon Tyne, since 1971; *b* Coventry, 27 Feb. 1919; *o s* of Arthur and Elsie Randall Matthews; *m* 1941, Mira Howe (marr. diss., 1960); one *s* three *d*; *m* 1963, Brenda McDermott; one *s* one *d*. *Educ:* Warwick. Thalberg Scholar, 1935, Blumenthal Composition Scholar, 1937, at RAM; studied with Harold Craxton and William Alwyn; Worshipful Co. of Musicians' Medal, 1938; first public appearances in London at Queen's Hall and National Gallery, 1939; has broadcast frequently, made records, given talks on musical subjects; soloist at Royal Philharmonic Society's concerts, May and Nov. 1945; toured USA and visited Potsdam with Royal Air Force Orchestra, 1944-45; Vienna Bach Festival, 1950; Canada, 1951, 1957, 1963; South Africa, 1953, 1954, 1962; Poland, 1956, 1960; Egypt and Far East, 1963; World Tour, 1964; N Africa, 1966; W and E Africa, 1968; Latin America, 1968, 1970. Mem., Arts Council of GB, 1972-73. Favourite composers: Bach, Mozart, Beethoven, Wagner. Hon. DMus St Andrews, 1973. Cobbett Medal, Musicians' Co., 1973. *Publications:* piano pieces, works for violin, 'cello; In Pursuit of Music (autobiog.), 1966; Keyboard Music, 1972. *Recreations:* astronomy, filing-systems, reading aloud. *Address:* Department of Music, University of Newcastle upon Tyne, NE1 7RU.

MATTHEWS, Dr Drummond Hoyle, VRD 1967; FRS 1974; Reader in Marine Geology, University of Cambridge, since 1971; *b* 5 Feb. 1931; *s* of late Captain C. B. and late Mrs E. M. Matthews; *m* 1963, Elizabeth Rachel McMullen; one *s* one *d*. *Educ:* Bryanston Sch.; King's Coll., Cambridge. BA 1954, MA 1959, PhD 1962. RNVR, 1949-51, retd 1967. Geologist, Falkland Islands Dependencies Survey, 1955-57; returned to Cambridge (BP student), 1958; Research Fellow, King's Coll., 1960; Sen. Asst in Research, Dept of Geophysics, 1960; Asst Dir of Research, 1966. *Publications:* papers on marine geophysics in jls and books. *Recreations:* walking, sailing. *Address:* Department of Geodesy and Geophysics, Madingley Rise, Madingley Road, Cambridge. *T:* Cambridge 51686. *Clubs:* Naval, Antarctic, Cruising Association.

MATTHEWS, Edwin James Thomas, TD 1946; Master of the Supreme Court (Taxing Office) since 1965; *b* 2 May 1915; *s* of Edwin Martin Matthews (killed in action, 1917); *m* 1939, Katherine Mary Hirst, BA (Oxon.), Dip. Soc. Sc. (Leeds); two *d*. *Educ:* Sedbergh Sch., Yorks. Admitted as Solicitor of Supreme Court, 1938; practice on own account in Middlesbrough, 1938-39. Served in Royal Artillery, 1939-46, UK, France and Belgium (Dunkirk 1940); released with rank of Major. Partner, Chadwick Son & Nicholson, Solicitors, Dewsbury, Yorks, 1946-

50; Area Sec., No. 6 (W Midland) Legal Aid Area Cttee of Law Soc., 1950-56; Sec. of Law Soc. for Contentious Business (including responsibility for administration of Legal Aid and Advice Schemes), 1956-65. Toured Legal Aid Offices in USA for Ford Foundation and visited Toronto to advise Govt of Ontario, 1963. Mem., Council, British Academy of Forensic Sciences, 1965-68. Special Consultant to NBPI on Solicitors' Costs, 1967-68. Mem., Lord Chancellor's Adv. Cttee on Legal Aid, 1971. *Publications:* contrib. Halsbury's Laws of England, 1961 and Atkins Encyclopaedia of Forms and Precedents, 1962; (with Master Graham-Green) Costs in Criminal Cases and Legal Aid, 1965; (jointly) Legal Aid and Advice Under the Legal Aid and Advice Acts, 1949 to 1964, 1971; (ed jtly) Supreme Court Practice; contribs to journals. *Recreations:* trout fishing, theatre, gardening, French wines. *Address:* Romany Cottage, Greenhill Road, Otford, Kent. *T:* Otford 3467.

MATTHEWS, Prof. Ernest, DDS, PhD, MSc, ARCS, DIC, FDS, RCS; Director of Prosthetics, University of Manchester, 1935-70, now Professor Emeritus; *b* 14 Dec. 1904; *s* of James Alfred Matthews, Portsmouth; *m* 1928, Doris Pipe; one *d* (two *s* decd). *Educ:* Imperial Coll., London; Cambridge; Guy's Hospital, London. Demonstrator and Lecturer, Guy's Hospital Medical and Dental Schs, 1926-34; Prosthetic Dental Surgeon, Manchester Royal Infirmary, 1937; Dean and Dir, Turner Dental Sch., 1966-69; Cons. Dental Surgeon, Christie Hosp., 1945; Hon. Adviser in Dental Surgery to Manchester Regional Hospital Board, 1951. *Publications:* 40 papers on scientific and dental subjects. *Recreation:* gardening. *Address:* 8 Hale Green Court, Hillside Road, Hale, Cheshire. *T:* 061-980 2204.

MATTHEWS, Ven. Frederick Albert John; Archdeacon of Plymouth since 1962; Vicar of Plympton St Mary, Devon, since 1961; *b* 4 Jan. 1913; *s* of Albert and Elizabeth Anne Matthews; *m* 1941, Edna Stacey; one *d*. *Educ:* Devonport High Sch.; Exeter Coll., Oxford. Curate of Stoke Damerel, Plymouth, 1936-44; Vicar of Pinhoe, Devon, 1944-61; Rural Dean of Aylesbeare, 1957-61. *Recreations:* Association football (spectator), walking, photography. *Address:* St Mary's Vicarage, Plympton, Plymouth PL7 4LD. *T:* Plymouth 36157.

MATTHEWS, Prof. Geoffrey, MA, PhD; FIMA; Shell Professor of Mathematics Education, Centre for Science Education, Chelsea College, University of London, 1968-77; *b* 1 Feb. 1917; *s* of Humphrey and Gladys Matthews; *m* 1st, 1941, Patricia Mary Jackson; one *s* one *d*; 2nd, 1972, Julia Comber. *Educ:* Marlborough; Jesus Coll., Cambridge (MA); PhD (London). Wiltshire Regt, Intelligence Officer 43rd (Wessex) Div., 1939-45, Captain (dispatches, 1945; US Bronze Star, 1945). Teacher: Haberdashers' Aske's Sch., 1945-50; St Dunstan's Coll., 1950-64, Dep. Head and head of mathematics dept; Organiser, Nuffield Mathematics Teaching Project, 1964-72. Pres., Mathematical Assoc., 1977-78. *Publications:* Calculus, 1964; Matrices I & II, 1964; Mathematics through School, 1972; papers in Proc. Kon. Akad. Wetensch. (Amsterdam); numerous articles in Math. Gaz., etc. *Recreations:* sculpture, travel. *Address:* 50 Sydney Road, Bexleyheath, Kent DA6 8HG. *T:* 01-303 4301.

MATTHEWS, George Lloyd; Head of Press and Publicity Department, Communist Party of Great Britain, since 1974; *b* 24 Jan. 1917; *s* of James and Ethel Matthews, Sandy, Beds; *m* 1940, Elisabeth Lynette Summers; no *c*. *Educ:* Bedford Modern Sch.; Reading Univ. Pres., Reading Univ. Students Union, 1938-39; Vice-Pres., Nat. Union of Students, 1939-40; Vice-Pres., University Labour Fedn, 1938-39. County Chm., Nat. Union of Agricultural Workers, 1945-49; Mem. Exec. Cttee, Communist Party, 1943-; Asst Gen. Sec., Communist Party, 1949-57; Asst Editor, 1957-59, Editor, 1959-74, Daily Worker, later Morning Star. *Recreation:* music. *Address:* c/o Communist Party, 16 King Street, WC2E 8HY. *T:* 01-836 2151.

MATTHEWS, Gordon (Richards), CBE 1974; FCA; *m* ; one *s* one *d* (and one *d* decd). *Educ:* Repton Sch. Chartered Accountant, 1932. Contested (U) General Election, Deritend, 1945, and Yardley, 1950; MP (C) Meriden Division of Warwicks, 1959-64; PPS to the Postmaster-General, 1960-64. Hon. Treas., Deritend Unionist Assoc., 1937-45; Hon. Sec., Birmingham Unionist Association, 1948-53. Pres. City of Birmingham Friendly Soc., 1957-64; Mem. Board of Management, Linen and Woollen Drapers Institution and Cottage Homes, 1950-65 (Pres. of Appeal, 1954-55); Chm. of Exec. Cttee, Birmingham Area of YMCA, 1951-59; Mem., Nat. Council and Nat. Exec. Cttee, YMCA, 1968-71; Chm., Finance Cttee, YWCA, Birmingham Area, 1965-72. Chm., West Midlands Cons. Council, 1970-73 (Dep. Chm., 1967-70). *Recreations:* fly-fishing and foreign travel. *Address:* Windrush Cottage, Old Minster Lovell, Oxon OX8 5RN.

MATTHEWS, Sir (Harold Lancelot) Roy, Kt 1967; CBE 1943; *b* 24 April 1901; *s* of Harold Hamilton and Jeanie Matthews; *m* 1927, Violet Mary, *d* of T. L. Wilkinson, Solicitor, Liverpool and Dublin; one *s* one *d*. *Educ:* Preparatory Sch., Eastbourne; The Leys, Cambridge. Was abroad, 1919-22; articled to Matthews & Goodman, Chartered Surveyors, 1923; qualified, 1925; Partner Matthews & Goodman, 1927. Emergency R of O, 1938. Served War of 1939-45 (temp. Brigadier) (despatches four times); France (BEF), 1939-40; War Office, 1940-43; N Africa, Middle East, Italy, 1943-44; Normandy, 1944; Belgium, Holland, Germany, 1945. Resumed City activities, 1946; Dep. Chm. 1963, Chm. 1964-72, Abbey National Building Soc.; Dir, Lloyds Bank, 1948-72. Legion of Merit (USA) Degree of Officer, 1945; Order of Orange Nassau (Holland) Degree of Commander, 1945. *Recreation:* gardening. *Address:* Road End, Ramsey, Isle of Man. *T:* Ramsey 812663. *Club:* Ellan Vannin (Douglas, IoM).

MATTHEWS, Horatio Keith, CMG 1963; MBE 1946; JP; HM Diplomatic Service, 1948-74; *b* 4 April 1917; *s* of late Horatio Matthews, MD and of Ruth Matthews (*née* McCurry); *m* 1940, Jean Andrée Batten; two *d*. *Educ:* Epsom Coll.; Gonville and Caius Coll., Cambridge. Entered Indian Civil Service, 1940, and served in Madras Presidency until 1947; appointed to Foreign Service, 1948; First Sec., 1949; Lisbon, 1949; Bucharest, 1951; Foreign Office, 1953; Imperial Defence Coll., 1955; Political Office with Middle East Forces, Cyprus, 1956; Counsellor, 1958; Counsellor, UK High Commission, Canberra, 1959; Political Adviser to GOC Berlin, 1961; Corps of Inspectors, Diplomatic Service, 1964; Minister, Moscow, 1966-67; High Commissioner in Ghana, 1968-70; UN Under-Sec.-Gen. for Admin and Management, 1971-72; Asst Under-Sec. of State, MoD (on secondment), 1973-74. Mem., Bd of Visitors, HM Prison, Albany, 1976-. JP IoW 1975. *Address:* Elm House, Bembridge, IoW. *T:* Bembridge 2327. *Club:* Travellers'.

MATTHEWS, Sir James (Henry John), Kt 1966; JP; retired as District Secretary, Workers' Educational Association; *b* 25 March 1887; *s* of James Alfred and Mary Matthews; *m* 1919, Clara Collin; one *d*. *Educ:* Higher Grade Sch., Portsmouth. Shipbuilding, Portsmouth Dockyard and Admty, 1901-24; Officer of WEA, 1924-52. Vice-Chm. of Council, University of Southampton; Mem. Southampton County Council, 1934-67, Alderman, 1945-67. JP Hants, 1942-. Hon. Freeman, City of Southampton, 1958. Hon. MA, Bristol Univ., 1949; Hon. LLD, Southampton Univ., 1962. *Publications:* articles on local government and adult education. *Recreation:* gardening. *Address:* 56 Ethelburt Avenue, Southampton. *T:* Southampton 557334.

MATTHEWS, Prof. James Robert, CBE 1956; LLD; MA, FRSE, FLS; Regius Professor of Botany, University of Aberdeen, and Keeper of Cruickshank Botanic Garden, 1934-59; Chm. Macaulay Institute for Soil Research, 1947-59; Chm. Scottish Horticultural Research Inst., 1952-59; Member, Nature Conservancy (Scottish Cttee) (ex-Chm.), 1949-61; Gov., North of Scotland Coll. of Agriculture, 1937-59; Member: Aberdeen Coll. of Education Cttee, 1945-55; Cttee for Brown Trout Research, 1948-59; Governing Body, Rowett Research Institute, 1955-59; Vice-Pres. Royal Society of Edinburgh, 1958-61; *b* 8 March 1889; *yr s* of Robert Matthews, Dunning, Perthshire, and Janet McLean; *m* 1st, 1916, Helen Donaldson, Milnathort (*d* 1926); 2nd, 1928, Christine Young Blackhall, Edinburgh; two *s*. *Educ:* Perth Acad.; Edinburgh Univ. Lecturer in Botany, Birkbeck Coll., London, 1913-16; Temp. Protozoologist at Liverpool Sch. of Tropical Medicine (Western Command), 1916-19; Lecturer in Botany, University of Edinburgh, 1920-29; Prof. of Botany, University of Reading, 1929-34. Veitch Memorial Medal in Horticulture, 1958; Neill Prize and Medal for Natural History, Royal Society Edinburgh, 1964. *Publications:* Origin and Distribution of the British Flora, 1955; various papers on the Taxonomy of British Plants (especially Rosa), on Plant Distribution, and on Plant Morphology; also numerous papers on the Protozoology of Dysentery. *Recreations:* gardening, music. *Address:* Duncrib, Banchory, Kincardineshire AB3 3SQ.

MATTHEWS, Jessie, OBE 1970; actress; singer; *b* Soho, London, 11 March 1907; *d* of late George Ernest Matthews and late Jane Townshend; *m* 1st, 1926, Lord Alva Lytton (Henry Lytton Jr) (from whom she obt. a div., 1929, and who *d* 1965); 2nd, 1931, John Robert Hale Monro (Sonnie Hale) (from whom she obt. a div., 1944, and who *d* 1959); one *d* (one *s* decd); 3rd, 1945, Brian Lewis (from whom she obt. a div., 1959); one *s* decd. *Educ:* Pulteney St (LCC) Sch. for Girls, Soho. Trained as a classical ballet dancer under Mme Elise Clerc, and Miss Terry Freedman of Terry's Juveniles; first London appearance, in Bluebell in Fairyland, Metropolitan, 1919. Early successes in: The Music Box Revue, Palace, 1923; The Charlot Show of 1926,

Prince of Wales, 1926. Then (C. B. Cochran contract) starred in (London Pavilion): One Dam Thing After Another, 1927; This Year of Grace, 1928; Wake Up and Dream, 1929; Ever Green, Adelphi, 1930 (during these years she originated songs, incl.: Noel Coward's A Room with a View; Cole Porter's Let's Do It; Harry Woods' Over My Shoulder; Richard Rodgers' My Heart Stood Still and Dancing on the Ceiling. London stage (cont.) in: Hold my Hand, Gaiety, 1931; Sally Who?, Strand, 1933; Come Out to Play, Phœnix, 1940; Wild Rose, Princes, 1942; Maid to Measure, Cambridge, 1948; Sweethearts and Wives, Wyndhams, 1949; Sauce Tartare, Cambridge, 1949-50; Five Finger Exercise, Unity, 1960; A Share in the Sun, Cambridge, 1966; The Water Babies, Royalty, 1973; The Jessie Matthews Show, Shaftesbury, 1976. First New York appearance, in André Charlot's Revue of 1924, Times Square, 1924; then in Wake Up and Dream, Selwyn, 1929-30; The Lady Comes Across, Shubert, 1941; toured: in Larger than Life, Aust. and NZ, 1952-53, S Africa, 1955-56; in Janus, Aust. and NZ, 1956-57. Films (1923-) include: This England, The Beloved Vagabond, Straws in the Wind, Out of the Blue, There Goes the Bride, The Man from Toronto, The Midshipmaid, The Good Companions, Friday the Thirteenth, Waltzes from Vienna, Evergreen, First a Girl, It's Love Again, Head Over Heels, Gangway, Sailing Along, Climbing High, Forever and a Day (in Hollywood), Candles at Nine, Victory Wedding (as director) Making the Grade, Life is Nothing without Music, Tom Thumb. Starred in two seasons of cabaret, Society, London, 1964. Tribute to Jessie Matthews, Festival, NY, 1965. Recording star, 1926-, on many labels. Television: many appearances in plays, programmes, etc., UK and Canada. Radio: Mrs Dale in serial, The Dales, 1963-69. *Publication:* Over My Shoulder (autobiog.), 1974; *relevant publication:* Jessie Matthews, by Michael Thornton, 1974. *Recreations:* drawing, gardening, motoring. *Address:* c/o CCA Personal Management Ltd, 29 Dawes Road, SW6 7DT. *T:* 01-381 3551.

MATTHEWS, L(eonard) Harrison, FRS 1954, MA, ScD; Scientific Director, Zoological Society of London, 1951-66; *b* 12 June 1901; *s* of Harold Evan Matthews and Ruby Sarah Matthews (*née* Harrison); *m* 1924, Dorothy Hélène Harris; one *s* one *d. Educ:* Bristol Grammar Sch.; King's Coll., Cambridge. BA Hons 1st Class Nat. Sci. Trip., 1922; Vintner Exhibitioner King's Coll., University Frank Smart Prize. Has carried out biological researches in Africa, S America, Arctic and Antarctic, etc. Mem. of scientific staff "Discovery" Expedition, 1924; special lectr in Zoology, Univ. of Bristol, 1935; Radio Officer, Anti-Aircraft Command, 1941; Sen. Scientific Officer, Telecommunications Research Establishment, 1942; Radar liaison duties with RAF, 1943-45; Research Fell. Univ. of Bristol, 1945. Pres. Section D, British Assoc. for the Advancement of Science, 1959; President: British Academy of Forensic Science, 1962; Ray Soc., 1965; Chm., Seals Sub-Cttee, NERC, 1967-71. Member Council: Marine Biological Assoc. of UK, 1944-51; Zoological Soc. of London, 1943-45, 1946-49, 1950-51 (Vice-Pres., 1944-45, 1947-49, 1950-51); Inst. of Biology, 1954-57; Linnean Soc., of London, 1953-57; Sec., 1947-48, Pres., 1960, Assoc. of British Zoologists; Chm., World List of Scientific Periodicals, 1959-66. Has made numerous sound and TV broadcasts. *Publications:* South Georgia, the Empire's Subantarctic Outpost, 1931; Wandering Albatross, 1951; British Mammals (New Naturalist), 1952; Amphibia and Reptiles, 1952; Sea Elephant, 1952; Animals in Colour, 1959; The Senses of Animals (with Maxwell Knight), 1963; (ed) The Whale, 1968; The Life of Mammals, Vol. I, 1969, Vol. II, 1971; Introd., Darwin's Origin of Species, 1972; Introd. and explanatory notes, Waterton's Wanderings in South America, 1973; Man and Wildlife, 1975 (pbk, with Foreword by HRH The Duke of Edinburgh, 1977); numerous scientific papers on zoological subjects in jls of learned socs, Discovery Reports, Philosophical Transactions, Encyclopædia Britannica, etc. *Address:* The Old Rectory, Stansfield, via Sudbury, Suffolk.

MATTHEWS, Mrs Pamela Winifred, (Mrs Peter Matthews), BSc (Econ.); Principal, Westfield College (University of London), 1962-65; *b* 4 Dec. 1914; *d* of Lt-Col C. C. Saunders-O'Mahony; *m* 1938, H. P. S. Matthews (*d* 1958); one *s* one *d. Educ:* St Paul's Girls' Sch.; London Sch. of Economics. Royal Institute of International Affairs, 1938-39; Foreign Office, 1939-40; The Economist Newspaper, 1940-43; Foreign Office, 1943-45; Reuters, 1945-61; Nat. Inst. for Social Work Trg, 1961-62. Independent Mem., Advertising Standards Authority, 1964-65. Governor, Northwood Coll., Middlesex, 1962-. *Publications:* diplomatic correspondence for Reuters. *Recreations:* travel, theatre. *Address:* 1 Edwardes Place, Kensington High Street, W8. *T:* 01-603 8458.

MATTHEWS, Paul Taunton, CBE 1975; MA, PhD; FRS 1963; Vice-Chancellor, Bath University, since 1976; *b* 19 Nov. 1919; *s* of Rev. Gordon Matthews and Janet (*née* Viney); *m* 1947,

Margit Zohn; two *s* two *d. Educ:* Mill Hill Sch.; Clare Coll., Cambridge. Research Fellow, Inst. for Advanced Study, Princeton, USA, 1950-51; ICI Research Fellow, Cambridge, 1951-52; Lectr, Univ. of Birmingham, 1952-57; Visiting Prof., Univ. of Rochester, USA, 1957; Imperial College, London: Reader in Theoretical Physics, 1957-62; Prof. of Theoretical Physics, 1962-76; Head of Dept of Physics, 1971-76; Dean, RCS, 1972-75. Mem., SRC, 1970-74; Chm., SRC Nuclear Physics Bd, 1972-74; Mem., Scientific Policy Cttee, CERN, Geneva, 1972-. *Publications:* Quantum Mechanics, 1963 (USA); Nuclear Apple, 1971; papers on elementary particle physics in Proc. Royal Soc., Phil. Mag., Phys. Review, Nuovo Cimento, Review Mod. Phys., Annals of Physics. *Address:* Bath University, Claverton Down, Bath, Avon BA2 7AY.

MATTHEWS, Percy; Director, Phoenix Assurance Co. Ltd, since 1971; *b* 24 July 1921; *s* of Samuel and Minnie Matthews; *m* 1946, Audrey Rosenthal; one *s* two *d. Educ:* Parmiters Sch., London. Hon. Fellow, St Peter's Coll., Oxford. Chm., Whitechapel Art Gall.; Trustee, Ravenswood Foundn; Mem. Management Cttee, Royal Postgrad. Med. Sch., Hammersmith Hosp.; Pres., Aston Villa Football Club; Freeman, City of London. *Recreations:* painting, golf. *Address:* Flat 4, 21 York Terrace East, Regent's Park, NW1.

MATTHEWS, Mrs Peter; see Matthews, Mrs Pamela W.

MATTHEWS, Sir Peter (Alec), Kt 1975; Managing Director, Vickers Ltd, since 1970; Director: Canadian Vickers Ltd, since 1971; Vickers Australia Ltd, since 1971; Lloyds Bank, since 1974; British Electric Traction Co. Ltd, since 1976; *b* 21 Sept. 1922; *s* of Major Alec Bryan Matthews and Elsie Lazarus Barlow; *m* 1946, Sheila Dorothy Bunting; four *s* one *d. Educ:* Shawnigan Lake Sch., Vancouver Island; Oundle Sch. Served Royal Engineers (retired as Major), 1940-46. Joined Stewarts and Lloyds Ltd, 1946; Director of Research and Technical Development, 1962; Member for R&D, BSC, 1968-70, Dep. Chm., 1973-76. Member: Council, CBI; British Overseas Trade Bd, 1973-; Export Guarantees Adv. Council, 1973-; NRDC, 1974-; Engineering Industries Council, 1976; Adv. Council for Applied R&D, 1976-. Vice-Pres., Engineering Employers Fedn. *Recreations:* sailing, gardening. *Address:* Vickers House, Millbank Tower, SW1P 4RA. *T:* 01-828 7777.

MATTHEWS, Peter Bryan Conrad, FRS 1973; MD, DSc; University Lecturer in Physiology since 1961 and Tutor and Student of Christ Church since 1958, University of Oxford; *b* 23 Dec. 1928; *s* of Prof. Sir Bryan Matthews, *qv*; *m* 1956, Margaret Rosemary Blears; one *s* one *d. Educ:* Marlborough Coll.; King's Coll., Cambridge; Oxford Univ. Clinical School. Sir Lionel Whitby Medal, Cambridge Univ., 1959; Robert Bing Prize, Swiss Acad. of Med. Science, 1971. *Publications:* Mammalian Muscle Receptors and their Central Actions, 1972; papers on neurophysiology in various scientific jls. *Address:* University Laboratory of Physiology, Parks Road, Oxford OX1 3PT. *T:* Oxford 57451; 3 Dean Court Road, Cumnor Hill, Oxford OX2 9JL.

MATTHEWS, Peter Jack, OBE 1974; QPM 1970; Chief Constable of Surrey, since 1968; *b* 25 Dec. 1917; *s* of Thomas Francis Matthews and Agnes Jack; *m* 1944, Margaret, *er d* of Cecil Levett, London; one *s . Educ:* Blackridge Public Sch., West Lothian. Joined Metropolitan Police, 1937; Flt-Lt (pilot) RAF, 1942-46; Metropolitan Police, 1946-65; seconded Cyprus, 1955; Chief Supt P Div. 1963-65; Chief Constable: of East Suffolk, 1965-67; of Suffolk, 1967-68. Pres. British Section, Internat. Police Assoc., 1964-70, Internat. Pres. 1966-70; Pres., Assoc. of Chief Police Officers of England, Wales and NI, 1976-77. *Address:* Police Headquarters, Mount Browne, Sandy Lane, Guildford, Surrey. *T:* Guildford 71212. *Club:* Royal Air Force.

MATTHEWS, Richard Bonnar, CBE 1971; QPM 1965; Chief Constable, Warwickshire, 1964-76 (Warwickshire and Coventry, 1969-74); *b* 18 Dec. 1915; *er s* of late Charles Richard Matthews, Worthing; *m* 1943, Joan, *d* of Basil Worsley, Henstridge, Som; two *d. Educ:* Stowe School. Served War of 1939-45, Lieut, RNVR. Joined Metropolitan Police, 1936; Asst Chief Constable, E Sussex, 1954-56; Chief Constable of Cornwall and Isles of Scilly, 1956-64. Chm., Traffic Cttee, Assoc. of Chief Police Officers, 1973-76. *Recreations:* ski-ing, fishing, gardening. *Address:* Lily Grove, Brighstone, Isle of Wight PO30 4DJ. *T:* Brighstone 740625. *Club:* Naval.

MATTHEWS, Prof. Richard Ellis Ford, ScD, FRS 1974, FRSNZ, FNZIC; Professor of Microbiology, since 1962, and Head of Department of Cell Biology, University of Auckland, New Zealand, 1962-76; *b* Hamilton, NZ, 20 Nov. 1921; *s* of Gerald Wilfrid Matthews and Ruby Miriam (*née* Crawford); *m*

1950, Lois Ann Bayley; three *s* one *d. Educ:* Mt Albert Grammar Sch.; Auckland University Coll.; Univ. of Cambridge. MSc (NZ), PhD, ScD (Cantab). Postdoctoral Research Fellow, Univ. of Wisconsin, 1949. Plant Diseases Div., DSIR, Auckland, NZ: Mycologist, 1950-53; Sen. Mycologist, 1954-55; (on leave from DSIR as a visiting worker at ARC Virus Research Unit, Molteno Inst., Cambridge, 1952-56); Sen. Principal Scientific Officer, DSIR, 1956-61. *Publications:* Plant Virus Serology, 1957; Plant Virology, 1970; over 100 original papers in scientific jls. *Recreations:* gardening, sea fishing, bee keeping. *Address:* 3 Sadgrove Terrace, Mt Albert, Auckland 3, New Zealand. *T:* 866005, Auckland; (summer residences) Rural Delivery 4, Hikurangi; 1019 Beach Road, Long Bay, Auckland.

MATTHEWS, Robert Charles Oliver, CBE 1975; FBA 1968; Master of Clare College, Cambridge, since 1975; *b* 16 June 1927; *s* of Oliver Harwood Matthews, WS, and Ida Finlay; *m* 1948, Joyce Hilda Lloyds; one *d. Educ:* Edinburgh Academy; Corpus Christi Coll., Oxford (Hon. Fellow, 1976). Student, Nuffield Coll., Oxford, 1947-48; Lectr, Merton Coll., Oxford, 1948-49; University Asst Lectr in Economics, Cambridge, 1949-51, and Univ. Lectr, 1951-65. Fellow of St John's Coll., Cambridge, 1950-65. Visiting Prof., University of California, Berkeley, 1961-62; Drummond Prof. of Political Economy, Oxford, and Fellow of All Souls Coll., 1965-75. Chm., SSRC, 1972-75. Managing Trustee, Nuffield Foundn. Member: Council, Royal Econ. Soc., 1973-; Exec. Cttee NIESR, 1975-; Central Adv. Council on Sci. and Tech., 1967-70; Council, British Academy, 1972-75; OECD Expert Group on Non-inflationary Growth, 1975-77. Pres., British Chess Problem Soc., 1971-72. *Publications:* A Study in Trade Cycle History, 1954; The Trade Cycle, 1958; articles in learned journals. (With M. Lipton and J. M. Rice) Chess Problems: Introduction to an Art, 1963. *Address:* The Master's Lodge, Clare College, Cambridge. *Club:* Reform.

MATTHEWS, Ronald Sydney; Deputy Secretary, Department of Health and Social Security, since 1976; *b* 26 July 1922; *s* of George and Louisa Matthews; *m* 1945, Eleanor Bronwen Shaw; one *s* one *d*. *Educ:* Kingsbury County School. RAF, 1940-46. Clerical Officer, Min. of Health, 1939; Principal 1959; Private Sec. to Minister of Health, 1967-68; Private Sec. to Sec. of State for Social Services, 1968-69; Asst Sec. 1968; Under-Sec., DHSS, 1973-76. *Recreations:* walking, gardening, reading. *Address:* 12 Gainsborough Avenue, St Albans, Herts. *T:* St Albans 57065.

MATTHEWS, Sir Roy; *see* Matthews, Sir (H. L.) R.

MATTHEWS, Rt. Rev. Seering John, OBE 1967; *b* 26 March 1900; *s* of Seering Frederick and Sarah Jane Matthews; *m* 1944, Barbara, *d* of Rev. H. G. Browning, Althorne, Essex; three *s* two *d. Educ:* St John's Coll., Auckland; Fort Street High Sch., Sydney; Moore Theol Coll., Sydney. ThL 1925. Deacon, 1925; Priest, 1926. Curate, Christ Church, Sydney, 1925-29; permission to officiate Dio. Canterbury, 1930; Priest-in-Charge, St Mary's Fitzroy, Melbourne, 1931-32; Vicar, St James', Calcutta, 1933-38; Principal, Bp Westcott Sch., Namkum, 1938-42; Chap. RAF (India), 1942-46; Vicar, St Bartholomew's, Ipswich, Suffolk, 1946-51; Chap. Southport Sch., Brisbane, 1951-54; Rector, St Paul's Cathedral, Rockhampton, 1954-60; Archdeacon of Rockhampton, 1954-60; Bishop of Carpentaria, 1960-68. *Recreation:* fishing. *Address:* 71 Kalimna Drive, Moana Park, Qld 4217, Australia. *Club:* United Service (Brisbane).

MATTHEWS, Sir Stanley, Kt 1965; CBE 1957; professional footballer; *b* Hanley, Stoke-on-Trent, 1 Feb. 1915; *s* of late Jack Matthews, Seymour Street, Hanley; *m* 1935, Elizabeth Hall Vallance (marr. diss. 1975); one *s* one *d. Educ:* Wellington Sch., Hanley. Played in first Football League match, 1931; first played for England, 1934, and fifty-five times subsequently; Blackpool FC, 1947-61 (FA Cup, 1953); Stoke City FC, 1961-65. Freedom of Stoke-on-Trent, 1963. *Publication:* The Stanley Matthews Story, 1960. *Recreations:* golf, tennis. *Club:* National Sporting.

MATTHEWS, Thomas Stanley; journalist; *b* 16 Jan. 1901; *s* of late Rt Rev. Paul Matthews, sometime Bishop of New Jersey, and late Elsie Procter; *m* 1st, 1925, Juliana Stevens Cuyler (*d* 1949); four *s*; 2nd, 1954, Martha Gellhorn; 3rd, 1964, Pamela, *widow* of Lt-Col V. Peniakoff. *Educ:* Park Hill, Lyndhurst, Hants; Shattuck Sch. (Minn.); St Paul's Sch. (Concord, NH); Princeton Univ.; New Coll., Oxford (MA). Doctor of Humane Letters, Kenyon Coll., Ohio; Doctor of Letters, Rollins Coll., Florida. Editorial staff: The New Republic, 1925-29; Time, 1929; Exec. Editor, Time, 1942; Managing Editor Time, 1943-50, Editor, 1950-53. *Publications:* To the Gallows I Must Go, 1931; The Moon's No Fool, 1934; The Sugar Pill, 1957; Name and Address, 1960; O My America!, 1962; The Worst Unsaid (verse), 1962; Why So Gloomy? (verse), 1966; Great Tom: notes

towards the Definition of T. S. Eliot, 1974; Jacks or Better, 1977. *Address:* Cavendish Hall, Cavendish, Suffolk. *T:* Clare 296. *Clubs:* Athenæum, Buck's, Brooks's, Garrick; Century Association, Coffee House (New York); Reading Room (Newport, RI).

MATTHEWS, Rt. Rev. Timothy John, CD 1963; BA, LST, STh, DD; *Educ:* Bishop's Univ., Lennoxville. Deacon 1932, priest 1933, Edmonton; Curate of Viking, 1933-37; Incumbent of Edson, 1937-40; Rector of Coaticook, 1940-44; Lake St John, 1944-52; Rector and Archdeacon of Gaspé, 1952-57; Rector of Lennoxville, 1957-71; Archdeacon of St Francis, 1957-71; Bishop of Quebec, 1971-77. *Address:* 36 rue des Jardins, Québec, Qué G1R 4L5, Canada. *Clubs:* University, Hole-in-One, Royal (Quebec).

MATTHEWS, Victor Collin, FIOB, FRSA; Deputy Chairman since 1973, and Group Managing Director since 1968, Trafalgar House Ltd; Chairman: Beaverbrook Newspapers, since 1977; The Cunard Steam-Ship Co. Ltd, since 1971; Trafalgar House Developments Holdings Ltd, since 1970; Trafalgar Offshore Ltd, since 1975; Trollope & Colls Holdings Ltd, since 1968; Whitbread Trafalgar Properties Ltd, since 1969; Ideal Building Corporation Ltd, since 1968; Glamford Finance Co. Ltd, since 1969; Eastern International Investment Trust Ltd, since 1974; The Ritz Hotel (London) Ltd, since 1976; Cementation International Ltd, since 1976; *b* 5 Dec. 1919; *s* of A. and J. Matthews; *m* 1942, Joyce Geraldine (*née* Pilbeam); one *s. Educ:* Highbury. Served RNVR, 1939-45. Director: Overline (Richmond) Ltd; Overline (Wimbledon) Ltd; Paternoster Developments Ltd; Associated Container Transportation (Australia) Ltd; Cunard Crusader World Travel Ltd; ATV. *Recreations:* racehorse owner, cricket, golf. *Address:* Trafalgar House Ltd, 1 Berkeley Street, W1X 6NN. *T:* 01-499 9020. *Clubs:* Marylebone Cricket, Royal Automobile.

MATTHEWS, Prof. Walter Bryan; Professor of Clinical Neurology, University of Oxford, since 1970; *b* 7 April 1920; *s* of Very Rev. Dr Walter Robert Matthews; *m* 1943, Margaret Forster; one *s* one *d. Educ:* Marlborough Coll.; University Coll., Oxford. MA, DM, FRCP. RAMC, 1943-46. Senior Registrar, Oxford, 1948; Chief Asst, Dept of Neurology, Manchester Royal Infirmary, 1949-52; Senior Registrar, King's College Hosp., 1952-54; Consultant Neurologist, Derbyshire Royal Infirmary, 1954-68; Consultant Neurologist, Manchester Royal Infirmary and Crumpsall Hosp., 1968-70. *Publications:* Practical Neurology, 1963 (3rd edn 1975); (with H. G. Miller) Diseases of the Nervous System, 1972 (2nd edn 1975); (ed) Recent Advances in Clinical Neurology, 1975; papers in Brain, Quarterly Jl of Medicine, etc. *Recreation:* walking. *Address:* Sandford House, Sandford-on-Thames, Oxford.

MATTINGLY, Alan; Secretary of the Ramblers' Association, since 1974; *b* 19 May 1949; *s* of Alexander and Patricia Mattingly; *m* 1973, Sylvia Granger. *Educ:* The Latymer Sch., Edmonton; St John's Coll., Cambridge (BA). Vice-Chm., Standing Cttee on Nat. Parks, 1977-. *Recreations:* walking, orienteering, swimming. *Address:* 5 Margaret Court, Vicars Moor Lane, N21 2QL.

MATTINGLY, Dr Stephen, TD 1964; FRCP; Consultant Physician, Middlesex Hospital, since 1958; Consultant Physician since 1956, and Medical Director since 1972, Garston Manor Rehabilitation Centre; Hon. Consultant in Rheumatology and Rehabilitation to the Army, since 1976; *b* 1 March 1922; *s* of Harold Mattingly and Marion Grahame Meikleham; *m* 1945, Brenda Mary Pike; one *s. Educ:* Leighton Park Sch.; UCH (MB, BS); Dip. in Physical Med., 1953. FRCP 1970. House-surg., UCH, 1947; Regtl MO, 2/10 Gurkha Rifles, RAMC Far East, 1947-49; House-surg. and Registrar, UCH, 1950-55; Sen. Registrar, Mddx Hosp., 1955-56. Reg. Med. Consultant for London, S-Eastern, Eastern and Southern Regions, Dept of Employment, 1960-74. Lt-Col RAMC TA, 1952-67. *Publications:* (contrib.) Progress in Clinical Rheumatology, 1965; (contrib.) Textbook of Rheumatic Diseases, ed Copeman, 1969; (contrib.) Fractures and Joint Injuries, ed Watson Jones, 1976; (ed) Rehabilitation Today, 1977. *Recreation:* swimming. *Address:* Pipers Barn, 55 Copperkins Lane, Amersham, Bucks. *T:* Amersham 3509.

MATTURI, Sahr Thomas, CMG 1967; BSc, PhD; Ambassador of the Republic of Sierra Leone to Republics of Italy, Austria and Yugoslavia; Permanent Representative to the UN Specialised Agencies in Rome, Geneva and Vienna; *b* 22 Oct. 1925; *s* of Sahr and Konneh Matturi; *m* 1956, Anna Adella Stephens; two *s* one *d. Educ:* University Coll., Ibadan; Hull Univ. School Teacher, 1944-47, 1954-55; University Lecturer, 1959-63; Principal, Njala Univ. Coll., 1963-76; Vice-Chancellor, Univ. of Sierra Leone,

1968-70; Acting Vice-Chancellor and Pro Vice-Chancellor, 1972-74, Pro Vice-Chancellor, 1966-68, 1970-72, 1973-75. Chm., W African Exams Council, 1971-76. Mem., British Mycol. Soc. FRSA. *Recreations:* cricket, lawn tennis, shooting. *Address:* Embassy of the Republic of Sierra Leone, Via Paola Frisi 44, 00197, Rome, Italy. *T:* 802 173, 878 263.

MAUCHLINE, Lord; Michael Edward Abney-Hastings; ranger with New South Wales Pastures Protection Board; *b* 22 July 1942; *s* and *heir* of Countess of Loudoun (13th in line), *qv* and *s* of Captain Walter Strickland Lord (whose marriage to the Countess of Loudoun was dissolved, 1945; his son assumed, by deed poll, 1946, the surname of Abney-Hastings in lieu of his patronymic); *m* 1969, Noelene Margaret McCormick, 2nd *d* of Mr and Mrs W. J. McCormick, Barham, NSW; one *s* three *d* (of whom one *s* one *d* are twins). *Educ:* Ampleforth. *Address:* 74 Coreen Street, Jerilderie, NSW 2716, Australia.

MAUCHLINE, Rev. Prof. John, MA, BD (Glasgow), DD (Edinburgh); Professor of Old Testament Language and Literature, University of Glasgow, 1935-72, and Principal of Trinity College, Glasgow, 1953-72; *b* 5 July 1902; *m* 1930, Helen Brisbane Paterson, MA; three *s*. *Educ:* Hutchesons' Grammar Sch.; Glasgow Univ. (First Class Hons in Semitic Langs); British Sch. of Archæology, American Sch. of Oriental Research, and l'Ecole St Etienne, Jerusalem. Maclean Scholar, 1926; Faulds Fellow, 1926-29; Minister of South Dalziel Church, Motherwell, 1929-34; Prof. of Old Testament Language and Literature, Trinity Coll., Glasgow, 1934. Principal Pollok Lecturer in Pine Hill Divinity Hall, Halifax, Nova Scotia, 1949. *Publications:* God's People Israel; The Balaam-Balak Songs and Saga, in W. B. Stevenson Anniversary Volume; Hosea in The Interpreter's Bible; 1st and 2nd Kings, in Peake's Commentary on The Bible (new and revised edn); Isaiah 1-39 (Torch Bible Commentary); (ed) An Introductory Hebrew Grammar, by A. B. Davidson, 26th edn, 1967; 1 and 2 Samuel (New Century Bible), 1971; articles in periodicals. *Address:* 31 Manse Road, Bearsden, Glasgow G61 3PR. *T:* 041-942 4993.

MAUD; *see* Redcliffe-Maud.

MAUD, Hon. Humphrey John Hamilton; HM Diplomatic Service; Head of Financial Relations Department, Foreign and Commonwealth Office, since 1975; *b* 17 April 1934; *s* of Baron Redcliffe-Maud, *qv*; *m* 1963, Maria Eugenia Gazitua; three *s*. *Educ:* Eton; King's Coll., Cambridge (Classics and History); MA; Nuffield Coll., Oxford (Econs). Instructor in Classics, Univ. of Minnesota, 1958-59; entered Foreign Service, 1959; FO, 1960-61; Madrid, 1961-63; Havana, 1963-65; FO, 1966-67; Cabinet Office, 1968-69; Paris, 1970-74. Nuffield Coll., Oxford, 1974-75. *Recreation:* music ('cellist). *Address:* c/o Foreign and Commonwealth Office, SW1A 2AH; 28 Whittlesey Street, SE1. *T:* 01-928 6502. *Club:* United Oxford & Cambridge University.

MAUDE, family name of **Viscount Hawarden.**

MAUDE, Col Alan Hamer, CMG 1919; DSO 1917; TD; *b* Highgate, 18 Aug. 1885; *e s* of Edmund Maude and Claudine Ina, *d* of G. A. Pridmore, JP, Coventry; *m* 1910, Dorothy Maude (*d* 1960), *o d* of Frederic Upton; one *s*. *Educ:* Rugby (scholar); Oriel Coll., Oxford (exhibitioner, MA). Sub-Editor Daily Chronicle, 1912-14; on Editorial Staff of The Times, 1920-50. Joined Army Service Corps (TF), 1909; served in France and Belgium, 1915-19 (despatches twice, CMG, DSO); Commanded 47th (London) Divl Train, 1918-19 and 1924-29, and 59th Divl Train, 1919; Bt-Col 1928; Col (TA), 1929; ADS&T, GHQ, BEF, 1939; AQMG and Controller, Central Purchase Bd, BEF, 1940; CRASC, Bordon District, 1940-43, and Kent District, 1943-45; Hon. Col 56th (London) Armoured Divl Column, RASC, TA, 1947-53. Pres. Old Rugbeian Soc., 1952-53. DL London, 1937-76. *Publications:* Edited War History of the 47th Division, 1914-19; Rugby School Register, 1911-46; and many special numbers of The Times. *Recreations:* formerly rifle-shooting (Captain, Rugby and Oxford teams); gardening, photography, genealogy. *Address:* Stone House, Petworth, West Sussex. *T:* Petworth 42314.
See also A. E. U. Maude.

MAUDE, Angus Edmund Upton, TD; MP (C) Stratford-upon-Avon Division of Warwickshire, since Aug. 1963; author and journalist; a Deputy Chairman of Conservative Party, and Chairman of Research Department, since 1975; *b* 8 Sept. 1912; *o c* of Col Alan Hamer Maude, *qv*; *m* 1946, Barbara Elizabeth Earnshaw, *o d* of late John Earnshaw Sutcliffe, Bushey; two *s* two *d*. *Educ:* Rugby Sch. (Scholar); Oriel Coll., Oxford (MA). Financial journalist, 1933-39: The Times, 1933-34; Daily Mail, 1935-39. Commissioned in RASC (TA), May 1939; served in RASC 1939-45, at home and in North Africa (PoW, Jan. 1942-

May 1945); Major 56th (London) Armd Divl Column RASC (TA), 1947-49; TARO, 1950. Engaged in economic and social research, 1946-48; Dep. Dir of PEP, 1948-50; MP (C) Ealing (South), 1950-57, (Ind. C), 1957-58; Dir, Conservative Political Centre, 1951-55. Editor of the Sydney Morning Herald, 1958-61. Contested S Dorset, by-election, Nov. 1962. *Publications:* (with Roy Lewis) The English Middle Classes, 1949; Professional People, 1952; (with Enoch Powell) Biography of a Nation, 1955; Good Learning, 1964; South Asia, 1966; The Common Problem, 1969. *Recreations:* home brewing and gardening. *Address:* South Newington House, near Banbury, Oxon.

MAUDE, Evan Walter, CB 1968; a Deputy Secretary, Ministry of Agriculture, Fisheries and Food, since 1970; *b* 11 Feb. 1919; *s* of late Sir E. John Maude, KCB, KBE; *m* 1949, Jennifer, *d* of Sir Edward Stanley Gotch Robinson, CBE, FSA, FBA, and of Pamela, *o d* of Sir Victor Horsley, CB, FRS, and *widow* of Capt. O. T. Bulmer; three *d*. *Educ:* Rugby; New Coll., Oxford. Served in RNVR (Fleet Air Arm), 1940-45 (despatches). Entered HM Treasury, 1946; Asst Private Sec. to Chancellor of the Exchequer and Economic Sec., 1947-48; Private Sec. to Sec. of State for Co-ordination of Transport, Fuel and Power, 1951-53; Principal Private Sec. to Chancellor of Exchequer, 1956-58; Asst Under-Sec. of State, Dept of Economic Affairs, 1964-66; Dep. Under-Sec. of State, 1966-67; Economic Minister in British Embassy, Washington, 1967-69; Third Sec., Treasury, 1969-70. Mem. ARC, 1974-. *Recreations:* sailing, ski-ing, music. *Address:* 5 Downshire Hill, NW3. *Club:* United Oxford & Cambridge University.

MAUDE, His Honour John Cyril, QC 1942; *b* 3 April 1901; *s* of Cyril Maude and Winifred Emery; *m* 1st, 1927, Rosamond Willing Murray (from whom he obtained a divorce, 1955), *d* of late Dr T. Morris Murray, Boston, Mass, USA; one *d*; *m* 2nd, 1955, Maureen Constance (who *m* 1st, 1930, 4th Marquess of Dufferin and Ava, killed in action, 1945; one *s* two *d*; 2nd, 1948, Major (Harry Alexander) Desmond Buchanan, MC (from whom she obtained a divorce, 1954)), 2nd *d* of late Hon. Arthur Ernest Guinness. *Educ:* Eton; Christ Church, Oxford. Joined Gen. Staff, War Office, temporary civil asst, 1939; Intelligence Corps, actg Major, 1940; offices of War Cabinet, 1942. Barrister, Middle Temple, 1925; KC 1943; Bencher, 1951; Mem., Bar Council, 1952. Counsel to PO at Central Criminal Court, 1935-42; Jun. Counsel to Treasury at Central Criminal Court, 1942-43; Recorder of Devizes, 1939-44, of Plymouth, 1944-54; Additional Judge, Mayor's and City of London Court, 1954-65; Additional Judge, Central Criminal Court, 1965-68. MP (C) Exeter, 1945-51. Chancellor of the Diocese of Bristol, 1948-50. Dir, Old Vic Trust Ltd, 1951-54; Chairman of the British Drama League, 1952-54; Governor, Royal Victoria Hall Foundn, 1953. Chm., Family Service Units, 1954; Mem. Bd, Middlesex Hosp., 1951-62. *Address:* Great Maynham Hall, Rolvenden, Kent. *T:* Rolvenden 512.
See also Marquess of Dufferin and Ava.

MAUDE-ROXBY, John Henry; Director General, Institute of Grocery Distribution, since 1974; *b* 4 March 1919; *m* 1966, Katherine Jewell; one *s*. *Educ:* Radley Coll.; Hertford Coll., Oxford (BA). ACIS. Regular Army Officer, Royal Artillery, 1939-59; Allied Suppliers Ltd, 1959-73; Dir, Cavenham Ltd, 1972-73; Dep. Chm. and Man. Dir, Morgan Edwards Ltd, 1973-74. *Recreations:* shooting, golf, gardening. *Address:* Bramleys, Wood End, Tingrith, Bucks. *T:* Toddington 2028. *Clubs:* Army and Navy; Vincent's (Oxford).

MAUDLING, Rt. Hon. Reginald, PC 1955; MP (C) Barnet, Chipping Barnet, since 1974 (Herts, Barnet, 1950-74); Hon. Fellow Merton College, Oxford, 1958; *b* 7 March 1917; *m* 1939, Beryl Laverick; three *s* one *d*. *Educ:* Merchant Taylors'; Merton Coll., Oxford. 1st Class in Greats. Called to the Bar, Middle Temple, 1940. Contested Borough of Heston and Isleworth, 1945. Parly Sec. to Minister of Civil Aviation, 1952; Economic Sec. to the Treasury, Nov. 1952-April 1955; Minister of Supply, April 1955-Jan. 1957; Paymaster-Gen., 1957-59; Pres. of the Board of Trade, 1959-61; Sec. of State for the Colonies, Oct. 1961-July 1962; Chancellor of the Exchequer, July 1962-Oct. 1964; Home Secretary, 1970-72. Pres., Nat. Union of Cons. and Unionist Assocs, 1967. *Address:* Bedwell Lodge, Essendon, Herts.

MAUDSLAY, Major Sir (James) Rennie, KCVO 1972 (CVO 1967); MBE 1945; Keeper of the Privy Purse and Treasurer to the Queen, since 1971 (Assistant Keeper, 1958-71); Extra Equerry to the Queen, since 1973; *b* 13 Aug. 1915; *o s* of late Joseph Maudslay and of Mrs Ruth Maudslay (*née* Partridge), Pinewood Copse, Boundstone, Farnham, Surrey; *m* 1951, (Jane) Ann, *d* of A. V. McCarty, Helena, Arkansas; two *s* one *d*. *Educ:* Harrow Sch. 2nd Lt, KRRC, 1938; served 1938-45 (despatches five times); Hon. Major, 1945. Chm., Mid-Southern Water Co.; Director: Airkem Inc.; Lyon, Lohr & Sly Ltd; Mem. of Lloyds. Pres., Farnham Conservative Assoc., 1954-57; Pres., Maudslay Soc., 1963-65; Hon. Mem., Jun. Instn of Engineers. Employed Lord Chamberlain's Office, 1952-53. Holds Order of: Verdienst (Germany), 1958; Taj (Iran), 1959; Dakshuna Bahu (Nepal), 1960; Legion of Honour (France), 1960; Crown of Thai (Thailand), 1960; Phœnix (Greece), 1963; Al Kawkab (Jordan), 1966; Ordine al Merito della Repubblica (Italy), 1969; Order of Kroonorde (Netherlands), 1972; Order of Merit (Germany), 1972; Order of Star (Afghanistan), 1972; Order of Dannebrog (Denmark), 1974. *Recreations:* shooting, gardening. *Address:* Frensham Vale, Rowledge, Surrey. *T:* Frensham 2854; 15 St James' Palace, SW1. *T:* 01-930 4110. *Clubs:* White's, MCC.

MAUGHAM, family name of **Viscount Maugham.**

MAUGHAM, 2nd Viscount, *cr* 1939, of Hartfield; **Robert Cecil Romer Maugham;** author (as Robin Maugham); barrister-at-law; *b* 17 May 1916; *o s* of 1st Viscount Maugham, PC, KC, and Helen Mary (*d* 1950), *d* of Rt Hon. Sir Robert Romer, GCB; *S* father 1958. *Educ:* Eton; Trinity Hall, Cambridge. Served War of 1939-45; Inns of Court Regt, 1939; commissioned Fourth County of London Yeomanry, 1940; Western Desert, 1941-42 (despatches, wounded); Middle East Intelligence Centre, 1943; invalided out, 1944. Called to Bar, Lincoln's Inn, 1945. *Publications:* Come to Dust, 1945; Nomad, 1947; Approach to Palestine, 1947; The Servant, 1948 (dramatised 1963; filmed, 1965); North African Notebook, 1948; Line on Ginger, 1949; Journey to Siwa, 1950; The Rough and the Smooth, 1951; Behind the Mirror, 1955; The Man With Two Shadows, 1958; The Slaves of Timbuktu, 1961; November Reef, 1962; The Joyita Mystery, 1962; Somerset and all the Maughams, 1966; The Green Shade, 1966; The Second Window, 1968; The Link, 1969; The Wrong People, 1970; The Last Encounter, 1972; Escape from the Shadows (autobiog.), 1972; The Barrier, 1973; The Black Tent and other stories, 1973; The Sign, 1974; Search for Nirvana, 1975; Knock on Teak, 1976; Lovers in Exile, 1977; *plays:* The Last Hero; Odd Man In (adaptation); Its in the Bag (adaptation); The Lonesome Road (in collaboration with Philip King); The Claimant, 1964; Enemy!, 1969. *Recreations:* reading and travel. *Address:* 5 Clifton Road, Brighton BN1 3HP. *Club:* Garrick.

MAUGHAN, Air Vice-Marshal Charles Gilbert, CB 1976; CBE 1970; AFC; Senior Air Staff Officer, RAF Strike Command, since 1975; *b* 3 March 1923. *Educ:* Sir George Monoux Grammar Sch.; Harrow County Sch. Served War, Fleet Air Arm (flying Swordfishes and Seafires), 1942-46. Joined RAF, 1949, serving with Meteor, Vampire and Venom sqdns in Britain and Germany; comd No 65 (Hunter) Sqdn, Duxford, Cambridgeshire (won Daily Mail Arch-to-Arc race, 1959). Subseq. comd: No 9 (Vulcan) Sqdn; flying bases of Honington (Suffolk) and Waddington (Lincs); held a staff post at former Bomber Cmd, Air Staff (Ops), Strike Command, 1968-70; Air Attaché, Bonn, 1970-73; AOA Strike Command, 1974-75. *Address:* Strike Command, RAF High Wycombe, Bucks HP14 4UE.

MAUND, Rt. Rev. John Arthur Arrowsmith, CBE 1975; MC 1946; *b* 1909; *s* of late Arthur Arrowsmith and Dorothy Jane Maund, Worcester, England; *m* 1948, Catherine Mary Maurice, Bromley, Kent; no *c*. *Educ:* Worcester Cathedral King's Sch.; Leeds Univ.; Mirfield Theological Coll. BA Leeds 1931; Asst Priest, All Saints and St Laurence, Evesham, Worcs, 1933-36; Asst Priest, All Saints, Blackheath, London, 1936-38; Asst Priest, Pretoria Native Mission, Pretoria, South Africa, 1938-40; CF 1940-46 (despatches, 1942); Asst Priest, Pretoria Native Mission, in charge Lady Selborne, Pretoria, 1946-50; Bishop of Lesotho, 1950-76 (diocese known as Basutoland, 1950-66). Fellow Royal Commonwealth Society. *Recreation:* horse riding. *Address:* Hengrave Hall Centre, Bury St Edmunds, Suffolk IP28 6LZ.

MAUNDER, Prof. Leonard, OBE 1977; BSc; PhD; ScD; CEng; FIMechE; Professor of Mechanical Engineering, since 1967 (Professor of Applied Mechanics, 1961), and Dean of the Faculty of Applied Science, since 1973, University of Newcastle upon Tyne; Head of Department, 1967-73; *b* 10 May 1927; *s* of Thomas G. and Elizabeth A. Maunder; *m* 1958, Moira Anne Hudson; one *s* one *d. Educ:* Grammar Sch., Swansea; University Coll. of Swansea (BSc); Edinburgh Univ. (PhD); Massachusetts Institute of Technology (ScD). Instructor, 1950-53, and Asst Prof., 1953-54, in Dept of Mech. Engrg, MIT; Aeronautical Research Lab., Wright Air Development Center, US Air Force, 1954-56; Lecturer in Post-Graduate Sch. of Applied Dynamics, Edinburgh Univ., 1956-61. Member: Requirements Bd for Mechanical Engrg and Machine Tools, 1973-76; NRDC, 1976-;

Council, IMechE, 1963-66, 1969-70, 1973- (Vice-Pres., 1976-); Pres., Internat. Fedn Theory of Machines and Mechanisms. *Publications:* (with R. N. Arnold) Gyrodynamics and Its Engineering Applications, 1961; scientific papers in the field of applied mechanics. *Recreations:* squash rackets, gardening. *Address:* Stephenson Building, The University, Newcastle upon Tyne NE1 7RU.

MAUNDRELL, Rev. Wolseley David; Vicar of Icklesham, East Sussex, since 1972; *b* 2 Sept. 1920; *s* of late Rev. William Herbert Maundrell, RN, and Evelyn Helen Maundrell; *m* 1950, Barbara Katharine Simmons; one *s* one *d. Educ:* Radley Coll.; New Coll., Oxford. Deacon, 1943; Priest, 1944; Curate of Haslemere, 1943; Resident Chaplain to Bishop of Chichester, 1949; Vicar of Sparsholt and Lainston, Winchester, 1950; Rector of Weeke, Winchester, 1956; Residentiary Canon of Winchester Cathedral, 1961-70 (Treasurer, 1961-70; Vice-Dean, 1966-70). Examining Chaplain to Bishop of Winchester, 1962-70; Asst Chaplain of Holy Trinity Church, Brussels, 1970-71. *Address:* Icklesham Vicarage, Winchelsea, East Sussex. *T:* Icklesham 207.

MAUNSELL, Mark Stuart Ker, CBE 1952 (OBE 1944); DSO 1943; Vice-Chairman, Brooke-Bond Liebig Ltd, since 1973; Director, Liebig Meat Co., since 1974; Baxters Ltd, since 1975; *b* 24 July 1910; *s* of Ernest Oliver Henry Maunsell, Flamsteadbury, Redbourn; *m* 1939, Ruth Hunter Mason, *d* of T. A. C. Mason, Headley, Surrey; one *s* one *d. Educ:* Cheltenham; RMA, Woolwich. Commissioned, RA, 1930; RHA Palestine (Clasp, 1934-35). Served War of 1939-45, Burma; Chief of Staff, Control Commn, Saigon, FIC, 1945; Asst Comdt, RMA, Sandhurst, 1946; Chief of Staff, Allied Forces Hong Kong, 1949; Chief of Staff, 1 (Br) Corps, 1954. Dir of Trading, John Lewis Partnership, 1957; Dir, Gallaher Ltd, 1963-76. Inspector-General of Prisons, 1967-70. Croix de Guerre (France); Commandeur, Légion d'Honneur, 1947. *Address:* Hurst Lodge, Hurstbourne Tarrant, near Andover, Hants SP11 0AH. *T:* Hurstbourne Tarrant 304. *Clubs:* Jockey, Royal Over-Seas League.

MAURICE, Dr Rita Joy; Director of Statistics, Home Office, since 1977; *b* 10 May 1929; *d* of A. N. Maurice and F. A. Maurice (*née* Dean). *Educ:* East Grinstead County Sch.; University Coll., London. BSc (Econ) 1951; PhD 1958. Asst Lectr, subseq. Lectr in Economic Statistics, University Coll., London, 1951-58; Statistician, Min. of Health, 1959-62; Statistician, subseq. Chief Statistician, Central Statistical Office, 1962-72; Head of Economics and Statistics Div. 6, Depts of Industry, Trade and Prices and Consumer Protection, 1972-77. *Publications:* articles in statistical jls. *Address:* 10 Fairfax Place, Swiss Cottage, NW6 4EH. *T:* 01-624 5797.

MAVOR, Air Marshal Sir Leslie (Deane), KCB 1970 (CB 1964); AFC 1942; FRAeS; DL; Principal, Home Office Home Defence College, since 1973; *b* 18 Jan. 1916; *s* of William David Mavor, Edinburgh; *m* 1947, June Lilian Blackburn; four *s. Educ:* Aberdeen Grammar Sch. Commissioned RAF 1937. Dir of Air Staff Briefing, Air Ministry, 1961-64; AOC, No 38 Group, 1964-66; Asst CAS (Policy), 1966-69; AOC-in-C, RAF Training Comd, 1969-72; retd Jan. 1973. DL N Yorks, 1976. *Recreations:* golf, fishing, shooting, gliding. *Address:* Barlaston House, Alne, Yorks. *Club:* Royal Air Force.

MAVOR, Ronald Henry Moray, CBE 1972; author; *b* 13 May 1925; *s* of late Dr O. H. Mavor, CBE (James Bridie) and Rona Bremner; *m* 1959, Sigrid, *d* of late Arne Bruhn, Copenhagen, and Fru Marie-Louise Backer; one *s* one *d* (and one *d* decd). *Educ:* Merchiston Castle Sch.; Glasgow Univ. MB, ChB 1948, MRCP(Glas) 1955. In medical practice until 1957, incl. periods in RAMC, at American Hosp., Paris, and Deeside Sanatoria. Drama Critic, The Scotsman, 1957-65; Dir, Scottish Arts Council, 1965-71. Vice-Chm., Edinburgh Festival Council and Chm. Programme Adv. Panel, 1975-; Mem. Gen. Adv. Council, BBC, 1971-76; Mem. Drama Panel, British Council. Vis. Lectr on Drama, Guelph, Ontario, and Minneapolis, 1976, Saskatoon, 1977. *Plays:* The Keys of Paradise, 1959; Aurelie, 1960; Muir of Huntershill, 1962; The Partridge Dance, 1963; A Private Matter (originally A Life of the General), 1973; The Quartet, 1974; The Doctors. *Publications:* Art the Hard Way, in Scotland, 1972; A Private Matter (play), 1974. *Address:* 5 Gloucester Place, Edinburgh. *T:* 031-225 1751. *Club:* Scottish Arts (Edinburgh).

MAVROGORDATO, John George, CMG 1952; *b* 9 May 1905; 2nd *s* of late George Michel and Irene Mavrogordato. *Educ:* Charterhouse; Christ Church, Oxford (BA 1927). Called to Bar, Gray's Inn, 1932; practised at Chancery Bar, 1932-39. Asst Dir, Ministry of Aircraft Production, 1943. Advocate-Gen., Sudan Government, 1946; Legal Adviser to Governor-Gen. of the Sudan, 1953; Senior Legal Counsel, Ministry of Justice, Sudan,

1958-61; retired, 1961. MBOU. *Publications:* A Hawk for the Bush, 1960; A Falcon in the Field, 1966. *Recreations:* falconry, ornithology, wild life conservation.

MAW, (John) Nicholas; composer; *b* 5 Nov. 1935; *s* of Clarence Frederick Maw and Hilda Ellen (*née* Chambers); *m* 1960, Karen Graham; one *s* one *d. Educ:* Wennington Sch., Wetherby, Yorks; Royal Academy of Music. Studied in Paris with Nadia Boulanger and Max Deutsch, 1958-59. Fellow Commoner in Creative Arts, Trinity Coll., Cambridge, 1966-70. Compositions include: *operas:* One-Man Show, 1964; The Rising of The Moon, 1970; *for orchestra:* Sinfonia, 1966; Sonata for Strings and Two Horns, 1967; Serenade, for small orchestra, 1973, 1977; Life Studies, for 15 solo strings, 1973; Odyssey, 1974; *for voice and orchestra:* Nocturne, 1958; Scenes and Arias, 1962; *chamber music:* String Quartet, 1965; Chamber Music for wind and piano quintet, 1962; *instrumental music:* Sonatina for flute and piano, 1957; Essay for organ, 1961; *vocal music:* Five Epigrams for chorus, 1960; Round for chorus and piano, 1963; The Voice of Love, for mezzo soprano and piano, 1966; Five Irish Songs, for mixed chorus, 1972. *Address:* c/o Boosey & Hawkes Ltd, 295 Regent Street, W1A 1BR.

MAWBY, Colin (John Beverley); Master of Music, Westminster Cathedral, since 1961; *b* 9 May 1936; *e s* of Bernard Mawby and Enid Mawby (*née* Vaux); unmarried. *Educ:* St Swithun's Primary Sch., Portsmouth; Westminster Cathedral Choir Sch.; Royal Coll. of Music. Organist and Choirmaster of Our Lady's Church, Warwick St, W1, 1953; Choirmaster of Plymouth Cath., 1955; Organist and Choirmaster of St Anne's, Vauxhall, 1957; Asst Master of Music, Westminster Cath., 1959. Conductor: Westminster Chamber Choir; Westminster Cathedral String Orchestra; New Westminster Chorus and Orchestra. Prof. of Harmony, Trinity Coll. of Music, 1975-. Director (Catholic) Publisher, L. J. Cary & Co., 1963; Vice-Pres., Brit. Fedn of *Pueri Cantores,* 1966; Member: Council, Latin Liturgical Assoc., 1969; Adv. Panel, Royal Sch. of Church Music, 1974; Music Sub-Cttee, Westminster Arts Council, 1974. Broadcaster and recording artist; occasional free lance journalism. *Publications:* Church music including five Masses, Anthems, Motets and Holy Week music. *Recreations:* politics and psychology. *Address:* 16 Stafford Mansions, Stafford Place, SW1. *T:* 01-828 8124; 01-834 4928.

MAWBY, Raymond Llewellyn; MP (C) Totnes Division of Devon since 1955; *b* 6 Feb. 1922; *m* 1944; one *d* (one *s* decd). *Educ:* Long Lawford Council Sch., Warwicks. One-time Pres. Rugby branch Electrical Trades Union; one-time mem. of Rugby Borough Council. Asst Postmaster-Gen., 1963-64. *Address:* 29 Applegarth Avenue, Newton Abbot, S Devon.

MAWER, Air Cdre Allen Henry, DFC 1943; General Manager, Basildon Development Corporation, since 1975; *b* 16 Dec. 1921; *s* of Gordon Mawer and Emily Naomi Mawer (*née* Block); *m* 1947, Pamela Mitchell, *d* of David Thomas; one *s* one *d. Educ:* Bancroft's School. Joined RAF, 1940; bomber and special duties ops, 1941-45; psc 1956; Stn Comdr, RAF Scampton, 1965-68; idc 1968; Comdt RAF Coll. of Air Warfare, 1969-71; Air Cdre Plans, HQ Strike Comd, RAF, 1971-73; Air Cdre, Malta, 1973-75, retd. Croix de Guerre, France, 1944. *Recreations:* painting, golf, shooting. *Address:* Richmond Cottage, Fambridge Road, Althorne, Essex CM3 6BZ. *Clubs:* Royal Air Force; Royal Burnham Yacht.

MAWER, Ronald K.; *see* Knox-Mawer.

MAWSON, Christian; *see* Barman, Christian.

MAWSON, David, RIBA; JP; Partner, Feilden and Mawson, Architects, Norwich, since 1957; *b* 30 May 1924; *s* of John William Mawson and Evelyn Mary Mawson (*née* Bond); *m* 1951, Margaret Kathlyn Norton; one *s* one *d. Educ:* Merchant Taylors' Sch., Sandy Lodge; Wellington Coll., NZ; Auckland Univ., NZ; Kingston-upon-Thames Coll. of Art. Royal Navy, 1945-47. Chartered Architect, 1952-. Chm., Norfolk Soc. (CPRE), 1971-76, Vice Pres. 1976-; Hon. Sec., Friends of Norwich Museums, 1967-; Founder and Chm., British Assoc. of Friends of Museums, 1973-; Founder Pres., World Fedn of Friends of Museums, 1975-; Mem., Cttee of Nat. Heritage, 1973-; Mem., Norfolk Assoc. of Architects, 1952- (Vice-Pres., 1977-). JP Norwich, 1972. *Publication:* paper on British Museum Friends Socs in Proc. of First Internat. Congress of Friends of Museums, Barcelona, 1972. *Recreations:* tennis, yachting. *Address:* Gonville Hall, Wymondham, Norfolk NR18 9JG. *T:* Wymondham 602166. *Club:* Norfolk (Norwich).

MAWSON, Stuart Radcliffe; Consultant Surgeon, Ear Nose and Throat Department, King's College Hospital, London, since 1951, Head of Department since Dec. 1973; *b* 4 March 1918; *s* of late Alec Robert Mawson, Chief Officer, Parks Dept, LCC, and Ena (*née* Grossmith), *d* of George Grossmith Jr, Actor Manager; *m* 1948, June Irene, *d* of George Percival; two *s* two *d. Educ:* Canford Sch.; Trinity Coll., Cambridge; St Thomas's Hosp., London. BA Cantab 1940; MRCS, LRCP 1943; MB, BChir Cantab 1946; FRCS 1947; DLO 1948. House Surg., St Thomas's Hosp., 1943; RMO XIth Para. Bn, 1st Airborne Div., Arnhem, POW, 1943-44; Chief Asst, ENT Dept, St Thomas's Hosp., 1950; Consultant ENT Surgeon: King's Coll. Hosp., 1951; Belgrave Hosp. for Children, 1951; Recog. Teacher of Oto-Rhino-Laryngology, Univ. of London, 1958. Chm., KCH Med. Cttee and Dist Management Team, 1977-. FRSocMed (Pres. Section of Otology, 1974-75); Liveryman, Apothecaries' Soc.; former Mem. Council, Brit. Assoc. of Otolaryngologists. *Publications:* Diseases of the Ear, 3rd edn 1974; (jtly) Essentials of Otolaryngology, 1967; (contrib.) Scott-Brown's Diseases of the Ear, Nose and Throat, 3rd edn 1971; (contrib.) Modern Trends in Diseases of the Ear, Nose and Throat, 1972; numerous papers in sci. jls. *Address:* Department of Otolaryngology, King's College Hospital, Denmark Hill, SE5 9RS. *T:* 01-274 6222; 4 Offley Road, SW9. *T:* 01-735 4895; Whinbeck, Knodishall, Saxmundham, Suffolk. *Clubs:* Aldeburgh Golf, Aldeburgh Yacht.

MAXWELL, family name of Baroness de Ros and Baron Farnham.

MAXWELL, Hon. Lord; Peter Maxwell; a Senator of the College of Justice in Scotland, since 1973; *b* 21 May 1919; *s* of late Comdr and late Mrs Herries Maxwell, Munches, Dalbeattie, Kirkcudbrightshire; *m* 1941, Alison Susan Readman; one *s* two *d* (and one *s* decd). *Educ:* Wellington Coll.; Balliol Coll., Oxford; Edinburgh Univ. Served Argyll and Sutherland Highlanders, and late RA, 1939-46. Called to Scottish Bar, 1951; QC (Scotland) 1961; Sheriff-Principal of Dumfries and Galloway, 1970-73. Mem., Royal Commn on Legal Services in Scotland, 1976-. *Address:* 1c Oswald Road, Edinburgh EH9 2HE. *T:* 031-667 7444.

MAXWELL, Colonel (Arthur) Terence, TD; British Representative, Investments Committee, International Labour Office; *b* 19 Jan. 1905; *s* of late Brig.-Gen. Sir Arthur Maxwell, KCB, CMG, DSO, and late Eva Jones; *m* 1935, Beatrice Diane, *d* of late Rt Hon. Sir J. Austen Chamberlain, KG, PC, MP, and late Ivy Muriel Dundas, GBE; two *s* one *d. Educ:* Rugby; Trinity Coll., Oxford, MA. Travelled in Africa as James Whitehead travelling student, 1926-27, and in South America; Barrister-at-Law, 1929; served 7th City of London Regt Post Office Rifles, 1923-35; Captain TA Reserve of Officers, 1935. Capt. KRRC 1940; Staff Coll., 1941; Leader Ministry of Economic Warfare Mission to the Middle East with rank of Counsellor, 1941-42; Col General Staff, AFHQ, 1943-44; Deputy Chief, Military Government Section; attached SHAEF etc. A Managing Dir, Glyn, Mills & Co., bankers, until 1945; Chm., Powers-Samas Accounting Machines Ltd, 1952-70; Dep. Chm., International Computers and Tabulators Ltd, 1959-67, Chm., 1967-68; Chm., International Computers (Holdings) Ltd, 1968, Dep. Chm. 1969; Chm. Computer Leasings Ltd, 1963-69; Director: Vickers Ltd, 1934-75; Aust. and NZ Banking Group Ltd, and its predecessors, 1935-76; Steel Co. of Wales, 1948-67; English Steel Corp. Ltd, 1954-67. Vice-Chm. Cttee on Rural Bus Services (1959), Ministry of Transport; Vice-Pres. and Treas. City and Guilds of London Institute, 1959-67; Mem. Delegacy of City and Guilds Coll., Imperial Coll., University of London, 1959-64. *Recreations:* forestry, golf, shooting. *Address:* Roveries Hall, Bishop's Castle, Salop. *T:* Bishop's Castle 402; Flat 7, 52 Onslow Square, SW7. *T:* 01-589 0321. *Club:* Carlton.

MAXWELL, Sir Aymer, 8th Bt of Monreith, *cr* 1681; Hon. Captain Scots Guards; *b* 7 Dec. 1911; *s* of late Lt-Col Aymer Maxwell, Royal Naval Div., Captain Grenadier Guards and Lovat Scouts, and Lady Mary Percy, 5th *d* of 7th Duke of Northumberland; *S* grandfather 1937. *Educ:* Eton; Magdalene Coll., Cambridge. BA (Hon.); JP Wigtownshire. *Heir:* nephew Michael Eustace George Maxwell, *b* 28 Aug. 1943. *Address:* Monreith, Wigtownshire. *T:* Portwilliam 248; Lansdowne House, W1A. *T:* 01-727 6394; Katounia, Limni, Euboea, Greece. *Club:* Boodle's.

MAXWELL of Ardwell, Col Frederick Gordon, CBE 1967; TD; FCIT; DL; *b* 2 May 1905; *s* of late Lt-Col Alexander Gordon Maxwell, OBE, Hon. Corps of Gentlemen-at-Arms; *m* 1st, 1935, Barbara Margaret, *d* of late Edward Williams Hedley, MBE, MD, Thursley, Surrey; two *s* one *d*; 2nd, 1965, True Hamilton Exley, *d* of Francis George Hamilton, Old Blundells Cottage, Tiverton, Devon. *Educ:* Eton. OC 2nd Bn The London Scottish, 1939-42; GSO1, 52nd (Lowland) Div., 1943-44, served in

Holland and Germany (despatches); GSO1, Allied Land Forces SE Asia, 1945; OC 1st Bn The London Scottish, 1947-50. Joined London Transport, 1924; Operating Manager (Railways), London Transport, 1947-70, retired 1971. Mem., Co. of London T&AFA, 1947-68; Lt-Col RE (T&AVR, IV), 1956-70; Regimental Col, The London Scottish, 1969-73. DL, Co. of London, 1962; DL, Greater London, 1966. OStJ 1969. *Address:* 41 Cheyne Court, Cheyne Place, SW3 5TS. *T:* 01-352 9801. *Clubs:* Naval and Military, Highland Brigade.

MAXWELL, Herbert William; *b* 24 March 1888; *s* of James Ward Maxwell and Charlotte Eleanor Morris; *m* 1915, Winifred J. Coysh (*d* 1961); one *s* one *d. Educ:* Kent Coll., Canterbury. Surveyor and Land Agent, 1906-14; Sergeant 1/25th London Cyclist Battalion, 1908-16; Lieut Royal Engineers, 1916-19; Secretary: British Institute of Industrial Art; Palace of Arts, BEE Wembley; Exhibition of Flemish and Belgian Art; Advisory Cttee, Royal Mint, 1920-27; Curator, Stoke-on-Trent Museums, 1927-30; Dir Bristol Museum and Art Gallery, 1930-45; Fellow, Royal Society of Arts; Mem. of Council, Museum Association, 1930-32; Pres., South-western group of Museums and Art Galleries 1931-32; Hon. Sec., Council for the Preservation of Ancient Bristol; Hon. Gen. Sec. Theatre Royal, Bristol, Preservation Fund, 1938-48. In South America with exhibition of British Contemporary Art for British Council, 1943-44; Mem. Advisory Council, Victoria and Albert Museum, 1945-50, Acting Hon. Sec. Royal West of England Academy, 1946-51; Dir, City Art Gallery, Bristol, 1945-52; Curator, Snowshill Manor, Glos (The National Trust), 1952-62. Elected to Morden Coll., 1967. *Publications:* Exhibition Catalogues, Magazine articles, etc. *Address:* Morden College, Blackheath, SE3 0PW.

MAXWELL, (Ian) Robert; MC 1945; Founder, Publisher and Chairman of Board, Pergamon Press, Oxford, London and New York; Co-Chairman, Scottish News Enterprises Ltd, 1975; *b* 10 June 1923; *s* of Michael and Ann Hoch; *m* 1945, Elisabeth (*née* Meynard); three *s* four *d* (and one *s* decd). *Educ:* self-educated. Served War of 1939-45 (MC). In German Sect. of Foreign Office (Head of Press Sect., Berlin), 1945-47. Chm., Robert Maxwell & Co. Ltd, 1948-; Dir, Computer Technology Ltd, 1966-77; Chm. and Chief Exec., Internat. Learning Systems Corp. Ltd, 1968-69; Dir, Gauthier-Villars (Publishers), Paris, 1961-70. MP (Lab) Buckingham, 1964-70. Chm., Labour Nat. Fund Raising Foundn, 1960-69; Chm., Labour Working Party on Science, Govt and Industry, 1963-64; Mem., Council of Europe (Vice-Chm., Cttee on Science and Technology), 1968. Contested (Lab) Buckingham, Feb. and Oct. 1974. Treasurer, The Round House Trust Ltd (formerly Centre 42), 1965-. Kennedy Fellow, Harvard Univ., 1971. Hon. Mem., Acad. of Astronautics, 1974. Co-produced films: Mozart's Don Giovanni, Salzburg Festival, 1954; Bolshoi Ballet, 1957; Swan Lake, 1968. *Publications:* (ed) Information USSR, 1963; The Economics of Nuclear Power, 1965; Public Sector Purchasing, 1968; (jt author) Man Alive, 1968. *Recreations:* chess, mountain-climbing. *Address:* Headington Hill Hall, Oxford. *T:* 64881.

MAXWELL, Surgeon Rear-Adm. Joseph Archibald, CB 1950; CVO 1939; CBE 1944 (OBE 1938); *b* 1890; *s* of Thomas Henry Maxwell, KC, LLD; *m* 1919, Dorothy Anna, ARRC, *d* of John Arthur Perkin, The Grange, Matfield, Kent; two *s* two *d. Educ:* Trinity Coll., Dublin (MB, BCh 1912); FRCS Edinburgh 1926. Surgeon Rear-Adm. 1946; in charge: Hospital Ship Oxfordshire, 1943-44; RN Aux. Hosp. Sydney, 1944-46; RN Aux. Hosp. Sherborne, 1946-48; RN Hosp. Haslar, 1948-49; formerly Surgical Specialist, RN Hosps, Haslar, Malta, Chatham, and Plymouth; retired, 1949; CStJ 1949, KHS 1946-49. Medical Superintendent, St Mary's Hospital, Portsmouth, retired 1955. *Address:* The Old Vicarage, Compton Chamberlayne, Salisbury, Wilts.

MAXWELL, Maurice William; President, Associated Book Publishers, since 1976 (chairman, 1974-76); *b* 11 March 1910; *s* of William Harold Maxwell and Hilda Maxwell (*née* Cox); *m* 1936, Margaret Lucy Carnaham (marr. diss. 1958); one *d. Educ:* Dean Close, Cheltenham. Joined Sweet & Maxwell, 1928, Man. Dir 1948, Chm. 1952-72; Vice-Chm., Associated Book Publishers, 1963-73; Pres., Carswell Co., Canada, 1958-74. Served in RAFVR, 1940-45 (Sqdn Ldr); RAuxAF, 1947-57 (AEM 1953). *Recreations:* reading, listening to music, motoring, travel. *Address:* 2 Orchard Green, Homefield Road, Bromley, Kent. *T:* 01-460 2955; Apt 11K, Le Lavallière, Res. le Roi Soleil, 06600 Antibes, France. *Clubs:* Reform, Royal Air Force.

MAXWELL, Patrick; Resident Magistrate; Solicitor; *b* 12 March 1909; *e s* of late Alderman Patrick Maxwell, Solicitor, Londonderry; *m* 1st, 1935 (wife *d* 1962); two *d*; 2nd, 1969. *Educ:* Convent of Mercy, Artillery Street, Londonderry;

Christian Brothers Sch., Brow-of-the-Hill, Londonderry; St Columb's Coll., Londonderry. Solicitor, 1932; entered Londonderry Corporation as Councillor, 1934; resigned as protest against re-destribution scheme, 1937; Leader of Anti-Partition Party in Londonderry Corporation from 1938; did not seek re-election, 1946; first Chairman of Irish Union Association, 1936; Chairman of Derry Catholic Registration Association, 1934-52. MP (Nat) Foyle Division of Londonderry City, Northern Ireland Parliament, 1937-53. Resident Magistrate, 1968-. President: Law Society of Northern Ireland, 1967-68 (Vice-Pres., 1966-67); Londonderry Rotary Club, 1958-59; Chm. Rotary in Ireland, 1963-64; Mem., Council, International Bar Association, 1968. *Address:* 3 Talbot Park, Londonderry. *T:* Londonderry 51425.

MAXWELL, Sir Patrick I. Heron-; *see* Heron-Maxwell.

MAXWELL, Peter; *see* Maxwell, Hon. Lord.

MAXWELL, Robert; *see* Maxwell, I. R.

MAXWELL, Sir Robert (Hugh), KBE 1961 (OBE 1942); *b* 2 Jan. 1906; *s* of William Robert and Nancy Dockett Maxwell; *m* 1935, Mary Courtney Jewell; two *s*. Comdr of Order of George I of Greece, 1961; Order of Merit of Syria. *Clubs:* Travellers'; Athens (Athens).

MAXWELL, Col Terence; *see* Maxwell, Col A. T.

MAXWELL, Rear-Adm. Thomas Heron, CB 1967; DSC 1942; idc, jssc, psc; Director-General of Naval Training, Ministry of Defence, 1965-67; retired, 1967; *b* 10 April 1912; *s* of late H. G. Maxwell; *m* 1947, Maeve McKinley; two *s* two *d. Educ:* Campbell Coll., Belfast; Royal Naval Engineering Coll. Cadet, 1930; Commander, 1946; Captain, 1956; Rear-Adm., 1965. *Recreation:* fishing. *Address:* Middle Twinhoe, Bath, Avon. *T:* Combe Down 832242.

MAXWELL, William Wayland, MA (Cantab); CEng, FIMechE, FIEE; FCIT; Board Member for Engineering, London Transport Executive, since 1973; *b* 10 March 1925; *s* of Somerset Maxwell and Molly Cullen; *m* 1963, Eugenie Pamela Cavanagh, *d* of Leslie Crump and Eugenie Thurlow; no *c. Educ:* Bedales Sch.; Trinity Hall, Cambridge (Mech. Scis Tripos). Entered London Transport, 1947; Development Engr (Victoria Line), 1963; Mechanical Engr, Development: Railways, 1964; Mechanical Engr, Running: Railways, 1969; Chief Operating Manager (Railways), 1970. Dir, Whelpdale, Maxwell & Codd Ltd, piano and harpsichord makers. Chm., Rly Div., IMechE, 1977. Lt-Col, Engr and Railway Staff Corps RE (T&AVR). SBStJ 1975. *Publications:* papers in Proc. IMechE and Proc. IEE. *Recreations:* reading, music, theatre and gardening. *Address:* 40 Elm Bank Gardens, Barnes, SW13 0NT. *T:* 01-876 9575. *Club:* Naval and Military.

MAXWELL-HYSLOP, Robert John, (Robin); MP (C) Tiverton Division of Devon since 1960; *b* 6 June 1931; 2nd *s* of Capt. A. H. Maxwell-Hyslop, GC, RN, and late Mrs Maxwell-Hyslop; *m* 1968, Joanna Margaret, er *d* of Thomas McCosh; two *d. Educ:* Stowe; Christ Church, Oxford (MA). Hons Degree in PPE Oxon, 1954. Joined Rolls-Royce Ltd Aero Engine Div., as graduate apprentice, Sept. 1954; served 2 years as such and then joined Export Sales Dept; apptd PA to Dir and GM (Sales and Service), 1958; left Rolls-Royce Aug. 1960. Contested (C) Derby (North) General Election, 1959. Vice-Chm., Anglo-Brazilian Parly Gp, 1971-; Jt Sec., Cons. Parly Aviation Cttee, 1970-. Member: Trade and Industry Sub-Cttee on Public Expenditure, 1971-; Standing Orders Cttee. Governor, Casa do Brazil. *Recreations:* motoring, swimming, tennis. *Address:* 4 Tiverton Road, Silverton, Exeter, Devon.

MAXWELL SCOTT, Sir Michael Fergus, 13th Bt *cr* 1642; *b* 23 July 1921; *s* of Rear-Adm. Malcolm Raphael Joseph Maxwell Scott, DSO (*d* 1943), and Fearga Victoria Mary (*d* 1969) *e d* of Rt Hon. Sir Nicholas Roderick O'Conor, PC, GCB, GCMG; *S* to baronetcy of kinsman, Sir Ralph (Raphael) Stanley De Marie Haggerston, 1972; *m* 1963, Deirdre Moira, *d* of late Alexander McKechnie; two *s* one *d*. *Educ:* Ampleforth; Trinity College, Cambridge. *Publication:* Stories of Famous Scientists, 1965. *Recreations:* sailing, fishing, gardening. *Heir:* s Dominic James Maxwell Scott, *b* 22 July 1968. *Address:* 100 Eaton Terrace, SW1W 8UG.

MAY, family name of **Baron May.**

MAY, 3rd Baron, *cr* 1935, of Weybridge; **Michael St John May;** 3rd Bt, *cr* 1931; late Lieut, Royal Corps of Signals; *b* 26 Sept. 1931; *o s* of 2nd Baron May and *d* of George Ricardo Thomas; *S* father 1950; *m* 1st, 1958, Dorothea Catherine Ann (marr. diss. 1963), *d* of Charles McCarthy, Boston, USA; 2nd, 1963, Jillian Mary, *d* of Albert Edward Shipton, Beggars Barn, Shutford, Oxon; one *s* one *d. Educ:* Wycliffe Coll., Stonehouse, Glos; Magdalene Coll., Cambridge. 2nd Lieut, Royal Signals, 1950. *Recreations:* flying, travel. *Heir: s* Hon. Jasper Bertram St John May, *b* 24 Oct. 1965. *Address:* Gautherns Barn, Sibford Gower, Oxon.

MAY, Surgeon Vice-Adm. Sir Cyril; *see* May, Surgeon Vice-Adm. Sir R. C.

MAY, Graham; Under-Secretary, and Principal Finance Officer, Property Services Agency, Department of the Environment, since 1972; *b* 15 Dec. 1923; *s* of Augustus May; *m* 1952, Marguerite Lucy Griffin; four *s. Educ:* Gravesend County Sch. for Boys; Balliol Coll., Oxford (BA). War Service, Royal Artillery, 1942-46. Asst Principal, Min. of Works, 1948, Principal 1952; seconded to Treasury, 1961-63; Asst Sec., MPBW, 1963. *Address:* 7 Hunter Road, Wimbledon, SW20 8NZ. *T:* 01-946 5710.

MAY, Harry Blight, MD, FRCP, retired; Director of Clinical Laboratories, The London Hospital, 1946-74; Consultant Pathologist to Royal Navy, 1950-74; *b* 12 Nov. 1908; *s* of John and Isobel May, Plymouth, Devon; *m* 1949, Dorothy Quartermaine; no *c. Educ:* Devonport; St John's Coll., Cambridge (Scholar). 1st cl. Natural Science Tripos, 1929. Postgraduate study Harvard Medical Sch., 1936. Dean, Faculty of Medicine, Univ. of London, 1960-64; Dean of Med. and Dental Sch., The London Hosp. Med. Coll., 1953-68; Mem. Senate, Univ. of London; Mem. Governing Body, Royal Veterinary Coll.; Examiner, Royal College of Physicians of London and Univ. of Oxford. *Publications:* Clinical Pathology (6th edn), 1951; papers on Antibacterial Agents and other medical subjects. *Address:* 3 Littlemead, Littleworth Road, Esher, Surrey. *T:* Esher 62394. *Club:* Athenæum.

MAY, Hon. Sir John (Douglas), Kt 1972; **Hon. Mr Justice May;** a Judge of the High Court, Queen's Bench Division, since 1972; Presiding Judge, Midland and Oxford Circuit, 1973-77; *b* 28 June 1923; *s* of late E. A. G. May, Shanghai, and of Mrs May, Whitelands House, SW3; *m* 1958, Mary, *er d* of Sir Owen Morshead, GCVO, KCB, DSO, MC, and Paquita, *d* of J. G. Hagemeyer; two *s* one *d. Educ:* Clifton Coll.; Balliol Coll., Oxford. Lieut (SpSc) RNVR, 1944-46. Barrister-at-Law, Inner Temple, 1947, Master of the Bench, 1972; QC 1965; Recorder of Maidstone, 1971; Leader, SE Circuit, 1971. *Address:* c/o Royal Courts of Justice, Strand, WC2. *Club:* Vincent's (Oxford).

MAY, John Otto, CBE 1962 (OBE 1949); HM Diplomatic Service; retired; *b* 21 April 1913; *s* of late Otto May, FRCP, MD; *m* 1939, Maureen McNally, one *d. Educ:* Sherborne; St John's Coll., Cambridge. Apptd to Dept of Overseas Trade, 1937. Private Sec. to Comptroller-General, 1939; Asst Commercial Secretary: Copenhagen, 1939; Helsinki, 1940; Ministry of Economic Warfare (Representative in Caracas), 1942-44; First Sec. (Commercial): Rome, 1945, Bucharest, 1948; Foreign Office, 1950-53; First Sec., Helsinki, 1954. Acted as Chargé d'Affaires in 1954, 1955, and 1956; Counsellor (Commercial) and Consul-General, HM Embassy, Athens, 1957-60; Consul-General: Genoa, 1960-65; Rotterdam, 1965-68; Gothenburg, 1968-72. *Recreations:* travel, photography, walking, philately. *Address:* 6 Millhedge Close, Cobham, Surrey KT11 3BE. *T:* Cobham 4645. *Club:* United Oxford & Cambridge University.

MAY, Paul, CBE 1970; retired 1970; *b* 12 July 1907; *s* of William Charles May and Katharine Edith May; *m* 1st, 1933, Dorothy Ida Makower (*d* 1961); two *s* one *d*; 2nd, 1969, Frances Maud Douglas (*née* Tarver); two step *s. Educ:* Westminster; Christ Church, Oxford (MA). United Africa Co. Ltd, 1930-32; John Lewis Partnership, 1932-40; Min. of Aircraft Production, 1940-45; John Lewis Partnership, 1945-70 (Dep. Chm., 1955-70). Mem. Exec. Cttee, Land Settlement Assoc. Ltd, 1962-71. *Recreations:* walking, reading, etc. *Address:* Chesterford, Whittingham, Northumberland. *T:* Wittingham 642.

MAY, Peter Barker Howard; Lloyd's Insurance Broker since 1953; Underwriting Member of Lloyd's, 1962; Director, Willis Faber & Dumas Ltd, since 1976; *b* 31 Dec. 1929; *m* 1959, Virginia, *er d* of A. H. H. Gilligan; four *d. Educ:* Charterhouse; Pembroke Coll., Cambridge (BA). Cambridge cricket and football XIs v. Oxford, 1950, 1951 and 1952; Surrey County Cricket Cap, 1950; played cricket for England v. S Africa 1951, v. India 1952, v. Australia 1953, v. W Indies 1953, v. Pakistan, Australia and New Zealand 1954; captained England 41 times, incl. v. S Africa, 1955, v. Australia 1956, v. S Africa 1956-57, v. W Indies, 1957, v. New Zealand 1958, v. Australia, 1958-59, v.

India, 1959, v. West Indies, 1959-60, v. Australia, 1961. *Publication:* Peter May's Book of Cricket, 1956. *Recreation:* golf. *Address:* Franklins, Shamley Green, Surrey. *T:* Bramley 3183. *Clubs:* MCC, Surrey County Cricket, Forty.

MAY, Surgeon Vice-Adm. Sir (Robert) Cyril, KBE 1958 (OBE 1942); CB 1956; MC 1918; FRCS 1957; Medical Director-General of the Navy, 1956-60; *b* 12 June 1897; *yr s* of Robert May, Belgrave Road, London; *m* 1925, Mary (*d* 1977), *d* of Patrick James Robertson, Cupar, Fife; one *s. Educ:* Westminster Sch.; Guy's Hospital. Served European War, 1916-18; 2nd Lieut RGA 1915; Actg Major 1917; comd 139 Siege Battery. MRCS, LRCP 1925. Surgeon Lieut RN, 1925; Surgeon Comdr, 1937; Asst to Med. Dir.-Gen., 1938-46; Surgeon Capt., 1946; Senior Medical Officer (Surgical Sect) RN Hosp., Chatham, 1946-49 and 1951-53; Fleet Medical Officer, Home Fleet, 1949-50; Surgeon Rear-Adm., 1953; Medical Officer-in-Charge, RN Hosp., Malta, and Medical Adviser to C-in-C, AFMed., 1953-56; QHS, 1953-60; Surg. Vice-Adm., 1956. KStJ 1959. *Recreations:* cricket, lawn tennis, golf. *Address:* 45 Belsize Court, Lyndhurst Gardens, NW3. *T:* 01-435 5233. *Club:* Army and Navy.

MAY, Valentine Gilbert Delabere, CBE 1969; Director, Yvonne Arnaud Theatre, Guildford, since 1975; *b* 1 July 1927; *s* of Claude Jocelyn Delabere May and Olive Gilbert; *m* 1955, Penelope Sutton; one *d. Educ:* Cranleigh Sch.; Peterhouse Coll., Cambridge. Trained at Old Vic Theatre Sch. Director: Ipswich Theatre, 1953-57; Nottingham Playhouse, 1957-61; Bristol Old Vic Company, 1961-75. Plays directed for Bristol Old Vic which subseq. transf. to London incl.: War and Peace, 1962; A Severed Head, 1963 (which he also dir. as his first Broadway prodn, 1964); Love's Labour's Lost, 1964 (which also went on a British Council European tour); Portrait of a Queen, 1965; The Killing of Sister George, 1965; The Italian Girl, 1968; Mrs Mouse, Are You Within, 1968; Conduct Unbecoming, 1969; It's a Two-Foot-Six Inches Above the Ground World, 1970; Poor Horace, 1970; Trelawny, 1972, The Card, 1973; (prod. for Arnaud Theatre, subseq. transfer to London) Baggage 1976, Banana Ridge, 1976. Other prodns seen in New York incl.: Romeo and Juliet and Hamlet, (followed by a tour of USA, Berlin and Israel); Portrait of a Queen; The Killing of Sister George; Conduct Unbecoming. Hon. MA Bristol, 1975. *Recreations:* reading, architecture, music, astronomy. *Address:* Yvonne Arnaud Theatre, Millbrook, Guildford, Surrey GU1 3UX. *T:* Guildford 64571.

MAYALL, Sir (Alexander) Lees, KCVO 1972 (CVO 1965); CMG 1964; HM Diplomatic Service, retired; Ambassador to Venezuela, 1972-75; *b* 14 Sept. 1915; *s* of late Alexander Mayall, Bealings End, Woodbridge, Suffolk, and husband, *d* of F. J. R. Hendy; *m* 1st, 1940, Renée Eileen Burn (marr. diss., 1947); one *d*; 2nd, 1947, Hon. Mary Hermione Ormsby Gore, *e d* of 4th Baron Harlech, KG, PC, GCMG; one *s* two *d. Educ:* Eton; Trinity Coll., Oxford (MA). Entered HM Diplomatic Service, 1939; served with armed forces, 1940; transferred to HM Legation, Berne, 1940-44; First Secretary: HM Embassy, Cairo, 1947-49, Paris, 1952-54; Counsellor, HM Embassy: Tokyo, 1958-61; Lisbon, 1961-64; Addis Ababa, 1964-65; Vice-Marshal of the Diplomatic Corps, 1965-72. *Recreations:* travelling, reading. *Address:* Sturford Mead, Warminster, Wilts. *T:* Chapmanslade 219. *Clubs:* Travellers', Pratt's, Beefsteak.

MAYBRAY-KING, family name of **Baron Maybray-King.**

MAYBRAY-KING, Baron *cr* 1971 (Life Peer), of the City of Southampton; **Horace Maybray Maybray-King,** PC 1965; DL; Deputy Speaker of the House of Lords, since 1971; *b* 25 May 1901; *s* of John William and Margaret Ann King; changed name by deed poll to Maybray-King, 1971; *m* 1st, 1924, Victoria Florence Harris (*d* 1966); one *d*; 2nd, 1967, Una Porter. *Educ:* Norton Council Sch.; Stockton Secondary Sch.; King's Coll., University of London. BA 1st Class Hons 1922, PhD 1940. Head of English Dept, Taunton's Sch., Southampton, 1930-47; Headmaster, Regent's Park Secondary Sch., 1947-50. MP (Lab): Test Div. of Southampton, 1950-55; Itchen Div. of Southampton, 1955-65 (when elected Speaker); Chairman of Ways and Means and Deputy Speaker, 1964-65; MP Itchen Division of Southampton and Speaker of the House of Commons, 1965-70. Mem., BBC Complaints Commn, 1971-74. Hon. Treasurer, Help the Aged, 1972-; Pres., Spina Bifida Assoc., 1971-. FKC; Hon. FRCP. Hon. DCL Durham, 1968; Hon. LLD: Southampton, 1967; London, 1967; Bath Univ. of Technology, 1969; Hon. DSocSci Ottawa, 1969; Hon. DLitt Loughborough Univ. of Technology, 1971. Hants County Hon. Alderman; Freeman of Southampton and Stockton-on-Tees. DL Hants, 1975. *Publications:* Selections from Macaulay, 1930; Selections from Homer, 1935; (ed) Sherlock Holmes Stories,

1950; Parliament and Freedom, 1953; State Crimes, 1967; Songs in the Night, 1968; Before Hansard, 1968; The Speaker and Parliament, 1973. *Recreations:* music and the entertainment of children. *Address:* 37 Manor Farm Road, Southampton. *T:* Southampton 555884. *Club:* Farmers'.

MAYCOCK, Rev. Francis Hugh; Principal of Pusey House, Oxford, 1952-70; Tutor, St Augustine's College, Canterbury, 1970-74; *b* 4 Oct. 1903; *s* of Canon H. W. Maycock and Mrs M. M. Maycock; unmarried. *Educ:* Tonbridge Sch.; Christ Church, Oxford; Cuddesdon Theological Coll. Christ Church, Forest Hill, SE 23, 1927-29; Corpus Christi Mission, Camberwell, 1929-31; Chaplain, Sidney Sussex Coll., Cambridge, 1931-36; Diocese of Borneo, 1936-40; Chaplain of Westcott House, Cambridge, 1940-44; Vicar of St Mary's the less, Cambridge, 1944-52. Examining Chaplain to the Bishop of Ripon, 1959-70. *Publication:* Original Sin (Mirfield Series), 1948. *Address:* S Bernard, Burwash, East Sussex.

MAYCOCK, William d'Auvergne, CBE 1970 (MBE 1945); MVO 1961; MD, FRCP, FRCPath; Director of Blood Products Laboratory, Lister Institute of Preventive Medicine, Elstree, Herts; *b* 7 Feb. 1911; *s* of William Perren Maycock, MIEE, and Florence Marion, *d* of Alfred Hart; *m* 1940, Muriel Mary, *d* of Duncan Macdonald, Toronto; two *s. Educ:* The King's School, Canterbury; McGill Univ., Montreal. MD McGill, 1935; FRCP, MRCS, FRCPath. Demonstrator in Pathology, McGill Univ., 1935; Leverhulme Scholar, RCS of Eng., 1936-39; Dept of Physiology, St Thomas's Hosp. Med. Sch., 1939. Served in RAMC, 1939-45: Temp. Col, AMS, 1945. Mem. Staff of Lister Inst., London, 1946-48; Consultant Adviser in Transfusion, Min. of Health (later Dept of Health and Social Security), 1946-; Hon. Cons. in Transfusion and Resuscitation to War Office (later Min. of Defence), 1946-. Oliver Memorial Award for Blood Transfusion, 1955; Pres., Brit. Soc. for Haematology, 1966-67. *Publications:* scientific and other papers. *Recreations:* various. *Address:* 59 Ivinghoe Road, Bushey, Herts. *Club:* Athenæum.

MAYER, Sir Robert, CH 1973; Kt 1939; FRCM; FTCL (Hon.); Hon. GSM; Hon. RAM; Founder: Robert Mayer Concerts for Children; Transatlantic Foundation Anglo-American Scholarships; Founder and Co-Chairman, Youth and Music; Member Council: National Music Council; English Chamber Orchestra; Wind Music Society; Anglo-Israel Association; Live Music; International Music Seminar; *b* Mannheim, 1879; *s* of Emil Mayer; *m* 1919, Dorothy Moulton Piper (*d* 1974), *d* of George Piper; two *s* one *d. Educ:* Mannheim Conservatoire. Hon. LLD Leeds, 1967; Hon. DSc City University, 1968; Hon. Dr of Music, Cleveland, O, 1970. Grand Cross, Order of Merit (Germany), 1967; Ordre de la Couronne (Belgium), 1969. *Publications:* Young People in Trouble; Crescendo. *Recreations:* philanthropy, music. *Address:* (office) 22 Blomfield Street, EC2. *T:* 01-588 4714; (home) 2 Mansfield Street, W1. *TA:* Robmayer. *T:* 01-636 1204. *Club:* Athenæum.

MAYER BROWN, Prof. Howard; see Brown, Prof. H. M.

MAYERS, Norman, CMG 1952; *b* 22 May 1895; 2nd *s* of late S. A. Mayers, Bolton, and Mary Alice, *e d* of late Charles Ditchfield. *Educ:* King's Coll., London; Caius Coll., Cambridge; abroad. Served in India, 1914-19, Middlesex and Hampshire Regts (Territorials). Entered Levant Consular Service, 1922, and served in Lebanon and Saudi Arabia; Asst Oriental Sec. at the Residency, Cairo, 1927-34; Oriental Sec., Addis Ababa, 1935-37; Consul at Alexandria, 1937; Bucharest, 1938; Shiraz and Isfahan, 1941; Mersin, 1941; served at Foreign Office, 1943-44; Chargé d'Affaires at San José, Costa Rica, 1944-45; Minister to El Salvador, 1945-48; Consul-Gen., São Paulo, 1948-51; Ambassador to Ecuador, 1951-55; retired. Consul (Hon.) Palma de Mallorca, 1957-63. *Recreations:* drawing, painting. *Address:* Calle Virgen de la Bonanova, 11 Genova, Palma de Mallorca, Spain. *Clubs:* United Oxford & Cambridge University, Travellers'.

MAYHEW, Christopher Paget; *b* 12 June 1915; *e s* of late Sir Basil Mayhew, KBE; *m* 1949, Cicely Elizabeth Ludlam; two *s* two *d. Educ:* Haileybury Coll. (Scholar); Christ Church, Oxford (Open Exhibitioner, MA). Junior George Webb-Medley Scholar (Economics), 1937; Pres., Union Soc., 1937. Gunner Surrey Yeomanry RA; BEF Sept. 1939-May 1940; served with BNAF and CMF; BLA 1944 (despatches); Major, 1944. MP (Lab) S Norfolk, 1945-50; MP (Lab) Woolwich East, later Greenwich, Woolwich East, June 1951-July 1974; PPS to Lord Pres. of the Council, 1945-46; Parly Under-Sec. of State for Foreign Affairs, 1946-50; Minister of Defence (RN), 1964, resigned 1966; MP (L) Greenwich, Woolwich East, July-Sept. 1974; Liberal Party Spokesman on Defence, 1974; contested (L) Bath, Oct. 1974;

Prospective Parly Cand. (L) Bath, Nov. 1974-. Chairman: Middle East International (Publishers) Ltd; ANAF Foundn; Liberal Action Group for electoral reform; former Chm., MIND (Nat. Assoc. for Mental Health). *Publications:* Planned Investment-The Case for a National Investment Board, 1939; Socialist Economic Policy, 1946; "Those in Favour..." (television play), 1951; Dear Viewer..., 1953; Men Seeking God, 1955; Commercial Television: What is to be done?, 1959; Coexistence Plus, 1962; Britain's Role Tomorrow, 1967; Party Games, 1969; (jtly) Europe: the case for going in, 1971; Publish It Not...: the Middle East cover-up, 1975; The Disillusioned Voter's Guide to Electoral Reform, 1976. *Recreations:* music, golf. *Address:* 39 Wool Road, Wimbledon, SW20 0HN.

MAYHEW, Patrick Barnabas Burke, QC 1972; MP (C) Royal Tunbridge Wells, since Feb. 1974; *b* 11 Sept. 1929; *o surv. s* of A. G. H. Mayhew, MC; *m* 1963, Jean Elizabeth Gurney *d* of John Gurney; four *s. Educ:* Tonbridge; Balliol Coll., Oxford (MA). President, Oxford Union Society, 1952. Commnd 4th/7th Royal Dragoon Guards, national service and AER, captain. Called to Bar, Middle Temple, 1955. Contested (C) Camberwell and Dulwich, in Gen. Election, 1970. *Address:* House of Commons, SW1.

MAYHEW-SANDERS, John Reynolds, FCA; Director since 1972, and Chief Executive since 1975, John Brown and Company Ltd; *b* 25 Oct. 1931; *e s* of Jack Mayhew-Sanders, FCA; *m* 1958, Sylvia Mary, *d* of George S. Colling; three *s* one *d . Educ:* Epsom Coll.; RNC, Dartmouth; Jesus Coll., Cambridge (MA Engrg). FCA 1958. RN, 1949-54. Mayhew-Sanders & Co., Chartered Accountants, 1954-58; P-E Consulting Gp Ltd, 1958-72. Mem. Management Bd, Engineering Employers' Fedn, 1977-. *Recreations:* fishing, shooting, gardening, music. *Address:* Earlstone House, Burghclere, Hants. *T:* Burghclere 288.

MAYLE, Norman Leslie, CMG 1951; Assistant Secretary, Colonial Office, 1944-59; *b* 1899; *m* 1934, Dorothy, *d* of William Whalley; one *s.* Served European War, 1917-19 (Lieut, RFC and RAF). Appointed Colonial Office, 1917; asst principal, 1928; Private Sec. to Under-Sec. of State for the Colonies, 1932; principal, 1936; Mem. British delegation to United States bases Conference, 1941. Federal Service Comr, Aden, 1959-60; Salaries Comr, Fiji and W Pacific, 1961. *Address:* 310 Hood House, Dolphin Square, SW1V 3LX. *T:* 01-834 3800.

MAYNARD, Brian Alfred, FCA, FCMA, FBIM; Partner, Coopers & Lybrand, Chartered Accountants, since 1950, and Chairman, Coopers & Lybrand Associates, Management Consultants; *b* 27 Sept. 1917; *s* of late Alfred A. Maynard and Clarissa (*née* Shawe); *m* 1946, Rosemary Graham, *y d* of late Col E. C. Maynard; two *s . Educ:* Leighton Park Sch.; Cambridge Univ. (MA). Commnd RNVR, served Middle East and Europe, 1939-46. Member: Oxford Univ. Appts Cttee, 1959-; Cttee of Duke of Edinburgh's Award Scheme, 1961-67; Mem. Council, Inst. of Chartered Accountants in England and Wales, 1968- (Pres., 1977); Chairman: London and Dist Soc. of Chartered Accountants, 1966-67; Management Consultants Assoc., 1970; Pres., Inst. of Management Consultants, 1974; Vice-Pres., European Fedn of Management Consultants Assoc., 1972-75; Pres., OECD Mission to USA, on Computers, 1960. *Publications:* Manual of Computer Systems, 1964; numerous contribs to professional and management press in UK and overseas. *Recreations:* farming, golf, shooting. *Address:* Cowage, Hilmarton, Calne, Wilts SN11 8RZ. *T:* Hilmarton 222; 34 Smith Street, Chelsea, SW3 4EP. *T:* 01-352 6777.

MAYNARD, Edwin Francis George; HM Diplomatic Service; Deputy High Commissioner, Calcutta, since 1976; *b* 23 Feb. 1921; *s* of late Edwin Maynard, MD, FRCS, DPH, and late Nancy Frances Tully; *m* 1945, Patricia Baker; one *s* one *d ; m* 1963, Anna McGettrick; two *s. Educ:* Westminster. Served with Indian Army (4/8th Punjab Regt and General Staff) (Major, GSO II), Middle East and Burma, 1939-46. BBC French Service, 1947; Foreign Office, 1949; Consul and Second Sec., Jedda, 1950; Second, later First, Sec., Benghazi, 1952; FO 1954; Bogota, 1956; Khartoum, 1959; FO, 1960; Baghdad, 1962; Founder Dir, Diplomatic Service Language Centre, 1966; Counsellor, Aden, 1967; Counsellor, New Delhi, 1968-72; Minister (Commercial), Buenos Aires, 1972-76. *Recreations:* shooting, fishing, languages, gardening. *Address:* c/o Foreign and Commonwealth Office, SW1; 115 Cheyne Walk, SW10. *Club:* Brooks's.

MAYNARD, Brig.-Gen. Francis Herbert, CB 1937; DSO 1937; MC 1916; Squadron Leader RAFVR; *b* Ottawa, Canada, 21 Dec. 1881; *s* of M. W. Maynard, Canadian Civil Service, and Ellen, *d* of Senator Hon. R. B. Dickey, Father of Confederation;

m 1914, Ethel Bates; three *d. Educ:* RMC Kingston, Canada (Hon. DScMil 1976). Commissioned to Indian Staff Corps; joined 2nd Battalion Oxf. and Bucks in Bombay, 1902, 25th Bombay Rifles, 1903; served in European War with 5/6 Rajputana Rifles, 57th Wildes Rifles, 4th Suffolks, 4th Black Watch, 2/30th Punjabis (despatches twice, MC); 3rd Afghan War; with Wana Column, operations in Waziristan, 1936-37 (CB); Waziristan, 1937 (despatches twice, DSO); operations Waziristan, 1938 (despatches); Commanded 5/6 Rajputana Rifles; held appointment Inspector of PT India; Commander Bannu Brigade, Bannu, NWFP, India, 1934-38; ADC to the King, 1937-38; retired, 1938, awarded good service pension; Hon. Col 5/6 Rajputana Rifles, 1939; Jubilee medal; Coronation medal; served as Flt-Lieut, RAFVR, 1939-40; successively PO, Sqn Ldr and Wing Comdr, RAF, 1940-45. *Recreations:* riding, shooting, and golf. *Address:* 6 York Place Mansions, 117 Baker Street, W1.
See also M . W . Ponsonby .

MAYNARD, Geoffrey Walter; Director of Economics, Chase Manhattan Bank, since 1977 (Economic consultant, 1974); Director, Chase Manhattan Ltd, since 1977; *b* 27 Oct. 1921; *s* of Walter F. Maynard and Maisie Maynard (*née* Bristow); *m* 1949, Marie Lilian Wright; two *d. Educ:* London School of Economics. BSc(Econ); PhD. Lectr and Sen. Lectr, UC of S Wales, Cardiff, 1951-62; Economic Consultant, HM Treasury 1962-64; Economic Advr, Harvard Univ. Devel Adv. Gp in Argentina, 1964-65; University of Reading: Reader, 1966-68; Prof. of Economics, 1968-76; Vis. Prof. of Economics, 1976-. Editor, Bankers' Magazine, 1968-72; Under-Sec. (Econs), HM Treasury, 1972-74 (on leave of absence); Dep. Chief Economic Advr, HM Treasury, 1976-77; occasional consultant, IBRD, Overseas Devel Administration of FCO. *Publications:* Economic Development and the Price Level, 1962; (jtly) International Monetary Reform and Latin America, 1966; (jtly) A World of Inflation, 1976; chapters in: Development Policy: theory and practice, ed G. Papanek, 1968; Commonwealth Policy in a Global Context, ed Streeten and Corbet, 1971; Economic Analysis and the Multinational Enterprise, ed J. Dunning, 1974; Special Drawing Rights and Development Aid (paper), 1972; articles in Economic Jl, Oxford Economic Papers, Jl of Development Studies, World Development, etc. *Address:* 14 Cintra Avenue, Reading, Berks RG2 7AU. *T:* Reading 82261. *Club:* Reform.

MAYNARD, Joan; see Maynard, V. J.

MAYNARD, Air Chief Marshal Sir Nigel (Martin), KCB 1973 (CB 1971); CBE 1963; DFC 1942; AFC 1946; Commander-in-Chief, RAF Strike Command, and Commander-in-Chief, UK Air Forces, 1976-77; *b* 28 Aug. 1921; *s* of late Air Vice-Marshal F. H. M. Maynard, CB, AFC, and of Irene (*née* Pim); *m* 1946, Daphne, *d* of late G. R. P. Llewellyn, Baglan Hall, Abergavenny; one *s* one *d. Educ:* Aldenham; RAF Coll., Cranwell. Coastal Comd, UK, Mediterranean, W Africa, 1940-43; Flt-Lieut 1942; Sqdn-Ldr 1944; Mediterranean and Middle East, 1944; Transport Comd, 1945-49; comd 242 Sqdn on Berlin Air Lift; Air Staff, Air Min., 1949-51; Wing Comdr 1952; psa 1952; Staff Officer to Inspector Gen., 1953-54; Bomber Comd, 1954-57; jssc 1957; Gp Capt. 1957; SASO 25 Gp, 1958-59; CO, RAF Changi, 1960-62; Gp Capt. Ops, Transport Comd, 1963-64; Air Cdre 1965; Dir of Defence Plans (Air), 1965; Dir of Defence Plans and Chm. Defence Planning Staff, 1966; idc 1967; Air Vice-Marshal, 1968; Commandant, RAF Staff College, Bracknell, 1968-70; Commander, Far East Air Force, 1970-71; Air Marshal, 1972; Dep. C-in-C, Strike Command, 1972-73; C-in-C RAF Germany, and Comdr, 2nd Allied Tactical Air Force, 1973-76; Air Chief Marshal 1976. *Recreations:* tennis, squash, shooting. *Address:* Manor House, Piddington, Bicester, Oxon. *T:* Brill 270. *Clubs:* Naval and Military, Royal Air Force; MCC.

MAYNARD, (Vera) Joan; MP (Lab) Sheffield, Brightside, since Oct. 1974; *b* 1921. Mem. Labour Party Nat. Exec. Cttee, 1972-; Sec., Yorks Area, Nat. Union of Agricl and Allied Workers, 1956-, sponsored as MP by the Union. *Address:* House of Commons, SW1A 0AA.

MAYNARD SMITH, Prof. John, FRS 1977; Professor of Biology, University of Sussex, since 1965; *b* 6 Jan. 1920; *s* of Sidney Maynard Smith and Isobel Mary (*née* Pitman); *m* 1941; two *s* one *d. Educ:* Eton Coll.; Trinity Coll., Cambridge (BA Engrg, 1941); UCL (BSc Zool., 1951). Aircraft stressman, 1942-47; Lectr in Zool., UCL, 1952-65; first Dean of Biol Sciences, Univ. of Sussex, 1965-72. *Publications:* The Theory of Evolution, 1958, 3rd edn 1975; Mathematical Ideas in Biology, 1968; On Evolution, 1972; Models in Ecology, 1974. *Recreations:* gardening, fishing, talking. *Address:* The White House, Kingston Ridge, Lewes, East Sussex. *T:* Lewes 4659.

MAYNE, Dr Gerald Outram; Deputy Chief Medical Adviser, Department of Health and Social Security, since 1973; *b* 29 May 1919; *s* of W. J. F. Mayne, MD and Cora Mayne, ARRC; *m* 1943, Hon. Helena Stewart Keith, *d* of late Baron Keith of Avonholm, PC (Life Peer); two *s. Educ:* Leeds Grammar Sch.; Univ. of Edinburgh. MB, ChB 1942, DPH 1948, MFCM 1972. House Phys., Edinburgh Royal Infirmary, 1942-43; commnd in RAMC, 1943-47; Asst Med. Officer of Health, County of Roxburgh, 1949-50; Asst Physician, Edinburgh Royal Infirmary, 1950-58; Med. Officer and Sen. Med. Officer, DHSS, 1958-73. *Publications:* papers in BMJ, Brit. Jl Venereal Diseases, etc. *Recreations:* hill walking, gardening. *Address:* 47B Fairdene Road, Coulsdon, Surrey CR3 1RG. *T:* Downland 56944. *Clubs:* Civil Service; University Union (Edinburgh).
See also Baron Keith of Kinkel .

MAYNE, John Fraser; Assistant Under Secretary (Air Staff), Ministry of Defence, since 1976; *b* 14 Sept. 1932; *s* of John Leonard Mayne and Martha Laura (*née* Griffiths); *m* 1958, Gillian Mary (*née* Key); one *s* one *d. Educ:* Dulwich Coll.; Worcester Coll., Oxford. National Service, Royal Tank Regt, 1951-53. Air Min., 1956-64; HM Treasury, 1964-67; MoD, 1967-70; Asst Private Sec. to Sec. of State for Defence, 1968-70; Cabinet Office and Central Policy Rev. Staff, 1970-73; MoD, 1973; Private Sec. to Sec. of State for Def., 1975-76. *Recreations:* music, fell-walking, cooking, work. *Address:* 4 Lawrie Park Crescent, SE26 6HD. *T:* 01-778 4601.

MAYNE, Richard (John), PhD; writer; Head of UK Office, Commission of the European Communities, since 1973; *b* 2 April 1926; *s* of John William Mayne and Kate Hilda (*née* Angus); *m* 1st, Margot Ellingworth Lyon; 2nd, Jocelyn Mudie Ferguson; two *d. Educ:* St Paul's Sch., London; Trinity Coll., Cambridge (1st Cl. Hons Pts I and II, Hist. Tripos; MA and PhD). War service, Royal Signals, 1944-47. Styring, Sen., and Res. Scholar, and Earl of Derby Student, Trinity Coll., Cambridge, 1947-53; Leverhulme European Scholar, Rome, and Rome Corresp., New Statesman, 1953-54; Asst Tutor, Cambridge Inst. of Educn, 1954-56; Official: ECSC, Luxembourg, 1956-58; EEC, Brussels, 1958-63; Dir of Documentation Centre, Action Cttee for United States of Europe, and Personal Asst to Jean Monnet, Paris, 1963-66; Paris Corresp., Encounter, 1966-71; Vis. Prof., Univ. of Chicago, 1971; Dir of Federal Trust for Educn and Res., 1971-73. *Publications:* The Community of Europe, 1962; The Institutions of the European Community, 1968; The Recovery of Europe, 1970 (rev. edn 1973); The Europeans, 1972; (ed) The New Atlantic Challenge, 1975; (trans.) The Memoirs of Jean Monnet, 1978. *Recreations:* travel, sailing, fell-walking. *Address:* c/o Commission of the European Communities, 20 Kensington Palace Gardens, W8 4QQ. *T:* 01-727 8090. *Club:* Europe House.

MAYNE, Mrs Roger; see Jellicoe, P. A.

MAYNEORD, Prof. William Valentine, CBE 1957; FRS 1965; Emeritus Professor of Physics as Applied to Medicine, University of London; formerly Director of Physics Department, Institute of Cancer Research, Royal Cancer Hospital; *b* 14 Feb. 1902; *s* of late Walter Mayneord; *m* 1963, Audrey Morrell, Kingston-upon-Thames. *Educ:* Prince Henry's Grammar Sch., Evesham; Birmingham Univ. BSc 1921, MSc 1922, DSc 1933. Chairman: Hon. Adv. Scientific Cttee of Nat. Gallery, 1966-71 (Member, 1952-); Internat. Commn on Radiological Units, 1950-53; Med. Res. Coun. Cttee on Protection against Ionising Radiations, 1951-58; Member: Internat. Commn on Radiological Protection, 1950-58; UK Delegn to UN Scientific Cttee on the Effects of Atomic Radiation, 1956-57; MRC Cttee on Hazards to Man of Nuclear and Allied Radiations, 1955-60; President: British Inst. of Radiology, 1942-43; 1st Internat. Conf. on Medical Physics, 1965; Internat. Orgn for Medical Physics, 1965-69; Consultant: UKAEA, 1945-70; CEGB; WHO; Mem. Council and Scientific Cttee, Imp. Cancer Research Fund, 1965-73. A Trustee, National Gallery, 1966-71. Many awards and hon. memberships of British and foreign learned societies. Coronation Medal, 1953; Gold Medals: Royal Swedish Acad. of Science, 1965; Faculty of Radiologists, 1966; Univ. of Arizona, 1974. Sievert Award, Internat. Radiation Protection Assoc., 1977. Hon. LLD Aberdeen, 1969. *Publications:* Physics of X-Ray Therapy, 1929; Some Applications of Nuclear Physics to Medicine, 1950; Radiation and Health, 1964; Carcinogenesis and Radiation Risk, 1975; articles on chemical carcinogenesis, and on applications of physics to medicine and radiation hazards. *Recreation:* Italian Renaissance art and literature, particularly Dante. *Address:* 7 Downs Way Close, Tadworth, Surrey. *T:* Tadworth 2297. *Club:* Athenæum.

MAYO, 10th Earl of, *cr* 1785; **Terence Patrick Bourke;** Baron Naas, 1766; Viscount Mayo, 1781; Lieut RN (retired); Managing Director, Irish Marble Ltd, Merlin Park, Galway; *b* 26 Aug. 1929; *s* of Hon. Bryan Longley Bourke (*d* 1961) and Violet Wilmot Heathcote Bourke (*d* 1950); *S* uncle, 1962; *m* 1952, Margaret Jane Robinson Harrison; three *s*. *Educ:* St Aubyns, Rottingdean; RNC Dartmouth. Lieut, RN, 1952; Fleet Air Arm, 1952; Suez, 1956; Solo Aerobatic Displays, Farnborough, 1957; invalided, 1959. Mem., Gosport Borough Council, 1961-64; Pres., Gosport Chamber of Trade, 1962; Gov., Gosport Secondary Schs, 1963-64. Mem., Liberal Party, 1963-65; contested (L) Dorset South, 1964. *Recreations:* sailing, riding, shooting, fishing. *Heir: s* Lord Naas, *qv*. *Address:* Doon House, Maam, Co. Galway, Eire. *Clubs:* Naval; County Galway.

MAYO, Eileen; artist, author, printmaker and painter. *Educ:* Clifton High School; Slade School of Art. Exhibited Royal Academy, London Group, United Society of Artists, Festival of Britain, etc.; works acquired by British Council, British Museum, Victoria and Albert Museum, Contemporary Art Society, and public galleries in UK, USA, Australia and NZ. Designer of Australian mammals series of postage stamps, 1959-62, and Barrier Reef series, 1966; four Cook Bicentenary stamps, NZ, 1969, and other NZ stamps, 1970-75. *Publications:* The Story of Living Things; Shells and How they Live; Animals on the Farm, etc. *Recreations:* printmaking, gardening. *Address:* 140 Fisher Avenue, Christchurch, New Zealand.

MAYO, Rear-Adm. Robert William, CB 1965; CBE 1962; *b* 9 Feb. 1909; *s* of late Frank Mayo, Charminster; *m* 1942, Sheila (*d* 1974), *d* of late John Colvill, JP, of Cambeltown; one *s*. *Educ:* Weymouth Coll.; HMS Conway. Royal Naval Reserve and officer with Royal Mail Steam Packet Co., 1926-37; Master's Certificate; transferred to Royal Navy, 1937. Served War, 1939-45; Korea, 1952; Capt., 1953; Rear-Adm., 1964; retired, 1966. Hon. Sheriff Substitute of Renfrew and Argyll at Campbeltown. *Recreations:* gardening, fishing, yachting. *Address:* Bellgrove, Campbeltown, Argyll. *T:* Campbeltown 2101. *Club:* Royal Scottish Automobile.

MAYS, Colin Garth; HM Diplomatic Service; Counsellor (Commercial), Bucharest, since 1977; *b* 16 June 1931; *s* of William Albert Mays and late Sophia May Mays (*née* Pattinson); *m* 1956, Margaret Patricia, *d* of Philemon Robert Lloyd; one *s*. *Educ:* Acklam Hall Sch.; St John's Coll., Oxford (Heath Harrison Scholar). Served in Army, 1949-51; entered HM Foreign (subseq. Diplomatic) Service, 1955; FO, 1955-56; Sofia, 1956-58; Baghdad, 1958-60; FO, 1960; UK Delegn to Conf. of 18 Nation Cttee on Disarmament, Geneva, 1960; Bonn, 1960-65; FO, 1965-69; Prague, 1969-72; FCO, 1972-77; Head of Information Administration Dept, 1974-77. *Recreations:* swimming, travel. *Address:* c/o Foreign and Commonwealth Office, SW1A 2AL. *Club:* Travellers'.

MAZE, Paul Lucien, DCM 1919, MM 1916 and Bar 1917; Légion d'Honneur, Croix de Guerre; Painter; *b* Havre, 21 May 1887; *s* of Georges Henry Maze and Catherine Branchard; *m* 1st, 1921, Mrs T. A. Nelson (Margaret Balfour) (marr. diss., 1949; she *d* 1967); one *s* (one *d* decd); 2nd, 1950, Jessie Lawrie. *Educ:* Havre and England. Served War of 1914-18, unofficially with Royal Scots Greys, later with French Army on reconnaissance work (despatches thrice); served War of 1939-45 in Home Guard and as personal Staff Officer to Air Marshal Sir Arthur Harris. Rounded Cape Horn in square rigged ship; since when he has established international reputation as painter; Jubilee exhbn of over 100 paintings, Wildenstein Gallery, 1977. *Publication:* A Frenchman in Khaki, 1934. *Address:* Mill Cottage, Treyford, Midhurst, W Sussex. *T:* Harting 464.

MBEKEANI, Nyemba W.; General Manager, Malaŵi Housing Corporation, since 1973; *b* 15 June 1929; Malawi parentage; *m* 1950, Lois Mosses (*née* Chikankheni); two *s* three *d*. *Educ:* Henry Henderson Institute, Blantyre; London Sch. of Economics (Economic and Social Administration, 1963). Local Government Officer, 1945-58; political detention in Malawi and Southern Rhodesia, 1959-60; Business Executive, 1960-61; Local Govt Officer, 1963-64; Foreign Service, 1964-; High Commissioner for Malawi in London, 1964-67; Ambassador to USA and Permanent Rep. at the UN, 1967-72; Ambassador to Ethiopia, 1972-73. Farmer, company director, tea broker. *Recreations:* football, squash and flower gardening. *Address:* PO Box 414, Blantyre, Malaŵi.

M'BOW, Amadou-Mahtar; Director-General of Unesco, since Nov. 1974; *b* 20 March 1921; *s* of Fara-N'Diaye M'Bow and N'Goné Casset, Senegal; *m* 1951, Raymonde Sylvain; one *s* two *d*. *Educ:* Univ. of Paris. Teacher, Rosso Coll., Mauritania, 1951-53; Dir, Service of Fundamental and Community Educn,

Senegal, 1953-57; Prof., Ecole Normale Supérieure, Dakar, 1964-66; Minister of Educn, 1966-68; Mem. Nat. Assembly, Senegal, 1967-70; Minister of Culture, Youth and Sports 1968-70; Asst Dir-Gen. for Educn, UNESCO, 1970-74. Mem., Acad. des Sciences d'Outre-Mer, 1977; Hon Dr: Buenos Aires, 1974; Granada (Lit. and Phil.), 1975; Sherbrooke (Educn), 1975; West Indies (Laws), 1975; Open, 1976; Kliment Okhridski, Sofia, 1976; Nairobi (Lit.), 1976; Malaya (Lit.), 1977; Philippines (Laws), 1977. Comdr, Nat. Orders of Ivory Coast and Upper Volta; Comdr, Palmes académiques (France); Officer, Order of Merit (Senegal); Grand Croix de l'Ordre du Libérateur, Venezuela; Grand Croix de l'Ordre nat. M.A.C. y R. José Cuervo, Colombia; Grand Croix de l'Ordre de Stara Planina, Bulgaria; Grand Officier de l'Ordre nat., Ivory Coast; Order of Merit, Indonesia; Médaille de l'Ordre Manuel José Hurtado, Panama. *Publications:* numerous monographs, articles in educl jls, textbooks, etc. *Address:* 7 Place de Fontenoy, 75700 Paris, France. *T:* 577.16.10.

MEACHER, Michael Hugh; MP (Lab) Oldham (West) since 1970; Parliamentary Under-Secretary of State, Department of Trade, since 1976; *b* 4 Nov. 1939; *s* of George Hubert and Doris May Meacher; *m* 1962, Molly Christine (*née* Reid); two *s* two *d*. *Educ:* Berkhamsted Sch., Herts; New College, Oxford. Greats, Class 1. Sec. to Danilo Dolci Trust, 1964; Research Fellow in Social Gerontology, Univ. of Essex, 1965-66; Lecturer in Social Administration: Univ. of York, 1967-69; London Sch. of Economics, 1970. Parly Under-Secretary of State: DoI, 1974-75; DHSS, 1975-76. *Publications:* Taken for a Ride: Special Residential Homes for the Elderly Mentally Infirm, a study of separatism in social policy, 1972; Fabian pamphlets, The Care of the Old, 1969; Wealth: Labour's Achilles Heel, in Labour and Equality, ed P. Townsend and N. Bosanquet, 1972; numerous articles. *Recreations:* music, sport, reading. *Address:* 45 Cholmeley Park, N6. *T:* 01-340 5293.

MEAD, Sir Cecil, Kt 1967; Chairman, Software Sciences Ltd, since 1970; *b* 24 Dec. 1900; *s* of James Frederick Mead; *m* 1929, Anne Muriel (*d* 1977), *d* of William Tysoe Boyce; three *d*. Joined Guest, Keen & Nettlefolds Ltd, 1916. Served War of 1914-18, RNVR. The British Tabulating Machine Co. Ltd: joined Tech. Service org., 1924; Sales Man., 1939; Dep. Man. Dir, 1949-55; Man. Dir, 1955-59; ICT (formed by merger of Br. Tabulating Machine Co. Ltd and Powers-Samas Accounting Machines Ltd): Man. Dir, 1959-60, 1964; Dep. Chm., 1960-65; Chm. and Chief Exec., 1965-67. Dir, Internat. Tutor Machines, 1962. Chm., BIM, 1963-64. *Address:* 20 Wolsey Road, East Molesey, Surrey.

MEAD, Dr Margaret; American Anthropologist; Adjunct Professor of Anthropology, Columbia University; Curator Emeritus of Ethnology, American Museum of Natural History, New York (Curator, 1964-69); *b* Philadelphia, 16 Dec. 1901; *d* of Edward Sherwood Mead and Emily (*née* Fogg); *m* 1936, Gregory Bateson; one *d*. *Educ:* Doylestown High Sch. and New Hope Sch. for Girls, Pennsylvania; De Pauw Univ., Greencastle Indiana; Barnard Coll. (BA); Columbia Univ. (MA; PhD 1929). Nat. Research Council Fellow for Study of Adolescent Girls in Samoa, Associate at Bishop Museum, Honolulu, 1925; Asst Curator of Ethnology, Amer. Museum of Nat. History, 1926-42; Social Science Research Council Fellow for Study of Young Children, Admiralty Is., 1928-29, and extensive field work in New Guinea, etc., during subsequent years; Visiting Lectr in Child Study, Vassar Coll., 1939-41; Exec. Sec., Cttee on Food Habits, Nat. Research Council, 1942-45; Associate Curator of Ethnology, American Museum of Natural History, New York, 1942-64. Lectr, Teachers Coll., 1947-51; Dir Columbia Univ. Research in Contemporary Cultures, 1948-50; Adjunct Prof. of Anthropology, Columbia Univ., 1954-; Consultant, 1968, Chm. (and Prof. of Anthropology), 1969-71, Social Sciences Div., Fordham Univ. Liberal Arts Coll., Lincoln Center, NY; Pres. World Federation for Mental Health, 1956-57; Visiting Prof., Dept of Psychiatry, University of Cincinnati, 1957-; Sloan Prof., Menninger Foundation, 1959-63; Pres., Amer. Anthropological Assoc., 1960; Chairman of Board, Amer. Assoc. for Advancement of Sci., 1976; Mem., Nat. Acad. of Scis, 1975. TV film, Margaret Mead's New Guinea Journal 1928-68, 1968. Arches of Science Award, 1971; Kalinga Prize, 1971; Wilder Penfield Award, 1972. Hon. DSc of several univs. *Publications:* An Inquiry into the Question of Cultural Stability in Polynesia, 1928; Coming of Age in Samoa, 1928; Growing Up in New Guinea, 1930; The Changing Culture of an Indian Tribe, 1932; Sex and Temperament in Three Primitive Societies, 1935; Ed. Cooperation and Competition among Primitive Peoples, 1937; (with Gregory Bateson) Balinese Character: A Photographic Analysis, 1942; And Keep Your Powder Dry, 1942; Male and Female: A Study of the Sexes in a Changing World, 1949; Soviet Attitudes Toward Authority, 1951; (with Frances Macgregor)

Growth and Culture: a Photographic Study of Balinese Childhood, 1951; ed, (with Rhoda Metraux): Study of Culture at a Distance, 1953, also Themes in French Culture, 1954; (with Nicolas Calas) Primitive Heritage, 1953: ed Cultural Patterns and Technical Change, 1953; (with Martha Wolfenstein) Childhood in Contemporary Cultures, 1955; New Lives for Old: Cultural Transformation, Manus, 1928-1953, 1956; An Anthropologist at Work: Writings of Ruth Benedict, 1959; People and Places, 1959; Continuities in Cultural Evolution, 1964; Anthropologists and What They Do, 1965; (With Ken Heyman) Family, 1965; (ed, with Th. Dobzhansky and E. Tobach) Science and the Concept of Race, 1968; (with Paul Byers) The Small Conference: an innovation in communication, 1968; Culture and Commitment, 1969; (with Rhoda Metraux) A Way of Seeing, 1970; (with James Baldwin) A Rap on Race, 1971; Blackberry Winter: my earlier years (memoirs), 1972; Twentieth Century Faith, 1972; Ruth Benedict: an autobiography, 1974; (with Ken Heyman) World Enough: rethinking the future, 1975. *Address:* American Museum of Natural History, Central Park West at 79th Street, New Tork, NY 10024, USA.

MEAD, Stella; Journalist and Authoress; *d* of John Mead. *Educ:* Stewkley C of E School; Toulouse University; Deutsches Institut für Ausländer an der Universität Berlin. After two years at Toulouse, went to Paris, did journalism, and attended lectures at the Sorbonne; spent three years in Berlin, studied folklore, contributed to several German papers (children's sections), taught English, and told English stories in German schools; spent two years, 1933-35, travelling in British India, and also in various Native States; contributed to Statesman (Calcutta), Times of India, Illustrated Weekly of India; did series of broadcasts to Bengali children from Calcutta Broadcasting House in co-operation with late J. C. Bose; occasional contributor to English and American Journals. *Publications:* The Land of Legends and Heroes; The Land of Happy Hours; The Land where Stories Grow; The Land where Tales are Told; The Land where Dreams come true; Princes and Fairies; Great Stories from many Lands; The Land of Never-grow-old; Rama and Sita; The Shining Way; Morning Light; Golden Day; Under the Sun; Traveller's Joy; Magic Journeys. *Recreations:* reading, gardening. *Address:* c/o National Westminster Bank, Wembley Park, Mddx.

MEAD, William Howard Lloyd; *b* 14 April 1905; *yr s* of late F. J. Mead; *m* 1951, Mary Pattinson, *e d* of late L. Borthwick Greig, Kendrew, S Africa. *Educ:* Marlborough; London Univ. BSc (Econ.) Hons. Industrial and Commercial Law, 1925. Chartered Accountant, 1930; RNVR 1938. Served War of 1939-45: in HMS Orion, 1939-41; Flag Lt to Vice-Adm. at Dover, 1942-45. Lt-Comdr (Sp) RNVR, retired, 1950. Clerk to the Vintners' Co., 1947-69. Dir, Royal Insurance Gp (London Bd), 1967-69. *Address:* 8 Triph Court, St Mark Street, St Julians, Malta GC. *Clubs:* Royal Malta Yacht, Malta Union.

MEAD, Prof. William Richard; Professor and Head of Department of Geography, University College, London, since 1966; *b* 29 July 1915; *s* of William Mead and Catharine Sarah Stevens; unmarried. *Educ:* Aylesbury Gram. Sch.; London Sch. of Economics. DSc(Econ) London, 1968. Asst Lectr and Lectr, University of Liverpool, 1947-49; Rockefeller Fellowship, held in Finland, 1949-50; Lectr, 1950, Reader, 1953, University Coll., London. Chm., Anglo-Finnish Soc., 1966-; Pres., Inst. of British Geographers, 1971; Hon. Sec., Royal Geographical Society, 1967-77. Hon Member: Finnish Geog. Soc.; Fenno-Ugrian Soc.; Det norske Videnskaps. Akademi, 1976. Gill Memorial Award, RGS, 1951. Dr *hc,* University of Uppsala, 1966; DPhil *hc,* Univ. of Helsinki, 1969. Chevalier, Swedish Order of Vasa, 1962; Comdr, Orders of: Lion of Finland, 1963 (Chevalier, 1953); White Rose of Finland, 1976; Polar Star of Sweden, 1977. *Publications:* Farming in Finland, 1953; Economic Geography of Scandinavian States and Finland, 1958; (with Helmer Smeds) Winter in Finland, 1967; Finland (Modern Nations of the World Series), 1968; (with Wendy Hall) Scandinavia, 1972; The Scandinavian Northlands, 1973; (with Stig Jaatinen) The Aland Islands, 1974; other books on Norway, Canada and USA. *Recreations:* riding, music. *Address:* Flat 2, 1 Hornton Street, W8.

MEADE, family name of **Earl of Clanwilliam.**

MEADE, (Charles Alan) Gerald, CMG 1951; *b* 9 Aug. 1905; *s* of Charles Austin Meade; *m* 1936, Beatrix Audibert, Paris; one *s* two *d. Educ:* Leighton Park Sch., Reading; St John's Coll., Oxford. Entered Consular Service, 1927; Vice-Consul: Bangkok, 1927; Saigon, 1930; Barcelona, 1932; Chargé d'Affaires, Tegucigulpa, 1935; Consul: Savannah, Ga, 1936; Jacksonville, Florida, 1937; Second Sec., 1941, First Sec., 1943, Lima; First

Sec., Buenos Aires, 1946; Counsellor, Washington, 1948; Minister (Economic and Social) to UK Delegation to UN, 1952. Permanent UK Representative to Council of Europe with rank of Minister, and Consul Gen. at Strasbourg, 1955-59; British Ambassador to Ecuador, 1959-62; retired, 1963. *Address:* Casa de d'Alt, Capdepera, Mallorca, Spain. *T:* Capdepera 563295; 55 rue de la Fédération, 75015 Paris, France. *T:* 273 08 81.

MEADE, Sir Geoffrey; *see* Meade, Sir R. G. A.

MEADE, Gerald; *see* Meade, C. A. G.

MEADE, James Edward, CB 1947; FBA 1951; MA Oxon, MA Cantab; Hon. Dr, Universities of Basel, Bath, Essex, Hull and Oxford; Hon. Fellow: London School of Economics; Oriel College, Oxford; Hertford College, Oxford; Christ's College, Cambridge; *b* 23 June 1907; *s* of Charles Hippisley Meade and Kathleen Cotton-Stapleton; *m* 1933, Elizabeth Margaret, *d* of Alexander Cowan Wilson; one *s* three *d. Educ:* Malvern Coll. (Open Schol. in Classics); Oriel Coll., Oxford (Open Schol. in Classics); Trinity Coll., Cambridge. 1st Class Hon. Mods 1928; 1st Class Philosophy, Politics, and Economics, 1930. Fellow and Lecturer in Economics, 1930-37, and Bursar, 1934-37, Hertford Coll., Oxford; Mem. Economic Section of League of Nations, Geneva, 1938-40. Economic Asst (1940-45), and Dir (1946-47), Economic Section Cabinet Offices. Prof. of Commerce, with special reference to International Trade, London Sch. of Economics, 1947-57; Prof. of Political Economy, Cambridge, 1957-68; Nuffield Res. Fellow, 1969-74, and Fellow, Christ's Coll., Cambridge, 1957-74. Member: Coun. of Royal Economic Society, 1945-62 (Pres., 1964-66, Vice-Pres., 1966-); Council of Eugenics Soc., 1962-68 (Treasurer 1963-67). Visiting Prof., Australian National Univ., 1956. Pres. Section F, British Assoc. for the Advancement of Science, 1957; Chm. Economic Survey Mission, Mauritius, 1960. Trustee of Urwick, Orr and Partners Ltd, 1958-76. Governor: Nat. Inst. of Economic and Social Research, 1947-; LSE, 1960-74; Malvern Coll., 1972-. Chm., Cttee of Inst. for Fiscal Studies in UK Tax Structure, 1975-77. Hon. Mem., Amer. Economic Assoc., 1962; For. Hon. Mem. Amer. Acad. of Arts and Sciences, 1966. (Jtly) Nobel Prize for Economics, 1977. *Publications:* Public Works in their International Aspect, 1933; The Rate of Interest in a Progressive State, 1933; Economic Analysis and Policy, 1936; Consumers' Credits and Unemployment, 1937; League of Nations' World Economic Surveys for 1937-38 and 1938-39; The Economic Basis of a Durable Peace, 1940; (with Richard Stone) National Income and Expenditure, 1944; Planning and the Price Mechanism, 1948; The Theory of International Economic Policy, Vol. I, 1951, Vol. II, 1955; A Geometry of International Trade, 1952; Problems of Economic Union, 1953; The Theory of Customs Unions, 1955; The Control of Inflation, 1958; A Neo-Classical Theory of Economic Growth, 1960; Three Case Studies in European Economic Union, 1962 (Joint Author); Efficiency, Equality, and the Ownership of Property, 1964; Principles of Political Economy, Vol. 1, The Stationary Economy, 1965, Vol. 2, The Growing Economy, 1968, Vol. 3, The Controlled Economy, 1972, Vol. 4, The Just Economy, 1976; The Theory of Indicative Planning, 1970; The Theory of Externalities, 1973; The Intelligent Radical's Guide to Economic Policy, 1975. *Address:* 40 High Street, Little Shelford, Cambridge CB2 5ES. *T:* Shelford 2491.
See also Sir Geoffrey Wilson, Prof. R. C. Wilson, S. S. Wilson.

MEADE, Patrick John, OBE 1944; consultant in meteorology to various international organisations; Director of Services, and Deputy Director-General, Meteorological Office, 1966-73; *b* 23 Feb. 1913; *s* of late John Meade, Caterham, Surrey; *m* 1937, Winifred Jessie, *d* of Bertram Kent, Fawley, Hants; two *s* one *d. Educ:* Sir Joseph Williamson's Math. Sch., Rochester; Imperial Coll. of Science and Technology (Royal College of Science). ARCSc, BSc; Lubbock Mem. Prize in Maths, London Univ., 1933. Entered Met. Office, 1936; Southampton, 1937; Flt Lt RAFVR, Fr., 1939-40; Sqdn Leader, Sen. Met. Off., GHQ Home Forces, 1940-42; Wing Comdr (Gp Capt. 1944), Chief Met. Off., MAAF, 1943-45; Chief Met. Off., ACSEA, 1945-46; Head of Met. Office Trng Sch., 1948-52; London Airport, 1952-55; Research, 1955-60; idc 1958; Dep. Dir for Outstations Services, 1960-65. Hon. Sec., Royal Meteorological Society, 1956-61, Vice-Pres., 1961-63. *Publications:* papers in jls on aviation meteorology and on meteorological aspects of air pollution, atmospheric radioactivity and hydrology. *Recreations:* music, gardening. *Address:* Luccombe, Coronation Road, South Ascot, Berks. *T:* Ascot 23206.

MEADE, Sir (Richard) Geoffrey (Austin), KBE 1963; CMG 1953; CVO 1961; *b* 8 March 1902; *s* of late Austin Meade, MA; *m* 1929, Elizabeth Ord, MA Oxon, 2nd *d* of late G. J. Scott, JP; three *d. Educ:* Ecole Alsacienne, Paris; Balliol Coll., Oxford. BA

1925. Entered Consular Service, 1925; served at Tangier, 1927, Salonica, 1929, Aleppo, 1930, Athens, 1931, Salonica, 1933, Tangier, 1935, Valencia, 1939, Crete, 1940, FO, 1941, Dakar, 1943, Tetuan, 1943, Cassablanca, 1945; Istanbul, 1947; idc, 1950; Marseilles, 1951; Tangier, 1956; Düsseldorf, 1957; Milan, 1958-62. Retired, 1962. *Address:* Baker's Close, 104 Lower Radley, Abingdon, Oxon OX14 3BA. *T:* Abingdon 21327.

MEADE-KING, Charles Martin, MA; Headmaster, Plymouth College, 1955-73, retired; *b* 17 Aug. 1913; *s* of late G. C. Meade-King, solicitor, Bristol; *m* 1948, Mary (*née* Frazer); one *s* one *d*. *Educ:* Clifton Coll.; Exeter Coll., Oxford (Stapeldon Scholar). Asst Master, King's Sch., Worcester, 1935-38; Asst Master, Mill Hill Sch., 1938-40. Intelligence Corps, 1940-45. Housemaster, Mill Hill Sch., 1945-55. *Recreations:* history, arts, games. *Address:* Whistledown, Yelverton, near Plymouth. *T:* Yelverton 2237.

MEADEN, Rt. Rev. John Alfred, DD, MA, LTh. *Educ:* Queen's Coll., Newfoundland; University Coll., Durham, England. LTh Durham, 1916, BA 1917, MA 1935. Deacon, 1917, Nova Scotia for Newfoundland; Priest, 1918, Newfoundland. Incumbent of White Bay, 1917-21; Rector of Burin, 1921-29; Pouch Cove, 1929-34; Sec.-treasurer of Executive Cttee of Newfoundland Diocesan Synod, 1934-47; Examining Chaplain to the Bishop of Newfoundland, 1943-47; Canon of St John Baptist's Cathedral, St John's, Newfoundland, 1938-57. Principal of Queen's Coll., St John's, 1947-57. Bishop of Newfoundland, 1956-65. Hon. DCL, Bishop's Univ., Lennoxville, 1957; Hon. DD, Trinity Coll., Toronto, 1959; Hon. LLD, Memorial Univ. of Nfld, 1961. *Address:* Saint Luke's Homes, Topsail Road, St John's, Newfoundland, Canada.

MEADOWS, Bernard William; sculptor; Professor of Sculpture, Royal College of Art, since 1960; *b* Norwich, 19 Feb. 1915; *s* of W. A. F. and E. M. Meadows; *m* 1939, Marjorie Winifred Payne; two *d.* *Educ:* City of Norwich Sch. Studied at Norwich Sch. of Art, 1934-36; worked as Asst to Henry Moore, 1936-40; studied at Royal College of Art, 1938-40 and 1946-48. Served with RAF, 1941-46. Commissioned by Arts Council to produce a work for Festival of Britain, 1951. Rep. (Brit. Pavilion) in Exhib. of Recent Sculpture, Venice Biennale, 1952; in Exhib., Kassel, Germany, 1959, etc. Exhibited in International Exhibitions of Sculpture (Open Air): Battersea Park, 1951, 1960; Musée Rodin, Paris, 1956; Holland Park, 1957; in 4th International Biennial, São Paulo, Brazil, 1957; also in Exhibns (Open Air) in Belgium and Holland, 1953-. *One man exhibitions:* Gimpel Fils, London, 1957, 1959, 1963, 1965, 1967; Paul Rosenberg, New York, 1959, 1962, 1967. *Works in Collections:* Tate Gallery; Victoria and Albert Museum; Arts Council; British Council; Museum of Modern Art, New York; also in public collections in N and S America, Israel, Australia, and in Europe. Mem., Royal Fine Art Commn, 1971-76. Awarded Italian State Scholarship, 1956. *Publication:* 34 etchings and box (for Molloy by Samuel Beckett), 1967. *Address:* 34 Belsize Grove, NW3. *T:* 01-722 0772.

MEADOWS, Robert; company director, motor trade; Lord Mayor of Liverpool, May 1972-May 1973; *b* 28 June 1902; *m* 1st, 1926, Ivy L. Jenkinson (*d* 1963); three *s*; 2nd, 1967, Nora E. Bullen. *Educ:* locally and Bootle Technical Coll. Engineering, 1917-21. Liverpool: City Councillor, Fairfield Ward, 1945; City Alderman, Princes Park Ward, 1961-74. *Recreations:* motor vehicle development, property improvement, landscape gardening. *Address:* La Casita, Acrefield Road, Woolton, Liverpool L25 5JP. *T:* 051-428 1032.

MEADOWS, Swithin Pinder, MD, BSc, FRCP; Consulting Physician: Westminster Hospital; National Hospital, Queen Square; Moorfields Eye Hospital; Neurologist, British European Airways; *b* 18 April 1902; *er s* of late Thomas and late Sophia Florence Meadows; *m* 1934, Doris Steward Noble; two *s* two *d.* *Educ:* Wigan Grammar Sch.; University of Liverpool; St Thomas' Hosp. Kanthack Medal in Pathology; Owen T. Williams Prize; House Physician and House Surgeon, Liverpool Royal Infirmary; House Physician, Royal Liverpool Children's Hospital; Medical Registrar and Tutor, St Thomas' Hosp.; RMO National Hosp., Queen Square; Medical First Asst, London Hosp.; Examiner in Neurology and Medicine, University of London; Hosp. Visitor, King Edward's Hosp. Fund for London; Mem. of Assoc. of Physicians and Assoc. of British Neurologists; Hon. Mem., Aust. Assoc. of Neurologists; Hunterian Prof., Royal College of Surgeons, 1952; Pres., Section of Neurology, Royal Society of Medicine, 1965-66; Visiting Prof., University of California, San Francisco, 1954; Doyne Meml Lectr, Oxford Ophthalmological Congress, 1969. Hon. Neurologist, Newspaper Press Fund. *Publications:* contributions to medical literature. *Recreations:* walking, music, country life. *Address:* 142 Harley Street, W1. *T:* 01-935 1802.

MEAGHER, Sir Thomas, Kt 1947; MB, BS; JP; medical practitioner, Victoria Park, since 1927; *b* Menzies, W Australia, 26 March 1902; *s* of Philip Francis and Ann Agnes Meagher, Bendigo, Victoria, Australia; *m* 1927, Marguerite Winifred Hough (*d* 1952); four *s* two *d*; *m* 1953, Doris Ita Walsh. *Educ:* Christian Brothers Coll., Perth; University of Western Australia; Newman Coll.; Melbourne Univ. Graduated 1925; House Surg., Royal Perth Hospital and Children's Hosp., 1925-26; in practice Victoria Park since 1927; Councillor, City of Perth, 1937-38; Lord Mayor, City of Perth, 1939-45; Past-Pres. RAC, W Australia; Past-Pres. Australian Automobile Assoc.; Pres. and Life Mem., Amateur Athletic Assoc., WA; Olympic Fed. Brit. Empire and Commonwealth Games Assoc., Pentathlon Assoc.; Pres. Industrial Fund for Advancement of Science Education in Schools; Pres. King's Park Board; KStJ; Mem. of Chapter, Commandery of St John of Jerusalem and of Ambulance Assoc. of WA; Past Pres. Royal Commonwealth Society; Chm. Museum Bd of WA; Trustee and Past Pres. Coun., Justices' Assoc. of WA; Pres. Nat. Safety Council; Vice-Patron Nat. Rose Soc.; Trustee Police Boys' Clubs; Life Member, Old Aquinians, Ex-Naval-Men's Assoc., Greek Ex-Service Men's Assoc.; Hon. Mem. Rotary Club, Perth. *Recreations:* fishing, gardening, sport. *Address:* Boolah Mia, 787 Albany Highway, East Victoria Park, WA 6101, Australia; Saranna, The Esplanade, Rockingham, Qld.

MEANEY, Patrick Michael; Managing Director, Thomas Tilling Ltd, since 1973; *b* 6 May 1925; *m* Mary June Kearney; one *s.* *Educ:* Wimbledon College. HM Forces, 1941-47. Joined Thomas Tilling Ltd, 1961. *Recreations:* Rugby football, music, travel, motoring. *Address:* Stambourne House, Totteridge Village, N20 8JP. *T:* 01-445 9576. *Clubs:* Harlequins, British Sportsman's.

MEANY, George; President, American Federation of Labor and Congress of Industrial Organizations, since 1955; *b* 16 Aug. 1894; *s* of Michael Meany and Anne Cullen; *m* 1919, Eugenie A. McMahon; three *d.* *Educ:* American public schs. Mem., Journeymen Plumbers Union, 1915; Business Agent, Local 463 of Plumbers Union, 1922; Pres. NY State Federation of Labor, 1934-39; Sec.-Treasurer, American Federation of Labor, 1940-52, Pres., 1952-55. Chm. Mem., or Adviser numerous bds and cttees. Laetare Medallist, University of Notre Dame, Ind., 1955; Hon. Dr of Laws of several American Univs; Rerum Novarum Award, St Peter's Coll., Jersey City, NJ, 1956; Presidential Medal of Freedom, US, 1963. Holds, also, foreign decorations. *Recreations:* golf, painting. *Address:* AFL-CIO Building, 815 Sixteenth Street, NW, Washington, DC 20006, USA. *T:* 637-5213. *Clubs:* Columbia Country, University, International (Washington, DC).

MEARS, Lady; see Tempest, Margaret M.

MEARS, Brig. Gerald Grimwood, CBE 1945; DSO 1944; MC 1918; *b* 15 Oct. 1896; *o s* of late Sir Grimwood Mears, KCIE; *m* 1925, Margaret (MBE 1946), *y d* of late Maj.-Gen. Sir Gerald Giffard; two *d.* *Educ:* St Paul's Sch. RA temp. commission Sept. 1914, regular Oct. 1915; BEF France, 1915-19 (1914-15 Star, Gen. Service and Victory medals, MC and Bar); India Frontier, 1919; ADC to Viceroy, 1921-22; Razmak Field Force, 1923; Staff Coll., Quetta, 1928-29; GSO 3 Sch. of Army Co-operation, Old Sarum, 1931-33; Staff Officer RA Southern Command, 1933-35; GSO 2 War Office, 1936-39; GSO 2 Allied Military Cttee, 1939-40; GSO 1 War Office and Home Forces, 1940-41; BGS Northern Command, 1942-43; CRA 3rd British Infantry Div., 1943-45 (DSO, CBE); CCRA and Chief of Staff, 1st British Corps, BRA, ALFSEA, 1946; BRA Southern Command, 1947; Commandant, Sch. of Artillery, 1947-49; ADC to the King, 1947-49; retd 1949. *Recreations:* yachting, fly-fishing, shooting. *Address:* Driftway, Steeple Langford, Salisbury, Wilts. *T:* Stapleford 461.

MEATH, 14th Earl of, *cr* 1627; **Anthony Windham Normand Brabazon;** Baron Ardee, Ireland, 1616; Baron Chaworth, of Eaton Hall, Co. Hereford, UK, 1831; late Major Grenadier Guards; *b* 3 Nov. 1910; *o s* of 13th Earl of Meath, CB, CBE and Lady Aileen Wyndham-Quin (*d* 1962), *d* of 4th Earl of Dunraven; *S* father 1949; *m* 1940, Elizabeth Mary, *d* of late Capt. Geoffrey Bowlby, Royal Horse Guards, and of Hon. Mrs Geoffrey Bowlby, *qv*; two *s* two *d.* *Educ:* Eton; RMC Sandhurst. Joined Grenadier Guards, 1930. ADC to Governor of Bengal, 1936; Capt., 1938; served War of 1939-45, Grenadier Guards (wounded); Major, 1941; retired, 1946. *Heir:* *s* Lord Ardee, *qv. Address:* Kilruddery, Bray, Co. Wicklow, Ireland.

MEATH, Bishop of, (RC), since 1968; **Most Rev. John McCormack;** *b* 25 March 1921; *s* of Peter McCormack and Bridget Mulvany. *Educ:* St Finian's Coll., Mullingar; Maynooth

Coll.; Lateran Univ., Rome. Priest, 1946. Ministered: Multyfarnham, 1950-52; St Loman's Hosp., 1952-58; Mullingar, 1958-68; Diocesan Sec., 1952-68. *Address:* Bishop's House, Dublin Road, Mullingar, Co. Westmeath, Ireland. *T:* Mullingar 8841.

MEATH and KILDARE, Bishop of, since 1976; **Most Rev. Donald Arthur Richard Caird;** *b Dublin, 11 Dec. 1925; s* of George Robert Caird and Emily Florence Dreaper, Dublin; *m* 1963, Nancy Ballantyne, *d* of Prof. William Sharpe, MD, and Gwendolyn Hind, New York, USA; one *s* two *d*. *Educ:* Wesley Coll., Dublin, 1935-44; Trinity Coll., Dublin Univ., 1944-50. Sen. Exhibn, TCD, 1946; elected Schol. of the House, TCD, 1948; 1st cl. Moderatorship in Mental and Moral Science, 1949; Prizeman in Hebrew and Irish Language, 1946 and 1947; Lilian Mary Luce Memorial Prize for Philosophy, 1947; BA 1949; MA and BD 1955; HDipEd 1959. Curate Asst, St Mark's. Dundela, Belfast, 1950-53; Chaplain and Asst Master, Portora Royal Sch., Enniskillen, 1953-57; Lectr in Philosophy, University Coll. of St David's, Lampeter, 1957; Rector, Rathmichael Parish, Shankill, Co. Dublin, 1960-69; Asst Master, St Columba's Coll., Rathfarnham, Co. Dublin, 1960-67; Dept Lectr in Philosophy, Trinity Coll., Dublin, 1962-63; Lectr in the Philosophy of Religion, Divinity Hostel, Dublin, 1964-70; Dean of Ossory, 1969-70; Bishop of Limerick, Ardfert and Aghadoe, 1970-76. Fellow of St Columba's Coll., Dublin, 1971. Mem., Bord na Gaeilge, 1974. *Publication:* The Predicament of Natural Theology since the criticism of Kant, in Directions, 1970 (Dublin). *Recreations:* swimming, tennis. *Address:* Ivy House, Leixlip, Co. Kildare, Ireland.

MEDAWAR, Sir Peter (Brian), CH 1972; Kt 1965; CBE 1958; FRS 1949; MA, DSc (Oxford); Member, Scientific Staff, Medical Research Council, since 1962; *b* 28 Feb. 1915; *s* of Nicholas Medawar and Edith Muriel Dowling; *m* 1937, Jean Shinglewood, *d* of Dr C. H. S. Taylor; two *s* two *d*. *Educ:* Marlborough Coll.; Magdalen Coll., Oxford. Christopher Welch Scholar and Senior Demy of Magdalen Coll., 1935; Fellow of Magdalen Coll., 1938-44, 1946-47; Fellow of St John's Coll., 1944; Mason Prof. of Zoology, Birmingham Univ., 1947-51; Jodrell Prof. of Zoology and Comparative Anatomy, University Coll., London, 1951-62; Dir, Nat. Inst. for Medical Research, Mill Hill, 1962-71, Dir Emeritus, 1975. Croonian Lectr, Royal Society, 1958; Reith Lecturer, 1959; Dunham Lectr, Harvard Med. Sch., 1959; Romanes Lectr, 1968; Prof. of Experimental Medicine, Royal Institution, 1977-. Pres., Brit. Assoc. for the Advancement of Science, 1968-69; Member: Agricultural Research Council, 1952-62; University Grants Cttee, 1955-59; Royal Commn on Med. Educn, 1965-68; Cttee of Management, Inst. of Cancer Research; Bd of Scientific Consultants, Meml Sloan-Kettering Cancer Centre; Inst. of Cellular Pathology, Brussels. Foreign Member: New York Acad. of Sciences, 1957; Amer. Acad. Arts and Sciences, 1959; Amer. Philosophical Soc., 1961; National Acad. of Sciences, 1965; Indian Acad. of Sciences, 1967. Fellow of St Catherine's Coll., 1960; Hon. Fellow: Magdalen Coll., 1961; University Coll., London, 1971; London Sch. of Economics, 1975; American Coll. of Physicians, 1964; Royal College Physicians and Surgeons, Canada, 1966; RCS, 1967; RSE, 1965; RCPE, 1966; RCPath, 1971; RCP, 1974; Prof. at Large, Cornell Univ., 1965; Royal Medal of Royal Society, 1959; Copley Medal, 1969. Nobel Prize for Medicine, 1960. Hon. ScD Cambridge; Hon. D de l'Univ.: Liège; Brussels; Hon. DSc: Aston, Birmingham, Hull, Glasgow, Brazil, Alberta, Dundee, Dalhousie, British Columbia, Chicago, Exeter, Southampton. *Publications:* The Uniqueness of the Individual, 1957; The Future of Man, 1960; The Art of the Soluble, 1967; Induction and Intuition, 1969; The Hope of Progress, 1972; Life Science, 1977. *Address:* Clinical Research Centre, Watford Road, Harrow, Mddx HA1 3UJ; 25 Downshire Hill, NW3.
See also Sir Ian McAdam.

MEDD, Patrick William, OBE 1962; QC 1973; a Recorder of the Crown Court, since 1972 (Recorder of Abingdon, 1964-71); *b* 26 May 1919; *s* of E. N. Medd; *m* 1st, 1945, Jeananne Spence Powell (marr. diss.); three *d*; 2nd, 1971, Elizabeth Spink D'Albuquerque. *Educ:* Uppingham Sch.; Selwyn Coll., Cambridge. Served in Army, 1940-46, S Staffs Regt and E African Artillery, Major. Called to Bar, Middle Temple, 1947, Bencher 1969. Dep. Chm., Shropshire QS, 1967-71; Jun. Counsel to Comrs of Inland Revenue, 1968-73. *Publication:* Romilly, 1968. *Recreation:* gardening. *Address:* 2 Garden Court, Temple, EC4. *T:* 01-353 4621.

MEDLEY, Robert; Painter and Theatrical Designer; Chairman, Faculty of Painting, British School at Rome, 1966-77; *b* 19 Dec. 1905; *s* of late C. D. Medley, and A. G. Owen. *Educ:* Gresham's Sch., Holt. Studied art in London and Paris; Art Dir of the Group Theatre and designed the settings and costumes for plays by T. S. Eliot, W. H. Auden, Christopher Isherwood, Louis Macneice, and Verdi's Othello, Sadler's Wells Theatre, Coppelia, Sadler's Wells Theatre Ballet; exhibited in London and New York World's Fair; pictures bought by: Tate Gallery; V. & A. (collection of drawings); Walker Art Gallery, Liverpool; City Art Gallery, Birmingham, and other provincial galleries; National Gallery of Canada, Ontario; Contemporary Art Society; Arts Council for Festival of Britain, 1951. Official War Artist, 1940. Retrospective Exhibition, Whitechapel Art Gallery, 1963. Diocletian in Sebastiane (film), 1976. *Address:* 10 Gledhow Gardens, SW5 0AY.

MEDLICOTT, Prof. William Norton, DLit, MA (London); FRHistS; Stevenson Professor of International History, University of London, 1953-67; Professor Emeritus, 1967; Senior Editor of Documents on British Foreign Policy, 1919-39, since 1965; *b* 11 May 1900; *s* of William Norton Medlicott and Margaret Louisa McMillan; *m* 1936, Dr Dorothy Kathleen Coveney. *Educ:* Aske's Haberdashers' Sch., Hatcham; University College, London; Institute of Historical Research. Gladstone Prizeman, Hester Rothschild Prizeman, UCL; Lindley Student, Univ. of London; Lecturer, University Coll., Swansea, 1926-45; Visiting Prof., Univ. of Texas, USA, 1931-32; Principal, Board of Trade, 1941-42; official historian, Ministry of Economic Warfare, 1942-58; Prof. of History, University Coll. of the South West, 1945-53; Vice-Principal, 1953. Creighton Lectr, Univ. of London, 1968. Fellow of UCL. Hon. Fellow LSE. Travel and research in US, 1946, 1952, and 1957; Hon. Sec. Historical Association, 1943-46, Pres., 1952-55; Chm. editorial board, International Affairs, 1954-62; Mem. Institute for Advanced Studies, Princeton, 1952, 1957; Chm. British Co-ordinating Cttee for Internat. Studies. Hon. DLitt Wales, 1970; Hon. LittD Leeds, 1977. *Publications:* The Congress of Berlin and After, 1938, new edn 1963; British Foreign Policy since Versailles, 1940, new edn, 1968; The Economic Blockade, vol. i, 1952, vol. ii, 1959; Bismarck, Gladstone, and the Concert of Europe, 1956; The Coming of War in 1939, 1963; Bismarck and Modern Germany, 1965; Contemporary England, 1914-1964, 1967, revd edn 1976; Britain and Germany: The Search for Agreement, 1930-1937, 1969; (with D. K. Coveney) Bismarck and Europe, 1971; (with D. K. Coveney) The Lion's Tail, 1971; numerous articles and reviews. *Address:* 2 Cartref, Ellesmere Road, Weybridge, Surrey. *T:* Weybridge 43842. *Club:* Athenæum.

MEDLYCOTT, Sir (James) Christopher, 8th Bt, *cr* 1808; *b* 17 April 1907; *e s* of Sir Hubert Mervyn Medlycott, 7th Bt, and Nellie Adah (*d* 1964), *e d* of late Hector Edmond Monro, Edmondsham, Dorset; *S* father, 1964. *Educ:* Harrow; Magdalene Coll., Cambridge. BA 1930. *Heir: nephew* Mervyn Tregonwell Medlycott, *b* 20 Feb. 1947. *Address:* The Yard House, Milborne Port, near Sherborne, Dorset. *T:* Milborne Port 312.

MEDWAY, Lord; Gathorne Gathorne-Hardy; Editor of the Ibis, since 1973; *b* 20 June 1933; *er s* of 4th Earl of Cranbrook, *qv*; *m* 1967, Caroline, *o d* of Col Ralph G. E. Jarvis, Doddington Hall, Lincoln; two *s* one *d*. *Educ:* Eton; Corpus Christi Coll., Cambridge (MA); University of Birmingham (PhD). Asst, Sarawak Museum, 1956-58; Fellow, Yayasan Siswa Lokantara (Indonesia), 1960-61; Sr Lectr in Zoology, Univ. of Malaya, 1961-70. Skinner and Freeman of the City of London. FLS; FZS; MBOU. OStJ. *Publications:* Mammals of Borneo, 1965; Mammals of Malaya, 1969; (with D. R. Wells) Birds of the Malay Peninsula, 1976. *Heir: s* Hon. John Jason Gathorne-Hardy, *b* 26 Oct. 1968. *Address:* c/o National Westminster Bank, St James's Square, SW1Y 4JX.

MEDWIN, Robert Joseph G.; *see* Gardner-Medwin.

MEE, Mrs Ellen Catherine, CBE 1956; MA; *d* of William Henry and Rebecca Catherine Oakden; *m* 1945, Frederick George Mee, MC, BA (*d* 1971). *Educ:* Birmingham Univ. (MA, Arts Fellowship); Somerville Coll., Oxford (Research). Lecturer in English, Goldsmiths' Coll., London Univ., 1921-29; Exchange Lecturer in English, USA, 1924-25; HM Inspector of Schools, 1929; Staff Inspector (Training of Teachers), 1945; Chief Inspector of Schs, Min. of Education, 1952-58. Consultant, Schs Broadcasting Council, BBC, 1962-72. Mem. Advisory Cttee on Educn in the Colonies, Colonial Office, 1938-52. Asst Sec. McNair Cttee on Training of Teachers, 1942-44 (Min. of Education). *Address:* 112 Murray Avenue, Bromley, Kent. *T:* 01-460 0031.

MEECH, Sir John Valentine, KCVO 1967 (CVO 1963); JP (NZ); retired Civil Servant, New Zealand Government; *b* 25 Jan. 1907; *s* of Edwin Arthur Wilton Meech and Jane Meech; *m* 1938, Rachel Crease Anderson; no *c*. *Educ:* Island Bay and Eastern

Hutt Schs; Hutt Valley High Sch.; Public Service Coll. Sec. for Internal Affairs, Sec. of Civil Defence and Clerk of the Writs, NZ Govt, 1959-67; Mem. various Bds and Cttees, 1959-67; New Zealand Sec. to the Queen, 1962-63; Dir of Royal Visits, Heads of State etc., 1959-67. JP 1949-; Mem. Council of Duke of Edinburgh's Award in New Zealand, 1963-69. Chm. of Bd of Trustees, Nat. Sch. of Ballet, 1969-; Member: Music Advisory Cttee, Queen Elizabeth II Arts Council, 1967-; Electricity Distribution Commn, 1968- (Dep. Chm); Life Mem., NZ Inst. of Town Clerks and Municipal Treasurers. *Recreations:* golf, racing, gardening, reading, arts. *Address:* 205 Barnard Street, Highland Park, Wellington 1, NZ. *T:* 47-280. *Clubs:* Civil Service, Miramar Golf (Wellington).

MEEK, Charles Innes, CMG 1961; Chief Executive, since 1962, Chairman, since 1973, White Fish Authority; *b* 27 June 1920; *er s* of late Dr C. K. Meek; *m* 1947, Nona Corry Hurford; two *s* one *d. Educ:* King's Sch., Canterbury; Magdalen Coll., Oxford (MA). Demyship, Magdalen Coll., Oxford, 1939. Served in Army, 1940-41; District Officer, Tanganyika, 1941; Principal Asst Sec., Tanganyika, 1958; Permanent Sec., Chief Secretary's Office, 1959; Permanent Sec. to Prime Minister, Sec. to Cabinet, 1960; Government Dir, Williamson Diamonds; Head of the Civil Service, Tanganyika, 1961-62, retd. FRSA 1969. *Publications:* occasional articles in Journal of African Administration, etc. *Address:* 30 Heriot Row, Edinburgh EH3 6EN. *T:* 031-226 2777. *Club:* Royal Commonwealth Society.

MEEK, Prof. John Millar, CBE 1975; DEng; FInstP; FIEE; David Jardine Professor of Electrical Engineering, University of Liverpool, since 1946; Public Orator, 1973-76, and Pro-Vice-Chancellor, 1974-77, University of Liverpool; *b* Wallasey, 21 Dec. 1912; *s* of Alexander Meek and Edith Montgomery; *m* 1942, Marjorie, *d* of Bernard Ingleby; two *d. Educ:* Monkton Combe Sch.; University of Liverpool. College Apprentice, Metropolitan-Vickers Electrical Co. Ltd, 1934-36; Research Engineer, Metropolitan-Vickers Electrical Co. Ltd, 1936-38, 1940-46. Commonwealth Fund Research Fellow, Physics Dept, University of California, Berkeley, 1938-40. Mem. of Council, IEE, 1945-48, 1960-63 (Vice-Pres. 1964-68, Pres., 1968-69), Faraday Medal, 1975. Mem., IBA (formerly ITA), 1969-74. Hon. DSc Salford, 1971. *Publications:* The Mechanism of the Electric Spark (with L. B. Loeb), 1941; Electrical Breakdown of Gases (with J. D. Craggs), 1953; High Voltage Laboratory Technique (with J. D. Craggs), 1954; papers in various scientific journals concerning research on electrical discharges in gases. *Recreations:* golf, gardening, theatre. *Address:* Hendred, 13 Abbey Road, West Kirby, Merseyside. *T:* 051-625 5850. *Club:* Royal Commonwealth Society.

MEERE, Sir Frank, (Francis Anthony), Kt 1960; CBE 1955; FAIM; Comptroller General of Customs, Canberra, 1952-60; *b* 24 July 1895; *s* of Philip Francis and Harriet Charlotte Meere of Daylesford, Vic.; *m* 1st, 1920, Helena Agnes (decd), *d* of late Wm G. Doyle; two *s*; 2nd, 1970, Mary Irene Higgins. *Educ:* Christian Brothers Coll., East St Kilda, Vic. Joined Australian Commonwealth Public Service, 1913; Deputy Dir, Division of Import Procurement, Brisbane, 1942-45; Dir, Division of Import Procurement, Sydney, 1945-47; Asst Comptroller General of Customs, Canberra, 1947-52. *Recreation:* gardening. *Address:* 3 Meehan Gardens, Canberra, ACT 2603, Australia. *Club:* Commonwealth (Canberra).

MEERES, Norman Victor, CB 1963; Under-Secretary, Ministry of Defence, 1971-73, retired; *b* 1 Feb. 1913; *m* 1938, Elizabeth Powys Fowler; two *s* one *d. Educ:* Sloane Sch., Chelsea; Magdalene Coll., Cambridge. Asst Principal, Air Ministry, 1935; Principal, 1940, Asst Sec., 1944, Ministry of Aircraft Prod.; Asst Sec., Min. of Supply, 1946; Under Secretary: Min. of Supply, 1956; Min. of Aviation, 1959-67; seconded to Dipl. Service in Australia, with title Minister (Defence Research and Civil Aviation), 1965-68; Under-Sec., Min. of Technology, 1969-70. ARCM (piano teaching), 1974. *Recreations:* music, lawn tennis. *Address:* 89 Grove Way, Esher, Surrey. *T:* 01-398 1639.

MEGARRY, Hon. Sir Robert (Edgar), Kt 1967; FBA 1970; **Hon. Mr Justice Megarry;** Judge of the High Court of Justice, Chancery Division, since 1967, The Vice-Chancellor, since 1976; *b* 1 June 1910; *e s* of late Robert Lindsay Megarry, OBE, MA, LLB, Belfast, and of late Irene, *d* of Maj.-Gen. E. G. Clark; *m* 1936, Iris, *e d* of late Elias Davies, Neath, Glam; three *d. Educ:* Lancing Coll.; Trinity Hall, Cambridge (Hon. Fellow, 1973). MA, LLD (Cantab); Solicitor, 1935-41; taught for Bar and Solicitors' exams, 1935-39; Mem., Faculty of Law, Cambridge Univ., 1939-40; Certificate of Honour, and called to Bar, Lincoln's Inn, 1944, in practice, 1946-67; QC 1956-67; Bencher, Lincoln's Inn, 1962. Principal, 1940-44, and Asst Sec., 1944-46, Min. of Supply; Book Review Editor and Asst Ed., Law

Quarterly Review, 1944-67; Dir of Law Society's Refresher Courses, 1944-47; Sub-Lector, Trinity Coll., Cambridge, 1945-46; Asst Reader, 1946-51, Reader, 1951-67, Hon. Reader, 1967-in Equity in the Inns of Court (Council of Legal Educn); Member: Gen. Council of the Bar, 1948-52; Lord Chancellor's Law Reform Cttee, 1952-73; Senate of the Four Inns of Court, 1966-70, and several other legal cttees and councils; Consultant to BBC for Law in Action series, 1953-66; Chairman: Notting Hill Housing Trust, 1967-68; Bd of Studies, and Vice-Chm., Council of Legal Educn, 1969-71; Friends of Lancing Chapel, 1969-; Incorporated Council of Law Reporting, 1972-; President: Soc. of Public Teachers of Law, 1965-66; Lancing Club, 1974-; Selden Soc., 1976-. Visiting Professor: New York Univ. Sch. of Law, 1960-61; Osgoode Hall Law Sch., Toronto, 1964. Hon. LLD (Hull), 1963. Hon. Life Mem., Canadian Bar Assoc., 1971. *Publications:* The Rent Acts, 1939, 10th edn 1967; A Manual of the Law of Real Property, 1946, 5th edn (ed P. V. Baker QC), 1975; Lectures on the Town and Country Planning Act, 1947, 1949; Miscellany-at-Law, 1955; (with Prof. H. W. R. Wade QC) The Law of Real Property, 1957, 4th edn 1975; Lawyer and Litigant in England (Hamlyn Lectures, 1962); Arabinesque-at-Law, 1969; Inns Ancient and Modern, 1972; A Second Miscellany-at-Law, 1973; Editor, Snell's Equity, 23rd edn 1947, 27th edn (with P. V. Baker, QC), 1973; contrib. to legal periodicals. *Recreations:* heterogeneous. *Address:* The Royal Courts of Justice, Strand, WC2A 2LL. *T:* 01-405 7641; 5 Stone Buildings, Lincoln's Inn, WC2A 3XT. *T:* 01-242 8607.

MEGAW, Arthur Hubert Stanley, CBE 1951; MA Cantab; FSA; *b* Dublin, 1910; *s* of late Arthur Stanley Megaw; *m* 1937, Elene Elektra, *d* of late Helias Mangoletsi, Koritsa, Albania; no *c. Educ:* Campbell Coll., Belfast; Peterhouse, Cambridge. Walston Student (University of Cambridge), 1931. Macmillan Student, British School of Archæology at Athens, 1932-33, Asst Dir, 1935-36; Dir of Antiquities, Cyprus, 1936-60; Field Dir, Byzantine Institute, Istanbul, 1961-62; Dir, British Sch. of Archæology, Athens, 1962-68. CStJ, 1967. *Publications:* (with A. J. B. Wace) Hermopolis Magna-Ashmunein, Alexandria, 1959; various papers in archæological journals. *Recreation:* travel. *Address:* 27 Perrin's Walk, NW3; 4-6 Anapiron Polemou, Athens 140, Greece.

MEGAW, Rt. Hon. Sir John, PC 1969; Kt 1961; CBE 1956; TD 1951; **Rt. Hon. Lord Justice Megaw;** a Lord Justice of Appeal, since 1969; *b* 16 Sept. 1909; 2nd *s* of late Hon. Mr Justice Megaw, Belfast; *m* 1938, Eleanor Grace Chapman; one *s* two *d. Educ:* Royal Academical Institution, Belfast; St John's Coll., Cambridge Univ. (open schol. in classics; Hon. Fellow, 1967); Harvard Univ. Law Sch. (Choate Fellowship). Served War, 1939-45; Col, RA. Barrister-at-Law, Gray's Inn, 1934 (Certificate of Honour, Bar Final exam.); Bencher, 1958; Treasurer, 1976; QC 1953; QC (N Ire.) 1954; Recorder of Middlesbrough, 1957-61; Judge of the High Court of Justice, Queen's Bench Div., 1961-69; Pres., Restrictive Practices Court, 1962-68. Visitor, New Univ. of Ulster, 1976; Hon. LLD Queen's Univ., Belfast, 1968. Legion of Merit (US), 1946. *Address:* 14 Upper Cheyne Row, SW3.

MEGRAH, Maurice Henry; QC 1971; *b* 5 Feb. 1896; *e s* of Henry Barnard Megrah and Annie, *d* of H. Jepps; *m* 1917, Jessie Halstead (*d* 1977); one *d. Educ:* London Sch. of Economics. MCom. (London) 1931. Westminster Bank Ltd, 1914. Served European War, 1914-18, London Scottish, 1915; commissioned Royal Field Artillery, 1917. Returned Westminster Bank Ltd, 1919; Secretary, Inst. of Bankers, 1935-59, Hon. Fellow 1959. Called to Bar, Gray's Inn, 1937; Gilbart Lecturer, University of London, 1950, 1951, 1952, 1958, 1959, 1960, 1962, 1963, 1969. *Publications:* Bills of Exchange Act, 1882, 1929; The Banker's Customer, 1932; (ed) 8th Edition Paget's Law of Banking, 1972; (ed) 23rd Edn Byles on Bills of Exchange, 1972; 5th Edn, Gutteridge and Megrah on Law of Bankers' Commercial Credits, 1976; contributions to Halsbury's Laws of England, and to law and banking periodicals. *Recreation:* riding. *Address:* 5 Paper Buildings, EC4. *T:* 01-353 8494. *Clubs:* Athenæum, Overseas Bankers'.

MEHEW, Peter; Assistant Secretary, Defence Secretariat, Ministry of Defence, since 1977; *b* 22 Jan. 1931; *er s* of Oliver Mehew and Elsie (*née* Cox); *m* 1956, Gwyneth Sellors; one *s* one *d. Educ:* Bishop Wordsworth's Sch.; St Catharine's Coll., Cambridge (BA 1954). Asst Principal, Admiralty, 1954, Principal 1959; Asst Sec., CSD, 1970; MoD, 1973; Dep. Head, UK Delegn to Negotiations on Mutual and Balanced Force Reductions, 1975-77. *Recreations:* badminton, tennis. *Address:* Kincraig East, Hitchen Hatch Lane, Sevenoaks, Kent. *T:* Sevenoaks 55641. *Club:* Royal Commonwealth Society.

MEHROTRA, Prof. Ram Charan, MSc, DPhil, PhD, DSc; Vice-Chancellor, University of Delhi, since Dec. 1974; *b* 16 Feb. 1922; *s* of late R. B. Mehrotra; *m* 1944, Suman; one *s* two *d*. *Educ:* Allahabad Univ. (MSc 1943, DPhil 1948); London Univ. (PhD 1952, DSc 1964). Research Chemist, Vigyan Kala Bhawan, Meerut, 1943-44; Lectr, Allahabad Univ., 1944-54; Reader, Lucknow Univ., 1954-58; Prof., 1958-62, Dean, Faculty of Science, 1959-62, Gorakhpur Univ.; Prof., 1962-74, Dean, Faculty of Science, 1962-65, Chief Rector, 1965-67, Vice-Chancellor, 1968-69 and 1972-73, Rajasthan Univ., Jaipur. President: Chemistry Section, Indian Sci. Congress, 1967; Indian Chemical Soc., 1976-77; Indian Science Congress, 1978-; Vice-Pres., Indian Nat. Science Acad., 1977-78. Sir S. S. Bhatnagar award, 1965; Fedn of Indian Chambers of Commerce and Industry award, 1975; Prof. T. R. Seshadri's Birthday Commem. Medal, 1976. Hon. DSc Meerut, 1976. *Publications:* numerous research papers in nat. and internat. jls of chemistry; contribs to chemistry progress reports of Chem. Soc. London. *Recreation:* photography. *Address:* 32 Chhatra Marg, University of Delhi, Delhi 110007, India. *T:* (office) 224497, (home) 227646.

MEHTA, Dr Jivraj Narayan, MD (London), MRCP; Member for Amreli, in Lok Sabha, since March 1971; *b* 29 Aug. 1887; *m* 1924, Hansa Manubhai Mehta; one *s* one *d*. *Educ:* Amreli High Sch., Gujarat State; Grant Med. Coll., Bombay; London Hosp. Med. Coll., London. Actg Asst Dir, Hale Clinical Lab., London Hosp., 1914-15; Chief MO, Baroda State, 1923-25; Dean, Seth GS Med. Coll. and KEM Hosp., Bombay, 1925-42; Dir-Gen. of Health Services, and Sec. to Govt of India in Min. of Health, 1947-48; Dewan, Baroda State, 1948-49; Elected Pres., Indian Med. Assoc., 1930, 1943, 1945; Mem. Syndicate, University of Bombay, 1928-29; Mem. Academic Coun., University of Bombay, 1934-43; Mem. Syndicate, University of Baroda, 1949-60; Fellow, Shrimati Nathibhai Thackersey Univ. for Women, 1916-60; Pres., Indian Conf. on Social Work, 1950, 1952-54; Mem. Governing Body, Indian Research Fund Assoc., 1931-32, 1937-39, 1946-51; Mem. Scientific Adv. Bd, Indian Coun. of Med. Research, 1946-51, 1953-56; Mem. Bd of Trustees, Kamala Nehru Memorial Hosp., Allahabad, 1940-; Vice-Pres., Bombay Nurses, Midwives and Health Visitors Coun., 1942; Mem. Bd of Scientific and Industrial Research, India, 1944-63; Chm., Pharmaceutical and Drugs Cttee, Coun. of Scientific and Industrial Research, 1954-60; Mem. Atomic Research Cttee, Coun. of Scientific and Industrial Research, 1951-60; Mem. Adv. Cttee, All India Med. Inst., New Delhi, 1955-57; Mem. Governing Body, All India Inst. of Med. Sci., 1957-63, 1971-; Chm., Children's Aid Soc., Bombay, 1949; Vice-Chm., Gandhi Memorial Leprosy Foundn, 1952-; Chm. Executive Council: Central Drug Research Institute, Lucknow, 1958-63; Central Salt and Marine Chemicals Research Institute at Bhavnagar, 1961-63, 1967-. Vice-Pres., All India Prohibition Council, 1968-. Mem. Medical Council of India, 1938-43, 1947-64 (Chm. Post-Grad. Cttee, 1962-64); Mem. Constituent Assembly, New Delhi, 1948-49; MLA Bombay, 1946-47 and 1949-60; Minister for Public Works, Bombay Govt, 1949-51; Finance Minister, Bombay Govt, 1952-60; Chief Minister, Gujarat State, 1960-63; High Comr for India in UK, 1963-66. Mem. Nat. Cttee Mahatma Gandhi Centenary Celebrations, 1966-70. Imprisoned for participation in Nat. Independence movt, 1932 (for 2 years) and 1942 (for 2 years). Awarded Padma Vibhushan, India, 1972. *Publications:* articles in Lancet and Jl of Indian Med. Assoc. *Address:* Everest House, 14 Carmichael Road, Bombay 26, India. *T:* 364159. *Club:* National Sports; Willingdon Sports (Bombay).

MEHTA, Ved Parkash; Staff Writer on The New Yorker, since 1961; *b* Lahore, 21 March 1934; 2nd *s* of Dr Amolak Ram Mehta, MD, retired Dep. Director General of Health Services, Govt of India, and Shanti Devi Mehta (*née* Mehra); naturalized citizen of USA, 1975. *Educ:* Arkansas Sch. for the Blind; Pomona Coll.; Balliol Coll., Oxford; Harvard Univ. BA Pomona, 1956; BA Hons Mod. Hist. Oxon, 1959; MA Harvard, 1961. Phi Beta Kappa, 1955. Hazen Fellow, 1956-59; Harvard Prize Fellow, 1959-60; Guggenheim Fellow, 1971-72, 1977-78; Ford Foundn Travel and Study Grantee, 1971-76; Vis. Scholar, Case Western Reserve Univ., 1974. Hon. DLitt Pomona, 1972. *Publications:* Face to Face, 1957 (Secondary Educn Annual Book Award, 1958; BBC dramatization on Home prog., serial reading on Light prog., 1958); Walking the Indian Streets, 1960 (rev. edn 1971); Fly and the Fly-Bottle, 1963; The New Theologian, 1966; Delinquent Chacha (novel), 1967; Portrait of India, 1970; John Is Easy to Please, 1971; Daddyji, 1972; Mahatma Gandhi and his Apostles, 1977; The New India, 1977; numerous editions and translations; articles and stories in Amer., British and Indian newspapers and magazines from 1957. *Recreation:* listening to Indian and Western music. *Address:* c/o The New Yorker, 25 West 43rd Street, New York,

NY 10036, USA. *T:* 212-695-1414. *Clubs:* Savile; Century Association (NY) (Trustee, 1973-75).

MEHTA, Zubin; Music Director of Los Angeles Philharmonic Orchestra, 1962-78; Director, New York Philharmonic, since 1978; Musical Adviser, Israel Philharmonic Orchestra; *b* 29 April 1936; *s* of Mehli Mehta; *m* 1st, 1958, Carmen Lasky (marr. diss. 1964); one *s* one *d*; 2nd, 1969, Nancy Kovack. *Educ:* St Xavier's Coll., Bombay; Musikakademie, Vienna. First Concert, Vienna, 1958; first prize internat. comp., Liverpool, 1958; US debut, Philadelphia Orch., 1960; debut with Israel and Vienna Philharmonic Orchs, 1961; apptd Music Director, Montreal Symphony Orch., 1961; European tour with this orch., 1962; guest conducting, major European Orchs, 1962. Opera debut, Montreal, Tosca, 1964; debut Metropolitan Opera, Aida, 1965. Australian tour, Israel Philharmonic, 1966; World tour (incl. debut in India) with Los Angeles Philharmonic, 1967; European Festivals Tour, 1971; tour with Israel Philharmonic, S and N America, 1972. Operas at Metropolitan incl.: Tosca, Turandot, Otello, Carmen, Mourning becomes Elektra (world première), Trovatore, etc. Holds hon. doctorates, and numerous awards; Padma Bhusan (India), 1967, etc. *Address:* 135 North Grand Avenue, Los Angeles, Calif 90012, USA. *T:* MA6-5781.

MEIGGS, Russell, MA; FBA 1961; *b* 1902; *s* of William Herrick Meiggs, London; *m* 1941, Pauline Gregg; two *d*. *Educ:* Christ's Hospital; Keble Coll., Oxford. Fellow of Keble Coll., 1930-39; Fellow and Tutor in Ancient History, Balliol Coll., Oxford, 1939-70, Hon. Fellow, 1970; Univ. Lectr in Ancient History, 1939-70; Praefectus of Holywell Manor, 1945-69. Vis. Prof., Swarthmore Coll., 1960, 1970-71, 1974; Kipling Fellow, Marlborough Coll., Vermont, 1967. DHL Swarthmore Coll., 1971. *Publications:* Home Timber Production, 1939-1945, 1949; Roman Ostia, 1960, 2nd edn, 1974; The Athenian Empire, 1972; (ed) Bury's History of Greece, 3rd edn, 1951, 4th edn, 1975; (ed, jtly) Sources for Greek History between the Persian and Peloponnesian Wars, new edn, 1951; (ed, with David Lewis) Selection of Greek Historical Inscriptions to the end of the 5th century BC, 1969. *Recreations:* gardening, America. *Address:* The Malt House, Garsington, Oxford.

MEIKLE, Alexander, CBE 1964; CA; Chairman, 1969-76 (General Manager 1943-66, Director 1958), Woolwich Equitable Building Society; *b* 22 Oct. 1905; *s* of David and Marion Meikle; *m* 1935, Margaret Alice, *d* of Wilfred G. Wallis; three *s*. *Educ:* Shawlands Academy; Glasgow Univ. CA 1928. Asst Sec., Woolwich Equitable Building Soc., 1929. Vice-Pres. 1970 (Mem. Council, 1947-70, Chm., 1958-60), Building Societies Assoc.; Vice-President: Metropolitan Assoc. of Building Socs; Building Socs Inst.; Vice-Pres. and Mem. Council, Internat. Union of Building Socs; Vice-Pres., Nat. House Building Council. *Recreation:* golf. *Address:* Pilgrims, Church Road, Sundridge, near Sevenoaks, Kent. *T:* Westerham 62558. *Club:* Caledonian.

MEINERTZHAGEN, Daniel; Chairman, Lazard Brothers & Co. Ltd, since 1973; *b* 2 March 1915; *e s* of Louis Ernest Meinertzhagen, Theberton House, Leiston, Suffolk and Gwynedd, *d* of Sir William Llewellyn, PRA; *m* 1940, Marguerite, *d* of A. E. Leonard; two *s*. *Educ:* Eton; New Coll., Oxford. Served War of 1939-45, RAFVR (Wing Comdr). Joined Lazard Brothers, 1936; Man. Dir 1954; Dep. Chm. 1971; Chairman: Royal Insurance Co. Ltd; Liverpool London & Globe Insurance Co. Ltd; London & Lancashire Insurance Co. Ltd; Whitehall Trust; former Chm., Mercantile Credit Co. Ltd; Dep. Chm., Alexanders Discount Co. Ltd; Director: S. Pearson & Son Ltd; Pearson-Longman Ltd, Richard Costain Ltd, and other companies. *Address:* Bramshott Vale, Liphook, Hants. *T:* Liphook 723243. *Club:* White's.
See also Peter Meinertzhagen.

MEINERTZHAGEN, Peter, CMG 1966; General Manager, Commonwealth Development Corporation, since 1973; *b* 24 March 1920; *y s* of late Louis Ernest Meinertzhagen, Theberton House, Leiston, Suffolk; *m* 1949, Dido Pretty; one *s* one *d*. *Educ:* Eton, Served Royal Fusiliers, 1940-46 (Croix de Guerre, France, 1944). Alfred Booth & Co., 1946-57; Commonwealth Development Corporation, 1958-. Mem. Council, London Chamber of Commerce, 1968-69. *Address:* 59 Cleaver Square, SE11. *T:* 01-735 6263. *Club:* Muthaiga Country (Nairobi).
See also D. Meinertzhagen.

MEIR, Mrs Golda; Member of Mapai (Israel Labour Party) since 1939, and member of its Leadership Forum and Party Executive, since 1976; Prime Minister of Israel, 1969-74; Member of Parliament, 1948-74; *b* Kiev, SW Russia, 1898; one *s* one *d*. *Educ:* Teachers' Seminary, Milwaukee, Wis. Teacher, and leading mem. Poalei Zion (Zionist Labour Party), Milwaukee.

Delegate US section World Jewish Congress until 1921 when immigrated Palestine, joined Merhavia collective farm village; with Solel Boneh, Labour Federation (Histadruth) Contracting and Public Works Enterprise, 1924-26. Apptd Sec. Women's Labour Council of Histadruth, 1928; Mem. Exec. and Secretariat Fedn of Labour, 1929-34; Chm. Board of Directors Workers Sick Fund, also Head Political Department Fedn of Labour. Mapai (Labour Party) delegate Actions Cttee, World Zionist Organization, 1936; Mem. War Economic Advisory Council of Palestine Govt. Leading Mem. Hagana struggle. Head Political Dept Jewish Agency for Palestine, Jerusalem, 1946-48; Israel Minister to Moscow, Aug. 1948-April 1949; Minister of Labour and Social Insurance in Israeli cabinet, 1949-56; Minister for Foreign Affairs, 1956-66; Gen. Sec. of Mapai (Israel Labour Party), 1966-68. Leading figure at numerous Zionist, Internat. Labour and Socialist congresses. *Publications:* This is Our Strength (selected papers), 1962; My Life, 1975. *Address:* Tel-Aviv, Israel.

MEKIE, David Eric Cameron, OBE 1955; FRCSEd; FRSEd; FRCPEd; Conservator, Royal College of Surgeons of Edinburgh, 1955-74; *b* 8 March 1902; *s* of Dr D. C. T. Mekie and Mary Cameron; *m* 1930, Winifred Knott (*d* 1970); two *s* one *d*. *Educ:* George Watson's Coll., Edinburgh; University of Edinburgh. MB, ChB 1925; FRCSEd 1928; FRSEd 1962; MRCP 1962; FRCPEd, 1966. Tutor, Dept of Clinical Surgery, University of Edinburgh, 1928-33; Ernest Hart Scholar, 1931-33; Professor of Clinical Surgery and Surgery, University of Malaya, 1935-55 (now Prof. Emeritus). Dir, Postgrad. Bd for Medicine, Edinburgh, 1960-71; Postgrad. Dean of Medicine, Edinburgh Univ., 1970-71. Surgeon, Singapore General Hospital and Hon. Surgical Consultant, Far East Command. *Publications:* Handbook of Surgery, 1936; numerous surgical papers. *Recreations:* fishing, gardening. *Address:* 58 Findhorn Place, Edinburgh EH9 2NW. *T:* 031-667 6472.

MELANESIA, Archbishop of, since 1975; **Most Rev. Norman Kitchener Palmer,** MBE 1975; *b* 2 Oct. 1928; *s* of Philip Sydney and Annie Palmer; *m* 1960, Elizabeth Lucy Gorringe; three *s* one *d*. *Educ:* Kokeqolo, Pawa, Brit. Solomon Is Protectorate; Te Aute, NZ; Ardmore, NZ (Teachers' Cert.); St John's Theological Coll., NZ (LTh; ordained deacon, 1964). Appts in Brit. Solomon Is Protectorate: Deacon/Teacher, Pawa Secondary (Anglican), 1966; priest, Pawa, 1966; Priest/Headmaster: Alanguala Primary, 1967-69; St Nicholas Primary, 1970-72; Dean, St Barnabas Cathedral, 1973-75. Member, Public Service Advisory Bd, 1971-75. *Recreations:* swimming, athletics, Rugby, soccer, cricket, tennis. *Address:* Archbishop's House, PO Box 19, Honiara, Solomon Islands. *T:* 339.

MELBOURNE, Archbishop of, since 1977; **Most Rev. Robert William Dann,** *qv*.

MELBOURNE, Archbishop of, (RC), since 1974; **Most Rev. Thomas Francis Little,** KBE 1977; DD, STD; *b* 30 Nov. 1925; *s* of Gerald Thompson Little and Kathleen McCormack. *Educ:* St Patrick's Coll., Ballarat; Corpus Christi Coll., Werribee; Pontifical Urban Coll., Rome. STD Rome, 1953. Priest 1950; Asst Priest, Carlton, 1953-55; Secretary, Apostolic Deleg. to Aust., NZ and Oceania, 1955-59; Asst Priest, St Patrick's Cathedral, Melbourne, 1959-65; Dean, 1965-70; Episcopal Vicar for Lay Apostolate, 1969; Pastor, St Ambrose, Brunswick, 1971-73; Auxiliary Bishop, Archdiocese of Melbourne, 1972; Bishop, 1973. *Address:* St Patrick's Cathedral, Melbourne, Vic. 3002, Australia. *T:* 622.2233.

MELBOURNE, Bishops Coadjutor of; *see* Grant, Rt Rev. J. A., Muston, Rt Rev. G. B.

MELCHETT, 4th Baron *cr* 1928; **Peter Robert Henry Mond;** Bt 1910; Minister of State, Northern Ireland Office, since 1976; *b* 24 Feb. 1948; *s* of 3rd Baron Melchett and of Sonia Elizabeth, *er d* of Lt-Col R. H. Graham; *S* father, 1973. *Educ:* Eton; Pembroke Coll., Cambridge (BA); Keele Univ. (MA). Res. Worker, LSE and Addiction Res. Unit, 1973-74. A Lord in Waiting (Govt Whip), 1974-75; Parly Under-Sec. of State, DoI, 1975-76. Chm., working party on pop festivals, 1975-76. Mem., Friends of Release. *Address:* 14 Allcroft Road, NW5 4NE. *T:* 01-267 0619.

MELCHIOR-BONNET, Christian; author; Director and Editor-in-Chief, Historia, Journal de la France, since 1969; *b* Marseille, 10 April 1904; *s* of Daniel-Joseph Melchior-Bonnet and Geneviève (*née* de Luxer); *m* 1930, Bernardine Paul-Dubois-Taine; two *s* one *d*. *Educ:* St Jean de Béthune, Versailles; Ecole du Louvre, Faculté de droit de Paris. Secretary to Pierre de Nolhac, de l'Académie française, historian, at Jacquemart-

André museum, 1927-36; formerly, Editor-in-Chief, Petit Journal, 1936-45 and Flambeau; Dir, historical and religious series of Editions Flammarion, 1932-46; Literary Dir, Fayard editions, 1946-67; Director of the reviews: Oeuvres Libres, 1946-64; Historia, 1946-; A la Page, 1964-69; Co-dir, Jardin des Arts; Literary Adviser to Nouvelles Littéraires, 1946-70. Privy Chamberlain to Pope Paul VI. Membre du jury: Prix Historia; Prix de la Fondation de France; Prix des Ambassadeurs. Officier de la Légion d'honneur; Commandeur de l'Ordre national du Mérite; Officier des Arts et des Lettres, et décorations étrangères. Prix du Rayonnement, Académie française, 1963. *Publications:* Scènes et portraits historiques de Chateaubriand, 1928; Les Mémoires du Comte Alexandre de Tilly, ancien page de la reine Marie-Antoinette, 1929; Les Mémoires du Cardinal de Retz, 1929; Principes d'action de Salazar, 1956; Le Napoléon de Chateaubriand, 1969; et nombreuses éditions de mémoires historiques. *Address:* 17 Boulevard de Beauséjour, Paris XVIe, France.

MELDRUM, Andrew, CBE 1962 (OBE 1956); KPM; Chief Inspector of Constabulary for Scotland, 1966-69, retired; *b* 22 April 1909; *s* of late Andrew Meldrum, Burntisland, Fife; *m* 1937, Janet H., *d* of late Robert Crooks, Grangemouth; one *s* one *d*. *Educ:* Burntisland, Fife. Joined Stirlingshire Police, 1927; Deputy Chief Constable, Inverness Burgh, 1943, Chief Constable, 1946; Chief Constable, County of Angus, 1949; Chief Constable of Fife, 1955; Inspector of Constabulary for Scotland, 1965-66. King's Police Medal, 1952. *Recreation:* golf. *Address:* 2/6 Craigleith Avenue South, Edinburgh EH4 3LQ. *Club:* Royal Burgess Golfing Society of Edinburgh.

MELGUND, Viscount; Gilbert Timothy George Lariston Elliot-Murray-Kynynmound; *b* 1 Dec. 1953; *s* and *heir* of 6th Earl of Minto, *qv*. *Educ:* Eton. Commissioned Scots Guards, 1972.

MELHUISH, Michael Ramsay; HM Diplomatic Service; Head of North America Department, Foreign and Commonwealth Office, since 1976; *b* 17 March 1932; *s* of late Henry Whitfield Melhuish and of Jeanette Ramsay Pender Melhuish; *m* 1961, Stella Phillips; two *s* two *d*. *Educ:* Royal Masonic Sch., Bushey; St John's Coll., Oxford (BA). FO, 1955; MECAS, 1956; Third Sec., Bahrain, 1957; FO, 1959; Second Sec., Singapore, 1961; First Sec. (Commercial) and Consul, Prague, 1963; First Sec. and Head of Chancery, Bahrain, 1966; DSAO (later FCO), 1968; First Sec., Washington, 1970; Counsellor, Amman, 1973. *Recreations:* tennis, golf. *Address:* c/o Foreign and Commonwealth Office, SW1A 2AH. *Club:* United Oxford & Cambridge University.

MELINSKY, Rev. Canon (Michael Arthur) Hugh; Principal, North West Ordination Course, since 1978; *b* 25 Jan. 1924; *s* of late M. M. Melinsky and Mrs D. M. Melinsky; *m* 1949, Renate (*née* Ruhemann); three *d*. *Educ:* Whitgift Sch., Croydon; Christ's Coll., Cambridge (BA 1947, MA 1949); London Univ. Inst. of Education (TDip 1949); Ripon Hall, Oxford. Asst Master: Normanton Grammar Sch., 1949-52; Lancaster Royal Grammar Sch., 1952-57. Curate: Wimborne Minster, 1957-59; Wareham, 1959-61; Vicar of St Stephen's, Norwich, 1961-68; Chaplain of Norfolk and Norwich Hosp., 1961-68; Hon. Canon and Canon Missioner of Norwich, 1968-73; Chief Sec., ACCM, 1973-77. Chairman: C of E Commn on Euthanasia, 1972-75; Inst. of Religion and Medicine, 1973-77. *Publications:* The Modern Reader's Guide to Matthew, 1963; the Modern Reader's Guide to Luke, 1963; Healing Miracles, 1967; (ed) Religion and Medicine, 1970; (ed) Religion and Medicine 2, 1973; Patterns of Ministry, 1974; (ed) On Dying Well, 1975. *Address:* 75 Framingham Road, Brooklands, Sale, Cheshire M33 3RH. *T:* 061-962 7513.

MELLAART, James, FSA; Lecturer in Anatolian Archaeology, Institute of Archaeology, University of London, since 1964; *b* 14 Nov. 1925; *s* of J. H. J. Mellaart and A. D. Van Der Beek; *m* 1954, Arlette Meryem Cenani; one *s*. *Educ:* University College, London. BA Hons (Ancient Hist. and Egyptology) 1951. Archaeol field surveys in Anatolia as Scholar and Fellow of British Inst. of Archaeol. at Ankara, 1951-56; excavations at Hacilar, 1957-60; Asst Dir, British Inst. of Archaeol. at Ankara, 1959-61; excavations at Çatal Hüyük, Turkey, 1961-63 and 1965; Foreign Specialist, Lectr at Istanbul Univ., 1961-63. Corresp. Mem., German Archaeol Inst., 1961. *Publications:* Earliest Civilisations of the Near East, 1965; The Chalcolithic and Early Bronze Ages in the Near East and Anatolia, 1966; Çatal Hüyük, a Neolithic Town in Anatolia, 1967; Excavations at Hacilcar, 1970; The Neolithic of the Near East, 1975; chapters in Cambridge Ancient History; numerous articles in Anatolian Studies, etc. *Recreations:* geology, Turkish ceramics, clan history, Gaelic and classical music, Seljuk art. *Address:* 13 Lichen Court, 79 Queen's Drive, N4 2BH. *T:* 01-802 6984.

MELLANBY, Kenneth, CBE 1954 (OBE 1945); ScD Cantab; FIBiol; research, since 1974; *b* 26 March 1908; *s* of late Emeritus-Professor A. L. Mellanby; *m* 1933, Helen Neilson Dow, MD (marr. diss.); one *d*; *m* 1948, Jean Copeland, MA, JP; one *s. Educ:* Barnard Castle Sch.; King's Coll., Cambridge (Exhibitioner). Research Worker, London Sch. of Hygiene and Trop. Med., 1930-36 and 1953-55; Wandsworth Fellow, 1933; Sorby Research Fellow of Royal Society of London, 1936; Hon. Lecturer, University of Sheffield; CO (Sqdn Ldr RAFVR) Sheffield Univ. Air Sqdn. Dir Sorby Research Institute, 1941; first Principal, University Coll., Ibadan, Nigeria, 1947-53; Major, RAMC (Specialist in Biological Research), overseas service in N Africa, SE Asia, etc.; Dep. Dir, Scrub Typhus Research Laboratory, SEAC; Reader in Medical Entomology, University of London, 1945-47; Head of Dept of Entomology, Rothamsted Experimental Station, Harpenden, Herts, 1955-61; first Dir, Monks Wood Experimental Station, Huntingdon, 1961-74. Vice-Pres. and Mem. Council, Royal Entomological Soc. of London, 1953-56; Pres. Assoc. for Study of Animal Behaviour, 1957-60; Member: Inter-university Council for Higher Education Overseas, 1960-75; ARC Research Cttee on Toxic Chemicals; Council, and Chm., Tropical Group, Brit. Ecological Soc.; Nat. Exec., Cambs Br., CPRE (also Pres.); Council for Science and Technology Insts, 1976-77 (Chm.); Council for Environmental Science and Engrg, 1976-; Pres., Sect. D (Zoology), 1972, and Sect. X (General), 1973, British Assoc.; Vice-Pres. of the Institute of Biology, 1967, Pres., 1972-73; Hon. Professorial Fellow, University Coll. of S Wales; Hon. Prof. of Biology, Univ. of Leicester. Essex Hall Lectr, 1971. Fellow, NERC. Mem. Editorial Bd, New Naturalist series. Hon. DSc: Ibadan, 1963; Bradford, 1970; Leicester, 1972. *Publications:* Scabies, 1943, new edn 1973; Human Guinea Pigs, 1945, new edn 1973; The Birth of Nigeria's University, 1958, new edn 1975; Pesticides and Pollution, 1967; The Mole, 1971; The Biology of Pollution, 1972; Can Britain Feed Itself?, 1975; Talpa, the story of a mole, 1976; many scientific papers on insect physiology, ecology, medical and agricultural entomology; ed, Monographs on Biological Subjects; British Editor of Entomologia Experimentalis et Applicata; Editor, Environmental Pollution. *Recreation:* austere living. *Address:* Hill Farm, Wennington, Huntingdon. *T:* Abbots Ripton 392. *Club:* Athenæum.

MELLANBY, Lady; May; MA, ScD Cantab; Hon. DSc Sheffield, 1933; Hon. DSc Liverpool, 1934; Charles Mickle Fellow, Toronto University, 1935-36; Member of the Empire Marketing Board Research Grants Committee until disbanded; formerly Investigator for Medical Research Council; *b* London, 1882; *e d* of late Rosa and George Tweedy, London; *m* 1914, Sir Edward Mellanby, GBE, KCB, FRS, FRCP (*d* 1955). *Educ:* Hampstead and Bromley High Schs; Girton Coll., Cambridge. Natural Science Tripos Parts I and II; Research Scholar and Lecturer, London Univ. (Bedford Coll.), 1906-14; Hon. Fellow, Girton Coll., 1958; Hon. Member: Internat. Assoc. for Dental Research (Science Award of Assoc., 1975, in recognition of outstanding basic research in biological mineralization); British Dental Assoc.; Stomatological Soc. of Greece. *Publications:* many publications of a scientific nature principally dealing with conditions affecting the structure of the teeth and related tissues and their resistance to disease including MRC Special Report Series 140, 153 and 191. *Address:* 5 East Heath Road, Hampstead, NW3. *T:* 01-435 2874. *Club:* English-Speaking Union.

MELLERS, Prof. Wilfrid Howard, DMus; Composer; Professor of Music, University of York, since 1964; *b* 26 April 1914; *s* of Percy Wilfrid Mellers and Hilda Maria (*née* Lawrence); *m* 1950, Peggy Pauline (*née* Lewis); two *d. Educ:* Leamington Coll.; Downing Coll., Cambridge. BA Cantab 1939; MA Cantab 1945; DMus Birmingham 1962. Supervisor in English and College Lecturer in Music, Downing Coll., Cambridge, 1945-48; Staff Tutor in Music, Extra Mural Dept, University of Birmingham, 1949-60; Visiting Mellon Prof. of Music, University of Pittsburgh, USA, 1960-62. *Publications:* Music and Society, 1946; Studies in Contemporary Music, 1948; François Couperin and the French Classical Tradition, 1950; Music in the Making, 1951; Man and his Music, 1957; Harmonious Meeting, 1964; Music in a New Found Land, 1964; Caliban Reborn: renewal in 20th-century music, 1967 (US), 1968 (GB); Twilight of the Gods: the Beatles in retrospect, 1973. Published Compositions include: Canticum Incarnations, 1960; Alba in 9 Metamorphoses, 1962; Rose of May, 1964; Life-Cycle, 1967; Yeibichai, 1968; Canticum Resurrectionis, 1968; Natalis Invicti Solis, 1969; The Word Unborn, 1970; The Ancient Wound, 1970; De Vegetabilis et Animalibus, 1971; Venery for Six Plus, 1971; Sun-flower = the Quaternity of William Blake, 1972-73; The Key of the Kingdom, 1976; Rosae Hermeticae, 1977. *Address:* Department of Music, University of York, York.

MELLERSH, Air Vice-Marshal Francis Richard Lee, CB 1977; DFC 1943 and Bar 1944; Air Officer Flying and Officer Training, HQ Training Command, 1974-77; *b* 30 July 1922; *s* of Air Vice-Marshal Sir Francis Mellersh, KBE, AFC; *m* 1967, Elisabeth Nathalie Komaroff; two *s* one *d. Educ:* Winchester House Sch.; Imperial Service College. Joined RAFVR, 1940; Nos 29, 600 and 96 Sqdns, 1941-45; various staff and flying appts, 1946-57; Dirg Staff, RAF Staff Coll., 1957-59; Staff of Chief of Defence Staff, 1959-61; Dep. Dir Ops (F), 1961-63; OC RAF West Raynham, 1965-67; Chief Current Plans, SHAPE, 1967-68; RCDS 1969; SASO, RAF Germany, 1970-72; ACDS (Ops), 1972-74. *Address:* Rother Lea, Lossenham Lane, Newenden, Kent. *Club:* Royal Air Force.

MELLING, Cecil Thomas, CBE 1955; MScTech, CEng, FIEE, FIMechE, Sen. FInstF, FBIM; *b* Wigan, 12 Dec. 1899; *s* of late William and late Emma Melling; *m* 1929, Ursula Thorburn Thorburn; two *s* one *d* (and one *s* and one *d* decd). *Educ:* Manchester Central High Sch.; College of Technology, University of Manchester. 2nd Lieut RE 1918. Metropolitan Vickers Electrical Co. Ltd, 1920-34; Yorkshire Electric Power Co., 1934-35; Edmundson's Electricity Corporation Ltd, 1935-43. Borough Electrical Engineer, Luton, 1943-48. Mem. of British Electricity Authority, 1952-53, and 1957; Chm., Eastern Electricity Board, 1948-57; Full-Time Mem., Electricity Council, 1957-61. Chm. Utilization Sect., Institution of Electrical Engineers, 1949-50; Vice-Pres., IEE, 1957-62, Pres., 1962-63; Chm. of Council, British Electrical Development Association, 1951-52, Founder-Chm. 1945, and Pres. 1947, Luton Electrical Soc.; Pres. Ipswich & District Electrical Assoc., 1948-57; Chm. of Council, British Electrical and Allied Industries Research Assoc., 1953-55; Pres. Assoc. of Supervising Electrical Engineers, 1952-54; a Dep. Chm. Electricity Council, 1961-65; Chm., British Nat. Cttee for Electro-Heat, 1958-68; Vice-Pres. Internat. Union for Electro-Heat, 1964-68, Pres., 1968-72; Pres., British Electrotechnical Approvals Bd for Household Appliances, 1974- (Chm., 1964-73); Chm., Electricity Supply Industry Trg Bd, 1965-68; Vice-Pres., Union of Internat. Engineering Organisations, 1969-75. *Publications:* contribs to Proc. Engineering Instns and Confs. *Address:* Durham, The Grand, Folkestone. *Club:* Athenæum.

MELLISH, Rt. Hon. Robert Joseph, PC 1967; MP (Lab) Southwark, Bermondsey, since 1974 (Bermondsey, Rotherhithe, 1946-50; Bermondsey, 1950-74); Official, Transport and General Workers' Union; *b* 1913; *m*; five *s.* Served War of 1939-45, Captain RE, SEAC. PPS to Minister of Pensions, 1951 (to Minister of Supply, 1950-51); Jt Parly Sec., Min. of Housing, 1964-67; Minister of Public Building and Works, 1967-69; Parly Sec. to Treasury and Govt Chief Whip, 1969-70 and 1974-76; Opposition Chief Whip, 1970-74. Chm., London Regional Lab. Party, 1956-77. *Address:* c/o House of Commons, SW1.

MELLON, James; HM Diplomatic Service; Head of Trade Relations and Export Department, Foreign and Commonwealth Office, since 1976; *b* 25 Jan. 1929; *m* 1956, Frances Murray (*d* 1976); one *s* three *d. Educ:* Glasgow Univ. (MA). Dept of Agriculture for Scotland, 1953-60; Agricultural Attaché, Copenhagen and The Hague, 1960-63; FO, 1963-64; Head of Chancery, Dakar, 1964-66; UK Delegn to European Communities, 1967-72; Counsellor, 1970; Hd of Sci. and Technol. Dept, FCO, 1973-75; Commercial Counsellor, East Berlin, 1975-76. *Address:* c/o Foreign and Commonwealth Office, SW1. *Club:* Travellers'.

MELLON, Paul, Hon. KBE 1974; Trustee, National Gallery of Art, Washington, DC, since 1945 (President since 1963); *b* 11 June 1907; *s* of late Andrew William Mellon and late Nora McMullen Mellon; *m* 1st, 1935, Mary Conover (decd); one *s* one *d*; 2nd, 1948, Rachel Lambert. *Educ:* Choate Sch., Wallingford, Conn; Yale and Cambridge Univs. Trustee: Andrew W. Mellon Foundn (successor to merged Old Dominion and Avalon Foundns), 1969-; A. W. Mellon Educational and Charitable Trust, Pittsburgh, 1930-; Trustee, Virginia Mus. of Fine Arts, Richmond, Va, 1938-68, 1969-. Mem., Amer. Philosophical Soc., Pa, 1971. Hon. Citizen, University of Vienna, 1965. Yale Medal, 1953; Horace Marden Albright Scenic Preservation Medal, 1957; Distinguished Service to Arts Award, Nat. Inst. Arts and Letters, 1962; Benjamin Franklin Medal, Royal Society of Arts, 1965, Benjamin Franklin Fellow, 1969; Alumni Seal Prize Award, Choate Sch., 1966; Skowhegan Gertrude Vanderbilt Whitney Award, 1972. Hon. DLitt, Oxford Univ., 1961; Hon. LLD, Carnegie Inst. of Tech., 1967; Hon. DHL, Yale, 1967. Order of Homayoun, Iran, 1966. *Recreations:* fox-hunting, thoroughbred breeding and racing, sailing, swimming. *Address:* (office) 1729 H Street NW, Washington, DC 20006, USA; (home) Oak Spring, Upperville, Va 22176. *Clubs:* Buck's; Travellers (Paris); Jockey, Knickerbocker, Links, Racquet and

Tennis, River, Yale, Grolier (New York); Metropolitan, 1925 F Street (Washington); Duquesne, Fox Chapel, Golf, University, Rolling Rock (Pittsburgh).

MELLOR, Hugh Wright; Secretary, National Corporation for Care of Old People, since 1973; *b* 11 Aug. 1920; *s* of William Algernon and Katherine Mildred Mellor; *m* 1944, Winifred Joyce Yates. *Educ:* Leys Sch., Cambridge; London Univ. (BScEcon). Friends Relief Service, 1940-45; Sec., St Albans Council of Social Service, 1945-48; Community Develt Officer, Hemel Hempstead Develt Corp., 1948-50; Asst Sec., Nat. Corp. for Care of Old People, 1951-73. Chm., BSI Cttee on Alarm Systems for the Elderly; Vice-Chm., Age Concern Greater London; Trustee, Quaker Housing Trust; Mem. Management Cttee, Hanover Housing Assoc.; Mem., Exec. Cttee, Age Concern England; Mem. Adv. Council, Charities Aid Foundn; Hon. Sec., British Council for Ageing. *Recreations:* walking, reading, music. *Address:* Lark Rise, Risborough Road, Great Kimble, Aylesbury, Bucks HP17 0XS *Club:* Royal Commonwealth Society.

MELLOR, Brig. James Frederick McLean, CBE 1964 (OBE 1945); Norfolk County Commandant, Army Cadet Force, 1969-72; *b* 6 June 1912; *s* of late Col A. J. Mellor, RM, Kingsland, Hereford; *m* 1942, Margaret Ashley, *d* of Major F. A. Phillips, DSO, Holmer, Hereford; one *s* one *d*. *Educ:* Radley Coll.; Faraday House. C. A. Parsons, 1933; Yorkshire Electric Power, 1935. Commnd in Regular Army as Ordnance Mechanical Engr, 1936; France, Belgium, Dunkirk, 1940; Burma, Malaya, HQ, SEAC, 1944-47 (despatches, 1945); Brig. A/Q Northern Comd, 1961-64; Dir of Technical Trng and Inspector of Boys' Trng (Army), MoD, 1966-69; ADC to the Queen, 1963-69. Various appts in engineering and technical educn. Chm., IMechE Eastern Branch, 1971-72. DFH, FIMechE, FIEE. *Address:* Muckleburgh, Kelling, Holt, Norfolk. *T:* Weybourne 227. *Clubs:* Naval and Military, Royal Automobile; Norfolk (Norwich).

MELLOR, Sir John (Serocold Paget), 2nd Bt, *cr* 1924; *b* 6 July 1893; *er s* of 1st Bt and Mabel, *d* of G. E. Serocold Pearce-Serocold, of Cherryhinton, Torquay; *S* father, 1929; *m* 1st, 1922, Rachael Margaret (who obtained a divorce, 1937), *d* of Sir Herbert F. Cook, 3rd Bt, of Doughty House, Richmond; one *s*; 2nd, 1937, Mrs Raie Mendes (*d* 1965); 3rd, 1971, Mrs Jessica de Pass, *er d* of late Clarence de Sola, Montreal. *Educ:* Eton; New Coll., Oxford. Barrister, Inner Temple; formerly Capt. Prince Albert's Somerset LI. Served overseas 1914-18 (1914-15 Star, twice wounded, taken prisoner-of-war by Turks at Kut); rejoined Somerset LI, Sept. 1939; contested (C) Workington Division, 1929; adopted Conservative Candidate for Luton Division, 1931, but withdrew in favour of Liberal National Candidate; MP (C) Tamworth Division of Warwicks, 1935-45, Sutton Coldfield Division of Warwicks, 1945-55. Pres., Prudential Assurance Co. Ltd, 1972-77 (Dir, 1946-72; Dep. Chm., 1959-65; Chm., 1965-70); Director: City and International Trust Ltd; CLRP Investment Trust Ltd. *Heir: s* John Francis Mellor, *b* 9 March 1925. *Address:* Binley House, near Andover, Hants. *Club:* Carlton.

MELLOR, John Walter; *b* 24 Sept. 1927; *s* of William Mellor and Ruth (*née* Tolson); *m* 1957, Freda Mary (*née* Appleyard); one *s* three *d*. *Educ:* Grammar Sch., Batley; Leeds Univ. (LLB). Called to Bar, Gray's Inn, 1953. A Recorder of the Crown Court, 1972-74. *Recreations:* golf, sailing, visiting West Cork. *Address:* 171 Scotchman Lane, Morley, Leeds, W Yorks. *T:* Morley 4093. *Clubs:* Morley Rugby Union; Crookhaven Yacht.

MELLOR, Kenneth Wilson, QC 1975; a Recorder of the Crown Court, since 1972; *m* 1957, Sheila Gale; one *s* three *d*. *Educ:* King's College Cambridge (MA, LLB). RNVR (Sub Lieut). Called to the Bar, Lincoln's Inn, 1950. Dep. Chm., Hereford QS, 1969-71; Chm., Agricultural Land Tribunal (West Midlands). *Address:* 5 Fountain Court, Steelhouse Lane, Birmingham B4 6DR; 1 Paper Buildings, Temple, EC4.

MELLOWS, Prof. Anthony Roger, TD 1969; PhD, LLD; Solicitor of the Supreme Court, and Professor of the Law of Property in the University of London, since 1974; *b* 30 July 1936; *s* of L. B. and M. P. Mellows; *m* 1973, Elizabeth, *d* of Ven. B. G. B. Fox, *qv. Educ:* King's Coll., London. LLB (1st Cl. Hons) 1957; LLM (Mk of Distinction) 1959; PhD 1962; BD 1968; LLD 1973. Commissioned Intelligence Corps (TA), 1959, Captain 1964; served Intell. Corps (TA) and (T&AVR) and on the Staff, 1959-71; RARO, 1971-. Admitted a solicitor, 1960; private practice, 1960-; Sen. Partner, Messrs Alexanders. Asst Lectr in Law, King's Coll., London, 1962, Lectr, 1964, Reader, 1971; Dir of Conveyancing Studies, 1969. Mem. Council, KCL, 1972-; Trustee, Kincardine Foundn, 1972-. AKC, London,

1957; FRSA 1959. Freeman of the City of London, 1963. *Publications:* Local Searches and Enquiries, 1964 (2nd edn 1967); Conveyancing Searches, 1964 (2nd edn 1975); Land Charges, 1966; The Preservation and Felling of Trees, 1964; The Trustee's Handbook, 1965 (3rd edn 1975); Taxation for Executors and Trustees, 1967 (4th edn 1976); The Modern Law of Trusts (jt), 1966 (3rd edn 1975); The Law of Succession, 1970 (3rd edn 1977); Taxation of Land Transactions, 1973. *Address:* 22 Devereux Court, Temple Bar, WC2R 3JJ. *Club:* Athenæum.

MELLY, (Alan) George (Heywood); professional blues singer; with John Chilton's Feetwarmers, since 1974; *b* 17 Aug. 1926; *s* of Francis Heywood and Edith Maud Melly; *m* 1963, Diana Campion Dawson; one *s* and one step *s* one step *d*. *Educ:* Stowe School. Able Seaman, RN, 1944-47. Art Gallery Asst, London Gallery, 1948-50; sang with Mick Mulligan's Jazz Band, 1949-61. Wrote Flook strip cartoon balloons (drawn by Trog (Wally Fawkes)), 1956-71. Critic, The Observer: pop music, 1965-67; TV, 1967-71; films, 1971-73. Film scriptwriter: Smashing Time, 1968; Take a Girl Like You, 1970. Pres., British Humanist Assoc., 1972-74. Critic of the Year, IPC Nat. Press Awards, 1970. *Publications:* I Flook, 1962; Owning Up, 1965; Revolt into Style, 1970; Flook by Trog, 1970; Rum Bum and Concertina, 1977. *Recreations:* trout fishing, singing and listening to blues of 1920s, collecting modern paintings. *Address:* 102 Savernake Road, NW3. *Club:* Colony Room.

MELMOTH, Christopher George Frederick Frampton, CMG 1959; South Asia Department, International Bank for Reconstruction and Development, 1962-75; *b* 25 Sept. 1912; *s* of late George Melmoth and Florence Melmoth; *m* 1946, Maureen Joan (*née* Brennan); three *d*. *Educ:* Sandringham Sch., Forest Gate. Accountant Officer, Co-ordination of Supplies Fund, Malta, 1942-45; Administrative Officer, Hong Kong, 1946-55; Minister of Finance, Uganda, 1956-62. *Recreations:* tennis, golf, walking. *Address:* Hoptons Field, Kemerton, Tewkesbury, Glos.

MELONEY, Mrs W. B.; *see* Franken, Rose.

MELROSE, Prof. Denis Graham; Professor of Surgical Science, Royal Postgraduate Medical School and Consultant Clinical Physiologist to Hammersmith Hospital; *b* 20 June 1921; *s* of Thomas Robert Gray Melrose, FRCS and Floray Collings; *m* 1945, Ann, *d* of Kathleen Tatham Warter; two *s*. *Educ:* Sedbergh Sch.; University Coll., Oxford; UCH London. MA, BM, BCh, MRCP, FRCS. Junior appts at Hammersmith Hosp. and Redhill County Hosp., Edgware, 1945; RNVR, 1946-48; subseq. Lectr, later Reader, Royal Postgrad. Med. Sch.; Nuffield Travelling Fellow, USA, 1956; Fulbright Fellow, 1957; Associate in Surgery, Stanford Univ. Med. Sch., 1958. *Publications:* numerous papers in learned jls and chapters in books, particularly on heart surgery, heart lung machine and med. engrg. *Recreations:* sailing, ski-ing. *Address:* 1 Lower Common South, SW15. *T:* 01-788 0116. *Club:* Royal Naval Sailing Association.

MELVILLE, 9th Viscount *cr* 1802; **Robert David Ross Dundas;** Baron Duneira 1802; *b* 28 May 1937; *s* of Hon. Robert Maldred St John Melville Dundas (2nd *s* of 7th Viscount) (killed in action, 1940), and of Margaret Connell (who *m* 2nd, 1946, Gerald Bristowe Sanderson), *d* of late Percy Cruden Ross; *S* uncle, 1971. *Educ:* Wellington College. District Councillor, Lasswade, Midlothian. Lieutenant, Ayrshire Yeomanry; Captain (Reserve), Scots Guards. *Recreations:* golf, fishing. *Heir: cousin* Hugh McKenzie Dundas [*b* 3 June 1910; *m* 1939, Catherine Sanderson, *d* of late John Wallace; one *s* one *d*]. *Address:* Keltie Castle, Dunning, Perthshire. *T:* Dunning 208; Esk Cottage, Melville, Lasswade, Midlothian. *T:* Lasswade 3162. *Clubs:* Cavalry and Guards; Turf; Midlothian County.

MELVILLE; *see* Leslie Melville, family name of Earl of Leven and Melville.

MELVILLE, Alan; revue writer and author; *b* 9 April 1910. *Educ:* Edinburgh Academy. BBC features and drama producer and script-writer, 1936-40. Served War with RAF, 1940-46. *Publications: revues:* Rise Above It (Comedy), 1940; Sky High (Phoenix), 1941; Sweet and Low, Sweeter and Lower, Sweetest and Lowest (Ambassadors), 1943-46; A La Carte (Savoy), 1948; At the Lyric (Lyric, Hammersmith), 1953; Going to Town (St Martin's), 1954; All Square (Vaudeville), 1963; (jtly) Hulla Baloo (Criterion), 1972; Déjà Revue, 1975; *plays:* Jonathan (Aldwych), 1948; Top Secret (Winter Garden), 1949; Castle in the Air (Adelphi), 1949-50; Dear Charles (New), 1952-53; Simon and Laura, 1954; The Bargain (Ethel Barrymore Theatre, New York), 1953; Mrs Willie, 1955; Change of Tune, (Strand), 1959; Devil May Care, 1963; Fuender Bitte Melden (Stadt Theater, Baden-Baden), 1966; Demandez Vicky (Théatre des

Nouveautés, Paris), 1966; Content to Whisper (adaptation from French) (Theatre Royal, York); Darling You Were Wonderful (Richmond); *musical plays*: Gay's the Word (Saville), 1951; Bet Your Life (Hippodrome), 1952; Marigold (Savoy), 1959; *Films*: Derby Day, 1952; Hot Ice, 1952; As Long as They're Happy, 1954; All for Mary, 1955; Simon and Laura, 1955; *novels*: Weekend at Thrackley, 1935; Death of Anton, 1936; Quick Curtain, 1937; The Vicar in Hell, 1938; Warning to Critics, 1939; *war autobiography*: First Tide, 1945; *autobiography*: Myself When Young, 1956; Merely Melville, 1970. *TV series*: A-Z, Merely Melville, Melvilianity, What's My Line?, Parade, Raise Your Glasses, Whitehall Worrier, Before the Fringe, Misleading Cases, The Very Merry Widow, The Brighton Belle; also Titipu, Iolanthe; *radio*: The King's Favourite, 1972; The Sun King, 1973. *Recreations*: tennis, swimming. *Address*: c/o Eric Glass Ltd, 28 Berkeley Square, W1.

MELVILLE, Anthony Edwin; Headmaster, The Perse School, Cambridge, since 1969; *b* 28 April 1929; *yr s* of Sir Leslie Melville, *qv*; *m* 1964, Pauline Marianne Surtees Simpson, *d* of Major A. F. Simpson, Indian Army; two *d*. *Educ*: Sydney Church of England Grammar Sch.; Univ. of Sydney (BA); King's Coll., Cambridge (MA). Sydney Univ. Medal in English, 1950; Pt II History Tripos, 1st cl. with dist., 1952; Lightfoot Schol. in Eccles. History, 1954. Asst Master, Haileybury Coll., 1953. *Recreations*: reading, gardening. *Address*: 80 Glebe Road, Cambridge. *T*: Cambridge 47964. *Club*: East India, Devonshire, Sports and Public Schools.

MELVILLE, Archibald Ralph, CB 1976; CMG 1964; agricultural consultant; Member, Commonwealth Development Corporation, since 1977; *b* 24 May 1912; *e s* of late James Melville, MA, Edinburgh, and Mrs K. E. Melville, Lynton, Devon; *m* 1943, Theresa Kelly, SRN, SCM, QAIMNS (*d* 1976); two *d*. *Educ*: George Heriot's Sch., Edinburgh; University of Edinburgh; Royal College of Science, London; Imperial Coll. of Tropical Agriculture, Trinidad. BSc in Agriculture with Hons Zoology, Edinburgh, 1934; AICTA, Trinidad, 1936. Entomologist, Kenya Dept of Agriculture, 1936; Senior Entomologist, 1947; Chief Research Officer, 1956; Dir of Agriculture, 1960-64, Kenya Government Service; Agricultural Adviser, ODM, 1965-71; Chief Natural Resources Advr, 1971-76, Under Sec., 1972-76, ODM. Mem., Governing Body, Animal Virus Res. Inst., 1977-. Served 1939-44 with Kenya Regt and East African Army Medical Corps (Major). *Publications*: contributions to technical journals. *Recreations*: golf, gardening, natural history. *Address*: Spearpoint Cottage, Kennington, Ashford, Kent. *T*: Ashford 20056. *Club*: Farmers'.

MELVILLE, Sir Eugene, KCMG 1965 (CMG 1952); HM Diplomatic Service, retired; Director-General, British Property Federation, since 1974; *b* 15 Dec. 1911; *s* of George E. Melville; *m* 1937, Elizabeth, *d* of Chas M. Strachan, OBE; two *s* one *d*. *Educ*: Queen's Park Sch., Glasgow; St Andrews Univ. (Harkness Residential Scholar; 1st cl. Hons Classics; 1st cl. Hons Economics). Appointed to Colonial Office, 1936; Colonies Supply Mission, Washington, 1941-45; PS to Sec. of State for Colonies, 1945-46; Financial Adviser, Control Commission for Germany, 1949-52; Asst Under-Sec. of State, Colonial Office, 1952; Asst Under-Sec. of State, Foreign Office, 1961; Minister (Economic), Bonn, 1962-65; Permanent UK Delegate to EFTA and GATT, 1965; Ambassador and Permanent UK Representative to UN and other Internat. Organisations at Geneva, 1966-71; Special Advr, Channel Tunnel Studies, 1971-73. Sec-Gen., Malta Round Table Conf., 1955; Dir, Metropolitan Housing Trust; Mem. Corp., Framlingham Coll.; Hon. Treasurer, British Sailors' Soc.; Chm., Aldeburgh Festival, Snape Maltings Foundn, 1976-. *Address*: 51 Westminster Mansions, Little Smith Street, SW1; Longcroft, Aldeburgh, Suffolk. *Club*: Reform.

MELVILLE, Sir Harry (Work), KCB 1958; FRS 1941; FRIC; PhD Edinburgh and Cantab; DSc Edinburgh; MSc Birmingham; Principal, Queen Mary College, University of London, 1967-76; *b* 27 April 1908; *s* of Thomas and Esther Burnett Melville; *m* 1942, Janet Marian, *d* of late Hugh Porteous and Sarah Cameron; two *d*. *Educ*: George Heriot's Sch., Edinburgh; Edinburgh Univ. (Carnegie Res. Scholar); Trinity Coll., Cambridge (1851 Exhibitioner). Fellow of Trinity College, Cambridge, 1933-44. Meldola Medal, Inst. of Chemistry, 1936; Davy Medal, Royal Society, 1955; Colwyn Medal, Instn of the Rubber Industry. Asst Dir, Colloid Science Laboratory, Cambridge, 1938-40; Prof. of Chemistry, Univ. of Aberdeen, 1940-48; Scientific Adviser to Chief Superintendent Chemical Defence, Min. of Supply, 1940-43; Superintendent, Radar Res. Station, 1943-45; Mason Prof. of Chemistry, Univ. of Birmingham, 1948-56. Chief Scientific Adviser for Civil Defence, Midlands Region, 1952-56; Bakerian Lecture, Royal

Society, 1956. Member: Min. of Aviation Scientific Adv. Council, 1949-51; Adv. Council, Dept of Scientific and Industrial Res., 1946-51; Res. Council, British Electricity Authority, 1949-56; Royal Commn on Univ. Educn in Dundee, 1951-52; Res. Council, DSIR, 1961-65; Chm., Adv. Council on Research and Develt, DTI, 1970-74; Member: Nuclear Safety Adv. Cttee, DTI, 1972-; Cttee of Managers, Royal Institution, 1976-; Sec. to Cttee of the Privy Council for Scientific and Industrial Research, 1956-65; Chm., SRC, 1965-67. Mem., London Electricity Bd, 1968-75. Mem., Parly and Scientific Cttee, 1971-75; Pres., Plastics Inst., 1970-75. Hon. LLD Aberdeen; Hon. DCL Kent; Hon. DSc: Exeter; Birmingham; Liverpool; Leeds; Heriot-Watt; Essex; Hon. DTech Bradford. *Publications*: papers in Proceedings of Royal Society, etc. *Address*: Norwood, Dodds Lane, Chalfont St Giles, Bucks. *T*: 2222. *Club*: Athenæum.

MELVILLE, Dr James, CMG 1969; Director, Waite Agricultural Research Institute, University of Adelaide, 1956-73, retired; *b* 10 July 1908; *s* of Andrew Melville, Lovells' Flat, NZ; *m* 1938, Margaret, *d* of Charles Ogilvie, Christchurch, NZ; one *s* two *d* (and one *d* decd). *Educ*: Otago, London & Yale Univs. MSc (NZ) 1930, PhD (London) 1934. Commonwealth Fund Fellow, Yale Univ., 1934-36; Asst Chemist, Wheat Research Inst., NZ, 1936-38; Dir, Plant Chemistry Laboratory, DSIR, NZ, 1939-50. War Service: S and SW Pacific Areas, 1941-45. Dir, Grasslands Div., DSIR, NZ, 1951-55. Mem., CSIRO Exec., 1958-65. Chm., Bushfire Research Cttee, 1959-77; Chm., Aust. Wool Industry Conf., 1964-66. FRACI 1958; FAIAS 1968. *Publications*: contrib. scientific jls (agricultural and chemical). *Address*: Longwood, SA 5153, Australia.

MELVILLE, Sir Leslie Galfreid, KBE 1957 (CBE 1953); Member of the Board of the Reserve Bank, 1959-63, and 1965-74; Chairman of Commonwealth Grants Commission, 1966-74; *b* 26 March 1902; *s* of Richard Ernest Melville and Lilian Evelyn Thatcher; *m* 1925, Mary Maud Scales; two *s*. *Educ*: Sydney Church of England Grammar Sch. Bachelor of Economics, University of Sydney, 1925; Public Actuary of South Australia, 1924-28; Prof. of Economics, University of Adelaide, 1929-31; Economic Adviser to Commonwealth Bank of Australia, 1931-49; Asst Gov. (Central Banking) Commonwealth Bank of Australia, 1949-53; Mem. of Commonwealth Bank Bd, 1951-53; Exec. Dir of International Monetary Fund and International Bank for Reconstruction and Development, 1950-53. Mem. of Cttees on Australian Finances and Unemployment, 1931 and 1932; Financial Adviser to Australian Delegates at Imperial Economic Conference, 1932; Financial Adviser to Australian Delegate at World Economic Conference, 1933; Mem. of Financial and Economic Advisory Cttee, 1939; Chm. of Australian Delegation to United Nations Monetary Conf. at Bretton Woods, 1944; Mem. of Advisory Council of Commonwealth Bank, 1945-51; Chm. UN Sub-Commn on Employment and Economic Stability, 1947-50; Member: Immigration Planning Council, 1956-61; Develt Adv. Service of Internat. Bank, 1963-65; Chm. of Tariff Bd, Australia, 1960-62; Chm., Tariff Adv. Cttee of Papua and New Guinea, 1969-71. Vice-Chancellor Australian National Univ., Canberra, ACT, 1953-60. Hon. LLD Toronto, 1958. *Address*: 71 Stonehaven Crescent, Canberra, ACT 2600, Australia. *Clubs*: University (Sydney); Commonwealth.
See also A. E. Melville.

MELVILLE, Sir Ronald (Henry), KCB 1964 (CB 1952); Director: Electronic Components Board; Westland Aircraft; *b* 9 March 1912; *e s* of Henry Edward Melville; *m* 1940, Enid Dorcas Margaret, *d* of late Harold G. Kenyon, Ware; two *s* one *d*. *Educ*: Charterhouse; Magdalene Coll., Cambridge. 1st Class Classical Tripos, Pts I and II, Charles Oldham Scholarship. Civil Servant, Air Ministry, 1934-60; Dep. Under-Sec., War Office, 1960-63; Second Permanent Under-Sec. of State, Ministry of Defence, 1963-66; Permanent Sec., Ministry of Aviation, 1966-67; Secretary (Aviation), Min. of Technology, 1967-70; Permanent Sec., Min. of Aviation Supply, 1970-71; Permanent Sec., attached Civil Service Dept, 1971-72. Chm., Nat. Rifle Assoc., 1972- (Captain, GB Rifle Team, touring USA and Canada, 1976, and for Kolapore match in UK, 1977). Member: Council, Herts T&AVR Assoc; Herts Soc. *Recreations*: rifle shooting, painting, bird-watching, gardening. *Address*: c/o Midland Bank, 194 Strand, WC2. *Club*: Brooks's.

MELVIN, Air Cdre James Douglas, CB 1956; OBE 1947; idc 1956; retired; Property Manager, Coutts & Co.; *b* 20 Feb. 1914; *s* of William Adamson Melvin, The Square, Turriff, Aberdeenshire, and Agnes Fyffe, The Hunghar, Kirriemuir; *m* 1946, Mary Wills; one *d* (one *s* decd). *Educ*: Turriff Secondary Sch. Apprentice, Halton, 1930; Cadet, Cranwell, 1933. Dep. Dir Organization, Air Ministry, 1951-53; Group Capt.

Organization, MEAF, 1953-55; Dir of Organization, Air Ministry, 1957-61, retd. *Address:* Kyrenia Cottage, Old Bosham, Sussex. *Club:* Royal Air Force.

MELVIN, John Turcan, TD and star; MA Cantab; *b* 19 March 1916; *m* 1951, Elizabeth Ann Parry-Jones; one *s* three *d*. *Educ:* Stowe Sch.; Trinity Coll., Cambridge; Berlin Univ. (Schol.). Asst Master, Sherborne Sch., 1938. Served with Dorset Regt, 1939-46. Housemaster, Sherborne Sch., 1950; Headmaster, Kelly Coll., 1959-72; Hd of German Dept, Foster's Sch., Sherborne, 1972-75. *Recreations:* walking, reading, tennis, dramatics. *Address:* Culverhayes Lodge, Sherborne, Dorset. *Club:* East India, Devonshire, Sports and Public Schools.

MELVYN HOWE, Prof. George; *see* Howe, Prof. G. M.

MENAUL, Air Vice-Marshal Stewart William Blacker, CB 1963; CBE 1957; DFC 1941; AFC 1942; Director-General, Royal United Services Institute for Defence Studies, Whitehall, 1968-76; *b* 17 July 1915; 2nd *s* of late Captain W. J. Menaul, MC, and Mrs M. Menaul, Co. Armagh, N Ireland; *m* 1943, Hélène Mary, *d* of late F. R. Taylor; one *s* one *d*. *Educ:* Portadown; RAF Coll., Cranwell. Bomber Command Squadrons, 1936-39; on outbreak of war serving with No 21 Sqdn until 1940; Flying Instructor, 1940-41; No 15 Sqdn, 1941-42; Air Staff No 3 Gp, Bomber Command, 1943; Pathfinder Force, 1943-45; RAF Staff Coll., 1946; Air Ministry, 1947-49; Imperial Defence Coll., 1950-51; Air Ministry, Dep. Dir of Operations, 1951-54; Comd British Atomic Trials Task Forces, Monte Bello and Maralinga (Australia), 1955-56; Commanding Officer, Bombing Sch., Lindholme, 1957-58; Air Officer Administration, Aden, 1959-60; Senior Air Staff Officer, Headquarters Bomber Command, 1961-65; Commandant, Joint Services Staff Coll., 1965-67. *Recreations:* ornithology, painting. *Address:* The Lodge, Frensham Vale, Lower Bourne, Farnham, Surrey. *Club:* Royal Air Force.

MENDE, Dr Erich; Member of the Bundestag, German Federal Republic, since 1949; *b* 28 Oct. 1916; *m* 1948, Margot (*née* Hattje); three *s* one *d*. *Educ:* Humane Coll., Gross-Strehlitz; Universities of Cologne and Bonn (Dr jur). Military service in Infantry Regt 84, Gleiwitz. Served War of 1939-45, Comdr of a Regt (wounded twice, prisoner of war); Major, 1944. Co-founder of FDP (Free Democratic Party), 1945; Mem. Exec. Cttee, British Zone, FDP, 1947; Dep. Chm. FDP in North Rhine Westphalia, 1953-; Mem. 1949-, Dep. Chm. 1956-, Exec. Cttee of Federal Organisation of FDP; Mem. Exec. Cttee, German Council and Parliamentary Section of European Movement; Parliamentary Group of FDP; Whip, and Mem. Exec. Cttee, 1950-53; Dep. Chm., 1953; Chm., 1957; Chm. of FDP, 1960-68. Vice-Chancellor and Minister for All-German Affairs, Federal Republic of Germany, 1963-66. Mem., CDU Hessen, 1970. *Address:* Bundeshaus, 53 Bonn, Germany. *T:* 16 3255; (home) Am Stadtwald 62, 53 Bonn-Bad Godesberg, Germany.

MENDELSON, John Jakob; MP (Lab) for Penistone Division of West Riding of Yorkshire since June 1959; *b* 1917; *s* of late J. C. Mendelson. *Educ:* in London and abroad; University of London (BSc Econ). Lecturer in Economics and Public Administration, Extra Mural Studies, University of Sheffield, 1949-59; formerly, Vice-Pres., Sheffield Trades and Labour Council; Member: Public Accounts Cttee, 1964-66; Mr Speaker's Conf., 1973-. Mem. Consultative Assembly, Council of Europe, 1973-. *Publications:* (jointly) The History of the Sheffield Trades and Labour Council; (jt) The Growth of Parliamentary Scrutiny, 1970; articles in various national weekly papers. *Recreations:* book-collecting, music, Association football, chess. *Address:* House of Commons, SW1; 114 Riverdale Road, Ranmoor, Sheffield, S10 3FD; Flat 15a, Dunrobin Court, 391 Finchley Road, NW3. *T:* 01-794 5472.

MENDELSSOHN, Kurt Alfred Georg, FRS 1951; MA Oxon; MA, DPhil Berlin; Reader in Physics, Oxford University, 1955-73, Emeritus Reader, 1973; Emeritus Professorial Fellow of Wolfson College, 1973 (Professorial Fellow, 1971-73); *b* 7 Jan. 1906; *s* of Ernst Mendelssohn and Eliza Ruprecht, Berlin; *m* 1932, Jutta Lina Charlotte Zarniko, Heiligenbeil; one *s* four *d*. *Educ:* Goethe-Sch., Berlin; Berlin Univ. Research and teaching appointments: Berlin Univ., 1930; Breslau Univ., 1932; Oxford Univ., 1933; Fellow, Wolfson Coll., 1966. Visiting Professor: Rice Institute, Texas, 1952; Purdue Univ., 1956; Tokyo Univ., 1960; Kumasi, Ghana, 1964; Tata Inst., Bombay, 1969; Acad. Sinica, Peking, 1971; Penang Univ., 1972; Coimbra Univ., 1973; Cairo Univ., 1975. Pres., A2 Commn, Internat. Inst. of Refrigeration, 1972-76. Consultant, UKAEA, 1973-. Vice-Pres. Physical Soc., 1957-60; Chm., Internat. Cryogenic Engineering Cttee, 1969-. Editor, Cryogenics, 1960-. Hughes Medal, Royal Society, 1967; Simon Memorial Prize, 1968. *Publications:* What

is Atomic Energy?, 1946; Cryophysics, 1960; The Quest for Absolute Zero, 1966, 1977; In China Now, 1969; The World of Walther Nernst, 1973; The Riddle of the Pyramids, 1974; Science and Western Domination, 1976; in Proc. Royal Society and other scientific and med. jls, mainly on low temperature research, medical physics and Egyptology. *Recreations:* Egyptology, oriental art. *Address:* Wolfson College, Oxford; 235 Iffley Road, Oxford. *T:* 43747. *Club:* Athenæum.

MENDÈS FRANCE, Pierre; Commander of the Legion of Honour; Lawyer; *b* Paris, 11 Jan. 1907; *m* 1933, Lily Cicurel (*d* 1967); two *s*. Prof., Ecole Nationale d'Administration. Under-Sec. for the Treasury, 1938; tried by Vichy Administration, 1940, escaped to serve with Fighting French Air Force. Finance Minister, French Provisional Govt, 1943-44; Head of French Financial Missions, Washington and Breton Woods, 1944; Minister of National Economy, 1944-45; Governor for France of International Bank for Reconstruction and Development and Monetary Fund, 1946-58, resigned. Prime Minister and Minister of Foreign Affairs, France, June 1954-Feb. 1955; Minister of State without portfolio, France, Jan.-May 1956. Docteur en Droit (*hc*). *Publications:* L'Œuvre financière du gouvernement Poincaré, 1928; La Banque internationale, 1930; Liberté, liberté chérie..., 1942 (trans. Eng. as The Pursuit of Freedom, 1956); Gouverner c'est choisir, 1953; Sept mois, dix-sept jours, 1955; La Science économique et l'action (with Gabriel Ardant), 1954 (trans. Eng. and other langs); (with A. Bevan and P. Nenni) Rencontres, 1959; La Politique et la vérité, 1959; La République Moderne, 1962, trans. Eng. as A Modern French Republic, 1963, new edn, 1965; Pour préparer l'avenir, 1968; Dialogues avec l'Asie, 1972, trans. Eng. as Face to Face with Asia; Science économique et lucidité politique (with Gabriel Ardant), 1973; Choisir, 1974; La Vérité guidait leurs pas, 1975. *Address:* Les Monts, 27400 Louviers, France.

MENDIS, Vernon Lorraine Benjamin; High Commissioner for Sri Lanka in UK, since 1975; *b* 5 Dec. 1925; *m* 1953, Padma Rajapathirana; one *s*. *Educ:* Univ. of Ceylon (BA Hons History, 1948). Post Grad. Master of Philosophy, Sch. of Oriental and African Studies, Univ. of London, 1966. *Publication:* The Advent of the British to Ceylon 1760-1850, Colombo 1971. *Recreations:* hiking, bird watching. *Address:* 35 Avenue Road, NW8. *Club:* Travellers'.

MENDL, James Henry Embleton; His Honour Judge Mendl; a Circuit Judge since 1974; *b* 23 Oct. 1927; *s* of R. W. S. Mendl, barrister and author, and Dorothy Williams Mendl (*née* Burnett), and *g s* of late Sir S. F. Mendl, KBE; *m* 1971, Helena Augusta Maria Schrama, *d* of late J. H. and H. H. Schrama-Jekat, The Netherlands. *Educ:* Harrow; University Coll., Oxford (MA). Called to Bar, Inner Temple, 1953; South Eastern Circuit. Commissioned, Worcestershire Regt, 1947; served: Egypt, with 2nd N Staffs, 1947-48; with Royal Signals (TA), 1952-54, and Queen's Royal Regt (TA) (Captain, 1955), 1954-56. Councillor, Royal Borough of Kensington and Chelsea, 1964-74 (Vice-Chm., Town Planning Cttee, 1969; Chm. (Vice-Chm. 1970), Libraries Cttee, 1971). Contested (C) Gateshead East, 1966. *Recreations:* music, skiing. *Address:* 1 Wetherby Place, SW7 4NU. *T:* 01-373 1518.

MENDOZA, Maurice, MSM 1946; Director of Manpower and Management Services, Departments of the Environment and Transport; *b* 1 May 1921; *e s* of Daniel and Rachel Mendoza; *m* 1949, Phyllis Kriger. *Educ:* Sir Henry Raine's Foundation. Dip. Sociology London. Clerical Officer, HM Office of Works, 1938; served Royal Signals and Cheshire Yeo., 1941-46 (Sgt); Mil. Mission to Belgium, 1944-46; Organisation Officer, Treasury, 1956-61; Principal, MPBW, 1963; Asst Sec. 1968; DoE, 1970; Under-Sec., 1973. *Recreations:* theatre, walking, photography. *Address:* 45 Grange Grove, Canonbury, N1 2NP. *T:* 01-226 3250. *Club:* Civil Service.

MENDOZA, Vivian P.; *see* Pereira-Mendoza.

MENECES, Maj.-Gen. Ambrose Neponucene Trelawny, CB 1963; CBE 1944; DSO 1945; MD; *b* London, 19 March 1904; *s* of Joseph and Amy Meneces, London; *m* 1st, 1934, Elsie Gertrude Hunt (*d* 1976); 2nd, 1977, Cecilia Ethel Parker. *Educ:* St Benedict's; Westminster Cathedral Sch.; Univ. Coll. Hosp. MB, BS London 1928; MD London 1946; FRCP 1960; DTM&H London 1948. Commissioned into RAMC 1928; served on North-West Frontier, 1935-36; Burma, 1942-45 (despatches three times); Korea, 1952-54. Prof. of Tropical Medicine, Royal Army Medical College, 1949-52; Chief of Medical Divs, SHAPE, 1956; Dir of Medical Services, Western Command, 1958-61, BAOR, 1961-62; Commandant and Dir of Studies, Royal Army Medical College, 1963-66; MO, DHSS, 1966-71. Fellow of University Coll., London, 1964-. Fitzpatrick

Lectr, RCP, 1969-70. Chadwick Medal, 1964. OStJ 1954; QHP, 1960-66. *Publications:* Transport of Casualties by Air, 1949; Heat Stroke and Heat Exhaustion, 1950; First Aid for Nuclear Casualties, 1956; Life of Sir Edwin Chadwick, 1972; contribs to British Encyclopædia of Medicine, etc. *Recreation:* fishing. *Address:* 2 Bracken Road, Seaford, E Sussex BN25 4HR. *Club:* Athenæum.

MENEMENCIOGLU, Turgut; Ambassador of Turkey to the Court of St James's, since 1972; *b* Istanbul, 8 Oct. 1914; *s of* Muvatfak and Kadriye Menemencioğlu; *m* 1944, Nermin Moran; two *s. Educ:* Robert Coll., Istanbul; Geneva Univ. Joined Turkish Min. of Foreign Affairs, 1939; Permanent Delegate, European Office, UN Geneva, 1950-52; Counsellor, Turkish Embassy, Washington, 1952; Dir-Gen., Econ. Affairs, Min. of Foreign Affairs, 1952-54; Dep. Permanent Rep. to UN, 1954-60; Ambassador to Canada, 1960; Permanent Rep. to UN, 1960-62; Ambassador to USA, 1962-67; High Polit. Adviser, Mem., High Polit. Planning Bd, Min. of Foreign Affairs, 1967-68; Sec.-Gen., CENTO, 1968-72; Adviser, Min. of Foreign Affairs, 1972. *Address:* Turkish Embassy, 69 Portland Place, W1; Koryurek Sokak 11 Çankaya, Ankara, Turkey.

MENEVIA, Bishop of, (RC), since 1972; **Rt. Rev. Langton Douglas Fox,** DD; *b* 21 Feb. 1917; *s of* Claude Douglas Fox and Ethel Helen (*née* Cox). *Educ:* Mark Cross, Wonersh and Maynooth. BA 1938; DD 1945. Priest 1942. Lectr, St John's Seminary, Wonersh, 1942-55; Mem., Catholic Missionary Soc., 1955-59; Parish Priest, Chichester, 1959-65; Auxiliary Bishop of Menevia, 1965-72. *Recreations:* sailing, swimming. *Address:* Bishop's House, Wrexham, Clwyd. *T:* Wrexham 2054.

MENHENNET, Dr David; Librarian of the House of Commons, since 1976; *b* 4 Dec. 1928; *s of* Thomas William Menhennet and Everill Waters Menhennet, Redruth, Cornwall; *m* 1954, Audrey, *o d of* William and Alice Holmes, Accrington, Lancs; two *s. Educ:* Truro Sch., Cornwall; Oriel Coll., Oxford (BA 1st Cl. Hons 1952); Queen's Coll., Oxford. Open Scholarship in Mod. Langs, Oriel Coll., Oxford, 1946; Heath Harrison Trav. Scholarship, 1951; Bishop Fraser Res. Scholar, Oriel Coll., 1952-53; Laming Trav. Fellow, Queen's Coll., Oxford, 1953-54; Zaharoff Trav. Scholarship, 1953-54. MA 1956, DPhil 1960, Oxon. Library Clerk, House of Commons Library, 1954; Asst Librarian i/c Res. Div., 1964-67; Dep. Librarian, 1967-76. Member: Study of Parliament Gp, 1964-; Adv. Cttee, Bibliographic Services Divn, British Library, 1975-; Associate, Inst. of Cornish Studies, 1974-. FRSA 1966. *Publications:* (with J. Palmer) Parliament in Perspective, 1967; The Journal of the House of Commons: a bibliographical and historical guide, 1971; (ed with D. C. L. Holland) Erskine May's Private Journal, 1857-1882, 1972; articles in Libr. Assoc. Record, Parliamentarian, Parly Affairs, Polit. Quart., New Scientist. *Recreations:* walking, visiting old churches, music, watching sport. *Address:* (office) House of Commons Library, SW1A 0AA. *T:* 01-219 3635. *Club:* Athenæum.

MENNEER, Stephen Snow, CB 1967; retired, 1970, as Assistant Under-Secretary of State, Department of Health and Social Security; *b* 6 March 1910; *s of* Sydney Charles Menneer, LLD, and Minnie Elizabeth Menneer; *m* 1935, Margaret Longstaff Smith (*d* 1976); one *s* one *d. Educ:* Rugby Sch.; Oriel Coll., Oxford. Min. of Information, 1939; Min. of National Insurance, 1948; Under-Sec., Min. of Pensions and Nat. Insurance, then Min. of Social Security, 1961. *Address:* Cowlas, Burrington, Umberleigh, N Devon.

MENNELL, Peter, CMG 1970; MBE 1945; HM Diplomatic Service; High Commissioner in the Bahamas, since 1975; *b* 29 Aug. 1918; *s of* Dr James B. Mennell, London, and Elizabeth Walton Allen, St Louis, Mo.; *m* 1946, Prudence Helen Vansittart; two *s* two *d. Educ:* Oundle Sch.; King's Coll., Cambridge (MA). Served 67th Field Regt, RA, 1939-46 (despatches, MBE). Vice-Consul, New York (commercial), 1946-49; 1st Sec., Foreign Office, 1949-51; 1st Sec., Moscow, 1951-54; Foreign Office, 1954-57; Madrid, 1959-61; HM Consul-Gen., Cleveland, Ohio, 1961-64; Inspector, HM Diplomatic Service, 1964-66; Counsellor, Democratic Republic of the Congo, 1966-70; intermittently Chargé d'Affaires, there and in Burundi, 1966-70; Ambassador to Ecuador, 1970-74. Leader, UK Delegn to Econ. Commn for Latin America, 1973, and in Guatemala, 1977. Mem., Pilgrims Soc. Liveryman of Worshipful Company of Grocers, 1954; Col in Hon. Order of Kentucky Colonels, 1961; Visiting Cttee of Bd of Govs, Western Reserve Univ. for Lang. and Lit., 1964. Hon. Mem., Quito Br., Internat. Law Assoc. *Recreations:* usual outdoor sports and choral singing. *Address:* c/o Foreign and Commonwealth Office, SW1A 2AH. *Clubs:* United Oxford & Cambridge University; Lyford Cay (Nassau).

MENON, Prof. Mambillikalathil Govind Kumar, MSc, PhD; FRS 1970; Chairman, Electronics Commission and Secretary to the Government of India Department of Electronics, since 1971; Scientific Adviser to Minister of Defence, Director General of Defence Research and Development Organisation, and Secretary in the Ministry of Defence for Defence Research, since 1974; *b* 28 Aug. 1928; *s of* Kizhekepat Sankara Menon and Mambillikalathil Narayaniamma; *m* 1955, Indumati Patel; one *s* one *d. Educ:* Jaswant Coll., Jodhpur; Royal Inst. of Science, Bombay (MSc); Univ. of Bristol (PhD). Royal Commn for Exhibn of 1851 Senior Award, 1953-55; Tata Inst. of Fundamental Research: Reader, 1955-58; Associate Prof., 1958-60; Prof. of Physics and Dean of Physics Faculty, 1960-64; Senior Prof. and Dep. Dir (Physics), 1964-66, Dir, 1966-75. Mem., UN Sec.-Gen's Adv. Cttee on Application of Sci. and Technol. to Develt.; Mem., Nat. Cttee on Science and Technol., Govt of India; Chairman: Electronics Trade and Technol. Develt Corp. Ltd; Bharat Dynamics Ltd. Fellow: Indian Acad. of Sciences (Pres., 1974-76), Council Mem., 1977-79; Indian Nat. Science Acad.; Hon. Fellow, Nat. Acad. of Sciences, India; For. Hon. Mem., Amer. Acad. of Arts and Scis; Hon. Fellow, Instn Electronics and Telecomm. Engrs (India). Hon. DSc: Jodhpur Univ., 1970; Delhi Univ., 1973; Sardar Patel Univ., 1973; Shanti Swarup Bhatnagar Award for Physical Sciences, Council of Scientific and Industrial Research, 1960; Padma Shri, 1961; Padma Bhushan, 1968; Khaitan Medal, RAS, 1973. *Publications:* about 65, on cosmic rays and elementary particle physics; about 40 major lectures, talks etc. *Recreations:* photography, bird-watching. *Address:* Department of Electronics, Vigyan Bhavan Annexe, Maulana Azad Road, New Delhi 110011, India. *Clubs:* National Liberal; United Services (Bombay); Indian International Centre (New Delhi).

MENOTTI, Gian Carlo; Composer; Founder and President, Spoleto Festival; *b* Cadegliano, Italy, 7 July 1911. *Educ:* The Curtis Institute of Music, Philadelphia, Pa. Has been resident in the United States since 1928. Teacher of Composition at Curtis Inst. of Music, 1948-55. First performances of works include: Amelia Goes to the Ball (opera), 1936; The Old Maid and the Thief (radio opera), 1939 (later staged); The Island God, 1942; Sebastian (Ballet), 1943; Piano Concerto in F, 1945; The Medium (opera), 1946 (later filmed); The Telephone (opera), 1947; Errand into the Maze (ballet), 1947; The Consul (opera), 1950 (Pulitzer Prize); Apocalypse (orchestral), 1951; Amahl and the Night Visitors (television opera), 1951; Violin Concerto in A Minor, 1952; The Saint of Bleeker Street (opera), 1954 (Pulitzer Prize); The Unicorn, The Gorgon, and the Manticore, 1956; Maria Golovin (television opera), 1958; The Last Savage (opera), 1963; The Death of the Bishop of Brindisi (oratorio), 1963; Martin's Lie (opera), 1964; Canti della Lontananza (song cycle), 1967; Help, Help, the Globolinks (opera), 1968; The Leper (drama), 1970; Triplo Concerto a Tre (symphonic piece), 1970; The Most Important Man (opera), 1971. Wrote libretto for Vanessa (opera, by Samuel Barber), 1958. *Publications:* his major works have been published, also some minor ones; he is the author of all his libretti, most of which have been written in English. *Address:* 27 E 62nd Street, New York, NY 10021, USA.

MENSFORTH, Sir Eric, Kt 1962; CBE 1945; MA Cantab; CEng; FIMechE; FRAeS; FIProdE; Vice Lord-Lieutenant, South Yorkshire, since 1974; Deputy Chairman John Brown & Co. Ltd; Director: Westland Aircraft Ltd (Chairman, 1953-68, Vice-Chairman, 1968-71); Boddy Industries Ltd; *b* 17 May 1906; 2nd *s of* late Sir Holberry Mensforth, KCB, CBE; *m* 1934, Betty, *d of* late Rev. Picton W. Francis; three *d. Educ:* Altrincham County High Sch.; University Coll. Sch.; King's Coll., Cambridge (1st class mechanical sciences tripos). Engineering work at Woolwich Arsenal, Mather & Platt Ltd, Bolckow Vaughan Ltd, Kloecknerwerke A. G., Dorman Long Ltd, English Electric Ltd, Markham & Co. Ltd, T. Firth & John Brown Ltd, Chief Production Adviser to Chief Executive, Ministry of Aircraft Production, 1943-45. Master Cutler, Sheffield, 1965-66. Chairman: EDC for Electronics Industry, 1968-70; Cttee on Quality Assurance, 1968-70; Council of Engineering Instns, 1969-72; Governing Body, Sheffield Polytechnic, 1969-75; Member: British Productivity Council, 1964-69; Royal Ordnance Factories Bd, 1968-72; Council, RGS, 1968-70; Treasurer, British Assoc. for Advancement of Science, 1970-75; a Vice-Pres., Fellowship of Engineering, 1977; Pres., S Yorks Scouts' Assoc., 1969-76. Hon. DEng Sheffield, 1967; Hon. DSc Southampton, 1970. DL S (formerly WR) Yorks, 1971. *Address:* 3 Belgrave Drive, Fulwood, Sheffield S10 3LQ. *T:* Sheffield 307737. *Clubs:* Alpine; Sheffield (Sheffield).

MENTER, Sir James (Woodham), Kt 1973; MA, PhD, ScD Cantab; FRS 1966; FInstP; Principal, Queen Mary College, London University, since 1976; *b* 22 Aug. 1921; *s of* late Horace

Menter and late Jane Anne Lackenby; *m* 1947, Marjorie Jean, *d* of late Thomas Stodart Whyte-Smith, WS; two *s* one *d*. *Educ:* Dover Grammar Sch.; Peterhouse, Cambridge. PhD 1949, ScD 1960. Experimental Officer, Admty, 1942-45; Research, Cambridge Univ., 1946-54 (ICI Fellow, 1951-54; Sir George Beilby Mem. Award, 1954); Tube Investments Research Laboratories, Hinxton Hall, 1954-68; Dir of Research and Develt, Tube Investments Ltd, 1965-76. Director: Tube Investments Res. Labs, 1961-68; Tube Investments Ltd, 1965-; Round Oak Steelworks Ltd, 1967-76; British Petroleum Co., 1976-. Mem., SRC, 1967-72; a Vice-Pres., Royal Society, 1971-76, Treasurer, 1972-76. Extraordinary Fellow, Churchill Coll., Cambridge, 1966. President: Inst. of Physics, 1970-72; Metals Soc., 1976; Dep. Chm., Adv. Council Applied R&D, 1976-. Mem. (part-time), BSC, 1976-. Hon. DTech Brunel, 1974. Bessemer Medal, Iron and Steel Inst., 1973; Glazebrook Medal and Prize, Inst. of Physics, 1977. *Publications:* scientific papers in Proc. Royal Society, Advances in Physics, Jl Iron and Steel Inst., etc. *Recreation:* fishing. *Address:* 1 The Pierhead, Wapping High Street, E1. *T:* 01-488 3393.

MENTETH, Sir James (Wallace) Stuart-, 6th Bt, *cr* 1838; with Imperial Chemical Industries Ltd, Paints Division; *b* 13 Nov. 1922; *e s* of 5th Bt and Winifred Melville (*d* 1968), *d* of Daniel Francis and *widow* of Capt. Rupert G. Raw, DSO; *S* father, 1952; *m* 1949, Dorothy Patricia, *d* of late Frank Greaves Warburton; two *s*. *Educ:* Fettes; St Andrews Univ.; Trinity Coll., Oxford (MA). Served War of 1939-45, with Scots Guards, 1942-44; on active service in North Africa and Italy (Anzio) (severely wounded). *Recreations:* motoring, swimming, gardening, ornithology. *Heir: s* Charles Greaves Stuart-Menteth, *b* 25 Nov. 1950. *Address:* Broomhurst, Deepcut, Camberley, Surrey.

MENUHIN, Yehudi, KBE (Hon.) 1965; violinist; *b* New York, 22 April 1916; *s* of Moshe and Marutha Menuhin; *m* 1938, Nola Ruby, *d* of George Nicholas, Melbourne, Australia; one *s* one *d*; *m* 1947, Diana Rosamond, *d* of late G. L. E. Gould and Lady Harcourt (Evelyn Suart); two *s*. *Educ:* private tutors; studied music under Sigmund Anker and Louis Persinger, in San Francisco; Georges Enesco, Rumania and Paris; Adolph Busch, Switzerland. Made début with orchestra, San Francisco, aged 7, Paris, aged 10, New York, 11, Berlin, 13; since then has played with most of world's orchestras and conductors; has introduced among contemp. works Sonata for Violin alone, by Béla Bartók (composed for Mr Menuhin), as well as works by William Walton, Ben-Haim, Georges Enesco, Pizzetti, Ernest Bloch, etc. During War of 1939-45 devoted larger part of his time to concerts for US and Allied armed forces and benefit concerts for Red Cross, etc (500 concerts). Series of concerts in Moscow (by invitation), 1945; seven visits to Israel, 1950-; first tour of Japan, 1951; first tour of India (invitation of Prime Minister), 1952. Largely responsible for cultural exchange programme between US and Russia, 1955, and for bringing Indian music and musicians to West. Initiated his own annual music festival in Gstaad, Switzerland, 1957, and in Bath, 1959-68; Jt Artistic Dir, Windsor Festival, 1969-72. Founded Yehudi Menuhin Sch. of Music, Stoke d'Abernon, Surrey, 1963; Pres., Trinity Coll. of Music, 1971. Hon. Fellow, St Catharine's Coll., Cambridge, 1970; Hon. DMus: Oxford, 1962; Cambridge, 1970; Sorbonne, 1976, and 10 other degrees from Brit. Univs. Freedom of the City of Edinburgh, 1965; City of Bath, 1966. *Films:* Stage Door Canteen; Magic Bow; The Way of Light (biog.). He records for several companies, both as soloist and as Conductor of Menuhin Festival Orch., with which has toured USA, Australia, NZ and Europe; appears regularly on American and British Television. Gold Medal, Royal Philharmonic Soc., 1962; Jawaharlal Nehru Award for International Understanding, 1970; Sonning Music Prize, Denmark, 1972; Handel Medal, NY; City of Jerusalem Medal. Decorations include: Comdr, Legion of Honour, Order of Arts and Letters (France); Order of Leopold (Belgium); Ordre de la Couronne (Belgium); Order of Merit (W German Republic); Royal Order of the Phœnix (Greece); Comdr, Order of Orange-Nassau (Netherlands); Hon. Citizen of Switzerland, 1970. *Publications:* The Violin: six lessons by Yehudi Menuhin, 1971; Theme and Variations, 1972; Violin and Viola, 1976; Sir Edward Elgar: my musical grandfather (essay), 1976; (autobiography) Unfinished Journey, 1977; *Relevant Publication:* Yehudi Menuhin, The Story of the Man and the Musician, by Robert Magidoff, 1956 (USA). *Address:* (agents) Columbia Artists Management, 165 W 57th Street, New York City; Harold Holt, 134 Wigmore Street, W1, England. *Clubs:* Athenæum, Garrick.
See also *J . C . M . Benthall* .

MENZIES, John Maxwell; Chairman, John Menzies Holdings Ltd and subsidiary cos, since 1952; *b* 13 Oct. 1926; *s* of late John Francis Menzies; *m* 1953, Patricia Eleanor Dawson, *d* of late

Comdr Sir Hugh Dawson, Bt, CBE; four *d*. *Educ:* Eton. Lieut Grenadier Guards, released 1948. Berwickshire CC, 1954-57. Director: Atlantic Assets, 1973-; Independent Investment Trust, 1973-; Vidal Sassoon Inc., 1974-; Vidal Sassoon UK Ltd, 1974-; Gordon and Gotch Holdings Ltd, 1976-; Trustee, Newsvendors' Benevolent Instn, 1968- (Pres., 1968-74). Mem., Royal Co. of Archers, HM's Body Guard for Scotland. *Recreations:* farming, shooting, reading, travel. *Address:* Kames, Duns, Berwickshire. *T:* Leitholm 202. *Clubs:* Turf, Boodle's; New (Edinburgh).

MENZIES, Sir Laurence James, Kt 1962; Director, The Commercial Banking Co. of Sydney (London Board), since 1966; *b* 23 Dec. 1906; *yr s* of late James Menzies, Coupar Angus, Perthshire; *m* 1935, Agnes Cameron, *yr d* of John Smart; one *s* one *d*. *Educ:* Wandsworth Sch. Entered Bank of England, 1925; Asst Chief Cashier, 1943; Dep. Chief Cashier, 1952; Adviser to the Govs, 1957-58, 1962-64; Sec. of the Export Credits Guarantee Dept, 1958-61. Pres., Union d'Assureurs des Crédits Internationaux (Berne Union), 1960-61. *Recreation:* golf. *Address:* Timbers, Vincent Close, Esher, Surrey. *T:* Esher 64257. *Clubs:* Overseas Bankers', Bath, MCC.

MENZIES, Marie Ney; Actress Producer; *d* of William Fix and Agnes Rohan; *m* 1930, T. H. Menzies (marr. diss., 1949; remarried to T. H. Menzies, 1959, he *d* 1962). *Educ:* St Mary's Convent, Wellington, NZ. stage début in Melbourne, 1917; played in Australia until 1922, supporting among other visiting stars Marie Tempest; leading lady at the Old Vic 1924-25; parts included Ophelia, Lady Macbeth and Beatrice; visited Cairo 1927 with company invited by the Egyptian Government, parts included Desdemona, Portia and Viola; leading roles in London include Kate Hardcastle in Sir Nigel Playfair's production She Stoops To Conquer, Milady in The Three Musketeers, Miss Janus in John Van Druten's London Wall; leading part in J. B. Priestley's Dangerous Corner; star role in The Lake by Dorothy Massingham and Murray Macdonald; this play was especially written for her; leading role in Touch Wood; played leading role in Mrs Nobby Clark under her own management; Olga, in Anton Tchehov's Three Sisters (Old Vic); lead with Frank Vosper in Love from a Stranger; Mrs Alving in Ghosts; leading part in Sanctity, by Mrs Violet Clifton; leading roles in G. Bernard Shaw's The Millionairess (Dublin and Hull) and Candida (Dutch Tour 1939); Australian Season, Sydney and Melbourne, 1940-41; Ladies in Retirement, No Time for Comedy, Private Lives; Shakespearean Recitals, Australia, Malaya; with South African Broadcasting Corporation, Johannesburg Production, etc., 1942, 1943, 1944; African-Middle-East Tour, Shakespeare's Women, for British Council and ENSA; Italy and Holland, 1945, and performances for Arts Council; Hecuba in Trojan Women for Company of 4, Lyric Theatre; King of Rome, Fish in the Family, Native Son, Bolton's Theatre, SW10, 1947-48; Nurse Braddock in the Gioconda Smile, 1948; Lady Corbel in Rain on the Just, 1948; Sara Cantrey in The Young and Fair, St Martin's, 1949; Mrs Cortelyon in The Second Mrs Tanqueray, Haymarket, 1950; Martha in The Other Heart, Old Vic, 1952; Mary in Fotheringhay, Edinburgh Festival, 1953. Played in films including The Wandering Jew; Brief Ecstasy; Jamaica Inn; Uneasy Terms; Conspirators; Romantic Age; Seven Days to Noon; Lavender Hill Mob; Night was our Friend; Simba. Television: The Little Dry Thorn, The Infernal Machine, Family Reunion, The Lake, The Sacred Flame, Time and the Conways, The Wrong Side of the Park, Do you Remember the Germans. *Recreations:* reading, riding, walking, painting. *Address:* London Management, 235 Regent Street, W1. *Club:* Lansdowne.

MENZIES, Dame Pattie (Maie), GBE 1954; *b* 2 March 1899; *d* of late Senator J. W. Leckie; *m* 1920, Robert Gordon Menzies (*see* Rt Hon. Sir Robert Menzies); one *s* one *d* (and one *s* decd). *Educ:* Fintona Girls' Sch., Melbourne; Presbyterian Ladies' Coll., Melbourne. *Address:* 2 Haverbrack Avenue, Malvern, Melbourne, Vic 3144, Australia. *Club:* Alexandra (Melbourne).

MENZIES, Sir Peter (Thomson), Kt 1972; Director: National Westminster Bank Ltd since 1968; Commercial Union Assurance Co. Ltd since 1962; *b* 15 April 1912; *s* of late John C. Menzies and late Helen S. Aikman; *m* 1938, Mary McPherson Alexander, *d* of late John T. Menzies and late Agnes Anderson; one *s* one *d*. *Educ:* Musselburgh Grammar Sch.; University of Edinburgh. MA, 1st Class Hons Math. and Natural Philosophy, 1934. Inland Revenue Dept, 1933-39; Treasurer's Dept, Imperial Chemical Industries Ltd, 1939-56 (Asst Treas. 1947, Dep. Treas. 1952); Director: Imperial Chemical Industries Ltd, 1956-72 (Dep. Chm., 1967-72); Imperial Metal Industries Ltd, 1962-72 (Chm., 1964-72). Part-time Mem., CEGB, 1960-72; Chm., Electricity Council, 1972-77. A Vice-Pres., Siol na Meinnrich; President: UNIPEDE, 1973-76; District Heating

Assoc., 1975-. FInstP; CompIEE; Fellow, Inst. Dirs. *Address:* Kit's Corner, Harmer Green, Welwyn, Herts. *T:* Welwyn 4386. *Club:* Caledonian.

MENZIES, Rt. Hon. Sir Robert (Gordon), KT 1963; AK 1976; PC 1937; CH 1951; QC 1929; FRS 1965; LLM; MHR for Kooyong, 1934-66; Prime Minister, Australia, 1939-41 and 1949-66 (also Minister for External Affairs, 1960-61; led Mission to Pres. Nasser on Suez Canal, 1956); *b* Jeparit, 20 Dec. 1894; *s* of late James Menzies; *m* 1920, Pattie Maie (*see* Dame P. Menzies); one *s* one *d* (and one *s* decd). *Educ:* State Schs; Grenville Coll., Ballarat; Wesley Coll., Melbourne; Melbourne Univ. (first class Final Hons). First Australian Hon. LLD Melbourne Univ., also Hon. LLD: QUB, Bristol Univ., Universities of BC Sydney, McGill, Lavel, Montreal, Harvard, Royal University of Malta, Tasmania, Cambridge, Leeds, Adelaide, Edinburgh, Birmingham, Aust. Nat. Univ. Canberra, Sussex; Hon. DCL, Oxford and Univ. of Kent at Canterbury; Hon. DSc, University of NSW. Hon. Fellow, Worcester Coll., Oxford, 1968. Practised as a Barrister at the Victorian Bar; entered Victorian Parliament, 1928; MLC East Yarra, 1928-29; MLA Nunawading, 1929-34; Hon. Minister, McPherson Government, 1928-29; Attorney-Gen., Minister for Railways and Dep. Premier of Victoria, 1932-34; Attorney-Gen., Commonwealth of Australia, 1934-39; Treasurer, 1939-40; Minister: for Trade and Customs, Feb.-March 1940; for Co-ordination of Defence, 1939-42; for Information and for Munitions, 1940; Prime Minister, 1939-41; Leader of Opposition, 1943-49. Chancellor, Melbourne Univ., 1967-72. Freeman of Cities of Swansea, 1941; Edinburgh, 1948; London, 1952; Oxford, 1953; Athens, 1955; Melbourne, 1966; Hastings, 1966; Sandwich, 1967; Deal, 1969; Hon. Master of Bench, Gray's Inn, 1935; FRSA; Hon. FRACP, 1955; Hon. FRAIA, 1956; Hon. FInstM, 1957; Hon. FAA, 1958; Hon. FRCPEd 1960; Hon. FRCOG 1961; Hon. FRCS 1965; Hon. Freeman: Clothworkers' Co.; Goldsmiths' Co.; Trustee, Melbourne Cricket Ground. Constable of Dover Castle, Lord Warden of the Cinque Ports, 1965-; Pres., Dover Coll., 1966-; Pres., Kent County Cricket Club, 1969. Chief Commander, Legion of Merit (US), 1950; Order of Rising Sun, First Class (Japan), 1973. *Publications:* The Rule of Law during War, 1917; To The People of Britain at War from the Prime Minister of Australia, 1941; The Forgotten People, 1943; Speech is of Time, 1958; Afternoon Light (Memoirs), 1967; Central Power in the Australian Commonwealth, 1967; The Measure of the Years, 1970; (jt) Studies in Australian Constitution; contribs to contemporary art and legal jls. *Recreations:* walking and watching first-class cricket. *Address:* 2 Haverbrack Avenue, Malvern, Melbourne, Vic 3144, Australia; (Business) 95 Collins Street, Melbourne, Vic. 3000. *Clubs:* Athenæum, Savage, Pratt's, MCC, (Pres. 1962) Lord's Taverners'; Athenæum, Australian, Savage, (Pres.) Melbourne Scots, West Brighton (all Melbourne).

MENZIES ANDERSON, Sir Gilmour, Kt 1962; CBE 1956 (MBE 1943); solicitor; *b* 29 April 1914; *s* of William Menzies Anderson, DSO, MC, and Jessie Jack Gilmour; *m* 1943, Ivy Beryl Shairp (*née* Chadwick); one *d. Educ:* Glasgow High Sch.; Glasgow Univ. (LLB). Solicitor, 1939. Mem. Glasgow Corporation, 1938-39 and again, 1945-47. Commissioned 6th HLI (TA), 1939; served with "Chindits", India and Burma, 1942-45; in comd 16th Inf. Bde, 1945; demob., 1945, with rank Hon. Brig. Chm., Glasgow Unionist Assoc., 1954-57; Pres., Scottish Unionist Assoc., 1960-61; Chm. Conservative Party in Scotland, 1967-71 (Dep. Chm. 1965-67). *Recreations:* fishing and shooting. *Address:* Craigievern Cottage, Balfron Station, Glasgow G63 0NQ. *T:* Drymen 320. *Club:* Western (Glasgow).

MERCER, David; Playwright since 1961; *b* 27 June 1928; has one *d. Educ:* King's Coll., Newcastle upon Tyne. Writers' Guild Award (Best Teleplay): A Suitable Case for Treatment, 1962; In Two Minds, 1967; Let's Murder Vivaldi, 1968; Evening Standard Drama Award (Most Promising Dramatist): Ride a Cock Horse, 1965; British Film Academy Award (Best Screen Play): Morgan, 1965. *Publications:* The Generations, 1964; Three TV Comedies, 1966; Ride a Cock Horse, 1966; The Parachute and Other Plays, 1967; Belcher's Luck, 1967; The Governor's Lady, 1968; On the Eve of Publication and Other Plays, 1970; After Haggerty, 1970; Flint, 1970; Duck Song, 1974; The Bankrupt and other plays, 1974; Huggy Bear and other plays, 1977. *Recreation:* political studies. *Address:* c/o Margaret Ramsay Ltd, 14a Goodwin's Court, WC2.

MERCER, Rt. Rev. Eric Arthur John; *see* Exeter, Bishop of.

MERCER, John Charles Kenneth; a Recorder of the Crown Court, since 1975; *b* 17 Sept. 1917; *s* of late Charles Wilfred Mercer and Cecil Maud Mercer; *m* 1944, Barbara Joan, *d* of late Arnold Sydney Whitehead, CB, CBE, and Maud Ethel Whitehead; one *s* one *d. Educ:* Ellesmere Coll.; Law Sch., Swansea University Coll. (LLB). Solicitor. War Service, 1940-45, Captain RA. Partner, Douglas-Jones & Mercer, 1946-. Mem., SW Wales River Authority, 1960-74. *Recreations:* fishing, shooting, golf, watching sport. *Address:* 334 Gower Road, Killay, Swansea, West Glamorgan. *T:* Swansea 22931. *Clubs:* City and County, Clyne Golf (Swansea).

MERCER, Rt. Rev. Robert William Stanley; *see* Matabeleland, Bishop of.

MERCER NAIRNE PETTY-FITZMAURICE, family name of Marquess of Lansdowne.

MERCHANT, Vivien; actress since 1943; *b* 22 July 1929; *d* of William Thomson and Margaret McNaughton; *m* 1956, Harold Pinter, *qv*; one *s. Educ:* Bury Convent, Manchester. Principal Appearances: Stella in The Collection (TV), 1961; Sarah in The Lover (stage and TV), 1963; Ruth in The Homecoming (stage, London and NY), 1965-67; Natasha Petrovna in A Month in the Country (TV), 1966; Lady Macbeth in Macbeth (Royal Shakespeare Co.), 1967; Mixed Doubles, Comedy, 1969; Flint, Criterion, 1970; The Tea Party, Duchess, 1970; Exiles, Mermaid, 1970, Aldwych 1971; The Man of Mode, Old Times, Aldwych, 1971; The Maids, Greenwich, 1974; Gaslight, Guildford, 1974; The Ginger-bread Lady, Windsor, 1974; *films:* Alfie, 1966 (nominated for Academy Award); Accident, 1967; Under Milk Wood, 1972; Frenzy, 1972; The Offence, 1973; The Homecoming, 1974; The Maids, 1974; The Lover, 1976; Man in an Iron Mask, 1976. TV Actress of the Year award, 1963. *Recreations:* table tennis, listening to jazz, reading. *Address:* c/o International Creative Management, 22 Grafton Street, W1.

MERCHANT, Rev. Prof. William Moelwyn, FRSL; Professor of English, University of Exeter, since 1961; Vicar of Llanddewi Brefi, diocese of St Davids, since 1974; *b* 5 June 1913; *s* of late William Selwyn and Elizabeth Ann Merchant, Port Talbot, Glamorgan; *m* 1938, Maria Eluned Hughes, Llanelly; one *s* one *d. Educ:* Port Talbot Grammar Sch.; (Exhibnr) University Coll., Cardiff. BA, 1st Cl. English hons 1933; 2nd Cl. 1st div. Hist., 1934; MA 1950; DLitt 1960. Hist. Master, Carmarthen Grammar Sch., 1935; English Master, Newport High Sch., 1936; English Lectr, Caerleon Trg Coll., 1937; University Coll. Cardiff: Lectr in Eng. Lang. and Lit., 1939; Sen. Lectr, 1950; Reader, 1961. Fellow, Folger Shakespeare Library, Washington, DC, and Fulbright Fellow, 1957; Woodward Lectr, Yale Univ., 1957; Dupont Lectr, Sewanee Univ., Tenn, 1963; Willett Prof. of English and Theology, Univ. of Chicago, 1971. Founded Rougemont Press, 1970 (with Ted Hughes, Eric Cleave and Paul Merchant). Welsh Cttee of Arts Council of Gt Brit., 1960; Council, Llandaff Festival, 1958-61. Ordained to Anglican Orders, 1940; Examining Chaplain to the Bishop of Salisbury; Canon of Salisbury Cathedral, 1967-73, Canon Emeritus, 1973 (Chancellor, 1967-71). Founded Llanddewi Brefi Arts Fest., 1975. FRSL 1976; Hon. Fellow, University Coll. of Wales, Aberystwyth, 1975. Hon HLD Wittenberg Univ., Ohio, 1973. *Publications:* Wordsworth's Guide to the Lakes (illus. John Piper), 1952 (US 1953); Reynard Library Wordsworth, 1955 (US 1955); Shakespeare and the Artist, 1959; Creed and Drama, 1965; (ed) Merchant of Venice, 1967; (ed) Marlowe's Edward the Second, 1967; Comedy, 1972; Tree of Life (libretto, music by Alun Hoddinott), 1972; (ed) Essays and Studies, 1977; articles in Times Literary Supplement, Warburg Jl, Shakespeare Survey, Shakespeare Quarterly, Shakespeare Jahrbuch, Encyc. Britannica, etc. *Recreations:* theatre, typography, sculpting (one-man exhibns at Exeter, Cardiff, Swansea, Plymouth, Southampton, Aberystwyth, 1971-77). *Address:* Llanddewi Vicarage, Tregaron, Dyfed. *T:* Tregaron 359.

MEREDITH, George Patrick, MSc, MEd (Leeds); PhD (London); FBPsS; Professor of Psychophysics, University of Leeds, 1967-69; retired 1969; now Professor Emeritus; Director of Epistemic Communication Research Unit, retired 1969; *b* 10 May 1904; *s* of Edgar and Helen Meredith; *m* 1942, Gillian Tremaine; one *s. Educ:* Wolverley Sch.; University of Leeds; University Coll. and Institute of Education, University of London. Taught science in Switzerland, London and Gloucestershire, 1926-38; Lecturer in Educational Psychology and Visual Education, UC, Exeter, 1938-47; established and directed Visual Education Centre, Exeter; Research Grants: Leon Trust, 1945; DSIR, 1954; Dept of Educ. and Science, 1965; Dept of Environment, 1970. Lecturer in Educational Psychology, University of Leeds, 1947-49; Professor of Psychology, 1949-67. Editor-in-Chief, International Jl of the Educational Sciences, 1967-70. *Publications:* Visual Education and the New Teacher, 1946; Materials for Visual Aids, 1947; The Method of Topic Analysis, 1948; Algebra by Visual Aids (4 vols), 1948; The Modular Calculus, 1958; Semantic Matrices,

1959; Learning, Remembering and Knowing, 1961; Instruments of Communication, 1966; Dyslexia and the Individual, 1972; articles in Forum of Education, Occupational Psychology, New Era, Nature, Times Ed. Supp., Jl of Ed., Brit. Jl of Psychology, 20th Century, Proc. of Aristotelian Soc., BMJ, etc. *Recreations:* astronomy, walking, climbing, dramatics. *Address:* 7 Grosvenor Mount, LS6 2DX. *T:* Leeds 755997. *Club:* Athenæum.

MEREDITH, John Michael; barrister-at-law; a Recorder of the Crown Court, since 1976; *b* 23 Oct. 1934; *s* of late John Stanley Meredith and of Lily Meredith; *m* 1969, Penelope Ann Sykes; one *s* two *d*. *Educ:* Crossley and Porter Schs, Halifax, Yorks; Leeds Univ. (LLB Hons 1956). Called to the Bar, Gray's Inn, 1958. Chm., J. T. Meredith (Carbonisers) Ltd, Sowerby Bridge, W Yorks. *Recreations:* shooting, sailing. *Address:* Cooper House, Luddenden Foot, West Yorks. *T:* Calder Valley 3378. *Clubs:* Pwllheli Sailing (N Wales); Queen's Sports (Halifax).

MEREDITH, Richard Alban Creed, MA; Headmaster of Giggleswick School, since 1970; *b* 1 Feb. 1935; *s* of late Canon R. Creed Meredith; *m* 1968, Hazel Eveline Mercia Parry; one *s* one *d*. *Educ:* Stowe Sch.; Jesus Coll., Cambridge. Asst Master (Modern Langs), 1957-70, Housemaster, 1962-70, King's Sch., Canterbury. *Recreations:* walking, foreign travel, music, theatre, gardening. *Address:* Headmaster's House, Giggleswick School, Settle, N Yorks BD24 0DE. *T:* Settle 3545.

MEREDITH DAVIES, (James) Brian; see Davies.

MERITT, Benjamin Dean; Visiting Scholar, University of Texas, since 1973; *b* at Durham, North Carolina, 31 March 1899; *s* of Arthur Herbert Meritt and Cornelia Frances Dean; *m* 1st, 1923, Mary Elizabeth Kirkland; two *s*; 2nd, 1964, Lucy T. Shoe. *Educ:* Hamilton Coll. (AB 1920, AM 1923, LLD 1937); American Sch. of Class. Studies at Athens. AM Princeton 1923, PhD 1924, LittD 1947; DLitt Oxford, 1936; LLD Glasgow, 1948; LHD: University of Pennsylvania, 1967; Brown Univ., 1974; Dr *hc* Sch. of Philosophy, Univ. of Athens, 1970. Instr Greek Univ. of Vermont, 1923-24; Brown Univ., 1924-25; Asst Prof. Greek, Princeton, 1925-26; Asst Dir Am. Sch. of Class. Studies at Athens, 1926-28; Associate Prof. Greek and Latin, University of Michigan, 1928-29, Prof. 1929-33; Visiting Prof. Am. Sch. Class. Studies at Athens, 1932-33; Dir Athens Coll., 1932-33; Francis White Prof. of Greek, Johns Hopkins, 1933-35; lecturer at Oxford, 1935; Annual Prof. Am Sch. of Class. Studies at Athens, 1936, 1954-55, 1969-70; Eastman Prof., Oxford Univ., 1945-46; Sather Prof., University of California, 1959; Prof. of Greek Epigraphy, Inst. for Advanced Study, Princeton, NJ, 1935-69, Emeritus, 1969; Vis. Prof., Univ. of Texas, 1972; Member: American Philosophical Soc.; German Archae. Inst.; Fellow American Academy of Arts and Sciences; Corr. fellow British Academy; hon. councillor, Greek Archæ. Soc.; hon. mem. Michigan Acad. of Sciences, Arts and Letters, Society for the Promotion of Hellenic Studies; Assoc. Mem., Royal Flemish Acad.; Foreign Mem., Acad. of Athens; Pres. Amer. Philological Assoc., 1953. Commander: Order of the Phœnix (Greece); Order of George I (Greece). *Publications:* The Athenian Calendar in the Fifth Century, 1928; Supplementum Epigraphicum Graecum, Vol. V (with Allen B. West), 1931; Corinth, Vol. VIII, Part I-Greek Inscriptions, 1931; Athenian Financial Documents, 1932; The Athenian Assessment of 425 BC (with Allen B. West), 1934; Documents on Athenian Tribute, 1937; The Athenian Tribute Lists (with H. T. Wade-Gery and M. F. McGregor), Vol. I, 1939, Vol. II, 1949, Vol. III, 1950, Vol. IV, 1953; Epigraphica Attica, 1940; The Chronology of Hellenistic Athens (with W. K. Pritchett), 1940; The Athenian Year, 1961; (with J. S. Traill) The Athenian Councillors, 1974. *Address:* 712 W 16th Street, Austin, Texas 78701, USA.

MERLE, Robert; Croix du Combattant, 1945; Officier de l'Instruction publique, 1953; Professor of English Literature, University of Paris X, Nanterre, since 1965; Titular Professor: University of Rennes, Brittany, since 1944 (on leave, 1950-51); University of Toulouse since 1957; University of Caen-Rouen, since 1960; University of Algiers, since 1963; *b* 29 Aug. 1908; father an officer; *m* 1st; one *d*; *m* 2nd, 1969, three *s* one *d*; 3rd, 1965; one *s*. *Educ:* Lycée Michelet, Paris; Sorbonne, Paris. Professor, 1934. Mobilised, 1939; Liaison agent with BEF (prisoner, 1940-43). *Publications:* Oscar Wilde, 1948; Week-end à Zuydcoote, 1949 (awarded Prix Goncourt); La Mort est mon métier, 1953; L'Ile, 1962 (awarded Prix de la Fraternité) (translated, as The Island, 1964); Un Animal doué de raison, 1967 (translated, as The Day of the Dolphin, 1969); Derrière la vitre, 1970; Malevil, 1972; Les hommes protégés, 1974; Madrapour, 1976; *plays:* Flamineo (inspired by Webster's White Devil), 1953; Nouveau Sisyphe; *historical essays:* Moncada, 1965; Ben Bella, 1965; translations, articles. *Recreations:*

swimming, tennis, yachting. *Address:* Le Bousquet de la Malonie, Marquay, Dordogne, France.

MERMAGEN, Air Commodore Herbert Waldemar, CB 1960; CBE 1945 (OBE 1941); AFC 1940; retired, 1960; Director, Sharps, Pixley Ltd, retired, 1977; *b* 1 Feb. 1912; *s* of late L. W. R. Mermagen, Southsea; *m* 1937, Rosemary, *d* of late Maj. Mainwaring Williams, DSO and late Mrs Tristram Fox, Cheltenham; two *s*. *Educ:* Brighton Coll., Sussex. Joined RAF, 1930; Squadron Leader, 1938; served War of 1939-45 in Fighter Command, UK, Middle East, France and Germany (SHAEF); AOC British Air Command, Berlin, 1945-46; Sen. RAF Liaison Officer, UK Services Liaison Staff, Australia, 1948-50; AOC, RAF Ceylon, 1955-57; Air Officer i/c Administration, Headquarters, RAF Transport Command, 1958-60. Air Commodore, 1955. Comdr Legion of Merit (USA), 1946; Medal for Distinguished Services (USSR), 1945; Chevalier, Légion d'Honneur (France) 1951. *Recreations:* golf, gardening. *Address:* Tile House, Park Farm, Fairford, Glos.

MERMAGEN, Patrick Hassell Frederick, TD; MA Cantab; Headmaster, Ipswich School, 1950-72; *s* of late L. H. Mermagen, MA, Taunton; *m* 1st, 1934, Neva Sonia (*d* 1953), *d* of late E. Haughton James, Forton House, Chard, Somerset; two *s* one *d* (and one *s* decd); 2nd, 1965, Inge (*née* Schütt), Hamburg; one *s* one *d*. *Educ:* Sherborne Sch.; Pembroke Coll., Cambridge (Open Scholar in Mathematics). Asst master, Loretto Sch., 1933-39, Radley Coll., 1939-50. Served War of 1939-45, Sept. 1940-Feb. 1946, The Royal Berkshire Regt; Staff Coll., Camberley (sc), 1944; held appointments in NW Europe and in SE Asia. *Recreations:* cricket, golf, gardening. *Address:* The Old Rectory, Otley, Ipswich IP6 9NP. *T:* Helmingham 495.

MERRELLS, Thomas Ernest; Lord Mayor of Cardiff, May 1970-71; *b* 5 Aug. 1891; *s* of Thomas Arthur Merrells, OBE, JP, and Kate Merrells, Swansea; *m* 1922, Vera Pughe Charles; one *s* one *d*. *Educ:* Bishop Gore Grammar Sch., Swansea. Served European War, 1914-18, in France; commissioned in Welsh Regt; seconded to HQ Staff, Royal Engineers, 1917; War of 1939-45: Chm., S Wales Area Nat. Dock Labour Bd; Mem., Exec. Cttee, Regional Port Director of Bristol Channel. Dep. Chm., S Wales Fedn of Port Employers, 1926-47, and Chm., Jt Conciliation Cttee for S Wales Ports. Councillor, City of Cardiff, 1951-74; Alderman, 1966-74. Freeman of City of London, 1971. Chevalier, Order of Mérite Social (France), 1958. *Recreation:* golf. *Address:* 151 Cyncoed Road, Cardiff. *T:* Cardiff 753321. *Clubs:* Cardiff Athletic and Rugby; Cardiff Golf.

MERRIMAN, Dr Basil Mandeville; *b* 28 March 1911; *s* of Thomas Henry Merriman and Ida, *d* of Mandeville Blackwood Phillips; *m* 1938, Yvonne Flavelle (*d* 1974); one *s*. *Educ:* St Paul's School; St Bartholomew's Hospital Med. Coll.; MRCS, LRCP 1934. House Appointments, St Bartholomew's Hosp., 1934-36; post graduate studies, Berlin, Vienna, Prague, 1936-38; Medical Adviser, British Drug Houses, 1938; Med. Dir, Carter Foundn, 1950; Consultant, Home Office Prison Department, 1963. FRAS 1972; Fellow, Royal Soc. for Asian Affairs, 1973; FRAI 1974; FRGS 1976. *Publications:* contribs to medical and social jls on drug action and drug addiction and their relationship to crime, also various related aspects of social anthropology. *Recreation:* travel of all forms, particularly Asiatic (journeys mainly in Arab Asia, Central Asiatic region, and Japan). *Address:* 85 Holland Park, W11. *T:* 01-727 8228.

MERRIMAN, Air Cdre Henry Alan, CBE 1973; AFC 1957, and Bar 1961; Director of Operational Requirements (1), RAF, since 1977; *b* 17 May 1929; *s* of Henry Victor Merriman and Winifred Ellen Merriman; *m* 1965, Mary Brenda Stephenson; three *d*. *Educ:* Hertford Grammar Sch.; RAF Coll., Cranwell. Graduate, Empire Test Pilots Sch. MRAeS 1974. Commnd, 1951; Qual. Flying Instr, 263 F Sqdn, Empire Test Pilots Sch., Fighter Test Sqdn, A&AEE, Central Fighter Estabt, and RAF Staff Coll., 1952-63; Personal Air Sec. to Minister of Defence for RAF, 1964-66; Jt Services Staff Coll., 1966; OC Fighter Test Sqdn, A&AEE, 1966-69; HQ 38 Gp, 1969-70; Stn Comdr, RAF Wittering, 1970-72; RCDS, 1973; CO Empire Test Pilots Sch., 1974-75; Comdt, A&AEE, 1975-77. Queen's Commendation for Valuable Services in the Air, 1956. *Recreations:* sailing, gardening. *Address:* c/o Lloyds Bank Ltd, Cox's and King's Branch, 6 Pall Mall, SW1. *Clubs:* Royal Air Force; Poole Yacht.

MERRIMAN, James Henry Herbert, CB 1969; OBE 1961; MSc, MInstP, CEng, FIEE; Chairman, National Computing Centre, since 1977; Member for Technology, Post Office Corporation, 1969-76; *b* 1 Jan. 1915; *s* of Thomas P. Merriman, AMINA and A. Margaretta Jenkins; *m* 1942, Joan B. Frost; twin *s* one *d*. *Educ:* King's Coll. Sch., Wimbledon; King's Coll., University of London. BSc (Hons) 1935; MSc (Thesis) 1936. Entered GPO

Engrg Dept (Research), 1936; Officer i/c Castleton Radio Stn, 1940; Asst Staff Engr, Radio Br., 1951; Imp. Def. Coll., 1954; Dep. Dir, Organisation and Methods, HM Treasury, 1956; GPO: Dep. Engr-in-Chief, 1965; Sen. Dir Engrg, 1967. Mem., Nat. Electronics Council, 1969-76. Vis. Prof. of Electronic Science and Telecommunications, Strathclyde Univ., 1969. Governor, Imperial College, Univ. of London, 1971-; Chm., Inspec, 1975-; Dir, Infoline, 1976-; Member: Science Museum Adv. Council; Council, Spurgeon's Coll. Mem. Council, IEE, 1965 (Chm. Electronics Div. Bd, 1968; Vice-Pres., 1969-72, Dep. Pres., 1972; Pres., 1974-75; Faraday Lectr, 1969-70); Royal Instn Discourse, 1971. FKC 1972. Hon. DSc Strathclyde, 1974. *Publications:* contribs to scientific and professional jls on telecommunications subjects. *Recreations:* walking, organ playing, church work, cactus growing. *Address:* 5 Melville Avenue, Copse Hill, W Wimbledon, SW20. *T:* 01-946 9870. *Club:* Athenæum.

MERRISON, Sir Alexander Walter, (Sir Alec Merrison), Kt 1976; FRS 1969; DL; Vice-Chancellor, University of Bristol, since 1969; *b* 20 March 1924; *s* of late Henry Walter and Violet Henrietta Merrison; *m* 1st, 1948, Beryl Glencora Le Marquand (*d* 1968); two *s*; 2nd, 1970, Maureen Michèle Barry; one *s* one *d*. *Educ:* Enfield Gram. Sch.; King's Coll., London. BSc (London) 1944; PhD (Liverpool) 1957. Res. in Radio Wave Propagation, as Experimental Officer, Signals Research and Development Establishment, Christchurch, 1944-46; Research in Reactor and Nuclear Physics, as Sen. Scientific Officer, AERE, Harwell, 1946-51; Research in Elementary Particle Physics, as Leverhulme Fellow and Lecturer, Liverpool Univ., 1951-57; Physicist, European Organisation for Nuclear Research (CERN) Geneva, 1957-60; Prof. of Experimental Physics, Liverpool Univ., 1960-69, and Dir, Daresbury Nuclear Physics Lab., SRC, 1962-69. Chairman: Cttee of Inquiry into Design and Erection of Steel Box Girder Bridges, 1970-73; Cttee of Inquiry into the Regulation of the Medical Profession, 1972-75; Royal Commn on NHS, 1976-. Charles Vernon Boys Prizeman of Inst. of Physics and the Physical Soc., 1961, and Mem. Council, 1964-66; Member: Council for Scientific Policy, 1967-72; Adv. Bd for the Res. Councils, 1972-73; Nuclear Power Adv. Bd, 1973-76. Governor, Bristol Old Vic Trust, 1969-, Chm., 1971-. FRSA 1970; FKC 1973. DL Avon, 1974. Hon. LLD Bristol, 1971; Hon. DSc Ulster, 1976; Hon. DSc Bath, 1977. *Publications:* contrib. to scientific jls on nuclear and elementary particle physics. *Address:* The University, Senate House, Bristol, BS8 1TH. *T:* Bristol 24161, ext. 84. *Club:* Athenæum.

MERRITT, Prof. John Edward; Professor of Educational Studies, Open University, since 1971; *b* 13 June 1926; *s* of Leonard Merritt and Janet (*née* Hartford); *m* 1948, Denise Edmondson; two *s*. *Educ:* Univ. of Durham (BA); Univ. of London (DipEdPsychol). ABPsS. Sandhurst, 1945-46; Trng Officer, Border Regt, 1946-48. Educnl Psychologist, Lancs LEA, 1957-59; Sen. Educnl Psychologist, Hull LEA, 1959-63; Lectr, Inst. of Educn, Univ. of Durham, 1964-71. Pres., UK Reading Assoc., 1969-70; Chm., 5th World Congress on Reading, Vienna, 1974; Mem., Nat. Cttee of Inquiry into Reading and Use of English (Bullock Cttee), 1973-75. *Publications:* Reading and the Curriculum (ed), 1971; A Framework for Curriculum Design, 1972; (ed jtly) Reading Today and Tomorrow, 1972; (ed jtly) The Reading Curriculum, 1972; Perspectives on Reading, 1973; What Shall We Teach, 1974; numerous papers in educnl jls. *Recreations:* fell walking, climbing, theatre. *Address:* 35 Vicarage Street, Woburn Sands, Milton Keynes MK17 8RE. *T:* Milton Keynes 583546.

MERRIVALE, 3rd Baron, *cr* 1925, of Walkhampton, Co. Devon; **Jack Henry Edmond Duke;** *b* 27 Jan. 1917; *o s* of 2nd Baron Merrivale, OBE, and Odette, *d* of Edmond Roger, Paris; *S* father 1951; *m* 1st, 1939, Colette (marr. diss. 1974), *d* of John Douglas Wise, Bordeaux, France; one *s* one *d*; 2nd, 1975, Betty, *widow* of Paul Baron. *Educ:* Dulwich; Ecole des Sciences Politiques, Paris. Served War of 1939-45, RAF, 1940; Flight-Lieut, 1944 (despatches). President: Inst. of Traffic Administration, 1953-70; Railway Development Assoc., 1959; Chairman: Anglo-Malagasy Soc., 1961; British Cttee for Furthering of Relations with French-speaking Africa, 1973. FRSA 1964. Chevalier, Nat. Order of Malagasy, 1968. *Recreations:* sailing, riding, photography. *Heir: s* Hon. Derek John Philip Duke, *b* 16 March 1948. *Address:* 16 Brompton Lodge, SW7 2JA. *T:* 01-589 4111.

MERSEY, 3rd Viscount, *cr* 1916, of Toxteth; **Edward Clive Bigham;** DL; Baron, *cr* 1910; *b* 5 June 1906; *e s* of 2nd Viscount Mersey, PC, CMG, CBE, and Mary (*d* 1973), *d* of late Horace Seymour, CB (nominated, but not invested as KCB); *S* father 1956; *m* 1933, Lady Katherine Fitzmaurice, *er d* of 6th Marquess of Lansdowne (she succeeded Aug. 1944, on the death of her brother, 7th Marquess, to the Barony of Nairne); three *s*.

Educ: Eton Coll.; Balliol Coll., Oxford (BA). Served Irish Guards, 1940-45. Mem. LCC, 1955-65. DL West Sussex, 1977. *Heir: s* Master of Nairne, *qv*. *Address:* Bignor Park, Pulborough, W Sussex; Derreen, Lauragh, Killarney, Ireland. *Clubs:* Brooks's, Pratt's, MCC, White's, Beefsteak.
See also Baron Ponsonby.

MERTHYR, Barony of (*cr* 1911); title disclaimed by 4th Baron; *see under* Lewis, Trevor Oswin.

MERTON, John Ralph, MBE 1942; painter; *b* 7 May 1913; *s* of late Sir Thomas Merton, KBE, FRS; *m* 1939, Viola Penelope von Bernd; two *d* (and one *d* decd). *Educ:* Eton; Balliol Coll., Oxford. Served War of 1939-45 (MBE); Air Photo reconnaissance research, Lieut-Col 1944. Works include: Mrs Daphne Wall, 1948; The Artist's daughter, Sarah, 1949; Altar piece, 1952; The Countess of Dalkeith, 1958; A myth of Delos, 1959; Clarissa, 1960; Lady Georgina Pelham, Mrs Julian Sheffield, 1970, Sir Charles Evans, 1973; Susan and the Cat, 1975; Viscountess Wimborne, 1976. Legion of Merit (USA), 1945. *Recreations:* music, making things, underwater photography. *Address:* Pound House, Oare, Pewsey, Wilts; Fourth Floor, 50 Cadogan Square, SW1. *Club:* Garrick.

MERTON, Air Chief Marshal Sir Walter (Hugh), GBE 1963 (OBE 1941); KCB 1959 (CB 1953); Inspector General of Civil Defence, 1964-68; *b* 29 Aug. 1905; *s* of late G. R. Merton; *m* 1st, 1930, B. H. B. Kirby (from whom he obtained a divorce, 1932); one *s*; 2nd, 1938, Margaret Ethel Wilson, 2nd *d* of late J. C. Macro Wilson, Cossington Manor, Som. *Educ:* Eastbourne Coll.; RAF Cadet Coll., Cranwell. Commissioned, 1925; Wing Comdr, 1940; served War of 1939-45 (despatches thrice); Middle East, 1940-43: Directing Staff and Asst Comdt, RAF War Staff Coll., 1943-44; Dir of Organization, Air Ministry, 1944-45. Air Attaché, Prague, 1947-48; AOC and Head of RAF Delegation, Greece, 1949-50. AOC No. 63 (Western and Welsh) Group, 1951-52; AOC No. 22 Gp, Tech. Trg Comd, 1952-53; Chief of the Air Staff, Royal NZ Air Force, 1954-56; Air Officer in charge of Administration, Headquarters Bomber Command, RAF High Wycombe, 1956-59; Chief of Staff, Allied Air Forces, Central Europe, 1959-60; Air Mem. for Supply and Organisation, April 1960-Aug. 1963, retd. Air Cdre, 1949; Air Vice-Marshal, 1953; Air Marshal, 1959; Air Chief Marshal, 1961. Air ADC to the Queen, 1962-63. Gold Cross, Royal Order of George I, with crossed swords (Greece), 1941; Order of the Phœnix, Class I (Greece), 1963. *Address:* Hart House, Martin, Fordingbridge, Hants SP6 3LF. *T:* Martin Cross 237. *Club:* Royal Air Force.

MERVYN DAVIES, David Herbert; *see* Davies, D. H. M.

MESSEL, Prof. Harry, BA, BSc, PhD (NUI) 1951; Professor and Head of the School of Physics, and Director of Science Foundation for Physics, University of Sydney, Australia, since 1952; *b* 3 March 1922. *Educ:* Rivers Public High Sch., Rivers, Manitoba. Entered RMC of Canada, 1940, grad. with Governor-General's Silver Medal, 1942. Served War of 1939-45: Canadian Armed Forces, Lieut, Canada and overseas, 1942-45. Queen's Univ., Kingston, Ont., 1945-48; BA 1st Cl. Hons in Mathematics, 1948, BSc Hons in Engineering Physics, 1948; St Andrews Univ., Scotland, 1948-49; Institute for Advanced Studies, Dublin, Eire, 1949-51; Sen. Lectr in Mathematical Physics, University of Adelaide, Australia, 1951-52. Mem., Aust. Atomic Energy Commn, 1974-. *Publications:* Chap. 4, Progress in Cosmic Ray Physics, vol. 2, (North Holland Publishing Company), 1953; numerous papers published in: Proc. Physical Soc., London; Philosophical Magazine, London; Physical Review of America; Co-author and Editor of: A Modern Introduction to Physics (Horwitz-Grahame, Vols I, II, III, 1959, 1960, 1962); Selected Lectures in Modern Physics, 1958; Science for High School Students, 1964; Senior Science for High School Students, 1966; (jt) Electron-Photon Shower Distribution Function, 1970; editor of: From Nucleus to Universe, 1960; Space and the Atom, 1961; A Journey Through Space and the Atom, 1962; The Universe of Time and Space, 1963; Light and Life in the Universe, 1964; Time, 1965; Atoms to Andromeda, 1966; Apollo and the Universe, 1967; Man in Inner and Outer Space, 1968; Nuclear Energy Today and Tomorrow, 1969; Pioneering in Outer Space, 1970; Molecules to Man, 1971; Brain Mechanisms and the Control of Behaviour, 1972; Focus on the Stars, 1973; Solar Energy, 1974; (ed jtly and part author) Multistrand Senior Science for High School Students, 1975; (ed) Our Earth, 1975; Australian Animals and their Environment, 1977. *Recreations:* water ski-ing, hunting, fishing and photography. *Address:* University of Sydney, Sydney, NSW 2006, Australia. *T:* 692 2537, 692 3383.

MESSEL, Oliver Hilary Sambourne, CBE 1958; *b* 13 Jan. 1904; 2nd *s* of Lieut-Col Leonard Messel, OBE, TD, Homestead, Cuckfield, Sussex, and Maud Frances, *o d* of Edward Linley Sambourne. *Educ:* Eton; Slade School of Art. *Theatrical Productions: plays:* Cochran Revue, 1926, This Year of Grace, 1928, Wake Up and Dream, 1929, Cochran Revues, 1930-31, all at London Pavilion; Helen, Adelphi; The Miracle, Lyceum, 1932; Glamorous Night, Drury Lane, 1935; The Country Wife, Old Vic and New York, 1936; A Midsummer Night's Dream, Old Vic, 1937; The Tempest, Old Vic; The Infernal Machine, Arts, 1940; Big Top, His Majesty's, 1942; The Rivals, Criterion, 1945; Tough at the Top, Adelphi, The Lady's Not for Burning, Globe and New York, 1949; Ring Round the Moon, Globe, and Copenhagen, The Little Hut, Lyric and New York, 1950; Romeo and Juliet, New York, 1951; Under the Sycamore Tree, Aldwych, Letter from Paris, Aldwych, 1952; The Dark is Light Enough, Aldwych and New York, The House of Flowers, New York, 1954; The School for Scandal, Copenhagen, 1958; Rashomon, New York, 1958; costume designs for Gigi, 1973; *operas:* The Magic Flute, Covent Garden, 1947; Ariadne auf Naxos, Glyndebourne; Queen of Spades, Covent Garden, 1950; Idomeneo, Glyndebourne, 1951; La Cenerentola, Glyndebourne, 1952; Il Barbiere di Siviglia, Le Comte Ory, Glyndebourne, La Cenerentola, Glyndebourne, Berlin, 1954; Zemire et Azore, Bath Festival, Le Nozze di Figaro, 1955; Die Entführung aus dem Serail, Die Zauberflöte, Glyndebourne, 1956; Samson, Covent Garden, 1958; Der Rosenkavalier, Glyndebourne, 1959; Le Nozze di Figaro, Metropolitan, New York, 1959; Ariadne, Metropolitan, New York, 1962; *ballets:* Francesca da Rimini, Covent Garden and New York, 1937; Comus, New Theatre, 1942; Sleeping Beauty, Covent Garden and New York, 1946; Homage to the Queen, Covent Garden and New York, 1953. *Films:* Private Life of Don Juan, 1934; Romeo and Juliet, 1936; Caesar and Cleopatra, 1945; The Queen of Spades, 1949; Suddenly Last Summer, 1959. *Exhibitions:* Masks, Claridge Galls, 1925; Designs and Maquettes, Lefevre Galls, 1933; Leicester Galls, 1936; Portrait Paintings, Leicester Galls, 1938; Paintings and Designs, Carol Carstairs Galls, New York, 1938; Designs for film Queen of Spades, Leicester Galleries, 1949; Paintings and Designs, Redfern Galleries, 1951; Sagittarius Gallery, New York, 1959; O'Hana Gallery, 1962. *Decorations:* for Royal Command Performance, Covent Garden, for President of France, 1950, and Gala Performance for King of Sweden, 1954. *Architectural design:* reconstruction of Flaxley Abbey, Glos, 1958-65; Queen's Park Theatre, houses, and garden, Bridgetown, Barbados, 1967-75; designed all initial buildings for develt of island of Mustique, also about 15 houses, 1968-75. Served in HM Forces, Captain, 1940-44. Fellow of University Coll. London, 1956. Hon. Associate, Regional Coll. of Art, Manchester, 1960. *Publications:* Stage Designs and Costumes, 1933; Designs for (Batsford) Romeo and Juliet, 1936; Designs for (Folio Society) A Midsummer Night's Dream, 1957; Designs for (Adrianne Allen and Marjorie Salter) Delightful Food, 1958. *Recreation:* gardening. *Address:* Maddox, St James', Barbados, West Indies.

MESSER, Malcolm, CBE 1949; *b* 1901; *s* of late Andrew Messer, MB, ChM; *m* 1943, Mary (*d* 1951), *er d* of G. F. Grigs; one *d*. *Educ:* Edinburgh Univ. (MA); Oxford Univ. (BA). Research Asst, Agricultural Economics Research Institute, Oxford, 1927-34; Technical Editor, Farmers' Weekly, 1934-38; Editor, Farmers' Weekly, 1938-66, retired editorship, 1 July 1966. Chm., Farm Journals Ltd, 1966-69. *Address:* Manor Farm House, Tarlton, near Cirencester, Glos.

MESSERVY, Professor Albert; Professor of Veterinary Surgery, University of Bristol, 1953-73, now Emeritus Professor; *b* 8 Feb. 1908; 2nd *s* of late E. P. Messervy, Jersey; *m* May, *d* of late F. E. Luce, Jersey; two *s* one *d*. *Educ:* Victoria Coll., Jersey; Royal Veterinary Coll., London. Private practice, 1929-40; Lecturer. Dept of Veterinary Surgery, Royal Vet. Coll., 1941-45; private practice, 1945-53. Mem. of Council, RCVS, 1957-65; Pres., Royal Jersey Agric. and Hort. Soc., 1974. Hon. MSc, 1964. *Publications:* clinical veterinary. *Recreation:* fishing. *Address:* Ville à L'Eveque, Trinity, Jersey, Channel Islands. *T:* Jersey Central 62588.

MESSIAEN, Olivier; Grand Officier de la Légion d'Honneur; Grand Officier de l'Ordre national du Mérite; Commandeur des Arts et des Lettres; Member, Institut de France; composer and organist; *b* Avignon, 10 Dec. 1908; *s* of Pierre Messiaen and Cécile Sauvage; *m* 1st, Claire Delbos (*d* 1959); one *s*; 2nd, 1961, Yvonne Loriod (pianist). *Educ:* Lycées and Grenoble; Conservatoire Nat. supérieur de musique (7 1st prizes). Organist, Trinité, Paris, 1930; co-founder Jeune-France Movement, 1936. Professor: Ecole Normale and Schola Cantorum, 1936-39; of Harmony, Paris Conservatoire, 1941-47; of Analysis, Aesthetics and Rhythm, 1947-; of Composition,

1966-. Mem. Council, Order of Arts and Letters, 1975-. Member: Royal Academy; Acads of Brussels, Madrid, Stockholm. Erasmus Prize, 1971; Sibelius Prize, 1971, Van Siemens Prize, 1975, Léonie Sonning Prize, 1977. *Works for organ include:* Le Banquet Céleste, 1928; Le Diptyque, 1929; L'Ascension, 1933; La Nativité du Seigneur, 1935; Les Corps Glorieux, 1939; Messe de la Pentecôte, 1949; Livre d'Orgue, 1951; Méditations sur le Mystère de la Sainte Trinité, 1969; *other works include:* Préludes, 1929; Poèmes pour Mi, 1936; Chants de Terre et de Ciel, 1938; Quatuor pour la Fin du Temps, 1941; Visions de l'Amen, 1943; Vingt Regards sur l'Enfant Jésus, 1944; Trois Petites Liturgies de la Présence Divine, 1944; Harawi, 1945; Turangalila Symphonie, 1946-48; Cinq Rechants, 1949; Etudes de Rythme, 1949; Réveil des Oiseaux, 1953; Oiseaux exotiques, 1955; Catalogue d'Oiseaux, 1956-58; Chronochromie, 1959; Sept Haïkaï, 1963; Couleurs de la Cité Céleste, 1964; Et Exspecto Resurrectionem Mortuorum, 1965; La Transfiguration de Notre Seigneur, Jésus-Christ, 1969; Des Canyons aux Etoiles, 1970-74. *Address:* 230 rue Marcadet, 75018 Paris, France.

MESSITER, Air Commodore Herbert Lindsell, CB 1954; 2nd *s* of late Colonel Charles Bayard Messiter, DSO, OBE, Barwick Park, Yeovil, Som, and Alice Lindsell; *m* 1933, Lucy Brenda Short; one *d*. *Educ:* Bedford Sch. Served War of 1939-45 (despatches 4 times): Egypt, N Africa, Belgium, Germany. Command Engineer Officer, Far East Air Force, 1950-52; Senior Technical Staff Officer, Bomber Command, RAF, 1952-56; Senior Technical Staff Officer, Middle East Air Force, 1956-59, retired. *Address:* c/o Lloyds Bank Ltd, 6 Pall Mall, SW1; Lion Cottage, Grateley, Hants. *Club:* Royal Air Force.

MESSMER, Pierre Auguste Joseph; Commandeur de la Légion d'Honneur; Compagnon de la Libération; Croix de Guerre, 1939-45; Médaille de la Résistance; *b* Vincennes (Seine), 20 March 1916; *s* of Joseph Messmer, industrialist, and of Marthe (*née* Farcy); *m* 1947, Gilberte Duprez. *Educ:* Lycées Charlemagne and Louis-le Grand; Faculty of Law, Paris; Ecole Nationale de la France d'Outre-Mer. Pupil Administrator of Colonies, 1938. Served War of 1939-45: Free French Forces, 1940; African Campaigns (Bir-Hakeim), France, Germany; parachuted Tonkin; PoW of Vietminh, 1945. Sec.-Gen., Interministerial Cttee of Indochina, 1946; Dir of Cabinet of E. Bollaert (High Commissioner, Indochina), 1947-48; Administrator-in-Chief of France Overseas, 1950; Governor: of Mauritania, 1952, of Ivory Coast, 1954-56; Dir of Cabinet of G. Defferre (Minister, France Overseas), Jan.-April 1956; High Commissioner: Republic of Cameroon, 1956-58; French Equatorial Africa, 1958; French West Africa, July 1958-Dec. 1959; Minister of Armed Forces: (Cabinets: M. Debré, 5 Feb. 1958-14 April 1962; G. Pompidou, April-Nov. 1962, 6 Dec. 1962-7 Jan. 1966, 8 Jan. 1966-1 April 1967, 7 April 1967-10 July 1968; M. Couve de Murville, 12 July 1968-20 June 1969). Deputy (UDR), Moselle (8th circonscription: Sarrebourg, 23 June-12 Aug. 1968 and 19 Oct. 1969-March 1971); Minister of State in charge of Depts and Territories Overseas, Feb. 1971-72; Prime Minister, 1972-74. Pres., UDR Federal Cttee, Moselle, 1969-; Counsellor-Gen., Canton of Rechicourt-le-Château, 1970-. Officer, American Legion. *Recreations:* tennis, sailing. *Address:* 1 rue du Général Delanne, 92 Neuilly-sur-Seine, France.

MESTEL, Prof. Leon, PhD; FRS 1977; Professor of Astronomy, University of Sussex, since 1973; *b* 5 Aug. 1927; *s* of late Rabbi Solomon Mestel and Rachel (*née* Brodetsky); *m* 1951, Sylvia Louise Cole; two *s* two *d*. *Educ:* West Ham Secondary Sch., London; Trinity Coll., Cambridge (BA 1948, PhD 1952). ICI Res. Fellow, Dept of Maths, Univ. of Leeds, 1951-54; Commonwealth Fund Fellow, Princeton Univ. Observatory, 1954-55; University of Cambridge: Univ. Asst Lectr in Maths, 1955-58; Univ. Lectr in Maths, 1958-66; Fellow of St John's Coll., 1957-66; Vis. Mem., Inst. for Advanced Study, Princeton, 1961-62; J. F. Kennedy Fellow, Weizmann Inst. of Science, Israel, 1966-67; Prof. of Applied Maths, Manchester Univ., 1967-73. *Publications:* Magnetohydrodynamics (with N. O. Weiss), 1974 (Geneva Observatory); papers, revs and conf. reports on different branches of theoretical astrophysics. *Recreations:* reading, music. *Address:* 13 Prince Edward's Road, Lewes, E Sussex BN7 1BJ. *T:* Lewes 2731.

MESTON, family name of **Baron Meston.**

MESTON, 2nd Baron, *cr* 1919, of Agra and Dunottar; **Dougall Meston;** *b* 17 Dec. 1894; *s* of 1st Baron and Jeanie, CBE (*d* 1946), *o d* of James M'Donald; *S* father, 1943; *m* 1947, Diana Mary Came, *o d* of late Capt. O. S. Doll, 16 Upper Cheyne Row, Chelsea; two *s*. *Educ:* Charterhouse; RMA, Woolwich. Served European War, 1914-19; Capt., RA, 1917; N-W Frontier, India

(Afghan War, 1919, Waziristan, 1919-20); retired, 1922; Barrister, Lincoln's Inn, 1924. Hon. Mem. Incorporated Association of Architects and Surveyors. President, British Soc. of Commerce. Contested (L) Southend Bye-Election, 1927, and General Election, 1929. *Publications:* Law of Moneylenders; Law of Nuisances; The Restrictive Trade Practices Act, 1956; The Rent Act, 1957; The Rating and Valuation Act, 1961; The Betting, Gaming and Lotteries Act, 1963; The Offices, Shops and Railway Premises Act, 1963; Weights and Measures Act, 1963; Rent Act, 1965; Leasehold Reform Act, 1967; The Gaming Act, 1968; Industrial Relations Act, 1971; Consumer Credit Act, 1974; several works on Gaming, Landlord and Tenant, War Damage, Local Government, Town and Country Planning, Highways, Trade Wastes, Public Health and Housing Acts; Jt Ed. of Mather's Sheriff and Execution Law (3rd edn). *Heir: s* Hon. James Meston [*b* 10 Feb. 1950; *m* 1974, Anne, *yr d* of John Carder; one *s*]. *Address:* Hurst Place, Cookham Dene, Berks; Queen Elizabeth Building, Temple, EC4. *T:* 01-353 3911. *Club:* Reform.

METCALF, Malcolm, MC 1944; Vice-Chairman, Surrey County Council, since 1977; *b* 1 Dec. 1917; *s* of Charles Almond Metcalf and Martha Fatherly Atkins Metcalf; *m* 1945, Charis Thomas; two *s*. *Educ:* Merchant Taylors' Sch., Crosby. ACIS. Army service, 1939-46. Contested (C) Barrow-in-Furness, 1959; Mem., Surrey CC, 1965- (Leader, 1973-77); Member: Metrop. Water Board, 1965-74 (Vice-Chm. 1971-72); Thames Conservancy, 1970-74; Thames Water Authority, 1973-. Mem., Assoc. of County Councils, 1975-. *Address:* Linden, Clive Road, Esher, Surrey KT10 8PS. *T:* Esher 64476. *Clubs:* MCC, Ski Club of Great Britain; Burhill Golf (Walton-on-Thames).

METCALFE, Sir Theophilus (John), 8th Bt, *cr* 1802; *b* 14 Oct. 1916; *s* of late Lieut-Col Eric Debonnaire Theophilus Metcalfe, OBE, MC, Indian Army, half-brother of 7th Bt, and Winifred Crampton, *d* of E. Neild Shackle, Hayes, Middx; *S* uncle, 1950. *Educ:* Haileybury. *Heir:* none. *Address:* 3 Kensington House, 35 Kensington Court, W8.

METFORD, Prof. John Callan James; Professor of Spanish, since 1960, Head of Department of Hispanic and Latin American Studies, since 1973, Chairman, School of Modern Languages, since 1976, University of Bristol; *b* 29 Jan. 1916; *s* of Oliver Metford and Florence Stowe Thomas; *m* 1944, Edith Donald; one *d*. *Educ:* Porth Grammar Sch.; Universities of Liverpool, Yale and California. Commonwealth Fund Fellow, 1939-41; British Council Lecturer in Brazil, 1942-44; Regional Officer, Latin American Department of the British Council, 1944-46; Lectr in Latin American Studies, Univ. of Glasgow, 1946-55; Head of Dept of Spanish and Portuguese, Univ. of Bristol, 1955-73, Dean of Faculty of Arts, 1973-76. Vis. Prof., Lehigh Univ., USA, 1968-69. Vice-Chm., Council of Westonbirt Sch.; Mem., Central Cttee of Allied Schs; Governor, Coll. of St Matthias, Bristol; Professorial Mem., Council of Univ. of Bristol, 1972-74. *Publications:* British Contributions to Spanish and Spanish American Studies, 1950; San Martín the Liberator, 1950, 2nd edn 1970; Modern Latin America, 1964; The Golden Age of Spanish Drama, 1969; articles in Bulletin of Spanish Studies, Bulletin of Hispanic Studies, Liverpool Studies in Spanish, International Affairs, etc. *Recreations:* opera, iconography. *Address:* 2 Parry's Close, Bristol BS9 1AW. *T:* 682284. *Clubs:* Royal Commonwealth Society (London); Royal Commonwealth Society (Bristol).

METHUEN, family name of Baron Methuen.

METHUEN, 6th Baron *cr* 1838; **Anthony John Methuen,** ARICS; *b* 26 Oct. 1925; *s* of 5th Baron Methuen and Grace (*d* 1972), *d* of Sir Richard Holt, 1st Bt; *S* father, 1975. *Educ:* Winchester; Royal Agricultural Coll., Cirencester. Served Scots Guards and Royal Signals, 1943-47. Lands Officer, Air Ministry, 1951-62; QALAS 1954. *Recreations:* sailing, shooting, scouting. *Heir: b* Hon. Robert Alexander Holt Methuen [*b* 22 July 1931; *m* 1958, Mary Catharine Jane, *d* of Ven. C. G. Hooper, *qv*; two *d*.] *Address:* Corsham Court, Wilts. *Clubs:* Lansdowne, Royal Ocean Racing; Royal Motor Yacht (Poole).

METHVEN, (Malcolm) John; Director General, Confederation of British Industry, since 1976; *b* 14 Feb. 1926; *s* of late Lt-Col M. D. Methven, OBE and late Mrs H. M. Methven; *m* 1952, Margaret Field Nicholas; three *d*; *m* 1977, Karen Jane Caldwell. *Educ:* Mill Hill Sch.; Gonville and Caius Coll., Cambridge (Tapp Exhibn in Law; Tapp Post-Grad. Schol. in Law; MA, LLB). Admitted Solicitor, 1952; Solicitor, Birmingham Corp., 1952-57; ICI (Metals Div.), 1957; ICI (Legal Dept), 1957-68; Head of Central Purchasing Dept, ICI, 1968-70; Dep. Chm., ICI Ltd, Mond Div., 1970-73; Dir-Gen. of Fair Trading, 1973-76. Member: Monopolies Commn, 1972; NEDC, 1976. Custodian

Trustee, Nat. Assoc. of Citizens' Advice Bureaux. Vice Pres., Inst. of Trading Standards Admin. *Recreations:* music, sailing, gardening. *Address:* 20 Bushwood Road, Richmond, Surrey. *Club:* United Oxford & Cambridge University.

METSON, Gilbert Harold, MC 1940; MSc, PhD, DSc; Consulting Engineer; formerly Director of Research, Post Office; *b* 4 July 1907; British; *m* 1932, Una (*née* Pyke); two *d*. *Educ:* Mercers' Sch., Queen Elizabeth's Sch., Barnet. BSc (Eng.) London; MSc, PhD and DSc Queen's Univ. of Belfast. Post Office Engineer. Served War, in Royal Signals, 1939-45; comd 11th L of C Signals in N Africa and Italy; GSO1, War Office. *Publications:* wide range, mainly concerned with thermionic emission from oxide cathodes. *Recreation:* fly-fishing. *Address:* 38 Wheathampstead Road, Harpenden, Herts AL5 1ND.

MEXBOROUGH, 7th Earl of, *cr* 1766; **John Raphael Wentworth Savile,** DL; Baron Pollington, 1753; Viscount Pollington, 1766; *b* 11 Oct. 1906; *o s* of 6th Earl and Hon. Marjorie Knatchbull-Hugessen, *d* of 2nd Baron Brabourne; *S* father 1945; *m* 1930, Josephine, *d* of Capt. Fletcher of Saltoun; two *s* one *d*. *Educ:* Downside Sch.; Pembroke Coll., Cambridge (MA). JP North Riding of Yorks; DL, North Riding of Yorks, 1967. Capt., Intelligence Corps, 1942; in India, May 1941-Jan. 1945; ADC to Governor of Bihar, 1944-45. *Heir: s* Viscount Pollington, *qv*. *Address:* Arden Hall, Hawnby, York. *T:* Bilsdale 213. *Clubs:* Brooks's, All England Lawn Tennis.

MEYER, Prof. Alfred; Professor of Neuropathology in the University of London, Institute of Psychiatry, 1949-56, retired; *b* 3 Feb. 1895; *m* 1949, Nina Cohen. Assoc. Prof. of Neurology at University of Bonn, 1931; Rockefeller Research Fellow in Pathological Laboratory, Maudlsey Hosp., London, 1933; Neuropathologist in the Pathological Laboratory, Maudsley Hospital, 1943. *Publications:* (jt) Prefrontal Leucotomy and Related Operations: anatomical aspects, 1954; (jt) Neuropathology, 1958, 2nd edn 1963; Historical Aspects of Cerebral Anatomy, 1971; articles on neuroanatomical and neuropathological subjects. *Address:* 38 Wood Lane, N6 5UB.

MEYER, Sir Anthony John Charles, 3rd Bt, *cr* 1910; MP (C) West Flint since 1970; *b* 27 Oct. 1920; *o s* of Sir Frank Meyer, MP, 2nd Bt, Ayot House, Ayot St Lawrence, Herts; *S* father, 1935; *m* 1941, Barbadee Violet, *o c* of late A. Charles Knight, JP, and of Mrs Charles Knight, Herne Place, Sunningdale; one *s* three *d*. *Educ:* Eton (Capt. of Oppidans); New Coll., Oxford. Served Scots Guards, 1941-45 (wounded); HM Treasury, 1945-46; entered HM Foreign Service, 1946; HM Embassy, Paris, 1951; 1st Sec., 1953; transferred to HM Embassy, Moscow, 1956; London, 1958. MP (C) Eton and Slough, 1964-66. Cons. Research Dept, 1968. PPS to Chief Sec., Treasury, 1970-72; PPS to Sec. of State for Employment, 1972-74. Vice-Chm., Franco-British Parly Relations Cttee, 1975-. Trustee of Shakespeare National Memorial Theatre. Founder and Dir of political jl, Solon, 1969. *Publication:* A European Technological Community, 1966. *Heir: s* Anthony Ashley Frank Meyer [*b* 23 Aug. 1944; *m* 1966, Susan Mathilda, *d* of John Freestone; one *d*]. *Address:* Cottage Place, Brompton Square, SW3. *T:* 01-589 7416; Rhewl House, Llanasa, Flints. *Club:* Beefsteak.

MEYER, Ven. Conrad John Eustace; Archdeacon of Bodmin since 1969; Hon. Canon of Truro since 1966; *b* 2 July 1922; *s* of William Eustace and Marcia Meyer; *m* 1960, Mary Wiltshire; no *c*. *Educ:* Clifton Coll.; Pembroke Coll., Cambridge; Westcott House. BA 1946, MA 1948. Served War of 1939-45: Royal Navy (commissioned from lower deck), 1942-46. Lieut (S) RNVR, post war, until apptd Chaplain, RNVR, 1950-54. Deacon, 1948; Priest, 1949; Asst Curate: St Francis, Ashton Gate, Bristol, 1948-51; Kenwyn, Truro, 1951; Falmouth Parish Church, 1954; Vicar of Devoran, Truro, 1956-65; Diocesan Youth Chaplain, 1956; Asst Dir of Religious Educn, 1958; Diocesan Sec. for Educn, 1960-69; Examining Chaplain to Bishop of Truro, 1973-. Hon. Diocesan Sec., Nat. Soc., 1960-69. Mem. Governing Body, SPCK, 1972-; Chm., Cttee for Mission, SPCK, 1973-. Mem. Cornwall Community Health Council. Fellow, Woodard Corp. of Schools; Provost, Western Div., Woodard Corp., 1970-. Associate Fellow, Inst. of Civil Defence. *Recreations:* swimming, walking, military history, civil defence, archaeology. *Address:* Archdeacon's House, St Catherine's Hill, Launceston, Cornwall PL15 7EJ. *T:* Launceston 2714. *Club:* Royal Commonwealth Society.

MEYER, John Mount Montague, CBE 1967; Chairman and Managing Director, Montague L. Meyer Ltd; *b* 6 July 1915; *s* of late Montague L. Meyer and Muriel G. Meyer; *m* 1942, Denise Georgina Saunders; two *s*. *Educ:* Sherborne School. Joined Montague L. Meyer Ltd, 1933: Dir 1938; Asst Man. Dir and Gen. Man. 1939; Vice-Chm. 1951; Chm. and Man. Dir 1961.

Man. Dir, MacMillan Bloedel Meyer Ltd, 1966-; Director: MacMillan Bloedel Ltd, Vancouver, 1972-; Hallam Group of Nottingham Ltd, 1973-; Dep. Chm., Mercator Chartering Ltd, 1973-. Mem., Bd of Port of London Authority, 1961-, Vice-Chm., 1976-. British Soviet Chamber of Commerce: Mem. Exec. Council, 1947-52; Chm. 1952-62; Pres. 1962-77. *Recreations:* golf, fishing. *Address:* 52 Northgate, Regent's Park, NW8 7EH. *T:* 01-722 5678. *Club:* MCC.

MEYER, Matt; Newspaperman, USA; *b* Tilden, Ala, 28 Aug. 1904; *s* of Matthew Meyer and Julia Patterson; *m* 1931, Emily Cluett Dorlon; three *d. Educ:* New York University, USA (BCS). With Scripps-Howard Newspapers, 1932: Advertising Dir, Washington Daily News, 1938-47, Pres. and Business Manager, 1947-59; Asst Gen. Business Manager, Scripps-Howard Newspapers, 1959-62; Vice Pres., Business Manager, New York World-Telegram and Sun, 1962-65, Pres., 1965-66; Dir, Scripps-Howard Investment Co.; Pres., World-Journal-Tribune Inc., 1966-68. Chm., Publishers Association, New York City, 1963-65. Chm. and Pres., Scripps Howard Foundn, 1970-. *Recreations:* golf, photography, reading. *Address:* 69 Chase Road, Scarsdale, NY 10583, USA. *Clubs:* Union League (New York); Bald Peak Colony; Scarsdale Golf.

MEYER, Michael Leverson; free-lance writer since 1950; *b* London, 11 June 1921; 3rd and *y s* of Percy Barrington Meyer and Eleanor Rachel Meyer (*née* Benjamin); unmarried; one *d. Educ:* Wellington Coll.; Christ Church, Oxford (MA). Operational Res. Section, Bomber Comd HQ, 1942-45; Lectr in English Lit., Uppsala Univ., 1947-50. Mem. Editorial Adv. Bd, Good Food Guide, 1958-72. FRSL. Gold Medal, Swedish Academy, 1964. Knight Commander, Polar Star (1st class), 1977. *Publications:* (ed, with Sidney Keyes, and contrib.) Eight Oxford Poets, 1941; (ed) Collected Poems of Sidney Keyes, 1945; (ed) The Minos of Crete, by Sidney Keyes, 1948; The End of the Corridor (novel), 1951; The Ortolan (play), 1967; Henrik Ibsen: The Making of a Dramatist, 1967; Henrik Ibsen: The Farewell to Poetry, 1971; Henrik Ibsen: The Top of a Cold Mountain, 1971 (Whitbread Biography Prize, 1971); *translated:* The Long Ships, by Frans G. Bengtsson, 1954; Ibsen: Brand, The Lady from the Sea, John Gabriel Borkman, When We Dead Awaken, 1960; The Master Builder, Little Eyolf, 1961; Ghosts, The Wild Duck, Hedda Gabler, 1962; Peer Gynt, An Enemy of the People, The Pillars of Society, 1963; The Pretenders, 1964; A Doll's House, 1965; Rosmersholm, 1966; Strindberg: The Father, Miss Julie, Creditors, The Stronger, Playing with Fire, Erik the Fourteenth, Storm, The Ghost Sonata, 1964; A Dream Play, 1973; To Damascus, Easter, The Dance of Death, The Virgin Bride, 1975. *Recreations:* cricket, eating, sleeping. *Address:* 4 Montagu Square, W1H 1RA. *T:* 01-486 2573. *Clubs:* Savile, Garrick, MCC.

MEYER, Rollo John Oliver, (Jack Meyer), OBE 1967; Headmaster, since 1973, President and Member, Governing Body, since 1976, Campion School, Athens; *b* 15 March 1905; *s* of Canon Rollo Meyer and Arabella Ward; *m* 1931, Joyce Symons; two *d. Educ:* Haileybury Coll.; Pembroke Coll., Cambridge. MA 1926. Cottonbroker, Gill & Co., Bombay, 1926-29; Private Tutor, Limbdi, Porbandar, Dhrangadhra, 1929-35; Founder, and Headmaster of Millfield School, 1935-71; founded Edgarley Hall Preparatory Sch., Glastonbury, 1945. Planning other internat. public schs. *Recreations:* ornithology, any game with a ball in it, chess, gardens, writing, National Hunt racing, shooting. *Address:* Little Scotland, Bleadney, Wells, Somerset BA5 1PJ. *T:* Wedmore 712399; Campion School, Paleo Psychico, Athens, Greece. *Clubs:* MCC, English-Speaking Union, Royal Over-Seas League.

MEYJES, Sir Richard (Anthony), Kt 1972; Deputy Chairman, Coates Brothers and Co. Ltd, since 1977; Director: Portals Holdings Ltd; Foseco Minsep Ltd; *b* 30 June 1918; *s* of Anthony Charles Dorian Meyjes and Norah Isobel Meyjes; *m* 1939, Margaret Doreen Morris; three *s. Educ:* University College School, Hampstead. War Service, RASC, Sept. 1939-Jan. 1946 (temp. Captain). Qualified as Solicitor, June 1946; Legal Dept, Anglo-Saxon Petroleum Co., 1946-56; Manager, Thailand and Vietnam Division, Shell International Petroleum Co., 1956-58; Marketing Manager, Shell Co. of Philippines, Ltd, Manila, 1958-61; President, 1961-64; Head of Regional Marketing Div., Shell International Petroleum Co., London, 1964-66; Marketing Coordinator, 1966-70. Seconded to HM Govt (Mr Heath's Admin) as Head of Business Team, 1970-72; Dir and Group Personnel Co-ordinator, Shell International Petroleum Co. Ltd, 1972-76. FBIM, FRSA. Officer of Philippine Legion of Honour, 1964. *Recreations:* gardening, walking, golf. *Address:* Longhill House, The Sands, near Farnham, Surrey. *T:* Runfold 2601. *Clubs:* Junior Carlton, Institute of Directors; Farnham Golf.

MEYNELL, Dame Alix (Hester Marie); (Lady Meynell), DBE 1949; *b* 2 Feb. 1903; *d* of late Surgeon Commander L. Kilroy, RN, and late Hester Kilroy; *m* 1946, Sir Francis Meynell, RDI (*d* 1975); no *c. Educ:* Malvern Girls' Coll.; Somerville Coll., Oxford. Joined civil service, Board of Trade, 1925. Seconded to the Monopolies and Restrictive Practices Commission as Sec., 1949-52; Under-Sec., Board of Trade, 1946-55; resigned from the Civil Service, 1955. Called to the Bar, 1956. Chm. Consultative Council, South Eastern Gas Board, 1956-63. Member: Harlow New Town Corpn; Performing Right Tribunal; Cttees of Investigation for England, Scotland and Great Britain under Agricultural Marketing Acts, 1956-65; SE Gas Board, 1963-69; Monopolies Commn, 1965-68; Bd of Management, Theatre Royal, Bury; Cosford RDC, 1970-74. *Recreations:* family bridge, entertaining my friends. *Address:* The Grey House, Lavenham, Sudbury, Suffolk. *T:* Lavenham 526.

MEYNELL, Benedict; Director, Directorate General for External Relations, Commission of the European Communities (with responsibility for relations with North America, Japan and Australasia), since 1977; *b* 17 Feb. 1930; *s* of late Sir Francis Meynell, RDI, and of Lady (Vera) Meynell, MA; *m* 1st, 1950, Hildamarie (*née* Hendricks); two *d*; 2nd, 1967, Diana (*née* Himbury). *Educ:* Beltane Sch.; Geneva Univ. (Licencié-ès-sciences politiques); Magdalen Coll., Oxford (Doncaster schol.; MA). Asst Principal, Bd of Inland Revenue, 1954-56; Asst Principal, BoT, 1957-59, Principal, 1959-68; Principal British Trade Commissioner, Kenya, 1962-64; Board of Trade: Principal Private Sec. to Pres., 1967-68; Asst Sec., 1968-70; Commercial Counsellor, Brit. Embassy, Washington, DC, 1970-73; a Dir, EEC (responsible for relations with Far East, and for commercial safeguards and textiles negotiations), 1973-77. *Address:* 49 rue Père Eudore Devroye, 1040 Bruxelles, Belgium. *T:* 736 4916.

MEYNELL, Laurence Walter; (Robert Eton); Author; *b* Wolverhampton, 1899; *y s* of late Herbert and Agnes Meynell; *m* 1932, Shirley Ruth (*d* 1955), *e d* of late Taylor Darbyshire; one *d*; *m* 1956, Joan Belfrage (*née* Henley). *Educ:* St Edmund's Coll., Old Hall, Ware. After serving in the Honourable Artillery Company became successively schoolmaster, estate agent and finally professional writer; Royal Air Force in War of 1939-45 (despatches). Literary Editor, Time and Tide, 1958-60, Past Pres. Johnson Soc. *Publications:* as *Robert Eton:* The Pattern; The Dividing Air; The Bus Leaves for the Village; Not In Our Stars; The Journey; Palace Pier; The Legacy; The Faithful Years; The Corner of Paradise Place; St Lynn's Advertiser; The Dragon at the Gate; as *Laurence Meynell:* Bluefeather; Paid in Full; The Door in the Wall; The House in the Hills; The Dandy; Third Time Unlucky; His Aunt Came Late; The Creaking Chair; The Dark Square; Strange Landing; The Evil Hour; The Bright Face of Danger; The Echo in the Cave; The Lady on Platform One; Party of Eight; The Man No One Knew; Give me the Knife; Saturday Out; Famous Cricket Grounds; Life of Sir P. Warner; Builder and Dreamer; Smoky Joe; Too Clever by Half; Smoky Joe in Trouble; Rolls, Man of Speed; Young Master Carver; Under the Hollies; Bridge Under the Water; Great Men of Staffordshire; Policeman in the Family; James Brindley; Sonia Back Stage; The Young Architect; District Nurse Carter; The Breaking Point; One Step from Murder; The Abandoned Doll; The House in Marsh Road; The Pit in the Garden; Virgin Luck; Sleep of the Unjust; Airmen on the Run; More Deadly Than the Male; Double Fault; Die by the Book; Week-end in the Scampi Belt; Death of a Philanderer; The Curious Crime of Miss Julia Blossom; The End of the Long Hot Summer; Death by Arrangement; Little Matter of Arson; A View from the Terrace; The Fatal Flaw; The Thirteen Trumpeters; The Woman in Number Five; The Fortunate Miss East; The Fairly Innocent Little Man; The Footpath; Don't Stop For Hooky Hefferman; Hooky and the Crock of Gold; The Lost Half Hour; Hooky Gets the Wooden Spoon; as *A. Stephen Tring* (for children): The Old Gang; The Cave By the Sea; Penny Dreadful; Barry's Exciting Year; Penny Triumphant; Penny Penitent; Penny Dramatic; Penny in Italy; Penny Goodbye. *Recreations:* walking, trying to write a play. *Address:* 9 Clifton Terrace, Brighton BN1 3HA. *Club:* Authors'.

MEYNER, Robert Baumle; Lawyer since 1934; Governor, State of New Jersey, USA, 1954-62; *b* 3 July 1908; *s* of late Gustave H. Meyner and Sophia Baumle Meyner; *m* 1957, Helen Day Stevenson. *Educ:* Lafayette Coll. (AB); Columbia Univ. Law Sch. (LLB). State Senator from Warren County, 1948-52; Senate Minority (Democrat) Leader, 1950; Director: Prudential Insurance Co.; Engelhard Minerals & Chemicals Corp.; Phillipsburg (NJ) National Bank and Trust Co.; First National State Bank, First National State Bancorporation, Newark (NJ); Delaware and Bound Brook Railroad. Administrator, Cigarette

Advertising Code. Hon. degrees: Dr of Laws: Rutgers (The State Univ.) 1954; Lafayette Coll., 1954; Princeton Univ., 1956; Long Island Univ., 1958; Fairleigh Dickinson Univ., 1959; Syracuse Univ., 1960; Lincoln Univ., 1960; Colorado Coll., 1961. *Address:* (business) Suite 2500, Gateway 1, Newark, New Jersey 07102, USA; 16 Olden Lane, Princeton, NJ 08540, USA; 372 Lincoln Street, Phillipsburg, NJ 08865, USA. *Club:* River (New York).

MEYRICK, Lt-Col Sir George David Eliott Tapps-Gervis-, 6th Bt, *cr* 1791; MC 1943; *b* 15 April 1915; *o s* of Major Sir George Llewelyn Tapps-Gervis-Meyrick, 5th Bt, and Marjorie (*née* Hamlin) (*d* 1972); *S* father 1960; *m* 1940, Ann, *d* of Clive Miller; one *s* one *d. Educ:* Eton; Trinity Coll., Cambridge (BA). 2nd Lieut, 9th Queen's Royal Lancers, 1937. Served War of 1939-45 (wounded, MC): BEF, 1940; Middle East, 1941-43; Italy, 1945; Captain, 1940 Lt-Col, 1947; retired, 1952. Dir, Southampton FC, 1953-. *Recreations:* shooting, travel. *Heir: s* George Christopher Cadafael Tapps-Gervis-Meyrick [*b* 10 March 1941; *m* 1968, Jean Louise Montagu Douglas Scott, *d* of late Lt-Col Lord William Scott and of Lady William Scott, Beechwood, Melrose, Scotland; two *s*]. *Address:* Hinton Admiral, Christchurch, Dorset. *T:* Highcliff 72887; Bodorgan, Isle of Anglesey. *T:* Bodorgan 204. *Club:* Cavalry and Guards.

MEYRICK, Col Sir Thomas Frederick, 3rd Bt, *cr* 1880; TD; late 15th/19th Hussars; DL, JP, Pembrokeshire; *b* 28 Nov. 1899; *o s* of Brigadier-General Sir Frederick Charlton Meyrick, 2nd Bt; *S* father, 1932; *m* 1926, Ivy Frances (*d* 1947), *d* of late Lieut-Col F. C. Pilkington, DSO; three *s* three *d*; *m* 1951, Gladice Joyce (*d* 1977), *d* of late Bertram W. Allen, Cilrhiw, Narberth, Pembs; one *s.* Capt. 15/19 Hussars, 1927; Equitation Instructor, Weedon, 1922-27, and RMC, 1930-34; retd pay, 1934; Captain 102 (Pembroke and Cardigan), Field Brigade RA (TA), 1937; Major, 1939; Hon. Col 302 Pembroke Yeo. Field Regt, RA (TA), 1955-59. Sheriff of Pembrokeshire, 1938; Master Pembrokeshire Foxhounds, 1934-35, South Pembrokeshire, 1936-39; V. W. H., Lord Bathurst's, 1939, Pembrokeshire, 1946-58; President: Royal Welsh Agricultural Soc., 1955; Hunters Improvement Soc., 1972; Chm., Pembs Branch, NFU, 1968. *Heir: s* David John Charlton Meyrick [*b* 2 Dec. 1926; *m* 1962, Penelope Anne Marsden-Smedley; three *s*]. *Address:* Gumfreston, Tenby, Dyfed SA70 8RA. *Club:* English-Speaking Union.

See also T. O. Lewis.

MEYSEY-THOMPSON, Sir (Humphrey) Simon, 4th Bt *cr* 1874; *b* 31 March 1935; *s* of Guy Herbert Meysey-Thompson (*d* 1961), and of Miriam Beryl Meysey-Thompson; *S* kinsman, Sir Algar de Clifford Charles Meysey-Thompson, 1967. *Address:* 10 Church Street, Woodbridge, Suffolk. *T:* Woodbridge 2144.

MIALL, (Rowland) Leonard, OBE 1961; Research Historian; *b* 6 Nov. 1914; *e s* of late Rowland Miall and S. Grace Miall; *m* 1st, 1941, Lorna (*d* 1974), *o d* of late G. John Rackham; three *s* one *d*; 2nd, 1975, Sally Bicknell, *e d* of late Gordon Leith. *Educ:* Bootham Sch., York (Scholar); Freiburg Univ.; St John's Coll., Cambridge (Sizar), MA. Pres. Cambridge Union, 1936; Ed. Cambridge Review, 1936. Lectured in US, 1937; Sec. British-American Associates, 1937-39; joined BBC; inaugurated talks broadcast to Europe, 1939; BBC German Talks and Features Editor, 1940-42. Mem. British Political Warfare Mission to US, 1942-44 (Dir of News, San Francisco, 1943; Head of New York Office, 1944); Personal Asst to Dep. Dir-Gen., Political Warfare Exec., London, 1944; attached to Psychological Warfare Division of SHAEF, Luxembourg, 1945. Rejoined BBC: Special Correspondent, Czechoslovakia, 1945; Actg Diplomatic Corresp., 1945; Chief Corresp. in US, 1945-53; Head of Television Talks, 1954; Asst Controller, Current Affairs and Talks, Television, 1961; Special Asst to Dir of Television, planning start of BBC-2, 1962; Asst Controller, Programme Services, Television, BBC, 1963-66; BBC Rep. in US, 1966-70; Controller, Overseas and Foreign Relations, BBC, 1971-74. Inaugurated BBC Lunchtime Lectures, 1962; Advisor, Cttee on Broadcasting, New Delhi, 1965; Delegate to Commonwealth Broadcasting Confs, Jamaica, 1970, Kenya, 1972, Malta, 1974. Dir, Visnews Ltd; Overseas Dir, British Acad. of Film and Television Arts. Trustee, Broadcasting Foundn of Amer. FRSA. Cert. of Appreciation, NY City, 1970. *Publication:* Richard Dimbleby, Broadcaster, 1966. *Recreations:* bridge; doing it oneself. *Address:* Maryfield, Taplow, Maidenhead, Berks SL6 0EX. *T:* Burnham 4195. *Clubs:* Garrick; Metropolitan (Washington); Union (Cambridge).

MICHAEL, David Parry Martin, CBE 1972; MA; Headmaster, Newport High School, Gwent, 1960-76; Secretary (part-time) University College, Cardiff, Press Board, since 1976; *b* 21 Dec. 1910; *m* 1937, Mary Horner Hayward; one *s. Educ:* University Coll., Cardiff. Major, RAOC, combined ops, 1941-46 (despatches). Asst Master, Bassaleg Gram. Sch., Mon., 1935-41 and 1946-50; Headmaster, Cathays High Sch. for Boys, Cardiff, 1950-60. Member: Coun., University Coll., Cardiff, 1961-; Governing Body, Church in Wales, 1963-. Gov., Nat. Library of Wales, 1967-76; Mem., Broadcasting Council for Wales, 1969-73. Pres., Incorporated Assoc. of Headmasters, 1968; Mem., HMC, 1971-76; Pres., Welsh Secondary Schools Assoc., 1973. Editor, Welsh Secondary Schools' Review, 1965-76. *Publications:* The Idea of a Staff College, 1967; Guide to the Sixth Form, 1969; Arthur Machen, 1971; (jtly) Comprehensive School Case Studies, 1976; Town Walk, 1977; articles and reviews in educational and other jls. *Recreations:* collecting Victorian Staffordshire portrait figures; setting and solving crosswords. *Address:* 28 Fields Road, Newport, Gwent. *T:* Newport (Gwent) 62747.

MICHAEL, Ian (Lockie), CBE 1972; Deputy Director, Institute of Education, University of London, since 1973; *b* 30 Nov. 1915; 4th *c* of late Reginald Warburton Michael and Margaret Campbell Kerr; *m* 1942, Mary Harborne Bayley, *e c* of late Rev. William Henry Bayley; one *s* one *d. Educ:* St Bees Sch.; private study. BA (London) 1938; PhD (Bristol) 1963. Schoolmaster: St Faith's Sch., Cambridge, 1935-40; Junior Sch., Leighton Park, 1941-45, Headmaster, 1946-49; Lectr in Educn, Bristol Univ., 1950-63; Prof. of Educn, Khartoum Univ., 1963-64; Vice-Chancellor, Univ. of Malaŵi, 1964-73. Hon. DLitt Malaŵi, 1974. *Publication:* English Grammatical Categories and the Tradition to 1800, 1970. *Address:* 33 Tavistock Square, WC1H 9EZ.

MICHAELS, Michael Israel, CB 1960; Industrial Consultant; *b* 22 Dec. 1908; *m* 1932, Rosina, *e d* of late Joseph Sturges; one *s* one *d. Educ:* City of London College; London Sch. of Economics (Social Science Research Scholar, 1931). Asst Sec., New Survey London Life and Labour, 1932-34. Deputy Director, Programmes and Statistics, Ministry of Supply, 1940-45. Asst Sec., Ministry of Health, 1946-54; Under-Sec., Atomic Energy Office, 1955-59; Office of the Minister for Science (Atomic Energy Division), 1959-64; Under-Sec., Min. of Technology, 1964-71, retired. British Mem., Bd of Governors, Internat. Atomic Energy Agency, 1957-71. *Recreations:* music, gardening, history. *Address:* The Mill House, Kelsale, Saxmundham, Suffolk. *T:* Saxmundham 3142.

MICHALOPOULOS, André, CBE 1937 (OBE 1919); FRSA; Professor Emeritus of Classical Literatures and Civilizations, since 1964, Professor 1957-64, Fairleigh-Dickinson University; *b* 1897; *m* 1st, 1924, Aspasia Eliasco; one *s* two *d*; 2nd, 1964, Countess Eleanor von Etzdorf. Educ: St Paul's Sch., London; Oriel Coll., Oxford (Scholar). BA 1st Cl. Hons Litt Hum., 1920; MA 1927; Priv. Sec. to Eleutherios Venizelos, Prime Minister of Greece, 1917 and 1921-24; Mem. Greek Delegation, Lausanne Peace Conference, 1922-23; Civil Governor of Lemnos, Imbros, Tenedos, and Samothrace, 1918-19; Governor of Corfu and adjacent islands, 1924-25; left Public Service for business, 1925; Managing Dir of Athens-Piraeus Water Coy; Dir of several Banking, Industrial, and Commercial Corpns in Athens; Pres. of the Anglo-Hellenic League, Athens, 1935-45; broadcast nightly English news commentary from Athens during Greco-Italian War, 1940-41; joined Greek forces in Crete, April 1941; Gen. Sec. of Nat. Cttee of Greeks of Egypt for resistance, May 1941; followed Greek Govt to S Africa, Aug. 1941; Mem. Greek Cabinet (Minister of Information in London, Washington and Cairo), Sept. 1941-May 1943. Lectured and broadcast extensively in S Africa, Great Britain, USA, Canada, 1941-43; Minister Plenipotentiary for Greece i/c information in America, 1945-46; Special Adviser on American Affairs to Royal Greek Embassy in Washington, 1950-67; Mem., Supreme Educnl Council of Greek Orthodox Archdiocese in N and S America, 1962-70. Visiting Professor, Kansas City University, 1949. Participated as Chm. or panel-mem., in Invitation to Learning programme, Columbia Broadcasting System, 1947-65; Master of Ceremonies and political and literary commentator on weekly Hellenic Television Hour, New York, 1955-56. Broadcast to Greece on Voice of America programme, 1950-55. Participated in annual American Foreign Policy Conf., Colgate Univ., 1951-61; has lectured and broadcast in the 48 States of USA and in Canada. Archon, Order of St Andrew; Grand Protonotary of Oecumenical Patriarchate of Constantinople, 1967. Commander Order of George I (Greece) with swords, 1941; Commander Order of the Phœnix (Greece), 1936; Chevalier Legion of Honour (France), 1934; Commander Order of Orange Nassau (Netherlands), 1939. FRSA 1936; Mem. Academy of American Poets, 1956; Mem. Poetry Society of America, 1957. Fellow, Ancient Monuments Soc. (London), 1958. Hon. LittD Westminster Coll., Utah. *Publications:* Homer, an interpretative study of the Iliad and Odyssey, 1965; and Greek Fire: a collection of broadcasts, articles and addresses, 1943; two collections of Verse 1923 and 1928; contribs to Encyclopedia Americana and Funk & Wagnall's Reference Encyclopaedia; chapts and articles in Greek, English, Scottish, American, Canadian, Egyptian, French, and South African books, reviews and newspapers; weekly book reviews for King Features Syndicate (USA), 1959-75. *Address:* Grasshopper Hill, Irvington-on-Hudson, New York, NY 10533, USA. *T:* 914-591-8447.

MICHALOWSKI, Jerzy; Polish diplomat; *b* 26 May 1909; *s* of Andrzej and Maria Michalowski; *m* 1947, Mira Krystyna; two *s*. *Educ:* University of Warsaw. Asst In Polish Inst. of Social Affairs, 1933-36; Dir of Polish Workers Housing Organisation, 1936-39; Chief of Housing Dept of Warsaw City Council, 1945; Counsellor of Polish Embassy in London, 1945-46; Deputy Deleg. of Poland to UN, March-Nov. 1946; Ambassador of Republic of Poland to the Court of St James's 1946-53; Head of a department, Ministry of Foreign Affairs, Warsaw, 1953-54; Under Sec. of State for Educ., 1954-55; Deleg. of Poland to the Internat. Commn in Vietnam, 1955-56; Permanent Representative of Poland to UN, 1956-60; Dir-Gen., in Ministry of Foreign Affairs, Warsaw, 1960-67; Ambassador to USA, 1967-71. Pres. of ECOSOC, UN, 1962. *Publications:* Unemployment of Polish Peasants, 1934; Housing Problems in Poland (publ. by League of Nations), 1935; The Big Game for the White House, 1972. *Recreations:* tennis and winter sports. *Address:* Al. I Armii WP 16/20, Warsaw, Poland.

MICHELHAM, 2nd Baron, *cr* 1905, of Hellingly; **Herman Alfred Stern;** Bt, *cr* 1905; a Baron of Portugal; *b* 5 Sept. 1900; *e s* of 1st Baron Michelham; *S* father, 1919; *m* 1919, Berthe Isabella Susanna Flora (*d* 1961), *d* of Arthur Joseph Capel. *Educ:* Malvern Coll. *Heir: b* Hon. Jack Herbert Michelham [*b* 23 Dec. 1903; assumed by deed poll, 1928, the surname of Michelham. *Educ:* Harrow; Magdalen Coll., Oxford].

MICHELIN, Reginald Townend, CMG 1957; CVO 1953; OBE 1952; General Manager: Agualta Vale Estates, Jamaica, 1958-64; Jamaica Tourist Board, 1964-73; *b* 31 Dec. 1903; *s* of V. A. Michelin, Planter, Jamaica; *m* 1940, Nina Gladys Faulkner, Iffley, Oxford; one *s* one *d*. *Educ:* Exeter Sch., England. Sub-Inspector, Police, Jamaica, 1924; Inspector, Police, Leeward Islands, 1928; Asst Commissioner of Police, Nigeria, 1930; Comr of Police, Barbados, 1949; Commissioner of Police, Jamaica, 1953-58, retd. *Address:* After All, Runaway Bay, Jamaica, West Indies.

MICHELL, Alan, CMG 1966; HM Diplomatic Service; retired; *b* 11 Nov. 1913; *s* of late Pierre William Michell and late Mary Michell; *m* 1941, Glenys Enid Davies (*d* 1965); one *s* two *d*. *Educ:* Barry School; Jesus Coll., Oxford (Stanhope Univ. Prize, 1934). Served Royal Tank Regt, 1940-46. Asst Master, King's Sch., Canterbury, 1937-40; Foreign Office, 1947; Second Sec., Paris, 1952; Nicosia, 1954; Singapore, 1956; First Sec., Saigon, 1959; FO, later FCO, 1961-72. *Address:* Northwick House, Brabourne, near Ashford, Kent.

MICHELL, Francis Victor, CMG 1955; *b* 17 Jan. 1908; *s* of late Pierre William Michell and late Mary Michell; *m* 1943, Betty Enid Tempest, *d* of late William Tempest Olver, JP, Tamworth; no *c*. *Educ:* Barry Sch.; Jesus Coll., Oxford. Attaché British Embassy, Rio de Janeiro, 1943-46; First Sec., Istanbul, 1947-51; First Sec., Commissioner-General's Office, Singapore, 1951-53; Foreign Office, 1953-65. *Address:* Nettlesworth Farm, Vines Cross, Heathfield, East Sussex. *T:* Heathfield 2695. *Club:* Travellers'.

MICHELL, Keith; actor since 1948; Artistic Director, Chichester Festival Theatre, 1974-77; *b* Adelaide; *s* of Joseph Michell and Alice Maud (*née* Aslat); *m* 1957, Jeannette Sterke; one *s* one *d*. *Educ:* Port Pirie High Sch.; Adelaide Teachers' Coll.; Sch. of Arts and Crafts; Adelaide Univ.; Old Vic Theatre School. Formerly taught art. First stage appearance, Playbox, Adelaide, 1947; Young Vic Theatre Co., 1950-51; first London appearance, And So To Bed, 1951; Shakespeare Mem. Theatre Co., Australian tour, 1952-53, Stratford, 1954 and 1955 (Troilus and Cressida, Romeo and Juliet, Taming of the Shrew, All's Well That Ends Well, Macbeth, Twelfth Night); Don Juan, Royal Court, 1956; Old Vic Co., 1956 (Antony and Cleopatra, Much Ado about Nothing, Comedy of Errors); Irma La Douce, Lyric, 1958, Washington, DC, 1960 and Broadway, 1960-61; The Art of Seduction, Aldwych, 1962; Chichester Festival, 1962; The Rehearsal, NY, 1963; The First Four Hundred Years, Australia and NZ, 1964; Robert and Elizabeth, Lyric, 1964; The King's Mare, 1966; Man of La Mancha, 1968-69, NY, 1970; Abelard and Heloise, 1970, Los Angeles and NY, 1971; Hamlet, Globe, 1972; Dear Love, Comedy, 1973. Chichester, 1974:

Tonight We Improvise, Oedipus Tyrannus; Chichester, 1975: Cyrano de Bergerac, Othello; Chichester, 1976 (directed and designed): Twelfth Night; Chichester, 1977: The Apple Cart, (directed and designed) In Order of Appearance. Has appeared in films and on TV (played Henry VIII in series The Six Wives of Henry VIII, 1970, film, Henry VIII and his Six Wives, 1972; Keith Michell at Chichester, one man show, 1974) and made recordings. First exhibn of paintings, 1959; subseq. exhibns at John Whibley Gall., London and Wright Hepburn and Webster Gall., NY, Century Gall., Henley. *Recreations:* painting, photography, swimming, riding. *Address:* c/o Chatto & Linnit Ltd, Globe Theatre, W1.

MICHELMORE, Clifford Arthur, CBE 1969; Television Broadcaster and Producer; Managing Director, RM/EMI Visual Programmes, since 1971; Editorial Director, Barclaycard Magazine; *b* 11 Dec. 1919; *s* of late Herbert Michelmore and Ellen Alford; *m* 1950, Jean Metcalfe (Broadcaster); one *s* one *d*. *Educ:* Cowes Senior Sch., Isle of Wight. Entered RAF, 1935; commnd 1940; left RAF 1947. Head, Outside Broadcasts and Variety, BFN, 1948; Dep. Station Dir, BFN, also returned to freelance as Commentator and Producer, 1949. Entered Television, 1950. Has taken part in numerous radio and television programmes in Britain, Europe and the USA. Introduced "Tonight" series, 1957-65; 24 Hours series, 1965-68; General Election Results programmes, 1964, 1966, 1970; Our World, 1967; With Michelmore (interviews), 1968-; Talkback, 1968-; Apollo Space Programmes, 1960-70; Holiday, 1969-77; Chance to Meet, 1970-73; Wheelbase, 1972; Getaway, 1975; Globetrotter, 1975; Opinions Unlimited, 1977. Made film, Shaping of a Writer, 1977. FRSA, 1975. Television Society Silver Medal, 1957; Guild of TV Producers Award, Personality of the Year, 1958; TV Review Critics Award, 1959; Variety Club Award, 1961. *Publications:* various articles on television and broadcasting. *Recreations:* golf, reading and doing nothing. *Address:* White House, Reigate, Surrey; Brookfield, Bembridge, Isle of Wight. *Clubs:* Garrick, Royal Air Force; Cowes Corinthian Yacht.

MICHELMORE, Sir Walter Harold Strachan, Kt 1958; MBE 1945; Company Director; *b* Chudleigh, Devon, 4 April 1908; 2nd *s* of late Harold G. Michelmore; *m* 1933, Dorothy Walrond (*d* 1964), *o c* of late E. W. Bryant; one *d*; *m* 1967, Mrs Dulcie Mary Scott, *d* of late Leonard Haughton. *Educ:* Sherborne Sch.; Balliol Coll., Oxford. Joined Bird & Co., Calcutta, 1929. Served Indian Army (Staff), 1940-46 (MBE). Managing Dir, Bird & Co. (Pvt) Ltd and F. W. Heilgers & Co. (Pvt) Ltd, Calcutta, 1948-63; Dep. Chm., 1955, Chm. 1961; retired 1963. Pres. Bengal Chamber of Commerce and Industry and Associated Chambers of Commerce of India, 1957. Chm., Fund of Australia Services Ltd. *Recreations:* golf, fishing, gardening. *Address:* Derriwong, Derriwong Lane, Round Corner, via Dural, NSW 2158, Australia. *Clubs:* Oriental, Queen's; Bengal (Calcutta); Australian, Elanora Country (Sydney).

MICHELMORE, Maj.-Gen. Sir (William) Godwin, KBE 1953; CB 1945; DSO 1919; MC, TD; JP; DL; Solicitor and Notary Public; Deputy Diocesan Registrar, Bishop's Secretary; *b* 14 March 1894; 3rd *s* of late Henry William Michelmore of Exeter; *m* 1st, 1921, Margaret Phœbe (*d* 1965), *d* of late Sir F. G. Newbolt, KC; one *s* two *d*; 2nd, 1971, Maud Winifred, *widow* of Lt-Col William Holderness and *d* of late Rt Rev. Henry Hutchinson Montgomery, KCMG, DD. *Educ:* Rugby; London Univ.; LLB. Served European War, 1914-19 (despatches, MC, DSO); wounded at Passchendaele, 1917; commanded 43rd (Wessex) Div. Signals TA, 1919-29; Dep. Chief Signal Officer, Southern Command, 1929-33; Col 1933; commanded 4th Bn Devonshire Regt, 1936-39; commanded Infantry Brigade, 1939-41, Division Commander, 1941-45; ADC to the King, 1942-47; Mayor of Exeter, 1949-50. Chm. Devon T&AFA, 1948-58; Vice-Chm. Council of T&AFA, 1956-59. Resigned 1975: Chm. Devon Magistrates Courts Cttee; Chm. Govs, St Luke's Coll., Exeter; Gov., Blundell's Sch.; Mem. Coun., University Exeter. DL 1938, JP 1950, Devon. *Address:* 10 St Leonard's Road, Exeter, Devon EX2 46A. *T:* 59585.

MICHENER, James Albert; Author; *b* New York City, 3 Feb. 1907; *s* of Edwin Michener and Mabel (*née* Haddock); *m* 1st, 1935, Patti Koon (marr. diss. 1948); 2nd, 1948, Vange Nord (marr. diss., 1955); 3rd, 1955, Mari Yoriko Sabusawa; no *c*. *Educ:* Swarthmore Coll., Pennsylvania; St Andrews Univ., Scotland; Harvard Coll., Mass. Teacher, George Sch., Pa, 1933-36; Prof., Colorado State Coll. of Educn, 1936-41; Visiting Prof., Harvard, 1940-41; Associate Editor, Macmillan Co., 1941-49; Mem. advisory cttee on the arts, US State Dept, 1957. Served with USNR on active duty in South Pacific, 1944-45. Sec., Pennsylvania Constitutional Convention, 1968. Hon. DHL, LLD, and LittD, from numerous univs. *Publications:* Unit in the

Social Studies, 1940; Tales of the South Pacific (Pulitzer prize for fiction), 1947; The Fires of Spring, 1949; Return to Paradise, 1951; The Voice of Asia, 1951; The Bridges at Toko-ri, 1953; Sayonara, 1954; Floating World, 1955; The Bridge at Andau, 1957; (with A. Grove Day) Rascals in Paradise, 1957; Selected Writings, 1957; The Hokusai Sketchbook, 1958; Japanese Prints, 1959; Hawaii, 1959; Caravans, 1964; The Source, 1965; Iberia, 1968; Presidential Lottery, 1969; The Quality of Life, 1970; Kent State, 1971; The Drifters, 1971; Centennial, 1974; Michener on Sport, 1977; ed; Future of Social Studies for NEA, 1940. *Recreations:* photography, philately, tennis. *Address:* Pipersville, Pa 18947, USA.

MICHENER, Rt. Hon. Roland, CC, CMM, CD; Royal Victorian Chain, 1973; PC (Canada) 1962; QC (Canada) Governor-General and Commander-in-Chief of Canada, 1967-Jan. 1974; Barrister associated as Counsel with Lang, Michener, Cranston, Farquharson & Wright, Toronto, since 1974; Chancellor, Queen's University; Hon. Chairman of Board, Metropolitan Trust Co., Toronto; Chairman of Board, Teck Mining Corporation Ltd; Director, Pamour Porcupine Mines Ltd; etc; *b* Lacombe, Alta, 19 April 1900; *s* of late Senator Edward Michener and Mary Edith (*née* Roland), Lincoln Co., Ontario; *m* 1927, Norah Evangeline, *d* of Robert Willis, Manitoba; two *d* (and one *d* decd). *Educ:* Universities of Alberta and Oxford. BA (Alta) 1920; Rhodes Scholar for Alta, 1919; BA 1922, BCL 1923, MA 1929, Oxon. Served with RAF, 1918. Called to Bar, Middle Temple, 1923; Barrister, Ontario, 1924; KC (Canada) 1943. Practising lawyer with Lang, Michener & Cranston, Toronto, 1924-57. Mem. Ontario Legislature for St David, Toronto, 1945-48, and Provincial Sec. and Registrar for Ontario, 1946-48; elected to Canadian House of Commons, 1953; re-elected 1957 and 1958; elected Speaker, 1957 and May 1958; Canadian High Commissioner to India and Ambassador to Nepal, 1964-67. Gen. Sec. for Canada, Rhodes Scholarships, 1936-64. Mem. Bd of Governors, Toronto Stock Exchange, 1974-76. Formerly: Governor, Toronto Western Hosp.; Hon. Counsel, Chm. of Exec. Cttee (now President), Canadian Inst. of Internat. Affairs; Hon. Counsel, Red Cross Ont Div.; Chm. of Exec., Canadian Assoc. for Adult Educn; Officer and Dir of various Canadian mining and financial companies. Chancellor and Principal Companion, Order of Canada, 1967-74; Chancellor and Comdr, Order of Military Merit, 1972-74. KJStJ (Prior for Canada), 1967. Hon. Fellow: Hertford Coll., Oxford, 1961; Acad. of Medicine, Toronto, 1967; Trinity Coll., Toronto, 1968; Frontier Coll., Toronto, 1972; Hon. FRCP(C) 1968; Hon. FRAIC, 1968; Hon. FRSC, 1975. Hon. Mem., Canadian Medical Assoc., 1968; Hon. Bencher, Law Soc. of Upper Canada, 1968. Hon. LLD: Ottawa, 1948; Queen's, 1958; Laval, 1960; Alberta, 1967; St Mary's, Halifax, 1968; Toronto, 1968; RMC Canada, 1969; Mount Allison, 1969; Sackville, NB, 1969; Brock, 1969; Manitoba, 1970; McGill, 1970; York, Toronto, 1970; British Columbia, 1971; Jewish Theol Seminary of America, 1972; New Brunswick, 1972; Law Soc. of Upper Canada, 1974; Dalhousie, 1974; Hon. DCL: Bishop's, 1968; Windsor, 1969; Oxford Univ., 1970. *Address:* PO Box 10, First Canadian Place, Toronto, Ontario M5X 1A2, Canada; (home) 24 Thornwood Road, Toronto, Ontario M4W 2S1.

MICHIE, Charles Watt, CMG 1960; OBE 1943; Secretary: Scottish Universities Entrance Board, 1967-69 (Assistant to Secretary, 1963-67); Scottish Universities Council on Entrance, 1968-72; *b* 1 Sept. 1907; *s* of late Charles Michie and late Emily (*née* MacGregor); *m* 1935, Janet Leslie Graham Kinloch; two *d*. *Educ:* Aberdeen Gram. Sch.; Aberdeen Univ. Cadet, Colonial Admin. Service, 1930; Cadet, N Region of Nigeria, 1931; Consul for Spanish Territories of Gulf of Guinea and Labour Officer in Nigerian Department of Labour, 1940-42; Labour Officer on Nigerian tin minesfield, 1942; N Regional Secretariat, Kaduna, 1944; Chm. Labour Advisory Bd for Nigerian tin minesfield, 1947; District Administration, 1948; Sen. District Officer, and Asst Sec., Actg Principal, Nigerian Secretariat, 1949; returned to provincial administration and promoted Resident, 1954; Sen. Resident, 1954; Permanent Sec. to N Region Min. of Agriculture in Nigeria, 1957; retired 1960. Asst Teacher, Mod. Langs, Morgan Academy, Dundee, 1960-63. Defence Medal, 1945; Coronation Medal, 1953. *Recreations:* gardening, photography. *Address:* Nethermiln, Blebo Craigs, Cupar, Fife. *T:* Strathkinness 316.

MICHIE, David Alan Redpath, RSA 1972 (ARSA 1964); Vice-Principal, Edinburgh College of Art, since 1974; *b* 30 Nov. 1928; *s* of late James Michie and late Anne Redpath, OBE, ARA, RSA; *m* 1951, Eileen Anderson Michie; two *d*. *Educ:* Edinburgh Coll. of Art (DA). National Service, 1947-49; Edinburgh Coll. of Art, 1949-53 (studied painting); travelling scholarship, Italy, 1953-54; Lectr in Painting, Gray's Sch. of Art, Aberdeen, 1958-62; Lectr in Painting, Edinburgh Coll. of Art, 1962-69, Sen.

Lectr, 1969-73, Deputy Head, Sch. of Drawing and Painting, 1973-74. Member: Gen. Teaching Council for Scotland; Edinburgh Festival Soc. Pres., Soc. of Scottish Artists, 1961-63. One Man Exhibitions: Mercury Gallery, London, 1967, 1969, 1971, 1974. *Recreation:* fishing. *Address:* 17 Gilmour Road, Edinburgh EH16 5NS. *T:* 031-667 2684. *Club:* (Associate Mem.) University of Edinburgh Staff.

MICHIE, Prof. Donald, DPhil, DSc; FRSE; FBCS; Professor of Machine Intelligence, University of Edinburgh, since 1967; *b* 11 Nov. 1923; *s* of James Kilgour Michie and Marjorie Crain Michie; *m* 1st, 1949, Zena Margaret Davies (marr. diss.); one *s*; 2nd, 1952, Anne McLaren (marr. diss.); one *s* two *d*; 3rd, 1971, Jean Elizabeth Crouch. *Educ:* Rugby Sch.; Balliol Coll., Oxford. Open Class. Scholar, Balliol Coll., 1942; Balliol Coll. War Memorial Student, 1949; MA Human Anatomy and Physiol., 1949; DPhil Oxon, Mammalian Genetics, 1953; DSc Oxon, Biol Sciences, 1971. Sci. Fellow Zool Soc. of London, 1953; FRSE 1969; FBCS 1971. War Service in FO, Bletchley, 1942-45; Res. Associate, Univ. of London, 1952-58; Univ. of Edinburgh: Sen. Lectr, Dept of Surg. Science, 1958; Reader in Surg. Science, 1962; Founder and Dir of Expermtl Programming Unit, 1965; Founder and Chm. of Dept of Machine Intelligence and Perception, 1966; Bd Chm., Univ. Centre for Industrial Consultancy and Liaison, 1969; Dir, Machine Intelligence Res. Unit, 1974. Vis. Associate Prof. in Elec. Eng, Stanford Univ., 1962; Royal Soc. Lectr in USSR in Biomedical Computing, 1965; Vis. Prof. in Systems and Inf. Science, Syracuse Univ., 1970; Vis. Fellow, St Cross Coll., Oxford, 1971; Vis. Res. Prof. in Systems and Inf. Science, Syracuse Univ., 1971; William Withering Lectr, Univ. of Birmingham, 1972; Vis. Lectr in Math. Biol. and Artificial Intell., USSR Acad. of Sciences, 1973; Vis. Prof. in Computer Science and Stats, Virginia Polytech. Inst. and State Univ., 1974; George A. Miller Lectr, Univ. of Ill, 1974; Vis. Prof. in Inf. Sciences, Univ. of Calif, Santa Cruz, 1975; Vis. Res. Prof., Dartmouth Coll., USA, 1975; Vis. Prof. in Computer Sci., Univ. of Ill, 1976; Herbert Spencer Lectr, Univ. of Oxford, 1976; Vis. Lectr in Machine Intell., USSR Acad. of Sciences, 1976; Vis. Prof. in Computer Sci., Carnegie Mellon Univ., 1977. Chief Editor of series, Machine Intelligence. *Publications:* (jtly) An Introduction to Molecular Biology, 1964; Computing Science in 1964: a pilot study of the state of University based research in the UK, 1965; (jtly) Programming for Schools: first steps in ALGOL, 1968; On Machine Intelligence, 1974; various papers in tech. jls and conf. proc. *Recreations:* chess, travel. *Address:* 15 Hope Park Terrace, Edinburgh; Croft Cottage, Thame, Oxfordshire. *Club:* New (Edinburgh).

MICKLETHWAIT, Sir Robert (Gore), Kt 1964; QC 1956; Chief National Insurance Commissioner, 1966-75 (Deputy Commissioner, 1959; National Insurance Commissioner and Industrial Injuries Commissioner, 1961); *b* 7 Nov. 1902; 2nd *s* of late St J. G. Micklethwait, KC; *m* 1936, Philippa J., 2nd *d* of late Sir Ronald Bosanquet, QC; three *s* one *d*. *Educ:* Clifton Coll.; Trinity Coll., Oxford (2nd Class Lit. Hum., MA). Called to Bar, Middle Temple, 1925, Bencher, 1951; Autumn Reader, 1964; Dep. Treasurer, 1970, Treasurer, 1971. Oxford Circuit; Gen. Coun. of the Bar, 1939-40 and 1952-56; Supreme Court Rule Cttee, 1952-56. Royal Observer Corps, 1938-40; Civil Asst, WO, 1940-45; Recorder of Worcester, 1946-59. Deputy Chm., Court of Quarter Sessions for County of Stafford, 1956-59. Hon. LLD Newcastle upon Tyne, 1975. Hon. Knight, Hon. Soc. of Knights of the Round Table, 1972. *Publication:* The National Insurance Commissioners (Hamlyn Lectures), 1976. *Address:* 71 Harvest Road, Englefield Green, Surrey TW20 0QR. *T:* Egham 2521.

MIDDLEDITCH, Edward, MC 1945; RA 1973 (ARA 1968); ARCA 1951; painter; Head of Fine Art Department, Norwich School of Art, since 1964; *b* 23 March 1923; *s* of Charles Henry Middleditch and Esme Buckley; *m* 1947, Jean Kathleen Whitehouse; one *d*. *Educ:* Mundella School, Nottingham; King Edward VI Grammar Sch., Chelmsford; Royal College of Art. Served Army, 1942-47, France, Germany, India, W Africa; commissioned Middx Regt 1944. Eleven Exhibitions, London, 1954-74; contrib. to mixed exhibitions: Paris; Rome: Venice Biennale, 1956; Six Young Painters, 1957; Pittsburgh Internat., 1958; Whitechapel, 1959; English Landscape Tradition in the 20th Century, 1969; British Painting '74, 1974; 25 Years of British Painting, 1977, etc. Gulbenkian Foundn Scholarship, 1962; Arts Council of GB Bursary, 1964; Arts Council of NI Bursary, 1968. Paintings in private and public collections, including: Tate Gall.; Arts Council; V & A Museum; Contemporary Art Soc.; Manchester City Art Gall.; Ferens Art Gall., Hull; Nat. Gall. of Victoria; Nat. Gall. of S Aust.; Nat. Gall. of Canada; Chrysler Art Museum, Mass; Toledo Museum of Art, Ohio. *Address:* School House, Edwardstone, Boxford, near Colchester, Essex CO6 5PJ. *T:* Boxford (Suffolk) 210240; c/o New Arts Centre, 41 Sloane Street, SW1.

MIDDLEMISS, Prof. John Howard, CMG 1968; Professor of Radiodiagnosis, University of Bristol, and Director of Radiology, United Bristol Hospitals, since 1949; *b* 14 May 1916; *s* of Thomas Middlemiss, Monkseaton, Northumberland; *m* 1942, Isobel Mary, *d* of Ivan Pirrie, MC, MD, Maldon, Essex; one *s* two *d. Educ:* Repton; Durham Univ. MB, BS 1940; MD 1947; DMRD 1946; FFR 1948; MRCP 1964, FRCP 1972; FRCS 1976. Served with RAMC as Temp. Major and Actg Lieut-Col, 1941-46. Asst Radiologist, Royal Victoria Infirmary, Newcastle upon Tyne, 1946-48. Adviser in Radiology to Governments of: Burma, Iran, Laos, Malaysia, Nigeria, Pakistan, Philippines, South Vietnam, Tanzania, Turkey and Uganda, and to Universities of Ahmadu Bello, Ghana, Ibadan, Makerere, West Indies, for periods between 1953-76. Member: Med. Adv. Cttee, Min. of Overseas Develt; Inter-Univ. Council, 1969-; British Deleg. to 13th Internat. Congress of Radiology, 1973 (Chm.); Accident Service Review Cttee; Jt Consultants Cttee, 1972-76; Cons. to WHO; Past Chm., Bristol Standing Cttee on Disarmament; Examnr, FFR, UK 1958-60 and 1962-63, Aust. and NZ 1969, DM (Rad.) W Indies, 1973 and 1976. Harkness Fellow, US, 1964. Lectures: Long Fox, Bristol, 1962; Mackenzie Davidson, BIR, 1971; Litchfield, Oxford, 1972; Skinner, FR, 1972; Lindblom, Univ. of Stockholm, 1973; Edelstein, Johannesburg, 1975; Frimann-Dahl, Univ. of Oslo, 1976. Warden, Faculty of Radiologists, 1966-71, Pres. 1972-75, Pres., Royal Coll. of Radiologists, 1975-76; FRSocMed. Hon. FFR, RCSI, 1969; Hon. FACR, 1972; Mem., BIR (Past Chm. of Med. Cttee); Past Vice-Pres., Section of Radiol, RSM; Hon. Member: Soc. of Radiology, Luxembourg, 1971; W African Assoc. of Radiologists, 1971; Radiol Soc. of N America, 1976; Deutsche Röntgengesellschaft, 1977; Hon. Fellow, Royal Aust. Coll. of Radiologists, 1972. *Publications:* Radiology in Surgery, 1960; Tropical Radiology, 1961; numerous scientific papers in Clinical Radiology, British Jl of Radiology; contrib. Encyclopaedia Britannica. *Recreations:* international relations, arboriculture, travel. *Address:* 48 Pembroke Road, Clifton, Bristol BS8 3DT. *T:* Bristol 38553; White Cottage, Wellington Heath, Ledbury, Herefordshire. *Clubs:* Sesame, English-Speaking Union.

MIDDLEMORE, Sir William Hawkslow, 2nd Bt, *cr* 1919; *b* 10 April 1908; *s* of 1st Bt and Mary, *d* of late Rev. Thomas Price, Selly Oak, Birmingham; *S* father, 1924; *m* 1934, Violet Constance, *d* of Andrew Kennagh, Worcester. *Heir:* none. *Address:* St Joseph's, Shurdington Road, Cheltenham, Glos. *T:* Cheltenham 25414.

MIDDLESBROUGH, Bishop of, (RC), since 1967; **Rt. Rev. (John) Gerard McClean;** *b* Redcar, Yorks, 24 Sept. 1914; *s* of Robert and Elizabeth McClean. *Educ:* Marist Coll., Middlesbrough; Ushaw Coll., Durham. Ordained, 1942. Titular Bishop of Maxita and Coadjutor of Middlesbrough, Feb. 1967; Bishop of Middlesbrough, June 1967. *Recreation:* golf. *Address:* Bishop's House, 16 Cambridge Road, Middlesbrough, Cleveland. *T:* Middlesbrough 88253.

MIDDLESEX, Archdeacon of; *see* Perry, Ven. J. N.

MIDDLETON, 12th Baron *cr* 1711; **Digby Michael Godfrey John Willoughby,** MC 1945; DL; Bt 1677; *b* 1 May 1921; *er s* of 11th Baron Middleton, KG, MC, TD, and of Angela Florence Alfreda, *er d* of Charles Hall, Eddlethorpe Hall, Malton, Yorks; *S* father, 1970; *m* 1947, Janet, *o d* of General Sir James Marshall-Cornwall, *qv* ; three *s. Educ:* Eton; Trinity Coll., Cambridge. BA 1950; MA 1958. Served War of 1939-45: Coldstream Guards, 1940-46; NW Europe, 1944-45 (despatches, MC, Croix de Guerre); Hon. Col, 2nd Bn Yorkshire Volunteers, TAVR, 1976-. Land Agent, 1951-. DL 1963, JP 1958, CC 1964-74, ER of Yorks; CC N Yorks, 1974-77; Mem., Yorkshire and Humberside Economic Planning Council, 1968-. *Heir: s* Hon. Michael Charles James Willoughby [*b* 14 July 1948; *m* 1974, Hon. Lucy Sidney, *y d* of Viscount De L'Isle, *qv* ; one *s*]. *Address:* Birdsall House, Malton, N Yorks. *T:* North Grimston 202. *Club:* Boodle's.

MIDDLETON, Suffragan Bishop of, since 1959; **Rt. Rev. Edward Ralph Wickham;** *b* 3 Nov. 1911; *s* of Edward Wickham, London; *m* 1944, Dorothy Helen Neville Moss, *d* of Prof. Kenneth Neville Moss, Birmingham; one *s* two *d. Educ:* University of London (BD); St Stephen's House, Oxford. Deacon, 1938; Priest, 1939; Curate, Christ Church, Shieldfield, Newcastle upon Tyne, 1938-41; Chaplain, Royal Ordnance Factory, Swynnerton, 1941-44; Curate-in-charge, Swynnerton, 1943-44; Diocesan Missioner to Industry, Sheffield, 1944-59; Hon. Chaplain to Bishop of Sheffield, 1950-59; Canon Residentiary, Sheffield, 1951-59. Sir H. Stephenson Fellow, Sheffield University, 1955-57. Chm. Council, and Pro-Chancellor, Salford Univ., 1975-. Hon. DLitt Salford, 1973.

Publications: Church and People in an Industrial City, 1957; Encounter with Modern Society, 1964; Growth & Inflation, 1975; contributions to: Theology, The Ecumenical Review, Industrial Welfare, etc. *Recreations:* mountaineering, rock-climbing. *Address:* Maitland House, 1 Portland Road, Eccles, Manchester. *T:* 061-789 3144.

MIDDLETON, Donald King; HM Diplomatic Service; British High Commissioner, Papua New Guinea, since 1977; *b* 24 Feb. 1922; *s* of late Harold Ernest Middleton and Ellen Middleton; *m* 1945, Marion Elizabeth Ryder; one *d. Educ:* King Edward's Sch., Birmingham; Saltley Coll. Min. of Health, 1958-61; joined Commonwealth Relations Office, 1961; First Sec., British High Commn, Lagos, 1961-65; Head of Chancery, British Embassy, Saigon, 1970-72; British Dep. High Commissioner, Ibadan, 1973-75; HM Chargé d'Affaires, Phnom Penh, 1975; seconded to NI Office, Belfast, 1975-77. *Recreations:* music, sailing. *Address:* c/o Foreign and Commonwealth Office, SW1. *Club:* Royal Commonwealth Society.

MIDDLETON, Drew, OBE 1947 (Hon.); Military Correspondent of The New York Times, since 1970; *b* 14 Oct. 1914; *o s* of E. T. and Jean Drew Middleton, New York; *m* 1943, Estelle Mansel-Edwards, Dinas Powis, Glamorgan; one *d. Educ:* Syracuse Univ., Syracuse, New York. Correspondent: for Associated Press in London, 1939; for Associated Press in France, Belgium, London, Iceland, with the British Army and RAF, 1939-42; for The New York Times with US and British Forces in North Africa, Sicily, Britain, Normandy, Belgium and Germany, 1942-45; Chief Correspondent in USSR, 1946-47, in Germany, 1948-53, and in London, 1953-63; Chief Correspondent in Paris, 1963-65; Chief Correspondent, UN, 1965-69; European Affairs Correspondent, 1969-70. Correspondent at four meetings of Council of Foreign Ministers, also Potsdam and Casablanca Conferences. Medal of Freedom (US). English-Speaking Union Better Understanding Award, 1955. Doctor of Letters (*hc*) Syracuse Univ., 1963. *Publications:* Our Share of Night, 1946; The Struggle for Germany, 1949; The Defence of Western Europe, 1952; The British, 1957; The Sky Suspended, 1960; The Supreme Choice: Britain and the European Community, 1963; Crisis in the West, 1965; Retreat From Victory, 1973; Where Has Last July Gone?, 1974; Can America Win the Next War?, 1975; Submarine, 1976. *Recreations:* tennis, the theatre. *Address:* The New York Times, 229 W 43rd Street, New York, NY 10036, USA. *Clubs:* Beefsteak, Press, Garrick; Travellers' (Paris); The Brook, Century (New York).

MIDDLETON, Francis; Advocate; Sheriff of Glasgow and Strathkelvin (formerly of Lanarkshire) at Glasgow, since 1956; *b* 21 Nov. 1913; Scottish; *m* 1942, Edith Muir; two *s* one *d. Educ:* Rutherglen Academy; Glasgow Univ. MA, LLB 1937. Practising as Solicitor, 1937-39; volunteered Sept. 1939; Cameronian Scottish Rifles; commissioned to 6th Battn 11th Sikh Regt, Indian Army, 1940; Captain 1940; Major 1942, injured; Interpreter 1st Class in Hindustani, 1943; posted to Judge Advocate's Branch, 1944; released Dec. 1945. Admitted Faculty of Advocates in Scotland, 1946. Sheriff Substitute of Inverness, Moray, Nairn and Ross and Cromarty, 1949-52, Fife and Kinross, 1952-56. *Recreations:* reading, gardening, golf. *Address:* 23 Kirklee Road, Glasgow G12 0RQ.

MIDDLETON, Sir George (Humphrey), KCMG 1958 (CMG 1950); HM Diplomatic Service, retired; *b* 21 Jan. 1910; *e s* of George Close Middleton and Susan Sophie (*née* Harley, subsequently Elphinstone); *m* Marie Elisabeth Camille Françoise Sarthou, Bordeaux; one *s. Educ:* St Lawrence Coll., Ramsgate; Magdalen Coll., Oxford. Entered Consular Service, 1933, Vice-Consul, Buenos Aires; transferred to Asuncion, 1934, with local rank of 3rd Sec. in Diplomatic Service; in charge of Legation, 1935; transferred to New York, 1936; to Lemberg (Lwow), 1939; local rank of Consul; in charge of Vice-Consulate at Cluj, 1939-40; appointed to Genoa, 1940, to Madeira, 1940, to Foreign Office, 1943; 2nd Sec. at Washington, 1944; 1st Sec. 1945; transferred to FO, 1947; Counsellor, 1949; Counsellor, British Embassy, Tehran, Jan. 1951; acted as Chargé d'Affaires, 1951 and 1952 (when diplomatic relations severed); Dep. High Comr for UK, in Delhi, 1953-56; British Ambassador at Beirut, 1956-58; Political Resident in the Persian Gulf, 1958-61; British Ambassador to: Argentina, 1961-64; United Arab Republic, 1964-66. Mem. *Ad hoc* Cttee for UN Finances, 1966. Consultant, Industrial Reorganisation Corporation, 1967-68; Chairman: Michael Rice Ltd; C. E. Planning Ltd; Mears Bros Holdings; Geofran Ltd; Director: Liberty Life Assurance Co. Ltd; British Smelter Constructions Ltd; Britarge Ltd; Decor France Ltd; Johnson and Bloy Holdings. Chm., Exec. Cttee, British Road Fedn, 1972; Chief Executive, British Industry Roads Campaign, 1969-76. Chairman: Bahrain Soc.; Anglo-

Peruvian Soc. FRSA. Comdr, Order of Merit, Peru. *Recreations:* fishing, tennis, talking. *Address:* 53 Albert Hall Mansions, SW7. *T:* 01-589 8406. *Clubs:* Travellers', Pratt's, Royal Automobile.

MIDDLETON, Sir George (P.), KCVO 1962 (CVO 1951; MVO 1941); MB, ChB (Aberdeen); Medical Practitioner, retired 1973; Surgeon Apothecary to HM Household at Balmoral Castle, 1932-73; *b* Schoolhouse, Findhorn, Morayshire, 26 Jan. 1905; *s* of late A. Middleton, FEIS, Kincorth, Elgin; *m* 1931, Margaret Wilson (*d* 1964), *er d* of late A. Silver; one *s* one *d. Educ:* Findhorn; Forres Academy; Aberdeen Univ. Entered the Faculty of Medicine, 1921; Graduated, 1926, Bachelor of Medicine and Bachelor of Surgery, Ogston Prize and 1st medallist in Senior Systematic Surgery, 1st Medallist in Operative Surgery, House Surgeon Ward X, and House Physician Ward 4, Aberdeen Royal Infirmary, 1926; went to practice in Sheffield, 1927; Asst to late Sir Alexander Hendry, 1928; into partnership, 1929; partnership dissolved, 1931; taken into partnership, Dr James G. Moir, 1948. *Recreations:* golf, Association football, bowling. *Address:* Highland Home, Ballater, Aberdeenshire. *TA:* Highland Home, Ballater. *T:* Ballater 478.

MIDDLETON, Kenneth William Bruce; Sheriff of Lothian and Borders at Edinburgh; *b* Strathpeffer, Ross-shire, 1 Oct. 1905; 2nd *s* of W. R. T. Middleton; *m* 1938, Ruth Beverly (marr. diss. 1972), *d* of W. H. Mill; one *s* one *d. Educ:* Rossall Sch.; Merton Coll., Oxford; Edinburgh Univ. BA Oxford, LLB Edinburgh; called to Scottish Bar, 1931; Vans Dunlop Scholar in International Law and Constitutional Law and History, Edinburgh Univ.; Richard Brown Research Scholar in Law, Edinburgh Univ.; served War of 1939-45 with Royal Scots and Seaforth Highlanders; attached to Military Dept, Judge Advocate-Gen.'s Office, 1941-45. Sheriff-Substitute, subseq. Sheriff: Perth and Angus at Forfar, 1946-50; Lothians and Peebles, later Lothian and Borders, at Edinburgh, 1950-. *Publication:* Britain and Russia, 1947. *Address:* Sheriff Court House, Lawnmarket, Edinburgh.

MIDDLETON, Lawrence John, PhD; HM Diplomatic Service; Counsellor (Commercial), Belgrade, since 1974; *b* 27 March 1930; *s* of John James Middleton and Mary (*née* Horgan); *m* 1963, Sheila Elizabeth Hoey; two *s* one *d. Educ:* Finchley Catholic Grammar Sch.; King's Coll., London (BSc 1951, PhD 1954). Scientific Officer, ARC, 1954-60 and 1962-63; Cons. to FAO and to UN Cttee on Effects of Atomic Radiation, 1960-62; CENTO Inst. of Nuclear Science, 1963-65; Principal, Min. of Agriculture, 1966-68; First Sec., FO, 1968; Washington, 1969-71; Kuala Lumpur, 1971-74. *Publications:* articles on plant physiology and nuclear science in biology, 1954-63. *Address:* c/o Foreign and Commonwealth Office, King Charles Street, SW1A 2AH.

MIDDLETON, Lucy Annie; Vice-President, Trade Union, Labour and Co-operative Democratic History Society, since 1969; Director and Foundation Chairman of War on Want, 1958-68; *b* 9 May 1894; 2nd *d* of late Sydney J. Cox, Keynsham, Somerset; *m* 1936, James S. Middleton (*d* 1962), sometime Sec. of Labour Party. *Educ:* Elementary Sch.; Colston's Girls' High Sch., Bristol; Bristol Univ. Held teaching appts under Gloucester and Bristol Authorities until 1924 when she became Organising Sec. in the Peace Movement; political adviser to Hindu Minorities during sittings of Round Table Conferences; joined staff of Labour Party, 1934. Governor of Chelsea Polytechnic, 1936-57. Certificated Advertising Consultant. Attended Inter-Parliamentary Union Confs Brussels, Nice, Rome, Stockholm, presenting Reports on Maternity and Child Welfare, Family Allowances, and Safeguarding of Women in Employment throughout the World; formerly Mem. of House of Commons Estimates Cttee. MP (Labour) Sutton Div. of Plymouth, 1945-50 (re-elected for enlarged Div., 1950-51). *Recreations:* cooking, gardening, golf. *Address:* 7 Princes Road, Wimbledon, SW19 8RQ. *T:* 01-542 2791.

MIDDLETON, Michael Humfrey, CBE 1975; Director, Civic Trust, since 1969; *b* 1 Dec. 1917; *s* of Humfrey Middleton and Lilian Irene (*née* Tillard); *m* 1954, Julie Margaret Harrison; one *s* two *d. Educ:* King's Sch., Canterbury. Art Critic, The Spectator, 1946-56; Art Editor and Asst Editor, Picture Post, 1949-53; Exec. Editor, Lilliput, 1953-54; Editor, House and Garden, 1955-57; Sec. and Dep. Dir, Civic Trust, 1957-69; Mem. Council, Soc. of Industrial Artists and Designers, 1953-55, 1968-70; UK Sec.-Gen., European Architectural Heritage Year, 1972-75. FSIA; Hon. Fellow, RIBA, 1974. Film scripts include A Future for the Past, 1972. Council of Europe Pro Merito Medal, 1976. *Publications:* Soldiers of Lead, 1948; Group Practice in Design, 1967; contributor to many jls on Art and Design, at

home and abroad. *Recreation:* looking. *Address:* 46 Holland Park Avenue, W11. *T:* 01-727 9136.

MIDDLETON, Ronald George, DSC 1945; solicitor; Partner in Coward Chance (formerly Coward, Chance & Co.), since 1949; *b* 31 July 1913; *o s* of late Sir George Middleton; *m* 1959, Sybil Summerscale (*d* 1976); no *c. Educ:* Whitgift Middle Sch.; University Coll., London. Solicitor, 1936. RNVR, 1939-47 (Lt-Comdr); Radar Officer HMS Queen Elizabeth, 1944-45; Fleet Radar Officer, Indian Ocean, 1945. Dir, Morgan Crucible Co. Ltd. Part-time Mem., NBPI, 1965-68. *Recreation:* sailing. *Address:* Quin, Wineham, Henfield, W Sussex. *T:* Cowfold 236. *Clubs:* Reform, Royal Ocean Racing.

MIDDLETON, Stanley; novelist; Head of English Department, High Pavement College Nottingham, since 1958; *b* Bulwell, Nottingham, 1 Aug. 1919; *y s* of Thomas and Elizabeth Ann Middleton; *m* 1951, Margaret Shirley, *y d* of Herbert and Winifred Vera Welch; two *d. Educ:* High Pavement Sch.; University Coll., Nottingham (later Univ. of Nottingham). Served Army (RA and AEC), 1940-46. Hon. MA Nottingham, 1975. *Publications:* novels: A Short Answer, 1958; Harris's Requiem, 1960; A Serious Woman, 1961; The Just Exchange, 1962; Two's Company, 1963; Him They Compelled, 1964; Terms of Reference, 1966; The Golden Evening, 1968; Wages of Virtue, 1969; Apple of the Eye, 1970; Brazen Prison, 1971; Cold Gradations, 1972; A Man Made of Smoke, 1973; Holiday (jtly, Booker Prize 1974), 1974; Distractions, 1975; Still Waters, 1976; Ends and Means, 1977. *Recreations:* music, walking, listening, argument. *Address:* 42 Caledon Road, Sherwood, Nottingham NG5 2NG. *T:* Nottingham 623085. *Club:* PEN.

MIDDLETON, Sir Stephen Hugh, 9th Bt, *cr* 1662; *b* 1909; *s* of Lt Hugh Jeffery Middleton, RN, 3rd *s* of Sir Arthur Middleton, 7th Bt; *S* uncle 1942; *m* 1962, Mary (*d* 1972), *d* of late Richard Robinson. *Educ:* Eton; Magdalene Coll., Cambridge. *Heir: b* Lawrence Monck Middleton, *b* 1912. *Address:* Belsay Castle, Northumberland.

MIDGLEY, Eric Atkinson, CMG 1965; MBE 1945; HM Diplomatic Service, retired; *b* 25 March 1913; *s* of Charles Ewart Midgley, Keighley, Yorks; *m* 1937, Catherine Gaminara; two *d. Educ:* Christ's Hosp.; Merton Coll., Oxford. Indian Civil Service, 1937; Trade Commissioner at Delhi, 1947; Board of Trade, 1957; Commercial Counsellor at The Hague, 1960; Minister (Economic) in India, 1963-67; Minister (Commercial), Washington, 1967-70; Ambassador to Switzerland, 1970-73. *Recreation:* sailing. *Address:* 2 Wellington Place, Captains Row, Lymington, Hants. *Club:* Royal Lymington Yacht.

MIDLETON, 2nd Earl of, *cr* 1920; **George St John Brodrick,** MC; Viscount Midleton, *cr* 1717, of Midleton, Ireland; Viscount Dunsford of Dunsford, Surrey, 1920; Baron Brodrick, Midleton, Ireland, 1715; Baron Brodrick, Peper Harow, 1796; late Capt., Surrey Yeomanry; *b* 21 Feb. 1888; *e s* of 1st Earl of Midleton and Lady Hilda Charteris (*d* 1901), *d* of 9th Earl of Wemyss; *S* father, 1942; *m* 1st, 1917, Margaret (marr. diss. 1925), *d* of J. Rush, Cromer, Norfolk; 2nd, 1925, Guinevere (marr. diss. 1975), widow of George J. Gould and *d* of Alexander Sinclair, Dublin; 3rd, 1975, Irene Creese (Rene Ray). *Educ:* Eton; Balliol Coll., Oxford. Served World War I, 1914-17 (despatches, Legion of Honour, Military Cross). Served World War II, 1939-45 (ADC to C-in-C Home Forces). *Heir:* (to Viscountcy of Midleton and Barony of Brodrick only) *cousin,* Trevor Lowther Brodrick [*b* 7 March 1903; *m* 1940, Sheila Campbell, *d* of Charles Campbell Macleod]. *Address:* Martello Lodge, St Brelade's Bay, Jersey, Channel Islands. *T:* Central 41171.

MIERS, Rear-Adm. Sir Anthony (Cecil Capel), VC 1942; KBE 1959; CB 1958; DSO 1941; Royal Navy retired; joined National Car Parks as Director for Development Coordination, 1971; with London and Provincial Poster Group, since 1962, Consultant, since 1972; *b* 11 Nov. 1906; 2nd *s* of late Capt. D. N. C. C. Miers, Queen's Own Cameron Highlanders (killed in France, Sept. 1914); *m* 1945, Patricia Mary, *d* of late D. M. Millar, of the Chartered Bank of India, Australia and China; one *s* one *d. Educ:* Stubbington House; Edinburgh Academy; Wellington Coll. Special entry cadet RN 1924. Joined submarines, 1929; commanded HM Submarine L54, 1936-37 (Coronation medal at HM's review in 1937); HMS Iron Duke, 1937-38; naval staff course, 1938 (psc); on staff of Admiral of the Fleet Sir Charles Forbes, C-in-C Home Fleet, in HM Ships Nelson, Rodney, and Warspite (despatches), 1939-40; commanded HM Submarine Torbay, 1940-42 (DSO and Bar, VC); Staff of Fleet Adm. C. W. Nimitz, C-in-C US Pacific Fleet, 1943-44 (US Legion of Merit, degree of Officer, 1945); Comdr S/M 8th Submarine Flotilla in HMS Maidstone, 1944-45; Commanded HMS Vernon II (Ramillies and Malaya), 1946; jssc

1947; Comd HMS Blackcap (RN Air Station, Stretton), 1948-50; Comd HMS Forth and Capt. S/M, 1st Submarine Flotilla, 1950-52. Capt. of the RN Coll., Greenwich, 1952-54 (Coronation medal, 1953); Commanded HMS Theseus, 1954-55; Flag Officer, Middle East, 1956-59. With Mills and Allen Ltd, 1962-74. Obtained pilot's certificate ("A" License), 1948. Governor, Star and Garter Home, Richmond, 1970-76; Chm., RN Scholarship Fund, 1968-73. Nat. Pres., Submarine Old Comrades Assoc., 1967-. Chm., Hudsons Offshore Ltd, 1972-73. Burgess and Freeman of Burgh of Inverness, 1955; Mem., Royal Highland Soc., 1966. Councillor, Lawn Tennis Assoc., 1954-; Pres. RN Squash Rackets Assoc., 1960-70; Pres. RN Lawn Tennis Assoc., 1962-; FInstD 1960. Freeman of the City of London, 1966; Mem., Court of Assistants, Worshipful Company of Tin Plate Workers, 1969; Hon. Kt, Hon. Soc. of Knights of Round Table, 1967. Silver Jubilee Medal, 1977. *Recreation:* tennis. *Address:* 17 Dover Park Drive, Roehampton, SW15 5BT. *T:* 01-788 6863. *Clubs:* Army and Navy, Curzon House, Hurlingham, MCC, British Sportsman's; London Scottish Football; Royal Navy 1765 and 1785; Hampshire Hog Cricket; Coral Yacht (President); Anchorites (President 1968).

MIGDALE, Hon. Lord; James Frederick Gordon Thomson, MA; DL; a Lord Commissioner of Justiciary, Scotland, and a Senator of HM College of Justice in Scotland, 1953-73; Lord Lieutenant of Sutherland, 1962-72; *b* 22 June 1897; *s* of late William Thomson, advocate, and Emmeline E. Gordon; *m* 1938, Louise Carnegie (*d* 1947), *d* of Roswell Miller and Mrs Carnegie Miller, of NY and Skibo Castle, Dornoch; one *s* four *d*. *Educ:* Edinburgh Academy and Clayesmore; Edinburgh and Glasgow Univs. Served European War, 1914-19, Royal Scots; War of 1939-45, Lt-Col Home Guard. Mem. Faculty of Advocates, 1924; Advocate-Depute, 1939-40; Standing Counsel to Board of Inland Revenue in Scotland, 1944-45; QC (Scotland) 1945; Sheriff of Ayr and Bute, 1949-52; Home Advocate Depute, 1952-53. Life Trustee, Carnegie UK Trust. DL Sutherlandshire, 1959. *Address:* Ospisdale, Dornoch, Sutherland IV25 3RH. *Clubs:* New (Edinburgh); Highland (Inverness); Hon. Company of Edinburgh Golfers.
See also J. G. Milligan.

MIKARDO, Ian; MP (Lab) Tower Hamlets, Bethnal Green and Bow, since 1974 (Poplar, 1964-74); *b* 9 July 1908; *m* 1932, Mary Rosette; two *d*. *Educ:* Portsmouth. MP (Lab) Reading, 1945-50, South Div. of Reading, 1950-55, again Reading, 1955-Sept. 1959. Member: Nat. Exec. Cttee of Labour Party, 1950-59, and 1960- (Chm., 1970-71); Internat Cttee of Labour Party (Chm., 1973-); Chm., Parly Labour Party, March-Nov. 1974; Chm., Select Cttee on Nationalized Industries, 1966-70. Pres., ASTMS, 1968-73. *Publications:* Centralised Control of Industry, 1944; Frontiers in the Air, 1946; (with others) Keep Left, 1947; The Second Five Years, 1948; The Problems of Nationalisation, 1948; (joint) Keeping Left, 1950; The Labour Case, 1950; It's a Mug's Game, 1951; Socialism or Slump, 1959. *Address:* House of Commons, SW1A 0AA. *T:* 01-219 5007.

MIKES, George, LLD (Budapest); Author; President, PEN in Exile; *b* Siklós, Hungary, 15 Feb. 1912; *s* of Dr Alfred Mikes and Margit Gál; *m* 1st, 1941, Isobel Gerson (marr. diss.), one *s*; 2nd, 1948, Lea Hanak; one *d*. *Educ:* Cistercian Gymnasium, Pécs; Budapest Univ. Theatrical critic on Budapest newspapers, 1931-38; London correspondent of Budapest papers, 1938-41; working for Hungarian Service of BBC, 1941-51. *Publications:* How to be an Alien, 1946; How to Scrape Skies, 1948; Wisdom for Others, 1950; Milk and Honey, 1950; Down with Everybody!, 1951; Shakespeare and Myself, 1952; Uber Alles, 1953; Eight Humorists, 1954; Little Cabbages, 1955; Italy for Beginners, 1956; The Hungarian Revolution, 1957; East is East, 1958; A Study in Infamy, 1959; How to be Inimitable, 1960; Tango, 1961; Switzerland for Beginners, 1962, new edn 1975; Mortal Passion, 1963; Prison (ed), 1963; How to Unite Nations, 1963; Eureka!, 1965; (with the Duke of Bedford) Book of Snobs, 1965; How to be Affluent, 1966; Not by Sun Alone, 1967; Boomerang, 1968; The Prophet Motive, 1969; Humour-In Memoriam, 1970; The Land of the Rising Yen, 1970; (with Duke of Bedford) How to run a Stately Home, 1971; Any Souvenirs?, 1971; The Spy Who Died of Boredom, 1973; Charlie, 1976; How to be Decadent, 1977. *Recreations:* tennis, cooking, and not listening to funny stories. *Address:* 1B Dorncliffe Road, SW6. *T:* 01-736 2624. *Clubs:* Garrick, Hurlingham, PEN.

MIKOYAN, Anastas Ivanovich; five Orders of Lenin; Order of the October Revolution, 1970; Order of the Red Banner; Hero of Socialist Labour; Hammer and Sickle Gold Medal, etc; Member of the Presidium of the Supreme Soviet, USSR, since 1965; Member of the Presidium of the Central Committee of the Communist Party of Soviet Union, 1952-66; Member Supreme

Soviet since 1937; *b* Sanain, Armenia, 25 Nov. 1895; *m*; one *s*. *Educ:* Armenian Ecclesiastical Seminary, Tiflis. Joined Communist Party, 1915; fought in Revolution, Baku (imprisoned and escaped thrice), 1917-19; Mem. All-Russian Central Exec. Cttee, 1919-23; Mem. All-Union Central Exec. Cttee, 1923-27; Mem. Central Cttee, Communist Party, 1923-; Peoples' Commissar of Trade, 1926; Mem. Council of Labour and Defence, 1926; Peoples' Commissar of Supply, 1930-34, of the Food Supply Industry, 1934-38; Mem. Political Bureau of the Central Cttee, 1935- (Candidate, 1926-35); Dep. Chm., Council of People's Commissars, 1937-46; People's Commissar of Foreign Trade, 1938-46; Mem. State Defence Cttee, 1942-45; Vice-Chm., Council of Ministers of USSR, 1946 and simultaneously Minister of Foreign Trade, 1946-49; Minister of Trade, 1953; First Vice-Chm., Council of Ministers of the USSR, 1955-64; Chm., Presidium of the USSR Supreme Soviet, 1964-65. *Address:* Presidium of the Supreme Soviet of the USSR, Kremlin, Moscow, USSR.

MILBANK, Major Sir Mark (Vane), 4th Bt, *cr* 1882; KCVO 1962; MC 1944; Extra Equerry to the Queen since 1954; Master of HM's Household, 1954-67; *b* 11 Jan. 1907; *e s* of Sir Frederick Milbank, 3rd Bt; *S* father, 1964; *m* 1938, Hon. Verena Aileen (she *m* 1st, 1934, Charles Lambert Crawley who died 1935), *yr d* of 11th Baron Farnham, DSO; two *s*. *Educ:* Eton; RMC, Sandhurst. Coldstream Guards, 1927-36 and 1939-45; ADC to Governor of Bombay, 1933-38; Comptroller to Governor General of Canada, 1946-52; Dir, Norwich Union, London Advisory Board, 1964-74. *Heir:* *s* Anthony Frederick Milbank [*b* 16 Aug. 1939; *m* 1970, Belinda Beatrice, *yr d* of Brigadier Adrian Gore, Sellindge, Kent; two *s* one *d*]. *Address:* Barningham Park, Richmond, N Yorks. *T:* Barningham 202.

MILBORNE-SWINNERTON-PILKINGTON, Sir T. H.; *see* Pilkington.

MILBURN, Sir John (Nigel), 4th Bt *cr* 1905; *b* 22 April 1918; *s* of Sir Leonard John Milburn, 3rd Bt, and Joan, 2nd *d* of Henry Anson-Horton, Catton Hall, Derbs; *S* father 1957; *m* 1940, Dorothy Joan, *d* of Leslie Butcher, Dunholme, Lincoln; one *s* decd. *Educ:* Eton; Trinity Coll., Cambridge. Served War of 1939-45 with Northumberland Hussars. *Recreations:* Joint-Master West Percy Foxhounds, 1955-59, 1963-. *Heir:* nephew Anthony Rupert Milburn [*b* 17 April 1947. *Educ:* Eton; Royal Agric. Coll., Cirencester]. *Address:* Brainshaugh, Acklington, Northumberland. *T:* Shilbottle 631. *Club:* Northern Counties (Newcastle upon Tyne).

MILBURN, Very Rev. Robert Leslie Pollington, MA; Master of the Temple since 1968; *b* 28 July 1907; *er s* of late George Leslie and Elizabeth Esther Milburn; *m* 1944, Margery Kathleen Mary, *d* of Rev. Francis Graham Harvie; one *d* (one *s* decd). *Educ:* Oundle; Sidney Sussex Coll., Cambridge; New Coll., Oxford. Asst Master, Eton Coll., 1930-32; Select Preacher, University of Oxford, 1942-44; Fellow and Chaplain of Worcester Coll., Oxford, 1934-57, Tutor, 1945-57, Estates Bursar, 1946-57 (Junior Bursar, 1936-46). University Lectr in Church History, 1947-57; Bampton Lectr, 1952. Examining Chaplain to Bishop of St Edmundsbury and Ipswich, 1941-53, to Bishop of Southwark, 1950-57, to Bishop of Oxford, 1952-57; Dean of Worcester, 1957-68, now Emeritus. Mem. of Oxford City Council, 1941-47. A Trustee, Wallace Collection, 1970-76. Grand Chaplain, United Grand Lodge of England, 1969. OStJ. *Publications:* Saints and their Emblems in English Churches, 1949; Early Christian Interpretations of History, 1954; articles in Journal of Theological Studies and Church Quarterly Review. *Address:* The Master's House, Temple, EC4; Wallcroft, Bromyard, Herefordshire. *Club:* Athenæum.

MILCHSACK, Dame Lilo, Hon. DCMG 1972 (Hon. CMG 1968); Hon. CBE 1958; Initiator and Hon. Secretary of Deutsch-Englische Gesellschaft e.V., since its foundation in 1949; *b* Frankfurt/Main, *d* of Prof. Dr Paul Duden and Johanna Bertha (*née* Nebe); *m* Hans Milchsack; two *d*. *Educ:* Univs of Frankfurt, Geneva and Amsterdam. Awarded Grosses Bundesverdienstkreuz, 1959. *Recreations:* gardening, reading. *Address:* An der Kalvey 11, D-4000 Düsseldorf 31-Wittlaer, Germany. *T:* Düsseldorf 40 13 87. *Clubs:* Sesame Pioneer, Lyceum.

MILDON, Arthur Leonard, QC 1971; a Recorder, since 1972; *b* 3 June 1923; *er s* of late Rev. Dr W. H. Mildon, Barnstaple; *m* 1950, Iva, *er d* of late G. H. C. Wallis, Plymouth; one *s* one *d*. *Educ:* Kingswood Sch., Bath; Wadham Coll., Oxford (MA). Pres., Oxford Univ. Liberal Club, 1948. Army Service, 1942-46: Lieut, 138th (City of London) Field Regt, RA; Captain, 1st Army Group, RA. Called to Bar, Middle Temple, 1950; Mem., Bar Council, 1973-74; Member of Western Circuit. Dep. Chm.,

Isle of Wight QS, 1967-71. *Recreation:* sailing. *Address:* 2 Crown Office Row, Temple, EC4. *T:* 01-353 9272. *Clubs:* Reform; Hampshire (Winchester); Royal Solent Yacht.

MILEDI, Prof. Ricardo, MD; FRS 1970; Professor of Biophysics, University College London, since 1965; *b* 15 Sept. 1927. *Educ:* Univ. of Mexico City. BSc 1948; MD 1954. Engaged in research at Nat. Inst. of Cardiology, 1953-56; Rockefeller Travelling Fellowship at ANU, 1956-58; research work in Dept of Biophysics, UCL, 1958-63, Reader, 1963-65. Royal Society Foulerton Res. Prof., 1975-. *Address:* Department of Biophysics, University College, Gower Street, WC1E 6BT. *T:* 01-387 7050; 5 Park Crescent Mews East, W1N 5HB. *T:* 01-636 3240.

MILES, Prof. Albert Edward William, LRCP; MRCS; FDS; DSc; Professor of Dental Pathology at The London Hospital Medical College, 1950-76, retired; Hon. Curator, Odontological Collection, Royal College of Surgeons of England since 1955; *b* 15 July 1912; *m* 1939, Sylvia Stuart; one *s* decd. *Educ:* Stationers' Company Sch.; Charing Cross and Royal Dental Hosps. John Tomes Prize, RCS, 1954-56. Charles Tomes Lecturer, RCS, 1957; Evelyn Sprawson Lecturer, 1977. Howard Mummery Meml Prize, 1976. Exec. Editor, Archives of Oral Biology, 1969-. *Publications:* contrib. to scientific literature. *Address:* 1 Cleaver Square, Kennington, SE11. *T:* 01-735 5350; Ivy Cottage, Wisborough Green, Sussex. *Club:* Tetrapods.

MILES, Anthony John; Editorial Director, since 1975, and Deputy Chairman, since 1977, Mirror Group Newspapers; *b* 18 July 1930; *s* of Paul and Mollie Miles; *m* 1975, Anne Hardman. *Educ:* High Wycombe Royal Grammar Sch. On staff of (successively): Middlesex Advertiser; Nottingham Guardian; Brighton Evening Argus. Daily Mirror: Feature writer, 1953-66; Asst Editor, 1967-68; Associate Editor, 1968-71; Editor, 1971-74. Mem., Press Council, 1975-. *Address:* Mirror Group Newspapers, Holborn Circus, EC1P 1DQ. *Club:* Reform.

MILES, Sir (Arnold) Ashley, Kt 1966; CBE 1953; FRS 1961; MA, MD, FRCP, FRCPath, FInstBiol; Professor of Experimental Pathology, University of London, 1952-71, now Emeritus Professor; Director of the Lister Institute of Preventive Medicine, London, 1952-71; Deputy Director, Department of Medical Microbiology, London Hospital Medical College; *b* 20 March 1904; *s* of Harry Miles, York; *m* 1930, Ellen Marguerite, *d* of Harald Dahl, Cardiff; no *c*. *Educ:* Bootham Sch., York; King's Coll., Cambridge, Hon. Fellow, 1972; St Bartholomew's Hosp., London. Demonstrator in Bacteriology, London Sch. of Hygiene and Tropical Medicine, 1929; Demonstrator in Pathol., University of Cambridge, 1931; Reader in Bacteriology, British Postgraduate Medical Sch., London, 1935; Prof. Bacteriology, University of London, 1937-45; Acting Dir Graham Medical Research Laboratories, University Coll. Hosp. Medical Sch., 1943-45; London Sector Pathologist, Emergency Medical Services, 1939-44; Dir, Medical Research Council Wound Infection Unit, Birmingham Accident Hosp., 1942-46; Dep. Dir, 1947-52 and Dir of Dept of Biological Standards, 1946-52, National Institute for Medical Research, London. Biological Sec. and Vice-Pres., Royal Society, 1963-68. MRC grant holder, Clinical Res. Centre, 1971-76. Pres., Internat. Assoc. Microbiological Socs, 1974-. Trustee, Beit Memorial Fellowships, 1970-. For. Corresp., Acad. de Médecine de Belgique, 1972. Hon. DSc, Newcastle, 1969. *Publications:* (with G. S. Wilson), Topley and Wilson's Principles of Bacteriology and Immunity, 1945, 1955, 1964, 1975; various scientific papers. *Recreations:* various. *Address:* Department of Medical Microbiology, London Hospital Medical College, Turner Street, E1 2AD. *T:* 01-247 0644, ext. 51. *Club:* Athenæum.

MILES, Basil Raymond, CBE 1968; Puisne Judge, Kenya, 1957-67, retired; *b* 10 Oct. 1906; *s* of John Thomas Miles and Winifred Miles, Wrexham, Denbighshire; *m* 1944, Margaret Baldwin Neilson; one *s* one *d*. *Educ:* Harrow; Magdalen Coll., Oxford. Barrister, Inner Temple, 1931; appointed Resident Magistrate, Tanganyika, 1946; Judge of the Supreme Court, The Gambia, 1953-57. A part-time Chm. of Industrial Tribunals, 1967-74. *Recreation:* music. *Address:* Mbeya, Chesham Road, Bovingdon, Herts. *T:* 3187.

MILES, Sir Bernard, Kt 1969; CBE 1953; Actor; Founder, with his wife, of the Mermaid Theatre, Puddle Dock, EC4, 1959 (first opened in North London, 1950); *b* 27 Sept. 1907; *s* of Edwin James Miles and Barbara Fletcher; *m* 1931, Josephine Wilson; one *s* two *d*. *Educ:* Uxbridge County Sch.; Pembroke Coll., Oxford (Hon. Fellow, 1969). Hon. DLitt, City Univ., 1974. First stage appearance as Second Messenger in Richard III, New Theatre, 1930; appeared in St Joan, His Majesty's, 1931; spent 5 years in repertory as designer, stage-manager, character-actor,

etc; frequent appearances on West End Stage from 1938. Entered films, 1937, and has written for, directed, and acted in them. First went on Music-hall stage, London Palladium, etc., 1950. Mermaid Theatre seasons: Royal Exchange, 1953: Macbeth, Dido and Aeneas, As You Like It, Eastward Ho! Formed Mermaid Theatre Trust which built City of London's first theatre for 300 years, the Mermaid, Puddle Dock, EC4. Opened May 1959, with musical play Lock Up Your Daughters. *Publication:* Favourite Tales from Shakespeare, 1976. *Address:* Mermaid Theatre, Puddle Dock, Blackfriars, EC4V 3DB.

MILES, Mrs Caroline Mary; Member, Monopolies and Mergers Commission, since 1975; part-time Member, National Enterprise Board, since 1976; *b* 30 April 1929; *d* of Brig. A.J.R.M.Leslie, OBE. *Educ:* numerous schools; Somerville Coll., Oxford. HM Treasury, 1953-54; NIESR, 1954-56 and 1964-67; attached to UN Secretariat, NY, 1956-63. Associate Mem., Nuffield Coll., Oxford, 1972-74. Member: Textile Council, 1968-71; Inflation Accounting Cttee (Sandilands Cttee), 1974-75. *Recreations:* picnics, poohsticks. *Address:* c/o Messrs Coutts & Co., 162 Brompton Road, SW3 1HW.

MILES, Prof. Charles William Noel; Head of Department of Land Management and Development since 1968, and Dean of Faculty of Urban and Regional Studies, 1972-75, University of Reading; Chairman, Agricultural Wages Board, since 1972; *b* 3 Nov. 1915; 2nd *s* of late Lt-Col Sir Charles W. Miles, 5th Bt; *m* 1940, Jacqueline (Dickie) Cross; one *d* (one *s* decd). *Educ:* Stowe Sch.; Jesus Coll., Cambridge (MA). FRICS. Army Service, 1939-46; Univ. Demonstrator and Univ. Lectr, Dept of Estate Management, Cambridge, 1946-54; Chief Agent to Meyrick Estates in Hants and Anglesey, 1954-68; Agent to Bisterne Estate, 1957-68. Pres., Chartered Land Agents Soc., 1965-66; Mem., Cambs AEC, 1953-54; Mem., SE Region Adv. Cttee of Land Commn, 1967-70. *Publications:* Estate Finance and Business Management, 1953, 3rd edn 1972; Estate Accounts, 1960; Recreational Land Management, 1977. *Recreations:* walking, gardening, theatre. *Address:* Glebe Cottage, Mattingley, Basingstoke, Hants. *T:* Heckfield 357.
See also Sir W. N. M. Miles, Bt.

MILES, Maj.-Gen. Eric Grant, CB 1943; DSO 1917; MC 1915; *b* 1891; 2nd *s* of late George H. Miles, Homestall, Welwyn, Herts; *m* 1924, Lady Marcia Valda, (*d* 1972), *y d* of 7th Earl of Roden; one *d*. *Educ:* Harrow; RMC. Joined King's Own Scottish Borderers, 1911; served European War, 1914-19 (wounded, despatches 5 times, DSO, MC); Capt. KOSB, 1916; Brevet Major, 1919; psc 1922; GSO 3 War Office, 1923; Brigade Major Shanghai Defence Force, 1927-28; Major, 1928; General Staff Officer, 2; War Office, 1930-33; Bt Lt-Col 1931; Imperial Defence Coll., 1934; Lt-Col 1936; commanded 1st Bn Royal Berks Regt, 1936-38; Col 1934; Gen. Staff Officer, 1st Grade, Malaya, 1938-39; Brig., 1940; Maj.-Gen., 1940; served in Flanders, 1940 (despatches); North Africa, 1943 (wounded); commanded 126th Inf. Bde 1940, 42nd (East Lancs) Div. 1941, 56th (London) Div. 1941-43; GOC Kent and Sussex Districts, 1943-46; Actg Lt-Gen., Sept.-Nov. 1944, as GOC-in-C South-Eastern Command; retired pay, 1946; Col KOSB, 1944-54. A Mem. of the House of Laity, Church Assembly, 1955-60; Dep. Chm. Lichfield Diocesan Board of Finance, 1954-60, Chm., 1960-71. *Address:* The Rope Walk, Lyth Hill, Shrewsbury. *T:* Bayston Hill 2053.

MILES, (Frank) Stephen, CMG 1964; HM Diplomatic Service; High Commissioner, Zambia, since 1974; *b* 7 Jan. 1920; *s* of Harry and Mary Miles; *m* 1953, Margaret Joy (*née* Theaker); three *d*. *Educ:* John Watson's Sch., Edinburgh; Daniel Stewart's Coll., Edinburgh; St Andrews Univ.; Harvard Univ. (Commonwealth Fellowship). Served with Fleet Air Arm, 1942-46 (Lt (A) RNVR). Scottish Home Dept, 1948; FCO (previously CRO), 1948-; served in: New Zealand, 1949-52, E and W Pakistan, 1954-57; Ghana, 1959-62; Uganda, 1962-63; British Dep. High Commissioner, Tanzania, 1963-65 (Acting High Commissioner, 1963-64); Acting High Commissioner in Ghana, March-April 1966; Consul-Gen., St Louis, 1967-70; Dep. High Comr, Calcutta, 1970-74. *Recreations:* cricket, tennis. *Address:* c/o Foreign and Commonwealth Office, SW1A 2AH; Maytrees, 71 Park Road, Limpsfield, Oxted, Surrey RH8 0AN. *T:* Oxted 3132. *Clubs:* Travellers', Naval, Royal Commonwealth Society, MCC.

MILES, Geoffrey, OBE 1970; HM Diplomatic Service; Consul-General, Edmonton, since 1976; *b* 25 Oct. 1922; *s* of late Donald Frank Miles and Honorine Miles (*née* Lambert); *m* 1946, Mary Rozel Cottle; one *s* one *d*. *Educ:* Eltham College. Joined Home Civil Service (Min. of Shipping), 1939; War service as pilot in RAF, 1941-46 (commnd 1945); Min. of Transport, 1946-50; British Embassy, Washington 1951; Sec., Copper-Zinc-Lead

Cttee, Internat. Materials Conf., Washington 1952-53; BoT, 1953-55; Asst Trade Comr, Perth, 1955-59; Second Sec., Ottawa, 1960-63; First Sec., Salisbury, 1963-66, Dublin, 1967-71; Trade Comr (later Consul) and Head of Post, Edmonton, 1971-75. *Recreations:* music, golf, amateur radio. *Address:* c/o Foreign and Commonwealth Office, SW1. *Clubs:* Edmonton, Petroleum (Edmonton).

MILES, Adm. Sir Geoffrey John Audley, KCB 1945 (CB 1942); KCSI 1947; *b* 2 May 1890; 3rd *s* of Audley Charles Miles and Eveline Cradock-Hartopp; *m* 1918, Alison Mary Cadell; two *s. Educ:* Bedford; HMS Britannia. Joined the Royal Navy, served with Submarines and Destroyers during European War, 1914-18; later appointments include: Dep. Dir Staff Coll., Dir Tactical Sch.; Capt. HMS Nelson, 1939-41; Rear-Adm., 1941; Vice-Adm., 1944; Adm., 1948. Head of Mil. Mission in Moscow, 1941-43; Flag Officer Comdg Western Mediterranean, 1944-45; C-in-C, Royal Indian Navy, 1946-47. *Address:* Clunie, Rowledge, Farnham, Surrey. *Club:* Naval and Military.

MILES, Prof. Hamish Alexander Drummond; Barber Professor of Fine Arts and Director of the Barber Institute, University of Birmingham, since 1970; *b* 19 Nov. 1925; *s* of J. E. (Hamish) Miles and Sheila Barbara Robertson; *m* 1957, Jean Marie, *d* of T. R. Smits, New York; two *s* two *d. Educ:* Douai Sch.; Univ. of Edinburgh (MA); Balliol Coll., Oxford. Served War: Army, 1944-47. Asst Curator, Glasgow Art Gallery, 1953-54; Asst Lectr, then Lectr in the History of Art, Univ. of Glasgow, 1954-66; Vis. Lectr, Smith Coll., Mass, 1960-61; Prof. of the History of Art, Univ. of Leicester, 1966-70. Trustee, National Galleries of Scotland. *Publications:* sundry articles and catalogues. *Recreations:* beekeeping and woodland management. *Address:* 37 Carpenter Road, Birmingham B15 2JJ; Burnside, Kirkmichael, Blairgowrie, Perthshire.

MILES, Prof. Herbert William, MSc (Bristol), DSc (Manchester); Adviser and Lecturer in Entomology, University of Manchester, 1927-42; Advisory Entomologist, University of Bristol (Long Ashton Research Station), 1942-46; Deputy Provincial Director (West Midland Province), National Agricultural Advisory Service, 1946-47; Prof. of Horticulture, Wye Coll., London Univ., 1947-65, now Emeritus. Hon. Consultant in Horticulture to RASE, 1948-75. President: Lincolnshire Naturalists' Union, 1938; Assoc. of Applied Biology, 1956. Officier, Ordre du Mérite Agricole, 1974. *Publications:* (with Mary Miles, MSc) Insect Pests of Glasshouse Crops, revised edn 1947; original papers on Economic Entomology in leading scientific journals; original studies on the biology of British sawflies. *Address:* 2 Wood Broughton, Grange-over-Sands, Cumbria.

MILES, John Edwin Alfred, OBE 1961 (MBE 1952); British High Commissioner to Swaziland, since 1975; *b* 14 Aug. 1919; *s* of late John Miles and late Rose Miles (*née* Newlyn); *m* 1952, Barbara Fergus Ferguson; two *s* one *d. Educ:* Hornsey County Sch. Apptd to Dominions Office, 1937. Served War: joined Queen's Royal West Surrey Regt, 1940; commissioned in N Staffordshire Regt, 1941; attached Royal Indian Army Service Corps, 1942 (Maj. 1943); released, Sept. 1946, and returned to Dominions Office. Served in: Wellington, NZ, 1948-51; Calcutta, 1953-56; CRO, 1957-61; Trinidad (on staff of Governor-Gen.), 1961; Jamaica (Adviser to Governor, and later First Sec. in British High Commission), 1961-64; Wellington, NZ, 1964-68; Counsellor, 1968; Accra, Ghana, 1968-71; Dep. High Comr, Madras, India, 1971-75. *Address:* c/o Foreign and Commonwealth Office, SW1; Cartref, Ladyegate Road, Dorking, Surrey. *T:* Dorking 4346.

MILES, Dame Margaret, DBE 1970; BA; Headmistress, Mayfield School, Putney, 1952-73; *b* 11 July 1911; 2nd *d* of Rev. E. G. Miles and Annie Miles (*née* Jones). *Educ:* Ipswich High Sch., GPDST; Bedford Coll., University of London. Asst Mistress: Westcliff High Sch., 1935-39; Badminton Sch., 1939-44; Lectr, Dept of Educn, University of Bristol, 1944-46; Headmistress, Pate's Grammar Sch., Cheltenham, 1946-51. Chm., Campaign for Comprehensive Educn, 1972- (Mem. 1966); Member of Council: Bedford Coll.; Chelsea Coll.; British Assoc.; Life Mem., Assoc. of Headmistresses, 1973; Vice-Chm., Educnl Adv. Cttee of Nat. Commn for Unesco. Hon. DCL, Univ. of Kent at Canterbury, 1973. *Publications:* And Gladly Teach, 1965; Comprehensive Schooling, Problems and Perspectives, 1968. *Recreations:* theatre, opera, concerts and films, when time; reading, gardening, walking, golf. *Address:* 31 Grosvenor Gardens, Kingston upon Thames, Surrey. *T:* 01-546 9835. *Clubs:* University Women's; Aberdovey Golf; Home Park Golf.

MILES, Maurice Edward; Conductor; Professor of Conducting, Royal Academy of Music and Royal Military School of Music; *b* 1908; *s* of T. S. Miles; *m* 1936, Eileen Spencer Wood (*d* 1977); one *s* two *d. Educ:* Wells Cathedral Gram. Sch.; Royal Academy of Music, London. Employed BBC, 1930-36; Conductor of Buxton Municipal Orchestra and of Bath Municipal Orchestra, 1936-39. Served in RAC, 1940-43. Returned to BBC, 1943; Conductor: Yorks Symphony Orchestra, 1947-54; City of Belfast Orchestra and Belfast Philharmonic Society, 1955-66; Ulster Orchestra, 1966-67. FRAM. *Publication:* Are You Beating 2 or 4?, 1977. *Recreations:* walking, reading. *Address:* Fairwinds, Burrows Lane, Gomshall, near Guildford, Surrey. *T:* Shere 2062.

MILES, Maxine Frances Mary; lately Director of F. G. Miles Engineering Ltd, Riverbank Works, Old Shoreham Road, Shoreham, Sussex; *b* 22 Sept. 1901; *d* of late Sir Johnston Forbes-Robertson; *m* 1932, Frederick George Miles, FRAeS, MSAE; one *s* (and one *d* decd). *Address:* Batts, Ashurst, Steyning, W Sussex.

MILES, (Richard) Oliver; HM Diplomatic Service; Counsellor, British Embassy, Athens, since 1977; *b* 6 March 1936; *s* of George Miles and Olive (*née* Clapham); *m* 1968, Julia, *d* of Prof. J. S. Weiner, *qv*; three *s. Educ:* Ampleforth Coll.; Merton Coll., Oxford (Oriental Studies). Entered Diplomatic Service, 1960; served in Abu Dhabi, Amman, Aden, Mukalla, Nicosia, Jedda. *Recreations:* bird-watching, singing. *Address:* c/o Foreign and Commonwealth Office, SW1A 2AH; Little Cowfold, Mattingley, Hants. *T:* Hook 2805. *Club:* Travellers'.

MILES, Roger Steele, PhD, DSc; Head, Department of Public Services, British Museum (Natural History), since 1975; *b* 31 Aug. 1937; *s* of John Edward Miles and Dorothy Mildred (*née* Steele); *m* 1960, Ann Blake; one *s* one *d. Educ:* Malet Lambert High Sch., Hull; King's Coll., Univ. of Durham (BSc, PhD, DSc). Sen. Res. Award, DSIR, 1962-64; Sen. Res. Fellow, Royal Scottish Museum, 1964-66, Sen. Scientific Officer, 1966-68; Sen. Sci. Officer, BM (Nat. Hist.), 1968-71, Principal Sci. Officer, 1971-74. *Publications:* 2nd edn, Palaeozoic Fishes, 1971 (1st edn, J. A. Moy-Thomas, 1939); (ed, with P. H. Greenwood and C. Patterson) Interrelationships of Fishes, 1973; (ed, with S. M. Andrews and A. D. Walker) Problems in Vertebrate Evolution, 1977; papers and monographs on anatomy and palaeontology of fishes, in jls. *Recreations:* music, reading. *Address:* 1 Highfield Green, Epping, Essex CM16 5HB. *T:* Epping 74848.

MILES, Surgeon Rear-Adm. Stanley, CB 1968; FRCP, FRCS; Medical Director, Gaelic Healthguard Co. Ltd, since 1976; *b* 14 Aug. 1911; *s* of late T. C. Miles, Company Dir, Sheffield; *m* 1939, Frances Mary Rose; one *s* one *d. Educ:* King Edward VII Sch.; University of Sheffield. MSc Sheffield, 1934; MB, ChB, 1936; DTM&HEng, 1949; MD, 1955; FRCP 1971, FRCS 1971. Joined RN Medical Service, 1936; served in China, W Africa, Pacific and Mediterranean Fleets. Medical Officer-in-Charge, RN Medical Sch. and Dir of Medical Research, 1961; Consultant in Physiology; Med. Officer-in-Charge, Royal Naval Hosp., Plymouth, 1966-69. Surg. Captain 1960; Surg. Rear-Adm. 1966. Dean, Postgraduate Med. Studies, Univ. of Manchester, 1969-76. Gilbert Blane Medal, RCS, 1957. QHP 1966-69. CStJ 1968. *Publication:* Underwater Medicine, 1962. *Recreations:* tennis, golf. *Address:* Carlton, Woodburn Avenue, Aberdeen. *Club:* National Liberal.

MILES, Stephen; *see* Miles, F. S.

MILES, Sir William (Napier Maurice), 6th Bt, *cr* 1859; Chartered Architect; Consultant in firm Miles & Wills, Chartered Architects; *b* 19 Oct. 1913; *s* of Sir Charles William Miles, 5th Bt, OBE; *S* father, 1966; *m* 1946, Pamela, *d* of late Capt. Michael Dillon; one *s* two *d. Educ:* Stowe; University of Cambridge (BA). Architectural Assoc. Diploma, 1939. *Recreations:* swimming, sailing. *Heir:* *s* Philip John Miles, *b* 10 Aug. 1953. *Address:* Old Rectory House, Walton-in-Gordano, near Clevedon, Avon. *T:* Clevedon 873365; Hillcrest House, 1 Sandquay Road, Dartmouth. *T:* Dartmouth 2275. *Club:* Dartmouth Yacht.
See also Prof. C. W. N. Miles.

MILFORD, 2nd Baron *cr* 1939; **Wogan Philipps**; Bt 1919; farmer and painter; *b* 25 Feb. 1902; *e s* of 1st Baron Milford; *S* father, 1962; *m* 1st, 1928, Rosamond Nina Lehmann, *qv*; one *s* (and one *d* decd); 2nd, 1944, Cristina, Countess of Huntingdon (who *d* 1953); 3rd, 1954, Tamara Rust. *Educ:* Eton; Magdalen Coll., Oxford. Member of International Brigade, Spanish Civil War. Former Member of Henley on Thames RDC, Cirencester RDC; has taken active part in building up Nat. Union of Agric. Workers in Gloucestershire and served on its county cttee.

Contested (Com) Cirencester and Tewkesbury, 1950. Has held one-man exhibitions of paintings in London, Milan and Cheltenham and shown in many mixed exhibns. *Heir: s* Hon. Hugo John Laurence Philipps [*b* 27 Aug. 1929; *m* 1st, 1951 (marr. diss., 1958); one *d*; 2nd, 1959, Mary, *e d* of Baron Sherfield, *qv*; three *s* one *d*]. *Address:* Butler's Farm, Colesbourne, Cheltenham, Glos. *T:* Coberley 260
See also Hon. J. P. Philipps, Hon. R. H. Philipps.

MILFORD, Rev. Canon Campbell Seymour, MC 1918; Canon Residentiary of Bristol Cathedral, 1962-67; retired, 1967; *b* 20 July 1896; *s* of Robert Theodore and Elspeth Milford; *m* 1926, Edith Mary (*née* Sandys) (*d* 1974); one *s*. *Educ:* Marlborough; Brasenose, Oxford. Lieut R West Kent Regt, 1915-19. BA 1st Class Lit. Hum., 1921; Lecturer, S Paul's Coll., Calcutta, 1922-25; MA and Diploma in Theology, Oxford, 1926. Deacon 1926, Priest 1927; Curate, Christ Church, Hampstead, 1926-28; Vice-Principal, S Paul's Coll., Calcutta (CMS), 1928-44; Lecturer and Fellow, Calcutta Univ., 1937-44; Canon of Calcutta Cathedral, 1943-44; Sec. for West Asia, CMS, London, 1944-57; Incumbent, Christ Church, Colombo, 1957-62. *Publications:* India Revisited, 1952; Middle East, Bridge or Barrier, 1956. *Recreation:* music. *Address:* 2 Priory Road, Bristol BS8 1TX. *T:* Bristol 38566.
See also Rev. Canon T. R. Milford.

MILFORD, Rev. Canon Theodore Richard; Master of the Temple, 1958-68; *b* 10 June 1895; *e s* of Robert Theodore Milford, MA, and Elspeth Barter; *m* 1st, 1932, Nancy Dickens Bourchier Hawksley; two *d*; 2nd, 1937, Margaret Nowell Smith; two *d*. *Educ:* Denstone; Fonthill, East Grinstead; Clifton; Magdalen Coll., Oxford; Westcott House, Cambridge. Served European War, 1914-18, 19th Royal Fusiliers, 1914; Oxford & Bucks LI, 1915-19 (Mesopotamia, 1916-18); Magdalen Coll., Oxford, 1919-21; BA (1st Cl. Lit. Hum), 1921; Union Christian Coll., Alwaye, Travancore, 1921-23; St John's Coll., Agra, 1923-24, 1926-30, 1931-34; Sec. Student Christian Movement, 1924-26 and 1935-38; Westcott House, 1930-31; Deacon, 1931; Priest, 1934 (Lucknow); Curate All Hallows, Lombard Street, 1935-37; Vicar of St Mary the Virgin, Oxford (University Church), 1938-47; Canon and Chancellor of Lincoln, 1947-58; Canon of Norton Episcopi, Lincoln Cathedral, 1947-68, Canon Emeritus, 1968. Chm., Oxfam, 1942-47 and 1960-65. Greek Red Cross (Bronze), 1947. *Publications:* Foolishness to the Greeks, 1953; The Valley of Decision, 1961. *Recreations:* music, chess. *Address:* 1 Kingsman Lane, Shaftesbury, Dorset. *T:* Shaftesbury 2843.
See also Rev. Canon C. S. Milford.

MILFORD HAVEN, 4th Marquess of, *cr* 1917; **George Ivar Louis Mountbatten;** Earl of Medina, 1917; Viscount Alderney, 1917; *b* 6 June 1961; *s* of 3rd Marquess of Milford Haven, OBE, DSC, and of Janet Mercedes, *d* of late Major Francis Bryce, OBE; *S* father, 1970. *Heir: b* Lord Ivar Alexander Michael Mountbatten, *b* 9 March 1963. *Address:* Flat 2, 2 Wilton Terrace, SW1; Moyns Park, Birdbrook, Essex.
See also Earl Mountbatten of Burma.

MILINGO, Most Rev. Emanuel; *see* Lusaka, Archbishop of, (RC).

MILKINA, Nina, (Mrs A. R. M. Sedgwick); concert pianist; *b* Moscow, 27 Jan. 1919; *d* of Jacques and Sophie Milkine; *m* 1943, Alastair Robert Masson Sedgwick, Dir Williams Sedgwick International; one *s* one *d*. *Educ:* privately. Musical studies with the late Leon Conus of the Moscow Conservatoire and at the Paris Conservatoire, also with Profs Harold Craxton and Tobias Matthay, London. First public appearance at age of 11 with Lamoureux Orchestra, Paris; has since been broadcasting, televising, and touring in Great Britain and abroad. At inauguration of Third Programme, was commissioned by BBC to broadcast series of all Mozart's piano sonatas; invited to give Mozart recital for bicentenary celebration of Mozart's birth, Edinburgh Festival; recorded for Westminster Co. of New York, and Pye Record Co., London. Widely noted for interpretation of Mozart's piano works. *Publications:* works for piano. *Recreations:* reading, chess, fly fishing. *Address:* 20 Paradise Walk, SW3; Vicarage Cottage, Rogate, Petersfield, Hants.

MILKOMANE, G. A. M.; *see* Sava, George.

MILL, Rear-Adm. Ernest, CB 1960; OBE 1944; Director General, Aircraft, Admiralty, 1959-62; *b* 12 April 1906; *s* of Charles and Rosina Jane Mill; *m* 1939, Isobel Mary Neilson (*d* 1971). *Educ:* Merchant Venturers Sch. Fleet Engr Officer on staff of C-in-C, Mediterranean, 1957; Rear-Adm., 1958. *Recreations:* sailing, fishing. *Address:* Oak Royal, Crondall, Hants. *Club:* Army and Navy.

MILL, Laura Margaret Dorothea, OBE 1962; MB, ChB, Diploma Psych; Medical Commissioner, Mental Welfare Commission for Scotland, 1962-63, retired; *b* 28 Nov. 1897; *d* of Rev. William Alexander Mill, MA and Isabel Clunas. *Educ:* The Park Sch., Glasgow; Glasgow Univ. House Surg., Samaritan Hosp. for Women, and Royal Maternity Hospital, Glasgow, House Physician, Royal Hospital for Sick Children, and Senior Medical Officer Out-patient Dispensary, Glasgow; Resident Medical Officer, York General Dispensary; Asst Physician, Riccartsbar Mental Hosp., Paisley, and Murray Royal Mental Hosp., Perth; Clinical Medical Officer, Glasgow Public Health Dept. Dep. Medical Commissioner, Gen. Board of Control for Scotland, 1936; Medical Commissioner, Gen. Board of Control for Scotland (later Mental Welfare Commission), 1947, and Senior Medical Officer, Dept of Health for Scotland. *Address:* 7 Montpelier Terrace, Edinburgh EH10 4NE. *T:* 031-229 7982.

MILL IRVING, David Jarvis, CBE 1955; Founder Member, and Hon. President, 1966, Scottish National Party in East Lothian; Ambassador to Costa Rica, 1956-61, retired; *b* 11 April 1904; 2nd *s* of late W. Mill Irving, LDS, RCSE, Langholm and Edinburgh, and Mary Low Jarvis; *m* 1934, Margaret Estella Orchardson, *d* of late W. Moxon, Edinburgh and Tangier; one *s*. *Educ:* Daniel Stewart's Coll., Edinburgh; Edinburgh Univ.; Pembroke Coll., Cambridge. MA (Hons) Edinburgh, 1929. Entered HM Diplomatic Service as Probationer Vice-Consul in former Levant Consular Service, 1927; served in Egypt, 1929-32, and in Morocco, 1932-34; Vice-Consul at Suez, 1934; a Judge of HBM Consular Court for Egypt, 1934-37; Vice-Consul at Rabat, 1940; Asst Oriental Sec. at Cairo with rank of 1st Sec., 1941; Consul at Fez, 1945; served as 1st Sec. in Foreign Office, 1945-49. Mem. UK Deleg. to Internat. Conf. for revision of Conventions relating to War Victims, 1949; Special Ambassador for Inauguration of President of Hayti, 1950; Minister to Hayti, 1950-53; Ambassador, 1953-55; Consul-Gen. for Algeria, 1955. Special Ambassador for the Inauguration: of the President of Honduras, 1957; of the President of Costa Rica, 1958. Member: Saltire Soc.; Scottish Genealogy Soc.; Andrew Fletcher Soc.; Sir Walter Scott Club. FSAScot; FAMS. Coronation Medal, 1953. *Recreation:* Scottish historical research. *Address:* Langlaw, East Saltoun, Pencaitland, East Lothian EH34 5EB. *T:* Pencaitland 340266. *Club:* Scottish National (Edinburgh).

MILLAIS, Sir Ralph (Regnault), 5th Bt, *cr* 1885; *b* 4 March 1905; *s* of Sir Geoffroy William Millais, 4th Bt, and Madeleine Campbell (*d* 1963), *d* of C. H. Grace; *S* father, 1941; *m* 1st, 1939, Felicity Caroline Mary Ward Robinson (marr. diss.), *d* of late Brig.-Gen. W. W. Warner, CMG; one *s* one *d*; 2nd, 1947, Irene Jessie (marr. diss. 1971), *er d* of E. A. Stone, FSI; 3rd, 1975, Babette Sefton-Smith, *yr d* of Maj.-Gen. H. F. Salt, CB, CMG, DSO. *Educ:* Marlborough; Trinity Coll., Cambridge. Business career. Joined RAFVR at outbreak of war, 1939, Wing Comdr. *Recreations:* fishing, travel and the restoration of famous Vintage and Historic cars. *Heir: s* Geoffroy Richard Everett Millais, *b* 27 Dec. 1941. *Address:* Gate Cottage, Winchelsea, East Sussex.

MILLAN, Rt. Hon. Bruce, PC 1975; MP (Lab) Craigton Division of Glasgow since 1959; Secretary of State for Scotland, since 1976; *b* 5 Oct. 1927; *s* of David Millan; *m* 1953, Gwendoline May Fairey; one *s* one *d*. *Educ:* Harris Academy, Dundee. Chartered Accountant, 1950-59. Chm. Scottish Labour Youth Council, 1949-50. Contested: West Renfrewshire, 1951, Craigton Div. of Glasgow, 1955. Parly Under-Sec. of State: for Defence, (RAF), 1964-66; for Scotland, 1966-70; Minister of State, Scottish Office, 1974-76. *Address:* 46 Hardy Road, SE3. *T:* 01-858 5634.

MILLAND, Raymond Alton, (Ray Milland); film actor and director, US; *b* Wales, 3 Jan. 1907; *s* of Alfred Milland and Elizabeth Truscott; *m* 1932, Muriel Weber; one *s* one *d*. *Educ:* private schs in Wales and England; Monks Preparatory Sch.; University of Wales. Served with Household Cavalry, 1926-29; became actor in 1930; went to USA, 1930, and became naturalized citizen, 1938. *Films include:* The Flying Scotsman; Payment Deferred; Bolero; Four Hours to Kill; The Glass Key; Ebb Tide; Beau Geste; The Lost Weekend; French Without Tears; So Evil My Love; Circle of Danger; A Man Alone; Lisbon; The Safecracker (also directed); Kitty; Golden Earrings; It Happens Every Spring; Alias Nick Beal; Dial M for Murder; 3 Brave Men; Man Alone; Love Story; The House in Nightmare Park; Gold; The Swiss Conspiracy; The Last Tycoon. Received Motion Picture Acad. Award for best actor, for part in The Lost Weekend. Has also appeared on stage and television. *Publication:* Wide-Eyed in Babylon (autobiog.), 1975. *Address:* 118 South Beverly Drive No 222, Beverly Hills, California, USA.

MILLAR, family name of **Baron Inchyra.**

MILLAR, Betty Phyllis Joy; Regional Nursing Officer, South Western Regional Health Authority, since 1973; *b* 19 March 1929; *o d* of late Sidney Hildersly Millar and May Phyllis Halliday. *Educ:* Ursuline High Sch. for Girls; Dumbarton Academy; Glasgow Royal Infirm.; Glasgow Royal Maternity Hosp.; Royal Coll. of Nursing, London. RGN 1950; SCM 1953; NA (Hosp.) Cert. 1961. Theatre Sister, Glasgow Royal Infirm., 1953-54; Ward and Theatre Sister, Henry Brock Meml Hosp., 1954-55; Nursing Sister, Iraq Petroleum Co., 1955-57; Clinical Instructor, Exper. Scheme of Nurse Trng, Glasgow, 1957-60; Admin. Student, Royal Coll. of Nursing, 1960-61; 2nd Asst Matron, Glasgow Royal Infirm., 1961-62; Asst Nursing Officer, Wessex Regional Hosp. Bd, 1962-67; Matron, Glasgow Royal Infirm., 1967-69; Chief Regional Nursing Officer, SW Regional Hosp. Bd, 1969-73. WHO Fellowship to study nursing services in Scandinavia, 1967. Mem. Jt Bd of Clinical Nursing Studies, 1970-; Mem. Council, Royal Coll. of Nursing, 1973. *Address:* Pinedrift, 45 Stoneyfields, Easton-in-Gordano, Bristol BS20 0LL. *T:* Pill 2709.

MILLAR, Dame Elizabeth; see Hoyer-Millar.

MILLAR, Prof. Fergus Graham Burtholme, DPhil; FBA 1976; Professor of Ancient History, University College, University of London, since 1976; *b* 5 July 1935; *s* of late J. S. L. Millar and of Jean Burtholme (*née* Taylor); *m* 1959, Susanna Friedmann; two *s* one *d*. *Educ:* Edinburgh Acad.; Loretto Sch.; Trinity Coll., Oxford (1st Cl. Lit. Hum.). Fellow: All Souls Coll., Oxford, 1958-64; Queen's Coll., Oxford, 1964-76. Conington Prize, 1963. Vice-Pres., Soc. for the Promotion of Roman Studies, 1977-. Editor, Jl of Roman Studies, 1975-. *Publications:* A Study of Cassius Dio, 1964; The Roman Empire and its Neighbours, 1967; (ed with G. Vermes) E. Schürer, history of the Jewish people in the age of Jesus Christ (175 BC-AD 135), Vol. I, 1973; The Emperor in the Roman World (31 BC-AD 337), 1977. *Address:* Department of History, University College, Gower Street, WC1E 6BT. *T:* 01-387 7050; 80 Harpes Road, Oxford OX2 7QL. *T:* Oxford 55782.

MILLAR, George, DSO 1944; MC; farmer and writer; *b* 19 Sept. 1910; 2nd *s* of Thomas Andrew Millar, architect, and Mary Reid Morton; *m* 1945, Isabel Beatriz, *d* of Montague Paske-Smith, CMG, CBE; no *c*. *Educ:* Loretto; St John's, Cambridge. Architect, 1930-32; journalist, with Daily Telegraph and Daily Express, 1934-39; Paris correspondent Daily Express, 1939; served War of 1939-45, The Rifle Bde; escaped from German POW camp to England, then served as agent in France; Chevalier de la Légion d'Honneur; Croix de Guerre avec Palmes. Tenant farmer, 400 acres, 1962; increased to 1000 acres, 1966. *Publications:* Maquis, 1945; Horned Pigeon, 1946; My Past was an Evil River, 1946; Isabel and the Sea, 1948; Through the Unicorn Gates, 1950; A White Boat from England, 1951; Siesta, 1952; Orellana, 1954; Oyster River, 1963; Horseman, 1970; The Bruneval Raid, 1974. *Recreation:* sailing. *Address:* Sydling St Nicholas, Dorset. *T:* Cerne Abbas 205. *Clubs:* Royal Cruising; Royal Yacht Squadron (Cowes).

MILLAR, Ian Alastair D.; see Duncan Millar.

MILLAR, John, CBE 1977; FIOB; DL; Lord Provost and Lord Lieutenant of the City of Edinburgh, 1975-77; Member: Falkirk Town Council, 1938-44; Edinburgh Town Council, 1961-75; *b* 18 June 1905; *m* 1932, Janet Calder Williamson; three *s* one *d*. *Educ:* Falkirk High Sch. Retired; Director: Border Concrete Products Ltd; Lafarge Organisation Ltd. Chm., Edinburgh Festival Guild. DL Edinburgh, 1977. Royal Order de l'Etoile Polaire (Sweden), 1975; Commandeur de l'Ordre National du Mérite (France), 1976. *Recreations:* golf, walking. *Address:* 8 Northlawn Court, Easter Park Drive, Edinburgh EH4 6JR.

MILLAR, John Stanley; County Planning Officer, Greater Manchester Council, since 1973; *b* 1925; *s* of late Nicholas William Stanley Millar and Elsie Baxter Millar (*née* Flinn); *m* 1961, Patricia Mary (*née* Land); one *d*. *Educ:* Liverpool Coll.; Univ. of Liverpool. BArch, DipCD, PPRTPI, RIBA. Planning Asst, then Sen. Asst Architect, City of Liverpool, 1948-51; Sectional Planning Officer, then Dep. Asst County Planning Officer, Lancs CC 1951-61; Chief Asst Planning Officer, then Asst City Planning Officer, City of Manchester, 1961-64; City Planning Officer, Manchester, 1964-73. *Publications:* papers in professional and technical jls. *Recreations:* walking, listening to music, travel, the sea. *Address:* 17 Pownall Road, Pownall Park, Wilmslow, Cheshire SK9 5DR. *T:* Wilmslow 23616. *Club:* National Liberal.

MILLAR, Sir Oliver Nicholas, KCVO 1973 (CVO 1963; MVO 1953); FBA 1970; Surveyor of the Queen's Pictures, since 1972; *b* 26 April 1923; *er s* of late Gerald Millar, MC and late Ruth Millar; *m* 1954, Delia Mary, 2nd *d* of late Lt-Col Cuthbert Dawnay, MC; one *s* three *d*. *Educ:* Rugby; Courtauld Institute of Art, University of London (Academic Diploma in History of Art). Unable, for medical reasons, to serve in War of 1939-45. Asst Surveyor of the King's Pictures, 1947-49, Dep. Surveyor 1949-72. Trustee, Nat. Portrait Gallery, 1972-. Mem., Reviewing Cttee on Export of Works of Art, 1975-. A Governor, St Mary's Sch., Calne. FSA. *Publications:* Gainsborough, 1949; William Dobson, Tate Gallery Exhibition, 1951; English Art, 1625-1714 (with Dr M. D. Whinney). 1957; Rubens' Whitehall Ceiling, 1958; Abraham van der Doort's Catalogue, 1960; Tudor, Stuart and Early Georgian Pictures in the Collection of HM the Queen, 1963; Zoffany and his Tribuna, 1967; Later Georgian Pictures in the Collection of HM the Queen, 1969; Inventories and Valuations of the King's Goods, 1972; The Age of Charles I (Tate Gallery Exhibn), 1972; The Queen's Pictures, 1977; articles in the Burlington Magazine, etc; numerous catalogues. *Recreations:* drawing, gardening, cricket, golf. *Address:* Yonder Lodge, Penn, Bucks. *T:* Penn 2124. *Club:* Brooks's.

MILLAR of Orton, Maj.-Gen. Robert Kirkpatrick, CB 1954; DSO 1944; DL; late Royal Engineers; *b* 29 June 1901; *s* of late Professor John Hepburn Millar and late Margaret Wilhelmina, *e d* of late J. W. Wharton Duff, of Orton, Morayshire; *m* 1934, Frances Rhodes, *yr d* of late Col W. G. Beyts, CBE; two *s* (and one *s* decd). *Educ:* Edinburgh Academy; RMA Woolwich. 2nd Lt Royal Engineers, 1921; served in India and China, 1925-33; served War of 1939-45 (despatches 5 times, 1939-46, DSO); Field Co. 49 (WR) Div. (Norway), 1940; CRE 15 (Scottish) Div. 1942-45 (France and Germany); CE London District, 1949-51; CE Scottish Command, 1951-53; Engineer-in-Chief, Pakistan Army, 1953-57. DL Moray, 1959-. *Recreations:* golf, shooting, fishing. *Address:* Darnethills, Orton, By Fochabers, Moray. *T:* Orton 284.

MILLAR, Ronald Graeme; playright and screenwriter; Deputy Chairman, Theatre Royal Haymarket Ltd; *b* 12 Nov. 1919; *s* of Ronald Hugh Millar and Dorothy Ethel Dacre Millar (*née* Hill). *Educ:* Charterhouse; King's Coll., Cambridge. Served as Sub-Lt, RNVR, 1940-43 (invalided out). Began in the Theatre as an actor. First stage appearance, London, Swinging the Gate, Ambassadors', 1940, subseq. in Mr Bolfry, The Sacred Flame, Murder on the Nile, Jenny Jones, (own play) Zero Hour, 1944. Ealing Studios, 1946-48, worked on Frieda, Train of Events, etc; screenwriter, Hollywood, 1948-54: So Evil My Love, The Miniver Story, Scaramouche, Rose-Marie, The Unknown Man, Never Let Me Go, Betrayed. Plays produced in London: Frieda, 1946; Champagne for Delilah, 1948, Waiting for Gillian, 1954; The Bride and the Bachelor, 1956; The More the Merrier, 1960; The Bride Comes Back, 1960; The Affair (from C. P. Snow novel), 1961, The New Men (from C. P. Snow), 1962; The Masters (from C. P. Snow), 1963; (book and lyrics) Robert and Elizabeth (musical), 1964; Number 10, 1967; Abelard and Heloise, 1970; The Case in Question (from C. P. Snow), 1975. *Recreations:* all kinds of music, all kinds of people. *Address:* 7 Sheffield Terrace, W8. *T:* 01-727 8361. *Club:* Dramatists'.

MILLAR, Prof. William Malcolm, CBE 1971; MD; Crombie-Ross Professor of Mental Health, University of Aberdeen, 1949-77; *b* 20 April 1913; *s* of Rev. Gavin Millar, BD, Logiealmond, Perthshire, and Margaret Malcolm, Stanley, Perthshire; *m* 1941, Catherine McAuslin Rankin; two *s* four *d*. *Educ:* George Heriot's Sch., Edinburgh; Edinburgh Univ. MB, ChB (Edinburgh) 1936; MD (Edinburgh) 1939; Dip. Psych. (Edinburgh) 1939; MRCPE 1958; FRCPE 1962. Asst Physician, Royal Edinburgh Hospital for Mental Disorders, 1937-39. Served 1939-46 (Lieut, Captain, Major), Specialist in Psychiatry, RAMC. Senior Lecturer, Dept of Mental Health, Aberdeen Univ., 1946-49. Dean, Faculty of Medicine to 1977. Member: MRC, 1960-64; Mental Welfare Commn for Scotland, 1964-. FBPsS 1946. *Publications:* contributions to various learned journals. *Recreations:* golf, chess, gardening. *Address:* 16 The Chanonry, Aberdeen. *T:* Aberdeen 43845.

MILLAR-CRAIG, Hamish, CMG 1960; OBE 1958; *b* 25 Sept. 1918; *yr s* of late Captain David Millar-Craig and late Winifred Margaret Cargill; *m* 1953, Rose Ernestine Boohene. *Educ:* Shrewsbury; Keble Coll., Oxford. Served War of 1939-45, 2nd Lt Royal Scots, 1940; Colonial Civil Service, Gold Coast, 1940-57; Ghana Civil Service, 1957-62; Reader in Public Administration (UN Technical Assistance), Ghana Institute of Public Administration, 1962-65; Dir, E African Staff Coll., 1965-69; Adviser, Min. of Finance, Somalia, 1969-71; Bursar, UNITAR, 1972-77. Economic Development Institute,

Washington, 1957-58. *Recreation:* philately. *Address:* c/o Lloyds Bank Ltd, Taunton, Somerset TA1 1HN.

MILLARD, Sir Guy (Elwin), KCMG 1972 (CMG 1957); CVO 1961; HM Diplomatic Service, retired; *b* 22 Jan. 1917; *s* of Col Baldwin Salter Millard, and Phyllis Mary Tetley; *m* 1st, 1946, Anne, *d* of late Gordon Mackenzie; one *s* one *d*; 2nd, 1964, Mary Judy, *d* of late James Dugdale and of Pamela, Countess of Aylesford; two *s*. *Educ:* Charterhouse; Pembroke Coll., Cambridge. Entered Foreign Office, 1939. Served Royal Navy, 1940-41. Asst Private Sec., to Foreign Sec., 1941-45; British Embassy, Paris, 1945-49, Ankara, 1949-52; Imperial Defence Coll., 1953; Foreign Office, 1954, Counsellor, 1955; Private Sec. to Prime Minister, 1955-57; British Embassy, Tehran, 1959-62; Foreign Office, 1962-64; Minister, UK Delegation to NATO, 1964-67; Ambassador to Hungary, 1967-69; Minister, Washington, 1970-71; Ambassador to Sweden, 1971-74; Ambassador to Italy, 1974-76. *Address:* Fyfield Manor, Southrop, Glos. *T:* Southrop 234. *Club:* Boodle's.

MILLARD, Raymond Spencer, CMG 1967; PhD; FICE; FIStructE; Civil Engineer, World Bank, Washington, since 1976; *b* 5 June 1920; *s* of Arthur and Ellen Millard, Ashbourne, Derbs; *m*; one *s* one *d*. *Educ:* Queen Elizabeth Grammar Sch., Ashbourne; University Coll., London (BSc (Eng)). RE and civil engineering contracting, 1941-44. Road Research Laboratory, 1944-74: Hd of Tropical Section, 1955-63; Dep. Dir, 1965-74; Partner, Peter Fraenkel & Partners, Asia, 1974-76. *Publications:* scientific and technical papers on road planning and construction. *Recreations:* painting, travel. *Address:* 1629 Evers Drive, McLean, Va, USA.

MILLBOURN, Sir (Philip) Eric, Kt 1955; CMG 1950; MIMechE; Adviser on Shipping in Port to Minister of Transport, 1946-63; Chairman Council of Administration, Malta Dockyard, since 1963; *b* 1 June 1902; *s* of late Philip Millbourn, Brunswick Square, Hove, Sussex; *m* 1931, Ethel Marjorie, *d* of late Joseph E. Sennett; one *s* one *d*. *Educ:* privately; London Univ. Chm., The London Airport Development Cttee. Dep. Chm., Nat. Ports Council, 1964-67. *Address:* Conkwell Grange, Limpley Stoke, near Bath, Avon BA3 6HD. *T:* Limpley Stoke 3102. *Club:* Travellers'.

MILLER, Alan Cameron; MA; LLB; FCIT; advocate; Master at Fettes College, since 1974; *b* 10 Jan. 1913; *o s* of late Arthur Miller, Edinburgh; *m* 1945, Audrey Main; one *s* one *d*. *Educ:* Fettes Coll.; Edinburgh Univ. MA 1934; LLB 1936; Advocate, 1938; served War of 1939-45, RN; Interim Sheriff-Substitute at Dundee, 1946; Sheriff-Substitute of Inverness, Moray, Nairn, Ross and Cromarty, at Fort William, 1946-52; Legal Adviser (Scotland): British Transport Commn, 1952-62; BR Board, 1962-73. Chm., Inst. of Transport (Scotland), 1971-72. *Recreations:* golf and music. *Address:* 42 Great King Street, Edinburgh, Scotland. *Clubs:* Arts (Edinburgh); HCEG.

MILLER, Alan John McCulloch, DSC 1941, VRD 1950; Chairman, Low & Bonar, since 1977; *b* 21 April 1914; *s* of late Louis M. Miller and Mary McCulloch; *m* 1940, Kirsteen Ross Orr; three *s* one *d*. *Educ:* Kelvinside Academy; Strathclyde Univ. CEng, MRINA, MIESS, FBIM, FRSA. Family engrg business, 1933-39. Commnd RNVR (Clyde Div.), 1938; served RN, 1939-45: Far East, Indian Ocean, S Atlantic, HMS Dorsetshire, then destroyers; in comd, HMS Fitzroy, Wolverine, Holderness, St Nazaire, Dieppe raids, Russian convoys, 1943-44; psc 1944. Rejoined family business, 1945, until sold to Bestobell Ltd, 1951; Dir, Bestobell Ltd, 1951-73, Chm. and Man. Dir, 1965-73; Chm. and Man. Dir, Wm Simons & Co. Ltd, Shipbuilders, 1956-60; Chm., Dev West Ltd, 1973-; Chm., BNEC Southern Africa Cttee, 1970, until abolished. Member: Sports Council; Central Council of Physical Recreation. *Recreations:* sailing, golf, ski-ing, shooting. *Address:* The Forest House, Hatchet Lane, Winkfield, Berks SL4 2EG. *T:* Winkfield Row 2606. *Clubs:* Army and Navy, Royal Thames Yacht, Royal Ocean Racing, Royal Cruising; Royal and Ancient (St Andrews); Sunningdale Golf; Royal Northern Yacht.

MILLER, Alastair Cheape, MBE 1948; TD; Prison Governor, retired 1972; *b* 13 March 1912 (twin-brother); *s* of John Charles Miller, Banker, Glasgow, and Jessie Amelia Miller; *m* 1943, Elizabeth S. Hubbard (marr. diss. 1967); one *s* one *d*. *Educ:* Melville Coll., Edinburgh; Bedford Sch., Bedford. Territorial Army, 1930-46; War Service (Gibraltar and Italy); 5th Beds and Herts Regt, 1st Herts Regt and 4th KOYLI, 1948-51. Barclays Bank Ltd; Junior Clerk to Cashier, 1929-45. Housemaster, Approved Sch., April-Nov. 1946. Prison Service: Asst Governor, Wakefield, Dec. 1946-Jan. 1953; Governor: Dover, 1953-59; Winchester, 1959-62; Hindley Borstal, 1962-65; Parkhurst Prison, 1966-70; Pentonville, 1970-72. Associated

with St Mungo Community Trust i/c Old Charing Cross Hosp. project for homeless people, 1974-75. *Publication:* Inside Outside, 1976. *Recreations:* golf, sailing. *Address:* 3 White Hart Street, SE11; Skeagh, Schull, West Cork, Eire. *Clubs:* Civil Service; Bantry Golf; Hampstead Golf; Seaford Golf (Seaford); Corinthian; Royal London Yacht (Cowes); Royal Solent Yacht (Yarmouth).

MILLER, Alexander Ronald, CBE 1970; Chairman and Managing Director, Motherwell Bridge (Holdings) Ltd, since 1958; *b* 7 Nov. 1915; *s* of Thomas Ronald Miller and Elise Hay. *Educ:* Craigflower; Malvern Coll.; Royal Coll. of Science and Technology. Royal Engineers and Royal Bombay Sappers and Miners, 1940-46. Member: Scottish Council, CBI (formerly FBI), 1955- (Chm., 1963-65); Design Council (formerly CoID), 1965-71 (Chm. Scottish Cttee, 1965-67); Scottish Economic Planning Council, 1965-71 (Chm., Industrial Cttee, 1967-71); British Railways (Scottish) Board, 1966-70; British Rail Design Panel, 1966-; Gen. Convocation, Univ. of Strathclyde, 1967-; Steering Cttee, W Central Scotland Plan, 1970-75; Lanarkshire Area Health Bd (Chm., 1973-77); Oil Develt Council for Scotland, 1973-; Instn of Royal Engineers; BIM Adv. Bd for Scotland, 1974-; Coll. Council, Bell Coll. of Technology, Hamilton, 1976-; Management Cttee, Scottish Health Services Common Services Agency (Chm., 1977-); Lloyds Register of Shipping Scottish Cttee; Incorporation of Hammermen, Merchants' House of Glasgow. A Burgess of the City of Glasgow. FRSA; AIMechE; FBIM. *Address:* Lairfad, Auldhouse, by East Kilbride, Lanarks. *T:* East Kilbride 63275. *Clubs:* Directors; Royal Scottish Automobile (Glasgow), Western (Glasgow).

MILLER, Rear-Adm. Andrew John; Flag Officer Second Flotilla, 1972-73, retired; *b* 12 Dec. 1926; *s* of Major A. D. Miller, Baluch Regt, IA; *m* 1954, Elizabeth Rosanne Foster; one *s* two *d*. *Educ:* Craigflower, Fife; RNC Dartmouth. Midshipman 1944; Sub-Lt 1946; Lieut 1948; Lt-Comdr 1956; Comdr 1959; Captain 1965; Rear-Adm. 1972. Commanded ML3513, Asheldham, Grafton, Scorpion, Nubian. Dir Public Relations (Navy), 1970-71. *Recreation:* gardening. *Address:* Forge Cottage, Bosham, West Sussex. *T:* Bosham 572144.

MILLER, Archibald Elliot Haswell, MC; Hon. MA Edinburgh 1951; RSW; Keeper and Deputy Director, National Galleries of Scotland, 1930-52 (retired); Secretary, Royal Fine Art Commission for Scotland; 1930-52 (retired); Secretary (later Director) National Buildings Record, Scottish Council, 1945-53 (retired); *b* Glasgow, 10 June 1887; *s* of William Miller and Elizabeth Haswell; *m* 1916, E. Josephine Cameron (Josephine Haswell Miller, ARSA); one *d*. *Educ:* Glasgow Academy. Studied Munich, Berlin, Vienna and Paris; Asst Professor in Glasgow Sch. of Art, 1910-14 and 1919-30; war services 1914-19 with 7th Bn Highland Light Infantry (MC), and 1939-45 with Intelligence Corps. Represented by works in Glasgow Art Gallery, National Gallery of New South Wales, and Imperial War Museum (Series of drawings representing all types of dress and equipment of the 1914-18 war period); has made a special study of military uniforms and Highland dress. Retrospective Exhibn 1908-71, Imperial War Museum, 1971. Consultant Art Historian, Army Museums Ogilby Trust. Mem. of Soc. of Mural Decorators and Painters in Tempera; has carried out mural paintings in Livingstone Memorial Museum, Blantyre. *Publication:* Military Drawings and Paintings in the Royal Collection, vol i, 1966, vol ii, 1970. *Address:* Yew Tree Cottage, Kington Magna, Gillingham, Dorset. *T:* East Stour 326.

MILLER, Arjay; Dean, Graduate School of Business, Stanford University, since 1969; Vice-Chairman, Ford Motor Company, 1968-69 (President, 1963-68); *b* 4 March 1916; *s* of Rawley John Miller and Mary Gertrude Schade; *m* 1940, Frances Marion Fearing; one *s* one *d*. *Educ:* University of California at Los Angeles (BS with highest hons, 1937). Graduate Student and Teaching Asst, University of California at Berkeley, 1938-40; Research Technician, Calif. State Planning Bd, 1941; Economist, Federal Reserve Bank of San Francisco, 1941-43. Captain, US Air Force, 1943-46. Asst Treas, Ford Motor Co., 1947-53; Controller, 1953-57; Vice-Pres. and Controller, 1957-61; Vice-Pres. of Finance, 1961-62; Vice-Pres., Staff Group, 1962-63. Member, Board of Directors: Ford Motor Co.; Levi Strauss & Co.; Utah Internat. Inc.; The Washington Post Co.; Wells Fargo Bank; Trustee: Urban Inst.; Eisenhower Exchange Fellowships; Brookings Instn, Washington; The Conference Board, 1965; Internat. Exec. Service Corps. Member: Stanford Res. Inst. Bd of Dirs; Econ. Policy Council, UNA; Trilateral Commn. LLD: Univ. of California (LA), 1964; Whitman Coll., 1965; Univ. of Nebraska, 1965. *Address:* Graduate School of Business, Stanford University, Stanford, Calif, USA. *Clubs:* Bohemian, Pacific Union (San Francisco).

MILLER, Arthur; playwright; *b* 17 Oct. 1915; *s* of Isadore Miller and Augusta Barnett; *m* 1940, Mary Grace Slattery (marr. diss.); one *s* one *d*; *m* 1956, Marilyn Monroe (marr. diss. 1961; she *d* 1962); *m* 1962, Ingeborg Morath; one *d*. *Educ:* University of Michigan, USA (AB). Pres. of PEN Club, 1965-. *Publications:* Situation Normal (reportage), 1944; Focus (novel), 1945; All My Sons (play) (New York Drama Critics Award, 1948), 1947; Death of A Salesman (play) (New York Drama Critics Award, 1949, Pulitzer Prize, 1949), 1949; The Crucible (play), 1953; A View from the Bridge (play), 1955, filmed, 1962; A Memory of Two Mondays (play), 1955; Collected Plays, 1958; The Misfits (motion picture play), 1960; After the Fall (play), 1963; Incident at Vichy (play), 1964; I Don't Need You Anymore (collected stories), 1967; The Price (play), 1968; (jt author) In Russia, 1969; The Creation of the World and Other Business (play), 1972, musical version, Up From Paradise, 1974; (with Inge Morath) In the Country, 1977; contrib. stories and essays to Esquire, Colliers, Atlantic Monthly, etc. *Address:* ICM, 40 W 57th Street, New York, NY 10019, USA.

MILLER, Sir Bernard; see Miller, Sir O. B.

MILLER, Bruce; see Miller, John D. B.

MILLER, Desmond Campbell, QC 1961; TD; Chairman, Rossminster Group, since 1973; *b* 17 Dec. 1914; *y s* of late Robert Miller, DD, sometime Bishop of Cashel and Waterford, and of Mary Miller, *yr d* of Dean Potter of Raphoe; *m* Ailsa, *y d* of Hon. Allan Victor Maxwell, CMG, and Margaret (*née* Lawless); two *s* one *d*. *Educ:* Manor Sch., Fermoy; Dean Close Sch., Cheltenham; St Columba's Coll., Rathfarnham; Pembroke Coll., Oxford. Called to Bar, Inner Temple, 1939, Gray's Inn (*ad eundem*), 1960; Master of the Bench, Inner Temple, 1968; retired from practice at the Bar, 1976. Served War of 1939-45 (despatches): Middx Yeo.; Northants Yeo.; 2nd, 6th and 11th Armoured Divs; HQ 1 Corps; HQ, ALFSEA; Staff Coll., Camberley, 1942. Lt-Col TA. Mem. General Council of the Bar, 1964-68, 1971-73 (Chm., Taxation and Retirement Benefits Cttees). *Recreations:* golf, flyfishing, reading. *Address:* Vogue House, 1 Hanover Square, W1. *T:* 01-493 3671; 116 Rivermead Court, SW6. *T:* 01-736 5753. *Clubs:* Brooks's, MCC, Hurlingham; Royal Mid-Surrey Golf.

MILLER, Donald C.; see Crichton-Miller.

MILLER, Sir Douglas; see Miller, Sir I. D.

MILLER, Sir Douglas (Sinclair), KCVO 1972; CBE 1956 (OBE 1948); Development Adviser, Duke of Edinburgh's Award Scheme, since 1971; *b* 30 July 1906; British parentage; *m* 1933, Valerie Madeleine Carter; one *d*. *Educ:* Westminster Sch.; Merton Coll., Oxford. HM Overseas Colonial Service, 1930-61: Supt of Native Educn, N Rhodesia, 1930-45; Director of Education: Basutoland, 1945-48; Nyasaland, 1948-52; Uganda, 1952-58; Kenya, 1958-59; Dir of Educn and Permanent Sec., Min. of Educn, Kenya, 1959-60; Temp. Minister of Educn, Kenya, 1960-61; Sec., King George's Jubilee Trust, 1961-71. *Address:* The Lodge, 70 Grand Avenue, Worthing, Sussex. *T:* Worthing 501195. *Clubs:* Royal Commonwealth Society; Kampala (Uganda).

MILLER, Edward; Master, Fitzwilliam College, Cambridge, since 1971; *b* Acklington, Northumberland, 16 July 1915; *e s* of Edward and Mary Lee Miller; *m* 1941, Fanny Zara Salingar; one *s*. *Educ:* King Edward VI's Grammar Sch., Morpeth; St John's Coll., Cambridge (Exhibnr, Schol.). BA 1937; MA 1945; Strathcona Res. Student, 1937-39, Fellow, 1939-65, and Hon. Fellow, 1974, St John's Coll., Cambridge. Nat. Service, 1940-45 in Durham Light Inf., RAC and Control Commn for Germany; Major. Dir of Studies in History, 1946-55 and Tutor, 1951-57, St John's Coll., Cambridge; Asst Lectr in History, 1946-50 and Lectr, 1950-65, University of Cambridge; Warden of Madingley Hall, Cambridge, 1961-65; Prof. of Medieval Hist., Sheffield Univ., 1965-71. FRHistS; Chm., Victoria Co. Histories Cttee of Inst. Hist. Research; Mem., Council of Selden Soc.; Chm., Editorial Bd, History of Parliament Trust. Hon. LittD Sheffield 1972. *Publications:* The Abbey and Bishopric of Ely, 1951; Portrait of a College, 1961; (Jt Ed.) Cambridge Economic History of Europe, Vol. iii, 1963; Historical Studies of the English Parliament, 2 vols, 1970; articles in Victoria County Histories of Cambridgeshire and York, English Hist. Rev., Econ. History Rev., Trans Royal Historical Society, Past and Present, etc. *Recreations:* with advancing years watching any form of sport, especially Rugby and cricket. *Address:* Fitzwilliam College, Cambridge CB3 0DG. *T:* Cambridge 58657.

MILLER, Edward; Director of Education, Strathclyde, since 1974; *b* 30 March 1930; *s* of Andrew and Elizabeth Miller; *m* 1955; two *s*. *Educ:* Eastbank Academy; Glasgow Univ. (MA, MEd). Taught at Wishaw High Sch., 1955-57 and Whitehill Secondary Sch., 1957-59; Depute Dir of Educn. West Lothian, 1959-63; Sen. Asst Dir of Educn, Stirlingshire, 1963-66; Depute, later Sen. Depute Dir of Educn, Glasgow, 1966-74. *Recreations:* golf, reading, numismatics. *Address:* 11 Southview Drive, Bearsden, Glasgow G61 4HG. *T:* 041-942 6532.

MILLER, Lt-Gen. (retired) Sir Euan (Alfred Bews), KCB 1954 (CB 1949); KBE 1951; DSO 1945; MC 1918; DL; Lieutenant of the Tower of London, 1957-60; *b* 5 July 1897; *s* of Dr A. E. Miller; *m* 1926, Margaret (*d* 1969), *d* of late Captain H. C. R. Brocklebank, CBE; one *s* two *d*. *Educ:* Wellington Coll.; RMC Sandhurst. 2nd Lieut, KRRC, 1915. Served European War, France and Salonika, 1915-18 (despatches, MC). Staff Coll., 1926-27; Bt Lt-Col, 1936; served War of 1939-45, GSO1, GHQ, BEF, 1939; OC2 KRRC, 1940 (despatches, prisoner of war, DSO). Col, 1945; Brig., 1946; Dep. Mil. Sec., 1946; ADC to the King, 1946-48; Comdr Hanover Dist, 1948; Maj.-Gen., 1948; Chief of Staff, Middle East Land Forces, 1949-51; Lieut-Gen. 1951; Military Sec. to the Sec. of State for War, 1951; retired, 1955. Col Comdt, 1 KRRC, 1954-61. Chm. Kent T&AFA, 1956-61. DL Kent, 1958. *Address:* Farningham House Cottage, Farningham, Kent DA4 0DH. *T:* Farningham 863243. *Club:* Army and Navy.

See also J. M. Clay, E. W. F. Tomlin.

MILLER, Air Chief Marshal Frank Robert, CC (Canada) 1972; CBE 1946; CD; Director, United Aircraft of Canada Ltd; *b* Kamloops, BC, April 1908; *m* Dorothy Virginia Minor, Galveston, Texas. *Educ:* Alberta Univ. (BSc, Civil Engrg). Joined RCAF, 1931. Served War of 1939-45: commanded Air Navigation Schs at Rivers, Man., and Penfield Ridge, NB, and Gen. Reconnaisance Sch., Summerside, PEI; subseq. Dir of Trng Plans and Requirements and Dir of Trng, Air Force HQ; service overseas with Can. Bomber Gp as Station Comdr, later Base Comdr, 1944; Tiger Force, 1945 (despatches); Chief SO (later AOC), Air Material Comd, 1945; US Nat. War Coll., 1948; Air Mem. Ops and Trng, Air Force HQ, 1949; Vice Chief of Air Staff, 1951; Vice Air Deputy, SHAPE HQ, Paris, 1954; Dep. Minister, Dept of Nat. Defence, 1955; Chm., Chiefs of Staff, 1960; first Pres., NATO Mil. Cttee, 1963-64; Chief of Defence Staff, Canada, 1964-66. Air Chief Marshal, 1961. Hon. LLD Alta, 1965; Hon. DScMil, RMC Canada, 1968. *Recreations:* golf, fishing. *Address:* 2 Seneca, Ottawa, Ontario, Canada.

MILLER of Glenlee, Sir (Frederick William) Macdonald, 7th Bt *cr* 1788; Conservative Agent for Lowestoft since 1965; *b* 21 March 1920; *e s* of Sir Alastair George Lionel Joseph Miller of Glenlee, 6th Bt; *S* father, 1964; *m* 1947, Marion Jane Audrey Pettit; one *s* one *d*. *Educ:* Tonbridge. Conservative Agent for: Whitehaven, 1947-50; Wembley North, 1950-52; North Norfolk, 1952-65. County Councillor, Suffolk. A Dep. Traffic Comr, Eastern Region, 1976-. *Recreation:* gardening. *Heir: s* Dr Stephen William Macdonald Miller of Glenlee [*b* 20 June 1953. *Educ:* Rugby; St Bartholomew's Hosp. MB, BS, LMSSA. Houseman, Norfolk and Norwich Hospital]. *Address:* Ivy Grange Farm, Westhall, Halesworth, Suffolk. *T:* Ilketshall 265.

MILLER, Brigadier George Patrick Rose-, DSO 1940; MC; beef farmer; inventor and export salesman; *b* 20 July 1897; 3rd *s* of late John Gardner Miller, Mayfield, Perth; *m* 1929, Millicent Rose Lang-Rose; two *s* two *d*. *Educ:* Trinity Coll., Glenalmond; RMC, Sandhurst. Gazetted to Queen's Own Cameron Highlanders, 1915; served in France and Belgium, 1916-17 (MC); served with 1st Bn in India, Burma and Sudan; Commanded 1st Bn in France 1940 (DSO); Raised and Commanded 227 Brigade; Commanded 155 Brigade. Invented calf feeder, 1948. *Publications:* Articles on agricultural subjects. *Address:* Barevan, Cawdor, Nairnshire. *T:* Croy 218. *Club:* Naval and Military.

MILLER, Gerald Cedar, MC; MA; Headmaster Forest School, near Snaresbrook, 1936-60; *b* 11 May 1894; *s* of Rev. Ernest George and Emilie Miller; *m* 1st, 1930, Alice Rosemary Taylor (*d* 1957); three *d*; 2nd, 1960, Molly Sherry. *Educ:* University Sch., Victoria, BC; Ardingly Coll., Sussex; Keble Coll., Oxford. Served European War, 1914-19, Commission in Oxon. and Bucks Lt Infty, in France and Salonika; Asst Master Ardingly Coll., 1921-25; Sch. House Master, 1925-28; Second Master and Junior House Master, 1928-35. *Address:* Home Close, Gubblecote, near Tring, Herts. *Club:* East India, Devonshire, Sports and Public Schools.

MILLER, Henry (Valentine); author and painter; *b* New York City, 26 Dec. 1891; *m*; one *s* two *d* by former *ms. Educ:* City Coll., NY; Cornell Univ. Worked in US until 1930; lived in Paris and was employed on editorial work on Phoenix, Booster and Volontés, 1930-38; visited Greece, 1939; returned to US, 1940. Mem., Amer. Inst. of Arts and Letters, 1958. *Publications:* Tropic of Cancer, 1931 (US 1961, UK 1964); Aller Retour New York, 1935; Tropic of Capricorn, 1935 (US 1962, UK 1964); Black Spring, 1936 (UK 1965); Max and the White Phagocytes, 1938 (UK 1970); The Cosmological Eye, 1939 (UK 1946); The World of Sex, 1940 (US 1957, UK 1970); The Colossus of Maroussi, 1941; The Wisdom of the Heart, 1941 (UK 1947); Sunday After the War, 1944 (UK 1946); The Air-Conditioned Nightmare, 1945 (UK 1947); Murder the Murderer, 1946; Maurizius Forever, 1946; Remember to Remember, 1947 (UK 1952); The Smile at the Foot of the Ladder, 1948 (UK 1966); Rosy Crucifixion, 1965: Sexus, 1949; Plexus, 1953; Nexus, 1959; The Books in My Life, 1952; Quiet Days in Clichy, 1956 (UK 1966); The Time of the Assassins, 1956 (UK 1959); Big Sur and the Oranges of Hieronymous Bosch, 1956 (UK 1958); The Red Notebook, 1958; Reunion in Barcelona, 1959; Stand still like the Mockingbird, 1962; A Letter, 1962; Watercolours, 1962; Just Wild About Harry, 1963 (UK 1964); (with Lawrence Durrell) A Private Correspondence, 1963; (with M. Fraenkel) Hamlet: correspondence, 1963; Greece, 1964; Letters to Anais Nin, 1965; What are you going to do about Alf?, 1971; My Life and Times, 1972; The Immortal Bard, 1973; On Turning Eighty, 1973; First Impressions of Greece, 1974; Journey to an Antique Land, 1974; The Waters Reglitterized, 1974. Exhibition of paintings, Los Angeles, 1966. *Address:* c/o Grove Press, 80 University Place, New York, NY 10013, USA; c/o Edward P. Schwartz, Henry Miller Literary Society, 121 N 7th Street, Minneapolis, Minn 55403, USA.

MILLER, Hilary Duppa, (Hal Miller); MP (C) Bromsgrove and Redditch since 1974; *b* 6 March 1929; *s* of Lt-Comdr John Bryan Peter Duppa-Miller, *qv*; *m* 1st, 1956, Fiona Margaret McDermid; two *s* two *d*; 2nd, 1976, Jacqueline Rae, *d* of T. G. W. Roe and of Lady Londesborough. *Educ:* Eton; Merton Coll., Oxford; London Univ. MA (Oxon) 1956; BSc (Estate Management) (London), 1962. With Colonial Service, Hong Kong, 1955-68. Contested: (C), Barrow-in-Furness, 1970; Bromsgrove by-elec. May 1971. Fellow of Economic Development Inst. of World Bank, Washington. Company Director. *Recreations:* sailing, fell walking, cricket, Rugby refereeing. *Address:* House of Commons, SW1A 0AA. *Clubs:* St Stephen's; Vincent's (Oxford); Aston Fields British Legion (Bromsgrove); Eton Ramblers, Free Foresters, Blackheath Football.
See also Michael Miller.

MILLER, Mrs Hugh; *see* Katzin, Olga.

MILLER, Sir (Ian) Douglas, Kt 1961; FRCS; Hon. Consulting Neurosurgeon since 1960 (Hon. Neurosurgeon, 1948), St Vincent's Hospital, Sydney, and Repatriation General Hospital; Chairman of Board, St Vincent's Hospital, since 1966; Dean of Clinical School, St Vincent's Hospital, Sydney, 1931-64; *b* Melbourne, 20 July 1900; *m* 1939, Phyllis Laidley Mort; three *s* two *d. Educ:* Xavier Coll., Melbourne; University of Sydney. MB, ChM Sydney 1924; FRCS 1928. Hon. Asst Surgeon, St Vincent's Hosp., Sydney, 1929; Lectr in Surgical Anat., University, Sydney, 1930; Hon. Surg., Mater. Hosp. Sydney, 1934; Hon. Surg., St Vincent's Hosp., 1939; Major AIF, Surgical Specialist, 1940; Lt-Col (Surgical CO), 102 AGH, 1942; o/c Neurosurgical Centre, AIF. Chairman: Community Systems Foundn of Aust.; Foundn of Forensic Scis, Aust. Mem. Ct of Examrs 1946, Mem. Council, 1947, RACS; President: RACS, 1957-59; Asian Australasian Soc. of Neurological Surgeons, 1964-67. Chairman: Editorial Cttee, ANZ Jl of Surgery; Editorial Bd, Modern Medicine in Australia. Hon. AM 1964, Hon. LittD 1974, Singapore. *Publications:* contrib. Med. Jl of Aust., 1956, 1960; Earlier Days, 1970. *Recreation:* agriculture. *Address:* 149 Macquarie Street, Sydney, NSW 2000, Australia. *T:* BU 5077, JJ 2431. *Club:* Australian (Sydney).

MILLER, Dr Jacques Francis Albert Pierre, FRS 1970; FAA 1970; Head of Experimental Pathology Unit, Walter and Eliza Hall Institute of Medical Research, since 1966; *b* 2 April 1931; French parents; *m* 1956, Margaret Denise Houen. *Educ:* St Aloysius' Coll., Sydney. BSc (Med.) 1953, MB, BS 1955, Sydney; PhD 1960, DSc 1965, London. Sen. Scientist, Chester Beatty Res. Inst., London, 1960-66; Reader, Exper. Pathology, Univ. of London, 1965-66. For. Mem., Académie Royale de Médicine de Belgique, 1969. Langer-Teplitz Cancer Research Award (USA), 1965; Gairdner Foundn Award (Canada), 1966; Encyclopaedia Britannica (Australia) Award, 1966; Scientific Medal of Zoological Soc. of London, 1966; Burnet Medal,

Austr. Acad. of Scis, 1971; Paul Ehrlich Award, Germany, 1974. *Publications:* over 200 papers in scientific jls and several chapters in books, mainly dealing with thymus and immunity. *Recreations:* music, photography. *Address:* Walter and Eliza Hall Institute of Medical Research, Royal Melbourne Hospital PO, Parkville, Victoria 3050, Australia. *T:* 347-1511.

MILLER, James, RSA 1964; RSW 1934; Artist, Painter; *b* 25 Oct. 1893; *s* of William Miller and Margaret Palmer; *m* 1934, Mary MacNeill, MA (*d* 1973); no *c. Educ:* Woodside Sch.; Sch. of Art, Glasgow. Teaching, 1917-47. Commissioned by Artists' Adv. Coun. of Min. of Information to make drawings of buildings damaged by enemy action in Scotland, 1939-41; travelled extensively in Spain looking at buildings and making drawings; made drawings for Pilgrim Trust, 1942. Paintings have been bought by Bradford, Newport, Glasgow, Dundee, Hertford, Paisley, Nat. Gall. of S Australia, Melbourne, Arts Coun., Aberdeen, Dumbarton, Perth and Muirhead Bequest, Edinburgh. Has held several one-man shows in Glasgow. *Recreations:* listening to gramophone records, reading. *Address:* Tigh-na-bruaich, Dunvegan, Isle of Skye. *Club:* Art (Glasgow).

MILLER, Bt Col Sir James (MacBride), Kt 1958; MC; TD; DL; *b* 18 June 1896; *s* of Rev. John Miller, Eyemouth, Berwickshire; *m* 1925, Jane Elizabeth Simson Elliot, *d* of Francis Elliot, Middlestots, Duns, Berwickshire. *Educ:* Berwickshire; George Watson's Coll., Edinburgh. Royal Artillery, TA, 1915-36. Convener, Berwickshire County Council, 1949-61; President of the Association of County Councils of Scotland, 1956-58. DL Berwickshire, 1948. Hon. Sheriff Substitute, Duns. *Address:* Duneaton, West Bay Road, North Berwick.

MILLER, Lt-Comdr John Bryan Peter Duppa-, GC and King's Commendation 1941; *b* 22 May 1903; *er s* of Brian Stothert Miller, JP, Posbury Devon, and Mary (*née* Sadler); *m* 1st, 1926, Barbara, *d* of Stanley Owen, 1st Viscount Buckmaster, GCVO; three *s*; 2nd, 1944, Clare, *d* of Francis Egerton Harding, JP, Old Springs, Market Drayton; 3rd, 1977, Greta, *d* of B. K. G. Landby, Gothenburg. *Educ:* Rugby Sch.; Hertford Coll., Oxford. Dep. County Educn Officer, Hants, 1930-35; Asst Sec., Northants Educn Cttee, 1936-39; Torpedo and Mining Dept, Admty, 1940-45; a Dep. Dir-Gen., Trade and Econs Div., Control Commn for Germany, 1945; Inspector-Gen., Min. of Educn, Addis Ababa, 1945-47; Educn Dept, Kenya, 1947-57; Chm. of European Civil Servants' Assoc., and formation Chm. Staff Side, Central Whitley Coun. for Civil Service; Sec. to Kenya Coffee Marketing Bd, 1960-61; Sec. to Tanganyika Coffee Bd, 1961-62; Asst Sec. and Marketing Officer, Min. of Lands and Settlement, Kenya, 1963-65. *Publication:* Saints and Parachutes, 1951. *Recreations:* yachting, economics. *Address:* c/o Standard Bank, Adderley Street, Cape Town, South Africa. *Club:* Reform.
See also H. D. Miller, Michael Miller.

MILLER, Prof. J(ohn) D(onald) Bruce; Professor of International Relations, Research School of Pacific Studies, Australian National University, since 1962; Overseas Visiting Fellow, St John's College, Cambridge, 1977-78; Smuts Visiting Fellow, University of Cambridge, 1977-78; *b* 30 Aug. 1922; *s* of Donald and Marion Miller, Sydney, Australia; *m* Margaret Martin (*née* MacLachlan); one *s. Educ:* Sydney High Sch.; University of Sydney. BEc, 1944; MEc 1951. Announcer and Talks Officer, Australian Broadcasting Commission, Sydney and Canberra, 1939-46; Staff Tutor, Department of Tutorial Classes, University of Sydney, 1946-54; Asst Lecturer in Political Science and International Relations, London Sch. of Economics, 1953-55; Lecturer in Politics, University Coll., Leicester, 1955-57; Prof. of Politics, University of Leicester, 1957-62; Dean of Social Sciences, 1960-62; Public Orator, 1961-62. Visiting Professor: Indian Sch. of International Studies, 1959; Columbia Univ., New York, 1962, 1966; Yale, 1977; Macrossan Lectr, University of Queensland, 1966. Member: Aust. Population and Immigration Council, 1975-; Aust. Res. Grants Cttee, 1975-. Joint Editor, Journal of Commonwealth Political Studies, 1961-62; Editor, Australian Outlook, 1963-69; Chm., Editorial Adv. Bd for Austr. documents on foreign relations, 1971-77. FASSA 1967. *Publications:* Australian Government and Politics, 1954, 4th edn with B. Jinks 1970; Richard Jebb and the Problem of Empire, 1956; Politicians (inaugural), 1958; The Commonwealth in the World, 1958; The Nature of Politics, 1962; The Shape of Diplomacy (inaugural), 1963; Australia and Foreign Policy (Boyer Lectures), 1963; The Disintegrating Monolith (ed with T. H. Rigby), 1965; Britain and the Old Dominions, 1966; Australia, 1966; The Politics of the Third World, 1966; (ed) India, Japan, Australia: Partners in Asia?, 1968; Survey of Commonwealth Affairs: problems of expansion and attrition 1953-1969, 1974; (ed) Australia's Economic Relations, 1975; The EEC and Australia, 1976.

Recreations: books, garden, dachshund. *Address:* 16 Hutt Street, Yarralumla, ACT 2600, Australia. *T:* Canberra 813138. *Clubs:* National Press, Commonwealth (Canberra).

MILLER, Sir John Francis C.; *see* Compton Miller.

MILLER, John Harmsworth; architect in private practice; *b* 18 Aug. 1930; *s* of Charles Miller and Brenda Borrett; *m* 1957, Patricia Rhodes (marr. diss. 1975); two *d*. *Educ:* Charterhouse; Architectural Assoc. Sch. of Architecture (AA Dip. Hons 1957). ARIBA 1959. Private practice, Colquhoun and Miller, 1961-; works include: Forest Gate High Sch., West Ham (Newham), 1965; Chemistry Labs, Royal Holloway Coll., London Univ., 1970; Melrose Activity Centre, Milton Keynes Develt Corp. (Commendation, Steel Awards, 1975); Pillwood House, Feock, Cornwall (RIBA Regional Award, 1975). Tutor: RCA and AA, 1961-73; Cambridge Sch. of Arch., 1969-70; Prof. of Environmental Design, RCA, 1975. Vis. Critic: Cornell Univ. Sch. of Arch., Ithaca, 1966, 1968 and 1971; Princeton Univ. Sch. of Arch., NJ, 1970; Dublin Univ. Sch. of Arch., 1972-73. *Publications:* contribs to architect. jls. *Address:* 23 Regent's Park Road, NW1. *T:* 01-267 5800.

MILLER, Sir John Holmes, 11th Bt *cr* 1705, of Chichester, Sussex; *b* 1925; *er s* of 10th Bt and of Netta Mahalah Bennett; *S* father 1960; *m* 1950, Jocelyn Robson Edwards, Wairoa, NZ; two *d*. Heir: *b* Harry Holmes Miller [*b* 1927; *m* 1954, Gwynedd Margaret Sheriff; one *s* two *d*].

MILLER, John Ireland; Vice-President, Methodist Conference of Great Britain, 1973-74; *b* 20 June 1912; *s* of John William Miller and Emma Miller (*née* Minkley); *m* 1943, Vida Bertha Bracher; one *s* one *d*. *Educ:* Hardye's School, Dorchester; Taunton School, Taunton. Admitted Solicitor and Member of Law Society, 1933. HM Coroner: Poole Borough, 1972-74 (Deputy Coroner, 1939-72); East Dorset, 1974-. Director: Fleetworks Ltd; Burt & Vick Ltd; Farney Close School Ltd. Chm., Methodist Homes for the Aged. *Address:* 25 Merriefield Drive, Broadstone, Dorset BH18 8BW. *T:* Broadstone 694057. *Club:* National Liberal.

MILLER, Lt-Col Sir John (Mansel), KCVO 1974 (CVO 1966); DSO 1944; MC 1944; Crown Equerry since 1961; *b* 4 Feb. 1919; 3rd *s* of Brig.-Gen. Alfred Douglas Miller, CBE, DSO, DL, JP, Royal Scots Greys, and of Ella Geraldine Fletcher, Saltoun, E Lothian. *Educ:* Eton; RMA, Sandhurst. 2nd Lieut Welsh Guards, 1939; Adjt 1942-44; ADC to F-M Lord Wilson, Washington, DC, 1945-47; Regtl Adjt, 1953-56; Brigade Major 1st Guards Brigade, 1956-58; comd 1st Bn Welsh Guards, 1958-61. *Recreations:* hunting, shooting, polo, driving. *Address:* Shotover House, Wheatley, Oxon. *T:* Wheatley 450; The Crown Equerry's House, Buckingham Palace, SW1. *T:* 01-930 4832. *Clubs:* Cavalry and Guards, Pratt's, Buck's, White's.

MILLER, Dr Jonathan Wolfe; Director; *b* 21 July 1934; *s* of late Emanuel Miller, DPM, FRCP; *m* 1956, Helen Rachel Collet; two *s* one *d*. *Educ:* St Paul's Sch.; St John's Coll., Cambridge. MB, BCh 1959. Res. Fellow in Hist. of Med., UCL, 1970-73. Associate Director, Nat. Theatre, 1973-75. Mem., Arts Council, 1975-76. Vis. Prof. in Drama, Westfield Coll., London, 1977-. Co-author and appeared in Beyond the Fringe, 1961-64; Ed. BBC Monitor, 1965; directed films for BBC TV (incl. Alice in Wonderland), 1966; stage directing in London and New York, 1965-67; *directed plays:* School for Scandal, 1968; The Seagull, 1969, The Malcontent, 1973, Nottingham Playhouse; King Lear, The Merchant of Venice, Old Vic, 1970; The Tempest, Mermaid, 1970; Hamlet, Arts Theatre, Cambridge, 1970; Danton's Death, 1971, School for Scandal, 1972, Measure for Measure, 1974, Marriage of Figaro, 1974, The Freeway, 1974, Nat. Theatre; The Taming of the Shrew, 1972, The Seagull, 1973, Chichester; Family Romances, Greenwich, 1974; The Importance of Being Earnest, Greenwich, 1975; All's Well, Greenwich, 1975; Three Sisters, Cambridge, 1976; *film:* Take a Girl Like You, 1970; *operas:* Arden must die, Sadler's Wells Theatre, 1974; The Cunning Little Vixen, Glyndebourne, 1975 and 1977; Kent Opera: Cosi Fan Tutte, 1975; Rigoletto, 1975; Orfeo, 1976; Eugene Onegin, 1977. *Publications:* McLuhan, 1971; (ed) Freud: the man, his world, his influence, 1972. *Recreation:* deep sleep. *Address:* 63 Gloucester Crescent, NW1. *T:* 01-485 6973.

MILLER, Maj.-Gen. Joseph Esmond, MC 1943; Medical Officer to Army Careers Information Office, Sheffield; *b* 22 Sept. 1914; *s* of Col J. F. X. Miller, OBE; *m* 1946, Kathleen Veronica Lochée-Bayne; one *s*. *Educ:* St George's Coll., Weybridge; London Univ. (St Bartholomew's Hosp.). MRCS, LRCP; MRCGP; MFCM; MBIM. Qualified, July 1940. Fellow RoySocMed; Member: BMA; Sheffield Medico-Chirurgical Soc. Served War of 1939-

45: commissioned in RAMC, Dec. 1940 (ante-dated Sept. 1940); RAMC Depot, 1940-42; Airborne Forces, 1942-45: N Africa, Sicily, Italy, Holland, Germany. RAMC Depot, 1945-47; Staff Coll., 1948; DADMS, HQ MELF, Egypt, 1949-50; CO, 35 Field Amb., Tripoli and Egypt, 1950-54; SMO, RMA Sandhurst, 1954-57; CO, 4 Field Amb., Germany, 1957-59; CO, 10 Bde Gp Med. Co., Aden, 1959-61; ADMS, Middle East Command, Aden, 1961; Chief Instr, RAMC Depot, 1961-65; CO, BMH Hong Kong, 1965-68; ADMS, 4 Div., Germany, 1968-69; DDMS: HQ BAOR, 1969-71; HQ Scotland (Army), 1971-72; HQ UKLF, 1972-73; DMS, HQ UKLF, 1973-76. QHS 1973-76. CStJ 1975. *Recreations:* golf, gardening. *Address:* 17 Norton Green Close, Norton, Sheffield S8 8BP. *T:* Sheffield 748694. *Club:* The Club (Sheffield).

MILLER, Prof. Karl Fergus Connor; Lord Northcliffe Professor of Modern English Literature, University College London, since 1974; *b* 2 Aug. 1931; *s* of William and Marion Miller; *m* 1956, Jane Elisabeth Collet; two *s* one *d*. *Educ:* Royal High School, Edinburgh; Downing Coll., Cambridge. Asst Prin., HM Treasury, 1956-57; BBC TV Producer, 1957-58; Literary Editor, Spectator, 1958-61; Literary Editor, New Statesman, 1961-67; Editor, Listener, 1967-73. *Publications:* (ed) Poetry from Cambridge, 1952-54, 1955; (ed, with introd.) Writing in England Today: The Last Fifteen Years, 1968; (ed) Memoirs of a Modern Scotland, 1970; (ed) A Listener Anthology, August 1967-June 1970, 1970; (ed) A Second Listener Anthology, 1973; (ed) Henry Cockburn, Memorials of his Time, 1974; Cockburn's Millennium, 1975. *Recreation:* football. *Address:* 26 Limerston Street, SW10. *T:* 01-352 1735.

MILLER, Dame Mabel, DBE 1967; LLB; JP; Barrister; Australian Representative to Status of Women Commission, United Nations, since 1967; Member, Metric Conversion Board, since 1970; *b* Broken Hill, NSW; *d* of J. C. Goodhart, Victor Harbour, S Australia; *m* 1930, Alan Miller; one *d*. *Educ:* Girton House, Adelaide; University of Adelaide. Joined WAAAF, 1941; Dep. Dir, WAAAF, 1942-43 (Sqdn Officer); Staff Officer, WAAAF, North Eastern Area, 1944. Alderman, Hobart, 1952- (Dep. Lord Mayor, 1954-56, 1964-66, 1966-68); MHA for Franklin, Tasmania, 1955-64. Pres., Right to Life Assoc., Tasmania; Foundn Mem., Tasmanian Women's Air Trng Corps (Women's Vol. Auxiliary); Member: Interim Cttee, Austr. Nat. Gall. in Canberra; Aust.-Amer. Assoc.; Member Committee: Aust.-British Assoc.; Queen Alexandra Hospital Country Women's Assoc.; Red Cross; Girl Guides Assoc. (Exec. Mem.); Past Pres., Nat. Coun. of Women. *Recreations:* golf, reading. *Address:* 403 Sandy Bay Road, Hobart, Tasmania. *T:* 252084. *Clubs:* University Women's; Queen Mary, Air Force, Royal Automobile, Business and Professional Women's, (Assoc. Mem.) Naval, Military and Air Force (Hobart); Lyceum (Melbourne); Royal Over-Seas League, Tasmanian Assoc. of University Women Graduates (Tasmania).

MILLER of Glenlee, Sir Macdonald; *see* Miller of Glenlee, Sir F. W. M.

MILLER, Mrs Mary Elizabeth H.; *see* Hedley-Miller.

MILLER, Maurice Solomon, MB; MP (Lab) East Kilbride, since 1974 (Glasgow Kelvingrove, 1964-74); *b* 16 Aug. 1920; *s* of David Miller; *m* 1944, Renée, *d* of Joseph Modlin, Glasgow; two *s* two *d*. *Educ:* Shawlands Academy, Glasgow; Glasgow University. MB, ChB 1944. Mem. of Glasgow Corporation since 1950; Bailie of Glasgow, 1954-57; JP Glasgow, 1957. Asst Govt Whip, 1968-69. Medical Adviser in the Port of Glasgow to the British and Commonwealth Shipping Company Ltd. Visited Russia as mem. of medical delegation, 1955. *Publication:* Window on Russia, 1956. *Address:* House of Commons, SW1; 82 Springkell Avenue, Glasgow S1.

MILLER, Michael, RD 1966; QC 1974; Barrister since 1958; *b* 28 June 1933; 2nd *s* of John Bryan Peter Duppa-Miller, *qv*; *m* 1958, Mary Elizabeth, *e d* of Donald Spiers Monteagle Barlow, *qv*; two *s* two *d*. *Educ:* Dragon Sch., Oxford; Westminster Sch. (King's Scholar); Christ Church, Oxford (Westminster Scholar). BA Lit. Hum. 1955; MA 1958. Ord. Seaman, RNVR, 1950; Sub-Lt 1956; qual. submarines, 1956; Navigating Officer, HMS Solent, 1956; Armaments Officer: HMS Sturdy, 1956-57; HMS Tally Ho, 1957; Lt-Comdr RNR. Called to Bar, Lincoln's Inn, 1958; practice at Chancery Bar from 1958; Mem. Bar Council, 1972-74; Mem. Senate of Inns of Court and Bar, 1974-. *Recreations:* sailing, music, chess, football. *Address:* 8 Stone Buildings, Lincoln's Inn, WC2. *See also* H. D. Miller.

MILLER, Rev. Norman, MA; *s* of late E. Banbury Miller, Bristol; *m* 1942, Annette Daukes, *e d* of late Rt Rev. F. W. Daukes, sometime Bishop of Plymouth; two *s. Educ:* Clifton Coll.; Queen's Coll., Cambridge (Schol.); University Stewart of Rannoch Schol. for Classics. Sixth Form Master, Berkhamsted Sch.; ordained, 1914; Asst Master in Haileybury Coll.; House-Master, 1919-26; Headmaster of Kelly Coll., Tavistock, 1926-38; Vicar of St Albans, Bristol, 1939-51; Rector of Swanage, Dorset, 1951-61. *Address:* Barn Cottage, Quenington, Glos.

MILLER, Sir (Oswald) Bernard, Kt 1967; Chairman, John Lewis Partnership, 1955-72; *b* 25 March 1904; *s* of late Arthur Miller and of Margaret Jane Miller; *m* 1931, Jessica Rose Marie ffoulkes; three *s. Educ:* Sloane Sch.; Jesus Coll., Oxford (Hon. Fellow, 1968); Stanhope Prize, 1925; BA 1927; MA 1930. Joined John Lewis Partnership, 1927; Dir, 1935. Chm., Retail Distributors Assoc., 1953; Member: Council of Industrial Design, 1957-66; Monopolies Commission, 1961-69; EDC for Distributive Trades, 1964-71. Chm. Southern Region, RSA, 1974-. Treasurer, Southampton Univ., 1974-. *Publication:* Biography of Robert Harley, Earl of Oxford, 1927. *Recreations:* fishing, gardening, opera and theatre. *Address:* The Field House, Longstock, Stockbridge, Hants. *T:* Stockbridge 627. *Clubs:* Garrick; Royal Southampton Yacht.

MILLER, Peter Francis Nigel, RIBA, FSIAD; Senior Partner, Purcell Miller Tritton and Partners, Architects, Surveyors and Design Consultants, since 1973; *b* 8 May 1924; *s* of Francis Gerald Miller and Dorothy Emily (*née* Leftwich); *m* 1950, Sheila Gillian Branthwayt (*née* Stratton); one *s* two *d. Educ:* King's Sch., Canterbury; Sch. of Architecture, Coll. of Art, Canterbury. ARIBA 1952; FRIBA 1968; MSIA 1956; FSIA 1968. Served army, 1942-47; commnd Duke of Cornwall's LI, 1943. Private practice: Peter Miller and Sheila Stratton, 1954; Miller and Tritton, 1956; Purcell Miller and Tritton, 1965. Surveyor to the Fabric of Ely Cathedral, 1974-; Architect, Cathedral of St John the Baptist, Norwich, 1976-. Vice-Pres., SIAD, 1976. *Recreations:* shooting and wildfowling. *Address:* Old Hall Farmhouse, Swanton Novers, Melton Constable, Norfolk NR24 2RE. *T:* Melton Constable 305; 64 Bethel Street, Norwich NR2 1NR. *T:* Norwich 20438. *Club:* Norfolk (Norwich).

MILLER, Sir Richard Hope, Kt 1955; Hon. Secretary, Greater Manchester and Area Branch, Institute of Directors, since 1966; Chairman, North West Region, Arthritis and Rheumatism Council, since 1974; President: Knutsford Division Conservative Association, since 1975; David Lewis Epileptic Centre, 1977; Lymm Lawn Tennis and Croquet Club, since 1971; Vice-President, Cheshire County Lawn Tennis Association, 1977; *b* 26 July 1904; 2nd *s* of late Hubert James Miller, The Old Court House, Knutsford, Cheshire, and of Elsa Mary Colimann; unmarried. *Educ:* Wellington Coll.; Trinity Hall, Cambridge. BA 1925; MA 1930. Served War of 1939-46: commissioned in 7th Bn (TA) The Manchester Regt; Adjutant 1941; Major 1945; served in Staff appointments (Britain, Ceylon, and Singapore), 1942-46. *Recreations:* skiing, tennis. *Address:* West Court, Knutsford, Cheshire. *T:* Knutsford 3422; Lloyds Bank Ltd, Cox's & King's Branch, 6 Pall Mall, SW1; National Westminster Bank Ltd, Knutsford, Cheshire. *Club:* United Oxford & Cambridge University.

MILLER, Robert Sydney; Puisne Judge, British Guiana, 1959-63, retired; Judge Advocate, Guyana Defence Force, with rank of Colonel; Member, Judicial Service Commission; Chairman, Income Tax Board of Review, No I; *b* 23 April 1901; *o s* of late Dr Robert Sydney Miller, British Guiana Medical Service, and Alice Matilda Miller (*née* Dodson); *m* 1942, Kathleen Elaine (*née* Fraser); one *s* one *d. Educ:* Queen's Coll., British Guiana; Weybridge Grammar Sch.; Skerry's Coll.; Jesus Coll., Oxford University. Called to Bar, Inner Temple. Practised at the Bar, British Guiana; Magistrate, British Guiana; acted Crown Counsel, 1949-50; acted Registrar of Supreme Court and of Deeds, 1953; Coronation Medal, 1953; Senior Magistrate, 1956; acted Puisne Judge, 1955-59. Chm., Adv. Cttee on Treatment of Offenders; held public inquiry into accidents to Cessna aircraft, 1967; Arbitrator (Guyana Mine Workers Union and Reynolds (Guyana) Mines Ltd), 1968. National Insurance Commissioner. *Recreations:* walking and reading. *Address:* A-34 Arakaka Place East, Bel Air Park, Georgetown, Guyana. *T:* 66515. *Clubs:* Royal Commonwealth Society (West Indian); Corona; Guyana Defence Force Officers, Georgetown.

MILLER, Prof. Ronald, MA, PhD, FRSE, FRSGS; Professor of Geography, Glasgow University, 1953-76; Dean of the Faculty of Science, 1964-67; *b* 21 Aug. 1910; *o c* of late John Robert Miller and Georgina Park; *m* 1940, Constance Mary Phillips, SRN, SCM; one *s* one *d. Educ:* North Queensferry; Stromness Acad.; Edinburgh Univ. Silver Medal, Royal Scottish Geographical Soc.; MA 1st cl Hons Geog., 1931; Carnegie

Research Fellowship at Marine Laboratory of Scottish Home Dept, Aberdeen, 1931-33; PhD 1933; Asst Lecturer Manchester Univ., 1933-36; Education Officer, Nigeria, 1936-46; Royal West African Frontier Force, 1939-44; Lecturer, Edinburgh Univ., 1947-53. Guest Lecturer: University of Montpellier, 1957; University of Oslo and Handelshøyskole Bergen, 1966; Simon Fraser Univ., 1967; Ife, 1969. Pres., RSGS, 1974-77. *Publications:* (with MacNair) Livingstone's Travels; The Travels of Mungo Park; (with Tivy) ed. The Glasgow Region, 1958; (with Watson) Ogilvie Essays, 1959; Africa, 1967; Orkney, 1976; papers on geographical topics in journals. *Address:* Ruah, 20 South End, Stromness, Orkney. *T:* Stromness 594.

MILLER, Comdr Ronald S.; *see* Scott-Miller.

MILLER, Rudolph Valdemar Thor C.; *see* Castle-Miller.

MILLER, Stephen James Hamilton, MD, FRCS; Surgeon-Oculist: to the Queen, since 1974; to HM Household, 1965-74; Ophthalmic Surgeon: St George's Hospital since 1951; National Hospital, Queen Square, since 1955; King Edward VII Hospital for Officers, since 1965; Surgeon, Moorfields Eye Hospital, since 1954; Recognised Teacher in Ophthalmology, St George's Medical School and Institute of Ophthalmology, University of London; Civilian Consultant in Ophthalmology to Royal Navy and Ministry of Defence, since 1971; *b* 19 July 1915; *e s* of late Stephen Charles Miller and Isobel Hamilton; *m* 1949, Heather P. Motion; three *s. Educ:* Arbroath High Sch.; Aberdeen Univ. House Physician and Surgeon, Royal Infirmary, Hull, 1937-39. Surgeon Lieut-Comdr RNVR, 1939-46 (Naval Ophthalmic Specialist, RN Aux. Hosp., Kilmacolm and RN Hosp., Malta). Resident Surgical Officer, Glasgow Eye Infirmary, 1946; Registrar and Chief Clinical Asst, Moorfields Eye Hosp., 1947-50; Registrar St George's Hosp., 1949-51; Research Associate, Institute of Ophthalmology, 1949-. FRSocMed; Fellow Faculty of Ophthalmology; Editor, British Journal of Ophthalmology; Mem. Editorial Bd, Ophthalmic Literature; Ophthalmological Soc. of UK; Oxford Ophthalmological Congress (Master, 1969-70); Examiner in Ophthalmology for Royal Colls and Brit. Orthoptic Bd. Hon. Mem., Amer. Acad. of Ophthalmology. Doyne Medal, 1972; Montgomery, 1974. CStJ (Deputy Hospitaller). *Publications:* Modern Trends in Ophthalmology, 1973; Operative Surgery, 1976; Parsons Diseases of the Eye, 1977; articles in BMJ, Brit. Jl of Ophthalmology, Ophthalmic Literature. *Recreation:* golf. *Address:* 149 Harley Street, W1. *T:* 01-935 4444. *Clubs:* Garrick; Woking Golf.

MILLER, Terence George, TD 1960; MA Cantab; Director, Polytechnic of North London, since 1971; *b* 16 Jan. 1918; *o s* of late George Frederick Miller, Cambridge, and late Marion Johnston, Port William, Wigtownshire; *m* 1944, Inga Catriona, 3rd *d* of Austin Priestman, MD, Folkestone, Kent; one *s* three *d. Educ:* Perse (foundn schol.); Jesus Coll., Cambridge (schol.). Wiltshire Prizeman, 1939. Served War of 1939-45: RA, Special Forces, Glider Pilot Regt, TA, 1947-67. Harkness Scholar, 1948; Research Fellow, Jesus Coll., 1949-54. University Demonstrator, 1948; Lectr in Geology, Univ. of Keele, 1953; Sen. Lectr, 1963. Prof. of Geography, Univ. of Reading, 1965-67; Principal, University Coll. of Rhodesia, 1967-69; Vis. Prof., Reading Univ., 1969-71. Member: Inter-Univs Council for Higher Educn Overseas; EEC Council for Higher Education and Res. *Publications:* Geology, 1950; Geology and Scenery in Britain, 1953; scientific papers in various jls. *Recreations:* studies in military history, sailing, beachcombing, cutting and burning. *Address:* Polytechnic of North London, Holloway, N7.

MILLER, Comdr William Ronald; Royal Navy (retired); Clerk to the Worshipful Company of Haberdashers since 1966; *b* 6 Dec. 1918; *y s* of Col Joseph Sidney Miller, DSO and Florence Eva Drabble; *m* 1942, Betty Claelia Otto, Richmond, Natal; one *d. Educ:* Cranleigh Sch., Surrey. Entered RN, 1936. Sec. to Flag Officer (Submarines), 1955-57; Exec. Asst to Dep. Supreme Allied Comdr Atlantic (as Actg Capt.), 1958-60; Sec. to C-in-C Home Fleet (as Actg Capt.), 1960-62; Sec. to C-in-C Portsmouth (as Actg Capt.), 1963-65; retd from RN at own request, 1966. Called to Bar, Lincoln's Inn, 1958. Liveryman, Haberdashers' Co., 1969. *Recreations:* golf, tennis, gardening. *Address:* Dolphin House, Pewley Hill, Guildford, Surrey. *T:* Guildford 60846. *Club:* Naval.

MILLER JONES, Keith; Chairman, Board of Governors of the National Hospitals for Nervous Diseases, 1963-74; Solicitor; *b* 7 April 1899; *o s* of late Frank W. Jones, Headingley, Leeds; *m* 1950, Hon. Betty Ellen Askwith, *qv, o d* of late Baron Askwith, KCB, KC, LLD. *Educ:* privately; New Coll., Oxford (Hon. Exhibr); Leeds Univ. Admitted Solicitor, 1925; Mem., firm of Braby & Waller, 1925-62. Mem., Paddington Group HMC, 1948-60; Dep. Chm., Georgian Group, 1955-71 (Mem. Council);

Founder Mem., Hansard Soc. for Parly Govt, 1944 (Mem. Council, 1944-75); Founder Mem., Wildfowl Trust, 1946 (Mem. Coun., 1946-67). *Recreations:* music, golf. *Address:* Flat 9, 105 Onslow Square, SW7. *T:* 01-589 7126. *Clubs:* Brooks's; Richmond Golf.

MILLER PARKER, Agnes; *see* Parker, A. M.

MILLES-LADE, family name of **Earl Sondes.**

MILLETT, Peter Julian, QC 1973; *b* 23 June 1932; *s* of late Denis Millett and Adele Millett; *m* 1959, Ann Mireille, *d* of David Harris; two *s* (and one *s* decd). *Educ:* Harrow; Trinity Hall, Cambridge (MA). Nat. Service, RAF, 1955-57 (Flying Officer). Called to Bar, Middle Temple, 1955, *ad eundem* Lincoln's Inn 1959; at Chancery Bar, 1958-. Examnr and Lectr in Practical Conveyancing, Council of Legal Educn, 1962-76. Junior Counsel to Dept of Trade and Industry in Chancery matters, 1967-73. Mem., General Council of the Bar, 1971-75. *Publications:* contrib. to Halsbury's Laws of England, Encycl. of Forms and Precedents. *Recreations:* philately, bridge, Times crossword. *Address:* 18 Portman Close, W1H 9HJ. *T:* 01-935 1152; St Andrews, Kewhurst Avenue, Cooden, Sussex. *Club:* National Liberal.

MILLIGAN, James George, QC (Scot.) 1972; Advocate-Depute, since 1971; *b* 10 May 1934; *s* of Rt Hon. Lord Milligan; *m* 1961, Elizabeth Carnegie Thomson, *e d* of Hon. Lord Migdale, *qv*; two *s* three *d*. *Educ:* St Mary's Sch., Melrose; Rugby Sch.; Oxford Univ. (BA); Edinburgh Univ. (LLB). Admitted to Faculty of Advocates, 1959; Standing Junior Counsel to the Scottish Home and Health Dept and Dept of Health and Social Security in Scotland. *Publication:* (contrib. small part of) Armour on Valuation for Rating, 3rd edn, 1961. *Recreations:* golf, squash. *Address:* 36 Mansionhouse Road, Edinburgh EH9 2JD. *T:* 031-667 4858. *Clubs:* New (Edinburgh); Honourable Company of Edinburgh Golfers (Muirfield).

MILLIGAN, Patrick Ward, DL; Chairman: Sedgwick Collins & Co., 1967-72; Sedgwick Forbes (Holdings) Ltd, 1972-74; a General Commissioner for Income Tax, since 1975; *b* 27 May 1910; 2nd *s* of James Knowles Milligan, MRCS, LRCP and Arabella Milligan; *m* 1934, Betty Mavis, *yr d* of Frank Rogerson; one *s* one *d*. *Educ:* Winchester Coll. Joined Lloyd's, 1928; underwriting mem., 1932. Served War of 1939-45, Queen's Royal Regiment; AQMG, BTE, 1945, Lt-Col. Member: Cttee Non Marine Assoc., Lloyd's, 1949-62 (Chm., 1958); Cttee of Lloyd's, 1954-57 and 1959-62; Dep. Chm. of Lloyd's, 1957, 1960, Chm., 1962; Chm., Lloyd's Brokers' Assoc., 1967. Chm. Transport Users Consultative Cttee (SE Area), 1966-76. DL Surrey 1976. *Recreations:* golf, cricket. *Address:* The Coach House, Eashing, Surrey. *T:* Godalming 5459. *Club:* Gresham.

MILLIGAN, Terence Alan, (Spike Milligan); actor; author; *b* 16 April 1918; *s* of late Captain L. A. Milligan, MSM, RA retd, and of Florence Winifred Milligan; *m* ; one *s* three *d*. *Educ:* Convent of Jesus and Mary, Poona; Brothers de La Salle, Rangoon; SE London Polytechnic, Lewisham. Appearances (comedy) as Spike Milligan: *stage:* The Bed-Sitting Room; Son of Oblomov; Ben Gunn, in Treasure Island, Mermaid, 1973, 1974; *radio:* Goon Show (inc. special performance, 1972, to mark 50th Anniversary of BBC); Best British Radio Features Script, 1972; *TV:* Show called Fred, ITV; World of Beachcomber, BBC; Q5, BBC; Oh in Colour, BBC; A Milligan for All Seasons, BBC, 1972-73; Marty Feldman's Comedy Machine, ITV (writing and appearing; awarded Golden Rose and special comedy award, Montreux, 1972); The Melting Pot, BBC, 1975; Q7, BBC series, 1977; TV Writer of the Year Award, 1956; *films:* The Magic Christian, 1971; The Devils, 1971; The Cherry Picker, 1972; Digby the Biggest Dog in the World, 1972; Alice's Adventures in Wonderland, 1972; The Three Musketeers, 1973; The Great McGonagall, 1975. *Publications:* Dustbin of Milligan, 1961; Silly Verse for Kids, 1963; Puckoon, 1963; The Little Pot Boiler, 1965; A Book of Bits, 1965; Milliganimals, 1968; The Bedside Milligan, 1968; The Bed-Sitting Room (play), 1969; The Bald Twit Lion, 1970; Adolf Hitler, My Part in his Downfall, 1971 (filmed 1973); Milligan's Ark, 1971; Small Dreams of a Scorpion, 1972; The Goon Show Scripts, 1972; Rommel? Gunner Who?, 1973; (for children) Badjelly the Witch, 1973; (with J. Hobbs): The Great McGonagall Scrapbook, 1975; The Milligan Book of Records, Games, Cartoons and Commercials, 1975; Dip the Puppy, 1975; Transports of Delight, 1975; William McGonagal, the truth at last, 1976; Monty, His Part in my Victory, 1976. *Recreations:* restoration of antiques, oil painting, water colours, gardening, eating, drinking, talking, wine, jazz. *Address:* 9 Orme Court, W2. *T:* 01-727 1544.

MILLIGAN, Wyndham Macbeth Moir, MBE 1945; TD 1947; Principal of Wolsey Hall, Oxford, since 1968; *b* 21 Dec. 1907; *s* of Dr W. Anstruther Milligan, MD, London, W1; *m* 1941, Helen Penelope Eirene Cassavetti, London, W1; three *s* two *d*. *Educ:* Sherborne; Caius Coll., Cambridge. Asst Master, Eton Coll., 1932-, House Master, Eton Coll., 1946; Warden, Radley Coll., 1954-68. Served 1939-45, with Scots Guards, in NW Europe (Major). Chm., N Berks Area Youth Cttee. Governor: St Mary's, Wantage (Chm.); Reed's Sch., Cobham; Lay Chm., Berkshire Deanery Synod; Mem., Administrative Council, King George's Jubilee Trust. FRSA 1968. *Recreation:* gardening. *Address:* South Lodge, Pusey, by Faringdon, Oxon. *Club:* Bath.

MILLING, Sir Denis C.; *see* Crowley-Milling.

MILLING, Geoffrey; Chairman, Bowring Steamship Company, 1965-68; Deputy Chairman, Lloyd's Register of Shipping, 1963-72; *b* 1 Sept. 1901; *s* of Henry Milling, Warrington, Lancs; *m* 1928, Dorothy Gordon Baird, St John's, Newfoundland; one *s* one *d*. *Educ:* Radley; Merton Coll., Oxford (MA). In USA, 1923, as Sec. to Sir Wilfred Grenfell; joined Lever Brothers, England, 1924; Hudson's Bay Co., 1926 (2 years in Baffin Land, as Manager of trading post, etc.); Bowring Brothers Ltd, St John's, 1935-48, returning to parent firm, London, 1948. Chm., Royal Alfred Merchant Seamen's Soc., 1951-59; Chm., London General Shipowners' Soc., 1959-60; Mem. Port of London Authority, 1959-67. *Recreation:* golf. *Address:* Priory Cottage, Quay Lane, Brading, Isle of Wight. *Clubs:* Leander; Swinley Forest Golf.

MILLING, Peter Francis, MB, BChir, FRCS; formerly: Surgeon, Ear, Nose and Throat Department, University College Hospital; Surgeon in charge, Throat and Ear Department, Brompton Hospital; Consultant Ear, Nose and Throat Surgeon: Epsom District Hospital; Oxted and Limpsfield Cottage Hospital; Visiting Laryngologist Benenden Chest Hospital. *Educ:* Cambridge University. BA Hons, 1937; MRCS, LRCP, 1940; MA, MB, BChir, 1941; FRCS, 1946. Formerly Chief Assistant, Ear, Nose and Throat Department, St Thomas' Hospital; Chief Clinical Assistant and Registrar, Ear, Nose and Throat Department, Guy's Hosp.; Surgical Registrar, Ear, Nose and Throat Dept, Royal Cancer Hospital. Member British Association of Otolaryngologists. FRSocMed. *Publications:* contributions to medical text-books and journals. *Address:* Hillcrest, Bradda West, Port Erin, Isle of Man.

MILLINGTON, Air Commodore Edward Geoffrey Lyall, CB 1966; CBE 1946; DFC 1943; Manager, Regional Defence Sales, SE Asia, Plessey Singapore Pte Ltd; *b* 7 Jan. 1914; *s* of late Edward Turner Millington, Ceylon CS; *m* 1st, 1939, Mary Bonynge (marr. diss. 1956), *d* of W. Heaton Smith, FRCS; 2nd, 1956, Anne Elizabeth, *d* of Robert Brennan. *Educ:* Nautical Coll., Pangbourne. Served Cameron Highlanders, Palestine, 1936 (despatches); War of 1939-45, RAF, in N Africa, Sicily, Italy (actg Gp Capt.; despatches); Air Cdre, 1960; Comdr, RAF Persian Gulf, 1964-66; Air Commander, Zambia Air Force, 1968-70; Air Defence Adviser, Singapore Air Defence Command, 1970-72. psc; idc; Order Mil. Valour (Poland). *Address:* c/o Williams & Glyn's Bank Ltd, Holt's Branch, 22 Whitehall, SW1. *Club:* Royal Air Force.

MILLINGTON, Wing Comdr Ernest Rogers, DFC 1945; Teacher in charge of Teachers' Centre, London Borough of Newham, since 1967; Editor, Project; *b* 15 Feb. 1916; *s* of Edmund Rogers Millington and Emily Craggs; *m* 1st, 1937 (marr. diss. 1974); four *d*; 2nd, 1975, Ivy Mary Robinson. *Educ:* Chigwell Sch., Essex; College of S Mark and S John, Chelsea; Birkbeck Coll., London Univ. Clerk; Accountant; Company Sec.; served War of 1939-45, soldier, gunner officer, pilot RAF, instructor and heavy bomber, CO of a Lancaster Sqdn. MP (Commonwealth) for Chelmsford, 1945-50. Re-joined Royal Air Force, 1954-57. Head of Social Educn, Shoreditch Comprehensive Sch., London, 1965-67. *Publication:* (ed) A Study of Film. *Recreations:* educational research; social curiosity. *Address:* 85 Upminster Road, Hornchurch, Essex. *T:* Hornchurch 43852.

MILLINGTON-DRAKE, James Mackay Henry; Managing Director, Inchcape & Co. Ltd, since 1976, Director since 1971; Director, Commonwealth Development Corporation, since 1972; *b* 10 Jan. 1928; *s* of Sir (John Henry) Eugen Vanderstegen Millington-Drake, KCMG and Lady Effie Millington-Drake; *m* 1953, Manon Marie Redvers-Bate; two *s* two *d*. *Educ:* Upper Canada Coll., Toronto; RNC Dartmouth. Joined Inchcape Group, London, 1956: Sydney, 1958-65; UK, 1965; now Exec. Dir, Inchcape & Co. Ltd, and Dir, Inchcape Overseas Ltd, with special responsibilities for Middle East and all marine ops in Group. Governor, Reed's Sch., Cobham. Chevalier, Royal

Order of Swedish Sword, 1949. *Recreations:* tennis, swimming, ski-ing, water ski-ing. *Address:* Manor House, Shepperton-on-Thames, Mddx. *T:* Walton-on-Thames 28762. *Clubs:* City of London, All England Lawn Tennis and Croquet; Union (Sydney).

MILLIS, Charles Howard Goulden, DSO 1918; OBE 1946; MC; *b* 1894; *e s* of C. T. Millis; *m* 1919, Violet, *o c* of late Herbert J. Gifford; one *s* one *d. Educ:* King's Coll. Sch.; Oxford, MA. Served European War, 1914-18, Brevet Major (despatches, DSO, MC and bar, Croix de Guerre with Palm, France); served War of 1939-45 (OBE). Managing Director, Baring Brothers & Co. Ltd, 1933-55; Vice-Chm., BBC, 1937-45; Mem., Nat. Res. Develt Corp., 1955-65; Rhodes Trustee, 1948-61. *Address:* 22 Belvedere Grove, SW19 7RL.

MILLIS, Sir Leonard (William Francis), Kt 1977; CBE 1970 (OBE 1948); JP; Secretary from 1939, subsequently Director and President, 1973, British Waterworks Association; *b* 1 Aug. 1908; *o s* of William John Millis and Jessie Millis, Hackney; *m* 1932, Ethel May, *o c* of John T. W. Willmott, Enfield; two *d* (and one *d* decd). *Educ:* Grocers' Company Sch., Hackney; London Sch. of Economics (BSc Econ). Called to Bar, Inner Temple, 1936; served with Metropolitan Water Board; Asst Sec., British Waterworks Assoc. Pres., Internat. Water Supply Assoc., 1974 (Sec.-Gen., 1947-72); Chm., North Surrey Water Co., 1956-; Thames Conservator, 1959-74; Chm., Sutton District Water Co., 1971-. Member: Council, Water Companies Assoc.; Nat. Water Council, 1973-; Water Services Staff Commn, 1973-; Commn on High Water Charges in Wales, 1974-. Sec., Public Works and Municipal Services Congress Council, 1965-; Vice-Pres., Freshwater Biological Assoc.; Vice-Chm. of Council, Water Research Assoc.; Master, Plumbers' Co.; Mem., Water Supply Industry Trng Board, 1966-74. Hon. MIWE 1966; Hon. Member: Amer. Water Works Assoc., 1969; Deutsche Verein von Gas- und Wasserfachmannern, 1974. JP Mddx (Barnet Div.). *Publications:* contribs to scientific and technical papers, also other papers about water supply. *Recreations:* reading, gardening, sport. *Address:* Covenden, 17 Beech Hill, Hadley Wood, Barnet, Herts. *T:* 01-449 6164. *Club:* Lansdowne.

MILLN, Rear-Adm. William Bryan Scott, CB 1969; *b* 15 March 1915; *e s* of late Surg.-Captain James Duff Scott Milln; *m* 1944, Maureen Alice Gardner; four *d. Educ:* Mount House, Plymouth; RNC Dartmouth. RNEC, 1933-36 and 1942-44; RNC Greenwich, 1937-39; served in HMS: Royal Oak, 1932-33; Apollo, 1936-37; Birmingham, 1939-42; Tumult, 1944-46; Glory, 1952-54; Thunderer, 1954-57; Victorious, 1957-59; Engr-in-Chief's Dept, Admty, 1946-52; Staff of C-in-C Far East, 1959-61; Dep. Dir of Marine Engrg, 1961-64; Captain, HMS Thunderer, 1964-67; Asst Chief of Staff (Logistics), SHAPE, 1967-69, retired. Lt 1937; Lt-Comdr 1944; Comdr 1948; Captain 1959; Rear-Adm. 1967. *Recreations:* practically everything, now reduced to golf. *Address:* Burhill Golf Club, Walton-on-Thames, Surrey.

MILLNER, Ralph; QC 1965; *b* 25 Jan. 1912; *o s* of Ralph Millner, Merchant, Manchester; *m* 1st, 1935, Bruna, *d* of Arturo Rosa, Este, Italy (marr. diss. 1949); one *d* decd; 2nd, 1949, Monica, *d* of Prof. P. W. Robertson, Wellington, NZ; one *s* two *d. Educ:* William Hulme's Gram. Sch., Manchester; Clare Coll., Cambridge (MA); Bedford Coll., London (BA, Italian). Called to English Bar, Inner Temple, 1934; Ghana Bar (Gold Coast), 1950; Sierra Leone Bar, 1957; Nigerian Bar and S Cameroons Bar, 1959; Guyana Bar (formerly British Guiana), 1961; has also appeared in courts of Aden and Kenya. Lectr in Italian, QUB, 1972-77. Member: Soc. for Italian Studies; Haldane Soc. *Address:* 10 King's Bench Walk, Temple, EC4.

MILLOTT, Prof. Norman; Director of the University Marine Biological Station, Millport, 1970-76; *b* 24 Oct. 1912; *s* of Reuben Tomlinson Millott and Mary Millott (*née* Thistlethwaite); *m* 1939, Margaret Newns; three *d. Educ:* The Brunts Sch., Mansfield, Notts; Univs of Sheffield, Manchester, Cambridge. BSc 1935, MSc 1936 (Sheffield); PhD 1944 (Cambridge). Demonstrator in Zoology, Manchester Univ., 1935-36; Rouse Ball Student, Trinity Coll., Cambridge, 1936-38; Lectr in Zoology, Manchester Univ., 1938-40 and 1945-47. Commissioned RAFVR Technical Branch, 1940-45. Prof. of Zoology, University Coll. of the West Indies, 1948-55; Prof. of Zoology, Bedford Coll., London Univ., 1955-70, Emeritus Prof., 1976. Staff Councillor, 1957-60, and Dean of Faculty of Science, Bedford Coll., 1958-60; Chm. of Board of Studies in Zoology, Univ. of London, 1961-65; Chm. Photobiology Group, UK, 1960-62; Chm. Academic Advisory Board, Kingston-upon-Thames Technical Coll., 1960-66; Vice-Pres., International Congress of Photobiology, 1964; Mem. Council, Scottish Marine Biological Assoc., 1971-76. Royal Society Vis. Prof., Univ. of

Malta, 1976-77. Governor, Bedford Coll., London Univ., 1976-. DSc (Sheffield), 1961. *Publications:* scientific papers chiefly on invertebrate morphology, histology, physiology, and biochemistry. *Address:* Dunmore House, Millport, Isle of Cumbrae, Scotland.

MILLS, family name of **Baron Hillingdon** and **Viscount Mills.**

MILLS, 2nd Viscount, *cr* 1962; **Roger Clinton Mills;** Bt 1953; Baron 1957; Company Executive since 1963; *b* 14 June 1919; *o s* of 1st Viscount Mills, PC, KBE, and Winifred Mary (*d* 1974), *d* of George Conaty, Birmingham; *S* father, 1968; *m* 1945, Joan Dorothy, *d* of James Shirreff; one *s* two *d. Educ:* Canford Sch.; Jesus Coll., Cambridge. Served War as Major, RA, 1940-46. Administrative Officer, Colonial Service, Kenya, 1946-63. Barrister, Inner Temple, 1956. *Heir: s* Hon. Christopher Philip Roger Mills, *b* 20 May 1956. *Address:* Whitecroft, Abbey Road, Knaresborough, N Yorks. *T:* Harrogate 866201.

MILLS, Maj.-Gen. Alan Oswald Gawler; Director-General of Artillery, Ministry of Defence (Army), 1967-69, retired; *b* 11 March 1914; *o s* of John Gawler Mills; *m* 1941, Beata Elizabeth de Courcy Morgan Richards; one *s* one *d. Educ:* Marlborough Coll.; RMA, Woolwich. Commissioned RA, 1934; Hong Kong, 1938-45; Br. Jt Services Mission, USA, 1951-53; Techn SO Grade I, Min. of Supply, 1955-57; Mil. Dir of Studies, RMCS, 1957-61; Sen. Mil. Officer, Royal Armament Research and Develt Estabt, 1961-62; BGS, WO, 1962-65; Dir, Guided Weapons Trials, Min. of Aviation, 1966. CEng, MRAeS. *Recreations:* sailing, ski-ing. *Address:* 3 Seafield Terrace, Seaview, IoW. *T:* Seaview 3166. *Clubs:* Royal Thames Yacht; Royal London Yacht, Island Sailing (Cowes); Seaview Yacht.

MILLS, Major Anthony David; Secretary and Treasurer, All England Lawn Tennis Club, since 1963; *b* 14 Dec. 1918; *s* of late Maj.-Gen. Sir Arthur Mills, CB, DSO; *m* 1948, Anne (*née* Livingstone); two *d. Educ:* Wellington Coll.; RMC, Sandhurst. Commnd Indian Army, 1939, 9th Gurkha Rifles; served War of 1939-45, NW Frontier and Burma, regimental duty and various staff appts; seconded Indian Para. Regt, 1944; retd from Army 1948. Apptd Asst Sec., All England Lawn Tennis Club and Wimbledon Championships, 1948. *Recreations:* golf, dog walking, consulting Who's Who. *Address:* 271 Church Road, Wimbledon SW19 5AF. *T:* 01-946 2244. *Clubs:* All England Lawn Tennis; Royal Wimbledon Golf.

MILLS, Prof. Bernard Yarnton, AC 1976; FRS 1963; FAA 1959; DSc Eng; Professor of Physics (Astrophysics), University of Sydney, since 1965; *b* 8 Aug. 1920; *s* of Ellice Yarnton Mills and Sylphide Mills. *Educ:* King's Sch., New South Wales; University of Sydney. BSc 1940, DSc Eng 1959 (Sydney). Joined the then Council for Scientific and Industrial Research and worked on Develt of mil. radar systems; after working for many years on radioastronomy he joined Sydney Univ. to form a radioastronomy group in Sch. of Physics, 1960; Reader in Physics, 1960-65; responsible for Mills Cross radio-telescope, near Hoskinstown, NSW. Lyle Medal of Australian Academy of Science, 1957. *Publications:* (jtly) A Textbook of Radar, 1946; many contrib. sci. jls in Australia, England and America, mainly on subject of radioastronomy. *Address:* c/o School of Physics, University of Sydney, Sydney, NSW 2006, Australia.

MILLS, (Charles) Ernest; Member, British Gas Corporation, since 1973 (Member for Economic Planning, Gas Council, 1968-72); *b* 9 Dec. 1916; *s* of late Charles and Mary Elizabeth Mills; *m* 1943, Irene Hickman; one *s* one *d. Educ:* Barnsley and District Holgate Grammar Sch.; Manchester Coll. of Technology. Administrative Staff Coll., Henley, 1958. Inspector of Naval Ordnance, 1939-45. Engrg Asst, Rochdale Corp. Gas Dept, 1945-51; East Midlands Gas Board: Asst Divisional Engr, 1951-54; Divisional Engr, 1954-58; Asst Chief Engr and Production Controller, 1958-61; Chief Engr and Production Controller, 1961-64; Dep. Chm., E Midlands Gas Bd, 1964-66, Chm., W Midlands Gas Bd, 1966-68. *Recreations:* travel, sports. *Address:* Long Rafters, Sheethanger Lane, Felden, Hemel Hempstead, Herts. *T:* Hemel Hempstead 55220.

MILLS, Vice-Adm. Sir Charles (Piercy), KCB 1968 (CB 1964); CBE 1957; DSC 1953; *b* 4 Oct. 1914; *s* of late Capt. Thomas Piercy Mills, Woking, Surrey; *m* 1944, Anne Cumberlege; two *d. Educ:* RN College, Dartmouth. Joined Navy, 1928; Comdr 1947; Capt. 1953; Rear-Adm. 1963; Vice-Adm. 1966. Served War of 1939-45, Home Waters, Mediterranean and Far East; Korea, 1951-52; Flag Officer, Second in Command, Far East Fleet, 1966-67; C-in-C Plymouth, 1967-69; Lieut-Governor and C-in-C Guernsey, 1969-74. US Legion of Merit, 1955. KStJ 1969. *Recreations:* golf, sailing. *Address:* Park Lodge, Aldeburgh, Suffolk. *T:* Aldeburgh 2115.

MILLS, Edward (David), CBE 1959; FRIBA; Architect and Design Consultant in private practice since 1937; *b* 19 March 1915; *s* of Edward Ernest Mills; *m* 1939, Elsie May Bryant; one *s* one *d. Educ:* Ensham Sch.; Polytechnic Sch. of Architecture. ARIBA 1937, FRIBA 1946. Mem. of RIBA Council, 1954-62 and 1964-69; Chm. RIBA Bd of Architectural Education, 1960-62 (Vice-Chm., 1958-60); Pres., Soc. of Architectural Illustrators. RIBA Alfred Bossom Research Fellow, 1953; Churchill Fellow, 1969. FSIA 1975; Mem., Uganda Soc. of Architects. Chm., Faculty Architecture, British School at Rome. Architect for British Industries Pavilion, Brussels Internat. Exhibn, 1958; works include: Nat. Exhibn Centre, Birmingham, churches, schools, industrial buildings, research centres, flats and houses in Great Britain and overseas. *Publications:* The Modern Factory, 1951; The New Architecture in Great Britain, 1953; The Modern Church, 1956; Architects Details, Vols 1-6, 1952-61; Factory Building, 1967; The Changing Workplace, 1971; Planning, 1972; The National Exhibition Centre, 1976; contribs to RIBA journal, Architectural Review, etc. *Recreations:* photography, foreign travel. *Address:* Gate House Farm, Newchapel, Lingfield, Surrey. *T:* Lingfield 832241.

MILLS, Eric Robertson; Registrar of the Privy Council since 1966; *b* 27 July 1918; *s* of late Thomas Piercy Mills, Woking, Surrey; *m* 1950, Shirley Manger; two *d. Educ:* Charterhouse; Trinity Coll., Cambridge (BA). Served Royal Artillery, 1939-46; Major 1944. Called to Bar, Inner Temple, 1947; Mem. of Western Circuit. Dep. Judge Advocate, 1955; Chief Clerk, Judicial Cttee of Privy Council, 1963. *Publications:* contribs to legal text books. *Address:* Lamber Green, St Catherines Drive, Guildford, Surrey GU2 5HE. *T:* Guildford 37218.

MILLS, Ernest; *see* Mills, C. E.

MILLS, Frank, CMG 1971; HM Diplomatic Service; High Commissioner to Ghana, since 1975; concurrently Ambassador to Togo, since 1976; *b* 3 Dec. 1923; *s* of Joseph Francis Mills and Louisa Mills; *m* 1953, Trilby Foster; one *s* two *d. Educ:* King Edward VI Sch., Nuneaton; Emmanuel Coll., Cambrdige. RAFVR, 1942-45. CRO, 1948; 2nd Sec., British High Commn in Pakistan, 1949-51; Private Sec. to Parly Under-Sec. of State, 1952-53; 1st Sec., British High Commn in S Africa, 1955-58; Principal Private Sec. to Sec. of State, 1960-62; British High Commn in Malaya, 1962-63; Counsellor, British High Commn in Malaysia (Kuala Lumpur and Singapore), 1963-65; Dep. High Comr in Singapore, 1965-66; Dep. Head of Personnel Operation Dept, DSAO and FCO, 1966-69; Hd of Personnel Policy Dept, FCO, 1969-71; RCDS, 1971-72; Counsellor and Head of Chancery, 1972-74, Minister, 1974-75, New Delhi. *Recreation:* golf. *Address:* c/o Foreign and Commonwealth Office, SW1. *Club:* Royal Commonwealth Society.

MILLS, Maj.-Gen. Giles Hallam, CB 1977; OBE 1964; *b* 1 April 1922; 2nd *s* of late Col Sir John Digby Mills, TD, Bisterne Manor, Ringwood, Hampshire, and of Lady Mills; *m* 1947, Emily Snowden Hallam, 2nd *d* of late Captain W. H. Tuck, Perrywood, Maryland, USA, and of Mrs Tuck; two *s* one *d. Educ:* Eton Coll. Served War: 2nd Lieut, KRRC, 1941; 1st Bn, KRRC, N Africa, Italy (Adjt, despatches), 1943-47. Staff Coll., 1951; Armed Forces Staff Coll. (US), 1959; Mil. Asst to CIGS, 1961-63; CO, 2 Green Jackets, KRRC, 1963-65; Admin. Staff Coll., Henley; 1965; Regtl Col, Royal Green Jackets, 1966-67; Comd, 8 Infty Bde, 1968-69; IDC 1970; Comd, British Army Staff and Mil. Attaché, Washington, 1971-73; Divl Brig., The Light Div., 1973-74; Dir of Manning (Army), 1974-77, retd. *Publication:* Annals of The King's Royal Rifle Corps, vol. VI (with Roger Nixon), 1971. *Recreations:* gardening, bird-watching, fishing, shooting, history. *Address:* Leeland House, Twyford, Winchester, Hants SO21 1NP. *T:* Twyford 713298. *Club:* Army and Navy.

MILLS, Herbert Horatio, MC 1944; Rector of the Edinburgh Academy, 1962-77; *b* Jan. 1919; *s* of Edward Charles and Sarah Mills. *Educ:* Marling Sch.; St Catharine's Coll., Cambridge (PhD). Commonwealth Fellow, University of Pennsylvania, USA, 1950. Asst Master, Sedbergh Sch., 1953-62. *Recreations:* mountaineering; Cambridge Rugby XV, 1947, 1948. *Clubs:* Alpine; Scottish Mountaineering; Scottish Arts (Edinburgh).

MILLS, Ivor Henry, FRCP; Professor of Medicine in the University of Cambridge since 1963; Fellow Churchill College, Cambridge; Hon. Consultant to United Cambridge Hospitals; *b* 13 June 1921; 3rd *s* of late J. H. W. Mills and late Priscilla Mills; *m* 1947, Sydney Elizabeth Puleston (*née* Roberts); one *s* one *d. Educ:* Selhurst Grammar Sch., Croydon; Queen Mary Coll., London; Trinity Coll., Cambridge. BSc (London) 1942; PhD (London) 1946; BA (Cantab) 1948; MB, BChir Cantab 1951;

MRCP 1953; MD Cantab 1956; MA Cantab 1963; FRCP 1964. Pres. Cambridge Univ. Medical Soc., 1947-48; Sen. Schol., Trinity Coll., Cambridge, 1948; MRC (Eli Lilly) Trav. Fellow, 1956; Vis. Scientist, Nat. Inst. of Health, 1957; Lectr in Medicine and Chem. Path., St Thomas's Hosp. Medical Sch., 1954; Reader in Medicine, St Thomas's Hosp. Medical Sch., London, 1962. Vis. Prof. in Physiology and Medicine, N Carolina Med. Sch., USA, 1972. Mem., Hunter Working Party on Medical Administrators, 1970-72. Sec., Soc. for Endocrinology, 1963-71; Mem. Council, RCP, 1971-74. Pro-Censor, RCP, 1974-75, Censor, 1975-76. Hon. FACP. *Publications:* Clinical Aspects of Adrenal Function, 1964; contrib. Lancet, Science Jl of Endocr., Clin. Science, etc. *Recreation:* gardening. *Address:* Addenbrooke's Hospital, Cambridge.

MILLS, John F. F. P.; *see* Platts-Mills.

MILLS, Sir John (Lewis Ernest Watts), Kt 1976; CBE 1960; Actor, Producer, Director; *b* 22 Feb. 1908; *m* 1941, Mary Hayley Bell, playwright; one *s* two *d. Educ:* Norwich. 1st appearance, stage, 1929. *Plays:* Cavalcade, London Wall, Words and Music, Five O'clock Girl, Give Me a Ring, Jill Darling, Floodlight, Red Night, We at the Cross Roads, Of Mice and Men, Men in Shadow, Duet for Two Hands, etc.; Old Vic Season, 1938; Top of the Ladder; Figure of Fun, Aldwych; Ross, New York, 1961; Power of Persuasion, Garrick, 1963; Veterans, Royal Court, 1972; At the End of the Day, Savoy, 1973; The Good Companions, Her Majesty's, 1974; Separate Tables, Apollo, 1977. *Films:* The Midshipmaid, Britannia of Billingsgate, Brown on Resolution, OHMS, Cottage To Let, The Young Mr Pitt, We Dive at Dawn, In Which We Serve, The Way to the Stars, Great Expectations, So Well Remembered, The October Man, Scott of the Antarctic, The History of Mr Polly, The Rocking Horse Winner, Morning Departure, Mr Denning Drives North, Gentle Gunman, The Long Memory, Hobson's Choice, The Colditz Story, The End of the Affair, Above Us the Waves, Town on Trial, Escapade, Its Great to be Young, The Baby and the Battleship, War and Peace, Around the World in Eighty Days, Dunkirk, Ice Cold in Alex, I Was Monty's Double, Summer of the Seventeenth Doll, Tiger Bay, Swiss Family Robinson, The Singer not the Song, Tunes of Glory, Flame in the Streets, The Valiant, Tiara Tahiti, The Chalk Garden, The Truth about Spring, King Rat, Operation X Bow, Red Waggon, Sky West and Crooked (directed), The Wrong Box, The Family Way, Chuka, Showdown, Oh What a Lovely War, The Return of the Boomerang, Ryan's Daughter (Best Supporting Actor Award, Oscar Award, 1971), Run Wild, Run Free, Emma Hamilton, Dulcima, Lamb, Young Winston; Oklahoma Crude; Trial by Combat; The Devil's Advocate; Great Expectations, stage, 1975. *TV series:* The Zoo Gang, 1974; The Human Factor, 1975. Member: SFTA (Vice-Pres.); RADA Council, 1965-; Chm., Stars Organization for Spastics, 1975. Patron Life Mem., Variety Club. *Recreations:* ski-ing, golf, painting. *Address:* c/o ICM, 22 Grafton Street, W1. *Club:* Garrick.

MILLS, Prof. John Norton, MA, DM Oxon, MD Cantab; Brackenbury Professor of Physiology, University of Manchester since October 1965; *b* 28 June 1914; *s* of George Percival Mills, Consultant Surgeon, and T. M. Cristabel (*née* Humphreys); *m* 1942, June Rosemary Jill Brenan; one *s* two *d. Educ:* Winchester; New Coll., Oxford; Christ Church, Oxford. Lecturer, New Coll., Oxford, 1941-46; Fellow and Lecturer, Jesus Coll., Cambridge, 1946-50; University of Manchester: Lecturer in Human Physiology, 1950; Sen. Lecturer, 1955; Reader in Physiology, 1959. *Publications:* (with R. T. W. L. Conroy) Human Circadian Rhythms, 1969; Chapters in: Recent Advances in Physiology (ed R. Creese), 1962; A Companion to Medical Studies (ed Passmore and Robson), 1968; Modern Trends in Physiology (ed C. B. B. Downman), 1972; Scientific Foundations of Paediatrics (ed Davis and Dobbing), 1974; ed and contrib. Biological Aspects of Circadian Rhythms, 1973; papers in Jl Physiol., Clin. Sci., Jl Endocrin., Brit. Med. Bulletin, Chronobiologia, Internat. Jl Chronobiol., etc. *Recreations:* rock climbing, walking, field botany. *Address:* 4 Lancaster Road, Didsbury, Manchester M20 8TY. *T:* 061-445 2949.

MILLS, John Robert, BSc, CEng, FIEE, MInstP; Under Secretary and Deputy Director (Systems) Royal Signals and Radar Establishment, Ministry of Defence, 1976-77; *b* 12 Nov. 1916; *s* of Robert Edward Mills and Constance H. Mills; *m* 1950, Pauline Phelps; two *s. Educ:* Kingston Grammar Sch., Kingston-upon-Thames; King's Coll., London (BSc 1939); MInstP; FIEE, 1971. Air Ministry Research Estab., Dundee, 1939; RAE Farnborough, 1940-42; TRE, later RRE, Malvern, 1942-60; Supt (Offensive), Airborne Radar, RRE, 1954-60; Asst Dir, Electronics R and D (Civil Aviation), Min. of Aviation,

1960-61; Head of Radio Dept, RAE Farnborough, 1961-65; Electronics Div., Min. of Technology, 1965-67; Dir, Signals R&D Establishment, MoD, 1967-76. *Publications:* (jointly) Radar article in Encyclopædia Britannica; various papers in journals. *Address:* Little Chewton, Chewton Farm Road, Highcliffe, Christchurch, Dorset.

MILLS, (John) Vivian G.; *b* 22 Sept. 1887; *s* of late Comdr J. F. Mills, ISO, RN (retd); *m* 1st, 1915, Lilian (*d* 1947), *d* of late A. Brisley; no *c*; 2nd, 1968, Marguerite Mélanie, *d* of late Jean Hoffman. Educ: privately; Merton Coll., Oxford; Classical Mods and Lit Hum; MA 1946; DLitt 1974. Barrister-at-law, Middle Temple, 1919; Cadet, Malayan Civil Service, 1911; qualified in Chinese, 1914; held various administrative, legal and judicial appointments, 1914-28; Solicitor-Gen., Straits Settlements, 1928-32; acting Attorney-Gen., and Mem. of the Executive and Legislative Councils, 1932; Commissioner of Currency, 1932; Puisne Judge, Straits Settlements, 1933; Judge, Johore, 1934; retired, 1940; Attached to office of Federal Attorney-Gen., Sydney, Australia, 1944-45; Additional Lecturer in Chinese Law, School of Oriental and African Studies, London, 1946-47; Pres. of Malayan Branch, Royal Asiatic Society, 1936; Joint Hon. Sec., Hakluyt Soc., 1950-53. *Publications:* Eredia's Malaca, Meridional India and Cathay, 1930; Malaya in the Wu-pei-chi Charts, 1937; (trans. and ed) Ma Huan: Ying-yai sheng-lan, The Overall Survey of the Ocean's Shores, 1970; various official publications. *Recreations:* Oriental research and watching first-class cricket. *Address:* Bellaria 62, 1814 La Tour de Peilz, Switzerland. *Club:* Athenæum.

MILLS, John William, OBE 1945; QC 1962; *b* 24 Oct. 1914; *s* of late John William Mills, OBE and Jessie Mills; *m* 1942, Phyllis Mary, *yr d* of late Arthur Gibson Pears; no *c*. *Educ:* Clifton; Corpus Christi Coll., Cambridge (MA). Called to Bar, Middle Temple, 1938; Bencher, 1968. Lt-Col, Royal Signals, 1944; Comdr, Royal Signals, 46 Div., 1944. Member: Bar Council, 1961-64; Clifton Coll. Council, 1967-. *Publications:* The Building Societies Act, 1960, 1961, Wurtzburg and Mills, Building Society Law, 1964-. *Recreations:* sailing, golf. *Address:* 38 Adam and Eve Mews, W8. *T:* 01-937 1259; 11 Old Square, Lincoln's Inn, WC2. *T:* 01-405 5243; Greenleas, Highleigh, Chichester, Sussex. *T:* Sidlesham 396.

MILLS, Laurence John; Member, National Coal Board since 1974; *b* 1 Oct. 1920; *s* of late Archibald John and Annie Ellen Mills; *m* 1944, Barbara May (*née* Warner); two *s. Educ:* Portsmouth Grammar Sch.; Birmingham Univ. BSc, CEng, FIMinE. Mining Student, Houghton Main Colliery Co. Ltd, 1939; Corps of Royal Engrs, 1942-46, Major 1946; various mining appts, Nat. Coal Bd: Man., Hemsworth Colliery, 1949; Man., South Kirkby Colliery, 1951; Agent, Frickley and South Elmsall Collieries, 1951; Dep. Area Prodn Man. (Reconstruction and Develt), No 3 Area, E Mids Div., 1954; Dep. Area Prodn Man. (Ops), No 7 Area, E Mids Div., 1957; Area Prodn Man., No 7 Area, E Mids Div., 1960; Asst Area Gen. Man., N Staffs Area, 1964; Dep. Dir (O) S Durham Area, 1967; Chief Mining Engr, HQ NCB, 1968; Area Dir, N Yorks Area, 1970; Area Dir, Doncaster Area, 1973. Member: Mining Qualifications Bd, 1975-; Adv. Council of Res. and Develt, 1975-. President: S Mids Br., NACM, 1961-62; Midland Counties Instn Engrs, 1962-63; IMinE, 1975. *Publications:* techn. papers in Trans IMinE. *Recreation:* coastal and inland waterway cruising. *Address:* Silver Birches, 33 Dove Park, Chorley Wood, Rickmansworth, Herts WD3 5NY. *T:* Chorley Wood 4281.

MILLS, Lawrence William Robert; Counsellor (Hong Kong Affairs), Hong Kong Office, UK Mission, Geneva, since 1976; *b* London, 7 May 1934; *s* of William H. Mills and E. May Mills; *m* 1964, Amy Kwai Lan (*née* Poon), Shanghai and Hong Kong; two *d. Educ:* Reigate Grammar Sch., Surrey. National Service: RN, 1953; Intell. Corps, 1954. Formerly, Jun. Exec., K. F. Mayer Ltd, London. Hong Kong Govt (Mem. of HMOCS): Exec. Officer, Cl. II, 1958; Asst Trade Officer, 1960; Trade Officer, 1964; Sen. Trade Officer, 1968; Principal Trade Officer, 1969; Asst Dir of Commerce and Industry, 1971; Chief Trade Negotiator, 1974-75. *Recreation:* music (classical jazz). *Address:* 20 Chemin d'Orbemont, 1260 Nyon, Vaud, Switzerland. *T:* Geneva 34 43 51; Queen's Gardens, Old Peak Road, Hong Kong. *T:* Hong Kong 22 63 63. *Clubs:* Hong Kong, Hong Kong Country (Hong Kong).

MILLS, Leif Anthony; General Secretary, National Union of Bank Employees, since 1972; *b* 25 March 1936; *s* of English father and Norwegian mother; *m* 1958, Gillian Margaret Smith; two *s* two *d. Educ:* Balliol Coll., Oxford. BA Hons PPE. Commnd in Royal Military Police, 1957-59. Trade Union Official, Nat. Union of Bank Employees, from 1960: Research

Officer, 1960; Asst Gen. Sec., 1962; Dep. Gen. Sec., 1968. Mem. various arbitration tribunals; Mem. TUC Non-Manual Workers Adv. Cttee, 1967-72; Office of Manpower Economics Adv. Cttee on Equal Pay, 1971. Mem., Cttee to Review the Functioning of Financial Institutions, 1977-. *Publication:* biography (unpublished), Cook: A History of the Life and Explorations of Dr Frederick Albert Cook, SPRI ms 883, Cambridge, 1970. *Recreations:* rowing, chess, squash. *Address:* 31 Station Road, West Byfleet, Surrey. *T:* Byfleet 42829. *Clubs:* Oxford University Boat, Weybridge Rowing; OT Squash.

MILLS, Leonard Sidney, CB 1970; Deputy Director General (2), Highways, Department of the Environment, 1970-74; *b* 20 Aug. 1914; *s* of late Albert Edward Mills; *m* 1940, Kathleen Joyce Cannicott; two *s. Educ:* Devonport High Sch.; London Sch. of Economics; Birkbeck Coll., University of London. Entered Exchequer and Audit Dept, 1933; transferred to Min. of Civil Aviation, 1946; Asst Sec., 1950; Min. of Transport: Under-Sec., 1959; Chief of Highway Administration, 1968-70. Commonwealth Fund Fellow, 1953-54. *Recreations:* walking and gardening. *Address:* Pine Rise, 7A Bedlands Lane, Budleigh Salterton, Devon.

MILLS, Neil McLay; Chairman, Bland Payne Holdings Ltd, since 1974; *b* 29 July 1923; *yr s* of L. H. Mills and Mrs Mills; *m* 1950, Rosamund Mary Kimpton, *d* of Col and Hon. Mrs A. C. W. Kimpton; two *s* two *d. Educ:* Epsom Coll.; London Univ. Served War, 1939-45: commnd RN; Lieut RNVR; Coastal Forces (mentioned in despatches, 1944). Joined Bland Welch & Co. Ltd, 1948; Exec. Dir, 1955; Chm., 1965. Underwriting Mem. of Lloyd's, 1955-. Director: Montagu Trust Ltd, 1966-74; Midland Bank Ltd, 1974-. Vice-President: Insurance Inst. of London, 1971-; Corp. of Insurance Brokers, 1972-. Member: Cttee, Lloyd's Ins. Brokers Assoc., 1974-; (Alternate), Cttee on Invisible Exports, 1975-; Church Army Board, 1957-64 (Vice-Chm., 1959-64); Council, Oak Hill Theol Coll., 1958-62. Trustee and Governor, Lord Mayor Treloar Trust, 1975-. Diocesan Lay Preacher, C of E, 1955-70. *Recreation:* farming. *Address:* Sackville House, 143/9 Fenchurch Street, EC3M 6BN; The Dower House, Upton Grey, near Basingstoke, Hants. *T:* Long Sutton 435. *Club:* Bath.

MILLS, Sir Peter (Frederick Leighton), 3rd Bt, *cr* 1921; *b* 9 July 1924; *s* of Major Sir Frederick Leighton Victor Mills, 2nd Bt, MC, RA, MICE, and Doris (*née* Armitage); *S* father 1955; *m* 1954, Pauline Mary, *d* of L. R. Allen, Calverton, Notts; one *s* one adopted *d. Educ:* Eastbourne Coll.; Cedara Coll. of Agriculture, University of Natal (BSc Agric.). Served HM Forces, 1943-47. CS, Fedn Rhodesia and Nyasaland, 1953; with Rhodesia Min. of Agric., 1964-. *Heir: s* Michael Victor Leighton Mills, *b* 30 Aug. 1957. *Address:* Henderson Research Station, P. Bag 222a, Salisbury, Rhodesia.

MILLS, Peter McLay; MP (C) Devon West, since 1974 (Torrington, 1964-74); Farmer; *b* 22 Sept. 1921; *m* 1948, Joan Weatherley; one *s* one *d. Educ:* Epsom; Wye Coll. Farmer since 1943. Parly Sec., MAFF, 1972; Parly Under-Sec. of State, NI Office, 1972-74. Mem., European Secondary Legislation Cttee, EEC, 1974-. *Recreations:* work and staying at home for a short time. *Address:* House of Commons, SW1. *T:* 01-219 4093.

MILLS, Peter William; *b* 22 July 1942; *s* of Joseph Roger Mills and Jane Eveyln (*née* Roscoe); *m* 1967, Eveline Jane (*née* Black); two *s. Educ:* Dalhousie Univ. Law Sch. (LLB); Dalhousie Univ. (BComm). Barrister and solicitor, Ont and NS, Canada; with McInnes, Cooper and Robertson, Halifax, 1967; Solicitor, Canadian Pacific Ltd, Montreal and Toronto, 1967-71; Dir, Cammell Laird Shipbuilders Ltd, 1971-76; Mem. Org. Cttee for British Shipbuilders, 1976-77. *Recreations:* golf, sailing, travel, reading. *Address:* Montana, Vyner Road South, Noctorum, Birkenhead, Merseyside L43 7PW. *T:* 051-652 8573. *Clubs:* Birkenhead Constitutional (Birkenhead); Royal Liverpool Golf (Holylake).

MILLS, Air Cdre Stanley Edwin Druce, CB 1968; CBE 1959; Royal Air Force, retired; *b* 1913; *s* of Edwin J. Mills; *m* 1938, Joan Mary, *d* of Robert Ralph James; one *s* one *d. Educ:* Collegiate Sch., Bournemouth, RAF Staff Coll. Entered RAF 1939; served RAF Middle East and Italy, 1942-45; Station Comdr, RAF Innsworth, 1957-60; Comd Accountant, RAF Germany, 1960-63; Dir of Personnel (Policy) (Air), MoD, 1963-65; Dir of Personal Services (Air), MoD, 1966-68. Bursar, Roedean Sch., 1968-73. FCA. *Recreations:* caravanning, gardening. *Address:* Orana, Cuckmere Road, Seaford, E Sussex. *Club:* Royal Air Force.

MILLS, Brig. Stephen Douglas, CBE 1943; MC; *b* 1892; *s* of late Stephen E. Mills, JP, Longmead, Havant, Hants; *m* 1923,

Rosamond, *d* of late W. R. Merk, CSI, CIE, ICS; one *s* one *d*. *Educ:* Bradfield Coll.; RMC, Sandhurst. Late Beds and Herts Regt, European War 1914-19, in France, Belgium, and Palestine (wounded, MC); Palestine, 1936-39 (despatches); War of 1939-45 in Middle East (despatches, CBE); retired pay, 1946. *Address:* Quidhams, Bowerchalke, near Salisbury, Wilts. *T:* Broadchalke 243.

MILLS, Stratton; *see* Mills, W. S.

MILLS, Vivian; *see* Mills, J. V. G.

MILLS, Wilbur Daigh; lawyer and politician, USA; Chairman of Ways and Means Committee, US House of Representatives, 1958-74 (Member House, 1939-76); *b* Kensett, Ark, 24 May 1909; *s* of Ardra Pickens Mills and Abbie Lois Daigh; *m* 1934, Clarine Billingsley; two *d*. *Educ:* Hendrix Coll. (AB); Harvard Law Sch. Admitted to State Bar of Arkansas, 1933; in private legal practice, Searcy; County and Probate Judge, White County, 1934-38; Cashier, Bank of Kensett, 1934-35. Democrat. *Address:* Kensett, Arkansas 72082, USA; Searcy, Arkansas 72143, USA.

MILLS, Maj.-Gen. William Graham Stead, CBE 1963; Warden of the Court, Liss, Home for Physically Disabled People; *b* 23 June 1917; *s* of William Stead Mills and Margaret Kennedy Mills; *m* 8 July 1941, Joyce Evelyn (*née* Ransom); three *s*. *Educ:* Merchiston Castle Sch., Edinburgh. Regtl duty, Royal Berks Regt, in India, 1938-43; Staff Coll., India, 1944; GSO2 and GSO1, Ops HQ 14th Army, Burma, 1944-45; WO and Washington, USA, 1946-50; Regtl duty with Parachute Regt, comdg 17th Bn, The Parachute Regt, 1958-60; GSO1, 2 Div. BAOR, 1956-58; Regtl Col The Parachute Regt, 1960-62; Comdg TA Brigade, Winchester, 1963-64; Brig. GS, HQ Middle East Comd, Aden, 1965-66; Imperial Defence Coll., Student, 1967; GOC West Midland District, 1968-70. *Recreations:* normal. *Address:* Broome House, Selborne, Hants. *T:* Selborne 305. *Club:* Army and Navy.

MILLS, (William) Stratton; Partner in Mills, Selig & Bailie, Solicitors, Belfast; Company Director: *b* 1 July 1932; *o s* of late Dr J. V. S. Mills, CBE, Resident Magistrate for City of Belfast, and Margaret Florence (*née* Byford); *m* 1959, Merriel E. R. Whitla, *o d* of Mr and Mrs R. J. Whitla, Belfast; three *s*. *Educ:* Campbell Coll., Belfast; Queen's Univ., Belfast (LLB). Vice-Chm., Federation of University Conservative and Unionist Assocs, 1952-53 and 1954-55; admitted a Solicitor, 1958. MP (UU) Belfast N, Oct. 1959-Dec. 1972; MP (Alliance) Belfast N, Apr. 1973-Feb. 1974; PPS to Parly Sec., Ministry of Transport, 1961-64; Member: Estimates Cttee, 1964-70; Exec. Cttee, 1922 Cttee, 1967-70, 1973; Hon. Sec. Conservative Broadcasting Cttee, 1963-70, Chm., 1970-73; Mem., Mr Speaker's Conference on Electoral Law, 1967. Mem., One Nation Gp, 1972-73. *Address:* (office) 20 Callender Street, Belfast 1. *T:* Belfast 43878; (home) 17 Malone Park, Belfast 9. *T:* Belfast 665210. *Clubs:* Junior Carlton; Ulster (Belfast).

MILLS BALDWIN, Nelson; *see* Baldwin, N. M.

MILLS-OWENS, Richard Hugh, CBE 1972; Puisne Judge, Hong Kong, 1967-71 (also 1961-64); Chief Justice, Fiji, 1964-67; *b* Jan. 1910; *s* of George Edward Owens and Jessie Mary Mills; *m* 1935, Elizabeth Ann Hiles (*d* 1968); two *s*. *Educ:* Rhyl Grammar Sch. Admitted Solicitor, 1932; Clifford's Inn Prizeman; Barrister-at-law, 1956, Middle Temple. Practised in Wales (including service with Carmarthenshire County Council) until 1949 when joined Colonial Legal Service as a Registrar of Titles; Principal Registrar, Kenya; Crown Counsel and Legal Draftsman, 1952; Magistrate, 1956, District Judge, 1958, Hong Kong. *Recreation:* golf. *Address:* Westwood, Hangersley, Ringwood, Hants.

MILLSON, John Albert; Assistant Under-Secretary of State (Organisation) (Air), Ministry of Defence, since 1976; *b* 4 Oct. 1918; *s* of late George Charles Millson and Annie Millson, London; *m* 1953, Megan Laura Woodiss; one *s* one *d*. *Educ:* St Olave's. Entered Air Min., 1936; Private Sec. to Parly Under-Sec. of State for Air, 1947-50; Principal, Air Min., 1955; Asst Sec., MoD, 1961; Asst Under-Sec. of State, 1972. Chm. of Governors, Homefield Prep. Sch., Sutton, 1975. *Recreations:* walking, listening to music. *Address:* 9 The Highway, Sutton, Surrey. *T:* 01-642 3967.

MILLWARD, William, CB 1969; CBE 1954; with Government Communications Headquarters, 1946-74, retired (Superintending Director, 1958-69); *b* 27 Jan. 1909; *s* of William John and Alice Millward; *m* 1937, Nora Florella Harper; one *s* one *d*. *Educ:* Solihull Sch.; St Catherine's Society, Oxford. Asst Master, Dulwich Coll., 1930-41; RAF, 1941-46. *Recreations:*

music, reading, walking. *Address:* Three Poplars, Evesham Road, Cheltenham, Glos. *T:* Cheltenham 25732.

MILMAN, Sir Dermot (Lionel Kennedy), 8th Bt, *cr* 1800; *b* 24 Oct. 1912; *e s* of Brig.-Gen. Sir Lionel Charles Patrick Milman, 7th Bt, CMG, and Marjorie Aletta, *d* of Col A. H. Clark-Kennedy, late Indian Civil Service; *S* father, 1962; *m* 1941, Muriel, *o d* of J. E. S. Taylor, King's Lynn; one *d*. *Educ:* Uppingham; Corpus Christi Coll., Cambridge. BA 1934, MA 1938. Served War of 1939-45, Royal Army Service Corps, in France, Belgium and Burma (despatches), Major. Hon. Major, RCT (formerly RARO, RASC). Assistant Dir, British Council Overseas Service (Bogota, Santiago, Lima, Milan, Peshawar), 1946-63; Liaison Officer for Hostel Develt, British Council, 1963-76. *Recreations:* Rugby football (Eng., 1937-38), cricket (Beds, Vice-Capt. 1935). *Heir:* *b* Malcolm Douglas Milman [*b* 18 May 1915; *m* 1940, Sheila Maud (marriage dissolved), *d* of Albert Maurice Dudeney; two *d*]. *Address:* 7 Old Westhall Close, Warlingham, Surrey. *T:* Upper Warlingham 4843.

MILMO, Hon. Sir Helenus Patrick Joseph, Kt 1964; DL; Hon. Mr Justice Milmo; Judge of High Court of Justice, Queen's Bench Division, since 1964; *b* 24 Aug. 1908; 3rd *s* of late Daniel Milmo, Furbough, Co. Galway, Eire; *m* 1933, Joan Frances, *d* of late Francis Morley, London; two *s* three *d* (and one *d* decd). *Educ:* Downside; Trinity Coll., Cambridge. Barrister, Middle Temple, 1931; Bencher, 1955; QC 1961; Dep. Treasurer, 1972; Treasurer 1973. Civil Asst, General Staff, War Office, 1940-45. Dep. Chm., West Sussex QS, 1960-64. DL Sussex, 1962. *Recreations:* hunting, fishing, wine. *Address:* Church Farm, Shipley, near Horsham, W Sussex. *T:* Coolham 261. *Clubs:* Pratts, Garrick, MCC.

MILNE, family name of **Baron Milne.**

MILNE, 2nd Baron, *cr* 1933, of Salonika and of Rubislaw, Co. Aberdeen; **George Douglass Milne;** *b* 10 Feb. 1909; *s* of 1st Baron Milne, GCB, GCMG, DSO, Field Marshal from 1928, and Claire Marjoribanks, MBE, DGStJ (*d* 1970), *d* of Sir John N. Maitland, 5th Bt; *S* father, 1948; *m* 1940, Cicely, 3rd *d* of late Ronald Leslie; two *s* one *d*. *Educ:* Winchester; New Coll., Oxford. Partner, Arthur Young McClelland Moores Co., 1954-73; Director: J. & W. Henderson Ltd; London & Northern Group Ltd; Oxo (UK) Ltd. Mem., Inst. of Chartered Accountants of Scotland. Master of the Grocers' Company, 1961-62. Served War of 1939-45, Royal Artillery (TA); prisoner of war, 1941; NWEF and MEF (wounded, despatches). *Recreation:* art: has exhibited RA, ROI, RP. *Heir:* *s* Hon. George Alexander Milne, *b* 1 April 1941. *Address:* 33 Lonsdale Road, Barnes, SW13. *T:* 01-748 6421; (business) Essex Hall, Essex Street, WC1.

MILNE, Alasdair David Gordon; Managing Director, BBC Television, since 1977; *b* 8 Oct. 1930; *s* of Charles Gordon Shaw Milne and Edith Reid Clark; *m* 1954, Sheila Kirsten Graucob; two *s* one *d*. *Educ:* Winchester Coll.; New Coll., Oxford. Commnd into 1st Bn Gordon Highlanders, 1949. Hon. Mods Oxon 1952; BA Oxon Mod. Langs, 1954. Joined BBC, 1954; Dep. Editor, 1957-61, Editor, 1961-62, of Tonight Programme; Head of Tonight Productions, 1963-65; Partner, Jay, Baverstock, Milne & Co., 1965-67; rejoined BBC, Oct. 1967; Controller, BBC Scotland, 1968-72; Dir of Programmes, BBC TV, 1973-77. *Recreations:* piping, salmon fishing, golf, tennis. *Address:* 30 Holland Park Avenue, W11. *T:* 01-229 3019. *Club:* Savile.

MILNE, Alexander Berkeley, OBE 1968; Counsellor, HM Diplomatic Service; *b* 12 Feb. 1924; *s* of George and Mary Milne; *m* 1952, Patricia Mary (*née* Holderness); one *s* two *d*. *Educ:* Keith Grammar and Buckie High Schs, Banffshire, Scotland; Univ. of Aberdeen (MA (Hons Mental Phil.) 1943); University Coll., Oxford (BA (Hons Persian and Arabic) 1949). 3/2nd Punjab Regt, Indian Army: service in India and Java, 1943-46. Scarborough Schol., Tehran Univ., 1950-51; Lectr in Persian, Edinburgh Univ., 1951-52. Foreign Office, 1952-53; BMEO, Cyprus, 1953-54; Third, later Second Sec., Tehran, 1954-57; FO, 1958-61; Second, later First Sec., Brussels, 1961-64; FO (later FCO), 1964-65; First Sec., British Residual Mission, Salisbury, Rhodesia, 1966-67; First Sec., Jedda, Saudi Arabia, 1968-70; FCO, 1971-74; Counsellor, Tehran, 1974-78. *Recreations:* gardening, reading; playing chamber music, preferably second violin in string quartets. *Address:* c/o Foreign and Commonwealth Office, SW1; (home) 120 York Road, Woking, Surrey GU22 7XS. *T:* Woking 73901. *Club:* Travellers'.

MILNE, Alexander George, CIE 1945; FICE, FIMechE; *b* Skene, Aberdeenshire, 27 July 1891; *s* of Alexander Milne; *m* 1927, Mary Agnes Murphy (*d* 1965), MB, BCh, DTM, *d* of P. J.

Murphy, Macroom, Cork; one d. *Educ:* Robert Gordon's Coll., Aberdeen. Pupil with late R. Gordon Nicol, OBE, MICE, MIMechE, Harbour Engineer, Aberdeen, 1908-13; in Admiralty Works Dept service HM Dockyard, Rosyth and Cromarty, 1913-18; Resident Engineer and Contractors' Agent various Public Works, England, 1918-23; Senior Asst Engineer and Exec. Engineer, Bombay Port Trust, 1923-27; from 1927 was engaged on opening up and development of Cochin Harbour, S India, as Exec. Engineer and Dep. Chief Engineer; Administrative Officer and Chief Engineer, Cochin Harbour, 1941-48. *Recreation:* golf. *Address:* c/o Bank of Scotland, Union Street, Aberdeen.

MILNE, Alexander Taylor; Fellow of University College London; Secretary and Librarian, Institute of Historical Research, University of London, 1946-71; *b* 22 Jan. 1906; *s* of late Alexander Milne and Shanny (*née* Taylor); *m* 1960, Joyce Frederica Taylor, Dulwich. *Educ:* Christ's Coll., Finchley; University Coll., London. BA History Hons 1927; Diploma in Education, 1928; MA (London), 1930; FRHistS, 1938; Vice-Pres., Historical Assoc., 1956-70, Pres., 1970-73; Asst Officer and Librarian, Royal Historical Society, 1935-40; Hon. Librarian, 1965-70. Fellow, Huntington Library, Calif, 1975. Served War of 1939-45: Buffs and Maritime Artillery, 1940-42; Army Bureau of Current Affairs, 1942-44; Research Dept, FO, 1944-46. Director, History Today, 1962-. *Publications:* History of Broadwindsor, Dorset, 1935; Catalogue of the Manuscripts of Jeremy Bentham in the Library of University College, London, 1937, 2nd edn 1961; Writings on British History, 1934-45: a Bibliography (8 vols), 1937-60; Centenary Guide to Pubns of Royal Historical Society, 1968; (part-author) Historical Study in the West, 1968; (ed) Librarianship and Literature, essays in honour of Jack Pafford, 1970; contribs to Cambridge History of the British Empire, Encyclopædia Britannica and learned journals. *Recreation:* golf. *Address:* 9 Frank Dixon Close, Dulwich, SE21 7BD. *T:* 01-693 6942. *Clubs:* Athenæum, Dulwich (1772).

MILNE, Archibald George, CBE 1975; CEng, FIMechE, FIEE; Chairman: British Approvals Service for Electric Cables, since 1974; British National Committee, International Conference on Electricity Distribution, since 1975; *b* 19 Feb. 1910; British; *m* 1937, Margaret Delia Salmon; two *s*. *Educ:* Faraday House Electrical Engrg Coll., London (Hons Dipl.). Asst Works Man., Thomas Firth & John Brown Ltd, Sheffield, 1934-36; various engrg posts, Yorks Electric Power Co., 1936-45; Techn. Supt, Blackburn Corp., 1945-46; Dep. City Electrical Engr, Bath, 1946-48; South Western Electricity Board: Man., Bath District, 1948-51; Dep. Chief Engr, 1951-58; Man., Bristol District, 1958-60; Chief Engr, London Electricity Bd, 1960-65; Dep. Chm., 1966-74, Chm., 1974-76, South Eastern Electricity Bd. Pres., IEE, 1973-74. *Publications:* numerous papers and lectures. *Recreations:* golf, sculpture, painting. *Address:* 2a Shirley Drive, Hove, E Sussex BN3 6UA. *T:* Brighton 504947. *Clubs:* West Hove Golf, Dyke Golf.

MILNE, Denys Gordon, (Tiny); Managing Director and Chief Executive, BP Oil Ltd, since 1976; *b* 12 Jan. 1926; *s* of late Dr George Gordon Milne and of Margaret (*née* Campbell); *m* 1951, Pamela Mary Senior; two *s* one *d*. *Educ:* Epsom Coll.; Brasenose Coll., Oxford (MA Hons Mod. History). Pilot Officer, RAF Regt, RAFVR, 1944-47. Colonial Admin. Service, Northern Nigeria, 1951-55; British Petroleum Company: Nigeria and Ghana, 1955-61; Marketing Dept, London, 1961-63; Gen. Man., BP Nigeria Ltd, 1963-65; Regional Coordinator, UK and Ireland, 1965-71; Dir, Shell Mex and BP Ltd, 1966-71; Chm. and Man. Dir, BP Southern Oil Ltd, Cape Town, 1971-75; Dep. Man. Dir, BP Oil Ltd, 1975-76. *Recreation:* gardening. *Address:* Westbury, Old Lane, St Johns, Crowborough, East Sussex. *T:* Crowborough 2634. *Club:* Vincent's (Oxford).

MILNE, Maj.-Gen. Douglas Graeme, QHS 1974; Deputy Director General Army Medical Services, since 1975; *b* 19 May 1919; *s* of George Milne and Mary Panton; *m* 1944, Jean Millicent Gove; one *d*. *Educ:* Robert Gordon's Coll.; Aberdeen Univ. MB, ChB, FFCM, DPH. Commnd into RAMC, 1943; service in W Africa, Malta, Egypt, BAOR, Singapore; Dir of Army Health and Research, 1973-75. *Recreations:* gardening, fishing. *Address:* 17 Stonehill Road, SW14 8RR. *T:* 01-878 2828.

MILNE, Edward James; Member, (Seaton Delaval Ward), Blyth Valley District Council, since 1976; *b* 18 Oct. 1915; *s* of Edward James Milne and Isabella Stewart; *m* 1939, Emily Constable; three *d*. *Educ:* George Street and Kittybrewster Primary; Sunnybank Intermediate; Robert Gordon's Coll., Aberdeen (Schol.). Lecturer and Organiser, National Council of Labour Colls, 1942-47; Area Organiser, Union of Shop Distributive and Allied Workers, 1952-61. MP (Lab) Blyth, Nov. 1960-Feb. 1974,

MP (Ind Lab) Blyth, Feb.-Sept. 1974; PPS to Sir Frank Soskice, Home Sec., 1964-65; Vice-Chm., Parly Labour Party, 1967-68; Secretary: Anglo-Norwegian Parly Gp, 1967-74; Anglo-Swedish Parly Gp, 1968-74. Grand Order of Star of Africa (Liberia), 1964. *Publication:* No Shining Armour, 1976. *Recreations:* walking, swimming. *Address:* Strathearn, Alston Grove, Seaton Sluice, Northumberland. *T:* Seaton Delaval 481510.

MILNE, Ian Innes, CMG 1965; OBE 1946; a Senior Clerk, House of Commons, 1969-76; *b* 16 June 1912; *e s* of Kenneth John Milne, CBE, and Maud Innes; *m* 1939, Marie Mange; one *d*. *Educ:* Westminster Sch.; Christ Church, Oxford. Advertising, 1935-40; RE, 1940-46 (Lieut-Col). FO, 1946-68; 2nd Sec., Teheran, 1948-51; 1st Sec., Berne, 1955-56; 1st Sec., Tokyo, 1960-63; retired 1968. US Leg. of Merit (Off.), 1946. *Recreations:* cricket, music, gardening. *Address:* c/o Lloyds Bank, 79 Brompton Road, SW3.

MILNE, James; General Secretary, Scottish Trades Union Congress, since 1975 (Assistant General Secretary, 1969-75); Member, General Council of Scottish TUC; Chairman, Scottish Business Education Council; patternmaker; *b* 1921. Secretary to Aberdeen Trades Council, 1948-69. Joined Young Communist League, 1939. *Address:* Scottish Trades Union Congress, 16 Woodlands Terrace, Glasgow G3 6DF. *T:* 041-332 4946.

MILNE, James L.; see Lees-Milne.

MILNE, Kenneth Lancelot, CBE 1971; JP; chartered accountant; non-executive Chairman, State Government Insurance Commission, since 1971; *b* 16 Aug. 1915; *s* of F. K. Milne, Adelaide; *m* 1941, Mary, *d* of E. B. Hughes; two *s* one *d*. *Educ:* St Peter's Coll., Adelaide. Entered Public Practice as a Chartered Acct, 1946; Elected to State Council, 1951, Chm. 1958-60, Mem. Gen. Council, 1956-60. Served with RAAF, 1940-45, attaining rank of Flt Lieut. Municipality of Walkerville: Councillor, 1960; Mayor, 1961-63; Municipal Assoc. 1961 (Pres. 1964-65); Pres. SA Br Aust. Inst. of Internat. Affairs, 1958-60; Mem. Faculty of Economics, University of Adelaide, 1963-65; Agent Gen. and Trade Comr for S Aust. in UK, 1966-71. Director: Lombard Australia Ltd; Malco Industries Ltd. President: SA Branch, Royal Overseas League, 1975-; Royal Life Saving Soc. Australia, 1977-. Mem., Commn on Advanced Educn, 1973-77. Freeman, City of London, 1970. JP SA, 1947. *Publications:* Ostrich Heads, 1937; Forgotten Freedom, 1952; The Accountant in Public Practice, 1959. *Recreations:* rowing, tennis, conchology. *Address:* (office) 32 Grenfell Street, Adelaide, South Australia 5000. *T:* 873125; (home) 7 Birch Road, Stirling, SA 5152. *T:* 79.7474. *Clubs:* Adelaide, Adelaide Rowing, Commerce (all in SA).

MILNE, Maurice, CB 1976; Deputy Director General of Highways, Department of the Environment, 1970-76; retired; *b* 22 July 1916; *s* of James Daniel Milne, stone mason, and Isabella Robertson Milne; *m* 1947, Margaret Elizabeth Stewart Monro; one *d* decd. *Educ:* Robert Gordon's Coll., Aberdeen; Aberdeen University. BScEng (1st cl. Hons); FICE, FIStructE, FIMunE, FIHE, FRTPI. Apprentice Civil Engr, City Engineer's Dept, Aberdeen, 1932-33; Aberdeen Univ., 1933-36; Asst Engineer: City Engr's Dept, Aberdeen, 1936-38; Aberdeen CC, 1938; Resident Engr and Asst in Charge, Main Drainage Dept, Aberdeen City Engineer's Dept, 1938-46; part-time lectr, Aberdeen Univ., 1941-43; Principal Planning Asst, Paisley Burgh Engr's Dept, 1946-47; Chief Asst, D. A. Donald & Wishart, Cons. Engrs, Glasgow, 1947-48; Sen. Engr and Chief Engr, Crawley Develt Corp., 1948-59; Engr, Weir Wood Water Board, 1953-57; County Engr and Surveyor, W Sussex CC, 1960-68; Dir, S Eastern Road Construction Unit, MoT, 1968-70. Rees Jeffreys Vis. Lectr, Univ. of Southampton, 1976-. Hon. Sec., County Surveyors' Soc., 1963-67; Pres., Instn Highway Engineers, 1974-75; Mem. Council, ICE, 1967-71 and 1972-75; Pres., Perm. Internat. Assoc. of Road Congresses, 1977. Mem. Court, Sussex Univ., 1974-. *Publications:* contributions to Jl Instn of Civil, Municipal and Highway Engrs. *Recreations:* gardening, camping, hill walking, photography. *Address:* Struan, Walton Lane, Bosham, Chichester, West Sussex. *T:* Bosham 573304. *Clubs:* Royal Automobile, St Stephen's, Civil Service; Bosham Sailing.

MILNE, Norman; Sheriff of North Strathclyde at Campbeltown and Oban, since 1975; *b* 31 Dec. 1915; *s* of William Milne and Jessie Ferguson; *m* 1947, Phyllis Cristina Philip Rollo; no *c*. *Educ:* Logie Central Sch., Dundee. Solicitor, 1939. Army, 1939-46: active service in Madagascar, Sicily, Italy, and Germany (despatches). Procurator Fiscal Depute: Perth, 1946-51; Edinburgh, 1951-55; Senior Depute Fiscal, Glasgow, 1955-58; Procurator Fiscal: Banff, 1959-64; Kirkcaldy, 1964-65; Paisley, 1965-71; Edinburgh, 1971-75. *Recreation:* sailing. *Address:* The

Anchorage, Machrihanish, Argyll. *Club:* Royal Scottish Motor Yacht.

MILNE HOME, Captain Archibald John Fitzwilliam, DL; RN, retired; Member of Queen's Body Guard for Scotland (Royal Company of Archers) since 1963; *b* 4 May 1909; *e s* of late Sir John Milne Home; *m* 1936, Evelyn Elizabeth, *d* of late Comdr A. T. Darley, RN; three *s* one *d. Educ:* RNC Dartmouth. Joined RN, 1923: Comdr 1946; Captain 1952; retd 1962; ADC to the Queen, 1961-62. Chm., Whitbread (Scotland), 1968-73. Chm., SE Region, Scottish Woodland Owners Assoc., 1966. DL Selkirkshire, 1970. Cross of Merit, SMO Malta, 1963. *Recreations:* shooting, fishing. *Address:* Elibank, Walkerburn, Peeblesshire. *T:* Walkerburn 218.

MILNE-WATSON, Sir (David) Ronald, 2nd Bt, *cr* 1937; *b* 15 July 1904; *s* of Sir David Milne-Watson, 1st Bt, and Olga Cecily (*d* 1952), *d* of Rev. George Herbert; *S* father, 1945. *Educ:* Trinity Coll., Glenalmond; Balliol Coll., Oxford; Capt. IA, 1942-45. *Recreation:* gardening. *Heir: b* Sir Michael Milne-Watson, *qv. Address:* The Stables, Oakfield, Mortimer, Berks; 38 Hugh Street, SW1. *T:* 01-834 5166. *Clubs:* Travellers', MCC.

MILNE-WATSON, Sir Michael, Kt 1969; CBE 1953; MA; Director: Commercial Union Assurance Co. Ltd; Industrial and Commercial Finance Corporation Ltd; Finance for Industry Ltd; Finance Corporation for Industry Ltd; Marine Oil Industry Repairs Ltd; Salvesen Offshore Holdings Ltd; Chairman, BUPA, since 1976; *b* 16 Feb. 1910; *yr s* of Sir David Milne-Watson, 1st Bt, and Lady Milne-Watson; *heir-pres.* to 2nd Bt; *m* 1940, Mary Lisette, *d* of late H. C. Bagnall, Auckland, New Zealand; one *s. Educ:* Eton; Balliol Coll., Oxford. Served War of 1939-45. RNVR, 1943-45. Joined Gas Light & Coke Co., 1933; Managing Dir, 1945; Governor, 1946-49; Chairman: North Thames Gas Board, 1949-64; Richard Thomas & Baldwins Ltd, 1964-67; The William Press Group of Companies, 1969-74; a Dep. Chm., BSC, 1967-69 (Mem. Organizing Cttee, 1966-67); Mem., Iron and Steel Adv. Cttee, 1967-69. President: Soc. of British Gas Industries Guild, 1970-71; Pipeline Industries Guild, 1971-72. Liveryman, Grocers' Co., 1947. Pres., Council, Reading Univ. Governor, Nuffield Nursing Homes Trust. *Address:* 39 Cadogan Place, SW1X 9RX; Oakfield, Mortimer, Berks. *T:* Burghfield Common 2200. *Clubs:* Athenæum, MCC; Leander.

MILNER, family name of **Baron Milner of Leeds.**

MILNER OF LEEDS, 2nd Baron, *cr* 1951; **Arthur James Michael Milner,** AE 1952; Partner, Milners, Curry & Gaskell, Solicitors, London; *b* 12 Sept. 1923; *o s* of 1st Baron Milner of Leeds, PC, MC, TD and of Lois Tinsdale, *d* of Thomas Brown, Leeds; *S* father, 1967; *m* 1951, Sheila Margaret, *d* of Gerald Hartley, Leeds; one *s* two *d. Educ:* Oundle; Trinity Hall, Cambridge (MA). Served: RAFVR, 1942-46, Flt Lt; 609 (W Riding) Sqn, RAuxAF, 1947-52, Flt Lt. Admitted Solicitor, 1951. Opposition Whip, House of Lords, 1971-74. Member: Clothworkers' Co.; Pilgrims; Hon. Treas, Soc. of Yorkshiremen in London, 1967-70. *Recreation:* water ski-ing. *Heir: s* Hon. Richard James Milner, *b* 16 May 1959. *Address:* 4 Carlyle Mansions, Cheyne Walk, SW3 5LS. *Club:* Royal Air Force.

MILNER, George; His Honour Judge Milner; a Circuit Judge, since 1974; *b* 11 Jan. 1927; *s* of Charles and Mary Elizabeth Milner; *m* 1952, Eileen Janet Blackett; two *s. Educ:* Tadcaster Grammar Sch.; Selwyn Coll., Cambridge (MA). Instructor Lieut RN, 1947-51. Called to Bar, Lincoln's Inn, 1951; practised in Sheffield from 1951. A Recorder of the Crown Court, 1972-74. *Recreations:* lawn tennis, squash rackets, gardening, music, history. *Address:* Crystal Cottage, Drumrauch Hall, Hutton Rudby, North Yorks. *T:* Hutton Rudby 700462. *Club:* The Club (Sheffield).

MILNER, Sir (George Edward) Mordaunt, 9th Bt *cr* 1716; *b* 7 Feb. 1911; *er s* of Brig.-Gen. G. F. Milner, CMG, DSO; *S* cousin (Sir William Frederick Victor Mordaunt Milner, 8th Bt) 1960; *m* 1st, 1935, Barbara Audrey (*d* 1951), *d* of Henry Noel Belsham, Hunstanton, Norfolk; two *s* one *d*; 2nd, 1953, Katherine Moodie Bisset, *d* of D. H. Hoey, Dunfermline. *Educ:* Oundle. Served War of 1939-45, Royal Artillery. Stipendiary Steward, Jockey Club of South Africa, 1954-59; Steward, Cape Turf Club, 1959-. *Publications:* (novels) Inspired Information, 1959; Vaulting Ambition, 1962; The Last Furlong, 1965. *Heir: s* Timothy William Lycett Milner, *b* 11 Oct. 1936. *Address:* Naite Vallei, Klapmuts, Cape, S Africa. *T:* 41. *Clubs:* Rand (Johannesburg); Jockey Club of SA.

MILNER, John Giddings; Consulting Surgeon, Moorfields Eye Hospital, since 1956; Consulting Ophthalmic Surgeon: Charing

Cross Hospital since 1966; St Andrew's Hospital, Dollis Hill, since 1966; *b* 7 Dec. 1900; 2nd *s* of late T. J. Milner, Blythwood, Radlett, and late Carrie, *d* of John Carpenter; *m* 1928, Monica Thrale, *d* of late Henry Mardall, Harpenden; one *s* two *d. Educ:* Marlborough Coll.; Trinity Coll., Cambridge; St Bartholomew's Hosp. MRCS, LRCP, 1925; MA, MB, BCh Cantab, 1929; FRCS, 1930. Ophthalmic Surgeon, Hertford County Hosp., 1929-46; Surgeon, Moorfields, Westminster and Central Eye Hosp., 1936-56; Wing Comdr RAFVR Medical Branch, 1940-45; Cons. Ophthalmic Surgeon, Hertford County Hosp., 1947; Surgeon Oculist to the late Queen Mary, 1948-53. Coronation Medal, 1953. *Publications:* Modern Treatment in General Practice (contribution), 1949; Brit. Jl Opth., 1934; Brit. Medical Jl, 1941, 1944. *Recreations:* golf, natural history. *Address:* Blythwood, Watford Road, Radlett, Herts. *T:* Radlett 5750.

MILNER, Joseph, CBE 1975; QFSM 1962; Chief Officer of the London Fire Brigade, 1970-76; *b* 5 Oct. 1922; *e s* of Joseph and Ann Milner; *m* 1943, Bella Grice (*d* 1976), *e d* of Frederick George Flinton; one *s* one *d. Educ:* Ladybarn Sch., Manchester. Served King's Regt (Liverpool), 1940-46: India/Burma, 1943-46 (Wingate's Chindits). Nat. Fire Service, 1946-48; North Riding Fire Bde, 1948-50; Manchester Fire Bde, 1950-51; Hong Kong Fire Bde, 1951-60; Dep. Dir, Hong Kong Fire Services, 1961-65; Dir, Hong Kong Fire Services, and Unit Controller, Auxiliary Fire Service, 1965-70. Mem., Hong Kong Council, Order of St John, 1965-70; JP Hong Kong, 1965-70. Regional Fire Commander (designate), 1970. Mem. Bd, Fire Service College, 1970; Mem., Central Fire Brigades Adv. Council, 1970; Adviser, Nat. Jt Council for Local Authority Fire Brigades, 1970; Chm., London Fire Liaison Panel, 1970; Mem., London Local Adv. Cttee, IBA; Fire Adviser, Assoc. of Metrop. Authorities. Fellow, Instn of Fire Engineers; Associate Mem., Inst. of British Engineers. OStJ 1971. *Recreations:* walking, poetry. *Address:* 6 Heathway, SE3. *Clubs:* Royal Over-Seas League; Hong Kong (Hong Kong).

MILNER, Sir Mordaunt; see Milner, Sir G. E. M.

MILNER, Ralph; see Millner, Ralph.

MILNER-BARRY, Sir (Philip) Stuart, KCVO 1975; CB 1962; OBE 1946; Ceremonial Officer, Civil Service Department (formerly Treasury), 1966-77; *b* 20 Sept. 1906; *s* of late Prof. E. L. Milner-Barry; *m* 1947, Thelma Tennant Wells; one *s* two *d. Educ:* Cheltenham Coll.; Trinity Coll., Cambridge (Major Schol.). 1st Class Hons, Classical Tripos (Pt I), Moral Science Tripos (Pt II). With L. Powell Sons & Co., Stockbrokers, 1929-38; Chess Correspondent, The Times, 1938-45; temporary civil servant, a Dept of the Foreign Office, 1940-45; Principal, HM Treasury, 1945; Asst Sec., 1947; Dir of Organisation and Methods, Treasury, 1954-58; Dir of Establishments and Organisation, Min. of Health, 1958-60; Under-Sec., Treasury, 1954-66. *Recreations:* Chess: British Boy Champion, 1923; British Championship Second, 1953; mem. British Internat. teams, 1937-61; Pres. British Chess Fedn, 1970-73; walking. *Address:* 43 Blackheath Park, SE3. *T:* 01-852 5808. *Club:* Brooks's.

MILNES, G. Turquet; see Turquet, Gladys.

MILNES COATES, Sir Robert (Edward James Clive), 3rd Bt *cr* 1911; DSO 1945; landowner and farmer; *b* 27 Sept. 1907; *s* of Captain Sir (Edward) Clive Milnes Coates, 2nd Bt, OBE and of Lady Celia Hermione, *d* of 1st Marquess of Crewe, KG, PC; *S* father, 1971; *m* 1945, Lady Patricia, *d* of 4th Earl of Listowel and widow of Lt-Col Charles Thomas Milnes-Gaskell, Coldstream Guards; one *s* one *d. Educ:* Harrow; RMC Camberley; Queens' College, Cambridge (MA). JP N Riding of Yorks, 1960; Patron of two livings. 2nd Lieut Coldstream Guards, 1927; ADC to Commander-in-Chief, India, 1930-33; served with Transjordan Frontier Force, 1937-40 (despatches); Italy, 1944-45 (despatches, DSO); retired, 1947. *Heir: s* Dr Anthony Robert Milnes Coates, *b* 8 Dec. 1948. *Address:* Moor House Farm, Helperby, York. *T:* Helperby 662. *Club:* Pratt's.

MILNES WALKER, Robert; see Walker, R. M.

MILOSLAVSKY, Dimitry T.; see Tolstoy, Dimitry.

MILSOM, Stroud Francis Charles, FBA 1967; Professor of Law, Cambridge University, and Fellow of St John's College, Cambridge, since 1976; Literary Director, Selden Society, since 1964; *b* 2 May 1923; *yr s* of late Harry Lincoln Milsom and of Isobel Vida Collins; *m* 1955, Irène, *d* of late Witold Szereszewski, Poland. *Educ:* Charterhouse; Trinity Coll., Cambridge. Admiralty, 1944-45. Called to the Bar, Lincoln's Inn, 1947, Hon. Bencher, 1970; Commonwealth Fund Fellow,

Univ. of Pennsylvania, 1947-48; Yorke Prize, Univ. of Cambridge, 1948; Prize Fellow, Fellow and Lectr, Trinity Coll., Cambridge, 1948-55; Fellow, Tutor and Dean, New Coll., Oxford, 1956-64; Prof. of Legal History, London Univ., 1964-76. Mem., Royal Commn on Historical Manuscripts, 1975-. Vis. Lectr, New York Univ. Law Sch., several times, 1958-70; Visiting Professor: Yale Law Sch., 1968, 1973, 1974, 1975, 1977; Harvard Law Sch. and Dept of History, 1973; Associate Fellow, Trumbull Coll., Yale Univ., 1974-; Charles Inglis Thomson Prof., Colorado Univ. Law Sch., 1977. Maitland Meml Lectr, Cambridge, 1972; Addison Harris Meml Lectr, Indiana Univ. Law Sch., 1974. Ames Prize, Harvard, 1972; Swiney Prize, RSA/RCP, 1974. *Publications:* Novae Narrationes (introd., trans. and notes), 1963; introd. reissue Pollock and Maitland, History of English Law, 1968; Historical Foundations of the Common Law, 1969; The Legal Framework of English Feudalism, 1976; articles in learned jls. *Address:* St John's College, Cambridge CB2 1TP; 23 Bentley Road, Cambridge CB2 2AW. *T:* Cambridge 54100. *Club:* Athenæum.

MILSTEIN, César, PhD, FRS 1975; Scientific Staff of Medical Research Council, since 1963; *b* 8 Oct. 1927; *s* of Lázaro and Máxima Milstein; *m* 1953, Celia Prilleltensky. *Educ:* Colegio Nacional de Bahia Blanca; Univ. Nacional de Buenos Aires; Cambridge Univ. Licenciado en Ciencias Quimicas 1952; Doctor en Quimica 1957; PhD Cantab 1960. British Council Fellow, 1958-60; Staff of Instituto Nacional de Microbiologia, Buenos Aires, 1957-63; Head of Div. de Biologia Molecular, 1961-63; Staff of MRC Laboratory of Molecular Biology, 1963-, Mem. Governing Bd, 1975; Jt Head of Sub-div. of Protein Chemistry, 1969. *Publications:* original papers and review articles on structure, evolution and genetics of immunoglobulins and phospheonzimes. *Recreations:* open air activities, cooking. *Address:* 292a Hills Road, Cambridge CB2 2QG. *Club:* Sefe (Cambridge).

MILSTEIN, Nathan; violinist; *b* Odessa, Russia, 31 Dec. 1904; *s* of Miron and Maria Milstein; *m* 1945, Thérèse Weldon; one *d.* *Educ:* St Petersburg Conservatory of Music. Studied under Eugène Isaye, Brussels. Many tours in Russia, 1920-26; left Russia, 1926; annual tours throughout Europe, also in North, Central and South America, from 1920, except for war years. Hon. Mem., Acad. of St Cecilia, Rome, 1963. Officier, Légion d'Honneur, 1967; Ehrenkreuz, Austria, 1963. *Address:* c/o Shaw Concerts Inc., 1995 Broadway, New York, NY 10023, USA; 17 Chester Square, SW1.

MILTHORPE, Prof. Frederick Leon, DSc London, MScAgr, DIC; FInstBiol; FRSA; Professor of Biology, Macquarie University, Sydney, New South Wales, since 1967; *b* 24 Sept. 1917; 2nd *s* of S. G. and Annie Milthorpe, Hillston, NSW; *m* 1941, Elma Joan, *o d* of R. K. Hobbs, Sydney; two *s.* *Educ:* McCaughey Memorial High Sch.; Univ. of Sydney; Imperial Coll. of Science, London. Walter and Eliza Hall Agricultural Fellow, 1940-42; Plant Pathologist, NSW Dept of Agriculture, 1942-46; Farrer Memorial Scholar, 1946-48; Leverhulme Research Fellow, 1948-49; Senior Plant Physiologist, Waite Agricultural Research Inst., University of Adelaide, 1949-54; Prof. of Agricultural Botany, University of Nottingham, 1954-67. Australian Medal of Agricultural Sciences, 1975. *Publications:* An Introduction to Crop Physiology (with J. Moorby), 1974; chapters, some jtly, on water relations and crop growth; various papers on plant physiology in scientific journals. *Address:* Macquarie University, North Ryde, NSW 2113, Australia.

MILVERTON, 1st Baron, *cr* 1947, of Lagos and of Clifton; **Arthur Frederick Richards,** GCMG 1942 (KCMG 1935; CMG 1933); KStJ 1945; Freedom Medal (USA), with silver palm, 1946; retired 1975; *b* 21 Feb. 1885; 2nd *s* of late W. Richards; *m* 1927, Noelle Benda Whitehead; two *s* one *d.* *Educ:* Clifton Coll.; Christ Church, Oxford. Cadet, Malayan Civil Service, 1908; in various district posts in the Federated Malay States, Kelantan and Kedah, 1910-20: 2nd Asst Colonial Sec., Straits Settlements, 1920; Sec. to Select Cttee on Constitution of Legislative Council, 1921; 1st Asst Colonial Sec. SS; and Clerk of Councils, Sec. to Trade Commissions, Straits Settlements and Federated Malay States; General Sec., Straits Settlements Retrenchment Cttee, 1922; Sec. to High Commissioner for Malay States, 1923; Chm., Executive Cttee, British Malaya, British Empire Exhibition, 1924; Sec., Opium Cttee, British Malaya; Sec. Cttee to enquire into organisation of Postal Services, Straits Settlements, Federated Malay States and Unfederated Malay States, 1924; Under-Sec. to Government FMS, 1926; Acting General Adviser to Government of Johore, 1929; Governor of North Borneo, 1930-33; Governor and Commander-in-Chief, Gambia Colony, 1933-36; Governor and Commander-in-Chief of Fiji and High Commissioner for Western Pacific, 1936-38; Capt.-Gen. and

Governor-in-Chief of Jamaica, 1938-43; Governor and C-in-C, Nigeria, 1943-47. A part-time Dir, Colonial Development Corp., 1948-51; Chm. of Council, London Sch. of Hygiene and Tropical Medicine, 1948-51; a Vice-Pres. of Royal Empire Society; Mem. of Board of Governors of Clifton Coll. Pres. Assoc. of British Malaya, 1948-50. Chairman: Empire Day Movement, 1948-50; British Empire Leprosy Relief Assoc., 1948-50; Royal African Soc., 1963-65; Director: West Indies Sugar Co. Ltd; Bank of West Africa, 1950-65; Kamuning (Perak) Rubber & Tin Co. Ltd, 1956-65. *Recreations:* golf, sailing. *Heir: s* Rev. Hon. Fraser Arthur Richard Richards [*b* 21 July 1930; *m* 1957, Mary Dorothy, *d* of Leslie Fly, Bickley, Kent; two *d*]. *Address:* The Lodge, Cox Green, Maidenhead, Berks. *T:* Maidenhead 20040. *Clubs:* Athenæum, United Oxford & Cambridge University, Royal Commonwealth Society (West Indian), Number 10.

MILWARD, Sir Anthony (Horace), Kt 1966; CBE 1960 (OBE 1945); FCIT; President, London Tourist Board, since 1976 (Chairman, 1971-76); *b* 2 March 1905; *s* of Henry T. and Elsie T. Milward, Redditch, Worcs; *m* 1931, Frieda Elizabeth Anne von der Becke; one *s* one *d.* *Educ:* Rugby Sch.; Clare Coll., Cambridge (BA). With Glazebrook, Steel & Co. Ltd, Manchester, 1926-40. Served Fleet Air Arm, RNVR, as Pilot, 1940-45, reaching rank of Lieut-Cdr. With BEA in various capacities, 1946-70, Chm., 1966-70; Mem. Bd, BOAC, 1964-70. Mem., Air Registration Board, 1964-70. *Recreations:* fishing, shooting, walking. *Address:* Dene House, Lower Slaughter, Cheltenham, Glos. *Club:* Royal Automobile.

MILWARD, John Frederic; JP; DL; Stipendiary Magistrate for Metropolitan County of West Midlands, since 1974 (for Birmingham, 1951-74); *b* 26 June 1908; *s* of late Charles Frederic and Emily Constantia Milward, Alvechurch, Worcs; *m* 1946, Doris Evelyn McMurdo, 2nd *d* of Aston E. McMurdo, Charlottesville, Va; two *s.* *Educ:* Bedales Sch.; Clare Coll., Cambridge. Called to Bar, Middle Temple, 1932. Associate of Oxford Circuit, 1942-51. JP Worcs, 1940-; Chm. of Worcs QS, 1964-71 (Dep. Chm., 1943-64); a Dep. Circuit Judge, 1972; DL Worcs 1972. A Life Governor of Birmingham Univ., 1952. Liveryman of Needlemakers' Company, Mem. Ct of Assistants, 1972. *Address:* Stable Door House, Alvechurch, Worcs. *T:* 021-445 1218. *Club:* Birmingham.

MIMPRISS, Trevor Walter, MS; FRCS; Hon. Consultant; retired, 1970, as: Surgeon to St Thomas' Hospital; Surgeon-in-Charge, Urological Division, St Peter's Hospital, Chertsey, Surrey; *b* 12 May 1905; *s* of late S. T. Mimpriss, Bromley, Kent; *m* 1938, Eleanor Joan, *d* of Gordon Innes; two *s* one *d.* *Educ:* Brighton Coll.; St Thomas' Hospital, London Univ. FRCS 1932; MS London 1935. Cheselden Medal for Surgery, St Thomas' Hospital, 1932; Louis Jenner Research Scholarship, 1936-37. Hunterian Professor of Royal College of Surgeons, 1938. *Publications:* various papers in medical journals. *Recreations:* shooting, fishing, golf. *Address:* Muskoka, Kingsley Green, Haslemere, Surrey.

MINCHINTON, Prof. Walter Edward; Professor and Head of Department of Economic History, University of Exeter, since 1964; *b* 29 April 1921; *s* of Walter Edward and Annie Border Minchinton; *m* 1945, Marjorie Sargood; two *s* two *d.* *Educ:* Queen Elizabeth's Hosp., Bristol; LSE, Univ. of London. 1st cl. hons BSc (Econ). FRHistS. War Service, RAOC, REME, Royal Signals (Lieut), 1942-45. UC Swansea: Asst Lectr, 1948-50; Lectr, 1950-59; Sen. Lectr, 1959-64. Rockefeller Research Fellow, 1959-60. Vis. Prof., Fourah Bay Coll., Sierra Leone, 1965. Chm., Confedn for Advancement of State Educn, 1964-67; Chm., British Agricultural History Soc., 1968-71; Chm., Export Research Group, 1971-72. Governor, Exeter Coll. of Further Education. Chm., Exeter Educn Cttee, 1972. Alexander Prize, RHistS, 1953. *Publications:* The British Tinplate Industry: a history, 1957; (ed) The Trade of Bristol in the Eighteenth Century, 1957; Politics and the Port of Bristol in the Eighteenth Century, 1963; Essays in Agrarian History, 1968; Industrial South Wales 1750-1914, essays in Welsh economic history, 1969; Mercantilism, System or Expediency?, 1969; The Growth of English Overseas Trade in the Seventeenth and Eighteenth Centuries, 1969; Wage Regulation in Pre-industrial England, 1972; Devon at Work, 1974; articles in Econ. History Review, Explorations in Entrepreneurial History, Mariner's Mirror, Trans RHistS, etc. *Recreations:* walking, music, industrial archaeology. *Address:* 53 Homefield Road, Exeter EX1 2QX. *T:* Exeter 77602.

MINHINNICK, Sir Gordon (Edward George), KBE 1976 (OBE 1950); Cartoonist, New Zealand Herald, 1930-76, retired; *b* 13 June 1902; *s* of Captain P. C. Minhinnick, RN, and Anne Sealy; *m* 1928, Vernor Helmore; one *s* (one *d* decd). *Educ:* Kelly Coll., Tavistock, Devon. Came to NZ, 1921; studied architecture for 4 years; Cartoonist: NZ Free Lance, 1926; Sun, Christchurch, and Sun, Auckland, 1927. Mem., MacKelvie Trust Bd. *Address:* 19c Killarney Street, Takapuna, Auckland, New Zealand. *T:* 495-390.

MINIO-PALUELLO, Lorenzo, FBA 1957; Reader in Medieval Philosophy, University of Oxford, 1956-75 (Senior Lecturer, 1948-56); Fellow of Oriel College, 1962-75, now Emeritus; *b* 21 Sept. 1907; *s* of Michelangelo Minio and Ersilia (*née* Bisson); *m* 1938, Magda Ungar; one *s* one *d* (and one *d* decd). *Educ:* Ginnasio-Liceo Foscarini, Venice; Univ. of Padua; Sorbonne and Ecole des Hautes Etudes, Paris. Dr of Philosophy (Padua), 1929; Asst Librarian, University of Padua, 1929-32; Fellow of Warburg Inst., Univ. of London, 1947-48; DPhil Oxon, MA Oxon, 1948; Barlow Lectr, Univ. of London, 1955; Prof. straord. of medieval and humanistic philology, Univ. of Padua, for 1956-57; Dir of Aristotles Latinus (Union Acad. Internat.), 1959-72; Mem., Inst. for Advanced Study, Princeton, 1969-70, 1974-76; Corresp. Fellow, Amer. Mediaeval Acad., 1970; Member: Amer. Philosophical Soc., 1971; Unione Accademica Nazionale (Pres., Corpus Philosophorum Medii Aevi), 1971-72; Corresp. Member: Koninklijke Academie voor Wetenschappen, Letteren en Schone Kunsten van Belgie, 1975; Accad. Patarina di Scienze, Lettere ed Arti, 1977. *Publications:* Education in Fascist Italy, 1946; editions of Aristotle's Categoriae and De interpretatione (1949, 1957), Plato's Phaedo (Medieval Latin trans., 1950), Aristotle's Categoriae, De interpretatione, Prior and Posterior Analytics, Topics (Ancient and Medieval Latin Trans. and paraphrases, 1953, 1954, 1961, 1962, 1965, 1967, 1969), Pseudo-Aristotle's De Mundo (Apuleius', Rinucio's, Sadoleto's trans, 1965), Porphyry's Isagoge (Boethius' trans, 1966); 'Liber VI Principiorum' (1966); co-ed Aristoteles Latinus Codices, vol. ii, and (ed) Supplementa Altera (1955, 1961), and Poetics (Latin trans., 1953, 1968); Twelfth Century Logic, vol. i, 1956, vol. ii, 1958; Opuscula: The Latin Aristotle, 1972; articles in The Classical Quart. Jl of Hellenic Studies, Mediaeval and Renaiss. Studies, Italian Studies, Studi Danteschi, Riv. di Filos. Neoscolastica, Studi Medievali, Rev. Philos. de Louvain, Traditio, Encyclopædia Britannica, Dizion. Biograf. degli Ital., Dictionary of Scientific Biography, etc. *Address:* 22 Polstead Road, Oxford. *T:* Oxford 57798.

MINION, Stephen, OBE 1954; JP; DL; Director and General Manager, The Lancashire & Cheshire Rubber Co. Ltd; *b* 2 June 1908; *s* of Stephen and Elizabeth Minion; *m* 1935, Ada, *d* of George and Jane Evans; no *c*. *Educ:* Liverpool Technical and Commercial Colleges. City Councillor 1940, Alderman 1961, Lord Mayor 1969-70, Liverpool. JP Liverpool, 1954; High Sheriff Merseyside, 1976; DL Merseyside, 1976. *Recreations:* outdoor sports, reading, history, theatre and music. *Address:* Glen Cairn, 223 Booker Avenue, Liverpool L18 9TA. *T:* 051-724 2671. *Clubs:* Athenæum, Racquet (Liverpool).

MINNEY, Rubeigh James; Novelist, Biographer, Playwright, Film Producer; *b* 29 Aug. 1895; *s* of late J. R. Minney; *m* 1st, Edith Fox (marr. diss.); one *s* one *d*; 2nd, Hetty (*née* Bolsom). *Educ:* King's Coll., London. Editorial Staff, Pioneer, Allahabad; Englishman, Calcutta; represented The Times in Calcutta; special representative with Duke of Connaught to India, 1920; Daily Express, London; Asst Editor, Sunday News, London; Editor, Everybody's Weekly, 1925-35; Dir Everybody's Publications, Ltd, until 1935; Dir Chapman and Hall, Ltd, 1934-36; Editor, Sunday Referee, 1935-39; Editor, The Era; Editor The War Weekly, 1939-41; Editor The Strand Magazine, 1941-42. In films since 1942. Hon. Pres. London Sch. of Economics Film Soc., 1948-49; Mem. of Executive and General Council, Association of Cine-Technicians, 1953-56; Vice-Chm. ACT Films Ltd, 1951-68, Chm. 1968-. Parly Candidate (Lab) for Southend East, 1950, for Bexley, 1955. Went to Peking to speak at George Bernard Shaw Centenary celebration, July 1956. *Publications: Novels:* Maki, 1921; The Road to Delhi, 1923; Distant Drums, 1935; Governor General, 1935; How Vainly Men..., 1940; A Woman of France, 1945; Nothing to Lose, 1946 (filmed as Time Gentlemen Please, 1952); Bring out the Drum, 1950; The Governor's Lady, 1951; (with Margot Duke) Anne of the Sealed Knot, 1972. *Biographies, etc:* Clive of India, 1931; Shiva, or The Future of India; Midst Himalayan Mists; Excursions in Ink; Across India by Air; The Journalist; Night Life of Calcutta; India Marches Past, 1933; Hollywood by Starlight, 1935; Talking of Films, 1947; Chaplin, The Immortal Tramp, 1954; Viscount Southwood, 1954; Carve Her Name with Pride, 1956 (filmed 1957); Next Stop Peking, 1957; Viscount Addison, Leader of the Lords, 1958; The Private Papers of Hore-Belisha, 1960; Fanny and the Regent of Siam, 1962; No 10 Downing Street: A House in History, 1963; The Film Maker and his World, 1964; The Edwardian Age, 1964; I Shall Fear No Evil: the story of Dr Alina Brewda, 1966; The Two Pillars of Charing Cross, 1967; The Bogus Image of Bernard Shaw, 1969

(US, Recollections of George Bernard Shaw); The Tower of London, 1970; Hampton Court, 1972; Rasputin, 1972; Puffin Asquith, 1973; Lola Montez, 1976. *Plays:* Clive of India (with W. P. Lipscomb), first prod. by village players of Great Hucklow in Derbyshire, 1933; filmed by Twentieth Century, Hollywood, 1934; They Had His Number (with Lady Rhys-Williams), first produced at Hippodrome, Bolton, 1942; Gentle Caesar (with Sir Osbert Sitwell), first produced Alexandra Theatre, Birmingham, 1943; The Voice of the People, first produced Southend, 1950. *Films:* (as producer): Madonna of the Seven Moons; Osbert Sitwell's A Place of One's Own; The Wicked Lady; The Magic Bow; The Idol of Paris; Terence Rattigan's The Final Test, etc. *Address:* Hook House, Cousley Wood, Wadhurst, Sussex. *Club:* Savage.

MINNITT, Robert John, CMG 1955; *b* 2 April 1913; *s* of Charles Frederick Minnitt and Winifred May Minnitt (*née* Buddle); *m* 1st, 1943, Peggy Christine Sharp (*d* 1973); one *s* two *d*; 2nd, 1975, Hon. Primrose Keighley Muncaster, *widow* of Claude Muncaster. *Educ:* Marlborough Coll.; Trinity Coll., Cambridge. Appointed to Colonial Administrative Service, Hong Kong, 1935; Chief Sec., Western Pacific High Commission, 1952-58, retired. Furniture designer and craftsman, 1960-66; temp. Civil Servant, CO, 1966; FCO, 1968-69. *Address:* Whitelocks, Sutton, Pulborough, W Sussex. *T:* Sutton 216.

MINOGUE, Hon. Sir John (Patrick), Kt 1976; QC; Law Reform Commissioner, Victoria, since 1977; *b* 15 Sept. 1909; *s* of John Patrick Minogue and Emma Minogue; *m* 1938, Mary Alicia O'Farrell. *Educ:* St Kevin's Coll., Melbourne; Univ. of Melbourne (LLB). Australian Army, 1940-46; GSO1 HQ 1 Aust. Corps and HQ New Guinea Force, 1942-43 (mentioned in despatches); GSO1 Aust. Mil. Mission, Washington, 1945-46. Solicitor, Bendigo, 1937-39; called to the Bar, Melbourne, 1939; QC Victoria 1957, NSW 1958; Papua New Guinea: Judge, Supreme Court, 1962; Chief Justice, 1970-74. Vice-Pres., Aust. Section, Internat. Commn of Jurists, 1965-. Member: Council and Faculty of Law, Univ. of Papua New Guinea, 1965-74 (Pro-Chancellor, 1972-74); Law Faculty, Melbourne Univ., 1975-. Hon. LLD Papua New Guinea, 1974. *Recreations:* reading, conversation, golf. *Address:* Marengo Vale, Seymour, Vic 3660, Australia. *T:* Seymour 922146. *Clubs:* Melbourne, Naval and Military, Royal Automobile of Victoria, Melbourne Cricket (Melbourne).

MINOGUE, Maj.-Gen. Patrick John O'Brien; Commander, Base Organisation, RAOC, 1975-78; *b* 28 July 1922; *s* of Col M. J. Minogue, DSO, MC, late East Surrey Regt, and Mrs M. V. E. Minogue; *m* 1950, June Elizabeth (*née* Morris); one *s* two *d*. *Educ:* Brighton Coll.; RMCS. FBIM, FBCS, FIWSP; jssc, psc, ato. Indian Army, 1942-46; East Surrey Regt, 1947; RAOC, 1951; served UK, BAOR, USA, Cyprus; Col, 1969; Brig., 1971; Insp. RAOC, 1971-73; Comdt, Central Ord. Depot, Bicester, 1973-75; Maj.-Gen. 1975. Hon. Col, RAOC (TAVR), 1975-. *Recreations:* cricket, sailing (Cdre Wayfarer Class, UK, 1975), golf, shooting, gun-dogs, athletics. *Address:* c/o Lloyds Bank Ltd, Parkstone, Poole, Dorset; 50 Los Marinos, Puerto del Carmen, Lanzarote, Canary Isles. *Clubs:* Army and Navy, MCC; Army Sailing Association; Milocarian Athletic; Staff College (Camberley); Bosham Sailing; Cortijo Grande Golf.

MINTO, 6th Earl of, *cr* 1813; **Gilbert Edward George Lariston Elliot-Murray-Kynynmound,** MBE 1955; Bt 1700; Baron Minto, 1797; Viscount Melgund, 1813; JP; late Captain Scots Guards; *b* 19 June 1928; *er s* of 5th Earl of Minto and Marion, OBE (*d* 1974), *d* of G. W. Cook, Montreal; *S* father, 1975; *m* 1st, 1952, Lady Caroline Child-Villiers (from whom he obtained a divorce, 1965), *d* of 9th Earl of Jersey; one *s* one *d*; 2nd, 1965, Mary Elizabeth, *d* of late Peter Ballantine and of Mrs Ballantine, Gladstone, New Jersey, USA. *Educ:* Eton; RMA, Sandhurst. Served Malaya, 1949-51; ADC to C-in-C FARELF, 1951, to CIGS, 1953-55, to HE Governor and C-in-C Cyprus, 1955; transferred to RARO, 1956. Brigadier, Queen's Body Guard for Scotland (Royal Company of Archers). Regional Councillor (Hermitage Div.), Borders Region, 1974-; Chm., Scottish Council on Alcoholism, 1973-. JP Roxburghshire, 1961-. *Heir: s* Viscount Melgund, *qv*. *Address:* Minto, Hawick, Scotland. *T:* Denholm 321. *Club:* Puffin's (Edinburgh).

MINTOFF, Dominic, MP; Prime Minister of Malta and Minister of Foreign Affairs, since 1971; Minister of the Interior, since 1976; Leader of Labour Party, since 1949; *b* 6 Aug. 1916; *s* of Lawrence Mintoff; *m* 1947, Moyra de Vere Bentinck; two *d*. *Educ:* Univ. of Malta (BSc; BE&A); Hertford Coll., Oxford (BA 1939; MA 1945); Mem., Malta Chamber of Architects and Civil Engrs. Practised as civil engineer in Britain, 1941-43, and as architect in Malta, 1943-. Gen. Sec. Malta Labour Party, 1936-37; Rejoined Maltese Labour Party, 1944; Mem., Council of

Govt and Exec. Council, 1945; MLA, 1947-; Dep. Leader, Labour Party, 1947; Dep. Prime Minister and Minister for Works and Reconstruction, 1947-49; Prime Minister and Minister of Finance, 1955-58; resigned office in 1958 to lead the Maltese Liberation Movement; Leader of Opposition, 1962-71. *Publications:* scientific, literary and artistic works. *Recreations:* riding, swimming, water skiing, boċċi. *Address:* Auberge de Castille, Valletta, Malta; The Olives, Tarxien, Malta.

MINTON, Yvonne Fay; mezzo-soprano; *b* 4 Dec. 1938; *er d* of R. T. Minton, Sydney; *m* 1965, William Barclay; one *s* one *d. Educ:* Sydney Conservatorium of Music. Elsa Stralia Scholar, Sydney, 1957-60; won Canberra Operatic Aria Competition, 1960; won Kathleen Ferrier Prize at s'Hertogenbosch Vocal Competition, 1961. Joined Royal Opera House as a Principal Mezzo-Soprano, 1965. Major roles include: Octavian in Der Rosenkavalier; Dorabella in Cosi Fan Tutte; Marina in Boris Godounov; Helen in King Priam; Cherubino in Marriage of Figaro; Orfeo in Gluck's Orfeo; Sextus in La clemenza di Tito; Dido in The Trojans at Carthage. Recordings include Octavian in Der Rosenkavalier, Mozart Requiem, Elgar's The Kingdom, etc. Guest Artist with Cologne Opera Company, Oct. 1969-. Hon. RAM 1975. *Recreations:* reading, gardening. *Address:* 57 Park View Road, Ealing, W5. *T:* 01-997 6087.

MIREPOIX, Duc de L.; *see* Lévis Mirepoix.

MIRÓ, Joan; artist; *b* Barcelona, 20 April 1893; *s* of Miguel and Dolores Miró; *m* 1929, Pilar. *Educ:* Barcelona Academy of Fine Art. Work includes paintings, ceramics, sculptures, engravings, lithographs. Guggenheim Award for ceramic mural in grounds of Unesco Building, Paris, 1958. Foundation Joan Miró, Parc Montjuï, Barcelona, opened in 1975 with exhibn of 92 paintings and sculptures dated 1917-74. *Exhibitions include:* Galerie Pierre, 1925; Goeman's Gallery, 1928; Galerie Maeght, Paris, 1948, 1953, 1956, 1961, 1970; Pierre Matisse Gallery, New York, 1947, 1953, 1956, 1961, 1965, 1967, 1970, 1972, 1973, 1975, 1976; Tate Gallery, London, 1964; Marlborough Fine Art Gallery, London, 1966; Tokyo, Kyoto, 1966; Barcelona, 1968; Maeght Foundn, St Paul de Vence, 1968; Munich, 1968; Museum of Modern Art, NY, 1974; Grand Palais, Paris, 1974. *Recreation:* walking. *Address:* Pierre Matisse Gallery, 41 East 57th Street, New York, NY 10022, USA; 13 rue de Téhéran, Paris, 8e, France.

MIRON, Wilfrid Lyonel, CBE 1969 (OBE 1945; MBE 1944); TD 1950; JP; DL; Regional Chairman (Midlands), National Coal Board, 1967 and Regional Chairman (South Wales), 1969; National Coal Board Member (with Regional responsibilities), 1971-76; *b* 27 Jan. 1913; *s* of late Solman Miron and late Minnie Pearl Miron; *m* 1958, Doreen (*née* Hill); no *c. Educ:* Llanelli Gram. Sch. Admitted Solicitor, 1934; private practice and Legal Adviser to Shipley Collieries and associated companies. TA Commn, Sherwood Foresters, 1939; served War of 1939-45: Home Forces, 1939; France and Dunkirk, 1940; IO 139 Inf. Bde and GSO3 Aldershot Dist, 1941-42; Staff Coll., Quetta, 1942 (SC); DAAG 17 Ind. Div., 1943-44, and AA&QMG 17 Ind. Div., 1944-45, Chin Hills, Imphal, Burma (despatches, 1944). E Midlands Div. NCB: Sec. and Legal Adviser, 1946-51; Dep. Chm., 1951-60; Chm., 1960-67. Pres. and Chm., Midland Dist Miners' Fatal Accident Relief Soc.; Chm., E Mids Regional Planning Council; Mem. Council and Law Adv. Cttee, Nottingham Univ.; Trustee, Leicester and Nottingham Trustee Savings Bank. Hon. Dir, Nottingham Theatre Trust Ltd. Freeman (by redemption) City of London, Renter Warden, Pattenmakers' Company. Hon. Lieut-Col; JP Notts, 1964; DL Notts, 1970. FRSA 1965. OStJ 1961. *Publications:* Bitter Sweet Seventeen, 1946; articles and papers in mining and other jls. *Recreations:* cricket, Rugby football, music, reading, crosswords. *Address:* Briar Croft, School Lane, Halam, Newark, Notts. *T:* Southwell 812446. *Clubs:* Army and Navy, MCC; XL; Nottingham and Notts United Services (Nottingham).

MIRRLEES, Prof. James Alexander; Edgeworth Professor of Economics, University of Oxford, and Fellow of Nuffield College, since 1968; *b* 5 July 1936; *s* of George B. M. Mirrlees; *m* 1961, Gillian Marjorie Hughes; two *d. Educ:* Douglas-Ewart High Sch., Newton Stewart; Edinburgh Univ.; Trinity Coll., Cambridge. MA Edinburgh Maths, 1957; BA Cantab Maths, 1959; PhD Cantab Econs, 1963. Adviser, MIT Center for Internat. Studies, New Delhi, 1962-63; Cambridge Univ. Asst Lectr in Econs and Fellow of Trinity Coll., 1963, University Lectr, 1965; Adviser to Govt of Swaziland, 1963; Res. Assoc., Pakistan Inst. of Develt Econs, Karachi, 1966-67. Vis. Prof., MIT, 1968, 1970, 1976. *Publications:* (joint author) Manual of Industrial Project Analysis in Developing Countries, 1969; (ed jtly) Models of Economic Growth, 1973; (jt author) Project Appraisal and Planning, 1974; articles in economic jls.

Recreations: reading detective stories and other forms of mathematics, playing the piano, travelling, listening. *Address:* Nuffield College, Oxford; 11 Field House Drive, Oxford OX2 7NT. *T:* Oxford 52436.

MIRRLEES, Robin Ian Evelyn Stuart de la Lanne-; Richmond Herald of Arms, 1962-67; *b* Paris, 13 Jan. 1925; godson of 11th Duke of Argyll; one *s. Educ:* Merton Coll., Oxford (MA). Several language diplomas. Served India, 1942-46; Captain RA, 1944; Gen. Staff, New Delhi, 1946; Embassy Attaché, Tokyo, 1947; Rouge Dragon Pursuivant of Arms, 1952-62 (and as such attended Coronation). Co-editor, Annuaire de France, 1966-. ADC to HM the King of Yugoslavia, 1963-70. Has raised substantial funds for humanitarian organisations; undertook restoration of Inchdrewer Castle, Scotland, and others; proprietor of Island of Bernera, pop. 350. Freeman of City of London, 1960. Succeeded to the title of Comte de Lalanne (France), 1962. Various foreign orders of knighthood. *Recreations:* foxhunting, piloting, travelling, painting, sculpture. *Address:* 25 Holland Park Avenue, W11; 115 Rue de la Pompe, Paris 16me; Inchdrewer Castle, Banff, Scotland; Villa Lambins-Lalanne, Le Touquet, France; Schloss Ratzenegg, Carinthia, Austria. *Clubs:* Buck's, Turf; Puffin's (Edinburgh); Travellers' (Paris).

MISCAMPBELL, Norman Alexander, QC 1974; MP (C) Blackpool North since 1962; barrister; a Recorder of the Crown Court, since 1977; *b* 20 Feb. 1925; *s* of late Alexander and Eileen Miscampbell; *m* 1961, Margaret Kendall; two *s* two *d. Educ:* St Edward's Sch., Oxford; Trinity Coll., Oxford. Called to Bar, Inner Temple, 1952; N Circuit. Mem., Hoylake UDC, 1955-61. Contested (C) Newton, 1955, 1959. *Address:* House of Commons, SW1; 7 Abbey Road, West Kirby, Cheshire.

MISCHLER, Norman Martin; Chairman: Hoechst UK Ltd, since 1975; Hoechst Ireland Ltd, since 1976; *b* 9 Oct. 1920; *s* of late Martin Mischler and Martha Sarah (*née* Lambert); *m* 1949, Helen Dora Sinclair; one *s* one *d. Educ:* St Paul's Sch., London; St Catharine's Coll., Cambridge (MA). Indian Army, 1940; served in Burma Campaign (mentioned twice in despatches); released, rank of Major, 1946. Joined Burt, Boulton & Haywood, 1947, Vice-Chm. 1963; Dep. Man. Dir, Hoechst UK Ltd, 1966; Director: Berger, Jenson & Nicholson Ltd; Ringsdorff Carbon Co. Ltd; Rochas Perfumes Ltd. Councillor, German Chamber of Industry and Commerce in London; Mem. Council, Chemical Industries Assoc. Ltd. Paviors Co.; Freeman, City of London. *Recreations:* cricket, opera, and theatre. *Address:* 45 Carlton Hill, NW8 0EL. *T:* 01-624 2906. *Clubs:* MCC; Hawks (Cambridge).

MISHCON, Victor, DL; Solicitor; Senior Partner, Victor Mishcon & Co.; *b* 14 Aug. 1915; *s* of Rabbi Arnold and Mrs Queenie Mishcon. *Educ:* City of London Sch. Mem. Lambeth Borough Coun., 1945-49 (Chm. Finance Cttee, 1947-49); Mem. London CC for Brixton, 1946-65 (Chairman: Public Control Cttee, 1947-52; Gen. Purposes Cttee, 1952-54; Council, April 1954-55; Supplies Cttee, 1956-57; Fire Brigade Cttee, 1958-65); Mem. GLC for Lambeth, 1964-67 (Chm., Gen. Purposes Cttee, 1964-67). Mem., Inner London Educn Authority, 1964-67. Chm. Governors, Cormont and Loughborough Secondary Schools, 1947-60; Governor: Stockwell Manor Sch., 1960- (Chm. of Governors, 1960-67, 1970-); JFS Comprehensive Sch., 1970-; Philippa Fawcett Coll. of Educn, 1970-. Member: Standing Joint Cttee, Co. of London Sessions, 1950-65 (Vice-Chm. 1959-61); Nat. Theatre Board, 1965-67, 1968- (Mem., Finance and General Purposes Cttee); London Orchestra Bd, 1966-67; Exec. Cttee, London Tourist Board, 1965-67; Government Cttee of Enquiry into London Transport, 1953-54; Departmental Cttee on Homosexual Offences and Prostitution, 1954-57. Vice-Pres., Bd of Deputies of British Jews, 1967-73; Hon. President, Brit. Technion Soc.; Mem. Bd of Governors, Technion, Israel; Vice-Pres. (Past Pres.) Assoc of Jewish Youth; Chm., British Council of the Shaare Zedek Hosp., Jerusalem; Vice Chm., Council of Christians and Jews; Chm. of Deputy Lieutenants' Cttee of Lambeth, 1956-68. Contested (Lab) NW Leeds, 1950, Bath, 1951, Gravesend, 1955, 1959. DL Co. London, 1954. Comdr Royal Swedish Order of North Star, 1954; Star of Ethiopia, 1954. *Address:* 12 Chelwood House, Gloucester Square, W2.

MISKIN, James William, QC 1967; **His Honour Judge Miskin;** Recorder of London, since 1975; *b* 11 March 1925; *s* of Geoffrey Miskin and late Joyce Miskin; *m* 1951, Mollie Joan Milne; two *s* two *d. Educ:* Haileybury; Brasenose Coll., Oxford (MA). Sub-Lt, RNVR, 1943-46. Oxford, 1946-49 (Sen. Heath Harrison Exhibnr). Called to Bar, Inner Temple, 1951; Bencher, 1976; Mem. of Bar Council, 1964-67, 1970-73. Dep. Chm., Herts QS 1968-71; a Recorder of the Crown Court, 1972-75; Leader of SE

Circuit, 1974-75. City of London Magistrate, 1976. Chm., Bd of Discipline, LSE, 1972-75. Appeals Steward, British Boxing Bd of Control, 1972-75; Mem., Inner London Probation After Care Cttee. One of HM Lieutenants, City of London, 1976-. Liveryman, Worshipful Co. of Curriers; Hon. Liveryman, Worshipful Co. of Cutlers. *Recreations:* golf, gardening. *Club:* Vincent's (Oxford).

MISSELBROOK, (Bertram) Desmond, CBE 1972; Chairman, Livingston Development Corporation, since 1972; *b* 28 May 1913; *s* of late C. J. and E. P. Misselbrook; *m* 1949, Anne, *er d* of late F. O. Goodman; two *s. Educ:* Chatham House, Ramsgate; Bristol Univ. Admiralty Psychologist, 1942-45. Lectr in Psychology and Dir, Unit of Applied Psychology, Edinburgh Univ., 1945-49; Senr Res. Fellow in Business Studies, 1970-71, Hon. Fellow, 1971. Personnel Adviser, 1949, Dir. 1955, Dep. Chm. 1963-70, British-American Tobacco Co. Ltd; Chm., Evershed and Vignoles Ltd, 1961-65; Chm., Mardon Packaging International Ltd, 1962-70; Dir, 1963, Dep. Chm. 1966-69, Wiggins Teape Ltd; Dir, Charterhouse Gp Ltd, 1969-72; Deputy Chairman: Standard Life Assurance Co., 1977- (Dir, 1970); Anderson Mavor Ltd, 1971-74; Chairman: Anderson Strathclyde Ltd, 1974-77; Seaforth Maritime Ltd, 1977-. Mem. Council, British Inst. of Management, 1967-72 (a Vice-Chm., 1969); Chairman: Bd of Governors, Oversea Service, 1963-70; Construction Ind. Trng Bd, 1970-73; Council, Scottish Business Sch., 1972-; Economic Development Cttees for Building and Civil Engineering Industries, 1969-72; Member: Adv. Council on Social Work (Scotland), 1970-74; Economic Consultant, Scottish Office, 1970-72. Hon. DSc Edinburgh, 1977. *Recreations:* fishing, gardening, walking. *Address:* Drumdewan, Aberfeldy, Perthshire PH15 2JQ. *T:* Aberfeldy 434.

MISSEN, Leslie Robert, CMG 1956; MC 1918; Research Consultant; *b* 2 May 1897; *e s* of Robert Symonds Missen, Chesterton, Cambs; *m* 1932, Muriel, *o d* of Robert Alstead, OBE, Gathurst, Lancs, formerly MP for Altrincham; two *s. Educ:* Perse Sch. and Christ's Coll., Cambridge. Served European War, Capt., 7th Bn N Stafford Regt, Mesopotamia, Persia and Caucasus, 1915-19. Asst Education Officer, Leeds, 1922-26; Dep. Chief Educ. Officer, Middlesbrough, 1926-30; Chief Educ. Officer: Wigan, 1930-36; East Suffolk County Council, 1936-62; Mem., Local Govt Commn for England, 1962-66. Educational Adviser to: Ministry of Education, 1950-57; Ministry of Agriculture, 1944-54; Colonial Sec., 1952-55; Royal Navy, 1958-64; Chairman: Working Party on Educn in Trinidad, BWI, 1954; Trustees of Homerton Coll., Cambridge, 1946-62; President: Assoc. of Education Officers, 1952; Old Persean Soc., 1953-55; Education Section of British Assoc., 1957; County Educn Officers' Soc., 1960; Chairman: Ipswich and District War Pensions Cttee, 1942-70; Suffolk War Pensions Cttee, 1971-. *Publications:* War History of 7th Bn N Stafford Regt, 1920; The Employment of Leisure, 1935; Anecdotes and After Dinner Stories, 1961; Quotable Anecdotes, 1966; Toptable Talk, 1968; contrib. Purnell's History of the First World War, 1971. *Recreations:* gardening, writing, piano. *Address:* 34 Saxmundham Road, Aldeburgh, Suffolk. *T:* Aldeburgh 3163.

MITCHELL, Adrian; writer; *b* 24 Oct. 1932; *s* of James Mitchell and Kathleen Fabian. *Educ:* Dauntsey's Sch.; Christ Church, Oxford. Worked as reporter on Oxford Mail, Evening Standard, 1955-63; subseq. free-lance journalist for Daily Mail, Sun, Sunday Times, New Statesman; Granada Fellow, Univ. of Lancaster, 1968-69; Fellow, Center for Humanities, Wesleyan Univ., 1972; Resident Writer, Sherman Theatre, Cardiff, 1974-75. *Plays:* Tyger, Nat. Theatre, 1971; Man Friday, 7:84 Theatre Co., 1973 (TV 1972, Screenplay 1975); Mind Your Head, Liverpool Everyman, 1973; (stage adaptation) Marat/Sade, Royal Shakespeare Co.; (TV) Daft as a Brush, 1975; A Seventh Man, Hampstead, 1976; White Suit Blues, Nottingham, Edinburgh and Old Vic, 1977; Houdini, Amsterdam, 1977. *Publications:* novels: If You See Me Comin', 1962; The Bodyguard, 1970; Wartime, 1973; *poetry:* Poems, 1964; Out Loud, 1968; Ride the Nightmare, 1971; The Apeman Cometh, 1975; also plays. *Address:* c/o Jonathan Cape, 30 Bedford Square, WC1B 3EL.

MITCHELL, Alec Burton, CEng, MIMechE, FRINA; Director, Admiralty Research Laboratory, since 1974; *b* 27 Aug. 1924; *er s* of Ronald Johnson Mitchell and Millicent Annie Mitchell; *m* 1952, Barbara, *d* of Arthur Edward and Katie Florence Jane Archer; three *s. Educ:* Purley County Sch.; St. John's Coll., Cambridge (MA). Mechanical Sciences Tripos, Cambridge, 1944. Aeronautical Engineer with Rolls Royce Ltd, Hucknall, 1944-46; Grad. apprentice and gas turbine design engr with English Electric Co Ltd, Rugby, 1946-48. Joined RN Scientific Service, 1948; Dep. Head of Hydrodynamic Research Div., Admty Research Lab., 1961; promoted Dep. CSO, 1966; Dep.

Dir, Admty Research Laboratory, 1973. *Publications:* numerous scientific papers on hydrodynamics and under-water propulsion systems. *Recreations:* golf, photography, wood-work. *Address:* 32 Ormond Crescent, Hampton, Mddx TW12 2TH. *T:* 01-979 6056.

MITCHELL, Alexander Graham, CBE 1973; DFM 1945; *b* 2 Nov. 1923; *s* of Alexander Mitchell and Evelyn Mitchell (*née* Green); *m* 1954, Pamela Ann Borman; three *d. Educ:* Dulwich College; Downing Coll., Cambridge (MA). Sudan Government Civil Service, 1951-55; HM Overseas Civil Service, 1955; Western Pacific High Commission: various posts in British Solomon Islands Protectorate and British Residency, New Hebrides, 1955-71; Sec., Financial Affairs, British Residency, 1968-71; Administrator, Turks and Caicos Is, 1971-73; Governor 1973-75; sabbatical, 1975-76, retired June 1977. *Recreations:* ancient and military history. *Address:* Apple Tree Cottage, The Row, Tottenhill, Norfolk. *Clubs:* Royal Over-Seas League, Farmers'.

MITCHELL, Angus; see Mitchell, J. A. M.

MITCHELL, Air Cdre Sir Arthur Dennis, KBE 1977; CVO 1961; DFC 1944, and Bar, 1945; AFC 1943; an Extra Equerry to the Queen since 1962; *b* 26 May 1918; 2nd *s* of Col A. Mitchell, DSO, Carrickfergus, Belfast, N Ireland; *m* 1949, Comtesse Mireille Caroline Cornet de Ways Ruart; one *s. Educ:* Nautical Coll., Pangbourne; RAF Coll., Cranwell. Joined RAF, 1936. Served 1939-45, India, Burma, UK and NW Europe. US Air Force, 1951-53. Captain of the Queen's Flight, 1956-59 and 1962-64; ADC to the Queen, 1958-62. Gen. Agent, Spantax SA; Man. Dir, Aero Systems SA. *Recreations:* riding, golf. *Address:* 8 chemin des Chasseurs, Ohain, Belgium. *T:* 653.13.01. *Clubs:* Royal Air Force, Naval and Military, Anglo-Belgian.

MITCHELL, Austin Vernon, DPhil; MP (Lab) Grimsby, since April 1977; *b* 19 Sept. 1934; *s* of Richard Vernon Mitchell and Ethel Mary Mitchell; *m* 1st, Patricia Dorothea Jackson; two *d;* 2nd, Linda Mary McDougall; one *s* one *d. Educ:* Woodbottom Council Sch.; Bingley Grammar Sch.; Manchester Univ. (BA, MA); Nuffield Coll., Oxford (DPhil). Lectr in History, Univ. of Otago, Dunedin, NZ, 1959-63; Sen. Lectr in Politics, Univ. of Canterbury, Christchurch, NZ, 1963-67; Official Fellow, Nuffield Coll., Oxford, 1967-69; Journalist, Yorkshire Television, 1969-71; Presenter, BBC Current Affairs Gp, 1972-73; Journalist, Yorkshire TV, 1973-77. *Publications:* New Zealand Politics In Action, 1962; Government By Party, 1966; The Whigs in Opposition 1815-1830, 1969; Politics and People in New Zealand, 1970; Yorkshire Jokes, 1971; The Half-Gallon Quarter-Acre Pavlova Paradise, 1974. *Recreation:* worriting (sic). *Address:* 1 Abbey Park Road, Grimsby, South Humberside; House of Commons, SW1. *T:* 01-219 4559. *Clubs:* Grimsby Labour (Grimsby); AEU (Saltaire, Shipley).

MITCHELL, Prof. Basil George; Nolloth Professor of the Philosophy of the Christian Religion, Oxford University, and Fellow of Oriel College, since 1968; *b* 9 April 1917; *s* of George William Mitchell and Mary Mitchell (*née* Loxston); *m* 1950, Margaret Eleanor Collin; one *s* three *d. Educ:* King Edward VI Sch., Southampton; Queen's Coll., Oxford (Southampton Exhibitioner. 1st cl. Lit Hum 1939). Served Royal Navy, 1940-46; Lt RNVR 1942, Instructor Lt RN 1945. Lectr, Christ Church, Oxford, 1946-47; Fellow and Tutor in Philosophy, Keble Coll., Oxford, 1947-67; Sen. Proctor, 1956-57; Hebdomadal Council, 1959-65. Vis. Prof., Princeton Univ., 1963; Stanton Lectr in Philosophy of Religion, Cambridge Univ., 1959-62; Edward Cadbury Lectr, University of Birmingham, 1966-67; Gifford Lectr, Glasgow Univ., 1974-76. Vis. Prof., Colgate Univ., 1976. Hon. DD Glasgow, 1977. *Publications:* (ed) Faith and Logic, 1957; Law, Morality and Religion in a Secular Society, 1967; Neutrality and Commitment, 1968; (ed) The Philosophy of Religion, 1971; The Justification of Religious Belief, 1973; articles in philosophical and theological periodicals. *Address:* Bridge House, Wootton, Woodstock, Oxford. *T:* Woodstock 811265; 26 Walton Street, Oxford. *T:* Oxford 53744.

MITCHELL, Bertram, CB 1963; retired as Chief Inspector, Board of Customs and Excise (1960-63); *b* 19 Sept. 1898; *s* of James and Mary A. Mitchell; *m* 1931, Dora M. Alway. *Educ:* Newton Abbot Grammar Sch. Collector, Customs and Excise, Manchester, 1956-58; Dep. Chief Inspector, Board of Customs and Excise, 1958-59. *Address:* 14 Mildenhall, West Cliff Road, Bournemouth, Dorset. *T:* Bournemouth 760400.

MITCHELL, Lt-Col Brian Granville Blayney, DSC 1940; RM (Retired); DL; *b* 14 March 1900; *er s* of William Blayney Mitchell, Drumreaske, Co. Monaghan, Eire; *m* 1937, Violet

Gwyndolin, *o d* of late Major Sir Charles Price, DL, Haverfordwest, Pembs; two *d. Educ:* King's Sch., Bruton, Somerset. Joined Royal Marines, 2nd Lt 1917; Lt 1919; HMS Erin, 1919; Emperor of India, Mediterranean, 1921-22; Hood, Atlantic and Round the World Cruise, 1923-24; Instructor, Sigs Portsmouth, 1925-27; HMS Champion, Home, 1928; Capt. 1928; Queen Elizabeth, Mediterranean, 1929-31; St Vincent (Boys' Training Estab.), 1932-33; Hermes, China, 1934-37; Coronation Review, Spithead, 1937; Supt of Sigs, RM, 1938-40; Major 1937; Actg Lt-Col 1940; Hook of Holland, 1940; The RM Div., 1941-42; Commando Group, Chief Signal Officer, 1943-44; Actg Col 1945; CO Molcab IV, 1945; retired, 1945. DL 1956, High Sheriff, 1959, County of Pembroke. Order of Orange Nassau with Crossed Swords (Netherlands), 1940. *Address:* Manor House, Wiston, Dyfed SA62 4PN. *T:* Clarbeston 258.

MITCHELL, Charles Julian Humphrey; *see* Mitchell, Julian.

MITCHELL, Lt-Col Colin (Campbell); *b* 17 Nov. 1925; *o s* of Colin Mitchell, MC, and Janet Bowie Gilmour; *m* 1956, Jean Hamilton Susan Phillips; two *s* one *d. Educ:* Whitgift Sch. Enlisted British Army, 1943; commissioned Argyll and Sutherland Highlanders, 1944, serving in Italy (wounded); Palestine, 1945-48 (wounded); Korea, 1950-51; Cyprus, 1958-59; Borneo, 1964 (brevet Lt-Col); Aden, 1967 (despatches). Qualified Camberley Staff Coll., 1955; subsequently: GSO2, 51st Highland Div. (TA); Bde Major, King's African Rifles, and GSO1 Staff of Chief of Defence Staff at MoD. Retired at own request, 1968; subseq. Special Correspondent, Vietnam; industrial management trainee. MP (C) W Aberdeenshire, 1970-Feb. 1974 (not seeking re-election); PPS to Sec. of State for Scotland, 1972-73. Hon. Pres., Scottish Military Collectors Soc.; Vice-Pres., Royal Scottish Country Dance Soc. *Publication:* Having Been A Soldier, 1969. *Recreations:* golf, shooting, squash, poetry, antiques, travel. *Address:* 901 Nelson House, Dolphin Square, SW1V 3NJ. *T:* 01-834 3800. *Clubs:* Caledonian, Carlton, Garrick.

MITCHELL, David Bower; MP (C) Basingstoke since 1964; *b* June 1928; *er s* of James Mitchell, Naval Architect; *m* 1954, Pamela Elaine Haward; two *s* one *d. Educ:* Aldenham. An Opposition Whip, 1965-67; PPS to Sec. of State for Social Services, 1970-74. Chm., Cons. Smaller Business Cttee, 1974-. Wine importer. *Address:* 46 Eaton Terrace, SW1. *T:* 01-730 4470; Berry Horn Cottage, Odiham, Hants. *T:* 2161.

MITCHELL, Sir Derek (Jack), KCB 1974 (CB 1967); CVO 1966; Executive Director, Guinness Mahon and Co. Ltd, since 1977; *b* 5 March 1922; *s* of late Sidney Mitchell, Schoolmaster, and Gladys Mitchell; *m* 1944, Miriam, *d* of late F. E. Jackson; one *s* two *d. Educ:* St Paul's Sch.; Christ Church, Oxford. Served War of 1939-45: Royal Armoured Corps and HQ London District, 1942-45. Asst Principal HM Treasury, 1947; Private Sec. to Economic Sec., 1948-49; Private Sec. to Permanent Sec. and Official Head of Civil Service (Sir Edward Bridges), 1954-56; Principal Private Sec. to: Chancellor of Exchequer (Mr Reginald Maudling), 1962-63; The Prime Minister (Mr Harold Wilson, previously Sir Alec Douglas-Home), 1964-66; Under-Sec., 1964; Dep. Under-Sec. of State, Dept of Economic Affairs, 1966-67; Dep. Sec., Min. of Agriculture, Fisheries and Food, 1967-69; Economic Minister and Head of UK Treasury and Supply Delegn, Washington, (also UK Executive Director for IMF and IBRD), 1969-72; Second Permanent Sec. (Overseas Finance), HM Treasury, 1973-77. *Recreations:* going to opera and concerts, travel. *Address:* 9 Holmbush Road, Putney, SW15 3LE. *T:* 01-788 6581. *Club:* Garrick.
See also E. F. Jackson.

MITCHELL, Douglas Svärd; Controller of Personnel and Administrative Services, Greater London Council, since 1972; *b* 21 Aug. 1918; *er s* of late James Livingstone Mitchell and Hilma Josefine (*née* Svärd); *m* 1943, Winifred Thornton Paterson, *d* of late William and Ellen Paterson; one *s* two *d. Educ:* Morgan Academy, Dundee. Royal Ordnance Factories, 1937-51; Principal, Min. of Supply, 1951-55; Dir of Personnel and Admin., in Industrial, Production and Engineering Groups, UKAEA, 1955-63; Authority Personnel Officer for UKAEA, 1963-64; Dir of Establishments, GLC, 1964-72. *Address:* Hatton Orchard, Yester Park, Chislehurst, Kent. *T:* 01-467 1393. *Club:* Athenæum.

MITCHELL, Prof. Edgar William John, CBE 1976; Professor of Physics, 1961-78, Deputy Vice-Chancellor, 1976-78, University of Reading; Dr Lee's Professor of Experimental Philosophy, Oxford University, from Oct. 1978; *b* Kingsbridge, S Devon, 25 Sept. 1925; *s* of late Edgar and Caroline Mitchell; *m* 1948; one *s. Educ:* Univs of Sheffield (BSc, MSc) and Bristol (PhD). FInstP. Metropolitan Vickers Research Dept, 1946-48, 1950-51; Univ.

of Bristol, 1948-50; Univ. of Reading, 1951-78: Dean, Faculty of Science, 1966-69. Mem., SRC, 1970-74 (Mem., 1965-70, Chm., 1967-70, Physics Cttee; Chm., 1966-74, Neutron Beam Res. Cttee); devised scheme for extensive University use of nuclear res. reactors for condensed matter res. Member: Sci. Council of Inst. Laue-Langevin, Grenoble; Comité de Direction, Solid State Physics Lab., École Normale and Univ. of Paris VI; Chm., SE Reg. Computing Cttee, 1974-76. *Publications:* numerous papers on solid state physics. *Recreations:* good food, opera, motoring, physics. *Address:* (until Oct. 1978) J. J. Thomson Physical Laboratory, The University, Whiteknights, Reading, Berks; (from Oct. 1978) Clarendon Laboratory, Oxford.

MITCHELL, Mrs Eric; *see* Shacklock, Constance.

MITCHELL, Ewan; *see* Janner, Hon. G. E.

MITCHELL, Rt. Rev. Frederick Julian, DD; *b* 30 July 1901; *s* of late Rev. R. J. Mitchell, MA, The Rectory, Trillick, Co. Tyrone; *m* Kathleen Louise, *d* of Rev. R. Watson, BD, Castle Archdale, Co. Fermanagh. *Educ:* Campbell Coll.; Trinity Coll., Dublin. Deacon, 1924, St Mary's, Belfast; Priest, 1925; Incumbent of S Polycarp, Finaghy, Belfast, 1928; Dean of Residences, QUB, 1934; Incumbent of Kilconriola and Ballyclug, 1936; Rural Dean of Ballymena, 1945; Canon and Prebendary of Kilroot in Chapter of S Saviour of Connor, and Bishop of Kilmore, Elphin and Ardagh, 1950-55; Bishop of Down and Dromore, 1955-69. *Publications:* A Pageant of the Book of Common Prayer (for Quater Centenary of 1549 Prayer Book); Pageant of the Holy Bible (in connection with Festival of Britain); Hail Caesar!; It Happened in Nazareth; Shreds and Patches (autobiog.), 1977. *Address:* Glen Lodge, Belmont Road, Belfast 4, Northern Ireland.

MITCHELL, Rear-Adm. Geoffrey Charles, CB 1973; retired 1975; Director, The Old Granary Art and Craft Centre, Bishop's Waltham, Hants; *b* 21 July 1921; *s* of William C. Mitchell; *m* 1955, Jocelyn Rainger, Auckland, NZ; one *s* two *d. Educ:* Marlborough College. Joined RN 1940; Captain 1961; Director Officer Recruiting, 1961-63; Captain (F), 2nd Frigate Sqdn, 1963-65; Director Naval Ops and Trade, 1965-67; Comdr, NATO Standing Naval Force Atlantic, 1968-69; Director Strategic Policy, to Supreme Allied Comdr Atlantic, 1969-71; Rear Adm. 1971; Dep. Asst Chief of Staff (Ops), SHAPE, 1971-74; Chm., RNR and Naval Cadet Forces Review Bd, 1974-75. *Recreations:* golf, tennis, painting, music, languages. *Address:* Willowpool, Lockhams Road, Curdridge, Southampton. *T:* Botley 2403.

MITCHELL, Prof. George Archibald Grant, OBE 1945; TD 1950; Professor of Anatomy and Director of Anatomical Laboratories, Manchester University, 1946-Sept. 1974, late Dean of Medical School and Pro-Vice-Chancellor; *b* 11 Nov. 1906; *s* of George and Agnes Mitchell; *m* 1933, Mary Cumming; one *s* two *d. Educ:* Fordyce Academy; Aberdeen Central Sch.; Aberdeen Univ. MB, ChB (1st Cl. Hons), 1929; ChM 1933; MSc (Manchester); DSc (Aberdeen) 1950; FRCS 1968. Lecturer in Anatomy, 1930-33, in Surgery, 1933-34, Aberdeen Univ.; Surgical Specialist, Co. Caithness, 1934-37; Sen. Lecturer in Anatomy, Aberdeen Univ., 1937-39. Chm., Internat. Anatomical Nomenclature Commn. Pres., 3rd European Anatomical Congress; Pres., S Lancs and E Cheshire BMA Br. Council; Mem. Ct of Examnrs, RCS, 1950-68; Mem. Bd of Governors, United Manchester Hosps, 1955-74; Past President: Anatomical Soc. of GB and Ireland; Manchester Med. Soc. Served War, 1939-45: Surgical Specialist, Officer i/c No. 1 Orthopædic Centre, MEF; Officer i/c Surgical Divs, Adviser in Penicillin and Chemotherapy, 21 Army Gp. Hon. Alumnus, Univ. of Louvain, 1944; Hon. Member: Société Med. Chir. du Centre; Assoc. des Anatomistes; Amer. Assoc. Anat. Chevalier First Class Order of the Dannebrog. *Publications:* The Anatomy of the Autonomic Nervous System, 1952; Basic Anatomy (with E. L. Patterson), 1954; Cardiovascular Innervation, 1956; ed Symposium, Penicillin Therapy and Control in 21 Army Group, 1945. Sections in: Penicillin (by Sir A. Fleming), 1946; Medical Disorders of the Locomotor System (by E. Fletcher), 1947; British Surgical Practice (by Sir Rock Carling and Sir J. Patterson Ross), 1951; Peripheral Vascular Disorders (by Martin, Lynn, Dible and Aird), 1956; Essentials of Neuroanatomy, 1966; Encyclopaedia Britannica, 15th edn; Editor, Nomina Anatomica, 1966. Numerous articles in Jl Anatomy, British Jl Surg., Jl Bone and Joint Surg., Brit. Jl Radiol., BMJ, Lancet, Acta Anat., Nature, Brit. Jl Urol., Edinburgh Medical Jl, Jl Hist. Med., Aberdeen Univ. Rev., Ann. Méd. Chir. du Centre, etc. *Recreations:* wood carving; studying antiques. *Address:* 596 Wilmslow Road, Manchester, M20 9DE. *T:* 061-445 1561.

MITCHELL, Prof. George Francis, FRS 1973; PRIA; Professor of Quaternary Studies, Trinity College, Dublin, since 1965; *b* 15 Oct. 1912; *s* of late David William Mitchell and late Frances Elizabeth Kirby; *m* 1940, Lucy Margaret Gwynn; two *d. Educ:* High Sch., Dublin; Trinity Coll., Dublin (MA, MSc); FTCD 1945. Various teaching and admin. posts, Trinity Coll., Dublin, 1934-. Pres., Internat. Union for Quaternary Research, 1969-73. MRIA 1939, PRIA 1976. DSc (*hc*): Queen's Univ., Belfast, 1976; NUI, 1977; fil.D(*hc*) Uppsala, 1977. *Publication:* The Irish Landscape, 1976. *Address:* Townley Hall, Drogheda, Co. Louth, Republic of Ireland. *T:* Drogheda 8218; Trinity College, Dublin. *T:* Dublin 772941.

MITCHELL, Sir George (Irvine), Kt 1976; CB 1970; QC (Scot.) 1972; Legal Secretary to Lord Advocate and First Parliamentary Draftsman for Scotland, 1969-76; an Assistant Legal Secretary and Parliamentary Draftsman, Lord Advocate's Department, since 1976; *b* 18 Feb. 1911; *e s* of late John Irvine Mitchell and Mrs L. J. Mitchell; *m* 1945, Elizabeth, *d* of late Charles Leigh Pemberton and Anna Norman; one *s* one *d. Educ:* George Watson's Coll.; Edinburgh Univ. MA 1932; LLB 1935; Vans Dunlop Scholarship in Law, 1937. Admitted to Faculty of Advocates, 1937; called to English Bar, Inner Temple, 1945. Served War of 1939-45, Border Regt, War Office. Draftsman in Lord Advocate's Dept, 1944. *Address:* 14 Rodway Road, Roehampton, SW15. *T:* 01-788 6649.

MITCHELL, Gladys (Maude Winifred); Writer; *b* 19 April 1901; *e d* of James Mitchell and Annie Julia Maude Simmonds. *Educ:* The Green Sch., Isleworth; Goldsmiths' and University Colls, University of London. First novel published, 1929; followed by other novels, short stories, BBC short detective plays, BBC excerpts from books, BBC Talks on Home Service. Member: Ancient Monuments Soc.; Soc. of Authors; Crime Writers' Assoc.; Detection Club. *Publications:* Speedy Death, 1929; and subsequently numerous other detective novels, including Dead Men's Morris; My Father Sleeps; Rising of the Moon; Dancing Druids; Tom Brown's Body; Groaning Spinney; The Devil's Elbow; The Echoing Strangers; Merlin's Furlong; Faintly Speaking; Watson's Choice; Twelve Horses and the Hangman's Noose; The Twenty-third Man; Spotted Hemlock; The Man Who Grew Tomatoes; Say It With Flowers, 1960; The Nodding Canaries, 1961; My Bones Will Keep, 1962; Adders on the Heath, 1963; Death of a Delft Blue, 1964; Pageant of Murder, 1965; The Croaking Raven, 1966; Skeleton Island, 1967; Three Quick and Five Dead, 1968; Dance to Your Daddy, 1969; Gory Dew, 1970; Lament for Leto, 1971; A Hearse on May-Day, 1972; The Murder of Busy Lizzie, 1973; A Javelin for Jonah, 1974; Winking at the Brim, 1974; Convent on Styx, 1975; Late, Late in the Evening, 1976; Noonday and Night, 1977; Fault in the Structure, 1977; Wraiths and Changelings, 1978; *as Stephen Hockaby:* Marsh Hay, 1934; Seven Stars and Orion, 1935; Shallow Brown, 1936; Grand Master, 1939; *as Malcolm Torrie:* Heavy As Lead, 1966; Late and Cold, 1967; Your Secret Friend, 1968; Churchyard Salad, 1969; Shades of Darkness, 1970; Bismarck Herrings, 1971; *children's books:* Outlaws of the Border, The Three Fingerprints, Holiday River, 1948; Seven Stones Mystery, 1949; The Malory Secret, 1950; Pam at Storne Castle, 1951; On Your Marks, 1954; Caravan Creek, 1954; The Light-Blue Hills, 1959. *Recreations:* reading, studying architecture, telling ghost stories. *Address:* 1 Cecil Close, Corfe Mullen, Wimborne, Dorset.

MITCHELL, Sir Godfrey Way, Kt 1948; Chairman of George Wimpey & Co., Ltd, 1930-73, Executive Director, since 1973; *b* 31 Oct. 1891; *s* of Christopher Mitchell and Margaret Mitchell (*née* Way); *m* 1929, Doreen Lilian Mitchell (*d* 1953); two *d. Educ:* Aske's Sch., Hatcham. Employed in father's business, Rowe & Mitchell, 1908, until European War, 1914-18; served in France; temp. commission RE; demobilized with rank Captain. Managing Dir of George Wimpey & Co. Ltd, 1919. Hon. Fellow, ICE, 1968; Hon. FIOB, 1971. *Address:* Copper Beech, 2 Curzon Avenue, Beaconsfield, Bucks HP9 2NN. *T:* Beaconsfield 3128.

MITCHELL, Graham Russell, CB 1957; OBE 1951; attached War Office, 1939-63, retired; *b* 4 Nov. 1905; *s* of late Capt. A. S. Mitchell; *m* 1934, Eleonora Patricia (*née* Robertson); one *s* one *d. Educ:* Winchester; Magdalen Coll., Oxford. *Recreations:* yacht racing, chess. *Address:* Barncote, Chobham, Woking, Surrey. *Clubs:* Bembridge Sailing (Bembridge, I of W); Royal Thames Yacht.

MITCHELL, Sir Hamilton, KBE 1969; Barrister and Solicitor, in private practice, New Zealand; *b* 24 Feb. 1910; *s* of Ernest Hamilton Mitchell and Catherine Mitchell; *m* 1938, Marion Frances Norman; two *s* one *d. Educ:* Auckland Grammar Sch.; New Zealand Univ. (LLM). Practice on own account, 1941-.

Served 2nd NZEF, 1943-46 (Captain, Egypt and Italy). President: Disabled Servicemen's Re-establishment League, 1959-63; NZ Returned Services Assoc., 1962-74; Vice-President: World Veterans' Fedn, 1964-66; British Commonwealth Ex-Services League, 1962-74; Judge, Courts Martial Appeal Court, 1962-; Dep. Chm., Winston Churchill Trust, 1966-76; Chairman: National Art Gallery Management Council, 1967-73; Canteen Fund Bd, 1967-; NZ Patriotic Fund, 1970-; Nat. War Meml Council, 1973-76; Dep. Chm., Rehabilitation League, NZ, 1970-. *Address:* 78 Orangikaupapa Road, Wellington, New Zealand. *T:* 757224. *Clubs:* Wellington, Wellesley, United Services (Wellington); Royal New Zealand Yacht Squadron.

MITCHELL, Harold Charles, CIE 1947; Indian Police (retired); *b* 7 March 1896; *s* of late Daniel Charles Mitchell and late Helen Mitchell; *m* 1923, Edna Evadne Bion; one *d. Educ:* Fairfield. RNVR, Bristol, 1912-19 (Pay Lt). Joined Indian Police, 1920; served as Dist Supt of Police, Bareilly, Benares, Cawnpore, Meerut and other UP districts; Central Intelligence Officer, UP and Ajmer, Home Dept Govt of India; Special Branch, CID, UP; Dep. Inspector-Gen. of Police, CID, UP; Personal Asst to Inspector-Gen. of Police, UP; Dep. Inspector-Gen. of Police, UP HQ and Railways. *Recreations:* golf, fishing. *Address:* Camber Cottage, Camberley, Surrey. *T:* Camberley 22675. *Clubs:* Naval; Camberley Heath.

MITCHELL, Col Sir Harold (Paton), 1st Bt, *cr* 1945; *b* 21 May 1900; *e s* of late Col. Alexander Mitchell, TD, JP, DL, of Tulliallan; *m* 1947, Mary, *d* of late William Pringle; one *d. Educ:* Eton; RMC, Sandhurst; University Coll., Oxford (MA), Hon. Fellow 1972; University of Geneva (Docteur ès Sciences Politiques). Vice-Chm. of Conservative Party, 1942-45; Contested (C) Clackmannan and East Stirlingshire in 1929; MP (C) Brentford and Chiswick Div. of Middlesex, 1931-45; Parliamentary Private Sec. to Rt Hon. John Colville, MP (Dept of Overseas Trade), 1931-35; Parliamentary Private Sec. to Rt Hon. Ralph Assheton, MP (Ministry of Labour, 1939-41, and Ministry of Supply, 1941); Mem. Departmental Cttee on Education and Training of Overseas Students, 1933-34; Mem. Selection Board for Consular Service, 1934-35; Mem. Company Law Amendment Cttee, 1943-45; Command Welfare Officer, AA Command, 1940-48, and Liaison Officer to Polish Forces (France, Belgium, Holland, 1944). Lectr, Hispanic American Studies, Stanford University 1959-65; Research Prof. of Latin American Studies, Rollins Coll. Hon. Col, 123 LAA Regt (City of London Rifles) TA, 1939-48; Hon. Col of 61st (City of Edinburgh) Signal Regt, TA, 1947-65. Chm. and Chief Exec., Luscar Ltd Group, Edmonton, Alberta; sometime Dir London and North Eastern Railway Co.; Joint Master Lauderdale Foxhounds, 1934-35; Mem. Queen's Body Guard for Scotland. DL Clackmannanshire, 1943-47. Hon. LLD Alberta, Rollins and St Andrews. KStJ; Knight Commander of Polonia Restituta; Polish Cross of Valour. *Publications:* Downhill Ski-Racing, 1930; Into Peace, 1945; In My Stride, 1951; Europe in the Caribbean, 1963; Caribbean Patterns, 1967, 2nd edn 1972; The Spice of Life, 1974. *Recreation:* ski-ing, represented Gt Britain, 1929, 1931, and 1933. *Address:* Maison Silence, 3920 Zermatt, Switzerland; Marshall's Island, Bermuda. *Clubs:* Alpine; Royal Bermuda Yacht.

MITCHELL, Harvey Allan; Director of Arts, Lothian Region, since 1975; *b* 23 Sept. 1932; *s* of Robert Mutter Mitchell and Margaret Massey Mitchell; *m* 1970, Karin Katharina Rapp, Tailfingen, Germany; two *s* one *d. Educ:* Edinburgh Univ. (MA Hons). Freelance Journalist, 1955-56; Press Officer, Rank Organization, 1956-58; Sen. Staff, Voice & Vision, 1958-60; Sen. Staff, Barnet & Reef (NY), 1961; Public Relations Administrator, Merck & Co., New York and Brussels, 1962-65; Asst to Vice-Pres., Massey-Ferguson (Toronto), 1965-67. Gen. Manager, New Philharmonia Orch., 1968-72; Dir of Develt, Tayside, 1972-75. Dir, Scottish Occupational Health Service, 1972-; Chm., Duntrune House Develts Ltd, 1972-. Dir, Royal Lyceum Theatre Co. *Publications:* articles on philosophy and the arts. *Recreations:* tennis, bridge, travel. *Address:* 10 Royal Terrace, Edinburgh. *T:* 031-556 1010. *Club:* Scottish Arts (Edinburgh).

MITCHELL, Ian Edward; Secretary, British Film Producers Association Ltd (formerly Film Production Association of Great Britain Ltd), since 1974; Secretary/Director, Central Casting Ltd, since 1970; Administrator, Federation of Specialised Film Associations, since 1970; *b* 24 Dec. 1932; *s* of George Thomas Mitchell and Lorna May Mitchell. *Educ:* Queensland, Australia. Local govt, Australia, 1953-65; Film Production Assoc. of Great Britain Ltd: Asst Dir of Labour Relations, 1966; Asst to Dir-Gen., 1971; Dep. Sec., 1972. *Recreations:* amateur theatricals, opera, swimming, tennis. *Address:* 80 Alexandra Road, Epsom, Surrey. *T:* Epsom 20982, (office) 01-734 2142.

MITCHELL, James; writer these many years; *b* South Shields, 12 March 1926; *s* of James Mitchell and Wilhelmina Mitchell; *m* 1968, Delia, *d* of Major and Mrs K. J. McCoy; two *s*. *Educ:* South Shields Grammar Sch.; St Edmund Hall, Oxford (BA 1948, MA 1950); King's Coll., Newcastle upon Tyne, Univ. of Durham (DipEd 1950). Worked in rep. theatre, 1948, then in shipyard, travel agency and Civil Service; taught for some fifteen years in almost every kind of instn from secondary modern sch. to coll. of art. Free-lance writer: novels; more than a hundred television scripts; several screenplays and a theatre play. *Publications:* Here's a Villain, 1957; A Way Back, 1959; Steady Boys, Steady, 1960; Among Arabian Sands, 1963; The Man Who Sold Death, 1964; Die Rich, Die Happy, 1965; The Money that Money can't Buy, 1967; The Innocent Bystanders, 1969; Ilion like a Mist, 1969; A Magnum for Schneider, 1969; The Winners, 1970; Russian Roulette, 1973; Death and Bright Water, 1974; Smear Job, 1975; When the Boat Comes In, 1976; The Hungry Years, 1976. *Recreations:* travel, military history, aristology. *Address:* 15 Zetland House, Marloes Road, W8 5LB. *Club:* Lansdowne.

MITCHELL, (James Lachlan) Martin, RD 1969; Sheriff of Lothian and Borders (formerly Lothians and Peebles) at Edinburgh since 1974 (as a floating Sheriff); *b* 13 June 1929; *o s* of late Dr L. M. V. Mitchell, OBE, MB, ChB and Harriet Doris Riggall. *Educ:* Cargilfield; Sedbergh; Univ. of Edinburgh. MA 1951, LLB 1953. Admitted Mem. Faculty of Advocates, 1957; Standing Junior Counsel in Scotland to Admty Bd, 1963-74. Nat. Service, RN, 1954-55; Sub-Lt (S) RNVR 1954; Perm. Reserve, 1956; Comdr RNR 1966, retd 1974. *Recreations:* fishing, photography, gramophone. *Address:* 3 Great Stuart Street, Edinburgh EH3 6AP. *T:* 031-225 3384. *Clubs:* New, Scottish Arts (Edinburgh).

MITCHELL, Jeremy George Swale Hamilton; Under Secretary, and Director, National Consumer Council, since 1977; *b* 25 May 1929; *s* of late George Oswald Mitchell and late Agnes Josephine Mitchell; *m* 1956, Margaret Mary Ayres; three *s* one *d*. *Educ:* Ampleforth; Brasenose and Nuffield Colls, Oxford (MA). Dep. Research Dir, then Dir of Information, Consumers' Assoc. (Which?), 1958-65; Asst Sec., Nat. Econ. Develt Office, 1965-66; Scientific Sec., then Sec., SSRC, 1966-74; Under Sec., and Dir of Consumer Affairs, Office of Fair Trading, 1974-77. *Publications:* (ed) SSRC Reviews of Research, series, 1968-73; (ed jtly) Social Science Research and Industry, 1971; Betting, 1972. *Recreations:* book collecting, Swinburne, writing, racing. *Address:* 32 Brookfield Park, NW5; Cleveland House, 26 Pound Lane, Isleham, Cambs.

MITCHELL, Dr Joan Eileen, (Mrs James Cattermole); Reader in Economics, University of Nottingham, since 1962; *b* 15 March 1920; *d* of late Albert Henry Mitchell, Paper Merchant, and Eva Mitchell; *m* 1956, James Cattermole; one *s* one *d*. *Educ:* Southend-on-Sea High Sch.; St Hilda's Coll., Oxford. Economist, Min. of Fuel and Power, 1942; Tutor, St Anne's Coll., Oxford, 1945; Economist, BoT, 1947; Research Officer, Labour Party, 1950; Lectr in Econs, Nottingham Univ., 1952. Mem., NBPI, 1965-68; personal economic adviser to Sec. of State for Prices and Consumer Protection, 1974-76. Mem., Cttee to Review the Functioning of Financial Institutions, 1977- (Chm. Res. Panel). *Publications:* Britain in Crisis 1951, 1963; Groundwork to Economic Planning, 1966; The National Board for Prices and Incomes, 1972. *Recreations:* gardening, cooking, highbrow music. *Address:* Economics Department, University of Nottingham; 15 Ranmoor Road, Gedling, Nottingham. *Club:* National Liberal.

MITCHELL, (John) Angus (Macbeth), CVO 1961; MC 1946; Secretary, Scottish Education Department, since 1976; *b* 25 Aug. 1924; *s* of John Fowler Mitchell, *qv*; *m* 1948, Ann Katharine Williamson; two *s* two *d*. *Educ:* Marlborough Coll.; Brasenose Coll., Oxford (Junior Hulme Scholar); BA Modern Hist. Served Royal Armoured Corps, 1943-46: Lieut, Inns of Court Regt, NW Europe, 1944-45; Captain East African Military Records, 1946. Entered Scottish Education Dept, 1949; Private Sec. to Sec. of State for Scotland, 1958-59; Asst Sec., Scottish Educn Dept, 1959-65; Dept of Agriculture and Fisheries for Scotland, 1965-68; Scottish Development Dept, 1968; Asst Under-Secretary of State, Scottish Office, 1968-69; Under Sec., Social Work Services Gp, Scottish Educn Dept, 1969-75; Under Sec., SHHD, 1975-76. Chairman: Scottish Marriage Guidance Council, 1965-69; Working Party on Social Work Services in NHS, 1976. Kt, Order of Oranje-Nassau (Netherlands), 1946. *Address:* 20 Regent Terrace, Edinburgh EH7 5BS. *T:* 031-556 7671. *Clubs:* Royal Commonwealth Society; New (Edinburgh).

MITCHELL, Prof. John David Bawden, CBE 1972; PhD; LLB (London); LLD (Edinburgh); Solicitor; Salvesen Professor of European Institutions, University of Edinburgh, since 1968; *b* 28 May 1917; *s* of A. Mitchell, OBE; *m* 1945, Jeanne Rosamund, *d* of late Maj-Gen. W. H. S. Nickerson, VC, CB, CMG; two *d*. *Educ:* Colfe's Grammar Sch.; London Sch. of Economics and Political Science, Univ. of London (Whittuck Schol.). Served War of 1939-45: commissioned North Staffs Regt, 1939; BEF 1940 (despatches); Staff Officer, 1943; released 1946. Admitted Solicitor, 1947; Lectr in Law, University Coll. of Wales, 1947-48; Lectr, Law Soc.'s Sch., 1948-49; Lectr 1949, Reader in English Law in the Univ. of London, 1952, at LSE; Prof. of Constitutional Law, Univ. of Edinburgh, 1954-68. Member: Vedel Cttee (EEC), 1971-72; Hansard Soc. Commn on Electoral Reform, 1975-76. Docteur de l'Université (*hc*), Lille, 1975. Hon. LLD Amsterdam, 1975. *Publications:* Contracts of Public Authorities, 1954; Constitutional Law, 1964 (2nd edn 1968). Articles in various legal periodicals. *Recreations:* talking and walking. *Address:* 28 Murrayfield Avenue, Edinburgh EH12 6AX. *T:* 031-337 6189. *Club:* New (Edinburgh).

MITCHELL, John Fowler, CIE 1935; Indian Civil Service, retired; *b* 30 Dec. 1886; *s* of William Mitchell and Janet Woodrow; *m* 1920, Sheila Macbeth; one *s* two *d*. *Educ:* Allan Glen's Sch., Glasgow; Royal College of Science, S Kensington; Glasgow Univ.; Merton Coll., Oxford; London Univ. (BSc 1st cl. Hons, Exptl Physics, 1908). Entered Indian Civil Service, 1910; from 1910-19 various posts as Asst Comr Punjab, including Magistrate and Sec. Municipal Cttee, Delhi; Subdivisional Officer, Fazilka; Superintendent Central Jail, Multan; Forest Settlement Officer, Kangra; from 1920-34 various finance and audit posts, including Under Sec. Finance, Punjab; Accountant General Madras, Central Provinces and Central Revenues; Dir of Audit Indian Railways; officiating Dep. Auditor General, India; retired 1937. Military Service, 1940-46; Allied Commission for Austria, 1946-47. *Publications:* (with Sheila Mitchell): Monumental Inscriptions in Kinross-shire, 1967; Monumental Inscriptions (pre-1855) in Clackmannanshire, 1968; similar volumes for West Lothian, 1969; Dunbartonshire, 1969; Renfrewshire, 1970; East Fife, 1971; West Fife, 1972; East Stirlingshire, 1972; West Stirlingshire, 1973; South Perthshire, 1974; North Perthshire, 1975. *Address:* 7 Randolph Cliff, Edinburgh EH3 7TZ. *T:* 031-225 6074.
See also J. A. M. Mitchell.

MITCHELL, John Gall, QC (Scot.) 1970; *b* 5 May 1931; *s* of late Rev. William G. Mitchell, MA; *m* 1959, Anne Bertram, *d* of John Jardine; three *s* one *d*. *Educ:* Royal High Sch., Edinburgh; Edinburgh Univ. (MA, LLB). Advocate 1957. Standing Junior Counsel, Customs and Excise, Scotland, 1964-70; Chairman: Industrial Tribunals, Scotland, 1966-; Legal Aid Supreme Court Cttee, Scotland, 1974-; Pensions Appeals Tribunal, Scotland, 1974-. Hon. Sheriff of Lanarkshire, 1970-74. *Address:* Advocates' Library, Parliament House, Edinburgh; Rosemount, Park Road, Eskbank, Dalkeith, Midlothian.

MITCHELL, John Matthew, CBE 1976; PhD; Controller, Education and Science Division, British Council, since 1977; *b* 22 March 1925; *s* of Clifford George Arthur Mitchell and Grace Maud Jamson; *m* 1952, Eva Maria von Rupprecht; three *s* one *d*. *Educ:* Ilford County High Sch.; Worcester Coll., Oxford; Queens' Coll., Cambridge (MA). PhD Vienna. Served War, RN, 1944-46. Lectr, Brit. Council, Austria, 1949-52 and Egypt, 1952-56; Brit. Council, Scotland, 1957-60; Dep. Rep., Japan, 1960-63; Reg. Dir, Zagreb, 1963-66; Reg. Rep., Dacca, 1966-69; Dep. Controller, Home Div., 1969-72; Vis. Fellow, Wolfson Coll., Cambridge, 1972-73; Brit. Council Rep., Federal Republic of Germany, 1973-77. Former Lectr, univs of Vienna, Cairo and Tokyo. *Publications:* verse, short stories and trans. from German. *Recreations:* ski-ing, golf, bridge. *Address:* 14 Woodclyffe Drive, Chislehurst, Kent. *T:* 01-467 6801. *Club:* Royal Commonwealth Society.

MITCHELL, John Newton; *b* Detroit, Michigan, 5 Sept, 1913; *s* of late Joseph Charles and Margaret Agnes McMahon Mitchell; *m* 1957, Martha (*née* Beall) (*d* 1976), Pine Bluff, Ark; one *d* (and one *s* one *d* of a previous marriage). *Educ:* public schs in New York; Jamaica High Sch., Jamaica, NY; Fordham Univ.; Fordham University Law Sch. (LLB); St John's University Law Sch. (post-grad.) Admitted to State Bar of New York, 1938. Served in US Navy, Comdr of Motor Torpedo Boats, 1943-46. Engaged in private practice of law in NYC, 1938-68: Caldwell & Raymond (associate), 1938-42; Caldwell, Trimble & Mitchell (partner), 1942-66; Nixon, Mudge, Rose, Guthrie, Alexander & Mitchell (partner), 1967-68. Attorney-General, US, 1969-72. Mem., NY State and American Bar Associations. Dir and Trustee of Amer. Council to Improve Our Neighbourhoods (ACTION) which later became part of Urban America, Inc.

(org. working on mod. city problems); Dir, Nat. Housing Conf., USA; Past President: Municipal Forum of New York; Municipal Bond Club.

MITCHELL, John Wesley, FRS 1956; PhD, DSc; William Barton Rogers Professor of Physics, University of Virginia; b 3 Dec. 1913; s of late John Wesley Mitchell and late Lucy Ruth Mitchell; m 1976, Virginia Hill; one step d of former marriage. Educ: Canterbury University Coll., Christchurch, NZ; Univ. of Oxford. BSc 1934. MSc 1935, NZ; PhD 1938, DSc 1960, Oxford. Reader in Experimental Physics in the Univ. of Bristol, Sept. 1945-Aug. 1959. Prof. of Physics, Univ. of Virginia, Sept. 1959-Sept. 1963; Dir of the National Chemical Laboratory, Oct. 1963-Aug. 1964. Publications: various on photographic sensitivity and on plastic deformation of crystals in scientific journals. Recreations: mountaineering, colour photography. Address: Department of Physics, University of Virginia, Charlottesville, Virginia 22901, USA. Clubs: Athenæum; Cosmos (Washington, DC).

MITCHELL, Joseph Rodney; Director General of Defence Accounts, Ministry of Defence, 1973, retired; b 11 March 1914; s of late Joseph William and Martha Mitchell, Sheffield; m 1936, Marian Richardson; two s three d. Educ: Sheffield Central Secondary School. FCCA, ACMA, ACIS. Works Recorder and Junior Costs Clerk, United Steel Cos Ltd, Sheffield, 1930-35; Senior Accounts Clerk, Cargo Fleet Iron Co. Ltd, Middlesbrough, 1936-39; Royal Ordnance Factories, 1940-55: Chief Exec. Officer, 1951-55; Min. of Supply/Aviation/Technology, 1956-71: Dir of Accounts, 1967-71; Dep. Dir Gen. of Defence Accounts, MoD, 1971-72. Recreation: hill-walking. Address: 4 Orchard Court, Hathersage Road, Grindleford, Sheffield S30 1HS.

MITCHELL, Prof. Joseph Stanley, CBE 1951; FRS 1952; Regius Professor of Physic in the University of Cambridge, 1957-75, now Emeritus; Director, Radiotherapeutic Centre, Addenbrooke's Hospital, Cambridge, 1943-Sept. 1976, and Professor of Radiotherapeutics, Cambridge University, 1946-57 and 1975-76; Fellow, St John's College, Cambridge, since 1936; Hon. Consultant, Atomic Energy Authority; b 22 July 1909; s of late Joseph Brown Mitchell and Ethel Maud Mary Arnold, Birmingham; m 1934, Dr Lilian Mary Buxton, MA, MB, ChB; one s one d. Educ: Marlborough Road Council Sch., Birmingham; King Edward's High Sch., Birmingham; University of Birmingham; St John's Coll., Cambridge. Nat. Sciences Tripos Part II, Class I, Physics, 1931; MB, BChir Cantab 1934; House Physician, Gen. Hosp., Birmingham; Beit Memorial Medical Research Fellowship; Colloid Science Laboratory, Cambridge, 1934-37; MA Cantab 1935; PhD Cantab 1937; Resident Radiological Officer, Christie Hosp., Manchester, 1937-38; Asst in Research in Radiotherapy, Dept of Medicine, University of Cambridge, 1938. Radiotherapist EMS, 1939; DMR (RCS), 1943; in charge of medical investigations, National Research Council Laboratory, Montreal, 1944-45. FFR, 1954; MRCP 1956; MD Cantab 1957; DSc (hc) Birmingham 1958; FRCP 1958. Foreign Fellow, Indian Nat. Science Acad., 1975. Linacre Lecturer, 1970. Pres. British Section, Anglo-German Medical Soc., 1959-68. Chm., Faith Courtauld Unit for Human Study of Cancer, King's College Hosp., London, 1971-. Hon. Mem., German Roentgen Soc., 1967; Pirogoff Medal, 1967. Publications: Studies in Radiotherapeutics, 1960; Cancer, if curable why not cured?, 1971; papers in scientific and medical journals on mechanism of therapeutic action of radiations, and the development of radioactive compounds. Recreations: walking, modern languages. Address: Thorndyke, Huntingdon Road, Girton, Cambridge CB3 0LG. T: Cambridge 76102. Club: Royal Overseas League.

MITCHELL, Julian; writer; b 1 May 1935; s of late William Moncur Mitchell and of Christine Mary (née Browne). Educ: Winchester; Wadham Coll., Oxford. Mem., Literature Panel, Arts Council, 1966-69. Governor, Chelsea Sch. of Art. John Llewellyn Rhys Prize, 1965; Somerset Maugham Award, 1966. Publications: novels: Imaginary Toys, 1961; A Disturbing Influence, 1962; As Far As You Can Go, 1963; The White Father, 1964; A Circle of Friends, 1966; The Undiscovered Country, 1968; biography: (with Peregrine Churchill) Jennie: Lady Randolph Churchill, 1974; plays: Half-Life, 1977; (adapted from Ivy Compton-Burnett): A Heritage and Its History, 1965; A Family and a Fortune, 1975. Television plays include: Shadow in the Sun; A Question of Degree; Rust; Abide With Me (Internat. Critics Prize, Monte Carlo, 1977); adaptations of: Persuasion; The Alien Corn; series, Jennie, Lady Randolph Churchill, 1974. Address: 16 Ovington Street, SW3 2JB. T: 01-589 1933.

MITCHELL, Leslie Herbert, CBE 1955 (OBE 1949); b 28 May 1914; s of J. W. and A. J. Mitchell; m 1937, Margaret Winifred Pellow; three s. Educ: Christ's Hospital. Served War of 1939-45 in HM Forces in NW Europe. 2nd Sec., British Embassy, Copenhagen, 1945-50; 1st Sec., British Embassy, Washington, 1953-56; 1st Sec., Bonn, 1956-57; FO, retd 1968. Order of Dannebrog (Denmark), 1947. Recreations: music, railways. Address: 63 Montpellier Terrace, Cheltenham, Glos. Club: Reform.

MITCHELL, Sir Mark (Ledingham), Kt 1957; BSc (Hons, Adelaide), MSc Cantab; FRACI; FACE; First Chancellor, Flinders University of South Australia, 1966-71; b Adelaide, South Australia, 13 June 1902; s of late Sir William Mitchell, KCMG. Educ: Queen's Sch., Adelaide, SA; University of Adelaide; Cambridge Univ. Lecturer in Biochemistry, University of Adelaide, 1927-38; Prof., 1938-63; Dep. Vice-Chancellor 1950-65. Editor-in-Chief, Australian Journal of Experimental Biology, 1935-63. Hon. DSc Flinders. Address: Fitzroy Terrace, Prospect, SA 5082, Australia. Clubs: Adelaide (Adelaide); Royal South Australian Yacht Squadron.

MITCHELL, Martin; see Mitchell, J. L. M.

MITCHELL, Very Rev. Patrick Reynolds; Dean of Wells, since 1973; b 17 March 1930; s of late Lt-Col Percy Reynolds Mitchell, DSO; m 1959, Mary Evelyn (née Phillips); three s one d. Educ: Eton Coll.; Merton Coll., Oxford (MA Theol); Wells Theol Coll. Officer in Welsh Guards (National Service), 1948-49. Deacon, 1954; priest, 1955; Curate at St Mark's, Mansfield, 1954-57; Priest-Vicar of Wells Cathedral and Chaplain of Wells Theological Coll., 1957-60; Vicar of St James', Milton, Portsmouth, 1961-67; Vicar of Frome Selwood, Somerset, 1967-73; Director of Ordination Candidates for Bath and Wells, 1971-74. Address: The Dean's Lodging, 25 The Liberty, Wells, Somerset. T: Wells 72192.

MITCHELL, Dr Peter Dennis, FRS 1974; Director of Research, Glynn Research Laboratories, since 1964; b 29 Sept. 1920; s of Christopher Gibbs Mitchell, Mitcham, Surrey; m 1958, Helen, d of Lt-Col Raymond P. T. ffrench, late Indian Army; three s one d. Educ: Queens Coll., Taunton; Jesus Coll., Cambridge. BA Cantab 1943; PhD Cantab 1950. Dept of Biochem., Univ. of Cambridge, 1943-55, Demonstrator 1950-55; Dir of Chem. Biol. Unit, Dept of Zoology, Univ. of Edinburgh, 1955-63, Sen. Lectr 1961-62, Reader 1962-63. For. Associate, Nat. Acad. of Scis, USA, 1977. Hon. Dr rer. nat. Tech. Univ., Berlin, 1976; Hon. DSc Exeter, 1977. CIBA Medal and Prize, Biochem. Soc., for outstanding research, 1973; (jtly) Warren Triennial Prize, Trustees of Mass Gen. Hosp., Boston, 1974; Louis and Bert Freedman Foundn Award, NY Acad. of Scis, 1974; Wilhelm Feldberg Foundn Prize, 1976; Lewis S. Rosenstiel Award, Brandeis Univ., 1977. Publications: Chemiosmotic Coupling in Oxidative and Photosynthetic Phosphorylation, 1966; Chemiosmotic Coupling and Energy Transduction, 1968; papers in scientific jls. Recreations: enjoyment of family life, home-building and creation of wealth and amenity, restoration of buildings of architectural and historical interest, music, thinking, understanding, inventing, making, sailing. Address: Glynn House, Bodmin, Cornwall PL30 4AU. T: Cardinham 381.

MITCHELL, Richard Charles; MP (Lab) Itchen Division of Southampton, since May 1971; b 22 Aug. 1927; s of Charles and Elizabeth Mitchell; m 1950, Doreen Lilian Gregory; one s one d. Educ: Taunton's Sch., Southampton; Godalming County Gram. Sch.; Southampton Univ. BSc(Econ) Hons 1951. Bartley County Sec. Sch.: Senior Master and Head of Maths and Science Dept, 1957-65; Dep. Headmaster, 1965-66. MP (Lab) Southampton Test, 1966-70. Mem., European Parlt, 1975-. Mem., Bureau of European Socialist Gp. Recreation: postal chess (rep. Brit. Correspondence Chess Assoc. against other countries). Address: 49 Devonshire Road, Polygon, Southampton. T: Southampton 21781.

MITCHELL, Robert; Stipendiary Magistrate, City of Glasgow, since 1974; b 24 June 1915; s of Robert Mitchell and Anne Mathie; m 1944, M. Dorothy Logan; two s. Educ: Dunbarton Acad.; Glasgow Univ. (MA, LLB 1939). LMRTPI 1962. Solicitor. Depute Town Clerk, Dumfries, 1944-53; Chief Exec., Eldoret, Kenya, 1953-55; general practice, Edinburgh, 1955-58; Town Clerk, Inverkeithing, 1958-65; Clerk to Glasgow City Courts, 1966-74. Recreations: walking and swimming. Address: 9 Dundonald Road, Glasgow G12 9LJ. T: 041-334 3230. Club: University of Glasgow College.

MITCHELL, Maj.-Gen. Robert Imrie, OBE 1958 (MBE 1945); retired; b 25 Jan. 1916; s of James I. Mitchell; m 1947, Marion

Lyell. *Educ:* Glasgow Academy; Glasgow Univ. BSc 1936, MB, ChB 1939. FFCM. 2/Lt 1937, Lieut 1938 (TA Gen. List); Lieut, RAMC, 1939; served war 1939-45 (despatches 1945); Captain 1940; Major 1947; Lt-Col 1958; Col 1962; Brig. 1968; DDMS, I (British) Corps, BAOR, 1968-69; Maj.-Gen. 1969; DDMS, Army Strategic Command, 1969-71; DMS, BAOR, 1971-73. QHP 1970-73. Hon. Colonel, Glasgow and Strathclyde Univs. OCT TAVR, 1977-. OStJ 1966. *Recreations:* skiing, shooting, fishing, golf. *Address:* Hallam, Gargunnock, Stirlingshire FK8 3BQ. *T:* Gargunnock 600. *Clubs:* Naval and Military; Royal Scottish Automobile (Glasgow).

MITCHELL, Dr Robert Lyell; Director, Macaulay Institute for Soil Research, Aberdeen, 1968-75, retired; *b* 3 June 1910; *s* of late David Hay Lyell Mitchell, marine engr, and late Agnes Davidson Brown, Edinburgh. *Educ:* Bathgate Academy; Univs of Edinburgh and Aberdeen. BSc Edinburgh, 1st cl. hons Chem., 1931; PhD Aberdeen, 1934; ETH Zürich; FRIC 1949; FRSE 1955. Macaulay Inst. for Soil Research: Head of Dept of Spectrochemistry, 1937-68; Dep. Dir, 1955-68. Research Medal, RASE, 1963; Gold Medal, Soc. for Analytical Chemistry, 1975. *Publications:* Spectrochemical Analysis of Soils, Plants and Related Materials, 1948; numerous contribs to scientific jls and internat. confs concerned with the soil, agriculture and analytical chemistry. *Recreations:* mountaineering, photography. *Address:* 125 Cranford Road, Aberdeen AB1 7NJ. *T:* Aberdeen 35916. *Clubs:* Alpine, Camera; Scottish Mountaineering (Edinburgh).

MITCHELL, Prof. Ross Galbraith, MD, FRCPE, DCH; Professor of Child Health, University of Dundee and Pædiatrician, Ninewells Hospital, Dundee, since 1973; Dean of the Faculty of Medicine and Dentistry, since 1978; *b* 18 Nov. 1920; *s* of late Richard Galbraith Mitchell, OBE and Ishobel, *d* of late James Ross, Broadford, Skye; *m* 1950, June Phylis Butcher; one *s* three *d*. *Educ:* Kelvinside Acad.; University of Edinburgh. MB, ChB Edinburgh, 1944. Surg-Lt, RNVR, 1944-47; Jun. hosp. posts, Liverpool, London, Edinburgh, 1947-52; Rockefeller Res. Fellow, Mayo Clinic, USA, 1952-53; Lectr in Child Health, Univ. of St Andrews, 1952-55; Cons. Pædiatrician, Dundee Teaching Hosps, 1955-63; Prof. of Child Health, Univ. of Aberdeen, Pædiatrician, Royal Aberdeen Children's and Aberdeen Maternity Hosps, 1963-73. Chairman: Scottish Adv. Council on Child Care, 1966-69; Specialist Adv. Cttee on Pædiatrics, 1975-; Academic Bd, British Pædiatric Assoc., 1975-. Jt Editor Developmental Medicine and Child Neurology. For. Corresp. Mem., Amer. Acad. of Cerebral Palsy. *Publications:* Disease in Infancy and Childhood, (7th edn) 1973; Child Life and Health (5th edn), 1970; Child Health in the Community, 1977; contribs to textbooks of medicine and obstetrics and articles in scientific and medical jls. *Recreations:* Celtic language and literature, fishing. *Address:* Department of Child Health, The University, Dundee, Angus.

**MITCHELL, Sir (Seton) Steuart (Crichton), KBE 1954 (OBE 1941); CB 1951; *b* 9 March 1902; *s* of A. Crichton Mitchell, DSc, FRSE; *m* 1929, Elizabeth (*née* Duke); no *c*. *Educ:* Edinburgh Acad.; RN Colls, Osborne and Dartmouth. Joined Royal Navy as Cadet, 1916; at sea in HMS Hercules, Grand Fleet, 1918, subsequently served in HM Ships Ramillies, Sportive, Tomahawk, Marlborough; qualified as Gunnery Specialist, 1927-29, subsequently Gunnery Officer of HM Ships Comus and Frobisher; Naval Ordnance Inspection Dept and Asst Supt of Design, 1931-39; War of 1939-45, Inspector of Naval Ordnance, in charge of Admiralty Ordnance contracts in Switzerland, 1939-40, in USA, 1940-44; Chief Engineer and Supt, in charge of Armament Design Establishment, Min. of Supply, 1945; Controller, Guided Weapons and Electronics, Min. of Supply, 1951-56; Controller, Royal Ordnance Factories, 1956-59; Controller, Guided Weapons and Electronics, Ministry of Aviation, 1959-62; Mem., BTC, Feb.-Nov. 1962; Vice-Chm., British Railways Bd, Nov. 1962-64; Chairman: Machine Tool Industry EDC, 1964-; Shipbuilding Industry Trng Bd, 1964-; Mem., Central Trng Council, 1965-; Adviser (part-time) to Min. of Technology, 1965-; Mem. Scottish Economic Planning Council, 1965-67; Mem. Nat. Economic Develt Council, 1967-70. Chm., Carrier Engineering Co., 1968-70; Director: Parkinson Cowan Ltd, 1964-71; Plessey Numerical Controls Ltd, 1970-73. Officer Legion of Merit (USA), 1945. *Recreations:* music, gardening, antiques. *Address:* 33 Marsham Court, Marsham Street, SW1. *T:* 01-828 6628. *Clubs:* English Speaking Union, Pilgrims.

MITCHELL, Sir Steuart Crichton; *see* Mitchell, Sir S. S. C.

MITCHELL, William Eric Marcus, MC; MB; BS London; FRCS; FRCSC; MRCP; DPH; Surgeon, genito-urinary specialist, Consulting Surgeon, Royal Jubilee Hospital, Victoria,

BC, retired; *b* 29 April 1897; *e s* of Dr J. F. Mitchell, formerly of Bangor, Co. Down; *m* 1922, Catherine, *d* of W. F. Hamilton, of Ashwick, NZ; one *d* ; *m* 1958, Margery, *d* of D. O. Thomas, Victoria, BC. *Educ:* Campbell Coll., Belfast; St Bartholomew's Hosp., University of London. Served as a Lt with the 11th Battalion Royal Irish Rifles in France, 1916 (wounded, MC); various prizes during sch. and Univ. career; House Surg., St Bartholomew's Hosp.; Chief Asst to a Surgical Unit, St Bartholomew's Hosp.; Clinical Asst, St Peter's Hosp., London; Pres., Abernethian Soc., St Bartholomew's Hosp. War of 1939-45, Lt-Col RAMC, Officer in Charge Surgical Div. No. 13 Gen. Hosp. MEF. *Publications:* Health, Wealth and Happiness, 1969; numerous papers on surgical subjects published in the Lancet, the Canadian Medical Association Journal, St Bartholomew's Hospital Journal. *Recreations:* fishing, ski-ing, mountaineering. *Address:* 2171 Granite Street, Oak Bay, Victoria, BC, Canada. *TA:* Victoria, BC. *Club:* Alpine Club of Canada.

MITCHELL, Yvonne; actress and novelist; Member, National Theatre Board, since 1976; *m* 1952, Derek Monsey; one *d*. *Educ:* St Paul's. First stage appearance as the child Estella in Great Expectations, 1940; plays include: Ophelia in Hamlet, Old Vic and Elsinore, 1950; Katherine in the Taming of the Shrew and Cordelia in King Lear, Stratford upon Avon, 1952; The Wall, Billy Rose Theatre, New York, 1960; Anna Petrovna in Ivanov, Phœnix, 1965; Children of the Wolf, Apollo, 1971; Pirandello's Henry IV, Her Majesty's, 1974; Bloomsbury, Phœnix, 1974; films include: Queen of Spades, 1949; The Divided Heart (Brit. Film Acad. Award), 1954; Woman in a Dressing-Gown (Berlin Fest. Award and Variety Club of Gt Britain Award), 1957; Sapphire, 1958; Trials of Oscar Wilde, 1959; Genghis Khan, 1965; Velvet House, 1968; many appearances on TV, incl. Chéri (BBC TV series), 1973. *Publications: plays:* The Same Sky (Produced Duke of York's Theatre, 1951) (Arts Council Award); Actress, 1957; (trans. from the French) Measure of Cruelty, 1964; *novels:* The Bedsitter, 1959; Frame for Julian, 1960; A Year in Time, 1964; The Family, 1967; Martha on Sunday, 1970; God is Inexperienced, 1974; But Answer Came There None, 1977; *for children:* Cathy Away, 1964; Cathy at Home, 1965; But Wednesday Cried, 1974; *biography:* Colette: a Taste for Life, 1975. *Address:* c/o Adza Vincent, 11a Ivor Place, NW1.

MITCHELL COTTS, Sir R. C.; *see* Cotts.

MITCHELL-THOMSON, family name of **Baron Selsdon.**

MITCHENSON, Francis Joseph Blackett, (Joe Mitchenson); Joint Founder and Director, The Raymond Mander and Joe Mitchenson Theatre Collection, since 1939 (Theatre Collection Trust, since 1977); *b* 4 Oct.; *s* of Francis William Mitchenson and Sarah Roddam. *Educ:* privately; Fay Compton Studio of Dramatic Art. First appeared on stage professionally in Libel, Playhouse, London, 1934; acted in repertory, on tour and in London, until 1946. With Raymond Mander, founded Theatre Collection, 1939; War Service with Royal Horse Artillery, invalided out, 1943; returned to stage, and collab. with Raymond Mander on many BBC progs. Collection subject of an Aquarius programme, 1971; many TV appearances on theatrical subjects. *Publications:* with Raymond Mander: Hamlet Through the Ages, 1952 (2nd rev. edn 1955); Theatrical Companion to Shaw, 1954; Theatrical Companion to Maugham, 1955; The Artist and the Theatre, 1955; Theatrical Companion to Coward, 1957; A Picture History of British Theatre, 1957; (with J. C. Trewin) The Gay Twenties, 1958; (with Philip Hope-Wallace) A Picture History of Opera, 1959; (with J. C. Trewin) The Turbulent Thirties, 1960; The Theatres of London, 1961, illus. by Timothy Birdsall (2nd rev. edn, paperback, 1963; 3rd rev. edn 1975); A Picture History of Gilbert and Sullivan, 1962; British Music Hall: A Story in Pictures, 1965 (rev. and enlarged edn 1974); Lost Theatres of London, 1968 (2nd edn, rev. and enlarged, 1976); Musical Comedy: A Story in Pictures, 1969; Revue: A Story in Pictures, 1971; Pantomime: A Story in Pictures, 1973; The Wagner Companion, 1977; Victorian and Edwardian Entertainments from Old Photographs, 1978; contribs to and revs in Encyc. Britannica, Theatre Notebook, and Books and Bookmen. *Recreations:* collecting anything and everything theatrical, sun bathing. *Address:* 5 Venner Road, Sydenham, SE26 5EQ. *T:* 01-778 6730.

MITCHESON, Prof. J(ames) Cecil, CBE 1961; BSc; Hon. ARSM; Fellow, Imperial College of Science and Technology; Professor Emeritus of Mining, London University, since 1963; *b* 18 May 1898; *s* of late G. A. Mitcheson; *m* 1928, Jean Hyndman, *d* of late D. S. Macpherson; one *s* one *d*. *Educ:* Bootham Sch.; RMA Woolwich; University of Birmingham. Lecturer in Coal Mining, Birmingham Univ., 1923-24; Agent and later Man. Dir, Morris & Shaw, Ltd, 1934-46; Dir of Production for Min. of

Fuel and Power, for Warwicks Coalfield, 1944-45; Divl Mining Development Engineer, W Midlands Div., NCB, 1947; Cons. Mining Engineer, 1947-52; Prof. of Mining, Imperial Coll., Royal School of Mines, London Univ., 1953-63. Mem., Mining Qualifications Board, 1950-69; Chm., Safety in Mines Research (Advisory) Bd., 1960-69. FInstME (Pres. 1953-54); FIMM. Chm., Geological Survey Board, 1961-65 (Mem. 1959-); Mem., Natural Environment Research Council, 1965-69. Lt RFA, with 33rd Div., France and Flanders, 1918. *Publications:* papers in Proceedings Instn of Mining Engineers and other technical jls. *Address:* The Croft, Knotty Green, Beaconsfield, Bucks.

MITCHISON, Dr Denis Anthony; Professor of Bacteriology, Royal Postgraduate Medical School, since 1971; Director, Medical Research Council's Unit for Laboratory Studies of Tuberculosis, since 1956; *b* 6 Sept. 1919; *e s* of Baron Mitchison, CBE, QC, and of Naomi Margaret Mitchison, *qv*; *m* 1940, Ruth Sylvia, *d* of Hubert Gill; two *s* two *d*. *Educ:* Abbotsholme Sch.; Trinity Coll., Cambridge; University Coll. Hosp., London (MB, ChB). House Physician Addenbrooke's Hosp., Royal Berkshire Hosp.; Asst to Pathologist, Brompton Hosp.; Prof. of Bacteriology (Infectious Diseases), RPGMS, 1968-71. FRCP; FRCPath. *Publications:* numerous papers on bacteriology and chemotherapy of tuberculosis. *Recreation:* computer programming. *Address:* 14 Marlborough Road, Richmond, Surrey. *T:* 01-940 4751.
See also J. M. Mitchison, N. A. Mitchison.

MITCHISON, Prof. John Murdoch, ScD; FRSE 1966; Professor of Zoology, University of Edinburgh, since 1963; *b* 11 June 1922; *s* of Lord Mitchison, CBE, QC, and of N. Haldane (*see* Naomi M. Mitchison); *m* 1947, Rosalind Mary Wrong; one *s* three *d*. *Educ:* Winchester Coll.; Trinity Coll., Cambridge. Army Operational Research, 1941-46; Sen. and Research Scholar, Trinity Coll., Cambridge, 1946-50; Fellow, Trinity Coll., Cambridge, 1950-54; Lectr in Zoology, Edinburgh, 1953-59; Reader in Zoology, Edinburgh, 1959-62. J. W. Jenkinson Memorial Lectr, Oxford, 1971-72. Member: Edinburgh Univ. Court, 1971-74; Council, Scottish Marine Biol. Assoc., 1961-67; Exec. Cttee, Internat. Soc. for Cell Biology, 1964-72; Biol Cttee, SRC, 1972-75; Royal Commn on Environmental Pollution, 1974-; Science Bd, SRC, 1977-; Pres., British Soc. for Cell Biology, 1974-77. FInstBiol 1963. *Publications:* The Biology of the Cell Cycle, 1971; papers in scientific jls. *Address:* Great Yew, Ormiston, East Lothian EH35 5NJ. *T:* Pencaitland 340530
See also D . A . Mitchison , N . A . Mitchison .

MITCHISON, Naomi Margaret, (Lady Mitchison since 1964, but she still wishes to be called Naomi Mitchison); *b* Edinburgh, 1 Nov. 1897; *d* of late John Scott Haldane, CH, FRS, and Kathleen Trotter; *m* 1916, G. R. Mitchison (*d* 1970), CBE, QC, created a Baron (Life Peer), 1964; three *s* two *d*. *Educ:* Dragon Sch., Oxford; home student, Oxford. Officier d'Académie Française, 1924; Argyll CC, 1945-65, on and off; Highland and Island Advisory Panel, 1947-65; Highlands and Islands Develt Consult. Council, 1966-; Tribal Advisor to Bakgatla, Botswana, 1963-. *Publications:* The Conquered, 1923; When the Bough Breaks, 1924; Cloud Cuckoo Land, 1925; The Laburnum Branch, 1926; Black Sparta, 1928; Anna Comnena, 1928; Nix-Nought-Nothing, 1928; Barbarian Stories, 1929; The Hostages, 1930; Comments on Birth Control, 1930; The Corn King and the Spring Queen, 1931; The Price of Freedom (with L. E. Gielgud), 1931; Boys and Girls and Gods, 1931; The Powers of Light, edited an Outline for Boys and Girls, 1932; The Delicate Fire, 1933; Vienna Diary, 1934; The Home, 1934; We Have Been Warned, 1935; Beyond this Limit, 1935; The Fourth Pig, 1936; Socrates (with R. H. S. Crossman), 1937; An End and a Beginning, 1937; The Moral Basis of Politics, 1938; The Kingdom of Heaven, 1939; As It was in the Beginning (with L. E. Gielgud), 1939; The Blood of the Martyrs, 1939; (ed) Re-educating Scotland, 1944; The Bull Calves, 1947; Men and Herring (with D. Macintosh), 1949; The Big House, 1950; Spindrift (play: with D. Macintosh), Citizens' Theatre, Glasgow, 1951; Lobsters on the Agenda, 1952; Travel Light, 1952; The Swan's Road, 1954; Graeme and the Dragon, 1954; The Land the Ravens Found, 1955; To the Chapel Perilous, 1955; Little Boxes, 1956; Behold your King, 1957; The Far Harbour, 1957; Five Men and a Swan, 1958; Other People's Worlds, 1958; Judy and Lakshmi, 1959; The Rib of the Green Umbrella, 1960; The Young Alexander, 1960; Karensgaard, 1961; The Young Alfred the Great, 1962; Memoirs of a Space Woman, 1962; (ed) What the Human Race is Up To, 1962; The Fairy who Couldn't Tell a Lie, 1963; When we Become Men, 1965; Ketse and the Chief, 1965; Return to the Fairy Hill, 1966; Friends and Enemies, 1966; The Big Surprise, 1967; African Heroes, 1968; Don't Look Back, 1969; The Family at Ditlabeng, 1969; The Africans: a history, 1970; Sun and Moon, 1970; Cleopatra's People, 1972; A Danish Teapot, 1973; Sunrise Tomorrow, 1973; Small Talk:

memoirs of an Edwardian childhood (autobiog.), 1973; A Life for Africa, 1973; Oil for the Highlands?, 1974; All Change Here (autobiog.), 1975; Solution Three, 1975; Snake!, 1976; The Two Magicians, 1977; The Cleansing of the Knife, 1977. *Recreation:* hard pruning. *Address:* Carradale House, Carradale, Campbeltown, Scotland.
See also D. A. Mitchison, J. M. Mitchison, N. A. Mitchison.

MITCHISON, Prof. Nicholas Avrion, FRS 1967; Jodrell Professor of Zoology and Comparative Anatomy, University College, London, since 1970; *b* 5 May 1928; 3rd *s* of Baron Mitchison, CBE, QC, and of Naomi Margaret Mitchison, *qv*; *m* 1957, Lorna Margaret, *d* of Maj.-Gen. J. S. S. Martin, CSI; two *s* three *d*. *Educ:* Leighton Park Sch.; New Coll., Oxford (MA 1949). Fellow of Magdalen College, 1950-52; Commonwealth Fund Fellow, 1952-54; Lecturer, Edinburgh Univ., 1954-61; Reader, Edinburgh Univ., 1961-62; Head of Div. of Experimental Biology, Nat. Inst. for Med. Research, 1962-71. *Publications:* articles in scientific journals. *Address:* 14 Belitha Villas, N1.
See also D. A. Mitchison, J. M. Mitchison.

MITFORD, family name of **Baron Redesdale.**

MITFORD, Jessica Lucy, (Mrs Jessica Treuhaft); author; *b* 11 Sept. 1917; *d* of 2nd Baron Redesdale; *m* 1st, Esmond Marcus David Romilly (*d* 1942); one *d*; 2nd, 1943, Robert Edward Treuhaft; one *s*. Distinguished Prof., San José State Univ., Calif, 1973-74. *Publications:* (as Jessica Mitford): Hons and Rebels, 1960; The American Way of Death, 1963; The Trial of Dr Spock, 1969; Kind and Usual Punishment, 1974; The American Prison Business, 1975; A Fine Old Conflict, 1977. *Address:* 6411 Regent Street, Oakland, Calif 94618, USA.

MITFORD, Rupert Leo Scott B.; *see* Bruce-Mitford.

MITFORD-SLADE, Col Cecil Townley; Lord-Lieutenant of Somerset, since 1968; *b* 19 April 1903; *s* of late Col William Kenyon Mitford, CMG, CVO; assumed additional name of Slade by deed poll, 1941; *m* 1931, Phyllis, *d* of late E. G. Buxton; two *s* one *d*. *Educ:* Eton; RMC; joined 60th Rifles, 1923; comd 8th Bn KRRC, 1943-44; 1st Bn KRRC, 1948-50; Comdt, WRAC Staff Coll., 1951; HM Bodyguard of Hon. Corps of Gentlemen-at-Arms, 1952-73. DL, Somerset, 1955; JP, 1953; CC, 1955; High Sheriff, 1963; Vice-Lieut, 1966-68. County Comr, St John Amb. Bde, 1954-68; Chm., Taunton Race Course Co. KStJ; Order of Mercy. *Recreations:* shooting, fishing. *Address:* Montys Court, Taunton, Somerset. *T:* Bishop's Lydeard 432255. *Club:* Naval and Military.

MITHEN, Dallas Alfred; Commissioner for Harvesting and Marketing, Forestry Commission, since 1977; *b* 5 Nov. 1923; *m* 1st, 1947, Peggy (*née* Clarke) (decd); one *s* one *d*; 2nd, 1969, Avril Teresa Dodd (*née* Stein). *Educ:* Maidstone Grammar Sch.; UC of N Wales, Bangor. BSc (Forestry). Fleet Air Arm, 1942-46. Joined Forestry Commission as District Officer, 1950; Dep. Surveyor, New Forest and Conservator SE (England), 1968-71; Senior Officer (Scotland), 1971-75; Head of Forest Management Div., Edinburgh, 1975-76. *Recreations:* cricket, swimming, sailing, walking. *Address:* Kings Knot, Bonnington Road, Peebles EH45 9HF. *T:* Peebles 20738.

MITMAN, Frederick S., CBE 1941; *b* 21 April 1900; *s* of late William and Elizabeth Mitman; *m* 1925, Helen McNary; one *s* one *d*. *Educ:* Lehigh Univ., USA (Deg. of Engineer of Mines, 1923). Dir of Light Alloys and Magnesium (Sheet and Strip) Control, Ministry of Aircraft Production, 1939-41; Co-ordinator of Aircraft Supplies for Fighter and Naval Aircraft, Ministry of Aircraft Production, 1940-41; Adviser on Light Metals Fabrication, Ministry of Aircraft Production, 1941-42. *Address:* 10 Campden House Close, Kensington, W8. *T:* 01-937 9071.

MITSAKIS, Prof. Kariofilis; Director, Institute for Balkan Studies, Thessaloniki; *b* 12 May 1932; *s* of Christos and Crystalli Mitsakis; *m* 1966, Anthoula Chalkia; two *s*. *Educ:* Univs of Pylaia (Thessaloniki), Oxford and Munich. Scientific Collaborator, Royal Research Foundn of Greece, 1959; Associate Prof. of Byzantine and Modern Greek Literature, Univ. of Maryland, 1966; Chm. of Dept of Comparative Literature, Univ. of Maryland, 1967; Sotheby and Bywater Prof. of Byzantine and Modern Greek Language and Literature, Univ. of Oxford, 1968-72. *Publications:* Problems concerning the text, the sources and the dating of the Achilleid, 1962 (in Greek); The Greek Sonnet, 1962 (in Greek); The Language of Romanos the Melodist, 1967 (in English); The Byzantine Alexander romance from the cod. Vindob. theol. gr. 244, 1967 (in German); Byzantine Hymnography, 1971 (in Greek); Academy, Universities and the Greek homophylophiloi, 1977 (in Greek);

contribs to Byzantinisch-Neugriechische Jahrbücher, Byzantinische Zeitschrift, Comparative Literature Studies, Glotta, Hellenika, Jahrbuch der Oesterreichischen Byzantinischen Gesellschaft, Nea Hestia, etc. *Recreations:* music, travelling, riding, boxing. *Clubs:* KKEx, Rotary, EKKE, Karfitsa, "Oulen 44".

MITTERRAND, François Maurice Marie; Officier Légion d'Honneur; Croix de Guerre (1939-45); French politician (Socialist Party); advocate; *b* Jarnac, Charente, 26 Oct. 1916; *s* of Joseph Mitterrand and Yvonne (*née* Lorrain); *m* 1944, Danielle Gouze; two *s. Educ:* Coll. Saint-Paul, Angoulême; Facultés de droit et des lettres, Univ. of Paris. Licencié en droit, Lic. ès lettres; Dip. d'études supérieures de droit public. Served War, 1939-40 (prisoner, escaped; Rosette de la Résistance). Missions to London and to Algiers, 1943; Sec.-Gen., Organisation for Prisoners of War, War Victims and Refugees, 1944-46. Deputy, 1946-58 and 1962-; Minister for Ex-Servicemen, 1947-48; Sec. of State for Information, attached Prime Minister's Office, 1948-49; Minister for Overseas Territories, 1950-51; Chm., UDSR, 1951-52; Minister of State, Jan.-Feb. 1952 and March 1952-July 1953; Deleg. to Council of Europe, July-Sept. 1953; Minister of the Interior, June 1954-Feb. 1955; Minister of State, 1956-57; Senator, 1959-62; Candidate for Presidency of France, 1965; Pres., Fedn of Democratic and Socialist Left, 1965-68; re-elected Deputy from Nièvre, 1967 and 1968; First Sec., Socialist Party, 1971-; Vice-Pres., Socialist International, 1972-. Again Candidate for the Presidency of France, May 1974. *Publications:* Aux frontières de l'Union française; La Chine au défi, 1961; Le Coup d'Etat permanent, 1964; Technique économique française, 1968; Ma part de vérité, 1969; Un socialisme du possible, 1971; La rose au poing, 1973; numerous contribs to the Press. *Recreations:* tennis, ping-pong. *Address:* (private) 22 rue de Bièvres, 75005 Paris, France.

MITTON, Rev. Dr Charles Leslie, BA; MTh; PhD; Principal of Handsworth College, Birmingham, 1955-70 (Tutor, 1951-55); *b* 13 Feb. 1907; *s* of Rev. Charles W. Mitton, Bradford, Yorks; *m* 1937, Margaret J. Ramage; one *s* one *d. Educ:* Kingswood Sch., Bath; Manchester Univ.; Didsbury Coll., Manchester. Asst Tutor at Wesley Coll., Headingley, 1930-33; Minister in Methodist Church at: Dunbar, 1933-36; Keighley, 1936-39; Scunthorpe, 1939-45; Nottingham, 1945-51; Tutor in New Testament Studies at Handsworth Coll., Birmingham, 1951-70. Editor of Expository Times, 1965-76. Hon. DD, Aberdeen Univ., 1964. *Publications:* The Epistle to the Ephesians: Authorship, Origin and Purpose, 1951; Pauline Corpus of Letters, 1954; Preachers' Commentary on St Mark's Gospel, 1956; The Good News, 1961; The Epistle of James, 1966; Jesus: the fact behind the faith, 1974; The Epistle to the Ephesians: a commentary, 1976. *Recreations:* Rugby football, Association football, cricket, tennis. *Address:* 14 Cranbrook Road, Handsworth, Birmingham B21 8PJ. *T:* 021-554 7892.

MOATE, Roger Denis; MP (C) Faversham since 1970; Insurance Broker; Director, Alexander Howden Insurance Brokers Ltd; *b* 12 May 1938; *m* 1960, Hazel Joy Skinner; one *s* one *d. Educ:* Latymer Upper Sch., Hammersmith. Joined Young Conservative Movement, in Brentford and Chiswick, 1954: Vice-Chm., Greater London area Young Conservatives, 1964; contested (C) Faversham, Gen. Elec., 1966. Hon. Sec., British Amer. Parly Gp; Vice Chm., Cons. Transport Cttee. *Recreations:* skiing, squash. *Address:* House of Commons, SW1; 23 Ponsonby Terrace, SW1. *Club:* St Stephen's.

MOBERLY, John Campbell, CMG 1976; HM Diplomatic Service; HM Ambassador in Amman, since 1975; *b* 27 May 1925; *s* of Sir Walter Moberly, GBE, KCB, DSO; *m* 1959, Patience, *d* of Major Sir Richard George Proby, Bt, *qv*; two *s* one *d. Educ:* Winchester College; Magdalen College, Oxford. War Service in Royal Navy, 1943-47 (despatches). Entered HM Foreign (now Diplomatic) Service, 1950; Political Officer, Kuwait, 1954-56; Political Agent, Doha, 1959-62; First Secretary, Athens, 1962-66; Counsellor, Washington, 1969-73; Dir, Middle East Centre for Arab Studies, 1973-75. *Recreations:* mountain walking and climbing, skiing, swimming. *Address:* c/o Foreign and Commonwealth Office, SW1; The Cedars, Temple Sowerby, Penrith, Cumbria. *T:* Kirkby Thore 437. *Clubs:* Travellers', Royal Automobile; Leander (Henley-on-Thames).

MOBERLY, Patrick Hamilton; HM Diplomatic Service; Assistant Under-Secretary of State, Foreign and Commonwealth Office, since 1976; *b* 2 Sept. 1928; *yr s* of G. H. Moberly; *m* 1955, Mary Penfold; two *s* one *d. Educ:* Winchester; Trinity Coll., Oxford (MA). HM Diplomatic Service, 1951-; diplomatic posts in: Baghdad, 1953; Prague, 1957; Foreign Office, 1959; Dakar, 1962; Min. of Defence, 1965;

Commonwealth Office, 1967; Canada, 1969; Israel, 1970; FCO, 1974. *Recreations:* tennis, skiing, opera. *Address:* c/o Foreign and Commonwealth Office, SW1A 2AH. *Clubs:* United Oxford & Cambridge University, Royal Commonwealth Society.

MOBERLY, Maj.-Gen. Richard James, CB 1957; OBE 1944; retired, 1960, and became Director, Communications Electronic Equipment, War Office, until 1964; *b* 2 July 1906; *m* 1st, 1935, Mary Joyce Shelmerdine (*d* 1964); three *d*; 2nd, 1971, Mrs Vivien Mary Cameron, *d* of Victor Bayley, CIE, CBE. *Educ:* Haileybury; Royal Military Academy, Woolwich. Commissioned Royal Signals, 1926; India, 1928-35; comd 1st Airborne Div. Signal Regt, 1942-43; CSO 1st Airborne Corps, 1943-45; Comdt Indian Signal Trng Centre, 1946-47; Dep. Comdt, Sch. of Signals, 1949-52; Dep. Dir of Signals, WO, 1952-54; CSO, Northern Army Gp, 1954-57; Signal Officer-in-Chief, War Office, 1957-60. Col Comdt, Royal Signals, 1960-66. Comr for Dorset, St John Ambulance, 1968-76. CStJ 1974. *Address:* Steeple Cottage, Westport Road, Wareham, Dorset BH20 4PR. *T:* Wareham 2697. *Club:* Army and Navy.

MOBERLY, Rt. Rev. Robert Hamilton; *b* 1884; *s* of Canon R. C. Moberly, DD, and Alice Sidney Moberly; *m* 1917, Rosamund Vere, *d* of late Rev. R. B. Smyth and late Grace Elizabeth Augusta Massy Smyth; one *s* (and one *s* killed in War, 1942). *Educ:* Winchester; Oxford, 1st class in Mods, Greats and Theology; Cuddesdon. Asst curate, St Margaret's-at-Cliffe, near Dover, 1909-14; Benoni, Transvaal, 1914-25; CF 1917-19; Principal, Bishops' Coll., Cheshunt, 1925-36; Bishop Suffragan of Stepney and Rector of St Margarets, Lothbury, 1936-52; Dean of Salisbury, 1952-60. White Lecturer, 1930. *Publication:* The Great Friendship, 1934. *Address:* Wadhurst, Pound Road, West Wittering, Sussex.

MOCATTA, Hon. Sir Alan Abraham, Kt 1961; OBE 1944; **Hon. Mr Justice Mocatta;** Judge of the High Court of Justice (Queen's Bench Division) since 1961; Member, Restrictive Practices Court, since 1961, President, since 1970; *b* 1907; *s* of Edward L. Mocatta and Flora Gubbay; *m* 1930, Pamela Halford, JP; four *s. Educ:* Clifton Coll.; New Coll., Oxford. Called to the Bar, Inner Temple, 1930; Bencher, 1960; Northern circuit; QC 1951. Served War of 1939-45: 2nd Lieut 12 LAA Regt, RA, TA, 1939; Bde Major, 56 AA Bde, 1940-41; GSO (2) AA HQ BTNI, 1941-42; Lt-Col GS, Army Council Secretariat, War Office, 1942-45. Chm., Council of Jews' Coll., 1945-61; Vice-Pres., Board of Elders, Spanish and Portuguese Jews' Congregation, Bevis Marks, 1961-67, Pres., 1967-; Chm. Treasury Cttee on Cheque Endorsement, 1955-56. Joint editor, 14th-18th editions of Scrutton on Charter parties. *Address:* 18 Hanover House, NW8 7DX. *T:* 01-722 2857; 10 Breakwater Road, Bude, Cornwall. *T:* Bude 2745. *Club:* MCC.

MOCKLER-FERRYMAN, Col (Hon. Brig.) Eric Edward, CB 1945; CBE 1941; MC; FZS; Hon. MA London; *b* 27 June 1896; *s* of late Col A. F. Mockler-Ferryman, 43rd LI; unmarried. *Educ:* Wellington; RMA, Woolwich. Commissioned RA, 1915; France and Flanders, 1915-19 (MC); seconded to AMF, 1937-39; served, 1939-45; Brig., 1940; Control Commission, Hungary, 1945-46; retired pay, 1947; Comdr Legion of Merit (US), Chevalier, Légion d'honneur and Fr. Croix de Guerre; Comdr Order of Leopold II and Belgian Croix de Guerre; Comdr Order of Orange Nassau. *Address:* c/o Lloyds Bank, 6 Pall Mall, SW1. *Club:* Army and Navy.

MOERAN, Edward Warner; *b* 27 Nov. 1903; *s* of E. J. Moeran. *Educ:* Christ's Coll., Finchley; University of London. Solicitor. MP (Lab) South Beds, 1950-51. Pres., W London Law Soc., 1970-71. Chm., Solicitors' Ecology Gp, 1972-74. *Publications:* Practical Conveyancing, 1949; Invitation to Conveyancing, 1962, enlarged edn 1977; Practical Legal Aid, 1970; (jtly) Social Welfare Law, 1977. *Recreations:* carpentry, travelling. *Address:* 1 Heath Street, Hampstead, NW3.

MOFFAT, Sir John Smith, Kt 1955; OBE 1944; MLC Northern Rhodesia, 1951-64; Member Federal Parliament, Salisbury, 1954-62; *b* N Rhodesia, April 1905; *s* of Rev. Malcolm Moffat; *m* 1930, Margaret Prentice; two *d. Educ:* Grey High Sch., Port Elizabeth, South Africa; Glasgow Univ. Cadet Northern Rhodesia Provincial Administration, 1927; District Officer, 1929. Served at Serenje, Fort Jameson, etc. Commissioner for National Development, 1945; retd from CS, 1951. Chm. Federal African Affairs Board, and leader Liberal Party until 1962, when disbanded. Farmer.

MOFFAT, Rennie John, CBE 1956 (MBE 1918); Consultant on development plans, Cawood, Wharton and Co., 1958-70, retired; *b* 23 May 1891; *o s* of late John and Susan Moffat; *m* 1918, Lottie May (*d* 1974), 4th *d* of late Robert and Edith Mizen; one *s.*

Educ: Central Foundation Sch., London; King's Coll., London. Entered Civil Service, (Patent Office), 1906; Ministry of Munitions, 1915-16; served European War, Inns of Court OTC, 1916-18. Sec., Road Transport Board, 1918; Coal Mines Dept (later Mines Dept), Bd of Trade, 1919-39 (latterly head of Inland Trade Branch); resigned from Civil Service, 1939. General Manager, Midland Coal Mines Schemes, 1939-46; Dep. Dir-Gen. of Marketing, NCB, 1946-55; Dir-Gen. of Marketing, 1955-58. *Address:* 6 Henley Court, Chase Side, Southgate, N14. *T:* 01-882 1233.

MOGG, Gen. Sir John, GCB 1972 (KCB 1966; CB 1964); CBE 1960; DSO 1944; Bar, 1944; Deputy Supreme Allied Commander, Europe, 1973-76; *b* 17 Feb. 1913; *s* of late Capt. H. B. Mogg, MC and late Alice Mary (*née* Ballard); *m* 1939, Cecilia Margaret Molesworth; three *s. Educ:* Malvern Coll.; RMC Sandhurst. Coldstream Guards, 1933-35; RMC Sandhurst (Sword of Honour) 1935-37; commissioned Oxfordshire and Buckinghamshire Light Infantry, 1937. Served War of 1939-45 (despatches); comd 9 DLI (NW Europe), 1944-45; Instructor, Staff Coll., 1948-50; Commander 10th Parachute Bn, 1950-52; Chief Instructor, School of Infantry, Warminster, 1952-54; Instructor (GSO1), Imperial Defence Coll., 1954-56; Comdr, Commonwealth Brigade Gp, Malaya, 1958-60; Meritorious Medal (Perak, Malaya); Dir of Combat Development, War Office, 1961-62; Comdt, Royal Military Academy, Sandhurst, 1963-66; Comdr 1st (British) Corps, 1966-68; GOC-in-C Southern Comd, 1968; GOC-in-C Army Strategic Comd, 1968-70; Adjutant-Gen., MoD (Army), 1970-73. ADC Gen. to the Queen, 1971-74. Col Comdt: Army Air Corps, 1963-74; The Royal Green Jackets, 1965-73; Hon. Col, 10th Parachute Bn, TA. Kermit Roosevelt Lectr, 1969. President: Army Cricket Assoc.; Army Saddle Club, 1969; Army Boxing Assoc., 1970; Army Parachute Assoc., 1971; BHS, 1972; Ex Services Mental Welfare Soc.; Chairman: Army Free Fall Parachute Assoc., 1970; Army Football Assoc., 1960-63; Army Benevolent Fund, 1976; Royal Soldiers' Daughters Sch., 1976; Pres., Council Services Kinema Corp., 1970; Dir, Lloyds Bank S Midland Regional Bd, 1976. Member Council: Wessex TA&VRA, 1976; British Atlantic Cttee, 1977. Comr, Royal Hospital Chelsea, 1976. Governor: Malvern College, 1967; Bradfield College, 1977. Hon. Liveryman, Fruiterers' Co. *Recreations:* cricket; most field sports. *Address:* Church Close, Watlington, Oxon. *Clubs:* Army and Navy, Flyfishers', MCC, Cavalry and Guards, Pitt.

MOGG, W. R.; *see* Rees-Mogg.

MOHAMED, Hon. Sir Abdool Razack, Kt 1970; Member, Legislative Council, Mauritius, since 1953; Minister of Housing, Lands and Town and Country Planning, since 1959; *b* Calcutta, India, 1906. *Educ:* India. Arrived in Mauritius, 1925; Municipal Councillor, 1943-56; Mayor of Port Louis, 1949, 1953 and 1956; Deleg. to London Constitutional Talks, 1955, 1957, 1961 and 1965. *Address:* Avenue Belle Rose, Quatre Bornes, Mauritius.

MOIR, Alan John, CMG 1971; Consultant to legal firm of Gillotts, since 1963; *b* 19 July 1903; *s* of George Allen Moir and Louise Elvina Moir (*née* Evans); *m* 1929, Eileen Walker; one *s* one *d. Educ:* Scotch Coll., Melbourne; Univ. of Melbourne. Barrister and Solicitor, Supreme Court of Victoria. Partner, Gillott Moir & Winneke, 1929-63, retd. *Recreations:* racing, bowls. *Address:* 27 Hopetoun Road, Toorak, Victoria 3142, Australia. *T:* 20-5267. *Clubs:* Athenæum (Melbourne); Victoria Racing, Victoria Amateur Turf, Moonee Valley Racing, Melbourne Cricket, Melbourne Rotary.

MOIR, Sir Ernest Ian Royds, 3rd Bt, *cr* 1916; *b* 9 June 1925; *o s* of Sir Arrol Moir, 2nd Bt, and Dorothy Blanche, *d* of Admiral Sir Percy Royds, CB, CMG; *S* father, 1957; *m* 1954, Margaret Hanham Carter; three *s. Educ:* Rugby; Cambridge Univ. (BA). Served War of 1939-45 in Royal Engineers. *Heir: s* Christopher Ernest Moir, *b* 22 May 1955. *Address:* Three Gates, 174 Coombe Lane West, Kingston, Surrey. *T:* 01-942 7394. *Club:* Royal Automobile.

MOIR, Rt. Rev. Francis Oag H.; *see* Hulme-Moir.

MOIR, George Guthrie, MA; with Thames Television; *b* 30 Oct. 1917; *s* of James William and May Flora Moir; *m* 1951, Sheila Maureen Ryan, SRN; one *s* two *d. Educ:* Berkhamsted; Peterhouse, Cambridge. Officer, 5th Suffolk Regt, 1940-46, POW Singapore, 1942. Chief Officer, St John Ambulance Bde Cadets, 1947-50; Dir, European Youth Campaign, 1950-52; Chm., later Pres., World Assembly of Youth, 1952-56; Education Adviser, Hollerith Tab. Machine Co., 1957; Asst Controller and Exec. Producer, Rediffusion TV, 1958-68; Controller of Educn and Religious Programmes, Thames TV,

1968-76. Serious damage under train in Sept. 1974, and in hospitals till 1976. Member: Gen. Synod (formerly House of Laity, Church Assembly), 1956-75; Bd of Church Army, 1973-; Mem. Council, Reading Univ. Mem. Cttee Athenæum, 1974-. Contested (L) Aylesbury Div., 1950. CC Bucks, 1949-75; President: Old Berkhamstedians Assoc., 1974; Ivinghoe Beacon Villages, 1973. Vice Pres., St John, Bucks. Papal Bene Merenti Medal 1970, for services to religious and educational broadcasting. OStJ. *Publications:* (ed) Why I Believe, 1964; (ed) Life's Work, 1965; (ed) Teaching and Television: ETV Explained, 1967; The Suffolk Regiment, 1969; Into Television, 1969; (ed) Beyond Hatred, 1969; contribs to Times, Times Ed. Supplement, Church Times, Contemporary Review, Frontier, etc. Many TV series, including This Week; Dialogue with Doubt; Royalist and Roundhead; Best Sellers; Treasures of the British Museum; (with Nat. Trust) A Place in the Country; A Place in History; A Place in Europe. *Recreations:* golf, poetry, churches, mountains. *Address:* The Old Rectory, Aston Clinton, Aylesbury, Bucks. *T:* Aylesbury 630393. *Clubs:* Athenæum, National Liberal, Nikaean.

MOIR, John Chassar, CBE 1961; MA, DM, FRCSE, FRCOG; Visiting Professor, Royal Postgraduate Medical School; Nuffield Professor of Obstetrics and Gynæcology, University of Oxford, 1937-67, now Emeritus; Fellow, Oriel College, 1937-67, Hon. Fellow, 1974; *b* 1900; *s* of late John and I. Moir (*née* Pirie), Montrose; *m* 1933, Grace Hilda Bailey; two *s* two *d. Educ:* Montrose Academy; Edinburgh University. MB, ChB (Edinburgh), 1922; MD, Gold Medal (Edinburgh), 1930; Asst Surgeon, East Surrey Hospital; 1st Asst Obstetric Unit, University Coll. Hospital, London; Reader in Obstetrics and Gynæcology, University of London (British Postgraduate Medical Sch.); Rockefeller Travelling Fellowship, 1932; Visiting Professor, Queen's Univ., Ontario, 1950; Examiner in Obstetrics and Gynæcology, University of Oxford, etc; late Pres., section Obstetrics and Gynæcology, Royal Society Medicine, Hon. Fellow, 1974; Hon. Fellow, American Association of Obstetricians and Gynecologists; Hon. Fellow, Amer. Gynecological Soc.; Corresponding Fellow, New York Acad. of Medicine; Hon. LLD Queen's Univ., Ont; Hon. DSc: Edinburgh, 1970; Manchester, 1972; Master of Midwifery, *hc,* Soc. Apothecaries, London. *Publications:* 5th edn, Munro-Kerr's Operative Obstetrics, 1949, 8th edn, 1967; The Vesicovaginal Fistula, 1961, 2nd edn, 1967; contributions to scientific journals, and to textbooks on obstetrics and gynæcology. *Address:* Farnmore, Woodstock Road, Charlbury, Oxford.

MOIR, Percival John; retired as Professor of Surgery and Dean of the Faculty of Medicine, University of Leeds, 1952-60; Emeritus Professor since 1960; *b* July 1893; 2nd *s* of late Frederick R. Moir; *m* 1926, Joan Evelyn Lander Whitehead; one *s. Educ:* Kelvinside, Glasgow; Univ. Glasgow; London Hospital. MB, ChB Glasgow Univ., 1914; FRCS, 1923; Capt. RAMC, 1914-18, served in Gallipoli, Egypt, Palestine, and France (despatches, MC). Formerly: Senior Hon. Surgeon, General Infirmary at Leeds; Surgeon Leeds Regional Hospital Board and United Leeds Hospitals Board; Mem. Board of Governors, Leeds United Hospitals; Mem., Leeds Regional Hospital Board; Mem., General Medical Council. Hon. Consulting Surgeon Dewsbury, Pontefract, Mirfield, and Ilkley Hospitals; Cons. Surg. WRCC; Prof. of Surgery, University of Leeds, 1940-46; Mem. Court of Examiners, Royal College of Surgeons of England, 1941-47. Fellow, Association of Surgeons of Great Britain and Ireland. *Publications:* contributed articles to Medical Journals. *Address:* 10 Windermere Avenue, SW19. *T:* 01-540 5505.

MOIR CAREY, D. M.; *see* Carey.

MOISEIWITSCH, Tanya, (Mrs Felix Krish), CBE 1976; designer for the theatre; *b* 3 Dec. 1914; *d* of late Benno Moiseiwitsch, CBE, and 1st wife, Daisy Kennedy, *qv; m* 1942, Felix Krish (*decd*). *Educ:* various private schs; Central School of Arts and Crafts, London; Scenic painting student at Old Vic, London. Abbey Theatre, Dublin, 1935-39; Q. Theatre, 1940; 1st West End prod. Golden Cuckoo, Duchess, 1940; Weekly Repertory, Oxford Playhouse, 1941-44. Stage designs include: Bless the Bride, Adelphi, 1947; Peter Grimes, Covent Garden, 1947; Beggar's Opera, English Opera Group, Aldeburgh Festival, 1948; Treasure Hunt, Apollo, 1949; Home at Seven, Wyndham's, 1950; The Holly and the Ivy, Lyric (Hammersmith) and Duchess, 1950; Captain Carvallo, St James's, 1950; Figure of Fun, Aldwych, 1951. Has designed for Old Vic Company since 1944; at Playhouse, Liverpool, 1944-45; at Theatre Royal, Bristol, 1945-46; productions for Old Vic Company include: (at New Theatre): Uncle Vanya, The Critic, Cyrano de Bergerac, 1945-46, The Cherry Orchard, 1948, A

Month in the Country, 1949; (at Old Vic): Midsummer Night's Dream, 1951, Timon of Athens, 1952, Henry VIII, 1953; Two Gentlemen of Verona, 1957. Has designed for Royal Shakespeare Theatre, Stratford upon Avon: Henry VIII, 1950; The History Cycle (assisted by Alix Stone), 1951; Othello, 1954; Measure for Measure, 1956; Much Ado about Nothing, 1958; All's Well that Ends Well, 1959; also for 1st, and subsequent seasons, Shakespearean Festival, Stratford, Ont; for The Matchmaker, Edinburgh Festival, 1954, and New York, 1955; for Cherry Orchard, Piccolo Teatro, Milan, 1955; for Merchant of Venice, Habimah Theatre, Israel, 1959; Tyrone Guthrie Theatre, Minneapolis, USA: 1963; Hamlet, The Miser, Three Sisters; 1964: St Joan, Volpone; 1965: The Way of the World; Cherry Orchard; 1966: As You Like It; Skin of our Teeth (with Carolyn Parker); 1967: The House of Atreus; Peter Grimes (Metropolitan Opera, New York), 1967; Volpone, Nat. Theatre, 1968; Macook's Corner, Ulster Players, Belfast, 1969; Caucasian Chalk Circle, Sheffield Playhouse, 1969; Swift, Abbey Theatre, Dublin, 1969; Uncle Vanya, Minneapolis, 1969; Cymbeline, Stratford, Ont., 1970; The Barber of Seville, Brighton Festival, 1971; cons. designer, Crucible Theatre, Sheffield, 1971-73; The Misanthrope, Nat. Theatre, 1973; The Government Inspector (with J. Jensen), USA, 1973; Australian Tour for Elizabethan Theatre Trust, 1974; The Imaginary Invalid, Stratford, Ont, 1974; The Misanthrope, St James' Theater, NY, 1975; Phaedra Britannica, Nat. Theatre, 1975; The Voyage of Edgar Allan Poe (world première), Minnesota Opera Co., USA, 1976; Rigoletto, NY Met., 1977. Diplôme d'Honneur, Canadian Conference of the Arts. Hon. DLitt: Birmingham, 1964; Waterloo, Ont, 1977. *Address:* c/o National Westminster Bank, 185 Sloane Street, SW1.

MOKAMA, Moleleki Didwell, BA, LLM; Barrister-at-Law; Advocate of the Supreme Court of Botswana; Attorney-General of Botswana, since 1969; *b* 2 Feb. 1933; *e s* of Mokama Moleleki and Baipoledi Moleleki, Maunatlala, Botswana; *m* 1962, Kgopodiso Vivien Robi; one *s. Educ:* Moeng; Fort Hare; London Univ.; Inner Temple. Crown Counsel to Botswana Govt, 1963-66; High Comr for Botswana in London, 1966-69; Botswana Ambassador Extraordinary and Plenipotentiary: to France, 1967-69; to Germany, 1967-69; to Sweden, 1968-69; to Denmark, 1968-69. Hon. Mem., American Soc. of International Law, 1965. *Recreations:* swimming, shooting, hunting. *Address:* Attorney-General's Chambers, Private Bag 9, Gaberones, Botswana.

MOLESWORTH, family name of Viscount Molesworth.

MOLESWORTH, 11th Viscount, *cr* 1716 (Ireland); **Richard Gosset Molesworth;** Baron Philipstown, 1716; secretarial work since 1959; *b* 31 Oct. 1907; *s* of 10th Viscount and Elizabeth Gladys Langworthy (*d* 1974); *S* father, 1961; *m* 1958, Anne Florence Womersley, MA; two *s. Educ:* Lancing Coll.; private tutors. Farmed for many years. Served War, in RAF, 1941-44 (Middle East, 1941-43). *Recreations:* foreign travel, music. *Heir:* *s* Hon. Robert Bysse Kelham Molesworth, *b* 4 June 1959. *Address:* Garden Flat, 2 Bishopswood Road, Highgate, N6. *T:* 01-348 1366.

MOLESWORTH, Hender Delves; *b* Raptsgate Park, Cirencester, 10 Feb. 1907; *s* of late Lionel Charles Molesworth and Saba Maud, *d* of Sir Henry Delves Broughton, 9th Bt; *m* 1934, Evelyn Carnegy, *d* of late M. W. and Edith Galloway, Shelley Hall, Ongar. *Educ:* Stubbington; Oundle; University Coll., Oxford. Joined staff of Victoria and Albert Museum, 1931; Curator of Institute of Jamaica, 1936-38; Ministry of Information, 1940; Press Attaché British Legation, Addis Ababa, 1942-45. Victoria and Albert Museum: Keeper of Sculpture, 1946; Keeper of Woodwork, 1954; retd 1966. *Publications:* European Sculpture, 1965; The Princes, 1969; (with J. Kenworthy-Browne) Three Centuries of Furniture Design, 1972; articles on art, etc. *Recreations:* travel, painting. *Address:* The Orangery, Langley Park, Wexham, Bucks. *T:* Slough 28815.

MOLESWORTH-ST AUBYN, Sir John, 14th Bt, *cr* 1689; CBE 1968; *b* 12 Jan. 1899; *s* of Sir Hugh Molesworth-St Aubyn, 13th Bt, and Emma Sybil (*d* 1929), *d* of Admiral Charles Wake; *S* father, 1942; *m* 1926, Celia Marjorie (*d* 1965), *e d* of late Lieut-Col Valentine Vivian, CMG, DSO, MVO; one *s* two *d. Educ:* Eton; Christ Church, Oxford. Flight Lieut, RAFVR, 1941. JP Cornwall, 1942; Sheriff of Cornwall, 1948. *Heir:* *s* John Arscott Molesworth-St Aubyn, *qv. Address:* Pencarrow, Washaway, Bodmin, Cornwall.
See also Earl of Morley.

MOLESWORTH-ST AUBYN, Lt-Col John Arscott, MBE 1963; DL; JP; *b* 15 Dec. 1926; *s* and *heir* of Sir John Molesworth-St

Aubyn, *qv*; *m* 1957, Iona Audrey Armatrude, *d* of late Adm. Sir Francis Loftus Tottenham, KCB, CBE; two *s* one *d. Educ:* Eton. 2nd Lieut KRRC 1946; Captain 1954; psc 1959; Major 1961; jssc 1964; served Malaya and Borneo, 1961-63 and 1965; Royal Green Jackets, 1966; Lt-Col 1967; retd 1969. County Comr, Scouts, Cornwall, 1969-. Mem., Cornwall River Authority, 1969-74; Chm. Devon Exec. Cttee, 1975-77, and Mem. Nat. Council, 1973-, Country Landowners Assoc.; Chm., West Local Land Drainage Cttee, SW Water Authority, 1974-. Pres., Royal Cornwall Agricl Assoc., 1976. JP Devon, 1971; DL Cornwall, 1971; High Sheriff Cornwall, 1975. *Recreations:* shooting, ornithology. *Address:* Tetcott Manor, Holsworthy, Devon. *T:* North Tamerton 220. *Clubs:* Army and Navy; Cornish 1768.

MOLEYNS; see Eveleigh-De-Moleyns.

MOLINE, Most Rev. Robert William Haines, MC; MA; DD (Lambeth), 1948; *b* Sudbury, Suffolk, 20 Oct. 1889; *s* of late Canon R. P. Moline and Alice Price; *m* 1929, Mirabel Mathilde, *d* of Thomas Rookley Parker, Townsville. *Educ:* King's Sch., Canterbury; Emmanuel Coll., Cambridge (Scholar). BA 1912, MA 1919. Asst Master, Cranleigh Sch., Surrey, 1912-14; served in Rifle Brigade and Machine Gun Corps, 1914-19; granted rank of Major on demobilisation, 1919; Bishop's Coll., Cheshunt, 1919. Deacon, 1920; Priest, 1921; Asst Curate, St Matthew's, Bethnal Green, 1920-22; joined Brotherhood of St Barnabas, North Qld, 1922; Warden of Brotherhood, 1925-27; Archdeacon of North Qld, 1926-29; Rector of North Cadbury, Som, 1929-34; Rector of Poplar, 1934-40; Vicar of St Paul's, Knightsbridge, 1940-47; Archbishop of Perth (Australia), 1947-62, resigned. *Address:* 70 Hipwood Road, Hamilton, Brisbane, Qld 4007, Australia.

MOLLAN, Maj.-Gen. Francis Robert Henry, CB 1950; OBE 1943; MC 1918; *b* 20 June 1893; *s* of late Rev. H. J. G. Mollan; *m* 1st, 1921, Violet Samana Desvoeux (*d* 1930); one *s* (and one *s* killed in action, Italy, 1944); 2nd, 1937, Alison Beatrice Hesmondhalgh; two *s* one *d. Educ:* Corrig Sch.; Royal College of Surgeons of Ireland. Served European War, 1915-18, France and Belgium (despatches twice, 1914-15 Star, British War Medal, Victory Medal, MC). Served North-West Frontier of India (Mohmand), 1933 (despatches, Medal and clasp). War of 1939-45 (despatches thrice, OBE, Africa Star and 8th Army clasp). Comdt and Dir of Studies, Royal Army Medical College, 1950-53; Maj.-Gen., 1951; retired 1953; re-employed as Pres., Standing Medical Boards SW District, 1954-61; Area Medical Officer, Taunton, 1961-68. QHS 1952-53 (KHS 1950-52). *Publications:* Contrib. to Jl of the RAMC. *Address:* 5a Mount Street, Taunton, Som. *T:* 3097.

MOLLER, Marjorie, MA; *b* 23 June 1899; *e d* of late C. G. C. Moller. *Educ:* Clapham High Sch.; St Hugh's Coll., Oxford (Honour School of Natural Science). Science mistress City of London Girls' Sch., 1923; Walter Page travelling scholarship, 1930; Head of Science dept, 1928, and House mistress at Wycombe Abbey Sch., 1930; Head Mistress of Headington Sch., Oxford, 1934-59; Warden of Denman Coll. (NFWI), 1959-64. *Address:* 26 Bickerton Road, Headington, Oxford.

MOLLISON, Prof. Patrick Loudon, MD; FRCP; FRCPath; FRS 1968; Professor of Hæmatology, St Mary's Hospital Medical School, London University, since 1962; Consultant Hæmatologist, St Mary's Hospital since 1960; Part-time Director, Medical Research Council Experimental Hæmatology Unit, since 1960; *b* 17 March 1914; *s* of William Mayhew Mollison, Cons. Surgeon (ENT), Guy's Hospital; *m* 1st, 1940, Dr Margaret D. Peirce (marr. diss., 1964); three *s*; 2nd, 1973, Dr Jennifer Jones. *Educ:* Rugby Sch.; Clare Coll., Cambridge; St Thomas' Hosp., London. MD Cantab 1944; FRCP 1959; FRCPath 1963. House Phys., Medical Unit, St Thomas' Hosp., 1939; Medical Officer, S London Blood Supply Depot, 1939-43; RAMC, 1943-46; Dir, MRC Blood Transfusion Res. Unit, Hammersmith Hosp., 1946-60; Hon. Lectr, then Sen. Lectr, Dept of Medicine, Post-grad. Medical Sch., 1948; Cons. Hæmatologist, Hammersmith Hosp., 1947-60. *Publications:* Blood Transfusion in Clinical Medicine, 1951 (5th edn, 1972); papers on red cell survival and blood group antibodies. *Recreations:* music, gardening, golf. *Address:* 60 King Henry's Road, NW3 3RR. *T:* 01-722 1947. *Club:* Savile.

MOLLO, Victor; Bridge Correspondent, The Evening Standard, 1970-75; Bridge Editor, Faber & Faber Ltd, since 1966; Bridge Cruise Director: P&O, 1973-74; Norwegian-America Line, 1975; *b* St Petersburg, 17 Sept. 1909; Russian parents; *m* 1952, Jeanne Victoria Forbes. *Educ:* privately in Paris; Cordwalles, Surrey (Prep. Sch.); Brighton Coll.; London School of Economics, London Univ. Free lance journalism, also reading

French and Russian texts for publishers, 1927-40; sub editor and editor, European Services (now External) BBC, 1940 till retirement in Oct. 1969. *Publications:* Streamlined Bridge, 1947; Card-Play Technique (in collab. with N. Gardener), 1955; Bridge for Beginners (in collab. with N. Gardener) 1956; Bridge Psychology, 1958; Will You Be My Partner?, 1959; Bridge: Modern Bidding, 1961; Success at Bridge, 1964; Bridge in the Menagerie, 1965; Confessions of an Addict, 1966; The Bridge Immortals, 1967; Victor Mollo's Winning Double, 1968; Bridge: Case for the Defence, 1970; (with E. Jannersten) Best of Bridge, 1972; Bridge in the Fourth Dimension, 1974; Instant Bridge, 1975; (with Aksel J. Nielson) Defence at Bridge, 1976; Bridge Unlimited, 1976; Bridge Course Complete, 1977; also Pocket Guides: ACOL: Winning Bidding, 1969 and Winning Defence, Winning Conventions. Contributing Editor to the Official Encyclopaedia of Bridge. Regular contributor to Bridge Magazines in USA, France, Denmark and Sweden and to Bridge Magazine in Britain. *Recreations:* gastronomy, conversation, bridge. *Address:* 801 Grenville House, Dolphin Square, SW1. *Clubs:* Royal Automobile, Eccentric, Curzon House.

MOLLOY, Michael John; Editor, Daily Mirror, since Dec. 1975; *b* 22 Dec. 1940; *s* of John George and Margaret Ellen Molloy; *m* 1964, Sandra June Foley; three *d*. *Educ:* Ealing School of Art. Sunday Pictorial, 1956; Daily Sketch, 1960; Daily Mirror, 1962-: Editor, Mirror Magazine, 1969; Asst Editor, 1970; Dep. Editor, 1975; Dir, Mirror Group Newspapers, 1976-. *Recreations:* reading, running. *Address:* Daily Mirror, 33 Holborn, EC1. *T:* 01-353 0246. *Club:* Reform.

MOLLOY, William John, FRGS; MP (Lab) Ealing North since 1964; *b* 26 Oct. 1918; *m* Eva Lewis; one *d*. *Educ:* elementary sch., Swansea; University Coll., Swansea (Political Economy, extra-mural). Served Field Coy, RE, 1939-46. Member: TGWU 1936-46; Civil Service Union, 1946-52; Co-op and USDAW, 1952. Chm., Staff-Side Whitley Council, Germany and Austria Sections, FO, and Staff-Side Lectr, 1946-52. Leader, Fulham Borough Council, 1959-62. Former Vice-Chm., Parly Labour Party Gp for Common Market and European Affairs; Parly Adviser, London Trades Council Transport Cttee, 1968-; Mem., House of Commons Estimates Cttee, 1968-70; PPS to Minister of Posts and Telecom., 1969-70. Mem. Assemblies, Council of Europe and WEU, 1969-73; Mem., European Parlt, 1976-. Chm., Parly Lab. Party Social Services Gp, 1974. Mem. Court, Reading Univ., 1968-; Mem. Council, RGS, 1976-. Governor, Holland Park Co-ed. Comp. Sch., 1958-64. *Recreations:* horse-riding, music. *Address:* 2a Uneeda Drive, Greenford, Middx.

MOLOHAN, Michael John Brew, CMG 1957; MBE 1936; formerly Member of HM Overseas Civil Service; *b* 30 May 1906; *s* of late George Brew Molohan, New Milton, Hants; *m* 1951, Alice Kathleen Branson Wilkinson; no *c*. *Educ:* Cheltenham Coll.; Trinity Coll., Oxford (BA). Entered Colonial Service (Tanganyika) as Administrative Officer, 1929; Labour Comr, Tanganyika, 1948-53; Senior Prov. Comr, 1953-61. *Recreations:* Rugby football, cricket, golf. *Address:* Hollies, 11 Pewley Hill, Guildford, Surrey. *Club:* Royal Commonwealth Society.

MOLONY, Sir Joseph (Thomas), KCVO 1970; Kt 1967; QC 1955; a Recorder, since 1972 (Recorder of Bristol, 1964-71); Judge of the Courts of Appeal, Jersey and Guernsey, 1972-75; *b* 8 Dec. 1907; 2nd *s* of Rt Hon. Sir T. F. Molony, 1st Bt, PC, Lord Chief Justice of Ireland; *m* 1936, Carmen Mary, *o d* of late Frankland Dent, PhD, MSc, FIC (Colonial Civil Service Singapore); two *s* two *d*. *Educ:* Downside; Trinity Coll., Cambridge (Senior Scholar). MA, LLM 1933; Barrister, Inner Temple, 1930 (Cert. of Honour, Barstow Scholar, Yarborough-Anderson Scholar); Master of the Bench, 1961. Leader of the Western Circuit, 1964-75; Mem. Bar Council, 1954-58, 1962; Commissioner of Assize: Midland and South-Eastern Circuits, 1958; North-Eastern Circuit, 1960; Western Circuit, 1968; Recorder: Devizes, 1951-54; Exeter, 1954-60; Southampton, 1960-64. Attorney General to the Duchy of Cornwall, 1960-69. Chairman: General Council of the Bar, 1963-64, 1964-65, 1965-66; Board of Trade Departmental Cttee on Consumer Protection, 1959; Code of Practice Cttee, Pharmaceutical Industry, 1967. Served War of 1939-45, Sqdn Leader, RAF, 1940-45. *Address:* 4 Parkside Gardens, Wimbledon Common, SW19. *T:* 01-946 3440.

MOLONY, Thomas Desmond, 3rd Bt. Does not use the title, and his name is not on the Official Roll of Baronets.

MOLOTOV, Vaycheslav Mikhailovich, (*pseudonym* of V. M. Skryabin); Soviet diplomat; *b* Kirov district (Vyatka), 9 March 1890; son of a ship assistant; as mem. of students' Marxist circles in Kazan, took part in first Revolution, 1905; joined Bolshevik section of Russian Social Democratic Labour Party and

organised students, 1906; arrested and deported to Vologda; organised Vologda railwaymen; graduated, 1909; organised students, Petrograd; contributed to Zvezda; part-founder with Stalin and sec. of Pravda, 1911; exiled from Petrograd for political activity, 1912; continued Party work from suburbs, organising elections and work of Party deputies in Duma, 1913; reorganised Moscow Bolshevik Party; exiled to Irkutsk, Siberia, 1915; escaped, returned to Petrograd and appointed mem. of Russian Bureau of Bolshevik Central Committee, 1916; mem. of executive of Petrograd Soviet and of military revolutionary cttee, 1917; chm. of People's Economy Council, Northern Region, 1918; chm. Nijegorodsky regional executive, 1919; sec. of Donets Regional Party cttee, 1920; elected mem. and sec. of Central Cttee of Communist Party of Soviet Union and candidate mem. of Political Bureau, 1921; mem. of Political Bureau of CPSU; worked against Zinovievists, Leningrad, 1926; elected mem. of Central Executive Cttee of Russian Soviet Socialist Republic, 1927; sec., Moscow cttee of CPSU; worked against Bukharinists in Moscow, 1928; elected mem. of Presidium of Central Executive Cttee of USSR, 1929; chm. of Council, of People's Commissars of USSR, 1930-41; 1st Dep. Chm., Council of People's Commissars, 1941-46; Dep. Chm., State Defence Cttee, 1941-45; took part in Teheran, Crimean, Potsdam and San Francisco Conferences; Leader of Soviet Delegn to Paris Peace Conf., 1946, to UN Gen. Assemblies, 1945-48; People's Commissar for For. Affairs, 1930-46, For. Min., 1946-49, 1953-56; First Dep. Chm. of USSR Council of Ministers, 1953-57; Min. of State Control, 1956-57; Dep. to Supreme Soviet, 1937-57; Soviet Ambassador to Mongolia, 1957-60; Chief Permanent Representative of the Soviet Union (rank Ambassador) to the International Atomic Energy Agency, Vienna, 1960-62. Hon. Mem. USSR Acad. of Sciences, 1946. Hero of Socialist Labour (and Hammer and Sickle Medal), 1943; Order of Lenin (4 awards). *Publications:* In the Struggle for Socialism, 1934; Articles and Speeches, 1935-36, 1937; Problems of Foreign Policy, 1948. *Address:* c/o Ministry of Social Security, 14 Shabolovka, Moscow, USSR.

MOLSON, family name of Baron Molson.

MOLSON, Baron, *cr* 1961, of High Peak (Life Peer); **(Arthur) Hugh (Elsdale) Molson,** PC 1956; President, Council for Protection of Rural England, since 1971 (Chairman, 1968-71); *b* 29 June 1903; *o surv. s* of late Major J. E. Molson, MP, Gainsborough, and Mary, *d* of late A. E. Leeson, MD; *m* 1949, Nancy, *d* of late W. H. Astington, Bramhall, Cheshire. *Educ:* Royal Naval Colleges, Osborne and Dartmouth; Lancing; New Coll., Oxford. Pres. of Oxford Union, 1925; 1st Class Hons Jurisprudence. Served 36 Searchlight Regt, 1939-41. Staff Captain 11 AA, Div., 1941-42. Barrister-at-Law, Inner Temple, 1931; Political Sec., Associated Chambers of Commerce of India, 1926-29; Contested Aberdare Div. of Merthyr Tydfil, 1929; MP (U) Doncaster, 1931-35. MP (U) The High Peak Div. of Derbyshire, 1939-61. Parly Sec., Min. of Works, 1951-53; Joint Parly Sec., Min. of Transport and Civil Aviation, Nov. 1953-Jan. 1957; Minister of Works, 1957-Oct. 1959. Mem., Monckton Commission on Rhodesia and Nyasaland, 1960; Chm., Commn of Privy Counsellors on the dispute between Buganda and Bunyoro, 1962. *Publications:* articles in various reviews on political and other subjects. *Recreation:* shooting. *Address:* Cherrytrees, Kelso, Roxburghshire. *T:* Yetholm 204; 14 Wilton Crescent, SW1. *T:* 01-235 3948. *Clubs:* Athenæum, Carlton.

MOLYNEAUX, James Henry; JP; MP (UU) South Antrim since 1970; *b* 27 Aug. 1920; *s* of late William Molyneaux, Seacash, Killead, Co. Antrim; unmarried. *Educ:* Aldergrove Sch., Co. Antrim. RAF, 1941-46. Vice-Chm., Eastern Special Care Hosp. Man. Cttee, 1966-73; Chm. Antrim Br., NI Assoc. for Mental Health, 1967-70; Hon. Sec., S Antrim Unionist Assoc., 1964-70; Vice-Pres., Ulster Unionist Council, 1974. Leader, UU Party, House of Commons, 1974-. Dep. Grand Master of Orange Order and Hon. PGM of Canada; Sovereign Grand Master, Commonwealth Royal Black Instn, 1971. JP Antrim, 1957; CC Antrim, 1964-73. *Recreations:* gardening, music. *Address:* Aldergrove, Crumlin, Co. Antrim, N Ireland. *T:* Crumlin 52545.

MOLYNEUX, John Anthony; HM Diplomatic Service, retired; *b* 1 Aug. 1923; *s* of late Mr and Mrs E. D. Molyneux; *m* 1958, Patricia Dawson; three *s* one *d*. *Educ:* Lancing; Worcester Coll., Oxford (MA). Royal Navy, 1941-46. Joined Commonwealth Relations Office, 1949; 2nd Sec., New Delhi, 1950-52; 1st Sec., Karachi, 1955-59, Canberra, 1959-62; Special Adviser to Governor of N Rhodesia, 1964; Dep. High Comr, Lusaka, 1964-66; Counsellor (Economic/Commercial), Belgrade, 1967-70; seconded to Birmingham Chamber of Commerce and Industry, 1971-72; Commercial Counsellor, The Hague, 1972-74; seconded to Dept of Energy, 1974-76. *Recreations:* gardening, golf. *Address:* The Old Farmhouse, Wroxton, near Banbury, Oxon. *Clubs:* Travellers'; Delhi Gymkhana; Karachi Yacht.

MOLYNEUX, Wilfrid, FCA; *b* 26 July 1910; *s* of Charles Molyneux and Mary (*née* Vose); *m* 1937, Kathleen Eleanor Young; one *s* one *d. Educ:* Douai Sch. With Cooper Brothers & Co., 1934-67; Finance Mem., BSC, 1967-71. *Address:* 105 Park Road, Brentwood, Essex CM14 4TT.

MOMIGLIANO, Prof. Arnaldo Dante, Hon. KBE 1974; DLitt (Turin); FBA 1954; Professor of Ancient History in the University of London at University College, 1951-75; Alexander White Visiting Professor, University of Chicago, 1959 and 1975-78; *b* 5 Sept. 1908; *s* of late Riccardo Momigliano and late Ilda Levi; *m* 1932, Gemma Segre; one *d. Educ:* privately, and at Univs of Turin and Rome. Professore Incaricato di Storia Greca, Univ. of Rome, 1932-36; Professore Titolare di Storia Romana, 1936-38, Professore Ordinario di Storia Romana in soprannumero, 1945-64, Univ. of Turin, *Id,* 1964-, Scuola Normale Superiore of Pisa. Lecturer in Ancient History, 1947-49, Reader in Ancient History, 1949-51, University of Bristol; research work in Oxford, 1939-47. Sather Prof. in Classics, Univ. of California, 1961-62; J. H. Gray Lectr, Univ. of Cambridge, 1963; Wingate Lectr, Hebrew Univ. of Jerusalem, 1964; Vis. Prof. and Lauro de Bosis Lectr, Harvard Univ., 1964-65; C. N. Jackson Lectr, Harvard Univ., 1968; Jerome Lectr, Michigan Univ., 1971-72; Vis. Schol., Harvard, 1972; Trevelyan Lectr, Cambridge Univ., 1973; Flexner Lectr, Bryn Mawr, 1974; Grinfield Lectr on the Septuagint, Oxford, 1977. Socio Nazionale: Accademia dei Lincei, 1961 (corresp. mem., 1947-61); Arcadia, 1967; Accademia delle Scienze di Torino, 1968; Istituto di Studi Romani, 1970 (corresp. mem., 1954-70); Istituto Studi Etruschi, 1973. Foreign Member: Royal Dutch Academy; Amer. Philosophical Soc.; Amer. Acad. of Arts and Scis; Corresp. Mem., German Archæological Institute, 1935; Hon. Mem., Amer. Hist. Assoc., 1964. Pres., Soc. for Promotion of Roman Studies, 1965-68. Hon. MA Oxford; Hon. DLitt: Bristol, 1959; Edinburgh, 1964; Oxford, 1970; Cambridge, 1971; London, 1975; Chicago, 1976; Leiden, 1977; Hon. DHL: Columbia, 1974; Brandeis, 1977; Hon. DPhil Hebrew Univ., 1974. Hon. Fellow: Warburg Inst., 1975; UCL, 1976. Premio Cantoni, Univ. of Florence, 1932; Premio Feltrinelli for historical res. (Accademia dei Lincei award), 1960; Kaplun Prize for historical res., Hebrew Univ., 1975. Co-editor of *Rivista Storica Italiana,* 1948-. *Publications:* La composizione della Storia di Tucidide, 1930; Prime Linee di storia della tradizione maccabaica, 1931 (2nd edn 1968); Claudius, 1934 (2nd edn 1961); Filippo il Macedone, 1934; La storiografia sull' impero romano, 1936; Contributo alla storia degli studi classici, 1955; Secondo Contributo alla storia degli studi classici, 1960; Terzo Contributo alla storia degli studi classici, 1966; Studies in Historiography, 1966; Paganism and Christianity in the Fourth Century, 1963; Quarto contributo alla storia degli studi classici, 1969; The Development of Greek Biography, 1971; Introduzione Bibliografica alla Storia Greca fino a Socrate, 1975; Quinto Contributo alla Storia degli studi classici, 1975; Alien Wisdom, the limits of Hellenization, 1975; Essays on Historiography, 1977; contribs to Cambridge Ancient History, Jl of Roman Studies, History and Theory, Jl of Warburg Inst., Daedalus, Enciclopedia Italiana, Encycl. Britannica, Encycl. Judaica. *Recreation:* walking. *Address:* All Souls College, Oxford.

MONAGHAN, Rt. Rev. James; Titular Bishop of Cell Ausaille and Bishop Auxiliary to Archbishop of St Andrews and Edinburgh since 1970; Parish Priest of Holy Cross, Edinburgh, since 1959; *b* Bathgate, 11 July 1914; *s* of Edward and Elizabeth Monaghan. *Educ:* St Aloysius' Coll., Glasgow; Blairs Coll., Aberdeen; St Kieran's Coll., Kilkenny, Ireland. Priest, 1940; Secretary, 1953; Vicar-Gen. for Archdio. St Andrews and Edinburgh, 1958-. *Address:* 252 Ferry Road, Edinburgh EH5 3AN. *T:* 031-552 3957.

MONAHAN, James Henry Francis, CBE 1962; Director, Royal Ballet School, since Sept. 1977; *b* 16 Dec. 1912; *s* of late George John Monahan, Indian Civil Service, and Helen Monahan (*née* Kennedy); *m* 1941, Joan Barker-Mill (*née* Eaden); two *s* three *d*; *m* 1965, Merle Park, *qv* (marr. diss. 1970); one *s*; *m* 1970, Gail Thomas; one *s* one *d*. *Educ:* Stonyhurst Coll.; Christ Church, Oxford. The Manchester Guardian: critic and reporter, London office, 1937-39; film critic, 1945-63; dance critic, 1945-. Government Service and attached to BBC German Service, 1939-42; Army Service: (despatches); Special Forces and No 10 Commando, 1942-45; Captain, 1944. British Broadcasting Corporation: Asst Head, West European Services, 1946; Head, West European Services, 1946-51; Controller, European Services, 1952-70; Dir of Programmes, External Services, 1971, retired. Part-time cons., Corp. for Public Broadcasting, USA,

1973. *Publications:* Far from the Land (poems), 1944; After Battle (poems), 1947; Fonteyn, 1958; report on Deutsche Welle, West Germany, 1972; The Nature of Ballet, 1976. *Recreations:* lawn tennis, squash rackets. *Address:* 6 Elm Bank Mansions, The Terrace, Barnes, SW13. *Club:* Hurlingham.

MONAHAN, Hon. Sir Robert (Vincent), Kt 1967; Supreme Court Judge, State of Victoria, Australia, 1955-70; *b* 11 April 1898; *s* of Patrick Martin Monahan, Victoria, and Mary Frances Monahan (*née* Nolan); *m* 1929, Lillie Elevia, *d* of Peter Donald Bowman, Adelaide; three *s* one *d. Educ:* St Patrick's Coll., Ballarat; Newman Coll., Univ. of Melbourne. Admitted to: Victorian Bar, 1922; New South Wales Bar, 1942; Tasmanian Bar, 1948; KC 1947; practised at Common Law and Criminal Law Bar throughout professional career. *Recreations:* golf, racing, fishing. *Address:* 99 Spring Street, Melbourne, Vic 3000, Australia. *T:* 26-2016. *Clubs:* Australian, Athenæum, Melbourne (Melbourne); Melbourne Cricket; Lawn Tennis Association of Victoria; all Melbourne racing; Victoria Golf.

MONCEL, Lt.-Gen. Robert William, OC 1968; DSO 1944; OBE 1944; CD 1944; retired 1966; *b* 9 April 1917; *s* of René Moncel and Edith Brady; *m* 1939, Nancy Allison, *d* of Ralph P. Bell; one *d. Educ:* Selwyn House Sch.; Bishop's Coll. Sch. Royal Canadian Regt, 1939; Staff Coll., 1940; Bde Major 1st Armd Bde, 1941; comd 18th Manitoba Dragoons, 1942; GSO1, HQ 2 Cdn Corps, 1943; comd 4th Armd Bde, 1944; Dir Canadian Armd Corps, 1946; Nat. War Coll., 1949; Canadian Jt Staff, London, 1949-54; Comdr 3 Inf. Bde, 1957; QMG, 1960; GOC Eastern Comd, 1963; Comptroller Gen., 1964; Vice-Chief of the Defence Staff, Canada, 1965-66. Col, 8th Canadian Hussars. Croix de Guerre, France, 1944; Légion d'Honneur, France, 1944. Hon. LLD Mount Allison Univ., 1968. *Recreations:* fishing, sailing, golf. *Address:* 174 Dufferin Road, Ottawa, Ontario. *T:* 745-5061; Windswept, Murder Point, Nova Scotia. *Clubs:* Royal Ottawa Golf; Royal St Lawrence Yacht; Royal Nova Scotia Yacht.

MONCK, family name of Viscount Monck.

MONCK, 6th Viscount *cr* 1800; **Henry Wyndham Stanley Monck,** OBE 1961; JP; DL; Baron Monck, 1797; Baron Monck (UK), 1866; formerly Coldstream Guards; formerly Company Director; Vice-Chairman, National Association of Boys' Clubs; *b* 11 Dec. 1905; *s* of Hon. Charles H. S. Monck (*d* 1914) and Mary Florence (*d* 1918), *d* of Sir W. Portal, 2nd Bt; *S* grandfather, 1927; *m* 1st, 1937, Eva Maria, Baroness Vreto (marr. diss. 1951), 2nd *d* of Prof. Zaunmüller-Freudenthaler, Vienna; 2nd, 1951, Brenda Mildred, *o d* of G. W. Adkins, Bowers Close, Harpenden; three *s. Educ:* Eton; RMC, Sandhurst. Member, Southern Gas Board, 1965-72. JP Hants, 1944; DL Hants 1973. *Heir: s* Hon. Charles Stanley Monck, BTech, *b* 2 April 1953. *Address:* Hurstbourne Priors House, Whitchurch, Hants RG28 7SB. *T:* Whitchurch, Hants, 2277. *Club:* MCC.

MONCKTON, family name of Viscount Galway, Viscount Monckton of Brenchley and Baroness Ruthven of Freeland.

MONCKTON OF BRENCHLEY, 2nd Viscount *cr* 1957; **Maj.-Gen. Gilbert Walter Riversdale Monckton,** CB 1966; OBE 1956; MC 1940; DL; retired, 1967; Director: Ransome, Hoffmann Pollard Ltd; United & General Trust Ltd; Crosswall Reinsurance Co. Ltd; Monckton Equities Ltd; *b* 3 Nov. 1915; *o s* of 1st Viscount Monckton of Brenchley, PC, GCVO, KCMG, MC, QC, and Mary A. S. (*d* 1964), *d* of Sir Thomas Colyer-Fergusson, 3rd Bt; *S* father, 1965; *m* 1950, Marianna Laetitia, Dame of Honour and Devotion, SMO Malta, OStJ, Pres., St John's Ambulance, Kent, 1975-, 3rd *d* of late Comdr Robert T. Bower; four *s* one *d. Educ:* Harrow; Trinity Coll., Cambridge. BA 1939, MA 1942. 2/Lt 5th Royal Inniskilling Dragoon Guards, SR 1938; Reg. 1939; France and Belgium, 1939-40; Staff Coll., 1941; Bde Major Armd Bde, 1942; Comd and Gen. Staff Sch., USA, 1943; Sqdn Ldr, 3rd King's Own Hussars, 1944, Italy and Syria; Sqdn Ldr, 5th Royal Inniskilling Dragoon Gds, 1945. RAF Staff Coll., 1949; GSO2, 7th Armd Div., 1949; Sqdn Ldr and 2 i/c 5th Royal Inniskilling Dragoon Gds, Korea and Egypt, 1951-52; GSO1, Mil. Ops, WO, 1954-56; Mil. Adv., Brit. Delegn, Geneva Confs on Indo-China and Korea, 1954; transf. 12th Royal Lancers and comd, 1956-58; Comdr Royal Armd Corps, 3rd Div., 1958-60; psc, idc 1961; Dep. Dir, Personnel Admin., WO, 1962; Dir of Public Relations, WO (subseq. MoD), 1963-65; Chief of Staff, HQ BAOR, 1965-67; Col 9th/12th Royal Lancers (Prince of Wales's), 1967-73; Hon. Col, Kent and Sharpshooters Yeomanry Sqdn, 1974-. Farms 400 acres in Kent. President: Kent Assoc. of Boys' Clubs, 1965; Inst. of Heraldic and Genealogical Studies, 1965; Kent Archæological Soc., 1968-75; Medway Productivity Assoc.,

1968-72; Kent Co. Rifle Assoc., 1970; Anglo-Belgian Union, 1973-; Chm., Thurnham Parish Council, 1968-70. DL Kent, 1970. Liveryman Broderers' Co., Warden 1977; KStJ; Chm., Council of Order of St John for Kent, 1969-75; Bailiff, Grand Cross of Obedience, SMO Malta (Chancellor of the British Assoc., 1963-68, Vice-Pres., 1968-74, Pres., 1974-); Comdr, Order of Crown (Belgium), 1965; Bailiff, Grand Cross of Justice, Constantinian Order of St George, 1975. *Recreations:* hunting, cricket, gardening. *Heir:* s Hon. Christopher Walter Monckton, b 14 Feb. 1952. *Address:* Runhams Farm, Runham Lane, Harrietsham, Maidstone, Kent ME17 1NJ. *T:* Ulcombe 313. *Clubs:* Brooks's, Cavalry and Guards, MCC; Casino Maltese (Valetta).
    See also Sir W. B. Goulding.

MONCKTON OF BRENCHLEY, the Dowager Viscountess; *see* Ruthven of Freeland, Lady.

MONCKTON-ARUNDELL, family name of **Viscount Galway.**

MONCREIFF, family name of **Baron Moncreiff.**

MONCREIFF, 5th Baron *cr* 1873; **Harry Robert Wellwood Moncreiff;** Bt, Nova Scotia 1626, UK 1871; Lt-Col (Hon.) RASC, retired; *b* 4 Feb. 1915; *s* of 4th Baron; *S* father, 1942; *m* 1952, Enid Marion Watson, *o d* of Major H. W. Locke, Belmont, Dollar; one *s*. *Educ:* Fettes Coll., Edinburgh. Served War of 1939-45 (despatches). Retired, 1958. *Recreations:* Rugby football, tennis, shooting. *Heir:* s Hon. Rhoderick Harry Wellwood Moncreiff, *b* 22 March 1954. *Address:* Tulliebole Castle, Fossoway, Kinross-shire, *T:* Fossoway 236.

MONCREIFF, Rt. Rev. Francis Hamilton; *b* North Berwick, 29 Sept. 1906; *s* of late James Hamilton Moncreiff. *Educ:* Shrewsbury Sch.; St John's Coll., Cambridge; Cuddesdon Theological Coll. Ordained, 1931; Curate at St Giles, Cambridge, 1931-35, at St Augustine's, Kilburn, 1935-41; Priest-in-charge, at St Salvador's, Edinburgh, 1941, Rector, 1947-51; Chaplain at HM Prison, Edinburgh, 1942-51; Canon of St Mary's Cathedral, Edinburgh, 1950; Diocesan Missioner in diocese of Edinburgh, 1951-52; Bishop of Glasgow and Galloway, 1952-74; Primus of the Episcopal Church in Scotland, 1962-74. Went on a Mission to European parishes in Northern Rhodesia, 1948 and 1951, to Pretoria and Johannesburg, 1953. Hon. DD Glasgow, 1967. *Address:* 19 Eglinton Crescent, Edinburgh EH12 5BY. *T:* 031-337 1523.

MONCREIFFE of that Ilk, Sir Iain; *see* Moncreiffe of that Ilk, Sir R. I. K.

MONCREIFFE of that Ilk, Sir (Rupert) Iain (Kay), 11th Bt, *cr* 1685; DL; author; *b* 9 April 1919; *s* of late Lt-Comdr Gerald Moncreiffe, Royal Navy, and Hinda (*d* 1960), *d* of late Frank Meredyth, styled Count de Miremont; *S* cousin (Sir David Moncreiffe of that Ilk, Bt, 23rd Laird of Moncreiffe), 1957; *m* 1st, 1946, Diana (marr. diss. 1964), *d* of 22nd Earl of Erroll (*see* Countess of Erroll); two *s* one *d*; 2nd, 1966, Hermione, *d* of late Lt-Col W. D. Faulkner, MC, Irish Guards and of the Countess of Dundee (*d* of late Lord Herbert Montagu-Douglas-Scott). *Educ:* Stowe; Heidelberg; Christ Church, Oxford (MA); Edinburgh Univ. (LLB, PhD). Capt. late Scots Guards; served 1939-46 (wounded in Italy): ADC to Gen. Sir Andrew Thorne (GOC-in-C Scottish Comd), 1944-45; Military Liaison Officer for Norway to Adm. Sir William Whitworth (C-in-C Rosyth), 1945. Private Sec. to Sir Maurice Peterson (Ambassador to USSR) and attaché at British Embassy in Moscow, 1946. Mem. Queen's Body Guard for Scotland (Royal Company of Archers), 1948-; called to Scottish Bar, 1950; Mem. of Lloyd's, 1952-. Mem. Advisory Cttee Scottish Nat. Portrait Gallery, 1957. Hon. Pres., Duodecimal Soc. of Great Britain, 1966-. Hon. Sheriff of Perth and Angus, 1958-. Albany Herald, 1961; DL Perth, 1961. FSA 1959. OStJ 1949. *Publications:* (with D. Pottinger) Simple Heraldry, 1953; Simple Custom, 1954; Blood Royal, 1956; Map of Scotland of Old, 1960; (with David Hicks) The Highland Clans, 1967. *Recreations:* shooting and travel. *Heir:* s Lord Hay, *qv*. *Address:* Easter Moncreiffe, by Perth. *T:* Bridge of Earn 338. *Clubs:* Turf, White's, Pratt's, Beefsteak; Royal and Ancient Golf (St Andrews); (Founder) Puffin's (Edinburgh).

MONCRIEFF; *see* Scott-Moncrieff.

MONCTON, Archbishop of, (RC), since 1972; **Most Rev. Donat Chiasson;** *b* Paquetville, NB, 2 Jan. 1930; *s* of Louis Chiasson and Anna Chiasson (*née* Godin). *Educ:* St Joseph's Univ., NB; Holy Heart Seminary, Halifax, NS; Theological and Catechetical studies, Rome and Lumen Vitae, Belgium. *Address:* PO Box 248, Chartersville, Moncton, NB, Canada. *T:* 389.9531.

MOND, family name of **Baron Melchett.**

MONDALE, Walter Frederick; Vice-President of the United States of America, since 1977; *b* Ceylon, Minnesota, 5 Jan. 1928; *s* of Rev. Theodore Sigvaard Mondale and Claribel Cowan (*née* Hope); *m* 1955, Joan Adams; two *s* one *d*. *Educ:* public schs, Minnesota; Macalester Coll., Univ. of Minnesota (BA *cum laude*); Univ. of Minnesota Law Sch. (LLB). Served with Army, 1951-53. Mem. Editorial Bd, Minn. Law Review, 1955-56. Admitted to Minn. Bar, 1956; private law practice, Minneapolis, 1956-60; Attorney-Gen., Minnesota, 1960-64; Senator from Minnesota, 1964-76. Past Member: President's Consumer Adv. Council, 1962-64; Exec. Bd of Nat. Assoc. of Attorneys General, etc. Democratic Candidate for Vice-Pres., USA, 1976. Averell Harriman Equal Housing Opportunity Award; Outstanding Young Man of Year in Minnesota, 1960. Member: Democratic Farm Labor Party; Minn. Safety Council; Amer. Legion; Amer. Assoc. UN; Amer., Minn., and Hennepin Co. Bar Assocs; service on numerous cttees. *Publications:* contrib. Minnesota Law Review. *Address:* The United States Senate, Washington, DC, USA; Old Executive Office Building, Washington, DC 20501, USA; (home) 3421 Lowell Street NW, Washington DC 20016, USA.

MONDAY, Horace Reginald, CBE 1967 (OBE 1958); Chairman: Management Committee, Banjul City Council, since 1971; Gambia Utilities Corporation, since 1972; *b* 26 Nov. 1907; *s* of late James Thomas Monday, Gambia Civil Servant, and late Rachel Ruth Davis; *m* 1932, Wilhelmina Roberta Juanita, *d* of late William Robertson Job Roberts, a Gambian businessman; one *s*. *Educ:* Methodist Mission Schools, in Banjul, The Gambia; correspondence course with (the then) London Sch. of Accountancy. Clerk, 1925-48; Asst Acct, Treasury, 1948-52; Acct and Storekeeper, Marine Dept, 1953-54; Acct-Gen., The Gambia Govt, 1954-65; Chm., Gambia Public Service Commn, 1965-68; High Comr for The Gambia in the UK and NI, 1968-71. Dir, Gambia Currency Bd, 1964-68; Governor, Gambia High Sch., 1964-68; Pres., Gambia Red Cross Soc., 1967-68. Comdr, National Order of Republic of Senegal, 1968. *Address:* Rachelville, 24 Clarkson Street, Banjul, The Gambia. *T:* Banjul 511.

MONEY, Ernle (David Drummond); Barrister-at-Law; *b* 17 Feb. 1931; *s* of late Lt-Col E. F. D. Money, DSO, late 4th Gurkha Rifles, and of Sidney, *o d* of D. E. Anderson, Forfar; *m* 1960, Susan Barbara, *d* of Lt-Col D. S. Lister, MC, The Buffs; two *s* two *d*. *Educ:* Marlborough Coll.; Oriel Coll., Oxford (open scholar). Served in Suffolk Regt, 1949-51, and 4th Bn, Suffolks Regt (TA), 1951-56; MA Hons degree (2nd cl.) in mod. hist., 1954. Tutor and lecturer, Swinton Conservative Coll., 1956. Called to Bar, Lincoln's Inn (Cholmeley Scholar), 1958. Mem., Bar Council, 1962-66. MP (C) Ipswich, 1970-Sept. 1974; Opposition Front Bench Spokesman on the Arts, 1974; Sec., Parly Cons. Arts and Amenities Cttee, 1970-73, Vice-Chm., 1974. Governor, Woolverstone Hall Sch., 1967-70; co-opted Mem., GLC Arts Cttee, 1972-73; Mem., GLC Arts Bd, 1974-76; Mem., Cttee of Gainsborough's Birthplace, Sudbury. Fine Arts Correspondent, Contemporary Review, 1968-. Pres., Ipswich Town Football Club Supporters, 1974-; Vice-Pres., E Suffolk and Ipswich Branch, RSPCA, 1974-. *Publications:* (with Peter Johnson) The Nasmyth Family of Painters, 1970; Margaret Thatcher, First Lady of the House, 1975; regular contrib. various periodicals and newspapers on antiques and the arts. *Recreations:* music, pictures and antiques, watching Association football. *Address:* 5 Paper Buildings, Temple, EC4. *T:* 01-583 3724; High House Farm, Rendlesham, near Woodbridge, Suffolk. *T:* Eyke 335. *Clubs:* Carlton; Ipswich and Suffolk (Ipswich).

MONEY, George Gilbert; Director, Barclays Bank International Ltd, since 1955 (Vice-Chairman, 1965-73); *b* 17 Nov. 1914; 2nd *s* of late Maj.-Gen. Sir A. W. Money, KCB, KBE, CSI and late Lady Money (*née* Drummond). *Educ:* Charterhouse Sch. Clerk, L. Behrens & Soehne, Bankers, Hamburg, 1931-32; Clerk, Barclays Bank Ltd, 1932-35, Dir 1972-73; joined Barclays Bank DCO (now Barclays Bank International Ltd), London, 1935; served in Egypt, Palestine, Cyprus, Ethiopia, Cyrenaica, E Africa, 1936-52; Local Dir, W Indies, 1952; Director: Barclays Bank of California, 1965; Bermuda Provident Bank Ltd, 1969; Banco Popular Antiliano NV, Aruba, 1970; Barclays Finance Corp. of Trinidad & Tobago Ltd, 1972; Barclays Bank of Trinidad & Tobago Ltd, 1972; Barclays Bank of Jamaica Ltd, 1972; Barclays Australia Ltd, 1972-75; New Zealand United Corp., 1972-75; Chairman: Bahamas Internat, Trust Co. Ltd, 1970-72; Cayman Internat. Trust Co. Ltd, 1970-72; Mem., E Caribbean and Bahamas Bds, Barclays Bank International Ltd. *Recreations:* tennis, water ski-ing, fishing, bridge. *Address:* 54 Lombard Street, EC3. *Clubs:* Crockfords, Royal Commonwealth Society (West Indian).

MONEY, Col Reginald Angel, CBE 1943; MC 1917; ED; FRCS; FRACS; MB, ChM (Sydney); RAAMC; *b* Sydney, Australia, 3 March 1897; *s* of late Angel Money, MD, FRCP, Harley Street, W1, and of late Mrs Amy Money, 138 Ocean Street, Edgecliff, Sydney; *m* 1937, Dorothy Jean Wilkinson, Strathfield, NSW; two *d. Educ:* Sydney Grammar Sch.; Univ. of Sydney. Enlisted in AIF and was abroad with Australian Field Artillery, 1916-19 (Lt, MC); CO 2/6 Australian Gen. Hosp., AIF, 1940-44 (Col, CBE); MB, ChM from Medical Sch. of Univ. of Sydney, 1923; House Surgeon, Registrar, and Medical Supt, Royal Prince Alfred Hosp., Sydney, 1923-28, Hon. Asst Surgeon, 1928; Hon. Neuro-Surgeon, 1937-57. FRCS 1932; FRACS 1931; Tutor in Surgery, Sydney Univ., 1933-37; Lecturer in Head and Spinal Injuries, 1935-57; Mem., Bd of Directors, Royal Prince Alfred Hospital, Sydney, 1953. Hon. Consulting Neuro-Surgeon, Royal Prince Alfred Hosp., Royal North Shore Hosp., and St George Hosp., Sydney; Visiting Neuro-Surgeon, NSW Masonic Hosp., Sydney. Postgraduate Professional Tours of Great Britain, Europe, USA, Canada, USSR, Mexico, South America, Japan, S Africa, Asia, in 1928, 1932, 1935, 1947, 1953, 1957, 1961, 1963, 1965, 1967, 1969, 1972, 1973, 1975. *Publications:* articles and case reports in med. and surgical jls, etc. *Recreations:* swimming, contract bridge, farming. *Address:* 175 Macquarie Street, Sydney, NSW 2000, Australia. *T:* 221-3964; 28 Bathurst Street, Woollahra, Sydney, NSW 2025. *T:* 387-2165. *Clubs:* Australian, Royal Sydney Golf, Australian Jockey (Sydney).

MONEY, Maj.-Gen. Robert Cotton, CB 1943; MC; psc; *b* 21 July 1888; *o c* of late Col R. C. Money, CMG, CBE; *m* 1917, Daphne Dorina (*d* 1968), 2nd *d* of Brig.-Gen. C. W. Gartside Spaight, Derry Castle, Killaloe, Ireland; (one *s* killed in action, 1940) one *d. Educ:* Arnold House, Llandulas; Wellington Coll.; RMC, Sandhurst. Joined Cameronians (Scottish Rifles), 1909; served with both battalions, European War and India; commanded 1st Bn 1931-34; commanded Lucknow Bde, 1936-39; Commandant Senior Officers' Sch., 1939; comd 15th (Scottish) Div., 1940-41; District Comdr, India, 1942-44; retired pay, 1944. Ministry of Transport, 1944-52; retired, 1952. *Recreation:* gardening. *Address:* The Old Vicarage, Cholesbury, Tring, Herts. *Club:* Army and Navy.

MONEY-COUTTS, family name of **Baron Latymer.**

MONEY-COUTTS, David Burdett; Managing Director since 1970, and Chairman since 1976, Coutts & Co.; *b* 19 July 1931; *s* of Hon. Alexander B. Money-Coutts (2nd *s* of 6th Baron Latymer, TD), and Mary E., er *d* of Sir Reginald Hobhouse, 5th Bt; *m* 1958, Helen Penelope June Utten Todd; one *s* two *d. Educ:* Eton; New Coll., Oxford (MA). National Service, 1st Royal Dragoons, 1950-51; Royal Glos Hussars, TA, 1951-67. Joined Coutts & Co., 1954; Dir, 1958. Director: National Discount Co., 1964-69; Gerrard & National Discount Co., 1969- (Dep. Chm. 1969-); United States & General Trust Corp., 1964-73; Charities Investment Managers (Charifund), 1964-; (Regional), SE Reg., National Westminster Bank, 1969-; National Westminster Bank, 1976-; Dun & Bradstreet, 1973-. Member: Kensington and Chelsea and Westminster AHA, 1974-; Health Educn Council, 1973-77. Middlesex Hospital: Governor, 1962-74 (Dep. Chm. Governors, 1973-74); Chm., Finance Cttee, 1965-74; Mem., Med. Sch. Council, 1963- (Chm., 1974-). Trustee, Multiple Sclerosis Soc., 1967-. Hon. Treas., Nat. Assoc. of Almshouses, 1960-; Hon. Sec., Old Etonian Trust, 1969-76, Chm. Council, 1976-. *Recreations:* odd jobs, living in the country. *Address:* Magpie House, Peppard Common, Henley-on-Thames, Oxon RG9 5JG. *T:* Rotherfield Greys 497. *Club:* Leander (Henley-on-Thames).

MONGER, George William; Under-Secretary, Electricity Division, Department of Energy, since 1976; *b* 1 April 1937; *s* of George Thomas Monger and Agnes Mary (*née* Bates). *Educ:* Holloway Sch.; Jesus Coll., Cambridge (PhD 1962). Min. of Power, Min. of Technol., DTI, and Dept of Energy; Principal, 1965; Asst Sec., 1972. Alexander Prize, RHistS, 1962. *Publication:* The End of Isolation: British Foreign Policy, 1900-1907, 1963. *Address:* Lochalsh, Christ Church Lane, Hadley Green, Barnet, Herts. *T:* 01-449 7887. *Club:* United Oxford & Cambridge University.

MONIER-WILLIAMS, Evelyn Faithfull; His Honour Judge Monier-Williams; a Circuit Judge since 1972; *b* 29 April 1920; *o s* of late R. T. Monier-Williams, OBE, Barrister-at-Law, and Mrs G. M. Monier-Williams; *m* 1948, Maria-Angela Oswald; one *s* one *d. Educ:* Charterhouse; University Coll., Oxford (MA). Admitted to Inner Temple, 1940; served Royal Artillery, 1940-46 in UK, Egypt, Libya, Tunisia, Sicily (8th Army), France, Low Countries and Germany; called to Bar, Inner Temple, 1948; South Eastern Circuit; Master of the Bench, Inner Temple, 1967; Mem. Senate of Four Inns of Court, 1969-

73; Mem. Council, Selden Soc., 1970; Mem., Council of Legal Educn, 1971, Vice Chm., 1974; Livery, Glaziers Company, 1974. *Recreation:* collecting old books. *Address:* 1 Temple Gardens, Temple, EC4Y 9BB. *T:* 01-583 5246; 73 Christchurch Road, SW14 7AT.

MONIZ DE ARAGÃO, José Joaquim de Lima e Silva; *b* Rio de Janeiro, Brasil, 12 May 1887; *m* 1926, Isabel Rodrigues Alves; two *s. Educ:* Faculty of Law, Rio de Janeiro. Attached to Ministry of Foreign Affairs, Rio de Janeiro, 1908; 2nd Sec., Washington, 1911; 1st Sec., Monte-Video, Madrid, Rome, 1913; Counsellor, Berlin, 1915-18; Counsellor, Brazilian Delegn Peace Conf., Versailles, 1919; Counsellor, Berlin, 1920-25; Minister, League of Nations, Geneva, 1926; Minister Delegate, Internat. Labour Office, Geneva, 1928-29; Minister, Copenhagen, Caracas, 1929-33; Under-Sec. of State for Foreign Affairs, Rio de Janeiro, 1934; Ambassador to Berlin, 1935-38; Brazilian Ambassador to Court of St James's, 1940-52. Brazilian Delegate to UNO Assembly in London, 1945; Chief Brazilian Delegate to: UNESCO Assembly, London, 1945, Paris, 1946; UNRRA Assembly, London, 1946; Internat. Cttee for Refugees in London, 1944, 1945, Paris, 1946. Mem. Royal Philatelic Society. Knight Grand Cross of the Royal Victorian Order, Gt Brit. (Hon. GCVO); Comdr Order of the British Empire (Hon. CBE). *Address:* Avenida Atlântica no 2242, 10 andar, Rio de Janeiro, Brazil. *Clubs:* Rotary, Jockey, Automovel (Rio de Janeiro).

MONK, Rear-Adm. Anthony John, CBE 1973; Rear-Admiral Engineering to Flag Officer Naval Air Command, since 1976; *b* 14 Nov. 1923; *s* of Frank Leonard and Barbara Monk; *m* 1951, Elizabeth Ann Samson; four *s* one *d. Educ:* Whitgift Sch.; RNC Dartmouth; RNEC Keyham. MSc, BScEng, FIMarE, MRAeS, MIMechE. Engr Cadet, 1941; served War of 1939-45, Pacific Fleet; flying trng, Long Air Engrg Course, Cranfield, 1946; RN Air Stn Ford; RNEC Manadon, 1950; Prodn Controller and Man., RN Aircraft Yard, Belfast, 1953-56; Mem. Dockyard Work Measurement Team, subseq. Engr Officer HMS Apollo, Techn. Asst to Dir-Gen. Aircraft, Sqdn Engr Officer to Flag Officer Aircraft Carriers, 1963-65; Asst Dir of Marine Engrg, 1965-68; Dir of Aircraft Engrg, 1968; Comd Engrg Officer to Flag Officer Naval Air Comd; Naval Liaison Officer for NI and Supt RN Aircraft Yard, Belfast, 1970; Port Admiral, Rosyth, 1974-75. Comdr 1956; Captain 1964; Rear-Adm. 1974. *Recreation:* swimming (ASA teacher). *Address:* Royal Naval Air Station, Yeovilton, Som; Wales House, Queen Camel, Som.

MONK BRETTON, 3rd Baron *cr* 1884; **John Charles Dodson;** *b* 17 July 1924; *o s* of 2nd Baron and Ruth (*d* 1967), 2nd *d* of late Hon. Charles Brand; *S* father, 1933; *m* 1958, Zoë Diana Scott; two *s. Educ:* Westminster Sch.; New Coll., Oxford (MA). *Recreations:* hunting, farming. *Heir:* *s* Hon. Christopher Mark Dodson, *b* 2 Aug. 1958. *Address:* Shelley's Folly, Cooksbridge, near Lewes, East Sussex. *T:* Barcombe 231. *Club:* Brooks's.

MONKS, Constance Mary, OBE 1962; JP; *b* 20 May 1911; *d* of Ellis Green and Bessie A. Green (*née* Burwell); *m* 1937, Jack Monks; one *s* (decd). *Educ:* Wheelton County Sch.; Chorley Grammar Sch.; City of Leeds Training Coll. Apptd Asst Teacher, 1931. Started retail business as partner with husband, 1945. Councillor (C), Chorley (N Ward), 1947-67, Alderman, 1967-74; Mayor of Chorley, 1959-60; Mem. Lancs CC, 1961-64. MP (C) Chorley, Lancs, 1970-Feb. 1974. JP Chorley, 1954. *Recreations:* reading, needlework. *Address:* 17 Sandridge Avenue, Chorley, Lancs. *T:* Chorley 6744.

MONKSWELL, Barony of (*cr* 1885); title disclaimed by 4th Baron; *see under* Collier, William Adrian Larry.

MONMOUTH, Bishop of, since 1972; **Rt. Rev. Derrick Greenslade Childs;** *b* 14 Jan. 1918; er *s* of Alfred John and Florence Theodosia Childs; *m* 1951, Elizabeth Cicely Davies; one *s* one *d. Educ:* Whitland Grammar Sch., Carmarthenshire; University Coll., Cardiff (BA Wales, 1st cl. Hons History); Sarum Theol College at Wells. Deacon 1941, priest 1942, Diocese of St David's; Asst Curate: Milford Haven, 1941-46; Laugharne with Llansadwrnen, 1946-51; Warden of Llandaff House, Penarth (Hall of Residence for students of University Coll., Cardiff), 1951-61; Gen. Sec., Provincial Council for Education of the Church in Wales, 1955-65; Director of Church in Wales Publications, 1961-65; Chancellor of Llandaff Cathedral, 1964-69; Principal of Trinity Coll. of Education, Carmarthen, 1965-72; Canon of St David's Cathedral, 1969-72. Member: Court University College, Cardiff; Council, St David's Univ. College, Lampeter; Court, Univ. of Wales; Chm., Church in Wales Provincial Council for Educn, 1972; Chm. of Council, Historical Soc. of Church in Wales, 1972; Vice-Chm., National Society, 1973; Chm. Bd, Church in Wales Publications. Sub-Prelate, Order of St John of Jerusalem, 1972. *Publications:*

Editor: Cymry'r Groes, 1947-49, Province, 1949-68, and regular contributor to those quarterly magazines; contrib.: E. T. Davies, The Story of the Church in Glamorgan, 1962; Religion in Approved Schools, 1967. *Recreations:* music, walking, and watching cricket and Rugby football. *Address:* Bishopstow, Stow Hill, Newport, Gwent NPT 4EA. *T:* Newport 63510.

MONMOUTH, Assistant Bishop of; *see* Gresford Jones, Rt Rev. E. M.

MONMOUTH, Dean of; *see* Jenkins, Very Rev. F. G.

MONNET, Jean; European political figure; *b* Cognac, Charente, 9 Nov. 1888; *s* of J. G. Monnet. *Educ:* Cognac Coll. French representative, Allied Exec. Cttees for re-allocation of common resources, European War; Dep. Sec.-Gen., League of Nations, 1918; returned to family business; took part in re-organisation of Chinese Railways, 1932; Chm., Franco-British Economic Co-ordination Cttee, 1939; took part in organisation of common defence programme, 1940; Mem. British Supply Council, Washington, 1940-43; Comr for Armament, Supplies and Reconstruction, French National Liberation Cttee, Algiers, 1943-44; created Plan Monnet, 1946; Gen. Comr, Plan for Modernisation and Equipment of France, 1946; Pres. Preparatory Conf. of Schuman Plan, 1950; Pres. European Coal and Steel Community, 1952-55; Chm., Action Cttee for the United States of Europe, 1956-75. Hon. Mem., RGS, 1972. Holds hon. doctorates of following universities: Columbia, 1953; Glasgow, 1956; Princeton, 1959; Yale, 1961; Cambridge, 1961; Oxford, 1963. Wateler Peace Prize, 1951; Charlemagne Prize, 1953; Grand Cross of Merit of German Federal Republic, 1958; Freedom Award, 1963; Prize of Foundation Gouverneur Emile Cornez, 1963; US Presidential Medal of Freedom, 1963. Hon. GBE 1947; Hon. CH 1972. *Publications:* Les Etats Unis d'Europe ont commencé (collection of extracts from speeches); Memoirs, 1976. *Address:* Houjarray, par Montfort l'Amaury (Seine-et-Oise), France.

MÖNNIG, Hermann Otto, BA, DrPhil, BVSc, DSc (*hc*); Chairman, Agricura Laboratoria Ltd, 1945-70, now Adviser; formerly Chairman, Science Advisory Council; Scientific Adviser to Prime Minister, 1962; National Parks Board, 1952; *b* Cape Town, 27 Jan. 1897; *s* of C. J. O. Mönnig and A. H. Schmidt; *m* 1923, Everdina Maria Koning; two *s*. *Educ:* Gymnasium, Paarl; Univs of Stellenbosch, Amsterdam, Zürich, Neuchâtel, SA. Research Officer at Onderstepoort, S Africa, 1922; Graduated in Veterinary Science, Univ. of South Africa, 1926; Pretoria Univ.: Lectr in Helminthology, 1928; Prof. of Parasitology, 1930; Mem. of Council, 1949-70. *Publications:* Veterinary Helminthology and Entomology, 1934; various scientific articles on parasitology. *Recreation:* wood-carving. *Address:* 246 Hay Street, Pretoria, Transvaal, South Africa. *TA:* Agrilab, Silverton. *T:* Pretoria 74-2674.

MONOD, Prof. Théodore, DèsSc; Officier de la Légion d'Honneur, 1958; Professor Emeritus at National Museum of Natural History, Paris (Assistant 1922, Professor, 1942-73); *b* 9 April 1902; *s* of Rev. Wilfred Monod and Dorina Monod; *m* 1930, Olga Pickova; two *s* one *d*. *Educ:* Sorbonne (Paris). Docteur ès-sciences, 1926. Sec.-Gen. (later Dir) of l'Institut Français d'Afrique Noire, 1938; Prof., Univ. of Dakar, 1957-59; Doyen, Science Faculty, Dakar, 1957-58. Mem., Academy of Sciences; Member: Acad. des Sciences d'Outre-Mer; Académie de Marine; Corresp. Mem., Académie des Sciences de Lisbonne and Académie Royale des Sciences d'Outre-Mer. Dr *hc* Köln, 1965, Neuchâtel, 1968. Gold Medallist, Royal Geographical Soc., 1960; Gold Medallist, Amer. Geographical Soc., 1961; Haile Sellassie Award for African Research, 1967. Comdr, Ordre du Christ, 1953; Commandeur, Mérite Saharien, 1962; Officier de l'Ordre des Palmes Académiques, 1966, etc. *Publications:* Méharées, Explorations au vrai Sahara, 1937; L'Hippopotame et le philosophe, 1942; Bathyfolages, 1954; (ed) Pastoralism in Tropical Africa, 1976; many scientific papers in learned jls. *Address:* 14 quai d'Orléans, 75004 Paris, France. *T:* 326 79.50; Muséum National d'Histoire Naturelle, 57 rue Cuvier, 75005 Paris, France. *T:* 331 40.10.

MONRO, Hector Seymour Peter; JP; DL; MP (C) Dumfries since 1964; Opposition Spokesman on Sport, since 1974; *b* 4 Oct. 1922; *s* of late Capt. Alastair Monro, Cameron Highlanders, and Mrs Monro, Craigcleuch, Langholm, Scotland; *m* 1949, Elizabeth Anne Welch, Longstone Hall, Derbs; two *s*. *Educ:* Canford Sch.; King's Coll., Cambridge. RAF, 1941-46, Flight Lt; RAuxAF, 1946-53 (AEM 1953). Mem. of Queen's Body Guard for Scotland, Royal Company of Archers. Dumfries CC, 1952-67 (Chm. Planning Cttee, and Police Cttee). Chm. Dumfriesshire Unionist Assoc., 1958-63; Scottish Cons. Whip, 1967-70; a Lord Comr of HM Treasury, 1970-71; Parly Under-

Sec. of State, Scottish Office, 1971-74; Opposition Spokesman on Scottish Affairs, 1974-75. Mem. Dumfries T&AFA, 1959-67; Mem., Area Executive Cttee, Nat. Farmers' Union of Scotland. JP 1963, DL 1973, Dumfries. *Recreations:* Rugby football (Mem. Scottish Rugby Union, 1958-77, Vice-Pres., 1975, Pres., 1976-77); golf, flying, vintage sports cars. *Address:* Williamwood, Kirtlebridge, Dumfriesshire. *T:* Kirtlebridge 213. *Clubs:* Caledonian, East India, Devonshire, Sports and Public Schools, MCC; Royal Scottish Automobile (Glasgow).

MONRO DAVIES, William Llewellyn, QC 1974; His Honour Judge Monro Davies; a Circuit Judge, since 1976; *b* 12 Feb. 1927; *s* of Thomas Llewellyn Davies and Emily Constance Davies; *m* 1956, Jean, *d* of late E. G. Innes; one *s* one *d*. *Educ:* Christ Coll., Brecon; Trinity Coll., Oxford (MA, LitHum). Served in RNVR, 1945-48 (Sub-Lt). Called to the Bar, Inner Temple, 1954. Mem., Gen. Council of the Bar, 1971-75. A Recorder of the Crown Court, 1972-76. *Recreations:* the theatre and cinema; watching Rugby football. *Address:* Farrar's Buildings, Temple, EC4Y 7BD. *T:* 01-583 9241. *Clubs:* Garrick; Bristol Channel Yacht (Mumbles).

MONROE, Elizabeth, (Mrs Humphrey Neame), CMG 1973; MA Oxon; Fellow of St Antony's College, Oxford, 1963-73, now Emeritus Fellow; Hon. Fellow of St Anne's College; *b* 16 Jan. 1905; *d* of late Canon Horace Monroe, Vicar of Wimbledon; *m* 1938, Humphrey Neame (*d* 1968). *Educ:* Putney High Sch., GPDST; St Anne's Coll., Oxford. Secretariat of League of Nations, Geneva, 1931; staff of Royal Institute of International Affairs, 1933; Rockefeller Travelling Fellowship, held in Middle East and French N Africa, 1936-37; Min. of Information, Dir, Middle East Div., 1940; Diplomatic correspondent, The Observer, 1944. UK rep. on UN Sub-Commn for Prevention of Discrimination and Protection of Minorities, 1947-52; staff of Economist Newspaper, London, 1945-58. Leverhulme Research Fellowship, 1969. *Publications:* (with A. H. M. Jones) A History of Abyssinia, 1935; The Mediterranean in Politics, 1938; Britain's Moment in the Middle East: 1914-1956, 1963; The Changing Balance of Power in the Persian Gulf, 1972; Philby of Arabia, 1973; (with Robert Mabro) Oil Producers and Consumers: conflict or cooperation, 1974. *Recreation:* entertaining. *Address:* 56 Montagu Square, W1H 1TG. *T:* 01-262 8141.
See also J. G. Monroe.

MONROE, Hubert Holmes, QC 1960; Special Commissioner, since 1973, Presiding Commissioner, since 1977; *b* 2 July 1920; *s* of James Harvey Monroe, KC, late of Dublin; *m* 1946, June Elsie, *d* of Harold Lawson Murphy, KC, late of London; one *s* two *d*. *Educ:* Rugby; Corpus Christi Coll., Oxford. Called to the Bar, Middle Temple, 1948; Bencher, 1965; Hon. Treasurer, Senate of the Inns of Court and the Bar, 1975-77. Commodore, Island Cruising Club, 1972. *Address:* 40 Cleaver Street, SE11 4DP. *T:* 01-735 9009. *Club:* Garrick.

MONROE, John George; National Insurance Commissioner since 1973; *b* 27 July 1913; *s* of late Canon Horace G. Monroe, Vicar of Wimbledon and Sub-dean of Southwark and of Frances Alice Monroe (*née* Stokes); *m* 1943, Jane Reynolds; one *s* two *d*. *Educ:* Marlborough Coll.; Oriel Coll., Oxford. Called to Bar, Middle Temple, 1937; Master of the Bench, 1967. *Publications:* (ed, with Judge McDonnell *qv*) Kerr on Fraud and Mistake, 7th edn; The Law of Stamp Duties, 1954 (5th edn, with R. S. Nock, 1976). *Address:* Highmead, Birchwood Grove Road, Burgess Hill, West Sussex. *T:* Burgess Hill 3350.
See also Elizabeth Monroe.

MONSARRAT, Nicholas John Turney, FRSL; author; *b* Liverpool, 22 March 1910; *s* of late K. W. Monsarrat; *m* 1st, 1939, Eileen Rowland (marr. diss. 1952); one *s*; 2nd 1952, Philippa Crosby (marr. diss. 1961); two *s*; 3rd, 1961, Ann Griffiths. *Educ:* Winchester Coll.; Trinity Coll., Cambridge (BA 1931). Heinemann Foundation Prize for Literature, 1951. Coronation Medal, 1953. War of 1939-45; in RN 1940-46; Lt-Comdr RNVR (despatches). Councillor, Kensington Borough Council, 1946. Dir, UK Information Office, Johannesburg, 1946-53; Ottawa, 1953-56. Chm. Nat. War Memorial Health Foundation (South Africa), 1951-53. Board of Governors, Stratford Shakespeare Fest. of Canada, 1956; Bd of Dirs, Ottawa Philharmonic Orchestra, 1956. Chevalier, Sovereign Order of St John of Jerusalem, 1973. *Publications:* Think of Tomorrow, 1934; At First Sight, 1935; The Whipping Boy, 1936; This is the Schoolroom, 1939; Three Corvettes, 1945; Depends What You Mean by Love, 1947; My Brother Denys, 1948; The Cruel Sea, 1951; HMS Marlborough Will Enter Harbour, 1952; The Story of Esther Costello, 1953; Boys' Book of the Sea, 1954; Canada Coast-to-Coast, Castle Garac, 1955; The Tribe that Lost its Head, 1956; Boys' Book of the Commonwealth, 1957; The Ship that Died of Shame, 1959; The Nylon Pirates, 1960; The White Rajah, 1961; The Time Before This, 1962; Smith and Jones, 1963; To Stratford with Love, 1963; A Fair Day's Work, 1964; The Pillow Fight, 1965; Something to Hide, 1965; Richer Than all His Tribe, 1968; The Kappillan of Malta, 1973; Monsarrat at Sea, 1975; The Master Mariner: vol. I Running Proud, 1978; *autobiography:* Life is a Four-Letter Word, Vol. I, 1966, Vol. II 1970; *play:* The Visitor (Daly's Theatre, 1936); *films:* The Cruel Sea, 1953; The Ship That Died of Shame, 1955; The Story of Esther Costello, 1957; The Way of a Ship (Narration), 1965; Something to Hide, 1972. *Recreations:* sailing, music. *Address:* c/o Campbell Thomson & McLaughlin Ltd, 31 Newington Green, N16 9PU. *T:* 01-249 2971; San Lawrenz, Gozo, Malta. *T:* 76977. *Clubs:* Naval, Lansdowne; Rideau (Ottawa).

MONSELL, 2nd Viscount *cr* 1935, of Evesham; **Henry Bolton Graham Eyres-Monsell;** *b* 21 Nov. 1905; *s* of 1st Viscount Monsell, PC, GBE, and Caroline Mary Sybil, CBE (*d* 1959), *d* of late H. W. Eyres, Dumbleton Hall, Evesham; *S* father, 1969. *Educ:* Eton. Served N Africa and Italy, 1942-45 (despatches); Lt-Col Intelligence Corps. US Medal of Freedom with bronze palm, 1946. *Recreation:* music. *Address:* The Mill House, Dumbleton, Evesham, Worcs. *Club:* Travellers'.
See also P . M . L . Fermor .

MONSEY, Mrs Derek; *see* Mitchell, Yvonne.

MONSON, family name of **Baron Monson.**

MONSON, 11th Baron *cr* 1728; **John Monson;** Bt *cr* 1611; *b* 3 May 1932; *e s* of 10th Baron and of Bettie Northrup (who *m* 1962, Capt. James Arnold Phillips), *d* of late E. Alexander Powell; *S* father, 1958; *m* 1955, Emma, *o d* of late Anthony Devas, ARA, RP; three *s*. *Educ:* Eton; Trinity Coll., Cambridge (BA). *Heir: s* Hon. Nicholas John Monson, *b* 19 Oct. 1955. *Address:* Manor House, South Carlton, near Lincoln. *T:* Scampton 263.

MONSON, Sir (William Bonnar) Leslie, KCMG 1965 (CMG 1950); CB 1964; HM Diplomatic Service, retired; Director, Overseas Branch, St John Ambulance, since 1975; *b* 28 May 1912; *o s* of late J. W. Monson and late Selina L. Monson; *m* 1948, Helen Isobel Browne. *Educ:* Edinburgh Acad.; Hertford Coll., Oxford. Entered Civil Service (Dominions Office) 1935; transferred to Colonial Office, 1939; Asst Sec., 1944; seconded as Chief Sec. to West African Council, 1947-51; Asst Under-Sec. of State, Colonial Office, 1951-64; British High Commissioner in the Republic of Zambia, 1964-66; Dep. Under-Sec. of State, Commonwealth Office, later FCO, 1967-72. KStJ 1975. *Address:* Golf House, Goffers Road, Blackheath, SE3. *Club:* United Oxford & Cambridge University.

MONTAGU; *see* Douglas-Scott-Montagu.

MONTAGU, family name of **Duke of Manchester, Earldom of Sandwich,** and **Baron Swaythling.**

MONTAGU OF BEAULIEU, 3rd Baron *cr* 1885; **Edward John Barrington Douglas-Scott-Montagu;** *b* 20 Oct. 1926; *o s* of 2nd Baron and Pearl (who *m* 2nd, 1936, Captain Hon. Edward Pleydell-Bouverie, RN, MVO, *s* of 6th Earl of Radnor), *d* of late Major E. B. Crake, Rifle Brigade, and Mrs Barrington Crake; *S* father, 1929; *m* 1st, 1959, Elizabeth Belinda (marr. diss. 1974), *o d* of late Capt. the Hon. John de Bathe Crossley, and late Hon. Mrs Crossley; one *s* one *d* ; 2nd, 1974, Fiona Herbert; one *s*. *Educ:* St Peter's Court, Broadstairs; Ridley Coll., St Catharines, Ont; Eton Coll.; New Coll., Oxford. Late Lt Grenadier Guards; released Army, 1948. Founded Montagu Motor Car Museum, 1952 and World's first Motor Cycle Museum, 1956; created Beaulieu Museum Trust, 1970, to administer new Nat. Motor Museum at Beaulieu, opened 1972. President: Historic Houses Assoc.; Southern Tourist Bd; Assoc. of Brit. Transport Museums; Vice-Pres., Transport Trust; Council Mem., Nat. Heritage. *Publications:* The Motoring Montagus, 1959; Lost Causes of Motoring, 1960; Jaguar, A Biography, 1961; The Gordon Bennett Races, 1963; Rolls of Rolls-Royce, 1966; The Gilt and the Gingerbread, 1967; Lost Causes of Motoring: Europe, vol. i, 1969, vol. ii, 1971; More Equal than Others, 1970; History of the Steam Car, 1971; The Horseless Carriage, 1975; Early Days on the Road, 1976; Behind the Wheel, 1977; Editor and Publisher of the Veteran and Vintage Magazine. *Heir: s* Hon. Ralph Douglas-Scott-Montagu, *b* 13 March 1961. *Address:* Palace House, Beaulieu, Hants. *T:* Beaulieu 612345; 3 Wyndham Place, W1. *T:* 01-262 2603. *Clubs:* Veteran Car, Vintage Sports-Car, Vintage Motor Cycle, Historical Commercial Vehicle (Pres.), Disabled Drivers Motor, Show Biz Car (Pres.), Steam Boat Assoc. of Gt Britain (Vice-Pres.), and many other motoring clubs.
See also Sir E. John Chichester, Bt, Viscount Garnock.

MONTAGU, Ainsley Marshall Rendall, CIE 1945; FCGI; FICE; MIWE; *b* 6 Nov. 1891; *s* of Alfred John Montagu and Hester Vaudrey (*née* Holland); *m* 1st, 1918, Margaret Violet Rumsby; two *s*; 2nd, 1940, Phyllis Henley Marion Moreton; one *d*. *Educ:* St Paul's Sch.; City and Guilds Engineering Coll., London. Joined PWD India, 1914; served European War, 1914-18, with KGO Bengal Sappers and Miners and RFC (despatches). Returned to PWD, 1920; Chief Engr and Sec. to Govt, Punjab PWD (Irrigation Br.), 1943; retd, 1947. Engineering Adviser to UNRWA for Palestine Refugees, 1950-52; Dep. Dir, Public Works Dept, Sudan Government, Khartoum, 1952-54; Consultant, Sir Murdoch MacDonald & Partners, 1954-68, retired. Fellow of City and Guilds of London Institute (FCGI), 1957. *Publications:* papers on hydraulics and hydraulic engineering for learned societies and journals. *Address:* c/o Lloyds Bank Ltd, 6 Pall Mall, SW1.

MONTAGU, (Alexander) Victor (Edward Paulet); *b* 22 May 1906; *S* father, 1962, as 10th Earl of Sandwich, but disclaimed his peerages for life, 24 July 1964; *m* 1st, 1934, Rosemary, *d* of late Major Ralph Harding Peto; two *s* four *d* ; 2nd, 1962, Anne, MBE, *y d* of Victor, 9th Duke of Devonshire, KG, PC. *Educ:* Eton; Trinity Coll., Cambridge. MA (Nat. Sciences). Lt 5th (Hunts) Bn The Northamptonshire Regt, TA, 1926; served France, 1940, and afterwards on Gen. Staff, Home Forces. Private Sec. to Rt Hon. Stanley Baldwin, MP, 1932-34; Treasurer, Junior Imperial League, 1934-35; Chm., Tory Reform Cttee, 1943-44. MP (C) South Dorset Div. (C 1941, Ind. C 1957, C 1958-62); contested (C) Accrington Div. Lancs, Gen. Elec., 1964. Pres., Anti-Common Market League, 1962-; Chm., Conservative Trident Gp, 1973-. *Publications:* Essays in Tory Reform, 1944; The Conservative Dilemma, 1970; articles in Quarterly Review, 1946-47. *Heir: (to disclaimed peerages):* s John Edward Hollister Montagu, *qv*. *Address:* Mapperton, Beaminster, Dorset. *Clubs:* Carlton, Brooks's.

MONTAGU, Ashley; *see* Montagu, M. F. A.

MONTAGU, Hon. David Charles Samuel; Chairman and Chief Executive, Orion Bank, and Chairman, Orion Termbank, since 1974; *b* 6 Aug. 1928; *e s* and *heir* of 3rd Baron Swaythling, *qv*, and Mary Violet, *e d* of Major Levy, DSO; *m* 1951, Christiane Françoise (Ninette), *d* of Edgar Dreyfus, Paris; one *s* two *d*. *Educ:* Eton; Trinity Coll., Cambridge. Exec. Dir, 1954, Chm., 1970-73, Samuel Montagu & Co. Ltd; Director: Trades Union Unit Trust Managers Ltd; Carreras Rothmans Ltd; United British Securities Trust Ltd; Derby Trust Ltd (Chm.); Drayton Commercial Investment Co. Ltd; Rothmans International Ltd; London Weekend Television Ltd; Standard Telephones and Cables. *Recreations:* shooting, racing, theatre. *Address:* 25 Kingston House South, Ennismore Gardens, SW7; The Kremlin, Newmarket. *T:* Newmarket 2467. *Clubs:* Turf, Portland, Pratt's.

MONTAGU, Hon. Ewen Edward Samuel, CBE 1950 (OBE mil. 1944); QC 1939; The Judge Advocate of the Fleet, 1945-73; Hon. Captain RNR, 1973; *b* 29 March 1901; 2nd *s* of 2nd Baron Swaythling; *m* 1923, Iris Rachel, *d* of late Solomon J. Solomon, RA; one *s* one *d*. *Educ:* Westminster Sch.; Harvard Univ.; Trinity Coll., Cambridge (MA, LLB). Called to Bar, Middle Temple, 1924, Bencher, 1948, Treas., 1968; Western Circuit. Recorder of Devizes, 1944-51, of Southampton, 1951-60; Chairman of Quarter Sessions: Hampshire, 1951-60 (Dep. Chm., 1948-51, and 1960-71); Middlesex, 1956-65 (Asst Chm., 1951-54; Dep. Chm., 1954-56); Middlesex Area of Gtr London, 1965-69; Judge, 1969; Chm. Central Council of Magistrates' Courts Cttees, 1963-71 (Vice-Chm., 1954-63). Pres. United Synagogue, 1954-62; Vice-President: Anglo-Jewish Assoc.; Nat. Addiction and Research Inst., 1969; Chm. Gen. Purposes Cttee, RYA, 1960-68; RYA Award, 1972. DL County of Southampton, 1953. RNVR, 1939-45. Order of the Crown, Yugoslavia, 1943. *Publications:* The Man Who Never Was, 1953; The Archer-Shee Case, 1974; Beyond "Top Secret U", 1977. *Recreations:* sailing, fly-fishing, shooting, beagling, golf, painting, grandchildren. *Address:* 24 Montrose Court, Exhibition Road, SW7 2QQ. *T:* 01-589 9999; Warren Beach, Beaulieu, Hants. *T:* Bucklers Hard 239. *Clubs:* Royal Ocean Racing, Bar Yacht (Hon. Commodore).
See also Ivor Montagu.

MONTAGU, Ivor; author; *b* 23 April 1904; 3rd *s* of 2nd Baron Swaythling; *m* 1927, Eileen, *d* of late Francis Anton Hellstern. *Educ:* Westminster Sch.; Royal Coll. of Science, London; King's Coll., Cambridge. Pres. and/or Chm., (Ping Pong Assoc., then Table Tennis Assoc., then) English Table Tennis Assoc., 1922-33, 1936-66, Life Vice-Pres., 1970-; Pres. and Chm., International Table Tennis Fedn, 1926-67, Life Founder Pres. 1967-; Chm., Film Soc., 1925-39; film critic, editor, director, writer, producer from 1925; Hon. Member: Assoc. of Cine and Television Technicians, 1970; Writers Guild, 1964; Editorial Staff, Daily Worker, 1932-33 and 1937-47; Mem. Secretariat and Bureau, World Council of Peace, 1948-67, Presidential Cttee, 1969-72; Pres., Soc. for Cultural Relations with USSR, 1973-. Order of Liberation, 1st Class (Bulgaria), 1952; Lenin Peace Prize, 1959; Order of Pole Star (Mongolia), 1963; Lenin Centenary Commemoration Medal, 1970; Dimitrov Anniv. Medal, 1972; Mongolian Peace Medal, 1973. *Publications:* Table Tennis Today, 1924; Table Tennis, 1936; The Traitor Class, 1940; Plot against Peace, 1952; Land of Blue Sky, 1956; Film World, 1964; Germany's New Nazis, 1967; With Eisenstein in Hollywood, 1968; The Youngest Son (Vol. I of memoirs), 1970; numerous scenarios, translations, pamphlets, articles on current affairs, contribs to Proc. Zool. Soc. London. *Recreations:* washing up, pottering about, sleeping through television. *Address:* Old Timbers, Verdure Close, Watford WD2 7NJ. *Clubs:* MCC; Hampshire County Cricket.

See also Hon. E. E. S. Montagu, Baron Swaythling.

MONTAGU, John Edward Hollister; (Viscount Hinchingbrooke, but does not use the title); *b* 11 April 1943; *er s* of Victor Montagu, *qv*, and *heir* to disclaimed Earldom of Sandwich; *m* 1968, Caroline, *o d* of Canon P. E. C. Hayman, Rogate, W Sussex; two *s* one *d*. *Educ:* Eton; Trinity College, Cambridge. *Address:* 69 Albert Bridge Road, SW11 4QE.

MONTAGU, Prof. (Montague Francis) Ashley; *b* 28 June 1905; *o c* of Charles and Mary Ehrenberg; *m* 1931, Helen Marjorie Peakes; one *s* two *d*. *Educ:* Central Foundation Sch., London; Univ. of London; Univ. of Florence; Columbia Univ. (PhD 1937). Research Worker, Brit. Mus. (Natural Hist.), 1926; Curator, Physical Anthropology, Wellcome Hist. Mus., London, 1929; Asst-Prof. of Anatomy, NY Univ., 1931-38; Dir, Div. of Child Growth and Develt, NY Univ., 1931-34; Assoc.-Prof. of Anat., Hahnemann Med. Coll. and Hosp., Phila, 1938-49; Prof. and Head of Dept of Anthropology, Rutgers Univ., 1949-55; Dir of Research, NJ Cttee on Growth and Develt, 1951-55. Chm., Anisfield-Wolf Award Cttee on Race Relations, 1950-. Vis. Lectr, Harvard Univ., 1945; Regent's Prof., Univ. of Calif, Santa Barbara, 1961. DSc, Grinnell Coll., Iowa, 1967; DLitt Ursinus Coll., Pa, 1972. *Publications:* Coming Into Being Among the Australian Aborigines, 1937, 2nd edn 1974; Man's Most Dangerous Myth: The Fallacy of Race, 1942, 5th edn 1974; Edward Tyson, MD, FRS (1650-1708): And the Rise of Human and Comparative Anatomy in England, 1943; Introduction to Physical Anthropology, 1945; Adolescent Sterility, 1946; On Being Human, 1950; Statement on Race, 1951; On Being Intelligent, 1951; Darwin, Competition, and Cooperation, 1952; The Natural Superiority of Women, 1953, 3rd edn 1974; Immortality, 1955; The Direction of Human Development, 1955, 2nd edn 1970; The Biosocial Nature of Man, 1956; Education and Human Relations, 1958; Anthropology and Human Nature, 1957; Man: His First Million Years, 1957, 2nd edn 1969; The Reproductive Development of the Female, 1957; The Cultured Man, 1958; Human Heredity, 1959, 2nd edn 1963; A Handbook of Anthropometry, 1960; Man in Process, 1961; The Humanization of Man, 1962; Prenatal Influences, 1962; Race, Science and Humanity, 1963; The Science of Man, 1964; Life Before Birth, 1964, 2nd edn 1978; The Human Revolution, 1965; The Idea of Race, 1965; Up the Ivy, 1966; The American Way of Life, 1967; The Anatomy of Swearing, 1967; Man Observed, 1968; Man: His First Two Million Years, 1969; Sex, Man and Society, 1969; Immortality, Religion and Morals, 1971; Touching: the human significance of the skin, 1971; The Elephant Man, 1971; (ed) The Endangered Environment, 1973; (ed) Frontiers of Anthropology, 1974; (ed) Culture and Human Development, 1974; (ed) The Practice of Love, 1974; (ed) Race and IQ, 1975; The Nature of Human Aggression, 1976; Anatomy and Physiology (with E. B. Steen), 2 vols, 1959; The Prevalence of Nonsense (with E. Darling), 1967; The Dolphin in History (with John Lilly), 1963; Man's Evolution (with C. Loring Brace), 1965; The Human Dialogue (with Floyd Matson), 1967; The Ignorance of Certainty (with E. Darling), 1970; Textbook of Human Genetics (with M. Levitan), 1971, 2nd edn 1977; Man and the Computer (with S. S. Snyder), 1972; The Nature of Human Aggression, 1976; Human Evolution (with C. L. Brace), 1977; Editor: Studies and Essays in the History of Science and Learning; The Meaning of Love, 1953; Toynbee and History, 1956; Genetic Mechanisms in Human Disease, 1961; Atlas of Human Anatomy, 1961; Culture and the Evolution of Man, 1962; International Pictorial Treasury of Knowledge, 6 vols, 1962-63; The Concept of Race, 1964; The Concept of the Primitive, 1967; Culture: Man's Adaptive Dimension, 1968; Man and Aggression, 1968; The Origin and Evolution of Man, 1973. *Recreations:* book collecting, gardening. *Address:* 321 Cherry Hill Road, Princeton, NJ 08540, USA. *T:* Area Code 609 924-3756.

MONTAGU, Victor; *see* Montagu, A. V. E. P.

MONTAGU DOUGLAS SCOTT, family name of **Duke of Buccleuch.**

MONTAGU-POLLOCK, Sir G. S.; *see* Pollock.

MONTAGU-POLLOCK, Sir William H., KCMG 1957 (CMG 1946); *b* 12 July 1903; *s* of Sir M. F. Montagu-Pollock, 3rd Bt; *m* 1st, 1933, Frances Elizabeth Prudence (marr. diss. 1945), *d* of late Sir John Fischer Williams, CBE, KC; one *s* one *d*; 2nd, 1948, Barbara, *d* of late P. H. Jowett, CBE, FRCA, RWS; one *s*. *Educ:* Marlborough Coll.; Trinity Coll., Cambridge. Served in Diplomatic Service at Rome, Belgrade, Prague, Vienna, Stockholm, Brussels, and at Foreign Office; British Ambassador, Damascus, 1952-53 (Minister, 1950-52); British Ambassador: to Peru, 1953-58; to Switzerland, 1958-60; to Denmark, 1960-62. Retired from HM Foreign Service, 1962. Governor, European Cultural Foundation; Dir, British Nat. Cttee for Cultural Co-operation in Europe; Hon. Treasurer, Soc. for Promotion of New Music. *Recreations:* music, more music. *Address:* 28 Drayton Gardens, SW10. *T:* 01-373 3685; Playa Blanca, Yaiza, Lanzarote, Canary Islands. *Club:* Athenæum.

MONTAGU-STUART-WORTLEY-MACKENZIE, family name of **Earl of Wharncliffe.**

MONTAGUE, family name of **Baron Amwell.**

MONTAGUE, Francis Arnold, CMG 1956; retired; *b* 14 June 1904; *s* of late Charles Edward Montague, OBE, author and journalist, and of Madeleine Montague (*née* Scott), Manchester; *m* 1939, Fanny Susanne, *d* of late E. S. Scorer and Mrs C. D. Scorer; one *d*. *Educ:* Cargilfield Sch., Edinburgh; Rugby Sch.; Balliol Coll., Oxford. Tanganyika: served in Game Preservation Dept, 1925-28; Cadet, Colonial Administrative Service, 1928; Dist Officer, 1938; Private Sec. to Governor, 1938-40; Asst Chief Sec., 1948; Administrative Sec., Sierra Leone, 1950-58; retired from Colonial Service, Jan. 1958. Deputy-Chairman: Public Service Commn, Uganda, 1958-63; Public Service Commn, Aden, 1963. Mem., Oxon CC, 1964-73, Witney (Oxon) RDC, 1966-74; W Oxon Dist. Council, 1973-76. *Recreation:* gardening. *Address:* Dolphin House, Westhall Hill, Fulbrook OX8 4BN. *T:* Burford 2147. *Club:* Lansdowne.

MONTAGUE, Leslie Clarence; Chairman, Johnson Matthey & Co. Ltd, 1966-71; *b* 28 May 1901; *s* of Albert Edward Montague and Clara Amelia Chapman; *m* 1926, Ellen Rose Margaret Keene; no *c*. *Educ:* Bancroft's School, Woodford. 50 years' service with Johnson Matthey & Co. Ltd; appointed Secretary, 1934, and a Director, 1946. *Recreations:* walking, gardening. *Address:* Jasmine Cottage, Piddinghoe, near Newhaven, East Sussex.

MONTAGUE, Michael Jacob, CBE 1970; Chairman: Valor Company Ltd since 1965 (Managing Director, 1963); Hospitality Hotels, since 1972; *b* 10 March 1932; *s* of David Elias Montague and Eleanor Stagg. *Educ:* High Wycombe Royal Grammar Sch.; Magdalen Coll. Sch., Oxford. Founded Gatehill Beco Ltd, 1958 (sold to Valor Co., 1962). Pres., Young European Management Assoc.; Gov., Nat. Inst. of Hardware; Chairman: Asia Cttee, BNEC, 1968-71; Immigration Cttee, Kent Social Service; Hon. Treas., British Assoc. for World Government. *Address:* Greywell House, The Hockering, Woking, Surrey.

MONTAGUE BROWNE, Anthony Arthur Duncan, CBE 1965 (OBE 1955); DFC 1945; a Managing Director, Gerrard and National Discount Co. Ltd, since 1974 (Director, since 1967); *b* 8 May 1923; *s* of late Lt-Col A. D. Montague Browne, DSO, OBE, Bivia House, Goodrich, Ross-on-Wye, and Violet Evelyn (*née* Downes); *m* 1st, 1950, Noel Evelyn Arnold-Wallinger (marr. diss. 1970); one *d*; 2nd, 1970, Shelagh Macklin (*née* Mulligan). *Educ:* Stowe; Magdalen Coll., Oxford; abroad. Pilot RAF, 1941-45. Entered Foreign (now Diplomatic) Service, 1946; Foreign Office, 1946-49; Second Sec., British Embassy, Paris, 1949-52; seconded as Private Sec. to Prime Minister, 1952-55; seconded as Private Sec. to Rt Hon. Sir Winston Churchill, 1955-65; Counsellor, Diplomatic Service, 1964; seconded to HM Household, 1965-67; Trustee and Vice-Chm., Winston Churchill Memorial Trust. *Address:* c/o R3 Section, Lloyds Bank Ltd, Cox's & King's Branch, 6 Pall Mall, SW1. *Clubs:* Boodle's, Pratt's.

MONTAGUE-JONES, Brigadier (retd) Ronald, CBE 1944 (MBE 1941); jssc; psc; *b* 10 Dec. 1909; *yr s* of late Edgar Montague Jones, until 1932 Headmaster of St Albans Sch., Herts, and of late Emmeline Mary Yates; *m* 1937, Denise

Marguerite (marr. diss.), y d of late General Sir Hubert Gough, GCB, GCMG, KCVO; one s; m 1955, Pamela, d of late Lieut-Col Hastings Roy Harington, 8th Gurkha Rifles, and the Hon. Mrs Harington; one s. Educ: St Albans Sch., Herts; RMA, Woolwich; St John's Coll., Cambridge (BA 1933, MA 1937). 2nd Lieut RE 1930; Temp. Brig. 1943; Brig. 1958. Egypt, 1935; Palestine, 1936-39 (despatches twice); War of 1939-45 (MBE, CBE, US Bronze Star, Africa Star, 1939-45 Star, Italy Star, Burma Star, General Service Medal with Clasps Palestine, SE Asia and Malaya). CC Dorset, for Swanage (East), 1964-74, Swanage, 1974-. Address: 10 Battlemead, Swanage, Dorset BH19 1PH. T: Swanage 3186.

MONTAGUE-SMITH, Patrick Wykeham; Editor of Debrett since 1962; b 3 Jan. 1920; o s of late Major Vernon Milner Montague-Smith, Richmond, Surrey, and Sybil Katherine, d of late William Wykeham Frederick Bourne, Kensington, and Fockbury House, Worcs; m 1974, Annabele Christina Calvert, o d of late Noel Newton, MA and Isabella Newton, 65 Abbotsbury Close, Kensington, W14. Educ: Lynfield, Hunstanton and Mercers' Sch. Served RASC, 8 Corps, 1940-46; in NW Europe, 1944-46. Asst Editor of Debrett, 1946-62. Dir, Debrett's Peerage Ltd. A Vice-Pres., English Genealogical Congress, Cambridge, 1975. Fellow, Soc. of Genealogists, 1969; Member: Heraldry Soc.; Soc. of Descendants of Knights of the Garter (Windsor); Sublime Soc. of Beefsteaks; Hon. Mem., Internat. Mark Twain Soc., Missouri. Freeman of the City of London. Publications: Royal Line of Succession, 1953; The Prince of Wales, 1958; Princess Margaret, 1961; Debrett's Correct Form, 1970, new edn 1976; Debrett's Royal Wedding: HRH Princess Anne and Captain Mark Phillips, 1973; The Royal Year, 1974, 1975, 1976; The Country Life Book of the Royal Silver Jubilee (1977), 1976; contribs to Encyclopædia Britannica and various journals and newspapers, principally on genealogy, heraldry, and historical subjects, also lectures, television and broadcasts. Recreations: genealogy, heraldry, British history, visiting country houses and browsing in bookshops. Address: Brereton, 197 Park Road, Kingston upon Thames, Surrey. T: 01-546 8807; Debrett's Peerage Ltd, 23 Mossop Street, SW3. T: 01-589 2463.

MONTALE, Eugenio; Italian poet; Literary and music critic, Corriere della Sera, since 1948; b Genoa, 12 Oct. 1896; s of Domenico Montale and Giuseppina (née Ricci); m Drusilla Tanzi (d 1963). Educ: studied opera singing under Ernesto Sivon; served as Infantry officer, 1917-18; jt founder Primo Tempo, 1922; on staff of Bemporad, Florence, 1927; curator of Gabinetto Vieusseux Library, 1928-38; poetry critic, La Fiera Letteraria, 1938-48. Life Mem., Italian Senate, 1967. Feltrinelli Prize, 1963-64; Calouste Gulbenkian Prize, Paris, 1971; Nobel Prize for Literature, 1975. Hon. degrees from Univs of Milan, Rome and Cambridge. Works trans. into English and other languages. Publications: poetry: Ossi di seppia, 1925; La casa dei doganieri, 1932 (Antico Fattore Poetry Prize); Quaterno di traduzione, 1948; Le occasioni, 1948; La bufèra e altro, 1956 (Premio Manzotto); Satura, 1962, Xenia, 1966, published together as Satura, 1971; Diario del '71 e del '72, 1973; prose: La farfalla di Dinard (autobiog), 1956; Auto da fé, 1966; Furori di casa, 1969; contribs to anthologies and jls. Recreations: music and art. Address: c/o Corriere della Sera, Milan, Italy; Via Bigli 11, Milan, Italy.

MONTANARO, Brig. Gerald Charles Stokes, DSO; MA, CEng, FICE, FIMechE, FIEE, AFRAeS, MBIM, FCIS, MNSE; company director; b 16 Sept. 1916; s of late Col C. A. H. Montanaro, OBE. Educ: Bedford Sch.; RMA and Cambridge Univ. Commissioned, RE, 1936; BEF, France, 1939-40; Commandos, Special Canoe Troop, 1940-42 (DSO); commissioned Lieut-Comdr, RN, 1942-45, in comd flotilla of submersible craft; Staff Coll., 1947; GSO2 and GSO1 (ops) GHQ, MELF, 1947-48; Tech. Staff Course, 1948-49; Mil. Comdg Officer RAE, 1949-52; OC Sqdn and Regt, Hong Kong and Korea, 1952-54; GSO1 War Office, 1954-57; Comd of Regt and CRE, BAOR, 1957-60; Asst Dir Devel., WO, 1960-61; Brig., Gen. Staff, WO, 1962-63; Brig., IDC, 1963-64; Brigadier A/Q HQ ME, Aden, 1964-65. Man. Dir Reed Develt Services Ltd, and Dep. Chm. Reed Transport Ltd, Reed Paper Gp, 1965-66; Dep. Man. Dir, Norton Villiers Ltd, 1967-68; Dir, Fairline Engineering Ltd, 1968-70; Man. Dir, Alistair McCowan & Associates, Nigeria. Recreations: deer stalking, shooting, sailing. Address: 131 Broad Street, PO Box 3402, Lagos, Nigeria. T: Lagos 23113 and 27538. Clubs: Naval and Military; Ikoyi (Lagos); Lagos Motor Boat.

MONTAND, Simone H. C.; see Signoret, Simone.

MONTEAGLE OF BRANDON, 6th Baron cr 1839; Gerald Spring Rice; late Captain, Irish Guards; b 5 July 1926; s of 5th

Baron and Emilie de Kosenko, d of Mrs Edward Brooks, Philadelphia, USA; S father 1946; m 1949, Anne, d of late Col G. J. Brownlow, Ballywhite, Portaferry, Co. Down; one s three d (of whom two are twins). Educ: Harrow. Heir: s Hon. Charles James Spring Rice, b 24 Feb. 1953. Address: 3 Elia Street, Islington, N1 8DE. Clubs: Cavalry and Guards, Pratt's; Kildare Street and University (Dublin).

MONTEATH, Robert Campbell, CBE 1964; County Clerk, Treasurer and Local Taxation Officer, Kirkcudbright, 1946-72, and Clerk to the Lieutenancy, since 1966; b 15 June 1907; s of Gordon Drysdale Monteath, Dumbarton; m 1936, Sarah McGregor, d of John Fenwick, Dumbarton; two s one d. Educ: Dumbarton Academy; Glasgow Univ. Dep. County Clerk, Dunbartonshire, 1937-46; Dep. Civil Defence Controller, 1939-46; Hon. Sheriff, Kirkcudbright, 1966-. Address: Gortonbrae, Townhead, Kirkcudbright. T: Townhead 251. Clubs: Royal Over-Seas League; Royal Scottish Automobile (Glasgow).

MONTEFIORE, Harold Henry S.; see Sebag-Montefiore.

MONTEFIORE, Rt. Rev. Hugh William; see Birmingham, Bishop of.

MONTEITH, Rt. Rev. George Rae, BA; b 14 Feb. 1904; s of John Hodge Monteith and Ellen (née Hall); m 1931, Kathleen Methven Mules; two s one d. Educ: St John's Coll., Auckland; Univ. of New Zealand. BA 1927. Deacon, 1928; priest, 1929; Curate: St Matthew's, Auckland, 1928-30; Stoke-on-Trent, 1931-33; Vicar of: Dargaville, NZ, 1934-37; Mt Eden, Auckland, NZ, 1937-49; St Mary's Cathedral Parish, Auckland, 1949-69; Dean of Auckland, 1949-69; Vicar-General, 1963-76; Asst Bishop of Auckland, NZ, 1965-76. Address: 7 Cathedral Place, Auckland 1, NZ. T: 374.449.

MONTEITH, Brig. John Cassels, CBE 1968; MC 1938; JP; Colonel, The Black Watch, since 1976; b 28 Sept. 1915; s of Lt-Col John Cassels Monteith (killed in action 1915), Moniaive, Dumfriesshire, and of Mrs Jane Robertson Monteith (née Wilson), Dunning, Perthshire; m 1st, 1949, Winifred Elisabeth (d 1968), d of Louis Cecil Breitmeyer, Kettering; one s one d; 2nd, 1973, Pamela Joan, d of Col Francis E. Laughton, MC, TD. Educ: Stowe; Trinity Coll., Cambridge (BA). 2nd Lieut Black Watch, 1935; served War 1939-45, ME, Italy and NW Europe; CO 1st Bn Black Watch, 1957-59; Col 1961; Comdr 155 (L) Inf. Bde, TA, 1962-65; Brig. 1963; Defence and Mil. Attaché, Bonn, 1965-68; Comdr Highland Area, 1968-70; retd 1970. Chm., Highland TAVR Assoc., 1971-76. Brig., Queen's Body Guard for Scotland (Royal Company of Archers), 1972. JP Perthshire, 1972. Recreations: shooting, gardening. Address: Essendy House, Blairgowrie, Perthshire. T: Essendy 260. Clubs: Army and Navy; Royal Perth.

MONTEITH, Prof. John Lennox, FRS 1971; FRSE 1972; Professor of Environmental Physics, University of Nottingham, since 1967; b 3 Sept. 1929; s of Rev. John and Margaret Monteith; m 1955, Elsa Marion Wotherspoon; four s one d. Educ: George Heriot's Sch.; Univ. of Edinburgh; Imperial Coll., London. BSc, DIC, PhD. Mem. Physics Dept Staff, Rothamsted Experimental Station, 1954-67. FInstP, FIBiol. Governor, Grassland Res. Inst., 1976-. Vice Pres., British Ecological Soc., 1977-. Publications: Instruments for Micrometeorology (ed), 1972; Principles of Environmental Physics, 1973; (ed with L. E. Mount) Heat Loss from Animals and Man, 1974; (ed) Vegetation and the Atmosphere, 1975; papers on Micrometeorology and Crop Science in: Quarterly Jl of RMetSoc.; Jl Applied Ecology, etc. Recreations: music, photography. Address: School of Agriculture, Sutton Bonington, Loughborough, Leics LE12 5RD. T: Kegworth 2386.

MONTEITH, Lt-Col Robert Charles Michael, MC 1943; TD 1945; JP; Vice Lord-Lieutenant of Lanarkshire since 1964; Land-owner and Farmer since 1950; b 25 May 1914; s of late Major J. B. L. Monteith, CBE, and late Dorothy, d of Sir Charles Nicholson, 1st Bt; m 1950, Mira Elizabeth, e d of late John Fanshawe, Sidmount, Moffat; one s. Educ: Ampleforth Coll., York. CA (Edinburgh), 1939. Served with Lanarkshire Yeomanry, 1939-45: Paiforce, 1942-43; MEF, 1943-44; BLA, 1944-45. Contested (U) Hamilton Division of Lanarkshire, 1950 and 1951. Member: Mental Welfare Commn for Scotland, 1962-; E Kilbride Develt Corp., 1972-76. DL 1955, JP 1955, CC 1949-64, 1967-74, Lanarkshire; Chm., Lanark DC, 1974-. Mem. Queen's Body Guard for Scotland, Royal Company of Archers. Mem. SMO of Knights of Malta; OStJ 1973. Recreations: shooting, curling. Address: Cranley, Cleghorn, Lanark. T: Carstairs 330. Clubs: New, Puffins (Edinburgh).

MONTGOMERIE, family name of **Earl of Eglinton.**

MONTGOMERIE, Lord; Hugh Archibald William Montgomerie; *b* 24 July 1966; *s* and *heir* of 18th Earl of Eglinton and Winton, *qv.*

MONTGOMERY, family name of **Viscount Montgomery of Alamein.**

MONTGOMERY OF ALAMEIN, 2nd Viscount *cr* 1946, of Hindhead; **David Bernard Montgomery,** CBE 1975; Director, Terimar Services (Overseas Trade Consultant), since 1974; *b* 18 Aug. 1928; *s* of 1st Viscount Montgomery of Alamein, KG, GCB, DSO, and Elizabeth (*d* , 1937), *d* of late Robert Thompson Hobart, ICS; *S* father, 1976; *m* 1st, 1953, Mary Connell (marr. diss. 1967); one *s* one *d* ; 2nd, 1970, Tessa, *d* of late Gen. Sir Frederick Browning, GCVO, KBE, CB, DSO, and of Lady Browning, DBE (*see* Dame Daphne du Maurier). *Educ:* Winchester, Trinity Coll., Cambridge (MA). Shell International, 1951-62; Yardley International (Director), 1963-74; Director of various companies, 1974-. Chm., Economic Affairs Cttee, Canning House, 1973-75; Pres., British Industrial Exhibition, Sao Paulo, 1974. Councillor, Royal Borough of Kensington and Chelsea, 1974. Hon. Consul, Republic of El Salvador, 1973. Governor, Amesbury Sch., 1976. *Recreations:* golf, sailing. *Heir:* s Hon. Henry David Montgomery, *b* 2 April 1954. *Address:* Isington Mill, Alton, Hants. *T:* Bentley 3126. *Clubs:* Bath, Royal Fowey Yacht.

MONTGOMERY, Sir (Basil Henry) David, 9th Bt, *cr* 1801, of Stanhope; JP; DL; landowner; *b* 20 March 1931; *s* of late Lt-Col H. K. Purvis-Montgomery, OBE, and of Mrs C. L. W. Purvis-Russell-Montgomery (*née* Maconochie Welwood); *S* uncle, 1964; *m* 1956, Delia, *o d* of Adm. Sir (John) Peter (Lorne) Reid, GCB, CVO; one *s* four *d* (and one *s* decd). *Educ:* Eton. National Service, Black Watch, 1949-51. Member: Nature Conservancy Council, 1973-; Tayside Regional Authority. DL Kinross-shire, 1960, Vice-Lieutenant 1966-74; JP 1966; DL Perth and Kinross, 1975. *Heir:* s James David Keith Montgomery, *b* 13 June 1957. *Address:* Kinross House, Kinross. *T:* Kinross 63416.

MONTGOMERY, (Charles) John, CBE 1977; Director since 1972, and Chief General Manager, 1973-May 1978, Lloyds Bank Ltd; *b* 18 Feb. 1917; *s* of late Rev. Charles James Montgomery; *m* 1950, Gwenneth Mary McKendrick; two *d*. *Educ:* Colwyn Bay Grammar School. Served with RN, 1940-46. Entered Lloyds Bank, 1935; Jt Gen. Man. 1968; Asst Chief Gen. Man. 1970; Dep. Chief Gen. Man. 1973. Pres., Inst. of Bankers, 1976-77, Vice Pres., 1977. Chm., Chief Exec. Officers' Cttee, Cttee of London Clearing Bankers, 1976-. *Recreations:* walking, photography. *Address:* High Cedar, 6 Cedar Copse, Bickley, Kent. *T:* 01-467 2410. *Clubs:* Naval, Overseas Bankers.

MONTGOMERY, Fergus; *see* Montgomery, (William) Fergus.

MONTGOMERY, Prof. George Lightbody, CBE 1960; TD 1942; MD, PhD, FRCPE, FRCPGlas, FRCPath, FRCSE; FRSE; Professor of Pathology, University of Edinburgh, 1954-71, now Emeritus; *b* 3 Nov. 1905; *o s* of late John Montgomery and Jeanie Lightbody; *m* 1933, Margaret Sutherland, 3rd *d* of late A. Henry Forbes, Oban; one *s* one *d*. *Educ:* Hillhead High Sch., Glasgow; Glasgow Univ. MB, ChB, 1928; Commendation and RAMC Memorial Prize; PhD (St Andrews), 1937; MD Hons and Bellahouston Gold Medal (Glasgow), 1946. House Physician, House Surgeon, Glasgow Royal Infirmary, 1928-29; Lecturer in Clinical Pathology, Univ. of St Andrews, 1931-37; Lecturer in Pathology of Disease in Infancy and Childhood, Univ. of Glasgow, 1937-48; Asst Pathologist, Glasgow Royal Infirmary, 1929-31; Asst Pathologist, Dundee Royal Infirmary, 1931-37; Pathologist, Royal Hospital for Sick Children, Glasgow, 1937-48; Professor of Pathology (St Mungo-Notman Chair), Univ. of Glasgow, 1948-54. Chm. Scottish Health Services Council, 1954-59. Hon. Member: Pathological Soc. Gt Britain and Ireland; BMA. Col (Hon.) Army Medical Service. *Publications:* Textbook of Pathology, 1965; General Pathology for Students of Dentistry, 3rd edn 1965; numerous contribs to medical and scientific journals. *Recreation:* music. *Address:* 2 Cumin Place, Edinburgh EH9 2JX. *T:* 031-667 6792. *Club:* New (Edinburgh).

MONTGOMERY, Group Captain George Rodgers, CBE 1946; RAF (Retired); Secretary, Norfolk Naturalists' Trust, 1963-75; Hon. Appeal Secretary, and Member of the Court, University of East Anglia, since Nov. 1966; *b* 31 May 1910; *s* of late John Montgomery, Belfast; *m* 1932, Margaret McHarry Heslip, *d* of late William J. Heslip, Belfast; two *s*. *Educ:* Royal Academy, Belfast. Commnd in RAF, 1928; retd 1958. Served in UK and ME, 1928-38. War of 1939-45: Bomber Comd, NI, Air Min. and

ME. Served UK, Japan and W Europe, 1946-58: Comdr RAF Wilmslow, 1946-47; Air Adviser to UK Polit. Rep. in Japan, and Civil Air Attaché, Tokyo, 1948-49; Chief Instr RAF Officers' Advanced Trg Sch., 1950; Comdt RAF Sch. of Admin, Bircham Newton, 1951-52; Comdr RAF Hednesford, 1953-54; DDO (Estabts) Air Min. and Chm. RAF Western European Estabts Cttee, Germany, 1955-57. On retirement, Organising Sec. Friends of Norwich Cathedral, 1959-62; Appeal Sec., Univ. of East Anglia, 1961-66; Member: Norfolk Naturalists' Trust Council; Great Bustard Trust Council; Broads Soc. Cttee. *Recreations:* river cruising, gardening. *Address:* 24 Cathedral Close, Norwich, Norfolk. *T:* Norwich 28024. *Clubs:* Royal Air Force; Prince Albert (Brussels).

MONTGOMERY, John; *see* Montgomery, C. J.

MONTGOMERY, John Matthew; Clerk of the Salters' Company, since 1975; *b* 22 May 1930; *s* of Prof. George Allison Montgomery, QC, and Isabel A. (*née* Morison); *m* 1956, Gertrude Gillian Richards; two *s* one *d*. *Educ:* Rugby Sch.; Trinity Hall, Cambridge (MA). Various commercial appointments with Mobil Oil Corporation and First National City Bank, 1953-74. *Recreations:* various natural history interests (Chm., Surrey Trust for Nature Conservation Ltd, 1973-). *Address:* Dunedin, Red Lane, Claygate, Esher, Surrey KT10 0ES. *T:* Esher 64780.

MONTGOMERY, Col John Rupert Patrick, MC 1943; Secretary, Anti-Slavery Society, since 1963; *b* 25 July 1913; *s* of George Howard and Mabella Montgomery, The Green, Bromyard; *m* 1940, Alice Vyvyan Patricia (*d* 1976), *d* of Vyvyan James and Catherine Mitchell; one *s* two *d*. *Educ:* Wellington Coll.; RMC, Sandhurst. Commissioned, Oxfordshire and Buckinghamshire LI (now First Royal Green Jackets), 1933; Regimental Service in India, 1935-40 and 1946-47. Served War, in Middle East, N Africa and Italy, 1942-45. Commanded 17 Bn Parachute Regt (9 DLI), 1953-56; SHAPE Mission to Portugal, 1956-59; retired, 1962. Represents the Anti-Slavery Society at UN Economic and Social Council and its subordinate commissions on matters relating to slavery and similar institutions, violations of human rights and the well-being of indigenous peoples. *Address:* Anti-Slavery Society, 60 Weymouth Street, W1N 4DX. *T:* 01-935 6498; The Oast House, Buxted, Sussex. *Club:* Army and Navy.

MONTGOMERY of Blessingbourne, Captain Peter Stephen; Vice-Lieutenant of County of Tyrone, Northern Ireland, since 1971; *b* 13 Aug. 1909; 2nd *s* of late Maj.-Gen. Hugh Maude de Fellenberg Montgomery, CB, CMG, DL, RA, and late Mary, 2nd *d* of Edmund Langton and Mrs Massingberd, Gunby Hall, Lincs. *Educ:* Wellington Coll.; Trinity Coll., Cambridge (MA). Founder, 1927, and Conductor until 1969, of Fivemiletown Choral Soc.; employed with BBC in N Ireland and London, 1931-47; Asst Music Dir and Conductor, BBC Northern Ireland Symphony Orchestra, 1933-38. Served War of 1939-45: Captain, Royal Intelligence Corps, ADC to Viceroy of India (FM Earl Wavell), 1945-46. Mem. BBC Northern Ireland Advisory Council, 1952-71, and BBC Gen. Adv. Council, 1963-71. Hon. ADC to Governor of Northern Ireland (Lord Wakehurst), 1954-64; Member: National Trust Cttee for NI; Bd of Visitors, HM Prison, Belfast (Chm. 1971); Friends of National Collections of Ireland; Bd of Arts Council of NI (Pres., 1964-74). JP 1959, DL 1956, Co. Tyrone; High Sheriff of Co. Tyrone, 1964. Hon. LLD Queen's Univ. Belfast, 1976. *Address:* Blessingbourne, Fivemiletown, Co. Tyrone, Northern Ireland. *Clubs:* Oriental; Ulster (Belfast); Tyrone County (Omagh).

MONTGOMERY, (William) Fergus; MP (C) Altrincham and Sale, since Oct. 1974; *b* 25 Nov. 1927; *s* of William Montgomery and late Winifred Montgomery; *m* Joyce, *d* of George Riddle. *Educ:* Jarrow Grammar Sch.; Bede Coll., Durham. Served in Royal Navy, 1946-48; Schoolmaster, 1950-59. Nat. Vice-Chm. Young Conservative Organisation, 1954-57, National Chm., 1957-58; contested (C) Consett Division, 1955; MP (C): Newcastle upon Tyne East, 1959-64; Brierley Hill, Apr. 1967-Feb. 1974; contested Dudley W, Feb. 1974; PPS to Leader of the Opposition, 1975-76. Councillor, Hebburn UDC, 1950-58. Has lectured extensively in the USA. *Recreations:* bridge, reading. *Address:* 30 Laxford House, Cundy Street, SW1. *T:* 01-730 2341; 3 Groby Place, Altrincham, Cheshire. *T:* 061-928 1983.

MONTGOMERY CUNINGHAME, Sir John Christopher Foggo, 12th Bt *cr* 1672, of Corsehill, Ayrshire and Kirktonholm, Lanarkshire; Director, Morgan Grenfell & Co. Ltd, since 1973; *b* 24 July 1935; 2nd *s* of Col Sir Thomas Montgomery-Cuninghame, 10th Bt, DSO (*d* 1945), and of Nancy Macaulay (his 2nd wife), *d* of late W. Stewart Foggo, Aberdeen (she *m* 2nd, 1946, Johan Frederik Christian Killander); *b* of Sir Andrew

Mongtomery-Cuninghame, 11th Bt; *S* brother, 1959; *m* 1964, Laura Violet, *d* of Sir Godfrey Nicholson, Bt, *qv*; three *d. Educ:* Fettes; Worcester Coll., Oxford (BA). 2nd Lieut, Rifle Brigade (NS), 1955-56; Lieut, London Rifle Brigade, TA, 1956-. *Recreation:* fishing. *Heir:* none. *Address:* 52 Scarsdale Villas, W8. *T:* 01-937 9935.

MONTGOMERY WATT, Prof. William; *see* Watt.

MONTMORENCY, Sir Reginald de; *see* de Montmorency.

MONTREAL, Archbishop of, (RC), since 1968; **Most Rev. Paul Grégoire;** *b* Verdun, 24 Oct. 1911. *Educ:* Ecole Supérieure Richard; Séminaire de Ste-Thérèse; Univ. of Montreal. Priest, 1937; became Professor, but continued his studies: PhD, STL, LèsL, MA (Hist.), dip. in pedagogy. Subseq. became Director, Séminaire de Ste-Thérèse; Prof. of Philosophy of Educn at l'Ecole Normale Secondaire and at l'Institut Pédagogique; Chaplain of the Students, Univ. of Montreal, 1950-61; consecrated Bishop, 1961, and became auxiliary to Archbishop of Montreal; Vicar-General and Dir of Office for the Clergy; Apostolic Administrator, Archdiocese of Montreal, Dec. 1967-Apr. 1968. Pres., Episcopal Commn on Ecumenism (French sector), 1965. Has presided over several Diocesan Commns (notably Commn for study of the material situation of the Clergy), 1965-68. Dr *hc*: Univ. of Montreal, 1969; St Michael's Coll., Winooski, Vt, 1970. *Address:* Archbishop's House, 1071 Cathedral Street, Montreal H3B 2V4, Quebec, Canada.

MONTREAL, Bishop of, since 1975; **Rt. Rev. Reginald Hollis;** *b* 18 July 1932; *s* of Jesse Farndon Hollis and Edith Ellen Lee; *m* 1957, Marcia Henderson Crombie; two *s* one *d. Educ:* Selwyn Coll., Cambridge; McGill Univ., Montreal. Chaplain and Lectr, Montreal Dio. Theol Coll., 1956-60; Chaplain to Anglican Students, McGill Univ.; Asst Rector, St Matthias' Church, Westmount, PQ, 1960-63; Rector, St Barnabas' Church, Pierrefonds, PQ, 1963-70; Rector, Christ Church, Beaconsfield, PQ, 1971-74; Dir of Parish and Dio. Services, Dio. Montreal, 1974-75. Hon. DD 1975. *Address:* 3630 Mountain Street, Montreal, PQ, Canada.

MONTROSE, 7th Duke of, *cr* 1707; **James Angus Graham;** *cr* Baron Graham before 1451; Earl of Montrose, 1505; Bt (NS) 1625; Marquis of Montrose, 1645; Duke of Montrose, Marquis of Graham and Buchanan, Earl of Kincardine, Viscount Dundaff, Baron Aberuthven, Mugdock, and Fintrie, 1707; Earl and Baron Graham (Peerage of England), 1722; Hereditary Sheriff of Dunbartonshire; *b* 2 May 1907; *e s* of 6th Duke of Montrose, KT, CB, CVO, VD, and Lady Mary Douglas-Hamilton, OBE (*d* 1957), *d* of 12th Duke of Hamilton; *S* father, 1954; *m* 1st, 1930, Isobel Veronica (marr. diss. 1950), *yr d* of late Lt-Col T. B. Sellar, CMG, DSO; one *s* one *d*; 2nd, 1952, Susan Mary Jocelyn, *widow* of Michael Raleigh Gibbs and *d* of Dr J. M. Semple; two *s* two *d. Educ:* Eton; Christ Church, Oxford. Lt-Comdr RNVR. MP for Hartley-Gatooma in Federal Assembly of Federation of Rhodesia and Nyasaland, 1958-62; Minister of Agriculture, Lands, and Natural Resources, S Rhodesia, 1962-63; Minister of Agric., Rhodesia, 1964-65; (apptd in Rhodesia) Minister of External Affairs and Defence, 1966-68. *Heir: s* Marquis of Graham, *qv. Address:* Derry Farm, PB 309B, Salisbury, Rhodesia; (Seat) Auchmar, Drymen, Glasgow.

MOODY, Helen Wills; *see* Roark, H. W.

MOODY, John Percivale, OBE 1961; Joint Artistic Director, Welsh National Opera Co.; *b* 6 April 1906; *s* of Percivale Sadleir Moody; *m* 1937, Helen Pomfret Burra; one *s* decd. *Educ:* Bromsgrove; Royal Academy Schools. In publishing in the City, 1924-26; Painting; Academy Schs, 1927-28, various London Exhibitions; taught at Wimbledon Art Sch., 1928-29. Studied opera Webber Douglas Sch. Derby Day under Sir Nigel Playfair, Lyric, Hammersmith, 1931. West End plays include: The Brontës, Royalty, 1932; Hervey House, His Majesty's, 1935; After October, Criterion, 1936; played in Old Vic seasons 1934, 1937; Ascent of F6, Dog Beneath the Skin, Group Theatre, 1935; Dir Old Vic Sch., 1940-42. AFS Clerkenwell, 1940 (wounded and discharged). Producer Old Vic Co., Liverpool, 1942-44; Birmingham Repertory Theatre, 1944-45; Carl Rosa Opera Co., 1945; Sadler's Wells Opera Co., 1945-49; Drama Dir, Arts Council of Great Britain, 1949-54; Dir, Bristol Old Vic Co., 1954-59. First productions in England of Verdi's Simone Boccanegra, 1948, Nabucco, 1952, and The Battle of Legnano, 1960; Rimsky's May Night, 1960; also for Welsh Nat. Opera: Rossini's William Tell, 1961; Macbeth, 1963; Moses, 1965; Carmen, 1967; Boris Godunov, 1968; Simone Boccanegra, 1970; Rigoletto, 1972; The Pearl Fishers, 1973; What the Old Man Does is Always Right, Fishguard Festival, 1977. With wife, new translations of Carmen, Simone Boccanegra, La Traviata, The

Pearl Fishers, and Prince Igor. *Recreations:* swimming, gardening. *Address:* 2 Richmond Park Road, Bristol BS8 3AT. *T:* Bristol 34436.

MOODY, Sydney, CMG 1942; OBE 1932; Colonial Secretary, Mauritius, 1939-48; *b* 1889; *s* of Jonathan Moody; *m* 1921, Flora Marion, *e d* of late Rev. William Ewing, MC, DD, Edinburgh; two *d. Educ:* Oxford (BA). Served European War, 1914-20. *Address:* The Brae, Alyth, Perthshire.

MOODY, Prof. Theodore William, MA, PhD; Professor of Modern History, Dublin University, and Senior Fellow of Trinity College, Dublin, 1939-77, now Fellow Emeritus; *b* 26 Nov. 1907; *o s* of William J. Moody, Belfast, and Ann I. Dippie; *m* 1935, Margaret C. P. Robertson, LLB, Bristol; one *s* four *d. Educ:* Royal Academical Instn, Belfast; Queen's Univ., Belfast (BA Mediæval and Modern Hist., 1930); Inst. of Historical Research, Univ. of London, 1930-32 (PhD 1934). FRHistS 1934; MRIA 1940. Queen's Univ., Belfast: Asst in History, 1932-35; Lectr in History, 1935-39. Trinity Coll., Dublin: Fellow, 1939; Tutor, 1939-52 (MA 1941); Sen. Tutor, 1952-58; Sen. Lectr, 1958-64; first Dean, Faculty of Arts, 1967-69. Hon. Treasurer, Social Service Co., TCD, 1942-53, Chm. 1953-. Member: Irish MSS Commn, 1943-; Adv. Cttee on Cultural Relations, Dept of External Affairs, Ireland, 1949-63; Govt Commn on Higher Educn in Ireland, 1960-67; Comhairle Radio Eireann (Irish Broadcasting Council), 1953-60; Irish Broadcasting Authority, 1960-72. Leverhulme Res. Fellow, 1964-66. Mem., Sch. of Historical Studies, Inst. for Advanced Study, Princeton, 1965. Jt Editor, Irish Historical Studies, 1937-; Editor, Studies in Irish History, 1st series, 1944-56, 2nd series, 1960-75; Chm., Bd of Editors, A New History of Ireland, 1968-. Corresp. FBA, 1977. Hon. DLit, Queen's Univ., Belfast, 1959. *Publications:* The Londonderry Plantation, 1609-41: the City of London and the plantation in Ulster, 1939; The Irish Parliament under Elizabeth and James I: a general survey (Proc. of RIA, vol xiv, sect C, no 6), 1939; Thomas Davis, 1814-45, 1945; (with J. C. Beckett) Queen's, Belfast, 1845-1949: the history of a university, 1959; The Ulster Question 1603-1973, 1974; *Editor and contributor:* (with H. A. Cronne and D. B. Quinn) Essays in British and Irish History in honour of J. E. Todd, 1949; (with J. C. Beckett) Ulster since 1800, 1st series, 1955, 2nd series, 1957; (with F. X. Martin) The Course of Irish History, 1967; Historical Studies vi, 1968; The Fenian Movement, 1968; Irish Historiography 1936-70, 1971; Early Modern Ireland, 1534-1691 (A New History of Ireland, vol. iii), 1976; Nationality and the Pursuit of National Independence, 1977; *Editor:* Ulster Plantation Papers, 1608-13 (Analecta Hibernica, no 8), 1938; An Irish Countryman in the British Navy, 1809-1815: the memoirs of Henry Walsh (The Irish Sword, iv-v, nos 16-21), 1960-62; (with J. G. Simms) The Bishopric of Derry and the Irish Society of London, 1602-70, 1968; Michael Davitt's Leaves from a Prison Diary, repr. 1972; various contribs on modern Irish history, the Irish in America, the Irish university question, and especially on Michael Davitt 1846-1906 (in Irish Historical Studies, Studies, History, Trans of Royal Hist. Soc., Hermathena). *Recreations:* listening to music, walking. *Address:* Trinity College, Dublin.

MOOKERJEE, Sir Birendra Nath, Kt 1942; MA Cantab, MIE (India); Partner of Martin & Co. and Burn & Co., Managing Director, Martin Burn Ltd, Engineers, Contractors, Merchants, Shipbuilders, etc; Chairman Steel Corporation of Bengal Ltd; President Calcutta Local Board of Imperial Bank of India; Director Darjeeling Himalayan Railway Co. Ltd and many other companies; *b* 14 Feb. 1899; *s* of late Sir Rajendra Nath Mookerjee, KCIE, KCVO, MIE (India), FASB, DSc (Eng); *m* 1925, Ranu Priti Adhikari, *d* of Phani Bhusan Adhikari, late Professor Benares Hindu Univ.; one *s* two *d. Educ:* Bishop's Collegiate Sch., Hastings House, Calcutta; Bengal Engineering Coll.; Trinity Coll., Cambridge. Mem., Viceroy's Nat. Defence Council; Adviser, Roger Mission; Mem., Munitions Production Adv. Cttee. Fellow Calcutta Univ.; Sheriff of Calcutta 1941. *Address:* Martin Burn Ltd, Martin Burn House, 12 Mission Row, Calcutta 1, India; 7 Harington Street, Calcutta 16. *Clubs:* National Liberal; Calcutta, Calcutta Polo, Royal Calcutta Turf, Calcutta South, Cricket Club of India (Calcutta), etc.

MOON, Maj.-Gen. Alan Neilson, CB 1966; CBE 1961; Director, Army Dental Service, 1963-66; *b* 10 June 1906; *s* of late E. W. Moon, Weston-super-Mare; *m* 1st, 1933, Joyce Beatrix (marr. diss., 1943), *d* of E. E. Searles, Bristol; one *d*; 2nd, 1961, Dorothy Mary, ARRC, *d* of W. H. Wilson, Blairgowrie. *Educ:* Queen's Coll., Taunton; Univ. of Bristol. LDS 1930; commnd Lieut, The Army Dental Corps, 1931; Captain 1934; Major 1941; Lt-Col 1948; Col 1956; Brig. 1959; Maj.-Gen. 1963. Served: India, 1939-45; Middle East, 1950-53; Dep. Dir Dental Service Western Command, 1956, Southern Command, 1957;

Asst Dir, War Office, 1958-63. OStJ 1961. *Address:* Fulwood, Torphins, Aberdeenshire AB3 4JS. *T:* Torphins 384.

MOON, Sir (Edward) Penderel, Kt 1962; OBE 1941; Assistant Editor, India Office Records on the Transfer of Power, since 1972; *b* 13 Nov. 1905; *s* of Dr R. O. Moon, FRCP; *m* 1966, Pauline Marion (marr. diss.), *d* of Rev. W. E. C. Barns. *Educ:* Winchester; New Coll., Oxford (MA). Fellow of All Souls College, Oxford, 1927-35. Entered ICS, 1929, resigned, 1944; Sec., Development Board and Planning Advisory Board, Govt of India; Min. of Revenue and Public Works, Bahawalpur State; Chief Comr, Himachal Pradesh; Chief Comr, Manipur; Adviser, Planning Commission. *Publications:* Strangers in India; The Future of India; Warren Hastings and British India; Divide and Quit; Gandhi and Modern India; Disbelief in God; (ed) Wavell: the Viceroy's Journal. *Recreations:* hunting, shooting and singing. *Address:* Manor Farm, Wotton Underwood, Aylesbury, Bucks.

MOON, Prof. Harold Philip, MA Cantab; Professor of Zoology, University of Leicester, 1950-70, now Professor Emeritus; *b* 15 Jan. 1910; *er s* of Harold Joseph Moon, LRCP, MRCS, and Beatrice Sarah, *yr d* of George Greenwood; *m* 1939, Ruth Hannah, *er d* of late Capt. E. Rivenhall Goffe, RAOC (Retd); three *s* one *d.* *Educ:* Bootham Sch., York; King's Coll., Cambridge. Asst Naturalist, Freshwater Biological Assoc., 1933-35; Asst Research Officer, Avon Biological Research, University Coll., Southampton, 1936-39 (on leave of absence, Percy Sladen expedn to Lake Titicaca, S America, 1937); Asst Lecturer, Dept of Zoology, Manchester, 1939; Demonstrator, Bedford Coll. for Women, Univ. of London, 1941; Junior Scientific Officer, Operational Research, MAP, 1942; Insect Infestation Branch, MOF, 1943-45; promoted Sen. Inspector, 1944; Lecturer in Charge, Dept of Zoology, University Coll., Leicester, 1945-50. *Publications:* papers on freshwater biology in scientific journals. *Recreation:* walking. *Address:* The Beeches, 48 Elmfield Avenue, Stoneygate, Leicester LE2 1RD. *T:* Leicester 707625.

MOON, Sir John (Arthur), 4th Bt, *cr* 1887; Master (retired) Merchant Navy; *b* 27 Oct. 1905; 3rd *s* of Reginald Blakeney Moon (*d* 1927; *g s* of 1st Bt) and Lucy Annie (*d* 1935), *d* of J. Crowther; *S* brother, Sir Richard Moon, 3rd Bt, 1961; *m* 1939, René Henriette Maria Dolores (*d* 1949), *o d* of late Joseph Amédée Amedet, Le Mans, France; no *c. Heir: b* Robert Blakeney Moon [*b* 3 March 1908; *m* 1st, 1936, Margaret (marr. diss. 1941), *d* of W. H. Law; 2nd, 1945, Helen Everard Collier (marr. diss., 1968), *d* of late Col C. H. Wiley, Royal Engineers; 3rd, 1968, Dorothy Mary, *d* of late Walter Hill]. *Address:* BP 2710, Papeete, Tahiti, French Polynesia.

MOON, Sir Penderel; *see* Moon, Sir E. P.

MOON, Peter James Scott; HM Diplomatic Service; Counsellor, Cairo, since 1975; *b* 1 April 1928; *m* 1955, Lucile Worms; three *d.* Home Office, 1952-54; CRO, 1954-56; Second Sec., Cape Town/Pretoria, 1956-58; Principal, CRO, 1958-60; First Sec., Colombo, 1960-63; Private Sec. to Sec. of State for Commonwealth Relations, 1963-65; First Sec., UK Mission to UN, New York, 1965-69; Counsellor, FCO, 1969-70; Private Sec. to Prime Minister, 1970-72; NATO Defence Coll., 1972; seconded to NATO Internat. Staff, Brussels, 1972-75. *Address:* c/o Foreign and Commonwealth Office, SW1.

MOON, Sir Peter Wilfred Giles Graham-, 5th Bt, *cr* 1855; *b* 24 Oct. 1942; *s* of Sir (Arthur) Wilfred Graham-Moon, 4th Bt, and 2nd wife, Doris Patricia, *yr d* of Thomas Baron Jobson, Dublin; *S* father, 1954; *m* 1967, Sarah Gillian Chater (formerly *m* Major Antony Chater; marr. diss. 1966), *e d* of late Lt-Col Michael Lyndon Smith, MC, MB, BS, and Mrs Michael Smith; two *s. Recreations:* shooting, golf. *Heir: s* Rupert Francis Wilfred Graham-Moon, *b* 29 April 1968. *Address:* Littlebrook House, Little Tew, Oxfordshire. *T:* Great Tew 249. *Club:* Royal Cork Yacht.

MOON, Philip Burton, FRS 1947; Poynting Professor of Physics in the University of Birmingham, 1950-74, now Emeritus; Dean of the Faculty of Science and Engineering, 1969-72; *b* 17 May 1907; *o s* of late F. D. Moon; *m* 1st, 1937, Winifred F. Barber (*d* 1971); one *s* one *d*; 2nd, 1974, Lorna M. Aldridge. *Educ:* Leyton County High Sch.; Sidney Sussex Coll., Cambridge. *Publications:* Artificial Radioactivity, 1949; various papers on physics. *Address:* 42 Serpentine Road, Selly Park, Birmingham B29 7HU. *T:* 021-472 5615.

MOON, Lieut (Hon. Captain) Rupert Vance, VC 1917; Director, Queensland Stations Ltd; *b* Bacchus Marsh, 1892; *s* of Arthur Moon, of the Nat. Bank of Australasia, Melbourne; *m* 1931,

Susan Alison May, *yr d* of R. T. Vincent, Prospect House, Geelong; one *s* one *d. Educ:* Kyneton Grammar Sch. Served European War (VC). Formerly Accountant, National Bank of Australasia Ltd, Geelong; Gen. Manager, Dennys Lascelles Ltd, retd 1960, and Dir, retd 1975. *Address:* Calder Park, Mount Duneed, Belmont, Vic 3216, Australia. *Clubs:* Melbourne, Naval and Military, Victorian Racing, Moonee Valley Racing (Melbourne); Geelong, Geelong Racing (Geelong); Victoria Amateur Turf (Caulfield).

MOONMAN, Eric; MP (Lab) Basildon, since 1974; *b* 29 April 1929; *s* of Borach and Leah Moonman; *m* 1962, Jane; two *s* one *d. Educ:* Rathbone Sch., Liverpool; Christ Church, Southport; Univs of Liverpool and Manchester. Dipl. in Social Science, Liverpool, 1955. Human Relations Adviser, British Inst. of Management, 1956-62; Sen. Lectr in Industrial Relations, SW Essex Technical Coll., 1962-64; Sen. Research Fellow in Management Sciences, Univ. of Manchester, 1964-66. MSc Manchester Univ., 1967. MP (Lab) Billericay, 1966-70; PPS to Minister without Portfolio and Sec. of State for Educn, 1967-68. Chairman: All-Party Parly Mental Health Information Unit, 1968-70 and 1974; New Towns and Urban Affairs Cttee, Parly Labour Party, 1974-. Member: Stepney Council, 1961-65 (Leader, 1964-65); Tower Hamlets Council, 1964-67. Governor, BFI, 1974-; Mem. Court, Brunel Univ.; Council Mem., Toynbee Hall Univ. Settlement (Chm., Finance Cttee); Chm., Zionist Fedn, 1975. *Publications:* The Manager and the Organization, 1961; Employee Security, 1962; European Science and Technology, 1968; Communication in an Expanding Organization, 1970; Reluctant Partnership, 1970; articles on management-trade union relations in American and British literature. *Recreations:* football, theatre, cinema. *Address:* 1 Beacon Hill, N7.

MOORBATH, Dr Stephen Erwin, FRS 1977; Senior Research Officer, Oxford University, since 1962; Fellow of Linacre College, since 1970; *b* 9 May 1929; *s* of Heinz Moosbach and Else Moosbach; *m* 1962, Pauline Tessier-Varlêt; one *s* one *d. Educ:* Lincoln Coll., Oxford Univ. (MA 1957, DPhil 1959). DSc Oxon 1969. Asst Experimental Officer, AERE, Harwell, 1948-51; Undergrad., Oxford Univ., 1951-54; Scientific Officer, AERE, Harwell, 1954-56; Research Fellow: Oxford Univ., 1956-61; MIT, 1961-62. Wollaston Fund, Geol Soc. of London, 1968; Liverpool Geol Soc. Medal, 1968. *Publications:* contribs to scientific jls and books. *Recreations:* music, philately, travel, linguistics. *Address:* 53 Bagley Wood Road, Kennington, Oxford OX1 5LY. *T:* Oxford 739507.

MOORCRAFT, Dennis Harry; Under-Secretary, Inland Revenue, since 1975; *b* 14 Aug. 1921; *s* of late Harry Moorcraft and Dorothy Moorcraft (*née* Simmons); *m* 1945, Ingeborg Utne, Bergen, Norway; one *s* one *d. Educ:* Gillingham County Grammar Sch. Tax Officer, Inland Revenue, 1938. RNVR, 1940-46. Inspector of Taxes, 1948; Sen. Inspector of Taxes, 1956; Principal Inspector of Taxes, 1963. *Recreations:* gardening, garden construction, croquet. *Address:* Board of Inland Revenue, Somerset House, WC2R 1LB.

MOORE, family name of Earl of Drogheda.

MOORE, Viscount; Henry Dermot Ponsonby Moore; photographer; *b* 14 Jan. 1937; *o s* and *heir* of 11th Earl of Drogheda, *qv*; *m* 1968, Eliza Lloyd (marr. diss. 1972), *d* of Stacy Barcroft Lloyd, Jr, and Mrs Paul Mellon. *Educ:* Eton; Trinity College, Cambridge. *Address:* 40 Warwick Avenue, W9.

MOORE, Alexander Wyndham Hume S.; *see* Stewart-Moore.

MOORE, Antony Ross, CMG 1965; *b* 30 May 1918; *o s* of late Arthur Moore and late Eileen Maillet; *m* 1st, 1941, Philippa Weigall (marr. diss.); two *d*; 2nd, 1963, Mary, *yr d* of late Prof. V. H. Galbraith, FBA, and of Dr Georgina Rosalie Galbraith (*née* Cole-Baker); one *s. Educ:* Rugby; King's Coll., Cambridge. Served in Friends Ambulance Unit, 1939-40; HM Forces, 1940-46. Apptd Mem. Foreign (subseq. Diplomatic) Service, Nov. 1946; transf. to Rome, 1947; FO, Nov. 1949; 1st Sec., 1950; transf. to Tel Aviv, 1952; acted as Chargé d'Affaires, 1953, 1954; apptd Consul, Sept. 1953; FO, 1955; UK Perm. Delegn to UN, NY, 1957; Counsellor and transf. to IDC, 1961; FO, 1962-64; Internat. Fellow, Center for Internat. Affairs, Harvard Univ., 1964-65; Regional Information Officer, Middle East, British Embassy, Beirut, 1965-67; Head of Eastern Dept, FO, 1967; retd from HM Diplomatic Service, Dec. 1968. Dir, Iranian Selection Trust, 1969-72. *Address:* Touchbridge, Boarstall, Aylesbury, Bucks. *T:* Brill 247.

MOORE, Archie Murrell Acheson, FRCS; Hon. FICS, 1962; FRSH; formerly Senior Surgeon and Associate Director,

Surgical Unit, London Hospital, Hon. Consultant Surgeon, since 1968; Hon. Consultant Surgeon: Poplar Hospital; King George Hospital, Ilford; Dr Barnardo's Homes; St Luke's Nursing Home for the Clergy; Arthur Stanley Institute for Rheumatism; *b* 14 Aug. 1904; *s* of Archie Moore, Aughnacloy, NI; *m* Marjorie Aitken (*d* 1977); one *s* two *d. Educ:* Boys' High Sch., Pretoria, SA; London Hosp. (Surgical Scholar; Buxton, Lethby and minor surgical prize); King's Coll. FRCS 1930; MRCS, LRCP 1927; FDSRCS 1973. Formerly: Surgeon Southend Gen. Hosp. and Essex CC. Examiner in Surgery: Univs of London and Durham; RCS; GDC. Past Mem. Bd of Examiners for primary FRCS; Vice-Pres. and Fellow and Past Treas., BMA; Past Pres. Metropolitan Counties Br. and Chm. Marylebone Div. BMA; Past Chm. Conf. of Consultants and Specialists, and Chm. Adv. Cttee, Commonwealth Medical Adv. Bureau; Chm. Library sub-Cttee BMA; Chm. Cttee on Accidents in Home. Pres. Bd of Registration of Medical Auxiliaries; Mem. Statutory Chiropodists' Bd; Mem. Governing Body British Post Graduate Medical Fedn; Mem. Bd of Governors, London Hosp.; Past Pres., British Supporting Gp, World Medical Assoc.; Past Hon. Pres. British Medical Students Assoc. Chairman: Academic Bd, London Hosp. Medical Coll.; Cttee of Management Medical Insurance Agency; British Medical Students Trust. Mem., Academy of Forensic Sciences; Visitor for GDC. James Sherren Centenary Meml Lectr, 1972. Gen. Comr of Income Tax. Past Master, Worshipful Soc. of Apothecaries, 1961-62, and Hon. Treas.; Liveryman Worshipful Co. of Barbers; Freeman City of London. Hon. Mem. Assoc. of Police Surgeons; FRSM; Fellow: Assoc. of Surgeons; Medical Soc. London. FZS. CStJ 1968. *Publications:* contribs to medical jls. *Recreation:* fencing. *Address:* 42 Crag Path, Aldeburgh, Suffolk. *T:* Aldeburgh 2598. *Clubs:* Athenæum, City Livery.

MOORE, Bobby; *see* Moore, Robert.

MOORE, Brian; novelist; *b* 25 Aug. 1921; *s* of James Bernard Moore, FRCS, Northern Ireland, and Eileen McFadden; *m* Jean Denney. Guggenheim Fellowship (USA), 1959; Canada Council Senior Fellowship (Canada), 1960. National Institute of Arts and Letters (USA) Fiction Award 1960; Governor-Gen. of Canada's Award for Fiction, 1960, etc. *Publications:* novels: The Lonely Passion of Judith Hearne, 1955; The Feast of Lupercal, 1956; The Luck of Ginger Coffey, 1960; An Answer from Limbo, 1962; The Emperor of Ice-Cream, 1965; I am Mary Dunne, 1968; Fergus, 1970; The Revolution Script, 1972; Catholics, 1972 (W. H. Smith Literary Award, 1973); The Great Victorian Collection, 1975 (James Tait Black Meml Award, 1976; Governor Gen. of Canada's Award for Fiction, 1976); The Doctor's Wife, 1976; *non -fiction:* Canada (with Editors of Life), 1964. *Address:* c/o Collins-Knowlton-Wing, 60 East 56th Street, New York, NY 10022, USA. *T:* Plaza 54200.

MOORE, Air Vice-Marshal Charles Stuart, CB 1962; OBE 1945; *b* London, 27 Feb. 1910; *s* of late E. A. Moore and late E. B. Moore (née Druce); *m* 1st, 1937, Anne (*d* 1957), *d* of Alfred Rogers; 2nd, 1961, Jean Mary, *d* of John Cameron Wilson; one *d. Educ:* Sutton Valence Sch.; RAF Coll., Cranwell. Commissioned in General Duties Branch, Dec. 1930; served in Egypt, 1932-34 and 1936-41; Sqdn Ldr 1936; Sudan, 1941-42; Wing Comdr 1940; 11 Group, 1943-44; Gp Capt. 1943; OC, OTU, 1944-45; Gp Capt. Org., HQFC, 1945-46; Staff Coll., Bracknell, 1946-47; Dep. Dir Plans, Air Ministry, London, 1947-49; Student, US National War Coll., Washington, 1949-50; Staff of USAF Air War Coll., Alabama, 1950-53; Air Commodore, 1953; AOC 66 Group, 1953-55; Dir of Intelligence, Air Ministry, London, 1955-58; AOA, NEAF, 1958-62; Actg Air Vice-Marshal, 1960; retired, 1962. Joined HM Foreign Service, Oct. 1962; posted to British Embassy, Tehran, Iran; left HM Diplomatic Service, March 1969. *Recreations:* music, photography and travelling. *Address:* Ferndene, The Avenue, Crowthorne, Berks. *T:* Crowthorne 2300. *Club:* Royal Air Force.

MOORE, Maj.-Gen. Denis Grattan, CB 1960; DL; retired; *b* 15 March 1909; *s* of Col F. G. Moore, CBE and Marian, *d* of Very Rev. W. H. Stone, Dean of Kilmore; *m* 1st, 1932, Alexandra, *d* of W. H. Wann; two *d*; 2nd, 1946, Beatrice Glynn, *d* of W. S. Williamson; one adopted *d. Educ:* Wellington Coll.; Royal Military College, Sandhurst. Commissioned 1929, Royal Inniskilling Fusiliers; GSO1, HQ Tenth Army, 1943; Asst Dir of Artillery (Weapons), HQ Eighth Army, 1944; GSO1, War Office, 1946; GSO1 (Col) War Office, 1952-54; comd 47 Infantry Bde, TA, 1954-57; Dir of Weapons and Development, War Office, 1958-60; Dir of Equipment Policy, War Office, 1960-61; Chief, Jt Services Liaison Staff, BAOR, 1961-63. Col, The Royal Inniskilling Fusiliers, 1960-66. Chm., Ulster Timber Growers Organisation, 1965-. High Sheriff, Co. Tyrone, 1969; DL Co. Tyrone, 1974. *Recreations:* shooting, fishing. *Address:*

Mountfield Lodge, Omagh, Co. Tyrone, N Ireland. *T:* Mountfield 206. *Club:* Naval and Military.

MOORE, Mrs D(oris) Langley, OBE 1971; FRSL; Founder (1955) and former Adviser, Museum of Costume, Assembly Rooms, Bath; author. Has done varied literary work in connection with films, television, and ballet, and has specialized in promoting the study of costume by means of exhibns and lectures in England and abroad. Designer of clothes for period films. *Publications: fiction:* A Winter's Passion, 1932; The Unknown Eros, 1935; They Knew Her When..., 1938 (subseq. re-published as A Game of Snakes and Ladders); Not at Home, 1948; All Done by Kindness, 1951; My Caravaggio Style, 1959; *non-fiction:* Anacreon: 29 Odes, 1926; The Technique of the Love Affair, 1928; Pandora's Letter Box, A Discourse on Fashionable Life, 1929; E. Nesbit, A Biography, 1933 (rev. 1966); The Vulgar Heart, An Enquiry into the Sentimental Tendencies of Public Opinion, 1945; The Woman in Fashion, 1949; The Child in Fashion, 1953; Pleasure, A Discursive Guide Book, 1953; The Late Lord Byron, 1961; Marie and the Duke of H, The Daydream Love Affair of Marie Bashkirtseff, 1966; Fashion through Fashion Plates, 1771-1970, 1971; Lord Byron: Accounts Rendered, 1974 (Rose Mary Crawshay Prize, awarded by British Academy, 1975); Ada, Countess of Lovelace, 1977; (with June Langley Moore): Our Loving Duty, 1932; The Pleasure of Your Company, 1933. *Recreation:* Byron research. *Address:* 5 Prince Albert Road, NW1.

MOORE, Dudley Stuart John; actor (stage, films, TV and radio); composer (film music and incidental music for plays, etc); *b* 19 April 1935; *s* of Ada Francis and John Moore; *m* Suzy Kendall (marr. diss.); *m* Tuesday Weld; one *s. Educ:* County High Sch., Dagenham, Essex; Magdalen Coll., Oxford (BA, BMus). *Stage:* Beyond the Fringe, 1960-62 (London), 1962-64 (Broadway, New York); Vic Lewis, John Dankworth Jazz Bands, 1959-60; composed incidental music, Royal Court Theatre (various plays), 1958-60. *BBC TV:* own series with Peter Cook: Not only... but also, 1964, 1966, 1970; in the sixties, *ITV:* Goodbye again; Royal Command Performance. Play it again Sam, Woody Allen, Globe Theatre, 1970. *BBC TV Series:* It's Lulu, not to mention Dudley Moore, 1972. Behind the Fringe, Cambridge Theatre, 1972-73; Good Evening, Broadway, New York, 1973-74; Tour of USA, 1975. Various TV and radio guest spots with Jazz piano trio. *Films* 1966-73: The Wrong Box, 30 is a dangerous age Cynthia, Bedazzled, Monte Carlo or Bust, The Bed-sitting room, Alice in Wonderland. *Film music* composed for: Bedazzled, 30 is a dangerous age Cynthia, The Staircase and various TV films. *Publication:* Dud and Pete: The Dagenham Dialogues, 1971. *Recreations:* films, theatre, music. *Address:* c/o Oscar Beuselinck, Wright & Webb, 10 Soho Square, W1. *T:* 01-734 9641; c/o Mrs M. Walker. *T:* 01-352 4404. *Club:* White Elephant.

MOORE, Rt. Rev. Edward Francis Butler; *see* Kilmore and Elphin and Ardagh, Bishop of.

MOORE, Sir Edward Stanton, 2nd Bt *cr* 1923; OBE 1970; *b* 1910; *s* of Major E. C. H. Moore (killed, Vimy Ridge, 1917) and Kathleen Margaret (*d* 1970), *d* of H. S. Oliver, Sudbury, Suffolk; *S* grandfather, 1923; *m* 1946, Margaret, *er d* of T. J. Scott-Cotterell. *Educ:* Mill Hill Sch.; Cambridge. RAF 1940-46; Wing Cdr Special Duties; Managing Director, Spain and Western Mediterranean, BEA, 1965-72. Pres., British Chamber of Commerce in Spain, 1969-71; Dir, European British Chambers of Commerce, 1970-72. FCIT. *Heir: u* Eric Edward James Moore, DSO [*b* 24 Sept. 1894; *m* 1928, Gertrude, *d* of F. F. Vanderhoef, New York; one *d*]. *Address:* Church House, Sidlesham, Sussex. *T:* Sidlesham 369. *Clubs:* Special Forces; Royal Yachting Association, Chichester Yacht.

MOORE, (the Worshipful Chancellor the Rev.) E(velyn) Garth; barrister-at-law; Chancellor, Vicar-General and Official Principal of Diocese of Durham since 1954, of Diocese of Southwark since 1948 and of Diocese of Gloucester since 1957 (and Official Principal of Archdeaconries of Lewisham, Southwark, Kingston-on-Thames and Ely); Vicar, Guild Church of St Mary Abchurch, London, since 1972; Fellow of Corpus Christi College, Cambridge, since 1947, and formerly Lecturer in Law (Director of Studies in Law, 1947-72); High Bailiff of Ely Cathedral since 1961; Member Governing Body of St Chad's College, Durham, since 1955; President, Churches' Fellowship for Psychical and Spiritual Studies, since 1963; Church Commissioner since 1964; *b* 6 Feb. 1906; *y s* of His Honour the late Judge (Robert Ernest) Moore and late Hilda Mary, *d* of Rev. John Davis Letts; unmarried. *Educ:* The Hall, Belsize Sch.; Durham Sch.; Trinity Coll., Cambridge (MA); Cuddesdon Theol Coll., 1962. Deacon, 1962; Priest, 1962. Called to Bar, Gray's Inn, 1928; SE Circuit. Formerly: Tutor of

Gray's Inn; Lector of Trinity Coll., Cambridge; Mem. Gen. Council of Bar and of Professional Conduct Cttee. Commnd 2nd Lt RA, 1940; Major on staff of JAG; served at WO and throughout Great Britain, N Ireland, Paiforce, Middle East (for a time local Lt-Col), Greece, etc. Mem. of Church Assembly (for Dio. Ely), 1955-62. JP and Dep. Chm. of QS, Hunts, 1948-63 and Cambs, 1959-63; Lectr in Criminal Procedure, Council of Legal Educn, 1957-68, Lectr in Evidence, 1952-68. Council, St David's Coll., Lampeter, 1949-65 and Westcott House, 1961-65. Legal Assessor to Disciplinary Cttee, RCVS, 1963-68. Pres., Sion Coll., 1977-78. Vis. Prof., Khartoum Univ., 1961. Mere's Preacher, Cambridge Univ., 1965. *Publications:* An Introduction to English Canon Law, 1966; 8th Edn (with Suppl.) of Kenny's Cases on Criminal Law; (jt) Ecclesiastical Law, in Halsbury's Laws of England (3rd edn); Believe it or Not: Christianity and psychical research, 1977; various contribs mainly to legal and theological jls. *Recreations:* travel, architecture, furniture, etc, psychical research. *Address:* Corpus Christi College, Cambridge. *T:* 59418; 1 Raymond Buildings, Gray's Inn, WC1. *T:* 01-242 3734; St Mary Abchurch, EC4. *T:* 01-626 0306. *Clubs:* Gresham; Pitt (Cambridge).

MOORE, Maj.-Gen. (retired) Frederick David, CB 1955; CBE 1954; *b* 27 Nov. 1902; *s* of Sir Frederick W. Moore; *m* 1932, Anna Morrell Hamilton (*d* 1974), *d* of Col T. H. M. Clarke, CMG, DSO; one *s. Educ:* Wellington Coll.; RMA Woolwich. Commnd in RFA, 1923. Served War of 1939-45: BEF 1940, 5th Regt RHA; BLA, 1944-45, CO 5th Regt RHA and CRA 53rd (W) Div.; GOC 5th AA Group, 1953-55; retd, 1956. DL Beds, 1958, Vice-Lieutenant, 1964-70. Officer Order of Crown (Belgian); Croix de Guerre (Belgian), 1940, with palm, 1945. *Recreations:* country pursuits. *Address:* Riverview, Bunclody, Co. Wexford, Ireland. *T:* Enniscorthy 7184. *Club:* Army and Navy.

MOORE, Frederick Thomas, OBE 1943; FRCS, FRCSE; Consulting Plastic Surgeon to King's College Hospital, London, since 1948; Plastic Unit East Grinstead since 1948; *b* 19 Oct. 1913; *s* of Francis Moore and Rose Perry; *m* 1957; Margrethe Johanne Holland (actress, as Greta Gynt); one *d. Educ:* St Bartholomew's Hosp. MRCS, LRCP 1936; FRCSE 1939; FRCS 1945. Served War of 1939-45 (OBE): RAF, Plastic Surgeon, 1939-48. Mem. Council, British Assoc. Plastic Surgeons, 1949. Founder Mem., British Hand Club. Legion of Honour, 1948. *Publications:* numerous on surgical problems. *Recreations:* golf, sailing, writing, research (medical). *Address:* Flat 1, 30 Harley Street, W1N 1AB. *T:* 01-636 0955. *Clubs:* Royal Thames Yacht; Monaco Yacht.

MOORE, Prof. Geoffrey Herbert; Professor of American Literature and Head of the Department of American Studies, University of Hull, since 1962; *b* 10 June 1920; *e s* of late Herbert Jonathan Moore, Norwich; *m* 1947, Pamela Marguerite (marr. diss. 1962), *d* of Bertram Munn, Twickenham; one *s* one *d. Educ:* Mitcham Grammar Sch.; Emmanuel Coll., Cambridge; Univ. of Paris. 1st Cl. English Tripos, Cambridge, 1946; MA 1951. War Service (Air Ministry and RAF), 1939-43. Instr in English, Univ. of Wisconsin, 1947-49; Vis. Prof. of English, Univs of Kansas City and New Mexico, 1948, 1949; Asst Prof. of English, Tulane Univ., 1949-51; Vis. Prof. of English, Univ. of Southern California and Claremont Coll., 1950; Extra Mural Lectr, London and Cambridge Univs, 1951-52 and 1953-54; Editor and Producer, BBC Television Talks, 1952-53; Rose Morgan Prof., Univ. of Kansas, 1954-55; Lectr in Amer. Lit., Manchester Univ., 1955-59; Vis. Lectr, Univs of Mainz, Göttingen and Frankfurt, 1959; Rockefeller Fellow, Harvard Univ., 1959-60; Sen. Lectr in Amer. Lit., Manchester Univ., 1960-62; Dean, Faculty of Arts, Univ. of Hull, 1967-69. Visiting Lecturer: Univs of Montpellier, Aix-en-Provence and Nice, 1967, 1971; Univs of Frankfurt, Heidelberg, Mainz, Saarbrücken, Tübingen, 1967, 1968; Univs of Perpignan, Turin, Florence, Pisa, Rome, New Delhi, Hyderabad, Madras, Bombay, Calcutta, 1971; Fellow, Sch. of Letters, Indiana Univ., Summer 1970; Visiting Professor: York Univ., Toronto, 1969-70; Univ. of Tunis, Spring 1970, 1971; Harvard, 1971; Univs of Düsseldorf, Heidelberg, Freiburg, Mainz, 1972; Res. Fellow, Univ. of California at San Diego, 1974. Mem. Cttee, British Assoc. for Amer. Studies, 1957-60. Sen. Scholar Award, Amer. Coun. of Learned Socs, 1965. Ed. and Founder, The Bridge (Cambridge lit. mag.), 1946. *Publications:* Voyage to Chivalry (under pseud.), 1947; Poetry from Cambridge in Wartime, 1947; The Penguin Book of Modern American Verse, 1954; (ed) 58 Short Stories by O. Henry, 1956; Poetry Today, 1958; American Literature and the American Imagination, 1964; American Literature, 1964; The Penguin Book of American Verse, 1977; articles in TLS, Amer. Mercury, BBC Quarterly, Kenyon Review, Review of English Lit., The Year's Work in English Studies, and other scholarly and literary jls. *Recreations:*

swimming, driving. *Address:* The University, Hull, HU6 7RX. *T:* Hull 46311. *Club:* Savile.

MOORE, George; Under Secretary and Regional Industrial Director, North West Regional Office, Department of Industry, since 1976; *b* 7 Oct. 1923; *s* of George Moore and Agnes Bryce Moore; *m* 1946, Marjorie Pamela Davies; three *s. Educ:* Coatbridge Secondary School; University Coll. and Royal Technical Coll., Cardiff (Jt Engineering Diploma); Hull Univ. (Post Graduate Diploma in Economics). Graduate Engineer, Electricity Authority, 1948-50; Development Engineer, Anglo-Iranian Oil Co., Abadan, 1950-52; Chief Electrical Engineer, Distillers' Solvents Div., 1952-58; Management Consultant, Urwick, Orr & Partners, 1958-64; Executive Dir, Burton Group, 1964-66; Group Managing Dir, Spear & Jackson International Ltd and Chm., USA Subsidiary, 1966-75; Dir of cos in Sweden, France, India, Australia, Canada, S Africa, 1966-75. *Recreations:* golf, sailing. *Address:* 56 Common Lane, Sheffield S11 7TG. *T:* Sheffield 303818. *Clubs:* Reform; Manchester (Manchester).

MOORE, Rear-Adm. (retired) George Dunbar, CBE 1944; *b* 10 Oct. 1893; *s* of Dr John Irwin and Susan Moore; *m* 1923, Doretta Ziele Russell; one *d. Educ:* The Southport Sch., Queensland; Brisbane Grammar Sch.; HMS Conway. Sub-Lt RAN 1914; Lt 1916; Comdr 1928; Capt. 1935; Commodore, 1942; Acting Rear-Adm., 1944; commanded: HMS Dunoon, 1932-33; HMAS Penguin, 1934-35; HMAS Yarra, 1936-37; HMAS Stuart, 1937-38; HMS Curaçoa, 1939; HMS Dauntless, 1939-41; HMAS Australia, 1941; HMAS Canberra, 1942. 2nd Naval Mem., Australian Commonwealth Naval Board, 1942-44; Flag Officer-in-Charge, New South Wales, 1944-50; Minister for Australia in the Philippines, 1950-55, retired. *Address:* Bank of New South Wales, King Street and George Street, Sydney, NSW 2000, Australia. *Club:* Royal Sydney Golf (Sydney).

MOORE, His Honour George Edgar; HM First Deemster and Clerk of the Rolls, Isle of Man, 1969-74; *b* 13 July 1907; *er s* of Ramsey Bignall Moore, OBE, formerly HM Attorney-General for Isle of Man, and Agnes Cannell Moore; *m* 1937, Joan Mary Kissack; one *s* one *d. Educ:* Rydal School. Served in RAF, 1940-45 (Sqdn Ldr). Admitted to Manx Bar, 1930; Attorney-General for Isle of Man, 1957-63; HM Second Deemster, 1963-69; MLC; Chairman: IoM Criminal Injuries Compensation Tribunal, 1967-69; IoM Income Tax Appeal Comrs, 1969-74; Tynwald Common Market Select Cttee, 1970-74; Mem., Exec. Council Manx Museum and Nat. Trust, 1970-74; Chm. of Directors: Commercial Bank of Wales (IoM) Ltd, 1975-; Securicor (IoM) Ltd, 1975-; Chm., Trustees of Manx Blind Welfare Soc.; Pres., Isle of Man Badminton Assoc., 1953-72; Chm., Manx War Work Trust; Hon. County Representative of Royal Air Force Benevolent Assoc., 1948-72. *Address:* Hillcrest, Alexander Drive, Douglas, Isle of Man. *Club:* Ellan Vannin (IoM).

MOORE, George Herbert, MSc; FPS; FRIC; *b* 1 June 1903; *s* of late R. Herbert Moore and Mabel Moore, Bath; *m* 1931, Dora, *d* of Frederick and Emily Blackmore, Bath; one *d. Educ:* King Edward's Sch., Bath; Bath Coll. of Chemistry and Pharmacy. FPS 1928, FRIC 1943; MSc Bristol 1953. Merchant Venturers' Technical Coll., Bristol; Lectr in Pharmaceutical Chemistry, 1929-38; Head of Science Dept, 1938-50; Vice-Principal, Bristol Coll. of Technology, 1950-54; Principal, Bristol Coll. of Science and Technology, 1954-66; Vice-Chancellor, Bath Univ., 1966-69. Vice-Pres. Royal Inst. of Chemistry, 1955-57. Hon. LLD Bath, 1968. *Recreations:* music, photography. *Address:* Hilcot, Horsecombe Vale, Combe Down, Bath BA2 5QR. *T:* Bath 837417. *Club:* Bristol Savages (Bristol).

MOORE, Gerald, CBE 1954; pianoforte accompanist; *b* Watford, Herts, 30 July 1899; *e s* of David Frank Moore, Tiverton, Devon; *m* Enid Kathleen, *d* of Montague Richard, Beckenham, Kent. *Educ:* Watford Grammar Sch.; Toronto Univ. Studied piano in Toronto; toured Canada as a boy pianist; returning to England, devoted himself to accompanying and chamber music. Associated with world's leading singers and instrumentalists. Festivals of Edinburgh, Salzburg, Holland, etc. Retired from concert platform 1967, but continues to make records and to lecture and gives broadcasts and television talks on music and the art of accompanying; Ensemble Classes in USA, Tokyo, Stockholm, Helsinki, Dartington Hall, Salzburg Mozarteum, London S Bank Fest. Awarded Cobbett Gold Medal, 1951, for services to Chamber Music; Pres. Incorporated Soc. of Musicians, 1962. Hon. RAM 1962. Grand Prix du Disque: Amsterdam, 1968, 1970; Paris, 1970; Granados Medal, Barcelona, 1971; Hugo Wolf Medal, Vienna, 1973. Hon. DLitt Sussex, 1968; Hon. MusD Cambridge, 1973. *Publications:* The Unashamed Accompanist, 1943 (rev. edn 1957); Careers in Music, 1950; Singer and Accompanist, 1953; Am I Too Loud?,

1962; The Schubert Song Cycles, 1975; Farewell Recital, 1978; arrangements of songs and folk songs. *Recreations:* reading, bridge, gardening. *Address:* Beechwood Cottage, Penn Bottom, Penn, Bucks. *T:* Penn 2507. *Clubs:* Savile, MCC.

MOORE, Gordon Charles; Chief Executive, City of Bradford Metropolitan Council, since 1974; *b* 23 July 1928; *s* of John Edward and Jessie Hamilton Moore; *m* 1956, Ursula Rawle; one *s* two *d*. *Educ:* Uppingham; St Catharine's Coll., Cambridge (MA, LLB). Solicitor. FBIM. Legal Asst, Cambs CC, 1955-56; Asst Solicitor: Worcester CB, 1956-58; Bath CB, 1958-60; Sen. Asst Solicitor: Bath CB, 1960-63; Croydon CB, 1963-65; Asst Town Clerk, Croydon LB, 1965; Dep. Town Clerk, Bradford CB, 1965-68, Town Clerk, 1968-73. Silver Jubilee Medal, 1977. *Recreations:* music, railways, supporting Yorkshire County Cricket. *Address:* City Hall, Bradford, West Yorks BD1 1HY. *T:* Bradford 29577.

MOORE, Brig. Guy Newton, CBE 1941; DFC; ED; Chartered Accountant; Senior Partner, A. Capper Moore & Sons; *b* 13 Jan. 1893; *s* of A. Capper and Alice Eleanor Moore; *m* 1922, Marguerite Thompson; three *d*. *Educ:* Wesley Coll., Melbourne. Served with Royal Flying Corps and Royal Air Force (Capt.), 1916-18; Hon. Sqdn Leader, Citizens Air Force (Australia); Chief Paymaster, AIF. Dir of Finance Administration, Australian Commonwealth Forces, 1939-45. *Recreations:* golf, swimming, bowls. *Address:* 34 Queen's Road, Melbourne, Victoria 3004, Australia. *Clubs:* Naval and Military, Emerald Country, RACV (Melbourne).

MOORE, Harry T(hornton); Research Professor, Southern Illinois University, since 1957; *b* Oakland, California, 2 Aug. 1908; *s* of Lt-Col H. T. Moore, US Army; *m* 1st, Winifred Sheehan; one *s* one *d*; 2nd, 1946, Beatrice Walker. *Educ:* Univ. of Chicago (PhB); Northwestern Univ. (MA); Boston Univ. (PhD). Instructor: Ill. Inst. of Techn., 1940-41; Inst., Northwestern Univ., 1941-42. Served USAAF, 2nd World War, now Lt-Col USAF Reserve. Dept of Hist. and Lit., Babson Inst., 1947-57 (now Babson Coll.); Prof. of English, Southern Illinois Univ., 1957-. Visiting Professor: Univ. of Colorado, 1959 and 1963-64; Columbia Univ. and New York Univ., 1961; Staff Mem., Univ. of Nottingham Lawrence Summer Sch., 1971 and 1975. Pres. of Coll. English Assoc., 1961. Editor: series: Crosscurrents/Modern Critiques; Crosscurrents: Modern Fiction; on editorial adv. boards of Virginia Woolf Qly, D. H. Lawrence Rev., and English Language Notes. FRSL 1952-; Guggenheim Fellowships, 1958, 1960. *Publications:* The Novels of John Steinbeck, 1939; The Life and Works of D. H. Lawrence, 1951; The Intelligent Heart, 1955; Poste Restante, 1956; E. M. Forster, 1965; 20th Century French Literature (2 vols), 1966; The Age of the Modern, 1971; The Priest of Love: a life of D. H. Lawrence, 1974; Henry James and his World, 1974; Co-author: D. H. Lawrence and his World: a Pictorial Biography, 1966; 20th Century German Literature, 1967; (jtly) 20th Century Russian Literature, 1974; Co-Editor: The Achievement of D. H. Lawrence, 1953; The Human Prospect (by Lewis Mumford), 1956; Phœnix II: Uncollected, Unpublished and other Prose Works by D. H. Lawrence, 1968; The Richard Aldington-Lawrence Durrell Letters, 1977; Co-Translator: Tragedy is Not Enough (by Karl Jaspers); Editor: D. H. Lawrence's Letters to Bertrand Russell, 1948; D. H. Lawrence's Essays on Sex, Literature, and Censorship, 1953; A D. H. Lawrence Miscellany, 1959; Selected Letters of Rainer Maria Rilke, 1960; The World of Lawrence Durrell, 1962; The Collected Letters of D. H. Lawrence, 1962 (2 vols); Contemporary American Novelists, 1964; The Elizabethan Age, 1965; contributed NY Times Book Review; Saturday Review; Kenyon Review; New Republic, etc. *Recreation:* listening to Shakespearean recordings. *Address:* 922 South Division Street, Carterville, Illinois 62918, USA. *T:* 618-985-2014. *Clubs:* Cliff Dwellers (Chicago); PEN.

MOORE, Henry, OM 1963; CH 1955; FBA 1966; Hon. FRIBA; sculptor; *b* Castleford, Yorks, 30 July 1898; *s* of Raymond Spencer Moore and Mary Baker; *m* 1929, Irene Radetzky; one *d*. *Educ:* Castleford Grammar Sch. After serving European War, 1917-19, in Army, studied at Leeds Sch. of Art and Royal College of Art. Official War Artist, 1940-42. A Trustee: Tate Gallery, 1941-48 and 1949-56; National Gallery, 1955-63 and 1964-74; Member: Arts Council, 1963-67; Royal Fine Art Commn, 1947-71. Formed Henry Moore Foundation, 1977. *Major exhibitions of his work held:* London 1928, 1931, 1933, 1935, 1936, 1940, 1945, 1946, 1948, 1951, 1953, 1955, 1960, 1961, 1963, 1965, 1967, 1968, 1974, 1975, 1976; Leeds, 1941; New York, 1946; Chicago, 1947; San Francisco, 1947; Australia Tour, 1947; Venice Biennale, 1948 (of which he was awarded First Prize for Sculpture); Europe Tour, 1949-51; Cape Town, 1951; Scandinavian Tour, 1952-53; Rotterdam, 1953; Antwerp,

1953; São Paulo, 1953 (of which he was awarded 1st Prize in Foreign Sculpture); Germany Tour, 1953-54; USA Tour, 1955; Basle, 1955; Yugoslavia Tour, 1955; Canada, New Zealand, Australia, RSA Tour, 1955-58; Paris, 1957; Arnhem, 1957; Japan Tour, 1959; Spain and Portugal Tour, 1959; Poland Tour, 1959; Europe Tour, 1960-61; Edinburgh, 1961; USA Tour, 1963; Latin America Tour, 1964-65; USA Tour, 1966-68; East Europe Tour, 1966; Israel Tour, 1966; Canada Tour, 1967-68; Holland and Germany Tour, 1968; Japan Tour, 1969-70; New York, 1970; Iran Tour, 1971; Munich, 1971; Paris, 1971; Florence, 1972; Luxembourg, 1973; Los Angeles, 1973; Toronto, 1974; Scandinavia Tour, 1975-76; Zurich, 1976; Paris, 1977. *Examples of work are in:* the Tate Gallery, British Museum, the Museum of Modern Art, New York, the Allbright Knox Art Gallery, Buffalo, and other public galleries in the UK, USA, Germany, Italy, Switzerland, Holland, Sweden, Denmark, Norway, France, Australia, Brazil, Israel, South Africa and Japan. Foreign Corresp. Mem., Acad. Flamande des Sciences; For. Mem., Acad. Lettres et Beaux Arts de Belgique; For. Mem., Swedish Royal Academy of Fine Arts; For. Hon. Mem., Amer. Acad. of Arts and Sciences; Mem. de l'Institut, Acad. des Beaux-Arts, Paris, 1975; Hon. Fellow, Churchill Coll., Cambridge. Hon. Degrees: Dr of Lit: Leeds, London, Reading, Oxford, Hull, York, Durham; Dr of Arts: Yale, Harvard; Dr of Law: Cambridge, St Andrews, Sheffield, Toronto, Manchester; Dr of Letters: Sussex, Warwick, Leicester, York (Toronto), Columbia; Dr of Engineering, Berlin; Hon. Dr, RCA, 1967; Hon. Prof. Emeritus of Sculpture, Carrara Acad. of Fine Arts, 1967. Feltrinelli Foundn Internat. Sculpture Prize, 1963; Erasmus Prize, 1968; Einstein Prize, 1968. Biancoumano Prize, 1973; Goslar Prize, 1975. Order of Merit, West Germany, 1968; Order of Merit, Italy, 1972; Commandeur de l'Ordre des Arts et des Lettres, Paris, 1973. *Publications:* Heads, Figures and Ideas, 1958; Henry Moore on Sculpture (with Philip James), 1966; Catalogues Raisonné: Sculpture, 4 vols; Graphics, 2 vols; principal monographs by Will Grohmann, John Russell, Robert Melville, Kenneth Clark, (drawings) David Finn, John Hedgecoe, G. C. Argan, Henry Seldis. *Address:* Hoglands, Perry Green, Much Hadham, Herts. *T:* Much Hadham 2566. *Club:* Athenæum.

MOORE, Henry Roderick, CBE 1971; Director, Hill Samuel Group Ltd, since 1949; Chairman: Associated Engineering Ltd, 1955-75; Associated Engineering (SA) Ltd, 1967-76; Staveley Industries, since 1970; Vice-Chairman, Philip Hill Investment Trust Ltd, since 1949; Director: Stone-Platt Industries Ltd, since 1967; Estates House Investment Trust Ltd, 1975-76; *b* 19 Aug. 1915; *er s* of late Roderick Edward Moore; *m* 1944, Beatrice Margaret, *d* of late Major J. W. Seigne; one *s* one *d*. *Educ:* Malvern Coll.; Pembroke Coll., Cambridge. Qualified as mem. of Institute of Chartered Accountants, 1939. Served War of 1939-45: North Africa, Italy, Europe; 2nd Lt Royal Fusiliers, 1939; Lt-Col, 1944. Chm., Bd of Governors, The London Hospital, 1960-74; Mem. Council, British Heart Foundn; Dep. Chm., Adv. Panel on Institutional Finance in New Towns; Chm., North East Thames RHA, 1974-; Mem., Adv. Gp on Commercial Property Develt, 1975-76. High Sheriff of Bucks, 1966. *Address:* Bourton Grounds, near Buckingham. *T:* Buckingham 2241; 70 Chesterfield House, Chesterfield Gardens, W1Y 5TD. *T:* 01-492 0666. *Clubs:* White's, Pratt's; Leander; Rand (Johannesburg).

MOORE, Adm. Sir Henry Ruthven, GCB 1946 (KCB 1942; CB 1939); CVO 1937; DSO 1916; DL; *b* 29 Aug. 1886; *e s* of late Col Henry Moore, JP, late King's Own Royal Regiment; *m* 1908, Katherine Henley Joan (*d* 1945), *d* of late H. J. Gillespie, barrister-at-law, The Gables, Windsor; one *s* one *d*; *m* 1948, Catherine Harlow Wilkinson, *widow* of Vice-Adm. T. S. Wilkinson, USN, and *d* of late Richard Austin Harlow, Hockley, Arlington, Virginia. *Educ:* Sherborne. Entered HMS Britannia as Naval Cadet, 1902; Lt, 1908; Comdr, 1919; Capt., 1926; Rear-Adm., 1938; Vice-Adm., 1941; Adm., 1945; served on staff of Royal Naval Staff Coll., 1919-21; Naval Asst Sec. to the Cttee of Imperial Defence, 1921-24; Asst Sec. to British Delegation to Conference for Limitation of Armament, Washington, 1921-22, and at Geneva, 1927; attended Imperial Defence Coll., 1927; Dep. Dir of Plans Div., Admiralty, 1930-32; Dir, 1932-33; HMS Neptune, 1933-35; Cdre 1st Class and Chief of Staff to C-in-C Home Fleet, 1936-38; ADC to the King, 1937-38; Chief of Staff to Comdr-in-Chief, Portsmouth, 1938-39; Rear-Adm. Commanding 3rd Cruiser Sqdn, 1939-40; Asst Chief of Naval Staff (Trade), 1940-41; Vice-Chief of Naval Staff, 1941-43; Second-in-Command Home Fleet, 1943-44; C-in-C Home Fleet, 1944-45; Head of British Naval Mission, Washington, DC, Dec. 1945-Sept. 1948; Naval Representative of British Chiefs of Staff on Military Staff Cttee of Security Council, UN, 1946-48; Comdr-in-Chief, The Nore, 1948-50; First and Principal Naval ADC to the King, 1948-51; retired list, 1951.

Served in Grand Fleet in European War of 1914-18 (despatches, DSO); War of 1939-45 (despatches). DL Kent, 1957; High Sheriff of Kent, 1959-60. OStJ. Chief Comdr, Legion of Merit (USA). *Address:* The Beck, Wateringbury, Kent. *T:* Maidstone 812566.

MOORE, Rear-Adm. Humfrey John Bradley, CBE 1951; RI 1955; *b* 16 May 1898; *s* of Harry Farr Bradley and Mabel Clara Adelaide Moore; *m* 1925, Doris May Best; one *s* one *d. Educ:* Rugby Sch. Served European War, Grand Fleet, 1916-18. Thereafter various afloat and administrative posts, including Royal Naval Engineering Coll., Devonport staff, Admiralty (Engineer-in-Chief's and Naval Ordnance Depts) and Manager, Engineering Depts at Rosyth and Devonport and Staff of C-in-C, The Nore; retired 1952. *Recreations:* painting, music. *Address:* Prestons Cottage, Ightham, Kent. *T:* Borough Green 882668. *Club:* Arts.

MOORE, Gen. Sir (James Newton) Rodney, GCVO 1966 (KCVO 1959); KCB 1960 (CB 1955); CBE 1948; DSO 1944; PMN 1961; Chief Steward, Hampton Court Palace, since 1975; *b* 9 June 1905; *s* of late Maj.-Gen. Sir Newton Moore, KCMG, Perth, WA; *m* 1st, 1927, Olive Marion (marr. diss., 1947), *d* of late Lt-Col Sir Thomas Bilbe Robinson, GBE, KCMG; one *s* two *d*; 2nd, 1947, Patricia Margery Lillian, *d* of late James Catty, New York. *Educ:* Harrow; RMC, Sandhurst. Gazetted to Grenadier Guards, 1925, and served with Regt in England until 1933, then served in Egypt until 1936. Returned to England, 1936, and at outbreak of European War was at staff Coll., Camberley. Served War of 1939-45 (despatches, DSO): at GHQ Home Forces, 1940; Bde Major 30th Guards Bde and 6th Guards Armd Bde, 1940-42; GSO1, Guards Armd Div., 1942-44; Comd 2nd Armd Bn Gren. Guards in campaign NW Europe, 1944-45. Brig. comdg 8th Brit. Inf. Bde, Germany, Egypt and Palestine, 1945-46; Comd 1st Guards Bde, Palestine, 1946-47; Chief of Staff, HQ London Dist, 1948-50; idc 1950; Dep. Adjt Gen. HQ BAOR, 1951-53; Chief of Staff, Allied Forces, Northern Europe, 1953-55; GOC, 1st Infantry Div., MELF, 1955; GOC, 10th Armoured Div., 1955-57; Gen. Officer Commanding, London Dist; Maj.-Gen. Commanding Household Brigade, 1957-59; Chief of the Armed Forces Staff and Dir of Border Operations, Federation of Malaya, 1959-64; Defence Services Sec., Min. of Defence, 1964-66, retd. ADC Gen., 1965-66; Gentleman Usher to the Queen, 1966-75, Extra Gentleman Usher, 1975-. Col Comdt, HAC, 1966-76. Officer Order of Crown of Belgium and Belgian Croix de Guerre with Palm, 1944. Panglima Mangku Negara, 1961. *Recreations:* hunting, polo, fishing. *Address:* Hampton Court Palace, East Molesey, Surrey. *Clubs:* Cavalry and Guards, Turf.

MOORE, Miss Jocelyn A. M., (Mrs David Symon), FRCS; FRCOG; retired; Professor of Obstetrics and Gynæcology, Ahmadu Bello University Hospital, Zaria, Nigeria, 1969-73; Hon. Consultant Obstetrician and Gynæcologist, Royal Free Hospital; Emeritus Consultant, South London Hospital for Women; *b* 29 Aug. 1904; *e d* of Maj.-Gen. Sir John Moore, KCMG, CB, FRCVS; *m* 1941, David Symon (decd); no *c. Educ:* Wycombe Abbey Sch., Bucks; Royal Free Hospital School of Medicine. Served RAMC, 1941-45, as Specialist in Gynaecology, in the UK, Belgium and Germany. Mem. BMA; Mem. Medical Women's Fedn. *Address:* The Boot, 6 Upper Street, Quainton, Aylesbury, Bucks. *T:* Quainton 229.

MOORE, Hon. Sir John (Cochrane), Kt 1976; President, Australian Conciliation and Arbitration Commission, since 1973; *b* 5 Nov. 1915; *s* of E. W. Moore and L. J. Moore; *m* 1946, Julia Fay, *d* of Brig. G. Drake-Brockman; two *s* two *d. Educ:* N Sydney Boys' High Sch.; Univ. of Sydney (BA, LLB). Private, AIF, 1940; R of O Hon. Captain 1945. Admitted NSW Bar, 1940; Dept of External Affairs, 1945; 2nd Sec., Aust. Mission to UN, 1946; practice, NSW Bar, 1947-59; Dep. Pres., Commonwealth Conciliation and Arbitration Commn, 1959-72, Actg Pres. 1972-73. Chm. (Pres.), Aust. Council of Nat. Trusts, 1969-; President: Nat. Trust of Aust. (NSW), 1966-69; Ind. Relations Soc. of NSW, 1972-73; Ind. Relations Soc. of Aust., 1973-74. *Recreations:* swimming, reading. *Address:* Law Courts Building, Queen's Square, Sydney, NSW 2000, Australia. *T:* 238-0344. *Club:* Athenæum (Melbourne).

MOORE, John Edward Michael; MP (C) Croydon Central since 1974; Chairman, Dean Witter (International) Ltd, since 1975, Director since 1968; *b* 26 Nov. 1937; *s* of Edward O. Moore; *m* 1962, Sheila Sarah Tillotson; two *s* one *d. Educ:* London Sch. of Economics (BSc Econ). Nat. Service, Royal Sussex Regt, Korea, 1955-57 (commnd). Chm. Conservative Soc., LSE, 1958-59; Pres. Students' Union, LSE, 1959-60. Took part in expedn from N Greece to India overland tracing Alexander's route, 1960. In Banking and Stockbroking instns, Chicago, 1960-65;

Democratic Precinct Captain, Evanston, Ill, USA, 1962; Democratic Ward Chm. Evanston, Illinois, 1964. Conservative Councillor, London Borough of Merton, 1971-74; Chm., Stepney Green Conservative Assoc., 1968; a Vice-Chm., Conservative Party, 1975-. *Address:* House of Commons, SW1A 0AA.

MOORE, Captain John Evelyn, RN; Editor, Jane's Fighting Ships, since 1972; *b* Sant Ilario, Italy, 1 Nov. 1921; *s* of William John Moore and Evelyn Elizabeth (*née* Hooper); *m* 1st, 1945, Joan Pardoe; one *s* two *d*; 2nd, Barbara (*née* Kerry). *Educ:* Sherborne Sch., Dorset. Served War: entered Royal Navy, 1939; specialised in hydrographic surveying and submarines, 1943. Commanded HM Submarines: Totem, Alaric, Tradewind, Tactician, Telemachus. RN Staff course, 1950-51; Comdr, 1957; attached to Turkish Naval Staff, 1958-60; subseq. Plans Div., Admty; 1st Submarine Sqdn, then 7th Submarine Sqdn in comd; Captain, 1967; served as: Chief of Staff, C-in-C Naval Home Command, Defence Intell. Staff; retired list at own request, 1972. FRGS 1942. *Publications:* Jane's Major Warships, 1973; The Soviet Navy Today, 1975; Seapower and Politics, 1976; Submarine Development, 1976; articles in: Navy International, Nato's 15 Nations. *Recreations:* gardening, riding, swimming, archaeology. *Address:* Elmhurst, Rickney, Hailsham, Sussex BN27 1SF. *T:* Eastbourne 763294. *Clubs:* Naval, MCC, Anchorites.

MOORE, John Michael, CB 1974; DSC 1944; Deputy Secretary, Civil Service Department, since 1972; *b* 2 April 1921; *m . Educ:* Whitgift Middle Sch.; Selwyn Coll., Cambridge. Royal Navy, 1940-46. Royal Humane Society Bronze Medal, 1942. Ministry of Transport, 1946; Joint Principal Private Sec. to Minister (Rt Hon. Harold (later Lord) Watkinson), 1956-59; Asst Sec., 1959; Under-Sec., 1966; Under-Sec., DoE, 1970-72. Sec. to Jack Cttee on Rural Bus Services and Geddes Cttee on Carriers' Licensing; Chm. Cttee, Admin Trainee Review, CSD, 1977-. Mem., Council, Inst. of Manpower Studies. *Recreations:* making things, walking hills and mountains. *Address:* High Spinney, Old Coach Road, Wrotham, Kent. *T:* Fairseat 822340. *Club:* Royal Automobile.

MOORE, Prof. Leslie Rowsell, BSc, PhD, DSc, CEng, FIMinE, FGS; Professor of Geology, University of Sheffield, 1949-77; *b* 23 June 1912; *m* 1946, Margaret Wilson MacRae; one *s. Educ:* Midsomer Norton Grammar Sch.; Bristol Univ. Univ. of Bristol, 1930-37; Lecturer and Senior Lecturer, Cardiff, 1939-46; Research Dir, Univ. of Glasgow, 1946-48; Reader in Geology, Univ. of Bristol, 1948-49. *Publications:* contributions to: Quarterly Journal Geol. Soc., London; Geological Magazine; S Wales Inst. Engineers. *Recreations:* soccer, cricket, golf. *Address:* Moorside, The Bent, Curbar, near Sheffield S30 1YD.

MOORE, Noel Ernest Ackroyd; Under-Secretary, Civil Service Department, since 1975; *b* 25 Nov. 1928; *s* of late Rowland H. Moore and of Hilda Moore (*née* Ackroyd); *m* 1954, Mary Elizabeth Thorpe; two *s . Educ:* Penistone Grammar Sch., Yorks; Gonville and Caius Coll., Cambridge (MA); Half-Blue for chess. Asst Principal, Post Office, 1952; Asst Private Sec. to Postmaster General, 1955-56; Private Sec. to Asst PMG, 1956-57; Principal, 1957; Sec., Cttee of Inquiry on Decimal Currency, 1961-63; Treasury, 1966; Asst Sec., 1967; Sec., Decimal Currency Bd, 1966-72; Civil Service Dept, 1972. *Publication:* The Decimalisation of Britain's Currency (HMSO), 1973. *Address:* 30 Spurgate Hutton, Brentwood, Essex CM13 2LA. *T:* Brentwood 216988.

MOORE, (Sir) Norman Winfrid (3rd Bt *cr* 1919; has established his claim but does not use the title); Senior Principal Scientific Officer, Nature Conservancy, since 1965 (Principal Scientific Officer, 1958-65); *b* 24 Feb. 1923; *s* of Sir Alan Hilary Moore, 2nd Bt; *S* father 1959; *m* 1950, Janet, *o d* of late Mrs Phyllis Singer; one *s* two *d. Educ:* Eton; Trinity Coll., Cambridge. Served War, 1942-45, Germany and Holland (wounded, POW). *Heir: s* Peter Alan Cutlack Moore, *b* 21 Sept. 1951. *Address:* The Farm House, Swavesey, Cambridge.

MOORE, Patrick, OBE 1968; free-lance author since 1968; *b* 4 March 1923; *s* of late Capt. Charles Caldwell-Moore, MC, and of Mrs Gertrude Lilian Moore. *Educ:* privately (due to illness). Served with RAF, 1940-45: Navigator, Bomber Command. Concerned in running of a school, 1945-52; free-lance author, 1952-65; Dir of Armagh Planetarium, 1965-68. TV Series, BBC, The Sky at Night, 1957-; radio broadcaster. Composed and performed in Perseus and Andromeda (opera), 1975. Vice-Pres., British Astronomical Assoc., 1976. Hon. Mem., Astronomic-Geodetic Soc. of USSR, 1971. Editor, Year Book of Astronomy, 1962-76. Lorimer Gold Medal, 1962; Goodacre Gold Medal, 1968; Arturo Gold Medal (Italian Astronomical Socs), 1969;

Jackson-Guitt Medal, RAS, 1977. Hon. DSc Lancaster, 1974. *Publications:* More than 60 books, mainly astronomical, including Moon Flight Atlas, 1969; Space, 1970; The Amateur Astronomer, 1970; Atlas of the Universe, 1970; Guide to the Planets, 1976; Guide to the Moon, 1976; Can You Speak Venusian?, 1977; Guide to the Stars, 1977; Guide to Mars, 1977. *Recreations:* cricket, chess, tennis, amateurish playing of piano and xylophone. *Address:* Farthings, 39 West Street, Selsey, West Sussex. *Club:* Pathfinder.

MOORE, Very Rev. Peter Clement; Dean of St Albans, since 1973; *b* 4 June 1924; *s* of Rev. G. G. Moore and Vera (*née* Mylrea); *m* 1965, Mary Claire, *o d* of P. A. M. Malcolm and Celia (*née* Oldham); one *s* one *d. Educ:* Cheltenham Coll.; Christ Church, Oxford (MA, DPhil); Cuddesdon Coll., Oxford. Minor Canon of Canterbury Cathedral and Asst Master, Cathedral Choir School, 1947-49; Curate of Bladon with Woodstock, 1949-51; Chaplain, New Coll., Oxford, 1949-51; Vicar of Alfrick with Lulsley, 1952-59; Hurd Librarian to Bishop of Worcester, 1953-62; Vicar of Pershore with Pinvin and Wick, 1959-67; Rural Dean of Pershore, 1965-67; Canon Residentiary of Ely Cathedral, 1967-73; Vice-Dean, 1971-73. Member: Archbishops' Liturgical Commission, 1968-76; Council, RSCM; Governing Body, SPCK; Liveryman, Worshipful Co. of Glaziers and Painters of Glass; Trustee, Historic Churches Preservation Trust. *Publication:* Tomorrow is Too Late, 1970. *Recreations:* gardening, music, fishing, barrel organs. *Address:* The Deanery, St Albans, Herts. *T:* St Albans 52120; Thruxton House, Thruxton, Hereford. *T:* Wormbridge 376. *Club:* Athenæum.

MOORE, Rt. Hon. Sir Philip (Brian Cecil), PC 1977; KCVO 1976; CB 1973; CMG 1966; Private Secretary to the Queen and Keeper of the Queen's Archives, since 1977; *b* 6 April 1921; *s* of late Cecil Moore, Indian Civil Service; *m* 1945, Joan Ursula Greenop; two *d. Educ:* Dragon Sch.; Cheltenham Coll. (Scholar); Oxford Univ. Classical Exhibitioner, Brasenose Coll., Oxford, 1940. RAF Bomber Command, 1940-42 (prisoner of war, 1942-45). Brasenose Coll., Oxford, 1945-46. Asst Private Sec. to First Lord of Admiralty, 1950-51; Principal Private Sec. to First Lord of Admiralty, 1957-58; Dep. UK Commissioner, Singapore, 1961-63; British Dep. High Comr in Singapore, 1963-65; Chief of Public Relations, MoD, 1965-66; Asst Private Secretary to the Queen, 1966-72, Dep. Private Secretary, 1972-77. *Recreations:* golf; Rugby football (Oxford Blue, 1945-46; International, England, 1951), hockey (Oxford Blue, 1946), cricket (Oxfordshire). *Address:* Wren House, Kensington Palace, W8. *T:* 01-937 2272. *Club:* MCC.

MOORE, Richard Valentine; GC 1940; CBE 1963; BSc (Eng); FIMechE; FIEE; Managing Director (Reactor Group), UK Atomic Energy Authority, 1961-76; Member, 1971-76; *b* 14 Feb. 1916; *s* of Randall and Ellen Moore; *m* 1944, Ruby Edith Fair; three *s. Educ:* Strand Sch., London; London Univ. County of London Electric Supply Co., 1936-39. RNVR, 1939-46; HMS Effingham, 1939-40; HMS President, 1940-41; HMS Dido, 1942-44; British Admiralty Delegn, Washington, DC, 1944-46; Lieut-Comdr 1944. AERE Harwell, 1946-53; Dept of Atomic Energy, Risley, 1953; Design and Construction of Calder Hall, 1953-57; Chief Design Engineer, 1955; UKAEA, 1955; Dir of Reactor Design, 1958-61. Mem., Nuclear Power Adv. Bd., 1973-. Faraday Lectr, 1966. Hon. DTech Bradford, 1970. *Publications:* various papers to technical institutions. *Recreations:* golf, gardening. *Address:* Culleen House, Cann Lane, Appleton, Ches. *T:* Warrington 61023. *Club:* Naval.

MOORE, Robert, (Bobby Moore), OBE 1967; professional footballer; *b* 12 April 1941; *m* 1962, Christina Elizabeth Dean; one *s* one *d.* Captained: England Youth, at 17 years old (18 caps); England Under 23 (8 caps); has made 108 appearances for England (the record number), 90 as Captain (equalling Billy Wright's record). League debut for West Ham against Manchester United, Sept. 1958; England debut against Peru, 1962; played in World Cup, in Chile, 1962; Captained England for first time, against Czechoslovakia, 1963. Footballer of the Year, 1963-64; Holder of: FA Cup Winners' medal, 1964; European Cup Winners' medal, 1965; named Player of Players in World Cup (England the Winner), 1966; transferred to Fulham Football Club, 1974-77; played 1,000 matches at senior level. *Publication:* Bobby Moore (autobiog.). *Address:* 136 Greengate Street, E13. *T:* 01-472 2434.

MOORE, Robert, CBE 1973; Commissioner for Local Administration in Scotland, since 1976; *b* 2 Nov. 1915; *m* 1940, Jean Laird Dick; two *s. Educ:* Dalziel High Sch., Motherwell; Glasgow Univ. (BL). Admitted solicitor, 1939. Town Clerk, Port Glasgow, 1943-48; Secretary, Eastern Regional Hosp. Bd, 1948-60; Principal Officer: Scottish Hosp. Administrative Staffs Cttee, 1960-74; Manpower Div., Scottish Health Service, 1974-

75. Lectr in Administrative Law, St Andrews Univ., 1960-65; External Examr in Administrative Law, Glasgow Univ., 1967-71. Mem., Scottish Cttee, Council on Tribunals, 1964-. *Address:* (home) 93 Greenbank Crescent, Edinburgh EH10 5TB. *T:* 031-447 5493; (office) 125 Princes Street, Edinburgh EH2 4AD. *T:* 031-226 2823. *Club:* New (Edinburgh).

MOORE, Gen. Sir Rodney; *see* Moore, Gen. Sir J. N. R.

MOORE, Roger; actor; *b* London, 14 Oct. 1927; *m* 1st, Doorn van Steyn (marr. diss. 1953); 2nd, 1953, Dorothy Squires (marr. diss. 1969); 3rd, 1969, Luisa Mattioli; two *s* one *d. Educ:* RADA. Stage début, Androcles and the Lion. *TV series include:* Ivanhoe, 1958; Maverick, 1961; The Alaskans, 1960-61; The Saint, 1962-69 (dir some episodes); The Persuaders, 1972-73; *films include:* The Last Time I Saw Paris, 1954; The Interrupted Melody, 1955; The King's Thief, 1955; Diane, 1956; The Miracle, 1959; Sins of Rachel Cade, 1961; Gold of the Seven Saints, 1961; The Rape of the Sabine Women, 1961; The Man Who Haunted Himself, 1970; Gold, 1974; That Lucky Touch, 1975; Save Us From Our Friends; Street People, 1975; Shout at the Devil, 1975; Sherlock Holmes in New York, 1976; as James Bond: Live and Let Die, 1973; The Man with the Golden Gun, 1974; The Spy Who Loved Me, 1976. *Address:* c/o London Management Ltd, 235 Regent Street, W1.

MOORE, Roy, CBE 1962; *b* 10 Jan. 1908; *s* of Harry Moore and Ellen Harriet Post; *m* 1st, 1934, Muriel Edith (*d* 1959), *d* of late C. E. E. Shill; two *s*; 2nd, 1963, Lydia Elizabeth Newell Park, widow of David Park, Berkeley, Calif. *Educ:* Judd Sch., Tonbridge; King's Coll., London. 2nd Cl. Hons English, 1928; AKC 1928; MA 1931; Carter Prize for English Verse. Chief English Master, Mercers' Sch., London, 1931-40. Served War of 1939-45, Squadron Leader RAF Bomber Command, 1941-45. Head Master: Lawrence Sheriff Sch., Rugby, 1945-51; Mill Hill Sch., 1951-67. Fellow King's Coll., London, 1956. *Address:* 138 Santo Tomas Lane, Santa Barbara, Calif. 93103, USA. *Club:* Athenæum.

MOORE, Prof. Stanford; Member and Professor, Rockefeller Institute, since 1952; *b* 4 Sept. 1913; *s* of John Howard and Ruth Fowler Moore. *Educ:* Vanderbilt and Wisconsin Univs. BS Vanderbilt, 1935; PhD Wisconsin, 1938. Rockefeller Inst. for Med. Research: Asst, 1939-42; Associate, 1942-49; Associate Mem., 1949-52. Techn. Aide, Office of Scientific R&D, Nat. Defense Research Cttee, 1942-45. Vis. Prof. (Francqui Chair), Univ. of Brussels, 1950-51; Vis. Investigator, Cambridge, 1950; Vis. Prof., Vanderbilt, 1968. Mem., US Nat. Acad. of Sciences, 1960. Richards Medal, Amer. Chem. Soc., 1972; Linderstrøm-Lang Medal, Copenhagen, 1972; Nobel Prize in Chemistry, 1972. Hon. MD Brussels, 1954; Hon. Dr Paris, 1964; Hon. DSc Wisconsin, 1974. *Publications:* technical articles on chemistry of proteins and carbohydrates. *Address:* The Rockefeller University, 66th Street and York Avenue, New York, NY 10021, USA. *T:* 212-360-1220.

MOORE, Thomas, OBE 1968; formerly, Chief Constable of City of Nottingham, and Deputy Chief Constable of Nottinghamshire; *b* 16 March 1903; *s* of Alfred and Fanny Moore; *m* 1932, Norah Carruthers; two *s. Educ:* The Hickling Sch., Loughborough. *Recreations:* shooting and fishing. *Address:* Lowcroft, Manvers Grove, Radcliffe-on-Trent, Notts. *T:* Radcliffe 2108.

MOORE, Thomas William, JP; Chairman (since inception) of Trojan Plant Ltd, Trojan (Civil Engineering) Ltd, Trojan (Demolition) Ltd, Carseview Holdings Ltd; *b* 9 Aug. 1925; Scottish; *m* 1945, Mary Kathleen Thompson; four *s* two *d. Educ:* Stobswell Secondary Sch.; Leicester Coll. of Art and Technology. MBIM. Contested (Lab) Perth and East Perthshire, 1959. Lord Provost of Dundee, and Lord Lieutenant of County of City of Dundee, 1973-75; Chairman: Tay Road Bridge Jt Cttee, 1973; Tayside Steering Cttee. FInstD. *Recreations:* golf, reading. *Address:* 85 Blackness Avenue, Dundee. *T:* Dundee 69839. *Club:* Royal Automobile.

MOORE, Sir William Samson, 2nd Bt, *cr* 1932; *b* 17 April 1891; *s* of Rt Hon. Sir William Moore, 1st Bt, PC, LLD, DL, JP; *S* father, 1944; *m* 1915, Ethel (Grig) (*d* 1973), *d* of W. L. Wheeler, Lennoxvale, Belfast; one *s* (one *d* decd). *Educ:* RNA, Gosport; Marlborough. Served European War, 1914-18. High Sheriff, Co. Antrim, 1944. DL, JP, Co. Antrim. *Heir:* *s* William Roger Clotworthy Moore, TD [*b* 17 May 1927; *m* 1954, Gillian, *d* of John Brown, Co. Antrim; one *s* one *d. Educ:* Marlborough. High Sheriff, Co. Antrim, 1964]. *Address:* Moore Lodge, Ballymoney, Northern Ireland. *T:* Kilrea 322.

MOORE-BRABAZON, family name of **Baron Brabazon of Tara.**

MOORE-COULSON, Maj.-Gen. Samuel, CB 1959; ERD 1948; *b* 26 May 1908; *s* of late Samuel Coulson and Laura Elizabeth Moore, Leicestershire; *m* 1936, Joan Hardy, *d* of late J. R. H. Watkiss, London; one *s* two *d. Educ:* Wyggeston, Leicester; University Coll., Nottingham. Commnd Royal Leicestershire Regt (SRO), 1930; Asst Master, Queen Elizabeth Gram. Sch., Barnet, 1932-39; served with 2nd Bn Royal Leicestershire Regt, Palestine, 1939-40; Western Desert, 1940-41; Crete, 1941; Syria, 1941; Staff Officer, Lebanon, 1941-43; Canal Zone, 1943-44; War Office (AG1), 1945-46; transferred to RAEC, 1946; War Office (AE7/8), 1946-48; Regular Commn, 1948; SO1 Education, Far East, 1949-52; Dep. Dir of Army Education, 1952-55; Chief Education Officer, Eastern Command, 1955-57; Dir of Army Education, 1957-62; Maj.-Gen., 1957; retired, 1962. Head of Educn and Research Div., FBI, 1962-65; Asst Dir, Educn and Training, CBI, 1965-69; Chief Training and Develt Adviser, Dunlop Co. Ltd, 1969-70. Vice-Chm. Governors, Brit. Soc. for Internat. Understanding, 1964-70; Chm., Internat. Youth Science Fortnight, 1963-65, Vice-Pres., 1967-72. Hon. Fellow, Corporation of Secretaries, 1966; Mem., Adv. Cttee, Duke of Edinburgh Award, 1958-62 and 1968-70. Former Chairman: Army Rugby Referees Soc., Army Chess Soc.; MoD Foreign Language Trng Cttee; Standing Cttee on Educn of Service Children Overseas. Member: Min. of Education Cttee on R&D in Modern Languages; Co-ord. Cttee on Overseas Vol. Service; Comr Duke of York's Royal Mil. Sch.; Governor, Centre for Inf. on Language Teaching, SOAS. *Recreations:* gardening and photography. *Address:* Broadley Lodge, Sway, Lymington, Hants. *T:* Sway 2517.

MOOREHEAD, Alan McCrae, CBE 1968 (OBE 1946); *b* 22 July 1910; 2nd *s* of Richard Moorehead, Croydon, Vic., Aust.; *m* 1939, Lucy, *yr d* of Dr Vincent Milner, Torquay; two *s* one *d. Educ:* Scotch Coll., Melbourne; Melbourne Univ. Editor Melbourne Univ. Magazine, 1929. Worked on various newspapers in Australia and England, mostly as war correspondent, 1930-46, when retired from active journalism to write books. *Publications:* Mediterranean Front, 1941; A Year of Battle, 1943; The End in Africa, 1943; African Trilogy, 1944; Eclipse, 1945; Montgomery, 1946; The Rage of the Vulture, 1948; The Villa Diana, 1951; The Traitors, 1952; Rum Jungle, 1953; A Summer Night, 1954; Gallipoli, 1956 (Sunday Times 1956 Book Prize and Duff Cooper Memorial Award); The Russian Revolution, 1958; No Room in the Ark, 1959; The White Nile, 1960; The Blue Nile, 1962, 2nd edn 1972; Cooper's Creek, 1963 (Royal Society of Literature Award); The Fatal Impact, 1966; Darwin and the Beagle, 1969; A Late Education: episodes in a life, 1970. *Address:* c/o National Bank of Australasia, Australia House, Strand, WC2.

MOORER, Admiral Thomas Hinman; US Navy; Defense Distinguished Service Medal, 1973; DSM 1965, 1967, 1968, 1970; Silver Star 1942; Legion of Merit, 1945; DFC 1942; Purple Heart, 1942; Presidential Unit Citation, 1942; Chairman, Joint Chiefs of Staff, USA, 1970-74; *b* Mount Willing, Alabama, 9 Feb. 1912; *s* of Dr R. R. Moorer and Hulda Hill Hinson, Eufaula, Ala; *m* 1935, Carrie Ellen Foy Moorer; three *s* one *d. Educ:* Cloverdale High Sch., Montgomery, Ala; USN Acad.; Naval Aviation Trg Sch.; Naval War Coll. First ship, 1933; serving at Pearl Harbour in Fleet Air Wing, Dec. 1941; Pacific and East Indies areas, 1942; Mining Observer, C-in-C, US Fleet in UK, 1943; Strategic Bombing Survey in Japan, 1945; Naval Aide to Asst Sec. of Navy (Air), 1956; CO, USS Salisbury Sound, 1957; Special Asst to CNO, 1959; Comdr, Carrier Div. Six, 1960; Dir, Long Range Objectives Group, CNO, 1962; Comdr Seventh Fleet, 1964; C-in-C: US Pacific Fleet, 1965; Atlantic and Atlantic Fleet, and Supreme Allied Commander, Atlantic, 1965-67; Chief of Naval Operations, 1967-70. Captain 1952; Rear-Adm. 1958; Vice-Adm. 1962; Adm. 1964. Holds seventeen foreign decorations. Hon. LLD Auburn, 1968; Hon. DH Samford, 1970. *Recreations:* golfing, fishing, hunting. *Address:* 402 Barbour Street, Eufaula, Alabama 36027, USA. *Clubs:* US Naval Inst. (Annapolis, Md); Army-Navy Country (Arlington, Va); Princess Anne Country (Virginia Beach, Va); Chevy Chase (Chevy Chase, Md).

MOORES, Hon. Frank Duff; MHA (Progressive C) Humber West, Newfoundland, since 1971 (MP for Bonavista-Trinity-Conception, 1968-71); Premier of the Province of Newfoundland since 1972; *b* 18 Feb. 1933; *s* of Silas Wilmot Moores and Dorothy Duff Moores; *m* 1973, Janis Johnson, Winnipeg; two *s* six *d* by a former marriage. *Educ:* United Church Academy, Carbonear; St Andrew's Coll., Aurora, Ont. Pres., Progressive Conservative Party in Canada, 1969. Is a Freemason. Hon. LLD, Meml. Univ. of Newfoundland, 1975. *Recreations:* tennis, reading, fishing, hunting, golf. *Address:*

Mount Scio House, St John's, Newfoundland, Canada. *Club:* Coral Beach (Bermuda).

MOOREY, (Peter) Roger (Stuart), DPhil; FBA 1977; FSA; Senior Assistant Keeper, Department of Antiquities, Ashmolean Museum, Oxford, since 1973; Fellow of Wolfson College, since 1976; *b* 30 May 1937; *s* of late Stuart Moorey and Freda (*née* Harris). *Educ:* Mill Hill Sch.; Corpus Christi Coll., Oxford (MA, DPhil). FSA 1967. Asst Keeper, Ashmolean Museum, Oxford, 1961-73. Editor of Levant, 1968-. *Publications:* Catalogue of the Ancient Persian Bronzes in the Ashmolean Museum, 1971; Ancient Persian Bronzes in the Adam Collection, 1974; Biblical Lands, 1975; museum booklets and articles in learned jls. *Recreations:* travel, walking. *Address:* Ashmolean Museum, Oxford. *T:* Oxford 57522.

MOORHOUSE, Geoffrey; writer; *b* 29 Nov. 1931; *s* of Richard and Gladys Moorhouse; *m* 1st, 1956, Janet Marion Murray; two *s* two *d;* 2nd, 1974, Barbara Jane Woodward. *Educ:* Bury Grammar School. Royal Navy, 1950-52; editorial staff: Bolton Evening News, 1952-54; Grey River Argus (NZ), Auckland Star (NZ), Christchurch Star-Sun (NZ), 1954-56; News Chronicle, 1957; (Manchester) Guardian, 1958-70 (Chief Features Writer, 1963-70). FRGS 1972. *Publications:* The Other England, 1964; The Press, 1964; Against All Reason, 1969; Calcutta, 1971; The Missionaries, 1973; The Fearful Void, 1974; The Diplomats, 1977. *Recreations:* music, cricket, hill-walking, looking at buildings. *Address:* c/o A. P. Watt & Son, 26-28 Bedford Row, WC1R 4HC. *T:* 01-405 1057.

MOORMAN, Rt. Rev. John Richard Humpidge, MA, DD, Cambridge; LittD: Leeds; St Bonaventure, USA; FSA; Hon. Fellow of Emmanuel College; *b* Leeds, 4 June 1905; 2nd *s* of late Professor F. W. Moorman; *m* 1930, Mary Caroline, *d* of late G. M. Trevelyan, OM; no *c. Educ:* Gresham's School, Holt; Emmanuel College, Cambridge. Curate of Holbeck, Leeds, 1929-33; of Leighton Buzzard, 1933-35; Rector of Fallowfield, Manchester, 1935-42; Hon. and Examining Chaplain to Bishop of Manchester, 1940-44; Vicar of Lanercost, 1945-46, and Examining Chaplain to Bishop of Carlisle, 1945-59; Principal of Chichester Theological Coll. and Chancellor of Chichester Cathedral, 1946-56; Prebendary of Heathfield in Chichester Cathedral, 1956-59; Bishop of Ripon, 1959-75. Delegate-observer to 2nd Vatican Council, 1962-65. Hale Memorial Lectr, Evanston, USA, 1966. Chairman: Anglican members, Anglican-Roman Catholic Preparatory Commn, 1967-69; Advisory Council for Religious Communities, 1971-. Member, Jt Internat. Commn of the Roman Catholic Church and the Anglican Communion, 1969-. *Publications:* Sources for the Life of S Francis of Assisi, 1940; Church Life in England in the Thirteenth Century, 1945; A New Fioretti, 1946; B. K. Cunningham, a Memoir, 1947; S Francis of Assisi, 1950, new edn 1976; The Grey Friars in Cambridge (Birkbeck Lectures), 1952; A History of the Church in England, 1953; The Curate of Souls, 1958; The Path to Glory, 1960; Vatican Observed, 1967; A History of the Franciscan Order, 1968; The Franciscans in England, 1974; Richest of Poor Men, 1977. *Recreations:* country life, music. *Address:* 22 Springwell Road, Durham. *T:* Durham 63503.

MOOSONEE, Archbishop of, since 1974; **Most Rev. James Augustus Watton,** BA, DD; Metropolitan of Ontario; *b* 23 Oct. 1915; *s* of Geo. A. Watton and Ada Wynn; *m* 1941, Irene A. Foster; one *s* two *d. Educ:* Univ. of Western Ontario (BA); Huron Coll. (STh); Post graduate Univ. of Michigan. Deacon 1938; Priest 1939. Bishop of Moosonee, 1963. DD (*jure dig.*), 1955. *Address:* Bishopstope, Schumacher, Ont., Canada. *T:* Timmins AM-4-0641.

MOOTHAM, Sir Orby Howell, Kt 1962; *b* 17 Feb. 1901; *s* of Delmé George Mootham, ARIBA; *m* 1st, 1931, Maria Augusta Elizabeth Niemöller (*d* 1973); one *s* one *d;* 2nd, 1977, Mrs Beatrix Douglas Ward, *widow* of Basil Ward, FRIBA. *Educ:* Leinster House Sch., Putney; London Univ. MSc (Econ). Called to Bar, Inner Temple, 1926 (Yarborough-Anderson Schol., 1924; hon. Bencher, 1958). An Advocate of Rangoon High Court, 1927-40; DJAG, Army in Burma, 1940-41, thereafter service in Dept of JAG in India and as Chief Judicial Officer, Brit. Mil. Admin. (despatches). Actg Judge, Rangoon High Court, 1945-46; Judge, Allahabad High Court, 1946-55; Chief Justice, 1955-61. Chm., Allahabad Univ. Enquiry Cttee, 1953-54; Legal Adviser's Dept, CRO, 1961-63. Deputy-Chairman of QS: Essex, 1964-71; Kent, 1965-71; Surrey, 1970-71; a Recorder of the Crown Court, 1972. Chm., Med. Appeals Tribunal, 1963-73; Mem. Governing Body, Froebel Educational Inst. *Publications:* Burmese Buddhist Law, 1939. Articles in Brit. Year Book of Internat. Law and other legal jls. *Recreation:* map collecting. *Address:* 3 Paper Buildings, Temple, EC4Y 7EU. *T:* 01-353 1310. *Club:* Athenæum.

MORAES, Dom; Indian poet and author; Chief Information Officer, United Nations Fund for Population Activities, on loan to Government of India; *b* 1938; *s* of Frank Moraes (Editor of the Indian Express and biographer of Nehru); *m* 1970, Leela Naidu. *Educ:* Jesus Coll., Oxford. Read English, 1956-59. Took up residence in England at age of 16, after world-wide travel and a 2-yr stay in Ceylon. *Publications:* A Beginning (poems), 1957 (Hawthornden Prize, 1958); Gone Away (Travel), 1960; Poems, 1960; John Nobody (poems), 1965; The Brass Serpent (trans. from Hebrew poetry), 1964; Poems 1955-65 (collected poems), 1966; My Son's Father (autobiography), 1968; The People Time Forgot, 1972; The Tempest Within, 1972; A Matter of People, 1974; (ed) Voices for Life (essays), 1975. *Recreeation:* thinking. *Address:* UNFPA, 485 Lexington Avenue, 20th Floor, New York, NY 10017, USA; c/o UNDP, 55 Lodi Estate, New Delhi, India.

MORAN, 2nd Baron *cr* 1943; **Richard John McMoran Wilson,** CMG 1970; HM Ambassador to Portugal, since 1976; *b* 22 Sept. 1924; *er s* of 1st Baron Moran, MC, MD, FRCP, and of Dorothy, MBE, *d* of late Samuel Felix Dufton, DSc; *S* father, 1977; *m* 1948, Shirley Rowntree Harris; two *s* one *d*. *Educ:* Eton; King's Coll., Cambridge. Served War of 1939-45; Ord. Seaman in HMS Belfast, 1943; Sub-Lt RNVR in Motor Torpedo Boats and HM Destroyer Oribi, 1944-45. Foreign Office, 1945; Third Sec., Ankara, 1948; Tel-Aviv, 1950; Second Sec., Rio de Janeiro, 1953; First Sec., FO, 1956; Washington, 1959; FO 1961; Counsellor, British Embassy in South Africa, 1965; Head of W African Dept, FCO, 1968-73; Ambassador to Chad, 1970-73; Ambassador to Hungary, 1973-76. *Publication:* C. B.: a life of Sir Henry Campbell-Bannerman, 1973 (Whitbread Award, 1973). *Recreations:* fishing, fly-tying, bird-watching. *Heir: s* Hon. James McMoran Wilson, *b* 6 Aug. 1952. *Address:* British Embassy, Lisbon, Portugal; 26 Church Row, Hampstead, NW3. *T:* 01-435 8717; Llewelyn House, Aberedw, Radnorshire. *T:* Erwood 257. *Clubs:* Beefsteak, Flyfishers'.
See also Baron Mountevans.

MORAN, Prof. Frances Elizabeth; Regius Professor of Laws, Trinity College, Dublin, 1944-63, retired; Professor of Equity Pleading and Practice, King's Inns, Dublin, 1932-68, retired; Professorial Representative on Board of Trinity College, 1958-62; Senior Counsel; Past President, International Federation of University Women; *b* Dublin, 6 Dec. 1893; 2nd *d* of late Senator James and late Elizabeth Moran, St James', Clontarf, Dublin; unmarried. *Educ:* Dominican Coll. and Trinity Coll., Dublin. Called to Bar, 1924; took silk, 1941; Reid Prof. in Law Sch., Trinity Coll., 1925-30; Lecturer in Law, 1930-34; Prof. of Laws, 1934-44; Hon. Fellow, 1968. Hon. Bencher, King's Inns, 1969. Hon. LLD, Queen's Univ., Belfast, 1957. *Recreations:* walking, reading, and foreign travel. *Address:* St James', Howth Road, Clontarf, Dublin 3. *T:* 339516.

MORAN, Joseph Michael, QC (Scot.) 1976; Legal Secretary to the Lord Advocate and First Parliamentary Draftsman for Scotland since 1976; *b* 27 June 1925; *s* of late Michael Moran and Catherine Stevenson; *m* 1959, Margaret, *d* of late John Barry, Sugarstown House, Co. Kilkenny; one *s* two *d*. *Educ:* St Aloysius' Coll., Glasgow; Holy Cross Acad., Edinburgh; Univ. of Edinburgh (MA 1945, LLB (with distinction) 1947). Admitted to Faculty of Advocates and called to Scottish Bar, 1948; entered Lord Advocate's Dept, 1949. Dep. Legal Sec. to Lord Advocate, 1969-76. *Recreations:* reading, bridge, golf. *Address:* 1 Coombe Gardens, West Wimbledon, SW20 0QU. *T:* 01-946 7421.

MORAN, Prof. Patrick Alfred Pierce, FRS 1975; FAA; Professor of Statistics, Australian National University, since 1952; *b* 14 July 1917; *s* of late Herbert Michael Moran and of Eva Moran; *m* 1946, Jean Mavis Frame; two *s* one *d*. *Educ:* St Stanislaus Coll., Bathurst, NSW; Univs of Sydney (DSc) and Cambridge (ScD). Exper. Officer, Min. of Supply, 1940-42; Australian Sci. Liaison Officer, London, 1942-45; Baylis Student, Cambridge, 1945-46; Sen. Res. Officer, Oxford Inst. of Statistics, 1946-51; Lectr in Maths, Trinity Coll., Oxford, 1949-51; Univ. Lectr in Maths, Oxford, 1951. Mem. Council, Australian Acad. of Scis, 1971-74; Vice-Pres., Internat. Statistical Inst., 1971-73. Lyle Medal, Australian Acad. of Scis, 1963. Hon. FSS. *Publications:* The Theory of Storage, 1960; The Random Processes of Evolutionary Theory, 1962; (with M. G. Kendall) Geometrical Probability, 1963; Introduction to the Theory of Probability, 1968. *Address:* 17 Tennyson Crescent, Forrest, Canberra, ACT 2603, Australia. *T:* Canberra 731140.

MORAN, Thomas, CBE 1946; ScD; DSc; Scientific Adviser, Home Grown Cereals Authority, 1966-69; Director of Research, Research Association of British Flour Millers, 1939-66; *b* 1899; *s* of late Thomas Moran; *m* 1st, 1924, Elizabeth Ann Flynn (*d*

1952); one *s* two *d*; 2nd, 1959, June Patricia Martin. *Educ:* St Francis Xavier's Coll., Liverpool; Liverpool Univ.; Gonville and Caius Coll., Cambridge. Sir John Willox Schol., 1920, Univ. Scholar, 1920, Liverpool Univ.; served European War, 1914-18, with Liverpool Scottish (KLR), 1917-19; with DSIR at Low Temperature Station, Cambridge, 1922-39. Mem. Advisory Scientific Cttee, Food Defence Plans Dept, 1938-39; Dir of Research and Dep. Scientific Adviser, Min. of Food, 1940-46; UK delegate, Quadripartite Food Conf., Berlin, Jan. 1946. Mem. Council, British Nutrition Foundation, 1967-70. *Publications:* Bread (with Lord Horder and Sir Charles Dodds); papers on different aspects of Food Science in scientific and medical journals, 1922-; reports on applied food research published by HM Stationery Office. *Address:* 5 Amhurst Court, Grange Road, Cambridge. *T:* Cambridge 54548.

MORANT, Dame Mary (Maud), DBE 1969, (**Sister Mary Regis**) (to be addressed as Sr Mary Regis, DBE); Headmistress, Roman Catholic Schools, 1933-70; retired, 1970, to Convent of Notre Dame, Battersea, to give social service; *b* 21 Dec. 1903; *d* of Stephen Augustus and Mary Morant. *Educ:* Notre Dame High Sch. and Notre Dame Coll. of Educn, Mt Pleasant. Asst, Notre Dame Demonstration Sch., 1924; Asst, St Mary's, Battersea, 1929; Headmistress, St John's, Wigan, 1933; Headmistress, Central Sch., Embakwe Mission, S Rhodesia, 1938; Vice-Pres., Chikuni Trg. Coll., N Rhodesia, 1946; Headmistress: St Peter Claver, Kroonstad, 1948; Lowe House, St Helens, Lancs, 1956; Our Lady's, Eldon St, Liverpool, 1961; Preparatory School, Convent of Notre Dame, Birkdale, 1969-70. Pro Pontifice et Ecclesia Medal, 1969, from HH Pope Paul VI. *Recreations:* drama, music. *Address:* Convent of Notre Dame, 118 St George's Road, Southwark, SE1. *T:* 01-928 7069.

MORAVIA, Alberto; Italian author; *b* 28 Nov. 1907; *s* of Carlo and Teresa de Marsanich; *m* 1941, Elsa Morante. Chevalier de la Légion d'Honneur (France), 1952. *Publications: novels:* Gli indifferenti, 1929 (Eng. trans.: The Time of Indifference, 1953); Le ambizioni sbagliate, 1935; La mascherata, 1941 (Eng. trans.: The Fancy Dress Party, 1948); Agostino, 1944 (Eng. trans.: Agostino, 1947); La Romana, 1947 (Eng. trans.: The Woman of Rome, 1949); La disubbidienza, 1948 (Eng. trans: Disobedience, 1950); L'amore Coniugale, 1949 (Eng. trans.: Conjugal Love, 1951); Il Conformista, 1951 (Eng. Trans.: The Conformist, 1952); La Ciociara, 1957 (Eng. trans.: Two Women, 1958); La Noia, 1961 (Viareggio Prize) (Eng. trans.: The Empty Canvas, 1961); The Fetish, 1965; L'attenzione, 1965 (Eng. trans.: The Lie, 1966); *short stories:* (and selections in Eng.); La bella vita, 1935; L'imbroglio, 1937; I sogni del pigro, 1940; L'amante infelice, 1943; L'epidemia, 1945; Racconti, 1952 (Eng. trans.: Bitter Honeymoon, and the Wayward Wife, 1959); Racconti romani, 1954 (Eng. trans.: Roman Tales, 1956); Nuovi racconti romani, 1959; L'automa, 1964; Una cosa è una cosa, 1966; Il Paradiso, 1970 (Eng. trans.: Paradise, 1971); Io e lui, 1971 (Eng. trans.: The Two of Us, 1971); Un'altra vita, 1973 (Eng. trans.: Lady Godiva and Other Stories, 1975); *essays:* L'uomo come fine e altri saggi, 1964 (Eng. trans.: Man as an End, 1966); *plays:* Beatrice Cenci, 1955; Il mondo è quello che è, 1966; Il dio Kurt, 1967; La Vita è Gioco, 1970; *travel:* La rivoluzione culturale in Cina, 1967 (Eng. trans: The Red Book and The Great Wall, 1968); Which Tribe Do You Belong To?, 1974. *Address:* Lungotevere della Vittoria 1, Rome, Italy. *T:* 386349.

MORAY, 20th Earl of, *cr* 1562; **Douglas John Moray Stuart;** Lord Abernethy and Strathearn, 1562; Lord Doune, 1581; Baron of St Colme, 1611; Baron Stuart (GB), 1796; *b* 13 Feb. 1928; *e s* of 19th Earl of Moray and Mabel Helen Maud Wilson (*d* 1968); *S* father, 1974; *m* 1964, Lady Malvina Murray, *er d* of 7th Earl of Mansfield and Mansfield; one *s* one *d*. *Educ:* Trinity Coll., Cambridge (BA), FLAS 1958. Trustee, Nat. Museum of Antiquities of Scotland, 1970-. *Heir: s* Lord Doune, *qv*. *Address:* Doune Park, Doune, Perthshire. *T:* Doune 333; Darnaway Castle, Forres, Moray, Scotland. *Club:* New (Edinburgh).

MORAY, ROSS and CAITHNESS, Bishop of, since 1970; **Rt. Rev. George Minshull Sessford;** *b* Aintree, Lancs, 7 Nov. 1928; *o s* of Charles Walter Sessford and Eliza Annie (*née* Minshull); *m* 1952, Norah, *y d* of David Henry Hughes and Ellen (*née* Whitely); three *d*. *Educ:* Warbreck Primary Sch.; Oulton High and Liverpool Collegiate Schs; St Andrews Univ. (MA). Curate, St Mary's Cathedral, Glasgow, 1953; Chaplain, Glasgow Univ., 1955; Priest-in-Charge, Cumbernauld New Town, 1958; Rector, Forres, Moray, 1966. *Recreations:* Lanchester motor cars, donkey breeding, sailing. *Address:* Spynie House, 96 Fairfield Road, Inverness, Scotland IV3 5LL. *T:* Inverness 31059.

MORAY, Edward Bruce D.; *see* Dawson-Moray.

MORCOM, Rev. Canon Anthony John; a Residentiary Canon of Ely Cathedral, since 1974; *b* 24 July 1916; *s* of late Dr Alfred Farr Morcom and Sylvia Millicent Morcom (*née* Birchenough); *m* 1st, 1955, Pamela Cappel Bain (*d* 1963); 2nd, 1965, Richenda, *widow* of Frederick Williams. *Educ:* Repton; Clare Coll., Cambridge; Cuddesdon Coll. Curate: St Mary Magdalene, Paddington, 1939-42; St Mary the Virgin, Pimlico, 1942-47; Domestic Chaplain to the Bishop of London, 1947-55; Archdeacon of Middx, 1953-66; Vicar of St Cyprian's, Clarence Gate, 1955-66; Vicar of St Mary the Less, Cambridge, 1966-73; Rural Dean of Cambridge, 1971-73. *Recreation:* travel. *Address:* Powchers Hall, Ely, Cambs. *T:* Ely 2336. *Clubs:* United Oxford & Cambridge University, MCC.

MORCOS-ASAAD, Prof. Fikry Naguib; Professor of Architecture, Department of Architecture and Building Science, University of Strathclyde, since 1970; *b* 27 Sept. 1930; *s* of Naguib and Marie A. Morcos-Asaad; *m* 1958, Sarah Ann (*née* Gribben); three *s*. *Educ:* Cairo Univ. (BArch); Georgia Inst. of Techn. (MArch); MIT (SM); IIT (PhD). M.ASCE; RIBA; FRIAS. Lectr in Architecture, Fac. of Engrg, Cairo Univ., 1952-54 and 1958-63; Dir of Structural Studies, Sch. of Arch., Univ. of Liverpool, 1963-70; Design Critic and Vis. Prof. in Arch. Engrg, Calif State Polytechnic Univ., 1969, 1970 and 1973. Comr, Royal Fine Art Commn for Scotland; Mem. Educn Cttee, Architects Registration Council of UK; Mem. Council, Glasgow Inst. of Architects (Mem. Educn, Professional Practice and Competitions Cttees); Mem. Council, Royal Incorp. of Architects in Scotland. *Publications:* Circular Forms in Architecture, 1955; High Density Concretes for Radiation Shielding, 1956; Structural Parameters in Multi-Storey Buildings under Dynamic Loading, 1956; The Egyptian Village, 1956; Architectural Construction, vol. 1 1960, vol. 2 1961; various papers on structural form in architecture. *Recreations:* renovation of antique clocks, gardening, reading, travelling. *Address:* Staneacre House, Townhead Street, Hamilton ML3 7BP. *T:* Hamilton 20644, (office) 041-552 4400, ext 3000. *Clubs:* Glasgow Art (Glasgow); Hamilton Civic Society (Hamilton).

MORDAUNT, Lt-Col Sir Nigel John, 13th Bt, *cr* 1611; MBE 1945; RA; Member of London Stock Exchange, since 1929; *b* 9 May 1907; *e s* of late E. C. Mordaunt and Cicely Marion, 2nd *d* of Henry Tubb; *S* uncle 1939; *m* 1938, Anne, *d* of late Arthur F. Tritton, Denford Mill, Hungerford, Berks; three *s* one *d*. *Educ:* Wellington Coll.; Christ Church, Oxford. Served War of 1939-45 (MBE). *Heir:* s Richard Nigel Charles Mordaunt [*b* 12 May 1940; *m* 1964, Myriam Atchia; one *s* one *d*]. *Address:* Elsenham Place, Bishops Stortford, Herts. *T:* Stansted 2344. *Clubs:* City of London, Buck's.

MORDECAI, Sir John Stanley, Kt 1962; CMG 1956; formerly Secretary, Development Planning, University of the West Indies; *b* 21 Oct. 1903; *s* of Segismund T. and Marie A. Mordecai; *m* 1st, 1929, Pearl K. Redmond (*d* 1947); two *s* four *d*; 2nd, 1951, Phyllis M. Walcott; two *s*. *Educ:* Wolmer's Boys' High Sch., Jamaica; Syracuse Univ., New York, USA. MSc (Pub. Adm.). Entered public service as clerical asst in Treasury, Jamaica, 1920; Finance officer, 1942; asst treasurer, 1944; asst sec. in charge of local government secretariat, 1946; trade administrator and sec. trade control board, 1949; principal, seconded to Colonial Office, 1950; Executive Sec. Regional Economic Cttee of the West Indies, British Guiana and British Honduras, with headquarters in Barbados, 1952-56; Federal Sec., West Indies Federation, 1956-60 (Special work on preparatory arrangements for Federation, 1955-58); Dep. Gov.-Gen., WI Fedn, 1960-62; Gen. Manager, Jamaica Industrial Develt Corp., 1962-63. Fellow, Princeton Univ., NJ, 1964-66. Chairman: Jamaica Public Services Commn, 1962; Cttee of Inquiry into Sugar Ind., 1969. *Publication:* The West Indies, 1968. *Recreations:* horse racing, music. *Address:* 34 Mona Road, Kingston 6, Jamaica.

MORE, Jasper, JP, DL; MP (C) Ludlow since 1960; *b* 31 July 1907; *s* of Thomas Jasper Mytton More and Lady Norah, *d* of 5th Marquess of Sligo; *m* 1944, Clare Mary Hope-Edwardes, Netley, Shropshire, *d* of Capt. Vincent Coldwell, 4th Indian Cavalry; no *c*. *Educ:* Eton (Schol.); King's Coll., Cambridge. Barrister, Lincoln's Inn, 1930, and Middle Temple, 1931; Harmsworth Law Schol., 1932; in practice, 1930-39. Served War of 1939-45: in Min. of Economic Warfare, MAP and Light Metals Control, 1939-42; commissioned as legal officer in Military Govt, 1943; with Allied Commission (Italy), 8th Army and 5th Army, 1943-45; Legal Adviser, Military Govt, Dodecanese, 1946. An Asst Government Whip, Feb.-Oct. 1964; Asst Opposition Whip, 1964-70; Vice-Chamberlain, HM Household, 1970-71. JP Salop, 1950; DL Salop, 1955; CC Salop, 1958-70. *Publications:* The Land of Italy, 1949; The Mediterranean, 1956. *Recreations:* shooting, fishing, riding,

building, travel and landscape gardening. *Address:* Linley Hall, Bishop's Castle, Salop. *Clubs:* Travellers', Brooks's.

MORE, Kenneth (Gilbert), CBE 1970; actor; *b* Gerrards Cross, Bucks, 20 Sept. 1914; *s* of Charles Gilbert More and Edith Winifred (*née* Watkins); *m* 1st, 1940, Beryl Johnstone (marr. diss.) (she *d* 1969); one *d*; 2nd, 1952, Mabel Edith Barkby (marr. diss.); one *d*; 3rd, 1968, Angela McDonagh Douglas. *Educ:* Victoria Coll., Jersey. First appeared on stage in a revue sketch, Windmill Theatre, 1936. Served War of 1939-45, Lieut RNVR. Returned to stage and took part of Rev. Arthur Platt in revival of And No Birds Sing, Aldwych, Nov. 1946; Eddie, in Power Without Glory, New Lindsey and Fortune, 1947; George Bourne, in Peace In Our Time, Lyric, 1948; John, in The Way Things Go, Phoenix, 1950; Freddie Page, in The Deep Blue Sea, Duchess, 1952; Peter Pounce, in Out of the Crocodile, Phoenix, 1963; Crichton, in Our Man Crichton, Shaftesbury, 1964; Hugh, in The Secretary Bird, Savoy, 1968; Sir Robert Morton in The Winslow Boy, New, 1970; George in Getting On, Queen's, 1971; Andrew Perry in Signs of the Times, Vaudeville, 1973; Duke in On Approval, Vaudeville, 1977. First appeared in films, 1948, in Scott of the Antarctic. Films include: Chance of a Lifetime; Genevieve; Doctor in the House (Brit. Film Acad. Award as best actor, 1954); Raising a Riot; The Deep Blue Sea (Venice Volpi Cup, as best actor, 1955); Reach for the Sky (Picturegoer annual award for best male performance, as Douglas Bader, also Belgian Prix Femina), 1956; The Admirable Crichton, 1957; Next to No Time, 1958; A Night to Remember, 1958; The Sheriff of Fractured Jaw, 1958; The Thirty Nine Steps, 1959; North West Frontier, 1959; Sink the Bismarck!, 1960; Man in the Moon, 1960; The Greengage Summer, 1961; The Longest Day, 1962; Some People, 1962 (For the Duke of Edinburgh's Award Scheme); We Joined the Navy, 1962; The Comedy Man, 1963; Dark of the Sun, 1967; Oh! What A Lovely War, 1968; Battle of Britain, 1969; Scrooge, 1970; The Slipper and the Rose, 1976; Journey to the Centre of the Earth, 1976; Leopard in the Snow, 1977. First Eurovision Production by BBC: Heart to Heart, 1963. Played Young Jolyon in The Forsyte Saga, BBC TV, 1966-67; Richard Drew in Six Faces, 1973; Father Brown, ATV, 1974. *Publications:* Happy Go Lucky (autobiography), 1959; Kindly Leave the Stage, 1965. *Recreation:* golf. *Address:* Bute House, 9 Ladbroke Terrace, W11. *Clubs:* Garrick, Green Room.

MOREAU, Jeanne; actress; *b* 23 Jan. 1928; *d* of Anatole-Désiré Moreau and Kathleen Moreau (*née* Buckley); *m* 1949, Jean-Louis Richard (marr. diss.); one *s*; *m* 1977, William Friedkin. *Educ:* Collège Edgar-Quinet; Conservatoire national d'art dramatique. Comédie Française, 1948-52; Théâtre National Populaire, 1953. Over 60 films including: Les amants, 1958; Les liaisons dangereuses, 1959; Le dialogue des Carmelites, 1959; Moderato cantabile, 1960; Jules et Jim, 1961; La Baie des Anges, 1962; Journal d'une femme de chambre, 1963; Viva Maria, 1965; Mademoiselle, 1965; The Sailor from Gibraltar, 1965; The Immortal Story, 1966; Great Catherine, 1967; The Bride wore Black, 1967; Monte Walsh, 1969; Chère Louise, 1971; Nathalie Granger, 1972; La Race des Seigneurs, 1974; Mr Klein, 1976. Chevalier des Arts et des Lettres, 1966. *Recreation:* reading. *Address:* 9 rue du Cirque, Paris 8e, France. *T:* Elysées 13-33.

MORECAMBE, Eric; *see* Bartholomew, J. E.

MORELL, Mrs A.; *see* Greenwood, Joan.

MORETON, family name of **Earl of Ducie.**

MORETON, Lord; David Leslie Moreton; *b* 20 Sept. 1951; *s* and heir of 6th Earl of Ducie, *qv*; *m* 1975, Helen, *er d* of M. L. Duchesne. *Educ:* Cheltenham College; Wye Coll., London Univ. (BSc 1973). *Address:* Talbots End Farm, Cromhall, Glos.

MORETON, Sir John (Oscar), KCVO 1976; CMG 1966; MC 1944; HM Diplomatic Service, retired; *b* 28 Dec. 1917; *s* of Rev. C. O. Moreton; *m* 1945, Margaret Katherine, *d* of late Sir John Fryer, KBE, FRS; three *d*. *Educ:* St Edward's Sch., Oxford; Trinity Coll., Oxford (MA). War Service with 99th (Royal Bucks Yeomanry) Field Regt RA, 1939-46: France, Belgium, 1940; India, Burma, 1942-45. Colonial Office, 1946; Private Sec. to Perm. Under-Sec. of State, 1949-50; seconded to Govt of Kenya, 1953-55; Private Sec. to Sec. of State for Colonies (Rt Hon. Alan Lennox-Boyd), 1955-59; transf. to CRO, 1960; Counsellor, British High Commn, Lagos, 1961-64; IDC 1965; Asst Under-Sec. of State, CRO, 1965-66, CO 1966-68, FCO 1968-69; Ambassador to Vietnam, 1969-71; High Comr, Malta, 1972-74; Dep. Perm. Representative, with personal rank of Ambassador, UK Mission to UN, NY, 1974-75; HM Minister, British Embassy, Washington, 1975-77. *Recreations:* tennis; formerly athletics (Oxford Blue and International, 880 yds,

1939). *Address:* Woodside House, Woodside Road, Cobham, Surrey. *Club:* Travellers'.

MOREY, Rev. Dom Adrian, MA, DPhil, LittD; FRHistS; Superior, Downside House of Studies, Cambridge; *b* 10 April 1904; *s* of late John Morey and Charlotte Helen Morey (*née* Nelson). *Educ:* Latymer Upper Sch.; Christ's Coll., Cambridge (Schol.); Univ. of Munich. 1st cl. hons Hist. Tripos Pts I and II, Cambridge. Housemaster, Downside Sch., 1934; Bursar, Downside Abbey and Sch., 1946-50; Headmaster, Oratory Sch., Reading, 1953-67; Rector, St Wulstan's, Little Malvern, Worcs, 1967-69. *Publications:* Bartholomew of Exeter, 1937; (with Prof. C. N. Brooke) Gilbert Foliot and His Letters, 1965; The Letters and Charters of Gilbert Foliot, 1967; The Catholic Subjects of Elizabeth I, 1977; articles in English Hist. Review, Jl Eccles. History, Cambridge Hist. Jl. *Address:* Benet House, Mount Pleasant, Cambridge. *T:* Cambridge 54637.

MORFEE, Air Vice-Marshal Arthur Laurence, CD; CB 1946; CBE 1943; retired; *b* 27 May 1897; *s* of George Thomas Morfee; *m* Estelle Lillian, *d* of William Edward Hurd of South Carolina, USA; one *s* one *d. Educ:* Finchley County Sch. Canadian Army from 1915; served France and Belgium, 19th Can. Inf. (wounded); joined RAF 1918; Air board (Civil Service), 1921-24; appointed RCAF 1924; psa Andover, Eng., 1933; Air Vice-Marshal, 1945; retd 1949. Dir of Air Cadet League; Vice-Chm., Nova Scotia Div., Corps of Commissionaires. US Legion of Merit (Comdr), 1949. *Address:* 380 St George Street, Annapolis Royal, NS, Canada.

MORGAN; *see* Vaughan-Morgan.

MORGAN, Alun Michael, CMG 1957; Member, Committee of Independent Experts, European Social Charter, since 1976; Under-Secretary, Overseas Division, Department of Employment, 1966-75; UK Government Representative on ILO Governing Body, 1971-75; *b* 31 March 1915; *s* of Richard Michael Morgan, Rhayader; *m* 1958, Hilary Jane, *d* of late Eric Wilkinson, OBE, Kelsale, Suffolk. *Educ:* St Paul's Sch.; Magdalen Coll., Oxford. Min. of Labour, 1937; Served with Royal Fusiliers, 1940; with Special Forces, 1942-45 (Lieut-Col); Dep. Chief, Manpower Div., CCG, 1946. Asst Sec., Min. of Labour and Nat. Service, 1947; Manpower Counsellor, OEEC, 1948; Counsellor and Labour Attaché, HM Embassy, Washington, 1957-60; Under-Sec., Min. of Labour, 1964. *Address:* 15 Hasker Street, SW3. *Club:* United Oxford & Cambridge University.

MORGAN, Arthur William Crawford, (Tony Morgan); Director: Morgan, Hemingway & Co. Ltd; HMS Selection Services Ltd; Lease Equipment Management Ltd; Penrad Group Ltd, since 1976; *b* 24 Aug. 1931; *s* of Arthur James and Violet Morgan; *m* 1955, Valerie Anne Williams; three *s. Educ:* Hereford High Sch.; Westcliff High Sch. Chairman and Man. Dir, Purle Bros Holdings Ltd, 1964-72; Redland Purle Ltd, 1971-73. Governor, BBC, 1972-77; Chm., Nat. Assoc. of Waste Disposal Contractors, 1968; Mem., Staudinger Cttee on Plastic Wastes, 1968. Sailed Olympic Games, Tokyo; Silver Medal, Flying Dutchman, 1964; Jt Yachtsman of the Year, 1965; Member: British Olympic Yachting Appeal, 1970; Royal Yachting Assoc. Council, 1968-72. FRSA. *Publications:* various technical papers. *Recreations:* squash, skiing, sailing. *Address:* Orsett Hall, Orsett, Essex. *T:* Grays Thurrock 891402; Berg Fried, Zermatt, Switzerland. *T:* Zermatt 77101. *Clubs:* Royal Thames Yacht, Royal Ocean Racing.

MORGAN, Rear-Adm. Brinley John, CB 1972; Director, Administration, Social Science Research Council, since 1975; *b* 3 April 1916; *s* of Thomas Edward Morgan and Mary Morgan (*née* Parkhouse); *m* 1945, Margaret Mary Whittles; three *s. Educ:* Abersychan Grammar Sch.; University Coll., Cardiff (BSc 1937). Entered Royal Navy as Instr Lt, 1939. Served War of 1939-45: Cruisers Emerald and Newcastle, 1939-41; Aircraft Carrier Formidable, 1941-43; Naval Weather Service (Admty Forecast Section), 1943-45. Staff of C-in-C Medit., 1945-48; HQ, Naval Weather Service, 1948-50; Staff of Flag Officer Trg Sqdn in HM Ships Vanguard, Indefatigable and Implacable, 1950-52; Instr Comdr, 1951; Lectr, RN Coll., Greenwich, 1952-54; Headmaster, RN Schools, Malta, 1954-59; Instr Captain, 1960; Staff of Dir, Naval Educn Service, 1959-61 and 1963-64; Sen. Officers' War Course, 1961; HMS Ganges, 1961-63; Dean, RN Engineering Coll., Manadon, 1964-69; Instr Rear-Adm., 1970; Dir, Naval Educn Service, 1970-75, retired. *Recreations:* tennis, squash. *Address:* 11 Selwyn House, Manor Fields, Putney Hill, SW15. *T:* 01-789 3269. *Club:* Hurlingham.

MORGAN, Rev. Chandos Clifford Hastings Mansel, CB 1973; MA; Chaplain, Dean Close School, Cheltenham, since 1976;

Chaplain of the Fleet and Archdeacon of the Royal Navy, 1972-75; *b* 12 Aug. 1920; *s* of Llewelyn Morgan, Anglesey; *m* 1946, Dorothy Mary (*née* Oliver); one *s. Educ:* Stowe; Jesus Coll., Cambridge (MA); Ridley Hall, Cambridge. Curate of Holy Trinity, Tunbridge Wells, 1944-51; staff of Children's Special Service Mission, 1947-51; Chaplain, RN, 1951; served in HM Ships: Pembroke, 1951; Vengeance and Ceylon, 1952; Drake, 1954; Theseus, 1956; Ocean, 1957; Caledonia, 1958; Adamant, 1960; Jufair, 1961; Heron, 1963; Ark Royal, 1965; Collingwood, 1967; Royal Arthur, 1969. QHC 1972-75. *Recreations:* riding, shooting, sailing, gardening, etc. *Address:* Westwood Farmhouse, West Lydford, Somerton, Somerset. *T:* Wheathill 301. *Club:* Naval.

MORGAN, Mrs Charles (L.); *see* Vaughan, Hilda.

MORGAN, Clifford Isaac, OBE 1977; Head of Outside Broadcasts Group, BBC Television, since 1975; *b* 7 April 1930; *m* 1955, Nuala Martin; one *s* one *d. Educ:* Tonyrefail Grammar School, South Wales. Played International Rugby Union for Wales, British Lions and Barbarians. Joined BBC, 1958, as Sports Organiser, Wales; Editor, Sportsview and Grandstand, 1961-64; Producer, This Week, 1964-66; freelance writer and broadcaster, 1966-72; Editor, Sport Radio, 1972-74; Head of Outside Broadcasts, Radio, 1974-75. *Recreation:* music. *Address:* BBC Television, W14.

MORGAN, Sir Clifford Naunton, Kt 1966; MS; FRCS; FRCOG; Hon. FRCSI; Hon. FACS; Commander of the Order of the Star of the North (Sweden); Hon. Consulting Surgeon: St Bartholomew's Hospital; St Mark's Hospital for Diseases of the Rectum and Colon; Hospital for Tropical Diseases; Surgeon, King Edward VII's Hospital for Officers; Consulting Surgeon: RAF; (Colon and Rectum) RN; *b* 20 Dec. 1901; *s* of late Thomas Naunton Morgan, Penygraig; *m* 1930, Ena Muriel Evans; two *s* one *d. Educ:* Royal Masonic Sch.; University Coll., Cardiff; Univ. of London (St Bartholomew's Hosp.). MB 1924; FRCS 1926. Surgeon: Metropolitan Hosp., 1930; Royal Masonic Hosp.; St Bartholomew's Hospital: Demonstrator of Anatomy, Med. Coll., 1929; Chief Asst to a Surgical Unit, 1930; Casualty Surgeon, 1936; Asst Dir of Surgery, Professorial Unit, 1937. Lectr and Examr in Surgery, Univ. of London; Examr in Surgery, Univs of Cambridge, Glasgow, and Edinburgh. Officer i/c Surgical Divs, MEF, 1941-43 (despatches); Cons. Surgeon: Persia-Iraq Force, 1943-45; E Africa Comd, 1945; Hon. Col and late Brig., AMS. Twice Pres., Section of Proctology, Royal Soc. of Medicine; Mem. Council, RCS of England, 1953-68 (Vice-Pres., 1963-65); Past Vice-Chm., Imperial Cancer Research Fund. Sims Commonwealth Travelling Prof., 1963; Bradshaw Lectr, RCS, 1964; Vicary Lectr, 1967. Fellow, Assoc. of Surgeons of Great Britain and Ireland (Pres., 1968); Hon. Fellow: Amer. Surgical Assoc.; Amer. Protologic Soc.; For. Mem., Académie de Chirurgie; Hon. Member: Pennsylvania Proctologic Soc.; Société Nationale Française de Proctologie; Sociedades Argentina, Brasileira and Chilena de Proctologie; Med. Assoc. of Thessaloniki; Burmese Med. Assoc. *Publications:* various chapters in British Surgical Practice and other surgical Text Books. Contributor St Mark's Hosp. Centenary Vol., 1935. Many articles on Surgery of the Colon and Rectum in Brit. and Amer. Jls. *Recreation:* farming. *Address:* Rolfe's Farm, Inkpen, Berks RG15 0PZ. *T:* Inkpen 259. *Club:* Royal Air Force.

MORGAN, (Dafydd) Elystan; *b* 7 Dec. 1932; *s* of late Dewi Morgan and late Mrs Olwen Morgan; *m* 1959, Alwen, *d* of William E. Roberts; one *s* one *d. Educ:* Ardwyn Grammar Sch., Aberystwyth; UCW, Aberystwyth. LLB Hons Aberystwyth, 1953. Research at Aberystwyth and Solicitor's Articles, 1953-57; admitted a Solicitor, 1957; Partner in N Wales (Wrexham) Firm of Solicitors, 1958-68; Barrister-at-law, Gray's Inn, 1971. MP (Lab) Cardiganshire, 1966-Feb. 1974; Chm., Welsh Parly Party, 1967-68, 1971-74; Parly Under-Secretary of State, Home Office, 1968-70. Contested (Lab) Cardigan, Oct. 1974. Pres., Welsh Local Authorities Assoc., 1967-73. *Address:* Carreg Afon, Dolau, Bow Street, Dyfed.

MORGAN, (David) Dudley; Senior Partner, Theodore Goddard & Co., Solicitors, since 1974; *b* 23 Oct. 1914; *y s* of Thomas Dudley Morgan; *m* 1948, Margaret Helene, *o d* of late David MacNaughton Duncan, Loanhead, Midlothian; two *d. Educ:* Swansea Grammar Sch.; Jesus Coll., Cambridge (MA, LLB). War Service with RAF in Intell. Br., UK, 1940-42 and Legal Br., India, 1942-46; Wing Comdr 1945. Admitted Solicitor, 1939, with Theodore Goddard & Co.; Partner 1948. Director: Associated Fisheries Ltd; Crown House Ltd; Francis Industries Ltd; Turner Curzon Ltd, and other companies. An Underwriting Member of Lloyds. *Recreation:* gardening. *Address:* St Leonard's House, St Leonard's Road, Nazeing,

Waltham Abbey, Essex EN9 2HG. *T:* Nazeing 2124. *Club:* Carlton.

MORGAN, David Gethin; County Treasurer, Avon County Council, since 1973; *b* 30 June 1929; *s* of Edgar and Ethel Morgan; *m* 1955, Marion Brook. *Educ:* Jesus Coll., Oxford (MA Hons English). IPFA, FInstAM(Dip). Graduate Accountancy Asst, Staffordshire CC, 1952-58; Computer Systems Officer, Sen. O&M Officer, Cheshire CC, 1958-62; County Management Services Officer, Durham CC, 1962-65; Leicestershire CC: Asst County Treasurer, 1965-68; Dep. County Treasurer, 1968-73. *Publication:* Vol. XV Financial Information Service (IPFA). *Recreations:* local history, church architecture. *Address:* 6 Wyecliffe Road, Henleaze, Bristol, Avon BS9 4NH. *T:* Bristol 629640.

MORGAN, David Glyn; a Recorder of the Crown Court, since 1974; *b* 31 March 1933; *s* of late Dr Richard Glyn Morgan, MC, and of Nancy Morgan; *m* 1959, Ailsa Murray Strang; three *d*. *Educ:* Mill Hill Sch.; Merton Coll., Oxford (MA). Called to Bar, Middle Temple, 1958; practised Oxford Circuit, 1958-70; Wales and Chester Circuit, 1970-. 2nd Lieut, The Queen's Bays, 1955; Lieut and Captain (AER) The Queen's Bays and 1st The Queen's Dragoon Guards, 1956-62; Dep. Col, 1st The Queen's Dragoon Guards, 1976. *Recreations:* riding, fishing, Rugby football, gardening. *Address:* 2 Harcourt Buildings, Temple, EC4Y 9DB. *T:* 01-353 8549; 55 Park Place, Cardiff. *T:* Cardiff 41121. *Clubs:* Cavalry and Guards; Newport (Mon) Constitutional.

MORGAN, Sir David John H.; *see* Hughes-Morgan.

MORGAN, Rev. Dewi, (David Lewis); Rector, St Bride's Church, Fleet Street, EC4, since 1962; a Prebendary of St Paul's Cathedral, since 1976; *b* 5 Feb. 1916; *s* of David and Anne Morgan; *m* 1942, Doris, *d* of Samuel and Ann Povey; two *d*. *Educ:* Lewis Sch., Pengam; University Coll. Cardiff (BA); St Michael's Coll., Llandaff. Curate: St Andrew's, Cardiff, 1939-43; Aberdare, 1943-46; Aberavon, 1946-50. Soc. for the Propagation of the Gospel: Press Officer, 1950-52, Editorial and Press Sec., 1952-62; Editor, St Martin's Review, 1953-55; Associate Editor: Church Illustrated, 1955-67; Anglican World, 1960-67. Freeman of City of London, 1963. *Publications:* Expanding Frontiers, 1957; The Bishops Come to Lambeth, 1957; Lambeth Speaks, 1958; The Undying Fire, 1959; 1662 And All That, 1961; But God Comes First, 1962; Agenda for Anglicans, 1963; Seeds of Peace, 1965; Arising From the Psalms, 1965; God and Sons, 1967. Edited: They Became Anglicans, 1959; They Became Christians, 1966; The Church in Transition, 1970; The Phoenix of Fleet Street, 1973. *Recreation:* sleeping. *Address:* St Bride's Rectory, Fleet Street, EC4. *T:* 01-353 1301. *Clubs:* Athenæum; Press (Hon. Chaplain), Publicity (Hon. Chaplain).

MORGAN, Dudley; *see* Morgan, David D.

MORGAN, Rt. Rev. Edmund Robert, DD; resigned as Bishop of Truro (1951-Oct. 1959); *b* London, 28 July 1888; *s* of Joseph John Morgan, solicitor, and Adelaide Holberton; *m* 1916, Isabel Charlotte (*d* 1964), *y d* of Joseph Jupp of Mowbray House, Malvern; one *s* (and two who died in the war). *Educ:* Winchester; New Coll., Oxford; Liverpool Univ. (Dip. in Educn). Curate, Farnham, 1913-15; Eastleigh, 1915-19; Domestic Chaplain to Bishop Talbot of Winchester, 1919-23; Warden, Coll. of the Ascension, Selly Oak, Birmingham, 1923-36; Rector of Old Alresford, 1936-42; Archdeacon of Winchester, 1936-43; Suffragan Bishop of Southampton, 1943-51; Canon of Winchester Cathedral, 1942-51. DD (Lambeth) 1955. Editor, The East and West Review, 1935-46. *Publications:* (ed) Essays Catholic and Missionary, 1928; The Catholic Revival and Missions, 1933; The Mission of the Church, 1946; (ed) The Mission of the Anglican Communion, 1948; The Undiscovered Country, 1962; Reginald Somerset Ward: A Memoir, 1963; The Ordeal of Wonder, 1964. *Recreations:* music, gardening, carpentry. *Address:* Moor Farm, Whiteparish, Salisbury, Wilts.

MORGAN, Hon. Sir Edward James Ranembe, Kt 1952; *b* Warwick, Queensland, 25 March 1900; *s* of Edward Ranembe Morgan, Adelaide, and Jean McMillan, *d* of John Brown, Culver Lodge, Much Hadham, Herts; *m* 1924, Dorothy Millar, *o c* of James Waite, MBE; two *s* one *d*. *Educ:* St Peter's Coll., Adelaide; The University of Adelaide (LLB). Called to South Australian Bar, 1921; Stipendiary Magistrate, Adelaide Police Court, 1934-41; Pres. of Industrial Court (South Australia), 1941-52; Judge of Commonwealth Court of Conciliation and Arbitration, 1952-56; Judge, Commonwealth Industrial Court, 1956-60; Judge, Supreme Court of Australian Capital Territory,

1958-60. Mem., Board of Trustees, Art Gallery of S Australia, 1940-44, and 1961-63, Chm., 1944-55, and 1963-70; Pres. Nat. Trust of S Australia, 1960-62; *Publications:* The Adelaide Club, 1863-1963; (with S. H. Gilbert) Victorian Adelaide, 1968; (with S. H. Gilbert) Early Adelaide Architecture, 1969. *Address:* 155 Kermode Street, North Adelaide, SA 5006, Australia. *Clubs:* Adelaide (Adelaide), Melbourne (Melbourne).

MORGAN, Prof. Edwin George; Titular Professor of English, University of Glasgow, since 1975; *b* 27 April 1920; *s* of Stanley Lawrence Morgan and Margaret McKillop Arnott. *Educ:* Rutherglen Academy; High Sch. of Glasgow; Univ. of Glasgow. MA 1st Cl. Hons, Eng. Lang. and Lit., 1947. Served War, RAMC, 1940-46. University of Glasgow: Asst, 1947, Lectr, 1950, Sen. Lectr, 1965, Reader, 1971, in English. Cholmondeley Award for Poets, 1968; Hungarian PEN Meml Medal, 1972; Scottish Arts Council Book Awards, 1968, 1973, 1975, 1977. Visual/concrete poems in many internat. exhibns, 1965-. Opera librettos (unpublished): The Charcoal-Burner, 1969; Valentine, 1976; Columba, 1976. *Publications: poetry:* The Vision of Cathkin Braes, 1952; Beowulf, 1952; The Cape of Good Hope, 1955; Poems from Eugenio Montale, 1959; Sovpoems, 1961; (ed) Collins Albatross Book of Longer Poems, 1963; Starryveldt, 1965; Emergent Poems, 1967; Gnomes, 1968; The Second Life, 1968; Proverbfolder, 1969; Penguin Modern Poets 15, 1969; Twelve Songs, 1970; The Horseman's Word, 1970; (co-ed) Scottish Poetry 1-6, 1966-72; Glasgow Sonnets, 1972; Wi the Haill Voice, 1972; Instamatic Poems, 1972; The Whittrick, 1973; From Glasgow to Saturn, 1973; Fifty Renascence Love-Poems, 1975; Rites of Passage, 1976; The New Divan, 1977; *prose:* Essays, 1974. *Recreations:* photography, scrapbooks, walking in cities. *Address:* 19 Whittingehame Court, Glasgow G12 0BG. *T:* 041-339 6260.

MORGAN, Ellis, CMG 1961; HM Diplomatic Service, retired; Counsellor, Foreign and Commonwealth Office (formerly Foreign Office), 1966-73; *b* 26 Dec. 1916; *s* of late Ben Morgan and of Mary Morgan, The Grove, Three Crosses, Gower, S Wales; *m* 1st, 1948, Molly Darby (marr. diss.); three *d*; 2nd, 1975, Mary, *d* of late Slade Baker Stallard-Penoyre; one *s*. *Educ:* Swansea Grammar Sch. (Bishop Gore Sch.). Dep. Librarian, County Borough of Swansea, 1937-39. Commissioned Royal Artillery, 1941; served War of 1939-45, in India, Burma, Malaya, 1943-47. Entered Foreign (subseq. Diplomatic) Service, 1948; 3rd Sec., 1948-50, 2nd Sec., 1951-53, subseq. 1st Sec., British Embassy, Rangoon; 1st Sec., British Embassy, Bangkok, 1954-55; 1st Sec., Office of Commissioner-Gen., Singapore, 1957-60; Student at Imperial Defence Coll., 1961; Counsellor, UK High Commission, New Delhi, 1964. *Recreations:* walking and books. *Addrrss:* Penhenllan, Cusop, Hay-on-Wye, Hereford. *T:* Hay 826. *Club:* East India, Devonshire, Sports and Public Schools.

MORGAN, Elystan; *see* Morgan, D. E.

MORGAN, Sir Ernest (Dunstan), ORSL; KBE 1971 (OBE 1951; MBE 1940); DCL; JP; *b* 17 Nov. 1896; *s* of Thomas William Morgan and Susan Barnett; *m* 1st, 1918, Elizabeth Mary Agnes Collier; one *d*; 2nd, 1972, Monica Fredericka Davies; one *s* three *d*. *Educ:* Zion Day School, Freetown; Methodist Boys' High School, Freetown. Government Dispenser, 1914-20; Druggist, 1917-. MHR Sierra Leone, 1956-61; Member: Freetown City Council, 1938-44; Fourah Bay Coll. Council, 1950-54; Chairman: Blind Welfare Soc., 1946-52; Public Service Commn, 1948-52. JP Sierra Leone, 1952. *Recreation:* tennis. *Address:* 15 Syke Street, Freetown, Sierra Leone. *T:* Freetown 23155 and 22366. *Club:* Freetown Dinner.

MORGAN, Col Farrar Robert Horton, DSO 1940; OBE 1946; late Border Regiment; *b* 12 Sept. 1893; *e s* of late Robert Upton Morgan, MBE; *m* 1st, 1915, Alice Winifred May (*d* 1955), *d* of late Thomas R. Cross; two *s* two *d*; 2nd, 1957, Frances Maud (*d* 1977), 4th *d* of late Harold and Ida Blackborow and *widow* of Sidney Turner. *Educ:* University Coll. Sch.; Sch. of Oriental Studies, London Univ. First commissioned, 1914, Border Regt; served in France, 1915-16 (despatches, 1915 Star, British War and Victory Medals); King's African Rifles, E Africa, 1917-24; Somaliland, 1920 (Medal and Clasp); Adjt Glasgow and Aberdeen Univs OTC, 1931-35; Lt-Col 1940; Col, 1941; served in China, 1927; Palestine, 1937-39 (Medal and Clasp); war of 1939-45, France, 1939-40 (despatches, DSO); Comd British Troops in Syria, 1944-46 (OBE); retired pay, 1946. Syrian Order of Merit (1st Class). Principal Control Officer, Germany, 1946-49. *Recreation:* painting. *Address:* Greystones, Bath Road, Bradford-on-Avon, Wilts. *T:* Bradford-on-Avon 3418.

MORGAN, Col Frank Stanley, CBE 1940; ERD 1954; DL; JP; *b* 10 Jan. 1893; *s* of F. A. Morgan, Commissioner Imperial

Chinese Customs; *m* 1918, Gladys Joan (*d* 1953), *d* of Lt-Col H. M. Warde, CBE, DL Kent; no *c*; *m* 1956, Minnie Helen Pine, MBE, TD, DL, Lt-Col WRAC, The Manor House, Great Barrow, Cheshire. *Educ:* Marlborough; Christ Church, Oxford. Served European War, 1914-19; public work in Wales; Territorial and Reserve Service, 1919-39; Air Formation Signals, France, North Africa, Italy, Middle East, 1939-45; DL, Glamorgan, 1946; JP 1951; Hon. Col 50 and 81 AF Signal Regts, 1952-60. *Address:* Herbert's Lodge, Bishopston, Swansea. *T:* Bishopston 4222.

MORGAN, Graham, CMG 1954; FICE; Chartered Civil Engineer; *b* 12 July 1903; *m* 1931, Alice Jane Morgan; three *d*. *Educ:* King Henry VIII Grammar Sch., Abergavenny; University Coll., Cardiff. BSc Civil Engineering, Wales, 1923; Asst Engineer: Newport, Mon., 1924; Devon CC, 1924; Federated Malay States, 1926; Sen. Exec. Engineer, Malayan Public Works Service, 1941; State Engineer, Johore, 1948; Dir of Public Works, Tanganyika, 1950-Sept. 1954, retired. FICE (Mem. of Council, 1953-55). *Address:* 36 Sandfield Road, Oxford.

MORGAN, Guy, FRIBA; AIStructE; FRSA; BA; Senior Partner, in architectural practice; *b* 14 June 1902; *s* of late Francis Morgan and Miriam Hanley; *m* 1937, Violet Guy; one *d* (one *s* decd). *Educ:* Mill Hill; Cambridge; University Coll., London. Andrew Taylor Prizeman, 1923. Lecturer and Year Master, Architectural Assoc., 1931-36. In practice, 1927-; principal works include: large blocks of flats and offices in London and Provinces; aircraft factories and air bases; town planning schemes and housing in England and abroad; agricultural buildings and country houses; ecclesiastical and hospital works; film studios; racing and sports stadia. Past Joint Master, Cowdray Foxhounds. Past Master of Worshipful Company of Woolmen. *Recreations:* foxhunting, sailing, travel; music. *Address:* Lower House Farm, Fernhurst, Haslemere, Surrey. *T:* Fernhurst 222; 12A Eaton Square, SW1. *T:* 01-235 5101. *Clubs:* Royal Thames Yacht, Bath.

MORGAN, Gwenda, RE 1961; Wood Engraver; *b* 1 Feb. 1908; *d* of late William David Morgan, JP, and late Mary Morgan. *Educ:* Brighton and Hove High Sch. Studied Art at Goldsmiths' Coll. Sch. of Art, and at Grosvenor Sch. of Modern Art under Iain Macnab. Women's Land Army, 1939-46. Mem., Soc. of Wood Engravers. Exhibited in London, provincial and foreign exhibitions. Work represented in Victoria and Albert Museum and Brighton Art Gallery. *Address:* Ridge House, Petworth, West Sussex.

MORGAN, Gwyn; *see* Morgan, J. G.

MORGAN, Prof. Henry Gemmell; Professor of Pathological Biochemistry, University of Glasgow, since 1965; *b* 25 Dec. 1922; *s* of John McIntosh Morgan, MC, MD, FRCPE, and Florence Ballantyne; *m* 1949, Margaret Duncan, BSc, MB, ChB; one *d*. *Educ:* Dundee High Sch.; Merchiston Castle Sch., Edinburgh; Univ. of St Andrews at University Coll., Dundee. BSc 1943; MB, ChB (distinction), 1946; FRCPE 1962; FRCPGlas 1968; FRCPath 1970; FRSE 1971. Hon. Consultant, Eastern District, Glasgow, 1966-. Chm., Post-Grad. Cttee on Chem. Pathology, West of Scotland; Ext. Examnr, Biochemistry, Univ. of Dundee; Examnr in primary FRCS and MRCP, RCPGlas. Chm., Scottish Br., Nutrition Soc., 1967-68. Adviser to Scottish Home and Health Dept. *Publications:* chapters; papers in medical jls. *Recreations:* golf, foreign travel, history. *Address:* Royal Infirmary, Glasgow G4 0SF; Firwood House, 8 Eaglesham Road, Newton Mearns, Glasgow. *T:* 041-639 4404.

MORGAN, Hugh Travers, CMG 1966; HM Diplomatic Service; Ambassador to Austria, since 1976; *b* 3 Aug. 1919; *s* of Dr Montagu Travers Morgan, CMG, MC; *m* 1959, Alexandra Belinoff; two *s* one *d*. *Educ:* Winchester Coll.; Magdalene Coll., Cambridge. RAF, 1939-45, prisoner-of-war in Germany, 1941-45. Entered HM Diplomatic Service, 1945, and served: New York, 1946-48; Moscow, 1948-50; Foreign Office, 1950-53; Canadian National Defence Coll., 1953-54; Mexico City, 1954-57; Foreign Office, 1957-58; UK Delegation to Conference on Nuclear Tests, Geneva, 1958-61; Peking (Counsellor), 1961-63; Political Adviser to the British Commandant, Berlin, 1964-67; FCO, 1967-70; Ambassador, Peru, 1970-74; Asst Under-Sec. of State, FCO, 1974-75. *Address:* c/o Foreign and Commonwealth Office, SW1.

MORGAN, Irvonwy, MA, BD Cantab, PhD (London); Secretary, Department of the London Mission of the Methodist Church, since 1951; *b* 11 April 1907; *s* of Rev. Llewelyn Morgan and Alice Anna Davies; *m* 1942, Florence Mary Lewis; two *d*

decd. *Educ:* Kingswood Sch.; Wesley House, Cambridge (1st cl. hons Theol., Schofield Univ. Prize). PhD London, 1949; BD Cantab 1957. Asst at Poplar Mission; in charge of Poplar Mission from 1937. Methodist Delegate, World Council of Churches, Evanston, 1954; Guest Preacher, Methodist Church of Australasia, 1959; visited US on behalf of World Coun. of Churches, 1962 and 1966. Pres. of the Methodist Conference, 1967-68; Moderator, Free Church Federal Council, 1972-73. Chm., Bible Lands Soc. *Publications:* The Nonconformity of Richard Baxter, 1949; Twixt the Mount and Multitude, 1955; Prince Charles' Puritan Chaplain, 1957; The Godly Preachers of the Elizabethan Church, 1965; Puritan Spirituality, 1973; A Rent for Love, 1973. *Recreation:* gardening. *Address:* (Home) 12 Heathdene Road, Wallington, Surrey. *T:* Wallington 9418; (Office) 1 Central Buildings, Westminster, SW1H 9NH. *T:* 01-930 1453. *Club:* Reform.

MORGAN, John Albert Leigh; HM Diplomatic Service; Head of Cultural Relations Department of Foreign and Commonwealth Office since 1972; *b* 21 June 1929; *s* of John Edward Rowland Morgan, Bridge, Kent; *m* 1st, 1961, Hon. Fionn Frances Bride O'Neill (marr. diss. 1975), *d* of 3rd Baron O'Neill's, Shane's Castle, Antrim; one *s* two *d*; 2nd, 1976, Angela Mary Eleanor, *e d* of Patrick Warre Rathbone, Woolton, Liverpool. *Educ:* London School of Economics. Served in Army, 1947-49; entered Foreign Service, 1951; FO, 1951-53; 3rd Sec. and Private Sec. to HM Ambassador, Moscow, 1953-56; 2nd Sec., Peking, 1956-58; FO, 1958-63; 1st Sec., 1960; Head of Chancery, Rio de Janeiro, 1963-64; FO, 1964-65; Chargé d'Affaires, Ulan Bator, 1965; Moscow, 1965-67; FO, 1968; Counsellor, 1970; Head of Far Eastern Dept, FCO, 1970-72. Served on Earl Marshal's Staff for State Funeral of Sir Winston Churchill, 1965, and for Investiture of Prince of Wales, 1969. Governor, LSE, 1971-. *Recreations:* one *s* two *d*. *Address:* 41 Hugh Street, SW1V 1QJ. *T:* 01-821 1037. *Club:* Travellers'.

MORGAN, (John) Gwyn(fryn); Head of the Welsh Information Office of the European Economic Community, since 1975; a Director, Development Corporation for Wales, since 1976; *b* 16 Feb. 1934; *s* of Arthur G. Morgan, coal miner, and Mary Walters; *m* 1960, Joan Margaret Taylor; one *d*. *Educ:* Aberdare Boys' Grammar Sch.; UCW Aberystwyth. MA Classics 1957; Dip. Educn 1958. Senior Classics Master, The Regis Sch., Tettenhall, Staffs, 1958-60; Pres., National Union of Students, 1960-62; Sec.-Gen., Internat. Student Conf. (ISC), 1962-65; Head of Overseas Dept, British Labour Party, 1965-69; Asst Gen. Secretary, British Labour Party, 1969-72; Chef de Cabinet to Mr George Thomson, 1973-75. Mem., Hansard Commn on Electoral Reform, 1975-76. *Publications:* contribs to numerous British and foreign political jls. *Recreations:* cricket, Rugby football, crosswords, wine-tasting. *Address:* c/o 4 Cathedral Road, Cardiff CF1 9SG. *Clubs:* Royal Commonwealth Society, Reform; Cardiff and County.

MORGAN, Kenneth; Joint Secretary, Press Council, since 1977 (Consultative Member, since 1970); *b* 3 Nov. 1928; *s* of Albert E. and Lily M. Morgan; *m* 1950, Margaret Cynthia, *d* of Roland E. Wilson; three *d*. *Educ:* Stockport Grammar School. Reporter, Stockport Express, 1944; Army, 1946; journalism, 1949; Central London Sec., NUJ, 1962; Nat. Organiser, NUJ, 1966; Gen. Sec., NUJ, 1970-77. Mem. Exec. Cttee: Printing and Kindred Trades Fedn, 1970-73; Nat. Fedn of Professional Workers, 1970-77; Bureau, Internat. Fedn of Journalists, 1970. Member: Printing Industries Cttee, TUC, 1974-77; Printing and Publishing Industries Trng Bd, 1975-77; Jt Standing Cttee, Nat. Newspaper Industry, 1976-77. *Recreations:* theatre, military history. *Address:* 174 Overhill Road, Dulwich, SE22 0PS. *T:* 01-693 6585. *Club:* Press.

MORGAN, Leslie James Joseph; a Recorder of the Crown Court, since 1975; a Deputy Circuit Judge, 1973-75; *b* Ballina, NSW, 2 June 1922; *er s* of late Bertram Norman Morgan and Margaret Mary Morgan, MA (*née* Meere); *m* 1949, Sheila Doreen Elton Williamson; one *s* one *d*. *Educ:* Bournemouth Sch.; University Coll., Southampton. LLB (London) 1943. Served, Home Guard, 1940, Radio Security Service, 1941-43. Solicitor (Distinction) 1944; general law practice, 1944-. Chairman: Southern Area Legal Aid Cttee, 1973-74; Bournemouth Exec. Council (NHS), 1962-74; Dorset Family Practitioner Cttee, 1974-77; Mem. Council, Law Society, 1973-; President: Bournemouth and Dist Law Soc., 1972-73; Soc. of Family Practitioner Cttees, 1975-76. *Publications:* articles on aspects of short wave radio. *Recreations:* music, reading, wine, amateur radio (licensed as G2HNO, 1939-). *Address:* 4 Tree Tops, Martello Park, Canford Cliffs, Poole, Dorset BH13 7BA. *T:* Canford Cliffs 708405. *Clubs:* Junior Carlton; Hampshire (Winchester), Constitutional (Bournemouth).

MORGAN, Michael Hugh; HM Diplomatic Service; High Commissioner, Sierra Leone, since 1977; b 18 April 1925; s of late H. P. Morgan; m 1957, Julian Bamfield; two s. Educ: Shrewsbury Sch.; Downing College, Cambridge; School of Oriental and African Studies, London Univ. Army Service 1943-46. HMOCS Malaya, 1946-56. Foreign Office, 1956-57; First Secretary, Peking, 1957-60; Belgrade 1960-64; attached to Industry, 1964; First Secretary, FCO, 1964-68; Counsellor and Head of Chancery, Cape Town/Pretoria, 1968-72; Counsellor, Peking, 1972-75; Inspector, FCO, 1975-77. Address: c/o Foreign and Commonwealth Office, SW1; Strefford House, Strefford, Craven Arms, Salop SY7 8DE.

MORGAN, Sir Morien Bedford, Kt 1969; CB 1958; MA; FRS 1972, CEng, Hon. FRAeS; Master, Downing College, Cambridge, since 1972; b 20 Dec. 1912; s of late John Bedford and Edith Mary Morgan, Bridgend, Glam; m 1941, Sylvia Axford; three d. Educ: Rutlish, Merton; St Catharine's Coll., Cambridge (Hon. Fellow, 1973). John Bernard Seely Prize in Aeronautics, 1934; apprenticed to Mather & Platt Ltd, 1934-35; joined Aerodynamics Dept, Royal Aircraft Establishment, 1935, and for some years was engaged on flight research and develt, specialising in problems of aircraft stability and control. Pilot's "A" licence, 1944. Head of Aero. Flight Section, RAE, 1946-48. Head of Guided Weapons Dept, RAE, 1948-53; Dep. Dir, RAE, 1954-59; Scientific Adviser, Air Ministry, 1959-60; Dep. Controller of Aircraft (R&D), Min. of Aviation, 1960-63; Controller of Aircraft, 1963-66; Controller of Guided Weapons and Electronics, Min. of Technology, 1966-69; Dir, RAE, 1969-72. Member: Airworthiness Requirements Bd, 1973-; Air Warfare Adv. Bd, 1974-; PO Bd (part time), 1975-. Chm., Air Traffic Control Bd, 1975-; Pres., Royal Aeronautical Society, 1967-68, Hon. Fellow, 1976. Founder Fellow, Fellowship of Engineering, 1976. Hon. DSc: Cranfield, 1976; Southampton, 1976. Silver Medal of the Royal Aeronautical Society, 1957, Gold Medal 1971, Busk Prize 1972. Publications: Reports and Memoranda of Aeronautical Research Council. Lectures to Royal Aeronautical Society. Recreation: music. Address: The Master's Lodge, Downing College, Cambridge. T: Cambridge 56338. Club: Athenæum.

MORGAN, Oswald Gayer, MA, MCh Cantab; FRCS; Consultant Surgeon Emeritus; Past President, Ophthalmological Society of UK; b 1889; m 1926, Jessie Campbell (d 1938), yr d of Colin MacDonald, 38 Abbey Road, NW; two d. Educ: Epsom Coll.; Clare Coll., Cambridge; Guy's Hosp. Surgeon in charge Duchess of Sutherland's Hosp., France, 1914-18; Ophthalmic House Surg. at Moorfield's Eye Hosp., 1920. Vice-Pres., BMA, 1965. Publications: The Wounded in Namur; Some Aspects of the Treatment of Infected War Wounds, British Journal of Surgery, 1916; Ophthalmology in General Practice. Address: The Oaks, West Byfleet, Surrey.

MORGAN, Rear-Adm. Sir Patrick (John), KCVO 1970; CB 1967; DSC 1942; Flag Officer, Royal Yachts, 1965-70, retired; b 26 Jan. 1917; s of late Vice-Adm. Sir Charles Morgan, KCB, DSO; m 1944, Mary Hermione Fraser-Tytler, d of late Col Neil Fraser-Tytler, DSO, Aldourie Castle, Inverness, and of Mrs C. H. Fraser-Tytler, qv; three s one d. Educ: RN College, Dartmouth. Served War of 1939-45 (despatches, DSC). Naval Attaché, Ankara, 1957-59; Imperial Defence Coll. 1960; Asst Chief of Staff, Northwood, 1961-62; Commanding Officer, Commando Ship, HMS Bulwark, 1963-64. Recreations: sports. Address: Swallow Barn, Well Road, Crondall, Farnham, Surrey GU10 5PW. T: Aldershot 850107.

MORGAN, Peter Trevor Hopkin, QC 1972; His Honour Judge Hopkin Morgan; a Circuit Judge, since 1972; b 5 Feb. 1919; o s of Cyril Richard Morgan and Muriel Arceta (née Hole); m 1942, Josephine Mouncey, d of Ben Travers, qv; one s three d. Educ: Mill Hill Sch.; Magdalen Coll., Oxford (BA). Called to Bar, Middle Temple, 1949; Wales and Chester Circuit; Lectr in Law, Univ. of Wales (Cardiff and Swansea), 1950-55; Mem., Mental Health Review Tribunal for Wales; Queen's Proctor's Panel, 1968-72. Liveryman, Fishmongers' Company. Recreation: rivers. Address: Itton Court, Chepstow NP6 6BW. T: Chepstow 3935. Club: Garrick.

MORGAN, Robin Milne; Principal, Daniel Stewart's and Melville College, Edinburgh, since 1977; b 2 Oct. 1930; o s of Robert Milne Morgan and Aida Forsyth Morgan; m 1955, Fiona Bruce MacLeod Douglas; three s one d. Educ: Mackie Academy, Stonehaven; Aberdeen Univ. (MA); London Univ. (BA, External). Nat. Service, 2nd Lieut The Gordon Highlanders, 1952-54; Asst Master: Arden House Prep. Sch., 1955-60; George Watson's Coll., 1960-71; Headmaster, Campbell Coll., Belfast, 1971-76. Recreations: music, archaeology, fishing, climbing, deer-stalking. Address: Daniel

Stewart's and Melville College, Queensferry Road, Edinburgh EH4 3EZ. Club: Watsonian (Edinburgh).

MORGAN, Roger Hugh Vaughan Charles; Librarian, House of Lords, since 1977; b 8 July 1926; s of late Charles Langbridge Morgan, FRSL, and of Hilda Vaughan, qv; m 1st, 1951, Harriet Waterfield (marr. diss. 1965), d of Gordon Waterfield; one s one d (and one s decd); 2nd, 1965, Susan Vogel Marrian, d of Hugo Vogel, Milwaukee, USA; one s. Educ: Downs Sch., Colwall; Phillips Acad., Andover, USA; Eton Coll.; Brasenose Coll., Oxford. MA. Grenadier Guards, 1944-47 (Captain, 1946). House of Commons Library, 1951-63; House of Lords Library, 1963-. Recreations: photography, cooking. Address: 30 St Peter's Square, W6 9UH. T: 01-741 0267. Club: Garrick.
See also Marchioness of Anglesey.

MORGAN, Tony; see Morgan, A. W. C.

MORGAN, Walter Thomas James, CBE 1959; FRS 1949; Director, Lister Institute of Preventive Medicine, London, 1972-75 (Deputy Director, 1952-68); b London, 5 Oct. 1900; s of Walter and Annie E. Morgan; m 1930, Dorothy Irene Price; one s two d. Educ: Univ. of London. Grocers' Company Scholar, 1925-27; Beit Memorial Med. Res. Fellow, 1927-28; First Asst and Biochemist, Lister Institute Serum Dept (Elstree), 1928-37; Rockefeller Research Fellow (Eidgenössiche Tech. Hochschule, Zürich), 1937. Reader, 1938-51, Lister Inst.; Prof. of Biochemistry, Univ. of London, 1951-68, now Prof. Emeritus. PhD 1927, DSc 1937, London Univ.; DrSc (Tech.) Zürich, 1938; FRIC 1929. Hon. Secretary: Biochemical Soc., 1940-45; Biological Council, 1944-47. Chm. Bd of Studies, Biochem., Univ. of London, 1954-57; Mem. of Scientific Advisory Council, 1956-60; Mem. of Medical Research Council, 1966-70. Guest Lecturer, 100th meeting of Gesellschaft Deutscher Naturforscher und Ärzte, Germany, 1959; Croonian Lecturer of Royal Soc., 1959; Vice-Pres., Royal Soc., 1961-64; Royal Medal, Royal Soc., 1968. MD hc Basel, 1964; DSc hc Michigan, 1969. Conway Evans Prize (Royal College of Physicians, London), 1964. (Jointly) Landsteiner Memorial Award (USA), 1967. (Jointly) Paul Ehrlich and Ludwig Darmstädter Prizes (Germany), 1968. Publications: papers on biochemistry, immunology and pathology. Address: Division of Immunochemical Genetics, Medical Research Council, Clinical Research Centre, Watford Road, Harrow, Mddx HA1 3UJ. T: 01-844 5311; 57 Woodbury Drive, Sutton, Surrey. T: 01-642 2319. Club: Athenæum.

MORGAN, William Geraint Oliver, QC 1971; MP (C) Denbigh, since Oct. 1959; a Recorder of the Crown Court, since 1972; b Nov. 1920; m 1957, J. S. M. Maxwell; two s two d. Educ: University Coll. of Wales, Aberystwyth; Trinity Hall, Cambridge. Served War of 1939-45 with Royal Marines; demobilised with Rank of Major, 1946. Called to the Bar, Gray's Inn, 1947; Squire Law Scholar; Holt Scholar; Northern Circuit. Contested: Merioneth, 1951; Huyton, 1955. Address: House of Commons, SW1; 13 Owen Road, Prescot, Lancs L35 0PJ.

MORGAN, Air Vice-Marshal William Gwyn, CB 1968; CBE 1960 (OBE 1945); RAF, retired 1969; b 13 Aug. 1914; s of T. S. Morgan; m 1962, Joan Russell. Educ: Pagefield Coll., Swansea. Joined Royal Air Force, 1939; Group Capt., 1958; Command Acct, HQ, FEAF, 1962; Air Commodore, 1965; DPS (2), RAF, 1965-66; AOA Technical Training Comd, 1966-68, Training Comd, 1968-69. Air Vice-Marshal, 1967; jssc; psc; FCCA; ACMA. Recreation: fell walking. Address: c/o Lloyds Bank, 6 Pall Mall, SW1. Club: Royal Air Force.

MORGAN, Rt. Hon. William James, PC (Northern Ireland) 1961; JP; Member (UUUC), for North Belfast, Northern Ireland Constitutional Convention, 1975-76; b 1914; m 1942; two s one d. Transport contractor. MP, Oldpark Div. of Belfast, 1949-58, Clifton Div. of Belfast, 1959-69, NI Parlt; Minister: of Health and Local Government, Northern Ireland, 1961-64; of Labour and National Insurance, 1964; of Health and Social Services, 1965-69; Mem. (U), N Belfast, NI Assembly, 1973-75. Address: Rhanbuoy, Carrickfergus, Co. Antrim. T: Carrickfergus 62236.

MORGAN, William Stanley, CMG 1965; Colonial Administrative Service, retired; b 29 April 1908; s of late J. W. Morgan; m 1957, Joan Ruth Dixon Williams; two s one d. Educ: Rendcomb Coll.; (Open Scholar in History) Queens' Coll., Cambridge (MA). Malayan Education Service, 1931-50; Colonial Administrative Service, 1950-57; Malaya, 1931-47; Sec., Commn on Univ. Educn in Malaya, 1947; Principal, Colonial Office, 1947-50; Sierra Leone, Ministerial Sec., 1950-57; Asst Adviser to Qatar Govt, 1957-60; Chm., Public and Police Service Commns, Mauritius, 1960-69. Publication: Story of Malaya, 1938. Recreations: tennis, travel and music. Address: Old Vicarage, Maughold, Isle of Man. T: Ramsey 2863.

MORGAN-GILES, Rear-Adm. Morgan Charles, DSO 1944; OBE 1943 (MBE 1942); GM 1941; MP (C) for Winchester since May 1964; *b* 19 June 1914; *e s* of late F. C. Morgan-Giles, OBE, MINA, Teignmouth, Devon; *m* 1946, Pamela (*d* 1966), *d* of late Philip Bushell, Sydney, New South Wales; two *s* four *d* ; *m* 1968, Marigold, *d* of late Percy Lowe. *Educ:* Clifton Coll. Entered Royal Navy, 1932; served on China Station, and in destroyers. War Service: Atlantic convoys and Mediterranean; Tobruk garrison and Western Desert, 1941; with RAF, 1942; Sen. Naval Officer, Vis. (Dalmatia) and liaison with Commandos and Marshal Tito's Partisan Forces, 1943-44. Captain 1953; Chief of Naval Intelligence, Far East, 1955-56; Captain (D) Dartmouth Training Sqdn, 1957-58; HMS Belfast, in command, 1961-62; Rear-Adm. 1962; Adm. Pres., Royal Naval Coll., Greenwich, 1962-64; retd 1964. Vice-Chm., Conservative Defence Cttee, 1965-75. Chm., HMS Belfast Trust; Member: Management Cttee, RNLI; Council Navy League; Governor, Heathfield Sch. Liveryman, Shipwrights' Company. *Recreations:* sailing, country pursuits. *Address:* Upton Park, Alresford, Hants. *T:* Alresford 2443; 93 West Eaton Place Mews, SW1. *T:* 01-235 8413. *Clubs:* Carlton; Royal Yacht Squadron; Australian (Sydney).
See also Baron Killearn.

MORGAN HUGHES, David; *see* Hughes, David M.

MORGAN-OWEN, John Gethin, MBE 1945; Vice Judge Advocate General since 1972; *b* 22 Aug. 1914; *o s* of late Maj.-Gen. L. I. G. Morgan-Owen, CB, CMG, CBE, DSO, West Dene, Beech, Alton; *m* 1950, Mary, *d* of late F. J. Rimington, MBE, Master Mariner; two *s* one *d.* *Educ:* Shrewsbury; Trinity Coll., Oxford (BA). Called to Bar, Inner Temple, 1938; Wales and Chester Circuit, 1939; practised at Cardiff, 1939-52. 2nd Lieut Suppl. Reserve, S Wales Borderers, 1939; served 2nd Bn SWB, 1939-44: N Norway, 1940; NW Europe, 1944; DAA&QMG, 146 Inf. Bde, 1944-45; Hon. Major. Dep. Judge Advocate, 1952: Germany, 1953-56; Hong Kong, 1958-60; Cyprus, 1963-66; AJAG, 1966; DJAG, Germany, 1970-72. *Recreations:* bad tennis, inland waterways, beagling. *Address:* Burninghams, Kingsley, Bordon, Hants GU35 9NW. *T:* Bordon 2040. *Club:* Army and Navy.

MORI, Haruki; Adviser to Japanese Foreign Office, since 1975; *b* 1911; *m* 1940, Tsutako Masaki; four *s.* *Educ:* Univ. of Tokyo. Ministry of Foreign Affairs, served USA and Philippines, 1935-41; Head of Economic Section, Dept of Political Affairs, 1950-53; Counsellor, Italy, 1953-55, Asian Affairs Bureau, 1955-56; Private Sec. to Prime Minister, 1956-57; Dep. Dir-Gen., Economic Affairs Bureau, 1957; Dir-Gen., American Affairs Bureau, 1957-60; Minister Plenipotentiary to UK, 1960-63, to France, 1963-64; Ambassador to OECD, 1964-67; Dep. Vice-Minister for Foreign Affairs, 1967-70; Vice-Minister for Foreign Affairs, 1970-72; Japanese Ambassador to the Court of St James's, 1972-75. *Recreation:* golf. *Address:* c/o Ministry of Foreign Affairs, Tokyo, Japan.

MORIARTY, Gerald Evelyn, QC 1974; a Recorder of the Crown Court, since 1976; *b* 23 Aug. 1928; *er s* of Lt-Col G. R. O'N. Moriarty and Eileen Moriarty (*née* Moloney); *m* 1961, Judith Mary, *er d* of Hon. William Robert Atkin; four *s.* *Educ:* Downside Sch.; St John's Coll., Oxford (MA). Called to the Bar, Lincoln's Inn, 1951. *Address:* 20 Addison Gardens, W14 8BQ. *T:* 01-602 1253. *Club:* Reform.

MORIARTY, Brig. Joan Olivia Elsie, RRC 1977; Matron-in-Chief and Director of Army Nursing Services, since Dec. 1976; *b* 11 May 1923; *d* of late Lt-Col Oliver Nash Moriarty, DSO, RA, and Mrs Georgina Elsie Moriarty (*née* Moore). *Educ:* Royal Sch., Bath; St Thomas' Hosp. (nursing); Queen Charlotte's Hosp. (midwifery). SRN. VAD, Somerset, 1941-42; joined QAIMNS (R), 1947; Reg. QAIMNS (later QARANC), 1948-; appts incl.: Staff Captain, WO; Instr, Corps Trng Centre; Liaison Officer, MoD; served in UK, Gibraltar, BAOR, Singapore, Malaya, Cyprus; Matron, Mil. Hosp., Catterick, 1973-76; Comdt, QARANC Trng Centre, Aldershot, 1976. Major 1960; Lt-Col 1971; Col 1973; Brig. 1977. QHNS, 1977-. OStJ 1977. *Recreation:* country pursuits. *Address:* Ministry of Defence (AMD 4), Lansdowne House, Berkeley Square, W1X 6AA. *Club:* VAD Ladies.

MORIARTY, Michael John; Assistant Under-Secretary of State, Criminal Policy Department, Home Office, since 1975; *b* 3 July 1930; *er s* of Edward William Patrick Moriarty, OBE, and May Lilian Moriarty; *m* 1960, Rachel Milward, *d* of J. S. Thompson and Isobel F. Thompson; one *s* two *d* . *Educ:* Reading Sch., Reading; St John's Coll., Oxford (Sir Thomas White schol.; MA Lit. Hum.). Entered Home Office as Asst Principal, 1954; Private Sec. to Parliamentary Under-Secretaries of State, 1957-

59; Principal, 1959; Civil Service Selection Bd, 1962-63; Cabinet Office, 1965-67; Asst Sec., 1967; Private Sec. to Home Sec., 1968; Head of Crime Policy Planning Unit, 1974-75. UK Representative, and Chm., 1978-, Council of Europe Cttee on Crime Problems. *Recreations:* music, walking, family pursuits. *Address:* 36 Willifield Way, Hampstead Garden Suburb, NW11 7XT. *T:* 01-455 8439.

MORICE, Prof. Peter Beaumont, DSc, PhD; FICE, FIStructE; Professor of Civil Engineering, University of Southampton, since 1958; *b* 15 May 1926; *o s* of Charles and Stephanie Morice; *m* 1952, Margaret Ransom; one *s* two *d.* *Educ:* Barfield Sch.; Farnham Grammar Sch.; University of Bristol; University of London. Surrey County Council, 1947-48; Research Div., Cement and Concrete Assoc., 1948-57. *Publications:* Linear Structural Analysis, 1958; Prestressed Concrete, 1958; papers on structural theory in various learned journals. *Recreations:* sailing, reading, listening to music. *Address:* 65 Shaftesbury Avenue, Highfield, Southampton. *T:* 556624.

MORINI, Erica; concert violinist; *b* Vienna, 5 Jan. 1910; *m* 1938, Felice Siracusano; no *c.* *Educ:* at age of 4 years under father, Prof. Oscar Morini, and then under Prof. Ottocar Sevcik, masterclass of Viennese Conservatory, at age of 8. Debut under Arthur Nikisch, at age of 9, in Leipzig Gewandhaus (Beethoven Festival); from there on Concert-tours to: Australia, Asia, Africa, Europe; to USA, 1920. Hon. Mem., Sigma Alpha Beta. Hon. MusD: Smith Coll., Mass, 1955; New England Conservatory of Music, Mass, 1963. *Recreations:* mountain climbing and chamber music. *Address:* 1200 Fifth Avenue, New York, NY 10029, USA.

MORISHIMA, Prof. Michio; Professor of Economics, London School of Economics and Political Science, since 1970; *b* 18 July 1923; *s* of Kameji and Tatsuo Morishima; *m* 1953, Yoko; two *s* one *d.* *Educ:* Univ. of Kyoto (BAEcon). Assistant Professor: Kyoto Univ., 1950-51; Osaka Univ., 1951-63; Prof., Osaka Univ., 1963-69; Sen. Visiting Fellow, All Souls Coll, 1963-64; Visiting Prof., Stanford Univ., 1964; Temp. Prof. and Keynes Visiting Prof., Univ. of Essex, 1968-70. Associate Editor, Econometrica, 1959-69; Co-editor and Editor, Internat. Economic Review, 1960-67; Board of Editors: Economica, 1975-; Jl of Economic Lit., 1976-; Fellow, Econometric Soc., 1958-, Vice-Pres., 1964, Pres., 1965; For. Hon. Mem., Amer. Acad. of Arts and Sciences, 1975-; For. Hon. Mem., Amer. Economic Assoc., 1976-. *Publications:* Equilibrium, Stability and Growth, 1964; Theory of Economic Growth, 1969; The Working of Econometric Models, 1972; Marx's Economics, 1973; Theory of Demand: real and monetary, 1973; The Economic Theory of Modern Society, 1976; Walras' Economics, 1977. *Recreation:* playing baseball with children. *Address:* Ker, Greenway, Hutton Mount, Brentwood, Essex CM13 2NP. *T:* Brentwood 219956.

MORISON, Alastair Malcolm; QC (Scotland), 1968; *b* 12 Feb. 1931; 2nd *s* of Sir Ronald Peter Morison, QC (Scotland); *m* 1957, Lindsay Balfour Oatts; one *s* one *d.* *Educ:* Cargilfield; Winchester Coll.; Edinburgh Univ. Admitted to Faculty of Advocates, 1956. *Recreation:* golf. *Address:* 6 Carlton Terrace, Edinburgh EH7 5DD. *T:* 031-556 6766. *Club:* New.

MORISON, Air Vice-Marshal Richard Trevor, CBE 1969 (MBE 1944); RAF retired; President, Ordnance Board, 1971-72; *s* of Oscar Colin Morison and Margaret Valerie (*née* Cleaver); *m* 1964, Rosemary June Brett; one *s* one *d.* *Educ:* Perse Sch., Cambridge; De Havilland Sch. of Aeronautical Engineering. Commnd in RAF, 1940; RAF Staff Coll., 1952; Sen. Techn. Officer, RAF Gaydon, 1955-57; HQ Bomber Comd, 1958-60; STSO HQ 224 Group, Singapore, 1960-61; Dir of Techn. Services, Royal NZ Air Force, 1961-63; Comd Engrg Officer, HQ Bomber Comd, 1963-65; Air Officer i/c Engrg, HQ Flying Training Comd, 1966-68; Air Officer i/c Engrg, HQ Training Comd RAF, 1968-69; Vice-Pres. (Air) Ordnance Bd, 1969-70. *Recreation:* cabinet making. *Address:* Meadow House, Chedgrave, Loddon, Norfolk. *Club:* Royal Air Force.

MORITA, Akio; Chairman of the Board and Chief Executive Officer, Sony Corporation, since 1976; *b* Nagoya, Japan, 26 Jan. 1921; *m* 1950, Yoshiko Kamei; two *s* one *d* . *Educ:* Osaka Imperial Univ. (BSc Physics). Sony Corporation, Tokyo: co-founder, 1946; Man. Dir, 1947-55; Sen. Man. Dir, 1955-56; Exec. Vice-Pres., 1959-71; Pres., 1971-76; Sony Corporation of America: Pres., 1960-66, Chm., 1966-72; Chm. Finance Cttee, 1972-74; Chm. Exec. Cttee, 1974-. Dir, IBM World Trade Americas/Far East Corp., 1972-77; Member: Internat. Council, Morgan Guaranty Trust Co.; Rockefeller Univ. Council. *Publications:* Gakureki Muyooron (Never Mind Education Records), 1966; Shin Jitsuryoku Shugi (A New Merit System),

1969. *Recreations:* music, golf. *Address:* Sony Corporation, 6-7-35 Kitashinagawa, Shinagawa-ku, Tokyo 141, Japan. *T:* 03-448-2002.

MORLAND, Martin Robert; HM Diplomatic Service; Head of Maritime and General Department, Foreign and Commonwealth Office, since 1977; *b* 23 Sept. 1933; *e s* of Sir Oscar Morland, *qv*; *m* 1964, Jennifer Avril Mary Hanbury-Tracy; two *s* one *d. Educ:* Ampleforth; King's Coll., Cambridge (BA). Nat. Service, Grenadier Guards, 1954-56; British Embassy, Rangoon, 1957-60; News Dept, FO, 1961; UK Delegn to Common Market negotiations, Brussels, 1962-63; FO, 1963-65; UK Disarmament Delegn, Geneva, 1965-67; Private Sec. to Lord Chalfont, 1967-68; European Integration Dept, FCO, 1968-73; Counsellor (Economic), 1973-76, Head of Chancery, 1973-77, Rome (seconded temporarily to Cabinet Office to head EEC Referendum Information Unit, 1975). *Address:* 3 Westover Road, SW18.

MORLAND, Michael, QC 1972; a Recorder of the Crown Court, since 1972; *b* 16 July 1929; *e s* of Edward Morland, Liverpool, and Jane Morland (*née* Beckett); *m* 1961, Lillian Jensen, Copenhagen; one *s* one *d. Educ:* Stowe; Christ Church, Oxford (MA). 2nd Lieut, Grenadier Guards, 1948-49; served in Malaya. Called to Bar, Inner Temple, 1953; practises on Northern Circuit. *Address:* 12 King's Bench Walk, Temple, EC4Y 7EL. *T:* 01-353 5892.

MORLAND, Sir Oscar Charles, GBE 1962; KCMG 1959 (CMG 1949); HM Ambassador to Japan, 1959-63, retired; *b* 23 March 1904; *s* of Harold John Morland, MA, FCA; *m* 1932, Alice, *d* of late Rt Hon. Sir F. O. Lindley, PC, GCMG; four *s. Educ:* Leighton Park Sch.; King's Coll., Cambridge. Joined HM Consular Service, 1927. Served in Japan, Manchuria, London. Under Sec., Cabinet Office, 1950-53; Ambassador to Indonesia, 1953-56; Asst Under-Sec., FO, 1956-59. Mem., Leeds Regional Hosp. Bd, 1965-74 (Chm. Mental Health and Geriatrics Cttee, 1972-74). *Address:* The High Hall, Thornton-le-Dale, Pickering, North Yorks. *T:* Thornton-le-dale 371. *Club:* Travellers'. *See also M. R. Morland.*

MORLEY; *see* Headlam-Morley.

MORLEY, 6th Earl of, *cr* 1815; **John St Aubyn Parker,** JP; DL; Lt-Col, Royal Fusiliers; Chairman: Farm Industries Ltd, Truro, since 1970; Plymouth Sound Ltd, since 1974; Director, Lloyds Bank, since 1974; *b* 29 May 1923; *e s* of Hon. John Holford Parker (*y s* of 3rd Earl), Pound House, Yelverton, Devon; *S* uncle, 1962; *m* 1955, Johanna Katherine, *d* of Sir John Molesworth-St Aubyn, Bt, *qv*; one *s* one *d. Educ:* Eton. 2nd Lt, KRRC, 1942; served NW Europe, 1944-45; Palestine and Egypt, 1945-48; transferred to Royal Fusiliers, 1947; served Korea, 1952-53; Middle East, 1953-55 and 1956; Staff Coll., Camberley, 1957; Comd, 1st Bn Royal Fusiliers, 1965-67. Mem., Devon and Co. Cttee, Nat. Trust, 1969-; President: Plymouth Incorporated Chamber of Trade and Commerce, 1970-; Cornwall Fedn of Chambers of Commerce and Trader Assocs, 1972; West Country Tourist Bd, 1971-. Governor: Seale-Hayne Agric. Coll., 1973; Plymouth Polytechnic, 1975- (Chm., 1977-). DL Devon, 1973. JP Plymouth, 1972. *Heir: s* Viscount Boringdon, *qv. Address:* Pound House, Yelverton, Devon. *T:* Yelverton 3162.

MORLEY, Cecil Denis, CBE 1967; Secretary General, The Stock Exchange, London, 1965-71; *b* 20 May 1911; *s* of Cornelius Cecil Morley and Mildred Irene Hutchinson; *m* 1936, Lily Florence Younge; one *s. Educ:* Clifton; Trinity Coll., Cambridge. Solicitor. Asst Sec., Share & Loan Dept, Stock Exchange, 1936; Sec. to Coun. of Stock Exchange, 1949. Served War of 1939-45, Major RA (TA). *Recreations:* travel, gardening. *Address:* 17a Eldon Road, W8. *T:* 01-937 8383.

MORLEY, Eric Douglas; Chairman since 1969 and Managing Director since 1968, Mecca Ltd, world's largest leisure complex; Director, Grand Metropolitan Hotels, since 1969; Director of numerous other companies; Managing Director, Outward Bound, since 1976; *b* 26 Sept. 1918; *s* of William Joseph Morley and Bertha Emily Menzies; *m* 1958, Julia Evelyn Pritchard; four *s* one *d. Educ:* Whitstable Grammar Sch.; St Martin-in-the-Fields; British Army School. Royal Fusiliers, 1934; RASC Motor Boats, 1943; demobilised 1946 (Captain). Joined Mecca, 1946; Dancing Dir, 1951; Dir, 1954; Asst Man. Dir, 1961; Jt Man. Dir, 1967. Mem., Outward Bound Council. Chm., main trade assocs in leisure industry. Responsible for introd. of commercial bingo to UK, 1961; creator of Miss World contest, 1951, and BBC TV series Come Dancing, 1950. President, Variety Club Internat., 1977-; formerly Chief Barker, Variety Club of GB. Contested (C) Southwark, Dulwich, Oct. 1974. *Publication:* Miss World Story, 1967. *Recreations:* music

(French horn), all forms of sport. *Address:* 11 College Road, SE21 7HL. *Club:* MCC.

MORLEY, Sir Godfrey (William Rowland), Kt 1971; OBE 1944; TD 1946; *b* 15 June 1909; *o s* of late Arthur Morley, OBE, KC, and late Dorothy Innes Murray Forrest; *m* 1st, 1934, Phyllis Dyce (*d* 1963), *d* of late Sir Edward Duckworth, 2nd Bt; two *s* two *d*; 2nd, 1967, Sonia Gisèle, *d* of late Thomas Ritchie; two *s. Educ:* Westminster; Christ Church, Oxford (MA). Solicitor, 1934; Partner in Allen & Overy, 1936, Senior Partner, 1960-75. Joined Territorial Army, 1937; served War of 1939-45, Rifle Bde and on Staff in Middle East and Italy (despatches); Lt-Col 1944. Law Society: Mem. Council, 1952-73; Vice-Pres., 1969-70; Pres., 1970-71. Member: Lord Chancellor's Law Reform Cttee, 1957-73; Cttee of Management, Inst. of Advanced Legal Studies, 1961-77; Law Adv. Panel, British Council, 1974-; Council, Selden Soc., 1975-. Dir, Bowater Corp. Ltd. Hon. Mem., Canadian Bar Assoc., 1970. Bronze Star Medal (US), 1945. *Address:* Hunter's Lodge, Warren Drive, Kingswood, Tadworth, Surrey KT20 6PT. *T:* Mogador 2485. *Clubs:* Athenæum, Boodle's, City of London.
See also Sir William Lindsay.

MORLEY, Gordon H.; *see* Hope-Morley.

MORLEY, Herbert, CBE 1974; Chairman: Bridon Wire Ltd, since 1977; Templeborough Rolling Mills Ltd, since 1977; Director, Bridon Ltd, since 1973; *b* 19 March 1919; *s* of George Edward and Beatrice Morley; *m* 1942, Gladys Hardy; one *s* one *d. Educ:* Almondbury Grammar Sch., Huddersfield; Sheffield Univ. (Assoc. Metallurgy); Univ. of Cincinnati (Post-Grad. Studies in Business Admin). Dir and Gen. Works Man., Samuel Fox & Co. Ltd, 1959-65; Dir and Gen. Man., Steel Peech Tozer, 1965-68; Dir, United Steel Cos, 1966-70; British Steel Corporation: Dir, Northern Tubes Gp, 1968-70; Man. Dir, Gen. Steel Div., 1970-73; Man. Dir, Planning and Capital Develt, 1973-76. *Recreations:* music, cricket lover, weekend golfer. *Address:* 73 Carr Hill Lane, Sleights, Whitby, North Yorkshire. *T:* Whitby 810310.

MORLEY, Robert, CBE 1957; Actor-Dramatist; *b* Semley, Wilts, 26 May 1908; *s* of Major Robert Morley and Gertrude Emily Fass; *m* 1940, Joan North Buckmaster, *d* of Dame Gladys Cooper, DBE; two *s* one *d. Educ:* Wellington Coll. Originally intended for diplomatic career; studied for stage at RADA. First appearance in Treasure Island, Strand Theatre, 1929; appeared in provinces; established repertory (with Peter Bull) at Perranporth, Cornwall; parts include: Oscar Wilde in play of that name, Gate, 1936, and Fulton (first New York appearance), 1938; Alexandre Dumas in The Great Romancer, Strand, 1937; Higgins in Pygmalion, Old Vic, 1937; Sheridan Whiteside in The Man Who Came to Dinner, Savoy, 1941; Prince Regent in The First Gentleman, New, 1945, and Savoy; Arnold Holt in Edward My Son, His Majesty's and Lyric, 1947, Martin Beck Theatre, New York, 1948; toured Australia, 1949-50; The Little Hut, Lyric, 1950; Hippo Dancing, Lyric, 1954; A Likely Tale, Globe, 1956; Fanny, Drury Lane, 1957; Hook, Line and Sinker, Piccadilly, 1958; A Majority of One, Phœnix, 1960; A Time to Laugh, Piccadilly, 1962; Halfway Up The Tree, Queen's, 1968; How the Other Half Loves, Lyric, 1970; A Ghost on Tiptoe, Savoy, 1974; Banana Ridge, Savoy, 1976. Directed: The Tunnel of Love, Her Majesty's Theatre, 1957; Once More, with Feeling, New Theatre, 1959. Entered films, 1937; *films:* Marie Antoinette; Major Barbara; Young Mr Pitt; Outcast of the Islands; The African Queen; Curtain Up; Mr Gilbert and Mr Sullivan; The Final Test; Beat the Devil; The Rainbow Jacket; Beau Brummell; The Good Die Young; Quentin Durward; Loser Takes All; Law and Disorder; The Journey; The Doctor's Dilemma; Libel; The Battle of the Sexes; Oscar Wilde; Go to Blazes; The Young Ones; The Boys; The Road to Hong Kong; Nine Hours to Rama; The Old Dark House; Murder at the Gallop; Take her, She's Mine; Hot Enough for June; Sold in Egypt; Topkapi; Of Human Bondage; Those Magnificent Men in Their Flying Machines; Ghengis Khan; ABC Murders; The Loved One; Life at the Top; A Study in Terror; Way Way Out; Finders Keepers; Hotel Paradiso; Le Tendre Voyou; Hot Millions; Sinful Davey; Song of Norway; Oliver Cromwell; When Eight Bells Toll; Doctor in Trouble; Theatre of Blood. *Publications:* Short Story, 1935; Goodness How Sad, 1937; Staff Dance, 1944; (with Noel Langley) Edward My Son, 1948; (with Ronald Gow) The Full Treatment, 1953; Hippo Dancing, 1953; (with Dundas Hamilton) Six Months Grace, 1957; (with Sewell Stokes) Responsible Gentleman (autobiography), 1966; A Musing Morley, 1974; Morley Marvels, 1976. *Recreations:* conversation, horse racing. *Address:* Fairmans, Wargrave, Berks. *Clubs:* Buck's, Garrick.

MORLEY, Very Rev. William Fenton; Dean Emeritus of Salisbury, since 1977; *b* 5 May 1912; *s* of Arthur Fenton and Margaret Morley; *m* 1937, Marjorie Rosa, *d* of Joseph Temple Robinson, Frinton; one *s* one *d*. *Educ:* St David's, Lampeter; Oriel Coll., Oxford; Wycliffe Hall, Oxford; University of London. Ordained, 1935; curate of: Ely, Cardiff, 1935-38; Porthcawl, S Wales, 1938-43; Officiating Chaplain to the Forces, 1941-43; Vicar of Penrhiwceiber, 1943-46; Rector of Haseley, Oxon, 1946-50; Director of Music and Lecturer in Hebrew at Cuddesdon Coll., Oxon, 1946-50; Examiner in Hebrew and New Testament Greek, 1947-59 and External Lecturer in Biblical and Religious Studies, 1950-61, Univ. of London; Chaplain and Lecturer of St Gabriel's Training Coll., 1956-61; Education Sec. to Overseas Council of Church Assembly, 1950-56; Warburton Lectr, Lincoln's Inn, 1963-65; Chairman: Church of England Deployment and Payment Commission, 1965-68; Church of England Pensions Bd, 1974-. Public Preacher to Diocese of Rochester, 1950-56; Canon Residentiary and Precentor of Southwark Cathedral, 1956-61; Vicar of Leeds, Rural Dean of Leeds and Hon. Canon of Ripon, 1961-71; Dean of Salisbury, 1971-77. Editor, East and West Review, 1953-64. Chaplain to HM's Household, 1965-71; Church Comr, 1968-. *Publications:* One Church, One Faith, One Lord, 1953; The Church to Which You Belong, 1955; The Call of God, 1959; Preaching through the Christian Year, 1974. *Recreations:* music, writing. *Address:* 5 Cavendish Place, Bath, Avon BA1 5UB. *Club:* Royal Commonwealth Society.

MORLEY-JOHN, Michael, RD 1970; **Hon. Mr Justice Morley-John;** Judge of the Supreme Court of Hong Kong, since 1973; *b* 22 May 1923; *s* of late Clifford Morley-John and Norah (*née* Thompson); *m* 1951, Sheila Christine Majendie; one *s* one *d*. *Educ:* Wycliffe Coll.; Univ. of Bristol (LLB). Called to the Bar, Gray's Inn, 1950. Hong Kong: Crown Counsel, 1951; Dir of Public Prosecutions, 1961; Acting Solicitor Gen., 1966-67; Dist Judge, 1967; Judicial Comr, State of Brunei, 1974. Acting Comdr, RNR, 1973. *Recreations:* tennis, stamp collecting, sailing. *Address:* Courts of Justice, Hong Kong. *T:* Hong Kong 96486; White House, Blissford, Fordingbridge, Hants SP6 2JG. *T:* Fordingbridge 53054. *Clubs:* East India, Devonshire, Sports and Public Schools, Royal Ocean Racing; Bar Yacht; Hong Kong, Royal Hong Kong Jockey, (former Pres.) Hong Kong Kennel (Hong Kong).

MORLING, Col Leonard Francis, DSO 1940; OBE 1946; TD 1942; Architect; *b* 2 Nov. 1904, British; 2nd *s* of late Ernest Charles Morling and Frances Ruth Baldwin; unmarried. *Educ:* Brighton Hove and Sussex Grammar Sch. Architect, 1927-36; Mem. of firm, C. Morling Ltd, Builders and Contractors, Seaford, 1936-39; social work, in London, 1948-50, Malaya, 1950-55; Personnel and Welfare Work, London, 1956-59, Australia, 1960-63, London, 1964. Comnd, Terrtl Army, 1924; Capt. 1930; Major, 1934; Lt-Col, 1943; Col 1946; served France and Flanders (despatches, DSO); Persia, Iraq and India. *Publication:* Sussex Sappers, 1972. *Address:* c/o Lloyds Bank Ltd, Seaford, East Sussex.

MORLING, Norton Arthur; Member, Civil Aviation Authority, 1972-75; *b* 13 Feb. 1909; *o s* of Norton and Edith Morling, Hunsdon, Herts; *m* 1942, Rachel Paterson, *d* of James and Elizabeth Chapman, Johannesburg, SA; one *s* one *d*. *Educ:* Hertford Grammar Sch.; Cambridge Univ. (MA); Birmingham Univ. (MCom). Joined Turner & Newall Ltd as Management Trainee, 1931. War Service, N Africa and Italy, 1942-45 (despatches); Lt-Col 1944; ADS&T, AFHQ, 1944-45. Dir, and in some cases Chm., of various subsid. and associated companies, UK and overseas, 1946-64, including Turner Brothers Asbestos Co. Ltd and Ferodo Ltd: Gp Dir, 1957-67; Financial Dir, 1964-67; seconded as Industrial Advr to Nat. Economic Develt Office, 1967-70; Mem., Air Transport Licensing Bd, 1971-72. Vis. Fellow, Univ. of Lancaster Business Sch., 1969-. *Recreations:* gardening, tennis. *Address:* Little Brook House, Over Wallop, Stockbridge, Hants SO20 8HT. *T:* Wallop 296. *Club:* Royal Automobile.

MORO, Aldo; Prime Minister of Italy, 1963-68 and 1974-76; President, Christian Democrat Party, since 1976; *b* 23 Sept. 1916; *s* of Aida and Renato Moro. *Educ:* Bari University. Member: Italian Constituent Assembly, 1946; Co-ordination Cttee for drafting of new Constitution of Republic of Italy; elected to Chamber of Deputies, 1948, reelected 1953, 1958, 1963, 1968, 1976; Under-Sec. of State, Foreign Affairs, 1949; Pres., Christian Democrat Party Gp, Chamber of Deputies, 1953-55; Minister of Justice, 1955-57; Minister of Educn, 1957-59; Political Sec., Christian Democrat Party, 1959-63; Minister of Foreign Affairs, Italy: Dec. 1965-Feb. 1966; Aug. 1969-June 1972; July 1973-Oct. 1974; Chm., Council of Ministers of the Common Market, July-Dec. 1971; Pres., Foreign Affairs Commn, Chamber of Deputies, Italy, 1972-73. *Publications:* La capacità giuridica penale, 1939; Lo Stato, 1943; L'Antigiuridicità, 1947; Unita e pluralitá de reati, 1951. *Address:* Camera dei Deputati, Rome, Italy.

MORO, Peter, CBE 1977; FRIBA, FSIAD; Architect in private practice with partners, Michael Mellish, RIBA and Michael Heard, RIBA, since 1952; *b* 27 May 1911; *s* of Ernst Moro and Grete Hönigswald; *m* 1940, Anne Vanneck; three *d*. *Educ:* Stuttgart, Berlin and Zurich. Swiss Dip. Architecture, 1936; FRIBA 1948; FSIA 1957. Practice with Tecton, 1937-39; Mem. Exec. Cttee, Mars Gp, 1938; Lectr, Sch. of Arch., Regent Street Polytechnic, 1941-47; LCC Associated Architect, Royal Festival Hall, 1948-51. Architect: Fairlawn Sch., LCC, 1957; Nottingham Playhouse, 1964; alterations, Royal Opera House, Covent Garden, 1964; Birstall Sch., Leics, 1964; housing schemes, GLC and Southwark, 1967-77; theatre, Hull Univ., the Gulbenkian Centre, 1970; additions and alterations, Bristol Old Vic, 1972; theatre, New Univ. of Ulster, 1976. Member: (Founder), Assoc. of British Theatre Technicians; Council, RIBA, 1967-73; Housing the Arts Cttee, Arts Council of GB. Lectures in UK, Finland and Norway. Bronze Medal, RIBA, 1964; 4 Civic Trust Awards and Commendations. *Publications:* contribs to technical jls in UK, Germany, France, Italy, Portugal and Japan. *Address:* 20 Blackheath Park, SE3 9RP. *T:* 01-852 0250.

MORONY, Maj.-Gen. Thomas Lovett, OBE 1969; Director, Royal Artillery, since Oct. 1975; *b* 23 Sept. 1926; *s* of Thomas Henry Morony, CSI, CIE, and Evelyn Myra (*née* Lovett); *m* 1961, Elizabeth, *d* of G. W. N. Clark; two *s*. *Educ:* Eton. Commissioned, 1947. BM, King's African Rifles, 1958-61; GSO1 (DS) at Camberley and RMCS, 1963-65; GSO1, HQ Northern Army Gp, 1966-67; commanded 22 Light Air Defence Regt, RA, 1968-69; Comdr, 1st Artillery Bde, 1970-72; Dep. Comdt, Staff Coll., Camberley, 1973-75. Mem. Bd of Governors, Sherborne Sch. *Recreations:* country pursuits, big game photography, music. *Address:* c/o Bank of Scotland, 8 Morningside Road, Edinburgh EH10 4DD. *Club:* Army and Navy.

MORPETH, Viscount; George William Beaumont Howard; *b* 15 Feb. 1949; *s* and *heir* of 12th Earl of Carlisle, *qv*. *Educ:* Balliol Coll., Oxford. 9th/12th Royal Lancers, 1967-; Lieut 1970 (Intelligence Officer, 16th/5th Queen's Royal Lancers, 1972); Captain, 1974. *Recreations:* reading, talking, travel, parachuting, croquet. *Address:* Naworth Castle, Brampton, Cumbria. *Clubs:* Beefsteak, Turf.

MORPETH, Douglas Spottiswoode, TD 1959; FCA; Partner, Touche Ross & Co., Chartered Accountants, since 1958; Chairman, Touche Ross Board of Partners, 1975; *b* 6 June 1924; *s* of Robert Spottiswoode Morpeth and Louise Rankine Morpeth (*née* Dobson); *m* 1951, Anne Rutherford, *yr d* of Ian C. Bell, OBE, MC, Edinburgh; two *s* two *d*. *Educ:* George Watson's Coll., Edinburgh; Edinburgh Univ. (BCom). Commissioned RA; served 1943-47, India, Burma, Malaya. Qualified as Mem. of Inst. of Chartered Accountants in England and Wales, 1952, Fellow, 1957 (Council of Inst., 1964, Vice-Pres., 1970, Dep. Pres., 1971, Pres., 1972). Dir, Clerical Medical and General Life Assurance Soc., 1973, Dep. Chm., 1974; Dir, Brixton Estate Ltd, 1977. Member: Accountants Advisory Cttee, 1969; Investment Grants Advisory Cttee, 1968-71; Chm., Inflation Accounting Steering Gp, 1976; Vice-Chm., Accounting Standards Cttee. Chm., Taxation Cttee, CBI, 1973-76. Honourable Artillery Company: Member, 1949-; commanded 'B' Battery, HAC, 1958-61; Lt-Col, comdg 1st Regt HAC, RHA, 1964-66; Master Gunner within the Tower of London, 1966-69. *Publication:* Practitioners Own Taxation Problems (Inst. of Chartered Accts in Eng. and Wales), 1967. *Recreations:* golf, tennis, gardening. *Address:* Summerden House, Shamley Green, near Guildford, Surrey. *T:* Bramley 2689. *Clubs:* City, Honourable Artillery Company, Royal Automobile.

MORPURGO, Jack Eric; Professor of American Literature, University of Leeds, since 1969; author; *b* 26 April 1918; *s* of late Mark Morpurgo, Islington; *m* 1946, Catherine Noel Kippe, *d* of late Prof. Emile Cammaerts; three *s* one *d*. *Educ:* Christ's Hosp.; Univ. of New Brunswick; Coll. of William and Mary, USA (BA); Durham Univ. Enlisted RA, 1939; served as regimental and staff officer in India, Middle East, Greece and Italy; GSO 2, Public Relations Directorate, War Office. Editorial Staff, Penguin Books, 1946-49; Editor Penguin Parade; General Editor, Pelican Histories, 1949-61; Asst Dir, Nuffield Foundation, 1950-54; Dir-Gen., Nat. Book League, 1955-69, Dep. Chm., 1969-71, Vice-Pres., 1971-; Prof. of American Studies, Univ. of Geneva, 1968-70; Visiting Prof., Michigan State Univ., 1950, George Washington Univ., 1970; Schol.-in-residence, Rockefeller Res. Centre, Italy, 1974; Vis. Fellow, Australian Nat. Univ., 1975; has lectured in USA, Canada, Germany, India, Burma, etc. Dir of Unesco Seminar on Production of Reading Materials, Rangoon, 1957, Madras, 1959. Donation Governor and Almoner, Christ's Hospital; Chm. Working Pty on Medical Libraries; Dir, William and Mary Historical Project, 1970-76. Phi Beta Kappa, 1948; Hon. Fellow, Coll. of William and Mary, 1949. Hon. LitD Maine, 1961; Hon. DLitt Elmira, 1966; Hon. DHL William and Mary, 1970. *Publications:* American Excursion, 1949; Charles Lamb and Elia, 1949; The Road to Athens, 1963; Barnes Wallis, 1972; Treason at West Point, 1975; Their Majesties Royall Colledge, 1976; contributor to: The Impact of America, 1951; joint author of: History of The United States (with Russel B. Nye), 1955; Venice (with Martin Hürlimann), 1964; edited: Leigh Hunt: Autobiography, 1949; E. J. Trelawny: Last Days of Shelley and Byron, 1952; Poems of John Keats, 1953; Rugby Football: An Anthology (with Kenneth Pelmear), 1958; Cobbett: a year's residence in USA, 1964; Cooper: The Spy, 1968. *Recreation:* watching Rugby football. *Address:* Cliff Cottage, 51 Cliff Road, Leeds LS6 2EZ. *Clubs:* Army and Navy, Pilgrims.

MORRAH, Ruth, (Mrs Dermot Morrah), JP; Chairman, Metropolitan Juvenile Courts, 1945-64; *b* 21 Aug. 1899; *d* of Willmott Houselander; *m* 1923, Dermot Michael Macgregor Morrah (*d* 1974); two *d*. *Educ:* convent schs; St Anne's Coll., Oxford. JP 1944. Pro Ecclesia et Pontifice, 1964. *Recreations:* travelling, needlework. *Address:* 3 Kennington Palace Court, Sancroft Street, SE11. *T:* 01-582 1894.
See also T. E. Utley.

MORRELL, A(rthur) Claude, CBE 1952; MC 1917; Chairman, John Morrell & Co. Ltd, 1929-69; *b* 3 April 1894; *s* of Alfred Morrell, CBE, Liverpool; *m* 1931, Laura May (*d* 1976), *d* of Andrew D. Mearns, Blundellsands, Lancs; no *c. Educ:* Malvern Coll. Served European War, 1914-19 (MC): with the King's (Liverpool) Regt and on General Staff, Fourth Army, Dir, Martins Bank, 1944-68. JP (Cheshire), 1945. *Recreations:* golf, music. *Address:* Cloverly Nursing Home, Brimstage Road, Bebington, Merseyside L63 6HF. *T:* 051-342 3816.

MORRELL, Frances Maine; Special Adviser to Tony Benn (as Secretary of State for Industry, then as Secretary of State for Energy), since 1974; Chairman, Islington South and Finsbury Constituency Labour Party, since 1976; *b* 28 Dec. 1937; *d* of Frank and Beatrice Galleway; *m* 1964, Brian Morrell; one *d. Educ:* Queen Anne Grammar Sch., York; Hull Univ. BA (Hons) English Lang. and Lit. Secondary Sch. Teacher, 1960-69; Press Officer, Fabian Soc. and NUS, 1970-72; Research into MPs' constituency role, 1973. Mem., Oakes Cttee, Enquiry into Payment and Collection Methods for Gas and Electricity Bills (report publ. 1976). Mem. Nat. Children's Bureau. Contested (Lab) Chelmsford, Feb. 1974. *Publications:* (with Tony Benn and Francis Cripps) A Ten Year Industrial Strategy for Britain, 1975; (with Francis Cripps) The Case for a Planned Energy Policy, 1976; From the Electors of Bristol: the record of a year's correspondence between constituents and their Member of Parliament, 1977. *Address:* c/o Department of Energy, Thames House South, Millbank, SW1P 4QJ. *T:* 01-211 3580.

MORRELL, Col (Herbert) William (James), OBE 1954; MC 1944; TD; DL; JP; *b* 1 Aug. 1915; *er s* of James Herbert Morrell, MA, Headington Hill, Oxford; *m* 1947, Pamela Vivien Eleanor, *d* of Richard Stubbs, Willaston, Cheshire; one *s* two *d. Educ:* Eton; Magdalen Coll., Oxford (MA). 2nd Lt RA, 1936; served War of 1939-45 (France, Madagascar, Burma); retired 1948. DL 1961, JP 1959, High Sheriff 1960, Oxon. *Recreations:* hunting, sailing. *Address:* Caphill, Sandford St Martin, Oxon. *T:* Great Tew 291.

MORRELL, Rt. Rev. James Herbert Lloyd; Canon and Prebend of Heathfield in Chichester Cathedral since 1959; Provost of Lancing (Southern Division Woodard Schools), since 1961; an Assistant Bishop, Diocese of Chichester, since 1978; *b* 12 Aug. 1907; *s* of George Henry and Helen Adela Morrell. *Educ:* Dulwich Coll.; King's Coll., London; Ely Theological Coll. Deacon, 1931; Priest, 1932; Curate of St Alphage, Hendon, 1931-35; Curate of St Michael and All Angels, Brighton, 1935-39; Bishop of Chichester's Chaplain for men, 1939-41; Lecturer for The Church of England Moral Welfare Council, 1941-44; Vicar of Roffey, 1944-46; Archdeacon of Lewes, 1946-59; Bishop Suffragan of Lewes, 1959-77. Fellow of King's Coll., London, 1960. *Publications:* Four Words (broadcast talks to the Forces), 1941; The Heart of a Priest, 1958; A Priest's Notebook of Prayer, 1961; The Catholic Faith Today, 1964. *Recreations:* walking, photography. *Address:* 83 Davigdor Road, Hove BN3 1RA. *T:* Brighton 733971. *Club:* English-Speaking Union.

MORRELL, Leslie James; Member (U), for Londonderry, Northern Ireland Assembly, 1973-75; Head of Department of Agriculture, Northern Ireland Executive, 1974; *b* 26 Dec. 1931; *s* of James Morrell; *m* 1958, Anne Wallace, BSc; two *s* one *d. Educ:* Portora Royal Sch., Enniskillen; Queen's Univ., Belfast. BAgric 1955. Dep. Leader, UPNI, 1974-. Coleraine RDC, 1961; Londonderry CC, 1969; JP 1970; Coleraine District Council, 1973-77. Chm., James Butcher Housing Assoc. (NI) Ltd, 1976-. *Address:* Dunboe House, Castlerock, Coleraine, N Ireland. *T:* Castlerock 352.

MORRELL, Col William; see Morrell, Col H. W. J.

MORRELL, William Bowes; Vice-Chairman, Westminster Press Ltd (formerly Westminster Press Provincial Newspapers Ltd), since 1976; *b* York, 18 Feb. 1913; *s* of J. B. Morrell, LLD, JP and Bertha Morrell (*née* Spence Watson); *m* 1939, Kate Lisa, *d* of Prof. E. and Elisabeth Probst; three *s. Educ:* Bootham Sch., York; St John's Coll., Cambridge (MA). Served War of 1939-45 (2 stars, 2 medals), RA; Capt. 1945. Birmingham Gazette and Despatch Ltd: Dir and Manager, 1948-53; Man. Dir, 1953-57; Westminster Press Provincial Newspapers Ltd: Dir and Gen. Man., 1957-58; Advertisement Dir, 1958-64; Dep. Man. Dir, 1964-65; Man. Dir, 1965-76. Chairman: Joseph Rowntree Social Service Trust Ltd; Joseph Rowntree Social Service Trust (Investments) Ltd; Turret Press (Holdings) Ltd; York Conservation Trust Ltd; York Common Good Trust; Dir, Southern Publishing Co. Ltd; Mem., Court of Univ. of York. Liveryman, Co. of Stationers and Newspaper Makers. *Recreation:* swimming. *Address:* 99 South End Road, NW3 2RJ. *T:* 01-435 0785; Flat 1, Ingram House, 90 Bootham, York. *T:* York 23197. *Club:* Lansdowne.

MORRIS; see Temple-Morris.

MORRIS, family name of **Barons Killanin, Morris, Morris of Borth-y-Gest, Morris of Grasmere** and **Morris of Kenwood.**

MORRIS, 3rd Baron *cr* 1918 **Michael David Morris;** *b* 9 Dec. 1937; *s* of 2nd Baron Morris and of Jean Beatrice (now Lady Salmon), *d* of late Lt-Col D. Maitland-Makgill-Crichton; *S* father, 1975; *m* 1st, 1959, Denise Eleanor (marr. diss. 1962), *o d* of Morley Richards; 2nd, 1962, Jennifer (marr. diss. 1969), *o d* of Squadron Leader Tristram Gilbert; two *d. Educ:* Downside. FCA. *Heir: yr twin b* Hon. Edward Patrick Morris [*b* 9 Dec. 1937; *m* 1963, Mary Beryl, *e d* of Lt-Col D. H. G. Thrush; one *s* one *d*].

MORRIS OF BORTH-Y-GEST, Baron (Life Peer) *cr* 1960; **John William Morris,** PC 1951; CH 1975; Kt 1945; CBE 1945; MC; *b* 11 Sept. 1896; *s* of Daniel and Ellen Morris, Liverpool and Portmadoc. *Educ:* Liverpool Institute, Liverpool; Trinity Hall, Cambridge (MA, LLB, Hon. Fellow, 1951); Harvard Law Sch., Harvard Univ., USA. Served in Royal Welch Fusiliers, 1916-19; two years in France (Captain); Pres. Cambridge Union Soc., 1919; Joseph Hodges Choate Memorial Fellowship, Harvard Univ., USA, 1920-21; called to Bar, Inner Temple, 1921; Bencher, 1943; Reader, 1966; Treasurer, 1967; Northern Circuit; KC 1935; Judge of Appeal, IOM, 1938-45; a Judge of the High Court, King's Bench Division, 1945-51; a Lord Justice of Appeal, 1951-60; a Lord of Appeal in Ordinary, 1960-75. Contested Ilford Div. (L) in 1923, 1924; Hon. Standing Counsel to the Univ. of Wales, 1938-45; HM Commissioner of Assize, Northern Circuit, 1942, and at Birmingham, Dec. 1944; Dep. Chm., Home Office Adv. Cttee, under Defence Regns, 1940-45; prepared Report for Treasury on Requisitioning, 1941; Chm., Home Office Cttee on War Damaged Licensed Houses, 1942-43; Chm., Cttee on the Selling Price of Houses, 1945; Chm., Courts of Inquiry into Engineering and Shipbuilding Wages Disputes, 1954; acted as Referee to decide the wage questions upon Settlement of Railway Strike, 1955; Chm. of National Reference Tribunal under the Coal-Mining Industry Conciliation Scheme, 1955-65; Chm., Home Office Cttee on Jury Service, 1963-64. Pres., London Welsh Assoc., 1951-53; Hon. Mem., Canadian and American Bar Assocs; Member: Pilgrims Soc.; Univ. Grants Cttee, 1955-69; Charing Cross Hosp. Council of Management, 1941-48 and of Board of Governors of Group, 1948-68; Pro-Chancellor of Univ. of Wales, 1956-74; Mem., the Gorsedd. Commissary of the Univ. of Cambridge, 1968-. JP 1939, DL 1951, Caernarvonshire; Dep.-Chm., Caernarvonshire QS, 1939-43, and Chm., 1943-69. Hon. LLD: Wales, 1946; British Columbia, 1952; Liverpool, 1966; Cambridge, 1967. *Address:* House of Lords, SW1; Bryn Gauallt, Portmadoc, Gwynedd. *Clubs:* Athenæum, Reform, MCC.

MORRIS OF GRASMERE, Baron *cr* 1967 (Life Peer), of Grasmere; **Charles Richard Morris,** KCMG 1963; Kt 1953; MA Oxon; Hon. LLD: Manchester, 1951; Aberdeen, 1963; Leeds,

1964; Malta, 1964; Hull, 1965; Hon. DLitt: Sydney, 1954; Lancaster, 1967; Hon. DTech Bradford, 1970; *b* 25 Jan. 1898; *s* of M. C. Morris, Sutton Valence, Kent; *m* 1923, Mary de Selincourt; one *s* one *d*. *Educ:* Tonbridge Sch.; Trinity Coll., Oxford. Lt RGA 1916-19; Fellow and Tutor of Balliol Coll., 1921-43; for one year, 1926-27 (while on leave of absence from Balliol), Prof. of Philosophy, Univ. of Michigan, USA; Senior Proctor, 1937-38; Mem. of Council of Girls Public Day Sch. Trust, 1933-38; Oxford City Councillor, 1939-41; Ministry of Supply, 1939-42; Under-Sec., Min. of Production, 1942-43; Head Master, King Edward's Sch., Birmingham, 1941-48; Chm., Cttee of Vice-Chancellors and Principals, 1952-55; Central Joint Adv. Cttee on Tutorial Classes, 1948-58; Commonwealth Univ. Interchange Cttee and Recruitment Sub-Cttee of British Council, 1951; Sch. Broadcasting Council, 1954-64; Inter-Univ. Council for Higher Education Overseas, 1957-64; Independent Chm., Jt Adv. Cttee for Wool Textile Industry, 1952; Pres., Council of Coll. of Preceptors, 1954-63. Vice-Chancellor of Leeds Univ., 1948-63; Pro-Chancellor, Univ. of Bradford, 1966-69. Member: Royal Commn on Local Govt in Greater London, 1957; Cttee of Inquiry on Australian Univs, 1957; Chairman: Adv. Bd Of Univs Quarterly, 1960; Local Govt Training Bd, 1967-75; President: Brit. Student Tuberculosis Foundn, 1960; Assoc. of Teachers in Colls and Depts of Educn, 1961-64. *Publications:* A History of Political Ideas (with Mary Morris), 1924; Locke, Berkeley, Hume, 1931; Idealistic Logic, 1933; In Defence of Democracy (with J. S. Fulton), 1936; British Democracy, 1939; various essays and papers to learned societies. *Recreation:* fell walking. *Address:* Ladywood, White Moss, Ambleside, Cumbria LA22 9SF. *T:* 286. *Club:* Athenæum.

MORRIS OF KENWOOD, 2nd Baron *cr* 1950, of Kenwood; **Philip Geoffrey Norris,** JP; Company Director; *b* 18 June 1928; *s* of 1st Baron Morris of Kenwood, and Florence, *d* of Henry Isaacs, Leeds; *S* father, 1954; *m* 1958, Ruth, *o d* of Baron Janner, *qv*; one *s* three *d*. *Educ:* Loughborough Coll., Leics. Served RAF, Nov. 1946-Feb. 1949; July 1951-Oct. 1955. JP Inner London, 1967. *Recreations:* tennis, golf, ski-ing. *Heir: s* Hon. Jonathan David Morris, *b* 5 Aug. 1968. *Address:* Lawn Cottage, Orchard Rise, Kingston, Surrey. *T:* 01-942 6321.

MORRIS, Alfred; MP (Lab and Co-op) Manchester (Wythenshawe) since 1964; Parliamentary Under-Secretary of State, Department of Health and Social Security, with special responsibility for disabled people, since 1974; *b* 23 March 1928; *s* of late George Henry Morris and Jessie Morris (*née* Murphy); *m* 1950, Irene (*née* Jones); two *s* two *d*. *Educ:* elem. and evening schs, Manchester; Ruskin Coll., Oxford; St Catherine's, Univ. of Oxford (MA); Univ. of Manchester (Postgrad. certif. in Educn). Employed in office of a Manchester brewing firm from age 14 (HM Forces, 1946-48); Schoolmaster and Adult Educn Lectr, Manchester, 1954-56; Asst Sec., NW & Merseyside and N Wales Dist Jt Adv. Councils for Electricity Supply Industry, 1956-59; Asst Sec., Nat. Jt Adv. Coun. for El. Supply Ind., 1959-61; Asst Labour Relations Officer, The Electricity Coun., London, 1961-64. Nat. Chm., Labour League of Youth, 1950-52; contested Liverpool (Garston), Gen. Elec. 1951; Mem., Bureau and Chm. Control Commn, Internat. Union of Socialist Youth, 1951-54; Observer, Coun. Socialist Internat. and Coun. of Europe, 1952-53; PPS to Minister of Agric., Fisheries and Food, 1964-67, and to Lord President of the Council and Leader of House of Commons, 1968-70; Opposition Front Bench Spokesman on Social Services, 1970-74. Mem. Exec. Cttee British Group, Inter-Parly Union, 1966-74; Treasurer, 1971-74; Mem., UK Parly Delegn to UN Gen. Assembly, 1966; Vice-Chm., Food and Agriculture Gp of Parly Lab. Party, 1970-71, Chm., 1971-74; Representative of Privy Council on Council of RCVS, 1969-74; promoted Chronically Sick and Disabled Persons Act, 1970, Food and Drugs (Milk) Act, 1970, Police Act, 1972, as a Private Member; Vice-Chm., Co-operative Parly Group, 1970-71, Chm., 1971-72; Vice-Chm., All-Party Parly Retail Trade Gp, 1972-74. Mem., Gen. Adv. Council, BBC, 1968-74; Patron of Disablement Income Group, 1970-74; Parly Adviser to the Police Federation, 1971-74; Mem., Exec. Cttee, Central Council for the Disabled and Nat. Fund for Research into Crippling Diseases, 1970-74. Field Marshal Lord Harding Award, 1971, for services to the disabled; Grimshaw Meml Award of Nat. Fedn of the Blind, 1971. *Publications:* Value Added Tax: a tax on the consumer, 1970; The Growth of Parliamentary Scrutiny by Committee, 1970; (with A. Butler) No Feet to Drag, 1972; Ed. lectures (Human Relations in Industry), 1958; Ed. Jl (Jt Consultation) publ. Nat. Jt Adv. Coun. Elec. Supply Ind., 1959-61. *Recreations:* gardening, walking, snooker, chess. *Address:* House of Commons, SW1A 0AA.

MORRIS, Air Vice-Marshal Arnold Alec; Director General Strategic Electronic Systems, Ministry of Defence (PE), since 1976; *b* 11 March 1926; *s* of late Harry Morris; *m* 1946, Moyna Patricia, *d* of late Norman Boyle; one *s* one *d* (twins). *Educ:* King Edward VI Sch., East Retford; King's Coll., Univ. of London; Univ. of Southampton. Commnd RAF, 1945; radar duties, No 90 (Signals) Gp, 1945-50; Guided Weapons Dept, RAE, 1953-56; exchange duty, HQ USAF, 1958-60; space res., Min. of Supply, 1960-63; DS, RAF Staff Coll., 1963-65; OC Eng, No 2 Flying Trng Sch., Syerston, 1966-68; Asst Dir, Guided Weapons R&D, Min. of Tech., 1968-70; OC RAF Central Servicing Develt Estabt, Swanton Morley, 1970-72; SASO, HQ No 90 (Signals) Gp, 1972-74; RCDS, 1974; Dir of Signals (Air), MoD, 1975-76. Pres., Soc. of Electronic and Radio Technicians, 1975- (Vice-Pres., 1973-75). *Recreations:* tennis, squash, gardening. *Address:* 6 Liverpool Road, Kingston-upon-Thames, Surrey KT2 7SZ. *T:* 01-549 3437. *Club:* Royal Air Force.

MORRIS, Brig. Arthur de Burgh, CBE 1949 (OBE 1948); DSO 1944; retired; *b* 11 Dec. 1902; *s* of late Lt-Col G. M. Morris, 8th Gurkha Rifles; *m* 1928, Doreen, *d* of late Sir Henry Miller, Londonderry; one *d*. *Educ:* Wellington Coll.; RMC, Sandhurst. Commissioned 2nd Lt, into 1st Sherwood Foresters, 1922; Adjt, 8th Sherwood Foresters, 1930-34; transferred to 8th Gurkha Rifles, 1936; Bde Major, Thal Bde NWFP, 1941-42; Temp. Lt-Col and Comd 1/8 Gurkha Rifles, 1943; served in Arakan and Burma, 1944 (DSO); Temp. Col and 2nd i/c 37 Inf. Bde (Gurkha), 1945; Temp. Brig. and Comd 49 Indian Inf. Bde, Nov. 1945; served in Java, 1946-47 (OBE); Comd North Malaya Sub. Dist, 1947-48 (CBE); Comdr Kowloon Inf. Bde, 1948; Brigade of Gurkhas, 1948; Comdr 48 Gurkha Inf., Bde, Malaya, 1950-53 (despatches); Perak Meritorious Service Medal (Malaya), 1953; retired, 1953. High Sheriff, City of Londonderry, 1964. *Recreations:* hunting and shooting. *Address:* Moyola Park, Castledawson, County Londonderry, Northern Ireland.
See also N. G. Morris.

MORRIS, Prof. Benjamin Stephen; Professor of Education, University of Bristol, 1956-75, now Emeritus; *b* 25 May 1910; *s* of Rev. B. S. Morris, Sherborne, Dorset, and Annie McNicol Duncan, Rothesay, Bute; *m* 1938, Margaret, *d* of Mr and Mrs Lamont, Glasgow; two *s* one *d*. *Educ:* Rothesay Academy; Glasgow Univ. BSc 1933, MEd 1937 (Glasgow). Trained as teacher, Jordanhill Training Coll., Glasgow; teacher, primary and secondary schs, 1936-39; Lecturer: in Psychology, Logic and Ethics, Jordanhill Trng Coll., 1939-40; in Educn, Univ. of Glasgow, 1940-46. Temp. Civil Servant, Min. of Food, 1941; Army Psychologist, 1942-46; Sen. Psychologist (WOSB), 1945-46; Hon. Lt-Col 1946. Student at Inst. of Psychoanalysis, London, 1946-50; Senior staff, Tavistock Institute of Human Relations, 1946-50 (Chm. Management Cttee, 1947-49); Dir Nat. Foundation for Educl Research in England and Wales, 1950-56. Vis. Prof. of Education, Harvard Univ., 1969-70. *Publications:* Objectives and Perspectives in Education, 1972; contributed to: The Function of Teaching, 1959; How and Why Do We Learn?, 1965; Study of Education, 1966; Higher Education, Demand and Response, 1969; Towards a Policy for the Education of Teachers, 1969; Towards Community Mental Health, 1971; The Sciences, The Humanities and the Technological Threat, 1975; articles in educational and psychological jls. *Recreation:* living in the country. *Address:* Bracken Hill, Wrington, Bristol BS18 7PN.

MORRIS, C. J.; *see* Morris, John.

MORRIS, Sir Cedric Lockwood, 9th Bt, *cr* 1806, of Clasemont, Glamorganshire; painter and horticulturist; Principal of The East Anglian School of Painting and Drawing, Hadleigh, Suffolk; President, South Wales Art Society; *b* Sketty, Glamorganshire, 11 Dec. 1889; *s* of Sir George Lockwood Morris, 8th Bt; *S* father, 1947; unmarried. *Educ:* Charterhouse; on the Continent. In early years worked as a farmer in Canada; studied art in Paris, Berlin, and Rome; works in most public galleries; served in the ranks, 1914-15; later with Remounts; International Exhibitor at Venice, Chicago, Brussels, etc; Exhibitions at Rome, 1922; New York, 1923; London (private), 1923; New York, 1924; Paris, 1925; London, 1928; The Hague, 1928; London, 1931, 1934, 1936, 1940, 1944, and 1952. RCA (Wales), 1930. Lectr in Design, RCA (London), 1950-53. Vice-Pres., Contemporary Art Soc. for Wales, 1967. *Publications:* reproductions of works in art and general periodicals; illustrations to books treating of plant and bird life; articles and poems. *Heir: c* Robert Byng Morris [*b* 25 Feb. 1913; *m* 1947, Christine Kathleen, *d* of Archibald Field, Toddington, Glos; one *s* three *d*]. *Address:* Benton End, Hadleigh, Suffolk.

MORRIS, Charles Alfred, RWS 1949 (ARWS 1943); RBA 1948; retired as Vice-Principal Brighton College of Art (1952-59); Vice-President, RWS, 1957-60; *b* 5 Sept. 1898; *s* of G. W. Morris and Susan (*née* Lee); *m* 1927, Alice Muriel Drummond, *d* of

Rev. Dr W. H. Drummond; one *s* two *d*. *Educ:* Royal Academy Schs and Brighton Coll. of Art. Served with HAC, 1916-19. Teacher of advanced drawing and painting, Liverpool Coll. of Art, 1926; Senior Asst, County Sch. of Art, Worthing, 1931, Principal, 1942. Examples of work in following public collections: Birkenhead, Blackburn, Brighton, Eastbourne, Hove, Worthing. *Recreation:* gardening. *Address:* Hillside Cottage, Burpham, Arundel, West Sussex. *T:* Arundel 883019.

MORRIS, Charles Richard; MP (Lab) Openshaw Division of Manchester since Dec. 1963; Minister of State, Civil Service Department, since Oct. 1974; *b* 14 Dec. 1926; *s* of George Henry Morris, Newton Heath, Manchester; *m* 1950, Pauline, *d* of Albert Dunn, Manchester; two *d*. *Educ:* Brookdale Park Sch., Manchester. Served with Royal Engineers, 1945-48. Pres., Clayton Labour Party, 1950-52. Mem. of Manchester Corporation, 1954-64: Chm. of Transport Cttee, 1959-62; Dep. Chm. of Establishment Cttee, 1963-64. Mem., Post Office Workers Union (Mem. Nat. Exec. Council, 1959-63). Contested (Lab) Cheadle Div. of Cheshire, 1959. PPS to the Postmaster-General, 1964; Govt Asst Whip, 1966-67; Vice-Chamberlain, HM Household, 1967-69; Treasurer, HM Household (Deputy Chief Whip), 1969-70; PPS to Rt Hon. H. Wilson, MP, 1970-74; Minister of State, DoE, March-Oct. 1974. *Address:* 24 Buxton Road West, Disley, Stockport, Cheshire. *T:* Disley 2450.

MORRIS, Rev. Dr Colin; General Secretary, Overseas Division of the Methodist Church, since 1973; President of the Methodist Conference, 1976-77; Member of the Council on International Development; Member of the Central Religious Advisory Committee of the BBC and IBA, since 1975; Presenter, Saints Alive, Associated Television, since 1977; *b* 13 Jan. 1929; *o s* of Daniel Manley Morris and Mary Alice Morris, Bolton, Lancs; *m* 1970, Shirley-Anne Benka. *Educ:* Bolton County Grammar Sch.; Univs of Oxford and Manchester. Student, Nuffield Coll., Oxford, 1953-56; Missionary, Northern Rhodesia, 1956-60; President: United Church of Central Africa, 1960-64; United Church of Zambia, 1965-68; Minister of Wesley's Chapel, London, 1969-73. Chm., Community and Race Relations Unit, BCC, 1974-76. Presenter, Anno Domini, BBC TV, 1974-76. Lectures: Willson, Univ. of Nebraska, 1968; Cousland, Univ. of Toronto, 1972; Voigt, S Illinois Conf. United Methodist Church, 1973; Hickman, Duke University, North Carolina, 1974; Palmer, Pacific NW Univ.; Select Preacher, Univ. of Cambridge, 1975, Oxford, 1976; holds several hon. degrees. Officer-Companion, Order of Freedom (Zambia), 1966. *Publications:* Black Government (with President K. D. Kaunda), 1960; Hour After Midnight, 1961; Out of Africa's Crucible, 1961; End of the Missionary, 1961; Church and Challenge in a New Africa, 1965; Humanist in Africa (with President K. D. Kaunda), 1966; Include Me Out, 1968; Unyoung, Uncoloured, Unpoor, 1969; What the Papers Didn't Say, 1971; Mankind My Church, 1971; The Hammer of the Lord, 1973; Epistles to the Apostle, 1974; The Word and the Words, 1975. *Recreations:* writing, walking, music. *Address:* 25 Marylebone Road, NW1 5JR. *T:* 01-935 2541.

MORRIS, Prof. Colin John Owen Rhonabwy, MSc, PhD; Professor of Experimental Biochemistry, London Hospital Medical College, University of London, since 1954; *b* 3 May 1910; *s* of John Jenkin Morris and Annie Margaret (*née* Thomas); *m* 1946, Peggy (*née* Clark); two *d* decd. *Educ:* Cowbridge Grammar Sch.; University Coll., Cardiff (MSc Wales). Lister Institute, London, 1932-36 (PhD London); Kaiser Wilhelm Institute, Heidelberg, 1936-37; London Hospital and London Hospital Med. Coll., 1937-; Reader in Chemical Pathology, 1947. *Publications:* (with Mrs P. Morris) Separation Methods in Biochemistry, 1964, 2nd edn 1976; numerous scientific papers in Journal of Chem. Soc., Biochem. Jl, etc. *Recreation:* sailing. *Address:* 14 Trowlock Avenue, Teddington, Mddx. *T:* 01-977 4853.

MORRIS, David Edward; Chief Scientist, Civil Aviation Authority, since 1972; *b* 23 July 1915; *m* 1950, Heather Anne Court; one *s* two *d*. *Educ:* University Coll. of North Wales, Bangor; Trinity Coll., Cambridge. Aerodynamics Dept, RAE, 1938-56; Chief Supt, A&AEE, 1956-59; Chief Supt, RAE, Bedford, 1959-61; Dir-General, Development (RAF), Min. of Aviation, 1961-65; Dir-Gen., Civil Aircraft and Gen. Services Research and Develt, 1965-69; Scientific Adviser (Civil Aviation), BoT, later DTI, 1969-72. FRAeS 1956. *Publications:* various reports and memoranda. *Recreations:* walking, bridge. *Address:* 38 Days Lane, Biddenham, Bedford. *T:* 66644.

MORRIS, David Elwyn; Registrar of the Principal Registry of the Family Division of the High Court of Justice, since 1976; *b* 22 May 1920; *s* of Rev. Samuel Mordecai Morris and Kathleen Winifred Morris; *m* 1947, Joyce Hellyer (*d* 1977); one *s* one *d*.

Educ: Mill Hill Sch.; Brasenose Coll., Oxford (Hulme Exhibnr; MA). With Friends' Ambulance Unit in China, 1942-44; served British Army in India, 1944-46. Called to Bar, Inner Temple, 1949; admitted Solicitor of the Supreme Court, 1955; Mem., Matrimonial Causes Rule Cttee, 1967-75. Partner, Jaques & Co. until 1975. *Publications:* China Changed My Mind, 1948; The End of Marriage, 1971; contrib. Marriage For and Against, 1972; Pilgrim through this Barren Land, 1974. *Recreation:* reading. *Address:* Woodstock, 5 Bois Avenue, Chesham Bois, Amersham, Bucks HP6 5NS. *T:* Amersham 7574.

MORRIS, Denis Edward, OBE 1958; Member, Public Relations and Promotion Sub-Committee, Test and County Cricket Board, 1968-75; Head, and ultimately Controller of Light Programme, BBC, 1960-67; *b* 29 June 1907; *s* of Philip and Edith Morris; *m* 1st, 1931, Angela Moore (marr. diss., 1942); one *s*; 2nd, 1943, Catharine Garrett (*née* Anderton); one *s*. *Educ:* Tonbridge Sch. BBC Talks Producer, 1936; BBC Midland Public Relations Officer, 1938; BBC Empire Public Relations Officer, 1939; MOI Dir, Midland Region, 1940-42; BBC Midland Regional Programme Dir, 1943-48; Head of Midland Regional Programmes, 1948-60. Leicester City Council, 1933-36; Chm., Findon Parish Council, 1971-74; Chm., Lord Mayor of Birmingham's War Relief Fund Publicity and Appeals Cttee, 1942-48; Chm., Shoreham Cons. Assoc., 1971-75; Member: Hosp. Management Cttee, St Francis Hosp. and Lady Chichester Hosp., 1966-71; Exec. Cttee, Nat. Cricket Assoc., 1969-74 (Chm., Public Relations Standing Cttee, 1969-72); Dep. Chm., Lord's Taverners' Council, 1963-65 (Mem., 1962-67); Public Relations Advisor to MCC and the Counties, 1967-68. *Publications:* Poultry-Keeping for Profit, 1949; The French Vineyards, 1958; A Guide to the Pleasures of Wine-Drinking, 1972. *Recreations:* swimming, golf, drinking wine and writing about it (for Daily Telegraph and Field). *Address:* Little Nepcote, Findon, Worthing, West Sussex BN14 0SN. *T:* Findon 3256. *Clubs:* MCC; Incogniti CC; Sussex Martlets CC; Gentlemen of Leicestershire CC; Blackheath Rugby Football; Sussex Rugby Football.

MORRIS, Desmond John, DPhil; writer on animal and human behaviour; Research Fellow, Wolfson College, Oxford, since 1973; *b* 24 Jan. 1928; *s* of Capt. Harry Howe Morris and Dorothy Marjorie Fuller Morris (*née* Hunt); *m* 1952, Ramona Baulch; one *s*. *Educ:* Dauntsey's Sch.; Birmingham Univ. (BSc); Magdalen Coll., Oxford (DPhil). Postdoctoral research in Animal Behaviour, Dept of Zoology, Oxford Univ., 1954-56; Head of Granada TV and Film Unit at Zool. Soc. of London, 1956-59; Curator of Mammals, Zool. Soc. of London, 1959-67; Dir, Inst. of Contemp. Arts, London, 1967-68. Chm. of TV programmes: Zootime (weekly), 1956-67; Life (fortnightly), 1965-68. *Publications:* (Jt Ed.) International Zoo Yearbook, 1959-62; The Biology of Art, 1962; The Mammals: A Guide to the Living Species, 1965; (with Ramona Morris) Men and Snakes, 1965; (with Ramona Morris) Men and Apes, 1966; (with Ramona Morris) Men and Pandas, 1966; The Naked Ape, 1967; (ed) Primate Ethology, 1967; The Human Zoo, 1969; Patterns of Reproductive Behaviour, 1970; Intimate Behaviour, 1971; Manwatching: a field guide to human behaviour, 1977; numerous papers in zoological jls. *Recreations:* painting, archæology. *Address:* Wolfson College, Oxford.

MORRIS, Air Marshal Sir Douglas (Griffith), KCB 1962 (CB 1954); CBE 1945; DSO 1945; DFC 1941; AOC-in-C, RAF Fighter Command, 1962-66; *b* 3 Dec. 1908; 2nd *s* of D. G. Morris, late of Natal, South Africa; *m* 1936, Audrey Beryl Heard; one *s* one *d*. *Educ:* St John's Coll., Johannesburg, South Africa. Commissioned RAF, 1930; trained as pilot, 1930-31; No. 40 (B) Sqdn, 1931-32; Fleet Air Arm, 1932-34; qualified as Flying Instructor, Central Flying Sch., 1934; on instructor duties, 1934-40; RAF Staff Coll., 1940; Air Ministry, 1940-41; on night fighting ops, 1941-42; Comdg No. 406 RCAF Sqdn, 1941-42, as Wing Comdr; Comd RAF North Weald, as Group Capt., 1942-43; on staff of Allied Exped. Air HQ, 1943-44; Comd No. 132 (F) Wing, 1944-45, in Normandy, Belgium, Holland; SASO No 84 Gp HQ, as Air Cdre, Feb.-Nov. 1945; in W Africa, Nov. 1945-46; Jt Planning staff, Min. of Defence, 1946-47; Nat. War Coll., Washington, 1947-48; on staff of Brit. Jt Services Mission, Washington, DC, 1948-50; Sector Comdr, Southern Sector, 1950-52; Sector Comdr, Metropolitan Sector, Fighter Comd, 1952-53; idc 1954; Air Vice-Marshal, 1955, and SASO, 2nd TAF; ACAS (Air Defence), Air Ministry, 1957-59; Chief of Staff, Allied Air Forces, Central Europe, 1960-62. Comdr Order of St Olav, 1945; Comdr Order of Orange-Nassau, 1947; ADC to King George VI, 1949-52; ADC to the Queen, 1952. Retired, 1966. *Recreations:* golf, ski-ing. *Address:* Friar's Côte, Northiam, Rye, East Sussex. *Club:* Royal Air Force.

MORRIS, Edward Allan, CMG 1967; OBE 1961; *b* 8 Sept. 1910; *s* of John Morris, Twickenham; *m* 1937, Phyllis, *d* of late Francis Guise, Twickenham; one *d* (one *s* decd). *Educ:* Hampton Grammar Sch.; Univ. of London (BCom). Entered Crown Agents' Office, 1928. RAFVR, 1942-46; Sqdn Leader (King's Commendation, 1946). Crown Agents' Office: Asst Head of Dept, 1956; Head of Dept, 1958; Asst Crown Agent, 1964; Crown Agent for Oversea Governments and Administrations, 1968-70. *Recreations:* cricket, Rugby Union football, church bells and change-ringing, preserving the riverside area of Twickenham. *Address:* 56 Lebanon Park, Twickenham, Mddx. *T:* 01-892 5856. *Clubs:* Royal Air Force, MCC, Corona (Hon. Treas.); Middlesex County Cricket, Harlequin Football.

MORRIS, Air Commodore Edward James, CB 1966; CBE 1959; DSO 1942; DFC 1944; RAF, retired 1968; *b* 6 April 1915; *s* of late D. G. Morris, and late Mrs E. Morris, Bulawayo, Southern Rhodesia; *m* 1945, Alison Joan, *d* of Sir Charles Henderson, KBE; two *s*. *Educ:* Michaelhouse, Natal, S Africa. Commnd, 1937; Fighter Comd, 1938-41; Desert Air Force, 1941-45; Staff Coll., 1945-46; BAFO Germany, 1946-49; Old Sarum, 1949-52; Caledonian Sector, Fighter Command, 1952-53; RAF Flying Coll., 1953-54; Exchange Posting with USAF, Florida, 1954-56; SASO HQ 12 Group, 1956-58; OC Wattisham, 1958-59; HQ Fighter Command, 1959-60; Air Ministry, 1960-64; Chief of Staff, Headquarters Middle East Command, 1964-66; AOC Air Cadets, and Comdt Air Training Corps, 1966-68. American DFC 1945. MBIM. *Recreations:* golf, shooting, fishing, ski-ing. *Address:* 26 Edgecliff Drive, Kloof, Natal, South Africa.

MORRIS, Gareth (Charles Walter); Principal Professor of the Flute, Royal Academy of Music, since 1945; *b* Clevedon, Som, 13 May 1920, *e s* of Walter and Enid Morris; *m* 1954; one *d* ; *m* 1975, Patricia Mary, *y d* of Neil and Sheila Murray, Romsey, Hampshire; one *s*. *Educ:* Bristol Cathedral Sch.; Royal Academy of Music, London. First studied the flute at age of twelve under Robert Murchie and later won a scholarship to RAM. Career since then has been as soloist, chamber music and symphonic player, teacher and lecturer; Principal Flautist, 1949-72, Chm., 1966-72, New Philharmonia Orch. (formerly Philharmonia Orch.). Has been mem. Arts Council Music Panel, and Warden of Incorporated Soc. of Musicians Soloists Section; Adjudicator, International Flute playing Competitions, Geneva, 1973, Munich, 1974. Played at Her Majesty's Coronation in Westminster Abbey in 1953. ARAM 1945; FRAM 1950; FRSA 1967. *Recreations:* reading and collecting books; astronomy, antiquarian horology. *Address:* 4 Alwyne Place, Canonbury, N1. *T:* 01-226 4752.

MORRIS, Sir Geoffrey N.; *see* Newman-Morris.

MORRIS, Captain George Horace Guy, CBE 1960; retired; *b* 21 Feb. 1897; *o s* of late H. W. T. Morris of Litherland, County of Lancaster; *m* 1919, Nancy (*d* 1963), *o c* of late Josiah Meir, Tunstall, Staffs; one *s* one *d*. *Educ:* Liverpool. Went to sea as apprentice with W. Lowden & Co., Liverpool, 1912; served as Lt RNR, 1916-20; joined Cunard Line as Junior Officer, 1922; Captain, 1947. Commanded: SS Vasconia, SS Arabia, SS Assyria, RMS Parthia, RMS Media, RMS Scythia, RMS Georgic, RMS Britannic, RMS Caronia, RMS Mauretania. Appointed Relieving Captain Queen Liners, 1956; Captain RMS Queen Mary, 1957; Captain RMS Queen Elizabeth, 1958; Commodore Cunard Line, 1958; retired, 1960. *Recreation:* motoring. *Address:* 6 Archers Court, Arrowe Park, Birkenhead, Merseyside. *T:* 051-677 6723.

MORRIS, Gwyn Rhyse Francis, QC 1959; **His Honour Judge Gwyn Morris;** a Circuit Judge, Central Criminal Court, since 1972; *b* 1910; *s* of late Wm John Morris, Co. Pembroke; *m* 1st, 1933, Margaret, *d* of late Ridley Mackenzie, MD; one *s* one *d* (and one *s* decd); 2nd, 1945, Lady Victoria Audrey Beatrice, *d* of Viscount Ingestre and *sister* of 21st Earl of Shrewsbury, *qv*. *Educ:* New Coll., Oxford. Called to Bar, Middle Temple, 1937. Mem. Gen. Council of the Bar, 1964-67; Master of the Bench, Middle Temple, 1966. Mem., Commn at CCC, 1971. *Address:* Penylan Hall, Llechryd, Dyfed. *T:* Llechryd 335; Goldsmith Building, Temple, EC4. *T:* 01-353 7881; (residence) Carpmael Building, Temple, EC4. *T:* 01-353 1373. *Club:* Travellers'.

MORRIS, Harry Frank Grave, CMG 1958; *b* 11 May 1907; *e s* of late Frank Morris; unmarried. *Educ:* Harrow; Balliol Coll., Oxford. MA Oxon 1928. Solicitor, 1931-41. Joined Foreign Service, 1943, Madrid, Lisbon, Budapest, Rome; retired, Dec. 1962. *Address:* 32 Pont Street, SW1. *T:* 01-584 0883. *Club:* Garrick.

MORRIS, Ivor Gray, CMG 1974; Chairman and Managing Director, Morris Woollen Mills (Ipswich) Pty Ltd, since 1934; *b* 28 March 1911; *s* of John and Annie Morris, Talybont, Cards, and Ipswich, Qld; *m* 1944, Jessie Josephine Halley; two *d*. *Educ:* Scotch Coll., Melbourne; Scots Coll., Warwick, Qld; Ipswich Grammar Sch., Qld; Leeds Univ. Founded Morris Woollen Mills (Ipswich) Pty Ltd, 1934. Mem. Exec., Wool Textile Manufrs Assoc. of Australia; Life Mem., Nuclear Physics Foundn; Mem., Trade Develt Council, Canberra. Chm. of Trustees, Ipswich Grammar Sch., 1970-; Vice-Pres., Qld Museum Trust, 1970-; Patron, St David's Welsh Soc.; Foundn Mem. and District Governor, Ipswich Apex Club (1st Apex Club formed in Austr.), 1938. *Recreations:* music, reading. *Address:* River Road, Redbank, Queensland 4301, Australia. *T:* 88-29-35. *Clubs:* Tattersall's (Brisbane); Ipswich, Ipswich North Rotary (Ipswich, Qld).

MORRIS, James; *see* Morris, Jan.

MORRIS, James Peter; *b* 17 Sept. 1926; *s* of Frank Morris and Annie (*née* Collindridge); *m* 1st, Peggy Giles (marr. diss.); 2nd, Margaret Law. *Educ:* Barnsley Grammar Sch.; Manchester Univ. (BA, Teaching Dip.). Served RAF, 1945-48; Research Dept, Labour Party, 1952-59; Govt Information Services, 1960-73, serving in COI, Treasury, LOB, DEA; Chief Information Officer, MoT, 1968-71; Dep. Dir of Information, DoE, 1971-72; Chief Information Officer, Industrial Develt Exec., DTI, 1972-73; Dir of Information, GLC, 1973-77. *Publication:* Road Safety: a Study of Cost Benefit in Public Service Advertising, 1972. *Recreations:* painting, theatre, brewing. *Address:* 88 Ridgmount Gardens, WC1E 7AY. *T:* 01-637 2141. *Clubs:* MCC, Reform.

MORRIS, James Richard Samuel; Group Tehnical Director, Courtaulds Ltd, since 1976 (Director, since 1967); *b* 25 Nov. 1925; *o s* of James John Morris and Kathleen Mary Morris (*née* McNaughton); *m* 1958, Marion Reid Sinclair; two *s* two *d*. *Educ:* Ardingly Coll.; Birmingham Univ. BSc, 1st cl. hons Chem. Engrg; Vice-Chancellor's Prize, 1955; CEng, FIChemE. Captain Welsh Guards, 1944-48. Courtaulds Ltd, 1950-: Man. Dir, National Plastics Ltd, 1959-64; Dep. Chm., British Cellophane Ltd, 1967-70; Chm., British Celanese Ltd, 1970-72; Chm., Northgate Gp Ltd, 1971-76; Chm., Meridian Ltd, 1972-76; Dir, British Nuclear Fuels Ltd, 1971-. Member: Nuclear Power Adv. Bd, 1973; Adv. Council for Energy Conservation, 1974-. Mem. Council, 1974, Vice-Pres., 1976, Pres., 1977, IChemE. Fellow, Fellowship of Engineering, 1977. *Recreations:* ski-ing, gardening, music. *Address:* Breadsall Manor, Derby. *T:* Derby 831368.

MORRIS, Jan, FRSL; writer; Commonwealth Fellow, USA, 1953; Editorial Staff, The Times, 1951-56; Editorial Staff, The Guardian, 1957-62. Mem., Yr Academi Gymreig. *Publications:* (as James Morris): Coast to Coast, 1956; Sultan in Oman, 1957; The Market of Seleukia, 1957; Coronation Everest, 1958; South African Winter, 1958; The Hashemite Kings, 1959; Venice, 1960, rev. edn, 1974; The Upstairs Donkey, 1962 (for children); The World Bank, 1963; Cities, 1963; The Presence of Spain, 1964; Oxford, 1965, rev. edn 1978; Pax Britannica, 1968; The Great Port, 1970; Places, 1972; Heaven's Command, 1973; Farewell the Trumpets, 1978; (as Jan Morris): Conundrum, 1974; Travels, 1976; The Oxford Book of Oxford, 1978. *Address:* Trefan Morys, Llanystumdwy, Cricieth, Gwynedd, Wales; Trefan Bach, Fforest, Abergafenni, Gwent, Wales. *T:* Crucorney 466.

MORRIS, Prof. Jeremy Noah, CBE 1972; FRCP; Professor of Community Health, University of London, at London School of Hygiene and Tropical Medicine, since 1967; *b* 6 May 1910; *s* of Nathan and Annie Morris; *m* 1939, Galina Schuchalter; one *s* one *d*. *Educ:* Hutcheson's Grammar Sch., Glasgow; Univ. of Glasgow; University Coll. Hosp., London; London School of Hygiene and Tropical Medicine. MA, DSc, DPH. Qual., 1934; hosp. residencies, 1934-37; general practice, 1937-38; Asst MOH, Hendon and Harrow, 1939-41; Med. Spec., RAMC, 1941-46 (Lt-Col 1944-46); Rockefeller Fellow, Prev. Med., 1946-47; Dir, MRC Social Med. Unit, 1948-75; Prof., Social Med., London Hosp., 1959-67; Visiting Prof., Yale, 1957, Berkeley, 1963. Lectures: Ernestine Henry, RCP London; Gibson, RCP Edinburgh; Fleming, RCPS Glasgow; Carey Coombs, Univ. of Bristol; Brontë Stewart, Univ. of Glasgow; St Cyres, Nat. Heart Hosp.; Alumnus, Yale; Delamar, Johns Hopkins Univ. Member: Royal Commission on Penal Reform; Cttee, Personal Social Services, Working Party Med. Admin, 1964-72; Chief Scientist's Res. Cttee, DHSS, 1973-; Med. Adv. Cttees, Sports Council, OPCS. Hon. MD Edinburgh, 1974; Hon. Mem. Amer. Epid. Soc., 1976; Hon. FFCM, 1977. *Publications:* Uses of Epidemiology, 1957, 3rd edn 1975; papers on coronary disease and exercise, and on health and prevention. *Recreations:* walking, swimming, piano music. *Address:* 3 Briardale Gardens, NW3. *T:* 01-435 5024. *Club:* RAC.

MORRIS, Rt. Hon. John, PC 1970; QC 1973; MP (Lab) Aberavon Division of Glamorgan since Oct. 1959; Secretary of State for Wales, since 1974; *b* Nov. 1931; *s* of late D. W. Morris, Penywern, Talybont, Cardiganshire; *m* 1959, Margaret M., *d* of late Edward Lewis, OBE, JP, of Llandysul; three *d*. *Educ:* Ardwyn, Aberystwyth; University Coll. of Wales, Aberystwyth; Gonville and Caius Coll., Cambridge; Academy of International Law, The Hague; Holker Senior Exhibitioner, Gray's Inn. Commissioned Royal Welch Fusiliers and Welch Regt. Called to the Bar, Gray's Inn, 1954. Parly Sec., Min. of Power, 1964-66; Jt Parly Sec., Min. of Transport, 1966-68; Minister of Defence (Equipment), 1968-70. Formerly Dep. Gen. Sec. and Legal Adviser, Farmers' Union of Wales. Member: UK Delegn Consultative Assembly Council of Europe and Western European Union, 1963-64; N Atlantic Assembly, 1970-74. Chairman: Nat. Pneumoconiosis Jt Cttee, 1964-66; Joint Review of Finances and Management, British Railways, 1966-67; Nat. Road Safety Advisory Council, 1967; Mem. Courts of University Colls, Aberystwyth, Swansea and Cardiff. *Address:* House of Commons, SW1.

MORRIS, John, (C. J. Morris), CBE 1957; *b* 27 Aug. 1895; *e s* of late Frank Morris. *Educ:* King's Coll., Cambridge (MA, MSc, Diploma in Anthropology). Served with Leicestershire Regt and 3rd QAO Gurkha Rifles, 1915-34; served European War: France and Belgium, 1915-17 (wounded), Palestine, 1918; Afghanistan, 1919; Waziristan and NW Frontier of India, 1919-21 and 1921-24; travelled extensively in Central Asia, Tibet, Nepal, Bhutan, Africa, the Far East, etc; mem. of 1922 and 1936 Mount Everest Expeditions; Murchison Memorial of Royal Geographical Society, for explorations in Chinese Turkestan, 1929; William Wyse studentship in Social Anthropology, Univ. of Cambridge, 1934-37. Prof. of English Literature at Keio Univ., Tokyo, and Lecturer at Imperial and Bunrika Univs, Tokyo; concurrently adviser on English language to Japanese Dept of Foreign Affairs, 1938-42; BBC: Head of Far Eastern Service, 1943-52; Controller, Third Programme, 1952-58. *Publications:* The Gurkhas (with Major W. Brook Northey), 1928; Handbooks for the Indian Army: Gurkhas, 1935; Living with Lepchas, 1938; Traveller from Tokyo, 1943; The Phœnix Cup, 1947; From the Third Programme (Edited), 1956; Hired to Kill, 1960; A Winter in Nepal, 1963; Eating the Indian Air, 1968. *Recreations:* travel, reading, music. *Address:* 21 Friday Street, Henley-on-Thames, Oxon. *T:* Henley-on-Thames 4369. *Clubs:* Savile, Alpine; University Alpine (Cambridge); Japan Alpine (Tokyo); Himalayan (Calcutta).

MORRIS, Maj.-Gen. John Edward Longworth, CB 1963; CBE 1956; DSO 1945; Director of Recruiting, War Office, 1960-64, retired; *b* 1 June 1909; *s* of Col A. E. Morris and M. E. Stanyon; *m* 1939, Pamela Gresley Ball; two *d*. *Educ:* Cheltenham Coll. Commissioned Regular Army, 1929; served War of 1939-45: India, Middle East and NW Europe, Col Comdt, RA, 1966-74. *Recreations:* sailing, climbing, photography, music. *Address:* Marshgate, Tolleshunt D'Arcy, Essex. *Clubs:* Royal Ocean Racing, Royal Artillery Yacht (Admiral).

MORRIS, John Evan A.; *see* Artro Morris.

MORRIS, Dr John Humphrey Carlile, FBA 1966; DCL; Fellow of Magdalen College, Oxford, 1936-77, Hon. Fellow, 1977; University Reader in Conflict of Laws, 1951-77; *b* 18 Feb. 1910; *e s* of H. W. Morris, Solicitor, and J. M. Morris; *m* 1939, Mercy Jane Kinch; no *c*. *Educ:* Charterhouse; Christ Church, Oxford. DCL Oxford, 1949. Barrister-at-Law, 1934; Fellow and Tutor in Law, Magdalen Coll., Oxford, 1936; All Souls Lecturer in Private Internat. Law, 1939-51. Lt-Comdr RNVR, 1940-45. Visiting Prof., Harvard Law Sch., 1950-51; Assoc. Mem. Amer. Acad. of Arts and Sciences, 1960. *Publications:* Cases in Private International Law, 4th edn, 1968; The Conflict of Laws, 1971; (with Prof. W. Barton Leach) The Rule against Perpetuities, 2nd edn, 1962; Editor, 9th, 10th and 11th edns of Theobald on Wills, 1939-54; Gen. Editor: Dicey's Conflict of Laws, 6th to 9th edns, 1949-73; Chitty on Contracts, 22nd edn, 1961; title Conflict of Laws in Halsbury's Laws of England, 4th edn, 1974. *Recreation:* yacht cruising. *Address:* Tubney Lodge, near Abingdon, Oxon. *T:* Oxford 390734. *Club:* Royal Cruising.

MORRIS, Rev. (John) Marcus (Harston); Managing Director, The National Magazine Co. Ltd, since 1964; *b* 25 April 1915; *er s* of late Rev. Canon W. E. H. Morris and Edith (*née* Nield); *m* 1941, Jessica, *d* of late John Hamlet Dunning and Alice (*née* Hunt-Jones); one *s* three *d*. *Educ:* Dean Close Sch., Cheltenham; Brasenose Coll., Oxford (Colquitt Exhibnr; BA Lit. Hum. 1937). Wycliffe Hall, Oxford (BA Theol. 1939, MA 1947). Deacon 1939, priest 1940. Curate: St Bartholomew's, Roby, 1939-40; Great Yarmouth, 1940-41; Chaplain, RAFVR, 1941-43; Rector of Weeley, 1943-45; Vicar of St James's,

Birkdale, 1945-50; Editor, The Anvil, 1946-50; Founder and Editor, Eagle, Girl, Swift, and Robin, 1950-59; Man. Editor, Housewife, 1954-59; Editorial Dir, The National Magazine Co. Ltd, 1960-64. Hon. Chaplain, St Bride's, Fleet Street, 1952-. *Publications:* Stories of the Old Testament, 1961; Stories of the New Testament, 1961; (ed) The Best of Eagle, 1977. *Recreation:* golf three times a year. *Address:* 82 Narrow Street, E14. *T:* 01-987 6831. *Club:* Savile.

MORRIS, Hon. Sir Kenneth (James), KBE 1968; CMG 1964; Senator, Australian National Parliament, 1963-68, retired; *b* 22 Oct. 1903; *s* of J. R. Morris; *m* 1931, Ettie L., *d* of W. H. Dunlop; three *s* one *d* (and one *s* decd). *Educ:* Brisbane Gram. Sch. Business Company Dir prior to 1939. Enlisted AIF, 1939; served in England with 6th Australian Division, then original mem. of 9th Australian Division; served Tobruk, Alamein, New Guinea; transferred to R of O, Major, 1944. Elected Qld Parliament, 1944, as MLA Enoggera (later Mt Coot-tha); served as Whip, 1944-49; Deputy Leader, 1949-53, Leader, 1953-62. Parliamentary Liberal Party; Deputy Premier, Minister of Labour and Industry, 1957-63. *Recreations:* bowls, fishing. *Address:* 20/45 Moray Street, New Farm, Brisbane, Qld 4005, Australia. *T:* 358 1289. *Clubs:* United Service, Masonic (Brisbane).

MORRIS, Rev. Marcus; *see* Morris, Rev. J. M. H.

MORRIS, Michael Sachs; Under-Secretary, Department of Trade, since 1973; *b* 12 June 1924; *s* of late Prof. Noah Morris, MD, DSc, and of Hattie Michaelis; *m* 1952, Vera Leonie, *er d* of Paul and Lona Heller; one *s* one *d*. *Educ:* Glasgow Academy; St Catharine's Coll., Cambridge. Wrangler, 1948. Scientific Officer, Admty Signals Estabt, 1943-46; Asst Principal, BoT, 1948; Asst Sec. 1966; idc 1970. Hon. Officer, New London Synagogue, 1971-74. *Recreation:* sitting in the sun. *Address:* 53 Westbury Road, Finchley, N12 7PB. *T:* 01-445 5234. *Club:* United Oxford & Cambridge University.

MORRIS, Michael Wolfgang Laurence; MP (C) Northampton South since 1974; Director, Benton & Bowles Ltd, since 1971; Chairman, Roy Friedlander and Partners, since 1975; *b* 25 Nov. 1936; *m* 1960, Dr Ann Appleby (Dr Ann Morris, MB, BS, MRCS, MRCP); two *s* one *d*. *Educ:* Bedford Sch.; St Catharine's Coll., Cambridge (MA). BA Hons Econs, MIPA, MInstM. Management Trainee to Marketing Manager, UK, India and Ceylon, Reckitt & Colman Gp, 1960-63; Service Advertising Ltd, 1964-68; Marketing Exec. to Account Supervisor, Horniblow Cox-Freeman Ltd, 1968-71, Dir 1969-71. Contested (C) Islington North, 1966. Islington Council: Councillor, 1968-70; Alderman, 1970-74; Chm. of Housing, 1968; Leader, 1969-71. Secretary: Cons. Housing and Local Govt Cttee, 1974-76; Cons. Trade Cttee, 1974-76. *Publications:* (jtly) Helping the Exporter, 1967; (contrib.) Marketing below the Line: Studies in Management, 1972. *Recreations:* restoration work, clocks, squash. *Address:* Caesar's Camp, Sandy, Beds. *T:* Sandy 80388. *Clubs:* Carlton, Wellington; George Row, Conservative, Whitworth, Billing Road, (Northampton); John O'Gaunt Golf (Beds).

MORRIS, Nigel Godfrey, CMG 1955; MVO 1966; QPM 1954; *b* 11 Nov. 1908; 2nd *s* of late Lt-Col G. M. Morris, 2/8th Gurkha Rifles and late Mrs Morris; *m* 1941, Mrs G. E. Baughan (*widow*), *e d* of late J. C. Sidebottom; one *d* and one step *d*. *Educ:* Wellington Coll. Asst Superintendent SS Police, 1928; Chinese language course, Amoy, China, 1929; Asst Supt of Police, Singapore CID 1931; Special Branch, 1935; Asst Supt of Police, Town Penang, 1939; interned by Japanese, 1942; repatriated to UK, 1945; Asst Dir, Malayan Security Service, 1946; Dir, Special Branch, Singapore, 1948; Dep. Commissioner, CID, Singapore, 1950, Comr, 1952; Deputy Inspector-General of Colonial Police, Colonial Office, 1957-63; Commissioner of Police, Bahamas, 1963-68, retired. Colonial Police Medal, 1949. *Recreation:* golf. *Address:* Blenheim House, Watlington, Oxon. *T:* Watlington 2228.

See also Brigadier Arthur de Burgh Morris.

MORRIS, Prof. Norman Frederick, MD, FRCOG; Professor of Obstetrics and Gynæcology, University of London, Charing Cross Hospital Medical School, since 1958; Dean, Faculty of Medicine, University of London, 1971-76; Deputy Vice-Chancellor, University of London, since 1976; *b* Luton, 26 Feb. 1920; *s* of F. W. Morris, Luton; *m* 1944, Lucia Xenia Rivlin; two *s* two *d*. *Educ:* Dunstable Sch., Dunstable; St Mary's Hospital Medical Sch. MRCS, LRCP 1943; MRCOG 1949; MB, BS (London) 1943; MD (London) 1949; FRCOG 1959. House appts St Mary's Hosp., Paddington and Amersham, 1944-46; Res. Obstetrician and Surg. Officer, East Ham Memorial Hosp., E6; Surg. Specialist RAF (Sqdn Ldr), 1946-48; Registrar, St

Mary's Hosp., W2, and East End Maternity Hosp., E1, 1948-50; Sen. Registrar (Obst. and Gynæcol.), Hammersmith Hosp., 1950-52; First Asst, Obstetric Unit, Univ. Coll. Hosp., WC1, 1953-56; Reader, Univ. of London in Obst. and Gynæcol., Inst. of Obstetrics and Gynæcology, 1956-58; Member: Court and Senate, Univ. of London, 1972-; Bd of Governors, Wye Coll., 1973-; Pres., Internat. Soc. of Psychosomatic Obstetrics and Gynaecology; Dep. Chm., NW RHA. External Examiner, Univs of Sheffield, Leeds, Dundee and Liverpool. Formerly Chairman: Assoc. of University Clinical Academic Staff; 3rd World Congress of Psychosomatic Medicine in Obst. and Glynæcol. (Editor, Proceedings, 1972). Editor, Midwife and Health Visitor Jl. *Publications:* The Baby Book, 1957; Non-Toxæmic Hypertension in Pregnancy (jtly), 1958; Sterilisation, 1976; contrib. Lancet, 1960; various articles in medical jls related to obstetric problems, 1952-. *Recreations:* arguing, collecting antiques, music. *Address:* 16 Provost Road, NW3. *T:* 01-722 4244. *Clubs:* Athenæum, 1942.

MORRIS, Owen Humphrey, CB 1977; CMG 1967; Deputy Under-Secretary of State, Welsh Office; *b* 15 June 1921; *o c* of late David Humphreys Morris, Ton Pentre, Rhondda, Glam., and Mrs Amy Ann Morris (*née* Jones); *m* 1972, Mair Annetta Evans, *d* of late Capt. Daniel Evans, DSC, Tynllys, Morfa Nefyn. *Educ:* Public Elem. Schs; King's Coll. Sch., Wimbledon (Schol.); Balliol Coll., Oxford (Schol.; MA). Served War of 1939-45: The Welch Regt and King's African Rifles, 1941-45 (Capt.). Asst Princ., Colonial Office, 1946; seconded Sierra Leone Administration, 1952-53; Asst Sec., 1955; Dept of Techn. Cooperation, 1962; Min. of Overseas Development, 1964; Min. of Housing and Local Govt, 1966; Welsh Office, 1969; Asst Under-Sec., 1970; Dep. Sec., 1974. *Address:* c/o Welsh Office, Cathays Park, Cardiff.

MORRIS, Prof. Peter John; Nuffield Professor of Surgery, Oxford University, since 1974; Fellow of Balliol College, since 1974; *b* 17 April 1934; *s* of Stanley Henry and Mary Lois Morris; *m* 1960, Mary Jocelyn Gorman; three *s* two *d.* *Educ:* Xavier Coll., Melbourne; Univ. of Melbourne (MB, BS, PhD). FRCS, FRACS, FACS. Jun. surg. appts at St Vincent's Hosp., Melbourne, Postgrad. Med. Sch., London, Southampton Gen. Hosp. and MGH Boston, 1958-64; Research Fellow, Harvard Med. Sch., 1965-66; Asst Prof. in Surgery, Med. Coll. of Virginia, 1967; 2nd Asst in Surgery, Univ. of Melbourne, 1968-69, 1st Asst 1970-71; Reader in Surgery, Univ. of Melbourne, 1972-74. WHO Consultant, 1970-; Cons. to Walter and Eliza Hall Inst. of Med. Res., 1969-74. Selwyn Smith Prize, Univ. of Melbourne, 1971. Hunterian Prof., RCS, 1972. *Publications:* numerous sci. articles and chapters in books concerned mainly with transplantation and surgery. *Recreations:* golf, tennis, cricket. *Address:* 19 Lucerne Road, Oxford OX2 7QB. *Clubs:* Frilford Heath Golf (Oxford); Yarra Yarra Golf (Australia).

MORRIS, Sir Philip (Robert), KCMG 1960; Kt 1946; CBE 1941; MA Oxon; Hon. LLD: Rhodes, 1950; Bristol, 1951; McGill, 1955; Windsor, 1958; NUI, W Ontario, 1960; London, 1965; Bath, 1966; Hon. ARCVS 1958; FRSA 1961; Hon. FRCS 1966; Vice-Chancellor Bristol University, 1946-66; *b* 6 July 1901; 2nd *s* of late M. C. Morris, HM Inspector, and late J. Morris, Sutton Valence; *m* 1926, Florence Redvers Davis, 2nd *d* of Walford Davis Green, Barrister-at-law, and Annie L. Green; two *s* one *d* (and one *d* decd). *Educ:* Tonbridge Sch.; St Peter's, York; Trinity Coll., Oxford. Modern Greats, 1923; Teachers' Diploma, London Univ., 1924; Lectr in History and Classics, Westminster Trng Coll., 1923-25; Administrative Officer, Kent Education Cttee, Asst Dir, 1932; Dir, 1938-43; Dir-Gen. of Army Education, 1944-46; Educational Adviser, HM Prison, 1938-44; Mem. Board of Education Cttee on Training of Teachers and Youth Leaders, 1942-44. Life Trustee of Carnegie UK Trust; UK Deleg. First Conf. of UNESCO, 1946; Chm., Army Educ. Advisory Bd, 1946-48; Vice-Chm., British Council, 1946-59; Chm., Secondary Sch. Examinations Council, 1948-51 (Actg Chm. 1947-48); Chairman: Nat. Advisory Council on Training and Supply of Teachers, 1946-59; Cttee of Vice-Chancellors and Principals, 1955-58; Miners' Welfare Nat. Scholarship Scheme Selection Cttee, 1948-49; Anglo-Czechoslovak Cultural Commn, 1949; Chm. Conference on African Education, 1952; Theatre Royal, Bristol, Management Cttee, 1946-63; Chm. Bristol Old Vic Trust, 1946-71, Pres., 1971-; Chm. Commonwealth Education Conference, 1959; Chm. Commonwealth Education Liaison Cttee, 1959-62; Vice-Chm., United Bristol Hosps Bd of Govs, 1948-66; Member: BBC Gen. Adv. Council, 1947-52; Vice-Chm. of BBC, 1954-60 (a Governor, 1952-60); BBC West Reg. Adv. Council, 1961-68 (Chm. 1947-52); SW Regional Hosp. Bd, 1948-53; Central Adv. Council for Educn (England), 1944-48; Adv. Cttee for Educn in the Colonies, 1945-48 and 1949-52, 1953-56, 1959-62; General Nursing Council, 1954-55; Advisory Cttee on Recruiting, 1958;

Cttee on Higher Education, 1961-64. Mem. Council, Boy Scouts' Assoc., 1946-59; Vice-Chm. Assoc. Univs of British Commonwealth, 1951-55; Pres., Library Association, 1955; Mem., Governing Bd of National Institute for Research in Nuclear Science, 1957-58; Hon. Mem., Bristol Medico-Chirurgical Soc., 1963-. Hon. Fellow, Bristol Univ., 1966. *Publications:* Christianity and the World of Today, 1961; articles, published addresses etc, on educational subjects. *Recreations:* music, golf. *Address:* Bryncoedifor Vicarage, Rhydymain, Dolgellau, Gwynedd LL40 2AN. *T:* Rhydymain 237. *Club:* Athenæum.

MORRIS, Dr Richard Murchison, CMG 1958; OBE 1949; *b* 14 Sept. 1898; *s* of Richard Henry Morris, Capetown, S Africa; *m* 1928, Kathleen, *d* of Lt-Col C. H. Divine, DSO; one *d* (and one *s* decd). *Educ:* Diocesan Coll., Rondebosch, Cape; London Hospital, Univ. of London. 2nd Lt (Pilot) RAF, 1918. MRCS, LRCP, 1923; House-Surgeon, Poplar Hosp.; MB, BS, 1924; House Physician, etc, London Hosp.; House Physician, Tropical Diseases Hosp.; MD (Gold Medal), 1926; DTM and H, 1926; S Rhodesian Medical Service, 1926; DPH (London, 1932); Sen. Govt MO, 1934; DMS, 1946; Sec. for Health, 1948; Sec. to Ministry of Health, Fedn of Rhodesia and Nyasaland, 1954-58, retired. Councillor, Salisbury City Council, 1961-75; Alderman, City of Salisbury, Rhodesia, 1971. Surg.-Col British S Africa Police, 1946; Col and ADMS Matabeleland, 1939-45; Consultant Physician, RAF Training Group, S Rhodesia, 1940-45. External Examiner in Medicine, Univ. of Capetown, 1950-51. Vice-Chm. Council, University of Rhodesia, 1968-. KStJ 1963. Hon. LLD, Univ. of Rhodesia, 1977. *Publications:* medical papers in Lancet and Central African Jl of Medicine. *Address:* 2 Denmark Avenue, PO Belvedere, Salisbury, Rhodesia. *T:* Salisbury 21351. *Clubs:* Bulawayo (Bulawayo); Salisbury (Salisbury).

MORRIS, Air Vice-Marshal Ronald James Arthur, CB 1974; Principal Medical Officer, RAF Strike Command, 1974-75; retired; *b* 27 Nov. 1915; *s* of late Dr James Arthur Morris, Ladybank, Fife; *m* 1945, Mary Kerr Mitchell; one *s* two *d.* *Educ:* Madras Coll., St Andrews; St Andrews Univ. MB, ChB 1939; DPH Edinburgh, 1953; MFCM 1972. Commnd RAF, 1939; served on Fighter Comd Stns, 1940-41; India and Burma Campaign, 1941-45; HQ Techn. Trng Comd, 1946-48; SMO, HQ Air Forces Western Europe, 1948-50; Sen. Trng Officer and Comdt Med. Trng Estabt, 1950-52; Exchange Officer, Sch. of Aviation Medicine (USAF), 1955-56; Dept MA7, Air Min., 1956-60; OC RAF Chessington, 1960-61; OC RAF Hosp. Wroughton, 1961-63; PMO, Signals Comd, 1963-65; Dep. PMO, Far East Air Forces, 1965-69; PMO, Maintenance Comd, 1969-70; DDGMS (RAF), 1971-73. QHS, 1971-75. CStJ 1974. *Recreations:* golf, fishing. *Address:* 2 Cairnsden Gardens, St Andrews, Fife KY16 8SQ. *T:* St Andrews 5326.

MORRIS, Prof. Terence Patrick, JP; Professor of Sociology (with special reference to Criminology), University of London, since 1969; *b* 8 June 1931; *s* of Albert and Norah Avis Morris; *m* 1954, Pauline Jeannette Peake (*née* Morris) (marr. diss. 1973); one *d*; *m* 1973, Penelope Jane, *y d* of Stanley and Alexandra Tomlinson. *Educ:* John Ruskin Grammar Sch., Croydon; LSE, Univ. of London (Leverhulme Schol.). BSc (Soc) 1953, PhD (Econ) 1955. Lectr in Sociology, LSE, 1955-63; Reader in Sociology (with special ref. to Criminology), 1963-69. Vis. Prof. of Criminology, Univ. of California, 1964-65. Mem., Adv. Mission on Treatment of Offenders (Western Pacific, British Honduras, Bahamas), 1966. Member: Magistrates' Assoc. Treatment of Offenders Cttee (co-opted), 1969-77; Council, Inst. for Study of Drug Dependence. Man. Editor, British Jl of Sociology, 1965-74. JP Inner London, 1967. *Publications:* The Criminal Area, 1957; (with Pauline Morris) Pentonville: a sociological study of an English prison, 1963; (with L. J. Blom-Cooper) A Calendar of Murder, 1964; Deviance and Control: the secular heresy, 1976; contribs to Brit. Jl Criminology, Brit. Jl Sociology, Encycl. Britannica. *Recreation:* sailing and maintenance of small boats. *Address:* c/o London School of Economics, Houghton Street, WC2A 2AE. *Clubs:* Royal Automobile; Royal Solent Yacht.

MORRIS, Most Rev. Thomas; see Cashel and Emly, Archbishop of, (RC).

MORRIS, Thomas Gwilym, CBE 1974; QPM 1968; DL; Chief Constable, South Wales Constabulary, since 1971; *b* 16 Oct. 1913; *m* 1940, Mair Eluned Williams; one *s* one *d.* *Educ:* Swansea Grammar Sch. Certif. of Educn (1st cl.) of Civil Service Commn. Joined Metropolitan Police Force, 1933; Sergt, and Asst to Police War Duty Officer, 1940-43. Joined HM Forces, 1943; served War: commissioned 2nd Lieut, Suffolk Regt, 1944; Captain, and comd Infty Company, 1945; Staff Captain G3 and

ADC to Governor-Gen. of Jamaica, 1946; Major and Dep. Asst Adjt and QMG, N Caribbean Area, 1946. Rejoined Metropolitan Police, after War (Admin., and CID), 1947; Station Sergt (Actg Inspector), 1951; Course at Police Coll., Ryton-on-Dunsmore, 1953; Inspector, and in charge Divl Office, 1954; Chief Inspector: in charge Special Detachments at Buckingham Palace, Houses of Parliament, etc; Sen. Officers Course, Ryton and at Bramshill, 1956; Supt (Grade 2), Dist HQ, opl duties (specially selected to organise air reconnaissance for traffic problems), 1957; Supt (Grade 1) and comd of Police in Borough of Willesden, 1958; Dist Supt, No 2 Dist HQ, Paddington, 1959; Asst Chief Constable, Cardiff, 1962, Chief Constable, Dec. 1963; Dep. Chief Constable, S Wales Constabulary, 1969. Pres., Vice-Pres., etc, various Socs. Admitted as Druid, Bardic Circle, National Eisteddfod, 1973. DL South Glamorgan 1972. Comr, E Glam Dist, Order of St John; CStJ 1970. *Recreations:* Rugby football (Chm., S Wales RFC), golf. *Address:* Pen Llain, 114 Heol Isaf, Radyr, Cardiff CF4 8EA. *T:* Cardiff 843074. *Clubs:* (Hon. Mem.) Cardiff and County (Cardiff); Radyr Golf; (Vice-Pres.) Cardiff Athletic; (Vice-Pres.) Glamorgan Wanderers; Bridgend RF.

MORRIS, Walter Frederick, LLB London; ACII; MBIM; Senior Partner, Morris, Scott & Co., Solicitors, Highcliffe, Christchurch, Dorset and Barton-on-Sea, New Milton, Hants; *b* 15 Oct. 1914; *s* of late Captain Frederick James Morris and Elsie Eleanor (*née* Williams); *m* 1945, Marjorie Vaughan, *o d* of late Thomas Vaughan Phillips and Eleanor Mirren (*née* Jones); one *s* one *d*. *Educ:* Cardiff High Sch.; University Coll., Cardiff (Law Prizeman), Legal practice, 1936-39; Served RA (TA), 1939-45: GHQ Home Forces (Intelligence); WO Sch. of Military Administration; Certificate of Merit, Western Comd; GSO1 (Lt-Col), HQ 21st Army Gp, BLA (later BAOR); commanded Legal Aid Organisation, which provided legal assistance to all British Army and RAF personnel in Europe; legal practice (and Hon. District Army Welfare Officer), 1945-47; entered Administrative Home Civil Service, 1947; Min. of Social Security, 1947-68 (Prin., Dep. Chief Insce Off., Asst Sec.); Admin. Staff Coll., Henley, 1953; on loan to Export Credits Guarantee Dept, 1955-57; Manchester Business Sch., 1968; trans. to HM Diplomatic Service, 1968; HM Consul-Gen., Cairo, 1968-70; ME Centre for Arab Studies, Shemlan, Lebanon, 1969; Head of Claims Dept, FCO, 1970-72; Dep. High Comr, later Consul-Gen., Lahore, 1972-73; retired from HM Diplomatic Service, 1973. Mem., Law Soc. Liveryman, City of London Solicitors' Co. *Recreations:* yachting, golf, photography. *Address:* 13 Royston Place, Becton Lane, Barton-on-Sea, New Milton, Hants BH25 7AJ. *T:* New Milton 616970. *Clubs:* Royal Lymington Yacht; Barton-on-Sea Golf; Royal Eastbourne Golf; Punjab (Lahore).

MORRIS, William Alexander, CMG 1956; *b* 15 June 1905; *e s* of late William G. Morris, Cheam, Surrey; *m* 1938, Cecilia Mary, *d* of late James M. Anderson, of Istamboul, and Oxted, Surrey; four *d*. *Educ:* St Paul's Sch.; Univ. of London. BSc (Econ.) Hons 1929. Economic Asst to High Comr for Australia, 1935-39; entered Bd of Trade, 1940; transferred to Colonial Office, 1942; seconded to Foreign Office, 1963; HM Consul-Gen., Rotterdam, 1963-65; Dept of Economic Affairs and Cabinet Office, 1966-70, retired 1970. *Address:* 30 Bridewell Street, Devizes, Wilts. *T:* Devizes 5249.

MORRIS, His Honour Sir William (Gerard), Kt 1972; Honorary Recorder of Manchester, since 1972; *b* 20 June 1909; *s* of Joseph Thomas and Ellen Morris; *m* 1935, Mollie Broadbent; three *s*. *Educ:* Bolton Sch.; Gonville and Caius Coll., Cambridge. Called to Bar, 1931; practised on Northern Circuit till 1961; County Court Judge, 1961-66. Served in RAFVR, 1940-45, rank Sqdn Leader. Asst Recorder of Salford, 1956-61; Recorder of Liverpool, 1966-67; Recorder of Manchester, and Judge of the Crown Court at Manchester, 1967; a Circuit Judge, 1972-77. *Recreation:* golf. *Address:* Kingslea, Chorley New Road, Bolton, Lancs. *T:* Bolton 40900.

MORRIS, Prof. William Ian Clinch; Professor of Obstetrics and Gynaecology, University of Manchester, 1949-72, Professor Emeritus since 1972; *b* 10 May 1907; *s* of Dr J. M. Morris, Neath; *m* 1938, Mary Farquharson (*d* 1976); one *d*. *Educ:* Royal High Sch., Edinburgh; Edinburgh Univ. Obstetrician to Ayr County Council, 1937-46; Sen. Lectr in Obstetrics and Gynaecology, Univ. of Edinburgh, 1946-49. RAMC (TA) 1935; war service, 1939-43. *Publications:* (jointly) A Combined Textbook of Obstetrics and Gynaecology, 1950; contribs to Jl of Obstetrics and Gynaecology of British Commonwealth, Lancet, Edinburgh Med. Jl, etc. *Address:* 19 Linden Avenue, Newport-on-Tay, Fife. *T:* Newport-on-Tay 5412425.

MORRIS, Rev. William James, JP; Minister of Glasgow Cathedral since 1967; a Chaplain to the Queen in Scotland, since 1969; Chaplain to the Lord High Commissioner, since 1975; *b* Cardiff, 22 Aug. 1925; *o s* of William John Morris and Eliza Cecilia Cameron Johnson; *m* 1952, Jean Daveena Ogilvy Howie, MBE, *o c* of Rev. David Porter Howie and Veena Christie, Kilmarnock; one *s*. *Educ:* Cardiff High Sch.; Univ. of Wales; Edinburgh Univ. BA 1946, BD 1949, Wales; PhD Edinburgh, 1954; Hon. LLD Strathclyde 1974. Ordained, 1951. Asst, Canongate Kirk, Edinburgh, 1949-51; Minister, Presbyterian Church of Wales, Cadoxton and Barry Is, 1951-53; Buckhaven (Fife): St David's, 1953-57; Peterhead Old Parish, 1957-67; Chaplain to the Lord High Comr to the General Assembly of the Church of Scotland, 1975-76; Chaplain: Peterhead Prison, 1963-67; The High Sch. of Glasgow, 1974-76; Glasgow Acad., 1976-; Strathclyde Police, 1977-; Hon. Chaplain, The Royal Scottish Automobile Club; Moderator, Presbytery of Deer, 1965-66; Convener Adv. Bd, Church of Scotland, 1977-. President: Rotary Club of Peterhead, 1965-66; Peterhead and Dist Professional and Business Club, 1967; Chairman: Iona Cath. Trust, 1976 (Trustee, 1967); Council, Soc. of Friends of Glasgow Cath., 1967; Club Service Cttee, Dist 101, RIBI, 1964-66; Prison Chaplaincies Bd (Church of Scotland Home Bd); Vice-Pres., St Andrew's Soc., Glasgow; Member: Scottish Cttee, British Sailors' Soc.; Bd of Management, W of Scotland Convalescent Home; Council of Management, Quarriers' Homes; Bd of Management, Glasgow YMCA; Gen. Convocation, Strathclyde Univ.; Scottish Council on Crime. JP: Co. of Aberdeen, 1963-71; Co. of City of Glasgow, 1971. *Recreations:* fishing, gardening. *Address:* 60 Dalziel Drive, Glasgow G41 4PA. *T:* 041-427 2757. *Clubs:* New (Edinburgh); RNVR (Scotland) (Hon.); University of Strathclyde Staff (Hon.); Rotary of Dennistoun (Hon.).

MORRIS, Sir Willie, KCMG 1977 (CMG 1963); HM Ambassador, Cairo, since 1975; *b* 3 Dec. 1919; *m* 1959, Ghislaine Margaret Trammell; three *s*. *Educ:* Batley Grammar Sch., Yorks; St John's Coll., Oxford. Served in Royal Navy, 1940-45. Joined Foreign Service, 1947; Third Sec., Middle East Centre for Arab Studies, 1947; Second Sec., Cairo, 1948; First Sec., 1951; transferred to Foreign Office, 1952; attended course at Canadian Defence Coll., 1954; transferred to Washington, 1955; Counsellor, Amman (Chargé d'Affaires, 1960, 1961 and 1962), 1960-63; Head of Eastern Dept, FO, 1963-67; Fellow, Center for Internat. Affairs, Harvard Univ., 1966-67; Ambassador: Jedda, 1968-72; (non-resident) Yemen Arab Republic, 1971; Addis Ababa, 1972-75. *Address:* c/o Foreign and Commonwealth Office, SW1. *Club:* Travellers'.

MORRIS, Wyn, FRAM; Chief Conductor or Musical Director of Symphonica of London; *b* 14 Feb. 1929; *s* of Haydn Morris and Sarah Eluned Phillips; *m* 1962, Ruth Marie McDowell; one *s* one *d*. *Educ:* Llanelli Grammar Sch.; Royal Academy of Music; Mozarteum, Salzburg. August Mann's Prize, 1950; Apprentice Conductor, Yorkshire Symph. Orch., 1950-51; Musical Dir, 17th Trg Regt, RA Band, 1951-53; Founder and Conductor of Welsh Symph. Orch., 1954-57; Koussevitsky Memorial Prize, Boston Symph. Orch., 1957; (on invitation George Szell) Observer, Cleveland Symph. Orch., 1957-60; Conductor: Ohio Bell Chorus, Cleveland Orpheus Choir and Cleveland Chamber Orch., 1958-60; Choir of Royal National Eisteddfod of Wales, 1960-62; London debut, Royal Festival Hall, with Royal Philharmonic Orch., 1963; Conductor: Royal Choral Society, 1968-70; Huddersfield Choral Soc., 1969-74; Ceremony for Investiture of Prince Charles as Prince of Wales, 1969; Royal Choral Soc. tour of USA, 1969. FRAM 1964. Specialises in conducting of Mahler; has recorded Des Knaben Wunderhorn (with Dame Janet Baker and Sir Geraint Evans), Das klagende Lied, Symphonies 1, 2, 5, 8 and 10 in Deryck Cooke's final performing version. Mahler Memorial Medal (of Bruckner and Mahler Soc. of Amer.), 1968. *Recreations:* chess, Rugby football, climbing, cynghanedd and telling Welsh stories. *Address:* Symphonica Music Ltd, c/o Norton Warburg Investments, 103 Cannon Street, EC4.

MORRIS-JONES, Prof. Huw; Professor, University College of North Wales, Bangor; Head of Department of Social Theory and Institutions, University College, since 1966; *b* 1 May 1912; *s* of William Oliver Jones and Margaret Jones; *m* 1942, Gwladys Evans; one *s* one *d*. *Educ:* Alun Grammar Sch., Mold, Flintshire; University Coll. of North Wales, Bangor; Oriel Coll., Oxford. Educn Officer, S Wales Council of Social Service, 1937-39; Tutor and Lectr, Dept of Extra-Mural Studies, Univ. of Nottingham, 1939-42; Lectr, Sen. Lectr and Prof., Bangor, 1942-. Mem., IBA. *Publications:* Y Gelfyddyd Lenyddol yng Nghymru, 1957; contrib. Aesthetics in the Modern World (ed Osborne), 1968; Philosophy, Jl of Royal Inst. Philosophy, Monist, Efrydiau Athronyddol. *Address:* Ceredigion, Pentraeth Road, Menai Bridge, N Wales. *T:* Menai Bridge 712522. *Club:* United Oxford & Cambridge University.

MORRIS-JONES, Ifor Henry, QC 1969; **His Honour Judge Morris-Jones;** a Circuit Judge, since 1977; *b* 5 March 1922; *s* of late Rev. Prof. and Mrs D. Morris-Jones; *m* 1950, Anne Diana, *d* of S. E. Ferris, Blundellsands; one *s* two *d. Educ:* Taunton Sch.; Sidney Sussex Coll., Cambridge. Called to the Bar, Lincoln's Inn, 1947. Joined Northern Circuit, 1947; Assistant Recorder, Carlisle, 1962; Dep. Chm., Cumberland Sessions, 1969; a Recorder, 1972-76. Mem., Bar Council, 1972. *Recreation:* golf. *Address:* 5 Essex Court, Temple, EC4. *T:* 01-353 4365, 01-353 8273; Trewarren, Dowhills Road, Blundellsands, Liverpool L23 8SP. *T:* 051-924 4848. *Clubs:* Athenæum (Liverpool); County (Carlisle).

MORRIS-JONES, Prof. Wyndraeth Humphreys; Professor of Commonwealth Affairs and Director, Institute of Commonwealth Studies, University of London, since 1966; *b* 1 Aug. 1918; *s* of late William James Jones, Carmarthen, and Annie Mary Jones (*née* Morris); *m* 1953, Graziella Bianca Genre; one *s* two *d. Educ:* University Coll. Sch., Hampstead; London Univ. London Sch. of Economics, BSc(Econ.) First Class, 1938; Leverhulme Research Grant, 1939; Christ's Coll., Cambridge Research Schol., 1940; Indian Army, 1941-46 (Lt-Col, Public Relations Directorate, 1944); Constitutional Adviser to Viceroy of India, 1947; Lecturer in Political Science, London Sch. of Economics, 1946-55; Prof. of Political Theory and Instns, Univ. of Durham, 1955-65. Rockefeller Travel Grants, 1954, 1960 and 1967. Vis. Prof. of Commonwealth Hist. and Instns, Indian Sch. of Internat. Studies, New Delhi, 1960; Visiting Professor: Univ. of Chicago, 1962; Univ. of California, Berkeley, 1964-65. Editor, JI of Commonwealth and Comparative Politics (formerly Commonwealth Polit. Studies), 1964-. *Publications:* Parliament in India, 1957; Government and Politics of India, 1964, 3rd edn, 1971; articles in Polit. Studies, Asian Survey, Modern Asian Studies, etc. *Address:* Institute of Commonwealth Studies, 27 Russell Square, WC1. *T:* 01-580 5876.

MORRISH, John Edwin, (Jack); General Secretary, Customs and Excise Group, Society of Civil and Public Servants, since 1972; *b* 23 Sept. 1915; *s* of Henry Edwin Morrish and Ada Minnie (*née* Tapping); *m* 1st, 1938, Norah Lake; one *d*; 2nd, 1944, Violet Saunders; one *s* one *d. Educ:* Fleet Road, Hampstead, Elem. Sch.; University Coll. Sch.; Northampton Polytechnic, London; various work-faces. Post Office Techn. Officer, 1932-54; coalminer, 1944-45. Trade Union Official: Civil Service Union, 1954-72; Customs/Excise Group, Soc. of Civil Servants, 1972-. *Publications:* The Future of Forestry, 1971; contrib. Trade Union jls. *Recreations:* passive culture, thinking, pursuit of justice. *Address:* 2 Brookland Hill, NW11 6DX. *T:* 01-242 6171 (office). *Clubs:* The nearest 'local' and the world at large.

MORRISON, 2nd Baron *cr* 1945, of Tottenham; **Dennis Morrison;** Manufacturing Executive with The Metal Box Co. Ltd, 1957-72, retired; *b* 21 June 1914; *e* and *o* surv. *s* of 1st Baron Morrison, PC, and Grace, *d* of late Thomas Glossop; *S* father 1953; *m* 1940, Florence Alice Helena (marr. diss. 1958), *d* of late Augustus Hennes, Tottenham; *m* 1959, Joan (marr. diss. 1975), *d* of late W. R. Meech. *Educ:* Tottenham County Sch. Employed by The Metal Box Co. Ltd on research work, 1937-51; Quality Controller, 1952-57. Lord Lieutenant's Representative for Tottenham, 1955-. FSS 1953-57. Vice-Pres., Acton Chamber of Commerce, 1972 (Mem., Exec. Cttee, 1962). Hon. President: Robert Browning Settlement, 1967-; 5th Acton Scout Group, 1969. *Recreations:* gardening, football. *Heir:* none. *Address:* 7 Ullswater Avenue, Felixstowe, Suffolk. *T:* Felixstowe 77405.

MORRISON, Maj.-Gen. (retd) Albert Edward, CB 1956; OBE 1942; *b* 17 March 1901; *s* of late Major A. Morrison; *m* 1926, Esther May Lacey. *Educ:* Dover Coll.; RMA Woolwich. Royal Artillery, 1922-26; Royal Signals, 1926-57. Retired as Chief Signal Officer, AFHQ, March 1957. Col Commandant, Royal Corps of Signals, 1959-. Legion of Merit (US), 1946; Order of Rafidain (Iraq), 1940. *Recreation:* golf. *Address:* Wesley House, 68 Fairways, Ferndown, Wimborne, Dorset BH22 8BB.

MORRISON, Alexander, CBE 1976; Chief Executive, Thames Water Authority, since 1973; *b* 25 Jan. 1917; *e s* of late Alexander Morrison and Sarah (*née* Drummond); *m* 1941, Jennie, *o d* of late Henry and Ellen Mason; one *s* one *d. Educ:* Boroughmuir Sch., Edinburgh. Tax Officer, Inland Revenue, Edinburgh, 1934-36; Excise Off., Customs and Excise, Edinburgh, 1936; Royal Ordnance Factories: Jun. Exec. Off., Royal Arsenal, Woolwich, 1937-40; Higher Exec. Off.: Wigan, 1940-41; Poole, 1941-43; Sen. Exec. Off., Fazakerley, 1943-49; Chief Exec. Off., London, 1949-50; Overseas Food Corp., E Africa: Stores Controller, 1950-51; Chief Internal Auditor, 1951-52; Chief Accountant, 1952-54; Nat. Coal Board: Stores Controller, London, 1955-58; Purchasing and Stores Controller:

W Mids Div., 1958-59; N Eastern Div., 1959-61; Chief Officer of Supplies, LCC, 1961-64; GLC: Dir of Supplies, 1964-67; Exec. Dir, Highways and Transportation, 1967-69; Traffic Comr and Dir of Develt, 1969-70; Controller of Operational Services, 1970-73. Pres., Purchasing Officers' Assoc., 1966-67; Mem., Nat. Council for Quality and Reliability, 1963-71. FCMA (Mem. Council, 1971-, Vice-Pres., 1975, Pres., 1977); FInstPS; FCIT; FBIM. Swinbank Medal, Inst. of Purchasing and Supply, 1968. *Publication:* Storage and Control of Stock, 1962. *Recreations:* bowls, painting. *Address:* 70 Park Avenue, Bromley, Kent. *T:* 01-464 1460.

MORRISON, Alexander John Henderson; Barrister-at-Law; a Recorder of the Crown Court, since 1972; Regional Chairman of Industrial Tribunals, Sheffield; *b* 16 Nov. 1927; *yr s* of Dr Alexander Morrison and late Mrs A. Morrison. *Educ:* Derby Sch.; Emmanuel Coll., Cambridge. MA, LLB. Called to the Bar, Gray's Inn, 1951. Mem. of Midland Circuit; Dep. Chm., Derbyshire QS, 1964-71. *Recreations:* golf, music. *Address:* 17 Eastwood Drive, Littleover, Derby. *T:* Derby 45376. *Club:* The Club (Sheffield).

MORRISON, Hon. Charles Andrew; MP (C) Devizes since May 1964; *b* 25 June 1932; 2nd *s* of 1st Baron Margadale, *qv*; *m* 1954, Hon. Sara Long (*see* Hon. Sara Morrison); one *s* one *d. Educ:* Eton. Nat. Service in The Life Guards, 1950-52; Royal Wilts Yeo. (TA), 1952-66. County Councillor (Wilts), 1958-65; Chairman: Wilts Educn Cttee, 1963-64; South West Regional Sports Council, 1966-68; Young Volunteer Force Foundn, 1971-74; British Trust for Conservation Volunteers; Member: Council, Salmon and Trout Assoc.; Game Conservancy (Vice-Chm.). A Vice-Chm., 1922 Cttee, 1974- (Mem. Exec., 1972-74). *Recreations:* gardening, shooting. *Address:* 45 Westminster Gardens, Marsham Street, SW1. *T:* 01-834 8608; Fyfield Manor, Pewsey, Wilts. *T:* Pewsey 3438. *Clubs:* White's, Pratt's.

See also Hon. M. A. Morrison, Hon. P. H. Morrison.

MORRISON, Donald Alexander Campbell; Assistant Under-Secretary of State, Home Office, 1972-76; *b* 30 Nov. 1916; *s* of George Alexander Morrison, sometime MP for Scottish Univs, and Rachel Brown Morrison (*née* Campbell); *m* 1st, 1951, Elma Margaret Craig (*d* 1970); two *s* one *d*; 2nd, 1973, Jane Margaret Montgomery; one step *s. Educ:* Fettes Coll.; Christ Church, Oxford (BA). Home Office, 1939; Asst Sec., 1955. War Service, 1940-45: 79th (Scottish Horse) Medium Regt, RA, 1942-45. *Recreation:* music. *Address:* 97 Ridgway, SW19. *T:* 01-946 6176.

MORRISON, Air Vice-Marshal Ian Gordon, CB 1965; CBE 1957 (OBE 1946); RNZAF (retired); Development Director, A. S. Cornish Group; *b* 16 March 1914; *s* of W. G. Morrison; *m* 1938, Dorothy, *d* of W. H. Franks; one *s* two *d. Educ:* Christchurch Boys' High Sch., NZ. RAF 1935; RNZAF 1939; No 75 Sqdn, UK, 1939; Comd RNZAF, Omaka, 1941; Comd RNZAF, Gisborne, 1942; SASO, Islands Gp, 1943; Comd No 3 BR Sqdn Pacific, 1944-45; jssc, UK, 1950; Comd RNZAF, Ohakea, 1952; Air Mem. for Supply, 1954; idc, 1958; AOC, RNZAF, HQ London, 1959-60; Air Mem. for Personnel, 1961-62; Chief of the Air Staff, Royal New Zealand Air Force, 1962-66. Nat. Pres., Scout Assoc. of NZ, 1967-. *Recreations:* golf and angling. *Address:* 2 Taungata Road, York Bay, Eastbourne, New Zealand. *T:* Wellington 664293. *Clubs:* Wellington, Wellington Golf (both in NZ).

MORRISON, Prof. James, OBE 1963; BSc, NDA; Professor of Crop and Animal Husbandry, The Queen's University of Belfast, 1944-65, also Director, Agricultural Research Institute, Hillsborough, NI, 1934-65; retired; *b* 11 Aug. 1900; *m* 1934, Grace F. Stockdale, Clogher, Co. Tyrone; three *d. Educ:* Fordyce Academy, Banffshire, Scotland; Marischal Coll., Aberdeen Univ. Instructor in Agriculture, Co. Tyrone and Co. Down, 1925 and 1926; Sec. and Agric. Organiser, Co. Armagh, 1927-30; Inspector, Min. of Agric. for N Ireland, 1931-33; Lectr in Crop and Animal Husbandry, QUB, 1934. *Recreation:* gardening. *Address:* Loxwood, 35 Lisburn Road, Hillsborough, Co. Down BT26 6HW. *T:* Hillsborough (Co. Down) 682208.

MORRISON, John Lamb Murray, CBE 1957; DSc; FIMechE; Formerly Professor of Mechanical Engineering, University of Bristol, Emeritus 1971; *b* 22 May 1906; *s* of late Latto A. Morrison, Biggar, Lanarkshire; *m* 1936, Olga, *d* of late M. Nierenstein, DSc; two *s. Educ:* Biggar High Sch.; Univ. of Glasgow. Lecturer in Mechanical Engineering; Reader in Mechanical Engineering, Univ. of Bristol. Pres., IMechE, 1970-71. Hon. DSc Salford, 1972. *Publications:* An Introduction to the Mechanics of Machines, 1964; various papers on strength of materials and design of machines. *Recreations:* gardening, golf. *Address:* Dreva, Rayleigh Road, Bristol BS9 2AU. *T:* 681193.

MORRISON, John Sinclair; President, Wolfson College (formerly University College), Cambridge, since 1966; *b* 15 June 1913; *s* of Sinclair Morrison (and *g s* of William Morrison, NY and Stagbury, Chipstead, Surrey) and Maria Elsie, *d* of William Lamaison, Salmons, Kenley, Surrey; *m* 1942, Elizabeth Helen, *d* of S. W. Sulman, Bexhill, Sussex; three *s* two *d*. *Educ:* Charterhouse; Trinity Coll., Cambridge. Fellow Trinity College, Cambridge, 1937-45; Asst Lecturer Manchester University, 1937-39; Editor of Cambridge Review, 1939-40. Ordinary Seaman (Volunteer), 1940-41. In service of British Council, Cairo, Zagazig, Baghdad, 1941-42; British Council Rep. in Palestine and Transjordan, 1942-45; Pres. Jerusalem Rotary Club, 1945; Prof. of Greek and Head of Dept of Classics and Ancient History at the Durham Colls of Univ. of Durham, 1945-50; Fellow Tutor and Senior Tutor of Trinity Coll., Cambridge, 1950-60; Vice-Master and Sen. Tutor of Churchill Coll., Cambridge, 1960-65, now Hon. Fellow. Leverhulme Fellow, 1965. Mellon Prof., Reed Coll., Oregon, USA, 1976-77. Mem. of Council: Hellenic Soc., 1948, 1952; Classical Assoc., 1949; Member: Sierra Leone Educn Commission, 1954; Annan Cttee on Teaching of Russian, 1961; Hale Cttee on University Teaching Methods, 1961; Schools Council, 1965-67; Jt Working Party on 6th Form Curriculum and Examinations, 1968-72; Governing Bodies Assoc., 1965; Governor: Bradfield Coll., 1963; Wellington Coll., 1963; Culford Sch., 1969; Charterhouse Sch., 1970. Jt Editor, Classical Review, 1968-75. Trustee, National Maritime Museum, 1975-. *Publication:* (with R. T. Williams) Greek Oared Ships, 1968. *Address:* Wolfson College, Cambridge. *T:* Cambridge 64811. *Club:* Naval and Military.

MORRISON, Hon. Mary Anne, CVO 1970; Woman of the Bedchamber to the Queen since 1960; *b* 17 May 1937; *o d* of Baron Margadale, *qv. Educ:* Heathfield School. *Address:* Fonthill House, Tisbury, Wilts. *T:* Tisbury 202; Islay House, Bridgend, Isle of Islay, Argyllshire. *T:* Bowmore 223.
See also Hon . C . A . Morrison , Hon . P . H . Morrison .

MORRISON, Sir Nicholas (Godfrey), KCB 1974 (CB 1967); Permanent Under-Secretary of State, Scottish Office, since 1973; *b* 31 March 1918; *y s* of late John Wheatley Morrison and Kathleen King, Shotley Bridge, Co. Durham; *m* 1959, Rosemary, widow of E. H. U. de Groot; two step *d. Educ:* Cheltenham Coll.; Clare Coll., Cambridge. Entered War Office, 1939; Asst Private Sec. to Sec. of State for War, 1942-44. Served War of 1939-45, in HM Forces, 1944-46. Private Sec. to Minister of Defence, 1952-53; Asst Sec., War Office, 1955; Asst Under-Sec. of State (Dir of Establishments), War Office, 1960; Asst Under-Sec. of State, Min. of Defence, 1964; Under-Sec., HM Treasury, 1967-68; Civil Service Dept: Under-Sec., 1968-69; Dep. Sec., 1969-72; Dep. Under-Sec. of State, Scottish Office, 1972-73. FBIM, 1974; FIPM, 1976. *Recreations:* travel, opera, gardening, horseracing. *Address:* 5 Randolph Crescent, Edinburgh EH3 7TH. *T:* 031-225 6596; 10 Thomas More House, Barbican, EC2. *T:* 01-588 6851. *Clubs:* Athenæum; New (Edinburgh).

MORRISON, Hon. Peter Hugh; MP (C) City of Chester since 1974; *b* 2 June 1944; 3rd *s* of 1st Baron Margadale, *qv. Educ:* Eton; Keble Coll., Oxford (Hons Law). Personal Asst to Rt Hon. P. Walker, MP, 1966-67; Investment Manager, 1968-70; independent business, 1970-74. Sec., NW Cons. Members' Gp, 1974-76; Jt Sec., Cons. Smaller Businesses Cttee, 1974-76. An Opposition Whip, 1976-. *Address:* 81 Cambridge Street, SW1V 4PS. *T:* 01-828 8228; The Garden Cottage, Puddington, Chester; Fonthill House, Tisbury, Wilts; Islay House, Bridgend, Islay, Argyll. *Clubs:* White's, Pratt's, Turf.
See also Hon. C. A. Morrison, Hon. M. A. Morrison.

MORRISON, Maj.-Gen. Reginald Joseph Gordon, CB 1969; CBE 1959; MD, FRCP; Physician, The Royal Hospital, Chelsea, since 1969; Director of Medicine, Ministry of Defence (Army), and Consulting Physician to the Army, 1965-68; *b* 29 March 1909; *s* of R. Morrison; *m* 1947, Norma Jacqueline Nicholson; two *s. Educ:* Dulwich Coll.; St Joseph's Coll., SE19; St Bartholomew's Hosp. House Phys., St Bart's Hosp., 1934; Res. MO, Hove Gen. Hosp. Commnd RAMC, 1936; served as Med. Specialist, RAMC. Adviser in Medicine, EA Command, 1947-50; OC, Med. Div., QA Mil. Hosp., 1950-56; Cons. Phys., Far East, 1956-59; Prof. of Trop. Med., Royal Army Medical College, 1959-65. QHP 1963-68. *Publications:* (with W. H. Hargreaves) The Practice of Tropical Medicine, 1965; chapter in: Exploration Medicine, 1965; Medicine in the Tropics, 1974; various articles in Lancet, BMJ, Proc. RSM, etc. *Recreations:* rose growing, golf. *Address:* Gordon House, The Royal Hospital, Chelsea, SW3.

MORRISON, Hon. Sara Antoinette Sibell Frances, (Hon. Mrs Charles Morrison); General Electric Company since 1975; *b* 9 Aug. 1934; *d* of 2nd Viscount Long and of Laura, Duchess of Marlborough; *m* 1954, Hon. Charles Andrew Morrison, *qv* ; one *s* one *d . Educ:* in England and France. County Councillor, then Alderman, Wilts, 1961-71; Chairman: Wilts Assoc. of Youth Clubs, 1958-63; Wilts Community Council, 1965-70; Nat. Council Social Service, 1977- (Vice-Chm., 1970-77); Vice-Chairman: Nat. Assoc. Youth Clubs, 1969-71; Conservative Party Organisation, 1971-75; Member: Governing Bd, Volunteer Centre, 1972-; Annan Cttee of Enquiry into Broadcasting, 1974-77; Nat. Consumer Council, 1975-. *Recreations:* conserving physical energy, looking, listening, talking. *Address:* Fyfield Manor, Pewsey, Wilts. *T:* Pewsey 3438; 45 Westminster Gardens, SW1. *T:* 01-834 8608.

MORRISON, Prof. Stuart Love; Professorial Fellow in Community Medicine, Centre for Medical Research, University of Sussex, since 1976; *b* 25 Nov. 1922; *o s* of late William James Morrison, Ironfounder, Glasgow and late Isabella Murdoch, Edinburgh; *m* 1947, Dr Audrey Butler Lornie, *yr d* of late Lt-Col W. S. Lornie, MC, TD, MRCVS, Perth; one *d. Educ:* Glasgow Acad.; Dundee High Sch.; St Andrews and London Univs. MB, ChB (St Andrews) 1951; DPH (London) 1954; MRCP Edinburgh, 1966; FRCP Edinburgh, 1968. Served in RAF, 1939-46; Hosp. and gen. practice, 1951-53; Public Health appts, 1954-56; Mem., Scientific Staff, MRC Social Medicine Research Unit, 1956-62; Vis. Fellow, Epidemiology and Statistics, Univ. of N Carolina, 1961-62; Sen. Lectr in Social Med., Univ. of Edinburgh, 1962-64, Prof. of Community Medicine, Univ. of Edinburgh, 1964-75. FSS; Mem., WHO Expert Adv. Panel on Organisation of Medical Care. *Publications:* contribs to med. jls on epidemiology, organisation of medical care and medical administration. *Recreations:* hill walking, shooting. *Address:* March House, Little Dene, Glynde, Lewes, Sussex BN8 6AL. *T:* Glynde 369.

MORRISON, Rear-Adm. Thomas Kenneth, CB 1967; CBE 1962 (OBE 1941); DSC; Royal Australian Navy; *b* 31 Oct. 1911; *s* of late L. N. Morrison, Sydney, Australia; *m* 1938, Dorothy C., *d* of late W. M. Hole; one *s* three *d. Educ:* Jervis Bay Sch.; Royal Australian Naval College. Served War, 1939-45: Indian Ocean, Red Sea, Pacific (despatches, OBE, DSC). Qualified (Short Staff Course) RNC, Greenwich, 1945. Dir, Training and Staff Requirements, Navy Office, Melbourne, 1946-47; Comdr, Royal Australian Naval Coll., 1948-49; Capt., HMAS Tobruk, on commissioning, 1950-51; Dir of Manning, Navy Office, 1951-52; Dep. Chm., Naval Personnel, 1952-53; Commanding: 1st Frigate Squadron, Royal Australian Navy, 1954-55; HMAS Melbourne, 1959; Royal Australian Naval Air Stn, Nowra, NSW, 1961-62; Dep. Chief of the Naval Staff, Royal Australian Navy, 1962-64; Flag Officer Commanding the Australian Fleet, 1965; Flag Officer-in-Charge, East Australia Area, 1966-68. Australian Comr-Gen. for Osaka Exposition, 1970. *Recreation:* golf. *Address:* 38A The Crescent, Vaucluse, NSW 2030, Australia. *Club:* Royal Sydney Golf.

MORRISON-BELL, Sir William (Hollin Dayrell), 4th Bt *cr* 1905; *b* 21 June 1956; *s* of Sir Charles Reginald Francis Morrison-Bell, 3rd Bt and of Prudence Caroline, *d* of late Lt-Col W. D. Davies, 60th Rifles (she *m* 2nd, Peter Gillbanks); *S* father, 1967. *Educ:* Eton; St Edmund Hall, Oxford. *Heir:* *b* Julian Francis Tarret Morrison-Bell, *b* 14 Feb. 1959. *Address:* Highgreen, Tarset, Hexham, Northumberland. *T:* Greenhaugh 223; South Scarletts, Kiln Green, Twyford, Berks. *T:* Wargrave 3521.

MORRISON-LOW, Sir James; *see* Low.

MORRISON-SCOTT, Sir Terence Charles Stuart, Kt 1965; DSC 1944; FLS; Director, British Museum (Natural History), 1960-68 (Director, Science Museum, 1956-60); National Trust: Member, Properties Committee, since 1968; Chairman, Nature Conservation Panel, since 1970; Chairman, Architectural Panel, since 1973; *b* Paris, 24 Oct. 1908; *o s* of late R. C. S. Morrison-Scott, DSO, and Douairière Jhr. R. Quarles van Ufford; *m* 1935, Rita, 4th *d* of late E. J. Layton. *Educ:* Eton; Christ Church (MA of the House, 1947), Oxford; Royal College of Science (1st Class Hons Zoology, BSc, ARCS 1935, MSc 1939). Asst Master, Eton, 1935; Scientific Staff, Brit. Museum (Natural Hist.) in charge of Mammal Room, 1936-39, 1945-55 and part of 1956. DSc London, 1952. Served War of 1939-45, with Royal Navy (DSC). Lt-Comdr RNVR. Treas., Zoological Soc. of London, 1950-76; Treas., XVth Internat. Congress of Zoology, 1958. Trustee, Imp. War Museum, 1956-60; Dir, Arundel Castle Trustees Ltd, 1976-. Governor, Imperial Coll. of Science and Technology, 1956-76 (Fellow, 1963); Mem., Standing Commn on Museums and Galleries, 1973-76. Goodwood Flying Sch. (solo), 1975. *Publications:* Palaearctic and Indian Mammals (with J. R. E.), 1951; Southern African

Mammals (with J. R. E. and R. W. H.), 1953; papers in scientific jls on taxonomy of mammals. *Address:* Upperfold House, Fernhurst, Haslemere, Surrey GU27 3JH. *Clubs:* Athenæum, Brooks's; Vincent's (Oxford); Leander.

MORRITT, (Robert) Andrew, QC 1977; *b* 5 Feb. 1938; *s* of Robert Augustus Morritt and Margaret Mary Morritt (*née* Tyldesley Jones); *m* 1962, Sarah Simonetta Merton, *d* of John Ralph Merton, *qv* ; two *s* . *Educ:* Eton Coll.; Magdalene Coll., Cambridge (BA 1961). 2nd Lieut Scots Guards, 1956-58. Called to the Bar, Lincoln's Inn, 1962; Mem., Gen. Council of the Bar, 1969-73. Junior Counsel: to Sec. of State for Trade in Chancery Matters, 1970-77; to Attorney-Gen. in Charity Matters, 1972-77. Mem., Adv. Cttee on Legal Educn, 1972-76. *Recreations:* fishing, shooting. *Address:* 7 Stone Buildings, Lincoln's Inn, WC2A 3SZ. *T:* 01-405 3886. *Club:* Garrick.

MORROCCO, Alberto, RSA 1963 (ARSA 1952); Head of School of Painting, Duncan of Jordanstone College of Art, Dundee, since 1950; *b* 14 Dec. 1917; *m* 1941, Vera Cockburn Mercer; two *s* one *d.* *Educ:* Gray's Sch. of Art, Aberdeen. Carnegie Schol., 1937; Brough Schol., 1938. In the Army, 1940-46. Guthrie Award, 1943; San Vito Prize, Rome, 1959. Pictures in: Scottish Modern Arts Coll.; Contemporary Arts Soc.; Scottish Arts Council Coll.; Hull, Aberdeen, Glasgow, Perth and Dundee Art Galleries. *Recreations:* travel, swimming, eating. *Address:* Binrock, 456 Perth Road, Dundee. *T:* Dundee 69319. *Club:* Scottish Arts.

MORROGH, Henton, CBE 1969; FRS 1964; Director of the British Cast Iron Research Association since 1959; *b* 29 Sept. 1917; *s* of Clifford and Amy Morrogh; *m* 1949, Olive Joyce Ramsay; one *d.* Distinguished for his work on the microstructure and solidification of cast iron and for the development of ductile cast iron. Visiting Prof., Dept of Industrial Engineering and Management Univ. of Technology, Loughborough, 1967-72. DSc (*hc*), Univ. of Birmingham, 1965; Iron and Steel Inst. Andrew Carnegie Gold Medal, 1946; E. J. Fox Medal Inst. of Brit. Foundrymen, 1951; McFadden Gold Medal, Amer. Foundrymen's Soc., 1952; Robert Hadfield Medal, Iron & Steel Inst., 1956; Gold Medal, Amer. Gray Iron Founders' Soc., 1961; Bessemer Gold Medal, Metals Soc., 1977. President: Instn of Metallurgists, 1967-68; Inst. of British Foundrymen, 1972-73. *Address:* British Cast Iron Research Association, Alvechurch, Birmingham. *T:* Redditch 66414; Cedarwood, Penn Lane, Tanworth-in-Arden, Warwicks. *T:* Tanworth-in-Arden 2414.

MORROW, Sir (Arthur) William, Kt 1959; DSO 1942; ED 1949; FRCP, FRACP; Hon. Consultant Physician, Royal Prince Alfred Hospital, Sydney, since 1963 (Hon. Physician, 1951-63); *b* 12 July 1903; *s* of Arthur John Morrow and Helonar (*née* Harkin); *m* 1st, 1937, Jean Buchanan Brown (*d* 1970); three *d* ; 2nd, 1974, Margaret Mary, *d* of late Dr E Wilfred Fairfax and Mary Fairfax (*née* Lamb). *Educ:* Newington Coll., Sydney; Sydney Univ. MB, BS Sydney 1927; FRCP 1949; FRACP 1938; Hon. FACP 1968. First Cl. Hons in Medicine at graduation, 1927; RMO, Royal Prince Alfred Hospital, Sydney, 1927; Dep. Supt 1932; Hon. Asst Phys., 1934. Hon. Cons. Phys., Canterbury District Memorial Hosp., Sydney, 1938; Marrickville Dist Hosp., 1939; Western Suburb Hosp., 1937; Lectr in Therapeutics, Univ. of Sydney, 1938-63. Served in AIF, War of 1939-45 (finishing rank Col); final posting, Cons. Phys. Advanced HQ (despatches, DSO). Now RAAMC Reserve. Pres. NSW Branch, BMA, 1958-59. Council, RACP, 1957- (Censor, 1953-, Censor-in-Chief, 1962-66, Pres. 1966-68). *Publications:* numerous medical scientific articles, mainly applied to gastroenterology. *Recreation:* golf. *Address:* 7 Rupertswood Avenue, Bellevue Hill, NSW 2023, Australia; (professional) 187 Macquarie Street, Sydney, NSW 2000. *T:* 221 1539. *Clubs:* Australian, Royal Sydney Golf (Sydney); Australian Jockey.

MORROW, Sir Ian (Thomas), Kt 1973; CA; FCMA, JDipMA, FBIM; CompIEE (Hon.); Deputy Chairman and Managing Director, UKO International Ltd (formerly UK Optical & Industrial Holdings Ltd), and Chairman of subsidiary companies; Chairman: The Laird Group Ltd; Mills and Allen International Ltd; J. H. Vavasseur Group Ltd; E. B. Meyer Brokers Ltd; Harlow & Jones Brokers Ltd; Harlow & Jones (Foreign Exchange) Ltd; Deputy Chairman, Siebe Gorman Holdings Ltd; Director: Hambros Ltd; Hambros Industrial Management Ltd; Vision Screening Ltd; James North (Africa) Pty Ltd; James North (Japan) Co. Ltd; International Harvester Co. of Great Britain Ltd; Lindustries Ltd; Martin Black Ltd; *b* 8 June 1912; *er s* of late Thomas George Morrow and Jamesina Hunter, Pilmour Links, St Andrews; *m* 1940, Elizabeth Mary Thackray (marr. diss. 1967); one *s* one *d* ; *m* 1967, Sylvia Jane Taylor; one *d* . *Educ:* Dollar Academy, Dollar. Chartered

Accountant 1935; FCMA 1945; Asst Accountant, Brocklehurst-Whiston Amalgamated Ltd, 1937-40; Partner, Robson, Morrow & Co., 1942-51; Financial Dir, 1951-52, Dep. Man. Dir, 1952-56, Joint Man. Dir, 1956-57, Man. Dir, 1957-58, The Brush Electrical Engineering Co. Ltd (now The Brush Group Ltd); Jt Man. Dir, H. Clarkson & Co. Ltd, 1961-72; Chairman: Associated Fire Alarms Ltd, 1965-70; Rowe Bros & Co. (Holdings) Ltd, 1960-70; Kenwood Manufacturing Co. Ltd, 1961-68; Crane Fruehauf Trailers Ltd, 1969-71; Deputy Chairman, Rolls Royce Ltd, 1970-71, Rolls Royce (1971) Ltd, 1971-73 (Man. Dir, 1971-72). Led Anglo-American Council on Productivity Team on Management Accounting to US, 1950. Council Member: British Electrical & Allied Manufacturers' Assoc., 1957-58; British Internal Combustion Engine Manufacturers' Assoc., 1957-58; Member: Grand Council, FBI, 1953-58; Council, Production Engineering Research Assoc., 1955-58; Council, Inst. of Cost and Works Accountants (now Inst. of Cost and Management Accountants), 1952-70 (Pres. 1956-67, Gold Medallist 1961); Performing Right Tribunal, 1968-74; Council, Inst. of Chartered Accountants of Scotland, 1968-72 (Vice-Pres. 1970-72); Inflation Accounting Steering Gp, 1976-; Lay Member, Press Council, 1974-; Freeman, City of London; Liveryman, Worshipful Co. of Spectaclemakers. *Publications:* papers and addresses on professional and management subjects. *Recreations:* reading, music, golf, ski-ing. *Address:* 23 Chester Terrace, Regent's Park, NW1 4ND. *T:* 01-486 4250. *Clubs:* National Liberal, Royal Automobile; Royal and Ancient (St Andrews).

MORROW, Martin S.; Stipendiary Magistrate, Glasgow, since 1972; *b* 16 Nov. 1923; *s* of late Thomas Morrow and Mary Lavery; *m* 1952, Nancy May, BMus, LRAM; one *s* two *d* . *Educ:* St Aloysius' Coll., Glasgow; Glasgow Univ. Solicitor. Private practice, 1951-56; Asst Procurator Fiscal, 1956-72. *Recreations:* music, golf, reading. *Address:* 14 Queen's Gate, Glasgow G12 9DN. *T:* 041-334 1324. *Club:* St Mungo (Glasgow).

MORROW, Sir William; *see* Morrow, Sir A. W.

MORSE, Sir Christopher Jeremy, KCMG 1975; Chairman of Lloyds Bank, since 1977 (Deputy Chairman, 1975-77); Director: Legal & General Assurance Society Ltd; Alexanders Discount Co. Ltd; *b* 10 Dec. 1928; *s* of late Francis John Morse, and of Kinbarra (*née* Armfield-Marrow); *m* 1955, Belinda Marianne, *d* of Lt-Col R. B. Y. Mills; three *s* one *d. Educ:* Winchester; New Coll., Oxford. 1st Class Lit. Hum. 1953. 2nd Lt KRRC, 1948-49. Trained in banking at Glyn, Mills & Co., and made a director in 1964; Executive Dir, Bank of England, 1965-72; Alternate Governor for UK of IMF, 1966-72; Chm. of Deputies of Cttee of Twenty, IMF, 1972-74. Mem., NEDC, 1977-. Fellow: All Souls Coll., Oxford, 1953-68; Winchester Coll., 1966-. FIDE Internat. Judge for chess compositions, 1975-. *Recreations:* family, problems and puzzles, golf. *Address:* 102a Drayton Gardens, SW10. *T:* 01-370 2265. *Club:* United Oxford & Cambridge University.

MORSE, David A.; partner, law firm of Surrey, Karasik & Morse (Washington DC, New York City, Paris, London); *b* New York City, 31 May 1907; *m* 1937, Mildred H. Hockstader. *Educ:* Somerville Public Schs, NJ; Rutgers Coll., NJ; Harvard Law Sch. LittB (Rutgers), 1929, LLB (Harvard), 1932. Admitted to New Jersey Bar, 1932, NY Bar, Washington DC Bar; Chief Counsel Petroleum Labor Policy Bd, Dept of Interior, 1934-35. US Dept of Interior; Special Asst to US Attorney-Gen., 1934-35; Regional Attorney, National Labor Relations Bd (Second Region), 1935-38. Impartial Chm., Milk Industry Metropolitan Area of New York, 1940-42, when entered Army. Lectr on Labor Relations, Labor Law, Administrative Law, various colleges and law schools, 1938-47. Gustav Pollak Lectr on Research in Govt, Harvard Univ., 1955-56. Formerly: Perm. US Govt Mem. on Governing Body of Internat. Labor Office; US Govt Deleg. to Internat. Labor Confs; Statutory Mem. Bd of Foreign Service; Dep. Chm. Interdepartmental Cttee on Internat. Social Policy; Mem., Bd of Educn, Somerville, NJ; Mem., Cttee for Conservation of Manpower in War Industry, State of NJ; served in N Africa, Sicily and Italy, 1943-44 (Chief of Labor Div., Allied Mil. Govt); arrived in England, 1944. Major, 1944; Chief of Labor Section, US Group Control Council for Germany and prepared Labor Policy and Program for Germany; also advised and assisted SHAEF in preparation of Labor Policy and Program for France, Belgium, Holland, etc; Lt-Col and Dir Labor for Mil. Govt Group, 1945; returned to US; Gen. Counsel, Nat. Labor Relations Bd, 1945-46; Asst Sec. of Labor, 1946-47; Under-Sec. of Labor, 1947-48; Actg Sec. of Labor, June-Aug. 1948; Dir-Gen., Internat. Labor Office, Geneva, 1948-70; Adviser to Administrator, UN Develt Programme. Member: Amer. Bar Assoc.; Council on Foreign Relations; World Rehabilitation Fund; NY Foundation; Nat.

Council of UN Assoc. of USA; Amer. Arbitration Assoc.; US Cttee of Dag Hammarskjöld Foundn; American Legion; Trustee, Rutgers Univ.; Impartial Chm., Coat and Suit Ind. of Metropolitan Area of NY, 1970. Hon. LLD: Rutgers, 1957; Geneva, 1962; Strasbourg, 1968; Hon. DSc, Laval, Quebec, 1969; Hon. DHL Brandeis Univ., 1971. Sidney Hillman Foundn Award, 1969; Rutgers Univ. Alumni Award, 1970; Internat. League for Rights of Man Award, 1970; Three Bronze Battle Stars; Legion of Merit; Officier de l'Etoile Equatoriale (Gabon); Ordre de la valeur (Cameroon); Order of Merit of Labour (Brazil); Grand Officer (Simon Bolivar) (Columbia), 1970; Grand Officer, French Legion of Honour, 1971; Orden El Sol, Peru, 1972; Grand Officer of Italy. *Address:* 14 East 75th Street, New York, NY 10021, USA. *Clubs:* Metropolitan (Washington DC); Century Association (New York).

MORSE, Sir Jeremy; *see* Morse, Sir C. J.

MORSE-BOYCOTT, Rev. Desmond; Co-founder with his wife, in 1932, and Hon. Principal and Director of the Music, of St Mary-of-the-Angels Song School, now Administrator of the Trust's Morse-Boycott Bursaries relative to Choir Schools; Assistant Curate of St Mary the Virgin, Somers Town, 1919-35; *b* 10 Dec. 1892; *y s* of late Frederic Augustus Morse-Boycott, Sennowe, Norfolk, and Octavia Mary, 5th *d* of Matthew John Anketell, Anketell Grove, JP and DL Co. Monaghan; *m* Marguerite Harriet Sandford (*d* 1959), Chailey, Sussex; one *d. Educ:* privately; Lichfield Theological Coll. At the age of 16 entered the service of the West Sussex County Education Cttee; during this period studied commercial subjects and became an expert shorthand teacher; became asst curate at Mayfield in Sussex; Bognor; then Somers Town; entered journalism, teaching himself the craft; became a contributor to all the leading newspapers; conducted a Test Centre for 'young aspirants to the ministry. Has supplied boys' choirs for various films as well as for Church and secular occasions of importance. LTh (Durham); FRSA. Hon. Fellow, Tonic Sol-Fa Coll. of Music, 1969. *Publications:* Alleluia; Three Holy Fruits; Seven Words of Love; Simplicitas and His Brethren, 1920; The Pilgrim's Way; Holy Communion; Ten Years in a London Slum, 1929; God and Everyman; Mystic Glow; Wayside Words; We do see Life; Saith the Preacher, 1931; Fields of Yesterday, 1932; Lead, Kindly Light; Credo, etc; The Secret Story of the Oxford Movement, 1933; Is it a Sin?, 1935; Great Crimes of the Bible, 1936; A Tramping Parson's Message, 1936; How can I be Happy?, 1937; Fear Not, 1939; They Shine Like Stars, 1948; A Golden Legend of the Slums, 1951; A Tapestry of Toil (autobiog.), 1970; A Pilgrimage of Song, 1972. Edits The Angel. *Recreations:* painting, music, philately. *Address:* Walnut Tree Cottage, 79 Ashacre Lane, Offington, Worthing, West Sussex. *T:* Worthing 60927.

MORSON, Basil Clifford, VRD 1963; MA, DM Oxon; FRCS; FRCPath; MRCP; Consultant in Pathology to the Royal Navy, since 1975; Consultant Pathologist to St Mark's Hospital since 1956; Director of the Research Department, since 1958; Director, WHO International Reference Centre for intestinal Tumours, since 1969; *b* 13 Nov. 1921; *s* of late A. Clifford Morson, OBE, FRCS; *m* 1950, Pamela Elizabeth Gilbert; one *s* two *d. Educ:* Beaumont Coll.; Wadham Coll., Oxford; Middlesex Hosp. Medical Sch. House Surg., Middlesex Hosp., 1949; House Surg., Central Middlesex Hosp., 1950; Asst Pathologist, Bland-Sutton Institute of Pathology, Middlesex Hosp., 1950. Sub-Lt RNVR, 1943-46; Surgeon-Comdr RNR (London Div.). Visiting Prof. of Pathology, Univ. of Chicago, 1959; Hon. Lectr in Pathology, 1965, Hon. Sen. Lectr, 1970, Royal Postgraduate Medical Sch. of London. Lettsomian Lectures, Med. Soc., 1970; Sir Arthur Hurst Meml Lectr, British Soc. Gastroenterology, 1971; Wade Prof. of Pathology, RCSE, 1971. (Scientific) FZS 1959; FRCS 1972; MRCP 1973. *Publications:* chap. Pathology of Alimentary tract in Systemic Pathology, ed G. Payling Wright and W. St C. Symmers, 1966; (ed) Diseases of the Colon, Rectum and Anus, 1969; Textbook of Gastrointestinal Pathology, 1972; numerous articles in medical journals. *Recreations:* tennis, gardening, ornithology, travel. *Address:* 52 Gordon Place, W8. *T:* 01-937 7101. *Club:* Hurlingham.

MORT, Rt. Rev. John Ernest Llewelyn, CBE 1965; Canon Residentiary and Treasurer of Leicester Cathedral, since 1970; Assistant Bishop, Diocese of Leicester, since 1972; *b* 13 April 1915; *s* of late Trevor Ll. Mort, JP, and Ethel Mary Mort; *m* 1953, Barbara Gifford. *Educ:* Malvern Coll.; St Catharine's Coll., Cambridge (BA Hist. Tripos 1938; MA 1942); Westcott House, Cambridge. Asst Curate, Dudley, 1940-44; Worcester Diocesan Youth Organiser, 1944-48; Private Chaplain to Bishop of Worcester, 1943-52; Vicar of St John in Bedwardine, Worcester, 1948-52; Bishop of N Nigeria, 1952-69. Hon. LLD

Ahmadu Bello Univ., 1970. *Recreations:* riding, tennis, Rugby football. *Address:* 7 St Martin's East, Leicester LE1 5FX. *T:* Leicester 52580.

MORTIMER, Chapman; *see* Chapman-Mortimer, W. C.

MORTIMER, Clifford Hiley, FRS 1958; DSc, DrPhil; Distinguished Professor in Zoology, University of Wisconsin-Milwaukee, since 1966; *b* Whitchurch, Som, 27 Feb. 1911; *er s* of Walter Herbert and Bessie Russell; *m* 1936, Ingeborg Margarete Closs, Stuttgart, Germany; two *d. Educ:* Sibford and Sidcot Schs; Univ. of Manchester. BSc (Manchester) 1932, DSc (Manchester) 1946; Dr Phil (Berlin) 1935. Served on scientific staff of Freshwater Biological Assoc., 1935-41 and 1946-56. Seconded to Admiralty scientific service, 1941-46. Sec. and Dir, Scottish Marine Biological Assoc., 1956-66; Dir, Center for Great Lakes Studies, Univ. of Wisconsin-Milwaukee, 1966-76. *Publications:* scientific papers on lakes and the physical and chemical conditions which control life in them. *Recreations:* music, travel. *Address:* 2501 E Menlo Boulevard, Shorewood, Wisconsin 53211, USA.

MORTIMER, James Edward; Chairman, Advisory Conciliation and Arbitration Service (formerly Conciliation and Arbitration Service), since 1974; *b* 12 Jan. 1921; *m*; two *s* one *d. Educ:* Junior Techn. Sch., Portsmouth; Ruskin Coll., Oxford; London Sch. of Economics. Worked in Shipbuilding and Engrg Industries as Ship Fitter Apprentice, Machinist and Planning Engr; TUC Schol., Oxford, 1945-46; TUC Economic Dept, 1946-48; full-time Trade Union Official, Draughtsmen's and Allied Technicians' Assoc., 1948-68. Dir, London Co-operative Soc., 1968-71. Mem., NBPI, 1968-71; LTE, 1971-74. Member: Wilberforce Ct of Inquiry into the power dispute, 1970; Armed Forces Pay Review Body, 1971-74; EDC for Chemical Industry, 1973-74; Chm. EDC for Mechanical and Electrical Engineering Construction, 1974-. Vis. Fellow, Admin. Staff Coll., Henley, 1976-. *Publications:* A History of Association of Engineering and Shipbuilding Draughtsmen, 1960; (with Clive Jenkins) British Trade Unions Today, 1965; (with Clive Jenkins) The Kind of Laws the Unions Ought to Want, 1968; Industrial Relations, 1968; Trade Unions and Technological Change, 1971; History of the Boilermakers' Society, vol. 1, 1973. *Recreation:* camping. *Address:* 9 Blenheim Court, Stanmore Road, Richmond, Surrey.

MORTIMER, John Barry, QC 1971; a Recorder of the Crown Court, since 1972; Chancellor of Diocese of Ripon, since 1971; *b* 7 Aug. 1931; *s* of John William Mortimer and Maud (*née* Snarr) Mortimer; *m* 1958, Judith Mary (*née* Page); two *s* two *d. Educ:* St Peters' School, York, (Headmasters' Exhibitioner 1945); Emmanuel College, Cambridge; BA 1955, MA 1959. Commissioned into 4 RTR, 1951; served in Egypt, 1951-52; 45/51 RTR (TA), 1952-57. Called to the Bar, Middle Temple, 1956; Harmsworth Law Scholar 1957; Prosecuting Counsel on NE Circuit: to Post Office, 1965-69; to Inland Revenue, 1969-71. Member of Bar Council, 1970-. *Recreations:* reading, shooting, cricket, golf. *Address:* 5 King's Bench Walk, Temple, EC4. *T:* 01-353 2882; 2 Park Square, Leeds. *T:* 33277; The Grange, Staveley, near Knaresborough. *T:* Copgrove 265.

MORTIMER, John (Clifford), QC 1966; barrister; playwright and author; *b* 21 April 1923; *s* of Clifford Mortimer and Kathleen May (*née* Smith); *m* 1st, 1949, Penelope Ruth Fletcher; one *s* one *d* ; 2nd, Penelope (*née* Gollop); one *d. Educ:* Harrow; Brasenose Coll., Oxford. Called to the Bar, 1948; Master of the Bench, Inner Temple, 1975. Mem. Nat. Theatre Bd, 1968-. Won the Italia Prize with short play, The Dock Brief, 1958; another short play What Shall We Tell Caroline, 1958. Full-length plays: The Wrong Side of the Park, 1960; Two Stars for Comfort, 1962; (trans.) A Flea in Her Ear, 1966; The Judge, 1967; (trans.) Cat Among the Pigeons, 1969; Come as You Are, 1970; A Voyage Round My Father, 1970; (trans.) The Captain of Köpenick, 1971; I, Claudius (adapted from Robert Graves), 1972; Collaborators, 1973; Mr Luby's Fear of Heaven (radio), 1976; Heaven and Hell, 1976; The Bells of Hell, 1977. Film Script: John and Mary, 1970. *Publications:* novels: Charade, 1947; Rumming Park, 1948; Answer Yes or No, 1950; Like Men Betrayed, 1953; Three Winters, 1956; Will Shakespeare: an entertainment, 1977; *travel:* (in collab. with P. R. Mortimer) With Love and Lizards, 1957; *plays:* The Dock Brief and Other Plays, 1959; The Wrong Side of the Park, 1960; Lunch Hour and Other Plays, 1960; Two Stars for Comfort, 1962; (trans.) A Flea in Her Ear, 1965; A Voyage Round My Father, 1970; (trans.) The Captain of Köpenick, 1971; Five Plays, 1971; Collaborators, 1973; writes TV plays; contribs to periodicals. *Recreations:* working, cooking, going to the theatre. *Address:* Turville Heath Cottage, Henley on Thames, Oxon. *Club:* Garrick.

MORTIMER, Penelope (Ruth); writer; *b* 19 Sept. 1918; *d* of Rev. A. F. G. and Amy Caroline Fletcher; *m* 1st, 1937, Charles Dimont (marr. diss. 1949); four *d*; 2nd, 1949, John Clifford Mortimer, QC (marr. diss. 1972); one *s* one *d. Educ:* Croydon High Sch.; New Sch., Streatham; Blencathra, Rhyl; Garden Sch., Lane End; St Elphin's Sch. for Daughters of Clergy; Central Educnl Bureau for Women; University Coll., London. *Publications:* Johanna (as Penelope Dimont), 1947; A Villa in Summer, 1954; The Bright Prison, 1956; (with John Mortimer) With Love and Lizards, 1957; Daddy's Gone A-Hunting, 1958; Saturday Lunch with the Brownings, 1960; The Pumpkin Eater, 1962; My Friend Says It's Bulletproof, 1967; The Home, 1971; Long Distance, 1974. *Address:* c/o Deborah Rogers Ltd, 5-11 Mortimer Street, W1.

MORTIMER, Raymond, CBE 1955; Officier de la Légion d'Honneur; *b* 25 April 1895; *s* of Charles Edward Mortimer and Marion Josephine Cantrell. *Educ:* Malvern; Balliol Coll., Oxford. *Publications:* Channel Packet, 1942; Manet's Bar aux Folies-Bergère, 1944; Duncan Grant, 1944. *Recreation:* travel. *Address:* 5 Canonbury Place, N1. *T:* 01-226 3548; Long Crichel House, Wimborne, Dorset. *T:* Tarrant Hinton 250. *Clubs:* Travellers', Beefsteak.

MORTIMER, Air Vice-Marshal Roger, CBE 1972; Officer Commanding RAF Institute of Pathology and Tropical Medicine and Consultant Adviser in Pathology and Tropical Medicine, 1969-76; Dean of Air Force Medicine, 1975-76; *b* 2 Nov. 1914; *s* of Henry Roger Mortimer, tea planter, Dooars, India and Lily Rose (*née* Collier); *m* 1942, Agnes Emily Balfour; two *d. Educ:* Uppingham; St Mary's Hosp. Med. School. MB, BS London, FRCPath, DCP, DTM&H. Joined RAF, 1942; Sqdn Med. Officer to Nos 23 and 85 Sqdns, 1942-44; Service Narrator and Editor to Official RAF Medical History of the War, 1944-47; specialised in Pathology and Tropical Medicine from 1947. Founder Mem. RCPath; Assoc. Editor and Council Mem., British Div. of Internat. Academy of Pathology, 1967-73; Editor, International Pathology, 1970-73; Mem. Council, Royal Soc. Trop. Med. and Hygiene, 1970-73. QHS 1973-76. *Publications:* papers on approved laboratory methods, practical disinfection, blood transfusion and infusion. *Recreations:* cars, anything mechanical, do-it-yourself, laboratory design. *Address:* The Old Forge, Askett, Aylesbury, Bucks. *T:* Princes Risborough 5566.

MORTIMER, William Charles C.; *see* Chapman-Mortimer.

MORTON, 22nd Earl of, *cr* 1458 (*de facto* 21st Earl, 22nd but for the Attainder); **John Charles Sholto Douglas;** Lord Aberdour, 1458; *b* 19 March 1927; *s* of Hon. Charles William Sholto Douglas (*d* 1960) (2nd *s* of 19th Earl) and of Florence, *er d* of late Major Henry Thomas Timson; *S* cousin, 1976; *m* 1949, Sheila Mary, *d* of late Rev. Canon John Stanley Gibbs, MC, Didmarton House, Badminton, Glos; two *s* one *d. Recreation:* polo. *Heir:* *s* Lord Aberdour, *qv. Address:* Dalmahoy, Kirknewton, Midlothian. *Clubs:* Edinburgh Polo, Dalmahoy Country.

MORTON, Alastair; *see* Morton, S. A.

MORTON, Rev. Andrew Queen; Minister of Culross Abbey since 1959; *b* 4 June 1919; *s* of Alexander Morton and Janet Queen; *m* 1948, Jean, *e d* of George Singleton and late Jean Wands; one *s* two *d. Educ:* Glasgow Univ. MA 1942, BD 1947, BSc 1948. Minister of St Andrews, Fraserburgh, 1949-59. Dept of Computer Science, Univ. of Edinburgh, 1965-. FRSE 1973. *Publications:* The Structure of the Fourth Gospel, 1961; Authorship and Integrity in the New Testament, 1963; (with G. H. C. Macgregor) The Structure of Luke and Acts, 1965; Paul the Man and the Myth, 1965; The Computer in Literary Research, 1973; contrib. Jl Royal Phil Soc., Mind, NT Studies, Class. Qly, Jl Royal Soc. Edinburgh, Jl Royal Statist. Soc., Zeit. für Pap. und Epi., etc. *Recreations:* thinking, talking. *Address:* The Abbey Manse, Culross, Dunfermline, Fife KY12 8JD. *T:* Newmills 231.

MORTON, Vice-Adm. Anthony Storrs; Vice-Chief of Defence Staff, 1977-78; *b* 6 Nov. 1923; *s* of late Dr Harold Morton. *Educ:* Loretto School. Joined RN 1941; war service in Atlantic, Mediterranean and Far East (despatches, HMS Wrangler, 1945); Commander 1956; Comd HMS Appleton and 100th MSS 1957-58; HMS Undine 1960; HMS Rocket 1960-62; Captain 1964; Captain (F) 20th Frigate Squadron, 1964-66; Chief Staff Officer, Plans and Policy, to Commander Far East Fleet, 1966-68; Senior Naval Officer, Northern Ireland, 1968-70; Senior Naval Mem., RCDS, 1971-72; ACDS (Policy), 1973-75; Flag Officer, First Flotilla, 1975-77. *Recreations:* fishing, sailing, shooting. *Address:* c/o Barclays Bank, Alresford, Hants. *Clubs:*

Army and Navy; Royal Yacht Squadron; Royal Cruising; Irish Cruising.

MORTON, Sir Brian, Kt 1973; FRICS; Chairman, Harland & Wolff, since 1975; *b* 24 Jan. 1912; *s* of Alfred Oscar Morton and Margaret Osborne Hennessy; *m* 1937, Hilda Evelyn Elsie Hillis; one *s* (and one *s* decd). *Educ:* Campbell Coll., Belfast. Estate Agency, Brian Morton & Co., Belfast, 1936; retired, 1964. Elected Councillor (U) Cromac Ward, Belfast Corp., 1967; apptd Mem. Craigavon Development Commn, 1968; Chm., Londonderry Develt Commn, 1969-73. *Recreations:* golf, sailing, landscape painting, fishing. *Address:* Rolly Island, Strangford Lough, Co. Down, N Ireland. *T:* Killinchy 541472. *Clubs:* Ulster Reform (Belfast); Royal County Down Golf (Newcastle); Northern Counties (Londonderry).

MORTON, Air Commodore Crichton Charles, CBE 1945; Command Electronics Officer, HQ Bomber Command, 1962-66, retired; *b* 26 July 1912; *s* of late Charles Crichton Morton, Ramsey, IOM; *m* 1956, Diana Yvonne, *d* of late Maj.-Gen. R. C. Priest, CB, RMS and *widow* of Group Captain N. D. Gilbart-Smith, RAF; no *c. Educ:* King William's Coll., IOM; RAF Coll., Cranwell. Various flying duties, 1932-36; RAF Officers Long Signals Course, Cranwell, 1936-37; signals duties, 1937-39; radar duties at HQ Fighter Comd, No 5 Signals Wing France, HQ 60 Signals Gp, Air HQ Iceland, HQ Air Comd SE Asia, 1939-45; Dir of Radar and Dep. Dir of Signals, Air Min., 1945-49; jssc Latimer, 1949-50; OC No 3 Radio Sch., RAF Compton Bassett, 1950-52; OC Communications Gp, Allied Air Forces Central Europe, 1952-55; Inspector of Radio Services, 1955-58; Dep. Chief Signals Office, HQ, SHAPE, 1958-60; Chm. of Brit. Jt Communications Electronics Board, Ministry of Defence, 1960-62. AMIEE 1955; AFRAeS 1965; MIERE 1965; CEng 1966. *Address:* Apartamento 102, Torre Tramontana, Apartado 50, Playa de Aro, Gerona, Spain.

MORTON, Digby; *see* Morton, H. D.

MORTON, Prof. Frank, CBE 1976 (OBE 1968); DSc 1952, PhD 1936 (Manchester); MSc Tech; FRIC; MIChemE; Professor of Chemical Engineering, University of Manchester, 1956-73, now Professor Emeritus; a Pro-Vice-Chancellor, 1968-72; *b* Sheffield, 11 Aug. 1906; *s* of late Joseph Morton, Manchester; *m* 1936, Hilda May, *d* of John W. Seaston, Withington, Manchester; one *s. Educ:* Manchester Univ. Demonstrator in Chemical Technology, 1931-36; Research Chemist, Trinidad Leaseholds Ltd, 1936-40; Superintendent of Research and Development, Trinidad Leaseholds, Trinidad, 1940-45; Chief Chemist, Trinidad Leaseholds Ltd, UK, 1945-49; Prof. of Chemical Engineering, Univ. of Birmingham, 1949-56. Actg Principal, Manchester Coll. of Science and Technology, 1964-65; Dep. Principal, Univ. of Manchester Inst. of Science and Technology, 1966-71. Member: Council, Manchester Business Sch., 1964-72; Chemical and Allied Products Training Board, 1968-71; European Fedn of Chemical Engineering, 1968-72. Pres., IChemE, 1963-64. Society of Chemical Industry: Vice-Pres., 1967-; Jubilee Memorial Lectr, 1967; Medal, 1969. *Publications:* Report of Inquiry into the Safety of Natural Gas as a Fuel (Ministry of Technology), 1970; various papers on petroleum, organic chemistry, chemical engineering and allied subjects. *Recreation:* golf. *Address:* 47 Penrhyn Beach East, Llandudno, Gwynedd. *T:* Llandudno 48037. *Club:* Savage.

MORTON, Rev. Harry Osborne; General Secretary, British Council of Churches, since 1973; *b* 28 June 1925; *s* of John William Morton and Alice Morton (*née* Betteridge); *m* 1954, Patricia Mary McGrath; two *s* two *d* (and one *d* decd). *Educ:* The King's Sch., Pontefract, Yorks; King's Coll., Cambridge (MA Cantab); Hartley Victoria Methodist Coll., Manchester. Marconi's Wireless Telegraph Co. Ltd, 1945; Gen. Sec., Order of Christian Witness, 1947; entered Methodist Ministry, 1949; ordained Deacon, Church of South India, 1954, Presbyter, 1955; Sec. for Scholarships, World Council of Churches, Geneva, 1960; Sec. for East and Central Africa, Methodist Missionary Soc., 1963, Gen. Sec. 1972-73. Pres., Methodist Conf., 1972. Select Preacher, Cambridge Univ., 1972 and 1975. *Recreations:* fell walking, music, theatre, coarse gardening. *Address:* 2 Eaton Gate, SW1W 9BL. *T:* 01-730 9611.

MORTON, (Henry) Digby; consultant designer (independent); *b* 26 Nov. 1906; *e s* of Digby Berkeley Morton, Dublin; *m* 1936, Phyllis May, *d* of James Harwood Panting, London. *Educ:* Dublin. Trained in Art and Architecture, Metropolitan Sch. of Art, Dublin, 1923-29. Opened Couture Establishment in London, 1930; worked in USA, 1953-57; Founder Mem., Incorporated Soc. of London Fashion Designers, 1939 (Vice-Pres. 1955-56). *Recreation:* moving.

MORTON, Henry Vollam, FRSL; author and journalist. Entered journalism, Birmingham Gazette and Express, 1910; assistant editor, 1912; edited Empire Magazine, London, 1913; sub-editor, Daily Mail, 1913-14; served in Warwicks Yeomanry during War; joined editorial staff Evening Standard in 1919; Daily Express, 1921; special writer, Daily Herald, 1931-42. Comdr, Order of the Phœnix (Greece), 1937; Cavaliere, Order of Merit (Italy), 1965. *Publications:* The Heart of London, 1925; The London Year, 1926; London, 1926; The Spell of London, 1926; The Nights of London, 1926; In Search of England, 1927; The Call of England, 1928; In Search of Scotland, 1929; In Search of Ireland, 1930; In Search of Wales, 1932; Blue Days at Sea, 1932; In Scotland Again, 1933; In the Steps of The Master, 1934; Our Fellow Men, 1936; In the Steps of St Paul, 1936; Through Lands of the Bible, 1938; Ghosts of London, 1939; Women of the Bible, 1940; H. V. Morton's London, 1940; Middle East, 1941; I, James Blunt, 1942; I Saw Two Englands, 1942; Atlantic Meeting, 1943; In Search of South Africa, 1948; In Search of London, 1951; In the Steps of Jesus, 1953; A Stranger in Spain, 1954; A Traveller in Rome, 1957; This is Rome, 1960; This is the Holy Land, 1961; A Traveller in Italy, 1964; The Waters of Rome, 1966; A Traveller in Southern Italy, 1969; H. V. Morton's England, 1975; The Splendour of Scotland, 1976. *Address:* PO Box 67, Somerset West, Cape Province, South Africa.

MORTON, Hugh Drennan Baird, QC 1974; *b* 10 April 1930; *s* of late Rev. T. R. Morton, DD, and of J. M. M. Morton (*née* Baird); *m* 1956, Muriel Miller; three *s. Educ:* Glasgow Academy; Glasgow Univ. (BL). Admitted Faculty of Advocates, 1965. *Address:* 25 Royal Circus, Edinburgh EH3 6TL. *T:* 031-225 5139.

MORTON, John Cameron Andrieu Bingham, (J. B. Morton), CBE 1952; Journalist; Beachcomber of the Daily Express, 1924-75; *b* 7 June 1893; *s* of Edward Morton, journalist and dramatist, and Rosamond, *d* of Capt. Devereux Bingham, Wartnaby Hall, Leics; *m* 1927, Dr Mary O'Leary (decd), Cappoquin, Co. Waterford. *Educ:* Park House, Southborough; Harrow; Worcester Coll., Oxford. Enlisted, 1914; fought in France; Commission, 1916; Intelligence, MI7b, 1917; received into Catholic Church, 1922. *Publications:* The Barber of Putney, 1919; Enchanter's Nightshade, 1920; Penny Royal, 1921; Tally-Ho!, 1922; Old Man's Beard, 1923; The Cow Jumped Over the Moon, 1924; Gorgeous Poetry, 1924; Mr Thake, 1929; Mr Thake Again, 1930; By the Way, 1931; Maladetta, 1932; Drink Up, Gentlemen, 1932; 1933 and Still Going Wrong; Sobieski, King of Poland, 1932; Hag's Harvest, 1933; Morton's Folly, 1933; Who's Who at the Zoo, 1933; The Adventures of Mr Thake, 1934; The Death of the Dragon, and other fairy tales, 1934; Skylighters, 1934; Vagabond, 1935; Stuff and Nonsense, 1935; Mr Thake and the Ladies, 1935; The Bastille Falls (Studies of the French Revolution), 1936; Gallimaufry, 1936; The Dauphin (Louis XVII), 1937; Sideways through Borneo (an Unconventional Journey), 1937; The New Ireland, 1938; A Diet of Thistles, 1938; The Dancing Cabman (Collected Verse), 1938; Pyrenean, 1938; Saint-Just, 1939; A Bonfire of Weeds, 1939; I Do Not Think So, 1940; Fool's Paradise, 1941; Captain Foulenough & Company, 1944; The Gascon, 1946; Brumaire; The Rise of Bonaparte, 1948; Here and Now, 1948; The Misadventures of Dr Strabismus, 1949; The Tibetan Venus, 1951; Camille Desmoulins: and Other Studies of the French Revolution, 1951; St Thérèse of Lisieux: The Making of a Saint, 1954; Hilaire Belloc: A Memoir, 1955; Springtime: Tales of the Cafe Rieu, 1956; Marshal Ney, 1958; Merry-go-Round, 1959; The Best of Beachcomber (selected by Michael Frayn), 1963. TV Series: The World of Beachcomber, BBC, 1969-70. *Address:* Melleray, Sea Lane, Ferring, West Sussex. *Club:* St Stephen's Green (Dublin).

MORTON, John Percival, CMG 1965; OBE 1946; Indian Police Medal for gallantry, 1935, Bar 1940; retired; *b* 15 May 1911; *e s* of late Henry Percy Dee Morton; *m* 1939, Leonora Margaret Sale, *d* of late Hon. Mr Justice S. L. Sale, ICS; one *s* one *d. Educ:* Bedford Modern Sch. Indian Police, Punjab, 1930-47 (Dist Supt Police Jullundur; Central Int. Officer, Govt of India, Punjab and Delhi Provinces; seconded HQ British Troops (Egypt); Senior Supt Police, Lahore Dist.); Principal, War Office, 1947; seconded to Air Min., as Civil Asst, Staff of AOC RAF Iraq, 1947-49; seconded as Counsellor, to Office of Comr-Gen., SE Asia, 1949-52; seconded as Dir of Int., Govt of Malaya, 1952-54; Asst Sec., War Office, 1954-59; IDC 1959; Sec. of State's Adv. Staff, Colonial Office, 1961-65; Asst Under-Sec. of State, MoD, 1968-71; retired 1971. Advisory missions for FCO to Jordan, Pakistan and E Caribbean, 1972-73, for MoD to N Ireland, 1973; Consultant, The De La Rue Co. Ltd, 1972-75; Panel Chm., Civil Service Commn Selection Bd, 1973-77. *Recreations:* golf, gardening. *Address:* Courtlands Cottage, Green Lane,

Pangbourne, Berks. *T:* Pangbourne 3908. *Clubs:* East India, Devonshire, Sports and Public Schools; Huntercombe (Oxon).

MORTON, Kenneth Valentine Freeland, CIE 1947; OBE 1971; Secretary East Anglian Regional Hospital Board, 1947-72, retired; *b* 13 May 1907; *s* of Kenneth John Morton; *m* 1936, Mary Hadwin Hargreaves; four *s* one *d. Educ:* Edinburgh Academy; University Coll., Oxford. Joined ICS, 1930; Under-Sec. (Political) Punjab Govt, 1934-36; Deputy Commissioner, 1936-39; Colonisation Officer, 1939-43; Deputy Sec., Development Dept, 1943-46; Sec. Electricity and Industries Depts, 1946-47; retired, 1947. *Recreations:* shooting and fishing. *Address:* Mulberry House, Little Wilbraham, Cambs CB1 5LE. *T:* Cambridge 811355. *Club:* East India, Sports and Public Schools.

MORTON, Sir Ralph (John), Kt 1960; CMG 1954; OBE 1947; MC 1918; Judge of High Court of Southern Rhodesia, 1949-59; *b* 2 Aug. 1896; *yr s* of John Morton, Wotton-under-Edge, Glos; *m* 1923, Cato Marie van den Berg; one *d. Educ:* Bishop's Stortford; Cambridge Univ. Served European War, RFA, 1915-19. Southern Rhodesia: Solicitor General, 1934; Attorney General, 1944. *Address:* 3 Dundalk Avenue, Parkview, Johannesburg 2193, South Africa.

MORTON, Robert Alastair Newton; Managing Director, British National Oil Corporation, since 1976; *b* 11 Jan. 1938; *s* of late Harry Newton Morton and of Elizabeth Martino; *m* 1964, Sara Bridget Stephens; one *s* one *d. Educ:* St John's Coll. and Witwatersrand Univ., Johannesburg (BA); Worcester Coll., Oxford (MA). Special grad. student, MIT, 1964. Anglo American Corp. of SA (mining finance), London and Central Africa, 1959-63; Internat. Finance Corp., Washington, 1964-67; Industrial Reorganisation Corp., 1967-70; Exec. Dir, 117 Group of investment trusts, 1970-72; Chm., Draymont Securities, 1972-76. Chm. or Dir, various public engineering groups, 1970-76; Mem., Royal Ordnance Factories Bd, 1974-76. Mem., City and East London AHA, 1974-77; Governor: London Hosp., Whitechapel, 1971-74 (Special Trustee, 1974-77); St Peter's Hosps, 1973-76. *Address:* 19 Oppidans Road, NW3.

MORTON, (Stephen) Alastair, TD 1949; JP; His Honour Judge Morton; a Circuit Judge (formerly Deputy Chairman, Greater London Quarter Sessions), since 1971; *b* 28 July 1913; *o s* of Philip Morton, Dune Gate, Dorchester; *m* 1939, Lily Yarrow Eveline, *o d* of J. S. P. Griffith-Jones, Drews, Beaconsfield, Bucks; one *s* one *d. Educ:* private sch.; Trinity Hall, Cambridge. Commnd Dorset Heavy Bde, RA, TA, 1932; served War of 1939-45, Royal Artillery. Called to the Bar, Middle Temple, 1938; Western Circuit, 1938; Master of the Bench, 1964. Counsel to the Crown at County of London Sessions, 1954-59; Central Criminal Court: First Junior Treasury Counsel, 1959-64; Senior Treasury Counsel, 1964-71; Recorder of Devizes, 1957-71; Dep.-Chm. Quarter Sessions: Dorset, 1957-71; Norfolk, 1969-71. JP Dorset, 1957. *Recreation:* painting. *Address:* 53 Eaton Terrace, SW1. *T:* 01-730 7730; Cringles, Overy Staithe, near King's Lynn, Norfolk. *T:* Burnham Market 339. *Clubs:* White's, Pratt's.

MORTON, Prof. W. E., MSc Tech; FTI; Dean of the Faculty of Technology in the University of Manchester, 1964-66; Vice-Principal of the Manchester College of Science and Technology, 1957-65; Professor of Textile Technology in the University of Manchester, 1926-57, and Arkwright Professor, 1957-67, now Professor Emeritus; Pro-Vice-Chancellor, 1963-65; *b* 1902; *s* of J. Morton, LDS Edinburgh, Penrith; *m* 1927, Elsie Maud, *d* of Charles Harlow, Fallowfield, Manchester; two *s* two *d. Educ:* St Bees Sch., Cumberland; Manchester Univ.; BScTech, 1922; MScTech 1923; Research Studentship, British Cotton Industry Research Assoc., 1923; Technical Asst to the Dir BCIRA, 1924; Technical Adviser to Dir of Narrow Fabrics, Min. of Supply, 1941-45. Chm., Heightside Housing Assoc., 1967-75. Hon. Fellow, UMIST. Textile Inst. Medal, 1952; Warner Medal, 1957. *Publications:* An Introduction to the Study of Spinning, 1938; (with J. W. S. Hearle) Physical Properties of Textile Fibres, 1963; papers read before the Textile Institute, and contribs to technical journals. *Recreation:* croquet. *Address:* Solway, Delahays Drive, Hale, Cheshire. *T:* 061-980 4520.

MORTON, Sir (William) Wilfred, KCB 1966 (CB 1958); Chairman, Board of Customs and Excise, 1965-69; *b* 14 April 1906; *s* of late William Morton; *m* 1939, Jacqueline Harriet, *d* of late H. P. B. Newman, Grenfell, New South Wales. *Educ:* Hutchesons' Grammar Sch.; Glasgow Univ. Entered Inland Revenue, 1927. Consultant to Govt of Bolivia, 1952-54; Comr of Inland Revenue and Dir of Establishments, 1955-58; Third Sec., HM Treasury, 1958-65. Mem., Transport Tribunal, 1971-. *Address:* Brook House, Bagnor, Newbury, Berks. *Club:* Athenæum.

MORTON-SANER, Robert, CVO 1966; CBE 1962 (OBE 1946; MBE 1941); HM Diplomatic Service, retired; *b* 30 December 1911; *o s* of late Major A. E. Saner; *m* 1943, Katharine Mary Gordon; two *d. Educ:* Westminster Sch.; Christ Church, Oxford. ICS, 1935; served in United Provinces; Under Sec., Defence Department, Government of India, 1940; Deputy Secretary and Chief Administrative Officer, General Headquarters, New Delhi, 1943-45; served with Resettlement Directorate, 1945-47. Retired from Indian Civil Service and entered Foreign (subseq. Diplomatic) Service, 1947. Served in Madras, 1947-50; Foreign Office, 1950-52; Budapest, 1953-55; NATO Defence College, 1955; Counsellor and Consul-General, Djakarta, 1955-59; Counsellor, Buenos Aires, 1960-64; Consul-General, Antwerp, 1964-70. Acted as Chargé d'Affaires, 1953, 1954, 1956, 1958, 1959, 1960. Member, Skinners' Company. Commander, Order of Leopold II (Belgium). *Recreations:* riding, golf. *Address:* Hethe Cottage, Hethe, Oxon. *Club:* Anglo-Belgian.

MOSDELL, Lionel Patrick; Judge of the High Court of Kenya, 1966-72, Tanganyika, 1960-64; Chairman: Surrey and Sussex Rent Assessment Panel, since 1972; National Insurance Local Tribunal, London South Region, since 1974; Legal Member: Immigration Appeal Tribunal, since 1975; Pensions Appeals Tribunals, since 1976; *b* 29 Aug. 1912; *s* of late William George Mosdell and late Sarah Ellen Mosdell (*née* Gardiner); *m* 1945, Muriel Jean Sillem; one *s* one *d. Educ:* Abingdon Sch.; St Edmund Hall, Oxford (MA). Solicitor, England, 1938. Served War of 1939-45, Gunner, Sussex Yeomanry RA, 1939-41; Commnd Rifle Bde, 1941; Libyan Arab Force; Force 133; No 1 Special Force; Egypt, Cyrenaica, Eritrea, Abyssinia, Italy (Capt.). Registrar of Lands and Deeds, N Rhodesia, 1946; Resident Magistrate, 1950; Senior Resident Magistrate, 1956. Barrister, Gray's Inn, 1952. *Recreations:* walking, cycling. *Address:* 27 Lloyd Road, Hove, East Sussex BN3 6NL. *Clubs:* Special Forces, Royal Commonwealth Society; Mombasa (Kenya).

MOSELEY, George Walker; Deputy Secretary, Department of the Environment, since 1976; *b* 7 Feb. 1925; *o c* of late William Moseley, MBE, and Bella Moseley; *m* 1950, Anne Mercer; one *s* one *d. Educ:* High Sch., Glasgow; St Bees Sch., Cumberland; Wadham Coll., Oxford (MA). Pilot Officer, RAF Levies, Iraq, 1943-48. Asst Principal, Min. of Town and Country Planning, 1950; Asst Private Sec. to Minister of Housing and Local Govt, 1951-52; Private Sec. to Parly Sec., 1952-54; Principal Private Sec. to Minister of Housing and Local Govt, 1963-65; Asst Sec. 1965; Under-Sec. 1970-76; Dep. Sec., 1976. *Recreation:* music. *Address:* 1 Howard Close, Hampton, Mddx. *Club:* United Oxford & Cambridge University.

MOSER, Sir Claus (Adolf), KCB 1973; CBE 1965; FBA 1969; Director, Central Statistical Office, and Head of Government Statistical Service, since 1967; *b* 24 Nov. 1922; *s* of Dr Ernest Moser and late Lotte Moser; *m* 1949, Mary Oxlin; one *s* two *d. Educ:* Frensham Heights Sch.; LSE, Univ. of London. RAF, 1943-46. London Sch. of Economics: Asst Lectr in Statistics, 1946-49; Lectr, 1949-55; Reader in Social Statistics, 1955-61; Prof. of Social Statistics, 1961-70; Vis. Prof. of Social Statistics, 1970-75. Dir, Higher Educn Research Unit, LSE, 1964-74. Statistical Adviser, Cttee on Higher Educn, 1961-64. Vis. Fellow, Nuffield Coll., Oxford, 1972-; Chm., Bd of Dirs, Royal Opera House, Covent Garden, 1974-; Member: Governing Body, Royal Academy of Music, 1967-; BBC Music Adv. Cttee, 1971-; Council, Centre for Studies in Social Policy; Exec. Cttee, PEP. Hon. FRAM, 1970. Hon. Fellow, LSE, 1976; Hon. DSocSci Southampton, 1975; Hon. DSc Leeds, 1977; Hon. DUniv Surrey, 1977. Comdr de l'Ordre National du Mérite (France), 1976. *Publications:* Measurement of Levels of Living, 1957; Survey Methods in Social Investigation, 1958; (jtly) Social Conditions in England and Wales, 1958; (jtly) British Towns, 1961; papers in statistical jls. *Recreation:* music. *Address:* 3 Regent's Park Terrace, NW1 7EE. *T:* 01-485 1619. *Club:* Garrick.

MOSES, Sir Charles (Joseph Alfred), Kt 1961; CBE 1954; Secretary-General, Asian Broadcasting Union, 1965-77; General Manager, Australian Broadcasting Commission, 1935-65; Company Director; *b* 21 Jan. 1900; *s* of Joseph Moses and Lily (*née* Henderson); *m* 1922, Kathleen, *d* of Patrick O'Sullivan, Bruree, Co. Limerick; one *s* (one *d* decd). *Educ:* Oswestry Grammar Sch.; RMC Sandhurst. Lt 2nd Border Regt, 1918-22, serving in Germany and Ireland; fruitgrower, Bendigo, Australia, 1922-24; in motor business in Melbourne, 1924-30; in radio, ABC: Announcer/Commentator, 1930-32; Talks and Sporting Editor, Sydney, 1933-34; Federal Talks Controller, 1934-35. War of 1939-45 (despatches): AIF in Malaya and Singapore, Major, 1941-42, in New Guinea, Lt-Col, 1942-43.

Leader of Austr. Delegn to UNESCO Annual Gen. Conf., Paris, 1952; Chm. Commonwealth Jubilee Arts Cttee, 1951; Vice-Pres., Royal Agricultural Society of NSW, 1951-; Vice-Pres., Elizabethan Theatre Trust; Remembrance Driveway (NSW). Hon. Dir, Postgraduate Med. Foundn (NSW). Member Council: Internat. Broadcasting Inst., London; Internat. Inst. for Youth and childrens' TV, Munich; Royal NSW Instn for Deaf and Blind Children; Australian-American Assoc.; Asian Mass Communications and Inf. Centre, Singapore. *Recreations:* walking, tree-felling, music. *Address:* 78 New Beach Road, Darling Point, NSW 2027, Australia. *T:* 32 4224. *Clubs:* Australian, Tattersall's, Rugby Union (Sydney).

MOSES, Eric George Rufus, CB 1973; Solicitor of Inland Revenue, since 1970; *b* 6 April 1914; *s* of Michael and Emily Moses; *m* 1940, Pearl Lipton; one *s. Educ:* University Coll. Sch., London; Oriel Coll., Oxford. Called to Bar, Middle Temple, 1938. Served Royal Artillery, 1940-46 (Major). Asst Solicitor, Inland Revenue, 1953-65, Principal Asst Solicitor, 1965-70. *Recreations:* mountains, opera.

MOSES, Ven. John Henry, PhD; Archdeacon of Southend, since 1977; *b* 12 Jan. 1938; *s* of late Henry William Moses and of Ada Elizabeth Moses; *m* 1964, Susan Elizabeth (*née* Wainwright); one *s* two *d. Educ:* Ealing Grammar School; Nottingham Univ. (Gladstone Meml Prize 1958, BA History 1959, PhD 1965); Trinity Hall and Dept of Education, Cambridge (Cert. in Education 1960); Lincoln Theological Coll. Deacon 1964, priest 1965; Asst Curate, St Andrew, Bedford, 1964-70; Priest-in-Charge, St Peter, Coventry, and Rector-designate of Coventry East Team Ministry, 1970-73; Priest-in-Charge, St Mark with St Barnabas, Coventry, 1971-73; Rector of Coventry East Team Ministry, 1973-77; Rural Dean of Coventry East, 1973-77; Examining Chaplain to Bishop of Coventry, 1972-. Bishops' Selector for ACCM, 1977-. *Address:* 144 Alexandra Road, Southend-on-Sea SS1 1HB. *T:* Southend-on-Sea 45175.

MOSLEY, family name of **Baron Ravensdale.**

MOSLEY, Nicholas; *see* Ravensdale, 3rd Baron.

MOSLEY, Sir Oswald Ernald, 6th Bt, *cr* 1781; late 16th Lancers; *b* 16 Nov. 1896; *e s* of Sir Oswald Mosley, 5th Bt; *S* father, 1928; *m* 1st, 1920, Lady Cynthia Curzon (*d* 1933), 2nd *d* of late Marquess Curzon of Kedleston; two *s* one *d* ; 2nd, 1936, Hon. Diana Mitford, 3rd *d* of 2nd Baron Redesdale; two *s. Educ:* Winchester; RMC, Sandhurst. Served in France during European War with his regt and also the RFC; MP (CU) Harrow Division of Middx, Dec. 1918-22; (Ind) 1922-24; (Lab) 1924; Smethwick 1926-31; Chancellor of Duchy of Lancaster, 1929-30. Founded British Union of Fascists 1932, imprisoned under Regulation 18B during Second World War. Appears on TV in Britain, Germany and America. *Publications:* The Greater Britain, 1932; My Answer, 1946; The Alternative, 1947; Europe: Faith and Plan, 1958; 300 Questions Answered, 1961; (autobiography) My Life, 1968; pamphlets, articles. *Heir:* s 3rd Baron Ravensdale, *qv. Address:* 1 Rue des Lacs, 91400 Orsay, Essonne, France. *T:* (Paris) 0104211. *Club:* White's.

MOSQUERA-CHAUX, Dr Victor; Senator of Republic of Colombia, 1958-70; *b* 1 Oct. 1919; *m* 1951, Señora Cecilia Paz de Mosquera; two *s* three *d. Educ:* Facultad de Derecho, Universidad del Cauca, Colombia. Princ. Rep. to Departmental Assembly of Cauca, 1942-47; Department of Cauca: Princ. Mem., Liberal Directory, 1942-60; Sec. of Govt, 1944-45; Governor, 1959-60; Head of Liberal Party, 1960-62; Rep. for Cauca to House of Commons, 1947-51; Nat. Directive of Liberal Party: Pres. of Exec. Cttee, 1960-62; Princ. Mem., 1962-67; Colombian Ambassador to London, 1967-70. Deleg. to 19th Conf. of UN. *Address:* c/o Partido Liberal, Bogotá, Colombia. *Clubs:* Curzon, Hurlingham, Belfry, Travellers'; Popayán, Campestre (Popayán, Colombia).

MOSS, Dr Alfred Allinson; Keeper of Minerals, British Museum (Natural History), 1968-74; *b* 30 Dec. 1912; *o s* of Frank Allinson and Alice Moss; *m* 1938, Sheila Mary, *o d* of Charles H. Sendell; two *d. Educ:* Ilfracombe Grammar Sch.; University Coll., Exeter. BSc London; PhD London. Chemist: War Dept, 1936; Govt Laboratory, 1937-39; Asst Keeper, Brit. Mus., 1939-40; Chemist, Chief Chemical Inspectorate, Min. of Supply, 1940-45; Asst Keeper, Brit. Mus., 1945-49; Principal Scientific Officer: Brit. Mus. 1949-53; Brit. Mus. (Nat. Hist.), 1953-59; Dep. Keeper of Minerals, Brit. Mus. (Nat. Hist.), 1959; Keeper, 1968. Treas., Mineralogical Soc., 1966-73; FSA. *Publications:* papers on archaeological and mineralogical subjects in various jls. *Recreations:* horology, chess, photography, squash rackets. *Address:* 12 Somerfields, Lyme Regis, Dorset DT7 3EZ. *T:* Lyme Regis 3443.

MOSS, Very Rev. Basil Stanley; Provost of Birmingham Cathedral since 1973; Rector, Cathedral parish of St Philip, since 1973; *b* 7 Oct. 1918; *e s* of Canon Harry George Moss and Daisy Violet (*née* Jolly); *m* 1950, Rachel Margaret, *d* of Dr Cyril Bailey and Gemma (*née* Creighton); three *d*. *Educ:* Canon Slade Grammar Sch., Bolton; The Queen's Coll., Oxford. Asst Curate, Leigh Parish Church, 1943-45; Sub-Warden, Lincoln Theological Coll., 1946-51; Sen. Tutor, St Catharine's Cumberland Lodge, Windsor Gt Pk, 1951-53; Vicar of St Nathanael with St Katharine, Bristol, 1953-60; Dir, Ordination Training, Bristol Dioc., 1956-66; Residentiary Canon of Bristol Cath., 1960-66, Hon. Canon, 1966-72; Chief Secretary, Advisory Council for the Church's Ministry, 1966-72; Chaplain to Church House, Westminster, 1966-72; Examining Chaplain to Bishop of Bristol, 1956-72. Chm., Birmingham Community Relations Council, 1973-. *Publications:* Clergy Training Today, 1964; (Edited) Crisis for Baptism, 1966. *Recreations:* walking, music. *Address:* Cathedral Office, St Philip's Place, Birmingham B3 2PP. *Club:* Birmingham Rotary.

MOSS, Charles James, CBE 1977; Head of Engineering Department, International Rice Research Institute, Los Banos, Philippines, since 1977; *b* 18 Nov. 1917; *s* of James and Elizabeth Moss; *m* 1939, Joan Bernice Smith; two *d*. *Educ:* Queen Mary Coll., London Univ. (BSc). CEng, FIMechE, FIAgE. Rotol Ltd, Gloucester, 1939-43; RAE Farnborough, 1943-45; CIBA Ltd, Cambridge, 1945-51; ICI Ltd, Billingham, 1951-58; Central Engineering Estabt, NCB, Stanhope Bretley, 1958-61; Process Develt Dept, NCB, London, 1961-63; Dir, NIAE, 1964-77. Vis. Prof., Dept of Agric. Engrg, Univ. of Newcastle upon Tyne, 1972-75. *Publications:* papers in learned jls, confs, etc. *Recreations:* gardening, walking. *Address:* The International Rice Research Institute, PO Box 933, Manila, Philippines. *T:* 88-48-69.

MOSS, Edward Herbert St George; Under-Secretary, University Grants Committee, since 1971; *b* 18 May 1918; *s* of late Sir George Moss, KBE, HM Consular Service in China, and late Lady (Gladys Lucy) Moss; *m* 1948, Shirley Evelyn Baskett; two *s* one *d*. *Educ:* Marlborough; Pembroke Coll., Cambridge. Army Service in UK and Middle East, 1940-45; entered HM Foreign (subseq. Diplomatic) Service, 1945; served in Japan, FO, Belgrade (Head of Chancery 1951-55), St Louis, Detroit, FO; transf. to Home Civil Service (MoD), 1960; Asst Sec. 1961; Dept of Educn and Science, 1969. *Recreations:* writing, gardening. *Address:* Prospect, 29 Guildown Avenue, Guildford, Surrey. *T:* Guildford 66984.

MOSS, Sir Eric (de Vere), Kt 1952; CIE 1943; late ICS; subsequently posts in Pakistan and lately Northern Rhodesia; *b* 13 April 1896; *s* of F. J. Moss; *m* 1919, Monica Meriton-Reed; one *s* three *d*. *Educ:* Victoria Coll., Jersey. Various appointments in ICS; District Magistrate and Collector of Gorakhpur, UP, 1940-42; War Production Comr, UP, 1943-46; Commissioner Jhansi Division, UP, 1946; Sec. to Min. of Industries and Commerce, Govt of Pakistan, 1947; Pakistan Refugees Commissioner; Sec. to Ministry of Refugees and Rehabilitation, Govt of Pakistan, 1948-49; Sec. to Ministry of Health and Works, Government of Pakistan, 1950; Road Traffic Commissioner, Government of Northern Rhodesia, 1952-62. *Recreations:* shooting and fishing. *Address:* Bracken Lodge, Brookside Close, Runcton, Chichester, West Sussex PO20 6PY. *Club:* East India, Devonshire, Sports and Public Schools.

MOSS, James Richard Frederick, OBE 1955; FRINA; FInstW; RCNC; Chief Executive, Balaena Structures (North Sea), 1974-77, retired; *b* 26 March 1916; *s* of late Lt-Cdr J. G. Moss, RN, and late Kathleen Moss (*née* Steinberg); *m* 1941, Celia Florence Lucas; three *d*. *Educ:* Marlborough College; Trinity Coll., Cambridge (1st Cl. Hons Mech. Sci. Tripos and Maths Pt I); RCNC, 1941; Asst Constructor, Admiralty Mission, Washington, 1941-44; Constructor Commander, Admiralty Tech. Mission, Ottawa, 1944-46; Admiralty Experimental Works, Haslar, 1946-49; Constructor Comdr to C-in-C, Far East Fleet, 1949-52; Aircraft Carrier design, Admiralty, Bath, 1952-55; Chief Constructor, HM Dockyard, Singapore, 1955-58; Chief Constructor, HM Dockyard, Devonport, 1958-62; Management Techniques, Dockyard HQ, Bath, 1962-63; Asst Director, R&D, Ship Dept, Bath, 1963-65; Supt, Naval Construction Research Estab., Dunfermline, 1965-68; Dir, Naval Ship Production, 1968-74. *Recreations:* yachting and dinghies, music. *Address:* 25 Church Street, Stapleford, Cambridge CB2 5DS. *T:* Shelford 3108. *Clubs:* Royal Naval Sailing Association; Royal Naval and Royal Albert Yacht (Portsmouth).

MOSS, Sir John H. T. E.; *see* Edwards-Moss.

MOSS, John Ringer, CB 1972; Deputy Secretary, Ministry of Agriculture, Fisheries and Food, since 1970; *b* 15 Feb. 1920; 2nd *s* of late James Moss and Louisa Moss; *m* 1946, Edith Bland Wheeler; two *s* one *d*. *Educ:* Manchester Gram. Sch.; Brasenose Coll., Oxford (MA). War Service, mainly India and Burma, 1940-46; Capt., RE, attached Royal Bombay Sappers and Miners. Entered Civil Service (Min. of Agric., Fisheries and Food) as Asst Princ., 1947; Princ. Private Sec. to Minister of Agric., Fisheries and Food, 1959-61; Asst Sec., 1961; Under-Sec., Gen. Agricultural Policy Gp, Min. of Agric., Fisheries and Food, 1967-70. Mem., Economic Develt Cttee for Agriculture, 1969-70. *Recreations:* music, travel. *Address:* 16 Upper Hollis, Great Missenden, Bucks. *T:* Great Missenden 2676.

MOSS, Norman J.; *see* Jordan-Moss.

MOSS, Rosalind Louisa Beaufort, FSA; Editor of Porter-Moss Topographical Bibliography of Ancient Egyptian Hieroglyphic Texts, Reliefs, and Paintings, 1924-72; *b* 21 Sept. 1890; *d* of Rev. H. W. Moss, Headmaster of Shrewsbury Sch., 1866-1908. *Educ:* Heathfield Sch., Ascot; St Anne's Coll., Oxford. Diploma in Anthropology (distinction), 1917, BSc Oxon 1922. Took up Egyptology, 1917. FSA 1949. Hon. DLitt, Oxon, 1961. Hon. Fellow, St Anne's Coll., Oxford, 1967. *Publications:* Life after Death in Oceania, 1925; Topographical Bibliography (see above); articles in Journal of Egyptian Archæology, etc. *Recreation:* travel. *Address:* 10 Glyn Garth Court, Menai Bridge, Gwynedd. *T:* Menai Bridge 713455.

MOSS, Stirling, OBE 1959; FIE; Racing Motorist, 1947-62, retired; Managing Director, Stirling Moss Ltd; Director: Designs Unlimited Ltd; SM Design & Interior Decorating Co.; America St Garage Ltd; Lema Laundrettes Ltd; Michael Farr (Design Integration) Ltd; Stirling Moss International Export; Motoring Broadcasts Ltd; Goblin Hill Hotels Ltd; Development Consultant, passenger vehicle evaluation, Chrysler Australia; Motoring Editor, Harpers & Queen Magazine; *b* 17 Sept. 1929; *m* 1st, 1957, Kathleen Stuart (marr. diss. 1963), *y d* of F. Stuart Moison, Montreal, Canada; 2nd, 1964, Elaine (marr. diss. 1968), 2nd *d* of A. Barbarino, New York; one *d*. *Educ:* Haileybury and Imperial Service Coll. Brit. Nat. Champion, 1950, 1951, 1952, 1954, 1955, 1956, 1957, 1958, 1959, 1961; Tourist Trophy, 1950, 1951, 1955, 1958, 1959, 1960, 1961; Coupe des Alpes, 1952, 1953, 1954; Alpine Gold Cup (three consecutive wins), 1954. Only Englishman to win Italian Mille Miglia, 1955. Competed in 466 races, rallies, sprints, land speed records and endurance runs, and won 194 of these. Successes include Targa Florio, 1955; Brit. Grand Prix, 1955, 1957; Ital. GP, 1956, 1957, 1959; NZ GP, 1956, 1959; Monaco GP, 1956, 1960, 1961; Leguna Seca GP, 1960, 1961; US GP, 1959, 1960; Aust. GP, 1956; Bari GP, 1956; Pescara GP, 1957; Swedish GP, 1957; Dutch GP, 1958; Argentine GP, 1958; Morocco GP, 1958; Buenos Aires GP, 1958; Melbourne GP, 1958; Villareal GP, 1958; Caen GP, 1958; Portuguese GP, 1959; S African GP, 1960; Cuban GP, 1960; Austrian GP, 1960; Cape GP, 1960; Watkins Glen GP, 1960; German GP, 1961; Modena GP, 1961. Twice voted Driver of the Year, 1954 and 1961. *Publications:* Stirling Moss's Book of Motor Sport, 1955; In the Track of Speed, 1957; Stirling Moss's Second Book of Motor Sport, 1958; Le Mans, 1959; My Favourite Car Stories, 1960; A Turn at the Wheel, 1961; All But My Life, 1963; Design and Behaviour of the Racing Car, 1964; How to Watch Motor Racing, 1975; *relevant publication:* Stirling Moss, by Robert Raymond, 1953. *Recreations:* snow-ski-ing, water ski-ing, dancing, spear-fishing, model making, the theatre, and designing. *Address:* (business) Stirling Moss Ltd, 46 Shepherd Street, W1; (residence) 44 Shepherd Street, W1. *Clubs:* White Elephant; British Racing Drivers', British Automobile Racing, British Racing and Sports Car, Road Racing Drivers of America, 200 mph, Lord's Taverners, Royal Automobile; Internationale des Anciens Pilotes; Chm. or Pres. of 28 motoring clubs.

MÖSSBAUER, Rudolf L., PhD; Professor of Experimental Physics; Director of the Institute Max von Laue-Paul Langevin, and of the French-German-British High-Flux-Reactor at Grenoble, since 1972; on five years' leave of absence from Technical University of Munich; *b* Munich, 31 Jan. 1929; *m* 1957, Elisabeth Pritz; one *s* two *d*. *Educ:* High Sch. and Inst. of Technology, Munich (equiv. Bachelor's and Master's degrees). PhD (Munich) 1958. Research Asst Max Planck Inst., Heidelberg, 1955-57; Research Fellow: Inst. of Techn., Munich, 1958-60, and at Caltech, 1960, Sen. Research Fellow, Caltech, 1961; Prof. of Experimental Physics, Munich, 1964. Hon. DSc Oxford, 1973. Research Corporation Award, New York, 1960; Röntgen award, Univ. of Giessen, Germany, 1961; Elliot Cresson Medal, Franklin Inst., Philadelphia, 1961; Nobel Prize for Physics, 1961, etc. Bavarian Order of Merit, 1962. *Publications:* Nobel Lecture, Rückstossfreie Kernresonanzabsorption von Gammastrahlung, 1961 (Stockholm); papers on Recoilless Nuclear Resonance Absorption in learned jls and proc. societies, etc. *Recreations:* photography, music, archæology. *Address:* Institut Max von Laue-Paul Langevin, BP 156, avenue des Martyrs, 38042 Grenoble Cedex, France.

MOSTYN, 5th Baron, cr 1831; **Roger Edward Lloyd Lloyd-Mostyn,** Bt 1778; MC 1943; *b* 17 April 1920; *e s* of 4th Baron Mostyn; *S* father, 1965; *m* 1943, Yvonne Margaret Stuart (marr. diss., 1957), *y d* of A. Stuart Johnston, Henshall Hall, Congleton, Cheshire; one *s* one *d*; 2nd, 1957, Mrs Sheila Edmondson Shaw, *o c* of Major Reginald Fairweather, Stockwell Manor, Silverton, Devon, and of Mrs Fairweather, Yew Tree Cottage, Fordcombe, Kent. *Educ:* Eton; Royal Military College, Sandhurst. 2nd Lt, 9th Queen's Royal Lancers, 1939. Served War 1939-45, France, North Africa, and Italy (wounded, despatches, MC). Temp. Major, 1946. *Heir: s* Hon. Llewellyn Roger Lloyd Lloyd-Mostyn [*b* 26 Sept. 1948; *m* 1974, Denise Suzanne, *d* of Roger Duvarel; one *d*. *Educ:* Eton. Called to the Bar, Middle Temple, 1973]. *Address:* Mostyn Hall, Mostyn, Clwyd, North Wales. *T:* Mostyn 222.

MOSTYN, Sir Jeremy (John Anthony), 14th Bt cr 1670; Senior Partner, Mostyn & Co., Estate Agents, Woodstock, Oxford; *b* 24 Nov. 1933; *s* of Sir Basil Anthony Trevor Mostyn, 13th Bt and Anita Mary, *d* of late Lt-Col Rowland Charles Feilding, DSO; *S* father 1956; *m* 1963, Cristina, *o d* of Marchese Orengo, Turin; one *s* two *d*. *Educ:* Rhodesia and Downside. Contested: Ealing South (L) General Election, 1959; Cities of London and Westminster, LCC Elections, 1960. Green Staff Officer, Investiture of the Prince of Wales, 1969. FRSA. Kt of Honour and Devotion, SMO Malta. *Recreation:* saving and restoring old houses. *Heir: s* William Basil John Mostyn, *b* 15 Oct 1975. *Address:* The Manor House, Lower Heyford, Oxon; 29 Aynhoe Road, W14. *Club:* Travellers'.

MOTE, Harold Trevor, DL, JP; Member for Harrow East, Greater London Council, since 1965; company director, company consultant and engineer; *b* 28 Oct. 1919; *s* of late Harold Roland Mote; *m* 1944, Amplias Pamela, *d* of late Harold Johnson, Oswestry; three *s* one *d*. *Educ:* Upper Latymer Sch.; St Paul's Sch.; Regent Street Polytechnic; Army Staff Coll. RE, TA, 1936; served War, Royal Signals, 1940-46 (Lt-Col); Royal Signals, TA, 1954. Councillor, Harrow, 1953-67, Alderman 1967; 1st Mayor, London Bor. of Harrow, 1965-66; Opposition Leader, Harrow Council, 1971-73, Leader, 1973-77. Greater London Council: Dep. Leader, Planning and Communications Gp, 1977-; Chm., Public Transport Cttee, 1977-; formerly, Chm., Scrutiny Cttee, and Vice-Chm., Public Services Cttee; formerly, Opposition Leader, Fire Bde Cttee, W Area Planning Cttee, and Transportation Cttee. Mem., Thames Water Authority, 1973- (Chm., Personnel Sub-Cttee, 1973-). JP Mddx 1965; DL Greater London 1967. *Address:* Parkville House, 8 Red Lion Parade, Pinner, Mddx. *T:* 01-868 3171; Mecury, London Road, Rickmansworth, Herts. *T:* Rickmansworth 74366.

MOTHERWELL, Bishop of, (RC), since 1964; **Rt. Rev. Francis Thomson;** Hon. Canon of St Andrews and Edinburgh, since 1961; *b* 15 May 1917; *s* of late Francis Thomson, MA and late Winifred Mary Clare (*née* Forsyth). *Educ:* George Watson's Coll., Edinburgh; Edinburgh Univ.; Christ's Coll., Cambridge; St Edmund's Coll., Ware; Angelicum Univ., Rome. MA Edinburgh 1938; BA Cambridge 1940; Priest, 1946; STL (Angelicum, Rome) 1949. Asst Priest: St Patrick's, Kilsyth, 1946-48; St James', St Andrews, 1949-52; St Cuthbert's, Edinburgh, 1952-53; Prof. of Dogmatic Theology, St Andrew's Coll. Drygrange, Melrose, 1953-60; Rector of St Mary's Coll., Blairs, Aberdeen, 1960-64. *Address:* Bishop's House, Bothwell, Glasgow. *T:* Bothwell 853115.

MOTT, John Charles Spencer, CEng, FICE, FIStructE; Chairman and Chief Executive, J. L. Kier Ltd, since 1976; Chairman: French Kier Holdings Ltd, 1974 (Director, on merger, 1973); Charles Brand & Son Ltd; W. C. French (Construction) Ltd; Kier Ltd; Kier International Ltd; *b* Beckenham, Kent, 18 Dec. 1926; *m* 1953, Patricia Mary (*née* Fowler); two *s*. *Educ:* Balgowan Central Sch., Beckenham, Kent; Brixton Sch. of Building; Battersea Polytechnic; Rutherford Coll. of Technology, Newcastle upon Tyne. Served war, Lieut, Royal Marines, 1943-46. Indentured as Engr under agreement with L. G. Mouchel & Partners, 1949-52; joined Kier Ltd, as engr, 1952; Agent on heavy civil engrg contracts, 1952-63. Director: Kier Ltd, 1963; J. L. Kier Ltd (Holding Co.), 1968. Past Member: Council, Instn Civil Engrs; Bragg Cttee of Falsework. *Recreations:* golf, gardening. *Address:* (home) 91 Long Road, Cambridge; (office) Tempsford Hall, Sandy, Beds SG19 2BD. *T:* Bedford 55111. *Club:* Danish.

MOTT, Sir John (Harmar), 3rd Bt, cr 1930; Regional Medical Officer, Department of Health and Social Security; *b* 21 July 1922; *s* of 2nd Bt and Mary Katherine (*d* 1972) *d* of late Rev. A. H. Stanton; *S* father, 1964; *m* 1950, Elizabeth (*née* Carson); one *s* two *d*. *Educ:* Radley Coll.; New Coll., Oxford. MA Oxford, 1948; BM, BCh, 1951. Served War of 1939-45: Pilot, Royal Air Force, 1943-46. Middlesex Hospital: House Physician, 1951; House Surgeon, 1952. Mem., RCGP. *Recreations:* sailing, photography. *Heir: s* David Hugh Mott, *b* 1 May 1952. *Address:* Daffodil Lodge, Park Road, Waterloo Park, Liverpool L22 3XG. *T:* 051-928 3112.

MOTT, Sir Nevill (Francis), Kt 1962; FRS 1936; MA Cantab; Cavendish Professor of Physics, Cambridge University, 1954-71; Senior Research Fellow, Imperial College, London, 1971-73; *b* 30 Sept. 1905; *s* of C. F. Mott, late Dir of Educn, Liverpool, and Lilian Mary Reynolds; *m* 1930, Ruth Horder; two *d*. *Educ:* Clifton Coll.; St John's Coll., Cambridge. Lecturer at Manchester Univ., 1929-30; Fellow and Lecturer, Gonville and Caius Coll., Cambridge, 1930-33; Melville Wills Prof. of Theoretical Physics in the Univ. of Bristol, 1933-48; Henry Overton Wills Prof. and Dir of the Henry Herbert Wills Physical Laboratories, Univ. of Bristol, 1948-54. Master of Gonville and Caius Coll., Univ. of Cambridge, 1959-66. Corr. mem., Amer. Acad. of Arts and Sciences, 1954; Pres., International Union of Physics, 1951-57; Pres., Mod. Languages Assoc., 1955; Pres., Physical Soc., 1956-58; Mem. Governing Board of Nat. Inst. for Research in Nuclear Science, 1957-60; Mem. Central Advisory Council for Education for England, 1956-59; Mem. Academic Planning Cttee and Council of University Coll. of Sussex; Chm. Ministry of Education's Standing Cttee on Supply of Teachers, 1959-62; Chairman: Nuffield Foundation's Cttee on Physics Education, 1961; Physics Education Cttee (Royal Society and Inst. of Physics), 1965-71. Chairman, Taylor & Francis, Scientific Publishers, 1970-75, Pres., 1976-. Foreign Associate, Nat. Acad. of Sciences of USA, 1957; Hon. Member: Akademie der Naturforscher Leopoldina, 1964; Société Française de Physique, 1970; Inst. of Metals, Japan, 1975; Hon. Fellow, UMIST. Hon. DSc (Louvain, Grenoble, Paris, Poitiers, Bristol, Ottawa, Liverpool, Reading, Sheffield, London, Warwick, Lancaster, Heriot-Watt, Oxon, East Anglia); Hon. Doctorate of Technology, Linköping, Sweden. Hon. FInstP 1972. Hughes Medal of Royal Society, 1941; Royal Medal, 1953; Grande Médaille de la Société Française de Métallurgie, 1970; Copley Medal, 1972; Faraday Medal, IEE, 1973; (jtly) Nobel Prize for Physics, 1977. Chevalier, Ordre Nat. du Mérite, France, 1977. *Publications:* An Outline of Wave Mechanics, 1930; The Theory of Atomic Collisions (with H. S. W. Massey), 1933; The Theory of the Properties of Metals and Alloys (with H. Jones), 1936; Electronic Processes in Ionic Crystals (with R. W. Gurney), 1940; Wave Mechanics and its Applications (with I. N. Snedden), 1948; Elements of Wave Mechanics, 1952; Atomic Structure and the Strength of Metals, 1956; Electronic Processes in Non-Crystalline Materials (with E. A. Davis), 1971; Elementary Quantum Mechanics, 1972; Metal-Insulator Transitions, 1974; various contribs to scientific periodicals about Atomic Physics, Metals, Semi-conductors and Photographic Emulsions and Glasses. *Recreations:* numismatics, photography. *Address:* The Cavendish Laboratory, Madingley Road, Cambridge CB3 0HE; 31 Sedley Taylor Road, Cambridge CB2 2PN. *Club:* Athenæum.

MOTT, Norman Gilbert, CMG 1962; retired, 1969; *b* 7 Sept. 1910; *s* of late Albert Norman Mott and late Ada Emily Kilby; *m* 1941, Betty Mary, *d* of late Sidney Hugh Breeze; two *s*. *Educ:* Christ's Coll., Finchley. Served in HM Forces (Intelligence Corps), 1940-47. Joined HM Diplomatic Service, 1948; served since in Foreign Office and at Trieste. *Recreations:* gardening, photography. *Address:* 34 Ferndale Road, Chichester, West Sussex. *T:* Chichester 527960.

MOTT-RADCLYFFE, Sir Charles (Edward), Kt 1957; DL; Captain Rifle Brigade, Reserve of Officers; *b* 1911; *o s* of Lt-Col C. E. Radclyffe, DSO, Rifle Brigade (killed in action 1915), Little Park, Wickham, Hants, and Theresa Caroline, *o d* of John Stanley Mott, JP, Barningham Hall, Norfolk; *m* 1940, Diana (*d* 1955), *d* of late Lt-Col W. Gibbs, CVO, 7th Hussars; three *d*; *m* 1956, Stella, *d* of late Lionel Harrisson, Caynham Cottage, Ludlow, Salop. *Educ:* Eton; Balliol Coll., Oxford. Hon. Attaché Diplomatic Service, Athens and Rome, 1936-38; Mem. Military Mission to Greece, 1940-41; served as Liaison Officer in Syria, 1941, and with Rifle Brigade in Middle East and Italy, 1943-44; MP (C) Windsor, 1942-70; Parliamentary Private Sec. to Sec. of State for India (Rt Hon. L. S. Amery), Dec. 1944-May 1945; Junior Lord of the Treasury, May-July 1945; Conservative Whip, Aug. 1945-Feb. 1946; Chm. Conservative Parly Foreign Affairs Cttee, 1951-59. Mem., Plowden Commn on Overseas Representative Services, 1963-64. A Governor of Gresham's

Sch., Holt; Mem., Historic Buildings Council for England, 1962-70; President: Country Landowners Assoc. (Norfolk Branch), 1972-; Norfolk CCC, 1972-74 (Chm., 1976-). High Sheriff, 1974, DL 1977, of Norfolk. Comdr, Order of Phoenix (Greece). *Publication:* Foreign Body in the Eye (a memoir of the Foreign Service), 1975. *Recreations:* cricket, shooting. *Address:* Barningham Hall, Matlaske, Norfolk. *T:* Matlaske 250; Flat 1, 38 Cadogan Square, SW1. *T:* 01-584 5834. *Clubs:* Turf, Buck's, Pratt's, MCC.

MOTTELSON, Prof. Ben R., PhD; Danish physicist; Professor, Nordic Institute for Theoretical Atomic Physics, Copenhagen, since 1957; *b* Chicago, Ill, USA, 9 July 1926; *s* of Goodman Mottelson and Georgia Mottelson (*née* Blum); *m* 1948, Nancy Jane Reno; three *c*; became a Danish citizen, 1971. *Educ:* High Sch., La Grange, Ill; Purdue Univ. (officers' trng, USN, V12 program; BSc 1947); Harvard Univ. (grad. studies, PhD 1950). Sheldon Trav. Fellowship from Harvard at Inst. of Theoretical Physics, Copenhagen (later, the Niels Bohr Inst.), 1950-51. His Fellowship from US Atomic Energy Commn permitted continuation of work in Copenhagen for two more years, after which he held research position in CERN (European Organization for Nuclear Research) theoretical study group, formed in Copenhagen. Visiting Prof., Univ. of Calif at Berkeley, Spring term, 1959. Nobel Prize for Physics (jtly), 1975; awarded for work on theory of Atomic Nucleus, with Dr Aage Bohr (3 papers publ. 1952-53). *Publications:* Nuclear Structure, vol. I, 1969; vol. II, 1975 (with A. Bohr); contrib. Rev. Mod. Phys (jt), etc. *Address:* Nordita, Copenhagen, Denmark.

MOTTERSHEAD, Frank William, CB 1957; Deputy Secretary, Department of Health and Social Security (formerly Ministry of Health), 1965-71; *b* 7 Sept. 1911; *o s* of late Thomas Hastings and Adeline Mottershead; unmarried. *Educ:* King Edward's Sch., Birmingham; St John's Coll., Cambridge. BA 1933, MA 1973. Entered Secretary's Dept of Admiralty, 1934; Principal Private Sec. to First Lord, 1944-46; idc 1949; Under Sec., 1950; Transferred to Ministry of Defence, 1956; Deputy Sec., 1958; Deputy Under-Sec. of State, 1964. *Address:* Old Warden, Grevel Lane, Chipping Campden, Glos. *T:* Evesham 840548. *Club:* United Oxford & Cambridge University.

MOTTISTONE, 4th Baron, *cr* 1933, of Mottistone; **David Peter Seely;** Director, Cake and Biscuit Alliance, since 1975; *b* 16 Dec. 1920; 4th *s* of 1st Baron Mottistone; *S* half brother, 1966; *m* 1944, Anthea, *er d* of T. V. W. McMullan, Bangor, Co. Down, N Ireland; two *s* two *d* (and one *d* decd). *Educ:* RN Coll., Dartmouth. Convoy escorting, Atlantic and Mediterranean, 1941-44; qualified in Communications, 1944; Served in Pacific, 1945; in comd HMS Cossack, FE Flt, 1958-59; in comd HMS Ajax and 24th Escort Sqdn, FE Flt (offensive ops against Indonesian confrontation) (despatches), 1963-65; Naval Advr to UK High Comr, Ottawa, 1965-66; retired at own request as a Captain, 1967. Dir of Personnel and Training, Radio Rentals Gp, 1967-69; Dir, Distributive Industry Trng Bd, 1969-75. FIERE; FIPM; MBIM. *Recreation:* yachting. *Heir: s* Hon. Peter John Philip Seely [*b* 29 Oct. 1949; *m* 1972, Joyce (marr. diss. 1975), *d* of Mr and Mrs Cairns, Stirling; one *s*]. *Address:* The Old Parsonage, Mottistone, Isle of Wight. *Clubs:* Royal Commonwealth Society; Royal Yacht Squadron, Royal Cruising, Island Sailing, Royal Navy Sailing Association.

MOTYER, Rev. John Alexander; Principal and Dean of College, Trinity College, Bristol, since Oct. 1971; *b* 30 Aug. 1924; *s* of Robert Shankey and Elizabeth Maud Motyer; *m* 1948, Beryl Grace Mays; two *s* one *d*. *Educ:* High Sch., Dublin; Dublin Univ. (MA, BD); Wycliffe Hall, Oxford. Curate: St Philip, Penn Fields, Wolverhampton, 1947-50; Holy Trinity, Old Market, Bristol, 1950-54; Tutor, Clifton Theol Coll., Bristol, 1950-54, Vice-Principal, 1954-65; Vicar, St Luke's, Hampstead, 1965-70; Dep. Principal, Tyndale Hall, Bristol, 1970-71. *Publications:* The Revelation of the Divine Name, 1959; After Death, 1965; The Richness of Christ (Epistle to the Philippians), 1966; The Tests of Faith (Epistle of James), 1970, 2nd edn 1975; (Old Testament Editor) New Bible Commentary Revised, 1970; The Day of the Lion (Amos), 1975; contributor: New Bible Dictionary; Expositor's Bible Commentary; New International Dictionary of New Testament Theology. *Recreations:* reading, odd-jobbing. *Address:* Trinity College, Stoke Hill, Bristol BS9 1JP. *T:* Bristol 684472.

MOTZ, Prof. Hans; Professor of Engineering, University of Oxford, 1972-77, now Emeritus; Emeritus Fellow of St John's College, Oxford; Consultant, Culham Laboratory, United Kingdom Atomic Energy Authority, since 1977; *b* 1 Oct. 1909; *s* of Karl and Paula Motz; *m* 1959, Lotte Norwood-Edlis; one *d*. *Educ:* Technische Hochschule, Vienna; Besançon Univ. (Schol.); Trinity Coll., Dublin (Schol.). Dipl. Ing 1932, Dr Techn. Sc.

1935, MSc TCD, MA Oxon; FInstP. Research Engr, Standard Telephones & Cables, 1939-41; Demonstrator, Dept of Engrg Science, Oxford, 1941; Lectr in Engrg Physics, Sheffield Univ., 1946-48; Research Assoc., Microwave Lab., Stanford Univ., 1949; Donald Pollock Reader in Engrg Science, Oxford, 1954; Professorial Fellow, St Catherine's Coll., Oxford, 1963, Emeritus Fellow, 1977-. Internat. Fellow, Stanford Res. Inst., 1956; Vis. Prof., Brown Univ., 1959; Guest Prof., Paris Univ. (Saclay), 1964; Vis. Prof., Brooklyn Polytech., 1965; Vis. Prof., Innsbruck Univ., 1976. *Publications:* Problems of Microwave Theory, 1951; many papers in sci. jls. *Recreations:* ski-ing, yachting, silversmith, and enamel work. *Address:* 16 Bedford Street, Oxford. *T:* Oxford 41895.

MOULD-GRAHAM, Colonel Robert, OBE 1944; MC 1918; TD 1930; DL; FCA; Consultant, Graham Proom & Smith, Chartered Accountants, Newcastle upon Tyne and Sunderland, 1966-76; Secretary, Royal British Legion Attendants Co. Ltd; Director: Cold Rolling Mills Ltd; A. M. Forster Ltd, 1951-76; Guardian Assurance Co. Ltd (Local Board), 1930-68; Northern Rock Building Society, 1939-71 (Chairman, 1954-67); W. E. Moffett and Co. Ltd, 1946-69 (Chairman); Part-time Member North Eastern Electricity Board, 1956-65; President Tyneside Chamber of Commerce, 1963-65; *b* 1895; *s* of late Joseph Graham, BSc, Corbridge, Northumberland; *m* 1st, 1922, Beatrice (*d* 1931), *d* of late H. S. Vincent; (one *d* decd); 2nd, 1937, Jocelyn Edith Katherine, MBE 1946, Col Comdt, Church Girls Brigade, 1967-, *d* of late Comdr F. P. Saunders, RN; one *s* one *d* (and one *d* decd). *Educ:* Rutherford Coll., Newcastle upon Tyne. Served European War, 1914-18, with 72 Field Regt, RA (France and Belgium); War of 1939-45 (despatches twice); with 272 Field Regt, RA (TA) and Staff, France, Belgium, N Africa and Italy. Hon. Col 272 Field Regt, 1949-65. A mem. of House of Laity Church Assembly, 1952-60; Newcastle Diocesan Soc., and Diocesan Bd of Finance, 1948-66; Mem., Salisbury Diocesan Bd of Finance, 1967-73. Chm., Buckland Newton Br., Brit. Legion, 1966-; Mem., Dorset County Cttee, 1967-, Vice-Pres., 1974. Alderman of Newcastle upon Tyne, 1949-61; Pres. Newcastle Central Br., Royal Brit. Legion, 1948-65; Tyne Improvement Comr, 1947-58; Sheriff of Newcastle upon Tyne, 1951-52, Lord Mayor 1954-55. JP 1948; DL Northumberland, 1953, Tyne and Wear, 1974. *Address:* The Manor House, Alton Pancras, Dorchester, Dorset DT2 7RW. *T:* Piddletrenthide 354. *Clubs:* Army and Navy; Northern Counties (Newcastle).

MOULE, Rev. Prof. Charles Francis Digby, FBA 1966; Lady Margaret's Professor of Divinity in the University of Cambridge, 1951-76; Fellow of Clare College, Cambridge, since 1944; Canon Theologian (non-residentiary) of Leicester, 1955-76, Canon Emeritus, since 1976; Honorary Member of Staff, Ridley Hall, Cambridge, since 1976; *b* 3 Dec. 1908; *s* of late Rev. Henry William Moule and Laura Clements Pope; unmarried. *Educ:* Weymouth Coll., Dorset; Emmanuel Coll., Cambridge (scholar) (Hon. Fellow 1972); Ridley Hall, Cambridge. 1st Cl. Classical Tripos Part I, 1929; BA (1st Cl. Classical Tripos Part II), 1931; Evans Prize, 1931; Jeremie Septuagint Prize, 1932; Crosse Scholarship, 1933; MA 1934. Deacon, 1933, priest, 1934; Curate, St Mark's, Cambridge, and Tutor of Ridley Hall, 1933-34; Curate, St Andrew's, Rugby, 1934-36; Vice-Principal, Ridley Hall, 1936-44, and Curate of St Mary the Great, Cambridge, 1936-40. Dean of Clare Coll., Cambridge, 1944-51; Faculty Asst Lecturer in Divinity in the Univ. of Cambridge, 1944-47; Univ. Lecturer, 1947-51. Burkitt Medal for Biblical Studies, British Acad., 1970. Hon. DD Univ. of St Andrews, 1958. *Publications:* An Idiom Book of New Testament Greek, 1953; The Meaning of Hope, 1953; The Sacrifice of Christ, 1956; Colossians and Philemon (Cambridge Greek Testament Commentary), 1957; Worship in the New Testament, 1961; The Birth of the New Testament, 1962; The Phenomenon of the New Testament, 1967; (co-editor) Christian History and Interpretation, 1968; The Origin of Christology, 1977; contrib., Encyclopædia Britannica, Interpreter's Dictionary of the Bible, Biblisch-Historisches Handwörterbuch. *Address:* Ridley Hall, Cambridge.

MOULE-EVANS, David, DMus Oxon; Composer; Conductor; Professor of Harmony, Counterpoint and Composition, Royal College of Music, 1945-74; *b* 21 Nov. 1905; *s* of John Evans, MA Cantab, and Emily Blanche Evans (*née* Cookson); *m* 1935, Monica Warden Evans, *d* of Richardson Evans, ICS; no *c*. *Educ:* The Judd Sch.; Royal College of Music. Mem. of Queen's Coll., Oxford. Open Scholarship in Composition, RCM, 1925 (Senior Composition Scholar); Mendelssohn Scholarship, 1928; DMus Oxford, 1930. Carnegie Publication Award (for Concerto for String Orchestra), 1928. Symphony in G Major awarded £1,000 Prize offered by Australian Govt, 1952. Many public and broadcast performances of orchestral and other works. *Publications: Published orchestral works include:* Overture: The

Spirit of London, 1947; Vienna Rhapsody, 1948; The Haunted Place (for String Orchestra), 1949; Old Tupper's Dance, 1951; chamber works: instrumental pieces and songs. *Recreations:* reading and studying subjects other than music; perambulating the countryside and looking at old churches. *Address:* Merry Down, Harrow Road West, Dorking, Surrey RH4 3BA. *T:* Dorking 4080.

MOULTON, Alexander Eric, CBE 1976; RDI; Managing Director, Moulton Developments Ltd, since 1956; Director: Moulton Bicycles Ltd since 1967; Alex Moulton (formerly Moulton Consultants) Ltd since 1967; Bicycle Consultants Ltd since 1967; *b* 9 April 1920; *s* of John Coney Moulton, DSc, The Hall, Bradfield on Avon, and Beryl Latimer Moulton. *Educ:* Marlborough Coll.; King's Coll., Cambridge (MA). Bristol Aeroplane Co., 1939-44: Engine Research Dept; George Spencer, Moulton & Co. Ltd, 1945-56; became Techn. Dir; estab. Research Dept (originated work on rubber suspensions for vehicles, incl. own design Flexitor); formed Moulton Developments Ltd, 1956 to do develt work on own designs of rubber suspensions for BLMC incl. Hydrolastic and Hydragas (Queen's Award to Industry, 1967); formed Moulton Bicycles Ltd to produce own design Moulton Bicycle, 1962 (Design Centre Award, 1964); designer of Moulton Coach. FRSA, 1968; Hon. Dr, RCA, 1967; Hon. DSc Bath, 1971. RDI 1968; SIAD Design Medal, 1976. *Publications:* numerous articles and papers on engineering and education. *Recreations:* canoeing, steam boating, shooting. *Address:* The Hall, Bradford-on-Avon, Wilts. *T:* Bradford-on-Avon 2991. *Clubs:* Brooks's; Royal Thames Yacht; Royal Southern Yacht (Hamble).

MOULTON, Maj.-Gen. James Louis, CB 1956; DSO 1944; OBE 1950; retired; *b* 3 June 1906; *s* of Capt. J. D. Moulton, RN; *m* 1937, Barbara Aline (*née* Coode); one *s* one *d*. *Educ:* Sutton Valence Sch. Joined Royal Marines, 1924; Pilot, Fleet Air Arm, 1930; Staff Coll., Camberley, 1938; served War of 1939-45: GSO3 GHQ, BEF, 1940; GSO1, Force 121 (Madagascar), 1942; Commanding Officer, 48 Commando, NW Europe, 1944-45 (DSO); Comd 4th Commando Bde, NW Europe, 1945; CO Commando Sch., 1947-49; Comd 3rd Commando Bde, Middle East, 1952-54; Maj.-Gen. Royal Marines, Portsmouth, 1954-57; Chief of Amphibious Warfare, 1957-61. Rep. Col Comdt RM, 1971-72. Editor, Brassey's Annual, 1969-73. *Publications:* Haste to the Battle, 1963; Defence in a Changing World, 1964; The Norwegian Campaign of 1940, 1966; British Maritime Strategy in the 1970s, 1969; The Royal Marines, 1972; Battle of Antwerp, 1977. *Address:* Fairmile, Woodham Road, Woking, Surrey GU21 4DN. *T:* Woking 5174. *Club:* Royal Automobile.

MOULTON, Air Vice-Marshal Leslie Howard, CB 1971; DFC 1941; with The Plessey Co., since 1971; *b* 3 Dec. 1915; *s* of late Peter Moulton, Nantwich, Cheshire; *m* Lesley, *d* of late P. C. Clarke, Ilford; two *s* two *d*. *Educ:* Nantwich and Acton School. Joined RAF, 1932; served War of 1939-45, Pilot; Operations with 14 Sqdn in Africa, 1940-42; CFS, 1942-44; specialised in Signals, 1945; Staff Coll., 1950; USAF, Strategic Air Comd, 1954-56; Dep. Dir Radio, Air Min., 1958-61; Comdt RAF Cosford, 1961-63; CSO Fighter Comd, 1963-65; Min. of Technology, 1965-68. Wing Comdr 1955; Gp Captain 1959; Air Cdre 1964; Air Vice-Marshal 1969; AOC No 90 (Signals) Group, RAF, 1969-71; retired 1971. FIERE, CEng, 1959; FRSA, 1974. *Recreations:* gardening, golf, hill walking. *Address:* Plessey Radar, Addlestone, Surrey; Childs Acre, Church Lane, Three Mile Cross, Berks. *T:* Reading 883327. *Club:* Royal Air Force.

MOUNSEY, John Patrick David, MA, MD, FRCP; Provost, Welsh National School of Medicine, since Oct. 1969; *b* 1 Feb. 1914; *s* of late John Edward Mounsey and late Christine Frances Trail Robertson; *m* 1947, Vera Madeline Sara King; one *s* one *d*. *Educ:* Eton Coll.; King's Coll., Cambridge; King's Coll. Hosp., London. Sherbrook Res. Fellow, Cardiac Dept, London Hosp., 1951; Royal Postgraduate Medical School: Lectr, 1960; Sen. Lectr and Sub-Dean, 1962; Cons. Cardiologist, Hammersmith Hosp., 1960; Dep. Dir, British Postgrad. Med. Fedn, 1967; Member: GMC, 1970; GDC, 1973; South Glamorgan AHA (T); Council, British Heart Foundn; British Cardiac Soc.; Assoc. of Physicians; Soc. of Physicians in Wales. Corresp. Mem., Australasian Cardiac Soc.; late Asst Ed., British Heart Jl. *Publications:* articles on cardiology mainly in British Heart Jl. *Recreations:* gardening, music. *Address:* St Quintins, Llanblethian, Cowbridge, South Glamorgan. *T:* Cowbridge 2415. *Clubs:* Athenæum; Cardiff and County.

MOUNT, Air Cdre Christopher John, CBE 1956; DSO 1943; DFC 1940; retired; *b* 14 Dec. 1913; *s* of Capt. F. Mount; *m* 1947, Audrey Mabel Clarke; two *s*. *Educ:* Eton; Trinity Coll., Oxford. Royal Auxiliary Air Force, 1935; Royal Air Force, 1938. Vice-

Chm. (Air) Eastern Wessex T&AVR. Partner with C. R. Thomas & Son, Solicitors, Maidenhead. *Address:* Garden House, Bagshot Road, Sunninghill, Ascot, Berks.

MOUNT, Sir William (Malcolm), 2nd Bt, *cr* 1921; Lieutenant-Colonel Reconnaissance Corps; *b* 28 Dec. 1904; *s* of Sir William Mount, 1st Bt, CBE, and Hilda Lucy Adelaide (*d* 1950), OBE, *y d* of late Malcolm Low of Clatto, Fife; *S* father, 1930; *m* 1929, Elizabeth Nance, *o d* of Owen John Llewellyn, Badminton Vicarage, Glos; three *d*. *Educ:* Eton; New Coll., Oxford. Berkshire: DL 1946; High Sheriff, 1947-48; Vice-Lieutenant, 1960-76. *Recreations:* fishing, shooting. *Heir: nephew* William Robert Ferdinand Mount [*b* 2 July 1939; *m* 1968, Julia Margaret, twin *d* of Archibald Julian Lucas; two *s* two *d*]. *Address:* Wasing Place, Aldermaston, Berks.
See also Sir W. S. Dugdale, Bt.

MOUNT CHARLES, Earl of; Henry Vivian Pierpoint Conyngham; *b* 23 May 1951; *s* and *heir* of 7th Marquess Conyngham, *qv*; *m* 1971, Juliet Ann, *yr d* of Robert Kitson; one *s* one *d*. *Educ:* Harrow; Harvard Univ. *Heir: s* Viscount Slane, *qv*. *Address:* Slane Castle, Co. Meath, Eire. *Club:* Kildare Street and University (Dublin).

MOUNT EDGCUMBE, 7th Earl of, *cr* 1789; **Edward Piers Edgcumbe;** Viscount Mount Edgcumbe and Valletort, 1781; Baron Edgcumbe of Mount Edgcumbe, Co. Cornwall (UK), 1742; *b* 13 July 1903; *s* of George Valletort Edgcumbe (*d* 1947) and Georgina Mildred (*d* 1941), *d* of T. A. Bell; *S* cousin 1965; *m* 1944, Victoria Effie Warbrick (widow), *y d* of late Robert Campbell, N Ireland and NZ. *Heir: nephew* Robert Charles Edgcumbe [*b* 1 June 1939; *m* 1960; five *d*]. *Address:* Mount Edgcumbe, Plymouth.

MOUNTAIN, Sir Denis Mortimer, 3rd Bt *cr* 1922; Chairman and Managing Director, Eagle Star Insurance Co. Ltd, since 1959; *b* 2 June 1929; *er s* of Sir Brian Edward Stanley Mountain, 2nd Bt, and of Doris Elsie, *e d* of late E. C. E. Lamb; *S* father, 1977; *m* 1958, Hélène Fleur Mary Kirwan-Taylor; two *s* one *d*. *Educ:* Eton. Late Lieut, Royal Horse Guards. Chairman: English Property Corporation Ltd; Australian Eagle Insurance Co. Ltd; South African Eagle Insurance Co. Ltd, and other companies both in UK and overseas; Director: Rank Organisation Ltd; Grovewood Securities Ltd (Dep. Chm.); Philip Hill Investment Trust Ltd and other UK and overseas companies. *Recreations:* fishing, shooting. *Heir: s* Edward Brian Stanford Mountain, *b* 19 March 1961. *Address:* Shawford Park, Shawford, near Winchester, Hants. *T:* Twyford 712289; 12 Queens Elm Square, Old Church Street, Chelsea SW3 6ED. *T:* 01-352 4331.

MOUNTAIN, Surgeon Rear-Adm. (D) William Leonard, CB 1966; OBE 1953; LDSRCS 1931; Director of Naval Dental Services, Ministry of Defence, 1964-68; *b* 29 Feb. 1908; *s* of William Mountain, LDS, Cowes, IoW; *m* 1946, Glenda Fleming, *d* of late Cyril Fleming, Groombridge, Sussex; one *d*. *Educ:* Sherborne Sch.; Guy's Hosp. Joined Royal Navy in rank of Surg.-Lt (D), 1933; Surg. Lt-Comdr (D) 1939. Served in HM Ships: Glasgow, Woolwich, Duke of York, Furious and Rodney, 1939-45; Fleet Dental Surg., Home Fleet, 1943-45; Surg. Comdr (D), 1948; Asst Dep. Dir-Gen. Dental Services, 1948-55; Surg. Captain (D), 1955; Command Dental Surg., The Nore, 1955-59; Fleet Dental Surg., Mediterranean, 1960; Command Dental Surg., Portsmouth, 1961-64; Surg. Rear-Adm. (D) 1964. QHDS, 1961-68. *Recreation:* golf. *Address:* 20 Yew Tree Road, Southborough, Tunbridge Wells, Kent. *T:* Tunbridge Wells 28378. *Club:* Royal Ashdown Forest.

MOUNTBATTEN, family name of **Marquess of Milford Haven** and **Earl Mountbatten of Burma.**

MOUNTBATTEN OF BURMA, 1st Earl, *cr* 1947; Baron Romsey, *cr* 1947; Viscount Mountbatten of Burma, *cr* 1946; **Admiral of the Fleet Louis (Francis Albert Victor Nicholas) Mountbatten,** KG 1946; PC 1947; GCB 1955 (KCB 1945; CB 1943); OM 1965; GCSI 1947; GCIE 1947; GCVO 1937 (KCVO 1922; MVO 1920); DSO 1941; FRS 1966; Hon. DCL (Oxford); Hon. LLD (Cambridge, Leeds, Edinburgh, Southampton, London, Sussex); Hon. DSc (Delhi and Patna); AMIEE 1927; AMRINA 1939; Governor of the Isle of Wight, 1965; Lord-Lieutenant of the Isle of Wight, since 1974; Personal ADC to the Queen since 1953 (Personal Naval ADC to King Edward VIII, 1936, and to King George VI, 1937-52); Col of the Life Guards, 1965; Col Commandant of the Royal Marines, 1965; Hon. Lt-Gen. and Air Marshal, 1942, and Hon. Colonel: Calcutta Light Horse, 1947; 292 Airborne Field Regt, 1947-55; 428th The Princess Beatrice IoW Rifles Heavy AA Regt, RA(TA), 1950-55; 289 Parachute Regt, RHA(TA), 1956; 4/5th Bn The Royal

Hampshire Regiment (TA), 1964-71; an Elder Brother of Trinity House; Grand President: Brit. Commonwealth Ex-Services League, 1946-74; Royal Life Saving Society; Royal Over-Seas League; Pres. of Council of SSAFA; King George's Fund for Sailors; Royal Naval Film Corporation, Royal Naval Saddle Club, Sailors Home and Red Ensign Club, Gordon Smith Inst., Liverpool, Training Ship Mercury and Commando Benevolent Fund; Society of Genealogists; Britain-Burma Soc.; Past Pres., Soc. of Film and Television Arts; Mem. and Past Pres., Inst. of Electronic and Radio Engineers; Chm. and Founder, National Electronics Research Council; Commodore Sea Scouts; Mem. and Past Prime Warden Shipwrights' Company; Hon. Mem. Honourable Company of Master Mariners; Mem. Mercers', Vintners' and Grocers' Companies; Royal Swedish Naval Soc.; Inner Magic Circle; Sword of Honour and Freedom of City of London, 1946; High Steward, 1940, and First Freeman, 1946, of Romsey; Freedom of City of Edinburgh, 1954; Freedom of Paimpol, 1961; *b* Frogmore House, Windsor, 25 June 1900; *yr s* of Adm. of the Fleet 1st Marquess of Milford Haven and Princess Victoria, *d* of Louis IV, Grand Duke of Hesse, KG, and of Princess Alice, Queen Victoria's Daughter; was known as Prince Louis Francis of Battenberg until, in 1917, his father relinquished title and assumed surname of Mountbatten; *m* 1922, Hon. Edwina Cynthia Annette Ashley (*d* 1960, in North Borneo, on tour as Superintendent-in-Chief, St John Ambulance Brigade), *d* of Lord Mount Temple, PC (Countess Mountbatten of Burma, CI, GBE, DCVO, LLD); two *d. Educ:* Locker's Park; Osborne and Dartmouth; Christ's Coll., Cambridge (Hon. Fellow, 1946). Naval Cadet, 1913; Midshipman, 1916; Sub-Lt, 1918; Lt, 1920; Lt-Comdr, 1928; Comdr, 1932; Capt., 1937; Cdre 1st Cl., 1941; Actg Vice-Adm., 1942; Actg Adm., 1943; Rear-Adm., 1946; Vice-Adm., 1949; Actg Adm., 1952; Adm. 1953; Adm. of the Fleet, 1956. Served in HMS Lion, 1916; HMS Queen Elizabeth, 1917; HM Sub. K6, 1918; HMS P31, 1918; HMS Renown, 1920 (Prince of Wales' Tour, Australia and New Zealand); HMS Repulse, 1921; HMS Renown, 1921 (Prince of Wales' Tour to India, Japan, and the Far East); HMS Revenge, 1923; Signal Sch., Portsmouth, 1924; RN Coll., Greenwich, 1925; Reserve Fleet Wireless and Signal Officer, 1926; Asst Fleet Wireless Officer, Mediterranean Fleet, 1927-28; 2nd Destroyer Flotilla Signal and Wireless Officer, 1928-29; Senior Wireless Instructor, Signal Sch., Portsmouth, 1929-31; Fleet Wireless Officer, Mediterranean Fleet, 1931-33; qualified as interpreter in French and German, 1933; in command of HMS Daring, 1934; and of HMS Wishart, 1935; Admiralty (Naval Air Div.), 1936; in command of HMS Kelly, and of the 5th Destroyer Flotilla, 1939 (despatches twice); in command of HMS Illustrious, 1941; Commodore Combined Ops, 1941-42; Chief of Combined Ops, 1942-43, and mem. of British Chiefs of Staff Cttee, 1942-43; Supreme Allied Comd, SE Asia, 1943-46; Viceroy of India, March-Aug. 1947; Governor-Gen. of India, Aug. 1947-June 1948; Flag Officer, Commanding 1st Cruiser Sqdn, Mediterranean Fleet, 1948-49; Fourth Sea Lord, 1950-52; Comdr-in-Chief, Mediterranean, 1952-54; concurrently C-in-C, Allied Forces, Mediterranean, 1953-54; First Sea Lord, 1955-59; Chief of UK Defence Staff and Chm. of Chiefs of Staff Cttee, 1959-65. Designated by the Home Sec. to examine into and report on prison security, Oct. 1966-. Chm., Council of Atlantic Colls, 1968-. For War Service: Legion of Merit, 1943, DSM, 1945 (US); Greek Mil. Cross (Crete), 1941; Grand Cross of Order of George I (Greece), 1946; Special Grand Cordon of the Cloud and Banner (China), 1945; Grand Cross of the Legion of Honour and Croix de Guerre (France), 1946; Grand Cross of: Star of Nepal, 1946; Order of White Elephant of Siam, 1946; Order of the Lion of the Netherlands, 1947. Not for War Service: KStJ 1943; Grand Cross of: Isabella Catolica (Spain), 1922; Crown of Rumania, 1924; Star of Rumania, 1937; Mil. Order of Avis (Portugal), 1951; The Seraphim (Sweden), 1952; Agga Maha Thiri Thudhamma (Burma), 1956; Grand Cross, Order of Dannebrog (Denmark), 1962; Grand Cross of the Order of the Seal of Solomon of Ethiopia, 1965. *Publications:* Time only to Look Forward (Speeches), 1949; Report to the Combined Chiefs of Staff by the Supreme Allied Commander SE Asia (1947), 1950; Reflections on the Transfer of Power and Jawaharlal Nehru, 1968. *Recreations:* polo, shooting and underwater-fishing. *Heir:* (by special remainder to the Earldom) *d* Lady Patricia Mountbatten [*b* 14 Feb. 1924; *m* 1946, 7th Baron Brabourne, *qv*; five *s* two *d*]. *Address:* 2 Kinnerton Street, SW1. *T:* 01-235 0081; Broadlands, Romsey, Hants. *T:* Romsey 3333; Classiebawn Castle, Cliffoney, County Sligo. *T:* Cliffoney 6. *Clubs:* Royal Automobile (Pres.), Royal Thames Yacht (Admiral of the Cumberland Fleet, Cdre, 1944-69), Royal Motor Yacht (Vice-Adm.), Naval and Military, Royal Air Force, East India, Devonshire, Sports and Public Schools, Savage, MCC, Buck's; Royal Yacht Squadron; Royal Southampton Yacht (Admiral); Royal and Ancient; Hampshire Aeroplane (Pres.); Hawks, Cambridge Union.
See also David Hicks, Marquess of Milford Haven.

MOUNTEVANS, 3rd Baron *cr* 1945, of Chelsea; **Edward Patrick Broke Evans;** Promotion Services Manager, British Tourist Authority, since 1976; *b* 1 Feb. 1943; *s* of 2nd Baron Mountevans and of Deirdre Grace, *d* of John O'Connell, Cork; *S* father, 1974; *m* 1973, Johanna Keyzer. *Educ:* Rugby; Trinity Coll., Oxford. Reserve Army Service, 1961-66; 74 MC Regt RCT, AER; Lt 1964. Joined management of Consolidated Gold Fields Ltd, 1966; British Tourist Authority, 1972; Manager, Sweden and Finland, 1973. *Heir: b* Hon. Jeffrey de Corban Richard Evans [*b* 13 May 1948; *m* 1972, Juliet, *d* of Baron Moran, *qv*; one *s*]. *Address:* c/o 13 Quick Street, N1. *Club:* Naval.

MOUNTFIELD, Alexander Stuart; *b* 5 Dec. 1902; *s* of Robert Mountfield and Caroline (*née* Appleyard); *m* 1934, Agnes Elizabeth Gurney; two *s. Educ:* Merchant Taylors' Sch., Crosby. Entered service of Mersey Docks and Harbour Board as Apprentice, 1918; served through clerical grades and in various administrative capacities. Gen. Man. and Sec., Mersey Docks and Harbour Bd, 1957-62; retd 1962. FCIT. *Recreations:* gardening, reading. *Address:* Lanthwaite, Hightown, near Liverpool. *T:* 051-929 2115. *Club:* Athenæum (Liverpool).

MOUNTFORD, Sir James (Frederick), Kt 1953; MA Oxon, DLitt Birmingham, Hon. DCL Oxon; Vice-Chancellor, University of Liverpool, 1945-63, retired; *b* 15 Sept. 1897; *s* of Alfred Mountford, West Bromwich, Staffs; *m* 1922, Doris May, *e d* of Harry Edwards, Handsworth, Birmingham; three *d. Educ:* West Bromwich Grammar Sch.; Univ. of Birmingham and (as a research student) Oriel College, Oxford; Cromer Greek Prize (British Academy), 1919; Fereday Fellow, St John's Coll., Oxford, 1924-27; Lecturer in Classics, King's Coll., Newcastle, 1918; Lecturer in Latin, Edinburgh Univ., 1919-24; Schiff Lecturer, Cornell Univ., 1924; Prof. of the Classics, Cornell Univ., 1924-27; Prof. of Latin, University Coll. of Wales, Aberystwyth, 1928-32; Prof. of Latin, Univ. of Liverpool, 1932-45, and Dean of Faculty of Arts, 1941-45; sometime External Examiner to Univs of Durham, Leeds, Manchester, St Andrews, and Wales; Chm. Cttee Vice-Chancellors and Principals, 1948-49; Mem. Advisory Cttee, Leverhulme Research Awards, 1948-70 (Chm., 1958-70); Chm. of Governors, Birkenhead Sch., 1944-49; Chm. of Governors, Birkenhead High Sch. for Girls, 1953-60; Chm., Northern Univs. Jt Matric. Board, 1947-49; Vice-Chm. Liverpool Regional Hosp. Board, 1948-70; Chm. of Govs, Burton Manor Residential Coll., 1946-66; Chm. of Govs, Malayan Federation Teachers' Training Coll., Kirby, 1951-63; Gov., Shrewsbury Sch., 1951-62; Dir, Liverpool Playhouse, 1952-66; Mem., Governing Bd of National Institute for Research in Nuclear Science, 1957-61. President: Classical Assoc., 1962-63; Virgil Soc., 1966-69. Hon. LittD, TCD; Hon. DLitt, Hull, Keele; Hon. LLD, Alberta, Birmingham, Liverpool, London, Manchester, Wales. *Publications:* Quotations from Classical Authors in Medieval Latin Glossaries, 1925; 'Abavus' Glossarium, 1926; Greek Music in Papyri and Inscriptions (in New Chaps in Greek Lit.), 1929; The Scholia Bembina to Terence, 1934 (repr. 1969); British Universities, 1966; Keele: an historical critique, 1972; edn of Kennedy's Revised Latin Primer, 1930; edn of Arnold's Latin Prose Composition (and Latin Versions), 1938-40; edn of Sidgwick's Greek Prose Composition, 1951; joint author of: Glossarium Ansileubi, 1926; Post-Classical Latin Unseens, 1928; Index to Scholia of Servius and Donatus, 1930 (German reprint, 1962); Outline of Latin Prose Composition, 1942; contributions to learned periodicals and articles on education. *Recreations:* music, the theatre, and photography. *Address:* 11 The Serpentine, Liverpool L19 9DT. *T:* 051-427 3199.

MOUNTFORT, Guy Reginald, OBE 1970; retired as Director, Ogilvy & Mather International Inc., New York (1964-66); and as Managing Director, Ogilvy and Mather Ltd, London (1964-66); *b* 4 Dec. 1905; *s* of late Arnold George Mountfort, artist, and late Alice Edith (*née* Hughes); *m* 1931, Joan Hartley (*née* Pink); two *d. Educ:* Grammar Sch. General Motors Corporation (France), 1928-38. War service, 1939-46, 12 Regt HAC and British Army Staff (Washington) Lt-Col; service in N Africa, Italy, Burma, Pacific, Germany. Procter & Gamble Inc., USA, 1946-47; Mather & Crowther Ltd, 1947, Dir, 1949; Vice-Chm., Dollar Exports Bd Advertising Cttee, 1948-49. Trustee, World Wildlife Fund; Scientific FZS (Stamford Raffles Award, 1969); Medal of Société d'Acclimatation, 1936. Hon. Sec. Brit. Ornithologists' Union, 1952-62, Pres. 1970-75 (Union Medal, 1967); Leader of scientific expedns to Coto Doñana, 1952, 1955, 1956; Bulgaria, 1960; Hungary, 1961; Jordan, 1963, 1965; Pakistan, 1966, 1967. *Publications:* A Field Guide to the Birds of Europe (co-author), 1954; The Hawfinch, 1957; Portrait of a Wilderness, 1958; Portrait of a River, 1962; Portrait of a Desert, 1965; The Vanishing Jungle, 1969; Tigers, 1973; So Small a World, 1974; Back from the Brink, 1977; contribs to ornithological and other scientific jls; television and radio broadcasts on ornithology and exploration. *Recreations:* ornithology, gardening, photography, travel. *Address:* Plovers Meadow, Possingworth Park, Blackboys, East Sussex. *T:* Heathfield 3416.

MOUNTGARRET, 17th Viscount (Ireland) *cr* 1550; Baron (UK) *cr* 1911; **Richard Henry Piers Butler;** *b* 8 Nov. 1936; *s* of 16th Viscount; *S* father, 1966; *m* 1st, 1960, Gillian Margaret (marr. diss. 1970), *o d* of Cyril Francis Stuart Buckley, London, SW3; two *s* one *d*; 2nd, 1970, Mrs Jennifer Susan Melville Fattorini, *o d* of Captain D. M. Wills, Barley Wood, Wrington, near Bristol. *Educ:* Eton; RMA, Sandhurst. Commissioned, Irish Guards, 1957; retd rank Capt., 1964. *Recreations:* shooting, stalking, cricket. *Heir: s* Hon Piers James Richard Butler, *b* 15 April 1961. *Address:* Stainley House, South Stainley, Harrogate, North Yorks. *T:* Harrogate 770087; Wyvis, Evanton, Ross-shire, Scotland. *Clubs:* White's, Pratt's.

MOURANT, Arthur Ernest, DM, FRCP; FRS 1966; formerly Director, Serological Population Genetics Laboratory; Conseiller Scientifique Etranger, Institut d'Hématologie, Immunologie et Génétique Humaine, Toulouse, since 1974; *b* 11 April 1904; *er s* of Ernest Charles Mourant and Emily Gertrude (*née* Bray); unmarried. *Educ:* Victoria Coll., Jersey; Exeter Coll., Oxford; St Bartholomew's Hosp. Medical Coll. London. BA 1925, DPhil (Geol.) 1931, MA 1931, BM, BCh 1943, DM 1948, Oxford; FRCP 1960; FRCPath 1963. 1st cl. hons Chem., 1926; Sen. King Charles I Schol., Exeter Coll., Oxford, 1926; Burdett-Coutts Schol., Oxford Univ., 1926. Demonstrator in Geology, Univ. of Leeds, 1928-29; Geol Survey of Gt Brit., 1929-31; teaching posts, 1931-34; Dir, Jersey Pathological Lab., 1935-38; Med. Student, 1939-43; House med. appts, 1943-44; Med. Off., Nat. Blood Transfusion Service, 1944-45; Med. Off., Galton Lab. Serum Unit, Cambridge, 1945-46; Dir, Blood Gp Reference Lab., Min. of Health and MRC, 1946-65 (Internat. Blood Gp Reference Lab., WHO, 1952-65); Hon. Adviser, Nuffield Blood Gp Centre, 1952-65; Hon. Sen. Lectr in Haematology, St Bartholomew's Hospital Medical Coll., 1965-77. Vis. Prof., Columbia Univ., 1953. Pres., Section H (Anthropology), Brit. Assoc., 1956; Vice-Pres.: Soc. for the Study of Human Biology, 1960-63; Mineralogical Soc., 1971-73; Mem. Hon. and Vice-Pres., Société Jersiaise; Corresp. Mem., Académie des Sciences, Inscriptions et Belles-Lettres, Toulouse; Honorary Member: Internat. Soc. of Blood Transfusion; British Soc. for Haematology; Peruvian Pathological Soc. Past or present Mem. Ed. Bd of seven British, foreign and internat. scientific jls. Oliver Meml Award, 1953; Huxley Memorial Medal, Royal Anthropological Institute, 1961; Landsteiner Meml Award, Amer. Assoc. of Blood Banks, 1973. *Publications:* The Distribution of the Human Blood Groups, 1954, (jtly) 2nd edn, 1976; (jtly) The ABO Blood Groups: Comprehensive Tables and Maps of World Distribution, 1958; (ed jtly) Man and Cattle, 1963; (jtly) Blood Groups and Diseases, 1977; numerous papers in scientific jls on blood groups and other biol subjects, geology and archæology. *Recreations:* photography, geology, archæology, travel, reading in sciences other than own, alpine gardening. *Address:* Maison de Haut, Longueville, St Saviour, Jersey, Channel Islands. *T:* Jersey Central 53840. *Club:* Athenæum.

MOVERLEY, Rt. Rev. Gerald, JCD; Titular Bishop of Tinisa in Proconsulari; Domestic Prelate to HH Pope Paul VI since 1965; Bishop Auxiliary of Leeds (RC) since 1968; *b* 9 April 1922; *s* of William Joseph Moverley and Irene Mary Moverley (*née* Dewhirst). *Educ:* St Bede's Grammar Sch., Bradford; Ushaw Coll., Durham; Angelicum Univ., Rome. Priest, 1946; Sec. to Bishop Poskitt, Leeds, 1946-51; Angelicum Univ., 1951-54; Chancellor, Dio. Leeds, 1958-68; elected Bishop, Dec. 1967. *Address:* Quarters, Carsick Hill Way, Sheffield, S10 3LT. *T:* Sheffield 301596.

MOWAT, John Stuart; Sheriff of Glasgow and Strathkelvin (formerly Lanark and Glasgow), since 1974; *b* 30 Jan. 1923; *s* of George Mowat and Annie Barlow; *m* 1956, Anne Cameron Renfrew; two *s* two *d*. *Educ:* Glasgow High Sch.; Belmont House; Merchiston Castle Sch.; Glasgow Univ. (MA, LLB). Served RAF Transport Comd, 1941-46; Flt-Lt 1944. Journalist, 1947-52; Advocate, 1952; Sheriff-Substitute, then Sheriff, of Fife and Kinross at Dunfermline, 1960-72; Sheriff of Fife and Kinross at Cupar and Kinross, 1972-74. Contested (L) Caithness and Sutherland, 1955; Office-bearer, Scottish Liberal Party, 1954-58; Life Trustee: Carnegie Dunfermline Trust, 1967-73; Carnegie UK Trust, 1971-73. *Recreations:* golf, curling, watching football. *Address:* 31 Westbourne Gardens, Glasgow G12 9PF. *T:* 041-334 3743. *Club:* Royal and Ancient (St Andrews).

MOWBRAY (26th Baron *cr* 1283), **SEGRAVE** (27th Baron *cr* 1283), and **STOURTON,** of Stourton, Co. Wilts (23rd Baron *cr* 1448); **Charles Edward Stourton;** a Conservative Whip, House of Lords, since 1974; *b* 11 March 1923; *s* of William Marmaduke Stourton, 25th Baron Mowbray, 26th Baron Segrave and 22nd Baron Stourton, MC, and Sheila (*d* 1975), *er d* of Hon. Edward Gully, CB; *S* father, 1965; *m* 1952, Hon. Jane de Yarburgh Bateson, *o c* of 5th Baron Deramore, and of Nina Lady Deramore, OBE, *d* of Alastair Macpherson-Grant; two *s*. *Educ:* Ampleforth; Christ Church, Oxford. Joined Army, 1942; Commissioned Gren. Guards, 1943; served with 2nd Armd Bn Gren. Gds, as Lt, 1943-44 (wounded, France, 1944; loss of eye and invalided, 1945). Mem. of Lloyd's 1952; Mem. Securicor, 1961-64; Dir, Securicor (Scotland) Ltd, 1964-70. Mem., Nidderdale RDC, 1954-58. A Conservative Whip in House of Lords, 1967-70; a Lord in Waiting (Govt Whip), and Spokesman for DoE, 1970-74. Chancellor, Primrose League, 1974-. Hon. Pres., Safety Glazing Assoc., 1975-. Bicentennial Year Award of Baronial Order of Magna Charta, USA, 1976. Kt of Hon. and Devotion, SMO Malta, 1947; Kt Gr. Cross, Mil. Order of St Lazarus, 1970. *Recreations:* reading, shooting, gardening. *Heir: s* Hon. Edward William Stephen Stourton, *b* 17 April 1953. *Address:* Marcus, by Forfar, Angus DD8 3QH. *T:* Finavon 219; 23 Warwick Square, SW1V 2AB. *Clubs:* Turf, White's, Pratt's, Beefsteak, Pilgrims.
See also F. P. Crowder, Hon. J. J. Stourton.

MOWBRAY, Sir John Robert, 6th Bt *cr* 1880; *b* 1 March 1932; *s* of Sir George Robert Mowbray, 5th Bt, KBE, and of Diana Margaret, *d* of Sir Robert Heywood Hughes, 12th Bt; *S* father, 1969; *m* 1957, Lavina Mary, *d* of late Lt-Col Francis Edgar Hugonin, OBE, Stainton House, Stainton in Cleveland, Yorks; three *d*. *Educ:* Eton; New College, Oxford. *Address:* Hunts Park, Great Thurlow, Suffolk. *T:* Thurlow 232.

MOWBRAY, William John, QC 1974; *b* 3 Sept. 1928; *s* of James Nathan Mowbray, sugar manufr and E. Ethel Mowbray; *m* 1960, Shirley Mary Neilan; one *s* three *d*. *Educ:* Upper Canada Coll.; Mill Hill Sch.; New Coll., Oxford. BA 1952. Called to Bar, Lincoln's Inn, 1953; called to Bahamian Bar, 1971. *Publications:* Lewin on Trusts, 16th edn, 1964; Estate Duty on Settled Property, 1969, etc; articles in jls. *Recreations:* music, gardening. *Address:* 12 New Square, Lincoln's Inn, WC2A 3SW. *T:* 01-405 3808/9, 01-405 0988/9.

MOWLEM, Rainsford, FRCS; Emeritus Cons. Plastic Surgeon, Middlesex Hospital; Surgeon i/c Department for Plastic Surgery, Middlesex Hospital, 1939-62, retired; Surgeon i/c North West Regional Centre for Plastic Surgery, Mount Vernon Hospital; Consulting Plastic Surgeon to King Edward VII Hospital, Windsor, Luton and Dunstable Hospital, Birmingham Accident Hospital; *b* 21 Dec. 1902; *s* of Arthur Manwell Mowlem, New Zealand; *m* 1933, Margaret West Harvey; two *d*. *Educ:* Auckland Grammar Sch.; Univ. of New Zealand. MB, ChB, NZ 1924, FRCS 1929. Asst Med. Officer i/c Plastic Surgery Unit, LCC, 1933-37; Asst Plastic Surgeon, St Andrews Hosp., Dollis Hill, 1937-39; Surgeon i/c NW Centre Plastic Surgery, Hill End Hosp., 1939-53. Fellow: Assoc. Surgeons of GB and Ireland; RSM; Brit. Orthopædic Assoc.; Past-Pres. Brit. Assoc. of Plastic Surgeons (1950 and 1959); Pres. Internat. Congress on Plastic Surgery, 1959; Mem. Editorial Cttee, British Assoc. of Plastic Surgeons; Hon. Member: Netherlands Assoc. of Plastic Surgeons, Amer. Soc. of Plastic and Reconstructive Surgery; French Soc. of Plastic and Reconstructive Surgery; Sociedad Española de Cirugia Plastica y Reparadora; Hon. Fellow Amer. Assoc. Plastic Surgeons. Corresp. Mem. Italian Soc. of Plastic Surgery. Hunterian Prof., RCS, 1940. Hon. ScD (Trinity Coll., Hartford). *Publications:* various on scientific subjects. *Address:* La Morena, Mijas, Malaga, Spain.

MOYA, (John) Hidalgo, CBE 1966; RIBA 1956; architect; *b* Los Gatos, Calif, 5 May 1920; *s* of Hidalgo Moya; *m* 1947, Janiffer Innes Mary Hall; one *s* two *d*. *Educ:* Oundle Sch.; Royal West of England Coll. of Art; AA Sch. of Architecture; AA Dip., 1943. Qualified, 1944; in practice with Philip Powell, 1946-61; with Sir Philip Powell, Robert Henley and Peter Skinner, 1961-; major works include: Churchill Gardens Flats, Westminster, 1948-62; Houses at Chichester, 1950; Toys Hill, 1954; Oxshott, 1954; Mayfield Sch., Putney, 1955; Mental Hosp. extensions at Fairmile, 1957, Borocourt, 1964; Brasenose Coll., Oxford, extensions, 1961; Chichester Festival Theatre, 1962; Christ Church, Oxford, Picture Gallery and undergraduate rooms, 1967; St John's Coll., Cambridge, new buildings, 1967; Public Swimming Baths, Putney, 1967; General Hosps at Swindon, High Wycombe and Wythenshawe, British Nat. Pavilion, Expo 1970, Osaka; Wolfson Coll., Oxford, 1974. Pimlico Housing Scheme, Winning Design in Open Competition, 1946; Skylon, Festival of Britain Winning Design, 1950; RIBA London

Architecture Bronze Medal, 1950; Festival of Britain Award, 1951; Mohlg Good Design in Housing Award, 1954; RIBA Bronze Medal, 1958, 1961 (Bucks, Berks, Oxon); Civic Trust Awards (Class I and II), 1961; Architectural Design Project Award, 1965; RIBA Architectural Award, (London and SE Regions), 1967; Royal Gold Medal for Architecture, RIBA, 1974. *Address:* Powell, Moya and Partners, Architects, 30 Percy Street, W1P 0BA. *T:* 01-636 7292; Day's Farm, Lippitt's Hill, High Beech, Loughton, Essex. *T:* 01-508 5272.

MOYERS, Bill D., BJ, BD; journalist; editor and chief reporter, CBS Reports; *b* 5 June 1934; *s* of John Henry Moyers and Ruby Moyers (*née* Johnson); *m* 1954, Judith Suzanne Davidson; two *s* one *d. Educ:* High Sch., Marshall, Texas; Univ. of Texas; Univ. of Edinburgh; Southwestern Theological Seminary. BJ 1956; BD 1959. Personal Asst to Senator Lyndon B. Johnson, 1959-60; Executive Asst, 1960; US Peace Corps: Associate Dir, 1961-63; Dep. Dir, 1963. Special Asst to President Johnson, 1963-66; Press Sec., 1965-67; Publisher of Newsday, Long Island, 1967-70; Editor-in-chief, Bill Moyers' Journal, Public Broadcasting Service, 1970-76; Contributing Editor, Newsweek Magazine. Three Emmy Awards, inc. most outstanding broadcaster, 1974; Lowell Medal, 1975; ABA Gavel Award for distinguished service to American system of law, 1974; ABA Cert. of Merit, 1975; Peabody Award, 1977. *Publication:* Listening to America, 1971. *Address:* 76 Fourth Street, Garden City, Long Island, New York 11530, USA.

MOYES, Lt-Comdr Kenneth Jack, RN retd; MBE (mil.) 1960; Under-Secretary, Department of Health and Social Security, since 1975; *b* 13 June 1918; *s* of Charles Wilfrid and Daisy Hilda Moyes; *m* 1943, Norma Ellen Outred Hillier; one *s* two *d. Educ:* Portsmouth Northern Grammar Sch. FCIS. Royal Navy, 1939-63. Principal, Dept of Health and Social Security, 1963; Asst Secretary, 1970. *Recreations:* gardening, tennis, squash, bridge. *Address:* Garden House, Darwin Road, Birchington, Kent CT7 9JL. *T:* Thanet 42015.

MOYLAN, John David FitzGerald; His Honour Judge Moylan; a Circuit Judge (formerly Judge of the County Courts), since 1967; *b* 8 Oct. 1915; *s* of late Sir John FitzGerald Moylan, CB, CBE, and late Lady Moylan (*née* FitzGerald); *m* 1946, Jean, *d* of F. C. Marno-Edwards, Lavenham, Suffolk; one *s* two *d. Educ:* Charterhouse; Christ Church, Oxford. Served War of 1939-45, with Royal Marines. Inner Temple, 1946; practised on the Western Circuit. *Recreations:* travel and music. *Address:* 29 Lennox Gardens, SW1. *T:* 01-584 4726.

MOYLE, Roland (Dunstan); MP (Lab) Lewisham East, since 1974 (Lewisham North, 1966-74); Minister of State for the Health Service, since 1976; *b* 12 March 1928; *s* of late Baron Moyle, CBE; *m* 1956, Shelagh Patricia Hogan; one *s* one *d. Educ:* Infants' and Jun. Elem. Schs, Bexleyheath, Kent; County Sch., Llanidloes, Mont.; UCW Aberystwyth (LLB); Trinity Hall, Cambridge (MA, LLB); Gray's Inn. Barrister-at-Law. Commnd in Royal Welch Fusiliers, 1949-51. Legal Dept, Wales Gas Bd, 1953-56; Asst Industrial Relations Officer, Wales Gas Board, 1956; Asst Industrial Relations Officer, Gas Coun., 1956-62 (Jt Sec., Nat. Jt Industrial Coun., Gas Industry; Jt Sec., Nat Jt Coun. for Gas Staffs); Conciliation Research Officer, Electricity Coun., 1962-65; Jt Sec., Nat. Coun. for Admin. and Clerical Staff in Electricity Supply, Electricity Coun., 1965-66. PPS to Chief Secretary to the Treasury, 1966-69, to Home Secretary, 1969-70; Parly Sec., MAFF, 1974; Min. of State, NI Dept, 1974-76. Mem., Select Cttee on Race Relations and Immigration, 1968-72; Vice-Chm., Parly Lab. Party Defence Group, 1968-72; Opposition Spokesman on higher educn and science, 1972-74; Sec., British Amer. Parly Gp, 1971-74. *Recreations:* gardening, motoring, swimming, reading. *Address:* House of Commons, SW1.

MOYNE, 2nd Baron, *cr* 1932, of Bury St Edmunds; **Bryan Walter Guinness,** MA; FRSL; poet, novelist and playwright; Pro-Chancellor, Trinity College, Dublin; Vice-Chairman of Arthur Guinness, Son and Co.; Chairman, Iveagh (Housing) Trust, Dublin; Barrister-at-Law; *b* 27 Oct. 1905; *e s* of 1st Baron Moyne (3rd *s* of 1st Earl of Iveagh) and Lady Evelyn Erskine (*d* 1939), (3rd *d* of 14th Earl of Buchan; *S* father 1944; *m* 1st, 1929, Diana Freeman-Mitford (marr. diss. 1934); two *s*; 2nd, 1936, Elisabeth Nelson; four *s* five *d. Educ:* Eton; Christ Church, Oxford. Called to Bar, 1930. Capt., Royal Sussex Regiment, 1943; A Governor National Gallery of Ireland, 1955; Mem., Irish Acad. of Letters, 1968. Hon. LLD: TCD, 1958; NUI, 1961. *Publications:* (as Bryan Guinness): 23 Poems, 1931; Singing out of Tune, 1933; Landscape with Figures, 1934; Under the Eyelid, 1935; Johnny and Jemima, 1936; A Week by the Sea, 1936; Lady Crushwell's Companion, 1938; The Children in the Desert, 1947; Reflexions, 1947; The Animals' Breakfast, 1950; Story of a

Nutcracker, 1953; Collected Poems, 1956; A Fugue of Cinderellas, 1956; Catriona and the Grasshopper, 1957; Priscilla and the Prawn, 1960; Leo and Rosabelle, 1961; The Giant's Eye, 1964; The Rose in the Tree, 1964; The Girl with the Flower, 1966; The Engagement, 1969; The Clock, 1973; Dairy Not Kept, 1975; *plays:* The Fragrant Concubine, 1938; A Riverside Charade, 1954. *Recreation:* travelling. *Heir: s* Hon. Jonathan Bryan Guinness, *qv. Address:* Biddesden House, Andover, Hants. *T:* Ludgershall (Wilts) 237; Knockmaroon, Castleknock, Co. Dublin. *Clubs:* Athenæum, Carlton; Kildare Street and University (Dublin).

MOYNIHAN, family name of Baron Moynihan.

MOYNIHAN, 3rd Baron, *cr* 1929; **Antony Patrick Andrew Cairnes Berkeley Moynihan;** Bt 1922; *b* 2 Feb. 1936; *s* of 2nd Baron Moynihan, OBE, TD, and of Ierne Helen Candy; *S* father 1965; *m* 1st, 1955, Ann Herbert (marr. diss., 1958); 2nd, 1958, Shirin Roshan Berry (marr. diss., 1967); one *d*; 3rd, 1968, Luthgarda Maria Fernandez; three *d. Educ:* Stowe. Late 2nd Lt Coldstream Guards. *Recreation:* dog breeding. *Heir: half-b* Hon. Colin Berkeley Moynihan, *b* 13 Sept. 1955.

MOYNIHAN, Senator (Daniel) Patrick; US Senator from New York State, since 1977; *b* Tulsa, Oklahoma, 16 March 1927; *s* of John Henry and Margaret Ann Phipps Moynihan; *m* 1955, Elizabeth Therese Brennan; two *s* one *d. Educ:* City Coll., NY; Tufts Univ.; Fletcher Sch. of Law and Diplomacy. MA, PhD. Gunnery Officer, US Navy, 1944-47. Dir of Public Relations, Internat. Rescue Commn, 1954; successively Asst to Sec., Asst Sec., Acting Sec., to Governor of NY State, 1955-58; Mem., NY Tenure Commn, 1959-60; Dir, NY State Govt Res. Project, Syracuse Univ., 1959-61; Special Asst to Sec. of Labor, 1961-62; Exec. Asst to Sec., 1962-63, Asst Sec. of Labor, 1963-65; Dir, Jt Center Urban Studies, MIT and Harvard Univ., 1966-69; Prof. of Govt, 1972-77 and Senior Mem., 1966-77, Harvard (Prof. of Education and Urban Politics, 1966-73). Asst to Pres. of USA for Urban Affairs, 1969-70; Counsellor to Pres. (with Cabinet rank), 1969-70; Consultant to Pres., 1971-73; US Ambassador to India, 1973-75; US Permanent Rep. to the UN and Mem. of Cabinet, 1975-76. Democratic Candidate for the Senate, NY, 1976. Mem., US delegn 26th Gen. Assembly, UN, 1971. Fellow, Amer. Acad. Arts and Scis; Member: Amer. Philosophical Soc.; AAAS (formerly Vice-Pres.); Nat. Acad. Public Admin; President's Sci. Adv. Cttee, 1971-73. Hon. Fellow, London Sch. of Economics, 1970. Holds numerous hon. degrees. *Publications:* (co-author) Beyond the Melting Pot, 1963; (ed) The Defenses of Freedom, 1966; (ed) On Understanding Poverty, 1969; Maximum Feasible Misunderstanding, 1969; (ed) Toward a National Urban Policy, 1970; (jt ed) On Equality of Educational Opportunity, 1972; The Politics of a Guaranteed Income, 1973; Coping: On the Practice of Government, 1974; (jt ed) Ethnicity: Theory and Experience, 1975. *Address:* Apt 42a, Waldorf Towers, 50th Street and Park Avenue, New York, USA; 1107 Dirksen Office Building, Washington, DC 20510, USA. *Clubs:* Century, Harvard (NYC); Federal City (Washington).

MOYNIHAN, Martin John, CMG 1972; MC; HM Diplomatic Service, retired; Associate Member in South African Studies, Clare Hall, Cambridge, since 1977; Administering Officer, The Kennedy Scholarships and Knox Fellowships, since 1977; *b* 17 Feb. 1916; *e s* of William John Moynihan and late Phoebe Alexander; *m* 1946, Monica Hopwood; one *s* one *d. Educ:* Birkenhead Sch.; Magdalen Coll., Oxford (MA). India Office, 1939. War of 1939-45: Indian Army, 1940; QVO Corps of Guides; served with Punjab Frontier Force Regt, N-W Frontier, Assam and Burma (MC); UK High Commission, Delhi, Madras and Bombay, 1946-48; Principal, CRO, 1948-52; Jt Sec., Commonwealth Supply and Production Meeting, 1951; UK High Commission, Karachi, 1952; Dep. High Commissioner: Peshawar, 1954-56; Lahore, 1956-58; Head of Technical Assistance Dept, Commonwealth Relations Office, 1959; Dep. High Commissioner: Kuala Lumpur, 1961-63; Port of Spain, 1964-66; HM Consul-General, Philadelphia, 1966-70; Ambassador to Liberia, 1970-73; High Comr in Lesotho, 1973-76. Member: Council, Hakluyt Soc., 1976; Council, USPG, 1976; Africa Cttee, Oxfam, 1976; Pres., Lesotho Assoc., 1976. Fellow, Internat. Scotist Congress, Padua, 1976. Knight Grand Band of Humane Order of African Redemption (Liberia), 1973. *Publications:* The Strangers, 1946; South of Fort Hertz, 1956. *Recreation:* riding. *Address:* The Gatehouse, 5 The Green, Wimbledon Common, SW19 5AZ. *T:* 01-946 7964. *Clubs:* Athenæum, Travellers'.

MOYNIHAN, Rodrigo, CBE 1953; Artist; lately Professor of Painting at the Royal College of Art; *b* 17 Oct. 1910; *s* of Herbert James Moynihan and late Maria de la Puerta; *m* 1931, Elinor

Bellingham Smith; one s; m 1960, Anne, d of Sir James Hamet Dunn, 1st Bt; one s. *Educ:* UCS, London, and in USA. Slade Sch., 1928-31; Mem. of London Group, 1933; one-man shows at Redfern Gall., 1940, 1958, 1961; Leicester Gallery, 1946; Hanover Gallery, 1963, 1967; New York: Egan Gallery, 1966; Tibor de Nagy, 1968. Army Service, 1940-43; Official War Artist, 1943-44. Pictures purchased by Chantrey Bequest, Tate Gallery, Contemporary Art Soc., War Artists' Advisory Cttee. ARA 1944, RA 1954-56 (resigned). Hon. Dr RCA 1969; Fellow UCL, 1970-. Editor (jtly with wife), Art and Literature, 1960-. *Publication:* Goya, 1951. *Address:* 70 Avenue du Léman, Lausanne, Switzerland.

MOYOLA, Baron cr 1971 (Life Peer), of Castledawson; **James Dawson Chichester-Clark,** PC (Northern Ireland) 1966; DL; b 12 Feb. 1923; s of late Capt. J. L. C. Chichester-Clark, DSO and bar, DL, MP, and Mrs C. E. Brackenbury; m 1959, Moyra Maud Haughton (*née* Morris); two d one step s. *Educ:* Eton. Entered Army, 1942; 2nd Lieut Irish Guards, Dec. 1942; wounded, Italy, 1944; ADC to Governor-General of Canada (Field-Marshal Earl Alexander of Tunis), 1947-49; attended Staff Coll., Camberley, 1956; retired as Major, 1960. MP (U), S Derry, NI Parlt, 1960-72; Asst Whip, March 1963; Chief Whip, 1963-67; Leader of the House, 1966-67; Min. of Agriculture, 1967-69; Prime Minister, 1969-71. DL Co. Derry, 1954. *Recreations:* shooting, fishing, ski-ing. *Address:* Moyola Park, Castledawson, Co. Derry, N Ireland. *Club:* Cavalry and Guards. See also Sir R. Chichester-Clark.

MTEKATEKA, Rt. Rev. Josiah; b 1903; s of Village Headman; m 1st, 1925, Maude Mwere Nambote (d 1940); one s four d; 2nd, 1944, Alice Monica Chitanda; six s two d (and five c decd). *Educ:* Likoma Island School; S Michael's Teachers' Training Coll., Likoma; St Andrew's Theological Coll., Likoma. Deacon, 1939; Priest, 1943. Asst Priest, Nkhotakota, Nyasaland Dio., 1943-45; Chiulu, Tanganyika, 1945-50; Priest, Mlangali, Tanganyika, Nyasaland Dio., 1950-52; Mlangali, SW Tanganyika Dio., 1952-60; rep. SW Tanganyika Dio. at UMCA Centenary Celebrations in England, 1957; Canon of SW Tanganyika Dio., 1959; Priest-in-charge, Manda, 1960-64; Njombe, 1964-65, SW Tanganyika Dio.; Archdeacon of Njombe, 1962-65; Suffragan Bishop, Nkhotakota, Dio. Malawi, 1965-71; Bishop of Lake Malawi, 1971-77. *Address:* c/o Bishop's House, Chanzi, PO Box 24, Nkhotakota, Malawi.

MUDD, (William) David; MP (C) Falmouth and Camborne, since 1970; b 2 June 1933; o s of Capt. W. N. Mudd and Mrs T. E. Mudd; m 1965, Helyn Irvine Smith; one s one d (and one step d). *Educ:* Truro Cathedral Sch. Journalist, Broadcaster, TV Commentator; work on BBC and ITV (Westward Television). Became Editor of The Cornish Echo; Staff Reporter, Western Morning News and Tavistock Gazette, 1954-. Mem., Tavistock UDC, 1963-65. Secretary: Conservative West Country Cttee, 1973-76; Conservative Party Fisheries Sub-Cttee, 1974-75. *Publications:* Cornishmen and True, 1971; Murder in the West Country, 1975; Facets of Crime, 1975; The Innovators, 1976. *Recreation:* jig-saw puzzles. *Address:* Field End, South Tehidy, Camborne, Cornwall. *T:* Camborne 712141. *Clubs:* Athenæum; Falmouth.

MUELLER, Anne Elisabeth; Under-Secretary, Department of Industry, since 1974; b 15 Oct. 1930; d of late Herbert Constantin Mueller and Phoebe Ann Beevers; m 1958, James Hugh Robertson; no c. *Educ:* Wakefield Girls' High Sch.; Somerville Coll., Oxford. Entered Min. of Labour and Nat. Service, 1953; served with OEEC, 1955-56; Treasury, 1962; Dept of Economic Affairs, 1964; Min. of Technology, 1969; DTI 1970; Under-Sec., DTI, later Dept of Industry, 1972-. *Address:* 21 Phillimore Place, W8 7BY. *T:* 01-937 9766.

MUFF, family name of **Baron Calverley.**

MUGGERIDGE, Douglas; Director of Programmes, BBC Radio, since 1976; b 2 Dec. 1928; s of Col Harry Douglas Muggeridge, OBE, and Bertha Ursula Rutland; m 1953, Diana Marguerite Hakim; two d. *Educ:* Shrewsbury; London Sch. of Economics. Sub-Editor and Leader-Writer, Liverpool Daily Post, 1953; joined BBC as Talks Producer, 1956; Senior Producer, 1959; Chief Publicity Officer, Overseas, 1961; Chief Asst, Publicity, 1964; Head of Overseas Talks and Features, 1965; Controller, Radio 1 and 2, 1969-75. Pres., Radio Industries Club, 1977. *Recreations:* music, fishing, vintage cars. *Address:* Castle Hill Cottage, Rotherfield, Sussex. *T:* Rotherfield 2770.

MUGGERIDGE, Malcolm; b 24 March 1903; s of late H. T. Muggeridge; m 1927, Katherine, d of G. C. Dobbs; two s one d (and one s decd). *Educ:* Selhurst Grammar Sch.; Selwyn Coll., Cambridge. Lecturer at Egyptian Univ., Cairo, 1927-30;

Editorial Staff, Manchester Guardian, 1930-32; Manchester Guardian correspondent, Moscow, 1932-33; Asst Editor, Calcutta Statesman, 1934-35; Editorial staff, Evening Standard, 1935-36. Served in War of 1939-45, in East Africa, North Africa, Italy and France, Intelligence Corps, Major (Legion of Hon., Croix de Guerre with Palm, Médaille de la Reconnaissance Française). Daily Telegraph Washington Correspondent, 1946-47; Dep. Editor Daily Telegraph, 1950-52; Editor of Punch, Jan. 1953-Oct. 1957. Rector, Edinburgh Univ., 1967-68. *Publications:* Three Flats, produced by the Stage Society, 1931; Autumnal Face, 1931; Winter in Moscow, 1933; The Earnest Atheist, a life of Samuel Butler, 1936; In A Valley of this Restless Mind, 1938; The Thirties, 1940; edited English edn Ciano's Diary, 1947; Ciano's Papers, 1948; Affairs of the Heart, 1949; Tread Softly for you Tread on my Jokes, 1966; London à la Mode (with Paul Hogarth), 1966; Muggeridge through the Microphone (Edited by C. Ralling); Jesus Rediscovered, 1969; Something Beautiful for God, 1971; Paul: envoy extraordinary (with A. R. Vidler), 1972; Chronicles of Wasted Time (autobiog.), vol. 1, 1972, vol. 2, 1973; Malcolm's Choice, 1972; Jesus: the man who lives, 1975; A Third Testament, 1977. *Recreation:* walking. *Address:* Park Cottage, Robertsbridge, East Sussex.

MUGNOZZA, Carlo S.; see Scarascia-Mugnozza.

MUIL, Maj.-Gen. David John, CB 1956; OBE 1945; b 18 Oct. 1898; s of David Muil, Kirkintilloch, Scotland; m 1924, Ruth, d of Mark Burgess, Alderley Edge, Cheshire; one d. *Educ:* Aston Grammar Sch.; Birmingham Univ. Served European War, 1917-19, with London Scottish, Royal Warwickshire Regt and RFC (France and Belgium). Joined Royal Army Dental Corps, 1923, and served with them War of 1939-45, in India and Far East; Col, 1949. Dir Army Dental Service, 1955-58. QHDS 1955. *Address:* 4 Courtslands, Court Downs Road, Beckenham, Kent. *T:* 01-650 9060.

MUIR, Air Commodore Adam, CB 1967; retired, 1977; b 4 Aug. 1908; s of George Muir and Mary Gillies Ferguson; m 1938, Isobel Janet Arbuckle Turnbull (d 1967); one s one d. *Educ:* Greenock Acad.; Glasgow Univ. MA 1929; BSc 1931; MB, ChB (Commend.) 1934; DTM&H (Eng) 1954; MRCPE 1955; FRCPE 1963. Joined RAF Medical Branch, 1937, retd 1967; served War of 1939-45, Iceland and Mediterranean Theatres (despatches twice); Dir of Hygiene and Research, RAF, 1959-63; PMO, RAF Germany, 1963-67; Officer i/c Reception, BMH Rinteln, 1967-70; MO, Army Careers Information Office, Glasgow, 1970-77. CStJ 1966. *Recreation:* music. *Address:* Clachan, Tighnabruaich, Argyll. *T:* Tighnabruaich 378. *Club:* Royal Air Force.

MUIR, Alec Andrew, CBE 1968; QPM 1961; DL; Chief Constable of Durham Constabulary, 1967-70; b 21 Aug. 1909; s of Dr Robert Douglas Muir, MD, and Edith Muir, The Limes, New Cross, SE14; m 1948, Hon. Helen (who m 1st, 1935, Wm Farr; marr. diss., 1948), e d of 1st and last Baron du Parcq (d 1949); one s one d (and one step s one step d). *Educ:* Christ's Hosp.; Wadham Coll., Oxford (MA). Receivers' Office, Metropolitan Police, 1933; Metropolitan Police Coll., 1934; Supt, 1948; Chief Constable, Durham Co. Constabulary, 1950. DL, Co. Durham, 1964. OStJ 1957. *Recreations:* cricket, bowls, squash, sailing. *Address:* Windywalls, Gatehouse-of-Fleet, Kirkcudbrightshire. *T:* Gatehouse 249. *Clubs:* United Oxford & Cambridge University; County (Durham).

MUIR, (Charles) Augustus; author and journalist; b Carluke, Ontario, Canada; s of late Rev. Walter Muir and Elizabeth Carlow; m Jean Murray Dow Walker (d 1972); m 1975, Mair Davies. *Educ:* George Heriot's Sch. and Edinburgh Univ.; contributor to various dailies, weeklies, and monthlies; Asst Editor and subsequently Editor, the World; served 1914-19 in Royal Scots, King's Own Scottish Borderers, and on Staff. *Publications:* The Third Warning; The Blue Bonnet; The Black Pavilion; The Shadow on the Left; The Silent Partner; Birds of the Night; The House of Lies; Beginning the Adventure; Scotland's Road of Romance; The Green Lantern; The Riddle of Garth; Raphael, MD; The Crimson Crescent; Satyr Mask; The Bronze Door; The Red Carnation; The Man Who Stole the Crown Jewels; Castles in the Air; The Sands of Fear; The Intimate Thoughts of John Baxter, Bookseller; Heather-Track and High Road; Joey and the Greenwings; Scottish Portrait; The Story of Jesus for Young People; The History of The Fife Coal Company; The History of the Shotts Iron Company; The History of Michael Nairn and Company; 75 Years, The History of Smith's Stamping Works (Coventry) Ltd and Smith-Clayton Forge Ltd, Lincoln; The History of Blyth, Greene, Jourdain & Co. Ltd, Merchant Bankers; Andersons of Islington, The History of C. F. Anderson & Son Ltd; The History of Churchill

& Sim Ltd; The Kenyon Tradition, The History of James Kenyon & Son Ltd; The History of Baker Perkins Ltd; In Blackburne Valley, The History of Bowers Mills; The Life of the Very Rev. Dr John White, CH; Candlelight in Avalon, A Spiritual Pilgrimage; How to Choose and Enjoy Wine; The First of Foot, The History of The Royal Scots (The Royal Regiment) 1633-1961; The Vintner of Nazareth, a study of the early life of Christ; History of British Paper & Board Makers Association. Joint-Editor The George Saintsbury Memorial Volume and A Last Vintage. *Recreations:* nearly anything except golf. *Address:* Parkhill, Stansted-Mountfitchet, Essex. *T:* Bishops Stortford 812289. *Clubs:* Savage, Saintsbury; Royal Scots, Scottish Arts (Edinburgh).

MUIR, Sir David (John), Kt 1961; CMG 1959; FCIS, FASA, FAIM, AAUQ; Chairman, Queensland Public Services Board, since 1977; *b* 20 June 1916; *s* of John Arthur and Grace Elizabeth Muir, Brisbane; *m* 1942, Joan Howarth; one *s* one *d*. *Educ:* Kangaroo Point State Sch.; State Commercial High Sch., Brisbane. Entered Qld Public Service, 1932, as Clerk in Dept of Public Lands; transf. to Premier's Dept, 1938. Made special study of problems associated with production and marketing of sugar. Permanent Under Sec., Premier and Chief Secretary's Dept, 1948-51; also Clerk of Exec. Council of Qld and Mem. of State Stores Bd. Agent General for Qld in London and Australian Govt Rep. on Internat. Sugar Council, 1951-63 (Chm. 1958); Dir, Industrial Develt, Queensland, and Chm., Industries Assistance Bd, 1964-77; Pres., Chartered Institute of Secretaries, 1964. Chm., Queensland Theatre Co. Bd, 1969-. James N. Kirby Medal, InstProdE, Australia, 1969. JP. *Recreations:* gardening and golf. *Address:* Executive Building, 100 George Street, Brisbane, Qld 4000, Australia; 28 Buena Vista Avenue, Coorparoo, Qld 4151, Australia.

MUIR, Sir Edward (Francis), KCB 1956 (CB 1950); FSA 1959; *b* 29 June 1905; *o s* of late W. E. Muir, JP; *m* 1928, Evelyn Mary Whitfield (*d* 1964); one *s* one *d*. *Educ:* Bradfield Coll.; Corpus Christi Coll., Oxford. BA, 1927, MA 1930; entered HM Office of Works, 1927; Under-Sec., 1946-51; Deputy Sec., Ministry of Materials, 1951-54; Ministry of Works, 1954-56; Permanent Secretary: Ministry of Works, 1956-62; Ministry of Public Building and Works, 1962-65. Chm., Assoc. of First Div. Civil Servants, 1948-49; Liveryman of the Worshipful Company of Fan Makers, 1936; Master, 1958. Governor, Central Foundation Schs of London, 1958-68. Pres., Haslemere Educational Museum, 1964; Mem. Standing Commission on Museums and Galleries, 1965-72; Chairman: Ancient Monuments Board for England, 1966-; Conf. on Training Architects in Conservation, 1969; A Trustee, Oxford Historic Buildings Fund, 1967; Vice-Pres., Fedn of Sussex Amenity Socs, 1977- (Vice-Chm., 1968-77); Mem., Redundant Churches Fund, 1969-76. Hon. Fellow Corpus Christi Coll., Oxford, 1965-. *Address:* Muirfield, Haslemere, Surrey. *T:* Haslemere 2931. *Clubs:* Athenæum, United Oxford & Cambridge University.

MUIR, Frank; writer and broadcaster; *b* 5 Feb. 1920; *s* of Charles James Muir and Margaret Harding; *m* 1949, Polly McIrvine; one *s* one *d*. *Educ:* Chatham House, Ramsgate; Leyton County High Sch. Served RAF, 1940-46. Wrote radio comedy-series and compered TV progs, 1946. With Denis Norden, 1947-64; collaborated for 17 years writing comedy scripts, including: (for radio): Take it from Here, 1947-58; Bedtime with Braden, 1950-54; (for TV): And so to Bentley, 1956; Whack-O,! 1958-60; The Seven Faces of Jim, 1961, and other series with Jimmy Edwards; resident in TV and radio panel-games; collaborated in film scripts, television commercials, and revues (Prince of Wales, 1951; Adelphi, 1952); joint Advisors and Consultants to BBC Television Light Entertainment Dept, 1960-64; jointly received Screenwriters Guild Award for Best Contribution to Light Entertainment, 1961; together on panel-games My Word!, 1956-, and My Music, 1967-. Asst Head of BBC Light Entertainment Gp, 1964-67; Head of Entertainment, London Weekend Television, 1968-69, resigned 1969, and reverted to being self-unemployed; resumed TV series Call My Bluff, 1970; began radio series Frank Muir Goes Into..., 1971; The Frank Muir Version, 1976. Pres., Johnson Soc., Lichfield, 1975-76. Rector, Univ. of St Andrews, 1977-. (With Simon Brett) Writers' Guild Award for Best Radio Feature Script, 1973. *Publications:* (with Patrick Campbell) Call My Bluff, 1972; (with Denis Norden) You Can't Have Your Kayak and Heat It, 1973; (with Denis Norden) Upon My Word!, 1974; Christmas Customs and Traditions, 1975; The Frank Muir Book: an irreverant companion to social history, 1976; What-a-Mess, 1977. *Recreations:* book collecting, staring silently into space. *Address:* Anners, Thorpe, Egham, Surrey TW20 8UE. *T:* Chertsey 62759. *Club:* Savile.

MUIR, (Isabella) Helen (Mary), MA, DPhil, DSc; FRS 1977; Head of the Division of Biochemistry, Kennedy Institute of Rheumatology, London, since 1966; *b* 20 Aug. 1920; *d* of late G. B. F. Muir, ICS, and Gwladys Muir (*née* Stack). *Educ:* Downe House, Newbury; Somerville Coll., Oxford. MA 1944, DPhil (Oxon) 1947, DSc (Oxon) 1973. Research Fellow, Dunn's Sch. of Pathology, Oxford, 1947-48; Scientific Staff, Nat. Inst. for Med. Research, 1948-54; Empire Rheumatism Council Fellow, St Mary's Hosp., London, 1954-58; Pearl Research Fellow, St Mary's Hosp., 1959-66. Scientific Mem. Council, Med. Research Council (first woman to serve), Oct. 1973-Sept. 1977; Member, Editorial Board: Biochemical Jl, 1964-69; Annals of the Rheumatic Diseases, 1971-. *Publications:* many scientific papers, mainly on biochem. of connective tissues in reln to arthritis and inherited diseases in Biochem. Jl, Biochim. et Biophys. Acta, Nature, etc; contribs to several specialist books. *Recreations:* gardening, music, horses and hunting, natural history and science in general. *Address:* Biochemistry Division, Mathilda and Terence Kennedy Institute of Rheumatology, Bute Gardens, W6 7DW. *T:* 01-748 9966.

MUIR, Jean Elizabeth, (Mrs Harry Leuckert), RDI, FRSA; Designer-Director and Co-Owner, Jean Muir Ltd, since 1967; *d* of Cyril Muir and Phyllis Coy; *m* 1955, Harry Leuckert. *Educ:* Dame Harper Sch., Bedford. Selling/sketching, Liberty & Co., 1950; Designer, Jaeger Ltd, 1956, then Jane & Jane; with Harry Leuckert as co-director, formed own company, 1966. Awards: Dress of the Year, British Fashion Writers' Gp, 1964; Ambassador Award for Achievement, 1965; Harpers Bazaar Trophy, 1965; Maison Blanche Rex Internat. Fashion Award, New Orleans, 1967, 1968 and 1974 (also Hon. Citizen of New Orleans); Churchman's Award as Fashion Designer of the Year, 1970; Neiman Marcus Award, Dallas, Texas, 1973. *Address:* 22 Bruton Street, W1X 7DA. *T:* 01-499 4214.

MUIR, John Cochran, CMG 1951; OBE 1944; retired; Colonial Agricultural Service; Member for Agriculture and Natural Resources, Tanganyika, 1949; *b* 1902; *m* 1936, Cathey, *d* of Maurice Hincks; one *s* two *d*. *Educ:* Allan Glen's Sch.; West of Scotland Agricultural Coll.; Univ. of Glasgow. BSc (agric.); National Diploma in Agriculture; National Diploma in Dairying, Asst Superintendent, Agriculture, Gold Coast, 1925; Senior Agricultural Officer, Zanzibar, 1935; Dir of Agriculture, 1941; Trinidad, 1944; Tanganyika, 1948. *Address:* Peacock Farm, Wicken, Ely, Cambs.

MUIR, John Gerald Grainger, CBE 1975; DSC 1944; Controller, Overseas Division (Europe), British Council, since 1976; *b* 19 Jan. 1918; *s* of George Basil Muir, ICS and Gladys Stack; *m* 1945, Lionella Maria Terni; three *d*. *Educ:* Rugby Sch.; Corpus Christi Coll., Oxford (MA). Bd of Educn Studentship, 1938. RN, Norway, Medit., Channel and Germany, 1939-46. British Council: Italy, 1946-49; Asst, Leeds, 1949-50; Asst Rep., Syria, 1950-55; Representative: Arab Gulf, 1955-60; Portugal, 1960-64; Iraq, 1964-67; Dep. Controller, Educn, 1968-72; Rep., Spain, 1972-76. *Publications:* contribs to Mariner's Mirror, Bull. SOAS, and Soc. de Geographia, Lisbon. *Recreations:* music, nautical research, sailing, travel, flowers, bee-keeping. *Address:* c/o Lloyds Bank Ltd, 6 Pall Mall, SW1Y 5NH. *Club:* Naval.

MUIR, Sir John (Harling), 3rd Bt, *cr* 1892; TD; DL; Director: James Finlay & Co. Ltd, since 1946 (Chairman, 1961-75); London and Lancashire Insurance Co. Ltd; Royal Insurance Co. Ltd; National and Grindlay's Holdings Ltd; Scottish United Investors Ltd; Star Offshore Services Ltd, etc; Member, Queen's Body Guard for Scotland (The Royal Company of Archers); *b* 7 Nov. 1910; *s* of James Finlay Muir (*d* 1948), Braco Castle, Perthshire, and of Charlotte Escudier, *d* of J. Harling Turner, CBE; *S* uncle 1951; *m* 1936, Elizabeth Mary, *e d* of late Frederick James Dundas, Dale Cottage, Cawthorne, near Barnsley; five *s* two *d*. *Educ:* Stowe. With James Finlay & Co. Ltd, in India, 1932-40. Served War of 1939-45; joined 3rd Carabiniers, Sept. 1940, Lieut; transferred 25th Dragoons, 1941, Capt.; Major, 1942; transferred RAC Depot, Poona, i/c Sqdn, 1942; transferred to Staff, HQ 109 L of C Area, Bangalore; held various Staff appointments terminating as AA and QMG with actg rank of Lt-Col; demobilised, 1946, with rank of Major. DL, Perthshire, 1966. *Recreations:* shooting, fishing, gardening. *Heir: s* Richard James Kay Muir [*b* 25 May 1939; *m* 1965, Susan Elizabeth (marr. diss.), *d* of G. A. Gardner, Leamington Spa; two *d*; *m* 1975, Lady Linda Mary Cole, *d* of 6th Earl of Enniskillen, *qv*; one *d*]. *Address:* Bankhead, Blair Drummond, by Stirling, Perthshire. *T:* Doune 207. *Clubs:* Oriental, English-Speaking Union; Western (Glasgow); Tollygunge (Calcutta).
See also Sir G. J. Aird, Bt.

MUIR, Prof. Kenneth, FBA 1970; King Alfred Professor of English Literature, University of Liverpool, 1951-74, now

Professor Emeritus; *b* 1907; *s* of Dr R. D. Muir; *m* 1936, Mary Ewen; one *s* one *d*. *Educ:* Epsom Coll.; St Edmund Hall, Oxford. Lectr in English, St John's Coll., York, 1930-37; Lectr in English Literature, Leeds Univ., 1937-51; Liverpool University: Public Orator, 1961-65; Dean of the Faculty of Arts, 1958-61. Visiting Professor: Univ. of Pittsburgh, 1962-63; Univ. of Connecticut, 1973; Univ. of Pennsylvania, 1977. Editor, Shakespeare Survey, 1965-; Chm., Internat. Shakespeare Assoc., 1974-. Leeds City Councillor, 1945-47, 1950-51; Chm. of Leeds Fabian Soc., 1941-46; Pres., Leeds Labour Party, 1951; Birkenhead Borough Councillor, 1954-57. Docteur de l'Université: de Rouen, 1967; de Dijon, 1976. *Publications:* The Nettle and the Flower, 1933; Jonah in the Whale, 1935; (with Sean O'Loughlin) The Voyage to Illyria, 1937; English Poetry, 1938; Collected Poems of Sir Thomas Wyatt, 1949; Arden edn Macbeth, 1951; King Lear, 1952; Elizabethan Lyrics, 1953; (ed) Wilkins' Painful Adventures of Pericles, 1953; John Milton, 1955; The Pelican Book of English Prose I, 1956; Shakespeare's Sources, 1957; (ed with F. P. Wilson) The Life and Death of Jack Straw, 1957; (ed) John Keats, 1958; Shakespeare and the Tragic Pattern, 1959; trans. Five Plays of Jean Racine, 1960; Shakespeare as Collaborator, 1960; editor Unpublished Poems by Sir Thomas Wyatt, 1961; Last Periods, 1961; (ed) U. Éllis-Fermor's Shakespeare the Dramatist, 1961; (ed) Richard II, 1963; Life and Letters of Sir Thomas Wyatt, 1963; Shakespeare: Hamlet, 1963; (ed) Shakespeare: The Comedies, 1965; Introduction to Elizabethan Literature, 1967; (ed) Othello, 1968; (ed) The Winter's Tale, 1968; (ed with Patricia Thomson) Collected Poems of Sir Thomas Wyatt, 1969; The Comedy of Manners, 1970; (ed) The Rivals, 1970; (ed) Double Falsehood, 1970; (ed with S. Schoenbaum) A New Companion to Shakespeare Studies, 1971; Shakespeare's Tragic Sequence, 1972; Shakespeare the Professional, 1973; (ed) Essays and Studies, 1974; (ed) Three Plays of Thomas Middleton, 1975; The Singularity of Shakespeare, 1977; The Sources of Shakespeare, 1977. *Recreations:* acting, producing plays, local government. *Address:* 6 Chetwynd Road, Oxton, Birkenhead, Merseyside. *T:* 051-652 3301. *Club:* Athenæum (Liverpool).

MUIR, Percival Horace; Managing Director, Elkin Mathews Ltd, since 1939, Director since 1930; *b* 17 Dec. 1894; *s* of Charles Henry Muir and Annie Hancock; *m* 1935, Barbara Kenrick Gowing (pen-name Barbara Kaye); one *s* one *d*. *Educ:* LCC primary and secondary Schs. After varied career in business and as lecturer, journalist and actor, set up on own account as antiquarian bookseller, 1920; joined Dulau & Co. Ltd, as Dir, 1927; Elkin Mathews Ltd, 1930. Chm., Collector Ltd. President: Antiquarian Booksellers' Assoc., 1945-47 (Hon. Life Mem.); Internat. League of Antiquarian Booksellers, 1948-50, thereafter life Pres. of Honour; Hon. Life Member: Nat. Book League; Société de la Librairie Ancienne et Moderne. *Publications:* Points, being extracts from a bibliographer's scrapbook, 1931, 2nd series 1934; Book Collecting, Vol. I, 1944, Vol. II, 1949; English Children's Books, 1954 (new edn, 1969); Minding My Own Business, 1956; Printing and the Mind of Man, 1967; Victorian Illustrated Books, 1971; ed, and part-author, Talks on Book Collecting, 1952; Some Printers and Publishers of Conjuring Books 1800-1850. *Recreations:* bibliography, music, gardening. *Address:* Scriveners, Blakeney, Holt, Norfolk. *T:* Cley 974475.

MUIR, Thompson; Counsellor (Industry and Energy), UK Permanent Representation to the European Communities, Brussels, since 1975; *b* 19 Feb. 1936; *s* of William and Maria Muir; *m* 1968, Brenda Dew; one *s* one *d*. *Educ:* King Edward VI Sch., Stafford; Univ. of Leeds. BA 1962. With English Electric Co. Ltd, 1954-59; joined BoT as Asst Principal, 1962, Principal, 1965; seconded to HM Diplomatic Service as First Sec., UK Permanent Delegn to OECD, Paris, 1968-71; Cabinet Office, 1971-72; DTI, later DoI, 1972-74; Asst Sec., 1972. *Recreations:* travel, reading, football and Rugby, cinema. *Address:* c/o Foreign and Commonwealth Office, SW1.

MUIR BEDDALL, Hugh Richard; *see* Beddall.

MUIR MACKENZIE, Sir Alexander (Alwyne Henry Charles Brinton), 7th Bt *cr* 1805; *b* 8 Dec. 1955; *s* of Sir Robert Henry Muir Mackenzie, 6th Bt and Charmian Cecil de Vere (*d* 1962), *o d* of Col Cecil Charles Brinton; *S* father, 1970. *Educ:* Eton; Trinity Coll., Cambridge. *Address:* Sunderland Hall, near Galashiels, Selkirkshire; Park Hall, near Kidderminster, Worcestershire.

MUIR WOOD, Alan Marshall, FICE; Partner, Sir William Halcrow & Partners, since 1964; Director, Halcrow Fox & Associates, since 1977; *b* 8 Aug. 1921; *s* of Edward Stephen Wood and Dorothy (*née* Webb); *m* 1943, Winifred Leyton Lanagan; three *s*. *Educ:* Abbotsholme Sch.; Peterhouse,

Cambridge Univ. (MA). FICE 1957; Fellow, Fellowship of Engrg, 1977. Engr Officer, RN, 1942-46. Asst Engr, British Rail, Southern Reg., 1946-50; Res. Asst, Docks and Inland Waterways Exec., 1950-52; Asst Engr, then Sen. Engr, Sir William Halcrow & Partners, 1952-64. Principally concerned with studies and works in fields of tunnelling, geotechnics, coastal engrg, roads and railways; major projects include: (Proj. Engr) Clyde Tunnel and Potters Bar railway tunnels; (Partner) Cargo Tunnel at Heathrow Airport, and road crossing of River Orwell; studies and works for Channel Tunnel (intermittently from 1958 to cancellation in 1975); Dir, Orange-Fish Consultants, resp. for 80 km irrigation tunnel. President: (first), Internat. Tunnelling Assoc., 1975-77; ICE, 1977-78. Telford Medal, ICE, 1976. *Publications:* Coastal Hydraulics, 1969; papers, mainly on tunnelling and coastal engrg, in Proc. ICE, and Geotechnique. *Address:* Franklands, Bere Court Road, Pangbourne, Berks. *T:* Pangbourne 2833.

MUIRHEAD, Sir David (Francis), KCMG 1976 (CMG 1964); CVO 1957; HM Diplomatic Service; HM Ambassador to Belgium, since 1974; *b* 30 Dec. 1918; *s* of late David Muirhead, Kippen, Stirlingshire; *m* 1942, Hon. Elspeth Hope-Morley, *d* of 2nd Baron Hollenden, and of Hon. Mary Gardner, *d* of 1st Baron Burghclere; two *s* one *d*. *Educ:* Cranbrook Sch. Commissioned Artists Rifles (Rifle Brigade), 1937; passed Officers Exam., RMC Sandhurst; apptd to Bedfs and Herts Regt, 1939; served War of 1939-45 in France, Belgium and SE Asia. Hon. Attaché, Brit. Embassy, Madrid, 1941. Passed Foreign Service Exam., 1946; appointed to Foreign Office, 1947; La Paz, 1948; Buenos Aires, 1949; Brussels, 1950; Foreign Office, 1953; Washington, 1955; Foreign Office, 1959; Head of Personnel Dept, DSAO, 1965; Under-Sec., Special Planning Duties, Foreign Office, 1966-67; HM Ambassador: Peru, 1967-70; Portugal, 1970-74. Kt Grand Cross, Military Order of Christ (Portugal). *Recreations:* tennis, badminton. *Address:* c/o Foreign and Commonwealth Office, SW1; 16 Pitt Street, W8. *T:* 01-937 2443. *Club:* Travellers'.

MUIRSHIEL, 1st Viscount, *cr* 1964, of Kilmacolm; **John Scott Maclay,** KT 1973; PC 1952; CH 1962; CMG 1944; Lord-Lieutenant of Renfrewshire since 1967; *b* 26 Oct. 1905; *s* of 1st Baron Maclay, PC; *m* 1930, Betty L'Estrange Astley (*d* 1974). *Educ:* Winchester; Trinity Coll., Cambridge. MP (Nat. L and C) for Montrose Burghs, 1940-50, for Renfrewshire West, 1950-64. Head of Brit. Merchant Shipping Mission, Washington, 1944; Parliamentary Sec., Min. of Production, May-July 1945; Minister of Transport and Civil Aviation, 1951-52; Minister of State for Colonial Affairs, Oct. 1956-Jan. 1957; Sec. of State for Scotland, Jan. 1957-July 1962. Pres., National Liberal Council, 1957-67; Chm., Joint Exchequer Board for Northern Ireland, 1965-72. Dir, Clydesdale Bank, 1970-. Hon. LLD: Edinburgh, 1963; Strathclyde, 1966; Glasgow, 1970. *Heir:* none. *Address:* Knapps, Kilmacolm, Renfrewshire. *T:* Kilmacolm 2770. *Clubs:* Boodle's; Western (Glasgow); Royal Yacht Squadron.

MUKHERJEE, Tara Kumar; District Manager, Save & Prosper Group, since 1970; President, Confederation of Indian Organisations (UK), since 1975; *b* 20 Dec. 1923; *s* of Sushil Chandra Mukherjee and Sova Moyee Mukherjee; *m* 1951, Betty Patricia Mukherjee; one *s* one *d*. *Educ:* Scottish Church Collegiate Sch., Calcutta, India; Calcutta Univ. (matriculated 1939). Shop Manager, Bata Shoe Co. Ltd, India, 1941-44; Buyer, Brevitt Shoes, Leicester, 1951-56; Sundries Buyer, British Shoe Corp., 1956-66; Prodn Administrator, Priestley Footwear Ltd, Great Harwood, 1966-68; Head Stores Manager, Brit. Shoe Corp., 1968-70. Pres., India Film Soc., Leicester. Member: Brit. Europ. Movement, London; Exec. Council, Leics Europ. Movement; Trustees, Haymarket Theatre, Leicester. *Recreation:* cricket (1st Cl. cricketer; played for Bihar, Ranji Trophy, 1941; 2nd XI, Leics CCC, 1949). *Address:* Tallah, 42 Shirley Avenue, Leicester LE2 3NA. *T:* Leicester 703255. *Club:* (Gen. Sec.) Indian National (Leicester).

MULDOON, Rt. Hon. Robert David, PC 1976; CH 1977; MP Tamaki, since 1960; Prime Minister of New Zealand, and Minister of Finance, since 1975; Leader of the National Party, since 1974; *b* 25 Sept. 1921; *s* of James Henry and Mamie R. Muldoon; *m* 1951, Thea Dale Flyger; one *s* two *d*. *Educ:* Mt Albert Grammar School. FCANZ, CMANZ, FCIS, FCWA. Chartered Accountant. Pres., NZ Inst. of Cost Accountants, 1956. Parly Under-Sec. to Minister of Finance, 1963-66; Minister of Tourism, 1967; Minister of Finance, 1967-72; Dep. Prime Minister, Feb.-Nov. 1972; Dep. Leader, National Party and Dep. Leader of the Opposition, 1972-74; Leader of the Opposition, 1974-75. *Publications:* The Rise and Fall of a Young Turk, 1974; Muldoon, 1977. *Recreation:* horticulture. *Address:* 290 Kohimarama Road, Auckland 5, New Zealand. *Clubs:* Wellington, Professional (New Zealand).

MULGRAVE, Earl of; Constantine Edmund Walter Phipps; *b* 24 Feb. 1954; *s* and *heir* of 4th Marquis of Normanby, *qv*. *Educ:* Eton (Oppidan Scholar); Worcester Coll., Oxford. *Address:* Mulgrave Castle, Whitby, N Yorks.

MULHOLLAND, family name of **Baron Dunleath.**

MULHOLLAND, Hon. Mrs John, (Olivia Vernon), DCVO 1971 (CVO 1958); Woman of the Bedchamber to Queen Elizabeth The Queen Mother since 1950; Chairman, Elizabeth Garrett Anderson Hospital, 1945-72; Vice-Chairman, Royal Free Hospital Group, 1950-61; Member: North London Group Hospital Management Committee, 1961-72; King Edward's Hospital Fund Management Committee, 1961; *b* 1902; 2nd *d* of 1st Viscount Harcourt and Mary Ethel, Viscountess Harcourt, GBE, *o d* of Walter Haynes Burns, New York and North Mymms Park, Hatfield; *m* 1923, Hon. (Godfrey) John A. M. L. Mulholland (*d* 1948), *y s* of 2nd Baron Dunleath, Ballywalter Park, Co. Down, N Ireland; one *s* two *d*. *Educ:* Notting Hill High Sch.; Lady Margaret Hall, Oxford. *Address:* Weston Mark, Upton Grey, Basingstoke, Hants. *T:* Long Sutton 429.

MULHOLLAND, Major Sir Michael (Henry), 2nd Bt *cr* 1945; retired; *b* 15 Oct. 1915; *s* of Rt Hon. Sir Henry George Hill Mulholland, 1st Bt, and of Sheelah, *d* of Sir Douglas Brooke, 4th Bt; *S* father, 1971; *m* 1st, 1942, Rosemary Ker (marr. diss. 1948); 2nd, 1949, Elizabeth, *d* of Laurence B. Hyde; one *s*. *Educ:* Eton; Pembroke College, Cambridge (BA). Regular Army Commission, 1937, Oxford and Bucks Light Infantry; retired, 1951, with rank of Major. *Heir: s* Brian Henry Mulholland, *b* 25 Sept. 1950. *Address:* Storbrooke, Massey Avenue, Belfast 4. *T:* Belfast 63394. *Clubs:* MCC; Light Infantry (Shrewsbury).

MULKEARNS, Most Rev. Ronald Austin; *see* Ballarat, Bishop of, (RC).

MULKERN, John, FCIT; Managing Director and Member of Board, British Airports Authority, since 1977; *b* 15 Jan. 1931; *s* of late Thomas Mulkern and of Annie Tennant; *m* 1954, May Egerton (*née* Peters); one *s* three *d*. *Educ:* Stretford Grammar Sch. Dip. in Govt Admin. FCIT 1973. Ministries of Supply and Aviation, Civil Service, 1949-65: Exec. Officer, finally Principal, Audit, Purchasing, Finance, Personnel and Legislation branches; British Airports Authority, 1965-: Dep. Gen. Man., Heathrow Airport, 1970-73; Dir, Gatwick Airport, 1973-77. *Recreations:* family pursuits, classical recorded music, destructive gardening. *Address:* 2 Holmwood Close, Maidenhead, Berks. *T:* Maidenhead 25150.

MULLALY, Terence Frederick Stanley; Art Critic of The Daily Telegraph since 1958; *b* 14 Nov. 1927; *s* of late Col B. R. Mullaly (4th *s* of Maj.-Gen. Sir Herbert Mullaly, KCMG, CB, CSI) and Eileen Dorothy (*née* Stanley); *m* 1949, Elizabeth Helen (*née* Burkitt). *Educ:* in India, England, Japan and Canada; Downing Coll., Cambridge (MA). Archæological studies in Tripolitania, 1948, and Sicily, 1949; has specialised in study of Italian art, particularly Venetian and Veronese painting of 16th and 17th centuries; lecturer and broadcaster. Pres. Brit. Section, Internat. Assoc. of Art Critics, 1967-73; Mem., Adv. Cttee: Cracow Art Festival, 1974; Palermo Art Festival, 1976. FRSA 1969; FSA 1977. Commendatore, Order Al Merito, Italy, 1974 (Cavaliere Ufficiale, 1964); l'Ordre du Mérite Culturel, Poland, 1974. *Publications:* Ruskin a Verona, 1966; catalogue of exhibition, Disegni veronesi del Cinquecento, 1971; contrib. to catalogue of exhibition Cinquant' anni di pittura veronese: 1580-1630, 1974; contrib on history of art, to Burlington Magazine, Master Drawings, Arte Illustrata, Antologia di Belle Arti, The Minneapolis Inst. of Arts Bulletin, etc. *Recreations:* collecting and travel. *Address:* 74 Greencroft Gardens, Hampstead, NW6. *T:* 01-624 8531.

MULLAN, Charles Heron, VRD; DL; Resident Magistrate; Lieutenant-Commander RNVR; retired, 1951; *b* 17 Feb. 1912; *s* of Frederick Heron Mullan, BA, DL, Solicitor, and Minnie Mullan; *m* 1940, Marcella Elizabeth Sharpe, *er d* of J. A. McCullagh, Ballycastle, Co. Antrim; one *s*. *Educ:* Castle Park, Dalkey; Rossall Sch., Fleetwood; Clare Coll., Cambridge. Hons Degree Law, Cambridge, 1934; MA 1939. Joined Ulster Div. RNVR, 1936; called up for active service with Royal Navy, Aug. 1939; served throughout the war (King Haakon VII War Decoration), HMS Rodney 1939-40; destroyers and escort vessels, Channel, North Sea, North Atlantic, etc, 1940-44 (with Royal Norwegian Navy, 1941-43). MP (UU) Co. Down, 1946-50, Imperial Parlt; contested S Down, 1945, for NI Parlt. Mem. Ulster Unionist Council, 1946-60. Solicitor 1948; Resident Magistrate, 1960; JP 1960; Chm., Belfast Juvenile Courts, 1964. Mem., N Ireland Section of British Delegn to 3rd UN Congress on Prevention of Crime and Treatment of Offenders, Stockholm,

1965; Mem. Exec. Cttee, British Juvenile Courts Soc., 1973; NI Rep. to 9th Congress of Internat. Assoc. of Youth Magistrates, Oxford, 1974; Mem., Internat. Assoc. of Youth Magistrates, 1974-. Hon. Governor, South Down Hospitals Gp, 1965-. DL Co. Down, 1974. *Recreations:* tennis, shooting, walking, boating. *Address:* Cairn Hill, Newry, Co. Down, Northern Ireland. *T:* 2003; Casanbarra, Ballycastle, Co. Antrim, Northern Ireland. *T:* 62323. *Club:* Naval.

MULLENS, Sir Harold (Hill), Kt 1963; FIEE; FRSA; President, Reyrolle Parsons Ltd; Deputy Chairman, The Nuclear Power Plant Co. Ltd; *b* 19 Feb. 1900; *s* of Harry Joseph Mullens and Gertrude Charlotte (*née* Hill); *m* 1932, Winifred McConnell; one *s* one *d*. *Educ:* Merchant Taylors' Sch.; Durham Univ. (BSc). Joined North Eastern Electric Supply Co. Ltd, 1926 and held various appointments from asst engineer to deputy General Manager until nationalisation of electricity supply industry. Chm. of North Eastern Electricity Board, 1948-54, when resigned to become Managing Dir of A. Reyrolle & Co. Ltd; Chairman: A. Reyrolle & Co. Ltd, 1958-68; C. A. Parsons & Co. Ltd, 1960-68; Reyrolle Parsons Ltd, 1968; Anglo Great Lakes Corp. Ltd, 1959-68; Sir Howard Grubb Parsons & Co. Ltd, 1960-66; The Bushing Co. Ltd, 1958-70; Director: Parolle Electrical Plant Co. Ltd, 1959-68; Pyrotenax Ltd, 1959-67; Dorman Long & Co. Ltd, and subsids, 1955-67; Internat. Research & Develt Co., 1963-68; The Nuclear Power Group Ltd, 1965-68. Mem. of British Electricity Authority, 1952-53. Vice-Pres. of British Electrical Development Assoc., 1956-59. Pres., British Electrical and Allied Manufacturers' Association, 1962-63; Pres., British Electrical Power Convention, 1963-64. Chm. Governors, Rutherford Coll., 1959-61. Hon. Col 105 Corps Engineer Regt Royal Engineers (TA), 1955-57. *Publications:* technical papers. *Recreations:* gardening and golf. *Address:* 4 Westfield Grove, Gosforth, Newcastle upon Tyne. *T:* Gosforth 854297. *Club:* Northern Counties (Newcastle).

MULLER, Franz Joseph; a Recorder of the Crown Court, since 1977; *b* England, 19 Nov. 1938; *s* of Wilhelm Muller and Anne Maria (*née* Ravens). *Educ:* Mount St Mary's Coll.; Univ. of Sheffield (LLB). Called to the Bar, Gray's Inn, 1961. Graduate Apprentice, United Steel Cos, 1960-61; Commercial Asst, Workington Iron and Steel Co. Ltd, 1961-63. Commenced practice at the Bar, 1964. Non-Executive Director: Richards of Sheffield (Holdings) Ltd, 1969-77; Joseph Rodgers and Son Ltd and Rodgers Wostenholm Ltd, 1975-77. *Recreations:* squash, fell walking, being in Greece, listening to music. *Address:* 18 Laurel Court, Endcliffe Vale Road, Sheffield S10 3DU. *T:* Sheffield 669187; 11 King's Bench Walk, Temple, EC4Y 7EQ. *T:* 01-353 3337.

MULLER, Dr Hilgard; director of companies and farmer; MP for Beaufort West, 1964-77; *b* 4 May 1914; *s* of C. J. Muller; *m* 1943, Anita Dyason; one *s*. *Educ:* Pretoria Univ.; Oxford Univ.; DLitt Pretoria, BLitt Oxon., LLB S Africa. Rhodes Scholar, 1937; Univ. Lecturer, Pretoria, 1941-47. Solicitor, 1947-61; Dir of Companies and farmer. Mayor of Pretoria, 1953-55; MP for Pretoria East, 1958-61; High Commissioner for Union of South Africa in the UK, Jan.-May, 1961; South African Ambassador to the Court of St James's, 1961-63; Minister of Foreign Affairs, South Africa, 1964-77. Chancellor of the Univ. of Pretoria, 1965-, formerly Pres. of Convocation. DPhil (*hc*) Pretoria; PhD (*hc*) Stellenbosch. Mem. RSA. Grand Cross, Order of Merit (Paraguay), 1966; Grand Cross, Order of Christ (Portugal), 1968; Grand Cross of Order of Infante Dom Henrique (Portugal), 1973; Grand Officer of Order of Merit of Central African Republic, 1976; Decoration for Meritorious Service (South Africa), 1976. *Recreations:* golf, farming, reading. *Address:* PO Box 793, Pretoria, South Africa. *Clubs:* various in South Africa.

MULLER, Mrs Robert; *see* Whitelaw, Billie.

MULLETT, Leslie Baden; Deputy Director, Transport and Road Research Laboratory, Department of the Environment/Department of Transport, since 1974; *b* 22 Aug. 1920; *s* of Joseph and Edith Mullett; *m* 1st, 1946, Katherine Lear (marr. diss. 1968); no *c*; 2nd, 1971, Gillian Pettit. *Educ:* Gram. Sch., Hales Owen, Worcs; Birmingham Univ. BSc (Hons Physics) 1941. Telecommunications Research Estab., 1941-46; AEA, 1946-60 (Head of Accelerator Div., 1958); Asst Dir, Rutherford High Energy Lab., SRC, 1960-; on secondment to Res. Gp, Min. of Technology, 1966-68; CSO, Min. of Transport, 1968; CSO, Res. Requirements, DoE, 1970-74. *Publications:* papers in learned jls on particle accelerators. *Recreations:* fishing, caravanning. *Address:* 22 Wellington Court, Spencers Wood, Reading, Berks. *T:* (business) Crowthorne 3131.

MULLEY, Rt. Hon. Frederick William, PC 1964; MP (Lab) Park Division of Sheffield since 1950; Secretary of State for Defence, since 1976; barrister-at-law and economist; *b* 3 July 1918; *er s* of late William and M. A. Mulley, Leamington Spa; *m* 1948, Joan D., *d* of Alexander and Betty Phillips; two *d. Educ:* Bath Place Church of England Sch.; Warwick Sch. (Schol.); Christ Church, Oxford (Adult Scholar, 1945). 1st Class Hons Philosophy, Politics and Economics, 1947; Research Studentship, Nuffield Coll., Oxford, 1947; Fellowship (Economics), St Catharine's Coll., Cambridge, 1948-50. Called to Bar, Inner Temple, 1954. Son of general labourer; clerk, National Health Insurance Cttee, Warwicks; joined Labour Party and Nat. Union of Clerks, 1936. Served War of 1939-45, Worcs Regt; Lance-Sgt 1940 (prisoner of war in Germany, 1940-45, meanwhile obtaining BSc (Econ.) and becoming Chartered Sec.). Contested (Lab) Sutton Coldfield Division of Warwicks, 1945. Parliamentary delegation to Germany, 1951, and to Kenya, 1957; PPS to Minister of Works, 1951; National Exec. Cttee, Labour Party, 1957-58, 1960-64, 1965-; Chm., Labour Party, 1974-75. Delegate to Council of Europe and WEU, 1958-61, also Vice-Pres. Economic Cttee and Vice-Pres. WEU Assembly, 1960. Deputy Defence Sec. and Minister for the Army, 1964-65; Minister of Aviation, Dec. 1965-Jan. 1967; Jt Minister of State, FCO (formerly FO), 1967-69; Minister for Disarmament, 1967-69; Minister of Transport, 1969-70; Minister for Transport, DoE, 1974-75; Sec. of State for Educn and Science, 1975-76. *Publications:* The Politics of Western Defence, 1962; articles on economic, defence and socialist subjects. *Address:* 192 Sutherland Avenue, W9.

MULLIGAN, Col Hugh Waddell, CMG 1954; MD, DSc; *b* 13 Nov. 1901; *s* of late Rev. J. A. W. Mulligan and Jem Anderson; *m* Rita, *d* of late J. E. Armstrong; two *s* one *d. Educ:* Robert Gordon's Coll., Aberdeen; Aberdeen Univ. MB, ChB 1923; MD (Hons) Aberdeen 1930; DSc, 1934, IMS, 1923-47. Served War of 1939-45 (active service, 1940-43). Commonwealth Fund Fellow, Univ. Chicago, 1933-35. Dir Pasteur Inst. of Southern India, 1938-40; Dir, Central Research Inst., Kasauli, 1944-47; Dir, West African Inst. for Trypanosomiasis Research (Colonial Research Service), 1947-54; Dir and Head of Biological Division, Wellcome Research Laboratories, Beckenham, Kent, 1954-66. *Publications:* (ed) The African Trypanosomiases, 1970; papers on protozoology, immunology, pathology, etc. *Recreations:* fishing, shooting, gardening. *Address:* 5 Thorngrove Road, Wilmslow, Cheshire. *T:* Wilmslow 22579.

MULLIGAN, Most Rev. Patrick; *see* Clogher, Bishop of, (RC).

MULLIKEN, Prof. Robert S., PhD; Professor of Physics and Chemistry, University of Chicago; *b* Newburyport, Mass, 7 June 1896; *s* of Samuel Parsons Mulliken, Prof. of Organic Chemistry, and Katherine (*née* Mulliken); *m* 1929, Mary Helen von Noé; two *d. Educ:* Massachusetts Inst. of Technology; Univ. of Chicago. BS (MIT), 1917; PhD (Chicago), 1921. Nat. Research Coun. Fellow, Univ. of Chicago, and Harvard Univ., 1921-25; Guggenheim Fellow, Europe, 1930 and 1932-33; Fulbright Scholar, Oxford Univ., 1952-53; Vis. Fellow, St John's Coll., Oxford, 1952-53. Jun. Chem. Engr, Bureau of Mines, US Dept of Interior, Washington, 1917-18; Chemical Warfare Service, US Army, 1918 (Pte First-Class); Asst in Rubber Research, New Jersey Zinc Co., Penn., 1919; Asst Prof. of Physics, Washington Sq. Coll., New York Univ., 1926-28; Univ. of Chicago: Assoc. Prof. of Physics, 1928-31; Prof. of Physics, 1931-61 and Chemistry, 1961; Ernest de Witt Burton Distinguished Service Prof., 1956-61; Distinguished Service Prof. of Physics and Chemistry, 1961-; Distinguished Research Prof. of Chemical Physics, Florida State Univ., (Jan.-March) 1965-72. Dir, Editorial Work and Information, Plutonium Project, Univ. of Chicago, 1942-45; Scientific Attaché, US Embassy, London, 1955. Baker Lectr, Cornell Univ., 1960; Silliman Lectr, Yale Univ., 1965; Visiting Professor: Bombay, 1962; Kampur, 1962; Jan van Geuns Vis. Prof., Amsterdam Univ., 1965. Member: Amer. Acad. of Arts and Sciences; Nat. Acad. of Sciences; Amer. Philosophical Soc.; Amer. Chem. Soc.; Fellow: Amer. Physical Soc.; Amer. Acad. for Advancement of Science; Internat. Acad. of Quantum Molecular Science; Hon. Fellow: Chem. Soc. of Gt Britain; Indian Nat. Acad. of Science; Foreign Mem., Royal Soc.; Hon. Mem., Soc. de Chimie Physique, Paris; Corresp. Mem., Soc. Royale des Sciences de Liège. Hon. Mem., Royal Irish Acad.; Hon. ScD: Columbia, 1939; Marquette, 1966; Cantab, 1966; Hon. PhD Stockholm, 1960. Nobel Prize for Chemistry, 1966; other medals and awards. *Publications:* (with Willis B. Person) Molecular Complexes; Selected Papers; over 200 contributions (1919-; in recent years dealing extensively with structure and spectra of molecular complexes) to various American and foreign journals including: Jl Am. Chem. Soc.; Jl Chem. Phys; Rev. Mod. Phys; Phys Rev.; Chem. Rev.; Nature; also contributions: Proc. Nat. Acad. Sci.; Trans Faraday Soc. *Recreations:* driving a car,

Oriental rugs, art. *Address:* (home) 5825 Dorchester Avenue, Chicago, Ill 60637, USA; (office) Department of Chemistry, University of Chicago, 5735 South Ellis Avenue, Chicago, Ill 60637. *Clubs:* Quadrangle (Chicago); Cosmos (Washington).

MULLIN, Prof. John William, DSc, PhD, CEng, FRIC, FIChemE; Professor of Chemical Engineering, University College London, since 1969; *b* Rock Ferry, Cheshire, 22 Aug. 1925; *er s* of late Frederick Mullin and Kathleen Nellie Mullin (*née* Oppy); *m* 1952, Averil Margaret Davies, Carmarthen; one *s* one *d. Educ:* Hawarden County Sch.; UCW Cardiff; University Coll. London. 8 yrs in organic fine chemicals industry; Lectr 1956, Reader 1961, Dean, Faculty of Engrg, 1975-77, University Coll. London. Vis. Prof., Univ. New Brunswick, 1967. Chm. Bd of Staff Examrs, Chem. Eng, Univ. London, 1965-70. Hon. Librarian, IChemE, 1965-77; Mem. Cttee of Management, Inst. of Child Health, 1970-; Founder Mem., Brit. Assoc. for Crystal Growth; Mem. BS and ISO Cttees on metrication, sieves, industrial screens, particle sizing, etc. Moulton Medal, IChemE, 1970. *Publications:* Crystallization, 1961, 2nd edn 1972; (ed) Industrial Crystallization, 1976; papers in Trans IChemE, Chem. Engrg Sci., Jl Crystal Growth, etc. *Address:* 4 Milton Road, Ickenham, Mddx. *Club:* Athenæum.

MULLINS, Brian Percival, PhD; Director of Research and Laboratory Services and Head of Safety in Mines Research Establishment, Health and Safety Executive, (Under-Secretary), since 1975; *b* 5 Aug. 1920; *s* of Thomas Percival Mullins and Lillian May Mullins; *m* 1944, Margaret Fiona Howell, MA; one *s* one *d. Educ:* Shooters' Hill Sch., London; Woolwich Polytechnic Evening Inst. BSc Nat. Sciences (London), 1940; PhD Fuel Techn. (Extern. London), 1951. Clerical Officer, Air Ministry, 1937-40; Research Scientist, Engine Dept, Royal Aircraft Estabt, 1941-42; seconded to Univ. of Cambridge for high vacuum gas analysis research, 1943; fuels, combustion and aero-engine research at Power Jets (R&D) Ltd and at Nat. Gas Turbine Estabt, 1944-60; Head of Chemistry Dept, RAE, 1960-62; Head of Chemistry, Physics and Metallurgy Dept, RAE, 1962-65; idc (seconded), 1966; Head of Structures Dept, RAE, 1967-74. Chm., Combustion Panel, AGARD-NATO, 1954-57; Sen. UK Mem., Structures and Materials Panel, AGARD-NATO, 1967-74. *Publications:* Spontaneous Ignition of Liquid Fuels, 1955; (jtly) Explosions, Detonations, Flammability and Ignition, 1959; numerous scientific research papers. *Recreation:* oriental languages. *Address:* 1 St Michael's Road, Farnborough, Hants GU14 8ND. *T:* Farnborough (Hants) 42137.

MULLINS, Rt. Rev. Daniel Joseph; Titular Bishop of Stowe, and Auxiliary Bishop in Cardiff (RC), since 1970; *b* 10 July 1929; *s* of Timothy Mullins. *Educ:* Mount Melleray; St Mary's, Aberystwyth; Oscott Coll.; UC of S Wales and Mon, Cardiff. Priest, 1953. Curate at: Barry, 1953-56; Newbridge, 1956; Bargoed, 1956-57; Maesteg, 1957-60; Asst Chaplain to UC Cardiff, 1960-64; Sec. to Archbp of Cardiff, 1964-68; Vicar General of Archdiocese of Cardiff, 1968. *Recreation:* golf. *Address:* St Joseph's Presbytery, Penarth, South Glam CF6 1RL. *T:* Penarth 708247.

MULLINS, Leonard, CMG 1976; PhD, DSc; Director of Research, Malaysian Rubber Producers' Research Association, Brickendonbury, Hertford, since 1962; *b* 21 May 1918; *s* of Robert and Eugenie Alice Mullins; *m* 1943, Freda Elaine Churchouse; two *d. Educ:* Eltham Coll.; University Coll., London; Inst. of Educn, London. BSc (Hons), PhD, DSc. Experimental Officer, Min. of Supply, 1940-44; Scientific Officer, finally Head of Physics Gp, Research Assoc. of British Rubber Manufrs, 1944-49; Malaysian (previously British) Rubber Producers' Research Assoc., 1950-; Foundn Lectr, Instn of Rubber Industry, 1968. Chairman: Council of Plastics and Rubber Inst., 1976-; Adv. Cttee, Nat. Coll. of Rubber Technology, 1976-; Vice-Pres., Plastics and Rubber Inst., 1977-. Discovered Mullins Effect, relating to elastic behaviour of rubber. Governor of local schools. Colwyn Medal, IRI, 1966; Comdr, Malaysian Order of Chivalry, JMN, 1975. *Publications:* numerous original scientific papers in field of rubber physics. *Address:* 32 Sherrardspark Road, Welwyn Garden City, Herts AL8 7JS. *T:* Welwyn Garden 23633. *Club:* Athenæum.

MUMFORD, Sir Albert (Henry), KBE 1963 (OBE 1946); CEng, FIEE; Engineer-in-Chief, GPO, 1960-65, retd; *b* 16 April, 1903; *s* of late George Mumford; *m* 1927, Eileen Berry; two *s* two *d. Educ:* Bancroft's Sch.; Queen Mary Coll., Univ. of London. BSc (Eng) 1st Class Hons (London) 1923. Entered GPO Engineering Dept, 1924; Staff Engineer radio branch, 1938; Imperial Defence Coll., 1948; Asst Engineer-in-Chief, 1951; Dep. Engineer-in-Chief, 1954. Treasurer, Instn of Electrical Engineers, 1969-72 (Chm. Radio Section, 1945-46; Vice-Pres. 1958-63; Pres. 1963-64); Pres. Assoc. Supervising Electrical Engineers, 1964-66;

Treas., Instn of Electrical and Electronic Technician Engineers, 1967-. Fellow, Queen Mary Coll., Dec. 1962; Hon. Mem., City and Guilds of London Inst. *Publications:* many scientific papers. *Address:* 27 Grendon Gardens, Wembley Park, Mddx. *T:* 01-904 2360.

MUMFORD, L(awrence) Quincy; Librarian of Congress, 1954-75, retd; *b* 11 Dec. 1903; *s* of Jacob Edward Mumford and Emma Luvenia (*née* Stocks); *m* 1930, Permelia Catharine Stevens (*d* 1961); one *d*; *m* 1969, Betsy Perrin Fox. Educ; Duke Univ. (AB *magna cum laude;* AM); Columbia Univ. (BS). Mem. staff, Duke Univ. Library, 1922-28; Head of Circulation Dept, 1926; Chief of Reference and Circulation, 1927-28; Student Asst, Columbia Univ. Library, 1928-29; Mem. staff, New York Public Library, 1929-45; General Asst in charge of Director's Office, 1932-35; Executive Asst and Chief of Preparation Div., 1936-43; Exec. Asst and Coordinator Gen. Services Divs, 1943-45; on leave from New York Public Library to serve as dir Processing Dept, Libary of Congress, 1940-41; Asst Dir, Cleveland Public Library, 1945-50, Dir, 1950-54. Hon. degrees: LittD: Bethany Coll. (WVa), 1954; Rutgers Univ. (NJ), 1956; Duke Univ. (NC), 1957; Belmont Abbey Coll. (NC), 1963; LLD: Union Coll. (NY), 1955, Bucknell Univ. (Pa), 1956; Univ. of Notre Dame (Ind.), 1964; Univ. of Pittsburgh (Pa), 1964; Michigan Univ., 1970; Hon. DrHum King's Coll. (Pa), 1970. President: Ohio Library Assoc., 1947-48; Amer. Library Assoc., 1954-55; Manuscript Soc., 1968-69. Chairman: Federal Library Cttee; Bd of Visitors, Duke Univ. Library. Member: Lincoln Sesquicentennial Commn, 1958-60; Sponsors Cttee, Papers of Woodrow Wilson; Board of Advisors, Dumbarton Oaks Research Library and Collection; US Nat. Book Cttee. Corresponding Mem. for the US of Unesco's Internat. Advisory Cttee on Bibliography, Documentation and Terminology. Benjamin Franklin Fellow, Royal Soc. for Encouragement of Arts, Manufactures and Commerce (London); President's Commn on Libraries, 1966-68. Chm. or Mem. ex officio of various cttees, bds, etc. *Publications:* contributions to library periodicals. *Address:* (home) 3721 49th Street NW, Washington, DC 20016, USA. *Club:* Cosmos (Washington).

MUMFORD, Lewis, Hon. KBE 1975; Writer; *b* 19 Oct. 1895; *s* of Lewis Mumford and Elvina Conradina Baron; *m* 1921, Sophia Wittenberg; (one son killed in action 1944) one *d. Educ:* Coll. of the City of New York, Columbia Univ. Radio operator (USN) 1918; Associate editor Fortnightly Dial, 1919; Acting Editor Sociological Review (London), 1920; Co-editor American Caravan, 1927-36. Member: National Inst. of Arts and Letters 1930-; Amer. Academy of Arts and Letters, 1956- (Pres., 1962-65); Amer. Philosophical Soc., Amer. Academy of Arts and Sciences; Bd of Higher Educn, City of New York, 1935-37; Commn on Teacher Educn, Amer. Council on Educn, 1938-44; Prof. of Humanities, Stanford Univ., 1942-44. Hon. LLD Edinburgh 1965; Hon. Dr Arch., Rome, 1967. Hon. Phi Beta Kappa, 1957; Hon. Fellow, Stanford Univ., 1941. Hon. FRIBA (Hon. ARIBA, 1942); Hon. MRTPI (Hon. Mem. TPI, 1946); Hon. Member: Amer. Inst. of Architects, 1951; Town Planning Inst. of Canada, 1960; Amer. Inst. of Planners, 1955; Colegio del Arquitectas del Peru; Prof. of City Planning, Univ. of Pennsylvania, 1951-56; Vis. Prof., MIT, 1957-60; Ford Prof., Univ. of Pennsylvania, 1959-60; Univ. of Calif., 1961; Fellow, Wesleyan Univ. Center for Advanced Studies, 1963; MIT: Vis. Lectr, 1973-74; Charles Abrams Prof., 1975. Co-chairman Wenner-Gren Foundation Conf. on Man's Use of the Earth, 1955. Made six documentary films on City for National Film Board, Canada, 1964. Hon. Fellow, Royal Inst. of Architects of Ireland. Townsend Harris Medal, 1939; Ebenezer Howard Memorial Medal, 1946; Medal of Honour, Fairmount Park Art Assoc., 1953; TPI (later RTPI) Gold Medal, 1957; RIBA Royal Gold Medal for Architecture, 1961; Presidential Medal of Freedom, 1964; Emerson-Thoreau Medal, Amer. Acad. of Arts and Sciences, 1965; Gold Medal, Belles Lettres, Nat. Inst. of Arts and Letters, 1970; Leonardo da Vinci Medal, Soc. for Hist. of Technology, 1969; Hodgkins Medal, Smithsonian Instn, 1971; Thomas Jefferson Meml Foundn Medal, 1972; Nat. Medal for Literature, 1972; Prix Mondial del Duca, 1976. *Publications:* The Story of Utopias, 1922; Sticks and Stones, 1924; The Golden Day, 1926; Herman Melville, 1929; The Brown Decades, 1931; Technics and Civilization, 1934; The Culture of Cities, 1938; Whither Honolulu?, 1938; Men Must Act, 1939; Faith for Living, 1940; The South in Architecture, 1941; The Condition of Man, 1944; City Development, 1945; Values for Survival, 1946 (Programme for Survival (Eng.), 1946); Green Memories: The Story of Geddes Mumford, 1947; The Conduct of Life, 1951; Art and Technics, 1952; In the Name of Sanity, 1954; The Human Prospect, 1955; From the Ground Up, 1956; The Transformations of Man, 1956; The City in History, 1961; Highway and City, 1962; Herman Melville (rev. edn), 1963; The Myth of the Machine, 1967; The Urban Prospect, 1968; The Van

Wyck Brooks-Lewis Mumford Letters, 1970; The Pentagon of Power, 1971; The Letters of Lewis Mumford and Frederic J. Osborn, 1971; Interpretations and Forecasts, 1973; Findings and Keepings: analects for an autobiography, 1975. Editor, Roots of Contemporary Architecture, 1952. *Recreations:* gardening and sketching. *Address:* Amenia, New York 12501, USA.

MUMFORD, Rt. Rev. Peter; *see* Hertford, Bishop Suffragan of.

MUMFORD, William Frederick; Assistant Secretary General for Defence Planning and Policy, NATO, Brussels, since Sept. 1976; *b* 23 Jan. 1930; *s* of late Frederick Charles Mumford and Hester Leonora Mumford; *m* 1958, Elizabeth Marion, *d* of Nowell Hall; three *s* one *d . Educ:* St Albans Sch.; Lincoln Coll., Oxford (MA PPE). Nat. Service commission, Royal Artillery, 1949-50. Appointed to Home Civil Service, 1953; Asst Principal, 1953-58, Principal, 1958-60, Air Ministry; First Secretary, UK Delegn to NATO, Paris, 1960-65; Principal, 1965-67, Asst Sec., 1967-73, Defence Secretariat, MoD; Dep. Head of UK Delegn to MBFR Exploratory Talks, Vienna, 1973; Principal Private Sec. to Secretaries of State for Defence: Rt Hon. Lord Carrington, 1973-74, Rt Hon. Ian Gilmour, MP and Rt Hon. Roy Mason, MP, 1974-75; Under-Sec., Machinery of Govt Div., CSD, 1975-76. *Recreations:* antique book collecting, mini-Rugby coaching. *Address:* c/o Barclays Bank Ltd, 366 Strand, WC2R 0JQ. *Club:* United Oxford & Cambridge University.

MUMMERY, H. E. L.; *see* Lockhart-Mummery.

MUNFORD, William Arthur, MBE 1946; PhD; FLA; Director-General, National Library for the Blind, since 1954; *b* 27 April 1911; *s* of late Ernest Charles Munford and Florence Margaret Munford; *m* 1934, Hazel Despard Wilmer; two *s* one *d . Educ:* Hornsey County Sch.; LSE (BScEcon, PhD). Asst, Hornsey Public Libraries, 1927-31; Chief Asst, Ilford Public Libraries, 1931-34; Borough Librarian, Dover, 1934-45 (Food Exec. Officer, 1939-45); City Librarian, Cambridge, 1945-53. Hon. Sec., Library Assoc., 1952-55, Hon. Fellow 1977. *Publications:* Books for Basic Stock, 1939; Penny Rate: aspects of British public library history, 1951; William Ewart, MP, 1960; Edward Edwards, 1963; (with W. G. Fry) Louis Stanley Jast, 1966; James Duff Brown, 1968; A History of the Library Association, 1877-1977, 1976; contribs to Librarianship, 1933-. *Recreations:* reading, rough gardening, wood sawing, cycling, serendipity. *Address:* 11 Manor Court, Pinehurst, Grange Road, Cambridge CB3 9BE. *T:* Cambridge 62962. *Club:* National Liberal.

MUNGO, Rear-Adm. Brian Byrne, CB 1975; FRAeS, MIMechE; Rear-Admiral Engineering to Flag Officer Naval Air Command, 1973-76; *b* 20 Feb. 1922; *s* of James and Ethel Langley Mungo; *m* 1945, Mary (*née* Hansford); one *s . Educ:* Colchester Royal Grammar Sch.; RNC, Dartmouth; RN Engineering Coll., Keyham. Served War, HMS Indomitable, 1943-45. Flying training, 1945-48; Royal Aircraft Establishment, Farnborough, 1950-52; Development Project Officer, Scimitar, 1954-58; British Joint Services Mission, Washington, 1958-61; Dir, Guided Weapons Research and Develt, 1965-67; Faculty Adviser, NATO Defence Coll., Rome, 1970-72. Comdr, 1954; Captain, 1964; Rear-Adm., 1973. *Address:* Castle House, Membury, Axminster, Devon EX13 7TE. *T:* Stockland 231. *Club:* Army and Navy.

MUNN, James, OBE 1976; MA; Rector, Cathkin High School, Cambuslang, Glasgow, since 1970; *b* 27 July 1920; *s* of Douglas H. Munn and Margaret G. Dunn; *m* 1946, Muriel Jean Millar Moles; one *d . Educ:* Stirling High Sch.; Glasgow Univ. (MA (Hons)). Entered Indian Civil Service, 1941; served in Bihar, 1942-47. Taught in various schools in Glasgow, 1949-57; Principal Teacher of Modern Languages, Falkirk High Sch., 1957-62, Depute Rector, 1962-66; Rector, Rutherglen Acad., 1966-70. Mem., Consultative Cttee on Curriculum, 1968-, University Grants Cttee, 1973-; Chm., Cttee to review structure of curriculum at SIII and SIV, 1975-77. Chevalier des Palmes Académiques, 1967. *Recreations:* reading, bridge. *Address:* 4 Kincath Avenue, High Burnside, Glasgow G73 4RP. *T:* 041-634 4654.

MUNN, Rear-Adm. William James, CB 1962; DSO 1941; OBE 1946; *b* 15 July 1911; *s* of late Col R. G. Munn, CMG, FRGS, and late Mrs R. G. Munn; *m* 1940, Susan Astle Sperling, Teviot Bank, Hawick, Scotland; two *s. Educ:* Britannia Royal Naval College, Dartmouth. Cadet and Midshipman in HMS Nelson, 1929-31. Flag Lt (Battle Cruiser Sqdn during Spanish Civil War); served War of 1939-45 (despatches, DSO): First Lt Destroyer HMS Mohawk; Comd Destroyer HMS Hereward (Battle of Matapan, evacuation of Crete), 1941. POW in Italy and Germany, 1941-45. Comd HMS Venus (Mediterranean during Palestine trouble, OBE), 1945-47; Comdr 1946; psc 1949;

Exec. Officer, Cruiser HMS Kenya (Far East Station, Korean War, despatches), 1949-51; Capt., 1951; Capt. of the Britannia Royal Naval College, Dartmouth, 1956-58; Capt. of HMS Gambia, Nov. 1958-Dec. 1960; Rear-Adm. 1960; Chief of Staff to the Comdr-in-Chief, Home Fleet, 1961-63, retd. *Recreations:* golf, sailing. *Address:* The Old Rectory, Langham, near Bury St Edmunds, Suffolk. *T:* Walsham-le-Willows 234. *Club:* Royal Worlington Golf.

MUNRO, Alan Gordon; HM Diplomatic Service; Foreign and Commonwealth Office, since 1977; *b* 17 Aug. 1935; *s* of late Sir Gordon Munro, KCMG, MC and Lilian Muriel Beit; *m* 1962, Rosemary Grania Bacon; twin *s* two *d*. *Educ:* Wellington Coll.; Clare Coll., Cambridge (MA). MIPM. Mil. Service, 4/7 Dragoon Guards, 1953-55; Middle East Centre for Arab Studies, 1958-60; British Embassy, Beirut, 1960-62; Kuwait, 1961; FO, 1963-65; Head of Chancery, Benghazi, 1965-66 and Tripoli, 1966-68; FO, 1968-73; Consul (Commercial), 1973-74, Consul-Gen., 1974-77, Rio de Janeiro. *Recreations:* historic buildings, gardening, music, history. *Address:* c/o Foreign and Commonwealth Office, SW1A 2AL; Eynham House, Chiswick Mall, W4 2PJ. *T:* 01-994 5022. *Club:* Travellers'.

MUNRO, Alison (Mrs), CBE 1964; Chairman, Merton, Sutton and Wandsworth Area Health Authority (T), since 1974; Member (part-time): Board of British Library, since 1973; British Tourist Authority, since 1973; Central Transport Consultative Committee, since 1974; *d* of late John Donald, MD; *m* 1939, Alan Lamont Munro (killed on active service, 1941); one *s*. *Educ:* Queen's Coll., Harley Street; Wynberg Girls' High Sch., South Africa; St Paul's Girls' Sch.; St Hilda's Coll., Oxford (MA). Ministry of Aircraft Production, 1942-45; Principal, Ministry of Civil Aviation, 1945; Asst Sec., 1949; Under-Sec., Ministry of Transport and Civil Aviation, 1958; Under-Sec., Ministry of Aviation, 1960; High Mistress, St Paul's Girls' Sch. Hammersmith, 1964-74. Chairman: Training Council for Teachers of the Mentally Handicapped, 1966-69; Cttee of Inquiry into Children's Footwear, 1972; Mem., Bd, BEA, 1966-73. Governor, Charing Cross Group of Hospitals, 1967-74; Mem., Chairmen's Panel, Civil Service Selection Bd, 1974-. *Recreations:* gardening, tennis, sailing. *Address:* Harbour Way, Ellanore Lane, West Wittering, West Sussex PO20 8AN. *T:* West Wittering 3274. *Club:* University Women's.

MUNRO, Charles Rowcliffe; *b* 6 Nov. 1902; *s* of Charles John Munro, CA, Edinburgh, Hon. Sheriff Substitute, County of Selkirk, and of Edith Rowcliffe; *m* 1942, Moira Rennie Ainslie, *d* of Dr Alexander Cruickshank Ainslie; two *s*. *Educ:* Merchiston Castle Sch., Edinburgh. Hon. Treasurer W Edinburgh Unionist Assoc., 1945-61, Hon. Treas. Scottish Nat. Cttee English-Speaking Union of the Commonwealth 1952-64; Pres. Edinburgh Union of Boys' Clubs, 1957-66. *Recreation:* fishing. *Address:* 17 Succoth Place, Edinburgh EH12 6BJ. *T:* 031-337 2139.

MUNRO, Colin William Gordon R.; *see* Ross-Munro.

MUNRO, Ian Arthur Hoyle, MB; Editor of The Lancet, since 1976; *b* 5 Nov. 1923; *o s* of Gordon Alexander and Muriel Rebecca Munro; *m* 1948, Olive Isabel, MRCS, LRCP, *o d* of Ernest and Isabella Jackson; three *s* two *d*. *Educ:* Huddersfield Coll.; Paston Sch., North Walsham; Royal Liberty Sch., Romford; Guy's Hosp. (MB 1946). Served with RAMC, 1947-50. Joined staff of The Lancet, 1951, Dep. Editor, 1965-76. *Recreations:* cricket, crosswords. *Address:* Oakwood, Bayley's Hill, Sevenoaks, Kent TN14 6HS. *T:* Sevenoaks 54993. *Clubs:* Athenæum; Yorkshire CC.

MUNRO of Foulis-Obsdale, Sir Ian Talbot, 15th Bt *cr* 1634; *b* 28 Dec. 1929; *s* of Robert Hector Munro (*d* 1965) (*n* of 12th and 13th Bts) and Ethel Amy Edith, *d* of Harry Hudson; *S* cousin, Sir Arthur Herman Munro, 14th Bt, 1972. *Heir: uncle* Malcolm Munro [*b* 24 Feb. 1901; *m* 1931, Constance, *d* of William Carter; one *d* (one *s* decd)]. *Address:* 38 Clarence Gate Gardens, NW1.

MUNRO, John Bennet Lorimer, CB 1959; CMG 1953; *b* 20 May 1905; *s* of late Rev. J. L. Munro; *m* 1st, 1929, Gladys Maie Forbes Simmons (*d* 1965); three *s*; 2nd, 1965, Margaret Deacy Ozanne, Blackfort House, Foxford, County Mayo. *Educ:* Edinburgh Academy; Edinburgh University; Corpus Christi Coll., Oxford. ICS: entered, 1928; Under-Sec. Public Dept, Fort St George, 1934; HM Treasury, 1939; Min. of Supply, 1943; idc, 1949; Div. of Atomic Energy Production, 1950; Chief Administrative Officer, UK High Commission for Germany, 1951; Under-Sec.: Min. of Supply, 1953; Bd of Trade, 1955-62; Export Credits Guarantee Dept, 1962-65; Consultant, Export Council for Europe, 1966-67. *Address:* 77 Shirley Drive, Hove, Sussex BN3 6UE. *T:* Brighton 556705.

MUNRO OF FOULIS, Captain Patrick, TD 1958; DL 1949; 30th Chief of Clan Munro; landowner and farmer; Vice-Lieutenant of Ross and Cromarty, 1968-77; *b* 30 Aug. 1912; *e s* of late Col C. H. O. Gascoigne, DSO, Seaforth Highlanders, and Eva Marion, *d* of Sir Hector Munro of Foulis, 11th Bt; assumed arms and designation of Munro of Foulis on death of his grandfather; *m* 1947, Eleanor Mary, *d* of Capt. Hon. William French, French Park, Co. Roscommon, Eire; three *s* one *d*. *Educ:* Imperial Service Coll., Windsor; RMC Sandhurst. 2nd Lt Seaforth Highlanders, 1933; Capt. 1939. Served War of 1939-45, France (POW). Mem. Ross and Cromarty T&AFA, 1938. Hon. Sheriff of Ross and Cromarty, 1973. *Address:* Foulis Castle, Evanton, Ross-shire. *T:* Evanton 212; Ardullie, Dingwall, Ross-shire. *Club:* MCC.

MUNRO, Sir Robert (Lindsay), Kt 1977; CBE 1962; President of the Senate, Fiji, since 1970; *b* NZ, 2 April 1907; *s* of Colin Robert Munro and Marie Caroline Munro; *m* 1937, Lucie Ragnhilde Mee; two *s* one *d*. *Educ:* Auckland Grammar Sch.; Auckland University Coll. (LLB). Barrister and Solicitor, 1929. Served War, 1940-46; 1st Lieut., FMF. Founder Chairman, Fiji: Town Planning Bd, 1946-53; Broadcasting Commn, 1953-61. Member: Educn Bd and Educn Adv. Council, 1943-70; Legislative Council, 1945-46; Nat. Health Adv. Cttee, 1976-. President: Law Soc., 1960-62 and 1967-69; Family Planning Assoc. of Fiji, 1963-. Internat. Planned Parenthood Federation: formerly Mem., Governing Body; Regional Vice-Pres., 1973-. Govt Representative: Bangkok reg. pre-consultation World Population Conf., ECAFE, 1974; World Pop. Conf., Bucharest, 1974; E Asian and Pacific Copyright Seminar, Sydney, 1976. Order of St Olav, Norway, 1966. Rifle shooting Blue; Captain, NZ Hockey Team, 1932. *Recreations:* literature, garden, music. *Address:* Foulis, 6 Milne Road, Suva, Fiji. *T:* 22166. *Club:* Fiji (Suva).

MUNRO, Robert Wilson, CMG 1967; *b* 21 Jan. 1915; *yr s* of late J. S. Munro and late Mrs E. G. Munro, Dunedin, NZ; *m* 1946, Annette Kilroy; two *s*. *Educ:* Otago Boys' High Sch., Univ. of Otago, New Zealand, MSc 1936, and Univ. of London, BSc(Econ), 1950. Research Chemist, NZ Dept of Agriculture, 1938-40. Served with 2 NZEF and UK Forces, 1941-45. Sudan Civil Service, 1945-52; HM Diplomatic Service, 1952-74; served in London, Warsaw, Paris, Baghdad and Khartoum; Inspector, Diplomatic Service, 1967-69; Dep. High Comr, Nairobi, 1969-71; RN College, Greenwich, 1971-72; Dep. High Comr, Wellington, 1972-74. Order of Nilein, 1965. *Recreations:* camping, shooting. *Address:* 20 Bisham Gardens, Highgate Village, N6.

MUNRO, Sir Sydney Douglas G.; *see* Gun-Munro, S. D.

MUNRO, Sir (Thomas) Torquil (Alfonso), 5th Bt, *cr* 1825; JP Angus; *b* 7 Feb. 1901; *e s* of 4th Bt and Selina Dorothea (*d* 1902), *d* of Major-General T. E. Byrne; *S* father, 1919; *m* 1st, 1925, Beatrice (who obtained a divorce, 1932), *d* of late Robert Sanderson Whitaker; one *s*; 2nd, 1934, Averil Moira Katharine, *d* of Kenneth Owen Hunter; one *s* one *d*. *Educ:* Winchester. *Heir: s* Alasdair Thomas Ian Munro [*b* 6 July 1927; *m* 1954, Marguerite Lillian, *d* of late Franklin R. Loy, Dayton, Ohio, USA; one *s* one *d*]. *Address:* Lindertis, Kirriemuir, Angus. *TA:* Munro, Lindertis, Kirriemuir, Angus. *T:* Craigton 209. *See also Baron Colyton.*

MUNRO, William, QC (Scotland) 1959; *b* 19 April 1900; *s* of William Munro, JP, Kilmarnock, and Janet Thomson Munro; *m* 1950, Christine Frances, *d* of W. B. Robertson, MC, DL, Colton, Dunfermline; three *d*. *Educ:* Glasgow High Sch.; Glasgow Univ. (MA, LLB). Called to Scottish Bar, 1925; called to Bar of Straits Settlements, 1927; Johore, 1927. Practised in Singapore and Malaya, 1927-57; Partner, Allen & Gledhill, Singapore. 1933-57 (Prisoner of war, Feb. 1942-Aug. 1945). Resumed practice Scottish Bar, 1958. *Recreations:* golf, gardening. *Address:* 9 The Hawthorns, Muirfield Park, Gullane EH31 2DZ. *T:* Gullane 84 2398. *Clubs:* Caledonian; New (Edinburgh), Hon. Company of Edinburgh Golfers.

MUNRO-LUCAS-TOOTH of Teananich, Sir Hugh (Vere Huntly Duff), 1st Bt, *cr* 1920; Lieutenant-Colonel Queen's Own Cameron Highlanders; *b* 13 Jan. 1903; *er s* of Major Hugh Munro Warrand of Bught and Beatrice Maud Lucas, *e c* of late Sir Robert Lucas Lucas-Tooth, Bt, of Holme Lacy, Co. Hereford, and *co-heiress* with her sisters in the lordship of the Manor of Holme Lacy; *m* 1925, Laetitia Florence, OBE 1958, *er d* of Sir John R. Findlay, 1st Bt; one *s* two *d*. *Educ:* Eton; Balliol Coll., Oxford. Called to Bar, Lincoln's Inn, 1933; MP (C) Isle of Ely, 1924-29, Hendon South, 1945-70; Parliamentary Under-Sec. of State, Home Office, 1952-55. Mem., Nat. Water Council, 1973-76. Sir Robert Lucas-Tooth, 1st Bt, having died, and all his three sons having lost their lives in France during the European War, HM the King was graciously pleased to grant a re-creation of the baronetcy in favour of Sir Robert's eldest grandson, H. V. H. D. Warrand, who assumed the name and arms of Lucas-Tooth in place of Warrand by Royal Letters Patent; changed name by Deed Poll from Lucas-Tooth to Munro-Lucas-Tooth of Teananich, 1965. *Heir: s* Hugh John Lucas-Tooth [*b* 20 Aug. 1932; *m* 1955, Caroline, *e d* of 1st Baron Poole, *qv*; three *d*]. *Address:* Burgate Court, Fordingbridge, Hants. *Club:* Brooks's. *See also Sir Michael Oppenheimer.*

MUNROW, William Davis, CBE 1963; Chief Inspector of Audit, Ministry of Housing and Local Government, 1965-68; *b* 28 April 1903; 2nd *s* of Alexander Gordon Davis and Charlotte Munrow; *m* 1927, Constance Caroline Moorcroft; one *s*. *Educ:* Council Schs; Birkbeck Coll.; and London Sch. of Economics (BSc(Econ)). District Auditor for London, 1954; Dep. Chief Inspector of Audit, 1958. *Recreation:* golf. *Address:* 60 Withyham Road, Cooden, Bexhill-on-Sea, East Sussex. *T:* Cooden 2543.

MUNSTER, 6th Earl of, *cr* 1831; **Edward Charles FitzClarence;** Viscount FitzClarence, Baron Tewkesbury, 1831; *b* 3 Oct. 1899; *s* of Brig.-Gen. Charles FitzClarence, VC (*g s* of 1st Earl) (killed in action, 1914), and Violet (*d* 1941), *d* of Lord Alfred Spencer-Churchill; *S* cousin, 1975; *m* 1st, 1925, Monica Shiela Harrington (marr. diss. 1930; she *d* 1958), *d* of Lt-Col Sir Henry Mulleneux Grayson, 1st Bt, KBE; one *s* one *d*; 2nd, 1939, Mrs Vivian Schofield, *d* of late Benjamin Schofield, JP, and step *d* of late Judge A. J. Chotzner (MP Upton Div., West Ham, 1931-34). *Educ:* Eton; RMC Sandhurst. Captain Irish Guards, retired. Served 1st Bn Irish Guards, Narvik, Norway, 1940; No 8 Commando, Western Desert, 1941. *Heir: s* Viscount FitzClarence, *qv*. *Address:* 98 Whitelands House, Cheltenham Terrace, SW3.

MUNTZ, (Frederick) Alan (Irving), FRAeS; Consultant; *b* 7 June 1899; *s* of Major Irving Muntz and Jessie Challoner; *m* 1st, 1923, Mary Lee (marr. diss., 1934), 3rd *d* of Canon W. L. Harnett; one *s* two *d*; 2nd, 1934, Lady Margaret Frances Anne (marr. diss., 1939), 2nd *d* of 7th Marquess of Londonderry; 3rd, 1948, Marjorie Mary Helena, 2nd *d* of Edward Strickland, Ceylon; one *d*. *Educ:* Winchester; Trinity Coll., Cambridge. (BA Mech. Sciences). Served in France; 2nd Lt 432nd Field Co. RE, 1918; British Petroleum Co., Ltd, 1922-26; Anglo-Iranian Oil Co., Ltd, 1926-28; with Sir Nigel Norman founded Airwork Ltd, and Heston Airport, 1928; with Talaat Harb Pasha, Banque Misr, Cairo, founded Misr Airwork SAE, 1932; with R. E. Grant Govan, Delhi, helped found Indian National Airways Ltd, 1933; founded: Alan Muntz & Co. Ltd and Alan Muntz Consultants, 1965, to develop Pescara free piston engine system and other inventions, 1937; Alan Muntz Consultants, 1965. *Recreations:* golf, fishing, travelling. *Address:* La Rouvière, Seillans, 83440 Fayence, Var, France. *T:* (94) 76 05 47. *Club:* Bath.

MUNTZ, (Isabelle) Hope, FSA; FRHistS; mediaevalist; *b* Toronto, Canada, 8 July 1907; *er d* of late Rupert Gustavus Muntz and 2nd wife, Lucy Elsie Muntz; unmarried. *Educ:* private schs, Bournemouth and Eastbourne. Commercial Art, aircraft engineering; secretarial work and free-lance journalism, to 1931; work and research on novel, 1931-39. ARP, driving, precision-engineering, 1939-45. Spare-time on research and book, 1943-45; novel completed, 1947. FAMS 1958; FSA 1969; FRHistS 1972. *Publications:* The Golden Warrior, England and Commonwealth, 1948, USA, 1949, Sweden, 1950, Norway, 1951, Germany, 1952, Denmark 1954 (also published in Braille and Talking Books); Battles for the Crown, 1966; (ed with Catherine Morton MA, FSA; FRHistS) Carmen de Hastingae Proelio, 1972. Script: The Norman Conquest in the Bayeux Tapestry (film), 1966. Articles, sketches, etc. to journals; contributions to Graya (magazine for members of Gray's Inn). *Recreations:* travel, driving, riding, reading, music, drama. *Address:* c/o Chatto & Windus Ltd, 40/42 William IV Street, WC2. *Club:* University Women's.

MUNTZ, Thomas Godric Aylett, CMG 1951; OBE 1948; retired; *b* 31 May 1906; *s* of R. A. Muntz, Tansor Manor, Peterborough; *m* 1st, 1932, Marjorie (*d* 1968), *d* of Sir Charles Statham; two *s*; 2nd, 1969, June Robertson. *Educ:* Lancing; Pembroke Coll., Oxford. Appointed to Dept of Overseas Trade, 1929; served at office of HM Trade Commissioner, New Zealand, 1931-38; Embassy, Warsaw, 1938-39; Board of Trade, 1939-40; Montreal, 1940-42; Embassy, Rio de Janeiro, 1942-43; Lisbon, 1944-47; Ankara, 1947-50; Head of Economic Relations Dept, Foreign Office, 1950-51; Tangier, 1952-55; Antwerp, 1957-59. *Address:* Barns, King's Cliffe, near Peterborough.

MURCHIE, John Ivor; His Honour Judge Murchie; a Circuit Judge, since 1974; *b* 4 June 1928; *s* of Captain Peter Archibald Murchie, OBE, RD, RNR; *m* 1953, Jenifer Rosalie Luard; one *s* two *d*. *Educ:* Edinburgh Academy; Rossall Sch.; Exeter Coll., Oxford (MA). Called to the Bar, Middle Temple, 1953; Harmsworth Scholarship, 1956. Dep. Chm., Berkshire QS, 1969-71; a Recorder of the Crown Court, 1972-74. *Recreations:* versifying and diversifying. *Address:* Brook House, Warren Row, Wargrave, Reading RG10 8QS.

MURCHISON, Very Rev. Thomas Moffat, DD; *b* 27 July 1907; *s* of Malcolm Murchison and Ann Moffat; *m* 1940, Mary Black Morton Philp; one *s* two *d*. *Educ:* Portree High Sch.; University and Trinity Coll., Glasgow. DD Glasgow, 1964. Minister of Glenelg, Inverness-shire, 1932-37; St Columba Copland Road Church, Glasgow, 1937-66; St Columba Summertown Church, Glasgow, 1966-72. Member: BBC National Broadcasting Council for Scotland, 1952-57; Scottish National Parks Cttee, 1946-47; Panel of Religious Advisers, ITA, 1966-70; Pres., Highland Development League; Convener, Church of Scotland Home Board, 1959-64; Convener, Church of Scotland Adv. Board, 1967-72; Moderator of Gen. Assembly of Church of Scotland, 1969-70. Internat. Pres., Celtic Congress, 1966-71. Chm. Dirs, Scottish Jl of Theology, 1970-74. Crowned Bard of the National Mod, 1958; Chief of Gaelic Society of Inverness, 1961; Bard of the Gorseth of the Bards of Cornwall, 1969. *Publications:* The Plight of the Smallholders, 1935; (Jt Editor) Alba: A Miscellany, 1948; (ed) The Golden Key, 1950; Gaelic Prose writings of Donald Lamont, 1960; Editor, The Gael, 1946-57; Editor, Gaelic Supplement, Life and Work, 1951-; numerous English and Gaelic articles and broadcasts. *Recreations:* Gaelic literature, highland history. *Address:* Kylerhea, Isle of Skye, by Kyle, Ross-shire; 10 Mount Stuart Street, Glasgow G41 3YL. *T:* 041-632 4276.

MURDOCH, Air Marshal Sir Alister Murray, KBE 1966 (CBE 1946); CB 1960; *b* 9 Dec. 1912; *s* of Brig. T. Murdoch, DSO, Melbourne; *m* 1937, Florence Eilene, *d* of Charles Herbert Miller, Sydney; one *d*. *Educ:* Caulfield Grammar Sch.; RMC Duntroon, Canberra. Attached to Directorate of Operations and Intelligence, 1938-39. Served War of 1939-45 (CBE). Senior Air Staff Officer, RAAF HQ, 1944; Dir, Air Staff Plans and Policy, 1949-52; AOC RAAF Pt Cook, and Comdt RAAF Coll., Pt Cook, 1952-53; AOC Training Command, 1954-58; Dep. Chief of the Air Staff, 1958-59; RAAF Representative in London, 1959-62; AOC, HQ Operational Command, 1962-65; idc; Chief of the Air Staff, RAAF, 1965-70. *Recreations:* golf and tennis. *Address:* 2131 Pittwater Road, Church Point, NSW 2105, Australia.

MURDOCH, Charles; Chief Executive, City of Glasgow District Council, since 1974; *b* 16 June 1925; *s* of Charles and Christina Murdoch; *m* 1950, Irene Moffat Shannon. *Educ:* Whitehill Sch.; Glasgow Univ. Served War: RNVR, 1943-47. Corporation of Glasgow, 1941-75 (Town Clerk Depute, 1965-75). *Recreations:* sailing, walking, reading. *Address:* 21 Merrylee Road, Glasgow G43 2SH. *T:* 041-637 2022. *Club:* RNVR (Scotland).

MURDOCH, Dame Elisabeth (Joy), DBE 1963 (CBE 1961); *b* 1909; *d* of Rupert Greene and Marie (*née* de Lancey Forth); *m* 1928, Sir Keith (Arthur) Murdoch (*d* 1952); one *s* three *d*. *Educ:* Clyde Sch., Woodend, Victoria. Pres., Royal Children's Hospital, Melbourne, Victoria, Australia, 1953-65. Trustee, National Gallery, Victoria, 1968-76. *Recreations:* gardening. *Address:* Cruden Farm, Langwarrin, Victoria 3910, Australia. *Clubs:* Alexandra, Lyceum (Melbourne). *See also K. R. Murdoch.*

MURDOCH, Iris; see Murdoch, J. I.

MURDOCH, (Jean) Iris, (Mrs J. O. Bayley), CBE 1976; novelist and philosopher; Fellow of St Anne's College, Oxford, since 1948, Hon. Fellow, 1963; Lecturer at Royal College of Art, 1963-67; *b* Dublin, 15 July 1919; *d* of Wills John Hughes Murdoch and Irene Alice Richardson; *m* 1956, John Oliver Bayley, *qv. Educ:* Froebel Educational Inst., London; Badminton Sch., Bristol; Somerville Coll., Oxford (Lit. Hum. 1st Class 1942), Hon. Fellow 1977. Asst Principal, Treasury, 1942-44; Administrative Officer with UNRRA, working in London, Belgium, Austria, 1944-46; Sarah Smithson studentship in philosophy, Newnham Coll., Cambridge, 1947-48. Mem., Irish Academy, 1970; Hon. Mem., Amer. Acad. of Arts and Letters, 1975. *Publications:* Sartre, Romantic Rationalist, 1953; Under the Net, 1954; The Flight from the Enchanter, 1955; The Sandcastle, 1957; The Bell, 1958; A Severed Head, 1961 (play, Criterion, 1963); An Unofficial Rose, 1962; The Unicorn, 1963; The Italian Girl, 1964 (play, Criterion, 1967); The Red and the Green, 1965; The Time of The Angels,

1966; The Nice and The Good, 1968; Bruno's Dream, 1969; A Fairly Honourable Defeat, 1970; The Sovereignty of Good, 1970; An Accidental Man, 1971; The Black Prince, 1973 (James Tait Black Meml Prize); The Sacred and Profane Love Machine, 1974 (Whitbread Prize); A Word Child, 1975; Henry and Cato, 1976; plays: The Servants and the Snow (Greenwich), 1970; The Three Arrows (Arts, Cambridge), 1972; papers in Proc. Aristotelian Soc., etc. *Recreation:* learning languages. *Address:* Cedar Lodge, Steeple Aston, Oxford.

MURDOCH, (Keith) Rupert; Publisher; Group Chief Executive, News Ltd, Australia; Chairman, News International Ltd, UK; Chairman and President, News America Publishing Inc.; Publisher and Editor-in-Chief, New York Post; *b* 11 March 1931; *s* of late Sir Keith Murdoch and of Dame Elisabeth (Joy) Murdoch, *qv*; *m* 1967, Anna Torv; two *s* two *d*. *Address:* 30 Bouverie Street, EC4; New York Post, 210 South Street, New York, NY 10002, USA.

MURDOCH, Richard Bernard; Actor (stage, films, broadcasting, television); *b* Keston, Kent; *s* of late Bernard Murdoch and late Amy Florence Scott, both of Tunbridge Wells; *m* 1932, Peggy Rawlings; one *s* two *d*. *Educ:* Charterhouse; Pembroke Coll., Cambridge. Commenced theatrical career in chorus of musical comedies, after which played dancing, light comedy and juvenile rôles in musical comedy and revue. Productions include: The Blue Train; Oh, Kay; That's a Good Girl; The Five O'Clock Girl; C. B. Cochran's 1930 Revue; Stand Up and Sing; Ballyhoo; various Charlot revues; Over She Goes. The advent of broadcasting brought firstly several appearances as an early television star and then the famous partnership with Arthur Askey. At outbreak of War, 1939, was playing in Band Waggon at London Palladium and also making films; these include; The Terror; Over She Goes; Band Waggon; Charlie's Big-Hearted Aunt; The Ghost Train; I Thank You. In Jan. 1941 joined RAF as Pilot-Officer in Admin. and Special Duties Branch; one year at Bomber Command HQ (Intelligence Br.) and subs. Intelligence Officer at various stations all over the country; towards end of War became Sqdn Ldr under Wing-Comdr Kenneth Horne in Directorate of Administrative Plans, Air Ministry. In off-duty hours at Air Ministry during this period Much-Binding-in-the-Marsh was evolved with Kenneth Horne. Released from RAF Oct. 1945; went on tour with George Black's revue, Strike a New Note. Dame in Emile Littler's Pantomime, Little Miss Muffet, London Casino, Dec. 1949. 20 weeks in Australia for ABC recordings, 1954. Other films include: Three Men and a Girl. BBC radio series, Men from the Ministry, 1961-. Season with Shaw Festival of Canada and tour of USA, 1973. TV appearances include: David Frost Show; David Nixon Show; Call My Bluff; Looks Familiar; Hazell; The Avengers; In the Looking Glass, etc. *Recreations:* sailing, golf. *Address:* The End Cottage, Walton-on-the-Hill, Tadworth, Surrey. *Clubs:* Royal Automobile; Walton Heath Golf.

MURDOCH, Robert, (Robin Murdoch), TD 1946; MD; FRCSGlas, FRCOG; Consultant Obstetrician and Gynaecologist, Royal Maternity and Royal Samaritan Hospitals, Glasgow, 1946-76; *b* 31 July 1911; *s* of late James Bowman Young Murdoch and Christina Buntin Murdoch (*née* Wood); *m* 1941, Nora Beryl (*née* Woolley); three *s*. *Educ:* Hillhead High Sch., Glasgow; Glasgow Univ. MB ChB 1934, MD 1955; MRCOG 1940; FRCSGlas 1959; FRCOG 1961. Pres., Glasgow Univ. Union, 1933. Served War, 1939-45; Major RAMC. Examiner in Obstetrics and Gynaecology, Univs of Glasgow and Cambridge. Royal College of Gynaecologists: Examiner; Mem. Council, 1954-60, 1968-74; Jun. Vice-Pres., 1974-75; Sen. Vice-Pres., 1975-77. Pres., Scottish AAA, 1956; Mem., British Amateur Athletic Bd, 1956. *Publications:* contribs to medical jls. *Recreations:* angling, golf, gardening, athletics (rep. Scotland (British Empire Games, 1934), and GB (1931, 1933, 1934, 1935, 1938) in 220 yds). *Address:* Carrick Arden, 22 Drymen Road, Bearsden, Glasgow G61 2RD. *T:* 041-942 3677. *Clubs:* Oriental; Royal Scottish Automobile (Glasgow).

MURDOCH, Rupert; see Murdoch, K. R.

MURDOCH, William Ridley Morton, CBE 1963; DSC 1940 and Bar, 1942; VRD 1949; Sheriff of Grampian, Highland and Islands (formerly Ross and Cromarty), at Dingwall and Tain since 1971; *b* 17 May 1917; *s* of William Ridley Carr Murdoch and Margaret Pauline Mackinnon; *m* 1941, Sylvia Maud Pearson; one *s* one *d*. *Educ:* Kelvinside Academy, Glasgow; Glasgow Univ. (MA, LLB). War Service in Navy, 1939-45; Captain, RNR, 1959. Solicitor in private practice, 1946-71; Dir, Glasgow Chamber of Commerce, 1955-71; Dean, Royal Faculty of Procurators in Glasgow, 1968-71. DL, County of City of Glasgow, 1963-75. *Recreations:* sailing, gardening. *Address:* Aird House, Gairloch, Ross-shire. *T:* Badachro 243. *Clubs:* Western, Naval (Glasgow).

MURE, Geoffrey Reginald Gilchrist, Hon. LLD (St Andrews); Warden of Merton College, Oxford, 1947-63; Hon. Fellow, Merton College, since 1963; Fellow of Wye College; *b* 8 April 1893; *s* of Reginald James Mure and Anna Charlotte Neave; *m* 1927, Kathleen Mary Seton (marr. diss. 1963), *d* of Seton de Winton; one *d* decd; *m* 1964, Mrs Josephine Browne (*d* 1974). *Educ:* Eton Coll.; Merton Coll., Oxford. 1st Cl. Hon. Mods, 1913; Warwicks RHA (T), 1914-19; served France and Belgium, 1915-18 (MC, despatches, Chevalier Ordre de la Couronne, Croix de Guerre); Fellow and Tutor of Merton Coll., 1922; University Lecturer in Philosophy, 1929-37. Served on Gen. Staff War Office, 21 Army Group, SHAEF in connexion with propaganda, 1939-45; Pro-Vice-Chancellor, Univ. of Oxford, 1957. *Publications:* Translation of Aristotle, Posterior Analytics, 1925; Aristotle, 1932; Josephine, a Fairy Thriller, 1937; The Boots and Josephine, 1939; Introduction to Hegel, 1940; A Study of Hegel's Logic, 1950; Retreat from Truth, 1958; The Philosophy of Hegel, 1965. Articles. *Recreations:* formerly rowing, fox-hunting and miscellaneous ball games, now sketching. *Address:* 105 Bryanston Court, W1. *T:* 01-262 5724. *Clubs:* Savile, Leander.

MURGATROYD, Prof. Walter; Professor of Thermal Power, Imperial College of Science and Technology, since 1968; Member: British-Greek Mixed Commission, since 1963; British-Belgian Mixed Commission, since 1964; British-Austrian Mixed Commission, since 1965; *b* 15 Aug. 1921; *s* of Harry G. Murgatroyd and Martha W. Strachan; *m* 1952, Denise Geneviève, *d* of Robert Adolphe Schlumberger, Paris and Bénouville; two *s* one *d*. *Educ:* St Catharine's Coll., Cambridge. Hawker Aircraft Ltd, 1942-44; Rolls Royce Ltd, 1944-46; Univ. of Cambridge (Liquid Metal and Reactor heat transfer research), 1947-54; UK Atomic Energy Authority, Harwell, 1954-56; Head of Dept of Nuclear Engineering, Queen Mary Coll., Univ. of London, 1956-67, and Dean of Engineering, 1966-67. *Publications:* contrib. to various scientific and technical journals. *Recreation:* music. *Address:* 90 Princes' Way, SW19. *T:* 01-788 7516.

MURISON, Maj.-Gen. Charles Alexander Phipps, CB 1944; CBE 1940; MC; *b* Grenfell, Sask, Canada, 7 Oct. 1894; *s* of late W. J. H. Murison, Montreal and Vancouver, and Alice Lepel, *d* of late Major C. E. Phipps; *m* 1920, Mary Pope Shirley, *d* of late Hon. Mr Justice W. H. P. Clement, of Supreme Court of British Columbia; one *d*. *Educ:* Vancouver High Sch.; Trinity Coll. Sch., Ont.; McGill Univ. 2nd Lt Royal Field Artillery, 1914; Brevet Major, 1932; Major, 1934; Brevet Lt-Col and Lt-Col 1939; Col, 1940; Brig., 1940; Temp. Maj.-Gen. 1943; Maj.-Gen. 1945; pac; psc; various Staff Appointments; served European War, 1914-18 (wounded, despatches, MC); War of 1939-45, France (CBE, CB); retired, 1949. Freedom, Municipality of North Cowichan, 1973. *Publications:* sundry articles in military journals. *Recreations:* riding, shooting, fishing, golf, etc. *Address:* 2352 Arnhem Road, Duncan BC V9L 3A6, Canada.

MURLESS, Sir (Charles Francis) Noel, Kt 1977; Trainer of racehorses, Newmarket, 1953-76; Owner: Woodditton Stud, Cambridgeshire; Cliff Stud, Yorkshire; *b* 1910; *m* 1940, Gwen Carlow; one *d*. Leading Trainer on the flat for ninth year at end of British flat racing season, 1973 (former years being 1948, 1957, 1959, 1960, 1961, 1967, 1968, 1970); The Queen's trainer until flat racing season of 1969. He made a new record in earnings (£256,899) for his patrons, 1967. Has trained the Derby winning horse three times: 1957 (Crepello); 1960 (St Paddy); 1967 (Royal Palace); over £2,500,000 in winning stakes; many successes in other classic races; has trained the record number of winners in Britain. Mem., Jockey Club, 1977-. *Address:* Woodditton Stud, near Newmarket, Suffolk.

MURLEY, John Tregarthen, DPhil; Counsellor, Washington, since 1976; *b* 22 Aug. 1928; *s* of John Murley and Dorothea Birch; *m* 1954, Jean Patricia Harris; one *d*. *Educ:* University College, London (BA 1st Cl. Hons History); St Antony's Coll., Oxford (DPhil). Entered FO, 1955. *Publication:* The Origin and Outbreak of the Anglo-French War of 1793, 1959. *Recreations:* tennis, squash, piano. *Address:* c/o Foreign and Commonwealth Office, SW1; 8213 Beech Tree Road, Bethesda, Md 20034, USA. *T:* 301-365-7298. *Club:* United Oxford & Cambridge University.

MURLEY, Reginald Sydney, TD 1946; FRCS; President, Royal College of Surgeons, since 1977; *b* 2 Aug. 1916; *s* of Sydney Herbert Murley and Beatrice Maud Baylis; *m* 1947, Daphne, 2nd *d* of Ralph E. and Rowena Garrod; three *s* two *d* and one step *d*. *Educ:* Dulwich Coll.; Univ. of London; St Bartholomew's Hosp. (MB, BS 1939, MS 1948). MRCS, LRCP 1939; FRCS 1946. Served War, RAMC, 1939-45: ME, E Africa, N Africa, Sicily, Italy and NW Europe; regtl and fld ambulance MO; Surgical Specialist, No 1 and 2 Maxillo-Facial Units and

Fld Surg. Units; Major. St Bartholomew's Hospital: Jun. Scholarship, 1935; Sen. Schol., and Sir William Dunn Exhibn in Anat., Univ. of London, 1936; House Surg., 1939; Anat. Demonstrator, 1946; Surg. Chief Asst, 1946-49; Cattlin Res. Fellow and Mackenzie Mackinnon Res. Fellow, RCP and RCS, 1950-51; Surgeon: St Albans Hosp., 1947; Royal Northern Hosp., London, 1953. Royal Coll. of Surgeons: formerly Tutor and Reg. Adviser; Mem. Council, 1970-77. FRSM; Fellow, Assoc. of Surgeons of GB and Ireland. Member: Hunterian Soc. (former Pres.); Med. Soc. of London (former Mem. Council); Harveian Soc. (former Mem. Council); Osler Club; BMA (former Councillor); European and internat. cardiovascular socs. Associate Mem., Brit. Assoc. of Plastic Surgs. *Publications:* (contrib.) Financing Medical Care, 1962; contrib. surg. textbooks; articles in med. literature on breast, thyroid and vascular diseases; articles on med. politics and econs. *Recreations:* golf, swimming, cricket, tennis, gardening, sailing, music, reading history and economics. *Address:* (home) Cobden Hill House, Radlett, Herts. *T:* 01-779 6532; (office) 95 Harley Street, W1N 1DF. *T:* 01-935 5050. *Clubs:* Royal Automobile; Fountain and Vicarage, St Bart's Hospital.

MURPHY, Prof. Alfred John, CBE 1964; DSc; FIM, FRAeS; Vice-Chancellor, Cranfield Institute of Technology, 1969-70, retired; *b* 26 Feb. 1901; *s* of late William and Martha Murphy; *m* 1927, Helen Eulalie Blanche (*d* 1974), *d* of late Rev. Herbert Findlay Millar, Jamaica, British West Indies; two *s*. *Educ:* Altrincham High Sch.; Univ. of Manchester. 1st Cl. Hons Chemistry, Manchester, 1920. Metallurgical Research, Univ. Coll., Swansea, 1920-23 and National Physical Laboratory, 1923-31; Chief Metallurgist, J. Stone & Co. Ltd, London, 1931-49; Dir, J. Stone & Co. Ltd, Light-Metal Forgings Ltd, Chm. Stone-Fry Magnesium Ltd, 1946-49; Prof. of Industrial Metallurgy, Univ. of Birmingham, 1950-55, and Dir of the Depts of Metallurgy, 1953-55; Principal, Coll. of Aeronautics, Cranfield, Bedford, 1955-69. Past Pres. Instn of Metallurgists; Past Pres. Inst. of Metals (Platinum Medallist, 1971); Pres., Brit. Cast Iron Res. Assoc., 1968-70; Vice-Chm., British Non-Ferrous Metals Research Assoc.; Member Council: Inter-Service Metallurgical Research Council, 1949-55 (Chm.), 1962-65; Aeronautical Research Council, 1961-64 (Materials Sub-Cttee, 1968-71). *Publications:* Non-Ferrous Foundry Metallurgy, 1954; numerous papers on metallurgical subjects. *Recreation:* music. *Address:* 4 Riverside Towers, St Mary's Street, Bedford. *T:* Bedford 59938. *Clubs:* Athenæum, Savage.

MURPHY, Rear-Adm. Anthony Albert, CBE 1976; Vice President and Senior Naval Member, Ordnance Board, since 1977; *b* 19 May 1924; *s* of Albert Edward Murphy and Jennie (*née* Giles); *m* 1954, Antonia Theresa (*née* Rayner); four *s*. *Educ:* Sir George Monoux Grammar Sch. National Provincial Bank, 1940-42; joined RN, 1942; commnd, 1944; Western Approaches, 1944-45; HMS Vanguard (Royal Tour of S Africa), 1945-49; HMS Bulwark (Suez); Comdr 1960; HMS Yarmouth/6th Frigate Sqdn, Kuwait, 1961-63; HMS Eagle, 1965-67; Captain 1967; Dir, Naval Guided Weapons, 1970-73; in comd HMS Collingwood, 1973-76; Rear-Adm. 1977. *Recreations:* cricket, soccer (Chm. RNFA, 1973-76), country activities. *Address:* Mill Farm, Mill Road, Slindon, West Sussex. *T:* Slindon 530. *Club:* Naval.

MURPHY, Mrs Brian Taunton; see Hufton, Prof. Olwen.

MURPHY, Cornelius McCaffrey, MA; Editor of Building (formerly The Builder), since 1974; Director, Building (Publishers) Ltd, since 1974; *b* 31 May 1936; 2nd *s* of Edward and Annie Murphy, Glasgow; *m* 1963, Joan Anne, *o d* of William Tytler, master carpenter, retd; two *d*. *Educ:* Holyrood Sch.; Univ. of Glasgow (MA 1958). Teaching, Glasgow, 1958-59, London, 1959-60; Unilever management trainee, 1961-62; Editorial assistant, The Builder, 1962; Editor, Official Architecture and Planning, 1970; re-joined Building as Executive Editor, 1972-74. *Recreations:* reading, racing. *Address:* 42 St John's Park, Blackheath, SE3 7JH. *T:* 01-853 2625.

MURPHY, Sir Ellis; see Murphy, Sir O. E. J.

MURPHY, Lt-Col Gerald Patrick, CIE 1943; IA and Indian Political Service (retired); *b* 8 May 1888; *y s* of Lt-Col Patrick Murphy, IMS, and Helen, *d* of Surgeon James McCraith, FRCS, RN; *m* 1926, Charlotte, *d* of Charles Nelson, Gloucester, Mass, USA; one *s*. *Educ:* Brighton Coll.; RMC, Sandhurst. 2nd Lt IA 1908; Political Service, 1913; reverted to military employ for European War, 1914-19; served NW Frontier 1915 and in Mesopotamia, 1916-18; held various appointments as Asst Political Agent and Asst Resident till 1926; HBM Consul, Muscat, 1926-30; Political Agent, West India States and Orissa

States, 1930-37; Resident Kolhapur and the Deccan States, 1937-38; for the Madras States, 1939-43; retired. *Address:* 13 Millais Park, St Helier, Jersey, CI.

MURPHY, Sheriff James Patrick; Sheriff of North Strathclyde, since 1976; *b* 24 Jan. 1932; *s* of Henry Francis Murphy and Alice (*née* Rooney); *m* 1956, Maureen Coyne; two *s* one *d*. *Educ:* Notre Dame Convent; St Aloysius' Coll., Glasgow; Univ. of Glasgow (BL 1953). Admitted Solicitor, 1953; assumed partner, R. Maguire Cook & Co., Glasgow, 1959; founded firm of Ross Harper & Murphy, Glasgow, 1961. President: Glasgow Juridical Soc., 1962-63; Glasgow Bar Assoc., 1966-67; Mem. Council, Law Soc. of Scotland, 1974-76. *Recreations:* photography, hill walking, caravanning, canoeing, cycling, supporting Partick Thistle. *Address:* 4 West End, Bearsden, Dunbartonshire.

MURPHY, Most Rev. John A.; see Cardiff, Archbishop of, (RC).

MURPHY, (John) Pelly; Resident Judge of HM Court of The Sovereign Base Areas of Akrotiri and Dhekelia, Cyprus, 1969-72, retired 1972; *b* 19 March 1909; *s* of late J. J. L. and late Anne Murphy. *Educ:* Mount St Mary's Coll.; Trinity Coll., Dublin. Barrister-at-Law: King's Inns, Dublin; Inner Temple. Asst Crown Solicitor, Hong Kong, 1936; Attorney-General: Gambia, 1947; Zanzibar, 1950; Puisne Judge, Supreme Court, Kenya, 1956-64; Asst Legal Adviser, FO, 1966-69. *Recreation:* idling. *Address:* c/o Allied Irish Banks, 8 Throgmorton Avenue, EC2. *Clubs:* East India, Devonshire, Sports and Public Schools; Royal Irish Yacht (Dun Laoghaire).

MURPHY, Leslie Frederick; Chairman, National Enterprise Board, since 1977 (Deputy Chairman, 1975-77); *b* 17 Nov. 1915; *s* of Frederick Charles and Lillian Annie Murphy; *m* 1940, Marjorie Iris Cowell; one *s* one *d*. *Educ:* Southall Grammar Sch.; Birkbeck Coll., Univ. of London. Principal Private Sec. to Minister of Fuel and Power, 1947-49; Asst Sec., Min. of Fuel and Power, 1949-52; Chm., Mobil Supply Co. Ltd and Mobil Shipping Co. Ltd, 1955-59; Finance Dir, Iraq Petroleum Co. Ltd, 1959-64; Dir, J. Henry Schroder Wagg & Co. Ltd, 1964-75 (Dep. Chm. 1972-73); Dep. Chm., Schroders Ltd, 1973-75; Dir, Unigate Ltd, 1968-75. Mem., NEDC, 1977-. Mem. Royal Commn on Distribution of Income and Wealth, 1974-76; Chm., Church Army Housing Ltd, 1973-. *Recreations:* music, golf. *Address:* Rosapenna, Manor Lane, Gerrards Cross, Bucks.

MURPHY, Hon. Mr Justice Lionel Keith; Justice of the High Court of Australia, since 1975; *b* 31 Aug. 1922; *s* of William and Lily Murphy; *m* 1969, Ingrid Gee; two *s* one *d*. *Educ:* Sydney Boys' High Sch.; Univ. of Sydney (BSc, LLB). Admitted to NSW Bar, 1947, to Victoria Bar, 1958; QC, NSW 1960, Vic 1961. Senator in Federal Parlt, 1962-75; Leader of Opposition in Senate, 1967-72; Leader of Govt in Senate, 1972-75; Attorney-General of Australia and Minister for Customs and Excise, 1972-75. Initiated reforms in legislative areas of human rights, family law, anti-trust, consumer protection. Mem. Executive, Australian section, Internat. Cttee of Jurists; Delegate to UN Conf. on Human Rights, Teheran, 1968; represented Australia, Nuclear Tests Case, Internat. Court of Justice, 1973-74. *Address:* c/o High Court of Australia, Taylor Square, Darlinghurst, NSW, Australia. *T:* 31.5720.

MURPHY, Sir (Oswald) Ellis (Joseph), Kt 1963; MB, ChM, FRCP, FRACP; Chairman, Queensland Cardiac Board, 1962-76; *b* 2 April 1895; *s* of Miles Murphy, Sydney; *m* 1924, May Beirne; one *s* two *d* (and one *s* decd). *Educ:* Christian Brothers High Sch., Lewisham, and Univ. of Sydney, Australia. Grad. in Med., First Cl. Hons and Univ. Medal, 1919; Hon. Phys. to Out-patients, Mater Misericordiæ Hosp., Brisbane, 1923-28; London Hosp., 1928, MRCP, Sen. Phys., MM Hosp., 1928-38; Phys., Brisbane Gen. Hosp., 1939-50; Acting Prof. of Medicine, Univ. of Qld, 1950-54. (Foundation) FRACP 1938; Mem. Council, RACP 1958-64; Mem., Qld State Cttee, CSIRO; Trustee, Qld Art Gallery. Hon. Col RAAMC. *Publications:* contributed to Australian Journal of Medicine. *Recreation:* yachting. *Address:* Camden, Toorak Road, Hamilton, Brisbane, Queensland 4007, Australia. *Clubs:* Queensland, United Service, Royal Queensland Yacht Squadron (Brisbane).

MURPHY, Richard Holmes; Chairman, Industrial Tribunals, since 1972; *b* 9 July 1915; *o s* of Harold Lawson Murphy, KC, and Elsie, 4th *d* of Rt Hon. Lord Justice Holmes; *m* 1967, Irene Sybil, *e d* of Reginald and Elizabeth Swift. *Educ:* Charterhouse; Emmanuel Coll., Cambridge (MA, LLB). Called to Bar, Inner Temple, 1939. Enlisted Inns of Court Regt, 1939; Commissioned 3rd County of London Yeomanry, 1940; served Middle East and Italy, 1941-45; Judge Advocate-Gen.'s Dept, WO, 1945-46; released, rank of Major. Resident Magistrate, Tanganyika, 1948; Chief Registrar, Gold Coast Supreme Ct and Registrar of W

African Ct of Appeal, 1951; Sen. Magistrate, Gold Coast, 1955; Puisne Judge, Ghana, 1957-60; Judge of High Court, Tanganyika, 1960-64; Senior Lectr in Law, Polytechnic of Central London (formerly Holborn Coll.), 1965-72. *Address:* 9 Vyvyan Terrace, Clifton, Bristol 8. *Club:* Royal Automobile.

MURPHY, Robert Daniel; Statesman; Chairman, Intelligence Oversight Board; Member, President's Foreign Intelligence Advisory Board; *b* Milwaukee, Wisconsin, 28 Oct. 1894; *s* of Francis Patrick Murphy and Catherine Louise Schmitz; *m* 1921, Mildred Claire Taylor; three *d. Educ:* Marquette Academy and Univ.; George Washington Univ., LLB 1920; LLM 1928; clerk Post Office Dept, 1916-17; clerk American Legation, Bern, 1917-19; Asst Chief Treas. Dept, 1919-20; vice-consul, Zürich, 1921; Munich, 1921-25; Consul, Seville, 1925; Dept of State, 1926-30; Consul, Paris, 1930-36; First Sec. Paris, 1936-39; Counsellor, Paris, 1940; Chargé d'Affaires, Vichy, July 1940; detailed Nov. 1940 by President Roosevelt to investigate conditions in French N Africa; concluded economic accord with General Maxime Weygand, Feb. 1941; effected preparations for Allied landings in N Africa, Nov. 1942; conducted negotiations for entry of French W Africa into war, Dec. 1942; appointed President's Personal Rep. with rank of Minister to French N Africa; chief civil affairs officer on staff of Supreme Commander Allied Forces HQ, 1942; DSM (American), 1942; participated in negotiations for Italian armistice, July-Aug. 1943; mem. Mediterranean Advisory Commission with rank of Ambassador, Sept. 1943; US Polit. Adviser with rank of Ambassador, Allied Forces HQ 1943; US Polit. Adviser for Germany with rank of Ambassador, SHAEF, 1944; Political Adviser to the Office of Military Government for Germany (US), 1945-49; Dir, Office of German and Austrian Affairs, US, 1949; US Ambassador in Brussels, 1949-52; US Ambassador in Tokyo, 1952-53; Asst Sec. of State for UN Affairs, 1953; Deputy Under Sec. of State, US, 1954-59; Under Sec. of State for Political Affairs, 1959. Hon. Chm., Corning Glass International, 1967. *Publication:* Diplomat among Warriors, 1964. *Recreations:* golf, etc. *Clubs:* Metropolitan (Washington); University, Links (New York); Chevy Chase (Maryland).

MURPHY, Stephen Dunlop; Programme Officer, Independent Broadcasting Authority, since 1976; *b* Glasgow, 28 Aug. 1921; *s* of Stephen Dunlop Murphy and Jean Irwin; *m* 1944, Jean Marian Smith, Burnley; two *s* one *d. Educ:* Royal Grammar Sch., Newcastle upon Tyne; Manchester Grammar Sch.; Balliol Coll., Oxford (BA). Asst Master, Manchester Grammar Sch., 1943; BBC Educn Officer, 1951; BBC Producer, 1955; ITA Regional Officer North, 1961; Senior Programme Officer, ITA, 1966; Secretary, British Bd of Film Censors, 1971-75. *Address:* 204 London Road, Twickenham, Mddx. *T:* 01-892 6794.

MURPHY, Thomas A.; Chairman, General Motors Corporation, since 1974; *b* Hornell, NY, 10 Dec. 1915. *Educ:* Leo High Sch., Chicago; Univ. of Illinois. Joined General Motors Corporation, 1938; Asst Treas., 1959; Comptroller, 1967; Treas., 1968-70; Vice-Pres., 1970-72; Vice-Chm., 1972-74. *Address:* General Motors Corporation, General Motors Building, Detroit, Mich 48202, USA.

MURPHY, William Parry, AD, MD; Lecturer on Medicine, Harvard Medical School, 1948-58, Lecturer Emeritus, 1958; Senior Associate in Medicine, Peter Bent Brigham Hospital, 1935-58, Senior Associate Emeritus in Medicine and Consultant in Hematology since 1958; Consultant Hematologist: Melrose Hospital, Melrose, Mass; Quincy City Hospital, Quincy, Mass; Emerson Hospital, Concord, Mass; Consultant in Internal Medicine, Delaware State Hospital, Farnhurst, Delaware; *b* 6 Feb. 1892; *s* of Thomas Francis Murphy and Rose Anna Parry; *m* 1919, Pearl Harriett Adams; one *s* (one *d* decd). *Educ:* Univ. of Oregon (AB); Harvard Med. Sch. (MD). Army, enlisted Medical Reserve, 1917-18; acted as House Officer at the Rhode Island Hosp., 1920-22; as Asst Resident Physician, 1922-23; Junior Associate in Medicine, 1923-28; Associate in Medicine, 1928-35 at Peter Bent Brigham Hospital; Asst in Medicine, 1923-28; Instructor in Medicine, 1928-35; Associate in Medicine, Harvard Medical Sch., 1935-48; has been engaged in the practice of Medicine since 1923, and carried on research at the Peter Bent Brigham Hospital in Boston; Diplomate in Internal Medicine, 1937. Mem. many American and foreign medical and scientific socs; co-discoverer of the liver treatment for pernicious anemia; was awarded the Cameron Prize in Medicine by the Univ. of Edinburgh Medical Faculty in 1930, the Bronze Medal of the American Medical Association in 1934, and the Nobel Prize in Physiology and Medicine in 1934. Hon. Dr of Science, Gustavus Adolphus Coll., 1963; Hon. Member: Univ. of Oregon Med. Alumni Assoc., 1964; Internat. Soc. for Research on Civilisation Diseases and Vital Substances, 1969. Mem. Bd of Dirs of Cordis Corp., 1960-70. Commander of the

first rank, Order of the White Rose, Finland, 1934; gold medal, Mass Humane Soc., 1935; National Order of Merit, Carlos J. Finlay, Official, Havana, Cuba, 1952; Dist. Achievement Award, City of Boston, 1965; Internat. Bicentenial Symposium Award, Boston, 1972; Gold Badge, Mass Med. Soc. 50th Anniv., 1973. *Publications:* Anemia in Practice: Pernicious Anemia, 1939; about 75 papers published in medical journals, especially on diseases of the blood. *Recreation:* collector of rare old firearms. *Address:* 1101 Beacon Street, Brookline, Mass 02146, USA. *T:* Longwood 6-4445; 97 Sewall Avenue, Brookline, Mass 02146, USA. *Clubs:* Sigma xi (Harvard); Harvard (Boston); Rotary (Brookline, Mass).

MURPHY-O'CONNOR, Rt. Rev. Mgr. Cormac; Rector, English College, Rome, since 1971; *b* 24 Aug. 1932; *s* of late Dr P. G. Murphy-O'Connor and Nellie (*née* Cuddigan). *Educ:* Prior Park Coll., Bath; English Coll., Rome; Gregorian Univ. PhL, STL. Ordained Priest, 1956. Asst Priest, Portsmouth and Fareham, 1957-66; Sec. to Bp of Portsmouth, 1966-70; Parish Priest, Parish of the Immaculate Conception, Southampton, 1970-71. *Recreations:* music, sport. *Address:* Venerable English College, Via Monserrato 45, Rome 00186, Italy. *T:* 6541829.

MURRAY; see Erskine-Murray.

MURRAY, family name of **Duke of Atholl,** of **Earl of Dunmore,** of **Earl of Mansfield and Mansfield** and of **Barons Murray of Gravesend** and **Murray of Newhaven.**

MURRAY OF GRAVESEND, Baron *cr* 1976 (Life Peer), of Gravesend; **Albert James Murray;** Member, European Parliament, since 1976; *b* 9 Jan. 1930; *s* of Frederick Clifton Murray and Catherine Murray; *m* 1960, Margaret Anne (*née* Wakeford); one *s* one *d. Educ:* Elementary. LCC Southwark Borough Council, 1953-62; LCC 1958-65 (Chm., LCC Schs Planning Cttee, 1961-65). MP (Lab) Gravesend, 1964-70; Mem., Estimates Cttee, 1966-; PPS to: Minister of Defence (Navy), 1965-66; Minister of State, Board of Trade, 1966-68; Minister of State, Min. of Technology, 1968-69; Parly Sec., Min. of Transport, Oct. 1969-June 1970. Mem., Governing Council, Nat. Soc. of Operative Printers and Assistants, 1971-73. Private Sec. to the Prime Minister, 1974-76. *Recreations:* reading, fishing, watching Association football. *Address:* 13 Parrock Road, Gravesend, Kent. *T:* Gravesend 65958.

MURRAY OF NEWHAVEN, Baron *cr* 1964 (Life Peer); **Keith Anderson Hope Murray,** KCB 1963; Kt 1955; Chancellor, Southampton University, 1964-74; Visitor, Loughborough University of Technology, since 1968; *b* 28 July 1903; 2nd *surviving s* of late Rt Hon. Lord Murray, PC, CMG, LLD. *Educ:* Edinburgh Academy; Edinburgh Univ. (BSc); Ministry of Agriculture, 1925-26; Commonwealth Fund Fellowship, 1926-29, at Cornell Univ., New York (PhD); Oriel Coll. and Agricultural Economics Research Institute, 1929-32, University of Oxford (BLitt and MA); Research Officer, 1932-39; Fellow and Bursar, Lincoln Coll., 1937-53, and Rector, 1944-53; Chm., Univ. Grants Cttee, 1953-63. Oxford City Council, 1938-40; Min. of Food, 1939-40; RAFVR 1941-42; Dir of Food and Agriculture, Middle East Supply Centre, GHQ, MEF, 1942-45; Oxfordshire Education Cttee, 1946-49; JP, City of Oxford, 1950-53; Chm., Vice-Chancellor's Commission of Enquiry on Halls of Residence, 1947; Mem. of Commission of Enquiry into Disturbances in the Gold Coast, 1948; Development Commissioner, 1948-53; Chairman: Advisory Cttee on Colonial Colleges of Arts, Science and Technology, 1949-53, RAF Education Advisory Cttee, 1947-53; National Council of Social Service, 1947-53. Advisory Cttees on Agricultural Colls, 1954-60, Harkness Fellowship Cttee of Award, 1957-63, Cttee on Provincial Agricultural Economics Service, 1949-57, Cttee on Australian Univs, 1957; World Univ. Service, 1957-62; Dartmouth Review Cttee, 1958; Pres. Agric. Economics Soc., 1959-60; Pres. Agricultural History Soc., 1959-62; Chairman: Colonial Univ. Grants Cttee, 1964-66; London Conf. on Overseas Students, 1963-67; Academic Adv. Cttee for Stirling Univ., 1967-75. Vice-Pres., Wellington Coll., 1966-69; Governor, The Charterhouse, 1957-69. Mem. Bd, Wellcome Trustees, 1965-73; Dir, Leverhulme Trust Fund, 1965-72; Hon. Pres., Nat. Union of Students, 1967-70. Chairman: Cttee of Enquiry into Governance of London Univ., 1970-72; Royal Commn for Exhibition of 1851, 1962-71. Director: Bristol Aeroplane Co., 1963-67; Metal Box Co., 1964-68. Hon. Fellow: Downing Coll., Cambridge; Oriel Coll., Oxford; Lincoln Coll., Oxford; Birkbeck Coll., London. Hon. LLD: Western Australia and of Bristol, 1963; Cambridge, Hull, Edinburgh, Southampton, Liverpool and Leicester, 1964; Calif., 1966; London and Strathclyde, 1973; Hon. DCL Oxford, 1964; Hon. DLitt Keele, 1966; Hon. DUniv. Stirling, 1968; Hon. DU Essex, 1971; Hon. FDSRCS, 1964; Hon. FUMIST, 1965. *Address:* 224

Ashley Gardens, SW1. *Club:* United Oxford & Cambridge University.

MURRAY, Bishop of The, since 1970; **Rt. Rev. Robert George Porter,** OBE 1952; *b* 7 Jan. 1924; *s* of Herbert James and Eileen Kathleen Porter; *m* 1954, Elizabeth Mary Williams; two *d.* *Educ:* Canterbury Boys' High School; St John's Theological Coll., Morpeth, NSW; Moore College, Sydney (ThL Hons). Served with AIF, 1942-44. Deacon 1947, priest 1948; Assistant Curate, Christ Church Cathedral, Ballarat, Victoria, 1947-49; Assistant Curate, St Paul's, Burwood, Sydney, 1949-50; Priest in charge of Isivita and Agenehambo, Diocese of New Guinea, 1950-57; Archdeacon of Ballarat, 1957-70; Assistant Bishop of Ballarat, 1967-70. *Recreations:* gardening, reading. *Address:* 48 Eleanor Terrace, Murray Bridge, SA 5253, Australia. *T:* 32 2240.

MURRAY of Blackbarony, Sir Alan (John Digby), 14th Bt, *cr* 1628; Hereditary Secretary for Scotland; engaged in livestock-raising and agriculture in Argentina; *b* 22 June 1909; *s* of late Alan Digby Murray and late Eileen Muriel Shaw; *S* cousin, Sir Kenelm Bold Murray, 13th Bt, 1959; *m* 1943, Mabel Elisabeth, *d* of Arthur Bernard Schiele, Arias, Argentina; four *s. Educ:* Brighton Coll., Sussex. *Recreations:* golf, tennis, riding. *Heir:* s Nigel Andrew Digby Murray, *b* 15 Aug. 1944. *Address:* (Residences): Estancia La Linda Mora, Arias, Argentina; Four Winds, Los Cocos, Sierras de Cordoba, Argentina. *Clubs:* English, Tigre Boat, Dorado Fishing (Buenos Aires); Strangers' (Rosario).

MURRAY, Dame (Alice) Rosemary, DBE 1977; MA, DPhil; JP; President, New Hall, Cambridge, since 1964 (Tutor in Charge, 1954-64); Deputy Vice-Chancellor, Cambridge University, 1973-75 and since 1977 (Vice-Chancellor, 1975-77); *b* 28 July 1913; *d* of late Adm. A. J. L. Murray and Ellen Maxwell Spooner. *Educ:* Downe House, Newbury; Lady Margaret Hall, Oxford (Hon. Fellow, 1968). MA (Oxon and Cantab); BSc, DPhil (Oxon). Lecturer in chemistry: Royal Holloway Coll., 1938-41; Sheffield Univ., 1941-42. Served War of 1939-45, Experimental Officer, Admiralty Signals Establishment, 1941; WRNS, 1942-46, successively Wren, 3rd, 2nd, 1st and Chief Officer. Lectr in Chemistry, Girton Coll., Cambridge, 1946-54, Fellow, 1949, Tutor, 1951, Hon. Fellow, 1976; Demonstrator in Chemistry, Univ. of Cambridge, 1947-52. Member: Lockwood Cttee on Higher Educn in NI, 1963-65; Wages Councils, 1968-; Council, GPDST, 1969-; Armed Forces Pay Review Body, 1971-. JP City of Cambridge, 1953-. Hon. DSc: New Univ. of Ulster, 1972; Leeds, 1975; Pennsylvania, 1975; Wellesley Coll., 1976; Hon. DCL Oxon, 1976; Hon. DL Univ. Southern California, 1976; Hon. LLD Sheffield, 1977. *Recreations:* sailing, foreign travel, gardening. *Address:* New Hall, Cambridge. *T:* 51721. *Club:* University Women's, English-Speaking Union.

MURRAY, Catherine Joan Suzette; *see* Gauvain, C. J. S.

MURRAY, Cecil James Boyd, MS; FRCS; Emeritus Consultant Surgeon, Middlesex Hospital, since 1975 (Surgeon, 1946-75); Surgeon, Royal Masonic Hospital, London, 1958-75; *b* 8 Jan. 1910; *s* of Richard Murray, MIEE; *m* 1940, Bona (*d* 1974), *o d* of Rev. William Askwith, MA, Ripon; two *s. Educ:* Warriston Sch., Moffat; King's Sch., Canterbury; Middlesex Hospital Medical Sch. MB, BS, 1935; MS 1936; MRCS, LRCP, 1933, FRCS 1936. Formerly: Surgeon, King Edward Memorial Hospital, Ealing; Lecturer in Operative Surgery, Middlesex Hospital Medical Sch. Served War of 1939-45 (despatches), temp. Lt-Col RAMC. Mem., Court of Examiners, Royal College of Surgeons of England; Fellow, Assoc. of Surgeons of Great Britain; FRSocMed. *Publications:* papers in medical journals. *Recreation:* fly-fishing. *Address:* Conifera, Comrie, Perthshire PH6 2LT. *T:* Comrie 395. *Clubs:* Flyfishers', MCC.

MURRAY, Colin Robert Baillie, CIE 1946; *b* 1892; *s* of late A. A. Murray, Kilcoy, Black Isle, Ross-shire; *m* 1917, Margaret (*d* 1971), *d* of E. G. Drake-Brockman, ICS; one *s* one *d. Educ:* Cargilfield Sch., Edinburgh; Clifton. Entered Indian Police, 1911; served European War, 8th Cavalry, Indian Army, 1915-19. Deputy Dir of Intelligence, Govt of India, 1938; Inspector-General of Police, Orissa, India, 1944-46; retired, 1947. *Address:* 51 Seabrook Road, Hythe, Kent. *T:* 67008.

MURRAY, Hon. Donald Bruce; Hon. Mr Justice Murray; Judge of the High Court of Justice in Northern Ireland, since 1975; *b* 24 Jan. 1923; *y s* of late Charles Benjamin Murray and late Agnes Mary Murray, Belfast; *m* 1953, Rhoda Margaret, *o c* of late Thomas and Anna Parke, Londonderry; two *s* one *d. Educ:* Belfast Royal Acad.; Queen's Univ. Belfast (LLB Hons); Trinity Coll. Dublin (BA). 1st Cl., Certif. of Honour, Gray's Inn Prize,

English Bar Final Exam., 1944; Called to Bar, Gray's Inn, 1945. Asst Parly Draftsman to Govt of NI, 1945-51; Asst Lectr, Faculty of Law, QUB, 1951-53. Called to NI Bar, 1953, and to Inner Bar, NI, 1964; Bencher, Inn of Court, NI, 1971; Chm., Gen. Council of Bar of NI, 1972-75. Dep. Chm., Boundary Commn for NI, 1976-. Mem. 1971, Chm. 1974, Incorporated Council of Law Reporting for NI; Dir, NI Legal Quarterly; Member: UK Delegn to Commn Consultative des Barreaux des Pays des Communautés Européennes, 1972-75; Jt Standing Cttee of Bars of UK and Bar of Ireland, 1972-75; Deptl Cttee on Registration of Title to Land in N Ireland. Chm., Deptl Cttee on Reform of Company Law in NI; Inspector apptd to report on siting of new prison in NI. Mem., Legal Adv. Cttee of Standing Cttee of General Synod of Church of Ireland; Lay Mem., Diocesan Court of Connor. Governor, Belfast Royal Academy. *Publications:* articles in various legal periodicals. *Recreation:* playing the piano. *Address:* 40 Cadogan Park, Belfast, N Ireland. *Club:* Ulster (Belfast).

MURRAY, Donald Frederick, CMG 1973; HM Diplomatic Service; Assistant Under Secretary of State, Foreign and Commonwealth Office, since 1977; *b* 14 June 1924; *s* of A. T. Murray and F. M. Murray (*née* Byfield); *m* 1949, Marjorie Culverwell; three *s* one *d. Educ:* Colfe's Grammar Sch.; King's Sch., Canterbury (King's and Entrance Schols); Worcester Coll., Oxford. Royal Marines, 1943-46. Entered Foreign Office, 1948; served in Warsaw, Vienna, Cyprus, Stockholm and Saigon; Counsellor: FCO, 1965-69; Tehran, 1969-72; RCDS, 1973; Ambassador to Libya, 1974-76. *Publication:* article in Seaford House Papers, 1973. *Recreations:* gentle sports, gardening. *Address:* c/o Foreign and Commonwealth Office, SW1; Oxney House, Wittersham, Kent; 10 St Mary's Walk, SE11. *Club:* Travellers'.

MURRAY, Edward C.; *see* Croft-Murray.

MURRAY, Sir (Francis) Ralph (Hay), KCMG 1962 (CMG 1950); CB 1957; Chairman: McAlpine Sea Tank Ltd; SAFT (UK) Ltd; *b* 3 March 1908; *s* of Rev. Charles Hay Murray and Mabel Umfreville; *m* 1935, Mauricette, *d* of Count Bernhard Kuenburg; three *s* one *d. Educ:* Brentwood Sch.; St Edmund Hall, Oxford. BBC, 1934-39; Foreign Office, 1939-45; Allied Commission for Austria, 1945-46; Special Commissioner's Staff, SE Asia, 1946-47; Foreign Office, 1947-51; Counsellor, HM Embassy, Madrid, 1951-54; Minister, HM Embassy, Cairo, 1954-56; Asst Under-Sec. of State, FO, 1957-61; Dep. Under-Sec. of State, FO, 1961-62; Ambassador to Greece, 1962-67. A Governor of the BBC, 1967-73. *Address:* The Old Rectory, Stoke Hammond, Bletchley, Bucks. *T:* Soulbury 247. *Club:* Travellers'.

MURRAY, George Raymond B.; *see* Beasley-Murray.

MURRAY, Gen. Sir Horatius, GCB 1962 (CB 1945); KBE 1956; DSO 1943; Colonel of The Cameronians (Scottish Rifles), 1958-64, now retired; *b* 18 April 1903; *s* of late Charles Murray; *m* 1953, Beatrice, *y d* of Frederick Cuthbert. *Educ:* Peter Symonds Sch., Winchester; RMC, Sandhurst. Gazetted to Cameronians, 1923; transferred to Camerons, 1935. Served War of 1939-45, North Africa, Sicily, Italy, France (DSO, CB); GOC 6 Armoured Division, 1944-45; Dir of Personal Services, War Office, 1946-47; GOC 1st Infantry Division, 1947-50; GOC Northumbrian District, 1951-53; Commander, Commonwealth Division in Korea, 1953-54; GOC-in-C, Scottish Command and Governor of Edinburgh Castle, 1955-58; Commander-in-Chief, Allied Forces, Northern Europe, 1958-61, retired. Commander Legion of Merit (US); Knight Commander, Order of the Sword (Sweden). *Recreations:* golf, cricket. *Club:* Royal Commonwealth Society.

MURRAY, Prof. Jack Keith, OBE 1959; ED; BA, BScAgr, NDD, DipMilSc; retired as Administrator, Territory of Papua and New Guinea, (1949-52), and President Executive Council, also of Legislative Council of Papua and New Guinea; Hon. Life Member, RSSAILA; *b* Brighton, Vic., 8 Feb. 1889; *s* of late John Murray, Coburg, Melbourne; *m* 1924, Evelyn, BSc Agr., *d* of late Ernest Andrews. *Educ:* Univ. of Sydney; Dairy Sch. for Scotland. Formerly Lecturer in Bacteriology and Dairy Technology, Hawkesbury Agric. Coll., NSW; Principal Qld Agric. Coll., 1923-45; Prof. of Agric., Univ. of Queensland, 1927-45, Emeritus Prof., 1975; Mem. Federal Dairy Investigation Cttee, 1930; Fellow Aust. Nat. Research Council; Fellow, Aust. and NZ Assoc. for Advancement of Science (Pres. Section "K" Melbourne meeting, 1935); Pres. Royal Society of Queensland, 1936. Served with 1st and 2nd AIF: Lt-Col, CO 25th (Darling Downs) Bn, AMF, 1940; Lt-Col, GSO2 (Training) Northern Command, 1940; Col comdg AIF Training Depots, Northern Comd, 1941-42; Col Comdg 5th Aust.

Training Bde, 1943; Research Officer, Directorate of Research, HQ, Allied Land Forces, 1944; Chief Instructor, Allied Land Forces Sch. of Civil Affairs, Duntroon, 1945. Hon. Col, retired list, 1951. Administrator, Provisional Administration of Papua-New Guinea, 1945-49. Macrossan Memorial Lecturer, Univ. of Queensland, 1946. Mem. Australian Delegation to South Seas Conference (South Pacific Commn), 1947. Adviser, under Colombo Plan, in Agricultural Education to Ceylon Dept of Agriculture, 1956-57; Actg Warden, Internat. House, Univ. of Melbourne, 1959; Mem. of Senate, Univ. of Queensland, 1953-68; Mem. Nat. Council, Australian Boy Scouts Assoc., 1959-70. Hon. Life Member: Royal Society Queensland; Queensland Univ. Union; FAIAS. Hon. DSc Queensland. *Recreation:* walking. *Address:* 49 Dell Road, St Lucia, Qld 4067, Australia. *Clubs:* United Services (Brisbane); Public Service, Konedobu (both at Port Moresby, Papua).

MURRAY, James, CMG 1966; HM Diplomatic Service; Minister and Deputy Permanent Representative to the United Nations, since 1974; *b* 3 Aug. 1919; *er s* of late James Hamilton Murray, King's Cross, Isle of Arran, and Hester Macneill Buie. *Educ:* Bellahouston Acad.; Glasgow Univ. Royal Regt of Artillery, 1939; Served India and Burma, 1943-45; Staff Coll., Quetta, 1945; Bde Major (RA) 19 Ind. Div.; GSO II (RA) ALFSEA; GSO II War Office. HM Foreign (subseq. Diplomatic) Service, 1947; Foreign Office, 1947-49; First Sec. (Information), HM Embassy, Cairo, 1949-54; Foreign Office, 1954-56; attached National Defence Coll. of Can., 1956-57; First Sec., HM Embassy, Paris, 1957-61; HM Consul in Ruanda-Urundi, 1961-62; Special Ambassador for Independence celebrations in Ruanda, July 1962, and in Burundi, Sept. 1962; Ambassador to Rwanda and Burundi, 1962-63; Deputy Head of UK Delegation to European Communities, 1963-65; Counsellor, Djakarta, 1965-67; Head of Far Eastern Dept, FCO, 1967-70; Consul-Gen., San Francisco, 1970-73; Asst Under-Sec. of State, FCO, 1973-74. *Recreations:* horses, lawn tennis. *Address:* c/o Foreign and Commonwealth Office, SW1. *Clubs:* Beefsteak, Queen's.

MURRAY, James Dalton, CMG 1957; HM Diplomatic Service, retired; *b* Edinburgh, 6 March 1911; *s* of late Dr James Murray, Edinburgh, and late Eleanor (*née* Mercer); *m* 1st, 1949, Dora Maud (Denny) Carter (*d* 1958); one *s* two *d*; 2nd, 1959, Merriall Rose, 2nd *d* of Sir Timothy Eden, 8th Bart; two *s*. *Educ:* Stowe; Magdalene Coll., Cambridge (Exhibitioner). Entered HM Consular Service, 1933; Vice-Consul: San Francisco, 1933, Mexico City, 1936; 2nd Sec., Embassy, Washington, 1939; 1st Sec. and Consul, La Paz, 1943; Foreign Office, 1945; Office of Comr-Gen. for SE Asia, Singapore, 1948; Counsellor, HM Foreign Service, and apptd to FO, 1950; seconded to CRO, 1952; Dep. High Comr for UK, Karachi, 1952; returned FO, 1955; Counsellor, British Embassy, Lisbon, 1959-61; Minister, 1961-63, Ambassador, 1963-65, Rumania; British High Comr, Jamaica, 1965-70, and Ambassador to Haiti (non-resident), 1966-70; retired 1970. Re-employed, 1970-76, as First Secretary and Consul (Chargé d'Affaires) resident in Port-au-Prince, Haiti. *Recreations:* golf, relaxing. *Address:* c/o Foreign and Commonwealth Office, SW1. *Club:* Travellers'.

MURRAY, Prof. James Greig; Professor of Surgery, University of London, since 1964; Hon. Consultant Surgeon, King's College Hospital, London; *b* 1 April 1919; *s* of J. A. F. Murray and Christina (*née* Davidson); *m* 1946, Cecilia (*née* Mitchell Park); one *s* one *d*. *Educ:* Peterhead Acad.; Aberdeen Univ. MB, ChB 1942; FRCS Edinburgh 1950; ChM (Aberdeen) 1961; FRCS 1964. Surg.-Lt, RNVR, 1943-46. Lectr in Anatomy Dept, Univ. Coll., London, 1950-54; Clinical Research Fellow, MRC, RCS of England, 1954-56; Sen. Lectr in Surgery, Univ. of Aberdeen, 1958-59. Chm., Cancer Res. Campaign Study on Breast Cancer. *Publications:* Scientific Basis of Surgery, 1965; Gastric Secretion: Mechanism and Control, 1965; After Vagotomy; articles in scientific and clinical jls on composition of vagus nerves, regeneration of nerves, physiology of gastric secretion and treatment of peptic ulceration, etc. *Recreations:* fishing, golf. *Address:* Six Pillars, Crescent Wood Road, Sydenham Hill, SE26. *T:* 01-693 3160.

MURRAY, James Patrick, CMG 1958; *b* 1906; *m* 1934, Margaret Ruth Buchanan; three *s*. *Educ:* St Edward's Sch., Oxford; Christ Church, Oxford. Cadet, Northern Rhodesia, 1929; District Officer, Northern Rhodesia, 1931; Provincial Commissioner, Northern Rhodesia, 1950; Senior Provincial Commissioner, Northern Rhodesia, 1955; Commissioner for Northern Rhodesia in London, 1961-64 (Country became Independent, as Zambia, 1964). Vice-Chm., Royal African Soc. *Address:* Trewen, Shaftesbury Road, Woking, Surrey. *T:* Woking 61988. *Club:* Royal Commonwealth Society.

MURRAY, John, QC (Scotland) 1974; *b* 8 July 1935; *o s* of J. H. Murray, farmer, Stranraer; *m* 1960, Bridget Jane, *d* of Sir William Godfrey, 7th Bt, and of Lady Godfrey; three *s*. *Educ:* Cairnryan Sch.; Park Sch., Stranraer; Stranraer High Sch.; Edinburgh Academy; Corpus Christi Coll., Oxford; Edinburgh Univ. BA Oxon 1959, LLB Edinburgh 1962. Advocate, 1962. Chm., Scottish Lawyers' European Gp; Vice-Chm., Agricultural Law Assoc. *Publications:* articles in legal and ornithological jls. *Recreations:* gardening, birdwatching, opera, field sports. *Address:* 6 Moray Place, Edinburgh EH3 6DS. *T:* 031-225 1881; Fell Cottage, Craigcaffie, Stranraer. *T:* Stranraer 3356. *Club:* New (Edinburgh).

MURRAY, John (Arnaud Robin Grey), CBE 1975 (MBE 1945); Senior Director of Publishing House of John Murray since 1968; *b* 22 Sept. 1909; *o s* of late Thomas Robinson Grey and Dorothy Evelyn Murray; *m* 1939, Diana Mary, 3rd *d* of late Col Bernard Ramsden James and Hon. Angela Kay-Shuttleworth; two *s* two *d*. *Educ:* Eton; Magdalen Coll., Oxford (BA Hist). Joined publishing firm of John Murray, 1930; Asst Editor, Cornhill Magazine, 1931; Asst Editor, Quarterly Review, 1933. Served with Royal Artillery and Army-Air Support, War Office, 1940-45. Relaunched Cornhill Magazine with Peter Quennell, 1945. Member: Council, Publishers' Assoc., to 1976; Council, RGS; Pres., English Assoc., 1976. *Publication:* (editor, with Peter Quennell) Byron: A Self-Portrait, 1950. *Recreations:* Byron, archives, forestry, music. *Address:* (office) 50 Albemarle Street, W1X 4BD. *T:* 01-493 4361; (home) Cannon Lodge, 12 Cannon Place, NW3. *T:* 01-435 6537. *Clubs:* Pratt's, Beefsteak, Brooks's; Roxburghe.
See also Master of Nairne.

MURRAY, Katherine Maud Elisabeth, MA, BLitt, FSA; Principal, Bishop Otter College, Chichester, 1948-70; *b* 3 Dec. 1909; *d* of Harold J. R. Murray (former HMI of Schools) and Kate M. Crosthwaite. *Educ:* Colchester County High Sch.; Somerville Coll., Oxford. Tutor and Librarian, Ashburne Hall, Manchester, 1935-37; Mary Somerville Research Fellow, Somerville Coll., Oxford, 1937-38; Asst Tutor and Registrar, 1938-44, Domestic Bursar, 1942-44, and Junior Bursar, 1944-48, Girton Coll., Cambridge. Chairman of Council, Sussex Archæological Soc., 1964-77, Pres., 1977-. Mem., Chichester District Council, 1973-, Vice-Chm. Planning Cttee, 1976-. *Publications:* The Constitutional History of the Cinque Ports, 1935; Register of Daniel Rough, Kent Record Soc., 1945; Caught in the Web of Words: James A. H. Murray and the Oxford English Dictionary, 1977; articles in Sussex Notes and Queries, Transactions of the Royal Historical Society, Archæologia Cantiana, English Historical Review. *Recreations:* walking, archæology. *Address:* Upper Cranmore, Heyshott, Midhurst, West Sussex. *T:* Midhurst 2325.

MURRAY, Keith (Day Pearce), MC 1917; RDI 1936; FRIBA, 1939; retired; *b* 5 July 1892; *s* of Charles Murray, Auckland, NZ; *m* 1948, Mary Beatrice de Cartaret Hayes, *d* of Lt-Col R. Malet; one *d*. *Educ:* King's Coll., Auckland, NZ; Mill Hill Sch., London. Served RFC and RAF in France, 1915-19 (MC, Croix de Guerre Belge, despatches 5 times); OC No 10 Sqdn, 1917-19; Major. Served in RAF, 1939-41. Studied at Architectural Association School. Commenced practice as partner with C. S. White, 1936. Designed pottery, glass and silver during the thirties; Master of the Faculty of Royal Designers for Industry, 1945-47. Gold Medal, 5th Triennale of Milan, 1933. Principal works: Wedgwood Factory at Barlaston; Hong Kong Air Terminal; BEA Engineering Base at London Airport; various industrial and office buildings. *Recreation:* trout fishing. *Address:* Stephouse, Tarrant Gunville, Blandford, Dorset. *T:* Tarrant Hinton 339.

MURRAY, Sir Kenneth, Kt 1958; JP, DL (Ross and Cromarty); *b* 23 Aug. 1891; *o s* of T. M. Murray, Geanies, Fearn, Ross-shire; *m* 1919, Edith Maud, *y d* of W. J. Tustin; one *s* three *d*. *Educ:* Winchester; New College, Oxford (BA). Served European War, 1914-18, with Lovat Scouts; discharged early 1918 with rank of Captain on account of ill-health caused by wounds. Mem. of HM's Body Guard for Scotland (Royal Company of Archers). Chm. of the Court, Royal Bank of Scotland, 1946-55 (Dir, 1935-57); Chm. and Dir of various other institutions and companies, 1930-67. Succeeded, in 1936, to the property of Geanies, Fearn, Ross-shire. *Recreations:* shooting, golf, gardening. *Address:* Geanies, Fearn, Ross-shire. *T:* Portmahomack 247. *Club:* New (Edinburgh).

MURRAY, Kenneth Alexander George, CB 1977; MA, BEd; Special Adviser to the Home Office on Police Service, Prison Service, and Fire Service selection, since 1977; Director, Civil Service Selection Board, and Civil Service Commissioner, 1964-77; *b* 16 June 1916; *s* of late George Dickie Murray and Isabella

Murray; *m* 1942, Elizabeth Ward Simpson; one *d. Educ:* Skene Street and Central Schools, Aberdeen; Aberdeen Univ. (MA English (1st Cl. Hons), BEd Psychol. (1st Cl. Hons)). RAMC and War Office Selection Bd, 1940-45, Captain. Psychological Adviser, Govt of India, 1945-47; Lectr in Psychology, Univ. of Hull, 1948-50; Principal Psychologist and Chief Psychologist, CS Selection Bd, 1951-63. Adviser to Police Service in high-grade selection, 1963-, also to Fire and Prison Services; Adviser (earlier) to Govts of Pakistan and Western Nigeria through their Public Service Commns. *Recreations:* reading, walking, watching cricket and Rugby League. *Address:* 15 Melvinshaw, Leatherhead, Surrey KT22 8SX. *T:* Leatherhead 72995. *Clubs:* MCC, Royal Commonwealth Society.

MURRAY, Rt. Hon. Lionel (Len Murray), PC 1976; OBE 1966; General Secretary of the Trades Union Congress, since 1973; *b* 2 Aug. 1922; *m* 1945, Heather Woolf; two *s* two *d. Educ:* Wellington (Salop) Gram. Sch.; Univ. of London, 1940-41; NCLC; New Coll., Oxford, 1945-47 (Hon. Fellow, 1975). Economic Dept, TUC, 1947, Head of Dept, 1954-69; Asst Gen. Sec., TUC, 1969-73. Mem., NEDC, 1973-; Cttee to Review the Functioning of Financial Institutions, 1977-; Vice-President: ICFTU, 1973; European Trade Union Confedn, 1974; Governor: Nat. Inst. of Economic and Social Research, 1968; LSE, 1970. Vis. Fellow, Nuffield Coll., Oxford, 1974. *Publication:* Contrib. to Economics and Technical Change. *Address:* Trades Union Congress, 23-28 Great Russell Street, WC1. *T:* 01-636 4030.

MURRAY, (Malcolm) Patrick, CB 1954; *b* 10 July 1905; *s* of late Sir Oswyn Murray, GCB, and Lady Mildred Octavia Murray; *m* 1st, 1934, Betty (*d* 1955), *er d* of A. M. Black, Richmond, Surrey; one *s* one *d* (and one *s* decd); 2nd, 1956, Richilda, *d* of Walter Hemingway, Wakefield, Yorks. *Educ:* Uppingham; Exeter Coll., Oxford (Open History Scholar). MA Honour Schools of Modern History and of Jurisprudence. Entered Home Civil Service as Asst Principal, Air Ministry, 1929; Private Sec. to Permanent Sec., 1931-37; graduated Imperial Defence Coll., 1938; Asst Sec., 1939; seconded for special duty, 1943; transferred to Ministry of Fuel and Power, 1946; Under-Sec., Electricity Division, Ministry of Fuel and Power, 1947-59; Dir of Establishments, Ministry of Power, 1959-61; a Deputy Sec., Ministry of Power, 1961-65, retd. *Address:* 26 Templemere, Oatlands Drive, Weybridge, Surrey KT13 9PB. *Club:* Special Forces.

MURRAY, Patrick; *see* Murray, M. P.

MURRAY, Peter, CMG 1959; HM Diplomatic Service, retired; *b* 18 July 1915; *m* 1960, E. M. Batchelor. *Educ:* Portsmouth Gram. Sch.; Merton Coll., Oxford. Burma Commission, 1937-49, Foreign Service, 1947; HM Ambassador to Cambodia, 1961-64; Ambassador to Ivory Coast, Upper Volta and Niger, 1970-72. *Address:* Brae Cottage, Lion Lane, Haslemere GU27 1JR. *Club:* East India, Devonshire, Sports and Public Schools.

MURRAY, Peter (John), PhD (London), FSA; Professor of the History of Art at Birkbeck College, University of London, since 1967; *b* 23 April 1920; *er s* of John Knowles Murray and Dorothy Catton; *m* 1947, Linda Bramley. *Educ:* King Edward VI Sch., Birmingham; Robert Gordon's Coll., Aberdeen; Gray's Sch. of Art, Aberdeen; Slade Sch. and Courtauld Inst., Univ. of London. Sen. Research Fellow, Warburg Inst., 1961; Pres., Soc. of Architectural Historians of GB, 1969-72. Rhind Lecturer, Edinburgh, 1967. *Publications:* Watteau, 1948; Index of Attributions... before Vasari, 1959; Dictionary of Art and Artists (with Linda Murray), 1959 (4th edn 1976); History of English Architecture (with P. Kidson), 1962 (with P. Kidson and P. Thomson), 1965; The Art of the Renaissance (with L. Murray), 1963; The Architecture of the Italian Renaissance, 1963; Renaissance Architecture, 1971; contribs to New Cambridge Mod. Hist., Encycl. Britannica, etc.; translations; articles in Warburg and Courtauld Jl, Burlington Mag., Apollo, foreign jls. *Recreation:* driving fast cars. *Address:* 24 Dulwich Wood Avenue, SE19 1HD. *T:* 01-670 4808.

MURRAY, Sir Ralph; *see* Murray, Sir F. R. H.

MURRAY, Rt. Hon. Ronald King, PC 1974; QC (Scotland) 1967; MP (Lab) Leith Division of Edinburgh since 1970; Lord Advocate, since 1974; *b* 15 June 1922; *s* of James King Murray, MIEE, and Muriel (*née* Aitken), Glasgow; *m* 1950, Sheila Winifred Gamlin; one *s* one *d. Educ:* George Watson's Coll., Edinburgh; Univ. of Edinburgh; Jesus Coll., Oxford. MA (1st cl. hons Phil) Edinburgh, 1948; LLB Edinburgh, 1952. Served HM Forces, 1941-46; commnd in REME, 1942; India and SEAC, 1943-46. Asst in Moral Philosophy, Edinburgh Univ., 1949; called to Scottish Bar, 1953; Standing Jun. Counsel to BoT

(Scotland), 1961-64; Advocate-Depute, 1964-67; Senior Advocate-Depute, 1967-70. *Publications:* articles in various jls. *Recreation:* boating. *Address:* 31 Boswall Road, Edinburgh EH5 3RP. *T:* 031-552 5602. *Clubs:* Royal Forth Yacht, Forth Corinthian Yacht.

MURRAY, Dr Ronald Ormiston, MBE (mil.) 1945; MD; FRCPE, DMR, FRCR; Consultant Radiologist: Royal National Orthopaedic Hospital, 1956-77; Lord Mayor Treloar's Orthopaedic Hospital, Alton, and Heatherwood Hospital, Ascot, 1951-77; *b* 14 Nov. 1912; *y s* of late John Murray and Elizabeth MacGibbon; *m* 1940, Catherine Joan Suzette Gauvain, *qv*; one *s* two *d. Educ:* Glasgow Acad.; Loretto Sch.; St John's Coll., Cambridge (MA); St Thomas's Hosp. Med. Sch. Casualty Officer and Ho. Surg., St Thomas' Hosp., 1938-39; RAMC (TA), 1939-45, MO 2nd Bn The London Scottish, Hon. Lt-Col. Associate Prof., Radiology, Amer. Univ. Hosp., Beirut, 1954-56. Sen. Lectr in Orthopaedic Radiology, Inst. of Orthopaedics, London Univ., 1963; Robert Jones Lectr, RCS, 1973; Baker Travelling Prof. in Radiology, Australasia, 1974; Caldwell Lectr, Amer. Roentgen Ray Soc., 1975, also Corresp. Mem. of the Soc., 1973-; other eponymous lectures. Associate Editor, Brit. Jl of Radiology, 1959-71. Founder Vice-Pres., Internat. Skeletal Soc., 1973. Fellow: Brit. Orthopaedic Assoc.; RSocMed; Hon. Fellow, Amer. Coll. of Radiology, 1969; Hon. Member: Mexican and Peruvian Rad. Socs, 1968; Rad. Soc. of N Amer., 1975. *Publications:* Chapters in: Modern Trends in Diagnostic Radiology, 1970; D. Sutton's Textbook of Radiology, 1969, 2nd edn 1975; (jtly) Radiology of Skeletal Disorders: exercises in diagnosis, 1971, 2nd edn 1977; papers in med. jls, mainly concerning radiological aspects of orthopaedics. *Recreations:* golf; formerly: Rugby football (Cambridge XV 1934-35, Scotland XV 1935), swimming (Cambridge Univ. Team 1933-34, British Univs Team, Turin, 1934). *Address:* 25 Wimpole Street, W1M 7AD. *T:* 01-935 4747; Pond House, Well, Long Sutton, Basingstoke RG25 1TL. *T:* Long Sutton (Hants) 297. *Clubs:* United Oxford & Cambridge University; Hawks (Cambridge), Berkshire Golf, Rye Golf.

MURRAY, Dame Rosemary; *see* Murray, Dame A. R.

MURRAY, Sir Rowland William Patrick, 14th Bt *cr* 1630; General Manager, Miles Motor Inn, Augusta, Georgia; *b* 26 Oct. 1910; *s* of late Rowland William Murray, 2nd *s* of 12th Bt, and Gertrude Frances McCabe; *S* uncle 1958; *m*; four *s* two *d.* Served in US Army during War of 1939-45. Captain. *Heir: s* Rowland William Murray, *b* 22 Sept. 1947. *Address:* 239 Kenlock Place NE, Atlanta, Ga 30305, USA.

MURRAY-BROWN, Gilbert Alexander, CIE 1942; OBE 1918; BSc; FICE; *b* 24 Jan. 1893; *m* 1928, Norah Frances, *e d* of late F. H. Burkitt, CIE; two *s. Educ:* Glasgow Univ. Joined RE (TF) 1914; served European War, 1914-19; Capt. 1916; Major, AIRO 1928. Joined Indian Service of Engineers, 1919; Chief Engr and Sec. to Govt, PWD, NWFP, India, 1940-46. Pres., Central Bd of Irrigation, India, 1943. *Recreations:* golf, fishing, shooting. *Address:* Kinnelhook, Lockerbie, Dumfriesshire. *T:* Lochmaben 211.

MURRIE, Sir William (Stuart), GCB 1964 (CB 1946); KBE 1952; Permanent Under-Secretary of State for Scotland, 1959-64, retired; *b* Dundee, 19 Dec. 1903; *s* of Thomas Murrie and Catherine Burgh; *m* 1932, Eleanore Boswell (*d* 1966). *Educ:* S America; Harris Acad., Dundee; Edinburgh Univ.; Balliol Coll., Oxford. Entered Scottish Office, 1927; transferred to Dept of Health for Scotland, 1935; Under-Sec., Offices of War Cabinet, 1944; Deputy Sec. (Civil), Cabinet Office, 1947; Deputy Under-Sec. of State, Home Office, 1948-52; Sec. to the Scottish Education Dept, 1952-57; Sec., Scottish Home Dept, 1957-59. Chm., Board of Trustees for Nat. Galls of Scotland, 1972-75; Member: Council on Tribunals, 1965-77; Adv. Cttee on Rhodesian Travel Restrictions. General Council Assessor, Edinburgh Univ. Court, 1967-75. Hon. LLD, Dundee Univ., 1968. *Address:* 7 Cumin Place, Edinburgh EH9 2JX. *T:* 031-667 2612.

MURSELL, Sir Peter, Kt 1969; MBE 1941; Vice-Lord-Lieutenant, West Sussex, since 1974; *b* 20 Jan. 1913; *m* 1938, Cicely, *d* of late Mr and Mrs M. F. North; two *s* two *d. Educ:* Bedales Sch.; Downing Coll. Cambridge. Fruit growing, 1934. War Service: Air Transport Auxiliary, 1940-44, Sen. Comdr. West Sussex County Council: Mem., 1947-74; Chm., 1962-67 and 1969-74. Member: Cttee on Management in Local Govt, 1965-66; Royal Commn on Local Govt in England, 1966-69; Water Space Amenity Commn, 1973-76; Inland Waterways Amenity Adv. Council, 1974-77. DL West Sussex, 1962. *Recreations:* sailing, mountain walking, skiing, squash, canal cruising. *Address:* Dounhurst Farm, Wisborough Green, Billingshurst, West Sussex. *T:* Kirdford 209. *Club:* Farmers'.

MURTAGH, Miss Marion; Chairman: Stats (MR) Ltd; Midas Research Ltd; CSB Data Processing Ltd. *Educ:* Waverley Gram. Sch., Birmingham. Qualified as: Certified Accountant, 1947; Chartered Secretary, 1948. Proprietor, The Calculating Bureau, 1938-51, Joint Owner, 1951-61. Member: Anglo-Thai Soc.; West Midlands Bridge Club (Pres.). *Recreation:* bridge. *Address:* 116 Chessetts Wood Road, Lapworth, Solihull, West Midlands B94 6EL. *T:* Lapworth 2089.

MURTON, Rt. Hon. (Henry) Oscar, PC 1976; OBE 1946; TD 1947 (Clasp 1951); JP; MP (C) Poole since 1964; Deputy Speaker and Chairman of Ways and Means, House of Commons, since 1976; *b* 8 May 1914; *o s* of late H. E. C. Murton, and of E. M. Murton (*née* Renton), Hexham, Northumberland; *m* 1939, Constance F. Murton (*née* Connell) (*d* 1977), *e d* of late F. O'L. Connell, Low Fell, Co. Durham; one *s* one *d. Educ:* Uppingham Sch. Commissioned, TA, 1934; Staff Coll., Camberley, 1939; active service, Royal Northumberland Fusiliers, 1939-46; GSO1, HQ Salisbury Plain Dist, 1942-44; GSO1, SD1, War Office, 1944-46. Managing Dir, Henry A. Murton Ltd, Departmental Stores, Newcastle-upon-Tyne and Sunderland, 1949-57. Dep. Sec. Northern Div. Nat. Coal Board, 1947-49. Mem., Wessex Provincial Area Exec. Cttee of Conservative Party, 1964, etc.; Sec., Cons. Parly Cttee for Housing, Local Government and Land, 1964-67, Vice-Chm., 1967-70; Chm., Cons. Parly Cttee for Public Building and Works, 1970; introduced Highways (Amendment) Act, 1965; PPS to Minister of Local Government and Development, 1970-71; an Asst Govt Whip, 1971-72; a Lord Comr, HM Treasury, 1972-73; Second Dep. Chm., 1973-74, First Dep. Chm., 1974-76, of Ways and Means, House of Commons. Member: Exec. Cttee, Inter-Parliamentary Union British Group, 1970-71; Panel of Chairmen of Standing Cttees, 1970-71; a former Vice-Pres., Assoc. of Municipal Corporations; Mem. Herrison (Dorchester) Hosp. Group Management Cttee, 1963-74. Governor, Canford Sch., 1972-76. JP, Poole, 1963. *Recreation:* sailing. *Address:* 343 Cromwell Tower, Barbican, EC2Y 8DD. *T:* 01-588 2577; Flat 5 Seaview Court, North Road, Parkstone, Poole, Dorset. *T:* Bournemouth 730243. *Clubs:* Royal Motor Yacht, Poole Yacht, Parkstone Yacht (Poole).

MUSCHAMP, Rt. Rev. Cecil Emerson Barron, MA, ThL; *b* Wing, Bucks, England, 16 June 1902; *s* of late Canon E. G. Muschamp, Launceston, Tasmania; *m* 1931, Margaret Warren Crane; two *s* two *d. Educ:* Church Grammar Sch., Launceston, Tasmania; Univ. of Tasmania; Univ. of Oxford; St Stephen's House, Oxford. BA Univ. of Tasmania, 1924, Oxon (Hon. Sch. of Theology), 1927; ThL Australian Coll. of Theology, 1925; MA Oxon, 1934. Schoolmaster, 1920-25, Hutchins Sch., Hobart, and St Peter's Coll., Adelaide. Deacon, 1927; Priest, 1928. Curate of St Luke, Bournemouth, 1927-30; in charge of St Albans and St Aidan's, Aldershot, 1930-32; Curate, Withycombe Raleigh (in charge of All Saints, Exmouth), 1932-37; Vicar of St Michael and All Angels, City and Diocese of Christchurch, NZ, 1937-50; Asst Bishop of Perth, 1950-55; Bishop of Kalgoorlie, 1950-67; Dean of Brisbane, 1967-72; retired 1972. Served War of 1939-45: Chaplain in Royal New Zealand Air Force, 1942-45; Sen. Chaplain, 1944, S Pacific Comd. Pres., WCC in WA, 1953-55; Councillor, Royal Flying Doctor Service, Kalgoorlie Base, 1955-67. *Publications:* Table Manners, 1945; Sin and its Remedy, 1961; The Church of England and Roman Catholicism, 1962. *Recreations:* golf, gardening. *Address:* 9 Samson Street, Mosman Park, WA 6012, Australia. *Club:* Rotary (Mosman Park).

MUSCROFT, Harold Colin; a Recorder of the Crown Court, since 1972; *b* Leeds, 12 June 1924; *s* of Harold and Meta Catrina Muscroft; *m* 1958; three *d. Educ:* Dept of Navigation, Southampton Univ.; home; Exeter Coll., Oxford (MA). Volunteer, Royal Corps of Signals, 1942; commnd RA, 1943; served in India, Burma (wounded), Malay and Java; demobilised 1947 (Captain). Oxford, 1947-51. Called to Bar, Inner Temple, 1953; practised NE Circuit. Huddersfield Town Councillor, 1958-59. *Recreations:* reading science fiction, mathematics, playing the pianoforte. *Address:* 15 Arthington Avenue, Harrogate, North Yorks. *T:* Harrogate 65032.

MUSGRAVE, Sir Christopher (Patrick Charles), 15th Bt *cr* 1611; *b* 14 April 1949; *s* of Sir Charles Musgrave, 14th Bt and of Olive Louise Avril, *o d* of Patrick Cringle, Norfolk; *S* father, 1970. *Recreations:* sailing, tennis, table-tennis, painting. *Heir: b* Julian Nigel Chardin Musgrave, *b* 8 Dec. 1951. *Address:* c/o Mrs Nelson, Tans End, Church Street, Wells-next-the-Sea, Norfolk.

MUSGRAVE, Clifford, OBE 1958; Director Brighton Public Libraries, Art Gallery, Museums and the Royal Pavilion, 1939-68; *b* 26 July 1904; *s* of William Francis Musgrave, bookseller; *m* 1928, Margaret Esther, *d* of Walter Meakin, journalist; two *s.* Director: Birkenhead Public Libraries and Williamson Art Gallery, 1937-39. Member Council of Museum Association, 1951-54; Pres. South-East Federation of Museums and Art Galleries, 1947-48-49; Mem. Cttee for 18th Century English Taste Exhibition, Royal Academy, 1955-56; Mem. Cttee for Le Siècle de l'Elégance Exhibition, Paris, 1959; Hon. Mem., Georgian Group; Mem. Advisory Council of Victoria and Albert Museum, 1957-69; Vice-Pres., Regency Soc.; FLA; Fellow Museums Assoc. Hon. DLitt Sussex, 1969. *Publications:* Late Georgian Architecture 1760-1810, 1956; Sussex, 1957; Regency Architecture 1810-1830 (The Connoisseur Period Guides, 1956-58), 1958; Royal Pavilion: an episode in the romantic, 1959; Regency Furniture, 1961, 2nd edn 1971; Adam and Hepplewhite Furniture, 1965; Life in Brighton, 1969; articles and reviews in various jls. *Recreations:* music, travel, architectural photography. *Address:* 33 Prince Regent's Close, Kemp Town, Brighton. *T:* Brighton 63100.

MUSGRAVE, Sir (Frank) Cyril, KCB 1955 (CB 1946); retired; *b* 21 June 1900; *s* of late Frank Musgrave; *m* 1st, Elsie Mary, *d* of late Christopher Williams; one *s* one *d* ; 2nd, Jean Elsie, *d* of late John Soulsby; two *s. Educ:* St George's Coll., London. Entered Civil Service, 1919; served Inland Revenue, 1920-37; Air Ministry, 1937-40; Ministry of Aircraft Production, 1940-46; Min. of Supply, 1946-59, Permanent Sec., 1956-59. Chm., Iron and Steel Bd, 1959-67; Mem. (part time), BSC, 1967-70; Dir various companies, 1960-76. *Recreations:* music, gardening. *Address:* Willows House, Walsham-le-Willows, Bury St Edmunds, Suffolk IP31 3AH. *T:* Walsham-le-Willows 486.

MUSGRAVE, Sir Richard James, 7th Bt, *cr* 1782; *b* 10 Feb. 1922; *s* of Sir Christopher Norman Musgrave, 6th Bt, OBE, and Kathleen (*d* 1967), 3rd *d* of late Robert Chapman, Co. Tyrone; *S* father 1956; *m* 1958, Maria, *d* of late Col M. Cambanis, and Mrs Cambanis, Athens, Greece; two *s* four *d. Educ:* Stowe. Capt., The Poona Horse (17th Queen Victoria's Own Cavalry), 1940-45. *Recreation:* shooting. *Heir: s* Christopher John Shane Musgrave, *b* 23 Oct. 1959. *Address:* Riverstown, Tara, Co. Meath. *T:* Drogheda 25121. *Club:* Kildare Street and University (Dublin).

MUSGRAVE, Thea; composer; *b* 1928; *d* of James P. Musgrave and Joan Musgrave (*née* Hacking); *m* 1971, Peter, *s* of Irving Mark, NY. *Educ:* Moreton Hall, Oswestry; Edinburgh Univ.; Paris Conservatoire; privately with Nadia Boulanger. *Works include:* Cantata for a summer's day, 1954; The Abbot of Drimock (Chamber opera), 1955; Triptych for Tenor and orch., 1959; Colloquy for violin and piano, 1960; The Phoenix and the Turtle for chorus and orch., 1962; The Five Ages of Man for chorus and orch., 1963; The Decision (opera), 1964-65; Nocturnes and arias for orch., 1966; Chamber Concerto No. 2, in homage to Charles Ives, 1966; Chamber Concerto No 3 (Octet), 1966; Concerto for orchestra, 1967; Music for Horn and Piano, 1967; Clarinet Concerto, 1968; Beauty and the Beast (ballet), 1968; Night Music, 1969; Memento Vitae, a concerto in homage to Beethoven, 1970; Horn concerto, 1971; From One to Another, 1972; Viola Concerto, 1973; The Voice of Ariadne (opera), 1972-73; Rorate Coeli, for chorus, 1974; Space Play, 1974; Orfeo I and Orfeo II, 1975; Mary, Queen of Scots (opera), 1976-77. Performances and broadcasts: UK, France, Germany, Switzerland, Scandinavia, USA, USSR, etc., Edinburgh, Cheltenham, Aldeburgh, Zagreb, Venice and Warsaw Festivals. Hon. MusDoc, CNAA. *Address:* c/o Novello & Co. Ltd, Borough Green, Kent.

MUSGRAVE, Prof. William Kenneth Rodgerson, PhD, DSc (Birmingham); Professor of Organic Chemistry, since 1960, Head of Department of Chemistry, 1968-71, and 1974-77, Pro-Vice-Chancellor and Sub-Warden, since 1973, University of Durham; *b* 16 Sept. 1918; *s* of late Charles Musgrave and late Sarah Alice Musgrave; *m* 1944, Joyce Cadman; two *s. Educ:* Stanley Grammar Sch., Co. Durham; Univ. of Birmingham. British-Canadian Atomic Energy Project, 1944-45; Univ. of Durham: Lecturer in Chemistry, 1945-56; Senior Lecturer, 1956-60; Second Pro-Vice-Chancellor, 1970-73. Personal Readership in Organic Chemistry, 1960. *Publications:* (joint) Advances in Fluorine Chemistry, Vol. I, edited by Stacey, Tatlow and Sharpe, 1960; Rodd's Chemistry of Carbon Compounds, vols Ia and IIIa, edited by Coffey; scientific papers in chemical journals. *Recreations:* gardening, rough shooting. *Address:* The Orchard, Potter's Bank, Durham City. *T:* Durham 3196.

MUSGROVE, Prof. Frank; Sarah Fielden Professor and Head of the Department of Education, University of Manchester, since 1970; Dean of the Faculty of Education, since 1976; *b* 16 Dec. 1922; *e s* of late Thomas and Fanny Musgrove, New Brinsley,

Nottingham; *m* 1944, Dorothy Ellen (*née* Nicholls); one *d*. *Educ:* Henry Mellish Grammar Sch., Nottingham; Magdalen Coll., Oxford; Univ. of Nottingham. BA Oxon, PhD Nottingham, MEd Manchester. Served War, RAFVR, Navigator, Bomber Command (Flying Officer), Ops 149 Sqdn, 1942-45 (tour of bombing missions completed 1944). Educational appts in England and in the Colonial Educn Service, E Africa, 1947-57; Lectureships in Univs of Leicester and Leeds, 1957-65; Vis. Prof. of Educn, Univ. of British Columbia, 1965; Prof. of Research in Educn, Univ. of Bradford, 1965-70; Vis. Prof. of Sociology, Univ. of California, 1969; The Chancellor's Lectr, Univ. of Wellington, NZ, 1970; Raymond Priestley Lectr, Univ. of Birmingham, 1975. Co-editor, Research in Education, 1971-76. FRSA 1971. *Publications:* The Migratory Elite, 1963; Youth and the Social Order, 1964; The Family, Education and Society, 1966; Society and the Teacher's Role (with P. H. Taylor), 1969; Patterns of Power and Authority in English Education, 1971; Ecstasy and Holiness, 1974; Margins of the Mind, 1977; research papers in: Africa; Sociological Review; Brit. Jl of Sociology; Brit. Jl of Educational Psychology; Economic History Review; Brit. Jl of Social and Clinical Psychology, etc. *Recreations:* fell walking, fly fishing. *Address:* 11 Oakwood Drive, Prestbury, Cheshire. *T:* Prestbury 48637. *Club:* Macclesfield Flyfishers'.

MUSGROVE, Prof. John, RIBA; Professor of Architecture in the University of London at University College, since 1970; *b* 20 June 1920; *s* of James Musgrove and Betsy (*née* Jones); *m* 1941, Gladys Mary Webb; three *s*. *Educ:* Univ. of Durham (King's Coll.) (BArch, 1st Cl. Hons). Asst to late Baron Holford, RA, 1952-53; Research Architect, Nuffield Foundn, 1953-60; Sen. Lectr and Reader in Architecture, University Coll. London, 1960-70. Hon. Fellow, Inst. of Architects, Sri Lanka, 1972. *Publications:* (jtly) The Function and Design of Hospitals, 1955; (jtly) The Design of Research Laboratories, 1960; numerous articles and papers in Architects' Jl, RIBA Jl, and reviews. *Recreations:* painting in oils, gardening. *Address:* Netherby, Green End Road, Boxmoor, Hemel Hempstead, Herts HP1 1QW.

MUSHIN, Prof. William W(oolf), CBE 1971; MA Oxon, 1946; MB, BS (Hons) London, 1933; FRCS 1966; FFARCS 1948; Professor and Director of Anaesthetics, Welsh National School of Medicine, University of Wales, 1947-75, now Emeritus; *b* London, Sept. 1910; *y s* of Moses Mushin and Jesse (*née* Kalmenson); *m* 1939, Betty Hannah Goldberg; one *s* three *d*. *Educ:* Davenant Sch.; London Hosp. Med. Sch. Buxton Prize in Anatomy, Anderson Prize in Clinical Medicine; Various resident hosp. posts; formerly: Anaesthetist, Royal Dental Hosp.; first Asst, Nuffield Dept of Anaesthetists, Univ. of Oxford. Lectures: Clover, RCS, 1955; Kellogg, George Washington Univ., 1950; Guedel, Univ. of Calif, 1957; John Snow, 1964; Baxter Travenol, Internat. Anaesth. Research Soc., 1970; Macgregor, Univ. of Birmingham, 1972; Rovenstine, Amer. Soc. of Anesthesiol., 1973. Visiting Professor or Consultant to univs, academic and other bodies in USA, Argentine, Uruguay, Brazil, Denmark, NZ, Australia, India, Germany, Ghana, S Africa, and Holland. Examiner: Univ. of Oxford for MD and PhD; FFARCS, 1953-73; FRCSI, 1962-67. Welsh Regional Hospital Board: Cons. Adviser in Anaesthetics, 1948-74; Mem., 1961-74. Member: Central Health Services Council, 1962-72; Safety of Drugs Cttee, Dept of Health and Social Security, 1964-76; Medicines Commn, 1976-; Assoc. of Anaesthetists, 1936- (Mem. Council, 1946-59 and 1961-73; Vice-Pres., 1953-56); Anaesthetists Group Cttee, BMA, 1950-69; Bd of Governors, United Cardiff Hosps, 1956-65; Court, Univ. of Wales, 1957-58; Commonwealth Scholarships Commn, 1969-. Welsh National School of Medicine: Mem. Senate, 1947-75; Mem. Council, 1957-58; Vice-Provost, 1958-60; Royal College of Surgeons: Mem. Bd, Faculty of Anaesthetists, 1954-71; Mem. Council, 1961-64; Dean, Faculty of Anaesthetists, 1961-64. Mem. Bd of Management and Consulting Editor, British Jl of Anaesthesia, 1947-75. Hon. Mem., various societies of anaesthetists. Hon. FFARACS 1962; Hon. FFA(SA) 1962; Hon. FFARCSI 1962. John Snow Silver Medal, 1974. *Publications:* Anaesthesia for the Poor Risk, 1948; (with Sir R. Macintosh) Local Analgesia: Brachial Plexus, 1954, 4th edn 1967; Physics for the Anaesthetist, 1946, 3rd edn 1964; Automatic Ventilation of Lungs, 1959, 2nd edn 1969; (ed) Thoracic Anaesthesia, 1963. Numerous papers on anaesthesia and allied subjects in British and foreign jls. *Address:* 30 Bettws-y-Coed Road, Cardiff CF2 6PL. *T:* Cardiff 751002. *Club:* United Oxford & Cambridge University.

MUSKER, Sir John, Kt 1952; Banker; Director, Cater, Ryder & Co., Ltd, Bankers (Chairman, 1960-71); Hon. Treasurer, London Municipal Society, since 1936; *b* 25 Jan. 1906; *o s* of late Capt. Harold Musker, JP, Snarehill Hall, Thetford, Norfolk; *m*

1932, Elizabeth (decd), *d* of Captain Loeffler, 51 Grosvenor Square, W1; two *d*; *m* 1955, Mrs Rosemary Pugh, *d* of late Maj.-Gen. Merton Beckwith-Smith. *Educ:* privately; St John's Coll., Cambridge (BA). Mem. LCC for City of London, 1944-49. Lt, RNVR, 1940. *Address:* Shadwell Park, Thetford, Norfolk. *T:* Thetford 3257; 71 Cadogan Gardens, SW3. *Clubs:* White's; Royal Yacht Squadron.

MUSKERRY, 8th Baron (Ireland), *cr* 1781; **Hastings Fitzmaurice Tilson Deane**; 13th Bt (Ireland), *cr* 1710; Radiologist to Regional Health Authority, Limerick, since 1961; *b* 12 March 1907; 3rd and *o surv. s* of 7th Baron Muskerry and Mabel Kathleen Vivienne (*d* 1954), *d* of Charles Henry Robinson, MD, FRCSI; *S* father, 1966; *m* 1944, Betty Fairbridge, *e d* of George Wilfred Reckless Palmer, South Africa; one *s* one *d*. *Educ:* Sandford Park Sch., Dublin; Trinity Coll., Dublin; MA, MB, BCh, BAO; DMR London. Served War of 1939-45, S African Army (Western Desert; seconded RAMC, Italy, Greece). Specialised in Radiology, London Univ., 1946-48; Consultant Radiologist to Transvaal Administration, 1949-57. *Heir: s* Hon. Robert Fitzmaurice Deane, BA, BAI [*b* 26 March 1948; *m* 1975, Rita Brink, Pietermaritzburg. *Educ:* Sandford Park Sch., Dublin; Trinity Coll. Dublin]. *Address:* Springfield Castle, Drumcollogher, Co. Limerick. *T:* Drumcollogher 5.

MUSKETT, Prof. Arthur Edmund, OBE 1957; DSc London, ARCS, MRIA; FIBiol; Professor of Plant Pathology and Head of Department of Mycology and Plant Pathology, The Queen's University, Belfast, 1945-65; Professor Emeritus, since 1966; Head of Plant Pathology Division, Ministry of Agriculture, N Ireland, 1938-65; *b* 15 April 1900; *s* of late Arthur Muskett, Wood Farm, Ashwellthorpe, Norwich, Norfolk; *m* 1926, Hilda Elizabeth, *d* of late Henry Smith, Manor Farm, Fundenhall, Norwich; three *s* one *d*. *Educ:* City of Norwich Sch., Norwich; Imperial Coll. of Science, London. BSc, ARCS (Botany); MSc (London) 1931; MRIA 1933; DSc (London) 1938. RAF Flight Cadet A, 1918-19. Asst in Plant Pathology, Min. of Agr., NI and QUB, 1923-26, Junior Lectr QUB 1926; Dep. Head Plant Pathology Div., Min. of Agric. NI and Lectr QUB, 1931; Dean of Faculty of Agriculture, Queen's Univ., Belfast, 1950-57. Pres. British Mycological Soc., 1948; Vice-Pres., Assoc. Applied Biologists, 1954-55. Chairman: Central Gardens Assoc. for Northern Ireland; Ulster Countryside Cttee, 1965-72; N Ireland Amenity Council; Ulster Tree Cttee. *Publications:* Diseases of the Flax Plant, 1947; A. A. McGuckian: A Memorial Volume, 1956; Autonomous Dispersal: Plant Pathology (An Advanced Treatise), Vol. III, 1960; Ulster Garden Handbook (annually); numerous papers in Annals of Applied Biology, Annals of Botany, Trans Brit. Mycological Soc., etc. *Recreations:* horticulture; extra work. *Address:* The Cottage, 29 Ballynahinch Road, Carryduff, Belfast. *T:* Carryduff 812350.

MUSKIE, Edmund Sixtus; lawyer and politician, USA; US Senator from Maine since 1959; Senate Assistant Majority Whip since 1966; Chairman, Senate Budget Committee; *b* Rumford, Maine, 28 March 1914; *s* of Stephen Muskie and Josephine Czarnecki; *m* 1948, Jane Frances Gray; two *s* three *d*. *Educ:* Bates Coll., Maine (AB); Cornell Law Sch., Ithaca, New York (LLB). Served War, Lt USNR, 1942-45. Admitted to Bar: Massachusetts, 1939; Maine, 1940, and practised at Waterville, Maine, 1940 and 1945-55; Federal District Court, 1941. Mem., Maine House of Reps, 1947-51; Democratic Floor Leader, 1949-51; Dist. Dir for Maine, Office of Price Stabilisation, 1951-52; City Solicitor, Waterville, Maine, 1954-55; Governor of State of Maine, 1955-59. Cand. for Vice-Presidency of US, 1968. Former Mem., Senate Foreign Relations Cttee, and its Sub-Cttees on Arms Control, Internat Organization and Surveillance; Former Chm., and Mem. *ex officio*, Democratic Senatorial Campaign Cttee; Chairman, Senate Sub-Cttees on: Environmental Pollution, Senate Environment and Public Wks Cttee; Intergovtl Relations, Senate Governmental Affairs Cttee; Member: Special Cttee on Aging; Exec. Cttee, Nat. Governors' Conf.; Chm., Roosevelt Campobello Internat. Park Commn. Mem, Amer. Acad. of Arts and Sciences. Has several hon. doctorates. Phi Beta Kappa; Phi Alpha Delta. *Publication:* Journeys, 1972. *Address:* Senate Office Buildings, Washington, DC 20510, USA.

MUSSEN, Surgeon Rear-Adm. Robert Walsh, CB 1954; CBE 1949; MD; FRCP; retired; *b* 13 May 1900; *s* of Hugh Harper Mussen, JP, Belfast, late Crown Solicitor, N Ireland; *m* 1932, Mary Katherine Anne, *d* of late Surgeon Rear-Adm. H. E. R. Stephens; two *s* two *d*. *Educ:* Campbell Coll., Belfast; Queen's Univ., Belfast; Charing Cross Hosp., London. Entered Royal Navy, 1922. Served in ships and Naval hosps at home and abroad; specialized in Clin. Pathology and Internal Medicine. MD (Belfast); MRCP 1935; FRCP 1949. Sqdn MO, 1st Battle Sqdn, 1938; Brit. Naval Med. Liaison Officer with US Navy,

1943-45; Surgeon Capt., 1944; MO i/c and Dir Med. Studies, RN Medical Sch., 1945-48. Surgeon Rear-Adm., 1952; QHP 1952-55; Medical Officer in Charge, RN Hosp., Chatham, and Command MO on staff of Comdr-in-Chief, the Nore, 1952-55; Min. of Health, 1955-65. Chm., Chailey RDC, 1972-74. Comdr Order of St John, 1954. *Publications:* various papers on medical subjects and on naval medical history. *Recreations:* golf, walking, reading and writing. *Address:* Cleves, Ditchling, Sussex. *T:* Hassocks 2920. *Clubs:* Army and Navy; Royal Naval and Royal Albert Yacht (Portsmouth); Ulster (Belfast).

MUSSON, Maj.-Gen. Alfred Henry, CB 1958; CBE 1956; pac; late RA; President, Ordnance Board, 1957-58, retired (Vice-President, 1955-57); *b* 14 Aug. 1900; *s* of Dr A. W. Musson, Clitheroe, Lancs; *m* 1932, Joan Wright Taylor; three *s. Educ:* Tonbridge Sch.; RMA Woolwich. Served War of 1939-45. *Address:* Lyndon, The Ridgeway, Tonbridge, Kent. *T:* 64978.

MUSSON, Gen. Sir Geoffrey (Randolph Dixon), GCB 1970 (KCB 1965; CB 1959); CBE 1945; DSO 1944; BA; *b* 9 June 1910; *s* of late Robert Dixon Musson, Yockleton, Shrewsbury; *m* 1939, Hon. Elspeth L. Bailey, *d* of late Hon. Herbert Crawshay Bailey; one *s* one *d. Educ:* Shrewsbury; Trinity Hall, Cambridge. 2nd Lt KSLI, 1930. Served War of 1939-45, North Africa and Italy; Comdr 2nd Bn DCLI, 1943-44; Comdr 36th Infantry Bde, 1944-46. Comdr Commonwealth Forces in Korea, 1954-55; Comdt Sch. of Infantry, 1956-58, Comdr 7th Armoured Div., BAOR, 1958; Maj.-Gen. 1958; Comdr of the 5th Div., 1958-59. Chief of Staff, GHQ, Near East Land Forces, 1959-62; Vice-Adjutant-Gen., War Office, subseq. Min. of Defence, 1963-64; GOC-in-C, N Command, 1964-67; Adjutant-General, 1967-70, retired. Colonel: King's Shropshire Light Infantry, 1963-68; The Light Infantry, 1968-72. A Vice-Chm., Nat. Savings Cttee, 1970-77; Chm., HM Forces Savings Cttee, 1970-77. Mem., Royal Patriotic Fund Corporation, 1977-. *Address:* (home) Provost Hill, Hurstbourne Tarrant, Andover, Hants SP11 0AT. *T:* Hurstbourne Tarrant 323. *Club:* Army and Navy.

MUSSON, John Nicholas Whitaker; Warden, Trinity College, Glenalmond, since 1972; *b* 2 Oct. 1927; *s* of late Dr J. P. T. Musson, OBE and Gwendoline Musson (*née* Whitaker); *m* 1953, Ann Priest; one *s* three *d. Educ:* Clifton (Schol.); Brasenose Coll., Oxford (MA). Served with Welsh Guards and Lancs Fusiliers, 1945-48; BA Hons Mod. Hist., Oxford, 1951; HM Colonial Admin. Service, 1951-59; District and Provincial Administration, N Nigeria; Lectr, Inst. of Administration, N Nigeria; Staff Dept, British Petroleum, London, 1959-60; Asst Master and Housemaster, Canford Sch., 1961-72. *Recreations:* hill walking, history, fine arts. *Address:* Trinity College, Glenalmond, Perthshire. *T:* Glenalmond 205. *Club:* East India, Devonshire, Sports and Public Schools.

MUSSON, Samuel Dixon, CB 1963; MBE 1943; Chief Registrar of Friendly Societies and Industrial Assurance Commissioner, 1963-72; *b* 1 April 1908; *e s* of late R. Dixon Musson, Yockleton, Salop; *m* 1949, Joan I. S., 2nd *d* of late Col D. Davies-Evans, DSO, Penylan, Carmarthenshire. *Educ:* Shrewsbury Sch.; Trinity Hall, Cambridge. Called to Bar (Inner Temple), 1930; practised as Barrister, 1930-46; commnd, Pilot Officer, RAFVR, 1941; served Egypt, N Africa, Italy, 1942-45 (despatches). Ministry of Health: Senior Legal Asst, 1946; Asst Solicitor, 1952; Principal Asst Solicitor, 1957. Vice-Pres., Building Socs Assoc., 1972-77; Mem., Trustee Savings Bank Inspection Cttee. *Recreations:* golf, country pursuits. *Address:* Prospect Hill Farm, Headley, Bordon, Hants. *T:* Headley Down 3183. *Club:* Savile.

MUSTILL, Michael John, QC 1968; a Recorder of the Crown Court, since 1972; Chairman, Civil Service Appeal Tribunal, since 1971; *b* 10 May 1931; *o s* of Clement William and Marion Mustill; *m* 1960, Beryl Reid Davies. *Educ:* Oundle Sch.; St John's Coll., Cambridge. Royal Artillery, 1949-51 (commissioned, 1950). Called to Bar, Gray's Inn, 1955, Bencher, 1976. Dep. Chm., Hants QS, 1971. *Recreation:* cricket. *Address:* 8 Prior Bolton Street, N1. *T:* 01-226 3032. *Club:* Travellers'.

MUSTON, Rt. Rev. Gerald Bruce; Bishop Coadjutor, Diocese of Melbourne, since 1971; *b* 19 Jan. 1927; 3rd *s* of Stanley John and Emily Ruth Muston; *m* 1951, Laurel Wright; one *s* one *d. Educ:* N Sydney Chatswood High School; Moore Theological College, Sydney. ThL (Aust. Coll. of Theology). Rector, Wallerawang, NSW, 1951-53; Editorial Secretary, Church Missionary Society (Aust.), 1953-58; Rector, Tweed Heads, NSW, 1958-61; Vicar, Essendon, Vic, 1961-67; Rural Dean of Essendon, 1963-67; Rector of Darwin, NT, and Archdeacon of Northern Territory, 1967-69; Federal Secretary, Bush Church Aid Society of Aust., 1969-71. *Recreations:* golf, reading. *Address:* 20 Hall Street, Brighton, Victoria 3186, Australia. *T:* 927514. *Clubs:* Melbourne, Royal Automobile of Victoria (Melbourne).

MUTCH, Nathan, MA, MD Cantab, FRCP (London); Consulting Physician, Guy's Hospital; formerly Staff Examiner in Applied Pharmacology, London University; Examiner in Therapeutics, Cambridge University; Lecturer in Pharmacology, London University; Director of Department of Pharmacology, Guy's Hospital; originator of medicinal Magnesium Trisilicate; Member of the first Editorial Board, British Journal of Pharmacology and Chemotherapy; Sector Adviser in Medicine, Emergency Medical Service; Consulting Physician to American Red Cross Society in Europe; *b* 22 May 1886; *s* of Nathan Mutch, Rochdale, and Helen Hollinshead; *m* 1913, Eileen Caroline Arbuthnot, 3rd *d* of Sir W. Arbuthnot Lane, 1st Bt, CB; one *d* (one *s* decd). *Educ:* Manchester Grammar Sch. (The King's prize for Chemistry); Emmanuel Coll., Cambridge (Senior Scholar and Research Student); 1st class Parts I and II, Nat. Science Tripos, 1906-07; Guy's Hosp. Medical Sch., (Univ. Scholar). Mem. of Physiological Soc.; founder Mem. of British Pharmacological Soc.; FRSM. *Publications:* articles on pathology and treatment of intestinal disorders, in scientific journals; also on magnesium trisilicate, other medicinal silicates, alumina and clays. *Address:* Pitt-White, Uplyme, Devon. *T:* Lyme Regis 2094.

MUTI, Riccardo; Principal Conductor, Philharmonia (formerly New Philharmonia) Orchestra and Orchestra Maggio Musicale Fiorentino; *b* 28 July 1941; *m* 1969, Christina Mazzavillani; one *s* one *d. Educ:* Diploma in pianoforte, Conservatorio di Napoli; Diploma in composition and conducting, Milan. Principal Guest Conductor, Philadelphia Orchestra, 1975-. Concert tours in USA: with Boston, Cleveland, Chicago, Philadelphia, and New York orchestras; concerts at Edinburgh Festival, and concerts and one opera at Salzburg Festival, concerts with Berlin Philharmonic; concerts in London as Principal Conductor, New Philharmonia Orchestra; Covent Garden Opera, 1977; opera in Florence and Vienna. Accademico dell' Accademia di Santa Cecilia. Verdienstkreuz, 1st class (Germany), 1976. *Address:* Via Corti Alle Mura 25, Ravenna, Italy. *T:* 38428.

MWENDWA, Maluki Kitili; Chief Justice of Kenya, 1968-71; Chairman: United Nations Association, Kenya; Chania Enterprises Ltd; Trans-African Highway Services Ltd; ExpoAfrica Ltd; Consultant General, Mugie Ltd; *b* 24 Dec. 1929; *s* of Senior Chief M. Kitavi Mwendwa and Mrs Kathuka Mwendwa; *m* 1964, Winifred Nyiva Mangole (Hon. Mrs Winifred Mwendwa, MP Kitui West; one of first four Kenya women MPs, Oct. 1974); one *s* three *d. Educ:* Alliance High Sch., Kenya; Makerere University Coll.; London Univ.; Exeter Univ.; St Catherine's Coll., Oxford. DipEd 1950; LLB 1955 (Sir Archibald Bodkin Prize for Criminal Law, 1953); DPA 1956; BA 1959, MA 1963. President: Cosmos Soc., 1959; Jowett Soc., 1959; St Catherine's Debating Soc., 1959, Oxford. Called to the Bar, Lincoln's Inn, 1961. Lectr Kagumo Teacher Training Coll., 1951. Asst Sec., Min. of Commerce and Industry, 1962, Min. of Works and Communications, 1962; Sen. Asst Sec., Min. of Tourism, Forests and Wild Life, 1962-63; Perm. Sec., Min. of Social Services, 1963, and Min. of Home Affairs, 1963-64; Solicitor Gen., 1964-68 (acting Attorney Gen., 1967). Leader, Kenya Delegn: Commonwealth and Empire Law Conf., Sydney, 1965; World Peace through Law Conf., Washington, 1965; Conf. on Intellectual Property, Stockholm, 1967 (Vice-Pres. of Conf.); UN Special Cttee on Friendly Relations, Geneva, 1967; Conf. on Law of Treaties, Vienna, 1968; Kenya Rep. on 6th Cttee, 21st Session, and on 2nd and 6th Cttees (Vice-Chm. of 6th Cttee), 22nd Session, UN Gen. Assembly; Ambassador to 22nd Session, UN Gen. Assembly, 1967 (Vice-Chm., Kenya Delegn to April/May 1967 Special Session); Mem., UN Internat. Trade Law Commn, 1967-74; Mem., Executive Council: African Inst. of Internat. Law, Lagos; Kenya Farmers' Assoc.; Donovan Maule Theatre, Nairobi; Agricultural Soc. of Kenya, Nairobi, 1970-73; African Automobile Assoc., Nairobi. Chm., Bd of Governors: Ngara Sch., 1965-73; Parklands Sch., 1967-73; Kitui Sch., 1972-74. *Publication:* Constitutional Contrasts in the East African Territories, 1965. *Recreations:* hunting, swimming, cycling, walking. *Address:* c/o Gigi House, Gigiri Road, PO Box 40198, Nairobi, Kenya. *T:* Nairobi 23450. *Clubs:* Executive (Nairobi), Mount Kenya Safari (Nanyuki).

MYDDELTON, Lt-Col Ririd, MVO 1945; JP; Extra Equerry to The Queen since 1952; Vice-Lieutenant of Denbighshire, 1968-74; *b* 25 Feb. 1902; *e s* of late Col Robert Edward Myddelton, TD, DL, JP, Chirk Castle, and late Lady Violet, *d* of 1st Marquess of Abergavenny; *m* 1931, Margaret Elizabeth Mercer Nairne (now Lady Margaret Elizabeth Myddelton; granted rank as *d* of a Marquess, 1946), *d* of late Lord Charles Mercer Nairne; two *s* one *d. Educ:* Eton; RMC Sandhurst. 2nd Lt Coldstream Guards, 1923; Adjutant, 3rd Bn, 1928-31; Staff Capt., London District, 1934-37; seconded as Dep. Master of the Household to King George VI, 1937-39; DAAG London District, 1939-40;

Staff Coll., Camberley, War Course, 1942; Commanded: 1st (Armd) Bn, Coldstream Guards, 1942-44 (Normandy); retired, 1946. JP 1948, DL 1949, High Sheriff, 1951-52, Denbigh. KStJ 1961. *Recreations:* hunting, shooting. *Address:* Chirk Castle, North Wales. *T:* Chirk 2460. *Club:* Turf.
See also Captain A. S. Aird.

MYER, Dame (Margery) Merlyn Baillieu, DBE 1960 (OBE 1948); *b* Queenscliff, Vic., 8 Jan. 1900; *d* of George Francis Baillieu and Agnes Sheehan; *m* 1920, Sidney Myer (*d* 1934); two *s* two *d*. *Educ:* Cromarty Girls' Sch., Victoria; Melbourne Univ. Interest in The Myer Emporium Ltd enterprises throughout Australia and abroad (founded by her late husband, Sidney Myer). Member: Cttee of Management of Royal Melbourne Hospital for 42 years; Victorian Council and Nat. Council of Australian Red Cross Soc. for 10 years; Sidney Myer Music Bowl Trust, which administers Sidney Myer Music Bowl. Collector of Jade, Porcelain and Objects d'Art. *Recreations:* garden lover, agricultural and musical interests, travel. *Address:* Cranlana, 62 Clendon Road, Toorak, Victoria 3142, Australia. *T:* 244966.

MYERS, Dr David Milton, CMG 1974; Vice-Chancellor, La Trobe University, Melbourne, 1965-76; *b* 5 June 1911; *s* of W. H. Myers, Sydney; *m* 1937, Beverley A. H., *d* of Dr T. D. Delprat; three *s*. *Educ:* Univs of Sydney and Oxford. BSc, BE, DScEng; FIE Aust., FIEE, FInstP. 1st Chief of Div. of Electrotechnology, CSIR, 1939-49; P. N. Russell Prof. of Elec. Engrg, Univ. of Sydney, 1949-59; Dean, Faculty of Applied Science, and Prof. of Elec. Engrg, Univ. of British Columbia, 1960-65. Mem. Adv. Council, CSIRO, 1949-55; Mem. Nat. Res. Council of Canada, 1965; Chm., Cttee on Overseas Professional Qualifications, 1969-. *Publications:* various research papers in sci. jls. *Recreations:* golf, tennis, music. *Address:* 76 Glenard Drive, Heidelberg, Vic. 3084, Australia. *T:* 459 9629. *Clubs:* Melbourne (Melbourne); Green Acres Golf.

MYERS, Brig. (Retired) Edmund Charles Wolf, CBE 1944; DSO 1943; BA Cantab; MICE; *b* 12 Oct. 1906; *er s* of late Dr C. S. Myers, CBE, FRS; *m* 1943, Louisa, *er d* of late Aldred Bickham Sweet-Escott; one *d*. *Educ:* Haileybury; Royal Military Academy, Woolwich; Caius Coll., Cambridge. Commissioned into Royal Engineers, 1926. Served Palestine, 1936 (despatches); War of 1939-45; Comdr, British Mil. Mission to Greek Resistance Forces, 1942-43; Middle East, including Balkans, until 1944 (African Star, Italy Star, DSO, CBE); North-West Europe, 1944-45 (France and Germany Star, Dutch Bronze Lion, Norwegian Liberty Medal); Far East, 1945; Korea, 1951-52 (despatches, American Legion of Merit). Chief Engineer, British Troops in Egypt, 1955-56; Dep. Dir, Personnel Administration in the War Office, 1956-59; retired 1959. Chief Civil Engineer Cleveland Bridge & Engineering Co. Ltd, 1959-64. Construction Manager, Power Gas Corp. Ltd, Davy-Ashmore Group, 1964-67. Regional Sec., British Field Sports Soc., 1968-71. *Publication:* Greek Entanglement, 1955. *Recreations:* horse training and riding, sailing, flying (1st Sec. RE Flying Club, 1934-35), fishing. *Address:* Wheatsheaf House, Broadwell, Moreton-in-Marsh, Glos GL56 0TY. *T:* Stow-on-the-Wold 30183. *Clubs:* Naval and Military, Special Forces.

MYERS, Geoffrey Morris Price; Under-Secretary, Agricultural Research Council, since 1973; *b* 8 May 1927; *o s* of Sam Price Myers, Liverpool and Deptford, and M. E. (Nancy) Price Myers, London. *Educ:* Reigate Grammar Sch.; King's Coll., London. BSc 1st cl. hons Botany 1947, MSc Plant Physiology 1950. Captain, RAEC, 1947-49; Asst Principal, Home Civil Service, 1950; UKAEA, 1959-67, Private Sec. to Chm.; Nat. Econ. Develt Office, 1967-69; Agric. Research Council, 1970; Asst Sec., Plants and Soils Research, 1970-73. *Address:* 160 Great Portland Street, W1N 6DT. *Club:* Athenæum.

MYERS, Gordon Elliot; Minister (Agriculture), Office of UK Permanent Representative to the European Economic Community, since 1975; *b* 4 July 1929; *s* of William Lionel Myers and Yvonne (*née* Arthur); *m* 1963, Wendy Jane Lambert; two *s* one *d*. *Educ:* Kilburn Grammar Sch.; University Coll., Oxford (BA 1st Cl. Hons Modern History). Asst Principal, MAFF, 1951; Principal, 1958; Asst Sec., 1966; Head successively of Land Drainage Div., Sugar and Tropical Foods Div., and EEC Div., 1966-74. *Address:* Karel van Lorreinen Laan 30, 1980 Tervuren, Belgium. *T:* 767.54.54.

MYERS, Harry Eric, QC 1967 (Gibraltar 1977); *b* 10 Jan. 1914; *s* of Harry Moss Myers and Muriel Serjeant; *m* 1951, Lorna Babette Kitson (*née* Blackburn); no *c*. *Educ:* Bedford Sch. Admitted Solicitor of Supreme Court, 1936; called to Bar, Middle Temple, 1945. Prosecuting Counsel to Bd of Inland Revenue on SE Circuit, 1965. *Address:* 3 Hare Court, Temple, EC4. *T:* 01-353 7741.

MYERS, Sir Kenneth (Ben), Kt 1977; MBE 1944; FCA; Chairman of Directors, South British Insurance Co. Ltd, since 1945; *b* 5 March 1907; *s* of Hon. Sir Arthur Myers and Lady (Vera) Myers (*née* Levy); *m* 1933, Margaret Blair Pirie; one *s* two *d*. *Educ:* Marlborough Coll.; Gonville and Caius Coll., Cambridge (BA 1928). FCA 1933. Returned to NZ, 1933; served War with 2nd NZEF, ME and Italy, 1940-45. Dir, cos in NZ, Australia and S Africa. President: Auckland Div., NZ Cancer Soc.; Auckland Medical Res. Foundn; other charities. *Recreations:* looking after my business connections and my family. *Address:* 21 Upland Road, Auckland 5, New Zealand. *T:* Auckland 545499. *Clubs:* Boodle's; Northern (Auckland).

MYERS, Mark, QC 1977; *b* 22 July 1930; *s* of Lewis Myers and Hannah Myers; *m* 1964, Katherine Ellen Desormeaux Waldram; one *s* one *d*. *Educ:* King's Sch., Ely; Trinity Coll., Cambridge (Exhibnr; MA). Called to the Bar, Gray's Inn, 1954. Sublector in Law, Trinity Coll., Cambridge, 1954-61; Part-time Lectr in Law, Southampton Univ., 1959-61. Mem., Consumers Cttee for England and Wales, and Consumers Cttee for GB, 1974-. *Publications:* articles in legal jls. *Recreations:* music and country life. *Address:* 73 Cholmeley Crescent, Highgate, N6 5EX. *T:* 01-340 7623; 11 King's Bench Walk, Temple, EC4Y 7EQ. *T:* 01-353 9281.

MYERS, Prof. Rupert Horace, CBE 1976; Vice-Chancellor and Principal, The University of New South Wales, since 1969, and Foundation Professor of Metallurgy since 1952; *b* 21 Feb. 1921; *s* of Horace Alexander Myers and Dorothy (*née* Harris); *m* 1944, Io Edwina King; one *s* three *d*. *Educ:* Melbourne High Sch.; Univ. of Melbourne. BSc 1942; MSc 1943; PhD 1947. Commonwealth Res. Fellow, Univ. of Melbourne, 1942-47; Principal Res. Officer, CSIRO, AERE Harwell, 1947-52; Univ. of New South Wales: Dean, Faculty of Applied Science, 1956-61; Pro-Vice-Chancellor, 1961-69. Chm. (part time), NSW State Pollution Control Commn, 1971-; Mem., Sydney Opera House Trust, 1976-. Hon. LLD Strathclyde, 1973; Hon. DSc Wollongong, 1976. *Publications:* numerous on metallurgy and atomic energy (also patents). *Recreations:* tennis, music. *Address:* University of New South Wales, PO Box 1, Kensington, NSW 2033, Australia. *T:* 663-0351.

MYERSON, Arthur Levey, QC 1974; a Recorder of the Crown Court since 1972; *b* 25 July 1928; *o s* of Bernard and Eda Myerson; *m* 1960, Elaine Shirley Harris; two *s*. *Educ:* Blackpool Grammar Sch.; Queens' Coll., Cambridge. BA 1950, LLB 1951. Called to the Bar, 1952. RAF, 1946-48. *Recreations:* reading, sailing, golf. *Address:* 25 Sandmoor Drive, Leeds LS17 2RE. *T:* Leeds 684169. *Clubs:* Moor Allerton Golf (Leeds), Leeds Sailing.

MYERSON, Aubrey Selwyn, QC 1967; a Recorder of the Crown Court, since 1972; *b* Johannesburg, S Africa, 10 Dec. 1926; *o s* of late Michael Colman Myerson, MRCSI, LRCPI, and late Lee Myerson; *m* 1955, Helen Margaret, *d* of Hedley Lavis, Adelaide, S Austr.; one *s* one *d*. *Educ:* Cardiff High Sch.; University Coll. of S Wales and Mon. Called to Bar, Lincoln's Inn, 1950, Bencher, 1975. *Recreations:* squash, fencing, tennis, gardening. *Address:* 8 Sloane Court East, Chelsea, SW3. *T:* 01-730 4707; Laurustina Cottage, Inkpen, Berks. *T:* Inkpen 468; 1 Dr Johnson's Buildings, Temple, EC4. *T:* 01-353 9328. *Clubs:* Reform; Bristol Channel Yacht.

MYINT, Prof. Hla; Professor of Economics, London School of Economics, since 1966; *b* Bassein, Burma, 20 March 1920; *m* 1944, Joan (*née* Morris); no *c*. *Educ:* Rangoon Univ.; London Sch. of Economics. Prof. of Econs, Rangoon Univ., and Econ. Adviser to Govt of Burma, 1946-49; Univ. Lectr in Econs of Underdeveloped Countries, Oxford Univ., 1950-65; Rector of Rangoon Univ., 1958-61. Vis. Prof., Univs of Yale, Cornell and Wisconsin; has served on UN Expert Cttees; Hon. DLitt, Rangoon, 1961. Order of Sithu (Burma), 1961. *Publications:* Theories of Welfare Economics, 1948; The Economics of the Developing Countries, 1964; Economic Theory and the Underdeveloped Countries, 1971; Southeast Asia's Economy: development policies in the 1970s, 1972; many papers in learned jls. *Recreations:* walking, garden watching. *Address:* 12 Willow Drive, Barnet, Herts. *T:* 01-449 3028.

MYLLENT, Peter; see Hamylton Jones, K.

MYNETT, George Kenneth, QC 1960; JP; **His Honour Judge Mynett**; a Circuit Judge, Oxford Crown Court, since 1972; *b* 16 Nov. 1913; *s* of E. Mynett, Wellington, Salop; *m* 1940, Margaret Verna Bass-Hammonds; two *s*. *Educ:* Adams Grammar Sch., Newport, Salop; London Univ. Admitted solicitor of Supreme Court, 1937; LLB Hons (London) 1938. Served War of 1939-45, RAF, 1940-46; Dep. Judge Advocate Staff, Dept of JAG, 1945,

1946. Barrister, Middle Temple, 1942, 1st Cl. Hons, Certificate of Honour; after demobilisation practised on Oxford Circuit. Master of the Bench, Middle Temple, 1967. Recorder of Stoke-on-Trent, 1961-71, Honorary Recorder 1972-; JP Stoke-on-Trent, 1961; JP Oxon, 1969-71; Dep. Chm., Oxfordshire QS, 1969-71; Comr of Assize: SE Circuit, 1970; Oxford Circuit, 1971. UK Representative, Conferences of Judges of Supreme Administrative Courts of EEC Countries in Berlin, Rome, The Hague, Luxembourg etc. Member: Council for the Training of Magistrates, 1967; Gen. Council of the Bar, 1968; Court of Governors, Univ. of Keele, 1961-. *Recreations:* landscape painting, golf, travel. *Address:* Tanglewood House, Boar's Hill, Oxford. *T:* Oxford 730439; 12 King's Bench Walk, Temple, EC4. *T:* 01-353 7008.

MYNORS, Sir Humphrey (Charles Baskerville), 1st Bt, *cr* 1964; *b* 28 July 1903; 2nd *s* of Rev. A. B. Mynors, rector of Langley Burrell, Wilts; *m* 1939, Lydia Marian, *d* of late Sir Ellis Minns, LittD, FSA, FBA; one *s* four *d*. *Educ:* Marlborough; Corpus Christi Coll., Cambridge. Fellow of Corpus Christi Coll., Cambridge, 1926-33; Hon. Fellow, 1953. Entered the service of the Bank of England, 1933; a Dir, 1949-54; Dep. Governor, 1954-64. Chm., Panel on Take-overs and Mergers, 1968-69; Dep. Chm., 1969-70. Hon. DCL Durham. *Heir: s* Richard Baskerville Mynors [*b* 5 May 1947; *m* 1970, Fiona Bridget, *d* of Rt Rev. G. E. Reindorp, *qv*; one *d*]. *Address:* Treago, St Weonards, Hereford. *T:* St Weonards 208.

MYNORS, Sir Roger (Aubrey Baskerville), Kt 1963; FBA 1944; *b* 28 July 1903; *s* of Rev. A. B. Mynors, Rector of Langley Burrell, Wilts; *m* 1945, Lavinia Sybil, *d* of late Very Rev. C. A. Alington, DD. *Educ:* Eton; Balliol College, Oxford. Fellow and Classical Tutor of Balliol, 1926-44 (Hon. Fellow 1963); Kennedy Prof. of Latin in the Univ. of Cambridge and Fellow of Pembroke Coll., 1944-53 (Hon. Fellow, 1965); Corpus Christi Prof. of Latin Language and Literature, Oxford, 1953-70 (Hon. Fellow, Corpus Christi Coll., 1970). Vis. Lectr, Harvard, 1938. Temp. Principal, HM Treasury, 1940. Longman Vis. Fellow, Leeds Univ., 1974. Pres., Classical Assoc., 1966. Hon. DLitt: Edinburgh; Durham; Hon. LittD: Cambridge; Sheffield. Hon. Mem., Amer. Acad. of Arts and Sciences. *Publications:* Cassiodori Senatoris Institutiones, 1937; Durham Cathedral MSS before 1200, 1939; Catulli Carmina, 1958; Catalogue of Balliol MSS, 1963; Plinii Epistulae, 1963; Panegyrici Latini, 1964; Vergilii Opera, 1969. *Address:* Treago, St Weonards, Hereford HR2 8QB. *T:* St Weonards 208.

MYRDAL, Alva; former Swedish Cabinet Minister, diplomatist, sociologist and author; Ambassador at large since 1961; Member of Swedish Parliament, 1962-70; Minister without Portfolio (in charge of disarmament and Church affairs) in Swedish Government, 1967-73; *b* 31 Jan. 1902; *d* of Albert and Lova Reimer; *m* 1924, Dr Gunnar Myrdal, *qv*; one *s* two *d*. *Educ:* Stockholm Univ. (AB); Uppsala Univ. (AM); USA; Geneva. Founder 1936, and Dir, 1936-48, Training Coll. for Pre-Sch. Teachers, Stockholm; Principal Dir, UN Dept of Social Affairs, 1949-50; Dir, Unesco Dept of Social Sciences, 1951-55; Minister to India, Burma, Ceylon and Nepal, 1955-56, Ambassador, 1956-61. Delegate to: ILO Conf., Paris, 1945, Geneva, 1947; Unesco Conf., Paris, 1946, New Delhi, 1956; UN General Assemblies, 1962, 1963, 1965-73. Chief Swedish Delegate to UN Disarmament Cttee, Geneva, 1962-73. Fellow, Center for Study of Democratic Instns, Santa Barbara, Calif., 1974. Vis. Professor: MIT 1974, 1975; Wellesley Coll., 1976. Chairman: Internat. Inst. for Peace Research, Stockholm, 1965-66; UN Expert Group on South Africa, 1964; Swedish Govt Cttees: on relations between State and Church, 1968-72; on Research on the Future, 1971-72; UN Expert Gp on Disarmament and Development, 1972. World Council on Pre-School Educn, 1947-49; Board Member: World Fedn of UN Assocs; Internat. Fedn of Univ. Women; Swedish Organisation for Cultural Relief in Europe; Swedish Fedn of Business and Professional Women (Chm. 1935-38, 1940-42). Hon. LLD: Mount Holyoke Coll., USA, 1950; Edinburgh Univ., 1964; Dr Humane Letters, Columbia Univ., 1965; Temple Univ., 1968; Hon. PhD, Leeds Univ., England, 1956; Hon. DD: Gustavus Adolphus, Miami, 1971; Brandeis, 1974; Gothenburg, 1975; East Anglia, 1976. West German Peace Prize (with G. Myrdal), 1970; Wateler Peace Prize, Hague Acad., 1973; Royal Inst. of Technology award, Stockholm, 1975. *Publications:* (with G. Myrdal) Crisis in the Population Problem, 1934; City Children, 1935; Nation and Family, 1941; Postwar Planning, 1944; Are We Too Many?, 1950; (with V. Klein) Women's Two Roles, 1956; Towards Equality, 1970; Game of Disarmament, 1976, etc.; numerous contribs to newspapers, periodicals, books and reports. *Recreations:* travel, theatre, cooking, reading. *Address:* Vaesterlaanggatan 31, Stockholm, Sweden.

MYRDAL, Prof. (Karl) Gunnar; Swedish economist; *b* 6 Dec. 1898; *s* of Carl Adolf Pettersson and Anna Sofia Carlsdotter; *m* 1924, Alva Reimer (*see* Alva Myrdal); one *s* two *d*. *Educ:* Stockholm Univ. Studied in Germany and Britain, 1925-29; Rockefeller Fellow, US, 1929-30; Assoc. Prof., Post-Grad. Inst. of Internat. Studies, Geneva; Lars Hierta Prof. of Polit. Econ. and Public Finance, Stockholm Univ., 1933; Mem. Swedish Senate (Social Democrat), 1934; directed study of Amer. Negro problem for Carnegie Corp., NY, 1938; returned to Sweden, 1942, re-elected to Senate, Mem. Bd of Bank of Sweden, Chm. Post-War Planning Commn; Minister of Commerce, 1945-47; Exec. Sec., UN Econ. Commn for Europe, 1947-57; directed study of econ. trends and policies in S Asian countries for Twentieth Century Fund, 1957-67; Prof. of Internat. Econs, Stockholm Univ., 1961; founded Inst. for Internat. Econ. Studies, Stockholm Univ., 1961; past Chm., Bd of Stockholm Internat. Peace Research Inst. (Mem. Bd) and Bd of Latin Amer. Inst., Stockholm; Vis. Res. Fellow, Center for Study of Democratic Instns, Santa Barbara, 1973-74; Distinguished Vis. Prof., New York City Univ., 1974-75. Member: British Acad.; Amer. Acad. of Arts and Scis; Royal Swedish Acad. of Scis; Hungarian Acad. of Scis; Fellow, Econometric Soc.; Hon. Mem., Amer. Econ. Assoc. Holds numerous hon. degrees and has received many awards, incl. Nitti Prize, 1976 and Nobel Prize for Economics (jtly), 1974. *Publications:* numerous sci. works, incl: The Cost of Living in Sweden 1830-1930, 1933; Monetary Equilibrium, 1939; An American Dilemma: The Negro Problem and Modern Democracy, 1944; The Political Element in the Development of Economic Theory, 1953; An International Economy: Problems and Prospects, 1956; Econimic Theory and Underdeveloped Regions, 1957; Value in Social Theory, 1958; Beyond the Welfare State: Economic Planning and its International Implications, 1960; Challenge to Affluence, 1963; Asian Drama: An Inquiry into the Poverty of Nations, 1968; Objectivity in Social Research, 1969; The Challenge of World Poverty: A World Anti-Poverty Program in Outline, 1970; Against the Stream: Critical Essays on Economics, 1973. *Address:* Västerlånggatan 31, 111 29 Stockholm, Sweden. *T:* (08) 21-36-41.

MYRES, John Nowell Linton, CBE 1972; LLD, DLitt, DLit, MA; FBA 1966; FSA; President, Society of Antiquaries, 1970-75 (Vice-President, 1959-63; Director, 1966-70), now Hon. Vice-President; Bodley's Librarian, University of Oxford, 1947-65; Hon. Student of Christ Church, 1971 (Student 1928-70), and Fellow of Winchester College; *b* 27 Dec. 1902; *yr s* of late Emeritus Prof. Sir John Linton Myres, OBE; *m* 1929, Joan Mary Lovell, *o d* of late G. L. Stevens, Jersey; two *s*. *Educ:* Winchester Coll. (Scholar); New Coll., Oxford (Scholar), Hon. Fellow, 1973. 1st Class Lit Hum., 1924; 1st Class Modern History, 1926; BA 1924; MA 1928; Lecturer, 1926, Student and Tutor, 1928-48, Librarian, 1938-48, of Christ Church; Univ. Lectr in Early English History, 1935-47; served in Min. of Food, 1940-45 (Head of Fruit and Veg. Products Div., 1943-45); mem. of Council of St Hilda's Coll., Oxford, 1957-72; Pres. Oxford Architectural and Historical Soc., 1946-49. Mem. Institute for Advanced Study, Princeton, 1956; Pres. Council for British Archæology, 1959-61; Member: Ancient Monuments Board (England), 1959-76; Royal Commn on Historical Monuments (England), 1969-74; Chm. Standing Conference of National and Univ. Libraries, 1959-61. Pres: Library Assoc., 1963; Soc. for Medieval Archæology, 1963-66. Lectures: Ford's, in English History, 1958-59; O'Donnell, Edinburgh Univ., 1961; Oxford 1966-67; Rhind, Edinburgh, 1964-65; Raleigh, British Acad., 1970. Hon. Mem., Deutsches Archäologisches Institut. Hon. LLD Toronto, 1954; Hon. DLitt Reading, 1964; Hon DLit Belfast, 1965. Has supervised excavations at Caerleon Amphitheatre, 1926, St Catharine's Hill, Winchester, 1925-28, Colchester, 1930, Butley Priory, 1931-33, Aldborough, 1934-35 and elsewhere. Gold Medal, Soc. of Antiquaries, 1976. Hon. Foreign Corresp. Mem. Grolier Club, New York. *Publications:* part-author: St Catharine's Hill, Winchester, 1930; Roman Britain and the English Settlements, 1936; Anglo-Saxon Pottery and the Settlement of England, 1969; A Corpus of Anglo-Saxon Pottery, 1977; articles and reviews in learned periodicals. *Recreations:* growing of vegetables and fruit; bibliophily, study of antiquities. *Address:* Manor House, Kennington, Oxford. *T:* Oxford 735353.

N

NAAS, Lord; Charles Diarmuidh John Bourke; *b* 11 June 1953; *e s* and *heir* of 10th Earl of Mayo, *qv*; *m* 1975, Marie Antoinette Cronnelly; one *d*. *Educ:* St Aubyn's, Rottingdean; Portora Royal Sch., Enniskillen; QUB; Bolton Street Coll. of Technology, Dublin. *Address:* Doon House, Maam, Co. Galway, Eire.

NABARRO, Prof. Frank Reginald Nunes, MBE 1946; FRS 1971; City of Johannesburg Professor of Physics since 1970, Professor and Head of Department of Physics since 1953, University of the Witwatersrand (Dean of Faculty of Science, 1968-70); Representative of Senate on Council, since 1967; *b* 7 March 1916; *s* of late Stanley Nunes Nabarro and Leah Nabarro; *m* 1948, Margaret Constance, *d* of late James Dalziel, ARAM; three *s* two *d*. *Educ:* Nottingham High Sch.; New Coll., Oxford (MA, BSc). DSc Birmingham. Sen. Exper. Officer, Min. of Supply, 1941-45; Royal Soc. Warren Research Fellow, Univ. of Bristol, 1945-49; Lectr in Metallurgy, Univ. of Birmingham, 1949-53. Vis. Prof., Nat. Research Council, Ottawa, 1956; Vice-Pres., S African Inst. of Physics, 1956-57; Republic Steel Vis. Prof., Dept of Metallurgy, Case Inst. of Techn., Cleveland, Ohio, 1964-65; Overseas Fellow of Churchill Coll., Cambridge, 1966-67; Gauss Prof., Akademie der Wissenschaften, Göttingen, 1970; Professeur-associé, Univ. Paris-Sud, 1971, Montpellier II, 1973; Vis. Prof. Dept of Material Science, Univ. of Calif., Berkeley, 1977. Hon. FRSSAf 1973. Beilby Memorial Award, 1950; South Africa Medal, 1972. *Publications:* Theory of Crystal Dislocations, 1967; scientific papers, mainly on solid state physics. *Recreation:* gardening. *Address:* 32 Cookham Road, Auckland Park, Johannesburg, South Africa. *T:* 726-7745.

NADER, Ralph; author, lecturer, lawyer; *b* Winsted, Conn, USA, 27 Feb. 1934; *s* of Nadra Nader and Rose (*née* Bouziane). *Educ:* Gilbert Sch., Winsted; Woodrow Wilson Sch. of Public and Internat. Affairs, Princeton Univ. (AB *magna cum laude*); Law Sch. of Harvard Univ. (LLB). Admitted to Bar of Connecticut, 1958; to Bar of Massachusetts, 1959, and US Supreme Court; US Army, 1959; Law practice in Hartford, Conn, 1959-. Member: Amer. Bar Assoc.; AAAS; Phi Beta Kappa. Lectr in History and Govt, Univ. of Hartford, 1961-63; Lectr, Princeton Univ., 1967-68. Has pursued, actively, better consumer protection; improving the lot of the American Indian, etc; lobbyed in Washington for safer gas pipe-lines and nuclear reactors, also played a very important role in work for the passing of: National Traffic and Motor Vehicle Safety Act, 1966; Wholesome Meat Act, 1967. Niemen Fellows Award, 1965-66; named one of the Ten Outstanding Young Men of the Year by US Junior Chamber of Commerce, 1967. *Publications:* Unsafe at Any Speed: The Designed-in Dangers of the American Automobile, 1965; (ed) The Consumer and Corporate Accountability, 1974; (ed jtly) Taming the Giant Corporation, 1976; contrib. articles to New Republic, etc. *Address:* (home) 53 Hillside Avenue, Winsted, Conn. 06098, USA.

NADESAN, Pararajasingam, CMG 1955; OBE 1954; Governor, Rotary International, District 321; Director: The Galle Face Hotel; Cargills (Ceylon) Ltd; Associated Hotels Co. Ltd; Colonial Motors Ltd; Hire Purchase Co. Ltd; Chairman, The Nuwara Eliya Hotels Co. Ltd; Past Chairman, Low Country Products Association; Member: Central Bd of Agriculture; Tea & Coconut Research Institutes; Ceylon Tea Propoganda Bd; *b* 20 Dec. 1917; *s* of Sir Sangarapillai Pararajasingam, *qv*; *m* 1st, 1941, Gauri Nair (decd); one *s* one *d*; 2nd, 1953, Kamala Nair; three *d*. *Educ:* Royal College, and Ceylon Univ. Coll.; Univ. of London (BA Hons). Tutor, Ceylon Univ. Coll., 1940; entered Ceylon Civil Service, 1941; held various appts in sphere of provincial administration, 1941-47; Asst Permanent Sec., Min. of Transport and Works, 1948-53; Dir of Civil Aviation in addition to duties as Asst Sec. Min. of Transport and Works, 1954-56; Sec. to the Prime Minister and Information Officer, Ceylon, 1954-56; Member: Ceylon Delegation to the Bandung Conf.; Commonwealth Prime Minister's Conf.; ICAO Gen. Assembly; ILO Cttee on Plantations. FCIT. Officer Order of Merit (Italy), 1954; Knight Comdr Order of the Crown, Thailand, 1955; Comdr Order of Orange Nassau, Netherlands, 1955; Defence Medal, 1947; Coronation Medal, 1953; Ceylon Armed Services Inauguration Medal, 1956. *Recreations:* golf, tennis, gardening, collecting antiques. *Address:* Six 28th Lane A, Inner Flower Road, Colombo 3, Sri Lanka. *T:* 28202 (Residence), 25919 (Office). *Clubs:* Colombo, Orient, Rotary (Colombo); Gymkhana.

NAGEON de LESTANG, Sir (Marie Charles Emmanuel) Clement, Kt 1960; *b* 20 Oct. 1910; *e s* of late M. F. C. Nageon de Lestang, Solicitor and Simone Savy; *m* 1933, Danielle Sauvage;

one *s* three *d* (and one *s* decd). *Educ:* St Louis' Coll., Seychelles; King's Coll., London. LLB (Hons) London, 1931. Called to the Bar, Middle Temple, 1931. Private practice, Seychelles, 1932-35; Legal Adviser and Crown Prosecutor to Govt of Seychelles, 1936-39; Actg Chief Justice, Seychelles, 1939-44; Resident Magistrate, Kenya, 1944-47; Puisne Judge, Kenya, 1947-56; Federal Justice, Federal Supreme Court of Nigeria, 1956-58; Chief Justice of the High Court of Lagos, 1958-64, and of the Southern Cameroons, 1958-60; Justice of Appeal, Court of Appeal for Eastern Africa, 1964, Vice-Pres., 1966-69. Chm., Industrial Tribunals. *Recreations:* yachting, fishing, tennis. *Address:* Pennies, Court Drive, Shillingford, Oxon.

NAGOGO, Alhaji Hon. Sir Usuman; Emir of Katsina, KBE 1962 (CBE 1948); CMG 1953; President, Council of Chiefs, North-Central State (formerly Minister without Portfolio, Northern Region of Nigeria, and Member, House of Assembly). Hon. DCL Ife Univ., 1973. *Address:* Katsina, Northern Nigeria.

NAGY, János L.; *see* Lörincz-Nagy, J.

NAIPAUL, Vidiadhar Surajprasad; author; *b* 17 Aug. 1932; *m* 1955, Patricia Ann Hale. *Educ:* Queen's Royal Coll., Trinidad; University Coll., Oxford. *Publications:* The Mystic Masseur, 1957 (John Llewelyn Rhys Memorial Prize, 1958); The Suffrage of Elvira, 1958; Miguel Street, 1959 (Somerset Maugham Award, 1961); A House for Mr Biswas, 1961; The Middle Passage, 1962; Mr Stone and the Knights Companion, 1963 (Hawthornden Prize, 1964); An Area of Darkness, 1964; The Mimic Men, 1967 (W. H. Smith Award, 1968); A Flag on the Island, 1967; The Loss of El Dorado, 1969; In a Free State, 1971 (Booker Prize, 1971); The Overcrowded Barracoon, and other articles, 1972; Guerrillas, 1975; India: a wounded civilization, 1977. *Address:* c/o André Deutsch Ltd, 105 Great Russell Street, WC1.

NAIRAC, Hon. Sir André (Lawrence), Kt 1963; CBE 1953; QC (Mauritius); *b* 1905. *Educ:* Royal Coll., Mauritius; Balliol Coll., Oxford Univ. Called to the Bar, Middle Temple, 1929. Formerly: Minister of Industry, Commerce and External Communications; Mem. of Legislative Council and Mem. of Executive Council, Mauritius. *Address:* Reunion Road, Vacoas, Mauritius.

NAIRN, Bryce James Miller, CBE 1960 (OBE 1944); Consul-General, Tangier, 1957-63, retired; *b* 9 July 1903; *s* of Cuthbert and Mary Nairn; *m* 1928, Margaret Mary, *d* of T. R. White, Orkney; one *d* (and one *d* decd). *Educ:* Pollokshields Academy, Glasgow. After taking MRCVS, farmed in French Morocco, 1926-32; joined Foreign Service, 1933; served Marrakesh and Tangier, 1933-40; Brazzaville, 1941-43; Marrakesh and Casablanca, 1943-44; Consul: Bordeaux, 1944-48, Madeira, 1948-50, St Paul-Minneapolis, 1950-53; Consul-General, Lourenço-Marques, 1953-57. *Recreations:* riding, shooting, fruit farming, golf. *Address:* BP511, Marrakesh, Morocco. *T:* Dar Tounsi 109.

NAIRN, Sir George; *see* Nairn, Sir M. G.

NAIRN, Air Vice-Marshal Kenneth Gordon, CB 1945; chartered accountant; *b* 9 Nov. 1898; *m* 1920, Mary Fleming Martin; two *s* one *d*. *Educ:* George Watson's Coll., Edinburgh; Univ. of Manitoba. Lived in Edinburgh till 1911; proceeded to Canada; service in Strathcona Horse and transferred to RFC 1916-19; Pilot, rank Lt; moved to Vancouver from Winnipeg, 1921; retired. Hon. Wing Commander of 111 Aux. Squadron RCAF 1933; Active Service, 1939-45; on Air Council as Air Mem. Accounts and Finance till Oct. 1944, then Special Adviser to Minister for Air on Finance. Hon. ADC for Province of BC to the Governor-General, Viscount Alexander, 1947. Norwegian Cross of Liberation, 1948. *Recreations:* golf, fishing, yachting. *Address:* 1611 Drummond Drive, Vancouver, BC. *T:* 224-1500. *Clubs:* Royal Air Force; Vancouver, Royal Vancouver Yacht (Vancouver).

NAIRN, Margaret, RGN, SCM; Chief Area Nursing Officer, Greater Glasgow Health Board, since 1974; *b* 20 July 1924; *d* of James R. Nairn and Anne G. Nairn. *Educ:* Aberdeen Academy. Nurse Training: general: Aberdeen Royal Infirmary, to 1945 (RGN); midwifery: Aberdeen Maternity Hosp., until 1948 (State Certified Midwife); Health Visitors: Aberdeen Coll. for Health Visitors, until 1952 (Health Visitors Cert.); administrative: Royal Coll. of Nursing, London, to 1959 (Nursing Admin. Cert.); 6 months study in USA as British Commonwealth and Empire Nurses Scholar, 1956. Ward Sister and Night Supt, Aberdeen Maternity Hosp., 1945-52; Director of Nursing Services in Aberdeen and Glasgow, 1952-74. *Publications:* articles in medical and nursing press: A Study of 283 Families with Rent Arrears; Liaison Services between Hospital and Community Nursing Services; Health Visitors in General Practice. *Recreations:* reading, gardening, swimming. *Address:* Flat 18, 20 Kensington Road, Glasgow G12 9UX. *T:* 041-339 1150.

NAIRN, Sir (Michael) George, 3rd Bt, *cr* 1904; TD 1948; *b* 30 Jan. 1911; *s* of Sir Michael Nairn, 2nd Bt, and Mildred Margaret, *e d* of G. W. Neish; *S* father 1952; *m* 1936, Helen Louise, *yr d* of late Major E. J. W. Bruce, Melbourne, Aust., and late Mrs L. Warre Graham-Clarke; two *s. Educ:* Trinity Coll., Glenalmond. Chairman: Kirkcaldy and Dist Trustee Savings Bank, 1952-71; Michael Nairn & Greenwich Ltd, 1958-62; Nairn Williamson (Holdings) Ltd, 1962-70. Served War of 1939-45, with The Black Watch (wounded); Major, 1939. Mem. of the Queen's Body Guard for Scotland (Royal Company of Archers). *Heir: s* Michael Nairn [*b* 1 July 1938; *m* 1972, Diana, *er d* of Leonard Bligh; two *s*]. *Address:* Pitcarmick, Bridge of Cally, Blairgowrie, Perthshire. *T:* Strath Ardle 214. *Club:* Caledonian. *See also Sir W. G. N. Walker.*

NAIRN, Sir Robert Arnold S.; *see* Spencer-Nairn.

NAIRNE, 12th Baroness, *cr* 1681; **Katherine Evelyn Constance Bigham;** *b* 22 June 1912; *d* of 6th Marquess of Lansdowne and Elizabeth (she *m* 2nd, Lord Colum Crichton-Stuart, who *d* 1957; she *d* 1964); *S* to brother's Barony of Nairne, 1944; *m* 1933, Hon. Edward Bigham (now Viscount Mersey, *qv*); three *s. Heir: s* Master of Nairne, *qv. Address:* Bignor Park, Pulborough, W Sussex. *T:* Sutton (Sussex) 214.

NAIRNE, Master of; Hon. Richard Maurice Clive Bigham; film director; *b* 8 July 1934; *e s* of 3rd Viscount Mersey, *qv,* and of 12th Baroness Nairne, *qv*; *m* 1961, Joanna, *d* of John A. R. G. Murray, *qv*; one *s. Educ:* Eton and Balliol. Irish Guards, 1952-54 (final rank Lt). Films: The Name of the Cloud is Ignorance, 1965 (Plaque, Lion of St Mark, and Premio San Giorgio, Venice; Main Award, Salerno); The Threat in the Mind, 1968 (Golden Rocket and Dip. of Honour, Rome; Gold Award, BISFA; Brit. Film Acad. award for best specialised film); Cast Us Not Out, 1969 (Silver Award, BISFA); Caring for History, 1973 (John Grierson Award, SFTA). *Address:* 1 Rosmead Road, W11. *T:* 01-727 5057. *Clubs:* Brooks's, Pratt's.

NAIRNE, Sir Patrick (Dalmahoy), KCB 1975 (CB 1971); MC 1943; Permanent Secretary, Department of Health and Social Security, since 1975; *b* 15 Aug. 1921; *s* of late Lt-Col C. S. and Mrs E. D. Nairne; *m* 1948, Penelope Chauncy Bridges, *d* of Lt-Col R. F. and Mrs L. C. Bridges; three *s* three *d. Educ:* Radley Coll.; University Coll., Oxford (Exhibr). Seaforth Highlanders, 1941-45 (Capt.). 1st cl. hons Mod. Hist. (Oxon), 1947. Entered Civil Service and joined Admty, Dec. 1947; Private Sec. to First Lord of Admty, 1958-60; Asst Sec., 1960; Private Sec. to Sec. of State for Defence, 1965-67; Assistant Under-Sec. of State (Logistics), MoD, 1967-70; Dep. Under-Sec. of State, MoD, 1970-73; Second Perm. Sec., Cabinet Office, 1973-75. *Recreations:* watercolour painting, calligraphy. *Address:* South Lodge, Knipp Hill, Cobham, Surrey. *T:* Cobham 2401. *Club:* United Oxford & Cambridge University.

NAIROBI, Archbishop of, (RC), since 1971; **H. E. Cardinal Maurice Otunga;** *b* Jan. 1923. Priest, 1950; Titular Bishop of Tacape, 1957; Bishop of Kisii, 1960; Titular Archbishop of Bomarzo, 1969; Cardinal 1973. *Address:* Archbishop's House, PO Box 14231, Nairobi, Kenya.

NAISBY, John Vickers, MC 1918; TD 1935; QC 1947; *b* 1894; *m* 1954, Dorothy Helen, *d* of late J. H. Fellows. *Educ:* Rossall; Emmanuel Coll., Cambridge. Called to Bar, Inner Temple, 1922. Lt-Col and Brevet Col. *Address:* 3 Westmoreland Place, SW1V 4AB. *T:* 01-828 8917.

NALDER, Hon. Sir Crawford David, Kt 1974; farmer; active in voluntary and charitable organisations; *b* Katanning, WA, 14 Feb. 1910; *s* of H. A. Nalder, Wagin; *m* 1st, 1934, Olive May (*d* 1973), *d* of S. Irvin; one *s* two *d* ; 2nd, 1974, Brenda Wade. *Educ:* State Sch., Wagin; Wesley Coll., Perth, WA. Sheep, wheat and pig farmer, 1934-; Country rep. for Perth butchers. Entered parliament, 1947; MLA (CP) for Katanning, Parliament of Western Australia, 1950-73 (for Wagin, 1947-50); Dep. Leader, Country Party, 1956; Minister: for War Service Land Settlement, 1959-66; for Agriculture, 1959-71; for Electricity, 1962-71; Leader, Parly Country Party, 1962-73. Chm., Girls College Council. Knighted for services to the state and in local govt. *Recreations:* tennis, gardening. *Address:* 7 Morriett Street, Attadale, WA 6156, Australia.

NALDER, Major-General Reginald Francis Heaton, CB 1944; OBE 1941; BSc; retired; *b* 2 Feb. 1895; *s* of late Francis Henry Nalder; *m* 1916, Kathleen, *d* of late William Heaton Jacob; one *s* one *d. Educ:* Dulwich Coll.; London University. Commissioned Loyal North Lancashire Regt, 1914; E Surrey Regt, 1915; served European War, France, Belgium and Italy, 1916-18; transferred to Royal Signals, 1922; North-West Frontier of India, 1930-31; at War Office, 1935-39; served War of 1939-45: in France and Belgium, 1939-40; Chief Signal Officer, Allied Armies in Italy, 1943-45, and AFHQ, 1945 (despatches, OBE, CB, Commander Legion of Merit, Officer Legion of Honour, French Croix de Guerre). Signal Officer-in-Chief, India, 1946-47; retired, 1947; Colonel Commandant Royal Signals, 1955-60. Princess Mary Medal (Royal Signals Institution), 1966. *Publications:* British Army Signals in the Second World War, 1953; The Royal Corps of Signals, 1958. *Address:* 23 Alexandra Road, Epsom, Surrey KT17 4BP. *T:* Epsom 22041. *Clubs:* Naval and Military, Royal Automobile.

NALL, Sir Michael (Joseph), 2nd Bt *cr* 1954; DL; *b* 6 Oct. 1921; *er s* of Colonel Sir Joseph Nall, 1st Bt; *S* father, 1958; *m* 1951, Angela Loveday Hanbury, *e d* of Air Chief Marshal Sir Alec Coryton, *qv*; two *s. Educ:* Wellington College, Berks. Joined Royal Navy, 1939. Served War of 1939-45 (at sea); psm 1949; Lt-Comdr, 1950-61, retired. General Manager, Guide Dogs for the Blind Association, 1961-64. Pres., Nottingham Chamber of Commerce and Industry, 1972-74. DL Notts, 1970-; High Sheriff, Notts, 1971. *Recreations:* field sports, flying. *Heir: s* Edward William Joseph Nall, 13th/18th Royal Hussars (QMO), *b* 24 Oct. 1952. *Address:* Hoveringham Hall, Nottingham NG14 7JR. *T:* Lowdham 3634.

NALL-CAIN, family name of **Baron Brocket.**

NANCE, Francis James, LLM; **His Honour Judge Nance;** a Circuit Judge (formerly a Judge of County Courts and Commissioner, Liverpool and Manchester Crown Courts), since 1966; *b* 5 Sept. 1915; *s* of late Herbert James Nance, South Africa, and of Margaret Ann Nance, New Brighton; *m* 1943, Margaret Gertrude Roe; two *s. Educ:* St Francis Xavier's College, Liverpool; University of Liverpool (LLM 1938). Called to the Bar, Gray's Inn, 1936. Served War of 1939-45, Royal Corps of Signals (Captain): Normandy invasion, NW Europe (despatches). Practised on Northern Circuit, 1936-66. Deputy Chairman, Lancashire QS, 1963-71. *Recreation:* chess. *Address:* 37 Warren Drive, Wallasey, Merseyside L45 0JW. *T:* 051-639 2915. *Club:* Athenæum (Liverpool).

NANDY, Dipak; Deputy Chief Executive, Equal Opportunities Commission, since 1976; *b* 21 May 1936; *s* of B. C. Nandy and Leela Nandy; *m* 1st, 1964, Margaret Gracie; 2nd, 1972, Hon. Luise Byers; one *d. Educ:* St Xavier's Coll., Calcutta; Univ. of Leeds BA 1st Cl. Hons English Literature, 1960; C.E. Vaughan Research Fellowship, 1960-62. Lectr, English Literature, Univ. of Leicester, 1962-66; Lectr and Fellow of Rutherford College, Univ. of Kent at Canterbury, 1966-68; founder-Director, The Runnymede Trust, 1968-73; Vis. Fellow, Adlai Stevenson Inst. of International Affairs, Chicago, 1970-73; Research Fellow, Social and Community Planning Research, 1973-75. Mem., Cttee of Inquiry into Future of Broadcasting, 1974-77. *Publications:* numerous essays in books, periodicals and newspapers on literature, political thought, race relations, urban problems, and equality for women. *Recreations:* collecting records, opera, mathematics. *Address:* c/o Equal Opportunities Commission, Overseas House, Quay Street, Manchester M3 3HN. *T:* 061-833 9244. *Club:* Film Exchange (Manchester).

NANKIVELL, Owen; Assistant Director, Central Statistical Office, since 1972; *b* 6 April 1927; *s* of John Hamilton Nankivell and Sarah Ann Mares; *m* 1956, Mary Burman Earnshaw; one *s* two *d. Educ:* Torquay Grammar Sch.; Univ. of Manchester. BA (Econ) 1951, MA (Econ) 1963. FRSS. Admty, 1951-52; Colonial Office, 1952-55; Central Statistical Office, 1955-65; DEA, 1965-69; HM Treasury, 1969-72. *Recreations:* Christian, tennis, choral music, singing. *Address:* 20 Hillway, N6 6QA. *T:* 01-340 0897.

NAPIER, family name of **Barons Napier and Ettrick** and **Napier of Magdala.**

NAPIER, 14th Lord, of Merchistoun, *cr* 1627 (Scotland), **and ETTRICK, 5th Baron,** *cr* 1872 (UK); **Francis Nigel Napier;** a Bt of Nova Scotia, 1666, 11th Bt of Thirlestane; DL; Major, Scots Guards (Reserve of Officers); Private Secretary, Comptroller and Equerry to HRH the Princess Margaret, Countess of Snowdon, since 1973; *b* 5 Dec. 1930; *e s* of 13th Baron Napier and 4th Ettrick, TD, and Muir, *e d* of Sir Percy Newson, Bt; *S* father 1954; *m* 1958, Delia Mary, *yr d* of A. D. B. Pearson; two *s* two *d. Educ:* Eton; RMA, Sandhurst. Commissioned, 1950; served Malaya, 1950-51; Adjt 1st Bn Scots Guards, 1955-57. Equerry to His late Royal Highness The Duke of Gloucester, 1958-60, retd, 1960. Deputy Ceremonial and Protocol Secretary, CRO, 1962-66. A Cons. Whip, House of Lords, 1970-71; Mem. Royal Co. of Archers (Queen's Body Guard for Scotland), 1953-. Pres., St John Ambulance Assoc. and Brigade for County of London, 1975-. DL Selkirk, 1974, Ettrick and Lauderdale, 1975. Freeman, City of London; Liveryman, Worshipful Company of Grocers. Hon. Treasurer, PDSA. *Heir: s* Master of Napier, *qv. Address:* Laidlawstiel, Galashiels, Ettrick and Lauderdale TD1 1TJ. *T:* Clovenfords 216; Apartment 2, St James's Palace, SW1A 1BA. *T:* 01-930 0242. *Clubs:* White's, Pratt's, Cavalry and Guards.

NAPIER OF MAGDALA, 5th Baron (UK), *cr* 1868; **Robert John Napier,** OBE 1944; MICE; late Royal Engineers; Brigadier, Chief Engineer, HQ, Scottish Command, retd; *b* 16 June 1904; *o s* of 4th Baron and Florence Martha *d* (*d* 1946), *d* of Gen. John Maxwell Perceval, CB; *S* father, 1948; *m* 1939, Elizabeth Marian, *y d* of E. H. Hunt, FRCS; three *s* two *d. Educ:* Wellington. Served Waziristan, 1936-37 (despatches); War of 1939-45, Sicily (OBE). *Heir: s* Hon. Robert Alan Napier [*b* 6 Sept. 1940; *m* 1964, Frances Clare, *er d* of A. F. Skinner, Monks Close, Woolpit, Suffolk; one *s* one *d*]. *Address:* 8 Mortonhall Road, Edinburgh EH9 2HW. *Club:* New (Edinburgh).

NAPIER, Master of; Hon. Francis David Charles Napier; *b* 3 Nov. 1962; *s* and *heir* of 14th Baron Napier (and 5th Baron Ettrick), *qv.*

NAPIER, Barbara Langmuir, OBE 1975; JP; Senior Tutor to Women Students in the University of Glasgow, 1964-Sept. 1974; Member, the Industrial Arbitration Board (formerly Industrial Court), 1963-76; *b* 21 Feb. 1914; *y c* of late James Langmuir Napier, Consultant Engineer, and late Siblie Agnes Mowat. *Educ:* Hillhead High Sch., Glasgow; Univ. of Glasgow (MA); Glasgow and West of Scotland Coll. of Domestic Science. Org. Sec. Redlands Hosp., Glasgow, 1937-41; Univ. of Glasgow: Warden, Queen Margaret Hall, 1941-44; Gen. Adv. to Women Students, 1942-64; Appts Officer (Women), 1942-65. Founder Mem. Assoc. of Principals, Wardens and Advisers to Univ. Women Students, 1942 (Pres. 1965-68); Local Rep. and later Mem. Coun., Women's Migration and Overseas Appts Soc., 1946-64; Winifred Cullis Lecture Fellowship (midwest USA) of Brit. Amer. Associates, 1950; Governor: Westbourne Sch., Glasgow, 1951- (Chm. 1969-); Notre Dame Coll. of Educn, Glasgow, 1959-64; Founder Dir, West of Scotland Sch. Co. Ltd, 1976-. Member, Tribunal under National Insurance Acts, 1954-60; President, Standing Conference of Women's Organisations (Glasgow), 1955-57; Member: Scottish Committee, ITA, 1957-64; Executive Cttee, Nat. Advisory Centre on Careers for Women, (formerly Women's Employment Fedn), 1963-68, 1972-; Indep. Member: Flax and Hemp Wages Council (GB), 1962-70 (Dep. Chm. 1964-70); Hat, Cap and Millinery Wages Council (GB), 1963-70; Laundry Wages Council (GB), 1968-70. JP Glasgow 1955-75, Stirling 1975-. *Publications:* (with S. Nisbet) Promise and Progress, 1970; contrib. University Women's Review, etc. *Recreations:* reading, walking, travel, gardening, painting, being with cats. *Address:* Benview, Gartmore, Stirling FK8 3RJ. *T:* Aberfoyle 206. *Club:* College (Glasgow).

NAPIER, Charles (Goddard), RSW; artist; *b* 1 Aug. 1889; 2nd *s* of late Andrew Nelson Napier, herbalist, Edinburgh; *m* 1934, Hazel May Eadie (*d* 1960), *d* of late Arthur William Ballance, Herringswell. *Educ:* George Watson's Coll., Edinburgh. Studied Edinburgh College of Art; works mostly in water-colours; attracted by architectural subjects; did a series of black and white drawings of prominent Edinburgh buildings; painted in Holland, France and Italy; exhibited RSA, Glasgow Institute, USA, Canada, and New Zealand; first London exhibition of water-colours, Brook Street Art Gallery, Feb. 1934; exhibition of water colours, British Council, Oxford, 1949; second exhibition of water colours, Phantasy and Dream, British Council, 1952. Marlborough in Wiltshire purchased 1937, and In Wells Harbour, Norfolk, 1940, for Scottish Modern Arts, Edinburgh. *Address:* 4 East Castle Street, Edinburgh EH10 5AR. *T:* 031-229 5281.

NAPIER, Hon. Sir (John) Mellis, KCMG 1945; Kt 1943; KStJ; Chief Justice of South Australia, 1942-67; Lieutenant-Governor of South Australia, 1942-73; Chancellor of the University of Adelaide, 1948-61; *b* Dunbar, Scotland, 24 Oct. 1882; *s* of late Alexander Disney Leith Napier, MD, MRCP, FRSE; *m* 1908, Dorothy Bell (*d* 1959), *d* of Edward Kay, Adelaide; two *s* (and one missing, presumed died, on active service). *Educ:* City of London School; Adelaide University; LLB 1902; LLD (*hc*)

Melbourne 1956; LLD (*aeg*) 1959. Called SA Bar, 1903; KC 1922; Puisne Judge of Supreme Court of S Australia, 1924-42; Chairman of Royal Commission on Monetary and Banking Systems of Australia, 1936-37. *Address:* 49 Kanmantoo Road, Aldgate, South Australia.

NAPIER, Sir Joseph William Lennox, 4th Bt, *cr* 1867; OBE 1944; *b* 1 Aug. 1895; *s* of 3rd Bt and Mabel Edith Geraldine (*d* 1955), *d* of late Rev. Charles Thornton Forster, Vicar of Hinxton, Cambridgeshire; *S* father, 1915; *m* 1931, Isabelle Muriel, *yr d* of late Maj. H. Siward B. Surtees, DL, JP; two *s. Educ:* Rugby; Jesus College, Cambridge. Served European War in South Wales Borderers, 1914-18; re-employed 1939, Lt-Col HQ Staff, Eastern Command and Italy. *Heir: s* Robert Surtees Napier [*b* 5 March 1932; *m* 1971, Jennifer Beryl, *d* of H. Warwick Daw; one *s*]. *Address:* 17 Cheyne Gardens, Chelsea, SW3; Berystede Cottage, Ascot, Berks. *Club:* Alpine.
See also Brigadier V. J. L. Napier.

NAPIER, Oliver John; Member (Alliance) of Northern Ireland Constitutional Convention for East Belfast, 1975-76; *b* 11 July 1935; *e s* of James J. and Sheila Napier; *m* 1962, Brigid (*née* Barnes); three *s* five *d* (and one *s* decd). *Educ:* Ballycruttle Public Elem. Sch., Downpatrick; St Malachy's Coll., Belfast; Queen's Univ., Belfast (LLB). Qual. Solicitor, NI, 1959; Lectr and Mem. Bd of Examrs, Incorp. Law Soc. of NI, 1965-71. Mem. Exec., Ulster Liberal Party, 1962-69; Founder Mem., New Ulster Movt, 1969; Founder Mem., Alliance Party, 1970, Leader 1973-. Mem. (Alliance), E Belfast, NI Assembly, 1973-75; Minister of Legal Affairs, NI Executive, Jan.-May 1974. Prospective Parly Cand. (Alliance), E Belfast, 1977-. *Recreations:* many and varied. *Address:* 83 Victoria Road, Holywood, Co. Down.

NAPIER, Brigadier Vivian John Lennox, MC 1918; late S Wales Borderers; Vice-Lieutenant, Brecknock, 1964-74; *b* 13 July 1898; 3rd *s* of Sir William Lennox Napier, 3rd Bt; *m* 1958, Marion Avis, OBE, *d* of late Sir John and Lady Lloyd. *Educ:* Uppingham; RMC. Served European War, 1914-18: France and Belgium (wounded, MC); served War of 1939-45: HQ Cairo Bde and 1 Bn Welch Regt, North Africa (despatches, prisoner). Brig. Comdg Mombasa Area, 1948-49; Dep. Comdr S-W District, UK, 1949-51; retd, 1952. Commissioner, St John Ambulance, Breconshire, 1957-62. DL Brecknock, 1958. Order of Leopold (Belgium), 1925; OStJ 1959. *Recreation:* fishing. *Address:* Ty Nant, Groesffordd, Brecon, Powys.
See also Sir Joseph Napier, Bt.

NAPIER, Sir William Archibald, 13th Bt, of Merchiston, *cr* 1627; *b* 19 July 1915; *s* of Sir Robert Archibald Napier, 12th Bt and Violet Payn; *S* father 1965; *m* 1942, Kathleen Mabel, *d* of late Reginald Greaves, Tafelberg, CP; one *s. Educ:* Cheam School; Stowe. Captain S African Engineers, Middle East, 1939-45. Mechanical Engineer. AM Inst. of (SA) Mech. Engineers; AM Inst. of Cert. Engineers (Works); Fellow, Inst. of Matériel Handling. *Recreations:* shooting, golf, squash. *Heir: s* John Archibald Lennox Napier [*b* 6 Dec. 1946; *m* 1969, Erica, *d* of late Kurt Kingsfield; one *s* one *d*]. *Address:* Merchiston Croft, PO Box 65177, Benmore, Transvaal, 2010, S Africa. *T:* 7832651. *Clubs:* Junior Carlton; Rand, Johannesburg Country, Wanderers' (Johannesburg).

NAPLEY, Sir David, Kt 1977; Solicitor; Partner in Kingsley, Napley & Co. since 1937; President of the Law Society, 1976-77 (Vice-President, 1975-76); *b* 25 July 1915; *s* of late Joseph and Raie Napley; *m* 1940, Leah Rose, *d* of Thomas Reginald Saturley; two *d. Educ:* Burlington College. Solicitor, 1937. Served with Queen's Royal (W Surrey) Regt, 1940; commnd 1942; Indian Army, 1942; Captain 1942; invalided 1945. Contested (C): Rowley Regis and Tipton, 1951; Gloucester, 1955. Pres., London (Criminal Courts) Solicitors Assoc., 1960-63; Chm. Exec. Council, British Academy of Forensic Sciences, 1960-74 (Pres. 1967; Director, 1974-); Mem. Council, Law Soc., 1962-; Mem. Judicial Exchange with USA, 1963-64; Chm., Law Soc's Standing Cttee on Criminal Law, 1963-; Pres., City of Westminster Law Soc., 1967-68; Mem. Editorial Bd, Criminal Law Review, 1967-; Chairman: Contentious Business, Law Soc., 1972-75; Legal Aid Cttee, 1969-72; Mem. Home Office Law Revision Cttee, 1971-. Chm., Mario & Franco Restaurants Ltd, 1968-77. *Publications:* Law on the Remuneration of Auctioneers and Estate Agents, 1947; (ed) Bateman's Law of Auctions, 1954; The Law of Auctioneers and Estate Agents Commission, 1957; Crime and Criminal Procedure, 1963; Guide to Law and Practice under the Criminal Justice Act, 1967; The Technique of Persuasion, 1970, 2nd edn 1975; a section, Halsbury's Laws of England; contrib. legal and forensic scientific jls, press, legal discussions on radio and TV. *Recreations:* painting, reading, writing, music, eating. *Address:* 24 Moore Street, Chelsea, SW3. *T:* 01-589 2068. *Club:* Garrick.

NAPOLITAN, Leonard, CB 1970; Director of Economics and Statistics, Ministry of Agriculture, Fisheries and Food, since 1965; *b* 9 April 1919; *s* of late Domenic and of Rose G. Napolitan; *m* 1945, Dorothy Laycock; two *d*. *Educ:* Univ. of London (BSc Econ. 1944); LSE (MSc Econ. 1946). Asst Agric. Economist, Univ. of Bristol, 1947-48; joined Min. of Agric. and Fisheries as Agric. Economist, 1948; Chief Agric. Economist, 1958. Chm., Conf. of Provincial Agric. Economists, 1956-68; Chm., Nat. Food Survey Cttee, 1965-77. Pres., Agric. Econs Soc., 1974-75. *Address:* 4 The Strand, Rye, East Sussex.

NAPPER, Prof. Jack Hollingworth, CBE 1968; Professor of Architecture and Head of the School of Architecture in the University of Newcastle upon Tyne, 1963-70, now Emeritus; *b* 23 Dec. 1904; *s* of Frederick George Napper, Headmaster, and Edna Napper; *m* 1935, Mary Whitehead; two *s* one *d*. *Educ:* Oldham High Sch.; Univ. of Manchester. Clerk in cotton industry 1918-31; Architectural Assistant (Oldham, Bolton, London), 1935; Lecturer in Architecture, Hull, 1935-38; University of Durham, King's College, Newcastle upon Tyne: Lectr in Architecture, 1938-59; personal chair of Architecture, 1959-60; Head of School of Architecture, 1960-70. Private Practice, 1944-. President, Northern Architectural Association, 1958-59; Mem. Council, RIBA, 1958-63, 1963-69, and 1970-74, Vice-Pres., 1973-74. *Publications:* (with Prof. W. Fisher Cassie) Structure in Building, 1952; reviews in Jl of RIBA. *Address:* 15 Brandling Park, Newcastle upon Tyne NE2 4RR. *T:* Newcastle upon Tyne 810724.

NAPPER, John (Pelham); painter; *b* 17 Sept. 1916; *e s* of late John Mortimer Napper and late Dorothy Charlotte (*née* Hill); *m* 1st, 1935, Hedvig Sophie Armour; 2nd, 1945, Pauline Davidson. *Educ:* Frensham Heights, Surrey and privately; Dundee Sch. of Art; Royal Acad. Schs of Art. Served War of 1939-45: commnd RA, 1941; Ceylon, 1942, War Artist to Ceylon comd, 1943-44; seconded to RNVR, 1944, E Africa, 1944; demobilised, 1945. One-man exhibitions: Leicester Galleries, London, 1949, 1961, 1962; The Adams Gallery, London, 1957 and 1959; The Walker Art Gallery, Liverpool, 1959; La Maison de la Pensée Française, Paris, 1960; Galerie Lahumière, Paris, 1963; Galleries Hervé and Lahumière, Paris, 1965; Larcada Gallery, New York, 1968, 1970, 1972, 1975, 1977; represented in many public and private collections. Vis. Prof. of Fine Arts, Southern Illinois Univ., USA, 1968-69. Awarded prize at International Exhibition of Fine Arts, Moscow, 1957; Awarded International Assoc. of Art Critics Prize, 1961. *Address:* Steadvallets Farm, Bromfield, Ludlow, Salop. *T:* Bromfield 247.

NARAIN, Sase, OR 1976; CMG 1969; JP (Guyana); solicitor; Speaker of the National Assembly, Guyana, since 1971; Chairman, Berger Paints (Guyana) Ltd; *b* 21 Jan. 1925; *s* of Oudit and Sookdai Naraine; *m* 1952, Shamshun Narain (*née* Rayman); four *s*. *Educ:* Modern Educational Inst.; Gibson and Weldon Law Tutors. Solicitor, admitted in England and Guyana, 1957. Town Councillor, City of Georgetown, 1962-70; Member: History and Arts Council, 1969-; Republic Cttee of Guyana, 1969; Pres., Guyana Sanatan Dharma Maha Sabha, 1963-. Comr for Oaths to Affidavits, 1961; Notary Public, 1968. Dep. Chm., Public Service Commn, Guyana, 1966-71; Mem., Police Service Commn, 1961-71. Mem., Nat. Awards Cttee of Guyana. JP 1962. *Recreations:* golf, cricket, swimming. *Address:* 217 South Street, Lacytown, Georgetown, Demerara, Guyana. *T:* 66611. *Clubs:* Georgetown, Georgetown Cricket, Lusignan Golf, Everest Cricket (Guyana).

NARASIMHAN, Chakravarthi Vijayaraghava; Under-Secretary-General for Inter-Agency Affairs and Co-ordination, since 1973, United Nations, New York; *b* 21 May 1915; *s* of Chakravarthi V. and Janaki Vijayaraghavachari; *m* 1938, Janaki, *d* of Dr M. T. Chari; two *d*. *Educ:* University of Madras (BA); Oxford (MA). Indian Civil Service, 1936; Dep. Sec., Development Dept, Government of Madras, 1945-48; Min. of Agriculture, Govt of India, 1950-53; Joint Sec., Economic Affairs Dept, Ministry of Finance, 1953-56; Executive Sec., UN Economic Commission for Asia and Far East, 1956-59; Under-Sec. for Special Political Affairs, UN, 1959-62; Chef de Cabinet of the Sec.-Gen., UN, 1961-73; Under-Sec., 1962-67, Under-Sec.-Gen. 1967-69, for Gen. Assembly Affairs, UN; Dep. Administrator, UN Develt Prog., 1969-72. Hon. Doctor of Laws, Williams Coll. Williamstown, Mass, 1960; Hon. Dr of Humane Letters, Colgate Univ., 1966. *Recreations:* Sanskrit literature, South Indian classical music, tennis. *Address:* 300 East 33rd Street, New York, NY 10016, USA. *T:* (212)-686-2398.

NARAYAN, R. K.; Author; *b* Madras, India, 1907. *Educ:* Maharaja's College, Mysore, India. Padma Bushan award for distinguished services to literature. Hon. LittD Leeds, 1967. *Publications: novels:* (several published in England); Swami and Friends, 1935; (followed by): The Bachelor of Arts, 1937; The Dark Room, 1939; The English Teacher, 1945; Mr Sampath, 1947; The Financial Expert, 1952; Waiting for the Mahatma, 1955; The Guide, 1958; The Man-Eater of Malgudi, 1961; Gods, Demons and Others, 1964; The Sweet Vendor, 1967; The Painter of Signs, 1977; (ed) The Ramayana, 1973; Reminiscences, 1973; *autobiography:* My Days, 1975; *short stories:* An Astrologer's Day; The Lawley Road; A Horse and Two Goats, 1970, etc; *essays:* Next Sunday, 1955 (India); My Dateless Diary, 1960 (India). *Address:* c/o David Higham Associates, Ltd, 5/8 Lower John Street, Golden Square, W1R 4HA; Yadavagiri, Mysore 2, India.

NASH, (Denis Frederic) Ellison, FRCS; Consultant Surgeon: St Bartholomew's Hospital, since 1947; Chailey Heritage Hospital, since 1952; *b* 10 Feb. 1913; *m* 1938, Joan Mary Andrew; two *s* two *d*. *Educ:* Dulwich College; St Bartholomew's Medical College. MRCS, LRCP, 1935; FRCS 1938. Served war of 1939-45, RAFVR, Wing-Comdr (Air Efficiency Award, 1943). Hunterian Professor, 1949 and 1956. Arris and Gale Lecturer, 1950. Dean, St Bartholomew's Hospital Medical College, 1957-62; Special Trustee, St Bartholomew's Hosp., 1974-; Regional Postgraduate Dean, and Asst Dir, British Postgraduate Medical Fedn, Univ. of London, 1948-74. Special interest in the education and care of the physically handicapped; Hon. Med. Advr, Shaftesbury Soc. Member, British Assoc. of Urological Surgeons. Senior Fellow, British Orthopædic Assoc.; Fellow, Assoc. of Surgeons of GB. Chm., Dulwich Coll. Preparatory Sch. Trust. *Publications:* The Principles and Practice of Surgery for Nurses and Allied Professions, 6th revised edn, 1976; scientific papers in medical journals particularly concerned with surgery of childhood. *Recreation:* photography. *Address:* 10 Kingswood Drive, SE19 1UT. *T:* 01-670 2281. *Club:* City of London Guild of Freemen.

NASH, John Edward; Director, S. G. Warburg & Co. Ltd, since 1977; Director and Deputy Chairman, Banque de Gestion Financière, Zürich, since 1977; Director, Reckitt & Colman, Ltd, 1960-73 and since 1977; *b* 25 June 1925; *s* of Joseph and Madeleine Nash; *m* 1947, Ralda Everard Herring; two *s* two *d*. *Educ:* Univ. of Sydney (BEc); Balliol Coll., Oxford (BPhil). Teaching Fellow in Economics, Sydney Univ., 1947. Exec. Dir, Samuel Montagu & Co. Ltd, 1956; also Director, 1960-73: British Australian Investment Trust; Montagu Trust Ltd; Midland Montagu Industrial Finance Ltd; Cape Court Corp. (in Melb.); resigned all directorships on appt to Brussels, 1973; Dir of Monetary Affairs, EEC, 1973-77. Dir, Oxford Univ. Business Summer Sch., 1965; Research Fellow, Nuffield Coll., Oxford (part-time), 1966-69. *Recreations:* golf, skiing, horse-racing, music. *Address:* Gartenstrasse 26, 8039 Zürich, Switzerland; Chalet Gstelli, Gsteig bei Gstaad, Switzerland. *T:* (030) 51162. *Clubs:* Turf, Buck's, MCC, University (Sydney).

NASH, Prof. John Kevin Tyrie Llewellyn; Professor of Civil Engineering and Assistant Principal, King's College, University of London; *b* 24 April 1922; *s* of George Llewellyn Nash and Menie Tyrie; *m* 1947, Margaret Elizabeth Littleboy; one *s* three *d*. *Educ:* Newtown Sch., Waterford; Trinity Coll., Dublin. BA, BAI 1944, MA, MAI 1947, DSc (Eng) London 1975; FKC 1972; FICE, FASCE, FGS. Asst Engrg with K. C. D. Gp on Phoenix Caissons for Mulberry Harbour, 1943-44; Jun. Sci. Officer, Road Res. Lab. in Soil Mechs Div., 1944-46; King's Coll., London: Lectr, 1946-51; Reader, 1951-61; Prof. of Civil Engrg, 1961-; Head of Civil Engrg Dept, 1971-; Asst Principal, 1973-77. Cons. to Nigerian Govt on engrg educn in Nigeria, 1963; soil mechs cons. on Kainji dam, Nigeria, 1961-69 and various earth and rock-fill dams and dykes in Nigeria, Jordan, Israel, Cyprus, Portugal, Greece, Sudan and Britain; expert witness for NCB at Aberfan Tribunal, 1966-67 and for BP at Sea Gem enquiry, 1967; cons. for foundns of London Bridge and Humber Bridge. Mem. Council, ICE, 1959-62 and 1963-68; Chm., British Geotechnical Soc., 1959-61; Sec.-Gen., Internat. Soc. for Soil Mechs and Foundn Engrg, 1967-; Chm. Editorial Panel, Géotechnique, 1960-66. *Publications:* Elements of Soil Mechanics, 1951; Civil Engineering, 1957; sci. papers on soil mechs in Proc. Int. Soc. Soil Mechs and Foundn Engrg, specialist symposia and confs, Géotechnique, etc. *Recreations:* music, photography, bird-watching. *Address:* King's College, Strand, WC2R 2LS. *T:* 01-836 5454; Shandon, Jordans, Beaconsfield, Bucks HP9 2ST. *T:* Chalfont St Giles 3295. *Club:* Athenæum.

NASH, Kenneth Twigg; Academic Registrar and Secretary, University of Exeter, since 1976; *b* Rotherham, 15 Sept. 1918; *s* of Albert Nash, AIC, AMIChemE, chemical engineer, and Marjorie Nora Twigg; *m* 1960, Patricia Mary Kate Batchelor; two *s*. *Educ:* Rotherham Grammar Sch.; Gonville and Caius Coll., Cambridge. War of 1939-45: 67th (York and Lancs) and

62nd (1st/3rd E Riding) HAA Regts, RA. Admiralty, 1948; Private Sec. to Sir John Lang; Prin. Private Sec. to three First Lords (Cilcennin, Hailsham, Selkirk); service in civil establishments, finance and as a Head of Military Branch of Admiralty. Called to Bar, Inner Temple, 1955. IDC, 1964; Defence Counsellor, British Embassy, Washington, 1965; Asst Under-Sec. (Policy), MoD, 1968; Asst Sec. Gen., NATO, 1969-72; Asst Under-Sec. (Defence Staff), 1972-74; Dep. Under-Sec. of State, MoD (PE), 1974-75. *Address:* West Riding, West Avenue, Exeter.

NASH, Thomas Arthur Manly, CMG 1959; OBE 1944; Dr (Science); retired; *b* 18 June 1905; *s* of late Col L. T. Nash, CMG, RAMC; *m* 1930, Marjorie Wenda Wayte; (one *s* decd). *Educ:* Wellington Coll.; Royal Coll. of Science. Entomologist, Dept Tsetse Research and Reclamation, Tanganyika Territory, 1927; Entomologist, Sleeping Sickness Service, Med. Dept, Nigeria, 1933. Doctorate of Science, 1933. In charge Anchau Rural Development Scheme, 1937-44; seconded as Chief Entomologist, W African Institute for Trypanosomiasis Research, 1948; Deputy Director, WAITR, 1953; Director, 1954-59; Dir, Tsetse Research Lab., Univ. of Bristol, Veterinary Field Station, Langford, 1962-71. *Publications:* Tsetse Flies in British West Africa, 1948; Africa's Bane, The Tsetse Fly, 1969; numerous scientific publications on tsetse and trypanosomiasis. *Recreation:* fishing. *Address:* Spring Head Farm, Upper Langford, near Bristol. *T:* Churchill 852321.

NASIR, Rt. Rev. Eric Samuel; *see* Delhi, Bishop of.

NASMITH; *see* Dunbar-Nasmith.

NATAL, Bishop of, since 1974; **Rt. Rev. Philip Welsford Richmond Russell;** *b* 21 Oct. 1919; *s* of Leslie Richmond Russell and Clarice Louisa Russell (*née* Welsford); *m* 1945, Violet Eirene, *d* of Ven. Dr O. J. Hogarth, sometime Archdeacon of the Cape; one *s* three *d*. *Educ:* Durban High Sch.; Rhodes Univ. College (Univ. of South Africa), BA 1948; LTh 1950. Served War of 1939-45; MBE 1943. Deacon, 1950; Priest, 1951; Curate, St Peter's, Maritzburg, 1950-54; Vicar: Greytown, 1954-57; Ladysmith, 1957-61; Kloof, 1961-66; Archdeacon of Pinetown, 1961-66; Bishop Suffragan of Capetown, 1966-70; Bishop of Port Elizabeth, 1970-74. *Recreations:* caravanning, fishing. *Address:* Bishop's House, 5 Chaceley Place, Morningside, Durban 4001, South Africa.

NATALI, Lorenzo; politician and lawyer, Italy; Vice-President, Commission of the European Communities, since 1977; *b* 2 Oct. 1922. *Educ:* Collegio d'Abruzzo dei Padri Gesuiti; Univ. of Florence. MP (Christian Democrat); Under-Secretary of State: for the Press and Information, 1955-57; Min. of Finance, 1957-59; Treasury, 1960-64; Minister: for Merchant Marine, 1966-68; of Public Works, 1968; of Tourism and Entertainments, 1968-69; of Agriculture, 1970-73. *Recreations:* sport, scholasticism. *Address:* 200 rue de la Loi, 1040 Brussels, Belgium; (home) Via Nibby 18, Rome, Italy.

NATHAN, family name of **Baron Nathan.**

NATHAN, 2nd Baron, *cr* 1940; **Roger Carol Michael Nathan;** *b* 5 Dec. 1922; *s* of 1st Baron Nathan, PC, TD, and Eleanor Joan Clara (*d* 1972), *d* of C. Stettauer; *S* father, 1963; *m* 1950, Philippa Gertrude, *d* of Major J. B. Solomon, MC; one *s* two *d*. *Educ:* Stowe Sch.; New Coll., Oxford (MA). Served War of 1939-45: Capt., 17/21 Lancers (despatches, wounded twice). Admitted Solicitor (Hons), 1950. Associate Mem., Bar Assoc. of City of New York 1975-; FSA; FRSA; FRGS. Dir, Kleeman Industrial Holdings Ltd; Chm. Pharmitalia (UK) Ltd. Pres., Jewish Welfare Board, 1967-71; Chm., Central British Fund for Jewish Relief and Rehabilitation, 1971-; Chm. Exec. Cttee, British Empire Cancer Campaign, 1970-75; a Vice-Pres., The Jewish Museum; Chm., Working Party on Energy and the Environment (reported 1974); Vice Chm., Cttee on Charity Law and Practice (reported 1976); Vice-Pres., Geographical Assoc.; Chm., RSA, 1975-. Chm., City Festival of Flowers, 1964; Master, Worshipful Company of Gardeners, 1963-64. *Heir: s* Hon. Rupert Harry Bernard Nathan, *b* 26 May 1957. *Address:* 20 Copthall Avenue, EC2. *T:* 01-628 9611. *TA:* Client, London; Collyers Farm, Lickfold, Petworth, West Sussex. *T:* Lodsworth 284. *TA:* Ronath, Lodsworth. *Clubs:* Athenæum, Cavalry and Guards.

NATHAN, Sir Maurice (Arnold), KBE 1963 (CBE 1957); Chairman and Managing Director, Patersons (Australia) Ltd and associated cos.; *b* Kew, Vic, 17 July 1914; *s* of late Harold B. Nathan, Melbourne; *m* 1942, Margaret Frances, *d* of David McKay; one *s*. *Educ:* Geelong C of E Gram. Sch. Served War of 1939-45, Capt. AIF, Pres., Victorian Industries Confederation,

Furnishers Soc. of Victoria and Aust. Retail Furnishers Assoc., 1951-53; Mem. Melbourne City Council, 1952-72; Lord Mayor of Melbourne, 1961-63; Founder and Chm., Victoria Promotion Cttee; Chm., Olympic Park Cttee of Management; Founder and Chairman, Australian World Exposition Project; Pres., Victorian Football League. *Recreations:* gardening, racing, squash, football, tennis, golf. *Address:* c/o Patersons Pty Ltd, 152 Bourke Street, Melbourne 3000, Australia. *T:* 66.6025; 20 St Georges Road, Toorak, Vic 3142. *T:* 24.2282. *Clubs:* Victoria Amateur Turf, Victoria Racing, Moonee Valley Racing, Melbourne Cricket, Lawn Tennis Assoc. of Vic, Kelvin, Green Room.

NATTA, Prof. Giulio; Director, Institute of Industrial Chemistry, Polytechnic of Milan, since 1938; *b* 26 Feb. 1903; *m* 1936, Rosita Beati; one *s* one *d*. *Educ:* Polytechnic Institute of Milan. Degree in Chemical Engineering, 1924; Professor in General Chemistry, 1927. Assistant Prof. in Analytical Chemistry, Polytechnic of Milan, 1925-32; Full Prof. and Director, Inst. of General Chemistry, Univ. of Pavia, 1933; Full Prof. of Physical Chemistry, Univ. of Rome, 1935-37; Full Prof. of Industrial Chemistry, Polytechnic of Turin, 1937-38. Doctor *hc* in Chemistry, Univ. of Turin, 1962; also holds honorary doctorates from foreign universities, etc; 16 gold medals from Italian and foreign Chemical Societies, among them Nobel Prize for Chemistry (jtly), 1963. *Publications:* about 450 articles mainly published in: Die Makromol. Chemie; Jl of Polymer Science; Chimica e Industria; Jl of Amer. Chem. Soc.; Tetrahedron; Rend. Accademia Nazionale Lincei. *Address:* Via S Sebastiano 11, 24100 Bergamo, Italy. *T:* 221100. *Club:* Rotary (Milan).

NATTRASS, Frederick John, MD Durham, FRCP; Emeritus Professor of Medicine, Universities of Durham and Newcastle upon Tyne; Hon. Consulting Physician, Royal Victoria Infirmary, Newcastle upon Tyne; Hon. Life President, formerly Chairman, Muscular Dystrophy Group of Great Britain; *b* 6 August 1891; *s* of Rev. J. Conder Nattrass, BA, BD; *m* 1st, 1915, Gladys (*d* 1951), *d* of Benjamin Vickers, Lincoln; two *d* (one *s* decd); 2nd, 1963, Helen Byrne Bryce (*d* 1971), Burford, Oxford. *Educ:* King Edward's Sch., Birmingham; Univ. of Durham, MB, BS (1st Class Honours) Durham, 1914; MD (gold medal), 1920; Capt., RAMC, 1915-20 (BEF, France; POW). Physician, Royal Victoria Infirmary, Newcastle, 1921-56; Prof. of Medicine, Univ. of Durham, 1941-56; Prof. of Medicine, Univ. of Lagos, Nigeria, 1962-63. Sometime Examiner in Medicine, University of Bristol, Trinity College, Dublin, Univs. of Manchester, Queen's Belfast, St Andrews, Nat. Univ. of Ireland. Censor Royal College of Physicians, 1950-52; Senior Censor, 1955-56; Lumleian Lecturer, RCP, 1948; Pres., Newcastle and Northern Counties Med. Soc., 1948-49. President: Assoc. of Physicians of GB and Ireland, 1953-54; Assoc. of British Neurologists, 1957-59; Section of Neurology, Royal Society of Medicine, 1954-55. Pres., 3rd Internat. Congress on Muscle Diseases, 1974. Hon. DCL Newcastle, 1974. *Publications:* The Commoner Nervous Diseases, 1931; section on nervous diseases in Chamberlain's Textbook of Medicine, 1951; papers and addresses chiefly on disorders of the nervous and muscular systems. *Recreations:* ornithology, music. *Address:* Little Cocklands, Burford, Oxford. *T:* Burford 2110.

NATWAR-SINGH, Kanwar; High Commissioner for India in Zambia and Botswana, since 1977; *b* 16 May 1931; *s* of Govind Singh and Prayag Kaur; *m* 1967, Princess Heminder Kumari, *e d* of Maharaja of Patiala; one *s* one *d*. *Educ:* St Stephen's Coll., Delhi Univ.; Corpus Christi Coll., Cambridge; Peking Univ. 1st cl. hons History Delhi. Joined Indian Foreign Service, 1953; 3rd Sec., Peking, 1956-58; Adviser, Indian Delegn to UN, NY, 1961-66; Rapporteur, UN Cttee on Decolonisation, 1962-66; Rapporteur, UN Trusteeship Council, 1965; Alt. Deleg. of India to UN Session for 1962; Rep. of India on Exec. Bd of UNICEF, NY, 1962-65; Dep. Sec. to Prime Minister of India, 1966-67; Dir, Prime Minister's Secretariat, New Delhi, 1967-70; Jt Sec. to Prime Minister, 1970-71; Ambassador to Poland, 1971-73; Dep. High Comr in London, 1973-77; attended Commonwealth Heads of Govt Meeting, Jamaica, 1975; Mem., Commonwealth Cyprus Cttee, 1977. Hon. Res. Fellow, UCL. *Publications:* E. M. Forster: A Tribute, 1964; The Legacy of Nehru, 1965; Tales from Modern India, 1966; Stories from India, 1971; book reviews for NY Times, New Statesman, Saturday Review. *Recreations:* tennis, reading, writing, playing with own children and silence. *Address:* High Commission of India, Lusaka, Zambia. *Clubs:* Garrick, Queen's, Royal Over-Seas League; Delhi Gymkhana (Delhi).

NAUNTON MORGAN, Sir Clifford; *see* Morgan, Sir C. N.

NAYLOR, Arthur Holden, MSc; FICE; FIMechE; Emeritus Professor; *b* 1897; *er s* of Rev. John and Eunice Naylor; *m* 1925,

Edith Riley; one *s* one *d*. RE, 1916-19 and 1940-43; Aeroplane Research under DSIR 1919; engaged on construction of Johore Causeway and Prai Power Station, Malaya, 1921-24; Sir Lawrence Guillemard Service Reservoir, Penang, 1925-29; Severn Barrage Investigation, 1930-31; Lochaber Water Power Scheme, 1931-34; Kenya and Uganda Hydro-Electric Investigations, 1934-35; Research Officer, Institution of Civil Engineers, 1935-38; Professor of Civil Engineering, Queen's University, Belfast, 1938-63; Professor of Civil Engineering, Ahmadu Bello University, Nigeria, 1963-66; Visiting Lecturer, 1966-67, Senior Research Fellow, School of Engineering, 1967-70, University College of Swansea. *Publication:* Siphon Spillways, 1935. *Address:* 2 Hael Lane, Southgate, near Swansea.

NAYLOR, Rev. Canon Charles Basil; Chancellor and Canon Residentiary of Liverpool Cathedral since 1956; *b* 29 Oct. 1911; *s* of Charles Henry Naylor and Eva Garforth. *Educ:* Rugby School; Keble College, Oxford. BA 2nd class Lit. Hum., 1934; MA 1939. Deacon, 1939, priest, 1940, Liverpool; Asst Master, Llandovery Coll., 1935-39; Asst Master, Chaplain and Housemaster, Liverpool College, 1939-43; Chaplain RNVR, 1943-46, East Indies Station and Fleet. Curate, St Peter le Bailey Oxford, 1946-56; Chaplain of St Peter's Coll., 1946-56, Dean, 1946-52, Fellow, 1950-56; Tutor in Theology, 1952-56. Examining Chaplain: to Bishop of Blackburn, 1951-; and to Bishop of Liverpool, 1954-; Senior Proctor of Univ. of Oxford, 1952-53. Exchanged duties with Dean of Christchurch, New Zealand, Dec. 1960-April 1961. Dir of Ordination Candidates and Dir of Post-Ordination Training, Liverpool dio., 1956-72; Dir of In-service Trng, Liverpool dio., 1973-. Librarian, Radcliffe Library, Liverpool Cathedral, 1958-. Mem., Liturgical Commn, 1962-66. Trustee, St Peter's Coll., Oxford, 1971-. *Publication:* Why Prayer Book Revision at all, 1964; contrib. Theological Collections: The Eucharist Then and Now, 1968; Ground for Hope, 1968; contrib. Arias of J. S. Bach, 1977. *Recreations:* music, walking. *Address:* Liverpool Cathedral, St James' Mount, Liverpool L1 7AZ. *T:* 051-645 6271. *Clubs:* National Liberal; Athenæum (Liverpool).

NAYLOR, Peter Brian; Representative of the British Council, Brazil, since 1975; *b* 10 July 1933; *s* of Eric Sydney Naylor and Phyllis Marian Jolly; *m* 1958, Barbara Pearson; three *s* one *d*. *Educ:* Grange High Sch., Bradford; Selwyn Coll., Cambridge (Open Exhibnr; BA 1957). Wool Top Salesman, Hirsch, Son & Rhodes, Bradford, 1957; British Council: Asst Rep., Bangkok, 1959; Courses Dept and E Europe Dept, London, 1962; Asst Rep., Warsaw, 1967; Reg. Rep., Dacca, E Pakistan, 1969; Actg Rep., Athens, 1971; Rep., Argentina, 1972. *Recreations:* painting, music, books, games. *Address:* 48 Gilmerton Court, Long Road, Cambridge. *T:* Trumpington 3138.

NAYLOR, William Maurice, CBE 1973; FHA; JP; Regional Administrator, Trent Regional Health Authority, since 1974; *b* 1920; *s* of late Thomas Naylor; *m* 1948, Maureen Ann, *d* of John Walsh; one *s* two *d*. *Educ:* St Joseph's Coll., Market Drayton; Manchester Univ. (BA). FHA 1956. Asst Sec., Manchester Regional Hosp. Bd, 1955-57; Dep. Sec., Sheffield Regional Hosp. Bd, 1957-63, Sec., 1963-73. *Address:* 9 Derriman Close, Sheffield S11 9LB.

NAYLOR-LEYLAND, Sir Vivyan (Edward), 3rd Bt, *cr* 1895; *b* 5 March 1924; *e s* of Sir Edward Naylor-Leyland, 2nd Bt, and Marguerite Helene (*d* 1945), 2nd *d* of late Baron de Belabre; *S* father 1952; *m* 1st, 1952, Elizabeth Anne (marr. diss. 1960), *yr d* of 2nd Viscount FitzAlan of Derwent, OBE; one *s*; 2nd, 1967, Starr Anker-Simmons (marr. diss. 1975); one *d*. *Educ:* Eton; Christ Church, Oxford; Royal Agricultural Coll., Cirencester. Grenadier Guards, 1942-47. *Heir: s* Philip Vyvyan Naylor-Leyland, *b* 9 August 1953. *Address:* 6 Harbour Mews, Nassau, Bahamas. *T:* Nassau 77523. *Club:* White's (overseas mem.).

NEAGLE, Dame Anna, (Dame Marjorie Wilcox), DBE 1969 (CBE 1952); Hon. Vice-President, FANY Corps, 1972 (Hon. Ensign 1950); actress, producer; Member: Executive Council, King George VI Memorial Foundation; Council Edith Cavell Homes of Rest for Nurses; Council, King George's Pension Fund for Actors and Actresses; *b* Forest Gate, Essex; *d* of late Captain Herbert William Robertson, RNR, and Florence Neagle Robertson; *m* 1943, Herbert Wilcox, CBE (*d* 1977). *Educ:* High School, St Albans, Herts; Wordsworth's Physical Training College. Theatre Royal, Drury Lane, Charlot and Cochran revues, London and New York, 1926-30; Stand up and Sing, with Jack Buchanan, 1931; Open Air Theatre-Rosalind and Olivia, 1934; Peter Pan, 1937; Jane Austen's Emma, 1944-45; *later plays include:* The Glorious Days, Palace Theatre, 1952-53; The More the Merrier, Strand, 1960; Person Unknown, 1964; Charlie Girl, Adelphi, 1965-71, Aust. and NZ

presentation 1971-72; No, No, Nanette, Drury Lane, 1973; The Dame of Sark, Duke of York's and O'Keefe Centre, Toronto, 1975; The First Mrs Fraser; Maggie, Shaftesbury, 1977. Has appeared in plays on television. *Films:* Good Night, Vienna, 1931; Bitter Sweet, 1933; Nell Gwyn, 1934; Peg of Old Drury, 1935; Victoria The Great, 1937; Sixty Glorious Years, 1938; Hollywood: Edith Cavell, 1939; Irene, No, No, Nanette, Sunny, 1939-40; England: They Flew Alone, 1941; Yellow Canary, 1943; I Live in Grosvenor Square, 1944; Piccadilly Incident, 1946; The Courtneys of Curzon Street, 1947; Spring in Park Lane, Elizabeth of Ladymead, 1948; Maytime in Mayfair, 1949; Odette, 1950; The Lady With The Lamp, 1951; Derby Day, 1951; Lilacs in the Spring, 1954; King's Rhapsody, 1955; My Teenage Daughter, 1956; No Time for Tears, 1957; The Man Who Wouldn't Talk, 1957; The Lady is a Square, 1958. *Produced:* These Dangerous Years, 1957; Wonderful Things, 1958; Heart of a Man, 1959. Has received numerous awards both international and national. *Publication:* There's Always Tomorrow (autobiog.), 1974. *Recreations:* walking, travel, reading. *Address:* 117b Hamilton Terrace, NW8. *Club:* FANY Regimental.

NEAL, Prof. Bernard George, MA, PhD, ScD; Professor of Engineering Structures, Imperial College of Science and Technology, since 1972; Head of Civil Engineering Department, since 1976; *b* 29 March 1922; *s* of late Horace Bernard Neal, Wembley, and Hilda Annie Webb; *m* 1948, Elizabeth Ann, *d* of late William George Toller, Woodbridge, and Bertha Catharine Toller; one *s* one *d*. *Educ:* Merchant Taylors'; Trinity College, Cambridge (Schol.). MA Cantab, 1947; PhD Cantab 1948; ScD Cantab 1965; FInstCE 1960; FIMechE 1961; FIStructE 1966. Temp. Experimental Officer, Admiralty, 1942-45; Research Student, Univ. of Cambridge, 1945-48; Research Associate, Brown University, USA, 1948-49; Demonstrator, 1949-51, Lecturer, 1951-54, Univ. of Cambridge; Research Fellow, 1947-50, Staff Fellow, 1950-54, Trinity Hall, Cambridge; Prof. of Civil Engineering, University Coll. of Swansea, 1954-61; Prof. of Applied Science (with special reference to Engineering), Imperial College, 1961-72, Pro-Rector, 1972-74; Dean of City and Guilds Coll., 1964-67; Visiting Prof., Brown Univ., USA, 1959-60. Telford Premium, 1951, Manby Premium, 1952, Instn Civil Engineers. *Publications:* The Plastic Methods of Structural Analysis, 1956; Structural Theorems and their Applications, 1964; technical papers on theory of structures, strength of materials; contrib. to Proc. Roy. Soc., Proc. Instn of Civil Engineers, The Structural Engineer, Jl of Mechanical Engineering Science, etc. *Recreations:* lawn tennis, croquet. *Address:* Imperial College of Science and Technology, South Kensington, SW7. *T:* 01-589 5111.

NEAL, Frederick Albert, FIL; Counsellor (Economic and Commercial), Ottawa, since 1975; *b* 22 Dec. 1932; *s* of Frederick William George Neal and Frances Elizabeth (*née* Duke); *m* 1958, Gloria Maria Moirano. *Educ:* Royal Grammar Sch., High Wycombe; Birkbeck Coll., London (BA). Min. of Supply, 1953; Asst Defence Supply Attaché, Bonn, 1958-64; Principal, Min. of Technology (subseq. DTI), 1967; Asst Sec., DTI, 1974. *Recreations:* golf, bridge, music. *Address:* c/o Foreign and Commonwealth Office, King Charles Street, SW1. *Clubs:* Naval and Military, Royal Over-Seas League; Royal Ottawa Golf.

NEAL, Sir Leonard (Francis), Kt 1974; CBE 1971; FCIT; Industrial Relations Consultant to Marks & Spencer, Ranks Hovis McDougall, and a number of other industrial and commercial companies; *b* 27 Aug. 1913; *s* of Arthur Henry Neal and Mary Neal; *m* 1939, Mary Lilian Puttock; one *s* one *d*. *Educ:* London School of Economics; Trinity College, Cambridge (MA). Labour Manager, Esso, 1956; Employee Relations Manager, Fawley Refinery, 1961; Labour Relations Adviser, Esso Europe Inc. Mem., British Railways Board, 1967-71; Chm., Commn on Industrial Relations, 1971-74. Prof. (part-time) of Industrial Relations, UMIST, 1970-76; Vis. Fellow, Univ. of Lancaster Sch. of Business and Organisational Studies, 1970-76. Chm., MAT Transport International Gp Ltd, 1974-; Director: Allied Breweries Pension Trust, 1975-; (non-exec.) Pilkington Bros., 1976-. Pres., Assoc. of Supervisory and Executive Engineers, 1974-. Mem. Council, Open Univ. FCIT (MInstT 1969); CIPM 1973. *Publications:* (with A. Robertson) The Managers Guide to Industrial Relations. *Recreations:* reading, gardening, motoring. *Address:* Brightling, Sussex. *Club:* United Oxford & Cambridge University.

NEAL, Michael David; Headmaster, Cranborne Chase School, since 1969; *b* 27 Jan. 1927; *s* of David Neal, FCA; *m* 1952, Barbara Lisette, *d* of late Harold Carter, MA; two *s* two *d*. *Educ:* Winchester; University Coll., Oxford (BA). Rifle Bde, 1945-48 (Captain); Asst Master, RNC Dartmouth, 1952-54; Eton Coll., 1954-69 (Housemaster, 1963-69). Mem., Eton UDC, 1960-63.

Address: Wardour Castle, Tisbury, Salisbury, Wilts. *T:* Tisbury 464.

NEALE, Sir Alan (Derrett), KCB 1972 (CB 1968); MBE 1945; Permanent Secretary, Ministry of Agriculture, Fisheries and Food, since 1973; *b* 24 Oct. 1918; *o s* of late W. A. Neale and Florence Emily (*née* Derrett); *m* 1956, Joan, *o d* of Harry and Hilda Frost, Wisbech; one *s. Educ:* Highgate School; St John's College, Oxford. War Service, Intelligence Corps, 1940-45. Board of Trade, 1946-68; Second Sec., 1967; Dep. Sec., Treasury, 1968-71, Second Permanent Sec., 1971-72. Commonwealth Fund Fellowship, USA, 1952-53; Fellow of Center for Internat. Affairs, Harvard Univ., 1960-61. *Publications:* The Anti-Trust Laws of the USA, 1960; The Flow of Resources from Rich to Poor, 1961. *Recreations:* music, bridge. *Address:* 37 Stormont Road, N6. *T:* 01-340 5236. *Club:* Reform.

NEALE, Rt. Rev. John Robert Geoffrey; *see* Ramsbury, Bishop Suffragan of.

NEALE, Kenneth James, OBE 1959; FSA; Assistant Under Secretary of State, Home Office, since 1976; *b* 9 June 1922; *s* of late James Edward and Elsie Neale; *m* 1943, Dorothy Willett; three *s* one *d. Educ:* Hackney Downs (Grocers') Sch., London. Entered Civil Service as Clerical Officer, Tithe Redemption Commn, 1939. Lieut, RNVR, 1941-46. Exec. Officer, Min. of Nat. Insce, 1947-51; Asst Princ., 1951-55, Principal, 1955-62, Colonial Office; Sec. for Interior and Local Govt, Cyprus, 1957; Dep. Admin Sec., Cyprus, 1958-59; Central African Office, 1962-64; Asst Sec., Commonwealth Office, Diplomatic Service, 1964-67; Asst Sec., Home Office, 1967-70; Dir, Industries and Supply, Home Office, 1970-75. Member: Prisons Bd, 1967-69, 1976-; European Cttee on Crime Problems, 1976-. *Publications:* Discovering Essex in London, 1970; Victorian Horsham, 1975; Work in Penal Institutions, 1976; Essex in History, 1977; various articles and papers on local history. *Recreations:* reading, local history, natural history. *Address:* The Forge Cottage, West Chiltington, West Sussex. *T:* West Chiltington 3410.

NEALON, Mrs Catherina Theresa, (Rina); JP; Chairman, Lothian Health Board, since 1973; *d* of John and Margaret O'Reilly, Glasgow; *m* 1940, James Patrick Nealon; one *s. Educ:* Convent of Mercy, Garnethill, Glasgow. Mem., Edinburgh Town Council for Pilton Ward, 1949-74; served as Magistrate, 1954-57; Judge of Police, 1957-62; Chm., Health Cttee, 1972-73. Member: Royal Infirmary and Associated Hosp's Bd of Management, 1952-56; NHS Exec. Council for City of Edinburgh, 1953-74 (Vice-Chm., May 1966-74); Exec. Cttee of Scottish Assoc. of Exec. Councils, 1967-74 (Vice-Pres., 1971, Pres., 1972); SE Regional Hosp. Bd, Scotland, 1966-74 (Chm., 1969-74); Med. Educn Cttee, 1969-74 (Chm., 1972-74); Scottish Health Service Planning Council, 1974-; Common Services Agency, Management Cttee, and Convenor, Estabt and Accommodation Sub-Cttee, Scottish Health Service, 1974-77; Univ. Liaison Cttee, 1974- (Chm., 1974-76; Vice-Chm., 1976-); Edinburgh and SE District Cttee, Scottish Gas Consultative Council, 1967-74 (Chm., 1970-74; Mem. Council, 1969-74); Clean Air Council for Scotland, 1966-; Nat. Soc. for Clean Air, Scottish Div., 1963-74 (Vice-Pres., 1970-72, Pres., 1972-74); Chm., Scottish Hosp. Supplies Steering Cttee, 1972-74. Former Member: Edin. and Lothian Probation Cttee; Animal Disease Res. Assoc.; Nat. Assoc. for Maternal and Child Welfare; Nat. Council on recruitment of Nurses and Midwives; Scottish Assoc. for Mental Health; Assoc. of Sea and Airport Authorities; Edin. and Lothians Tourist Assoc.; Bd of Governors, Moray House Coll. of Educn. Mem. Extra-Mural Cttee, Edin. Univ., 1960-65; Mem. Bd of Governors: Napier Coll. of Science and Technology, 1964-73 (Vice-Chm., 1971-73); Telford Coll. for Further Education, 1969-72. JP Edinburgh, 1957; Mem. Justices Cttee, 1975; Justice on District Court, 1975; Mem. Extra-Parliamentary Panel, 1976. Member, Church of Scotland. Hon. Dr Edinburgh. *Recreations:* dancing, dressmaking. *Address:* 34 Learmonth Crescent, Edinburgh EH4 1DE.

NEAME, Captain Douglas Mortimer Lewes, DSO 1940, Bar 1942; RN retired; *b* Oct. 1901; *s* of late Douglas John Neame; *m* 1937, Elizabeth Ogilvy Carnegy; one *s* two *d. Educ:* RN Colleges, Osborne and Dartmouth. Served European War, 1917-19; Fleet Air Arm, 1927-31; Commander, 1936; Capt. 1940. Commanded HM Ships Carlisle and Vengeance in War of 1939-45; Commodore 2nd Class, 1947-50; retd 1950. Member of Olympic Team, Amsterdam, 1928, British Empire Games, Canada, 1930. Vice-Patron AAA; Vice-Pres. LAC. *Recreation:* gardening. *Address:* de Vaux Lodge, Salisbury, Wilts. *Clubs:* Naval; Milocarian, London Athletic.

NEAME, Mrs Humphrey; *see* Monroe, E.

NEAME, Lt-Gen. Sir Philip, VC 1914; KBE 1946; CB 1939; DSO 1916; psc; idc; DL; Colonel Commandant, RE, 1945-55; Hon. Colonel 131 Airborne Regiment RE (T), 1948-58; Hon. Colonel Kent ACF Regiment RE, 1952-58; President of the Institution of Royal Engineers, 1954-57; *b* 12 December 1888; *y s* of late F. Neame, JP, of Luton, Selling, Faversham; *m* 1934, H. Alberta Drew; three *s* one *d. Educ:* Cheltenham Coll.; RMA Woolwich. Entered Army, 1908; Capt. 1914; Bt Major 1917; Bt Lt-Col 1922; Major, 1925; Col 1926; Maj.-Gen. 1937; Temp. Lt-Gen., 1940; Lt-Gen., 1947; served European War, 1914-18, 15th Field Coy, RE, Adjt Divl Engineers; Brig.-Maj. Inf. Bde, Gen. Staff of Division, Corps and Army (despatches five times, VC, DSO, Chevalier of the Legion of Honour, French Croix de Guerre, Belgian Croix de Guerre); on the Directing Staff, Staff College, Camberley, 1919-23; served in India with KGO Bengal Sappers and Miners, 1925-29; Imperial Defence College, 1930; General Staff Officer, 1st Grade, Waziristan District, India, 1932-33; Brigadier, General Staff, Eastern Command, India, 1934-38; went to Lhasa, Tibet, with political-military mission, 1936; Commandant Royal Military Academy, Woolwich, 1938-39; Deputy Chief of the General Staff, BEF France, 1939-40; Commander 4th Indian Division, Western Desert, 1940; GOC (Lt-Gen.) Palestine, Transjordan, Cyprus, 1940; GOC-in-C and Military Governor, Cyrenaica, 1941 (despatches twice); Commanded British, Australian, and Indian Forces against Rommel's first attack in Cyrenaica, Mar.-Apr. 1941; prisoner of war, 1941, escaped from Italy 1943; retired pay, 1947. Lieutenant-Governor and Commander-in-Chief of Guernsey and its dependencies, Channel Islands, 1945-53. Mem., Governing Body of Gordon Boys School; Vice-Pres., Nat. Rifle Assoc.; Pres. North London Rifle Club. DL Kent, 1955. FRGS. KStJ; Knight of Order of White Lion, Czechoslovakia. *Publications:* German Strategy in the Great War, 1923; Autobiography, Playing with Strife, 1946; also various articles on big-game shooting, Tibet, North West Frontier, etc. *Recreations:* gardening and fruit growing, polo, hunting, point to point racing, big and small game shooting, rifle and revolver shooting (in British Olympic Sporting Rifle Team, Gold and Bronze Medals, France, 1924; in Army Revolver VIII and Army Rifle Twenty). *Address:* The Kintle, Selling Court, Faversham, Kent.

NEAME, Ronald; film producer and director; *b* 23 Apr. 1911; *s* of Elwin Neame and Ivy Close; *m* 1933, Beryl Yolanda Heanly; one *s. Educ:* University College School; Hurstpierpoint College. Entered film industry, 1928; became Chief Cameraman, 1934. In charge of production on: In Which We Serve, This Happy Breed, Blithe Spirit, Brief Encounter, 1942-45; produced: Great Expectations, Oliver Twist, The Magic Box; directed: Take My Life, The Card, 1945-51; The Million Pound Note, 1953; The Man Who Never Was, 1954; Windom's Way, 1957; The Horse's Mouth, 1958; Tunes of Glory, 1960; I Could Go On Singing, 1962; The Chalk Garden, 1963; Mr Moses, 1964; Gambit, 1966; The Prime of Miss Jean Brodie, 1968; Scrooge, 1970; The Poseidon Adventure, 1972; Odessa File, 1973. *Address:* 194 Old Brompton Road, SW5 0AS. *Club:* Savile.

NEARY, Martin Gerard James; Organist and Master of Music, Winchester Cathedral, since 1972; Organ Recitalist and Conductor; Founder and Conductor, Martin Neary Singers, since 1972; Conductor, Waynflete Singers, since 1972; *b* 28 March 1940; *s* of Leonard Walter Neary and Jeanne Marguerite (*née* Thébault); *m* 1967, Penelope Jane, *d* of Sir Brian Warren, *qv*, and Dame A. J. M. T. Barnes, *qv*; one *s* two *d. Educ:* HM Chapels Royal, St James's Palace; City of London Sch.; Gonville and Caius Coll., Cambridge (Organ Schol., MA). FRCO. St Margaret's, Westminster: Asst Organist, 1963-65; Organist and Master of Music, 1965-71; Prof. of Organ, Trinity Coll., London, 1963-72. Organ Advr to dio. of Winchester, 1975-. Conductor, Twickenham Musical Soc., 1966-72; Founder and Conductor, St Margaret's Westminster Singers, 1967-71; Dir, Southern Cathedrals Festival, 1972, 1975, 1978. Many organ recitals and broadcasts in UK, incl. Royal Festival Hall and music festivals; toured US and Canada, 1963, 1968, 1971, 1973, 1975, 1977; many European tours and recordings. Hon. FTCL, 1969. Hon. Citizen of Texas, 1971. Prizewinner, St Alban's Internat. Organ Festival, 1963; Conducting Scholarship, Berkshire Music Center, USA, 1963; Diploma, J. S. Bach Competn, Leipzig, 1968. *Publications:* edns of early organ music; contribs to organ jls. *Recreation:* cricket. *Address:* 10 The Close, Winchester, Hants. *T:* Winchester 4392.

NEAVE, Airey Middleton Sheffield, DSO 1945; OBE 1947; MC 1942; TD (with 1st clasp) 1945; MP (C) Abingdon Division of Berkshire since July 1953; Director, Clarke Chapman Services Limited, since 1971; Barrister-at-Law; *b* 23 January 1916; *e s* of late Dr Sheffield Neave, CMG, OBE; *m* 1942, Diana Josceline Barbara, *d* of Thomas A. W. Giffard, MBE, JP, of Chillington Hall, Wolverhampton; two *s* one *d*. *Educ:* Eton; Merton Coll., Oxford. BA (Hons) Jurisprudence, 1938, MA 1955. Called to the Bar, Middle Temple, 1943. Served War of 1939-45 (despatches, MC, DSO); with RA (TA) in France, 1940; wounded and prisoner, 1940; escaped, 1942; MI9, 1942-44; GSO(2) (I), 21 Army Group, 1944-45. Lieut-Col AAG, British War Crimes Executive, 1945-46; served indictments on Goering and major Nazi War Criminals, 1945; Comr for Criminal Organizations. Internat. Mil. Tribunal, Nuremburg, 1946; OC Intell. Sch. no 9 (TA), 1949-51. Contested Thurrock (C), 1950, Ealing North (C) 1951; PPS to Minister of Transport and Civil Aviation, 1954; PPS to Secretary of State for Colonies, 1954-56; Joint Parly Sec., Min. of Transport and Civil Aviation, 1957-59; Parly Under-Sec. of State for Air, 1959. Dep. Chm., Parly and Scientific Cttee, 1971-74; Mem., Select Cttee of House of Commons on Science and Technology, 1965-75 (Chm., 1970-74); Head of Leader of Opposition's private office, 1975-; opposition spokesman on N Ireland, 1975-. Hon. Sec., Assoc. of British Chambers of Commerce, 1960-62; a Governor, Imperial College of Science and Technology, 1963-71. UK delegate to UN High Comr for Refugees, 1970-75; Chm., Standing Conf. of British orgns for aid to refugees, 1972-74. French Croix de Guerre, American Bronze Star and Officer Order Orange Nassau, Holland, 1945; Knight, Order Polonia Restituta (Poland), 1977 (Comdr, 1971). *Publications:* They Have Their Exits, 1953; Little Cyclone, 1954; Saturday at MI9, 1969; The Flames of Calais, 1972. *Address:* c/o Clarke Chapman Ltd, Tavistock House East, Woburn Walk, Tavistock Square, WC1. *T:* 01-387 9393. *Club:* Carlton.

NEAVE, Sir Arundell Thomas Clifton, 6th Bt, *cr* 1795; JP; late Major Welsh Guards; *b* 31 May 1916; *e s* of Col Sir Thomas Lewis Hughes Neave, 5th Bt, and Dorina (*d* 1955) (author of 26 years on the Bosphorus, Remembering Kut, 1937, Romance of the Bosphorus, 1950), *d* of late George H. Clifton; *S* father, 1940; *m* 1946, Richenda Alice Ione, *o c* of Sir Robert J. Paul, 5th Bt; two *s* two *d*. *Educ:* Eton. Served in 1939-45 war, Welsh Guards (Major); Dunkirk, 1940, retired 1947. JP for Anglesey, 1950. *Heir: s* Paul Arundell Neave, *b* 13 December 1948. *Clubs:* Carlton, Cavalry and Guards; Pratt's; Kildare Street and University (Dublin).
See also Sir Richard Williams-Bulkeley.

NEDEN, Sir Wilfred (John), Kt 1955; CB 1949; CBE 1946; retired as Chief Industrial Commissioner, Ministry of Labour and National Service, (1954-58); Deputy Chairman, BOAC, 1960-63; *b* 24 August 1893; *s* of John Thomas and Margaret Neden; *m* 1st, 1925, Jean Lundie (*d* 1965); one *s* one *d*; 2nd, 1967, Mrs L. Violet Ryan, Hove, Sussex. *Educ:* St Olave's Gram. Sch. Army, 1914-22, Lieut RFA (Regular Commission); served European War, 1914-18, severely wounded, 1918 (despatches). Entered Ministry of Labour, 1922; Under Secretary, 1946; Director of Organisation and Establishments, 1948-54.

NEEDHAM, family name of **Earl of Kilmorey.**

NEEDHAM, Dorothy Mary Moyle, FRS 1948; ScD Cantab; Research Worker, Biochemical Laboratory, Cambridge, 1920-63; *b* London, 22 Sept. 1896; *d* of John Moyle and Ellen Davies; *m* 1924, Joseph Needham, *qv*; no *c*. *Educ:* Claremont Coll., Stockport; Girton Coll., Cambridge. Research for DSIR, 1920-24; Gamble Prize, 1924; Beit Meml Research Fellow, 1925-28. Specialised in biochemistry of muscle, carbohydrate metabolism and phosphorylations; carried out research and teaching at Cambridge and in laboratories in USA, France, Germany, Belgium, etc., 1928-40; Research Worker for Ministry of Supply (Chemical Defence), 1940-43; Chemical Adviser and Acting Director, Sino-British Science Cooperation Office, Chungking, China, 1944-45; Research Worker for MRC 1946-52; Research grant from Broodbank Fund, Univ. of Cambridge, 1952-55; Research Worker for ARC, 1955-62; Foulerton Gift Donation, Royal Society, 1961-62; Leverhulme Award, 1963. *Publications:* Biochemistry of Muscle, 1932; Science Outpost (ed jtly), 1948; Machina Carnis: the biochemistry of muscle contraction in its historical development, 1971; numerous original papers in biochemical journals and Proc. Royal Soc. *Address:* 42 Grange Road, Cambridge CB3 9DG.

NEEDHAM, Prof. John, MA (Sheffield); FRIBA, DipArch (Leeds); Professor of Architecture, The University, Sheffield, 1957-72, now Professor Emeritus; *b* 2 April 1909; British; *s* of P. Needham; *m* 1934, Bessie Grange; three *d*. *Educ:* Belle Vue Grammar School, Bradford; Leeds School of Architecture. Diploma in Architecture, Leeds, 1931; ARIBA 1931, FRIBA 1948; RIBA; Alfred Bossom Silver Medal, 1937; Alfred Bossom Gold Medal, 1938; Soane Medal, 1938; Athens Bursar, 1949.

Head, Dundee School of Architecture, 1938-57. 1st Premium in Open Architectural Competition for new County Buildings, Cupar, Fife, 1947. Mem. Amenity Cttee set up by Sec. of State for Scotland under Hydro Electric (Scotland) Development Acts. Hon. Editor, Quarterly Jl of Royal Incorporation of Architects in Scotland, 1946-50. *Address:* Contrast, Elterwater, Ambleside, Cumbria LA22 9HW.

NEEDHAM, Joseph, MA, PhD, ScD (Cantab); FRS 1941; FBA 1971; Director, East Asian History of Science Library, Cambridge, since 1976; Master of Gonville and Caius College, 1966-76; Hon. Counsellor, UNESCO; *b* 1900; *s* of late Joseph Needham, MD, of Harley Street and Clapham Park, and Alicia A. Needham; *m* 1924, Dorothy Mary (*see* D. M. M. Needham), *d* of John Moyle, Babbacombe, Devon. *Educ:* Oundle School. Fellow Gonville and Caius Coll., 1924-66 (Librarian, 1959-60, Pres., 1959-66); Univ. Demonstrator in Biochem., 1928-33; Sir William Dunn Reader in Biochemistry, 1933-66, now Emeritus; Vis. Prof. of Biochem. at Stanford Univ., California, USA, 1929; Hitchcock Prof., Univ. of California, 1950; Visiting Professor: Univ. of Lyon, 1951; Univ. of Kyoto, 1971; Collège de France, Paris, 1973; Univ. of British Columbia, Vancouver, 1975. Lectures: Terry and Carmalt, Yale Univ.; Goldwin-Smith, Cornell Univ.; Mead-Swing, Oberlin College, Ohio, USA, 1935; Oliver Sharpey, RCP, 1935-36; Herbert Spencer, Oxford, 1936-37; for Polskie Towarzystwo Biologicznej in the Universities of Warsaw, Lwów, Kraków and Wilno, 1937; Comte Memorial, London, 1940; Conway Memorial, London, 1947; Boyle, Oxford, 1948; Noguchi, Johns Hopkins Univ., 1950; Hobhouse, London Univ., 1950; Dickinson, Newcomen Soc., 1956; Colombo, Singapore, Peking and Jaipur Universities, 1958; Wilkins, Royal Society, 1958; Wilde, Manchester, 1959; Earl Grey, Newcastle upon Tyne, 1960-61; Henry Myers, Royal Anthropological Institute, 1964; Harveian, London, 1970; Rapkine, Paris, 1971; Bernal, London, 1971; Ballard Matthews, Bangor, 1971; Fremantle, Oxford, 1971; Irvine, St Andrews, 1973; Dressler, Leeds, 1973; Carr-Saunders, London, Gerald Walters, Bath, First John Caius, Padua, 1974; Bowra, Oxford, 1975; Danz, Seattle, 1977. Head of the British Scientific Mission in China and Counsellor, British Embassy, Chungking, and Adviser to the Chinese National Resources Commission, Chinese Army Medical Administration and Chinese Air Force Research Bureau, 1942-46; Director of the Dept of Natural Sciences, UNESCO, 1946-48. Chm. Ceylon Government University Policy Commission, 1958. Pres., Internat. Union of Hist. of Science, 1972-75. Foreign Member: Amer. Acad. Arts and Sciences; National Academy of China (Academia Sinica); Mem. Internat. Academies of Hist. of Science and of Med.; Hon. Member Yale Chapter of Sigma Xi. Hon. Fellow, UMIST. Hon. DSc Brussels and Norwich; Hon. LLD Toronto and Salford; Hon. LittD Hongkong, Newcastle upon Tyne, Hull and Chicago; DUniv Surrey. Sir William Jones Medallist, Asiatic Society of Bengal, 1963; George Sarton Medallist, Soc. for History of Science, 1968; Leonardo da Vinci Medallist, Soc. for History of Technology, 1968. Order of the Brilliant Star (China). *Publications:* Science, Religion and Reality (ed), 1925; Man a Machine, 1927; The Sceptical Biologist, 1929; Chemical Embryology (3 vols), 1931; The Great Amphibium, 1932; A History of Embryology, 1934; Order and Life, 1935; Christianity and the Social Revolution (ed), 1935; Adventures before Birth (tr.), 1936; Perspectives in Biochemistry (Hopkins Presentation Volume; ed), 1937; Background to Modern Science (ed), 1938; Biochemistry and Morphogenesis, 1942; The Teacher of Nations, addresses and essays in commemoration of John Amos Comenius (ed), 1942; Time, the Refreshing River, 1943; History is on Our Side, 1945; Chinese Science, 1946; Science Outpost, 1948; Hopkins and Biochemistry (ed), 1949; Science and Civilisation in China (7 vols), 1954-: vol. I, Introductory Orientations, 1954; vol. II, History of Scientific Thought, 1956; vol III, Mathematics and the Sciences of the Heavens and the Earth, 1959; vol. IV, Physics and Physical Technology, part 1, Physics, 1962, part 2, Mechanical Engineering, 1965, part 3, Civil Engineering and Nautics, 1971; vol. V, Chemistry and Chemical Technology, part 2, Spagyrical Discovery and Invention, 1974; The Development of Iron and Steel Technology in China, 1958; Heavenly Clockwork, 1960; Within the Four Seas, 1970; The Grand Titration, 1970; Clerks and Craftsmen in China and the West, 1970; (ed) The Chemistry of Life, 1970; Moulds of Understanding, 1976. Chart to illustrate the History of Physiology and Biochemistry, 1926; original papers in scientific, philosophical and sinological journals. *Address:* 42 Grange Road, Cambridge; East Asian History of Science Library, Shaftesbury Road, Cambridge. *Club:* United Oxford & Cambridge University.

NEEDHAM, N. J. T. M.; *see* Needham, Joseph.

NEEDHAM, Richard Francis; (6th Earl of Kilmorey, but does not use the title); *b* 29 Jan. 1942; *e s* of 5th Earl of Kilmorey (*d* 1977), and of Helen Bridget, *y d* of Sir Lionel Faudel-Phillips, 3rd and last Bt; *m* 1965, Sigrid Juliana Thiessen-Gairdner, *o d* of late Ernst Thiessen and of Mrs John Gairdner, Hamburg; two *s* one *d*. *Educ:* Eton College. Chairman, R. G. M. Print Holdings Ltd. Member, Slade Art Union. CC Somerset, 1967-74. Contested (C): Pontefract and Castleford, Feb. 1974; Gravesend, Oct. 1974; Personal Asst to Rt Hon. James Prior, MP, Shadow Minister of Employment, 1974-. Prospective Parly Candidate (C) Chippenham, 1976-. *Heir:* s Viscount Newry and Morne, *qv. Address:* The Croft House, Somerford Keynes, near Cirencester, Glos. *T:* Ashton Keynes 333; Flat 41, Belgravia Court, Ebury Street, SW1. *T:* 01-730 6494. *Club:* Buck's.

NEEL, Dr Louis Boyd, OC 1973; CBE 1953; MA (Cantab); Hon. RAM; MRCS, LRCP; international conductor; musical director; Founder and Conductor, Boyd Neel Orchestra; Dean Royal Conservatory of Music of Toronto, Canada, 1953-71; radio speaker on musical subjects; *b* 19 July 1905; *s* of Louis Anthoine Neel and Ruby le Couteur; unmarried. *Educ:* RNC, Osborne and Dartmouth; Caius Coll., Cambridge. Originally destined for Navy, but took up a medical career on leaving Dartmouth; qualified as a doctor, 1930; House Surgeon and Physician, St George's Hospital, London; resident doctor, King Edward VII's Hosp. for Officers, 1931. Founded Boyd Neel Orchestra, 1932, and owing to success of this, forsook medicine for music; conducted the orchestra all over Europe, incl. the Salzburg Festival, 1937, and made many recordings, incl. several important firsts; has also conducted other famous English orchestras on many occasions; conducted first performance at Glyndebourne, 1934, soon after the theatre was built; conducted Robert Mayer Children's Concerts, 1938-39 and 1947-53. On outbreak of war in 1939 returned to medical work, and was engaged in the fitting of artificial limbs. Later in the war, undertook a lecture tour of the Mediterranean area at the request of the Admiralty. Conductor Sadler's Wells Opera Co., 1944-45, and two London seasons D'Oyly Carte Opera Co., 1948-49. In 1947 took his orchestra to Paris, then to Australia and New Zealand under auspices of British Council; entire orchestra, instruments and music transported by air across Atlantic and Pacific, thus making history. In 1948-49 his orchestra toured Holland, Germany and Portugal (2nd time) and gave ten concerts at Edinburgh Festival; in 1950, visited France, Denmark, Norway, Sweden and Finland. In 1951 toured Italy, gave concerts in Berlin, and again appeared at Edinburgh Festival. In 1952, gave two concerts at Aix-en-Provence Festival, and took orchestra on tour in Canada and USA. In 1953 toured France and Switzerland and gave concerts at Strasbourg Festival. Founded Hart House Orchestra of Toronto, 1955; toured with it Canada and USA; brought it to Europe, 1958 (Brussels World Fair), 1966 (Aldeburgh and Bergen Festivals); week of Canadian music, Expo '67, 1967; orchestra has made numerous recordings. World tour, 1971; conducted ballet and opera seasons in S Africa. Jury Mem., internat. music competitions. *Publication:* The Story of an Orchestra, 1950. *Address:* c/o York Club, 135 St George Street, Toronto, Ontario, Canada.

NÉEL, Prof. Louis Eugène Félix, Grand Croix de la Légion d'Honneur; Croix de Guerre avec Palme; Président d'Honneur, Institut National Polytechnique de Grenoble; *b* Lyon, 22 Nov. 1904; *m* 1931, Hélène Hourticq; one *s* two *d*. *Educ:* Ecole Normale Supérieure. Agrégé de l'Université; DèsS. Prof. of Science, Strasbourg, 1937-45. Dir, Centre d'Etudes Nucléaires, Grenoble, 1956-71, and Delegate of High Comr for Atomic Energy at the centre, 1971-; rep. France at Scientific Council, NATO. Mem., Acad. of Science, Paris, 1953; For. Member: Acad. of Science, USSR, 1959 and Rumania, 1965; Royal Netherlands Acad., 1959; Deutsche Akademie der Naturforscher Leopoldina, 1964; Royal Society, 1966; Amer. Acad. of Arts and Sciences, 1966; Pres., Internat. Union of Pure and Applied Physics, 1963-66. Gold Medal, CNRS, 1965; Nobel Prize for Physics, 1970. Hon. Dr: Graz, 1948; Nottingham, 1951; Oxford, 1958; Louvain, 1965; Newcastle, 1965; Coimbra, 1966; Sherbrooke, 1967. *Publications:* numerous on magnetism. *Address:* 15 rue Marcel-Allégot, 92190 Meudon-Bellevue, France. *T:* (1) 027 36 51.

NEELY, Air Vice-Marshal John Conrad, CB 1957; CBE 1952; DM; FRCS; retired; Senior Consultant, 1955, and Consultant in Ophthalmology, RAF Central Medical Establishment, 1950-59; *b* 29 Mar. 1901; *s* of late William Neely; *m* 1st, 1938, Marjorie Monica (*d* 1964), *d* of Dr Ernest Bramley, Eastbourne; 2nd, 1966, Roma, *widow* of Group Capt. Neil McKechnie, GC. *Educ:* Stonyhurst; Oxford Univ.; Guy's Hosp. MRCS, LRCP, 1927; MA, BM, BCh, 1928, DO (Oxon) 1935, DM 1945, Oxford; DOMS London, 1933. Joined RAF 1928; served War of

1939-45; Middle East (despatches); RAF Hosp., Halton. KHS 1951. Wing Comdr, 1940; Air Cdre, 1950; Air Vice-Marshal, 1955; retired, 1959. FRCS 1958. CStJ 1955. *Address:* 27 Vicarage Drive, Eastbourne, East Sussex.

NEEP, Edward John Cecil, QC; *b* 13 Oct. 1900; *e s* of late Rev. Edward Neep, Rector of St George's, Southwark, and Florence Emma Neep; *m* 1926, Evelyn, *e d* of late Sir Harry Pritchard. *Educ:* Westminster School (King's Scholar). Works chemist, 1917-20; tutor and journalist, 1920-23; called to Bar, Middle Temple, 1923; practised for twenty-nine years at the Bar and at the Patent and Parliamentary Bars for twenty years. Contested (Lab) Woodbridge 1922 and 1923, Central Leeds 1924, Lowestoft 1931; KC 1946; QC 1952. Deputy Speaker and Chairman of Committees, Kenya Legislative Council, 1952. *Publications:* Seditious Offences; (part author of): A Handbook of Church Law; Pons Asinorum, or the Future of Nonsense; Horatio Nelson; Gladstone: a spectrum. *Address:* 31 Rua de Santo Antonio à Estrela, Lisbon, Portugal; Quinta Monte de Cruz, Cintra, Portugal. *Club:* Royal British (Lisbon).

NEGUS, Arthur George; Partner, Messrs Bruton, Knowles & Co., Gloucester, since 1972; *b* 29 March 1903; *s* of Arthur George Negus and Amy Julia Worsley; *m* 1926, Irene Amy Hollett; two *d*. *Educ:* Reading Sch. Dealer in Antiques, 1920-40; Police War Reserve, 1941-45; joined Messrs Bruton, Knowles & Co., Fine Art Auctioneers, as Appraiser, 1946. BBC Television, 1966-, and BBC Radio, 1968-. *Publication:* Going for a Song: English furniture, 1969 (5th edn 1977). Freeman of the City of London, 1976. *Recreations:* watching sport, philately. *Address:* 31 Queens Court, Cheltenham, Glos GL50 2LU. *T:* Cheltenham 45696. *Club:* Lord's Taverners.

NEHRU, Braj Kumar; Indian High Commissioner in London, 1973-77; *b* Allahabad, 4 Sept. 1909; *s* of Brijlal and Rameshawri Nehru; *m* 1935, Magdalena Friedmann; three *s*. *Educ:* Allahabad Univ.; LSE (Fellow); Balliol Coll., Oxford. BSc; BSc(Econ.). Called to Bar, Inner Temple. Joined ICS, 1934; Asst Comr, 1934-39; Under-Sec., Dept of Education, Health and Lands, 1939; Officer on special duty, Reserve Bank of India, and Under-Sec., Finance Dept, 1940; Jt Sec., 1947; Exec. Dir, IBRD, and Minister, Indian Embassy, Washington, 1949-54; Sec., Dept of Econ. Affairs, 1957-58; Comr-Gen. for Econ. Affairs, Min. of Finance, 1958-61; Ambassador to USA, 1961-68; Governor: Assam and Nagaland, 1968-73; Meghalaya, Manipur and Tripura, 1972-73. Rep. of India: Reparations Conf., 1945; Commonwealth Finance Ministers Confs, UN Gen. Assembly, 1949-52, and 1960; FAO Confs, 1949-50; Sterling Balance Confs, 1947-49; Bandung Conf., 1955; deputed to enquire into Australian Fed. Finance, 1946; Mem., UN Adv. Cttee on Admin and Budgetry Questions, 1951-53; Advr to Sudan Govt, 1955; Mem., UN Investments Cttee, 1962-. Hon. LLD Mo Valley Coll.; Hon. LittD Jacksonville. *Publications:* Australian Federal Finance, 1947; Speaking of India, 1966. *Recreations:* bridge, reading, conversation. *Address:* c/o E. J. Nehru, House no 230, Sector IX, Chandigarh, India.

NEIDPATH, Lord; Hon. James Donald Charteris, Lord Douglas of Neidpath; *b* 22 June 1948; *s* and *heir* of 12th Earl of Wemyss and March, *qv. Educ:* Eton; University College, Oxford (BA 1969, MA 1974); St Antony's Coll., Oxford (DPhil 1975). Page of Honour to HM Queen Elizabeth the Queen Mother, 1962-64. *Address:* Stanway, Cheltenham, Glos. *Clubs:* Pratt's; Puffin's (Edinburgh).

NEIL, Prof. Eric; John Astor Professor of Physiology in the University of London, at the Middlesex Hospital Medical School, since 1956; *b* 15 Feb. 1918; *s* of George Neil, MC, and Florence Neil; *m* 1946, Anne Baron, *d* of late T. J. M. B. Parker and of Evelyn Maud Parker; two *d*. *Educ:* Heath Grammar School; University of Leeds. BSc Hons (Physiology) (Leeds), 1939; MB, ChB, 1942; MD (Dist.), 1944 and DSc, 1953 (Leeds). Demonstrator and Lecturer in Physiology, Univ. of Leeds, 1942-50; Sen. Lecturer and later Reader in Physiology, Middx Hosp. Med. School., 1950-56. Hon. Treas., Physiological Soc.; Chm., European Editorial Bd of Physiological Reviews; Mem., Brit. Nat. Cttee of Physiological Sciences. Examiner in Physiology, Univs of London, Aberdeen, Leeds, Manchester and Cambridge. *Publications:* (with Prof. C. Heymans) Reflexogenic Areas in the Cardiovascular System, 1958; (with Prof. C. A. Keele) 11th edn of Wright's Applied Physiology, 1964; papers on physiological topics in British and foreign med. scientific jls. *Recreations:* pianoforte, golf. *Address:* 53 Talbot Road, Highgate, N6. *T:* 01-340 0543.

NEIL, Matthew, CBE 1976; Secretary and Chief Executive, Glasgow Chamber of Commerce, since 1954; *b* 19 Dec. 1917; *er s* of John Neil and Jean Wallace. *Educ:* John Neilson High Sch.,

Paisley; Glasgow Univ. (MA, LLB). Served War, 1939-46: Far East, ME, Mediterranean and Western Europe; RHA, RA and Air Op. Pilot; RAuxAF, 1950-57. Admitted solicitor, 1947. *Recreations:* skiing, golf, music. *Address:* 39 Arkleston Road, Paisley PA1 3TH. *T:* 041-889 4975. *Clubs:* East India, Devonshire, Sports and Public Schools; Western (Glasgow); Erskine Golf, Lamlash Golf.

NEIL, Thomas, CMG 1962; TD 1951; Director, Thomson Foundation since 1963; *b* 23 December 1913; *s* of late W. R. Neil; *m* 1939, Phyllis Selina Gertrude Sargeant; one *d. Educ:* King's College, University of Durham (now University of Newcastle upon Tyne) (BSc, NDA). Lectr in Agriculture, Devon County Council, 1936-39; Chief Technical Officer, 1946. Colonial Service: District Officer, Kenya, 1947; Assistant Chief Secretary, 1957; Permanent Secretary, 1957; Permanent Secretary, Ministry of State, Kenya, 1959-63. Director, Kenya Famine Relief, 1961-63. Directed Africanisation of CS. Served War of 1939-45 with Devonshire Regiment (TA), Lieutenant-Colonel, in UK, E Africa, Middle East. *Recreation:* country life. *Address:* 16th Floor, London International Press Centre, 76 Shoe Lane, EC4A 3JB; Summerhill, Bourne End, Bucks. *T:* Bourne End 20403.

NEIL, Rev. William, MA, BD, PhD, DD; Warden of Hugh Stewart Hall, 1953-75, Reader in Biblical Studies 1965-75, in the University of Nottingham; *b* 13 June 1909; *s* of William Maclaren Neil and Jean Chalmers Hutchison; *m* 1936, Effie Lindsay Park, *d* of late Rev. Graham Park, MA, and Euphemia Lindsay, MA; two *s. Educ:* Glasgow Acad.; Univs of Glasgow and Heidelberg. Black Fellow, 1932-33, Faulds Fellow, 1934-37, Univ. of Glasgow. Minister at Bridge of Allan, 1937-46. Chaplain to 4/5 Royal Scots, 1940-43, and 5 Survey Regt RA, CMF 1943-45 (despatches, Italy). Head of Dept of Biblical Study, Univ. of Aberdeen, 1946-53. Croall Lecturer, Univ. of Edinburgh, 1967. Hon. DD Glasgow, 1961. *Publications:* St Paul's Epistles to the Thessalonians (Moffatt Commentaries), 1950; The Rediscovery of the Bible, 1954; The Epistle to the Hebrews, 1955; The Plain Man Looks at the Bible, 1956; I and II Thessalonians (Torch Commentaries), 1957; One Volume Bible Commentary, 1962; Jeremiah and Ezekiel (Bible Guides), 1964; The Life and Teaching of Jesus, 1965; Apostle Extraordinary: The Life and Letters of St Paul, 1966; The Christian Faith in Art (with Eric Newton), 1966; Galatians (Cambridge Bible Commentaries), 1967; The Truth About Jesus, 1968; The Truth about the Early Church, 1970; The Bible Story, 1971; The Truth about the Bible, 1972; The Acts of the Apostles (New Century Bible), 1973; Concise Dictionary of Religious Quotations, 1974; The Difficult Sayings of Jesus, 1975; Good News in Corinthians, 1977; translations: The Bible as History, 1956; Jesus Lived Here, 1958; Editor, The Bible Companion, 1959; General Editor, Knowing Christianity, 1964-; contributor to: Interpreter's Dictionary of the Bible, Peake's Commentary on the Bible, Cambridge History of the Bible, etc. *Address:* 590 Derby Road, Adams Hill, Nottingham NG4 2GZ. *T:* Nottingham 781818.

NEILD, Prof. Robert Ralph; Professor of Economics, University of Cambridge, since 1971; Fellow of Trinity College, Cambridge; *b* 10 Sept. 1924; *o s* of Ralph and Josephine Neild, Letchmore Heath, Hertfordshire; *m* 1960, Elizabeth Walton Griffiths; one *s* four *d* (incl. twin *d*). *Educ:* Charterhouse; Trinity Coll., Cambridge. Royal Air Force, 1943-44; Operational Research, 1944-45. Secretariat of United Nations Economic Commission for Europe, Geneva, 1947-51; Economic Section, Cabinet Office and Treasury, 1951-56; Lecturer in Economics, and Fellow, Trinity College, Cambridge, 1956-58; National Institute of Economic and Social Research: at first as Editor of its Quarterly Economic Review; then as Deputy Director of the Institute, 1958-64; MIT Center for International Studies, India Project, New Delhi, 1962-63; Economic Adviser to HM Treasury, 1964-67; Dir, Stockholm Internat. Peace Research Inst., 1967-71. Mem., Fulton Cttee on Reform of CS, 1966-68. *Publications:* Pricing and Employment in the Trade Cycle, 1964; various articles. *Address:* 5 Cranmer Road, Cambridge. *T:* Cambridge 56902.

NEILL, Brian Thomas, QC 1968; a Recorder of the Crown Court, since 1972; *b* 2 Aug. 1923; *s* of late Sir Thomas Neill and of Lady (Annie) Neill (*née* Bishop); *m* 1956, Sally Margaret, *d* of late Sydney Eric Backus and late Marguerite Backus; three *s. Educ:* Highgate Sch.; Corpus Christi Coll., Oxford. Rifle Brigade, 1942-46 (Capt.). MA Oxford. Called to the Bar, Inner Temple, 1949, Bencher, 1976. Mem., Departmental Cttee to examine operation of Section 2 of Official Secrets Act, 1971. Governor, Highgate Sch., 1969. *Address:* 48 Ham Street, Ham, Richmond, Surrey. *T:* 01-940 9309. *Clubs:* MCC, Hurlingham.
See also F. P. Neill.

NEILL, Prof. Derrick James, DFC 1943; Professor of Prosthetic Dentistry, University of London, since 1969; Sub-Dean of Dental Studies, Guy's Hospital Dental School, 1969-76; Consultant Dental Surgeon, Guy's Hospital, since 1960; *b* 14 March 1922; *s* of Jameson Leonard Neill, MBE, and Lynn Moyle; *m* 1st, 1952, Iris Jordan (*d* 1970); one *s* one *d* ; 2nd, 1971, Catherine Mary Daughtry. *Educ:* East Sheen County Grammar Sch.; Guy's Hosp. Dental Sch., Univ. of London. LDSRCS 1952; FDSRCS 1955; MDS London, 1966. Served RAFVR, 1941-46, 150 Sqdn, Bomber Comd (Sqdn Ldr). Dept of Dental Prosthetics, Guy's Hosp. Dental School: Lectr, 1954; Sen. Lectr, 1959; Univ. Reader in Dental Prosthetics, 1967. Examr, Univs of Bristol, Edinburgh and Newcastle. Council Member, Odontological Section, Royal Soc. of Medicine, 1966-73; Past Pres., British Soc. for Study of Prosthetic Dentistry. *Publications:* (jtly) Complete Dentures, 1968; Partial Denture Construction, 1976; numerous papers in dental jls. *Recreations:* gardening, golf, music. *Address:* Hurst, Clenches Farm Road, Kippington, Sevenoaks, Kent. *T:* Sevenoaks 52374. *Club:* Royal Automobile.

NEILL, Francis Patrick, QC 1966; Warden of All Souls College, Oxford, since 1977; a Judge of the Court of Appeal of Jersey and Guernsey, since 1977; a Recorder of the Crown Court, 1975; *b* 8 Aug. 1926; *s* of late Sir Thomas Neill, JP, and of Lady (Annie Strachan) Neill (*née* Bishop); *m* 1954, Caroline Susan, *d* of late Sir Piers Debenham, 2nd Bt, and Lady (Angela) Debenham; four *s* two *d. Educ:* Highgate Sch.; Magdalen College, Oxford. Gibbs Law Scholar, 1949; Eldon Law Scholar, 1950. BA 1950; BCL 1951; MA 1972. Served Rifle Brigade, 1944-47 (Captain); GSO III (Training), British Troops Egypt, 1947. Fellow of All Souls, 1950-, Sub-Warden 1972-74. Called to the Bar, Gray's Inn, 1951; Bencher, 1971; Member, Bar Council, 1967-71, Vice-Chm., 1973-74, Chm., 1974-75; Chm., Senate of the Inns of Court and the Bar, 1974-75. *Recreations:* music and forestry. *Address:* All Souls College, Oxford OX1 4AL. *T:* Oxford 722251; 8 Milborne Grove, SW10. *T:* 01-373 6775; Blackdown House, Briantspuddle, Dorset. *T:* Bere Regis 231.
See also B. T. Neill.

NEILL, Major Rt. Hon. Sir Ivan, Kt 1973; PC (N Ireland) 1950; DL; *b* Belfast 1 July 1906; *m* 1928, Margaret Helena Allen. *Educ:* Ravenscroft Nat. Sch., Belfast; Shaftesbury House Tutorial Coll., Belfast; Queen's Univ., Belfast (BSc Econ). FRGS. Served War of 1939-45: RE in UK and FE, 1939-46; Major. Sen Dir, Ivan Neill and Co., Building and Engineering Contractors, 1928-. MP Ballynafeigh Div. of Belfast, Parlt of Northern Ireland, 1949-73; Government of Northern Ireland: Minister of Labour and National Insurance, 1950-62; Minister of Home Affairs, Aug.-Oct. 1952; Minister of Education, 1962-64; Minister of Finance, 1964-65; Leader of House of Commons, Oct. 1964; resigned from Govt, April 1965; Minister of Develt, Dec. 1968-March 1969; Speaker of House of Commons, 1969-73. Represented N Ireland at Internat. Labour Confs, 1950-61. Councillor and Alderman in Belfast Corp., 1946-50 (specialised in educn, housing and youth welfare). DL Belfast, 1966. *Address:* Greenlaw, Ballywilliam, Donaghadee, Co. Down, Northern Ireland.

NEILL, Very Rev. Ivan Delacherois, CB 1963; OBE 1958; Provost of Sheffield and Vicar of the Cathedral Church of St Peter and St Paul, 1966-74, now Emeritus; Chaplain to the Queen, 1962-66; *b* 10 July 1912; *s* of Rev. Robert Richard Neill and Bessie Montrose (*née* Purdon); *m* 1938, Enid Eyre Godson (*née* Bartholomew); one *s* one *d. Educ:* St Dunstan's College; Jesus College, Cambridge (MA); London College of Divinity. Curate: St Mary, West Kensington, 1936-38; Christ Church, Crouch End, 1938-39. CF 4th Cl., Chatham; served BEF and UK with 3rd Div., Orkneys, Sandhurst, 1941-43; Sen. Chaplain, N Aldershot, 1943; 43rd (Wessex) Div., 1943-45 (despatches); DACG, 1st British Corps, 1945-46; Sen. Chaplain, Guards Depot, Caterham, 1947-50; DACG, N Canal, Egypt, 1950-53; Catterick, 1953; Warden, Royal Army Chaplains Dept Trg Centre Depot, 1954-57; Sen. Chaplain, SHAPE 1957-58; Asst Chaplain-Gen., Middle East Land Forces, 1958-60; QHC 1960; Chaplain General to HM Forces, 1960-66. Chairman of Governors: Monkton Combe Sch., Bath, 1969-; St Mary's C of E Coll. of Educn, Cheltenham, 1974-. Knight Officer, Order of Orange Nassau (with Swords) 1946. *Address:* Rodborough Crest, Rodborough Common, Stroud, Glos GL5 5BT. *T:* Amberley 3224; Churchtown, Broadway, Co. Wexford, Republic of Ireland.

NEILL, James Hugh, CBE 1969; TD 1950; DL; Chairman and Chief Executive, James Neill Holdings Ltd, since 1963; Member, Eastern Regional Board, National Westminster Bank Ltd; *b* 29 March 1921; *o s* of Col Sir Frederick Neill, CBE, DSO, TD, DL, JP, and Lady (Winifred Margaret) Neill (*née* Colver); *m* 1943, Jane Margaret Shuttleworth; two *d. Educ:* Rugby School. War service with RE and Royal Bombay Sappers and Miners, UK, Norway, Burma and Germany, 1939-46 (despatches, Burma, 1945). Mem., British Overseas Trade Bd, 1973-; Pres., European Tool Cttee, 1972-76; Mem., Trent Regional Health Authority, 1974-; Chm. Exec. Cttee, Sheffield Council of Social Service, 1953-; Mem. Council, CBI, 1965-; Chm., E and W Ridings Regional Council, FBI, 1962-64; Pres., Nat. Fedn of Engrs Tool Manufrs, 1963-65; Pres., Fedn of British Hand Tool Manufrs, 1960-61; Vice-Pres., Inst. of Export. FBIM. Master Cutler of Hallamshire, 1958; High Sheriff of Hallamshire, 1971; DL South Yorkshire, 1974. *Recreations:* golf, racing, shooting. *Address:* Lindrick Lodge, Woodsetts, near Worksop, S81 8AZ. *T:* Dinnington 2806. *Clubs:* East India, Devonshire, Sports and Public Schools; Sheffield (Sheffield); Royal and Ancient (St Andrews).

NEILL, Patrick; *see* Neill, F. P.

NEILL, Rt. Rev. Stephen Charles, FBA 1969; *b* 31 Dec. 1900; *s* of Rev. Charles Neill, MB, and of Margaret, *d* of late James Monro, CB. *Educ:* Dean Close School; Trinity College, Cambridge (MA 1926). Fellow of Trinity College, Cambridge, 1924-28; Missionary in dioceses of Tinnevelly and Travancore, 1924-30; Warden, Bishop's Theological College, Tirumaraiyur, Nazareth, S India, 1930-38; Bishop of Tinnevelly, 1939-45; Chaplain of Trinity Coll., Cambridge; Univ. Lecturer in Divinity, 1945-47; Co-Director Study Dept of World Council of Churches, 1947-48; Asst Bishop to Archbishop of Canterbury, 1947-50; Associate Gen. Sec. of World Council of Churches, 1948-51; General Editor, World Christian Books, 1952-62; Director, 1962-70; Prof. of Missions and Ecumenical Theology, Univ. of Hamburg, 1962-67; Prof. of Philosophy and Religious Studies, Nairobi Univ., 1969-73. Lectures: Hulsean, Cambridge, 1946-47; Birkbeck, Trinity Coll., Cambridge, 1949-50; Godfrey Day in Missions, TCD, 1950; Earle, Pacific School of Religions, Berkeley, California, 1950; Cody Meml, Toronto, 1956; Carnahan, Faculty of Theology, Buenos Aires, 1958; Duff in Missions, Edinburgh and Glasgow, 1958-59; Moorhouse, Melbourne, 1960; Firth, Nottingham, 1962; Bampton, Oxford, 1964; Ziskind, Dartmouth Coll., NH, 1966; Westcott-Teape, Delhi and Madras, 1972; Livingstone Meml, Blantyre, Malawi, 1973. Visiting Professor: of Missions, Hamburg Univ., 1956-57, 1961; of Theol., Colgate-Rochester Divinity Sch., 1961-62; of Theol., Wycliffe Coll., Toronto, 1962; Drew Univ., NJ, 1967; of Religion, Univ. Coll., Nairobi, 1968: of Science of Religion, Durban-Westville Univ., SA, 1975. Hon. DD: Trinity Coll., Toronto, 1950; Culver-Stockton, 1953; Glasgow, 1961; Acadia, 1976; Hon. ThD: Hamburg, 1957; Uppsala, 1965; Hon. LittD St Paul's Univ., Tokyo, 1960. *Publications:* Out of Bondage, 1928; Builders of the Indian Church, 1933; Beliefs, 1940; Foundation Beliefs, 1942; The Challenge of Jesus Christ, 1944; Christ, His Church and His World, 1948; The Cross over Asia, 1948; On the Ministry, 1952; The Christian Society, 1952; Christian Partnership, 1952; Towards Church Union, 1937-1952, 1952; Under Three Flags, 1954; The Christian's God, 1954; Christian Faith To-day, 1955; The Christian Character, 1955; Who is Jesus Christ?, 1956; The Unfinished Task, 1957; Anglicanism, 1958; A Genuinely Human Existence, 1959; Creative Tension, 1959; Christian Holiness, 1960; Men of Unity, 1960; Christian Faith and other Faiths, 1961; The Eternal Dimension, 1963; The Interpretation of the New Testament, 1964; A History of Christian Missions, 1964; Colonialism and Christian Missions, 1966; The Church and Christian Union, 1968; Christianity in India and Pakistan, 1970; Bible Words and Christian Meanings, 1970; What do we know of Jesus?, 1970; Bhakti Hindu and Christian, 1974; Salvation Tomorrow, 1976; Jesus Through Many Eyes, 1976. (Editor) Twentieth Century Christianity, 1961; (ed jtly) A History of the Ecumenical Movement, 1517-1948, 1951-54; (ed jtly) The Layman in Christian History, 1963; (ed jtly) The Concise Dictionary of the Christian World Mission, 1970; contrib. to: Encyclopædia Britannica; Chambers's Encyclopædia; Die Religion in Geschichte und Gegenwart; Evangelisches Kirchenlexikon; Weltkirchenlexikon. *Address:* Wycliffe Hall, Oxford.

NEILL, Ian (Godfrey), DFC 1944; TD 1951; Clerk to: Governors of the Cripplegate Foundation, Cripplegate Educational Foundation, Trustees of St Giles and St Luke's Joint Parochial Charities, and Governors of the Cripplegate Schools Foundation, since 1974; *b* 4 Dec. 1918; *er s* of James Wilson Neilson, solicitor, Glasgow; *m* 1945, D. Alison St Clair Aytoun, Ashintully; one *s* one *d. Educ:* Glasgow Acad.; Glasgow Univ. (BL). Legal Trng, Glasgow, 1935-39; Territorial Army, 1938; War Service, 1939-45: Field Artillery; Air Observation Post, 1941; RA Staff, 1944; Lt-Col comdg War Crimes Investigation Unit, Germany, 1945-46. Enrolled Solicitor, 1946. Royal Institution of Chartered Surveyors; Scottish Sec., Edinburgh, 1946-53; Asst Sec., London, 1953-61;

Under-Sec., 1961-65; Brigade Sec., The Boys' Brigade, 1966-74 (officer, 5th Mid-Surrey Co., 1972-). Hon. Treasurer, Thames Youth Venture Adv. Council (City Parochial Foundn), 1968-76. Vice-Chm., British Council of Churches Youth Dept, 1971-74; Mem., Nat. Council for Voluntary Youth Services, 1966-74; Chm. of Governors, Lucas-Tooth Training Fund for Boys, 1976-. Elder, United Reformed Church, St Andrew's, Cheam, 1972-; Lay Mem., Provincial Ministerial Cttee, URC, 1974-. MBIM 1975, Hon. Sec., City of London Branch, 1976-. Sen. Instr, Royal Yachting Assoc., 1977-. Chm., Epsom Choral Soc., 1977-. Freeman, Guild of Air Pilots and Air Navigators, 1976-; Freeman, City of London, 1975. *Recreations:* golf, music, gardening, sailing. *Address:* 103 Longdown Lane South, Epsom Downs, Epsom, Surrey KT17 4JJ. *T:* Epsom 20670. *Club:* Athenæum.

NEILSON, Hon. William Arthur; Agent-General for Tasmania, in London, since 1978; *b* 27 Aug. 1925; *s* of late Arthur R. Neilson; *m* 1948, Jill, *d* of A. H. Benjamin; one *s* three *d. Educ:* Ogilvie Commercial High Sch., Hobart. When first elected to Tasmanian Parlt in 1946, aged 21, youngest MP in British Commonwealth and youngest member ever elected to any Australian parlt. Re-elected, 1948, 1950, 1955, 1956, 1959, 1964, 1969 and 1972, resigned 1977. Labor Party Whip, Dec. 1946-Feb. 1955; Minister for Tourists and Immigration and Forests, Oct. 1956-Aug. 1958; Attorney-Gen. and Minister for Educn, Aug.-Oct 1968; Minister for Educn, until April 1959, then Treasurer and Minister for Educn, April-May 1959; Minister for Educn, 1959-69 and May 1972-March 1974; Attorney-Gen., also Dep. Premier, Minister for Environment and Minister administering Police Dept and Licensing Act, April 1974-March 1975; Premier and Treasurer, 1975-77. *Recreations:* reading, writing, chess, Australian Rules football, amateur theatre. *Address:* Tasmania House, 458/9 Strand, WC2R 0RJ. *T:* 01-839 2291.

NELIGAN, Desmond West Edmund, OBE 1961; National Insurance Commissioner, 1961-76, retired; *b* 20 June 1906; *s* of late Rt Rev. M. R. Neligan, DD (one time Bishop of Auckland, NZ), and Mary, *d* of Edmund Macrory, QC; *m* 1st, 1936, Penelope Ann, *d* of Henry Mason (marr. diss., 1946); two *s*; 2nd, 1947, Margaret Elizabeth, *d* of late Captain Snook, RN; one step *d. Educ:* Bradfield Coll.; Jesus Coll., Cambridge. BA Cantab, 1929; Barrister, Middle Temple, 1940. Practising Barrister until 1961. Appointed Umpire under National Service Acts, Nov. 1955. Dep. Comr for National Insurance, 1955-61. Served War of 1939-45, in 2 NZ Division, in Greece, Crete and Western Desert. *Publications:* (ed) 6th, 7th and 8th Editions Dumsday's Parish Councils Handbook; (with Sir A. Safford, QC) Town and Country Planning Act, 1944, and *ibid,* 1947. *Recreations:* formerly: hockey, cricket (Mem. MCC), tennis and hunting. *Address:* Frobishers, Danhill Cross Roads, West Chiltington, Pulborough, West Sussex. *T:* Coolham 434.

NELSON, family name of **Earl Nelson** and **Baron Nelson of Stafford.**

NELSON, 8th Earl *cr* 1805, of Trafalgar and of Merton; **George Joseph Horatio Nelson;** Baron Nelson of the Nile and of Hilborough, Norfolk, 1801; Viscount Merton, 1805; retired; *b* 20 April 1905; 4th *s* of 5th Earl Nelson and Geraldine (*d* 1936), *d* of Henry H. Cave, Northampton; *S* brother, 1972; *m* 1945, Winifred Mary, *d* of G. Bevan, Swansea; one *d. Educ:* Ampleforth. FCA (resigned). *Heir: nephew* Peter John Horatio Nelson [*b* 9 Oct. 1941; *m* 1969, Maureen Quinn; one *s* one *d*]. *Address:* 9 Pwlldu Lane, Bishopston, Swansea SA3 3HA. *T:* Bishopston 2682.

NELSON OF STAFFORD, 2nd Baron, *cr* 1960; **Henry George Nelson,** Bt 1955; MA, CEng, FICE, Hon. FIMechE, FIEE, FRAeS; Chairman, The General Electric Company Ltd, since 1968, Director: Bank of England; National Bank of Australasia Ltd (London Board of Advice); International Nickel Company of Canada; Chancellor of Aston University; *b* Manchester, 2 Jan. 1917; *s* of 1st Baron Nelson of Stafford and late Florence Mabel, *o d* of late Henry Howe, JP; *S* father, 1962; *m* 1940, Pamela Roy Bird, *yr d* of late Ernest Roy Bird, formerly MP for Skipton, Yorks; two *s* two *d. Educ:* Oundle; King's Coll., Cambridge. Exhibnr 1935; Mechanical Sciences Tripos, 1937. Practical experience in England, France and Switzerland, 1937-39. Joined the English Electric Co. Ltd, 1939; Supt, Preston Works, 1939-40; Asst Works Man., Preston, 1940-41; Dep. Works Man., Preston, 1941-42; Man. Dir, D. Napier & Son Ltd, 1942-49; Exec. Dir, The Marconi Co. Ltd, 1946-58; Dep. Man. Dir, 1949-56, Man. Dir, 1956-62, Chm. and Chief Exec., 1962-68, The English Electric Co. Ltd. Outside Lectr, Univ. of Cambridge (Mech. Sciences Tripos course on Industrial Management), 1947-49. Member: Govt. Adv. Council on Scientific Policy,

1955-58; Adv. Council on Middle East Trade, 1958-63 (Industrial Leader and Vice-Chm., 1959-63); Civil Service Commn (Part time Mem. Final Selection and Interview Bds), 1956-61; Engrg Adv. Council, 1958-61; Engrg Employers' Fedn, 1956- (Vice-Pres., 1963, Gen. Council, 1956-. and Management Bd, 1956-); Council, Inst. Electrical Engineers, 1959- (Vice-Pres. 1957-62 and 1965-70, Pres., 1970-71); Internat. Electrical Assoc., 1953-57 (Chm. 1955) and 1959-74; Middle East Assoc. (Vice-Pres., 1962-); Gen. Bd of NPL, 1959-66; Council, SBAC, 1943-64 (Pres. 1961-62); Council Foundn on Automation and Employment Ltd, 1963-68; Council, BEAMA, 1964- (Pres., 1966); Adv. Council, Min. of Technology, 1964-70; Engineering Industries Council, 1975-. World Power Conference: Mem., British Nat. Cttee, 1954-71, Chm., 1971-74. Mem., Nat. Def. Industries Council, 1969- (Chm., 1971-); Pres. Locomotive and Allied Manufacturers Assoc., 1964-66; Pres., British Electrical Power Convention, 1965-67. President: Orgalime (Organisme de Liaison des Industries Métalliques Européennes), 1968-70; Sino-British Trade Council, 1973-. Liveryman: Worshipful Co. of Coachmakers and Coach Harness Makers of London, 1944; Worshipful Co. of Goldsmiths, 1961. Lord High Steward of Borough of Stafford, 1966-71. Hon. DSc: Aston, 1966; Keele, 1967; Cranfield, 1972; Hon. LLD Strathclyde, 1971; Fellow, Imp. Coll. of Science and Technology, 1969. Benjamin Franklin Medal, RSA, 1959. Recreations: shooting, tennis, ski-ing, riding. Heir: s Hon. Henry Roy George Nelson [b 26 Oct. 1943; m 1968, Dorothy, yr d of Leslie Caley, Tibthorpe Manor, Driffield, Yorks; one s]. Address: 8 Carlton Lodge, 37 Lowndes Street, SW1X 9HX. T: 01-235 6551. Clubs: Carlton, Hurlingham.

NELSON, NZ, Bishop of, since 1965; **Rt. Rev. Peter (Eves) Sutton;** b Wellington, NZ, 7 June 1923; m 1956, Pamela Cherrington, e d of R. A. Dalley, Patin House, Kidderminster; one s one d. Educ: Wellesley Coll.; Nelson Coll.; University of New Zealand. BA 1945; MA 1947; LTh 1948. Deacon, 1947; Priest, 1948 (Wellington); Curate of Wanganui, New Zealand, 1947-50; St John the Evangelist, Bethnal Green, 1950-51; Bishops Hatfield, Diocese of St Albans (England), 1951-52; Vicar of St Cuthberts, Berhampore (NZ), 1952-58; Whangarei, Diocese of Auckland, New Zealand, 1958-64; Archdeacon of Waimate, 1962-64; Dean of Dunedin and Vicar of St Paul's Cathedral, Dunedin, 1964-65. Publication: Freedom for Convictions, 1971. Recreations: golf (Canterbury Univ. Blue), tennis. Address: Bishopdale, Nelson, New Zealand.

NELSON, Anthony; see Nelson, R. A.

NELSON, Bertram, CBE 1956; FCA; b 1905; s of W. E. Nelson, Liverpool; m 1954, Eleanor Kinsey; one s one d. Educ: The Leys School, Cambridge. Hon. Sec. Merseyside Civic Soc. 1938-53. Chm. Liverpool Chamber of Commerce, 1951-53, Treas., 1953-60; a Vice-Pres. of Assoc. of British Chambers of Commerce, 1956. Pres. Soc. of Incorporated Accountants, 1954-56; Mem. Council of Inst. of Chartered Accountants, 1957-75 (Chairman of Education Committee, 1961-66). Chm., Liverpool Daily Post and Echo Gp, 1972-76. BBC North Regional Council, 1947-57. Mem. Board of Trade Consultative Cttee on Companies, 1954-73, and of Bd of Trade Treas. Cttee on Export Credit Guarantees Dept., 1958; Part-time Mem., Merseyside and N Wales Electricity Bd 1967-76. Treas. of Liverpool Univ., 1948-57, Vice-Pres., 1957-63, Pres. and Pro-Chancellor, 1963-67, Senior Pro-Chancellor, 1967-73; Chm., Univ. Develt Cttee, 1961-68; Governor: The Leys Sch., Cambridge (Vice-Chm., 1970); Staff Coll. for Further Education; Mem. Mersey Docks and Harbour Bd, 1951-65; Chm. Liverpool Youth Welfare Advisory Cttee, 1952-65; Dir, the Playhouse, Liverpool, 1949-63; Chm. of Appeals Cttee on Gradings and Salaries in Colls of Advanced Technology, 1964-65. Trustee, Civic Trust for NW. JP Liverpool, 1944. Hon. LLD Liverpool, 1972. Publication: Tables of Procedure, 1933. Address: Tyddyn Rossa, Prion, Denbigh, Clwyd LL16 4RP. Clubs: Reform, Athenæum (Pres. 1962); University Staff House (Liverpool).

NELSON, Air Cdre Eric Douglas Mackinlay, CB 1952; DL; retired, Sept. 1963; b 2 Jan. 1912; e s of late Rear-Adm. R. D. Nelson, CBE, and the late Ethel Nelson (née MacKinlay); m 1939, Margaret Yvonne Taylor; one s one d. Educ: Dover Coll.; RAF Coll., Cranwell. Commissioned RAF, 1932; served War of 1939-45 (despatches); CO 103 (HB) Sqdn Elsham Wolds, 1943-44; Group Capt., 1944; ADC to the Queen, 1953-57; Air Commodore, 1956; Commandant, RAF, Halton, 1956-58; Commandant, Royal Air Force Staff College, Andover, 1958-60; AOA Transport Command, 1960-61; Air Officer Commanding and Commandant, Royal Air Force College, Cranwell, 1961-63. DL Lincs, 1966, Hon. Clerk to Lieutenancy, 1973-. Recreations: boxed for RAF, 1933-39; sailing, hunting. Address: (permanent) Jasmine Cottage, Carlton-le-Moorland, Lincoln. T: Bassingham 309. Club: Royal Air Force.

NELSON, Maj.-Gen. Sir (Eustace) John (Blois), KCVO 1966 (MVO 1953); CB 1965; DSO 1944; OBE 1948; MC 1943; b 15 June 1912; s of late Roland Hugh Nelson and late Hylda Letitia Blois; m 1936, the Lady Jane FitzRoy (granted rank and precedence of d of a duke, 1931), er d of (William Henry Alfred FitzRoy) Viscount Ipswich; two d. Educ: Eton; Trinity College, Cambridge. BA (Hons) History. Commissioned Grenadier Guards, Sept. 1933; served 1939-45 with 3rd and 5th Bns, Belgium, N Africa, Italy (wounded three times, despatches); comd 3rd Bn Grenadier Guards, 1944-45, Italy. Contested (C) Whitechapel, 1945. Comd 1st Guards Parachute Bn, 1946-48, Palestine; comd 1st Bn Gren. Gds, 1950-52, Tripoli, N Africa. Planning Staff Standing Group, Washington, DC, 1954-56, Imperial Defence College, 1958; comd 4th Guards Bde, 1959-61, Germany; GOC London District, and Maj.-Gen. comdg Household Brigade 1962-65; GOC Berlin (British Sector), 1966-68. Chm., Internat. Students' House; Vice-Pres., Nat. Playing Fields Assoc. (Gen. Sec. 1969-72). Silver Star (USA), 1944. Recreations: the countryside, sailing. Address: Tigh Bhaan, Appin, Argyll. T: Appin 252. Club: Cavalry and Guards.

NELSON, Geoffrey Sheard, CBE 1970; Director: Leased Hotels Ltd; Sociedade Portuguesa de Resina-Dismutada SARL; b 1 Jan. 1909; s of late William Nelson and Sarah Nelson (née Sheard); m 1932, Gladys, d of late C. W. Brown; two d. Educ: Leeds Central High Sch. Chartered Accountant (Incorporated Accountant, 1931). Min. of Supply (Costing Br.), 1942-45. Subseq. with Finance Corp. for Industry Ltd., Gen. Manager, 1948-73. FCA, ACMA. Recreations: golf, photography, travel. Address: 4 Norman Way, Southgate N14 6NA. T: 01-886 0442.

NELSON, Henry Ince, QC 1945; BA, LLB; Commissioner of National Insurance, 1968-69 (Deputy Commissioner, 1959-68); retired; b 29 May 1897; s of late Henry Nelson, OBE, and of late Ada Bell Nelson; m 1933, Mary Howard Cooper; three s one d. Educ: Aldenham School; Pembroke Coll., Cambridge. RFA 1915-19, rank Lt (twice wounded); served on Western Front with VI Divisional Artillery. Called to Bar, Inner Temple, 1922; Bencher 1952. Judge of Salford Hundred Court of Record, 1947-48; Judge of Liverpool Court of Passage, 1948-50; Recorder of Liverpool, 1950-54. Recreations: gardening and golf. Address: Brackendene, Hockering Road, Woking, Surrey. T: Woking 61210. Club: Golf (Woking).

NELSON, John Howard; Deputy Under-Secretary of State (Air), Ministry of Defence, since 1976; b 23 May 1925; s of late Rev. S. T. Nelson and of Mrs Nelson; m 1949, Hazel Dent; one s one d. Educ: Methodist Coll., Belfast; Pembroke Coll., Cambridge (Scholar). BA 1948. War Service 1943-46, Sub-Lt RNVR. Asst Principal, Air Ministry, 1949; Principal, 1954; Asst Sec., 1962; attended Imperial Defence Coll. course, 1968; Asst Under-Sec. of State, 1972. Recreations: unremarkable. Address: 2 Ingleside Grove, Blackheath, SE3. T: 01-858 2716.

NELSON, Air Marshal Sir Richard; see Nelson, Air Marshal Sir S. R. C.

NELSON, (Richard) Anthony; MP (C) Chichester, since Oct. 1974; b 11 June 1948; o s of Gp Captain R. G. Nelson, BSc, CEng, FRAeS, MICE, and Mrs J. M. Nelson; m 1974, Caroline Victoria Butler. Educ: Harrow Sch.; Christ's Coll., Cambridge (MA (Hons) Economics and Law). State Scholarship to Harrow, 1961; Churchill Prize, 1962; Head of School, 1966; Rothschild Scholar, 1966. Chm., Cambridge Univ. Management Gp, 1968. Merchant banker, 1969-75. Mem., Nat. Assoc. for Care and Resettlement of Offenders, 1971; Founder Mem., Nat. Victims Assoc., 1972; Mem., Bow Gp Council, 1973. Contested (C) E Leeds, Feb. 1974. Mem., Select Cttee on Science and Technology, 1975-; Jt Sec., Cons. Parly Industry Cttee and All Party Penal Reform Gp, 1975-. Publications: various papers on internat. relations and economic affairs. Recreations: music, travel, rugby. Address: The Old Vicarage, Easebourne, Midhurst, Sussex.

NELSON, St Elmo Dudley, CMG 1964; Permanent Secretary, Military Governor's Office, Kano, 1968-76; Acting Secretary to Military Government, Kano, 1970, 1972 and 1975; b 18 March 1919; s of Dudley Nelson and Dorothy Maida (née Browne), Highton, Victoria, Australia; m 1958, Lynette Margaret, o d of Philip Anthony Browne, Yarram and Frankston, Victoria, Australia. Educ: privately; Geelong School; Oxford University; Sorbonne. Served War of 1939-45 (despatches): 2/7 Australian Infantry Bn (Major); campaigns N Africa, Greece, Crete, New Guinea; Instructor Staff Coll., Cabalah, 1944. Joined HM Colonial Administrative Service. Nigeria: Cadet 1947; Administrative Officer (Class II), 1957; Resident, Plateau Province, 1961; Resident and Provincial Sec., Kabba Province, 1962; Provincial Sec., Kano Province, 1963-67, Sokoto, 1967-68.

Chm., Cttee which divided assets of Northern Region between the six Northern States, 1967. *Recreations:* fishing, polo, squash. *Address:* East Cottage, Faulstone House, Bishopstone, near Salisbury, Wilts.

NELSON, Air Marshal Sir (Sidney) Richard (Carlyle), KCB 1963 (CB 1962); OBE 1949; Director-General, Royal Air Force Medical Services, 1962-67; Director of Research and Medical Services, Aspro-Nicholas Ltd, 1967-72; *b* Ponoka, Alberta, Canada, 14 Nov. 1907; *s* of M. O. Nelson, BA; *m* 1939, Christina Elizabeth Powell; two *s. Educ:* University of Alberta (MD). Commissioned in RAF, 1935; served: England 1935-36; Egypt and Western Desert, 1936-42; Fighter Command, 1943; UK Delegation (Canada), 1943-44; British Jt Services Mission (Washington), 1945-48; RAF Staff Coll., 1949; Air Ministry, 1949-52; Comd RAF Hosp., Nocton Hall, 1953-55; SMO British Forces, Arabian Peninsula, 1956-57; PMO Technical Training Comd, 1957-59; Bomber Comd, 1959-62, QHP 1961-67. *Recreations:* fishing, golf. *Address:* Caffyn's Copse, Shappen Hill Lane, Burley, Hants. *T:* Burley 3308. *Clubs:* Royal Air Force; Royal Lymington Yacht.

NELSON, Sir William Vernon Hope, 3rd Bt, *cr* 1912; OBE 1952; Major (retired) late 8th Hussars; *b* 25 May 1914; *s* of late William Hope Nelson (2nd *s* of 1st Bt); *S* uncle, Sir James Hope Nelson, 2nd Bt, 1960; *m* 1945, Elizabeth Ann Bevil, *er d* of Viscount Falkland, *qv*; three *s* three *d. Educ:* Beaumont; Royal Military College, Sandhurst. Commissioned 2nd Lt, 8th Hussars, 1934. Served in Palestine, 1936-39 (despatches, medal with clasp). Served War of 1939-45; served Korea, 1950-51 (OBE). *Heir: s* Jamie Charles Vernon Hope Nelson, *b* 23 Oct. 1949. *Address:* c/o Hoare & Co., 16 Waterloo Place, SW1.

NEMON, Oscar; Sculptor; *b* 13 March 1906; *s* of Mavro and Eugenia Nemon, Yugoslavia; *m* 1939, Patricia Villiers-Stuart; one *s* two *d. Educ:* Osijek; Brussels; Paris. Exhibitions held in principal capitals of Europe. Examples of his work are in: House of Commons; Windsor Castle; The Guildhall, London; The Union, Oxford. His sitters include: HM The Queen, Rt Hon. Sir Winston Churchill, Rt Hon. Harold Macmillan, Lord Beaverbrook, Sigmund Freud, Sir Max Beerbohm, Lord Montgomery, President Eisenhower; other work: Lord Portal, 1975. *Recreation:* searching for lost opportunities. *Address:* Pleasant Land, Boars Hill, Oxford. *T:* Oxford 735583.
See also Sir George Young, Bt.

NEPEAN, Lt-Col Sir Evan Yorke, 6th Bt, *cr* 1802; late Royal Signals; *b* 23 Nov. 1909; *s* of Sir Charles Evan Molyneux Yorke Nepean, 5th Bt, and Mary Winifred, *o d* of Rev. William John Swayne, formerly Vicar of Heytesbury, Wilts, and Custos of St John's Hospital, Heytesbury; *S* father 1953; *m* 1940, (Georgiana) Cicely, *o d* of late Major Noel Edward Grey Willoughby, Middlesex Regiment, of Chancel End House, Heytesbury, Wilts; three *d. Educ:* Winchester; Downing College, Cambridge. BA 1931, MA 1946. North West Frontier of India (Mohmand), 1935. Served War of 1939-45: GSO3, War Office, 1939-40; with Royal Signals (Lt-Col 1943), UK, and Middle East, Major 1946; on Staff Southern Command, 1947; GSO1 Royal Signals, Ministry of Defence, 1950-53; Lt-Col 1952; Cmdg 11 Air Formation Signal Regt, BAOR, 1955-56, retired. Civil Servant, 1957-59; CSO's branch at HQ Southern Command (Retired Officers' Staff appt), 1959-73. MIEE. *Recreations:* cricket, sailing. *Heir:* none. *Address:* Goldens, Teffont, Salisbury, Wilts. *T:* Teffont 275.

NERINA, Nadia; (*née* Nadine Judd); Prima Ballerina; Ballerina with Royal Ballet, 1951-69; *b* Cape Town, Oct. 1927; *m* 1955, Charles Gordon. Joined Sadler's Wells Sch., 1946; after two months joined Sadler's Wells Theatre Ballet; transferred Sadler's Wells Ballet, Royal Opera House (now Royal Ballet), as soloist, 1967. *Rôles:* Princess Aurora in The Sleeping Beauty; Ondine; Odette-Odile in Swan Lake; Swanhilda in Coppelia; Sylvia; Giselle; Cinderella; Firebird; Can Can Dancer in La Boutique Fantasque; Ballerina in Petrushka; Colombine in Carnaval; Mazurka, Little Waltz, Prelude, in Les Sylphides; Mam'zelle Angot; Ballet Imperial; Scènes de Ballet; Flower Festival of Genzano; Les Rendezvous; Polka in Façade; The Girl in Spectre de la Rose; Casse Noisette; Laurentia; Khadra; Vagabonds; The Bride in A Wedding Bouquet; *creations:* Circus Dancer in Mardi Gras; Fairy Spring in Cinderella; Queen of the Earth in Homage to the Queen; Faded Beauty in Noctambules; Variation on a Theme; Birthday Offering; Lise in La Fille Mal Gardée; Electra; The Girl in Home; Clorinda in Tancredi. Appeared with Royal Ballet: Europe; South Africa; USA; Canada; USSR; Bulgaria; Romania. Recital Tours with Alexis Rassine: South Africa, 1952-55; England, 1956-57; concert performances, Royal Albert Hall and Royal Festival Hall, 1958-60. *Guest appearances include:* Turkish Nat. Ballet, 1957; Bolshoi Ballet, Kirov Ballet,

1960; Munich Ballet, 1963; Nat. Finnish Ballet, Royal Danish Ballet, 1964; Stuttgart Ballet, 1965; Ballet Theatre, Opera House Chicago, 1967; Royal Command Variety Performances, 1963-66. Mounted, dir. and prod three Charity Gala performances, London Palladium, 1969, 1971, 1972. Many TV appearances, UK and USA. Hon. Consultant on Ballet, Ohio Univ., 1967-69. Fellow, 1959, Patron, 1964, Cecchetti Soc. Mem. Council, RSPCA, 1969-74. *Publications:* contrib: La Fille Mal Gardée, 1960; Ballet and Modern Dance, 1974; *relevant publication:* Ballerina, ed Clement Crisp, 1975. *Address:* c/o Royal Opera House, Covent Garden, WC2.

NERVI, Pier Luigi; Structural engineer, Italy; Partner of and consultant adviser to Nervi & Bartoli, Engineers, since 1932; *b* 21 June 1891; *s* of late Antonio and Luisa Bartoli; *m* 1924, Irene Calosi; four *s. Educ:* Univ. of Bologna (Degree in Civil Engineering). Engineer, Società per Costruzione Cementizie, Bologna, 1913-15, and 1918-23; Officer, Engineering Corps, 1915-18; Partner, Nervi & Nebbiosi, Engineers, 1923-32. Prof. of Technology and Technique of Construction, Faculty of Architecture, Rome, 1947-61; Charles E. Norton Prof., Harvard, 1961-62. Life Mem., Internat. Inst. Arts and Letters, Zürich, 1961; Hon. Member: Amer. Acad.-Inst. of Arts and Letters, 1957; Amer. Acad. Arts and Sciences, 1960; Foreign Mem., Royal Acad. of Fine Arts, Stockholm, 1957; Corresponding Member: Academia Nacionale de Ciencias Exactas Fisicas y Naturales, Buenos Aires, 1959; Bayrische Akademie der Schönen Künste, 1960; Accademico Nazionale, and Accad. di San Luca, Roma, 1960; Special Mem., Architectural Section, Academy of Arts of Berlin, 1964. Holds Hon. Degrees at Universities of Buenos Aires, 1950, Edinburgh, 1960, Warsaw, 1961, Harvard, 1962, at Technische Hochschule, München, 1960, and at Dartmouth Coll., 1962, Univ. of London, 1969. Hon. FAIA 1956; Hon. RA (London), 1967. Alfred Lindau Award, Amer. Concrete Inst., 1963; E. Mörsch Award, Deutsche Beton Verein, 1963; Feltrinelli Award, Rome, 1968. Frank P. Brown Medal, 1957; Royal Gold Medal for Architecture, 1960; Gold Medal: AIA, 1964; IStructE, 1968. Cavaliere di Gran Croce al Merito della Repubblica Italiana; Cavaliere al Merito del Lavoro, Rome, 1962. *Publications:* Arte o scienza del costruire, 1945; El linguaje arquitectonico (Buenos Aires), 1952; Costruire correttamente, 1954; New Structures, 1963; Aesthetics and Technology in Building, 1965; various articles on architecture in Italian, French, English and American technical journals. *Recreation:* sailing. *Address:* Lungo Tevere Arnaldo da Brescia 9, Rome, Italy. *T:* 350292. *Club:* Rotary (Rome).

NESBITT, Cathleen; actress; *b* 24 Nov. 1888; *d* of Captain T. Nesbitt, RN, and Mary Catherine Parry; *m* 1921, Captain C. B. Ramage, *qv*; one *s* one *d. Educ:* Belfast; Lisieux; Paris. 1st London appearance as Perdita in Granville Barker's production of The Winter's Tale, 1912; subsequently played lead in Quality Street, Justice, Hassan, Spring Cleaning, The Case of the Frightened Lady, Children in Uniform, Our Betters, Medea, The Uninvited Guest, and Goneril in Granville Barker's all star production of Lear, 1940. Later appearances in: The Cocktail Party; Gigi (New York); Sabrina Fair (New York and London); My Fair Lady (New York); The Sleeping Prince, NY; Anastasia, NY, etc. *Films:* An Affair to Remember, So Long At The Fair, Three Coins in the Fountain, Separate Tables, The French Connection II, Hitchcock's Family Plot, etc. TV series in Hollywood. *Publication:* A Little Love and Good Company (autobiog.), 1974. *Address:* c/o ICM, 22 Grafton Street, W1X 3LD.

NESS, Air Vice-Marshal Charles Ernest, CBE 1967 (OBE 1959); Director General, Personnel Management (RAF), since 1976; *s* of late Charles W. Ness and Jessica Ness; *m* 1951, Audrey, *d* of late Roy and Phyllis Parker; one *s. Educ:* George Heriot's Sch.; Edinburgh Univ. MBIM, MIPM. Joined RAF, 1943; Commander, British Skybolt Trials Force, Florida, 1962-63; Station Commander, Royal Air Force, Steamer Point, Aden, 1965-67; Air Comdr, Gibraltar, 1971-73; Director of Organisation and Administrative Plans (RAF), MoD, 1974-75; Comdr, Southern Maritime Air Region, 1975-76. *Address:* Cottingham Lodge, Loosley Row, Aylesbury, Bucks HP17 0NY. *T:* Princes Risborough 4652. *Club:* Royal Air Force.

NETHERTHORPE, 1st Baron, *cr* 1959; **James Turner;** Kt 1949; Director: Fisons Ltd (Chairman 1962-73); Lloyds Bank Ltd; Abbey National Building Society; Steetley Co. Ltd; Film Development and Research Ltd; Unigate (Vice-Chairman, since 1976); J. H. Fenner & Co. (Holdings) Ltd; The National Bank of New Zealand Ltd; *b* 6 Jan. 1908; *s* of late Albert Edward Mann Turner, Anston, Sheffield, and Lucy, *d* of Henry Helliwell; *m* 1935, Margaret Lucy, *d* of James Arthur Mattock; three *s* (and one *s* decd). *Educ:* Knaresborough; Leeds University. BSc

Leeds, 1928. Chairman of Notts County Branch, NFU, 1937; Notts Council Deleg., NFU, 1943; Vice-Pres., NFU, 1944; Pres., NFU, 1945-60. Pres. Internat. Fedn of Agricultural Producers, 1946-48; Member: Brit. Productivity Council (Chm., 1963); Commn of Inquiry into Industrial Representation, 1971-72; NEDC, 1971-75; Pay Bd, 1974; Animal Health Trust; Council, Royal Assoc. of British Dairy Farmers (Pres. 1964); Council Royal Agricultural Society of England (Pres. 1965); Liveryman of Painter-Stainers Co. and of Farmers Co. LLD (Hon.), Leeds, 1952; LLD (Hon.) Birmingham, 1959. *Recreations:* shooting and golf. *Heir: s* Hon. James Andrew Turner, *qv. Address:* Hadley Hurst, Hadley Common, Barnet, Herts EN5 5QG. *Club:* Farmers'.

NEUBERGER, Albert, CBE 1964; PhD (London), MD (Würzburg); FRCP; FRS 1951; FRIC; Professor of Chemical Pathology, St Mary's Hospital, University of London, 1955-73, now Emeritus Professor; Physician-in-Chief (*Pro Tem.*), at Peter Bent Brigham Hospital, Boston, and Visiting Lecturer on Biological Chemistry, Harvard Univ., 1964; *b* 15 April 1908; *s* of late Max Neuberger and Bertha Neuberger; *m* 1943, Lilian Ida, *d* of late Edmond Dreyfus and of Marguerite Dreyfus, London; four *s* one *d. Educ:* Gymnasium, Würzburg; Univs of Würzburg and London. Beit Memorial Research Fellow, 1936-40; Research at the Biochemistry Department, Cambridge, 1939-42; Mem. of Scientific Staff, Medical Research Council, 1943; Adviser to GHQ, Delhi (Medical Directorate), 1945; Head of Biochemistry Dept, Nat. Inst. for Medical Research, 1950-55; Principal of the Wright Fleming Institute of Microbiology, 1958-62. Visiting Lectr on Medicine, Harvard Univ. 1960. Mem. of Editorial Bd Biochemical Jl, 1947-55, Chm., 1952-55; Associate Man. Editor, Biochimica et Biophysica Acta, 1968-. Member: MRC, 1962-66; Council of Scientific Policy, 1968-69; ARC, 1970-; Indep. Cttee on Smoking and Health, 1973-; Chm., Jt ARC/MRC Cttee on Food and Nutrition Res., 1971-73; Chairman: Governing Body, Lister Inst., 1971- (Mem., 1968-); Advisory Board, Beit Memorial Fellowships, 1967-73; Biochemical Soc., 1967-69 (Hon. Mem., Biochemical Soc., 1973). Pres., Assoc. of Clinical Biochemists, 1972-73. For. Hon. Mem., Amer. Acad. Arts and Sciences, 1972. FRCPath 1964; FRCP 1966. William Julius Mickle Fellowship of Univ. of London, 1946-47; Heberden Medal, 1959; Frederick Gowland Hopkins Medal, 1960; Kaplun Prize, 1973. Hon. LLD, Aberdeen, 1967; Hon. PhD, Jerusalem, 1968. *Publications:* papers in Biochemical Jl, Proceedings of Royal Society and other learned journals. *Address:* 37 Eton Court, Eton Avenue, NW3 3HJ. *T:* 01-586 5470; Department of Biochemistry, Charing Cross Hospital Medical School, Fulham Palace Road, W6 8RF. *Club:* Athenæum.

NEUBERT, Michael Jon; MP (C) Havering, Romford, since Feb. 1974; *b* 3 Sept. 1933; *s* of Frederick Henry and Mathilda Marie Louise Neubert; *m* 1959, Sally Felicity Bilger; one *s. Educ:* Queen Elizabeth's Sch., Barnet; Bromley Grammar Sch.; Royal Coll. of Music; Downing Coll., Cambridge. MA (Cantab) Modern and Medieval Langs. Travel consultant. Councillor, Borough of Bromley, 1960-63; London Borough of Bromley: Councillor, 1964-68; Alderman, 1968-74; Leader of the Council, 1967-70; Mayor, 1972-73. Prospective Parly Candidate (C), N Hammersmith, 1965; contested (C): N Hammersmith, Gen. Elec., 1966; Romford (Prosp. Cand., 1969), Gen. Elec., 1970. Chm., Bromley Conservative Assoc., 1968-69. *Publication:* Running Your Own Society, 1967. *Recreations:* music, literature, cinema, theatre, tennis, spectator sports. *Address:* 12 Greatwood, Chislehurst, Kent BR7 5HU. *T:* 01-467 0040. *Club:* Romford Conservative and Constitutional.

NEUMANN, Dr Bernhard Hermann, FACE 1970; FAA 1964; FRS 1959; Honorary Research Fellow, CSIRO Division of Mathematics and Statistics, since 1978; *b* Berlin-Charlottenburg, 15 Oct. 1909; *s* of late Richard Neumann and late Else (*née* Aronstein); *m* 1st, 1938, Hanna Neumann (*née* von Caemmerer) (*d* 1971), DPhil, DSc, FAA, formerly Prof. and Head of Dept of Pure Mathematics, Sch. of Gen. Studies, ANU; three *s* two *d* ; 2nd, 1973, Dorothea Neumann (*née* Zeim). *Educ:* Herderschule, Berlin; Univs of Freiburg, Berlin, Cambridge. Dr phil Berlin, 1932; PhD Cambridge 1935; DSc Manchester 1954. Asst Lectr, University Coll, Cardiff, 1937-40. Army Service, 1940-45. Lectr, University Coll., Hull, 1946-48; Lectr, Senior Lectr, Reader, Univ. of Manchester, 1948-61; Prof. and Hd of Dept of Maths, Inst. of Advanced Studies, ANU, Canberra, 1962-74, Emeritus Prof., 1975-; Sen. Res. Fellow, CSIRO Div. of Maths and Stats, 1975-77. Visiting Lecturer: Australian Univs, 1959; Univ. of Cambridge, 1970; Visiting Professor: Tata Inst. of Fundamental Research, Bombay, 1959; New York Univ., 1961-62; Univ. of Wisconsin, 1966-67; Vanderbilt Univ., 1969-70; G. A. Miller Vis. Prof., Univ. of Illinois at Urbana-Champaign, 1975; Vis. Fellow, Fitzwilliam

Coll., Cambridge, 1970. Adams Prize, Univ. of Cambridge, 1952-53. Chm., Aust. Subcommn, Internat. Commn Math. Instruct., 1967-75; Mem.-at-large, Internat. Commn Math. Instruct., 1975-; Mem. Programme Adv. Cttee, Congress Math. Educn, Karlsruhe, 1976. Member Council: London Math. Society, 1954-61 (Vice-Pres., 1957-59); Aust. Math. Society, 1963- (Vice-Pres., 1963-64, 1966-68, 1971-73, Pres., 1964-66); Aust. Acad. of Science, 1968-71 (a Vice-Pres., 1969-71). Mem. Aust. Nat. Cttee for Mathematics, 1963-75 (Chm., 1966-75); (Foundation) Pres., Aust. Assoc. Math. Teachers, 1966-68, Vice-Pres., 1968-69, Hon. Mem., 1975-; (Foundn) Pres., Canberra Math. Assoc., 1963-65, Vice-Pres., 1965-66, Hon. Mem., 1975-; Hon. Mem., NZ Math. Soc., 1975-. Hon. DSc, Univ. of Newcastle, NSW, 1974; Hon. Fellow, Dept of Maths, Inst. of Advanced Studies, ANU, 1975-79. Hon. Editor, Proc. London Math. Soc., 1959-61; Assoc. Editor, Pacific Jl Math., 1964-; (Foundation) Editor, Bulletin of Aust. Math. Soc., 1969-; Member Editorial Board: Communications in Algebra, 1973-; Houston Math. Jl, 1974-; Indian Jl Math. Educn, 1974-; Mem., Adv. Bd, Zentralblatt Didaktik Math. 1970-; Founder Editor and Publisher, IMU Canberra Circular, 1972-. *Publications:* Appendix to German and Hungarian translations of A. G. Kuroš: Teoriya Grupp, 1953, 1955: Topics in the Theory of Infinite Groups, Bombay, 1961; Special Topics in Algebra, Vol. I: Universal Algebra, Vol. II: Order Techniques, New York, 1962; papers, mainly on theory of groups, in various mathematical journals. *Recreations:* chess, cycling, music. *Address:* 20 Talbot Street, Forrest, ACT 2603, Australia. *T:* (062) Canberra 733447.

NEVILE, Henry Nicholas; Lord-Lieutenant of Lincolnshire, since 1976; *b* 1920; *s* of Charles Joseph Nevile, Wellingore, Lincoln; *m* 1944, Jean Rosita Mary, *d* of Cyril James Wenceslas Torr; two *s* three *d. Educ:* Ampleforth; Trinity Coll., Cambridge. Served war, Scots Guards, in France and Germany, 1940-46. JP 1950, DL 1962, Lincs; High Sheriff of Lincolnshire, 1963. *Address:* Aubourn Hall, Lincoln. *T:* Bassingham 224.

NEVILL, family name of **Marquess of Abergavenny.**

NEVILL, Air Vice-Marshal Sir Arthur de Terrotte, KBE 1950 (CBE 1941); CB 1946; CEng; FRAeS; engaged in research administration, University Grants Committee; Director of Civil Aviation, New Zealand, 1956-65, retired; Royal New Zealand Air Force; *b* 29 April 1899; *s* of late H. G. Nevill; *m* 1927, Mary Seton, *d* of E. T. Norris; two *d. Educ:* Auckland Grammar School; Royal Military College, Duntroon. BSc 1921; MSc 1952. Chief of Air Staff, NZ, 1946-51; Member Air Licensing Authority, 1952; Deputy Director of Civil Aviation, New Zealand, 1952-56, Director, 1956-65. President NZ Div., RAeS, 1949-52. Member: NZ Univ. Grants Cttee, 1955-68 (Dep.-Chm., 1961-68); Research and Scholarships Cttee, UGC; US Educational Foundation in NZ, 1958-70; NZ Architects Educn and Registration Board, 1964-; President: Air Force Association, 1967-72; Air Cadet League, 1972-76. Hon. D Waikato Univ., 1969. Legion of Merit (USA). *Address:* 29 Moana Road, Kelburn, Wellington 5, New Zealand. *Club:* United Services (Wellington).

NEVILL, Maj.-Gen. Cosmo Alexander Richard, CB 1958; CBE 1954; DSO 1944; War Office, 1958-60; Colonel, Royal Fusiliers, 1959-63, retired; *b* 14 July 1907; *s* of late Maj. Cosmo Charles Richard Nevill, DSO, OBE, Eccleston, Leamington Spa; *m* 1934, Grania, *d* of late Maj. G. V. Goodliffe, MC, Birdstown, co. Donegal; one *s* one *d. Educ:* Harrow; Royal Military College. Commissioned as Second Lieutenant, Royal Fusiliers, 1927; served War of 1939-45 (DSO, OBE): on staff, India; commanded 2nd battalion Devonshire Regiment, Normandy; Lieutenant-Colonel, 1944. A General Staff Officer, Military Staff Committee, United Nations, New York, 1946-48; commanded 1st battalion Royal Fusiliers, 1950-51; temporary Brigadier, 1951; a Brigade Commander, 1951-54; Commandant School of Infantry, 1954-56; Major-General 1957; GOC 2nd Infantry Division, 1956-58. CC West Suffolk, 1962. *Address:* Holt, Edwardstone, Boxford, Suffolk. *T:* Boxford 210428. *Club:* Army and Navy.

NEVILL, Lord Rupert Charles Montacute, JP; DL; Member of London Stock Exchange; Treasurer, since 1970, and Private Secretary, since 1976, to the Duke of Edinburgh; *b* 29 Jan. 1923; 2nd *s* of 4th Marquess and *b* and *heir-pres* of 5th Marquess of Abergavenny, *qv* ; *m* 1944, Lady Anne Camilla Eveline Wallop, *e d* of 9th Earl of Portsmouth, *qv* ; two *s* two *d. Educ:* Eton. JP 1953, DL 1960, Sussex; High Sheriff of Sussex, 1952-53. Captain, Life Guards, ADC to Lt-Gen. Sir Brian Horrocks, 1945-47. Director: Sun Life Assurance Society (a Vice-Chm., 1971-); Owners of Middlesbrough Estates Co.; Australian Estates, 1968-75; Household and General Insurance Co. Ltd,

1965-72; Kent & Sussex Courier, 1974-. President: S Eastern Area Building Socs, 1960-72; S Eastern Area Trustee Savings Bank, 1964-72; Vice-Pres., London and SE Trustee Savings Bank, 1972-; Vice-Pres., Building Societies Assoc., 1960. Pres. Metropolitan Union of YMCAs, 1956-71; Mem., World Council of YMCAs, 1956; Pres., Nat. Council of YMCAs, 1966-; Pres., British Olympic Assoc., 1977- (Chm., 1966-77); Vice-Chm., Nat. Playing Fields Assoc., 1963-; Chairman: Invalid Children's Aid Assoc., 1969-; Sussex Army Cadets, 1951-68; Greater London and SE Regional Sports Council, 1969-; Greater London and SE Regional Council for Sport and Recreation, 1976-77; Mem., Sports Council, 1971-; Pres., BSJA, 1973-75; Vice-Pres., Sussex Boy Scouts, 1950-74, Pres., E Sussex Boy Scouts, 1974-; Vice-Pres., Sussex Boys' Clubs; Pres., Sussex St John Ambulance Cadets, 1952-61; Commander, Sussex St John Ambulance Bde, 1969-77 (Pres. 1961-69); Mem., Sussex St John's Council, 1952, Chm., 1966-. Member: E Sussex CC, 1954-67; Uckfield RDC, 1949-67. KStJ 1972. *Address:* Horsted Place, Uckfield, East Sussex. *T:* Isfield 315; 30B St James's Palace, SW1. *T:* 01-839 7206. *Clubs:* White's, Bucks, Beefsteak.

NEVILL, Rev. Thomas Seymour, FRSA; Part-time Chaplain, Royal Masonic Hospital, since 1973; *b* 30 Oct. 1901; *s* of late T. G. Nevill, FSA and late Mrs Nevill; *m* 1966, Muriel Pite (*née* Tasker), *widow* of A. G. Pite. *Educ:* Dover Coll.; Jesus Coll., Cambridge. Westcott House, Cambridge, 1956. BA, 1923; MA, 1926; 2nd Class Honours Mod. and Med. Languages Tripos and Historical Tripos; Asst Masterships at Llandovery Coll., Dover Coll. and Weymouth Coll.; Assoc. Member of Headmasters' Conference; Welsh Hockey XI, 1927, 1929 and 1930; Schools' Secretary of Student Christian Movement, 1934-37; Headmaster of Wellingborough School, 1940-56. Ordained Deacon, 1956; Priest, 1957. Curate at Fareham Parish Church, 1956-58; Charterhouse Missioner in Southwark, 1958-62; Master of Charterhouse, 1962-73; Speaker's Chaplain, 1969-72. Pres., Sion College, 1967-68. *Recreations:* rock-climbing and photography. *Address:* 12 Cowper Road, Hanwell, W7 1EH. *Club:* Hawks (Cambridge).

NEVILLE, family name of **Baron Braybrooke.**

NEVILLE, Prof. Adam Matthew, MC 1944; TD 1963; Head of Department of Civil Engineering, University of Leeds, since 1968; *b* 5 Feb. 1923; *m* 1952, Mary Hallam Cousins; one *s* one *d.* BSc 1st cl. Hons, MSc, PhD, DSc (Eng) London; FICE, FIStructE, FIHE, FAmSCE, MSocCE (France); FIArb. Lectr, Southampton Univ., 1950-51; Engr, Min. of Works, NZ, 1951-54; Lectr, Manchester Univ., 1955-60; Prof. of Civil Engrg, Nigerian Coll. of Technology, 1960-62; Dean of Engrg, Calgary Univ., 1963-67, also Dean of Graduate Studies, 1965-66; Vis. Prof., Swiss Federal Inst. of Technology, 1967-68. Consultant on concrete and structural failures. Chairman: Commn of European Concrete Cttee; CGLI Cttee; former Chm., Permanent Concrete Commn, RILEM (Internat. Union of Testing and Res. Labs for Materials and Structures); Mem., BSI and Govt Cttees; Mem., Exec. Cttee, British Gp, Internat Assoc. for Bridge and Structural Engineering; Dir, Petroleum Recovery Res. Inst. Advr to Canadian Govt on management of concrete research. Member Council: Concrete Soc., 1968-77, Pres., 1974-75; IStructE, 1976; Faculty of Building, 1976. Mem. Editorial Boards: Magazine of Concrete Research; Internat. Jl Mechanical Sciences; Jl Cement and Concrete Research; Leeds Review. Fellow, Amer. Concrete Inst., 1973; Hon. Fellow, Assoc. of Concrete Technologists, 1976; For. Mem., Académie Royale des Sciences d'Outre-Mer, Belgium, 1974. Queen Mary Coll. Prize, 1950; Univ. of London Postgraduate Scholarship, 1950; NZ Instn of Engineers Prize, 1952; IStructE Research Award, 1960; Reinforced Concrete Assoc. Medal, 1961; Senior Research Fellowship, Nat. Research Council of Cananda, 1967. Stanton Walker Award (US) 1968; IStructE (Yorkshire) Prize, 1970; Medal of Univ. of Liège (Belgium), 1970; Arthur R. Anderson Award, Amer. Concrete Inst., 1972; Lectures: C. L. Robertson Meml, Rhodesian Instn of Engrs, 1972; George Hondros Meml, W Australia, 1973. *Publications:* Properties of Concrete, 1963; (with J. B. Kennedy) Basic Statistical Methods, 1964; (ed) Symposium on Creep of Concrete, 1964; (ed) Bibliography on Creep of Concrete, vol. I, 1967, vol II, 1972; Creep of Concrete: plain, reinforced and prestressed, 1970; (with A. Ghali) Structural Analysis: a unified classical and matrix approach, 1971; Hardened Concrete: physical and mechanical aspects, 1971; chapter in Reinforced Concrete Engineering, 1974; High Alumina Cement Concrete, 1975; (ed) series of books on structural design and materials, 1975; (ed) Fibre-reinforced Cement and Concrete, 1975; numerous research papers on concrete and concrete structures. *Recreations:* ski-ing, travel. *Address:* Spring House, Spring Hill, Tile Lane, Adel, Leeds LS16 8EA; Fluage Deux, Les Marecottes, Valais, Switzerland; Creep Three, 31 Archbishops Place, SW2. *Club:* Athenæum.

NEVILLE, (Eric) Graham; a Recorder of the Crown Court, since 1975; *b* 12 Nov. 1933; *s* of late Frederick Thomas Neville and Doris Winifred (*née* Toye); *m* 1966, Jacqueline Catherine, *d* of late Major Francis Whalley and Alexandrina Whalley (*née* MacLeod). *Educ:* Kelly Coll.; Sidney Sussex Coll., Cambridge. Served Royal Air Force. Called to Bar, Middle Temple, 1958. *Recreations:* sailing, fishing. *Address:* 4 Pump Court, Temple, EC4Y 7AN. *T:* 01-353 2656; Trillow House, Nadderwater, Exeter EX4 2LD. *T:* Exeter 54403. *Clubs:* Exeter and County (Exeter); Royal Western Yacht (Plymouth); Brixham Yacht (Brixham).

NEVILLE, Lt-Col Sir (James) Edmund (Henderson), 2nd Bt, *cr* 1927; MC 1918; *b* 5 July 1897; *er s* of Sir Reginald James Neville Neville, 1st Bt and Ida (*d* 1913), 4th *d* of Lt-Col Sir Edmund Y. W. Henderson, KCB, RE; *S* father 1950; *m* 1932, Marie Louise *o d* of C. E. Pierson, Flesk, Burnham, Somerset; two *d. Educ:* Eton; RMC Sandhurst. Served European War, 1914-19 (wounded, MC); joined 52nd Light Infantry, 1916; with 43rd Light Infantry to North Russia, 1919 (wounded); captain and adjutant, 1923; Regular Reserve of Officers, 1925; served in 12th London Regt (Rangers), 1931-36; Major; Master Worshipful Company of Bowyers, 1936-38; War of 1939-45, recalled, Aug. 1939; in command Light Infantry Training Centre, 1941-44; trooping, 1945-46; retd as Lt-Col, July 1946. Prime Warden, Fishmongers' Co., 1958. *Publication:* History of 43rd Light Infantry, 1914-19. *Heir:* half-b Richard Lionel John Baines Neville [*b* July 1921. *Educ:* Eton; Trinity College, Cambridge (MA). Served Burma, 1943-45, as Captain Oxford and Bucks LI, and West African Frontier Force]. *Address:* Sloley Old Hall, Norwich, NR12 8HA. *T:* Swanton Abbott 232. *Clubs:* Army and Navy, Greenjackets, Light Infantry.

NEVILLE, John, OBE 1965; actor, stage and film; Hon. Professor in Drama, Nottingham University, since 1967; Artistic Director: Citadel Theatre, Edmonton, Canada, 1973-78; Neptune Theatre, Halifax, Nova Scotia, from May 1978; *b* Willesden, 2 May 1925; *s* of Reginald Daniel Neville and Mabel Lillian (*née* Fry); *m* 1949, Caroline Hooper; three *s* three *d. Educ:* Willesden and Chiswick County Schools; Royal Academy of Dramatic Art. Worked as a stores clerk before studying at RADA. First appearance on stage, walking-on part in Richard II; subseq. parts at Open Air Theatre, in repertory at Lowestoft, and with Birmingham Repertory Co.; Bristol Old Vic Co., 1950-53; Old Vic Co., London, 1953-61; Nottingham Playhouse, 1961-63; Theatre Director, Nottingham Playhouse, 1963-68; Dir, Park Theatre Co., Fortune, 1969. Parts with Old Vic include: Ferdinand in The Tempest, Macduff, Richard II, Orlando in As You Like It, Henry Percy in Henry IV, Part I, Mark Antony; during Old Vic tour of Europe, 1958, Hamlet, Sir Andrew Aguecheek. Played lead in Irma La Douce, Lyric, 1959-60; produced Henry V, Old Vic, 1960; The Lady From the Sea, Queen's, 1961; The School for Scandal, Haymarket, 1962; Alfie, Mermaid and Duchess, 1963. Acted in: The Chichester Festival Theatre, 1962; Beware of the Dog, St Martin's, 1967; Iago in Othello, Nottingham Playhouse, 1967; Mr and Mrs, Palace, 1968; The Apple Cart, Mermaid, 1970; The Beggar's Opera, The Doctor's Dilemma, Chichester, 1972; Sherlock Holmes, NY, 1975; Happy Days, Nat. Theatre, 1977. Tour W Africa (Jt Dir and acting), 1963. *Films:* Oscar Wilde; Topaze; Billy Budd; A Study in Terror. Has appeared on television, incl. The First Churchills, series for BBC 2. *Address:* c/o Larry Dalzell Associates, 3 Goodwin's Court, St Martin's Lane, WC2.

NEVILLE, Maj.-Gen. Sir Robert Arthur Ross, KCMG 1952; CBE 1948; late RM; *b* 17 Dec. 1896; *s* of late Col William Neville, DSO, Cheshire Regt; *m* 1943, Doris Marie (*d* 1977), *y d* of late Capt. Philip Collen, 14th Sikh Regiment; one *s* one *d. Educ:* Cheltenham College. Joined Royal Marines, 1914, served European War, 1914-18, Grand Fleet and France (despatches); Lt-Col, 1940; served War of 1939-45, Admlty, as Asst Dir of Naval Intelligence, Combined Ops, and in Mediterranean; Colonel, 1945; ADC to the King, 1946-48; Maj.-Gen., 1948. Governor and C-in-C, Bahamas, 1950-Dec. 1953. *Address:* Oak Hanger, Reeds Lane, Liss, Hants. *T:* Liss 3325. *Club:* White's.

NEVILLE, Royce Robert; Agent-General for Tasmania, in London, 1971-78; Governing Director, Neville Constructions Pty Ltd, Burnie; *b* 5 Oct. 1914; *s* of R. P. Neville, Launceston, Tasmania; *m* 1941, Joan, *d* of G. A. Scott; two *s* two *d. Educ:* Launceston Technical Coll. Served War, Sqdn Ldr (OC Flying, Chief Flying Instr, Gen Reconnaissance Sqdn), RAAF, 1941-45. OC Air Trg Corps, Burnie, 1947. Past President: Air Force Assoc., 1947; Tas. Apex, 1948; Tas. Master Builders' Assoc., 1965-67; Master Builders' Fedn of Aust., 1965-66; Pres. Fedn of Emigrants and Families Assoc. of the Commonwealth, 1971; Comr of Oaths for Tasmania, 1971; Liaison Officer in London for Federal Council of Aust. Air Force Assoc., 1971; Rep. on

Central Council for Disabled, London, 1971; Member: Baltic Exchange, London; Australia Soc., London; Aust. Musical Assoc., London; Commonwealth Producers' Org., London (Vice-Pres.); Council, Rotary Club of London; Inst. of Directors, London; Royal Commonwealth Soc.; Royal Over-Seas League; Council, Victoria League for Commonwealth Friendship, 1974-; Council, British Australian Soc., 1973-; Life Mem., Tasmanian Master Builders' Assoc. FInstD, FRAIB, AFAIM, Fellow, Inst. of Dirs, Aust., 1971; MIEx 1973; FFB 1976. Freeman, City of London, 1975; Freeman, Guild of Air Pilots and Air Navigators, 1976. JP 1974. *Recreations:* boating, fishing, water skiing, painting, tennis. *Address: c/o* The ANZ Bank, 73 Wilson Street, Burnie, Tasmania 7320, Australia. *Clubs:* Naval and Military, Royal Automobile, No 10, Wig and Pen, Royal Air Force (all in London); Naval, Military and Air Force (Hobart); Royal Yacht Club of Tasmania.

NEVIN, Robert Wallace, TD 1948; FRCS; Consulting Surgeon: St Thomas' Hospital; Treloar's Hospital, Alton, Hants; Chief Surgeon to the Metropolitan Police since 1957; *b* Burton-on-Trent, Nov. 1907; *s* of Robert Nevin, medical practitioner, and Florence, *d* of Joseph Chamberlain, Burton-on-Trent; *m* 1947, Rosalind Audrey Leeson, *d* of late Rt Rev. Spencer Leeson, DD, Bishop of Peterborough, 1949-56; one *s* two *d. Educ:* Clifton; Emmanuel College, Cambridge. BA (Nat. Scis tripos) Cantab, 1929; MB, BChir Cantab, 1932; MRCS, LRCP 1932; FRCS 1933; MA Cantab 1933. Teacher of Surgery in Univ. of London, 1949; Dean, St Thomas's Hosp. Med. Sch., 1957-68; Member: Bd of Governors, St Thomas' Hosp., 1955-70; Senate, Univ. of London, 1966-69. Examiner in Surgery, Universities of Cambridge, London, Glasgow, Oxford; Mem. Ct of Examrs, RCS; Hunterian Professor Royal College of Surgeons, 1947; Col RAMC (TA), 1947. *Publications:* numerous papers in medical and surgical jls. *Recreations:* gardening, fishing. *Address:* The Old Forge, Greywell, Basingstoke, Hants. *T:* Odiham 2217. *Club:* Athenæum.

NEVIN, Samuel, FRCP; retired as Physician, Maida Vale Hospital, and Neurologist, King's College Hospital; *s* of Samuel Nevin, District Inspector, Royal Ulster Constabulary; *m* 1950, Margaret Esch; one *s* one *d. Educ:* Methodist College, Belfast, Queen's Univ., Belfast. BSc (1st Cl. Hons) 1929; MB, BCh, BAO (1st Cl. Hons) Belfast 1927; MD (Gold Medal) 1930; MRCP 1934; FRCP 1941. Formerly: House Physician, National Hospital, Queen Square; Director Research Laboratory, Inst. Psych., Maudsley Hosp.; Prof. Mental Pathology, Univ. of London. Hon. Lt-Col RAMC. *Publications:* contributions to medical journals. *Address:* 17 Malmains Way, Beckenham, Kent.

NEVIN, Thomas Richard, TD 1949 (and Bar), LLB; JP; **His Honour Judge Nevin;** a Circuit Judge and Crown Court Liaison Judge (formerly Judge of County Courts), since 1967; Member, County Courts Rule Committee, since 1974; *b* 9 Dec. 1916; *e s* of late Thomas Nevin, JP, and Phyllis (*née* Strickland), Ebchester Hall and Mirfield; *m* 1955, Brenda Micaela, *e d* of Dr B. C. Andrade-Thompson, MC, Scarborough; one *s* (and one *s* decd). *Educ:* Bilton Grange; Shrewsbury School; Leeds University. LLB 1939. 2nd Lt, W Yorks Regt (Leeds Rifles) TA, 1935. Served London Bombardment, India and Burma, 1939-46; Indian Artillery, Lt-Col 1944 (despatches), SEAC; DJAG, XII Army, 1945. Major, TARO, 1951. WR Special Constab., 1938-66. Articled Clerk to Sir A. M. Ramsden, CB, Solicitor, 1935. Called to Bar, Inner Temple, 1948; practised 19 years on NE Circuit; Law Lectr, Leeds Coll. of Commerce, 1949-51; Asst Recorder of Leeds, 1961-64; Recorder of Doncaster, 1964-67; Dep. Chm., Quarter Sessions: W Riding, 1965-71; E Riding, 1968-71, Yorkshire. Chm., Northern Agricultural Land Tribunal, 1963-67 (Dep. Chm. 1961-63); a special Divorce Comr, 1967-72; a Deputy High Court Judge, 1974-. Director, Bowishott Estates Ltd; Member: Leeds Gp Hospital Management Cttee, 1965-67; Thoresby Soc.; Yorks Archæological Soc.; President, Yorks Numismatic Soc., 1968; Life Member: Guild of Freemen of London; British Numismatic Soc.; Vice-Pres. Leeds Univ. Law Graduates; Associate OStB Nashdom Abbey. FRNS; FRSA; FRGS; Fellow, Inst. of Arbitrators. Freeman of City of London. JP West Yorks 1965-. *Publications:* Hon. Editor, Yorkshire Numismatic Soc.; and various articles. *Recreations:* coinage, our past, gardening, and rest therefrom. *Address:* Rawdon Hall, Rawdon, Yorks; Wooley Park, Allendale; Coomboots, Scalby, Yorks; 11 King's Bench Walk, Temple, EC4. *T:* 01-236 3337.

NEW WESTMINSTER, Archbishop of, since 1975; **Most Rev. Thomas David Somerville;** Metropolitan of Ecclesiastical Province of British Columbia; *b* 11 Nov. 1915; *s* of Thomas Alexander Somerville and Martha Stephenson Scott; unmarried. *Educ:* King George High Sch., Vancouver; Univ. of British

Columbia (BA 1937); Anglican Theological Coll. of BC (LTh 1939, BD 1951). Deacon, 1939; priest, 1940; Incumbent of: Princeton, 1940-44; Sardis with Rosedale, 1944-49; Curate of St. James, Vancouver, 1949-52, Rector, 1952-60; Chapter Canon, Dio. of New Westminster, 1957; Dean of Residence, Anglican Theological Coll. of BC, 1960-65; Gen. Sec., Gen. Bd of Religious Education, Anglican Church of Canada, 1965-66; Director of Planning and Research, Anglican Church of Canada, 1966-69; Coadjutor Bishop of New Westminster, 1969-71; Bishop of New Westminster, 1971. Hon. DD Anglican Theol. Coll. of BC, 1969. *Recreations:* music, botany. *Address:* 692 Burrard Street, Vancouver V6C 2L1, Canada. *T:* 684 6306.

NEW ZEALAND, Primate and Archbishop of, since 1972; Bishop of Waikato since 1969; **Most Rev. Allen Howard Johnston,** LTh; *b* Auckland, NZ, 1912; *s* of Joseph Howard Johnston; *m* 1937, Joyce Rhoda, *d* of John A. Grantley, Auckland; four *d. Educ:* Seddon Memorial Technical College; St John's College, Auckland; Auckland Univ. College. Deacon, 1935; Priest, 1936. Assistant Curate of St Mark's, Remuera, 1935-37; Vicar of Dargaville, 1937-42; Vicar of Northern Wairoa, 1942-44; Vicar of Otahuhu, 1944-49; Vicar of Whangarei, 1949-53; Archdeacon of Waimate, 1949-53; Bishop of Dunedin, 1953-69. Fellow, St John's Coll., Auckland, 1970. Hon. LLD Otago, 1969. ChStJ 1974. *Address:* Bishop's House, 322 Cobham Drive, Hamilton, Waikato, NZ.

NEWALL, family name of **Baron Newall.**

NEWALL, 2nd Baron, *cr* 1946; **Francis Storer Eaton Newall;** company director; Chairman of several companies; *b* 23 June 1930; *o s* of 1st Baron (Marshal of the RAF Lord) Newall, GCB, OM, GCMG, CBE, AM; *S* father, 1963; *m* 1956, Pamela Elizabeth, *e d* of E. H. L. Rowcliffe, Pinkney Park, Malmesbury, Wilts; two *s* one *d. Educ:* Eton College; RMA Sandhurst. Commissioned into 11th Hussars (Prince Albert's Own), 1950; served in: Germany, 1950-53; Malaya, 1953-55; on staff of GHQ FarELF, Singapore, 1955-56; Adjt Royal Gloucestershire Hussars, 1956-58; retired 1961. Introduced Farriers Registration Bill in House of Lords and saw it into law. Cons. Whip and front bench spokesman, 1976-. *Recreations:* shooting, travel, meeting people. *Heir: s* Hon. Richard Hugh Eaton Newall, *b* 19 Feb. 1961. *Address:* 18 Lennox Gardens, SW1X 0DG; Wotton Underwood, near Aylesbury, Bucks. *Club:* Cavalry and Guards.

NEWARK, Archdeacon of; *see* Woodhams, Ven. Brian Watson.

NEWBIGGING, David Kennedy; Chairman and Managing Director, Jardine Matheson & Co. Ltd, Hong Kong, since 1975; Chairman: Hongkong Land Co. Ltd, City Hotels Ltd, Jardine Fleming & Co. Ltd, since 1975; Hongkong & Kowloon Wharf & Godown Co. Ltd, since 1970; Director, Hongkong & Shanghai Banking Corporation Ltd, since 1975; *b* 19 Jan. 1934; *s* of late David Locke Newbigging, CBE, MC, and Lucy Margaret; *m* 1968, Carolyn Susan (*née* Band); one *s* two *d. Educ:* in Canada; Oundle Sch., Northants. Joined Jardine, Matheson & Co. Ltd, 1954; Man. Dir, 1970. JP (unofficial) Hong Kong, 1971. *Recreations:* most outdoor sports; Chinese art. *Address:* Bangour, 35 Mount Kellett Road, The Peak, Hong Kong. *T:* 5-96334. *Clubs:* Hurlingham, Turf; Hongkong (Hong Kong).

NEWBIGIN, Rt. Rev. James Edward Lesslie, CBE 1974; DD; Lecturer in Theology, Selly Oak Colleges, Birmingham, since 1974; *b* 8 Dec. 1909; *s* of Edward Richmond Newbigin, Shipowner, Newcastle, and Annie Ellen Newbigin (*née* Affleck); *m* 1936, Helen Stewart, *d* of Rev. Robert Henderson; one *s* three *d. Educ:* Leighton Park Sch.; Queens' Coll., Cambridge; Westminster Coll., Cambridge. Intercollegiate Secretary, Student Christian Movement, Glasgow, 1931-33. Ordained by Presbytery of Edinburgh and appointed to Madras Mission of Church of Scotland, 1936; served as missionary in Chingleput and Kancheepuram, 1936-46; Bishop in Madura and Ramnad, Church of South India, 1947. Chairman, Advisory Cttee on Main Theme for Second Assembly, World Council of Churches, 1954; Vice-Chairman, Commission on Faith and Order, 1956; Chairman, International Missionary Council, 1958. Resigned from See of Madura, 1959. General Secretary, International Missionary Council, 1959; Associate General Secretary, World Council of Churches, 1959-65; Bishop in Madras, 1965-74. Moderator, Gen. Assembly of URC, 1978. Hon. DD: Chicago Theological Seminary, 1954; St Andrews Univ., 1958; Hamburg, 1960; Basel, 1965. *Publications:* Christian Freedom in the Modern World, 1937; The Reunion of the Church, 1948; South India Diary, 1951; The Household of God, 1953; Sin and Salvation, 1956; A Faith for This One World?, 1962; Honest Religion for Secular Man, 1966; The Finality of Christ, 1969; The Good Shepherd, 1977. *Recreations:* music, walking. *Address:* Selly Oak Colleges, Birmingham B29 GEL.

NEWBOLD, Sir Charles Demorée, KBE 1970; Kt 1966; CMG 1957; QC (Jamaica) 1947; President, Court of Appeal for East Africa, 1966-70; *b* 11 June 1909; *s* of late Charles Etches and Laura May Newbold; *m* 1936, Ruth, *d* of Arthur L. Vaughan; two *d*. *Educ:* The Lodge Sch., Barbados; Keble Coll., Oxford (BA). Called to Bar, Gray's Inn, 1931. Private practice at the Bar, Trinidad, 1931-35; joined Colonial Legal Service, 1936, as Principal Officer, Supreme Court Registry, Trinidad; Magistrate, Trinidad, 1937; Legal Draftsman, Jamaica, 1941; Solicitor-General Jamaica, 1943; Member of Commission of Enquiry into Land Taxation, Jamaica, 1942-43; represented Jamaica at Quarantine Conf. in Trinidad, 1943; at US Bases Conf. in Trinidad, 1944; at Washington, USA, for labour contracts, 1945; Actg Attorney-Gen., 1946; Legal Secretary, East Africa High Commn, 1948-61. Mem. of East Africa Central Legislative Assembly, 1948-61 (Chm. of Committee of Supply, 1948-61); Commissioner for Revision of High Commn Laws, 1951; Vice-Chm. Governing Council of Royal Technical Coll., 1954-59; Justice of Appeal, Court of Appeal for Eastern Africa, 1961-65; Vice-Pres., 1965-66. Star of Africa (Liberia). *Publications:* Joint Editor of Trinidad Law Reports, 1928-33; Editor of East African Tax Cases Reports, 1948-61. *Recreations:* cricket, tennis, croquet, reading. *Address:* Woodvale, Harpsden, Henley-on-Thames, Oxon.

NEWBOROUGH, 7th Baron, *cr* 1776; **Robert Charles Michael Vaughan Wynn**, Bt 1742; DSC 1942; *b* 24 April 1917; *er s* of 6th Baron Newborough, OBE, JP, DL, and Ruby Irene (*d* 1960), 3rd *d* of Edmund Wigley Severne, of Thenford, Northamptonshire and Wallop, Shropshire; *S* father, 1965; *m* 1st, 1945, Rosamund Lavington Barbour (marr. diss. 1971); one *s* two *d*; 2nd, 1971, Jennifer, *y d* of late Captain C. C. A. Allen, RN, and Lady Morgan. *Educ:* Oundle. Served as 2nd Lt, SR, 1935-39, with 9th Lancers, 5th Inniskilling Dragoon Guards, then as Lt with 16th/5th Lancers after 6 months attachment with Royal Dragoon Guards; invalided out of Army, 1940. Took command of vessel attached to Fleet Air Arm, 1940, as civilian, and took part in Dunkirk evacuation; then joined RNVR as Sub Lieut; later had command of MTB 74 and took part in St Nazaire raid, 1942 (wounded, despatches, DSC, POW, escaped 1944). High Sheriff of Merionethshire, 1963. *Recreation:* yachting. *Heir: s* Hon. Robert Vaughan Wynn, *b* 11 Aug. 1949. *Address:* Rhug, Corwen, Clwyd, North Wales. *T:* Corwen 2510. *Clubs:* Goat, Naval and Military; Bembridge Sailing.

NEWBURGH, 11th Earl of, *cr* 1660; **Don Giulio Cesare Taddeo Cosimo Maria Rospigliosi**; Viscount Kynnaird, Baron Levingston, 1660; 10th Prince Rospigliosi (Holy Roman Empire), 10th Duke of Zagarolo, 13th Prince of Castiglione, Marquis of Giuliana, Count of Chiusa, Baron of La Miraglia and Valcorrente, Lord of Aidione, Burgio, Contessa and Trappeto, and Conscript Roman Noble, Patrician of Venice, Genoa and Pistoia; *b* 26 Oct. 1907; *s* of Prince Giambattista Rospigliosi (*d* 1956) and Ethel (*d* 1924), *d* of Isaac Bronson; *S* cousin, 1977; *m* 1940, Donna Giulia, *d* of Don Guido Carlo dei Duchi Visconti di Mondrone, Count of Lonate Pozzolo; two *s*. *Educ:* Corpus Christi College, Cambridge (Engineering Tripos, MA). *Heir: s* Viscount Kynnaird, *qv*. *Address:* Via Corridoni 3, 20. 122 Milan, Italy.

NEWBY, (George) Eric, MC 1945; FRSL 1972; FRGS 1975; writer; Travel Editor, The Observer, and General Editor, Time Off Books, 1964-73; *b* 6 Dec. 1919; *o s* of George Arthur Newby and Hilda Pomeroy, London; *m* 1946, Wanda, *d* of Viktor Skof and Gisella Urdih, Trieste; one *s* one *d*. *Educ:* St Paul's School. With Dorland Advertising, London, 1936-38; apprentice and ord. seaman, 4-masted Finnish barque, Moshulu, 1938-39; served War of 1939-45, The Black Watch and Special Boat Service, POW 1942-45; Women's Fashion Business, 1946-56 (with Worth Paquin, 1955-56); explored in Nuristan and made unsuccessful attempt to climb Mir Samir, Afghan Hindu Kush, 1956; with Secker & Warburg, 1956-59; with John Lewis Partnership (Central Buyer, Model Dresses), 1959-63; descended Ganges with wife, 1963. Mem., Assoc. of Cape Horners. *Publications:* The Last Grain Race, 1956; A Short Walk in the Hindu Kush, 1958; Something Wholesale, 1962; Slowly Down the Ganges, 1966; Time Off in Southern Italy, 1966; Grain Race: Pictures of Life Before the Mast in a Windjammer, 1968; (jointly) The Wonders of Britain, 1968; (jointly) The Wonders of Ireland, 1969; Love and War in the Apennines, 1971; (jointly) The World of Evelyn Waugh, 1973; Ganga (with photographs by Raghubir Singh), 1973; World Atlas of Exploration, 1975; Great Ascents, 1977. *Recreations:* walking, running, cycling, gardening. *Address:* Pear Tree Court, Harbertonford, Totnes TQ9 7TA. *T:* Harbertonford 312. *Club:* Garrick.

NEWBY, (Percy) Howard, CBE 1972; novelist; Managing Director BBC Radio, since 1975; *b* 25 June 1918; *o s* of Percy Newby and Isabel Clutsam (*née* Bryant); *m* 1945, Joan Thompson; two *d*. *Educ:* Hanley Castle Grammar Sch., Worcester; St Paul's Coll., Cheltenham. Served War of 1939-45, RAMC, 1939-42; BEF, France, 1939-40; MEF, 1941-42; seconded as Lecturer in English Literature, Fouad 1st University, Cairo, 1942-46. Joined BBC, 1949; Controller: Third Programme, 1958-69; Radio Three, 1969-71; Dir of Programmes, Radio, 1971-75. Atlantic Award, 1946; Somerset Maugham Prize, 1948; Yorkshire Post Fiction Award, 1968; Booker Prize, 1969 (first recipient). *Publications:* A Journey to the Interior, 1945; Agents and Witnesses, 1947; The Spirit of Jem, 1947; Mariner Dances, 1948; The Snow Pasture, 1949; The Loot Runners, 1949; Maria Edgeworth, 1950; The Young May Moon, 1950; The Novel, 1945-50, 1951; A Season in England, 1951; A Step to Silence, 1952; The Retreat, 1953; The Picnic at Sakkara, 1955; Revolution and Roses, 1957; Ten Miles from Anywhere, 1958; A Guest and his Going, 1959; The Barbary Light, 1962; One of the Founders, 1965; Something to Answer For, 1968; A Lot to Ask, 1973; Kith, 1977. *Address:* Upton House, Cokes Lane, Chalfont St Giles, Buckinghamshire. *T:* Little Chalfont 2079. *Club:* Savile.

NEWCASTLE, 9th Duke of, *cr* 1756; **Henry Edward Hugh Pelham-Clinton-Hope**, OBE 1945; Earl of Lincoln, 1572; Wing Comdr, retd; *b* 8 April 1907; *o s* of 8th Duke and Olive Muriel (*d* 1912), *d* of George Horatio Thompson, banker, Melbourne, formerly wife of Richard Owen; *S* father 1941; *m* 1st, 1931, Jean (from whom he obtained a divorce 1940), *d* of D. Banks, Park Avenue, New York; 2nd, 1946, Lady Mary Diana Montagu-Stuart-Wortley (marr. diss., 1959), 2nd *d* of 3rd Earl of Wharncliffe; two *d*; 3rd, 1959, Mrs Sally Ann Wemyss Hope (Jamal), *d* of Brig. John Henry Anstice, DSO. *Educ:* Eton; Cambridge. Sqdn Ldr Comdg No 616 Sqdn, 1938-39; served War of 1939-45 in RAF at home and overseas. *Heir: cousin* Edward Charles Pelham-Clinton, *b* 18 Aug. 1920. *Address:* 5 Quay Hill, Lymington, Hants SO4 9AB.

NEWCASTLE, Bishop of, since 1973; **Rt. Rev. Ronald Oliver Bowlby**; *b* 16 August 1926; *s* of Oliver and Helena Bowlby; *m* 1956, Elizabeth Trevelyan Monro; three *s* two *d*. *Educ:* Trinity College, Oxford (MA); Westcott House, Cambridge. Curate of St Luke's, Pallion, Sunderland, 1952-56; Priest-in-charge and Vicar of St Aidan, Billingham, 1956-66; Vicar of Croydon, 1966-72. *Publication:* contrib. Church without Walls, ed Lindars, 1969. *Recreations:* hill-walking, music. *Address:* Bishop's House, 29 Moor Road South, Gosforth, Newcastle upon Tyne NE3 1PA.

NEWCASTLE, Provost of; *see* Spafford, Very Rev. C. G. H.

NEWDEGATE, Francis Humphrey Maurice F.; *see* FitzRoy Newdegate.

NEWE, Rt. Hon. Gerard Benedict, PC (N Ireland) 1971; CBE 1977 (OBE 1961); Chairman, Personal Social Services Advisory Committee for Northern Ireland, since 1974; *b* 5 Feb. 1907; *s* of Patrick Newe and Catherine Newe (*née* McCanny); unmarried. *Educ:* St Malachy's Coll.; Belfast; Belcamp Coll., Dublin. Editor, The Ulster Farmer, 1931-67. Area Admin. Officer, Min. of Health and Local Govt, NI, 1941-48; Regional Officer and Dir, NI Council of Social Service, 1948-72. First Roman Catholic Minister of State, Govt of NI, 1971-72. Last Minister to be appointed to old HM Privy Council in Northern Ireland. Hon. MA The Queen's Univ. of Belfast, 1967; Hon. DLitt New Univ. of Ulster, Coleraine, 1971. *Publications:* The Catholic in the Community, 1958, 2nd edn 1965; The Story of the Northern Ireland Council of Social Service, 1963; contribs to Tablet, The Furrow, Christus Rex, Aquarius. *Recreations:* reading, trying to be lazy. *Address:* Prospect House, 28 Coast Road, Cushendall, Ballymena, Co. Antrim BT44 0RY. *T:* Cushendall 219.

NEWELL, Rev. Canon John Philip Peter; Vicar of Goudhurst, since 1975; Chaplain to the Queen, since 1975; *b* 4 Dec. 1911; *s* of late Joseph Newell and Edith Newell; *m* 1955, Mary, *d* of William and Alice Forbes; one *s*. *Educ:* Shrewsbury Sch.; Magdalen Coll., Oxford. Classical Upper Sixth Form Master, Repton Sch., 1935-36; Asst Priest, Ashbourne Parish Church, and Organizing Sec., Derby Diocesan Youth Council, 1936-39; Asst Master and Chaplain, Diocesan Coll., Rondebosch, Cape Town, 1939-43; Classical Upper Sixth Form Master and Chaplain, Sedbergh School, 1943-53; Headmaster: Bradford Grammar School, 1953-62; The King's School, Canterbury, 1962-75. Select Preacher, University of Oxford, 1956, 1960, 1977. Hon. Canon, Canterbury Cathedral, 1963. *Recreations:* hills and rivers and village churches. *Address:* Goudhurst Vicarage, Kent TN17 1AN. *T:* Goudhurst 332. *Club:* East India, Devonshire, Sports and Public Schools.

NEWELL, Philip Staniforth, CB 1961; *b* 1903; *m* 1927, Sylvia May Webb; two *s* one *d*. *Educ:* Uppingham; Emmanuel College, Cambridge (Scholar). First Class Part I, Mathematical Tripos, First Class Mechanical Sciences Tripos; Assistant Master at Uppingham; Chief Mathematical Master, Repton; Headmaster of Gresham's School, Holt, 1935-44; Admiralty, 1944-64; Imperial Defence College, 1955; Under-Secretary, 1956; Principal Finance Officer, 1961-65. Director, Greenwich Hosp., 1964-69; a Maths Master, Pierrepont Sch., Surrey, 1969-72. *Address:* Dawson's, Tilford, Surrey. *T:* Frensham 2787. *Club:* Athenæum.

NEWENS, (Arthur) Stanley; MP (Lab and Co-op) Harlow, since 1974; *b* 4 Feb. 1930; *s* of Arthur Ernest and Celia Jennie Newens, Bethnal Green; *m* 1st, 1954, Ann (*d* 1962), *d* of J. B. Sherratt, Stoke-on-Trent; two *d*; 2nd, 1966, Sandra Christina, *d* of J. A. Frith, Chingford; two *d*. *Educ:* Buckhurst Hill County High Sch.; University Coll., London (BA Hons History); Westminster Training Coll. (Post-Graduate Certificate of Education). Coal face worker in N Staffs mines, 1952-55. Secondary Sch. Teacher, 1956-65, 1970-74. MP (Lab) Epping, 1964-70 (NUT sponsored). Chm., Eastern Area Gp of Lab MPs, 1974-; Vice-Chairman: E Reg. Council, Lab. Party; Parly Lab Party Foreign Affairs Gp. Active Member: Labour Party, holding numerous offices, 1949-; NUM, 1952-55; NUT, 1956-. Chm., Liberation (Movement for Colonial Freedom), 1967-. Dir, London Co-operative Soc., 1971- (Pres., 1977-); Mem. Central Exec., Co-op. Union, 1974-. *Publications:* numerous pamphlets and articles, incl. The Case Against NATO, 1972; Nicolae Ceausescu, 1972; Third World: change or chaos, 1977. *Recreations:* local historical research, family, reading. *Address:* The Leys, 18 Park Hill, Harlow, Essex. *T:* Harlow 20108.

NEWEY, John Henry Richard, QC 1970; a Recorder of the Crown Court, since 1972; Commissary General of the City and the Diocese of Canterbury, since 1971; *b* 20 Oct. 1923; *s* of Lt-Col T. H. Newey; *m* 1953, Mollie Patricia (*née* Chalk); three *s* two *d*. *Educ:* Ellesmere Coll.; Queens' Coll., Cambridge. Served Central India Horse, Indian Army, 1942-47 in India, Middle East, Italy and Greece; Captain, last British Adjt (US Bronze Star, 1944). Foundn Schol., Queens' Coll., Cambridge, 1941-43 and 1947-49 (MA, LLB). Called to Bar, Middle Temple, 1948, Bencher 1977. Prosecuting Counsel to Post Office, South Eastern Circuit, 1964-65; Standing Counsel to Post Office at Common Law, 1965-70; Personal Injuries Junior to Treasury, 1968-70; Dep. Chm., Kent County QS, 1970-71. Legal Assessor, GMC, 1973-. Contested (C) Cannock Div. of Staffs, 1955. Alternate Chm., Burnham and other Teachers' Remuneration Cttees, 1969-. *Recreation:* excursions with family. *Address:* St David's, The Drive, Sevenoaks, Kent. *T:* Sevenoaks 54597.

NEWFOUNDLAND, Archbishop of, since 1975; **Most Rev. Robert Lowder Seaborn**; Metropolitan of Ecclesiastical Province of Canada; Bishop of Eastern Newfoundland and Labrador (of Newfoundland, 1965-75); *b* 9 July 1911; *s* of Rev. Richard Seaborn and Muriel Kathleen Reid; *m* 1938, Mary Elizabeth Gilchrist; four *s* one *d*. *Educ:* Univ. of Toronto Schs; Trinity Coll., Univ. of Toronto (MA); Oxford Univ. Deacon, 1934; Priest, 1935; Asst Curate, St Simon's, Toronto, 1934-36; Asst Curate, St James's Cathedral, Toronto, 1937-41; Rector, St Peter's, Cobourg, Ont., 1941-48; Chaplain, Canadian Army, 1942-45 (Padre Canadian Scottish Regt); Dean of Quebec and Rector of Parish of Quebec, 1948-57; Rector, St Mary's, Kerrisdale, Vancouver, BC, 1957-58; Asst Bishop of Newfoundland, 1958-65, Coadjutor, June-Dec. 1965. Croix de Guerre avec étoile de vermeil (French), 1945. DD, (*jure dignitatis*), Trinity Coll., 1948; DCL (*hc*), Bishop's Univ., 1962; Hon. LLD Meml Univ. of Newfoundland, 1972. *Publication:* Faith in our Time, 1963. *Recreations:* camping, golf. *Address:* 67 Portugal Cove Road, St John's, Newfoundland A1B 2M2, Canada.

NEWFOUNDLAND, CENTRAL, Bishop of, since 1976; **Rt. Rev. Mark Genge**; *b* 18 March 1927; *s* of Lambert and Lily Genge; *m* 1959, Maxine Clara (*née* Major); five *d*. *Educ:* Queen's Coll. and Memorial Univ., Newfoundland; Univ. of Durham (MA); BD Gen. Synod of Canada. Deacon, Corner Brook, Newfoundland, 1951; priest, Stephenville, 1952; Durham, 1953-55; Vice-Principal, Queen's Coll., St John's, Newfoundland, 1955-57; Curate, St Mary's Church, St John's, 1957-59; Rector: Foxtrap, 1959-64; Mary's Harbour, 1964-65; Burgeo, 1965-69; Curate, Marbleton, PQ, 1969-71; Rector, South River, Port-de-Grave, 1971-73; District Sec., Canadian Bible Soc., 1973-76. *Recreations:* badminton, swimming. *Address:* Roe Street, Gander, Newfoundland.

NEWFOUNDLAND, EASTERN, AND LABRADOR, Bishop of; *see* Newfoundland, Archbishop of.

NEWFOUNDLAND, WESTERN, Bishop of, since 1976; **Rt. Rev. William Gordon Legge**, DD; *b* 20 Jan. 1913; *s* of Thomas Legge and Jane (*née* Gill); *m* 1941, Hyacinth Florence Richards; one *s* one *d*. *Educ:* Bishop Feild and Queen's Colls, St John's, Newfoundland. Deacon 1938, priest 1939; Curate, Channel, 1938-41; Incumbent of Botwood, 1941-44; Rector, Bell Island, 1944-55; Sec., Diocesan Synod, 1955-68; Archdeacon of Avalon, 1955-68; Canon of Cathedral, 1955-76; Diocesan Registrar, 1957-68; Suffragan Bishop, 1968. DD *hc* , Univ. of King's College, Halifax, NS, 1973. *Address:* 13 Cobb Lane, Corner Brook, Newfoundland. *T:* 639 9987; (office) Suite 311, Millbrook Mall, Corner Brook, Nfld. *T:* 639 8712.

NEWHOUSE, Ven. Robert John Darrell; Archdeacon of Totnes and Canon Residentiary of Exeter Cathedral, 1966-76, now Archdeacon Emeritus and Canon Emeritus; Treasurer of Exeter Cathedral, 1970-76; *b* 11 May 1911; *s* of Rev. R. L. C. Newhouse; *m* 1938, Winifred (*née* Elton); two *s*. *Educ:* St Edward's Sch.; Worcester Coll., Oxford; Cuddesdon College. Ordained, 1936. Curate of: St John's, Peterborough, 1936-40; St Giles, Cambridge, 1940-46; Chaplain, RNVR, 1941-46; Rector of Ashwater, Devon, 1946-56; Rural Dean of Holsworthy, 1954-56; Vicar of Littleham-cum-Exmouth, 1956-66; Rural Dean of Aylesbeare, 1965-66. *Recreation:* gardening. *Address:* Pound Cottage, Northlew, Okehampton, Devon. *T:* Beaworthy 532.

NEWINGTON, Michael John; HM Diplomatic Service; Counsellor and Consul-General, Tel Aviv, since 1975; *b* 10 July 1932; *er s* of J. T. Newington, Halmer House, Spalding, Lincs; *m* 1956, Nina Gordon-Jones; one *s* one *d*. *Educ:* Stamford Sch.; St John's Coll., Oxford. MA. Joined Foreign Office, 1955; Economic Survey Section, Hong Kong, 1957-58; resigned 1958. ICI, 1959-60. Rejoined FO, 1960; Second, later First Sec. (Economic), Bonn, 1961-65; First Sec., Lagos, 1965-68; Asst Head of Science and Technology Dept, FCO, 1968-72; Counsellor (Scientific), Bonn, 1972-75. *Recreations:* skiing, golf, gardening. *Address:* The Clock House, Lindfield, Sussex. *T:* Lindfield 3018.

NEWIS, Kenneth, CB 1967; CVO 1970 (MVO 1958); *b* 9 Nov. 1916; *o s* of late H. T. and G. Newis, Manchester; *m* 1943, Kathleen, *o d* of John Barrow, Davenport, Cheshire; two *d*. *Educ:* Manchester Grammar Sch.; St John's Coll., Cambridge (Scholar). BA 1938, MA 1942. Entered HM Office of Works, 1938; Private Sec. to Minister of Works (Rt Hon. C. W. Key), 1948-49; Asst Sec., 1949; Under-Sec., 1959; Dir of Management Services, MPBW, 1969-70; Under-Sec., Scottish Develt Dept, 1970-73, Sec., 1973-76. Member: Council, Scottish Fedn of Housing Assocs; Management Cttee, Edinvar Housing Assoc. (Edinburgh); Board, Methodist Homes for the Aged; Management Cttee, MHA Housing Assoc. Ltd. Mem. Cttee, Churchill and Greenhill Assoc., Edinburgh; Dir, Cockburn Conservation Co. Ltd; Conservator of Wimbledon and Putney Commons, 1963-70. Crown Estate Paving Comr. Mem. Bd, RSAMD; Dir, Scottish Philharmonic Soc. Ltd; Chm., Scottish Philharmonic Club. Governor: Farrington's School; Richmond College, 1964-70. Mem. Pres's Council, Methodist Church, 1977-. *Recreation:* music. *Address:* 11 Abbotsford Park, Edinburgh EH10 5DZ. *Clubs:* Royal Commonwealth Society; New (Edinburgh).

NEWITT, Dudley Maurice, MC 1918; FRS 1942; DSc, PhD; Professor Emeritus of Chemical Engineering in the University of London; *b* 1894. *Address:* Imperial College of Science, South Kensington, SW7. *Club:* Athenæum.

NEWLAND, Prof. David Edward, CEng, FIMechE, MIEE, FIMA; Professor of Engineering (1875), University of Cambridge, since 1976; Fellow, Selwyn College, Cambridge, since 1976; consulting engineer (part-time), since 1963; *b* 8 May 1936; *s* of Robert W. Newland and Marion A. Newland (*née* Dearman); *m* 1959, Patricia Frances Mayne; two *s*. *Educ:* Alleyne's Sch., Stevenage; Selwyn Coll., Cambridge (MA); Massachusetts Inst. of Technol. (ScD). English Electric Co., 1957-61; MIT, 1961-64; Imperial Coll. of Science and Technol., 1964-67; Sheffield Univ., 1967-76. *Publications:* An Introduction to Random Vibrations and Spectral Analysis, 1975; technical papers, mostly in British and Amer. engrg jls. *Recreations:* golf, cycling, engineering memorabilia. *Address:* c/o University Engineering Department, Trumpington Street, Cambridge CB2 1PZ. *T:* Cambridge 66466.

NEWLEY, Edward Frank, CBE 1960; Member, National Savings Committee, Southern Region, since 1976; *b* 9 June 1913; *s* of Frederick Percy Newley; *m* 1946, Sybil Madge Alvis; two *s* one *d*. *Educ:* King's Coll., London. 1st class hons BSc; MSc. GPO Engrg Dept, Radio Research Br, 1937-44; GPO Factories Dept, 1944-49; Royal Naval Scientific Service, 1949-55; joined

UKAEA, 1955; Dep. Dir, AWRE, 1959; Dir, Atomic Weapons Establishment, Aldermaston, 1965-76. *Publications:* sundry scientific and technical papers. *Address:* Reades, Heads Hill, Newbury, Berks. *T:* Headley 371.

NEWLEY, (George) Anthony; actor since 1946; author, composer; *b* 24 Sept. 1931; *m* 1956, Ann Lynn; *m* 1963, Joan Collins; one *s* one *d*. *Educ:* Mandeville Street Sch., Clapton, E5. Appeared on West End stage in: Cranks, 1955; Stop the World, I Want to Get Off (co-author and co-composer, with Leslie Bricusse), 1961-62; subseq. starred in New York production, 1962-63; The Good Old Bad Old Days (co-author and co-composer with Leslie Bricusse), 1972; The Roar of the Greasepaint-the Smell of the Crowd (co-author and composer, with Leslie Bricusse, star and director), New York, 1965. Has acted in over 40 films in last 17 years. *Films include:* Adventures of Dusty Bates; Oliver Twist; Up To His Neck; Cockleshell Heroes; High Flight; Idle on Parade; Jazz Boat; The Small World of Sammy Lee; Dr Doolittle; Sweet November; (wrote, produced and acted) Can Heironymus Merkin ever forget Mercy Humppe and find True Happiness?; (directed) Summertree, 1970; (score) Willy Wonka and the Chocolate Factory (Academy Award nomination, 1972); Quilp, 1974; It Seemed Like a Good Idea at the Time, 1974. *TV appearances include:* Anthony Newley Shows; The Strange World of Gurney Slade, 1960-61; Johnny Darling Show, 1962; Lucy in London, 1966; appears on TV in USA. He is also a successful recording star. *Recreations:* photography, painting, fishing. *Address:* c/o Katz-Gallin, 9255 Sunset Boulevard, Los Angeles, Calif 90069, USA.

NEWMAN, Charles, CBE 1965; MD (Cantab); FRCP; retired; Emeritus Dean, Postgraduate Medical School (now Royal Postgraduate Medical School); Harveian Librarian, since 1962, Royal College of Physicians; *b* 16 March 1900; *s* of Charles Arnold Newman and Kate Beck; *m* 1971, Anne, *d* of G. W. Stallard, engineer. *Educ:* Shrewsbury Sch.; Magdalene Coll., Cambridge (Scholar); King's College Hospital (Scholar). Murchison Scholar RCP, 1926; FRCP 1932; Volunteer Asst to Prof. Aschoff, Univ. of Freiburg i B. 1930; Hon. Treas., RSocMed, 1946-50; Fellow Medical Society of London (Orator, 1961); Hon. Member Assoc. of Physicians, 1965. Hon. Secretary, 1942-47. Hon. Treasurer, 1948-58; Mem., British Gastro-enterological Soc. (Pres., 1964); Governor, St Clement Dane's Sch., 1955-76, Vice-Chm., 1958-76; Mem. Cttee of Management of Con-joint Board in England, 1958-68 (Chm., 1965-68). Goulstonian Lectr, 1933; FitzPatrick Lectr, 1954, 1955 and 1968; Linacre Fellow, 1966; Harveian Orator, 1973; Assistant Registrar, RCP, 1933-38; Sub-Editor, EMS, Official Medical History of the War, 1942-47; late Physician, Medical Tutor and Vice-Dean, King's College Hospital and Asst Physician, Belgrave Hospital for Children. *Publications:* Medical Emergencies, 1932, 3rd edn 1946, repr. 1948; Evolution of Medical Education in the Nineteenth Century, 1957; articles in medical text-books and encyclopædias; papers on diseases of the liver and gall-bladder, medical history and education. *Address:* Basset, South Road, Oundle, Peterborough, Northants. *T:* Oundle 3310. *Club:* Athenæum.

NEWMAN, Sir Geoffrey (Robert), 6th Bt, *cr* 1836; *b* 2 June 1947; *s* of Sir Ralph Alured Newman, 5th Bt, and Ann Rosemary Hope, *d* of late Hon. Claude Hope-Morley; *S* father, 1968. *Educ:* Heatherdown, Ascot; Kelly Coll., Tavistock. 1st Bn, Grenadier Guards, 1967-70. *Recreations:* shooting, sailing, all sports. *Heir:* *b* Richard Claude Newman, *b* 2 May 1951. *Address:* Blackpool House, Dartmouth, Devon. *Club:* Cavalry and Guards.

NEWMAN, Sir Gerard (Robert Henry Sigismund), 3rd Bt, *cr* 1912; *b* 19 July 1927; *s* of Sir Cecil Gustavus Jacques Newman, 2nd Bt, and Joan Florence Mary, CBE (*d* 1969), *e d* of late Rev. Canon Hon. Robert Grimston; *S* father, 1955; *m* 1960, Caroline Philippa, *d* of late Brig. Alfred Geoffrey Neville, CBE, MC; three *s* one *d*. *Educ:* Eton; Jesus Coll., Oxford. *Recreation:* shooting. *Heir:* *s* Francis Hugh Cecil Newman, *b* 12 June 1963. *Address:* Burloes, Royston, Herts; 27 Bloomfield Terrace, SW1. *T:* 01-730 7540. *Club:* Boodle's.

NEWMAN, Sir Jack, Kt 1977; CBE 1963; FCIT 1955; JP; Chairman, TNL Group Ltd, Nelson, New Zealand, since 1938; *b* 3 July, 1902; *s* of Thomas Newman and Christina Thomson; *m* 1926, Myrtle O. A. Thomas; four *d*. *Educ:* Nelson Coll. for Boys, NZ. Joined Newman Bros Ltd (family business), 1922; Manager, 1927; Managing Director, 1935. Director: Zip Holdings Ltd; L & M Oil (NZ) Ltd; NZ Motor Bodies Ltd; Moller Holdings Ltd. Past President and Life Member: NZ Cricket Council; NZ Travel Assoc.; Pres., NZ Cricket Foundn; former Dir, Pacific Area Travel Assoc. Represented: NZ, at cricket, 1931-33; Nelson, Canterbury and Wellington, at cricket; Nelson, at Rugby football, golf, and lawn bowls. JP Nelson, 1950. *Recreations:* lawn bowls, golf. *Address:* (home) 36 Brougham Street, Nelson, New Zealand; (office) TNL Group Ltd, PO Box 48, Nelson, NZ. *Clubs:* MCC; Wellesley (Wellington); Nelson (Nelson).

NEWMAN, Karl Max; Under-Secretary, Lord Chancellor's Office, since 1972; *b* 26 March 1919; *s* of Karl Neumann, DrJur, and Licie Neumann; *m* 1952, Annette, *d* of late Ronald Cross Sheen; one *s* one *d*. *Educ:* Ottershaw Coll., Surrey; Christ Church, Oxford (MA). Bacon Scholar of Gray's Inn, 1939. Served War in Army, 1940-42. Called to Bar, Gray's Inn, 1946; joined Lord Chancellor's Office, 1949; Asst Solicitor, 1962; Under-Sec., 1972; part-time Legal Adviser to European Unit of Cabinet Office, 1972-. Member: UK delegns to Internat. Diplomatic Confs on Nuclear Liability, 1962-63; expert Cttees of Council of Europe, 1961-68; 10th and 11th Session of Hague Conf. on Private Internat. Law, 1964-68. *Publications:* Das Englisch-Amerikanische Beweisrecht, 1949 (Heidelberg); contribs to legal publications on internat. jurisdiction and recognition of judgments. *Recreations:* philately, looking at paintings. *Address:* 17 Marryat Road, Wimbledon, SW19 5BB. *Club:* United Oxford & Cambridge University.

NEWMAN, Kenneth Leslie; Chief Constable, Royal Ulster Constabulary, since 1976; *s* of John William Newman and Florence Newman; *m* 1949, Eileen Lilian. *Educ:* London Univ. (LLB Hons). Served War, RAF, 1942-46. Palestine Police, 1946-48; Metropolitan Police, 1948-73; Comdr, New Scotland Yard, 1972; Royal Ulster Constab., 1973-; Sen. Dep. Chief Constable, 1973. *Recreations:* squash, riding.

NEWMAN, Maxwell Herman Alexander, MA, FRS 1939; Professor Emeritus, University of Manchester; *b* 7 Feb. 1897; *m* 1st, 1934, Lyn (*d* 1973), *d* of Rev. J. A. Irvine; two *s*; 2nd, 1973, Margaret, *widow* of Prof. L. S. Penrose, FRS. *Educ:* City of London School; St John's College, Cambridge; Vienna Univ., 1922-23. MA 1924; Fellow of St John's College, Cambridge, 1923-45 (Hon. Fellow, 1973); Rockefeller Research Fellow at Princeton, 1928-29; University Lecturer in Mathematics, Cambridge University, 1927-45; Fielden Professor of Mathematics, Manchester Univ., 1945-64; Visiting Professor in Australian National Univ., 1964-65 and 1967; in Univ. of Wisconsin and Rice Univ., 1965-66. Royal Soc. Council, 1946-47; Pres., London Mathematical Soc., 1950-51; Pres. Mathematical Assoc., 1959. Hon. DSc Hull, 1968. Sylvester Medal of Royal Society, 1959; De Morgan Medal, 1962. *Publications:* Topology of Plane Sets of Points, 1939, 2nd edn 1951; papers on mathematics in various journals. *Address:* Cross Farm, Comberton, Cambridge.

NEWMAN, Philip Harker, CBE 1976; DSO 1940; MC; FRCS; Hon. Consulting Orthopædic Surgeon, Middlesex Hospital, Royal National Orthopædic Hospital, King Edward VII's Hospital for Officers, W1; *b* 22 June 1911; *s* of John Harker Newman, Mannofield, Ingatestone, Essex; *m* 1943, Elizabeth Anne, *er d* of Rev. G. H. Basset, Turners, Belchamp St Paul, Suffolk; two *s* one *d*. *Educ:* Cranleigh; Middlesex Hospital Medical School (Senior Broderip Scholar and 2nd Year Exhibitioner), MRCS, LRCP, 1934; FRCS, 1938; Hunterian Prof., RCS, 1954; late Lt-Col RAMC; Served War of 1939-45 (DSO, MC); FRSM (formerly Pres., Section of Orthopaedics); Fellow Brit. Orthopædic Assoc. (Pres., 1975-76); Chm., British Editorial Soc. of Bone and Joint Surgery, 1973-75; Chm., Medical Br., St John; Member British Medical Association. *Publications:* The Prisoner of War Mentality, 1944; Early Treatment of Wounds of the Knee Joint, 1945; Sacroiliac Arthrodesis, 1946; The Etiology of Spondylolisthesis, 1962; The Spine, the Wood and the Trees, 1968; Spinal Fusion, Operative Surgery, 1969; Orthopædic Surgery, Medical Encyclopædia, 1956. *Address:* 107 Harley Street, W1. *T:* 01-935 2776; 72A Saxmundham Road, Aldeburgh, Suffolk.

NEWMAN, Ronald William; HM Diplomatic Service; Consul General, Casablanca, since 1977; *b* 6 April 1921; *s* of William James Newman and Louisa Ellen Taylor; *m* 1943, Victoria Brady; three *d*. *Educ:* Wandsworth Sch. Served War, RAF, 1940-46. Min. of Agriculture and Fisheries, later MAFF, 1946-58; Statistical Org. Adviser to Central Bureau of Statistics, Jerusalem, 1958; O&M Adviser to Basutoland, Bechuanaland and Swaziland, 1959-61; MAFF, 1962-65; CRO, 1965-67; First Secretary: (Econs), Accra, 1967; (Capital Aid), Nairobi, 1968-72; (Econs), Islamabad, 1973-75; Counsellor, Khartoum, 1975-76. *Recreations:* squash, swimming, diving, flying. *Address:* c/o Foreign and Commonwealth Office, SW1A 2AL; Dene Bank, Cranley Close, Guildford, Surrey GU1 2JN. *T:* Guildford 76728. *Club:* Churchill (Casablanca).

NEWMAN, Sydney Cecil; film and television producer and executive; Special Advisor on Film to the Secretary of State for Canada, since 1975; *b* Toronto, 1 April 1917; *m* 1944, Margaret Elizabeth, *d* of Rev. Duncan McRae, DD; three *d. Educ:* Ogden Public School and Central Technical School, Toronto. Painter, stage, industrial and interior designer; still and cinema photographer, 1935-41. Joined National Film Board of Canada under John Grierson as splicer-boy, 1941. Editor and Director of Armed Forces training films and war information shorts, 1942. Producer of Canada Carries On, 1945. Exec. Producer in charge of all films for cinemas, including short films, newsreels, films for children and travel, 1947-52. Over 300 documentaries, including: Suffer Little Children (UN), It's Fun to Sing (Venice Award), Ski Skill, After Prison What? (Canada Award). For Canadian Govt to NBC in New York to report on American television techniques, 1949-50. Joined Canadian Broadcasting Corporation as Television Director of Features and Outside Broadcasts, 1953. Superviser of Drama and Producer of General Motors Theatre, On Camera, Ford Theatre, Graphic, 1954. Produced first plays by Arthur Hailey, inc. Flight Into Danger, Course for Collision. Ohio State Award for Religious Drama; Liberty Award, Best Drama Series. Superviser of Drama and Producer Armchair Theatre, ABC Television, England, 1958-62 (devised, The Avengers, 1961); Head of Drama Group, TV, BBC, 1963-67 (devised, Adam Adamant Lives!, 1966); Producer, Associated British Productions Ltd, Elstree, 1968-69; Special Advisor to Chm. and Dir, Broadcast Programmes Branch, Canadian Radio and Television Commn, 1970; Canadian Govt Film Comr and Chm., Nat. Film Bd of Canada, 1970-75. Producer: Stephen D, 1963; The Rise and Fall of the City of Mahagonny, 1965; The Tea Party, 1965. Commissioned and prod. first on-air plays of Alun Owen, Harold Pinter, Angus Wilson, Robert Muller, Peter Luke; also plays by Clive Exton and David Perry. Trustee, Nat. Arts Center, Ottawa, 1970-75; Director: Canadian Film Develt Corp., Montreal, 1970-75; Canadian Broadcasting Corp., 1972-75. FRSA 1970; Fellow Soc. of Film and Television Arts. Desmond Davis Award, 1967, Soc. of Film and Television Arts; President's Award, 1969, and Zeta Award, 1970, Writers Guild of Great Britain; Canadian Picture Pioneers Special Award, 1973; Special Recognition Award, SMPTE, 1975. Kt of Mark Twain, USA. *Address:* 3 Nesbitt Drive, Toronto, Ont., Canada.

NEWMAN-MORRIS, Sir Geoffrey, Kt 1969; ED 1946; Chairman, Australian Red Cross Society, since 1958; *b* 14 May 1909; *s* of John and Eleanor Annie Newman-Morris; *m* 1945, Sheila, *d* of Martin Brown; two *s* one *d. Educ:* Melbourne Church of England Grammar Sch.; Trinity Coll., Univ. of Melbourne. MB BS Melbourne 1932, MS Melbourne 1936, FRCS 1937, FRACS 1938. Lt-Col, RAAMC (Ret.); served 1939-45, Mid. East and New Guinea (despatches 1944). Hon. Cons. Surg. Prince Henry's Hosp., Melbourne. Pres., 5th Aust. Med. Congress, 1974. Mem., Standing Commn, Internat. Red Cross, 1965-73 (Chm., 1973-77); Vice-Chm., League of Red Cross Socs, 1969-73; Pres., Confedn Medical Assocs of Asia and Oceania, 1975-77. KStJ 1964. *Publications:* contrib. med. jls. *Recreation:* bowls. *Address:* Flat 1, 111 Kooyong Koot Road, Hawthorn, Vic 3122, Australia. *T:* 81 84769. *Clubs:* Melbourne, Melbourne Cricket (Australia).

NEWNHAM, Captain Ian Frederick Montague, CBE 1955; RN Retired; *b* 20 Feb. 1911; *s* of late John Montague Newnham, OBE, DL, JP, and Hilda Newnham; *m* 1947, Marjorie Warden; no *c. Educ:* RN College, Dartmouth. Served War of 1939-45 (despatches). Captain, 1952; retd 1961. Lent to Indian Navy as Chief of Material, 1952-55; Chief of Staff to Admiral, British Joint Service Mission, and Naval Attaché, Washington, 1959-61. Gen. Manager, Precision Engineering Div., Short Brothers and Harland, Belfast, 1961-68. *Recreations:* golf, fishing. *Address:* Elsted Green, near Midhurst, West Sussex.

NEWNS, Sir (Alfred) Foley (Francis Polden), KCMG 1963 (CMG 1957); CVO 1961; MA Cantab; *b* 30 Jan. 1909; *s* of late Rev. Alfred Newns, AKC; *m* 1936, Jean, *d* of late A. H. Bateman, MB, BS; one *s* one *d. Educ:* Christ's Hospital; St Catharine's College, Cambridge. Colonial Administrative Service, Nigeria, 1932; served E Reg. and Colony; Enugu Secretariat, 1947; Lagos Secretariat, 1949; attached Cabinet Office, London, 1951; Resident, 1951; Secretary to Council of Ministers, 1951; Secretary to Governor-General and the Council of Ministers, Federation of Nigeria, 1955-59; Dep. Governor, Sierra Leone, 1960-61; Acting Gov. during 1960; Adviser to the Government of Sierra Leone after Independence, 1961-63; Sec. to Cabinet, Govt of the Bahamas, 1963-71. FRSA 1969. *Publications:* various papers on Cabinet procedure and government machinery, circulated in Commonwealth. *Recreations:* astronomy, natural history, photography. *Address:* Cedar House, Caxton Lane, Foxton, Cambs. *T:* Cambridge 870629.
See also J. Ounsted.

NEWNS, George Henry, MD, FRCP; Physician, The Hospital for Sick Children, Great Ormond Street, WC1, 1946-73; Hon. Consulting Physician since 1974; Dean, Institute of Child Health, University of London, 1949-73, Emeritus Dean, 1974; Pædiatrician to Barnet General Hospital, 1946-67; Civilian Pædiatric Consultant to the Admiralty, 1962-74; Hon. Consultant in Pædiatrics to the Army, 1966-74; *b* 27 July 1908; *s* of late George Newns, Dartford, Kent; *m* 1936, Deirdre, *d* of late Lawrence Kenny, Clonmel, Tipperary, Eire; one *s* one *d. Educ:* Whitgift School; King's Coll., and King's Coll. Hosp., London. MB, BS (London) 1931; MRCP 1932; MD (London), 1933; FRCP 1951. Registrar: Roy. Northern Hosp., 1933-34; to Children's Dept, King's Coll. Hosp., 1934-35; Med. Registrar and Pathologist, Hosp. for Sick Children, Gt Ormond St, 1935-38; Physician: Bolingbroke Hosp., London, 1938-45; Queen Elizabeth Hosp. for Children, 1939-46. Mem., British Pædiatric Assoc., 1945-; Pres., Pædiatric Section, RSM, 1966-67. *Publications:* contributor to Medical Annual, 1953-61; (with Dr Donald Paterson) Modern Methods of Feeding in Infancy and Childhood, 10th edn, 1955; contrib. to Pædiatric Urology (ed D. I. Williams), 1968; Urology in Childhood, 1974; numerous contributions to med. journals. *Recreations:* reading and looking at paintings. *Address:* 12 Milborne Grove, SW10 9SN. *T:* 01-373 2011; 34 Great Ormond Street, WC1N 3JH. *T:* 01-405 1306.

NEWPORT, Viscount; Richard Thomas Orlando Bridgeman; *b* 3 Oct. 1947; *s* and *heir* of 6th Earl of Bradford, *qv. Educ:* Harrow; Trinity College, Cambridge. Owner of The Caviar Bar and Bewicks Restaurant; Director: Ringingham Ltd; T/A Bombacha; Tenihurst Ltd; Aristocrat Discotheques Inc.; Harvey White Properties Ltd. *Address:* 15 Simpson Street, SW11. *T:* 01-223 5770; Weston Park, Shifnal, Salop. *T:* Weston-under-Lizard 218.

NEWRY and MORNE, Viscount; Robert Francis John Needham; *b* 30 May 1966; *s* and *heir* to Earl of Kilmorey (*see* R. F. Needham).

NEWSAM, Peter Anthony; Education Officer, Inner London Education Authority, since 1977; *b* 2 Nov. 1928; *s* of late W. O. Newsam and of Mrs D. E. Newsam; *m* 1953, Elizabeth Joy Greg; four *s* one *d. Educ:* Clifton Coll.; Queen's Coll., Oxford (MA, DipEd). Asst Principal, BoT, 1952-55; teacher, 1956-63; Asst Educn Officer, N Riding of Yorks, 1963-66; Asst Dir of Educn, Cumberland, 1966-70; Dep. Educn Officer: W Riding of Yorks, 1970-72; ILEA, 1972-76. *Address:* 48 Dartmouth Row, Greenwich, SE10.
See also R. W. Newsam.

NEWSAM, Richard William, CVO 1961; HM Diplomatic Service, retired; *b* 23 June 1918; *s* of late W. O. Newsam, ICS; *m* 1952, Joan Rostgard; one *s. Educ:* St Paul's; Trinity Coll., Oxford. Commnd RASC; served War of 1939-45: with East African Forces, Kenya, Abyssinia, Ceylon and Burma. Temporary Administrative Assistant, Colonial Office, 1946; Assistant Principal, Colonial Office, 1947; Principal, 1948; Nigeria secondment, 1952-53; joined Commonwealth Relations Office, 1957; served in: Ceylon, 1958; Pakistan, 1960; Dept of Technical Co-operation, 1963; Ministry of Overseas Development, 1964; Deputy High Commissioner, Dar es Salaam, 1965; Accra, 1967-69. *Recreations:* golf, sailing. *Address:* 43A Underhill Road, SE22. *Club:* Dulwich and Sydenham Hill Golf.

NEWSOM, George Harold, QC 1956; Chancellor: Diocese of St Albans, since 1958; Diocese of London, since 1971; Diocese of Bath and Wells, since 1971; *b* 29 Dec. 1910; *e s* of late Rev. G. E. Newsom, Master of Selwyn Coll., Cambridge; *m* 1939, Margaret Amy, *d* of L. A. Allen, OBE; two *s* one *d. Educ:* Marlborough; Merton College, Oxford. 2nd Class Lit Hum, 1931; 1st Class Jurisprudence, 1932; Harmsworth Senior Scholar; Merton College, 1932; Cholmeley Student, 1933, called to Bar, 1934; Lincoln's Inn; Bencher, 1962. Min. of Economic Warfare, 1939-40; Trading with the Enemy Dept, Treasury and Bd of Trade, 1940-45; Junior Counsel to Charity Comrs, 1947-56; Conveyancing Counsel to PO, 1947-56; Dep. Chm., Wilts QS, 1964-71; a Recorder of the Crown Court, 1972-74. Member Gen. Council of the Bar, 1952-56. Vis. Prof. in Law, Auckland Univ., NZ, 1971. *Publications:* Restrictive Covenants affecting freehold land, 1st edn (with late C. H. S. Preston), 1940, 6th edn 1976; Limitation of Actions, 1st edn (with late C. H. S. Preston), 1939, 2nd edn 1943, 3rd edn (with L. Abel-Smith), 1953; The Discharge and Modification of Restrictive Covenants, 1957; (with J. G. Sherratt) Water Pollution, 1972. *Recreations:* lawn tennis, walking. *Address:* The Old Vicarage, Bishop's Cannings, Devizes, Wilts. *T:* Cannings 660. *Club:* Athenæum.

NEWSOME, David Hay, MA, LittD Cantab; Headmaster of Christ's Hospital, since 1970; *b* 15 June 1929; *s* of Captain C. T. Newsome, OBE; *m* 1955, Joan Florence, *d* of Lt-Col L. H. Trist, DSO, MC; four *d. Educ:* Rossall Sch., Fleetwood; Emmanuel Coll., Cambridge (Scholar). First Cl. in Hist. Tripos Parts I and II, 1952, 1953. Asst Master, Wellington Coll., 1954-59 (Head of History Dept, 1956-59); Fellow of Emmanuel Coll., Cambridge, 1959-70; Asst Lectr in Ecclesiastical History, Univ. of Cambridge, 1961-66; Univ. Lectr, 1966-70; Sen. Tutor, Emmanuel Coll., Cambridge, 1965-70. Lectures: Gore Memorial, Westminster Abbey, 1965; Bishop Westcott Memorial, Cambridge, 1968; Birkbeck, Univ. of Cambridge, 1972. Council of: Ardingly Coll., 1965-69; Eastbourne Coll., 1966-70; Epsom Coll., 1966-70. FRHistS, 1970. *Publications:* A History of Wellington College, 1859-1959, 1959; Godliness and Good Learning, Four Studies in a Victorian Ideal, 1961; The Parting of Friends, a study of the Wilberforces and Henry Manning, 1966; Bishop Westcott and the Platonic Tradition, 1969; Two Classes of Men: Platonism and English Romantic Thought, 1974; articles in Jl of Theological Studies, Jl of Ecclesiastical History, Theology, History Today, Historical Jl. *Recreations:* music, fell-walking. *Address:* Christ's Hospital, Horsham, West Sussex. *T:* Horsham 63248. *Clubs:* Athenæum, MCC.

NEWSOME, William Antony; Director-General, Association of British Chambers of Commerce, since 1974; Member, Simplification of International Trade Procedures Board (SITPRO), since 1972; *b* 8 Nov. 1919; *s* of William F. Newsome and Elizabeth (*née* Thompson); *m* 1951, Estella Ann (*née* Cope); one *s. Educ:* King Henry VIII Sch., Coventry; Bedford Modern Sch. Student Engineer, W. H. Allen, Sons & Co. Ltd, Bedford, 1937-40. Served War, Royal Engineers: N Africa, Sicily, Italy campaigns, 1940-47. Engrg Dept, Crown Agents for Oversea Governments and Administrations, 1949-61; Principal: Home Office, 1961-64; Min. of Technology, 1964-70; Dept of Trade and Industry, 1970-71; Asst Sec., Dept of Trade, 1971-74. *Recreations:* photography, swimming, lawn tennis. *Address:* Bourdon Lacey, Old Woking Road, Woking, Surrey GU89 8HR. *T:* Woking 62237.

NEWSON-SMITH, Sir John (Kenneth), 2nd Bt *cr* 1944; DL; Member of HM Commission of Lieutenancy for City of London, since 1947; Deputy Chairman, London United Investments Ltd, since 1971 (Chairman, 1968-71); *b* 9 Jan. 1911; *s* of Sir Frank Newson-Smith, 1st Bt and Dorothy (*d* 1955), *d* of late Sir Henry Tozer; *S* father, 1971; *m* 1st, 1945, Vera Margaret Allt (marr. diss. 1971); one *s* two *d*; 2nd, 1972, Anne, *d* of late Harold Burns. *Educ:* Dover Coll.; Jesus Coll., Cambridge (MA). Joined Newson-Smith & Co, 1933, Partner 1938. Served War, Royal Navy, 1939-40; RNVR 1940. Rejoined Newson-Smith & Co, 1946 (which subseq. became Fielding Newson-Smith & Co.). Master of Turners Co., 1969-70; Liveryman: Merchant Taylors' Co.; Spectaclemakers. Elected to Court of Common Council, 1945; Deputy, Ward of Bassishaw, 1961. DL City of London, 1947. *Recreations:* travelling, gardening. *Heir: s* Peter Frank Graham Newson-Smith [*b* 8 May 1947; *m* 1974, Mrs Mary-Ann Owens, *o d* of Cyril C. Collins; one *s*]. *Address:* 39 Godfrey Street, SW3. *T:* 01-352 0722. *Clubs:* Royal Automobile, Naval.

NEWTH, Brig. Arthur Leslie Walter, CBE 1938; DSO 1919; MC; TD; DL; JP; *b* 1897; *s* of late Arthur Edward Newth, Westbury-on-Trym, Bristol; *m* 1926, Ruth Buchanan, *d* of P. Steadman, JP; two *s* one *d. Educ:* Bristol Grammar School. 2nd Lieut, 4th Gloucestershire Regt, 1914; proceeded to France, March 1915; served there until transferred to Italian Expeditionary Force, Nov. 1917; returned to France, April 1918; after holding various Staff appointments, commanded 6th Bn Cheshire Regiment and 2/23rd Bn The London Regiment (DSO, MC, despatches four times); Adjutant 4th Gloucestershire Regiment, 1924-28; Captain, 1915; Major, 1917; Lieut-Colonel, 1929; Bt Colonel, 1933; Colonel, 1934; Brigadier, 1937; commanded 4th (City of Bristol) Bn Gloucestershire Regt, 1929-34; Commander 144th (Glos and Worcs) Infantry Brigade TA, 1934-38; Commander 135 Infantry Brigade, 1939-42; 1942-43 North African Campaign (despatches, Legion of Merit, Degree of Officer); Served at Allied Force HQ, 1943-45, N Africa and Italy (despatches). Chm., BEM Exports Ltd, 1965-75. DL Glos, 1950-74, Somerset, 1974; JP 1952-64. Chairman South Western Regional Board for Industry, 1956-65. Governor Bristol Grammar Sch.; Fellow Royal Commonwealth Society. Hon. Colonel 5th Bn The Gloucestershire Regiment, 1961-67. Master, Furniture Makers' Co., 1975-76. Hon. Freeman, City of London. La Médaille d'honneur d'or de l'éducation physique (France), 1946. *Recreation:* gardening. *Address:* Shepton House, Shepton Montague, Wincanton, Somerset. *T:* Bruton 2258. *Club:* Naval and Military.

NEWTH, Prof. David Richmond; Regius Professor of Zoology, University of Glasgow, since 1965; *b* 10 Oct. 1921; *s* of Herbert Greenway Newth and Annie Munroe (*née* Fraser); *m* 1946, Jean Winifred (*née* Haddon); two *s* one *d. Educ:* King Edward VI High Sch., Birmingham. Entered University Coll., London, 1938; graduated in Zoology, 1942. Served War of 1939-45, REME, commnd 1943. Asst Lectr in Zoology at University Coll., London, 1947; Lectr, 1949; Prof. of Biology as Applied to Medicine in the Univ. of London, at the Middlesex Hospital Medical Sch., 1960-65. Pres., Scottish Marine Biol. Assoc., 1973-. FRSE 1966. Editor, Journal of Embryology and Experimental Morphology, 1960-69. *Publications:* Animal Growth and Development, 1970; original articles in scientific journals, translations, and contrib. (popular) scientific works. *Recreation:* resting. *Address:* Department of Zoology, The University, Glasgow G12 8QQ.

NEWTON, 4th Baron, *cr* 1892; **Peter Richard Legh;** *b* 6 April 1915; *er s* of 3rd Baron Newton, TD, DL, JP, and Hon. Helen Meysey-Thompson (*d* 1958); *S* father 1960; *m* 1948, Priscilla, *yr d* of late Capt. John Egerton-Warburton and *widow* of William Matthew Palmer, Visc. Wolmer; two *s. Educ:* Eton; Christ Church, Oxford (MA). 2nd Lt, Grenadier Guards (SR), 1937; Captain, 1941; Major, 1945. JP 1951; CC Hampshire, 1949-52 and 1954-55. Chairman East Hampshire Young Conservatives, 1949-50. MP (C) Petersfield Division of Hants, Oct. 1951-June 1960; PPS to Fin. Sec. to Treasury, 1952-53; Asst Govt Whip, 1953-55; a Lord Comr of Treasury, 1955-57; Vice-Chamberlain of the Household, 1957-59; Treasurer of the Household, 1959-60; Capt. Yeomen of the Guard and Govt Asst Chief Whip, 1960-62; (Joint) Parly Sec., Min. of Health, 1962-64; Min. of State for Education and Science, April-Oct. 1964. *Recreations:* photography, clock repairing, making gadgets. *Heir: s* Hon. Richard Thomas Legh, *b* 11 Jan. 1950. *Address:* Vernon Hill House, Bishop's Waltham, Hampshire. *T:* Bishop's Waltham 2301. *Clubs:* Carlton, Constitutional, Pratt's; Hampshire (Winchester).
See also Major Hon. Sir F. M. Legh, Earl of Selborne.

NEWTON, Antony Harold; MP (C) Braintree since Feb. 1974; economist; *b* Aug. 1937; *m* ; two *c. Educ:* Friends' Sch., Saffron Walden; Trinity Coll., Oxford. Hons PPE. Pres., OU Conservative Assoc., 1958. Formerly Sec. and Research Sec., Bow Group. Head of Conservative Research Dept's Economic Section, 1965-70; Asst Dir, Conservative Research Dept, 1970-74. Chm. Coningsby Club, 1962-66. Contested (C) Sheffield, Brightside, 1970. Vice-Chm., Fedn of Univ. Conservative and Unionist Assocs. Governor, City Literary Inst.; Past Gov., City of Westminster Coll. Interested in education and social services. *Address:* 17 Warner Road, N8. *T:* 01-340 7706; House of Commons, SW1A 0AA.

NEWTON, Douglas Anthony, CB 1976; Senior Registrar, Principal Registry, Family Division of High Court, 1972-75, retired; *b* 21 Dec. 1915; *s* of John and Janet May Newton; *m* 1946, Barbara Sutherland; one *s* one *d. Educ:* Westminster Sch. Joined Civil Service, 1934. Served War, British and Indian Armies, 1940-46. Apptd Registrar, 1959; Sen. Registrar, 1972. *Recreations:* beer, boats, building. *Address:* 12 Lakeside, Oatlands Drive, Weybridge, Surrey KT13 9JB. *T:* Walton-on-Thames 22664; Resthaven, Hamm Court, Weybridge, Surrey KT13 8YF. *T:* Weybridge 45280.

NEWTON, Sir Gordon; see Newton, Sir L. G.

NEWTON, Sir (Harry) Michael (Rex), 3rd Bt, *cr* 1900; Director Thos Parsons & Sons Ltd; *b* 7 Feb. 1923; 2nd and *e* surv. *s* of Sir Harry K. Newton, 2nd Bt, OBE, DL, and Myrtle Irene (*d* 1977), *e d* of W. W. Grantham, Balneath Manor, Lewes; *S* father, 1951; *m* 1958, Pauline Jane, *o d* of late R. J. F. Howgill, CBE; one *s* ; three adopted *d. Educ:* Eastbourne College. Served War of 1939-45, with KRRC, in 8th Army and Middle East, 1941-46 (wounded). Master, Girdlers' Company, 1975-76; Freeman of City of London. *Recreations:* shooting, sailing (winner of 1953 Fastnet Race), ski-ing, fencing. *Heir: s* George Peter Howgill Newton, *b* 26 March 1962. *Address:* Weycroft Hall, near Axminster, Devon. *T:* 3169. *Clubs:* Bath, Royal Ocean Racing.

NEWTON, Sir Hubert, Kt 1968; Chairman, Britannia Building Society, since 1976; *b* 2 Sept. 1904; *s* of Joe Newton and Gertrude Elizabeth Newton; *m* 1931, Elsie (*née* Wilson); one *d. Educ:* Burnley Gram. School. Burnley Building Soc., 1918-23; Mortgage Dept Controller, Northampton Town Building Soc., 1923-26; Controller of Investment Dept, Leeds Perm. Building Soc., 1926-30; Asst Sec., Bristol & West Building Soc., 1930-33; Leek and Moorlands Building Soc.: Sec., 1933-40; Gen. Man., 1940-63; Chm. and Man. Dir, 1963-66, when Leek and Moorlands amalgamated with Westbourne Park Building Soc.

to form Leek and Westbourne Building Soc.; Man. Dir, 1966-69, Chm., 1966-74, Leek and Westbourne Building Soc.; on further amalgamation, Jt Dep. Chm., Leek Westbourne and Eastern Counties Building Soc. (name changed to Britannia Building Soc., 1975), 1974-76. Hd Office Dir, Liverpool Bd, Royal Insce Co. Ltd. Former Member Council: Building Socs Assoc. of Gt Britain (Chm., 1952-54); and Mem., Exec. Cttee, Internat. Union of Building Socs and Savings Assocs (Dep. Pres., Washington Congress, 1962; Pres., London Congress, 1965); Vice-President: Building Socs Inst., 1962; Building Socs Assoc. of Jamaica Ltd, 1967; Midland Assoc. of Building Socs, 1969; Pres., N Staffs Chamber of Commerce, 1964-65. Former Mem., Skelmersdale Devalt Corp. Past Mem., Central Housing Adv. Cttee; Mem. Council, Nat. House-Building Council (Vice-Pres.); Liveryman, Gold and Silver Wyre Drawers' Company. Hon. MA Keele, 1971. Coronation Medal, 1953. *Publications:* contribs to Building Socs Gazette. *Recreations:* golf, travel. *Address:* Birchall, Leek, Staffs ST13 5RA. *T:* Leek 382397.

NEWTON, Ivor, CBE 1973; FRCM; Pianoforte Accompanist; *b* London, 15 Dec. 1892; *s* of William and Gertrude Newton. Studied the piano with Arthur Barclay (Dir of Music, Brompton Oratory), York Bowen, and Isidore Snook (Amsterdam); studied Art of Accompanying and Repertoire with Raimund von zur Muhlen and Coenraad Bos (Berlin). Associated as accompanist with Kirsten Flagstad, Melba, Clara Butt, Tetrazzini, Conchita Supervia, Lily Pons, Lotte Lehmann, Elisabeth Schumann, Victoria de los Angeles, Joan Hammond, Kathleen Ferrier, Chaliapine, Gigli, Tito Schipa, John McCormack, Jussi Björling, Tito Gobbi, Ysaye, Yehudi Menuhin, Milstein, Casals, Piatigorsky, Suggia, di Stefano and Maria Callas. Toured extensively in Europe, United States, Canada, Africa, Australia, New Zealand and the Orient. Salzburg, Edinburgh and Aldeburgh Festivals. Organised first concert in aid of British War Relief in United States at British Embassy, Washington, 1940; toured Egypt, Irak, and the Persian Gulf giving concerts to forces, 1943; concerts to Royal Navy and Soviet Fleet in Scapa Flow, 1944; toured Germany and Austria with Grace Moore on invitation of American C-in-C, 1946; British Council Tours, Scandinavia with Henry Holst, 1946; France with Maggie Teyte, 1947, Persia, Turkey and Austria with Leon Goossens, 1955. Adviser on music for HM Prisons. *Publication:* At the Piano-Ivor Newton (autobiog.), 1966. *Address:* Kirsten House, Kinnerton Street, Belgrave Square, SW1. *T:* 01-235 2882. *Clubs:* Garrick, Chelsea Arts; Royal Naval and Royal Albert Yacht (Portsmouth).

NEWTON, John Mordaunt, CB 1964; retired from Post Office Central HQ, 1973; *b* 24 April 1913; *o s* of late Wallis and Mabel Newton; *m* 1939, Pamela Frances, *e d* of late Sir E. John Maude, KCB, KBE; five *d. Educ:* Manchester Gram. Sch.; CCC, Cambridge (Scholar). BA 1st Cl. History Tripos, 1935. Assistant Principal, Post Office, 1936; Principal: Ministry of Home Security, 1941; Home Office, 1943; Treasury, 1945-47; Post Office 1947-73: Assistant Secretary, 1949; Under Secretary, 1957; Director of Personnel, GPO, 1957-67; Dir, Management Develt, 1967-73. Hon. Secretary, Abbeyfield Chiswick Soc. *Address:* Thames Bank, Chiswick Mall, W4 2PR. *T:* 01-994 1803.

NEWTON, Sir Kenneth (Garnar), 3rd Bt *cr* 1924; OBE 1970 (MBE 1944); TD; Managing Director, since 1961 and Chairman, since 1972, Garnar Scotblair Ltd; *b* 4 June 1918; *s* of Sir Edgar Henry Newton, 2nd Bt, and Gladys Maud (*d* 1966), *d* of late Sir James Garnar; *S* father, 1971; *m* 1944, Margaret Isabel, *d* of Rev. Dr George Blair, Dundee; two *s. Educ:* Wellington College, Berks. Served War of 1939-45 (MBE); Lt-Col, RASC (TA). General Commissioner for Income Tax, 1961-. Pres., Internat. Council of Tanners, 1972-; Past President, British Leather Federation (1968-69); Liveryman and Member of Court of Assistants, and Second Warden, 1976-77, Master, 1977-78, Leathersellers' Company and Feltmakers' Company. *Heir: s* John Garnar Newton, *b* 10 July 1945. *Address:* Whitebeams, Beech Avenue, Effingham, Surrey. *T:* Bookham 58551.

NEWTON, Sir (Leslie) Gordon, Kt 1966; Chairman, London Broadcasting Co. until 1977; Deputy Chairman, Mills & Allen (International); Director, Trust Houses Forte Ltd; *b* 1907; *s* of John and Edith Newton; *m* 1935, Peggy Ellen Warren; one *s. Educ:* Blundell's School; Sidney Sussex College, Cambridge. Editor, 1950-72, Dir, 1967-72, The Financial Times. Hannen Swaffer Award for Journalist of the Year, 1966; Granada Television special award, 1970. *Address:* Little Basing, Vicarage Walk, Bray-on-Thames, Berks.

NEWTON, Prof. Lily, DSc, PhD; Professor of Botany, University College of Wales, Aberystwyth, 1930-58, Prof.

Emeritus since 1959; Vice-Principal, 1951-52; Acting Principal, May 1952-Sept. 1953; *b* 26 Jan. 1893; *d* of George Batten and Melinda Batten (*née* Casling); *m* 1925, William Charles Frank Newton (*d* 1927). *Educ:* Colston's Girls' School, Bristol; University of Bristol. Assistant Lecturer in Botany, University of Bristol, 1919-1920; Lecturer in Botany, Birkbeck Coll., Univ. of London, 1920-23; research worker, Imperial College of Science and British Museum, Natural History, 1923-25; Lecturer in Botany, University College of Wales, Aberystwyth, 1928-30. President: Section K, British Association, 1949; British Phycological Soc., 1955-57; UK Fedn for Educn in Home Economics, 1957-63. Hon. LLD Wales, 1973. *Publications:* Handbook of British Seaweeds, 1931; Plant distribution in the Aberystwyth district, 1935; (jointly) A Study of certain British Seaweeds and their utilisation in the preparation of agar, 1949; Utilisation of Seaweeds, 1951. Papers in Jl of Linnean Soc., Jl of Ecology, Annals of Applied Biology, Vistas in Botany and others. *Recreations:* cookery, needlework, gardening. *Address:* Banc-y-Rhos, Cae Melyn, Aberystwyth, Dyfed. *T:* Aberystwyth 3490.

NEWTON, Margaret; Headmistress, Westonbirt School, since 1965; *b* 20 Dec. 1927; 2nd *d* of F. L. Newton, KStJ, MB, ChB, and Mrs A. C. Newton, MBE, BA. *Educ:* Sherborne School for Girls; St Andrews Univ.; Oxford University. MA Hons St Andrews, 1950; Educn Dip. Oxon 1951. Asst Mistress, King Edward VI Grammar School, Handsworth, Birmingham, 1951-54; Classics Mistress, Queen Margaret's Sch., York, 1954-60 (House Mistress, 1957); House Mistress, Malvern Girls' College, 1960-64 (Head of Classics Dept, 1962). *Address:* Westonbirt School, Tetbury, Gloucestershire; 2 West Court, Westfield Road, Budleigh Salterton, Devon.

NEWTON, Sir Michael; see Newton, Sir H. M. R.

NEWTON, Robert, CMG 1953; retired as Colonial Secretary, Mauritius, 1961; *b* Newcastle upon Tyne, 12 Oct. 1908; *m* 1933, Muriel Winifred, *d* of late Mr and Mrs R. P. Chinneck; one *s* two *d. Educ:* Aysgarth School; Malvern College; Pembroke College, Cambridge. Joined Colonial Administrative Service as Administrative Officer (Cadet), Nigeria, 1931; served there as an Assistant District Officer until 1937; served Palestine until 1946; IDC 1947; seconded for duty in Colonial Office, 1948; Financial Secretary, Jamaica, 1949. Member, British Ornithologists Union. PhD (Exon) 1966. FRSA 1972. *Publications:* Tarnished Brocade, 1937; Swords of Bronze, 1939; Victorian Exeter, 1968; The Northumberland Landscape, 1972. *Recreations:* ornithology, walking. *Address:* 14 Howell Road, Exeter, Devon. *Club:* United Oxford & Cambridge University.

NEWTON-CLARE, Herbert Mitchell, CBE 1976; MC 1943; Director, FMC Ltd, since 1976; Managing Director, FMC Harris Products Division, since 1976; *b* 5 May 1922; *s* of Herbert John and Eileen Margaret Newton-Clare; *m* 1970, Maureen Mary Thorp; three *d. Educ:* Cheltenham Coll. TA, Middlesex Regt, 1938; served War of 1939-45: mobilised, 1939; commnd, Wiltshire Regt, 1941; wounded, Normandy, 1944; demobilised, 1945 (Major). Joined Bowyers (Wiltshire) Ltd, as trainee, 1945; Factory Manager, 1955, Gen. Manager, 1957, Man. Dir, 1960, Chm., 1966; following take-over by Unigate of Scot Bowyers (formerly Bowyers (Wiltshire) Ltd), became Director of Unigate, 1973, Vice-Chm., 1974-76. Director: Agricultural Database Ltd; Dunmow Flitch Bacon Co. Ltd; C. & T. Harris (Calne) Ltd; Harris (Calne) Trustee Corp. Ltd; Marsh & Baxter Ltd; Marsh & Baxter Trustee Corp. Ltd; Oake Woods & Co. Ltd; Vale of Mowbray Bacon Co. Ltd; Winsford Bacon Co. Ltd. Chm., Meat Manufrs Assoc.; Mem. Council, Food Manufrs Fedn. *Recreations:* golf, fishing. *Address:* Hurtmore Holt, Shackleford, near Godalming, Surrey GU8 6AY. *T:* Godalming 7116. *Club:* Sunningdale Golf.

NEY, Marie; see Menzies, M. N.

NGAIZA, Christopher Pastor; Tanzania's Ambassador to the Arab Republic of Egypt, since 1972; *b* 29 March 1930; parents decd; *m* 1952, Thereza; three *s* two *d* (and one *s* decd). *Educ:* Makerere University Coll.; Loughborough Co-operative College. Local Courts Magistrate, 1952-53; Secretary/Manager, Bahaya Co-operative Consumer Stores, 1955-57; Loughborough Co-operative Coll., 1957-59; Auctioneer and Representative of Bukoba Native Co-operative Union, Mombasa, 1959-61; Foreign Service, 1961-; Counsellor, Mission to UN, 1961-62; Counsellor, Tanganyika High Commn, London, 1962-63; High Commissioner for United Republic of Tanganyika and Zanzibar in London, 1964-65; Tanzanian Ambassador to Netherlands, 1965-67; Mem., E African Common Market Tribunal, 1968-69; Tanzania's first High Comr to Zambia, 1969-72. *Recreations:* music, tennis. *Address:* Tanzania Embassy, 9 Abdul Hamid

Lotfy Street, Mohandession City, Dokki, Cairo, Arab Republic of Egypt.

NG'ETHE NJOROGE; High Commissioner for Kenya in London since Oct. 1970; *m* 1972, Dr Njeri Ng'ethe Njoroge; one *s*. *Educ:* Kenya and Uganda (Cambridge Sch. Cert., 1949); United States: Central State Coll., Wilberforce, Ohio (BSc (Gen. Sci.) 1955); Univ. of Dayton, Dayton, Ohio (Sociology, 1955-56); Boston Univ. (MSc (Pol. Sci. and Journalism) 1962). Began as journalist, Patriot Ledger, Quincy, Mass; subseq., Kenya Govt: Asst Sec. (Admin), in Min. of Lands and Settlement, and Min. of Works, 1963-64; Min. of Foreign Affairs, 1964; Head of Africa Div., 1964-67; Counsellor, Kenya Embassy, Bonn, 1968-70. Delegate: Commonwealth Conf., 1965, 1966, 1971; Organization of African Unity Confs, 1964-67; UN Gen. Assembly, 1964, 1965, 1966. *Recreations:* music (collector of jazz and classical records), photography (colour slides), reading; interest in current public and international issues. *Address:* Kenya High Commission, 45 Portland Place, W1. *T:* 01-636 2371/5.

NGONDA, Putteho Muketoi; Permanent Secretary, Ministry of Foreign Affairs, Republic of Zambia, since 1975; *b* 16 Aug. 1936; *m* 1965, Lungowe Mulala; three *s*. *Educ:* Mongu and Munali Secondary Schs, Zambia; UC of Rhodesia and Nyasaland, Salisbury. BScEcon (Hons). District Officer, 1963-64; 2nd Sec., Zambia Perm. Mission to US, 1964-65; 1st Sec., Zambian Embassy, Washington, 1967-68; Asst Sec. (Political), Min. of Foreign Affairs, 1968-70; Under-Sec., Min. of Foreign Affairs, 1970-72; Ambassador to Ethiopia, 1972-74; High Comr to UK, 1974-75. *Recreation:* mainly tennis. *Address:* Ministry of Foreign Affairs, PO Box RW69, Lusaka, Zambia.

NIALL, Sir Horace Lionel Richard, Kt 1974; CBE 1957 (MBE 1943); Civil Servant (retd); *b* 14 Oct. 1904; *s* of late Alfred George Niall and Jane Phyllis Niall; *m* 1965, Una Lesley Niall (née de Salis); one *d*. *Educ:* Mudgee High Sch., NSW; Sydney Univ., NSW. Served War of 1939-45: with AIF, four yrs in New Guinea, rank Major, No NGX 373, all campaigns in New Guinea. NSW Public Service (Water Conservation Commn), 1923-27. Public Service of Papua, New Guinea, 1927-64: joined as a Cadet and retd as Dist Comr; rep. PNG at South Pacific Commn, 1954, and UN Trusteeship Council, 1957; Mem. for Morobe in first House of Assembly and Speaker First House, 1964. *Recreations:* golf, surfing. *Address:* 9 Commodore, 50 Palm Beach Road, Palm Beach, NSW 2108, Australia. *T:* 919 5462. *Clubs:* Royal Commonwealth Society; Palm Beach Golf, RSL Palm Beach (NSW).

NIARCHOS, Stavros Spyros; Grand Cross of Order of the Phœnix (Greece), 1957; Commander of Order of George I of Greece, 1954; Commander of Order of St George and St Constantine (Greece), 1964; Head of Niarchos Group of Shipping Companies which controls over 5.75 million tons of shipping (operational and building); *b* 3 July 1909; *s* of late Spyros Niarchos and of Eugenie Niarchos; *m* 1st, 1939, Melpomene Capparis (marr. diss., 1947); no *c*; 2nd, 1947, Eugenie Livanos (*d* 1970); three *s* one *d*; 3rd, 1965, Charlotte Ford (marr. diss., 1967); one *d*; 4th, 1971, Mrs Athina Livanos (*d* 1974). *Educ:* Univ. of Athens (Dr of Laws). On leaving Univ. joined family grain and shipping business; started independent shipping concern, 1939. Joined Royal Hellenic Navy Volunteer Reserve, 1941; served on destroyer engaged in North Atlantic convoy work (despatches). Demobilised, 1945, with rank of Lieut-Comdr. Returned to Shipping business. Pioneered super-tankers. *Recreations:* yachting, ski-ing. *Address:* c/o Niarchos (London) Ltd, 41/43 Park Street, W1. *T:* 01-629 8400. *Clubs:* Athenian, Royal Yacht Club of Greece (both in Athens).

NIBLETT, Prof. William Roy, CBE 1970; BA, BLitt; Professor of Higher Education, University of London, 1967-73, Professor Emeritus, 1973; *b* 25 July 1906; *m* 1938, Sheila Margaret, OBE, *d* of A. C. Taylor, Peterborough; one *s* one *d*. *Educ:* Cotham Sch., Bristol; University of Bristol (1st cl. hons English); St Edmund Hall, Oxford. Lectr in Educn, King's Coll., Newcastle, 1934-45 (Registrar of Univ. Durham, 1940-44); Prof. of Educn, University Coll., Hull, 1945-47; Prof. of Education, and Dir, Inst. of Education, Univ. of Leeds, 1947-59. Dean, Univ. of London Inst. of Education, 1960-68; Mem., UGC, 1949-59; Hibbert Lectr, 1965; Kellogg International Fellow, 1954; sometime Visiting Professor, Universities of California, Melbourne, Otago and Univs of Japan. Chairman: UGC Sub-Cttee on Halls of Residence, 1956 (Report 1957); Educn Dept, BCC, 1965-71; Commn on C of E Colls of Higher Educn, 1976-. Member: Nat. Advisory Coun. on Trng and Supply of Teachers, 1950-61; Council, Royal Holloway College, 1963-76; Council, Cheltenham Ladies' College, 1967-; Council, Soc. for Research in Higher Educn, 1974-; Governing Body, Bristol Polytechnic,

1976-; Trustee, St Luke's Foundn, 1977-. Mem. Editorial Bd, Studies in Higher Education, 1975-. *Publications:* Education and the Modern Mind, 1954; Christian Education in a Secular Society, 1960; Universities Between Two Worlds, 1974; (with D. Humphreys and J. Fairhurst) The University Connection, 1975; (ed) Moral Education in a Changing Society; (ed) Higher Education: Demand and Response, 1969; (ed with R. F. Butts) World Year Book of Education, 1972-73; (ed) The Sciences, The Humanities and the Technological Threat, 1975; contribs to periodicals. *Address:* Pinfarthings, Amberley, Stroud, Glos GL5 5JJ. *Club:* Athenæum.

NIBLOCK, Henry, OBE 1972; HM Diplomatic Service, retired; HM Consul-General, Strasbourg, 1968-72; *b* 25 Nov. 1911; *s* of Joseph and Isabella Niblock, Belfast; *m* 1940, Barbara Mary Davies, *d* of late Captain R. W. Davies, Air Ministry; two *s*. Vice-Consul: Bremen, 1947-50; Bordeaux, 1951; Second Sec. (Commercial), Copenhagen, 1951-53; Consul, Frankfurt-on-Main, 1954-57; First Sec. and Consul, Monrovia, 1957-58; Consul, Houston, 1959-62; Chargé d'Affaires, Port-au-Prince, 1962-63; First Sec. and Consul, Brussels, 1964; Consul (Commercial), Cape Town, 1964-67. *Recreations:* walking, photography. *Address:* 5 Kewhurst Avenue, Cooden, Bexhill-on-Sea, East Sussex. *T:* Cooden 4630. *Club:* Royal Over-Seas League.

NICCOL, Dame Sister Mary Leo, (Kathleen Agnes Niccol), DBE 1973 (MBE 1963), of Auckland, New Zealand; Member of the Sisters of Mercy, Auckland. Specialised in vocal training. Entered Order of Sisters of Mercy, 1923. Has been a singing teacher for over 40 years; pupils who have gained international success include Kiri Te Kanawa (Mrs Kiri J. Park, OBE), now living in London, Heather Begg, and Mina Foley. TV Documentary on her life and work, NZ, 1975. *Address:* St Mary's Convent, PO Box 47025, Ponsonby, Auckland 1, New Zealand.

NICHOL, Mrs Muriel Edith; JP; *e d* of late R. C. Wallhead, MP Merthyr Tydfil, 1922-34; *m* James Nichol, MA; one *s*. Onetime Chm., Welwyn Garden City UDC (1937-45); formerly Dep. Chm., Welwyn Magistrates' Court. MP (Lab) North Bradford, 1945-50; Mem. Parly Delegation to India, Jan.-Feb. 1946; Mem. "Curtis" Cttee (Home Office) on Care of Children, 1945-46. JP Herts, 1944. *Recreations:* local government, social welfare, education. *Address:* 8 Elmwood, Welwyn Garden City, Herts. *T:* Welwyn Garden 22277.

NICHOLAS, Sir Alfred James, Kt 1967; CBE 1960 (OBE 1954); Chairman: Aberdare Holdings Ltd, 1963-70; South Wales Switchgear Ltd, 1965-70; Glyn John Transport Ltd; *b* 1900; *s* of George and Harriet Nicholas; *m* 1927, Ethel, *d* of Thomas Platt; one *s*. *Educ:* Bishop's Castle Sch.; Wellington Sch., Salop; Manchester Coll. of Technology. With Metropolitan Vickers Ltd, and Ferguson-Pailin Ltd until 1941. Formerly Chm. and Man. Director: Aberdare Cables Ltd; Aberdare Engineering Ltd; Erskine Heap & Co. Ltd; South Wales Group (Pty) Ltd South Africa; South Wales Electric (Pvt) Ltd Rhodesia; South Wales Electric Australia (Pty) Ltd; South Wales Electric Zambia Ltd; Director, Electric Switchgear Co. Montreal. Founder Mem. and former Chm., Develt Corp. for Wales, President, 1971-; founder Mem. and former Pres., Industrial Assoc. of Wales and Monmouthshire; a Vice-Chm., Welsh Economic Council, 1966-68; Vice-Pres., Welsh Council, 1968-71; Past Pres., Cardiff Chamber of Commerce and Industry. Member: Council and Court of Governors, University Coll., Cardiff; Court of Governors, UWIST; Governor, Christ's Coll., Brecon. Assoc. Mem. Manchester Coll. of Technology; FIEE; MIEEE (USA); CEng; FBIM. Freeman of the City of London; Liveryman, Worshipful Co. of Tin Plate Workers. Hon. LLD Wales. CStJ (Pres., East Mon area). *Recreations:* photography, gardening. *Address:* Bovil House, Machen, Gwent NP1 8SN. *Club:* Cardiff and County (Cardiff).

NICHOLAS, Prof. Barry; *see* Nicholas, Prof. J. K. B. M.

NICHOLAS, Sir Harry; *see* Nicholas, Sir Herbert Richard.

NICHOLAS, Prof. Herbert George, FBA 1969; Rhodes Professor of American History and Institutions, Oxford University, 1969-Sept. 1978; Fellow of New College, Oxford, since 1951; *b* 8 June 1911; *s* of late Rev. W. D. Nicholas. *Educ:* Mill Hill Sch.; New Coll., Oxford (1st cl. Lit. Hum., 1934). Jessie Teresa Rowden Schol., New Coll., 1934. Commonwealth Fund Fellow in Modern History, Yale, 1935-37; MA Oxon, 1938; Exeter College, Oxford: Lectr, 1938, Fellow, 1946-51; Amer. Div., Min. of Information, and HM Embassy, Washington, 1941-46; Faculty Fellow, Nuffield Coll., Oxford, 1948-57; Nuffield Reader in the Comparative Study of

Institutions at Oxford Univ., 1956-69. Chm., British Assoc. for American Studies, 1960-62; Vice-Pres., British Academy, 1975-76. Vis. Prof., Brookings Instn, Washington, 1960; Albert Shaw Lectr in Diplomatic History, Johns Hopkins, 1961; Vis. Fellow, Inst. of Advanced Studies, Princeton, 1964; Vis. Faculty Fellow, Inst. of Politics, Harvard, 1968. Hon. DCL Pittsburgh, 1968. *Publications:* The American Union, 1948; The British General Election of 1950, 1951; To the Hustings, 1956; The United Nations as a Political Institution, 1959, 5th edn 1975; Britain and the United States, 1963; The American Past and The American Present, 1971; The United States and Britain, 1975; Editor, Tocqueville's De la Démocratie en Amérique, 1961; articles. *Recreations:* gardening, listening to music. *Address:* 3 William Orchard Close, Old Headington, Oxford. *T:* Oxford 63165. *Clubs:* Athenæum; Lotos (New York).

NICHOLAS, Sir Herbert Richard, (Sir Harry Nicholas), Kt 1970; OBE 1949; General Secretary of the Labour Party, 1968-72; *b* 13 March 1905; *s* of Richard Henry and Rosina Nicholas; *m* 1932, Rosina Grace Brown. *Educ:* Elementary sch., Avonmouth, Bristol; Evening Classes; Correspondence Courses. Clerk, Port of Bristol Authority, 1919-36. Transport and Gen. Workers Union: District Officer, Gloucester, 1936-38; Regional Officer, Bristol, 1938-40; National Officer, London: Commercial Road Transport Group, 1940-42; Chemical Section, 1942-44; Metal and Engineering Group, 1944-56; Asst Gen. Sec., 1956-68 (Acting Gen. Sec., Oct. 1964-July 66). Mem., TUC General Council, 1964-67. Mem., Labour Party Nat. Exec. Cttee, 1956-64, 1967-; Treasurer, Labour Party, 1960-64. *Publications:* occasional articles in press on Industrial Relations subjects. *Recreations:* Rugby football, fishing, reading, gardening. *Address:* 33 Madeira Road, Streatham, SW16. *T:* 01-769 7989.

NICHOLAS, Prof. (John Keiran) Barry (Moylan); Professor of Comparative Law, University of Oxford, 1971-78; Principal of Brasenose College, Oxford, from Aug. 1978 (Fellow, 1947-78); *b* 6 July 1919; *s* of Archibald John Nicholas and late Rose (*née* Moylan); *m* 1948, Hildegart, *d* of late Prof. Hans Cloos, Bonn; one *s* one *d. Educ:* Downside; Brasenose Coll., Oxford (Scholar). 1st cl. Class. Mods, 1939 and Jurisprudence, 1946. Royal Signals, 1939-45: Middle East, 1941-45; Major, 1943. Called to Bar, Inner Temple, 1950. Tutor, 1947-71 and Vice-Principal, 1960-63, Brasenose Coll.; All Souls Reader in Roman Law, Oxford Univ., 1949-71. Vis. Prof.: Tulane Univ., 1960; Univ. of Rome Inst. of Comparative Law, 1964; Fordham Univ., 1968. *Publications:* Introduction to Roman Law, 1962; Jolowicz's Historical Introduction to Roman Law, 3rd edn, 1972. *Address:* Brasenose College, Oxford. *T:* Oxford 48641.

NICHOLAS, John William; HM Diplomatic Service; Consul General, Melbourne, since 1976; *b* 13 Dec. 1924; *m* 1947, Rita (*née* Jones); two *s. Educ:* Birmingham Univ. Served 7th Rajput Regt, Indian Army, 1944-47; joined Home Civil Service, 1949; War Office, 1949-57; transf. to CRO 1957; First Sec., Brit. High Commn, Kuala Lumpur, 1957-61; Economic Div., CRO, 1961-63; Dep. High Comr in Malawi, 1964-66; Diplomatic Service Inspector, 1967-69; Dep. High Comr and Counsellor (Commercial), Ceylon, 1970-71; Dir, Establishments and Finance Div., Commonwealth Secretariat, 1971-73; Hd of Pacific Dependent Territories Dept, FCO, 1973-74; Dep. High Comr, Calcutta, 1974-76. *Address:* c/o Foreign and Commonwealth Office, SW1. *Clubs:* Royal Over-Seas League, Travellers'.

NICHOLAS, Reginald Owen Mercer, CB 1956; retired as Commissioner of Inland Revenue and Secretary, Board of Inland Revenue (1954-65); *b* 20 June 1903; *e s* of Reginald John Nicholas, mining engineer, Gold Coast, and Margaret Mary (*née* Trice); *m* 1929, Joan Estelle, *d* of E. S. Friend, Uplyme, Devon; two *s* one *d. Educ:* Royal Masonic Sch.; Gonville and Caius Coll., Cambridge (Scholar). Entered Inland Revenue Dept, 1925. Mem. War Damage Commn, 1962-64. *Address:* Thornton Cottage, Higher Metcombe, Ottery-St-Mary, Devon.

NICHOLAS, William Ford, OBE 1954; Director, London Chamber of Commerce and Industry, since 1974; *b* 17 March 1923; *s* of William and Emma Nicholas; *m* 1954, Isobel Sybil Kennedy; two *s. Educ:* Stockport Grammar School. Called to Bar, Middle Temple, 1965. Joined S Rhodesia Civil Service, 1947; Private Sec. to Prime Minister, S Rhodesia, 1950; Private Sec. to Prime Minister, Fedn of Rhodesia and Nyasaland, 1953; Counsellor, High Comr's Office, London, 1960; retd 1963. Dir, UK Cttee, Fedn of Commonwealth Chambers of Commerce, 1964; Dep. Dir, London Chamber of Commerce, 1966. *Address:* 2 Lime Close, Frant, Tunbridge Wells, Kent. *T:* Frant 428. *Club:* Gresham.

NICHOLETTS, Air Marshal Sir Gilbert (Edward), KBE 1956; CB 1949; AFC 1931 and Bar, 1933; retired; *b* 9 Nov. 1902; *s* of Edward Cornewall Nicholetts and Ellen Fanny Hollond; *m* 1956, Nora Beswick, *d* of Francis John Butt, MB, Chester. *Educ:* RN Colleges, Osborne and Dartmouth. Cranwell Cadet Coll., 1921-22; Calshot, Lee-on-Solent, 1922-24; HMS Eagle (Med. Fleet), 1924-26; Far East Flight and 205 Sqdn, 1927-30; 209 Sqdn, 1931-32; long distance flight (World Record, 5309 miles non-stop), 1933; Air Staff, 23 Group HQ, 1934; Staff Coll., 1935; Air Staff, AHQ Iraq, 1936-38; Air Ministry organization, 1938-39; War of 1939-45, OC 228 Sqdn, 1939-41; Haifa, Shallufa, 1941; POW Far East, 1942-45; AOC Central Photographic Establishment, 1946-48; Dir of Organization, Air Ministry, 1948-51; SASO Coastal Command, 1951; AOC No. 21 Group, Flying Training Command, 1953; SASO Flying Training Command, March-Dec. 1955; AOC Malta, and Dep. C-in-C (Air), Allied Forces, Mediterranean, Jan. 1956-Dec. 1957; Inspector-Gen., Royal Air Force, Jan. 1958-June, 1959; retired, 1959. *Address:* Stoborough Croft, Wareham, Dorset. *T:* Wareham 2992. *Club:* Royal Air Force.

NICHOLLS; *see* Harmar-Nicholls.

NICHOLLS, Donald James, QC 1974; *b* 25 Jan. 1933; *yr s* of William Greenhow Nicholls and late Eleanor Jane (*née* Looney); *m* 1960, Jennifer Mary, *yr d* of late W. E. C. Thomas, MB, BCh, MRCOG, JP; two *s* one *d. Educ:* Birkenhead Sch.; Liverpool Univ.; Trinity Hall, Cambridge (Foundn Schol.). LLB 1st cl. hons Liverpool, BA 1st cl. hons with dist., Pt II Law Tripos Cantab, LLB 1st cl. hons with dist. Cantab. Certif. of Honour, Bar Final, 1958; called to Bar, Middle Temple, 1958; in practice, Chancery Bar, 1958-. Mem., Senate of Inns of Court and the Bar, 1974-76. *Recreations:* gardening, music. *Address:* Little Blakeney, Leigh Hill Road, Cobham, Surrey. *T:* Cobham 4740. *Club:* Athenæum.

NICHOLLS, Pastor Sir Douglas (Ralph), KCVO 1977; Kt 1972; OBE 1968; Governor of South Australia, 1976-77; *b* Cummeragunja, NSW, 9 Dec. 1906; *s* of H. Nicholls, Cummeragunja; *m* 1942, Gladys, *d* of M. Bux; one *s* one *d. Educ:* at Cummeragunja. Formerly one of the best-known aborigines of Australia in the field of athletics and football; Pastor, Churches of Christ Aborigines' Mission, Fitzroy, Victoria; Dir, Aborigines Advancement League, 1969-76. KStJ 1977. *Publications:* contribs AAL quarterly magazines. *Recreations:* formerly running (won Nyah Gift and Warracknabeal Gift, 4th Melbourne Thousand, 1929); football (rep. Vic. in interstate matches). *Address:* 688 Canterbury Road, Vermont, Vic 3133, Australia.

NICHOLLS, Rear-Adm. Francis Brian Price B.; *see* Brayne-Nicholls.

NICHOLLS, Air Marshal John Moreton, CBE 1970; DFC 1953; AFC 1965; Air Member for Supply and Organisation, since 1977; *b* 5 July 1926; *s* of Alfred Nicholls and Elsie (*née* French); *m* 1945, Enid Jean Marjorie Rose (*d* 1975); two *d*; *m* 1977, Shelagh Joyce Hall (*née* Strong). *Educ:* Liverpool Collegiate; St Edmund Hall, Oxford. RAF Coll., 1945-46; No 28 Sqdn, 1947-49; No 257 Sqdn, 1949-52; 335th Ftr Sqdn USAF, Korea, 1952; CFE, 1953-56 and 1962-64; 435th and 83rd Ftr Sqdns USAF, 1956-58; attached British Aircraft Co., Lightning Project, 1959-61; psa 1961; jssc 1964; MoD, 1964-67; comd RAF Leuchars, 1967-70; idc 1970; SASO 11 Gp, 1971; Principal Staff Officer to CDS, 1971-73; SASO, Strike Comd, 1973-75; ACAS (Op. Requirements), 1976-77. DFC (USA) and Air Medal (USA), 1953. *Recreations:* fishing, hill walking. *Address:* Barclay's Bank, 301 Aigburth Road, Liverpool L17 0BN. *Club:* Royal Air Force.

NICHOLLS, Philip, CB 1976; a Special Adviser to the Royal Commission on Gambling; *b* 30 Aug. 1914; *yr s* of late W. H. Nicholls, Radlett; *m* 1955, Sue, *yr d* of late W. E. Shipton; two *s. Educ:* Malvern; Pembroke Coll., Cambridge. Asst Master, Malvern, 1936; Sen. Classical Master, 1939; resigned, 1947. Served in Army, 1940-46: 8th Bn, The Worcestershire Regt; HQ, East Africa Command; Allied Commn for Austria. Foreign Office (German Section), 1947; HM Treasury, 1949; a Forestry Commissioner (Finance and Administration), 1970-75. Member Council: Malvern Coll. (Vice-Chm., 1963); Malvern Girls' Coll. *Address:* 24 Rivermead Court, SW6. *T:* 01-736 1919. *Clubs:* Athenæum, Hurlingham.

NICHOLLS, Rt. Rev. Vernon Sampson; *see* Sodor and Man, Bishop of.

NICHOLS, Beverley; author and composer; *y s* of late John Nichols, Solicitor, of Bristol; unmarried. *Educ:* Marlborough

Coll.; Balliol Coll., Oxford (Pres. of the Union, Editor of the Isis, Founder and Editor of the Oxford Outlook). *Publications:* Prelude (a public school novel), 1920; Patchwork, 1921; Self, 1922; Twenty-Five (an autobiography), 1926; Crazy Pavements, 1927; Are They the Same at Home?, 1927; The Star Spangled Manner, 1928; Women and Children Last, 1931; Evensong, 1932; Down the Garden Path, 1932; For Adults Only, 1932; Failures, 1933; Cry Havoc, 1933; A Thatched Roof, 1933; A Village in a Valley, 1934; The Fool Hath Said, 1936; No Place Like Home, 1936; News of England, 1938; Revue, 1939; Green Grows the City, 1939; Men do not Weep, 1941; Verdict on India, 1944; The Tree that Sat Down, 1945; The Stream that Stood Still, 1948; All I Could Never Be, 1949; Uncle Samson, 1950; The Mountain of Magic, 1950; Merry Hall, 1951; A Pilgrim's Progress, 1952; Laughter on the Stairs, 1953; No Man's Street, 1954; The Moonflower, 1955; Death to Slow Music, 1956; Sunlight on the Lawn, 1956; The Rich Die Hard, 1957; The Sweet and Twenties, 1958; Murder by Request, 1960; Beverley Nichols' Cats ABC, 1960; Beverley Nichols' Cats XYZ, 1961; Garden Open Today, 1963; Forty Favourite Flowers, 1964; Powers That Be, 1966; A Case of Human Bondage, 1966; The Art of Flower Arrangement, 1967; Garden Open Tomorrow, 1968; The Sun in My Eyes, 1969; The Wickedest Witch in the World, 1971; Father Figure (autobiog.), 1972; Down the Kitchen Sink, 1974; *plays:* (Musical and otherwise): The Stag, 1929; Cochran's 1930 Revue, 1930; Avalanche, 1931; Evensong, 1932; When The Crash Comes, 1933; Dr Mesmer, 1934; Floodlight, 1937; Song on the Wind (Operette), 1948; Shadow of the Vine, 1949; Lady's Guide, 1950. *Address:* Sudbrook Cottage, Ham Common, Surrey. *Club:* Garrick.

NICHOLS, Clement Roy, CMG 1970; OBE 1956; Chairman, Alpha Spinning Mills Pty Ltd and associated companies; *b* 4 Jan. 1909; *s* of C. J. Nichols, Melbourne; *m* 1933, Margareta, *d* of A. C. Pearse, Melbourne; one *s* one *d. Educ:* Scotch Coll., Melbourne. ATI. Lifetime in wool worsted manufacturing. Past Pres., Wool Textile Mfrs of Australia; Vice-Pres., Internat. Wool Textile Organisation; President: Victorian Chamber of Mfrs, 1970-72, 1977-; Associated Chambers of Mfrs of Australia, 1971-74. Mem., World Scouts' Cttee, 1959-65, 1967-73; Chm., Asia Pacific Region, 1962-64; Chief Comr, Scout Assoc., 1963-66; Chief Comr, Victorian Br., 1952-58; Nat Chm., 1973-. *Address:* 82 Studley Park Road, Kew, Victoria 3101, Australia. *Clubs:* Australian, Royal Automobile of Victoria (Melbourne); Rotary (Heidelberg).

NICHOLS, Sir Edward (Henry), Kt 1972; TD; Town Clerk of City of London, 1954-74; *b* 27 Sept. 1911; *o s* of Henry James and Agnes Annie Nichols, Notts; *m* 1941, Gwendoline Hetty, *d* of late Robert Elgar, Leeds; one *s. Educ:* Queen Elizabeth's Gram. Sch., Mansfield; Selwyn Coll., Cambridge (BA, LLB). Articled Town Clerk, Mansfield, 1933; Asst Solicitor, Derby, 1936-40. Served War of 1939-45, Hon. Lt-Col RA. Dep. Town Clerk, Derby, 1940-48, Leicester, 1948-49; Town Clerk and Clerk of the Peace, Derby, 1949-53. Hon. DLitt City Univ., 1974. Chevalier, Order of N Star of Sweden; holds other foreign orders. *Address:* Hillrise, Park Close, Esher KT10 8LG. *T:* Esher 65102. *Club:* City Livery.

NICHOLS, John Winfrith de Lisle, BSc (Eng); CEng; FIEE; Director, National Maritime Institute, since 1976; *b* 7 June 1919; *er s* of late John F. Nichols, MC, PhD, FRHistS, FSA, Godalming; *m* 1942, Catherine, *er d* of Capt. A. V. Grantham, RNR, Essex; two *s* two *d. Educ:* Sir Walter St John's Sch., Battersea; London Univ. Royal Navy, 1940-46; GPO, Dollis Hill, 1946-47; RN Scientific Service, 1947-55; Chief Research Officer, Corp. of Trinity House, 1955-59; UKAEA, 1959-65; Min. of Technology, later DTI and Dept of Industry, 1965-; Under-Sec., and Chm., Requirement Bd for Computers, Systems and Electronics, 1972-74; Under Sec., Research Contractors Div., DoI, 1974-76. *Recreations:* gardening, sailing, caravanning. *Address:* West House, Leybourne, Wormley, Godalming, Surrey. *T:* Wormley 3252. *Club:* Athenæum.

NICHOLS, Kenneth John Heastey; Metropolitan Stipendiary Magistrate, since 1972; *b* 6 Sept. 1923; *s* of Sidney Kenneth Nichols, MC and Dorothy Jennie Heastey Richardson; *m* 1st, 1946, Audrey Heather Powell; one *d*; 2nd, 1966, Pamela Marjorie Long, *d* of late John Holywell Long, AMICE and Emily McNaughton. *Educ:* Westminster School. Served War of 1939-45: 60th Rifles, 1941-43; Parachute Regt, NW Europe, SE Asia Comd, 1943-46 (Captain). Admitted Solicitor, 1949; Partner, Speechly, Mumford & Soames (Craig), 1949-69. Mem. Council of Law Soc., 1959-68. *Recreations:* cricket, music, seafishing. *Address:* Flat 1, 36 Buckingham Gate, SW1; Duck Street, Mousehole, Cornwall. *Club:* MCC.

NICHOLS, Peter Richard; playwright since 1959; *b* 31 July 1927; *s* of late Richard George Nichols and Violet Annie Poole; *m* 1960, Thelma Reed; one *s* two *d* (and one *d* decd). *Educ:* Bristol Grammar Sch.; Bristol Old Vic Sch.; Trent Park Trng Colle. Actor, mostly in repertory, 1950-55; worked as teacher in primary and secondary schs, 1958-60. Mem., Arts Council Drama Panel, 1973-75. Playwright in residence, Guthrie Theatre, Minneapolis, 1976. *TV plays:* Walk on the Grass, 1959; Promenade, 1960; Ben Spray, 1961; The Reception, 1961; The Big Boys, 1961; Continuity Man, 1963; Ben Again, 1963; The Heart of the Country, 1963; The Hooded Terror, 1963; The Brick Umbrella, 1964; When the Wind Blows, 1964 (later adapted for radio); Daddy Kiss It Better, 1968; The Gorge, 1968; Hearts and Flowers, 1971; The Common, 1973; *films:* Catch Us If You Can, 1965; Georgy Girl, 1967; Joe Egg, 1971; The National Health, 1973; *stage plays:* A Day in The Death of Joe Egg, 1967 (Evening Standard Award, Best Play); The National Health, 1969 (Evening Standard Award, Best Play); Forget-me-not Lane, 1971; Chez Nous, 1973; The Freeway, 1974; Privates on Parade, 1977. *Publications:* some TV plays in anthologies; all above stage plays published. *Recreations:* listening to jazz, looking at cities. *Address:* Margaret Ramsay Ltd, 14 Goodwin's Court, WC2. *T:* 01-240 0691.

NICHOLS, William Henry, CB 1974; *b* 25 March 1913; *s* of William and Clara Nichols. *Educ:* Owens School. Entered Inland Revenue, 1930; Exchequer and Audit Dept, 1935, Secretary, 1973-75, retired. *Address:* 17 Park House, Winchmore Hill Road, N21 1QL. *T:* 01-886 4321.

NICHOLS, William Reginald, CBE 1975; TD; MA; Clerk of the Worshipful Company of Salters, 1946-75; *b* 23 July 1912; *s* of late Reginald H. Nichols, JP, FSA, Barrister-at-Law; *m* 1946, Imogen, *d* of late Rev. Percy Dearmer, DD, Canon of Westminster, and of Nancy (who *m* 1946, Sir John Sykes, KCB; he died, 1952); one *s* one *d. Educ:* Harrow; Gonville and Caius Coll., Cambridge (Sayer Classical Scholar). MA 1938. Called to the Bar, Gray's Inn, 1937. Served War of 1939-45 with Hertfordshire Regt (despatches) and on staff 21st Army Group. Governor of Christ's Hospital; Governor of Grey Coat Hospital Foundation. *Address:* The Farriers Cottage, St Nicholas-at-Wade, Birchington, Kent.

NICHOLSON, Air Commodore Angus Archibald Norman, CBE 1961; Deputy Secretary-General, International Shipping Secretariat, since 1971; *b* 8 March 1919; *s* of Major Norman Nicholson and Alice Frances Nicholson (*née* Salvidge), Hoylake, Cheshire; *m* 1943, Joan Mary, *d* of Ernest Beaumont, MRCVS, DVSM; one *s* one *d. Educ:* Eton; King's Coll., Cambridge. Cambridge Univ. Air Sqn, 1938-39; commissioned, 1939. Served War 1939-45: flying duties in Bomber Command and Middle East. Air Cdre, 1966; Dir of Defence Plans (Air), Min. of Defence, 1966-67; Defence Adviser to British High Comr in Canada and Head of British Defence Liaison Staff, 1968-70; retired from RAF, 1970. MBIM 1967. *Recreations:* sailing, ski-ing, golf, fishing. *Address:* 12 Captain's Row, Lymington, Hants. *Clubs:* Royal Automobile; Leander (Henley); Royal Lymington Yacht.

NICHOLSON, Sir Arthur (William), Kt 1968; OBE 1962; Mayor of City of Ballarat, 1952-53, 1960-61, 1967-68, and 1974-75; Chairman of Ballarat Water Commissioners and Ballarat Sewerage Authority, for 21 years; *b* 1 June 1903; *s* of A. H. Nicholson; *m* 1932, Jessie Beryl, *d* of H. A. Campbell; one *s. Educ:* Humffray Street State School; Ballarat High School and School of Mines. Master Builder-family business. Hon. Life Mem. Master Builders' Assoc. (twice Pres.); Mem., Western Moorabool Water Board; Mem., Water Resources Council of Victoria; Chm., Provincial Sewerage Authorities Assoc. of Victoria, 1959-68; Chm., Waterworks Trusts Assoc. of Victoria. Councillor, City of Ballarat, 1946-; Past Pres., Queen Elizabeth Home, Ballarat; Past Pres., National Board YMCAs, Australia; Mem., National Board, YMCA; Mem. Council, Ballarat School of Mines and Industries; Govt Nominee on Ballarat Coll. of Advanced Education Council; Dir of Ballarat Television Station. Past Pres., Assoc. of Victorian Homes and Hospitals for the Aged and Infirm; twice Pres., Ballarat Caledonian Soc. Mem. Ebenezer Presbyterian Church, Ballarat. *Recreations:* bowls, photography and farming. *Address:* 103 Wendouree Parade, Ballarat, Victoria 3350, Australia. *T:* Ballarat 311375. *Club:* Old Colonists (Ballarat).

NICHOLSON, Ben, OM 1968; painter; *b* 10 April 1894; *s* of late Sir William and Mabel Nicholson; *m* 1st, Winifred Roberts, painter and writer (marr. diss.); two *s* one *d*; 2nd, Barbara Hepworth (Dame Barbara Hepworth, DBE, *d* 1975) (marr. diss.); one *s* two *d*; 3rd, Dr Felicitas Vogler. *Educ:* Heddon Court, Cockfosters; Gresham Sch. (one term); Slade School of

Art (one term); Tours; Milan. Awarded 1st prize Carnegie International, Pittsburgh, 1952; Ulissi prize, Venice Biennale, 1954; Governor of Tokyo prize at 3rd International Exhibition, Japan, 1955; Grand Prix at 4th Lugano International, 1956; 1st Guggenheim Foundation Award, 1957; 1st Internat. Prize, 4th S Paulo Biennial, 1957; Rembrandt Prize, 1974. Works included in following public collections: Tate Gallery; British Council; Arts Council; Contemporary Art Society; Victoria and Albert Museum, London; City Art Galleries: Leeds; Manchester; Birmingham; Bristol; Glasgow; Nottingham City Museum; Bedford Museum; Museum of Modern Art, New York; Guggenheim Museum, New York; Carnegie Institute, Pittsburgh; Walker Art Centre, Minneapolis; Allbright Museum, Buffalo; San Francisco Art Museum; Philadelphia Museum; Phillips Gallery and American University, Washington; Kunstmuseum, Zürich; Kunstmuseum, Berne; Wintherthur, Kunstmuseum; Kunsthalle, Hamburg; Musée des Beaux Arts, Antwerp; Museum of Fine Arts, Rotterdam; Palais des Beaux Arts, Brussels; Australian National Gallery; Canadian National Gallery; Museum of Fine Arts, Tel-Aviv, Israel; Museo de Arte Moderno, Rio de Janeiro; Museo Nacional de Buenos Aires; Centre National d'Art Moderne; Ohara Museum, Japan, etc. Retrospective one-man exhibitions include: Venice Biennale, 1954; Stedilijk Museum, Amsterdam, 1954; Musée Nationale d'Art Moderne, Paris, 1955; Palais des Beaux Arts, Brussels, 1955; Kunsthalle, Zürich, 1955; Tate Gallery, London, 1955, 1956, 1969, 1970; in German Cities, 1959; Kunsthalle, Bern, 1961; Marlborough New London Gallery, 1967; Crane Kalman Gall., 1968; Galerie Beyeler, Basle, 1968; Marlborough Gall., 1971. *Publications:* (co-editor) Circle international survey of constructive art, 1937, repr. 1971; monographs: Ben Nicholson (introduction Sir John Summerson), Penguin, 1948; Notes on Abstract Art (by Ben Nicholson), included in Ben Nicholson (introduction Sir Herbert Read), Lund Humphries, vol. 1, 1911-, 1948, vol. 2, Work from 1948-1955; Ben Nicholson, The Meaning of His Art (introd. Dr J. P. Hodin), 1957; Ben Nicholson (introd. Sir Herbert Read), 1962; Ben Nicholson (introd. D. Baxandall), 1962; Ben Nicholson (introd. Ronald Alley), 1962; Ben Nicholson: Drawings, Paintings and Reliefs, 1911-1968 (introd. John Russell), 1969; Ben Nicholson (ed Maurice de Sausmarez), 1969. *Recreations:* painting, tennis, golf, table tennis, etc. *Address:* c/o Banca della Svizzera, Locarno, Ticino, Switzerland.
See also Alan Bowness .

NICHOLSON, General Sir Cameron Gordon Graham, GCB 1954 (KCB 1953, CB 1945); KBE 1950 (CBE 1943); DSO 1940; MC 1918; Governor of the Royal Hospital, Chelsea, 1956-61; Master Gunner, St James's Park, 1956-60; Colonel Commandant, Royal Artillery, 1950-60; Colonel Commandant Royal Horse Artillery, 1956-60; *b* 30 June 1898; *s* of late Brig.-General G. H. W. Nicholson, CB, CMG; *m* 1926, Evelyn Odell Westropp; one *s* two *d. Educ:* Northaw Place; Wellington; RMA, Woolwich. 2nd Lieut, RA, 1915; European War, 1915-18 (MC and Bar); RHA, 1917-27 (France, India, Iraq, Palestine, Egypt); Instructor, RMA, Woolwich, 1927-30; Staff Coll., Camberley, 1930-32; Bde Major, RA 2nd Div., 1934-36; MO War Office, 1936-37; Instructor, Staff Coll., Camberley, 1938-39; served War of 1939-45 (DSO and Bar, CBE, CB); GSO1, 45 Div., 1940; GSO1, Sickleforce, Norway, 1940; GSO1, 18 Div., 1940; DCGS Home Forces, 1941; Comd Support Group, 42 Armoured Div., 1941-42; Second-in-Command 6 Armoured Div., 1942; BGS First Army 1943; Commander 44 Indian Armoured Div., 1943-44; Commander 2 British Div., 1945-46; Director of Artillery, War Office, 1946; General Officer Commanding-in-Chief, West Africa Command, 1948-51; General Officer Commanding-in-Chief, Western Command, 1951-53; C-in-C Middle East Land Forces, 1953; Adjutant-General to the Forces, 1953-56; ADC General to the Queen, 1954-56; retired 1956. Hon. Colonel Travel Control Security Group (TA), 1955-60. Governor, Wellington Coll., 1956-68; Governor, Welbeck Coll., 1956-61. Received Order of Legion of Merit and Silver Star, USA, in North Africa. *Recreation:* gardening. *Address:* Greyhayes, St Breward, Bodmin, Cornwall.

NICHOLSON, Charles Gordon Brown; Sheriff of Lothian and Borders, since 1976; *b* 11 Sept. 1935; *s* of William Addison Nicholson, former Director, Scottish Tourist Board, and late Jean Brown; *m* 1963, Hazel Mary Nixon; two *s. Educ:* George Watson's Coll., Edinburgh; Edinburgh Univ. MA Hons (English Lit.) 1956, LLB 1958. 2nd Lieut Queen's Own Cameron Highlanders, 1958-60. Admitted Faculty of Advocates, Edinburgh, 1961; in practice at Bar; Standing Junior Counsel, Registrar of Restrictive Trading Agreements, 1968; Advocate-Depute, 1968-70; Sheriff of South Strathclyde, Dumfries and Galloway, 1970-76; Sec. Sheriffs' Assoc., 1975-. Member: Scottish Council on Crime, 1972-75; Dunpark Cttee on

Reparation by Offenders, 1974-77; Chm., Scottish Assoc. for Study of Delinquency, 1974-. *Recreations:* golf, philately. *Address:* 23 Lennox Street, Edinburgh EH4 1PY. *T:* 031-332 5861. *Club:* New (Edinburgh).

NICHOLSON, Hon. Sir David (Eric), Kt 1972; company director; Speaker of the Legislative Assembly of Queensland, 1960-72; MLA (CP) for Murrumba, 1950-72; *b* 26 May 1904; *s* of J. A. Nicholson; *m* 1934, Cecile F., *d* of M. E. Smith; two *s* two *d. Recreations:* bowls, swimming, gardening. *Address:* 23 Griffiths Street, New Farm, Qld 4005, Australia. *Clubs:* Redcliffe Trotting (Life Mem.), Redcliffe Agricl, Horticultural and Industrial Soc. (Life Mem.); Returned Servicemen's (Caboolture); New Farm Bowls.

NICHOLSON, Douglas; see Nicholson, F. D.

NICHOLSON, (Edward) Max, CB 1948; CVO 1971; Director-General of the Nature Conservancy 1952-66; Convener, Conservation Section, International Biological Programme, 1963-74; Chairman, Land Use Consultants, since 1966; *b* 1904; *m* 1st, 1932, Eleanor Mary Crawford (marr. diss., 1964); two *s*; 2nd, Marie Antoinette Mauerhofer; one *s. Educ:* Sedbergh; Hertford Coll., Oxford. Head of Allocation of Tonnage Division, Ministry of War Transport, 1942-45; Secretary of Office of The Lord President of the Council, 1945-52. Member Advisory Council on Scientific Policy, 1948-64; Secretary, Duke of Edinburgh's Study Conference on the Countryside in 1970, 1963; Albright Lecturer, Univ. of California, 1964. Vice-President: PEP; Council for Nature and Wildfowlers' Assoc. of Great Britain and Ireland; Trustee: Fair Isle Bird Observatory; Simon Population Trust; Mem. Bd, Inst. of Environment and Develt. Mem. Bd and Editorial Cttee, Birds of the Western Palearctic, 1965-. Chm., Environmental Cttee, London Celebrations for the Queen's Silver Jubilee, 1976-77; Chm., London Looks Forward Conf., 1977. FRSA. Hon. Mem., World Wildlife Fund and RTPI. Scientific Fellow Zoological Society of London; Corr. Fellow, American Ornithologists' Union. Hon. Fellow RIBA; Hon. LLD Aberdeen, 1964; Hon. Dr, RCA, 1970. John C. Phillips Medallist International Union for Conservation of Nature and Natural Resources, 1963; Europa Preis für Landespflege, 1972. Comdr, Order of Golden Ark, Netherlands, 1973. *Publications:* Birds in England, 1926; How Birds Live, 1927; Birds and Men, 1951; Britain's Nature Reserves, 1958; The System, 1967; The Environmental Revolution, 1970 (Premio Europeo Cortina-Ulisse, 1971); The Big Change, 1973; and other books, scientific papers and articles. *Address:* 13 Upper Cheyne Row, SW3. *Club:* Athenæum.

NICHOLSON, Edward Rupert, FCA; Partner, Peat Marwick Mitchell & Co. (UK), 1949-77; *b* 17 Sept. 1909; *s* of late Alfred Edward Nicholson and late Elise (*née* Dobson); *m* 1935, Mary Elley; one *s* one *d. Educ:* Whitgift Sch., Croydon. Articled to father, 1928-33; joined Peat Marwick Mitchell & Co., 1933. Apptd by BoT, jointly, Inspector of Majestic Insurance Co. Ltd and two others, 1961; apptd Liquidator, Davies Investments Ltd, 1967; apptd Receiver, Rolls-Royce Ltd, 1971; Receiver, Northern Developments (Holdings), 1975. Chm., Techn. Adv. Cttee, Inst. Chartered Accountants, 1969-70; Liquidator, Court Line Ltd, 1974; Mem., Post Office Review Cttee, 1976; Governor, Whitgift Foundn, 1976. *Publications:* articles in learned jls. *Address:* Grey Wings, The Warren, Ashtead, Surrey. *T:* Ashtead 72655. *Clubs:* Reform, Caledonian.

NICHOLSON, (Frank) Douglas, TD; MA Cantab; JP; DL; President, Vaux Breweries Ltd and subsidiary cos (Chairman, 1953-76; Joint Managing Director, 1937-52; Director 1928-77); Vice-President, The Brewers' Society (Chairman 1970-71); *b* 30 July 1905; *o s* of late Sir Frank Nicholson, CBE; *m* 1937, Pauline, *y d* of late Sir Thomas Lawson Tancred, 9th Bt, Borobridge; five *s. Educ:* Harrow; Clare Coll., Cambridge. Scottish Horse (TA), 1928; served in Scottish Horse and RA, War of 1939-45, in charge of British and American Supply Mission to Saudi Arabia, 1944. Contested (C) Spennymoor, at 1945 Election. Chm., Durham Police Authority, 1955-64. Pres. and Treasurer, Durham Co. Assoc. of Boys' Clubs, 1952-. High Sheriff Durham County, 1948-49; DL 1948; JP 1949. British Team Winner, World Driving Championship, Munster, W Germany, 1972. *Recreations:* farming, etc. *Address:* Southill Hall, near Chester-le-Street, Co. Durham DH3 4EQ. *T:* Chester-le-Street 882286. *Club:* Cavalry and Guards.

NICHOLSON, Sir Godfrey, 1st Bt, *cr* 1958; Distiller; *b* 9 Dec. 1901; *s* of late Richard Francis Nicholson of Woodcott, Hants, and late Helen Violet Portal; *m* 1936, Lady Katharine Constance Lindsay (*d* 1972), 5th *d* of 27th Earl of Crawford; four *d. Educ:* Winchester; Christ Church, Oxford. MP (Nat. C)

Morpeth, 1931-35; Royal Fusiliers, 1939-42; MP (C) Farnham Division of Surrey, 1937-66; retired. Chairman, Estimates Cttee, 1961-64. Pres., British Assoc. of Parascending Clubs, 1973-. FSA. *Address:* Bussock Hill House, Newbury, Berks. *T:* Chieveley 260. *Clubs:* Athenæum, Pratt's.
See also *R. N. Luce, Sir J. C. F. Montgomery Cuninghame.*

NICHOLSON, Dr Howard, FRCP; Physician, University College Hospital, since 1948; Physician, Brompton Hospital, since 1952; Fellow of University College, London, since 1959; *b* 1 Feb. 1912; *s* of Frederick and Sara Nicholson; *m* 1941, Winifrid Madeline Piercy. *Educ:* University Coll., London, and University Coll. Hospital. MB, BS, London, 1935; MD London 1938; MRCP 1938, FRCP 1949. House appointments and Registrarship, UCH, 1935-38; House Physician at Brompton Hosp., 1938. Served War, 1940-45, RAMC; Physician to Chest Surgical Team and Officer i/c Medical Div. (Lt-Col). Registrar, Brompton Hosp., and Chief Asst, Inst. of Diseases of Chest, 1945-48. Goulstonian Lecturer, RCP, 1950. *Publications:* sections on Diseases of Chest in The Practice of Medicine (ed J. S. Richardson), 1961, and in Progress in Clinical Medicine, 1961; articles in Thorax, Lancet, etc. *Recreations:* reading, going to the opera. *Address:* 22 Hamilton Terrace, NW8 9UG.

NICHOLSON, Sir John (Charles), 3rd Bt, *cr* 1859; TD 1954; FRCS 1934; BM, BCh; Consulting Surgeon; Senior Surgeon, Bethnal Green, St Leonard's and St Matthew's Hospitals, London, retired 1969; *b* 10 Jan. 1904; *s* of Sir Charles Nicholson, 2nd Bt, and Evelyn Louise (*d* 1927), *d* of Rev. H. Oliver; *S* father, 1949; *m* 1928, Caroline Elizabeth, *d* of late Rt Rev. John Frederick McNeice, Bishop of Down; no *c. Educ:* Brighton Coll.; New Coll., Oxford; St Bartholomew's Hospital. Major, RAMC, TA (commissioned 1932); Temp. Lieut-Colonel, RAMC, 1942; Hon. Lieut-Colonel 1945. Late Surgical Registrar, Royal National Orthopædic Hospital, etc.; Clinical Fellow in Surgery, Harvard Univ., 1947-48. Qualified 1929; BM, BCh, Oxford, 1929. *Publications:* various on professional subjects in British Medical Journal and other periodicals. *Recreation:* yachting. *Heir:* none. *Address:* Thames Cottage, Thames Street, Sunbury-on-Thames. *T:* Sunbury 82148.

NICHOLSON, Brigadier John Gerald, CMG 1961; CBE 1945; DL; retired; *b* 17 Jan. 1906; *er s* of late Lieut-Colonel Walter Adams Nicholson, RA (killed in action, 1917); *m* 1940, Emmeline Mary, *d* of late Henry Barrington Tristram; two *s* one *d* (and one *s* decd). *Educ:* Wellington Coll.; RMC, Sandhurst. Commnd into The Buffs, 1925; Adjt, 1930; Staff Coll., 1934. Served War of 1939-45 (wounded, despatches, CBE). DAAG, AHQ, India, 1939; DAAG 52 Div., 1940; AA and QMG, 15 Div., 1941; Comd 2nd Bn The Buffs, Western Desert, 1942; GSO1, Cyrenaica Dist., 1943; GSO1, GHQ, MEF, 1943; Brig. GS, Plans, AFHQ, CMF, 1944; DDI, SACSEA, 1945; seconded to Foreign Office, 1946. Retired from Army and entered Foreign Service, 1948; appointed to Political Office, MEF, 1948-51, when transferred to FO; retired, 1966. Dep. Colonel, The Buffs, 1956-58; DL Kent, 1958. Officer of the Legion of Merit (USA), 1944; Comdr Royal Danish Order of the Dannebrog, 1956. *Recreation:* horticulture. *Address:* Ashets, Stone Cross, Crowborough, East Sussex. *T:* Crowborough 61401. *Club:* Army and Navy.

NICHOLSON, (John) Leonard; Senior Fellow, Centre for Studies in Social Policy, since 1977; *b* 18 Feb. 1916; *er s* of late Percy Merwyn Nicholson and late Jane Winifred Nicholson (*née* Morris). *Educ:* Stowe; Institute of Actuaries; London School of Economics. MSc(Econ). Oxford University Inst. of Statistics, 1940-47; Statistician with Ministry of Home Security, 1943-44; Statistician, 1947-52, Chief Statistician, 1952-68, Central Statistical Office; Chief Economic Advr to DHSS, 1968-76. Simon Research Fellow, Manchester Univ., 1962-63; Assoc. Prof. of Quantitative Econs, Brunel Univ., 1972-74. *Publications:* The Beveridge Plan for Social Security (jtly), 1943; Variations in Working Class Family Expenditure, 1949; The Interim Index of Industrial Production, 1949; Redistribution of Income in the United Kingdom, 1965; contrib. D. Wedderburn, Poverty, Inequality and Class Structure, 1974; contrib. A. B. Atkinson, The Personal Distribution of Incomes, 1976; contrib. V. Halberstadt and A. J. Culyer, Public Economics and Human Resources, 1977; various papers mainly concerned with national income, family expenditure and economic welfare in academic journals. *Recreations:* listening to music, looking at paintings; real and lawn tennis, skiing. *Address:* 53 Frognal, NW3 6YA.

NICHOLSON, Rev. John Malcolm; *b* 26 May 1908; 2nd *s* of John and Madeleine Nicholson; *m* 1939, Dorothy Lisle Preston; one *s* two *d. Educ:* Whitgift Sch.; King's Coll., Cambridge; Cuddesdon Theological Coll. Asst Curate, St John's, Newcastle upon Tyne, 1932-36; Vicar, St Mary's, Monkseaton, 1936-38;

Vicar, Sugley, 1938-46; Vicar, St George's, Cullercoats, 1946-55; Archdeacon of Doncaster, 1955-59; Vicar of High Melton, 1955-59; Headmaster, The King's School, Tynemouth, 1959-70. Examining Chaplain: to Bishop of Newcastle, 1944-55; to Bishop of Sheffield, 1955-59; Select Preacher, Cambridge Univ., 1959. *Address:* Lynnhurst, Elvaston Drive, Hexham, Northumberland. *T:* Hexham 3729.

NICHOLSON, Sir John (Norris), 2nd Bt, *cr* 1912; KBE 1971; CIE 1946; JP; Vice Lord-Lieutenant and Keeper of the Rolls of the Isle of Wight, since 1974; Director: Barclays Bank Ltd; Royal Insurance Co. Ltd; *b* 19 Feb. 1911; *o c* of late Captain George Crosfield Norris Nicholson, RFC, and Hon. Evelyn Izme Murray, *y d* of 10th Baron and 1st Viscount Elibank (she *m* 2nd 1st Baron Mottistone, PC); *S* grandfather, 1918; *m* 1938, Vittoria Vivien, *y d* of late Percy Trewhella, Villa Sant' Andrea, Taormina; two *s* two *d. Educ:* Winchester Coll., Trinity Coll., Cambridge. Captain 4th Cheshires (TA), 1939-41. BEF Flanders 1940 (despatches). Min. of War Transport, India and SE Asia, 1942-46. Chairman: Ocean Steam Ship Co. Ltd, 1957-71; Liverpool Port Employers Assoc., 1957-61; Martins Bank Ltd, 1962-64 (Dep. Chm., 1959-62); Management Cttee, HMS Conway, 1958-65; British Liner Cttee, 1963-67; Cttee, European Nat. Shipowners' Assoc., 1965-69; Mem., Shipping Advisory Panel, 1962-64; Pres., Chamber of Shipping of the UK, 1970-71; Mem., Economic and Social Cttee, EEC, 1973-74. Mem., IoW AHA, 1974-. Governor, IoW Technical Coll. Silver Jubilee Medal, 1977. *Heir: s* Charles Christian Nicholson [*b* 15 Dec. 1941; *m* 1975, Martie, *widow* of Niall Anstruther-Gough-Calthorpe and *d* of Stuart Don]. *Address:* Mottistone Manor, Isle of Wight. *T:* Brightstone 322. *Clubs:* Brooks's; Royal Yacht Squadron.

NICHOLSON, Leonard; see Nicholson, J. L.

NICHOLSON, Lewis Frederick, CB 1963; Vice Controller Aircraft, Procurement Executive, Ministry of Defence, since 1969; *b* 1 May 1918; *s* of Harold and May Nicholson; *m* 1947, Diana Rosalind Fear; one *s* two *d. Educ:* Taunton Sch.; King's Coll., Cambridge. Research Laboratories of GEC, 1939; Royal Aircraft Establishment, 1939-59; Head of Aerodynamics Dept, RAE, 1953-59; Imperial Defence Coll., 1956; Director-General of Scientific Research (Air), Ministry of Aviation, 1959-63; Dep. Director (Air) Royal Aircraft Establishment, 1963-66; Chief Scientist, RAF, 1966-69. *Publications:* (Joint) Compressible Airflow-Tables; Compressible Airflow-Graphs; papers on aerodynamic subjects. *Address:* Ravenswood, Charles Hill, Tilford, Farnham, Surrey. *T:* Elstead 2376.

NICHOLSON, Max; see Nicholson, E. M.

NICHOLSON, Norman Cornthwaite; poet and critic; *b* Millom, Cumberland, 8 Jan. 1914; *s* of Joseph and Edith Nicholson; *m* 1956, Yvonne Edith Gardner. *Educ:* local schools. Literary criticism in weekly press. FRSL 1945; MA (Hon.): Manchester Univ., 1959; Open Univ., 1975. Cholmondley Award for Poetry, 1967; Grant from Northern Arts Assoc., 1969; Soc. of Authors Travelling Award, 1972. *Publications: poetry:* Five Rivers, 1944 (Heinemann Prize, 1945); Rock Face, 1948; The Pot Geranium, 1954; Selected Poems, 1966; A Local Habitation, 1973; *verse drama:* The Old Man of the Mountains (produced Mercury Theatre), 1946; A Match for the Devil, 1955; Birth by Drowning, 1960; *criticism:* Man and Literature, 1943; William Cowper, 1951; *topography:* Cumberland and Westmorland, 1949; The Lakers, 1955; Provincial Pleasures, 1959; Portrait of the Lakes, 1963; Greater Lakeland, 1969; *autobiography:* Wednesday Early Closing, 1975; *anthology:* The Pelican Anthology of Modern Religious Verse, 1943; A Choice of Cowper's Verse, 1975; The Lake District, 1977. *Address:* 14 St George's Terrace, Millom, Cumbria. *T:* Millom 2024.

NICHOLSON, Otho William, TD 1942; DL; *b* 1891; *e s* of late Colonel Rt Hon. William Graham Nicholson, PC; *m* 1927, Elisabeth (who obtained a divorce, 1932), *er d* of late Frederick C. Bramwell, Clerk of the Journals, House of Commons; two *d* ; *m* 1976, Joan, *widow* of Col K. F. W. Thomas. *Educ:* Harrow; Magdalene Coll., Cambridge. Served World War, 1914-19, in France with the Rifle Brigade and in the Wireless Intelligence, Royal Engineers; late Hon. Colonel 1st Anti-Aircraft Divisional Signals, Royal Corps of Signals (TA); Brigadier Comdg 40th and 51st Anti-Aircraft Brigade; Asst Comdt, School of AA Artillery, Shrivenham. LCC, 1922-25; Mayor of Finsbury, 1923-24; MP (C) Westminster (Abbey Division), March 1924-32; Chm., Finsbury Cons. Assoc. DL Mddx, 1938. CStJ. *Recreations:* cricket, shooting. *Address:* Whitecroft, Burley, near Ringwood, Hants. *Club:* Carlton.

NICHOLSON, Robert; publisher, designer, artist, writer; *b* Sydney, Australia, 8 April 1920; *m* 1951, Kate Poulter, ARCA (marr. diss. 1976); one *s* one *d. Educ:* Troy Town Elementary Sch., Rochester; Rochester Tech. Sch.; Medway Sch. of Art. Served War 1939-45, RAMC (mainly pathology in Middle East). Responsible with brother for major design projects during post-war design boom, 1945-55: Festival of Britain in Edinburgh, 1951; British Council exhibn in Zürich; Jamestown centenary exhibn, British Heritage; extensive redecoration of public rooms, Caledonian Hotel, Edinburgh; wallpapers, furniture and industrial design; the Design Centre, Haymarket, for CoID, 1956. Founded and ran small advertising agency, 1963-66: main client, Palladio wallpapers (WPM). Writer and publisher of guide books, 1966-, including: Nicholson's London Guide; Street Finder; Guide to Great Britain. Benjamin Franklin medal, 1960. First one man exhibn of paintings, Patrick Seale Gallery, Knightsbridge, 1976. *Recreations:* collecting, travelling to hot places-preferably volcanic, loves Spain, Wales, his own cooking and travelling by foot in out of way places. *Address:* (home) Little Horden Oast, Husheath Hill, Goudhurst, Kent.

NICHOLSON, Rupert; *see* Nicholson, E. R.

NICHOLSON, William Ewart, CBE 1941; BA, FRAI; *b* 29 Dec. 1890; *s* of Robert Francis Nicholson, Leeds; *m* 1920, Alice Elgie, *d* of W. E. Cork; one *d. Educ:* Leeds Grammar Sch.; Jesus Coll., Oxford. Education Dept, N Nigeria, 1914; Lieut, Nigeria Regt, 1917; Principal, Katsina Coll., 1934; Director of Education, Sierra Leone, 1935-45; Member Fourah Bay College Commission, 1938; Member of Exec. Council, JP, Sierra Leone; Educational Adviser to Government of The Gambia, 1944-45; Secretary Commission of Enquiry into the system of Education of the Jewish Community in Palestine, 1945-46; Director of Training, Ministry of Food, 1946-48. Hon. Keeper of Ethnography, Leeds City Museum, 1959-74. *Address:* 4 Weetwood Crescent, Leeds LS16 5NS.

NICHOLSON-LAILEY, John Raymond, FRCS; retired as Consultant Surgeon and Gynæcologist to Taunton and Somerset Hospital (from 1930); Vice-President, British Medical Association, 1968 (Chairman Council, 1962-66); *b* 11 April 1900; *s* of Henry George and Ann Blanche Nicholson-Lailey; *m* 1932, Penelope Alice Peach, MB, BS; one *s* two *d. Educ:* Trowbridge High Sch.; Bristol Univ. Served with Artists Rifles, April-Aug. 1918; Royal Artillery, Aug. 1918-Jan. 1919; commissioned 2nd Lieut, RA, on demob. MRCS, LRCP, 1923; MB, ChB, Bristol 1924; FRCS 1925. Res. Surgical Officer: Royal Devon and Exeter Hospital, 1926; Salford Royal Hospital, 1927; Gloucester Royal Infirmary, 1929. Hon. Surgeon, Taunton and Somerset Hospital, 1930. Past President, Bath, Bristol and Somerset Branch, BMA; Fellow, BMA. President, South-West Obstetric Society, 1960; Vice-Chairman Council, World Medical Assoc., 1964. Hon. LLD (Manchester) 1964. FRCOG 1965. Officer, Order of Merit, Grand Duchy of Luxembourg, 1964. *Address:* Orchard Rise, Trull, Taunton, Somerset. *T:* Taunton 7270.

NICKERSON, Albert Lindsay; Chairman, 1961-69, and Chief Executive Officer, 1958-69, Mobil Oil Corporation; *b* 17 Jan. 1911; *s* of Albert Lindsay Nickerson and Christine (*née* Atkinson); *m* 1936, Elizabeth Perkins; one *s* three *d. Educ:* Noble and Greenough Sch., Mass; Harvard. Joined Socony-Vacuum Oil Co. Inc. as Service Stn Attendant, 1933; Dist. Man., 1940; Div. Manager, 1941; Asst General Manager, Eastern Marketing Div., 1944; Director, 1946; name of company changed to Socony Mobil Oil Co. Inc., 1955; President, 1955-61; Chairman Exec. Cttee, 1958; name of company changed to Mobil Oil Corporation, 1966. Chairman, Vacuum Oil Co. Ltd, London (later Mobil Oil Co. Ltd), 1946. Director, Placement Bureau War Manpower Commission, Washington, 1943. Chm., Federal Reserve Bank of NY, and Federal Reserve Agent, 1969-71; Mem., The Business Council (Chm. 1967-69). Director: American Management Assoc., NY, 1948-51, 1953-56, 1958-61; Federal Reserve Board of NY, 1964-67; Metrop. Life Insurance Co.; Mobil Oil Corp., 1946-75; Raytheon Co.; State Street Investment Corp.; Federal Street Fund Inc.; Transportation Assoc. of America, 1969; Partner, State Street Exchange Fund; Trustee: International House, NY City, 1952-62; Cttee for Economic Development, NY, 1961-65; Peter Bent Brigham Hosp., Boston; Rockefeller Univ.; Boston Symphony Orch.; American Museum of Natural History, 1958-62, 1964-69; Mem. of Corp., Woods Hole Oceanographic Instn, Mass; former Director and Treas., American Petroleum Institute; former Member: Council on Foreign Relations; National Petroleum Council; Harvard Corp., 1965; Fellow, Harvard Univ., 1965-75; Overseer Harvard Univ., 1959-65. Hon. LLD: Hofstra Univ., 1964; Harvard Univ., 1976. Comdr, Order of Vasa (Sweden),

1963; Grand Cross of the Republic (Italy), 1968. *Recreations:* golfing, fishing, sailing, camping, bird-hunting. *Address:* (office) Room 3540, 150 East 42nd Street, New York, NY 10017, USA. *T:* 212 883-5225; (home) Lexington Road, Lincoln, Mass 01773, USA. *T:* (617) 259-9664. *Clubs:* Thames Rowing; Harvard Varsity, Cambridge Boat (Cambridge, Mass); Country (Brookline, Mass); Harvard (NY City); 25 Year Club of Petroleum Industry.

NICKLIN, Hon. Sir (George) Francis (Reuben), KCMG 1968; MM 1918; retired; Premier of Queensland, 1957-68; *b* 6 Aug. 1895; *s* of George Francis Nicklin and Edith Catherine Nicklin, *née* Bond; *m* 1922, Georgina (decd), *d* of R. Fleming. *Educ:* Murwillumbah State Sch.; Highfield Coll., Turramurra, NSW. Engaged in tropical fruit culture since leaving school; took leading part in organisation of Queensland fruit industry. MLA for Murrumba, Queensland, 1932-50, for Landsborough, Queensland, 1950-68; Secretary, Parliamentary Country Party, 1935-41; Leader of the Opposition, 1941-57; Premier and Minister for State Development, Queensland, 1957-68. Hon. LLD Queensland, 1961. *Recreations:* cricket, bowls, gardening, Surf Life Saving movement. *Address:* 13 Upper Gay Terrace, Caloundra, Queensland 4551, Australia. *T:* Caloundra 911075. *Clubs:* Queensland Cricketers', Queensland Masonic, Caloundra Services.

NICOL, Claude Scott, CBE 1977; TD; Hon. Physician, Genitourinary Medicine Department, St Thomas' Hospital, London; Hon. Consultant to the Army; Adviser in Genitourinary Medicine to Department of Health and Social Security; *b* 1914; *s* of late Dr C. G. Nicol, barrister-at-law (Lincoln's Inn); *m* 1939, Janet Wickham Bosworth Smith; one *s* two *d. Educ:* Harrow Sch.; St Mary's Hospital; St John's Coll., Oxford. MRCS, LRCP, 1936; MB, BS, 1938; MD 1946; MRCP, 1946; FRCP, 1962. Formerly: Physician in charge of Venereal Diseases Dept, St Bartholomew's Hosp., London; Physician, Whitechapel Clinic, London Hospital; Fellow in Medicine, Johns Hopkins Hospital, Baltimore; House Physician, St Mary's Hosp., London. Former Asst Dist Surgeon, St John Amb. Assoc. and Brigade. Ex-Pres., Medical Soc. for Study of Venereal Diseases; FRSM. QHP 1967-69. *Publications:* contributions to medical textbooks and journals. *Recreations:* squash racquets, tennis. *Address:* 40 Fernroft Avenue, NW3 7PE. *T:* 01-435 1310; The Albert Embankment Consulting Rooms, 199 Westminster Bridge Road, SE1 7EH. *T:* 01-928 5485.

NICOL, Davidson Sylvester Hector Willoughby, CMG 1964; MA, MD, PhD (Cantab); FRCPath; Under-Secretary-General of the United Nations and Executive Director, United Nations Institute for Training and Research (UNITAR), since 1972; Hon. Consultant Pathologist, Sierra Leone Government; *b* 14 Sept. 1924, of African parentage; *m* 1950, Marjorie Esme Johnston, MB, ChB; three *s* two *d . Educ:* Schools in Nigeria and Sierra Leone; Cambridge and London Univs. Science Master, Prince of Wales Sch., Sierra Leone, 1941-43. Cambridge: Foundation Schol., Prizeman, 1943-47, Fellow and Supervisor in Nat. Sciences and Med., 1957-59, Christ's Coll. (Hon. Fellow, 1972); BA 1946; 1st Cl. Hons (Nat. Sciences), 1947; Beit Meml Fellow for Medical Research, 1954; Benn Levy Univ. Studentship, Cambridge, 1956; Univ. Schol., House Physician (Medical Unit and Clinical Pathology), Receiving Room Officer, and Research Asst (Physiology), London Hosp., 1947-52; Univ. Lectr, Medical School, Ibadan, Nigeria, 1952-54; Visiting Lecturer: Univs of Toronto, California (Berkeley), Mayo Clinic, 1958; Aggrey-Fraser-Guggisberg Meml Lectr, Univ. of Ghana, 1963; Danforth Fellowship Lectr in African Affairs, Assoc. of Amer. Colls, USA, 1968-71. Sen. Pathologist, Sierra Leone, 1958-60; Principal, Fourah Bay Coll., Sierra Leone, 1960-68, and first Vice-Chancellor, Univ. of Sierra Leone, 1966-68; Perm. Rep. and Ambassador for Sierra Leone to UN, 1969-71 (Security Council, 1970-71, Pres. Sept. 1970; Chm., Cttee of 24 (Decolonisation); Mem., Economic and Social Council, 1969-70); High Comr for Sierra Leone in London, and Ambassador to Norway, Sweden and Denmark, 1971-72. Margaret Wrong Prize and Medal for Literature in Africa, 1952; Chm., Sierra Leone Nat. Library Bd, 1959-65; Member: Governing Body, Kumasi Univ., Ghana; Public Service Commn, Sierra Leone, 1960-68; W African Council for Medical Research, 1959-62; Exec. Council, Assoc. of Univs of British Commonwealth, 1960 and 1966; Commn for proposed Univ. of Ghana, 1960; Chm., Univ. of E Africa Visiting Cttee, 1962; Chm., UN Mission to Angola, July 1976. Director: Central Bank of Sierra Leone; Consolidated African Selection Trust Ltd (London); Davesme Corp. President: W African Science Assoc., 1964-66; Sierra Leone Red Cross Soc., 1962-66; Chm., W African Exams Council, 1964-69; Conference Delegate to: WHO Assembly, 1960; UNESCO Higher Educn Conf., Tananarive, 1963;

Commonwealth Prime Ministers' Conf., London, 1965 and 1969, Singapore 1971. Hon. Fellow: Christ's Coll., Cambridge, 1972; Ghana Acad. of Scis. Hon. LLD Leeds; Hon. DSc: Newcastle upon Tyne; Kalamazoo, Mich; Hon. DLitt Davis and Elkins Coll., W Va. Independence Medal, Sierra Leone, 1961. Grand Commander: Order of Rokel, Sierra Leone, 1974; Star of Africa, Liberia, 1974. *Publications:* Africa, A Subjective View, 1964; contribs to: Malnutrition in African Mothers and Children, 1954; HRH the Duke of Edinburgh's Study Conference, Vol. 2, 1958; The Mechanism of Action of Insulin, 1960; The Structure of Human Insulin, 1960; Africanus Horton and Black Nationalism (1867), 1969; New and Modern Rôles for Commonwealth and Empire, 1976; also to Jl Trop. Med., Biochem. Jl, Nature, Jl of Royal African Soc., Times, Guardian, New Statesman, Encounter, West Africa, etc. *Recreations:* numismatics, creative writing, old maps. *Address:* UNITAR, 801 United Nations Plaza, New York, NY 10017, USA. *T:* 754-1234, ext. 4285. *Clubs:* United Oxford & Cambridge University, Royal Commonwealth Society; Senior Dinner (Freetown).

NICOL, Prof. Donald MacGillivray; Koraës Professor of Modern Greek and Byzantine History, Language and Literature, University of London, King's College, since 1970; *b* 4 Feb. 1923; *s* of late Rev. George Manson Nicol and Mary Patterson (*née* MacGillivray); *m* 1950, Joan Mary Campbell; three *s*. *Educ:* King Edward VII Sch., Sheffield; St Paul's Sch., London; Pembroke Coll., Cambridge (MA, PhD). Friends' Ambulance Unit, 1942-46; Scholar at British Sch. of Archæology, Athens, 1949-50; Lectr in Classics, University Coll., Dublin, 1952-64; Vis. Fellow, Dumbarton Oaks, Washington, DC, 1964-65; Vis. Prof. of Byzantine History, Indiana Univ., 1965-66; Sen. Lectr and Reader in Byzantine History, Univ. of Edinburgh, 1966-70. Birkbeck Lectr, Cambridge, 1976-77. Pres., Ecclesiastical Hist. Soc., 1975-76. MRIA 1960; FRHistS 1971. Editor, Byzantine and Modern Greek Studies, 1973-. *Publications:* The Despotate of Epiros, 1957; Meteora, the Rock Monasteries of Thessaly, 1963, rev. edn, 1975; The Byzantine Family of Kantakouzenos (Cantacuzenus) ca 1100-1460: a genealogical and prosopographical study, 1968; The Last Centuries of Byzantium, 1261-1453, 1972; Byzantium: Its Ecclesiastical History and Relations with the Western World, 1972; articles in Byzantine, classical and historical jls. *Recreation:* bookbinding. *Address:* 19 Highshore Road, SE15 5AA. *T:* 01-732 6164. *Club:* Athenæum.

NICOL, Dr Joseph Arthur Colin, FRS 1967; Professor of Zoology, University of Texas Institute of Marine Science, since 1967; *b* 5 Dec. 1915; *s* of George Nicol and Noele Petrie; *m* 1941, Helen Wilhelmina Cameron; one *d*. *Educ:* Universities of McGill, Western Ontario and Oxford. BSc (hons Zool.) 1938, McGill; MA 1940, Western Ontario; DPhil 1947, DSc 1961, Oxford. Canadian Army, RCCS, 1941-45. Asst Professor in Zoology, University of British Columbia, 1947-49; Experimental Zoologist, Marine Biological Assoc., UK, 1949 (research on marine animals, comparative physiology, luminescence, vision, at Plymouth Laboratory, 1949-66). Guggenheim Fellow, Scripps Inst. Oceanography, 1953-54. Vis. Prof., Univ. of Texas, 1966-67. *Publications:* Biology of Marine Animals, 1960; papers on comparative physiology and anatomy in Jl Marine Biol. Assoc. UK, Proc. Royal Soc, Jl Exp. Biol., Biol. Review, etc. *Recreation:* English literature. *Address:* Port Aransas, Texas 78373, USA.

NICOL, Prof. Thomas, MD, DSc (Glasgow and London); FRCS; FRCSE; FRSE; FKC; Emeritus Professor of Anatomy, University of London; Professor of Anatomy and Head of Anatomical Department, King's College, University of London, 1936-67 (Senior Professor in all Faculties, 1966-67); Director of Department of Clinical Anatomy, Institute of Laryngology and Otology; Member: New York Academy of Sciences; Anatomical Society of Great Britain and Ireland; American Assoc. of Anatomists; International Reticulo-Endothelial Society; Society of Endocrinology; Hon. Member, Mark Twain Society, in succession to Sir Alexander Fleming; *b* 4 Aug. 1900; *s* of Wm. Nicol and Mary Wilson Gilmour; *m* 1927, Evelyn Bertha (*d* 1966), *d* of Thomas Keeling, MICE, Engineer-in-Chief late Glasgow and South Western Railway; one *s* one *d*. *Educ:* University of Glasgow. Honours and Bellahouston Gold Medal for MD Thesis, University of Glasgow, 1935; Struthers Gold Medal and Prize, University of Glasgow, 1935. Sen. House Surgeon to Sir William Macewen, FRS (the discoverer of asepsis), Western Infirmary, Glasgow, 1921; Demonstrator of Anatomy, 1922-27, Senior Lecturer in Anatomy, 1927-35, University of Glasgow. Pioneer of experimental stimulation of phagocytes as suggested by Bernard Shaw in The Doctor's Dilemma; succeeded in doing this with oestrogen in late twenties; later discovered that body defence is under hormone control and that 17β-oestradiol is the principal stimulant in both sexes. Lately: Dean of Faculty of Medicine, King's Coll., Univ. of London; Chm., Board of Studies in Human Anatomy and Morphology, Univ. of London; Examiner, Univs of London, Birmingham, Durham, Glasgow, and St Andrews, RCS England, Edinburgh and Ireland, and RCP; John Hunter Lectr in Applied Anatomy, St George's Hosp. Med. Sch.; Malcolm McHardy Lectr, Royal Eye Hosp. Lord of the Manor of Heveningham, Suffolk. *Publications:* research articles on raising body defence against infection and cancer, in British Jl of Surgery, Jl of Obstetrics and Gynaec. of British Empire, Jl of Anatomy, Trans. and Proc. Royal Society of Edinburgh, BMJ, Nature, Jl of Endocrinology, Jl of Reticuloendothelial Soc. *Recreations:* music, golf, swimming. *Address:* 18 Penn House, Moor Park, Northwood, Mddx. *T:* Northwood 25081.

NICOL, William Allardyce, CA, FCIS; President, Midland Assurance Ltd, since 1975 (Chairman, 1964-75); Director: Eagle Star Insurance Co. Ltd (Isle of Man), since 1975; Barclays Finance Co. (Isle of Man) Ltd, since 1975; Chairman, Isle of Man & General Life Assurance Co. Ltd, since 1977; *s* of William Nicol and Mary Wilson Gilmour; *m* 1st, 1933, Elizabeth (*d* 1967), *d* of James Miller; one *s* one *d*; 2nd, 1970, Sally Philippa, *d* of Robert Patrick Vernon Brettell; one *s* one *d*. *Educ:* Glasgow University. Guest, Keen & Nettlefolds: Asst to Man. Dir, 1939-48; Group Sec., 1948-60; Dir, 1958-77; full-time Exec. Admin. Dir, 1960-68; Dep. Chm., Eagle Star Insurance Co. Ltd, 1968-75; Director: Powell Duffryn Ltd, 1968-75; Barclays Bank Ltd (Birmingham Bd), 1961-75; Stait Carding Gp Ltd (Chm., 1973-75); Chm., John Stait Gp, 1972-75. Chm., Assoc. Scottish Chartered Accountants in Midlands, 1953-68; Mem. Grand Council, CBI, 1965-67. *Recreations:* golf, fishing, music. *Address:* Longmead, Ballakillowey, Colby, Isle of Man. *T:* Port Erin 832005.

NICOLL, Sir John (Fearns), KCMG 1953 (CMG 1946); *b* 26 April 1899; *s* of late John Nicoll; *m* 1939, Irene, *d* of Major J. D. Lenagan, MBE; one *s*. *Educ:* Carlisle Grammar Sch.; Pembroke Coll., Oxford. S Lancs Regt, 1918-19; Administrative Officer, British N Borneo, 1921-25; Administrative Officer, Tanganyika Territory, 1925-37; Dep. Colonial Sec., Trinidad, 1937-44; Colonial Sec., Fiji, 1944-49; Colonial Sec., Hong-Kong, 1949-52; Governor and Comdr-in-Chief, Singapore, 1952-55, retired. KStJ. *Club:* East India, Devonshire, Sports and Public Schools.

NICOLL, Prof. Ronald Ewart, MSc, FRTPI, FRICS; Professor of Urban and Regional Planning, University of Strathclyde, since 1966; *b* 8 May 1921; *s* of William Ewart Nicoll and Edith May Choat; *m* 1943, Isabel Christina McNab; one *s* one *d*. *Educ:* Southend Municipal Coll.; Hammersmith Sch. of Architecture and Building; Royal College of Science and Technology, Glasgow. Served War, Royal Navy, 1939-46. Planning Asst, 1949-53: Southend CB; Derbyshire CC; Northamptonshire CC. Dep. Dir of Planning, Glasgow City, 1953-64; Chief Planning Officer, Scottish Development Dept, 1964-66. Member: Scottish Social Advisory Council, 1970; Scottish Council on Crime, 1971; Scottish Council (Develt and Industry), 1971; Glasgow Chamber of Commerce, 1971; Royal Commn on Environmental Pollution, 1973-. RICS Gold Medal, 1975. *Publications:* Oceanspan, 1970; Energy and the Environment, 1975; contribs to: The Future of Development Plans, 1965 (HMSO); How Do You Want to Live?, 1972 (HMSO); A Future for Scotland, 1973. *Recreations:* travel, photography, hill walking. *Address:* 78 Victoria Park Drive North, Glasgow G14 9PJ. *T:* 041-959 7854. *Club:* Carrick (Glasgow).

NICOLL, William, CMG 1974; Under Secretary, Department of Prices and Consumer Protection, since 1975; *b* 28 June 1927; *s* of Ralph Nicoll and Christina Mowbray Nicoll (*née* Melville); *m* 1954, Helen Morison Martin; two *d*. *Educ:* Morgan Acad., Dundee; St Andrews Univ. Entered BoT, 1949; British Trade Comr: Calcutta, 1955-56; New Delhi, 1957-59; Private Sec. to Pres. of BoT, 1964-67; Commercial Inspector, Foreign and Commonwealth Office, 1967-69; DTI, 1969-72; Counsellor, later Minister, Office of UK Perm. Rep. to European Communities, 1972-75. *Address:* 95 Beechwood Road, South Croydon CR2 0AF. *T:* 01-657 7030.

NICOLSON, family name of Baron Carnock.

NICOLSON, Benedict; see Nicolson, L. B.

NICOLSON, Sir David (Lancaster), Kt 1975; Chairman, BTR Ltd, since 1969 (Deputy Chairman, 1965-69); Chairman, since 1975, and Chief Executive, since 1976, Rothmans International Ltd; Director: Delta Metal Co. Ltd; Bank of Montreal; Richard Costain Ltd; Tradewinds Airways Ltd; MEPC; Todd Shipyards Corp.; Société de Banque et de participations; Rothmans of Pall Mall (Australia) Ltd; Alfred Dunhill Ltd; *b* 20 Sept. 1922; *s* of

Charles Tupper Nicolson, consulting engineer, and Margaret Lancaster Nicolson; *m* 1945, Joan Eileen, *d* of Major W. H. Griffiths, RA; one *s* two *d*. *Educ:* Haileybury; Imperial Coll., London Univ., Hon. Fellow 1971. FCGI; BSc, CEng, FIMechE, FIProdE; FIAM; FBIM; FRSA. Constructor Lt, Royal Corps Naval Constructors, 1942-45; served N Atlantic and Normandy, 1944 (despatches). Management Consultant, Production-Engineering Ltd, 1946-50; Production Manager, Bucyrus Erie Co., Milwaukee, 1951-52; Manager, later Dir, Production-Engineering Ltd, 1953-62; Chairman: P-E Consulting Gp, 1963-68; Associated British Maltsters Ltd, 1965-71; Howden Gp Ltd, 1971-72; Chm., British Airways Board, 1971-75. Chm. NEDC Cttee for Hosiery and Knitwear 1966-68; Mem. Council: Inst. of Directors, 1971-76; Brit. Inst. of Management, 1964-69; Inst. of Production Engrs 1966-68; City and Guilds of London Inst. 1968-76; Member: SRC, 1970-71; SRC Engineering Bd, 1969-71; Governor of Imperial Coll., London Univ., 1966-77; Chm. Management Consultants Assoc., 1964; Mem. Brit. Shipbuilding Mission to India, 1957; Vice-Chm., BNEC Cttee for Canada, 1967, Chm., 1970-71. *Publications:* contribs to technical jls; lectures and broadcasts on management subjects in UK, USA, Australia, etc. *Recreation:* sailing. *Address:* Howicks, Dunsfold, Surrey. *T:* Dunsfold 296. *Clubs:* Carlton; Royal Thames Yacht.

NICOLSON, Lionel Benedict, CBE 1971; MVO 1947; FBA 1977; Editor of The Burlington Magazine since 1947; *b* 6 Aug. 1914; *s* of late Hon. Sir Harold Nicolson, KCVO, CMG and Hon. V. Sackville-West, CH; *m* 1955, Luisa Vertova, Florence (marr. diss. 1962); one *d*. *Educ:* Eton Coll.; Balliol Coll., Oxford. Dep. Surveyor of the King's Pictures, 1939, resigned, 1947. Served War of 1939-45; Commn, 1942, in Intelligence Corps; Interpreter in Italian POW Camps, 1943; Middle East (Egypt, Palestine, Syria), 1943-44, Italy, 1944-45, Instr in Photo-Intelligence; Capt. 1944. Mem. Exec. Cttee, Nat. Art Collections Fund, 1972-. Hon. Dr RCA 1971. *Publications:* The Painters of Ferrara, 1950; Hendrick Terbrugghen, 1958; Wright of Derby: Painter of Light, 1968; The Treasures of the Foundling Hospital, 1972; Courbet: The Studio of the Painter, 1973; (with C. Wright) Georges de La Tour, 1974. *Recreations:* reading, travel. *Address:* 45b Holland Park, W11. *T:* 01-229 2799. *Clubs:* Brooks's, Beefsteak.

See also N. Nicolson.

NICOLSON, Nigel, MBE 1945; FSA; FRSL; author; Director of Weidenfeld and Nicolson Ltd since 1947; *b* 19 Jan. 1917; 2nd *s* of late Hon. Sir Harold Nicolson, KCVO, CMG and Hon. V. Sackville-West, CH; *m* 1953, Philippa Janet (marr. diss. 1970), *d* of Sir Gervais Tennyson d'Eyncourt, 2nd Bt; one *s* two *d*. *Educ:* Eton Coll.; Balliol Coll., Oxford. Capt. Grenadier Guards. Served War of 1939-45 in Tunisian and Italian Campaigns (MBE). Contested (C) NW Leicester, 1950, and Falmouth and Camborne, 1951; MP (C) Bournemouth East and Christchurch, Feb. 1952-Sept. 1959. Chm. Exec. Cttee, UNA, 1961-66. *Publications:* The Grenadier Guards, 1939-45, 1949 (official history); People and Parliament, 1958; Lord of the Isles, 1960; Great Houses of Britain, 1965; (editor) Harold Nicolson: Diaries and Letters, 1930-39, 1966; 1939-45, 1967; 1945-62, 1968; Great Houses, 1968; Alex (FM Alexander of Tunis), 1973; Portrait of a Marriage, 1973; (ed) Letters of Virginia Woolf, 1975-; The Himalayas, 1975; Mary Curzon, 1977. *Recreation:* archæology. *Address:* Sissinghurst Castle, Kent. *T:* Sissinghurst 250. *Club:* Beefsteak.

See also L. B. Nicolson.

NIDDITCH, Prof. Peter Harold; Professor and Head of Department of Philosophy, since 1969, Dean, Faculty of Arts, 1977-, University of Sheffield; *b* 15 Sept. 1928; *o s* of Lazarus Nidditch and Matilda Nidditch (*née* Freeman); *m* 1951, Bridget Veronica McDonnell; no *c*. *Educ:* Clifton Coll.; Birkbeck Coll., Univ. of London. BA (External) 1949, MA 1951, PhD 1953. Asst, Birkbeck Coll., 1953-54; Asst Lectr, Queen's Univ., Belfast, 1955-56; Lectr, Univ. of Liverpool, 1956-59; Univ. of Bristol, 1959-63; Univ. of Sussex: Sen. Lectr, 1963-64; Reader in Phil. and History of Science, and Chm. of Logic, History, and Policy of Science Div., Sch. of Math. and Phys. Scis, 1964-70; Editor, official pubns of Univ. of Sussex, 1965-69. Gen. Editor, Clarendon Edn of Works of John Locke (30 vols), in progress. *Publications:* Introductory Formal Logic of Mathematics, 1957; Elementary Logic of Science and Mathematics, 1960; Propositional Calculus, 1962; Russian Reader in Pure and Applied Mathematics, 1962; The Development of Mathematical Logic (in C. K. Ogden's Basic English), 1962; (ed) Philosophy of Science, 1968; The Intellectual Virtues, 1970; A Bibliographical and Text-Historical Study of the Early Printings of Locke's Some Thoughts concerning Education, 1972; Locke's Essay concerning Human Understanding, with Introd., Critical Apparatus, and Glossary, 1975; revd edn of Selby-Bigge:

Hume's Enquiries, 1975; An Apparatus of Variant Readings for Hume's Treatise of Human Nature, 1976; chapters in several other books; articles in The Locke Newsletter and other learned jls. *Address:* Sparlands, Grindleford, Derbyshire S30 1HQ. *T:* Hope Valley 30670.

NIELD, Hon. Sir Basil Edward, Kt 1957; CBE 1956 (MBE 1945); DL; **Hon. Mr Justice Nield;** Judge of High Court of Justice, Queen's Bench Division, since 1960; *b* 7 May 1903; *yr s* of late Charles Edwin Nield, JP, and Mrs F. E. L. Nield, MBE, LLA, Upton-by-Chester. *Educ:* Harrow Sch.; Magdalen Coll., Oxford (MA). Officers Emergency Reserve, 1938; served War of 1939-45: commnd Captain, 1940; 1941; GHQ MEF (Major), HQs E Africa Force, Abyssinia, Palestine and Syria; Pres., Palestine Military Courts in Jerusalem; 1942; HQs Eritrea and 8th Army; 1943: HQ Persia and Iraq; Asst Dep. Judge Advocate-Gen., ME (Lt-Col; despatches); Home Estab.; 1944: 21 Army Gp; HQ Lines of Communication, BLA, Normandy; HQ 2nd Army, France, Belgium, Holland and Germany (MBE); Home Estab., 1945; RARO until 1948. Called to Bar, Inner Temple, 1925, Reader, 1976, Treasurer, 1977; Northern Circuit, Chambers in Liverpool; KC 1945; Recorder of Salford, 1948-56; Recorder and first permanent Judge of Crown Court at Manchester, 1956-60. MP (U) City of Chester, 1940-56; sponsored as Private Member's Bill the Adoption of Children Act, 1949; Hon. Parly Chm., Dock and Harbour Authorities Assoc., 1944-50; Mem., Special Cttee under Reorganisation Areas Measure for Province of York, 1944. Mem., Gen. Council of Bar, 1951; Master of Bench of Inner Temple, 1952-. Member: Magistrates' Rules Cttee, 1952-56; Legal Bd, Church Assembly, 1952-56; Home Secretary's Adv. Cttee on Treatment of Offenders, 1957. Chancellor, Diocese of Liverpool, 1948-56. Vice-President: Nat. Chamber of Trade, 1948-56; Graduate Teachers Assoc., 1950-56; Corp. of Secretaries, 1950; Assoc. of Managers of Approved Schools, 1956; Cheshire Soc. in London; Spastics Soc., Manchester. Chm., Chester Conservative Assoc., 1930-40. Member: Court, Liverpool Univ., 1948-56; Adv. Council, E-SU, 1951; Oxford Soc.; Imperial Soc. of Knights Bachelor; Life Mem., Royal Soc. of St George. Governor, Harrow Sch., 1961-71. FAMS. JP Co. Lancaster, 1956; DL County Palatine of Chester, 1962-. Freeman, City of London, 1963. *Publication:* Farewell to the Assizes, 1972. *Address:* 7 King's Bench Walk, Temple, EC4. *T:* 01-353 3488; The Stable House, Christleton, near Chester. *T:* Chester 35607. *Clubs:* Carlton, Garrick, Royal Automobile; City, Grosvenor (Chester).

NIELD, Sir William (Alan), GCMG 1972; KCB 1968 (CB 1966); Deputy Chairman, Rolls Royce (1971) Ltd, 1973-76; *b* 21 Sept. 1913; *s* of William Herbert Nield, Stockport, Cheshire, and Ada Nield; *m* 1937, Gwyneth Marion Davies; two *s* two *d*. *Educ:* Stockport Gram. Sch.; St Edmund Hall, Oxford. Research and Policy Dept of Labour Party, 1937-39; K-H News Letter Service, 1939. Served Royal Air Force and Royal Canadian Air Force, 1939-46 (despatches, 1944); demobilised as Wing Comdr, 1946. Min. of Food, 1946-47; HM Treasury, 1947-49; Min. of Food and Min. of Agric., Fisheries and Food, 1949-64 (Under-Sec., 1959-64); Dept of Economic Affairs: Under-Sec., 1964-65; Dep. Under-Sec., 1965-66; a Dep. Sec., Cabinet Office, 1966-68; Permanent Under-Sec. of State, DEA, 1968-69; Permanent Secretary: Cabinet Office, 1969-72; NI Office, 1972-73. *Address:* South Nevay, Stubbs Wood, Chesham Bois, Bucks. *T:* Amersham 3869. *Club:* Farmers'.

NIEMEYER, Oscar; architect; *b* Rio de Janeiro, 15 Dec. 1907; *s* of Oscar Niemeyer Soares; *m* Anita Niemeyer; one *d*. *Educ:* Escola Nacional de Beles Artes, Univ. of Brazil. Joined office of Lúcio Costa, 1935; worked on Min. of Education and Health Building, Rio de Janeiro, Brazilian Pavilion, NY World Fair, etc., 1936-41. Major projects include: Pamphulha, Belo Horizonte, 1941-43; also Quintandinha, Petrópolis; Exhibition Hall, São Paulo, 1953; Brasilia (Dir of Architecture), 1957-. Brazilian Rep., UN Bd of Design Consultants, 1947. Lenin Peace Prize, 1963; Prix Internat. de l'Architecture Aujourd'hui, 1966.

NIEMÖLLER, Rev. Dr (Friedrich Gustav Emil) Martin; a President of the World Council of Churches, 1961-68; Church President of Evangelical Church in Hesse and Nassau, Germany, 1947-64, retired; *b* Lippstadt, Westphalia, 14 Jan. 1892; *s* of Pastor Heinrich Niemoeller; *m* 1st, 1919, Else (*née* Bremer) (*d* 1961); three *s* two *d* (and one *s* one *d* decd); 2nd, 1971, Sibylle (*née* von Sell). *Educ:* Gymnasium, Elberfeld. Midshipman in German Navy, 1910; retd 1919, as Kapitänleutnant; studied Theology, Münster, Westfalen; Pastor, 1924; Pastor of Berlin-Dahlem, 1931; creator of Pastors' Union and Confessing Church; prisoner in concentration camps at Sachsenhausen and Dachau, 1937-45; Pres. Office of Foreign

Affairs of Evangelical Church in Germany, 1945-56. Holds Hon. DD of Univ. of Göttingen (Germany), and several foreign hon. doctorates. *Publications:* Vom U-Boot zu Kanzel (Berlin), 1934;... Dass wir an Ihm bleiben: Sechzehn Dahlemer Predigten (Berlin), 1935; Alles und in allem Christus; Fünfzehn Dahlemer Predigten (Berlin), 1935; Fran U-Bat till Predikstol (trans.) (Stockholm), 1936; Dennoch getrost: Die letzten 28 Predigten (Switzerland), 1939; Ach Gott vom Himmel sieh darein: Sechs Predigten (Munich), 1946;... Zu verkündigen ein Gnädiges: Jahr des Herrn: Sechs Dachauer Predigten (1944-45), (Munich), 1946; Herr ist Jesus Christus: Die letzten 28 Predigten (Gütersloh), 1946; Herr, wohin sollen wir gehen? Ausgewählte Predigten (Munich), 1956; some hundred articles about theological, cultural and political themes. *Address:* Brentanostrasse 3, Wiesbaden, Germany. *T:* 85097.

NIGHTINGALE, Sir Charles (Manners Gamaliel, 17th Bt *cr* 1628; Higher Executive Officer, Department of Health and Social Security, since 1977; *b* 21 Feb. 1947; *s* of Sir Charles Athelstan Nightingale, 16th Bt, and of Evelyn Nadine Frances, *d* of late Charles Arthur Diggens; *S* father, 1977. *Educ:* St Paul's School. Entered DHSS as Executive Officer, 1969; Higher Executive Officer, 1977. Heir: cousin Edward Lacy George Nightingale, *b* 11 May 1938. *Address:* 2 Ferncroft, Basire Street, N1 8PJ.

NIGHTINGALE, Edward Humphrey, CMG 1955; Farmer in Kenya since 1954; *b* 19 Aug. 1904; *s* of Rev. Edward Charles Nightingale and Ada Mary Nightingale; *m* 1944, Evelyn Mary Ray; three *s* one *d. Educ:* Rugby Sch.; Emmanuel Coll., Cambridge. Joined Sudan Political Service, 1926; Dep. Civil Sec., Sudan Government, 1951-52; Gov., Equatoria Province, Sudan, 1952-54. Order of the Nile, 4th Class, 1940. *Recreations:* polo, ski-ing, photography. *Address:* Nunjoro Farm, PO Box 100, Naivasha, Kenya. *T:* Naivasha 53Y1. *Clubs:* Rift Valley Sports (Nakuru); Muthaiga Country (Nairobi).

NIGHTINGALE, Sir John (Cyprian), Kt 1975; CBE 1970; BEM 1941; QPM 1965; DL; Chief Constable, Essex, 1962-69 and since 1974 (Essex and Southend-on-Sea Joint Constabulary, 1969-74); *b* 16 Sept. 1913; *s* of Herbert Paul Nightingale, Sydenham, London; *m* 1947, Patricia Mary, *d* of Norman Maclaren, Glasgow University. *Educ:* Cardinal Vaughan Sch., Kensington; University Coll., London. Joined Metropolitan Police, 1935; Asst Chief Constable, Essex, 1958. Chm., Police Council, 1976-. Served with RNVR, 1943-45. DL Essex 1975. *Publications:* various police. *Address:* Springfield Court, Chelmsford, Essex.

NIGHTINGALE of Cromarty, Michael David, OBE 1960; BSc; BLitt; FSA; Baron of Cromarty; Chairman, The Anglo-Indonesian Corporation Ltd; Esquire Bedell, University of London, since 1953; *b* 6 Dec. 1927; *s* of late Victor Russell John Nightingale, Wormshill, Kent; *m* 1956, Hilary Marion Olwen, *d* of late John Eric Jones, Swansea; two *s* three *d. Educ:* Winchester; Wye Coll.; Magdalen Coll., Oxford. Organised Exhibition from Kent Village Churches, Canterbury, 1951; Asst to Investment Manager, Anglo-Iranian Oil Co., 1951-53; Asst to Principal, Univ. of London, 1953-54; Investment Adviser, Univ. of London, 1954-66; Dir, Charterhouse Japhet Ltd, 1965-70. Secretary: Museums Assoc. (and Editor of Museums Jl), 1954-60; Museum Cttee, Carnegie UK Trust, 1954-60; Member: Advisory Council on Export of Works of Art, 1954-60; British Cttee of International Council of Museums, 1956-60; Canterbury Diocesan Advisory Cttee, 1964-; Exec. Cttee, S E Arts Assoc., 1974-77; Area Archaeol. Adv. Cttee for SE England, 1975-. Mem., Kent CC, 1973-77; Chm., Planning Cttee, Maidstone Borough Council, 1973-77, Leader, 1976-77. Vice-Pres., Swale & North Downs Soc.; Chm., Churches Cttee, Kent Archaeological Soc. Dep. Steward, Royal Manor of Wye, 1954-. *Publications:* articles on agrarian and museum subjects. *Address:* Wormshill Court, Sittingbourne, Kent. *T:* Wormshill 235; Perceval House, 21 Dartmouth Row, Greenwich, SE10. *T:* 01-692 6033; Cromarty House, Ross and Cromarty. *T:* Cromarty 265. *Club:* Athenæum.

NIGHTINGALE, Percy Herbert, CMG 1957; *b* 22 Dec. 1907; *s* of late Rev. S. J. Nightingale and late Mrs Nightingale; *m* 1935, Doris Aileen Butcher; one *s* one *d. Educ:* St Michael's, Limpsfield, Surrey; Monkton Combe Sch., near Bath; Christ's Coll., Cambridge. BA Cantab, 1928. Colonial Administrative Service, Fiji, 1930-52; District Commissioner, 1940; Asst Colonial Sec., 1947; Financial Sec., Zanzibar, 1952-60. Appeal Organiser, Monkton Combe Sch., 1960-64; Lay Asst to Bishop of Salisbury, 1964-73. Coronation Medal, 1953; Order of Brilliant Star, Zanzibar (2nd Class), 1960. *Recreation:* gardening. *Address:* Little Croft, Netherhampton, Salisbury, Wilts. *T:* Wilton 3454.

NIKLASSON, Frau Bertil; *see* Nilsson, Birgit.

NIKLAUS, Prof. Robert, BA, PhD London; LèsL Lille; DrUniv Rennes, *hon. causa,* 1963; Officier de l'Ordre National du Mérite, 1972; Professor of French, 1956-75, now Emeritus, Head of Department of French and Spanish, 1958-64, French and Italian, 1964-75, University of Exeter; *b* 18 July 1910; *s* of late Jean Rodolphe and Elizabeth Niklaus; *m* 1st, 1935, Thelma (*née* Jones) (*d* 1970); two *s* one *d* ; 2nd, 1973, Kathleen (*née* Folta). *Educ:* Lycée Français de Londres; University Coll., London; Univ. of Lille. Sen. Tutor, Toynbee Hall, London, 1931-32; Asst and Asst Lecturer at University Coll., 1932-38; Asst Lecturer, Lecturer, Univ. of Manchester, 1938-52; Prof. of French, UC of the SW, 1952-56. Dean of the Faculty of Arts, Exeter, 1959-62; Dep. Vice-Chancellor, 1965-67. Visiting Professor: Univ. of Calif., Berkeley, 1963-64; Univ. of British Columbia, 1975-76; Univ. of Nigeria, Nsukka, 1977-78. Pres., Assoc. of Univ. Teachers, 1954-55, Mem. Executive Cttee, 1948-62; Pres. Internat. Assoc. of Univ. Profs and Lecturers, 1960-64 (Vice-Pres., 1958-60, 1964-66); Member: Cttee of Modern Humanities Research Association, 1956-71; Cttee, Soc. for French Studies, 1965-72 (Vice-Pres., 1967-68 and 1970-71, Pres. 1968-70; Pres., British Soc. for XVIIIth Century Studies, 1970-72; Treasurer, Internat. Soc. for Eighteenth-century Studies, 1969; Post-graduate Awards Cttee of Min. of Education, 1956-61; Management Cttee, British Inst., Paris, 1965-67. Gen. Editor, Textes Français Classiques et Modernes, Univ. of London Press. *Publications:* Jean Moréas, Poète Lyrique, 1936; The Nineteenth Century (Post-Romantic) and After (in The Year's Work in Modern Language Studies, VII-XIII), 1937-52; Diderot and Drama, 1942; Beaumarchais, Le Barbier de Séville, 1968; A Literary History of France, the Eighteenth Century, 1970; critical editions of: J.-J. Rousseau, Les Rêveries du Promeneur Solitaire, 1942; Denis Diderot, Pensées Philosophiques, 1950; Denis Diderot, Lettre sur les Aveugles, 1951; Marivaux, Arlequin poli par l'Amour, 1959 (in collab. with Thelma Niklaus); Sedaine, La Gageure imprévue, 1970; articles in Encyclopaediæ and learned journals; textbooks for schools and universities. *Recreations:* aviculture, the theatre, the cinema. *Address:* 17 Elm Grove Road, Topsham, Exeter, Devon. *T:* Topsham 3627.

NIKOLAYEVA-TERESHKOVA, Valentina Vladimirovna; Hero of the Soviet Union; Order of Lenin; Gold Star Medal; Order of October Revolution; Joliot-Curie Peace Medal; Soviet cosmonaut; *b* Maslennikovo, 6 March 1937; *d* of late Vladimir and of Elena Fyodorovna Tereshkova; *m* 1963, Andrian Nikolayev; one *d.* Formerly textile worker, Krasny Perekop mill, Yaroslavl; served on cttees; Sec. of local branch, Young Communist league, 1960; joined Yaroslavl Air Sports Club, 1959, and started parachute jumping; Mem., Communist Party of Soviet Union, 1962; joined Cosmonaut Training Unit, 1962. Became first woman in the world to enter space when she made 48 orbital flights of the earth in spaceship Vostok VI, 16-19 June 1963. Mem. Central Cttee, CPSU, 1971. Nile Collar (Egypt), 1971; holds honours and citations from other countries. *Address:* Soviet Women's Committee, 23 Pushkinskaya Street, Moscow, USSR.

NILSSON, Birgit, (Fru Bertil Niklasson); Swedish operatic soprano; *b* Karup, Kristianstadslaen, 1922. *Educ:* Stockholm Royal Academy of Music. Debut as singer, 1946; with Stockholm Opera, 1947-51. Has sung at Glyndebourne, 1951; Bayreuth, 1953, 1954, 1957-70; Munich, 1954-58; Hollywood Bowl, Buenos Aires, Florence, 1956; La Scala, Milan, 1958-; Covent Garden, 1957, 1960, 1962, 1963, 1973 and 1977; Edinburgh, 1959; Metropolitan, New York, 1959-; Moscow, 1964; also in most leading opera houses and festivals of the world. Particularly well-known for her Wagnerian rôles. Austrian Kammersängerin, 1968; Bavarian Kammersängerin, 1970. Swedish Royal Acad. of Music's Medal for Promotion of Art of Music, 1968. Comdr of the Vasa Order, Sweden, 1968.

NIMMO, Hon. Sir John (Angus), Kt 1972; CBE 1970; Justice of the Federal Court of Australia, since 1977; Justice of Australian Industrial Court, since 1969; *b* 15 Jan. 1909; *s* of John James Nimmo and Grace Nimmo (*née* Mann); *m* 1935, Teanie Rose Galloway; two *s. Educ:* Univ. of Melbourne. Admitted to practise at Victorian Bar, 1933. QC 1957. Mem., Commonwealth Taxation Bd of Review No 2, 1947-54; Actg Supreme Court Justice, Victoria, 1963; Dep. Pres., Commonwealth Conciliation and Arbitration Commn, 1964-69; Chm., Health Insce Cttee of Enquiry, 1968-69. Dep. Pres., Trade Practices Tribunal, 1966-73, also a Justice of Supreme Courts of ACT and NT, 1966-74; on secondment as Chief Justice of Fiji, 1972-74. Royal Comr into future of Norfolk Is, 1975-76. OStJ 1945. *Recreations:* reading, bowls, walking. *Address:* 11 Abernethy Street, Weetangera, ACT 2614,

Australia. *T:* 542791. *Clubs:* Australian (Melbourne); Melbourne Cricket.

NIMMO, Sir Robert, Kt 1944; JP; *b* 11 June 1894; *s* of Robert Nimmo, Brewer, Perth; *m* 1922, Dorothy Wordsworth, *d* of Walter Gillies; two *s* one *d.* Lord Provost of Perth, 1935-45. Hon. Sheriff, Perth. *Address:* 8 Anderson Drive, Perth.

NIND, Philip Frederick, TD 1946; Director, Foundation for Management Education, since 1968; Secretary, Council of Industry for Management Education, since 1969; *b* 2 Jan. 1918; *s* of W. W. Nind, CIE; *m* 1944, Fay Allardice Crofton (*née* Errington); two *d. Educ:* Blundell's Sch.; Balliol Coll., Oxford (MA). War service, 1939-46, incl. Special Ops in Greece and Albania (despatches), 1943-44, Mil. Govt Berlin, 1945-46 (Major). Shell Gp of Cos in Venezuela, Cyprus, Lebanon, Jordan and London, 1939-68. Educn and Trng Cttee, CBI (formerly FBI), 1961-68; OECD Working Gp on Management Educn, 1966-69; Nat. Adv. Council on Educn for Industry and Commerce, 1967-70; UGC Management Studies Cttee, 1968-; NEDO Management Educn Trng and Develt Cttee, 1968-; Chm., NEDO Management Teacher Panel, 1969-72; Council for Techn. Educn and Trng for Overseas Countries, 1970-75; CNAA Management Studies Bd, 1971-; Oxford Univ. Appts Cttee, 1967-; Exec. Cttee, Royal Academy of Dancing, 1970-; Governor: Univ. of Keele, 1961-; Bedford Coll., London Univ., 1967-. Chevalier, Order of Cedars of Lebanon, 1959; Grand Cross, Orders of St Mark and Holy Sepulchre, 1959. *Publications:* (jtly) Management Education and Training Needs of Industry, 1963; Fourth Stockton Lecture, 1973; articles in various jls. *Address:* Foundation for Management Education, Management House, Parker Street, WC2B 5PT. *T:* 01-405 3456. *Clubs:* Travellers', Special Forces.

NINEHAM, Rev. Dennis Eric, MA, BD; Warden of Keble College, Oxford, since 1969; *b* 27 Sept. 1921; *o c* of Stanley Martin and Bessie Edith Nineham, Shirley, Southampton; *m* 1946, Ruth Corfield, *d* of Rev. A. P. Miller; two *s* two *d. Educ:* King Edward VI Sch., Southampton; Queen's Coll., Oxford. Asst Chaplain of Queen's Coll., 1944; Chaplain, 1945; Fellow and Praelector, 1946; Tutor, 1949; Prof. of Biblical and Historical Theology, Univ. of London (King's Coll.), 1954-58; Prof. of Divinity, Univ. of London, 1958-64; Regius Prof. of Divinity, Cambridge Univ., and Fellow, Emmanuel Coll., 1964-69. FKC 1963. Examining Chaplain: to Archbishop of York and to Bishop of Ripon; to Bishop of Sheffield, 1947-54; to Bishop of Norwich, 1964-73. Select Preacher to Univ. of Oxford, 1954-56, 1971, and to Univ. of Cambridge, 1959; Proctor in Convocation of Canterbury: for London Univ., 1955-64; for Cambridge Univ., 1965-69. Mem. General Synod of Church of England for Oxford Univ., 1970-76; Mem., C of E Doctrine Commn. Roian Flack Resident-in-Religion, Bryn Mawr Coll., Pa, 1974. Governor of Haileybury, 1966-. Hon. DD: Berkeley Divinity Sch., Yale, 1965; Birmingham, 1972. *Publications:* The Study of Divinity, 1960; A New Way of Looking at the Gospels, 1962; Commentary on St Mark's Gospel, 1963; The Use and Abuse of the Bible, 1976; Explorations in Theology, 1977; (Editor) Studies in the Gospels: Essays in Honour of R. H. Lightfoot, 1955; The Church's Use of the Bible, 1963; The New English Bible Reviewed, 1965; contrib. to: Studies in Ephesians (editor F. L. Cross), 1956; On the Authority of the Bible, 1960; Religious Education, 1944-1984, 1966; Theologians of Our Time, 1966; Christian History and Interpretation, 1967; Christ for us To-day, 1968; Christian Believing, 1976; The Myth of God Incarnate, 1977. *Recreation:* reading. *Address:* Keble College, Oxford. *T:* Oxford 59201.

NINIS, Ven. Richard Betts; Archdeacon of Stafford and Treasurer of Lichfield Cathedral, since 1974; *b* 25 Oct. 1931; *s* of George Woodward Ninis and Mary Gertrude Ninis; *m* 1967, Penelope Jane Harwood; one *s* one *d. Educ:* Lincoln Coll., Oxford (MA); Bishop's Hostel, Lincoln (GOE). Curate, All Saints, Poplar, 1955-62; Vicar of: St Martins, Hereford, 1962-71; Bullinghope and Dewsall with Callow, 1966-71. Diocesan Missioner for Hereford, 1971-74. *Recreations:* gardening, viticulture, travel. *Address:* 24 The Close, Lichfield, Staffs. *T:* Lichfield 23535. *Club:* Royal Over-Seas League.

NIRENBERG, Dr Marshall Warren; Research Biochemist; Chief, Laboratory of Biochemical Genetics, National Heart, Lung and Blood Institute, National Institutes of Health, Bethesda, Md, since 1966; *b* New York, 10 April 1927; *m* 1961, Perola Zaltzman; no *c. Educ:* Univs of Florida (BS, MS) and Michigan (PhD). Univ. of Florida: Teaching Asst, Zoology Dept, 1945-50; Res. Associate, Nutrition Lab., 1950-52; Univ. of Michigan: Teaching and Res. Fellow, Biol Chemistry Dept, 1952-57; Nat. Insts of Health, Bethesda: Postdoctoral Fellow of Amer. Cancer Soc., Nat. Inst. Arthritis and Metabolic Diseases,

1957-59, and of Public Health Service, Section of Metabolic Enzymes, 1959-60; Research Biochemist, Section of Metabolic Enzymes, 1960-62 and Section of Biochem. Genetics, 1962-66. Member: Amer. Soc. Biol Chemists; Amer. Chem. Soc.; Amer. Acad. Arts and Sciences; Biophys. Soc.; Nat. Acad. Sciences; Washington Acad. Sciences; Sigma Xi; Soc. for Study of Development and Growth; (Hon.) Harvey Soc.; Leopoldina Deutsche Akademie der Naturforscher; Neurosciences Research Program, MIT; NY Acad. Sciences; Pontifical Acad. Science, 1974. Robbins Lectr, Pomona Coll., 1967; Remsden Mem. Lectr, Johns Hopkins Univ., 1967. Numerous awards and prizes, including Nobel Prize in Medicine or Physiology (jtly), 1968. Hon. Dr Science: Michigan, Yale, and Chicago, 1965; Windsor, 1966; Harvard Med. Sch., 1968. *Publications:* numerous contribs to learned jls and chapters in symposia. *Address:* Laboratory of Biochemical Genetics, National Heart, Lung and Blood Institute, Bethesda, Md 20014, USA; 7001 Orkney Parkway, Bethesda, Maryland, USA.

NISBET, Prof. John Donald, MA, BEd, PhD; Professor of Education, Aberdeen University, since 1963; *b* 17 Oct. 1922; *s* of James Love Nisbet and Isabella Donald; *m* 1952, Brenda Sugden; one *s* one *d. Educ:* Dunfermline High Sch.; Edinburgh Univ. (MA, BEd); PhD (Aberdeen); Teacher's Certif. (London). Royal Air Force, 1943-46. Teacher, Fife, 1946-48; Lectr, Aberdeen Univ., 1949-63. Editor, British Jl of Educnl Psychology, 1967-74; Chairman: Educnl Research Bd, SSRC, 1972-75; Scottish Central Cttee on Primary Educn, 1974-; Scottish Council for Research in Educn, 1975-; Pres., British Educnl Research Assoc., 1975. *Publications:* Family Environment, 1953; Age of Transfer to Secondary Education, 1966; Transition to Secondary Education, 1969; Scottish Education Looks Ahead, 1969; Educational Research Methods, 1970; Educational Research in Action, 1972; papers in jls on educnl psychology and curriculum develt. *Recreation:* golf. *Address:* 5 The Chanonry, Aberdeen AB2 1RP. *T:* Aberdeen 44375.

See also S . D . Nisbet .

NISBET, Prof. Robin George Murdoch, FBA 1967; Corpus Christi Professor of Latin, Oxford, since 1970; *b* 21 May 1925; *s* of R. G. Nisbet, Univ. Lecturer, and A. T. Husband; *m* 1969, Anne, *d* of Dr J. A. Wood. *Educ:* Glasgow Academy; Glasgow Univ.; Balliol Coll., Oxford (Snell Exhibitioner). Fellow and Tutor in Classics, Corpus Christi College, Oxford, 1952-70. *Publications:* Commentary on Cicero, *in Pisonem,* 1961; (with M. Hubbard) on Horace, *Odes I,* 1970; articles and reviews on Latin subjects. *Recreation:* 20th century history. *Address:* 80 Abingdon Road, Cumnor, Oxford. *T:* Cumnor 2482.

NISBET, Prof. Stanley Donald; Professor of Education, University of Glasgow, 1951-77; *b* 26 July 1912; *s* of Dr J. L. and Isabella Nisbet; *m* 1942, Helen Alison Smith; one *s* one *d. Educ:* Dunfermline High Sch., Edinburgh Univ. MA (1st Cl. Hons Classics), 1934; Diploma in Education, 1935; BEd (with distinction in Education and Psychology), 1940. Taught in Moray House Demonstration Sch., Edinburgh, 1935-39. Served War in RAF, 1940-46; research officer at Air Ministry, 1944-46. Lecturer in Education, Univ. of Manchester, Feb.-Sept. 1946; Prof. of Education, Queen's Univ. of Belfast, 1946-51. FRSE 1955; FEIS 1976. *Publications:* Purpose in the Curriculum, 1957; (with B. L. Napier) Promise and Progress, 1970; articles in psychological and educational journals. *Recreations:* walking, sailing. *Address:* 6 Victoria Park Corner, Glasgow G14 9NZ.

See also J . D . Nisbet .

NISSAN, Alfred Heskel, PhD, DSc (Chem. Eng, Birmingham), MIMechE, MIChemE, MAIChE, MASME; MACS; Member Sigma XI; Vice-President since 1967, and Corporate Director of Research, since 1962, WESTVACO (formerly West Virginia Pulp and Paper), New York; *b* 14 Feb. 1914; *s* of Heskel and Farha Nissan, Baghdad, Iraq; *m* 1940, Zena Gladys Phyllis, *o d* of late Phillip and Lillian Frances Pursehouse-Ahmed, Birmingham; one *d. Educ:* The American Sch. for Boys, Baghdad, Iraq; Univ. of Birmingham. Instn of Petroleum Scholarship, 1936; first cl. Hons BSc 1937; Sir John Cadman Medal, 1937; Instn of Petroleum Medal and Prize and Burgess Prize, 1937; Research Fellow, 1937, Lectr, 1940, Univ. of Birmingham; Head of Central Research Laboratories, Bowater Paper Corporation Ltd, 1947; Technical Director in charge of Research, Bowaters Development and Research Ltd, 1950; Research Prof. of Wool Textile Engineering, the Univ. of Leeds, 1953; Prof. of Chemical Engineering, Rensselaer Polytechnic Inst., Troy, NY, USA, 1957. Hon. Vis. Prof., Uppsala Univ., 1974. Schwarz Memorial Lectr, Amer. Soc. of Mech. Engrs, 1967. Member: Adv. Council for Advancement of Industrial R&D, State of NY, 1965-; Board of Directors: Technical Assoc. of Pulp & Paper Industry, 1968-71 (R&D Div. Award, 1976);

Industrial Res. Inst., 1973-77. *Publications:* (ed) Textile Engineering Processes, 1959; (ed) Future Technical Needs and Trends in the Paper Industry, 1973; Lectures on Fiber Science in Paper, 1977; papers on physical chemistry and chemical engineering problems of petroleum, paper and textile technology in scientific jls. *Address:* WESTVACO, Westvaco Building, 299 Park Avenue, New York, NY 10017, USA. *Club:* University (New York).

NISSEN, Karl Iversen, MD, FRCS; retired Surgeon, Royal National Orthopædic Hospital, W1, 1946-71; Orthopædic Surgeon: Harrow Hospital 1946-71; Peace Memorial Hospital, Watford, 1948-71; *b* 4 April 1906; *s* of Christian and Caroline Nissen; *m* 1935, Margaret Mary Honor Schofield; one *s* one *d*. *Educ:* Otago Boys' High Sch., Dunedin, NZ; Univ. of Otago, NZ. BSc (NZ) 1927; MB, ChB (NZ) 1932; MD (NZ) 1936; FRCS 1936. Served as Orthopædic Specialist, RNVR, 1943-46. Corresp. mem. Belgian, French, Swiss, German, Scandinavian, Norwegian, Finnish Socs of Orthopædics. *Recreation:* foreign travel. *Address:* Prospect House, The Avenue, Sherborne, Dorset. *T:* Sherborne 3539. *Club:* Naval.

NIVEN, Sir (Cecil) Rex, Kt 1960; CMG 1953; MC 1918; *b* 20 Nov. 1898; *o s* of late Rev. Dr G. C. and Jeanne Niven, Torquay, Devon; *m* 1925, Dorothy Marshall (*d* 1977), *e d* of late D. M. Mason, formerly MP (Coventry and E Edinburgh); one *d* (and one *d* decd.) *Educ:* Blundell's Sch., Tiverton; Balliol Coll. Oxford (MA Hons). Served RFA 1917-19, France and Italy. Colonial Service Nigeria, 1921-54; served Secretariats, and Provinces; PRO, Nigeria, 1943-45; Senior Resident; twice admin. Northern Govt; Mem. Northern House of Assembly, 1947-59 (Pres. 1952-58; Speaker, 1958-59); Mem., Northern Executive Co., 1951-54; Commissioner for Special Duties in Northern Nigeria, 1959-62; Dep. Sec., Southwark Diocesan Board of Finance, 1962-68. Life Mem., BRCS; Member: Council, RSA, 1963-69; Council, Northern Euboea Foundation; Council, Imp. Soc. of Knights Bachelor, 1969-; Gen. Synod of C of E; St Charles's (formerly Paddington) Group Hosp. Management Cttee, 1963-72. FRGS. *Publications:* A Short History of Nigeria, 1937; Nigeria's Story, 1939; Nigeria: the Outline of a Colony, 1946; How Nigeria is Governed, 1950; West Africa, 1958; Short History of the Yoruba Peoples, 1958; You and Your Government, 1958; Nine Great Africans, 1964; Nigeria (in Benn's Nations of the Modern World), 1967; The War of Nigerian Unity, 1970; (collab.) My Life, by late Sardauna of Sokoto, 1962. *Recreations:* walking, architecture. *Address:* The Old Cottage, Hope Road, Deal, Kent. *T:* Deal 5104. *Club:* Royal Over- Seas League.

NIVEN, David; see Niven, J. D. G.

NIVEN, Ian; see Niven, J. R.

NIVEN, (James) David (Graham); Actor-producer (international); author; *b* 1 March 1910; *s* of late William Graham Niven and late Lady Comyn-Platt, Carswell Manor, Abingdon, Berks; *m* 1st, Primula (*d* 1946), *d* of Hon. William and Lady Kathleen Rollo; two *s*; 2nd, Hjördis Tersmeden, Stockholm; two *d*. *Educ:* Stowe; RMC Sandhurst. Commissioned HLI, 1929, Malta and Home Service; resigned commission, 1932; roamed Canada, USA, West Indies and Cuba till 1935. Journalist; Whisky Salesman; indoor pony-racing promoter; delivery of laundry; etc. Arrived California; became "extra" in films in Hollywood, 1935 ("English Type No. 2008"); played bits and small parts; first starring rôle, Bachelor Mother, 1938, with Ginger Rogers. Returned to England at outbreak of War of 1939-45; rejoined Army; commissioned Rifle Brigade, later to Phantom Reconnaissance Regt; served Normandy, Belgium, Holland, Germany (usual campaign decorations, American Legion of Merit). Important films: Wuthering Heights, Dawn Patrol, Raffles, The First of the Few, The Way Ahead, A Matter of Life and Death, The Bishop's Wife, Bonnie Prince Charlie, The Elusive Pimpernel, Enchantment, Soldiers Three, Happy Go Lovely, The Moon is Blue, The Love Lottery, Happy Ever After, Carrington VC, Around the World in 80 Days, The Birds and the Bees, Silken Affair, The Little Hut, Oh, Men, Oh, Women, Bonjour Tristesse, My Man Godfrey, Separate Tables, Ask Any Girl, Please don't eat the Daisies, The Guns of Navarone, The Best of Enemies, Guns of Darkness, 55 Days at Peking, The Pink Panther, The King of the Mountain, Bedtime Story, Lady L., Where the Spies Are, Eye of the Devil, Casino Royale, Extraordinary Seaman, Prudence and the Pill, The Impossible Years, Before Winter Comes, The Brain, The Statue; King, Queen, Knave; Vampira, Paper Tiger, No Deposit No Return, Murder by Death, Candleshoe. Formed Four Star Television, 1952, which has since produced over 2000 films for TV. Winner Academy Award, 1959; New York Critics' Award, 1960. *Publications:* Round the Rugged Rocks, 1951; The

Moon's a Balloon (autobiog.), 1971; Bring on the Empty Horses, 1975. *Recreations:* ski-ing, skin diving, oil painting. *Address:* c/o Coutts & Co., 440 Strand, WC2. *Club:* White's.

NIVEN, John Robertson, (Ian Niven); Under-Secretary, Department of the Environment, formerly Ministry of Housing and Local Government, since 1974; *b* 11 May 1919; *s* of Robert Niven and Amelia Mary Hill; *m* 1946, Jane Bicknell; three *s*. *Educ:* Glasgow Academy; Jesus Coll., Oxford. Entered Min. of Town and Country Planning, 1946; Sec., Royal Commn on Local Govt in Greater London, 1957-60. *Address:* 14 Anglefield Road, Berkhamsted, Herts. *T:* Berkhamsted 3034.

NIVEN, Margaret Graeme, ROI 1936; Landscape and Portrait Painter; *b* Marlow, 1906; *yr d* of William Niven, FSA, ARE, JP, Marlow Place, Marlow, Bucks, and Eliza Mary Niven. *Educ:* Prior's Field, Godalming. Studied at Winchester Sch. of Art, Heatherley Sch. of Fine Art, and under Bernard Adams, RP, ROI; Mem. of National Soc. Painters, Sculptors, and Engravers, 1932. Exhibitor at Royal Academy and Royal Soc. of Portrait Painters. Works purchased by Bradford Art Gallery, The Ministry of Works, Homerton Coll., Cambridge, and Bedford Coll., London. Served with WRNS, 1940-45. *Address:* Broomhill, Sandhills, Wormley, near Godalming, Surrey.

NIVEN, Sir Rex; see Niven, Sir C. R.

NIVEN, Col Thomas Murray, CB 1964; TD 1941; DL; FICE; FIMechE; *b* 20 Aug. 1900; *s* of Thomas Ogilvie Niven, Civil Engineer, Glasgow. *Educ:* Glasgow Academy; Glasgow Univ. Served War of 1939-45 with Royal Signals: comdg 52 (Lowland) Div. Signals, 1938-40; comdg Royal Signals Mobilisation Centre, 1941-43; Dep. Chief Signal Officer, Northern Command, 1944. Comdg 6 Glasgow Home Guard Bn, 1952-56; Hon. Col 52 (Lowland) Signal Regt (TA), 1950-66; Chm., Glasgow T & AFA, 1959-62. Formerly Dir of Mechans Ltd, Engineers, Scotstoun Iron Works, Glasgow. DL Glasgow, 1949. *Recreation:* walking.

NIVISON, family name of **Baron Glendyne.**

NIXON, Sir (Charles) Norman, Kt, *cr* 1946; Governor of the National Bank of Egypt until 1946; *b* 8 June 1891; *m* Catherine Marwood Ranson (*d* 1954); two *s*. Served European War, 1914-18, Indian Army (despatches). *Address:* 1 The Garden, Lady Street, Dulverton, Som.

NIXON, Major Sir Christopher John Louis Joseph, 3rd Bt, *cr* 1906; MC; Royal Ulster Rifles; *b* 21 March 1918; *s* of Major Sir Christopher Nixon, 2nd Bt, DSO, and Louise, *y d* of Robert Clery, JP, The Glebe, Athlacca, Limerick; *S* father, 1945; *m* 1949, Joan Lucille Mary, *d* of R. F. M. Brown, London; three *d*. Served War of 1939-45, Burma. Gurkha Bde (despatches, MC); Palestine, Egypt, 1945-48; UK, attached London Irish Rifles, 1948-50; Korea (despatches). 1950-51. *Heir: b* Rev. Kenneth Michael John Basil Nixon, SJ. [*b* 22 Feb. 1919; in Holy Orders of Church of Rome]. *Address:* c/o Lloyds Bank Ltd, Cox's & King's Branch, 6 Pall Mall, SW1.

NIXON, Edwin Ronald, CBE 1974; Managing Director since 1965: IBM United Kingdom Holdings Ltd; IBM United Kingdom Ltd; IBM United Kingdom Rentals Ltd; Chairman of IBM United Kingdom Laboratories Ltd, since 1965; Director, IBM Information Services Ltd, since 1967; *b* 21 June 1925; *s* of William Archdale Nixon and Ethel (*née* Corrigan); *m* 1952, Joan Lilian (*née* Hill); one *s* one *d*. *Educ:* Alderman Newton's Sch., Leicester; Selwyn Coll., Cambridge; MA. Dexion Ltd, 1950-55; IBM United Kingdom Ltd, 1955-; Dir, National Westminster Bank Ltd, 1975-. Mem. Council: Foundn for Automation and Employment, 1967-77; Electronic Engineering Assoc., 1965-76; CBI, 1971 (Chm. Standing Cttee on Marketing and Consumer Affairs); Foundn for Management Educn, 1973; Member: British Cttee of Awards for Harkness Fellowships, 1976-; Adv. Council, Business Graduates Assoc., 1976-; Board of Governors, United World Coll. of Atlantic, 1977-; Council: Manchester Business Sch., 1974- (Chm., Finance and Gen. Purposes Cttee, 1975-); Westfield Coll., London, 1969; William Temple Coll., Manchester, 1972; Oxford Centre for Management Studies, 1973. *Recreations:* music, tennis, squash, golf, sailing, ski-ing. *Address:* Starkes Heath, Rogate, Petersfield, Hants. *T:* Rogate 504. *Clubs:* Athenæum, Reform.

NIXON, Rear-Adm. Harry Desmond, CB 1973; MVO 1958; Member, Public Inquiries Panel for Department of the Environment, since 1974; *b* 6 May 1920; *s* of Harry Earle Nixon and Ethel Maude Nixon; *m* 1946, Elizabeth June Witherington; one *s* two *d*. *Educ:* Brigg. CEng, FIMechE, MIMarE, FInstPet. Joined RN as Cadet, 1938; RNEC, 1939-42; HMS: Suffolk,

1942; Indomitable, 1943-45; HM Dockyard, Malta, 1954-55; HM Yacht Britannia, 1956-58; Ship Dept, Admty, Bath, 1958-60; RNEC, 1960-62; Naval District Engr Overseer Midlands, 1962-64; CO, HMS Sultan, 1964-66; idc 1967; Dir of Fleet Maintenance, 1968-71. Comdr 1953; Captain 1962; Rear-Adm. 1971; Vice-Pres. (Naval), 1971-73, Pres., 1973-74, Ordnance Board. *Address:* Ashley Cottage, Ashley, Box, Corsham, Wilts. *Club:* Army and Navy.

NIXON, Howard Millar, FSA; Librarian, Westminster Abbey, since 1974; *b* 3 Sept. 1909; *s* of Rev. Leigh H. Nixon, MVO, and Harrie (*née* Millar); *m* 1951, Enid Dorothy Bromley; three *s*. *Educ:* Marlborough; Keble Coll., Oxford. BA 1931; MA 1974. Served in Army, 1939-46 (Major, RA). Asst Cataloguer, Dept of Printed Books, British Museum, 1936; Asst Keeper, 1946, Dep. Keeper, 1959-74. Lectr in Bibliography, Sch. of Library Studies, University Coll., London, 1959-76; Sandars Reader in Bibliography, Univ. of Cambridge, 1967-68. Pres., Bibliographical Soc., 1972-74. Editor, British Library Jl, 1974-. Chm., Panel for allocation of Printed Books received in lieu of Death Duties, 1976-. Hon. Fellow, Pierpont Morgan Library, NY. *Publications:* Twelve Books in Fine Bindings, 1953; Broxbourne Library, 1956; Bookbindings from the Library of Jean Grolier, 1965; Sixteenth-century Gold-tooled Bookbindings in the Pierpont Morgan Library, 1971; English Restoration Bookbindings, 1974; articles in The Library, Book Collector, etc. *Recreation:* golf. *Address:* 4A Little Cloister, Westminster Abbey, SW1P 3PL. *T:* 01-222 6428. *Club:* Grolier (New York).

NIXON, Sir Norman; *see* Nixon, Sir C. N.

NIXON, Richard M.; President of the United States of America, 1969-74, resigned 10 Aug. 1974; *b* 9 Jan. 1913; *s* of Francis A. and Hannah Milhous Nixon; *m* 1940, Patricia Ryan; two *d*. *Educ:* Whittier Coll., Whittier, California (AB); Duke University Law Sch., Durham, North Carolina (LLB). Lawyer, Whittier, California, 1937-42; Office of Price Administration, 1942; Active duty, US Navy, 1942-46. Member 80th, 81st Congresses, 1947-50; US Senator from California, 1950-53. Vice-President of the USA, 1953-61; Republican candidate for the Presidency of the USA, 1960. Lawyer, Los Angeles, 1961-63, NY, 1963-68. Republican Candidate for Governor of California, 1962. Member: Board of Trustees, Whittier Coll., 1939-68; Society of Friends; Order of Coif. *Publication:* Six Crises, 1962. *Address:* La Casa Pacifica, Avenida de Presidente, San Clemente, California 92672, USA.

NIXON, Rev. Robin Ernest, MA; Principal, St John's College, Nottingham, since 1975; *b* 5 Dec. 1931; *s* of Ernest Nixon and Helen Louisa Nixon (*née* Smallwood); *m* 1958, Ruth Mary, *d* of Arthur Eric Jarvis Vickers and Katherine Vickers (*née* Wood); three *d*. *Educ:* Ascham House Sch., Newcastle upon Tyne; Winchester Coll.; Trinity Hall, Cambridge; Ridley Hall, Cambridge. Pt I Law, Pts II and III Theol., MA 1958, Cantab. Asst Curate, Holy Trinity Church, Hull, 1957-60; Tutor, St John's Coll., Univ. of Durham, 1960-63, Sen. Tutor, 1963-75. Editor, The Churchman, 1972-. *Recreations:* family, reading, current affairs. *Address:* St John's College, Bramcote, Nottingham NG9 3DS. *T:* Nottingham 251114.

NOAD, Sir Kenneth (Beeson), Kt 1970; Consulting Physician since 1931; Patron, Australian Postgraduate Federation in Medicine; *b* 25 March 1900; *s* of James Beeson and Mary Jane Noad; *m* 1935, Eileen Mary Ryan; no *c*. *Educ:* Maitland, NSW; Sydney University. MB, ChM 1924, MD 1953, Sydney; MRCP 1929; FRCP 1948; Foundn FRACP 1938 (PRACP 1962-64). Hon FACP 1964; Hon. FRCPE 1968. Served War of 1939-45, Palestine, Egypt, Greece, Crete, New Guinea; Lt-Col Comdr Medical Div. of an Australian General Hospital. Hon. DLitt and Hon. AM Singapore. *Publications:* papers in Brain, Med. Jl of Australia. *Recreations:* golf, gardening. *Address:* 22 Billyard Avenue, Elizabeth Bay, NSW 2011, Australia. *Clubs:* Australian (Sydney); Royal Sydney Golf.

NOAKES, Col Geoffrey William, OBE 1958; TD 1948; JP; DL; Past Managing Director, William Timpson Ltd, Footwear Retailers; *b* 1913; *s* of Charles William Noakes; *m* 1936, Annie, *d* of Albert Hough, Peel Green; two *s* two *d*. *Educ:* Wyggeston Sch. Commissioned RA, 1936. Served War: in France, 1940; Burma, 1940-46 (despatches); Staff Coll., Quetta, 1944; AQMG, Fourteenth Army, 1944-45. In command 252 Field Regt RA, 1951-57; DCRA, 42 Div., 1957-62. Past Pres., Multiple Shoe Retailers' Assoc.; Past Pres. and Vice-Chm., Footwear Distributors' Fedn; Leader and Sec., Employer's side, Boot and Shoe Repairing Wages Council; Past Pres., Nat. Assoc. of Shoe Repair Factories. Past Chm., Publicity and Recruiting Cttee, and Vice-Chm., NW of England and IOM TAVR Assoc.; Pres.,

Burma Star Assoc., Altrincham; Past Mem., Bd of Examiners, Sch. of Business Studies, Manchester Polytechnic; Mem. Exec. Cttee, Manchester and Dist Boys' Clubs; Governor, Manchester Univ.; formerly Rep. Col Comdt, RA Uniformed Staff. JP Manchester, 1963; DL Lancs 1974. FIBM, FIWM, MIPM, ABSI. *Recreations:* hunting, shooting, fishing (Pres. Altrincham Angling Club), golf. *Address:* The Mill House, Bickley, near Malpas, Cheshire SY14 8EG. *T:* Hampton Heath 309. *Club:* Army and Navy.
See also P. R. Noakes.

NOAKES, Michael, PROI, RP; artist; portrait painter; *b* 28 Oct. 1933; *s* of late Basil and of Mary Noakes; *m* 1960, Vivien Noakes (*née* Langley), writer; two *s* one *d*. *Educ:* Downside; Royal Academy Schs, London. Nat. Dipl. in Design, 1954; Certificate of Royal Academy Schools, 1960. Commnd: National Service, 1954-56. Has broadcast and televised on art subjects in UK and USA; Art Correspondent, BBC TV programme Town and Around, 1964-68. Member Council: ROI, 1964- (Vice-Pres. 1968-72; Pres., 1972-); RP, 1969-71 and 1972-74; NS, 1962-76 (Hon. Mem., 1976-); Chm., Contemp. Portrait Soc., 1971. Governor, Fedn of British Artists, 1972-. *Exhibited:* Royal Acad.; Royal Inst. Oil Painters; Royal Soc. Portrait Painters; Contemp. Portrait Soc.; Nat. Society; Young Contemporaries, Grosvenor Galleries, Upper Grosvenor Galls, Woodstock Galls, Royal Glasgow Inst. of Fine Arts, Nat. Portrait Gall.; Roy. Soc. of British Artists; Grafton Gall.; Art Exhibitions Bureau, touring widely in Britain, USA and Canada. Judge, Miss World Contest, 1976. Platinum disc, 1977 (record sleeve design Portrait of Sinatra). *Portraits include:* The Queen (unveiled Silver Jubilee year, for Manchester); Lord Aberconway; Lord Amory; Princess Anne (for Saddlers' Co.); Sir Henry Benson; Lord Barnetson; Lord Boothby; Lady Boothby; Lord Bowden; Lord Boyd; FM Sir Michael Carver; Lord Chuter-Ede; Lord Elwyn-Jones; Archbishop Lord Fisher; Lord Fulton; Sir Alec Guinness; Sir H. John Habakkuk; Gen. Sir John Hackett; Gilbert Harding; Robert Hardy; Lord Iveagh; Sir Henry Jones; Sir Douglas Logan; Lord Selwyn-Lloyd; Bishop Lunt; Cliff Michelmore; Eric Morley; Robert Morley; Malcolm Muggeridge; Sir Gerald Nabarro; Valerie Profumo; J. B. Priestley; Sir Ralph Richardson; Sir Martin Roth; Edmund de Rothschild; Dame Margaret Rutherford; Very Rev. M. Sullivan; Lord Todd; Sir Arthur Vick; Dennis Wheatley; Sir Mortimer Wheeler; Lord Wolfenden; Sir Donald Wolfit; *major group portraits:* Royal Family, with Lord and Lady Mayoress, for Guildhall; Members and Officers, Metropolitan Water Board (47 figures); Lords of Appeal in Ordinary (for Middle Temple). *Represented in collections:* The Prince of Wales; British Mus.; Nat. Portrait Gall. (Hugill Fund Purchase, RA, 1972); numerous Oxford and Cambridge colleges; County Hall, Westminster; various livery companies and Inns of Court; House of Commons; Bradford Art Gall.; London Univ.; Nottingham Univ.; Frank Sinatra. *Publications:* A Professional Approach to Oil Painting, 1968; contributions to various art journals. *Recreation:* idling. *Address:* 146 Hamilton Terrace, St John's Wood, NW8 9UX. *T:* 01-328 6754.

NOAKES, Philip Reuben, OBE 1962; HM Diplomatic Service, retired; *b* 12 Aug. 1915; *y s* of late Charles William and Elizabeth Farey Noakes; *m* 1940, Moragh Jean Dickson; two *s*. *Educ:* Wyggeston Grammar Sch.; Wycliffe Coll.; Queens' Coll., Cambridge (Open Schol.). Mod. Langs Tripos Part I, Hist. Tripos Part II; BA 1937; MA 1945; Pres., Cambridge Union Soc., 1937. Served War, 1940-46; Capt.-Adjt 2nd Fife and Forfar Yeomanry, RAC (despatches). Public Relations Officer, Royal Over-Seas League, 1947-48; Sen. Information Officer, Colonial Office, 1948; Prin. Information Officer, CO, 1953; Information Adviser to Governor of Malta, 1960-61; Chief Information Officer, CO, 1963-66; Commonwealth Office, 1967; Counsellor (Information), Ottawa, 1967-72; Consul-Gen., Seattle, 1973-75. *Recreations:* bird-watching, fishing, ski-ing. *Address:* Eaton Hey, The Drive, Eaton Park, Cobham, Surrey. *Club:* Royal Over-Seas League.
See also G. W. Noakes.

NOAKES, His Honour Sidney Henry; a Circuit Judge (formerly County Court Judge), 1968-77; *b* 6 Jan. 1905; *s* of Thomas Frederick Noakes (Civil Servant) and Ada Noakes. *Educ:* Merchant Taylors' Sch.; St John's Coll., Oxford (MA). Called to Bar, Lincoln's Inn, 1928; SE Circuit; Bencher, 1963. War Service, Lt-Col., Intelligence Corps, England and NW Europe. Deputy Chairman: Surrey QS, 1963; Herts QS, 1964; Recorder of Margate, 1965-68. *Publication:* Fire Insurance, 1947. *Recreations:* regretfully now only golf, walking and gardening. *Address:* 14 Meadway Crescent, Hove, E Sussex BN3 7NL. *T:* Brighton 736143.

NOBES, (Charles) Patrick; Headmaster of Bedales School, since 1974; *b* 17 March 1933; *o c* of Alderman Alfred Robert Nobes, OBE, JP, and Marguerite Violet Vivian (*née* Fathers), Gosport, Hants; *m* 1958, Patricia Jean (*née* Brand); three *s. Educ:* Price's Sch., Fareham, Hants; University Coll., Oxford. MA. With The Times, reporting and editorial, 1956-57; Head of English Dept, King Edward VI Grammar Sch., Bury St Edmunds, 1959-64; Head of English and General Studies and Sixth Form Master, Ashlyns Comprehensive Sch., Berkhamsted, 1964-69; Headmaster, The Ward Freman Sch., Buntingford, Herts, 1969-74. Chm., HMC Co-ed Schs Gp, 1976-. General Editor and adapter, Bulls-Eye Books (series for adults and young adults with reading difficulties), 1972-. *Recreations:* cricket and hockey, King Arthur, Hampshire, music, First World War. *Address:* The Headmaster's House, Bedales School, Petersfield, Hants GU32 2DG. *T:* Petersfield 2970. *Club:* Athenæum.

NOBLE, family name of **Baron Glenkinglas.**

NOBLE, Comdr Rt. Hon. Sir Allan (Herbert Percy), PC 1956; KCMG 1959; DSO 1943; DSC 1941; DL; a Member of Lloyd's; *b* 2 May 1908; *s* of late Admiral Sir Percy Noble, GBE, KCB, CVO, and Diamantina Campbell; *m* 1938, Barbara Janet Margaret, *o d* of late Brigadier Kenneth Gabbett. *Educ:* Radley College. Entered Royal Navy, 1926; ADC to Viceroy of India (Lord Linlithgow), 1936-38; commanded HM Destroyers Newport, Fernie and Quentin, 1940-42; Commander, 1943. Attended Quebec and Yalta Conferences. Served War of 1939-45 (despatches, DSC, DSO); retired list, 1945. MP (C) for Chelsea, 1945-59; Government Observer, Bikini Atomic Bomb Tests, 1946; PPS to Mr Anthony Eden, 1947-51; Parly and Financial Sec., Admiralty, 1951-55; Parly Under-Sec. of State for Commonwealth Relations, Dec. 1955-Nov. 1956; Minister of State for Foreign Affairs, Nov. 1956-Jan. 1959; Leader, UK Delegation: to UN Gen. Assembly, 1957-58; to UN Disarmament Sub-Cttee, 1957; Special Ambassador, Ivory Coast, 1961. Dir and Chm., Tollemache & Cobbold Breweries Ltd, 1960-73; Dir, Colonial Mutual Life Assurance Soc. Ltd (UK Br.), 1960-76. Member Cttee of Management, Inst. of Cancer Research, Royal Cancer Hosp., 1959-67. Mem., Advisory Cttee on Service Parly Candidates, 1963-74. President: Chelsea Cons. Assoc., 1962-66; Cambridgeshire Cons. Assoc., 1967-72; a Mem. of Radley Coll. Council, 1947-63; Chm., National Trainers' Assoc., 1963-66. Hon. Freeman: Chelsea, 1963; Royal Borough of Kensington and Chelsea, 1965. DL Suffolk, 1973. Inter Services Athletics (Hurdles), 1931. *Address:* Troston Cottage, Bury St Edmunds, Suffolk IP31 1EX. *T:* Honington 250; 3 Culford Gardens, SW3. *T:* 01-589 0649. *Club:* White's.

NOBLE, Sir Andrew Napier, 2nd Bt, *cr* 1923; KCMG 1954 (CMG 1947); *b* 16 Sept. 1904; *s* of Sir John Henry Brunel Noble, 1st Bt, and Amie (*d* 1973), *d* of S. A. Walker Waters; *S* father, 1938; *m* 1934, Sigrid, 2nd *d* of M. Michelet, of Royal Norwegian Diplomatic Service; two *s* one *d. Educ:* Eton; Balliol Coll., Oxford. Counsellor of the British Embassy, Buenos Aires, 1945-47; Assistant Under-Secretary of State, Foreign Office, 1949; HM Minister at Helsinki, 1951-54; HM Ambassador: Warsaw, 1954-56; Mexico, 1956-60; Netherlands, 1960-64, retired. Member Executive Committee: Oxford Soc.; Genealogical Soc. *Publications:* (jt author) Centenary History, OURFC, 1969; History of the Nobles of Ardmore and of Ardkinglas, 1971. *Heir: s* Ian Andrew Noble, *b* 1935. *Address:* 11 Cedar House, Marloes Road, W8 5LA. *Club:* Boodle's.
See also Baron Glenkinglas.

NOBLE, Col Sir Arthur, KBE 1972; CB 1965; DSO 1943; TD; DL; Deputy Chairman, W. & C. French Ltd, 1966-68 (Director, 1953-68); President, Harlow and District Sports Trust, 1976 (Chairman, 1957-76); *b* 13 Sept. 1908; *s* of F. M. Noble, Chipping Ongar, Essex; *m* 1935, Irene Susan, OBE 1970, JP, *d* of J. D. Taylor, Wimbledon; three *s* two *d. Educ:* Felsted School. Chartered Quantity Surveyor, 1934; joined W. & C. French Ltd, 1945. Essex Regt (Territorial Army), 1927; Served Middle East and Italy, 1939-45; Commanded 4th Essex, 1941-44 and 1947-51; Chief Instructor, Sch. of Infantry, 1944-45. Hon. Col, TA and T&AVR Bn, The Essex Regt, 1955-71; a Dep. Hon. Col, The Royal Anglian Regt (Essex), T&AVR, 1971-73. Chm. Essex County Playing Fields Assoc., 1956-61; Chm., County of Essex T&AF Assoc., 1958-66; Vice-Chm., Council of TA&VRA, 1966-72. Mem. of Council, Federation of Civil Engineering Contractors, 1963-68, Mem., Eastern Sports Council, 1966-72; Vice-Pres., Nat. Playing Fields Assoc., 1968. DL (Essex) 1946. *Recreations:* many. *Address:* Marchings, Chigwell, Essex. *T:* Hainault 5302. *Club:* Army and Navy.

NOBLE, Sir Fraser; see Noble, Sir T. A. F.

NOBLE, Kenneth Albert, CBE 1975; Member, Price Commission, since 1973 (Deputy Chairman, 1973-76); Director, 1954-73, Vice-Chairman, since 1966, Co-operative Wholesale Society Ltd; Director of associated organisations and subsidiaries. Member: CoID, 1957-65; Post Office Users Nat. Council, 1965-73; Monopolies Commn, 1969-73. Served War, 1940-46 (despatches); Major RASC. *Address:* 23 St Augustine's Avenue, Southend-on-Sea, Essex SS1 3JH.

NOBLE, Major Sir Marc (Brunel), 5th Bt, *cr* 1902; *b* 8 Jan. 1927; *er s* of Sir Humphrey Brunel Noble, 4th Bt, MBE, MC, and Celia, *d* of late Captain Stewart Weigall, RN; *S* father, 1968; *m* 1956, Jennifer Lorna, *yr d* of late John Mein-Austin, Flint Hill, West Haddon, Northants; two *s* one *d* (and one *d* decd). *Educ:* Eton. Commissioned into King's Dragoon Guards as 2nd Lieut, 1947; on amalgamation, transferred Royal Dragoons, 1958. Training Major and Adjutant, Kent and County of London Yeomanry (Sharpshooters), 1963-64; retired, rank of Major, RARO, 1966. Commonwealth Comr, Scout Assoc., 1972-. *Heir: er s* David Brunel Noble, *b* 25 Dec. 1961. *Address:* Deerleap House, Knockholt, Sevenoaks, Kent TN14 7NP. *T:* Knockholt 3222. *Club:* Cavalry and Guards.

NOBLE, Michael Alfred (Mike); MP (Lab) Rossendale since Oct. 1974; *b* 10 March 1935; *s* of Alfred and Olive Noble; *m* 1956, Brenda Kathleen Peak; one *s* two *d. Educ:* Hull Grammar Sch.; Sheffield Univ. (BA); Hull Univ. (DipEd). Secondary Sch. Teacher, Hull, 1959-63; WEA Tutor in Industrial Relations, 1963-73; Consultant in Industrial Relations and Trng, 1973-74. *Recreations:* golf, fishing, reading. *Address:* 21 Mill Hill Lane, Hapton, Burnley, Lancs. *T:* Burnley 74416. *Club:* Workingmen's (Ramsbottom).

NOBLE, Sir Peter (Scott), Kt 1967; Principal of King's College, University of London, 1952-July 1968; *b* 17 Oct. 1899; *s* of Andrew Noble and Margaret Trail; *m* 1928, Mary Stephen; two *s* one *d. Educ:* Aberdeen Univ.; St John's Coll., Cambridge. First Bursar at Aberdeen Univ., 1916, MA, with 1st Class Honours in Classics 1921, Simpson Prize and Robbie Gold Medal in Greek, Seafield Medal and Dr Black prize in Latin, Jenkyns Prize in Comparative Philology, Liddell Prize in Greek Verse, Fullerton Scholarship in Classics, 1921, Croom Robertson Fellow (1923-26); Scholar of St John's Coll., Cambridge; 1st class Classical Tripos Part I (1922) Part II (1923), 1st Class Oriental Langs Tripos Part I (1924) Part II (1925), Bendall Sanskrit Exhibition (1924), (1925), Hutchison Student (1925); Lecturer in Latin at Liverpool Univ., 1926-30; Professor of Latin Language and Literature in the University of Leeds, 1930-37; Fellow of St John's Coll., Cambridge, 1928-31; Regius Professor of Humanity, University of Aberdeen, 1938-52; Member of University Grants Cttee, 1943-53; Vice-Chancellor, University of London, 1961-64; Member of General Dental Council, 1955; Member of Educational Trust, English-Speaking Union, 1958; Governor of St Thomas' Hospital, 1960. Hon. LLD Aberdeen, 1955. *Publications:* Joint editor of Kharosthi Inscriptions Vol. III; reviews, etc, classical journals. *Address:* 17 Glenorchy Terrace, Edinburgh EH9 2DG.

NOBLE, Robert More Hilary; a Recorder of the Crown Court since 1972; Chairman: National Health Service Tribunal for England and Wales, since 1970; West Sussex Supplementary Benefits Appeal Tribunal, since 1970; Industrial Tribunals, since 1975 (part-time); *b* 23 Aug. 1909; *s* of late Mr Justice Noble, KCSG, Colonial Legal Service, and of late Mrs Robert Noble; *m* 1936, Faith (*née* Varley); two *s* three *d* (and one *d* decd). *Educ:* Beaumont Coll.; Balliol Coll. (BA Hons). Admitted Solicitor, 1934. Served War, 1939-45. Commissioned RAFVR, Air Force Dept of Judge Advocate General's Office, France and Middle East, also Accidents Investigation Br., 1940-41, ranks Sqdn Ldr, Actg Wing Comdr. Partner: Underwood & Co., 1946-59, Vernor Miles & Noble, 1959-70 (both of London). Trustee of a number of Charitable Trusts (concerned with educn and the disabled). *Publications:* short stories and contrib. legal jls. *Recreations:* riding, swimming. *Address:* Peartree Cottage, Blackboys, Sussex. *T:* Framfield 337. *Club:* Oriental.

NOBLE, Sir (Thomas Alexander) Fraser, Kt 1971; MBE 1947; Principal and Vice-Chancellor, University of Aberdeen, since 1976; *b* 29 April 1918; *s* of late Simon Noble, Grantown-on-Spey and Jeanie Graham, Largs, Ayrshire; *m* 1945, Barbara A. M. Sinclair, Nairn; one *s* one *d. Educ:* Nairn Acad; Univ. of Aberdeen. After military service with Black Watch (RHR), entered Indian Civil Service, 1940. Served in NW Frontier Province, 1941-47, successively as Asst Comr, Hazara; Asst Polit. Agent, N Waziristan; Controller of Rationing, Peshawar; Under-Sec., Food Dept and Develt Dept; Sec., Home Dept; Joint Dep. Comr, Peshawar; Civil Aide to Referendum Comr. Lectr in Political Economy, Univ. of Aberdeen, 1948-57; Sec.

and Treas., Carnegie Trust for Univs of Scotland, 1957-62; Vice-Chancellor, Leicester Univ., 1962-76. Mem. and Vice-Chm., Bd of Management, Aberdeen Mental Hosp. Group, 1953-57. Sec., Scottish Economic Soc., 1954-58; Vice-Pres., 1962-. Chm., Scottish Standing Conf. of Voluntary Youth Organisations, 1958-62; Vice-Chm., Standing Consultative Council on Youth Service in Scotland, 1959-62. Mem., Departmental Cttee on Probation Service, 1959-62; Chairman: Probation Advisory and Training Board, 1962-65; Television Research Cttee, 1963-69; Advisory Council on Probation and After-Care, 1965-70; Univs Council for Adult Education, 1965-69; Min. of Defence Cttee for Univ. Assistance to Adult Educn in HM Forces, 1965-70; Advisory Board, Overseas Students' Special Fund, 1967-71, Fees Awards Scheme, 1968-75; Cttee of Vice-Chancellors and Principals of Univs of UK, 1970-72; British Council Cttee on Exchanges between UK and USSR, 1973-. Member: Academic Advisory Cttee, Univs of St Andrews and Dundee, 1964-66; E Midlands Economic Planning Council, 1965-68; Council, Assoc. Commonwealth Univs, 1970-; Exec. Cttee, Inter-Univ. Council for Higher Educn Overseas, 1972-; Exec. Cttee, British Council, 1973-; British Council Cttee for Commonwealth Univ. Interchange, 1973-; US-UK Educnl Commn, 1973-. Hon. LLD Aberdeen, 1968. *Publications:* articles in economic journals. *Recreation:* golf. *Address:* Chanonry Lodge, Old Aberdeen.

NOCK, Rt. Rev. Frank Foley; *see* Algoma, Bishop of.

NOCK, Sir Norman (Lindfield), Kt 1939; Chairman of Directors, Nock & Kirby Ltd, Sydney; *s* of Thomas Nock, Stanhope Road, Killara, Sydney; *m* 1927, Ethel Evelina Bradford; one *s. Educ:* Sydney Church of England Grammar Sch. Alderman for Gipps Ward, City of Sydney, 1933-41; Lord Mayor of Sydney, 1938-39; Chairman, Federal Australian Comforts Fund, 1939-43; Chairman, Australian Comforts Fund, NSW Division, 1939-45; President of the National Roads and Motorists Association, 1954-69; Chairman Royal North Shore Hospital of Sydney, 1940-69; Member National Health and Medical Research Council, 1946-69. JP for New South Wales. *Recreations:* golf, sailing and motoring. *Address:* Box 4250, GPO Sydney, NSW 2001, Australia. *Club:* Royal Sydney Golf (Sydney).

NOCKOLDS, Stephen Robert, FRS 1959; PhD; Reader in Geochemistry in the University of Cambridge, 1957-72, now Emeritus Reader; *b* 10 May 1909; *s* of Stephen Nockolds; *m* 1932, Hilda Jackson (*d* 1976). *Educ:* Felsted; University of Manchester (BSc); University of Cambridge (PhD). Fellow of Trinity Coll. and formerly Lectr in Petrology, Univ. of Cambridge. Murchison Medal, Geol Soc., 1972. Hon. Fellow, Geol. Soc. of India. *Publications:* various papers in mineralogical and geological journals. *Recreation:* gardening. *Address:* The Bell House, Castle Street, Saffron Walden, Essex CB10 1BD.

NODDER, Timothy Edward; Under-Secretary, Department of Health and Social Security, since 1972; *b* 18 June 1930; *s* of Edward Nodder; *m* 1952, Sylvia Broadhurst; two *s* two *d. Educ:* St Paul's Sch.; Christ's Coll., Cambridge. *Recreation:* natural history. *Address:* Hamsey, Lewes, E Sussex.

NOEL, family name of **Earl of Gainsborough.**

NOËL, Sir Claude; *see* Noël, Sir M. E. C.

NOEL, Rear-Adm. Gambier John Byng, CB 1969; retired; *b* 16 July 1914; *s* of late G. B. E. Noel; *m* 1936, Miss Joan Stevens; four *d. Educ:* Royal Naval Coll., Dartmouth. Joined Royal Navy, 1931; Served in War of 1939-45, HMS Aurora and HMS Norfolk (despatches twice). Captain 1959; Imperial Defence Coll., 1962; Staff of Commander Far East Fleet, 1964-67; Rear-Admiral 1967; Chief Staff Officer (Technical) to C-in-C, Western Fleet, 1967-69. *Recreations:* gardening, golf. *Address:* Woodpeckers, Church Lane, Haslemere, Surrey. *T:* Haslemere 3824. *Club:* Anglo-Belgian.

NOEL, Major Geoffrey Lindsay James; Metropolitan Stipendiary Magistrate, since 1975; *b* 19 April 1923; *s* of Major James Noel and Maud Noel; *m* 1st, 1947, Beryl MacGregor; two *d* ; 2nd, 1966, Eileen Pickering (*née* Cooper); two step *s. Educ:* Crewkerne Sch., Somerset; Glasgow Univ.; Cambridge Univ. Enlisted Royal Regt of Artillery, 1941; commnd, 1942; attached 9th Para Bn, 6 Airborne Div., 1944, Captain; regular commn, 1946; BAOR and British Mil. Mission to Denmark, 1946-50; RWAFF, 1952-55; Major 1957; retd 1960. Called to Bar, Middle Temple, 1962; practised London and SE circuit. *Recreations:* sailing, military history. *Address:* Patchings, Henfield, Sussex. *T:* Henfield 2098.

NOEL, Hon. Gerard Eyre Wriothesley; author; *b* 20 Nov. 1926; *s* of 4th Earl of Gainsborough, OBE, TD, and Alice (*née* Eyre); *m* 1958, Adele Julie Patricia, *d* of Major V. N. B. Were; two *s* one *d. Educ:* Georgetown, USA; Exeter Coll., Oxford (MA, Modern History). Called to Bar, Inner Temple, 1952. Dir, Herder Book Co., 1959-66; Chm., Sands & Co. (Publishers) Ltd, 1967-. Literary Editor, Catholic Times, 1958-61; Catholic Herald: Asst Editor, 1968; Editor, 1971-76; Editorial Dir, 1976-. Mem. Exec. Cttee, Council of Christians and Jews, 1974-. Contested (L) Argyll, 1959. Liveryman, Co. of Stationers and Newspapermakers. Freeman, City of London. *Publications:* Paul VI, 1963; Harold Wilson, 1964; Goldwater, 1964; The New Britain, 1966; The Path from Rome, 1968; Princess Alice: Queen Victoria's Forgotten Daughter, 1974; The Great Lock-Out of 1926, 1976; The Anatomy o the Roman Catholic Church, 1978; contrib. The Prime Ministers, 1974; *translations:* The Way to Unity after the Council, 1967; The Holy See and the War in Europe (Official Documents), 1968; articles in: Church Times, Catholic Times, Jewish Chronicle, Baptist Times, Catholic Herald, Universe. *Recreations:* walking, travel, exploring London. *Address:* 105 Cadogan Gardens, SW3. *T:* 01-730 8734; Westington Mill, Chipping Campden, Glos. *T:* Evesham 840240. *Clubs:* Beefsteak, Garrick, Royal Automobile.

NOËL, Sir (Martial Ernest) Claude, Kt 1976; CMG 1973; Director and Chairman of sugar and other companies; *b* 1 Feb. 1912; *m* 1937, Héléne Fromet de Rosnay; three *s* three *d. Educ:* College du St Esprit, Mauritius. Maths teacher, 1930; joined sugar industry, 1931; Manager sugar estate, 1939-. Chairman: Central Cttee of Estate Managers on several occasions; Mauritius Sugar Producers; Mauritius Employers Fedn, 1962-63; Mauritius Chamber of Agriculture, 1971-72 (Pres., 1974-). Citoyen d'Honneur Escalier Village. *Address:* Floréal, Mauritius. *T:* Curepipe 2235. *Clubs:* Dodo, Mauritius Turf (Mauritius).

NOEL-BAKER, family name of **Baron Noel-Baker.**

NOEL-BAKER, Baron *cr* 1977 (Life Peer), of the City of Derby; **Philip John Noel-Baker,** PC 1945; *b* Nov. 1889; *s* of late J. Allen Baker, MP; *m* 1915, Irene (*d* 1956), *o d* of Frank Noel, British landowner, of Achmetaga, Greece; one *s. Educ:* Bootham School, York; Haverford Coll., Pa; King's Coll., Cambridge, MA. Historical Tripos, Part I, Class II, 1910; Economics Tripos, Part II, Class I, 1912; University Whewell Scholar, 1911 (continued, 1913); President CUAC, 1910-12; President Cambridge Union Society, 1912; Vice-Principal, Ruskin Coll., Oxford, 1914; First Commandant Friend's Ambulance Unit, Aug. 1914-July 1915; Officer First British Ambulance Unit for Italy, 1915-18; Mons Star; Silver Medal for Military Valour (Italy), 1917; Croce di Guerra, 1918; League of Nations Section of British Delegation during Peace Conference, 1919; League of Nations Secretariat till 1922; contested (Lab) Handsworth Division of Birmingham, 1924; MP (Lab), for Coventry, 1929-31, for Derby, 1936-50, for Derby South, 1950-70; PPS to the Sec. of State for Foreign Affairs, 1929-31; Parly Sec. to Min. of War Transport, 1942-45; Minister of State, FO, 1945-46; Sec. of State for Air, 1946-47; Sec. of State for Commonwealth Relations, 1947-50; Minister of Fuel and Power, 1950-51. Chairman, Foreign Affairs Group, Parly Labour Party, 1964-70. Late Fellow, King's Coll., Cambridge; Hon. Fellow, since 1961; Sir Ernest Cassel Prof. of International Relations in the Univ. of London, 1924-29; Member of British Delegation to the 10th Assembly of the League of Nations, 1929 and 1930; Principal Asst to the Pres. of the Disarmament Conference at Geneva, 1932-33; British Delegate to UN Preparatory Commn, 1945; Mem., British Delegn to Gen. Assembly of UN, 1946-47; Delegate to Colombo Conf. on Economic Aid, 1950. Dodge lecturer, Yale Univ., 1934; President, International Council on Sport and Physical Recreation, UNESCO, 1960-; Howland Prize for distinguished work in the sphere of Government, Yale Univ., 1934; Nobel Peace Prize, 1959; Albert Schweitzer Book Prize, 1960; Olympia Diploma of Merit, 1975. Officer, Legion of Honour, 1976; Papal Knight, Order of St Sylvester, 1977. *Hon* . *Degrees:* Birmingham Univ.; Nottingham Univ.; Manchester Univ.; Univ. of Colombo; Queen's Univ., Ontario; Haverford Coll., USA; Brandeis Univ., USA. *Publications:* The Geneva Protocol, 1925; Disarmament, 1926; The League of Nations at Work, 1926; Disarmament and the Coolidge Conference, 1927; J. Allen Baker, MP, a Memoir (with E. B. Baker); The Juridical Status of the British Dominions in International Law, 1929; The Private Manufacture of Armaments, Vol. I, 1936; The Arms Race: A Programme for World Disarmament, 1958; pamphlets and articles. *Address:* 16 South Eaton Place, SW1. *T:* 01-730 5377.

See also Hon . Francis Noel -Baker .

NOEL-BAKER, Hon. Francis Edward; Director, Fini Fisheries, Cyprus, since 1976; *b* 7 Jan. 1920; *s* of Baron Noel-Baker, *qv; m* 1957, Barbara Christina, *yr d* of late Joseph Sonander, Sweden; four *s* one *d. Educ:* Westminster Sch.; King's Coll., Cambridge (Exhibitioner). Left Cambridge to join Army, summer 1940, as Trooper, Royal Tank Regt; Commissioned in Intelligence Corps and served in UK, Middle East (despatches); returned to fight Brentford and Chiswick Div.; MP (Lab) Brentford and Chiswick Div. of Mddx, 1945-50; PPS Admiralty, 1949-50; MP (Lab) Swindon, 1955-69; Sec., 1955-64, Chm., 1964-68, UN Parly Cttee. Chm., Advertising Inquiry Council, 1951-68. Chm., North Euboean Foundation Ltd; Hon. Pres., Union of Forest Owners of Greece, 1968-. Mem., Freedom from Hunger Campaign UK Cttee Exec. Cttee, 1961. Governor, Campion Sch., Athens, 1973-. *Publications:* Greece, the Whole Story, 1946; Spanish Summary, 1948; The Spy Web, 1954; Land and People of Greece, 1957; Nansen, 1958; Looking at Greece, 1967. *Address:* Sisini 13, Athens 612, Greece. *Telex:* 214707; Achmetaga Estate, Prokopion, Euboea, Greece. *TA:* Noelbaker, Mantoudion, Greece. *T:* 0227 41204. *Clubs:* Travellers'; Athens.

NOEL-BUXTON, 2nd Baron, *cr* 1930, of Aylsham; **Rufus Alexander Buxton;** writer and painter; *b* 13 Jan. 1917; *s* of 1st Baron Noel-Buxton and Lucy Edith (MP (Lab) North Norfolk, 1930-31, Norwich, 1945-50; *d* 1950), *e d* of late Major Henry Pelham Burn; *S* father, 1948; *m* 1st, 1939, Nancy (marr. diss. 1947; she *d* 1949), *yr d* of late Col K. H. M. Connal, CB, OBE; two *s*; 2nd, 1948, Margaret Elizabeth, *er d* of Stephanus Abraham Cloete, Pretoria, SA; one *s* one *d.* Assumed names of Rufus Alexander Buxton in lieu of those of Noel Alexander Noel-Buxton, 1944. *Educ:* Harrow; Balliol Coll., Oxford (BA). Invalided from 163 OCTU (the Artists Rifles), 1940; Research Asst, Agricultural Economics Research Inst., Oxford, 1941-43; Lecturer to Forces, 1943-45; Producer, BBC North American Service, 1946-48; editorial staff of The Farmer's Weekly, 1950-52. *Publications:* The Ford, 1955; Westminster Wader, 1957. *Heir: s* Hon. Martin Connal Noel-Buxton (assumed by deed poll, 1964, original surname of Noel-Buxton) [*b* 8 Dec. 1940; *m* 1964, Miranda Mary (marr. diss. 1968), *er d* of H. A. Chisenhale-Marsh, Gaynes Park, Epping, and Lady Buxton, Woodredon, Waltham Abbey; *m* 1972, Sarah Margaret Surridge, *d* of N. C. W. Barrett; one *s* one *d*]. *Address:* House of Lords, SW1.

NOEL-PATON, family name of **Baron Ferrier.**

NOGUEIRA, Albano Pires Fernandes; Secretary General, Ministry for Foreign Affairs, Lisbon, since 1976; *b* 8 Nov. 1911; *m* 1937, Alda Maria Marques Xavier da Cunha. *Educ:* Univ. of Coimbra. 3rd Sec., Washington, 1944; 2nd Sec., Pretoria, 1945; 1st Sec., Pretoria, 1948; Head of Mission, Tokyo, 1950; Counsellor, London, 1953; Consul-Gen., Bombay, 1955; Consul-Gen., NY, 1955; Asst Perm. Rep. UN, NY, 1955; Asst Dir-Gen., Econ. Affairs, Lisbon, 1959; Dir Gen., Econ. Affairs, Lisbon, 1961; Ambassador to: European Communities, Brussels, 1964; NATO, 1970; Court of St James's, 1974-76. Grand Cross, Order of Infante Don Henrique (Portugal), 1963; Merito Civil (Spain), 1961; Isabel la Católica (Spain), 1977; Grand Officer, Order of: Cruzeiro do Sul (Brazil), 1959; White Elephant (Thailand), 1960. *Publications:* Imagens em espelho Côncavo (essays); Portugal na Arte Japonesa (essay); Uma Agulha no Céu (novel); contrib. leading Portuguese papers and reviews. *Recreations:* reading, writing. *Address:* 18 Avenue Gaspar C. Real, 4-Ap-Dlt 2T, Cascais, Portugal. *Clubs:* Grémio Literário, Automóvel de Portugal (Lisbon).

NOLAN, Brig. Eileen Joan, CB 1976; Director, Women's Royal Army Corps, 1973-77; Hon. ADC to the Queen, 1973-77; *b* 19 June 1920; *d* of late James John and Ethel Mary Nolan. *Educ:* King's Norton Grammar Sch. for Girls. Joined ATS, Nov. 1942; commissioned, 1945. Lt-Col, 1967; Col, 1970; Brig., 1973. *Address:* 25 Devonport, Southwick Street, W2. *T:* 01-402 7995.

NOLAN, Michael Patrick, QC 1968; QC (NI) 1974; a Recorder of the Crown Court, since 1975; *b* 10 Sept. 1928; *yr s* of James Thomas Nolan and Jane (*née* Walsh); *m* 1953, Margaret, *yr d* of Alfred Noyes, CBE, and Mary (*née* Mayne); one *s* four *d. Educ:* Ampleforth; Wadham Coll., Oxford. Served RA, 1947-49; TA, 1949-55. Called to Bar, Middle Temple, 1953; Bencher, 1975. Member: Bar Council, 1973-74; Senate of Inns of Court and Bar, 1974- (Treasurer, 1977-); called to Bar, NI, 1974; Sandilands Cttee on Inflation Accounting, 1973-75. Mem. Governing Body, Convent of the Sacred Heart, Woldingham, 1973-; Governor, Combe Bank Sch., 1974-. *Recreations:* fishing, shooting. *Address:* Tanners, Brasted, Westerham, Kent. *T:* Westerham 63758. *Club:* Reform.

NOLAN, Sidney Robert, CBE 1963; artist; *b* Melbourne, 22 April 1917; *s* of late Sidney Henry Nolan; *m* 1939, Elizabeth Patterson (marr. diss. 1942); *m* 1948, Cynthia Hansen (*d* 1974). *Educ:* State and technical schools, Melbourne; National Art Gallery Sch., Victoria. Italian Government Scholar, 1956; Commonwealth Fund Fellow, to USA, 1958; Fellow: ANU, 1965 (Hon. LLD, 1968); York Univ., 1971; Bavarian Academy, 1971. Hon. DLit London, 1971. Exhibited: Paris, 1948, 1961; New Delhi, 1953; Pittsburgh International, 1953, 1954, 1955, 1964, 1967, 1970; Venice Biennale, 1954; Rome, 1954; Pacific Loan Exhibition, 1956; Brussels International Exhibition, 1958; Documenta II, Kassel, 1959; Retrospective, Art Gallery of New South Wales, Sydney, 1967; Retrospective, Darmstadt, 1971; Ashmolean Museum, Oxford, 1971; Retrospective, Royal Dublin Soc., 1973. Exhibits Tate Gallery, Marlborough New London Gallery, Marlborough Gallery, New York. Ballet Designs for Icare, Sydney, 1941; Orphée (Cocteau), Sydney, 1948; The Guide, Oxford, 1961; Rite of Spring, Covent Garden, 1962; The Display, Adelaide Festival, 1964. Works in Tate Gallery, Museum of Modern Art, New York, Australian national galleries, Contemporary Art Society and Arts Council of Great Britain, etc. *Publication:* Paradise Garden (poems, drawings and paintings), 1972; *Illustrated:* Near the Ocean, by Robert Lowell, 1966; The Voyage, by Bendelaire, trans. Lowell, 1968; Children's Crusade, by Benjamin Britten, 1973; *Relevant publications:* Kenneth Clark, Colin MacInnes, Bryan Robertson: Nolan, 1961; Robert Melville: Ned Kelly, 1964; Elwyn Lynn: Sydney Nolan: Myth and Imagery, 1967; Melville and Lynn: The Darkening Ecliptic: Ern Malley Poems, Sidney Nolan Paintings, 1974; Cynthia Nolan: Open Negative 1967; Sight of China, 1969; Paradise, and yet, 1971. *Address:* c/o Bank of New South Wales, 9 Sackville Street, W1.

NONWEILER, Prof. Terence Reginald Forbes, BSc; PhD; CEng; FRAeS; FIMA; Professor of Mathematics, Victoria University of Wellington, since 1975; *b* 8 Feb. 1925; *s* of Ernest James Nonweiler and Lilian Violet Amalie Nonweiler (*née* Holfert); *m* 1949, Patricia Hilda Frances (*née* Neame); four *s* one *d. Educ:* Bethany Sch., Goudhurst, Kent; University of Manchester, BSc 1944, PhD 1960. Scientific Officer, Royal Aircraft Establishment, Farnborough, Hants, 1944-50; Scientific Officer, Scientific Advisor's Dept, Air Ministry, 1950-51; Senior Lecturer in Aerodynamics, College of Aeronautics, Cranfield, Beds, 1951-57; Senior Lecturer in Aeronautical Engineering, The Queen's Univ. of Belfast, 1957-61; Mechan Prof. of Aeronautics and Fluid Mechanics, Glasgow Univ., 1961-75. Consultant: to Admiralty, 1951; to Ministry of Aviation, 1959; to Ministry of Agriculture, 1966; to Wellington City Corp., 1977. Member, International Academy of Astronautics. *Publications:* Jets and Rockets, 1959. Numerous technical papers on aeronautics, space flight, and submarine motion. *Recreations:* acting and stage production. *Address:* 7 Donald Street, Karori, Wellington 5, New Zealand.

NORBURY, 6th Earl of, *cr* 1827; **Noel Terence Graham-Toler;** Baron Norwood, 1797; Baron Glandine, 1800; Viscount Glandine, 1827; *b* 1 Jan. 1939; *s* of 5th Earl and Margaret Greenhalgh; *S* father 1955; *m* 1965, Anne Mathew; one *s* one *d. Heir: s* Viscount Glandine, *qv. Address:* Stock Exchange, EC2.

NORCROSS, Lawrence John Charles; Headmaster, Highbury Grove School, since 1975; *b* 14 April 1927; *s* of Frederick Marshall Norcross and Florence Kate (*née* Hedges); *m* 1958, Margaret Wallace; three *s* one *d. Educ:* Ruskin Coll., Oxford; Univ. of Leeds (BA Hons English). Training Ship, Arethusa, 1941-42; RN, 1942-49 (E Indies Fleet, 1944-45); clerical asst, 1949-52; Asst Teacher: Singlegate Sch., 1957-61; Abbey Wood Sch., 1961-63; Housemaster, Battersea County Sch., 1963-74; Dep. Headmaster, Highbury Grove Sch., 1974-75. Member: Headmasters' Assoc.; NAS/UWT. Founder and Hon. Sec., John Ireland Soc.; former Chm., Contemp. Concerts Co-ordination. Occasional broadcasts and television appearances. *Publications:* occasional articles. *Recreations:* talking to friends, playing bridge badly, watching cricket, listening to music. *Address:* 17 Devereux Road, SW11 6JR. *T:* 01-228 8478.

NORDEN, Denis; scriptwriter and broadcaster; *b* 6 Feb. 1922; *s* of George Norden and Jenny Lubell; *m* 1943, Avril Rosen; one *s* one *d. Educ:* Craven Park Sch., London; City of London Sch. Theatre Manager, 1939-42; served RAF, 1942-45; staff-writer in Variety Agency, 1945-47. With Frank Muir, 1947-64: collaborated for 17 years writing comedy scripts, including: (for radio): Take it from Here, 1947-58; Bedtime with Braden, 1950-54; (for TV): And so to Bentley, 1956; Whack-O!, 1958-60; The Seven Faces of Jim, 1961, and other series with Jimmy Edwards; resident in TV and radio panel-games; collaborated in film scripts, television commercials, and revues; joint Advisors and Consultants to BBC Television Light Entertainment Dept, 1960-

64; jointly received Screenwriters Guild Award for Best Contribution to Light Entertainment, 1961; together on panel-games My Word!, 1956-, and My Music, 1967-. Since 1964, solo writer for television and films; Chm., Looks Familiar (Thames TV), 1973-. Film Credits include: The Bliss of Mrs Blossom; Buona Sera, Mrs Campbell; The Best House in London; Every Home Should Have One; Twelve Plus one; The Statue. *Publications:* (with Frank Muir) You Can't Have Your Kayak and Heat It, 1973; Upon My Word, 1974. *Recreations:* reading, loitering. *Address:* 16 Neal's Yard, Monmouth Street, WC2. *Club:* Queen's.

NORDMEYER, Hon. Sir Arnold (Henry), KCMG 1975 (CMG 1970); JP; Leader of the Opposition (Labour), New Zealand, 1963-65; *b* Dunedin, New Zealand, 7 Feb. 1901; *s* of Arnold and Martha Nordmeyer; *m* 1931, Frances Maria Kernahan; one *s* one *d. Educ:* Waitaki Boys' High Sch.; Otago Univ. (BA, DipSocSci.). Presbyterian Minister for 10 years. Entered New Zealand Parliament, 1935; MP for Oamaru, 1935-49, for Brooklyn, 1951-54, for Island Bay, 1954-69; Minister of: Health, 1941-47; Industries and Commerce, 1947-49; Finance, 1957-60. JP 1970. Hon. LLD Otago, 1970. *Recreations:* shooting, fishing. *Address:* 53 Milne Terrace, Wellington, New Zealand.

NORFOLK, 17th Duke of, *cr* 1483; **Miles Francis Stapleton Fitzalan-Howard,** CB 1966; CBE 1960; MC 1944; DL; Earl of Arundel, 1139; Baron Beaumont, 1309; Baron Maltravers, 1330, Earl of Surrey, 1483; Baron FitzAlan, Clun, and Oswaldestre, 1627; Earl of Norfolk, 1644; Baron Howard of Glossop, 1869; Earl Marshal and Hereditary Marshal and Chief Butler of England; Premier Duke and Earl; a Director of Robert Fleming Holdings Ltd, since 1969; *b* 21 July 1915; *s* of 3rd Baron Howard of Glossop, MBE, and Baroness Beaumont (11th in line), OBE, *S* to barony of mother, 1971, and of father, 1972, and to dukedom of cousin, 1975; *m* 1949, Anne Mary Teresa, *e d* of late Wing Commander Gerald Joseph Constable Maxwell, MC, DFC, AFC; two *s* three *d. Educ:* Ampleforth Coll.; Christ Church, Oxford (MA). 2nd Lieut, Grenadier Guards, 1937. Served War of 1939-45, France, North Africa, Sicily, Italy (despatches, MC), NW Europe. Appointed Head of British Military Mission to Russian Forces in Germany, 1957; Commanded 70 Bde KAR, 1961-63; GOC, 1 Div., 1963-65 (Maj.-Gen.); Dir, Management and Support Intelligence, MoD, 1965-66; Director, Service Intelligence, MoD, 1966-67; retd 1967. Chm., Arundel Castle Trustees, Ltd. DL West Sussex, 1977. Knight of the Sovereign Order of Malta. *Heir: s* Earl of Arundel and Surrey, *qv. Address:* Arundel Castle, Sussex; *T:* Arundel 882173; Carlton Towers, Goole, North Humberside. *T:* Goole 860 243; Bacres House, Hambleden, Henley-on-Thames, Oxfordshire. *T:* Hambleden 350. *Clubs:* Turf, Pratt's.
See also Lord Michael Fitzalan -Howard .

NORFOLK, Lavinia Duchess of; Lavinia Mary Fitzalan-Howard, CBE 1971; Lord-Lieutenant of West Sussex, since 1975; *b* 22 March 1916; *d* of 3rd Baron Belper and of Eva, Countess of Rosebery, DBE; *m* 1937, 16th Duke of Norfolk, KG, PC, GCVO, GBE, TD (*d* 1975); four *d. Educ:* Abbothsill, Hemel Hempstead, Herts. President: Sussex Branch, BRCS, 1957-75; Riding for the Disabled Assoc., 1970-; Nat. Canine Defence League, 1969-; Pony Riding for the Disabled Trust, Chigwell, 1964-. Vice-President: ASBAH, 1970-; Spastic Soc., 1969-; NSPCC, 1967-. Chairman, King Edward VII Hosp., Midhurst, 1975-. Steward, Goodwood, 1976-. BRCS Certificate of Honour and Badge, Class 1, 1969. Silver Jubilee Medal, 1977. *Address:* Arundel Park, Sussex. *T:* Arundel 882041.
See also Earl of Ancram , Lady Herries .

NORFOLK, Archdeacon of; *see* Dawson, Ven. Peter.

NORFOLK, Leslie William, CBE 1973 (OBE 1944); TD 1946; CEng; engineering consultant; *b* 8 April 1911; *e s* of late Robert and Edith Norfolk, Nottingham; *m* 1944, A. I. E. W. (Nancy) Watson (then WRNS), *d* of late Sir Hugh Watson, IFS (retd); two *s* one *d. Educ:* Southwell Minster Grammar Sch., Notts; University Coll., Nottingham. Assistant and later Partner, E. G. Phillips, Son & Norfolk, consulting engineers, Nottingham, 1932-36. Served with RE, France, Gibraltar, Home Forces, 1939-45, Lt.-Col. Engineer, Dyestuffs Div., ICI Ltd, 1945-53; Resident Engineer, ICI of Canada, Kingston, Ont., 1953-55; Asst Chief Engr, Metals Div., ICI Ltd, 1955-57; Engineering Manager, Severnside Works, ICI Ltd, 1957-59; Engineering Director, Industrias Quimicas Argentinas Duperial SAIC, Buenos Aires, 1959-65; Director, Heavy Organic Chemicals Div., ICI Ltd, 1965-68; retired from ICI, 1968; Chief Exec., Royal Dockyards, MoD, 1969-72. *Recreations:* golf, sailing, caravanning. *Address:* Beechwoods, Beechwood Road, Combe Down, Bath, Avon. *T:* Combe Down 832104. *Club:* Bath & County (Bath).

NÖRLUND, Niels Erik, PhD (Copenhagen), Hon. DSc (London), Hon. DEng (Darmstadt); Hon. PhD (Lund); Hon. DSc (Dijon); Hon. PhD (Oslo); Hon. DASc (Copenhagen); Formerly Professor of Mathematics in University of Copenhagen; Director Danish Geodetic Institute; Editor Acta Mathematica; *b* Slagelse, Denmark, 26 Oct. 1885; *m* 1912, Agnete Weaver (*d* 1959); two *d. Educ:* University of Copenhagen, Paris and Cambridge. Formerly Pres., International Council of Scientific Unions; Formerly Pres. Rask-Orsted Foundation; lately Pres., Royal Danish Academy of Science; formerly Pres. Baltic Geodetic Commission; formerly Rector of Univ. of Copenhagen; Foreign Mem. Royal Soc., Royal Astronomical Soc., Acad. Science Paris, Rome, Stockholm, Oslo, Helsingfors, Uppsala and Naples; Hon. Member Royal Institution, London. *Publications:* Vorlesungen über Differenzenrechnung (Berlin), 1924; Leçons sur les séries d'interpolation (Paris), 1926; Sur la somme d'une fonction (Paris), 1927; Leçons sur les équations aux différences finies (Paris), 1929; The map of Iceland (Copenhagen), 1944. *Address:* Copenhagen, Malmögade 6, Denmark. *TA:* Copenhagen. *T:* Obro 3046.

NORMAN, Baroness (Priscilla), CBE 1963; JP; *b* 1899; *o d* of late Major Robert Reyntiens and late Lady Alice Bertie; *m* 1st, 1921, Alexander Koch de Gooreynd (marr. diss. 1929); two *s*; 2nd, 1933, 1st Baron Norman, PC, DSO (*d* 1950). Member: London County Council, 1925-33; Chelsea Borough Council, 1928-31; Bethlem Royal and the Maudsley Hospital Board, 1951-75; South-East Metropolitan Regional Board, 1951-74; Hon. Pres., World Fedn for Mental Health, 1972. Vice-Chm., Women's Voluntary Services for Civil Defence, 1938-41; Vice-Pres., Royal College of Nursing. JP 1944. *Address:* Aubrey Lodge, Aubrey Road, W8 7JJ.
See also S. P. E. C. W. Towneley, P. G. Worsthorne.

NORMAN, (Alexander) Vesey (Bethune); Master of the Armouries, HM Tower of London, since 1977; *b* 10 Feb. 1930; *s* of Lt-Col A. M. B. Norman and Sheila M. Maxwell; *m* 1954, Catherine Margaret Barne; one *s. Educ:* Alford Sch.; Trinity Coll., Glenalmond; London Univ. (BA Gen.). Asst Curator, Scottish United Services Museum, Edinburgh Castle, 1957; Hon. Curator of Arms and Armour, Abbotsford, 1957; Asst to Dir, Wallace Collection, 1963, Inspector of Armouries, 1977. *Publications:* Arms & Armour, 1964 (also foreign edns); (with Don Pottinger) Warrior to Soldier, 449-1660, 1966 (USA edn as A History of War and Weapons, 449-1660); Small Swords and Military Swords, 1967; The Medieval Soldier, 1971 (also USA); Arms and Armour in the Royal Scottish Museum, 1972; A Catalogue of Ceramics, Wallace Collection, Pt I, 1976; articles in learned jls. *Recreation:* study of arms and armour. *Address:* 19 Highgate High Street, N6.

NORMAN, Archibald Percy, MBE 1945; FRCP; MD; Physician, Hospital for Sick Children, since 1950; Paediatrician, Queen Charlotte's Maternity Hospital, since 1951; *b* 19 July 1912; *s* of Dr George Percy Norman and Mary Margaret MacCallum; *m* 1950, Aleida Elisabeth M. M. R. Bisschop; five *s. Educ:* Charterhouse; Emmanuel Coll., Cambridge. Served War of 1939-45, in Army, 1940-45. *Publications:* (joint) Fibrocystic Disease of the Pancreas, 1952; (ed) Congenital Abnormalities, 1962, 2nd edn 1971; (ed) Moncreiff's Nursing and Diseases of Sick Children, 1966; contributions to medical journals. *Recreations:* fishing and family. *Address:* White Lodge. Heather Close, Kingswood, Surrey. *T:* Mogador 2626.

NORMAN, Sir Arthur (Gordon), KBE 1969 (CBE 1966); DFC 1943; and Bar 1944; Chairman, The De La Rue Company, since 1964 (Chief Executive, 1972-77); *b* N Petherton, Som, 18 Feb. 1917; *m* 1944, Margaret Doreen Harrington; three *s* two *d. Educ:* Blundell's Sch. Joined Thomas De La Rue & Co., 1934. RAF 1939-45 (DFC and Bar); Wing-Comdr, 1943. Rejoined Thomas De La Rue & Co., 1946; Director, 1951; Managing Director, 1953. Director: Sun Life Assurance Society; SKF (UK) Ltd, 1970-; Bank of New Zealand (London Board), 1977. Pres., CBI, 1968-70. Trustee, Royal Air Force Museum; Chm., World Wildlife Fund (British Nat. Appeal), 1977-. *Recreations:* tennis, golf, country life. *Address:* De La Rue House, 84/86 Regent Street, W1A 1DL. *T:* 01-734 8020.

NORMAN, Sir Edward (James), Kt 1958; Chief Inspector of Taxes, 1956-64, retired; *b* Bridport, Dorset, 8 Jan. 1900; *s* of Edward Robert Norman; *m* 1923, Lilian May Sly (*d* 1974); three *d. Educ:* Weymouth Grammar Sch. Entered Inland Revenue Department, 1917; Assistant Inspector of Taxes, 1920; Principal Inspector, Somerset House, 1947; Assistant Secretary, Board of Inland Revenue, 1948; Dep. Chief Inspector of Taxes, 1950-55. Member, and later Dep. Chm., Housing Corporation, 1964-69. Financial Advr, 1964-72, Indep. Chm., Building & Civil

Engineering Holidays Scheme Management Ltd., 1972-, Benefits Scheme Trustee Ltd, 1975-. *Address:* Bourn Cottage, Westhumble, Dorking, Surrey.

NORMAN, Rt. Rev. Edward Kinsella; see Wellington, Bishop of.

NORMAN, Rev. Dr Edward Robert; Dean of Peterhouse, Cambridge, since 1971; Lecturer in History, University of Cambridge, since 1965; *b* 22 Nov. 1938; *o s* of Ernest Edward Norman and Yvonne Louise Norman. *Educ:* Chatham House Sch.; Monoux Sch.; Selwyn Coll., Cambridge (MA, PhD, BD). FRHIstS. Deacon, 1965; Priest, 1971. Asst Master, Beaconsfield Sec. Mod. Sch., Walthamstow, 1957-58; Fellow of Selwyn Coll., Cambridge, 1962-64; Fellow of Jesus Coll., Cambridge, 1964-71. NATO Res. Fellow, 1966-68. Asst Chaplain, Addenbrooke's Hosp., Cambridge, 1971-. Reith Lectr, 1978. *Publications:* The Catholic Church and Ireland, 1965; The Conscience of the State in North America, 1968; Anti-Catholicism in Victorian England, 1968; The Early Development of Irish Society, 1969; A History of Modern Ireland, 1971; Church and Society in Modern England, 1976. *Recreation:* watching television. *Address:* Peterhouse, Cambridge. *T:* Cambridge 50256. *Club:* Athenæum.

NORMAN, Vice-Admiral Sir (Horace) Geoffrey, KCVO 1963; CB 1949; CBE 1943; retired, 1950; *b* 25 May 1896; *m* 1924, Noreen Frances, *o d* of late Brig.-General S. Geoghegan; one s one d. *Educ:* Trent Coll.; RN Coll., Keyham. HMS Queen Elizabeth and destroyers, 1914-18; Long Gunnery Course, 1921; passed RN Staff Coll., 1929; Commander, 1932; Captain, 1938; idc 1939; Rear-Admiral, 1947; Chief of Staff to C-in-C, Mediterranean Station, 1948-50; Admiralty, 1950; Vice-Admiral (retired), 1950. *Recreations:* fishing and outdoor sports. *Address:* Chantry Cottage, Wickham, Hants. *T:* Wickham 832248.

NORMAN, Brig. Hugh Ronald, CBE 1970; DSO 1944; *b* 17 Oct. 1905; *e s* of late R. C. Norman; *m* 1937, Margaret, *d* of late Scott Griffin, Toronto; three s one d. *Educ:* Eton; RMC, Sandhurst. Joined Coldstream Guards, 1925; served in China, 1927, Palestine, 1936; Adjutant, 3rd Bn, 1934-37; War of 1939-45, on staff of AA Command, 1939; 128 Inf. Bde, 1940; GHQ Home Forces, 1941; HQ London District, 1942; Comd 2nd Bn Coldstream Guards, Africa, 1943, and Italy, 1944 (wounded); Comd 201 Guards Bde (UK), 1945-46, and Victory Parade Camps; retired (from disability), 1947. Kent County Cadet Comdt, 1948-52; Chairman: Territorial Assoc., 1962-68; South East TA&VR Assoc., 1968-69. Member Kent Agricultural Exec. Cttee, 1952-58 (Vice-Chm., 1957); Chm., Kent Branch Country Landowners Assoc. (CLA), 1958-62, Pres., 1967-72. JP 1949; DL 1952; High Sheriff of Kent, 1957. *Address:* Lower St Clere, Kemsing, Sevenoaks, Kent. *T:* Sevenoaks 61250. *Clubs:* Cavalry and Guards, White's.

NORMAN, Sir Mark (Annesley), 3rd Bt, *cr* 1915; Director, IU Europe Ltd, and other companies; *b* 8 Feb. 1927; *s* of Sir Nigel Norman, 2nd Bt, CBE, and Patricia Moyra (who *m* 2nd, 1944, Sir Robert Perkins, *qv*), *e d* of late Lieut-Colonel J. H. A. Annesley, CMG, DSO; *S* father, 1943; *m* Joanna Camilla, *d* of late Lt-Col I. J. Kilgour, Bampton, Oxon; two s one d. *Educ:* Winchester Coll. Late Lieut, Coldstream Guards. Flying Officer, 601 (County of London) Squadron Royal Auxiliary Air Force, 1953-56. *Recreations:* gardening, skiing. *Heir:* s Nigel James Norman, *b* 5 Feb. 1956. *Address:* Wilcote Manor, Charlbury, Oxfordshire. *T:* Ramsden 357. *Clubs:* White's, MCC; St Moritz Tobogganing.
See also N. D. Norman, W. R. Norman.

NORMAN, Mark Richard, CBE 1977 (OBE 1945); Managing Director of Lazard Brothers & Co. Ltd, 1960-75; Chairman, Gallaher Ltd, 1963-75; Director of other public companies, 1947-75; Deputy Chairman, National Trust, since 1977 (Chairman, Finance Committee, since 1969); *b* 3 April 1910; *s* of late Ronald C. Norman; *m* 1933, Helen, *d* of late Thomas Pinckney Bryan, Richmond, Virginia; two s three d. *Educ:* Eton; Magdalen Coll., Oxford. With Gallaher Ltd, 1930-32; Lazard Brothers & Co. Ltd, 1932-39. Served War of 1939-45: Hertfordshire Yeomanry; wounded Greece, 1941; an Asst Military Secretary, War Cabinet Offices, 1942-45 (Lieut-Colonel). Partner Edward de Stein & Co., 1946-60. *Address:* Garden House, Moor Place, Much Hadham, Herts. *T:* Much Hadham 2703. *Club:* Brooks's.

NORMAN, Nigel Desmond, CBE 1970; Director, NDN Aircraft Ltd, Chichester, since 1977; *b* 13 Aug. 1929; 2nd *s* of Sir Nigel Norman, 2nd Bt (*d* 1943), CBE, and Patricia Moyra (who *m* 2nd, 1944, Sir Robert Perkins, *qv*); *m* 1st, Anne Fogg-Elliott; two s ; 2nd, 1965, Mrs. Boel Elizabeth Holmsen; two s two d.

Educ: Eton; De Havilland Aeronautical Technical Sch. (1946-49). RAF GD Pilot, thereafter 601 Sqdn, RAuxAF Fighter Sqdn, until disbandment, 1948-57. Export Asst at SBAC, 1951-53; Founder of Britten-Norman Ltd with F. R. J. Britten, 1954, Jt Man. Dir, 1954-71; Dir, Britten-Norman (Bembridge) Ltd, 1971-77; Dir, Fairey SA (Belgium), 1972-76; Marketing Dir, Fairey Britten-Norman, 1973-76. *Recreations:* aviation, sailing, shooting. *Address:* NDN Aircraft Ltd, Goodwood Aerodrome, Chichester, Sussex. *T:* Chichester 84337; Kingates Farm, Whitwell, near Niton, IoW. *T:* Niton 730287. *Clubs:* Bath, Royal Air Force, Royal Yacht Squadron.
See also Sir Mark Norman, Bt, W. R. Norman.

NORMAN, Prof. Richard Oswald Chandler, DSc; FRS 1977; CChem, FRIC; Professor of Chemistry, University of York, since 1965; *b* 27 April 1932; *s* of Oswald George Norman and Violet Maud Chandler. *Educ:* St Paul's Sch.; Balliol Coll., Oxford (MA, DSc). CChem; FRIC 1963. Jun. Res. Fellow, Merton Coll., Oxford, 1956-58, Fellow and Tutor, 1958-65; Univ. Lectr in Chemistry, Oxford, 1958-65. *Publications:* Principles of Organic Synthesis, 1968; papers in Jl Chem. Soc. *Recreations:* cricket, music, gardening. *Address:* 129 The Mount, York YO2 2DA. *T:* York 53900. *Club:* Athenæum.

NORMAN, Sir Robert (Wentworth), Kt 1970; JP; Director, Bank of New South Wales, since 1970 (Chief General Manager, 1964-77); *b* 10 April 1912; *s* of William Henry Norman and Minnie Esther Brown; *m* 1942, Grace Hebden, *d* of Sidney Percy Hebden; one s one d. *Educ:* Sydney Grammar Sch. Served Army 1940-46: Captain, AIF. Joined Bank of New South Wales, 1928; Manager, Head Office, 1961; Dep. Gen. Manager, 1962. Director: Australian Guarantee Corp. Ltd; Australian Gas Light Co. Ltd; Reckitt & Colman Australia Ltd; Ciba-Geigy Australia Ltd; Chrysler Australia Ltd; Partnership Pacific Ltd; Borthwick Australia Ltd. Vice-Pres., Australian-American Assoc.; Australian-Japan Business Co-operation Cttee; Councillor: Science Foundn for Physics within Univ. of Sydney; Inst. of Public Affairs; Senator and Life Mem., Junior Chamber Internat.; Chm., Sydney Opera House. FAIM (Vice-Pres.). JP NSW, 1956. *Recreations:* bowls, reading. *Address:* 432 Edgecliff Road, Edgecliff, NSW 2027, Australia. *T:* 32 1900. *Clubs:* Imperial Service, Union, Australian, Tattersalls, Royal Sydney Golf, Australian Jockey (Sydney).

NORMAN, Vesey; see Norman, A. V. B.

NORMAN, Willoughby Rollo; Hon. President, The Boots Co. Ltd, since 1972 (Chairman, 1961-72); Deputy Chairman, English China Clays Ltd; 2nd *s* of Major Rt Hon. Sir Henry Norman, 1st Bt; *m* 1st, 1934, Hon. Barbara Jacqueline Boot, *er d* of 2nd and last Baron Trent, KBE; one s two d ; 2nd, 1973, Caroline Haskerd, *d* of William Greville and Lady Diana Worthington. *Educ:* Eton; Magdalen Coll., Oxford. Served War of 1939-45, Major, Grenadier Guards. Director: National Westminster Bank (Chm. Eastern Region); Guardian Royal Exchange Assurance; Sheepbridge Engineering Ltd. Underwriting member of Lloyd's. Vice-Chairman Boots Pure Drug Co. Ltd, 1954-61. High Sheriff of Leicestershire, 1960. *Recreations:* shooting, farming, gardening. *Address:* Hurst Mill, Petersfield, Hants; 28 Ranelagh House, Elystan Place, SW3. *T:* 01-584 9410. *Clubs:* White's, Pratt's.
See also Sir Mark Norman, Bt, N. D. Norman.

NORMAN-WALKER, Sir Hugh (Selby), KCMG 1966 (CMG 1964); OBE 1961; *b* 17 Dec. 1916; *s* of late Colonel J. N. Norman-Walker, CIE; *m* 1948, Janet Baldock; no c. *Educ:* Sherborne; Corpus Christi Coll., Cambridge. MA. Indian Civil Service, 1938-48; Colonial Administrative Service, 1949; Development Secretary, Nyasaland, 1954; Secretary to the Treasury, Nyasaland, 1960-64; Malawi, 1964-65; HM Commissioner, Bechuanaland, 1965-66; Governor and C-in-C, Seychelles, and Comr, British Indian Ocean Territory, 1967-69; Colonial Sec., Hong Kong, 1969-74. KStJ 1967. *Recreations:* sailing, shooting, bridge. *Address:* Houndwood, Farley, Wilts. *Clubs:* East India, Devonshire, Sports and Public Schools; Island Sailing (Cowes), etc.

NORMANBY, 4th Marquis of, *cr* 1838; **Oswald Constantine John Phipps,** CBE 1974 (MBE (mil.) 1943); Baron Mulgrave (Ireland), 1767; Baron Mulgrave (Great Britain), 1794; Earl of Mulgrave and Viscount Normanby, 1812; Lord-Lieutenant of North Yorkshire, since 1974 (of North Riding of Yorkshire, 1965-74); *b* 29 July 1912; *o s* of Rev. the 3rd Marquess and Gertrude Stansfeld, OBE, DGStJ (*d* 1948), *d* of Johnston J. Foster of Moor Park, Ludlow; *S* father, 1932; *m* 1951, Hon. Grania Maeve Rosaura Guinness, *d* of 1st Baron Moyne; two s five d. *Educ:* Eton; Christ Church, Oxford. Served War of 1939-45, The Green Howards (wounded, prisoner, repatriated). PPS to Sec. of State for Dominion Affairs, 1944-45, to Lord President of the Council, 1945; a Lord-in-Waiting to the King, 1945. Chairman: KCH, 1948-74; Council of St John for N Yorks (for NR Yorks, 1950-74); Pres., Nat. Library for the Blind, 1977-; Member: Cttee of Management, RNLI; Council of St Dunstans; Gen. Council, King Edward's Hosp. Fund; Council and Chapter-Gen., OStJ. Hon. Col Comdt, The Green Howards, 1970-; Dep. Hon. Col, 2nd Bn Yorks Volunteers, 1971-72; Pres., TA&VRA for N of England, 1971-74 (Vice-Pres., 1968-71). KStJ. Hon. DCL Durham Univ. *Heir:* s Earl of Mulgrave, *qv.* *Address:* Mulgrave Castle, Whitby; Argyll House, 211 King's Road, SW3. *T:* 01-352 5154. *Club:* Yorkshire (York).

NORMAND, Sir Charles William Blyth, Kt 1945; CIE 1938; MA, DSc; *b* 10 Sept. 1889; *m* 1920, Alison MacLennan (*d* 1953); one *s* (and one *s* decd). *Educ:* Royal High School and University, Edinburgh. Research Scholar at Edinburgh, 1911-13; Imperial Meteorologist, Simla, India, 1913-15 and 1919-27; joined IARO and served in Mesopotamia, 1916-19; Director-General of Observatories in India, 1927-44; on special duty with Govt of India, 1944-45; Symons Gold Medal, Royal Met. Soc., 1944; President, Royal Met. Society, 1951-53; Member, Met. Research Cttee, Air Ministry, 1945-58, Chairman, 1955-58; Secretary International Ozone Commn, 1948-59. *Publications:* articles, mainly on meteorological subjects, in scientific journals. *Address:* 23 St Thomas' Street, Winchester, Hants. *T:* Winchester 2550.

NORMANTON, 6th Earl of, *cr* 1806; **Shaun James Christian Welbore Ellis Agar;** Baron Mendip, 1794; Baron Somerton, 1795; Viscount Somerton, 1800; Baron Somerton (UK), 1873; Royal Horse Guards, 1965; Blues and Royals, 1965; left Army, 1972, Captain; *b* 21 Aug. 1945; *er s* of 5th Earl of Normanton; *S* father, 1967; *m* 1970, Victoria Susan, *o d* of J. H. C. Beard, Hookswood House, Farnham, Shaftesbury; one *d.* *Educ:* Eton. *Recreations:* shooting, power boat racing. *Heir:* brother Hon. Mark Sydney Andrew Agar, late Lieut, Blues and Royals [*b* 2 Sept. 1948; *m* 1973, Rosemary, *d* of Major Philip Marnham]. *Address:* Somerley, Ringwood, Hants. *T:* Ringwood 3253. *Clubs:* White's; Royal Yacht Squadron.

NORMANTON, Tom, TD; BA (Com); MP (C) Cheadle since 1970; Member, European Parliament, since 1973; chairman of a group of companies; *b* 12 March 1917; *m* 1942, Annabel Bettine (*née* Yates); two *s* one *d.* *Educ:* Manchester Grammar Sch.; Manchester Univ. (BA (Com); Chm., Cons. Assoc., 1937-38; Vice-Pres. Students' Union, 1938). Joined family group of textile cos, 1938. Served War of 1939-45: Army (commnd TA 1937) Europe and N Africa; GS appts, GHQ BEF, HQ First and Eighth Armies; HQ 21 Army Gp (wounded, Calais, 1940; despatches, 1944); demob., rank Major, 1946. Chm., Rochdale YC, 1948; Mem. Rochdale CB Council, 1950-53; contested (C) Rochdale, 1959 and 1964. Hon. Sec., Cons. Backbencher Industry Cttee, 1972-74; Mem., Expenditure Cttee, 1972-73; opposition front bench spokesman on energy, 1975-; European Parliament: Member: Commn on Energy and Research, 1973-; Commn on Economic and Monetary Affairs, 1973-; Commn EP/ACP States, 1975-; spokesman on Competition Policy, 1975; Deleg. to US Congress, 1975-. Manager, Lancashire Fusiliers Compassionate Fund, 1964-; Trustee, Cotton Industry War Memorial Fund, 1965; apptd Employer panel, NBPI, 1966-68; Member: Council, CBI, 1964-76 (Mem. Europe Cttee, 1964-); Stockport Chamber of Commerce, 1970-; Central Training Council, 1968; Exec., UK Automation Council, 1966- (Vice-Chm., 1970-73); Exec. Council, British Textile Confederation, 1972-76; Vice-Chm. Manchester Br. of Inst. of Dirs, 1969-71; Chm., European Textile Industries Cttee; President: British Textile Employers Assoc., 1970-71; Internat. Fedn of Cotton & Allied Textiles Industries, 1976- (Vice-Pres., 1972-76). Director: Industrial Training Services Ltd, 1972-; N Reg. Bd, Commercial Union Assurance Ltd, 1974-; Manchester Chamber of Commerce, 1970-. AMBIM. *Recreations:* sailing, walking, gardening. *Address:* Bollin Court, Macclesfield Road, Wilmslow, Cheshire. *T:* Wilmslow 24930; Rivermill, Grosvenor Road, SW1. *Clubs:* Beefsteak, House of Commons Yacht (Hon. Treasurer, 1972-74, Commodore, 1976-); St James's (Manchester).

NORREYS, Lord; Henry Mark Willoughby Bertie; *b* 6 June 1958; *s* and *heir* of Earl of Lindsey (14th) and Abingdon (9th), *qv.* *Educ:* Eton. *Address:* Hunsdonbury, Hunsdon, Ware, Herts.

NORRIE, family name of **Baron Norrie.**

NORRIE, 2nd Baron, *cr* 1957; **George Willoughby Moke Norrie;** Director, Fairfield Nurseries (Hermitage) Ltd; *b* 27 April 1936; *s* of 1st Baron Norrie, GCMG, GCVO, CB, DSO, MC, and

Jocelyn Helen (*d* 1938), *d* of late R. H. Gosling; *S* father, 1977; *m* 1964, Celia Marguerite, *d* of John Pelham Mann, MC; one *s* two *d.* *Educ:* Eton College; RMA Sandhurst. Commissioned 11th Hussars, 1956; ADC to C-in-C Middle East Comd, 1960-61; GSO 3 (Int.) 4th Guards Brigade, 1967-69; retired, 1970. Pres. Royal British Legion (Newbury Branch). *Recreations:* skiing, tennis. *Heir:* s Hon. Mark Willoughby John Norrie, *b* 31 March 1972. *Address:* Henwick Old Farm, Newbury, Berks RG16 9EP. *T:* Thatcham 62808. *Clubs:* Cavalry and Guards, MCC.

NORRINGTON, Sir Arthur (Lionel Pugh), Kt 1968; MA; JP; President of Trinity College, Oxford, 1954-70; Vice-Chancellor, Oxford University, 1960-62; Warden of Winchester College, 1970-74; *b* 27 Oct. 1899; *o s* of late Arthur James Norrington; *m* 1st, 1928, Edith Joyce (*d* 1964), *d* of William Moberly Carver; two *s* two *d*; 2nd, 1969, Mrs Ruth Margaret Waterlow, *widow* of Rupert Waterlow, and *y d* of Edmund Cude. *Educ:* Winchester; Trinity Coll., Oxford (Scholar). Served in RFA, 1918. Joined Oxford University Press, 1923. Secretary to Delegates of Oxford University Press, 1948-54. Chm., Adv. Cttee on the Selection of Low-priced Books for Overseas, 1960-. JP City of Oxford. Hon. Fellow, Trinity, St Cross and Wolfson Colleges. Officier de la Légion d'Honneur, 1962. *Publication:* (with H. F. Lowry and F. L. Mulhauser), The Poems of A. H. Clough, 1951. *Recreations:* music, gardening. *Address:* Grenville Manor, Haddenham, Bucks; 3 Beach Cottages, Fishguard. *Club:* United Oxford & Cambridge University. *See also R. A. C. Norrington.*

NORRINGTON, Roger Arthur Carver; Musical Director: Kent Opera, since 1966; London Baroque Players, since 1975; *b* 16 March 1934; *s* of Sir Arthur Norrington, *qv*; *m* 1964, Susan Elizabeth McLean May; one *s* one *d.* *Educ:* Dragon Sch., Oxford; Westminster; Clare Coll., Cambridge (BA); Royal Coll. of Music. Freelance singer, 1962-72. Dir, Heinrich Schütz Choir, 1962-73; Schütz Choir of London, 1973-; BBC radio debut, 1964, TV 1967. Conducted BBC Symphony, Royal Philharmonic, Sadler's Wells Opera, English Chamber, London Mozart Players, Gulbenkian, Lisbon, Lyrique de ORTF Paris, and Symphonia di Como orchestras, etc; appeared at Proms, City of London, Bath, Aldeburgh, English Bach and Harrogate festivals; broadcasts regularly at home and abroad. Debuts: Germany, Austria, Denmark, Finland, 1966; Portugal, 1970; Italy, 1971; France and Belgium, 1972; USA, 1974; Holland, 1975; Switzerland, 1976. Many gramophone recordings. *Publications:* articles in Musical Times, Music and Musicians. *Recreations:* reading, walking, sailing. *Address:* 52 King Henry's Road, NW3. *T:* 01-722 0945.

NORRIS, Dame Ada (May), DBE 1976 (OBE 1954); CMG 1969; *b* 28 July 1901; *d* of Allan Herbert Bickford and Alice Hannah (*née* Baggs); *m* 1929, John Gerald Norris; two *d.* *Educ:* Melbourne High Sch.; Melbourne Univ. (MA, DipEd). Teacher, 1925-29. Vice-Chm., Victorian Council on the Ageing, 1951-; Vice-Pres., Victorian Soc. for Crippled Children and Adults, 1951-; Pres., Australian Adv. Council for the Physically Handicapped, 1955-57; Mem., Exec. Cttee, Internat. Council of Women, 1966-; Pres., Nat. Council of Women of Australia, 1967-70; Chm., Nat. Cttee for Internat. Women's Year, 1974-76. Australian Rep., UN Commn on Status of Women, 1961-63. Chm., Appeal Cttee, Hall of Residence for Women Students, Univ. of Papua New Guinea, 1969-73. UN Peace Medal, 1975. *Publications:* The Society: history of the Victorian Society for Crippled Children and Adults, 1974; papers on status of women and social welfare matters. *Recreations:* gardening, travel. *Address:* 10 Winifred Crescent, Toorak, Vic 3142, Australia. *T:* Melbourne 03245166. *Club:* Lyceum.

NORRIS, Alan Hedley; Chairman, North Eastern Electricity Board, 1969-77 (Deputy Chairman, 1968-69); *b* 15 July 1913; *s* of Hedley Faithfull Norris, Solicitor; *m* 1941, Rachel Mary Earle; one *s* two *d.* *Educ:* Bradfield; Clare Coll., Cambridge. Served with RAF, 1940-45. HM Inspector of Factories, 1937-46; Min. of Power: Asst Principal, 1946-48; Principal, 1948-52; Asst Secretary, 1952-65; Under Secretary, 1965-68. *Recreation:* fishing. *Address:* Ednam East Mill, Kelso, Roxburghshire. *T:* Kelso 2000. *Club:* Flyfishers'.

NORRIS, Sir Alfred (Henry), KBE 1961; *b* 27 April 1894; *s* of late Alfred James Norris, Hornchurch, Essex, and Charlotte Norris; *m* 1925, Betty K. R. Davidson (decd); *m* 1936, Winifred Gladys, *d* of late Archibald Henry Butler; three *s.* *Educ:* Cranbrook Sch., Kent. Served War of 1914-18, King's Own Royal (Lancaster) Regt. Retired Company Director and Chartered Accountant; formerly of Brazil. *Recreations:* social work, gardening. *Address:* Rua Dr Antonio Martins 20, Estoril, Portugal. *Clubs:* Canning (London); Royal British (Lisbon).

NORRIS, Vice-Adm. Sir Charles (Fred Wivell), KBE 1956; CB 1952; DSO 1944; *b* 16 Dec. 1900; *m* 1924, Violet Cremer; one *s. Educ:* RNC Osborne and Dartmouth. Comdr, 1934; RN Staff Course, 1935; commanded HMS Aberdeen, 1936-39; Captain, 1941; commanded HMS Bellona, 1943-45; commanded HMS Dryad (Navigation and Direction School), 1945-46; Imperial Defence Coll., 1947; Captain of the Fleet, Home Fleet, 1948-50; Rear-Admiral, 1950; Director of Naval Training, and Deputy Chief of Naval Personnel, 1950-52; Vice-Admiral, 1953; Flag Officer (Flotilla), Mediterranean, 1953-54. Commander-in-Chief, East Indies Station, 1954-56, retired, 1956. Director of the British Productivity Council, 1957-65. *Address:* Clouds, 56 Shepherd's Way, Liphook, Hants. *T:* Liphook 722456.

NORRIS, Air Chief Marshal Sir Christopher Neil F.; *see* Foxley-Norris.

NORRIS, Rt. Rev. Mgr David Joseph; Prelate of Honour to the Pope; General Secretary to RC Bishops' Conference of England and Wales, since 1967; *b* 17 Aug. 1922; *s* of David William and Anne Norris. *Educ:* Salesian Coll., Battersea; St Edmund's Coll., Ware; Christ's Coll., Cambridge (MA). Priest, 1947; teaching at St Edmund's Coll., Ware, 1948-53; Cambridge, 1953-56; Private Secretary to Cardinal Godfrey, 1956-64; National Chaplain to Catholic Overseas Students, 1964-65; Private Secretary to Cardinal Heenan, 1965-72; Vicar General of Westminster Diocese, 1972-. *Recreations:* reading, music, sport. *Address:* Archbishop's House, Westminster, SW1P 1QJ. *T:* 01-834 4717.

NORRIS, Sir Eric (George), KCMG 1969 (CMG 1963); HM Diplomatic Service, retired; *b* 14 March 1918; *s* of late H. F. Norris, Bengeo, Hertford; *m* 1941, Pamela Crane; three *d. Educ:* Hertford Grammar Sch.; St Catharine's Coll., Cambridge. Served Royal Corps of Signals, 1940-46 (Major). Entered Dominions Office, 1946. Served in British Embassy, Dublin, 1948-50; UK High Commission in Pakistan, 1952-55; UK High Commission in Delhi, 1956-57; Dep. High Commissioner for the UK, Bombay, 1957-60; IDC 1961; British Dep. High Comr, Calcutta, 1962-65; Commonwealth Office, 1966-68; High Comr, Kenya, 1968-72; Dep. Under Sec. of State, FCO, 1972-73; High Comr, Malaysia, 1974-77. *Address:* Melton Half, Newdigate, Surrey. *T:* Rusper 323. *Club:* East India, Devonshire, Sports and Public Schools.

NORRIS, Maj.-Gen. Sir (Frank) Kingsley, KBE 1957 (CBE 1943); CB 1953; DSO; ED; MD; Hon. Consultant Pædiatrician, Alfred Hospital, Melbourne, since 1948; *b* 25 June 1893; *s* of Dr W. Perrin Norris; *m* 1920, Dorothy Leonard Stevenson; two *d. Educ:* Melbourne Church of England Grammar Sch.; Trinity Coll., Melbourne Univ. Served Australian Imperial Forces, ME, 1914-16; CO 1 CCS, AIF, 1939; ADMS 7 Australian Div. AIF, 1940-43; DDMS 1 Australian Corps AIF, 1943; Service in Middle East, Libya, 1940; Palestine 1941; Syria, 1941; Java, 1942; New Guinea, 1942-44; Korea, 1951-53. DGMS Commonwealth Military Forces, 1948-55; President: Royal Empire Soc., Vic. Br., 1948-54; BMA, Vic. Br., 1947; Good Neighbour Council, Vic., 1958-63; Alcoholic Foundn of Vic., 1961-68. Comr St John's Ambulance Bde, 1956, Chief Comr, 1963-; Chief Comr, Priory of St John Ambulance in Australia. Medical Adviser, Civil Defence, Australia, 1956-61. KStJ 1961 (CStJ 1959). KHP 1948; QPH 1953-55. *Publications:* The Syrian Campaign, 1944; The New Guinea Campaign, 1946; Major-General Sir Neville Howse, VC, 1965; No Memory for Pain (autobiography), 1970; various papers to medical journals. *Recreations:* bridge, chess, golf, model-ship building, cooking. *Address:* 19 Currajong Avenue, Camberwell, Victoria 3124, Australia. *Clubs:* MCC; Beefsteak, Melbourne, Naval and Military (Melbourne).

NORRIS, Gilbert Frank; Chief Road Engineer, Scottish Development Department, 1969-76; *b* 29 May 1916; *s* of Ernest Frank Norris and Ada Norris; *m* 1941, Joan Margaret Catherine Thompson; one *s. Educ:* Bemrose Sch., Derby; UC Nottingham. FICE, FInstHE. Served with Notts, Bucks and Lindsey County Councils, 1934-39; Royal Engineers, 1939-46; Min. of Transport: Highways Engr in Nottingham, Edinburgh and Leeds, 1946-63; Asst Chief Engr, 1963-67; Dep. Chief Engr, 1967; Dir, NE Road Construction Unit, 1967-69. *Recreations:* motoring, photography. *Address:* 17 Suffolk Road, Edinburgh EH16 5NJ. *T:* 031-667 1422.

NORRIS, Col Graham Alexander, OBE (mil.) 1945; JP; company director and management consultant, since 1972; Vice Lord-Lieutenant of County of Greater Manchester, since 1975; *b* 14 April 1913; *er s* of late John O. H. Norris and Beatrice H. Norris (née Vlies), Manchester; *m* 1st, 1938, Frances Cicely, *d* of late Walter Gorton, Minchinhampton, Glos; one *d;* 2nd, 1955, Muriel, *d* of late John Corris, Manchester. *Educ:* William

Hulme's Grammar Sch.; Coll. of Technology, Manchester; Regent St Polytechnic, London; Merchant Venturers Techn. Coll., Bristol. CEng, FIMechE, FIMI. Trng as automobile engr, Rolls Royce Ltd, Bristol Motor Co. Ltd; Joseph Cockshoot & Co. Ltd: Auto Engr, Works Man., 1937, Works Dir 1946, Jt. Man. Dir 1964, Chm. and Man. Dir, 1968; Dir, Lex Garages Ltd, 1968-70; Dir, Red Garages (N Wales) Ltd, 1973-. War service, RAOC and REME, UK, ME and Italy, 1940-46 (Lt-Col); Comdr REME 22 (W) Corps Tps (TA), 1947-51; Hon. Col, 1957-61. Mem., NEDC for Motor Vehicle Distrib. and Repair, 1966-; Pres., Motor Agents Assoc., 1967-68; Vice-Pres., Inst. of Motor Industry, 1973; Mem., Industrial Tribunal Panel, 1976. Pres., Manchester and Dist Fedn of Boys' Clubs, 1968-74; Vice-Pres., NABC, 1972-; Chm. Council and Mem. Court, UMIST; Mem. Court, Univ. of Manchester. Master, Worshipful Co. of Coachmakers and Coach Harness Makers, 1961-62; Freeman, City of London, 1938. JP, Lancashire 1963; DL Co. Palatine of Lancaster, 1962. *Recreations:* gardening, walking, social service activities. *Address:* Silver Ridge, Waterhead, Ambleside, Cumbria LA22 0HE; 4A, 281 Washway Road, Sale, Manchester M33 4BP. *Club:* East India, Devonshire, Sports and Public Schools.

NORRIS, Herbert Walter; Regional Director, South East Region, National Westminster Bank Ltd, 1969-73; Deputy Chief General Manager, 1962-65, Director, 1965-68, Westminster Bank Ltd; *b* 9 Dec. 1904; *s* of Walter Norris, Widnes, Lancs; *m* 1935, Laura Phyllis Tardif, *d* of A. Tardif, St Martin's, Guernsey; no *c. Educ:* Liverpool Collegiate School. Joined Westminster Bank, Liverpool Office, 1921; Joint General Manager, Westminster Bank Ltd, 1949. Member Council, Institute of Bankers, 1952-65; (Dep. Chairman, 1959-61). Master of Coopers' Company, 1973-74. *Recreations:* gardening, fishing, music. *Address:* The Coach House, Ballards, Goudhurst, Cranbrook, Kent. *T:* Goudhurst 501.

NORRIS, Prof. John Robert, PhD; Director, Agricultural Research Council Meat Research Institute, since 1973; Professor of Applied Microbiology, University of Bristol, since 1974; *b* 4 March 1932; *s* of Albert Norris and Winifred May Perry; *m* 1956, Barbara Jean Pinder; two *s* one *d* (and one *s* decd). *Educ:* Depts of Bacteriology and Agriculture, Univ. of Leeds (BSc 1st Cl. Hons 1954, PhD 1957). Lectr in Bacteriology, Univ. of Glasgow, 1957-63; Microbiologist, Shell Research Ltd, 1963-73 (Dir, Borden Microbiol Lab., 1970-73). Editor, Methods in Microbiology, 1969-. *Publications:* papers in microbiol jls. *Recreations:* walking, wood carving, Yoga. *Address:* 32 Redland Grove, Bristol BS6 6PR. *T:* Bristol 47175. *Club:* Farmers.

NORRIS, Maj.-Gen. Sir Kingsley; *see* Norris, Maj.-Gen. Sir F. K.

NORRISH, Ronald George Wreyford, FRS 1936; ScD, PhD (Cantab); FRIC; Professor Emeritus of Physical Chemistry; Director of Department of Physical Chemistry, Cambridge University, 1937-65; Fellow of Emmanuel College, Cambridge; *b* 9 Nov. 1897; *e s* of Herbert Norrish; *m* 1926, Annie, *e d* of Albert E. Smith, Heaton Mersey, near Manchester; two *d. Educ:* Perse Sch.; Malvern Girls' Coll.; Emmanuel Coll., Cambridge (Foundation Scholar, 1915); 1st Class Hons Natural Sciences Tripos, I and II, 1920, 1921. Served European War, 1916-19 (POW 1918). Research Fellow of Emmanuel Coll., 1925-31; Humphrey Owen Jones Lecturer in Physical Chemistry, Cambridge Univ.; Meldola Medal of Institute of Chemistry, 1926; Leverhulme Research Fellow, 1935; Council of Chem. Soc. and of Faraday Soc., 1933-36; Council of Senate, Univ. of Cambridge, 1938-41; Scientific Adv. Council of the Min. of Supply, 1942-45; Pres., Faraday Soc., 1953-55; Vice-Pres., Royal Inst. of Chemistry, 1957-59; Liversidge Lecture and Medal, Chem. Soc., 1958; Davy Medal, Royal Soc., 1958; Lewis Medal of Combustion Inst., 1964; Faraday Memorial Lecture and Medal, Chem. Soc., 1965; Longstaff Medal, Chem. Soc., 1969; Bakerian Lecture, Royal Soc., 1966. Nobel Laureate (Jt) for Chemistry, 1967. Pres. British Assoc., Section B (Chemistry), 1960-61. Liveryman, Worshipful Company of Gunmakers, 1961. Hon. Ddel'U Sorbonne (Paris), 1958; Hon. Member Polish Chemical Soc., 1959; Corr. Mem. Acad. of Sciences, Göttingen, 1960; Corr. Mem., Royal Soc. of Sciences, Liège, 1960; Foreign Mem. Polish Acad., of Sciences, 1962; Hon. Member: Royal Soc. of Sciences, Uppsala, Sweden, 1964; Faraday Soc., 1966; NY Acad. of Sciences, 1968; Bulgarian Acad. of Sciences, 1970; Société de Chimie Physique, Paris; Belgian Acad of Sciences, 1975. Hon. DSc: Leeds, Sheffield, 1965; Liverpool, Lancaster, 1968; British Columbia, 1969. Hon. FRSE 1972. Chevalier Commandeur de la confrérie des Chevaliers du Tastevin, 1971; Knight's Cross, Order of Polonia Restituta, 1974; Order of Cyril and Methodus of Bulgaria, 1974.

Publications: Scientific papers in Proceedings of Royal Society, Journal of Chemical Soc., Transactions of Faraday Soc., etc. *Recreations:* recollections of tennis and golf. *Address:* Emmanuel College, Cambridge. *T:* Cambridge 65411; Department of Physical Chemistry, Lensfield Road, Cambridge. *T:* Cambridge 66499; 7 Park Terrace, Cambridge. *T:* 55147. *Club:* Savage.

NORSTAD, Gen. Lauris, DSM (US) with Oak Leaf Cluster and Silver Star; Legion of Merit (US) with Cluster; Air Medal; United States Air Forces, retired; Hon. Chairman (formerly Chairman and Chief Executive Officer, 1967-72), Owens-Corning Fiberglas Corporation (President, Owens-Corning Fiberglas International, January-December 1963); Director: United Air Lines; Abitibi Paper Co.; *b* Minneapolis, USA, 24 March 1907; *s* of Martin Norstad; *m* 1935, Isabelle Helen Jenkins; one *d. Educ:* US Military Academy (BS). 2nd Lieut, Cavalry, 1930; graduated, Air Corps Sch., 1931. Served in various branches of Air Force; duty at GHQ Air Force, Langley Field, Va., 1940; Assistant Chief of Staff for Operations, 12th Air Force, 1942, served with 12th Air Force, England and Algiers; Director of Operations, Allied Air Forces, Mediterranean, Dec. 1943; Chief of Staff, 20th Air Force, Washington, 1944; Asst Chief of Staff for Plans, Army Air Force HQ, 1945; Director of Plans and Operations Div., War Dept, Washington, 1946; Dep. Chief of Staff for Operations, USAF, 1947; Acting Vice Chief of Staff, Air Force, May 1950; C-in-C US Air Forces in Europe and C-in-C Allied Air Forces Central Europe, 1951; Deputy (Air) to Supreme Allied Commander, Europe, 1953; C-in-C, US European Comd, 1956-62, and Supreme Allied Commander, Europe, 1956-62; retired, 1963. Has several hon. degrees. Hon. CBE (GB). Holds other foreign orders. *Address:* (business) 717 Fifth Avenue, New York, NY 10022, USA.

NORTH, family name of **Earl of Guilford.**

NORTH, Lord; Piers Edward Brownlow North; *b* 9 March 1971; *s* and *heir* of Earl of Guilford, *qv.*

NORTH, Rt. Hon. Sir Alfred Kingsley, PC 1966; KBE 1964; Kt 1959; Judge of the Court of Appeal, New Zealand, 1957-72 (President of the Court, 1963-72); first Chairman, New Zealand Press Council, since 1972; *b* 17 Dec. 1900; *s* of late Rev. J. J. North, DD; *m* 1924, Thelma Grace Dawson; two *s* one *d. Educ:* Canterbury Coll., Christchurch, New Zealand (LLM). Was, for many years, in the legal firm of Earl Kent and Co., Auckland, New Zealand. One of HM Counsel (KC 1947); Judge of the Supreme Court of New Zealand, 1951-57. Past President Auckland Rotary Club; Past Chairman Auckland Branch of Crippled Children's Society, etc. Hon. Bencher, Gray's Inn. *Recreation:* trout-fishing. *Address:* 28 Mahoe Avenue, Remuera, Auckland, NZ. *Club:* Northern (Auckland, NZ).

NORTH, Brig. Francis Roger, CB 1942; MC and Bar, 1918; ED 1937; Solicitor, Member of firm of Roberts Leu & North, Solicitors, Townsville, N Queensland; *b* 13 April 1894; *s* of Robert Dundas North, Brisbane; *m* 1929, Margaret May, *d* of Robert Lawrence Craddock; two *d. Educ:* The Southport School. Served War of 1914-18 (wounded twice, despatches twice); commissioned 1914, served 9th, 15th and 47th Inf., AIF, Egypt, Gallipoli, France and Flanders; Captain, 1916, Major, 1927, 31st Bn, Lt-Col, 1927; comd 31st Bn, 1924-29 and 1933-40. War of 1939-45; comd 11th Inf. Bde, 1940-42 (temp. Brig.); comd 1st Australian L of C Sub Area, 1942-45; Col R of O 1945; Brig., retired. Chancellor to Bishop of North Queensland, 1928-70; Chancellor to Bishop of Carpentaria, 1930-70; Pres., N Qld br., RSSAILA, 1932-39; Alderman of Townsville City Council, 1936-39. Pres., N Qld Golf Assoc., 1928-38; Trustee Scartwater Trust; Vice-Consul for Sweden. Knight of the Royal Order of Vasa (Sweden), 1953. *Address:* 54 Denham Street, Townsville, North Queensland 4810, Australia. *Clubs:* North Queensland, RSSAILA (Townsville); United Services (Brisbane).

NORTH, Sir Jonathan; see North, Sir W. J. F.

NORTH, Dr Peter Machin, DCL; a Law Commissioner, since 1976; Fellow of Keble College, Oxford, since 1965; *b* Nottingham, 30 Aug. 1936; *o s* of late Geoffrey Machin North and Freda Brunt (*née* Smith); *m* 1960, Stephanie Mary, *e d* of T. L. Chadwick; two *s* one *d. Educ:* Oakham Sch.; Keble Coll., Oxford (BA 1959, BCL 1960, MA 1963, DCL 1976). National Service, Royal Leics Regt, 2nd Lieut, 1955-56. Teaching Associate, Northwestern Univ. Sch. of Law, Chicago, 1960-61; Lecturer: University Coll. of Wales, Aberystwyth, 1961-63; Univ. of Nottingham, 1963-65; Tutor in Law, Keble Coll., Oxford, 1965-76. Vis. Professor: Univ. of Auckland, 1969; Univ. of BC, 1975-76. Dir of Studies, Hague Acad. of Internat. Law,

1970; Mem., Lord Chancellor's Adv. Cttee on Legal Educn, 1973-75. *Publications:* Occupiers' Liability, 1971; The Modern Law of Animals, 1972; (ed) Cheshire's Private International Law, 9th edn 1974; Private International Law of Matrimonial Causes, 1977; (ed jtly) Chitty on Contracts,24th edn 1977; articles and notes in legal jls. *Recreations:* children, gardening, cricket (both playing and sleeping through). *Address:* 66 Eynsham Road, Oxford. *T:* Cumnor 2001; Law Commission, Conquest House, 37-38 John Street, Theobald's Road, WC1N 2BQ. *T:* 01-242 0861.

NORTH, Roger, JP; a Recorder of the Crown Court, 1971-73; Chairman West Norfolk Valuation Panel, since 1949; *b* 10 Dec. 1901; *s* of F. K. North, Rougham Hall, King's Lynn, and Grace, *d* of Gen. Sir Percy Feilding; *m* 1934, Pamela Susan, *d* of Rev. H. W. L. O'Rorke, North Litchfield, Hants; one *s* three *d. Educ:* Eton; Trinity Coll., Cambridge. Called to the Bar, 1925. Began farming at Rougham, Norfolk, 1932. Dep. Chm., Norfolk QS, 1962-71 (apptd by Royal Warrant); Chm., King's Lynn QS, 1942-71. Late Chm. Tractor Users' Assoc. and Oxford Farming Conf. Cttee; Council Mem. Instn of Agricultural Engineers, 1954-58; Chm., Norfolk Br., Mathematical Assoc. JP Norfolk, 1941. *Publication:* The Art of Algebra, 1965. *Recreations:* veteran motor cars and mathematics. *Address:* Rougham Hall, Rougham, King's Lynn, Norfolk. *T:* Weasenham St Peter 230. *Clubs:* Royal Institution; Norfolk.

NORTH, Sir (William) Jonathan (Frederick), 2nd Bt, *cr* 1920; *b* 6 Feb. 1931; *s* of Muriel Norton (2nd *d* of 1st Bt) and Hon. John Montagu William North (who *m* 2nd, 1939, Marion Dyer Chase, Boston, Mass); *g s* of Sir William Hicking, 1st Bt; *S* grandfather, 1947 (under special remainder); *m* 1956, Sara Virginia, *d* of Air Chief Marshal Sir Donald Hardman, *qv*; one *s* two *d. Educ:* Marlborough Coll. *Heir: s* Jeremy William Francis North, *b* 5 May 1960. *Address:* Frogmore, Weston-under-Penyard, Herefordshire.

NORTHAMPTON, 6th Marquess of, *cr* 1812; **William Bingham Compton;** DSO 1919; Earl of Northampton, 1618; Earl Compton, Baron Wilmington, 1912; *b* 6 Aug. 1885; *e* surv. *s* of 5th Marquess and Hon. Mary Florence Baring (*d* 1902), *o d* of 2nd Lord Ashburton; *S* father, 1913; *m* 1st, 1921, Lady Emma Thynne, OBE 1943 (marr. diss., 1942), 2nd *d* of 5th Marquess of Bath, KG, PC, CB; 2nd, 1942, Virginia (marr. diss., 1958), *d* of Lt-Col David Heaton, DSO, two *s* two *d*; 3rd, 1958, Elspeth, Lady Teynham (*d* 1976). *Educ:* Eton; Balliol Coll., Oxford. BA. Northamptonshire Yeomanry, 1903-06; 2nd Lieut, Royal Horse Guards, 1907; Captain and Adjutant, 1913; served European War, 1914-19 (DSO, wounded, despatches twice); commanded Warwickshire Yeomanry, 1933. JP Northants; DL Northants; late Chairman Northants CC; resigned, 1955. Owns about 10,000 acres. *Heir: s* Earl Compton, *qv*. *Address:* Chadstone Old Rectory, Castle Ashby, Northampton. *Club:* Turf.
See also Baron Loch.

NORTHAMPTON, Bishop of, (RC), since 1967; **Rt. Rev. Charles Alexander Grant,** MA; LCL; *b* 25 Oct. 1906; *s* of Frank and Sibylla Christina Grant. *Educ:* Perse Sch., Cambridge; St Edmund's, Ware; Christ's Coll., Cambridge; Oscott Coll., Birmingham; Gregorian Univ., Rome. Curate, Cambridge, 1938; Parish Priest: Ely, 1943; Kettering, 1945. Bishop-Auxiliary of Northampton, 1961-67. *Address:* Bishop's House, Northampton NN2 6AW. *T:* Northampton 715635.

NORTHAMPTON, Archdeacon of; see Marsh, Ven. Bazil Roland.

NORTHBOURNE, 4th Baron, *cr* 1884; **Walter Ernest Christopher James,** Bt, 1791; *b* 1896; *o* surv. *s* of 3rd Baron and Laura Gwenllian (who *m* 2nd, 1935, William Curtis Green, RA; he *d* 1960), *d* of late Admiral Sir Ernest Rice, KCB; *S* father, 1932; *m* 1925, Katherine Nickerson, *d* of Hon. Lady Hood, and late George A. Nickerson, Boston, Mass; one *s* four *d. Educ:* Eton; Magdalen Coll., Oxford. Chairman, Kent Agricultural Executive Cttee, 1946-57. Fellow, Wye Coll., 1967. *Publications:* Look to the Land, 1940; Religion in The Modern World, 1963; Looking Back on Progress, 1970. *Heir: s* Hon. Christopher George Walter James [*b* 18 Feb. 1926; *m* 1959, Marie Sygne, *e d* of M and Mme Henri Claudel; three *s* one *d*]. *Address:* Northbourne Court, Deal, Kent. *T:* Deal 4617. *Clubs:* Leander, Farmers'.
See also T. J. Hemsley.

NORTHBROOK, 5th Baron, *cr* 1866; **Francis John Baring,** Bt 1793; DL; *b* 31 May 1915; *s* of 4th Baron Northbrook and Evelyn Gladys Isabel (*d* 1919), *d* of J. G. Charles; *S* father 1947; *m* 1951, Rowena Margaret, 2nd *d* of late Brig-General Sir William Manning, and of Lady Manning, Hampton Court

Palace; one *s* three *d*. *Educ:* Winchester; Trinity Coll., Oxford. JP 1955, DL 1972, Hants. *Heir: s* Hon. Francis Thomas Baring, *b* 21 Feb. 1954. *Address:* East Stratton House, East Stratton, Winchester, Hants.

NORTHCHURCH, Baroness (Life Peer); *see* under Davidson, Dowager Viscountess.

NORTHCOTE, family name of **Earl of Iddesleigh.**

NORTHCOTE, Prof. Donald Henry, FRS 1968; Master of Sidney Sussex College, Cambridge, since 1976; Professor of Plant Biochemistry, University of Cambridge, since 1972 (Reader, 1965-72); *b* 27 Dec. 1921; *m* Eva Marjorie Mayo; two *d*. *Educ:* Sir George Monoux Grammar Sch., London; London Univ.; Cambridge Univ. Fellow, St John's College, Cambridge, 1960-76. Hon. Fellow, Downing Coll., Cambridge, 1976. *Publication:* Differentiation in Higher Plants, 1974. *Recreations:* sitting and chatting; strolling about. *Address:* The Master's Lodge, Sidney Sussex College, Cambridge. *T:* Cambridge 55860.

NORTHCOTE, Peter Colston; His Honour Judge Northcote; a Circuit Judge since 1973; *b* 23 Oct. 1920; *s* of late William George Northcote and late Edith Mary Northcote; *m* 1947, Patricia Bickley; two *s*. *Educ:* Ellesmere Coll.; Bristol Univ. Called to Bar, Inner Temple, 1948. Chm., Nat. Insce Tribunal; Chm., W Midland Rent Tribunal; Dep. Chm., Agric. Land Tribunal. Commnd KSLI, 1940; served 7th Rajput Regt, Far East (Major). *Recreations:* music, travel, ski-ing. *Address:* Wroxeter Grange, Wroxeter, Shrewsbury, Salop. *T:* Cross Houses 279. *Clubs:* Army and Navy; Union and County (Worcester).

NORTHCOTE-GREEN, Roger James, MC 1944; TD 1950; JP; Headmaster, Worksop College, Notts, 1952-70; *b* 25 July 1912; *s* of Rev. Edward Joseph Northcote-Green and Mary Louisa Catt; *m* 1941, Joan, *d* of Ernest Greswell and Grace Lillian (*née* Egerton); three *s* one *d*. *Educ:* St Edward's Sch. and The Queen's Coll., Oxford (MA). Served with Oxford and Bucks Light Infantry, 1939-44, in India and Burma; Staff Coll., Quetta, 1944-45; Bde Major, 53rd Ind. Inf. Bde, Malaya, 1945. Assistant Master, St Edward's Sch., 1936-39, 1946-52; Housemaster, 1947. Representative OURFC on RU Cttee, 1946-52. S Western Sec., Independent Schs Careers Orgn. JP Nottinghamshire, 1964. *Recreations:* shooting, fishing. *Address:* Manor Cottage, Woolston, Williton, Som. *T:* Williton 32445. *Clubs:* East India, Devonshire, Sports and Public Schools, MCC; Vincent's (Oxford).

NORTHCOTT, Rev. Cecil; *see* Northcott, Rev. (William) C.

NORTHCOTT, Prof. Douglas Geoffrey, FRS 1961; MA, PhD, Cambridge; Town Trust Professor of Mathematics, University of Sheffield, since 1952; *b* London, 1916; *m* 1949, Rose Hilda Austin, Twickenham, Middlesex; two *d*. *Educ:* Christ's Hospital; St John's Coll., Cambridge. *Publications:* Ideal Theory, 1953; An Introduction to Homological Algebra, 1960; Lessons on Rings, Modules and Multiplicities, 1968; A First Course of Homological Algebra, 1973; Finite Free Resolutions, 1976. *Address:* Department of Pure Mathematics, The University, Sheffield; 25 Parkhead Road, Ecclesall, Sheffield S11 9RA.

NORTHCOTT, Rev. (William) Cecil, MA; PhD; Religious Affairs Adviser and Churches Correspondent, Daily Telegraph, since 1967; Editorial Secretary United Society for Christian Literature and Editor, Lutterworth Press, 1952-72; Editor-at-large, Christian Century of USA, 1945-70; *b* Buckfast, Devon, 5 April 1902; *s* of William Ashplant Northcott and Mary Nance; *m* 1930, Jessie Morton, MA, 2nd *d* of J. L. Morton, MD, Hampstead and Colyford, Devon; one *s* one *d*. *Educ:* Hele's Sch., Exeter; Fitzwilliam Coll., and Cheshunt Coll., Cambridge. 2nd Class Hons Historical and Theological Triposes; BA 1927; MA 1930; PhD London Univ. (School of Oriental and African Studies), 1961. Three years social work East End of London; Member Cambridge delegation to League of Nations, Geneva, 1926; Joint Proprietor and Editor The Granta, 1927-28; Asst Minister Ormskirk Street Congregational Church, St Helens, 1929-32; Minister Duckworth Street Congregational Church, Darwen, Lancs, 1932-35; Home Secretary and Literary Superintendent London Missionary Society, 1935-50; General Secretary and Editor United Council for Missionary Education (Edinburgh House Press), 1950-52; Chairman London Missionary Society, 1954-55; Delegate World Conferences, Amsterdam, 1948, Willingen, 1952, Evanston, 1954, New Delhi, 1961, Uppsala, 1968, Nairobi, 1975. Member, World Council of Churches Information Cttee, 1954-61; Member, British Council of Churches Christian Aid Cttee, 1946-64. Select Preacher,

Cambridge, 1958; Danforth Foundation Lecturer, USA, 1961; Visiting Lecturer, Garrett Theological Seminary, USA, 1965, 1967, 1969, 1971. British Information Services, USA 1944; editor, Congregational Monthly, 1953-58. Leverhulme Research Award, 1958. *Publications:* Time to Spare (Collab. BBC Talks), 1935; Southward Ho!, 1936; Guinea Gold, 1937; Who Claims the World?, 1938; John Williams Sails On, 1939; Change Here for Britain, 1942; Glorious Company, 1945; Whose Dominion?, 1946; Religious Liberty, 1948; Venturers of Faith, 1950; Voice Out of Africa, 1952; Robert Moffat: Pioneer in Africa, 1961; Christianity in Africa, 1963; David Livingstone: his triumph, decline and fall, 1973; Slavery's Martyr, 1976; ed Encyclopedia of the Bible for Children, 1964; People of the Bible, 1967. *Recreation:* walking. *Address:* 34 Millington Road, Cambridge. *T:* Cambridge 62905. *Clubs:* National Liberal, Royal Commonwealth Society; Union (Cambridge).

NORTHERN TERRITORY, AUSTRALIA, Bishop of the, since 1968; **Rt. Rev. Kenneth Bruce Mason;** *b* 4 Sept. 1928; *s* of Eric Leslie Mason and Gertrude Irene (*née* Pearce); unmarried. *Educ:* Bathurst High Sch.; Sydney Teachers' Coll.; St John's Theological Coll., Morpeth; Univ. of Queensland. Deacon, 1953; Priest, 1954. Primary Teacher, 1948-51; St John's Theological Coll., Morpeth, 1952-53 (ThL); Member, Brotherhood of the Good Shepherd, 1954; Parish of: Gilgandra, NSW, 1954-58; Darwin, NT, 1959-61; Alice Springs, NT, 1962; University of Queensland, 1963-64 (BA, Dip Div); resigned from Brotherhood, 1965; Trinity Coll., Melbourne Univ.: Asst Chaplain, 1965; Dean, 1966-67. *Recreations:* listening to music, railways. *Address:* The Lodge, PO Box 2267, Darwin, NT 5794, Australia.

NORTHESK, 13th Earl of, *cr* 1647; **Robert Andrew Carnegie;** Lord Rosehill and Inglismaldie, 1639; Landowner, Farmer; *b* 24 June 1926; *yr s* of 12th Earl of Northesk and Dorothy Mary (*d* 1967), *er d* of late Col Sir William Robert Campion, KCMG, DSO; *S* father, 1975; *m* 1949, Jean Margaret, *yr d* of Captain (John) Duncan George MacRae, Ballimore, Otter Ferry, Argyll; one *s* two *d* (and one *s* decd). *Educ:* Pangbourne RNR Coll.; Tabor Naval Acad., USA. Served with Royal Navy, 1942-45. Mem., Council, Fédération Internationale des Assocs d'éléveurs de la race bovine Charolaise. *Heir: s* Lord Rosehill, *qv*. *Address:* Fair Oak, Rogate, Sussex; Springwaters, Ballamodha, Isle of Man.

NORTHFIELD, Baron *cr* 1975 (Life Peer), of Telford, Salop; **(William) Donald Chapman;** Visiting Fellow, Centre for Contemporary European Studies, University of Sussex, since 1973; Chairman: Development Commission, since 1974; Telford Development Corporation, since 1975; *b* 25 Nov. 1923; *s* of Wm H. and Norah F. E. Chapman, Barnsley. *Educ:* Barnsley Grammar Sch.; Emmanuel Coll., Cambridge, MA (1st Cl. Hons) Economics, also degree in Agriculture; Senior Scholar of Emmanuel Coll. Research in Agric. Economics, Cambridge, 1943-46; Cambridge City Councillor, 1945-47; Sec., Trades Council and Labour Party, 1945-57; MP (Lab) Birmingham (Northfield), 1951-70. Research Sec. of the Fabian Soc., 1948-49, Gen. Sec., 1949-53. Gwilym Gibbon Fellow, Nuffield Coll., Oxford, 1971-73. Mem., Noise Adv. Council, 1976-. *Publications:* The European Parliament: the years ahead, 1973; The Road to European Union, 1975; articles and Fabian pamphlets. *Recreation:* travel. *Address:* The Development Commission, 11 Cowley Street, SW1P 3NA. *T:* 01-222 9134. *Club:* Reform.

NORTHOLT, Archdeacon of; *see* Southwell, Ven. Roy.

NORTHROP, Filmer S(tuart) C(uckow), PhD, LittD, LLD; Sterling Professor of Philosophy and Law Emeritus, the Law School and the School of Graduate Studies, Yale University, USA, since 1962; *b* 27 Nov. 1893; *s* of Marshall Ellsworth Northrop and Ruth Cuckow; *m* 1st, 1919, Christine Johnston; two *s*; 2nd, 1969, Marjorie Carey. *Educ:* Beloit Coll. (BA 1915, LittD 1946); Yale (MA 1919); Harvard (MA 1922, PhD 1924); Imperial Coll. of Science and Technology, London; Trinity Coll., Cambridge. Instr. at Yale, 1923-26; Asst Prof., Yale, 1926-29; Associate Prof., Yale, 1929-32, Prof., 1932-47; Master of Silliman Coll., 1940-47; Sterling Prof. of Philosophy and Law, Yale, 1947-62; Visiting Prof., summer session, Univ. of Iowa, 1926; Univ. of Michigan, 1932; Univ. of Virginia, 1931-32; Visiting Prof. and Mem. of East-West Conf. on Philosophy at Univ. of Hawaii, 1939; Prof. Extraordinario, La Universidad Nacional Autonoma de Mexico, 1949; Fellow: American Acad. of Arts and Sciences, 1951; American Acad. of Political and Social Science, 1957; Pres., American Philosophical Assoc. (Eastern Div.), 1952. Hon. Founder: Macy Foundn Conferences, 1944-53; Amer. Soc. of Cybernetics, 1964; Mem., SEATO Round Table, Bangkok, 1958. Hon. LLD: Univ. of

Hawaii, 1949, Rollins Coll., 1955; Hon. LittD: Beloit Coll., 1946; Pratt Inst., 1961. Order of the Aztec Eagle (Mexican), 1946, *Publications:* Science and First Principles, 1931; The Meeting of East and West, 1946; The Logic of the Sciences and the Humanities, 1947; The Taming of the Nations, A Study of the Cultural Bases of International Policy, 1952 (Wilkie Memorial Building Award, 1953); European Union and United States Foreign Policy, 1954; The Complexity of Legal and Ethical Experience, 1959; Philosophical Anthropology and Practical Politics, 1960; Man, Nature and God, 1962; Co-Editor, Cross-cultural Understanding: Epistemology in Anthropology, 1964; Chapter 5 in Contemporary American Philosophy, second series, 1970; (with J. Sinões da Fonseca) Interpersonal Relations in Neuropsychological and Legal Science, 1975; ed, Ideological Differences and World Order, 1949. *Recreations:* travel, baseball. *Address:* 68 Front Street, Exeter, NH 03833, USA. *Clubs:* Century (New York); Beaumont, Berzilius, Elizabethan, Graduates, Mory's (New Haven); American Academy of Arts and Sciences (Philosophy Section) (Boston).

NORTHROP, John Howard; Member Rockefeller University (formerly Institute), 1924, Emeritus 1962; Visiting Professor of Bacteriology, University of California, 1949, Emeritus, 1959; Professor Biophysics, 1958, Emeritus 1959; Research Biophysicist, Donner Laboratory, 1958; *b* Yonkers, NY, 5 July 1891; *s* of Dr John I. Northrop, of Department of Zoology, Columbia Univ., and Alice Rich Northrop, of Dept of Botany, Hunter Coll., NY City; *m* 1917, Louise Walker, NY City; one *s* one *d. Educ:* Columbia Univ. BS 1912; AM 1913; PhD 1915; W. B. Cutting Travelling Fellow, Columbia Univ. (year in Jacques Loeb's laboratory at Rockefeller Inst.), 1915; on staff of Rockefeller Inst. 1916; Member, 1924; Stevens prize, Coll. of Physicians and Surgeons, Columbia Univ., 1931; Captain, Chemical Warfare Service, 1917-18; discovered and worked on fermentation process for manufacturing acetone; ScD Harvard 1936, Columbia 1937, Yale 1937, Princeton 1940, Rutgers 1941; LLD, University of California, 1939; Chandler Medal, Columbia Univ., 1937; DeLamar Lectr, Sch. of Hygiene and Public Health, Johns Hopkins, 1937; Jesup Lectr, Columbia Univ., 1938; Hitchcock Lectr, Univ. of California, 1939; Thayer Lectr, Johns Hopkins, 1940; Daniel Giraud Elliot Medal for 1939 of National Acad. of Science, 1944; Consultant, OSRD, 1941-45. Shared Nobel Prize in Chemistry, 1946. Certificate of Merit, USA, 1948. Alex. Hamilton Medal, Columbia Univ., 1961. Member: Sons of the American Revolution; Delta Kappa Epsilon fraternity, Sigma Xi, Phi Lambda Upsilon; American Society of Biological Chemists; National Acad. of Sciences, Halle Akademie der Naturforscher; Société Philomathique (Paris); American Philosophical Society; Society of General Physiologists; Chemical Society (Hon. Fellow); Fellow World Academy; Benjamin Franklin Fellow, RSA. *Publications:* Crystalline Enzymes, 1939; numerous papers on physical chemistry of proteins, agglutination of bacteria, kinetics of enzyme reactions, and isolation and chemical nature of enzymes; editorial board of Journal of General Physiology, Experimental Biology Monographs; Contrib. Editor, Funk & Wagnell's Encyclopedia. *Recreations:* field shooting, salmon fishing. *Address:* PO Box 1387, Wickenburg, Arizona 85358, USA. *Club:* Century Association (New York).

NORTHUMBERLAND, 10th Duke of, *cr* 1766; **Hugh Algernon Percy;** KG 1959; PC 1973; TD 1961; FRS 1970; JP; Earl of Northumberland, Baron Warkworth, 1749; Earl Percy, 1776; Earl of Beverly, 1790; Lord Lovaine, Baron of Alnwick, 1784; Bt, *cr* 1660; Baron Percy (by writ), 1722; Lord Steward of HM Household, since 1973; Lord-Lieutenant and Custos Rotulorum of Northumberland since 1956; Chancellor of University of Newcastle since 1964; Chairman, Medical Research Council, since 1969; *b* 6 April 1914; 2nd *s* of 8th Duke of Northumberland, KG, CBE, MVO (*d* 1930), and Lady Helen Gordon-Lennox (Helen, Dowager Duchess of Northumberland, who *d* 1965), *y d* of 7th Duke of Richmond and Gordon; *S* brother (killed in action), 1940; *m* 1946, Lady Elizabeth Diana Montagu-Douglas-Scott, *er d* of 8th Duke of Buccleuch and Queensberry, KT, PC, GCVO; three *s* three *d. Educ:* Eton; Oxford. Lieut, Northumberland Hussars, 1936; RA, 1940; Captain, 1941; Captain, Northumberland Hussars, 1947; TARO, 1949-64; Chm., T&AFA, 1950-56; Pres., Northumberland T&AFA, 1956-68; Pres., TA&VR Assoc. for North of England, 1968-71; Hon. Col, 6th (V) Bn, Royal Regt of Fusiliers, T&AVR, 1975-. A Lord in Waiting, May-July 1945. Mem., Northumberland CC, 1944-55, Alderman, 1955-67. President: Northern Area, British Legion; Northumberland Boy Scouts' Assoc., 1946-; Northumb. Assoc. of Boys' Clubs, 1942-; British Horse Soc., 1950; North of England Shipowners' Assoc., 1952-; Hunters Improvement and Light Horse Breeding Soc., 1954; Royal Agricultural Soc. of England, 1956, 1962; BSJA, 1959; The Wildfowl Trust, 1968-72. Chairman: Departmental

Cttee on Slaughter of Horses, 1952; Court of Durham Univ., 1956-64; Border Forest Park Cttee, 1956-68; ARC, 1958-68; Departmental Cttee for Recruitment of Veterinary Surgeons, 1964; Cttee of Enquiry on Foot-and-Mouth Disease, 1968-69; Agricultural EDC, 1971-. Member: Agricultural Improvement Council, 1953-62; National Forestry Cttee for England and Wales, 1954-60; Hill Farming Advisory Cttee for England and Wales, 1946-60; County Agricultural Exec. Cttee, 1948-59; Royal Commn on Historical Manuscripts, 1973-. Chm. Council, RASE, 1971-74. Hon. Treasurer, RNLI; Associate, RCVS, 1967. Master of Percy Foxhounds, 1940-. KStJ 1957. Hon. DCL Durham, 1958. *Heir: s* Earl Percy, *qv. Address:* Alnwick Castle, Northumberland NE66 1NQ. *T:* Alnwick 2456; Syon House, Brentford. *T:* Isleworth 2353; Clive Lodge, Albury Park, Guildford. *T:* Shere 2695. *Clubs:* Boodle's, Northern Counties, Turf.
See also Duke of Hamilton and Brandon, Sir Aymer Maxwell, Bt, Lord Richard Percy, Duke of Sutherland.

NORTHUMBERLAND, Archdeacon of; *see* Unwin, Ven. C. P.

NORTON, family name of **Barons Grantley** and **Rathcreedan.**

NORTON, 7th Baron, *cr* 1878; **John Arden Adderley,** OBE 1964; *b* 24 Nov. 1915; *s* of 6th Baron Norton; *S* father, 1961; *m* 1946, Betty Margaret, *o d* of late James Mckee Hannah; two *s. Educ:* Radley; Magdalen Coll., Oxford (BA). Oxford University Greenland Expedition, 1938; Assistant Master, Oundle School, 1938-39. Served War, 1940-45 (despatches); RE (N Africa, Europe). Major, 1944. Asst Secretary, Country Landowners Assoc., 1947-59. *Recreations:* mountaineering, shooting, heraldry and genealogy. *Heir: s* Hon. James Nigel Arden Adderley [*b* 2 June 1947; *m* 1971, Jacqueline Julie Willett, *e d* of Guy W. Willett, Woking, Surrey]. *Address:* Fillongley Hall, Coventry, West Midlands. *T:* Fillongley 303.

NORTON, Sir Clifford John, KCMG 1946 (CMG 1933); CVO 1937; *b* 17 July 1891; *o* surv. *s* of late Rev. George Norton and Clara, *d* of late John Dewey; *m* 1927, Noel Evelyn (*d* 1972), *d* of late Sir Walter Charleton Hughes, CIE, MInstCE; no *c. Educ:* Rugby Sch.; Queen's Coll., Oxford, MA 1915. Suffolk Regt, 1914, Gallipoli, Palestine; Captain, General Staff EEF, 1917; Political Officer, Damascus, Deraa, Haifa, 1919-20; entered Diplomatic Service, 1921; Private Secretary to the Permanent Under-Secretary of State for Foreign Affairs, 1930-37; First Secretary, 1933; Counsellor British Embassy, Warsaw, 1937-39; Foreign Office, 1939-42; Minister, Berne, 1942-46; HM Ambassador in Athens, 1946-51; retired, 1951; Hon. Citizen of Athens, 1951. UK Delegate (alternate) to United Nations Assembly, 1952 and 1953. Past President, Anglo-Swiss Society. Hon. Fellow, Queen's Coll., Oxford, 1963. *Address:* 21a Carlyle Square, SW3; Bothamstead Farm, Hampstead Norris, Berks.

NORTON, Maj.-Gen. Cyril Henry, CB 1952; CBE 1945; DSO 1943; Colonel Commandant RA, 1958-63; *b* 4 Nov. 1898; *s* of late F. H. Norton, Tilehurst, Caterham, Surrey; *m* 1934, Ethel, *d* of Kapten R. E. G. Lindberg, Stockholm, Sweden; one *s* one d. *Educ:* Rugby Sch.; RMA, Woolwich. 2nd Lieut, RFA, 1916; Captain, 1929; Major, 1938; Lieut-Colonel, 1945; Colonel, 1946. Brig., 1950; Maj.-Gen., 1951; GOC 5th Anti-Aircraft Group, 1950-53; retired Nov. 1953. Served European War, 1914-19 (Salonika); Palestine, 1937-39 (despatches); War of 1939-45: in Middle East, Sicily and NW Europe. *Address:* Dunn House, Long Melford, Sudbury, Suffolk. *Club:* Army and Navy.
See also Viscount Colville of Culross .

NORTON, Donald; Regional Administrator, Oxford Regional Health Authority, since Oct. 1973; *b* 2 May 1920; *s* of Thomas Henry Norton and Dora May Norton (née Prentice); *m* 1945, Miriam Joyce, *d* of Herbert and Florence Mann; two *s* one *d. Educ:* Nether Edge Grammar Sch., Sheffield; Univs of Sheffield and London. LLB, DPA; FHA. Senior Administrator Sheffield Regional Hosp. Bd, 1948-51; Sec. Supt, Jessop Hosp. for Women and Charles Clifford Dental Hosp., Sheffield, 1951-57; Dep. Sec., Archway Gp of Hosps, London, 1957-60; Gp Sec., Dudley Road Gp of Hosps, Birmingham 1960-70; Sec., Oxford Regional Hosp. Bd, 1970-73. *Recreations:* marriage, golf, gardening. *Address:* The Squirrels, 14 Pullens Field, Headington, Oxford OX3 0BU. *T:* Oxford 67291. *Clubs:* Victory; Management (Oxford); Frilford Heath.

NORTON, Captain Gerard Ross, VC 1944; MM; 1/4th Hampshire Regiment; *b* S Africa, 7 Sept. 1915; *m* 1942, Lilia Morris, East London, S Africa; one *d. Educ:* Selborne Coll., East London, S Africa. Bank clerk. *Recreations:* Rugger-provincial, tennis, cricket. *Address:* Minnehaha, PO Raffingora, Rhodesia.

NORTON, Admiral of the Fleet Sir Peter John H.; *see* Hill-Norton.

NORTON, **Roger Edward**, CMG 1948; OBE 1943; *b* 15 June 1897; *s* of late Henry Turton Norton; *m* 1924, Priscilla Anne Mary, *d* of late J. R. C. Deverell; one *s* two *d*. *Educ:* Eton College. Served European War, 1914-18, with BRCS (despatches, OStJ, Cav. Order of Crown of Italy, Italian Croce di Guerra). Started farming in E Africa, 1919. Joined Kenya Govt Service, 1938, as Sec. Standing Board of Economic Development; Chm. E African War Supplies Board, 1942; Dir Produce Disposal, 1943; Dep. Chm. EA Production and Supply Council, 1944; East African Comr in London, 1945-51; Regional Controller, East Africa, Colonial Development Corporation, 1951-59, retired. *Address:* 23 Ashley Gardens, SW1. *T:* 01-834 6731.

NORTON-GRIFFITHS, **Sir Peter**, 2nd Bt, *cr* 1922; Barrister-at-Law, Inner Temple, 1931; *b* 3 May 1905; *e s* of late Sir John Norton-Griffiths, 1st Bt, KCB, DSO; *S* father, 1930; *m* 1935, Kathryn, *e d* of late George F. Schrafft, Boston, Massachusetts, USA; two *s* one *d*. *Educ:* Eton; Magdalen Coll., Oxford. Asst to President, Shell Union Oil Corporation, NY, 1936-39; enlisted Intelligence Corps, 1940; Asst Military Attaché, British Embassy, Madrid (GSO2) 1941-42; Instructor School of Military Intelligence, GSO3, 1943-44; GSO3, Intelligence Staff, SHAEF, 1944-45. Asst to General Manager, Deutsche Shell AG, 1948-50; General Manager, Shell Co. of Portugal Ltd, 1950-53; Managing Director, Belgian Shell Co., SA, 1953-60; retired from business. Officier de l'Ordre de la Couronne (Belgium); Officier de l'Ordre de la Couronne de Chêne (Luxembourg). *Recreations:* music, sight-seeing. *Heir: s* John Norton-Griffiths [*b* 4 Oct. 1938; *m* 1964, Marilyn Margaret, *er d* of Norman Grimley]. *Address:* Quinta do Torneiro, Paço d'Arcos, Portugal. *Clubs:* Boodle's; Eça de Queiroz (Lisbon). *See also* Rt Hon. J. J. Thorpe.

NORWICH, **2nd Viscount**, *cr* 1952, of Aldwick; **John Julius Cooper;** writer and broadcaster; *b* 15 Sept. 1929; *s* of 1st Viscount Norwich, PC, GCMG, DSO, and of Lady Diana Cooper, *qv*, *d* of 8th Duke of Rutland; *S* father, 1954; *m* 1952, Anne (Frances May), *e d* of late Hon. Sir Bede Clifford, GCMG, CB, MVO; one *s* one *d*. *Educ:* Upper Canada Coll., Toronto, Canada; Eton; University of Strasbourg; New Coll., Oxford. Served 1947-49 as Writer, Royal Navy. Entered Foreign Office, 1952; Third Secretary, British Embassy, Belgrade, 1955-57; Second Secretary, British Embassy, Beirut, 1957-60; worked in Foreign Office (First Secretary from 1961) and in British Delegation to Disarmament Conference, Geneva, from 1960 until resignation from Foreign Service 1964. Chairman: Venice in Peril Fund; British Theatre Museum, 1966-71; Member: Exec. Cttee, National Trust, 1969-; Properties Cttee, 1970-. Makes historical documentary films for BBC TV. Chm., Serenissima Travel Ltd. *Publications:* Mount Athos (with Reresby Sitwell), 1966; The Normans in the South (as The Other Conquest, US), 1967; Sahara, 1968; The Kingdom in The Sun, 1970; Gen. Editor, Great Architecture of the World, 1975; A History of Venice, vol. I, The Rise to Empire, 1977. *Recreation:* sight-seeing. *Heir: s* Hon. Jason Charles Duff Bede Cooper, *b* 27 Oct. 1959. *Address:* 24 Blomfield Road, W9. *T:* 01-286 5050. *Club:* Beefsteak.

NORWICH, **Diana, Viscountess;** *see* Cooper, Lady Diana.

NORWICH, **Bishop of**, since 1971; Rt Rev. Maurice Arthur Ponsonby Wood, DSC 1944; MA; RNR; *b* 26 Aug. 1916; *o s* of late Arthur Sheppard Wood and of Jane Elspeth Dalzell Wood (*née* Piper); *m* 1st, 1947, Marjorie (*née* Pannell) (*d* 1954); two *s* one *d*; 2nd, 1955, M. Margaret (*née* Sandford); two *s* one *d*. *Educ:* Monkton Combe Sch.; Queens' Coll., Cambridge (MA); Ridley Hall, Cambridge. Curate, St Paul's, Portman Square, 1940-43. Royal Naval Chaplain, 1943-47 (still a Chap. to Commando Assoc.); attached RM Commandos, 1944-46; Chaplain, RNR, 1971. Rector, St Ebbe's, Oxford, 1947-52; Vicar and RD of Islington, and Pres. Islington Clerical Conf., 1952-61; Principal, Oak Hill Theological Coll., Southgate, N14, 1961-71; Prebendary of St Paul's Cathedral, 1969-71. Proctor in Convocation of Canterbury and Mem. House of Clergy and Gen. Synod of Church of England (formerly Church Assembly), 1954-; Member: various standing cttees on Liturgical Reform; Archbishops' Council on Evangelism. Chm., Theological Colls Principals' Conf., 1970-71. Governor: Monkton Combe Sch., Bath; Gresham's Sch., Holt. Abbot of St Benet's; Visitor, Langley Sch., Norfolk. *Publications:* Like a Mighty Army, 1956; Comfort in Sorrow, 1957; Your Suffering, 1959; Christian Stability, 1968; To Everyman's Door, 1968. *Recreations:* hockey, tennis, swimming, painting; supporting Norwich City FC. *Address:* The Bishop's House, Norwich NR3 1SB. *T:* Norwich 29001. *Club:* Royal Commonwealth Society.

NORWICH, **Archdeacon of;** *see* Dudley-Smith, Ven. T.

NORWOOD, **Suzanne Freda, (Mrs John Lexden Stewart); Her Honour Judge Norwood;** a Circuit Judge, since 1973; *b* 24 March 1926; *d* of Frederic Francis Norwood and Marianne Freda Norwood (*née* Thomas); *m* 1954, John Lexden Stewart (*d* 1972); one *s*. *Educ:* Lowther Coll., Bodelwyddan; St Andrews Univ. MA English, MA Hons History. Called to Bar, Gray's Inn, 1951; practised at Bar, SE Circuit. *Recreations:* walking, housekeeping, opera. *Address:* 69 Lee Road, SE3. *T:* 01-852 1954.

NORWOOD, **Sir Walter (Neville)**, Kt 1971; Chairman, New Zealand Motor Corporation; Chairman and Managing Director, C. B. Norwood Ltd; Director: General Finance Ltd; Otago Metal Industries Ltd; *b* 14 July 1907; *s* of late Sir Charles Norwood; *m* 1935, Rana Muriel, *d* of David Redpath; two *s* one *d*. *Educ:* Wellington and Wanganui. Trustee: Nuffield Trust for Crippled Children; Laura Fergusson Trust for Disabled Persons; Norwood Cricket Trust. Past Pres., Wellington Rotary Club; Pres., Wellington Racing Club. *Recreations:* racing, farming, sailing. *Address:* Hillcrest, 24 Mataroa Avenue, Wellington, New Zealand. *Clubs:* Wellesley, Wellington (Wellington, NZ).

NOSER, **Most Rev. Adolf;** *b* Belleville, Ill, 4 July 1900. *Educ:* Angelicum Univ., Rome. Ordained Priest, 1925. Seminary Professor, US, 1927-34; Seminary Rector, US, 1934-39; Superior of Accra, Ghana, 1939-47; Bishop of Accra, 1947; transferred to Alexishafen, 1953; Archbishop of Madang, 1966-76. Dr of Sacred Theology, 1927. *Publications:* pamphlets and magazine articles. *Address:* PO Alexishafen, via Madang, Papua New Guinea.

NOSSAL, **Sir Gustav (Joseph Victor)**, Kt 1977; CBE 1970; PhD; Director, Walter and Eliza Hall Institute of Medical Research, Melbourne, since 1965; Professor of Medical Biology, University of Melbourne, since 1965; *b* 4 June 1931; *m* 1955, Lyn B. Dunnicliff; two *s* two *d*. *Educ:* Sydney Univ. (MB, BS, BScMed); Melbourne Univ. (PhD 1960). Jun., then Sen. Resident Officer, Royal Prince Alfred Hosp., Sydney, 1955-56; Res. Fellow, Walter and Eliza Hall Inst. of Med. Res., 1957-59; Asst Prof., Dept of Genetics, Stanford Univ. Sch. of Medicine, Calif, 1959-61; Dep. Dir, Walter and Eliza Hall Inst. of Med. Res., 1961-65. Special Consultant, Tropical Disease Res. Prog., WHO, 1976. Emil von Behring Prize, Philipps Univ., Marburg, Germany, 1971; Rabbi Shai Shacknai Memorial Prize, Univ. of Jerusalem, 1973. *Publications:* Antibodies & Immunity, 1968 (rev. edn 1977); Antigens Lymphoid Cells & The Immune Response, 1971; Medical Science & Human Goals, 1975. *Recreations:* golf, literature. *Address:* 46 Fellows Street, Kew, Vic 3101, Australia. *T:* 86 8256. *Clubs:* Melbourne (Melbourne); Rosebud Country.

NOSWORTHY, **Harold George**, CMG 1965; *b* 15 March 1908; *m* 1941, Marjorie Anjelique; two *d*. *Educ:* Kingston Technical High Sch.; private tuition. Entered Jamaica Civil Service, 1929; 2nd class Clerk, 1938; Examiner of Accounts, 1943; Asst Commissioner, Income Tax, 1947; Asst Trade Administrator, 1950; Trade Administrator and Chairman Trade Control Board, 1953; Principal Asst Secretary, Ministry of Finance, 1955; Auditor-General, 1957-66; Dir, Internal Audit Service, UN, 1966-68. Queen's Coronation Medal, 1953; Jamaica Independence Medal, 1962. *Recreations:* reading, billiards, bridge, swimming. *Address:* 18 Hyperion Avenue, PO Box 127, Kingston 6, Jamaica. *T:* 937-9889. *Club:* Kingston Cricket (Jamaica).

NOTT, **Charles Robert Harley**, CMG 1959; OBE 1952; retired, New Zealand; *b* 24 Oct. 1904; *e s* of late John Harley Nott, JP, Leominster, Herefordshire and late Mrs Nott, formerly of Bodenham Hall, Herefordshire; *m* 1935, Marion (*née* Macfarlane), Auckland, NZ; one *s* one *d*. *Educ:* Marlborough; Christ's Coll., Cambridge (MA). Colonial Administrative Service: Fiji, 1926; Administrative Officer (Grade II), 1938, (Grade I), 1945. Member of the Legislative Council, Fiji, 1950; HBM's Agent and Consul, Tonga, 1954-57; Sec. for Fijian Affairs, 1957-59; MLC, MEC, retired, 1960. *Recreation:* fishing. *Address:* Matakana, Havelock North, New Zealand.

NOTT, **John William Frederic;** farmer and businessman; MP (C) St Ives Division of Cornwall since 1966; *b* 1 Feb. 1932; *s* of Richard William Kandahar Nott, Bideford, Devon, and Phyllis (*née* Francis); *m* 1959, Miloska Sekol, Maribor, Yugoslavia; two *s* one *d*. *Educ:* King's Mead, Seaford; Bradfield Coll.; Trinity Coll., Cambridge. Lieut, 2nd Gurkha Rifles (regular officer), Malayan emergency, 1952-56; Trinity Coll., Cambridge, 1957-59 (BA Hons Law and Econs); Pres., Cambridge Union, 1959; called to the Bar, Inner Temple, 1959; Gen. Manager, S. G.

Warburg & Co. Ltd, Merchant Bankers, 1960-66; Chairman: Imperial Eastman (UK) Ltd; Andrew Hydraulics International Ltd, 1976-; Dir, Clarkson International Tools Ltd, and other cos. Sec., Cons. Parly Finance Cttee, 1969-70; Minister of State, HM Treasury, 1972-74; Cons. front bench spokesman on: Treasury and Economic Affairs, 1975-76; Trade, 1976-. *Address:* House of Commons, SW1. *T:* 01-219 4157.

NOTT, Very Rev. Michael John, BD; FKC; Provost of Portsmouth since 1972; *b* 9 Nov. 1916; *s* of Frank and Ann Nott; *m* 1942, Elisabeth Margaret Edwards; one *s* one *d*. *Educ:* St Paul's; King's Coll., London, FKC 1972; Lincoln Theological Coll. Curate of: Abington, Northampton, 1939-45; St Mary, Reading, 1945-46; Vicar of St Andrew, Kettering, 1946-54; Rural Dean of Kettering, 1952-54; Warden and Chaplain, Heritage Craft Sch. and Hospital, Chailey; Vicar of Seaford, 1957-64; Rural Dean of Seaford, 1961-64; Senior Chaplain to Archbishop of Canterbury, 1964-65; Archdeacon of Maidstone, 1965-67; Archdeacon of Canterbury, 1967-72; Canon Residentiary of Canterbury Cathedral, 1965-72. *Recreations:* reading, walking, travel. *Address:* Provost's House, Portsmouth, Hants. *T:* Portsmouth 24400. *Club:* Royal Naval (Portsmouth).

NOTT, Rt. Rev. Peter John; *see* Taunton, Bishop Suffragan of.

NOTTAGE, Raymond Frederick Tritton, CMG 1964; Director-General, Royal Institute of Public Administration, since 1949; *b* 1 Aug. 1916; *s* of Frederick and Frances Nottage; *m* 1941, Joyce Evelyn, *d* of Sidney and Edith Philpot; three *d*. *Educ:* Hackney Downs Secondary Sch. Civil servant, Post Office Headquarters, 1936-49; Editor of Civil Service Opinion, and Member Exec. Cttee, Soc. of Civil Servants, 1944-49; Mem. Hornsey Borough Council, 1945-47; Mem. Cttee on Training in Public Admin. for Overseas Countries, 1961-63; Vice-Pres. Internat. Inst. of Admin. Sciences, 1962-68; Mem. Governing Body, Inst. of Development Studies, Univ. of Sussex, 1966-76; travelled abroad as Consultant and Lectr. Treasurer, Arkwright Arts Trust, Hampstead. *Publications:* Sources of Local Revenue (with S. H. H. Hildersley), 1968; Financing Public Sector Pensions, 1975; articles in Public Administration and similar jls. *Recreations:* enjoying music, taking exercise. *Address:* 36e Arkwright Road, NW3. *T:* 01-794 7129. *Club:* Reform.

NOTTINGHAM, Bishop of, (RC), since 1974; **Rt. Rev. James Joseph McGuinness;** *b* 2 Oct. 1925; *s* of Michael and Margaret McGuinness. *Educ:* St Columb's College, Derry; St Patrick's College, Carlow; Oscott College, Birmingham. Ordained, 1950; Curate of St Mary's, Derby, 1950-53; Secretary to Bishop Ellis, 1953-56; Parish Priest, Corpus Christi Parish, Clifton, Nottingham, 1956-72; Vicar General of Nottingham Diocese, 1969; Coadjutor Bishop of Nottingham and Titular Bishop of St Germans, 1972-74. *Recreations:* gardening, golf. *Address:* Bishop's House, 27 Cavendish Road East, The Park, Nottingham NG7 1BB.

NOURSE, Martin Charles, QC 1970; Attorney General of the Duchy of Lancaster, since 1976; a Judge of the Court of Appeal of Jersey and Guernsey, since 1977; *b* 3 April 1932; *yr s* of Henry Edward Nourse, MD, MRCP, Cambridge, and late Ethel Millicent, *d* of Rt Hon. Sir Charles Henry Sargant, Lord Justice of Appeal; *m* 1972, Lavinia, *yr d* of Comdr D. W. Malim, RN(retd), Welwyn, Herts; one *s* one *d*. *Educ:* Winchester; Corpus Christi Coll., Cambridge. National Service as 2nd Lieut, Rifle Bde, 1951-52; Lieut, London Rifle Bde Rangers (TA), 1952-55. Called to Bar, Lincoln's Inn, 1956; Mem., General Council of the Bar, 1964-68; a Junior Counsel to BoT in Chancery matters, 1967-70. *Address:* North End House, Grantchester, Cambridge; 1 Stone Buildings, Lincoln's Inn, WC2; 2 New Square, Lincoln's Inn, WC2. *Clubs:* Brooks's; Cambridge County (Cambridge).
See also Sir Edmund Sargant.

NOVA SCOTIA, Bishop of, since 1975; **Rt. Rev. George Feversham Arnold,** DD; *b* 30 Dec. 1914; *s* of Arnold Feversham and Elsie Mildred Arnold; *m* 1940, Mary Eleanor Sherman Holmes; one *s* one *d*. *Educ:* Univ. of King's Coll., Halifax, NS (LTh 1937, BD 1944); Dalhousie Univ. (BA 1935, MA 1938). Rector: Louisbourg, 1938-41; Mahone Bay, 1941-50; St John's, Fairview, 1950-53; Windsor, 1953-58; Clerical Sec. and Diocesan Registrar, 1958-67; Exam. Chaplain to Bishop of Nova Scotia, 1947-70; Hon. Canon of All Saints Cathedral, 1959-63, Canon, 1963-67; Bishop Suffragan of Nova Scotia, 1967-75, Bishop Coadjutor, May-Sept. 1975. Hon. DD, King's Coll., Halifax, 1968. *Recreation:* yachting. *Address:* 5732 College Street, Halifax, NS B3H 1X3, Canada. *T:* 423-8301.

NOVE, Prof. Alexander; Professor of Economics and Director of Institute of Soviet and East European Studies, University of Glasgow, since 1963; *b* Leningrad, 24 Nov. 1915; *s* of Jacob Novakovsky; *m* 1951, Irene MacPherson; three *s*. *Educ:* King Alfred Sch., London; London Sch. of Economics. BSc (Econ) 1936. Army, 1939-46. Civil Service (mainly BoT), 1947-58; Reader in Russian Social and Economic Studies, Univ. of London, 1958-63. Hon. Dr.agr Giessen, 1977. *Publications:* The Soviet Economy, 1961 (3rd edn 1969); (with J. A. Newth) The Soviet Middle East, 1965; Was Stalin Really Necessary?, 1965; Economic History of the USSR, 1969; (ed, with D. M. Nuti) Socialist Economics, 1972; Efficiency Criteria for Nationalised Industries, 1973; Stalinism and After, 1976; The Soviet Economic System, 1977. *Recreations:* walking in Scottish hills, travel, music, theatre, exotic dishes. *Address:* 55 Hamilton Drive, Glasgow G12 8DP. *T:* 041-339 1053. *Club:* Royal Commonwealth Society.

NOWAR, Maj.-Gen. Ma'an Abu, Jordanian Star 1st Class; Mayor of Amman; *b* 26 July 1928; *m* Vivian Ann Richards; two *s* seven *d*; *m* 1976, Susan Ann Coombs, Bath, Som. *Educ:* London Univ. (Dip. World Affairs, 1963). Joined Jordanian Armed Forces, 1943; comd Regt, 1956; comd Bde, 1957; Counsellor, Jordan Embassy, London, 1963; Dir of Civil Defence, 1964; Dir of Public Security, 1967; Asst Chief of Staff, Jordan Armed Forces, 1969; Minister of Culture and Information, 1972-73; Ambassador of Jordan to the Court of St James's, 1973-76. *Publications:* The Battle of Karameh, 1968; For Jerusalem, 1969; 40 Armoured Brigade, 1970; The State in War and Peace, 1971; History of the Jordan Army, 1972. *Recreation:* swimming. *Address:* Mayor's Office, Amman, Jordan.

NOWELL-SMITH, Prof. Patrick Horace, AM (Harvard); MA (Oxon); Professor of Philosophy, York University, Toronto, since 1969; *b* 17 Aug. 1914; *s* of Nowell Charles Smith; *m* 1st, 1946, Perilla Thyme (marr. diss. 1968), *d* of Sir Richard Vynne Southwell; three *s* one *d*; 2nd, 1968, Felicity Margret, *d* of Dr Richard Leonard Ward; two *d*. *Educ:* Winchester Coll.; New College, Oxford. Commonwealth Fellow, Harvard Univ., 1937-39. Served War of 1939-45, in Army, 1939-45. Fellow and Lecturer, Trinity Coll., Oxford, 1946-57, Estates Bursar, 1951-57. Professor of Philosophy: University of Leicester, 1957-64; University of Kent, 1964-69. *Publications:* Ethics, 1954; articles in Mind, Proc. Aristotelian Soc., Theoria, etc. *Address:* Department of Philosophy, York University, Downsview, Ont, Canada.
See also S. H. Nowell-Smith.

NOWELL-SMITH, Simon Harcourt, FSA; *b* 5 Jan. 1909; *s* of late Nowell Charles Smith, sometime Headmaster of Sherborne; *m* 1938, Marion Sinclair (*d* 1977), *d* of late W. S. Crichton, Liverpool; two *s* one *d*. *Educ:* Sherborne; New Coll., Oxford (MA). Editorial Staff of The Times, 1932-44; Assistant Editor, Times Literary Supplement, 1937-39; attached to Intelligence Division, Naval Staff, 1940-45; Secretary and Librarian, The London Library, 1950-56; Secretary, Hospital Library Services Survey, 1958-59; President, Bibliographical Society, 1962-64; Lyell Reader in Bibliography, Oxford Univ., 1965-66. Pres., Oxford Bibliographical Soc., 1972-76. Trustee, Dove Cottage Trust, 1974-. OStJ. *Publications:* Mark Rutherford, a bibliography, 1930; The Legend of the Master (Henry James), 1947; The House of Cassell, 1958; (ed) Edwardian England, 1964; Letters to Macmillan, 1967; International Copyright Law and the Publisher, 1968; Postscript to Autobiography of William Plomer, 1975. *Address:* Quarry Manor, Headington, Oxford OX3 8JN.
See also Prof. P. H. Nowell-Smith.

NSEKELA, Amon James; High Commissioner for Tanzania in London, since 1974; *b* 4 Jan. 1930; *s* of Ngonile Reuben Nsekela and Anyambilile (*née* Kalinga); *m* 1957, Christina Matilda Nsekela; two *s*. *Educ:* Rungwe Dist Sch.; Malangali Secondary Sch.; Tabora Govt Sen. Sec. Sch.; Makere UC (DipEd); Univ. of Pacific (Scholar, MA). Entered Civil Service as DO, Moshi, 1960; Perm. Sec., Min. of External Affairs and Defence, 1963; Perm. Sec. to Min. of Commerce, 1964; Prin. Sec. to Treasury, 1966-67. MP 1973-75, and Mem. E African Legis. Assembly, 1967-70. Chm. or Dir of many cos and corporations, 1967-, incl.: Chm. and Man. Dir, Nat. Bank of Commerce, 1967-74; Chm., Nat. Ins. Corp. of Tanzania, 1967-72; Director: Nat. Develt Corp. (past Chm. when Tanganyika Develt Corp.); Bd of Internal Trade; E African Airways Corp. Mem./Sec., Presidential Commn on Estabt of Democratic One-Party State in Tanzania. Chm. Council, Inst. of Finance Management, 1971-; Chm. Council, UC, Dar es Salaam; Past Pres., Economic Soc. of Tanzania. *Publications:* Minara ya Historia ya Tanganyika: Tanganyika hadi Tanzania, 1965, new edns 1966 and 1971; Demokrasi Tanzania, 1973; (with A. L. Nhonoli) The Development of Health Services in Mainland Tanzania:

Tumetoka Mbali, 1973; Socialism and Social Accountability in a Developing Nation, 1977. *Recreations:* squash, table tennis, swimming. *Address:* Tanzania High Commission, 43 Hertford Street, W1. *Club:* Simba Sports (Tanzania).

NTIWANE, Nkomeni Douglas; Permanent Secretary, Ministry of Commerce and Co-operatives, Swaziland, since 1977; *b* 16 Feb. 1933; *s* of Isaiah Myotha and Jane Dlamini; *m* 1960, Sophia Pulane Kali; three *s*. *Educ:* DOT Coll., Middelburg, Transvaal, SA; Columbia Univ. (1967-68; Carnegie Fellow in Dipl.). Teacher, East Transvaal, 1955-61; Headmaster (Swaziland): Mponono Sch., 1961-62; Mbekelweni Sch., 1962-63; Mhlume Central Sch., 1964-66; Lozitha Central Sch., Jan.-Sept. 1967. High Commissioner in London, 1968-71; Ambassador: Federal Republic of Germany, March 1969; Republic of France, April 1969. Permanent Secretary: Dept of Foreign Affairs, Swaziland, 1971-72; Ministry of Health, 1972-77. *Publication:* Vakala Ngwane (siSwati poetry). *Address:* PO Box 526, Mbabane, Swaziland.

NUGEE, Edward George, TD 1964; QC 1977; *b* 9 Aug. 1928; *o s* of late Brig. George Travers Nugee, CBE, DSO, MC, RA, and of Violet Mary (*née* Richards, now Brooks); *m* 1955, Rachel Elizabeth (JP, MA Oxon, Central Pres. Mothers' Union 1977-), *e d* of John Moritz Makower, MBE, MC, and Adelaide Gertrude Leonaura, *d* of Sir Leonard Franklin, OBE, MP; four *s*. *Educ:* Brambletye; Radley Coll. (Open Scholar); Worcester Coll., Oxford (Open Exhibnr; Law Mods, Distinction, 1950; 1st Cl. Hons Jurisprudence, 1952; Eldon Law Scholar, 1953; MA 1956). National Service, RA, 1947-49 (Office of COS, GHQ, FARELF); service with 100 Army Photographic Interpretation Unit, TA, 1950-64 (retd Captain, Intell. Corps, 1964). Read as pupil with Mr Justice Templeman and Mr Justice Brightman; called to the Bar, Inner Temple, 1955, Bencher 1976; *ad eundem* Lincoln's Inn, 1968. Jun. Counsel to Land Commn (Chancery and Conveyancing), 1967-71; Counsel for litigation under Commons Registration Act, 1965, 1968-77; Conveyancing Counsel to Treasury, WO, MAFF, Forestry Commn, MoD (Admiralty), and DoE, 1972-77; Conveyancing Counsel of Court, 1976-77. Poor Man's Lawyer, Lewisham CAB, 1954-72. Member: CAB Adv. Cttee, Family Welfare Assoc., 1969-72; Management Cttee, Greater London Citizens Advice Bureaux Service Ltd, 1972-74; Man. Cttee, Forest Hill Advice Centre, 1972-76; Bar Council, 1962-66 (Mem., External Relations Cttee, 1966-71); Council of Legal Educn, 1967- (Vice-Chm. 1976-, and Chm. of Bd of Studies, 1976-); Adv. Cttee on Legal Educn, 1971-; Common Professional Exam. Bd, 1976-; Lord Chancellor's Law Reform Cttee, 1973-; various working parties and consultative groups of Law Commn, 1966-; Inst. of Conveyancers, 1971-. Chm. Governors, Brambletye Sch., 1972-77; Mem. Council, Radley Coll., 1975-. *Publications:* (jtly) Nathan on the Charities Act 1960, 1962; (ed jtly) titles Landlord and Tenant, Real Property in Halsbury's Laws of England, 3rd edn 1958-60; contribs to legal jls. *Address:* 3 New Square, Lincoln's Inn, WC2A 3RS. *T:* 01-405 5296; 10 Heath Hurst Road, Hampstead, NW3 2RX. *T:* 01-435 9204.

NUGENT, family name of **Earl of Westmeath** and **Baron Nugent of Guildford.**

NUGENT OF GUILDFORD, Baron, *cr* 1966 (Life Peer), of Dunsfold; **George Richard Hodges Nugent;** Bt 1960; PC 1962; Chairman, National Water Council, since 1973; *b* 6 June 1907; *s* of late Colonel George H. Nugent, RA; *m* 1937, Ruth, *d* of late Hugh G. Stafford, Tilford, Surrey. *Educ:* Imperial Service Coll., Windsor; RMA, Woolwich. Commissioned RA, 1926-29. MP (C) Guildford Division of Surrey, 1950-66. Parliamentary Secretary: Ministry of Agriculture, Fisheries and Food, 1951-57; Min. of Transport, 1957-Oct. 1959. A Dep. Speaker, House of Lords. JP Surrey; CC and sometime Alderman, Surrey, 1944-51. Chairman: Thames Conservancy Board, 1960-74; House of Commons Select Cttee for Nationalised Industries, 1961-64; Agricultural Market Development Cttee, 1962-68; Animal Virus Research Institute, 1964-77; Standing Conf. on London and SE Regional Planning, 1962-; President, Assoc. of River Authorities, 1965-74. Mem., Guildford Diocesan Synod, 1970-. FRSA 1962. Hon. FIPHE. DUniv Surrey, 1968. *Address:* Blacknest Cottage, Dunsfold, Surrey. *Clubs:* Junior Carlton, Royal Automobile (Vice-Pres., 1974).

NUGENT of Clonlost, David James Douglas (7th Baron Nugent, Austrian title *cr* 1859, confirmed by Royal Warrant of Edward VII, 1908; HSH Prince Nugent, Austrian Empire, *cr* 1816); *b* 24 Nov. 1917; 2nd *s* of Albert Beauchamp Cecil Nugent (5th Baron) and Frances Every Douglas, niece of 3rd Lord Blythswood, KCB, CVO; *S* brother, 1944; *m* 1968, Mary Louise (*d* 1975), *er d* of William Henry Wroth, Bigbury Court, Devon. *Educ:* Lancing Coll. *Recreations:* gardening, historical research.

Address: Longbridge Deverill House, Wiltshire; 4 Gloucester Place Mews, Portman Square, W1.

NUGENT, Sir Hugh Charles, 6th Bt, *cr* 1795; Count of the Holy Roman Empire; *b* 26 May 1904; *s* of late Charles Hugh Nugent, *o s* of 5th Bt and Anna Maria (she *m* 2nd, Edwin John King, Danemore Park, Speldhurst, Kent), *d* of Edwin Adams; *S* grandfather, 1927; *m* 1931, Margaret Mary Lavallin, *er d* of late Rev. H. L. Puxley, The White House, Chaddleworth, Newbury, Berks; two *s*. *Educ:* Stonyhurst Coll. Knight of Malta. *Heir: s* John Edwin Lavallin Nugent [*b* 16 March 1933; *m* 1959, Penelope Ann, *d* of late Brig. R. N. Hanbury, of Braughing, Hertfordshire; one *s* one *d*]. *Address:* Ballinlough Castle, Clonmellon, Co. Westmeath, Ireland. *T:* Trim 33135.

NUGENT, Sir Peter Walter James, 5th Bt, *cr* 1831; *b* 26 Jan. 1920; *s* of Sir Walter Richard Nugent, 4th Bt and of Aileen Gladys, *y d* of late Middleton Moore O'Malley, JP, Ross, Westport, Co. Mayo; *S* father, 1955; *m* 1947, Anne Judith, *o d* of Major Robert Smyth, Gaybrook, Mullingar, Co. Westmeath; two *s* two *d*. *Educ:* Downside. Served War of 1939-45; 2nd Lieut, Hampshire Regt, 1941; Major, 1945. *Heir: s* Walter Richard Middleton Nugent, *b* 15 Nov. 1947. *Address:* Bay Bush, Straffan, Co. Kildare, Eire.

NUGENT, Sir Robin (George Colborne), 5th Bt *cr* 1806; *b* 11 July 1925; *s* of Sir Guy Nugent, 4th Bt and of Maisie, Lady Nugent, *d* of J. A. Bigsby; *S* father, 1970; *m* 1st, 1947, Ursula Mary (marr. diss. 1967), *d* of late Lt-Gen. Sir Herbert Fothergill Cooke, KCB, KBE, CSI, DSO; two *s* one *d*; 2nd, 1967, Victoria Anna Irmgard, *d* of late Dr Peter Cartellieri. *Educ:* Eton; RWA School of Architecture. Lt Grenadier Guards, 1943-48; served Italy, 1944-45. ARIBA 1959. *Recreations:* golf, skiing, travel. *Heir: s* Christopher George Ridley Nugent, *b* 5 Oct. 1949. *Address:* Bannerdown House, Batheaston, Bath, Avon. *T:* Bath 858481. *Club:* Cavalry and Guards.

NUNBURNHOLME, 4th Baron *cr* 1906; **Ben Charles Wilson;** Major, Royal Horse Guards, retired; *b* 16 Jan. 1928; *s* of 3rd Baron Nunburnholme, and Lady Mary Thynne, *y d* of 5th Marquess of Bath, KG, PC, CB; *S* father, 1974; *m* 1958, Ines Dolores Jeanne, *d* of Gerard Walravens, Brussels; four *d* (including twin *d*). *Educ:* Eton. *Heir: b* Hon. Charles Thomas Wilson [*b* 27 May 1935; *m* 1969, Linda Kay, *d* of Cyril James Stephens; one *d*]. *Address:* Shillinglee Park, Chiddingfold, Surrey.

NUNN, Janet; *see* Suzman, J.

NUNN, Jean Josephine, CB 1971; CBE 1966; Deputy Secretary, Cabinet Office, 1966-70; *b* 21 July 1916; *d* of late Major John Henry Nunn, RHA, and Mrs Doris Josephine Nunn (*née* Gregory); unmarried. *Educ:* The Royal School for Daughters of Officers of the Army, Bath; Girton Coll., Cambridge, Hon. Fellow 1971. Entered Home Office, 1938; Secretary, Royal Commission on the Press, 1947-49; Private Secretary to the Secretary of State, 1949-51; Assistant Secretary, 1952; Assistant Under-Secretary of State, 1961-63; Under-Secretary, Cabinet Office, 1963-66. *Recreations:* gardening, bird-watching, reading. *Address:* Garden Cottage, School Lane, Washington, Pulborough, West Sussex. *T:* Ashington 892280. *Club:* Royal Commonwealth Society.

NUNN, John Francis, PhD; MD; FFARCS; Head of Division of Anaesthesia, Medical Research Council Clinical Research Centre, since 1968; *b* 7 Nov. 1925; *s* of Francis Nunn, Colwyn Bay; *m* 1949, Sheila, *d* of late E. C. Doubleday; one *s* two *d*. *Educ:* Wrekin Coll.; Birmingham Univ. MO, Birmingham Univ. Spitzbergen Expedition, 1948; Colonial Med. Service, Malaya, 1949-53; University Research Fellow, Birmingham, 1955-56; Leverhulme Research Fellow, RCS, 1957-64; Part-time Lectr, Postgrad. Med. Sch., Univ. of London, 1959-64; Consultant Anæsth., Hammersmith Hosp., 1959-64; Prof. of Anaesthesia, Univ. of Leeds, 1964-68. Member: Board, Faculty of Anaesthetists, RCS (Vice-Dean, 1977-79); Council, Assoc. of Anaesthetists, 1973-76; Hunterian Professor, RCS, 1960; Visiting Professor to various American Universities, 1960-; British Council Lecturer: Switzerland, 1962; USSR, 1963; Czechoslovakia, 1969; China, 1974. Joseph Clover Lectr, RCS, 1968. Mem., Egypt Exploration Soc. *Publications:* Applied Respiratory Physiology, 1969, 2nd edn 1977; Jt Editor, General Anaesthesia, 3rd edn, 1971; several chapters in medical text-books, and publications in Journal appl. Physiol., Lancet, Nature, British Journal Anæsth., etc. *Recreations:* archaeology and ski-ing. *Address:* MRC Clinical Research Centre, Northwick Park, Harrow, Middx; 3 Russell Road, Moor Park, Northwood, Mddx. *T:* Northwood 26363.

NUNN, Trevor Robert; Artistic Director, Royal Shakespeare Company, since 1968; *b* 14 Jan. 1940; *s* of Robert Alexander Nunn and Dorothy May (*née* Piper); *m* 1969, Janet Suzman, *qv*. *Educ:* Northgate Grammar Sch., Ipswich; Downing Coll., Cambridge (BA). Producer, Belgrade Theatre, Coventry; subseq. Associate Dir, Royal Shakespeare Company. *Address:* c/o Aldwych Theatre, WC2.

NUNNELEY, John Hewlett, FCIT; Managing Director, British Transport Advertising Ltd, since 1969; Director, British Posters Ltd; *b* 26 Nov. 1922; *o s* of Lt-Col Wilfrid Alexander Nunneley, Sydney, NSW, Aust., and Audrey Mary Nunneley (*née* Tebbitt); *m* 1945, Lucia, *e d* of Enrico Ceruti, Milan, Italy; one *s* one *d*. *Educ:* Lawrence Sheriff Sch., Rugby. Served War of 1939-45: Somerset LI, seconded KAR; Abyssinia, Brit. Somaliland, 1942; Burma campaign, 1944 (wounded, despatches); Captain and Adjt. Various management posts in aircraft, shipping, printing and publishing industries, 1946-55. Exec., Beaverbrook Newspapers, 1955-62; joined BTC, 1962: Chief Publicity Officer, 1962-63; Chief Development Officer (Passenger) BR Bd, 1963-64; Chief Passenger Manager, 1964-69; Pres. and Chm., BR-Internat. Inc., New York, USA, 1966-69; Member: Paddington Borough Council, 1951-53; Passenger Co-ordination Cttee for London, 1964-69; Outdoor Advertising Council, 1969-. Internat. Four Day Marches, Nijmegen, five times, (Medal). FRSA. *Publications:* numerous articles on transport and advertising subjects. *Recreations:* walking, gliding. *Address:* 6 Ashfield Close, Petersham, Surrey.

NUNNS, Hector Matthew, MBE 1976; Member, West Yorkshire Metropolitan County Council, since 1973 (first Chairman of Council, 1973-75); *b* 9 Nov. 1905; *s* of George Thomas Nunns and Susan Ethel (*née* Ellis); *m* 1930, Gladys, (*née* Whimpenny); two *d*. *Educ:* Thornhill Sch., Dewsbury. Mem. Dewsbury Co. Borough Council, 1945-74; Mem., Nat. Exec., Union of Shop, Distributive and Allied Workers, 1959-71. Hon. Freeman of Dewsbury, 1972. JP Dewsbury, 1949-76 (Chm., Dewsbury Bench, 1972-76). *Address:* Ash Grove, Overthorpe Road, Dewsbury, W Yorkshire. *T:* Dewsbury 463192. *Clubs:* Thornhill Edge Working Men's; Dewsbury Textile.

NUREYEV, Rudolph Hametovich; ballet dancer and choreographer; *b* Ufa, E Siberia, 1939, of a farming family. Joined Kirov Ballet School and at age 17 appeared with the Company in 1959; when on tour, in Paris, sought political asylum, May 1961. Joined Le Grand Ballet du Marquis de Cuevas Company and has made frequent appearances abroad; London debut at Royal Academy of Dancing Gala Matinée, organised by Dame Margot Fonteyn, Dec. 1961; debut at Covent Garden in Giselle with Margot Fonteyn, Feb. 1962; Choreographic productions include: La Bayadère, Raymonda, Swan Lake, Tancredi, Sleeping Beauty, Nutcracker, Don Quixote, Romeo and Juliet; guest artist in England and America in wide variety of rôles. Has danced in many countries of the world. Gold Star, Paris, 1963. *Films:* Romeo and Juliet, 1965; I am a Dancer, 1972; Don Quixote, 1974; Valentino, 1977. *Publication:* Nureyev, 1962. *Recreations:* listening to and playing music. *Address:* c/o S. A. Gorlinsky Ltd, 35 Dover Street, W1X 4NJ.

NURJADIN, Air Chief Marshal Roesmin; Indonesian Ambassador to the United States of America, since 1974; *b* 31 May 1930; *m* 1962, Surjati Subali; two *s* one *d*. *Educ:* Indonesian Air Force Academy; Techn. Coll., Univ. Gadjahmada. Student Army, 1945-50. Comdr 3rd Fighter Sqdn, 1953; RAF CFS, England, 1954; Law Sch., 1956; Instructor, Jet Sqdn, 1957-59; Junior Staff Sch., 1959; Defence Services Staff Coll., Wellington, India, 1960-61; Dir Operation AF HQ, 1961-62; Dep. Comdr Operational Comd, Chief of Staff Air Defence Comd, 1962-64; Air Attaché: Bangkok, 1964-65; Moscow, 1965-66; Minister/C-in-C/Chief of Staff, Indonesian Air Force, 1966-70; Ambassador to the UK, 1970-74. 2nd Lieut 1952; 1st Lieut 1953; Captain 1956; Major 1959; Lt-Col 1961; Col 1962; Cdre 1965; Air Vice-Marshal 1966; Air Marshal 1966; Air Chief Marshal 1967. *Recreations:* golf, swimming. *Address:* Indonesian Embassy, 2020 Massachusetts Avenue, Washington, DC 20036, USA. *Clubs:* Highgate Golf; Djakarta Golf.

NURSAW, William George; investment consultant since 1961; financial writer and company director; *b* 5 Sept. 1903; *s* of George Edward Nursaw and Amy Elizabeth (*née* Davis); *m* 1931, Lilian May (*née* Howell); one *s* two *d*. *Educ:* Rushmore Road LCC Primary Sch.; Holloway Grammar Sch. (Schol.). Insurance, 1920-61: Trustee Man., Atlas Assce Co.; subseq. Dir Throgmorton Management (Man. Dir, 1962-71) and Hogg Robinson Gardner Mountain Pensions Management (Chm., 1963-71); Hon. Financial Adviser, RAF Escapers Soc, 1965-, and National Birthday Trust, 1950- (and Hon. Treas.); Co-

founder and Dep. Chm., Covenanters Educational Trust and Perry Foundn, 1947-; Freeman, City of London; Liveryman, Loriners' Co.; Deacon, Chingford Congregational Church, 1944-62; Youth Leader, 1942-67; Chm., Waltham Forest Playing Fields Assoc.; Exec., Greater London Playing Fields. Civil Defence (Post Warden), 1938-65. FSS; FInstD; ACII; FCIS (Mem. Council, 1962-70, Chm., London, 1968-69); Fellow, Inst. of Arbitrators (Mem. Council, 1968-74); Mem. Soc. of Investment Analysts. *Publications:* Investment in Trust: problems and policies, 1961; Art and Practice of Investment, 1962, 4th edn 1974; Purposeful Investment, 1965; Principles of Pension Fund Investment, 1966, 2nd edn 1976; Investment for All, 1972; articles for national press on investment and insurance, incl. over 200 articles for The Guardian, Observer, etc. *Recreations:* rose-growing, cricket, writing, portrait painting, playing-fields movement, 1934- (Duke of Edinburgh award). *Address:* 603 Mountjoy House, Barbican, EC2Y 8BP. *T:* 01-628 7638; 6 Carlton Road East, Westgate, Kent. *T:* Thanet 32105. *Clubs:* City Livery, Royal Over-Seas League, MCC, Pen International.

NURSE, Ven. Charles Euston, MA; Archdeacon of Carlisle, 1958-70, now Archdeacon Emeritus; Canon Residentiary of Carlisle Cathedral, 1958-73; *b* 12 June 1909; *s* of Rev. Canon Euston John Nurse, MA, and Mrs Edith Jane Robins Nurse, Windermere Rectory. *Educ:* Windermere Grammar Sch.; Gonville and Caius Coll., Cambridge. Assistant Curate, Holy Trinity, Carlisle, 1932; Vicar of St Nicholas, Whitehaven, 1937; Vicar of St George, Barrow-in-Furness, 1948; Rural Dean of Dalton, 1949; Hon. Canon of Carlisle Cathedral, 1950-58. Examining Chaplain to the Bishop of Carlisle, 1959-. *Recreations:* fell-walking, fishing, entomology. *Address:* 76 Croft Road, Stanwix, Carlisle, Cumbria. *T:* Carlisle 24991.

NURSTEN, Prof. Harry Erwin, PhD, DSc; FRIC, FIFST; Professor and Head of Department of Food Science, Reading University, since 1976; *s* of Sergius Nursten and Helene Nursten; *m* 1950, Jean Patricia Frobisher. *Educ:* Ilkley Grammar Sch.; Leeds Univ. (BSc 1st Cl. Hons Colour Chemistry, 1947; PhD 1949; DSc 1973). FRIC 1957; FIFST 1972. Bradford Dyers Assoc. Res. Fellow, Dept of Colour Chem. and Dyeing, Leeds Univ., 1949-52; Lectr in Textile Chem. and Dyeing, Nottingham and Dist Tech. Coll., 1952-54; Lectr 1955-65, Sen. Lectr 1965-70, and Reader 1970-76, Procter Dept of Food and Leather Science, Leeds Univ. Res. Associate, Dept of Nutrition, Food Science and Technol., MIT, 1961-62; Vis. Prof., Dept of Food Science and Technol., Univ. of Calif, Davis, 1966. Pres., Soc. of Leather Technologists and Chemists, 1974-76. Bill Littlejohn Memorial Medallion Lectr, Brit. Soc. of Flavourists, 1974. *Publications:* papers in Jl Sci. Food Agric., Jl Soc. Leather Technol. Chem., and Jl Chem. Soc. *Address:* Department of Food Science, University of Reading, London Road, Reading, Berks RG1 5AQ. *T:* Reading 85234.

NUTMAN, Dr Phillip Sadler, FRS 1968; Head of Department of Soil Microbiology, Rothamsted Experimental Station, Harpenden, since 1957; *b* 10 Oct. 1914; *s* of John William Nutman and Elizabeth Hester Nutman (*née* Hughes); *m* 1940, Mary Meta Stanbury; two *s* one *d*. *Educ:* Teignmouth Grammar Sch.; Imperial Coll., London Univ. Research Asst, Rothamsted Experimental Station, 1940; Senior Research Fellow, Canberra, Australia, 1953-56; Rothamsted, 1956-. Huxley Medal, 1959. *Publications:* research papers in plant physiological, genetical and microbiological journals. *Recreations:* music, woodworking. *Address:* 2 Lyndhurst Drive, Harpenden, Herts. *T:* Harpenden 4249.

NUTT, Albert Boswell, FRCS; Ophthalmic Surgeon, United Sheffield Hospitals, 1948-63; *b* 7 July 1898; *s* of late Ernest Smith Nutt; *m* 1926, Olive Margaret Robson; two *s* one *d*. *Educ:* King Edward VII Sch., Sheffield; University of Sheffield; University of London. MSc Sheffield, 1922; MB, ChB Sheffield (Clinical Gold Medal in Medicine and Surgery), 1923; MB, BS London, 1923; FRCS 1949. Formerly Ophthalmic Registrar, House Surgeon and Senior Ophthalmic House Surgeon, Sheffield Royal Infirmary; Hon. Ophthalmic Surgeon, 1927-48; Hon. Ophthalmic Surgeon to Children's Hospital, Sheffield, 1938-48, Opth. Surgeon, 1948-63; Hunterian Professor, RCS, 1954; Member: Council, RCS, 1953-58 (Rep. of Ophthalmology); Standing Ophth. Advisory Cttee to Min. of Health; Council of Faculty of Ophthalmology, 1947-68 (Pres. 1963-65, Vice-Pres. 1951-53, Treasurer 1949-51); Council of Ophthalmic Soc. of UK, 1941-44 (Vice-Pres. 1950-53); Member Court of Examiners, RCS, 1957-63; External Examiner to University of Belfast, 1960-63; Chairman, British Orthoptic Board, 1958-70; Vice-Chm., British Orthoptists' Bd, 1966-70. Hon. Lecturer in Ophthalmology, Univ. of Sheffield, 1960-61; Master of Oxford Ophthalmol. Congress, 1961-62; Mem.

Council, Court, and Convocation Univ. of Sheffield (Chm. of Convocation, 1964-67); Mem. Court, Univ. of Bradford. Mem. Sheffield Town Trust. Fellow: Royal Society of Medicine; Hunterian Society; Mem. Soc. Franc. d'Ophthalmologie; Hon. Mem., Australian Coll. of Ophthalmology (Guest Lecturer, 1954, 1963). Past Pres., Sheffield Medico and Chirurgical Soc. Liveryman, Soc. of Apothecaries of London; Freeman, City of London. OStJ. Hon. LLD Sheffield, 1974. *Publications:* contributions to medical journals, including BMJ, Trans. Ophth. Soc. of UK, Trans. Ophth. Soc. of Australia, British Orthoptic Journal, The Practitioner, etc. *Recreations:* masonry, golf, gardening. *Address:* 249 Glossop Road, Sheffield S10 2GZ. *T:* Sheffield 24876. *Clubs:* Sheffield (Sheffield); Lindrick Golf; Royal and Ancient (St Andrews).

NUTT, A. E. W.; *see* Woodward-Nutt.

NUTTALL, Dr Geoffrey Fillingham; Ecclesiastical historian, retired; Visiting Professor, King's College, London, since 1977; *b* Colwyn Bay, Wales, 8 Nov. 1911; *s* of Harold Nuttall and Muriel Fillingham (*née* Hodgson); *m* 1944, Mary (*née* Preston), *widow* of George Philip Powley. *Educ:* Bootham Sch., York; Balliol Coll., Oxford (MA 1936); Mansfield Coll., Oxford (BD 1938, DD 1945). Ordained Congregational Minister, 1938; Warminster, Wilts, 1938-43; Fellow, Woodbrooke, Selly Oak Colls, Birmingham, 1943-45; Lectr in Church Hist., New Coll. (Sch. of Divinity), London Univ., 1945-77; Chm., Bd of Studies in Theol., Univ. of London, 1957-59; Dean, Faculty of Theol., 1960-64; FKC 1977. University Preacher: Leeds, 1950; Cambridge, 1958; London, 1968; Oxford, 1972. Lectures: Friends of Dr Williams's Library, 1951; Drew, New Coll., London, 1956; Hibbert, 1962; W. M. Llewelyn, Memorial Coll., Swansea, 1966; Charles Gore, Westminster Abbey, 1968; Owen Evans, Aberystwyth, 1968; F. D. Maurice, King's Coll., London, 1970; R. T. Jenkins, Bangor, 1976. External Examiner: Belfast, Birmingham, Cambridge, Canterbury, Durham, Edinburgh, Leeds, McMaster, Manchester, Nottingham, Oxford, Wales. President: Friends' Hist. Soc., 1953; Congregational Hist. Soc., 1965-72; London Soc. for Study of Religion, 1966; Eccles. History Soc., 1972; United Reformed Church History Soc., 1972-. Vice-Chm., Christian Econ. and Social Res. Foundn. Trustee, Dr Daniel Williams's Charity. Mem., Adv. Editorial Bd, Jl of Eccles. History, 1950-. Hon. DD Wales, 1969. *Publications:* (ed) Letters of John Pinney 1679-1699, 1939; The Holy Spirit in Puritan Faith and Experience, 1946 (2nd edn 1947); The Holy Spirit and Ourselves, 1947 (2nd edn 1966); Studies in Christian Enthusiasm illustrated from Early Quakerism, 1948; (ed) Philip Doddridge 1702-1751: his contribution to English religion, 1951; Richard Baxter and Philip Doddridge: a study in a tradition, 1951; The Reality of Heaven, 1951; James Nayler: a fresh approach, 1954; (contrib.) Studies in Christian Social Commitment, 1954; Visible Saints: the Congregational Way 1640-1660, 1957; The Welsh Saints 1640-1660: Walter Cradock, Vavasor Powell, Morgan Llwyd, 1957; Christian Pacifism in History, 1958 (2nd edn 1971); (ed with Owen Chadwick) From Uniformity to Unity 1662-1962, 1962; Better Than Life: the lovingkindness of God, 1962; (contrib.) Man's Faith and Freedom: the theological influence of Jacobus Arminius, 1962; (contrib.) The Beginnings of Nonconformity, 1964; (contrib.) Choose your Weapons, 1964; Richard Baxter (Leaders of Religion), 1965; Howel Harris 1714-1773: the last enthusiast, 1965; The Puritan Spirit: essays and addresses, 1967; Congregationalists and Creeds, 1967; (contrib.) A Declaration of Faith (Congregational Church in England and Wales), 1967; The Significance of Trevecca College 1768-91, 1969; The Faith of Dante Alighieri, 1969; Christianity and Violence, 1972; (contrib.) Violence and Oppression: a Quaker Response, 1973; (contrib.) Christian Spirituality: essays in honour of Gordon Rupp, 1975; (contrib.) Der Pietismus in Gestalten und Wirkungen: Martin Schmidt zum 65 Geburtstag, 1975; New College, London and its Library, 1977; contrib. Studies in Church History: Vol. VII, 1971; Vol. X, 1973; contrib. Dict. of Nat. Biog., Encyc. Brit., Dict. d'Histoire et de Géog. Ecclés., Evang. Kirchenlexikon; articles and revs in Jl Eccles. History and Jl Theol Studies; *Festschrift:* Reformation, Conformity and Dissent: essays in honour of Geoffrey Nuttall, 1977. *Recreations:* walking, motoring (as passenger), languages, piano. *Address:* 2 Brim Hill, N2 0HF. *T:* 01-455 3198. *Club:* Penn.

NUTTALL, Rt. Rev. Michael; *see* Pretoria, Bishop of.

NUTTALL, Sir Nicholas Keith Lillington, 3rd Bt, *cr* 1922; Chairman, Edward Nuttall Ltd, since 1967; *b* 21 Sept. 1933; *s* of Lieut-Colonel Sir E. Keith Nuttall, 2nd Bt, RE (who died on active service, Aug. 1941), and Gytha Primrose Harrison (*d* 1967), *e d* of Sidney H. Burgess, of Heathfield, Bowdon, Cheshire; *S* father, 1941; *m* 1st, 1960, Rosemary Caroline (marr.

diss. 1971), *e d* of Christopher York, *qv* ; one *s* one *d* ; 2nd, 1971, Julia Jill Beresford (marr. diss. 1975), *d* of Thomas Williamson; 3rd, 1975, Miranda, *d* of Richard St John Quarry and of Lady Mancroft; two *d* . *Educ:* Eton; Royal Military Academy, Sandhurst. Commissioned Royal Horse Guards, 1953; Captain, 1959; Major 1966; retd 1968. *Heir: s* Harry Nuttall, *b* 2 Jan. 1963. *Address:* c/o Edmund Nuttall Ltd, 22 Grosvenor Gardens, SW1. *Club:* White's.

NUTTALL, Major William F. Dixon; *see* Dixon-Nuttall.

NUTTER, Rt. Rev. Harold Lee; *see* Fredericton, Bishop of.

NUTTGENS, Patrick John; Director, Leeds Polytechnic, since 1969; *b* 2 March 1930; 2nd *s* of Joseph Edward Nuttgens, stained glass artist, and Kathleen Mary Nuttgens (*née* Clark); *m* 1954, Bridget Ann Badenoch; five *s* three *d* . *Educ:* Ratcliffe Coll., Leicester; Univ. of Edinburgh; Edinburgh Coll. of Art. MA, PhD, DA(Edin), ARIBA. Lectr, Dept of Architecture, Univ. of Edinburgh, 1956-61; Dir, Inst. of Advanced Architectural Studies, Univ. of York, 1962-68; Prof. of Architecture, Univ. of York, 1968-69; Hoffman Wood Prof. of Architecture, Univ. of Leeds, 1968-70. Member: Royal Commn on Ancient and Historical Monuments of Scotland, 1967-76; Ancient Monuments Bd, 1975-; Chairman: BBC North Region Adv. Council, 1970-75; BBC Further Educn Adv. Council, 1977-. *Publications:* Reginald Fairlie, a Scottish Architect, 1959; York, City Building Series, 1971; The Landscape of Ideas, 1972; York: the continuing city, 1976; contrib. Spirit of the Age, 1975; regular contributor to jls on architecture, planning and environmental studies. *Recreations:* drawing, painting. *Address:* Providence House, High Street, Clifford, Wetherby, West Yorks. *T:* Boston Spa 842507. *Club:* Yorkshire (York).

NUTTING, Rt. Hon. Sir (Harold) Anthony, 3rd Bt *cr* 1902; PC 1954; *b* 11 Jan. 1920; 3rd and *y s* of Sir Harold Stansmore Nutting, 2nd Bt, and Enid Hester Nina (*d* 1961), *d* of F. B. Homan-Mulock; *S* father, 1972; *m* 1st, 1941, Gillian Leonora (marr. diss., 1959), *d* of Edward J. Strutt, Hatfield Peverel, Essex; two *s* one *d* ; 2nd, 1961, Anne Gunning Parker. *Educ:* Eton; Trinity College, Cambridge. Leics. Yeo., 1939; invalided, 1940. In HM Foreign Service, 1940-45; MP (C) Melton Division of Leics, 1945-56, resigned. Chairman: Young Conservative and Unionist Movement, 1946; National Union of Conservative and Unionist Associations, 1950; Conservative National Executive Cttee, 1951. Parliamentary Under-Secretary of State for Foreign Affairs, 1951-54; Minister of State for Foreign Affairs, 1954-56, resigned. Leader, UK Delegn to UN General Assembly and to UN Disarmament Commn, 1954-56. *Publications:* I Saw for Myself, 1958; Disarmament, 1959; Europe Will Not Wait, 1960; Lawrence of Arabia, 1961; The Arabs, 1964; Gordon, Martyr and Misfit, 1966; No End of a Lesson, 1967; Scramble for Africa: the Great Trek to The Boer War, 1970; Nasser, 1972. *Recreation:* fishing. *Heir: s* John Grenfell Nutting [*b* 28 Aug. 1942; *m* 1973, Diane Countess Beatty; one *s* one *d*]. *Address:* 1½ Disbrowe Road, W6. *Club:* Booodle's.

NUTTING, Prof. Jack, MA, ScD, PhD; Professor of Metallurgy, Houldsworth School of Applied Science, University of Leeds, since 1960; *b* 8 June 1924; *o s* of Edgar and Ethel Nutting, Mirfield, Yorks; *m* 1950, Thelma Kippax, *y d* of Tom and Florence Kippax, Morecambe, Lancs; one *s* two *d* . *Educ:* Mirfield Grammar School, Yorks; Univ. of Leeds. BSc Leeds, 1945; PhD Leeds, 1948; MA Cantab, 1952; ScD Cantab, 1967. Research at Cavendish Laboratory, Cambridge, 1948-49; University Demonstrator, 1949-54, University Lecturer, 1954-60, Department of Metallurgy, Cambridge University. Pres., Metals Soc.; Vice-Pres., Instn of Metallurgists. Awarded Beilby medal and prize, 1961; Hadfield medal and prize, 1964. Hon. DSc, Acad. of Mining and Metallurgy, Cracow, 1969. *Publications:* numerous papers in Journal of Iron and Steel Institute and Institute of Metals. *Recreations:* foreign travel, mountain walking. *Address:* St Mary's, 57 Weetwood Lane, Headingley, Leeds LS16 5NP. *T:* Leeds 51400.

NYE, Prof. John Frederick, FRS 1976; Professor of Physics, University of Bristol, since 1969; *b* 26 Feb. 1923; *s* of Haydn Percival Nye and Jessie Mary, *d* of Anderson Hague, painter; *m* 1953, Georgiana Wiebensen; one *s* two *d* . *Educ:* Stowe; King's Coll., Cambridge (Maj. Schol.; MA, PhD 1948). Research, Cavendish Laboratory, Cambridge, 1944-49; Univ. Demonstrator in Mineralogy and Petrology, Cambridge, 1949-51; Bell Telephone Laboratories, NJ, USA, 1952-53; Lectr, 1953, Reader, 1965, Univ. of Bristol; Visiting Professor: in Glaciology, California Inst. of Technol., 1959; of Applied Sciences, Yale Univ., 1964; of Geophysics, Univ. of Washington, 1973. President: Internat. Glaciological Soc., 1966-69; Internat. Commn of Snow and Ice, 1971-75. For. Mem., Royal Swedish

Acad. of Scis, 1977. Kirk Bryan Award, Geol. Soc. of Amer., 1961; Seligman Crystal, Internat. Glaciol Soc., 1969; Antarctic Service Medal, USA, 1974. *Publications:* Physical Properties of Crystals, 1957, rev. edn 1972; papers on physics of crystals and on glaciology in scientific jls. *Address:* 45 Canynge Road, Bristol BS8 3LH. *T:* Bristol 33769.
See also P . H . Nye .

NYE, Ven. Nathaniel Kemp; Archdeacon of Maidstone, since 1972; *b* 4 Nov. 1914; *s* of Charles Frederick and Evelyn Nye; *m* 1941, Rosa Jackson; two *s* one *d. Educ:* Merchant Taylors' Sch.; King's College London (AKC 1935); Cuddesdon College, Oxford. Ordained 1937 to St Peter's, St Helier Estate, Morden, Surrey; Chaplain RAF, 1940-46 (POW 1941-43; escaped from Italy at liberation); Rector, Holy Trinity, Clapham, 1946-54; Vicar, St Peter's, St Helier Estate, 1954-60; Vicar, All Saints, Maidstone (Parish Church), Canon, and Rural Dean, 1960-66; Tait Missioner, Canterbury Diocese, 1966-72. Hon. Canon of Canterbury, 1960. *Recreations:* painting, sailing, travel; family life! *Address:* Archdeacon's House, Charing, Kent. *T:* Charing 2294.

NYE, Peter Hague; Reader in Soil Science, University of Oxford, since 1961; Fellow of St Cross College, since 1966; *b* 16 Sept. 1921; *s* of Haydn Percival Nye and Jessie Mary (*née* Hague); *m* 1953, Phyllis Mary Quenault; one *s* two *d . Educ:* Charterhouse; Balliol Coll., Oxford (MA, BSc (Domus Exhibnr)); Christ's Coll., Cambridge. Agricl Chemist, Gold Coast, 1947-50; Lectr in Soil Science, University Coll. of Ibadan, Nigeria, 1950-52; Sen. Lectr in Soil Science, Univ. of Ghana, 1952-60; Res. Officer, Internat. Atomic Energy Agency, Vienna, 1960-61; Vis. Professor, Cornell Univ., 1974. Pres., British Soc. Soil Science, 1968-69; Mem. Council, Internat. Soc. Soil Science, 1968-74. *Publications:* The Soil under Shifting Cultivation, 1961; Solute Movement in the Soil-Root System, 1977; articles, mainly in Jl of Soil Science, Plant and Soil, Jl of Agricl Science. *Recreations:* gardening; formerly cricket, tennis, squash. *Address:* 13 Mill Lane, Marston, Oxford OX3 0PY. *T:* Oxford 42446.
See also J . F . Nye .

NYERERE, Julius Kambarage; President, United Republic of Tanzania (formerly Tanganyika and Zanzibar), since 1964; President, Tanganyika African National Union, since 1954; Chancellor, University of Dar es Salaam, since 1970; *b* 1922; *m* 1953, Maria Magige; five *s* two *d. Educ:* Tabora Secondary School; Makerere University College; Edinburgh University (MA). Began as Teacher; became President African Association, Dar es Salaam, 1953; formed Tanganyika African National Union, left teaching and campaigned for Nationalist Movement, 1954; addressed Trusteeship Council, 1955, and Cttee of UN Gen. Assembly, 1956. MLC Tanganyika, July-Dec. 1957, resigned in protest; elected Mem. for E Prov. in first elections, 1958, for Dar es Salaam, 1960; Chief Minister, 1960; Prime Minister of Tanganyika, 1961-62; President, Tanganyika Republic, 1962-64. First Chancellor, Univ. of East Africa, 1963-70. Holds hon. degrees. *Publications:* Freedom and Unity-Uhuru Na Umoja, 1966; Freedom and Socialism-Uhuru na Ujamaa, 1969; Essays on Socialism, 1969; Freedom and Development, 1973; Swahili trans of Julius Caesar and The Merchant of Venice, 1969. *Address:* State House, Dar es Salaam, United Republic of Tanzania.

O

OAKELEY, Sir (Edward) Atholl, 7th Bt *cr* 1790; retired; *b* 31 May 1900; *s* of late Major E. F. Oakeley, South Lancashire Regiment, and late Everilde A. Oakeley, *d* of Henry Beaumont; *S* cousin (Sir Charles Richard Andrew Oakeley, 6th Bt), 1959; *m* 1st, 1922, Ethyl Felice O'Coffey (marr. diss.); 2nd, (Patricia) Mabel Mary (*née* Birtchnell) (marr. diss.); one *s* ; 3rd, Doreen (*née* Wells) (marr. diss.); 4th, 1960, Shirley Church; one *d. Educ:* Clifton and Sandhurst. Lieutenant, Oxfordshire and Buckinghamshire Light Infantry, 1919-23; then Chief Contact to late Sir Charles Higham in Advertising; Captain, Amateur International Wrestling Team, 1928-29; Heavyweight wrestling Champion of Europe, 1932; Heavyweight Wrestling Champion of Gt Britain, 1930-35; Manager to World Heavyweight Wrestling Champion, Jack Sherry, 1935-39; Promoter of Championship Wrestling, Harringay Arena, 1949-54. *Publications:* The Facts on which R. D. Blackmore based Lorna Doone, 1969; Blue Blood on the Mat, 1971. *Recreations:* cricket; hunting; athletics; sailing; wrestling; boxing; weight-lifting. *Heir:*

s John Digby Atholl Oakeley [*b* 27 Nov. 1932; *m* 1958, Maureen, *d* of John and Helen Cox, Hamble, Hants; one *s* one *d*]. *Address:* Nomad, Lynton, Devon.
See also M. Oakeley.

OAKELEY, Mary, MA Oxon; Headmistress, St Felix School, Southwold, 1958-April 1978; *b* 2 April 1913; *d* of Maj. Edward Francis Oakeley, S Lancs Regt, and Everilde Anne (*née* Beaumont). *Educ:* St John's Bexhill-on-Sea; St Hilda's Coll., Oxford. MA Hons History. Asst Mistress: St James's, West Malvern, 1935-38; St George's, Ascot, 1938-39; Headmistress, Craighead Diocesan Sch., Timaru, NZ, 1940-55; Head of American Section, La Châtelainie, St Blaise, Switzerland, 1956-58. *Recreations:* ski-ing, gardening, embroidery. *Address:* Cherwell Lodge, Eynsham, Oxon. *T:* Evenlode 759. *Club:* Royal Over-Seas League.
See also Sir Atholl Oakeley, Bt.

OAKES, Sir Christopher, 3rd Bt, *cr* 1939; *b* 10 July 1949; *s* of Sir Sydney Oakes and Greta, *yr d* of Gunnar Victor Hartmann, Copenhagen, Denmark; *S* father, 1966. *Educ:* Bredon, Tewkesbury; Georgia Mil. Acad., USA. *Heir:* uncle Harry Philip Oakes [*b* 30 Aug. 1932; *m* 1958, Christiane, *o d* of Rudolf Botsch, Hamburg; three *s* one *d*]. *Address:* PO Box 1002, Nassau, Bahamas.

OAKES, Gordon James; MP (Lab) Widnes, since Sept. 1971; Minister of State, Department of Education and Science, since 1976; *b* 22 June 1931; *o s* of James Oakes and Florence (*née* Hewitt), Widnes, Lancs; *m* 1952, Esther O'Neill, *e d* of Councillor Joseph O'Neill; three *s. Educ:* Wade Deacon Gram. Sch., Widnes; Univ. of Liverpool. BA (Hon.) English, 1952; Admitted Solicitor, 1956. Entered Widnes Borough Council, 1952 (Mayor, 1964-65). Chm Widnes Constituency Labour Party, 1953-58; contested (Lab): Bebington, 1959; Moss Side (Manchester) by-election, 1961; MP (Lab) Bolton West, 1964-70; PPS, Home Office, 1966-67, Dept of Education and Science, 1967-70; Front Bench Opposition spokesman on local govt and the environment, 1970-74; Parly Under-Secretary of State: DoE, 1974-76; Dept of Energy, 1976. British Deleg., NATO Parliamentarians, 1967-70; Mem., Select Cttee on Race Relations, 1969-70. Mem. Executive, NW Region of Labour Party, 1971-. Vice-President: Rural District Councils Assoc., 1972-74; Inst. of Public Health Inspectors, 1973-; Jt Chm., Nat. Waste Management Adv. Council, 1974-76. *Publications:* various articles. *Recreations:* conversation, motoring with the family. *Address:* Upton Bridle Path, Widnes, Cheshire.

OAKES, Joseph Stewart; a Recorder of the Crown Court, since 1975; barrister-at-law; *b* 7 Jan. 1919; *s* of Laban Oakes and Mary Jane Oakes; *m* 1950, Irene May Peasnall. *Educ:* Royal Masonic Sch., Bushey; Stretford Grammar Sch.; Manchester Univ., 1937-40 (BA Hons). Royal Signals, 1940-48, Captain. Called to Bar, Inner Temple, 1948; practised on Northern Circuit, 1948-. *Recreations:* horticulture, photography, music. *Address:* 38 Langley Road, Sale, Greater Manchester M33 5AY. *T:* 061-962 2068; 12th Floor, Sunlight House, Quay Street, Manchester M3 3LA. *T:* 061-834 8418. *Club:* Freemasons' (Manchester).

OAKESHOTT, Michael Joseph, FBA 1966; MA; Professor Emeritus, University of London, 1969; *b* 11 Dec. 1901; *s* of Joseph Francis Oakeshott and Frances Maude Hellicar. *Educ:* St George's School, Harpenden; Gonville and Caius College, Cambridge. Fellow: Gonville and Caius College, 1925-; Nuffield College, Oxford, 1949-50 University Prof. of Political Science at LSE, Univ. of London, 1951-69. Served in British Army, 1940-45. Muirhead Lecturer, Univ. of Birmingham, 1953. *Publications:* Experience and its Modes, 1933: A Guide to the Classics (with G. T. Griffith), 1936, 1947; Social and Political Doctrines of Contemporary Europe, 1939; Hobbes's Leviathan, 1946; The Voice of Poetry in the Conversation of Mankind, 1959; Rationalism in Politics and other Essays, 1962; Hobbes on Civil Association, 1975; On Human Conduct, 1975. *Address:* 16 New Row, WC2.

OAKESHOTT, Walter Fraser, MA; FBA 1971; FSA; Hon. LLD (St Andrews); Rector of Lincoln College, Oxford, 1953-72, Hon. Fellow, 1972; a Trustee of the Pilgrim Trust, 1949-77; *b* 11 Nov. 1903; *s* of Walter Field Oakeshott, MD, and Kathleen Fraser; *m* 1928, Noël Rose (*d* 1976), *d* of R. O. Moon, MD, FRCP; twin *s* two *d. Educ:* Tonbridge; Balliol Coll., Oxford. Class. Mods 1924; Lit. Hum. 1926; Hon. Fellow, 1974. Assistant Master, Bec School, SW17, 1926-27; Assistant Master Merchant Taylors', 1927-30; Kent Education Office, 1930-31; Assistant Master Winchester College, 1931-38; released for 15 months (1936-37) for membership of Pilgrim Trust Unemployment Enquiry; High Master of St Paul's School, 1939-46; Headmaster of Winchester College, 1946-54. Vice-Chancellor, Oxford University, 1962-64;

Pro-Vice-Chancellor, 1964-66. President, Bibliographical Society, 1966-68. Rhind Lecturer, Edinburgh Univ., 1956. Master, Skinners' Co., 1960-61. *Publications:* Men Without Work (joint), 1938; The Artists of the Winchester Bible, 1945; The Mosaics of Rome, Fourth to Fourteenth Centuries, 1967; Sigena Wall Paintings, 1972; various semi-popular books on literature and medieval art. *Recreations:* pictures, books. *Address:* The Old School House, Eynsham, Oxford. *Club:* Roxburghe.

OAKHAM, Archdeacon of; *see* Fernyhough, Ven. B.

OAKLEY, Kenneth (Page), FBA; Deputy Keeper (Anthropology) British Museum (Natural History), 1959-69, retired; *b* 7 April 1911; *s* of Tom Page Oakley, BSc, LCP, and Dorothy Louise Oakley (*née* Thomas); *m* 1941, Edith Margaret Martin; two *s. Educ:* Challoner's Grammar School, Amersham; University College School, Hampstead; University College, London. BSc in Geology (1st cl. Hons), 1933; PhD 1938, DSc 1955. Geologist in Geological Survey, GB, 1934-35; Asst Keeper Dept of Geology (Palæontology), Brit. Mus. (Nat. Hist.), 1935 (seconded to Geological Survey for war-time service); Principal Scientific Officer, 1947-55; Senior Principal, 1955-69; head of Anthropology Sub-Dept, 1959-69. Rosa Morison Memorial Medal, University Coll., London, 1933; Wollaston Fund, 1941; Prestwich Medal, Geological Soc. of London, 1963; Henry Stopes Memorial Medal, Geologists' Assoc., 1952. Sec. Geol. Soc. Lond., 1946-49. Pres., Anthropological Section, British Assoc. for Advancement of Science, 1961. Collecting and research expeditions to East Africa, 1947, and South Africa, 1953. Viking Fund (Wenner-Gren Foundn) Lectures, New York, 1950, 1952; Royal Institution Discourse, 1953; Visiting Professor in Anthropology, University of Chicago, 1956. Corresponding Member, Istituto Italiano di Paleontologia Umana, 1955; Hon. Mem., British Acad. of Forensic Sciences, 1959; FSA 1953; FBA 1957; Fellow of University Coll., London, 1958. *Publications:* Man the Tool-maker, Brit. Mus. Nat. Hist., 1949 (6th edn 1972; repr. Chicago, 1957, 1976; Japanese edn 1971); The Fluorine-dating Method (in Year-book of Physical Anthropology for 1949), 1951; (part-author) The Solution of the Piltdown Problem (Bull. Brit. Mus. Nat. Hist.), 1953; Frameworks for Dating Fossil Man, 1964 (3rd edn 1969; Cronologia del hombre fosil, 1968; Die Datierung menschlicher Fossilien, 1971); The Problem of Man's Antiquity (Brit. Mus. Nat. Hist.), 1964; (Co-ed) Catalogue of Fossil Hominids (Brit. Mus. Nat. Hist.), part 1, Africa, 1967, rev. repr. 1977, part 2, Europe, 1971, part 3, Americas, Asia, Australasia, 1975; Decorative and Symbolic Uses of Vertebrate Fossils (Pitt Rivers Mus.), 1975; contrib. chapter, Skill as a Human Possession, in A History of Technology, vol. I (ed Singer et al), 1954, rev. version in festschrift, Perspectives on Human Evolution, 2 (ed Washburn and Dolhinow), 1972. *Recreations:* listening to music, art, pursuit of the unusual, folklore. *Address:* 2 Islip Place, Summertown, Oxford OX2 7SR. *T:* Oxford 56524; 2 Chestnut Close, Amersham, Bucks.

OAKLEY, Wilfrid George, MD, FRCP; Hon. Consulting Physician, King's College Hospital, 1971; Vice President, British Diabetic Association, since 1971; *b* 23 Aug. 1905; *s* of late Rev. Canon G. D. Oakley and Mrs Oakley; *m* 1931, Hermione Violet Wingate-Saul; one *s. Educ:* Durham School; Gonville and Caius College, Cambridge; St Bartholomew's Hospital. Tancred studentship in Physic, Gonville and Caius Coll., 1923; Bentley Prize and Baly Research Schol., St Bart's Hosp., 1933. Formerly Physician i/c Diabetic Dept, King's College Hosp., 1957-70. Examr, Cambridge and Glasgow Univs. MD (Hon. Mention) Cantab 1934; FRCP 1942. FRSocMed; Pres., Med. Soc., London, 1962; Mem. Assoc. of Physicians of Great Britain; Vice-Pres., British Diabetic Assoc., 1971. *Publications:* (jtly) Clinical Diabetes and its Biochemical Basis, 1968; Diabetes and its Management, 1973; scientific articles and chapters in various text-books on diabetes. *Address:* 149 Harley Street, W1. *T:* 01-935 4444.

OAKSEY, 2nd Baron *cr* 1947 (properly **TREVETHIN,** 4th Baron *cr* 1921, **AND OAKSEY); John Geoffrey Tristram Lawrence;** Racing Correspondent to Daily Telegraph since 1957, to Horse and Hound since 1959 and to Sunday Telegraph since 1960; *b* 21 March 1929; *o s* of 1st Baron Oaksey and 3rd Baron Trevethin and of Marjorie, *d* of late Commander Charles N. Robinson, RN; *S* father, 1971; *m* 1959, Victoria Mary, *d* of Major John Dennistoun, MBE; one *s* one *d. Educ:* Horris Hill; Eton; New College, Oxford (BA); Yale Law School. *Publications:* History of Steeplechasing (jointly), 1967; The Story of Mill Reef, 1974. *Recreations:* hunting, skiing, tennis, riding. *Heir: s* Hon. Patrick John Tristram Lawrence, *b* 29 June 1960. *Address:* Hill Farm, Oaksey, Malmesbury, Wilts. *T:* Crudwell 303. *Club:* Brooks's.
See also H . S . L . Dundas .

OAKSHOTT, Hon. Sir Anthony (Hendrie), 2nd Bt *cr* 1959; *b* 10 Oct. 1929; *s* of Baron Oakshott, MBE (Life Peer), and of Joan, *d* of Marsden Withington; *S* to baronetcy of father, 1975; *m* 1965, Mrs Valerie de Pret-Roose, *d* of Jack Vlasto. *Educ:* Rugby. *Heir: b* Hon. Michael Arthur John Oakshott [*b* 12 April 1932; *m* 1957, Christina Rose Methuen, *d* of late Thomas Banks; three *s*]. *Address:* New House, Idbury, Oxford OX7 6RU. *T:* Shipton under Wychwood 830 044. *Clubs:* White's, Turf.

OATES, John Claud Trewinard, FBA 1976; Reader in Historical Bibliography, since 1972 and Deputy Librarian, since 1975, University of Cambridge; Fellow of Darwin College, Cambridge, since 1964; *b* 24 June 1912; *s* of Claud Albert Oates and Clarissa Alberta Wakeham; *m* 1960, Helen Cooke (*née* Lister). *Educ:* Crypt Sch., Gloucester; Trinity Coll., Cambridge (Scholar; 1st Cl. Class. Tripos Pt I 1933, Pt II 1935; BA 1935, MA 1938). Sch. of Tank Technol., Mil. Coll. of Science, 1941-46. Univ. of Cambridge: Walston Student, 1935; Asst Under-Librarian, 1936, Under-Librarian, 1949, Univ. Library; Sandars Reader in Bibliography, 1952, 1965. Pres., Bibliograph. Soc., 1970-72; Vice-Pres., Cambridge Bibliograph. Soc., 1975-; Trustee, Laurence Sterne Trust, 1968-; Mem., Brotherton Library Adv. Cttee, Univ. of Leeds, 1974-. Editor, The Library (Trans Bibliograph. Soc.), 1953-60. *Publications:* A Catalogue of the Fifteenth-Century Printed Books in the University Library, Cambridge, 1954; (contrib.) The English Library before 1700 (ed F. Wormald and C. E. Wright), 1958; Shandyism and Sentiment 1760-1800 (bicentenary lecture), 1968; contrib. bibliograph. jls. *Recreation:* walking the dog. *Address:* 144 Thornton Road, Cambridge. *T:* Cambridge 76653.

OATES, Sir Thomas, Kt 1972; CMG 1962; OBE 1958 (MBE 1946); Governor and Commander-in-Chief of St Helena, 1971-76; *b* 5 November 1917; *er s* of Thomas Oates, Wadebridge, Cornwall; unmarried. *Educ:* Callington Grammar School, Cornwall; Trinity College, Cambridge (MA). Mathematical Tripos (Wrangler). Admiralty Scientific Staff, 1940-46; HMS Vernon, Minesweeping Section, 1940-42; British Admiralty Delegn, Washington, DC, 1942-46; Temp. Lieut, RNVR Colonial Administrative Service, Nigeria, 1948-55; seconded to HM Treasury, 1953-55; Adviser to UK Delegn to UN Gen. Assembly, 1954. Financial Sec. to Govt of: British Honduras, 1955-59, Aden, 1959-63; Dep. High Comr, Aden, 1963-67; Permanent Sec., Gibraltar, 1968-69; Dep. Governor, Gibraltar, 1969-71. *Recreations:* photography, walking, ski-ing. *Clubs:* East India, Devonshire, Sports and Public Schools; Royal Commonwealth Society, Naval.

OATLEY, Sir Charles (William), Kt 1974; OBE 1956; MA; FRS 1969, FIEE, FIEEE; Professor of Electrical Engineering, University of Cambridge, 1960-71, now Emeritus; Fellow of Trinity College, Cambridge, since 1945; *b* 14 Feb. 1904; *s* of William Oatley and Ada Mary Dorrington; *m* 1930, Dorothy Enid West; two *s. Educ:* Bedford Modern Sch.; St John's Coll., Cambridge. Demonstrator, later lecturer, Dept of Physics, KCL, 1927-39. Min. of Supply, Radar Research and Development Establishment, 1939-45. Actg Superintendent in charge of scientific work, 1944-45. Lecturer, later Reader, Dept of Engineering, Cambridge Univ., 1945-60. Director, English Electric Valve Company, 1966. Member: Council, Inst. of Electrical Engineers, 1954-56, 1961-64 (Chm. of Radio Section, 1954-55); Council, Royal Society, 1970-72. Hon. Fellow, Royal Microscopical Soc., 1970; FKC 1976. Hon. DSc Heriot-Watt, 1974. Achievement Award, Worshipful Co. of Scientific Instrument Makers, 1966; Duddell Medal, Inst. of Physics and Physical Soc., 1969; Royal Medal, Royal Soc., 1969; Faraday Medal, Inst. of Electrical Engineers, 1970; Mullard Award, Royal Soc., 1973. *Publications:* Wireless Receivers, 1932; The Scanning Electron Microscope, 1972; Electric and Magnetic Fields, 1976; papers in scientific and technical journals. *Recreation:* gardening. *Address:* 16 Porson Road, Cambridge. *T:* Cambridge 56194. *Club:* Athenæum.

OBAN, Provost of (St John's Cathedral); *see* Copland, Very Rev. C. McA.

O'BEIRNE, Cornelius Banahan, CBE 1964; QC; Senior Legal Assistant, Council on Tribunals, since 1971; *b* 9 September 1915; *e s* of late Captain C. B. O'Beirne, OBE; *m* 1949, Ivanka, *d* of Miloc Tupanjanin, Belgrade; one *s* one *d. Educ:* Stonyhurst Coll. Solicitor (Eng.), 1940. Served War, 1940-46; Maj. RA, Eur., Mid. E; Polit. Adviser's Office, Brit. Emb., Athens, 1945-46. Colonial Office, 1947-48. Called to Bar, Lincoln's Inn, 1952. Crown Counsel: Nigeria, 1949-53; High Commn Territories, SA, 1953-59; Solicitor-Gen., 1959; Attorney-General, High Commission Territories, South Africa, 1961-64; Counsellor (Legal), British Embassy, SA, 1964-65; Lord Chancellor's Office, 1966-71; seconded as Attorney-Gen., Gibraltar, 1966-70.

QC: Basutoland, Bechuanaland and Swaziland, 1962; Gibraltar, 1967. Member: RIIA; Justice; Plowden Soc.; Statute Law Soc. *Publication:* Laws of Gibraltar, rev. edn 1968. *Recreations:* photography, modern languages. *Address:* Nanhoran Cottage, Claremont Lane, Esher, Surrey.

OBERON, Merle, (Estelle Merle O'Brien Thompson); Film Actress; *b* Tasmania, 19 Feb. 1917; British; *m* 1st 1939, Sir Alexander Korda (*d* 1956) (marr. diss.); 2nd, 1945, Lucien Ballard (marr. diss. 1949); 3rd, 1958, Bruno Pagliai (marr. diss. 1973); 4th, 1975, Robert Wolders. *Educ:* La Martinere College, Calcutta; France. Films include: Henry VIII, Wuthering Heights, Night in Paradise, Temptation, Night Song, Berlin Express, Dark Angel, Song to Remember, Of Love and Desire, Hotel. *Recreations:* riding, swimming, fishing, and reading. *Address:* c/o Allan & Ingersoll, 1901 Avenue of Stars, Los Angeles, Calif 90067, USA.

OBERT de THIEUSIES, Vicomte Alain; Grand Officier de la Couronne; Grande Croix de l'Ordre de Léopold II; Grand Cordon de la Couronne de Chêne, etc.; Comdr de la Légion d'Honneur; *b* 10 March 1888; *s* of Vicomte Obert de Thieusies and Vicomtesse Obert de Thieusies (*née* Comtesse de Ribaucourt); *m* 1927, Yolanda, *d* of Baron Romano-Avezzana; three *s*. *Educ:* Maredsous Abbey; Stoneyhurst College (Doctor of Law). Entered diplomatic service, 1911, as Attaché de Légation; Secrétaire de Légation, Madrid, 1912; Chargé d'Affaires, ad interim, Belgrade, 1913, Sofia, 1913; Secrétaire de Légation (1st Cl.), 1915, Rio de Janiero, 1919; Counsellor, Paris, 1921; Minister Plenipotentiary, 1930; Consul General, Tangiers, 1930; Minister, Prague, 1932, Belgrade, 1938-41; Directeur Général du Commerce Extérieur in London, 1941; Chairman of Liquidation Cttee of Belgian Govt Service in London, 1944; Head of Belgian Economic Mission, 1945; Belgian Ambassador to the Court of St James's, 1946-53. *Recreations:* golf, shooting. *Heir: s* Martel, *b* 30 Apr. 1928. *Address:* Château de Thoricourt, Hainaut, Belgium.

OBOLENSKY, Prof. Dimitri, MA, PhD; FBA 1974; FSA; FRHistS; Professor of Russian and Balkan History in the University of Oxford since 1961, and Student of Christ Church since 1950; *b* Petrograd, 1 April 1918; *s* of late Prince Dimitri Obolensky and late Countess Mary Shuvalov; *m* 1947, Elisabeth Lopukhin. *Educ:* Lycée Pasteur, Paris; Trinity College, Cambridge. Cambridge: 1st Class Modern and Medieval Langs Tripos Parts I and II; Amy Mary Preston Read and Allen Schol.; Fellow of Trinity Coll., 1942-48; Faculty Asst Lecturer, 1944; Lecturer, Trinity Coll., 1945; Univ. Lecturer in Slavonic Studies, 1946. Reader in Russian and Balkan Medieval History in Univ. of Oxford, 1949-61; Vis. Schol., Dumbarton Oaks Center for Byzantine Studies, Harvard Univ., 1952, 1964, 1977; Vis. Prof. of Russian History, Yale Univ., 1957; Birkbeck Lecturer in Ecclesiastical History, Trinity Coll., Cambridge, 1961; Gen. Sec. Thirteenth Internat. Congress of Byzantine Studies, Oxford, 1966; Vis. Prof. of European History, Univ. of California, Berkeley, 1973. British Co-Chairman: Anglo-Bulgarian Conf. of Historians, 1973; Anglo-Romanian Conf. of Historians, 1975. *Publications:* The Bogomils, A Study in Balkan Neo-Manichaeism, 1948; (ed) The Penguin Book of Russian Verse, 1962; (jointly) The Christian Centuries, vol. 2: The Middle Ages, 1969; Byzantium and the Slavs, 1971; The Byzantine Commonwealth, 1971; (ed jtly) Companion to Russian Studies, 3 vols, 1976-77; articles in Oxford Slavonic Papers, Dumbarton Oaks Papers, Slavonic and East European Review, etc.; contrib. to Encyc. Brit. and Chambers's Encyc. *Recreations:* lawn tennis, motoring. *Address:* 29 Harbord Road, Oxford; Christ Church, Oxford. *T:* 58989. *Club:* Athenæum.

Ó BRIAIN, Hon. Barra, MSM; President of the Circuit Court and, *ex officio,* Judge of High Court in Ireland 1959-73 (seconded as President of the High Court of Justice, Cyprus, 1960-62); appointed a Member of Committee of Inquiry into the operation of the Courts in Ireland, 1962; *b* 19 September 1901; *s* of Dr Christopher Michael and Mary Theresa O Briain, Merrion Square, Dublin; *m* 1928, Anna Flood, Terenure, Dublin (*d* 1968); three *s* eight *d*. *Educ:* Belvedere College; University Coll., Dublin; Paris University. Served in IRA in Irish War of Independence, 1920-21; National Army, 1922-27; Mil. Sec. to Chief of Staff, 1926-27. Called to Irish Bar, 1926; Hon. Bencher, King's Inns, 1974. Sen. Counsel, 1940; Circuit Judge, 1943 (S Western Circuit). *Publication:* The Irish Constitution (1927). *Recreations:* fishing, gardening, walking. *Address:* Gúgán Barra, Enniskerry, Co. Wicklow. *T:* 867493.

O'BRIEN, family name of **Barons Inchiquin** and **O'Brien of Lothbury.**

O'BRIEN OF LOTHBURY, Baron *cr* 1973 (Life Peer), of the City of London; **Leslie Kenneth O'Brien,** PC 1970; GBE 1967; President, British Bankers' Association, since 1973; *b* 8 Feb. 1908; *e s* of late Charles John Grimes O'Brien; *m* Isabelle Gertrude Pickett; one *s*. *Educ:* Wandsworth School. Entered Bank of England, 1927; Deputy Chief Cashier, 1951; Chief Cashier, 1955; Executive Director, 1962-64; Deputy Governor, 1964-66; Governor, 1966-73; Director, Commonwealth Develt Finance Co. Ltd, 1962-64. Hon. Fellow and Vice-President, Inst. of Bankers; Chm., Cttee of Inquiry into export of animals for slaughter, 1973. Director: The Prudential Assurance Co. Ltd, 1973-; The Rank Organisation, 1974-; Bank for International Settlements, 1974-; Saudi Internat. Bank, 1975-. Mem., Adv. Bd, Unilever Ltd, 1973-; Consultant to J. P. Morgan & Co. 1973-; Chm., Internat. Council of Morgan Guaranty Trust Co., NY, 1974-; Mem. Adv. Council, Morgan Grenfell & Co. Ltd, 1974-. Member: Finance and Appeal Cttee, RCS, 1973-; Council, RCM, 1973-; Bd of National Theatre, 1973-; Financial Adv. Cttee, Royal Acad. of Arts, 1973-; Council, Marie Curie Meml Foundn, 1963-; Investment Adv. Cttee, Mercers' Co., 1973-; City of London Savings Cttee, 1966-. A Trustee of Glyndebourne Arts Trust, 1974-. Pres., United Banks' Lawn Tennis Assoc., 1958-. One of HM Lieutenants for City of London; Freeman, City of London in Co. of Mercers; Hon. Liveryman, Leathersellers Co. Hon. DSc City Univ., 1969; Hon. LLD, Univ. of Wales, 1973. Cavaliere di Gran Croce al Merito della Repubblica Italiana, 1975; Grand Officier, Ordre de la Couronne (Belgium), 1976. *Address:* 33 Lombard Street, EC3P 3BH. *T:* 01-283 8888. *Clubs:* Athenæum, Garrick, Boodle's, Grillions, MCC, All England Lawn Tennis.

O'BRIEN, Bryan Justin, CMG 1950; *b* 21 Jan. 1902; *s* of late Rev. G. E. O'Brien, Bosley Vicarage, Cheshire; *m* 1937, Maro, *d* of late Cleanthis Constantinides, Famagusta, Cyprus; one *s*. *Educ:* Uppingham; Queen's College, Oxford. First class honour Mods, second class literæ humaniores; Laming Fellow. Assistant Secretary, Colonial Secretary's Office, Cyprus, 1927; Commissioner, 1936; Assistant Colonial Secretary, Mauritius, 1939; Principal Assistant Colonial Secretary, 1943; Under-Secretary, Trinidad, 1943-47; Colonial Secretary, Gibraltar, 1947-53; Chief Secretary, North Borneo, 1953-56; retired. Mem. Commn on Salaries and Wages, Ghana, 1956-57. Jt Editor, Handbook of Cyprus, 1930 edn. *Club:* Travellers'.

O'BRIEN, Charles Michael, MA; FIA, FSS; Manager and Actuary, Royal National Pension Fund for Nurses, since 1955; *b* 17 Jan. 1919; *s* of late Richard Alfred O'Brien, CBE, MD, and Nora McKay; *m* 1950, Joy, *d* of late Rupert Henry Prebble and Phyllis Mary Langdon; two *s*. *Educ:* Westminster Sch.; Christ Church, Oxford (MA). Commissioned, Royal Artillery, 1940 (despatches, 1945). Asst Actuary, Equitable Life Assce Soc., 1950; Royal National Pension Fund for Nurses: Asst Manager, 1953; Manager and Actuary, 1955. Institute of Actuaries: Fellow, 1949; Hon. Sec., 1961-62; Vice-Pres., 1965-68; Pres., 1976-78. Mem., Governing Body, Westminster Sch. *Recreations:* lawn tennis, Eton fives, training gundogs. *Address:* Furzedown, Grubb Street, Limpsfield, Surrey RH8 0SH. *T:* Limpsfield Chart 2197.

O'BRIEN, Conor Cruise; Member of the Senate, Republic of Ireland, since 1977; Pro-Chancellor, University of Dublin, since 1973; *b* 3 November 1917; *s* of Francis Cruise O'Brien and Katherine Sheehy; *m* 1st, 1939, Christine Foster (marr. diss. 1962); one *s* two *d*; 2nd, 1962, Máire Mac Entee; one adopted *s* one adopted *d*. *Educ:* Sandford Park School, Dublin; Trinity College, Dublin (BA, PhD). Entered Department of External Affairs of Ireland, 1944; Counsellor, Paris, 1955-56; Head of UN section and Member of Irish Delegation to UN, 1956-60; Asst Sec., Dept of External Affairs, 1960; Rep. of Sec.-Gen. of UN in Katanga, May-Dec. 1961; resigned from UN and Irish service, Dec. 1961. Vice-Chancellor, Univ. of Ghana, 1962-65; Albert Schweitzer Prof. of Humanities, New York Univ., 1965-69. TD (Lab) Dublin North-East, 1969-77; Minister for Posts and Telegraphs, 1973-77. Vis. Fellow, Nuffield Coll., Oxford, 1973-75. Mem., Royal Irish Acad. Hon. DLitt: Bradford, 1971; Ghana, 1974. *Publications:* Maria Cross (under pseud. Donat O'Donnell), 1952 (reprinted under own name, 1963); Parnell and his Party, 1957; (ed) The Shaping of Modern Ireland, 1959; To Katanga and Back, 1962; Conflicting Concepts of the UN, 1964; Writers and Politics, 1965; The United Nations: Sacred Drama, 1967 (with drawings by Felix Topolski); Murderous Angels, 1968; (ed) Power and Consciousness, 1969; Conor Cruise O'Brien Introduces Ireland, 1969; (ed) Edmund Burke, Reflections on the Revolution in France, 1969; Camus, 1969; A Concise History of Ireland, 1972; (with Máire Cruise O'Brien) The Suspecting Glance, 1972; States of Ireland, 1972. *Recreation:* travelling. *Address:* Whitewater, Howth Summit, Dublin, Ireland. *T:* Dublin 322474. *Club:* Athenæum.

O'BRIEN, Sir David (Edmond), 6th Bt *cr* 1849; *b* 19 Feb. 1902; *s* of Edmond Lyons O'Brien (*y b* of 3rd Bt) and Audrey Townshend, *d* of late David Crawford, New York; *S* brother, 1969; *m* 1927, Mary Alice (*d* 1974), *y d* of Sir Henry Foley Grey, 7th Bt; two *s* one *d. Educ:* Oratory School. *Recreations:* fishing, gardening. *Heir: er s* John David O'Brien [*b* 9 June 1928; *m* 1957, Sheila Winifred, *o d* of Sir Charles Arland Maitland Freake, 4th Bt; two *s* two *d*]. *Address:* Salisbury, Clonmel, Co. Tipperary. *T:* Clonmel 110. *Club:* Kildare Street and University (Dublin).

O'BRIEN, Edna; writer; *b* 15 Dec. 1936; marr. diss.; two *s. Educ:* Irish convents; Pharmaceutical Coll. of Ireland. Yorkshire Post Novel Award, 1971. *Publications:* The Country Girls, 1960; The Lonely Girl, 1962; Girls in Their Married Bliss, 1963; August is a Wicked Month, 1964; Casualties of Peace, 1966; The Love Object, 1968; A Pagan Place, 1970; (play) A Pagan Place, 1971; Night, 1972; (short stories) A Scandalous Woman, 1974; Mother Ireland, 1976; Johnnie I hardly knew you, 1977. *Recreations:* cooking, dancing. *Address:* c/o A. M. Heath & Co., 40-42 King William IV Street, WC2N 4DD.

O'BRIEN, Frederick William Fitzgerald, QC (Scotland) 1960; Sheriff-Principal of North Strathclyde, since 1975; *b* 19 July 1917; *s* of Dr Charles Henry Fitzgerald O'Brien and Helen Jane; *m* 1950, Audrey Muriel Owen; two *s* one *d. Educ:* Royal High Sch.; Univ. of Edinburgh; MA 1938; LLB 1940. Admitted Faculty of Advocates, 1947. Member of Legal Aid Central Cttee, 1961-64; Comr, Mental Welfare Commission of Scotland, 1962-65; Home Advocate Depute, 1964-65; Sheriff-Principal of Caithness, Sutherland, Orkney and Shetland, 1965-75; Interim Sheriff-Principal of Aberdeen, Kincardine and Banff, 1969-71; Hon. Sheriff, Lothians and Peebles, 1962-. Member: Scottish Medical Practices Cttee, 1973-76; Scottish Records Adv. Council, 1974-; Convener of Sheriffs Principal; Chm., Sheriff Court Rules Council. Pres., Royal High Sch. Former Pupils Club, 1975-76. Mem., Inst. of Advanced Motorists. *Recreations:* golf, music. *Address:* 1/6 Barcapel Avenue, Newton Mearns, Renfrewshire G77 6QD. *T:* 041-639 6808. *Clubs:* Bruntsfield Golf, Scottish Arts.

O'BRIEN, Prof. John W., PhD, DCL, LLD; Rector and Vice-Chancellor, Concordia University (incorporating Loyola College and Sir George Williams University, Montreal), since 1969; Professor of Economics, since 1965; *b* 4 Aug. 1931; *s* of Wilfred Edmond O'Brien and Audrey Swain; *m* 1956, Joyce Helen Bennett; two *d. Educ:* McGill Univ., Montreal, Que. BA 1953, MA 1955, PhD 1962. Sir George Williams Univ.: Lectr in Economics, 1954; Asst Prof. of Economics, 1957; Associate Prof. of Economics and Asst Dean, 1961; Dean, Faculty of Arts, 1963; Vice-Principal (Academic), 1968-69. *Publication:* Canadian Money and Banking, 1964 (2nd edn, with G. Lermer, 1969). *Address:* Concordia University, 1455 de Maisonneuve Boulevard West, Montreal, Que H3G 1M8, Canada. *T:* 879-2862.

O'BRIEN, Rt. Rev. Mgr. Michael Joseph; Principal Chaplain (RC), Royal Air Force, 1967-71; *b* 13 April 1913; *s* of John O'Brien and Anastasia (*née* Corbett). *Educ:* De La Salle, Waterford; Rockwell Coll.; Cashel; St John's Coll., Waterford. Ordained, 1936; Curate: Corpus Christi, Weston-super-Mare, 1936-40; St John the Evangelist, Bath, 1940-41; joined RAF Chaplain's Branch, 1941. *Recreation:* golf. *Address:* Lisieux, 25 Rockfield Park, Waterford, Ireland. *T:* Waterford 3117. *Club:* Royal Air Force.

O'BRIEN, (Michael) Vincent; trainer of horses for flat and National Hunt racing, England and Ireland; *b* 9 April 1917; *s* of Daniel P. O'Brien and Kathleen (*née* Toomey); *m* 1951, Jacqueline (*née* Wittenoom), Perth, Australia; two *s* three *d. Educ:* Mungret Coll., Ireland. Started training in Co. Cork, 1944; moved to Co. Tipperary, 1951. Won all principal English and Irish steeple-chases, incl. 3 consecutive Grand Nationals, Gold Cups and Champion Hurdles. From 1959 has concentrated on flat racing and has trained winners of 13 English classics, incl. 5 Derbys; trainer of Nijinsky, first triple crown winner since 1935; also 2 Irish Derbys, Prix de l'Arc de Triomphe and Washington International. *Recreations:* shooting, fishing, golf. *Address:* Ballydoyle House, Cashel, Co. Tipperary, Ireland. *T:* 062-61222; Telex 8214. *Club:* St Stephen's Green (Dublin).

O'BRIEN, Owen; General Secretary, National Society of Operative Printers, Graphical and Media Personnel, since 1975; *b* Stepney, 22 June 1920; *m* ; two *s* two *d. Educ:* Tower Hill Sch., E1. Entered printing industry, 1934. Served War: Merchant Navy, 1939-41; RAF, 1941-46. Elected: Asst Sec., London Machine Br. of Union, Dec. 1951; (unopposed) Sec. of Br., Nov.

1952; Sec. of Union's London Jt Branches, 1952-63; Nat. Asst Sec., 1964. Past Mem., local Labour Party and London Labour Party; Mem., Stepney Borough Council, 1947-50; Printing and Publishing Industry Training Board: Mem. Exec. Cttee and Chm., Levy and Grant Cttee since Bd's constitution in 1968; Chm., 1977; Mem. Council, Industrial Soc. Governor, London Coll. of Printing, 1964- (Chm., Governors, 1969, 1977). *Recreations:* walking, reading, swimming. *Address:* Caxton House, 13-16 Borough Road, SE1 0AL. *T:* 01-928 1481.

O'BRIEN, Raymond Francis; Chief Executive, Merseyside Metropolitan County Council, since 1978; *b* 13 Feb. 1936; *s* of Ignatius and Anne O'Brien; *m* 1959, Mary Agnes (Wendy) Alcock; two *s* two *d. Educ:* St Mary's Coll., Great Crosby, Liverpool; St Edmund Hall, Oxford. BA Hons 1959, MA 1962; IPFA. Accountant, Cheshire CC, 1959-65; Head of Data Processing, Staffs CC, 1965-67; Asst County Treas., Notts CC, 1967-70; Dep. Clerk, Notts CC, 1970-73; Clerk of CC and Chief Executive, Notts, 1973-77. *Recreations:* cricket, rugby, gardening, music, reading. *Address:* Anfield, Cow Lane, Bramcote, Nottingham. *T:* Nottingham 253113.

O'BRIEN, Richard, DSO 1944, MC 1942 (Bar 1944); Chairman, Manpower Services Commission, since 1976; *b* 15 Feb. 1920; *s* of late Dr Charles O'Brien and Marjorie Maude O'Brien; *m* 1951, Elizabeth M. D. Craig; two *s* three *d . Educ:* Oundle Sch.; Clare Coll., Cambridge (MA). Served, 1940-46, with Sherwood Foresters and Leicesters, N Africa, ME, Italy and Greece; transf. to Personal Staff C-in-C, 21st Army Gp, 1945. Develt Officer, Nat. Assoc. of Boys' Clubs, 1946-48; Richard Sutcliffe Ltd, Wakefield (latterly Prodn Dir), 1948-58; Dir and Gen. Man., Head Wrightson Mineral Engrg Ltd, 1958-61; Dir, Industrial Relns, British Motor Corp., 1961-66; Industrial Adviser (Manpower), DEA, 1966-68; Delta Metal Co. Ltd (subseq. Dir of Manpower, and Dir 1972-76), 1968-76. Chm., CBI Employment Policy Cttee, 1971-76; Mem., NEDC, 1977-. Mem. Council, Industrial Soc., 1962-; Mem. Council, Univ. of Birmingham, 1969-. JP Wakefield, 1955-61. *Publications:* contrib. Conflict at Work (BBC pubn), 1971; articles in various jls. *Recreations:* reading, squash. *Address:* 24 Argyll Road, W8. *T:* 01-937 8944.

O'BRIEN, Terence John, CMG 1971; MC 1945; HM Diplomatic Service; Ambassador to Burma, since 1974; *b* 13 Oct. 1921; *s* of Joseph O'Brien; *m* 1950, Phyllis Mitchell (*d* 1952); *m* 1953, Rita Emily Drake Reynolds; one *s* two *d. Educ:* Gresham's Sch., Holt; Merton Coll., Oxford. Ayrshire Yeo., 1942-45. Dominions Office, 1947; CRO, 1947-49; British High Comr's Office, Ceylon, 1950-52; Princ., Treasury, 1953-56; 1st Sec. (Financial), Canberra, 1956-58; Planning Officer, CRO, 1958-60; 1st Sec., Kuala Lumpur, 1960-62; Sec. to Inter-Governmental Cttee, Jesselton, 1962-63; Head of Chancery, New Delhi, 1963-66; Imp. Def. Coll., 1967; Counsellor, FCO (formerly FO), 1968-70; Ambassador, Nepal, 1970-74. *Recreations:* fishing, trekking. *Address:* c/o Foreign and Commonwealth Office, SW1; Beaufort House, Woodcutts, Dorset. *Clubs:* Reform, Royal Commonwealth Society.

O'BRIEN, Turlough Aubrey, CBE 1959; Public Relations Consultant, since 1972; *b* 30 Sept. 1907; *er s* of late Lieut-Colonel A. J. O'Brien, CIE, CBE; *m* 1945, Phyllis Mary, twin *d* of late E. G. Tew; two *s* one *d. Educ:* Charterhouse; Christ Church, Oxford. Assistant to Director of Public Relations, Board of Trade, 1946-49; Public Relations Officer: Home Office, 1949-53; Post Office, 1953-64; Chief Public Relations Officer, 1964-66; Director, Public Relations, 1966-68; Public Relations Manager, Bank of London and South America, 1968-72. President, Institute of Public Relations, 1965. *Recreation:* fishing. *Address:* Clare Place, Goose Rye Road, Worplesdon, Guildford, Surrey. *T:* Worplesdon 3151. *Club:* United Oxford & Cambridge University.

O'BRIEN, Vincent; see O'Brien, M. V.

O'BRIEN, Adm. Sir William (Donough), KCB 1969 (CB 1966); DSC 1942; Commander-in-Chief, Western Fleet, Feb. 1970-Sept. 71, retd Nov. 1971; *b* 13 Nov. 1916; *s* of late Major W. D. O'Brien, Connaught Rangers and I. R. Caroe (*née* Parnis); *m* 1943, Rita Micallef, Sliema, Malta; one *s* two *d. Educ:* Royal Naval Coll., Dartmouth. Served War of 1939-45: HM Ships Garland, Wolsey, Witherington, Offa, 1939-42; Cottesmore i/c, 1943-44; Arakan Coast, 1945. HMS Venus i/c, 1948-49; Commander 1949; HMS Ceylon, 1952; Admiralty, 1953-55; Captain, 1955; Captain (D) 8th DS in HMS Cheviot, 1958-59; HMS Hermes i/c, 1961-64; Rear-Admiral 1964; Naval Secretary, 1964-66; Flag Officer, Aircraft Carriers, 1966-67; Comdr, Far East Fleet, 1967-69; Admiral 1969. Mem., Inland Waterways Amenity Adv. Council, 1974-. Chairman: Kennet and Avon Canal Trust, 1974; King George's Fund for Sailors, 1974. *Address:* Drew's Mill, Potterne Road, Devizes, Wilts. *T:* Devizes 3243. *Club:* Army and Navy.

OCHOA, Dr Severo; Distinguished Member, Roche Institute of Molecular Biology, New Jersey, since 1974; *b* Luarca, Spain, 24 Sept. 1905; *s* of Severo Ochoa and Carmen (*née* Albornoz); *m* 1931, Carmen G. Coblan. *Educ:* Malaga Coll.; University of Madrid. AB, Malaga, 1921; MD, Madrid, 1929. Lecturer in Physiology, University of Madrid Medical School, 1931-35; Head of Physiology Div., Institute for Medical Research, 1935-36; Guest Research Asst, Kaiser Wilhelm Inst., Heidelberg, 1936-37; Marine Biological Lab., Plymouth, July-Dec. 1937; Demonstrator and Nuffield Research Assistant in Biochemistry, University of Oxford Medical School, 1938-41; Instructor and Research Assoc. in Pharmacology, Washington Univ. School of Medicine, St Louis, 1941-42; New York University School of Medicine: Research Assoc. in Medicine, 1942-45; Asst Professor of Biochemistry, 1945-46; Professor of Pharmacology, and Chairman of Dept of Pharmacology, 1946-54; Prof. of Biochemistry, and Chm. of Dept of Biochemistry, 1954-74. Carlos Jimenez Diaz lectr, Madrid Univ., 1969. Pres., Internat. Union of Biochemistry, 1961-67. Member: US National Academy of Sciences; American Academy of Arts and Sciences; American Philosophical Society; Deutsche Akademie der Naturforscher (Leopoldina), etc. Nobel Prize (joint) in Physiology and Medicine, 1959. Hon. degrees from universities and colleges in Argentina, Brazil, England, Italy, Philippines, Scotland, Spain and USA. Foreign Member: Royal Society, 1965; USSR Academy of Science, 1966; Polish Acad. of Science; Acad. of Science, DDR, 1977; Hon. Mem., Royal Acad. Med., Sevilla, 1971. Gold Medal, Madrid Univ., 1969; Queredo Gold Medal, Madrid, 1969; Albert Gallatin Medal, NY Univ., 1970. Order of Rising Sun, 2nd class, 1967. *Publications:* papers on biochemistry and molecular biology. *Recreations:* colour photography and swimming. *Address:* 530 East 72nd Street, New York, NY 10021, USA. *T:* Trafalgar 9-1480.

O'COLLINS, Most Rev. James Patrick; *b* Melbourne, Australia, 31 March 1892. *Educ:* St Columba's, Springwood; St Patrick's, Sydney; Urban Coll., Rome. Ordained Priest, Rome, 1922 for the Diocese of Melbourne; RC Bishop of Geraldton, 1930-42; Bishop of Ballarat, 1942-71. Nominated Asst Bishop at the Papal Throne, 1955. *Address:* 1444 Sturt Street, Ballarat, Victoria 3350, Australia.

O'CONNELL, Sir Bernard Thomas, Kt 1972; Deputy Chairman, New Zealand Breweries Ltd, since 1970; *b* 31 Dec. 1909; *s* of Bernard O'Connell and Mary Walker, Yorkshire, England; *m* 1939, Margaret Mary Collins; three *s*. *Educ:* Christian Brothers Schools in Australia and New Zealand. New Zealand Breweries Ltd, Wellington, New Zealand: Sec. 1939; Gen. Manager, 1946; Man. Dir, 1958; Dep. Chm., 1970. FCA. *Recreations:* golf, racing. *Address:* 7 Wai-te-ata Road, Wellington, New Zealand. *T:* Wellington 726-704. *Clubs:* Wellesley, Wellington Golf, Wellington Racing (all in Wellington, NZ).

O'CONNELL, Prof. Daniel Patrick, RD; LLD; DCL; QC 1977; Chichele Professor of Public International Law, Oxford University, since 1972, and Fellow of All Souls; *b* 7 July 1924; *s* of Daniel Patrick O'Connell, Howick, New Zealand, and of Magdalen Roche; *m* 1957, Renate von Kleist, Drenow; three *s* two *d*. *Educ:* Auckland Univ.; Trinity Coll., Cambridge (PhD, LLD). Comdr, RNR. Barrister-at-Law, Middle Temple; Reader in Law, 1952-62, Prof. of International Law, 1962-72, Univ. of Adelaide. Dir of Studies, Internat. Law Assoc., 1973-. Pres., Assoc. of Aust. and NZ Law Schools, 1964; Rapporteur, State Succession Cttee, Internat. Law Assoc., 1961-72; Rockefeller Fellow, Harvard Univ., 1957; Visiting Prof.: Georgetown Univ., 1960; Inst. Hautes Etudes Internat., Geneva, 1965; Associé de l'Institut de Droit Internat., 1967; Legal Adviser to several Commonwealth Govts. Mem., St John's Council, S Aust. FRHistS. Kt of Grace and Devotion, Order of Malta, 1958. *Publications:* The Law of State Succession, 1956; International Law, 1965 (2nd edn 1970); International Law in Australia, 1966; State Succession in Municipal Law and International Law, 1967; Richelieu, 1968; Opinions on Imperial Constitutional Law, 1972; The Influence of Law on Seapower, 1975; numerous articles in British, US and foreign, legal, political, literary and historical jls. *Recreations:* art, music, history, sailing. *Address:* All Souls College, Oxford. *T:* Oxford 722251; Powder Hill House, Youlbury, Boar's Hill, Oxford. *T:* Oxford 730148; 2 Katoomba Road, Beaumont, Adelaide, Australia. *Clubs:* Athenæum; Naval, Military and Air Force of SA (Adelaide).

O'CONNELL, John Eugene Anthony, MS (London), FRCS; Consulting Neurological Surgeon, St Bartholomew's Hospital; *b* 16 Sept. 1906; *s* of Thomas Henry and Catherine Mary O'Connell; *m* Marjorie Hutchinson Cook. *Educ:* Clongowes Wood and Wimbledon Colleges; St Bartholomew's Hospital. Held posts of House Surgeon, Senior Demonstrator of Anatomy, and Surgical Chief Assistant, St Bartholomew's Hospital, 1931-39; Studied at Universities of Michigan and Chicago on Rockefeller Foundation Travelling Fellowship, 1935-36; Surgeon in charge of an EMS Neurosurgical Unit, 1941-46; Surgeon i/c Dept of Neurol Surgery, St Bartholomew's Hosp., 1946-71; Hunterian Professor, Royal College of Surgeons, 1943 and 1950. Member: Soc. of Brit. Neurol Surgeons (ex-Pres.); RSM (ex-Vice-Pres.); Hon. Member: Neurosurgical Soc. Australasia; Deutsche Gesellschaft für Neurochirurgie; Corresp. Mem., Amer. Assoc. Neurol Surgeons. *Publications:* papers in neurological, surgical and other journals and books. *Recreations:* fly-fishing, bird watching. *Address:* Fishing Cottage, Itchen Abbas, Winchester, Hants. *T:* Itchen Abbas 227; 149 Harley Street, W1. *T:* 01-935 4444. *Club:* Athenæum.

O'CONNELL, Sir Morgan (Donal Conail), 6th Bt, *cr* 1869; *b* 29 Jan. 1923; *o s* of Captain Sir Maurice James Arthur O'Connell, 5th Bt, KM, MC, and Margaret Mary, *d* of late Matthew J. Purcell, Burton Park, Buttevant; *S* father, 1949; *m* 1953, Elizabeth, *o d* of late Major and Mrs John MacCarthy O'Leary, Lavenders, West Malling, Kent; two *s* four *d*. *Educ:* The Abbey School, Fort Augustus, Scotland. Served War of 1939-45, in Royal Corps of Signals, 1943-46; BLA, 1944-46. *Recreations:* fishing and shooting. *Heir:* *s* Maurice James Donagh MacCarthy O'Connell, *b* 10 June 1958. *Address:* Lakeview, Killarney, Co. Kerry. *T:* 31845.

O'CONNOR, Surgeon Rear-Adm. Anthony, MVO 1967; Deputy Director, Red Cross Blood Transfusion Service, Western Australia, since 1975; *b* 8 Nov. 1917; *s* of Armel John O'Connor and Lucy Violet O'Connor (*née* Bullock-Webster); *m* 1946, Catherine Jane (*née* Hayes); three *d*. *Educ:* Kings Coll., Strand, London; Westminster Hosp. Med. Sch. MRCS, LRCP, MB, BS, FFARCS, MFCM. Qualified Medical Practitioner, 1941; joined Royal Navy (RNVR), 1942; Permanent Commn, 1945; Dep. Medical Director General (Naval), 1969; MO i/c, Inst. of Naval Med. and Dean of Naval Med., 1972-75. QHP 1970-75. *Recreations:* gardening, photography. *Address:* c/o Lloyds Bank, 237 Old Brompton Road, SW5 0DZ.

O'CONNOR, Cormac Murphy; *see* Murphy-O'Connor.

O'CONNOR, Professor Daniel John; Professor of Philosophy, Trinity College, Dublin, since 1975; *b* 2 April 1914. *Educ:* Birkbeck Coll., University of London. Entered Civil Service, 1933; Commonwealth Fund Fellow in Philosophy, University of Chicago, 1946-47; Professor of Philosophy, University of Natal, SA, 1949-51; Professor of Philosophy, University of the Witwatersrand, Johannesburg, 1951-52; Lecturer in Philosophy, Univ. Coll. of North Staffordshire, 1952-54; Professor of Philosophy: University of Liverpool, 1954-57; University of Exeter, 1957-75; Visiting Professor, University of Pennsylvania, 1961-62. *Publications:* John Locke, 1952; Introduction to Symbolic Logic (with A. H. Basson), 1953; Introduction to Philosophy of Education, 1957; A Critical History of Western Philosophy (ed), 1964; Aquinas and Natural Law, 1968; Free Will, 1971; (ed jtly) New Essays in the Philosophy of Education, 1973; The Correspondence Theory of Truth, 1975; various papers in philosophical journals. *Address:* Trinity College, Dublin 2.

O'CONNOR, Lt-Gen. Sir Denis (Stuart Scott), KBE 1963 (CBE 1949; OBE 1946); CB 1959; DL; *b* Simla, 2 July 1907; *s* of Lieut-Colonel Malcolm Scott O'Connor and Edith Annie (*née* Rees); *m* 1936, Martha Neill Algie (*née* Johnston), Donaghadee, Co. Down; two *s* one *d*. *Educ:* Glengorse, Eastbourne; Harrow School; RMA Woolwich. Commnd 2nd Lieut, Royal Artillery, 1927; India, 1929-35; France, 1939, Captain; Student Staff Coll., 1940; Major Instructor, Staff Coll., 1941, Lieut-Colonel GSO 1, 11th Armoured Division, 1942-44; N.W. Europe, CO Artillery Regt, 1944 (despatches); Colonel, 14th Army, 1945; Brigadier, Director of Plans, Supreme Allied Commander, South East Asia, 1945-46; Middle East, BGS, 1946-49; Student, IDC 1950; School of Artillery, 1951-52; CRA, 11th Armoured Division, BAOR, 1953-54; Director of Plans, War Office, 1955-56; Maj.-General, Commander, 6th Armoured Division, BAOR, 1957-58; Chief Army Instructor, Imperial Defence Coll., London, 1958-60; GOC, Aldershot District, 1960-62; Vice Chief of Defence Staff, Ministry of Defence, 1962-64; Commander British Forces, Hong Kong, 1964-66, retired. Colonel Commandant, RA, 1963-72. Member of Administrative Board of Governors, Corps of Commissionaires, 1964-75, Life Governor, 1975. DL Surrey, 1968. *Recreations:* shooting, fishing, golf. *Address:* Springfield Lodge, Camberley, Surrey.

O'CONNOR, Sir Kenneth Kennedy, KBE 1961; Kt 1952; MC 1918; QC (Kenya) 1950; *b* 21 Dec. 1896; *s* of Rev. William O'Connor and Emma Louisa O'Connor; *m* 1928, Margaret Helen (*née* Wise); two *s*. *Educ:* Abbey Sch., Beckenham; St Columba's Coll., near Dublin. Indian Army, 14th (KGO) Sikhs, 1915-18 (despatches, MC). Pol. Dept, Mesopotamia, 1919. Foreign and Pol. Dept, Government of India, 1920-22; resigned, 1922. Called to Bar, Gray's Inn, 1924; practised at Bar, London and Singapore, 1924-41. President, Straits Settlements Assoc., 1938, 1939, 1940. Colonial Legal Service, 1943; Acting Attorney-General, Nyasaland, 1944; Colonel, 1945; Attorney-General, Malaya, 1946-48; Attorney-General, Kenya, 1948-51; Chief Justice, Jamaica, 1951-54; Chief Justice of Kenya, 1954; President, Court of Appeal for Eastern Africa, 1957-62, retired. *Publications:* Index Guide to the Law of Property Act, 1925, 1926. Editor Straits Settlements Law Reports. Contributions to legal journals. *Recreations:* cricket, lawn tennis, golf. *Address:* 7 Westfield Close, Wimborne, Dorset. *Club:* Royal Over-Seas League.

O'CONNOR, Air Vice-Marshal Patrick Joseph, CB 1976; OBE 1943; MD; FRCPE, FRCPsych; Senior Consultant to the RAF, at Central Medical Establishment, RAF, since 1975 (Consultant Adviser in Neurology and Psychiatry, to the RAF, since 1964); *b* 21 Aug. 1914; *s* of Charles O'Connor, Straffan, Co. Kildare, Eire, farmer; *m* 1946, Elsie, *o d* of David Craven, Leeds, Yorks; one *s* two *d* (and one *d* decd). *Educ:* Roscrea Coll.; University of Dublin. MB, BCh 1938. Joined RAF, 1940; Air Cdre 1966; Air Vice-Marshal 1971. MD 1950; MRCPE 1950; DPM 1953; FRCPE 1960; MRCP 1960; FRCPsych 1970. QHP 1967. Member: Med. Council to Migraine Trust; Med. Council on Alcoholism; The EEG Soc.; Assoc. of British Neurologists; Internat. Acad. of Aviation and Space Med., 1977; Internat. League against Epilepsy; Flying Personnel Res. Cttee. Fellow, Aerospace Med. Assoc; FRSM. *Publications:* contrib.: Journal Neurology, Psychiatry and Neurosurgery; British Journal Psychiatry; BMJ. *Recreations:* gardening, shooting. *Address:* Central Medical Establishment, RAF, Kelvin House, Cleveland Street, WC1. *T:* 01-636 4651; St Benedicts, Bacombe Lane, Wendover, Bucks. *T:* Aylesbury 623329. *Club:* Royal Air Force.

O'CONNOR, Hon. Sir Patrick McCarthy, Kt 1966; **Hon. Mr Justice O'Connor;** Judge of the High Court of Justice, Queen's Bench Division, since 1966; *b* 28 Dec. 1914; *s* of late William Patrick O'Connor; *m* 1938, Mary Garland, *d* of William Martin Griffin, KC, of Vancouver, BC; two *s* two *d*. *Educ:* Downside; Merton Coll., Oxford. Called to the Bar, Inner Temple, 1940; Master of the Bench, 1966. Junior Counsel to the Post Office, 1954-60; QC 1960; Recorder: of King's Lynn, 1959-61; of Southend, 1961-66; Dep. Chairman, IoW QS, 1957-71. Vice-Chm., Parole Bd, 1974-75. A Governor of Guy's Hospital, 1956-60. *Recreation:* yachting. *Address:* Royal Courts of Justice, Strand, WC2; 17 Eldon Road, Kensington, W8. *T:* 01-937 9198. *Club:* Royal Solent Yacht.

O'CONNOR, General Sir Richard Nugent, KT 1971; GCB 1947 (KCB 1941; CB 1940); (Scottish Rifles) DSO 1917; MC; *b* 1889; *s* of Major Maurice Nugent O'Connor, Royal Irish Fusiliers; *m* 1st, 1935, Jean (*d* 1959), *d* of Sir Walter Ross, KBE, of Cromarty; 2nd, 1963, Dorothy, widow of Brigadier Hugh Russell, DSO. *Educ:* Wellington Coll.; Royal Military Coll., Sandhurst. Served European War, 1914-18 (despatches 9 times, DSO, bar, MC, Italian Silver medal for valour); GSO 2nd Grade, War Office, 1932-34; Imperial Defence College Course, 1935; Commander Peshawar Brigade, India, 1936-38; Military Governor of Jerusalem, 1938-39; served War of 1939-45; commanded Western Desert Corps in successful Libyan campaign, 1940-41 (prisoner, escaped Dec. 1943); a Corps Commander in France, 1944 (despatches, 1939-45 Star, France and Germany Star, Legion of Honour, Commander, Croix de Guerre with palm); GOC-in-C Eastern Command, India, Jan. 1945; GOC-in-C N. Western Army, India, 1945-46; General, 1945; Adjutant-General to the Forces, 1946-47; ADC General to the King, 1946; retired, 1948. Commandant Army Cadet Force, Scotland, 1948-59; Colonel, The Cameronians (Scottish Rifles), 1951-54. Lord Lieutenant County of Ross and Cromarty, 1955-64. Lord High Commissioner, Church of Scotland General Assembly, 1964. JP Ross and Cromarty, 1952. *Address:* Kincurdie House, Rosemarkie, Ross-shire.

O'CONNOR HOWE, Mrs Josephine Mary; HM Diplomatic Service; Counsellor, Foreign and Commonwealth Office, since 1974; *b* 25 March 1924; *d* of late Gerald Frank Claridge and late Dulcie Agnes Claridge (*née* Waldegrave); *m* 1947, John O'Connor Howe (decd); one *d*. *Educ:* Wychwood Sch., Oxford; Triangle Coll. (course in journalism). Inter-Allied Information Cttee, later, United Nations Information Office, 1942-45; Foreign Office: The Hague, 1945-46; Internat. News Service and

freelance, 1946-50; FO, 1952-. *Recreations:* theatre, gardening, grandchildren. *Address:* c/o Foreign and Commonwealth Office, SW1A 2AH; Dering Cottage, Little Chart, Ashford, Kent TN27 0PT. *T:* Pluckley 328.

Ó DÁLAIGH, Cearbhall; Uachtarán na hÉireann (President of Ireland), 1974-76; *b* 12 Feb. 1911; *m* 1934, Máirín Nic Dhiarmada. *Educ:* National Sch., Bray; Scoil na Leanbh sa Rinn; Christian Brothers' Sch., Synge Street, Dublin; University College Dublin. BA (Celtic Studies); BL King's Inns 1934. Studied Irish, An Rinn, An Blascaod, Dún Chaoin, Comineoil; studied Italian, Università per stranieri, Perugia. Irish Editor, Irish Press, 1931-40; called to Bar, 1934; admitted to Inner Bar, 1945; Attorney General of Republic of Ireland, 1946-48, 1951-53; Judge of the Supreme Court, 1953, Chief Justice and Pres. Supreme Court, 1961-73; Judge of Court of Justice of European Communities, Luxembourg, 1973, Pres. First Chamber of Court of Justice of European Communities, 1974. Formerly Chairman: Commn on Industrial Taxation; Commn on Income Tax; Commn on Accommodation Needs of Constituent Colls of NUI; Commn on Higher Education; Cultural Relations Cttee of Dept of Foreign Affairs; Irish Nat. Council on Alcoholism; Council for Overseas Students; special interest in refugee problems. MRIA. Hon. FRSCI. Hon. LLD Dublin; Hon. DLittCelt NUI. *Recreations:* Irish literature, Italian and French languages, art, education, theatre, horse-riding, bird-watching. *Address:* Caoindroim, Cill Chomhaid, Baile O gCearnaigh, An Chloch Liath, Ireland.

ODDIE, Christopher Ripley; His Honour Judge Oddie; a Circuit Judge, since 1974; *b* Derby, 24 Feb. 1929; *o s* of Dr and Mrs J. R. Oddie, Uttoxeter, Staffs; *m* 1957, Margaret Anne, *d* of Mr and Mrs J. W. Timmis; one *s* three *d*. *Educ:* Giggleswick Sch.; Oriel Coll., Oxford (MA). Called to Bar, Middle Temple, 1954, Oxford Circuit. Contested (L) Ludlow, Gen. Election, 1970. A Recorder of the Crown Court, 1972-74. *Recreations:* reading, opera, fishing. *Address:* 89 The Vineyard, Richmond, Surrey. *T:* 01-940 4135; Woodside Cottage, Clun, Craven Arms, Salop.

ODDIE, Prof. Guy Barrie; Robert Adam Professor of Architecture and Head of Department of Architecture, University of Edinburgh, since 1968; *b* 1 Jan. 1922; *o s* of Edward Oddie and Eleanor Pinkney; *m* 1952, Mabel Mary Smith; no *c*. *Educ:* Hookergate Grammar Sch.; Univ. of Newcastle upon Tyne. BArch, DipTP, RIBA, FRIAS. Demonstrator, Univ. of Newcastle upon Tyne, 1944; Sen. Lectr, Birmingham Sch. of Architecture, 1950-52; Research Architect, Building Res. Stn, 1947-50; Develt Gp, Min. of Educn, 1952-58; Staff architect, UGC, 1958-63; Consultant to OECD, 1963-66; Dir, Laboratories Investigation Unit, DES, 1966-68. Sen. Advr to OECD Prog. on Educnl Bldg, 1972-; Mem., Bldg Res. Estabt Scottish Adv. Cttee. *Publications:* School Building Resources and their Effective Use, 1966; Development and Economy in Educational Building, 1968; Industrialised Building for Schools, 1975; contrib. Architects Jl, Architectural Rev., RIBA Jl. *Recreations:* dry-fly fishing, gardening. *Address:* The Causeway, Edinburgh EH15 3QA. *T:* 031-661 5492.

O'DEA, Mrs Denis; see McKenna, Siobhan.

O'DEA, Sir Patrick Jerad, KCVO 1974; Secretary for Internal Affairs, Wellington, New Zealand, 1967-78; *b* 18 April 1918; 2nd *s* of late Patrick O'Dea; *m* 1945, Jean Mary, *d* of Hugh Mulholland; one *s* three *d*. *Educ:* St Paul's Coll. and Univ. of Otago, Dunedin, NZ; Victoria Univ., Wellington, NZ. Joined NZ Public Service, 1936; served in Agriculture Dept, 1936-47. Served War in Royal New Zealand Artillery of 2 NZEF, 1941-45. With Industries and Commerce Dept, 1947-49; subseq. served with Dept of Internal Affairs in various posts interrupted by 2 years' full-time study at Victoria Univ. of Wellington (DPA). Group Exec. Officer, Local Govt, 1959-64; Dep. Sec., 1964-67. Also, 1967-: Sec. for: Local Govt; Civil Defence; Sec. of Recreation and Sport; Clerk of the Writs; NZ Sec. to the Queen. *Publications:* several papers on local govt in New Zealand. *Recreations:* gardening, golf, bowls. *Address:* 1 Tensing Place, Khandallah, Wellington, New Zealand. *T:* Wellington 792-424. *Clubs:* United Services Officers' (Wellington, NZ); Shandon Golf (Petone, NZ); Khandallah Bowling (Khandallah, NZ).

O'DEA, William Thomas, FIEE; FMA; formerly founder Director-General, Ontario Science Centre, 1966-70; *b* 27 Jan. 1905; *s* of late William O'Dea, MBE; *m* 1933, Kathleen Alice Busby; no *c*. *Educ:* Manchester University (BSc). Entered Science Museum from industry, 1930, as Assistant Keeper; transferred 1939, to Air Ministry (later MAP); Asst Director, Engine Accessories Production, 1940; Acting Director, Propeller Production, 1941; Dep. Regional Controller, London and SE England, Ministry of Production, 1942-44; Dep.

Controller of Storage, Board of Trade, 1944-46. Keeper, Dept of Aeronautics, and Sailing Ships, Science Museum, SW7, 1948-66. Unesco adviser to Governments of Ceylon and India on establishment of Science Museums, 1956-60; Adviser to Government of UAR, 1962. Chairman, Cttee for Museum of Science and Technology, International Council of Museums, 1966-71. Hon. Citizen, Quincy, Mass, 1965. *Publications:* The Meaning of Engineering, 1961; The Social History of Lighting, 1958; Science Museum Handbooks on Electric Power, 1933, Radio Communication, 1934, Illumination, 1936, 1948 and 1959; papers in Journals of IEE and IMechE; contributor, Festival Lectures, Royal Society of Arts, 1951, and to various societies on history of engineering and illumination. *Address:* Pippins, Lower Farm Road, Effingham, Surrey KT24 5JL.

ODELL, John William, OBE 1969; Deputy Chairman, Lesney Products & Co. Ltd, Diecasting Engineers, London E9, since 1973 (Joint Managing Director, 1947-73). *Address:* Lesney Products & Co. Ltd, Lee Conservancy Road, Hackney Wick, E9. *T:* 01-985 5533/0664.

ODELL, Prof. Peter Randon; Professor of Economic Geography, Erasmus University, Rotterdam, since 1968; *b* 1 July 1930; *s* of Frank James Odell and late Grace Edna Odell; *m* 1957, Jean Mary McKintosh; two *s* two *d*. *Educ:* County Grammar Sch., Coalville; Univ. of Birmingham (BA, PhD); Fletcher Sch. of Law and Diplomacy, Cambridge, Mass. (AM). RAF 1954-57. Economist, Shell International Petroleum Co., 1958-61; Lectr, LSE, 1961-65; Sen. Lectr, LSE, 1965-68. Stamp Meml Lectr, London Univ., 1975. *Publications:* An Economic Geography of Oil, 1963; Natural Gas in Western Europe, 1969; Oil and World Power, 1970, 4th edn 1975; (with D. A. Preston) Economics and Societies in Latin America, 1973, 2nd edn 1978; Energy: Needs and Resources, 1974, 2nd edn 1977; (with K. E. Rosing) The North Sea Oil Province, 1975; The West European Energy Economy: the case for self-sufficiency, 1976; (with K. E. Rosing) The Optimal Development of the North Sea Oilfields, 1976. *Address:* Oudorpweg 9, Rotterdam 16, The Netherlands. *T:* Rotterdam 119341.

ODEY, George William, CBE 1945; DL; Honorary President, Barrow, Hepburn Group Ltd, Tanners and Leather Merchants, since 1974 (Chairman, 1937-74); *b* 21 April 1900; *s* of late George William Odey; *m* 1st, 1926, Dorothy Christian (*d* 1975), *d* of late James Moir; one *s*; 2nd, 1976, Mrs Doris Harrison-Broadley. *Educ:* Faversham Grammar Sch.; University College, London. President Union Society, UCL, 1921-22. University of London Union Society, 1922. Fellow, UCL 1953; Assistant Secretary, University of London Appointments Board, 1922-25. Joined firm of Barrow, Hepburn & Gale, Ltd, 1925; Board of Barrow, Hepburn & Gale, Ltd, 1929, Managing Director, 1933. Representative Ministry of Supply in Washington for negotiations in connection with joint purchase of hides between UK and USA, 1941; Member joint UK and USA Mission on Hides and Leather to S. America, 1943; Chairman: Board of Governors, National Leathersellers Coll., 1951-; United Tanners' Federation, 1951. MP (C) Howdenshire Division of E Yorks, Nov. 1947-Feb. 1950, Beverley Division of the East Riding of Yorkshire, 1950-55; CC East Riding, Yorkshire, 1964-74. Leathersellers' Company Livery, 1939. Hon. Air Commodore (RAuxAF), retired. Commodore House of Commons Yacht Club, 1954. President: International Tanners' Council, 1954-67; British Leather Manufacturers Research Assoc., 1964; British Leather Federation, 1965; Federation of Gelatine and Glue Manufacturers, 1955-57; British Gelatine and Glue Research Assoc., 1950-. Member: Western Hemisphere Export Council, 1960-64; Cttee for Exports to the US, 1964; Member of Lloyd's. DL Humberside, 1977. *Recreations:* farming, yachting, tennis. *Address:* Keldgate Manor, Beverley, North Humberside. *T:* Beverley 882418. *Clubs:* Carlton, Royal Automobile; Royal Yorkshire Yacht; Lloyds Yacht; Scarborough Yacht; House of Commons Yacht.

ODGERS, Graeme David William; Associate Director, General Electric Co., since 1977; *b* 10 March 1934; *s* of William Arthur Odgers and Elizabeth Minty (*née* Rennie); *m* 1957, Diana Patricia Berge; one *s* three *d*. *Educ:* St John's Coll., Johannesburg; Gonville and Caius Coll., Cambridge (Mech. Scis Tripos); Harvard Business Sch. (MBA, Baker Scholar). Investment Officer, Internat. Finance Corp., Washington DC, 1959-62; Management Consultant, Urwick Orr and Partners Ltd, 1962-64; Investment Executive, Hambros Bank Ltd, 1964-65; Director: Keith Shipton and Co. Ltd, 1965-72; C. T. Bowring (Insurance) Holdings Ltd, 1972-74; Chm., Odgers and Co. Ltd (Management Consultants), 1970-74; Dir, Industrial Develt Unit, DoI, 1974-77. *Recreations:* tennis, swimming. *Address:* The Limes, Frant Green, Frant, Sussex. *T:* Frant 214. *Club:* City of London.

ODGERS, Lindsey Noel Blake, MC 1916; *b* 21 Dec. 1892; *s* of late William Blake Odgers, KC, LLD, and Frances (*née* Hudson); *m* 1923, Constance Attneave (*d* 1969). *Educ:* Rugby; St John's Coll., Cambridge. Served European War in Middlesex Regt, 1914-18, and Royal Engineers, 1918-19. Entered Home Office, 1919; seconded to Chief Secretary's Office, 1920-22; Principal, Home Office, 1926; Assistant Secretary, 1937; Assistant Under Secretary of State, Home Office, 1949-54. *Recreation:* gardening.

ODGERS, Paul Randell, CB 1970; MBE 1945; TD 1949; Deputy Secretary, Department of Education and Science, 1971-75; *b* 30 July 1915; *e s* of late Dr P. N. B. Odgers and Mrs M. A. Odgers (*née* Higgins); *m* 1944, Diana, *d* of late R. E. F. Fawkes, CBE; one *s* one *d*. *Educ:* Rugby; New Coll., Oxford. Entered CS, Board of Education, 1937. Army Service, 1939-45 (despatches three times). Asst Secretary: Min. of Educn, 1948; Cabinet Office, 1956; Under-Secretary: Min. of Educn, 1958; Office of First Secretary of State, 1967; Office of Lord President of the Council, 1968; Office of Sec. of State for Social Services, 1968; Cabinet Office, 1970. Treasurer, Soc. for Promotion of Roman Studies; Mem. Council, GPDST. *Address:* Stone Walls, Aston Road, Haddenham, Bucks. *T:* Haddenham 291830.

ODLING, Thomas George, CB 1974; *b* 18 Sept. 1911; *yr s* of late Major W. A. Odling, Paxford, Glos and late Mary Bennett Odling (*née* Case); *m* 1st, Camilla Haldane Paterson (marr. diss.); two *s*; 2nd, Hilary Katharine, *d* of late W. J. Palgrave-Ker, Lilliput, Dorset. *Educ:* Temple Grove; Rugby Sch.; New Coll., Oxford (MA). House of Commons: Asst Clerk, 1935; Clerk of Private Bills, Examr of Petitions for Private Bills and Taxing Officer, 1961-73; Clerk of Select Cttee on Parly Comr for Admin, 1969-73; Clerk of Committees, 1974-76, retired 1976. Temp. attached to Consultative Assembly of Council of Europe during 1949 and later sessions. *Recreations:* music, gardening. *Address:* Paxford, Campden, Glos. *Clubs:* Athenæum, MCC. *See also Maj.-Gen. W. Odling.*

ODLING, Maj.-Gen. William, CB 1963; OBE 1951; MC; DL; various offices in English Speaking Union, since 1965; *b* 8 June 1909; *s* of late Major W. A. Odling, Middlesex Regt, and of Mrs W. A. Odling, Paxford, Campden, Gloucestershire; *m* 1939, Margaret Marshall (*née* Gardner); one *s* two *d*. *Educ:* Temple Grove; Wellington Coll.; RMA, Woolwich. Commissioned Royal Artillery, 1929; Subaltern RHA and RA, chiefly in India until 1938; Captain, 1938; Major, 1946; Lieut-Colonel, 1951; Colonel, 1953; Brigadier 1957; Maj.-General, 1961; Adjutant, TA, 1939; CRA, Madagascar Force, 1942 (MC); GSO 1, RA, COSSAC, Planning Staff for Operation Overlord, 1943; N.W. Europe Campaign (despatches), 1944; GSO 1, War Office, 1945; GSO 1, Training, GHQMELF, 1948; AQMG, MELF, 1950; AAG Colonel, War Office, Nov. 1953; CRA, E. Anglian Div., 1957; Brigadier, AQ Headquarters, Eastern Command, 1959; Maj.-General in charge of Administration, General Headquarters, Far East Land Forces, 1961-62; Chief of Staff, General Headquarters, Far East Land Forces, 1962-64. DL Essex, 1975. *Publication:* Soldier's Bedside Book, 1945. *Recreations:* various offices in the Church of England, beagling, sailing, print collecting. *Address:* Gun House, Fingringhoe, Colchester CO5 7AL. *T:* Peldon 320. *Club:* Army and Navy. *See also T. G. Odling.*

ODLUM, Dr Doris Maude; Hon. Consultant, since 1955, formerly Senior Physician for Psychological Medicine, Elizabeth Garrett Anderson (Royal Free) Hospital, London; Consultant Emeritus, Marylebone Hospital for Psychiatry and Child Guidance, London; Consultant Emeritus, Bournemouth and East Dorset Hospital Group; Fellow, British Medical Association, 1959; *b* 26 June 1890; *d* of Walter Edward and Maude Gough Odlum. *Educ:* Talbot Heath, Bournemouth; St Hilda's Coll., Oxford; St Mary's Hospital and London School of Medicine for Women. MA Oxon; BA London; MRCS; LRCP, Foundn Fellow, Royal Coll. Psychiatrists, 1971; DPM; DipEd. Hon. Consultant Phys., Lady Chichester Hospital for Nervous Diseases, Hove, 1928-48; Hon. Phys. for Psychiatry, Royal Victoria and W. Hants Hospital, Bournemouth, 1928-48; President, British Med. Women's Federation, 1950-53; President, European League for Mental Hygiene, 1953-56; Vice-President, International Med. Women's Assoc., 1950-54; Vice-President, National Assoc. for Mental Health, 1946-; Member Exec. World Federation for Mental Health, 1948-51; Hon. Cons. Psychiatrist to the Samaritans Inc., 1961-, Life Pres., 1973-. Corresponding Member Swiss Psychiatric Assoc., 1946-; Member Home Office Cttee on Adoption, 1954. *Publications:* You and Your Children, 1948; Psychology, the Nurse and the Patient (3rd edn 1959, US edn 1960); Journey Through Adolescence, 1957 (2nd edn, 1965, 3rd edn 1977); The Mind of Your Child, 1959; L'Età Difficile, 1962 (2nd edn 1968); Puber

Puberteit, 1965; The Male Predicament, 1975; Understanding Your Child, 1976; articles in British Medical Journal, Lancet, Practitioner, etc. *Recreations:* painting, golf, swimming, travel. *Address:* (Residence) 11 Golden Gates, Ferry Way, Sandbanks, Poole, Dorset BH13 7QH. *T:* Canford Cliffs 707915; 56 Wimpole Street, W1.

O'DOHERTY, Most Rev. Eugene; *b* 4 Feb. 1896. Ordained priest, 1921. Formerly President of St Columb's College, Londonderry; Bishop of Dromore (RC), 1944-76. *Address:* c/o Bishop's House, Newry, Co. Down, N Ireland.

O'DONNELL, Most Rev. Patrick Mary; *b* Fethard, Co. Tipperary, 2 Feb. 1897; *y* s of Thomas O'Donnell and Johanna Sheehan. *Educ:* Mungret College, Limerick; Pontificio Collegio Urbano, Rome. Priest, 1922; staff of St Mary's Cathedral, Sale, Victoria; Administrator of St Mary's Cathedral, Sale, 1928-37; Pastor, Leongatha, 1937-46; Pastor, Warragul, 1946-49; Vicar General of Sale Dio., 1941; Domestic Prelate to the Pope, 1944; Titular Archbishop of Pelusium and Coadjutor Archbishop of Brisbane, 1949-65; Archbishop of Brisbane, 1965-73. Member Senate, University of Queensland, 1965-73. *Recreations:* walking, reading. *Address:* Glengariff, Derby Street, Hendra, Brisbane, Qld 4011, Australia. *T:* Brisbane 2682327.

O'DONNELL, Peadar; Member Irish Academy of Letters. *Educ:* St Patrick's, Dublin. *Publications:* Storm; Islanders, 1925; Adrigoole, 1928; The Knife, 1930; The Gates Flew Open; On The Edge of the Stream, 1934; Salud; An Irishman in Spain, 1937; The Big Windows, 1955; Proud Island, 1976. *Address:* 44 Charlston Road, Ranelagh, Dublin.

O'DONNELL, Hon. Turlough; Hon. Mr Justice O'Donnell; Puisne Judge of the High Court of Justice in Northern Ireland, since Aug. 1971; *b* 5 Aug. 1924; *e* s of Charles and Eileen O'Donnell; *m* 1954, Eileen McKinley; two *s* two *d*. *Educ:* Abbey Grammar Sch., Newry; Queen's Univ., Belfast (LLB). Called to Bar of Northern Ireland, 1947; called to Inner Bar, 1964; Chairman, NI Bar Council, 1970-71. *Recreations:* golf, folk music. *Address:* 155 Glen Road, Belfast 11. *T:* 613965; Royal Courts of Justice (Ulster), Belfast BT1 3JF.

OESTREICHER, Rev. Paul; Vicar, Church of the Ascension, Blackheath, since 1968; Chairman of British Section, Amnesty International, since 1974; journalist; Hon. Secretary for East-West Relations, British Council of Churches; *b* Germany, 29 Sept. 1931; *s* of Paul Oestreicher and Emma (*née* Schnaus); *m* 1958, Lore Feind; two *s* two *d*. *Educ:* King's High Sch., Dunedin; Otago and Victoria Univs, NZ; Bonn Univ. (Humboldt Res. Fellow); Lincoln Theol College. BA Mod. Langs Otago 1953; MA Hons Polit. Sci. Victoria 1955. Ordained 1959. Fled to NZ with refugee parents, 1939; returned to Europe, 1955. Fraternal worker with German Lutheran Church at Rüsselsheim, trng in problems of industrial soc. (Opel, Gen. Motors), 1958-59; Curate, Dalston, E London, 1959-61; Producer, Relig. Dept, BBC Radio, 1961-64; Assoc. Sec., Dept of Internat. Affairs, Brit. Council of Churches with special resp. for East-West Relations, 1964-69; Dir of (Lay) Trng, Dio. Southwark, 1969-72. Hon. Chaplain to Bp of Southwark, 1975-. Mem. Gen. Synod of C of E, 1970-; Mem. Brit. Council of Churches working parties on Southern Africa and Eastern Europe. Editor, Critic (Otago Univ. newspaper), 1952-53; subseq. free-lance journalist and broadcaster. *Publications:* (ed English edn) Helmut Gollwitzer, The Demands of Freedom, 1965; (trans.) H. J. Schultz, Conversion to the World, 1967; (ed, with J. Klugmann) What Kind of Revolution: A Christian-Communist Dialogue, 1968; (ed) The Christian Marxist Dialogue, 1969. *Address:* 40 Dartmouth Row, SE10 8AP. *T:* 01-692 4051.

O'FAOLAIN, Sean; writer. *Publications:* Midsummer Night Madness, 1932; A Nest of Simple Folk, 1933; Constance Markievicz: a biography, 1934; Bird Alone, 1936; A Purse of Coppers, 1937; King of the Beggars: a biography, 1938; She Had to Do Something (play), 1938; An Irish Journey, 1940; Come Back to Erin, 1940; The Great O'Neill: a biography, 1942; Teresa, 1946; The Short Story, 1948; Summer in Italy, 1949; Newman's Way, 1952; South to Sicily, 1953; The Vanishing Hero, 1956; The Stories of Sean O'Faolain, 1958; I Remember! I Remember!, 1962; Vive Moi!, 1965; The Heat of the Sun, 1966; The Talking Trees, 1970; Foreign Affairs and Other Stories, 1976. *Address:* 17 Rosmeen Park, Dunlaoire, Dublin.

O'FERRALL, Ven. Basil Arthur, QHC 1975; MA; Chaplain of the Fleet and Archdeacon of the Royal Navy, since 1975; Hon. Canon of Gibraltar, since 1977; *b* 25 Aug. 1924; *s* of Basil James and Mabel Violet O'Ferrall, Dublin; *m* 1952, Joyce Forbes (*née* Taylor); one *s* two *d*. *Educ:* St Patrick's Cathedral Gram. Sch.,

Dublin; Trinity Coll., Dublin (BA 1948, MA 1966). Curate Assistant, St Patrick's, Coleraine, 1958; Chaplain RN, 1951; served: HMS Victory, 1951; Ganges, 1952; Gambia, 1952-54; Curlew, 1955; Daedalus, 1956; Amphibious Warfare Sqdn, 1956-58; HMS Adamant, 1958-60; 40 Commando, RM, 1960-62; RN Hosp., Bighi, 1962; HMS Victorious, 1963-64; Condor, 1964-66; Maidstone, 1966-68; St Vincent, 1968; Commando Training Centre, RM, 1969-71; HM Naval Base, Portsmouth, 1971-74; CTC, RM, 1975. *Recreations:* sailing, ornithology. *Address:* Ministry of Defence (Navy), Lacon House, Theobalds Road, WC1X 8RY. *Club:* Royal Commonwealth Society.

OFFALY, Earl of; Thomas FitzGerald; *b* 12 Jan. 1974; *s* of Marquess of Kildare, *qv*.

OFFICER, Maj.-Gen. William James, CB 1962; CBE 1959 (OBE 1945); MB, ChB; late RAMC; *b* 24 August 1903; *s* of John Liddell Officer, OBE, WS, Edinburgh; *m* 1934, Doris, *d* of William Charles Mattinson, Keswick, Cumberland; three *d*. *Educ:* Edinburgh Acad.; Durham School; Edinburgh University. MB, ChB, Edin., 1927. Joined RAMC, 1929; Major, 1939; Commanding Officer British Military Hosp., Deolali, and Officer-in-Charge RAMC Records, India and Burma, 1939-41; Served War of 1939-45 (despatches twice); in Burma, 1941-45; ADMS, 17th Indian Division and 2nd British Division; DDMS, Chindits Special Force and 33rd Indian Corps. Lt-Col, 1946; Asst Commandant, RAMC Depot and Training Establishment; Commanding Officer, British Military Hospital, Fayid (T/Col), 1949; Col 1951; ADMS, Hannover Dist, 1952; ADMS, N Midland Dist, 1954; DDMS (Actg Brig.), 2 (Br) Corps (Suez), 1956; Brig., 1957; Dir of Medical Services (temp. Maj.-Gen.), Middle East Land Forces, 1957-60; Maj.-Gen., 1960; Dir of Medical Services, Far East Land Forces, 1960-63; QHS 1961-63, retired 1963. *Address:* c/o Williams & Glyn's Bank Ltd, Kirkland House, SW1. *Club:* Naval and Military.

OFFICER BROWN, Sir (Charles) James; *see* Brown, Sir C. J. O.

OFFLER, Prof. Hilary Seton, MA; FBA 1974; Professor of Medieval History in the University of Durham, 1956-Sept. 1978; Chairman, Board of Studies in Modern History, 1965-68 and 1971-75; *b* 3 Feb. 1913; *s* of Horace Offler and late Jenny Whebby; *m* 1951, Betty Elfreda, *d* of late Archibald Jackson, Sawbridgeworth; two *s*. *Educ:* Hereford High School; Emmanuel College, Cambridge. 1st Cl. Historical Tripos Pt I, 1932, Part II, 1933, Theological Tripos Pt II, 1934; Lightfoot Schol., Cambridge, 1934; Research Fellow, Emmanuel Coll., 1936-40. Served with RA in N Africa, Sicily and NW Europe, 1940-46, commissioned 1942. Lecturer, Univ. of Bristol, 1946; Reader in Medieval History, Univ. of Durham, 1947. Sec., Surtees Society, 1950-66. *Publications:* edited: Ockham, Opera politica, vol. i (jtly) 1940, *ed. altera* 1974; vol. ii (jtly) 1963; vol. iii 1956; (with E. Bonjour and G. R. Potter) A Short History of Switzerland, 1952; Medieval Historians of Durham, 1958; Durham Episcopal Charters 1071-1152, 1968; articles in English and foreign hist. jls. *Address:* 28 Old Elvet, Durham.

OFFORD, Albert Cyril, FRS 1952; DSc London; PhD Cantab; FRSE; Senior Research Fellow, Imperial College of Science; Emeritus Professor of Mathematics, University of London; Professor, London School of Economics and Political Science, 1966-73; *b* 9 June 1906; *s* of Albert Edwin and Hester Louise Offord; *m* 1945, Marguerite Yvonne Pickard; one *d*. *Educ:* Hackney Downs School, London; University Coll. London (Fellow, 1969); St John's Coll., Cambridge. Fellow of St John's Coll., Cambridge, 1937-40; Lectr, UC N Wales, Bangor, 1940-41; Lectr, King's Coll., Newcastle upon Tyne, 1941-45; Professor: King's College, Newcastle upon Tyne, 1945-48; Birkbeck Coll., Univ. of London, 1948-66. *Publications:* papers in various mathematical journals. *Address:* 70 Elms Road, Harrow, Mddx HA3 6BS.

O'FIAICH, Most Rev. Tomás Séamus; *see* Armagh, Archbishop of, (RC).

O'FLAHERTY, Dr Coleman Anthony; First Assistant Commissioner, National Capital Development Commission, Australia, since 1974; *b* 8 Feb. 1933; *s* of Michael and Agnes O'Flaherty; *m* 1957, Nuala Rose Silke. *Educ:* Nat. Univ. of Ireland (BE); Iowa State Univ. (MS, PhD). FIMunE; FIEI; FIHE; FCIT. Engineer: Galway Co. Council, Ireland, 1954-55; Canadian Pacific Railway Co., Montreal, 1955-56; M. W. Kellogg Co., USA, 1956-57; Asst Prof., Iowa State Univ., 1957-62; Leeds University: Lectr, 1962-66; Prof. of Transport Engineering, Inst. for Transport Studies and Dept of Civil Engineering, 1966-74. Vis. Prof., Univ. of Melbourne, 1973. *Publications:* Highways, 1967, 2nd edn 1974; (jtly) Passenger Conveyors, 1972; (jtly) Introduction to Hovercraft and

Hoverports, 1975; contribs to professional jls. *Recreations:* walking, squash. *Address:* 10 Gundara Street, Aranda, Canberra, ACT 2614, Australia. *T:* Canberra 511700.

O'FLAHERTY, Liam; novelist; *b* Aran Islands, Co. Galway. *Educ:* Rockwell College; Blackrock College; University College, Dublin. *Publications:* Thy Neighbour's Wife, a novel; The Black Soul, a novel; Spring Sowing, short stories; The Informer, a novel; The Tent, and other stories, 1926; Mr Gilhooley, 1926; The Life of Tim Healy, 1927; The Assassin, 1928; Return of the Brute, 1929; The Mountain Tavern, and other stories, 1929; A Tourist's Guide to Ireland, 1929; The House of Gold, 1929; Two Years, 1930; I went to Russia, 1931; The Puritan, 1932; Skerrett, 1932, repr. 1977; The Martyr, 1933; Shame the Devil, 1934; Hollywood Cemetery, 1935; Famine, 1937; Short Stories of Liam O'Flaherty, 1937; Land, 1946; Two Lovely Beasts, short stories, 1948; Insurrection, 1950; The Short Stories of Liam O'Flaherty, 1956; The Pedlar's Revenge and other stories, 1976. *Address:* c/o A. D. Peters, 10 Buckingham Street, Adelphi, WC2.

O'FLYNN, Brigadier (Retd) Dennis John Edwin, CBE 1960 (MBE 1937); DSO 1945; Army Officer retired; *b* 2 Aug. 1907; *s* of late Patrick Horace George O'Flynn and of Katie Alice (*née* Pye); *m* 1936, Winifred Madge Cairn Hogbin; (one *s* and one *d* decd). *Educ:* St Paul's School; RMC Sandhurst. Commissioned 2nd Lieut, Royal Tank Corps, 1928; served in Trans-Jordan Frontier Force, 1932-36; commanded: Westminster Dragoons (2nd Co. Lond. Yeo.), 1947-48; 3rd Royal Tank Regiment, 1948-50. Brigade Commander, 1953-60; retired 1960. Area Comr, St John Ambulance Brigade, 1966-69. OStJ 1967. *Recreations:* golf, gardening, photography. *Address:* High Copse, Pinemount Road, Camberley, Surrey. *T:* Camberley 63736. *Club:* Army and Navy.

of MAR, family name of **Countess of Mar.**

OGDEN, Sir Alwyne (George Neville), KBE 1948 (OBE 1927); CMG 1946; retired; *b* Simla, India, 29 June 1889; *s* of William Ogden, Indian Government Railways, and Emily Mary Stowell; *m* 1922, Jessie Vera (*d* 1969), *d* of Albert Bridge (Adviser to Chinese Government); one *s* one *d. Educ:* Dulwich College; Corpus Christi College, Cambridge (Scholar, BA (Hons) in Classics and History). Student-Interpreter in China Consular Service, 1912; special service (War Office) with Chinese Labour Corps, 1917-18, and on Tibetan Frontier, 1922; Actg Consul-General at Chengtu 1922-23, and Tientsin, 1929-30; Consul (Grade II) 1929, (Grade I), 1934. Served at Peking, Tientsin, Tsinanfu, Chengtu, Hankow, Changsha, Kiukiang, Chefoo, Wei-Hai-Wei, Nanking, Shanghai; Consul-General at Tientsin, 1941, Kunming, 1942-45, Shanghai, 1945-48; retired from Foreign Service, 1948. Acting Judge of HBM Supreme Court for China, 1942-43. FRSA 1952. *Address:* Kingsbury, 51 Ridgway Road, Farnham, Surrey. *T:* Farnham 5461. *Clubs:* Junior Carlton, Royal Automobile.

OGDEN, (Edward) Michael, QC 1968; Barrister since 1950; a Recorder (formerly Recorder of Hastings), since 1971; *b* 9 Apr. 1926; *er s* of late Edward Cannon Ogden and Daisy (*née* Paris); *m* 1951, Joan Kathleen, *er d* of late Pius Charles Brodrick and Kathleen (*née* Moran); two *s* two *d. Educ:* Downside Sch.; Jesus Coll., Cambridge (MA). Served in RAC (Royal Glos Hussars and 16th/5th Lancers), 1944-47 (Capt.); Inns of Court Regt (TA) 1950-56. Jesus Coll., Cambridge, 1948-49; called to Bar, Lincoln's Inn, 1950; Bencher, 1977. Mem. Bar Council, 1960-64, 1966-70, 1971- (Treasurer, 1972-74); Mem. Senate of the Inns of Court, 1966-70, 1972-75. Leader, SE Circuit, 1975-. Member: Council of Union Internationale des Avocats, 1962-; Council of Legal Educn, 1969-74; Chm., Criminal Injuries Compensation Bd, 1975- (Mem., 1968-); Mem., Lord Chancellor's Adv. Cttee on Legal Education, 1972-74. *Address:* 2 Crown Office Row, Temple, EC4Y 7HJ. *T:* 01-353 9337.

OGDEN, Eric; MP (Lab) West Derby Division of Liverpool since 1964 (NUM sponsored candidate); *b* 23 Aug. 1923; *s* of Robert and Jane Lillian Ogden, Rhodes, Co. Lancaster; *m* ; one *s* ; *m* Marjorie (*née* Smith); two *s* two step *d . Educ:* Queen Elizabeth's Grammar School, Middleton, Lancs; Leigh Tech. Coll.; Wigan Mining and Tech. Coll. Merchant Service, 1942-46. Textiles, 1946-52; NCB, 1952-64. Mem., Nat. Union of Mineworkers. Councillor, Borough of Middleton, 1958-65. NUM sponsored candidate, West Derby, Liverpool, 1962. Parly Advisor, Council of Pharm. Soc.; Hon. Vice-Pres., Socialist Medical Assoc.; Jt Hon. Chm., Parly Channel Tunnel Gp; Mem., PO Stamps Adv. Cttee. *Recreations:* painting, gardening, motoring. *Address:* House of Commons, SW1. *T:* 01-219 5201.

OGDEN, Frank Collinge, CBE 1956; FRGS; *b* 30 Mar. 1907; *s* of Paul and Nora Ogden; *m* 1944, Margaret, *o d* of Fred and Elizabeth Greenwood; one *s* two *d* (and one *d* decd). *Educ:* Manchester Grammar School; King's College, Cambridge. Entered Levant Consular Service, 1930; served in Cairo, Alexandria, Bagdad and Damascus; served War, 1941-42; Min. of Information, 1942; Tabriz, 1942; 1st Sec., Bogotá, 1944, Chargé d'Affaires, 1945; Consul, Shiraz, 1947; transferred to Seattle, 1949; Consul-General, Seattle, 1952; Basra, 1953; Gothenburg, 1955; Couns., Brit. Emb. in Libya, 1958; Chargé d'Affaires, 1958, 1959; Counsellor and Consul-General, Brit. Emb., Buenos Aires, 1960-65; retired. *Recreations:* swimming, motoring. *Address:* Yellow Sands, Thorney Drive, Selsey, Chichester, West Sussex. *Club:* Royal Automobile.

OGDEN, Sir George (Chester), Kt 1973; CBE 1966; DL; Chief Executive, Greater Manchester Metropolitan County Council, 1973-76; *b* 7 June 1913; *s* of late Harry and Florence A. Ogden, Burnley, Lancs; *m* 1942, Nina Marion (*née* Lewis); one *s* two *d. Educ:* Burnley Gram. Sch.; Giggleswick Sch.; Corpus Christi Coll., Oxford (MA). Asst Solicitor, Middlesbrough Corp., 1940. Served in Royal Marines, Middle East, Sicily and NW Europe, 1941-45 (Major). Dep. Town Clerk: Middlesbrough, 1947-53; Leicester, 1953-54; Town Clerk, Leicester, 1955-66; Town Clerk, Manchester, 1966-73. Dep. Chm., Police Complaints Bd, 1977-. DL Greater Manchester (formerly Co. Palatine of Lancaster), 1971. FBIM, Hon. LLD Manchester, 1976. *Recreations:* golf, fell walking. *Address:* Agecroft, Prestbury Road, Wilmslow, Cheshire. *Club:* National Liberal.

OGDEN, Michael; see Ogden, E. M.

OGDON, John (Andrew Howard); Pianist, Composer; Professor in his Music Department, University of Indiana, since 1977; *b* 27 Jan. 1937; *s* of late John Andrew Howard Ogdon, Schoolmaster, and Dorothy Louise (*née* Mutton); *m* 1960, Brenda Mary Lucas; one *s* one *d. Educ:* Manchester Gram. Sch.; Royal Manchester Coll. of Music. Concert Appearances include: Michelangeli Festival, Brescia, 1966; Festivals of Spoleto, Edinburgh, Prague Spring, Zagreb Biennale, Cheltenham. Founded Cardiff Festival (with Alun Hoddinott), 1967, Jt Artistic Dir. Two-piano recitals with Brenda Lucas; concert appearances, USA, USSR, Australia, Far East, European capitals. Awards: Liverpool, 1959; Liszt Prize, 1961; Tschaikovsky Prize (*ex aequo* with Vladimir Ashkenazy), Moscow, 1962; Harriet Cohen International Award. *Compositions:* large and small, mainly for piano. *Recreations:* history, literature, P. G. Wodehouse, reading Peter Simple. *Address:* c/o Music Department, University of Indiana, Bloomington, Indiana 47401, USA. *Clubs:* Savage; Savage (Bristol); Scottish Arts (Edinburgh).

OGG, Sir William Gammie, Kt 1949; Director of Rothamsted Experimental Station, 1943-58, retired; *b* 2 Nov. 1891; *s* of late James Ogg, Cults, Aberdeenshire, farmer; *m* 1922, Helen, *y d* of late Henry Hilbert, Halifax; one *s* one *d. Educ:* Robert Gordon's College; Aberdeen University; Christ's College, Cambridge. MA, BSc, BSc (Agr.), Aberdeen Univ., PhD Cantab, LLD Aberdeen, FRSE. Res. Fellow, Bd of Agr. for Scotland, studying in Canada and USA, 1919-20; Researcher, Christ's College, Cambridge, 1920-24; Advisory Officer in Soils, Edinburgh, and East of Scotland College of Agriculture, 1924-30; first Director of the Macaulay Institute for Soil Research, Craigiebuckler, Aberdeen, 1930-43, and research lecturer in Soil Science in the University of Aberdeen; Pres. Soc. of Chem. Industry, 1953-55. Hon. Fellow of the Royal Agric. Soc. of England; For. Corresp. of French Acad. of Agriculture; For. Member of Roy. Acad. of Agriculture of Sweden; Foreign Member of All-Union Academy of Agric. Sciences of the USSR. Hon. Coun. Consejo Superior de Investigaciones Cientificas, Spain. Raffaele Piria medal of Societa Chimica Italiana, 1958. *Publications:* Jt Editor, with G. V. Jacks, Nelson's Agricultural Series; publications on soil chemistry, soil surveys, land reclamation and peat. *Address:* Arnhall, by Edzell, Angus. *T:* Edzell 400. *Club:* Athenæum.

OGILVIE, Sir Alec (Drummond), Kt 1965; Chairman, Powell Duffryn Ltd, since 1969 (Deputy Chairman, 1967-69); *b* 17 May 1913; *s* of late Sir George Drummond Ogilvie, KCIE, CSI; *m* 1945, Lesley Constance, *d* of E. B. Woollan; two *s. Educ:* Cheltenham College. Served War of 1939-45; 2/2nd Gurkha Rifles (Indian Army), 1940-45; Captain 1941; PoW, Singapore, 1942-45. Joined Andrew Yule & Co. Ltd, Calcutta, 1935, Man. Dir, 1956, and Chm., 1962-65. Director: Westinghouse Brake & Signal Co. Ltd, 1966-; Lindustries Ltd, 1973-; J. Lyons & Co. Ltd, 1977-. Pres., Bengal Chamber of Commerce and Industry, 1964-65; Pres., Associated Chambers of Commerce and Industry of India, 1964-65. *Recreations:* golf, walking. *Address:* Brakelands, Warninglid, near Haywards Heath, West Sussex. *T:* Warninglid 270. *Clubs:* Oriental, MCC; Bengal (Calcutta).

OGILVIE, Lady, (Mary Helen); Principal of St Anne's College, Oxford, 1953-66; *b* 22 March 1900; *e d* of late Rev. Professor A. B. Macaulay, DD, of Glasgow; *m* 1922, (Sir) Frederick Wolff Ogilvie, LLD (*d* 1949), Principal of Jesus College, Oxford, 1945-49; two *s* (and one *s* decd). *Educ:* St George's, Edinburgh; Somerville College, Oxford. BA Hon. Sch. of Mod. Hist., Oxford, 1922, MA 1937. Member: Royal Commission on Population, 1944-49; Archbp's Commn on Church and State, 1967-70. Tutor of Women Students, University of Leeds, 1949-53. Member of Arts Council of Great Britain, 1953-58; on Governing Board of Cheltenham Ladies' College, 1951-75; Governing Board of Clifton College, 1960-72. Hon. LLD: Wilson College, Pa, 1956, QUB 1960; Leeds Univ., 1962; Trent Univ., Ont, 1972; Hon. DCL Stirling, 1973. Hon. Fellow: St Anne's College, Oxford, 1966; Lucy Cavendish Collegiate Soc., 1971. *Recreation:* travel. *Address:* Flat 5, Fairlawn, First Turn, Wolvercote, Oxford. *T:* 58137. *Club:* University Women's.

OGILVIE, Prof. Robert Maxwell, FBA 1972; MA, DLitt; Professor of Humanity, University of St Andrews, since 1975; *b* 5 June 1932; *y s* of late Sir Frederick Ogilvie and of Lady Ogilvie, *qv*; *m* 1959, Jennifer Margaret, *d* of D. W. Roberts, Lymington; two *s* one *d*. *Educ:* Rugby; Balliol College, Oxford. First class Hon. Mods, 1952; first class, Lit. Hum., 1954; Harmsworth Sen. Schol. Merton Coll., 1954-55; Fellow and Dir of Studies in Classics, Clare Coll., Cambridge, 1955-57; Fellow of Balliol, 1957-70; Sen. Tutor, 1966-70; Mem., Gen. Board of the Faculties, 1967-70; Mem., Hart Cttee on Relations with Junior Members, 1968; Headmaster, Tonbridge Sch., 1970-75. Visiting Special Lecturer, University Coll., Toronto, 1965-66; Vis. Prof., Yale Univ., 1969; Hofmeyr Vis. Fellow, Wits Univ., 1969. Vice-Pres., Soc. for Roman Studies, 1976. Mem. Council, Trinity Coll., Glenalmond, 1976-. Mem. Scottish Council, Queen's Silver Jubilee Appeal. Editor, Classical Qly, 1977-. DLitt Oxon, 1967; FSA 1968; FSAScot 1972. *Publications:* Latin and Greek: a history of the influence of the classics on English life, 1964; A Commentary on Livy, 1-5, 1965; Tacitus, *Agricola* (with Sir Ian Richmond), 1967; The Ancient World (Oxford Children's Reference Library), 1969; The Romans and Their Gods, 1970; Livy 1-5 (Oxford Classical Texts), 1974; Early Rome and the Etruscans, 1975. *Recreations:* music, climbing, golf. *Address:* Department of Humanity, University of St Andrews, St Andrews, Fife KY16 9AJ; Errachd, By Fort William, Inverness-shire.

OGILVIE-GRANT, family name of **Earl of Seafield.**

OGILVY, family name of **Earl of Airlie.**

OGILVY, Lord; David John Ogilvy; *b* 9 March 1958; *s* and *heir* of 13th Earl of Airlie, *qv*. *Educ:* Eton and Oxford. *Address:* 13 St Leonards Terrace, Chelsea, SW3. *T:* 01-730 8741.

OGILVY, Hon. Angus James Bruce; company director; *b* 14 Sept. 1928; *s* of 12th (*de facto* 9th) Earl of Airlie, KT, GCVO, MC; *m* 1963, HRH Princess Alexandra of Kent; one *s* one *d*. *Educ:* Eton Coll.; Trinity Coll., Oxford. Captain, Scots Guards, 1946-48. Patron: Scottish Wildlife Trust; Nat. Assoc. of Ladies' Circles; Pres., Imperial Cancer Research Fund, 1964-; Pres., National Association of Youth Clubs; Vice-Pres., The Friends of the Poor and Gentlefolk's Help, 1963-; Patron, British Rheumatism and Arthritis Assoc., 1963-; Vice-Patron, Toc H, 1963-. *Address:* Thatched House Lodge, Richmond Park, Surrey. *T:* 01-546 8833. *Club:* White's.
See also under Royal Family.

OGILVY, Sir David (John Wilfrid), 13th Bt, *cr* 1626; DL; farmer and landowner; *b* 3 February 1914; *e s* of Gilbert Francis Molyneux Ogilvy (*d* 1953) (4th *s* of 10th Bt) and Marjory Katharine, *d* of late M. B. Clive, Whitfield, Herefordshire; *S* uncle, Sir Herbert Kinnaird Ogilvy, 12th Bt, 1956; *m* 1966, Penelope Mary Ursula, *d* of Arthur Lafone Frank Hills, White Court, Kent; one *s*. *Educ:* Eton; Trinity College, Oxford. Served in the RNVR in War of 1939-45. JP 1957, DL 1971, East Lothian. *Heir: s* Francis Gilbert Arthur Ogilvy, *b* 22 April 1969. *Address:* Winton House, Pencaitland, East Lothian EH34 5AT. *T:* Pencaitland 340222. *Club:* New (Edinburgh).

OGILVY, David Mackenzie, CBE 1967; Chairman, Ogilvy and Mather, International, 1965-75; *b* 23 June 1911; *s* of Francis John Longley Ogilvy and Dorothy Fairfield. *Educ:* Fettes College, Edinburgh; Christ Church, Oxford (Scholar). British Security Coordination, 1942; Second Secretary, British Embassy, Washington, 1944. Trustee, World Wildlife Fund. Dr of letters (*hc*), Adelphi Univ., USA, 1977. *Publication:* Confessions of an Advertising Man, 1964. *Recreation:* gardening. *Address:* Château de Touffou, 86300 Bonnes, France. *Club:* Brook (NY).

OGILVY-WEDDERBURN, Sir Andrew John Alexander, 13th and 7th Bt *cr* 1704 and 1803; Captain, The Black Watch (Royal Highland Regiment); *b* 4 Aug. 1952; *s* of Sir (John) Peter Ogilvy-Wedderburn, 12th and 6th Bt, and of Elizabeth Katharine, *e d* of late John A. Cox, Drumkilbo; *S* father, 1977. *Educ:* Gordonstoun. *Heir: cousin* Caryl Eustace Wedderburn Ogilvy, ARIBA [*b* 10 Dec. 1925; *m* 1953, Ktharine Mary, *o d* of William Steele; one *s* two *d*]. *Address:* Silvie, Alyth, Perthshire.

OGLE-SKAN, Peter Henry, CVO 1972; TD 1948; Director, Scottish Services, Department of the Environment, 1970-75; *b* 4 July 1915; 2nd *s* of Dr H. W. Ogle-Skan, Hendon; *m* 1941, Pamela Moira Heslop; one *s* one *d*. *Educ:* Merchant Taylors' Sch., London. Clerk with Arbuthnot-Latham & Co. Ltd, London, 1933-39. Commnd into Royal Engineers (TA), 1936; War Service, 1939-46; England, 1939-42; India, 1942-45. Min. of Works: Temp. Principal, 1946; Principal, 1948; Asst Sec., 1955; Under-Sec., Scottish HQ, MPBW, 1966-70. *Recreations:* golf, walking, photography. *Address:* 44 Ravelston Garden, Edinburgh EH4 3LF. *T:* 031-337 6834.

OGLESBY, Peter Rogerson; Under-Secretary, Department of Health and Social Security, since 1974; *b* 15 July 1922; *s* of late Leonard William Oglesby and of Jessie Oglesby (*née* Rogerson); *m* 1947, Doreen Hilda Hudson; three *d*. *Educ:* Woodhouse Grove Sch., Apperley Bridge. Clerical Officer, Admlty, 1939-47; Exec. Officer, Min. of Nat. Ins., 1947-56; Higher Exec. Officer, MPNI, 1956-62, Principal 1962-64; Principal Private Secretary: to Chancellor of Duchy of Lancaster, 1964-66; to Minister without Portfolio, 1966; to First Sec. of State, 1966-68; to Lord President, 1968; Asst Sec., Cabinet Office, 1968-70, Asst Sec., DHSS, 1970-73; Sec., Occupational Pensions Bd, 1973-74. *Address:* 41 Draycot Road, Wanstead, E11 2NX. *T:* 01-989 5526.

OGMORE, 2nd Baron *cr* 1950, of Bridgend; **Gwilym Rees Rees-Williams;** *b* 5 May 1931; *er s* of 1st Baron Ogmore, PC, TD, and of Constance, *er d* of W. R. Wills; *S* father, 1976; *m* 1967, Gillian Mavis, *d* of M. K. Slack; two *d*. *Educ:* Mill Hill School; St Luke's Coll., Exeter. *Heir: b* Hon. Morgan Rees-Williams [*b* 19 Dec. 1937; *m* 1964, Patricia (marr. diss. 1970), *o d* of C. Paris Jones; *m* 1972, Roberta (marr. diss. 1976), *d* of Captain Alec Cunningham-Reid, DFC]. *Address:* 4 Foster Road, Chiswick, W4.

OGNALL, Harry Henry, QC 1973; a Recorder of the Crown Court since 1972; *b* 9 Jan. 1934; *s* of Leo and Cecilia Ognall; *m* 1962, Jean Mary Stalker; two *s* one *d*. *Educ:* Leeds Grammar Sch.; Lincoln Coll., Oxford (MA (Hons)); Univ. of Virginia, USA (LLM). Called to Bar (Gray's Inn), 1958. Joined NE Circuit. *Recreations:* photography, music, travel. *Address:* 5 King's Bench Walk, Temple, EC4Y 7DN; 2 Park Square, Leeds LS1 2NE.

O'GORMAN, Rev. Brian Stapleton; President of the Methodist Conference, 1969-70; *b* 4 March 1910; *s* of William Thomas and Annie Maria O'Gorman; *m* 1939, Margaret, *d* of William and Margaret Huggon, Carlisle; two *d*. *Educ:* Bowdon College, Cheshire; Handsworth Theological College, Birmingham. Porlock, 1931-32; Handsworth College, 1932-35; Manchester Mission, 1935-40; Islington Mission, London, 1940-43; Longton Mission, Stoke on Trent, 1943-50; Sheffield Mission, 1950-57; Chm., Wolverhampton and Shrewsbury Dist of Methodist Church, 1957-75. *Address:* 9 Trysull Gardens, Wolverhampton WV3 7LD. *T:* Wolverhampton 762167.

OGSTON, Alexander George, FRS 1955; MA, DSc; President of Trinity College, Oxford, 1970-78; Fellow, 1937, and Bedford Lecturer, 1950, Balliol College; *b* 30 January 1911; *s* of late Walter Henry Ogston and late Josephine Elizabeth Ogston (*née* Carter); *m* 1934, Elizabeth Wicksteed; one *s* three *d*. *Educ:* Eton College (King's Scholar); Balliol College, Oxford. DPhil 1936, MA 1937, DSc 1970. Demonstrator, Balliol College, 1933; Freedom Research Fellow, London Hospital, 1935; Departmental Demonstrator (Biochemistry), 1938; University Demonstrator, 1944. Oxford; Reader in Biochemistry, University of Oxford, 1955-59; Prof. of Physical Biochemistry, John Curtin School of Medical Research, ANU, 1959-70, Prof. Emeritus, 1970. Chairman, Editorial Bd, Biochemical Journal, 1955-59 (Member of Board, 1951-55). Vice-Chm., Central Council, Selly Oak Colleges, Birmingham, 1976-. Fellow, Australian Acad. of Science, 1962; Hon. Fellow, Balliol Coll., Oxford, 1969; Hon. Mem. American Soc. of Biological Chemists, 1965; Hon. DMed Uppsala. *Publications:* scientific papers on physical chemistry and biochemistry. *Address:* c/o Trinity College, Oxford OX1 3BH.

OGSTON, Prof. Derek, MD, PhD, DSc; FRCP; Regius Professor of Physiology, University of Aberdeen, since 1977; *b* 31 May 1932; *s* of Frederick John Ogston and Ellen Mary Ogston; *m* 1963, Cecilia Marie Clark; one *s* two *d*. *Educ:* King's Coll. Sch., Wimbledon; Univ. of Aberdeen (MA, MD, PhD, DSc). FRCP Edin 1973; FRCP 1977. Univ. of Aberdeen: Res. Fellow, 1959-62; Lectr in Medicine, 1962-69; Sen. Lectr in Med., 1969-75; Reader in Med., 1975-76. MRC Trav. Fellow, 1967-68. *Publications:* scientific papers on haemostasis. *Recreation:* home maintenance. *Address:* 64 Rubislaw Den South, Aberdeen AB2 6AX. *T:* Aberdeen 36587.

O'HAGAN, 4th Baron, *cr* 1870; **Charles Towneley Strachey;** *b* 6 Sept. 1945; *s* of Hon. Thomas Anthony Edward Towneley Strachey (*d* 1955; having assumed by deed poll, 1938, the additional Christian name of Towneley, and his mother's maiden name of Strachey, in lieu of his patronymic) and of Lady Mary Strachey, *d* of 3rd Earl of Selborne, PC, CH; *S* grandfather, 1961; *m* 1967, Princess Tamara Imeretinsky; one *d*. *Educ:* Eton; (Exhibitioner) New College, Oxford. Page to HM the Queen, 1959-62. Independent Member, British Delegation to European Parliament, 1973-75; joined Conservative Party, 1976. *Heir: b* Hon. Richard Towneley Strachey, *b* 29 Dec. 1950. *Address:* Sutton Court, Stowey, Pensford, Bristol, Avon. *T:* Chew Magna 2933. *Clubs:* Beefsteak, Pratt's.

O'HAGAN, Desmond, CMG 1957; *b* 4 Mar. 1909; *s* of Captain Claud O'Hagan, Nyeri, Kenya and Eva O'Hagan (*née* Napier Magill); *m* 1942, Pamela, *d* of Major A. H. Symes-Thompson, DSO, Kiambu, Kenya; one *s* two *d*. *Educ:* Wellington Coll.; Clare Coll., Cambridge. Entered Colonial Administrative Service, Kenya, 1931. Called to Bar, Inner Temple, 1935. Private Secretary to British Resident, Zanzibar, 1937; served with E African Forces in N Province, Kenya, 1940-42; Native Courts Adviser, 1948-51; Provincial Commissioner, Coast Province, Kenya, 1952-59; Chairman, Transport Licensing Authority, Tanganyika, 1959-63. *Recreations:* bridge, golf. *Address:* Kianjibbi, Kiambu, Kenya. *Clubs:* East India, Devonshire, Sports and Public Schools; Muthaiga (Nairobi).

O'HALLORAN, Michael Joseph; MP (Lab) Islington North since Oct. 1969 (NUR sponsored Member of Parliament); *b* 20 Aug. 1929; British; *m* 1956, Stella Beatrice McDonald; three *d* (one *s* decd). *Educ:* Clohanes National School, Eire; self-educated. Railway worker, 1948-63; building works manager, 1963-69. Mem., TGWU. Chm., Islington Soc. for Mentally Handicapped Children; Mem., NI Civil Rights Assoc. *Recreations:* boxing, football, fishing. *Address:* 40 Tytherton Road, N19. *Clubs:* Finsbury Park Railwaymen's, Irish Centre, Irish, Challoner.

O'HARA, Bill; National Governor of the BBC for Northern Ireland, since 1973; *b* 26 Feb. 1929; *s* of William P. O'Hara and Susanna Agnes O'Hara (*née* Gill); *m* 1953, Anne Marie Finn; two *s* two *d*. *Address:* Ashvale, 14 Raglan Road, Bangor, Co. Down, N Ireland. *T:* Bangor 60869. *Clubs:* Royal Ulster Yacht, Royal Belfast Golf, Sunnyland Beagles.

O'HARA, Frank; Director-General Equipment, Procurement Executive, Ministry of Defence, 1973-77; *b* 1 Oct. 1917; *s* of Francis O'Hara and Lily Mary O'Hara (*née* Slaven); *m* 1943, Mhuire Wheldon Hattle; one *s* three *d*. *Educ:* Alloa Academy; Edinburgh Univ.; Christ's Coll., Cambridge. MA Hons Maths and Nat. Phil., Edinburgh, 1938; BA Hons Maths 1940, MA Cantab 1944. Marine Aircraft Experimental Estab., 1940; Airborne Forces Exper. Estab., 1942; Aircraft and Armament Exper. Estab., 1950; RAE Bedford, 1954; Head, 3' Supersonic Tunnel, 1956; Head, Aero Flight, 1959; Chief Supt and Head Flight Group, 1966. Dir-Gen. Civil Aircraft, MoD, 1970-73. FRAES 1966. Alston Medal for Flight Testing, 1970; Busk Prize, 1965. *Publications:* papers in Reports and Memoranda of ARC, and various jls. *Recreations:* literature and the arts, gardening. *Address:* Welcroft, 11 Glasgow Street, Helensburgh, Dunbartonshire.

O'HIGGINS, Hon. Thomas Francis, SC (Ireland) 1954; Chief Justice of Ireland, since 1974; *b* 23 July 1916; *e s* of Dr Thomas F. O'Higgins and Agnes McCarthy; *m* 1948, Thérèse Keane; five *s* two *d*. *Educ:* St Mary's Coll., Rathmines, Clongowes Wood Coll.; University Coll., Dublin (BA, BL); King's Inns, Dublin. Called to Irish Bar, 1938; Bencher of King's Inns, 1967; Judge of High Court, 1973. Elected to Dail Eireann, 1948; Minister for Health, 1954; contested Presidency, 1966 and 1973. *Recreations:* fishing, golf. *Address:* Jerpoint, Elton Park, Sandycove, Co. Dublin. *T:* 803605. *Clubs:* Stephen's Green, Miltown Golf.

OHLSON, Sir Eric James, 2nd Bt, *cr* 1920; *b* 16 March 1911; *s* of Sir Erik Ohlson, 1st Bt, and Jennie (*d* 1952), *d* of J. Blakeley; *S*

father 1934; *m* 1935, Marjorie Joan, *d* of late C. H. Roosmale-Cocq, Dorking, Surrey; two *s* one *d*. *Heir: s* Brian Eric Christopher Ohlson, *b* 27 July 1936. *Address:* Belvedere House, Esplanade, Scarborough, Yorks.

OISTRAKH, Igor Davidovich; Russian Violinist; *b* Odessa, 1931; *s* of late David Oistrakh. *Educ:* Music Sch. and State Conservatoire, Moscow. Many foreign tours (USSR, Europe, South America, Japan); many gramophone records; many concerts with father. 1st prize, Violin Competition, Budapest, 1952, Wieniawki Competition, Poznan, 1952; Honoured Artist of RSFSR. *Address:* State Conservatoire, 13 Ulitsa Herzen, Moscow, USSR.

OKEDEN, Richard Godfrey Christian; *see* Parry-Okeden.

O'KEEFE, John Harold; Head of Industrial Relations, Thames Television, since 1974; *b* 25 Dec. 1938; *s* of Terence Harold O'Keefe and Christian Frances (*née* Foot); *m* 1959, Valerie Anne Atkins; two *s* two *d*. *Educ:* Acton County Grammar School. Dir, Newspaper Publishers Assoc., 1974. *Address:* 189 Kingshall Road, Beckenham, Kent. *T:* 01-778 8010.

O'KEEFFE, Georgia; artist; *b* Sun Prairie, Wisconsin, USA, 15 Nov. 1887; *d* of Francis O'Keeffe and Ida Totto; *m* 1924, Alfred Stieglitz. *Educ:* Sacred Heart Acad., Madison, Wis; Chatham (Va) Episcopal Inst.; Art Inst., Chicago; Art Students' League, NY; Univ. of Va; Columbia Univ. Head of Art Dept, West Texas State Normal Coll., Canyon, 1916-18. Painting, only, 1918-; annual one-man shows, 1923-46, in Stieglitz galls. Retrospective exhibitions: Brooklyn Museum, 1927; Art Inst. of Chicago, 1943; Museum of Modern Art (New York), 1946; Worcester Art Museum, USA, 1960; Whitney Mus. of Mod. Art, 1970; Art Inst. of Chicago, 1971; San Francisco Mus. of Art, 1971. Paintings in permanent collections of many museums and galleries in USA. Member National Institute of Arts and Letters; Benjamin Franklin Fellow, Royal Soc. for Encouragement of Arts, Manufactures and Commerce, 1969. Holds many hon. degrees. Creative Arts Award, Brandeis Univ., 1963; Wisconsin Governor's Award, 1966; Gold Medal, Nat. Inst. of Arts and Letters, 1970; M. Carey Thomas Award, Bryn Mawr Coll., 1971; Nat. Assoc. of Schs of Art award, 1971; Skowhegan Sch. of Painting and Sculpture award, 1973. *Publication:* Georgia O'Keeffe (portfolio of 12 reproductions with text), 1937. *Address:* Abiquiu, Rio Arriba County, New Mexico, USA.

O'KEEFFE, Peter Laurence, CVO 1974; HM Diplomatic Service; Director-General, British Information Services, and Deputy Consul General (Information), New York, since 1976; *b* 9 July 1931; *s* of Richard O'Keeffe and Alice (*née* Chase); *m* 1954, Suzanne Marie Jousse; three *d*. *Educ:* St Francis Xavier's Coll., Liverpool; University Coll., Oxford (schol.). HM Customs and Excise, 1953-62; 2nd, later 1st Sec. (Economic), Bangkok, 1962-65; FO, 1965-68; 1st Sec. and Head of Chancery, Athens, 1968-72; Commercial Counsellor, Jakarta, 1972-75; Head of Hong Kong and Indian Ocean Dept, FCO, 1975-76. *Recreations:* gardening, music. *Address:* c/o Foreign and Commonwealth Office, SW1.

OKEOVER, Col Sir Ian P. A. M. W.; *see* Walker-Okeover.

OKOGIE, Most Rev. Anthony Olubunmi; *see* Lagos, Archbishop of, (RC).

OKORO, Godfrey; *see* Benin, Oba of.

OLAGBEGI II, The Olowo of Owo, (Sir Olateru), Kt 1960; Oba Alaiyeluwa, Olagbegi II, Olowo of Owo, since 1941; Minister of State, Western Region (now Western Provinces) of Nigeria, 1952; President of the House of Chiefs, Western Region (now Western Provinces), 1965; *b* 1910; *s* of Oba Alaiyeluwa, Olagbegi I, Olowo of Owo; married; many *s* and *d* (some decd). *Educ:* Owo Government School. A Teacher in Owo; Treasury Clerk in Owo Native Administration, 1935-41. Queen's Medal, 1957. *Recreations:* lawn tennis, squash racquets. *Address:* PO Box 1, Afin Oba Olowo, Owo, Western Provinces of Nigeria. *T:* Owo 1.

OLANG', Most Rev. Festo Habakkuk; *see* Kenya, Archbishop of.

OLDENBOURG-IDALOVICI, Zoë; writer (as Zoë Oldenbourg); *b* 31 March 1916; *d* of Sergius Oldenbourgh, writer and historicist, and of Ada (*née* Starynkevitch); *m* 1948, Heinric Idalovici; one *s* one *d*. *Educ:* Lycée Molière and Sorbonne, Paris. Prix Fémina, 1953. *Publications:* Argile et cendres, 1946 (The World is Not Enough, 1949); La Pierre angulaire, 1953 (The Cornerstone, 1954); Merveilles de la Vie,

1956 (The Awakened, trans. E. Hyams, 1957); Les Irréductibles, 1958 (The Chains of Love, 1959); Bûcher de Montségur, 1959 (Massacre at Montségur, 1962); Les Brûlés, 1961 (Destiny of Fire, trans. P. Green, 1961); Les Cités charnelles, 1961 (Cities of the Flesh, 1963); Les Croisades: un essai historique, 1963 (The Crusades, trans. Anne Carter, 1966); Catherine de Russie, 1965 (Catherine the Great, 1965); Saint Bernard, 1969; La Joie des pauvres, 1970 (The Heirs of the Kingdom, trans. Anne Carter, 1972); L'Epopée des cathédrales, 1973; Que vous a donc fait Israël?, 1974; Visages d'un autoportrait (autobiog.), 1977. *Recreation:* painting. *Address:* c/o Victor Gollancz Ltd, 14 Henrietta Street, WC2; 5 rue Isabey, 75016 Paris, France.

OLDFIELD, John Richard Anthony; *b* July 1900; *s* of late Major H. E. Oldfield; *m* 1953, Jonnet Elizabeth, *d* of late Maj. H. M. Richards, DL, JP. *Educ:* Eton; Trinity College, Cambridge; Served in: Coldstream Guards, 1918-20; RN, 1939-45. MP (Lab) South-East Essex, 1929-31; Parliamentary Private Secretary to Sec. of State for Air, 1929-30. Mem. LCC, 1931-58 (Vice-Chairman, 1953). CC Kent, 1965. *Address:* Doddington Place, near Sittingbourne, Kent. *Club:* Cavalry and Guards.

OLDFIELD, Sir Maurice, KCMG 1975 (CMG 1964); CBE 1956 (MBE 1946); HM Diplomatic Service; *b* 16 Nov. 1915; *e s* of late Joseph and Ada Annie Oldfield, Over Haddon. *Educ:* Lady Manners School, Bakewell; Manchester Univ. 1st Cl. Hons History; MA 1938. Served War of 1939-45, Intelligence Corps, Middle East, 1941-46 (Lt-Col; MBE). Jones Fellow in History and Tutor, Hulme Hall, Manchester, 1938-39. Attached to Foreign Office, 1947-49; Office of Commissioner-General for UK in South East Asia, Singapore, 1950-52; Foreign Office 1953-55; First Secretary, Singapore, 1956-58; Foreign Office, 1958-59; Counsellor: Washington, 1960-64; FO, subseq. FCO, 1965-75. *Recreation:* farming. *Address:* c/o Foreign and Commonwealth Office, SW1. *Clubs:* Athenæum; Metropolitan (Washington, DC).

OLDFIELD-DAVIES, Alun Bennett, CBE 1955; MA; Controller, Wales, British Broadcasting Corporation, 1945-67; *b* 1905; *s* of Rev. J. Oldfield-Davies, Wallasey, Cheshire; *m* 1931, Lilian M. Lewis, BA. *Educ:* Porth County Sch., Rhondda; University College, Aberystwyth. Schoolmaster and Lecturer to University Extension Classes in Ammanford, Carmarthenshire, and Cardiff, 1926-37. British Broadcasting Corporation: Schools Asst, 1937-40; Welsh Executive, 1940-44; Overseas Services Establishment Officer, 1944-45. Member: Court and Council of University of Wales; President, National Museum of Wales, 1972-; President, Welsh Council for Education in World Citizenship. Formerly Warden, University of Wales Guild of Graduates. Hon. LLD, Univ. of Wales, 1967. *Address:* Ty Gwyn, Llantrisant Road, Llandaff, Cardiff. *T:* 565920.

OLDHAM, Rev. Canon Arthur Charles Godolphin; *b* 5 Apr. 1905; *s* of late Sidney Godolphin and Lilian Emma Oldham; *m* 1934, Ursula Finch Wigham Richardson, *d* of late George and Isabel Richardson, Newcastle upon Tyne; one *s* two *d*. *Educ:* King's College School; King's College, London. Business, music and journalism to 1930. Ordained, to Witley, Surrey, 1933; Vicar of Brockham Green, 1936; Rector of Merrow, 1943; Rural Dean of Guildford, 1949; Vicar of Godalming, 1950; Rural Dean of Godalming, 1957; Director of Ordination Training, and Bishop's Examining Chaplain, 1958; Hon. Canon of Guildford, 1959; Canon Residentiary of Guildford Cathedral, 1961-71, retired. *Recreations:* music, sketching. *Address:* Dora Cottage, Beech Hill, Hambledon, Surrey. *T:* Wormley 2087.

OLDHAM, Arthur Joseph Percy; Senior Principal Medical Officer, Department of Health and Social Security, 1970-75; Consulting Psychiatrist, Guy's Hospital, 1965-75; *b* 1 Oct. 1920; *s* of Arthur Oldham and Emily Sherston-Baker; *m* 1948, Elsa Harhalaki. *Educ:* Brighton Coll.; Guy's Hosp., London Univ. MRCS, LRCP, MB, BS, DPM, MD, FRCPsych.

OLDMAN, Col Sir Hugh (Richard Deare), KBE 1974 (OBE 1960); MC 1942; retired; *b* 24 June 1914; *s* of late Maj.-Gen. R. D. F. Oldman, CB, CMG, DSO, and Mrs Helen Marie Oldman (*née* Pigot); *m* 1947, Agnes Fielding Murray Oldman (*née* Bayles); no *c*. *Educ:* Wellington Coll.; RMC Sandhurst. CO 8th Bn Durham LI, 1944-45; psc 1945; Chief Instructor, Quetta Staff Coll.; comd Bn, Aden Protectorate Levies, 1957-60; comd Sultan's Armed Forces, Oman, 1961-64; Staff, HQ Allied Forces Southern Europe (NATO), 1965-67; retd from Army, 1967; subseq. Sec. for Defence, Sultanate of Oman. Croix de Guerre (Palme), 1944; Order of Merit 1st cl., Oman, 1972. *Recreations:* polo, yachting, golf. *Address:* Stroud Cottage, Grayswood, Haslemere, Surrey GU27 2DJ. *T:* Haslemere 2870. *Clubs:* Royal Lymington Yacht; Liphook Golf.

OLDROYD, Prof. James Gardner, MA, PhD, ScD (Cantab); Professor of Applied Mathematics since 1965 and Head of Department of Applied Mathematics and Theoretical Physics since 1973, University of Liverpool; *b* 25 April 1921; *o s* of late H. and R. Oldroyd; *m* 1946, Marged Katryn, *e d* of late Rev. J. D. Evans; three *s*. *Educ:* Bradford Grammar Sch.; Trinity Coll., Cambridge (Schol.). Min. of Supply (PDE), 1942-45; Fundamental Research Lab., Courtaulds Ltd, Maidenhead, 1945-53; Fellow, Trinity Coll., Cambridge, 1947-51; Prof. of Applied Maths, UC Swansea, Univ. of Wales, 1953-65; Dean, Faculty of Science, UC Swansea, 1957-59. Pres., Brit. Soc. of Rheology, 1955-57. Adams Prize, 1963-64. *Publications:* papers on mathematical theory of deformation and flow in Proc. Royal Soc., Proc. Cambridge Phil. Soc., etc. *Address:* Department of Applied Mathematics and Theoretical Physics, University of Liverpool, Liverpool L69 3BX. *T:* 051-709 6022; Ardenmohr, Graham Road, West Kirby, Wirral, Merseyside L48 5DN. *T:* 051-632 2684.

O'LEARY, Patrick; *see* Guerisse, A. M. E.

O'LEARY, Terence Daniel; HM Diplomatic Service; Deputy High Commissioner and Counsellor, Wellington, since 1974; *b* 18 Aug. 1928; 2nd *s* of late Daniel O'Leary; *m* 1960, Janet Douglas Berney, *d* of Dr H. B. Berney, Masterton, NZ; twin *s* one *d*. *Educ:* Dulwich; St John's Coll., Cambridge. BA 1950. Army, commnd Queen's Royal Regt, 1946-48. Commerce, 1951-53; Asst Principal, CRO, 1953; 2nd Sec., British High Commn, Wellington, 1956-58; Principal, PSO's Dept, CRO, 1958; 1st Sec., New Delhi, 1960-63; 1st Sec., Dar es Salaam, 1963-64; CRO, 1964-65; 1st Sec. and Defence Sec., Canberra, 1965-68; Actg Head, S Asia Dept, FCO, 1969; Asst Sec., Cabinet Office, 1970-72; Counsellor, Pretoria/Cape Town, 1972-74. *Recreations:* walking, tennis, reading, family expeditions. *Address:* c/o Foreign and Commonwealth Office, SW1; 3 Glenconner, Old Avenue, St George's Hill, Weybridge, Surrey. *Clubs:* Travellers'; Wellington (New Zealand).

OLIPHANT, Air Vice-Marshal David Nigel Kington B.; *see* Blair-Oliphant.

OLIPHANT, Sir Mark, (Marcus Laurence Elwin), AC 1977; KBE 1959; FRS 1937; Governor of South Australia, 1971-76; *b* Adelaide, 8 Oct. 1901; *e s* of H. G. Oliphant; *m* 1925, Rosa Wilbraham, Adelaide, S Australia; one *s* one *d*. *Educ:* Unley and Adelaide High Schools; University of Adelaide; Trinity Coll., Cambridge (1851 Exhibitioner, Overseas 1927, Senior 1929; PhD 1929). Messel Research Fellow of Royal Society, 1931; Fellow and Lecturer St John's Coll., 1934. Hon. Fellow, 1952; Assistant Director of Research, Cavendish Laboratory, Cambridge, 1935, Poynting Professor of Physics, University of Birmingham, 1937-50; Dir, Research Sch. of Physical Sciences, ANU, Canberra, 1950-63; Prof. of Physics of Ionised Gases, Inst. of Advanced Studies, ANU, 1964-67, now Professor Emeritus. Pres., Aust. Acad. of Sciences, 1954-57. Hon. DSc (Toronto, Belfast, Melbourne, Birmingham, New South Wales, ANU, Adelaide, Flinders); Hon. LLD (St Andrews). KStJ 1972. *Publications:* Rutherford: recollections of the Cambridge days, 1972; various papers on electricity in gases, surface properties and nuclear physics. *Address:* 37 Colvin Street, Hughes, ACT, Australia. *Club:* Athenæum.

OLIPHANT, Patrick James, TD 1945; Deputy Keeper of Her Majesty's Signet, 1964-75; *b* 19 March 1914; 2nd *s* of Kenneth M. Oliphant, MC, WS, and Florence Agnes, *d* of late Abram Lyle; *m* 1938, Margaret Kemp, *er d* of late James Brown, Ironfounder, Stirling; no *c*. *Educ:* Edinburgh Academy; Trinity Coll., Oxford (BA); Edinburgh Univ. (LLB). Admitted WS, 1938. Served RA, 1939-45 (US Bronze Star, 1945). Commanded 278 (City of Edinburgh) Regt RATA, 1948-51; Hon. Colonel, 1961-64. Director: Royal Bank of Scotland Ltd; Norwich Union Life Insurance Society Ltd; Scottish American Investment Co. Ltd. *Recreations:* shooting, fishing, golf. *Address:* 79 Ravelston Dykes Road, Edinburgh EH4 3NU. *T:* 031-337 3091. *Clubs:* Caledonian; New (Edinburgh).

OLIVER, Benjamin Rhys; a Recorder of the Crown Court, since 1972; *b* 8 June 1928; *m* 1955; one *s* one *d*. *Educ:* Llandovery and Aberystwyth. Called to the Bar, Inner Temple, 1954. *Recreation:* golf. *Address:* 86 St Helen's Road, Swansea, West Glamorgan. *T:* Swansea 52988.

OLIVER, Sir (Frederick) Ernest, Kt 1962; CBE 1955; TD 1942; DL; Chairman, George Oliver (Footwear) Ltd, 1950-73; *b* 31 Oct. 1900; *s* of late Colonel Sir Frederick Oliver and late Lady Oliver, CBE; *m* 1928, Mary Margaret, *d* of late H. Simpson, two *d* (one *s* decd). *Educ:* Rugby School. Member Leicester City Council, 1933-73, Lord Mayor, 1950. Officer, Territorial Army,

1922-48. Served UK and Burma, 1939-45. President: Multiple Shoe Retailers' Assoc., 1964-65; Leicester YMCA, 1955-76; Leicester Conservative Assoc., 1952-66. Leicester: DL 1950; Hon. Freeman, 1971. *Recreation:* shooting. *Address:* 6 Westminster Road, Leicester. *T:* 705310. *Club:* Leicestershire (Leicester).

OLIVER, Admiral Sir Geoffrey (Nigel), GBE 1955; KCB 1951 (CB 1944); DSO 1941; *b* 22 Jan. 1898; *er s* of late Prof. F. W. Oliver; *m* 1933, Barbara, *o d* of late Sir Francis Jones, KBE, CB; one *s* (and one *s* one *d* decd). *Educ:* Rugby. Cadet, 1915; Mid. and Sub-Lieut, HMS Dreadnought, 1916; HMS Renown, 1917-20; specialised in Gunnery, 1923; HMS Carlisle, China Station, 1925-27; HMS Rodney, 1930-32; Commander, 1932; commanded HMS Diana and HMS Veteran, 1st Destroyer Flotilla, Mediterranean, 1934-36; Captain, 1937; served War of 1939-45 (DSO and two Bars, CB); commanded HMS Hermione, 1940-42, Western Mediterranean, Malta, Madagascar, Eastern Mediterranean; Commodore, 2nd class, 1942; Senior Officer Inshore Squadron, North Africa, 1942-43; British Assault Force Commander, Salerno, 1943; Commodore, 1st class, 1944; Commander, Force J, Assault Force, Normandy, 1944; 21st Aircraft Carrier Squadron, 1944-45; Rear-Admiral, 1945; Admiral (Air), 1946; a Lord Comr of the Admiralty and Asst Chief of Naval Staff, 1947-48; Vice-Admiral, 1949; President, RN Coll., Greenwich, 1948-50; Commander-in-Chief, East Indies Station, 1950-52; Admiral, 1952; Commander-in-Chief, the Nore, 1953-55; retired, Dec. 1955. *Address:* Batts, Henfield, West Sussex.

OLIVER, Henry John Callard, BSc; Assistant Master, Kingsmead School, Hoylake, since 1974; Member, Headmasters' Association; *b* 28 April 1915; *s* of late H. J. Oliver, Master Mariner, Wallington, Surrey; *m* 1939, Megan Eluned, *d* of late D. J. Edwards; two *s* one *d*. *Educ:* Sutton County School; King's Coll., London. 1st class Hons Physics, 1936. Physics Master, St Paul's Sch., 1936; Scientific Officer, MAP, 1940; Senior Science Master, Warwick Sch., 1951; Headmaster, Maidenhead Grammar Sch., 1954; Headmaster, Wallasey Grammar Sch., 1960; Headmaster, Northampton Grammar Sch., 1965-74. *Recreation:* dinghy sailing. *Address:* Hesny, 88 Birkenhead Road, Meols, Wirral, Merseyside. *T:* Hoylake 4203.

OLIVER, Henry Sherrard; Director, Ulster Office in Great Britain, since May 1977; *b* 2 March 1917; *s* of Robert John Oliver, Limavady, Co. Londonderry, and Martha Sherrard, Magilligan, Co. Londonderry; *m* 1948, Betty Wigley; two *s*. *Educ:* St Jude's Elementary Sch., Belfast. Served War of 1939-45; Major, RA, 1940-46 (despatches). Entered Northern Ireland Civil Service, 1936; Dept of Agriculture, 1946-73; Dir of Industrial Development Organisation, Dept of Commerce, 1973-77. *Recreations:* golf, gardening, soccer. *Address:* Ulster Office, 11 Berkeley Street, W1X 6BU. *T:* 01-493 0601; Yew Tree Cottage, Folly Lane, South Cadbury, Somerset.

OLIVER, Brig. James Alexander, CB 1957; CBE 1945; DSO 1942 (and Bar to DSO 1943); TD; Vice-Lieutenant, County of Angus, since 1967; *b* 19 March 1906; *s* of Adam Oliver, Arbroath, Angus; *m* 1932, Margaret Whytock Scott; no *c*. *Educ:* Trinity Coll., Glenalmond. 2nd Lieut, Black Watch (TA), 1926; commanded: 7th Black Watch, 1942; 152 Infantry Bde (Highland Div.), 1943; 154 Infantry Bde (Highland Div.), 1944; served War of 1939-45 in N Africa, Sicily and NW Europe (despatches). DL (Angus) 1948; ADC to the Queen, 1953-63; Hon. Colonel, 6/7th Black Watch, 1960-67; Hon. Colonel, 51st Highland Volunteers, 1967-70. Member, Angus and Dundee T&AFA, 1938- (Chairman, 1945-59). Chm., 1972-73, Vice-Pres., 1973, The Earl Haig Fund, Scotland. Hon. LLD Dundee, 1967. *Address:* West Newton, Arbroath, Angus, Scotland. *T:* Arbroath 72579. *Club:* Naval and Military.

OLIVER, Dr John Andrew, CB 1968; *b* 25 Oct. 1913; *s* of Robert John Oliver, Limavady, Co. Londonderry and Martha Sherrard, Magilligan, Co. Londonderry; *m* 1943, Stella Ritson; five *s*. *Educ:* Royal Belfast Academical Institution; Queen's Univ., Belfast; Bonn Univ.; Königsberg Univ.; Zimmern School of International Studies, Geneva; Imperial Defence Coll., London. BA 1936; DrPhil, 1951; IDC, 1954. Ministry of Development, NI: Second Sec., 1964-71; Permanent Sec., 1971-74; Permanent Sec., Housing, Local Govt and Planning, NI, 1974-75; Chief Adviser, NI Constitutional Convention, 1975-76. Hon. Sec., Assoc. of Governing Bodies of Voluntary Grammar Schs in NI, 1964-; Chm., Bd of Governors, Royal Belfast Academical Instn, 1970-77. Hon. MRTPI, 1964; Hon. Member, Assoc. for Housing and Town Planning, W Germany, 1966. *Recreations:* walking, maps, languages. *Address:* 107 Circular Road, Belfast 4, N Ireland. *T:* Belfast 768101. *Club:* Royal Over-Seas League.

OLIVER, John Laurence; Journalist; *b* 14 Sept. 1910; *s* of late Harold Oliver and of Mrs Teresa Oliver; *m* 1946, Renée Mary Webb; two *s*. *Educ:* Haberdashers' Aske's Hampstead School. Publicity Manager, The Book Society, 1934; Art Editor, The Bystander, 1935-39. War of 1939-45: served in the Field Security Corps; commissioned 1941, The Suffolk Regt (transferred The Cambridgeshire Regt). Joined staff of The Sphere, 1946; Art Editor, 1947; Assistant Editor, 1956; Editor, 1960-64; Editor, The Tatler, 1961-65. *Publications:* Saint John's Wood Church (with Rev. Peter Bradshaw), 1955; occasional short stories and articles. *Recreations:* reading, theatre going, watching cricket. *Address:* 10 Wellington Place, NW8 9JA. *T:* 01-286 5891. *Clubs:* Garrick, MCC.

OLIVER, Group Captain John Oliver William, CB 1950; DSO 1940; DFC 1940; RAF retired; *b* 1911; *e s* of William Oliver; *m* 1935 (marr. diss., 1951); one *s* two *d*; *m* 1962, Anne Fraser Porteous; one *s* two *d* (of whom *s* and *yr d* are twins). *Educ:* Christ's Hospital; Cranwell. Commissioned from Cranwell, GD Pilot Branch p., 1931; served 43 (F) Squadron and 55 (B) Squadron, Iraq; qualified CFS. Served War of 1939-45 (despatches thrice); commanded 85 (F) Squadron, 1940; Fighter Command and Tactical Air Force; Wing Commander, 1940; Group Captain, 1942. Assistant Commandant, RAF Coll., Cranwell, 1948-50; ACOS Ops, Allied Forces Northern Europe, 1958-60; retired, 1961. Personnel Officer, ENV (Engineering) Ltd, 1961; Staff Institute Personnel Management, 1962; Personnel Manager, Humber Ltd, 1963; Manager, Training and Administrative Service, Rootes, Coventry, 1965; Senior Training Officer, Engineering Industry Training Board, 1968; Personnel and Trng Manager, Goodmans Loudspeakers Ltd, Thorn Gp, 1970-76, retired. *Address:* 9 Magdala Road, Hayling Island, Hants. *Club:* Mengham Sailing.

OLIVER, Leslie Claremont, FRCS; FACS; Consulting Neurosurgeon: Charing Cross Hospital; Westminster Hospital; West London Hospital; Royal Northern Hospital; Founder, Neurosurgical Centre, Oldchurch Hospital, Romford. *Educ:* Latymer Sch.; Guy's Hospital. LRCP, MRCS, 1933; MB, BS, London, 1953; FRCS England, 1935; FACS 1957. Formerly: 1st Assistant and Registrar, Dept of Neurosurgery, London Hospital; Resident Asst Surgeon, W London Hospital; Surgical Registrar and Teacher in Surgery, Bristol General Hospital. Member Society British Neurological Surgeons; Corr. Member Soc. de Neurochirurgie de Langue Française. Formerly Chm. Court of Examiners, RCS. *Publications:* Essentials of Neurosurgery, 1952; Parkinson's Disease and its Surgical Treatment, 1953; (ed and contrib.) Basic Surgery, 1958; Parkinson's Disease, 1967; Removable Intracranical Tumours, 1969. *Recreation:* travel. *Address:* 94 Harley Street, W1. *T:* 01-935 5896. *Clubs:* Royal Society of Medicine, Hurlingham.

OLIVER, Martin Hugh, PhD, CEng; Director General, Research Electronics, Procurement Executive, Ministry of Defence, 1972-76; *b* 9 July 1916; *s* of late Thomas Frederick Oliver and late Jessie Oliver (*née* Gibson), Peterborough; *m* 1963, Barbara Rivcah, *d* of late Richard Burgis Blakeley, Worcester; one *d*. *Educ:* King's Sch., Peterborough; Imperial Coll. (City and Guilds Coll.), Univ. of London. BSc (Eng) 1937, PhD (Eng) 1939; ACGI, DIC, MIEE. Metropolitan Vickers Electrical Co. Ltd, Manchester, 1938-41; National Physical Laboratory, Teddington, 1941-43; RRE, Malvern, 1943-65; Head of Radio Dept, RAE, Farnborough, 1965-68; Dir, Services Electronics Res. Lab., MoD, 1968-72.

OLIVER, Hon. Sir Peter (Raymond), Kt 1974; Hon. Mr Justice Oliver; Judge of the High Court of Justice, Chancery Division, since 1974; Member, Restrictive Practices Court, since 1976; *b* 7 March 1921; *s* of David Thomas Oliver, Fellow of Trinity Hall, Cambridge, and Alice Maud Oliver; *m* 1945, Mary Chichester Rideal, *d* of Sir Eric Keightley Rideal, MBE, FRS; one *s* one *d*. *Educ:* The Leys, Cambridge; Trinity Hall, Cambridge. Military Service, 1941-45, 12th Bn RTR (despatches). Called to Bar, Lincoln's Inn, 1948, Bencher 1973; QC 1965. *Recreations:* gardening, music. *Address:* 24 Westbourne Park Road, W2. *T:* 01-229 1058.

OLIVER, Peter Richard, CMG 1965; HM Diplomatic Service, retired; Ambassador to Uruguay, 1972-77; *b* 3 June 1917; *yr s* of William Henry Oliver and Muriel Daisy Elisabeth Oliver (*née* Widdicombe); *m* 1940, Freda Evelyn Gwyther; two *s* two *d*. *Educ:* Felsted Sch.; Hanover; Berlin; Trinity Hall, Cambridge. Indian Civil Service, 1939-47; served in Punjab and Bahawalpur State. Transferred to HM Foreign (subsequently Diplomatic) Service, 1947; served in Karachi, 1947-49; Foreign Office, 1949-52; The Hague, 1952-56; Havana, 1956-59; Foreign Office, 1959-61; Djakarta, 1961-64; Bonn, 1965-69; Dep. High Comr, Lahore, 1969-72. *Recreations:* tennis, golf, sailing. *Address:*

(permanent) c/o Grindlays Bank, 13 St James's Square, SW1. *Clubs:* United Oxford & Cambridge University; Hawks (Cambridge); Union (Cambridge).

OLIVER, Prof. Richard Alexander Cavaye; Professor of Education and Director of the Department of Education in the University of Manchester, 1938-70, now Emeritus Professor; Dean of Faculty of Education, 1938-48, 1962-65; Dean of Faculty of Music, 1952-62, 1966-70; *b* 9 Jan. 1904; *s* of Charles Oliver and Elizabeth Oliver (*née* Smith); *m* 1929, Annabella Margaret White; one *s* one *d. Educ:* George Heriot's Sch.; University of Edinburgh; Stanford Univ., California, USA. Held Commonwealth Fund Fellowship at Stanford Univ., 1927-29; research educational psychologist in Kenya, 1929-32; Asst Master Abbotsholme Sch. and on staff of Edinburgh Education Cttee, 1933-34; University Extension Lecturer, 1933-34; Asst Director of Education, Wilts Education Cttee, 1934-36; Dep. Secretary, Devon Education Cttee, 1936-38. Director, University of Manchester School of Education, 1947-51; Pro Vice-Chancellor, 1953-57 and 1960-61; Presenter of Hon. Graduands, 1959-64, 1966. Member National Advisory Council on Training and Supply of Teachers, 1949-59; Chairman, Northern Universities Joint Matriculation Board, 1952-55; Member Secondary School Examinations Council, 1958-64. FBPsS. Hon. Research Fellow, Princeton Univ., 1961. *Publications:* General Intelligence Test for Africans, 1932; (with others) The Educational Guidance of the School Child, 1936; Research in Education, 1946; The Content of Sixth Form General Studies, 1974; Joint Matriculation Board Occasional Publications; contrib. to Africa, British Journal of Psychology, Yearbook of Education, Universities Quarterly, Research in Education, etc. *Recreations:* gardening, painting. *Address:* Waingap, Crook, Kendal, Cumbria LA8 9HT. *T:* Staveley 277. *See also* H. A. Hetherington.

OLIVER, Vice-Admiral Robert Don, CB 1948; CBE 1942; DSC 1918; DL; *b* 17 March 1895; *s* of Colonel William James Oliver, CBE, and Margaret Oliver; *m* 1928, Torfrida Lois Acantha Huddart (*d* 1961); no *c; m* 1965, Mrs M. J. Glendinning van der Velde. *Educ:* Osborne and Dartmouth Naval Colleges. Commander, 1930; Captain, 1936; Commanded: HMS Iron Duke, 1939; HMS Devonshire, 1940-42; HMS Excellent, 1943; HMS Swiftsure, 1944; Rear-Admiral, 1945; Asst Chief of Naval Staff (Weapons), 1945-46; Dep. Chief of Naval Staff, 1946-47; Flag Officer Commanding 5th Cruiser Squadron, 1947-48; Vice-Admiral, retired list, 1948. DL Roxburghshire, 1962. *Address:* Lochside House, Kelso, Roxburghshire. *T:* Yetholm 275.

OLIVER, Prof. Roland Anthony, MA, PhD (Cantab); Professor of the History of Africa, London University, since 1963; *b* Srinagar, Kashmir, 30 March 1923; *s* of late Major D. G. Oliver and of Lorimer Janet (*née* Donaldson); *m* 1947, Caroline Florence, *d* of late Judge John Linehan, KC; one *d. Educ:* Stowe; King's Coll., Cambridge. Attached to Foreign Office, 1942-45; R. J. Smith Research Studentship, King's Coll., Cambridge, 1946-48; Lecturer, School of Oriental and African Studies, 1948-58; Reader in African History, University of London, 1958-63; Francqui Prof., University of Brussels, 1961; Visiting Professor: Northwestern Univ., Illinois, 1962; Harvard Univ., 1967; travelled in Africa, 1949-50 and 1957-58; org. international Conferences on African History and Archæology, 1953-61; Haile Sellassie Prize Trust Award, 1966. Pres., African Studies Assoc., 1967-68; Member: Perm. Bureau, Internat. Congress of Africanists, 1973-; Council, Royal African Society; Chm., Minority Rights Group. Corresp. Member, Académie Royale des Sciences d'Outremer, Brussels. *Publications:* The Missionary Factor in East Africa, 1952; Sir Harry Johnston and the Scramble for Africa, 1957; (ed) The Dawn of African History, 1961; A Short History of Africa (with J. D. Fage), 1962; A History of East Africa (ed with Gervase Mathew), 1963; Africa since 1800 (with A. E. Atmore), 1967; (ed) The Middle Age of African History, 1967; Ed. (with J. D. Fage) The Journal of African History, 1960-73; (with B. M. Fagan) Africa in the Iron Age, 1975; Gen. Editor (with J. D. Fage), Cambridge History of Africa, 8 vols, 1975-. *Address:* 7 Cranfield House, Southampton Row, WC1. *T:* 01-636 5343; Frilsham Woodhouse, Newbury, Berks. *T:* Hermitage 201407.

OLIVER, Lt-Gen. Sir William (Pasfield), GBE 1965 (OBE 1945); KCB 1956 (CB 1947); KCMG 1962; DL; late Infantry; *b* 8 Sept. 1901; *e s* of late Captain P. V. Oliver, Royal Navy; *m* 1938, Elizabeth Margaret, *o d* of late General Sir J. E. S. Brind, KCB, KBE, CMG, DSO; one *s* one *d. Educ:* Radley Coll.; RMC, Sandhurst. Chief of General Staff, GHQ, ME (Maj.-Gen.), 1945-46; Maj.-Gen., 1949; Chief Army Instructor, Imperial Defence Coll., 1949-50; Chief of Staff, Eastern Command, Jan. 1951-Dec. 1952; Principal Staff Officer to High Commissioner, Federation

of Malaya, 1953-54; General Officer Commanding Berlin (British Sector), 1954-55; Vice-Chief of Imperial General Staff, 1955-57, retired; Principal Staff Officer to Secretary of State for Commonwealth Relations, 1957-59; British High Commissioner in the Commonwealth of Australia, 1959-65; UK Commissioner General for 1967 Exhibition, Montreal, Canada, 1965-67. Dir, Viyella International Ltd, 1968-69. Mem., Adv. Cttee on Rhodesian Travel Restrictions. Colonel, The Queen's Own Royal W. Kent Regt, 1949-59. DL Kent. Governor, Corps of Commissionaires. Hon. DCL, Bishop's Univ., Quebec Province. Commander Legion of Merit (USA), 1946; Knight Grand Cross Royal Order Phoenix (Greece) 1949. *Address:* Little Crofts, Sweethaws, Crowborough, East Sussex.

OLIVIER, family name of **Baron Olivier.**

OLIVIER, Baron *cr* 1970 (Life Peer), of Brighton; **Laurence Kerr Olivier,** Kt 1947; Actor; Director, 1962-73, Associate Director, 1973-74, National Theatre; Member, South Bank Theatre Board, since 1967 (South Bank Theatre and Opera House Board, 1962-67); *b* 22 May 1907; *s* of late Rev. G. K. Olivier and Agnes Louise Crookenden; *m* 1st, 1930, Jill Esmond (marr. diss., 1940); one *s*; 2nd, 1940, Vivien Leigh (marr. diss., 1961; she *d* 1967); 3rd, 1961, Joan Plowright, *qv*; one *s* two *d. Educ:* St Edward's Sch., Oxford. MA Hon. Tufts, Mass, 1946; Hon. DLitt, Oxon, 1957; Hon. LLD: Edinburgh 1964; Manchester, 1968; Hon. DLit London, 1968; Commander, Order Dannebrog, 1949; Officier Legion d'Honneur, 1953; Grande Ufficiale dell' Ordino al Merito della Repubblica (Italian), 1953; Order of Yugoslav Flag with Golden Wreath, 1971. First appeared in 1922 at Shakespeare Festival, Stratford-on-Avon special boys' performance, as Katherine in Taming of the Shrew; played in Byron, King Henry IV, toured in sketch Unfailing Instinct, with Ruby Miller, Season with Lena Ashwell, King Henry VIII, 1924-25; Played with Birmingham Repertory Company till 1928; Stanhope in Journey's End, for Stage Society; Beau Geste; Circle of Chalk, Paris Bound, The Stranger Within; went to America, 1929; returned 1930 and played in The Last Enemy, After All and in Private Lives; New York, 1931, played Private Lives, 1933; Rats of Norway, London; Green Bay Tree, New York; returned London, 1934, Biography, Queen of Scots, Theatre Royal; Ringmaster under his own management, Golden Arrow, Romeo and Juliet, 1935; Bees on the Boat Deck and Hamlet at Old Vic, 1936; Sir Toby Belch in Twelfth Night, and Henry V, Hamlet at Kronborg, Elsinore, Denmark, 1937; Macbeth, 1937; Iago in Othello, King of Nowhere, and Coriolanus, 1938; No Time for Comedy, New York, 1939; under his own management produced and played Romeo and Juliet with Vivien Leigh. Lieut (A) RNVR until released from Fleet Air Arm, 1944, to co-direct The Old Vic Theatre Company with Joan Burrell and Ralph Richardson, at New Theatre; played in Old Vic, 1944-45 Season; Peer Gynt, Arms and the Man, Richard III, Uncle Vanya; toured Continent in May 1945 with Peer Gynt, Arms and the Man, Richard III; Old Vic Season, 1945-46; Henry IV, Parts I and II, Oedipus, The Critic, Uncle Vanya, Arms and the Man; six weeks' season in New York with Henry IV, Parts I and II, Oedipus, The Critic and Uncle Vanya; Old Vic, 1946-47 Season, produced and played King Lear. Made a tour of Australia and New Zealand, 1948, with Old Vic Company, in Richard III, School for Scandal, Skin of our Teeth, Old Vic, 1949 Season, Richard III, The School for Scandal, Antigone. Directed A Street Car Named Desire, Aldwych, 1949; St James's, 1950-51; produced and acted in Venus Observed, under own management, produced Captain Carvallo, 1950, Antony in Antony and Cleopatra, Caesar in Caeser and Cleopatra, 1951; also in US, 1951-52; The Sleeping Prince, Phoenix, 1953; Stratford Season, 1955; Macbeth, Malvolio in Twelfth Night, Titus in Titus Andronicus; Archie Rice in The Entertainer, Royal Court Theatre, 1957; presented The Summer of the Seventeenth Doll, 1957; toured Europe in Titus Andronicus, 1957; Titus in Titus Andronicus, Stoll, 1957; Archie Rice in The Entertainer (revival), Palace Theatre, 1957, and New York, 1958; Coriolanus in Coriolanus, Stratford, 1959; directed The Tumbler, New York; Berenger in Rhinoceros, Royal Court Theatre and Strand Theatre, 1960; Becket in Becket, New York, 1960; Henry II in Becket, US Tour and New York, 1961; Fred Midway in Semi-Detached, Saville Theatre, 1962. Apptd Dir of National Theatre (first, as Old Vic): 1963: (produced) Hamlet; 1963-64; acted in Uncle Vanya and in The Recruiting Officer, 1964; acted in Othello and in The Master Builder, 1964-65. Chichester Festival: first Director, also acted, 1962 (Uncle Vanya; The Broken Heart; also Director, The Chances), 1963 (Uncle Vanya, also Director); National Theatre (produced) The Crucible; in Love for Love, Moscow and London, 1965; Othello, Moscow and London, 1965; Othello, Love for Love, (dir.) Juno and the Paycock, 1966; Edgar in The Dance of Death, Othello, Love for Love (dir.) Three Sisters, National Theatre, 1967; A Flea in Her Ear, 1968; Home and

Beauty, Three Sisters (directed and played Chebutikin), 1968-69; Shylock in Merchant of Venice, 1970, Long Day's Journey into Night, 1971, 1972; Saturday, Sunday, Monday, 1973; The Party, 1974; (dir.) Eden End, 1974; *films:* Potiphar's Wife, The Yellow Passport, Perfect Understanding, No Funny Business, Moscow Nights, Fire Over England, As You Like It, The First and the Last, Divorce of Lady X, Wuthering Heights, Rebecca, Pride and Prejudice, Lady Hamilton, 49th Parallel, Demi-Paradise; produced, directed, played Henry V; produced, directed, played Hamlet (International Grand Prix, 1948, Oscar award, 1949); Carrie (Hollywood), 1950; Macheath in film The Beggar's Opera, 1953; produced, directed, played Richard III (British Film Academy's Award), 1956; produced, directed and played in The Prince and the Showgirl, 1957; General Burgoyne in The Devil's Disciple, 1959; The Entertainer; Spartacus; Term of Trial; Bunny Lake is Missing; Othello; Khartoum; The Power and The Glory, 1961, (TV) USA; Dance of Death; Shoes of the Fisherman; Oh! What a Lovely War; Battle of Britain; David Copperfield; directed and played Chebutikin in Three Sisters; Nicholas and Alexandra; Lady Caroline Lamb; Sleuth (NY Film Critics Award, Best Actor, 1972); Seven-per-cent Solution; Marathon Man (Variety Club of GB Award, 1977); A Bridge Too Far; The Betsy; Boys from Brazil; *television:* John Gabriel Borkmann, 1959; Long Day's Journey Into Night, 1972 (Emmy Award, 1973); The Merchant of Venice, 1973; Love Among The Ruins, USA, 1974 (Emmy Award, 1975); Jesus of Nazareth, 1976; The Collection, 1976; Cat on a Hot Tin Roof, 1976; Hindle Wakes, 1976; Come Back Little Sheba, Daphne Laureola, Saturday Sunday Monday, 1977. Narrated World at War (TV), 1963. Sonning Prize, Denmark, 1966; Gold Medallion, Swedish Acad. of Literature, 1968; Special Award for directorship of Nat. Theatre, Evening Standard, 1973; Albert Medal, RSA, 1976. *Recreations:* tennis, swimming, motoring, flying, gardening. *Address:* 33-34 Chancery Lane, WC2A 1EN. *Clubs:* Garrick, Green Room, MCC.

OLIVIER, George B.; *see* Borg Olivier.

OLIVIER, Henry, CMG 1954; MScEng, PhD London, DEng; FICE, FASCE, Beit Fellow; specialist consulting engineer in water resources engineering, Henry Olivier & Associates, since 1973; *b* 25 Jan. 1914; *s* of J. Olivier, Umtali, S Rhodesia; *m* 1940, Lorna Renée, *d* of Robert and F. M. Collier, Haywards Heath, Sussex; one *d* (one *s* decd). *Educ:* Umtali High Sch.; Cape Town Univ.; University College, London. BSc (Cape), 1936. MSc (Cape), 1947; PhD (London), 1953. Beit Engineering Schol., 1932-38; Beit Fellow for two Rhodesias, 1939. Engineering post-grad. training with F. E. Kanthack & Partners, Consulting Engineers, Johannesburg, 1937; Sir Alex. Gibb & Partners, Cons. Engineers, London: training 1938, Asst Engineer, 1939. Experience covers design and construction of steam-electric power-stations, hydro-electric, floating harbour, irrigation, and water resources development schemes in UK, Africa, Middle East, and USA; Chief Engineer in charge civil engineering contracts, Owen Falls Hydro-Electric Scheme, Uganda, 1950-54; Partner in firm of Sir Alexander Gibb and Partners (Africa), 1954-55; Resident Director and Chief Engineer (Rhodesia), in firm of Gibb, Coyne & Sogei (Kariba), 1955-60; Consultant (mainly in connection with Indus Basin Project in Pakistan) to Sir Alexander Gibb and Partners, London, 1960-69 (Sen. Consultant, 1967); Partner, Gibb Hawkins and Partners, Johannesburg, 1963-69; Chm. LTA Ltd and LTA Engineering Ltd, 1969-73. FRSA. DEng, Witwatersrand, 1967; Hon. DSc: Cape, 1968; Rhodesia, 1977. *Publications:* Irrigation and Climate, 1960; Irrigation and Water Resources Engineering, 1972; Damit, 1975; Great Dams in Southern Africa, 1977; Papers to Institution Civil Engineering Journal; Int. Commn on Irrigation and Drainage; Water for Peace Conference, Washington, DC. *Recreation:* tennis. *Address:* Henry Olivier and Associates, PO Box 6844, Johannesburg, South Africa. *Clubs:* Salisbury (Rhodesia); Rand (Johannesburg).

OLIVIER, Lady, (Joan); *see* Plowright, Joan.

OLLERENSHAW, Dame Kathleen (Mary), DBE 1971; MA, DPhil; FIMA, FCP; Member, Manchester City Council, since 1956, Leader of Conservative Opposition, since 1977 (Alderman, 1970-74, Lord Mayor, 1975-76, Deputy Lord Mayor, 1976-77); Chairman of Court, Royal Northern College of Music, Manchester, since 1968; *b* 1 Oct. 1912; *d* of late Charles Timpson, JP, and late Mary Elizabeth Timpson (*née* Stops); *m* 1939, Robert Ollerenshaw; one *s* (one *d* decd). *Educ:* Ladybarn House Sch., Manchester; St Leonards Sch., St Andrews; (open schol. in maths) Somerville Coll., Oxford. BA (Hons) 1934, MA 1943, DPhil 1945; Foundation Fellow, Institute of Mathematics and its Applications (FIMA), 1964 (Mem. Council, 1973-75, Vice-Pres., 1976-77, Pres., 1978-). Research Assistant, Shirley Institute, Didsbury, 1937-40.

Chairman: Educn Cttee, Assoc. of Municipal Corporations, 1968-71; Assoc. of Governing Bodies of Girls' Public Schs, 1963-69; Manchester Educn Cttee, 1967-70 (Co-opted Mem., 1954-56); Manchester Coll. of Commerce, 1964-69; Member: Central Adv. Council on Educn in England, 1960-63; CNAA, 1964-74; SSRC, 1971-75; Tech. Educn Council, 1973-75; (Vice-Pres.,) British Assoc. for Commercial and Industrial Educn (Mem. Delegn to USSR, 1963); Exec., Assoc. of Educn Cttees, 1967-71; Nat. Adv. Council on Educn for Industry and Commerce, 1963-70; Gen. Adv. Council of BBC, 1966-72; Schools Council, 1968-71; Management Panel, Burnham Cttee, 1968-71; Nat. Foundn of Educnl Res., 1968-71; Layfield Cttee of Inquiry into Local Govt Finance, 1974-76; Council of Univ. of Salford, 1967-; Court, Univ. of Manchester, 1964-; Manchester Polytechnic, 1968-(Chm., 1969-72; Dep.-Chm., 1972-75); Court, UMIST, 1971- (Vice-Pres., 1976-); Council, Lancaster Univ., 1975-; Council, CGLI, 1972-; Sen. Res. Fellow (part-time), 1972-75, Hon. Res. Fellow, 1975-77, Lancaster Univ.; Rep. Governor: Union of Lancashire and Cheshire Institutes, 1967-73; Manchester and Dist Adv. Council for Further Educn, 1967-71; Associated Local Educn Authorities of Lancashire, 1967-70; NW Reg. Council for Further Educn, 1959-63, 1967-71; Univ. of Manchester Sch. of Educn Delegacy for the Trng of Teachers, 1967-70; Royal Coll. of Advanced Technol., Salford, 1959-67; Governor: St Leonards Sch., St Andrews, 1950-72; Manchester High Sch. for Girls, 1959-69; Ladies Coll., Cheltenham, 1966-68; Chethams Hosp. Sch., Manchester, 1967-; Further Educn Staff Coll., Blagdon, 1960-74; Hon. Mem., Manchester Technology Assoc., 1976-; Hon. Col, Manchester and Salford OTC, 1977-. Dir, Manchester Independent Radio, Ltd, 1972-. Winifred Cullis Lecture Fellow to USA, 1965; Fourth Cockroft Lecture, UMIST and Manchester Tech. Assoc., 1977. OStJ (Chm. Council for Greater Manchester, 1974-). Hon. LLD CNAA, 1975; Hon. DSc Salford, 1975; Hon LLD Manchester, 1976. Mancunian of the Year, Jnr Chamber of Commerce, 1977. *Publications:* Education of Girls, 1958; Education for Girls, 1961; The Girls' Schools, 1967; Returning to Teaching, 1974; The Lord Mayor's Party, 1976; First Citizen, 1977; papers in mathematical journals on Geometry of Numbers, 1945-54; articles on education and local govt in national and educational press. *Address:* 2 Pine Road, Didsbury, Manchester M20 0UY. *T:* 061-445 2948. *Club:* English-Speaking Union.

OLLIS, Prof. William David, BSc, PhD; FRS 1972; Professor of Organic Chemistry, since 1963, Head of Department of Chemistry, since 1973, University of Sheffield; *b* 22 Dec. 1924; *s* of Albert George and Beatrice Charlotte Ollis; *m* 1951, Sonia Dorothy Mary Weekes; two *d*. *Educ:* Cotham Grammar Sch., Bristol; University of Bristol. Assistant Lecturer in Organic Chemistry, University of Bristol, 1946-49, Lecturer, 1949-62, Reader, 1962-63. Visiting Research Fellow, Harvard, 1952-53; Visiting Professor: University of California, Los Angeles, 1962; University of Texas, 1966; Nat. Science Foundn Sen. Fellowship, 1970-71; Hon. Prof., Universidade Federal Rural do Rio de Janeiro, Brasil, 1969. Robert Gnehm Lecture, 1965; Chemical Soc. Tilden Lectr, 1969. *Publications:* Recent Developments in the Chemistry of Natural Phenolic Compounds, 1961; scientific papers mainly in Journal of Chemical Society. *Address:* 640 Fulwood Road, Fulwood, Sheffield S10 3QL. *T:* 302685. *Club:* Athenæum.

O'LOGHLEN, Sir Colman (Michael), 6th Bt, *cr* 1838; Judge of the Supreme Court of Papua New Guinea; *b* 6 April 1916; *s* of Henry Ross O'Loghlen (*d* 1944; 6th *s* of 3rd Bt) and of Doris Irene, *d* of late Major Percival Horne, RA; *S* uncle 1951; *m* 1939, Margaret, *d* of Francis O'Halloran, Melbourne, Victoria; six *s* two *d*. *Educ:* Xavier Coll., Melbourne; Melbourne Univ. (LLB). Formerly Captain AIF. *Heir:* s Michael O'Loghlen, *b* 21 May 1945. *Address:* 98 Williamsons Road, Doncaster, Victoria 3108, Australia.

OLUWASANMI, Hezekiah Adedunmola, MA, PhD Harvard; Vice-Chancellor, University of Ife, Nigeria, 1966-74; *b* 12 Nov. 1919; *s* of John Oluwasanmi and Jane Ola Oluwasanmi; *m* 1959, Edwina Marie Clarke; one *s* two *d*. *Educ:* Morehouse Coll. (BA); Harvard University. Secondary School Teacher, 1940-41; Meteorological Observer, 1941-44; Clerk, Shell Oil Co., 1944-47; Student, 1948-55; Lectr, Sen. Lectr, and Prof. of Agricultural Economics, Univ. of Ibadan, 1955-66, Dean, Faculty of Agriculture, 1963-66. Member: W Nigeria Economic Planning Cttee, 1961-62; W Nigeria Economic Adv. Cttee, 1966-71. Chairman: Cttee of Vice-Chancellors of Nigerian Univs, 1970-72; Univ. of Zambia Grants Cttee; Member: Council, Univ. of Ghana; Assoc. of Commonwealth Univs; Bd of Governors, Internat. Develt Res. Centre, Ottawa; Bd of Trustees, Internat. Inst. of Tropical Agriculture, 1970-72. Member: Nigerian Econ. Soc.; Agricultural Soc., Nigeria; Internat. Assoc. Agricultural Economists. Hon DSc, Univ. of Nigeria, Nsukka, 1971; Hon.

LLD, Univ. of Wisconsin, 1974; Hon. LHD, Morehouse Coll., Georgia, USA, 1974. *Publications:* Agriculture and Nigerian Economic Development, 1966; (jt author) Uboma, a socioeconomic and nutritional survey of a rural community in Eastern Nigeria, 1966; various reports, contribs to symposia and papers in learned jls. *Recreations:* reading, walking, listening to music.

OLVER, Sir Stephen (John Linley), KBE 1975 (MBE 1947); CMG 1965; HM Diplomatic Service, retired; *b* 16 June 1916; *s* of late Rev. S. E. L. Olver and Mrs Madeleine Olver (*née* Stratton); *m* 1953, Maria Morena, Gubbio, Italy; one *s. Educ:* Stowe. Indian Police, 1935-44; Indian Political Service, Delhi, Quetta, Sikkim and Bahrain, 1944-47; Pakistan Foreign Service, Aug.-Oct. 1947; Foreign Service, Karachi, 1947-50; Foreign Office, 1950-53; Berlin, 1953-56; Bangkok, 1956-58; Foreign Office, 1958-61; Washington, 1961-64; Foreign Office, 1964-66; The Hague, 1967-69; High Comr, Freetown, 1969-72; High Comr, Nicosia, 1973-75. *Recreations:* golf, photography, painting. *Address:* Tanglewoods, Heath Ride, Wokingham, Berks. *Club:* MCC.

OLYOTT, Ven. Leonard Eric; Archdeacon of Taunton and Prebendary of Milverton, since 1977; *b* 11 Jan. 1926; *s* of Thomas Olyott and Maude Ann Olyott (*née* Purser); *m* 1951, Yvonne Winifred Kate Keele; two *s* one *d. Educ:* Colchester Royal Grammar School; London Univ. (BA 1950); Westcott House, Cambridge. Served RNVR, 1944-47; commissioned, 1945. Asst Curate, St George, Camberwell, 1952-55; Priest-in-Charge, St Michael and All Angels, Birchwood, Hatfield, Herts, 1955-60; Vicar of Chipperfield, Herts, 1960-68; Vicar of Crewkerne, 1968-71; Rector of Crewkerne with Wayford, 1971-77; Rural Dean of Crewkerne, 1972-77; Prebendary of Timberscombe, 1976. *Recreations:* sailing, gardening, elkhounds, music. *Address:* Summerhayes, Higher Street, Curry Mallet, Taunton, Somerset. *T:* Hatch Beauchamp 758.

OMAN, Carola Mary Anima, (Lady Lenanton), CBE 1957; FSA; FRSL; FRHistS; Writer; *b* 11 May 1897; *d* of late Sir Charles Oman, KBE; *m* 1922, Sir Gerald Lenanton (*d* 1952). *Educ:* Wychwood Sch., Oxford. Served BRCS, 1916-19 and 1938-58 (Co. President, Hertfordshire Branch, 1947-58). *Publications:* The Menin Road (poetry); Britain Against Napoleon (history); Ayot Rectory; *historical novels:* The Road Royal; Princess Amelia; Crouchback; The Empress; King Heart; Major Grant; The Best of His Family; Over the Water; Miss Barrett's Elopement; *children's books:* Ferry the Fearless; Robin Hood; Johel; Alfred, King of the English; Baltic Spy; *historical biographies:* Prince Charles Edward; Henrietta Maria; Elizabeth of Bohemia; Nelson (awarded Sunday Times annual prize for English literature, 1948); Sir John Moore (James Tait Black Memorial Prize for biography, 1953); David Garrick, 1958; Mary of Modena, 1962; Napoleon's Viceroy; Eugène de Beauharnais, 1966; The Gascoyne Heiress, Diaries of 2nd Marchioness of Salisbury, 1968; The Wizard of the North: The Life of Sir Walter Scott, 1973; *autobiography:* An Oxford Childhood 1892-1914, 1976. *Address:* Bride Hall, Welwyn, Hertfordshire AL6 9DB. *T:* Wheathampstead 3160. *Club:* VAD Ladies.

OMAN, Charles Chichele; *b* 5 June 1901; *s* of late Sir Charles Oman, KBE; *m* 1929, Joan Trevelyan (*d* 1973); one *s* one *d. Educ:* Winchester; New Coll., Oxford; British School at Rome. Entered Victoria and Albert Museum, 1924; lent to Ministry of War Transport, 1939-44; Keeper of Department of Metalwork, Victoria and Albert Museum, 1945-66. Hon. Vice-Pres., Royal Archaeological Inst. Hon. Mem., Hispanic Soc. of America. Liveryman of Company of Goldsmiths, 1946. *Publications:* English Domestic Silver, 1934; English Church Plate, 1957; English Silver in the Kremlin, 1961; Golden Age of Hispanic Silver, 1968; Caroline Silver 1625-1688, 1971; British Rings 800-1914, 1974; English Engraved Silver, 1978. *Address:* 13 Woodborough Road, Putney, SW15. *T:* 01-788 2744.
See also Julia Trevelyan Oman.

OMAN, Julia Trevelyan, (Mrs Roy Strong), RDI 1977; designer; Director, Oman Productions Ltd; *b* 11 July 1930; *d* of Charles Chichele Oman, *qv*; *m* 1971, Roy Colin Strong, *qv. Educ:* Royal College of Art, London. Royal Scholar, 1953 and Silver Medal, 1955, RCA. Designer: BBC Television, 1955-67; Alice in Wonderland, BBC TV Film, 1966; Brief Lives, London and New York, 1967; Country Dance, London and Edinburgh, 1967; Art Director (England), The Charge of the Light Brigade, 1967; Art Director, Laughter in the Dark, 1968; Designer: The Enigma Variations (for the Royal Ballet), 1968; 40 Years On, 1968; (Production designer) Julius Caesar, 1969; The Merchant of Venice, National Theatre, 1970; Eugene Onegin, Covent Garden, 1971; The Straw Dogs (film), 1971; Othello, Stratford,

1971; Samuel Pepys Exhibn, Nat. Portrait Gall., 1971; Getting On, Queen's, 1971; Othello, RSC, Aldwych, 1972; Un Ballo in Maschera, Hamburgische Staatsoper, 1973; La Bohème, Covent Garden, 1974; A Month in the Country (for Royal Ballet), 1976; The Importance of Being Ernest, Burgtheater, Vienna, 1976. Des RCA (1st class), 1955; FSIA. Designer of the Year Award for Alice in Wonderland, 1967. *Publications:* Street Children (photographs by Julia Trevelyan Oman; text by B. S. Johnson), 1964; (with Roy Strong) Elizabeth R, 1971; (with Roy Strong) Mary Queen of Scots, 1972; introd. The Merchant of Venice, Folio Soc. edn, 1975; contrib. Architectural Review (photographs), Vogue (text and photographs). *Address:* c/o London Management, 235/241 Regent Street, W1A 2JT.

OMMANNEY, Francis Downes; *b* 22 April 1903; *s* of Francis Frederick Ommanney and Olive Caroline Owen; unmarried. *Educ:* Aldenham Sch.; Royal College of Science. ARCS, PhD (London), FLS, FRSL, FRSA. Polar Medal (Bronze), 1942. Lecturer in Zoology, Queen Mary Coll., 1926-29; Scientific Staff of Discovery Cttee, 1929-39; RNVR, 1940-46; British Council, 1946-47; Mauritius-Seychelles Fisheries Survey, 1947-49; Colonial Research Service, 1951-57; Reader in Marine Biology in the Univ. of Hong Kong, 1957-60. *Publications: scientific:* Discovery Reports, 1932, 1933, 1936; Colonial Office Fishery Publications, Vol. I, Nos 3, and 18; *non-scientific:* South Latitude, 1938; North Cape, 1939; The House in the Park, 1944; The Ocean, 1949; The Shoals of Capricorn, 1952; Isle of Cloves, 1955; Eastern Windows, 1960; Fragrant Harbour, 1962; A Draught of Fishes, 1965; The River Bank, 1966; Collecting Sea Shells, 1968; Lost Leviathan: Whales and Whaling, 1971. *Club:* Travellers'.

O'MORCHOE, David Nial Creagh, MBE 1967; (The O'Morchoe); Chief of O'Morchoe of Oulartleigh and Monamolin; Commander, Sultan of Oman's Land Forces, since 1977; *b* 17 May 1928; *s* of Nial Creagh O'Morchoe and Jessie Elizabeth, *d* of late Charles Jasper Joly, FRS, FRIS, MRIA, Astronomer Royal of Ireland; *S* father as Chief of the Name (O'Morchoe), 1970; *m* 1954, Margaret Jane, 3rd *d* of George Francis Brewitt, Cork; two *s* one *d. Educ:* St Columba's Coll., Dublin; RMA Sandhurst. Commissioned Royal Irish Fusiliers, 1948; served in Egypt, Jordan, Gibraltar, Germany, Kenya, Cyprus, Oman; psc 1958, jssc 1966; CO 1st Bn RIrF, later 3rd Bn Royal Irish Rangers, 1967-68; Directing Staff, Staff Coll., Camberley, 1969-71; RCDS 1972; Brigade Comdr, 1973-75; Brig. GS, BAOR, 1975-76; promoted Major General, 1977. Dep. Col, 1971-76, Col 1977-, The Royal Irish Rangers. *Recreations:* sailing and most sports. *Heir:* s Dermot Arthur O'Morchoe, *b* 11 Aug. 1956. *Address:* c/o Williams and Glyn's Bank Ltd, Holt's Branch, Kirkland House, Whitehall, SW1. *Clubs:* Naval and Military, Cruising Association, Royal Yachting Association; Royal Cork Yacht.

O'NEIL, Most Rev. Alexander Henry, MA, DD; *m* 1931, Marguerite (*née* Roe); one *s. Educ:* Univ. of W Ontario; BA 1928, BD 1936, MA 1943; Huron Coll., London, Ont; LTh 1929. Deacon, 1929; Priest, 1930; Principal, Huron Coll., London, Ont, 1941-52; Gen. Sec., British and Foreign Bible Soc. in Canada, 1952-57; Bishop of Fredericton, 1957-63; Archbishop of Fredericton and Metropolitan of the Province of Canada, 1963-71. Hon. DD: Univ. of W Ontario, 1945; Wycliffe Coll., Toronto, 1954; King's Coll., Halifax, 1958; Hon. LLD: W Ontario, 1962; St Thomas Univ., Fredericton, 1970; Hon. DCL Bishop's Univ., Lennoxville, 1964. *Address:* Apt 807 Grosvenor Gates, 1 Grosvenor Street, London N6A 1Y2, Ont, Canada.

O'NEILL, family name of **Barons O'Neill, O'Neill of the Maine, and Rathcavan.**

O'NEILL, 4th Baron *cr* 1868; **Raymond Arthur Clanaboy O'Neill,** TD 1970; DL; Chairman, since 1975, Member, since 1973, Northern Ireland Tourist Board; *b* 1 Sept. 1933; *s* of 3rd Baron and Anne Geraldine (she *m* 2nd, 1945, 2nd Viscount Rothermere, *qv*, and 3rd, 1952, late Ian Fleming), *e d* of Hon. Guy Charteris; *S* father, 1944; *m* 1963, Georgina Mary, *er d* of Lord George Montagu Douglas Scott; three *s. Educ:* Eton; Royal Agricultural Coll. 2nd Lieut, 11th Hussars, Prince Albert's Own; Major, North Irish Horse, AVR; Lt-Col, RARO. Chm., Ulster Countryside Cttee, 1971-75. Trustee, Ulster Folk and Transport Mus., 1969-. DL Co. Antrim. *Recreations:* vintage motoring, railways, gardening. *Heir:* s Hon. Shane Sebastian Clanaboy O'Neill, *b* 25 July 1965. *Address:* Shane's Castle, Antrim, Ireland. *T:* Antrim 3264. *Clubs:* Turf, Ulster.
See also J. A. L. Morgan.

O'NEILL OF THE MAINE, Baron *cr* 1970 (Life Peer), of Ahoghill, Co. Antrim; **Terence Marne O'Neill,** PC (N Ireland) 1956; DL; *b* 10 Sept. 1914; *s* of Capt. Hon. Arthur O'Neill, MP (killed in action, 1914; *s* of 2nd Baron O'Neill, Shane's Castle Antrim) and of late Lady Annabel Crewe-Milnes, *e d* of 1st and last Marquis of Crewe, KG; *m* 1944, Katherine Jean, *y d* of late W. I. Whitaker, Pylewell Park, Lymington, Hants; one *s* one *d*. *Educ:* Eton. Served, 1939-45, Irish Guards. MP (Unionist) Bannside, Parlt of N Ireland, 1946-70; Parl. Sec., Min. of Health, 1948; Deputy Speaker and Chairman of Ways and Means, 1953; Joint Parl. Sec., Home Affairs and Health, 1955; Minister: Home Affairs, 1956; Finance, 1956; Prime Minister of N Ireland, 1963-69. Mem., Hansard Soc. Commn on Electoral Reform, 1975-76. Director: S. G. Warburg & Co.; International Holdings Ltd; Phoenix Assurance, 1969-. Chm. Council, Winston Churchill Meml Trust. DL Co. Antrim, 1948; High Sheriff County Antrim, 1953. Hon. LLD, Queen's Univ., Belfast, 1967. *Publications:* Ulster at the Crossroads, 1969; The Autobiography of Terence O'Neill, 1972. *Address:* House of Lords, SW1. *Clubs:* Brooks's; Ulster (Belfast).

O'NEILL, Alan Albert; Clerk to the Drapers' Company and Hon. Clerk to the Governors, Howell's School, Denbigh, since 1973; *b* 11 Jan. 1916; *o s* of late Albert George O'Neill; *m* 1939, Betty Dolbey; one *s*. *Educ:* Sir George Monoux Grammar Sch., Walthamstow. Joined staff Drapers' Co., 1933, Dep. Clerk 1967. Clerk to Governors, Bancroft's School, 1951-73; Governor, Queen Mary Coll., 1959-. Served War of 1939-45, Royal Navy: Telegraphist, RNV(W)R, 1939; DEMS Gunnery Officer, SS Aquitania and SS Nieuw Amsterdam; Lt-Comdr, RNVR, 1943; DEMS Staff Officer, Aberdeen and NE Coast Scotland, 1945. *Recreations:* tennis, gardening. *Address:* Drapers' Hall, Throgmorton Avenue, EC2N 2DQ. *T:* 01-588 5002; Wickenden Farm, Plaxtol, Sevenoaks, Kent. *T:* Plaxtol 334.

O'NEILL, Hon. Sir Con (Douglas Walter), GCMG 1972 (KCMG 1962; CMG 1953); Director, Unigate Ltd, since 1974; *b* 3 June 1912; 2nd *s* of 1st Baron Rathcavan, *qv*; *m* 1st, 1940, Rosemary (marriage dissolved 1954), *d* of late H. Pritchard, MD; one *s* one *d*; 2nd, 1954, Baroness Mady Marschall von Bieberstein (*d* 1960), *d* of late Baron von Holzing-Berstett; 3rd, 1961, Mrs Anne-Marie Lindberg, Helsinki. *Educ:* Eton College; Balliol Coll., Oxford (History Scholar). BA 1934 (1st Class, English), MA 1937; Fellow, All Souls College, Oxford, 1935-46; called to Bar, Inner Temple, 1936; entered Diplomatic Service, 1936; Third Secretary, Berlin, 1938; resigned from Service, 1939. Served War of 1939-45 in Army (Intelligence Corps), 1940-Nov. 1943; temp. employed in Foreign Office, 1943-46; Leader-writer on staff of Times, 1946-47; returned to Foreign Office, 1947; re-established in Foreign Service, 1948; served in Frankfurt and Bonn, 1948-53; Counsellor, HM Foreign Service, 1951; Imperial Defence College, 1953; Head of News Department, Foreign Office, 1954-55; Chargé d'Affaires, Peking, 1955-57; Asst Under-Sec., FO, 1957-60; Ambassador to Finland, 1961-63; Ambassador to the European Communities in Brussels, 1963-65; Dep. Under-Sec. of State, FO, 1965-68; Dir, Hill, Samuel & Co. Ltd, 1968-69; Dep. Under-Sec. of State, FCO, and Leader at official level of British delegn to negotiate entry to EEC, 1969-72; Chm., Intervention Bd for Agricl Produce, 1972-74. Dir, Britain in Europe Campaign, 1974-75. *Publication:* Our European Future, 1972 (Stamp Meml Lecture). *Recreations:* shooting, fishing. *Address:* 37 Flood Street, SW3. *Club:* Travellers'.

O'NEILL, Denis, CB 1957; formerly Under-Secretary, Ministry of Transport, retired 1968; *b* 26 Feb. 1908; *e surv. s* of late Very Rev. F. W. S. O'Neill, DD and Mrs O'Neill, Belfast and Manchuria; *m* 1st, 1930, Pamela (marr. diss. 1936), *d* of John Walter; one *s*; 2nd, 1944, Barbara, *d* of Mrs W. E. Norton; one adopted *d*. *Educ:* Royal Academical Institution, Belfast; Oriel Coll., Oxford (scholar). Entered Ministry of Transport, Oct. 1931; successively Private Secretary to following Ministers of Transport: Rt Hon. Leslie (later Lord) Hore-Belisha, MP 1935-37; Leslie Burgin, MP, 1937-39; Euan Wallace, MP, 1939-40; Sir John (Lord) Reith, MP, 1940; Lt-Col J. T. C. Moore-Brabazon, MP (later Lord Brabazon of Tara), 1940-41, and (with F. H. Keenlyside) Lord Leathers (Minister of War Transport), Asst Sec., 1943; Under-Sec., Min. of Transport, 1951. *Recreations:* reading, gardening, walking. *Address:* c/o Malta Union Club, Sliema, Malta GC. *Clubs:* Savile; Union (Malta).

O'NEILL, Michael; *b* 7 Oct. 1909; *s* of Michael and Sarah O'Neill; *m* 1936, Kathleen O'Connor, Ballinasloe, Co. Galway; three *s* three *d*. *Educ:* Dromore NS; Bellisle Academy. Draper's Asst, 1923-29; Haulage Contractor, 1929-31; Tillage Contractor, 1931-45; Farmer, 1945-52. Mem. Exec. Ulster Farmers' Union, 1945-48; Exec. Irish Anti-Partition League, 1946-57; Omagh RDC, 1945-57; Tyrone CC, 1950-57; Tyrone Co. Educ. Cttee, 1950-52; Tyrone Co. Health Cttee, 1950-52; Tyrone Co. Welfare Cttee, 1950-52; Entertainments Officer, Tyrone and Fermanagh Hosp., 1960-74. MP (Irish Republican) Mid-Ulster, 1951-55.

Recreations: amateur dramatics, Gaelic football. *Address:* 24 Centenary Park, Omagh, Co. Tyrone, N Ireland. *T:* Omagh 2461.

O'NEILL, Most Rev. Michael Cornelius, OBE 1945; MM 1918; *b* 15 Feb. 1898; Irish Canadian. *Educ:* St Michael's College, University of Toronto; St Augustine's Seminary, Toronto. Overseas Service, Signaller, CFA, European War, 1916-19. St Joseph's Seminary, Edmonton; Professor, 1928-39; Rector, 1930-39. Overseas Service, Canadian Chaplain Services, War of 1939-45; Principal Chaplain (Army) Overseas, (RC), 1941-45; Principal Chaplain (Army), (RC), 1945-46. Archbishop of Regina, 1948-73. Hon. Chaplain, Saskatchewan Comd, Royal Canadian Legion, 1973. Nat. Lutheran Merit Award, 1974. Hon. LLD: Toronto, 1952; Univ. of Saskatchewan (Regina Campus), 1974. *Address:* 67 Hudson Drive, Regina, Sask, Canada. *Club:* East India, Devonshire, Sports and Public Schools.

O'NEILL, Prof. Patrick Geoffrey, BA, PhD; Professor of Japanese, University of London, since 1968; *b* 9 Aug. 1924; *m* 1951, Diana Howard; one *d*. *Educ:* Rutlish Sch., Merton; Sch. of Oriental and African Studies, Univ. of London. Lectr in Japanese, Sch. of Oriental and African Studies, Univ. of London, 1949. *Publications:* A Guide to Nō, 1954; Early Nō Drama, 1958; (with S. Yanada) Introduction to Written Japanese, 1963; A Programmed Course on Respect Language in Modern Japanese, 1966; Japanese Kana Workbook 1967; A Programmed Introduction to Literary-style Japanese, 1968; Japanese Names, 1972; Essential Kanji, 1973. *Recreations:* tennis, photography. *Address:* School of Oriental and African Studies, University of London, WC1E 7HP.

O'NEILL, Rt. Hon. Phelim Robert Hugh, PC (N Ireland) 1969; Major, late RA; *b* 2 Nov. 1909; *s* and *heir* of 1st Baron Rathcavan, *qv*; *m* 1st, 1934, Clare Désirée (from whom he obtained a divorce, 1944), *d* of late Detmar Blow; one *s* one *d*; 2nd, 1953, Mrs B. D. Edwards-Moss, *d* of late Major Hon. Richard Coke; three *d* (and one *d* decd). *Educ:* Eton. MP (UU) for North Antrim (UK Parliament), 1952-59; MP (U) North Antrim, Parliament of N Ireland, 1959-72; Minister, N Ireland: Education, 1969; Agriculture, 1969-71. *Address:* Lizard Manor, Aghadowey, Londonderry, N Ireland.

O'NEILL, Robert James; HM Diplomatic Service; Head of South Asian Department, Foreign and Commonwealth Office, since 1975; *b* 17 June 1932; *m* 1958, Helen Juniper; one *s* two *d*. *Educ:* King Edward VI Sch., Chelmsford; Trinity Coll., Cambridge (Schol.). 1st cl. English Tripos Pts I and II. Entered HM Foreign (now Diplomatic) Service, 1955; FO, 1955-57; British Embassy, Ankara, 1957-60; Dakar, 1961-63; FO, 1963-68, Private Sec. to Chancellor of Duchy of Lancaster, 1966, and to Minister of State for Foreign Affairs, 1967-68; British Embassy, Bonn, 1968-72; Counsellor Diplomatic Service, 1972; seconded to Cabinet Office as Asst Sec., 1972-75. *Recreation:* hill-walking. *Address:* c/o Foreign and Commonwealth Office, SW1A 2AH. *Club:* Travellers'.

O'NEILL, Thomas P(hilip), Jr; Speaker, House of Representatives, USA, since Nov. 1976; *b* Cambridge, Mass, 9 Dec. 1912; *s* of Thomas P. O'Neill and Rose Anne (*née* Tolan); *m* 1941, Mildred Anne Miller; three *s* two *d*. *Educ:* St John's High Sch.; Boston Coll., Mass. Grad. 1936. In business, insurance, in Cambridge, Mass. Mem., State Legislature, Mass, 1936-52: Minority Leader, 1947 and 1948; Speaker of the House, 1948-52. Member, Camb. Sch. Cttee, 1946, 1949. Member of Congresses: 83rd-87th, 11th Dist, Mass; 88th-93rd, 8th Dist, Mass. Democrat: Majority Whip, 1971-73, Majority Leader, 1973-. *Address:* Rayburn House Office Building, Washington, DC 20515, USA.

ONIANS, Richard Broxton, MA (Liverpool), PhD (Cantab); Hildred Carlile Professor of Latin in University of London, 1936-66; now Emeritus; *b* 11 January 1899; *s* of late Richard Henry Onians, Liverpool; *m* 1937, Rosalind, *d* of late Lt-Col Ernest Browning Lathbury, OBE, MD, RAMC, Chipperfield, Herts; two *s* four *d*. *Educ:* Liverpool Inst.; Liverpool Univ. (1st Class Hons Classics); Trinity Coll. Cambridge (Senior Scholarship Examination, Open Research Studentship, Hooper English Oration Prize); Craven Grant for archæological research in Greece, and Hare Prize (Univ. of Cambridge). Member Council Assoc. of Univ. Teachers, 1945-53; Exec. Cttee 1946-51; Chm. London Consultative Cttee (AUT), 1946-48; Chm., Nat. Campaign Cttee for Expansion of Higher Educ., 1947-Feb. 1948 and June 1948-53; Chm. Joint Standing Cttee and Conf. on Library Cooperation, 1948-60; Mem. Exec. Cttee and Finance Committee of National Central Library, 1947-53. Formerly 4th South Lancs and RAF (1917-18); Lecturer in

Latin, Univ. of Liverpool, 1925-33; Professor of Classics, Univ. of Wales (Swansea), 1933-35. *Publications:* The Origins of European Thought about the Body, the Mind, the Soul, the World, Time, and Fate: new interpretations of Greek, Roman, and kindred evidence, also of some basic Jewish and Christian beliefs, 1951 (further enl. edn 1977); articles and reviews in Classical Journals. *Recreation:* walking. *Address:* Stokesay, 21 Luard Road, Cambridge. *T:* Cambridge 44250.

ONION, Francis Leo, CMG 1968; JP; Director, NZ Co-operative Dairy Co. Ltd (Chairman, 1961-69); Chairman, NZ Dairy Board, 1968-76 (Deputy Chairman, 1964-68); *b* 10 July 1903; *s* of Edwin Joseph Onion, Blenheim, NZ; *m* 1931, *d* of D. Ross, Otorohanga, NZ; two *s* one *d. Educ:* Hamilton High School. Farmer and Company Director; Chairman: Waipa County Council, NZ, 1947-61; New Zealand Counties Ward, 1947-61; Central Waikato Electric Power Board, 1947-61; Maramurua Coalfields Ltd, 1961-69; Auckland Farm Products Ltd, 1967-; New Zealand Dairy Exporter Newspaper, 1963-; Mem. Bd, NZ Meat Producers, 1969-75. JP Hamilton, 1961. Coronation Medal, 1953. *Recreations:* shooting and bowls. *Address:* Te-Kowhai, RD8, Frankton, New Zealand. *T:* HOT 832 NZ. *Club:* National (Hamilton, NZ).

ONIONS, Mrs Oliver; *see* Ruck, Berta.

ONSLOW, family name of **Earl of Onslow.**

ONSLOW, 7th Earl of, *cr* 1801; **Michael William Coplestone Dillon Onslow,** Bt 1660; Baron Onslow, 1716; Baron Cranley, 1776; Viscount Cranley, 1801; *b* 28 Feb. 1938; *s* of 6th Earl of Onslow, KBE, MC, TD, and of Hon. Pamela Louisa Eleanor Dillon, *o d* of 19th Viscount Dillon, CMG, DSO; *S* father, 1971; *m* 1964, Robin Lindsay, *o d* of Major Robert Lee Bullard III, US Army, and of Lady Aberconway; one *s* two *d. Educ:* Eton; Sorbonne. Life Guards, 1956-60, served Arabian Peninsula. Farmer. *Heir: s* Viscount Cranley, *qv. Address:* Temple Court, Clandon Park, Guildford, Surrey. *Clubs:* White's, Beefsteak.
See also A . A . Waugh .

ONSLOW, Cranley Gordon Douglas; MP (C) Woking since 1964; *b* 8 June 1926; *s* of late F. R. D. Onslow and Mrs M. Onslow, Effingham House, Bexhill; *m* 1955, Lady June Hay, *yr d* of 13th Earl of Kinnoull; one *s* three *d. Educ:* Harrow; Oriel Coll., Oxford; Geneva Univ. Served in RAC, Lieut 7th QO Hussars, 1944-48, and 3rd/4th Co. of London Yeo. (Sharpshooters) (TA) as Captain, 1948-52. Joined HM Foreign Service, 1951; Third Sec. Br. Embassy, Rangoon, 1953-55; Consul at Maymyo, N Burma, 1955-56; resigned, 1960. Served on Dartford RDC, 1960-62, and Kent CC, 1961-64. Mem. Exec. 1922 Cttee, 1968-72. Chm., Cons. Aviation Cttee, 1970-72. Parly Under-Sec. of State, Aerospace and Shipping, DTI, 1972-74; an Opposition spokesman on health and social security, 1974-75, on defence, 1975-76. Mem., UK delegn to N Atlantic Assembly, 1977. Council Member: Nat. Rifle Assoc.; Salmon & Trout Assoc.; Anglers' Co-operative Assoc. *Publication:* Asian Economic Development (ed), 1965. *Recreations:* fishing, shooting, watching cricket. *Address:* Chobham Park House, Chobham, Woking, Surrey. *Club:* English-Speaking Union.

ONSLOW, Maj.-Gen. Sir Denzil M.; *see* Macarthur-Onslow.

ONSLOW, Sir John (Roger Wilmot), 8th Bt, *cr* 1797; *b* 21 July 1932; *o s* of Sir Richard Wilmot Onslow, 7th Bt, TD, and Constance (*d* 1960), *o d* of Albert Parker; *S* father, 1963; *m* 1955, Catherine Zoia, *d* of Henry Atherton Greenway, The Manor, Compton Abdale, near Cheltenham, Gloucestershire; one *s* one *d. Educ:* Cheltenham College. *Heir: s* Richard Paul Atherton Onslow, *b* 16 Sept. 1958. *Address:* c/o Barclays Bank Ltd, Fowey, Cornwall.

ONSLOW, William George, CB 1970; Chairman Yorkshire and Humberside Economic Planning Board, 1965-71; *b* 12 June 1908; *s* of Albert Edward and Ann Onslow; *m* Joyce Elizabeth Robson; two *s* one *d. Educ:* Medway Technical College; London University. Board of Trade: Patent Examiner, 1930-39; Principal, 1942-46; Assistant Secretary, 1946-65; Under Secretary, Department of Economic Affairs, 1965, Min. of Housing and Local Govt, 1969, DoE, 1970-71. *Recreation:* golf. *Address:* 9 Elmete Avenue, Leeds, West Yorkshire. *T:* Leeds 659706.

ONTARIO, Metropolitan of; *see* Moosonee, Archbishop of.

ONTARIO, Bishop of, since 1975; **Rt. Rev. Henry Gordon Hill;** *b* 14 Dec. 1921; *s* of Henry Knox Hill and Kathleen Elizabeth (*née* Cunningham); unmarried. *Educ:* Queen's Univ., Kingston, Ont. (BA 1945); Trinity Coll., Toronto (LTh 1948); St John's Coll.,

Cambridge (MA 1952). Deacon, Dio. Ont., 1948; Priest (Bp of Ely for Ontario), 1949; Curate, Belleville, Ont., 1950; Rector of Adolphustown, Ont., 1951; Chaplain, St John's Coll., Cambridge, Eng., 1952; Curate, Wisbech, Cambs, 1955; Rector, St Thomas, Reddendale, Ont., 1957; Asst Prof., Canterbury Coll., Univ. of Windsor, 1962-68; (Vice-Principal, 1965-68); Associate Prof. of History, Univ. of Windsor, Ont., 1968-74. Hon. DD: Trinity Coll., Toronto, 1976; Montreal Dio. Theol Coll., 1976; Hon. LLD Univ. of Windsor, 1976; Hon. Dr, Theological Inst., Bucharest, 1977. CLJ 1976. Patriarchal Cross of Romanian Orthodox Church, 1969. *Publications:* articles in Cdn Jl of Theology, Sobornost, Jl Fellowship of St Alban and St Sergius. *Recreations:* walking, reading. *Address:* 90 Johnson Street, Kingston, Ontario, Canada K7L 1X7. *T:* 613-544-4774.

OPENSHAW, William Harrison, DL; **His Honour Judge Openshaw;** a Circuit Judge (formerly Chairman Lancashire Quarter Sessions), since 1958; *b* 11 Dec. 1912; *s* of late Sir James Openshaw, OBE, JP, DL; *m* 1945, Joyce Lawford; two *s* one *d. Educ:* Harrow; St Catharine's, Cambridge. Called to Bar, Inner Temple, 1936; practised on Northern Circuit; Recorder of Preston, 1958-71, Hon. Recorder, 1971-; Judge and Assessor of the Borough Court of Pleas, Preston, 1958-72. DL Lancs, 1968. *Address:* Park House, Broughton, Lancs.

OPHER, William David, CBE 1963; CEng, FIMechE; Joint Managing Director, Vickers Limited, 1967-68, retired; *b* 30 May 1903; *s* of William Thomas Opher, London, and Margaret Mary Carson, Belfast; *m* 1930, Marie Dorothy, 3rd *d* of William Fane; one *s. Educ:* Borough Polytechnic, London. Apprenticed Arnold Goodwin & Son, Bankside; joined Vickers, 1928; Director: Vickers Ltd, Shipbuilding Group, 1955; Vickers Ltd, 1959; Rolls-Royce & Associates Ltd, 1959; Vickers & Bookers Ltd, 1959; British Hovercraft Corporation, 1966; Chairman Vickers, Ltd, Engineering Group, 1962-67. Mem. Council, Lancaster Univ., 1968; Governor, Polytechnic of the South Bank (formerly Borough Polytechnic), 1969-73. Freeman, City of London, 1949. Serving Brother, Order of St John, 1962, Officer Brother, 1973. *Recreations:* golfing, fishing, shooting. *Address:* The Garth, Grange-over-Sands, Cumbria LA11 6BG. *T:* (Home) Grange-over-Sands 3151. *Club:* Bexleyheath Golf.

OPIE, Evelyn Arnold; Matron, King's College Hospital, SE5, 1947-60; *b* 21 Aug. 1905; *d* of George and Annie Opie. *Educ:* Wentworth School for Girls, Bournemouth. Westminster Sick Children's Hosp., 1924-26 (sick children's trng); Guy's Hosp., SE1, 1926-29; SRN Oct. 1929. Midwifery Trng SCM, 1930, Sister, 1930-32, Guy's Hosp.; private nursing, Bournemouth, 1932-33; Sister (Radium Dept and Children's Ward), 1933-39, Administrative Sister, Asst Matron, Dep. Matron, 1939-47, Guy's Hosp. Diploma in Nursing of London Univ., 1935. *Recreations:* music, gardening. *Address:* 63 Windrush Way, Hythe, Southampton SO4 6JF. *T:* Hythe 842232.

OPIE, Iona Margaret Balfour; folklorist; *b* 13 Oct. 1923; *d* of late Sir Robert Archibald, CMG, DSO, MD, and of Olive Cant; *m* 1943, Peter Mason Opie, *qv* ; two *s* one *d. Educ:* Sandecotes Sch., Parkstone. Served 1941-43, WAAF meteorological section. Hon. Mem., Folklore Soc., 1974. Coote-Lake Medal (jtly with husband), 1960. Hon. MA Oxon, 1962. *Publications:* (all with Peter Opie): I Saw Esau, 1947; The Oxford Dictionary of Nursery Rhymes, 1951; The Oxford Nursery Rhyme Book, 1955; Christmas Party Games, 1957; The Lore and Language of Schoolchildren, 1959; Puffin Book of Nursery Rhymes, 1963 (European Prize City of Caorle); Children's Games in Street and Playground, 1969 (Chicago Folklore Prize); The Oxford Book of Children's Verse, 1973; Three Centuries of Nursery Rhymes and Poetry for Children (exhibition catalogue), 1973, enl. edn 1977; The Classic Fairy Tales, 1974. *Recreations:* reading, walking. *Address:* Westerfield House,West Liss, Hants.

OPIE, Peter Mason; author; *b* 25 Nov. 1918; *o s* of late Major Philip Adams Opie, RAMC and Margaret Collett-Mason; *m* 1943, Iona Margaret Balfour Opie, *qv* ; two *s* one *d. Educ:* Eton. Served Royal Fusiliers, 1939; commnd Royal Sussex Regt, 1940, invalided 1941. Engaged in research with wife from 1944. Pres. Anthropology Section, British Assoc., 1962-63; Pres., Folklore Soc., 1963-64. Silver Medal, RSA, 1953; Coote-Lake Medal (jtly with wife), 1960. Hon. MA Oxon, 1962. *Publications:* I Want to Be, 1939; Having Held the Nettle, 1945; The Case of Being a Young Man, 1946 (joint-winner Chosen Book Competition); works on child life and literature (with Iona Opie): I Saw Esau, 1947; The Oxford Dictionary of Nursery Rhymes, 1951; The Oxford Nursery Rhyme Book, 1955; Christmas Party Games, 1957; The Lore and Language of Schoolchildren, 1959; Puffin Book of Nursery Rhymes 1963 (European Prize City of Caorle); Children's Games in Street and Playground, 1969 (Chicago Folklore Prize); The Oxford Book of Children's Verse, 1973;

Three Centuries of Nursery Rhymes and Poetry for Children (exhibition catalogue), 1973, enl. edn 1977; The Classic Fairy Tales, 1974; contrib. Encycl. Britannica, Chambers Encycl., New Cambridge Bibliog. of English Lit., etc. *Recreations:* book collecting, blackberry picking. *Address:* Westerfield House, West Liss, Hants.

OPIE, Redvers, CMG 1944; MA (Oxon and Harvard); PhD (Harvard); Director: Business International (New York), since 1954; Fomentadora Rural SA (Mexico); Economic Counsellor to American Chamber of Commerce of Mexico, Mexico City, since 1966, and publisher of report on Mexico, Economic Analysis for Company Planning (monthly), since 1974; *b* 20 January 1900; *s* of late James Reid and Bessie Hockaday Opie; naturalised US citizen, 1948; *m* 1st, 1929, Catharine Crombie Taussig (marr. diss., 1948), Cambridge, Mass; one *s* one *d*; 2nd, 1971, Blanca Bolaños Aceves, México, DF. *Educ:* Rutherford Coll.; Univ. of Durham. Lectr in Economics, Univ. of Durham, 1919-23, Wellesley Coll. (USA), 1923-24, Harvard Univ. 1924-30; Fellow of Magdalen College, Oxford, 1931-45, Home Bursar, 1935-40 (on leave of absence for National Service from Sept. 1939); University Lecturer in Economic Science, 1936-39; Counsellor and Economic Adviser to British Embassy, Washington, DC (resigned 1946). Adviser, UK Delegation, International Food Conference, 1943; UK Delegate, International Monetary and Financial Conference, 1944; Member US Govt Mission, on Private Foreign Investment, to Turkey, 1953; Senior Staff Mem., Brookings Institution, Washington, DC, 1947-53. President, American Ligurian Company Inc., New York, 1947-54. Gen. Editor, Oxford Economic Papers, 1938-39. *Publications:* (joint) Major Problems of US Foreign Policy, annually, 1947-52; Anglo-American Economic Relations, 1950; Current Issues in Foreign Economic Assistance, 1951; The Search For Peace Settlements, 1951; American Foreign Assistance, 1953; Selected papers on the Mexican and International Economies, 1966-68, 1968. *Recreations:* tennis and music. *Address:* Reforma 368-503, Mexico 6, DF. *T:* 5288845. *Clubs:* Harvard (New York); Metropolitan (Washington, DC); Churubusco, University (Mexico).

OPIE, Roger Gilbert, CBE 1976; Member, Monopolies and Mergers Commission, since 1968; Fellow and Lecturer in Economics, New College, Oxford, since 1961; *b* Adelaide, SA, 23 Feb. 1927; *o s* of late Frank Gilbert Opie and late Fanny Irene Grace Opie (*née* Tregoning); *m* 1955, Norma Mary, *o d* of Norman and Mary Canter; two *s* one *d*. *Educ:* Prince Alfred Coll. and Adelaide Univ., SA; Christ Church and Nuffield Coll., Oxford. BA 1st Cl. Hons 1948, MA Adelaide 1950; SA Rhodes Schol., 1950; Boulter Exhibnr, 1952; George Webb Medley Jun. Schol., 1952, Sen. Schol., 1953; PPE 1st Cl. 1953; Nuffield Coll. Studentship, 1954; BPhil 1954. Asst Lectr and Lectr, LSE, 1954-61; Econ. Adviser, Econ. Section, HM Treasury, 1958-60; Asst Dir, HM Treasury Centre for Administrative Studies, 1964; Asst Dir, Planning Div., Dept of Economic Affairs, 1964-66; Economic Adviser to Chm., NBPI, 1967-70; Special Univ. Lectr in Econs, Oxford, 1970-75. City Councillor, Oxford, 1972-74; Oxford Dist Councillor, 1973-76. Economic Correspondent, New Statesman, 1967-71, 1974-76; Editor: The Bankers' Magazine, 1960-64; International Currency Review, 1970-71. Governor, Bryanston Sch. *Publications:* co-author of a number of works in applied economics. *Recreations:* sailing, reading, disorganised philately. *Address:* 8 New College Lane, Oxford OX1 3BL. *T:* Oxford 41769. *Clubs:* Reform; Lilliput Sailing (Dorset).

OPPENHEIM, Tan Sri Sir Alexander, Kt 1961; OBE 1955; FRSE; MA, DSc (Oxon); PhD (Chicago); Visiting Professor, University of Benin, Nigeria, 1973-77; Vice-Chancellor, University of Malaya, 1957-65 (Acting Vice-Chancellor, 1955); *b* 4 Feb. 1903; *o s* of late Rev. H. J. and Mrs F. Oppenheim; *m* 1930, Beatrice Templer, *y d* of Dr Otis B. Nesbit, Indiana, USA; one *d*. *Educ:* Manchester Grammar Sch.; Balliol Coll., Oxford (Scholar). Sen. Mathematical Schol., Oxf., 1926; Commonwealth Fund Fell., Chicago, 1927-30; Lectr, Edinburgh, 1930-31; Prof. of Mathematics, 1931-42, 1945-49; Dep. Principal, 1947, 1949, Raffles Coll., Singapore; Prof. of Mathematics, 1949-57; Dean, Faculty of Arts, 1949, 1951, 1953. Hon. degrees: DSc (Hong Kong) 1961; LLD: (Singapore) 1962; (Leeds) 1966; DLitt (Malaya) 1965. L/Bdr, SRA(V), POW (Singapore, Siam), 1942-45; Dean POW University, 1942; Pres. Malayan Mathematical Soc., 1951-55, 1957. Pres. Singapore Chess Club, 1956-60; Pres., Amer. Univs. Club, 1956. Chm. Bd of Management, Tropical Fish Culture Research Institute (Malacca), 1962; Member: Unesco-International Assoc. of Universities Study of Higher Education in Development of Countries of SE Asia, 1962; Academic Adv. Cttee, Univ. of Cape Coast, 1972. Visiting Professor: Univ. of Reading, in Dept of

Mathematics, 1965-68; Univ. of Ghana, 1968-73. Panglima Mangku Negara (Fedn of Malaya), 1962; FWA, 1963. *Publications:* papers on mathematics in various periodicals. *Recreations:* chess, bridge, walking, swimming. *Address:* 664 Finchley Road, NW11. *T:* 01-458 2863. *Clubs:* Royal Commonwealth Society; Selangor (Kuala Lumpur).

OPPENHEIM, Sir Duncan (Morris), Kt 1960; Adviser to British-American Tobacco Co. Ltd, 1972-74 (Chairman 1953-66, President, 1966-72); Chairman, Tobacco Securities Trust Co. Ltd, 1969-74; Deputy Chairman, Commonwealth Development Finance Co., 1968-74; *b* 6 Aug. 1904; *s* of Watkin Oppenheim, BA; TD; and Helen, 3rd *d* of Duncan McKechnie; *m* 1st, 1932, Joyce Mary (*d* 1933), *d* of Stanley Mitcheson; no *c*; 2nd, 1936, Susan May (*d* 1964), *e d* of Brig.-Gen. E. B. Macnaghten, CMG, DSO; one *s* one *d*. *Educ:* Repton Sch. Admitted Solicitor of the Supreme Court, 1929; Messrs Linklaters & Paines, London, Assistant Solicitor, 1929-34; joined British-American Tobacco Ltd group as a Solicitor, 1934; Director: British-American Tobacco Co. Ltd, 1943; Lloyds Bank Ltd, 1956-75; Equity and Law Life Assurance Society. Chairman: Council, Royal College of Art, 1956-72; Council of Industrial Design, 1960-72 (Mem. 1959); British Nat. Cttee of Internat. Chamber of Commerce, 1963-74; Overseas Investment Cttee CBI, 1964-74; Chm. and Mem. Council, RIIA, 1968-73; Member: Adv. Council, V&A Mus., 1967- (Chm. V&A Associates, 1976-); Crafts Adv. Cttee and British Crafts Centre, 1972- (acting Chm., 1977); Governing Body of Repton School, 1959; Chm. Court of Governors, Admin. Staff Coll., 1963-71. Hon. Dr and Senior Fellow, Royal College of Art; Hon. FSIA, 1972. Bicentenary Medal, RSA, 1969. *Recreations:* painting, sailing. *Address:* 43 Edwardes Square, Kensington, W8. *T:* 01-603 7431. *Clubs:* Athenæum; Royal Yacht Squadron.

OPPENHEIM, Mrs Henry M.; *see* Oppenheim, Sally.

OPPENHEIM, Sally, (Mrs Henry M. Oppenheim); MP (C) Gloucester since 1970; *b* 26 July 1930; *d* of Mark and Jeanette Viner; *m* 1949, Henry M. Oppenheim; one *s* two *d*. *Educ:* Sheffield High Sch.; Lowther Coll., N Wales. Formerly: Exec. Dir, Industrial & Investment Services Ltd; Social Worker, School Care Dept, ILEA. Trustee, Clergy Rest House Trust. Vice Chm., 1971-73, Chm., 1973-74, Cons. Party Parly Prices and Consumer Protection Cttee; Opposition Spokesman on Prices and Consumer Protection, 1974-; Mem. Shadow Cabinet, 1975-. Nat. Vice-President: Nat. Mobile Home Residents Assoc; Nat. Union of Townswomen's Guilds; Pres., Glos. Dist Br., BRCS; Vice-President: S Wales and the West Fire Liaison Panel; Wester Centre of Public Health Inspectors; Member: Exec. Cttee and Management Cttee, Nat. Council for the Single Woman and her Elderly Dependents; Adv. Council, 1971-, Business Cttee, 1974-, BBC; Soc. of Cons. Lawyers. *Recreations:* tennis, bridge. *Address:* 1 Ardmore Close, Tuffley, Gloucester; House of Commons, SW1. *Clubs:* (Pres.) Conservative (Gloucester).

OPPENHEIMER, Harry Frederick; Chairman: Anglo-American Corporation of SA Ltd; De Beers Consolidated Mines, Ltd, and other producing, marketing and investment companies in the De Beers Group; AE&CI Ltd; Director: Barclays Bank International; General Mining and Finance Corp. Ltd; and other investment, mining, colliery and development companies; *b* Kimberley S Africa, 28 Oct. 1908; *s* of late Sir Ernest Oppenheim, DCL; LLD; *m* 1943, Bridget, *d* of late Foster McCall; one *s* one *d*. *Educ:* Charterhouse; Christ Church, Oxford (MA). MP (SA) Kimberley City, 1948-58. Served 4th SA Armoured Car Regt 1940-45. Chancellor, Univ. of Cape Town; Hon. DEcon, Univ. of Natal; Hon. DLaws, Univs of Leeds, Rhodes and Witwatersrand. Instn MM Gold Medal, 1965. *Recreations:* racing, golf, riding. *Address:* Brenthurst, Parktown, Johannesburg, South Africa. *Clubs:* Brooks's; Rand, Inanda (Johannesburg); Kimberley (SA); Salisbury (Rhodesia).

OPPENHEIMER, Sir Michael (Bernard Grenville), 3rd Bt, *cr* 1921; BLitt, MA; *b* 27 May 1924; *s* of Sir Michael Oppenheimer, 2nd Bt, and Caroline Magdalen (who *m* 2nd, 1935, late Sir Ernest Oppenheimer), *d* of Sir Robert G. Harvey, 2nd Bt; *S* father, 1933; *m* 1947, Laetitia Helen, BPhil, MA, *er d* of Sir Hugh Munro-Lucas-Tooth of Teananich, *qv*; three *d*. *Educ:* Charterhouse; Christ Church, Oxford. Served with South African Artillery, 1942-45. Lecturer in Politics: Lincoln Coll., Oxford, 1955-68; Magdalen Coll., Oxford, 1966-68. *Heir:* none. *Address:* L'Aiguillon, Rue des Cotils, Grouville, Jersey. *Clubs:* Victoria (Jersey); Kimberley (Kimberley).

OPPENHEIMER, Peter Morris; Student of Christ Church, Oxford, and University Lecturer in Economics, since 1967; *b* 16

April 1938; s of Friedrich Rudolf and Charlotte Oppenheimer; m 1964, Catherine, er d of Dr Eliot Slater, qv, and Dr Lydia Pasternak; two s one d. Educ: Haberdashers' Aske's Sch.; The Queen's Coll., Oxford (BA 1961). National Service, RN, 1956-58. Bank for International Settlements, Basle, 1961-64; Research Fellow, Nuffield Coll., Oxford, 1964-67; Vis. Prof., London Graduate Sch. of Business Studies, 1976-77. Dir, Investing in Success Equities Ltd, 1975-. Mem., Royal Commn on Legal Services, 1976-. Publications: contribs to symposia, conference procs, prof. jls, bank reviews, etc. Recreations: music, opera, amateur dramatics (including broadcasting), skiing. Address: 8 Lathbury Road, Oxford OX2 7AU. T: Oxford 58226.

OPPENHEIMER, Sir Philip (Jack), Kt 1970; Chairman, The Diamond Trading Co. (Pty) Ltd; Deputy Chairman, Charter Consolidated Ltd; b 29 Oct. 1911; s of Otto and Beatrice Oppenheimer; m 1935, Pamela Fenn Stirling; one s one d. Educ: Harrow; Jesus Coll., Cambridge. Bronze Cross of Holland, 1943; Commandeur, Ordre de la Courronne (Belgium) 1971. Recreations: golf, horse-racing and breeding. Address: 39 Egerton Terrace, SW3 2BU. Clubs: Jockey, Portland, White's.

OPPENHEIMER, Raymond Harry, CBE 1959; b 13 Nov. 1905; s of Louis Oppenheimer and Charlotte Emily Pollak. Educ: Harrow; Christ Church, Oxford. Served in RAFVR, 1940-45 (Fighter Controller). Recreations: golf, dog breeding (bull terriers). Address: White Waltham Place, Berkshire. T: Maidenhead 103. Clubs: Royal and Ancient; Royal Lytham, etc.

OPPERMAN, Hon. Sir Hubert (Ferdinand), Kt 1968; OBE 1952; Australian High Commissioner in Malta, 1967-72; b 29 May 1904; Australian; m 1928, Mavys Paterson Craig; one s (one d decd). Educ: Armadale, Vic.; Bailieston, Vic. Served RAAF 1940-45; commissioned 1942. Commonwealth Public Service: PMG's Dept, 1918-20; Navigation Dept, Trade and Customs, 1920-22. Cyclist: Australian Road Champion, 1924, 1926, 1927, 1929; Winner French Bol d'Or, 1928, and Paris-Brest-Paris, 1931; holder, numerous world's track and road unpaced and motor paced cycling records. Director, Allied Bruce Small Pty Ltd, 1936-60. MHR for Corio, Vic., 1949-67; Convenor: Commonwealth Jubilee Sporting Sub-Cttee, 1951; Mem. Australian Delegn to CPA Conf., Nairobi, 1954; Chief Govt, Whip, 1955-60; Minister for Shipping and Transport, 1960-63; Minister for Immigration, 1963-66. OStJ 1974. Medal of City of Paris, 1971. Publication: Pedals, Politics and People (autobiog.), 1977. Recreations: cycling, swimming. Address: c/o Bruce Small Enterprises, 12 Marine Parade, St Kilda, Vic 3182, Australia. T: 940711. Clubs: USI, Air Force (Victoria).

ORAM, family name of **Baron Oram.**

ORAM, Baron cr 1975 (Life Peer), of Brighton, E Sussex; **Albert Edward Oram;** a Lord in Waiting (Government Whip), since 1976; b 13 Aug. 1913; s of Henry and Ada Edith Oram; m Frances Joan, d of Charles and Dorothy Barber, Lewes; two s. Educ: Burgess Hill Element. Sch.; Brighton Grammar Sch.; University of London (London School of Economics and Institute of Education). Formerly a teacher. Served War 1942-45; Royal Artillery, Normandy and Belgium. Research Officer, Co-operative Party, 1946-55. MP (Lab and Co-op) East Ham South, 1955-Feb. 1974; Parly Secretary, ODM, 1964-69. Co-ordinator, Develt Programmes, Internat. Co-operative Alliance, 1971-73; Develt Administrator, Intermediate Technol. Develt Gp. Mem., Commonwealth Develt Corp., 1975-76. Recreations: country walking, cricket, chess. Address: 19 Ridgeside Avenue, Patcham, Brighton BN1 8WD. T: Brighton 505333.

ORAM, Rt. Rev. Kenneth Cyril; see Grahamstown, Bishop of.

ORAM, Samuel, MD (London); FRCP; Senior Physician, and Director, Cardiac Department, King's College Hospital; Censor, Royal College of Physicians; Medical Adviser, Rio Tinto Zinc Corporation Ltd; Consulting Medical Officer, Sun Life Assurance Co. of Canada; b 11 July 1913; s of Samuel Henry Nathan Oram, London; m 1940, Ivy, d of Raffaele Amato; two d. Educ: King's College, London; King's College Hospital, London. Senior Scholar, KCH, London; Sambrooke Medical Registrar, KCH. Served War of 1939-45, as Lt-Col, RAMC. Examiner in Medicine for RCP and Univ. of London; Examiner: in Pharmacology and Materia Medica, The Conjoint Bd; in Medicine, The Worshipful Soc. of Apothecaries. Member: Assoc. of Physicians; Br. Cardiac Society; American Heart Assoc.; Canada Club; Corresp. Member Australasian Cardiac Soc. Publications: Clinical Heart Disease (textbook), 1971; various cardiological and medical articles in Quart. Jl Med., British Heart Jl, BMJ, Brit. Encyclopaedia of Medical Practice, The Practitioner, etc. Recreation: golf (execrable). Address: 73 Harley Street, W1. T: 01-935 9942. Club: Athenæum.

ORANMORE and BROWNE, 4th Baron (Ireland), cr 1836; Baron Mereworth of Mereworth Castle (UK), cr 1926; **Dominick Geoffrey Edward Browne;** b 21 Oct. 1901; e s of 3rd Baron and Lady Olwen Verena Ponsonby (d 1927), e d of 8th Earl of Bessborough; S father, 1927; m 1st, 1925, Mildred Helen (who obtained a divorce, 1936), e d of Hon. Thomas Egerton; two s two d; 2nd, 1936, Oonagh (marr. diss., 1950), d of late Hon. Ernest Guinness; one s (and two s decd); 3rd, 1951, Sally Gray, 5b Mount Street, London, W. Educ: Eton; Christ Church, Oxford. Heir: s Hon. Dominick Geoffrey Thomas Browne [b 1 July 1929; m 1957, Sara Margaret (marr. diss. 1974), d of late Dr Herbert Wright, 59 Merrion Square, Dublin, and of Mrs C. A. West, Cross-in-Hand, Sussex]. Address: 52 Eaton Place, SW1. Club: Kildare Street and University (Dublin).
See also Hon. M. A. R. Cayzer.

ORBACH, Maurice; MP (Lab) Stockport South since 1964; General Secretary Trades Advisory Council since 1940; b 13 July 1902; s of late Hiam M. and Millicent Orbach, Cardiff and New York; m 1935, Ruth Beatrice Huebsch; one s one d. Educ: Cardiff; New York City. Engineer. Member St Pancras Board of Guardians, 1924; Member, South West St Pancras, LLC, 1937-46; MP (Lab) Willesden East, 1945-Sept. 1959. Governor, Central Foundation Schools; Mem. London Town Planning Committee; Governor, St Paul's, St Peter's, St Barts and St Philip's Hospitals, 1969-; Chm., British Emigrants Families Assoc. Lecturer on Industry and Commerce and the American Scene. Publication: Mission to Madrid, Austria, 1946. Address: 76 Eton Hall, Eton College Road, NW3. T: 01-722 4696, 01-452 8287.

ORCHARD, Edward Eric, CBE 1966 (OBE 1959); Director of Research, Foreign and Commonwealth Office, 1970-76; b 12 Nov. 1920. Educ: King's Sch., Grantham; Jesus Coll., Oxford (MA). War Service, 1941-46; FO, and HM Embassy, Moscow, 1948-51; Lectr in Russian, Oxford, 1951-52; FO, 1953-57, 1959-63; First Sec. and Head of Russian Secretariat, Moscow, 1957-59, 1963-65; FCO, 1965-76. Vice-Pres., Royal Soc. for Asian Affairs. Publications: various articles. Recreations: swimming, skating, chess, gardening. Address: Sturt Meadow House, Haslemere, Surrey. T: Haslemere 3034. Club: Athenæum.

ORCHARD-LISLE, Aubrey Edwin, CBE 1973; Consultant Partner, Healey & Baker, Surveyors, London, Amsterdam, Paris and Brussels (Senior Partner until 1973); b 12 March 1908; s of late Edwin Orchard-Lisle and late Lucy Ellen Lock; m 1934, Phyllis Muriel Viall; one s one d. Educ: West Buckland Sch., N Devon; Coll. of Estate Management. FRICS. Joined Healey & Baker, 1926. Governor, Guy's Hosp. 1953-74; Vice-Chm. of Bd, 1963-74; Governor, Guy's Hosp. Med. Sch.; Chm., Special Trustees, Guy's Hosp., 1974-; Mem., Lambeth, Southwark, Lewisham, AHA (Teaching), 1974-; Property Consultant, NCB Superannuation Schemes, 1953-; Mem. Bd, Gen. Practice Finance Corp., 1966-; Chm., Adv. Panel for Institutional Finance in New Towns, 1969-; part-time Mem., Nat. Bus Co., 1971-77. Recreations: gardening, swimming, travel. Address: 2 Aldford Street, Park Lane, W1Y 5PT. T: 01-499 6470; White Walls, Quarry Wood Road, Marlow, Bucks. T: Marlow 2573. Clubs: Buck's, St Stephen's, MCC.

ORD, Andrew James B.; see Blackett-Ord.

ORD JOHNSTONE, Morris Mackintosh, CB 1960; Chairman, Tobacco Advisory Committee, 1968-77; Independent Member, Home Grown Timber Advisory Committee; b 10 Oct. 1907; s of late James Ord Johnstone and Emily Morrison; m 1935, Violet Springett; one d. Educ: Uppingham; Wadham Coll., Oxford. Board of Trade, 1941-67; Under-Secretary, 1955-67. Address: 5 Campden Grove, W8. T: 01-937 7654.

ORDE, Alan C. C.; see Campbell Orde.

ORDE, Sir Charles William, KCMG cr 1940 (CMG 1931); b 25 Oct. 1884; e s of late William Orde, DL, of Nunnykirk. Morpeth, Northumberland; m 1914, Frances Fortune (d 1949), o d of James Davidson, Dunedin, New Zealand; two s two d. Educ: Eton; King's College, Cambridge. Minister to Baltic States, 1938-40; Ambassador to Chile, 1940-45. Recreations: fishing, music. Address: Nunnykirk, Morpeth, Northumberland. T: Hartburn 250.

ORDE, Denis Alan; a Recorder of the Crown Court since 1972; Barrister-at-Law; b 28 Aug. 1932; s of John Orde, CBE, Littlehoughton Hall, Northumberland, and late Charlotte Lilian Orde, County Alderman; m 1961, Jennifer Jane, d of Dr John Longworth, Masham, Yorks; two d. Educ: Oxford Univ. (MA). Served Army, 1950-52, 2nd Lieut 1951; TA, 1952-64 (RA), Lieut 1952, Captain 1958. Pres., Oxford Univ. Conserv. Assoc.,

1954; Mem. Cttee, Oxford Union, 1954-55; Vice-Chm., Fedn of Univ. Conserv. Assocs., 1955. Called to Bar, Inner Temple, 1956; Pupil Studentship, 1956; Profumo Prize, 1959. North-Eastern Circuit, 1958; Northern Area Legal Aid Cttee, 1969-. Asst Recorder: Kingston upon Hull, 1970; Sheffield, 1970-71. Contested (C): Consett, Gen. Elec. 1959, Newcastle upon Tyne West, Gen. Elec. 1966, Sunderland South, Gen. Elec. 1970. *Recreations:* listening to music; cricket, golf, painting. *Address:* Fulbeck House, Fulbeck, Morpeth, Northumberland. *T:* Morpeth 2295; 60 Grainger Street, Newcastle upon Tyne; 11 King's Bench Walk, Temple, EC4. *Clubs:* Carlton, Coningsby, United and Cecil.

ORDE, Sir John (Alexander) Campbell-, 6th Bt *cr* 1790, of Morpeth; *b* 11 May 1943; *s* of Sir Simon Arthur Campbell-Orde, 5th Bt, TD, and of Eleanor, *e d* of Col. Humphrey Watts, OBE, TD, Haslington Hall, Cheshire; *S* father, 1969; *m* 1973, Lacy Ralls, *d* of Grady Gallant, Nashville, USA; two *d*. *Educ:* Gordonstoun. *Heir: b* Peter Humphrey Campbell-Orde [*b* 18 June 1946; *m* 1976, Perdita Bennett (*née* Watts)]. *Address:* 228 West Hillwood Drive, Nashville, Tennessee, USA. *Clubs:* Caledonian, Lansdowne.

ORDE-POWLETT, family name of **Baron Bolton.**

O'REILLY, Anthony John Francis, (Tony O'Reilly); President and Chief Operating Officer, H. J. Heinz Co. Inc., since 1973; *b* Dublin, 7 May 1936; *o c* of J. P. O'Reilly, former Inspector-General of Customs; *m* 1962, Susan, *d* of Keith Cameron, Australia; three *s* three *d* (of whom two *s* one *d* are triplets). *Educ:* Belvedere Coll., Dublin; University Coll., Dublin. BCL 1958. Admitted Solicitor, 1958. Industrial Consultant, Weston Evans UK, 1958-60; PA to Chm., Suttons Ltd, Cork, 1960-62; Gen. Man., Irish Dairy Bd, 1962-66; Man. Dir, Irish Sugar Bd, 1966-69; Man. Dir, Erin Foods Ltd, 1966-69; Jt Man. Dir, Heinz-Erin, 1967-70; Man. Dir, H. J. Heinz Co. Ltd, UK, 1969-71; Sen. Vice-Pres., N America and Pacific, H. J. Heinz Co., 1971-72; Exec. Vice-Pres. and Chief Op. Off., H. J. Heinz Co., 1972-73. Lectr in Business Management, UC Cork, 1960-62. Director: Robt McCowen & Sons Ltd, 1961-62; Agricl Credit Corp. Ltd, 1965-66; Nitrigin Eireann Teoranta, 1965-66; Allied Irish Investment Bank Ltd, 1968-71; Thyssen-Bornemisza Co., 1970-71; Ulster Bank Ltd, 1973; Independent Newspapers, 1973-77; Nat. Mine Service Co.; Chm., Fitzwilliam Securities Ltd, 1971-; Deputy Chairman: Crowe Wilson & Co. Ltd, 1971-72; Fitzwilton Ltd, 1972-. Member: Incorp. Law Soc.; Council, Irish Management Inst.; Pres., Irish Work Study Inst. FBIM; FInstD. Hon. Dr Laws. *Publications:* Prospect, 1962; Developing Creative Management, 1970; The Conservative Consumer, 1971; Food for Thought, 1972. *Recreations:* Rugby (played for Ireland 29 times), tennis. *Address:* 835 Fox Chapel Road, Pittsburgh, Pa 15238, USA; Castlemartin, Kilcullen, Co. Kildare, Ireland. *Clubs:* Annabels; Stephen's Green (Dublin); Union League (New York); Duquesne, Allegheny, Fox Chapel, Pittsburgh Golf (Pittsburgh); Rolling Rock (Ligonier); Lyford Cay (Bahamas).

ORESCANIN, Bogdan; Ambassador of Yugoslavia to the Court of St James's, 1973-76; *b* 27 Oct. 1916; *m* 1947, Sonja Dapcevic; no *c. Educ:* Faculty of Law, Zagreb; Higher Mil. Academy. Organised uprising in Croatia; i/c various mil. and polit. duties in Nat. Liberation Struggle, War of 1939-45; Asst, then DCGS and Asst Defence Sec. of State, Yugoslav People's Army (Col General); formerly Mem. Fed. Parlt, Mem. Council of Fedn, Chm. Parly Cttee for Nat. Defence, Mem. For. Affairs Cttee of Fed. Parlt and Mem. Exec. Bd, Yugoslav Gp of IPU; Mil. Attaché in Gt Britain, 1952-54; Yugoslav Ambassador, People's Republics of China, Korea and Vietnam, 1970-73. Holds various Yugoslav and foreign decorations. *Publications:* articles on military-political theory; (study) Military Aspects of the Struggle for World's Peace, National Independence and Socialism. *Address:* Federal Secretariat for Foreign Affairs, Kneza Milosa 24, 11000 Belgrade, Yugoslavia.

ORGAN, (Harold) Bryan; painter; *b* Leicester, 31 Aug. 1935; *o c* of late Harold Victor Organ and Helen Dorothy Organ; *m* 1959, Elizabeth Jane Waters. *Educ:* Wyggeston Sch., Leicester; Coll. of Art, Loughborough; Royal Academy Schs, London. Lectr in Drawing and Painting, Loughborough Coll. of Art, 1959-65. One-man exhibns: Leicester Museum and Art Gallery, 1959; Redfern Gallery, 1967, 1969, 1971, 1973, 1975; Leicester 1973, 1976; New York, 1976. Represented: Kunsthalle, Darmstadt, 1968; Mostra Mercatao d'Arte Contemporanea, Florence, 1969; 3rd Internat. Exhibn of Drawing, Germany, 1970; Sao Paolo Museum of Art, Brazil. Works in public and private collections in England, USA, Germany, France, Canada, Italy. Portraits include: Malcolm Muggeridge, 1966; Sir Michael Tippett, 1966; David Hicks, 1968; Mary Quant, 1969; Nadia Nerina, 1969;

Princess Margaret, 1970; Dr Roy Strong, 1971; Elton John, 1973; Lester Piggott, 1973; Lord Ashby, 1975. Hon. MA Loughborough, 1974. *Address:* c/o Redfern Gallery, 20 Cork Street, W1. *T:* 01-734 1732. *Club:* Vintage Motor Cycle.

ORGANE, Sir Geoffrey (Stephen William), Kt 1968; MD, FFARCS; FRCS; Emeritus Professor of Anæsthetics, University of London, Westminster Medical School; formerly: Civilian Consultant in Anæsthetics to Royal Navy; Consultant Adviser in Anæsthetics, Ministry of Health; *b* Madras, 25 Dec. 1908; *er s* of Rev. William Edward Hartland Organe, K-i-H, and Alice (*née* Williams); *m* 1935, Margaret Mary Bailey, *e d* of Rev. David Bailey Davies, MC; one *s* two *d. Educ:* Taunton Sch.; Christ's Coll., Cambridge; Westminster Med. Sch. MRCS, LRCP, 1933; DA, RCP&S, 1937; MA, MD Cantab 1941; FFARCS 1948; FRCS 1965. Various resident appointments and first Anæsthetic Registrar (1938-39), Westminster Hospital; two years in general practice. Hon. Secretary, Medical Research Council's Anæsthetics Sub-Committee of Committee on Traumatic Shock, 1941-47; formerly Hon. Sec. Anæsthetics Cttee, Cttee on Analgesia in Midwifery; Vice-Pres., BMA Sect. Anæsthetics, Harrogate, 1949, Toronto, 1955; Pres., World Fedn of Socs. of Anæsthesiologists, 1964-68 (Sec.-Treas., 1955-64); Mem. Coun., RCS, 1958-61, Joseph Clover Lectr, Fac. of Anæsthetics; Royal Society of Medicine: Mem. Council; Hon. Sec. 1953-58; Hon. Fellow, 1974; Pres. Sect. of Anæsthetics, 1949-50 (Hon. Mem.); Assoc. of Anæsthetists of Gt Brit. and Ire.: Hon. Sec. 1949-53; Vice-Pres. 1953-54; Mem. Council, 1957-59; Pres. 1954-57; Hon. Mem., 1974; John Snow Silver Medal, 1972; Mem. Cttee of Anæsthetists' Group of BMA (Chm. 1955-58); Pres. SW Metropolitan Soc. of Anæsthetists, 1957-59; Dean, Faculty of Anæsthetists, 1958-61; Examr in Anæsthetics, Conjoint Bd; Examiner for FFARCS. Visited Italy, Turkey, Greece, Syria, Lebanon for Brit. Council; Denmark, Norway for WHO; also Portugal, France, Switzerland, Spain, Belgium, Netherlands, Germany, Finland, USA, Canada, Argentina, Australia, Venezuela, Mexico, Uganda, Peru, Japan, Hong Kong, Philippines, Brazil, Ceylon, Egypt, India, Iran, Israel, Malaysia, Uruguay, Austria, Sweden, Poland, USSR, Bulgaria, Czechoslovakia, Malta. Hon. or Corr. Mem., Danish, Argentine, Australian, Austrian, Brazilian, Canadian, Greek, Portuguese, French, German, Italian, Philippine, Spanish, Venezuelan Societies of Anæsthetists; Hon. FFARACS 1957; Hon. FFARCSI 1960; Hon. FFARCS 1975. *Publications:* various articles and chapters in medical journals and textbooks. *Recreations:* travel, gardening, photography, competitive sports; (formerly Pres., Vice-Pres., Hon. Treas., Capt. 1933) United Hospitals Athletic Club. *Address:* 38 Newlands Park, Seaton, Devon. *T:* Seaton 20266.

ORGEL, Leslie Eleazer, DPhil Oxon, MA; FRS 1962; Senior Fellow, Salk Institute, La Jolla, California, USA, and Adjunct Professor, University of California, San Diego, Calif, since 1964; *b* 12 Jan. 1927; *s* of Simon Orgel; *m* 1950, Hassia Alice Levinson; two *s* one *d. Educ:* Dame Alice Owen's Sch., London. Reader, University Chemical Laboratory, Cambridge, 1963-64, and Fellow of Peterhouse, 1957-64. *Publication:* An Introduction to Transition-Metal Chemistry, Ligand-Field Theory, 1960; The Origins of Life: molecules and natural selection, 1973. *Address:* Salk Institute, PO Box 1809, San Diego, Calif 92112, USA.

ORIGO, Marchesa Iris, DBE 1977; FRSL; author; *b* Birdlip, Glos, 15 August 1902; *o d* of W. Bayard Cutting, Westbrook, Long Island, USA, and Lady Sybil Cuffe; *m* 1924, Marchese Antonio Origo (*d* 1976); two *d. Educ:* privately, mostly in Florence. Holds honorary doctorates from Smith College and Wheaton College, USA; Isabella d'Este medal for essays and historical studies, Mantua, Italy, 1966. *Publications:* Leopardi, a biography, 1935 (revised 1953); Allegra, 1935; Tribune of Rome, 1938; War in Val d'Orcia, 1947; Giovanna and Jane, 1948; The Last Attachment, 1949; The Merchant of Prato, 1957; A Measure of Love, 1957; The World of San Bernardino, 1963; Images and Shadows, Part of a Life, 1970; The Vagabond Path: an anthology, 1972. *Recreations:* travel, gardening. *Address:* La Foce, Chianciano (Siena), Italy.

ORKNEY, 8th Earl of, *cr* 1696; **Cecil O'Bryen Fitz-Maurice;** Viscount of Kirkwall and Baron of Dechmont, 1696; *b* 3 July 1919; *s* of Douglas Frederick Harold FitzMaurice (*d* 1937; *g g s* of 5th Earl) and Dorothy Janette (who *m* 2nd, 1939, Commander E. T. Wiggins, DSC, RN), *d* of late Capt. Robert Dickie, RN; *S* kinsman 1951; *m* 1953, Rose Katharine Durk, *yr d* of late J. W. D. Silley, Brixham. Joined RASC, 1939; served in North Africa, Italy, France and Germany, 1939-46, and in Korea, 1950-51. *Heir: kinsman* Oliver Peter St John [*b* 27 Feb. 1938; *m* 1963, Mary Juliet, *d* of W. G. Scott-Brown, *qv*; one *s* three *d*]. *Address:* Summerlands, Princes Road, Ferndown, Dorset.

ORLEBAR, Michael Keith Orlebar S.; *see* Simpson-Orlebar.

ORMANDY, Eugene, KBE (Hon.) 1976; MusD; Conductor and Music Director of Philadelphia Orchestra since 1936; *b* 18 Nov. 1899; Hungarian; *s* of Benjamin and Rosalie Ormandy; *m* 1st, 1922, Steffy Goldner (marr. diss. 1947; decd), harpist, NY Philharmonic Orchestra; no *c*; 2nd, 1950, Margaret Frances Hitsch. *Educ:* Royal State Acad. of Music, BA 1914; state diploma for art of violin playing, 1916, and as prof., 1917; Grad. Gymnasium; student Univ. of Budapest, 1917-20. Hon. MusD: Hamline Univ., St Paul, 1934; Univ. of Pennsylvania, 1937; Philadelphia Academy of Music, 1939; Curtis Inst. of Music, 1946; Temple Univ., 1949; Univ. of Michigan, 1952; Lehigh Univ., 1953; Villanova Univ., 1968; Rensselaer Polytechnic Inst., 1968; Peabody Inst., 1968; Univ. of Illinois, 1969; Doctor of Letters: Clark Univ., 1956, Miami Univ., 1959, Rutgers Univ., 1960, Long Island Univ., 1965; Lafayette Coll., 1966; Jefferson Medical Coll., 1973; Moravian Coll., 1976; holds many other hon. degrees. Toured Hungary as child prodigy; Head of master classes, State Conservatorium of Music, Budapest, at age of 20; arrived in United States, 1921, naturalised 1927; substituted for Toscanini as Conductor Philadelphia Orchestra; Conductor Minneapolis Symphony Orch., 1931-36; toured Australia, 1944, S America, 1946, Europe, 1950, 1951, 1952, 1953, 1954, 1955, 1957, 1958. Appeared Edinburgh Festival, 1955, 1957. Caballero, Order of Merit of Juan Pablo Duarte, Dominican Republic, 1945; Commandeur, French Legion of Honour, 1958; Knight, Order of Dannebrog, 1st cl., 1952; Knight 1st cl., Order of the White Rose, Finland, 1955; Comdr, Order of Lion of Finland, 1966; Honor Cross for Arts and Sciences, Austria, 1967; Golden Medallion, Vienna Philharmonic Orch., 1967; Freedom Medal, USA, 1970; Commendatore, Italy, 1972. *Address:* 1420 Locust Street, Philadephia, Pa 19102, USA.

ORMATHWAITE, 6th Baron, *cr* 1868; **John Arthur Charles Walsh,** Bt 1804; Farming since 1950; *b* 25 December 1912; *s* of 5th Baron Ormathwaite and Lady Margaret Jane Douglas-Home (*d* 1955), 3rd *d* of 12th Earl of Home; *S* father, 1944; unmarried. *Educ:* Eton College; Trinity College, Cambridge. *Heir:* none. *Address:* Pen-y-Bont Hall, Llandrindod Wells, Powys. *T:* Pen-y-Bont 228.

ORME, Ion G.; *see* Garnett-Orme.

ORME, John Samuel, CB 1963; OBE 1945; Research Student, Department of Social Administration, London School of Economics, since 1975; *b* 7 May 1916; *m* 1940, Jean Harris; three *s* one *d*. *Educ:* The High School, Newcastle under Lyme; St John's College, Oxford; Ecole des Sciences Politiques, Paris. BA 1937, 1st Cl. Hons, Sch. of Mod. Hist.; MA 1957. Air Ministry, 1938; served RAF, 1941-45; Wing Comdr, 1944 (despatches, OBE); Air Ministry, 1945; Internat. Staff of NATO, Paris, 1954-57; Assistant Under Secretary of State, Air Ministry, 1957-58, and again 1960-64; Under-Secretary; Cabinet Office, 1958-60; Min. of Transport, 1964-66; Assistant Under-Secretary of State: Welsh Office, 1966-70; DHSS, 1970-75. Cleveland, Ohio Foundation Fellow, 1977. *Address:* Broom House, Seer Green, Bucks HP9 2UH. *T:* Beaconsfield 5920; Dalyhill House, Ballyconneely, Co. Galway. *Clubs:* Reform; Connemara Golf.

ORME, Rt. Hon. Stanley, PC 1974; MP (Lab) Salford West since 1964; Minister for Social Security, since 1976; *b* 5 April 1923; *s* of Sherwood Orme, Sale, Cheshire; *m* 1951, Irene Mary, *d* of Vernon Fletcher Harris, Worsley, Lancashire. *Educ:* elementary and technical schools; National Council of Labour Colleges and Workers' Educational Association classes. Warrant Officer, Air-Bomber Navigator, Royal Air Force Bomber Command, 1942-47. Joined the Labour party, 1944; contested (Lab) Stockport South, 1959. Minister of State: NI Office, 1974-76; DHSS, 1976. Member of Sale Borough Council, 1958-65; Member: AEU; District Committee, Manchester; shop steward; ASE, Altrincham. *Address:* House of Commons, SW1; 47 Hope Road, Sale, Cheshire. *Club:* Ashfield Labour (Salford).

ORMEROD, Major Sir (Cyril) Berkeley, KBE 1960 (CBE 1954, OBE 1946); Director, Public Relations, British Information Services, New York, 1945-62 (Financial Adviser, British Press Service, 1940-45); formerly Chairman, Director and Trustee of public companies and trusts, now retired; *b* London, 3 Oct. 1897; *s* of late Ernest Berkeley Ormerod, Ashton-under-Lyne, Lancs, and late Alice Heys; *m* 1962, Beatrice, *widow* of Frederick Sigrist, Nassau, Bahamas. *Educ:* Colet Court; St Paul's Sch.; Royal Military Academy. Royal Regt of Artillery, 1916-26; European War, active service in France and Belgium, 1917-18. London Stock Exchange (Foster and Braithwaite), 1929-39. Regular contributor to Financial Times, Investor's Chronicle, Barron's (New York), 1934-39. Member UK Delegation, UN organizational Conference, San Francisco, 1945; Public Relations Adviser to Secretary of State (late Ernest Bevin) Foreign Ministers' Conference, New York, 1946. Specially attached to the Ambassador's Staff as Press Adviser to the Royal Party during American visit of the Queen and the Duke of Edinburgh, Oct. 1957; Press Advisor to the Governor of the Bahamas during Nassau talks between Prime Minister Macmillan and late President Kennedy, Dec. 1962. Member of The Pilgrims; RIIA (Chatham House); FIPR. *Publications:* Dow Theory Applied to the London Stock Exchange, 1937. *Recreations:* cricket (Oxfordshire, The Army, RA, MCC, I Zingari, Free Foresters, etc), golf (won Army Championship, 1924), bridge. *Address:* PO Box N 969, Nassau, Bahamas. *Clubs:* Cavalry and Guards, Boodle's, MCC; Royal and Ancient (St Andrews); Berkshire Golf; Knickerbocker, Lotos, Dutch Treat (New York); Travellers' (Paris); Lyford Cay (Nassau).

ORMEROD, Richard Caton; HM Diplomatic Service, retired; *b* 22 Jan. 1915; *s* of late Prof. Henry Arderne Ormerod and Mildred Robina Ormerod (*née* Caton); *m* 1947, Elizabeth Muriel, *yr d* of late Sheriff J. W. More, St Andrews; two *s* two *d*. *Educ:* Winchester Coll.; New Coll., Oxford (BA). India Office, 1938. War Service, 1941-45: Indian Army, 7th Light Cavalry; active service in Imphal and Burma (wounded). Asst Private Secretary to Secretary of State for India and Burma, 1945-46; Principal, Burma Office, 1946; CRO, 1948; First Secretary, British High Commn: Bombay, 1951-53; Wellington, 1956-59; Asst Secretary, 1960; Counsellor, British High Commn, Calcutta, 1962-65; Ministry of Overseas Development, 1965; Consul-Gen., Marseilles, 1967-71. Member: Wiltshire Branch, CPRE; Wiltshire Archaeol. Soc. *Publication:* Ferns in the Waste, 1943. *Recreations:* music, gardening, archaeology. *Address:* Chequers, 44 The Street, Marden, Devizes, Wilts SN10 3RQ; La Gourguette, 84750 Viens, France.

ORMESSON, Comte Jean d'; Chevalier des Palmes académiques 1962; Commandeur des Arts et Lettres 1973; Chevalier de la Légion d'honneur 1973; Membre Académie française 1973; Secretary-General, International Council for Philosophy and Humanistic Studies (UNESCO), since 1971 (Deputy, 1950-71); writer and journalist; *b* 16 June 1925; 2nd *s* of Marquis d'Ormesson, French diplomat and Ambassador; *m* 1962, Françoise Béghin; one *d*. *Educ:* Ecole Normale Supérieure. MA (History), Agrégé de philosophie. Mem. French delegns to various internat. confs, 1945-48; Mem. staff of various Govt Ministers, 1958-66; Mem. Council ORTF, 1960-62; Mem. Control Cttee of Cinema, 1962-69; Mem. TV Programmes Cttee, ORTF, 1973-74. Journalist, 1946-50; Dep. Editor, Diogenes, 1952-72, Mem. Managing Cttee, 1972; Dir, 1974-77, Editor-in-Chief, 1975-77, Le Figaro. *Publications:* L'Amour est un plaisir, 1956; Du côté de chez Jean, 1959; Un amour pour rien, 1960; Au revoir et merci, 1966; Les Illusions de la mer, 1968; La Gloire de l'Empire, 1971 (Grand Prix du Roman de l'Académie française), Amer. edn 1975; Au Plaisir de Dieu, 1974; articles and essays, columns in Le Figaro, Le Monde, Le Point, La Revue des Deux Mondes, La Nouvelle Revue Française. *Recreation:* ski-navigation. *Address:* CIPSH-UNESCO, 1 rue Miollis, 75732 Paris Cedex 15, France; 37 rue du Louvre, 75002 Paris. *T:* 2334400; (home) 10 avenue du Parc Saint-James, 92200 Neuilly-sur-Seine, France.

ORMOND, Sir John (Davies Wilder), Kt 1964; BEM 1940; JP; Chairman: Shipping Corporation of New Zealand Ltd, since 1973; New Zealand Meat Producers Board, 1951-72; Chairman, Exports and Shipping Council, since 1964; *b* 8 Sept. 1905; *s* of J. D. Ormond and Gladys Wilder; *m* 1939, Judith Wall; four *s* one *d*. *Educ:* Christ's Coll., Christchurch, New Zealand. Chairman, Waipukurau Farmers Union, 1949; President, Waipukurau Jockey Club, 1950; Member, New Zealand Meat Producers Board, 1934-72. Active Service Overseas (Middle East), 1940. JP, NZ, 1945. *Recreations:* tennis, polo, Rugby Union football. *Address:* Wallingford, Waipukurau, New Zealand. *T:* Waipukurau 542M. *Club:* Hawke's Bay (New Zealand).

ORMONDE, 7th Marquess of, *cr* 1825; **James Hubert Theobald Charles Butler,** MBE 1921; Earl of Ormonde, 1328; Viscount Thurles, 1525; Earl of Ossory, 1527; Baron Ormonde (UK), 1821; 31st Hereditary Chief Butler of Ireland; retired; *b* 19 April 1899; *s* of Lord Theobald Butler (4th *s* of 2nd Marquess) and Annabella Brydon (*d* 1943), *o d* of Rev. Cosmo Reid Gordon, DD; *S* cousin, 1971; *m* 1st, 1935, Nan Gilpin (*d* 1973); two *d*; 2nd, 1976, Elizabeth Liles. *Educ:* Haileybury College; RMC Sandhurst. Commissioned Dec. 1917, King's Royal Rifle Corps; resigned commission, May 1926 (Lieut). Various business connections in USA. *Address:* 17W 718 Butterfield Road, Apt 118, Oakbrook Terrace, Ill 60181, USA. *Club:* Naval and Military.

ORMROD, Rt. Hon. Sir Roger (Fray Greenwood), PC 1974; Kt 1961; **Rt. Hon. Lord Justice Ormrod;** a Lord Justice of Appeal, since 1974; *b* 20 Oct. 1911; *s* of Oliver Fray Ormrod and Edith Muriel (*née* Pim); *m* 1938, Anne, *d* of Charles Lush; no *c. Educ:* Shrewsbury Sch.; The Queen's Coll., Oxford. BA Oxon (Jurisprudence) 1935. Called to Bar, Inner Temple, 1936; QC 1958; Judge of High Court of Justice, Family Division (formerly Probate, Divorce and Admiralty Division), 1961-74. Hon. Fellow, Queen's Coll., Oxford, 1966. BM, BCh Oxon, 1941; FRCP 1969. House Physician, Radcliffe Infirmary, Oxford, 1941-42. Served in RAMC, 1942-45, with rank of Major. DADMS 8 Corps. Lecturer in Forensic Medicine, Oxford Medical Sch., 1950-59. Hon. Prof. of Legal Ethics, Univ. of Birmingham, 1973-74. Governor, Bethlem Royal Hosp. and Maudsley Hosp. Chairman: The London Marriage Guidance Council; Lord Chancellor's Cttee on Legal Education, 1968; Notting Hill Housing Trust, 1968-. Pres., British Acad. of Forensic Science, 1970-71; Chm., Cttee of Management, Institute of Psychiatry. Visitor, Royal Postgrad. Med. Sch., 1975-. Hon. Fellow, Manchester Polytechnic, 1972; Hon. FRCPsych 1975. *Publications:* ed, (with E. H. Pearce) Dunstan's Law of Hire-Purchase, 1938; (with Harris Walker) National Health Service Act 1946, 1949. *Address:* 4 Aubrey Road, W8. *T:* 01-727 7876. *Club:* Garrick.

ORMSBY GORE, family name of **Baron Harlech.**

OROWAN, Egon, DrIng; FRS 1947; Professor of Mechanical Engineering, Massachusetts Institute of Technology, Cambridge, Massachusetts, USA, 1950-67, now Emeritus; Senior Lecturer, MIT, 1967-73; *b* Budapest, 2 Aug. 1902; *s* of Berthold Orowan and Josephine Ságvári; *m* 1941, Yolande Schonfeld; one *d. Educ:* University of Vienna; Technical Univ., Berlin-Charlottenburg. Demonstrator Technical Univ., Berlin-Charlottenburg, 1928; i/c Krypton Works, United Incandescent Lamp and Electrical Co. Ltd, Ujpest, Hungary, 1936; Research in Physics of Metals, Physics Dept, University of Birmingham, 1937, and Cavendish Laboratory, Cambridge, 1939; Reader in the Physics of Metals, University of Cambridge. Alcoa Vis. Prof., Univ. of Pittsburgh, 1972-73. Mem., Nat. Acad. of Sciences; Corresp. Mem., Akademie der Wissenschaften, Göttingen. Thomas Hawksley Gold Medal, MechE, 1944; Bingham Medal, Society of Rheology, 1959; Carl Friedrich Gauss Medal, Braunschweigische Wissenschaftliche Gesellschaft, 1968; Vincent Bendix Gold Medal, Amer. Soc. of Engrg Educn, 1971; Paul Bergsøe Medal, Dansk Metallurgisk Selskab, 1973. DrIng (*hc*) Technische Universität, Berlin, 1965. *Publications:* Papers in scientific and engineering journals. *Address:* Department of Mechanical Engineering, Massachusetts Institute of Technology, Cambridge, Mass 02139, USA.

ORR, Rt. Hon. Sir Alan (Stewart), PC 1971; Kt 1965; OBE 1944; **Rt. Hon. Lord Justice Orr;** A Lord Justice of Appeal, since 1971; *b* 21 Feb. 1911; *s* of late William Orr and Doris Kemsley, Great Wakering, Essex; *m* 1933, Mariana Frances Lilian, *d* of late Captain J. C. Lang, KOSB; four *s. Educ:* Fettes; Edinburgh Univ. (1st Class Hons Classics); Balliol Coll., Oxford (1st Class Hons Jurisprudence). Barrister Middle Temple, 1936 (Cert. Hon.); Master of the Bench, 1965; Barstow Law Scholar; Harmsworth Scholar. RAF, 1940-45 (despatches, OBE), Wing Comdr. Lectr in Laws (pt-time), UCL, 1948-50. Member of General Council of the Bar, 1953-57; Junior Counsel (Common Law) to Commissioners of Inland Revenue, 1957-63; QC 1963; Recorder of: New Windsor, 1958-65; Oxford, Jan.-Aug. 1965; Dep. Chairman, Oxford Quarter Sessions, 1964-71; Judge of High Court of Justice, Probate, Divorce and Admiralty Division, 1965-71; Presiding Judge, North-Eastern Circuit, 1970-71. Mem., Chancellor's Law Reform Cttee, 1966- (Chm., 1973). Chm., Court of Governors, Mill Hill Sch., 1976. *Recreation:* golf. *Address:* Highfield, Harmer Green, Welwyn, Herts. *T:* Welwyn 4250; Royal Courts of Justice, Strand, WC2. *Club:* United Oxford & Cambridge University.

ORR, Sir David (Alexander), Kt 1977; MC and bar 1945; LLB; Chairman, Unilever Ltd, and Vice-Chairman, Unilever NV, since 1974; *b* 10 May 1922; *s* of late Canon Adrian William Fielder Orr and Grace (*née* Robinson); *m* 1949, Phoebe Rosaleen Davis; three *d. Educ:* High Sch., Dublin; Trinity Coll., Dublin. Served Royal Engineers attached QVO Madras Sappers and Miners, 1941-46. With various Unilever companies from 1948: Hindustan Lever, 1955-60; Mem. Overseas Cttee, Unilever, 1960-63; Lever Bros Co., New York, 1963, Pres. 1965-67; Dir, 1967-, Vice-Chm. 1970-74, Unilever Ltd. Co-Chm., Netherlands British Chamber of Commerce. Trustee: Leverhulme Trust; Civic Trust. A Vice-Pres., Liverpool Sch. of Tropical Medicine. FRSA. *Recreations:* golf, Rugby, travel. *Address:* Unilever House, Blackfriars, EC4P 4BQ; 8 Lyall Mews

West, SW1; Oakhill, Enton Green, Godalming, Surrey. *T:* Godalming 7032. *Club:* Blind Brook (New York).

ORR, James Bernard Vivian, CVO 1968 (MVO 1962); Secretary, Medical Commission on Accident Prevention, since 1970; *b* 19 Nov. 1917; *s* of Dr Vivian Bernard Orr and Gladys Constance Orr (*née* Power); unmarried. *Educ:* Harrow; Gordonstoun; RMC, Sandhurst. British South Africa Police, Southern Rhodesia, 1939-46. Attached occupied Enemy Territory Administration in Ethiopia and Eritrea Police Forces, 1941-49; Kenya Police, 1954-57. Private Secretary to HRH The Duke of Edinburgh, 1957-70, an Extra Equerry, 1970-. *Recreations:* horse racing, watching cricket. *Address:* 5 Lancelot Place, SW7.

ORR, Dr James Henry; Director of Prison Medical Services, and Member of Prisons Board, since 1976; *b* 2 Feb. 1927; *s* of Hubert Orr and Ethel Maggs; *m* 1950, Valerie Elizabeth Yates; two *s* one *d. Educ:* Bristol Grammar Sch.; Bristol Univ. (MB, ChB 1955). DPM; MRCPsych. Enlisted, 1944; commnd RE, 1947; demobilised, 1949. Hosp. appts, 1955-56; gen. practice, 1956-58; Medical Officer, HM Prison: Leeds, 1958; Winchester, 1962; Lincoln, 1966; SMO, Leeds, 1967; Asst Dir, Prison Med. Services, 1973. *Recreation:* gardening. *Address:* c/o Home Office, 89 Eccleston Square, SW1V 1PU. *T:* 01-828 9848.

ORR, Jean Fergus Henderson; Director, Office of Manpower Economics, since 1973; *b* 3 April 1920; *yr d* of late Peter Orr, OBE and Janet Muir Orr (*née* Henderson). *Educ:* privately; University Coll., London (BA). Min. of Aircraft Prodn, temp. Asst Principal, 1942; Min. of Supply: Asst Principal, 1946; Principal, 1949; HM Treasury, 1954: Principal, Official Side Sec. to Civil Service Nat. Whitley Council negotiations on Report of Royal Commn on Civil Service, 1953-55; Asst Sec. 1961; on loan to Office of Manpower Econs as Sec. to Top Salaries Review Body, 1971. *Recreations:* music, travel, natural history. *Address:* 27 Primrose Hill Road, NW3 3DG. *T:* 01-722 2933. *Club:* United Oxford & Cambridge University.

ORR, John Henry; OBE 1972; QPM 1977; Chief Constable, Lothian and Borders Police, since 1975; *b* 13 June 1918; *m* 1942, Isobel Margaret Campbell; one *s* one *d. Educ:* George Heriot's Sch., Edinburgh. Edinburgh City Police, 1937; served in RAF 1943-45 (Flying Officer; Defence and War Medals); Chief Constable: of Dundee, 1960; of Lothians and Peebles, 1968. Hon. Sec., Assoc. of Chief Police Officers (Scotland), 1974. Coronation Medal, 1953; Police Long Service and Good Conduct Medal, 1959; Jubilee Medal, 1977; OStJ, 1975. Comdr, Polar Star, class III, Sweden, 1975; Legion of Honour, France, 1976. *Recreations:* Rugby (capped for Scotland; Past Pres., Scottish Rugby Union); golf. *Address:* 12 Lanark Road West, Currie, Midlothian EH14 5ET.

ORR, Prof. John Washington; Professor of Pathology and Director of Cancer Research, University of Birmingham, and Hon. Pathologist, United Birmingham Hospitals, 1948-66; Professor Emeritus, 1967; *b* 5 Aug. 1900; *er s* of Frederick William and Elizabeth Orr, Belfast; *m* 1932, Nora Margaret (*d* 1965), 2nd *d* of David James and Margaret Carmichael; one *s* one *d. Educ:* Royal Academical Institution, Belfast; Queen's University of Belfast. MB, BCh, BAO, Belfast, 1923; BSc (1st class Hons) Belfast, 1924, DPH 1924; MD (Gold Medal) Belfast, 1926; MRCP London, 1940; MD Birmingham, 1948; FRCP London, 1950. Hon. MD Perugia, 1961. Riddell Demonstrator of Pathology, Belfast, 1924; Musgrave student in Pathology, Belfast, 1925; First Assistant Pathologist and Asst Curator of the Museum, St Mary's Hospital, W2, 1926; Lecturer in Exp. Pathology and Asst Director of Cancer Research, University of Leeds, 1932; Reader in Exp. Pathology, 1937; President of Leeds Pathological Club, 1946-47. Senior Research Pathologist, Detroit Institute of Cancer Research, 1966-67; Research Pathologist, Royal Victoria Hosp., Bournemouth, 1967-69. Served War of 1939-45 as Pathologist in EMS and Battalion MO, Home Guard. *Publications:* articles on medical subjects in Journal of Pathology and Bacteriology, British Journal of Exp. Pathology, British Journal of Cancer, Lancet, American Journal of Cancer, etc, especially papers on experimental cancer research. *Address:* c/o Lloyds Bank, 359 Bristol Road, Birmingham B5 7SS.

ORR, Captain Lawrence Percy Story; Director, Associated Leisure Ltd, since 1972; *b* 16 Sept. 1918; *s* of late Very Rev. W. R. M. Orr, MA, LLD, sometime Dean of Dromore; *m* 1939, Jean Mary, *d* of late Frederick Cairns Hughes, Donaghadee; four *s* one *d. Educ:* Campbell Coll., Belfast; Trinity Coll., Dublin. Served with East Lancashire Regt, Royal Armoured Corps, and Life Guards, 1939-46. Organiser Iveagh Unionist Association, 1947-49; Secretary County Down Unionist Association, 1949; MP (UU) South Down, 1950-Sept. 1974;

Vice-Chairman, Conservative Broadcasting Cttee, 1959-62; was Chm., Ulster Unionist Parly Party, and Vice-Pres., Ulster Unionist Council. Co-founder, Middle Class Assoc. (later Voice of the Independent Centre), 1974. *Recreations:* fishing and painting.

ORR, Prof. Robin, (Robert Kemsley Orr), CBE 1972; MA, MusD (Cantab); FRCM; Hon. RAM; Hon. DMus, Hon. LLD; Composer; Professor of Music, Cambridge University, and Fellow of St John's College, 1965-76; *b* Brechin, Scotland, 2 June 1909; *s* of Robert Workman Orr and Florence Mary Kemsley; *m* 1937, Margaret, *er d* of A. C. Mace; one *s* two *d. Educ:* Loretto Sch.; Royal Coll. of Music; Pembroke Coll., Cambridge (Organ Scholar); Accademia Musicale Chigiana, Siena. Studied privately with Casella and Nadia Boulanger. Dir of Music, Sidcot Sch., Somerset, 1933-36; Asst Lecturer in Music, Univ. of Leeds, 1936-38. Served War of 1939-45, RAFVR, Photographic Intelligence (Flight Lieut). Organist and Dir of Studies in Music, St John's Coll., 1938-51, and Fellow, 1948-56, Univ. Lecturer in Music, 1947-56, Cambridge; Prof. of Theory and Composition, RCM, 1950-56; Gardiner Prof. of Music, Univ. of Glasgow, 1956-65. Vice-Chm. Carl Rosa Trust, 1958; Chm., Scottish Opera, 1962-76; Dir, Arts Theatre, Cambridge, 1970-75. Compositions include: Sonatina for violin and piano, 1941; Three Chinese Songs, 1943; Sonata for viola and piano, 1947; Winter's Tale (Incidental Music), BBC, 1947; Overture, The Prospect of Whitby, 1948; Oedipus at Colonus (Cambridge Univ. Greek Play), 1950; Four Romantic Songs (for Peter Pears), 1950; Festival Te Deum, 1950; Three Pastorals for soprano, flute, viola and piano, 1951; Deirdre of the Sorrows (Incidental Music), BBC, 1951; Italian Overture, 1952; Te Deum and Jubilate in C, 1953; Motet, I was glad, 1955; Spring Cantata, 1955; Sonata for violin and clavier, 1956; Rhapsody for string orchestra; Antigone (Bradfield College Greek Play), 1961; Symphony in one movement, 1963; Full Circle (Opera), 1967; From the Book of Philip Sparrow, 1969; Journeys and Places (mezzo-sop. and strings), 1971; Symphony No 2, 1971; Hermiston (Opera), 1975; ed, The Kelvin Series of Scots Songs. Hon DMus Glasgow, 1972; Hon. LLD Dundee, 1976. *Address:* West House, Wick, Mid Glamorgan. *T:* Wick 215.

ORR-EWING, family name of **Baron Orr-Ewing.**

ORR-EWING, Baron *cr* 1971 (Life Peer), of Little Berkhamsted; **(Charles) Ian Orr-Ewing**, OBE 1945; 1st Bt *cr* 1963; Consultant and Director various companies; Chairman, Metrication Board, 1972-77 (Deputy Chairman, 1971-72); *b* 10 Feb. 1912; *s* of Archibald Ian Orr Ewing and Gertrude (*née* Runge); *m* 1939, Joan McMinnies; four *s. Educ:* Harrow; Trinity Coll., Oxford. MA (Physics). Apprenticeship to radio firm, 1934, 1937 (EMI Hayes); BBC Television Service, 1938-39, 1946-49. Served RAFVR, 1939-46, N Africa, Italy, France and Germany, Wing Comdr, 1941; Chief Radar Officer, Air Staff, SHAEF, 1945 (despatches twice); BBC Television Outside Broadcasts Manager, 1946-48. Adopted prospective Conservative Candidate N Hendon, 1946; MP (C) North Hendon, 1950-70; Joint Secretary, Parliamentary Scientific Cttee, 1950; Vice-Chm., Civil Air Cttee, 1955-57; Vice-Pres., Parliamentary and Scientific Cttee, 1965-68; Vice-Chm., 1922 Cttee, 1966-70 (Secretary, 1957); Vice-Chairman, Defence Cttee, 1966-70. Parliamentary Private Secretary to Sir Walter Monckton, Minister of Labour and National Service, Nov. 1951-May 1955. Parliamentary Under-Secretary of State, for Air, Air Ministry, 1957-59; Parliamentary and Financial Secretary to Admiralty, 1959; Civil Lord of the Admiralty, 1959-63. Mem., Royal Commn on Standards of Conduct in Public Life, 1975-76. Pres. and Chm. of Council, Electronic Engineering Assoc., 1969-70. Pres., Nat. Ski Fedn of GB, 1972-76. FIEE. *Recreations:* tennis, light-hearted cricket and ski-ing. *Heir* (to baronetcy only): *s* (Alistair) Simon Orr-Ewing [*b* 10 June 1940; *m* 1968, Victoria, *er d* of Keith Cameron, Fifield House, Milton-under-Wychwood, Oxon; two *s* one *d*]. *Address:* The Old Manor, Little Berkhamsted, near Hertford, Herts. *Clubs:* Carlton, MCC; Vincents' (Oxford).

ORR EWING, Major Sir Ronald Archibald, 5th Bt, *cr* 1886; Major (retired) Scots Guards; *b* 14 May 1912; *e s* of Sir Norman Orr Ewing, 4th Bt, CB, DSO, and Lady Orr Ewing (*née* Robarts), Tile House, Buckingham; *S* father, 1960; *m* 1938, Marion Hester, *yr d* of late Colonel Sir Donald Walter Cameron of Lochiel, KT, CMG, and of Lady Hermione Cameron of Lochiel, *d* of 5th Duke of Montrose, KT; two *s* two *d. Educ:* Eton; RMC, Sandhurst. Scots Guards, 1932-53, Major. Served War of 1939-45, Middle East (POW 1942). JP Perthshire, 1956; DL Perthshire, 1963. Grand Master Mason of Scotland, 1965-69. *Recreation:* shooting. *Heir: s* Archibald Donald Orr Ewing [*b* 20 Dec. 1938; *m* 1st, 1965, Venetia Elizabeth (marr. diss. 1972), *y d* of Major and Mrs Richard Turner, Co. Dublin; 2nd,

1972, Nicola Jean-Anne, *d* of Reginald Baron Black, Co. Cork]. *Address:* Cardross, Port of Menteith, Stirling. *T:* Port of Menteith 220. *Clubs:* Army and Navy; New (Edinburgh).

ORR-LEWIS, Sir (John) Duncan, 2nd Bt, *cr* 1920; Major RASC; *s* of 1st Bt and Maud Helen, *o d* of William Booth, London, Ontario, Canada; *b* 21 Feb. 1898; *S* father, 1921; *m* 1st, 1921; one *d*; 2nd, 1929; 3rd, 1940; 4th, 1950; 5th, 1965. *Educ:* Eton; Cambridge. Military Service: 10th Army, Persia MEF, 1942-43; 2nd Army, France, Germany, Aug. 1944-45. *Heir:* none. *Address:* 8 rue Du Bois, 77 Cély-en-Bière, France; Ir-Razzett, Malta. *Clubs:* White's; Travellers' (Paris).

ORSON, Rasin Ward, FSS; Member, The Electricity Council, since 1976; Director, Chloride Silent Power Ltd, since 1974; *b* 16 April 1927; *s* of Rasin Nelson Orson and Blanche Hyre; *m* 1950, Marie Goodenough; two *s. Educ:* Stratford Grammar Sch.; London School of Economics (BScEcon 1948). Asst Statistician, Min. of Civil Aviation, 1948, Statistician, 1953; Electricity Council: Head of Economics and Forecasting Branch, 1963; Dep. Commercial Adviser, 1968; Commercial Adviser, 1972. *Recreations:* music, pottering. *Address:* 12 Shelley Grove, Loughton, Essex IG10 1BY. *T:* 01-508 5994.

ORTOLI, François-Xavier; Vice-President, Commission of the European Communities, since 1977 (President, 1972-76); *b* 16 Feb. 1925. *Educ:* Hanoi Faculty of Law; Ecole Nationale d'Administration. Inspector of Finances, 1948-51; Tech. Adv., Office of Minister of Econ. Affairs and Information, 1951-53; Asst Dir to Sec. of State for Econ. Affairs and Sec.-Gen., Franco-Italian Cttee of EEC, 1955; Head, Commercial Politics Service of Sec. of State for Econ. Affairs, 1957; Dir-Gen. Internal Market Div., EEC, 1958; Sec.-Gen., Inter-Ministerial Cttee for Questions of European Econ. Co-operation, Paris, 1961-; Dir of Cabinet to Prime Minister, 1962-66; Comr-Gen. of the Plan, 1966-67; Minister: of Works, 1967-68; of Educn, 1968; of Finance, 1968-69; of Industrial and Scientific Develt, 1969-72. Hon. DCL Oxon, 1975; Hon Dr Sch. of Political Scis, Athens, 1975. Officier de la Légion d'Honneur; Médaille Militaire; Croix de Guerre, 1945; Médaille de la Résistance. *Address:* 18 rue de Bourgogne, 75007 Paris, France.

OSBORN, Sir Danvers (Lionel Rouse), 8th Bt, *cr* 1662; *b* 31 Jan. 1916; *s* of Sir Algernon K. B. Osborn, 7th Bt, JP and Beatrice Elliot Kennard, *d* of William Bunce Greenfield, JP, DL; *S* father, 1948; *m* 1943, Constance Violette, JP, SSStJ, *d* of late Major Leonard Frank Rooke, KOSB; one *s* one *d* (one *s* and one *d* decd). *Educ:* Eton; Magdalene Coll., Cambridge. Employed as Civil Assistant in Intelligence Dept of War Office, 1940-45. Joined Spicers Ltd, 1955. Director of two Picture Galleries. *Recreations:* golf, tennis, bridge. *Heir: s* Richard Henry Danvers Osborn, *b* 12 Aug. 1958. *Address:* The Dower House, Moor Park, Farnham, Surrey. *T:* Runfold 2658. *Club:* MCC.

OSBORN, Sir Frederic (James), Kt 1956; Hon. FRTPI; Hon. FRIBA; Hon. Member: American Institute of Planners; Community Planning Association of Canada; Mark Twain Society, USA; President, Town and Country Planning Association; Hon. Vice-President, Royal Town Planning Institute; Vice-President and Hon. Member, International Federation for Housing and Planning; Corresponding Member, Akademie für Raumforschung und Landesplanung, Hannover; *b* 26 May 1885; *e s* of T. F. Osborn; *m* 1st, 1916, Margaret Paterson Robb, Glasgow (*d* 1970); one *s* one *d*; 2nd, 1974, Shirley Catherine Stephens. *Educ:* London private and Council Schools. Estate Manager, Welwyn Garden City, 1919-36; Hon. Sec. and Chm., Town and Country Planning Assoc., 1936-61; Director, Murphy Radio Ltd, 1936-60; Member New Towns Cttee, 1946. Hon. Editor, Town and Country Planning, 1949-65; Chairman, Welwyn Drama Festival, 1929-65. Silver Medal, American Society of Planning Officials, 1960; Gold Medal, Town Planning Institute, 1963; Ebenezer Howard Memorial Medal, 1968. *Publications:* New Towns after the War, 1918, 1942; Green-Belt Cities, 1946, 1969; Can Man Plan? and Other Verses, 1959; New Towns: The Answer to Megalopolis (with A. Whittick), 1963, 1974, 1977; Transatlantic Dialogue (with Lewis Mumford), 1971, etc. *Recreations:* literature, drama, music, gardening, travel. *Address:* 16 Guessens Road, Welwyn Garden City, Herts AL8 6QR. *T:* Welwyn Garden 22317.

OSBORN, John Holbrook; MP (C) (NL and U, 1959-64), Hallam Division of Sheffield, since 1959; Steel Company Director; *b* 14 Dec. 1922; *s* of Samuel Eric Osborn and Aileen Decima, *d* of Colonel Sir Arthur Holbrook, KBE, MP; *m* 1st, 1952, Molly Suzanne (*née* Marten) (marr. diss.); two *d*; 2nd, 1976, Joan Mary MacDermot (*née* Wilkinson). *Educ:* Rugby; Trinity Hall, Cambridge. MA Cantab; Part 2 Tripos in Metallurgy; Diploma in Foundry Technology, National

Foundry Coll., 1949. Served in Royal Corps of Signals, West Africa, 1943-47 (Captain); served in RA (TA) Sheffield, 1948-55, Major. Director of Samuel Osborn & Co. Ltd, and associated companies, 1951-. Chairman, Hillsborough Divisional Young Conservatives and Liberal Association, 1948-53. PPS to the Secretary of State for Commonwealth Relations and for the Colonies, 1963-64. Mem., UK Delegn to Council of Europe and WEU, 1972-75; Mem., European Parlt, 1975-; an Hon. Sec., 1922 Cttee, 1968-. Asst Searcher, Co. of Cutlers in Hallamshire, 1950-. Fellow, Institute of British Foundrymen (Member Council, Sheffield Branch, 1954-64); Fellow, Institute of Directors; Member Council: Sheffield Chamber of Commerce, 1956-; Assocs British Chambers of Commerce Council, 1960-62 (Hon. Secretary, 1962-64); Industrial Society; British Iron and Steel Res. Association, 1965-68; CBI and Yorks and WR Br., CBI, 1968-; Member: Metals Soc.; Court and Cttee of Sheffield Univ.; Council, East and West Riding Br., CBI, 1969-. *Recreations:* golf, tennis, squash, sailing, photography, gardening. *Address:* Folds Head Close, Calver, Sheffield S30 1XJ. *T:* Hope Valley 30253; Flat 13, 102 Rochester Row, SW1. *T:* 01-799 5932. *Clubs:* Carlton; Sheffield.

OSBORN, Margaret, MA; High Mistress of St Paul's Girls' School, Hammersmith, 1948-63, retired; *b* 23 April 1906; *d* of Rev. G. S. Osborn, late Rector of Milton, Cambridge. *Educ:* St Leonard's Sch., St Andrews, Fife; St Hugh's Coll., Oxford. Graduated 1929; MA Hons Lit Hum Oxon. Pelham Student at British School at Rome, 1931; Headmistress of St George's School for Girls, Edinburgh, 1943-48. *Publication:* A Latin Epithet, article in Mnemosyne (Leyden Journal), 1932. *Recreations:* music and reading. *Address:* 15 Wold's End, Chipping Camden, Glos GL55 6AB.

OSBORNE, Sir Basil, Kt 1967; CBE 1962; Lord Mayor of Hobart, Tasmania, 1959-70, Alderman, 1952-76; Chairman, Metropolitan Transport Trust, since 1971; business administrator; *b* 19 April 1907; *s* of late Alderman W. W. Osborne, MBE; *m* 1934, Esma, *d* of late T. Green; one *s*. *Educ:* Metropolitan Business Coll. Chairman: Board of Management, Royal Hobart Hospital, 1968- (Vice-Chairman, 1952-68); Ambulance Commn, Tasmania, 1960. Royal Life Saving Society: Pres., Tasmanian Branch; Austr. Dep. Pres.; Life Governor, Commonwealth Council; Pres., Hobart Orpheus Club. Hon. Fellow, Inst. Sales and Marketing. OStJ 1972. *Recreations:* music, sport. *Address:* 6 Myella Drive, Chigwell, Tasmania 7011, Australia. *Club:* Royal Autocar (Tasmania).

OSBORNE, Charles (Thomas); author; Literature Director, Arts Council of Great Britain, since 1971; *b* 24 Nov. 1927; *s* of Vincent Lloyd Osborne and Elsa Louise Osborne; *m* 1970, Marie Korbelářová (marr. diss. 1975). *Educ:* Brisbane State High Sch. Studied piano and voice, Brisbane and Melbourne; acted in and directed plays, 1944-53; wrote poetry and criticism, published in Aust. and NZ magazines; co-owner, Ballad Bookshop, Brisbane, 1947-51; actor, London, provincial rep. and on tour, also TV and films, 1953-57; Asst Editor, London Magazine, 1958-66; Asst Lit. Dir, Arts Council of GB, 1966-71. Broadcaster, musical and literary progs, BBC, 1957-; Dir, Poetry International, 1967-; Sec., Poetry Book Soc., 1971-. Mem. Editorial Board: Opera, 1970-; Annual Register, 1971-. *Publications:* (ed) Australian Stories of Today, 1961; (ed) Opera 66, 1966; (with Brigid Brophy and Michael Levey) Fifty Works of English Literature We Could Do Without, 1967 (USA 1968); Kafka, 1967; Swansong (poems), 1968; The Complete Operas of Verdi, 1969 (USA 1970; Italian trans. 1975); Ned Kelly, 1970; (ed) Australia, New Zealand and the South Pacific, 1970; (ed) Letters of Giuseppe Verdi, 1971 (USA 1972); (ed) The Bram Stoker Bedside Companion, 1973 (USA 1974); (ed) Stories and Essays by Richard Wagner, 1973 (USA 1974); The Concert Song Companion, 1974; Masterpieces of Nolan, 1976; Masterpieces of Drysdale, 1976; Masterpieces of Dobell, 1976; Wagner and his World, 1977 (USA 1977); Verdi, 1977; The Opera House Album, 1977; (ed) Dictionary of Composers, 1977; The Complete Operas of Mozart, 1978; poems in: The Oxford Book of Australian Verse, 1956; Australian Poetry, 1951-52, etc; The Queensland Centenary Anthology, 1959; Australian Writing Today, 1968; various jls; contrib.: TLS, Observer, Sunday Times, Times, Guardian, Spectator, London Mag., Encounter, Opera, Chambers Encyc. Yearbook, and Enciclopedia dello spettacolo; also cassettes. *Recreations:* travel, reading, theatre and opera-going, watching old movies on TV, visiting Austrian baroque churches, writing. *Address:* c/o Richard Scott Simon Ltd, 32 College Cross, N1 1PR.

OSBORNE, Maj.-Gen. the Rev. Coles Alexander, CIE 1945; Indian Army, retired; *b* 29 July 1896; *s* of late W. E. Osborne, formerly of Dover, Kent; *m* 1930, Joyce, *o d* of late R. H. Meares of Forbes and Sydney, NSW, Australia; two *d*. *Educ:* Dover

County Sch. European War, 1914-18 served with HAC, Royal West Kent Regt, and RFC (wounded); transferred to 15th Sikhs, 1918; served in Afghan War 1919 and in NW Frontier Operations 1920-22 and 1939; Palestine 1938; Middle East 1940. Tactics Instructor at Royal Military Coll., Duntroon, Australia, 1928-30; Bt Major 1933; General Staff (Operations), War Office, 1934-38; Bt Lieut-Col 1936; Comd 1 Bombay Grenadiers, 1940; Deputy Director Military Training, India, 1940; Colonel, 1940; Commandant, Staff Coll., Quetta, 1941-42; Brigadier, 1941; Director Military Operations, GHQ, India and Burma, 1942-43; Temp. Maj.-Gen. 1942; Comd Kohat District, 1943-45; retired 1946. Student at Moore Theological Coll., Sydney, 1947; ordained, 1947; Hon. Asst Minister St Andrew's Cathedral, Sydney, Australia, 1947-53; Hon. Asst Minister, St Mark's Church, Darling Point, 1953-66; Personal Chaplain to Anglican Archbishop of Sydney, 1959-66. Director, Television Corp., 1956-75. Fellow of St Paul's Coll., Sydney Univ., 1953-69. Chairman, Freedom from Hunger Campaign, NSW, 1970-72. *Address:* 126 Hopetown Avenue, Vaucluse, NSW 2030, Australia. *T:* 337-2969. *Club:* Australian (Sydney).

OSBORNE, Prof. John; (First) Professor of Dental Prosthetics, University of Birmingham, 1948-73; *b* 6 April 1911; *s* of John W. and Gertrude Osborne; *m* 1937, Virginia Preston, *d* of W. H. Fruish; one *s* one *d*. *Educ:* Bishop Vesey Grammar Sch.; Birmingham Univ. LDS Birmingham, 1933; PhD Sheffield, 1945; MDS 1948; FDS, RCS, 1948; FFD, RCSI, 1964; House Surgeon and junior staff appointments at Birmingham Dental Hospital, 1933-37; also private practice during same period; Lecturer in Dental Prosthetics, University of Sheffield, 1937; Lecturer in Dental Prosthetics, University of Birmingham, 1946; Dir of Dental Studies, Univ. of Birmingham, 1965-69 (Dep. Dir, 1953-65). Visiting Professor: NW University, Chicago, 1956-57; Univ. of Adelaide, 1971; Univ. of Malaya, 1973-74. Guest lecturer, Australian Dental Assoc., 1962. External Examiner to Universities of Malaya, Liverpool, Durham, London, Manchester, Glasgow, Dundee, Bristol, Edinburgh, Sheffield, Belfast, Lagos, Singapore, and to Royal College of Surgeons of England and of Ireland. President: British Dental Students Assoc., 1956-58; Central Counties Branch, British Dental Assoc., 1958-59; Hospitals Group, 1968-69. *Publications:* Dental Mechanics for Students, 1939, 6th edn 1970; Acrylic Resins in Dentistry, 1942, 3rd edn 1948; Partial Dentures (with Dr G. A. Lammie), 1954, 4th edn, 1974; scientific papers in leading dental journals. *Recreations:* philately, gardening, sailing. *Address:* Vesey Cottage, Warlands Lane, Shalfleet, Isle of Wight. *T:* Calbourne 384. *Clubs:* Island Sailing (Cowes); Royal Solent Yacht; Osborne Golf (E Cowes).

OSBORNE, John (James); dramatist and actor; Director of Woodfall Films; *b* 12 Dec. 1929; *s* of Thomas Godfrey Osborne and Nellie Beatrice Grove; *m* 1st, 1951, Pamela Elizabeth Lane (marr. diss. 1957); 2nd, 1957, Mary Ure (marr. diss. 1963, she *d* 1975); 3rd, 1963, Penelope Gilliatt (marr. diss. 1968); 4th, 1968, Jill Bennett, *qv* (marr. diss. 1977). *Educ:* Belmont Coll., Devon. First stage appearance at Lyceum, Sheffield, in No Room at the Inn, 1948; toured and in seasons at: Ilfracombe, Bridgwater, Camberwell, Kidderminster, Derby, etc; English Stage Company season at Royal Court: appeared in Death of Satan, Cards of Identity, Good Woman of Setzuan, The Making of Moo, A Cuckoo in the Nest; Directed Meals on Wheels, 1965; appeared in: The Parachute (BBC TV), 1967; First Night of Pygmalion (TV), 1969; First Love (film, as Maidanov), 1970; Get Carter (film), 1971; Lady Charlotte (TV), 1977. First play produced, 1949, at Theatre Royal, Huddersfield; other plays include: Personal Enemy, Opera House, Harrogate, 1955; The Blood of the Bambergs, 1962; Under Plain Cover, 1962; The Right Prospectus (TV), 1969. *Plays filmed:* Look Back in Anger, 1958; The Entertainer, 1959, 1975; Inadmissible Evidence, 1965; Luther, 1971. *Publications:* Look Back in Anger (play), 1957 (produced 1956); The Entertainer (play), 1957 (also produced); Epitaph for George Dillon (with A. Creighton), 1958 (produced 1957); The World of Paul Slickey (comedy of manners with music), 1959 (produced 1959); Luther (play), 1960 (produced 1961, New York, 1964); A Subject of Scandal and Concern (TV play), 1960; Plays for England, 1963; Inadmissible Evidence (play), 1964 (produced 1965); A Patriot for Me (play), 1964 (produced 1965); A Bond Honoured, 1966 (produced 1966); The Hotel in Amsterdam, 1967 (produced 1968); Time Present, 1967 (produced 1968); Hedda Gabler (adaptation), 1970 (produced 1972); The Right Prospectus and Very Like a Whale (TV plays), 1971; West of Suez, 1971 (produced 1971); The Gift of Friendship (TV play), 1971; A Sense of Detachment, 1972 (produced 1972); A Place Calling Itself Rome, 1972; The Picture of Dorian Gray (play), 1973; The Gift of Friendship (TV play), 1974; Jill and Jack (TV play), 1974; The End of Me Old Cigar (play), 1975; Watch it come down (play), 1975; contrib. to Declaration (a symposium), 1957; various newspapers, journals.

Film: Tom Jones, 1964 (Oscar for best screenplay). Hon. Dr RCA, 1970. *Address:* 124 Finchley Road, NW3. *Clubs:* Savile, Garrick.

OSBORNE, Kenneth Hilton, QC (Scot.) 1976; *b* 9 July 1937; *s* of Kenneth Osborne and Evelyn Alice (*née* Hilton); *m* 1964, Clare Ann Louise Lewis; one *s* one *d*. *Educ:* Larchfield Sch., Helensburgh; Merchiston Castle Sch., Edinburgh; Edinburgh Univ. (MA, LLB). Admitted to Faculty of Advocates in Scotland, 1962; Standing Junior Counsel to Min. of Defence (Navy) in Scotland, 1974-76. Chm., Disciplinary Cttee, Potato Marketing Bd, 1975-. *Recreations:* skiing, fishing, gardening, music, cooking. *Address:* 11 Ann Street, Edinburgh EH4 1PL. *T:* 031-332 1455; Primrose Cottage, Bridgend of Lintrathen, by Kirriemuir, Angus DD8 5JH. *Clubs:* New (Edinburgh), Scottish Arts (Edinburgh).

OSBORNE, Surgeon Rear-Admiral (D) Leslie Bartlet, CB 1956; *b* 16 Sept. 1900; *s* of late Rev. Joseph Osborne, MA, and of Miriam Duke James; *m* 1929; two *s* one *d*; *m* 1955, Joan Mary Williams (*née* Parnell). *Educ:* Caterham Sch.; Guy's Hospital. LDS, RCS England 1923; FDS, RCS (Edinburgh) 1955. Dental House Surgeon, Guy's Hospital, 1923. Entered Royal Navy, Surgeon Lieutenant (D), 1923; Surgeon Commander (D), 1936; Surgeon Captain (D), 1948; Surgeon Rear-Admiral (D), 1954; Deputy Director-General for Dental Services in the Royal Navy, 1954-57, retired. Served War of 1939-45. KHDS 1951; QHDS 1953-58. *Recreations:* Rugby Football (rep. RN, Sussex and Devonport Services; Hon. Manager British Isles Rugby Union Team to New Zealand and Australia, 1950; Chairman Rugby Football Union Selection Cttee, 1949-51; President, Rugby Football Union, 1956); gardening. *Address:* 4 Westbourne Court, Cooden Drive, Cooden Beach, Bexhill-on-Sea, East Sussex TN39 3AA. *T:* Cooden 4431.

OSBORNE, Lithgow; President, Auburn (NY) Cablevision; *b* 2 April 1892; *s* of Thos Mott Osborne and Agnes Devens; *m* 1918; three *s*. *Educ:* Harvard Class of 1915. US Diplomatic Service, 1915-19 (Berlin, Copenhagen, Paris Peace Conference); Assistant Secretary, General Conference on Disarmament, 1921-22; Editor Auburn (NY) Citizen-Advertiser, 1922-33; Conservation Commissioner, State of New York, 1933-42; Delegate-at-large, NY State Constitutional Convention, 1938; Office of Foreign Relief and Rehabilitation, Washington, 1942-43; Deputy Director-General, Dept of Services and Areas, UNRRA European Regional Office, 1943-44; American Ambassador to Norway, 1944-46. *Recreation:* fishing. *Address:* 32 Owasco Street, Auburn, NY 13021, USA. *Clubs:* Harvard, Century (NY).

OSBORNE, Sir Peter (George), 17th Bt, *cr* 1629; *b* 29 June 1943; *s* of Lt-Col Sir George Osborne, 16th Bt, MC, and Mary (Grace), *d* of C. Horn; *S* father, 1960; *m* 1968, Felicity, *d* of Grantley Loxton-Peacock; three *s*. *Educ:* Wellington Coll., Berks; Christ Church Coll., Oxford. *Heir: s* Gideon Oliver Osborne, *b* 23 May 1971. *Address:* 36 Porchester Terrace, W2. *T:* 01-402 3903.

O'SHEA, Alexander Paterson, CMG 1962; North American Director, New Zealand Meat Producers' Board, USA, 1964-68, retired, 1968; *b* 29 Dec. 1902; *s* of John O'Shea; *m* 1935; one *d*. *Educ:* Otago Boys' High Sch.; Victoria University College (now Victoria Univ. of Wellington). (BCom). Farming, 1919-27. Wellington City Corporation, 1928-35; Secretary, Farmers' Union, 1935-46 (later Federated Farmers of NZ Inc.); General Secretary, Federated Farmers of New Zealand Inc., Wellington, NZ, 1946-64. Fellow (Chartered Accountant) New Zealand Society of Accountants. *Publication:* The Public Be Damned, 1946. *Recreation:* onlooker, Rugby football. *Address:* Herbert Gardens, The Terrace, Wellington 1, New Zealand. *Clubs:* Civil Service, Wellesley (Wellington, NZ).

O'SHEA, David Michael; Deputy Solicitor to the Metropolitan Police, since 1976; *b* 27 Jan. 1927; *s* of late Francis Edward O'Shea and Helen O'Shea; *m* 1953, Sheila Winifred; two *s*. *Educ:* St Ignatius Coll., London; King's Coll., London Univ. (LLB). Served RN, 1946-48. Articled H.C.L. Hanne & Co., London, 1949-52; admitted solicitor, 1952; in practice with H. C. L. Hanne & Co., 1952-56; joined Solicitor's Dept, Metropolitan Police Office, 1956. *Recreations:* continental travel; school football and Rugby spectator. *Address:* 55 Northey Avenue, Cheam, Surrey. *T:* 01-642 4862. *Club:* Sutton and Epsom Rugby Football.

OSIFELO, Sir Frederick (Aubarua), Kt 1977; MBE 1972; Speaker of Legislative Assembly, Solomon Islands, since 1974; Chairman, Public Service Commission, since 1975; *b* 15 Oct. 1928; *s* of Paul Iromea and late Joy Ngangale Iromea; *m* 1949,

Margaret Tanai; three *s* three *d*. *Educ:* Torquay Technical Coll., England (Dip. Public Admin). Office cleaner, 1945; clerk, 1950; 1st Cl. Magistrate, 1967; Admin. Officer, Cl. B, 1967; Admin. Officer, Cl. A, 1972; Sen. Sec., 1973; Comr of Lands, 1974. Pres., Amateur Sports Assoc., 1975-. Lay Canon, 1977. *Address:* PO Box 548, Honiara, Solomon Islands. *T:* 705 or 759.

OSMAN, Sir (Abdool) Raman (Mahomed), GCMG 1973; CBE 1963; Governor-General of Mauritius, since 1972; *b* 29 Aug. 1902, of Mauritian parents; unmarried. *Educ:* Royal College, Mauritius; Inns of Court, London. District Magistrate, Mauritius, 1930-38; Additional Substitute Procureur and Advocate General, 1938-50; Actg Procureur and Advocate-General, 1950-51; Actg Chief Justice, Apr.-Nov. 1958; Puisne Judge, Supreme Court of Mauritius, 1950-59, Sen. Puisne Judge, 1959-60, retired. Hon. DCL Mauritius, 1975. *Address:* Government House, Le Réduit, Mauritius. *Club:* Port Louis Gymkhana.

OSMAN, Louis, BA (Arch.); FRIBA; architect, artist, and goldsmith; *b* 30 January 1914; *s* of Charles Osman, Exeter; *m* 1940, Dilys Roberts, *d* of Richard Roberts, Rotherfield, Sussex; one *d*. *Educ:* Hele's School, Exeter; London University. Open exhibn at Bartlett School of Architecture, University Coll. London, 1931, and at Slade School; Donaldson Medallist of RIBA, 1935. With British Museum and British School of Archæology Expeditions to Syria, 1936, 1937; designed private and public buildings, 1937-39. Served War of 1939-45, Major in Intelligence Corps: Combined Ops HQ and Special Air Service as specialist in Air Photography, Beach Reconnaissance Cttee, prior to invasion of Europe. Resumed practice in London, 1945, designed buildings, furniture, tapestries, glass, etc; work in Westminster Abbey, Lincoln, Ely and Exeter Cathedrals; Staunton Harold for National Trust; Bridge, Cavendish Square, with Jacob Epstein; Newnham Coll., Cambridge; factory buildings for Cambridge Instrument Co., aluminium Big Top for Billy Smart's Circus, two villages on Dartmoor, etc; consultant architect to British Aluminium Co.; executed commissions as goldsmith and jeweller, 1956-; commissioned by De Beers for 1st Internat. Jewellery Exhibn, 1961; designed and made Prince of Wales' crown for investiture, 1969; British Bicentennial Gift to America housing Magna Carta, 1976; work in precious metals exhibited GB, Denmark, Holland, Germany, American, S Africa, Australia, Japan, etc; one-man retrospective exhibn, Goldsmiths' Hall, 1971. Mem. Exec. Cttee The Georgian Group, 1952-56. *Publications:* reviews and contributions to learned jls. *Recreations:* music, riding. *Address:* Canons Ashby, Northants NN12 6SD. *T:* Blakesley 275.

OSMAN, Dr Mohammed Kheir; Ambassador of Sudan to the Court of St James's, 1975-76; consultant to UNESCO, since 1976; *b* 1928; *s* of Khalifa Taha Osman and Khadija el Sharif; *m* 1953, Sara Ahmed; three *s* four *d*. *Educ:* Khartoum Univ. (BA); London Univ. (MA); Univ. of California (PhD). Director: Educational Research, 1970-71; Productivity Centre, Khartoum, 1972; Minister of Education, 1972-75. *Recreation:* reading. *Address:* c/o UNESCO, Place de Fontenoy, 75700 Paris, France. *Club:* Athenæum.

OSMAN, Sir Raman; *see* Osman, Sir A. R. M.

OSMOND, Sir Douglas, Kt 1971; CBE 1968 (OBE 1958); QPM; Chief Constable, Shropshire, 1946-62, Hampshire, 1962-77. OStJ 1971. *Address:* Cygnet House, Martyr Worthy, Winchester, Hants.

OSMOND, Mervyn Victor; Secretary, Council for the Protection of Rural England, 1966-77 (Assistant Secretary, 1946; Deputy Secretary 1963); *b* 2 July 1912; *s* of Albion Victor Osmond and Florence Isabel (*née* Edwards), Bristol; *m* 1940, Aimée Margaret Moir; one *d*. *Educ:* Clifton Coll. (Schol.); Exeter Coll., Oxford (Schol.). 1st cl. Hon. Class. Mods.; 2nd cl. Lit. Hum.; 2nd cl. Jurisprudence; Poland Prizeman (Criminal Law), 1937; called to Bar (Inner Temple), 1938; MA 1939. Practising Barrister, Western Circuit, 1938-40. Joined Gloucestershire Regt, TA, 1931; served war of 1939-45; Royal Fusiliers; DAAG (Major) 352 L of C Sub-Area and 303 L of C Area (Calcutta). *Recreations:* reading, enjoying rural England. *Address:* 39 Stonehill Road, East Sheen, SW14 8RR. *T:* 01-876 7138.

OSMOND, Michael William Massy, CB 1977; Solicitor to the Department of Health and Social Security, and to the Office of Population Censuses and Surveys, and the General Register Office, since 1974; *b* 1918; *s* of late Brig. W. R. F. Osmond, CBE, and Mrs C. R. E. Osmond; *m* 1943, Jill Ramsden; one *s* one *d*. *Educ:* Winchester; Christ Church, Oxford. 2nd Lieut Coldstream Guards, 1939-40. Called to Bar, Inner Temple, 1941; Asst Principal, Min. of Production, 1941-43;

Housemaster, HM Borstal Instn, Usk, 1943-45; Legal Asst, Min. of Nat. Insce, 1946; Sen. Legal Asst, 1948; Asst Solicitor, Min. of Pensions and Nat. Insce, 1958; Principal Asst Solicitor, DHSS, 1969. *Recreations:* music, fishing, sailing, travel. *Address:* Hollybank, The Warren, Ashtead, Surrey. *T:* Ashtead 75147. *Club:* United Oxford & Cambridge University.

OSMOND, (Stanley) Paul, CB 1966; Secretary to the Church Commissioners, since 1975; *b* 13 May 1917; *o s* of late Stanley C. and Susan Osmond; *m* 1942, Olivia Sybil, *yr d* of late Ernest E. Wells, JP, Kegworth, Leicestershire; two *s. Educ:* Bristol Grammar School; Jesus College, Oxford. 2nd Cl. Final Hons School of Modern History, Oxford, 1939. Served War of 1939-45, in Army (Gloucestershire Regiment and staff), 1940-46. Home Civil Service, 1939-75: Ministry of Education, 1946-48; Private Secretary to Prime Minister, 1948-51; Admiralty, 1951, Asst Secretary, 1954; Under-Secretary, 1959; HM Treasury, 1962, Third Secretary, 1965; Deputy Secretary: Civil Service Dept, 1968-70; Office of the Lord Chancellor, 1970-72; DHSS, 1972-75. A Manager of the Royal Institution, 1966-69, 1970-73. *Recreations:* theatre, unavoidable gardening. *Address:* 20 Beckenham Grove, Bromley, Kent BR2 0JU. *T:* 01-460 2026. *Club:* Athenæum.

OSMOND, Thomas Edward, BA (hons), MB Cantab; MRCS, LRCP; late Hon. Consulting Venereologist to the British Army; *b* Thorpe-le-Soken, 7 Oct. 1884; *s* of Edward Osmond, JP; *m* 1920, Daisy Stewart Mathews (*d* 1963); one *s* one *d. Educ:* King's Sch., Rochester; Emmanuel Coll., Cambridge; St Bart.'s Hospital. MB Cantab 1912; joined RAMC; service in India and Mesopotamia, 1914-18 (despatches); transferred to RARO 1920 and appointed Pathologist VD Dept St Thomas' Hospital; recalled to Army 1 Sept. 1939; served in France; late Brig. RAMC; adviser in venereology to the Army, 1939, Consultant 1943-45; late MO i/c Male VD Dept and Marlborough Path. Lab. Royal Free Hospital, London; late Pres. Med. Society for the Study of Venereal Diseases; Fellow Med. Society of London; President Middlesex Partial County Committee and Ashford (Middlesex) Branch British Legion. *Publications:* Article, Venereal Disease, Encyclopædia Britannica, Book of the Year, 1939; Aids to the diagnosis and treatment of Venereal Diseases, 1946; articles, Venereal Disease and Social Implications of Venereal Disease, Chambers's Encyclopædia, 1947; Venereal Disease in Peace and War, British Journal of Venereal Diseases, 1949; contributions to British Medical Journal, The Practitioner, etc. *Recreations:* gardening, bridge. *Address:* Compton, 34 The Avenue, Clevedon, Avon BS21 7EA. *T:* 3697.

OSMOND-CLARKE, Sir Henry, KCVO 1969; CBE 1947; FRCS; Consulting Orthopædic Surgeon: London Hospital, E1 (Orthopædic Surgeon, 1946-70); Robert Jones and Agnes Hunt Orthopædic Hospital, Oswestry (Senior Visiting Surgeon, 1930-70); Hon. Civilian Consultant in Orthopædics, RAF, since 1946; Orthopædic Surgeon to Queen, 1965-73; *e s* of W. J. Clarke, Brookeborough, Co. Fermanagh, NI; *m* Freda, *e d* of Richard Hutchinson, Bury, Lancs; two *d. Educ:* Clones High School; Trinity College, Dublin University; Vienna, Bologna, New York, Boston, London. BA 1925; MB, BCh (stip. cond.) 1926; FRCSIre 1930; FRCS 1932; Surgical Travelling Prize, TCD 1930. Consultant Orthopædic Surgeon, Oldchurch, Black Notley, Tilbury and East Grinstead Hosps; Orthopædic Surgeon, King Edward VII Hosp. for Officers, London; Cons. King Edward VII Convalescent Home for Officers, Osborne; Hunterian Prof. RCS, 1936. Service Cons. in Orthop. Surg., Air Cdre, RAF, 1941-46; Mayo Clinic Foundation Lecturer, 1948; Orthop. Mem. WHO Mission to Israel, 1951, to India, 1953, to Persia, 1957. Past President, British Orthop. Assoc. (former Editorial Sec. and Acting Sec.); FRSocMed and several Brit. Med. Socs. Formerly: Clinical Tutor in Orthop. Surg., Manchester Roy. Infirmary and Lecturer in Surg. Pathology (Orthop.), Univ. of Manchester; Orthop. Surg., Crumpsall Hosp., Manchester, and Biddulph Grange Orthop. Hosp., Stoke-on-Trent; Sen. Ho. Surg. and Orthop. Ho. Surg. Ancoats Hosp., Manchester, and Royal Nat. Orthop. Hospital, London. Mem. Council, RCS, 1959-75, Vice-Pres. 1970-72. Chm. Accident Services Review Cttee of Great Britain and Ireland, 1960. Hon. Mem. American Orthop. Assoc.; American Acad. of Orthopædic Surgery; Australian, New Zealand and Canadian Orthopædic Assocs; Corresp. Mem., French Orthopædic Society and Surg. Soc. of Lyon; Mem. International Soc. of Orthopædics and Traumatology. *Publications:* papers on surgical and orthopædic subjects in leading surgical text-books and med. jls, including Half a Century of Orthopædic Progress in Great Britain, 1951. *Recreations:* travel, reading, fishing. *Address:* 46 Harley House, Marylebone Road, NW1 5HJ. *T:* 01-486 9975; Arunbrook, Wormley, near Godalming, Surrey. *T:* Wormley 2876. *Club:* Royal Air Force.

OSSORY, FERNS and LEIGHLIN, Bishop of; *see* Cashel, Waterford and Lismore, Ossory, Ferns and Leighlin.

OSSULSTON, Lord; Peter Grey Bennet; *b* 18 Oct. 1956; *s* and heir of 9th Earl of Tankerville, *qv.*

OSTLERE, Dr Gordon; *see* Gordon, Richard.

O'SULLEVAN, Peter John, OBE 1977; Daily Express Racing Correspondent, since 1950, and BBC Television Commentator; *b* 3 March 1918; *o s* of late Col John Joseph O'Sullevan, DSO, formerly Resident Magistrate, Killarney, and Vera, *o d* of Sir John Henry, DL, JP; *m* 1951, Patricia, *o d* of Frank Duckworth, Winnipeg, Manitoba, Canada. *Educ:* Hawtreys; Charterhouse; Collège Alpin, Switzerland. Specialised in ill-health in early life and not accepted for fighting forces in 1939-45 war, during which attached to Chelsea Rescue Services. Subsequently worked for John Lane, the Bodley Head, on editorial work and MSS reading. Joined Press Assoc. as Racing Correspondent, 1945, until appointed Daily Express, 1950, in similar capacity. Race-broadcasting 1946- (incl. Australia, S Africa, Italy, France, USA); in 1953 became first regular BBC TV and horse-racing commentator to operate without a race-reader. In Dec. 1967 commentated world's first televised electronic horse race from Atlas computer at Univ. of London, transmitted by BBC TV Grandstand. (With late Clive Graham) Derby Award for Racing Journalist of the Year, 1971; Racehorse Owner of the Year Award, Horserace Writers' Assoc., 1974. *Recreations:* racehorse owning, in minor way (happiest broadcasting experience commentating success of own horses, Be Friendly, 1966-67, and Attivo, 1974); travel, reading, art, food and wine. *Address:* 37 Cranmer Court, SW3 3HW. *T:* 01-584 2781.

O'SULLIVAN, Bernard John; journalist; Editor, The British Racehorse, 1959-67; *b* 22 Sept. 1915; *s* of late P. J. O'Sullivan, Valentia Island, Co. Kerry, and late Teresa McGough, Carlisle. *Educ:* Xaverian College. Joined staff of Raceform, 1936; Editor, 1940-46; Joint-founder and Editor, The Racehorse, 1944-46; Editor and Chief Contributor, The Bloodstock Breeders' Review, 1947-52. *Publications:* (ed) The International Family Tables of Racehorses, 1953; contrib. on Thoroughbred breeding and racing to various jls in England and overseas. *Recreations:* cricket, bridge.

O'SULLIVAN, (Carrol Austin) John (Naish), CB 1973; LLB (London); Public Trustee, 1971-75; *b* 24 Jan. 1915; *s* of late Dr Carrol Naish O'Sullivan and late Stephanie O'Sullivan (*née* Manning); *m* 1939, Lillian Mary, *y d* of Walter Frank Yate Molineux, Ulverston; one *s* one *d. Educ:* Mayfield College. Admitted Solicitor, 1936. Served War of 1939-45, Gordon Highlanders and HQ Special Force SEAC (Captain). Joined Public Trustee Office, 1945; Chief Administrative Officer, 1963-66; Asst Public Trustee, 1966-71. Pres., Holborn Law Soc., 1965-66. Chm. of Governors of St Thomas More High Sch. for Boys, Westcliff-on-Sea, 1964-66. *Publications:* articles in legal jls; short stories. *Recreations:* golf, photography, family history, grandchildren. *Address:* The Rowan Tree House, 3 The Leeway, Hopping Jack's Lane, Danbury, Chelmsford CM3 4PS. *T:* Danbury 3829.

O'SULLIVAN, Rt. Rev. Mgr. James, CBE 1973 (MBE 1963); Officiating Chaplain (RC), RAMC Depot and Training Centre, since 1973; *b* 2 Aug. 1917; *s* of Richard O'Sullivan and Ellen (*née* Ahern). *Educ:* St Finnbarr's Coll., Cork; All Hallows Coll., Dublin. Ordained, 1941; joined Royal Army Chaplain's Dept, 1942; 49 Infantry Div., Normandy, 1944; Senior RC Chaplain, Malaya, 1952-54 (despatches 1953); Chaplain Irish Guards, 1954-56; Senior RC Chaplain, Berlin, 1956-59; Staff Chaplain (RC), War Office, 1959-64; Senior RC Chaplain, BAOR, 1965-69; Principal RC Chaplain (Army), 1969-73. *Recreation:* golf. *Address:* Osgil, Vicarage Lane, Ropley, Alresford, Hants.

O'SULLIVAN, John; *see* O'Sullivan, C. A. J. N.

OSWALD, Maj.-Gen. Marshall St John, CB 1965; CBE 1961; DSO 1945; MC 1943; retired as Director of Management and Support Intelligence, Ministry of Defence, 1966; *b* 13 Sept. 1911; *s* of William Whitehead Oswald and Katharine Ray Oswald; *m* 1st, 1938, Mary Georgina Baker (*d* 1970); one *s* two *d*; 2nd, 1974, Mrs Barbara Rickards. *Educ:* Rugby Sch.; RMA, Woolwich. Commissioned RA, 1931; served in RHA and Field Artillery, UK and India, 1931-39. Served War of 1939-45 (despatches, MC, DSO): Battery Comdr 4 RHA and Staff Officer in Egypt and Western Desert, 1939-42; GSO1, Tactical HQ, 8th Army, 1942-43; 2nd in Comd Field Regt, Italy, 1943-44; CO South Notts Hussars, Western Europe, 1944-45; Col on staff of HQ 21 Army Group, 1945. Mil. Govt Comdr (Col) of Cologne Area, 1946-47; Staff Officer, War Office (Lt-Col) 1948-

49; Instructor (Col) Staff Coll., Camberley 1950-52; CO 19 Field Regt, Germany/Korea, 1953-55; GHQ, MELF (Col), 1955-56 (despatches 1957); IDC 1958; CCRA and Chief of Staff (Brig.) 1st Corps in Germany, 1959-62; DMI, War Office, 1962-64, Min. of Defence (Army), 1964-65. Council Mem., Salmon and Trout Assoc.; Mem. Bd of Directors, Test and Itchen Fishing Assoc. *Recreations:* fishing, shooting, ski-ing. *Address:* Eastfield House, Longparish, near Andover, Hants. *T:* Longparish 228. *Club:* Army and Navy.

OSWALD, Dr Neville Christopher, TD 1946; DL; MD Cantab 1946, FRCP 1947; retired 1975; formerly: Consultant Physician: St Bartholomew's Hospital; Brompton Hospital; King Edward VII's Hospital for Officers, London; King Edward VII's Hospital, Midhurst; *b* 1 Aug. 1910; *s* of late Col Christopher Percy Oswald, CMG; *m* 1st, 1941, Patricia Rosemary Joyce Cooke (*d* 1947); one *s* one *d* ; 2nd, 1948, Marjorie Mary Sinclair; one *d. Educ:* Clifton Coll.; Queens' Coll., Cambridge. Research Fellow, USA, 1938-39. Royal Army Medical Corps, 1939-45. Hon. Physician to the Queen, 1956-58; Hon. Consultant in Diseases of the Chest to the Army, 1972-75. Hon. Col, 17th (London) General Hospital RAMC (TA), 1963-70, 217 (Eastern) General Hospital RAMC (V), 1967-70. President: British Tuberculosis Assoc., 1965-67; Thoracic Soc., 1974. DL Greater London, 1973. RCP: Mitchell Lectr; Tudor Edwards Lectr. *Publications:* Recent Trends in Chronic Bronchitis, 1958; Diseases of the Respiratory System, 1962; many articles upon respiratory diseases. *Recreations:* travel, golf. *Address:* 2 The Old Rectory, Thurlestone, South Devon. *T:* Thurlestone 555.

OSWALD, Thomas; *b* 1 May 1904; *s* of John Oswald and Agnes Love, Leith; *m* 1933, Colina MacAskill, *d* of Archibald MacAlpine and Margaret MacAskill, Ballachulish, Argyllshire; three *s* one *d. Educ:* Yardheads and Bonnington Elementary Schools. Shipyard worker, transport worker. Official of Transport and General Workers' Union; Scottish Regional Trade Group Secretary, 1941-69. Contested (Lab) West Aberdeenshire, 1950. MP (Lab) Edinburgh Central, 1951-Feb. 1974; PPS to Secretary of State for Scotland, 1967-70. Sec. Treasurer, Scottish Parly Lab. Group, 1953-64; Sec., Members' Parly Cttee, 1956-66. Dir, St Andrew Animal Fund; Mem. Cttee, Scottish Soc. for Prevention of Vivisection; Nat. Pres., Scottish Old Age Pensions Assoc. *Recreations:* student economic and industrial history; swimming, camping, etc. *Address:* 28 Seaview Crescent, Joppa, Edinburgh EH15 2LU. *T:* 031-669 5569.

O'TOOLE, Peter; actor; *b* 1932; *s* of Patrick Joseph O'Toole; *m* Sian Phillips; two *d. Educ:* Royal Academy of Dramatic Art. With Bristol Old Vic Company, 1955-58; first appearance on London stage as Peter Shirley in Major Barbara, Old Vic, 1956. *Plays include:* Oh, My Papa!, Garrick, 1957; The Long and the Short and the Tall, Royal Court and New, 1959; season with Shakespeare Memorial Theatre Company, Stratford-on-Avon, 1960; Baal, Phœnix, 1963; Hamlet, National Theatre, 1963; Ride a Cock Horse, Piccadilly, 1965; Juno and the Paycock, Gaiety, Dublin, 1966; Uncle Vanya, Plunder, The Apple Cart, Bristol Old Vic, 1973. *Films include:* Kidnapped, 1959; The Day They Robbed the Bank of England, 1959; The Savage Innocents, 1960; Lawrence of Arabia, 1962; Becket, 1963; Lord Jim, 1964; What's New, Pussycat, 1965; How to Steal a Million, 1966; The Bible... in the Beginning, 1966; The Night of the Generals, 1967; Great Catherine, 1968; The Lion in Winter, 1968; Goodbye Mr Chips, 1969; Brotherly Love, 1970; Murphy's War, 1971; Under Milk Wood, 1971; The Ruling Class, 1972; Man of La Mancha, 1972; Rosebud, 1975; Man Friday, 1975; Foxtrot, 1975; Rogue Male (BBC TV), 1976. *Address:* c/o Keep Films, 5 Eaton Place, SW1. *T:* 01-235 6552. *Club:* Garrick.

OTTAWA, Archbishop of, (RC), since 1967; **Most Rev. Joseph Aurèle Plourde;** *b* 12 Jan. 1915; *s* of Antoine Plourde and Suzanne Albert. *Educ:* Bathurst Coll.; Bourget Coll.; Rigaud; Major Seminary of Halifax; Inst. Catholique, Paris, Gregorian Univ., Rome. Auxiliary Bishop of Alexandria, Ont., 1964. Hon. DEducn, Moncton Univ., 1969. *Address:* Archbishop's Residence, 145 Saint Patrick Street, Ottawa, Ont K1N 5K1, Canada. *T:* 237-4540.

OTTAWA, Bishop of, since 1970; **Rt. Rev. William James Robinson;** *b* 8 Sept. 1916; *s* of Thomas Albert Robinson and Harriet Mills; *m* 1946, Isobel Morton; one *s* three *d. Educ:* Bishop's Univ., Lennoxville, PQ. BA in Theology; DCL (*hc*) 1973. Deacon, 1939; Priest, 1940; Asst Curate in Trenton, 1939-41; Rector of: Tweed and Madoc, 1941-46, Tweed and N Addington, 1946-47; Napanee, 1948-53; St Thomas' Church, Belleville, 1953-55; St John's Church, Ottawa, 1955-62; Church of Ascension, Hamilton, 1962-67; St George's Church, Guelph, 1967-70. Canon of Christ Church Cathedral, Hamilton, 1964-

68; Archdeacon of Trafalgar (Niagara Diocese), 1968-70. *Recreation:* golf. *Address:* Bishop's Court, 24 Madawaska Drive, Ottawa K1S 3G6. *T:* 235-8823.

OTTAWAY, Prof. Christopher Wyndham, PhD, FRCVS; Research Professor of Veterinary Science, University of Bristol, 1973-75, now Emeritus; Chairman, Board of Veterinary Studies, 1955-59, 1965-67; *b* 6 June 1910; 3rd *s* of W. H. Ottaway; *m* 1938, Grace, *d* of E. Luckin, JP; two *s* one *d. Educ:* Owen's Sch.; Roy. Vet. Coll., London; King's College, Cambridge (Senior Wellcome Scholar). Veterinary Practitioner, 1931-34; Department of Anatomy, Royal Veterinary College, London: Demonstrator, 1934-38; Lecturer, 1938-41; Reader, 1941-45; Wellcome Scholar, 1945-48; Lecturer in Zoology, Cambridge University, 1949; Prof of Veterinary Anat., Bristol Univ., 1949-73. *Publications:* ed, Anatomy of the Horse (1938 edn); Locomotion, in Phys. Farm Animals (ed Hammond), 1955; scientific papers. *Recreations:* music, walking. *Address:* 59 High Kingsdown, Bristol BS2 8EP. *T:* Bristol 23330.

OTTER, Rt. Rev. Anthony, MA; an Assistant Bishop, Diocese of Lincoln, since 1965; *b* 8 Sept. 1896; *s* of Robert Charles and Marianne Eva Otter; *m* 1929, Dorothy Margaret Ramsbotham; no *c. Educ:* Repton; Trinity College, Cambridge. Served European War, 1914-18, in RNVR, 1914-19. BA (2nd cl. History Tripos), 1920; MA 1925. Cambridge Mission to Delhi, 1921-24; Westcott House, Cambridge, 1924-25; Deacon, 1925; Priest, 1926; Curate of Holy Trinity, St Marylebone, 1925-31; London Secretary of SCM, 1926-31; Vicar of Lowdham with Gunthorpe, Dio. of Southwell, 1931-49; Chaplain of Lowdham Grange Borstal Institution, 1931-45; Ed. of Southwell Diocesan Magazine, 1941-46; Hon. Canon of Southwell Cathedral, 1942-49; Rural Dean of Gedling, 1946-49; Bishop Suffragan of Grantham, 1949-65; Dean of Stamford, 1949-71. *Publications:* William Temple and the Universal Church, 1949; Beginning with Atoms, 1971. *Recreations:* country, birds; maintenance of domestic machinery. *Address:* The Old Rectory, Belton, Grantham, Lincs. *T:* Grantham 2061.

OTTER, Air Vice-Marshal Victor Charles, CBE 1967 (OBE 1945); Air Officer Engineering, Air Support Command Royal Air Force, 1966-69, retired; *b* 9 February 1914; *s* of Robert and Ada Annie Otter; *m* 1943, Iris Louise Dykes; no *c. Educ:* Weymouth Gram. School. RAF Aircraft Apprentice, 1929-32; flying duties, 1935-37; commissioned Engr. Br., 1940; SO (Techn) Controller Research and Development (MAP), 1942-47; Asst Air Attaché, Budapest, 1947-48; Officer Comdg Central Servicing Develt Establt, 1953-55; Chief Engrg Officer, Bomber Comd, 1956-59; OC No 32 Maintenance Unit, 1959-61; STSO Flying Trng Comd, 1961-63; Project Dir, P1154/P1127, 1963-66. CEng, FRAeS, FIMechE, MBIM, psc. *Recreation:* gliding. *Address:* Harpenden, 21 Keats Avenue, Littleover, Derby. *T:* Derby 52048. *Club:* Royal Air Force.

OTTLEY, Agnes May; retired as Principal, S Katharine's College, Tottenham, N17, Dec. 1959; *b* 29 June 1899; *d* of late Rev. Canon Robert Lawrence Ottley, Professor of Moral and Pastoral Theology, Oxford. *Educ:* privately; Society of Oxford Home Students. Final Honours School of Modern History, Oxford, 1921; MA Oxon; Assistant Mistress at S Felix School, Southwold, 1925; Lecturer in History, Avery Hill Training College, 1927. *Address:* 104 Lyndhurst Road, Hove, East Sussex BN3 6FD. *T:* Brighton 733958.

OTTLEY, Warner Herbert Taylor, CB 1945; retired; *b* 1889; *m* 1921, Hilda Mary Edwards; two *s. Educ:* Malvern; St John's College, Cambridge. Higher Division Clerk, War Office, 1913; Director of Finance, War Office, 1942; retired, 1949. *Address:* 14 Medrow Court, Hastings, East Sussex.

OTTON, Geoffrey John; Deputy Secretary, Department of Health and Social Security, since 1975; *b* 10 June 1927; *s* of late John Alfred Otton and Constance Alma Otton; *m* 1952, Hazel Lomas (*née* White); one *s* one *d. Educ:* Christ's Hosp.; St John's Coll., Cambridge (MA). Home Office: Asst Principal, 1950; Principal, 1954-64 (seconded to Cabinet Office, 1959-61); Principal Private Sec. to Home Sec., 1963-65; Asst Sec., 1964-70; Asst Under-Sec. of State, Home Office Children's Dept, 1970; transf. with that Dept to DHSS, 1971, Under-Sec., DHSS, 1971-75. Chief Advr to Supplementary Benefits Commn, 1976-. *Recreation:* music. *Address:* 72 Cumberland Road, Bromley, Kent. *T:* 01-460 9610.

OTTON, Philip Howard, QC 1975; a Recorder of the Crown Court, since 1972; Barrister-at-Law; *b* 28 May 1933; *o s* of H. A. Otton, Kenilworth; *m* 1965, Helen Margaret, *d* of late P. W. Bates, Stourbridge; two *s* one *d. Educ:* Bablake School, Coventry; Birmingham Univ. LLB 1954. Called to the Bar,

Gray's Inn, 1955. Dep. Chm., Beds QS, 1970-71; Junior Counsel to the Treasury (Personal Injuries), 1970-75. *Address:* 2 Crown Office Row, Temple, EC4Y 7HJ. *T:* 01-353 9337; 6 Parkmead, SW15 5BS. *T:* 01-789 6262. *Clubs:* Garrick, Roehampton.

OTUNGA, HE Cardinal Maurice; see Nairobi, Archbishop of, (RC).

OULD, His Honour Ernest; a Circuit Judge (formerly Judge of County Courts), Sheffield, Rotherham, Barnsley and Pontefract, 1955-75; *b* 9 Dec. 1901; *s* of Percy and Emily Ould, Leeds; *m* 1931, Sarah Ackroyd, Leeds; two *s. Educ:* City of Leeds School; Leeds University. Called to the Bar, Gray's Inn, 1937; practised Leeds and North Eastern Circuit. *Recreation:* golf. *Address:* 3/33a Shire Oak Road, Leeds LS6 2DD.

OULTON, Antony Derek Maxwell, MA, PhD; Deputy Secretary, Lord Chancellor's Office, since 1976, and Deputy Clerk of the Crown in Chancery, since 1977; barrister-at-law; *b* 14 Oct. 1927; *y s* of late Charles Cameron Courtenay Oulton and Elizabeth, *d* of T. H. Maxwell, KC; *m* 1955, Margaret Geraldine, *d* of late Lt-Col G. S. Oxley, MC, 60th Rifles; one *s* three *d. Educ:* St Edward's Sch., Oxford; King's Coll., Cambridge (scholar; BA (1st Cl.), MA; PhD 1974). Called to Bar, Gray's Inn, 1952; in private practice, 1952-60; Private Sec. to Lord Chancellor, 1961-65; Sec., Royal Commn on Assizes and Quarter Sessions, 1966-69. *Publication:* (jtly) Legal Aid and Advice, 1971. *Address:* 35 St John's Wood Terrace, NW8 6JL. *T:* 01-586 1555.

OULTON, Air Vice-Marshal Wilfrid Ewart, CB 1958; **CBE** 1953; **DSO** 1943; **DFC** 1943; FInst Nav; CEng; FIERE; Director: EMI (Electronics) Ltd; Emihus Ltd; Medsales Ltd; *b* 27 July 1911; *s* of Llewellin Oulton, Monks Coppenhall, Cheshire; *m* 1935, Sarah, *d* of Rev. E. Davies, Pitsea, Essex; three *s. Educ:* University Coll., Cardiff; Cranwell. Commissioned, 1931; Director, Joint Anti-Submarine School, 1946-48; Joint Services Staff College, 1948-50; Air Attaché, Buenos Aires, Montevideo, Asuncion, 1950-53; idc 1954; Director of Operations, Air Ministry, 1954-56; commanded Joint Task Force "Grapple" for first British megaton weapon tests in the Pacific, 1956-58; Senior Air Staff Officer, RAF Coastal Command, HQ, 1958-60; retd. *Recreations:* music, squash, golf, travel. *Address:* Denefield, Overstream, Rickmansworth, Herts. *T:* Rickmansworth 74258. *Club:* Naval and Military.

OUNSTED, John, MA Cantab; HM Inspector of Schools, since 1971; *b* London, 24 May 1919; *e s* of Rev. Laurence J. Ounsted, Dorchester Abbey, Oxon (ordained 1965; formerly with Sun Life Assurance); *m* 1940, Irene, 3rd *d* of late Rev. Alfred Newns; one *s* four *d. Educ:* Winchester (Scholar); Trinity College, Cambridge (Major Scholar). Math. Tripos Part I, 1st Class; Moral Science Tripos Part II, 1st Class; Senior Scholarship, Trinity College. Assistant Master, King Edward's School, Birmingham, 1940-48; Headmaster, Leighton Park School, 1948-70. First layman ever to be Select Preacher, Oxford Univ., 1964. Page Scholarship to visit USA, 1965. Liveryman, Worshipful Company of Mercers. *Publications:* verses from various languages in the 2 vols of Translation, 1945 and 1947; contributions to Watsonia, The Proceedings of the Botanical Society of the British Isles, and various other educational and botanical periodicals. *Recreations:* botany, camping, being overtaken when motoring. *Address:* Dumney Lane Cottage, Great Leighs, Chelmsford, Essex. *T:* Great Leighs 445.
See also Sir A. Foley Newns.

OUTERBRIDGE, Col Hon. Sir Leonard Cecil, Kt 1946; **CC** (Canada) 1967; **CBE** 1926; **DSO** 1919; **CD** 1954; Director, Harvey & Co., Ltd, and other Cos, St John's, Newfoundland; *b* 1888; *s* of late Sir Joseph Outerbridge; *m* 1915, Dorothy Winifred (*d* 1972), *d* of late John Alexander Strathy, Barrie, Ontario. *Educ:* Marlborough; Toronto Univ. (BA, LLB; Hon. LLD, 1950); Hon. LLD: Laval Univ., 1952; Memorial Univ. of Newfoundland, 1961. Solicitor and Barrister, Ontario, 1914; President, Newfoundland Board of Trade, 1923-24; Chairman, Newfoundland Committee arranging Exhibits at British Empire Exhibition (1924 and 1925) (CBE); served European War, 1914-19 (despatches twice, DSO). Hon. Private Sec. to the Governor of Newfoundland, 1931-44; Director of Civil Defence, 1942-45; Lieutenant-Governor of Newfoundland, 1949-57. Hon. Col, Royal Newfoundland Regt, 1950-75. KStJ 1951. *Address:* Littlefield, Pringle Place, St John's, Newfoundland.

OUTERIÑO, Felix C.; see Candela Outeriño.

OUTRAM, Sir Alan James, 5th Bt, *cr* 1858; MA; Assistant Master, Harrow School; *b* 15 May 1937; *s* of late James Ian Outram and Evelyn Mary Littlehales; *S* great-uncle, 1945; *m* 1976, Victoria Jean, *d* of George Dickson Paton, Bexhill-on-Sea; one *d. Educ:* Spyway, Langton Matravers, Swanage; Marlborough College, Wilts; St Edmund Hall, Oxford. Lt-Col TAVR. *Recreations:* golf, tennis, bridge. *Heir: kinsman* John Douglas Outram [*b* 24 June 1947; *m* 1970, Valerie Wilson; two *s*]. *Address:* Harrow School, Harrow-on-the-Hill, Middlesex.

OVENDEN, John Frederick; MP (Lab) Gravesend since 1974; *b* 17 Aug. 1942; *s* of late Richard Ovenden and Margaret Louise Ovenden (*née* Lucas); *m* 1963, Maureen (*née* White); one *d. Educ:* Salmestone County Primary Sch.; Chatham House Grammar Sch., Ramsgate. Asst Exec. Engr, Post Office, 1961-74. *Recreation:* football (as a spectator). *Address:* House of Commons, SW1. *Clubs:* Gillingham Labour (Gillingham); Gravesend Trades Hall (Gravesend).

OVENS, Maj.-Gen. Patrick John, OBE 1968; **MC** 1951; Commandant, Joint Warfare Establishment, since 1976; *b* 4 Nov. 1922; *s* of late Edward Alec Ovens and late Mary Linsell Ovens, Cirencester; *m* 1952, Margaret Mary White; one *s* two *d. Educ:* King's Sch., Bruton. Commnd into Royal Marines, 1941; HMS Illustrious, 1942-43; 46 Commando, 1945; HQ 3rd Commando Bde, 1946-48; 41 Indep. Commando, Korea, 1950-52; HQ Portsmouth Gp, 1952-55; psa 1955-56; Staff of CGRM, 1959-61; Amphibious Warfare Sqdn, 1961-62; 41 Commando, 1963-65, CO 1965-67; C-in-C Fleet Staff, 1968-69; Comdr 3 Commando Bde, 1970-72; RCDS 1973; COS to Comdt Gen., RM, MoD, 1974-76. *Recreations:* sailing, music, gardening. *Address:* Joint Warfare Establishment, Old Sarum, Salisbury SP4 6BN. *T:* Salisbury 22461.

OVERALL, Sir John (Wallace), Kt 1968; **CBE** 1962; **MC** and Bar; Principal, John Overall & Partners, since 1973; Director: CSR Ltd, since 1973; Land Lease Corporation Ltd, since 1973; Alliance Holdings Ltd, since 1975; General Property Trust, since 1976; *b* 15 July 1913; *s* of late W. Overall, Sydney; *m* 1943, Margaret J., *d* of C. W. Goodman; four *s. Educ:* Sydney Techn. College. AIF, 1940-45: CO, 1 Aust. Para. Bn (Lt-Col). Chief Architect, S Australian Housing Trust, 1946-48; private practice, Architect and Town Planner, 1949-52; Dir of Architecture, Commonwealth Dept of Works, 1952-57; Comr, Nat. Capital Develt Commn, 1958-72; Chm., Nat. Capital Planning Cttee, 1958-72; Comr, Cities Commn (Chm., Adv. Cttee), 1972-73. Chm. of Olympic Fine Arts Architecture and Sculpture Exhibn, Melb., 1956. Life Fellow, RAIA; FAPI, FRTPI; Pres., Austr. Inst. of Urban Studies, 1970-71. Past Pres., Canberra Legacy Club. Sydney Luker Meml Medal, 1970; Sir James Barrett Medal, 1970. *Publication:* Observations on Redevelopment Western Side of Sydney Cove, 1967; sundry papers to professional jls. *Recreations:* squash, golf, tennis. *Address:* 10 Wallaroy Road, Double Bay, NSW 2028, Australia. *T:* 362046. *Clubs:* Australian (Sydney); Royal Sydney Golf.

OVEREND, Douglas, CB 1965; Assistant Under-Secretary of State, Department of Health and Social Security, 1968-75; *b* 22 Nov. 1914; *s* of Simeon and Frances Overend, Rodley, Leeds. *Educ:* Leeds Grammar School; Queen's College (Hastings Scholar, Taberdar), Oxford. 1st cl. Classical Mods. 1936; Greats 1938. Army Service, 1939-46. Entered Min. of Nat. Insce as Principal, 1946; Asst Sec., 1953; Under-Sec., 1959; Min. of Pensions and Nat. Insce, 1959-66; Min. of Social Security, 1966-68. *Recreation:* golf. *Address:* 2 The Orchard, Tayles Hill, Ewell, Surrey. *T:* 01-394 0094.

OVEREND, Prof. William George; Professor of Chemistry in the University of London and Head of Department of Chemistry in Birkbeck College, since 1957; Vice-Master, Birkbeck College, since 1974; *b* 16 Nov. 1921; *e s* of Harold George Overend, Shrewsbury, Shropshire; *m* 1949, Gina Olava, *y d* of Horace Bertie Cadman, Birmingham; two *s* one *d. Educ:* Priory School, Shrewsbury; Univ. of Birmingham. BSc (Hons) 1943, PhD 1946, DSc 1954, Birmingham; CChem; FRIC, 1955. Asst Lecturer, Univ. Coll., Nottingham, 1946-47; Research Chemist with Dunlop Rubber Co. Ltd and subsequently British Rubber Producers' Assoc., 1947-49; Hon. Research Fellow, 1947-49, Lecturer in Chemistry, 1949-55, Univ. of Birmingham; Vis. Associate Prof., Pennsylvania State Univ., 1951-52; Reader in Organic Chemistry, Univ. of London, 1955-57. Univ. of London: Mem., Academic Council, 1963-67 and 1976-; Mem., University Entrance and Schools Examination Council, 1966-67; Chm., Bd of Studies in Chemistry, 1974-76; Mem., Senate, 1976-; Mem., Finance and General Purposes Cttee, 1976-; Mem., Jt Cttee of Court and Senate for collective planning; Mem. Council, Inst. of Educn. Royal Institute of Chemistry: Examiner, 1958-62; Assessor, 1959-72; Mem., Institutions and Examinations Cttee, 1969-75 (Chm., 1976-); Mem. Council, 1977-; Mem. Qual and Admissions Cttee, 1977-; Chemical

Society: Mem. Council, 1967-70, 1972-77; Mem. Publications Bd, 1967-; Hon. Sec. and Hon. Treasurer, Perkin Div., 1972-75; Vice-Pres., 1975-77; Mem., Interdivisional Council, 1972-75; Mem., Educn and Trng Bd, 1972-; Soc. of Chemical Industry: Mem., Council, 1955-65, Mem., Finance Committee, 1956-65, Mem., Publications Cttee, 1955-65 (Hon. Sec. for publications and Chairman of Publications Committee, 1958-65); Brit. Nat. Cttee for Chemistry, 1961-66, 1973-; Brit. Nat. Cttee for Biochemistry, 1975-; Chemical Council, 1960-63 and 1964-69 (Vice-Chm. 1964-69); European Cttee for Carbohydrate Chemists, 1970- (Chm.); Hon. Sec., Internat. Cttee for Carbohydrate Chemistry, 1972-75; Mem., Jt IUPAC-IUB Commn on Carbohydrate Nomenclature, 1971-. Jubilee Memorial Lecturer, Society of Chemical Industry, 1959-60; Lampitt Medallist, Society of Chemical Industry, 1965; Member: Pharmacopœia Commission, 1963-; Home Office Poisons Board. Governor: Polytechnic of the South Bank, 1970-; Thomas Huxley Coll., 1971-77. *Publications:* The Use of Tracer Elements in Biology, 1951; papers in Nature, and Jl of Chemical Soc. *Recreation:* gardening. *Address:* Department of Chemistry, Birkbeck College, Malet Street, WC1E 7HX. *T:* 01-580 6622; The Retreat, Nightingales Lane, Chalfont St Giles, Bucks HP8 4SR. *Club:* Athenæum.

OVERTON, Hugh Thomas Arnold, CMG 1975; HM Diplomatic Service; Minister (Economic), Bonn, since 1975; *b* 2 April 1923; *e s* of late Sir Arnold Overton, KCB, KCMG, MC; *m* 1948, Claire-Marie Binet; one *s* two *d. Educ:* Dragon Sch., Oxford; Winchester; Clare Coll., Cambridge. Royal Signals, 1942-45. HM Diplomatic Service, 1947-; served: Budapest; UK Delegn to UN, New York; Cairo; Beirut; Disarmament Delegn, Geneva; Warsaw; Bonn; Canadian Nat. Defence Coll.; Head of N America Dept, FCO, 1971-74; Consul-Gen., Düsseldorf, 1974-75. *Recreations:* reading, walking, sailing. *Address:* c/o Barclays Bank, 276 Kensington High Street, W8. *Clubs:* Royal Commonwealth Society, Royal Automobile.

OWEN, (Alfred) David; Chairman since 1975, and Managing Director since 1969, Rubery Owen Holdings Ltd; *b* 26 Sept. 1936; *m* 1966, Ethne (*née* Sowman); two *s* one *d. Educ:* Brocksford Hall; Oundle; Emmanuel Coll., Cambridge Univ. (MA). Joined Rubery Owen Gp, 1960; Gen. Man., Rubery Owen Motor Div., 1962-67; Dep. Man. Dir, Rubery Owen & Co. Ltd, 1967; Acting Chm., Rubery Owen Holdings Ltd, 1969. *Recreations:* hockey, squash, photography, music, industrial archaeology, local history, collecting books. *Address:* Mill Dam House, Mill Lane, Aldridge, Walsall, West Midlands. *T:* 021-353 1221. *Club:* National.

OWEN, Alun, MC 1945; Under-Secretary, Land Use Planning Group, Welsh Office, since 1975; *b* 14 March 1919; *s* of late Evan Thomas Owen and of Gwladys (*née* David); *m* 1946, Rhona Evelyn Griffiths; one *s* four *d. Educ:* West Monmouth Grammar Sch.; Bridgend Grammar Sch.; LSE (BScEcon). Mil. Service, 1939-46: Ches. Regt, 1940-46 (Captain); seconded to 1st Eritrean Refugee Working Bn; service in Sudan, Suez Canal Zone, W Desert, 1941-42; 2nd Bn, Ches. Regt, 1942-44, service in W Desert, N Africa, Sicily, NW Europe (despatches, Normandy, 1944); 6th Bn Royal Welch Fusiliers, 1945; Instr, Inf. Heavy Weapons Sch., 1945-46. Cadet Officer, Min. of Labour NW Region, 1946-48; Asst Principal, Min. of Fuel and Power, 1948-50; Customs and Excise, 1950-59, Principal 1951; Welsh Office, Min. of Housing and Local Govt, 1959-62; Admin. Mem., Welsh Bd of Health, 1962-69; Welsh Office: Asst Sec., hosp., health and social work services, 1969-72; Estabt Officer, 1972-73; Under-Sec., Health Services, 1974-75. *Recreation:* golf. *Address:* 78 Stanwell Road, Penarth, South Glamorgan. *T:* Penarth 709276. *Clubs:* Civil Service, National Liberal; Cardiff and County (Cardiff).

OWEN, Alun (Davies); writer since 1957; *b* 24 Nov. 1925; *s* of Sidney Owen and Ruth (*née* Davies); *m* 1942, (Theodora) Mary O'Keeffe; two *s. Educ:* Cardigan County School, Wales; Oulton High School, Liverpool. Worked as Stage Manager, Director and Actor, in theatre, TV and films, 1942-59. Awards: Screenwriters and Producers Script of the Year, 1960; Screenwriters Guild, 1961; Daily Mirror, 1961; Golden Star, 1967. *Acted in: stage:* Birmingham Rep., 1943-44; Humoresque, 1948; Snow White and the Seven Dwarfs, 1951; Old Vic season, 1953; Tamburlaine the Great, As You Like It, King Lear, Twelfth Night, The Merchant of Venice, Macbeth, The Wandering Jew, The Taming of the Shrew, 1957; Royal Court Season, 1957; Man with a Guitar, The Waiting of Lester Abbs, The Samson Riddle, 1972; *films:* Every Day Except Christmas, 1957; I'm All Right Jack, 1959; The Servant, 1963. *Author of productions: stage:* The Rough and Ready Lot, 1959 (Radio 1958), publ. 1960; Progress to the Park, 1959 (Radio 1958), publ. 1962; The Rose Affair, 1966 (TV 1961), publ. 1962; A

Little Winter Love, 1963, publ. 1964; Maggie May, 1964; The Game, 1965; The Goose, 1967; Shelter, 1971 (TV 1967), publ. 1968; There'll Be Some Changes Made, 1969; Norma, We Who Are About To (later title Mixed Doubles), 1969, publ. 1970; The Male of the Species, 1974 (TV 1969), publ. 1972; *screen:* The Criminal, 1960; A Hard Day's Night, 1964; Caribbean Idyll, 1970; *radio:* Two Sons, 1957; It Looks Like Rain, 1959; *television:* No Trams to Lime Street, 1959, After the Funeral, 1960, Lena, Oh My Lena, 1960, publ. as Three TV Plays, 1961; The Ruffians, 1960; The Ways of Love, 1961; Dare to be a Daniel, 1962, publ. in Eight Plays, Book 1, 1965; The Hard Knock, You Can't Wind 'em All, 1962; The Strain, Let's Imagine Series, The Stag, A Local Boy, 1963; The Other Fella, The Making of Jericho, 1966; The Wake, 1967, publ. in A Collection of Modern Short Plays, 1972; George's Room, 1967, publ. 1968; The Winner, The Loser, The Fantasist, Stella, Thief, 1967; Charlie, Gareth, Tennyson, Ah There You Are, Alexander, Minding the Shop, Time for the Funny Walk, 1968; Doreen, 1969, publ. in The Best Short Plays, 1971; The Ladies, Joan, Spare Time, Park People, You'll Be the Death of Me, Male of the Species, 1969; Hilda, And a Willow Tree, Just the Job, Female of the Species, Joy, 1970; Ruth, Funny, Pal, Giants and Ogres, The Piano Player, 1971; The Web, 1972; Ronnie Barker Show (3 scripts), Buttons, Flight, 1973; Lucky, Norma, 1974; Left, 1975; Forget Me Not (6 plays), 1976. *Recreations:* languages and history. *Address:* c/o Felix de Wolfe & Associates, 1 Robert Street, Adelphi, WC2N 6BH.

OWEN, David; *see* Owen, A. D.

OWEN, Rt. Hon. David Anthony Llewellyn, PC 1976; MP (Lab) Plymouth, Devonport, since 1974 (Plymouth, Sutton, 1966-74); Secretary of State for Foreign and Commonwealth Affairs, since 1977; *b* Plympton, South Devon, 2 July 1938; *s* of Dr John William Morris Owen and Mary Llewellyn; *m* 1968, Deborah Schabert; two *s. Educ:* Bradfield College; Sidney Sussex College, Cambridge; St Thomas' Hospital. BA 1959; MB, BChir 1962; MA 1963. St Thomas' Hospital: house appts, 1962-64; Neurological and Psychiatric Registrar, 1964-66; Research Fellow, Medical Unit, 1966-68. Contested (Lab) Torrington, 1964. PPS to Minister of Defence, Administration, 1967; Parly Under-Sec. of State for Defence, for RN, 1968-70; Opposition Defence Spokesman, 1970-72, resigned over EEC, 1972; Parly Under-Sec. of State, DHSS, 1974; Minister of State: DHSS, 1974-76; FCO, 1976-77. Sponsored 1973 Children's Bill; ministerially responsible for 1975 Children's Act. Chm., Decision Technology Internat., 1970-72. Governor of Charing Cross Hospital, 1966-68; Patron, Disablement Income Group, 1968-. Chairman of SW Regional Sports Council, 1967-71. Fellow Roy. Soc. Med. *Publications:* (ed) A Unified Health Service, 1968; The Politics of Defence, 1972; In Sickness and in Health, 1976; contrib. to Social Services for All, 1968; articles in Lancet, Neurology, and Clinical Science. *Recreation:* sailing. *Address:* 78 Narrow Street, Limehouse, E14. *T:* 01-987 5441; Castlehayes, Plympton, Plymouth, Devon. *T:* Plymouth 336130.

OWEN, Dr David Elystan, CBE 1972; Director, Manchester Museum, 1957-76; *b* 27 Feb. 1912; *s* of Dr John Griffith Owen, Kingston-on-Thames, and Mrs Gertrude Owen (*née* Heaton); *m* 1936, Pearl Jennings, Leicester; one *s* one *d. Educ:* The Leys Sch., Cambridge; King's Coll., London Univ. 1st cl. hons BSc 1933, PhD 1935. Keeper, Dept of Geology, Liverpool Museum, 1935-47; War Service, 1939-45 in Artillery (Major, RA); Dir, Leeds City Museums, 1947-57. Treas. 1956-61, Pres. 1968-69, Museums Assoc. *Publications:* The Story of Mersey and Deeside Rocks, 1939; A History of Kirkstall Abbey, 1955; Water Highways, 1967; Water Rallies, 1969; Water Byways, 1973; Canals to Manchester, 1977; numerous palaeontological papers in Palaeontology, Geological Jl, etc. *Recreation:* cruising the British canal and river system. *Address:* 9 Carleton Road, Higher Poynton, Cheshire. *T:* Poynton 2924.

OWEN, Maj.-Gen. David Lanyon Ll.; *see* Lloyd Owen.

OWEN, Sir Dudley H. C.; *see* Cunliffe-Owen.

OWEN, Rt. Rev. Edwin; *see* Limerick and Killaloe, Bishop of.

OWEN, Eric Hamilton; formerly Deputy Chairman, Grindlays Bank Ltd (1967-75); retired; *b* 4 Aug. 1903; *s* of Harold Edwin Owen and Hilda Guernsey; *m* 1937, Margaret Jeannie Slipper. Served Artists' Rifles, 1921-39; RASC, 8th Army, 1940-45; 21st SAS Regt (Artists), 1946-48 (despatches). Dir, Gabbitas-Thring Educational Trust Ltd. Member Board of Trade Mission to Ghana, 1959. *Recreations:* photography, travel. *Address:* Burnaston, 8 Silverdale Avenue, Oxshott, Surrey. *Club:* Army and Navy.

OWEN, Frank, (H. F. Owen), OBE (mil.); Journalist, Author, Broadcaster and Public Relations Consultant; *b* 1905; *s* of Thomas and Cicely Owen, Hereford; *m* 1939, Grace Stewart McGillivray (*d* 1968), Boston, USA. *Educ:* Monmouth Sch.; Sidney Sussex Coll., Cambridge (Schol.); 1st class hons, History Tripos. South Wales Argus, 1928-29; MP (L) Hereford Division, 1929-31; Daily Express, 1931-37; Editor, Evening Standard, 1938-41; served Royal Armoured Corps, 1942-43; South-East Asia Command, 1944-46; Lieut-Colonel (OBE); Editor, Daily Mail, 1947-50. Freeman of the City of London. *Publications:* (with Cemlyn Jones) Red Rainbow, 1931, novel; (with R. J. Thompson) His was the Kingdom, An Account of the Abdication, 1937; (with Michael Foot and Peter Howard) Guilty Men: an attack on Neville Chamberlain, Halifax, etc for collaboration with Hitler, 1938; The Three Dictators, 1940; The Campaign in Burma, 1946; Tempestuous Journey: Lloyd George, His Life and Times, 1954; The Eddie Chapman Story, 1956; Peron: His Rise and Fall, 1957; The Fall of Singapore, 1960. *Address:* 132 Elgin Avenue, W9. *T:* 01-289 1440. *Clubs:* Savage, Press.

OWEN, Gerald Victor, QC 1969; *b* London, 29 Nov. 1922; *m* 1946, Phyllis (*née* Ladsky); one *s* one *d*. *Educ:* Kilburn Grammar Sch.; St Catharine's Coll., Cambridge. Exhibr, St Catharine's Coll., Cambridge, 1940; Drapers' Company Science Schol., Queen Mary Coll., London, 1940. 1st cl. Maths Tripos I, 1941; Senior Optimes Tripos II, 1942; BA 1943, MA 1946, Cantab; Royal Statistical Soc. Certif., 1947; LLB London (Hons) 1949. Research Ballistics, Min. of Supply, 1942-45; Statistical Officer, LCC, 1945-49. Called to Bar, Gray's Inn, 1949; *ad eundem* Inner Temple, 1969. A Dep. Circuit Judge, 1971. Member, Cttees of Justice on: Legal Aid in Criminal Cases; Complaints against Lawyers, 1970; False Witness, the problem of perjury, 1973. *Recreations:* walking, theatre, concert going. *Address:* Wellington House, Eton Road, NW3; 3 Paper Buildings, Temple, EC4. *T:* 01-353 1182. *Club:* Maccabaeans.

OWEN, Prof. Gwilym Ellis Lane, FBA 1969; Laurence Professor of Ancient Philosophy, University of Cambridge, since 1973; Fellow of King's College, Cambridge, since 1973; *b* 18 May 1922; *o s* of Ellis William Owen, Portsmouth; *m* 1947, Sally Lila Ann Clothier; two *s*. *Educ:* Portsmouth Grammar Sch.; Corpus Christi Coll., Oxford. MA (Oxon) 1949; BPhil 1950; MA (Cantab) 1973. Res. Fellow in Arts, Univ. of Durham, 1950; Univ. Lectr in Ancient Philosophy, Univ. of Oxford, 1953; Reader in Ancient Philosophy, 1957; Fellow of Corpus Christi Coll., 1958; Prof. of Ancient Philosophy, 1963; Victor S. Thomas Prof. of Philosophy and the Classics, Harvard Univ., 1966-73. Visiting Professor of Philosophy: Pennsylvania, 1956; Harvard, 1959; California, 1964; Princeton, 1975. Fellow, Amer. Acad. of Arts and Sciences, 1967; For. Mem., Finnish Acad. of Arts and Letters, 1976. *Publications:* (ed, with I. Düring) Aristotle and Plato in the Mid-Fourth Century, 1960; (ed) Aristotle on Dialectic, 1968; Collected articles, 1977. *Address:* King's College, Cambridge; The Beeches, Lower Heyford, Oxford. *T:* Steeple Aston 40467.

OWEN, Maj.-Gen. Harry, CB 1972; Chairman, Medical Appeal Tribunal, since 1972; *b* 17 July 1911; *m* 1952, Maureen (*née* Summers); one *s* one *d*. *Educ:* University Coll., Bangor. BA Hons Philosophy, 1934. Solicitor of Supreme Court, 1939. Commissioned in Queen's Own Cameron Highlanders, 1940-43; joined Mil. Dept of Office of Judge Advocate General, 1943; served in: W Africa, 1945-46; Middle East, 1947-50; Austria, 1952-53; Dep. Dir of Army Legal Services: Far East, 1960-62; HQ, BAOR, 1962-67; Brig. Legal Staff, 1968-69; Maj.-Gen. 1969; Dir, Army Legal Services, 1969-71, retd. *Recreations:* philosophy, history of art, walking, gardening. *Address:* Clavering, 40 North Park, Gerrards Cross, Bucks. *T:* Gerrards Cross 86777.

OWEN, Captain Hilary Dorsett, CMG 1944; RN, retired; *b* 25 Aug. 1894; *s* of late J. D. Owen, JP, Plas-yn-Grove, Ellesmere, Shropshire; *m* 1924, Eileen Amy Hamilton (*d* 1952), *e d* of W. B. Dunlop, Seton Castle, Longniddry; one *s*. *Educ:* Belvedere, Brighton; RN Colleges, Osborne and Dartmouth. Midshipman, 1912; served at sea, War of 1914-18; Commander, 1930; Naval Attaché, Lisbon, 1938-44; SHAEF 1944-45; retired list, 1944.

OWEN, H. F.; *see* Owen, Frank.

OWEN, Sir Hugh (Bernard Pilkington), 5th Bt *cr* 1813; *b* 28 March 1915; *s* of Sir John Arthur Owen, 4th Bt and of Lucy Fletcher, *e d* of F. W. Pilkington; *S* father, 1973. *Educ:* Chillon Coll., Switzerland. *Heir: b* John William Owen [*b* 7 June 1917; *m* 1963, Gwenllian Mary, *er d* of late E. B. Phillips]. *Address:* 63 Dudsbury Road, Ferndown, Dorset.

OWEN, Idris Wyn; a director of a company in the construction industry; *b* 1912; *m*. *Educ:* Stockport Sch. and Coll. of Technology; Manchester Sch. of Commerce. Contested (C): Manchester Exchange, 1951; Stalybridge and Hyde, 1955; Stockport North 1966; MP (C) Stockport North, 1970-Feb. 1974; contested (C) Stockport North, Oct. 1974. Member, Stockport Borough Council, 1946; Mayor, 1962-63. Vice-Pres., Nat. Fedn of Building Trades Employers, 1965. FIOB. *Address:* Gawsworth Old Rectory, Cheshire.

OWEN, John Arthur Dalziel, QC 1970; a Recorder of the Crown Court, since 1972; *b* 22 Nov. 1925; *s* of late R. J. Owen and Mrs O. B. Owen; *m* 1952, Valerie, *d* of W. Ethell; one *s* one *d*. *Educ:* Solihull Sch.; Brasenose Coll., Oxford. MA, BCL 1949. Called to Bar, Gray's Inn, 1951. Dep. Chm., Warwickshire QS, 1967-71. Mem., General Synod of Church of England, Dio. Coventry, 1970-; Chancellor, Dio. Derby, 1973-, Dio. Coventry, 1976-. *Address:* Lansdowne House, Shipston-on-Stour, Warwicks. *T:* Shipston-on-Stour 61521.

OWEN, John Benjamin Brynmor, DSc (Oxon), MSc (Wales); CEng; John William Hughes Professor of Civil Engineering, University of Liverpool, 1950-77; *b* 2 Sept. 1910; *s* of David Owen (Degwyl) and Mary Alice Owen; *m* 1938, Beatrice Pearn (*née* Clark); two *d*. *Educ:* Universities of Oxford and Wales. Drapers Company Scholar, Page Prize and Medal, University College, Cardiff, 1928-31; Meyricke Scholar, Jesus Coll., Oxford, 1931-32; British Cotton Industry Research Association, 1933-35; Messrs A. V. Roe, Manchester, 1935-36; Royal Aircraft Establishment, Farnborough, 1936-48; Naval Construction Research Establishment, 1948-50. *Publications:* Light Structures, 1965; many contributions to learned journals on design of structures, on helicopters and on investigation of aircraft accidents. *Address:* Department of Civil Engineering, The University of Liverpool, PO Box 147, Brownlow Street, Liverpool L69 3BX. *T:* 051-709 6022.

OWEN, John Gethin M.; *see* Morgan-Owen.

OWEN, Maj.-Gen. John Ivor Headon, OBE 1963; Chef de Cabinet to Thomson McLintock & Co, Chartered Accountants, since 1974; Joint Secretary to McLintock Main Lafrentz International, since 1974; *b* 22 Oct. 1922; *s* of Major William H. Owen; *m* 1948, Margaret Jean Hayes; three *d*. *Educ:* St Edmund's Sch., Canterbury. MBIM; psm, jssc, idc. Joined Royal Marines (as Marine), 1942; temp. 2nd Lieut RM, 1942; 44 Commando RM, Far East, 1942-46; demobilised 1946 (Captain RM); Constable, Metropolitan Police, 1946-47; rejoined Royal Marines as Lieut, 1947; regimental service, 1948-55; Staff Coll., Camberley, 1956; Bde Major, HQ 3 Cdo Bde, 1959-62; Naval Plans, Admty/MoD, 1962-64; 42 Cdo RM, 1964-66; Instructor, Jt Services Staff Coll., 1966-67; CO 45 Cdo RM, 1967-68 (despatches); Col GS, Staff of CGRM, 1969-70; Royal Coll. of Defence Studies, 1971-72; Maj.-Gen, Commando Forces RM, Plymouth, 1972-73. Lt-Col 1966; Col 1970; Maj.-Gen. 1972. Mem., Clergy Orphan Corporation Cttee. *Publications:* Brassey's Infantry Weapons of the World; Brassey's NATO Infantry Weapons; Brassey's Warsaw Pact Infantry Weapons; contrib. Seaford House Papers, 1971. *Recreations:* woodworking, gardening. *Address:* c/o Midland Bank Ltd, 89 Queen Victoria Street, EC4V 4AQ. *Club:* Army and Navy.

OWEN, Prof. John V.; *see* Vallance-Owen.

OWEN, Prof. Paul Robert, CBE 1974; FRS 1971; Zaharoff Professor of Aviation, London University, at Imperial College of Science and Technology, since 1963; *b* 24 Jan. 1920; *s* of Joseph and Deborah Owen; *m* 1958, Margaret Ann, *d* of Herbert and Dr Lily Baron; two *s* two *d*. *Educ:* Queen Mary Coll., London Univ. BSc (London) 1940, MSc (Manchester), CEng, FRAeS, FRMetS. Aerodynamics Dept, RAE, Farnborough, 1941-53; Reader and Director of Fluid Motion Laboratory, Manchester Univ., 1953-56; Professor of the Mechanics of Fluids and Director of the Laboratory, Manchester Univ., 1956-62. Member: ARC, 1964-67, 1969- (Chm, 1971-); Safety in Mines Research Adv. Bd, 1956-73; Environmental Design and Engring Res. Cttee, DoE (Chm., 1973-); British Nat. Cttee for Theoretical and Applied Mechanics, 1971- (Chm., 1973-); Construction and Housing Res. Adv. Council, 1976-; Anglo-French Mixed Commn on Cultural Exchange, 1976-. Fellow, Queen Mary Coll., 1967. Founder Fellow, Fellowship of Engineering, 1976. Hon. Dr Aix-Marseille, 1976. *Publications:* papers on Aerodynamics in R & M series of Aeronautical Research Council, Journal of Fluid Mechanics, etc. *Recreations:* music, theatre. *Address:* 1 Horbury Crescent, W11. *T:* 01-229 5111.

OWEN, Peter Granville, CMG 1965; QPM 1964; CPM 1960; *b* 28 Oct. 1918; *s* of Walter Lincoln Owen, Highgate, and Ethel Belton, London, N6; *m* 1943, Mercia Louvaine Palmer; one *s* one *d. Educ:* Grove House Sch., Highgate; City of Norwich Sch. Great Yarmouth Borough Police, 1938-42; RAF, F/O, 1942-46; Public Prosecutor, Somalia Gendarmerie, 1946; Resident Magistrate, Mogadishu, Somalia, 1948; District Commissioner: Somalia, 1949-50; Eritrea, 1950; Tanganyika Police: Cadet, Asst Superintendent and Dep. Superintendent of Police, 1950; Somaliland Police: Superintendent and Senior Superintendent of Police, 1956; Commissioner of Police: Gibraltar, 1960; British Guiana, 1962; Aden, 1965; UN Police Adviser, Govt of Somali Republic, 1968. Adjudication Officer, Cadastral Surveys, British Virgin Is, 1971, Cayman Is, 1973, Blantyre, Malawi, 1976. OStJ 1960. *Recreations:* cricket, swimming, walking. *Address:* 141 Yarmouth Road, Thorpe St Andrew, Norwich, Norfolk. *Clubs:* Royal Commonwealth Society, MCC.

OWEN, Philip Loscombe Wintringham, TD 1950; QC 1963; JP; a Recorder of the Crown Court, since 1972; *b* 10 Jan. 1920; *er s* of Rt Hon. Sir Wintringham Stable, *qv*; assumed surname of Owen in lieu of Stable by deed poll, 1942; *m* 1949, Elizabeth Jane, *d* of late Lewis Trelawny Widdicombe, Effingham, Surrey; three *s* two *d. Educ:* Winchester; Christ Church, Oxford (MA). Served War of 1939-45, Royal Welch Fusiliers: W Africa, India, Ceylon, Burma, 1939-47; Major TARO. Received into Roman Catholic Church, 1944. Called to Bar, Middle Temple, 1949; Bencher, 1969; Mem., Gen. Council of the Bar of England and Wales, 1971-; a Deputy Chairman of Quarter Sessions: Montgomeryshire, 1959-71; Cheshire, 1961-71; Recorder of Merthyr Tydfil, 1971; Leader, Wales and Chester Circuit, 1975-. Chm., Adv. Bd constituted under Misuse of Drugs Act, 1974-. Legal Assessor to: Gen. Med. Council, 1970-; Gen. Dental Council, 1970-; RICS, 1970-. Contested (C) Montgomeryshire, 1945. JP Montgomeryshire, 1959; JP Cheshire, 1961. Vice-Pres., Montgomeryshire Cons. and Unionist Assoc.; Pres., Montgomeryshire Soc., 1974-75. Dir, Swansea City AFC Ltd. *Recreations:* shooting, fishing, forestry, music, Association football. *Address:* 1 Brick Court, Temple, EC4. *T:* 01-353 0777; 51 Hartington Road, Chiswick, W4. *T:* 01-994 0415; Plas Llwyn Owen, Llanbrynmair, Powys. *T:* 229. *Clubs:* Carlton; Hurlingham; Cardiff and County; Welshpool and District Conservative; Bristol Channel Yacht (Mumbles).
See also R. O. C. Stable.

OWEN, Rear-Adm. Richard Arthur James, CB 1963; *b* 26 Aug. 1910; *s* of late Captain Leonard E. Owen, OBE, JP; *m* 1941, Jean Sophia (*née* Bluett); one *s* two *d. Educ:* Sevenoaks Sch. Joined RN, 1927; Commander (S) 1945; Captain, 1954; Rear-Admiral, 1961; Director-General, Personal Services, Admiralty, 1962-64; retired. *Address:* High Bank, Martin, near Fordingbridge, Hants. *T:* Martin Cross 295.

OWEN, Robert Davies, CBE 1962; FRCS; FRCSE; Senior Ear and Throat Surgeon, Cardiff Royal Infirmary, 1928-64, retired; Lecturer in Oto-Laryngology, Welsh National School of Medicine, 1929-64, retired; *b* 8 May 1898; 2nd *s* of late Capt. Griffith Owen and late Mrs Jane Owen; *m* 1928, Janet Miles, Llantrisant; two *d. Educ:* Towyn Grammar Sch. Cadet, Harrison Line, Liverpool, 1916-18; University College, Cardiff, 1918-21; Guy's Hospital, London, 1921-27. BSc (Wales) 1921. MRCS, LRCP 1923; FRCS 1930; FRCSEd 1926. *Publications:* contrib. BMJ, Lancet, Proc. Royal Society of Medicine. *Recreations:* shooting, fishing. *Address:* 1 The Mount, Cardiff Road, Llandaff, Cardiff. *T:* Cardiff 568739. *Club:* Cardiff and County.

OWEN, Robert Penrhyn; Director and Secretary, The Water Companies Association; *b* 17 Dec. 1918; *s* of late Captain Richard Owen; *m* 1949, Suzanne, *d* of late L. H. West; one *s* one *d. Educ:* Friar's School. War service in Royal Welch Fusiliers, 1939-46, in Madagascar, India, The Arakan and North and Central Burma. Admitted Solicitor, 1947. Asst Solicitor: Berks CC, 1948-50; Leics CC, 1950-54; Chief Asst Solicitor, Lancs CC, 1954-60; 2nd Dep. Clerk and 2nd Dep. Clerk of the Peace, Lancs CC, 1960-63; Gen. Manager, Telford Develt Corp. (New Town), 1963-69; Sec., Chief Exec. Officer and Solicitor, Thames Conservancy, 1969-74. *Recreations:* all sport, reading. *Address:* Pilgrims Wood, Fawley Green, Henley-on-Thames, Oxon. *T:* Henley-on-Thames 2994. *Clubs:* Lansdowne, MCC.

OWEN, Ronald Hugh, FIA; Chairman, Prudential Assurance Co. Ltd, since 1975; *b* 2 June 1910; *er s* of late Owen Hugh Owen and late Jane Tegwedd Owen; *m* 1939, Claire May Tully; one *s. Educ:* King's College Sch., Wimbledon. FIA 1936. Served War of 1939-45: 52 Field Regt, RA (Major); Bde Major RA, 8 Ind. Division, Middle East and Italy. Joined Prudential, 1929: India, 1936-39; Dep. General Manager, 1959-67; Chief General

Manager, 1968-73; Director, 1974-75. Dep. Chm., British Insurance Assoc., 1971-72. Member, Governing Body and Chairman of Finance Cttee, King's College Sch., Wimbledon. *Recreation:* golf. *Address:* 110 Rivermead Court, Hurlingham, SW6. *T:* 01-736 4842. *Clubs:* Hurlingham; Royal Wimbledon Golf.

OWEN, Rowland Hubert, CMG 1948; Deputy Controller, HM Stationery Office, 1959-64, retired; *b* 3 June 1903; *s* of William R. and Jessie M. Owen, Armagh, NI; *m* 1st, 1930, Kathleen Margaret Evaline Scott (*d* 1965); no *c*; 2nd, 1966, Shelagh Myrle Nicholson. *Educ:* Royal Sch., Armagh; Trinity Coll., Dublin (BA, LLB). Entered Dept of Overseas Trade, 1926; Private Secretary to Comptroller-General, 1930; Secretary Gorell Cttee on Art and Industry, 1931; idc, 1934; Commercial Secretary, Residency, Cairo, 1935; Ministry of Economic Warfare, 1939; Rep. of Ministry in Middle East, 1942; Director of Combined (Anglo-American) Economic Warfare Agencies, AFHQ, Mediterranean, 1943; transferred to Board of Trade and appointed Senior UK Trade Commissioner in India, Burma and Ceylon, 1944; Economic Adviser to UK High Commissioner in India, 1946; Adviser to UK Delegation at International Trade Conf., Geneva, 1947. Comptroller-General, Export Credits Guarantee Dept, 1953-58; Member Managing Cttee, Union d'Assureurs des Crédits Internationaux, 1954-58. Vice-President, Tilford Bach Society, 1962-69; Organist: St Mary's, Bramshott, 1964-70; St John the Evangelist, Farncombe, 1970-75; St Luke's, Grayshott, 1975-; Pres., Surrey Organists' Assoc., 1976, Secretary, 1977-. Staff of National Playing Fields Assoc., 1964-68. US Medal of Freedom. *Publications:* Economic Surveys of India, 1949 and 1952; Insurance Aspects of Children's Playground Management, 1966; Children's Recreation: Statutes and Constitutions, 1967. *Recreations:* music, theatre, gardening. *Address:* Oak Tree Cottage, Holdfast Lane, Haslemere, Surrey.

OWEN, Samuel Griffith, CBE 1977; MD, FRCP; Second Secretary, Medical Research Council, since 1968; *b* 3 Sept. 1925; *e s* of late Rev. Evan Lewis Owen and of Marjorie Lawton; *m* 1954, Ruth, *e d* of Merle W. Tate, Philadelphia, Pa, USA; two *s* two *d. Educ:* Dame Allen's Sch.; Durham Univ. MB, BS Dunelm 1948; MRCP 1951; MD Dunelm 1954; FRCP 1965; clinical and research appts at Royal Victoria Infirmary, Newcastle upon Tyne, 1948-49 and 1950-53; RAMC, SMO, HM Troopships, 1949-50; Med. Registrar, Nat. Heart Hosp., 1953-54; Instr in Pharmacology, Univ. of Pennsylvania Sch. of Med., 1954-56; Reader in Med., Univ. of Newcastle upon Tyne, 1964-68 (First Asst, 1956, Lectr, 1960, Sen. Lectr, 1961); Hon. Cons. Physician, Royal Victoria Infirmary, Newcastle upon Tyne, 1960-68; Clin. Sub-Dean of Med. Sch., Univ. of Newcastle upon Tyne, 1966-68 (Academic Sub-Dean, 1964-66); Examr in Med., Univ. of Liverpool, 1966-68; Examr in Membership, RCP, 1967-68; Member: Research Cttee, RCP, 1968-; Assoc. of Physicians of GB, 1965-; Brit. Cardiac Soc., 1962-; Consultant to WHO, SE Asia, 1966 and 1967-68; Commonwealth Fund Fellow, Univ. of Illinois, 1966. Chm., Feldberg Foundn, 1974-. *Publications:* Essentials of Cardiology, 1961 (2nd edn 1968); Electrocardiography, 1966 (2nd edn 1973); numerous contribs to med. jls on heart disease, cerebral circulation, thyroid disease, med. educn, etc. *Recreations:* squash rackets, gastronomy. *Address:* 20 Park Crescent, W1; 60 Bath Road, Chiswick, W4. *T:* 01-636 5422. *Club:* Athenæum.

OWEN, Thomas Joseph, DL; Town Clerk, Nottingham, 1951-66; *b* 3 Nov. 1903; *s* of late Richard Owen, Sarn, Caernarvonshire; *m* 1935, Marjorie Ethel Tilbury. Articled to late Sir Hugh Vincent, 1921-26; admitted a Solicitor, 1926; Asst Solicitor with Town Clerk, Stoke-on-Trent, 1926-27; Asst Solicitor, Leeds, 1927-30; Asst Solicitor, Brighton, 1930-36; Deputy Town Clerk, Nottingham, 1936-50. President: Nottinghamshire Law Society, 1957-58; Commn of Income Tax for Nottingham Dist. Trustee: Nottingham Roosevelt Travelling Scholarship Fund; Holbrook Trust (Painting and Sculpture). DL Notts, 1966. *Recreations:* watching Rugby football and cricket; travel abroad, reading. *Address:* Woodlands, Sherwood, Nottingham. *T:* Nottingham 61767. *Club:* United Services (Nottingham).

OWEN, Commodore Trevor Lewis, OBE 1942; RD 1938; RNR, retired; *b* 21 Dec. 1895; 4th *s* of D. H. Owen, Wainhams, Shrewsbury; *m* 1920, Freda, 4th *d* of Rev. Prof. John Ramsey, Ballymoney, Co. Antrim; three *d. Educ:* Arnold House Sch., Chester. Joined Merchant Service, Oct. 1911; Sub-Lieut, RNR, 1918; Master's Certificate, 1919. Commander RNR, 1937; Captain, RNR, 1942; Commodore RNR (Acting), 1942 and served in Atlantic Convoys until 1943. Elder Brother of Trinity House, 1943-62 (Nether Warden 1958); retired as an Active Elder Brother, Aug. 1962. Vice-President, Marine Society, 1961 (Chairman 1960). *Recreations:* gardening, sailing. *Address:*

Sevenstones, Stoke Gabriel, Totnes, Devon. *T:* Stoke Gabriel 350.

OWEN, Prof. Walter Shepherd, PhD, DEng; Professor of Materials Science and Engineering and Head of Department of Materials Science and Engineering, Massachusetts Institute of Technology, since 1973; *b* 13 March 1920; *s* of Walter Lloyd and Dorothea Elizabeth Owen; *m* 1953, Carol Ann Wood; one *d.* *Educ:* Alsop High Sch.; University of Liverpool. Metallurgist, D. Napier and Sons and English Electric Co., 1940-46; Asst Lecturer and Lecturer in Metallurgy, 1946-54, Commonwealth Fund Fellow, Metallurgy Dept, Massachusetts Inst. of Technology, USA, 1951-52, on research staff, 1954-57; Henry Bell Wortley Professor of Metallurgy, University of Liverpool, 1957-66. Thomas R. Briggs Prof. of Engineering and Dir of Materials Science and Engineering, Cornell Univ., 1966-70; Dean of Technological Inst., Northwestern Univ., 1970-71; Vice Pres. for Science and Research, Northwestern Univ., 1971-73. Mem., Nat. Acad. of Engineering, USA, 1977. *Publications:* papers in British and American journals on aspects of physical metallurgy. *Address:* Massachusetts Institute of Technology, 77 Massachusetts Avenue, Room 8-307, Cambridge, Mass 02139, USA.

OWEN, William James; *b* 18 Feb. 1901; *m* 1930, Ann Smith; one *s* one *d.* *Educ:* Elementary Sch., Blaina, Mon; Central Labour Coll. Miner, 1914-20; College Student, 1921-23; Tutor-Organiser, National Council Labour Colleges, 1923-30; Urban District Councillor, Blaina, Mon, 1927-30; ILP Secretary, Leicester, 1930-35; City Councillor, Leicester, 1933-38; Education Secretary: Co-operative Society, Burslem, Staffs, 1937-40; London Co-op. Society, 1940-44; Bristol Co-op. Society, 1944-48; Community Welfare Officer, National Coal Board, 1948-51; contested (Lab and Co-op) Dover, 1950 and 1951; MP (Lab and Co-op) Morpeth Div. of Northumberland, 1954-70, retired. Chm., Sutton and Carshalton Constituency Labour Party, 1974-. Gen. Secretary, Assoc. of Clothing Contractors, 1960-70; class teacher and lecturer, adult education, 1970-. *Recreations:* walking, gardening, writing, painting. *Address:* 18a Woodstock Road, Carshalton, Surrey.

OWEN-JONES, John Eryl, CBE 1969; JP; DL; Clerk of Caernarvonshire County Council, 1956-74, and Clerk of Lieutenancy; *b* 19 Jan. 1912; *s* of late John Owen-Jones, Rhydwenfa, Old Colwyn; *m* 1944, Mabel Clara, *d* of Grant McIlvride, Ajmer, Rajputana; one *s* one *d.* *Educ:* Portmadoc Grammar Sch.; University Coll. of Wales, Aberystwyth; Gonville and Caius Coll., Cambridge. LLB Wales 1933; MA Cantab 1939. Admitted Solicitor, 1938; Asst Solicitor, Chester Corp., 1939. Sqdn Ldr, RAFVR, 1945; Legal Staff Officer, Judge Advocate General's Dept, Mediterranean. Dep. Clerk, Caernarvonshire CC, 1946; Clerk of the Peace, Caernarvonshire, 1956-71; formerly: Sec., N Wales Combined Probation and After-Care Cttee; Dep. Clerk, Snowdonia Jt Adv. Cttee; Dep. Clerk, Gwynedd Police Authority, 1967. Hon. Sec., Caernarvonshire Historical Soc. Mem., Gorsedd of Royal National Eisteddfod of Wales. DL Caernarvonshire, 1971; JP 1974, DL 1974, Gwynedd. *Recreations:* music, gardening, photography. *Address:* Rhiw Dafnau, Caernarvon, Gwynedd. *T:* Caernarvon 3370. *Club:* National Liberal.

OWENS, Frank Arthur Robert, CBE 1971; Editor, Birmingham Evening Mail, 1956-74; Director, Birmingham Post & Mail Ltd, 1964-75; *b* 31 Dec. 1912; *s* of Arthur Oakes Owens; *m* 1st, 1936, Ruby Lilian Long; two *s*; 2nd, Olwen Evans, BSc; one *s* one *d.* *Educ:* Hereford Cathedral School. Served with RAF, 1940-46 (despatches). Management Mem., Newspaper Mutual Insurance Soc.; Member: Deptl Cttee on Official Secrets Act 1911; Defence, Press and Broadcasting Cttee, 1964-75; West Midlands Econ. Planning Council, 1975-; Press Council, 1976-. Pres., Guild of British Newspaper Editors, 1974-75. *Address:* Fox Hill, 30 Linden Road, Bournville, Birmingham B30 1JU. *T:* 021-472 1509.

OWENS, Richard Hugh M.; *see* Mills-Owens.

OWER, Dr David Cheyne, TD 1975; Senior Principal Medical Officer, Department of Health and Social Security, since 1976; *b* 29 July 1931; *s* of Ernest Ower and Helen Edith Cheyne (*née* Irvine); *m* 1954, June Harris; two *s* two *d.* *Educ:* King's Coll. Sch., Wimbledon; King's Coll., London; King's Coll. Hosp. Med. Sch. (MB, BS 1954). DObstRCOG 1959; MFCM 1976. Jun. hosp. appts, King's Coll. Hosp. and Kingston Hosp., 1955; RAF Med. Br., 1956-58; gen. practice, 1959-64; DHSS (formerly Min. of Health) Med. Staff, 1965-. T&AVR, and RAMC(V), 1962-; Lt-Col RAMC(V); CO 221 (Surrey) Field Amb., 1973-75. *Recreations:* music, bridge, thinking about playing golf. *Address:* Merlewood, 94 Coombe Lane West, Kingston-upon-Thames, Surrey. *T:* 01-942 8552.

OWO, The Olowo of; *see* Olagbegi II.

OXBURY, Harold Frederick, CMG 1961; Deputy Director-General, British Council, 1962-66 (Assistant Director-General, 1959); *b* 11 Nov. 1903; *s* of Fredric Thomas Oxbury; *m* 1st, 1928, Violet Bennets (*d* 1954); one *s* one *d*; 2nd, 1954, Helen Shipley (*d* 1975), *d* of Amos Perry, FLS, VMH. *Educ:* Norwich Sch.; Trinity Coll., Cambridge (Senior Scholar). Entered Indian Civil Service, 1928; Chief Collector of Customs, Burma, 1940; Government of Burma Representative, Burma Office, 1942-44; Dep. Controller Finance (Colonel), Military Administration, Burma, 1945; Finance Secretary, Government of Burma, 1946; British Council: Director, Colonies Dept, 1947; Controller Finance, 1956. *Recreations:* gardening, writing, painting. *Address:* Huntersmoon, Horton-cum-Studley, Oxon.

OXFORD, CHRIST CHURCH, Dean of; *see* Chadwick, Very Rev. Henry.

OXFORD, Archdeacon of; *see* Witton-Davies, Ven. Carlyle.

OXFORD, Kenneth Gordon, QPM 1976; Chief Constable, Merseyside Police, since 1976; *b* Lambeth, 25 June 1924; *s* of Ernest George Oxford and late Gladys Violet (*née* Seaman); *m* 1954, Muriel (*née* Panton). *Educ:* Caldecot Sch., Lambeth. MBIM. RAF, 1942-47. Metropolitan Police, 1947-69, with final rank Det. Ch. Supt, following Intermed. Comd Course, 1966, Sen. Staff Course, 1968, The Police Coll., Bramshill; Asst Chief Constable (Crime), Northumberland Constabulary, 1969; Northumbria Police, 1974; Dep. Chief Constable, Merseyside Police, 1974-75. Member: Forensic Science Soc., 1970; Medico-Legal Soc., 1975; Vice-Chm., Merseyside Br., British Inst. of Management, 1975-; Merseyside County Dir, St John's Ambulance Assoc., 1976-. OStJ 1977. *Recreations:* cricket, music, books, roses. *Address:* 244 Prescot Road, St Helen's, Merseyside WA10 1HS. *T:* St Helen's 55965. *Clubs:* Royal Commonwealth Society; Surrey CCC; Liverpool Cricket.

OXFORD AND ASQUITH, 2nd Earl of, *cr* 1925; **Julian Edward George Asquith,** KCMG 1964 (CMG 1961); Viscount Asquith, *cr* 1925; Governor and Commander-in-Chief, Seychelles, 1962-67; Commissioner, British Indian Ocean Territory, 1965-67; *b* 22 April 1916; *o s* of late Raymond Asquith and Katharine Frances (*d* 1976), *d* of late Sir John Horner, KCVO; *S* grandfather, 1928; *m* 1947, Anne Mary Celestine, CStJ, *d* of late Sir Michael Palairet, KCMG; two *s* three *d.* *Educ:* Ampleforth; Balliol Coll., Oxford (Scholar). 1st Class Lit. Hum., 1938. Lieut, RE, 1941; Assistant District Commissioner, Palestine, 1942-48; Dep. Chief Secretary, British Administration, Tripolitania, 1949; Director of the Interior, Government of Tripolitania, 1951; Adviser to Prime Minister of Libya, 1952; Administrative Secretary, Zanzibar, 1955; Administrator of St Lucia, WI, 1958. KStJ. *Heir: s* Viscount Asquith, *qv. Address:* The Manor House, Mells, Frome, Somerset. *T:* Mells 812324. *Club:* Bath.

See also Baron Hylton .

OXFUIRD, 12th Viscount of, *cr* 1651; **(John) Donald (Alexander Arthur) Makgill;** Bt 1627; Lord Macgill of Cousland 1651; late Lt Coldstream Guards; RARO; *b* 31 Dec. 1899; *e s* of Sir George Makgill, 11th Bt (*de jure* 11th Viscount) and Frances Elizabeth (*d* 1947), *e d* of Alexander Innes Grant, of Merchiston, Otago, NZ; *S* father, 1926; claim to Viscountcy admitted by Committee for Privileges, House of Lords, 1977; *m* 1927, Esther Lilian (marr. diss. 1943), *y d* of late Sir Robert Bromley, KCMG; one *d*; *m* 1955, Mrs Maureen Gillington, *y d* of late Lt-Col A. T. S. Magan, CMG. *Recreation:* fishing. *Heir: nephew* George Hubbard Makgill [*b* 7 Jan. 1934; *m* 1967, Alison Campbell (marr. diss. 1977), *d* of late Neils Max Jensen, Randers, Denmark; three *s* (inc. twin *s*)]. *Address:* The Flat, Blairquhan, Maybole, Ayrshire. *T:* Straiton 278. *Club:* New (Edinburgh).

OXLEY, Humphrey Leslie Malcolm, CMG 1966; OBE 1956; HM Diplomatic Service, retired; *b* 9 Oct. 1909; *s* of W. H. F. Oxley, MRCS, LRCP, FRCOG, and Lily Malcolm; *m* 1945, Frances Olga, *d* of George Bowden, San Jose, Costa Rica; twin *s.* *Educ:* Epsom Coll. Admitted Solicitor, 1933; Junior Legal Assistant, India Office, 1933; Commissioner for Oaths, 1934; Assistant Solicitor, 1944; Commonwealth Relations Office, 1947; Assistant Legal Adviser, 1961; Legal Counsellor, Commonwealth Office, 1965-67; HM Diplomatic Service, 1967; Dep. Legal Adviser, FCO, 1967-69. Legal Consultant to HM Comr, Magistrate, various legal appts, Anguilla, 1971-72. *Recreations:* sailing, gardening. *Address:* Sandpipers, Crooked Lane, Birdham, Chichester, West Sussex. *Club:* Civil Service.

OXLEY, James Keith R.; *see* Rice-Oxley.

OXLEY, Maj.-General Walter Hayes, CB 1947; CBE 1941; MC 1916; *b* 2 Jan. 1891; *s* of late Edward Hayes Oxley and Bessie Eleanor Paton; *d* of late J. P. Hindley; *m* 1921, Margaret, *d* of late W. James Smith, JP, Gibraltar and Villa Viega, Algeciras; one *d*. *Educ:* Eastbourne Coll.; RMA, Woolwich. 2nd Lieut, RE, 1911; served European War, 1914-18, in Egypt, Palestine and Macedonia (despatches, MC, Bt Major); Egyptian Army, 1918-19; psc; Military Attaché HM Legations, Belgrade and Prague; Bt Lieut-Colonel, 1931; AQMG British Military Mission to Egyptian Army; Order of Nile, 3rd Class; Brigadier, i/c Admin., Malta; War of 1939-45, commanded 2nd Inf. Bde, Malta, then 7th Inf. Bde 3rd Division in UK; GOC Malta, 1943-44; Commissioner British Military Mission, Bulgaria, 1944-47. Acting Maj.-General, 1943; Temp. Maj.-General, 1944; ADC to the King, 1943-48; retired pay, 1948. *Recreations:* shooting, fishing and golf. *Address:* Charminster House, Dorchester, Dorset. *T:* Dorchester 238. *Club:* Naval and Military.

OXMANTOWN, Lord; William Brendan Parsons; Deputy Resident Representative of UN Development Programme in Bangladesh, since 1975; *b* 21 Oct. 1936; *s* and *heir* of 6th Earl of Rosse, *qv; m* 1966, Alison Margaret, *er d* of Major J. D. Cooke-Hurle, Startforth Hall, Barnard Castle, Co. Durham; one *s* one *d. Educ:* Eton; Grenoble Univ.; Christ Church, Oxford. BA 1961, MA 1964. 2nd Lieut, Irish Guards, 1955-57. UN Official appointed successively: Admin. Officer, UNTAB, Ghana, 1963-65; Asst Resident Rep., UNDP, Dahomey, 1965-68; Area Officer for Mid-West Africa, 1968-70; Asst Resident Rep., UNDP, Iran, 1970-75. *Heir: s* Hon. Laurence Patrick Parsons, *b* 31 March 1969. *Address:* (home) Birr Castle, Co. Offaly, Ireland. *T:* Birr 23.

P

PÄCHT, Otto Ernst, MA, DPhil; FBA 1956; Professor in the History of Art, and Director of the Kunsthistorisches Institut, Vienna University, 1963-72, now Professor Emeritus; *b* Vienna, 7 Sept. 1902; *s* of David and Josephine Pächt; *m* 1940, Jeanne Michalopulo (*d* 1971); one *s. Educ:* Vienna and Berlin Universities. Lecturer in History of Art: Heidelberg Univ., 1933; Oriel Coll., Oxford, 1945. Senior Lecturer in Medieval Art, 1952, Reader, 1962, Oxford Univ. Lyell Reader, Oxford, 1971. Membre de la Société Archéologique française. Wirkl. Mitgl. Oesterr. Akad. Wissenschaft, 1967. Hon. DLitt Oxon, 1971. *Publications:* Oesterreichische Tafelmalerei der Gotik, 1929; Master of Mary of Burgundy, 1948; The St Albans Psalter, 1960; The Rise of Pictorial Narrative in Twelfth-century England, 1962; Vita Sancti Simperti, 1964; (ed with J. J. G. Alexander) Illuminated Manuscripts in the Bodleian Library, 1973; (ed with D. Thoss) Illuminated Manuscripts in the Austrian National Library, French School, 1974; (ed with U. Jenni) Illuminated Manuscripts in the Austrian National Library, Dutch School, 1975; contrib. to Kritische Berichte, Kunstwissenschaftliche Forschungen, Burlington Magazine, Journal of the Warburg Institute, Revue des Arts; Jahrbuch der Kunsthistorischen Sammlungen, Wien. *Address:* Pötzleinsdorferstrasse 66, 1180 Vienna, Austria.

PACK, Prof. Donald Cecil, OBE 1969; MA, DSc, FIMA, FRSE, FEIS; Professor of Mathematics, University of Strathclyde, Glasgow, since 1953, Vice-Principal, 1968-72; *b* 14 April 1920; *s* of late John Cecil and late Minnie Pack, Higham Ferrers; *m* 1947, Constance Mary Gillam; two *s* one *d. Educ:* Wellingborough School; New Coll., Oxford. Lecturer in Mathematics, University College, Dundee, University of St Andrews, 1947-52; Visiting Research Associate, University of Maryland, 1951-52; Lecturer in Mathematics, University of Manchester, 1952-53. Member: Dunbartonshire Educn Cttee, 1960-66; Gen. Teaching Council for Scotland, 1966-73; Chairman: Scottish Certificate of Educn Examn Bd, 1969-77; Cttee of Inquiry into Truancy and Indiscipline in Schools in Scotland, 1974-77; Mem. of various Govt Scientific Cttees, 1952-; Hon. Treasurer of Institute of Mathematics and its Applications, 1964-72; Mem., British Nat. Cttee for Theoretical and Applied Mechanics, 1973-. Governor, Hamilton Coll. of Education, 1977-. *Publications:* Papers on fluid dynamics. *Recreations:* music, gardening, golf. *Address:* 3 Horseshoe Road, Bearsden, Glasgow. *T:* 041-942 5764.

PACK, Captain Stanley Walter Croucher, CBE 1957; RN, 1927-60; author since 1927; *b* 14 Dec. 1904; *s* of Walter Edward Pack and Beatrice Eleanor (*née* Croucher); *m* 1934, Dorothea Edna Mary (*née* Rowe); one *s* one *d. Educ:* St John's, Malta; Imperial College of Science. Whitworth Scholar, 1924; John Samuel Scholar, 1925; 1st class hons BSc (Engineering) 1926; ACGI 1926; MSc 1927; DIC 1927. Served War of 1939-45: HMS Formidable, 1940-41; British Commonwealth Secretary, Combined Meteorological Cttee, Washington, 1941-43; Chief Naval Met. Officer to SACSEA, 1945. Dep. Director, Naval Weather Service, Admiralty, 1951-54; Dep. Director, Naval Education Service, Admiralty, 1956-58; ADC to the Queen, 1957-60; retired RN, 1960. Sen. Lectr, Britannia RNC, Dartmouth, 1963-69. Member: Soc. of Authors; Council, Navy Records Soc.; Cttee, Old Centralians Assoc.; MIEE 1946; FRMetS 1950. Boyle Somerville Memorial Prize for Meteorology, 1938. Officer, Legion of Merit, USA, 1948. *Publications:* Anson's Voyage, 1947; Weather Forecasting, 1948; Admiral Lord Anson, 1960; Battle of Matapan, 1961; Windward of the Caribbean, 1964; The Wager Mutiny, 1965; Britannia at Dartmouth, 1966; Sea Power in the Mediterranean, 1971; Night Action off Cape Matapan, 1972; The Battle for Crete, 1973; Cunningham the Commander, 1974; The Battle of Sirte, 1975; The Allied Invasion of Sicily, 1977; contributions to Blackwood's Magazine, 1937- and to Daily Telegraph, Sunday Times, The Field, The Navy, etc. *Recreations:* music, painting. *Address:* Blossom's Pasture, Strete, Dartmouth, Devon. *T:* Stoke Fleming 254. *Club:* Royal Ocean Racing (Life Mem.; first qualified Fastnet Race, 1929, and Santander Race, 1930).

PACKARD, Lt.-Gen. Sir (Charles) Douglas, KBE 1957 (CBE 1945; OBE 1942); CB 1949; DSO 1943; retired as GOC-in-C Northern Ireland Command, 1958-61; *b* 17 May 1903; *s* of late Capt. C. T. Packard, MC, Copdock, near Ipswich; *m* 1937, Marion Lochhead; one *s* two *d. Educ:* Winchester; Royal Military Academy, Woolwich. 2nd Lieut, RA, 1923; served War of 1939-45, in Middle East and Italy (despatches, OBE, DSO, CBE); Dep.-Chief of Staff, 15th Army Group, 1944-45; Temp. Maj.-Gen. and Chief of Staff, Allied Commission for Austria (British Element), 1945-46; Director of Military Intelligence, WO, 1948-49; Commander British Military Mission in Greece, 1949-51; Chief of Staff, GHQ, MELF, 1951-53; Vice-Quarter-Master-General War Office, 1953-56; Military Adviser to the West African Governments, 1956-58. Lt-Gen. 1957. Col Comdt, RA, 1957-62. Officer Legion of Merit (USA). *Recreation:* sailing. *Address:* 103a Thoro'fare, Woodbridge, Suffolk IP12 1AS. *T:* Woodbridge 4729.

PACKARD, Vance (Oakley); Author; *b* 22 May 1914; *s* of Philip and Mabel Packard; *m* 1938, Mamie Virginia Mathews; two *s* one *d. Educ:* Pennsylvania State Univ.; Columbia Univ. Reporter, The Boston Record, 1938; Feature Editor, The Associated Press, 1939-42; Editor and Staff Writer, The American Magazine, 1942-56; Staff writer, Colliers, 1956; Distinguished Alumni Award, Pennsylvania State University, 1961; Outstanding Alumni Award, Columbia University Graduate School of Journalism, 1963. LittD Monmouth Coll., 1974. *Publications:* (books on social criticism): The Hidden Persuaders, 1957; The Status Seekers, 1959; The Waste Makers, 1960; The Pyramid Climbers, 1962; The Naked Society, 1964; The Sexual Wilderness, 1968; A Nation of Strangers, 1972; The People Shapers, 1977; numerous articles for The Atlantic Monthly. *Recreations:* reading, boating. *Address:* Mill Road, New Canaan, Conn 06840, USA. *T:* WO 6-1707.

PADLEY, Walter Ernest; MP (Lab) Ogmore Division of Mid-Glamorgan, since 1950; Member National Executive Committee of Labour Party, since 1956 (Chairman, Labour Party, 1965-66; Chairman, Overseas Cttee, 1963-71); *b* 24 July 1916; *s* of Ernest and Mildred Padley; *m* 1942, Sylvia Elsie Wilson; one *s* one *d. Educ:* Chipping Norton Grammar Sch.; Ruskin Coll., Oxford. Active in distributive workers' trade union, 1933-; President, Union of Shop, Distributive and Allied Workers, 1948-64. Member of National Council of Independent Labour Party, 1940-46. Minister of State for Foreign Affairs, 1964-67. *Publications:* The Economic Problem of the Peace, 1944; Am I My Brother's Keeper?, 1945; Britain: Pawn or Power?, 1947; USSR: Empire or Free Union?, 1948. *Address:* 73 Priory Gardens, Highgate, N6. *T:* 01-340 2969.

PADMORE, Sir Thomas, GCB 1965 (KCB 1953; CB 1947); MA; FCIT; Director, Laird Group Ltd; *b* 23 April 1909; *e s* of Thomas William Padmore, Sheffield; *m* 1st, 1934, Alice (*d* 1963), *d* of Robert Alcock, Ormskirk; two *d* (one *s* decd); 2nd, 1964, Rosalind Culhane, *qv. Educ:* Central Sch., Sheffield; Queens' Coll., Cambridge (Foundation Scholar; Hon. Fellow, 1961). Secretaries' Office, Board of Inland Revenue, 1931-34; transferred to Treasury, 1934; Principal Private Secretary to Chancellor of Exchequer, 1943-45; Second Secretary, 1952-62; Permanent Sec., Min. of Transport, 1962-68. *Address:* 39 Cholmeley Crescent, Highgate, N6. *T:* 01-340 6587. *Club:* Reform.

PADMORE, Lady (Thomas); *see* Culhane, Rosalind.

PAFFARD, Rear-Admiral (retired) Ronald Wilson, CB 1960; CBE 1943; *b* Ludlow, 14 Feb. 1904; 4th *s* of Murray Paffard and Fanny (*née* Wilson); *m* 1933, Nancy Brenda Malim; one *s* one *d*. *Educ:* Maidstone Grammar Sch. Paymaster Cadetship in RN, 1922; Paymaster Commander, 1940; Captain (S), 1951; Rear-Admiral, 1957. Secretary to Adm. of the Fleet Lord Tovey in all his Flag appointments, including those throughout the War of 1939-45; Supply Officer of HMS Vengeance, 1946-48; Portsmouth Division, Reserve Fleet, 1948-50; HMS Eagle, 1950-51; Asst Director-General, Supply and Secretarial Branch, 1952-54; Commanding Officer, HMS Ceres, 1954-56; Chief Staff Officer (Administration) on staff of Commander-in-Chief, Portsmouth, 1957-60, retired. *Recreations:* painting, golf. *Address:* 2 Little Green Orchard, Alverstoke, Hants PO12 2EY.

PAFFORD, John Henry Pyle, MA, DLit (London); FSA; FLA; Goldsmiths' Librarian of the University of London, 1945-67; *b* 6 March 1900; *s* of John Pafford and Bessie (*née* Pyle); *m* 1941, Elizabeth Ford, *d* of R. Charles Ford and Margaret Harvey; one *d* (and one *d* decd). *Educ:* Trowbridge High Sch.; University Coll., London (Fellow, 1956). Library Asst, University College, London, 1923-25; Librarian, and Tutor, Selly Oak Colleges, 1925-31; Sub-Librarian, National Central Library, 1931-45; Lecturer at University of London School of Librarianship, 1937-61. Editor, Year's Work in Librarianship, 1935-38 (jointly), and 1939-46; Library Adviser, Inter-Univ. Council for Higher Education Overseas, 1960-68. *Publications:* Bale's King Johan, 1931, and The Sodder'd Citizen, 1936 (Malone Society); Library Co-operation in Europe, 1935; Accounts of Parliamentary Garrisons of Great Chalfield and Malmesbury, 1645-46, 1940; Books and Army Education, 1946; W. P. Ker, A Bibliography, 1950; The Winter's Tale (Arden Shakespeare), 1963; Watts's Divine Songs for Children, 1971; L. Bryskett's Literary Works, 1972; (with E. R. Pafford) Employer and Employed, 1974. *Address:* Hillside, Allington Park, Bridport, Dorset DT6 5DD. *T:* Bridport 22829.

PAGAN, Brig. Sir John (Ernest), Kt 1971; CMG 1969; MBE (Mil.) 1944; ED; Chairman: P. Rowe Holdings Pty Ltd, since 1958; Associated National Insurance Co. Ltd, since 1973; Director: NSW Permanent Building Society Ltd; D. J. Properties Ltd; *b* 13 May 1914; *s* of late D. C. Pagan, Hay, NSW; *m* 1948, Marjorie Hoskins; one *s* two *d*. *Educ:* St Peter's Coll., Adelaide. Served RAA, AIF, Middle East, Papua/New Guinea, 1939-45, 2/1st AA Regt; 2/4th LAA Regt 9 Div. Finschhafen 1943; Citizen Military Forces, E Command; Lt-Col 1948, Brig. 1958; Hon. Col, Corps of School Cadets, 1970-72; Representative Col Comdt in Australia, Royal Regt of Australian Artillery. Hon. ADC to Governor of NSW, 1950-55; Member: Nat. Council, Scout Assoc. of Austr.; NSW Council, Girl Guides Assoc.; Mem. Board, NSW Soc. for Crippled Children, 1967-; Vice-Pres., Council, Big Brother Movement, 1947-; Mem. Board, Church of England Retirement Villages, 1961-; Mem., Commonwealth Immigration Adv. Council, 1959-70. Vice-Pres., Nat. Parks and Wildlife Foundn. Governor, Frensham Sch., 1968-70; Councillor, Nat. Heart Foundn, 1969-; Chm., Red Shield Appeal, 1975; Member: Bd, Royal Prince Alfred Hospital, 1974-; NSW Exec., Inst. of Public Affairs, 1975-. Pres., Australian Bobsleigh Assoc., 1974-. Liberal Party of Australia: State Pres., NSW, 1963-66; Federal Pres., 1966-70; Agent-General for NSW in London, 1970-72. Freeman, City of London, 1973. CStJ 1972. *Address:* 2 Lincoln Place, Edgecliff, NSW 2027, Australia; Kennerton Green, Mittagong, NSW 2575, Australia. *Clubs:* White's, MCC (London); Imperial Service, Union, Royal Sydney Golf (Sydney); Melbourne (Melbourne).

PAGE, Sir Alexander Warren (Sir Alex Page), Kt 1977; MBE 1943; Chairman, Metal Box Ltd since 1970 (Chief Executive, 1970-77); *b* 1 July 1914; *s* of Sydney E. Page and Phyllis (*née* Spencer); *m* 1940, Anne Lewis Hickman (marr. diss.); two *s* one *d*. *Educ:* Tonbridge; Clare Coll., Cambridge (MA). Served REME, with Guards Armoured Div., 1940-45, Lt-Col REME. Joined The Metal Box Co. Ltd, 1936; joined board as Sales Dir, 1957; Man. Dir 1966; Dep. Chm. 1969. Mem., IBA (formerly ITA), 1970-76; Mem., Food Science and Technology Bd., 1973-. FIMechE; FBIM. Governor, Colfe's Grammar Sch., Lewisham, 1977-. *Recreations:* golf, tennis, squash. *Address:* Merton Place, Dunsfold, Godalming, Surrey. *T:* Dunsfold 211. *Club:* Bath.

PAGE, Ven. Alfred Charles; Archdeacon of Leeds since 1969; Hon. Canon of Ripon since 1966; *b* 24 Dec. 1912; *s* of late Henry Page, Homersfield, Suffolk; *m* 1944, Margaret Stevenson, *d* of late Surtees Foster Dodd, Sunderland, Co. Durham. *Educ:* Bungay Grammar Sch.; Corpus Christi Coll., Cambridge (MA); Wycliffe Hall, Oxford. Curate: Wortley-de-Leeds, 1936; Leeds Parish Church, 1940 (Sen. Curate and Priest-in-charge of S Mary, Quarry Hill, 1941); Vicar: St Mark, Woodhouse, Leeds, 1944; Rothwell, Yorks, 1955. Rural Dean of Whitkirk, 1961-69; Surrogate, 1963; Vicar of Arthington, 1969-73. *Recreation:* photography. *Address:* 25 Church Lane, Adel, Leeds LS16 8DQ. *T:* Leeds 674501. *Club:* Leeds (Leeds).

PAGE, Col Alfred John, CB 1964; TD 1945; DL; Chairman, TA&VR Association for Greater London, 1968-71 (Chairman, County of London T&AFA, 1957-68); *b* 3 January 1912; *s* of Harry Gould Page, Surbiton, Surrey; *m* 1941, Sheila Margaret Aileen (marr. diss. 1966), *d* of Charles Skinner Wilson, Ugley, Essex; one *s* two *d*; *m* 1969, Margaret Mary Juliet Driver, widow of Harold Driver. *Educ:* Westminster School. 2nd Lt 19th London Regt (TA), 1931. Served 1939-45 with RA in AA Comd. Brevet Colonel 1952; ADC (TA) to the Queen, 1961-66; Hon. Col, Greater London Regt RA (Territorials), 1967-71; Dep. Hon. Col, 6th Bn, Queen's Regt, T&AVR, 1971-72. Master, Worshipful Co. of Pattenmakers, 1973-74. DL Co. of London, 1951; DL Greater London, 1965. *Address:* 66 Iverna Court, W8. *T:* 01-937 2590. *Club:* Army and Navy.

PAGE, Annette, (Mrs Ronald Hynd); Ballerina of the Royal Ballet, 1959-67, retired; Member, Arts Council of Great Britain, since 1976; *b* 18 Dec. 1932; *d* of James Lees and Margaret Page; *m* 1957, Ronald Hynd, *qv*; one *d*. *Educ:* Royal Ballet School. Audition and award of scholarship to Roy. Ballet Sch., 1944. Entry into touring company of Royal Ballet (then Sadler's Wells Theatre Ballet), 1950; promotion to major Royal Ballet Co. (Sadler's Wells Ballet), 1955. *Roles include:* The Firebird, Dec. 1958; Princess Aurora, May 1959; Odette-Odile, June 1959; Giselle, March 1960; Lise in La Fille Mal Gardée, 1963; Romeo and Juliet, 1965; Cinderella, 1966. *Recreations:* music, books.

PAGE, Anthony (Frederick Montague); *b* 21 Sept. 1935; *s* of Frederick Charles Graham Page and Pearl Valerie Montague Hall. *Educ:* Oakley Hall, Cirencester; Winchester Coll. (Schol.); Magdalen Coll., Oxford (Schol., BA); Neighborhood Playhouse Sch. of the Theater, NY. Asst, Royal Court Theatre, 1958: co-directed Live Like Pigs, directed The Room; Artistic Dir, Dundee Repertory Theatre, 1962; The Caretaker, Oxford and Salisbury; Women Beware Women, and Nil Carborundum, Royal Shakespeare Co., 1963; BBC Directors' Course, then several episodes of Z-Cars, Horror of Darkness and 1st TV prodn Stephen D; Jt Artistic Dir, Royal Court, 1964-65; directed Inadmissible Evidence (later Broadway and film), A Patriot for Me, 1st revival of Waiting for Godot, Cuckoo in the Nest; Diary of a Madman, Duchess, 1966; Artistic Dir, two seasons at Royal Court: Uncle Vanya, 1970; Alpha Beta (also film); Hedda Gabler; Krapp's Last Tape; Not I; Cromwell; other plays transf. from Royal Court to West End: Time Present; Hotel in Amsterdam; revival, Look Back in Anger; West of Suez; directed Hamlet, Nottingham, 1970; Rules of the Game, National Theatre; King Lear, Amer. Shakespeare Fest., 1975. TV prodns include: The Parachute; Emlyn; Hotel in Amsterdam; Speaking of Murder; You're Free; Pueblo (nominated for Emmy award); The Changeling; Headmaster; October Missiles (nominated for Emmy award); Scott Fitzgerald in Hollywood; Adam's Chronicle; I Never Promised You a Rose Garden (film). Directors' and Producers' Award for TV Dir of Year, 1966. *Recreations:* movies, reading, riding, travelling. *Address:* 68 Ladbroke Grove, W11.

PAGE, (Arthur) John; MP (C) Harrow West since March 1960; *b* 16 Sept. 1919; *s* of Sir Arthur Page, QC (late Chief Justice of Burma), and Lady Page, KiH; *m* 1950, Anne, *d* of Charles Micklem, DSO, JP, DL, Longcross House, Surrey; four *s*. *Educ:* Harrow, Magdalene College, Cambridge. Joined RA as Gunner, 1939, commissioned, 1940; served War of 1939-45, Western Desert (wounded), France, Germany; demobilised as Major, comdg 258 Battery Norfolk Yeomanry, 1945; various positions in industry and commerce, 1946-63. Chm. Bethnal Green and E London Housing Assoc., 1957-; contested (C) Eton and Slough, Gen. Election, 1959. PPS to Parly Under-Sec. of State, Home Office, 1961-63; Conservative Parly Labour Affairs Cttee: Sec., 1960-61, 1964-, Vice-Chm., 1964-69, Chm., 1970-74; Sec., Conservative Broadcasting Cttee, 1974-76. Pres., Cons. Trade Unionists Nat. Adv. Council, 1967-69; Member: Parly Select Cttee on Race Relations and Immigration, 1970-71; British Delegn to Council of Europe and WEU, 1972- (Chm. Budget Cttee, 1973-74, Social and Health Cttee, 1975-). Mem. Exec., IPU, British Gp, 1970 (Treasurer, 1974-77; Vice-Chm., 1977-); Pres., Independent Schools Assoc., 1971-; Chm., Council for Indep. Educn, 1974-. *Recreations:* painting and politics. *Address:* Hitcham Lodge, Taplow, Bucks. *T:* Burnham 5056. *Clubs:* Brooks's, MCC.

PAGE, Bertram Samuel; University Librarian and Keeper of the Brotherton Collection, University of Leeds, 1947-69, Emeritus Librarian, since 1969; *b* 1 Sept. 1904; *s* of Samuel and Catherine Page; *m* 1933, Olga Ethel, *d* of E. W. Mason. *Educ:* King Charles I School Kidderminster; University of Birmingham. BA 1924, MA 1926. Asst Librarian (later Sub-Librarian), Univ. of Birmingham, 1931-36; Librarian, King's College, Newcastle upon Tyne, 1936-47. Pres. Library Assoc., 1960 (Hon. Fellow, 1961); Chairman: Standing Conf. of Nat. and Univ. Libraries, 1961-63; Exec. Cttee, Nat. Central Library, 1962-72 (Trustee, 1963-75); Librarianship Bd, Council for Nat. Academic Awards, 1966-71. Mem. Court of Univ. of Birmingham, 1954-69. Hon. DUniv. York, 1968. *Publications:* contrib. to Stephen MacKenna's trans. of Plotinus, vol. 5, 1930 (revised whole trans. for 2nd, 3rd, 4th edns, 1958, 1962, 1969); A Manual of University and College Library Practice (jt ed.), 1940; articles and reviews in classical and library jls. *Address:* 24 St Anne's Road, Headington, Oxford. *T:* Oxford 65981.

PAGE, Maj.-Gen. Charles Edward, CB 1974; MBE 1944; Independent Telecommunications Consultant; *b* 23 Aug. 1920; *s* of late Sir (Charles) Max Page, KBE, CB, DSO, FRCS and Lady (Helen) Page; *m* 1948, Elizabeth Marion, *d* of late Sir William Smith Crawford, KBE; two *s* one *d. Educ:* Marlborough Coll.; Trinity Coll., Cambridge. BSc (Eng) London 1949; CEng, FIEE 1968. Commissioned 2nd Lieut Royal Signals from TA, 1941; regimental appts Guards Armd Divisional Signals, 1941-45; CO 19 Indian Div. Signals, 1945-46; GSO1 Air Formation Signals Far East, 1946-47; Student RMCS, 1947-49; psc 1951; GSO2 British Middle East Office, 1952-55; GSO2 Staff Coll., 1955-58; Sqdn Comdr 30 Signal Regt, 1959; GSO1 Combat Develt Directorate, WO, 1960-63; CO 1st Div. Signal Regt, 1963-65; Student NATO Defence Coll., 1965-66; CCR Signals 1 (BR) Corps, 1966-68; Sec., NATO Mil. Cttee, Brussels, 1968-70; DCD(A) MoD, 1971-74; retired 1974. Col Comdt, Royal Corps of Signals, 1974-. Hon. Col, Women's Transport Service (FANY), 1976. *Recreations:* shooting, golf, fishing, photography. *Address:* 6 Cheyne Gardens, SW3 5QU. *T:* 01-352 5674. *Club:* Bath.

PAGE, (Charles) James; QPM 1971; HM Inspector of Constabulary, since 1977; *b* 31 May 1925; *s* of Charles Page and Mabel Cowan; *m* 1st, 1947, Margaret Dobson; two *s* one *d*; 2nd, 1971, Shirley Marina Woodward. *Educ:* Sloane Grammar Sch., Chelsea. Served War, RAF, 1943-47. Blackpool Police, 1947-57; Metropolitan Police, 1957-67; City of London Police, 1967-77; apptd Asst Commissioner, 1969; Comr, 1971-77. Dir, Police Extended Interviews, 1975-. FBIM 1975. CStJ 1974. Officer of Légion d'Honneur, 1976, and other foreign decorations. *Recreations:* fell walking, photography. *Address:* Wild Goose Cottage, Rogerground, Hawkshead, Cumbria. *Club:* City Livery.

PAGE, Cyril Leslie, OBE 1965; Controller, Personnel, Television, BBC Television Service, 1971-76, retired; *b* 20 Oct. 1916; *s* of Cyril Herbert Page and Rosamund Clara Page; *m* 1939, Barbara Mary Rowland; one *s* one *d. Educ:* Sherborne Sch. Royal Air Force, 1936-46 (Wing Comdr). British Broadcasting Corporation, 1946-: Asst, Appts Dept, 1947; Asst Admin. Officer, Overseas Services, 1949; Asst Head of TV Admin., 1951; Establt Officer, TV, 1958; Head of TV Establt Dept, 1961; Asst Controller, TV Admin., 1964. Member: Ealing, Hammersmith and Hounslow AHA(T); Council, Royal Postgrad. Med. Sch., 1975; Cttee of Management, Inst. of Obstetrics and Gynaecology, 1973; Special Trustee, Hammersmith Hosp., 1974. *Recreations:* reading, gardening. *Address:* Fairfield, 96 Norbury Hill, SW16 3RT.

PAGE, Rt. Rev. Dennis Fountain; *see* Lancaster, Bishop Suffragan of.

PAGE, Sir Denys (Lionel), Kt 1971; LittD 1960; FBA 1952; Master of Jesus College, Cambridge, 1959-73, Hon. Fellow, 1976; Regius Professor of Greek, Cambridge University, 1950-73; Hon. Student of Christ Church, Oxford; Hon. Fellow of Trinity College, Cambridge; *b* 1908; *s* of F. H. D. Page, OBE, and late Elsie Page, MBE; *m* 1938, Katharine Elizabeth, *d* of late Joseph Michael and Edith Hall Dohan, Philadelphia, Pa, USA; four *d. Educ:* Newbury; Christ Church, Oxford (Schol.). 1st Cl. Hons Class. Mods, Chancellor's Prize for Latin Verse, Gaisford Prize for Greek Verse, de Paravicini Schol., Craven Schol., 1928; 1st Cl. Lit. Hum., Derby, Univ. and Goldsmiths' Company's senior Schols, 1930. Vienna Univ., 1930-31; Lecturer of Christ Church, 1931-32; Student and Tutor, 1932-50; Senior Proctor, 1948-49. Lectures: Dean West, Princeton Univ., US, 1939; Flexner, Bryn Mawr, 1954; Sather, Univ. of California, 1957-58; Jackson, Harvard, 1972. Dept of Foreign Office, 1939-46. Head of Command Unit, Intelligence Division, HQ South-East Asia,

1945-46. Pres., British Academy, 1971-74. Foreign Member: Academy of Athens; Amer. Acad. of Arts and Scis; Amer. Philosophical Soc.; Hon. Fellow: Archæological Soc. of Athens; Hellenic Soc. of Humanities. Kenyon Medal, British Academy. Hon. LittD: Trinity Coll., Dublin; Newcastle; Hull; Bristol; Hon. DLitt Oxon. Comdr, Order of Merit, Poland. *Publications:* Actors' Interpolations in Greek Tragedy, 1934; Euripides' Medea, 1938; Greek Literary Papyri, 1941; Alcman, 1951; Corinna, 1953; Sappho and Alcaeus, 1955; The Homeric Odyssey, 1955; (co-editor), Poetarum Lesbiorum Fragmenta, 1955; (co-editor), Aeschylus, Agamemnon, 1957; History and the Homeric Iliad, 1959; Poetae Melici Graeci, 1962; The Oxyrhynchus Papyri, vol. xxix, 1964; (co-editor), The Greek Anthology: Hellenistic Epigrams, 1965; The Garland of Philip, 1968; Melica Graeca Selecta, 1968; The Santorini Volcano and the Destruction of Minoan Crete, 1971; (ed) Aeschylus, 1972; Folk Tales in the Odyssey, 1973; (ed) Supplementum Lyricis Graecis, 1975; (ed) Epigrammata Graeca, 1975; Rufinus, 1978. *Address:* Thorneyburn Lodge, Tarset, Northumberland. *T:* Greenhaugh 40272.

PAGE, Derek; *see* Page, J. D.

PAGE, Brig. (Edwin) Kenneth, CBE 1951 (OBE 1946); DSO 1945; MC 1918; *b* 23 Jan. 1898; *s* of G. E. Page, Baldock, Herts; *m* 1921, Kate Mildred (*d* 1975), *d* of G. H. Arthur, Yorkshire, Barbados, BWI; two *s. Educ:* Haileybury College; RMA, Woolwich. 2nd Lt, RFA, 1916; BEF, France, 1916-18. Adjt TA, 1924-27; Staff College, Camberley, 1928-29; Staff Captain, India, 1931-35; GSO2, War Office, 1936-39; Lt-Col, 1939; served War of 1939-45: BEF, France, 1940; Col, 1945; Brig., 1946; Dep. Director, WO, 1946-48; Commander, Caribbean Area, 1948-51; employed War Office, 1951; retired pay, 1952. CC 1961-74, CA 1968-74, Dorset. *Address:* 12 De Maulley Road, Canford Cliffs, Poole, Dorset. *T:* Canford Cliffs 707181. *Club:* Army and Navy.
    See also Prof. J. K. Page.

PAGE, Frederick William, CBE 1961; CEng, FRAeS; Chairman and Chief Executive, Aircraft Group of British Aerospace, since 1977; *b* 20 Feb. 1917; *s* of Richard Page and Ellen Potter; *m* 1940, Kathleen Edith de Courcy; three *s* one *d. Educ:* Rutlish Sch., Merton; St Catharine's Coll., Cambridge (MA). Joined Hawker Aircraft Co., in Design Office, 1938; English Electric, 1945; became Chief Engr, 1950, and Dir and Chief Exec. (Aircraft), English Electric Aviation, 1959; Managing Dir, Mil. Aircraft Div. of BAC, 1965-72, Chm., 1967; apptd Managing Dir (Aircraft), BAC, and Chm., Commercial Aircraft Div., 1972. Jt Chm. of SEPECAT, the Anglo-French co. formed for management of Jaguar programme, 1966; relinquished this Jt Chmship, 1973, but remained a Dir of SEPECAT; apptd to Bd of Panavia Aircraft GmbH, 1969, Chm. 1977; relinquished Chmship of BAC Mil. Aircraft Div., but retains a Directorship of the Div.; apptd Chm. BAC Ltd (a co. of Brit. Aerospace), 1977. Mem. Council, Soc. of Brit. Aerospace Cos Ltd; apptd to Bd of BAC (Operating) Ltd, also made Dir and Chief Exec. of BAC (Preston) Ltd, 1963; Dir, BAC (USA) Inc., 1975-77. British Gold Medal for Aeronautics, 1962; Gold Medal of Royal Aeronautical Soc., 1974; Hon. Fellow, UMIST, 1970; Fellow, Fellowship of Engrg, 1977. *Recreation:* gardening. *Address:* Renvyle, 60 Waverley Lane, Farnham, Surrey GU9 8BN. *T:* Farnham 4999. *Clubs:* United Oxford & Cambridge University, Royal Automobile.

PAGE, Rt. Hon. Graham; *see* Page, Rt Hon. R. G.

PAGE, Sir Harry (Robertson), Kt 1968; Consultant, Butler Till Ltd; Chairman, National Transport Tokens Ltd; *b* 14 Apr. 1911; *s* of late Henry Page and Dora (*née* Robertson); *m* 1937, Elsie Dixon; two *s. Educ:* Manchester Grammar Sch.; Manchester University. BA (Admin) 1932; MA (Admin) 1934. IPFA. Appointed City Treasurer's Dept, Manchester, 1927, Dep. Treasurer, 1952; Treasurer, 1957-71. Sen. Hon. Financial Adviser to Assoc. of Municipal Corps, 1962-71; Chm., Chancellor's Cttee to review Nat. Savings, 1971-73. Hon. Fellow, Manchester Polytechnic, 1970. Hon. Simon Res. Fellow, Manchester Univ., 1974. Freeman, City of London, 1976. Haldane Medal (RIPA), 1933. *Publications:* Co-ordination and Planning in the Local Authority, 1936; Councillor's Handbook, 1945; Local Government up-to-date, 1946; contrib. to symposium of papers given to British Assoc., Leeds, 1968; contribs to Local Govt Finance, Bank Reviews, financial jls, etc. *Recreation:* collecting Victorian and other nineteenth century ephemera; heraldry. *Address:* 205 Old Hall Lane, Fallowfield, Manchester M14 6HJ. *T:* 061-224 2891. *Club:* Manchester (formerly Reform, Manchester).

PAGE, James; see Page, C. J.

PAGE, John; see Page, A. J.

PAGE, John Brangwyn; Chief Cashier of the Bank of England since 1970; *b* 23 Aug. 1923; *s* of late Sidney John Page, CB, MC; *m* 1948, Gloria Vail; one *s* one *d. Educ:* Highgate Sch. (Foundation Schol.); King's Coll., Cambridge (BA). RAF, 1942-46; Cambridge, 1946-48; Bank of England, 1948; seconded to IMF, 1953; worked in various depts of Bank; Asst Chief Cashier, 1966; Deputy Chief Cashier, 1967; 1st Deputy Chief Cashier, 1968. FIB; FBIM. *Recreations:* gardening, music, travel. *Address:* Bank of England, EC2.

PAGE, (John) Derek; Director: Cambridge Chemical Co. Ltd, since 1962; Buckmaster and Page Ltd, since 1970; *b* 14 Aug. 1927; *s* of John Page and Clare Page (*née* Maher); *m* 1948, Catherine Audrey Halls; one *s* one *d. Educ:* St Bede's College, Manchester; London University. External BSc (Soc). MP (Lab) King's Lynn, 1964-70; contested (Lab) Norfolk NW, Feb. 1974. Member: E Anglia Economic Planning Council; Council of Management, COSIRA. *Recreation:* private pilot. *Address:* The Vicarage, Whaddon, Royston, Herts. *T:* Arrington 209. *Club:* Reform.

PAGE, Maj.-Gen. John Humphrey, CB 1977; OBE 1967; MC 1952; Director of Personal Services (Army), Ministry of Defence, 1974-78; *b* 5 March 1923; *s* of Captain W. J. Page, JP, Devizes and Alice Mary Page (*née* Richards); *m* 1956, Angela Mary Bunting; three *s* one *d. Educ:* Stonyhurst. Commnd into RE, 1942; served in NW Europe, India, Korea, ME and UK, 1942-60; Instr, Staff Coll., Camberley, 1960-62; comd 32 Armd Engr Regt, 1964-67; idc 1968; CCRE 1st Br. Corps, 1969-70; Asst Comdt, RMA Sandhurst, 1971-74. *Address:* c/o Lloyds Bank, Cox & King's Branch, 6 Pall Mall, SW1.

PAGE, John Joseph (Joffre), OBE 1959; Chairman, National Ports Council, since 1977; *b* 7 Jan. 1915; 2nd *s* of late William Joseph and Frances Page; *m* 1939, Cynthia Maynard, *d* of late L. M. Swan, CBE; two *s. Educ:* Emanuel School. RAF, 1933-38 and 1939-46 (despatches, 1943); Group Captain. Iraq Petroleum Group of Cos, 1938-39 and 1946-70; served in Palestine, Jordan, Lebanon, Syria, Iraq, Qatar, Bahrain and Abu Dhabi; Head Office, London, 1958-61; Gen. Man., 1955-58; Chief Representative, 1961-70; Chm., 1972-77, and Chief Exec., 1975-77, Mersey Docks and Harbour Co. Dep. Chm., British Ports Assoc., 1974-77. *Recreations:* photography, fishing, music. *Address:* Spring Hill, Hill Road, Helsby, Cheshire WA6 9AG. *T:* Helsby 2994. *Clubs:* Oriental, MCC.

PAGE, Prof. John Kenneth; Professor of Building Science, University of Sheffield, since 1960; *b* 3 Nov. 1924; *s* of Brig. E. K. Page, *qv*; *m* 1954, Anita Bell Lovell; two *s* two *d. Educ:* Haileybury College; Pembroke College, Cambridge. Served War of 1939-45, Royal Artillery, 1943-47. Asst Industrial Officer, Council of Industrial Design, 1950-51; taught Westminster School, 1952-53; Sen. Scientific Officer, Tropical Liaison Section, Building Research Station, 1953-56; Chief Research Officer, Nuffield Div. for Architectural Studies, 1956-57; Lecturer, Dept. of Building Science, Univ. of Liverpool, 1957-60. Former Chm., Environmental Gp, and Mem., Econ. Planning Council, Yorks and Humberside Region. Former Chm., UK Section, Internat. Solar Energy Soc. *Publications:* papers on Energy policy, Environmental Design and Planning, Building Climatology and Solar Energy. *Address:* c/o Department of Building Science, University of Sheffield, Western Bank, Sheffield S10 2TN. *T:* Sheffield 78555.

PAGE, Kenneth; see Page, Edwin Kenneth.

PAGE, Richard Lewis; MP (C) Workington, since Nov. 1976; *b* 22 Feb. 1941; *s* of Victor Charles and Kathleen Page; *m* 1964, Madeleine Ann Brown; one *s* one *d. Educ:* Hurstpierpoint Coll.; Luton Technical Coll. Apprenticeship, Vauxhall Motors, 1959-64; HNC Mech Engineering; Director of family company, 1964-76. Young Conservatives, 1964-66; Councillor, Banstead UDC, 1968-71; contested (C) Workington, Feb. and Oct. 1974. *Recreation:* most sport. *Address:* Brook Cottage, Gomshall, Surrey. *Club:* Rotary (Epsom).

PAGE, Rt. Hon. R(odney) Graham, PC 1972; MBE 1944; LLB (London); MP (C) Crosby since Nov. 1953; solicitor (admitted 1934); Privy Council Appeal Agent; *b* 30 June 1911; *s* of Lt-Col Frank Page, DSO and bar, and Margaret Payne Farley; *m* 1934, Hilda Agatha Dixon; one *s* one *d. Educ:* Magdalen College School, Oxford; London University (External). Served War of 1939-45: Flt-Lt, RAFVR. Chm., Select Cttee on Statutory Instruments, 1964-70, 1974-; an Opposition Front Bench

spokesman on Housing and Land, 1965-70; Minister of State, Min. of Housing and Local Govt, June-Oct. 1970; Minister for Local Govt and Develt, DoE, 1970-74. Vice-Chm., Parly All-Party Solicitors Gp. Promoter: (Private Member's Bills) Cheques Act, 1957, Wages Bill, 1958, Pawnbrokers Act, 1960; Road Safety Bills 1960, 1964, 1965; Stock Transfer Act, 1963; National Sweepstakes Bill, 1966; Lotteries Bill, 1974. Director: United Real Property Trust Ltd; John Howard (Northern) Ltd. Vice-Pres., National Chamber of Trade. Formerly: A Governor of St Thomas' Hosp., London; Treas., Pedestrians' Assoc. for Road Safety. Hon. FCIS; Hon. FIPA; Hon. FIWSP. *Publications:* Law Relating to Flats, 1934; Road Traffic Courts, 1938; Rent Acts, 1966; contributions to legal journals. *Address:* 21 Cholmeley Lodge, Cholmeley Park N6 5EN. *T:* 01-340 3579.

PAGE, William Frank, CMG 1946; *b* 26 June 1894; *s* of late W. T. Page, civil engineer, Worcester; *m* 1932, Kathleen Margaret, *d* of late Rev. C. A. Stooke, Combe Down, Bath. *Educ:* Clifton. South Wales Borderers, 1914-19, Gallipoli and France, temp. commission, Capt.; farming (War Settlement) Southern Rhodesia, 1919-21; Provincial Administration, Tanganyika Territory, 1922-47; Provincial Commissioner, 1944; Director of Man Power, 1942-46; retired, 1947. *Address:* Le Douit, Sous l'Eglise, St Saviour's, Guernsey, CI. *T:* Guernsey 63995.
See also Sir George Stooke.

PAGE WOOD, Sir Anthony John, 8th Bt, *cr* 1837; *b* 6 Feb. 1951; *s* of Sir David (John Hatherley) Page Wood, 7th Bt and Evelyn Hazel Rosemary, *d* of late Captain George Ernest Bellville; *S* father 1955. *Heir:* uncle, Matthew Page Wood [*b* 13 Aug. 1924; *m* 1947; two *d*].

PAGET, family name of **Marquess of Anglesey** and **Baron Paget of Northampton.**

PAGET OF NORTHAMPTON, Baron *cr* 1974 (Life Peer), of Lubenham, Leics; **Reginald Thomas Paget,** QC 1947; *b* 2 Sept. 1908; *m* 1931. *Educ:* Eton; Trinity College, Cambridge. Barrister, 1934. Lt RNVR, 1940-43 (invalided). Contested Northampton, 1935; MP (Lab) Northampton, 1945-Feb. 1974. Hon. Sec., UK Council of European Movement, 1954. Master, Pytchley Hounds, 1958-71. *Publications:* Manstein-Campaigns and Trial, 1951; (with late S. S. Silverman, MP) Hanged—and Innocent?, 1958. *Address:* 9 Grosvenor Cottages, SW1. *T:* 01-730 4034.

PAGET, Sir John (Starr), 3rd Bt *cr* 1886; CEng, FIMechE; Chairman, Thermal Syndicate Ltd, Wallsend, since 1973; *b* 24 Nov. 1914; *s* of Sir Richard Paget, 2nd Bt and Lady Muriel Paget, CBE; *S* father 1955; *m* 1944, Nancy Mary Parish, JP, *d* of late Lieutenant-Colonel Francis Parish, DSO, MC; two *s* five *d. Educ:* Oundle; Chateau D'Oex; Trinity College, Cambridge (MA). Joined English Electric Co. Ltd, 1936; Asst Works Supt, English Electric, Preston, 1941; Joined D. Napier & Son Ltd, 1943; Assistant Manager, D. Napier & Son Ltd, Liverpool, 1945; Manager, D. Napier & Son Ltd, London Group, 1946; Works Director, Napier Aero Engines, 1961-62 (Dir and Gen. Man. D. Napier & Son Ltd, 1959-61). Director: Glacier Metal Group, 1963-65; Hilger & Watts, 1965-68; Rank Precision Industries Ltd, 1968-70. Hon. DTech Brunel, 1976. Silver Medal, Institution Production Engineers, 1950. *Recreations:* cabinet making, cooking. *Heir: s* Richard Herbert Paget, *b* 17 February 1957. *Address:* Haygrass House, Taunton, Somerset. *T:* Taunton 81779; 20 Marloes Road, W8. *T:* 01-373 9760. *Clubs:* Athenæum; Northern Counties (Newcastle upon Tyne).

PAGET, Lt-Col Sir Julian (Tolver), 4th Bt *cr* 1871; Gentleman Usher to the Queen, since 1971; author; Public Relations Officer, Strutt and Parker, since 1968; *b* 11 July 1921; *s* of General Sir Bernard Paget, GCB, DSO, MC (*d* 1961) (*g s* of 1st Bt), and of Winifred, *d* of Sir John Paget, 2nd Bt; *S* uncle, Sir James Francis Paget, 3rd Bt, 1972; *m* 1954, Diana Frances, *d* of late F. S. H. Farmer; one *s* one *d. Educ:* Radley College; Christ Church, Oxford (MA). Joined Coldstream Guards, 1940; served North West Europe, 1944-45; retired as Lt-Col, 1968. *Publications:* Counter-Insurgency Campaigning, 1967; Last Post: Aden, 1964-67, 1969; The Story of the Guards, 1976. *Recreations:* fishing, shooting, travel, writing. *Heir: s* Henry James Paget, *b* 2 Feb. 1959. *Address:* 4 Trevor Street, SW7. *T:* 01-584 3524. *Clubs:* Cavalry and Guards, Pratt's, Flyfishers'.

PAGET, Paul Edward, CVO 1971; FSA, FRIBA; Chairman, Norwich Diocesan Advisory Committee, 1973-76; Master, Art Workers Guild, 1971; Member: Redundant Churches Fund, 1969-76; Crafts Advisory Committee, 1971-75; Surveyor to the Fabric of St Paul's Cathedral, 1963-69; Senior Partner in Firm of Seely & Paget, Chartered Architects, 1963-69 (from death of late Lord Mottistone, OBE, FSA, FRIBA, in Jan. 1963); Architect to St George's Chapel, Windsor, and Portsmouth Cathedral, 1950-69; *b* 24 Jan. 1901; 2nd and *o surv s* of Bishop Henry Luke Paget and Elma Katie (*née* Hoare); *m* 1971, Verily, *d* of late Rev. F. R. C. Bruce, DD, and *widow* of Captain Donald Anderson. *Educ:* Winchester; Trinity Coll., Cambridge. Asst Private Sec. to 1st Viscount Templewood, PC, GCSI, GBE, CMG, 1924-26. Flight Lieutenant, RAuxAF, 1939-44. Asst Director, Emergency Works, 1941-44; Common Councilman, Corporation of London, 1949-55. CStJ 1962. *Principal Works:* Restorations: Eltham Palace; Lambeth Palace; Upper Sch., Eton Coll.; London Charterhouse, Deanery and Little Cloister, Westminster Abbey; Churches: Lee-on-Solent, Six Mile Bottom, All Hallows-by-the-Tower, City Temple, Stevenage New Town; Colleges of Education: Oxford, Norwich, Bristol, Culham. *Address:* Templewood, Northrepps, near Cromer, Norfolk. *T:* Overstrand 243. *Clubs:* Athenæum; Norfolk (Norwich).

PAICE, Karlo Bruce; Assistant Under-Secretary of State, Home Office, 1955-66; *b* 18 August 1906; *s* of H. B. Paice, Horsham, Sussex; *m* 1st, 1935, Islay (*d* 1965), *d* of late Paymaster Comdr Duncan Cook; four *s*; 2nd, 1966, Mrs Gwen Morris (*née* Kenyon). *Educ:* Collyer's School, Horsham; Jesus Coll., Cambridge (MA). Second Clerk, Metropolitan Police Courts, 1928; Assistant Principal, Home Office, 1929; Asst Sec. to the Poisons Bd, 1933-35; Private Sec. to successive Parliamentary Under-Secretaries of State for Home Affairs, 1935-39. Principal, 1936; Assistant Secretary, 1941, serving in London Civil Defence Region, Fire Service Department, and Aliens Department. Secretary to the Prison Commission and a Prison Commissioner, 1949-55. *Recreations:* walking, history, music. *Address:* Flat 5, Windsor Lodge, Third Avenue, Hove, East Sussex. *T:* Brighton 733194. *Clubs:* Athenæum.

PAIGE, Prof. Edward George Sydney, PhD; Professor of Engineering (Electrical), University of Oxford, since 1977; *b* 18 July 1930; *s* of Sydney and Maude Paige; *m* 1953, Helen Gill; two *s* two *d*. *Educ:* Reading University (BSc, PhD); FInstP. Junior Research Fellow to DCSO, Royal Radar Establishment, Malvern, 1955-77. *Address:* Department of Engineering Science, University of Oxford, Parks Road, Oxford. *T:* Oxford 59988.

PAIGE, Rear-Adm. Richard Collings, CB 1967; *b* 4 October 1911; *s* of Herbert Collings Paige and Harriet Pering Paige; *m* 1937, Sheila Brambles Ward, *d* of late Dr Ernest Ward, Paignton; two *s*. *Educ:* Blundell's School, Tiverton; RNE College, Keyham. Joined Navy, 1929. Served in HMS Neptune, Curaçao, Maori, King George V, Superb, Eagle (despatches twice); Captain, 1957; Commanding Officer, RNE College, 1960-62; Commodore Supt, HM Naval Base, Singapore, 1963-65; Admiral Supt HM Dockyard, Portsmouth, 1966-68. Rear-Adm. 1965.

PAIGE, Victor Grellier; Deputy Chairman, National Freight Corporation, since 1977; Member, Manpower Services Commission, since 1974; *b* 5 June 1925; *s* of Victor Paige and Alice (*née* Grellier); *m* 1948, Kathleen Winifred, 3rd *d* of Arthur and Daisy Harris; one *s* one *d*. *Educ:* East Ham Grammar Sch.; Univ. of Nottingham. CIPM, FCIT, FBIM. Roosevelt Mem. Schol. 1954. Dep. Personnel Manager, Boots Pure Drug Co. Ltd, 1957-67; Controller of Personnel Services, CWS Ltd, 1967-70; Dir of Manpower and Organisation, 1970-74, Exec. Vice-Chm. (Admin), 1974-77, Nat. Freight Corp. Member: Notts Educn Cttee, 1957-63; Secondary Schs Examn Council, 1960-63; UK Adv. Council for Educn in Management, 1962-65; Careers Adv. Bd, Univ. of Nottingham, 1975; Chairman: Regional Adv. Council for Further Educn, E Mids, 1967; Exec. Council, British Assoc. for Commercial and Industrial Educn, 1974; Adv. Council, Industrial Relations Trng Resource Centre, 1977. *Publications:* contrib. techn. press on management. *Recreations:* reading, sport generally, athletics in particular (Pres. Notts Athletic Club, 1962-67). *Address:* 1 Seeleys Close, Beaconsfield, Bucks. *T:* Beaconsfield 4647.

PAIN, Barry Newton, QPM 1976; Chief Constable of Kent, since 1974; *b* 25 Feb. 1931; *s* of Godfrey William Pain and Annie Newton; *m* 1951, Marguerite Agnes King; one *s* one *d*. *Educ:* Waverley Grammar Sch., Birmingham. Clerk to Prosecuting Solicitor, Birmingham, 1947-51; 2nd Lieut (Actg Captain) RASC, Kenya, 1949-51. Birmingham City Police, 1951-68; Staff Officer to HM Inspector of Constabulary, Birmingham, 1966-68; Asst Chief Constable, Staffordshire and Stoke-on-Trent Constabulary, 1968-74; JSSC 1970. Adviser to Turkish Govt on Reorganization of Police, 1972. *Recreations:* golf, shooting, boating. *Address:* c/o Kent Police HQ, Maidstone, Kent ME15 9BZ. *T:* Maidstone 65432.

PAIN, Lt-Gen. Sir (Horace) Rollo (Squarey), KCB 1975 (CB 1974); MC 1945; late 4th/7th Royal Dragoon Guards; Head of British Defence Staff, Washington, since 1975; *b* 11 May 1921; *s* of late Horace Davy Pain, Levenside, Haverthwaite, Ulverston, and Audrey Pain (*née* Hampson); *m* 1950, Denys Sophia (*née* Chaine-Nickson); one *s* two *d*. Commissioned into Reconnaissance Corps during War of 1939-45: served NW Europe (MC). After War, served for two years in E Africa and Brit. Somaliland before joining 4th/7th Royal Dragoon Gds in Palestine, 1947; attended Staff Coll., Camberley, 1951; subseq. served in Mil. Ops Directorate, in War Office; served with his Regt in BAOR, 1955-56; Mem. Directing Staff, Staff Coll., Camberley, 1957; GSO1, Brit. Army Staff, Washington, DC, 1960; commanded his Regt in BAOR, 1962; commanded one of the three divs, Staff Coll., Camberley, 1964; commanded 5 Inf. Bde in Borneo, 1965; IDC, 1968; ADC to the Queen, 1969; BGS, HQ, BAOR, 1969-70; GOC 2nd Div., 1970-72; Dir of Army Training, MoD, 1972-75; Col Comdt, Mil. Provost Staff Corps, 1974-. *Recreations:* agriculture, hunting. *Address:* Eddlethorpe Hall, Malton, North Yorkshire. *T:* Burythorpe 218. *Club:* Cavalry and Guards.

PAIN, Hon. Sir Peter (Richard), Kt 1975; **Hon. Mr Justice Pain;** a Judge of the High Court of Justice, Queen's Bench Division, since 1975; *b* 6 Sept. 1913; *s* of Arthur Richard Pain and Elizabeth Irene Pain (*née* Benn); *m* 1941, Barbara Florence Maude Riggs; two *s*. *Educ:* Westminster; Christ Church, Oxford. Called to the Bar, Lincoln's Inn, 1936, Bencher 1972. QC 1965. Chairman: Race Relations Board Conciliation Cttee for Greater London, 1968-; South Metropolitan Conciliation Cttee, 1971-73. Pres., Holiday Fellowship, 1977. *Publications:* Manual of Fire Service Law, 1951; The Law Relating to the Motor Trade (with K. C. Johnson-Davies), 1955. *Recreations:* forestry, cricket, mountain walking. *Address:* Loen, St Catherine's Road, Frimley, Surrey. *T:* Deepcut 5639.

PAIN, Sir Rollo; *see* Pain, Sir H. R. S.

PAINE, George, CB 1974; DFC 1944; Director, Office of Population Censuses and Surveys, and Registrar General for England and Wales, since 1972; *b* 14 Apr. 1918; 3rd *s* of late Jack Paine, East Sutton, and Helen Margaret Hadow; *m* 1969, Hilary (*née* Garrod), *widow* of Dr A. C. Frazer. *Educ:* Bradfield Coll.; Peterhouse, Cambridge. External Ballistics Dept, Ordnance Bd, 1941; RAF, 1942-46; Min. of Agriculture, 1948; Inland Revenue, 1949; Central Statistical Office, 1954; Board of Trade, 1957; Dir of Statistics and Intelligence, Bd of Inland Revenue, 1957-72. Hon. Treasurer, Royal Statistical Soc., 1974-. *Recreation:* beekeeping. *Address:* Springfield House, Broad Town, near Swindon, Wilts SN4 7RU. *T:* Broad Hinton 377. *Club:* Athenæum.

PAINE, Peter Stanley, DFC 1944; Managing Director, Tyne Tees Television Ltd, since 1974; *b* 19 June 1921; *s* of Arthur Bertram Paine and Dorothy Helen Paine; *m* 1942, Sheila Mary, *d* of Frederick Wigglesworth, MA; two *s* two *d*. *Educ:* King's Sch., Canterbury. Served 1940-46, 2 Gp RAF (Flt-Lt). Worked in Punch Publishing Office, 1945-47; Sales Promotion Man., Newnes Pearson, 1948-52, Odhams Press, then Sales Dir and Dir of Tyne Tees Television, 1958-67; Sales Dir and Dir of Yorkshire Television, 1967; Director: Trident Television Ltd, Trident Management Ltd, Castlewood Investments Ltd; Trident International Television Enterprises Ltd; Sport TV Ltd (Brussels); Watts & Corry Ltd; Sound Broadcasting (Teesside) Ltd; Mem. Council, Independent Television Companies Assoc. (4 yrs Chm. Marketing Cttee). *Recreations:* golf, sailing, theatre, music, reading. *Address:* Whitegates, Meadowfield Road, Stocksfield, Northumberland. *T:* Stocksfield 3143; Briarfield, Ashwood Road, Woking, Surrey. *T:* Woking 73143. *Clubs:* Thirty; West Hill Golf.

PAINE, Dr Thomas Otten; President and Chief Operating Officer, Northrop Corporation, since 1976; *b* 9 Nov. 1921; *s* of George Thomas Paine, Cdre, USN retd and Ada Louise Otten; *m* 1946, Barbara Helen Taunton Pearse; two *s* two *d*. *Educ:* Maury High, Norfolk, Va; Brown Univ.; Stanford Univ. Served War of 1939-45 (US Navy Commendation Ribbon 1944; Submarine Combat Award with two stars, 1943-45). Research Associate: Stanford Univ., 1947-49; General Electric Res. Lab., Schenectady, 1949-50; Manager: GE Meter & Instruments Lab., Lynn, 1951-58; Technical Analysis, GE R&D Center, Schenectady, 1959-62; TEMPO, GE Center for Advanced Studies, Santa Barbara, 1963-67; Dep. Administrator, US Nat. Aeronautics and Space Admin., Washington, 1968, Administrator 1968-70; Group Executive, GE, Power Generation Group, 1970-73, Sen. Vice-Pres., GE, 1974-76. MInstMet; Member: Newcomen Soc.; Nat. Acad. of Engineering; Acad. of Sciences, NY; Sigma Xi; Trustee: Occidental Coll.; Brown Univ. Outstanding Contribution to Industrial Science Award, AAS, 1956; NASA DSM, 1970;

Washington Award, Western Soc. of Engrs, 1972; John Fritz Medal, United Engrg Soc., 1976; Faraday Medal, IEE, 1976. Hon. Dr of Science: Brown, 1969; Clarkson Coll. of Tech., 1969; Nebraska Wesleyan, 1970; New Brunswick, 1970; Oklahoma City, 1970; Hon. Dr Engrg, Worcester Polytechnic Inst., 1970. Grand Ufficiale della Ordine Al Merito della Repubblica Italiana, 1972. *Publications:* various technical papers in Physical Review, Jl Applied Physics, Electrical Engrg, Powder Metallurgy, etc; general papers in National Geographic, Air Force and Space Digest, Public Administration Review, Ordnance, etc. *Recreations:* sailing, beachcombing, skin diving, photography, book collecting, oil painting. *Address:* (office) Northrop Corporation, 1800 Century Park East, Los Angeles, Calif 90067, USA; (home) 765 Bonhill Road, Los Angeles, Calif 90049. *Clubs:* Sky, Lotos, Explorers (New York); Army and Navy, Cosmos (Washington); California (Los Angeles).

PAINTER, George Duncan, OBE 1974; Biographer and Incunabulist; Assistant Keeper in charge of fifteenth-century printed books, British Museum, 1954-74; *b* Birmingham, 5 June 1914; *s* of George Charles Painter and Minnie Rosendale (*née* Taylor); *m* 1942, Isabel Joan, *d* of Samuel Morley Britton, Bristol; two *d. Educ:* King Edward's Sch., Birmingham; Trinity Coll., Cambridge (Schol.). Bell Exhibr; John Stewart of Rannoch Schol.; Porson Schol.; Waddington Schol.; 1st cl. hons Class. Tripos pts I and II; Craven Student; 2nd Chancellor's Class. Medallist, 1936; MA Cantab 1945. Asst Lectr in Latin, Univ. of Liverpool, 1937; joined staff of Dept of Printed Books, BM, 1938. FRSL 1965. *Publications:* André Gide, A Critical Biography, 1951, rev. edn 1968; The Road to Sinodun, Poems, 1951; André Gide, Marshlands and Prometheus Misbound (trans.), 1953; Marcel Proust, Letters to his Mother (trans.), 1956; Marcel Proust, A Biography, vol. 1, 1959, vol. 2, 1965 (Duff Cooper Memorial Prize); The Vinland Map and the Tartar Relation (with R. A. Skelton and T. E. Marston), 1965; André Maurois, The Chelsea Way (trans.), 1966; William Caxton, a Quincentenary Biography, 1976; Chateaubriand, A Biography, vol. 1, The Longed-for Tempests, 1977; articles on fifteenth-century printing in The Library, Book Collector, Gutenberg-Jahrbuch. *Recreations:* family life, walking, gardening, music. *Address:* 10 Mansfield Road, Hove, East Sussex. *T:* Brighton 416008.

PAINTER, Terence James; Under-Secretary, Board of Inland Revenue, since 1975; *b* 28 Nov. 1935; *s* of late Edward Lawrence Painter and Ethel Violet (*née* Butler); *m* 1959, Margaret Janet Blackburn; two *s* two *d. Educ:* City of Norwich Sch.; Downing Coll., Cambridge (BA (History)). Entered Inland Revenue as Asst Principal, 1959; Principal, 1962; seconded to Civil Service Selection Bd, 1967-68; Asst Sec., 1969; seconded to HM Treasury, 1973-75. *Recreations:* music, gardening. *Address:* 9 Grant Gardens, Harpenden, Herts AL5 4QD. *T:* Harpenden 60269.

PAISH, Frank Walter, MC 1918; MA; Professor Emeritus, University of London; *b* 15 January 1898; *e s* of late Sir George Paish; *m* 1927, Beatrice Marie, *d* of late G. C. Eckhard; two *s* one *d. Educ:* Winchester College; Trinity College, Cambridge. Served European War (RFA), 1916-19. Employed by Standard Bank of South Africa, Ltd, in London and South Africa, 1921-32. Lecturer, London School of Economics, 1932-38; Reader, 1938-49; Professor of Economics (with special reference to Business Finance), 1949-65; Hon. Fellow, 1970. Secretary, London and Cambridge Economic Service, 1932-41 and 1945-49; Editor, 1947-49. Deputy-Director of Programmes, Ministry of Aircraft Production, 1941-45. Consultant on Economic Affairs, Lloyds Bank Ltd, 1965-70. *Publications:* (with G. L. Schwartz) Insurance Funds and their Investment, 1934; The Post-War Financial Problem and Other Essays, 1950; Business Finance, 1953; Studies in an Inflationary Economy, 1962; Long-term and Short-term Interest Rates in the United Kingdom, 1966; (ed) Benham's Economics, 8th edn, 1967, (with A. J. Culyer) 9th edn, 1973; How the Economy Works, 1970; The Rise and Fall of Incomes Policy, 1969; articles in The Economic Journal, Economica, London and Cambridge Bulletin, etc. *Address:* The Old Rectory Cottage, Kentchurch, Hereford.

PAISLEY, Bishop of, (RC), since 1968; **Rt. Rev. Stephen McGill;** *b* Glasgow, 4 Jan. 1912; *s* of Peter McGill and Charlotte Connolly. *Educ:* St Aloysius', Glasgow; Blairs College, Aberdeen; Coutances, France; Institut Catholique, Paris. Ordained Priest of St Sulpice, 1936. STL Paris. St Mary's College, Blairs, Aberdeen: Spiritual Director, 1940-51; Rector, 1951-60. Bishop of Argyll and the Isles, 1960-68. *Address:* Bishop's House, Porterfield Road, Kilmacolm, Renfrewshire.

PAISLEY, Rev. Ian Richard Kyle; MP (Democratic Unionist) North Antrim, since 1974 (Prot U, 1970-74); Minister, Martyrs

Memorial Free Presbyterian Church, Belfast, since 1946; *b* 6 April 1926; 2nd *s* of late Rev. J. Kyle Paisley and Mrs Isabella Paisley; *m* 1956, Eileen Emily Cassells; two *s* three *d* (incl. twin *s*). *Educ:* Ballymena Model Sch.; Ballymena Techn. High Sch.; S Wales Bible Coll.; Reformed Presbyterian Theol. Coll., Belfast. Ordained, 1946. Moderator, Free Presbyterian Church of Ulster, 1951. Commenced publishing The Protestant Telegraph, 1966. Contested (Prot U) Bannside, NI Parlt, 1969; MP (Prot U), Bannside, Co. Antrim, NI Parlt, 1970-72; Leader of Opposition, 1972; Chm., Public Accounts Cttee, 1972. Mem. (Democratic Unionist), N Antrim, NI Assembly, 1973-75. Mem. (UUUC), N Antrim, NI Constitutional Convention, 1975-76. Hon. DD Bob Jones Univ., SC. FRGS. Mem., Internat. Cultural Soc., Korea, 1977. *Publications:* History of the 1859 Revival, 1959; Ravenhill Pulpit, Vol. 1, 1966, vol. 2, 1967; Exposition of the Epistle to Romans, 1968; Billy Graham and the Church of Rome, 1970; The Massacre of St Bartholomew, 1972; America's Debt to Ulster, 1976. *Address:* House of Commons, SW1; The Parsonage, 17 Cyprus Avenue, Belfast BT5 5NT.

PAISLEY, John Lawrence, CB 1970; MBE 1946; Consultant with L. G. Mouchel & Partners, Consulting Engineers, since 1971; *b* Manchester, 4 Sept. 1909; *e s* of J. R. and Mrs E. W. Paisley; *m* 1937, Angela Dorothy Catliff; three *d. Educ:* King George V Sch., Southport; Univ. of Liverpool. BEng 1930, MEng 1935. Asst Engineer: Siemens Bros & Co. Ltd, North Delta Transmission Lines, Egypt, 1930-34; Howard Humphreys & Sons, Cons. Engrs, Tunnels and Viaduct on A55, in N Wales, 1934-35; W Sussex CC, 1935-37; Asst Engr in Scotland, Min. of Transport, 1937-39. War Service with Royal Engineers, 1939-46: took part in Dunkirk evacuation and finally as Major, RE (now Hon. Major), commanded 804 Road Construction Co. in UK, France and Germany (MBE). Ministry of Transport: Engr in Scotland, 1946-52; Senr Engr in HQ, London, 1952-60; Divl Rd Engr, NW Div. at Manchester, 1960-64; Dep. Chief Engr, HQ, London, 1964-66; Chief Highway Engr, Min. of Transport, 1966-70. Vice-Pres., Permanent Internat. Assoc. of Road Congresses, 1972-76, and Chm., British Nat. Cttee, 1972-. FICE; FInstHE. *Publications:* contribs Proc. Instn of Civil Engrs, Proc. Instn of Highway Engrs. *Recreation:* fell walking. *Address:* Weybrook, Warren Road, Guildford, Surrey. *T:* Guildford 62798. *Clubs:* Civil Service, Victory; Rucksack (Manchester).

PAKENHAM, family name of **Earl of Longford.**

PAKENHAM, Elizabeth; *see* Longford, Countess of.

PAKENHAM, Henry Desmond Verner, CBE 1964; HM Diplomatic Service, retired; *b* 5 Nov. 1911; *s* of Hamilton Richard Pakenham and Emilie Willis Stringer; *m* 1st, 1946, Crystal Elizabeth Brooksbank (marr. diss., 1960); one *s* one *d* (and one *s* decd); 2nd, 1963, Venetia Maude; one *s* one *d. Educ:* Monkton Combe; St John Baptist College, Oxford. Taught modern languages at Sevenoaks School, 1933-40. Served in HM Forces, 1940-45. Entered Foreign Service, 1946; served in Madrid, Djakarta, Havana, Singapore, Tel Aviv, Buenos Aires and Sydney; retired 1971. *Recreations:* music and wild life. *Address:* Rose Farm, Brettenham, Suffolk.

PAKES, Ernest John, CBE 1954; Under-writing Member of Lloyd's, since 1956; *b* 28 Jan. 1899; *s* of Ernest William Pakes; *m* 1928, Emilie Pickering; one *s. Educ:* Hampton Gram. Sch. Served with London Scottish, 1917-19 (wounded). Admiralty, 1915-16; Gray Dawes & Co., 1916-21; Mackinnon Mackenzie & Co., India, 1921-40, Ceylon, 1940-44, India, 1945-54 (Chairman, 1951-54). Dep. Rep., Min. of War Transport, Karachi, 1945-46; Chairman: Karachi Chamber of Commerce, 1946-47; Allahabad Bank Ltd, India, 1951-54. Pres. Bengal Chamber of Commerce and Assocd Chambers of Commerce of India, 1953-54; Chm., Outward and Homeward UK and Continental/India and Pakistan Confs, 1956-58. Member of Council, Chamber of Shipping, 1956-62; Chairman, British India Steam Navigation Co. Ltd, 1960-62 (a Managing Director, 1954-62); Deputy Chairman, (1957-60); Director, Chartered Bank, London, 1958-62. Liveryman, Worshipful Co. of Shipwrights. *Recreation:* golf. *Address:* Staneway, Tyrrells Wood, Leatherhead, Surrey. *T:* Leatherhead 73243. *Club:* Walton Heath.

PAKINGTON, family name of **Baron Hampton.**

PAL, Dr Benjamin Peary, Padma Shri 1958; Padma Bhushan 1968; FRS 1972; Scientist Emeritus, Indian Council of Agricultural Research, since 1972; *b* 26 May 1906; *s* of Dr R. R. Pal; unmarried. *Educ:* Rangoon Univ.; Cambridge University. MSc hons, PhD Cantab. 2nd Economic Botanist, Imperial Agric. Research Inst., 1933; Imperial Economic Botanist, 1937;

Dir, Indian Agric. Res. Inst., 1950; Dir-Gen., Indian Council of Agric. Research, 1965; retd 1972. Hon. DSc: Punjab Agric. Univ.; Sardar Patel Univ.; UP Agric. Univ.; Haryana Agric. Univ.; Foreign Mem., All Union Lenin Acad. of Agric. Sciences; Hon. Member: Japan Acad.; Acad. d'Agriculture de France; Fellow: Linnean Soc. of London; Indian Nat. Science Acad. (Pres., 1975-76). *Publications:* Beautiful Climbers of India, 1960; Wheat, 1966; Charophyta, The Rose in India, 1966; Flowering Shrubs, 1967; All About Roses, 1973; Bougainvilleas, 1974. *Recreations:* rose gardening, painting. *Address:* P11, Hauz Khas Enclave, New Delhi 16, India. *T:* 626145.

PALADE, Prof. George Emil; scientist, USA; Professor of Cell Biology, Yale University, since 1973; *b* Jasesy, Roumania, 19 Nov. 1912; *s* of Emil Palade and Constanta Cantemir; *m* 1st, 1941, Irina Malaxa (decd); one *s* one *d* ; 2nd, 1970, Dr Marilyn Farquhar. *Educ:* Liceul Al. Hasdeu, Buzau, Roumania; Med. Sch., Univ. of Bucharest (MD). Arrived in US, 1946; naturalized US citizen, 1952. Instructor, Asst Prof., then Lectr in Anatomy, Sch. of Med., Univ. of Bucharest, 1940-45; Visiting Investigator, Rockefeller Inst. for Med. Research, 1946-48; continuing as an Assistant (later the Inst. became Rockefeller Univ., NYC); promoted to Associate, 1951, and Associate Mem., 1953; Prof. of Cell Biology, Rockefeller Univ. and full Member of Rockefeller Inst., 1956. Fellow, Amer. Acad. of Arts and Sciences; Member: Nat. Acad. of Sciences; Amer. Soc. Cell Biology; Amer. Assoc. for the Advancement of Science. Awards include: Albert Lasker Basic Research, 1966; Gairdner Award, 1967; Hurwitz Prize, 1970; Nobel Prize for Medicine, 1974. *Publications:* Editor: Jl of Cell Biology (co-founder); Jl of Membrane Biology; numerous contribs med. and sci. jls. *Address:* Section of Cell Biology, Yale University School of Medicine, 333 Cedar Street, New Haven, Conn. 06510, USA. *T:* (203) 436-2376.

PALETHORPE-TODD, Richard Andrew; *see* Todd, Richard.

PALETTE, John; General Manager, Southern Region, British Railways, since 1977; *b* 19 May 1928; *s* of Arthur and Beatrice Palette; *m* 1950, Pamela Mabel Palmer; three *s*. *Educ:* Alexandra Sch., Hampstead. MCIT. Gen. Railway Admin, 1942-69; Divl Manager, Bristol, 1969-72; Asst Gen. Manager, Western Region, 1972-74; Divl Manager, Manchester, 1974-76; Gen. Manager, Scottish Region, 1976-77, British Railways. Chm., British Transport Ship Management (Scotland) Ltd, 1976-. *Recreations:* walking, reading, gardening, watching sport. *Address:* 90 Wargrave Road, Twyford, Reading, Berks. *T:* Twyford (Berks) 340965.

PALFREY, William John Henry, CBE 1970 (OBE 1966); QPM 1960; DL; *b* 1 March 1906; *s* of late W. H. Palfrey, Exminster, Devon; *m* 1927, Dorothy, *d* of Henry Cowell, Kenton, Devon; one *s*. *Educ:* Hele's Sch., Exeter. Portsmouth City Police, 1926; Chief Constable, Accrington, 1940; seconded to Army, 1943-47; served with 1st American Army, Chief Public Safety Officer, Cherbourg, later Paris; Lt-Col i/c Central Register of War Criminals, 1945; War Crime Investigation, Germany, 1946-47; Asst Chief Constable (Operations), Lancs Constabulary, 1951; seconded to Thai Govt to carry out survey of Thai Police, 1955; Chief Constable, Lancs, 1969-72 (Dep. Chief Constable, 1962-69). Dep. Sec.-Gen., Internat. Fedn of Senior Police Officers, 1966-72. Lectured at Internat. Traffic Confs throughout Europe. Chm., Lancs Youth Clubs Assoc. DL Co. Palatine of Lancaster, 1971. Bronze Star (US) and Certif. of Merit (US Army), 1944. *Publications:* contribs to police jls throughout Europe. *Recreations:* motor sport, cinephotography, travel. *Address:* Netherside, Green Lane, Whitestake, Preston, Lancs.

PALING, Helen Elizabeth, (Mrs W. J. S. Kershaw); a Recorder of the Crown Court, since 1972; *b* 25 April 1933; *o d* of A. Dale Paling and Mabel Eleanor Thomas; *m* 1961, William John Stanley Kershaw, PhD; one *s* three *d*. *Educ:* Prince Henry's Grammar Sch., Otley; London Sch. of Economics. LLB London 1954. Called to Bar, Lincoln's Inn, 1955. *Address:* 46 Grainger Street, Newcastle upon Tyne. *T:* Newcastle upon Tyne 21980, 22392.

PALING, William Thomas; *b* 28 Oct. 1892; *s* of George Thomas Paling, Sutton-in-Ashfield, Notts; *m* 1919, Gladys Nellie, MBE, *d* of William Frith, James Street, Nuncar Gate, Nottinghamshire; one *s* one *d*. MP (Lab) Dewsbury, 1945-59, retired. *Address:* 3 Lancaster Close, Tickhill, near Doncaster, South Yorks. *T:* Doncaster 742875.

PALLEY, Prof. Claire Dorothea Taylor; Professor of Law, since 1973, Master of Darwin College, since 1974, University of Kent at Canterbury; *b* 17 Feb. 1931; *d* of Arthur Aubrey Swait, Johannesburg; *m* 1952, Ahrn Palley, advocate and medical

practitioner; five *s*. *Educ:* Durban Girls' Coll.; Univs of Cape Town and London. BA 1950, LLB 1952, Cape Town; PhD London 1965. Called to Bar, Middle Temple; Advocate, S Africa and Rhodesia. Lecturer: Cape Town Univ., 1953-55; UC Rhodesia and Nyasaland, 1960-65; QUB, 1966-67; Reader, QUB, 1967-70. Prof. of Public Law, 1970-73, and Dean of Faculty of Law, 1971-73. Chm., SE Area Cttee, Nat. Assoc. of Citizens' Advice Bureaux, 1974-; Mem. Council, Minority Rights Group, 1975-; Constitutional Adviser to African Nat. Council at Const. Talks on Rhodesia, 1976. Governor: Polytechnic of the South Bank, 1975-; King's Sch., Canterbury, 1977-. *Publications:* The Constitutional History and Law of Southern Rhodesia, 1966; contrib. learned jls. *Address:* Darwin College, University of Kent at Canterbury, Canterbury, Kent CT2 7NY.

PALLISER, Sir (Arthur) Michael, GCMG 1977 (KCMG 1973; CMG 1966); Permanent Under-Secretary of State, Foreign and Commonwealth Office, and Head of the Diplomatic Service, since 1975; *b* 9 Apr. 1922; *s* of late Admiral Sir Arthur Palliser, KCB, DSC, and of Lady Palliser (*née* Margaret Eva King-Salter); *m* 1948, Marie Marguerite, *d* of late Paul-Henri Spaak; three *s*. *Educ:* Wellington Coll.; Merton Coll., Oxford. Served with Coldstream Guards, 1942-47; Capt. 1944. Entered HM Diplomatic Service, 1947; SE Asia Dept, Foreign Office, 1947-49; Athens, 1949-51; Second Sec., 1950; Foreign Office: German Finance Dept, 1951-52; Central Dept, 1952-54; Private Sec. to Perm. Under-Sec., 1954-56; First Sec., 1955; Paris, 1956-60; Head of Chancery, Dakar, 1960-62 (Chargé d'Affaires in 1960, 1961 and 1962); Counsellor, and seconded to Imperial Defence College, 1963; Head of Planning Staff, Foreign Office, 1964; a Private Sec. to PM, 1966; Minister, Paris, 1969; Ambassador and Head of UK Deleg. to European Communities, Brussels, 1971; Ambassador and UK Permanent Representative to European Communities, 1973-75. Chevalier, Order of Orange Nassau, 1944; Chevalier, Légion d'Honneur, 1957. *Address:* Foreign and Commonwealth Office, SW1. *Club:* Buck's.

PALLOT, Arthur Keith, CMG 1966; Secretary and Director-General, Commonwealth War Graves Commission, since 1975 (Director of Finance and Establishments, 1956-75); *b* 25 Sept. 1918; *s* of Harold Pallot, La Tourelle, Jersey; *m* 1945, Marjorie, *d* of J. T. Smith, Rugby; two *d*. *Educ:* Newton College. Royal Navy, 1936; retired as Lt-Comdr, 1947. Commonwealth War Graves Commission, 1947. Awarded the Queen's Commendation for brave conduct, 1958. *Recreations:* walking, cricket and Rugby (watching and administration). *Address:* Northways, Stubbles Lane, Cookham Dean, Berks. *T:* Marlow 6529.

PALMAR, Derek James; Chairman and Chief Executive, Bass Charrington Ltd; Chairman: Rush & Tompkins Group Ltd; British Railways Advisory Board (Southern); Director: Grindlays Bank Ltd; Howard Machinery Ltd; *b* 25 July 1919; *o s* of Lt-Col F. J. Palmar; *m* 1946, Edith Brewster; one *s* one *d*. *Educ:* Dover College. Served RA and Staff, 1941-46; psc; Lt-Col 1945; Peat, Marwick, Mitchell & Co., 1937-57; Dir, Hill Samuel Group, 1957-70. Adviser, Dept of Economic Affairs, 1965-67. Mem., British Railways Bd, 1969-72. FCA; FBIM. *Address:* 7 Grosvenor Gardens, SW1. *T:* 01-834 3121. *Club:* Boodle's.

PALMER, family name of **Earl of Selborne, Baron Palmer** and **Baroness Lucas of Crudwell.**

PALMER, 3rd Baron, *cr* 1933, of Reading; **Raymond Cecil Palmer,** OBE 1968; Bt *cr* 1916; Director, Associated Biscuit Manufacturers Ltd; Chairman: Huntley & Palmers Ltd, since 1969; Huntley Boorne & Stevens Ltd, Reading, since 1956 (Deputy Chairman, 1948); *b* 24 June 1916; *er s* of 2nd Baron Palmer and Marguerite (*d* 1959), *d* of William McKinley Osborne, USA, Consul-General to Great Britain; *S* father 1950; *m* 1941, Victoria Ellen, *o c* of late Captain J. A. R. Weston-Stevens, Maidenhead; two *d* (and one *d* decd). *Educ:* Harrow; University Coll., Oxford. Joined Huntley & Palmers Ltd, 1938, Dep. Chm., 1966-69, Man. Dir, 1967-69. Served War of 1939-45 in Grenadier Guards as Lieut, in UK and North Africa, 1940-43 (invalided). Mem., Southern Electricity Bd, 1965-77. Pres., Nat. Savings S Region Ind. Council. *Recreations:* cricket, rackets, music and gardening; shooting. *Heir:* *b* Col Hon. Gordon William Nottage Palmer, *qv. Address:* Farley Hill House, Farley Hill, Reading, Berkshire. *T:* Eversley 732260. *Club:* Cavalry and Guards.
See also Lord Wodehouse.

PALMER, Arnold Daniel; professional golfer since 1954; *b* 10 Sept. 1929; *s* of Milfred J. and Doris Palmer; *m* 1954, Winifred Walzer; two *d*. *Educ:* Wake Forest Univ. Winner of numerous tournament titles, including: British Open Championship, 1961,

1962; US Open Championship, 1960; Masters Championship, 1958, 1960, 1962, 1964; Spanish Open Championship, 1975; Professional Golfers' Assoc. Championship, 1975. Hon. Dr of Laws, Wake Forest; Hon. Dr Hum, Thiel Coll. *Publications:* (all jointly) Arnold Palmer Golf Book, 1961; Portrait of a Professional Golfer, 1964; My Game and Yours, 1965; Situation Golf, 1970; Go for Broke, 1973; Arnold Palmer's Best 54 Golf Holes, 1977. *Recreations:* aviation (speed record for flying round world in twin-engine jet, 1976), bridge, tennis, hunting, fishing. *Address:* PO Box 52, Youngstown, Pa 15696, USA. *T:* (412) 537-7751. *Clubs:* (Owner and Pres.) Latrobe Country; (Pres. and Part-Owner) Bay Hill (Orlando, Fla); (Tournament Professional) Laurel Valley Golf; numerous other country, city, golf.

PALMER, Arthur Montague Frank, CEng, FIEE, FInstF; MP (Lab and Co-op) Bristol North East, since 1974 (Bristol Central, 1964-74); *b* 4 Aug. 1912; *s* of late Frank Palmer, Northam, Devon; *m* 1939, Dr Marion Ethel Frances Woollaston, medical consultant; two *d. Educ:* Ashford Gram. Sch.; Brunel Technical College (now Brunel Univ.). Is a Chartered Engineer and a Chartered Fuel Technologist. Studied electrical supply engineering, 1932-35, in London; Member technical staff of London Power Co., 1936-45; Staff Mem., Electrical Power Engineers Assoc. Member Brentford and Chiswick Town Council, 1937-45. MP (Lab) for Wimbledon, 1945-50; MP (Lab and Co-op) for Cleveland Div. of Yorks, Oct. 1952-Sept. 1959; Chairman: Parly and Scientific Cttee, 1965-68; House of Commons Select Cttee on Science and Technology, 1966-70, 1974-; Co-operative party Parly Gp, 1970-. *Publications:* The Future of Electricity Supply, 1943; Modern Norway, 1950; Law and the Power Engineer, 1959; articles on political, industrial, and economic subjects. *Recreations:* walking, motoring, reading novels, history and politics. *Address:* 14 Lavington Court, Putney, SW15. *T:* 01-789 1967; Hill Cottage, Charlcutt, near Calne, Wilts. *T:* Kellaways 653; (office) 140 Lower Marsh, SE1. *T:* 01-928 3825. *Club:* Royal Automobile.

PALMER, Bernard Harold Michael, MA; Editor of the Church Times since 1968; *b* 8 Sept. 1929; *e s* of late Christopher Harold Palmer; *m* 1954, Jane Margaret, *d* of late E. L. Skinner; one *s* one *d. Educ:* St Edmund's School, Hindhead; Eton (King's Scholar); King's College, Cambridge. BA 1952; MA 1956. Member of editorial staff, Church Times, 1952-; Managing Director, 1957-; Editor-in-Chief, 1960-68; Chm., 1962-. *Recreations:* cycling, penmanship. *Address:* 143 Bradbourne Vale Road, Sevenoaks, Kent. *T:* Sevenoaks 53327. *Club:* Royal Commonwealth Society.

PALMER, Charles Alan Salier, CBE 1969; DSO 1945; Chairman, Associated Biscuit Manufacturers Ltd, 1969-72 (Vice-Chm., 1963); *b* 23 Oct. 1913; *s* of late Sir (Charles) Eric Palmer, Shinfield Grange, near Reading; *m* 1939, Auriol Mary, *d* of late Brig.-Gen. Cyril R. Harbord, CB, CMG, DSO. *Educ:* Harrow; Exeter Coll., Oxford. Joined Huntley & Palmer's, 1934 (Bd, 1938; Dep.-Chm. 1955; Chm., Huntley & Palmer's, 1963). Served War of 1939-45: with Berks Yeo., Adjt, 1939-41; GSO3, HQ 61 Div., 1941-42; GSO2, HQ III Corps, 1942-43; Lt-Col; commanded SOE mission, Albania, 1943-45 (despatches). Pres., Reading Conservative Assoc., 1946-; Chm., Cake & Biscuit Alliance, 1967-70; Mem. Council, CBI 1967-70; Mem. British Productivity Council, 1970-73. *Recreations:* shooting, fishing, tropical agriculture. *Address:* Forest Edge, Farley Hill, Reading, Berks. *T:* Arborfield Cross 760233.

PALMER, Sir (Charles) Mark, 5th Bt, *cr* 1886; *b* 21 Nov. 1941; *s* of Sir Anthony Frederick Mark Palmer, 4th Bt, and of Henriette (*see* Lady Abel Smith); *S* father 1941. Heir: kinsman, Charles Lionel Palmer [*b* 7 Feb. 1909; *s* of late Capt. Lionel Hugo Palmer (6th *s* of 1st Bt) and 2nd wife, Blanche, *o d* of Walter Balmford, York; *m* 1937, Karoline, *d* of late Major Carl Gach, Vienna; two *d*]. *Address:* Quenington Old Rectory, Cirencester, Glos.

PALMER, Ven. Derek George; Archdeacon of Rochester and Canon Residentiary of Rochester Cathedral, since 1977; *b* 24 Jan. 1928; *s* of George Palmer, MBE and Edna Palmer; *m* 1952, June Cecilie Goddard; two *s* two *d. Educ:* Clifton Coll.; Selwyn Coll., Cambridge (MA); Wells Theological Coll. Deacon 1952, priest 1953; Priest in Charge, Good Shepherd, Bristol, 1954-58; first Vicar of Hartcliffe, 1958-68; Vicar of Christ Church, Swindon, 1968-77. Member: General Synod, 1971-77; Board of Education, 1974-. Canon of Bristol Cathedral, 1975-. *Publications:* All Things New, 1963; Quest, 1971. *Recreation:* canals. *Address:* The Archdeaconry, The Precinct, Rochester, Kent ME1 1SX. *T:* Medway 42527.

PALMER, Edward Hurry, CB 1972; retired Civil Servant; *b* 23 Sept. 1912; *s* of late Harold G. Palmer and late Ada S. Palmer; *m* 1940, Phyllis Eagle; no *c. Educ:* Haileybury. Dep. Chief Surveyor of Lands, Admty, 1942; Chief Surveyor of Lands, Admty, 1950; Chief Surveyor of Defence Lands, MoD, 1964; Comptroller of Defence Lands and Claims, MoD, 1968-72; Property Services Agency, DoE: Dir, Defence Lands Services, 1972-73; Dir, Estate Surveying Services, 1973-74. *Recreations:* gardening, walking. *Address:* 49 Paines Lane, Pinner, Middlesex. *T:* 01-866 5961.

PALMER, Felicity Joan; soprano; *b* 6 April 1944. *Educ:* Erith Grammar Sch.; Guildhall Sch. of Music and Drama. AGSM (Teacher/Performer), FGSM; Kathleen Ferrier Meml Prize, 1970; major appearances at concerts in Britain, America, Belgium, France, Germany, Italy and Spain; toured Europe with BBC Symphony Orchestra, May 1973; operatic début, Marriage of Figaro, Houston, USA, Oct. 1973; The Magic Flute, London, 1975; Don Giovanni, London, 1976; recitals in Amsterdam, Paris, Vienna, 1976-77; concert tours with BBC SO, Europe, Australasia and Far East, 1977-. Recordings include: Poèmes pour Mi, with Pierre Boulez; Holst Choral Symphony, with Sir Adrian Boult, and recitals, with John Constable, of songs by Poulenc, Ravel and Fauré. *Address:* 7 Bayham Road, W4 1BJ. *T:* 01-995 1291.

PALMER, Rev. Francis Harvey; Rector of Worplesdon, Surrey, since 1972; Diocesan Ecumenical Officer, Guildford, since 1974; *b* 13 Jan. 1930; *s* of Harry Hereward North Palmer and Ada Wilhelmina Annie Utting; *m* 1955, Mary Susan Lockhart; three *d. Educ:* Nottingham High Sch.; Jesus Coll., Cambridge (Exhibr); Wycliffe Hall, Oxford. MA. Deacon, 1955; Priest, 1956. Asst Curate: Knotty Ash, Liverpool, 1955-57; St Mary, Southgate, Crawley, 1958-60; Chaplain, Fitzwilliam House, Cambridge, 1960-64; Vicar of Holy Trinity, Cambridge and Chaplain to Cambridge Pastorate, 1964-71; Principal, Ridley Hall, Cambridge, 1971-72. *Publication:* (contrib.) New Bible Dictionary, 1959. *Recreation:* stamp collecting. *Address:* Worplesdon Rectory, Guildford, Surrey. *T:* Worplesdon 2012.

PALMER, Prof. Frank Robert, FBA 1975; Professor and Head of Department of Linguistic Science, University of Reading, since 1965; *b* 9 April 1922; *s* of George Samuel Palmer and Gertrude Lilian (*née* Newman); *m* 1948, Jean Elisabeth Moore; three *s* two *d. Educ:* Bristol Grammar Sch.; New Coll., Oxford (Ella Stephens Schol., State Schol.) 1942-43 and 1945-48; Merton Coll., Oxford (Harmsworth Sen. Schol.) 1948-49. MA Oxon 1948; Craven Fellow, 1948. Served war, E Africa, 1943-45. Lectr in Linguistics, Sch. of Oriental and African Studies, Univ. of London, 1950-60 (study leave in Ethiopia, 1952-53); Prof. of Linguistics, University Coll. of N Wales, Bangor, 1960-65; Dean of Faculty of Letters and Social Sciences, Univ. of Reading, 1969-72; Linguistic Soc. of America Prof., Buffalo, 1971. Professional visits to Canada, USA, Mexico, Venezuela, Peru, Chile, Argentine, Uruguay, Brazil, Indonesia, Morocco, Tunisia, Uganda, Kuwait and most countries of Europe. *Publications:* The Morphology of the Tigre Noun, 1962; A Linguistic Study of the English Verb, 1965; (ed) Selected Papers of J. R. Firth, 1968; (ed) Prosodic Analysis, 1970; Grammar, 1971; The English Verb, 1974; Semantics, 1976; articles and reviews on Ethiopian langs, English and linguistic theory, in learned jls. *Recreations:* gardening, crosswords. *Address:* Whitethorns, Roundabout Lane, Winnersh, Wokingham, Berks RG11 5AD. *T:* Wokingham 786214.

PALMER, Sir Geoffrey (Christopher John), 12th Bt, *cr* 1660; *b* 30 June 1936; *er s* of Lieutenant-Colonel Sir Geoffrey Frederick Neill Palmer, 11th Bt, and Cicely Katherine (who *m* 1952, Robert W. B. Newton), *o d* of late Arthur Radmall, Clifton, nr Watford; *S* father 1951; *m* 1957, Clarissa Mary, *er d* of Stephen Villiers-Smith, Knockholt, Kent; four *d. Educ:* Eton. *Recreations:* squash, racquets, cricket, shooting. Heir: *b* Jeremy Charles Palmer [*b* 6 May 1939; *m* 1968, Antonia, *d* of late Ashley Dutton; two *s*]. *Address:* Carlton Curlieu Hall, Leicestershire. *T:* Great Glen 2656. *Clubs:* Boodle's; MCC, I Zingari, Free Foresters, Eton Ramblers, Butterflies, Gentlemen of Leicestershire, Forty, Frogs, Pedagogues.

PALMER, Gerald Eustace Howell, Hon. DLitt Reading, 1957; farmer and iconographer; *b* 9 June 1904; *s* of late Eustace Exall Palmer, Chairman of Huntley and Palmers Ltd, and Madeline Mary Howell. *Educ:* Winchester; New College, Oxford (Scholar). MP (Nat. C) for Winchester Division of Hampshire, 1935-45. Served RA, Capt (despatches). President of the Council, Univ. of Reading, 1966-69; A Verderer of the New Forest, 1957-66; Chm., Forestry Commission Regional Adv. Cttee for South-East England, 1954-63; A Forestry Commissioner, 1963-65; Chm., Forestry Commn Nat. Cttee for

England, 1964-65. Hon. Fellow, Soc. of Foresters of GB. *Publications:* following translations (in collab. with E. Kadloubovsky): Writings from the Philokalia, 1951; Unseen Warfare, 1952; The Meaning of Icons, by Lossky and Ouspensky, 1952; Early Fathers, from the Philokalia, 1954. *Address:* Bussock Mayne, Newbury, Berks. *T:* Chieveley 265. *Club:* Brooks's.

PALMER, Col Hon. Gordon William Nottage, OBE 1957 (MBE 1944); TD 1950; Vice-Chairman, Associated Biscuit Manufacturers; Chairman and Managing Director, Associated Biscuits Ltd; Managing Director, Huntley & Palmers Ltd, 1959-65; Vice-Lord-Lieutenant, Berkshire, since 1976; *b* 18 July 1918; *yr s* of 2nd Baron Palmer and Marguerite Osborne, USA; *heir-pres.* to 3rd Baron Palmer, *qv*; *m* 1950, Lorna Eveline Hope, *d* of Major C. W. H. Bailie; two *s. Educ:* Eton Coll.; Christ Church, Oxford. Served War of 1939-45, with Berks Yeo., 1939-41; staff Capt. RA, HQ 61 Div., 1941; DAQMG, Malta, 1942; GSO2, Ops, GHQ Middle East, 1943-44; GSO2, HQ 5 Div., 1944-45; Lt-Col, Instructor Staff College, Camberley, 1945; Comd Berkshire Yeo., TA, 1954-56. Hon. Col Berkshire and Westminster Dragoons, 1966-67; Hon. Col, Royal Yeomanry, 1972-75. Dir, Huntley, Boorne & Stevens Ltd, 1948-69; Chm. Cake and Biscuit Alliance, 1957-59. Mem., British National Export Council, 1966-69. Dir, S Midlands Regional Bd, Lloyds Bank Ltd. Pres., Council, Reading Univ., 1973-75 (Mem. 1954-, Treas., 1955-59, Vice-Pres., 1966-73; Hon. LLD, 1975); Chm. Council, Royal Coll. of Music, 1973-; FRCM 1965; Mem. Council, Bradfield College; DL Berks, 1960; JP 1956; High Sheriff, 1965; Chairman, Berkshire T&AFA, 1961-68. *Recreations:* shooting, and gardening. *Address:* Harris House, Mortimer, Berkshire. *T:* Mortimer 332317; Edrom Newton, Duns, Berwickshire. *T:* Chirnside 292. *Club:* Cavalry and Guards.

PALMER, John; Under Secretary, Department of Transport, since 1976; *b* 13 Nov. 1928; 2nd *s* of William Nathaniel Palmer and Grace Dorothy May Palmer (*née* Proctor); *m* 1958, Lyliane Marthe Jeanjean, *o d* of René Jeanjean and Jeanne Jeanjean (*née* Larrouy); two *d. Educ:* Heath Grammar Sch., Halifax; The Queen's Coll., Oxford (Lit. Hum.) (MA). Entered Min. of Housing and Local Govt, 1952; Cabinet Office, 1963-65; Asst Sec., 1965; Under Sec., DoE, 1971. *Address:* 2 The Hermitage, Richmond, Surrey. *T:* 01-940 6536; 64 Escou, France. *Club:* United Oxford & Cambridge University.

PALMER, Sir John (Edward Somerset), 8th Bt, *cr* 1791; Consultant; *b* 27 Oct. 1926; *e s* of Sir John A. Palmer, 7th Bt; *S* father, 1963; *m* 1956, Dione Catharine Skinner; one *s* one *d. Educ:* Canford School; Cambridge Univ. (MA); Durham Univ. (MSc). Colonial Service, Northern Nigeria, 1952-61. Senior Executive, R. A. Lister & Co. Ltd, Dursley, Glos, 1962-63; Min. Overseas Develt, 1964-68. Mem. Amer. Soc. of Agric. Engrs; MIAgrE. *Heir: s* Robert John Hudson Palmer, *b* 20 Dec. 1960. *Address:* The Grange, Wavendon, near Milton Keynes, Bucks MK17 8LH. *T:* Woburn Sands 583248. *Clubs:* Junior Carlton, Farmers'.

PALMER, Leonard Robert; Professor of Comparative Philology, University of Oxford, and Fellow of Worcester College, 1952-71, Emeritus Professor, 1971, Emeritus Fellow, 1972; *b* 5 June 1906; *m* ; one *d. Educ:* High School, Canton, Cardiff; University College of South Wales and Monmouthshire; Trinity College, Cambridge; University of Vienna. BA Wales 1927; PhD Vienna 1931; PhD Cambridge 1936; MA Oxford 1952. Assistant Lecturer in Classics, 1931-35, Lecturer in Classics, 1935-41, Victoria University of Manchester; temp. Civil Servant in Foreign Office, 1941-45; Professor of Greek and Head of Dept of Classics at King's Coll., London, 1945-52. Hon. Secretary Philological Society, 1947-51, President, 1957-. Corresponding Member Deutsches Archäologisches Institut, 1958. *Publications:* Translation of E. Zeller: Outlines of the History of Greek Philosophy, 14th edn, 1931; Introduction to Modern Linguistics, 1936; A Grammar of the Post-Ptolemaic Papyri, Vol. 1 (Publications of the Philological Society), 1945; The Latin Language, 1954; Mycenaeans and Minoans, 1961, 2nd edn 1965 (trans. Minoici e Micenei, 1970); The Language of Homer (in A Companion to Homer), 1962; The Interpretation of Mycenaean Greek Texts, 1963; The Find Places of the Knossos Tablets, 1963; De Aegeische Wereld, 1963; Knossos och Mykene, 1963; A New Guide to the Palace of Knossos, 1969; The Penultimate Palace at Knossos, 1969; Descriptive and Comparative Linguistics: a critical introduction, 1972; Introduccion al Latin, 1974; Introduccion a la Linguistica Descriptiva y Comparada, 1975; La Lingua Latina, 1977; various articles in English and foreign learned journals. *Festschrift:* Studies in Greek, Italic, and Indo-European Linguistics, offered to Leonard R. Palmer on the occasion of his seventieth birthday, ed Anna M. Davies

and W. Meid, 1976. *Address:* A-60-73 Sistrans, Tyrol, Austria. *T:* Innsbruck 70702.

PALMER, Leslie Robert, CBE 1964; Hon. Treasurer and Chairman, Finance and Administration Department, United Reformed Church, since 1973; Director-General, Defence Accounts, Ministry of Defence, 1969-72; *b* 21 Aug. 1910; *s* of Robert Palmer; *m* 1937, Mary Crick; two *s* one *d. Educ:* Battersea Grammar School; London University. Entered Admiralty Service, 1929; Assistant Dir of Victualling, 1941; Dep. Dir of Victualling, 1954; Dir of Victualling, Admiralty, 1959-61; Principal Dir of Accounts, Admiralty, 1961-64; Principal Dir of Accounts (Navy) MoD, 1964-68. *Recreation:* music. *Address:* High Meadow, Upper Limpley Stoke, near Bath. *T:* Limpley Stoke 3308.

PALMER, Most Rev. Norman Kitchener; *see* Melanesia, Archbishop of.

PALMER, Brig. Sir Otho Leslie P.; *see* Prior-Palmer.

PALMER, Maj.-Gen. Peter Garwood, MBE 1944; FIMechE; MBIM; Deputy Secretary, Institution of Mechanical Engineers, since 1971; *b* 2 March 1914; *s* of H. G. Palmer, Great Yarmouth, Norfolk; *m* 1945, Isabel Mary Kinsley Boucher; one *s. Educ:* Haileybury College, Herts; Sheffield University (BEng). Petters Ltd, Yeovil, Som: Graduate Apprentice, 1933-35; Development Engineer, 1935-38. Regular Army Officer: RAOC, 1938-42; REME, 1942-71 (MBE); Dep. Dir of Electrical and Mechanical Engineering (Army), MoD, 1965-68; Comdt, Technical Gp, REME, Woolwich, 1968-71. Col Comdt, REME, 1973-. *Recreations:* gardening, photography, sport. *Address:* 127 Claygate Lane, Hinchley Wood, Esher, Surrey. *Club:* St Stephen's.

PALMER, Maj.-Gen. (Retd) Philip Francis, CB 1957; OBE 1945; Major-General late Royal Army Medical Corps; *b* 8 Aug. 1903. MB, BCh, BAO, Dublin, 1926; DPH 1936. Served North West Frontier of India, 1930-31 (medal and clasp). Adjutant Territorial Army, 1932-36. War of 1939-45 (OBE). Director of Medical Services, Middle East Land Forces, Dec. 1955; QHS, 1956-60, retired. Col Comdt, RAMC, 1963-67. *Address:* c/o Williams & Glyn's Bank Ltd, Whitehall, SW1.

PALMER, Robert Henry Stephen; a Recorder of the Crown Court, since 1972; *b* 13 Nov. 1927; *s* of Henry Alleyn Palmer and Maud (*née* Obbard); *m* 1955, Geraldine Elizabeth Anne Evens; one *s* two *d. Educ:* Charterhouse; University Coll., Oxford. Called to the Bar, 1950. Dep. Chm., Berks QS, 1970. *Publications:* Harris's Criminal Law, 1960; Guide to Divorce, 1965. *Recreations:* numismatics, surf-riding. *Address:* 44 Staveley Road, Chiswick, W4 3ES. *T:* 01-994 3394.

PALMER, Sidney John, CB 1972; OBE 1953; Deputy Director General, Ships, and Head of Royal Corps of Naval Constructors, 1968-73; *b* 28 Nov. 1913; *m* 1941, Mavis Beatrice Blennerhassett Hallett; four *s. Educ:* RNC Greenwich. WhSch 1937. Admty Experiment Works, Haslar, 1938; Portsmouth Dockyard, 1942; Chief Constructor, Sydney, 1945; Constructor Comdr, Hong Kong, 1946; Chief Constructor Aircraft Carriers, 1948; Prof. of Naval Architecture, RNC Greenwich, 1952; Asst Dir Dreadnought Project, 1959; Dep. Dir Polaris Programme, 1963; Dir Naval Ship Production, 1966; Dep. Dir General Ships, 1968. Mem. Council, RINA, 1960; Liveryman, Shipwrights' Co., 1968; Hon. Research Fellow, UCL, 1968. Mem., Cttee of Management, RNLI, 1974-. *Recreations:* tennis, golf, bridge. *Address:* Bloomfield Avenue, Bath, Avon. *T:* Bath 312592.

PALMER, William John, CBE 1973; Judge of Her Majesty's Chief Court for the Persian Gulf, 1967-72; a part-time Chairman of Industrial Tribunals, since 1975; *b* 25 April 1909; *o s* of late William Palmer and late Mary Louisa Palmer (*née* Dibb), Suffolk House, Cheltenham; *m* 1st, 1935, Zenaida Nicolaevna (*d* 1944), *d* of late Nicolai Maropoulo, Yalta, Russia; 2nd, 1949, Vanda Ianthe Millicent, *d* of late William Matthew Cowton, Kelvin Grove, Queensland; one *s* two *d. Educ:* Pate's Grammar School, Cheltenham; Christ's College, Cambridge (Lady Margaret Scholar). Barrister, Gray's Inn. Joined Indian Civil Service, 1932; Deputy Commissioner, Jalpaiguri, 1943, Chief Presidency Magistrate, Calcutta, 1945; retired from ICS, 1949. Joined Colonial Legal Service as Magistrate, Nigeria, 1950; Chief Registrar, High Court, Eastern Region, 1956; Judge, 1958; Acting Chief Justice of Eastern Nigeria, Oct.-Dec. 1963 and Aug.-Nov. 1965. Judge of HM's Court for Bahrain and Assistant Judge of the Chief Court for the Persian Gulf, 1965-67. *Recreations:* swimming, travel, history. *Address:* Guys Farm, Icomb, Glos GL54 1JD. *T:* Stow-on-the-Wold 30219. *Clubs:* East India, Devonshire, Sports and Public Schools; Union (Sydney, NSW).

PALUELLO, L. M.; see Minio-Paluello.

PANCKRIDGE, Surg. Vice-Adm. Sir (William) Robert
(Silvester), KBE 1962; CB 1960; Medical Director-General of
the Navy, 1960-63, retired; b 11 Sept. 1901; s of W. P.
Panckridge, OBE, MB, MRCS, LRCP, and Mrs Panckridge; m
1932, Edith Muriel, d of Sir John and Lady Crosbie, St John,
Newfoundland; one d. Educ: Tonbridge School; Middlesex
Hospital. FRSM 1955; QHP 1958. PMO, RN Coll., Dartmouth,
1948; Medical Officer-in-Charge; RN Hosp., Hong Kong, 1952;
RN Hosp., Chatham, 1958; Surgeon Captain, 1952; Surgeon
Rear-Admiral, 1958; Surgeon Vice-Admiral, 1960. QHP, 1958-
63. CStJ 1959. Recreations: shooting, fishing, gardening.
Address: Waterfall Lodge, Oughterard, Co. Galway. T: Galway
82168.

PANDIT, Vijaya Lakshmi, (Mrs Ranjit S. Pandit); Member of
Congress, Uttar Pradesh-Phulpur, India, 1964-68; b 18 August
1900; d of Motilal Nehru and Sarup Rani Nehru; m 1921, Ranjit
S. Pandit; three d. Educ: privately. Member Municipal Board,
Allahabad, and Chm. Education Cttee, 1935; MLA, UP, and
Minister of Local Govt and Health in Congress Cabinet of UP,
1937-39, and 1946-47. Leader India delegation to UN General
Assembly, 1946, 1947, 1948; Ambassador to Moscow, 1947-49;
Ambassador of India to the USA and Mexico, 1949-51; Member
of Indian Parliament, 1952-54; High Commissioner for India in
London, and Indian Ambassador to Ireland, 1954-61,
concurrently Indian Ambassador to Spain, 1958-61; Governor
of Maharashtra, 1962-64. Imprisoned three times for
participation in national movement, 1932, 1941, 1942. President
of the United Nations Assembly, 1953-54. Hon. DCL, Oxford,
1964, and numerous other Hon. degrees from Universities and
Colleges. Publication: The Evolution of India (Whidden
Lectures), 1958. Address: 181B Rajpur Road, Dehra Dun, Uttar
Pradesh, India.

PANET, Brig. Henri de Lotbinière, CBE 1943 (OBE 1941); b 21
Apr. 1896; s of late Brig.-Gen. A. E. Panet, CB, CMG, DSO; m
1931, Truda Buchanan Hope; one d. Educ: Loyola Coll.,
Montreal; Royal Military Coll., Canada. Served European War,
1915-18. Royal Engineers, France and Salonica (wounded,
despatches); Indian State Railways, 1920-34; served Egypt and
Palestine, 1935-36 (despatches); Hong Kong, 1938-41 (OBE);
Iraq and Persia, 1941-43 (CBE); BLA, 1944-45 (despatches);
Director of Fortifications and Works, War Office, 1947-49;
retired, 1949. Recreation: fishing. Address: 161 Wilton Road,
Salisbury, Wilts. T: Salisbury 3615.

PANKHURST, Air Vice-Marshal (Retd) Leonard Thomas, CB
1955; CBE 1944; b 26 August 1902; s of late Thomas William
Pankhurst, Teddington, Middlesex; m 1939, Ruth, d of late
Alexander Phillips, Cromer, Norfolk; one s two d. Educ:
Hampton Grammar School. Joined Royal Air Force, 1925;
Group Captain, 1942; Air Commodore, 1947; Actg Air Vice-
Marshal, 1954. Served War of 1939-45 (despatches, CBE);
Directorate of War Organisation, Air Ministry, 1938-41; Coastal
Command, 1941-42; Mediterranean Air Forces, 1942-45. Air
Officer Commanding 44 Group Transport Command, 1945-46;
Asst Comdt RAF Staff Coll., 1946; idc, 1947; Dir Staff Trg, Air
Ministry, 1948-50; Air Officer Commanding RAF E Africa,
1950-52; Dir of Postings, Air Ministry, 1953-54; Director-
General of Personnel (I), Air Ministry, 1954-57. Address: Earl's
Eye House, Sandy Lane, Chester. T: Chester 20993.

PANNELL, family name of Baron Pannell.

PANNELL, Baron cr 1974 (Life Peer), of the City of Leeds;
Thomas Charles Pannell, PC 1964; b 10 Sept. 1902; s of James
William and Mary Jane Pannell; m 1929, Lilian Maud Frailing;
one d. Hon. Secretary, Trade Union Group Parliamentary
Labour Party, 1953-64; Member AEU, 1918-; Member
Walthamstow Borough Council, 1929-36, Chief Whip of Labour
Group; Chairman: Rating and Valuation Cttee; Municipal
Entertainments Cttee; Erith Borough Council, 1938-55. Leader
of Council and Chairman of Finance and General Purposes
Cttee, until 1949; responsible Chairman during whole of War of
1939-45, for post-blitz services; Mayor, 1945-46, Alderman,
1944-55. Chairman of NW Kent Divisional Exec. for Education,
1944-55; Member and Dep. Leader, Kent County Council
Labour Group, 1946-49. Member Labour Party, 1918-; Past
Chairman Dartford Divisional Labour Party. MP (Lab) W
Leeds, 1949-74. Parliamentary Delegations, Inter-Parliamentary
Union: Berne, 1951; Belgium, 1952; NATO Conference of
Parliamentarians, 1955-56-57; Poland, 1958; W Germany, 1960;
Singapore, 1966 (Leader); NZ CPA, 1971; UAR, 1973 (Leader);
Deleg. Atlantic Congress, 1959. Member Select Cttee on:
Accommodation, 1953-54; Procedure, 1958-59; Law of
Privilege, 1967; Member Joint Select Cttee, Lords and

Commons, on House of Lords Reform, 1962; Minister of Public
Building and Works, 1964-66; British Delegate, CPA
Conference, Ottawa, 1966; Member, Cttee of Privileges, 1968-
74. Vice-Pres., Assoc. of Municipal Corporations. Hon. LLD
Leeds, 1975. Address: 159 Glenview, Abbey Wood, SE2. T: 01-
310 4180.

PANNETT, Juliet Kathleen, (Mrs M. R. D. Pannett), PS; FRSA;
Portrait Painter; Free Lance Artist to The Times, Daily
Telegraph, Radio Times, etc; Special Artist to Illustrated
London News, 1958-65; b Hove; 2nd d of Charles Somers and
May Brice, Hove, Sussex; m 1938, Major M. R. D. Pannett, late
the Devonshire Regt; one s one d. Educ: Wistons Sch., Brighton;
Brighton College of Art. Exhibitions: Royal Festival Hall, 1957,
1958; Qantas Gallery, 1959; New York, 1960; Cleveland, Ohio,
1960; Cooling Gallery, 1961; Coventry Cathedral Festival, 1962;
Gloucester Three Choirs Festival, 1962; Brighton Corporation
Gallery, Rottingdean, 1967; Arun Art Centre, 1967, 1969, 1972;
Fine Art Gall., 1969; Mignon Gall., Bath, 1970. Exhibitor:
Royal Academy; Royal Society of Portrait Painters; Royal Inst.
of Painters in Watercolours, etc. Official Artist on Qantas
Inaugural Jet Flight, London to Sydney, 1959, London to Hong
Kong, 1964; Air Canada Inaugural Flight, London to
Vancouver, 1968. Freeman: City of London; Painter Stainers'
Company. Work in Permanent Collections: portraits in:
National Portrait Gall., Brighton Art Gall.; Hove Art Gall.;
Worthing Art Gall.; Cambridge Colleges; Maudsley Hospital;
Army Phys. Training Sch., Aldershot; Painter Stainers' Hall,
London; Edinburgh Univ.; Portraits, many for official bodies,
include: HRH Prince Andrew, HRH Prince Edward, for HM
The Queen; HRH Princess Marina, Duchess of Kent, 1968;
Olave Lady Baden-Powell; Sir Bernard Lovell; Earl Spencer; Sir
Barnes Wallis; Lord Widgery; Sir John Glubb; Sir Edward
Howard; The Rt Rev. Norman Porteous; Sir Neville Mott;
Edward Heath; Sir Harold Wilson; David Ben Gurion; Lord
Goodman; Commemorative Stained Glass Window, Garrison
church, Münster, 1967. Publications: Illustr. articles in The
Artist; Leisure Painter; Illustr. for article in The Lancet;
portraits in: S. J. Goldsmith's 20 Twentieth Century Jews; A.
Frank's Svetlana Beriosova; action studies, Ballet Annual, 1956,
1957, 1958, 1959, 1960; cover portraits: Gerald Pawle's The War
and Colonel Warden; Law Guardian; Guardian Gazette;
frontispieces, etc. Recreations: watercolour landscape, travel,
music. Address: Pound House, Angmering Village, Sussex. T:
Rustington 4446. Club: Press.

PANT, Apasaheb Balasaheb; Padma Shri 1954; retired 1975; b 11
Sept. 1912; s of Pratinidhis of Aundh; m 1942, Nalini Pant, MB,
BS, FRCS; two s one d. Educ: Univ. of Bombay (BA); Univ. of
Oxford (MA). Barrister-at-Law, Lincoln's Inn. Educn Minister,
Aundh State; Prime Minister, 1944-48 (when State was merged
into Bombay State). Member, AICC, 1948; an alternate Deleg.,
of India, at UN, 1951 and 1952; Comr for Govt of India in Brit.
E Africa, 1948-54; apptd Consul-Gen. for Belgian Congo and
Ruanda-Urundi, Nov. 1950, and Comr for Central Africa and
Nyasaland, Dec. 1950; Officer on Special Duty, Min. of Ext.
Affairs, 1954-55; Polit. Officer in Sikkim and Bhutan with
control over Indian Missions in Tibet, 1955-61; Ambassador of
India: to Indonesia, Oct. 1961-June 1964; to Norway, 1964-66;
to UAR, 1966-69; High Comr in London, 1969-72; Ambassador
to Italy, 1972-75. Vis. Fellow, The Indian Institute of Advanced
Studies. Publications: Tensions and Tolerance, 1965; Aggression
and Violence: Gandhian experiments to fight them, 1968; Yoga,
1968 (Arabic edn); Surya Namaskar, 1969 (Italian edn);
Mahatma Gandhi; A Moment in Time; Mandala, An
Awakening; Progress, Power, Peace and India. Recreations:
photography, yoga, tennis, ski-ing, gliding. Address: Pant
Niwas, Bhandarkar Road, Deccan Gymkhana, Poona 4, India.
T: 58615.

PANTCHEFF, Theodore Xenophon Henry, CMG 1977; HM
Diplomatic Service, retired; b 29 Dec. 1920; s of Sophocles
Xenophon Pantcheff and Ella Jessie, d of Dr S. H. Ramsbotham,
Leeds; m 1954, Patricia Mary Tully; two s. Educ: Merchant
Taylors' Sch.; Gonville and Caius Coll., Cambridge (MA). HM
Forces, 1941-47; Control Commn for Germany, 1948-51; joined
Foreign Office, 1951; Vice-Consul, Munich, 1954-56; 1st Sec.,
Lagos, 1958-60; 1st Sec., Leopoldville, 1961-63; seconded MoD,
1969-71; Counsellor, FCO, 1971-77. Recreations: reading and
conversation. Address: Butes Cottage, Alderney. Clubs: Junior
Carlton; Alderney Society (Alderney).

PANTER-DOWNES, Mollie Patricia, (Mrs Clare Robinson);
London Correspondent The New Yorker, since 1939; b 25 Aug.
1906; o c of late Major Edward Panter-Downes, Royal Irish
Regt; m 1927, Clare, 3rd s of late Aubrey Robinson; two d.
Educ: mostly private. Wrote novel, The Shoreless Sea, at age of
16 (published John Murray, 1924); wrote in various English and

American publications. *Publications:* Letter from England (Atlantic Monthly Press), 1940; Watling Green (children's book) (Scribners), 1943; One Fine Day, 1947; Ooty Preserved, 1967; At the Pines, 1971; London War Notes, 1972; contributed to The New Yorker Book of War Pieces, 1947. *Address:* Roppelegh's, near Haslemere, Surrey.

PANTIN, Most Rev. Anthony; *see* Port of Spain, Archbishop of.

PANTON, Air Cdre Alastair Dyson, CB 1969; OBE 1950; DFC 1939; Provost Marshal and Director of RAF Security, 1968-71; retired; *b* 2 Nov. 1916; third *s* of William Dickson Panton, Aberdeen, and Mary Ethel Langley, Bedford; *m* 1939, Eileen Isabel Lumley, Bedford; three *s* (and one *s* decd). *Educ:* Bedford School; RAF Coll., Cranwell. Pilot Officer, No 53 Sqdn RAF, 1937; POW 1940-45; OC, Nos 58 and 540 Sqdns, 1946-47; Air Staff, Hong Kong, 1948-50; Wing Comdr Flying, RAF Coningsby, 1951-53; Staff Coll., 1953-54; Air Ministry, 1954-57; Station Comdr, RAF Cranwell, 1957-60, RAF Bircham Newton, 1961-62, RAF Tern Hill, 1963-64; HQ Far East Air Force, 1965-67. *Recreations:* gardening, poetry, Tchaikovsky. *Address:* Penrhyn Castle, Bangor, Gwynedd. *T:* Bangor 53084.

PANTON, Dr Francis Harry, MBE 1948; Director of Propellants, Explosives and Rocket Motor Establishment, Waltham Abbey and Westcott (formerly ERDE Waltham and RPE Westcott), and Head of Rocket Motor Executive, Ministry of Defence, since 1976; *b* 25 May 1923; 3rd *s* of George Emerson Panton and Annie Panton; *m* 1952, Audrey Mary (*née* Lane); two *s. Educ:* City Sch., Lincoln; University College and Univ. of Nottingham. PhD Nottingham 1952. Served War of 1939-45: commissioned, Bomb Disposal, Royal Eng., 1943-47. Pres., Univ. of Nottingham Union, 1950-51; Vice-Pres., Nat. Union of Students, 1952-54; Technical Officer, ICI, Billingham, 1952-53; Permanent Under-Secretary's Dept, FO, 1953-55; Office of Political Adviser, Berlin, 1955-57; Dep. Head, Technical Research Unit, MoD, 1957-58; Attaché, British Embassy, Washington, DC, 1958-59; Technical Adviser, UK Delegn to Conf. on Discontinuance of Nuclear Tests, Geneva, 1959-61; Permanent Under-Secretary's Dept, FO, 1961-63; Counsellor (Defence), British Embassy, Washington, DC, 1963-66; Head of Defence Science 6, MoD, 1966-68; Asst Chief Scientific Adviser (Nuclear), MoD, 1969-76; Dir Gen., Estabs, Resources and Programmes (B), MoD, April-Sept. 1976. FRIC 1961; FRSA 1973. *Recreations:* bridge, reading local history. *Address:* 1 St Peter's Lane, Canterbury, Kent. *T:* Canterbury 52902. *Club:* Reform.

PANUFNIK, Andrzej; composer and conductor; *b* 24 Sept. 1914; 2nd *s* of Tomasz Panufnik and Mathilda Thonnes Panufnik; *m* 1963, Camilla Ruth, *yr d* of Commander R. F. Jessel, DSO, OBE, DSC, RN (retired); one *s* one *d. Educ:* Warsaw State Conservatoire; Vienna State Acad. for Music (under Professor Felix von Weingartner). Diploma with distinction, Warsaw Conservatoire, 1936. Conductor of the Cracow Philharmonic, 1945-46; Director and Conductor of the Warsaw Philharmonic Orchestra, 1946-47. Conducting leading European orchestras such as L'Orchestre National, Paris, Berliner Philharmonisches Orchester, L'Orchestre de la Suisse Romande, Geneva, and all principal British orchestras, 1947-. Polish decorations: Standard of Labor 1st class (1949), twice State Laureate (1951, 1952). Left Poland and settled in England, 1954; naturalized British subject, 1961. Vice-Chairman of International Music Council of UNESCO, Paris, 1950-53; Musical Director and Conductor, City of Birmingham Symphony Orchestra, 1957-59. Hon. Member of International Mark Twain Society (USA), 1954; Knight of Mark Twain, 1966. The Sibelius Centenary Medal, 1965. *Ballets:* Elegy, NY, 1967; Cain and Abel, Berlin, 1968; Miss Julie, Stuttgart, 1970. *Publications:* Piano Trio, 1934; Five Polish Peasant Songs, 1940; Tragic Overture, 1942; Twelve Miniature Studies for piano, 1947; Nocturne for orchestra, 1947; Lullaby for 29 stringed instruments and 2 harps, 1947; Sinfonia Rustica, 1948; Hommage à Chopin-Five vocalises for soprano and piano, 1949; Old Polish Suite for strings, 1950; Concerto in modo antico, 1951; Heroic Overture, 1952; Rhapsody for orchestra, 1956; Sinfonia Elegiaca, 1957; Polonia-Suite for Orchestra, 1959; Piano Concerto, 1961; Autumn Music, 1962; Landscape, 1962; Two Lyric Pieces, 1963; Sinfonia Sacra, 1963 (first prize, Prix de Composition Musicale Prince Rainier III de Monaco, 1963); Song to the Virgin Mary, 1964; Katyn Epitaph, 1966; Jagiellonian Triptych, 1966; Reflections for piano, 1967; The Universal Prayer, 1969; Thames Pageant, 1969; Violin Concerto, 1971; Triangles, 1972; Winter Solstice, 1972; Sinfonia Concertante, 1973; Sinfonia di Sfere, 1974; String Quartet, 1976. *Address:* Riverside House, Twickenham, Middlesex.
See also O. R. Jessel, T. F. H. Jessel.

PAOLOZZI, Eduardo Luigi, CBE 1968; ARA 1972; Sculptor; Tutor, Royal College of Art; *b* 7 March 1924; *s* of Rudolpho Antonio Paolozzi and Carmella (*née* Rossi), both Italian; *m* 1951, Freda Elliott; three *d. Educ:* Edinburgh School of Art; Slade Sch. Worked in Paris, 1947-50; Instructor, Central School of Arts and Crafts, London, 1950-55; Lecturer, St Martin's School of Art, 1955-56. *One-man exhibitions:* first in London, Mayor Gallery, 1947; first in New York, Betty Parsons Gallery, 1960, also 1962; Tate Gallery, 1971; Marlborough Fine Art Gallery, 1976; Anthony d'Offay Gall., 1977. Retrospective: V&A, 1977. Work in permanent collections: Tate Gallery; Contemporary Art Society; Museum of Modern Art, New York, etc. Work exhibited in: British Pavilion, Venice Biennale, 1952; Documenta 2, Kassel, 1959; New Images of Man, New York, 1959; British Pavilion, 30th Venice Biennale; International Exhibition of Sculpture, Boymans Museum, Rotterdam; Open Air Sculpture, Battersea Park, London; Critics Choice, Tooths Gallery, London; City Art Gallery, Manchester, Oct. 1960; British Sculpture in the Sixties, Tate Gallery, March 1965; Chelsea School of Art, 1965; Hanover Gallery, 1967; Tate Gall., 1971. *Recreation:* music. *Address:* 107 Dovehouse Street, SW3; Landermere, Thorpe-le-Soken, Essex. *T:* Thorpe-le-Soken 210.

PAPADOPOULOS, Achilles Symeon, MVO 1972; MBE 1954; HM Diplomatic Service; HM Ambassador to El Salvador, since 1977; *b* 16 Aug. 1923; *s* of late Symeon Papadopoulos and of Polyxene Papadopoulos; *m* 1954, Joyce Martin (*née* Stark); one *s* two *d. Educ:* The English School, Nicosia, Cyprus. British Mil. Admin, Eritrea, 1943; HMOCS: Cyprus, 1953; Dar es Salaam, 1959; Malta, 1961; HM Diplomatic Service: Malta, 1965; Nairobi, 1965; FCO, 1968; Colombo, 1971; Washington, 1974; Havana, 1974. *Recreations:* golf, bridge, travelling. *Address:* c/o Foreign and Commonwealth Office, SW1A 2AH; 5 Lansdowne Close, Wimbledon, SW20 8AS. *Club:* Royal Commonwealth Society.

PAPE, Hon. Sir George (Augustus), Kt 1968; Judge of Supreme Court of Victoria, 1957-75, retired; *b* 29 Jan. 1903; *s* of George Frederick Pape and Minnie Maud Pape (*née* Bryan); *m* 1952, Mabel, *d* of Alfred Lloyd; no *c. Educ:* All Saints Grammar Sch., St Kilda; University of Melbourne (LLB). QC 1955. RAAF, 1940-46. *Recreations:* tennis, golf. *Address:* 146 Kooyong Road, Toorak, Victoria 3142, Australia. *T:* 20-6158. *Club:* Australian (Melbourne).

PAPE, Jonathan Hector Carruthers; Chief General Manager, National Dock Labour Board, since 1975 (General Manager and Secretary, 1970-75); *b* 8 March 1918; *er s* of Jonathan Pape, MA and Florence Muriel Myrtle; *m* 1944, Mary Sullins (*née* Jeffries); one *s. Educ:* Merchant Taylors' Sch., Crosby. Mercantile Marine, 1934-46; Master Mariner (FG), 1944 (Liverpool Qualif.). Manager, Master Stevedoring Co., Liverpool, 1947-51; National Dock Labour Board: Dep. Port Manager, London, 1952-57; Asst Gen. Manager, Bd HQ, 1957-69; Dep. Gen. Manager and Secretary, Bd HQ, 1969. Mem., Honourable Co. of Master Mariners, 1965. Freeman, City of London. FCIT. *Recreations:* swimming, gardening, and riding at anchor in what spare time is left. *Address:* 4 Knole Way, Sevenoaks, Kent. *T:* Sevenoaks 52820. *Club:* Wig and Pen.

PAPUA NEW GUINEA, Archbishop of, since 1976; Most Rev. Geoffrey David Hand, CBE 1975; *b* 11 May 1918; *s* of Rev. W. T. Hand. *Educ:* Oriel College, Oxford; Cuddesdon Theological College, BA 1941, MA 1946. Deacon, 1942; Priest, 1943. Curate of Heckmondwike, 1942-46; Missioner, Diocese of New Guinea, 1946-50; Priest in charge: Sefoa, 1947-48; Sangara, 1948-50; Archdeacon, North New Guinea, 1950-65; Bishop Coadjutor of New Guinea, 1950-63; Bishop of New Guinea (later Papua New Guinea), 1963-76. *Address:* PO Box 806, Port Moresby, Papua New Guinea.

PARARAJASINGAM, Sir Sangarapillai, Kt 1955; Senator, Ceylon, 1954-59; Chairman, Board of Directors, Colonial Motors Ltd, 1961-74; former Member, Board of Trustees, Ceylon Social Service League; *b* 25 June 1896; *s* of late W. Sangarapillai, social worker and philanthropist; *m* 1916, Padmavati, *d* of Sir Ponnambalam Arunachalam; one *s* one *d. Educ:* St Thomas' Coll., Mt Lavinia. Past President, Board of Directors, Manipay Hindu Coll., Manager, 1929-61; Past President Ceylon Poultry Club; Member National Savings Cttee; Past Chairman, Board Governors, Ceylon Inst. of Scientific and Industrial Research. Formerly Chairman: Board of Directors, Agricultural and Industrial Credit Corporation of Ceylon; Education Cttee, Ceylon Social Service League; Low Country Products Assoc., 1943-44 and 1944-45; Ceylon Coconut Board; Coconut Commn; Past Member: Textile Tribunal; Land Advisory Cttee; Ceylon Tea Propaganda Board; Coconut Research Scheme; Radio Advisory Board; Excise Advisory

Cttee; Central Board of Agriculture; Income Tax Board of Review; Rice Advisory Board; Services Standing Wages Board; Board for Approval of Credit Agencies; Commn on Broadcasting; Past President Vivekananda Society; Rotary Club of Colombo; Governor, Rotary Internat. District 320, 1951-52; formerly Trustee and Hon. Treasurer, Ceylon Society of Arts; formerly Manager, all Schools managed by Ceylon Social Service League. JP Ceylon 1923. Travelled widely in the UK, Europe, USA, India, Far East. Coronation Medals, 1937 and 1953. *Recreations:* gardening, agriculture and farming. *Address:* No 50, Pathmalaya, Flower Road, Colombo 7, Sri Lanka. *T:* 23159.
See also P. Nadesan.

PARBURY, George Mark; Chief Registrar of the High Court of Justice in Bankruptcy, since 1975; *b* 27 April 1908; *s* of Norman Cecil Parbury (living in Queensland) and late Ellen Parbury; *m* 1942, Roma Constance, *d* of late James Robert Raw, JP, New Zealand, and Clare Raw. *Educ:* Geelong, Australia; Jesus Coll., Cambridge. Called to Bar, Lincoln's Inn, 1934. Practised at Chancery Bar, 1934-39. Served War of 1939-45, 1940-45, Temp. Lt-Col, 1944; AAG, AG3e War Office, Mil. Govt 21 Army Group. Again practised at Chancery Bar, 1946-65; Mem. Bar Council, 1961-62. Registrar, High Court of Justice in Bankruptcy, 1965-75. *Recreations:* walking on the Downs; gardening. *Address:* The Orchard, Paine's Twitten, Lewes, East Sussex. *T:* Lewes 3529. *Club:* Army and Navy.

PARDOE, John George Magrath, CBE 1975; FRAeS; Director-General, Airworthiness, Civil Aviation Authority, since 1972. *Educ:* Coll. of Aeronautical Engineering. Entered design work in Aircraft Industry, 1935; joined Accidents Inspection Br. of Air Ministry, 1942; joined Staff, Air Registration Bd, 1945; Chief Technical Officer, 1969. *Address:* Civil Aviation Authority, Brabazon House, Redhill, Surrey RH1 1SQ.

PARDOE, John Wentworth; MP (L) Cornwall North since 1966; *b* 27 July 1934; *s* of Cuthbert B. Pardoe and Marjorie E. W. (*née* Taylor); *m* 1958, Joyce R. Peerman; two *s* one *d*. *Educ:* Sherborne; Corpus Christi Coll., Cambridge (MA). Television Audience Measurement Ltd, 1958-60; Osborne Peacock Co. Ltd, 1960-61; Liberal News, 1961-66. Treasurer of the Liberal Party, 1968-69. Consultant to Nat. Assoc. of Schoolmasters, 1967-73. Director: William Schlackman Ltd, 1968-71; Gerald Metals; Mem. London Metal Exchange. Mem., IBA Gen. Adv. Council, 1973-. *Recreations:* cricket, walking, singing. *Address:* House of Commons, SW1; Chy-an-Porth, Trevone, Padstow, Cornwall.

PARE, Rev. Philip Norris; Vicar of Cholsey, diocese of Oxford, since 1973; *b* 13 May 1910; *s* of Frederick William and Florence May Pare; *m* 1943, Nancy Eileen, *d* of late Canon C. Patteson; two *s* two *d*. *Educ:* Nottingham High Sch.; King's Coll., Cambridge; Cuddesdon Theological Coll. Curate, All Saints, W Dulwich, 1934-37; Chaplain and Vice-Principal, Bishops Coll., Cheshunt, 1937-39; Curate, St Mary the Less, Cambridge, 1939-40. Chaplain RNVR, 1940-46. Vicar of Cheshunt, Herts, 1946-57; Rural Dean of Ware, 1949-56; Examining Chaplain to Bishop of St Albans, 1952-56; Missioner Canon Stipendiary, Diocese of Wakefield, 1957-62; Diocesan Adviser for Christian Stewardship, 1959-68; Provost, and Vicar of Cathedral Church of All Saints, Wakefield, 1962-71. A Church Commissioner, 1968-71; Member Board of Ecclesiastical Insurance Office, 1966-; Provost of Woodward Schools (Northern Div.), 1977-. *Publications:* (with Donald Harris) Eric Milner-White, A Memoir, 1965; Re-Thinking Our Worship, 1967; articles in Theology, The Reader, etc. *Recreations:* modern stained glass and architecture; railways, motor cars; church music. *Address:* Cholsey Vicarage, Wallingford, Oxon. *T:* Cholsey 651216.

PARENT, Most Rev. Charles Eugène, ThD; former Archbishop of Rimouski, from 1970; Titular Archbishop of Vassinassa, 1967-70; *b* Les Trois-Pistoles, Qué, 22 April 1902; *s* of Louis Parent and Marie Lavoie. *Educ:* Rimouski Seminary; Laval University of Quebec; Institutum Angelicum, Rome. ThD 1929. Professor of Theology at Rimouski Seminary and Chaplain at St Joseph's Hospital of Rimouski, 1931-41; Rector of Saint Germain's Cathedral, 1941-45; Auxiliary Bishop at Rimouski, 1944-50; Capitulaire Vicaire, 1950-51; Archbishop of Rimouski, 1951-67. *Publication:* Mandements et circulaires au clergé et au peuple de l'archidiocèse de Rimouski, 3 vols, 1951-67. *Address:* Archevêché, PO Box 730, Rimouski, Québec G5L 7C7, Canada.

PARES, Peter; *b* 6 Sept. 1908; 2nd *s* of late Sir Bernard Pares, KBE, DCL, and late Margaret Pares (*née* Dixon); unmarried. *Educ:* Lancing Coll.; Jesus Coll., Cambridge (Scholar). Entered Consular Service, 1930; served in Philadelphia, 1930; Havana, 1932; Consul, Liberec and Bratislava, Czechoslovakia, 1936-39;

Budapest, 1939; Cluj, Rumania, 1940; New York, 1941; Washington, as First Secretary, 1944; Control Commission for Germany, 1946; Foreign Office, 1949; Casablanca, 1952; Strasbourg, 1956; Deputy Consul-General, Frankfurt, 1957; Consul-General, Asmara, Eritrea, 1957-59; Head of Education and Cultural Relations Dept, CRO, 1960-63. *Address:* 17 Beechwood Crescent, Eastbourne, East Sussex.

PARFITT, Rt. Rev. Thomas Richards; Assistant Bishop, diocese of Derby since 1962; Rector of Matlock with Tansley since 1962; *b* 24 May 1911; *s* of Charles Henry John and Maud Sarah Parfitt. *Educ:* S John Baptist Coll., Oxford. BA Oxon 1933 (2nd class Lit. Hum., 1933; 2nd class Theology, 1934); MA 1936. Cuddesdon Coll., 1934-35. Deacon, 1935; Priest, 1936; Asst Curate of New Mills, 1935-39; Curate of Rugby (in charge of Holy Trinity), 1939-43; Chaplain RNVR, 1943-46; Vicar of S Andrew, Derby, 1946-52; Rural Dean of Derby, 1951-52; Bishop in Madagascar, 1952-61. *Address:* Matlock Rectory, Derbyshire DE4 3BZ. *T:* Matlock 2199.

PARGETER, Edith; *b* 28 Sept. 1913; 3rd *c* of Edmund Valentine Pargeter and Edith Hordley; unmarried. *Educ:* Dawley C of E Elementary Sch.; County High School for Girls, Coalbrookdale. Worked as a chemist's assistant, and at twenty succeeded in finding a publisher for first-and unsuccessful-book. WRNS Aug. 1940, teleprinter operator (BEM 1944); dispersed from the Service, Aug. 1945. FIIAL 1962. Gold Medal and Ribbon, Czechoslovak Society for International Relations, 1968. *Publications:* Hortensius, Friend of Nero, Iron Bound, 1936; The City Lies Foursquare, 1939; Ordinary People, 1941; She Goes to War, 1942; The Eighth Champion of Christendom, 1945; Reluctant Odyssey, 1946; Warfare Accomplished, 1947; By Firelight, 1948; The Fair Young Phoenix, 1948; The Coast of Bohemia, 1949; Lost Children, 1950; Fallen Into the Pit, 1951; Holiday with Violence, 1952; This Rough Magic, 1953; Most Loving Mere Folly, 1953; The Soldier at the Door, 1954; A Means of Grace, 1956; Tales of the Little Quarter (trans. from the Czech of Jan Neruda), 1957; Don Juan (trans. from the Czech of Josef Toman), 1958; Assize of the Dying, 1958; The Heaven Tree, 1960; The Green Branch 1962; The Scarlet Seed, 1963; The Terezí Requiem (trans. from the Czech of Josef Bor), 1963; The Lily Hand and other stories, 1965; Close Watch on the Trains (trans from the Czech of Bohumil Hrabal), 1968; Report on my Husband (trans. from the Czech of Josefa Slánská), 1969; A Bloody Field by Shrewsbury, 1972; Sunrise in the West, 1974; The Dragon at Noonday, 1975; The Hounds of Sunset, 1976; Afterglow and Nightfall, 1977. *Recreations:* collecting gramophone records, particularly of voice; reading anything and everything; theatre. *Address:* Parkville, Park Lane, Madeley, Telford, Salop. *T:* Telford 585178.

PARGITER, family name of **Baron Pargiter.**

PARGITER, Baron, *cr* 1966 (Life Peer) of Southall; **George Albert Pargiter,** CBE 1961; *b* 16 March 1897; *s* of William Pargiter, Greens Norton; *m* 1919, Dorothy Woods; two *s* one *d*. *Educ:* Towcester Grammar Sch. Engineer by profession. Served 1914-16 Army, at Gallipoli. MP (Lab) Spelthorne Division of Middlesex, 1945-50, Southall, 1950-66; Member Middlesex County Council, 1934-65, County Alderman, 1946 (Chairman, 1959-60). Member several public bodies. Mayor of Southall, 1938-40 (three years); DL Middlesex 1953; DL County of London, later Greater London, 1965-76. *Address:* 190 Whyteleafe Road, Caterham, Surrey CR3 5ED. *T:* Caterham 45588.

PARGITER, Maj.-Gen. Robert Beverley, CB 1942; CBE 1945; *b* 11 July 1889; *s* of late F. E. Pargiter, ICS; *m* 1st, 1917, Muriel Huxley (*d* 1971); one *s* two *d*; 2nd, 1973, Mrs Colin C. Gulliland. *Educ:* Rugby; RMA, Woolwich. Commissioned RA 1909; served with RA, European War, 1914-18, on NWF, India, France, and Belgium (severely wounded, despatches); Military Mission to Baltic States, 1919-21 (Brevet of Major); psc Camberley, 1924; Instructor Staff Coll., Quetta, 1930-33; idc 1934; GSO 1 Operations, WO, 1936-38; War Service, 1939-45; Commander 1st AA Brigade; 4th, 7th and 5th AA Divisions; 3rd AA Group; Maj.-Gen. Anti-Aircraft, Allied Force HQ, N. Africa and Central Mediterranean Forces (despatches, CBE, Commander of Legion of Merit); retired, 1945; Commissioner, British Red Cross and St John's War Organisation, Middle East, 1945, Malaya, 1946. Colonel Comdt RA, 1951-54. *Publication:* (with late Colonel H. Eady) The Army and Sea Power, 1927. *Recreations:* fishing, gardening, braille. *Address:* The Dye House, Biddenden, Kent.

PARHAM, Adm. Sir Frederick Robertson, GBE 1959 (CBE 1949); KCB 1955 (CB 1951); DSO 1944; *b* 9 Jan. 1901; *s* of late Frederick James Parham, Bath, and late Jessie Esther Brooks

Parham (*née* Robertson), Cheltenham; *m* 1926, Kathleen Dobrée, (*d* 1973), *d* of Eugene Edward Carey, Guernsey; one *s*. *Educ*: RN Colleges, Osborne and Dartmouth. Joined HMS Malaya as Midshipman, 1917; specialised in gunnery, 1925; Commander, 1934. Commanded HMS Shikari, 1937, HMS Gurkha, 1938-40. Captain, 1939. Commanded HMS Belfast, 1942-44 (despatches), HMS Vanguard, 1947-49; Dep. Chief, Naval Personnel, 1949-51; Rear-Admiral, 1949; Vice-Admiral, 1952; Flag Officer (Flotillas) and 2nd in command, Mediterranean, 1951-52; a Lord Commissioner of the Admiralty, Fourth Sea Lord and Chief of Supplies and Transport, 1954-55; Commander-in-Chief, The Nore, 1955-58; retired list, 1959. Member British Waterways Board, Jan. 1963-1967, Vice-Chairman (part-time) Aug. 1963-1967. Naval ADC to the King, 1949. Grand Cross of Military Order of Avis (Portugal), 1955; Order of Al Rafidain (Class II, Mil., conferred by the King of Iraq), 1956; Ordine al merito della Repubblica, Grande Ufficiale (Italy) 1958. *Address*: The High House, Elsted, Midhurst, West Sussex. *T*: Harting 296.

PARHAM, Hedley John, CBE 1955; MA, LLB (Cantab); JP; *b* 29 Oct. 1892; *s* of late Leonard Parham, JP, Gosport, Hants; *m* 1921, Irene, *d* of late H. E. Phillips, JP, Kintbury, Berks; two *s*. *Educ*: Leys Sch., Cambridge; Trinity Hall, Cambridge. Served European War (RE), 1914-19 (despatches). Called to the Bar (Inner Temple), 1919. Joined Department of Director of Public Prosecutions, 1920; Asst Director of Public Prosecutions, 1949-56; retired. JP Glos, 1957. *Address*: 4 The Mead, Cirencester, Glos GL7 2BB.

PARIKIAN, Manoug; violinist; Professor of Violin, Royal Academy of Music, since 1959; *b* Mersin, Turkey, 15 Sept. 1920, of Armenian parentage; *s* of late Stepan Parikian and Vanouhi (*née* Bedelian); *m* 1957, Diana Margaret (*née* Carbutt); two *s*. *Educ*: Trinity College of Music, London (Fellow). Leader: Liverpool Philharmonic Orchestra, 1947-48; Philharmonia Orchestra, London, 1949, until resignation, 1957; has appeared in all European countries as solo violinist, and at following festivals: Aldeburgh, 1949-51, 1968, 1973, 1975; Edinburgh, 1950, 1964; Holland, 1951; Aix-en-Provence, 1954; Baalbek, 1957; Three Choirs, 1958; Cheltenham, 1959-60, 1962, 1963, 1965; Lisbon (Gulbenkian), 1960; Llandaff, 1961; Coventry, 1962; Oxford, 1963; York, 1966; Leeds Triennial, 1967; Salisbury, 1975; Promenade concerts, Royal Albert Hall, 1952-. Introduced Shostakovitch Violin Concerto to Scandinavia (Stockholm), 1956; first public performance of works by Iain Hamilton, Rawsthorne, Musgrave, Alexander Goehr, Elizabeth Maconchy, Gordon Crosse and Hugh Wood. Toured: USSR, April-May 1961, and Nov. 1965; Latin America, July-Aug. 1974. Member Jury, Tchaikovsky violin competition, Moscow, 1970. Dir, Yorkshire Sinfonia, 1976-. Sir Robert Mayer Vis. Lectr, Leeds Univ., 1974-75. Hon. RAM, 1963. *Recreations*: collecting early printed books in Armenian; backgammon. *Address*: The Old Rectory, Waterstock, Oxford. *T*: Ickford 603.

PARIS, Sir Edward (Talbot), Kt 1954; CB 1947; DSc (London), FInstP; *b* 23 Jan. 1889; *s* of late Edward and Eliza Paris; *m* 1925, Eveline Amy (*d* 1968), *d* of late J. W. Shortt, MD; three *d*. *Educ*: Dean Close Sch., Cheltenham; Imperial College of Science; University College, London. Fellow University College, London, 1921; served European War, 1914-18, RA, 1915-18; seconded to Ministry of Munitions, 1918; Signals Experimental Establishment, War Dept, 1919; Experimental Officer in Air Defence Experimental Establishment, 1923; Dep. Director of Scientific Research, WO, 1938; transferred Ministry of Supply, 1939; Controller of Physical Research, 1941; Controller of Physical Research and Signals Development, 1942; Principal Director of Scientific Research (Defence), Ministry of Supply, 1946; Chief Scientific Adviser, Home Office, 1948-54. US Medal of Freedom with Bronze Palm, 1947. *Publications*: various papers in scientific journals. *Address*: Lavender Cottage, Crazy Lane, Sedlescombe, Sussex. *T*: Sedlescombe 261.

PARIS, John; Director, National Army Museum, 1967-69; *b* Hove, 2 May 1912; *s* of Herbert Henry Paris, Comptroller of Telegraphs and Postmaster, Durban, during Boer War; *m* 1940, Beryl Maria Thomson; no *c*. *Educ*: Brighton Coll.; Brighton College of Art; Worcester Coll., Oxford. BA (English) 1936; MA 1938; BLitt 1938. Commissioned into RA, 1940; SO Fixed Defences Scottish Command, 1942; Major. Dep. Director, Walker Art Gallery, Liverpool, 1938-49; Director, National Gallery of S Africa, Cape Town, 1949-62. Hon. Life Vice-President, Friends of Italy; Past President, S African Museums Assoc.; Kolbe Memorial Lecturer, University of Cape Town, 1961. Has made broadcasts. *Publications*: English Water-Colour Painters, 1945; William Gilpin and the Cult of the Picturesque; introductions, catalogues and articles in learned journals; occasional poems, etc. *Address*: Brook House, Ardingly, Sussex. *T*: Ardingly 274.

PARISH, David (Elmer) Woodbine, CBE 1964; Chairman, City and Guilds of London Institute since 1967; *b* 29 June 1911; *o s* of late Walter Woodbine Parish and Audrey Makins; *m* 1939, Mona Blair McGarel, *o d* of late Charles McGarel Johnston, Glynn, Co. Antrim; two *d*. *Educ*: Sandroyd; Eton; Lausanne, Switzerland. Chm. and Man. Dir, Holliday and Greenwood Ltd, 1953-59; Man. Dir, Bovis Holdings Ltd, 1960-66; Dep. Chm., Marine and General Mutual Life Assurance Soc., 1976- (Dir, 1971-). Chm., Jt Mission Hosp. Equip. Bd (ECHO), 1973-. President: London Master Builders Assoc., 1952; Nat. Fedn of Building Trades Employers, 1960; Member: Regional Adv. Council for Technological Educn, London and Home Counties, 1952-69; Architects Registration Council, 1952-72; Nat. Adv. Council for Educn in Industry and Commerce, 1953-; BIM Council, 1953-62, Bd of Fellows, 1966-72; Nat. Council for Technological Awards, 1955-61; Bd of Building Educn, 1955-66; Building Res. Bd, 1957-60; Industrial Training Council, 1958-64; Council, British Employers' Confedn, 1959-65; Council Foundn for Management Educn, 1959-65; British Productivity Council, 1961-70; Human Sciences Cttee (SRC), 1963-66; Construction Industry Training Bd, 1964-70. Chairman: UK Nat. Cttee, Internat. Apprentice Competition, 1962-70; MPBW Working Party on Res. and Information, 1963; Nat. Examinations Bd for Supervisory Studies, 1964-73; Nat. Jt Consult. Cttee of Architects, Quantity Surveyors and Builders, 1966-68; Dept of Health and Social Security Cttee of Inquiry on Hosp. Building Maintenance and Minor Capital Works, 1968-70; Member: Court, Russia Co., 1937-; Court, City Univ., 1967-72; Bd of Governors, The Polytechnic, Regent Street, 1967-70; Court, Polytechnic of Central London, 1970-76; Governing Body, Imperial Coll. of Science and Technology, 1971-. Vice-Pres., Internat. Fedn of European Contractors of Building and Public Works, 1967-71. Vice-Chm., Bd of Governors, St Thomas' Hosp., 1968-74; Chm. Council, St Thomas's Hosp. Med. Sch., 1970-; Member: Nightingale Fund Council, 1974-; Bd of Governors, Bethlem Royal Hosp. and Maudsley Hosp., 1975-. Warden, 1962-64, Master, 1974-75, Clothworkers' Co. FIOB 1940; FRSA 1953; FBIM 1957. Fellow, Imperial Coll., 1976. Hon. LLD Leeds, 1975. *Publications*: contribs to technical jls concerned with construction. *Recreations*: travel and music. *Address*: The Glebe Barn, Pulborough, West Sussex RH20 2AF. *T*: Pulborough 2613; 5 Lurgan Mansions, Sloane Square, SW1W 8BH. *T*: 01-730 6512. *Club*: Boodle's.

PARK, Daphne Margaret Sybil Désirée, CMG 1971; OBE 1960; HM Diplomatic Service; serving in Foreign and Commonwealth Office, since 1973; *b* England, 1 Sept. 1921; British parents; unmarried. *Educ*: Rosa Bassett Sch.; Somerville Coll., Oxford. WTS (FANY), 1943-47 (Allied Commn for Austria, 1946-48). FO, 1948; UK Delegn to NATO, 1952; 2nd Sec., Moscow, 1954; FO, 1956; Consul and 1st Sec., Leopoldville, 1959; FO, 1961; Lusaka, 1964; FO, 1967; Consul-Gen., Hanoi, 1969-70; Hon. Res. Fellow, Univ. of Kent, 1971-72, on sabbatical leave from FCO; Chargé d'Affaires *a i*, Ulan Bator, Apr.-June 1972. Mem. RIIA. *Recreations*: good talk, politics, and difficult places. *Address*: c/o Foreign and Commonwealth Office, SW1; c/o National Westminster Bank, 121 High Street, Oxford. *Clubs*: Naval and Military, Royal Commonwealth Society.

PARK, George Maclean, JP; MP (Lab) Coventry North East since Feb. 1974; *b* 27 Sept. 1914; *s* of James McKenzie Park and Mary Gorman Park; *m* 1941, Joyce, *d* of Robert Holt Stead and Gertrude Stead; one *d*. *Educ*: Onslow Drive Sch., Glasgow; Coventry Techn. College. Sen. AEU Shop Steward, Chrysler UK Ltd, Ryton, 1968-73. Coventry City Councillor, 1961-74; Coventry District Councillor, 1973-74; Leader of Council Labour Gp, 1967-74; W Mids Metropolitan CC, 1973-77; Chm. Coventry and District Disablement Adv. Cttee, 1960-74; Leader, Coventry City and District Councils, 1972-74; Chm. Policy Adv. Cttee, 1972-74. PPS to Dr J. Gilbert, Minister for Transport, 1975-76; PPS to Sec. of State for Industry, 1976-. Chm., W Midland Group Labour MPs. Chm. Belgrade Theatre Trust, 1972-74. JP Coventry, 1961. AEU Award of Merit, 1967. *Recreations*: reading, walking. *Address*: 170 Binley Road, Coventry CV3 1HG. *T*: Coventry 458589.

PARK, Hon. Sir Hugh (Eames), Kt 1965; **Hon. Mr Justice Park**; Judge of the High Court of Justice, Queen's Bench Division, since 1973 (Family Division, 1965-73); *b* 24 April 1910; *er s* of late William Robert and late Helen Beatrice Park; *m* 1938, Beryl Josephine, *d* of late Joseph and Margery Coombe; three *d*. *Educ*: Blundell's; Sidney Sussex Coll., Cambridge (Hon. Fellow, 1968). Called to the Bar, Middle Temple, 1936; QC 1960; Bencher, 1965. Member Western Circuit. Served War, 1940-45; Sqdn Leader, 1945. Recorder of Penzance, 1959-60; of Exeter, 1960-64; of Southampton, 1964-65. Member, Court of Exeter Univ., 1961; Member, Board of Governors, Blundell's Sch., 1961. Commn of Assize, North East Circuit, 1963; Judge of the Courts of Appeal, Channel Islands, 1964-65; Chairman, County of Devon Quarter Sessions, 1964-71; Deputy Chairman, Cornwall County Quarter Sessions, 1959-71; Presiding Judge, Western Circuit, 1970-75. *Recreation:* fishing. *Address:* Royal Courts of Justice, Strand, WC2; 31 Ferncroft Avenue, Hampstead, NW3. *T:* 01-435 8909; Gorran Haven, Cornwall. *T:* Mevagissey 2333.

PARK, Ian Grahame, JP; Managing Director and Editor in Chief, Liverpool Daily Post and Echo Ltd, since 1972; *b* 15 May 1935; *s* of William Park and Christina (*née* Scott); *m* 1965, Anne Turner; one *s*. *Educ:* Lancaster Royal Grammar Sch.; Queens' Coll., Cambridge. 1st Bn Manchester Regt, Berlin (Nat. Service Commn), 1954-56. Trainee Journalist, Press and Journal, Aberdeen, 1959; Asst Lit. Editor, Sunday Times, 1960-63; various management posts, Thomson Newspapers, 1963-65; Liverpool Daily Post and Echo, 1965-. Mem. Council, Newspaper Soc., 1967-; Dir, Press Assoc., 1973-; Dir, Radio City (Sound of Merseyside Ltd), 1973-; Dir, Liverpool Playhouse, 1973-; Trustee, Blue Coat Soc. of Arts, Liverpool, 1973-. JP Liverpool 1975. *Recreations:* reading, theatre, visiting galleries. *Address:* Church Cottage, Green Lane, Formby, Liverpool. *Club:* Reform.

PARK, Kiri; see Te Kanawa, K.

PARK, Merle Florence, (Mrs Sidney Bloch), CBE 1974; Principal, Royal Ballet; *b* Salisbury, S Rhodesia, 8 Oct. 1937; *d* of P. J. Park, Eastlea, Salisbury, S Rhodesia, C Africa; *m* 1st, 1965, James Monahan, *qv* (marr. diss. 1970); one *s*; 2nd, 1971, Sidney Bloch. *Educ:* Elmhurst Ballet Sch. Joined Sadler's Wells Ballet, 1955; first rôle, a Mouse (Sleeping Beauty prologue); first solo, Milkmaid (Façade), 1955; Performed solos, 1956; principal soloist, 1959. First danced: Blue Bird (Act III, Sleeping Beauty), 1956; Swanhilda (Coppelia), 1958; Mamzelle Angot (Mamzelle Angot), 1958; Lise (Fille Mal Gardée), 1960; Cinderella, 1962; Juliet (Romeo and Juliet), 1965; Giselle, 1967; Clara (Nutcracker), 1968; Celestial (Shadow Play), 1967; Aurora (Sleeping Beauty), 1968; Odette (Swan Lake), 1971; A Walk to Paradise Garden, 1972; Firebird, 1973; Odette/Odile, Swan Lake, 1973; Dances at a Gathering, 1973; Manon, 1974; Emilia (The Moor's Pavane), 1974; Aureole, 1974; Terpsichore (Apollo), 1974; Elite Syncopations, 1974; Lulu, 1976; Kate (The Taming of the Shrew), La Bayadère, Tuesday's Child (Jazz Calendar), Triad, 1977. *Recreation:* teaching at her own ballet school. *Address:* Chiswick Mall, W4.

PARK, Trevor; Lecturer in Industrial Relations, Department of Adult Education and Extramural Studies, University of Leeds, since 1972; *b* 12 Dec. 1927; *s* of Stephen Clifford Park and Annie Park (*née* Jackson); *m* 1953, Barbara Black; no *c*. *Educ:* Bury Grammar Sch.; Manchester Univ. (MA). History Master, Bacup and Rawtenstall Grammar Sch., 1949-56; WEA, Tutor and Organiser (NW District), 1956-60; Lecturer, Extramural Dept, Univ. of Sheffield (politics and internat. relations), 1960-64; WEA Tutor and Organiser, Manchester, 1970-72. Parliamentary Labour Candidate: Altrincham and Sale, General Election, 1955; Darwen, General Election, 1959; MP (Lab) South East Derbyshire, 1964-70. Member: TGWU; Select Cttees on Nationalised Industries, 1966-68, and on Education and Science, 1968-70; Yorkshire and Humberside Economic Planning Council, 1977-. Chm. ATAE, 1972-75. *Recreation:* walking. *Address:* Department of Adult Education and Extramural Studies, The University, Leeds LS2 9JT.

PARK, William, OBE 1967; Keeper of Manuscripts, National Library of Scotland, 1946-72; *b* 14 April 1909; *s* of John Park and Isabella Stephenson Berridge; *m* 1935, Mary Allan (decd), *d* of Robert Wilson; two *d*. *Educ:* Hawick High Sch.; Edinburgh Univ. (MA); School of Librarianship, University College, London. Assistant, National Library of Scotland, 1932-46; seconded to Scottish Home Department, 1940-46. *Address:* 24 Liberton Drive, Edinburgh EH16 6NN. *T:* 031-664 3695.

PARKE, Prof. Dennis Vernon William, PhD, DSc; CChem, FRIC, FIBiol, FRCPath; (first) Professor and Head of Department of Biochemistry, University of Surrey, since 1967; *b* London, 15 Nov. 1922; *e s* of William Parke and Florence Parke; *m* 1943, Doreen Joan Dunn; two *s* one *d*. *Educ:* West Ham Municipal Secondary Sch. (Gurney Scholar); Chelsea and University Colls, Univ. of London 1940-48; St. Mary's Hosp. Med. Sch., London (PhD DSc). War Service, RA RAMC, 1942-47. Head, Dept of Microbiol Chem., Glaxo Labs Ltd, 1948-49; St. Mary's Hosp. Med. Sch., Univ. of London: Res. Asst to Prof. R. T. Williams, FRS, 1949-52; Lectr in Biochem., 1952-58, Sen. Lectr, 1958-62; Reader in Biochem., 1962-67; Dean, Faculty of Biol and Chem. Sciences, Univ. of Surrey, 1971-75. Sometime Examnr, Univs of Dublin (Trinity), Edinburgh, Glasgow, Liverpool, London, Newcastle upon Tyne, Reading,

Strathclyde, Wales, Auckland, Ibadan, Nairobi, Singapore, Sydney and Wellington. Member: Cttee on Safety of Drugs, 1968-70; Cttee on Safety of Medicines, 1970-; Cttee on Med. Aspects of Chemicals in Food and Environment, DHSS, 1972-; Food Additives and Contaminants Cttee, MAFF, 1972-; WHO Expert Panel on Food Additives, 1975-; WHO Sci. Gp on Toxicity Evaluation of Chemicals, 1975; WHO Cons. in Indust. Toxicol., Poland, 1974; Sci. Dir, NATO Workshop on Ecotoxicology, July-Aug. 1977. Editor, Xenobiotica, 1970-. *Publications:* The Biochemistry of Foreign Compounds, 1968; (ed) Enzyme Induction, 1975; chapters in books and res. papers in Biochem. Jl and Biochem. Pharmacol. *Recreations:* landscape gardening, music. *Address:* Trevelen, Poyle Road, Guildford, Surrey. *T:* Guildford 73667. *Club:* Athenæum.

PARKE, Herbert William, MA (Oxon); LittD (Dublin); Fellow Emeritus of Trinity College, Dublin, since 1973, Fellow, 1929-73; Professor of Ancient History, 1934-73, Vice-Provost, 1952-73, Librarian 1949-65, Curator, 1965-73; *b* Moneymore, Co. Londonderry, 7 Sept. 1903; *o s* of William and Bertha Blair Parke; *m* 1930, Nancy Bankart, *y d* of Arthur R. Gurney, Cracoe, Yorks; one *d*. *Educ:* Coleraine Academical Institution; Bradford Grammar Sch.; Wadham Coll., Oxford (Scholar). 1st Class Hon. Mods, 1924; 1st Class Lit. Hum. 1926; A. M. P. Read Scholar, 1927; Craven Fellow, 1928; Cromer Essay Prize, 1928; Member of Royal Irish Academy, 1933; L. C. Purser Lect. in Archæology, 1934; Temp. Principal, Board of Trade, 1942-44; FRNS, 1947. Member Institute for Advanced Study, Princeton, USA, 1960. Hon. DLit QUB, 1974. *Publications:* Greek Mercenary Soldiers, 1933; Delphic Oracle, 1939 (2nd edition with Professor D. E. W. Wormell, 1956); Oracles of Zeus, 1967; Greek Oracles, 1967; Festivals of the Athenians, 1977; contrib. to Journal of Hellenic Studies, Hermathena, etc, articles on Greek History and Mythology in Chambers's Encyclopædia, Encyclopædia Britannica, and Oxford Classical Dictionary. *Address:* 8 Christchurch Place, Christchurch Mount, Epsom, Surrey KT19 8RS. *Club:* Kildare Street and University (Dublin).

PARKE, Dr Mary, FRS 1972; Senior Phycologist, Marine Biological Association, Plymouth, 1947-73, retired; *b* 23 March 1908. *Educ:* Notre Dame Convent, Everton Valley; Univ. of Liverpool. DSc, PhD; FLS, FIBiol. Isaac Roberts Research Schol. in Biology, 1929; Phycologist, Marine Biological Stn, Port Erin, IoM, 1930-40; research on algae for Develt Commn and Min. of Supply, 1941-46. Corresp. Mem., Royal Botanical Soc. of Netherlands, 1970; Mem., Norwegian Acad. of Science and Letters, 1971. *Publications:* (with M. Knight) Manx Algae, 1931; papers in Jl of Marine Biol Assoc., Plymouth, etc. *Address:* 6 Alfred Street, Plymouth PL1 2RP. *T:* Plymouth 68609.

PARKER, family name of **Earls of Macclesfield** and **Morley.**

PARKER, Viscount; Richard Timothy George Parker; *b* 31 May 1943; *s* and *heir* of 8th Earl of Macclesfield, *qv*; *m* 1967, Tatiana Cleone, *d* of Major Craig Wheaton-Smith; one *d*. *Educ:* Stowe; Worcester Coll., Oxford.

PARKER, A(gnes) Miller, RE; Artist and Wood-engraver; *b* Irvine, Ayrshire, 25 March 1895; *d* of William McCall and Agnes Mitchell Parker; *m* 1918, William McCance, Artist (marr. diss. 1963, and she legally assumed maiden name); no *c*. *Educ:* Glasgow School of Art (Diploma, Haldane Scholar). Instructress, Glasgow School of Art, 1918-20; Art Mistress, Maltmans Green School, Gerrards Cross, 1920-28; Art Mistress, Clapham High School and Training Coll., 1928-30; Walter Brewster Prize, 1st International Exhibition of Engraving and Lithography, Chicago, 1929; Wood-engraver to Gregynog Press, Newtown, Montgomeryshire, 1930-33. *Publications:* Chief Illustrated Editions; Esopes Fables by Caxton, 1931; Daisy Matthews and three other tales by Rhys Davies, 1932; XXI Welsh Gypsy Folk-Tales, collected by John Sampson, 1933; The House with the Apricot by H. E. Bates, 1933; Forest Giant-translated from the French by J. H. Ross (Colonel T. E. Lawrence), 1935; Through the Woods by H. E. Bates, 1936; Down the River by H. E. Bates, 1937; Gray's Elegy written in a Country Church-yard (Limited Editions Club of NY), 1938; Richard II-Shakespeare (Limited Editions Club of NY), 1940; A Shropshire Lad by A. E. Housman, 1940; The Return of the Native by Thomas Hardy (Limited Editions Club of NY), 1942; Essays in Russet by Herbert Furst, 1944; Spring of the Year by Richard Jefferies, 1946; The Life of the Fields, 1947, Field and Hedgerow, 1948, The Open Air, 1948, The Old House at Coate, 1948, by Richard Jefferies; Animals Under the Rainbow by Aloysius Roche, 1952; The Faerie Queene by Edmund Spenser, vols I and II, 1953; Lucifer by J. C. Powys, 1956; Tess of the D'Urbervilles, 1956, and Far From the Madding Crowd, 1958, by Thomas Hardy (New York); The Tragedies of Shakespeare

(New York), 1959; The Mayor of Casterbridge by Thomas Hardy (Limited Editions Club of NY), 1964; Poems of Shakespeare (Limited Editions Club of NY), 1967; Jude the Obscure by Thomas Hardy (Limited Editions Club of NY), 1969. *Recreations:* fishing and cats. *Address:* Cladach, King's Cross, Brodick, Isle of Arran KA27 8RG, Scotland.

PARKER, Albert, CBE 1946; DSc; FRIC; FIChemE; Hon. FInstGasE; Hon. FInstFuel; Consulting Chemical Engineer; *b* 2 May 1892; *s* of late John Albert and Alice Parker, Manchester; *m* 1922, Lilian Maud (*d* 1972), *d* of late Albert Edward Midgley, Birmingham; one *d* (and one *d* decd). *Educ:* Manchester Grammar Sch.; Manchester Univ. First Class Hons Chemistry, Manchester, 1912; Grad. Schol. and Beyer Research Fellow, Manchester, 1912-14; DSc Birmingham, 1916. Lecturer in Phys. Chem. and Thermodynamics, Birmingham Univ., and Chemist Inspector on manufacture of high explosives for Midland area, 1914-19. Research Chem. to University of Leeds and Instn of Gas Engineers, 1919-28. Asst Director Water Pollution Research, DSIR, 1928-39, Director, 1939-43; Director of Fuel Research, DSIR, 1943-56. Lt-Col in charge of team of British and American experts investigating synthetic oil, etc in Germany, March-April 1945. Osborne Reynolds Medal, IChemE, 1941; Melchett Medal, Inst. of Fuel, 1955; Telford Premium, 1942, and Chadwick Medal, 1955, ICE; Mitchell Gold Medal, Stoke-on-Trent Assoc. of Engineers, 1956; Thomas Hawksley Lectr, IMechE, 1949; Cantor Lectures, RSA, 1960. Pres., Fuel Luncheon Club, 1953-55; Hon. Secretary, British National Cttee, World Power Conference, 1951-64, and Chm., Consultative Panel on Survey of Energy Resources, 1958-68; Chm. Council, RSH, 1955-56; Chm., Expert Cttee on Air Pollution, WHO, 1958; Pres., National Society for Clean Air, 1963-65 (Clean Air Award, 1973). *Publications:* Control of Industrial Air Pollution, 1977; contrib. various scientific and technical journals and books. *Recreation:* music. *Address:* Stanway, Wellesley Avenue, Northwood, Middlesex HA6 3HZ. *T:* Northwood 26435. *Club:* Athenæum.
See also Mrs B . A . Calvert .

PARKER, Prof. Alexander Augustine, MA, LittD; Professor of Spanish Literature, University of Texas, since 1970; *b* Montevideo, 1908; *er s* of Arthur Parker and Laura Bustamante; *m* 1941, Frances Ludwig; two *s* two *d. Educ:* Hawkesyard School (later Blackfriars School, Laxton); Gonville and Caius Coll., Cambridge (Exhibn. and scholar). First Class Mod. and Medieval Langs Tripos, Part I 1928, Part II 1930; Gibson Schol., 1931. Fellow of Gonville and Caius Coll., 1933-39. Lecturer and Head of Dept of Spanish, University of Aberdeen, 1939-49; Reader in Spanish, University of Aberdeen, 1949-53; Cervantes Professor of Spanish, University of London (King's Coll.), 1953-63; Prof. of Hispanic Studies, Univ. of Edinburgh, 1963-69. Seconded to University College of the West Indies as Prof. of Modern Languages, 1960-61; Andrew Mellon Visiting Prof., University of Pittsburgh, 1964, 1968, 1969-70. Gen. Editor, Edinburgh Bilingual Library of European Literature. Hon. Councillor of Consejo Superior de Investigaciones Cientificas, 1953. Corr. Member Royal Acad. of Letters of Seville, 1958; Corr. Member Hispanic Society of America, 1960, Member, 1960; Corr. Member Spanish Academy, 1964. Hon. DLitt Durham, 1975. Commander of the Order of Isabel la Católica, 1956. *Publications:* The Allegorical Drama of Calderón, An Introduction to the Autos Sacramentales, 1943; No hay más Fortuna que Dios, by Calderón, ed. with Introd. and notes, 1949; Literature and the Delinquent: the Picaresque Novel in Spain and Europe (1599-1753), 1967; Luis de Góngora, Fable of Polyphemus and Galatea: a study of a baroque poem, 1977; papers and articles in The Mod. Lang. Review, Bulletin of Spanish Studies, Revista de Filología Española, etc. *Recreations:* opera, horticulture and lepidoptera. *Address:* Department of Spanish and Portuguese, University of Texas, Austin, Texas 78712, USA; 9 West Castle Road, Edinburgh EH10 5AT. *T:* 031-229 1632.

PARKER, Christopher William Oxley, MA; JP; DL; *b* 28 May 1920; *s* of Lieut-Col John Oxley Parker, *qv; m* 1947, Jocelyn Frances Adeline, *d* of Colonel C. G. Arkwright, Southern Rhodesia; one *s* two *d. Educ:* Eton; Trinity Coll., Oxford. Local Director, Barclays Bank, Chelmsford Local Board; Director: Strutt and Parker (Farms) Ltd; Lord Rayleighs Farms Inc. Served War of 1939-45, with 147th Field Regt (Essex Yeomanry) Royal Artillery, 1939-42. JP Essex, 1952; High Sheriff of Essex, 1961; DL Essex 1972. *Recreations:* shooting, tennis, golf; estate management. *Address:* Faulkbourne Hall, Witham, Essex. *T:* Witham 513385. *Clubs:* Boodle's, MCC.

PARKER, Rt. Rev. Clement George St Michael; *b* 29 Sept. 1900; *s* of late Rev. W. H. Parker, Vicar of S Peter, Birmingham. *Educ:* Christ Church, Oxford. Ordained 1923; Asst Curate. S

Bartholomew and S Jude, Birmingham; Vicar of King's Heath, 1939-61; Rural Dean, King's Norton, 1943-61; Hon. Canon of Birmingham, 1944-61; Archdeacon of Aston, 1946-54; Bishop Suffragan of Aston, 1954-61; Bishop of Bradford, 1961-71. *Address:* Prospect Cottage, Old Road, Shipston on Stour, Warwickshire. *T:* Shipston on Stour 61024.

PARKER, Clifford Frederick, MA, LLB Cantab; JP; Bracton Professor of Law at the University of Exeter since 1957 (Deputy Vice-Chancellor, 1963-65); *b* 6 March 1920; *yr s* of late Frederick James Parker and Bertha Isabella (*née* Kemp), Cardiff; *m* 1945, Christine Alice (*née* Knowles); two *d. Educ:* Cardiff High Sch.; Gonville and Caius Coll., Cambridge. Royal Air Force, 1940-43. Solicitor of Supreme Court, 1947. Lecturer in Common Law, University of Birmingham, 1951-57; Senior Tutor and Asst Director of Legal Studies, Faculty of Law, University of Birmingham, 1956-57. Pres., Soc. of Public Teachers of Law, 1974-75. JP Devon, 1969. *Publications:* contrib. to legal periodicals. *Recreation:* touring. *Address:* Lynwood, Exton, Exeter EX3 0PR. *T:* Topsham 4051.

PARKER, Sir Douglas D.; *see* Dodds-Parker.

PARKER, Rear-Adm. Douglas Granger, CB 1971; DSO, DSC, AFC; Assistant Chief of Naval Staff (Operations and Air), 1969-71, retired; *b* 21 Nov. 1919; *s* of R. K. Parker; *m* 1953, Margaret Susan, *d* of late Col W. Cooper; one *s* one *d. Educ:* W Hartlepool Technical Coll. Joined Royal Navy, 1940; Command Fleet Air Arm Fighter Squadrons, 1948-51; Commanded: HMS Cavendish, 1961-62; RN Air Station, Lossiemouth, 1965-67; HMS Hermes, 1967-69. Captain 1959; Rear-Adm. 1969. *Address:* High Meadow, Walhampton, Lymington, Hants. *T:* Lymington 3259. *Club:* Royal Lymington Yacht.

PARKER, Sir Douglas William Leigh, Kt 1966; OBE 1954; retired as Director of Orthopædic Services, Tasmanian Government Health Dept, 1966. *Educ:* University of Sydney; University of Liverpool. MB, ChM (Sydney), 1923; FRCSEd 1925; MChOrth (Liverpool), 1930; FRACS, 1935. War of 1939-45: Surgeon, 2/9 AGH, 1940-42, 111 AGH, 1942-46. Senior Orthopædic Surgeon, Royal Hobart Hospital. Comr St John Ambulance Bde, Tasmania. Member Legacy, Hobart. OStJ. *Address:* 30 Fisher Avenue, Lower Sandy Bay, Hobart, Tasmania, Australia. *Clubs:* Tasmanian, Naval and Military and Air Force (Hobart).

PARKER, Sir Edmund; *see* Parker, Sir W. E.

PARKER, Geoffrey, CB 1966; Under-Secretary, Department of Industry, formerly Department of Trade and Industry, 1970-76; *b* 17 Jan. 1917; *m* 1942, Janet Crawford Chidley; two *s* one *d. Educ:* Hulme Grammar Sch., Oldham; New Coll., Oxford; Queen's Coll., Oxford; Universities of Berlin and Berne, MA, DPhil (Oxon). Entered Board of Trade as temp. Assistant Principal, May 1940; established as Principal, 1946. Counsellor (Commercial), HM Embassy, Washington, DC, 1952-55; Under-Sec., 1961; Principal Establishment and Organisation Officer, 1965-70. *Recreations:* reading, languages. *Address:* 5 Hove Court, Raymond Road, Wimbledon SW19 4AG. *T:* 01-946 9300.

PARKER, Gordon, CBE 1972; MM 1916; TEM 1924; Chairman: Favor Parker Ltd, since 1921; Stoke Ferry, since 1921; Felixstowe Dock & Railway Co., 1921-76, Life President since 1976; *b* 1892; *m* 1915 and 1925; two *s* two *d* (and one *s* decd). *Educ:* Thetford Grammar School. Farming, seed merchant, 1910-22; War Service, 1914-19; grain merchant, farming, fertiliser manufacturer, 1922-51; subseq. grain merchanting, Britain and overseas, with Felixstowe Dock & Rly Co., manufacturer animal feed. *Recreation:* now only shooting, earlier everything. *Address:* Stoke Ferry Hall, Kings Lynn, Norfolk. *T:* Stoke Ferry 360.

PARKER, Sir Harold, KCB 1949 (CB 1943); KBE 1946; MC 1918; *b* 27 May 1895; *s* of W. G. Parker; *m* 1926, Kathleen Maud Gibbs; two *s. Educ:* Haberdashers' School. Exchequer and Audit Department, 1914; Treasury, 1919; Principal Assistant Secretary, 1938; Deputy Secretary, Ministry of Pensions, 1941-45; Secretary, Ministry of Pensions, 1946-48; Permanent Secretary to the Ministry of Defence, 1948-56, retired; Chairman: Corp. of Insurance Brokers Society of Pension Consultants, 1958-70; Member, United Nations Civil Service Advisory Board, 1957-70. President Amateur Swimming Association, 1958. Served European War, 1914-18, Temporary Captain RFA. *Recreations:* golf, swimming. *Address:* 90 Rivermead Court, SW6. *T:* 01-736 6945; 9 Upper Third Avenue, Frinton, Essex. *T:* Frinton 4783. *Club:* Hurlingham.

PARKER, Herbert John Harvey; see Parker, John.

PARKER, Hugh; Senior Director, McKinsey & Co. (UK); *b* 12 June 1919; *s* of Ross Parker and Ruth Baker Parker; *m* 1957, Elsa del Carmen Mijares Osorio; one *s* one *d. Educ:* Tabor Academy; Trinity Hall, Cambridge; Massachusetts Inst. of Technology. North Carolina Shipbuilding Co., 1941-43; General Electric Co., 1945-46; Ludlow Manufacturing Co., 1947-50; McKinsey & Co. Inc., 1951-. Pres., American Chamber of Commerce (UK), 1976; Mem., Council of Management, Oxford Centre for Management Studies. Pres., MIT Alumni Club of GB. Mem. Council, St George's House; Mem. and Governor, Ditchley Foundn. *Recreations:* reading, sculling, cooking. *Address:* 9 Cheyne Walk, SW3. *T:* 01-352 9592. *Clubs:* Turf, American, The Pilgrims, United Oxford & Cambridge University; Leander (Henley-on-Thames); Racquet and Tennis (New York); Eastern Yacht (Mass).

PARKER, James Roland Walter, OBE 1968; HM Diplomatic Service; Governor and Commander-in-Chief, Falkland Islands and Dependencies, and High Commissioner, British Antarctic Territory, since 1977; *b* 20 Dec. 1919; *s* of late Alexander Roland Parker, ISM; *m* 1941, Deirdre Mary Ward. Served War of 1939-45: 1st London Scottish, 1940-41. Ministry of Labour, 1938-57; Labour Attaché, Tel Aviv, 1957-60; Labour Adviser: Accra, 1960-62; Lagos, 1962-64; seconded to Foreign Office, 1965-66; Dep. High Comr, Enugu, 1966-67; Commonwealth Office (later FCO), 1968-70; Head of Chancery, Suva, Fiji, 1970-71; High Comr in The Gambia, 1972-75; Consul-Gen., Durban, 1976. *Address:* Government House, Stanley, Falkland Islands. *Club:* Travellers'.

PARKER, John, CBE 1965; MP (Lab) Barking, Dagenham, since 1974 (Dagenham, 1945-74); Vice-President, Fabian Society, since 1972; Governor, London School of Economics, since 1949; *b* 15 July 1906; *s* of Capt. H. A. M. Parker, retired schoolmaster, and N. P. Parker; *m* 1943, Zena Mimardiere; one *s. Educ:* Marlborough; St John's College, Oxford. Chm., Oxford Univ. Labour Club, 1928; Asst to Director, Social Survey of Merseyside (Liverpool Univ.), 1929-32; Gen. Sec., New Fabian Res. Bureau, 1933-39; Fabian Society: Gen. Sec., 1939-45; Vice-Chm., 1946-50; Chm., 1950-53. MP (Lab) Romford, Essex, 1935-45; PPS to Miss Ellen Wilkinson, Min. of Home Security, 1940-42; Parly Under-Sec. of State, Dominions Office, 1945-46; Member: Speaker's Conferences, 1944, 1965-67, 1973-74; Procedure Cttee, 1966-73; Parly Delegation to USSR, 1945; National Executive Labour Party, 1943-44; Executive London Labour Party, 1942-47; Select Cttee Parliamentary Disqualifications, 1956; Parly Delegation to Ethiopia, 1964; Leader, Delegation to Windward Islands, 1965; contested (Lab) Holland-with-Boston, Lincolnshire, 1931. Hon. Sec., Webb Trustees; Member: Council, Essex Univ; Council, 1968-, Exec. Cttee, 1969-, Nat. Trust; Historic Buildings Council, 1974-; Inland Waterways Amenity Council, 1970-73, 1974-. Yugoslav Red Star, 1975. *Publications:* The Independent Worker and Small Family Business, 1931; Public Enterprise (Forestry Commission), 1937; Democratic Sweden (Political Parties); Modern Turkey, 1940; 42 Days in the Soviet Union, 1946; Labour Marches On, 1947; Newfoundland, 1950; (ed) Modern Yugoslav Novels (English edn), 1958-64; (comp. and ed) biographies, inc. Harold Wilson and Willy Brandt, 1964. *Recreations:* architecture and gardening. *Address:* 4 Essex Court, Temple, EC4. *T:* 01-353 8521. *Club:* Arts Theatre.

PARKER, Sir John; see Parker, Sir W. J.

PARKER, Sir John (Edward), Kt 1975; BCEng; FIEAust; retired; *b* 28 Sept. 1904; *s* of late Matthew Parker and Edith Florence Parker; *m* 1932, Winifred Mary Becher; two *s* one *d. Educ:* Wesley Coll., Melbourne, Vic.; Queen's Coll., Melbourne Univ. (BCE). Served War: RAE, AIF, in SW Pacific Area, rank Major, 1942-45. Dep. Dir of Works, Public Works Dept, Perth, WA, 1953-62; Dir of Engineering, PWD, Perth, WA, 1962-69. Chm., State Electricity Commn of WA, 1969-74. *Recreations:* golf, fishing, gardening. *Address:* 11 Hopetoun Street, South Perth, WA 6151, Australia. *T:* Perth 67 1272. *Clubs:* Weld (Perth, WA); Royal Perth Golf.

PARKER, Comdr (John) Michael (Avison), CVO 1957 (MVO 1953); RN (retired); Partner, Mann's Transport; Director, Travel Holdings (Australia) Pty Ltd; *b* 23 June 1920; *s* of late Capt. C. A. Parker, CBE, Royal Australian Navy, Melbourne; *m* 1st, 1943, Eileen Margaret Anne (*née* Allan) (marr. diss. 1958); one *s* one *d*; 2nd, 1962, Carol (marr. diss.; she *d* 1977), *d* of Sir Ivo Thomson, 2nd Bt, and Mrs Brian Whitmee; one *s* one *d*; 3rd, 1976, Mrs Jean Ramsay. *Educ:* Xavier College, Melbourne, Australia. Royal Navy, 1938-47. Equerry-in-Waiting to Princess Elizabeth and the Duke of Edinburgh, 1947-52; Private Sec. to Duke of Edinburgh, 1947-57. Member: Nat. Cttee, Aust.-Britain Soc.; Council for Res. and Rehabilitation of Retarded Children; Trustee: Australian Ballet Trust; Victorian Conservation Trust. *Recreations:* reading, tennis and sailing. *Address:* Santosa, 33 Albany Road, Toorak, Vic 3142, Australia.

PARKER, Lt-Col John Oxley, TD; MA; *b* 28 June 1886; *e s* of Christopher William Parker and Helen Cecilia, *d* of Sir William J. Farrer, Faulkbourne Hall, Essex; *m* 1916, Mary Monica (*d* 1958), *d* of Arnold F. Hills, Hammerfield, Penshurst; one *s* two *d. Educ:* Eton; Oriel Coll., Oxford. Local Director (retired) Barclays Bank; President Essex Agricultural Society, 1959. Served European War, 1914-18, Essex Yeo., Major, France (Croix de Guerre Belge); HG, 1940-45 (Lt-Col). Essex: JP 1921; DL 1926-72; High Sheriff, 1948-49. *Publication:* The Oxley Parker Papers, 1964. *Recreations:* shooting, estate management, gardening and forestry. *Address:* The Old Rectory, Faulkbourne, Witham, Essex. *T:* Witham 513221. *Club:* United Oxford & Cambridge University.

See also *C . W . O . Parker , Sir A . A . S . Stark .*

PARKER, Sir Karl T., Kt 1960; CBE 1954; MA, PhD; FBA 1950; Hon. DLitt Oxon, 1972; Hon. Antiquary to the Royal Academy, 1963; Keeper of the Ashmolean Museum, Oxford, 1945-62 (retired); Keeper of the Department of Fine Art, Ashmolean Museum, and of the Hope Collection of Engraved Portraits, 1934-62; Hon. Fellow, Oriel College, Oxford; *s* of late R. W. Parker, FRCS, and Marie Luling; *m* Audrey (*d* 1976), *d* of late Henry Ashworth James, of Hurstmonceux Place; two *d. Educ:* Bedford; Paris; Zürich. Studied art at most continental centres and at the British Museum; edited Old Master Drawings, a Quarterly Magazine for Students and Collectors, since its inception, 1926; late Asst Keeper, Dept of Prints and Drawings, British Museum; Trustee, National Gallery, 1962-69. *Publications:* North Italian Drawings of the Quattrocento; Drawings of the Early German Schools; Alsatian Drawings of the XV and XVI Centuries; Drawings of Antoine Watteau; Catalogue of Drawings in the Ashmolean Museum, Vol. I, 1938, Vol. II, 1956; Catalogue of Holbein's Drawings at Windsor Castle, 1945; The Drawings of Antonio Canaletto at Windsor Castle, 1948; Antoine Watteau: Catalogue Complet de son œuvre Dessiné, Vol. I (with J. Mathey), 1957, Vol. II, 1958; and articles, mostly on Old Master drawings, in various English and continental periodicals. *Address:* 4 Saffrons Court, Compton Place Road, Eastbourne.

PARKER, Kenneth Alfred Lamport; CB 1959; Receiver for the Metropolitan Police District, 1967-74; *b* 1 April 1912; *e s* of A. E. A. and Ada Mary Parker; *m* 1938, Freda Silcock (OBE 1975); one *s* one *d. Educ:* Tottenham Grammar Sch.; St John's College, Cambridge. Home Office, 1934; London Civil Defence Region, 1938-45; (Assistant Secretary, 1942, Deputy Chief Administrative Officer, 1943); Assistant Under-Secretary of State, Home Office, 1955-67 (Head of Police Dept, 1961-66). Imperial Defence College, 1947. *Address:* 18 Lichfield Road, Kew, Surrey. *T:* 01-940 4595. *Club:* United Oxford & Cambridge University.

PARKER, Margaret Annette McCrie Johnston, (Margaret Johnston); actress; *d* of James and Emily Dalrymple Johnston; *m* 1946, Albert E. W. Parker (*d* 1974). *Educ:* North Sydney and Neutral Bay High School; Sydney University, Australia. Student, RADA; studied with Dr Stefan Hock; in repertory and acted as understudies. *Plays:* Murder without Crime, 1943; Fifth Column, 1944; Last of Summer, 1944; Time of Your Life, 1946; Shouting Dies, 1946; Barretts of Wimpole Street, 1947; Always Afternoon, 1949; Summer and Smoke, 1950; Second Threshold, 1951; The Dark is Light Enough, 1954; Sugar in the Morning, 1959; The Ring of Truth, 1959; Masterpiece, 1961. Stratford Memorial Theatre, 1956 season: Othello, The Merchant of Venice, Measure for Measure; Chichester Festival Theatre, 1966 Season: Lady Macbeth. *Films:* Rake's Progress, 1945; Man About the House, 1946; Portrait of Clare, 1949; Magic Box, 1951; Knave of Hearts, 1953; Touch and Go, 1955; Nose on her Face; Life at the Top, 1965; Psychopath; Sebastian. Television plays. *Address:* 50 Mount St, W1. *T:* 01-499 4232, 01-499 3080.

PARKER, Dame Marjorie Alice Collett, DBE 1977; welfare worker, Tasmania; Deputy-Chairman, Australian National Council of Women, 1960-64 (Life Member, since 1974); *b* Ballarat; *d* of W. Shoppee, Ballarat, Vic; *m* 1926, Max Parker; one *s. Educ:* Ballarat State Sch. Announcer and Dir Women's Interests, Radio Launceston, 1941-69; Public Relations Adviser for Girl Guide Assoc., 1954-68; Pres. and Org., Red Cross Meals on Wheels, Launceston, Tas., 1961-71; State Exec. and Public Relations Officer, Good Neighbour Council, Tas., 1964-70; Nth Regional Pres., Aust. Red Cross Soc., Tas. Div., 1965-68; Pres., Victoria League, Launceston, 1966-69; Exec. Mem., Soc. for

Care of Crippled Children (Life Mem. 1973). Past Pres., N Tas. Branch, Royal Commonwealth Soc. Vice-Pres., United Nations Assoc., Launceston, 1964-68. *Recreation:* gardening. *Address:* Apsley, 5 Croydon Grove, Cypress Street, Launceston, Tasmania 7250, Australia. *Clubs:* Soroptomist (Pres. 1951), Royal Commonwealth Soc. (Launceston, Tas).

PARKER, Comdr Michael; see Parker, Comdr (J.) M. (A.).

PARKER, Michael Clynes, QC 1973; a Recorder of the Crown Court, since 1972; *b* 2 Nov. 1924; *s* of Herbert Parker and Elsie Vera Parker (sometime Pres., NUT); *m* 1950, Molly Leila Franklin; one *s* two *d*. *Educ:* City of London Sch.; Pembroke Coll., Cambridge (BA, LLB). Sec., Cambridge Union, 1943. Flt-Sgt/Air Gunner, RAF, 1943-47. Called to Bar, Gray's Inn, 1949; practised in London and SE Circuit. Contested (Lab) S Kensington, 1951. *Recreations:* theatre, watching cricket. *Address:* 93 Lansdowne Road, W11 2LE. *Club:* United Oxford & Cambridge University.

PARKER, Michael St J.; see St John Parker.

PARKER, Peter, MVO 1957; Chairman, British Rail Board, since 1976; Member British Airways Board, since 1971; *b* 30 Aug. 1924; *s* of late Tom and Dorothy S. Parker; *m* 1951, Gillian Rowe-Dutton, *d* of late Sir Ernest Rowe-Dutton, KCMG, CB, and of Lady Rowe-Dutton; three *s* one *d*. *Educ:* Bedford Sch.; London Univ.; Lincoln Coll., Oxford. Major, Intelligence Corps, 1943-47. Commonwealth Fund Fellowship to Cornell and Harvard, 1950-51. Contested (Lab) Bedford, 1951. Phillips Electrical, 1951-53; Head of Overseas Dept, Industrial Soc. 1953-54; Sec., Duke of Edinburgh's Study Conf. on Human Problems of Industry, 1954-56; joined Booker McConnell Ltd, 1956; Chairman: Bookers Engineering & Industrial Holdings Ltd, 1966-70; Associated British Maltsters Ltd, 1971-73; Rockware Group Ltd, 1971-76; Curtis Brown Ltd, 1971-76; Victoria Deep Water Terminal Ltd, 1971-76; Dawnay Day Group, 1971-76; H. Clarkson & Co. (Holdings) Ltd, 1975-76; Director: Booker Bros McConnell & Co. Ltd, 1960-70; Renold Group Ltd; Chm.-designate, Nat. Ports Authority, 1970; Member: BSC, 1967-70; British Tourist Authy Bd, 1969-75; Business Graduates Assoc.; Ct of London Univ. (Dep. Chm. 1970-); Political and Econ. Plannning Exec. (Hon. Treas.); Council, BIM (Vice-Chm.); Foundn on Automation & Human Develt, 1971-; Engineering Industries Council, 1975-76; Founder Mem., Council of Foundn for Management Educn; Chairman: Westfield College, 1969-76; Clothing EDC; Adv. Council, Business Graduates Assoc. *Recreations:* Rugby (played for Bedford and E Mids); swimming, browsing. *Address:* British Railways Board, 222 Marylebone Road, NW1. *Club:* Savile.

PARKER, Rev. Reginald Boden; *b* Wallasey, Cheshire, 4 June 1901; *s* of Joseph William and Ada Parker. *Educ:* Wallasey Grammar School; St Catherine's College, Oxford University; Ripon Hall, Oxford. BSc (London), 1923; MA (Oxon), 1938. Assistant Master, Ashton Gram. Sch., Lancs, 1925-30; Asst Master, Newton Gram. Sch., Lancs, 1930-32; Curate, Childwall, Liverpool, 1935-37; Curate, St Margaret's, Westminster, 1937-39; Asst Master and Chaplain, Oundle School, 1940-48; Headmaster, Igbobi College, Lagos, 1948-58; Bishop's Chaplain in Liverpool University, 1958-61; Residentiary Canon, Liverpool Cathedral, 1958-61; Precentor, Liverpool Cathedral, 1959-61; Asst Master, Wellington Coll., 1961-64; Rector of Bentham, dio. of Bradford, 1964-72. Hon. Lecturer in Hellenistic Greek, Liverpool University, 1959; Select Preacher, Oxford University, 1960. Member of Headmasters' Conference, 1950. *Publications:* (with J. P. Hodges): The Master and the Disciple, 1938 (SPCK); The King and the Kingdom, 1939 (SPCK); The Holy Spirit and The Kingdom, 1941 (SPCK). *Address:* 3 Yew Tree Cottages, Sheepscombe, Stroud, Glos GL6 7RB. *T:* Painswick 812650.

PARKER, Richard Eric, PhD (London), CChem, FRIC; Secretary and Registrar, Royal Institute of Chemistry, since 1962 (Member Council, 1959-62); *b* 6 May 1925; *e s* of late Leonard Parker and of Louisa Mary Parker (*née* Frearson); *m* 1969, Elizabeth Howgego; one *s* two step *d*. *Educ:* Wyggeston Sch., Leicester; University Coll., Leicester. Tutorial Student, King's Coll., London, 1946; Asst Lectr, 1947, and Lectr in Organic Chemistry, 1950-62, Univ. of Southampton. Hon. Treas., 1966-69, and Jt Hon. Sec., 1973-76, Parly and Scientific Cttee; Mem. Exec. Cttee, Fedn of European Chemical Socs, 1977- (Jt Hon. Sec., 1970-76); Chm., European Communities Chemistry Cttee, 1973-. FRSA 1970. *Publications:* papers and articles on physical organic chemistry, mainly in Jl Chem. Soc. *Recreations:* bridge, travel, swimming, Rugby football. *Address:* Royal Institute of Chemistry, 30 Russell Square, WC1B 5DT. *T:* 01-580 3482; 24 Kent Road, East Molesey, Surrey. *T:* 01-979 2148. *Club:* Savage.

PARKER, Sir Richard (William) Hyde, 12th Bt, *cr* 1681; *b* 5 April 1937; *o s* of Sir William Stephen Hyde Parker, 11th Bt, and Ulla Ditlef, *o d* of C. Ditlef Nielsen, Dr of Philosophy, Copenhagen; *S* father 1951; *m* 1972, Jean, *d* of late Sir Lindores Leslie, 9th Bt; three *d* (incl. twins). *Educ:* Millfield, Street, Somerset; Royal Agricultural College, Cirencester. *Heir: cousin* Laurence Edmond Hyde Parker [*b* 24 Feb. 1912; *m* 1953, Margarethe Van Thörne; two *s* one *d*]. *Address:* Melford Hall, Long Melford, Suffolk.

PARKER, Rear-Adm. Robert William, CBE 1954; JP; *b* 1902; *s* of Colonel W. F. Parker, Delamore, Cornwood, Devon; *m* 1935, Noemi Vyvian, *d* of C. V. Espeut; no *c*. *Educ:* Royal Naval Colleges Osborne and Dartmouth. Midshipman, 1918; served in Grand Fleet; specialised Engineering, 1922-24; served as Engineer Officer: HMS Rodney, 1942-44; HMS Indomitable (British Pacific Fleet), 1944-46; comd HMS Caledonia, RN Apprentices Training Establishment, Rosyth, 1949-52; Rear-Adm. (E), 1952, on staff of C-in-C, Plymouth; Deputy Engineer-in-Chief of the Fleet, 1953-55; retired 1955. JP Somerset, 1961. *Recreation:* model engineering. *Address:* The Hermitage, Freshford, near Bath, Avon. *T:* Limpley Stoke 3220.

PARKER, Hon. Sir Roger (Jocelyn), Kt 1977; **Hon. Mr Justice Parker;** a Judge of the High Court, Queen's Bench Division, since 1977; Judge of the Courts of Appeal, Jersey and Guernsey, since 1974; *b* 25 Feb. 1923; *s* of Captain Hon. T. T. Parker, DSC, RN (Retired) and Marie Louise Leonie (*née* Kleinwort); *m* 1948, Ann Elizabeth Frederika (*née* White); one *s* three *d*. *Educ:* Eton; King's Coll., Cambridge. Served Rifle Bde, 1941-46. Called to Bar, Lincoln's Inn, 1948, QC 1961; Bencher, 1969. Member, Bar Council, 1968-69, Vice-Chm., 1970-72, Chm., 1972-73. Vice-Pres., Senate of Four Inns of Court, 1972-73. Dep. Chm., Herts QS, 1969-71. Conducted Windscale Nuclear Fuel Reprocessing Inquiry, 1977. Chm., Court of Inquiry into Flixborough Explosion, 1974. *Address:* The Old Rectory, Widford, near Ware, Herts. *T:* Much Hadham 2593. *Clubs:* Lansdowne; Leander.

PARKER, Ronald William, CBE 1959; JP; *b* 21 Aug. 1909; *s* of late Ernest Edward Parker, MBE, Accountant of Court, and Margaret Parker (*née* Henderson); *m* 1937, Phyllis Mary (*née* Sherren); two *s*. *Educ:* Royal High School, Edinburgh. Chartered Accountant, 1933. Secretary, later Dir, Weston Group of Companies, 1935; Asst Dir of Finance, Ministry of Fuel and Power, 1942; Partner, J. Aikman, Smith & Wells, CA, 1946. National Coal Board: Finance Dir, Scottish Division, 1947; Dep. Chm., North Western Division, 1954; Chm., Scottish Division, 1955-67; Regional Chm., Scottish Region, 1967-68; Chm., Scottish Gas Region (formerly Scottish Gas Bd), 1968-74. JP City and County of Edinburgh, 1972. *Recreations:* golf, gardening, fishing. *Address:* Claremont, 3 South Lauder Road, Edinburgh EH9 2LL. *T:* 031-667 7666. *Clubs:* Caledonian; New (Edinburgh); Royal Northern (Aberdeen).

PARKER, Rev. Thomas Maynard, DD; Fellow and Praelector in Theology and Modern History, University College, Oxford, 1952-73; now Emeritus Fellow; University Lecturer in Theology, Oxford, 1950-73; *b* 7 March 1906; *s* of late Thomas Maynard and Emily Mary Parker; unmarried. *Educ:* King Edward VI School, Stratford-on-Avon; Exeter College, Oxford, (Scholar). 1st Class Hon. School of Modern History, 1927; BA 1927; 1st Cl. Hon. Sch. of Theology, 1929; Liddon Student, 1928-30; MA 1931; BD, DD 1956. St Stephen's House, Oxford, 1927-29. Liveryman of Butchers' Company, 1927 (Mem. Ct of Assistants, 1955-57, 1963-65; Warden, 1957-61; Providitor, 1960-61; Renter Asst, 1961-62; Master, 1962-63; Past Master, 1963-); Freeman of City of London, 1927. Deacon, 1930; Priest, 1931; Librarian and Tutor, Chichester Theological College, 1930-32; Curate of St Mary's, Somers Town, London, NW1, 1932-35; Librarian of Pusey House, Oxford, 1935-52; Custodian of the Pusey Memorial Library, 1946-52; Member, Faculty of Modern History, 1935-, Faculty of Theology, 1935-73, Oxford Univ. Bampton Lecturer, Univ. of Oxford, 1950; Acting Chaplain and Lecturer in Medieval History and Political Science, Pembroke College, Oxford, 1951-52; Assistant Chaplain, Exeter College, Oxford, 1946-52; Chaplain, University Coll., Oxford, 1952-70; Select Preacher, University of Cambridge, 1955; Lecturer in Theology, Pembroke Coll., Oxford, 1952-61; Chairman: Faculty of Theology, 1963-65; Board of Faculty of Theology, 1964-65; Examiner in: Honour School of Theology, 1963-65; Honour School of Mod. Hist., Oxford, 1953-55; Select Preacher, Oxford Univ., 1960-61. Examining Chaplain to Bishop of Bradford, 1943-55; Birkbeck Lecturer, Trinity College, Cambridge, 1956-57. External Examr: QUB, 1964-66; External Examr in Church History for BD, St David's Coll., Lampeter, 1968-70; Examr for BPhil in European History, Oxford Univ., 1972-74. Member Central Advisory

Council for Training of Ministry, 1948-55; Member Faith and Order Department of Brit. Council of Churches, 1949-55. FRHistS, 1956 (Mem. Council 1964-68); FSA, 1962. *Publications:* The Re-Creation of Man, 1940; The English Reformation to 1558, 1950 (2nd edn 1966); Christianity and the State in the Light of History (Bampton Lectures), 1955. Contributor to: Union of Christendom, 1938; The Apostolic Ministry, 1946; Ideas and Beliefs of the Victorians (Broadcast Talks), 1949, new edn 1966; Augustinus Magister, 1955; Oxford Dictionary of the Christian Church, 1957, 2nd edn, 1974; Miscellanea Historiæ Ecclesiasticæ, Congrès de Stockholm, 1960; Studies in Church History, vol. I, 1964; Trends in Mediæval Political Thought, 1965; Essays in Modern English Church History in Memory of Norman Sykes, 1966; Anglican Initiatives in Christian Unity, 1967; The Rediscovery of Newman, 1967; The New Cambridge Modern History, Vol. III, 1968; Encyclopædia Britannica, Chambers's Encycl., Journal Theol. Studies, English Historical Review, Journal of Eccles. Hist., Speculum, Medium Aevum, Church Quarterly Review, Time and Tide, Oxford Magazine, Proc. of British Academy. *Recreation:* study of railways. *Address:* 36 Chalfont Road, Oxford OX2 6TH. *T:* Oxford 58494. *Club:* Athenæum.

PARKER, Sir (Walter) Edmund, Kt 1974; CBE 1946; Partner in Price Waterhouse & Co., Chartered Accountants, 1944-71; *b* 24 June 1908; *er s* of late Col Frederic James Parker, CB, and Emily Margaret Joan Parker (*née* Bullock); *m* 1934, Elizabeth Mary Butterfield; one *s. Educ:* Winchester. Joined Price Waterhouse & Co., 1926; admitted Mem. Inst. of Chartered Accountants in England and Wales, 1931. 2nd Lieut 1/5 Essex Regt (TA), 1939. Bd of Trade: Chief Accountant, 1940; Asst Sec., 1941-45. Various Govt Cttees, 1946-50; Mem., Industrial Develt Adv. Bd, 1972-74. Mem. Council, Inst. of Chartered Accountants, 1957-69 (President, 1967); Chairman, Cinematograph Films Council, 1964-66. Auditor, Duchy of Cornwall, 1956-71; Chm., Local Employment Acts Financial Adv. Cttee, 1971-73. *Recreations:* garden and countryside. *Address:* Stable Cottage, Manuden, near Bishop's Stortford, Herts. *T:* Bishop's Stortford 812273.

PARKER, Vice-Adm. Sir (Wilfred) John, KBE 1969 (OBE 1953); CB 1965; DSC 1943; Chairman, Seven Seas Dredging, since 1974; *b* 12 Oct. 1915; *s* of Henry Edmond Parker and Ida Mary (*née* Cole); *m* 1943, Marjorie Stuart Jones, Halifax, NS, Canada; two *d. Educ:* RN College, Dartmouth. Joined Royal Navy, 1929; Imperial Defence College, 1957; Commodore West Indies, 1958-60; Captain RNC Dartmouth, 1961-63; an Asst Chief of Defence Staff, Min. of Defence, 1963-66; Flag Officer, Medway, and Adm. Supt HM Dockyard, Chatham, 1966-69, retd 1969. Commander 1949; Captain 1954; Rear-Adm., 1964; Vice-Adm., 1967. *Recreations:* tennis, ski-ing, sailing. *Address:* Nyewood Oaks, Rogate, Petersfield, Hants. *Clubs:* Anglo-Belgian, Royal Navy.

PARKER, Sir William Alan, 4th Bt *cr* 1844; *b* 20 March 1916; *er s* of Sir William Lorenzo Parker, 3rd Bt, OBE, and late Lady Parker; *S* father, 1971; *m* 1946, Sheelagh Mary, *o d* of late Dr Sinclair Stevenson; one *s* one *d. Educ:* Eton; New College, Oxford. Served War of 1939-45, RE (Captain); Middle East, 1941-45. *Heir: s* William Peter Brian Parker, *b* 30 Nov. 1950. *Address:* Apricot Hall, Sutton-cum-Beckingham, Lincoln LN5 0RE. *T:* Fenton Claypole 322.

PARKER, Rt. Rev. William Alonzo; *b* 31 Jan. 1897; *s* of late W. H. Parker, Alkrington, Lancs; *m* 1930, Ellen, *d* of Rev. Robert Hodgson, Hooton Roberts, Yorks; one *s. Educ:* Manchester University (MA). Royal Tank Corps, 1916-24; served European War (despatches); Ordained, 1929; Curate of Sheffield Cathedral; Chaplain of St George's Cathedral, Jerusalem, 1931-37; Vicar of St Matthew, Gosport, 1937-42; Vicar of St Chad, Shrewsbury, 1942-45; Rector of Stafford, 1945-55; Archdeacon of Stafford, 1945-59; Bishop Suffragan of Shrewsbury, 1959-69; Prebendary of Tachbrook, 1947-55; Canon Residentiary, Treasurer, and Prebendary of Offley in Lichfield Cathedral, 1955-59, Hon. Canon, 1968-. Prebendary of Freeford, 1959-68; Provost of Denstone, 1960-67. SCF, 1939-40. Pres., Shropshire and W Midland Agric. Soc., 1966-. Sub-Prelate OStJ. *Recreation:* fishing. *Address:* 104 Stretton Farm Road, Church Stretton, Salop SY6 6DX.

PARKER BOWLES, Dame Ann, DCVO 1977; CBE 1972; Chief Commissioner, Girl Guides, 1966-75; *b* 14 July 1918; *d* of Sir Humphrey de Trafford, 4th Bt, MC; *m* 1939, Derek Henry Parker Bowles; three *s* one *d.* County Comr, Girl Guides (Berkshire), 1959-64; Dep. Chief Comr, Girl Guides, 1962-66. *Recreation:* horse racing. *Address:* White Oak House, Highclere, Newbury, Berkshire. *T:* Highclere 253735.

PARKES, Sir Alan (Sterling), Kt 1968; CBE 1956; FRS 1933; MA, PhD, DSc, ScD; Fellow of Christ's College, Cambridge, 1961-69, Hon. Fellow 1970; Fellow of University College, London; Chairman, Galton Foundation, since 1969; *b* 1900; *y s* of E. T. Parkes, Purley; *m* 1933, Ruth, *d* of Edward Deanesly, FRCS, Cheltenham; one *s* two *d. Educ:* Willaston School; Christ's College, Cambridge; BA Cantab, 1921, ScD 1931; PhD Manchester, 1923; Sharpey Scholar, University College, London, 1923-24; Beit Memorial Research Fellow, 1924-30; MA Cantab 1925; Schäfer Prize in Physiology, 1926; DSc London 1927; Julius Mickle Fellowship, University of London, 1929; Hon. Lecturer, University College, London, 1929-31; Member of the Staff of the National Institute for Medical Research, London, 1932-61; Mary Marshall Prof. of the Physiology of Reproduction, Univ. of Cambridge, 1961-67, Professor Emeritus 1968. Consultant, Cayman Turtle Farm Ltd, Grand Cayman, BWI, 1971-. Foulerton Student of the Royal Society, 1930-34. Mem., Biol. and Med. Cttee, Royal Commn on Population, 1944-46. Lectures: Sidney Ringer, University College Hospital, 1934; Ingleby, Univ. of Birmingham, 1940; Galton, Eugenics Society, 1950; Addison, Guy's Hospital, 1957; Darwin, Inst. of Biology; Robert J. Terry, Washington Univ., Sch. of Medicine, 1963; Ayerst, Amer. Fertility Soc., 1965; Dale, Soc. for Endocrinology, 1965; Dick, Univ. of Edinburgh, 1969; Cosgrave, Amer. Coll. of Obstetricians and Gynaecologists, 1970; Tracy and Ruth Storer, Univ. of Calif, Davis, 1973. President: Section of Endocrinology, Roy. Soc. Med., 1949-50, Section of Comparative Medicine, 1962-63; Section D Brit. Assoc. for the Advancement of Science, 1958; Eugenics Soc., 1968-70; Inst. of Biology, 1959-61; Assoc. of Scientific Workers, 1960-62. Chairman: Soc. for Endocrinology, 1944-51; Soc. for Study of Fertility, 1950-52, 1963-66; Nuffield Unit of Tropical Animal Ecology, 1966-69; Breeding Policy Cttee, Zool Soc. of London, 1960-67; Scientific Adv. Cttee, Brit. Egg Mkting Bd, 1961-70. Mem. Adv. Cttee on Med. Research of the WHO, 1968-71. Executive Editor, Jl Biosocial Science, 1969-; Sec., Jls of Reproduction & Fertility Ltd, 1960-76. Consultant, IPPF, 1969-. Cameron Prize, 1962; Sir Henry Dale Medal, Soc. for Endocrinology, 1965; John Scott Award (jtly with Dr A. U. Smith and Dr C. Polge), City of Philadelphia, 1969; Marshall Medal, Soc. Stud. Fert., 1970; Oliver Bird Medal, FPA, 1970. *Publications:* The Internal Secretions of the Ovary, 1929; Sex, Science and Society, 1966; Patterns of Sexuality and Reproduction, 1976; papers on the Physiology of Reproduction, on Endocrinology and on the behaviour of living cells at low temperatures in Jl of Physiology, Proc. Royal Society, and other scientific jls. Ed. Marshall's Physiology of Reproduction, 3rd edn, 1952. *Address:* 1 The Bramleys, Shepreth, Royston, Hertfordshire SG8 6PY.

PARKES, Sir Basil (Arthur), Kt 1971; OBE 1966; JP; Chairman: Boston Deep Sea Fisheries Ltd, since 1962; *b* 20 Feb. 1907; *s* of late Sir Fred Parkes, Boston, Lincs, and Blackpool, Lancs, and late Gertrude Mary Parkes (*née* Bailey); *m* 1933, May Lewis McNeill; two *s* one *d. Educ:* Boston Grammar Sch., Lincs. Joined small trawler owning Co., 1924 (Dir, 1928; Man. Dir, 1946). French Consular Agent, 1954-; Belgian Consul in Hull, 1968, Humberside 1974-. Pres., United Towing Ltd, 1960-. Hon. Brother, Hull Trinity House. JP Hull, 1966. Mem., Worshipful Co. of Fishmongers; Mem., Worshipful Co. of Poulters; FInstM 1971; FBIM 1972. Officier de l'ordre du Mérite National Français, 1973. *Recreations:* golf, shooting. *Address:* Stockdove Wood, Tranby Park, Hessle, North Humberside. *Clubs:* City Livery, Constitutional.

PARKES, Dr Edward Walter; Vice-Chancellor, City University, since 1974; *b* 19 May 1926; *o s* of Walter Frederick Parkes; *m* 1950, Margaret, *d* of John Parr; one *s* one *d. Educ:* King Edward's, Birmingham; St John's College, Cambridge; Scholar; 1st cl. hons Mech. Sci. Tripos, 1945; MA, PhD, ScD; FIMechE, MICE. At RAE and in the aircraft industry, 1945-48; research student and subsequently Univ. Lecturer, Cambridge, 1948-59; Fellow and Tutor of Gonville and Caius College; Vis. Prof., Stanford Univ., 1959-60; Head of the Department of Engineering, Univ. of Leicester, 1960-65; Prof. of Mechanics, Cambridge, and Professorial Fellow, Gonville and Caius Coll., 1965-74 (Mem. Gen. Bd, Dep. head of Dept of Engineering). Member: Brynmor Jones Cttee, 1964-65; Adv. Bd for Res. Councils, 1974-; University and Polytechnic Grants Cttee for Hong Kong, 1974-. *Publications:* Braced Frameworks, 1965, 2nd edn 1974; papers on elasticity, dynamic plasticity or thermal effects on structures in Proc. and Phil. Trans. Royal Society and other jls. *Address:* The City University, EC1V 4PB. *Club:* Athenæum.

PARKES, Geoffrey, CMG 1947; FTI 1942; Deputy Chairman, National Westminster Bank Ltd, North Region, 1969-72; *b* 24 April 1902; *er s* of late Harry Clement Parkes, JP, and late Edith

Newton; *m* 1925, Marjorie Syddall (*d* 1976); no *c*. *Educ:* Clifton College; and L'Institut Technique, Roubaix. Director: Small & Parkes Ltd, 1927-64; Geigy (UK) Ltd, 1943-66; Director of Narrow Fabrics, Ministry of Supply, and Hon. Adviser to Board of Trade, 1939-44; Director-General Textiles & Light Industries Branch, CCG, 1944-46; Dep. Chief (Exec.) Trade and Industry Div., CCG, 1946. Director: District Bank Ltd, 1949-69; National Provincial Bank Ltd, 1963-69. Mem. Court, Manchester Univ., 1949-69. MA (*hc*) Manchester Univ., 1966. FRSA 1952. JP Manchester, 1949-65. *Recreation:* gardening. *Address:* Berth-y-Coed, Colwyn Bay, North Wales. *T:* Colwyn Bay 30377.

PARKES, Rev. James William, MA, DPhil; Hon. DHL; Hon. DLitt; *b* 22 Dec. 1896; *s* of late Henry Parkes, and Annie Katharine Bell; *m* 1942, Dorothy E., *d* of F. Iden Wickings, Hildenborough. *Educ:* Elizabeth College, Guernsey; Hertford Coll., Oxford, Open Classical Scholar. Private, Artists Rifles, 1916; 2nd Lieut, Queen's Royal West Surrey Regt, 1917; Captain and Adj., 19th Queen's 1918; BA (Aegrotat) Theology, 1923; MA 1926; Post-Graduate Schol. Exeter College, 1930; DPhil 1934; Internat. Study Sec. Student Christian Movement, 1923-26; Warden, Student Movement House, London, 1926-28; Study Sec. Internat. Student Service, Geneva, 1928-34; Chairman Nat. Com. Common Wealth, 1942-43, Vice-Pres. 1943; Charles William Eliot lecturer, Jewish Inst. of Religion, NY, 1946-47; Pres. Jewish Historical Soc. of England, 1949-51; Director, The Parkes Library, 1956-64; Deacon, 1925; Priest, 1926. Hon. Fellow, Hebrew Univ. of Jerusalem, 1970. *Publications:* The Jew and His Neighbour, 1930, 2nd and revised edn 1938; International Conferences, 1933; The Conflict of the Church and the Synagogue, 1934; Jesus, Paul and the Jews, 1936; The Jew in the Medieval Community, 1938; The Jewish Problem in the Modern World, 1939, 2nd (American) edn 1946, 3rd (German) edn 1948, 4th (Italian) edn, 1953; Oxford Pamphlets on World Affairs; Palestine, 1940; The Jewish Question, 1941; An Enemy of the People: Antisemitism, 1945, 2nd (German) edn 1948; The Emergence of the Jewish Problem, 1878-1939, 1946; Judaism and Christianity, 1948; A History of Palestine from 135 AD to Modern Times, 1949; The Story of Jerusalem, 1949; God at work, 1952; End of an Exile, 1954; The Foundations of Judaism and Christianity, 1960; A History of the Jewish People, 1962 (German, Dutch, Italian and Spanish trans.); Antisemitism, 1963 (German and Spanish trans.); Prelude to Dialogue, 1969; Voyage of Discoveries: an autobiography, 1969; Whose Land? The Peoples of Palestine, 1970; (as John Hadham) Good God, 1940 (US edn 1965, rev. edn 1966); God in a World at War, 1940; Between God and Man, 1942; God and Human Progress, 1944; Common Sense About Religion, 1961. *Relevant Publication:* A Bibliography of the Printed Works of James Parkes with selected quotations, by Sidney Sugarman and Diana Bailey, 1977. *Recreations:* architecture and gardening. *Address:* Netherton, Iwerne Minster, Blandford, Dorset. *T:* Fontmell Magna 367. *Club:* Athenæum.

PARKES, John Hubert; Deputy Secretary (Northern Ireland Civil Service), Northern Ireland Office, since 1973; *b* 1 Oct. 1930; 2nd *s* of Frank Hubert Parkes and Mary Edith (*née* Barnes), Birmingham; *m* 1956, Elsie Griffiths Henderson; two *s*. *Educ:* George Dixon Sch., Birmingham; Magdalen Coll., Oxford (MA). Joined NI Civil Service, 1953; Asst Sec. 1966; RCDS 1972. *Address:* 18 Wilton Grove, Wimbledon, SW19. *T:* 01-540 6370.

PARKES, Norman James, CBE 1976 (OBE 1960); Clerk of the Australian House of Representatives, 1971-76, retired; *b* 29 July 1912; *s* of Ernest William Parkes; *m* 1937, Maida Cleave, *d* of James Nicholas Silk; two *s*. *Educ:* Victorian State Schools. AASA. Parliamentary officer, 1934: with Reporting Staff, 1934-37; with House of Representatives, 1937-76. *Recreation:* bowls. *Address:* 3/3 Nuyts Street, Red Hill, Canberra, ACT 2603, Australia. *T:* Canberra 957320. *Club:* Canberra Bowling.

PARKHOUSE, Prof. James, MD, FFARCS; Professor of Anaesthetics, Manchester University, since 1970; Hon. Consultant Anaesthetist, Manchester and Salford Area Health Authorities (Teaching), since 1970; *b* 30 March 1927; *s* of Charles Frederick Parkhouse and Mary Alice Sumner; *m* 1952, Hilda Florence Rimmer; three *s* two *d*. *Educ:* Merchant Taylors' Sch., Great Crosby; Liverpool Univ. (MD 1955). MB ChB, 1950; MA Oxon 1960; MSc Manchester 1974. DA; FFARCS 1952. Anaesthetist, RAF Med. Br., 1953-55. Sen. Resident Anaesth., Mayo Clinic, 1957-58; First Asst, Nuffield Dept of Anaesths, Oxford, and Hon. Cons. Anaesth., United Oxford Hosps, 1958-66; Prof. and Head of Dept of Anaesths, Univ. of Manitoba, and Chief Anaesth., Winnipeg Gen. Hosp., 1967-68; Postgrad. Dean, Faculty of Med., Sheffield Univ., and

Hon. Cons. Anaesth., United Sheffield Hosps, 1969-70. Consultant, postgrad. med. trng, WHO, 1969-. Member: Sheffield Reg. Hosp. Bd, 1969-70; Bd, Faculty of Anaesthetists, 1971-. *Publications:* A New Look at Anaesthetics, 1965; contrib. to The Lancet, BMJ and specialist jls. *Recreations:* music, golf. *Address:* 10 Pownall Road, Wilmslow, Cheshire. *T:* Wilmslow 22661. *Club:* Royal Air Force.

PARKHOUSE, Peter; Director in Directorate-General for Agriculture, Commission of the European Communities, since 1973; *b* 22 July 1927; *s* of late William Richard Parkhouse, MBE, and of Alice Vera Parkhouse (*née* Clarke); *m* 1950, Mary Alison Holland; one *s* one *d*. *Educ:* Blundell's Sch.; Peterhouse, Cambridge; Cologne Univ. BA 1947, MA 1950. Instr Lieut, RN, 1947-50; Asst Master, Uppingham Sch., 1951-52; Asst Principal, Min. of Food, 1952; transf. to MAFF, 1955; served in private office of successive Ministers and Parly Secs, 1954-58; Principal 1958; Principal Private Sec. to Minister, 1966-67; Asst Sec. 1967; successively head of Fisheries Div., Planning Unit and EEC Div.; Under-Sec. 1973, i/c EEC Gp. *Recreations:* music, fishing, sailing. *Address:* 21 Terwenberglaan, Sterrebeek 1960, Belgium. *T:* Brussels 731-63-57.

PARKHURST, Raymond Thurston, BSc(Agr), MSc, PhD; Director of South Central Poultry Research Laboratory, State University, Mississippi, 1960-68, retired; *b* Everett, Massachusetts, USA, 24 April 1898; *o s* of Fred Lincoln and Celeste Elizabeth Parkhurst; *m* 1922, Norma F. Langroise; one *s* one *d*. *Educ:* Fitchburg (Massachusetts) High School; Universities of Massachusetts, Idaho and Edinburgh. Extension Poultryman, Iowa State College, 1919-21; Professor of Poultry Husbandry, Experiment Station Poultry Husbandman, and Head, Dept of Poultry Husbandry, University of Idaho, 1921-27; Director, Brit. Nat. Institute of Poultry Husbandry, 1927-32; Head, Department Agricultural Research, National Oil Products Co., 1932-38; Head, Dept of Poultry Husbandry, University of Massachusetts, Amherst, 1938-44; Director, Nutrition and Research, Flory Milling Co., Bangor, Pa, 1944-49; Director of Nutrition and Research, Lindsey-Robinson and Company, Roanoke, Va, USA, 1949-60; Member: Amer. Poultry Science Assoc.; Civic Coordinating Council; Mississippi Educnl TV; Amer. Assoc. of Retired Persons; Nat. Assoc. of Retired Persons, etc.; First President of British Poultry Education Association. *Publications:* Vitamin E in relation to Poultry; The Comparative Value of various Protein Feeds for Laying Hens; Factors Affecting Egg Size; Mixed Protein Foods for Layers; Ricketts and Perosis in Growing Chickens; Rexing the Rabbit; Corn Distillers By-Products in Poultry Rations; Calcium and Manganese in Poultry Nutrition; Crabmeal and Fishmeal in Poultry Nutrition; Commercial Broiler Raising; Gumboro Disease, etc. *Recreations:* educational television, stamps, coins. *Address:* 700 Sassafras Drive, Starkville, Miss 39759, USA. *Club:* Kiwanis International.

PARKIN, John Mackintosh; Assistant Under-Secretary of State, Ministry of Defence, since 1974; *b* 18 June 1920; *s* of Thomas and Emily Cecilia Parkin; *m* Biancamaria Giuganino, Rome; two *d*. *Educ:* Nottingham High Sch.; Emmanuel Coll., Cambridge (Sen. Schol.; MA). Royal Artillery, 1939-46 (Captain). Asst Principal, WO, 1949; Registrar, RMCS, 1957-60; Principal Private Sec. to Sec. of State for War, 1960-62; Asst Sec. 1962; Sen. Fellow, Harvard Univ., 1966-67; Comd Sec., BAOR, 1967-70. Mem., Royal Patriotic Fund Corpn, 1977-. *Recreation:* history of architecture and art. *Address:* 35 Little Bornes, Dulwich, SE21 8SD. *T:* 01-670 5564.

PARKINSON, Cecil Edward; MP (C) Hertfordshire South, since 1974 (Enfield West, Nov. 1970-1974); Partner in West, Wake, Price & Co., Chartered Accountants, London EC2, 1961-71; *b* 1 Sept. 1931; *s* of Sidney Parkinson, Carnforth, Lancs; *m* 1957, Ann Mary, *d* of F. A. Jarvis, Harpenden, Herts; three *d*. *Educ:* Royal Lancaster Grammar Sch., Lancaster; Emmanuel Coll., Cambridge. BA 1955, MA 1961. Joined Metal Box Company as a Management Trainee; joined West, Wake, Price, Chartered Accountants, 1956; qualified 1959; Partner, 1961; founded Parkinson Hart Securities Ltd, 1967; Director of several cos, 1965-69. Constituency Chm., Hemel Hempstead Conservative Assoc.; Chm., Herts 100 Club, 1968-69; contested (C) Northampton, 1970. PPS to Minister for Aerospace and Shipping, DTI, 1972-74; an Asst Govt Whip, 1974; an Opposition Whip, 1974-76; Opposition Spokesman on trade, 1976-. Sec., Cons. Parly Finance Cttee, 1971-72; Vice-Chm., Anglo-Swiss Parly Gp; Leader, Inst. of Dirs Parly Panel. *Recreations:* golf, skiing; ran for Oxford and Cambridge, 1954 and 1955; ran for Cambridge against Oxford, 1954 and 1955. *Address:* The Old Vicarage, Northaw, Potters Bar, Herts. *Club:* Hawks (Cambridge).

PARKINSON, Cyril Northcote, MA, PhD, FRHistS; author, historian and journalist; Seigneur of Anneville, Mauxmarquis and Beavoir; Professor Emeritus, Troy State University, Alabama, since 1970; Chairman, Leviathan House (Publishers), since 1972; *b* 30 July 1909; *yr s* of late W. Edward Parkinson, ARCA and late Rose Emily Mary Curnow; *m* 1st, 1943, Ethelwyn Edith Graves (marr. diss.); one *s* one *d* ; 2nd, 1952, Elizabeth Ann Fry; two *s* one *d*. *Educ:* St Peter's School, York; Emmanuel College, Cambridge; King's College, London. Fellow of Emmanuel Coll., Cambridge, 1935; Sen. History Master, Blundell's Sch., Tiverton, 1938; Master, RNC, Dartmouth, 1939. Commissioned as Captain, Queen's Roy. Regt, 1940; Instructor in 166 OCTU; attached RAF, 1942-43; Major, 1943; trans. as GSO2 to War Office (General Staff), 1944; demobilised, 1945; Lectr in History, Univ. of Liverpool, 1946; Raffles Professor of History, University of Malaya, Singapore, 1950-58. Visiting Professor: Univ. of Harvard, 1958; Univs of Illinois and California, 1959-60. Mem. French Académie de Marine and US Naval Inst.; Mem. Archives Commission of Govt of India. Hon. LLD Maryland, 1974. *Plays:* Helier Bonamy, Guernsey, 1967; The Royalist, Guernsey, 1969. *Publications:* many books including: Edward Pellew Viscount Exmouth, 1934; Trade in the Eastern Seas, 1937; (ed.) The Trade Winds, 1948; The Rise of the Port of Liverpool, 1952; War in the Eastern Seas, 1954; Britain in the Far East, 1955; Parkinson's Law, the Pursuit of Progress, 1958; The Evolution of Political Thought, 1958; British Intervention in Malaya, 1867-1877, 1960; The Law and the Profits, 1960; In-laws and Outlaws, 1962; East and West, 1963; Ponies Plot, 1965; A Law unto Themselves, 1966; Left Luggage, 1967; Mrs Parkinson's Law, 1968; The Law of Delay, 1970; The Life and Times of Horatio Hornblower, 1970; Devil to Pay, 1973; Big Business, 1974; The Fireship, 1975; Gunpowder Treason and Plot, 1977; (with H. Le Compte) The Law of Life, 1977; Britannia Rules, 1977; The Rise of Big Business, 1977; Touch and Go, 1977; contribs to Encyclopædia Britannica, Economist, Guardian, New York Times, Fortune, Saturday Evening Post, Punch and Foreign Policy. *Recreations:* painting, travel, sailing. *Address:* Les Câches Hall, St Martin's, Guernsey, CI. *Club:* Royal Channel Islands Yacht.

PARKINSON, Dr David Hardress; Director General, Establishments Resources and Programmes, A, Ministry of Defence, since 1973; *b* Liverpool, 9 March 1918; *s* of E. R. H. Parkinson; *m* 1st, 1944, Muriel Gwendoline Patricia (*d* 1971), *d* of Captain P. W. Newenham; two *s* ; 2nd, 1974, Daphne Margaret Scott-Gall. *Educ:* Gravesend County Grammar Sch.; Wadham Coll., Oxford (MA, DPhil). FInstP. Royal Artillery, 1939-45 (Major); Oxford Univ., 1937-39 and 1945-49; Civil Service: TRE, Malvern, 1949; Supt Low Temp. and Magnetics Div., RRE, Malvern, 1956-63; Head Physics Gp, RRE, 1963-68; Head Physics and Electronics Dept, RRE and Dep. Dir, 1968-72. Hon. Prof. Physics, Birmingham Univ., 1966-73. Chm. Midland Br., Inst. Physics, 1968-70; Vice-Pres. (Exhibns), Inst. Physics, 1973-. *Publications:* (with B. Mulhall) Generation High Magnetic Fields, 1967; many scientific papers and articles. *Recreations:* debating, talking, antiques. *Address:* South Bank, 47 Abbey Road, Great Malvern, Worcs WR14 3HH. *T:* Malvern 5423. *Club:* National Liberal.

PARKINSON, Desmond Frederick, CMG 1975; Counsellor, Foreign and Commonwealth Office; *b* 26 Oct. 1920; widower; two *s* two *d*. HM Forces, 1939-49; served FO, 1949-51; Rangoon, 1951-53; Jakarta, 1954-55; FO, 1955-57; Rabat, 1957-60; Lagos, 1960-61; FO, 1961-63; Singapore, 1965-67; FCO, 1967-. *Address:* c/o Foreign and Commonwealth Office, SW1A 2AH; Woodrow, Silchester, near Reading. *T:* Reading 700257. *Clubs:* Royal Commonwealth Society, MCC.

PARKINSON, Desmond John, OBE 1950; Under-Secretary, Agricultural Research Council, 1971-73; *b* 8 March 1913; *s* of late Frederick A. Parkinson, Rio de Janeiro; *m* 1st, 1940, Leonor Hughes (marr. diss. 1954); 2nd, 1955, Lorna Mary Britton (*née* Wood); no *c*. *Educ:* Hereford Cathedral Sch.; St John's Coll., Cambridge; Brasenose Coll., Oxford. BA Cantab 1935; Colonial Admin. Service, Gold Coast, Colonial Office, British Guiana, Nigeria; Principal, UK MAFF, 1960-63; ARC, 1963-73. *Recreation:* gardening. *Address:* Hartwellend Farm House, Stone, Aylesbury, Bucks. *T:* Stone 634. *Club:* United Oxford & Cambridge University.

PARKINSON, Ewart West, BSc, DPA, CEng, FICE, PPRTPI, FIMunE; Director of Environment and Planning, County of South Glamorgan, since 1973; *b* 9 July 1926; *s* of Thomas Edward Parkinson and Esther Lilian West; *m* 1948, Patricia Joan Wood; two *s* one *d*. *Educ:* Wyggeston Sch., Leicester; Coll. of Technology, Leicester (BSc, DPA). Miller Prize, Instn CE, 1953. After working with Leicester, Wakefield, Bristol and Dover Councils, he became Dep. Borough Engr, Chelmsford,

1957-60; Dep. City Surveyor Plymouth, 1960-64; City Planning Officer, Cardiff, 1964-73. Vice-Pres., RTPI, 1973-75, Pres., 1975-76, Chm. Internat. Affairs Bd, 1975-; Member: Sports Council for Wales, 1971- (Chm., Facilities Cttee); Internat. Soc. of City and Regional Planners, 1972; Govt Deleg. to UN Conf. on Human Settlements, 1976. *Publications:* The Land Question, 1974; And Who is my Neighbour?; articles in prof. jls. *Recreations:* camping, watching football, being with family. *Address:* County of South Glamorgan Headquarters, Newport Road, Cardiff.

PARKINSON, Maj.-Gen. (Retd) Graham Beresford, CBE 1945; DSO and Bar; *b* 5 Nov. 1896; *s* of Henry Ainslie Parkinson, MA, and Ethel Constance Young, Hobart, Tasmania; *m* 1925, Barbara Waiohine Howe. *Educ:* Wellington College, NZ, Royal Military College of Australia, Duntroon (graduated 1915). Proceeded overseas and served in France until the Armistice, proceeding to Germany. Internal security expedition to Fiji in 1920; various staff appts until attended Gunnery Staff Course, Woolwich, 1924; various staff appts until appointed Director of Artillery Army HQ, Wellington, 1936; proceeded overseas with 2 NZ Div. on outbreak of war and continued to serve until conclusion of hostilities with Germany; appointments included: Comdr 4th Field Regt; Comdr 6 Inf. Bde; Comdr RA 2 NZ Div.; GOC 2 NZ Div. for a period under NZ Corps; Quartermaster-General, Army HQ, NZ, 1946; NZ Jt Liaison Staff (London), Dec. 1946-Sept. 1949. Legion of Merit Degree of Officer (USA). *Recreation:* horticulture. *Address:* 27 Clifford Avenue, Fendalton, Christchurch, New Zealand.

PARKINSON, Dr James Christopher, MBE 1963; TD 1962; Deputy Director, Brighton Polytechnic, since 1970; *b* 15 Aug. 1920; *s* of late Charles Myers Parkinson, Pharmacist, Blackburn, Lancs.; *m* 1950, Gwyneth Margot, *d* of late Rev. John Raymond Harrison, Macclesfield, Ches.; three *s*. *Educ:* Queen Elizabeth's Gram. Sch., Blackburn; Univ. Coll., Nottingham. BPharm, PhD (London), FRIC, FPS. Served in Mediterranean area, Parachute Regt, 1943-46; Parachute Regt TA: 16 AB Div. and 44 Parachute Bde, 1949-63 (Major). Lectr, Sch. of Pharmacy, Univ. of London, 1948-54; Head of Sch. of Pharmacy, Brighton Coll. of Technology, 1954-64; Dep. Sec., Pharmaceutical Soc. of Gt Britain, 1964-67; Principal, Brighton Coll. of Technology, 1967-70. Mem. various pharmaceutical cttees of British Pharmacopœia, British Pharmaceutical Codex and British Veterinary Codex, 1956-64; Examr, Pharmaceutical Soc. of Gt Britain, 1954-64; Mem. Bds of Studies in Pharmacy and Librarianship, CNAA, 1965-75. Member, Gen. Synod and Bd of Educn of Church of England, 1970-75. *Publications:* research papers on applied microbiology in Jl Appl. Bact. and Jl Pharm. (London) and on pharmaceutical education in Pharm. Jl. *Recreation:* do-it-yourself. *Address:* 92 Wickham Hill, Hassocks, West Sussex BN6 9NR. *T:* Hurstpierpoint 833369.

PARKINSON, Sir Kenneth Wade, Kt 1957; MA; DL; *b* 1908; *e s* of late Bertram Parkinson, JP, Creskeld Hall, Arthington; *m* 1937, Hon. Dorothy Lane-Fox, OBE, *d* of 1st and last Baron Bingley, PC; one *d* (and one *d* decd). *Educ:* Uppingham; Clare College, Cambridge. Director: B. Parkinson and Co. Ltd; Yorkshire Post Newspapers Ltd; United Newspapers Ltd. High Sheriff of Yorkshire, 1963; DL West Yorks (formerly WR Yorks), 1967. *Address:* (business) 268 Thornton Road, Bradford; (home) Aketon Close, Follifoot, North Yorks. *T:* Spofforth 222.

PARKINSON, Norman; photographer; *b* 21 April 1913; *m* 1945, Wenda (*née* Rogerson); one *s*. *Educ:* Westminster School. Always a photographer of people old and young, horses, birds, still-life, active life, fashion, reportage and travel. Has recently photographed, together and separately, all members of the Royal Family (in particular 21st Birthday and Engagement pictures of HRH The Princess Anne). *Publications:* Life, Look Magazines, (USA); continually contributing to all the Vogues; his photographs have appeared in almost all the world's periodicals. *Recreations:* pig farming (manufactures the famous Porkinson banger in Tobago); sun worshipping, bird watching, breeding Creole racehorses. *Address:* Tobago, West Indies. *T:* none fortunately. *Clubs:* Annabel's; Union (Trinidad); Turf (Tobago).

PARKINSON, Thomas Harry, CBE 1972; DL; Town Clerk, 1960-72, Clerk of the Peace, 1970-72, Birmingham; *b* Bilston, 25 June 1907; *y s* of G. R. J. Parkinson; *m* 1936, Joan Catherine, *d* of C. J. Douglas-Osborn; two *s* one *d*. *Educ:* Bromsgrove; Birmingham University. LLB Hons 1929. Admitted Solicitor, 1930. RAF, 1939-45. Asst Solicitor, Birmingham Corp., 1936-49; Dep. Town Clerk, Birmingham, 1949-60. Pres., Birmingham Law Soc., 1969-70. Sec., W Midlands Passenger Transport Authority, 1969-72; Member: Water Services Staff Adv.

Commn, 1973-; W Midlands Rent Assessment Panel, 1972-; Sec., Nat Exhibn Centre Ltd, 1972-; Hon. Member: Birmingham Assoc. of Mech. Engrs; Inst. of Housing. DL Warwickshire, 1970. Hon. DSc Aston, 1972. *Recreations:* walking, sailing, gardening. *Address:* Stuart House, Middlefield Lane, Hagley, Worcs. *T:* Hagley 2422.

PARKS, Sir Alan (Guyatt), Kt 1977; MD; FRCS, FRCP; Consultant Surgeon to the London Hospital and St Mark's Hospital, since 1959; *b* 19 Dec. 1920; *s* of Harry Parks and Grace Parks; *m* 1956, Caroline Jean Cranston; three *s* one *d*. *Educ:* Epsom Coll.; Brasenose Coll., Oxford (Exhibnr; MA, MCh); Johns Hopkins Univ. Med. Sch. (Rockefeller Student; MD); Guy's Hosp. Med. Sch. FRCS 1948; FRCP 1976. Captain, RAMC, 1950-52. Med. Internship, Johns Hopkins Hosp., 1945-46; house appts, Guy's Hosp., 1946, registrar appts, 1952-59. Hon. Consultant in Proctology to the Army, 1974-. Hunterian Prof., RCS, 1965. Chm., Jt Consultants Cttee, 1974-. Mem. Council, RCS, 1971-. *Publications:* articles on various aspects of intestinal surgery in med. jls. *Recreations:* natural history, Japanese ceramic art; formerly Rugby and athletics for Oxford University. *Address:* 33 Alwyne Road, N1 2HW. *T:* 01-226 8045. *Club:* Athenæum.

PARKYN, Brian (Stewart); Principal, Glacier Institute of Management, since 1976; *b* 28 April 1923; *o s* of Leslie and Gwen Parkyn, Whetstone, N20; *m* 1951, Janet Anne, *o d* of Charles and Jessie Stormer, Eastbourne; one *s* one *d*. *Educ:* King Edward VI Sch., Chelmsford; technical colleges. Dir, Scott Bader Co. Ltd, 1953-. British Plastics Federation: Chm., Reinforced Plastics Gp, 1961-63; Mem. Council, 1959-75. Has travelled widely and lectured in N and S America, Africa, Australasia, India, Japan, USSR and China, etc.; Plastics Lectr, Worshipful Co. of Horners, 1967. Contested (Lab) Bedford, 1964; MP (Lab) Bedford, 1966-70; Mem., Select Cttee on Science and Technology, 1967-70; Chm., Sub-Cttee on Carbon Fibres, 1969; contested (Lab) Bedford, Oct. 1974. Member: Council, Cranfield Inst. of Technology, 1971-; Council, RSA, 1976-. FPRI. *Publications:* many on polyester resins and reinforced plastics throughout world. *Recreations:* writing; interested in industrial democracy. *Address:* 9 Clarendon Square, Leamington Spa, Warwicks. *T:* Leamington 30066.

PARMOOR, 4th Baron *cr* 1914; **Milo Cripps;** *b* 18 June 1929; *s* of 3rd Baron Parmoor, DSO, TD, DL, and of Violet Mary Geraldine, *d* of Sir William Nelson, 1st Bt; *S* father, 1977. *Educ:* Ampleforth; Corpus Christi College, Oxford. *Heir: cousin* (Matthew) Anthony Leonard Cripps, *qv*. *Address:* Manor House, Sutton Veny, Wilts.

PARNELL, family name of **Baron Congleton.**

PARNIS, Alexander Edward Libor, CBE 1973; Secretary of the Churches' Main Committee, since 1973; *b* 25 Aug. 1911; *s* of Alexander T. J. Parnis and Hetty Parnis (née Dams). *Educ:* Malvern Coll.; London Univ. BSc(Econ); MA (Cantab). Entered HM Consular Service, 1933: Acting British Vice-Consul, Paris, 1933-34; transferred to HM Treasury, 1937; Finance Officer, Friends' Ambulance Unit, 1941-45; returned to HM Treasury, 1945. Sec., Gowers Cttee on Houses of Outstanding Historic or Architectural Interest, 1950; Sec., Waverley Cttee on Export of Works of Art, etc, 1952; Treasurer, Univ. of Cambridge, 1953-62; Fellow, King's Coll., Cambridge, 1959-62; Asst Sec., Univ. Grants Cttee, 1962-72. *Recreations:* music, travel, cycling, walking. *Address:* 26 Ardilaun Road, N5 2QR. *T:* 01-226 2688. *Clubs:* Reform; Casino Maltese (Malta).

PARR, Martin Willoughby, CBE 1944 (OBE 1929); Executive Committee, Gordon Boys' School, Woking; *b* 22 Nov. 1892; *s* of Rev. Willoughby Chase Parr and Laura, *d* of Colonel Francklyn, Speen Hill Lodge, Newbury; unmarried. *Educ:* Winchester (Scholar); BNC Oxford (Scholar). Commissioned HLI (SR), 1914; served France 1914-15, Palestine 1917-18, France 1918 (wounded); Sudan Political Service, 1919; Private Secretary to Governor-General, 1927-33; Deputy Civil Secretary, 1933-34; Governor Upper Nile, 1934-36; Governor Equatoria, 1936-42; retired, 1942. Mem: NABC Council, 1944; Vice-President: B&FBS, CMS and NABC; Alderman, LCC, 1954-61. *Recreations:* rifle-shooting; played Rugby football for Oxford 1913-14, half-blue rifle shooting, 1913-14. Shot for Sudan and for England in Elcho Shield at Bisley on several occasions. *Address:* 11 Edith Road, W14. *T:* 01-603 6729. *Clubs:* Royal Commonwealth Society; Vincent's (Oxford).

PARR, Sir Robert, KBE 1950 (OBE 1927); CMG 1943; DèsL (*hc*) University of Lyons, 1956; *b* 15 May 1894; *e s* of Rev. Robert Edmund Parr (*d* 1938), Medomsley, Co. Durham, and of Harriet, *d* of Alfred William Nicholson; *m* Cicely Emily (*d*

1964), *d* of Henry David Shaw, Hadnall, Salop; one *d* (one *s* Robert Philip, Lieut, Grenadier Guards, killed in action at Minturno, 1944; and one *d* decd). *Educ:* Durham; Magdalen Coll., Oxford. Entered Levant Consular Service, 1919; Vice-Consul, 1926; Consul, 1933; Consul-General, 1940; retired, 1956. Chevalier Serbian Order of White Eagle (Mil.); Serbian Gold Medal for Valour and Alexander I Medal; Freedom of City of Lyons, 1945, of Villefranche-en-Beaujolais, 1949, of Tournus, 1951, of City of Dijon, 1952, of Vienne, 1954, of Grézieu-la-Varenne, 1955, and of La Mulatière, 1958; Médaille d'Honneur of City of Dijon, 1950, Médaille Bimillénaire of City of Lyons, 1958; Associate Member Acad. of Lyons, 1950, Acad. of Mâcon, 1955; Mem. various other learned societies in France; Hon. Dean of Consular Body of City of Lyons; Hon. President: Lyons Fédération des Amicales Régimentaires et d'Anciens Combattants; Union des Jouteurs et Sauveteurs de La Mulatière; Association des Rescapés de Montluc; The Lyons English Club. *Address:* c/o Mrs Michael Livingstone-Learmouth, Minchinhampton, Glos. *Clubs:* Brooks's, Royal Automobile; Salop (Shrewsbury); Rotary of Chalon-sur-Saône (Hon.)

PARR, Stanley, CBE 1975; QPM 1968; DL; Chief Constable of Lancashire, since 1972; *b* 14 July, 1917; *s* of Thomas Walmsley and Ada Parr; *m* 1943, Charlotte Lilian Wilson, St Helens; three *s*. *Educ:* St Helens, Lancashire. Joined Lancashire Constabulary, 1937. Served War: commissioned RNVR, 1942-46. Dep. Chief Constable, Blackpool, 1958; Chief Constable, Blackpool, 1962; Dep. Chief Constable, Lancashire, 1967. Pres., St John Ambulance Assoc., Lancashire, 1972. DL Lancs, 1976. OStJ 1970. *Address:* Police Headquarters, Hutton, Preston, Lancs. *T:* Longton 614444.

PARRINDER, Prof. (Edward) Geoffrey (Simons); Professor of Comparative Study of Religions, University of London, at King's College, 1970-77, Professor Emeritus, 1977; *b* 30 April 1910; *s* of William Patrick and Florence Mary Parrinder; *m* 1936, Esther Mary Burt; two *s* one *d*. *Educ:* private sch.; Richmond Coll., London Univ.; Faculté libre de théologie protestante, Montpellier. MA, PhD, DD London. Minister of Methodist Church, Dahomey and Ivory Coast, 1933; ordained 1936; Principal, Séminaire Protestant, Dahomey, 1936-40, 1945-46; Methodist Church: Redruth, 1940; Dahomey, 1943; Guernsey, 1946; Lectr in Religious Studies, 1949, Sen. Lectr, 1950-58, UC Ibadan; Reader in Comparative Study of Religions, Univ. of London, 1958-70; Dean, Faculty of Theology, KCL, 1972-74. Mem. Editorial Bd of Religious Studies and Jl of Religion in Africa. Hon. Sec., Internat. Assoc. for History of Religions, British Br., 1960-72, Pres., 1972-77. Lectures: Charles Strong (Australian Church), 1964; Wilde, in Natural and Comparative Religion, Oxford Univ., 1966-69; Teape, Delhi, Madras, 1973. Vis. Prof., Internat. Christian Univ., Tokyo, 1977-78. FKC 1972; Hon. DLitt Lancaster, 1975. *Publications:* West African Religion, 1949; Bible and Polygamy, 1950; West African Psychology, 1951; Religion in an African City, 1953; African Traditional Religion, 1954; Story of Ketu, 1956; Introduction to Asian Religions, 1957; Witchcraft, 1958; (ed) African Ideas of God, 1961; Worship in the World's Religions, 1961; Comparative Religion, 1962; Upanishads, Gitā and Bible, 1962; What World Religions Teach, 1963; The Christian Debate, 1964; The World's Living Religions, 1965; A Book of World Religions, 1965; Jesus in the Qur'ān, 1965; African Mythology, 1967; Religion in Africa, 1969 repr. as Africa's Three Religions, 1976; Avatar and Incarnation, 1970; Dictionary of Non-Christian Religions, 1971; (ed) Man and his Gods, 1971; The Indestructible Soul, 1973; Themes for Living, 1973; The Bhagavad Gita, a Verse Translation, 1974; Something after Death?, 1974; The Wisdom of the Forest, 1975; Mysticism in the World's Religions, 1976; The Wisdom of the Early Buddhists, 1977; articles and reviews in Times Lit. and Educnl Supplements, and jls of theology, African and Asian religions and Annual Register, 1958-. *Recreations:* travel, gardening, literature. *Address:* King's College, Strand, WC2. *T:* 01-836 5454; 31 Charterhouse Road, Orpington, Kent. *T:* Orpington 23887.

See also D. M. Boston.

PARRINGTON, Francis Rex, ScD; FRS 1962; Reader in Vertebrate Zoology, Cambridge, 1963-70, now Emeritus; Director, University Museum of Zoology, 1938-70; *b* 20 Feb. 1905; 2nd *s* of late Frank Harding Parrington and Bessie May Parrington (née Harding); *m* 1946, Margaret Aileen Knox Johnson (marr. diss., 1963); one *s* one *d*. *Educ:* Liverpool Coll.; Sidney Sussex Coll., Cambridge. BA 1927; ScD 1958. Asst Director, Museum of Zoology, 1927; Strickland Curator, 1928; Balfour Student, 1933; Demonstrator in Zoology, 1935; Lecturer in Zoology, 1938-63. Palæontological expeditions, East Africa, 1930, 1933. Served Royal Artillery, 1939-45, Major. Deputy Chairman, John Joule & Sons, Stone, Staffs, 1962-64

(Director, 1945-64). *Publications:* various on comparative anatomy and palæontology, Proc. Zoological Society, London, etc. *Recreation:* fly-fishing. *Address:* Stroma House, 40 Hanger Hill, Weybridge, Surrey.

PARROTT, Sir Cecil (Cuthbert), KCMG 1964 (CMG 1953); OBE 1947; MA; Hon. FIL; Professor of Central and South European Studies, University of Lancaster, 1971-76, now Emeritus Professor; Founder, and Hon. Pres., Comenius Centre, University of Lancaster (Director, 1968-76); *b* 29 Jan. 1909; *s* of Engineer Captain Jasper W. A. Parrott, RN, and Grace Edith West; *m* 1935, Ellen Julie, *d* of Hermann and Marie Matzow, Trondhjem, Norway; three *s. Educ:* Berkhamsted Sch.; Peterhouse, Cambridge. Asst Master at Christ's Hospital and at Edinburgh Acad., 1931-34. Tutor to King Peter of Yugoslavia, at Belgrade, 1934-39; HM Legation, Oslo, 1939-40; Stockholm, 1940-45; HM Embassy, Prague, 1945-48; Foreign Office, 1948-50; Head of UN Political Dept, 1950-52; Principal Political Adviser to UK Delegation to the United Nations, 1951-52; Counsellor, HM Embassy, Brussels, 1952-54; HM Minister, Moscow, 1954-57; Director of Research, Librarian and Keeper of the Papers, at the Foreign Office, 1957-60; Ambassador to Czechoslovakia, 1960-66; Prof. of Russian and Soviet Studies, Univ. of Lancaster, 1966-71. Vice-Chm., D'Oyly Carte Opera Trust, 1970-. Hon. FIL, 1968. *Publications:* The Good Soldier Švejk (first complete English trans.), 1973; The Tightrope (autobiog.), 1975; The Serpent and The Nightingale, 1977; The Bad Bohemian Mašek, 1977; various articles and broadcast talks on Slavonic history, music, art and literature. *Recreations:* music, theatre, literature, languages. *Address:* c/o University of Lancaster, Bailrigg, Lancaster LA1 4YN.

PARRY, family name of **Baron Parry.**

PARRY, Baron *cr* 1975 (Life Peer), of Neyland, Dyfed; **Gordon Samuel David Parry;** Warden, Pembrokeshire Teachers' Centre, since 1969; *b* 30 Nov. 1925; *s* of Thomas Lewis Parry and Anne Parry (*née* Evans); *m* 1948, Glenys Parry (*née* Incledon); one *d. Educ:* Neyland Board Sch.; Pembroke County Intermediate Sch.; Trinity Coll., Carmarthen; Univ. of Liverpool (Dipl. Advanced Educn). Teacher: Coronation Sch., Pembroke Dock, 1945-46; Llanstadwell Voluntary Primary Sch., Neyland, 1946-47; Barn St Voluntary Sch., Haverfordwest, 1947; County Primary Sch., Neyland, 1947-52; Librarian, Housemaster, County Sec. Sch., Haverfordwest, 1952-62 and 1963-68; Inst. of Educn, Univ. of Liverpool, 1962-63. Member: Welsh Develt Authority; Gen. Adv. Council, IBA; Fac. of Educn, Univ. Coll. of Wales Aberystwyth; Welsh Arts Council, Schs Council Cttee for Wales. President: Pembs Br., Multiple Sclerosis Soc.; Pembs Spastics Soc. Contested (Lab) Monmouth 1959, Pembroke 1970, and Feb. and Oct. 1974. Writer, broadcaster, and TV panel Chm. *Recreations:* travel; watching Welsh Rugby XV win the Grand Slam; reading. *Address:* 2 Neyland Terrace, Neyland, Milford Haven, Dyfed SA73 1PP. *T:* Neyland 600362.

PARRY, Claude Frederick, CIE 1947; OBE 1943; Indian Police (retired); Secretary, The Athenæum, 1951-62; *b* 9 March 1896; *s* of late F. W. Parry; *m* 1930, Sylvia Nancy Irene Kingsley; two *s* one *d. Educ:* St Bees Sch. Served European War, 1914-19 (Mons Star). Joined Indian Police, 1919; Principal, Police Coll., Saugor, CP, 1933-36; Inspector General of Police, Central Provinces, 1946; retired, 1947. Indian Police Medal, 1943; King's Police Medal, 1945. *Address:* Gambrel West, East Street, Coggeshall, Essex. *Club:* Athenæum.

PARRY, Prof. Clive, LLD (Cantab); LLD (Birmingham); Professor of International Law, University of Cambridge, since 1969; Fellow of Downing College; *b* 13 July 1917; 2nd *s* of Frank Parry, LRCPI, and Katharine Haughton Billington; *m* 1945, Luba Poole; one *s* one *d.* Barrister, Gray's Inn. Tagore Law Prof., Univ. of Calcutta, 1972. Associé de l'Institut de Droit International; Pres. Grotian Soc.; Member, Carlyle Club. *Publications:* Nationality and Citizenship Laws of the Commonwealth and of the Republic of Ireland, vol. 1 1957, vol. 2 1960; The Sources and Evidences of International Law, 1965; (ed) British Digest of International Law, 1965-; (ed) British International Law Cases, 1964-; (ed) Consolidated Treaty Series, 1969-. *Address:* Downing College, Cambridge; 5 The Cenacle, Cambridge. *T:* Cambridge 56187; 13 Old Square, Lincoln's Inn, WC2. *T:* 01-405 5441. *Club:* Athenæum.

PARRY, Captain Cuthbert Morris, CVO 1952; OBE 1947; Captain, RN (retired); *b* 24 April 1907; *s* of late Major and Mrs M. V. Parry; *m* 1943, Joan Stanton Iles; three *s. Educ:* RN Colleges, Osborne and Dartmouth. *Recreations:* various. *Address:* Gardener's Cottage, Titchfield Lane, Wickham, Hants-. *T:* Wickham 832224. *Club:* Army and Navy.

PARRY, Ernest J.; *see* Jones-Parry.

PARRY, Sir Hugh (Nigel), Kt 1963; CBE 1954; *b* 26 Aug. 1911; *s* of Charles Frank Parry and Lilian Maud Parry (*née* Powell); *m* 1945, Ann Maureen Forshaw; two *d. Educ:* Cheltenham Coll.; Balliol Coll., Oxford. Entered Colonial Administrative Service, 1939. Chief Secretary, Central African Council, Salisbury, S Rhodesia, 1951-53; Secretary, Office of Prime Minister and External Affairs, Federal Government of Rhodesia and Nyasaland, 1953-63; Ministry of Overseas Development, 1965; Acting Head, Middle East Develt Div., 1969-71, retd 1971. *Recreations:* sailing, motoring. *Address:* c/o Grindlays Bank, 13 St James's Square, SW1.

PARRY, Prof. John Horace, CMG 1960; MBE 1942; Professor of Oceanic History and Affairs, Harvard University, since 1965; *b* 26 April 1914; *s* of late Walter Austin Parry and Ethel Parry; *m* 1939, Joyce, *d* of Rev. H. C. and Mabel Carter; one *s* three *d. Educ:* King Edward's Sch., Birmingham; Clare Coll., Cambridge; Harvard University. Fellow of Clare Coll., Cambridge, 1938; served in RN, 1940-45. Asst Tutor, Clare Coll., Cambridge, and University Lecturer in History, 1945-49; Prof. of Modern History in University College of the West Indies, 1949-56; Principal of University College, Ibadan, Nigeria, 1956-60; Principal of University College, Swansea, 1960-65; Vice-Chancellor, University of Wales, 1963-65. Commander, Order of Alphonso X (Spain), 1976. *Publications:* The Spanish Theory of Empire, 1940; The Audiencia of New Galicia, 1948; Europe and a Wider World, 1949; The Sale of Public Office in the Spanish Indies, 1953; A Short History of the West Indies, 1956; The Age of Reconnaissance, 1963; The Spanish Seaborne Empire, 1966; Ed., The European Reconnaissance, 1968; Trade and Dominion, 1971; The Discovery of the Sea, 1974. Contributor to historical journals. *Recreations:* sailing, fishing, mountain walking, ornithology. *Address:* Widener 45, Cambridge, Mass 02138, USA. *Clubs:* Athenæum, United Oxford & Cambridge University; Harvard (New York).

PARRY, Mrs Margaret Joan; Headmistress of Heathfield School, Ascot, since 1973; *b* 27 Nov. 1919; *d* of W. J. Tamplin, Llantrisant, Glamorgan; *m* 1946, Raymond Howard Parry; two *s* one *d. Educ:* Howell's Sch., Llandaff, Cardiff; Univ. of Wales. Hons English Cl I. Married to a housemaster at Eton; taught and coached interesting people from time to time; Examiner for: Civil Service, LCC, Schools Examination Boards. *Recreations:* books, music, tapestry. *Address:* Westbury, Eton College, Windsor, Berks. *T:* Windsor 60902.

PARRY, Robert; MP (Lab) Liverpool, Scotland Exchange, since 1974 (Liverpool Exchange, 1970-74); *b* 8 Jan. 1933. *Educ:* Bishop Goss RC School, Liverpool. Became a building trade worker. Former full-time organizer for National Union of Public Employees; now Member of Transport and General Workers' Union. Member of Co-operative Party; specially interested in industrial law and industrial relations, housing, the aged and handicapped persons. Member, Liverpool City Council, 1963-74, Labour Group Whip, 1967-70. *Address:* House of Commons, SW1.

PARRY, Robert Hughes, MD (London), BS, FRCP, MRCS, DPH; Retired; formerly Principal Medical Officer to the Bristol City Council; formerly Professor of Preventive Medicine, University of Bristol; Past President Society of Medical Officers of Health; President Preventive Medicine Section, BMA (1949); Hon. FAPHA; *b* 3 Nov. 1895; *s* of J. Hughes-Parry, JP, Penllwyn, Pwllheli, and Anne Hughes, Cwmcoryn, Caernarvonshire; *m* Elsie Joan Williams, LRCP, MRCS, two *s* two *d. Educ:* Pwllheli (Chairman Scholar); University College of Wales, Aberystwyth; University of London, The Middlesex Hospital (Lyell Scholar and Gold Medallist, Junior Broderip Scholar). Lieut, RAF. MS; Asst to Professor of Experimental Pathology at the Middlesex Cancer Hospital, London, 1922-24; Medical Officer of Health of Bristol, 1930-56; Visiting Prof., Yale Univ., USA, 1956; formerly KHP to King George VI and QHP to the Queen. Medical Consultant, WHO, 1959. Member, Local Government Commission for England, 1959-63. High Sheriff of Caernarvonshire, 1958-59. *Publications:* Under the Cherry Tree (autobiography), 1969; Within Life's Span, 1973; various publications on cancer, health centres and other public health problems. *Recreation:* gardening. *Address:* 61 Downs Park East, Bristol.

PARRY, Thomas, MA, DLitt (Wales); FBA 1959; President, National Library of Wales, 1969-77; Principal of the University College of Wales, Aberystwyth, 1958-69; *b* 14 Aug. 1904; *e s* of Richard and Jane Parry, Carmel, Caernarvonshire; *m* 1936, Enid, *o d* of Picton Davies, Cardiff. *Educ:* Pen-y-groes Grammar

Sch.; University College of North Wales, Bangor. Assistant Lecturer in Welsh and Latin, University College, Cardiff, 1926-29; Lecturer in Welsh, University College, Bangor, 1929-47; Prof. of Welsh, 1947-53; Librarian of National Library of Wales, Aberystwyth, 1953-58; Vice-Chancellor, University of Wales, 1961-63, 1967-69; Chairman, UGC Cttee on Libraries, 1963-67. Hon. Professorial Fellow, University Coll. of Wales, 1971. Hon. DLitt Celt. NUI; Hon. LLD Wales. Cymmrodorion Medal, Cymmrodorion Soc., 1976. *Publications:* Peniarth 49, 1929; Theater du Mond, 1930; Awdl "Mam", 1932; Saint Greal, 1933; Baledi'r Ddeunawfed Ganrif, 1935; Mynegai i Weithiau Ifor Williams, 1939; Hanes Llenyddiaeth Gymraeg, 1945; Llenyddiaeth Gymraeg, 1900-45, 1945; Hanes ein Llên, 1946; Lladd wrth yr Allor (translation of T. S. Eliot's Murder in the Cathedral), 1949; Gwaith Dafydd ap Gwilym, 1952; Llywelyn Fawr (a play), 1954; (ed) Oxford Book of Welsh Verse, 1962; articles in Bulletin of Board of Celtic Studies, Trans. Hon. Society of Cymmrodorion, Y Traethodydd, Yr Athro, Yorkshire Celtic Studies. *Address:* Gwyndy, 2 Victoria Avenue, Bangor, Gwynedd. *T:* Bangor 4460.

PARRY BROWN, Arthur Ivor; see Brown, A. I. P.

PARRY-OKEDEN, Richard Godfrey Christian, CMG 1964; CBE 1961; JP; Director, John Lysaght (Australia) Ltd, 1936-70 (Chairman, 1946-67, Managing Director, 1946-65); *b* Blandford, Dorset, 25 Dec. 1900; *s* of Lt-Col U. E. Parry Okeden and Carolina Susan Hambro; *m* 1930, Florence, *d* of E. E. Brown, Pymble, Sydney, NSW; one *s* two *d. Educ:* Eton College. President: Chamber of Manufactures of NSW, 1951-53; Associated Chambers of Manufactures of Australia, 1952-53. JP New South Wales, 1934. Hon. DSc Sydney, 1957. FAIM; FInstD. *Recreation:* enjoying old age. *Address:* 1985 Pittwater Road, Bayview, NSW 2104, Australia. *T:* Sydney 99.2863. *Club:* Union (Sydney).

PARS, Dr Leopold Alexander, MA, ScD Cantab; Fellow, formerly President, of Jesus College, Cambridge; *b* 2 Jan. 1896; *o s* of late Albertus Maclean Pars and Emma Laura Pars (*née* Unwin). *Educ:* Latymer Upper School; Jesus Coll., Cambridge. Smith's Prizeman, 1921; Fellow of Jesus Coll., 1921-. University Lectr in Mathematics, Cambridge, 1926-61. Visiting Professor: Univ. of California, Berkeley, 1949; Florida Atlantic Univ., 1964; Univ. of Sydney, 1965. *Publications:* Introduction to Dynamics, 1953; Calculus of Variations, 1962; A Treatise on Analytical Dynamics, 1965. Papers on Mathematics in scientific jls. *Recreations:* rock climbing, travel, theatre. *Address:* Jesus College, Cambridge. *T:* Cambridge 68611. *Clubs:* Athenæum, United Oxford & Cambridge University.

PARSELLE, Air Vice-Marshal Thomas Alford Boyd, CB 1962; CBE 1950; psa; *b* 15 July 1911; *s* of late John Parselle, Salisbury, S Rhodesia; *m* 1st, 1936, Daphne (*d* 1970), *d* of late Lt-Col H. G. Lewis-Hall; two *s* one *d*; 2nd, 1974, Patricia Cato Catherine Duncan. *Educ:* Cheltenham Coll.; RAF Coll., Cranwell. Served Egypt, 208 Squadron, 1932-34; 601 Squadron, RAuxAF, 1935-36 and Japan, 1937-39. Middle East and E. Africa, 1940-42; Bomber Command, 1943 (POW). Staff Coll., 1946-47; Comd RAF Scampton, Hemswell, 1948-50; Air Ministry, 1951-53; Comd RAAF Staff Coll., Point Cook, Australia, 1954-56 (exchange posting); Commandant Royal Air Force College and Air Officer Commanding RAF Cranwell, Lincolnshire, 1956-58; Commander, Task Force "Grapple", 1958-59; Senior Air Staff Officer, Bomber Command, 1959-61; Deputy Air Secretary, Air Ministry, 1961-64. Air Commodore, 1956; Air Vice-Marshal, 1958; retired, 1964. *Address:* Casa Holanda, Mojacar, Almeria, Spain.

PARSHALL, Horace Field, TD 1947; Receiver-General, Venerable Order of St John of Jerusalem, 1968-72 (Chancellor, 1961-66); *b* 16 June 1903; *o s* of late Horace Field Parshall, DSc, and Annie Matilda Rogers; *m* 1st, 1929, Hon. Ursula Mary Bathurst (marr. diss., 1942), *o d* of 1st Viscount Bledisloe; one *s*; 2nd, 1953, Margaret Savage, MB, BS, DPH (*d* 1961), *d* of late Captain Philip Alcock, DL, JP, Wilton Castle, Enniscorthy, and Overton Lodge, Ludlow; one *s* two *d*; 3rd, 1965, Lady (Phyllis Gabrielle) Gore, *o d* of M. von den Porten, New York. *Educ:* Eton Coll.; New Coll., Oxford (MA). Barrister-at-Law, Inner Temple. Served War of 1939-45, with Oxford and Bucks Light Inf.; Hon. Major, TARO. Dep. Commissioner-in-Chief, St John Ambulance Brigade, 1950; Director-General, St John Ambulance Assoc., 1951-60; Vice-Chancellor, Order of St John, 1960. Member Court of Assistants, Merchant Taylors' Company (Master, 1958-59); Director, Pyrene Co. Ltd, 1947-68 (Dep.-Chairman, 1962-68). GCStJ 1960. *Recreations:* gardening, reading and travel. *Address:* Southridge House, near Streatley, Berks. *T:* Goring-on-Thames 2710; Flat 8, 51 Onslow Square, SW7. *T:* 01-589 3371. *Club:* Garrick.

PARSLOE, Charles Guy, MA; Secretary, Institute of Welding, 1943-67, Hon. Fellow, 1968; Vice-President, International Institute of Welding, 1966-69 (Secretary-General, 1948-66); *b* London, 5 Nov. 1900; *o surv s* of Henry Edward Parsloe; *m* 1929, Mary Zirphie Munro, *e d* of J. G. Faiers, Putney; two *s* one *d. Educ:* Stationers' Company's School and University College, London. First Class hons. History, 1921; Franks student in Archæology, 1922; Secretary and Librarian, Institute of Historical Research, 1927-43; Assistant in History, University Coll., 1925-27. Secretary OEEC Welding Mission to USA, 1953; organised Commonwealth Welding Conferences, 1957, 1965; President, Junior Institution of Engineers, 1967. Hon. Freeman, Founders' Company, 1964. Pres., John Evelyn Soc. for Wimbledon, 1975. Wheatley Medal, Library Association, 1965; Edstrom Medal, Internat. Inst. of Welding, 1971. *Publications:* The English Country Town, 1932; The Minute Book of the Corporation of Bedford, 1647-64, 1949; some 400 bibliographies in the Cambridge Bibliography of English Literature, 1940; Wimbledon Village Club and Lecture Hall, 1858-1958; Wardens' Accounts of the Worshipful Company of Founders of the City of London, 1497-1681, 1964; papers on historical and bibliographical subjects. *Recreation:* historical research. *Address:* 1 Leopold Avenue, SW19 7ET. *T:* 01-946 0764. *Club:* Athenæum.

PARSONS, family name of **Earl of Rosse.**

PARSONS, Adrian; see Parsons, C. A. H.

PARSONS, Sir Anthony (Derrick), KCMG 1975 (CMG 1969); MVO 1965; MC 1945; HM Ambassador to Iran, since 1974; *b* 9 Sept. 1922; *s* of late Col H. A. J. Parsons, MC; *m* 1948, Sheila Emily Baird; two *s* two *d. Educ:* King's Sch., Canterbury; Balliol Coll., Oxford. HM Forces, 1940-54; Asst Mil. Attaché, Baghdad, 1952-54; Foreign Office, 1954-55; HM Embassy: Ankara, 1955-59; Amman, 1959-60; Cairo, 1960-61; FO, 1961-64; HM Embassy, Khartoum, 1964-65; Political Agent, Bahrain, 1965-69; Counsellor, UK Mission to UN, NY, 1969-71; Under-Sec., FCO, 1971-74. Order of the Two Niles (Sudan), 1965. *Recreations:* modern poetry, ornithology, tennis. *Address:* c/o Foreign and Commonwealth Office, Whitehall, SW1. *Clubs:* MCC, English-Speaking Union.

PARSONS, (Charles) Adrian (Haythorne); Charity Commissioner since 1974; *b* 15 June 1929; *s* of Dr R. A. Parsons and Mrs W. S. Parsons (*née* Haythorne); *m* 1951, Hilary Sharpe; one *d. Educ:* Bembridge Sch.; Wadham Coll., Oxford. Called to Bar, Gray's Inn, 1964. Coutts & Co., Bankers, 1952-64; joined Charity Commn, 1964; Dep. Comr, 1972. *Recreations:* fine arts, music, inland waterways. *Address:* 3 St Georges Crescent, Queens Park, Chester CH4 7AR. *T:* Chester 49649. *Club:* United Oxford & Cambridge University.
See also R.E.C.F. Parsons.

PARSONS, Geoffrey Penwill, OBE 1977; concert accompanist; *b* 15 June 1929; *s* of Francis Hedley Parsons and Edith Vera Buckland. *Educ:* Canterbury High Sch., Sydney; State Conservatorium of Music (with Winifred Burston), Sydney. Winner ABC Concerto Competition, 1947; first tour of Australia, 1948; arrived England, 1950; has accompanied many of world's greatest singers and instrumentalists, incl. Elisabeth Schwarzkopf, Victoria de los Angeles, Nathan Milstein, Paul Tortelier, Janet Baker, in 40 countries of world on all six continents. Master Classes, South Bank Summer Festival, 1977. Harriet Cohen Internat. Music Award, 1968. Hon. RAM, 1975. *Address:* 176 Iverson Road, NW6 2HL. *T:* 01-624 0957.

PARSONS, Ian Macnaghten, CBE 1971 (OBE 1944); Chairman, Sprint Productions Ltd; Joint Chairman, Chatto, Bodley Head and Jonathan Cape Ltd; President, Society of Bookmen, since 1969; *b* 21 May 1906; *s* of late Edward Percival and Mabel Margaret Parsons, Pont Street, SW; *m* 1934, Marjorie Tulip Ritchie; no *c. Educ:* Winchester Coll.; Trinity Coll., Cambridge. Senior Scholar; 1st Class Eng. Lit. Joined Chatto & Windus, 1928, Partner, 1930-53; Director of Chatto & Windus Ltd, 1953, Chairman, 1954-74; Director: Scottish Academic Press, 1969-76; Sussex University Press, 1971-76. President, The Publishers Association, 1957-59. Hon. DLitt St Andrews, 1975. *Publications:* Shades of Albany, 1928. Editor: The Progress of Poetry, 1936; Poetry for Pleasure, 1956, 1977; Men Who March Away, 1965; Poems of C. Day Lewis, 1977; (with George Spater) A Marriage of True Minds, 1977. *Recreations:* reading, gardening. *Address:* Juggs Corner, Kingston, Lewes, East Sussex. *T:* Lewes 4707. *Clubs:* Garrick, Beefsteak, Royal Automobile, MCC, Blackheath Rugby Football.

PARSONS, Mrs J. D.; see Beer, Patricia.

PARSONS, Sir (John) Michael, Kt 1970; Managing Director, Inchcape & Co. Ltd, since 1976, Director since 1971; Chairman and Director, Assam Investments, since 1976; Director, Commonwealth Development Finance Co. Ltd, since 1973; *b* 29 Oct. 1915; *s* of late Rt Rev. Richard Godfrey Parsons, DD, Bishop of Hereford; *m* 1st, 1946, Hilda Mary Frewen (marr. diss. 1964); one *s* two *d*; 2nd, 1964, Caroline Inagh Margaret Frewen. *Educ:* Rossall Sch.; University Coll., Oxford. Barry & Co., Calcutta, 1937. Served in Royal Garhwal Rifles (Indian Army), 1939-45: Bde Major, 1942; POW, Singapore, 1942. Macneill & Barry Ltd, Calcutta, 1946-70; Chm. & Managing Dir., 1964-70; Chm., Macdonald Hamilton & Co. Pty Ltd, 1970-72. Vice-Chm., Indian Jute Mills Assoc., 1960-61; President: Bengal Chamber of Commerce, 1968-69; Associated Chambers of Commerce of India, 1969; Chm., UK Cttee, Fedn of Commonwealth Chambers of Commerce, 1974. Mem., Advisory Council on Trade, Bd of Trade, India, 1968-69; Chm. Council, Royal Commonwealth Soc., 1976; Pres., India, Pakistan and Bangladesh Assoc., 1973; Mem., British Overseas Trade Adv. Council, 1975. *Recreation:* golf. *Address:* 38 Barrie House, Lancaster Gate, W2 3QJ. *T:* 01-262 4365. *Clubs:* Oriental; Bengal, Tollygunge (Calcutta); Union (Sydney).

PARSONS, Kenneth Charles, CMG 1970; OBE 1962; Counsellor, HM Diplomatic Service; with HQ British Forces Hong Kong, since 1977; *b* 9 Jan. 1921; *m* 1949, Monica (*née* Howell) (decd); two *d*. *Educ:* Haverfordwest Grammar Sch.; Exeter Coll., Oxford. Served War of 1939-45: with Oxfordshire and Buckinghamshire LI, 1941-46. 1st Class Hons, Mod. Langs (at Oxford), 1948. Joined Diplomatic Service, 1949; served FO, Moscow, Tokyo, Rangoon and Athens, 1951-72; FCO, 1972-77. *Recreations:* rowing, swimming, walking. *Address:* Grove End, Lower Park Road, Chipstead, Surrey. *T:* Downland 53907. *Club:* Junior Carlton.

PARSONS, Sir Maurice (Henry), KCMG 1970; Kt 1966; Chairman: Billing & Sons Ltd, 1971-74; London Regional Industrial Committee National Savings Group, 1971-74; Director, Globtik Tankers Ltd, 1971-74; *b* 19 May 1910; *s* of late G. H. C. Parsons; *m* 1937, Daphne I. Warner; one *s* one *d*. *Educ:* University College School. Entered Bank of England, 1928; Private Secretary to Governor (Montagu Norman), 1939-43; Alternate Exec. Director for UK on International Monetary Fund, 1946-47; International Bank, 1947; Director of Operations International Monetary Fund, 1947-50; Dep. Chief Cashier, Bank of England, 1950; Asst to Governors, 1955; Executive Director, 1957; Alternate Governor for UK of International Monetary Fund, 1957-66; Dep. Governor, Bank of England, 1966-70. Chm., Bank of London and S America, July-Dec. 1970; Dir, John Brown & Co., 1970-72. Hon. Treasurer, Soc. of Internat. Develt, 1971-74. *Address:* Clifford House, Shalford, Surrey. *T:* Guildford 61523. *Club:* National.

PARSONS, Sir Michael; *see* Parsons, Sir J. M.

PARSONS, Peter John, FBA 1977; Lecturer in Papyrology, University of Oxford, since 1965; Student of Christ Church, Oxford, since 1964; *b* 24 Sept. 1936; *s* of Robert John Parsons and Ethel Ada (*née* Frary). *Educ:* Raynes Park County Grammar Sch.; Christ Church, Oxford (MA 1961). Oxford (MA 1961). Oxford University: Craven Scholar, 1955; 1st Cl. Hons Mods and de Paravicini Scholar, 1956; Chancellor's Prize for Latin Verse and Gaisford Prize for Greek Verse, 1st Cl. Lit. Hum., Derby Scholar, Dixon and Sen. Scholar of Christ Church, 1958; Passmore Edwards Scholar, 1959; Lectr in Documentary Papyrology, 1960-65. *Publications:* (jtly) The Oxyrhynchus Papyri XXXI, 1966, XXXIII and XXXIV, 1968; The Oxyrhynchus Papyri XLII, 1973; (with H. Lloyd-Jones) Supplementum Hellenisticum, 1978; articles in learned jls. *Recreations:* music, cinema, cooking and eating. *Address:* Christ Church, Oxford OX1 1DP. *T:* Oxford 43979.

PARSONS, Richard Edmund (Clement Fownes), CMG 1977; HM Diplomatic Service; Ambassador to Hungary, since 1976; *b* 14 March 1928; *s* of Dr R. A. Parsons; *m* 1960, Jenifer Jane Mathews; three *s*. *Educ:* Bembridge Sch.; Brasenose Coll., Oxford. Served in Army, 1949-51; joined HM Foreign (subseq. Diplomatic) Service, 1951; FO, 1951-53; 3rd Sec., Washington, 1953-56; 2nd Sec., Vientiane, 1956-58; FO, 1958-60; 1st Sec., Buenos Aires, 1960-63; FO, 1963-65; 1st Sec., Ankara, 1965-67; FO, 1967-69; Counsellor, Lagos, 1969-72; Head of Personnel Ops Dept, FCO, 1972-76. *Recreations:* reading, writing, music, travel. *Address:* c/o Foreign and Commonwealth Office, King Charles Street, SW1. *Club:* Travellers'.
See also C . A . H . Parsons .

PARSONS-SMITH, Basil Gerald, OBE 1945; MA, MD, FRCP; Hon. Consulting Physician, St Mary's Hospital Group; Hon. Consulting Neurologist, Charing Cross Hospital; Teacher in Medicine, London University; *b* 19 Nov. 1911; *s* of late Dr Basil Parsons-Smith, FRCP, and Marguerite, *d* of Sir David Burnett, 1st Bt; *m* 1939, Aurea Mary, *d* of late William Stewart Johnston, Sunningdale; two *s* one *d*. *Educ:* Harrow; Trinity Coll., Cambridge. St George's Hospital; Entrance Exhib., 1933; Brackenbury Prize in Medicine, 1936; House Surgeon, House Physician, Med. Registrar. Physician: Western Ophthalmic Hospital (St Mary's), 1938-60; Electro Encephalograph Dept, Middlesex Hospital Medical Sch., 1950-55; Dept of Neurology, Charing Cross Hosp., 1950-76; Gray Lingwell Hosp., Chichester, 1950; West End Hosp. for Neurology, 1951-72. MRCP 1939. Served War of 1939-45, as Blood Transfusion Officer, Chelsea EMS, then as medical specialist i/c medical divisions in RAF Hospitals in ME; Sqdn Leader RAFVR (despatches, OBE). MD (Cantab) 1949, Prox. Acc. Raymond Horton-Smith Prize; FRCP 1955. Examiner, RCP. FRSocMed. Member: Association of British Neurologists; Ophthalmic Society of UK. Liveryman, Society of Apothecaries. Appeared in Hospital 1922, TV, 1972. *Publications:* Electro Encephalographic Studies, 1949; contributed to scientific journals mostly in connection with diseases of the brain, the nervous system and the eye. *Recreations:* gardens and horses. *Address:* Roughets House, Bletchingley, Surrey RH1 4QX. *T:* Caterham 43929. *Clubs:* Army and Navy; Pitt (Cambridge).

PART, Sir Antony (Alexander), GCB 1974 (KCB 1966; CB 1959); MBE 1943; Chairman, Orion Insurance Company; Director: Debenhams; EMI; Life Association of Scotland; Lucas Industries; Metal Box Co. Ltd; Savoy Hotel Ltd; *b* 28 June 1916; *s* of late Alexander Francis Part and late Una Margaret Reynolds (*née* Snowdon); *m* 1940, Isabella Bennett; no *c*. *Educ:* Wellesley House, Broadstairs; Harrow; Trinity Coll., Cambridge. First Class Hons Modern and Mediæval Langs Tripos. Entered Board of Education, 1937; Asst Private Secretary to successive Ministers of Supply, 1939-40. Served War of 1939-45 (despatches); Army Service, 1940-44; Lt-Col GS(1), 21st Army Group, 1944. Principal Private Secretary to successive Ministers of Education, 1945-46; Home Civil Service Commonwealth Fellow to USA, 1950-51; Under-Secretary, Ministry of Education, 1954-60; Deputy Secretary: Ministry of Education, 1960-63; MPBW, 1963-65; Permanent Secretary: MPBW, 1965-68; BoT, 1968-70; DTI, 1970-74; DoI, 1974-76. FBIM 1972. Governor, Administrative Staff Coll., 1968-; Governor, LSE, 1968-. Hon. DTech Brunel, 1966; Hon. DSc: Aston, 1974; Cranfield, 1976. *Recreation:* travel. *Address:* Flat 5, 71 Elm Park Gardens, SW10. *T:* 01-352 2950. *Clubs:* MCC, United Oxford & Cambridge University.

PARTON, Prof. John Edwin; Professor of Electrical Engineering, University of Nottingham, since 1954; at University of Tennessee, Knoxville, USA, as Senior Visiting Scientist, National Science Foundation, 1965-66; *b* Kingswinford, Staffordshire, 26 Dec. 1912; *s* of Edwin and Elizabeth Parton; *m* 1940, Gertrude Brown; one *s* one *d*. *Educ:* Huntington Church of England Sch.; Cannock Chase Mining Coll.; University of Birmingham. BSc (1st Class Hons), 1936, PhD, 1938, Birmingham; DSc Glasgow, 1971. Training: Littleton Collieries, 1934; Electrical Construction Co., 1935; Asst Engineer, PO Engineering Dept, Dollis Hill Research Station, 1938-39; Part-time Lecturer: Cannock Chase Mining Coll., 1931-38; Northampton Polytechnic, 1938-39. Served RNVR Electrical Branch, Sub-Lt, 1939, to Lt-Comdr, 1943-45. Sen. Sci. Officer, British Iron and Steel Research Assoc., 1946; Lecturer, 1946-54. Senior Lecturer, 1954, University of Glasgow. Chairman, East Midland Centre Institution of Electrical Engineers, 1961-62. FIEE 1966; Sen. Mem. IEEE 1966; FIMechE 1967. *Publications:* Applied Electromagnetics (jtly), 1975; papers in Proc. IEE, Trans. IEEE, Trans. IES, Instrument Practice, International Journal of Electrical Engineering Education, etc. *Recreations:* golf, gardening. *Address:* 6 Coopers Green, Wollaton, Nottingham NG8 2RP. *T:* Nottingham 286942.

PARTRIDGE, Derek William; HM Diplomatic Service; First Secretary (Commercial and Economic), British High Commission, Colombo, since Oct. 1974; *b* 15 May 1931; *o s* of Ernest and Ethel Elizabeth Partridge (*née* Buckingham), Wembley. *Educ:* Preston Manor County Grammar Sch., Wembley. Entered Foreign Service (later Diplomatic Service), 1949. Royal Air Force, 1949-51. Served: Foreign Office, 1951-54; Oslo, 1954-56; Jedda, 1956; Khartoum, 1957-60; Sofia, 1960-62; Bangkok, 1962; Manila, 1962-65; Djakarta, 1965-67; FCO, 1967-70; Diplomatic Service Inspectorate, 1970-72; British Consul-General, Brisbane, 1972-74. *Address:* c/o Foreign and Commonwealth Office, SW1.

PARTRIDGE, Eric Honeywood; Author; *b* Waimata Valley, Gisborne, New Zealand, 1894; *s* of John and Ethel Partridge; *m*

1925, Agnes Vye-Parminter; one *d. Educ:* TGS; Queensland and Oxford Universities. School-teacher, 1910-13; served as private in Australian Infantry, 1915-18; Queensland Travelling Fellow at Oxford, 1921-23 (BLitt in Anglo-French Literature); lecturer Manchester and London Universities, 1925-27; founder and managing director of the Scholartis Press, 1927-31; since 1932 author, since 1963 partly revision, and partly work on A Dictionary of Catch Phrases; Army 1940-41; RAF Dec. 1942-Aug. 1945. *Publications:* The French Romantics' Knowledge of English Literature; Eighteenth Century English Romantic Poetry; English Prose; Three Personal Records of the War (with R. H. Mottram and John Easton); Songs and Slang of the British Soldier (with John Brophy); Slang To-day and Yesterday: a History and a Study; A Dictionary of Slang and Unconventional English, revised edn, 1970; The World of Words; A Dictionary of Clichés; Usage and Abusage; A Guide to Good English; A Dictionary of Abbreviations, 1943; Journey to the Edge of Morning, 1946; Shakespeare's Bawdy (a study and a glossary), 1947; (with Wilfred Granville and Frank Roberts) Forces' Slang (1939-45), 1948; English for Human Beings, 1949; A Dictionary of the Underworld, British and American, 1950; Here, There and Everywhere: essays on language, 1950; (with Prof. John W. Clark, University of Minnesota) A History of English in the 20th Century, 1951; From Sanskrit to Brazil, 1952; You Have a Point There (punctuation), 1953; The Concise Usage and Abusage, 1954; English Gone Wrong, 1957; Origins: An Etymological Dictionary of English, 1958 (4th edn 1966); Name This Child (Christian Names), 1959; A Charm of Words (essays), 1960; Adventuring among Words, 1961; Comic Alphabets, 1961; The Gentle Art of Lexicography, 1963; Catch Phrases, 1977. *Recreations:* reading, persons. *Address:* c/o Ronald Pearsall, Landscove, near Newton Abbot, Devon. *Club:* Saville.

PARTRIDGE, Sir (Ernest) John, KBE 1971; Chairman, Imperial Group Ltd (formerly Imperial Tobacco Group Ltd), 1964-75; *b* 18 July 1908; *s* of William Henry and Alice Mary Partridge; *m* 1st, 1934, Madeline Fabian (*d* 1944); one *s* one *d*; 2nd, 1949, Joan Johnson, MBE; one *s* one *d. Educ:* Queen Elizabeth's Hospital, Bristol. Joined Imperial Tobacco Co., 1923; Asst Secretary, 1944; Secretary, 1946; Dep. Chairman, 1960. Director: British-American Tobacco Co. Ltd, 1963-75; Tobacco Securities Trust Ltd, 1964-75; National Westminster Bank, 1968-; Dunlop Holdings Ltd, 1973-; Delta Metal Co. Ltd, 1973-; General Accident Fire & Life Assurance Corporation Ltd, 1973-; Finance for Industry, 1975-; Member: Tobacco Advisory Cttee, 1945-58; Cheque Endorsement Cttee, 1955-56; NEDC, 1967-75; BNEC, 1968-71; Internat. Adv. Bd, Chemical Bank, NY, 1972-; Chairman: Tobacco Manufacturers' Standing Cttee (now Tobacco Research Council), 1960-62; Industrial Management Research Assoc., 1964-67; Council of Industry for Management Education, 1967-71; Pres., CBI, 1970-72 (Dep. Pres., 1969-70, Vice-Pres., 1972-76; Chm., Educn Foundn, 1976-); President: Foundn for Management Educn, 1972-; Nat. Council of Social Service, 1973-. Vice-President: Industrial Participation Assoc., 1966-; Soc. of Business Economists, 1976-. Governor: Queen Elizabeth's Hospital; Clifton Coll.; Badminton Sch.; Ashridge Management Coll., 1963-73; Member: Governing Body, London Graduate School of Business Studies, 1967-75; Court of Patrons, RCS, 1971; The Queen's Silver Jubilee Appeal Council, 1976-. FBIM, 1963-. Hon. LLD Bristol, 1972; Hon. DSc Cranfield Inst. of Technology, 1974. *Recreations:* walking, gardening, listening to music. *Address:* Wildwood, Haslemere, Surrey. *T:* Haslemere 51002; 601 Carrington House, Hertford Street, W1. *T:* 01-499 3787. *Club:* Athenæum.

PARTRIDGE, Harry Cowderoy; Member of Civil Aviation Authority since 1974, Controller Finance and Administration since 1975; *b* 29 Aug. 1925; *y s* of late Harry Ewart Partridge and Edith Cowderoy; *m* 1st, 1950, Margaret Neill Cadzow (*d* 1967), *o d* of Charles J. M. Cadzow, OBE; two *s* one *d*; 2nd, 1973, Jeanne Margaret Henderson; one *s. Educ:* George Watson's Coll., Edinburgh; Edinburgh Univ. CA. Air-gunner, RAF, 1943-47. Company Accountant, McGrouther Ltd, 1955-59; Plant Controller, IBM UK Ltd, 1959-63; Sec., George Kent Ltd, 1963, Financial Dir 1965-71; Controller of Finance and Planning, CAA, 1972. *Recreations:* house and garden. *Address:* Rushey Ford House, Box End, Kempston, Beds. *T:* Bedford 851594. *Club:* Savile.

PARTRIDGE, Sir John; see Partridge, Sir E. J.

PARTRIDGE, Michael John Anthony; Under-Secretary, Department of Health and Social Security, since 1976; *b* 29 Sept. 1935; *s* of late Dr John Henry Partridge, DSc, PhD, and of Ethel Green; *m* 1968, Joan Elizabeth Hughes; two *s* one *d. Educ:* Merchant Taylors'; St John's Coll., Oxford. BA (1st Cl. Hons. Mods and Lit Hum) 1960, MA 1963. Entered Home Civil

Service (Min. of Pensions and Nat. Insce), 1960; Private Sec. to Permanent Sec., 1962-64; Principal, 1964-71 (MPNI, Min. of Social Security and DHSS); Asst Sec., 1971-76. *Recreations:* Do-it-Yourself, Greece, reading, skiing. *Address:* 27 High View, Pinner, HA5 3NZ. *T:* 01-868 0657. *Club:* United Oxford & Cambridge University.

PARTRIDGE, Prof. (Stanley) Miles, FRS 1970; Head of Department of Biochemistry and Physiology since 1968, ARC Meat Research Institute, Langford, Bristol; *b* Whangarei, NZ, 2 Aug. 1913; *s* of Ernest Joseph Partridge and Eve Partridge (later Eve McCarthy) (*d* 1977); *m* 1940, Ruth Dowling; four *d. Educ:* Harrow County Sch.; Battersea Coll. of Technology. PhD Chemistry 1937; MA 1946, ScD 1964, Cantab. Beit Memorial Fellow, Lister Inst. of Preventive Medicine, 1940; Techn. Adviser, Govt of India, 1944; returned to Low Temperature Stn, Cambridge, 1946; Principal Scientific Officer 1952; Dep. Chief Scientific Officer, ARC, 1964. Member: Biochemical Soc. Cttee, 1957-61; Nuffield Foundn Rheumatism Cttee, 1965-77. Fourth Tanner Lectr and Award, Inst. of Food Technologists, Chicago, 1964. *Publications:* scientific papers, mainly in Biochemical Jl. *Recreation:* gardening. *Address:* Millstream House, St Andrew's Road, Cheddar, Somerset. *T:* Cheddar 742130.

PARTRIDGE, Rt. Rev. William Arthur; Assistant Bishop of Hereford, 1963-75; Prebendary Emeritus, Hereford Cathedral, since 1977; *b* 12 Feb. 1912; *s* of Alfred and Sarah Partridge; *m* 1945, Annie Eliza Joan Strangwood; one *s. Educ:* Alcester Grammar Sch.; Birmingham Univ.; Scholæ Cancellarii, Lincoln. Curate of Lye, Worcs, 1935; SPG Studentship at Birmingham Univ. Education Dept, 1938-39; Educational Missionary, Dio. Madras, 1939-43; Chaplain, RAFVR, 1943-46; Lecturer Meston Training Coll., Madras, 1947-51; Metropolitan's Commissary and Vicar-General in Nandyal, 1951; Asst Bishop of Calcutta (Bishop in Nandyal), 1953-63; Vicar of Ludford, 1963-69. *Publication:* The Way in India, 1962. *Recreation:* the organ. *Address:* Lulworth, Roman Road, Three Elms, Hereford HR4 9QN. *T:* Hereford 3457.

PASCAL, Roy, MA, LittD; FBA 1970; Professor of German, Birmingham University, 1939-69; *b* 28 Feb. 1904; *s* of C. S. Pascal and Mary Edmonds, Birmingham; *m* 1931, Feiga Polianovska; two *d. Educ:* King Edward's Sch., Birmingham; Pembroke Coll., Cambridge (Scholar; Hon. Fellow 1976). Studied at Berlin and Munich; Fellow of Pembroke Coll., Cambridge, 1929-34 and 1936-39; Director of Modern Language Studies at Pembroke College, 1936-39; Lecturer in German in the University of Cambridge, 1934-39; President, Assoc. of University Teachers, 1944-45; Chm. Conference of Univ. Teachers of German, 1960-61. Hon. LLD Birmingham, 1974; Hon. DLitt Warwick, 1977. Goethe Medal, 1965; Shakespeare Prize, Hamburg, 1969. *Publications:* Martin Luther, The Social Basis of the German Reformation, 1933; The Nazi Dictatorship, 1934; Shakespeare in Germany 1740-1815, 1937; Ed. of the German Ideology by Marx and Engels, 1938; contributor to The German Mind and Outlook, 1944-45; Growth of Modern Germany, 1946; The German Revolution 1848, 1948; Goethe's Faust, in Essays on Goethe, 1949; The German Sturm und Drang, 1952; Moeller van den Bruck (in The Third Reich, ed Vermeil), 1955; The German Novel, 1956; The Art of Autobiography (in Stil und Formprobleme in der Literatur, ed Böckmann), 1959; Design and Truth in Autobiography, 1960; Realism (in Spätzeiten, ed Kohlschmidt), 1962; German Literature 1500-1700, 1967; From Naturalism to Expressionism, 1973; Culture and the Division of Labour, 1974; The Dual Voice, 1976; contributions to: Presentation Vols to R. L. G. Ritchie, 1949; L. A. Willoughby, 1952; H. A. Korff, 1957; J. Boyd, 1959; W. H. Bruford, 1962; K. Hoppe, 1962; P. Böckmann, 1964; Fr Martini, 1969; C. P. Magill 1974; Fr Beissner, 1974; Introduction to Nietzsche's Thus Spake Zarathustra, Everyman edition, 1958; articles in Modern Language Review, Goethe Society Publications, German Life and Letters. *Recreations:* angling, carpentry. *Address:* 102 Witherford Way, Birmingham B29 4AW.

PASCO, Richard Edward, CBE 1977; actor; Associate Artist, Royal Shakespeare Company; *b* 18 July 1926; *s* of Cecil George Pasco and Phyllis Irene Pasco; *m* 1st, Greta (*née* Watson) (marr. diss.); one *s*; 2nd, 1967, Barbara (*née* Leigh-Hunt). *Educ:* Colet Court; King's Coll. Sch., Wimbledon. Served HM Forces, 1944-48. 1st stage appearance, She Stoops to Conquer, 1943; 1st London appearance, Zero Hour, Lyric, 1944; 1st New York appearance, The Entertainer, 1958. London appearances include: leading roles, English Stage Co., Royal Court, 1957; The Entertainer, Palace, 1957; The Lady from the Sea, Queen's, 1961; Teresa of Avila, Vaudeville, 1961; Look Homeward, Angel, Phoenix, 1962; The New Men, Strand, 1962; The Private Ear and the Public Eye, Globe, 1963; Henry V (title role) and

Love's Labour's Lost, Bristol Old Vic, 1964; Ivanov, Phoenix, 1965; The Italian Girl, Wyndham's, 1968. Joined RSC, 1969; leading roles include: Becket, Murder in the Cathedral, Aldwych, 1972; (alternated with Ian Richardson) Richard and Bolingbroke in Richard II, Stratford-on-Avon, 1973, and Stratford and Aldwych, 1974; Jack Tanner in Man and Superman, tour and Savoy, 1977. Many foreign tours; film, radio and television appearances; records of poems and plays. *Recreations:* music, country life, the protection of rural England. *Address:* Lane End Cottage, Newnham, Aston Cantlow, Solihull, West Midlands.

PASHLEY, Dr Donald William, FRS 1968; Director of Research, Tube Investments Ltd and Director, Tube Investments Research Laboratories; *b* 21 Apr. 1927; *s* of late Harold William Pashley and Louise Pashley (*née* Clarke); *m* 1954, Glenys Margaret Ball; one *s* one *d. Educ:* Henry Thornton Sch., London; Imperial Coll., London (BSc). 1st cl. hons Physics, 1947; PhD 1950. Research Fellow, Imp. Coll., 1950-55; TI Res. Labs., Hinxton Hall: Res. Scientist, 1956-61; Gp Leader and Div. Head, 1962-67; Asst Dir, 1967-68; Dir, 1968-. Rosenhain Medal, Inst. of Metals, 1968. *Publications:* (jtly) Electron Microscopy of Thin Crystals, 1965; numerous papers on electron microscopy and diffraction, thin films and epitaxy in Phil. Mag., Proc. Roy. Soc., etc. *Address:* 32 Beeches Close, Saffron Walden, Essex CB11 4BT. *T:* Saffron Walden 23509; Tube Investments Research Laboratories, Hinxton Hall, near Saffron Walden, Essex. *T:* Cambridge 832381.

PASLEY, Maj.-Gen. Joseph Montagu Sabine, CB 1952; CBE 1944; MVO 1936; late RA; *b* 5 Sept. 1898; *s* of Montagu Wynyard Sabine and Grace Lillian Pasley; *m* 1st, 1926; one *d* ; 2nd, 1950, Mrs D. B. Parsons; one *s. Educ:* Christ's Hospital; RMA. Commissioned RA, 1916; served European War, France, 1918; War of 1939-45 (CBE); Maj.-Gen., 1949. Comdr, 1st Anti-Aircraft Group, 1949-52. Formerly Commissioner for Surrey, St John Ambulance Brigade. OStJ. *Address:* 1 Ryefield Close, Eastbourne, East Sussex. *T:* Eastbourne 51478. *Club:* Cavalry and Guards.

PASLEY, Sir Rodney (Marshall Sabine), 4th Bt, *cr* 1794; retired as Headmaster, Central Grammar School, Birmingham (1943-59); *b* 22 Feb. 1899; *s* of late Captain Malcolm Sabine Pasley, RN, and late Nona Marion Paine; *S* uncle, 1947; *m* 1922, Aldyth Werge Hamber; one *s* one *d. Educ:* Sherborne School; University Coll., Oxford. Served European War, 1914-18, 2nd Lt RFA. BA 1921, MA 1925; Asst Master, Alleyn's School, 1921-25; Vice-Principal, Rajkumar Coll., Rajkot, India, 1926-28; Asst Master, Alleyn's School, 1931-36; Headmaster, Barnstaple Grammar School, 1936-43. *Publication:* Private Sea Journals, 1778-1782, kept by Admiral Sir Thomas Pasley, 1931. *Heir: s* John Malcolm Sabine Pasley, Magdalen Coll., Oxford, [*b* 5 April 1926; *m* 1965, Virginia Killigrew Wait; two *s*]. *Address:* Hazel Cottage, Peaslake, Surrey.

PASMORE, (Edwin John) Victor, CBE 1959; MA; Artist; *b* Chelsham, Surrey, 3 Dec. 1908; *s* of late E. S. Pasmore, MD; *m* 1940, Wendy Blood; one *s* one *d. Educ:* Harrow School; attended evening classes, LCC Central School of Arts & Crafts. Local government service, LCC County Hall, 1927-37; joined the London Artists' Assoc., 1932-34, and the London Group, 1932-52. Associated with the formation of the Euston Road School, 1937-39, and the first post-war exhibitions of abstract art, 1948-53; joined the Penwith Society, St Ives, 1951-53. Visiting teacher, LCC Camberwell School of Art, 1945-49; Central School of Arts and Crafts, 1949-53. Master of Painting, Durham University, 1954-61; consultant architectural designer, South West Area, Peterlee New Town, 1955. *Retrospective Exhibitions at:* Venice Biennale, 1960; Musée des Arts Décoratifs, Paris, 1961; Stedelijk Museum, Amsterdam, 1961; Palais des Beaux Arts, Brussels, 1961; Louisiana Museum, Copenhagen, 1962; Kestner-Gesellschaft, Hanover, 1962; Kunsthalle, Berne, 1963; Tate Gallery, 1965; São Paolo Biennale, 1965; Marlborough New London Gallery, 1966, 1969, 1972. Carnegie Prize for painting, 1964. Works represented in Tate Gallery, Arts Council and other public collections in Gt Britain, Canada, Australia, Holland, Italy, Austria and the USA. Member of the Institute of Contemporary Art. Trustee, Tate Gall., 1963-66. *Address:* 12 St Germans Place, Blackheath, SE3. *T:* 01-858 0369.

PASMORE, Victor; *see* Pasmore, E. J. V.

PASQUILL, Frank, DSc; FRS 1977; retired from Meteorological Office, 1974; *b* 8 Sept. 1914; *s* of late Joseph Pasquill and Elizabeth Pasquill (*née* Rudd), both of Atherton, Lancs; *m* 1937, Margaret Alice Turnbull, West Rainton, Co. Durham; two *d* . *Educ:* Henry Smith Sch., Hartlepool; Durham Univ. BSc (1st

Cl. Hons Physics) 1935, MSc, 1949, DSc 1950. Meteorological Office, 1937-74, with posts at Chem. Defence Res. Estabt, Porton, 1937-46 (incl. overseas service in Australia); Sch. of Agric., Cambridge Univ., 1946-49; Atomic Energy Res. Estabt, Harwell, 1949-54; Chem. Defence Res. Estabt, Porton, 1954-61; Meterological Office HQ Bracknell, 1961-74 (finally Dep. Chief Scientific Officer, and Head of Boundary Layer Research Br.). Visiting Prof., Pennsylvania State Univ., Autumn, 1974, N Carolina State Univ., Spring, 1975; Visiting Scientist, Penn. State Univ., 1975, Winter, 1976, Winter, 1977, Savannah River Lab., S Carolina, Winter, 1976. Royal Meteorological Society: Editor, 1961-64; Pres., 1970-72; Chm., Aero Res. Council's Gust Res. Cttee, 1963-68; Chm., CEGB's Adv. Panel on Environmental Res. *Publications:* Atmospheric Diffusion, 1962, 2nd edn 1974; papers on atmospheric turbulence and diffusion in various jls. *Address:* Woodwell, 37 Arbor Lane, Winnersh, Wokingham, Berks RG11 5JE.

PASTERFIELD, Rt. Rev. Philip John; *see* Crediton, Bishop Suffragan of.

PASTON-BEDINGFELD, Sir Edmund George Felix, 9th Bt, *cr* 1661; Major late Welsh Guards; Managing Director, Handley Walker (Europe) Ltd, since 1969; *b* 2 June 1915; *s* of 8th Bt and Sybil, *e d* of late H. Lyne Stephens of Grove House, Roehampton; *S* father, 1941; *m* 1st, 1942, Joan Lynette (*née* Rees) (*d* 1965); one *s* one *d* ; 2nd, 1957, Agnes Kathleen (*d* 1974), *d* of late Miklos Gluck, Budapest; 3rd, 1975, Mrs Peggy Hannaford-Hill, Fort Victoria, Rhodesia. *Educ:* Oratory School; New College, Oxford. Under-Sec., Head of Agricultural Div., RICS, 1966-69. *Heir: s* Henry Edgar Paston-Bedingfeld [*b* 7 Dec. 1943; *m* 1968, Mary, *er d* of Brigadier R. D. Ambrose, CIE, OBE, MC; two *s* two *d*]. *Address:* Arundell House, Brettenham, Ipswich. *T:* Rattlesden 607. *Club:* Cavalry and Guards.

PASTON BROWN, Dame Beryl, DBE 1967; *b* 7 March 1909; *d* of Paston Charles Brown and Florence May (*née* Henson). *Educ:* Streatham Hill High School; Newnham Coll., Cambridge (MA); London Day Training College. Lecturer: Portsmouth Training Coll., 1933-37; Goldsmiths' Coll., Univ. of London, 1937-44 and 1946-51. Temp. Asst Lecturer, Newnham Coll., 1944-46. Principal of City of Leicester Training Coll., 1952-61; Principal, Homerton College, Cambridge, 1961-71. Chairman, Assoc. of Teachers in Colleges and Depts of Educn, 1965-66. *Address:* 21 Keere Street, Lewes, East Sussex. *T:* Lewes 3608.

PATCH, Air Chief Marshal Sir Hubert (Leonard), KCB 1957 (CB 1952); CBE 1942; *b* 16 Dec. 1904; *s* of late Captain Leonard W. Patch, RN (retd), St Margarets-on-Thames; *m* 1960, Claude Renée, *d* of Major Jean-Marie Botéculet (Légion d'Honneur, Croix de Guerre, Médaille Militaire, MC (British), killed in action in Morocco, 1925). *Educ:* Stonyhurst; RAF Coll., Cranwell, Lincs. Joined RAF, 1925; Group Captain, 1946; Air Cdre, 1947; Air Vice-Marshal, 1951. Served 1939-44 (despatches, CBE). Senior Air Staff Officer, HQ Far East Air Force, 1952-53; AOC No 11 Gp, Fighter Comd, Nov. 1953-Jan. 1956; Air Officer Commanding-in-Chief (Temp.), Fighter Command, Jan.-Aug. 1956; Commander-in-Chief, Middle East Air Force, 1956-58; Air Member for Personnel April-Sept. 1959; Commander-in-Chief, British Forces, Arabian Peninsula, October 1959-May 1960; Acting Air Marshal, 1956; Air Marshal, 1957; Air Chief Marshal, 1959. Retired from Royal Air Force, 1961. Representative of British Aircraft Corporation to the NATO countries, 1961-63. *Address:* Loma de Rio Verde, Marbella, Spain; *c/o* Barclays Bank, Colchester, Essex. *Club:* Royal Air Force.

PATEL, Ambalal Bhailalbhai, CMG 1949; *b* 1 May 1898; *e s* of late Bhailalbhai Dharamdas Patel, Changa, Gujarat; *m* Gangalaxmi Patel (decd); four *s* one *d. Educ:* Petlad High School; Baroda Coll. (BA); Bombay University (LLB). Barrister-at-Law, Lincoln's Inn, 1923. Advocate, Supreme Court of Kenya, 1924; as Kenya Indian Deleg. gave evidence before Joint Parl. Committee on Closer Union, London, 1931. Pres. E African Indian National Congress, 1938-42, and 1945-46; Pres. Kenya Indian Conf., 1942; Mem. standing and exec. Cttees of EAIN Congress, 1924-56; Chm. Indian Elected Members Organization, 1941-48; Hon. Sec. Coast Elected Members Organization, 1949-56; Mem. Makerere Coll. Assembly, 1938-48. Chm. Central Indian Advisory Man-Power Cttee and Indian E Dist Man-Power Cttee during War of 1939-45. Chm. Indian and Arab Land Settlement Bd, 1946-54; attended African Conf. in London, 1948; Mem. E African Central Legislative Assembly, 1948-52; Minister without Portfolio, Govt of Kenya, 1954-56, retired. MLC 1938-56, MEC Kenya, 1941-56. Mem. Royal Technical College Council, Nairobi, and Makerere University Coll. Council, 1954-56. Gen. Sec. and Treasurer, World Union, 1964-; Member: Emergency

Council for World Govt, World Union Movement (The Hague), 1974-; World Federal Authority Cttee (Oslo), 1975-; Co-pres., World Constitution and Parliament Assoc., 1977; First signatory, Constitution for Fedn of Earth, 1977. Pres. or trustee various political, social and cultural institutions at different times. Coronation Medal, 1953. *Publication:* Toward a New World Order, 1974. *Address:* c/o Sri Aurobindo Ashram, Pondicherry (via Madras), India.

PATEL, Praful Raojibhai Chaturbhai; Company Director; Investment Adviser in UK, since 1962; Hon. Secretary, All-Party Parliamentary Committee on UK Citizenship, since 1968; *b* Jinja, Uganda, 7 March 1939; *s* of Raojibhai Chaturbhai Patel, Sojitra, Gujarat, India, and Maniben Jivabhai Lalaji Patel, Dharmaj, Gujarat; unmarried. *Educ:* Government Sec. Sch., Jinja, Uganda; London Inst. of World Affairs, attached to University Coll., London (Extra Mural Dept). Sec., Uganda Students Union, 1956-58; Deleg. to Internat. Youth Assembly, New Delhi, 1958; awarded two travel bursaries for visits to E, Central and S Africa, and Middle East, to study and lecture on politics and economics; arrived in Britain as student, then commenced commercial activities, 1962; increasingly involved in industrial, cultural and educational projects affecting immigrants in Britain. Spokesman for Asians in UK following restriction of immigration resulting from Commonwealth Immigrants Act 1968; Council Mem., UK Immigrants Advisory Service, 1970-; Mem., Uganda Resettlement Bd, 1972-74; Hon. Sec., Uganda Evacuees Resettlement Advisory Trust, 1974-; Pres., Nava Kala India Socio-Cultural Centre, London, 1962-75; Chm. Bd of Trustees, Swaminarayan Hindu Mission, UK, 1970-76. *Publications:* articles in newspapers and journals regarding immigration and race relations. *Recreations:* cricket; campaigning and lobbying; current affairs; and inter-faith co-operation. *Address:* 60 Bedford Court Mansions, Bedford Avenue, Bedford Square, WC1B 3AD. *T:* 01-580 0897. *Club:* Royal Commonwealth Society.

PATEMAN, Jack Edward, CBE 1970; Managing Director, Marconi-Elliott Avionic Systems, since 1971; Director: Canadian Marconi Co., since 1971; GEC Computers Ltd, since 1971; Applications des Techniques de l'Electrique Industrielle SA, since 1974; *b* 29 Nov. 1921; *s* of William Edward Pateman and Lucy Varley (*née* Jetten); *m* 1949, Cicely Hope Turner; one *s* one *d. Educ:* Gt Yarmouth Grammar Sch. Served War of 1939-45, RAF, 1940-46. Research Engineer: Belling & Lee, 1946-48; Elliott Bros (London) Ltd, 1948-51. Formed Aviation Div. of EBL at Borehamwood, 1951-62; Dep. Chm. and Jt Man. Dir, Elliott Flight Automation Ltd, 1962-71. *Recreation:* sailing. *Address:* 40 Lyndhurst Drive, Sevenoaks, Kent. *T:* Sevenoaks 54390.

PATER, John Edward, CB 1953; Under Secretary, Ministry of Health and Department of Health and Social Security, 1947-73 (retired); *b* 15 March 1911; *s* of Edward Rhodes and Lilian Pater; *m* 1938, Margaret Anderson, *yr d* of M. C. Furtado; two *s* one *d. Educ:* King Edward VI School, Retford; Queens' College, Cambridge. Foundation Scholar, Queens' College; BA 1933, MA 1935. Assistant Principal, Ministry of Health, 1933; Principal, 1938; Assistant Secretary, 1943; Principal Assistant Secretary, 1945; Director of Establishments and Organisation, 1960-65. Treasurer: Methodist Church Dept of Connexional Funds and Finance Bd, 1959-73; Div. of Finance, 1973-; Central Finance Bd, 1968-74. *Recreations:* reading, archæology, walking (preferably on hills). *Address:* 22 Manor Way, South Croydon CR2 7BR. *T:* 01-688 0349.
See also R. A. Furtado.

PATERSON, Dr Alexander Brown; Director, Veterinary Laboratories and Veterinary Investigation Services, since 1969; *b* 19 Jan. 1917; *s* of Robert Paterson and Catherine Muir; *m* 1945, Margaret Birnie Paterson; one *s* two *d. Educ:* Woodside Sch.; Glasgow Veterinary College. ARC Research Fellow, 1942-45; Res. Officer, Biochemistry Dept, MAFF Weybridge, 1945-59; Head, Virology Dept, 1959-65; Dep. Dir, MAFF Lab., 1965-69. FRSocMed. *Publications:* papers in scientific jls. *Recreations:* tennis, geology. *Address:* Royston, 39 London Road, Guildford, Surrey. *T:* Guildford 73147.

PATERSON, Sir (Alexander) Swinton, KBE 1951 (OBE 1943); CMG, 1947; *b* 12 March 1893; *s* of late William Brockie Paterson, FFA, and Ethel M. Lamplough; *m* 1930, Iseult, *d* of late Theodore Charles Barclay; no *c. Educ:* Norwich School. Served European War, North Staffordshire Regt; entered Consular Service, 1920; Vice-Consul at Monrovia, 1921-24; Antwerp, 1924-27; Beira, 1927-29; New York, 1930-35; HM Minister Resident and Consul, Santo Domingo, Dominican Republic, 1935-43; Inspector-Gen. of Consular Establishments, Foreign Office, 1945-50; Senior Inspector, HM Foreign Service

Establishments, 1950-54; retd 1954. *Address:* 17 Boscombe Overcliff Drive, Bournemouth, Dorset. *Clubs:* Royal Automobile; Royal Motor Yacht (Sandbanks).

PATERSON, Arthur Spencer, MA (Oxon); MD; FRCPE, MRCP; FRCPsych; Consultant Psychiatrist; Physician in Charge, Department of Psychiatry, and Director Psychiatric Laboratory, West London Hospital, 1946-66; *b* 22 Feb. 1900; 4th *s* of late Professor W. P. Paterson, Edinburgh Univ., and late Jane Sanderson; *m* 1933, Antoinette, *d* of late Chas Baxter, WS; two *s* one *d. Educ:* Edinburgh Academy; Fettes (Scholar); 2nd Lt RHA 1919. Oriel, Oxford (Hon. Mods and Lit. Hum.; BA 1923); Edinburgh Univ. (MB, ChB 1928). Ho. Phys to Prof. of Medicine, Roy. Infirmary, Edinburgh, 1928-29; Asst Phys., Glasgow Royal Mental Hospital, 1929-30; Rockefeller Fellow, 1930-31; Pinsent-Darwin Research Student in Mental Pathology, Cambridge University, 1931-33; held research posts at: Johns Hopkins Univ., Baltimore, Md, USA, Research Inst. of Psychiatry, Munich; Maudsley Hosp., London. Asst Phys., Cassel Hosp., Penshurst, 1933-36; First Asst, Dept of Psychiatry, Middlesex Hosp., 1936-45, Psychiatrist, Sector V. EMS Metrop. Area, 1939-45. Honeyman-Gillespie Lectr, Edin. Univ., 1948. Membre d'honneur Soc. Méd. Ment. Belge, 1969; Membre Etranger, Soc. Méd.-Psychol., Paris, 1969; Corr. Member: American Psychiat. Association; American Pavlovian Soc. Hon. Secretary, Internat. Soc. for Experimental and Clin. Hypnosis, 1968-73. Hermann Goldman Lectr, NY Coll., Med., 1964. Foundation FRCPsych, 1971. FBPsS. *Publications:* Electrical and Drug Treatments in Psychiatry, 1963; Control of the Autonomic Nervous Functions by Conditioning and Hypnosis, in Hypnosis and Behaviour Therapy, ed E. Dengrove, 1975; numerous articles on psychiatric and allied subjects in British and foreign scientific periodicals. *Recreations:* travel, golf, chess. *Address:* Ely Hill House, Capel St Andrew, Woodbridge, Suffolk. *T:* Orford 355; 2 Devonshire Place, W1N 1PA. *Clubs:* Athenæum; Woodbridge Golf.

PATERSON, Betty Fraser Ross, CBE 1973; JP; Chairman: NW Thames Regional Health Authority, since 1973; National Staff Advisory Committee for England and Wales (Nurses and Midwives), since 1975; *b* 14 March 1916; *d* of Robert Ross Russell and Elsie Marian Russell (*née* Fraser); *m* 1940, Ian Douglas Paterson; one *s* one *d. Educ:* Harrogate Coll.; Western Infirmary, Glasgow. Mem. Chartered Soc. of Physiotherapy (MCSP). County Comr, Herts Girl Guides, 1950-57. Member: Herts CC, 1952-74 (Alderman 1959-74; Chm., 1969-73); NE Metropolitan Regional Hosp. Bd, 1960-74; Governing Body, Royal Hosp. of St Bartholomew, 1960-74; Commn for the New Towns, England and Wales, 1961-75 (Dep. Chm., 1971-75); Governing Body, Bishop's Stortford Coll., 1967-; Central Health Services Council, 1969-74; Gen. Council and Management Cttee, King Edward's Hosp. Fund for London, 1975-. JP Herts, 1950. *Recreations:* music, cooking, foreign travel. *Address:* Twyford Bury, Bishop's Stortford, Herts. *T:* Bishop's Stortford 53184.

PATERSON, Sir Dennis (Craig), Kt 1976; FRCS, FRACS; Director and Chief Orthopaedic Surgeon, Adelaide Children's Hospital, since 1970; Consultant Orthopaedic Surgeon: Royal Adelaide Hospital, since 1964; Queen Victoria Hospital, since 1968; *b* 14 Oct. 1930; *s* of Gilbert Charles Paterson and Thelma Drysdale Paterson; *m* 1955, Mary Mansell Hardy; one *s* three *d. Educ:* Collegiate Sch. of St Peter; Univ. of Adelaide (MB, BS 1953). FRCS 1958, FRACS 1961. Res. Med. Officer: Royal Adelaide Hosp., 1954; Adelaide Children's Hosp., 1956; Registrar, Robert Jones & Agnes Hunt Orthop. Hosp., Oswestry, Shropshire, 1958-60; Sen. Registrar, Royal Adelaide Hosp., 1960-62; Cons. Orthop. Surg., Repatriation Gen. Hosp., Adelaide, 1962-70; Adelaide Children's Hospital: Asst Hon. Orthop. Surg., 1964-66; Sen. Hon. Orthop. Surg., 1966-70. Amer./British/Canadian Trav. Prof., 1966. Royal Australasian Coll. of Surgeons: Mem., Bd of Orthop. Surg., 1974-; Mem., Court of Examnrs, 1974-; Mem., SA Cttee, 1974-. Fellow: British Orthopaedic Assoc.; RSocMed; Member: Aust. Orthopaedic Assoc., AMA; Internat. Scoliosis Res. Soc.; Scientific Internat. Soc. of Traumatol. and Orthopaedics. Pres., Crippled Children's Assoc. of South Australia Inc., 1970- (Mem. Council, 1966-70). *Publications:* over 30 articles in Jl of Bone and Joint Surg., Clin. Orthopaedics and Related Res., Aust. and NZ Jl of Surg., Med. Jl of Aust., Western Pacific Jl of Orthop. Surg. *Recreations:* golf, gardening. *Address:* 31 Myall Avenue, Kensington Gardens, SA 5068, Australia. *T:* 31 7865. *Clubs:* Adelaide, Naval, Military and Air Force, Kooyonga Golf (Adelaide).

PATERSON, Frank David; His Honour Judge Paterson; a Circuit Judge (formerly County Court Judge), since 1968; *b* 10 July 1918; *yr s* of late David Paterson and Dora Paterson,

Liverpool; *m* 1953, Barbara Mary, 2nd *d* of late Oswald Ward Gillow and Alice Gillow, Formby; one *s* two *d*. *Educ:* Calderstones Preparatory Sch. and Quarry Bank High Sch., Liverpool; Univ. of Liverpool (LLB). Called to Bar, Gray's Inn, 1941; Warden, Unity Boys' Club, Liverpool, 1941; Asst Warden, Florence Inst. for Boys, Liverpool, 1943. Practised on Northern Circuit. Chairman: Min. of Pensions and Nat. Insce Tribunal, Liverpool, 1957; Mental Health Review Tribunal for SW Lancashire and Cheshire, 1963. Asst Dep. Coroner, City of Liverpool, 1960. *Address:* Vailima, 2 West Lane, Formby, Liverpool L37 7BA. *T:* Formby 74345. *Club:* Athenæum (Liverpool).

PATERSON, Sir George (Mutlow), Kt 1959; OBE 1946; QC (Sierra Leone) 1950; Chairman, Industrial Tribunals, 1965; *b* 3 Dec. 1906; *e s* of late Dr G. W. Paterson; *m* 1935, Audrey Anita, *d* of late Major C. C. B. Morris, CBE, MC; one *s* two *d*. *Educ:* Grenada Boys' School; St John's College, Cambridge. Appointed to Nigerian Administrative Service, 1929. Called to the Bar, Inner Temple, 1933. Magistrate, Nigeria, 1936; Crown Counsel, Tanganyika, 1938. War of 1939-45: served with the King's African Rifles, 1939 (wounded 1940); Occupied Enemy Territories Admin., 1941; Lieutenant-Colonel 1945. Solicitor-General, Tanganyika, 1946; Attorney-General, Sierra Leone, 1949, Ghana, 1954-57; Chief Justice of Northern Rhodesia, 1957-61, retired 1961; appointed to hold an inquiry into proposed amendments to the Potato Marketing Scheme, 1962; appointed legal chairman (part-time), Pensions Appeal Tribunals, 1962; appointed chairman Industrial Tribunals, South Western Region, 1965. *Recreations:* shooting and gardening. *Address:* Buckshaw House, Sherborne, Dorset DT9 5LD. *T:* Bishop's Caundle 318. *Club:* East India, Devonshire, Sports and Public Schools.

PATERSON, Maj.-Gen. Herbert MacGregor, CB 1956; CBE 1954; retired; *b* 29 Nov. 1898; *s* of James Paterson, RSA; PRSW; *m* 1929, Kathleen Mary Tennent; one *d*. *Educ:* Fettes; RMA, Woolwich; Magdalene Coll., Cambridge. 2nd Lt, RA, 1918; Egypt and Palestine, 1918-20. Cambridge University, 1920-23; BA 1923; MA 1935. India, 1923-27; Military College of Science, 1927-34; War Office and Ministry of Supply, 1938-45; Comdt Military Coll. of Science, Bury, 1946-47; Director of Artillery, 1952; Director-General of Artillery, Ministry of Supply, 1953-56. Col 1946; Brig. 1952; Maj.-Gen. 1953; retired 1957. USA Medal of Freedom (Bronze Palm). *Recreation:* music. *Address:* Swan Cottage, Shillingford, Oxford.

PATERSON, Sqdn-Ldr Ian Veitch, CBE 1969; DL; JP; Deputy Chairman, Local Government Boundary Commission, since 1974; *b* 17 Aug. 1911; *s* of Andrew Wilson Paterson; *m* 1940, Anne Weir, *d* of Thomas Brown; two *s* one *d*. *Educ:* Lanark Grammar School; Glasgow University. Served RAF, 1940-45. Entered local govt service, Lanark, 1928; Principal Legal Asst, Aberdeen CC; Lanarkshire: Dep. County Clerk, 1949; County Clerk, 1956, resigned 1974. Chm., Working Party who produced The New Scottish Local Authorities Organisation and Management structures, 1973. DL Lanarkshire (Strathclyde), 1963; JP Hamilton (formerly Lanarkshire). *Address:* 35 Stewarton Drive, Cambuslang, Glasgow.

PATERSON, (James Edmund) Neil, MA; Author; *b* 31 Dec. 1915; *s* of late James Donaldson Paterson, MA, BL; *m* 1939, Rosabelle, MA, 3rd *d* of late David MacKenzie, MC, MA; two *s* one *d*. *Educ:* Banff Academy; Edinburgh Univ. Served in minesweepers, War of 1939-45, Lieut RNVR, 1940-46. Director Grampian Television; Chm. of Production, Films of Scotland Committee, 1954-; Vice-Chm., Scottish Arts Council; Mem., Arts Council of Great Britain, 1974; Governor: Nat. Film Sch.; Pitlochry Festival Theatre; British Film Institute, 1958-60; Atlantic Award in Literature, 1946; Award of American Academy of Motion Picture Arts and Sciences, 1960. *Publications:* The China Run, 1948; Behold Thy Daughter, 1950; And Delilah, 1951; Man on the Tight Rope, 1953; The Kidnappers, 1957; film stories and screen plays. *Recreations:* golf, fishing. *Address:* St Ronans, Crieff, Perthshire. *T:* 2615. *Clubs:* Naval; Scottish Arts (Edinburgh); Royal and Ancient (St Andrews).

PATERSON, Prof. James Ralston Kennedy, CBE 1949; MC 1917; MD (Edinburgh); FRCSEd; FRCS; FFR; Professor Emeritus of Radiotherapeutics, University of Manchester, since 1960; Director of Radiotherapy, Christie Hospital and Holt Radium Institute, 1931-62; *b* 21 May 1897; *s* of Rev. David Paterson; *m* 1930, Edith Isabel Myfanwy Irvine-Jones; two *s* one *d*. *Educ:* George Heriot's School, Edinburgh; Edinburgh University. Fellow in Radiology, Mayo Clinic, America, 1926. Acting Director, Radiological Department, Edinburgh, 1930. *Publication:* Treatment of Malignant Disease by Radium and X-

rays, 1962. *Recreations:* various. *Address:* Stenrieshill, Moffat, Scotland. *T:* Johnstone Bridge 221.

PATERSON, James Veitch; Sheriff of the Lothian and Borders (formerly Roxburgh, Berwick and Selkirk) at Jedburgh and Duns, since 1963; *b* 16 April 1928; *s* of John Robert Paterson, ophthalmic surgeon, and Jeanie Gouinlock; *m* 1956, Ailie, *o d* of Lt-Comdr Sir (George) Ian Clark Hutchison, *qv*; one *s* one *d*. *Educ:* Peebles High School; Edinburgh Academy; Lincoln College, Oxford; Edinburgh University. Admitted to Faculty of Advocates, 1953. *Recreations:* fishing, shooting, gardening. *Address:* Sunnyside, Melrose, Roxburghshire. *T:* Melrose 2502. *Club:* New (Edinburgh).

PATERSON, John Allan; Agent-General in London and Deputy Minister Abroad for Province of New Brunswick, 1968-75; *b* Montreal, 20 May 1909; *s* of William A. and M. Ethel Paterson; *m* 1935, Elizabeth Stewart Messenger; four *s*. *Educ:* Westmount, Quebec; Mount Allison Univ. (BSc 1932); Queen's Univ. Prudential Insurance Co. of America, 1934-46; RCAF 1941-45 (Sqdn Ldr); New Brunswick Dept of Industry, 1946-68 (Deputy Minister, 1956); Provincial Co-ordinator of Civil Defence, 1950-55; Bd of Comrs, Oromocto, 1956-63; Chm., Provincial Govts of Canada Trade and Industry Council, 1956-57, 1961-62 1964-65 and 1966-67.Mem. Bd of Regents, Mount Allison Univ., 1959-63; Pres. Oromocto Develt Corp., 1963-68. *Publication:* (co-author) The New Brunswick Economy, Past Present and Future, 1955. *Recreations:* golf, motoring, fishing.

PATERSON, Sir John (Valentine) J.; *see* Jardine Paterson.

PATERSON, Neil; *see* Paterson, James Edmund N.

PATERSON, Noel Kennedy, CIE 1947; OBE 1943; lately United Kingdom Trade Commissioner, Dublin; *b* 25 Dec. 1905; *s* of Rev. David Paterson, BD, Edinburgh; *m* 1934, Margaret Winifred Schreiber; two *s* two *d*. *Educ:* George Heriot's School, Edinburgh; Edinburgh University; St John's College, Cambridge. Entered Indian Civil Service, 1929; Asst Comr, 1929-34; Under Sec. to Govt of Central Provinces, 1934-36; Deputy Comr, 1936-37 and 1939-45; Under Sec. to Govt of India, 1937-38; Chief Comr, Andaman and Nicobar Islands, 1945-47. *Recreation:* travel. *Address:* Gabriel's Farm, Park Lane, Twyford, Hants. *T:* Twyford 713116.

PATERSON, Sir Swinton; *see* Paterson, Sir A. S.

PATEY, Very Rev. Edward Henry; Dean of Liverpool since 1964; *b* 12 Aug. 1915; *s* of Walter Patey, MD, and Dorothy Patey; *m* 1942, Margaret Ruth Olivia Abbott; one *s* three *d*. *Educ:* Marlborough College; Hertford College, Oxford; Westcott House, Cambridge. Assistant Curate, St Mary-at-the-Walls, Colchester, 1939; MA (Oxon) 1941; Assistant Curate Bishopwearmouth Parish Church, Sunderland, 1942; Youth Chaplain to the Bishop of Durham, 1946; Vicar of Oldland, with Longwell Green, Bristol, 1950; Secretary, Youth Department, The British Council of Churches, 1952; Assistant Gen. Secretary, The British Council of Churches, 1955; Canon Residentiary of Coventry Cathedral, 1958. *Publications:* Religion in the Club, 1956; Boys and Girls Growing Up, 1957; Worship in the Club, 1961; A Doctor's Life of Jesus, 1962; Young People Now, 1964; Enquire Within, 1966; Look out for the Church, 1969; Burning Questions, 1971; Don't Just Sit There, 1974; Christian Lifestyle, 1975; All in Good Faith, 1978. *Recreations:* reading, listening to music. *Address:* The Cathedral, Liverpool LI 7AZ.

PATON; *see* Noel-Paton, family name of **Baron Ferrier**.

PATON, Major Adrian Gerard Nigel H.; *see* Hadden-Paton.

PATON, Alan (Stewart); writer; was National President of the South African Liberal Party until it was made an illegal organisation in 1968; living at Botha's Hill, Natal; *b* Pietermaritzburg, 11 Jan. 1903; *s* of James Paton; *m* 1st, 1928, Doris Olive (*d* 1967), *d* of George Francis; two *s*; 2nd, 1969, Anne Hopkins. *Educ:* Natal Univ. (BSc, BEd). Formerly Principal Diepkloof Reformatory, 1935-48. Chubb Fellow, Yale Univ., 1973. Hon. LHD, Yale, 1954; Hon. DLitt: Kenyon Coll., 1962; Univ. of Natal, 1968; Trent Univ., 1971; Harvard, 1971; Rhodes, 1972; Williamette Univ., 1974; Michigan, 1977; Hon DD Edinburgh, 1971; Hon. LLB, Univ. of Witwatersrand, 1975. Freedom House Award (USA), 1960. *Publications:* Cry, the Beloved Country, 1948; Too Late the Phalarope, 1953; Land and People of South Africa, 1955; South Africa in Transition (with Dan Weiner), 1956; Debbie Go Home (short stories), 1961; Hofmeyr (biography), 1965; Instrument of Thy Peace, 1968; The Long View, 1969; Kontakion For You Departed, 1969;

Apartheid and the Archbishop, 1973; Knocking on the Door, 1975. *Address:* PO Box 278, Hillcrest, Natal, South Africa.

PATON, Col Alexander, DSO 1937; MC; RA, retired; *b* 13 Jan. 1897; *s* of Alexander Paton, Glasgow; *m* 1923, Sybil, *er d* of late Sir Grimwood Mears, KCIE; two *s. Educ:* Marlborough Coll.; RMA, Woolwich. Commissioned, 1915; served European War, France, 1916-19; Staff Captain, 1918; 15th Corps (despatches twice, MC and bar, General Service and Victory Medals); India, 1919-25; Staff Captain RA, Afghan War, 1919 (1908, General Service Medal, India, and clasp, 1919); Staff Officer RA, Simla, 1921-22; Chitral, NWF India, 1922-24; Home Service, 1925-36; Terr. Adj. 13th (Highland) Brigade, TA, Argyllshire, 1926-30; Company Officer at Royal Military Academy, Woolwich, 1932-34; Adjutant, 3rd Medium Brigade RA, Shoeburyness, 1934-36; India, NWF, 1937 (wounded, despatches, DSO, Medal and clasp); Burma, 1938-40; Comd 21 Mtn Regt NWF, 1940; Comdt MATC Ambala, Punjab, 1941-42; Comdt FATC Muttra, UP, 1942-44; Col 1943-44; Recruiting Staff, Rawalpindi, Punjab, 1944-45. Defence Medal, 1939-45, and War Medal (1939-45). Retd pay, 1947. *Recreation:* philately. *Address:* Willow Cottage, 33 Crofton Lane, Hillhead, Fareham, Hants. *T:* Stubbington 2116.

PATON, Sir Angus; *see* Paton, Sir T. A. L.

PATON, Brig. Charles Morgan, CVO 1944; CBE 1949; psc; *b* 5 Feb. 1896; *s* of late A. H. Paton; *m* 1920, Mabel Anne, *d* of J. M. Bathgate, JP; one *s. Educ:* Berkhamsted; Royal Military College, Sandhurst. Joined Essex Regiment 1914; Captain 1917; Staff College, 1927-28; Bt Major, 1934; Major, 1935; Lt-Col 1941; Col 1944. Served European War, 1914-18, France and Belgium; GSO for Weapon Training, W Comd, 1930-32; DAA & QMG W Comd, 1932-34; DAA & QMG S Comd, 1937-38; DAAG War Office, 1939-40; AAG Mid. East, 1941-42; DA and QMG, Palestine, 1943; DAG Allied Armies in Italy, 1944; retired, 1949. Colonel, The Essex Regiment, 1950-58; Associate Colonel, 3rd East Anglian Regiment (16/44 Foot), 1958-62; Dep. Col The Royal Anglian Regt, 1965-70. DL Essex, 1954-74. CStJ 1970. *Address:* c/o Lloyds Bank Ltd, 6 Pall Mall, SW1. *Club:* Army and Navy.

PATON, Rev. Canon David Macdonald; Chaplain to the Queen, since 1972; Rector of St Mary de Crypt and St John the Baptist, Gloucester, since 1970; Hon. Canon of Canterbury Cathedral, since 1966; *b* 9 Sept. 1913; *e s* of late Rev. William Paton, DD and Grace Mackenzie Paton (*née* Macdonald); *m* 1946, Alison Georgina Stewart; three *s. Educ:* Repton; Brasenose Coll., Oxford. BA 1936, MA 1939. SCM Sec., Birmingham, 1936-39; Deacon 1939, Priest 1941; Missionary in China, 1940-44 and 1947-50; Chaplain and Librarian, Westcott House, Cambridge, 1945-46; Vicar of Yardley Wood, Birmingham, 1952-56; Editor, SCM Press, 1956-59; Sec., Council for Ecumenical Co-operation of Church Assembly, 1959-63; Sec., Missionary and Ecumenical Council of Church Assembly, 1964-69; Chm., Gloucester Civic Trust, 1972-77. *Publications:* Christian Missions and the Judgement of God, 1953; (with John T. Martin) Paragraphs for Sundays and Holy Days, 1957; (ed) Essays in Anglican Self-Criticism, 1958; (ed) The Ministry of the Spirit, 1960; Anglicans and Unity, 1962; (ed) Reform of the Ministry, 1968; (ed) Breaking Barriers (Report of WCC 5th Assembly, Nairobi, 1975), 1976. *Recreations:* gardening, walking. *Address:* 17 Brunswick Road, Gloucester GL1 1HQ. *T:* Gloucester 22843. *See also* Bishop of Birmingham, Prof. W . D . M . Paton .

PATON, Douglas Shaw F.; *see* Forrester-Paton.

PATON, George Campbell Henderson, QC (Scotland) 1967; LLD Edin 1969; Reader in Scots Law, Edinburgh University, 1967-75; *b* 6 Aug. 1905; *s* of George Grieve Paton, MA, LLB, Solicitor, Glasgow and Mary Campbell Sclanders; *m* 1950, Eva French, *d* of David French Cranston, Edinburgh; two *d. Educ:* Glasgow Academy; Glasgow University. MA 1927; LLB (Distinction) 1930. Solicitor 1931; Advocate 1951. Served Admiralty, 1942-46. Faulds Fellow in Law, Glasgow Univ., 1931-34; Asst to Professor of Law, Glasgow, 1934-46. Lectr in History of Scots Law, Glasgow, 1951-59; Senior Lectr, Dept of Scots Law, Edinburgh, 1959-67. Literary Dir, Stair Soc., 1954-60. *Publications:* Ed., Baron Hume's Lectures (Stair Soc.), 1939-57; Ed. and Contrib., Introductory History of Scots Law (Stair Soc.), 1958; Asst Ed., A Source Book and History of Administrative Law in Scotland, 1956; (with J. G. S. Cameron) Law of Landlord and Tenant in Scotland, 1967; articles in various legal periodicals. *Recreations:* golf, tennis, walking. *Address:* 163 Colinton Road, Edinburgh EH14 1BE. *T:* 031-443 1660.

PATON, Sir George Whitecross, Kt 1957; Vice-Chancellor, University of Melbourne, 1951-68; *b* 16 August 1902; *s* of Rev. Frank H. L. Paton; *m* 1931, Alice Watson, CBE; one *s* three *d. Educ:* Scotch Coll., Melbourne; University of Melbourne; Magdalen College, University of Oxford. MA (Melb.), 1926; BA (Oxon.), 1928; BCL (Oxon.), 1929. Barrister-at-Law, Gray's Inn, 1929. Asst Lecturer, LSE, 1930; Professor of Jurisprudence, Univ. of Melbourne, 1931-51; Dean of Faculty of Law, 1946-51. Chairman Royal Commission on Television (Australia, 1953-54). LLD (Hon.): Glasgow, 1953; Sydney, 1955; Queensland, 1960; Tasmania, 1963; London, 1963; Monash, 1968; Melbourne, 1971; DCL (Hon.), Western Ontario, 1958. *Publications:* A Text Book of Jurisprudence, 1946, 4th edn 1972; Bailment in the Common Law, 1952; (with Barry and Sawer), Criminal Law in Australia, 1948. *Recreations:* tennis, walking, gardening. *Address:* Dunraven Avenue, Toorak, Victoria 3142, Australia. *T:* 24 1034. *Club:* Melbourne (Victoria, Aust.).

PATON, His Honour Harold William, DSC 1943; Judge of County Courts, Circuit No 54 (Bristol, etc) 1950-71; Chairman, Somerset Quarter Sessions, 1965-71; *b* 6 Oct. 1900; *s* of late Clifford James Paton; *m* 1947, Joan Orby, *d* of late Lt-Col Cecil Gascoigne, DSO, Seaforth Hldrs; one *d. Educ:* Winchester College; Christ Church, Oxford. Called to the Bar (Inner Temple), 1923 and practised at Common Law Bar. Served War of 1939-45 in RNVR (Coastal Forces); Lt-Comdr, 1944. *Recreations:* fishing, gardening. *Address:* Ardullie Farmhouse, Dingwall, Rossshire. *Club:* Royal Automobile.

PATON, Sir Leonard (Cecil), Kt 1946; CBE 1944; MC 1915; MA; Director, Harrisons & Crosfield Ltd (Chairman, 1957-62); *b* 7 May 1892; 4th *s* of John Paton, Dunfermline, Fife, Headmaster; *m* 1917, Muriel, *yr d* of William Searles, Maidstone; one *s* one *d. Educ:* George Watson's Coll.; Edinburgh University (MA, 1st Class Hons Classics, 1914); Christ Church, Oxford (Exhibitioner). European War, 1914-18, Captain Cameronians (MC, despatches). *Recreations:* fishing, golf. *Address:* 63 Woodland Court, Dyke Road Avenue, Hove, East Sussex BN3 6DQ.

PATON, Sir Stuart (Henry), KCVO 1965; CBE 1945; Captain RN, retired; *b* 9 July 1900; *s* of William Henry Paton and Winifred Powell, Norwood; *m* 1925, Dorothy Morgan, Shrewsbury; two *s* two *d. Educ:* Hillside, Godalming; RN Colleges, Osborne and Dartmouth. Served European War: Midshipman, HMS Marlborough, Grand Fleet, 1916; Sub-Lt, HMS Orcadia, English Channel, 1918. Specialised as Torpedo Officer; posts Lieut to Commander: Mediterranean and Home Fleets, Admiralty Plans Division, and New Zealand. War of 1939-45: HMS Vernon, Captain, 1940; Admiralty, Joint Intelligence Staff, 1941; Comd HMS Curacoa, E. Coast Convoys, 1942; Comd HMS Nigeria, Home Fleet and Eastern Fleet, 1942-44 (despatches Malta Convoy); Admiralty and served as a Dep.-Director, Admin. Planning, 1945-46; student, IDC, 1947; Comd HMS Newcastle, Mediterranean Fleet, 1948-49; Appointed ADC to King George VI, 1949; retired, 1950; General Secretary to King George's Fund for Sailors, 1950-65. *Recreations:* gardening, photography. *Address:* West Stroud, Grayswood, Haslemere, Surrey. *T:* Haslemere 3973.

PATON, Sir (Thomas) Angus (Lyall), Kt 1973; CMG 1960; FRS 1969; Senior Consultant, Sir Alexander Gibb & Partners, since 1977 (Senior Partner, 1955-77); *b* 10 May 1905; *s* of Thomas Lyall Paton and Janet (*née* Gibb); *m* 1932, Eleanor Joan Delmé-Murray (*d* 1964); two *s* two *d. Educ:* Cheltenham Coll.; University College, London. Fellow of University College. Joined Sir Alexander Gibb & Partners as pupil, 1925; after experience in UK, Canada, Burma and Turkey on harbour works, hydro-electric projects and industrial development schemes, was taken into partnership, 1938. Responsible for design and supervision of construction of many large industrial factories and for major hydro-electric and irrigation projects, including Owen Falls and Kariba Schemes, and for overall supervision of Indus Basin Project in W. Pakistan; also for economic surveys in Middle East and Africa on behalf of Dominion and Foreign Governments. Member UK Trade Mission to: Arab States, 1953; Egypt, Sudan and Ethiopia, 1955. Mem. NERC, 1969-72. Pres. ICE, 1970-71; Chm., Council of Engineering Instns, 1973; Past Chairman Assoc. of Consulting Engineers. FICE (Hon. FICE, 1975); FIStructE, Fellow Amer. Soc. of Civil Engineers, Past Pres., British Section, Soc. of Civil Engineers (France); a Vice-Pres., Royal Soc., 1977; FRSA. *Publications:* Power from Water, 1960; technical articles on engineering subjects. *Address:* 45 Richmond Hill Court, Richmond-on-Thames, Surrey. *T:* 01-940 1270. *Club:* Athenæum.

PATON, William Calder, CIE 1945; MC; Major-General IMS (retired); *b* 27 Jan. 1886; *s* of William and Isabella Paton; *m* 1st, 1915, Marian Bruce Williamson (*d* 1948); one *s* two *d*; 2nd, 1950, Isobel, MBE, *d* of R. Dean, JP, Beauly. *Educ:* Glasgow Academy; Edinburgh Univ. MB, ChB, Edinburgh, 1910; entered IMS, 1912; FRCS (Ed.), 1920; served European War, 1914-18 (MC and Brevet Major); various appointments on civil side of IMS, including Professor of Midwifery, Medical Coll., Madras, and Civil Surgeon, Delhi; Inspector-General of Civil Hospitals, N-WFP, 1939-41; Surgeon-General, Bengal, 1941-45; KHP; retired from IMS, 1945; Medical Superintendent, Royal Northern Infirmary, 1945-48; Medical Superintendent, Inverness Hospitals, 1948-54. *Publications:* articles in medical journals. *Recreations:* formerly riding, hunting; now walking, golf. *Address:* Sandymar, 5 Campbell Road, Longniddry, East Lothian EH32 0NP.

PATON, Prof. William Drummond Macdonald, CBE 1968; MA, DM; FRS 1956; FRCP 1969; JP; Professor of Pharmacology in the University of Oxford, and Fellow of Balliol College, since Oct. 1959; *b* 5 May 1917; 3rd *s* of late Rev. William Paton, DD, and Grace Mackenzie Paton; *m* 1942, Phoebe Margaret, *d* of Thomas Rooke and Elizabeth Frances (*née* Pearce); no *c*. *Educ:* Winchester House Sch., Brackley; Repton Sch.; New Coll., Oxford (Scholar); University College Hospital Medical Sch. BA (Oxon) Natural Sciences, Physiology, 1st class hons, 1938; Scholarships: Theodore Williams (Physiology), 1938; Christopher Welch, 1939; Jesse Theresa Rowden, 1939; Demonstrator in Physiology, Oxford, 1938-39; Goldsmid Exhibition, UCH Medical Sch., 1939; Ed. UCH Magazine, 1941; Fellowes Gold Medal in Clinical Med., 1941; BM, BCh Oxon, 1942; House physician, UCH Med. Unit, 1942. Pathologist King Edward VII Sanatorium, 1943-44; Member scientific staff, National Institute for Medical Research, 1944-52; MA 1948. Reader in Pharmacology, University College and UCH Med. Sch., 1952-54; DM 1953; Professor of Pharmacology, RCS, 1954-59. Delegate, Clarendon Press, 1967-72; Rhodes Trustee, 1968. Chm., Cttee for Suppression of Doping, 1970-71; Member: Pharmacological Soc. (Chm. Edtl Bd, 1969-74); Physiological Soc. (Hon. Sec. 1951-57); Med. Research Soc.; MRC, 1963-67; Council, Royal Society, 1967-69; Council, Inst. Study of Drug Dependence, 1969-75; Central Adv. Council for Science and Technology, 1970. Pres., Inst. of Animal Technicians, 1969-75, Vice-Pres., 1976-; Chm., Research Defence Soc., 1972-78; Wellcome Trustee, 1978. Hon. Member: Soc. Franc. d'Allergie; Australian Acad. Forensic Sci.; Corresp. Mem., German Pharmacological Soc.; Hon. Lectr, St Mary's Hosp. Med. Sch., 1950; Visiting Lecturer, Swedish Univs, 1953; Brussels, 1956. Robert Campbell Oration, 1957; Clover Lecture, 1958; Bertram Louis Abrahams Lecturer, RCP, 1962; Ivison Macadam Lecture, RCSE, 1973. Editor with R. V. Jones, Notes and Records of Royal Soc., 1971-. FRSA 1973; Hon FFARCS 1975. JP St Albans, 1956. Bengue Meml Prize, 1952; Cameron Prize, 1956; Gairdner Foundn Award, 1959; Gold Medal, Soc. of Apothecaries, 1976. *Publications:* (with J. P. Payne) Pharmacological Principles and Practice, 1968; papers on diving, caisson disease, histamine, synaptic transmission, drug action and drug dependence in physiological and pharmacological journals. *Recreations:* music, old books. *Address:* 13 Staverton Road, Oxford. *Club:* Athenæum.
See also Bishop of Birmingham , Rev. Canon D. M. Paton , Dr J . F . Stokes .

PATRICK, Graham McIntosh, CMG 1968; DSC 1943; Under Secretary, Department of the Environment, since 1971; Director, Scottish Services, Property Services Agency, since 1975; *b* 17 Oct. 1921; *m* 1945, Barbara Worboys; two *s*. *Educ:* Dundee High Sch.; St Andrews Univ. RNVR (Air Branch), 1940-46. Entered Ministry of Works, 1946; Regional Director: Middle East Region, 1965-67; South West Region, DoE, 1971-75; Chm., South West Economic Planning Bd, 1971-75. *Address:* c/o Argyle House, 3 Lady Lawson Street, Edinburgh. *Club:* Naval.

PATRICK, (James) McIntosh, ROI 1949; ARE; RSA 1957 (ARSA, 1949); Painter and Etcher; *b* 1907; *s* of Andrew G. Patrick and Helen Anderson; *m* 1933, Janet, *d* of W. Arnot Watterston; one *s* one *d*. *Educ:* Morgan Academy, Dundee; Glasgow School of Art. Awarded Guthrie Award RSA, 1935; Painting Winter in Angus purchased under the terms of the Chantrey Bequest, 1935; paintings purchased for National Gallery, Millbank; National Gallery of South Africa, Cape Town; National Gallery of South Australia; Scottish Contemp. Art Assoc.; and Municipal collections Manchester, Aberdeen, Hull, Dundee, Liverpool, Glasgow, Greenock, Perth, Southport, Newport (Mon.), Arbroath, also for Lady Leverhulme Art Gallery, etc.; etchings in British Museum and other print collections. Served War of 1939-46, North Africa and Italy;

Captain (General List). Hon. LLD Dundee, 1973. *Recreations:* gardening, music. *Address:* c/o Fine Art Society, New Bond Street, W1; The Shrubbery, Magdalen Yard Road, Dundee. *T:* Dundee 68561. *Club:* Scottish Arts (Edinburgh).

PATRICK, Brig. John, MC; *b* 10 June 1898; *s* of Lt-Col John Patrick, DL, and Florence Annie Rutherfoord; *m* (dissolved); two *s*. *Educ:* Harrow-on-the-Hill; RMA, Woolwich. 2nd Lieut, RFA, 1916; Chestnut Troop, RHA, 1919-28; Captain, 15/19th The King's Royal Hussars, 1928-38; psc 1934; retired, 1938; Lt-Col RA (SR), 1939; Brigadier, 1940-45; MP for Mid Antrim in Northern Ireland House of Commons, 1938-45. *Address:* Slemish, Preston, Hitchin, Herts. *T:* 2776.

PATRICK, John Bowman; Sheriff of North Strathclyde (formerly Renfrew and Argyll) at Greenock, since Oct. 1968; *b* 29 Feb. 1916; *s* of late John Bowman Patrick, Boot and Shoe maker, Greenock, and late Barbara Patrick (*née* James); *m* 1945, Sheina Struthers McCrea; one *d*. *Educ:* Greenock Academy; Edinburgh Univ.; Glasgow Univ. MA Edinburgh, 1937. Served War in Royal Navy, Dec. 1940-Dec. 1945; conscripted as Ordinary Seaman, finally Lieut RNVR. LLB Glasgow 1946. Admitted as a Solicitor in Scotland, June 1947; admitted to Faculty of Advocates, July 1956. Sheriff of Inverness, Moray, Nairn, Ross and Cromarty at Fort William and Portree (Skye), 1961-68. *Address:* 77 Union Street, Greenock, Renfrewshire. *T:* 20712.

PATRICK, Nigel Dennis Wemyss; Actor; *b* 2 May 1913; *s* of Charles Wemyss (Actor) and Dorothy Turner (Actress); *m* 1951, Beatrice Josephine Campbell; one *s* one *d*. *Educ:* privately. Started career as actor, Jan. 1932; first appeared West End stage, Oct. 1934, at Whitehall Theatre; played many parts in West End including Dudley in George and Margaret, Wyndham's, until 1939. Joined KRRC as Rifleman, 1939; discharged HM Forces, 1946, with rank of Lt-Col. Resumed career as actor, March 1946 at Lyric Hammersmith, in Tomorrow's Child; subsequently, among many plays, has appeared in: Noose, Saville, 1947; Who Goes There, Vaudeville, 1951; Escapade, St James's, 1953; The Remarkable Mr Pennypacker, New, 1955; The Egg, Saville, 1958; The Schoolmistress, Savoy, 1964; Reunion in Vienna, Chichester Festival, 1971, Piccadilly, 1972; Night Must Fall, Shaw, 1975; directed: Not in the Book, Criterion, 1958; Relatively Speaking, Duke of Yorks, 1967; The Others, Strand, 1967; Avanti, Booth Theatre, New York, 1968; Out of the Question, St Martin's, 1968; Blithe Spirit, Globe, 1970; Finishing Touches, Apollo, 1973; Dear Daddy, Ambassadors, 1976; directed and appeared in: The Pleasure of His Company, Haymarket, 1959; Settled Out of Court, Strand, 1960; Present Laughter, Queen's, 1965; Best of Friends, Strand, 1970; The Pay Off, Comedy, 1974. Has also appeared in many films, including Morning Departure, Trio, The Browning Version, Pandora and the Flying Dutchman, Sound Barrier, Pickwick Papers, Raintree County, Sapphire, League of Gentlemen, The Trials of Oscar Wilde, Johnny Nobody, The Informers, The Battle of Britain, The Virgin Soldiers, The Executioner, The Great Waltz, The Macintosh Man. *Recreations:* working, reading and travelling. *Address:* 54 Ovington Street, Chelsea, SW3. *T:* 01-589 4385. *Club:* Garrick.

PATRON, Sir Joseph, Kt 1961; OBE 1945; MC 1917; JP; Speaker of the Legislative Council, Gibraltar, 1958-64; *b* 19 Jan. 1896; *s* of late Joseph Armand Patron, CMG, OBE; *m* 1924, Emily Isham, *d* of John Maxwell Vaughan. *Educ:* Harrow. Served European War, 1914-18, Major; Yeomanry and Machine-Gun Corps (wounded, MC). Managing Director, Saccone and Speed, 1927-45; Company Director and Trustee, John Mackintosh Charitable Trust, Gibraltar; Member, Interdepartmental Cttee to Look After Evacuees, 1940-44. MEC Gibraltar, 1944-47; MLC 1950-58. JP Gibraltar, 1948. *Recreations:* golf, bridge, gardening. *Address:* 10 Calle Avila, Sotogrande, Prov. de Cadiz, Spain. *Clubs:* Boodle's; Royal Gibraltar Yacht.

PATTEN, Brian; poet; *b* 7 Feb. 1946. *Publications: poetry:* Penguin Modern Poets, 1967; Little Johnny's Confession, 1967; Notes to the Hurrying Man, 1969; The Irrelevant Song, 1971; The Unreliable Nightingale, 1973; Vanishing Trick, 1976; The Shabby Angel, 1978; *for younger readers:* The Elephant and the Flower, 1969; Jumping Mouse, 1971; *novel:* Mr Moon's Last Case, 1975; Emma's Doll, 1976; The Sly Cormorant and the Fish; adaptations of The Aesop Fables, 1977; *play:* The Pig And The Junkie, 1975; *records:* Brian Patten Reading His Own Poetry, 1969; British Poets Of Our Time, 1974; Vanishing Trick, 1976; The Sly Cormorant, 1977. *Address:* c/o Allen and Unwin Ltd, Publishers, 40 Museum Street, WC1.

PATTERSON, Arthur, CMG 1951; Assistant Secretary, Department of Health and Social Security, 1968-71; *b* 24 June

1906; 2nd *s* of late Alexander Patterson; *m* 1942, Mary Ann Stocks, *er d* of late J. L. Stocks; two *s* one *d. Educ:* Methodist Coll., Belfast; Queen's Univ., Belfast; St John's Coll., Cambridge. Entered Ministry of Labour, 1929; Assistant Secretary, 1941; transferred to Ministry of National Insurance, 1945; lent to Cyprus, 1953; Malta, 1956; Jamaica, 1963; Kuwait, 1971. *Address:* 42 Campden Hill Square, W8. *T:* 01-229 3894.

PATTERSON, Maj.-Gen. Arthur Gordon, CB 1969; DSO 1964; OBE 1961; MC 1945; Director of Army Training, 1969-72; retired; *b* 24 July 1917; *s* of late Arthur Abbey Patterson, Indian Civil Service; *m* 1949, Jean Mary Grant; two *s* one *d. Educ:* Tonbridge Sch.; RMC Sandhurst. Commnd, 1938; India and Burma, 1939-45; Staff Coll., Camberley, 1949; jssc 1955; CO 2nd 6th Queen Elizabeth's Own Gurkha Rifles, 1959-61; Comdr 99 Gurkha Inf. Brigade, 1962-64; idc 1965; GOC 17 Div. and Maj.-Gen., Bde of Gurkhas, 1965-69. Col, 6th Queen's Own Gurkha Rifles, 1969-73. *Address:* Burnt House, Benenden, Cranbrook, Kent. *Club:* Naval and Military.

PATTERSON, Rt. Rev. Cecil John, CMG 1958; CBE 1954; DD (Lambeth), 1963; DD (University of Nigeria, Nsukka), 1963; Commander of the Federal Republic (CFR) (Nigeria), 1965; *b* 9 Jan. 1908. *Educ:* St Paul's School; St Catharine's Coll., Cambridge; Bishop's Coll., Cheshunt. London Curacy, 1931-34; Missionary in S Nigeria, 1934-41; Asst Bishop on the Niger, 1942-45; Bishop on the Niger, 1945-69; Archbishop of West Africa, 1961-69; Representative for the Archbishops of Canterbury and York for Community Relations, 1970-72; Hon. Asst Bishop, Diocese of London, 1970-76. Hon. Fellow, St Catharine's Coll., Cambridge, 1963. *Address:* 6 High Park Road, Kew, Surrey. *T:* 01-876 4354.

PATTERSON, Mrs (Constance) Marie, OBE 1973; National Officer, Transport and General Workers' Union, since 1976 (National Woman Officer, 1963-76); Member of General Council of TUC since 1963 (Chairman, 1974-75 and 1977); *b* 1 April 1934; *d* of Dr Richard Swanton Abraham; *m* 1960, Thomas Michael Valentine Patterson (marr. diss. 1976). *Educ:* Pendleton High Sch.; Bedford Coll., Univ. of London (BA). Joined Staff of TGWU, 1957; serves on various negotiating cttees; Member: Exec., Confedn of Shipbuilding and Engrg Unions, 1966- (Pres., 1977-78); Hotel and Catering Trng Bd, 1966-; Food, Drink and Tobacco Trng Bd, 1968-; Industrial Injuries Adv. Council, 1973-77; Equal Opportunities Commn, 1975-; Central Arbitration Commn, 1976-. Dir of Remploy, 1966-. Lay Mem., Press Council, 1964-70. Hon. DSc Salford, 1975. *Recreations:* cooking, sight-seeing. *Address:* 15 Mackeson Road, NW3. *T:* 01-485 1327; Transport House, Smith Square, SW1. *T:* 01-828 7788.

PATTERSON, Geoffrey Crosbie, OBE 1975; Senior partner in firm of Scott-Moncrieff, Thomson & Shiells, Chartered Accountants; *b* 24 Sept 1912; *s* of late John George and late Elizabeth Louise Patterson; *m* 1939, Fay Mary, *d* of late James Wilson, solicitor; two *s. Educ:* Edinburgh Academy. Qualified as Chartered Accountant, 1935. Served War of 1939-45, Major, RA. Partner in firm of Scott-Moncrieff, Thomson & Shiells, 1936-. Pres., Inst. of Chartered Accountants of Scotland, 1971-72. Hon. Nat. Treasurer, The Royal British Legion, Scotland, 1958-77; Sec. and Treasurer, Scottish National War Memorial. *Recreations:* shooting, golf. *Address:* 17 Melville Street, Edinburgh EH3 7PH. *T:* 031-226 6281. *Clubs:* Caledonian; New (Edinburgh).

PATTERSON, Hugh Foggan; MA; Secretary, University of London King's College, since 1977; Clerk of the Senate, University of London, 1976; *b* 8 Nov. 1924; *s* of late Sir John Robert Patterson, KBE, CMG, and late Esther Margaret Patterson; *m* 1956, Joan Philippa Abdy Collins; one *s* two *d. Educ:* Royal Grammar Sch., Newcastle upon Tyne; King's Coll., Cambridge (MA). Served War, Royal Artillery, 1943-47. HM Oversea Civil Service, Nigeria, 1950-61; Universities of: Birmingham, 1962-63; Warwick, 1964-69; London, 1969-. *Recreations:* music, golf, badminton. *Address:* Lower Beechcroft, Chesham Road, Berkhamsted HP4 3AB. *T:* Berkhamsted 4353.

PATTERSON, Mrs Marie; *see* Patterson, Mrs C. M.

PATTIE, Geoffrey Edwin; MP (C) Chertsey and Walton since Feb. 1974; *b* 17 Jan. 1936; *s* of Alfred Edwin Pattie and Ada Olive (*née* Carr); *m* 1960, Tuëma Caroline (*née* Eyre-Maunsell); one *s* one *d. Educ:* Durham Sch.; St Catharine's Coll., Cambridge (MA). BA Cantab 1959. Called to Bar, Gray's Inn, 1964. Served: Queen Victoria's Rifles (TA), 1959-61; (on amalgamation) Queen's Royal Rifles (TA), now 4th Royal Green Jackets, 1961-65; Captain, 1964. MIPA (Mem. Council

1973). Dir, Collett, Dickenson, Pearce, International, 1966, Jt Man. Dir 1969-73. Mem. GLC, Lambeth, 1967-70; Chm. ILEA Finance Cttee, 1968-70. Chm. of Governors, London Coll. of Printing, 1968-69. Contested (C) Barking, 1966 and 1970. Sec., Cons. Parly Aviation Cttee, 1974-75, 1975-76, Vice Chm., 1976-77; Jt Sec., Cons. Parly Defence Cttee, 1975-76, 1976-77; Mem., Cttee of Public Accounts, 1976. Mem. General Synod of Church of England, 1970-75. *Publications:* Towards a New Defence Policy, 1976; (with James Bellini) A New World Role for the Medium Power: the British Opportunity. *Recreations:* travel, opera, cricket. *Address:* Terrington House, 15 College Road, Dulwich Village, SE21 7BG. *T:* 01-693 5131. *Clubs:* St Stephen's, Royal Green Jacket.

PATTINSON, Hon. Sir Baden, KBE 1962; LLB; Member, legal firm Pattinson, McLaughlin & Reid Smith; *b* 22 Dec. 1899; *m* 1926, Florence, *d* of T. A. Doman. Mayor of Maitland, 1928-30, and 1933; Mayor of Glenelg, 1944-47; MHA, South Australia: for Yorke Peninsula, 1930-38; for Glenelg, 1947-65; Minister of Education, SA, 1953-65. *Recreations:* horse riding, reading. *Address:* 12 Maturin Road, Glenelg, Adelaide, SA 5045, Australia.

PATTINSON, John Mellor, CBE 1943; MA; *b* 1899; *s* of late J. P. Pattinson, JP, Mobberley, Cheshire; *m* 1927, Wilhelmina, *d* of late W. J. Newth, Cheltenham; two *s. Educ:* Rugby Sch.; RMA; Cambridge Univ. RFA with BEF, 1918-19. Anglo-Iranian Oil Co., South Iran, 1922-45, General Manager, 1937-45. Director until 1969, British Petroleum Co. of Canada Ltd; Triad Oil Co. Ltd; BP Germany AG; Dep. Chm. 1960-65, and Man. Dir 1952-65, British Petroleum Co. Ltd; Dir, Chartered Bank, 1965-73. *Recreations:* gardening, travel. *Address:* Oakhurst, West Byfleet, Surrey. *Club:* East India, Devonshire, Sports and Public Schools.

PATTINSON, Peter L. F.; *see* Foden-Pattinson, P. L.

PATTINSON, William Derek; Secretary-General, General Synod of Church of England, since 1972; *b* 31 March 1930; *s* of late Thomas William Pattinson and of Mrs Elizabeth Pattinson. *Educ:* Whitehaven Grammar Sch.; Queen's Coll., Oxford (Stanhope Historical Essay Prize, 1951). BA 1952; MA 1956. Entered Home Civil Service, 1952; Inland Revenue Dept, 1952-62 and 1965-68; HM Treasury, 1962-65 and 1968-70; Assoc. Sec., General Synod, 1970-72. Chm., William Temple Assoc., 1966-70; Mem., Archbishops' Commn on Church and State, 1966-70; Mem., Governing Body, SPCK; Chm. of Governors, Liddon House, 1972-. *Address:* 4 Tufton Street, SW1P 3QY. *T:* 01-222 6307. *Clubs:* Athenæum, United Oxford & Cambridge University.

PATTISON, Prof. Bruce; Professor of Education, University of London Institute of Education, 1948-76, now Emeritus; *b* 13 Nov. 1908; *s* of Matthew and Catherine Pattison; *m* 1937, Dorothy Graham. *Educ:* Gateshead Grammar Sch.; King's Coll., Newcastle upon Tyne; Fitzwilliam House, Cambridge. Henry Mellish Sch., Nottingham, 1933-35; Hymers Coll., Hull, 1935-36; Lecturer in English, University College, London, 1936-48 (Reader, 1948). Board of Trade, 1941-43; Ministry of Supply, 1943-45. *Publication:* Music and Poetry of the English Renaissance, 1948, 2nd edn 1970. *Address:* Coombe Bank, Church Road, Kenley, Surrey CR2 5DU. *T:* 01-660 2991. *Clubs:* Athenæum, National Liberal.

PATTRICK, (William) Michael (Thomas), CBE 1975; FRIBA; AADipl; Principal, Central School of Art and Design, since 1961; *b* 25 Oct. 1913; *s* of late Arthur Devereux Pattrick and late Mrs Gilson Pattrick; *m* 1943, Joan Margaret Leech. *Educ:* Oundle School. Architectural Association School of Architecture, 1931-35; RIBA Howard Colls Scholarship; 1932. AA Studentship, 1934; Lecturer, Cambridge Univ., 1937; Architectural Assoc. Staff, 1945-61. Principal, The Architectural Association School of Architecture, 1951-61. *Recreation:* sailing. *Address:* Studio 1, St Peter's Wharf, Hammersmith Terrace, W6 9TR. *T:* 01-741 2745, (office) 01-242 7230.

PAUL VI, His Holiness Pope, (Giovanni Battista Montini); *b* Concesio, Brescia, 26 Sept. 1897; *s* of Giorgio Montini and Giuditta (*née* Alghisi). *Educ:* Istituto Arici, Brescia; Lombard Seminary, Pontifical Ecclesiastical Academy and Gregorian University, Rome. Ordained Priest, Roman Catholic Church, 1920; Attaché, Apostolic Nunciature in Warsaw, 1923; called to service of Secretariat of State, Vatican City, Oct. 1924; National Ecclesiastical Assistant to Italian Federation of Catholic University Students, 1925; Professor of History of Pontifical Diplomacy, 1931-37. Named Substitute of the Secretariat of State of His Holiness, 1937; accompanied the Papal Legate,

Cardinal Pacelli, to International Eucharistic Congress in Budapest, 1938. Appointed Pro-Secretary of State by Pope Pius XII, 1952; Archbishop of Milan, 1954-63. Created Cardinal, 1958. Elected Pope, 21 June 1963; solemn Coronation, 30 June 1963. *Address:* Apostolic Vatican Palace, Vatican City, Italy.

PAUL, Geoffrey David; Editor, Jewish Chronicle, since 1977; *b* 26 March 1929; *s* of Reuben Goldstein and Anne Goldstein; *m* 1st, 1952, Joy Stirling (marr. diss. 1972); one *d*; 2nd, 1974, Rachel Mann. *Educ:* Liverpool, Kendal, Dublin. Weekly newspaper and news agency reporter, 1947-57; asst editor, Jewish Observer and Middle East Review, 1957-62; Jewish Chronicle, 1962-: successively sub-editor, foreign editor, Israel corresp., deputy editor. *Recreations:* talking, listening to music, reading. *Address:* 25 Furnival Street, EC4A 1JT. *T:* 01-405 9252. *Club:* Press.

PAUL, Rt. Rev. Geoffrey John; *see* Hull, Bishop Suffragan of.

PAUL, Air Cdre Gerard John Christopher, CB 1956; DFC 1944; MA; CEng; FRAeS; *b* 31 Oct. 1907; *s* of E. W. Paul, FRCS; *m* 1937, Rosemary, *d* of Rear-Admiral H. G. E. Lane, CB; two *s* one *d*. *Educ:* Cheltenham Coll.; St John's Coll., Cambridge. Entered Royal Air Force, 1929; Fleet Air Arm, 1931-36; served War of 1939-45 in England and N.W. Europe; Commandant, Central Flying School, 1954-56; retired, 1958. Secretary-General of the Air League, 1958-71. Life Vice-Pres., RAF Gliding and Soaring Assoc.; Pres., Popular Flying Assoc. Croix de Guerre avec Palme (Belgium), 1944; Military Cross (Czechoslovakia), 1945. *Recreation:* flying. *Address:* Wearne House, Old Alresford, Hants. *Club:* Royal Air Force.

PAUL, Hugh Glencairn B.; *see* Balfour Paul.

PAUL, Sir John (Warburton), GCMG 1965 (KCMG 1962); OBE 1959; MC 1940; Lieutenant Governor of the Isle of Man, since 1974; *b* 29 March 1916; 2nd *s* of Walter George Paul and Phoebe (*née* Bull), Weymouth; *m* 1946, Kathleen Audrey, CStJ 1962, *d* of Dr A. D. Weeden, Weymouth; three *d*. *Educ:* Weymouth Coll., Dorset; Selwyn Coll., Cambridge (MA). Secretary, Maddermarket Theatre, Norwich, 1936. Commissioned Royal Tank Regt (Suppl. Res.), 1937; regular commission, RTR, 1938; BEF 1940 (despatches, prisoner-of-war); ADC and Private Secretary to Governor of Sierra Leone, 1945 (seconded). Called to the Bar, Inner Temple, 1947. Colonial Administrative Service, Sierra Leone, 1947; District Commissioner, 1952; Permanent Secretary, 1956; Provincial Commissioner, 1959; Secretary to the Cabinet, 1960; Governor and C-in-C, The Gambia, 1962-65; Governor-General of The Gambia, 1965-66; Governor and C-in-C: British Honduras, 1966-72; The Bahamas, 1972-73; Governor-General, The Bahamas, July-Oct. 1973. Member Board, West African Airways Corporation, 1954-56. KStJ 1962. *Recreation:* painting. *Address:* Government House, Isle of Man; Sherrens Mead, Sherfield-on-Loddon, Hampshire. *T:* Turgis Green 331. *Clubs:* Athenæum; Royal Dorset Yacht (Weymouth).

PAUL, Leslie (Allen); MA, FRSL; author; *b* Dublin, 1905. *Educ:* at a London Central School. Entered Fleet Street at age of 17; founded The Woodcraft Folk, a youth organisation, when 20; first Book (poems) when 21. Headed a delegation, on co-operation, to USSR, 1931; Editor, Plan, 1934-39; worked on Continent (refugees and underground movement); Tutor, WEA and LCC, 1933-40; called up, infantry, 1941; Middle East (AEC); Staff Tutor, Mount Carmel Coll. (MEF). Atlantic Award in Literature, 1946. Asst Director of Studies, Ashridge College of Citizenship, 1947-48; Director of Studies, at Brasted Place, Brasted, 1953-57. Leverhulme Research Fellow, 1957-59. Member Departmental Cttee on the Youth Service, 1958-60; Research Fellow, King George's Jubilee Trust and Industrial Welfare Society, 1960-61; Research Director, Central Advisory Council for the Ministry, for Church Assembly Enquiry into Deployment and Payment of the Clergy, 1962-64. Resident Fellow, Kenyon Coll., Ohio, 1964; Selwyn Lectr, St John's Coll., NZ, 1969; Lectr in Ethics and Social Studies, Queen's Coll., Birmingham, 1965-70. Scholar-in-Residence, Eastern Baptist Coll., Pa, USA, 1970. Mem., Gen. Synod of Church of England, 1970-75; Vice-Pres., Philosophical Soc., 1973-; Chm., Diocesan Council of Social Action (Hereford), 1972-. Hale Meml Lectr, and Hon. DCL, Seabury-Western, USA, 1970. *Publications:* (chief books, 1944-): Annihilation of Man, 1944; The Living Hedge, 1946; The Meaning of Human Existence, 1949; Angry Young Man, 1951; The English Philosophers, 1953; Sir Thomas More, 1953; The Boy Down Kitchener Street, 1957; Nature into History, 1957; Persons and Perception, 1961; Son of Man, 1961; The Transition from School to Work, 1962; Traveller on Sacred Ground, 1963; The Deployment and Payment of the Clergy, 1964; Alternatives to Christian Belief, 1967; The Death and

Resurrection of the Church, 1968; Coming to Terms with Sex, 1969; Eros Rediscovered, 1970; Journey to Connemara and other poems, 1972; A Church by Daylight, 1973; The Waters and the Wild, 1975; First Love, 1977. *Recreations:* bird-watching, photography, making lawns. *Address:* 6 Church Croft, Madley, Hereford HR2 9LT. *T:* Madley 598. *Club:* Royal Commonwealth Society.

PAUL, Noël Strange; Director, The Press Council, since 1976; *b* 1914; *y s* of late S. Evan Paul, SSC, and Susan, *d* of Dr Henry Habgood; *m* 1950, Mary, *yr d* of Philip J. Bone, FRSA, MRST, Luton. *Educ:* Kingston Grammar School. Journalist, Press Assoc., 1932; served War of 1939-45, Iran and Italy, Major seconded RAF (despatches). Home Counties Newspapers, 1949; Liverpool Daily Post, 1958; Asst Sec., Press Council, 1964, Sec., 1968-76. *Recreations:* sailing, photography. *Address:* Plummers, Fordham, Colchester, Essex. *T:* Colchester 240388. *Club:* Athenæum.

PAULET, family name of **Marquess of Winchester.**

PAULING, Linus (Carl); Research Professor, Linus Pauling Institute of Science and Medicine, since 1973; *b* 28 Feb. 1901; *s* of Herman William Pauling and Lucy Isabelle Darling; *m* 1923, Ava Helen Miller; three *s* one *d*. *Educ:* Oregon State Coll.; California Institute of Technology. BS Oregon State Coll., 1922; PhD California Inst. of Technology, 1925; Hon. DSc: Oregon State Coll., 1933; Univ. of Chicago, 1941; Princeton Univ., 1946; Yale, 1947; Cambridge, 1947; London, 1947; Oxford, 1948; Brooklyn Polytechnic Inst., 1955; Humboldt Univ. (Berlin), 1959; Melbourne, 1964; York (Toronto), 1966; LLD Reed Coll., 1959; LHD Tampa, 1949; Dr *hc*: Paris, 1948; Toulouse, 1949; Liège, 1955; Montpellier, 1958; Warsaw, 1969; Lyon, 1970; UJD, NB, 1950; DFA, Chouinard Art Inst., 1958. Asst in Chemistry and in Mechanics and Materials, Oregon State Coll., 1919-22; Graduate Asst, California Inst. Technology, 1922-23; Teaching Fellow, 1923-25; Research Associate, 1925-26; Nat. Res. Fellow in Chemistry, 1925-26; Fellow of John Simon Guggenheim Meml Foundn, 1926-27 (Univs of Munich, Zürich, Copenhagen); Asst Prof., California Inst. of Technology, 1927-29; Associate Prof., 1929-31; Prof. of Chemistry, 1931-63; Dir of Gates and Crellin Labs of Chemistry, and Chm., Div. of Chemistry and Chemical Engrg, 1936-58; Prof. of Chemistry, Stanford Univ., 1969-74. George Fisher Baker Lectr in Chemistry, Cornell Univ., Sept. 1937-Feb. 1938; George Eastman Prof., Oxford Univ., Jan.-June 1948, etc. Amer. Chem. Soc. Award in Pure Chemistry, 1931; William H. Nichols Medal, 1941; J. Willard Gibbs Medal, 1946; Theodore William Richards Medal, 1947; Davy Medal of Royal Society, 1947; Presidential Medal for Merit, 1948; Gilbert Newton Lewis Medal, 1951; Thomas Addis Medal, 1955; Amedeo Avogadro Medal, 1956; Pierre Fermat Medal, Paul Sabatier Medal, 1957; International Grotius Medal, 1957; Nobel Prize for Chemistry, 1954; Nobel Peace Prize for 1962, 1963; Linus Pauling Medal, 1966; Internat. Lenin Peace Prize, 1971; 1st Martin Luther King Jr Medical Award, 1972; Nat. Medal of Science, 1975. Member: Nat. Acad. of Sciences; Amer. Phil. Soc.; Amer. Acad. of Arts and Sciences, etc.; Hon. Fellow: Chemical Society (London), Royal Institution, etc.; For. Member: Royal Society, Akademia Nauk, USSR, etc.; Associé étranger, Acad. des Sciences, 1966. War of 1939-45, Official Investigator for projects of National Defense Research Cttee on Medical Research, and Office of Scientific Research and Development. Grand Officer, Order of Merit, Italian Republic. *Publications:* The Structure of Line Spectra (with S. Goudsmit), 1930; Introduction to Quantum Mechanics (with E. B. Wilson, Jun), 1935; The Nature of the Chemical Bond, 1939 (3rd ed., 1960); General Chemistry, 1947 (2nd ed., 1953); College Chemistry, 1950 (3rd ed., 1964); No More War!, 1958 (revised edn, 1962); The Architecture of Molecules (with Roger Hayward), 1964; The Chemical Bond, 1967; Vitamin C and the Common Cold, 1971; (with Peter Pauling) Chemistry, 1975; Vitamin C, the Common Cold and the Flu, 1976; also numerous scientific articles in the fields of chemistry, physics, and biology including the structure of crystals, quantum mechanics, nature of the chemical bond, structure of gas molecules, structure of antibodies and nature of serological reactions, etc. *Address:* Linus Pauling Institute of Science and Medicine, 2700 Sand Hill Road, Menlo Park, California 94025, USA.

PAULL, Sir Gilbert (James), Kt 1957; Judge of High Court of Justice, Queen's Bench Division, 1957-71; *b* 18 April 1896; *s* of Alan Paull, FSI, JP; *m* 1922, Maud Winifred, *d* of Charles Harris, Streatham; one *s* one *d*. *Educ:* St Paul's Sch.; Trinity Coll., Cambridge. Called to Bar, Inner Temple, 1920; QC, 1939; Bencher of Inner Temple 1946, Reader 1969, Treasurer 1970; Member of the Council of Legal Education, 1947-65; Recorder of Leicester, 1944-57. *Address:* Oatlands Park Hotel, Weybridge, Surrey. *Club:* Athenæum.

PAULSON, Godfrey Martin Ellis, CB 1966; CMG 1959; OBE (mil.) 1945; HM Diplomatic Service, retired 1970; *b* 6 July 1908; *s* of late Lt-Col P. Z. Paulson, OBE, Manchester Regt and Royal Signals, and late Mrs M. G. Paulson, *d* of late W. H. Ellis, Shipley Hall, Bradford, Yorkshire; *m* 1936, Patricia Emma, *d* of late Sir Hugh Murray, KCIE, CBE, and late Lady Murray, Englefield Green House, Surrey; one *s* one *d*. *Educ:* Westminster and Peterhouse, Cambridge. BA (Hons), 1930, MA 1940. Colonial Service; Assistant District Commissioner, Gold Coast Colony, 1930-32. Admitted Solicitor, 1936; practised in City of London until outbreak of war, 1939. Served 1939-45, Manchester Regt and on General Staff in Africa, UK, and North West Europe, including Military Mission to Free French; Lt-Col, 1945 (OBE 1945). Control Commn for Germany, 1945, for Austria, 1947-48. Joined Foreign Service, 1948, and served in Venice, Stockholm, Far East (Singapore), Beirut, Rome, Nice and Foreign Office. *Address:* Eastley House, Brightwalton, near Newbury, Berks. *T:* Chaddleworth 226. *Clubs:* United Oxford & Cambridge University, Bath, Garrick, MCC.

PAUNCEFORT-DUNCOMBE, Sir Philip; *see* Duncombe.

PAVITT, Laurence Anstice; MP (Lab and Co-op) Brent South, since 1974 (Willesden West, Oct. 1959-1974); *b* 1 Feb. 1914; *s* of George Anstice Pavitt and May (*née* Brooshooft); *m* 1937, Rosina (*née* Walton); one *s* one *d*. *Educ:* Elementary and Central Sch., West Ham. National Organising Secretary, British Fedn of Young Co-operators, 1942-46; Gen. Secretary, Anglo Chinese Development Soc., 1946-52; Regional Education Officer, Co-operative Union, 1947-52; UN Technical Assistance Programme, Asian Co-operative Field Mission, 1952-55; National Organiser, Medical Practitioners' Union, 1956-59. PPS to: Secretary for Education and Science, 1964-65; Secretary of State for Foreign Affairs, 1965-66; Secretary of State for Economic Affairs, 1966-67; an Asst Govt Whip, 1974-76. Chairman: Parly Labour Party's Health Gp, 1964-; British China All Party Gp; All Party Gp on Action on Smoking and Health; Member: MRC, 1969-72; Hearing Aid Council, 1968-74; Select Cttee on Overseas Aid, 1969-71; Exec. Cttee, Inter-Parly Union; Exec. Cttee, Commonwealth Parly Assoc. Vice-Pres., Brit. Assoc. for the Hard of Hearing. *Recreations:* reading, camping, walking. *Address:* House of Commons, SW1. *T:* 01-219 5225.

PAWLEY, Ven. Bernard Clinton; Archdeacon of Canterbury and Canon Residentiary of Canterbury Cathedral, since 1972; *b* 24 Jan. 1911; *s* of late Lt-Comdr S. G. Pawley, RN; *m* 1958, Margaret Grozier, *d* of late J. J. W. Herbertson, MVO, OBE; one *s* one *d*. *Educ:* Portsmouth Grammar School; Wadham College, Oxford; Wells Theological College. MA (Oxon), 1933. Deacon 1936, Priest 1936; Curate: Stoke on Trent Parish Church, 1934; Leeds Parish Church, 1937. CF (Emergency Commn), 1940-45 (despatches, 1945). Rector of Elland (dio. Wakefield), 1945-55; Diocesan Sec., Ely, 1955-59; Canon Residentiary, Vice-Dean and Treasurer, Ely, 1959-70; Canon Residentiary and Chancellor of St Paul's Cathedral, 1970-72. Proctor in Convocation, York, 1949-55, Canterbury, 1955-; Member: Church Assembly, 1949-70; General Synod, 1972-; Archbishops' Liaison with Vatican Secretariat for Unity, 1960-65; Vice-Chairman, Archbishops' Commission for RC Relations, 1966. Church Commissioner, 1963. Mem., British Council of Churches, 1966-; Delegate, World Council of Churches, 1968 and 1975. *Publications:* Looking at the Vatican Council, 1962; Anglican-Roman Relations, 1964; (ed) The Second Vatican Council, 1967; (with M. G. Pawley) Rome and Canterbury through Four Centuries, 1975. *Recreations:* music, foreign languages. *Address:* 29 The Precincts, Canterbury. *T:* Canterbury 63036.

PAWSON, Albert Guy, CMG 1935; retired as Secretary General, International Rubber Study Group, 1960; *b* 30 May 1888; *s* of Albert Henry and Alice Sarah Pawson; *m* 1917, Helen Humphrey Lawson; two *s*. *Educ:* Winchester College; Christ Church, Oxford. 2nd Class Honours School of History; joined Sudan Political Service, 1911; Governor, White Nile Province, 1927-31; Governor, Upper Nile Province, 1931-34. *Recreations:* fishing, cricket, tennis, Oxford Cricket Blue, 1908, 1909, 1910 and 1911, Captain 1910. *Address:* Flat 5, Greathed Manor, Lingfield, Surrey RH7 6PA.

PAWSON, Prof. Henry Cecil, MBE 1946; FRSE 1949; Emeritus Professor, Universities of Durham and Newcastle upon Tyne, since 1957; *b* 17 May 1897; *s* of late Rev. D. Ledger Pawson; *m* 1927, Edith Jean Sinclair; one *s* two *d*. *Educ:* Lady Manners Grammar School, Bakewell, Derbyshire; King's College later University, Newcastle. DSc 1959. University of Newcastle upon Tyne: Lecturer in Agriculture, 1917, Senior Tutor, 1945; Prof. of Agriculture, 1948-57. Methodist Local Preacher, 1917; Vice-

President Methodist Conference of Great Britain, 1951-52. *Publications:* The Study of Agriculture, 1921; Robert Bakewell, Pioneer Livestock Breeder, 1957; Cockle Park Farm, 1960; Agriculture of Northumberland, 1961; Personal Evangelism, 1968; Words of Comfort, 1968; Hand to the Plough (autobiog.), 1973; contrib. to God in Prayer, articles and papers on agricultural and religious subjects. *Address:* 56 Dunholme Road, Newcastle upon Tyne NE4 6XE. *T:* 33269. *Clubs:* University Union, YMCA (Newcastle upon Tyne).

PAXTON, John, PhD; Editor, The Statesman's Year-Book, since 1969; Chief Consultant Editor, Reference Book Division, The Macmillan Press Ltd; Director: Linolite Ltd (Deputy Chairman); *b* 23 Aug. 1923; *m* 1950, Joan Thorne; one *s* one *d*. Head of Economics department, Millfield, 1952-63. Asst Editor, 1964-68, and Dep. Editor, 1968, of The Statesman's Year-Book. *Publications:* (with A. E. Walsh) Trade in the Common Market Countries, 1965; (with A. E. Walsh) The Structure and Development of the Common Market, 1968; (with A. E. Walsh) Trade and Industrial Resources of the Common Market and Efta Countries, 1970; (with John Wroughton) Smuggling, 1971; (with A. E. Walsh) Into Europe, 1972; (ed) Everyman's Dictionary of Abbreviations, 1974; World Legislatures, 1974; (with C. Cook) European Political Facts 1918-1973, 1975; The Statesman's Year-Book World Gazetteer, 1975; (with A. E. Walsh) Competition Policy: European and International Trends and Practices, 1975; The Developing Common Market, 1976; (with C. Cook) European Political Facts 1848-1918, 1977; A Dictionary of the European Economic Community, 1977; (with C. Cook) Commonwealth Political Facts, 1978; (with S. Fairfield) A Calendar of Creative Man, 1978; A Directory of Common Markets and Free Trade Areas for Businessmen, 1978; (with C. Cook) European Political Facts 1789-1848, 1978; contrib. to Keesing's Contemporary Archives, TLS. *Address:* Moss Cottage, Hardway, Bruton, Somerset BA10 0LN. *T:* Bruton 3423. *Clubs:* National, Royal Over-Seas League, PEN.

PAYNE, Alan Jeffrey; HM Diplomatic Service; Counsellor, Mexico City, since 1975; *b* 11 May 1933; *s* of Sydney Ellis Payne and Lydia Payne; *m* 1959, Letitia Freeman; three *s*. *Educ:* Enfield Grammar Sch.; Queens' Coll., Cambridge (Exhibnr). RN, 1955-57. EMI, London, later Paris, 1957-62; Secretariat, NATO, Paris, 1962-64; joined Diplomatic Service, 1965; Commonwealth Relations Office (later FCO), 1965-67; British High Commn, Kuala Lumpur, 1967-70; FCO, 1970-72; British Embassy, Budapest, 1972-75. *Recreations:* music, theatre. *Address:* c/o Foreign and Commonwealth Office, King Charles Street, SW1A 2AH. *Club:* Royal Commonwealth Society.

PAYNE, Anson; *see* Payne, J. A.

PAYNE, Rev. Ernest Alexander, CH 1968; BA, BD (London), MA, BLitt (Oxon); Hon. DD St Andrews; Hon. LLD McMaster; a President, World Council of Churches, 1968-75; General Secretary of the Baptist Union of Great Britain and Ireland, 1951-67, Vice President, 1976-77, President, 1977-78; *b* 19 Feb. 1902; *er s* of late Alexander William Payne; *m* 1930, Winifred Mary Davies; one *d*. *Educ:* Hackney Downs Secondary Sch.; King's Coll., London; Regent's Park Coll.; St Catherine's and Mansfield College, Oxford; Marburg University. Bugbrooke Baptist Church, 1928-32; Headquarters Staff, Baptist Missionary Society, 1932-40; Senior Tutor, Regent's Park College, 1940-51; Lecturer in Comparative Religion and the History of Modern Missions, Oxford Univ., 1946-51; Editor, The Baptist Quarterly, 1944-50. Pres., Baptist Historical Soc.; Vice-Chm., Central Cttee World Council of Churches, 1954-68; Jt Pres. 1968-75; Moderator Free Church Federal Council, 1958-59; Vice-Pres., 1960-62, Chm., Executive Cttee, 1962-71, British Council of Churches; Vice-Pres. Baptist World Alliance, 1965-70. Examiner in the Univs of Oxford, Wales, Edinburgh and Bristol. *Publications:* The Saktas, 1933; The Church Awakes, 1942; The Free Church Tradition in the Life of England, 1944; The Fellowship of Believers, 1944; Henry Wheeler Robinson, 1946; The Anabaptists of the 16th Century (Dr Williams's Lecture), 1949; The Baptists of Berkshire, 1952; James Henry Rushbrooke, 1954. The Anabaptists (in New Cambridge Modern History, Vol. II), 1958; The Baptist Union: A short history, 1959; Veteran Warrior (a Memoir of B. Grey Griffith), 1962; Free Churchmen Unrepentant and Repentant, 1965; The World Council of Churches (Dr Williams's Lecture), 1970; Thirty Years of the British Council of Churches, 1942-72, 1972; Out of Great Tribulation: Baptists in the Soviet Union, 1974; contrib. to Twentieth Century Christianity, 1961; From Uniformity to Unity, 1962; The Churches and Christian Unity, 1963 and Journal of Theological Studies, Internat. Review of Missions, Congregational Quarterly, etc. *Recreations:* reading, writing and travel. *Address:* 9 Murray Court, 80 Banbury Road, Oxford. *Club:* Athenæum.

PAYNE, Maj.-Gen. George Lefevre, CB 1966; CBE 1963; Director of Ordnance Services, Ministry of Defence, 1964-68; retired, 1968; *b* 23 June 1911; *s* of Dr E. L. Payne, MRCS, LRCP, Brunswick House, Kew, Surrey; *m* 1938, Betty Maud, *d* of Surgeon Captain H. A. Kellond-Knight, RN, Eastbourne, Sussex; three *s. Educ:* The King's Sch., Canterbury; Roy. Mil. Coll., Sandhurst. Royal Leicestershire Regiment: England, Northern Ireland, 1931-33; India, 1933-37; Royal Army Ordnance Corps: England, 1938-39; France, 1939-40; England, 1941-. Deputy Director Ordnance Services: HQ, BAOR, 1952-54; War Office, 1955-57; Commandant, Central Ordnance Depot, Chilwell, 1957-59; Deputy Director Ordnance Services, War Office, 1959-63; Commander, Stores Organization, RAOC, 1963-64; Col Comdt, RAOC, 1968-72. *Recreations:* shooting, gardening. *Address:* 17 Highridge Court, Downs Avenue, Epsom, Surrey. *Club:* Royal Commonwealth Society.

PAYNE, Prof. Jack Marsh; Director, ARC Institute for Research on Animal Diseases, since 1973; *b* 9 March 1929; *m* 1952, Sylvia Bryant; two *s* two *d. Educ:* Royal Veterinary Coll., London; University Coll. Hosp. Med. Sch., London. PhD, BSc; MRCVS. Res. Fellowship under Sir Roy Cameron, FRS, 1952-57; apptd, 1957, to staff of IRAD, Compton, Newbury, Berks, where principal res. has involved investigation of metabolic disorders of dairy cattle; esp. interest has centred around the concept of prodn disease and the develt of the Compton Metabolic Profile Test; Head of Dept of Functional Pathology, IRAD, 1961-73. Member: British Veterinary Assoc.; Assoc. of Veterinary Teachers and Res. Workers; Pathological Soc. Chm., VETEC (round table of experts on vet. science in EEC). Veterinary Advr, British Council. G. Norman Hall Gold Medal, 1972; RASE Res. Gold Medal, 1972. *Publications:* numerous references in sci. jls, esp. on subject of metabolic disorders. *Recreations:* fell walking, music, painting. *Address:* ARC Institute for Research on Animal Diseases, Compton, Newbury, Berks RG16 0NN. *T:* Compton 411. *Club:* Veterinary Research.

PAYNE, Rev. James Richmond, ThL; JP; General Secretary, Bible Society in Australia, since 1968; Chairman, United Bible Societies World Executive Committee, since 1976; *b* 1 June 1921; *s* of late R. A. Payne, Sydney, New South Wales; *m* 1943, Joan, *d* of late C. S. Elliott; three *s. Educ:* Drummoyne High School; Metropolitan Business College, Moore Theological College, Sydney. Served War of 1939-45: AIF, 1941-44. Catechist, St Michael's, Surry Hills, NSW, 1944-47; Curate, St Andrew's, Lismore, NSW, 1947-50; Rector, St Mark's, Nimbin, NSW, 1950-52; Chaplain, RAAF, Malta and Amberley, Qld, 1952-57; Rector, St Stephen's, Coorparoo, Qld, 1957-62; Dean of Perth, Western Australia, 1962-68. JP, Queensland, 1960; JP, ACT, 1969. *Publication:* Around the World in Seventy Days, 1965. *Recreations:* sport, walking, reading, family. *Address:* PO Box 507, Canberra City, ACT 2601, Australia. *T:* 485188. *Clubs:* Weld (Perth); Commonwealth (Canberra).

PAYNE, (John) Anson, OBE 1945; Chairman, FMC, 1974-75 (Executive Vice-Chairman, 1972-74); formerly Director: FMC (Meat); C. & T. Harris (Calne); Marsh and Baxter, and other cos; *b* 19 May 1917; *yr s* of late Major R. L. Payne, DSO and of Mrs L. M. Payne (*née* Duncan); *m* 1949, Deirdre Kelly; one *s* one *d. Educ:* St Lawrence Coll., Ramsgate; Trinity Hall, Cambridge (MA). Entered Civil Service as Assistant Principal, 1939. Served War of 1939-45 (despatches twice, OBE): RAFVR, 1940-45; Wing Commander, 1943. Principal Private Secretary to Minister of Agriculture and Fisheries, 1947-51; Asst Secretary, 1951; seconded to Treasury, 1953-54; Under-Secretary, Min. of Agriculture, 1960-68. *Address:* Sandpit Cottage, 4 High Street, Ditchling, Sussex BN6 8TA. *T:* Hassocks 2310.

PAYNE, Warrant Officer Keith, VC 1969; Warrant Officer Instructor, 42 Battalion, Royal Queensland Regiment, Mackay, Queensland, Australia; *b* 30 Aug. 1933; *s* of Henry Thomas Payne and Remilda Payne (*née* Hussey); *m* 1954, Florence Catherine Payne (*née* Plaw); five *s. Educ:* State School, Ingham, North Queensland. Soldier, Department of Army, Aug. 1951-. Member: VC and GC Assoc.; Returned Services League; Korea and South East Asia Forces Assoc. Freeman City of Brisbane and of Shire of Hinchinbrook. Vietnamese Cross of Gallantry, with bronze star, 1969; US Meritorious Unit Citation; Vietnamese Unit Citation Cross of Gallantry with Palm. *Recreations:* football, fishing, hunting. *Address:* St Bees Avenue, Bucasia, via Mackay, Qld 4740, Australia. *T:* 96125.

PAYNE, Leonard Sidney; Director, J. Sainsbury Ltd, since 1974; *b* 16 Dec. 1925; *s* of Leonard Sydney Payne and Lillian May Leggatt; *m* 1944, Marjorie Vincent; two *s. Educ:* Woodhouse Grammar School. FCCA, MBIM, FCIT, MBCS. Asst Accountant, Peek Frean & Co. Ltd, 1949-52; Chief Accountant, Administrator of various factory units, head office appts, Philips

Electrical Industries, 1952-62; Dep. Gp Comptroller, Morgan Crucible Co. Ltd, 1962-64; British Road Services Ltd: Finance Dir, 1964-67; Asst Man. Dir, 1967-69; Man. Dir, 1969-71; Dir of Techn. Services and Develt, Nat. Freight Corp., 1971-74, Vice-Chm. Executive 1974. *Recreations:* gardening, swimming, squash, chess. *Address:* Wisley, Gills Hill Lane, Radlett, Herts.

PAYNE, Norman John, CBE 1976 (OBE 1956; MBE 1944); Chairman, British Airports Authority, since 1977 (Chief Executive, 1972-77); *b* 9 Oct. 1921; *s* of F. Payne, Folkestone; *m* 1946, Pamela Vivien Wallis; four *s* one *d. Educ:* Lower Sch. of John Lyon, Harrow; City and Guilds Coll., London. BSc Eng Hons; FCGI, FICE, MIHE, FCIT, MSocCE (France); Mem. Architectural Assoc. Royal Engrs (Captain), 1939-45 (despatches twice); Imperial Coll. of Science and Technology London (Civil), 1946-49; Sir Frederick Snow & Partners, 1949, Partner 1955; British Airports Authority: Dir of Engrg, 1965; Dir of Planning, 1969, and Mem. Bd 1971. Pres., West European Airports Assoc., 1975-77; Chm., Airports Assoc. Co-ordinating Council, 1976. FBIM 1975. *Publications:* various papers on airports and freight movement. *Recreation:* gardening. *Address:* Summer Meadow, Shamley Green, Guildford, Surrey. *T:* Bramley 2515. *Club:* Reform.

PAYNE, Peter Charles John, PhD; MScAgrEng; Visiting Professor, Cranfield Institute of Technology, and Consultant, since 1975; *b* 8 Feb. 1928; *s* of late C. J. Payne, China Clay Merchant, and of Mrs F. M. Payne; *m* 1961, Margaret Grover; two *s* one *d. Educ:* Plymouth Coll.; Teignmouth Grammar School; Reading University. BSc Reading 1948; Min. of Agriculture Scholar, Durham Univ., MSc (Agr. Eng.) 1950; Scientific Officer, Nat. Institute of Agricultural Engineering, 1950-55; PhD Reading 1954; Lecturer in Farm Mechanisation, Wye College, London Univ., 1955-60; Lecturer in Agricultural Engineering, Durham Univ., 1960-61; Principal, Nat. Coll. of Agricultural Engineering, Silsoe, 1962-75; Vis. Prof., Univ. of Reading, 1969-75. Vice-Pres., Section III, Commn Internationale du Génie Rural, 1969. FIAgrE 1968; FRAgSs 1971. *Publications:* various papers in agricultural and engineering journals. *Recreations:* sailing, gardening. *Address:* Garlidna Farm, Porkellis, Helston TR13 0JX. *T:* Constantine 301. *Club:* Farmers'.

PAYNE, Hon. Sir Reginald Withers, Kt 1962; **Hon. Mr Justice Payne;** Judge of the Family Division (formerly Probate, Divorce and Admiralty Division), High Court of Justice, since 1962; *b* 27 Sept. 1904; 2nd *s* of late John Herbert Payne, Solicitor, Hallgate House, Cottingham, E Yorks; *m* 1940, Alice, 3rd *d* of late Ernest Armstrong, Hankham Place, Pevensey; two *s. Educ:* Hymers Coll., Hull. LLB (London), 1927; admitted Solicitor, 1927; called to the Bar, Inner Temple, 1937 (North Eastern Circuit). Bencher, Inner Temple, 1962. Served, 1940-45, in RAFVR (Provost Marshal's Branch for Provost and Security Duties); Deputy Assistant Provost Marshal Yorkshire, Assistant Provost Marshal: Midlands; Karachi Area; Deputy Provost Marshal, Bengal and Assam; Squadron Leader, 1943; Wing Commander, 1945. Recorder of Pontefract, 1955-57; Recorder of Huddersfield, 1957-59; Judge of the County Courts (Circuit 14), Oct. 1959-May 1960; (Circuit 12), 1960-62. Chm., Lord Chancellor's Cttee on Enforcement of Judgments, 1965. *Recreations:* golf, shooting, gardening. *Address:* Royal Courts of Justice, Strand, WC2; 12 King's Bench Walk, Temple, EC4. *T:* 01-353 3114. *Clubs:* Reform, Garrick.
See also C. T. Evans.

PAYNE, Sir Robert (Frederick), Kt 1970; President, The Law Society, 1969-70; Principal in Payne & Payne, Solicitors, Hull; *b* 22 Jan. 1908; *s* of late Frederick Charles Payne and of Edith Constance Payne (*née* Carlton); *m* 1st, 1937, Alice Marguerite, *d* of William Sydney Cussons, one *s* one *d*; 2nd, 1951, Maureen Ruth, *d* of William Charles Walsh; one *s. Educ:* Hymers Coll., Hull. Solicitor, 1931. Served in RAF (Fighter Command), 1940-44, Sqdn Ldr, 2nd TAF. Chm., Cttee of Inquiry into Whittingham Hosp., 1971-72; Mem., Home Office Cttee on Liquor Licensing, 1971-72. Pres., Hull Incorporated Law Soc., 1954-55. Founder Mem., British Acad. of Forensic Sciences, 1959. Sheriff of Kingston-upon-Hull, 1957. *Recreations:* golf, music. *Address:* High Woodgates, North Ferriby, North Humberside. *T:* Hull 631533. *Club:* East India, Devonshire, Sports and Public Schools.

PAYNE-BUTLER, George William; County Treasurer, Surrey County Council, since 1973 (Assistant, 1962; Deputy, 1970); *b* 7 Oct. 1919; *s* of late George and Letitia Rachel Payne; *m* 1947, Joyce Louise Cockburn; one *s* two *d. Educ:* Woking Sch. for Boys. Joined Surrey CC, 1937. Served War, RAF, 1940-45. Chartered Municipal Treasurer, 1950 (CIPFA). *Recreations:* gardening, handicraft work in wood, reading. *Address:* Janston, Hillier Road, Guildford, Surrey GU1 2JQ. *T:* Guildford 65337.

PAYNE-GALLWEY, Sir Philip Frankland; *see* Gallwey.

PAYNTER, Dr John Frederick; Senior Lecturer, Department of Music, University of York, since 1974; *b* 17 July 1931; *s* of late Frederick Albert Paynter and late Rose Alice Paynter; *m* 1956, Elizabeth Hill; one *d*. *Educ:* Emanuel Sch., London; Trinity Coll. of Music, London (GTCL 1952). DPhil York, 1971. Teaching appts, primary and secondary schs, 1954-62; Lectr in Music, City of Liverpool C. F. Mott Coll. of Educn, 1962-65; Principal Lectr (Head of Dept of Music), Bishop Otter Coll., Chichester, 1965-69; Lectr, Dept of Music, Univ. of York, 1969. Composer and writer on music-educn. Dir, Schs Council Proj., Music in the Secondary School Curriculum, 1973-78. Gen. Editor, series, Resources of Music. *Publications:* Sound and Silence (with Peter Aston), 1970; Hear and Now, 1972; (with Elizabeth Paynter) The Dance and the Drum, 1974; All Kinds of Music, 1976; articles and revs in Music in Educn, Music Teacher, Times Educnl Sup., Music Now (Aust. Contemp. Music Qtly), Music Educn Rev.; scripts and commentaries for schs broadcasts and TV; *musical compositions:* choral and instrumental works including: Landscapes, 1972; The Windhover, 1972; May Magnificat, 1973; God's Grandeur, 1975; Sacraments of Summer, 1975; Incarnatus, 1976; Galaxies for Orchestra, 1977; solo vocal and instrumental works and music-theatre works for children. *Recreations:* walking, wine-making. *Address:* Westfield House, Newton on Derwent, York YO4 5DA.

PAYNTER, Air Cdre Noel Stephen, CB 1946; DL; retired; *b* 26 Dec. 1898; *s* of late Canon F. S. Paynter, sometime Rector of Springfield, Essex; *m* 1925, Barbara Grace Haagensen; one *s* one *d*. *Educ:* Haileybury; RMC, Sandhurst. Flying Brevet, 1917; France and Russia, 1918-19 (St Anne 3rd Class); North-West Frontier, 1919-21; North-West Frontier, 1925-30; Malta, 1934; Directorate of Intelligence, Air Ministry, 1936-39; Chief Intelligence Officer, Middle East, 1939-42 (despatches); Chief Intelligence Officer, Bomber Command, 1942-45 (CB); Directorate of Intelligence, Air Ministry, 1946. Chm. Buckinghamshire Playing Fields Assoc., 1958-65; Chm. Bucks Army Cadet Force (TA), 1962-65. High Sheriff, Bucks, 1965. DL Buckinghamshire, 1963. *Address:* Lawn House, Edgcott, near Aylesbury, Bucks. *T:* Grendon Underwood 238.

PAYNTER, (Thomas) William; Secretary, National Union of Mineworkers, 1959-68; Member, Arbitration Panel for the Advisory Arbitration and Conciliation Service (formerly the TUC-CBI Conciliation Panel), since 1972; *b* 6 Dec. 1903; *s* of a Miner; *m* 1st, 1937; two *s* (twins); 2nd, 1943; five *s* (one set of twins). *Educ:* Whitchurch (Cardiff) and Porth Elementary Schools. Left school at age of 13 to work on a farm, 1917; commenced work in Rhondda Pits; elected Checkweigher at Cymmer Colliery, Porth, 1929; removed by Court injunction, 1931. Took part in hunger marches, 1931, 1932, 1936. Elected to Executive Committee, South Wales Miners' Federation for Rhondda, 1936; joined International Brigade, 1937; Miners' agent for Rhymney Area, 1939; President South Wales Miners, 1951. Mem., Commn on Industrial Relations, 1969-70. *Publications:* British Trade Unions and the Problem of Change, 1970; My Generation (autobiog.), 1972. *Recreations:* reading and gardening. *Address:* 32 Glengall Road, Edgware, Mddx.

PAYTON, Stanley Walden, CMG 1965; Chief of Overseas Department, Bank of England, since 1975; *b* 29 May 1921; *s* of late Archibald Walden Payton and late Ethel May Payton (*née* Kirtland); *m* 1941, Joan (*née* Starmer); one *s* one *d*. *Educ:* Monoux School. Fleet Air Arm, 1940-46: Lieut, HMS Indomitable, HMS Illustrious. Entered Bank of England, 1946; UK Alternate on Managing Board of European Payments Union, Paris, 1957-59; First Governor of Bank of Jamaica, 1960-64; Dep. Chief, Overseas Dept, Bank of England, 1965-71; Senior Adviser, Bank of England, 1971-75. *Address:* Pollards Park House, Chalfont St Giles, Bucks. *Clubs:* Naval, Overseas Bankers.

PAYTON, Rev. Wilfred Ernest Granville, CB 1965; Vicar of Abingdon, since 1969; Rural Dean of Abingdon, since 1976; *b* 27 Dec. 1913; *s* of Wilfred Richard Daniel Payton and Alice Payton (*née* Lewin); *m* 1946, Nita Mary Barber; one *s* one *d*. *Educ:* Nottingham High School; Emmanuel College, Cambridge (MA); Ridley Hall, Cambridge. Ordained, 1938; Chaplain, RAF, 1941; Asst Chaplain-in-Chief, 1959; Chaplain-in-Chief, 1965-69; Archdeacon, Prebendary and Canon of St Botolph, Lincoln Cathedral, 1965-69. Hon. Chaplain to the Queen, 1965-69. *Recreations:* cricket (Cambridge Univ. 1937), hockey (Notts., 1938-39), tennis. *Address:* The Vicarage, Thames Street, Abingdon, Oxon. *T:* Abingdon 20144. *Clubs:* MCC; Hawks (Cambridge).

PAZ, Octavio; Mexican author; poet; Editor, Plural, a literary and political magazine; *b* Mexico City, 31 March 1914; *s* of Octavio Paz and Josefina Lozano; *m* Marie José Tramini; one *d*. *Educ:* National Univ. of Mexico. Founded and directed Mexican literary reviews: Barandal, 1931; Taller, 1939; El Hijo Pródigo, 1943. Guggenheim Fellowship, USA, 1944. Former Sec., Mexican Embassy, Paris; Chargé d'Affaires *ad interim*, Japan, 1951; posted to Secretariat for External Affairs; Ambassador to India, 1962-68, resigned. Simon Bolivar Prof. of Latin-American Studies, Cambridge, 1970; Fellow of Churchill Coll., Cambridge, 1970-71; Charles Eliot Norton Prof. of Poetry, Harvard Univ., 1971-72. Awarded International Poetry Grand Prix, 1963. *Publications: poetry:* Luna Silvestre, 1933; Raiz del Hombre, 1937; Entre la Piedra y la Flor, 1941; A la Orilla del Mundo, 1942; Libertad bajo palabra, 1949; Aguila o Sol?, 1951; Semillas para un Himno, 1956; Piedra de Sol, 1957 (trans. as Sun Stone, 1960); La Estación Violenta, 1958; Libertad bajo palabra (poetical works 1935-58), 1960; Salamandra, 1962; Blanco, 1967; Topoemas, 1967; Discos Visuales, 1968; Ladera Este, 1969; Renga, 1971; Vuelta, 1976; in English: Selected Poems (1935-57), 1963; Configurations (1958-69), 1971; *prose:* El Laberinto de la soledad, 1951 (trans. as Labyrinth of Solitude, 1960); El Arco y la Lira, 1956 (trans. as The Bow and The Lyre, 1974); Las Peras del Olmo, 1957; Cuadrivio, 1965; Puertas al campo, 1966; Corriente Alterna, 1967 (trans. as Alternating Current, 1972); Claude Levi-Strauss o el Nuevo Féstin de Esopo, 1967 (trans. as On Levi-Strauss, 1970); Marcel Duchamp o El Castillo de la Pureza, 1967 (trans. as Marcel Duchamp or the Castle of Purity, 1970); Conjunciones y Disyunciones (essay), 1969 (trans. as Conjunctions and Disjunctions, 1974); Postdata, 1970 (trans. as The Other Mexico, 1972); El Mono Gramático, 1971; Los Hijos del Limo, 1974 (trans. as Children of the Mire, 1974); El Signo y el Garabato, 1975. *Address:* c/o Plural, Reforma 12, desp. 505, Mexico 1, DF.

PEACH, Capt. C. L.; *see* Keighly-Peach.

PEACH, Denis Alan; Assistant Under Secretary of State (Principal Finance Officer), Home Office, since 1974; *b* 10 Jan. 1928; *s* of Richard Peach and Alice Ellen Peach; *m* 1957, Audrey Hazel Chamberlain. *Educ:* Selhurst Grammar Sch., Croydon. Home Office, 1946-: Asst Principal, 1951; Private Sec. to Perm. Under Sec of State, 1956; Principal, 1957; Sec. to Anglo-Egyptian Resettlement Bd, 1957-58; Prison Commn, 1958-62; Asst Sec., 1967. *Recreations:* painting, gardening. *Address:* 36 The Vale, Coulsdon, Surrey CR3 2AW. *T:* 01-660 6752.

PEACOCK, Prof. Alan Turner, DSC 1945; MA; Professor of Economics, and Principal-elect, University College at Buckingham, since 1978; *b* 26 June 1922; *s* of late Professor A. D. Peacock, FRSE and of Clara Mary (*née* Turner); *m* 1944, Margaret Martha Astell Burt; two *s* one *d*. *Educ:* Dundee High School; University of St Andrews (1939-42, 1945-47). Royal Navy, 1942-45 (Lieut RNVR). Lecturer in Economics: Univ. of St Andrews, 1947-48; London Sch. of Economics, 1948-51; Reader in Public Finance, Univ. of London, 1951-56; Prof. of Economic Science, Univ. of Edinburgh, 1957-62; Prof. of Economics, Univ. of York, 1962-78. Seconded from Univ. of York as Chief Economic Adviser, Dept of Industry, 1973-76. Visiting Prof. of Economics, Johns Hopkins Univ., 1958. Member: Commission of Enquiry into land and population problems of Fiji, 1959; Adv. Council, Inst. Economic Affairs, 1959-; Departmental Committee on Electricity in Scotland, 1961; Council, REconS, 1961-; Cttee of Enquiry on impact of rates, 1964; Commn on the Constitution, 1970-73; SSRC, 1972-73; Pres., Internat. Inst. of Public Finance, 1966-69; Chairman: Arts Council Enquiry on Orchestral Resources, 1969-70; Council, London Philharmonic Orch., 1975-. Hon. DUniv Stirling, 1974. *Publications:* Economics of National Insurance, 1952; (ed) Income Redistribution and Social Policy 1954; National Income and Social Accounting (with H. C. Edey), 1954, 3rd imp. 1967; The National Income of Tanganyika (1952-54) (with D. G. M. Dosser), 1958; The Growth of Public Expenditure in the UK, 1890-1955 (with J. Wiseman), 1961; Economic Theory of Fiscal Policy (with G. K. Shaw), 1971, 2nd edn, 1976; The Composer in the Market Place (with R. Weir), 1975; Welfare Economics: a liberal re-interpretation (with C. K. Rowley), 1975; articles on applied economics in Economic Jl, Economica and other journals. *Recreation:* music. *Address:* University College at Buckingham, Buckingham MK18 1EG. *T:* Buckingham 4161. *Clubs:* Reform, Naval.

PEACOCK, Hon. Andrew Sharp; MP (L) Kooyong, since 1966; Minister for Foreign Affairs, Australia, since 1975; *b* 13 Feb. 1939; *s* of late A. S. Peacock and Iris Peacock. *Educ:* Scotch Coll., Melbourne, Vic; Melbourne Univ. (LLB). Former Partner, Rigby & Fielding, Solicitors; Chm., Peacock and Smith

Pty Ltd, 1962-69. CMF Reserve (Captain), 1966. Pres., Victorian Liberal Party, 1965-66; Minister for Army and Minister assisting Prime Minister, 1969-71; Minister for Army and Minister asstg Treasurer, 1971-72; Minister for External Territories, Feb.-Dec. 1972; Mem., Opposition Exec., 1973-75; Oppos. Shadow Minister for For. Affairs, 1973-75. *Recreations:* horse racing and SCUBA diving. *Address:* 4 Treasury Place, Melbourne, Vic 3002, Australia. *T:* 633417. *Clubs:* Melbourne, Melbourne Cricket (Melbourne).

PEACOCK, David Henry, MA (Cantab); CChem, FRIC; DSc (London); IES (retired); *b* Dec. 1889; *s* of C. G. and Catherine Peacock; *m* 1915, Catherine Tait (*d* 1971); no *c. Educ:* Central Foundation School, London; Trinity Coll., Cambridge (Scholar); Gordon Wigan prize for research in Chemistry. Nobel's Explosives Factory Research Department, 1913-16; British Dyes Research Department, 1916-22; Chief Assistant Technical Department, Huddersfield, 1920-22; Professor of Chemistry, University of Rangoon, 1922-40; Special Chemical Adviser to the Government of Burma, 1938-40; Chemical Adviser, Bomber and Maintenance Commands, RAF, 1942-45; Chemical Consultant in Ministry of Supply, 1945-47; Lecturer in Organic Chemistry, University of Sheffield, 1947-55, also Tutor at Stephenson Hall; Demonstrator, Chemical Labs, Univ. of Cambridge. *Publications:* Life of Joseph Priestley; various papers in Journal of the Chemical Society, Journal of Physical Chemistry, Journal of the Society of Dyers and Colourists, Encyclopædia Britannica. *Address:* 32 London Road, Harston, Cambridge CB2 5QH.

PEACOCK, Geoffrey Arden, CVO 1977; MA; Remembrancer, City of London, since 1968; *b* 7 Feb. 1920; *s* of Warren Turner Peacock and Elsie (*née* Naylor); *m* 1949, Mary Gillian Drew, *d* of Dr Harold Drew Lander, Rock, Cornwall; two *d. Educ:* Wellington Coll.; Jesus Coll., Cambridge. Served in War, 1939-46; RA and Roy. Lincs. Regt; Lt-Col 1945; Pres. of War Crimes Court, Singapore. Called to the Bar, Inner Temple. Legal Asst, Treasury Solicitor's Dept, 1949; Princ., HM Treasury, 1954; Sen. Legal Asst, Treasury Solicitor's Dept, 1958. Member: Court of Assistants, Worshipful Co. of Pewterers; Co. of Watermen and Lightermen. Chm., Brighton and Storrington Beagles, 1970-73. Various foreign decorations. *Recreations:* beagling, sailing, rowing. *Address:* Cowfold Lodge, Cowfold, West Sussex. *T:* Cowfold 237. *Clubs:* Cruising Association, London Rowing, City Livery, Leander.

PEACOCK, (Ian) Michael; President, Video Arts Inc., since 1976; Managing Director, Warner Bros Television Ltd, since 1973; Chairman, Monitor Enterprises Ltd, since 1970; Director: Video Arts Ltd; Greater Manchester Independent Radio Ltd; *b* 14 Sept. 1929; *e s* of Norman Henry and Sara Barbara Peacock; *m* 1956, Daphne Lee; two *s* one *d. Educ:* Kimball Union Academy, USA; Welwyn Garden City Grammar School; London School of Economics (BSc Econ.). BBC Television: Producer, 1952-56; Producer Panorama, 1956-58; Asst Head of Television Outside Broadcasts, 1958-59; Editor, Panorama, 1959-61; Editor, BBC Television News, 1961-63; Chief of Programmes, BBC-2, 1963-65; Controller, BBC-1, BBC Television Service, 1965-67; Managing Dir, London Weekend Television Ltd, 1967-69. *Recreations:* theatre, cinema, concerts, gardening, sailing. *Address:* 21 Woodlands Road, Barnes, SW13. *T:* 01-876 2025. *Club:* Savile.

PEACOCK, John Atkins, CMG 1949; Chairman, Nurdin & Peacock Ltd, Raynes Park, SW20; Director of Eggs, Ministry of Food, 1940-54; *b* 8 Sept. 1898; *s* of Thomas Peacock; *m* 1925, Phyllis Evelyn Jones; two *s* one *d. Address:* Bushey Road, Raynes Park, SW20; Astra, Vicarage Lane, Send, Surrey. *Club:* Royal Automobile.

PEACOCK, (John) Roydon; Hon. Consultant Surgeon, Ear, Nose and Throat Department, St George's Hospital, SW1; *s* of late Ralph Peacock; *m* Olive Joan (*d* 1977), *d* of late Sir Arthur Blake, KBE. *Educ:* Westminster Sch.; Trinity Coll., Cambridge; St George's Hospital, University Entrance Schol.; Brackenbury Prize, Allingham Scholar. FRCS; BCh Cantab; MRCS, LRCP; 1st Class Hons Natural Sciences Tripos, Cambridge; late Hon. Asst Surgeon Throat, Nose and Ear Hospital, Golden Square, W1; late Hon. Surgeon in charge of Ear, Nose and Throat Dept, Metropolitan Hospital, Kingsland Road; late Hon. Aural Surgeon to Maida Vale Hospital for nervous diseases; late Hon. Laryngologist, King Edward's Memorial Hospital, Ealing; late Hon. Surgeon Royal National Throat, Nose and Ear Hospital; late Surgeon to Ear, Nose and Throat Dept, Canadian Red Cross Memorial Hospital, Taplow, Bucks; late Surgeon, Ear, Nose and Throat Dept, St George's Hospital, SW1; late recog. teacher in Otolaryngology, University of London. *Publications:* Alcoholic Labyrinthine Injection through the oval window in

the treatment of aural vertigo, Lancet, Feb. 1938; Meniere's Syndrome, an observation, Lancet, Dec. 1938. *Address:* Windrush, Bicknoller, Taunton, Somerset. *T:* Stogumber 265.

PEACOCK, Michael; see Peacock, I. M.

PEACOCK, Ronald, MA, LittD (Leeds), MA (Manchester), DrPhil (Marburg); Professor of German, Bedford College, University of London, 1962-75; *b* 22 Nov. 1907; *s* of Arthur Lorenzo and Elizabeth Peacock; *m* 1933, Ilse Gertrud Eva, *d* of Geheimer Oberregierungsrat Paul Freiwald; no *c. Educ:* Leeds Modern Sch.; Universities of Leeds, Berlin, Innsbruck, Marburg. Assistant Lecturer in German, University of Leeds, 1931-38; Lecturer, 1938-39; Professor, 1939-45; Henry Simon Professor of German Language and Literature, University of Manchester, 1945-62; Dean of the Faculty of Arts, 1954-56; Pro-Vice-Chancellor, 1958-62; Visiting Professor of German Literature, Cornell Univ. (USA), 1949; Visiting Professor of German Literature and Comparative Literature, University of Heidelberg, 1960-61; Professor of Modern German Literature, University of Freiburg, 1965, 1967-68. Hon. LittD Manchester, 1977. *Publications:* The Great War in German Lyrical Poetry, 1934; Das Leitmotiv bei Thomas Mann, 1934; Hölderlin, 1938; The Poet in the Theatre, 1946 (reprinted with additional essays, 1960); The Art of Drama, 1957; Goethe's Major Plays, 1959; Criticism and Personal Taste, 1972; various articles on literature contributed to reviews and periodicals. *Recreations:* music, theatre, travel. *Address:* Greenshade, Woodhill Avenue, Gerrards Cross, Bucks.

PEACOCK, Roydon; see Peacock, J. R.

PEACOCKE, Rt. Rev. Cuthbert Irvine, TD; MA; *b* 26 April 1903; *er s* of late Rt Rev. Joseph Irvine Peacocke, DD; *m* 1931, Helen Louise Gaussen; one *s* one *d. Educ:* St Columba's Coll., Dublin; Trinity Coll., Dublin; Curate, Seapatrick Parish, 1926-30; Head of Southern Mission, 1930-33; Rector, Derriaghy, 1933-35; Rector, St Mark's, Dundela, 1935-56; CF, 1939-45; Archdeacon of Down, 1950-56; Dean of St Anne's Cathedral, Belfast, 1956-69; Bishop of Derry and Raphoe, 1970-75. *Publication:* The Young Parson, 1936. *Recreations:* games, garden and reading. *Address:* Culmore House West, Culmore Point, Londonderry.

PEAKE, family name of **Viscount Ingleby.**

PEAKE, Air Cdre (retired) Dame Felicity (Hyde), (Lady Peake), DBE 1949 (MBE 1941); AE; JP; *b* 1 May 1913; *d* of late Colonel Humphrey Watts, OBE, TD, and Mrs Simon Orde; *m* 1st, 1935, John Charles Mackenzie Hanbury (killed on active service, 1939); no *c*; 2nd, 1952, Sir Harald Peake, *qv*; one *s. Educ:* St Winifreds, Eastbourne; Les Grands Huguenots, Vaucresson, Seine et Oise, France. Joined ATS Company of the RAF, April 1939; commissioned in the WAAF, Aug. 1939; served at home and in the Middle East; Director, Women's Auxiliary Air Force, 1946-49; Director Women's Royal Air Force, from its inception, 1949, until her retirement, 1950. Member Advisory Cttee, Recruitment for the Forces, 1958. Trustee, Imperial War Museum, 1963-; former Governor, London House; Mem. Council, RAF Benevolent Fund; Mem. Council Union Jack Club. Hon. ADC to King George VI, 1949-50. *Address:* 2 Shepherd's Close, Shepherd's Place, Upper Brook Street, W1. *T:* 01-629 1264; Court Farm, Tackley, Oxford OX5 3AQ. *T:* Tackley 221.

PEAKE, Sir Francis, Kt, *cr* 1951; *b* 31 Jan. 1889; *s* of late John Henry Hill Peake, Chingford, Essex; *m* 1914, Winifred Marie, *d* of late Thomas McKinnon Clark, Wood Green; two *d. Educ:* Tottenham Grammar Sch. Entered Civil Service, 1907. Called to Bar, Lincoln's Inn, 1915. Controller of Death Duties, Aug. 1948-31 July 1951. *Address:* 13 Brockswood Lane, Welwyn Garden City, Herts. *T:* Welwyn Garden 20456.

PEAKE, Sir Harald, Kt 1973; AE; MA; *b* 28 Oct. 1899; *s* of late G. H. Peake; *m* 1st, 1933, Countess Resy, OBE 1946 (marr. diss., 1944), *o d* of Count de Baillet Latour, Brussels; one *s*; 2nd, 1952, Dame Felicity Hanbury (*see* Dame Felicity Peake); one *s. Educ:* Eton; Trinity Coll., Cambridge. Served in Coldstream Guards during European War, and subsequently Yorkshire Dragoons Yeomanry; raised and commanded No. 609 (West Riding) Squadron, Royal Aux. Air Force, 1936; Director of the Auxiliary Air Force, Air Ministry, 1938; Director of Public Relations, Air Ministry, 1940-42; Director of Air Force Welfare, 1942-43; Special Duty List, Air Ministry, 1943-45; retired with rank of Air Commodore. Chairman: Steel Co. of Wales, 1955-62; Lloyds Bank Ltd, 1961-69 (Dep. Chm., 1961, Vice-Chm., 1947-61). Member, Nye Cttee on War Office Organisation, 1963. Chm., RAF Benevolent Fund, 1967-. Prime Warden,

Goldsmiths' Company, 1958-59. *Recreations:* rowed for Eton, Cambridge and England; Master of Rufford Hounds, 1931-32; Agriculture. *Address:* 2 Shepherd's Close, Shepherd's Place, Upper Brook Street, W1Y 3RT. *T:* 01-629 1264; Court Farm, Tackley, Oxford OX5 3AQ. *T:* Tackley 221. *Club:* Brooks's.

PEARCE, family name of **Baron Pearce.**

PEARCE, Baron (Life Peer) *cr* 1962, of Sweethaws; **Edward Holroyd Pearce,** PC 1957; Kt 1948; RBA 1940; Chairman of the Press Council, 1969-74; Chairman, Appeals Committee, Take-over Panel, 1969-76; *b* 9 Feb. 1901; *s* of late John W. E. Pearce and Irene, *d* of Holroyd Chaplin; *m* 1927, Erica, *d* of late Bertram Priestman, RA; two *s. Educ:* Charterhouse; Corpus Christi Coll., Oxford. Hon. Fellow, Corpus Christi Coll., 1950. Called to Bar, 1925; QC 1945; Bencher, Hon. Society of Lincoln's Inn, 1948; Treasurer, 1966. Deputy Chairman, East Sussex Quarter Sessions, 1947-48; Judge of High Court of Justice, Probate, Divorce and Admiralty Division, 1948-54; Queen's Bench Division, 1954-57; a Lord Justice of Appeal, 1957-62; a Lord of Appeal in Ordinary, 1962-69. Chairman, Cttee on Shipbuilding Costs, 1947-49; Mem., Royal Commission on Marriage and Divorce, 1951; Chairman: Commn to test Rhodesian approval of proposed British-Rhodesian settlements, 1971-72; Cttee for an organisation of Bar and Inns of Court, 1971-73; Indep. Chm., Press discussions on Charter of Press Freedom, 1976-77. Mem., Governing Body, Charterhouse Sch., 1943-64; Governor: Tonbridge Sch.; Sutton's Hospital in Charterhouse; Fedn of British Artists, 1970-73. Prof. of Law, Royal Acad. of Arts, 1971-. Past Master and Member of Court of Company of Skinners; President, Artists League of GB, 1950-74; Trustee, Chantrey Bequest; Hon. FRBS. One-man show of landscapes at The Mall Galleries, 1971 and (with wife) 1973, 1976; also in provinces; one-man show of Alpine landscapes at Chur, Switzerland, 1977. *Recreations:* painting and pictures. *Address:* House of Lords, SW1; Sweethaws, Crowborough. *T:* 61520. *Club:* Athenæum.
See also Hon. R. B. H. Pearce.

PEARCE, (Ann) Philippa, (Mrs M. J. G. Christie); freelance writer of children's fiction, since 1967; *d* of Ernest Alexander Pearce and Gertrude Alice (*née* Ramsden); *m* 1963, Martin James Graham Christie (decd); one *d. Educ:* Perse Girls' Sch., Cambridge; Girton Coll., Cambridge (MA Hons English Pt I, History Pt II). Temp. civil servant, 1942-45; Producer/Scriptwriter, Sch. Broadcasting, BBC Radio, 1945-58; Editor, Educn Dept, Clarendon Press, 1958-60; Children's Editor, André Deutsch Ltd, 1960-67. Also lectures. *Publications:* Minnow on the Say, 1955 (3rd edn 1974); Tom's Midnight Garden, 1958 (3rd edn 1976; Carnegie Medal, 1959); Mrs Cockle's Cat, 1961 (2nd edn 1974); A Dog So Small, 1962 (2nd edn 1964); (with Sir Harold Scott) From Inside Scotland Yard, 1963; The Strange Sunflower, 1966; (with Sir Brian Fairfax-Lucy) The Children of the House, 1968 (2nd edn 1970); The Elm Street Lot, 1969; The Squirrel Wife, 1971; What the Neighbours Did and other stories, 1972 (2nd edn 1974); (ed) Stories from Hans Christian Andersen, 1972; Beauty and the Beast (re-telling), 1972; The Shadow Cage and other stories of the supernatural, 1977; reviews in TLS and Guardian. *Address:* c/o Kestrel Books, 17 Grosvenor Gardens, SW1W 0BD.

PEARCE, Austin William, CBE 1974; PhD; Chairman, Esso Petroleum Company Ltd, since 1972; *b* 1 Sept. 1921; *s* of William Thomas and Florence Annie Pearce; *m* 1947, Maglona Winifred Twinn (*d* 1975); three *d. Educ:* Devonport High Sch. for Boys; Univ. of Birmingham. BSc (Hons) 1943, PhD 1945; Cadman Medallist. Joined Agwi Petroleum Corp., 1945 (later Esso Petroleum Co., Ltd): Asst Refinery Manager, 1954-56; Gen. Manager Refining, 1956-62; Dir, 1963; Man. Dir, 1968-71; Director: Esso Europe Inc., 1972-; Esso Africa Inc., 1972-; Pres., Esso Holding Co. UK Inc., 1971-; Chairman: Esso Pension Trust Ltd, 1972-; Irish Refining Co. Ltd, 1965-71; Dir, Williams & Glyns Bank Ltd. Part-time Mem., NRDC, 1973-76; Member: Adv. Council for Energy Conservation, 1974-; Energy Commn, 1977-; British Aerospace, 1977- (Mem., Organising Cttee, 1976); Chm., UK Petroleum Industry Adv. Cttee, 1977-. President: Inst. of Petroleum, 1968-70; The Pipeline Industries Guild, 1973-75; Pres., Oil Industries Club, 1975-77; Mem., Bd of Governors, English-Speaking Union, 1974-; Vice-Pres., RoSPA. *Recreations:* golf, woodwork. *Address:* Esso House, Victoria Street, SW1E 5JW. *T:* 01-834 6677. *Club:* Royal Wimbledon Golf.

PEARCE, Clifford James, CB 1974; Under Secretary (Local Government), Department of the Environment (formerly Ministry of Housing and Local Government), 1968-76; *b* 14 Aug. 1916; *s* of late Samuel Lightfoot Pearce and Maude Evelyn Neville; *m* 1946, Elaine Hilda (*née* Baggley); one *s* one *d. Educ:*

Strand Sch.; King's Coll., London; London Sch. of Economics. Entered Inland Revenue, 1935; served in RN, 1941-46 (Lieut, RNVR); entered Min. of Health, 1946; Asst Sec., Min. of Housing and Local Govt, 1957; Under Sec. 1968. Hon. Res. Fellow, Birmingham Univ., 1976-77. *Address:* 156 Burbage Road, Dulwich, SE21.

PEARCE, Most Rev. George; former Archbishop of Suva; *b* 9 Jan. 1921; *s* of George H. Pearce and Marie Louise Duval. *Educ:* Marist Coll. and Seminary, Framingham Center, Mass, USA. Entered Seminary, 1940; Priest, 1947; taught in secondary sch. in New England, USA, 1948-49; assigned as missionary to Samoa, 1949; consecrated Vicar Apostolic of Samoa, 1956; first Bishop of Apia, 1966; Archbishop of Suva, 1967-76; retired 1976. *Address:* Marist Fathers, 27 Isabella Street, Boston, Mass 02117, USA. *T:* 617-426-4448.

PEARCE, John Brian; Under-Secretary, Civil Service Department, since 1976; *b* 25 Sept. 1935; *s* of late George Frederic Pearce and Constance Josephine Pearce; *m* 1960, Michelle Etcheverry; four *s. Educ:* Queen Elizabeth Grammar Sch., Wakefield; Brasenose Coll., Oxford (BA). Asst Principal: Min. of Power, 1959; Colonial Office, 1960; Private Sec. to Parly Under-Sec. of State, 1963; Principal: Colonial Office, 1964; Dept of Economic Affairs, 1967; Principal Private Sec. to Sec. of State for Economic Affairs, 1968-69; Asst Sec., Civil Service Dept, 1969. *Recreations:* music, architecture, tennis. *Address:* 124 Court Lane, SE21 7EA.

PEARCE, John Dalziel Wyndham, MA, MD, FRCP, FRCPEd, FRCPsych, DPM, FBPsS; Consulting Psychiatrist: St Mary's Hospital; Queen Elizabeth Hospital for Children; Examiner in Medicine: Royal College of Physicians; University of London; Royal College of Psychiatrists; *b* 21 Feb. 1904; *s* of John Alfred Wyndham Pearce and Mary Logan Dalziel; *m* 1929, Grace Fowler (marr. diss., 1964), no *c; m* 1964, Ellinor Elizabeth Nancy Draper. *Educ:* George Watson's Coll.; Edinburgh Univ. Formerly: Physician-in-charge, Depts of Psychiatry, St Mary's Hosp. and Queen Elizabeth Hosp. for Children; Cons. Psychiatrist, Royal Masonic Hosp.; Hon. physician, Tavistock Clinic and West End Hospital for Nervous Diseases; Medical co-director Portman Clinic, Institute for Study and Treatment of Delinquency (ISTD); medico-psychologist, LCC remand homes; Mem. Academic Boards, Inst. of Child Health, and St Mary's Hosp. Med. Sch. (Univ. of London); Chm., Adv. Cttee on delinquent and maladjusted children, Internat. Union for Child Welfare; Mem., Army Psychiatry Adv. Cttee; Lt-Col, RAMC; adviser in psychiatry, Allied Force HQ, CMF (despatches). Member: Council, National Assoc. for Mental Health; Home Sec's Adv. Council on Treatment of Offenders. *Publications:* Juvenile Delinquency, 1952; technical papers in scientific journals. *Recreations:* golf, fishing, painting, breadmaking. *Address:* Stamford House, 4 Hampstead Square, NW3 1AB. *Club:* Caledonian.

PEARCE, John Trevor Archdall, CMG 1964; *b* 7 May 1916; *s* of late Rev. W. T. L. A. Pearce, Seven Hills, NSW, Australia, and late N. B. Pearce, Prahran, Victoria, Australia; *m* 1948, Isabel Bundey Rankine, Hindmarsh Island, S Australia; no *c. Educ:* The King's Sch., Parramatta, Australia; Keble Coll., Oxford, Eng. MA. District Officer, Tanganyika, 1939. War Service: Kenya, Abyssinia, Ceylon, India, Burma, 1940-46, Major RE. Tanganyika: District Commissioner, 1950; Provincial Commissioner, 1959; Permanent Secretary (Admin), Office of the Vice-President, 1961; Chairman, Public Service Commn, Basutoland, 1963, Swaziland, 1965; Registrar, Papua and New Guinea Univ. of Technology, 1969-73. *Recreations:* cricket, hill-walking, travel, the Law. *Address:* Clippings, Ferguson Avenue, Buderim, Qld 4556, Australia.

PEARCE, Kenneth Leslie; retired as Chairman, East Midlands Gas Region (formerly East Midlands Gas Board), 1968-74; *b* 2 May 1910; *s* of late George Benjamin Pearce and Eliza Jane Pearce; *m* 1940, Evlyn Sarah Preedy (*d* 1957); two *s. Educ:* Dudley Grammar Sch.; Birmingham Central Techn. Coll. Engr and Man., Bilston Gas Light & Coke Co., 1939-48; Engr and Man., City of Leicester Gas Dept, 1948-49; East Midlands Gas Board: Divisional Gen. Man., Leicester and Northants, 1949-50; Divisional Gen. Man., Notts and Derby, 1950-62; Chief Distribution Engr, 1962-67; Dep. Chairman, 1967-68. *Recreations:* fishing, gardening. *Address:* 48 Wergs Road, Tettenhall, Wolverhampton, West Midlands WV6 8TD. *T:* Wolverhampton 751105.

PEARCE, Maj.-Gen. Leslie Arthur, CB 1973; CBE 1971 (OBE 1964; MBE 1956); Chief of General Staff, NZ Army, 1971-73, retd; *b* 22 Jan. 1918; British parents; *m* 1944, Fay Mattocks, Auckland, NZ; two *s* one *d. Educ:* in New Zealand. Joined

Army, 1937; served War: Greece, Western Desert, Italy, 1939-45. Staff Coll., Camberley, 1948. Directing Staff, Australia Staff Coll., 1958-59; Commandant, Army Schools, NZ, 1960; Comdg Officer, 1 NZ Regt, in NZ and Malaysia, 1961-64; Dep. QMG, NZ Army, 1964-65; Dir of Staff Duties, NZ Army, 1966; IDC, 1967; QMG, 1968-69; Dep. Chief of Defence Staff, 1970. *Recreations:* golf, fishing, gardening; Provincial and Services Rugby representative, in youth. *Address:* 13 Stapleford Crescent, Browns Bay, Auckland, New Zealand.

PEARCE, Malcolm Arthur Fraser, CVO 1954; CBE 1946; AASA; *b* 19 April 1898; *s* of J. S. Pearce, Kapunda; *m* 1st, 1922, Gladys M. (*d* 1958), *d* of J. Green, Wayville, SA; one *s* one *d* (and one *d* decd); 2nd, 1959, Ivy, *widow* of Rev. F. V. Duffy, Kaniva, Victoria. *Educ:* Kapunda High Sch., SA. Entered Attorney-General's Dept, 1914; Private Secretary and later Official Secretary to Premiers of SA, 1926-54; Under-Secretary, State of SA, Secretary to Minister of Health, Clerk of Exec. Council, 1954-61; Chairman, State Bank Board, 1948-61; Chairman, SA Symphony Orch. Cttee, 1949-61; Member, SA Public Debt Commn, 1954-61; Agent-General and Trade Commissioner for South Australia in the UK, 1961-66. Visited England for Jubilee Celebrations, 1935; for Coronation Celebrations, 1953; South Australian State Director for Royal Visits, 1954 (CVO) and 1958. Vice-Pres., Meals on Wheels Organisation. *Recreations:* golf, bowls. *Address:* 10 Newcastle Street, Heathpool, Adelaide, SA 5068, Australia. *T:* 316371. *Clubs:* Royal Automobile; Glenelg Golf (Adelaide).

PEARCE, Philippa; *see* Pearce, A. P.

PEARCE, Hon. Richard Bruce Holroyd, QC 1969; a Recorder of the Crown Court, since 1972; *b* 12 May 1930; *s* of Lord Pearce, *qv*, and Erica, *d* of late Bertram Priestman, RA; *m* 1958, Dornie Smith-Pert; one *s* one *d*. *Educ:* Charterhouse; Corpus Christi Coll., Oxford (MA). Served HM Forces, 1949-56: RE and E African Engrs, 1949-50; 119 Field Engr Regt RE, TA, 1950-56. Called to Bar, Lincoln's Inn, 1955; *ad eund*. Mem., Middle Temple, 1958. A Legal Assessor to GMC, 1974-; GDC, 1974-; GNC, 1975-. Master, Skinner's Co., 1976-77. Governor, Tonbridge School. *Address:* Sweethaws, Crowborough, East Sussex. *T:* Crowborough 3888.

PEARCE-HIGGINS, Rev. Canon John Denis; Hon. Chaplain to the Forces; Residentiary Canon and Vice-Provost of Southwark, 1963-71, now Emeritus; *b* 1 June 1905; 2nd *s* of late Prof. Alexander Pearce Higgins and Mina MacLennan; *m* 1938, Margaret Edna, 2nd *d* of Harry and Marguerite Hodge, Kettering; two *s* three *d*. *Educ:* St Faith's Sch., Cambridge; Rugby Sch. (scholar); Gonville and Caius Coll., Cambridge (schol. and prizeman). Charles Winter Warr Research Schol. in Ancient Philosophy, 1928; 1st class hons Parts I and II Class. Tripos; Research at Vienna Univ., 1928-29; Ripon Hall Theological Coll., 1934-37. Priest, 1937; Curate: St Agnes, Cotteridge; Priory Church, Malvern, 1940. Chaplain in RAChD, Oct. 1940-Nov. 1945 (invalided; Overseas, Africa Star, Italy, Defence and Victory medals). Vicar of Hanley Castle, Worcs, 1945-53; OCF; Chaplain and Sen. Divinity Lecturer, City of Worcester Training Coll., 1946-53; Vicar of Putney, St Mary with St John and All Saints, Surrogate, 1953-63. Chairman, Modern Churchmen's Union, 1958-68. Vice-Chairman, Churches' Fellowship for Psychical and Spiritual Studies, 1961-. Member Society for Psychical Research. *Publications:* Resurrection, 1959; (ed) Life, Death and Psychical Research, 1973; articles in: Modern Churchman, Journal of SPR. *Recreations:* music, painting, swimming. *Address:* 37 Erpingham Road, Putney, SW15 1BQ. *T:* 01-788 4573.

PEARD, Rear-Admiral Sir Kenyon (Harry Terrell), KBE 1958 (CBE 1951); retired; *b* 1902; *s* of Henry T. Peard; *m* 1935, Mercy Leila Bone; one *s* one *d*. *Educ:* RN Colleges, Osborne and Dartmouth. Went to sea, 1919; Torpedo Specialist, 1929; transferred to Electrical Branch, 1946, Director, Naval Electrical Dept, Admiralty, 1955-58; retired 1958. *Address:* Finstead, Shorefield Crescent, Milford-on-Sea, Hants.

PEARKES, Maj.-Gen. Hon. George Randolph, VC 1918; CC (Canada) 1967; PC (Canada) 1957; CB 1943; DSO 1919; MC; Legion of Merit (US); Lieutenant-Governor, British Columbia, 1960-67, retired; *b* Watford, Herts, 26 Feb. 1888; *m* Constance Blytha, *o d* of W. F. U. Copeman, Sidney, BC; one *s*. *Educ:* Berkhamsted Sch. Went to Canada; farmed for three years; joined Royal N-W Mounted Police, 1909; enlisted in Canadian Expeditionary Force, 1914; arrived in France, Sept. 1915; Bombing Sgt, Dec. 1915; Lieut on the field, March 1916; Battalion Bombing Officer; Brigade Bombing Officer; Captain, Oct. 1916; Major, Nov. 1917; took command of Battalion, Dec. 1917 (VC, MC, despatches, wounded several times); passed Staff

Coll., Camberley, 1919; served on the General Staff of Permanent Force of Canada as GSO at Calgary, Winnipeg, Esquimalt and Kingston; DMT and SD; at Imperial Defence Coll., 1937; DOC, MD 13, Calgary, 1938-40; GOC First Canadian Division, 1940; GOC-in-C Pacific Command, Canada, 1942-45; retired April, 1945. Minister of National Defence, 1957-60. Hon. LLD, University of British Columbia. *Address:* 1268 Tattersall Drive, Victoria, BC, Canada. *Club:* Union (Victoria).

PEARMAN, Sir James (Eugene), Kt 1973; CBE 1960; Senior Partner, Conyers, Dill & Pearman; *b* 24 Nov. 1904; *o s* of Eugene Charles Pearman and Kate Trott; *m* 1929, Prudence Tucker Appleby (*d* 1976); two *s*; *m* 1977, Mrs Antoinette Trott, *d* of Dr and Mrs James Aigier, Philadelphia, Pa. *Educ:* Saltus Grammar Sch., Bermuda; Bromsgrove Sch., Worcs; Merton Coll., Oxford; Middle Temple. Law partnership with N. B. Dill, 1927-29; law partnership with Sir Reginald Conyers and N. B. Dill, 1929 and still continuing as firm of Conyers, Dill & Pearman. Member Colonial Parlt, Bermuda, 1943-72; MEC, 1955-63 and 1968-72; MLC, 1972-. Hon. Consul for Bolivia. *Recreations:* deep-sea fishing, bridge. *Address:* Tideway, Point Shares, Pembroke, Bermuda. *T:* 1-3029. *Clubs:* Bath; Royal and Ancient (St Andrews); Rod and Reel (Miami); Royal Bermuda Yacht.

PEARS, David Francis, FBA 1970; Student of Christ Church, Oxford, since 1960; Reader in Philosophy, Oxford University, since 1972; *b* 8 Aug. 1921; *s* of Robert and late Gladys Pears; *m* 1963, Anne Drew; one *s* one *d*. *Educ:* Westminster Sch.; Balliol Coll., Oxford. Research Lecturer, Christ Church, 1948-50; Univ. Lectr, Oxford, 1950-72; Fellow and Tutor, Corpus Christi Coll., 1950-60. Visiting Professor: Harvard, 1959; Univ. of Calif, Berkeley, 1964; Rockefeller Univ., 1967; Hill Prof., Univ. of Minnesota, 1970; Humanities Council Res. Fellow, Princeton, 1966. Governor, Westminster Sch., 1976; Delegate of Oxford Univ. Press, 1976. *Publications:* (trans. with B. McGuinness), Wittgenstein, Tractatus Logico-Philosophicus, 1961, repr. 1975; Bertrand Russell and the British Tradition in Philosophy, 1967, 2nd edn 1972; Ludwig Wittgenstein, 1971; What is Knowledge?, 1971; (ed) Russell's Logical Atomism, 1973; Some Questions in the Philosophy of Mind, 1975. *Address:* 31 Northmoor Road, Oxford. *T:* Oxford 54767.

PEARS, Harold Snowden; His Honour Judge Pears; a Circuit Judge (formerly Judge of County Courts, since 1971); *b* 21 April 1926; *s* of late Harold Pears and Florence Elizabeth (*née* Snowden); *m* 1960, Inge Haumann, *d* of late Heinrich Elvensø, and Agnes Elvensø, Denmark; no *c*. *Educ:* Dauntsey's Sch.; Emmanuel Coll., Cambridge (MA). Called to the Bar, Inner Temple, 1948; North Eastern Circuit, 1948-71. Dep. Chm., W Riding QS, 1967-71; Recorder of Doncaster, 1968-71, Hon. Recorder of Doncaster, 1972-75; Hon. Recorder of Sheffield, 1976. Legal Mem., Mental Health Review Tribunal, 1964-71. *Recreations:* boats, travel, fishing. *Address:* 35 Whirlow Park Road, Sheffield S11 9NN. *T:* Sheffield 366244. *Club:* Sheffield (Sheffield).

PEARS, Peter, CBE 1957; Tenor; *b* 22 June 1910; *s* of Arthur and Jessie Pears. *Educ:* Lancing; Oxford; Royal College of Music. BBC Singers, 1934-37; New English Singers, 1936-38; began American and European tours with Benjamin Britten, 1939, with Julian Bream, 1956, with Osian Ellis, 1972. Sadler's Wells Opera, 1943-46; Peter Grimes in Peter Grimes 1945 and 1960; English Opera Gp. 1947; Covent Garden Opera, 1948; Aschenbach in Death in Venice, NY Met., 1974; Co-Founder of Aldeburgh Festival, 1948. Pres., Incorporated Soc. of Musicians, 1970. First performed many new works by Britten, Tippett, Berkeley, etc. Cramb Lectr, Univ. of Glasgow, 1961. FRCM; Hon. RAM; DUniv York, 1969; Hon. DLitt Sussex, 1971; Hon. MusD Cantab, 1972; Hon. DMus Evansville (Indiana), 1976; Hon. DMus Edinburgh, 1976. *Publications:* (with Benjamin Britten) Purcell Edition, 1948-. *Address:* c/o Phipps, 8 Halliford Street, N1.

PEARS, Rear-Admiral Steuart Arnold, CBE 1950; DL; retired 1956; *b* 24 Feb. 1894; *e s* of S. D. Pears, President Municipality, Madras; *m* 1916, Anne Biggins; one *s* two *d*. *Educ:* RN Colleges, Osborne and Dartmouth. Sub-Lieut, 1914; Lieut, 1916; Lieut-Commander, 1924; Commander, 1934; Captain, 1947; Rear-Admiral, 1953. Served HMS Hercules, 1911; King George V, 1913; Falmouth, 1914; Oak, 1916; Excellent, 1919; Campbell, 1922; Reserve Fleet, 1924. Executive Officer Visit of Prince of Wales to S. America, 1925; lost right leg, 1926; transf. Inspection Research Design and Experimental Duties, 1927; Research Dept, 1928; Naval Ordnance Inspection Officer, Plymouth, 1932, Mediterranean, 1936; Supt. Experimental Establishment, Pendine, 1940; Chief Inspector, 1947; Vice-

President Ordnance Board, 1953; President, 1955; Master, Lord Leycester Hospital, Warwick, 1958-66. DL Warwickshire, 1959. *Recreation:* anything out-of-doors. *Address:* Chalcroft, Cliff Way, Compton, Winchester. *Club:* Royal Navy of 1765 and 1785 (United 1889).

PEARSE, Prof. Anthony Guy Everson, MA, MD (Cantab); FRCP, FRCPath; DCP (London); Professor of Histochemistry, University of London, Royal Postgraduate Medical School, since 1965; *b* 9 Aug. 1916; *o s* of Captain R. G. Pearse, DSO, MC, Modbury, Devon, and Constance Evelyn Steels, Pocklington, Yorks; *m* 1947, Elizabeth Himmelhoch, MB, BS (Sydney), DCP (London); one *s* three *d. Educ:* Sherborne Sch.; Trinity Coll., Cambridge. Kitchener Scholar, Raymond Horton-Smith prizeman, 1949-50. Posts, St Bart's Hospital, 1940-41; Surg.-Lt, RNVR, 1941-45. Registrar, Edgware General Hospital, 1946; Asst Lecturer in Pathol., PG Med. School, London, 1947-51, Lecturer, 1951-57; Cons. Pathol., Hammersmith Hospital, 1951; Fulbright Fellow and Visiting Prof. of Path., University of Alabama, 1953-54; Guest Instructor in Histochemistry, University of Kansas, 1957, 1958; Vanderbilt Univ., 1967; Reader in Histochemistry, University of London, 1957-65; Middleton Goldsmith Lectr, NY Path. Soc., 1976. Member: Path. Society (GB), 1949; Biochem. Society (GB), 1957; European Gastro Club, 1969; Hon. Member or Member various foreign societies incl. Deutsche Akademie der Naturforscher Leopoldina, 1973; Hon. Fellow, Royal Microscop. Society, 1964 (Vice-Pres., 1970-72; Pres., 1972-74). MD (Basel) *hc* 1960. Member Editorial Board: Histochemie, 1958-73; Jl Histochem. Cytochem., 1959-68; Enzymol. biol. clin., 1961-67; Brain Research, 1968-76; Cardiovascular Research, 1968-75; Virchow's Archiv 'B', 1968-; Histochemical Jl, 1968-; Jl of Royal Microscopical Soc., 1967-69; Jl Microscopy, 1969-; Jl of Neuro-visceral Relations, 1969-73; Jl of Molecular and Cellular Cardiology, 1970-; Histochem. Jl, 1970-; Scand. Jl Gastroenterol., 1971-; Jl Neural Transmission, 1973-76; Jl of Pathology, 1973-; Histochemistry, 1974-; Editor, Medical Biology, 1974-. *Publications:* Histochemistry Theoretical and Applied, 2nd edn, 1960, 3rd edn, vol. I, 1968, vol. II, 1972. Numerous papers on theoretical and applied histochemistry, esp. endocrinology. *Recreations:* horticulture (plant hybridization, Liliaceae); foreign touring (motoring, camping). *Address:* The Fortress, Letchmore Heath, Hertfordshire. *T:* Radlett 6466. *Club:* Naval.

PEARSE, Rear-Adm. John Roger Southey G.; *see* Gerard-Pearse.

PEARSON, family name of **Viscount Cowdray** and of **Baron Pearson.**

PEARSON, Baron (Life Peer), *cr* 1965; **Colin Hargreaves Pearson,** PC 1961; Kt 1951; CBE 1946; a Lord of Appeal in Ordinary, 1965-74; *b* 28 July 1899; 2nd *s* of Ernest William and Jessie Borland Pearson, Minnedosa, Manitoba, Canada; *m* 1931, Sophie Grace, *e d* of Arthur Hermann Thomas, LLD, DLitt, FSA, Worthing; one *s* one *d. Educ:* St Paul's Sch.; Balliol Coll., Oxford (Classical Scholar and Jenkyns Exhibitioner); Military service, Feb.-Dec. 1918; called to Bar, 1924; Yarborough Anderson Exhibition, Inner Temple, 1925, Reader, 1973, Treasurer, 1974; Junior Common Law Counsel to Ministry of Works, 1930-49; KC 1949; Recorder of Hythe, 1937-51; Judge of High Court of Justice, Queen's Bench Division, 1951-61; Judge of Restrictive Practices Court, 1957-61 (President, 1960-61); a Lord Justice of Appeal, 1961-65. Temporary member of Treasury Solicitor's Department, 1939-45. Member: Legal Cttee on Medical Partnerships, 1948; Supreme Court Rule Cttee, 1957-65; Exec. Council of the Inns of Court, 1962-65; Senate of Inns of Court, 1966-69. Chm., Royal Commn on Civil Liability and Compensation for Personal Injury, 1973-. Chairman: Cttee on Funds in Court, 1958; Law Reform Cttee, 1963-73. Chairman, Courts of Inquiry: into a dispute in the Electricity Supply Industry, 1964; into a dispute in the Shipping Industry, 1966-67; into a dispute in Civil Air Transport Industry, 1967-68; into a dispute in Steel Industry, 1968; the Dock Strike, 1970; Chm. Arbitral Body on Teachers' Renumeration, 1971, 1972. Visitor, Balliol Coll., Oxford, 1965-74; President, Old Pauline Club, 1960-63; Chairman, St Paul's School Building Appeal, 1966-; Member Council, Bedford Coll., University of London (Vice-Chairman, 1959-62, Chairman, 1962-63), 1958-66. President, Inc. Assoc. of Preparatory Schools, 1965-70. *Address:* 2 Crown Office Row, Temple, EC4. *T:* 01-353 5391. *Clubs:* Garrick, Roehampton.

PEARSON, Brig. Alastair Stevenson, CB 1958; DSO; OBE 1953; MC; TD; DL; Farmer; *b* 1 June 1915; *m* 1944, Mrs Joan Morgan Weld-Smith; three *d. Educ:* Kelvinside Acad.; Sedbergh. Coy. Director, 1936-39; served War of 1939-45 (MC, DSO, and three Bars); embodied 6th Bn Highland LI, TA, 1939; transferred to Parachute Regt, 1941; Lt-Col 1942. Commanding Officer 15th (Scottish) Bn The Parachute Regt (TA), 1947-53; Dep. Comd 46 Parachute Bde (TA), 1953-59. Comd Scotland Army Cadet Force, Brigadier, 1967-. ADC to the Queen, 1956-61. Hon. Colonel, 15th (Scottish) Bn The Parachute Regt (TA), 1963-77. DL Glasgow, 1951. *Address:* Tullochan, Gartocharn, By Alexandria, Dunbartonshire. *T:* Gartocharn 205.

PEARSON, Arthur, CBE 1949; JP; *b* 31 Jan. 1897; *s* of William Pearson, Pontypridd, Glamorgan. MP (Lab) Pontypridd, 1938-70, retired; Labour Whip, 1939-45; Comptroller of HM Household, 1945-46; Treasurer of HM Household, 1946-51; an Opposition Whip, 1951-64. JP 1939, CC 1928-46, Glamorgan. *Address:* 24 The Avenue, Pontypridd, Mid Glamorgan.

PEARSON, Bertram Lamb, CB 1947; DSO 1917; MC; *b* 1893; *y s* of late William Pearson of Wakefield, Yorkshire, and late Mary Ann Pearson; *m* 1920, Gladys Mary, *er d* of John Stewart of Yapham Hall, Pocklington, East Yorkshire. *Educ:* Bedford Grammar Sch.; Wakefield Grammar Sch.; The Queen's Coll., Oxford; 1st Hastings Exhibitioner and Honorary Scholar; 1st Class Honour (Classical) Moderations, 1913; 1st Class Literæ Humaniores, 1919. Served European War, 1914-19, as Captain, The Green Howards (wounded twice, despatches, MC, DSO); tutor, The Queen's Coll., Oxford, 1919-20; Private Sec. to Permanent Sec., Bd of Educn, 1924-28; Principal Private Sec. to President, Board of Educn, 1937; Accountant-General to Min. of Educn, 1944-55; Under-Secretary, 1946-55. Member Council: Central Council of Physical Recreation, 1956-; Girls' Public Day School Trust, 1958-69. *Recreations:* cricket, bowls, reading. *Address:* 15 Queen's Court, Queen's Road, Cheltenham, Glos GL50 2LU.

PEARSON, David Morris, OBE 1969 (MBE 1945); HM Diplomatic Service, retired; Ambassador to the Republic of Honduras, 1972-75; *b* 21 July 1915; *s* of late Bedlington Pearson and late Margaret Elizabeth Williams; *m* 1945, Camille Henriette Etey; no *c. Educ:* Kelvinside Academy, Glasgow; Sedbergh Sch.; Glasgow University. HM Forces, 1939-46 (Intell. Corps, then SOE in France, leading Pedagogy Mission). Personnel Manager, Gold Coast Main Reef Ltd, 1946-50; Sierra Leone Administrative Service, 1950-59; seconded to Foreign Service, in Consulate-General, Dakar, Senegal, 1954-59; entered Foreign Service, 1959; FO, 1960-62; Head of Chancery, Brazzaville, 1962-65; Rio de Janeiro, 1965-67; Kinshasa, 1967-69; Consul-Gen., Casablanca, 1969-72. French Croix de Guerre (with star), 1945. *Recreations:* music, reading, foreign travel. *Address:* 6 Wells Close, Tenterden, Kent. *Club:* Atlanta (Glasgow).

PEARSON, Sir Denning; *see* Pearson, Sir J. D.

PEARSON, Derek Leslie; Deputy Secretary, Cabinet Office, since 1975; *b* 19 Dec. 1921; *s* of late George Frederick Pearson and Edith Maud Pearson (*née* Dent); *m* 1956, Diana Mary, *d* of late Sir Ralph Freeman; no *c. Educ:* William Ellis Sch.; London Sch. of Economics. BSc (Econ). Observer, FAA, 1941-45. Colonial Office: Asst Principal, 1947; Principal, 1949; seconded to Kenya, 1954-56; Principal Private Sec. to Sec. of State for Colonies, 1959-61; Dept of Technical Cooperation, 1961; Asst Sec., 1962; ODM, 1964; Under Secretary: CSD, 1970-72; Min. of Overseas Develt, 1972-75. *Recreations:* none. *Address:* Hadlow, Hazelwood Lane, Chipstead, Surrey. *Clubs:* Naval, Civil Service.

PEARSON, Egon Sharpe, CBE 1946; FRS 1966; MA, DSc; Professor Emeritus, University of London; Statistical Consultant, British Standards Institution; *b* 11 Aug. 1895; *s* of late Karl Pearson, FRS; *m* 1st, 1934, Eileen (*d* 1949), *yr d* of Russell Jolly; two *d*; 2nd, 1967, Margaret Turner (*née* Scott) (*d* 1975), *widow* of L. B. Turner, ScD, MIEE. *Educ:* Dragon Sch., Oxford; Winchester Coll.; Trinity Coll., Cambridge. Lecturer in Statistics at University College, London, 1921-33; Reader, 1933-35, Professor, 1935-60. Managing Editor, Biometrika, 1936-66, and Editor of Auxiliary Publications, 1966-75. Attached to Ordnance Bd, Min. of Supply later MoD, 1939-46, Assoc. Mem., 1943-. President, Royal Statistical Society, 1955-57; Guy Medal in Gold of the Royal Statistical Society, 1955. Hon. Member Institute of Actuaries, 1956. Medal of Freedom with Bronze Palm, USA, 1947. *Publications:* Papers on the mathematical theory of statistics and its applications, in Biometrika and other journals; editor of several vols of Statistical Tables; pamphlet for the British Standards Institution on the application of statistical method in problems of standardisation and quality control, 1935. *Recreations:* classical music, 'match of the day'. *Address:* University College, Gower Street, WC1E 6BT.

PEARSON, Sir Francis Fenwick, 1st Bt, *cr* 1964; MBE 1945; JP; DL; Chairman, Central Lancashire New Town Development Corporation, since 1971; *b* 13 June 1911; *s* of Frank Pearson, solicitor, Kirby Lonsdale, and Susan Mary Pearson; *m* 1938, Katharine Mary Fraser; one *s* one *d. Educ:* Uppingham; Trinity Hall, Cambridge. 1st Gurkha Rifles, 1932; ADC to Viceroy of India, 1934-36; Indian Political Service, 1936; Under-Secretary, Political Dept, 1942-45; Chief Minister, Manipur State, 1945-47; retired, 1947. MP (C) Clitheroe, Oct. 1959-1970; Assistant Whip (unpaid), 1960-62; a Lord Commissioner of the Treasury, 1962-63; PPS to Prime Minister, Nov. 1963-Oct. 1964. JP Lancs, 1952; DL Co. Palatine of Lancaster, 1971. *Recreation:* fishing. *Heir: s* Francis Nicholas Fraser Pearson, *b* 28 Aug. 1943. *Address:* Gressingham Hall, Hornby, Lancs. *T:* Hornby 288. *Club:* Carlton.

PEARSON, Gerald Lionel, MC 1944; HM Diplomatic Service; Counsellor (Hong Kong Affairs), United Kingdom Mission to the Office of the United Nations and other International Organisations at Geneva, since 1971; *b* 11 Nov. 1918; *e s* of late Col H. S. I. Pearson, 5th (Royal) Mahratta LI; *m* 1st, 1945, Erica Mirrington-Mainwaring (marr. diss. 1963); one *s* one *d*; 2nd, 1964, Peggy Fallows. *Educ:* Wellington Coll.; Clare Coll., Cambridge (MA). Served War of 1939-45 (MC): S Wales Borderers and Parachute Regt; Captain 1940; discharged (wounded), 1945. BoT, 1945; British Trade Comr, Dublin, 1959-67; Counsellor (Commercial), Brit. Embassy, The Hague, 1967-71. *Recreations:* fishing, bird-watching. *Address:* c/o Foreign and Commonwealth Office, SW1; UK Mission, 37-39 rue de Vermont, Geneva, Switzerland. *T:* Geneva 34 90 40. *Clubs:* Junior Carlton, Royal Over-Seas League; Kildare Street and University (Dublin).

PEARSON, Air Commodore Herbert Macdonald, CBE 1944; RAF retired; *b* Buenos Aires, Argentina, 17 Nov. 1908; *s* of John Charles Pearson; *m* 1939, Jane Leslie; one *s* two *d. Educ:* Cheltenham Coll.; Cranwell. Left Cranwell, 1928; Malta, 1929-31; Central Flying Sch., 1932; Instructor, Cranwell, 1933-34; attached to Peruvian Government, 1935-36; Asst Air Attaché in Spain, 1936-38; comd No. 54 Sqdn, 1938-39. War of 1939-45, in Fighter Command; then France, Belgium and Germany; Air Attaché, Lima, Peru, 1946; Deputy Director Air Foreign Liaison, Air Ministry, 1949; Commanding Royal Air Force, Kai Tak, Hong Kong, 1951-53; Assistant Chief of Staff Intelligence, Headquarters of Allied Air Forces, Central Europe, 1953-55. Air Commodore, 1953; retired, 1955. *Address:* Mapleridge Barn, Horton, S Glos. *Club:* Naval and Military.

PEARSON, Sir (James) Denning, Kt 1963; JP; Consultant, Chairman and Chief Executive, Rolls-Royce Ltd, 1969-70; Chairman, Gamma Associates, since 1972; *b* 8 Aug. 1908; *s* of James Pearson and Elizabeth Henderson; *m* 1932, Eluned Henry; two *d. Educ:* Canton Secondary Sch., Cardiff; Cardiff Technical Coll. Senior Wh. Scholarship; BSc Eng. Joined Rolls-Royce Ltd, 1932; Technical Production Engineer, Glasgow Factory, 1941; Chief Quality and Service Engineer (resident in Canada for one year), 1941-45; Gen. Man. Sales and Service, 1946-49; Director, 1949; Director and Gen. Man., Aero Engine Division, 1950; Managing Director (Aero Engine Div.), 1954-65; Chief Exec. and Dep. Chm., 1957-68. President, SBAC, 1963; Member, NEDC, 1964-67. CEng; FRAeS, 1957-64; Hon. FRAeS, 1964; Hon. FIMechE; FBIM; DrIngEh Brunswick Univ., 1962. Member: Council, Manchester Business Sch.; Governing Body, London Graduate Sch. of Business Studies, 1968-70; Governing Body, Admin. Staff Coll., Henley, 1968-73; Council, Voluntary Service Overseas. Fellow, Imperial Coll. of Science and Technology, 1968-; Hon. Fellow, Manchester Univ. Inst. of Science and Technology, 1969; Hon. DSc: Nottingham, 1966; Wales, 1968; Cranfield Inst. of Technology, 1970; Hon. DTech: Loughborough, 1968; CNAA, 1969. Gold Medal, Royal Aero Club, 1969; Benjamin Franklin Medal, RSA, 1970. FRSA, 1970. *Recreations:* reading, golf, tennis, sailing. *Address:* Green Acres, Holbrook, Derbyshire. *T:* Derby 881137.

PEARSON, Prof. James Douglas; Professor of Bibliography, with reference to Asia and Africa, School of Oriental and African Studies, University of London, since 1972; *b* 17 Dec. 1911; *m* 1st, Rose Betty Burden (marr. diss.); one *s*; 2nd, Hilda M. Wilkinson; three *s. Educ:* Cambridge Univ. (MA). Asst Under-librarian, Cambridge Univ. Library, 1939-50; Librarian, Sch. of Oriental and African Studies, Univ. of London, 1950-72. Hon. FLA, 1976. *Publications:* Index Islamicus, 1958-; Oriental and Asian Bibliography, 1966; Oriental Manuscripts in Europe and North America, 1971. *Recreations:* natural history, walking. *Address:* 79 Highsett, Hills Road, Cambridge.

PEARSON, Sir (James) Reginald, Kt 1959; OBE 1950; DL; retired in Nov. 1962 as Deputy Chairman (1958) and Executive Assistant to Managing Director (1953), Vauxhall Motors Ltd, Luton, Beds; *b* 17 Nov. 1897; *s* of George Henry Pearson and Annie Pearson (*née* Stringer); *m* 1925, Nellie Rose Vittery (*d* 1977); one *d. Educ:* Dudley, Worcestershire. Apprenticed at Bullers Ltd, Tipton; National Projectile Factory, Dudley; Vauxhall Motors Ltd (1919); Craftsman, Journeyman, Foreman, Area Manager, Production Manager, Factory Manager, Director (1946). Chairman, Dawley Development Corporation, 1962-68. Vice-President, Royal Society for the Prevention of Accidents. High Sheriff of Bedfordshire, 1964; DL Beds, 1968. FIMechE; MIProdE. *Recreations:* golf, gardening; interested in all forms of sport; Hon. Life President, Vauxhall Motors Recreation Club. *Address:* 45 Bloomfield Road, Harpenden, Herts. *T:* Harpenden 3052.

PEARSON, Sir Neville, 2nd Bt *cr* 1916; *b* 13 Feb. 1898; *s* of 1st Bt, and Ethel Lady Pearson, DBE; *S* father, 1921; *m* 1st, 1922, Mary Angela (marr. diss. 1928, she *m* 1928, C. Willoughby Hordern and *d* 1937), 2nd *d* of 1st Baron Melchett; one *d* (one *s* decd); 2nd, 1928, Gladys Cooper (later Dame Gladys Cooper, DBE) (*d* 1971), (marr. diss. 1937; she *m* 1937, Philip Merivale); one *d*; 3rd, 1943, Mrs Anne Davis Elebash, New York. *Educ:* Eton. RFA, European War, 1917-18; subsequently entered firm of C. Arthur Pearson, Ltd; publishers; retired from all directorships, 1968. President St Dunstan's; President Fresh Air Fund. AA Artillery, War of 1939-45. *Heir:* none. *Address:* Chesham House, 30 Chesham Place, SW1. *Club:* Bath.
See also Baron Glenkinglas.

PEARSON, Norman Charles, OBE 1944; TD 1944; Lay Member, Restrictive Practices Court, since 1968; Director, United Kingdom Provident Institution since 1965; Deputy Chairman, Cincinnati Milacron Ltd, since 1972; *b* 12 Aug. 1909; *s* of late Max Pearson and Kate Pearson; *m* 1951, Olive May, *d* of late Kenneth Harper and Ruth Harper, Granston Manor, Co. Leix; one *s* one *d. Educ:* Harrow Sch. (Scholar); Gonville and Caius Coll., Cambridge (Sayer Scholar). Commnd Royal Signals (TA), 1932; Middx Yeomanry; served War of 1939-45, N Africa (despatches, OBE), Italy, Greece; Lt-Col 1942; comd 6th Armd Div. Signals, 1944; 10 Corps Signals; Mil. Comd Athens Signals; 4th Div. Signals, 1945; subseq. re-formed 56 Div. Signals Regt (TA). Boots Pure Drug Co. Ltd, 1931-37; Borax (Holdings) Ltd, 1937-69; Director, 1951. Mem., Air Transport Licensing Bd, 1971-72. *Recreation:* gardening. *Address:* 61 Albert Hall Mansions, SW7 2AG. *T:* 01-589 7595; Copt Heath, Cold Ash, Newbury, Berks. *Club:* Junior Carlton.

PEARSON, Mrs R. O'Neill; *see* Robins, Mrs Denise.

PEARSON, Sir Reginald; *see* Pearson, Sir J. R.

PEARSON, Rt. Rev. Thomas Bernard; Titular Bishop of Sinda, since 1949; Bishop Auxiliary in the Diocese of Lancaster, 1952-62, and since 1965; Episcopal Vicar for Cumbria (formerly Cumberland, Westmorland and Furness), since 1967; *b* Preston, Lancs, 18 January 1907; *s* of Joseph Pearson and Alice (*née* Cartmell). *Educ:* Upholland College; Ven. English College, Rome. Pontifical Gregorian University, Rome; PhD 1930; Bachelor of Canon Law, Licent. Sacred Theology, 1933. Priest, 1933; Assistant Priest, 1934-44; Parish Priest, St Cuthbert's, Blackpool, 1944-67. Mem., Order of Discalced Carmelites, 1974. *Recreation:* mountaineering. *Address:* Howard Lodge, 90 Warwick Road, Carlisle CA1 1JU. *T:* Carlisle 24952. *Clubs:* Alpine, Fell and Rock, English Lake District; Achille Ratti Climbing (Founder President).

PEARSON, Gen. Sir Thomas (Cecil Hook), KCB 1967 (CB 1964); CBE 1959 (OBE 1953); DSO 1940, and Bar, 1943; retired 1974; *b* 1 July 1914; *s* of late Vice-Admiral J. L. Pearson, CMG; *m* 1947, Aud, *d* of late Alf Skjelkvale, Oslo; two *s. Educ:* Charterhouse; Sandhurst. 2nd Lieutenant Rifle Bde, 1934. Served War of 1939-45, M East and Europe; CO 2nd Bn The Rifle Bde, 1942; Dep. Comdr 2nd Independent Parachute Bde Gp 1944; Dep. Comdr 1st Air-landing Bde 1945; GSO1 1st Airborne Div. 1945; CO 1st Bn The Parachute Regt 1946; CO 7th Bn The Parachute Regt 1947; GSO1 (Land Air Warfare), WO, 1948; JSSC, GSO1, HQ Malaya, 1950; GSO1 (Plans), FARELF, 1951; Directing Staff, JSSC, 1953; Comdr 45 Parachute Bde TA 1955; Nat. Defence Coll., Canada, 1956; Comdr 16 Indep. Parachute Bde 1957; Chief of Staff to Dir of Ops Cyprus, 1960; Head of Brit. Mil. Mission to Soviet Zone of Germany, 1960; Major-General Commanding 1st Division, BAOR, 1961-63; Chief of Staff, Northern Army Group, 1963-67; Comdr, FARELF, 1967-68; Military Sec., MoD, 1968-72; C-in-C, Allied Forces, Northern Europe, 1972-74; psc 1942; jssc 1950; ndc Canada 1957. ADC Gen. to the Queen, 1974-. Col Comdt, the Royal Green Jackets, 1973. Haakon VII Liberty Cross, 1948; Medal of Honour, Norwegian Defence Assoc.,

1973. *Recreations:* field sports, yachting. *Address:* Streete House, Weston under Penyard, Ross on Wye, Herefordshire HR9 7NY. *Clubs:* Naval and Military; Island Sailing, Kongelig Norsk Seilforenning.

PEARSON, William Thomas Shipston; Counsellor (Defence Research), British High Commission, Canberra, and Head of British Defence Research and Supply Staffs, Australia, since 1977; *b* 21 Aug. 1917; *s* of William Pearson and Alice (*née* Shipston); *m* 1948, Pauline Daphne Scott (*née* Wilkinson); one *s* two *d*. *Educ:* High Pavement Sch., Nottingham; University Coll., Nottingham (BSc). MRAeS, CEng. Appts at RAE, 1939-45; Hon. Commn, Flying Officer, RAFVR, 1944; Blind Landing Experimental Unit, Martlesham Heath, 1945-47; RAF Transport Comd Develt Unit, 1947-50; TRE, 1950-52; seconded to Australian Scientific Service, Long Range Weapons Estab., 1952-56; RAE, Farnborough, 1956-62; Asst Dir, Air Armaments, Min. of Aviation, 1962-65; Div. Head, Weapons Dept, RAE (concerned with various projs), 1965-76; seconded to FCO, 1977-. *Publications:* official reports. *Recreation:* photography. *Address:* 71 National Circuit, Deakin, Canberra, ACT 2600, Australia. *T:* 731013. *Club:* Commonwealth (Canberra).

PEART, family name of **Baron Peart.**

PEART, Baron *cr* 1976 (Life Peer), of Workington; **(Thomas) Frederick Peart,** PC 1964; Lord Privy Seal and Leader of the House of Lords, since 1976; *b* 30 Apr. 1914; *m* 1945, Sarah Elizabeth Lewis; one *s*. *Educ:* Crook Council; Wolsingham Grammar; Henry Smith Secondary, Hartlepool; Bede Coll., Durham Univ. (BSc); Inner Temple, Inns of Court. Pres. Durham University Union Soc. Councillor Easington RDC, 1937-40. Became a Schoolmaster. Served War of 1939-45, commissioned Royal Artillery, served in North Africa and Italy. MP (Lab) Workington Div. of Cumberland, 1945-76; PPS to Minister of Agriculture, 1945-51; Minister of Agriculture, Fisheries and Food, 1964-68 and 1974-76; Leader of the House of Commons, 1968-70; Lord Privy Seal, April-Oct. 1968; Lord President of the Council, Oct. 1968-1970; Opposition Spokesman; House of Commons Matters, 1970-71; Agriculture, 1971-72; Defence, 1972-74; British Delegate to Council of Europe, 1952-55 (Rep. Agriculture Cttee and Cttee for Culture and Science (Vice-Pres.)). Privy Council Rep. on Council of RCVS, Dir, FMC, 1971-74. Chm. Adv. Council for Applied R&D, 1976-. Hon. DSc Cranfield, 1977. *Address:* House of Lords, SW1.

PEART, Brian; Under-Secretary, Ministry of Agriculture, Fisheries and Food, since 1976; *b* 17 Aug. 1925; *s* of late Joseph Garfield Peart and Frances Hannah Peart (*née* English); *m* 1952, Dorothy (*née* Thompson); one *s* one *d*. *Educ:* Wolsingham Grammar Sch.; Durham Univ. (BA). Served War, RAF, 1943-47. Agricultural Economist, Edinburgh Sch. of Agric., 1950-57; Sen. Agricultural Economist, 1957-64; Regional Farm Management Adviser, MAFF West Midlands Region, 1964-67; Chief Farm Management Adviser, MAFF, 1967-71; Regional Manager, MAFF, Yorks/Lancs Region, 1971-74; Head of Intelligence and Trng Div., 1974-76. *Recreations:* golf, bridge, The Times crossword. *Address:* 18 Derwent Close, Claygate, Surrey KT10 0RS. *Clubs:* Farmers', Civil Service.

PEART, Donald Richard, MA, BMus Oxon, FRCM; composer, conductor, violinist; First Professor of Music, University of Sydney, New South Wales, 1948-74, Professor Emeritus, 1975; founder and President of Pro Musica Society, Sydney University; *b* Fovant, Wilts, 9 Jan. 1909; *s* of Herbert and Dorothy Peart, Welling Hill, Haslemere, Surrey; *m* Ellen Lilian, *d* of W. H. Germon; one *s* one *d*. *Educ:* Cheltenham College (Scholar); Queen's College, Oxford (Bible Clerk). Osgood Memorial Prizeman, University of Oxford, 1932; studied at Royal College of Music, 1932-35; Librarian, 1935-39. War service, 1939-46; commissioned into The Gloucestershire Regt, 1940; served in W Africa, Burma, and India, 1942-46. Mem., Australian UNESCO Cttee for Music, 1956-68, Chm., 1965-68; Founder-Pres., Internat. Soc. for Contemp. Music (Australian Section) and of Musicological Society of Australia. Works include: two symphonies; cantata Red Night; string quartets, etc. *Recreations:* travelling, mountain climbing, etc. *Address:* 14 Windward Avenue, Mosman, NSW 2088, Australia. *T:* 9694308.

PEART, Prof. William Stanley, MD; FRS 1969; Professor of Medicine, University of London, at St Mary's Hospital Medical School since 1956; *b* 31 March 1922; *s* of J. G. and M. Peart; *m* 1947, Peggy Parkes; one *s* one *d*. *Educ:* King's College School, Wimbledon; Medical School, St Mary's Hospital. MB, BS

(Hons), 1945; FRCP, 1959; MD (London), 1949. Lecturer in Medicine, St Mary's Hospital, 1950-56. Member: Adv. Bd for Res. Councils; Beit Fellowship Cttee. Trustee, Wellcome Trust, 1975-. Goulstonian Lectr, RCP, 1959. Stouffer Prize, 1968. *Publications:* chapters in: Cecil-Loeb, Textbook of Medicine; Renal Disease; Biochemical Disorders in Human Disease; articles in Biochemical Journal, Journal of Physiology, Lancet. *Recreations:* reading, tennis. *Address:* 5 Fordington Road, N6. *T:* 01-883 9346.

PEASE, family name of **Barons Daryngton, Gainford,** and **Wardington.**

PEASE, Sir (Alfred) Vincent, 4th Bt *cr* 1882; *b* 2 April 1926; *s* of Sir Alfred (Edward) Pease, 2nd Bt (*d* 1939), and of his 3rd wife, Emily Elizabeth (Dowager Lady Pease, JP); *S* half-brother, 1963; unmarried. *Educ:* Bootham School, York. *Heir: b* Joseph Gurney Pease [*b* 16 Nov. 1927; *m* 1953, Shelagh Munro, *d* of C. G. Bulman; one *s* one *d*]. *Address:* Baysdale Cottage, Pinchinthorpe, Guisborough, Cleveland. *T:* Guisborough 2578.

PEASE, Dr Rendel Sebastian, FRS 1977; Director, Culham Laboratory, UKAEA, since 1968; *b* 1922; *s* of Michael Stewart Pease and Helen Bowen (*née* Wedgwood); *m* 1952, Susan Spickernell; two *s* three *d*. *Educ:* Bedales Sch.; Trinity Coll., Cambridge (MA, ScD). Scientific Officer, Min. of Aircraft Prodn at ORS Unit, HQ, RAF Bomber Comd, 1942-46; research at AERE, Harwell, 1947-61; Div. Head, Culham Lab. for Plasma Physics and Nuclear Fusion, UKAEA, 1961-67; Vis. Scientist, Princeton Univ., 1964-65; Asst Dir, UKAEA Research Gp, 1967. Chairman: Adam Hilger Ltd, 1976-77; Plasma Physics Commn, Internat. Union of Pure and Applied Physics, 1975; Internat. Fusion Res. Council, Internat. Atomic Energy Agency, 1976. Member: Fabian Soc.; Inst. of Physics and Physical Soc. (Vice-Pres., 1973-77); Amer. Inst. of Physics. DUniv Surrey, 1973. *Publications:* articles in physics jls. *Recreation:* music. *Address:* The Poplars, West Ilsley, Newbury, Berks.

PEASE, Sir Richard (Thorn), 3rd Bt *cr* 1920; Vice-Chairman: Barclays Bank Ltd, since 1970; Barclays Bank UK Management, since 1971; *b* 20 May 1922; *s* of Sir Richard Arthur Pease, 2nd Bt, and Jeannette Thorn (*d* 1957), *d* of late Gustav Edward Kissel, New York; *S* father, 1969; *m* 1956, Anne, *d* of late Lt-Col Reginald Francis Heyworth; one *s* two *d*. *Educ:* Eton. Served with 60th Rifles, Middle East, Italy and Greece, 1941-46 (Captain). Director: Owners of the Middlesbrough Estate Ltd; First National Finance Corp. Ltd, 1975-; Bank of Scotland, 1977-; Yorkshire Bank Ltd, 1977. *Heir: s* Richard Peter Pease, *b* 4 Sept. 1958. *Address:* Hindley House, Stocksfield-on-Tyne, Northumberland.

PEASE, Sir Vincent; see Pease, Sir A. V.

PEAT, Charles Urie, MC; MA, FCA; *b* 1892; *s* of late Sir Wm Barclay Peat, CVO; *m* 1914, Ruth Martha, *d* of Rev. Henry John Pulley; two *s* four *d*. *Educ:* Sedbergh; Oxford. Served European War, 1914-19; MP (U) Darlington, 1931-45; Parliamentary Private Secretary to Mr Oliver Lyttelton, President of Board of Trade, 1941; Joint Parliamentary Secretary, Ministry of Supply, 1942-45; Parliamentary Secretary, Ministry of National Insurance, April 1945. Pres. Inst. of Chartered Accountants in England and Wales, 1959-60. *Address:* Wycliffe Hall, Barnard Castle, Co. Durham DL12 9TS. *T:* Whorlton 241. *Club:* Carlton.

PEAT, William Wood Watson, CBE 1972; JP; farmer; Director of F. M. C. Ltd; broadcaster; *b* 14 Dec. 1922; *o s* of William Peat and Margaret Hillhouse; *m* 1955, Jean Frew Paton McHarrie; two *s* one *d*. *Educ:* Denny Public School. Served with Royal Signals, Europe and India, 1941-46; Lieut 1944. Member: Nat. Council, Scottish Assoc. of Young Farmers' Clubs, 1949 (Chm., 1953-54; Vice-Pres., 1975); Stirling CC, 1959-75 (Vice-Convenor, 1967-70); Council, NFU Scotland, 1959 (Pres., 1966-67); Scottish River Purification Adv. Cttee, 1960; Bd of Management, Royal Scottish Nat. Hosp., 1962-72; Council, Hannah Research Inst., 1963; Council, Scottish Agricultural Organisation Soc. Ltd, 1963 (Pres. 1974); Bd of Management, British Farm Produce Council, 1964; Agric. Marketing Develt Exec. Cttee, 1966; Central Council for Agric. and Horticultural Co-operation, 1967; Bd of Management, Oatridge Agric. Coll., 1967-75; Gen. Comr of Income Tax, 1962; Governor, West of Scotland Agric. Coll., 1964- (Vice Chm., 1975); Dir, Agri-Finance (Scotland) Ltd, 1968; Chm., BBC Scottish Agric. Adv. Cttee, 1971-75; Chm., Scottish Adv. Cttee, Assoc. of Agriculture, 1974; Dir, Fedn of Agricultural Co-operatives (UK) Ltd, 1974. JP Stirlingshire, 1963. *Recreations:* amateur radio, flying. *Address:* Carbro, 61 Stirling Road, Larbert,

Stirlingshire FK5 4SG. *T:* Larbert 2420. *Clubs:* Farmers'; Stirling and County (Stirling); Turnhouse Flying (Edinburgh).

PEATE, Dr Iorwerth Cyfeiliog, FSA; Curator, Welsh Folk Museum, 1948-71; *b* 1901; *y s* of George Howard Peate and Elizabeth Peate, Llanbryn-Mair, Mont.; *m* 1929, Nansi, *d* of David and Rachel Davies, Eglwys-fach, Card.; one *s. Educ:* Llanbryn-Mair Sch.; Machynlleth Intermed. Sch.; Univ. Coll. of Wales, Aberystwyth. MA 1924; DSc 1941. Staff Tutor, Univ. Coll. of Wales, Aberystwyth, 1924-27; Nat. Mus. of Wales, Cardiff: Asst Keeper, Dept of Archæology, 1927-32; Asst Keeper i/c Sub-Dept of Folk Culture and Industries, 1932-36; Keeper, Dept of Folk Life, 1936-48. Ellis Gruffydd Prizeman, Univ. Wales, 1943; G. T. Clark Prizeman, Cambrian Archæol. Assoc., 1946; Pres., Sect. H (Anthrop.), Brit. Assoc. for Advancement of Science, 1958; Mem. Coun., British Assoc., 1961-66, 1970-74; Ed. of Gwerin, Internat. Jl of Folk Life, 1956-62; Pres., Soc. of Folk-Life Studies, 1961-66; a Vice-Pres., Hon. Soc. of Cymmrodorion; Pres., Cymrodoriaeth Powys. Hon. DLitt Celt., Nat. Univ. of Ireland, 1960; Hon. DLitt Wales, 1970. *Publications:* Y Cawg Aur, 1928; Welsh Bygones, 1929; Cymru a'i Phobl, 1931; Y Crefftwr yng Nghymru, 1933; Plu'r Gweunydd, 1933; Welsh Folk Crafts and Industries, 1935; Sylfeini, 1938; The Welsh House, 1940; Diwylliant Gwerin Cymru, 1942; Clock and Watch Makers in Wales, 1945; Y Deyrnas Goll, 1947; Ym Mhob Pen, 1948; Folk Museums, 1948; Canu Chwarter Canrif, 1957; Syniadau, 1969; Tradition and Folk Life, 1972; Rhwng Dav Fyd, 1976; *edited:* Studies in Regional Consciousness and Environment, 1930; Hen Gapel Llanbryn-Mair, 1939; Ysgrifau John Breese Davies, 1949; Cilhaul ac Ysgrifau eraill gan Samuel Roberts, 1961; John Cowper Powys: Letters 1937-54, 1974. *Address:* Maes-y-coed, St Nicholas, Cardiff, Glam. *T:* Peterston-super-Ely 760574.

PECHELL, Sir Ronald (Horace), 9th Bt *cr* 1797; *b* 4 June 1918; *o s* of Major Hugh Charles Pechell (and *g g s* of Commander Charles Pechell, *b* of 5th Bt), and Caroline Charlotte, *d* of G. A. Strickland; *S* kinsman, Sir Paul Pechell, 8th Bt, 1972; *m* 1949, Dora Constance, *d* of late John Crampthorne. *Educ:* St Paul's Sch.; HMS Worcester. Naval Cadet, Royal Air Force (Marine Craft Section) and Civil Aviation. Served War of 1939-45; Air-Sea Rescue five medals. Royal Humane Society Medal, 1950. *Recreations:* sailing and overseas travel. *Heir:* none. *Address:* c/o Child & Co., 1 Fleet Street, EC4.

PECK, Antony Dilwyn, CB 1965; MBE 1945; Deputy Secretary, Department of Trade and Industry, 1970-73; retired; *b* 10 April 1914; *s* of late Sir James Peck, CB, and late Lady Peck; *m* 1st, 1939, Joan de Burgh Whyte (*d* 1955); one *s* one *d*; 2nd, 1956, Sylvia Glenister; one *s* two *d. Educ:* Eton; Trinity College, Oxford. Fellow of Trinity College, 1938-46. Served War of 1939-45, Army, 1940-46 (Major). Joined Treasury as Principal, 1946; Asst Secretary, 1950; Under-Secretary, 1959; Dep. Under-Sec. of State, MoD, 1963-68; Second Sec., BoT, 1968-70. *Recreations:* tennis, bridge. *Address:* 45 Argyll Road, W8. *T:* 01-937 2869. *Club:* Hurlingham.

PECK, David (Edward); His Honour Judge Peck; a Circuit Judge (formerly Judge of County Courts), since Oct. 1969; *b* 6 April 1917; *m* 1st, 1950, Rosina Seton Glover Marshall (marr. diss.); one *s* three *d*; 2nd, 1973, Frances Deborah Redford (*née* Mackenzie; one *s. Educ:* Charterhouse School; Balliol College, Oxford. Served Army (Cheshire Regiment), 1939-46. Called to Bar, Middle Temple, 1949. *Address:* 8 New Square, Lincoln's Inn, WC2A 3QP.

PECK, Sir Edward (Heywood), GCMG 1974 (KCMG 1966; CMG 1957); HM Diplomatic Service, retired; British Permanent Representative to North Atlantic Council, 1970-75; *b* 5 Oct. 1915; *s* of Lt-Col Edward Surman Peck, IMS, and Doris Louise Heywood; *m* 1948, Alison Mary MacInnes; one *s* two *d. Educ:* Clifton College; The Queen's College, Oxford. 1st Cl. Hons (Mod. Langs), 1937; Laming Travelling Fellow, 1937-38. Entered Consular Service, 1938; served in Barcelona, 1938-39; Foreign Office, 1939-40; Sofia, 1940; Ankara, 1940-44; Adana, 1944; Iskenderun, 1945; Salonica, 1945-47; with UK Deleg. to UN Special Commn on the Balkans, 1947; Foreign Office, 1947-50; seconded to UK High Commissioner's Office, Delhi, 1950-52; Counsellor, Foreign Office, 1952-55; Dep. Comdt, Brit. Sector, Berlin, 1955-58; on staff of UK Commissioner-General for S-E Asia, 1959-60; Assistant Under-Secretary of State, Foreign Office, 1961-66; British High Commissioner in Kenya, 1966-68; Dep. Under-Secretary of State, FCO, 1968-70. Hon. Vis. Fellow in Defence Studies, Aberdeen Univ., 1976-. *Recreations:* mountaineering, ski-ing, reading: history and guide books. *Address:* Easter Torrans, Tomintoul, Banffshire. *Club:* Alpine.

PECK, Gregory; film actor, US, since 1943; *b* 5 April 1916; *s* of Gregory P. Peck and Bernice Ayres; *m* 1st, 1942, Greta Konen Rice (marr. diss. 1954); two *s* (and one *s* decd); 2nd, 1955, Veronique Passani; one *s* one *d. Educ:* Calif Public Schools; Univ. of Calif (BA). Broadway stage, 1941-43. *Films:* Days of Glory, 1943; Keys of the Kingdom, Valley of Decision, 1944; Spellbound, 1945; Duel in the Sun, The Yearling, 1946; The Macomber Affair, Gentlemen's Agreement, 1947; The Paradine Case, 1948; Yellow Sky, The Great Sinner, Twelve O'Clock High, 1949; The Gun Fighter, 1950; Only the Valiant, Captain Horatio Hornblower, David and Bathsheba, 1951; The World in his Arms, 1952; The Snows of Kilimanjaro, 1952; Roman Holiday, 1953; The Million Pound Note, 1953; Night People, 1954; The Purple Plain, 1954; The Man in the Grey Flannel Suit, 1956; Moby Dick, 1956; Designing Woman, 1957; The Bravados, 1958; The Big Country (co-producer), 1958; Pork Chop Hill, 1959; On the Beach, 1959; Guns of Navarone, 1960; Cape Fear, 1961; To Kill a Mocking Bird, 1962; Captain Newman, MD, 1963; Behold a Pale Horse, 1964; Mirage, 1965; Arabesque, 1965; Mackenna's Gold, 1967; The Chairman, 1968; The Stalking Moon, 1968; Marooned, 1970; I Walk the Line, 1971; Shoot Out, 1971; The Trial of the Catonsville Nine, 1972; Billy Two-Hats, 1974; *produced:* The Dove, 1974; The Omen, 1976; MacArthur, 1977. Nat. Chm., Amer. Cancer Soc., 1966. Mem., Nat. Council on Arts, 1965-67, 1968-; Pres., Acad. Motion Pictures Arts and Sciences, 1967-70; Chm., Board of Trustees, Amer. Film Inst., 1967-69. Medal of Freedom Award, 1969; Jean Hersholt Humanitarian Award, Acad. of Motion Picture Arts and Sciences, 1968. *Recreations:* riding, swimming, bicycling, gardening. *Address:* PO Box 49294, Los Angeles, Calif 90049, USA. *Club:* Players (New York).

PECK, Jasper Augustine, CMG 1965; *b* 14 July 1905; *s* of late John Herbert Peck, Lt-Col Indian Army, and late Margaret Jane Ada Batt; *m* 1939, Olwen, *d* of late Eliot Crawshay-Williams; no *c. Educ:* Westminster (King's Scholar); Univ. Coll., Oxford. Called to Bar, Inner Temple, 1930; practised, 1930-39. War Service, Gunner, 86th (HAC) HAA Regt, RA, TA, Major (DAAG), Mil. Dept., Judge Advocate-General's Office, 1939-45. Entered Colonial Office, Sept. 1945; Asst Legal Adviser, Colonial Office, 1950-65, retd. *Recreations:* ornithology, music. *Address:* 50 Saxmundham Road, Aldeburgh, Suffolk. *T:* Aldeburgh 2429. *Club:* Garrick.

PECK, Sir John (Howard), KCMG 1971 (CMG 1956); HM Diplomatic Service, retired; *b* Kuala Lumpur, 16 Feb. 1913; *o s* of late Howard and Dorothea Peck; *m* 1939, Mariska Caroline, *e d* of Josef Somlo; two *s. Educ:* Wellington College; CCC, Oxford. Assistant Private Secretary to First Lord of Admiralty, 1937-39; to Minister for Coordination of Defence, 1939-40; to the Prime Minister, 1940-46; transferred to Foreign Service, 1946; served in United Nations Dept, 1946-47; in The Hague, 1947-50; Counsellor and Head of Information Research Dept, 1951-54; Counsellor (Defence Liaison) and Head of Political Division, British Middle East Office, 1954-56; Director-General of British Information Services, New York, 1956-59; UK Permanent Representative to the Council of Europe, and Consul-General, Strasbourg, 1959-62; Ambassador to Senegal, 1962-66, and Mauritania, 1962-65; Asst Under-Sec. of State, FO, then FCO, 1966-70; Ambassador to the Republic of Ireland, 1970-73. Director: Irish Dunlop Ltd; Edward Dillon & Co. Ltd, Dublin. *Publications:* various essays and light verse. *Recreations:* photography, landscape gardening. *Address:* 4 Eglinton Park, Dun Laoghaire, Co. Dublin. *T:* Dublin 806315. *Club:* Stephen's Green (Dublin).

PECK, Stanley Edwards, CBE 1974; BEM 1954; QPM 1964; DL; HM Inspector of Constabulary, since 1964; *b* 1916; *er s* of late Harold Edwards Peck, Edgbaston and Shanghai; *m* 1939, Yvonne Sydney Edwards, *er d* of late John Edwards Jessop, LDS; two *s* two *d. Educ:* Solihull School; Birmingham University. Served with RAF, 1941-45 (Flt-Lt). Joined Metropolitan Police, 1935; Chief Inspector and Supt, New Scotland Yard, 1950-54; Asst Chief Constable, Staffs, 1954-61; Chief Constable, Staffs, 1961-64. DL Staffs, 1962. Pres., Royal Life Saving Soc., UK, 1969-74. OStJ. *Recreations:* shooting and sailing. *Address:* Lodge Gardens, Radcliffe-on-Trent, Nottinghamshire. *Club:* Royal Air Force.

PEDDER, Vice-Adm. Sir Arthur (Reid), KBE 1959; CB 1956; retired as Commander, Allied Naval Forces, Northern Europe (1957-59); *b* 6 July 1904; *s* of late Sir John Pedder, KBE, CB; *m* 1934, Dulcie, *d* of O. L. Bickford; two *s. Educ:* Osborne and Dartmouth. Served in various ships, 1921-; qualified as Naval Observer, 1930; promoted Commander and appointed Admiralty, 1937-40; Executive Officer, HMS Mauritius, 1940-42; Admiralty Asst, Dir of Plans (Air), 1942-45; Capt. 1944; comd HM Ships Khedive and Phoebe, 1945-47; idc 1948;

Admiralty (Dep. Dir of Plans), 1949-50; Fourth Naval Member of Australian Commonwealth Naval Board, 1950-52; Rear-Adm. 1953; Asst Chief of Naval Staff (Warfare), Admiralty, 1953-54; Flag Officer, Aircraft Carriers, December 1954-May 1956; Vice-Adm. 1956. *Recreation:* everything outdoors. *Address:* Langhurst, Hascombe, Godalming, Surrey. *T:* Hascombe 294. *Club:* Athenæum.

PEDDER, Air Vice-Marshal Ian Maurice, OBE 1963; DFC 1949; Deputy Controller, National Air Traffic Services, since 1977; *b* 2 May 1926; *s* of Maurice and Elsie Pedder; *m* 1949, Jean Mary (*née* Kellett); one *s* two *d*. *Educ:* Royal Grammar Sch., High Wycombe; Queen's Coll., Oxford. Service in Nos 28, 60, 81, 213 Sqdns, CFS, and with Burma Air Force, 1946-59; Staff Coll., Andover, and MoD, 1959-62; Far East, 1962-64; Staff appts, 1965-70; RCDS, 1971; Comdg RAF Chivenor, 1972-74; NATS, 1974-. *Publications:* contribs to Service jls, UK and US. *Recreations:* study of Victorian times, photography, riding (a bicycle). *Address:* Pilton, Barnstaple, North Devon. *Club:* Royal Air Force.

PEDDIE, Baron *cr* 1961, of City and County of Kingston upon Hull (Life Peer); **James Mortimer Peddie,** MBE 1944; JP; Chairman, National Board for Prices and Incomes, 1970-71 (Member, 1965-71, Deputy Chairman, 1968-70); Chairman, Agrément Board, since 1967; Director: TU Unit Trust, since 1965; Mid-Kent Water Board, since 1971; *b* 4 April 1907; *s* of Crofton and Ethel Peddie; *m* 1931, Hilda Mary Alice Bull; one *s* one *d* (and one *d* decd). *Educ:* St Paul's Church Sch.; Hull Technical Coll.; London Sch. of Economics. Lecturer in Economics and Industrial Admin., Coll. of Commerce, 1928-39; Dir and Publicity Manager, Hull Co-operative Soc. Ltd; Min. of Information, 1940-45. Director (1945-65): CWS Ltd and Co-op. Insurance Soc. Ltd.; Co-op. Permanent Building Soc.; West Norfolk Fertiliser Co.; British Luma Lamp Co.; Travco Hotels Ltd; Education Sciences Ltd, 1974; Chairman: Technical Laboratory Services Ltd, 1974; Enalon Plastics Ltd, 1975 (Dir, 1973-). Governor, British Film Institute, 1948-54; Member, Colonial Office Adv. Cttee, 1950-62; Member Exec. Cttee, Co-op. Union, 1957-65; Chairman, Brit. Co-op. Political Party, 1958-65; Pres., Brit. Co-op. Congress, 1958; Mem., Nat. Coun. of Labour, 1958-65; Vice-Chm., Reith Commn on Advertising, 1965. Trustee and Exec. Mem., Civic Trust for Manchester and the North West, 1961-; Gov., Manchester Coll. of Commerce, 1962-; Industrial Arbitrator, Film Industry, 1964; Chairman: Adv. Cttee, Dept of Technical Co-operation, 1962-65; Adv. Cttee, Min. of Overseas Development, 1965; Post Office Users Nat. Council, 1969-; Member: Consumer Council, 1963-68; Advertising Standards Authority, 1972-; Nat. Consumer Council, 1977-. Trustee: Denton Foundn, 1972; Attlee Meml Trust, 1967-; Chm., Attlee Meml Foundn, 1975; President: Industrial Police and Security Assoc., 1972; Yorkshire Kidney Res. Fund, 1974; Vice-Pres., British Waterworks Assoc., 1972. Member: Council of Europe, 1974; WEU, 1974; Budget Cttee; Jt Parly Statutory Instruments Cttee, 1973. Led Jt Parly delegations: Sweden, 1965; Finland, 1968. JP Cheshire, 1959-. LLD Manchester University, 1966. Hon. Citizen, Forth Worth, Texas, 1963; Freeman, City of London, 1972. *Publications:* Pricing in the Public Sector, 1975; frequent contributor to jls on Economics and Political subjects. *Recreation:* golf, as an excuse for walking. *Address:* House of Lords, SW1. *Clubs:* Royal Automobile; (Vice-Pres.) Springhead Park Golf (Hull).

PEDDIE, Maj.-Gen. Graham, CB 1959; DSO 1945; MBE 1941; *b* 15 Oct. 1905; *s* of late Graham Peddie and of Mrs Peddie; *m* 1937, Dorothy Mary Humfress (decd); one *s* one *d*; *m* 1959, Alexandra Mavrojani. *Educ:* Sherborne School, Royal Military Academy, Woolwich. Commissioned into RA, 1926; served in UK, 1926-30, in Egypt and Sudan, 1930-36; Instructor, RMA, Woolwich, 1937-39. War of 1939-45, in UK and NW Europe; 1st AA Group (Dep. Comd), 1948-50; idc, 1950-51. BAOR 1953-56; Director of Manpower Planning, War Office, 1957-60; retired, 1960. *Address:* Sundridge, Stratton, Cirencester, Glos GL7 2LJ. *Club:* Army and Navy.

PEDDIE, John Ronald, CBE 1937 (MBE 1918); MA 1909; DLitt 1927; FRSE 1942; FEIS 1947; Hon. LLD Glasgow, 1958; lately Secretary and Treasurer of the Carnegie Trust for the Universities of Scotland; retired December 1957; *b* 5 January 1887; *e s* of late Richard Dawes Peddie, Grangemouth; *m* 1914, Euphemia Scott Houston. *Educ:* Grangemouth High School; Glasgow University. Lecturer in English, Glasgow Univ., 1911-19; Official Adviser of Studies, Glasgow Univ. 1919-25; Executive Officer, National Committee for the Training of Teachers in Scotland, 1925-41; OC Glasgow University Contingent, Officers Training Corps, 1916-19; Examiner in English since 1911; a Governor of Heriot-Watt Univ., Edinburgh, 1957-68; Hon. Treas. Roy. Soc. of Edinburgh, 1957-

67; a Governor of Merchiston Castle School; Trustee of the Cross Trust. Trustee of National Library of Scotland, 1942-73; Vice-President and Trustee of Society of Scottish Artists; Chm., Sir J. Donald Pollock Trust; former Chm., Edinburgh Assoc. for the Provisions of Halls of Residence for Women Students. *Publications:* The Carnegie Trust; The First Fifty Years (1901-1951); Papers on literary and educational subjects. Editor, Glasgow University Roll of Honour. *Recreation:* gardening. *Address:* 7 Bruntsfield Terrace, Edinburgh EH10 4EX. *T:* 031-229 6055. *Club:* Mortonhall Golf.

PEDDIE, Robert Allan; Chairman, South Eastern Electricity Board, since 1977; *b* 27 Oct. 1921; *s* of Robert Allan Peddie and Elizabeth Elsie (*née* Sharp); *m* 1946, Ilene Ivy Sillcock; one *d*. *Educ:* Nottingham Univ. (BSc Eng). Electricity Dept, Hull Corp., 1946; joined nationalised electricity supply industry, 1948, and held various appts; Supt, Bradwell Nuclear Power Stn, 1958; Asst Reg. Dir, NW Region, 1962; Dep. Reg. Dir, Mids Region, 1967; Dir-Gen., SE Region, 1970; Mem. CEGB, 1972-77; part-time Mem., UKAEA, 1972-77. *Recreations:* swimming, golf, walking. *Address:* Torness, The Mount Drive, Reigate, Surrey. *T:* Reigate 44996. *Club:* Royal Automobile.

PEDDIE, Ronald, CBE 1971; JP; *b* 24 May 1905; *s* of Rev. James Peddie, BA and Elsie Mary, *d* of John Edward Corby; *m* 1931, Vera, *d* of W. G. Nicklin, Guildford; three *s* one *d*. *Educ:* Glasgow Academy; Leys Sch., Cambridge; St John's Coll., Cambridge (BA). CA 1930; Jt Dipl. Management Accounting, 1967. McClelland Ker & Co., CA, Glasgow, 1926-31; Accountant and Asst Sec., C. & J. Clark Ltd, Street, Som, 1931-43; The United Steel Cos Ltd, 1943-67 (Sec. from 1946, later Dir Finance and Admin); British Steel Corp.: Dir, Finance and Admin, Midland Group, 1967-69; Man. Dir, Administration, 1969-71, retd. Dir, Iron Trades Employers' Insurance Assoc. Ltd, 1970-75. Sec., Trevelyan Scholarships, 1958-; Governor, Ashorne Hill Management Coll., 1967-71. Past Mem., Cambridge and Leeds Univs Appt Bds. JP Sheffield, 1964. *Publications:* The United Steel Companies, 1918-1968: a History, 1968; The Trevelyan Scholarships, 1975; articles in Accountants Magazine and Accountancy. *Recreations:* gardening, reading, all games (now chiefly as a spectator). *Address:* Little Glebe, 15 Lime Close, West Clandon, Surrey. *T:* Guildford 222513.

PEDLER, Sir Frederick (Johnson), Kt 1969; Treasurer, School of Oriental and African Studies, University of London, since 1969; *b* 10 July 1908; *s* of Charles Henry Pedler and Lucy Marian (*née* Johnson); *m* 1935, Esther Ruth Carling; two *s* one *d*. *Educ:* Watford Grammar School; Caius College, Cambridge (MA). Colonial Office, 1930; seconded to Tanganyika, 1934; Secretary to Commission on Higher Educn in E Africa and Sudan, 1937; Sec. to Lord Privy Seal, 1938; Sec. to Lord Hailey in Africa, 1939, Congo, 1940; Chief Brit. Econ. Representative, Dakar, 1942; Finance Dept, Colonial Office, 1944. Joined United Africa Co., 1947, Director, 1951, Deputy Chairman, 1965-68. Director: Unilever Ltd and NV, 1956-68; William Baird Ltd, 1969-75. Chm., Council for Technical Educn and Training for Overseas Countries, 1962-73. Chm., E Africa and Mauritius Assoc., 1966-68; Mem., Inter-University Council, 1967-73. Hon. Fellow, SOAS, 1976. *Publications:* West Africa, 1951 (2nd edn 1959); Economic Geography of W Africa, 1955; The Lion and the Unicorn in Africa, 1974. *Recreations:* languages, history, ski-ing. *Address:* 36 Russell Road, Moor Park, Northwood, Mddx.

PEDLEY, Alan Sydney, DFC 1946; Lord Mayor of Leeds, 1975-1976; District Insurance Manager, since 1974; *b* 16 Aug. 1917; *s* of Herbert Leonard Pedley and Edith Mary (*née* Skipsey); *m* 1949, Evelyn Anderson (*née* Scott). *Educ:* Leeds Modern Sch. Entered Insurance, 1934; retd (Commercial Union), 1971; joined Barclays Insurance Services Co. Ltd, 1971. Elected: Leeds City Council, 1951; W Yorkshire Metropolitan CC, 1973; Dep. Lord Mayor, 1971-72. FCII 1949. *Recreations:* cricket, Association football, music, theatre, the Arts. *Address:* Sandylands, 44 Lidgett Lane, Leeds LS8 1PQ. *T:* Leeds 661666. *Club:* Brevet.

PEDLEY, Prof. Robin; Head of Department of Education, University of Southampton, since 1976; *b* 11 Aug. 1914; *s* of Edward and Martha Jane Pedley; *m* 1951, Jeanne Lesley Hitching, BA; one *s* one *d*. *Educ:* Richmond Sch., Yorks; Durham Univ. (MA, PhD, Teaching Dip.; Gibson Prize in Archaeology, Gladstone Meml Prize in Mod. Hist.). Research Fellow, Durham Univ., 1936-38; Teacher, Friends' Sch., Great Ayton, 1938-42, and Crossley and Porter Schs, Halifax, 1943-46. Lecturer: Coll. of St Mark and St John, Chelsea, 1946-47; Leicester Univ. Dept of Educn, 1947-63. Dir, Exeter Univ. Inst. of Educn, 1963-71; Head of Sch. of Educn and Dean, Faculty of Educn, Univ. of Southampton, 1971-75. *Publications:* Comprehensive Schools Today, 1955; Comprehensive

Education: a new approach, 1956; The Comprehensive School, 1963, 3rd edn 1978; The Comprehensive School (with J. Orring, publ. in Hebrew, Jerusalem), 1966; Towards the Comprehensive University, 1977; occasional articles various educational jls. *Recreations:* sport, reading. *Address:* Annerley, Waters Green, Brockenhurst, Hants, SO4 7RG. *T:* Brockenhurst 3001.

PEECH, Alan James; *b* 24 August 1905; *s* of late Albert Orlando Peech; *m* 1948, Betty Leese; no *c. Educ:* Wellington College; Magdalen College, Oxford (BA). Former Governor, Wellington College, retd 1975. Independent Chm., Cement Makers' Fedn, 1970-76; former Dep. Chm., Steetley Co. Ltd, retd 1976; Pres., British Iron and Steel Fedn, Jan.-June 1967; Jt Man. Dir, United Steel Cos Ltd, 1962-67, Chm., 1962-71; a Dep. Chm., BSC, 1967-70; Man. Dir, Midland Gp BSC, 1967-70. Hon. LLD Sheffield, 1966. *Recreations:* fishing and shooting. *Address:* High House, Blyth, Worksop, Notts. *T:* Blyth 255. *Clubs:* Carlton, MCC.

PEECH, Neil Malcolm; President, The Steetley Co. Ltd, since 1976 (Managing Director, 1935-68, Chairman, 1935-76); *b* 27 Jan. 1908; *s* of Albert Orlando Peech; *m* 1932, Margaret Josephine, *d* of late R. C. Smallwood, CBE, Worplesdon, Surrey; one *s* one *d. Educ:* Wellington College; Magdalen College, Oxford. Developed the production of magnesia from seawater and dolomite, 1939. Consul for Sweden, 1974-76 (Vice Consul, 1949-74). Underwriting member of Lloyd's, 1950-69; Director, Sheepbridge Engineering Ltd, 1949-, and Albright & Wilson Ltd 1958-. Chairman, Ministry of Power Solid Smokeless Fuel Committee, 1959. High Sheriff of Yorkshire, 1959. *Recreations:* fishing and shooting. *Address:* Park House, Firbeck, Worksop. *T:* Worksop 730338. *Club:* MCC.

PEEK, Sir Francis (Henry Grenville), 4th Bt, *cr* 1874; *b* 16 Sept. 1915; *o s* of 3rd Bt and Edwine Warner (*d* 1959), *d* of late W. H. Thornburgh, St Louis, USA; *S* father, 1927; *m* 1st, 1942, Ann (marr. diss., 1949), *d* of late Captain Gordon Duff and *widow* of Sir Charles Mappin, Bt (she *m* 1951, Sir William Rootes, later 1st Baron Rootes); 2nd, Marilyn (marr. diss., 1967; she *m* 1967, Peter Quennell), *d* of Dr Norman Kerr, London and Bahamas; one *s* decd; 3rd, Mrs Caroline Kirkwood, *d* of Sir Robert Kirkwood, *qv. Educ:* Eton; Trinity College, Cambridge. ADC to Governor of Bahamas, 1938-39; served Irish Guards, 1939-46. *Heir: cousin* William Grenville Peek [*b* 15 Dec. 1919; *m* 1950, Lucy Jane, *d* of late Major Edward Dorrien-Smith, DSO; one *s* three *d*]. *Address:* 60 Grosvenor Close, Nassau, Bahamas. *Club:* White's.

PEEK, Vice-Adm. Sir Richard (Innes), KBE 1972 (OBE 1944); CB 1971; DSC 1945; pastoralist; *b* 30 July 1914; 2nd *s* of late James Norman and Kate Doughty Peek; *m* 1943, Margaret Seinor (*née* Kendall) (*d* 1946); one *s* ; *m* 1952, Mary Catherine Tilley (*née* Stops); two *d. Educ:* Royal Australian Naval College. Joined RAN, 1928; served War of 1939-45 in HMS Royal Sovereign, HMAS Cerberus, Hobart, Australia, Navy Office; Korean War Service in HMAS Tobruk, 1951; Flag Officer Comdg HMA Fleet, 1967-68; Chief of Naval Staff, Australia, 1970-73. Legion of Merit (US), 1951. *Recreations:* gardening, golf. *Address:* Rothlyn, RMB, Monaro Highway, via Cooma, NSW 2630, Australia. *Clubs:* Imperial Service (Sydney); Royal Commonwealth Society (Canberra).

PEEL, family name of **Earl Peel.**

PEEL, 3rd Earl *cr* 1929; **William James Robert Peel;** Bt 1800; Viscount Peel, 1895; Viscount Clanfield, 1929; *b* 3 Oct. 1947; *s* of 2nd Earl Peel and Kathleen (*d* 1972), *d* of Michael McGrath; *S* father, 1969; *m* 1973, Veronica Naomi Livingston, *d* of Alastair Timpson; one *s . Educ:* Ampleforth; University of Tours; Cirencester Agric. Coll. *Heir: s* Viscount Clanfield, *qv . Address:* Gunnerside Lodge, Richmond, North Yorks; 49 Redcliffe Gardens, SW10. *Club:* Turf.

PEEL, Lady; (Beatrice); *see* Lillie, Beatrice.

PEEL, The Lady Delia (Adelaide Margaret), DCVO 1950 (CVO 1947); *b* 1889; *d* of 6th Earl Spencer, KG; *m* 1914, Col Hon. Sir Sidney Cornwallis Peel, 1st and last Bt, CB, DSO, TD (*d* 1938). A Woman of the Bedchamber, 1939-50; an Extra Woman of the Bedchamber, 1950, to the Queen; to Queen Elizabeth the Queen Mother, 1952. *Address:* Barton Turf, Norwich NR12 8AU.

PEEL, Prof. Edwin Arthur, DLit; Professor of Education, University of Birmingham, since 1950, and Chairman of School of Education, 1965-70; *b* 11 March 1911; *s* of late Arthur Peel and Mary Ann Miller; *m* 1939, Nora Kathleen Yeadon; two *s* two *d. Educ:* Prince Henry's Grammar School, Otley, Yorks; Leeds University; London University. Teaching in various

London Schools, 1933-38; LCC School of Building, 1938-41; MA London, 1938; Ministry of Supply, 1941-45; PhD London 1945; Part-time Lecturer London Univ. Institute of Education, 1945; Lecturer in Education, King's College, Newcastle, 1946; Reader in Psychology, Durham University, 1946-48; Professor of Educational Psychology, University of Durham, 1948-50. President British Psychological Society 1961-62. DLit, London, 1961. *Publications:* The Psychological Basis of Education, 1956; The Pupil's Thinking, 1960; The Nature of Adolescent Judgment, 1971; various in leading British and foreign journals of psychology; Editor and contrib., Educational Review. *Recreation:* painting. *Address:* 47 Innage Road, Birmingham B31 2DY. *T:* 021-475 2820.

PEEL, Captain Sir (Francis Richard) Jonathan, Kt 1959; CBE 1943; MC; KPM; *b* 10 Dec. 1897; *s* of late Walter Peel, CBE, JP; *m* 1932, Daphne Margaret Holwell, *d* of Commander A. McC. Pakenham, Bath; one *s* one *d. Educ:* Malvern College; Pembroke College, Cambridge. RFA, European War, 1915-19; Liverpool City Police, 1920-31; Chief Constable of Bath, 1931-33; Chief Constable of Essex, 1933-62, retired. DL County of Essex, 1959-72. King's Police Medal, 1952. CStJ 1959. *Address:* Cedarholme, 9 Lexden Road, Colchester, Essex.

PEEL, Jack Armitage, CBE 1972; DL; Director, Industrial Relations, in the Social Affairs Directorate, EEC, since 1973; *b* 8 Jan. 1921; *s* of Martha and George Henry Peel; *m* 1950, Dorothy Mabel Dobson; one *s* one *d. Educ:* elem. and modern sch.; Ruskin Coll., Oxford (Schol., Social Sci.), 1948-49. Railwayman, 1936-47. National Union of Dyers, Bleachers and Textile Workers: full-time Officer, 1950; Asst Gen.-Sec., 1957-66, Gen. Sec., 1966-73; Mem. Gen. Council of TUC, 1966-72. Part-time Director: British Wool Marketing Board, 1968-73; NCB, 1969-73. Served on several courts of inquiry, incl. Rochdale Cttee of Inquiry into Merchant Navy. DL West Yorks, 1971; JP Bradford, 1960-72. *Recreations:* cricket, painting, guitar music, swimming. *Address:* Kersenbomenlaan 55, Jezus-Eik, B-1900 Overyse, Belgium. *T:* Brussels 657-30-05; 21 Fitzroy Road, Bradford Moor, Bradford, West Yorkshire.

PEEL, Sir John; *see* Peel, Sir. W. J.

PEEL, Sir John (Harold), KCVO 1960; FRCP 1971; FRCS 1933; FRCOG 1944; Surgeon-Gynæcologist to the Queen, 1961-73; Consulting Obstetric and Gynæcological Surgeon, King's College Hospital, since 1969; Emeritus Consulting Gynæcologist, Princess Beatrice Hospital, since 1965; Member, Economic and Social Committee, European Economic Community, since 1973; *b* 10 December 1904; *s* of Rev. J. E. Peel; *m* 1947, Freda Margaret Mellish; one *d. Educ:* Manchester Grammar Sch.; Queen's Coll., Oxford. MA, BM, BCh Oxon 1932. King's College Hospital Med. Sch., qualified 1930; Obstetric and Gynæcological Surgeon: King's Coll. Hosp., 1936-69; Princess Beatrice Hosp., 1937; Queen Victoria Hosp., East Grinstead, 1941-69; Surgeon EMS, 1939-45. Director of Clinical Studies, King's College Hospital Medical School, 1948-67. Litchfield Lecturer, Oxford University, 1961 and 1969; Sir Kadar Nath Das Lecturer, Bengal O and G Soc., 1962; Sir A. Mudaliar Lecturer, Madras Univ., 1962; Vis. Prof., Cape Town Univ., 1963; Travelling Prof., S African Council, RCOG, 1968. Past Examiner, Universities of Oxford, Cambridge, London, Liverpool, Bristol, Glasgow, Newcastle, Nat. Univ. of Ireland, Birmingham, Dundee, Sheffield, Conjoint Board, RCOG and CMB. Nuffield visitor to Colonies, 1950 and 1953. President, RCOG, 1966-69 (Hon. Treasurer, 1961-66, Councillor, 1955-); President: Internat. Fedn of Obstetrics and Gynæcology, 1970-73; Chelsea Clinical Society, 1960; BMA 1970 (Chm., Bd of Science and Educn, 1972); Family Planning Assoc., 1971-74; Chm., DHSS Cttees of Enquiry: Domiciliary Midwifery and Bed Needs, 1971; The Use of Fetus and Fetal Material for Research, 1972. Hon. Fellow: American Association of Obstetricians and Gynæcologists, 1962 (Joseph Price Oration, 1961); Edinburgh Obstetrical Soc., 1971; RSM, 1973; Hon. Member: Canadian Assoc. of O and G, 1955; Italian Assoc O and G, 1960; Hon. Treas., GMC, 1972-75; Hon. FRCS (Canada), 1967; Hon. FCOG (SA), 1968; Hon. MMSA 1970; Hon. FACS 1970; Hon. FACOG 1971; Hon. Fellow, American Gynæcological Soc., 1974. Hon. DSc Birmingham, 1972; Hon. DM Southampton, 1974. *Publications:* Textbook of Gynæcology, 1943; Lives of the Fellows of Royal College of Obstetricians and Gynaecologists 1929-69, 1976; numerous contributions to Medical Journals. *Recreations:* fishing, golf. *Address:* Warren Court Farm, West Tytherley, Salisbury, Wilts. *Clubs:* Bath, Royal Automobile.

PEEL, Capt. Sir Jonathan; *see* Peel, Capt. Sir F. R. J.

PEEL, Prof. Ronald Francis Edward Waite, MBE 1945; MA (Cambridge) 1937; Professor of Geography, University of

Bristol, 1957-77; Dean of Science, 1968-70; *b* 22 Aug. 1912; *s* of late Albert Edward Peel, Bridgnorth, Shropshire, and Matilda Mary Peel (*née* Anderson), Helensburgh, Dunbartonshire; *m* 1938, Mary Annette Preston, MA Cantab, *o d* of H. Preston, Northampton; one *d. Educ:* Northampton Gram. Sch.; St Catharine's Coll., Cambridge (scholar). Lecturer in Geography, King's College, University of Durham, 1935-39; accompanied Brig. R. A. Bagnold, OBE, FRS, on exploring expedition in Libyan Desert, 1938. Served War of 1939-45, with RE; France, 1939-40; UK (staff appts), 1940-44; N Africa and Italy, 1944-45; UK, 1945. King's College, Newcastle, 1945-46; Department of Geography, Cambridge University, 1946, Lecturer in Geography, 1949; Prof. of Geography, University of Leeds, 1951-57, Head of Dept, 1953-57. Fellow of St Catharine's Coll., Cambridge, 1949. Cuthbert Peake Award of RGS, 1950; expeditions to Ruwenzori Mountains, 1952; W and C Sahara, 1961. President: Inst. British Geographers, 1965; Section E, British Assoc., 1967; Colston Research Soc., Bristol, 1973-76. FRGS, FRMetSoc. *Publications:* Physical Geography, 1951; articles on geographical subjects to technical jls, British and foreign. *Recreation:* travel. *Address:* 18 Porson Road, Cambridge. *Club:* Hawks (Cambridge).

PEEL, Sir (William) John, Kt 1973; Hon. Director, Conservative Party International Office, 1975-76; *b* 16 June 1912; *s* of late Sir William Peel, KCMG, KBE, and Violet Mary Drake, *er d* of W. D. Laing; *m* 1936, Rosemary Mia Minka, *er d* of Robert Readhead; one *s* three *d. Educ:* Wellington College; Queens' College, Cambridge. Colonial Administrative Service, 1933-51; on active service, 1941-45; British Resident, Brunei, 1946-48; Res. Comr, Gilbert and Ellice Is Colony, 1949-51. Personal Asst to Man. Dirs of Rugby Portland Cement Co. Ltd, 1952-54. Contested (C) Meriden Division of Warwickshire, 1955; MP (C) Leicester SE, 1957-Feb. 1974; Parliamentary Private Secretary to: Economic Secretary to the Treasury, 1958-59; Minister of State, Board of Trade, 1959-60; Asst Govt Whip (unpaid), 1960-61; a Lord Comr of the Treasury, Nov. 1961-Oct. 1964. Parly Delegate to: Assemblies of Council of Europe, 1961-74; WEU 1961-74 (Vice-Pres., 1967, Pres. 1972, Chm., Defence and Armaments Cttee, 1970-72, WEU); N Atlantic Assembly, 1959-74 (Leader, 1970-74; Pres., N Atlantic Assembly, Nov. 1972); Mem., British Delegn to European Parlt, Strasbourg, 1973-74. Mem. Council, Victoria League for Commonwealth Friendship, 1974 (Dep. Chm., 1976-); Chairman: Hospitality and Branches Cttee of Victoria League, 1974-; Jt Standing Cttee of Victoria League and Royal Commonwealth Soc., 1975-. Dato Seri Laila Jasa Brunei 1969; Dato Setia Negara Brunei 1971. *Recreations:* golf, walking. *Address:* 51 Cambridge Street, SW1. *T:* 01-834 8762. *Clubs:* Carlton; Hawks (Cambridge).

PEEL YATES, Lt-Gen. Sir David, KCB 1966 (CB 1963); CVO 1965; DSO 1943, and Bar, 1944; OBE 1943; DL; JP; *b* 10 July 1911; *er s* of late Lt-Col Hubert Peel Yates, DSO, late South Wales Borderers, and Gertrude Loetitia Molyneux (*née* Sarel); *m* 1947, Christine Hilary, *er d* of late Horatio Stanley-Williams, DSO, Irthlingborough, Northants; one *s* one *d. Educ:* Haileybury College; RMC Sandhurst. Commissioned S Wales Borderers, 1931; Waziristan operations, 1937; active service in N Africa, Italy and Greece as GSO1 HQ First Army, Comdg 6 Bn Lincolnshire Regt, GSO1 4th Div. and BGS (Ops) AFHQ, 1942-45. Commanded 1st Bn S Wales Borderers, 1953-55; Comdr 27 Infantry Bde, Hong Kong, 1955-57; Asst Commandant, Staff College, 1957-60; Chief of Staff, Eastern Command, 1960-62; GOC, Berlin (British Sector), 1962-66; GOC-in-C: Eastern Command, 1966-68; Southern Comd, 1968-69; retd 1969. Colonel: The South Wales Borderers, 1962-69; Royal Regt of Wales (24th/41st Foot), 1969-77. DL and JP Breconshire, 1970. Breconshire CC, 1970-74. Chm., ICP Ltd, 1973-. Legion of Merit, USA, 1946. *Recreations:* shooting, fishing, ski-ing. *Address:* Glyn Pedr, Llanbedr, Crickhowell, Breconshire. *T:* Crickhowell 810333. *Club:* Army and Navy.

PEERS, Rt. Rev. Michael Geoffrey; *see* Qu'Appelle, Bishop of.

PEET, Ronald Hugh, CBE 1974; Director and Chief Executive, Legal and General Assurance Society Ltd, since 1972; Deputy Chairman, Aviation & General Insurance Co. Ltd; *b* 12 July 1925; *s* of Henry Leonard and Stella Peet; *m* 1949, Winifred Joy Adamson; two *s* two *d. Educ:* Doncaster Grammar Sch.; Queen's Coll., Oxford (MA). Served in HM Forces, Captain RA, 1944-47. Joined Legal and General Assurance Soc. Ltd, 1952; emigrated to Australia, 1955; Sec., Legal and General's Australian Branch, 1955-59; Asst Life Manager, 1959-65; Manager and Actuary for Australia, 1965-69; returned to UK as General Manager (Ops), 1969. FIA. Director: City Arts Trust Ltd; Royal Philharmonic Orchestra Ltd. *Recreations:* music, theatre. *Address:* 83 Deodar Road, Putney, SW15. *T:* 01-874 9694. *Club:* Hurlingham.

PEGG, Arthur John, OBE 1951 (MBE 1946); AFRAeS 1953; Chief Test Pilot, Bristol Aeroplane Co., 1947-56; General Service Manager of Weston Works, retired; *b* 5 June 1906; *s* of Major S. Pegg, RAOC; *m* 1933, Eileen Mary Page; one *s* one *d. Educ:* Skinners, Tunbridge Wells. Joined Royal Air Force, 1921; learned to fly, 1925; granted permanent commission, 1930, and appointed test pilot at aeroplane and armament experimental establishments; resigned commission and appointed Asst Chief Test Pilot, Bristol Aeroplane Co., 1935. *Publication:* Sent Flying (autobiography), 1959. *Address:* Craigfoot No 1, 55 South Rd, Weston-super-Mare, Avon. *T:* Weston-super-Mare 3884.

PEGG, Michael Anstice, PhD; Librarian, University of Birmingham, since 1976; *b* 3 Sept. 1931; *s* of Benjamin and Rose Pegg; *m* 1955, Jean Williams; three *s. Educ:* Burton-on-Trent Grammar Sch.; Univ. of Southampton. BA (London), PhD (Southampton). Captain, Royal Army Education Corps, Educn Officer, SHAPE, Paris, 1958-60; Asst Keeper, Nat. Library of Scotland, Edinburgh, 1961-67; Sec. and Estabt Officer, Nat. Library of Scotland, Edinburgh, 1967-76. *Publications:* Les Divers Rapports d'Eustorg de Beaulieu (édn critique), 1964 (Geneva); Catalogue of German Reformation Pamphlets in Libraries of Great Britain and Ireland, 1973 (Baden Baden); Catalogue of Sixteenth-century German Pamphlets in Collections in France and England, 1977 (Baden Baden); Catalogue of Reformation Pamphlets in Swiss Libraries, 1978; occasional papers to learned jls. *Recreations:* cricket, tennis, squash, railway modelling. *Address:* Main Library, University of Birmingham, PO Box 363, Birmingham B15 2TT. *T:* 021-472 1301.

PEGGIE, Robert Galloway Emslie; Chief Executive, Lothian Regional Council, since 1974; *b* 5 Jan. 1929; *s* of John and Euphemia Peggie; *m* 1955, Christine Jeanette Simpson; one *s* one *d. Educ:* Lasswade High Sch. Certified accountant; Accountancy apprenticeship, 1946-52; Accountant in industry, 1952-57; Public Service, Edinburgh City, 1957-74. *Recreation:* golf. *Address:* 54 Liberton Drive, Edinburgh EH16 6NW. *T:* 031-664 1631.

PEGLER, Alfred Ernest; Engineering Inspector, Civil Service, since 1962; Councillor: Crawley Borough Council, since 1956; West Sussex County Council, since 1959; *b* 18 Jan. 1924; *s* of Frank Walter James Pegler and Violet Maud Pegler; *m* 1944, E. E. McDonald; one *s* one *d. Educ:* Cork Street Sch., Peckham; Oliver Goldsmith Sch., Peckham. Engrg apprentice, 1938-42; served War, RAF Air Crew, 1942-46; toolmaker, 1946-62. Chm., Crawley Council, 1959 and 1966; Chm. Housing Cttee, 1971-77. Leader, Labour Gp, W Sussex CC, 1977-. Mem., Crawley Cttee, New Towns Commn, 1962- (Chm., 1974-). Mem., Sussex Police Authority, 1973-77. Parly Candidate (Labour): twice, Horsham; Gloucester, 1974. *Recreations:* gardening, politics. *Address:* 7 Priors Walk, Three Bridges, Crawley, West Sussex RH10 1NX. *T:* Crawley 27330.

PEGLER, James Basil Holmes, TD; BA; FIA, FSS, FIS, FIMA; Professor of Actuarial Science, City University, since 1976; Director, Clerical, Medical and General Life Assurance Society (General Manager and Actuary, 1950-69, Managing Director, 1970-75); *b* 6 Aug. 1912; *s* of late Harold Holmes Pegler and late Dorothy Cecil (*née* Francis); *m* 1937, Enid Margaret Dell; one *s* three *d. Educ:* Charterhouse; Open Univ. Joined Clerical, Medical and Gen. Life Assce Soc., 1931. War service, Queen's Royal Regt and RA, 1939-45 (Major). Inst. of Actuaries: Fellow, 1939; Hon. Sec., 1955-57; Pres., 1968-70. Chm., Life Offices' Assoc., 1959-61; Chm., Life Gp of Comité Européen des Assurances, 1964-70. *Publications:* contribs to Jl Inst. Actuaries. *Recreations:* mathematics, music, languages, squash rackets. *Address:* Dormers, Deepdene Wood, Dorking, Surrey RH5 4BQ. *T:* Dorking 86076. *Clubs:* Army and Navy, Royal Automobile.

PEIERLS, Sir Rudolf (Ernst), Kt 1968; CBE 1946; FRS 1945; MA Cantab; DSc Manchester, DPhil Leipzig; Wykeham Professor of Physics, Oxford University, and Fellow, New College, Oxford, 1963-74, now Emeritus Fellow; Professor of Physics (part-time), University of Washington, Seattle, 1974-77; *b* Berlin, 5 June 1907; *s* of H. Peierls; *m* 1931, Eugenia, *d* of late N. Kannegiesser; one *s* three *d. Educ:* Humboldt School, Oberschöneweide, Berlin; Universities of Berlin, Munich, Leipzig. Assistant, Federal Institute of Technology, Zürich, 1929-32; Rockefeller Fellow, 1932-33; Honorary Research Fellow, Manchester University, 1933-35; Assistant-in-Research, Royal Society Mond Laboratory, 1935-37; Worked on Atomic Energy Project in Birmingham, 1940-43, in USA, 1943-46. Professor of Mathematical Physics (formerly Applied Mathematics), University of Birmingham, 1937-63. Member Governing Board of National Institute for Research in Nuclear

Science, 1957-62. Awarded Royal Medal of Royal Society, 1959; Lorentz Medal of Royal Netherlands Academy of Sciences, 1962; Max Planck Medal, Association of German Physical Societies, 1963; Guthrie Medal, IPPS, 1968. Hon. DSc: Liverpool, 1960; Birmingham, 1967; Edinburgh, 1969. Foreign Hon. Member, American Academy of Arts and Sciences, 1962; Hon. Associate, College of Advanced Technology, Birmingham, 1963; Foreign Associate, Nat. Acad. of Sciences, USA, 1970. *Publications:* Quantum Theory of Solids, 1955; The Laws of Nature, 1955; papers on Quantum Theory. *Address:* Farleigh, Orchard Lane, Old Boar's Hill, Oxford OX1 5JH; Nuclear Physics Laboratory, Keble Road, Oxford. *Club:* Athenæum.

PEILE, Vice-Admiral Sir Lancelot Arthur Babington, KBE 1960; CB 1957; DSO 1941; MVO 1947; DL; retired; *b* 22 Jan. 1905; *s* of late Basil Wilson Peile and Katharine Rosamond (*née* Taylor); *m* 1928, Gertrude Margaret (*née* Tolcher); two *s. Educ:* RN Colleges, Osborne and Dartmouth. Commander (E) 1939; Captain (E), 1947; Rear-Admiral, 1955; Vice-Admiral, 1958. Asst Engineer-in-Chief, 1948; Command of RN Engineering College, 1951; idc 1954. Asst Director of Dockyards, 1955-57; Admiral Superintendent, Devonport Dockyard, 1957-60; retired, 1960. DL Devon, 1969. *Address:* Strawberry How, Thurlestone, Kingsbridge, Devon. *T:* Thurlestone 209.

PEIRCE, Lt-Col Harold Ernest, CBE 1960 (OBE 1950); JP; Director of Public Companies, since 1929; *b* 7 Nov. 1892; *s* of Harry and Elizabeth Peirce. *Educ:* Croydon, Surrey. Served European War 1915-19, (Surrey Yeomanry, Queen's Royal W Surrey Regt). Joined Hall & Co. Ltd, 1907; Director, 1929; Managing Director, 1944. Director, Hall & Ham River Ltd, Holding Board, 1962; Chm., MPR Ltd; Director, Hall Aggregates Ltd, 1968, RMC Pension Nominees Ltd, 1968 (mems of Ready Mixed Concrete Gp of Cos). Founder Member, Ballast, Sand and Allied Trades Assoc. (now called Sand and Gravel Assoc. Ltd), 1930 (Chairman, 1943, now Pres.); Founder Member, National Council of Building Material Producers (Vice-President, 1955; Chairman Council, 1956; President, 1965); Member Indust. Development Mission to WI, 1952; Member Board of Trade Bankruptcy Acts Amendment Cttee, 1955. Appointed Member, Dollar Export Delegation to Canada, 1957. Comdr Bn of Home Guard, War of 1939-45, and also when later reformed. Chairman, Croydon Playing Fields Assoc. JP, Croydon, 1941-. *Recreations:* cricket and squash. Captain of Addiscombe Cricket Club for 26 years, now President of the Club. *Address:* Selsdon Park, Sanderstead, Surrey. *T:* 01-657 8811. *Clubs:* RAC, MCC; Surrey CCC (a Vice-Pres.).

PEIRIS, Dr Mahapitage Velin Peter, OBE 1956; *b* 28 July 1898; *s* of M. A. Peiris and H. D. Selestina, Panadura, Ceylon; *m* 1945, Edith Doreen Idona Carey, Negombo, Ceylon; three *s* one *d. Educ:* St John's Coll., Panadura; St Joseph's Coll., Colombo; Ceylon Medical Coll., Colombo. LMS Ceylon, 1926; MB, BS London, 1936; FRCS 1930; FICS 1957; FACS 1959. Served in Ceylon Army Med. Corps, 1930-45: Surg. to Mil. Hosps, Ceylon, 1940-45. Vis. Surgeon: Gen. Hosp., 1936-60; Children's Hosp., Colombo, 1951-60; Surg. to Orthop. Clinic, 1950-60; Cons. Orthop. Surg., Gen. Hosp., Colombo; Medico-Legal Adviser to Crown; Prof. of Surgery, Univ. of Ceylon, 1952-60. Senator, Ceylon Parlt, 1954-68: Minister of Health, 1960; Leader of Senate, and Minister of Commerce and Trade, 1965-68. Ambassador of Ceylon to USSR, 1968-69; High Comr for Ceylon in the UK, 1969-70. Mem. Coun., Univ. of Ceylon, 1960; President: Ceylon Med. Assoc., 1954; University Teachers' Assoc.; UNA of Ceylon, 1966-68. *Publications:* contribs to Indian and Ceylon medical jls. *Recreations:* swimming, photography. *Address:* 19 Beverley Court, Wellesley Road, W4 4LQ.

PEIRSE, Sir Henry G. de la P. B.; *see* Beresford-Peirse.

PELHAM, family name of **Earls of Chichester** and **Yarborough.**

PELHAM, Sir (George) Clinton, KBE 1957; CMG 1949; FRGS; HM Ambassador to Czechoslovakia, 1955-57, retired; *b* 20 May 1898; *s* of George Pelham; *m* 1930, Jeanie Adelina Morton; two *d. Educ:* privately. Served European War, 1915-18. Foreign Office, 1920; China Consular Service, 1923; HM Trade Commissioner and Commercial Secretary for South China, 1933; Acting Consul-General, Madagascar, 1943; First Secretary (Commercial), Bagdad, 1945; Counsellor (Commercial), Bagdad, 1946; Counsellor (Commercial), Madrid, 1948-51; HM Ambassador to Saudi Arabia, 1951-55. County Councillor, West Sussex, 1963-70. *Recreations:* music, painting, travel. *Address:* Crespin, Craigweil, Bognor Regis, West Sussex. *Club:* Junior Carlton.

PELHAM-CLINTON-HOPE, family name of **Duke of Newcastle.**

PELIZA, Hon. Major Robert John, ED 1955; Chief Minister, Gibraltar, 1969-72; Leader of the Opposition, 1972; *b* 16 Nov. 1920; *s* of late Robert Peliza; *m* 1950, Irma Risso; three *s* four *d. Educ:* Christian Brothers' Coll., Gibraltar. Served in Gibraltar Defence Force (now Gibraltar Regt), 1939-61. Company Director, 1962-. Founder Mem., Integration with Britain Party (first leader), 1967; apptd Chief Minister, following Gen. Elections, 1969. *Recreations:* walking, painting, reading, rowing. *Address:* Buena Vista Cottage, Buena Vista Road, Gibraltar. *Club:* Royal Gibraltar Yacht.

PELLEREAU, Maj.-Gen. Peter John Mitchell, MA, CEng, FIMechE, MBIM; Secretary, Association of Consulting Engineers, since 1977; *b* Quetta, British India, 24 April 1921; *s* of late Col J. C. E. Pellereau, OBE and of Mrs A. N. V. Pellereau (*née* Betham), Penshurst; *m* 1949, Rosemary, *e d* of S. R. Garnar, Old Palace, Wrotham; two *s. Educ:* Wellington Coll.; Trinity Coll., Cambridge. BA 1942, MA 1957. Commnd into Royal Engrs, 1942; War Service in NW Europe, 1942-45; OC 26 Armd Engr Sqdn, RE, 1946; ptsc, psc, 1950-51; Sec., Defence Research Policy Cttee, 1960; Asst Mil. Sec., WO, 1961; CO 131 Parachute Engr Regt RE TA, 1963; Mil. Dir of Studies, RMCS, 1965; Asst Dir RE Equipment Develt, 1967; Sen. Mil. Officer, Royal Armament R&D Estabt, 1970; Vice-Pres., 1973-75, Pres., 1975-76, Ordnance Board; retired 1976. *Recreations:* lawn tennis, ski-ing, hockey (as umpire; Pres., Oxted Hockey Club). Liveryman, Worshipful Co. of Plumbers, 1977. *Address:* Woodmans Folly, Crockham Hill, Edenbridge, Kent. *T:* Crockham Hill 309.

PELLETIER, Wilfrid, CC (Canada) 1967; CMG 1946; DM; *b* 20 June 1896; *m* 1936, Rose Bampton; two *s. Educ:* Montreal; Paris (France). Prix d'Europe, 1914; Assistant-conductor with Pierre Monteux, Albert Wolff and Louis Hasselmans at Metropolitan Opera House, New York City, 1916-19, Conductor, French and Italian Opera, to 1950; Ministère des Affaires Culturelles de la Province de Québec, 1942-70; Director Founder, Conservatoire de la Province de Québec, 1942-61. *Publication:* Une symphonie inachevée (autobiog.), 1972. *Recreations:* farm, collecting music manuscripts, autographs. *Address:* 322 East 57th Street, New York City, NY 10022, USA. *Cable:* Tierpelle Newyork. *Club:* Dutch Treat (New York City).

PELLEW, family name of **Viscount Exmouth.**

PELLING, Henry Mathison; Reader in Recent British History, Cambridge University, since 1976; Fellow of St John's College, since 1966; *b* 27 Aug. 1920; *s* of late D. L. Pelling, Prenton, Cheshire, and of Mrs M. M. Pelling; unmarried. *Educ:* Birkenhead School; St John's Coll., Cambridge. Class. Tripos Part I, 1941; History Tripos Part II, 1947 (MA 1945; PhD 1950; LittD 1975). Army service, 1941-45; Commnd RE, 1942; served NW Europe campaign, 1944-45. Fellow, Queen's Coll., Oxford, 1949-65; Tutor, 1950-65; Dean, 1963-64; Asst Dir of Research (History), Cambridge, 1966-76. Smith-Mundt Schol., University of Wisconsin, USA, 1953-54. *Publications:* Origins of the Labour Party, 1954; Challenge of Socialism, 1954; America and the British Left, 1956; British Communist Party, 1958; (with Frank Bealey) Labour and Politics, 1958; American Labor, 1960; Modern Britain, 1885-1955, 1960; Short History of the Labour Party, 1961; History of British Trade Unionism, 1963; Social Geography of British Elections, 1967; Popular Politics and Society in Late Victorian Britain, 1968; Britain and the Second World War, 1970; Winston Churchill, 1974; articles and reviews in learned journals. *Address:* St John's College, Cambridge CB2 1TP. *T:* Cambridge 61621. *Clubs:* National Liberal, Royal Commonwealth Society.

PELLIZZI, Camillo, DrJ (Pisa), DLit (London); Professor of Sociology, University of Florence, 1949-71, retired; *b* Collegno, Italy, 24 Aug. 1896; *s* of G. Battista Pellizzi and Giovanna Ferrari; *m* 1933, Raffaella Biozzi; two *s* one *d. Educ:* Pisa. Asst Lecturer, Reader then Professor of Italian at University College, University of London, 1920-40; Head of Division, then Councillor, on Training and Applied Social Sciences, OEEC, 1954-57. *Publications:* Problemi e realtà del Fascismo, 1924; Gli spiriti della vigilia, 1925; Le lettere italiane del nostro secolo, 1929; Il teatro inglese, 1934; Italy, 1939; Una rivoluzione mancata, 1948; Italian Sociology in our Century, 1957; Lineamenti di sistematica sociologica, 1964; Rito e linguaggio, 1964, etc. Editor, (Quarterly) Rassegna Italiana di Sociologia, 1960-. *Address:* 54 Via Gregoriana, 00187 Roma, Italy.

PELLOE, Rev. Canon John Parker; a Chaplain to the Queen, 1964-75; Hon. Canon of Ely Cathedral, 1952-53, and since 1965;

b 31 May 1905; *e s* of late Rev. E. P. Pelloe; *m* 1945, Kathleen, *d* of late Arthur Bland. *Educ:* Charterhouse; Queen's Coll., Oxford (MA); Cuddesdon Theological Coll. In business, 1922-32. Ordained 1936; Curate: St Columba, Sunderland, 1936-39; St Cuthbert, Kensington, 1939-42; Domestic Chaplain to Bishop of Ely, 1942-46; Vicar of Wisbech, 1946-60 (Rural Dean, 1946-53); Vicar of Stuntney, 1960-68; Archdeacon of Wisbech, 1953-64. *Recreation:* walking. *Address:* 14 Lynn Road, Ely, Cambs. *T:* Ely 2232.

PELLY, Sir Alwyne; *see* Pelly, Sir H. A.

PELLY, Cornelius James, CMG 1952; OBE 1944; *b* 8 April 1908; *e s* of Hyacinth Albert and Charity Mary Pelly, Benmore, Rushbrooke, Co. Cork, Eire; *m* 1949, Una O'Shea, *y d* of Patrick Seaborn O'Shea, Lismore, Co. Waterford; one *s* one *d. Educ:* Clongowes Wood Coll., Co. Kildare; Trinity Coll., Dublin. Entered Indian Civil Service by competitive examination, 1930; appointed to Punjab, 1931; Under-Secretary Punjab Government, 1935-36; transferred to Indian Political Service, 1936; Colonization Officer, Bahawalpur State, 1936-39; Political Agent and HM's Consul, Muscat, 1941-44; Consul, Bushire, 1946-47; Political Agent, Bahrain, 1947-51; Political Agent, Kuwait, 1951-55; Acting Political Resident, Persian Gulf, 1950 and 1952; Secretary for Financial Affairs, Sultanate of Muscat and Oman, 1968-70. *Recreations:* shooting, sailing. *Address:* 13 Leas Road, Warlingham, Surrey. *Clubs:* Travellers'; Royal Irish Yacht (Dun Laoghaire).

PELLY, Major Sir (Harold) Alwyne, 5th Bt, *cr* 1840; MC 1918; 7th Hussars, retired; *b* 27 Aug. 1893; *e s* of Sir Harold Pelly, 4th Bt, and Anna (*d* 1939), *d* of Robert Poore, Old Lodge, Salisbury; *S* father, 1950; *m* 1917, Carol (*d* 1976), *d* of late R. Heywood-Jones of Badsworth Hall, Yorkshire; three *s* one *d* (and one *s* decd). *Educ:* Wellington Coll.; Merton Coll., Oxford. Served European War, France and Mesopotamia (MC); Instructor Cavalry Sch., Netheravon, and Equitation Sch., Weedon, 1920-24; Adjutant, Leicestershire Yeomanry, 1927-31; retired, 1935. *Heir: s* Major John Alwyne Pelly, Coldstream Guards [*b* 11 Sept. 1918; *m* 1950, Elsie May, *d* of late L. Thomas Dechow, Rhodesia; one *d*. Served War of 1939-45 (prisoner of war); DL Hants]. *Address:* Preshaw House, Upham, Southampton SO3 1HP. *T:* Bishops Waltham 2531. *Club:* Cavalry and Guards. *See also Sir Thomas Lees, Bt.*

PELLY, Rear-Adm. Peter Douglas Herbert Raymond, CB 1958; DSO 1942; *b* 24 Sept. 1904; *s* of Rev. Douglas R. Pelly, DSO, and Verena Noellie (*née* Herbert); *m* 1932, Gwenllian Violet Edwardes; three *d. Educ:* RNC Osborne and Dartmouth. Joined Navy, 1918; normal peace-time services, except for appointment to Royal Yacht, 1939; served War of 1939-45; Commander, 1940; Comd Destroyer Windsor until 1940; 15th Cruiser Squadron, 1940-43; Plans Divison, Admiralty, 1943-45; Comd: Aircraft Carrier Ameer, 1945; HMS Raleigh, 1945-47; Captain, 1947; Admiralty, 1947-49; Reserve Fleet, Harwich, 1950; Captain (D) in Battleaxe, 1951-52; Chief Staff Officer, Gibraltar, 1952-54; Director of Ops Division, Admiralty, 1954-56; Rear-Admiral, 1956, Admiral Superintendent, HM Dockyard, Rosyth, Sept. 1956-Nov. 1957; Director-General of the Department of Dockyards and Maintenance, Admiralty, 1958-59; retired 1960. Sec., Assoc. of Consulting Engineers, 1960-69. Hon. Member, Smeatonian Society of Civil Engineers, 1965-70. Officer, Order of Orange Nassau (Holland), 1940. *Recreations:* normal. *Address:* Lowmersland, Les Rochers, Alderney, Channel Islands.

PELLY MURPHY, John; *see* Murphy, J. P.

PEMBERTON; *see* Leigh-Pemberton.

PEMBERTON, Sir Francis (Wingate William), Kt 1976; CBE 1970; FRICS; *b* 1 Oct. 1916; *s* of late Dr William Warburton Wingate (assumed Arms of Pemberton, by Royal Licence, 1921) and Viola Patience Campbell Pemberton; *m* 1941, Diana Patricia, *e d* of Reginald Salisbury Woods, *qv*, and late Irene Woods, CBE, TD; two *s. Educ:* Eton; Trinity Coll., Cambridge (MA). Senior Partner, Bidwells, Chartered Surveyors. Director: Agricultural Mortgage Corp. Ltd, 1969-; Barclays Bank UK Management Ltd, 1977-. Hon. Director: Royal Show, 1963-68; National Agricultural Centre, 1967-68 (Chm. Exec. Board, 1969-71); Member: Water Resources Board, 1964-74; Winston Churchill Meml Trust, 1965-; Economic Planning Council for East Anglia, 1965-74; National Water Council, 1974-; Council, RASE, 1951- (Pres., 1974-75; Dep. Pres., 1975-76). High Sheriff, Cambridgeshire and Isle of Ely, 1965-66. *Address:* Trumpington Hall, Cambridge. *T:* Trumpington 3157. *Club:* Farmers'.

PEMBERTON, Prof. John, MD London; FRCP, FFCM; DPH Leeds; Academic Co-ordinator, Northern Consortium, Trent Regional Health Authority; *b* 18 Nov. 1912; British; *m* 1937, Winifred Ethel Gray; three *s. Educ:* Christ's Hospital; University College and UCH, London. House Physician and House Surgeon, University College Hospital, 1936-37; Rowett Research Institute under the late Lord Boyd Orr, 1937-39; Rockefeller Travelling Fellow in Medicine, Harvard, Mass., USA, 1954-55; Director of MRC Group for research on Respiratory Disease and Air Pollution, and Reader in Social Medicine, University of Sheffield, 1955-58; Prof. of Social and Preventive Medicine, The Queen's Univ., Belfast, 1958-76. Mem., Health Educn Council, DHSS, 1973-76. Milroy Lectr, RCP, 1976. *Publications:* (with W. Hobson) The Health of the Elderly at Home, 1954; (ed) Recent Studies in Epidemiology, 1958; (ed) Epidemiology: Reports on Research and Teaching, 1963; Will Pickles of Wensleydale, 1970; articles in Lancet, BMJ, etc. *Recreations:* visual arts and fishing. *Address:* Iona, Cannon Fields, Hathersage, Sheffield S30 1AG.

PEMBROKE, 17th Earl of, *cr* 1551, and **MONTGOMERY,** 14th Earl of, *cr* 1605; **Henry George Charles Alexander Herbert;** Baron Herbert of Caerdiff, 1551; Baron Herbert of Shurland, 1605; Baron Herbert of Lea (UK), 1861; Hereditary Grand Visitor of Jesus College, Oxford; *b* 19 May 1939; *s* of 16th Earl of Pembroke and Montgomery, CVO, and of Mary Countess of Pembroke, *qv*; *S* father, 1969; *m* 1966, Claire Rose, *o d* of Douglas Pelly, Swaynes Hall, Widdington, Essex; three *d. Educ:* Eton Coll.; Oxford Univ. Royal Horse Guards, 1958-60 (National Service); Oxford University, 1960-63. *Recreations:* photography, gardening, horse racing. *Heir: uncle* Hon. David Alexander Reginald Herbert, *b* 3 Oct. 1908. *Address:* Wilton House, Salisbury, Wilts. *T:* Wilton 3211.

PEMBROKE, Mary Countess of; Mary Dorothea Herbert, CVO 1947; Extra Lady-in-Waiting to Princess Marina, Duchess of Kent, 1950-68 (Lady-in-Waiting, 1934-50); *o d* of 1st Marquess of Linlithgow; *m* 1936, Lord Herbert (later 16th Earl of Pembroke and Montgomery, who *d* 1969); one *s* one *d. Address:* The Old Rectory, Wilton, near Salisbury, Wilts. *T:* Wilton 3157.

PENDER, 3rd Baron, *cr* 1937; **John Willoughby Denison-Pender;** *b* 6 May 1933; *s* of 2nd Baron and Camilla Lethbridge, *o d* of late Willoughby Arthur Pemberton; *S* father, 1965; *m* 1962, Julia, *yr d* of Richard Nevill Cannon; one *s* two *d. Educ:* Eton. Formerly Lieut, 10th Royal Hussars and Captain, City of London Yeomanry (TA). *Heir: s* Hon. Henry John Richard Denison-Pender, *b* 19 March 1968. *Address:* North Court, Tilmanstone, Kent. *Clubs:* White's, Pratt's.

PENDERECKI, Krzysztof; Rector, State Academy of Music, Kraków, since 1972; Professor of Composition, School of Music, Yale University, New Haven, Conn, since 1973; *b* Debica, Poland, 23 Nov. 1933; *s* of Tadeusz Penderecki and Zofia Penderecki; *m* 1965, Elzbieta Solecka; one *s* one *d . Educ:* State Acad. of Music, Kraków, Poland (Graduate 1958). Compositions include: Threnody to the Victims of Hiroshima, 1959-61 (52 strings); Passion According to St Luke, 1965-66 (oratorio); Utrenja, 1969-71 (oratorio); Devils of Loudun, 1969 (opera); First Symphony, 1972; Magnificat, 1974 (oratorio); Awakening of Jacob, 1974 (orchestra); Paradise Lost, 1977 (rappresentazione for Chicago Lyric Opera; Milton libretto; Christopher Fry). Hon. Dr Univ. of Rochester, NY; Hon. Member: Kungl. Musikaliska Akademien, Sweden; Akademie der Künste, Germany; Royal Academy of Music, England; Accademia Nazionale di Santa Cecilia, Italy. Preis Nordrhein-Westfalen, 1966; Prix Italia, 1967/68. *Publications:* all works published. *Recreation:* collecting old furniture, clocks and paintings. *Address:* Cisowa 22, 30229 Kraków, Poland. *T:* 25760; 324 Livingston Street, New Haven, Conn 06511, USA. *T:* 203-777-3142.

PENDRED, Air Marshal Sir Lawrence Fleming, KBE 1954 (MBE 1933); CB 1947; DFC; DL; *b* 5 May 1899; *s* of Dr B. F. and Eleanor Pendred; *m* 1923, Nina Chour; two *s. Educ:* Epsom Coll. Served European War, 1914-18, with RNAS and RAF in France, 1918; Permanent Commission RAF, 1920; served in Egypt and Turkey (208 Squadron), 1920-23; Flying Instructor, including 4 years at Central Flying School, 1924-30; Staff Officer Intelligence, Transjordan and Palestine, 1930-34; psa Andover, 1935; Sqdn Leader, 1935; Chief Flying Instructor, Montrose, 1936-37; Air Ministry, 1937-40; Wing Comdr, 1938; Bomber Station Commander, 1940-41, Group Captain; Chief Intelligence Officer, Bomber Command, 1942; Director of Intelligence, Air Ministry, 1943; Air Commodore, Chief Intelligence Officer, AEAF, 1944; Asst Comdt RAF, Staff Coll., 1944-45; AOC 227 Group, India, 1945; Director of Intelligence to Supreme Commander, South East Asia, 1946; acting Air

Vice-Marshal, Dec. 1945; Air Vice-Marshal, 1948; Assistant Chief of Air Staff (Intelligence), 1947-49; Commandant, School of Land-Air Warfare, 1950-52; Air Officer Commanding-in-Chief, Flying Training Command, 1952-55; retired, 1955. Regional Director Civil Defence (Midland), 1955-63. DL Warwickshire, 1959. Grand Officer Polonia Restituta; Commander, Legion of Merit. *Address:* 13 Lansdowne Circus, Leamington Spa, Warwicks. *T:* Leamington Spa 23559.

PENDRY, Thomas; MP (Lab) Stalybridge and Hyde since 1970; *b* 10 June 1934; *m* 1966, Moira Anne Smith; one *d*. *Educ:* St Augustine's, Ramsgate; Oxford Univ. RAF, 1955-57. Full time official, Nat. Union of Public Employees, 1960-70; Mem., Paddington Borough Council, 1962-65; Chm., Derby Labour Party, 1966. An Opposition Whip, 1971-74; a Lord Comr of the Treasury and Govt Whip, 1974, resigned 1977. Member: Speaker's Conf., 1973; UK delegn to WEU and Council of Europe, 1973-; Industrial Law Soc. Pres., Stalybridge Public Band. *Recreations:* sport; football, cricket, boxing (sometime Middleweight Champion, Hong Kong; boxed for Oxford Univ.). *Address:* Chapel House, Gorsey Brow, Broadbottom, Cheshire. *Clubs:* Reform; Manchester Press; Stalybridge and Hyde Labour.

PENFOLD, Maj.-Gen. Robert Bernard, CB 1969; MVO 1957; General Manager, Royal Hong Kong Jockey Club, since 1972; *b* 19 Dec. 1916; *s* of late Bernard Hugh Penfold, Selsey, and late Ethel Ives Arnold; *m* 1940, Ursula, *d* of Lt-Col E. H. Gray; two *d*. *Educ:* Wellington; RMC, Sandhurst. Commnd into 11th Sikh Regt, Indian Army, 1936; served in NWFP and during War of 1939-45 in Middle East, Central Mediterranean Forces; Instructor, Staff Coll., Quetta, 1946-47; transf. to British Army, RA, 1947; RN Staff Coll., 1953; Secretary, British Joint Services Mission, Washington, 1957-59; comdg 6 King's African Rifles, Tanganyika, 1959-61; Comdr 127 Inf. Bde (TA), 1962-64; Security Ops Adviser to High Commissioner, Aden, 1964-65; Imperial Defence Coll., 1966; Chief of Defence Staff, Kenya, 1966-69; GOC South East District, 1969-72. *Recreations:* shooting, golf, gardening. *Address:* c/o Grindlays Bank, 13 St James's Square, SW1; Royal Hong Kong Jockey Club, Hong Kong. *Club:* Army and Navy.

PENGELLY, William Lister; Master of Supreme Court of Judicature, Chancery Division, 1950-64; *b* 21 Dec. 1892; *s* of Frederick Charles Goldsworthy Pengelly; *m* 1919; two *d*. *Educ:* Varndean, Brighton; Culham Coll., Culham, Oxfordshire. Lady Aubrey Fletcher Exhib. for violin, Brighton School of Music, 1908. Solicitor, 1921; Senior Partner in Pengelly & Co., 8 New Court, Lincoln's Inn, WC2, solicitors, until 1950. Served European War, 1914-18; 2nd Lieut, 2/5 Devon Regt, 1914; Lieut, 1915; in Egypt, 1915-16; in Mesopotamia, 1916 and 1917 with 4th Devon Regt (wounded); Asst Adjutant with 4th (R) Devon Regt, 1918-19; Captain, 1919. War of 1939-45, Major and Supervising Military Liaison Officer (Z Sector), Home Guard. Chairman of The Comedy Club, 1932-59; Captain London Solicitors Golfing Society, 1950-51; Founder Royal Courts of Justice Music Club, 1953. Member Worshipful Company of Musicians; Freeman of the City of London. *Recreations:* music and golf. *Address:* 11 West Hill Court, Budleigh Salterton, Devon. *Club:* East Devon Golf.

PENHALIGON, David Charles; MP (L) Truro since Oct. 1974; *b* 6 June 1944; *s* of late Robert Charles Penhaligon and of Sadie Jewell; *m* 1968, Annette Lidgey; one *s*. *Educ:* Truro Sch.; Cornwall Techn. College. CEng, MIMechE. R&D Engr, Holman Bros, Camborne, 1962-74. *Address:* 7 Fore Street, Chacewater, Truro, Cornwall. *T:* Threewaters 325. *Club:* National Liberal.

PENLEY, William Henry, CB 1967; CBE 1961; PhD; Controller, Research and Development Establishments, and Research, Ministry of Defence, 1976-77; *b* 22 March 1917; *s* of late William Edward Penley and late Clara (*née* Dodgson), Wallasey, Cheshire; *m* 1st, 1943, Raymonde Evelyn (*d* 1975), *d* of Frederick Richard Gough, Swanage, Dorset; two *s* one *d*; 2nd, 1977, Marion Claytor (*née* Airey). *Educ:* Wallasey Grammar Sch.; Liverpool Univ., BEng, 1937; PhD, 1940. FIEE (MIEE 1964); FRAeS, 1967; FRSA 1975. Head of Guided Weapons Department, Royal Radar Establishment, 1953-61; Director, Royal Radar Establishment, 1961-62; Director-General of Electronics Research and Development, Ministry of Aviation, 1962-64; Deputy Controller of Electronics, Ministry of Aviation, then Ministry of Technology, 1964-67; Dir, Royal Armament R&D Establishment, 1967-70; Chief Scientist (Army), 1970-75, Dep. Controller, Establishments and Res. B, 1971-75, MoD. *Address:* Beechwood, 13 Garth Road, Sevenoaks, Kent. *T:* Sevenoaks 54794.

PENMAN, Gerard Giles, MA, MD (Cantab), FRCS; Hon. Consulting Ophthalmic Surgeon, St Thomas' Hospital; Hon. Consulting Surgeon, Moorfields Eye Hospital; Consulting Ophthalmic Surgeon, Royal Hospital for Incurables, Putney; Fellow, Royal Society of Medicine and Hunterian Society; Member Ophthalmological Society of the UK and Oxford Ophthalmological Congress; Vice President, Dorset County Association for the Blind; *b* Port Elizabeth, 7 March 1899; *s* of late J. C. Penman and Grace Penman, Salisbury, Rhodesia, and Sherborne, Dorset; *m* 1928, Janet, *d* of late Dr J. Walter Carr, CBE; three *s*. *Educ:* Sherborne Sch.; Pembroke Coll., Cambridge; St Thomas' Hospital. Royal Field Artillery, 1917-19; Ophthalmic Surgeon, Royal Northern Hospital, 1926-31; Ophthalmic Surgeon, Hospital for Sick Children, Great Ormond Street, 1931-36; Examiner in Ophthalmology, Royal College of Physicians, 1962-65. *Publications:* The Projection of the Retina in the Lateral Geniculate Body (with W. E. le Gros Clark) (Proceedings of the Royal Society, 1934); The Position occupied by the Peripheral Retinal Fibres at the Nerve Head (with E. Wolff) (Internat. Ophthalmological Congress, 1950), etc. *Recreations:* archaeology, horticulture, philately. *Address:* Silversmiths, Newland, Sherborne, Dorset.

PENMAN, Dr Howard Latimer, OBE 1962; FRS 1962; Head of Physics Department, Rothamsted Experimental Station, 1955-74. Doctorate, Durham Univ., 1937. Has made physical studies of agricultural and botanical problems, particularly on transpiration and the irrigation of crops. *Publications:* Humidity (Monographs for Students, Inst. of Physics), 1955; Vegetation and Hydrology (Comm. Agric. Bur.), 1963. *Recreations:* music, golf. *Address:* 31 Dalkeith Road, Harpenden, Herts AL5 5PP. *T:* Harpenden 3366.

PENMAN, John, FRCP; Neurologist to: The Royal Marsden Hospital since 1954; The County Hospital, Hertford, and Haymeads Hospital, Bishop's Stortford; *b* 10 Feb. 1913; *er s* of late William Penman, FIA; *m* 1938, Joan, *d* of late Claude Johnson (marr. diss. 1976); one *s* two *d*; *m* 1976, Elisabeth Quin. *Educ:* Tonbridge Sch.; University College, Oxford (Senior Classical Scholar); Queen Mary Coll., E1; The London Hospital. MB, BS (London) 1944; MRCP 1948, FRCP 1969. Member of Association of British Neurologists. *Publications:* contributions to medical journals, mainly on tic douloureux and brain tumours; section on trigeminal injection, in Operative Surgery, 1957; chapters in Handbook of Clinical Neurology, 1968. *Recreations:* poetry; etymology; looking at Norman cathedrals. *Address:* Granard House, The Royal Marsden Hospital, Fulham Road, SW3; 4 Summerleigh, Gower Road, Weybridge, Surrey. *Club:* Royal Automobile.

PENN, Lt-Col Sir Eric, KCVO 1972; OBE 1960; MC 1944; Comptroller, Lord Chamberlain's Office, since 1964; Extra Equerry to the Queen since 1963; *b* 9 Feb. 1916; *o s* of Capt. Eric F. Penn (killed in action 1915), Grenadier Guards, and late Gladys Ebden; *m* 1947, Prudence Stewart-Wilson, *d* of late Aubyn Wilson and Muriel Stewart-Stevens, Balnakeilly, Pitlochry, Perthshire; two *s* one *d*. *Educ:* Eton; Magdalene Coll., Cambridge. Grenadier Guards, 1938-60. Assistant Comptroller, Lord Chamberlain's Office, 1960-64. CVO 1965. *Address:* Sternfield House, Saxmundham, Suffolk. *T:* Saxmundham 2456; St James's Palace, SW1; *T:* 01-839 3936. *Clubs:* Turf, White's.

PENNANT; see Douglas-Pennant.

PENNANT, David Edward Thornton; His Honour Judge Pennant; a Circuit Judge (formerly County Court Judge), since 1961; *b* 2 Aug. 1912; *s* of David Falconer Pennant, DL, JP, Barrister-at-law, late of Nantlys, St Asaph, N. Wales, and late Lilla Agnes Pennant; *m* 1938, Alice Catherine Stainer; three *s* one *d*. *Educ:* Charterhouse; Trinity Coll., Cambridge. Called to Bar, Inner Temple, 1935. Served, 1939-45, with Royal Signals (TA); OC, Signals Officers' Training Sch., Mhow, India, 1944-45. Chancellor, Dio. Monmouth, 1949-77. Governing, and Representative Bodies, Church in Wales, 1946-. Dep. Chairman, Brecknockshire QS, 1956-64; Joint Chairman, Medical Appeals Tribunal for Wales, 1957-61; Chairman, Radnorshire QS, 1962-64; Dep. Chairman, Flintshire QS, 1962-71; Mem., County Court Rule Cttee, 1970-. *Recreation:* gardening. *Address:* Parkbury, Balcombe Road, Branksome Park, Poole, Dorset. *T:* Bournemouth 765614.

PENNELL, Rev. Canon (James Henry) Leslie, TD and Bar, 1949; Rector of Foxearth and Pentlow (Diocese of Chelmsford), 1965-72, and of Borley and Lyston (Diocese of Chelmsford), 1969-72; Hon. Canon, Inverness Cathedral, since 1965 (Provost, 1949-65); *b* 9 Feb. 1906; *s* of late J. H. L. Pennell and late Elizabeth Esmé Gordon Steel; *m* 1939, Ursula Mary, *d* of Rev. A. E. Gledhill; twin *s* and *d*. *Educ:* Edinburgh Academy;

Edinburgh University (BL); Edinburgh Theological College. Precentor, Inverness Cathedral, 1929-32; Rector, St Mary's, Dunblane, and Offic. Chaplain to Queen Victoria School, 1932-49; Officiating Chaplain, Cameron Barracks, 1949-64. TA, 1934; BEF, 1940; SCF, 1943; DACG, 34th Ind. Corps, 1945; SCF Corps Troops, Scottish Comd, 1946-50. *Recreations:* reading and travel. *Address:* The Croft, Hundon, Clare, Suffolk. *T:* Hundon 221.

PENNELL, Montague Mattinson, CBE 1970; Deputy Chairman, since 1975 and Managing Director, since 1972, British Petroleum Co. Ltd; *b* 20 March 1916; *s* of F. M. S. Pennell; *m* 1945, Helen Williams; one *s* two *d. Educ:* Liverpool Univ. (BSc). Royal Corps of Signals, 1939-46; British Petroleum Co. Ltd, 1946-: Iran, E Africa, Sicily, USA, Libya and London. Member: Adv. Council for R&D in Fuel and Power, 1972-; Adv. Council for Applied R&D, 1976-. *Address:* 52 Onslow Square, SW7 3NX; Rushdens Farm, Stanford Dingley, Berks. *Club:* MCC.

PENNEY, family name of **Baron Penney.**

PENNEY, Baron, *cr* 1967, of East Hendred (Life Peer); **William George Penney,** OM 1969; KBE 1952 (OBE 1946); MA; PhD; DSc; FRS 1946; Rector of the Imperial College of Science and Technology, 1967-73; *b* 24 June 1909; *s* of W. A. Penney, Sheerness, Kent; *m* 1st, 1935, Adele Minnie Elms (decd); two *s*; 2nd, 1945, Eleanor Joan Quennell. *Educ:* Tech. School, Sheerness; Royal College of Science, London Univ. (BSc, PhD). Commonwealth Fund Fellowship. University of Wisconsin (MA), 1931-33; Senior Student of 1851 Exhibition, Trinity Coll., Cambridge, 1933-36; PhD (Cambridge), DSc (London), 1935; Stokes Student of Pembroke Coll., 1936; Assistant Professor of Mathematics at Imperial College of Science, London, 1936-45; on loan for scientific work to Ministry of Home Security and Admiralty, 1940-44; Principal Scientific Officer, DSIR, at Los Alamos Laboratory, New Mexico, 1944-45; Chief Superintendent, Armament Research, Ministry of Supply, 1946-52; Director Atomic Weapons Research Establishment, Aldermaston, 1953-59; Member for Weapons R&D, UKAEA, 1954-59; Member for Research, UKAEA, 1959-61; Dep. Chm., 1961-64; Chm., 1964-67. Director: Tube Investments, 1968-; Standard Telephones and Cables, 1971-. Treasurer, Royal Society, 1956-60 (Vice-President, 1957-60); Fellow, Imperial Coll.; Fellow, Winchester Coll., 1959; Supernumerary Fellow, St Catherine's Coll., Oxford, 1960; Hon Fellow: Manchester College of Science and Technology, 1962; Trinity Coll., Cambridge, 1969; Pembroke Coll., Cambridge, 1970; Hon FRSE, 1970; For. Assoc., National Academy of Sciences, USA, 1962. Hon. DSc: Durham, 1957; Oxford, 1959; Bath University of Technology, 1966; Hon. LLD Melbourne, 1956. Rumford Medal, Royal Society, 1966; Glazebrook Medal and Prize, 1969; Kelvin Gold Medal, 1971. *Publications:* articles in scientific journals on theory of molecular structure. *Recreations:* golf, cricket. *Address:* Orchard House, East Hendred, Wantage, Oxon. *Club:* Athenæum.

PENNEY, Reginald John; Assistant Under-Secretary of State, Ministry of Defence, 1964-73, retired; *b* 22 May 1919; *s* of Herbert Penney and Charlotte Penney (*née* Affleck); *m* 1941, Eileen Gardiner; one *s* two *d. Educ:* Westminster School. War Service, Royal West Kent Regt, 1939-46. Civil Servant, Air Ministry, until 1964, including service with Far East Air Force, Singapore, 1960-63. Chm., Sherborne Soc., CPRE, 1976. *Recreation:* golf. *Address:* Rumbow Cottage, Acreman Street, Sherborne, Dorset.

PENNINGTON, Prof. Robert Roland; Professor of Commercial Law, Birmingham University, since 1968; Special Legal Adviser to Commission of European Communities since 1972; *b* 22 April 1927; *s* of R. A. Pennington; *m* 1965, Patricia Irene; one *d. Educ:* Birmingham Univ. (LLB, LLD). Solicitor. Reader, Law Soc.'s Sch. of Law, 1951-62; Mem. Bd of Management, Coll. of Law, 1962; Sen. Lectr in Commercial Law, Birmingham Univ., 1962-68. Govt Adviser on Company Legislation, Trinidad, 1967 and Seychelles, 1977; UN Adviser on Commercial Law, 1970-. Editor, European Commercial Law Library, 1974-. *Publications:* Company Law, 1959, 4th edn 1978; Companies in the Common Market, 1962, 2nd edn 1970; The Investor and the Law, 1967; Stannary Law: A History of the Mining Law of Cornwall and Devon, 1973. *Recreations:* travel, walking, history, archaeology. *Address:* Gryphon House, Langley Road, Claverdon, Warwicks.

PENNINGTON-RAMSDEN, Major Sir (Geoffrey) William, 7th Bt, *cr* 1689; Major, Life Guards, retired; *b* 28 Aug. 1904; *yr* (but *o* surv.) *s* of Sir John Frecheville Ramsden, 6th Bt and Joan (*d* 1974), *d* of late G. F. Buxton, CB, Hoveton Hall; *S* father 1958; assumed by deed poll, 1925, surname of Pennington in lieu of

Ramsden; resumed surname of Ramsden after that of Pennington by deed poll, 1958; *m* 1927, Veronica Prudence Betty, *o d* of F. W. Morley, formerly of Biddestone Manor, Chippenham, Wilts; three *d. Educ:* Ludgrove; Eton; Jesus Coll., Cambridge (BA). Joined 11th Hussars, 1925; transferred Life Guards, 1927-38; served War of 1939-45; seconded to Provost Branch; APM 9th Armd Div. and APM 14th Army; Major, 1942. High Sheriff, Cumberland, 1962-63. *Heir: kinsman* Caryl Oliver Imbert Ramsden, *qv. Address:* Versions Farm, Brackley, Northants. *T:* Brackley 2412; Ardverikie, Newtonmore, Scotland; (seat) Muncaster Castle, Ravenglass, Cumberland. *T:* Ravenglass 203. *Club:* Lansdowne.

PENNISON, Clifford Francis, CBE 1977; *b* 28 June 1913; *s* of Henry and Alice Pennison; *m* 1940, Joan Margaret Hopkins; three *d. Educ:* Taunton Sch.; Bristol Univ. (BA, 1st Cl. Hons, Hist.). Barrister-at-Law, Inner Temple, 1951. Appointed senior management trainee, Unilever Ltd, 1938. Field Security Officer, Army, 1940-46 (Captain). Principal, Home Civil Service, 1946; Assistant Secretary, and Director of Organisation and Methods, Ministry of Food, 1949; Ministry of Agriculture: Director of Statistics Div., 1953; Director of Public Relations Div., 1958; Director of External Relations Div., 1961; FAO: Permanent UK representative, 1963-66; Director, Economic Analysis Div., 1966-67; Asst Dir-Gen., Admin and Finance, 1967-74; Consultant, EEC/FAO relations, 1974-76; retired 1976. *Recreations:* travel, reading, foreign languages, tennis. *Address:* Casa Scafati, Settefichi, Fisciano, Salerno, Italy. *Club:* Beaulieu Tennis.

PENNOCK, Raymond William; Deputy Chairman, Imperial Chemical Industries Ltd, since 1975; *b* 16 June 1920; *s* of Frederick Henry Pennock and Harriet Anne Pennock (*née* Mathieson); *m* 1944, Lorna Pearse; one *s* two *d . Educ:* Coatham Sch; Oxford Univ. (MA). 2nd cl. hons History, Dipl. Educn and Psychol. Royal Artillery (Captain), 1941-46 (despatches 1945). Joined ICI Ltd, 1947; Personnel Management and Commercial duties, 1947-61; Commercial Dir, Billingham Div., 1961-64; Dep. Chm., Billingham Div., 1964-68; Chm., Agric. (formerly Billingham) Div. 1968-72; Director, ICI Ltd, 1972. Chm., Economic Situation Cttee, CBI, 1977-. Governor, Durham Sch.; Mem. Nat. Council, Oxford Soc. *Recreations:* tennis, music, ballet, travel. *Address:* Imperial Chemical Industries Ltd, Imperial Chemical House, Millbank, SW1P 3JF. *Clubs:* Queen's, Royal Tennis Court.

PENNY, family name of **Viscount Marchwood.**

PENNY, Francis David, FRSE; Managing Director, Y-ARD Ltd, since 1969; Director, Yarrow & Co. Ltd; *b* 20 May 1918; *s* of late David Penny and Esther Colley; *m* 1949, Betty E. Smith, *d* of late Oswald C. Smith. *Educ:* Bromsgrove County High School; University Coll., London (BSc), Fellow 1973. Engineering Apprenticeship, Cadbury Bros Ltd, 1934-39; Armament Design Establishment, Ministry of Supply, 1939-53; Chief Development Engineer, Fuel Research Station, 1954-58; Dep. Dir, Nat. Engineering Laboratory, 1959-66, Dir, 1967-69. FIMarE; FIMechE; Member Council, IMechE, 1964- (a Vice-Pres., 1977-). *Publications:* various technical papers. *Recreations:* gardening, cricket, walking. *Address:* Forefaulds, East Kilbride, Glasgow. *T:* East Kilbride 20102.

PENNY, Sir James Downing, KCIE, *cr* 1943 (CIE 1937); CSI 1939; *b* 25 May 1886; *s* of late Edward Penny, MD, Medical Officer, Marlborough Coll.; *m* 1917, Margaret Mary Wilson (*d* 1962); one *d. Educ:* Marlborough Coll.; Magdalen Coll., Oxford (Classical Demy); 1st Class Classical Mods, 1907; 1st Class Lit. Hum. 1909; ICS 1910; Captain, IA Reserve of Officers, 1918; Deputy Secretary Government of India Finance Dept, 1926; Finance Secretary, Punjab Government, 1927-30; Officiating Commissioner, Multan Div., 1934, Lahore, 1935, Rawalpindi Div., 1936; Chief Secretary, 1937-41; Financial Commissioner, Development Dept and Secretary to Government of Punjab, 1941; retired, 1945. *Address:* 19 Five Mile Drive, Oxford.

PENNY, Joseph Noel Bailey, QC 1971; *b* 25 Dec. 1916; *s* of Joseph A. Penny, JP and Isabella Downie, JP; *m* 1st, 1947, Celia (*d* 1969), *d* of Mr and Mrs R. H. Roberts; three *s* one *d* ; 2nd, 1972, Sara Margaret, *d* of Sir Arnold France, *qv* ; one *d . Educ:* Worksop College; Christ Church, Oxford; MA (Oxon). Major, Royal Signals, 1939-46 (despatches). Called to Bar, Gray's Inn, 1948. A Nat. Insurance Comr, 1977-. *Recreations:* wine and song, travel and amateur dramatics. *Address:* Fair Orchard, Lingfield, Surrey. *T:* Lingfield 191.

PENNYBACKER, Joseph Buford, CBE 1967; Director, Department of Neurological Surgery, Radcliffe Infirmary, Oxford, 1954-71; *b* 23 Aug. 1907; *s* of Claude Martin

Pennybacker and Katherine Miller Mershon; *m* 1941, Winifrid Dean; one *s*. *Educ:* Universities of Tennessee and Edinburgh. BA (Tennessee) 1926; MB, ChB (Edinburgh) 1930; FRCS 1935; MA (Oxon) 1938; MD (Edinburgh) 1941. Resident appointments: Royal Infirmary, Edinburgh; Grimsby District Hospital; National Hospital, Queen Square; First Asst, Neurosurgical Dept, London Hospital; First Asst to Nuffield Prof. of Surgery, University of Oxford. Cross of Royal Order of George I, Greece, 1966. *Publications:* papers in neurological and surgical journals. *Recreations:* history, horticulture. *Address:* Creagandarraich, Tighnabruaich, Argyll. *T:* Tighnabruaich 260. *Club:* Athenæum.

PENNYCUICK, Rt. Hon. Sir John, PC 1974; Kt 1960; Judge of High Court of Justice, Chancery Division, 1960-74, Vice-Chancellor, 1970-74; *b* 6 Nov. 1899; *s* of late Colonel John Pennycuick, CSI, and Georgiana Grace Pennycuick; *m* 1930, Lucy Johnstone (*d* 1972); one *s* one *d. Educ:* Winchester; New Coll., Oxford. 2nd Lieut, Coldstream Guards, 1919; BA Oxford, 1922; Barrister, Inner Temple, 1925; KC 1947; Bencher, 1954. *Address:* Old Manor House, Maids Moreton, Buckingham. *T:* Buckingham 2249; 2 Harcourt Buildings, Temple, EC4. *T:* 01-583 1875. *Clubs:* Garrick; All England Lawn Tennis (Wimbledon).

PENRHYN, 6th Baron *cr* 1866; **Malcolm Frank Douglas-Pennant,** DSO 1945; MBE 1943; *b* 11 July 1908; 2nd *s* of 5th Baron Penrhyn and Alice Nellie (*d* 1965), *o d* of Sir William Charles Cooper, 3rd Bt; *S* father 1967; *m* 1954, Elisabeth Rosemary, *d* of late Brig. Sir Percy Laurie, KCVO, CBE, DSO, JP; two *d. Educ:* Eton; RMC, Sandhurst. Colonel (retd), KRRC. *Heir: b* Hon. Nigel Douglas-Pennant [*b* 22 Dec. 1909; *m* 1st, 1935, Margaret Dorothy (*d* 1938), *d* of T. G. Kirkham; one *s*; 2nd, 1940, Eleanor Stewart, *d* of late Very Rev. H. N. Craig; one *s* one *d*]. *Address:* Dean Farm, Bishops Waltham, Southampton. *T:* 2598. *Clubs:* Naval and Military, MCC.

PENRICE, Geoffrey; Director of Statistics, Department of the Environment, since 1973; *b* Wakefield, 28 Feb. 1923; *s* of Harry and Jessie Penrice; *m* 1947, Janet Gillies Allardice; three *s. Educ:* Thornes House Grammar Sch.; London Sch. of Economics. Control Commn for Germany, 1947; Asst Lectr in Statistics, LSE, 1952; Statistician, Inland Revenue, 1956; Statistician and Chief Statistician, Central Statistical Office, 1964; Chief Statistician, Min. of Housing and Local Govt, 1968; BoT, Min. of Technology, DTI, as Under-Sec., 1968-73. Statistical Adviser to Cttee on Working of Monetary System, 1957-59. *Publications:* articles on wages, earnings, financial statistics and housing statistics. *Address:* 10 Dartmouth Park Avenue, NW5. *T:* 01-267 2175.

PENRITH, Bishop Suffragan of, since 1970; **Rt. Rev. William Edward Augustus Pugh,** MA, LRAM (Singing); *b* 22 July 1909; *s* of William Arthur Augustus and Margaret Caroline Pugh; *m* 1937, Freda Mary, *er d* of Charles Frederick and Susannah Merishaw; no *c. Educ:* Leeds Univ.; College of the Resurrection, Mirfield. Assistant Curate: Staveley, Derbys, 1934-37; Edwinstowe, Notts, 1937-38; Rector of Bestwood Park, Notts, 1938-44; Vicar of Sutton-in-Ashfield, Notts, 1944-55; Hon. Canon of Southwell, 1954; Vicar of East Retford, Notts, 1955-59; Rector of Harrington, 1959-62; Vicar of Cockermouth, 1962-70, and Archdeacon of West Cumberland, 1959-70. *Recreations:* fishing, music. *Address:* Bishop's House, Clappersgate, Ambleside, Cumbria. *T:* Ambleside 3158.

PENROSE, Prof. Edith Tilton; Professor of Economics (with reference to Asia), School of Oriental and African Studies, University of London, since 1964; Professor, Institut Européen d'Administration des Affaires, Fontainebleau, since 1977; *b* 29 Nov. 1914; *d* of George Albert Tilton and Hazel Sparling Tilton; *m* 1st, 1934, David Burton Denhardt (*d* 1938); 2nd, 1944, Ernest F. Penrose; three *s* (and one *s* decd). *Educ:* Univ. of California, Berkeley (AB); Johns Hopkins Univ. (MA, PhD). Research Assoc., ILO, Geneva and Montreal, 1939-41; Special Asst, US Ambassador, London, 1941-46; US Delegn to UN, NY, 1946-47; research at Johns Hopkins Univ., 1948-50; Lectr and Res. Assoc., Johns Hopkins Univ., 1950-60; Vis. Fellow, Australian Nat. Univ., 1955-56; Assoc. Prof. of Econs, Univ. Baghdad, 1957-59; Reader in Econs, Univ. of London (LSE and SOAS), 1960-64; Actg Head, Dept of Econs and Polit. Studies, 1961-64; Head, Dept of Econs, SOAS, 1964-69; Visiting Professor: Univ. Dar Es Salaam, 1971-72; Univ. of Toronto, 1977. Member: Sainsbury Cttee of Enquiry into Relationship of Pharmaceutical Industry with Nat. Health Service, 1965-67; SSRC, 1974-76 (Econ. Cttee, 1970-76, Chm., 1974-76); Medicines Commn, 1975-; Dir, Commonwealth Develt Corp., 1975-; Mem. Council, Royal Economic Soc., 1975-; Governor, NIESR, 1974-. *Publications:* Food Control in Great Britain, 1940; Economics of

the International Patent System, 1951 (trans. Japanese, Spanish); The Theory of the Growth of the Firm, 1959 (trans. Japanese, French, Spanish, Italian); The Large International Firm in Developing Countries: The International Petroleum Industry, 1968 (trans. Japanese); The Growth of Firms, Middle East Oil and Other Essays, 1971; contrib. Amer. Econ. Rev., Bus. Hist. Rev., Econ. Jl, Economica, Jl Dev. Studies, Jl Econ. History, Yearbook of World Affairs, Etudes Internationales, Mondes en Développement. *Recreations:* travel, theatre, gardening. *Address:* 15 Chaldon Way, Coulsdon, Surrey. *T:* Downland 53421.

PENROSE, Maj.-Gen. (retd) John Hubert, OBE 1956; MC 1944; *b* 24 Oct. 1916; *e s* of late Brig. John Penrose, MC and late Mrs M. C. Penrose (*née* Hendrick-Aylmer); *m* 1941, Pamela Elizabeth, *d* of late H. P. Lloyd, Neath, Glam.; four *d. Educ:* Winchester Coll.; RMA Woolwich, 2nd Lieut, RA, 1936; war service in European Theatre, BEF, 1939-40, and BLA, 1944; subseq. service in India, Germany, Malaya and UK; idc 1964; Defence Adviser to British High Comr, New Delhi, 1968-71; retired 1972. *Address:* West Hoe House, Bishop's Waltham, Southampton SO3 1DT. *T:* Bishop's Waltham 2363.

PENROSE, Prof. Roger, FRS 1972; Rouse Ball Professor of Mathematics, University of Oxford, since 1973; *b* Colchester, Essex, 8 Aug. 1931; *s* of Lionel Sharples Penrose, FRS; *m* 1959, Joan Isabel Wedge; three *s. Educ:* University Coll. Sch.; University Coll., Univ. of London (BSc spec. 1st cl. Mathematics), Fellow 1975; St John's Coll., Cambridge (PhD). NRDC (temp. post, Feb.-Aug. 1956); Asst Lectr (Pure Mathematics), Bedford Coll., London, 1956-57; Research Fellow, St John's Coll., Cambridge, 1957-60; NATO Research Fellow, Princeton Univ. and Syracuse Univ., 1959-61; Research Associate King's Coll., London, 1961-63; Visiting Associate Prof., Univ. of Texas, Austin, Texas, 1963-64; Reader, 1964-66, Prof. of Applied Mathematics, 1966-73, Birkbeck Coll., London. Visiting Prof., Yeshiva, Princeton, Cornell, 1966-67 and 1969. Adams Prize (Cambridge Univ.), 1966-67; Dannie Heineman Prize (Amer. Phys. Soc. and Amer. Inst. Physics), 1971; Eddington Medal, RAS, 1975. Member: London Mathematical Soc.; Cambridge Philosophical Soc.; American Mathematical Soc. *Publications:* Techniques of Differential Topology in Relativity, 1973; many articles in scientific jls. *Recreations:* reading science fiction, 3 dimensional puzzles, making things with or for his three young sons. *Address:* 25 Aylmer Drive, Stanmore, Mddx HA7 3EJ. *T:* 01-954 3173; Mathematical Institute, 24-29 St Giles, Oxford OX1 3LB. *T:* Oxford 54295.

PENROSE, Sir Roland (Algernon), Kt 1966; CBE 1961; Chairman, Institute of Contemporary Arts, 1947-69, President, 1969-76; *b* 14 Oct. 1900; *s* of James Doyle Penrose and Hon. Elizabeth Josephine Peckover; *m* 1st, 1925, Valentine Andrée Boué; 2nd, 1947, Lee Miller (*d* 1977); one *s. Educ:* Leighton Park School, Reading; Queens' College, Cambridge. BA Cantab 1922; lived in France, studied and painted, 1922-34; returned to London, organised Internat. Surrealist Exhibition, 1936; painted and exhibited in London and Paris with Surrealist Group, 1936-39. Served War, 1940-45, WO Lecturer to Home Guard, 1940-42; commissioned Army, Gen. List, Capt. 1943-45. Founder, Inst. of Contemporary Arts; Fine Arts Officer, British Council, Paris, 1956-59; Member Fine Arts Panel: Brit. Coun., 1955-; Arts Coun., 1959-67; Trustee, Tate Gall., 1959-66; organised Exhibitions at Tate Gallery for Arts Council: Picasso, 1960; Max Ernst, 1962; Miró, 1964; Picasso (sculpture), 1967. *Publications:* The Road is Wider than Long, 1939; In the Service of the People, 1945; Picasso his Life and Work, 1958, rev. edn 1971; Portrait of Picasso, 1958, rev. edn 1971; Miró, 1970; (ed with John Golding) Picasso 1881-1973, 1973; Man Ray, 1975. *Recreation:* gardening. *Address:* Farley Farm, Chiddingly, nr Lewes, E Sussex. *T:* Chiddingly 308. *Club:* Garrick.

PENRUDDOCK, Sir Clement (Frederick), Kt 1973; CBE 1954; Senior Partner, Lawrance, Messer & Co., Solicitors, since 1947; *b* 30 Jan. 1905; *s* of Rev. Frederick Fitzpatrick Penruddock and Edith Florence Smith; *m* 1945, Philippa Mary Tolhurst; one *s* three *d. Educ:* Marlborough Coll.; Keble Coll., Oxford. BA 1927. Admitted Solicitor, 1931. Sec., Chequers Trust, 1941-72. Chairman: Atlanta Baltimore & Chicago Investment Trust Ltd; Channel Islands & Internat. Investment Trust Ltd; Paten & Co. (Peterborough) Ltd; Director: Save & Prosper Group Ltd; Illingworth Morris Ltd; Ocean Wilsons (Holdings) Ltd; London & Lancashire Investment Trust Ltd. *Recreations:* golf, ski-ing. *Address:* Venars, Nutfield, Redhill, Surrey. *T:* Nutfield Ridge 2218, (office) 01-606 7691. *Clubs:* City, United Oxford & Cambridge University.

PENSON, John Hubert, CB 1953; CMG 1942; MC; *b* 21 Jan. 1893; *s* of late Arthur A. Penson, formerly of Cirencester, Glos;

m 1st, 1929, Marjorie Doreen (*d* 1971), *d* of late Col F. H. Crawford, Belfast; one *s* two *d* ; 2nd, 1974, Ellen Mary, *d* of late James Cumming, Glasgow. Served European War, 1916-19 (Lieut 1918) RE (despatches, MC and bar). Commissioner for Finance, Commission of Government, Newfoundland, 1937-41. Secretary General, British Supply Mission in Washington, USA, 1944-45; Attaché British Embassy, Washington, 1947-53, Executive Secretary, International Materials Conference, Washington, 1953. *Address:* 173 Nithsdale Road, Glasgow G41 5QR. *T:* 041-423 1805.

PENTLAND, 2nd Baron, *cr* 1909, of Lyth, Caithness; **Henry John Sinclair,** BA; Member American IEE, MICE, MIEE; Director and Vice-President of the American British Electric Corporation (New York), and of Hunting Surveys Inc. (New York), etc.; *b* 1907; *o s* of 1st Baron and Lady Marjorie Gordon, DBE, JP (d 1970), *o d* of 1st Marquis of Aberdeen and *sister* of 2nd Marquis; *S* father, 1925; *m* 1941, Lucy Elisabeth, 3rd *d* of late Sir Henry Babington Smith, GBE, KCB, CH; one *d. Educ:* Cargilfield; Wellington; Trinity College, Cambridge; President, Cambridge Union Society, 1929; Asst Secretary Ministry of Production, and CPRB, Washington, 1944-45. *Recreation:* sailing. *Address:* 131 East 66th Street, New York, NY 10021, USA.

PENTNEY, Richard George; employed by Kent Education Committee, since 1973; *b* 17 Aug. 1922; *s* of late Rev. A. F. Pentney, MC; *m* 1953, Elisabeth, *d* of Sir Eric Berthoud, *qv* ; four *d. Educ:* Kingswood School, Bath; St John's Coll., Cambridge. RNVR (Lieut), 1942-46. Asst Master, Sedbergh School, 1947-58; Headmaster, St Andrew's Coll., Minaki, Tanzania, 1958-64; Asst Master, Oundle School, 1964-65; Headmaster, King's Coll., Taunton, 1965-69; Sec. for Appeals, St Christopher's Fellowship, 1969-70; Dir, Attlee House, Toynbee Hall, 1970-73. *Recreations:* walking, water-colour painting. *Address:* Poplar Farmhouse, Churn Lane, Horsmonden, Kent. *T:* Brenchley 2889.

PENTREATH, Rev. Canon Arthur Godolphin Guy Carleton, MA (Cambridge); Hon. Secretary, Hellenic Travellers' Club; Residentiary Canon, Rochester Cathedral, 1959-65, Emeritus, 1965; Headmaster of Cheltenham College, 1952-59, retired; *b* 30 March 1902; *s* of late Reverend Dr A. G. Pentreath, Royal Army Chaplains' Department, and Helen Guy Carleton, County Cork; *m* 1927, Margaret Lesley Cadman; two *s* one *d. Educ:* Haileybury College; Magdalene College, Cambridge. (Classical Scholar), 1st class Hon. with distinction in Classical Archæology, Class. Tripos Part II. Westcott House, Cambridge, 1925-26. Master at Oundle School, 1927; Deacon, 1928; Priest, 1929; Chaplain and Master at Michaelhouse School, Natal, 1928-30; Master of the King's Scholars, Westminster School, 1930-34; Headmaster St Peter's College, Adelaide, S Australia, 1934-43; Headmaster of Wrekin College, 1944-51. *Publication:* Hellenic Traveller, 1964. *Recreation:* sailing. *Address:* Wooden Walls, Dock Lane, Beaulieu, Hants. *T:* Beaulieu 612348.

PEPLOE, Denis (Frederic Neil), RSA 1966 (ARSA 1956); Teacher of drawing and painting at Edinburgh College of Art; *b* 25 March 1914; *s* of late Samuel John Peploe, RSA, and late Margaret Peploe (*née* Mackay); *m* 1957, Elizabeth Marion (*née* Barr); one *s* one *d. Educ:* Edinburgh Academy. Studied at Edinburgh College of Art and Académie André Lhote, 1931-37. Served War of 1939-45: Royal Artillery and Intelligence Corps. Appointed Lecturer at Edinburgh College of Art, 1954. *Recreations:* mah-jong, mycology. *Address:* 5 McLaren Road, Edinburgh EH9 2BE. *T:* 031-667 6219.

PEPPARD, Nadine Sheila, CBE 1970; Adviser on Race Relations, Home Office, since 1972; *b* 16 Jan. 1922; *d* of late Joseph Anthony Peppard and May Peppard (*née* Barber). *Educ:* Macclesfield High Sch.; Manchester Univ. (BA, Teacher's Dip.). French Mistress, Maldon Grammar Sch., 1943-46; Spanish Editor, George G. Harrap & Co. Ltd, 1946-55; Trg Dept, Marks and Spencer, 1955-57; Dep. Gen.-Sec., London Council of Social Service, 1957-64; Nat. Advisory Officer for Commonwealth Immigrants, 1964-65; Gen. Sec., Nat. Cttee for Commonwealth Immigrants, 1965-68; Chief Officer, Community Relations Commn, 1968-72. *Publications:* (trans.) Primitive India, 1954; (trans.) Toledo, 1955. *Recreations:* cookery, gardening. *Address:* 17 Kentmere Close, Hatherley, Cheltenham, Glos. *T:* Cheltenham 42583.

PEPPER, Claude Denson; Member of Congress, former United States Senator (Democrat); *b* Dudleyville, Alabama, USA, 8 Sept. 1900; *s* of Joseph Wheeler Pepper and Lena (*née* Talbot); *m* 1936, Irene Mildred Webster, St Petersburg, Fla; no *c. Educ:* University of Alabama (AB); Harvard Law School (LLB). Instr in Law, Univ. of Arkansas, 1924-25. Admitted to Alabama Bar,

1924; Florida Bar, 1925; began practice of law at Perry, Fla; House Mem. Fla State Legislature, 1929; began practice of law, Tallahassee, Fla, 1930; Mem. State Bd of: Public Welfare, 1931-32; Law Examiners, 1933-34; US Senator from Fla, 1936-51; Mem., various cttees; Chm., Middle East Sub-Cttee of Senate Foreign Relations Cttee (12 yrs) etc.; Chm. Fla Delegation to Dem. Nat. Convention, 1940-44; subseq. alternate Delegate, 1948, 1952, 1956, 1960, 1964, Delegate, 1968. Elected to: 88th Congress, 1962; 89th Congress, 1964; 90th Congress, 1966 (without opposition); 91st Congress, 1968; 92nd Congress, 1970; 93rd Congress, 1972; 94th Congress, 1974; 95th Congress, 1976; Member: (88th Congress) House Cttee on Banking and Currency, and sub cttees on Domestic Finance, Internat. Trade, and Internat. Finance; (89th, 90th, 91st, 92nd, 93rd, 94th and 95th Congress) House Rules Cttee; Chm. (91st-92nd Congress) House Select Cttee on Crime, Cttee on Internal Security; Chm. (95th Congress) House Select Cttee on Aging. Member: Board of Directors, Washington Federal Savings & Loan Assoc.; American Bar Assoc.; International Bar Association, etc. Albert Lasker Public Service Award, 1967. Holds hon. degrees. Member, American Legion; Baptist; Mason; Shriner; Elk; Moose, Kiwanian. *Publications:* contributor to periodicals. *Recreations:* hunting, golf, horseback riding, swimming. *Address:* (home) 2121 North Bayshore Drive, Miami, Florida, USA; 4201 Cathedral Avenue, Washington, DC, USA; (offices) 1701 Meridian Avenue, Miami Beach, Fla; 2239 Rayburn House Office Building, Washington, DC. *Clubs:* Harvard, Jefferson Island, Army-Navy, Columbia Country, Burning Tree, etc (Washington); various country (Florida).

PEPPER, Brig. Ernest Cecil, CMG 1967; CBE 1943 (OBE 1940); DSO 1944; *b* 3 Oct. 1899; *s* of W. E. Pepper, The Manor House, Nocton, Lincs; *m* 1929, Margaret, *d* of A. W. Allan, MD, Seacroft, Lincs; two *s. Educ:* Royal Military College, Sandhurst. Worcestershire Regt, Aug. 1918; India, 1925; ADC to Governor of UP, 1925-26; China, 1928; promoted Bedfordshire Regt, 1930; Adj. 1931; Staff College, 1935-36; Bde Major, Chatham, 1937-39; GSO2, France, 1939-40; GSO1, War Office, 1940-41; Bn Comdr, 1941-42; BGS Africa, 1942-43; BGS Washington, 1943-44; Brigade-Commander, Normandy, 1944-45; Comdt, School of Infantry, 1945; retd pay at own request, 1946. Warden, Dominion Students Hall Trust, 1945-70. Bd of Governors: Church of England Children's Society (Waifs and Strays); Victoria League. DL County of London, later Greater London, 1948-76. *Publication:* A Place to Remember, 1970. *Recreations:* cricket, golf. *Address:* Flat 1, Nutcombe Height, Portsmouth Road, Hindhead, Surrey. *T:* Hindhead 4644. *Club:* Army and Navy.

PEPPER, Kenneth Bruce, CB 1965; Commissioner of HM Customs and Excise, 1957-73; *b* 11 March 1913; *s* of late E. E. Pepper; *m* 1945, Irene Evelyn Watts; two *s. Educ:* County High Sch., Ilford; London Sch. of Economics. Joined HM Customs and Excise, 1932; Asst Sec., 1949; Commissioner, 1957. Lieutenant, Intelligence Corps, 1944. *Address:* Fairfield, Cae Mair, Beaumaris, Gwynedd.

PEPPERCORN, Trevor Edward, BA Oxon; *b* 4 June 1904; *s* of late William and Kate Peppercorn; *m* 1st, 1935, Sheila (*d* 1972), *d* of F. W. Ayre, St John's Newfoundland; one *s* ; 2nd, 1977, Mary Gertrude (*née* Cumming), widow of L. G. Williamson. *Educ:* Beaumont College; Balliol College, Oxford. Dunlop Rubber Co. Ltd, 1928; Dunlop Rubber Co. (India) Ltd, 1929; Dunlop South Africa Ltd, 1940 (Managing Director, 1943-52); Director, Dunlop Rubber Co. Ltd, 1957-76; Dir, Triplex Holdings, 1966-77 (Chm., 1966-75); Chairman: Weldall Engineering Ltd, 1971-77; Fibreglass-Pilkington Ltd, Bombay, 1972-77. Chm., Overseas Develt Inst., 1967-72. *Recreations:* gardening, shooting. *Address:* The Grange, Yattendon, Newbury, Berks. *Club:* Boodle's.

PEPPIATT, Sir Kenneth Oswald, KBE 1941; MC; *b* 25 March 1893; *s* of late W. R. Peppiatt; *m* 1929, Pamela, *d* of late Captain E. W. Carter, MC; two *s* one *d. Educ:* Bancrofts. Entered service of Bank of England, 1911; Principal of Discount Office, 1928-34; Chief Cashier, 1934-49; Exec. Dir, 1949-57. Dir, Coutts and Co., 1958-69. FIB 1934, Vice-Pres., 1949. Hon. Treasurer, Army Benevolent Fund, 1949-64. Served European War 1914-18, retd rank Major (despatches, MC and Bar, twice wounded). *Recreations:* shooting, fishing. *Address:* 7 Harvey Orchard, Beaconsfield, Bucks. *T:* Beaconsfield 3158. *Club:* Boodle's.

PEPPITT, John Raymond, QC 1976; Barrister-at-law; a Recorder of the Crown Court, since 1976; *b* 22 Sept. 1931; *s* of late Reginald Peppitt and of Phyllis Claire Peppitt; *m* 1960, Judith Penelope James; three *s. Educ:* St Paul's Sch.; Jesus Coll., Cambridge (BA Classical Tripos). Called to the Bar, Gray's Inn, 1958. *Recreations:* collecting water-colours, shooting. *Address:*

Stanton House, Romford Road, Pembury, Kent TN2 4AY. *T:* Pembury 2482.

PEPYS, family name of **Earl of Cottenham.**

PEPYS, Lady (Mary) Rachel, DCVO 1968 (CVO 1954); Lady-in-Waiting to Princess Marina, Duchess of Kent, 1943-68; *b* 27 June 1905; *e d* of 15th Duke of Norfolk, KG, PC, CVO (*d* 1917); *m* 1st, 1939, as Lady Rachel Fitz-Alan Howard, Lieutenant-Colonel Colin Keppel Davidson, CIE, OBE, RA (killed in action, 1943), *s* of Col Leslie Davidson, CB, RHA, and Lady Theodora, *d* of 7th Earl of Albemarle; one *s* one *d*; 2nd, 1961, Brigadier Anthony Hilton Percy Pepys, DSO (*d* 1967). *Address:* Highfield House, Crossbush, Arundel, W Sussex. *T:* Arundel 883158.

PERCEVAL, family name of **Earl of Egmont.**

PERCEVAL, Viscount; Thomas Frederick Gerald Perceval; *b* 17 Aug. 1934; *e s* of 11th Earl of Egmont, *qv.*

PERCEVAL, Robert Westby, TD 1968; Clerk Assistant, House of Lords, 1964-74; retired; *b* 28 Aug. 1914; *m* 1948, Hon. J. I. L. Littleton, *er d* of 5th Baron Hatherton; two *s* two *d*. *Educ:* Ampleforth; Balliol College, Oxford. Joined Parliament Office, House of Lords, 1938. Royal Artillery, 1939-44; General Staff, War Office, 1944-45. *Address:* Pillaton Hall, Penkridge, Staffs ST19 5RZ. *Clubs:* Beefsteak, Turf.

PERCIVAL, Allen Dain, CBE 1975; Principal, Guildhall School of Music and Drama, since 1965; *b* 23 April 1925; *s* of Charles and Gertrude Percival, Bradford; *m* 1952, Rachel Hay. *Educ:* Bradford Grammar Sch.; Magdalene Coll., Cambridge. MusB Cantab 1948. Served War of 1939-45, RNVR. Music Officer of British Council in France, 1948-50; Music Master, Haileybury and Imp. Service Coll., 1950-51; Dir of Music, Homerton Coll., Cambridge, 1951-62; Conductor, Cambridge Univ. Musical Soc., 1954-58; Dir of Music Studies, GSM, 1962-65. Also professional continuo playing, broadcasting and conducting. FRCM; FGSM. Hon. RAM 1966; Hon. FTCL 1967. *Publications:* The Orchestra, 1956; The Teach Yourself History of Music, 1961; Music at the Court of Elizabeth I, 1975; contribs to musical and educnl jls. *Recreation:* travel. *Address:* 7 Park Parade, Cambridge. *T:* 53953.

PERCIVAL, Sir Anthony (Edward), Kt 1966; CB 1954; Chairman: Gordon & Gotch Holdings Ltd, since 1971; Brameast Gotch, since 1972; Director: Simon Engineering Ltd, since 1971; Bank of Adelaide, since 1971; Switzerland (General) Insurance Co., since 1971; Trade Indemnity Co., since 1973; *b* 23 Sept. 1910; *m* 1935, Doris Cuff; one *d. Educ:* Manchester Gram. Sch.; Cambridge. Entered Board of Trade, 1933; Assistant Secretary, 1942; Commercial Counsellor, Washington, on secondment, 1946-49; Under-Secretary, Board of Trade, 1949-58; Sec., Export Credits Guarantee Dept, 1962-71. President: Berne Union of Export Credit Insurance Organisations, 1966-68; Export Credit Gp, OECD, Paris, 1967-70. *Address:* 16 Hayes Way, Beckenham, Kent. *T:* 01-650 2648.

PERCIVAL, Edgar Wikner, CEng, FRAeS, FIMechE, FIMarE, MSAE, MIAeS, AFIAeS, FRSA; engaged on Research and Design for national purposes; Founder, Chairman, Managing Director and Chief Designer, Percival Aircraft Ltd, Aircraft Manufacturers; Director: Valbank Ltd; Valco Ltd; Percival Power Units Ltd; Edgar Percival & Co.; *b* Albury, New South Wales; *s* of late William and Hilda Percival, Clarendon Park, Richmond, NSW; unmarried. *Educ:* Sydney Tech. Coll.; Sydney Univ. Served 7th Australian Light Horse, 60 Sqdn RFC and founder member 111 Sqdn RFC, RAF, 1914-18; RAFO, 1929-39; RAFVR, 1939-45. Built and flew gliders, 1912. Air Ministry approved test pilot on flying boats, seaplanes and land planes. Designer of Percival "Gull", EP9, and of all other Percival aeroplanes; is the first to have produced low-wing monoplanes in British Commonwealth; winner of numerous Air races and trophies, both national and international; won Melbourne Herald Air Race, Melbourne-Geelong-Melbourne, 1923; has flown fastest time in King's Cup Air Races for 6 years; holds record for fastest time ever flown in King's Cup; designed and built: King's Cup Air Race winners for the 3 consecutive years prior to world war II, and winners for 3 years since War; first civil aircraft in British Commonwealth to have a speed of over 200 m.p.h., the Percival Mew Gull, 1933; a group of lakes discovered in Australia in 1934 was named Percival Lakes in his honour; is the first person to have flown to Africa and back in a day (1935); winner of Johnstone Memorial Trophy and of Oswald Watt Memorial Gold Medal; three times winner of International Speed Trophy; designed and built the first aeroplane in the British Empire to carry 1000 pounds load for

1000 miles range. Founder Mem., Guild of Air Pilots and Air Navigators; Mem., Institute of Directors. Mem., Lloyd's of London, 1944-. *Recreations:* flying, horse riding and hunting, swimming, squash, shooting, ski-ing. *Address:* 72 Chesterfield House, Chesterfield Gardens, Curzon Street, W1. *T:* 01-499 2895. *Clubs:* Royal Air Force, Royal Automobile, Naval and Military.

PERCIVAL, George Hector, MD, PhD, FRCPE, DPH; Professor Emeritus of Dermatology, University of Edinburgh (Grant Professor, 1946); *b* 1901; *s* of late E. J. Percival, Kirkcaldy; *m* 1937, Kathleen, *d* of late John Dawson, MD, Buckhaven; one *s* one *d. Educ:* George Watson's Coll., Edinburgh; Univs of Edinburgh and Paris. Physician to the Skin Dept, Edinburgh Royal Infirmary, 1936. *Publications:* An Introduction to Dermatology; The Histopathology of the Skin; scientific articles in British Med. Journ., Lancet, etc., Encyclopædia of Med., System of Bacteriology (Med. Res. Council). *Recreations:* golf, fishing. *Address:* Woodcroft, Barnton Avenue, Edinburgh EH4 6JJ. *T:* 031-336 2438.

PERCIVAL, Ian, QC 1963; MP (C) Southport since Oct. 1959; Shadow Solicitor-General; a Recorder (formerly Recorder of Deal), since 1971; Barrister-at-Law; *b* 11 May 1921; *s* of Eldon and Chrystine Percival; *m* 1942, Madeline Buckingham Cooke; one *s* one *d. Educ:* Latymer Upper School; St Catharine's College, Cambridge (MA). Served HM Forces, 1940-46: 2nd Bn the Buffs, N Africa and Burma; Major. Called to the Bar, Inner Temple, 1948, Bencher, 1970. Sec., Cons. Parly Legal Cttee, 1964-68, Vice-Chm. 1968-70, Chm. 1970-74. Fellow, Inst. of Taxation (Chm., Parly Cttee, 1965-71); Mem., Royal Economic Soc. *Recreations:* golf and tennis. *Address:* 9 King's Bench Walk, Temple, EC4. *T:* 01-583 2939. *Club:* Rye Golf.

PERCIVAL, Prof. Ian Colin, PhD; Professor of Applied Mathematics, Queen Mary College, University of London, since 1974; *b* 27 July 1931; *m* 1955, Jill Cuff (*née* Herbert); two *s* one *d. Educ:* Ealing County Grammar Sch.; UCL (BSc, PhD). Lectr in Physics, UCL, 1957-61; Reader in Applied Maths, QMC, 1961-67; Prof. of Theoret. Physics, Univ. of Stirling, 1967-74. *Publications:* papers in learned jls on scattering theory, atomic and molecular theory, statistical mechanics and classical dynamics. *Address:* Queen Mary College, Mile End Road, E1 4NS. *T:* 01-980 4811.

PERCIVAL, Robert Clarendon, FRCS, FRCOG; Consulting Obstetric Surgeon, The London Hospital; *b* 16 Sept. 1908; British; *m* 1st, 1944, Beryl Mary Ind (*d* 1967); one *d*; 2nd, 1972, Beatrice Myfanwy Evans, FFARCS. *Educ:* Barker College, NSW; Sydney University; The London Hospital, Qualified, 1933. Resident appointments: Poplar Hospital; Hosp. for Sick Children, Gt Ormond St; The London Hosp.; Southend Gen. Hosp. Obstetric and Gynæcological 1st Asst, The London Hosp., 1937. Surgeon-Lt-Comdr, RNVR, 1941-45 (Surgical Specialist); Obstetric Surgeon, The London Hospital, 1947-73; Director, Obstetric Unit, 1968-73. Chm., Med. Adv. Cttee, NE Region Met. Hosp. Bd, 1967-73; President: Section of Obst. and Gyn., RSocMed, 1973-74; The London Hosp. Clubs' Union, 1965 (Treasurer, 1955-73); United Hosps RFC, 1969-72; London Hosp. Cricket Club, 1946-72. *Publications:* Ten Teachers' Midwifery, 1958, new edition as Ten Teachers' Obstetrics, 1972; Ten Teachers' Diseases of Women, 1965, new edition as Ten Teachers' Gynaecology, 1971; (jointly) British Obstetric Practice, 1963; (ed) Holland and Brews, Obstetrics, 1969; contrib. to Lancet. *Recreations:* fishing, tennis, golf, ski-ing. *Address:* Coker Wood Cottage, Pendomer, near Yeovil, Somerset BA22 9PD. *T:* Corscombe 328. *Club:* Royal Automobile.

PERCIVAL, (Walter) Ian; *see* Percival, Ian.

PERCY, family name of **Duke of Northumberland.**

PERCY, Earl; Henry Alan Walter Richard Percy; *b* 1 July 1953; *s* and *heir* of 10th Duke of Northumberland, *qv. Educ:* Eton; Christ Church, Oxford. *Address:* Alnwick Castle, Northumberland.

PERCY, Lord Richard Charles; Lecturer, Department of Zoology, in the University of Newcastle upon Tyne; *b* 11 February 1921; *s* of 8th Duke of Northumberland and Lady Helen Gordon-Lennox (who *d* 1965, as Dowager Duchess of Northumberland, GCVO, CBE); *m* 1966, Sarah Jane Elizabeth Norton, *o d* of Mr and Mrs Petre Norton, La Charca, Coin, Malaya, Spain; two *s. Educ:* Eton; Christ Church, Oxford; Durham University. BSc. Lieut-Colonel Comdg Northumberland Hussars, TA, 1959-61; late Capt. Gren. Guards. Served War, 1941-45. DL Northumberland, 1968.

Address: Department of Zoology, The University, Newcastle upon Tyne NE1 7RU; Lesbury House, Alnwick, Northumberland NE66 3PT. *T:* Alnmouth 330; 58 Woodsford Square, W14 8DS. *T:* 01-603 2220; Kirkville, Fochabers, Morayshire IV32 7DQ. *T:* Fochabers 820269. *Clubs:* Turf; Northern Counties (Newcastle upon Tyne).

PERCY, Rodney Algernon; a Recorder of the Crown Court, since 1972; *b* 15 May 1924; 3rd *s* of Hugh James Percy, Solicitor, Alnwick; *m* 1948, Mary Allen, *d* of late J. E. Benbow, Aberystwyth; one *s* three *d. Educ:* Uppingham; Brasenose Coll., Oxford (MA). Lieut, Royal Corps of Signals, 1942-46, served in Burma, India, Malaya, Java. Called to Bar, Middle Temple, 1950. Dep. Coroner, N Northumberland, 1957; Asst Recorder, Sheffield QS, 1964; Dep. Chm., Co. Durham QS, 1966-71. *Publications:* (ed) Charlesworth on Negligence, 4th edn 1962, 5th edn 1971 and 6th edn 1977. *Address:* (home) Brookside, Lesbury, Alnwick, Northumberland NE66 3AT. *T:* Alnmouth 326; (chambers) 11 King's Bench Walk, Temple, EC4. *T:* 01-236 3337; 60 Grainger Street, Newcastle upon Tyne NE1 5JP. *T:* Newcastle upon Tyne 21927 and 27975.

PERDUE, Rt. Rev. Richard Gordon; *see* Cork, Cloyne, and Ross, Bishop of.

PEREIRA, Arthur Leonard, FRCS; Consulting Ear, Nose and Throat Surgeon to St George's Hospital, London; *b* 10 March 1906; British; *m* 1973, Mrs Jane Wilson (*née* Lapworth). *Educ:* Merchant Taylors' School. MRCS, LRCP 1929; MB, BS London 1931; FRCS 1936. Otologist to: the Metropolitan Hospital, E8, 1941-47; St George's Hospital, 1946-71. *Address:* Leat Cottage, Old Bosham, Sussex. *T:* Bosham 572086. *Club:* Bosham Sailing.

PEREIRA, Sir Charles; *see* Pereira, Sir H. C.

PEREIRA, Helio Gelli, DrMed; FRS 1973; FIBiol 1975; Head of Department of Epidemiology and of World Reference Centre for Foot-and-Mouth Disease, Animal Virus Research Institute, since 1973; *b* 23 Sept. 1918; *s* of Raul Pereira and Maria G. Pereira; *m* 1946, Marguerite McDonald Scott; one *s* two *d. Educ:* Faculdade Fluminense de Medicina, also Instituto Oswaldo Cruz, Rio de Janeiro, Brazil. British Council Scholarship, Dept of Bacteriology, Manchester Univ. and Div. of Bacteriology and Virus Research, Nat. Inst. for Med. Research, London, 1945-47; Rickettsia Laboratory, Instituto Oswaldo Cruz, 1948-51; Asst to Prof. of Microbiology, Faculdade Fluminense de Medicina, 1943-45 and 1948-51. Nat. Inst. for Med. Research, Mill Hill, London: Mem. Scientific Staff, 1951-73; Head of Div. of Virology, 1964-73; Dir, World Influenza Centre, 1961-70. *Publication:* (with C. H. Andrewes) Viruses of Vertebrates (3rd edn), 1972. *Recreations:* skiing, music. *Address:* 3 Ducks Walk, Twickenham, Mddx TW1 2DD. *T:* 01-892 4511.

PEREIRA, Sir (Herbert) Charles, Kt 1977; DSc; FRS 1969; Chief Scientist, Ministry of Agriculture, Fisheries and Food, 1972-77, retired; *b* 12 May 1913; *s* of H. J. Pereira and Maud Edith (*née* Machin), both of London; *m* 1941, Irene Beatrice, *d* of David Sloan, Belfast; three *s* one *d. Educ:* Prince Albert Coll., Saskatchewan; St Albans Sch.; London Univ. Attached Rothamsted Expl Stn for Agric. PhD (London) 1941. Royal Engineers, 1941-46 (despatches). Colonial Agric. Service, Coffee Research Stn, Kenya, 1947-52; Colonial Research Service, established Physics Div. at East African Agriculture and Forestry Research Org., Kenya, 1952-61; DSc London 1961; Dir, ARC of Rhodesia and Nyasaland, 1961-63; Dir, ARC of Central Africa (Rhodesia, Zambia and Malawi), 1963-67; Chm., ARC of Malawi, 1967-74; Dir, East Malling Research Station, 1969-72. Member: Natural Environment Res. Council, 1971-; ARC, 1973-; ABRC, 1973-. FInstBiol; CompICE, 1971. Haile Selassie Prize for Research in Africa, 1966. *Publications:* (jtly) Hydrological Effects of Land Use Changes in East Africa, 1962; Land Use and Water Resources, 1973; papers in research jls; Founding Editor, Rhodesian Jl Agric. Research. *Recreations:* fencing, sailing. *Address:* Great East, East Malling, Maidstone, Kent. *T:* West Malling 840195. *Club:* Athenæum.

PEREIRA-MENDOZA, Vivian, MScTech, CEng, FIEE; Director, Polytechnic of the South Bank, since 1970; *b* 8 April 1917; *o s* of Rev. Joseph Pereira-Mendoza, Manchester; *m* 1942, Marjorie, *y d* of Edward Lichtenstein; two *d. Educ:* Manchester Central High Sch.; Univ. of Manchester. Asst Lectr, Univ. of Manchester, 1939. Served War, 1940-45, in Royal Corps of Signals; Major, and GSO II (War Office). Sen. Lectr, Woolwich Polytechnic, 1948; Head of Dept of Electrical Engrg, NW Kent Coll. of Technology, 1954; of Electrical Engrg and Physics, Borough Polytechnic, 1957; Vice-Principal, Borough

Polytechnic, 1964; Principal, Borough Polytechnic, and Dir of Nat. Coll. of Heating, Ventilating, and Refrigeration and Fan Engrg, 1966. Member: Regional Adv. Council for Tech. Educn (London and Home Counties) Cttee for Electrical Engrg, 1958-70, Regional Academic Bd, 1971-74; Jt Cttees for Nat. Certifs and Diplomas (in Electrical Engrg, 1969; in Food Technology, 1969); CNAA: Electrical Engrg Bd, 1964-68; Cttee for Arts and Social Studies, 1973-75; Jt Professional Gp for Educn and Trng, Instn of Electrical Engrs, 1966-69; Electricity Supply Industry: Trng Bd, 1971-73; Trng Cttee, 1974; Council for Educn and Trng of Health Visitors, 1971; Council, Chelsea Coll., Univ. of London, 1972. *Address:* 183 Salmon Street, Kingsbury, NW9. *T:* 01-205 0200.

PERELMAN, S(idney) J(oseph); author; *b* 1 Feb. 1904, New York; *s* of Joseph and Sophia Perelman; *m* 1929, Laura West (*d* 1970); one *s* one *d. Educ:* Brown Univ. Cartoonist and writer: Judge, 1925-29; College Humor, 1929-30; New Yorker, 1935-. Member: Screen Writer's Guild; Dramatist's Guild; Nat. Inst. Arts and Letters. Writer, 1930-: *film scripts:* Monkey Business, 1931; Horsefeathers, 1932; Sweethearts, 1938; Ambush, 1939; Around the World in Eighty Days (Best Screen Writer Award, NY Film Critics Award), 1956; *sketches for reviews:* Third Little Show, 1931; Walk a Little Faster, 1932; *plays:* (with Laura Perelman) All Good Americans, 1934; Night Before Christmas, 1941; (with Ogden Nash) One Touch of Venus, 1943; (with A. Hirschfeld) Sweet Bye and Bye, 1946; The Beauty Part, 1962. *Publications:* Dawn Ginsbergh's Revenge, 1929; Parlor, Bedlam and Bath, 1930; Strictly from Hunger, 1937; Look Who's Talking!, 1940; The Dream Department, 1943; Crazy Like a Fox, 1944, new edn 1973; Keep it Crisp, 1946; Acres and Pains, 1947; The Best of S. J. Perelman, 1947; Westward Ha!, 1948; Listen to the Mockingbird, 1949; Swiss Family Perelman, 1950; A Child's Garden of Curses, 1951; Ill-Tempered Clavichord, 1952; Perelman's Home Companion, 1955; The Road to Miltown, 1957; The Most of S. J. Perelman; The Rising Gorge, 1961; Chicken Inspector No 23, 1966; Baby, It's Cold Inside, 1970; Vinegar Puss, 1976. *Club:* Century Association (New York).

PEREN, Sir Geoffrey Sylvester, KBE 1959 (CBE 1953); BSA (Tor.); Brigadier (retired); Emeritus Professor of Agriculture, Massey University; *b* England; *m* 1923, Violet Essex, *d* of R. J. Surman, Worcester; one *s* one *d. Educ:* Toronto University. Four years Ontario Agric. Coll., Guelph; seven years mixed farming in Ontario and British Columbia; served European War with Canadian Field Artillery and RFA (despatches, Croix de Guerre); subsequently on staff of E Malling Agricultural Research Station, Kent; Inspector under Ministry of Agriculture; later at Agricultural and Horticultural Research Station, Long Ashton, Bristol; Prof. of Agriculture, Victoria Univ. Coll., Wellington, NZ, 1924-28; Principal, Massey Agricultural Coll., Univ. of NZ, 1928-59. During war of 1939-45 commanded 2nd Infantry Bde Group and later 4th NZ Division with rank of Brig. Colonel Comdt, 2 Armoured Regt, NZ Forces, 1954-56. Comr for Civil Defence, Central Region NZ, 1960-65. Hon. Life Member: Royal Agric. Soc. of NZ; Cheviot Sheep Soc. of NZ; Galloway Cattle Soc. of NZ; Perendale Sheep Soc. of NZ. DSc (*hc*) Massey. Silver Jubilee Medal, 1935; Coronation Medals, 1937, 1953. *Address:* 14 Collingwood Street, Palmerston North, NZ.

PERHAM, Dame Margery, DCMG 1965; CBE 1948; FBA 1961; DLitt Oxon; Hon. Fellow of Nuffield College since 1963; *b* 1895. *Educ:* St Stephens Coll., Windsor; St Anne's Sch., Abbots Bromley; St Hugh's College, Oxford, Modern History. Assistant Lecturer in History, Sheffield University; in Somaliland, 1922-23; Fellow and Tutor in Modern History and Modern Greats, St Hugh's College, Oxford, 1924-29; Rhodes Travelling Fellowship for travel and study of administration of coloured races in N America, Polynesia, Australia, Africa, 1929-31, and in West Africa, 1931-32; Research Fellow St Hugh's College, Oxford, 1930-39; Official Fellow, Nuffield College, 1939-63; Reader in Colonial Administration in the University of Oxford, 1939-48; Director of Oxford Univ. Institute of Colonial Studies, 1945-48. Rockefeller Travelling Fellowship of Int. Inst. of African Languages and Culture for travel and study in E Africa and Sudan, 1932; Research Lecturer in Colonial Administration, Oxford, 1935-39; Vice-Chairman, Oxford University Summer School of Colonial Administration, 1937-38; Member: Advisory Committee on Education in the Colonies, 1939-45; Higher Education Commission and West Indies Higher Education Cttee, 1944; Exec. Cttee of Inter-University Council on Higher Education Overseas, 1946-67; Colonial Social Science Research Council, 1947-61. Editor, Colonial and Comparative Studies, 1946-. Chairman, Oxford University Colonial Records Project, 1963-73. Reith Lecturer, BBC 1961; President, Universities' Mission to Central Africa, 1963-64. Mem., Amer. Acad. of Arts and Sciences, 1969. Hon. Fellow: St Hugh's College, Oxford, 1962; Makerere College, Uganda, 1963; School of Oriental and African Studies, 1964; Hon. LLD St Andrews Univ., 1952; Hon. DLitt: Southampton University, 1962; London University, 1964; Birmingham, 1969; Hon. LittD, Cambridge, 1966. Gold Wellcome Medal (Royal Africa Soc.). *Publications:* Major Dane's Garden, 1924; Josie Vine, 1925, new edn 1970; The Protectorates of South Africa (with Lionel Curtis), 1935; Ten Africans (ed), 1936; Native Administration in Nigeria, 1937; Africans and British Rule, 1941; African Discovery (with J. Simmons), 1943; Race and Politics in Kenya (with E. Huxley), 1944; The Government of Ethiopia, 1948, rev. edn 1969; Lugard-The Years of Adventure, 1956; The Diaries of Lord Lugard, 1889-1892 (ed with Mary Bull), 1959; Lugard-The Years of Authority, 1960; The Colonial Reckoning, The Reith Lectures for 1961, 1962; Colonial Sequence, Vol. I, 1967, Vol. II, 1970; African Apprenticeship, 1974; East African Journey, 1976; also articles in The Times, Africa, etc. *Relevant publication:* Essays in Imperial Government presented to Margery Perham, 1963. *Address:* 5 Rawlinson Road, Oxford.

PERINAT, Marqués de, Luis Guillermo; Spanish Ambassador to the Court of St James's, since 1976; *b* 27 Oct. 1923; *s* of Luis Perinat and Ana Maria, Marquesa de Campo Real; *m* 1955, Blanca Escriva de Romani, Marquesa de Alginet; two *s* one *d*. *Educ:* Univs of Salamanca and Valladolid. Barrister-at-law. Sec., Spanish Embassy, Cairo, 1949-51; Dep. Consul-Gen., New York, 1954-56; Counsellor, Spanish Embassy, Paris, 1962-65; Permanent Sec., Spanish-American Jt Defence Cttee, 1965-70; Dir-Gen., N American and Far Eastern Affairs, Min. of Foreign Affairs, Madrid, 1973-76. Grand Cross, Order of Civil Merit (Spain); Kt Comdr, Order of Isabel La Católica (Spain); Kt Comdr, Order of Merito Aeronautico (Spain); also holds foreign decorations. *Heir: s* Guillermo Perinat y Escriva de Romani. *Address:* Spanish Embassy, 24 Belgrave Square, SW1. *T:* 01-235 8363; Calle del Prado 26, Madrid, Spain. *Clubs:* White's, Travellers'; Puerto de Hierro, Nuevo (Madrid).

PERKINS, Bernard James; Chairman, Harlow Development Corporation, since 1972; *b* 25 Jan. 1928; *y s* of George and Rebecca Perkins; *m* 1956, Patricia (née Payne); three *d*. *Educ:* Strand School. Member: Lambeth Council, 1962-71 (Leader, 1968-71); Community Relations Commn, 1970-72; SE Econ. Planning Council, 1971-; Alderman, GLC, 1971-73; Chm., GLC Housing Cttee, 1972-73. *Recreation:* social service. *Address:* 25 Croxted Road, West Dulwich, SE21 8SZ. *T:* 01-670 9056. *Club:* Effra (Norwood).

PERKINS, Surg. Vice-Adm. Sir Derek Duncombe S.; *see* Steele-Perkins.

PERKINS, Dexter; Professor Emeritus, University of Rochester, USA, also of Cornell University; President, Salzburg Seminar in American Studies, 1950-62; Prof. of History from 1922 and Chairman, Department of History, 1925-54, University of Rochester; John L. Senior Prof. of American Civilization, Cornell University, 1954-59; City Historian of City of Rochester, 1936-48; *b* 20 June 1889; *s* of Herbert William Perkins and Cora Farmer, Boston, Mass; *m* 1918, Wilma Lois Lord, Rochester, NY; two *s*. *Educ:* Boston Latin School and Sanford School, Redding Ridge, Conn; Harvard University (AB 1909, PhD 1914). Instructor in history, Univ. of Cincinnati, 1914-15; instructor and asst prof. history, Univ. of Rochester, 1915-22; lecturer on Commonwealth Fund at University College, London, 1937; secretary of American Historical Assoc., 1928-39. Served as 1st lieut, later captain, inf. USA, 1918; attached to historical section, GHQ, Chaumont, France, Oct. 1918-Feb. 1919; work connected with the Peace Conf., Feb.-June 1919; gave Albert Shaw Lectures on Diplomatic History at Johns Hopkins Univ., 1932 and 1937; Professor of American History and Institutions, Cambridge Univ., 1945-46, MA Camb., 1946. Official historian for Overseas Branch of Office of War Information for San Francisco Conf. Lectures, Nat. War College, US, 1946-; Lectures, British Universities and RIIA, 1948 and 1952; Visiting Professor, University of Uppsala 1949; Chm. Council, Harvard Foundation for Advanced Study and Research, Harvard Univ., 1951-56. LLD, Union Coll., 1951, LittD, Harvard, 1953. Moderator of Unitarian Churches of US and Canada, 1952-54; Pres., Amer. Hist. Assoc., 1955-56. Pres., Salzburg Seminar in Amer. Studies, 1950-62. Member of Phi Beta Kappa. *Publications:* John Quincy Adams as Secretary of State; The Monroe Doctrine, 1823-26, 1927; The Monroe Doctrine, 1826-67, 1933; The Monroe Doctrine, 1867-1907, 1938; Hands Off! A History of the Monroe Doctrine, 1823-1940, 1941; America and Two Wars, 1944; The United States and the Caribbean, 1947; The Evolution of American Foreign Policy, 1948; The American Approach to Foreign Policy, 1952; The History of The Monroe Doctrine (revised edn, 1955); Charles

Evans-Hughes and American Democratic Statesmanship, 1956; Short Biography of Charles Evans Hughes; The New Age of Franklin Roosevelt, 1957; The American Way, 1957; The American Quest for Peace, 1960; The United States and Latin America, 1960; The United States of America: A History (with G. G. Van Deusen), 1962; The American Democracy: its rise to power, 1964; The Yield of the Years, 1969. *Recreations:* bridge and scrabble.

PERKINS, Prof. Donald Hill, FRS 1966; Professor of Elementary Particle Physics, Oxford University, since October 1965; *b* 15 Oct. 1925; *s* of George W. and Gertrude Perkins; *m* 1955, Dorothy Mary (née Maloney); two *d*. *Educ:* Malet Lambert High School, Hull. BSc London 1945; PhD London 1948; 1851 Senior Scholar, 1948-51. G. A. Wills Research Associate in Physics, Univ. of Bristol, 1951-55; Lawrence Radiation Lab., Univ. of California, 1955-56; Lectr in Physics, 1956-60, Reader in Physics, 1960-65, Univ. of Bristol. *Publications:* The Study of Elementary Particles by the Photographic Method (with C. F. Powell and P. H. Fowler), 1959; Introduction to High Energy Physics, 1972; about 50 papers and review articles in Nature, Physical Review, Philosophical Magazine, Physics Letters, Proc. Royal Soc., Nuovo Cimento, etc. *Recreations:* squash, tennis. *Address:* c/o Dept of Nuclear Physics, Keble Road, Oxford.

PERKINS, Dudley; *see* Perkins, G. D. G.

PERKINS, Francis Layton, CBE 1977; DSC 1940; Chairman, British Insurance Brokers' Association (since formation in 1976); Solicitor since 1937; *b* 7 Feb. 1912; *s* of Montague Thornton and Madge Perkins; *m* 1st, 1941, Josephine Brice Miller (marr. diss. 1971); one *s* two *d*; 2nd, 1971, Jill Patricia Greenish. *Educ:* Charterhouse. Served War of 1939-45, Comdr RNVR, in command of minesweepers. Partner in Clifford Turner & Co., 1946; Dir, Hogg Robinson & Capel-Cure Ltd, 1962; Chairman: Hogg Robinson and Gardner Mountain Ltd, 1967-74; Hogg Robinson Group Ltd (formerly Staplegreen Insurance Holdings Ltd), 1971-77; Dir, Transport Holding Co., 1971-73. Master of Skinners' Company, 1966; Dep. Pres., 1971, Pres., 1972-77, Corp. of Insurance Brokers; Chairman: UK Insurance Brokers European Cttee, 1973-; Common Mkt Cttee, Bureau International des Producteurs d'Assurances et de Réassurances, 1977; Dep. Chm., Cttee of Management, Inst. of Laryngology and Otology, 1976- (Mem., 1974-); Mem. Council, Industrial Soc., 1976- (Treasurer, 1976-). Governor: Tonbridge Sch.; Sutton's Hospital in Charterhouse, 1974-; Royal National Throat, Nose and Ear Hospital, 1974-; Chm., City of London and Thames Estuary Panel, Duke of Edinburgh's 1974 Commonwealth Conf. *Recreations:* tennis, golf, fishing. *Address:* Flat 18, 7 Princes Gate, SW7. *T:* 01-589 9438; The Dunes, Sandwich Bay, Kent. *T:* Sandwich 2832. *Clubs:* Boodle's, MCC, All England Lawn Tennis.

PERKINS, Rev. Canon Frederick Howard, MA; Canon Residentiary and Treasurer of Liverpool Cathedral, 1955-63, Canon Emeritus since 1964; Vicar of St Matthew and St James, Mossley Hill, Liverpool, 1936-63. *Educ:* St Catharine's College, Cambridge (MA); Ridley Hall, Cambridge. Lieut, RASC, 1915-19. Ordained deacon, 1922; priest, 1923. Curate: St John, Ladywood, Birmingham, 1922-26, St Martin, Birmingham, 1926-28; Vicar: St Christopher, Springfield, Worcs, 1928-36; Canon of Liverpool, 1951. Rural Dean of Childwall, 1947-63; Proctor in convocation, Liverpool, 1948-59; Chaplain, Ministry of Pensions Hosp., Mossley Hill, 1936-63; Bishop's Chaplain, Univ. of Liverpool, 1945-55; Examining Chaplain to Bishop of St Edmundsbury and Ipswich, 1960-65. *Address:* Abinger Lodge, Abbey Road, Worthing, West Sussex BN11 3RW.

PERKINS, Prof. George, MC; MCh; FRCS; Consultant Surgeon, Rowley Bristow Hospital, Pyrford. BA (1st cl. Hons), 1914; MA Oxon, 1921; MB, BCh 1916; MCh 1921; FRCS 1921. Formerly Professor of Surgery, St Thomas's Hospital Medical School, University of London; Consultant Orthopædic Surgeon, St Thomas' Hospital. Ex-president British Orthopædic Association. *Publications:* The Foundations of Surgery, 1954; Fractures and Dislocations, 1958; Orthopaedics, 1961; Ruminations of an Orthopaedic Surgeon, 1970. *Address:* Thorpe Lee, Denne Park, Horsham, W Sussex. *T:* Horsham 63759.

PERKINS, (George) Dudley (Gwynne), MA; Director-General of the Port of London Authority, 1964-71; *b* 19 March 1911; *s* of Gwynne Oliver Perkins and Sarah Perkins; *m* 1st, 1939, Enid Prys-Jones (*d* 1943); one *d*; 2nd, 1946, Pamela Marigo Blake; one *d*. *Educ:* Clifton College (Scholar); King's College, Cambridge (Choral Scholar; 1st cl. hons Eng. Lit.). Solicitor, 1937; Asst Legal Adviser, BBC, 1945-48; Asst Legal Adviser, National Coal Board, 1948-51; Chief Solicitor, PLA, 1955-62; Jt

Dep. General Manager, PLA, 1962-64. Member: Council of Law Society, 1954-62; Central Transport Consultative Cttee, 1962-69; SE Economic Planning Council, 1966-71; Performing Right Tribunal, 1974-. A Governor of Morley Coll., 1951-; Governor, Clifton Coll., 1969-. FCIT; FBIM. Regular broadcaster in Can I Help You and other broadcasts on law and current affairs, 1950-62. *Publications:* Can I Help You, 1959; Family Lawyer, 1962. *Recreations:* music, walking. *Address:* 63 Netherhall Gardens, Hampstead, NW3. *T:* 01-435 0609. *Clubs:* Garrick, MCC.

PERKINS, Air Vice-Marshal Irwyn Morse, MBE 1957; QHS; Principal Medical Officer, Royal Air Force Support Command, since 1977; *b* 15 Dec. 1920; *s* of William Lewis Perkins and Gwenllian Perkins; *m* 1948, Royce Villiers Thompson; one *s* one *d*. *Educ:* Pontardawe, Swansea; St Mary's Hospital, Paddington, W2. MRCS, LRCP 1945; MFCM 1973. Joined RAF, 1946; SMO: RAF Gibraltar, 1946-49; several flying stations in UK; RAF Laarbruch, Germany, 1958-61; RAF Khormaksar, Aden, 1964-66; DPMO, Bomber and Strike Commands, 1966-69; CO RAF Hospital, Ely, Cambs, 1969-72; PMO RAF Germany, 1972-75; CO PMRAF Hospital, Halton, 1975-77. QHS 1975. *Recreations:* sporting shooting, bodging. *Address:* 33 Park Lane, RAF Brampton, Huntingdon, Cambs PE18 8QL. *T:* Huntingdon 52151. *Club:* Royal Air Force.

PERKINS, James Alfred, MA, PhD; Chairman and Chief Executive Officer, International Council for Educational Development, since 1970; *b* 11 Oct. 1911; *s* of H. Norman Perkins and Emily (*née* Taylor); *m* 1st, 1938, Jean Bredin (*d* 1970); two *s* three *d*; 2nd, 1971, Ruth B. Aall; one step *s* three step *d*. *Educ:* Swarthmore Coll., Pa (AB); Princeton Univ., NJ (MA, PhD). Instructor Polit. Sci., Princeton Univ., 1937-39; Asst Prof. and Asst Dir, Sch. of Public and Internat. Affairs, Princeton, 1939-41; Dir, Pulp and Paper Div., Office of Price Admin., 1941-43; Asst to Administrator, For. Econ. Admin., 1943-45; Vice-Pres. Swarthmore Coll., 1945-50; Exec. Associate, Carnegie Corp. of NY, 1950-51; Dep. (on leave) Res. and Develt Bd, Dept of Defense, 1951-52; Vice-Pres., Carnegie Corp. of NY, 1951-63; Pres., Cornell Univ., 1963-69. Carnegie Foundn for the Advancement of Teaching: Sec. 1954-55; Vice-Pres., 1955-63. Chm., Pres. Johnson's Gen. Adv. Cttee on Foreign Assistance Prog., 1965-68; Trustee: Rand Corp., 1961-71; United Negro Coll. Fund (Chm. of Bd), 1965-69; Educl Testing Service, 1964-68; Council on Foreign Relations; Mem. Gen. Adv. Cttee of US Arms Control and Disarmament Agency, 1963-; Chm. NY Regents Adv. Cttee on Educational Leadership, 1963-67. Mem., Bd of Directors, Chase Manhattan Bank, 1967-75. Stevenson Memorial Fund, 1966-; Trustee, Aspen Inst., 1973-; Dir, Overseas Develt Council, 1969-. Mem. Society of Friends, Swarthmore, Pa. Hon. degrees: LLD: Centre Coll., 1958; Univ. of Akron, 1961; Brown Univ., Rutgers Univ., Swarthmore Coll., 1963; Princeton Univ., Lehigh Univ., Northwestern Univ., Syracuse Univ., 1964; Univ. of Rochester, 1965; Toronto Univ., 1965; Columbia Univ., 1966; Illinois Univ., 1967; Notre Dame, 1968; Yale, 1968; Yeshiva Univ., 1968; Univ. of Sydney, 1968; Florida Univ., 1974; LHD: Case Inst. of Tech., 1961; Ohio Univ., 1962; Hamilton Coll., 1966; Maine Univ., 1971. *Publications:* The University in Transition, 1966; Higher Education: from autonomy to systems, 1972; The University as an Organization, 1973; contrib. to: Public Admin. Review, Amer. Polit. Sci. Review, Educational Record, etc. *Address:* (home) North Road, Princeton, NJ, USA; (office) 680 Fifth Avenue, New York City, NY 10019, USA. *Clubs:* Century Association, Coffee House, University (NYC); Cosmos (Washington, DC).

PERKINS, John B. W.; *see* Ward-Perkins.

PERKINS, Maj.-Gen. Kenneth, CB 1977; MBE 1955; DFC 1953; Assistant Chief of Defence Staff (Operations), since 1977; *b* 15 Aug. 1926; *s* of George Samuel Perkins and Arabella Sarah Perkins (*née* Wise); *m* 1949, Anne Theresa Barry; three *d*. *Educ:* Lewes County Sch. for Boys; New Coll., Oxford. Enlisted 1944; commnd RA 1946; various appts in Middle and Far East, BAOR and UK until 1965; Staff Coll. Quetta 1958; Instructor, Staff Coll. Camberley, 1965-66; CO 1st Regt Royal Horse Artillery, 1967-69; GSO 1 Singapore, 1970; Comdr 24 Bde, 1971-72; RCDS 1973; Central Staff, MoD, 1974; Comdr, Sultan's Armed Forces, Oman, 1975-77. Selangor Distinguished Conduct Medal (Malaya), 1955; Order of Independence (Jordan), 1975; Order of Oman, 1977. *Publications:* articles in various Service jls. *Recreations:* painting, physical exercise. *Address:* c/o National Westminster Bank Ltd, Seaford, Sussex. *Club:* Army and Navy.

PERKINS, Air Vice-Marshal Maxwell Edmund Massy, CB 1962; CBE 1957; Director of Engineering, Aviation Division,

Smiths Industries Ltd, retired; *b* Portsmouth, Hants, 22 Aug. 1907; *s* of late Donald Maxwell Perkins; *m* 1st, 1934, Helena Joan Penelope (*d* 1973), *d* of Herbert John Newberry, Hitchin; one *s* two *d*; 2nd, 1974, Sylvia Mary, *widow* of Willson Gatward, Hitchin, Herts. *Educ:* Portsmouth College; London University (BA). Entered RAF, 1929; India. 1934-38. Served War of 1939-45, Bomber Command and Burma; America, 1952-54; STSO Fighter Command, 1954-56; Commandant, St Athan, 1956-58; Senior Technical Staff Officer, Bomber Command, 1958-61; Dir-Gen. of Engineering, Air Min., 1961-64, retired. Air Cdre, 1957; Air Vice-Marshal, 1961. CEng 1966, FIMechE (MIMechE 1957); FRaeS 1960. Co. Councillor, Herts, 1977-. *Recreation:* sailing. *Address:* Little Court, London Road, Hitchin, Herts. *Club:* Royal Air Force.

PERKINS, Sir Robert Dempster, Kt, *cr* 1954; *b* 1903; *s* of late W. Frank Perkins; *m* 1944, Lady Norman, *widow* of Sir Nigel Norman, 2nd Bt. *Educ:* Eton; Trinity Coll., Cambridge, MA. Mechanical Engineer. MP (C) Stroud (by-election May), 1931-45; MP (C) Stroud and Thornbury Division of Gloucestershire, 1950-55; Parliamentary Secretary, Ministry of Civil Aviation, 1945. *Recreations:* aviation and fishing. *Address:* The Manor House, Downton, Wilts.

PERKINS, Sir W. R. D.; *see* Perkins, Sir R. D.

PERKS, John Clifford, MC 1944; TD; His Honour Judge Perks; a Circuit Judge (formerly County Court Judge), since 1970; *b* 20 March 1915; *s* of John Hyde Haslewood Perks and Frances Mary Perks; *m* 1940, Ruth Dyke Perks (*née* Appleby); two *s* (one *s* two *d* decd). *Educ:* Blundell's; Balliol Coll., Oxford. Called to Bar, Inner Temple, 1938; joined Western Circuit; Chancellor, diocese of Bristol, 1950-71; Dep. Chm., Devon QS, 1965-71. *Recreation:* castles. *Address:* 32 Melbury Close, Chislehurst, Kent.

PERKS, Sir (Robert) Malcolm (Mewburn), 2nd Bt, *cr* 1908; retired Public Works Contractor, one time Chairman of Sir John Jackson Ltd, and Ford & Walton Ltd; *b* 29 July 1892; *s* of Sir Robert Wm Perks, 1st Bt, and Edith (*d* 1943), *y d* of late Wm Mewburn, DL; *S* father 1934; *m* 1917, Neysa Gilbert, *o c* of late Rev. Dr Cheney, New Rochelle, USA; two *d*. *Educ:* Leys Sch., Cambridge. Served European War, Lieut RNVR, Captain RAF. Director of Building Construction, Ministry of Supply, 1941-43. *Heir:* none. *Address:* 9 Esplanade Court, Worthing, Sussex. *See also* F. O. A. G. Bennett.

PERLMAN, Itzhak; violinist; *b* Tel Aviv, 31 Aug. 1945; *s* of Chaim and Shoshana Perlman; *m* 1967, Toby Lynn Friedlander; one *s* two *d*. Studied at Tel Aviv Acad. of Music with Ryvka Goldgart, and at Juilliard Sch., NY, under Dorothy Delay and Ivan Galamian. First solo recital at age of 10 in Israel; New York début, 1958. Leventritt Meml Award, NY, 1964. Has toured extensively in USA and played with all major American symphony orchestras; recital tours of Canada, South America, Europe, Israel, Far East and Australia; recorded many standard works for violin. *Recreations:* cooking Chinese style and watching basketball. *Address:* c/o Sheldon Gold, ICM Artists Ltd, 40 West 57th Street, New York, NY 10019, USA.

PEROWNE, Rear-Adm. Benjamin Cubitt; Director, Management and Support Intelligence, since 1976, also Chief Naval Supply and Secretariat Officer, since 1977; *b* 18 Feb. 1921; *s* of late Bernard Cubitt Perowne and of Gertrude Dorothy Perowne; *m* 1946, Phyllis Marjorie, *d* of late Cdre R. D. Peel, RNR, Southampton; two *s* one *d*. *Educ:* Culford Sch. Joined RN, 1939; Sec. to Adm. Sir Deric Holland-Martin, GCB, DSO, DSC, 1955-64; Acting Captain, 1957-64, Captain 1966; Staff, Chief of Personnel and Logistics, 1967-70; (Cdre, 1969-70); comd, HMS Cochrane, 1971-73; Dir of Defence Policy, 1973-75 (Cdre). *Recreations:* shooting, gardening. *Address:* Shortacre, Headley, Bordon, Hants. *T:* Bordon 2737. *Club:* Army and Navy.

PEROWNE, Dame Freya; *see* Stark, Dame Freya.

PEROWNE, Maj.-Gen. Lancelot Edgar Connop Mervyn, CB 1953; CBE 1945; Royal Engineers, retired; Company Director, retired; *b* 11 June 1902; 2nd and *o* surv. *s* of late Colonel Woolrych Perowne; *m* 1927, Gertrude Jenny Johanna Stein, Cologne, Germany; one *d*. *Educ:* Wellington Coll.; RMA, Woolwich. 2nd Lieut, RE, 1923; Temp. Brig., 1942; Col, 1945; Brig., 1951; Temp. Maj.-Gen., 1951; Maj.-Gen., 1952. Served France, 1940 (despatches); commanded 69 and 37 AA Bdes, AA Comd, 1940-43; commanded 23 Inf. Bde, India and Burma, 1943-45 (despatches, CBE); commanded Penang Sub-Area and 74 Indian Inf. Bde, SE Asia, 1945-46 (despatches); commanded 72 Inf. Bde, India, 1946-47; Comdt School of Combined

Operations, 1947-48; Comd 151 Northumberland and Durham Inf. Bde, TA, 1949-51; Commander British Miltary Mission to Greece, 1951-52; Commanded South Malaya District, 1952-55; GOC 17th Gurkha Division, 1952-55 (despatches); Maj.-Gen., The Brigade of Gurkhas, 1952-55, retired 1955. Colonel, The Gurkha Engineers, 1957-66. CEng; MIEE; KJStJ 1945; Star of Nepal (2nd Class), 1954. *Address:* Benfleet Hall, Green Lane, Cobham, Surrey KT11 2NN.

PEROWNE, Stewart Henry, OBE 1944; FSA; Orientalist and Historian; Colonial Administrative Service (retired); *b* 17 June 1901; 3rd *s* of late Arthur William Thomson Perowne, DD, Bishop of Worcester, and late Helena Frances Oldnall-Russell; *m* 1947, Freya Madeline Stark (*see* Dame Freya Stark). *Educ:* Haileybury Coll. (champion sprinter); Corpus Christi Coll., Cambridge; Harvard Univ., USA. BA 1923, MA 1931, Cambridge. Joined Palestine Government Education Service, 1927; Administrative Service, 1930 (Press Officer 1931); Asst District Commissioner, Galilee, 1934; Asst Secretary Malta, 1934 (pioneered Pasteurization); Political Officer, Aden Prot., 1937; recovered inscriptions and sculpture from Imadia and Beihan; Arabic Programme Organiser, BBC, 1938 (pioneered programme, English by Radio); Information Officer, Aden, 1939; Public Relations Attaché, British Embassy, Baghdad, 1941; Oriental Counsellor, 1944; Colonial Secretary, Barbados, 1947-51; seconded as Principal Adviser (Interior), Cyrenaica, 1950-51; retired 1951. Discovered ancient city of Aziris, 1951. Adviser, UK delegation to UN Assembly, Paris, Nov. 1951. Helped design stamps for Malta, 1936, Aden, 1938, Barbados, 1949, Libya, 1951; currency notes for W. Indies Federation, 1949, and Libya, 1951; Assistant to the Bishop in Jerusalem for Refugee work, 1952; designer and supervisor of Refugee model villages. FSA 1957. KStJ 1954. Coronation Medal, 1937; Iraq Coronation Medal, 1953; Metropolitan Police Mounted Officers certificate. Member, C. of E. Foreign Relations Council. *Publications:* The One Remains, 1954; Herod the Great, 1956; The Later Herods, 1958; Hadrian, 1960; Cæsars and Saints, 1962; The Pilgrim's Companion in Jerusalem and Bethlehem, 1964; The Pilgrim's Companion in Roman Rome, 1964; The Pilgrim's Companion in Athens, 1964; Jerusalem, 1965; The End of the Roman World, 1966; The Death of the Roman Republic: from 146 BC to the birth of the Roman Empire, 1969; Roman Mythology, 1969; (contrib.) Ancient Cities of the Middle East, 1970; The Siege within the Walls: Malta 1940-43, 1970; Rome, 1971; The Journeys of St Paul, 1973; The Caesars' Wives, 1974; The Archaeology of Greece and the Aegean, 1974; Holy Places of Christendom, 1976; articles in Encyclopædia Britannica, The Times, History Today, etc. *Recreations:* horses, the arts, archæology. *Address:* 44 Arminger Road, W12 7BB. *T:* 01-743 8363. *Clubs:* Travellers'; Casino Maltese; Savannah (Bridgetown); Phoenix-SK (Harvard).

PERREN, Edward Arthur, CB 1962; PhD; FRIC; *b* 13 June 1900; *s* of late Arthur Perren, London; *m* 1925, Muriel Davidge, Palmers Green; one *s* one *d* (and one *s* decd). *Educ:* Stationers' Sch., Hornsey; Imperial Coll., University of London. BSc Hons (London) 1919; PhD (London) 1922. Joined scientific staff of War Dept, 1922. Chief Superintendent, Suffield Experimental Station, Canada, 1949-51; Superintendent Research Division, CDEE, Porton, 1951-55; Director, CDEE, Porton (Chief Scientific Officer), 1955-61. *Publications:* various papers on Organic Chemistry. *Address:* Larchfield, Appleshaw, Andover, Hants. *T:* Weyhill 2434.

PERRETT, John, JP; **His Honour Judge Perrett;** a Circuit Judge (formerly a Judge of County Courts), since 1969; *b* 22 Oct. 1906; *er s* of late Joseph and Alice Perrett, Birmingham; *m* 1933, Elizabeth Mary, *y d* of late William Seymour, Nenagh, Co. Tipperary; two *s* two *d*. *Educ:* St Anne's RC and Stratford Road Schools, Birmingham; King's Coll., Strand, WC2. Entered office of Philip Baker & Co., Solicitors, Birmingham, 1922; joined late Alfred W. Fryzer, Solicitor, Arundel St, WC2, 1925; joined Herbert Baron & Co., Solicitors, Queen Victoria St, EC4, 1934. Served War of 1939-45: RAPC, 1939-45; RASC, 1945. Called to Bar, Gray's Inn, 1946; practised in London and on Midland Circuit; Dep. Chm., Warwicks QS, 1970-71; JP Warwicks, 1970. *Address:* 9 The Close, Lichfield, Staffs. *T:* Lichfield 52320; Farrar's Building, Temple, EC4. *T:* 01-583 9241.

See also G . H . Rooke .

PERRIN, John Henry; Director-General, British Agricultural Export Council, 1976-77; *b* 14 Jan. 1916; *s* of late William Perrin, Faringdon and Sonning, Berks, and Amelia (*née* Honey), Oxford; *m* 1940, Doris Winifred Barrington-Brider; two *s*. *Educ:* Minchenden Sch.; London Univ. HM Customs and Excise; Royal Navy, 1939-46; Min. of Agriculture, 1948-76: Principal Private Sec. to Minister (Lord Amory), 1955-57; Regional Controller, Eastern Region, 1957-68; Under Sec., 1968-76.

Member of Council, Royal Agricultural Soc. of England. *Recreations:* painting, Chinese porcelain, soccer, sailing. *Address:* Beeson End, Harpenden, Herts. *T:* Harpenden 61357. *Clubs:* Naval, Civil Service, Royal Yachting.

PERRIN, Sir Michael (Willcox), Kt 1967; CBE 1952 (OBE 1946); FRIC; Chairman, The Wellcome Foundation Ltd, 1953-70; Director: Inveresk Research International, 1961-74 (Chairman, 1971-73); Radiochemical Centre Ltd, 1971-75; *b* 13 Sept. 1905; *s* of late Bishop W. W. Perrin; *m* 1934, Nancy May, *d* of late Bishop C. E. Curzon; one *s* one *d*. *Educ:* Winchester; New Coll., Oxford (BA, BSc). Post-graduate research, Toronto Univ. (MA), 1928-29; Amsterdam Univ., 1929-33; ICI (Alkali) Research Dept, Northwich, 1933-38; Asst Director, Tube Alloys (Atomic Energy), DSIR, 1941-46; Dep. Controller, Atomic Energy (Technical Policy), Ministry of Supply, 1946-51; Research Adviser, ICI, 1951-52. Chm. (Treasurer) Bd of Governors, St Bartholomew's Hosp. and Pres., Med. Coll. of St Bartholomew's Hosp., 1960-69; Member: Council, Royal Veterinary Coll., London Univ., 1973-76 (Chm. 1967-72); Council, Sch. of Pharmacy, London Univ., 1963-76; Central Adv. Council for Science and Technology, 1969-70; Governing Body, British Postgrad. Med. Fedn, 1970-77 (Chm., 1972-77). Trustee, British Museum (National History), 1974-. Chm. Council, Roedean Sch., 1974-. Hon. DSc Univ. of British Columbia, 1969. *Publications:* papers in scientific and technical journals. *Address:* 14 Christchurch Hill, Hampstead, NW3 1LB. *T:* 01-794 3064; 8 Court Road Mansions, Eastern Terrace, Brighton BN2 1DJ. *T:* Brighton 689766. *Club:* Athenæum.

PERRING, John Raymond, TD 1965; Vice-Chairman, Perring Furnishings Ltd, since 1972; *b* 7 July 1931; *e s* and *heir* of Sir Ralph Perring, Bt, *qv*; *m* 1961, Ella Christine, *e d* of late A. G. Pelham and Mrs Ann Pelham; two *s* two *d*. *Educ:* Stowe School. Nat. Service, then TA, RA, 1949-60; Royal Fusiliers (City of London), 1960-65. Joined family furnishing business, 1951, Dir 1957, Jt Man. Dir 1964. One of HM Lieutenants of City of London, 1963-; Mem. Merchant Taylors' Co.; Mem. Court, Furniture Makers' Co.; Nat. Pres., Nat. Assoc. of Retail Furnishers, 1971-73; Chm., Retail Alliance, 1973-75; Mem. Council, Retail Consortium, 1972-; Mem. EDC (Distributive Trades), 1974-. *Recreations:* sailing, ski-ing, swimming, gardening. *Address:* 21 Somerset Road, Wimbledon, SW19. *T:* 01-946 8971. *Clubs:* City Livery, Royal Automobile; Royal Wimbledon Golf; Bembridge Sailing.

PERRING, Sir Ralph (Edgar), 1st Bt *cr* 1963; Kt 1960; Chairman, Perring Furnishings Ltd; *b* 23 March 1905; *yr s* of late Colonel Sir John Perring, DL, JP; *m* 1928, Ethel Mary, OStJ, *o d* of late Henry T. Johnson, Putney; two *s* (and one *s* decd). *Educ:* University College Sch., London. Lieut, RA (TA) 1938-40, invalided. Member Court of Common Council (Ward of Cripplegate), 1948-51; Alderman of City of London (Langbourn Ward), 1951-75, one of HM Lieutenants of the City of London, and Sheriff, 1958-59. Lord Mayor of London, 1962-63. Chairman, Spitalfields Market Cttee, 1951-52; JP County of London, 1943-; Member: LCC for Cities of London and Westminster, 1952-55; County of London Licensing Planning Cttee; New Guildford Cathedral Council; Consumer Advisory Council, BSI, 1955-59; Bd of Governors, E-SU, 1976-. Governor: St Bartholomew's Hospital, 1964-69; Imperial College of Science and Technology, 1964-67; Christ's Hospital; Vice-Chairman, BNEC Cttee for Exports to Canada, 1964-67, Chairman, 1968-70; Dir, Confederation Life Insurance Co. of Canada, 1969-. Vice-President, Royal Bridewell Hospital (King Edward's Sch., Witley, 1964-75); Master Worshipful Company of Tin Plate Workers, 1944-45; Master, Worshipful Company of Painters-Stainers, 1977-78; Mem. Court, Farmers' Co.; President Langbourn Ward Club, 1951-75. FRSA 1975. KStJ. Grand Cross of Merit (Republic of Germany), 1959; Order of Homayoun (Iran), 1959; Grand Officer, Order of Leopold (Belgium), 1963; Knight Commander, Royal Order of George I (Greece), 1963; Commander de la Valeur Camerounaise, 1963. *Heir: s* John Raymond Perring, *qv*. *Address:* 15 Burghley House, Somerset Road, Wimbledon, SW19. *T:* 01-946 3433. *Clubs:* Constitutional, Royal Automobile, City Livery (President, 1951-52).

PERRINS, Wesley, MBE 1952; an official of Municipal and General Workers' Union, Birmingham District Secretary; Member, Worcestershire County Council until 1974 (formerly Alderman); formerly Member, West Midlands Economic Planning Council; *b* 21 Sept. 1905; *s* of Councillor Amos Perrins, Stourbridge; *m* 1932, Mary, *d* of Charles Evans; one *s* one *d*. *Educ:* Wollescote Council Sch.; Upper Standard Sch., Lye. MP (Lab) Yardley Division of Birmingham, 1945-50. Member of: Lye & Wollescote UDC, 1928-31; Stourbridge Borough Council, 1931-46, 1971. Mem., Court of Governors,

Birmingham Univ. *Address:* Cromlech Cottage, 19 Walker Avenue, Wollescote, Stourbridge, West Midlands. *T:* Stourbridge 4640.

PERRIS, Sir David (Arthur), Kt 1977; MBE 1970; JP; Chairman, West Midlands Regional Health Authority, since 1974; Secretary, Trades Union Congress West Midlands Regional Council, since 1974; Secretary, Birmingham Trades Council, since 1966; Chairman, National Health Service National Training Council, since 1975; *b* 25 May 1929; *s* of Arthur Perris; *m* 1955, Constance Parkes, BPharm, FPS; one *s* one *d. Educ:* Sparkhill Commercial Sch., Birmingham. Film distribution industry, 1944-61; Reed Paper Group, 1961-65; Chm., Birmingham Regional Hosp. Bd, 1970-74; Mem. Bd of Governors: United Birmingham Hosps, 1965-74; Birmingham Coll. of Commerce, 1966-70; Mem., Birmingham Children's Hosp. House Cttee, 1958-71 (Chm. 1967-71); Vice-Chm., Birmingham Hosp. Saturday Fund, 1975-; Mem., W Mids Econ. Planning Council, 1968-70; Life Governor, Univ. of Birmingham, 1972; Mem. Convocation, Univ. of Aston in Birmingham, 1975-; Sec., Polytechnic Bursaries Cttee, 1966-; Mem., Midlands Postal Bd, 1974-; Chm. Magistrates' Assoc., Birmingham Bench, 1975-. JP Birmingham, 1962. *Recreations:* cinema, reading. *Address:* 24 Mayfield Road, Moseley, Birmingham B13 9HJ. *T:* 021-449 3652.

PERROTT, Sir Donald (Cyril Vincent), KBE 1949; *b* 12 April 1902; *s* of late Frederick John Perrott and of Alice Perrott, Southampton; *m* 1st, 1925, Marjorie May (*d* 1969), *d* of late William Holway, Taunton; one *s*; 2nd, 1969, Mrs L. L. Byre. *Educ:* Tauntons' Sch., Southampton; University College, Southampton. Inland Revenue Dept, 1920; Ministry of Aircraft Production, 1941; Ministry of Supply, 1942; Dep. Secretary Ministry of Food, 1947-49; Deputy Chairman, Overseas Food Corporation, 1949-51; Chairman: Queensland British Food Corporation, 1950-53; British Ministry of Supply, European Purchasing Commission, 1951-52; Interdepartmental Cttee, Woolwich Arsenal, 1953; Secretary, Department of Atomic Energy, 1954 and Member for Finance and Administration of Atomic Energy Authority, 1954-60; Member, Governing Board of National Institute for Research in Nuclear Science, 1957-60. *Recreations:* golf and bridge. *Address:* 5 Plane Tree House, Duchess of Bedford's Walk, W8 7QT. *Club:* Royal Automobile.

PERRY, Hon. Sir (Alan) Clifford, Kt 1976; Hon. Mr Justice Perry; Senior Puisne Judge, Supreme Court of New Zealand, since 1976 (Judge, 1962); *b* 10 July 1907; *s* of George Perry and Agnes Mary Jenkins; *m* 1943, Barbara Jean Head; two *s* one *d*. *Educ:* Hornby Primary Sch.; Christ's Coll., Christchurch; Canterbury University Coll., Univ. of NZ (LLM, 2nd Cl. Hons). Admitted barrister and solicitor, 1928; Partner, Wilding & Acland (legal firm), 1935-62; part-time Lectr in Commercial Law, Canterbury University Coll., 1939-47. Chairman Court of Enquiry: into fire on M. V. Holmburn, 1959; into loss of M. V. Holmglen, 1960. Pres., Canterbury Dist Law Soc., 1950; Chm., Council of Legal Educn, 1975- (Mem., 1954-62 and 1964-); Mem., Disciplin. Cttee, NZ Law Soc., 1952-62. Silver Jubilee Medal, 1977. Royal Danish Consul for S Island, NZ, 1948-62. Chevalier, Royal Order of Dannebrog, 1955. *Recreations:* reading; cottage in Arthur's Pass National Park. *Address:* 54 Mountain Road, Epsom, Auckland 3, New Zealand. *T:* 601-035. *Clubs:* Northern (Auckland); Canterbury (Christchurch).

PERRY, Charles Bruce; Medical Member, Pensions Appeals Tribunals; Professor of Medicine, University of Bristol, 1935-69, Emeritus since 1969; *b* 1903; *s* of Charles E. and Sarah Duthie Perry; *m* 1929, Mildred Bernice Harvey; three *d. Educ:* Bristol Grammar Sch.; University of Bristol, MB, ChB 1926; FRCP, 1936; MD Bristol, 1928; Physician, Bristol Royal Hospital for Sick Children and Women, 1928; Physician, Winford Orthopædic Hospital, 1930; Buckston Browne Prize, Harveian Society of London, 1929; Markham Skeritt Memorial Prize, 1931; Asst Physician, Bristol General Hospital, 1933. Lectures: Long Fox Memorial, 1943; Bradshaw, RCP, 1944; Lumleian, RCP, 1969; Carey Coombs, Univ. of Bristol, 1969; Cyril Fernando Meml, Ceylon, 1971. Pro-Vice-Chancellor, University of Bristol, 1958-61; President Assoc. of Physicians of Great Britain and Ireland, 1961-62; Chairman, British Cardiac Society, 1961-62; Censor, RCP, 1962-64. *Publications:* Bacterial Endocarditis, 1936; various papers in the Medical Press dealing with research in Diseases of the Heart. *Address:* Beechfield, 54 Grove Road, Coombe Dingle, Bristol BS9 2RR. *T:* Bristol 682713.

PERRY, Hon. Sir Clifford; *see* Perry, Hon. Sir A. C.

PERRY, Sir David Norman, Kt 1977; MBD; Chairman of Directors, Opotiki Textiles Ltd, St John Street, Opotiki, clothing manufacturers. Knighthood awarded for services to the community and the Maori people, New Zealand. *Address:* Woodlands, Opotiki, New Zealand. *T:* Opotiki 914; Opotiki Textiles Ltd, St John Street, PO Box 162, Opotiki, New Zealand. *T:* Opotiki 941.

PERRY, Ernest George; MP (Lab) Wandsworth, Battersea South, since 1974 (Battersea South, 1964-74); *b* 25 April 1908; British; *m* 1950, Edna Joyce Perks-Mankelow; one *s. Educ:* LCC secondary school. Textiles, 1923-33; Insurance, 1933-64. Member Battersea Borough Council, 1934-65 (Mayor of Battersea, 1955-56); Alderman, London Borough of Wandsworth, 1964-72. Asst Govt Whip, 1968-69; Lord Commissioner, HM Treasury, 1969-70; an Opposition Whip, 1970-74; an Asst Govt Whip, 1974-75. Served with Royal Artillery, 1939-46: Indian Army and Indian Artillery (Troop Sgt); Far East, 1942-45. *Recreations:* local government, sport, reading. *Address:* House of Commons, SW1; 30 Old Park Avenue, Balham, SW12.

PERRY, George Henry; *b* 24 Aug. 1920; *s* of Arthur and Elizabeth Perry; *m* 1944, Ida Garner; two *d. Educ:* elementary sch. and technical college. Engineering Apprentice, 1934-41. Naval Artificer, 1941-46 (Atlantic and Italy Stars; 1939-45 Star). Railway Fitter, 1946-66. Derby Town Councillor, 1955-66. Chairman: Derby Water Cttee, 1957-61; S Derbys Water Board, 1961-66; Derby Labour Party, 1961-62; Secretary, Derby Trades Council, 1961-66. Contested (Lab) Harborough, 1964; MP (Lab) Nottingham South, 1966-70. *Recreation:* walking. *Address:* 123 Hawthorn Street, Derby. *T:* Derby 44687.

PERRY, Ven. John Neville; Archdeacon of Middlesex, since 1975; *b* 29 March 1920; *s* of Robert and Enid Perry; *m* 1946, Rita Dyson Rooke; four *s* four *d*. *Educ:* The Crypt Gram. Sch., Gloucester; Univ. of Leeds (BA 1941), College of the Resurrection, Mirfield. Asst Curate, All Saints', Poplar, 1943-50; Vicar, St Peter De Beauvoir Town, Hackney, 1950-63; Vicar, St Dunstan with St Catherine, Feltham, Mddx, 1963-75; Rural Dean of Hounslow, 1967-75. Mem. Latey Cttee on the Age of Majority, 1966-67. *Recreations:* D-I-Y handyman. *Address:* 63 Alexandra Road, Hounslow, Middlesex TW3 4HP. *T:* 01-572 6984.

PERRY, Kenneth Murray Allan, MA, MD (Cantab), FRCP; Consulting Physician to: The London Hospital (Physician, 1946-72); the Royal Masonic Hospital (Physician, 1949-72); Medical Advisor to Central Advisory Council for Training for the Ministry of the Church of England, 1958-70; *b* 1 Feb. 1909; *s* of Major H. Perry, Ware, Herts; *m* 1938, Winifred, *d* of F. P. Grassi; no *c. Educ:* Christ's Hospital; Queens' Coll., Cambridge. Kitchener Scholar, 1927; Price University Entrance Scholarship, 1930; Medical Registrar, London Hospital, 1935-38; Dorothy Temple Cross Fellowship, Mass. General Hospital, Boston, 1938-39; Research Fellow, Harvard, 1939. Member of Scientific Staff, Medical Research Council, 1942-46. Ernestine Henry Lecturer, Royal College of Physicians, 1955. Visiting Physician, Papworth Village Settlement, 1946-72; Consulting Physician, Brentwood District and Warley Hospitals, 1947-72. Examiner in Medicine, Universities of Cambridge, London, Liverpool and Hong Kong; Royal College of Physicians, London; Society of Apothecaries of London. UK representative, International Society of Internal Medicine, 1969-72. Member: Assoc. of Physicians of Great Britain and Ireland, 1946-72; Thoracic Society, 1946-72. Miembro Correspondiente Extranjeo de Academia Nacional de Medicina de Buenos Aires. *Publications:* (with Sir Geoffrey Marshall) Diseases of the Chest, 1952; Pulmonary Œdema, in British Encyclopædia of Medical Practice, 1948; Industrial Medicine in Chambers's Encyclopædia, 1948; (with Sir Thomas Holmes Sellors) Chest Diseases, 1963. *Recreations:* travel, photography. *Address:* One Tower House, Old Portsmouth PO1 2JR. *T:* Portsmouth 21446. *Clubs:* Royal Over-Seas League, Royal Automobile; Royal Naval and Royal Albert Yacht (Portsmouth).

PERRY, Ven. Michael Charles, MA; Archdeacon of Durham and Canon Residentiary of Durham Cathedral since 1970; *b* 5 June 1933; *o s* of late Charlie Perry; *m* 1963, Margaret, *o d* of late John Middleton Adshead; two *s* one *d. Educ:* Ashby-de-la-Zouch Boys' Grammar Sch.; Trinity Coll., Cambridge (Sen. Schol.); Westcott House, Cambridge. Asst Curate of Berkswich, Stafford, 1958-60; Chaplain, Ripon Hall, Oxford, 1961-63; Chief Asst for Home Publishing, SPCK, 1963-70; Examining Chaplain to Bishop of Lichfield, 1965-74. Sec., Archbishops' Commn on Christian Doctrine, 1967-70. Diocesan Chm., 1970-, Mem. Council, 1975-, USPG. Lectures: Selwyn, NZ, 1976: Marshall Meml, Melbourne, 1976; Beard Meml, London, 1977. Editor, Church Quarterly, 1968-71; Review Editor, Parapsychologist, 1977-. *Publications:* The Easter Enigma,

1959; The Pattern of Matins and Evensong, 1961; (co-author) The Churchman's Companion, 1963; Meet the Prayer Book, 1963; (contrib.) The Miracles and the Resurrection, 1964; (ed) Crisis for Confirmation, 1967; (co-author) Declaring The Faith: The Printed Word, 1969; Sharing in One Bread, 1973; The Resurrection of Man, 1975; The Paradox of Worship, 1977; A Handbook of Parish Worship, 1977. *Address:* 7 The College, Durham DH1 3EQ. *T:* Durham 61891. *Club:* Royal Commonwealth.

PERRY, Peter George, JP; Under Secretary, Department of Health and Social Security, since 1975; *b* 15 Dec. 1923; *s* of late Joseph and Elsie Perry; *m* 1957, Marjorie Margaret Stevens; no *c*. *Educ:* Dartford Grammar Sch.; London Univ. (LLB). Normandy with Northants Yeomanry, 1944. Joined Min. of Health, 1947; Private Sec. to Minister of State, 1968-70; Asst Sec., 1971. JP City of London, 1974; Freeman, City of London, 1975. *Recreations:* sailing, squash, opera, wine. *Address:* 50 Great Brownings, College Road, Dulwich, SE21. *T:* 01-670 3387. *Club:* Little Ship.

PERRY, Lt-Col Robert Stanley Grosvenor, DSO 1943; DL; *b* 1909; *s* of late Robert Grosvenor Perry, CBE, Barton House, Moreton-in-Marsh, Glos; *m* 1937, Margaret Louisa Elphinstone, *o c* of Horace Czarnikow; one *s*. *Educ:* Harrow; RMC, Sandhurst. 2nd Lieut, 9th Lancers, 1929, Major, 1941; Adjutant, Cheshire Yeomanry, 1938-40; Commanding: 2nd Lothians and Border Yeomanry, 1943; 9th Lancers, 1944-45; served War of 1939-45, Palestine, Western Desert, N Africa, Italy (despatches, wounded twice); Commandant, RACOCTU, 1945-48. One of HM Bodyguard of Hon. Corps of Gentlemen at Arms from 1959. High Sheriff of Dorset, 1961. DL Dorset, 1962. Member British Olympic Yachting Team, Helsinki, 1952, Melbourne (Silver Medal), 1956; Winner: Cup of Italy with Vision (5.5 Metre), 1956; One Ton Cup with Royal Thames (6 Metre), 1958. *Recreations:* yacht racing, foxhunting, shooting. *Address:* Crendle Court, Purse Caundle, Sherborne, Dorset. *T:* Milborne Port 364. *Clubs:* Cavalry and Guards, Royal Yacht Squadron.

PERRY, Prof. Samuel Victor, BSc (Liverpool), PhD, ScD (Cantab); FRS 1974; Professor of Biochemistry, University of Birmingham, since Sept. 1959; *b* 16 July 1918; *s* of late Samuel and Margaret Perry; *m* 1948, Maureen Tregent Shaw; one *s* two *d*. *Educ:* King George V Sch., Southport; Liverpool Univ.; Trinity Coll., Cambridge. Served in War of 1939-45, home and N. Africa; Royal Artillery, 1940-46, Captain; POW 1942-45. Research Fellow, Trinity Coll., Cambridge, 1947-51; Commonwealth Fund Fellow, University of Rochester, USA, 1948-49; University Lecturer, Dept of Biochemistry, Cambridge, 1950-59. *Publications:* scientific papers in Biochemical Journal, Nature, Biochemica Biophysica Acta, etc. *Recreations:* gardening, pottery, Rugby football (Cambridge, 1946, 1947, England, 1947, 1948). *Address:* 64 Meadow Hill Road, King's Norton, Birmingham 30. *T:* 021-458 1511.

PERRY, Thomas Wilfred, CMG 1966; Director, Thomas Perry & Sons Ltd, since 1916; *b* 3 March 1899; *s* of Thomas and Florence Perry; *m* 1st, 1922, Winifred Newey Lucas (*d* 1960); four *s*; 2nd, 1962, Ada May Lucas. *Educ:* Technical Coll., Christchurch, NZ. Entered family business, 1916. Director and Chairman of many public companies, 1930-60. *Recreations:* farming, fishing. *Address:* 5 Coldstream Court, Fendalton, Christchurch, New Zealand. *T:* 517-817. *Club:* Canterbury (Christchurch).

PERRY, Sir Walter (Laing Macdonald), Kt 1974; OBE 1957; FRSE; Vice-Chancellor, The Open University, since 1969; *b* 16 June 1921; *s* of Fletcher S. Perry and Flora M. Macdonald; *m* 1st, 1946, Anne Elizabeth Grant (marr. diss. 1971); three *s*; 2nd, 1971, Catherine Hilda Crawley; one *s*. *Educ:* Ayr Acad.; Dundee High Sch. MB, ChB 1943, MD 1948, DSc, 1958 (University of St Andrews), MRCP (Edinburgh), 1963; FRCP (Edinburgh), 1967. Medical Officer, Colonial Medical Service (Nigeria), 1944-46; Medical Officer, RAF, 1946-47; Member of Staff, Medical Research Council, 1947-52; Director, Department of Biological Standards, National Institute for Medical Research, 1952-58. Prof. of Pharmacology, University of Edinburgh, 1958-68, Vice-Principal, 1967-68. Member, British Pharmacopœia Commission, 1952-68; Secretary, British Pharmacological Society, 1957-61. Hon. DSc Bradford, 1974; Hon. LLD Dundee, 1975. *Publications:* Open University, 1976; papers in Journal of Physiology, British Journal of Pharmacology and Chemotherapy, etc. *Recreations:* making music and playing games. *Address:* The Open University, Walton Hall, Milton Keynes. *T:* Milton Keynes 74066. *Clubs:* Savage; Scottish Arts.

PERRY-KEENE, Air Vice-Marshal Allan Lancelot Addison, CB 1947; OBE 1940; RAF (retired); *b* 10 Nov. 1898; *s* of late L. H.

A. and M. Perry-Keene; *m* 1923, K. L., *d* of late C. A. S. Silberrad, ICS; two *d*. *Educ:* Wolverley; King Edward's, Birmingham. Served European War, 1914-18; joined RFC, 1917; France, 1918-19; transferred RAF, 1918; Iraq, 1927-29; India, 1935-41; Burma and India, 1942; Director of Ground Training and Training Plans, Air Ministry, 1943-45; AOC 227 Group, India, and 3 (Indian) Group, 1946; Air Officer i/c Administration, Air HQ, India, 1946; Air Commander, Royal Pakistan Air Force, 1947-49. *Address:* Wayfarers Cottage, St Mary Bourne, Andover, Hants SP11 6AR. *T:* St Mary Bourne 210.

PERT, Maj.-Gen. Claude Ernest, CB 1947; CVO 1976; DSO 1945; retired; *b* 26 Sept. 1898; *s* of F. J. Pert, late ICS; *m* 1922, Lilian Katherine Nicolls. *Educ:* Royal Naval Coll., Osborne; Clifton Coll. Commissioned into Indian Army, 1917, and joined 15th Lancers; Comd Probyn's Horse, 1940-42; Comd 255 Indian Tank Bde in 14th Army, Burma; Comd 1st Indian Armoured Div., 1945-48; retired 1948. *Recreations:* polo and fishing. *Address:* Garden House, Ribblesdale Park, Ascot, Berks. *T:* Ascot 22976. *Clubs:* Cavalry and Guards, Buck's.

PERTH, 17th Earl of, *cr* 1605; **STRATHALLAN, 13th Viscount,** *cr* 1686; **John David Drummond,** PC 1957; Baron Drummond of Cargill, 1488; Baron Maderty, 1609; Baron Drummond, 1686; Lord Drummond of Gilston, 1685; Lord Drummond of Rickertoun and Castlemaine, 1686; Hereditary Thane of Lennox, and Hereditary Steward of Menteith and Strathearn; Representative Peer for Scotland, 1952-63; First Crown Estate Commissioner, 1962-77; Chairman, Ditchley Foundation, 1963-66; *b* 13 May 1907; *o s* of 16th Earl of Perth, PC, GCMG, CB, and Hon. Angela Constable-Maxwell (*d* 1965), *y d* of 11th Baron Herries; *S* father 1951; *m* 1934, Nancy Seymour, *d* of Reginald Fincke, New York City; two *s*. *Educ:* Downside; Cambridge Univ. Lieut. Intelligence Corps, 1940; seconded to War Cabinet Offices, 1942-43, Ministry of Production, 1944-45; Minister of State for Colonial Affairs, 1957-62 (resigned). Director: Royal Bank of Scotland; Tate & Lyle Ltd. Chm., Reviewing Cttee on Export of Works of Art, 1972-76. Member: Court of St Andrews Univ., 1967-; Adv. Council, V&A Museum, 1971-72; Trustee, Nat. Library of Scotland, 1968-. *Heir: s* Viscount Strathallan, *qv*. *Address:* 14 Hyde Park Gardens Mews, W2. *T:* 01-262 4667; Stobhall, by Perth.

PERTH, Provost of (St Ninian's Cathedral); *see* Watt, Very Rev. A. I.

PERTH (Australia), **Archbishop of,** and Metropolitan of Western Australia, since 1969; **Most Rev. Geoffrey Tremayne Sambell;** Chairman, National Consultative Council on Social Welfare, since 1976; *b* 28 Oct. 1914; *s* of E. Sambell, Violet Town, Vic.; single. *Educ:* Melbourne High Sch.; Melbourne University. ThL 1939; BA 1946. Deacon 1940; Priest, 1941. Army Chaplain, 1942-46 and 1949-58; Dir., Melbourne Diocesan Centre, 1947-62; Archdeacon of Essendon, 1955-61; Bishop Co-adjutor, Diocese of Melbourne, 1962-69; Archdeacon of Melbourne, 1961-69. Dir, Brotherhood of St Laurence, 1956-68. Pres., Victorian Coun. of Social Services, 1956-58. Fellow, Australian Coll. of Theology (Th.Soc.), 1962. *Recreation:* golf. *Address:* Bishop's House, Mounts Bay Road, Perth, WA 6000, Australia. *Clubs:* Melbourne, Royal Automobile of Victoria (Melbourne); West Australia, Weld, Lake Karrinyup (all Perth).

PERTH (Australia), **Archbishop of,** (RC), since 1968; **Most Rev. Launcelot John Goody,** KBE 1977; PhD, DD; *b* 5 June 1908; *s* of late Ernest John Goody and of Agnes Goody. *Educ:* Christian Brothers' College, Perth, WA; Urban University, Rome. PhD 1927, DD 1931. Ordained priest at Rome, 1930; Asst Parish Priest, Perth Cathedral, 1932-35, Kalgoorlie, 1935-37; Parish Priest, Toodyay, 1937; Director of Seminary, Guilford, 1940-47; Domestic Prelate to the Pope, 1947; Parish Priest, Bedford Park, 1947-51; Auxiliary Bishop of Perth, 1951; first RC Bishop of Bunbury, 1954-68. *Address:* St Mary's Cathedral, Perth, WA 6000, Australia. *T:* 259177.

PERTWEE, Captain Herbert Guy, CBE 1949; DSO 1919; RN, retired; *b* 28 July 1893; *s* of H. A. Pertwee, Great Yarmouth; *m* 1921, Carmen (*d* 1959), 2nd *d* of late T. Waddon-Martyn, Stoke, Devonport; two *s* one *d*. *Educ:* Gresham's Sch., Holt. Joined Royal Navy, 1911; Falkland Islands action in HMS Carnarvon, 1914; joined staff of Commodore Tyrwhitt in HMS Arethusa, 1915; subsequent flagships of the Harwich Force for 3 years (clasps); secretary to Commodore, Persian Gulf and Mesopotamia Division, and later the Caspian Naval Force, 1918-19 (clasps, DSO, Russian Order of St Anne, 3rd class, Russian Order of Stanislaus, 2nd class, with swords); naval secretary of Naval and Military Commission to Persia, 1920-21 (Naval GS medal and clasp); Staff of C-in-C, The Nore, 1921-24;

Naval Staff, Admiralty, 1924-26; secretary to Rear-Admiral, First Battle Squadron, 1926-27; Staffs of Cs-in-C, Portsmouth, Atlantic Fleet, and Mediterranean Fleet, 1928-31; secretary to Vice-Admiral, Commanding Battle Cruiser Squadron, 1932-34, to Deputy Chief of Naval Staff, 1935-38, and to C-in-C, Portsmouth, 1939-42; Staff Supply Officer, West Africa, 1943-44; ADC to the King, 1948; retired list, 1949. Chief Supplies Officer to the Groundnuts Scheme, 1949-51; Comdt, Government Hostel, Dar es Saalam, and Hon. ADC to the Governor, 1951-54; Divisional Comdt, Devon Special Constabulary, 1956-68. *Recreations:* gardening, local government. *Address:* Bickington, near Barnstaple, N Devon. *T:* Barnstaple 4360.

PERUTZ, Max Ferdinand, CH 1975; CBE 1963; FRS 1954; PhD; Chairman of the Medical Research Council Laboratory of Molecular Biology, 1962-79; *b* 19 May 1914; *s* of Hugo and Adèle Perutz; *m* 1942, Gisela Peiser; one *s* one *d*. *Educ:* Theresianum, Vienna; Univ. of Vienna; Univ. of Cambridge (PhD 1940). Hon. Fellow, Peterhouse, Cambridge, 1962. Dir, MRC Unit for Molecular Biology, 1947-62; Chm., European Molecular Biology Orgn, 1963-69. Reader, Davy Faraday Res. Lab., 1954-68, and Fullerian Prof. of Physiology, 1973-, Royal Instn. Mem., Royal Society of Edinburgh, 1976; Hon. Member American Academy of Arts and Sciences, 1963; Corresp. Member, Austrian Acad. of Sciences, 1963; Foreign Member: American Philosophical Society, 1968; French Acad. of Sciences, 1976; For. Associate, Nat. Acad. of Sciences, USA, 1970. Nobel Prize for Chemistry (jointly), 1962; Royal Medal, Royal Soc., 1971. Hon. degrees: in philosophy: Vienna, 1965; Salzburg, 1972; in science: Edinburgh, 1965; East Anglia, 1967. For. Mem., Royal Netherlands Acad., 1972. *Publication:* Proteins and Nucleic Acids, Structure and Function, 1962. *Address:* 42 Sedley Taylor Road, Cambridge; Laboratory of Molecular Biology, Hills Road, Cambridge.

PERY, family name of Earl of Limerick.

PESKETT, Stanley Victor, MA; Principal, Royal Belfast Academical Institution, since 1959; *b* 9 May 1918; *o s* of late Sydney Timber and late Mary Havard Peskett; *m* 1948, Prudence Eileen, OBE 1974, *o d* of late C. R. A. Goatly, Calcutta; two *s* two *d*. *Educ:* Whitgift Sch.; St Edmund Hall, Oxford. Served War, 1939-46 (despatches) in Royal Marines, Norway, Shetland, Normandy, India and Java; Lt-Col, 1944; two Admiralty awards for inventions. Senior English Master, 1946-59, Housemaster 1954-59, The Leys School. Mem. Cttee, Headmasters' Conf., 1976; Mem. Council, Headmasters' Assoc., and Pres., Ulster Headmasters' Assoc., 1973-75; Chm., Northern Ireland Cttee, Voluntary Service Overseas, 1969-78; Founder Pres., Irish Schools Swimming Assoc., 1968-69 (Chm., Ulster Branch, 1968-78); Chm., NI Branch, School Library Assoc., 1964-73; Governor, Belfast Sch. of Music, 1974-77; Mem. Adv. Council, UDR, 1975-78. *Address:* Fairy Hill, 6 Osborne Gardens, Belfast BT9 6LE; Huntsman and Hounds Cottage, Metfield, Harleston, Norfolk IP20 0LB. *Clubs:* Royal Commonwealth Society, East India, Devonshire, Sports and Public Schools.

PESTELL; *see* Wells-Pestell.

PESTELL, Catherine Eva; HM Diplomatic Service; Counsellor, East Berlin, since 1975; *b* 24 Sept. 1933; *d* of Edmund Ernest Pestell and Isabella Cummine Sangster. *Educ:* Leeds Girls' High Sch.; St Hilda's Coll., Oxford (MA). FO, 1956; Third Sec., The Hague, 1958; Second Sec., Bangkok, 1961; FO, 1964; First Sec., UK Delegn to OECD, Paris, 1969; FCO, 1971; St Antony's Coll., Oxford, 1974. *Address:* c/o Foreign and Commonwealth Office, SW1.
See also J. E. Pestell.

PESTELL, John Edmund; Under Secretary, Civil Service Department, since 1976; *b* 8 Dec. 1930; *s* of late Edmund Pestell and of Isabella (*née* Sangster); *m* 1958, Muriel Ada (*née* Whitby); three *s*. *Educ:* Roundhay Sch.; New Coll., Oxford (MA). National Service (Intell. Corps), 1949-50. Jt Intell. Bureau, 1953-57; Asst Principal, WO, 1957-60; Private Sec. to Parly Under Sec. of State for War, 1958-60; Principal, WO and MoD, 1960-70; Admin. Staff Coll., Henley, 1963; Private Sec. to Minister of Defence (Equipment), 1969-70; Asst Sec., MoD, 1970-72; Press Sec. (Co-ordination), Prime Minister's Office, 1972-74; Asst Sec., CSD, 1974-76. Governor: Cranleigh Sch.; Pennthorpe Sch., Rudgwick. *Address:* New House, Bridge Road, Cranleigh, Surrey. *T:* Cranleigh 3489.
See also C. E. Pestell.

PESTELL, Sir John Richard, KCVO 1969; an Adjudicator, Immigration Appeals, Harmondsworth, since 1970; *b* 21 Nov.

1916; *s* of late Lt-Comdr Frank Lionel Pestell, RN, and Winifred Alice Pestell; *m* 1951, Betty Pestell (*née* Parish); three *d*. *Educ:* Portsmouth Northern Secondary Sch. Joined British South Africa Police, Southern Rhodesia, 1939; retired, 1965, with rank of Asst Commissioner. Served, 1944-47, Gen. List, MELF, in Cyrenaica Defence Force. Secretary/Controller to Governor of S Rhodesia, Rt Hon. Sir H. V. Gibbs, 1965-69. *Recreations:* walking, golf. *Address:* Monks Walk, Ferry Lane, Medmenham, Marlow, Bucks.

PETCH, Barry Irvine, FCA; Finance Director, IBM United Kingdom Holdings Ltd and subsidiaries, since 1971; *b* 12 Oct. 1933; *s* of Charles Reginald Petch and Anne (*née* Fryer); *m* 1966, Anne Elisabeth (*née* Johannessen); two *s* one *d*. *Educ:* Doncaster Grammar Sch. FCA 1967. IBM United Kingdom Ltd, 1959-. Part-time Mem., Price Commn, 1973-. *Recreations:* tennis, sailing. *Address:* Hoevringen, Coombe Park, Kingston Hill, Surrey. *T:* 01-549 4778.

PETCH, Sir Louis, KCB 1968 (CB 1964); Chairman: Parole Board, since 1974; Wine Standards Board of Vintners' Company, since 1974; *b* 16 Aug. 1913; *s* of William and Rhoda Petch, Preston, Lancs; *m* 1939, Gwendoline Bolton; one *s* one *d*. *Educ:* Preston Grammar Sch.; Peterhouse, Cambridge. Entered Administrative Class of Home Civil Service, 1937; Secretaries' Office, Customs and Excise, 1937-40; Home Defence Executive, 1940-45; Treasury, 1945-68; Private Secretary to successive Chancellors of the Exchequer, 1953-56; Third Secretary and Treasury Officer of Accounts, 1962-66; Second Secretary, 1966-68; Second Permanent Sec., Civil Service Dept, 1968-69; Chairman: Bd of Customs and Excise, 1969-73; Civil Service Benevolent Fund, 1969-73; Civil Service Sports Council, 1973-77; Civil Service and PO Life-Boat Fund, 1972-77. *Address:* 15 Cole Park Road, Twickenham, Middlesex. *T:* 01-892 2089. *Club:* United Oxford & Cambridge University.

PETCH, Prof. Norman James, FRS 1974; Professor of Metallurgy, University of Strathclyde, since 1973; *b* 13 Feb. 1917; 3rd *s* of George and Jane Petch, Bearsden, Dunbartonshire; *m* 1949, Eileen Allen (*d* 1975); two *d*. *Educ:* Queen Mary Coll., London; Sheffield Univ. Research at Cavendish Lab., Cambridge, 1939-42; Royal Aircraft Establishment, 1942-46; Cavendish Laboratory, 1946-48; British Iron and Steel Research Assoc., Sheffield, 1948-49; Reader in Metallurgy, Leeds Univ., 1949-56; First Professor of Metallurgy, Leeds Univ., 1956-59; Cochrane Prof. of Metallurgy, 1959-73, a Pro-Vice-Chancellor, 1968-71, Univ. of Newcastle upon Tyne. *Address:* Abbotsford, Balfron, Stirlingshire. *T:* Balfron 249; Department of Metallurgy, University of Strathclyde, George Street, Glasgow G1 1XW.

PETERBOROUGH, Bishop of, since 1972; **Rt. Rev. Douglas Russell Feaver;** *b* 22 May 1914; *s* of late Ernest Henry Feaver, Bristol; *m* 1939, Katharine, *d* of late Rev. W. T. Stubbs; one *s* two *d*. *Educ:* Bristol Grammar School; Keble College, Oxford (Scholar; 1st cl. Hons. Mod. History, 1935; 1st cl. Hons. Theology, 1937; Liddon Student, 1935-37; MA); Wells Theological College. Deacon 1938, priest 1939, St Albans; Curate, St Albans Abbey, 1938-42. Chaplain, RAFVR, 1942-46. Canon and Sub-Dean of St Albans, 1946-58; Chaplain to St Albans School, 1946-58; Proctor in Convocation, 1951-58; Examining Chaplain to Bp of St Albans, 1948-58, to Bp of Portsmouth, 1960-72; Vicar of St Mary's, Nottingham and Rural Dean of Nottingham, 1958-72; Hon. Canon of Southwell, 1958-72; Treasurer, 1959-69; Proctor in Convocation for Southwell, 1970-72. Chairman of Trent House Boys' Probation Hostel, 1967-72; Governor of Nottingham Bluecoat School, 1958-72. *Publications:* reviews and articles in Church Times. *Address:* The Palace, Peterborough. *T:* Peterborough 62492.

PETERBOROUGH, Dean of; *see* Digby, Very Rev. R. S. Wingfield.

PETERKIEWICZ, Prof. Jerzy; novelist and poet; Professor of Polish Language and Literature, University of London, since 1972; *b* 29 Sept. 1916; *s* of late Jan Pietrkiewicz and Antonina (*née* Politowska); *m* 1952, Dr Christine Brooke-Rose, *qv* (marr. diss. 1975). *Educ:* Dlugosz Sch., Wloclawek; Univ. of Warsaw; Univ. of St Andrews (MA 1944); King's Coll., London (PhD 1947). Freelance writer until 1950; Reader (previously Lectr) in Polish Language and Literature, Sch. of Slavonic and East European Studies, Univ. of London, 1952-72, Head of Dept of E European Lang. and Lit., 1972-77. *Publications:* Prowincja, 1936; Wiersze i poematy, 1938; Pogrzeb Europy, 1946; The Knotted Cord, 1953; Loot and Loyalty, 1955; Polish Prose and Verse, 1956; Antologia liryki angielskiej, 1958; Future to Let, 1958; Isolation, 1959; (with Burns Singer) Five Centuries of Polish Poetry, 1960 (enlarged edn 1970); The Quick and the

Dead, 1961; That Angel Burning at my Left Side, 1963; Poematy londynskie, 1965; Inner Circle, 1966; Green Flows the Bile, 1969; The Other Side of Silence (The Poet at the Limits of Language), 1970; The Third Adam, 1975; essays, poems and articles in various periodicals. *Recreation:* travels, outward and inward. *Address:* 22 Russell Square, WC1E 7HU. *T:* c/o 01-637 4934.

PETERKIN, Ishbel Allan; *b* 2 March 1903; *d* of late J. Ramsay MacDonald and late Margaret Ethel Gladstone; *m* 1st, 1938, Norman Ridgley (*d* 1950); 2nd, 1953, James Peterkin (*d* 1956). *Educ:* City of London Sch.; North London Collegiate. Member of London County Council, 1928-34. Licensee at Plough Inn, Speen, 1936-53. *Address:* Hillocks, Moray Street, Lossiemouth, Moray IV31 6HX. *T:* Lossiemouth 3076.
See also Rt Hon. M. J. MacDonald.

PETERS, Adm. Sir Arthur M., KCB 1946 (CB 1943); DSC; *b* 1 June 1888; *o surv. s* of Maj.-Gen. W. H. B. Peters and of Hon. Mrs Peters, *d* of 24th Baron Dunboyne; *m* 1912, Agnes Vivien (*d* 1965), *d* of Colonel A. V. Payne, CMG; one *d*; *m* 1966, Mrs Sophie Maude Magnay (*d* 1976), *widow* of Brigadier A. D. Magnay. *Educ:* Stubbington House, Fareham, Hants; HMS Britannia. Went to sea 1904, served in North Sea throughout European War in HMS Southampton and Orion, present at Battle of Heligoland Bight, Dogger Bank, and Jutland (DSC, despatches); Captain, 1930; commanded HMS Southampton, 1936-38; Commodore in Charge of Naval Establishments, Hong Kong, 1939-40; Rear-Admiral, 1940; Naval Secretary to First Lord of the Admiralty, 1941-42; Mediterranean, 1943; Vice-Admiral, 1943; Flag Officer Commanding West Africa, 1943-45; retired, 1945; Admiral (retired), 1946. Since retirement interested in local affairs; Mem. for many years, St Thomas RDC and Lympstone Parish Council; formerly Chm., Sea Cadet Cttees of Exeter and Exmouth; President: Exmouth Branch, RNLI; Governors, Exeter Royal National Sch. for the Deaf; Devon Br., CLA; E Devon Hunt Cttee; Haldon Race Cttee; Chm., Ermsborough Nursing Home, Exeter, etc. *Address:* Somerton Lodge, Sidmouth, Devon EX10 8UH. *T:* Sidmouth 3927. *Club:* Naval and Military.

PETERS, John; Defence Counsellor, UK Delegation to NATO, Brussels, since 1975; *b* 5 Dec. 1929; *s* of Dr G. F. Peters and Mrs C. P. Peters; *m* 1955, Jane Catherine Mary Sheldon; one *s* two *d*. *Educ:* Downside Sch. (Scholar); Balliol Coll., Oxford (Exhibnr, MA). HM Forces, commissioned RAEC, 1948-49. Pres., Oxford Union Soc., 1953. Entered Administrative Class, Home Civil Service, Admiralty, 1953; PS to Civil Lord, 1956-59; Principal, 1959; PS to Navy Minister, 1964-67; PS to Minister of Defence (Equipment), 1967-68; Asst Sec., 1968; Dir of Naval Sales, 1968-72; Cabinet Office, 1974-75. *Address:* 60 Scotts Lane, Bromley, Kent. *T:* 01-650 0063. *Club:* United Oxford & Cambridge University.

PETERS, Kenneth Jamieson, JP; Managing Director, Aberdeen Journals Ltd, since 1960; Director, Thomson Regional Newspapers, since 1974; *b* 17 Jan. 1923; *s* of William Jamieson Peters and Edna Rosa Peters (*née* Hayman); *m* 1951, Arunda Merle Jane Jones. *Educ:* Aberdeen Grammar Sch.; Aberdeen Univ. Served War of 1939-45: last rank Captain/Adjutant, 2nd Bn King's Own Scottish Borderers. Editorial staff, Daily Record and Evening News Ltd, 1947-51; Asst Editor: Evening Express, Aberdeen, 1951-52; Manchester Evening Chronicle, 1952-53; Editor: Evening Express, Aberdeen, 1953-56; The Press and Journal, Aberdeen, 1956-60; Pres., Scottish Daily Newspaper Soc., 1964-66 and 1974-76; Mem., Press Council, 1974-77; Director: Highland Printers Ltd (Inverness), 1968-; Aberdeen Assoc. of Social Service, 1973-; Pres., Publicity Club of Aberdeen, 1972-; Member: Scottish Adv. Cttee of British Council, 1967-; Cttee, Films of Scotland, 1970-; Internat. Information Cttee, Scottish Council for Industry and Develt, 1969-, etc. JP City of Aberdeen, 1961. *Recreations:* cricket, Rugby football, cliff walking. *Address:* 47 Abergeldie Road, Aberdeen AB1 6ED. *T:* Aberdeen 27647. *Club:* Royal Northern (Aberdeen).

PETERS, Mary Elizabeth, MBE 1973; self employed; Managing Director, Mary Peters Sports Ltd, since 1971; *b* 6 July 1939; *d* of Arthur Henry Peters and Hilda Mary Peters. *Educ:* Portadown Coll., Co. Armagh; Belfast Coll. of Domestic Science (DipDomSc). Represented Great Britain: Olympic Games: 4th place, Pentathlon, 1964; 1st, Pentathlon (world record), 1972; Commonwealth Games: 2nd, Shot, 1966; 1st, Shot, 1st Pentathlon, 1970; 1st, Pentathlon, 1974. Member: Sports Council, 1974-; Northern Ireland Sports Council, 1974- (Vice-Chm., 1977). Director: Barwell Sports Management Ltd, 1974-; Churchill Foundn Fellowship Scholarship, Calif, 1972. Asst Sec., Multiple Sclerosis Soc., 1974-; Pres., Old-Age Pensioners'

Coal and Grocery Fund. Hon. Senior Athletic Coach, 1975-; BAAB Pentathlon Coach, 1976; Trustee, Ulster Sports Trust, 1977. Awards: BBC Sports personality, 1972; Athletic Writers', 1972; Sports Writers', 1972; Elizabeth Arden Visible Difference, 1976; Athletics, Dublin (Texaco), 1970 and 1972. Hon. DSc, New Univ. of Ulster, 1974. *Publication:* Mary P., an autobiography, 1974. *Recreations:* squash, swimming, parachuting. *Address:* Willowtree Cottage, River Road, Dunmurry, Belfast, N Ireland.

PETERS, Prof. Raymond Harry; Professor of Polymer and Fibre Science, University of Manchester, since 1955; *b* 19 Feb. 1918. *Educ:* County High Sch., Ilford; King's Coll., London Univ.; Manchester Univ. BSc (London) 1939, PhD (London), 1942, in Chemistry; BSc (Manchester), 1949, BSc (London), 1949, in Mathematics; DSc (London), 1968. Scientist at ICI Ltd, 1941-46 and 1949-55. President, Society of Dyers and Colourists, 1967-68. *Publications:* Textile Chemistry: Vol. I, The Chemistry of Fibres, 1963; Vol. II, Impurities of Fibres: Purification of Fibres, 1967; Vol. III, Physical Chemistry of Dyeing, 1975; contributions to Journals of Chemical Society, Society of Dyers and Colourists, Textile Institute, British Journal of Applied Physics, etc. *Recreation:* gardening. *Address:* University of Manchester Institute of Science and Technology, Manchester M60 1QD. *T:* 061-236 3311.

PETERS, Prof. Richard Stanley, BA (Oxon), BA (London), PhD (London); Professor of the Philosophy of Education, University of London Institute of Education, since 1962; Dean, Faculty of Education, London University, 1971-74; *b* 31 Oct. 1919; *s* of late Charles Robert and Mabel Georgina Peters; *m* 1943, Margaret Lee Duncan; one *s* two *d*. *Educ:* Clifton Coll., Bristol; Queen's Coll., Oxford; Birkbeck Coll., University of London. War service with Friends' Ambulance Unit and Friends' Relief Service in E. London, 1940-44. Classics Master, Sidcot School, Somerset, 1944-46; Birkbeck Coll., University of London: Studentship and part-time Lecturer in Philos. and Psychol., 1946-49; full-time Lecturer in Philos. and Psychol., 1949-58; Reader in Philosophy, 1958-62. Visiting Prof. of Education: Grad. School of Education, Harvard Univ., 1961; Univ. of Auckland, 1975; Visiting Fellow, Australian National Univ., 1969. Part-time lectureships, Bedford Coll., LSE; Tutor for University of London Tutorial Classes Cttee and Extension Cttee. Member, American National Academy of Education, 1966. *Publications:* (revised) Brett's History of Psychology, 1953; Hobbes, 1956; The Concept of Motivation, 1958; (with S. I. Benn) Social Principles and the Democratic State, 1959; Authority, Responsibility and Education, 1960; Ethics and Education, 1966; (ed) The Concept of Education, 1967; (ed) Perspectives on Plowden, 1969; (with P. H. Hirst) The Logic of Education, 1970; (ed with M. Cranston) Hobbes and Rousseau, 1971; (ed with R. F. Dearden and P. H. Hirst) Education and the Development of Reason, 1972; Reason and Compassion (Lindsay Meml Lectures), 1973; (ed) The Philosophy of Education, 1973; Psychology and Ethical Development, 1974; (ed) Nature and Conduct, 1975; (ed) The Role of the Head, 1976; Education and the Education of Teachers, 1977. *Address:* 16 Shepherd's Hill, N6.

PETERS, Sir Rudolph (Albert), Kt 1952; MC 1917 (Bar); FRS 1935; FRCP 1952; *b* 1889; *s* of Albert Edward Peters, MRCS, LRCP, and Agnes Malvina Watts; *m* 1917, Frances W. Vérel; two *s*. *Educ:* Warden House, Deal; Wellington Coll., Berks; King's Coll., London; Gonville and Caius Coll., Cambridge. MA Cantab, 1914; MD 1919, St Bartholomew's Hospital; MA Oxon (by decree), 1923; Hon. MD (Liège), 1950; Doctor *hc* (Paris), 1952; Hon. DSc (Cincinnati), 1953; Hon. MD (Amsterdam), 1954; Hon. DSc: London, 1954; Leeds, 1959; Australian National University, 1961; Hon. LLD (Glasgow), 1963; Hon. FRSE, 1957; late Drosier Fellow and Tutor Gonville and Caius Coll., Cambridge; Hon. Fellow Gonville and Caius Coll., Cambridge, 1951; Hon. Fellow Trinity Coll., Oxford, 1958; Thruston Medal, 1918; Royal Medal of Royal Society, 1949; Cameron Prize, Edinburgh, 1949; Hopkins Memorial Medal, 1959; British Nutrition Foundn Prize, 1972. Benn W. Levy Student of Biochemistry, Cambridge, 1912-13; formerly, Dunn Lecturer and Senior Demonstrator Biochemistry, Cambridge; Whitley Professor of Biochemistry, University of Oxford, 1923-54; Fellow Trinity Coll., Oxford, 1925-54; Scientific Staff, Agricultural Research Council, 1954-59. Mem., Biochemical and Physiological Societies, BMA. Assoc. Sci. Nat., Acad. Roy. Belg. For. Member Royal Nether. Acad. Sci. and Letters and Accademia Nazionale dei Lincei, Rome; For. Hon. Member American Academy of Arts and Sciences; Hon. Member: Finnish Biochem. Soc.; Assoc. Clin. Biochemists; Assoc. of Physicians; Biochemical Soc., Celer et Audax Club; Nutrition Soc.; Royal Acad. of Medicine, Belgium; American Inst. of Nutrition; Hon. Fellow: RSM; American Soc. Biological

Chemists; Physiological Soc. Lectures: Croonian, Royal Society; Dixon Meml, RSM, 1948; Louis Abrahams, RCP, 1952; Dunham, Harvard, 1946-47; Herman Leo Loeb, St Louis Univ., 1947; Christian Herter, New York Univ., 1947; Dohme, Johns Hopkins Univ., 1954; Linacre, Cambridge, 1962. Visiting Professor, Canadian MRC, Dalhousie Univ., Halifax, Nova Scotia, 1963. Member: MRC, 1946-50; Military College of Science Advisory Council, 1947-50; Sci. Adv. Council, Ministry of Supply, 1950-53. President, International Council of Scientific Unions, 1958-61. President, Cambridge Philosophical Society, 1965-67. RAMC (SR) 1915-18 (MC and bar, Brevet-Major, despatches). Hon. FCPath, 1967. Medal of Freedom with silver palm (USA), 1947. *Publications:* Biochemical Lesions and Lethal Synthesis, 1963; contributions to scientific journals. *Address:* University Department of Biochemistry, Tennis Court Road, Cambridge. *T:* Cambridge 51781; 3 Newnham Walk, Cambridge. *T:* Cambridge 50819.

PETERS, Theophilus, CMG 1967; HM Diplomatic Service; Consul-General, Antwerp, since 1973; *b* 7 Aug. 1921; *er s* of late Mark Peters and Dorothy Knapman; *m* 1953, Lucy Bailey Summers, *d* of late Lionel Morgan Summers, Winter Park, Fla; two *s* three *d. Educ:* Exeter Sch., Exeter; St John's Coll., Cambridge (MA). Served War of 1939-45: 2nd Lieut, Intelligence Corps, 1942; Captain, 8 Corps HQ, 1944; Normandy, 1944; Holland, 1944-45 (despatches); Germany; Major. Entered HM Foreign (subseq. Diplomatic) Service; Vice-Consul/2nd Secretary, Peking, 1948; FO, 1951-52; Tripoli and Benghazi (Libya), 1953; FO, 1956; Dep. Secretary-General, Cento, 1960; Head of Chancery, Manila, 1962; Counsellor (Commercial), Peking, 1965; Dir, Diplomatic Service Language Centre, 1968-71, and Head of Training Dept, FCO, 1969-71; Counsellor and Consul-Gen., Buenos Aires, 1971-73. *Address:* c/o Foreign and Commonwealth Office, SW1.

PETERS, Prof. Wallace, MD, DSc; Dean, Liverpool School of Tropical Medicine, since 1975; Walter Myers Professor of Parasitology, since 1966; *b* 1 April 1924; *s* of Henry and Fanny Peters; *m* 1954, Ruth (née Scheidegger). *Educ:* Haberdashers' Aske's Sch.; St Bartholomew's Hosp., London. MB BS, 1947; MRCP, MRCS, DTM&H. Served in RAMC, 1947-49; practised tropical medicine in West and East Africa, 1950-52; Staff Mem., WHO, Liberia and Nepal, 1952-55; Asst Dir (Malariology), Health Dept, Territory of Papua and New Guinea, 1956-61; Research Associate, CIBA, Basle, Switzerland, 1961-66. Vice-Pres. and Pres., Brit. Soc. Parasit., 1972-76; Pres., Brit. Sect., Soc. Protozool., 1972-75; Member: Editorial Bd, Ann. trop. Med. Parasit., 1966-; Expert Adv. Panel, WHO, 1967-; Trop. Med. Research Bd, MRC, 1973-; Vice-Pres., European Fedn Parasit., 1975-. *Publications:* A Provisional Checklist of Butterflies of the Ethiopian Region, 1952; Chemotherapy and Drug Resistance in Malaria, 1970; A Colour Atlas of Parasitology and Tropical Medicine (with H. M. Gilles), 1976; numerous papers in jls, on trop. med. and parasitology. *Recreation:* photography. *Address:* Liverpool School of Tropical Medicine, Pembroke Place, Liverpool L3 5QA. *T:* 051-709 7611. *Club:* Athenæum (Liverpool).

PETERS, William, MVO 1961; MBE 1959; HM Diplomatic Service; Ambassador to Uruguay, since 1977; *b* 28 Sept. 1923; *o s* of John William Peters and Louise (née Woodhouse), Morpeth, Northumberland; *m* 1944, Catherine B. Bailey; no *c. Educ:* King Edward VI Grammar Sch., Morpeth; Balliol Coll., Oxford. MA Lit. Hum. 1948. War Service, Queen's Royal Rifles, KOSB, and 9th Gurkha Rifles, 1942-46. Joined HMOCS as Asst District Comr, Gold Coast, 1950; served in Cape Coast, Bawku and Tamale; Dep. Sec., Regional Comr, Northern Region, 1958-59; joined CRO as Asst Prin., 1959; Prin., 1959; 1st Sec., Dacca, 1960-63; 1st Sec., Cyprus, 1963-67; Head of Zambia and Malawi Dept, CRO, 1967-68; Head of Central African Dept, FCO, 1968-69; Dir, Internat. Affairs Div., Commonwealth Secretariat, 1969-71; Counsellor and Head of Chancery, Canberra, 1971-73; Dep. High Comr, Bombay, 1974-77. *Publications:* contribs to Jl of African Administration, Illustrated Weekly of India; Diplomatic Service: Formation and Operation. *Recreations:* music, gardening, carpentry. *Address:* c/o Foreign and Commonwealth Office, SW1A 2AH. *Clubs:* United Oxford & Cambridge University, Royal Commonwealth Society.

PETERSEN, Jeffrey Charles, CMG 1968; HM Ambassador to Sweden, since 1977; *b* 20 July 1920; *s* of Charles Petersen and Ruby Petersen (née Waple); *m* 1962, Karin Kristina Hayward; two *s* four *d. Educ:* Westcliff High Sch.; London School of Economics. Served RN (Lieut, RNVR), 1939-46. Joined Foreign Office, 1948; 2nd Secretary, Madrid, 1949-50; 2nd Secretary, Ankara, 1951-52; 1st Secretary, Brussels, 1953-56; NATO Defence College, 1956-57; FO, 1957-62; 1st Secretary, Djakarta, 1962-64; Counsellor, Athens, 1964-68; Minister

(Commercial), Rio de Janeiro, 1968-71; Ambassador to Republic of Korea, 1971-74, to Romania, 1975-77. *Recreations:* painting, entomology, sailing. *Address:* 32 Longmoore Street, SW1. *T:* 01-834 8262; Crofts Wood, Petham, Kent.

PETERSHAM, Viscount; Charles Henry Leicester Stanhope; *b* 20 July 1945; *s* and *heir* of 11th Earl of Harrington, *qv; m* 1966, Virginia Alleyne Freeman Jackson, Mallow; one *s* one *d. Educ:* Eton. *Address:* c/o Greenmount, Patrickswell, Co. Limerick, Ireland.

PETERSON, Alexander Duncan Campbell, OBE 1946; Director: Department of Education, Oxford University, 1958-73; International Baccalaureate Office, 1968-77; *b* 13 Sept. 1908; 2nd *s* of late J. C. K. Peterson, CIE; *m* 1946, Corinna May, *d* of late Sir Arthur Cochrane, KCVO; two *s* one *d. Educ:* Radley; Balliol Coll., Oxford. Assistant master, Shrewsbury Sch., 1932-40; commissioned in MOI (SP), 1940; Deputy Director of Psychological Warfare, SEAC, 1944-46; Headmaster, Adams' Grammar Sch., 1946-52; Director-General of Information Services, Federation of Malaya, 1952-54; Headmaster, Dover College., 1954-57. Contested (L) Oxford City, 1966. Chm., Army Educn Adv. Bd, 1959-66. Chairman, Farmington Trust, 1963-71. *Publications:* The Far East, 1948; 100 Years of Education, 1952; Educating our Rulers, 1957; The Techniques of Teaching (ed), 1965; The Future of Education, 1968; International Baccalaureate, 1972; The Future of the Sixth Form, 1973. *Address:* 20A Warwick Avenue, W9. *T:* 01-289 0943; Rose Cottage, Stade Street, Hythe, Kent. *Club:* Special Forces.

PETERSON, Sir Arthur (William), KCB 1973 (CB 1963); MVO 1953; Chairman, Mersey Docks & Harbour Co., since 1977; *b* 22 May 1916; *s* of J. C. K. Peterson and F. Campbell; *m* 1940, Mary Isabel Maples; one *s* two *d. Educ:* Shrewsbury; Merton College, Oxford. Asst Principal, Home Office, 1938; Principal Private Secretary to Home Secretary, 1946-49; Secretary, Royal Commission on Betting and Lotteries, 1949-51; Asst Secretary, Home Office, 1951-56; Personal Assistant to Lord Privy Seal, 1957; Dep. Chm., Prison Commission, 1957-60, Chm., 1960-63; Asst Under-Sec. of State, Prison Dept, Home Office, 1963-64; Dep. Sec., DEA, 1964-68; Dir-Gen. and Clerk to GLC, 1968-72; Permanent Under-Sec. of State, Home Office, 1972-77. Hon. Fellow, Inst. of Local Government Studies, Birmingham Univ. *Address:* 7 Lincoln House, Basil Street, SW3. *T:* 01-589 2237. *Club:* Travellers'.

PETERSON, Colin Vyvyan; Secretary for Appointments to the Prime Minister and Ecclesiastical Secretary to the Lord Chancellor since 1974; *b* 24 Oct. 1932; *s* of late Sir Maurice Drummond Peterson, GCMG; *m* 1966, Pamela Rosemary Barry; two *s* two *d. Educ:* Winchester Coll.; Magdalen Coll., Oxford. Joined HM Treasury, 1959. *Recreation:* fishing. *Address:* 87 Christchurch Road, Winchester, Hants. *T:* Winchester 3784. *Club:* Brooks's.

PETERSON, John Magnus, MA (Oxon); *b* 18 Feb. 1902; *yr s* of late Rev. M. F. Peterson; *m* 1938, Rosemary (*d* 1944), *yr d* of late A. M. McNeile; two *s* one *d. Educ:* Shrewsbury Sch.; Oriel Coll., Oxford. Scholar of Shrewsbury School, 1915, and Oriel College, 1921; 1st Cl. Classical Mods, 1923; 1st Cl. Lit. Hum., 1925. Oxford Univ. Assoc. Football XI, 1924 and 1925 (Capt.); OU Authentics. Asst Master, Eton College, 1925-50, House Master, 1938-50; Headmaster of Shrewsbury School, 1950-63. *Address:* Lower Farm, Easton Royal, Pewsey, Wilts. *T:* Burbage 343. *Club:* Vincent's (Oxford).

PETERSON, Oscar Emmanuel, OC 1973; concert jazz pianist; *b* 15 Aug. 1925; *s* of Daniel Peterson and Kathleen Peterson; *m* 1947, Lillian Alice Ann; two *s* three *d. Educ:* (academic) Montreal High Sch.; (music) private tutors. 1st prize, amateur show, 1940; Carnegie Hall debut, 1950; 1950-: numerous jazz awards; TV shows; composer and arranger; yearly concert tours in N America, Europe, GB and Japan; has performed also in S America, Mexico, WI, Australia, NZ and Russia. Hon. LLD: Carleton Univ., 1973; Queen's Univ., Kingston, 1976. Civic Award of Merit, Toronto, 1972; Diplôme d'Honneur, Canadian Conf. of the Arts, 1974. *Publications:* Oscar Peterson New Piano Solos, 1965; Jazz Exercises and Pieces, 1965. *Recreations:* audio, photography, ham radio, sports. *Address:* 2421 Hammond Road, Mississauga, Ont. Canada. *T:* 416/255 5651.

PETHERICK, Maurice, MA; *b* 5 Oct. 1894; *s* of George Tallack and Edith Petherick. *Educ:* St Peter's Court, Broadstairs; Marlborough College; Trinity College, Cambridge. 2nd Lieutenant Royal 1st Devon Yeomanry 1914; invalided out, 1915; served in Foreign Office, 1916-17; recommissioned Royal Scots Greys, 1917; served in France, 1918; recommissioned

General List Army, Oct. 1939, Captain, Temp. Major. Contested (C) Penryn and Falmouth Division, 1929 and 1945; MP (C) Penryn and Falmouth, 1931-45; Financial Secretary, War Office, May-July, 1945; High Sheriff of Cornwall, 1957. Director, Prudential Assurance Co. Ltd, 1953-71. *Publications:* Captain Culverin, 1932; Victoire, 1943; Restoration Rogues, 1950. *Recreations:* racing, gardening. *Address:* Porthpean House, St Austell, Cornwall. *Club:* United Oxford & Cambridge University.

PETHICK, Brig. Geoffrey Loveston, CBE 1960; DSO 1944; *b* 25 Nov. 1907; *s* of late Captain E. E. Pethick, RN and May (*née* Brook); *m* 1939, Nancy Veronica Ferrand; one *d*. *Educ:* Newton College. Commissioned, Royal Artillery, 1927; RHA 1934; served War of 1939-45; CO, Field Regt, 1942; Far East, 1945. Comdr 3 Army Group, RA, 1951. Chief Instructor, 1949; idc, 1950. Commander, RA 3 Div. 1953; War Office, 1957; retired, 1960. Dir, British Paper Makers' Association, 1960-74. *Recreations:* golf, gardens. *Address:* Little Croft, Fireball Hill, Sunningdale, Ascot, Berks. *T:* Ascot 22018. *Club:* Army and Navy.

PETHYBRIDGE, Frank, CBE 1977; Regional Administrator, North Western Regional Health Authority, since 1973; *b* 19 Jan. 1924; *s* of Frank and Margaret Pethybridge; *m* 1947, Jean Ewing; one *s* one *d*. *Educ:* William Hulme's Grammar Sch., Manchester; Univ. of Manchester (BA Admin). FHA, FRSH. Served with RAF, 1942-47 (Flt-Lt). Town Clerk's Dept, Manchester CBC, 1940-42 and 1947-62; Manchester Regional Hosp. Bd, 1962-73. *Recreations:* gardening, woodwork, Rugby League football. *Address:* 31 Lullington Road, Pendleton, Salford M6 8GW. *T:* 061-736 5697.

PETIT, Sir Dinshaw Manockjee, 3rd Bt, *cr* 1890; *b* 24 June 1901; *s* of Sir Dinshaw Manockjee Petit, 2nd Bt, and Dinbai, *d* of Sir J. Jeejeebhoy, 3rd Bt; *S* father, 1933; *m* 1928, Sylla (*d* 1963), *d* of late R. D. Tata; one *s* one *d*. *Educ:* St Xavier's, Bombay; Trinity Hall, Cambridge. Called to Bar, Inner Temple, 1925. President: SPCA, Bombay; Petit Boys Sch., Poona; Petit Girls' Sch., Pali Hill, Bombay; Petit Sanatorium, Cumballa Hill, Bombay; Trustee: V.J.T. Technical Inst., Bombay; Parsee Gen. Hosp., Bombay. Pres., Northbrook Soc., London; Life Gov., Royal Hosp. for Incurables; Hon. Life Mem., RSPCA. Vice-Pres., British Assoc. of Riviera. Citizen of Honour of France. *Heir: s* Nasserwanjee Dinshaw Petit [*b* 13 Aug. 1934; *m* 1964, Nirmala Nanavatty; two *s*]. *Address:* Petit Hall, 66 Nepean Sea Road, Bombay, India; Savaric, 06 Eze-Village, France; 8 Mount Row, W1.

PETIT, Roland; Chevalier de la Légion d'honneur; Chevalier des Arts et des Lettres; French choreographer and dancer; *b* Villemomble, 13 Jan. 1924; *m* 1954, Renée Jeanmaire; one *s*. *Educ:* Ecole de Ballet de l'Opéra de Paris, studying under Ricaux and Lifar. Premier danseur, l'Opéra de Paris, 1940-44; founded Les Vendredis de la Danse, 1944, Les Ballets des Champs-Elysées, 1945, Les Ballets de Paris de Roland Petit, 1948. Choreographic works include: Les Forains, Le Jeune Homme et la Mort, Les Demoiselles de la nuit, Carmen, Deuil en 24 heures, Le Loup, L'éloge de la Folie, Les Chants de Maldoror, Notre Dame de Paris, Paradise Lost, Les Intermittences du coeur, La Symphonie fantastique, etc; choreographer and dancer: La Belle au Bois Dormant; Cyrano de Bergerac. Appeared in films Hans Christian Andersen; Un, Deux, Trois, Quartre (arr. ballets, for film, and danced in 3); 4 ballets, Black Tights. *Address:* 69 rue de Lille, 75007 Paris, France.

PETO, Brig. Sir Christopher (Henry Maxwell), 3rd Bt *cr* 1927; DSO 1945; DL; *b* 19 Feb. 1897; 2nd *s* of Sir Basil Peto, 1st Bt, and Mary Matilda Annie (*d* 1931), *d* of Captain T. C. Baird; *g s* of Sir Morton Peto, 1st Bt (*cr* 1855); *S* brother, 1971; *m* 1935, Barbara, *d* of E. T. Close, Camberley, Surrey; two *s* one *d*. *Educ:* Harrow. Joined 9th Lancers, 1915 (wounded, despatches); commanded 9th Lancers, 1938; War of 1939-45 (wounded, despatches thrice, DSO); Brig. 1941; Chief Liaison Officer 21 Army Group, 1944; retd pay, 1946. Col, 9th Lancers, 1950-60. MP (C) for North Div. of Devonshire, 1945-55. Chm., Wilts TA and AFA, 1957-61. Pres. Conservative Association of Devizes Division of Wilts, 1958-66. Legion of Honour, Croix de Guerre, Orders of Leopold I, Belgian Croix de Guerre. DL Devon, 1950-55; DL Wilts, 1956; High Sheriff of Wiltshire, 1966. *Recreations:* shooting, fishing. *Heir: s* Michael Henry Basil Peto [*b* 6 April 1938; *m* 1st, 1963, Sarah Susan (marr. diss. 1970), *y d* of Major Sir Dennis Stucley, Bt, *qv*; one *s* two *d*; 2nd, 1971, Lucinda Mary, *yr d* of Major Sir Charles Douglas Blackett, 9th Bt; two *s*]. *Address:* Lockeridge House, near Marlborough, Wilts. TA and *T:* Lockeridge 259. *Club:* Cavalry and Guards.

PETO, Comdr Sir Francis; *see* Peto, Comdr Sir (Henry) F. M.

PETO, Comdr Sir (Henry) Francis (Morton), 3rd Bt, *cr* 1855; RN, retired; *b* 18 Nov. 1889; *s* of late Morton Kelsall Peto and Olive Georgiana Elizabeth, *d* of late Hon. Francis Maude; *S* uncle 1938; *m* 1919, Edith (*d* 1945), *d* of late George Berners Ruck Keene; two *s*; *m* 1948, Rosemary Grizel (*d* 1976), *d* of late Rear-Adm. Archibald Cochrane, CMG, and widow of Major Thomas Clapton, DLI; one *s*. *Heir: s* Henry George Morton Peto [*b* 29 April 1920; *m* 1947, Frances Jacqueline, *d* of late Ralph Haldane Evers, Milan, and of Mrs Evers, Stow-on-the-Wold; two *s*]. *Address:* Balbeg, Straiton, Maybole, Ayrshire.

PETRE, family name of Baron Petre.

PETRE, 17th Baron, *cr* 1603; **Joseph William Lionel Petre;** Captain Essex Regiment; *b* 5 June 1914; *s* of 16th Baron and Catherine (who *m* 2nd, 1921, Sir Frederic Carne Rasch, 2nd Bt, TD, *d* 1963) *d* of late Hon. John and late Lady Margaret Boscawen, Tregye, Falmouth, Cornwall; *S* father, 1915; *m* 1941, Marguerite, *d* of late Ion Wentworth Hamilton, Westwood, Nettlebed, Oxfordshire; one *s*. *Heir: s* Hon. John Patrick Lionel Petre [*b* 4 Aug. 1942; *m* 1965, Marcia Gwendolyn, *o d* of Alfred Plumpton; two *s* one *d*]. *Address:* Ingatestone Hall, Essex.

PETRE, Prof. E. O. G. T.; *see* Turville-Petre.

PETRE, Francis Herbert Loraine; His Honour Judge Petre; a Circuit Judge, since 1972; *b* 9 March 1927; *s* of late Maj.-Gen. R. L. Petre, CB, DSO, MC and Mrs Katherine Sophia Petre; *m* 1958, Mary Jane, *d* of Everard White, Masterton, NZ; three *s* one *d*. *Educ:* Downside; Clare Coll., Cambridge. Called to Bar, Lincoln's Inn, 1952; Dep. Chm., E Suffolk QS, 1970; Dep. Chm., Agricultural Lands Tribunal (Eastern Area), 1972; a Recorder, 1972. *Address:* Colneford House, Earls Colne, near Colchester, Essex. *Club:* MCC.

PETRIE, Lady (Cecilia); *d* of late F. J. G. Mason, Kensington; *m* 1926, Sir Charles Petrie, 3rd Bt, *qv*; one *s*. Mem. Kensington Borough Council (Queen's Gate Ward), 1946-62; Alderman, 1965-71; Freeman, 1971; Mayor of the Royal Borough of Kensington, 1954-56. Member: (C) LCC, for S Kensington, 1949-65; Fulham & Kensington Hospital Management Committee, 1948-59 (Chairman, 1955-59); Chelsea and Kensington Hospital Management Cttee, 1959-72; Board of Governors, Charing Cross Hospital, 1959-68; Member Board of Governors of Hospital for Diseases of the Chest, 1951-73; Mem. Central Health Services Council, 1955-61; Dep.-Chm. of the London County Council, 1958-59; UK Delegate to United Nations Assembly, 14th Session, 1959; Member: SW Metropolitan Regional Hospital Board, 1959-65; London Exec. Council, Nat. Health Service, 1965-74; Family Practitioner Service, 1974-; Whitley Council Committee C, 1949-71. *Recreation:* reading detective stories. *Address:* 190 Coleherne Court, SW5. *T:* 01-373 9701.
See also P. C. Petrie.

PETRIE, Sir Charles (Alexander), 3rd Bt of Carrowcarden, *cr* 1918; CBE 1957; MA Oxon, FRHistS; *b* 28 Sept. 1895; *s* of 1st Bt and Hannah, *d* of late William Hamilton; *S* brother, 1927; *m* 1st, 1920, Ursula Gabrielle (marr. diss., 1925; decd), *er d* of late Judge Dowdall, QC; one *s*; 2nd, 1926, Cecilia (*née* Mason) (see Lady Petrie); one *s*. *Educ:* privately; Corpus Christi College, Oxford. Historian; Corresponding Mem. of the Royal Spanish Academy of History; Pres. of Military Hist. Soc. of Ireland. Foreign Editor of the English Review, 1931-37; Associate Editor of Empire Review, 1940-41, Editor, 1941-43; Managing Editor, New English Review, 1945-50; Editor, Household Brigade Magazine, 1945-76. Served with RGA, 1915-19; attached War Cabinet Office, 1918-19; Official Lecturer to HM Forces, 1940-45. Corresp. Member: Institución Fernando el Católico, Zaragoza; Hispanic Soc. of America. Doctor (*hc*) Valladolid University, 1964; Hon. LittD Nat. Univ. of Ireland, 1971. Comdr Order of Isabella the Catholic (Spain); Knight of Order of Civil Merit (Spain); Commendatore Order of Crown of Italy; Commander Order of George I (Greece). *Publications:* The History of Government, 1929; George Canning, 1930, new edn 1946; The Jacobite Movement, 1932, new edn, 1959; History of Spain (with Louis Bertrand), 1934 (new edn 1957); The Four Georges: A Revaluation, 1935; The Stuarts, 1937; Life and Letters of Sir Austen Chamberlain (2 vols), 1939-40; Diplomatic History, 1713-1933, 1946; Earlier Diplomatic History, 1492-1713, 1949; Chapters of Life, 1950; The Marshal Duke of Berwick, 1953; The Carlton Club, 1955; Wellington: a Reassessment, 1956; The Spanish Royal House, 1958; The Powers Behind the Prime Ministers, 1959; The Victorians, 1960; The Modern British Monarchy, 1961; Philip II of Spain, 1963; King Alfonso XIII, 1963; Scenes of Edwardian Life, 1965; Don

John of Austria, 1967; Great Beginnings, 1967; The Drift to World War, 1900-1914, 1968; King Charles III of Spain, 1971; A Historian Looks at his World, 1972; The Great Tyrconnel: a chapter in Anglo-Irish Relations, 1973; (ed) King Charles, Prince Rupert, and the Civil War, 1974; A Short History of Spain, 1976; contribs to Illustrated London News, 1958-. *Heir: s* Charles Richard Borthwick Petrie [*b* 19 Oct. 1921; *m* 1962, Jessie Ariana Borthwick Campbell]. *Address:* 190 Coleherne Court, SW5. *Clubs:* Carlton, 1900, Authors' (Pres.), Cavalry and Guards, Hurlingham; Kildare Street and University (Dublin).
See also P. C. Petrie.

PETRIE, Edward James, CMG 1955; *b* 1907; retired from HM Treasury, Nairobi. Assistant Revenue Officer, Kenya, 1933; Assistant Treasurer, 1934; Senior Accountant, 1943; Assistant Financial Secretary, 1946; Financial Secretary, Barbados, 1948; Accountant-General, Kenya, 1951; Sec. to Treasury, Kenya, 1953-56; retd 1956. *Address:* 19 Stirling Road, Edinburgh 5.

PETRIE, Joan Caroline, (Mrs M. E. Bathurst); HM Diplomatic Service, retired 1972; *b* 2 Nov. 1920; *d* of James Alexander Petrie, Barrister-at-law, and Adrienne Johanna (*née* van den Bergh); *m* 1968, Maurice Edward Bathurst, *qv*; one step *s*. *Educ:* Wycombe Abbey Sch.; Newnham Coll., Cambridge (Mary Ewart Schol.). 1st cl. Med. and Mod. Langs Tripos, 1942, MA 1964. Entered HM Foreign Service, 1947: FO, 1947-48; 2nd Sec., The Hague, 1948-50; FO, 1950-54; 1st Sec., 1953; Bonn, 1954-58; FO (later FCO), 1958-71; Counsellor 1969; Head of European Communities Information Unit, FCO, 1969-71. Mem., UK Delegn to Colombo Plan Consultative Cttee, Jogjakarta, 1959. Adviser, British Group, Inter-Parly Union, 1962-68. Officer, Order of Leopold (Belgium), 1966. *Recreation:* music. *Address:* Airlie, The Highlands, East Horsley, Surrey. *T:* East Horsley 3269. *Club:* United Oxford & Cambridge University.

PETRIE, Peter Charles; HM Diplomatic Service; Head of European Integration Department, Foreign and Commonwealth Office, since 1976; *b* 7 March 1932; *s* of Sir Charles Petrie, Bt, *qv* and Lady (Cecilia) Petrie, *qv*; *m* 1958, Countess Lydwine Maria Fortunata v. Oberndorff, *d* of Count v. Oberndorff, The Hague and Paris; two *s* one *d*. *Educ:* Westminster; Christ Church, Oxford. BA Lit. Hum., MA. 2nd Lieut Grenadier Guards, 1954-56. Entered HM Foreign Service, 1956; served in UK Delegn to NATO, Paris 1958-61; UK High Commn, New Delhi (seconded CRO), 1961-64; Chargé d'Affaires, Katmandu, 1963; Cabinet Office, 1965-67; UK Mission to UN, NY, 1969-73; Counsellor (Head of Chancery), Bonn, 1973-76. *Recreations:* fencing (Public Schs Fencing Champion (Foil), 1949, (Foil and Sabre), 1950; Captain OUFC, 1952-53); shooting, tennis. *Address:* 8 rue des Eaux, Paris 16e, France. *T:* 224-7294. *Clubs:* Brooks's, Hurlingham.

PETTINGELL, Sir William (Walter), Kt 1972; CBE 1965 (OBE 1959); General Manager, The Australian Gas Light Co., 1952-74; *b* Corrimal, NSW, 4 Sept. 1914; *s* of H. G. W. Pettingell, Cootamundra, NSW; *m* 1942, Thora M., *d* of J. Stokes; one *s* two *d*. *Educ:* Wollongong High Sch.; Univ. of Sydney. BSc (Sydney) 1st cl. hons, 1934. The Australian Gas Light Co.: Research Chemist, 1936; Production Engr, 1948; Works Manager, 1950; Asst Gen. Manager (Technical), 1951; Gen. Manager, 1952-74; Dir, 1974-. Deputy Chairman: Australian Consolidated Industries; Hammer Corp. Ltd; Manufacturers Mutual Insurance Ltd; Director: Howard Smith Ltd; Coal and Allied Industries Ltd; Leighton Holdings Ltd; Blackwood Hodge Ltd. FAIM, FIAM, FInstF, MInstGasE. *Recreation:* yachting (sails a 35 foot ocean racer and has taken part in annual Sydney to Hobart and other ocean yacht races). *Address:* 54 Linden Way, Castlecrag, NSW 2068, Australia. *T:* 95 1976. *Clubs:* Union, American, Royal Prince Alfred Yacht, Royal Sydney Yacht Squadron, Elanora Golf (all in NSW).

PETTIT, Sir Daniel (Eric Arthur), Kt 1974; Chairman, National Freight Corporation, since 1971; Member (Part-time), Board of National Ports Council, since 1971; *b* Liverpool, 19 Feb. 1915; *s* of Thomas Edgar Pettit and Pauline Elizabeth Pettit (*née* Kerr); *m* 1940, Winifred, *d* of William and Sarah Bibby; two *s*. *Educ:* Quarry Bank High Sch., Liverpool; Fitzwilliam House, Cambridge (MA). School Master, 1938-40 and 1946-47; War Service, Africa, India, Burma, 1940-46 (Major, RA); Unilever: Management, 1948-57; Associated Company Dir and Chm., 1958-70; Member: Bd (Part-time), Nat. Freight Corp., 1968-70; Freight Integration Council, 1971-; Bd, Foundn of Management Educn, 1971-; Waste Management Adv. Council, 1975-; Chm., EDC for Distributive Trades, 1974-; Director: Lloyds Bank Ltd, 1977- (Regional Dir, Birmingham & W Midlands Bd); Bransford Farmers Ltd; Mem. Council, British Road Fedn Ltd.

FBIM; FCIT (Pres. 1971-72); MIPM. *Publications:* various papers on transport and management matters. *Recreations:* cricket, Association football (Olympic Games, 1936; Corinthian FC, 1935-); fly-fishing. *Address:* Bransford Court, Worcester. *Clubs:* MCC; Hawks (Cambridge).

PETTY, Hon. Sir Horace (Rostill), Kt 1964; BCom, FASA; Agent-General for State of Victoria, in London, 1964-69; *b* 29 March 1904; *m* 1st, 1930 (marr. diss.); two *s* two *d*; 2nd, 1959, Beryl Anne Hoelter. *Educ:* South Yarra School; University High School; Melbourne University. Accountant and auditor (managerial appts in retail business field, etc.) from mid-twenties to 1939. Australian Army, 1940-44; Infty, Aust. Armd Div. and AHQ in North, rank Major. Mem. Municipal Council, City of Prahran, 1949- (Mayor, 1951-52). MLA for Toorak (Liberal) in Victorian Parl., 1952-64. (Victorian Govt) Minister of: Housing, July 1955-July 1961; Immigration, July 1956-Dec. 1961; Public Works, Victorian State Government, July 1961-Apr. 1964. Mem., RSSAILA. *Recreations:* golf, racing, motoring. *Address:* 593 Toorak Road, Toorak, Victoria 3142, Australia. *Clubs:* Stewards' (Henley); Naval and Military, Melbourne Cricket, Huntingdale Golf, Victoria Racing, Melbourne Rowing, RAC of Vic. (all Victorian).

PETTY, William Henry; County Education Officer, Kent, since 1973; *b* 7 Sept. 1921; *s* of Henry and Eveline Ann Petty, Bradford; *m* 1948, Margaret Elaine, *o d* of Edward and Lorna Bastow, Baildon, Yorks; one *s* two *d*. *Educ:* Bradford Grammar Sch.; Peterhouse, Cambridge; London Univ. MA 1950, BSc 1953. Served RA, India and Burma, 1941-45. Admin, teaching and lectrg in London, Doncaster and N R Yorks, 1946-57; Sen. Asst Educn Officer, W R Yorks CC 1957-64; Dep. County Educn Officer, Kent CC, 1964-73. Member: Council and Court, Univ. of Kent at Canterbury, 1974-; Local Govt Trng Bd, Careers Service Trng Cttee, 1975-; Careers Service Adv. Council, 1976-; Trng and Further Educn Cons. Gp, 1977-; Vital Skills Task Gp, 1977-. Prizewinner: Cheltenham Fest. of Lit., 1968; Camden Fest. of Music and Arts, 1969. *Publications:* No Bold Comfort, 1957; Conquest, 1967; contrib. educnl and lit. jls and anthologies. *Recreations:* literature, travel. *Address:* Godfrey House, Hollingbourne, Maidstone, Kent ME17 1TX. *T:* Hollingbourne 346. *Club:* United Oxford & Cambridge University.

PETTY-FITZMAURICE; *see* Mercer Nairne Petty-Fitzmaurice, family name of Marquess of Lansdowne.

PEVSNER, Sir Nikolaus (Bernhard Leon), Kt 1969; CBE 1953; FBA 1965; MA Cantab; MA Oxon; PhD; FSA; Hon. FRIBA; Hon. ARCA; Hon. FNZIA; Hon. Academician, Accademia di Belle Arti, Venice; Hon. Fellow, Royal Scottish Academy; Hon. Member, American Academy of Arts and Sciences; Hon. Fellow, Akademie der Wissenschaften Göttingen; Emeritus Professor of History of Art, Birkbeck College, University of London; *b* 30 Jan. 1902; *s* of late Hugo Pevsner; *m* 1923, Karola Kurlbaum (*d* 1963); two *s* one *d*. *Educ:* St Thomas's Sch., Leipzig; Univs of Leipzig, Munich, Berlin and Frankfort. PhD History of Art and Architecture, 1924; Asst Keeper, Dresden Gallery, 1924-28; Lectr, History of Art and Architecture, Goettingen Univ., 1929-33; Slade Prof. of Fine Art, Univ. of Cambridge, 1949-55; Fellow, St John's Coll., Cambridge, 1950-55, Hon. Fellow, 1967-; Slade Prof. of Fine Art, Univ. of Oxford, 1968-69. Former Chm., Victorian Soc. (to 1976); Member: Historic Buildings Council; Council, Wm Morris Soc.; (formerly) Adv. Bd for Redundant Churches (to 1977). Reith Lectr, BBC, 1955. Royal Gold Medal for Architecture (RIBA), 1967; Albert Medal, RSA, 1976; other medals: Howland, Yale, 1963; Hitchcock, London, 1966; Thomas Jefferson, Univ. of Virginia, 1975. Hon. Doctorates: Leicester, York, Leeds, Oxford, E Anglia, Zagreb, Keele, Open Univ., Heriot-Watt Univ., Edinburgh, Univ. of Pennsylvania. Grand Cross of Merit, Fed. Rep. of Germany. *Publications:* The Baroque Architecture of Leipzig, 1928; Italian Painting from the end of the Renaissance to the end of the Rococo (a vol. of the Handbuch der Kunstwissenschaft), 1927-30; Pioneers of the Modern Movement, from William Morris to Walter Gropius, 1936 (revised edn: Pioneers of Modern Design, Museum of Modern Art, New York, 1949; new edn 1972; also foreign edns); An Enquiry into Industrial Art in England, 1937; German Baroque Sculpture (with S. Sitwell and A. Ayscough), 1938; Academies of Art, Past and Present, 1940; An Outline of European Architecture, Pelican Books, 1942, most recent edn, 1973 (also edns in numerous foreign langs); High Victorian Design, 1951; The Buildings of England (46 vols), 1951-74; The Planning of the Elizabethan Country House, 1961; The Englishness of English Art, 1956; Sir Christopher Wren (in Italian), 1958; Sources of Modern Art, 1962 (re-issued as The Sources of Modern Architecture and Design, 1968); Dictionary of

Architecture (with John Fleming and Hugh Honour), 1966; Studies in Art, Architecture and Design (2 vols), 1968; (with J. M. Richards) The Anti-Rationalists, 1973; Some Architectural Writers of the Nineteenth Century, 1973; A History of Building Types, 1976 (Wolfson Literary Award). *Address:* 2 Wildwood Terrace, North End, NW3.

PEYREFITTE, (Pierre-) Roger; French author; *b* 17 Aug. 1907; *o s* of Jean Peyrefitte, landowner, and Eugénie Jamme; unmarried. *Educ:* Collège St Benoit, Ardouane, Hérault (Lazarist); Collège du Caousou, Toulouse, Hte. Garonne (Jesuit); Lycée de Foix, Ariège; Université de Toulouse; Ecole libre des Sciences Politiques, Paris. Bachelier de l'enseignement secondaire; Diplôme d'études supérieures de langue et de littérature française; Diplômé de l'Ecole libre des Sciences Politiques (major de la section diplomatique). Concours diplomatique, 1931; attached to Ministry of Foreign Affairs, 1931-33; Secretary, French Embassy, Athens, 1933-38; attached to Ministry of Foreign Affairs, 1938-40 and 1943-45. *Publications:* Les Amitiés Particulières, novel, 1944 (Prix Théophraste Renaudot, 1945); Mademoiselle de Murville, novel, 1947; Le Prince des neiges, play, 1947; L'Oracle, novel, 1948; Les Amours Singulières, 1949; La Mort d'une mère, 1950; Les Ambassades, novel, 1951; Du Vésuve à l'Etna, 1952; La Fin des Ambassades, novel, 1953; Les Clés de saint Pierre, novel, 1955; Jeunes Proies, 1956; Chevaliers de Malte, 1957; L'Exilé de Capri, novel, 1959; Le Spectateur Nocturne, play, 1960; Les Ambassades, play (adaptation of A. P. Antoine), 1961; Les Fils de la Lumière, 1962; La Nature du Prince, 1963; Les Juifs, 1965; Notre Amour, 1967; Les Américains, novel, 1968; Des Français, novel, 1970; La Coloquinte, novel, 1971; Manouche, 1972; Un Musée de l'Amour, 1972; La Muse garçonnière, 1973; Catalogue de la collection de monnais grecques et romains de l'auteur, 1974; Tableaux de chasse, ou la vie extraordinaire de Fernand Legros, 1976; Propos secrets, 1977. *Recreations:* travel, walks, collecting antiques. *Address:* 9 Avenue du Maréchal Maunoury, 75016 Paris, France.

PEYTON, Rt. Hon. John Wynne William, PC 1970; MP (C) Yeovil Division of Somerset since 1951; *b* 13 Feb. 1919; *s* of late Ivor Eliot Peyton and Dorothy Helen Peyton; *m* 1947, Diana Clinch (marr. diss., 1966); one *s* one *d* (and one *s* decd); *m* 1966, Mrs Mary Cobbold. *Educ:* Eton; Trinity College, Oxford. Commissioned 15/19 Hussars, 1939; Prisoner of War, Germany, 1940-45. Called to the Bar, Inner Temple, 1945. Parly Secretary, Ministry of Power, 1962-64; Minister of Transport, June-Oct. 1970; Minister for Transport Industries, DoE, 1970-74. Chm., Texas Instruments Ltd, 1974-. *Address:* The Old Malt House, Hinton St George, Somerset. *T:* Crewkerne 73618; 6 Temple West Mews, West Square, SE11. *T:* 01-582 3611. *Club:* Boodle's.

PEYTON, Sidney Augustus, PhD; Librarian of Sheffield University, 1941-56; *b* 1891; *e s* of late Sidney Peyton, Newbury; *m* Muriel Kathleen Pearse. *Educ:* University Coll., Reading. Lectr, University Coll., Reading, 1919; Univ. Librarian, Reading, 1922-41. Hon. LittD Sheffield. *Publications:* Oxfordshire Peculiars (Oxford Record Society); Kesteven Quarter Sessions Minutes (Lincoln Record Society); Kettering Vestry Minutes (Northamptonshire Record Society); Northamptonshire QS Records, Introduction; various historical papers. *Recreation:* music. *Address:* 14 Brincliffe Court, Nether Edge Road, Sheffield S7 1RX. *T:* Sheffield 52767.

PFEIFFER, Rudolf, MA Oxon, DPhil Munich; DPhil *hc* Vienna and Thessalonika; FBA 1949; Professor of Greek, University of Munich, 1929-37, and from 1951, Emeritus 1957; *b* 28 September 1889; *s* of late Carl Pfeiffer and late Elizabeth (*née* Naegele); *m* 1913, Lili (*d* 1969), *d* of late Sigmund and Mina Beer. *Educ:* Benedictine Abbey, St Stephan, Augsburg; Universities of Munich and Berlin. Sub-librarian, University Library, Munich, 1918; Lecturer, University of Munich, 1921; Professor extraordinarius, University of Berlin, 1923; Professor of Greek: Hamburg, 1923; Freiburg i. Br., 1927; Corpus Christi College, Oxford, 1938-51, University Lecturer, 1946, Senior Lecturer, 1948, Reader in Greek Literature, 1950. Ordinary Member of Bavarian Academy; Hon. Mem., Austrian Academy; For. Corresp. Member: Académie des Inscriptions et Belles-Lettres; Academy of Greece, 1973; Hon. Fellow of Athenian Scientific Society; Hon. Fellow Corpus Christi College, Oxford, 1959; Hon. Fellow Hellenic Society, 1961. Kenyon Medal, British Acad., 1977. Bavarian Order of Merit, 1959; Greek Order of Phœnix, 1959; Grand Cross of the Federal Republic of Germany, 1964. *Publications:* Augsburger Meistersinger und Homerübersetzer J. Spreng, 1914 and 1919; Callimachi Fragmenta nuper reperta, 1921, editio maior, 1923; Kallimachos-Studien, 1922; Humanitas Erasmiana, 1931; Die griechische Dichtung und die griechische Kultur, 1932; Die Diktyulkoi des Aischylos und der Inachos des Sophokles, 1937;

Callimachus (complete edn) vol. I Fragmenta, 1949 (reprinted 1965), vol. II Hymni et Epigrammata, 1953 (repr. 1966); Von der Liebe zu den Griechen, 1958; Ausgewählte Schriften: Aufsätze und Vorträge zur griechischen Dichtung und zum Humanismus, 1960; Philologia Perennis, 1961; History of Classical Scholarship: From the Beginnings to the End of the Hellenistic Age, 1968; Von der Liebe zur Antike; zum 80 Geburtstag von R.P., 1969; History of Classical Scholarship 1300-1850, 1976. Editor: U. von Wilamowitz, Kleine Schriften II, 1940. Numerous articles in periodicals on Greek and Latin literature, Erasmus, humanism. *Recreations:* music, walking. *Address:* Hiltenspergerstrasse 21, München 40, Germany. *T:* 372185.

PHALP, Geoffrey Anderson, CBE 1968; TD; Secretary, King Edward's Hospital Fund for London, since 1968; *b* 8 July 1915; *s* of late Charles Anderson Phalp and late Sara Gertrude Phalp (*née* Wilkie); *m* 1946, Jeanne Margaret, OBE, JP, *d* of late Emeritus Prof. G. R. Goldsborough, CBE, FRS; one *s* one *d*. *Educ:* Durham Sch.; Univ. of Durham (BCom). Served with RA (despatches), 1939-46. Asst Registrar, Med. Sch., King's Coll., Newcastle upon Tyne, 1946-49; Dep. House Governor and Sec., United Newcastle upon Tyne Hosps, 1949-51; Sec. and Principal Admin. Officer, United Birmingham Hosps, 1951-68. *Recreations:* fly fishing, gardening, music. *Address:* 86 Marryat Road, Wimbledon, SW19. *T:* 01-946 5132. *Club:* Savile.

PHELAN, Andrew James; His Honour Judge Phelan; a Circuit Judge, since 1974; *b* 25 July 1923; *e s* of Cornelius Phelan, Clonmel, Eire; *m* 1950, Joan Robertson McLagan; one *s* two *d*. *Educ:* Clongoweswood, Co. Kildare; National Univ. of Ireland (MA); Trinity Coll., Cambridge. Called to: Irish Bar, King's Inn, 1945; English Bar, Gray's Inn, 1949. Jun. Fellow, Univ. of Bristol, 1948-50; in practice at English Bar, 1950-74. *Publication:* The Law for Small Boats, 2nd edn, 1970. *Recreations:* sailing, mountain walking. *Address:* 17 Hartington Road, Chiswick, W4 1PD. *T:* 01-994 6109. *Club:* Bar Yacht.

PHELPS, Anthony John, CB 1976; Deputy Chairman, Board of Customs and Excise, since 1973; *b* 14 Oct. 1922; *s* of John Francis and Dorothy Phelps, Oxford; *m* 1st, 1949, Sheila Nan Rait (*d* 1967), *d* of late Colin Benton Rait, Edinburgh; one *s* two *d*; 2nd, 1971, Janet M. T., *d* of late Charles R. Dawson, Edinburgh. *Educ:* City of Oxford High Sch.; University Coll., Oxford. HM Treasury, 1946; Jun. Private Sec. to Chancellor of the Exchequer, 1949-50; Principal, 1950; Treasury Rep. in Far East, 1953-55; Private Sec. to the Prime Minister, 1958-61; Asst Sec., 1961; Under-Sec., 1968. Freeman, City of Oxford, 1971. *Recreations:* music, watching sport. *Address:* 22 Woodcrest Road, Purley, Surrey. *T:* 01-660 1545. *Club:* MCC.

PHELPS, Howard Thomas Henry Middleton; Group Personnel Director since 1972 and Board Member since 1973, British Airways Board; *b* 20 Oct. 1926; *s* of Ernest Henry Phelps, Gloucester, and Harriet (*née* Middleton); *m* 1949, Audrey (*née* Ellis); one *d*. *Educ:* Crypt Grammar Sch., Gloucester; Hatfield Coll.; Durham Univ. BA Hons Politics and Econs 1951. National Coal Board, Lancs, Durham and London, 1951-72, finally Dep. Dir-Gen. of Industrial Relations; Personnel Dir, BOAC, 1972. FIPM. Chm., Durham Univ. Soc. *Recreations:* gardening, musical appreciation, talking to trade unionists. *Address:* Littlecroft, Heathside Road, Woking, Surrey. *T:* Woking 62027.

PHELPS, Maj.-Gen. Leonard Thomas Herbert, CB 1973; OBE 1963; FBIM 1973; Director, The Warrior Group of Companies; *b* 9 Sept. 1917; *s* of Abijah Phelps; *m* 1945, Jean Irene, *d* of R. Price Dixon; one *s* one *d*. FBIM, FInstPS. Served War, Hong Kong, 1940-41; India/Burma, 1941-47. Student, Staff Coll., Quetta, 1946; DAQMG, HQ Land Forces Hong Kong, 1951-53; Second in Command, 4th Trng Bn, RAOC, 1955-57; War Office: DAAG, 1957-59; ADOS, 1961-63; AA & QMG Singapore Mil. Forces, 1963; Chief of Staff, 4th Malaysian Inf. Bde, 1964; ADOS, WO, 1965-67; Chief Inspector, Land Service Ammunition, 1967-70; Comdr, Base Organisation, RAOC, 1970; Dir, Ordnance Services, MoD (Army), 1971-73; retired 1973; Col Comdt, RAOC, 1976-. *Recreations:* shooting, golf. *Address:* South Port Cottage, Sutton Courtenay, Oxon; 2 Glebe House, Fitzroy Mews, W1P 5DQ. *Club:* Army and Navy.

PHELPS, Richard Wintour; General Manager, Central Lancashire New Town Development Corporation, since 1971; *b* 26 July 1925; *s* of Rev. H. Phelps; *m* 1955, Pamela Marie Lawson; two *d*. *Educ:* Kingswood Sch.; Merton Coll., Oxford (MA). 14th Punjab Regt, IA, 1944-46. Colonial Admin. Service, Northern Region and Fed. Govt. of Nigeria, 1948-57 and 1959-61; Prin., HM Treasury, 1957-59 and 1961-65; Sen. Administrator, Hants CC, 1965-67; Gen. Manager,

Skelmersdale New Town Devel Corp., 1967-71. Winston Churchill Trust Travelling Fellowship, 1971. *Recreations:* reading, travel, music. *Address:* 4 Sandringham Road, Birkdale, Southport, Merseyside. *T:* Southport 66607. *Club:* Royal Commonwealth Society.

PHELPS BROWN, Sir Ernest Henry; *see* Brown, Sir E. H. P.

PHEMISTER, James, MA, DSc, FRSE, FGS; FMSA; *b* 3 April 1893; 2nd *s* of John Clark Phemister and Elizabeth G. Crawford; *m* 1921, Margaret Clark, MA; two *s* one *d. Educ:* Govan High Sch.; Glasgow Univ. Served European War, RE and RGA; disabled 1917, and placed on retired list, 1918; teacher of Mathematics and Science, 1918-21; appointed Geological Survey, 1921; Petrographer, 1935-45; Curator, Museum of Practical Geology, 1945-46; Asst Dir Specialist Services, 1946-53; Pres. Mineralogical Soc., 1951-54; Pres. Glasgow Geol. Soc., 1961-64. Editor, Mineralogical Abstracts, 1959-66. *Publications:* papers on Petrological and Geophysical subjects. *Recreation:* swimming. *Address:* Murchison House, Edinburgh EH9 2LA.

PHEMISTER, Prof. Thomas Crawford, MSc (Chicago), PhD (Cantab), DSc (Glasgow); FRSE, FGS; Dr de l'Univ. de Rennes (hon. causa); Professor and Head of Department of Geology and Mineralogy, Aberdeen University, 1937-72, now Professor emeritus; *b* 25 May 1902; 4th *s* of John Clark Phemister and Elizabeth G. Crawford; *m* 1926, Mary Wood Reid, MA; three *d. Educ:* Allan Glen's School and University of Glasgow; St John's College, Cambridge; Chicago University. Assoc. Prof. of Geology and Mineralogy, Univ. of British Columbia, 1926-33; Field Officer, Geological Survey of Canada, 1928-30; University Demonstrator in Mineralogy and Petrology, Cambridge Univ., 1933-37. Served in Royal Engineers, War of 1939-45. Dean of Faculty of Science, 1945-48, Vice-Principal, 1963-66, Aberdeen University. Chm., Macaulay Inst. for Soil Research, 1958-. Chm., Robert Gordon's Colleges. *Publications:* papers on mineralogical and petrological subjects. *Address:* Department of Geology and Mineralogy, University of Aberdeen, Aberdeen AB9 1AS. *T:* Aberdeen 36489.

PHILBIN, Most Rev. William J.; *see* Down and Connor, Bishop of, (RC).

PHILIP, Alexander; General Manager, Scottish Region, British Railways, 1971-74; Chairman, British Transport Ship Management (Scotland) Ltd, 1971-74; *b* 4 June 1911; *s* of Alexander Philip and Elizabeth Milne Philip; *m* 1939, Isobel Thomson Morrison; one *s. Educ:* Robert Gordon's Coll., Aberdeen. FCIT, MIPM. Joined LNER, 1927; occupied various positions mainly on personnel and movements aspects of railway business in Aberdeen, Edinburgh and Glasgow. Mem., Lanarkshire Health Bd. *Recreations:* reading, golf, gardening. *Address:* 12 Dalmorglen Park, Stirling. *T:* Stirling 3672.

PHILIP, John Robert, DSc; FRS 1974; FAA 1967; Chief of Division of Environmental Mechanics, Commonwealth Scientific and Industrial Research Organization, Australia, since 1971; *b* 18 Jan. 1927; *e s* of Percival Norman Philip and Ruth (*née* Osborne), formerly of Ballarat and Maldon, Vic., Australia; *m* 1949, Frances Julia, *o d* of E. Hilton Long; two *s* one *d. Educ:* Scotch Coll., Melbourne; Univ. of Melbourne (Queen's Coll.). BCE 1946, DSc 1960. Research Asst, Melb. Univ., 1947; Engr, Qld Irrig. Commn, 1948-51; Research Staff, CSIRO, 1951-; Sen. Princ. Res. Scientist, 1961-63; Chief Res. Scientist and Asst Chief, Div. of Plant Industry, 1963-71. Visiting Scientist, Cambridge Univ., 1954-55; Res. Fellow, Calif. Inst. Techn., 1957-58; Vis. Prof., Univ. of Illinois, 1958 and 1961; Nuffield Foundn Fellow, Cambridge Univ., 1961-62; Res. Fellow, Harvard Univ., 1966-67; Vis. Prof., Univ. of Florida, 1969; Vinton-Hayes Fellow, Harvard Univ., 1972. Horton Award, Amer. Geophys. Union, 1957; David Rivett Medal, 1966. Mem. Council, Australian Acad. of Sci., 1972- (Biol. Sec., 1974-); ANZAAS: Pres. Section 1 (Physics), 1970; Pres. Sect. 8 (Maths), 1971. FRMetS. *Publications:* papers in scientific jls on soil and porous medium physics, fluid mechanics, hydrology, micrometeorology, mathematical and physical aspects of physiology and ecology. *Recreations:* reading, writing, architecture. *Address:* CSIRO Division of Environmental Mechanics, PO Box 821, Canberra City, ACT 2601, Australia. *T:* (062) 46-5645; 42 Vasey Crescent, Campbell, ACT 2601. *T:* (062) 47-8958.

PHILIP, Sir William (Shearer), Kt 1975; CMG 1961; MC 1918; President of Board of Management, Alfred Hospital, Melbourne, since 1948 (Member Board of Management, since 1935, Hon. Treasurer, 1939-48); Company Director; *b* Williamstown, Victoria, 18 Aug. 1891; *s* of Capt. William Philip, Aberdeen and Williamstown; *m* 1920, Irene Laura (*d* 1960), *d* of

William Cross; two *s* two *d. Educ:* Scotch College, Melbourne. Flack and Flack and Price Waterhouse & Co., Chartered Accountants, 1909-56, Partner, 1925-56. Member Charities Board of Victoria, 1942-48, Chairman, 1946-47. Business Adviser, AAMC, 1940-45. *Recreations:* golf and fishing. *Address:* Glenshee, No 1 Macquarie Road, Toorak, Victoria 3142, Australia. *T:* 20.3973. *Clubs:* Melbourne, Australian and Royal Melbourne Golf (Melbourne).

PHILIPPE, André J.; Luxembourg Ambassador to the Court of St James's, and Permanent Representative to Council of Western European Union, since 1972; concurrently Ambassador to Ireland and Iceland; *b* Luxembourg City, 28 June 1926. Dr-en-Droit. Barrister-at-Law, Luxembourg, 1951-52. Joined Luxembourg Diplomatic Service, 1952; Dep. to Dir of Polit. Affairs, Min. of Foreign Affairs, 1952-54; Dep. Perm. Rep. to NATO, 1954-61 and to OECD, 1959-61; Dir of Protocol and Legal Adviser, Min. of For. Affairs, 1961-68; Ambassador and Perm. Rep. to UN and Consul-Gen., New York, 1968-72 (Vice-Pres., 24th Session of Gen. Assembly of UN, 1969). Member: Bd of Dirs, Société Internationale de la Moselle, 1961-68 (sometime Vice-Pres.); Bd of Dirs, Société électrique de l'Our, 1961-68; Internat. Moselle Navigation Commn, 1961-68 (Chm., 1965 and 1968). Commander, Order of Adolphe Nassau (Luxembourg); holds foreign decorations, inc. GCVO (Hon.) 1972. *Address:* Luxembourg Embassy, 27 Wilton Crescent, SW1X 8SD.

PHILIPPS, family name of **Viscount St Davids** and **Baron Milford.**

PHILIPPS, Hon. Hanning; *see* Philipps, Hon. R. H.

PHILIPPS, Hon. James Perrott, TD; *b* 25 Nov. 1905; 3rd *s* of 1st Baron and *b* of 2nd Baron Milford, *qv*; *m* 1930, Hon. Elizabeth Joan, *d* of 1st Baron Kindersley; one *s* two *d. Educ:* Eton; Christ Church, Oxford. Chm., Dalham Farms Ltd. Mem., Jockey Club. Served War of 1939-45; Leicestershire Yeomanry and Shropshire Yeomanry (despatches). Major TA Reserve. High Sheriff of Suffolk, 1955-56. *Recreations:* breeding, racing. *Address:* Dalham Hall, Newmarket, Suffolk. *T:* Ousden 242. *Clubs:* Jockey; Turf, Royal Automobile.
See also Hon. R. H. Philipps.

PHILIPPS, Lady Marion (Violet), FRAgS; JP; farmer, since 1946; *b* 1 Feb. 1908; *d* of 12th Earl of Stair, KT, DSO; *m* 1930, Hon. Hanning Philipps, *qv*; one *s* one *d. Educ:* privately. FRAgS 1973. War Service: original Mem., WVS HQ Staff, i/c Canteen and Catering Information Services, 1938-41; Min. of Agriculture, 1942-45. Mem., Narberth Rural Dist Council, 1970-73. Chm., Picton Land & Investment Pty Ltd, WA. Trustee, Picton Castle Trust (Graham Sutherland Gallery), 1976-. Member: (Founder), British Polled Hereford Soc., 1950- (also first Pres.); Welsh Council, Historic Houses Assoc., 1975; Gardens Cttee, National Council of Historic Houses Assoc., 1975; Gardens Cttee, National Council of Historic Houses Assoc., 1976-. JP Dyfed (formerly Pembrokeshire), 1965. CStJ; Order of Mercy, 1926. *Recreation:* gardening. *Address:* Picton Castle, The Rhos, Haverfordwest, Dyfed. *T:* Rhos 201.

PHILIPPS, Hon. (Richard) Hanning, MBE 1945; JP; Hon. Major Welsh Guards; Lord-Lieutenant of Dyfed, since 1974 (HM Lieutenant of Pembrokeshire, 1958-74); Chairman, Milford Haven Conservancy Board, 1963-75; Chairman: Northern Securities Trust Ltd; Hon. President (formerly Chairman), Schweppes Ltd; *b* 14 Feb. 1904; 2nd *s* of 1st Baron and *b* of 2nd Baron Milford, *qv*; *m* 1930, Lady Marion Violet Dalrymple (*see* Lady Marion Philipps); one *s* one *d. Educ:* Eton. Contested (Nat) Brecon and Radnor, 1939. Served War of 1939-45, NW Europe, 1944-45 (MBE). Vice-Lieutenant of Pembrokeshire, 1957. Hon. Colonel Pembroke Yeomanry, 1959. *Recreations:* painting, forestry, gardening. *Address:* Picton Castle, Haverfordwest, Pembrokeshire SA62 4AS. *T:* Rhos 202; 5 Connaught Place, W2. *Clubs:* Boodle's, Pratt's.
See also Hon. J. P. Philipps.

PHILIPS, Prof. Sir Cyril (Henry), Kt 1974; Professor of Oriental History, University of London, since 1946; Director, School of Oriental and African Studies, London, 1957-76; Vice-Chancellor, University of London, 1972-76 (Deputy Vice-Chancellor, 1969-70); *b* Worcester, 27 Dec. 1912; *s* of William Henry Philips; *m* 1st, 1939, Dorcas (*d* 1974), *d* of John Rose, Wallasey; one *d* (one *s* decd); 2nd, 1975, Joan Rosemary, *d* of William George Marshall. *Educ:* Rock Ferry High School; Univs of Liverpool (MA) and London (PhD). Bishop Chavasse Prizeman; Gladstone Memorial Fellow. Frewen Lord Prizeman (Royal Empire Soc.); Alexander Prizeman (Royal Hist. Soc.); Sir Percy Sykes Meml Medal; Asst Lectr, Sch. of Oriental Studies, 1936. Served in Suffolk Infantry, Army Education

Corps, 1940-43; Commandant, Army School of Education, 1943. HM Treasury, Dept of Training, 1943-46. Colonial Office Mission on Community Development, Africa, 1947. Montague Burton Lectr, Univ. of Leeds, 1966; Creighton Lectr, Univ. of London, 1972. Chairman: UGC Cttee on Oriental, African and Slavonic Studies, 1965-70; UGC Cttee on Latin American Studies, 1966-70; India Cttee of Inter-University Council and British Council, 1972-; Member: Social Development Cttee, Colonial Office, 1947-55; Colonial Office Research Council, 1955-57; University Grants Cttee, 1960-69; Commonwealth Education Commn, 1961-70; Postgraduate Awards Cttee (Min. of Education), 1962-64; Modern Languages Cttee (Min. of Education), 1964-67; Inter-Univ. Council, 1967-; Court, London Univ., 1970-; Governor, Chinese Univ. of Hong Kong, 1965-. Hon. DLitt Warwick, 1967; Hon. LLD Hong Kong, 1971. *Publications:* The East India Company, 1940 (2nd edn 1961); India, 1949; Handbook of Oriental History, 1951 (2nd edn 1962); Correspondence of David Scott, 1951; Historians of India, Pakistan and Ceylon, 1961; The Evolution of India and Pakistan, 1962; Politics and Society in India, 1963; Fort William-India House Correspondence, 1964; History of the School of Oriental and African Studies, 1917-67, 1967; The Partition of India, 1970; The Correspondence of Lord William Bentinck, Governor General of India 1828-35, 1977. *Address:* School of Oriental and African Studies, Malet Street, WC1E 7HP. *T:* 01-637 2388.

PHILIPSON, Garry, DFC 1944; General Manager, Aycliffe and Peterlee Development Corporations, since 1974; *b* 27 Nov. 1921; *s* of George and Marian Philipson; *m* 1949, June Mary Miller Somerville; one *d. Educ:* Stockton Grammar Sch.; Durham Univ. (BA(Hons)). Jubilee Prize, 1947. Local Govt, 1937-40. Served War, RAFVR (2 Gp Bomber Comd), 1940-46. Colonial Service and Overseas Civil Service, 1949-60. Various Dist and Secretariat posts, incl. Clerk, Exec. Council and Cabinet Sec., Sierra Leone; Principal, Scottish Develt Dept, 1961-66; Under Sec., RICS, 1966-67; Dir, Smith and Ritchie Ltd, 1967-70; Sec., New Towns Assoc., 1970-74. *Publications:* Press articles and contribs to various jls. *Recreations:* country pursuits, history, archaeology. *Address:* Tunstall Grange, Tunstall, Richmond, North Yorks. *T:* Catterick Camp 3327; 12 Glebe Place, SW3. *T:* 01-352 0131. *Club:* East India, Devonshire, Sports and Public Schools.

PHILIPSON, Oliphant James; *b* 9 Sept. 1905; 2nd *s* of late Hylton Philipson; *m* 1946, Helen Mabel (*d* 1976), *d* of David Fell. *Educ:* Eton. Served War of 1939-45, RNVR. *Address:* Manor House, Everton, near Lymington, Hampshire. *Clubs:* Carlton; Royal Yacht Squadron.

PHILIPSON, Sir Robert James, (Sir Robin Philipson), Kt 1976; Hon. RA 1973 (ARA 1973); PRSA 1973 (RSA 1962; ARSA 1952); RSW 1954; Head of the School of Drawing and Painting, The College of Art, Edinburgh, since 1960; President, Royal Scottish Academy, since 1973 (Secretary, 1969-73); *b* 17 Dec. 1916; *s* of James Philipson; *m* 1949, Brenda Mark; *m* 1962, Thora Clyne (marr. diss. 1975); *m* 1976, Diana Mary Pollock. *Educ:* Whitehaven Secondary School; Dumfries Academy; Edinburgh College of Art, 1936-40. Served War of 1939-45: King's Own Scottish Borderers, 1942-46, in India and Burma; attached to RIASC. Member of teaching staff, Edinburgh College of Art, 1947. Exhibits with Roland, Browse and Delbanco and Scottish Gallery, Edinburgh. Mem., Royal Fine Art Commn for Scotland, 1965-. FRSA 1965; FRSE 1977. DUniv Stirling 1976; Hon. LLD Aberdeen 1977. *Address:* 23 Crawfurd Road, Edinburgh EH16 5PQ. *T:* 031-667 2373. *Club:* Scottish Arts (Edinburgh).

PHILIPSON-STOW, Sir Edmond (Cecil), 4th Bt *cr* 1907; MBE (mil.) 1946; retired; *b* 25 Aug. 1912; second *s* of Sir Elliot Philipson Philipson-Stow, 2nd Bt and Edith (*d* 1943), *y d* of late E. H. Pery-Knox-Gore, DL, JP; *S* brother, 1976. *Educ:* Malvern College; Royal Military College, Sandhurst. Served in The Duke of Cornwall's Light Infantry, 1932-52; Major (retd). *Heir:* cousin Christopher Philipson-Stow, DFC [*b* 13 Sept. 1920; *m* 1952, Elizabeth Nairn, *d* of late James Dixon Trees; two *s*]. *Address:* Cloonaghmore, Crossmolina, Co. Mayo.

PHILLIMORE, family name of **Baron Phillimore.**

PHILLIMORE, 3rd Baron, *cr* 1918, of Shiplake in County of Oxford; **Robert Godfrey Phillimore,** Bt, *cr* 1881; *b* 24 Sept. 1939; *s* of Capt. Hon. Anthony Francis Phillimore, 9th Queen's Royal Lancers (*e s* of 2nd Baron) and Anne, 2nd *d* of Maj.-Gen. Sir Cecil Pereira, KCB; *S* grandfather, 1947. *Heir:* *u* Major Hon. Claud Stephen Phillimore [*b* 15 Jan. 1911; *m* 1944, Anne Elizabeth, *e d* of Maj. Arthur Algernon Dorrien-Smith, DSO; one *s* one *d*]. *Address:* Coppid Hall, Henley-on-Thames, Oxon.

PHILLIMORE, John Gore, CMG 1946; a Managing Director of Baring Brothers & Co. Ltd, 1949-72; Director: Brascan Ltd, 1949 (formerly Brazilian Light & Power Co.); Commonwealth Development Finance Co. Ltd, 1967; Tribune Investment Trust Ltd; Adela Investment Co., since 1972; *b* 16 April 1908; 2nd *s* of late Adm. Sir Richard and Lady Phillimore, Shedfield, Hants; *m* 1951, Jill, *d* of late Captain Mason Scott, Royal Navy retd, Buckland Manor, Broadway, Worcs, and of Hon. Mrs Scott; two *s* two *d. Educ:* Winchester College; Christ Church, Oxford. Partner of Roberts, Meynell & Co., Buenos Aires, 1936-48; Representative of HM Treasury and Bank of England in South America, 1940-45. Prime Warden, Fishmongers' Co., 1974-75. High Sheriff of Kent, 1975. Commander, Orden de Mayo (Argentina). *Address:* The Postern, Tonbridge, Kent. *T:* 352178. *Clubs:* White's, Beefsteak, Overseas Bankers.

PHILLIPS, family name of Baroness Phillips.

PHILLIPS, Baroness *cr* 1964 (Life Peer); **Norah Phillips,** JP; Director, Association for the Prevention of Theft in Shops; Vice-President (and former General Secretary), National Association of Women's Clubs; President: Institute of Shops Acts Administration; Association for Research into Restricted Growth; Institute of Travel and Tourism; Vice-President: National Association of Local Councils; Pre-Retirement Association; Keep Fit Association; National Chamber of Trade; Chairman, Beatrice Webb House Trust; Member: National Consumer Council; Advertising Standards Authority; *b* 12 Aug. 1910; *d* of William and Catherine Lusher; *m* 1930, Morgan Phillips (decd); one *s* one *d* (*see* G. P. Dunwoody). *Educ:* Marist Convent; Hampton Training College. A Baroness in Waiting (Govt Whip), 1965-70. *Address:* 115 Rannoch Road, W6. *T:* 01-828 8889/0781.

PHILLIPS, Alan; *see* Phillips, D. A.

PHILLIPS, Arthur, OBE 1957; MA, PhD; JP; Barrister at Law (Middle Temple and Western Circuit); Chancellor, Diocese of Winchester; a Recorder of the Crown Court, since 1972; Professor Emeritus, University of Southampton; *b* 29 May 1907; *e s* of Albert William Phillips and Agnes Phillips (*née* Edwards); *m* 1934, Kathleen Hudson; two *s* two *d. Educ:* Highgate School; Trinity College, Oxford. In chambers in Temple, 1929; joined Colonial Service, 1931, and served in Kenya: Dist Officer, 1931; Actg Resident Magistrate, 1933-35; Crown Counsel, 1936; Actg Solicitor-Gen., 1940 and 1946; Judicial Adviser, 1945; Mem. of Kenya Leg. Council, 1940. Served in Kenya Regt, Somaliland and Abyssinia, 1940-42; Chm. War Claims Commn, Br. Somaliland, 1942; retd from Colonial Service on medical grounds and practised at Bar, England, 1947-49. Reader in Law, LSE, Univ. of London, 1949-56; Prof. of English Law, Univ. of Southampton, 1956-67; Dean of Faculty of Law, 1956-62; Deputy Vice-Chancellor, 1961-63. Dep. Chm., Hants QS, 1960-71. Director of Survey of African Marriage and Family Life, 1948-52. Chairman Milk and Dairies Tribunal, South-Eastern Region, 1961-; Pres., Southern Rent Assessment Panel, 1965-72. JP Hants.; Chairman Winchester County Magistrates' Court, 1956-61. Member, Church Assembly, 1965-70. Lay Reader, Diocese of Winchester, Counsellor to the Dean and Chapter of Winchester. *Publications:* Report on Native Tribunals (Kenya), 1945; (ed. and part-author) Survey of African Marriage and Family Life, 1953; (jt) Marriage Laws in Africa, 1971; principal contribr on Ecclesiastical Law, Halsbury's Laws of England, 1975. *Address:* Church Cottage, Compton, near Winchester, Hants. *T:* Twyford 713295. *Clubs:* Royal Commonwealth Society; Hampshire (Winchester).

PHILLIPS, Prof. Calbert Inglis, FRCS, FRCSE; Professor of Ophthalmology, University of Edinburgh and Ophthalmic Surgeon, Royal Infirmary, Edinburgh, since 1972; *b* 20 March 1925; *o s* of Rev. David Horner Phillips and Margaret Calbert Phillips; *m* 1962, Christina Anne Fulton, MB, FRCSE; one *s. Educ:* Glasgow High Sch.; Robert Gordon's Coll., Aberdeen; Aberdeen Univ. MB, ChB Aberdeen 1946; DPH Edinburgh 1950; FRCS 1955; MD Aberdeen 1957; PhD Bristol 1961; MSc Manchester 1969; FRCSE 1973. Lieut and Captain, RAMC, 1947-49. House Surgeon: Aberdeen Royal Infirmary, 1946-47 (House Phys., 1951); Aberdeen Maternity Hosp., 1949; Glasgow Eye Infirmary, 1950-51; Asst, Anatomy Dept, Glasgow Univ., 1951-52; Resident Registrar, Moorfields Eye Hosp., 1953-54; Sen. Registrar, St Thomas' Hosp. and Moorfields Eye Hosp., and Res. Asst, Inst. of Ophthalmology, 1954-58; Consultant Surg., Bristol Eye Hosp., 1958-63; Alexander Piggott Wernher Trav. Fellow, Dept of Ophthal., Harvard Univ., 1960-61; Consultant Ophthalmic Surg., St George's Hosp., 1963-65; Prof. of Ophthal., Manchester Univ., and Hon. Consultant Ophthalmic Surg. to United Manchester Hosps, 1965-72. *Publications:* papers in Brit. and Amer. Jls of Ophthal., Nature,

Brain, BMJ, etc, mainly on intra-ocular pressure and glaucoma, retinal detachments, ocular surgery and hereditary diseases. *Address:* Princess Alexandra Eye Pavilion, Chalmers Street, Edinburgh EH3 9HA. *T:* 031-229 2477.

PHILLIPS, Prof. Charles Garrett, FRS 1963; DM; FRCP; Dr Lee's Professor of Anatomy, University of Oxford, since 1975; Fellow of Hertford College; *b* 13 October 1916; *s* of Dr George Ramsey Phillips and Flora (*née* Green); *m* 1942, Cynthia Mary, *d* of late L. R. Broster, OBE, FRCS; two *d*. *Educ:* Bradfield; Magdalen College, Oxford; St Bartholomew's Hospital. Captain, RAMC, 1943-46. Reader in Neurophysiology, 1962-66, Prof., 1966-75, Oxford Univ.; Fellow, Trinity Coll., 1946-75. Hon. Sec., Physiological Society, 1960-66. Editor, Brain, 1975-. Hon. DSc Monash, 1971. Lectures: Ferrier, 1968; Hughlings Jackson (and Medal), 1973. Feldberg Prize, 1970. *Publications:* Papers on neurophysiology in Jl of Physiology, etc. *Address:* Department of Human Anatomy, Oxford. *T:* 58686. *Club:* United Oxford & Cambridge University.

PHILLIPS, Maj.-Gen. Charles George, CB 1944; DSO 1919, Bar 1940; MC; *b* 7 July 1889; *s* of Major George Edward Phillips, DSO, RE (killed in action Somaliland Expedition, 1902), and L. V. C. Alluaud; *m* 1924, Norah Butler; three *d*. *Educ:* Repton; RMC, Sandhurst. 2nd Lt West Yorkshire Regiment, 1909; Lieut 1910; seconded for service Merehan Somali Expedition, Jubaland, Kenya, 1912-14; European War, served in German East Africa; Captain, 1914; temp. Lt-Col, 1916-19; commanded 3/2 KAR; commanded Column, Philcol, Portuguese East Africa, 1918; wounded, Njangao, 1917 (German East Africa); temp. Major, 1919; temp. Lt-Col, 1919-23; commanded 1st Batt. 1st King's African Rifles and OC Troops in Nyasaland; Major, 1924; Lt-Col 1933; commanded 1st Battalion The West Yorkshire Regt (Prince of Wales Own), 1933-37; Bt Col, 1935; Commander 146th (1st West Riding) Infantry Brigade TA, 1938; (Medals, AGS, DSO, MC, 1914-15 Star, General Service Medal, Allied Victory Medal, French Croix de Guerre (avec palme), Officer Military Order of Aviz); War of 1939-45 (3 medals, Bar to DSO); Comdr British Troops, Namsos, Norway, 1940; Northern Iceland, 1940-41; Gambia and Sierra Leone areas, 1942-44; Maj.-Gen. 1942; retired pay, 1944. *Address:* PO Box 42370, Nairobi, Kenya. *Club:* Naval and Military.

PHILLIPS, (David) Alan; Stipendiary Magistrate for Mid-Glamorgan, since 1975; a Recorder of the Crown Court, since 1974; *b* 21 July 1926; *s* of Stephen Thomas Phillips and Elizabeth Mary Phillips; *m* 1960, Jean Louise (*née* Godsell); two *s*. *Educ:* Llanelli Grammar Sch.; University Coll., Oxford (MA). Left school, 1944. Served War, Army, 1944; commnd, 1946, RWF; Captain (GS), 1947; demobilised, 1948. Oxford, 1948-51. Lectr, 1952-59. Called to Bar, Gray's Inn, 1960. *Recreations:* music, chess, swimming. *Address:* 11 Greenfield Lane, Hoole, Chester CH2 2PA. *T:* Chester 24780.

PHILLIPS, Prof. David Chilton, FRS 1967; BSc, PhD (Wales); FInstP; Professor of Molecular Biophysics and Fellow of Corpus Christi College, Oxford, since Oct. 1966; Member, Medical Research Council, since 1974; *b* 7 March 1924; *o s* of late Charles Harry Phillips and Edith Harriet Phillips (*née* Finney), Ellesmere, Shropshire; *m* 1960, Diana Kathleen (*née* Hutchinson); one *d*. *Educ:* Ellesmere C. of E. Schools; Oswestry Boys' High Sch.; UCW, Cardiff. Radar Officer, RNVR, 1944-47. UCW, 1942-44 and 1947-51. Post-doctoral Fellow, National Research Council of Canada, 1951-53; Research Officer, National Research Laboratories, Ottawa, 1953-55; Research Worker, Davy Faraday Research Lab., Royal Institution, London, 1955-66; Member MRC External Staff, 1960-66. UK Co-ordinator, Internat. Science Hall, Brussels Exhibition, 1958; Member, European Molecular Biology Organization (EMBO), 1964, Mem. Council, 1972-78; Vice-Pres., 1972-73, 1976-77, Biological Sec., 1976-, Royal Society. For. Hon. Member, Amer. Academy of Arts and Sciences, 1968; Hon. Mem., Amer. Society of Biological Chemists, 1969 (Lecturer, 1965); Almroth Wright Memorial Lecturer, 1966; Plenary Lectures, Internat. Biochem. Congress, Tokyo, 1967, Hamburg, 1976, Internat. Crystallography Congress, Kyoto, 1972; Hassel Lecture, Oslo, 1968; Krebs Lecture and Medal, FEBS, 1971; Feldberg Prize, 1968; CIBA Medal, Biochem. Soc., 1971; Royal Medal, Royal Society, 1975. Hon. DSc: Leicester, 1974; Univ. of Wales, 1975. Member, Ed. Board, Journal of Molecular Biology, 1966-76. *Publications:* papers in Acta Cryst. and other journals. *Address:* Molecular Biophysics Laboratory, Zoology Department, South Parks Road, Oxford OX1 3PS. *T:* Oxford 56789; 3 Fairlawn End, Upper Wolvercote, Oxford OX2 8AR. *T:* Oxford 55828; Corpus Christi College, Oxford.

PHILLIPS, Prof. Dewi Zephaniah; Professor of Philosophy, University College, Swansea, since 1971; *b* 24 Nov. 1934; *s* of David Oakley Phillips and Alice Frances Phillips; *m* 1959, Margaret Monica Hanford; three *s*. *Educ:* Swansea Grammar Sch.; UC Swansea (MA); St Catherine's Society, Oxford (BLitt). Asst Lectr, Queen's Coll., Dundee, Univ. of St Andrews, 1961-62; Lectr: at Queen's Coll., Dundee, 1962-63; UC Bangor, 1963-65; UC Swansea, 1965-67; Sen. Lectr, UC Swansea, 1967-71. Vis. Prof., Univ. of Carleton, 1976. *Publications:* The Concept of Prayer, 1965; (ed) Religion and Understanding, 1967; (ed) Saith Ysgrif Ar Grefydd, 1967; (with H. O. Mounce) Moral Practices, 1970; Death and Immortality, 1970; Faith and Philosophical Enquiry, 1970; (with Ilham Dilman) Sense and Delusion, 1971; Athronyddu Am Grefydd, 1974; Religion Without Explanation, 1976; (General Editor) Studies in Ethics and the Philosophy of Religion; Values and Philosophical Enquiry; papers in philosophical jls. *Recreations:* lawn tennis, bowls, darts, supporting Swansea AFC (Sec., Swansea Welsh Schs Assoc.). *Address:* 45 Queen's Road, Sketty, Swansea. *T:* Swansea 23935.

PHILLIPS, Edwin William, MBE 1946; Director, Lazard Bros & Co. Ltd, since 1960; Chairman: Friends Provident Life Office, since 1968; Higgs and Hill, since 1975 (Deputy Chairman, 1974); *b* 29 Jan. 1918; *s* of C. E. Phillips, Chiswick; *m* 1951, P. M. Matusch; two *s*. *Educ:* Latymer Upper Sch. Joined Edward de Stein & Co., Merchant Bankers, 1934. Army, 1939-46; Major, Sherwood Rangers Yeomanry. Rejoined Edward de Stein & Co., 1946, Partner, 1954; merged into Lazard Bros & Co. Ltd, 1960. Director: British Rail Property Bd, 1970; Phoenix Assurance, 1975; Woolwich Equitable Building Soc., 1977. *Recreation:* cricket. *Address:* Send Barns, Send, Surrey. *T:* Guildford 223305. *Club:* MCC.

PHILLIPS, Eric Lawrance, CMG 1963; retired; *b* 23 July 1909; *s* of L. Stanley Phillips, London, NW1; *m* 1938, Phyllis Bray, Artist; two *s* one step *d*. *Educ:* Haileybury Coll.; Balliol Coll., Oxford (Scholar, BA). With Erlangers Ltd, 1932-39. Served War of 1939-45, Captain, RA. Principal, Bd of Trade, 1945, Monopolies Commn, 1949; Asst Secretary, Monopolies Commn, 1951, Bd of Trade, 1952; Under-Sec., Bd of Trade, 1964-69; Sec., Monopolies Commn, 1969-74; consultant to Monopolies and Mergers Commn, 1974-75. *Recreations:* looking at pictures, places and buildings. *Address:* 46 Platts Lane, NW3. *T:* 01-435 7873. *Club:* Royal Automobile.

PHILLIPS, Frank Coles, MA, PhD, FGS; Professor of Mineralogy and Petrology, University of Bristol, 1964-67, retired 1967; now Emeritus; *b* 19 March 1902; *s* of Nicholas Phillips and Kate Salmon; *m* 1929, Seonee Barker; one *s* one *d*. *Educ:* Plymouth Coll.; Corpus Christi Coll., Cambridge. 1st class, Natural Sciences Tripos, Part II (Geology), 1924; Amy Mary Preston Read Studentship, 1925; Fellow of Corpus Christi Coll., Cambridge, 1927-30; University Demonstrator in Mineralogy, 1928-32; Assistant Director of Studies in Natural Sciences, Corpus Christi College, 1931-46; University Lecturer in Mineralogy and Petrology, Cambridge, 1932-46; Lector in Mineralogy, Trinity Coll., 1945-46; Lecturer in Geology, University of Bristol, 1948-50; Reader in Petrology, 1950-64. Sedgwick Prize, 1937; Murchison Fund, Geological Society of London, 1937; Bolitho Gold Medal, Royal Geological Society of Cornwall, 1962. *Publications:* An Introduction to Crystallography, 1947 (4th edn 1971); The Use of Stereographic Projection in Structural Geology, 1954 (3rd edn 1971); revised (14th) edition of G. F. Herbert Smith's Gemstones, 1972; (with G. Windsor) trans. B. Sander, Einführung in die Gefügekunde der geologischen Körper, 1970. Papers on petrology and mineralogy communicated to scientific periodicals. *Recreations:* gardening, carpentry and mechanics. *Address:* Wains Way, Butt's Lawn, Brockenhurst, Hants. *T:* Brockenhurst 3000.

PHILLIPS, Sir Fred (Albert), Kt 1967; CVO 1966; Governor of St Kitts/Nevis/Anguilla, 1967-69; Special Representative, Cable and Wireless (West Indies); *b* 14 May 1918; *s* of Wilbert A. Phillips, Brighton, St Vincent. *Educ:* London Univ. (LLB); Toronto Univ.; McGill Univ. (MCL); Hague Acad. of International Law. Called to the Bar, Middle Temple. Legal Clerk to Attorney-General of St Vincent, 1942-45; Principal Officer, Secretariat, 1945-47; Windward Island: Chief Clerk, Governor's Office, 1948-49; District Officer/Magistrate of District III, 1949-53; Magistrate, Grenada, and Comr of Carriacou, 1953-56; Asst Administrator and MEC, Grenada, 1957-58 (Officer Administrating the Govt, April 1958); Senior Asst Sec., Secretariat, Fedn of W Indies (dealing with constitutional development), 1958-60; Permanent Sec. (Sec. to Cabinet), 1960-62 (when Fedn dissolved); actg Administrator of Montserrat, 1961-62; Sen. Lectr, Univ. of W Indies and Sen. Resident Tutor, Dept of Extra-mural Studies, Barbados, 1962-63; Registrar, Coll. of Arts and Science, Univ. of W Indies, 1963-64; Sen. Res. Fellow, Faculty of Law and Centre for Developing Area Studies, McGill Univ., 1964-65; Guggenheim Fellow,

1965; Administrator of St Kitts, 1966-67. Has attended numerous conferences as a Legal or Constitutional Adviser. KStJ 1968. *Publications:* Freedom in the Caribbean: a study in constitutional change, 1977; papers in various jls. *Recreations:* reading, bridge. *Address:* Chambers, Kingstown, St Vincent, West Indies; PO Box 206, Bridgetown, Barbados.

PHILLIPS, Surgeon Rear-Adm. George, CB 1961; retired 1961; *b* 1902; *s* of Dr G. Phillips; *m* 1930, Ernestine S., *d* of Surgeon Captain J. S. Orwin; one *s* one *d. Educ:* Dover Coll.; Edinburgh Univ. MB, ChB (Edinburgh), 1926; DLO England, 1936. Joined RN 1926; Surgeon Commander, 1938; MO i/c RN Hospital, Malta, 1943; Surgeon Captain, 1950; Surgeon Rear-Admiral, 1958; MO i/c RN Hospital, Trincomalee, 1950; MO i/c RN Hospital, Haslar, 1958; QHS 1958-61. CStJ 1960. *Recreations:* golf, fishing. *Address:* Whinacre, Yelverton, Devon. *T:* Yelverton 2519.

PHILLIPS, Rev. Gordon Lewis; Gresham Professor of Divinity, 1971-73; Chaplain to the English-Speaking Church in Luxembourg, 1972-74; *b* 27 June 1911; *s* of Herbert Lewis and Margaret Gertrude Phillips. *Educ:* Cathedral Sch., Llandaff; Dean Close Sch., Cheltenham; Brasenose Coll., Oxford (scholar; exhibitioner; BA 1st cl. Lit. Hum., 1933; 3rd cl. Theology, 1935; MA 1937); Kelham Theological Coll. Deacon 1937; Priest 1938; Curate, St Julian, Newport, Mon, 1937-40; Rector: Northolt, Mddx, 1940-55; Bloomsbury, Diocese of London, 1956-68; Anglican Chaplain, London Univ., 1955-68; Examg Chaplain to Bishop of St Albans, 1957; Prebendary of Hoxton in St Paul's Cathedral, 1960-68; Proctor, Convocation of London, 1960-65; Dean of Llandaff, 1968-71. Mem., Standing Cttee on Anglican and Roman Catholic Relations; Select Preacher: Univ. of Oxford, 1942, 1964; Univ. of Cambridge, 1963. Hon. Fellow, University Coll., Cardiff, 1970. *Publications:* Seeing and Believing, 1953; Flame in the Mind, 1957; contrib. to Studies in the Fourth Gospel, 1957. *Address:* Tŷ Comel, Cilycwm, Llandovery, Dyfed.

PHILLIPS, Sir Henry (Ellis Isidore), Kt 1964; CMG 1960; MBE 1946; Member, Civil Aviation Authority, since 1975; Director of Companies; *b* 30 Aug. 1914; *s* of late Harry J. Phillips, MBE; *m* 1st, 1941, Vivien Hyamson (marr. diss., 1965); two *s* one *d*; 2nd, 1966, Philippa Cohen. *Educ:* Haberdashers' Sch., Hampstead; University College, London. BA (London) 1936; MA 1939. Inst. of Historical Research, 1936-39. FRHistS. Commissioned in Beds and Herts Regt, 1939; served War of 1939-45, with 5th Bn, becoming Adjutant; POW, Singapore, 1942. Joined Colonial Administrative Service and appointed to Nyasaland, 1946 (until retirement in 1965); Development Secretary, 1952; seconded to Federal Treasury of Rhodesia and Nyasaland, 1953-57, Dep. Sec., 1956; Financial Sec., Nyasaland Govt, 1957-64, and Minister of Finance, 1961-64. Man. Dir, Standard Bank Finance and Development Corp., 1966-72. Hon. Treasurer, Stonham Meml Trust, 1977-. Active in the National Savings and Housing Association movements. *Address:* 34 Ross Court, Putney Hill, SW15. *T:* 01-789 1404. *Clubs:* MCC, Royal Commonwealth Society.

PHILLIPS, Herbert Moore, CMG 1949; Assistant Secretary, HM Civil Service, since 1942 (at present serving with UNESCO, formerly with Ministry of Labour); *b* 7 Feb. 1908; *s* of Herbert Phillips and Beatrice Moore; *m* 1934, Martha Löffler (marr. diss.); one *d. Educ:* St Olave's; Wadham Coll., Oxford. Entered Administrative Class of Home Civil Service, 1931; Principal, Ministry of Labour, 1937; Asst Secretary, 1942; seconded to Foreign Service for three years, 1946-49, as Counsellor to Permanent Delegation of UK at seat of UN; Member of UK Delegations to UNRRA, ILO, World Health Organisation, Economic and Social Council and UN Assembly and Delegate to Economic Commn for Latin America, 1947-50; resumed duty as Asst Secretary, Overseas Branch, Ministry of Labour, 1949; Consultant, Economic Commn for Latin America, 1950-51; Economic Adviser, UNESCO. *Address:* c/o UNESCO, Place Fontenoy, Paris. *Club:* United Oxford & Cambridge University.

PHILLIPS, Sir Horace, KCMG 1973 (CMG 1963); HM Diplomatic Service, retired; *b* 31 May 1917; *s* of Samuel Phillips; *m* 1944, Idina Doreen Morgan; one *s* one *d. Educ:* Hillhead High Sch., Glasgow. Joined Board of Inland Revenue, 1935. Served War of 1939-45, 1940-47. Transf. to FO, Oct. 1947; Acting Vice-Consul, Shiraz, Nov. 1947; Vice-Consul, Bushire, 1948 (Acting Consul, 1948); 1st Secretary and Consul, 1949; Kabul, Oct. 1949; Foreign Office, 1951; 1st Secretary, and Consul, Jedda, 1953; Counsellor, 1956; seconded to Colonial Office, Dec. 1956, as Protectorate Secretary, Aden, until Aug. 1960; Counsellor, British Embassy, Tehran, Oct. 1960; Deputy Political Resident in the Persian Gulf, at Bahrain, 1964-66; Ambassador to Indonesia, 1966-68; High Comr in Tanzania,

1968-72; Ambassador to Turkey, 1973-77. Hon. LLD Glasgow, 1977. *Recreations:* swimming, languages, long-distance car driving especially in the Middle East. *Address:* 34a Sheridan Road, Merton Park, SW19 3HP. *T:* 01-542 3836, 1780. *Clubs:* Travellers', Royal Commonwealth Society.

PHILLIPS, Ivan L.; *see* Lloyd Phillips.

PHILLIPS, Rev. Canon John Bertram, MA (Cantab) 1933; DD (Lambeth), 1966; writer and broadcaster since 1955; *b* 16 Sept. 1906; *e s* of late Philip William Phillips, OBE, and late Emily Maud Powell; *m* 1939, Vera May, *o d* of William Ernest and May Jones; one *d. Educ:* Emanuel Sch., London; Emmanuel Coll. and Ridley Hall, Cambridge. Asst Master, Sherborne Prep. School for boys, 1927-28; Curate, St John's, Penge, London, 1930-33; freelance journalist and Editorial Secretary, Pathfinder Press, 1934-36; Curate, St Margaret's, Lee, London, 1936-40; Vicar of Good Shepherd, Lee, London, 1940-44; Vicar of St John's, Redhill, Surrey, 1945-55; Wiccamical Prebendary of Exceit in Chichester Cathedral, 1957-60. Canon of Salisbury Cathedral, 1964. Hon. DLitt, Exeter, 1970. *Publications:* Letters to Young Churches, 1947; Your God is too Small, 1952; The Gospels in Modern English, 1952; Making Men Whole, 1952; Plain Christianity, 1954; When God was Man, 1954; Appointment with God, 1954; The Young Church in Action, 1955; New Testament Christianity, 1956; The Church under the Cross, 1956; St Luke's Life of Christ, 1956; The Book of Revelation, 1957; Is God at Home?, 1957; The New Testament in Modern English, 1958; A Man Called Jesus, 1959; God our Contemporary, 1960; Good News, 1963; Four Prophets, 1963; Ring of Truth, 1967; Through the Year with J. B. Phillips (ed Denis Duncan), 1974; Peter's Portrait of Jesus, 1976. *Recreations:* painting, photography, music, reading. *Address:* Golden Cap, 17 Gannetts Park, Swanage, Dorset. *T:* 3122.

PHILLIPS, John Fleetwood Stewart, CMG 1965; HM Diplomatic Service; Ambassador at Khartoum, 1973-77; *b* 16 Dec. 1917; *e s* of late Major Herbert Stewart Phillips, 27th Light Cavalry, and Violet Gordon, *d* of late Sir Alexander Pinhey, KCSI; *m* 1949, Mary Gordon Shaw, MB, BS; two *s* two *d. Educ:* Brighton; Worcester Coll., Oxford (Open Exhibition in Classics, MA). Represented Univ. and County intermittently at Rugby football, 1938-39. Served with 1st Bn, Argyll and Sutherland Highlanders in N Africa and Crete (wounded and captured, 1941). Appointed to Sudan Political Service, 1945; served in Kordofan and Blue Nile Provinces. HM Diplomatic Service, 1955, served in Foreign Office; Oriental Secretary in Libya, 1957; Consul-General at Muscat, 1960-63; Counsellor, British Embassy, Amman, 1963-66; Imperial Defence Coll., 1967; Dep. High Comr, Cyprus, 1968; Ambassador to Southern Yemen, 1969-70, to Jordan, 1970-72. *Recreations:* riding, fishing, birdwatching, shell-collecting. *Address:* Southwood, Gordon Road, Horsham, Sussex. *T:* Horsham 2894. *Clubs:* Travellers', Royal Commonwealth Society.

PHILLIPS, John Francis, CBE 1977 (OBE 1957); Deputy Chairman, Eggs Authority, since 1971; President, Institute of Chartered Secretaries and Administrators, 1977 (Secretary and Chief Executive, 1957-76; Member Council, 1976-); *b* 1911; *e s* of late F. W. Phillips and late Margaret (*née* Gillan); *m* 1937, Olive M. Royer; one *s* two *d. Educ:* Cardinal Vaughan Sch.; London Univ.; Trinity Hall, Cambridge. LLB (Hons) London; LLB (1st Cl. Hons), LLM Cantab. Barrister-at-law, Gray's Inn, 1944. Civil Servant (Lord Chancellor's Dept, Royal Courts of Justice), 1933-44; Parly Sec. and Asst Gen. Sec., Nat. Farmers' Union of England and Wales, 1945-57. Member: Council, Inst. of Arbitrators, 1969- (Vice-Pres., 1974-76; Pres., 1976-77); Gen. Cttee, Bar Assoc. for Commerce, Finance and Industry, 1967- (Vice-Chm., 1976-); Council for Accreditation of Correspondence Colls, 1969- (Hon. Treas., 1969-; Chm., 1975-); British Egg Marketing Bd, 1969-71; Departmental Cttee of Enquiry into Fowl Pest, 1971; Vice-Chm., Provident Assoc. for Medical Care (Private Patients' Plan), 1972- (Dir, 1958-); Vice-Chm. and Mem., Business Educn Council, 1974-; Chairman: Jt Cttee for Awards in Business Studies and Public Admin., 1968-75 (Mem. Jt Cttee for Awards, 1960-75); Associated Examining Bd, GCE, 1976- (Mem., 1958-; Vice-Chm., 1973-76); Houghton Poultry Res. Station, 1976- (Governor, 1973-); Governor: Christ's Hospital, 1957-; Crossways Trust, 1959-71 (Financial Advisor, 1966-71); Nuffield Nursing Homes Trust, 1975-; Mem. Council and Exec. Cttee, Animal Health Trust, 1976-; Deleg. to Internat. Labour Conf., 1950-56. FCIS 1958; FIArb 1966; FBIM (Council of Inst. 1969-74). *Publications:* The Agriculture Act, 1947, 1948; Heywood and Massey's Lunacy Practice, 1939; many articles on aspects of law relating to land and agriculture. *Recreation:* travel. *Address:* 17 Ossulton Way, Hampstead Garden Suburb, N2; (office) 16 Park Crescent, W1. *T:* 01-455 8460. *Clubs:* Athenæum, United Oxford & Cambridge University, City Livery.

PHILLIPS, Sir John (Grant), KBE 1972 (CBE 1968); Governor and Chairman of Board, Reserve Bank of Australia, 1968-75; *b* 13 March 1911; *s* of Oswald and Ethel Phillips, Sydney; *m* 1935, Mary W. Debenham; two *s* two *d*. *Educ:* C of E Grammar Sch., Sydney; University of Sydney (BEc). Research Officer, NSW Retail Traders' Assoc., 1932-35; Econ. Asst, Royal Commn Monetary and Banking Systems, 1936-37; Econ. Dept, Commonwealth Bank of Australia, 1937-51; Investment Adviser, Commonwealth Bank, 1954-60; Dep. Governor and Dep. Chairman of Board, Reserve Bank of Australia, 1960-68. Leader, Australian Delegation to 6th Conf. GATT, Geneva, 1951; Member: Council, Macquarie Univ., 1967-; Bd, Howard Florey Inst. of Experimental Physiology and Medicine, 1971-; Adv. Cttee, The Australian Birthright Movement, Sydney Br., 1971-; Dir, Lend Lease Corp. Ltd, 1976-. *Recreations:* lawn bowls, contract bridge. *Address:* 2/25 Marshall Street, Manly, NSW 2095, Australia. *Club:* University (Sydney).

PHILLIPS, Prof. John Guest, PhD, DSc; Professor of Zoology, University of Hull, since 1967; Director, Wolfson Laboratory for Research in Geronotology, since 1975; *b* 13 June 1933; *s* of Owen Gwynne Phillips and Dorothy Constance Phillips; *m* 1961, Jacqueline Ann Myles-White; two *s*. *Educ:* Llanelli Grammar Sch.; Univ. of Liverpool. BSc 1954, PhD 1957, Liverpool; DSc Hong Kong 1967; FIBiol; FRSocMed. Commonwealth Fund Fellow, Yale Univ., 1957-59; Fellow, Davenport Coll., Yale Univ., 1957-59; Lectr in Zoology, Univ. of Sheffield, 1959-62; Vis. Asst Prof., Univ. of BC, 1959; Milton Res. Assoc., Harvard Univ., 1960; Prof. of Zoology, Univ. of Hong Kong, 1962-67; Dean of Faculty of Science, Hong Kong, 1965-66, acting Vice-Chancellor, 1966. Vis. Prof. of Biology, Univ. of California, 1975. Member: Commonwealth Scholarships Commn, 1968-; Council, Marine Biological Assoc. of UK, 1969-71; Biology Cttee, SRC, 1975-; Cttee of Soc. for Endocrinology, 1971-74, 1975-; Treasurer, Soc. for Endocrinology, 1975-; Council of Management, Jl of Endocrinology, 1971-; Humberside AHA, 1974-; Humberside Area Nurse Educn Adv. Cttee (Chm., 1976-); Internat. Cttee for Comparative Endocrinology, 1974-; Internat. Cttee for Endocrinology, 1976-; Pres. Yorkshire Br., Inst. Biol., 1969-72; Governor: Endsleigh Coll. of Educn, Hull, 1967-77; St Anne's Special Sch., Hull, 1975-. Zoological Soc. of London Scientific Medal, 1970; Medal of Soc. for Endocrinology, 1971. *Publications:* Hormones and the Environment, 1971; Environmental Physiology, 1975; numerous papers in zoological, endocrinological and physiological jls. *Recreations:* gardening, squash rackets, music, travel. *Address:* Tremayne Lodge, Brough, N Humberside. *T:* Brough 668574. *Club:* Royal Commonwealth Society.

PHILLIPS, Rt. Rev. John Henry Lawrence; Priest-in-charge, West with East Lulworth, since 1975; *b* 2 Feb. 1910; *s* of Rev. H. L. Phillips, Wimborne, Dorset; *m* 1936, Morna, *d* of E. H. W. Winfield-King, OBE; one *s* three *d*. *Educ:* Weymouth Coll.; Trinity Hall, Cambridge, BA 1932; MA 1937; Ridley Hall, Cambridge, 1932-34. Deacon, 1934; priest, 1935. Curate of Christ Church, Harrogate, 1934-35; Curate of Methley, 1935-38; Rector of Farnley, Leeds, 1938-45; Surrogate, 1939-45; Chaplain RNVR, 1942-45; Director of Service Ordination Candidates, 1945-47; General Secretary Central Advisory Council of Training for the Ministry, 1947-49; Vicar of Radcliffe-on-Trent and of Shelford, 1949-57; Archdeacon of Nottingham, 1949-60; Rector of Clifton with Glapton, 1958-60; Bishop of Portsmouth, 1960-75. Chaplain to the Queen, 1959-60. Provincial Grand Master, Masonic Order, Hampshire and Isle of Wight, 1975. *Recreations:* cricket, golf, Rugby football, etc. *Address:* Finches, West Lulworth, Wareham, Dorset. *T:* West Lulworth 250. *Club:* Naval.

PHILLIPS, Hon. Sir (John) Raymond, Kt 1971; MC 1945; Hon. **Mr Justice Phillips;** Judge of High Court of Justice, Queen's Bench Division, since 1971; *b* 20 Nov. 1915; *o* surv. *s* of David Rupert and Amy Isabel Phillips, Radyr, Glam; *m* 1951, Hazel Bradbury Evans, *o d* of T. John Evans, Cyncoed, Cardiff; two *s*. *Educ:* Rugby; Balliol Coll., Oxford (MA, BCL). Barrister, Gray's Inn, 1939; Arden Scholar; Bencher, 1965; QC 1968. Served 3rd Medium Regt, RA, 1940-45 (despatches). Practised at Bar, 1946-71; Wales and Chester Circuit, 1939; Jun. Counsel, Inland Revenue (Rating Valuation), 1958-63; Jun. Counsel, Inland Revenue (Common Law), 1963-68. Dep. Chm., Glamorgan QS, 1964-71. Mem., Parole Bd, 1975-77, Vice-Chm., 1976; Pres., Employment Appeal Tribunal, 1976-. *Publication:* (ed) The Belsen Trial. *Address:* The Elms, Park Road, Teddington, Middx. *T:* 01-977 1584; Royal Courts of Justice, WC2A 2LL. *Clubs:* United Oxford & Cambridge University; Cardiff and County (Cardiff).

PHILLIPS, Sir Leslie (Walter), Kt 1962; CBE 1947; Chairman, Baltic Exchange, 1963-65 (Vice-Chairman 1961-63); *b* 12 Aug. 1894; 2nd *s* of late Charles Phillips; *m* 1915, Mary (*d* 1971), *d* of late John Corby; one *s*; *m* 1972, Patricia, *d* of late Claude Palmer. Chm., T. A. Jones Co. Ltd, Grain Brokers, 1943-70. President National Federation of Corn Trade Associations, 1949-52; President, London Corn Trade Assoc., 1959-60; Vice-Chairman, Sugar Board, 1966-68. Director of Freight, Ministry of Food, 1941-45; Controller of Freight and Warehousing, 1946-47. *Address:* 5 Newlands Avenue, Bexhill-on-Sea, E Sussex. *T:* Bexhill 935.

PHILLIPS, Air Cdre Manfred Norman; retired, RAF Medical Branch; Consultant Radiologist, RAF Hospital, Ely, 1968-77; *b* 6 Nov. 1912; *s* of Lewis and Norah Phillips, Portsmouth; *m* 1942, Dorothy Ellen (*née* Green); two *s*. *Educ:* Liverpool Coll.; Liverpool Univ. Med. Sch.; Middlesex Hospital. MB, ChB 1936; DMRD 1954. *Publications:* articles in Brit. Jl Clinical Practice and Brit. Jl Radiology. *Recreations:* gardening, golf, walking. *Address:* Quaney, 83C Cambridge Road, Ely, Cambs. *T:* Ely 3539. *Club:* Royal Air Force.

PHILLIPS, Captain Mark Anthony Peter, CVO 1974; ADC(P); 1st The Queen's Dragoon Guards; with Army Training Directorate, Ministry of Defence, since 1977; *b* 22 Sept. 1948; *s* of P. W. G. Phillips, MC, and Anne Patricia (*née* Tiarks); *m* 1973, HRH The Princess Anne; one *s*. *Educ:* Marlborough Coll.; RMA Sandhurst. Joined 1st The Queen's Dragoon Guards, July 1969; Regimental duty, 1969-74; Company Instructor, RMA Sandhurst, 1974-77. Personal ADC to HM the Queen, 1974-. In Three Day Equestrian Event, GB winning teams: Team Championships: World, 1970; European, 1971; Olympic Gold Medallists (Team), Olympic Games, Munich, 1972; Mem., Equestrian Team (Reserve), Olympic Games, Montreal, 1976. Liveryman; Farriers' Co.; Farmers' Co; Freeman: Saddlers' Co.; Loriners Co.; City of London. *Recreations:* riding, Rugby football, athletics. *Address:* Buckingham Palace, SW1. *Club:* (Hon. Mem.) Buck's.
See also under Royal Family.

PHILLIPS, Prof. Neville Crompton, CMG 1973; Research Professor (Vice-Chancellor and Rector, 1966-77), University of Canterbury, Christchurch, New Zealand; *b* 7 March 1916; 2nd *s* of Samuel and Clara Phillips, Christchurch, NZ; *m* 1940, Pauline Beatrice, 3rd *d* of Selby and Dorothy Palmer, Te Aratipi, Havelock North, NZ; one *s* two *d*. *Educ:* Dannevirke High Sch.; Palmerston North Boys' High Sch.; Canterbury University College; Merton Coll., Oxford. BA (NZ) 1936; MA 21938; Hon. LittD Cantuar 1977; NZ University Post-Grad. Schol. in Arts, Arnold Atkinson Prizeman, 1938; Journalist, Sun and Press, Christchurch, 1932-38; read PPE at Oxford, 1938-39; RA (Gunner, subseq. Major), 1939-46; service in Tunisia and Italy (despatches). Lecturer in History and Political Science, Canterbury University College, 1946-47; Senior Lecturer, 1948; Prof. of History and Political Science, 1949-62; Prof. of History, 1962-66; Emeritus Prof., 1966; Chairman, Canterbury Centennial Provincial Historical Cttee, 1948-66; Secondary Sch. Bds; 1st Pres., Canterbury Historical Assoc., 1953; Editorial Adviser, NZ War Histories, 1957-67; US Dept of State Leader Grantee, 1966; Member: Council, Canterbury Manufacturers' Assoc., 1967-77; Christchurch Teachers' Coll. Council, 1968-76; NZ Vice-Chancellors' Cttee, 1966-77 (Chm., 1973-74); Council, Assoc. of Commonwealth Univs, 1973-74; NZ Council Educational Research, 1973-77. Queen's Silver Jubilee Medal, 1977. *Publications:* Italy, vol. 1 (The Sangro to Cassino), 1957; Yorkshire and English National Politics, 1783-84, 1961; The Role of the University in Professional Education, 1970; (ed) A History of the University of Canterbury, 1873-1973, 1973; articles, mainly on eighteenth-century English politics, in English and NZ jls. *Recreations:* reading history, watching cricket, things Italian. *Address:* 122 Straven Road, Christchurch 1, New Zealand. *T:* 487-559. *Club:* University (Christchurch).

PHILLIPS, Prof. Owen Hood, DCL, MA, Oxon; MA, LLB, Dublin; LLM Birmingham; QC 1970; JP; Visiting Professor in English Law, University College at Buckingham, since 1974; *b* 30 Sept. 1907; *yr s* of late Surgeon-Captain J. E. Hood Phillips, RN, Portsmouth; *m* 1949, Lucy Mary Carden, 3rd *d* of late Arnold Philip, and formerly Lecturer in Physical Educn, Univ. of Birmingham. *Educ:* Weymouth Coll.; Merton Coll., Oxford. Asst Lecturer in Laws, King's Coll., London, 1931-35; Lectr in General Jurisprudence, Univ. of Dublin (Trinity Coll.), 1935-37; Reader in English Law, Univ. of London, 1937-46; Vice-Dean of Faculty of Laws, King's Coll., London, 1937-40; University of Birmingham: Barber Prof. of Jurisprudence, 1946-74; Dean, Faculty of Law, and Dir Legal Studies, 1949-68, Public Orator, 1950-62, Vice-Principal and Pro-Vice-Chancellor, 1971-74. Min. of Labour and National Service, 1940; Min. of Aircraft

Production, 1940-45; adviser to Singapore Constitutional Commn, 1953-54; delegate to Malta Round Table Conf., 1955, to Malta Constitutional Conf., 1958. Governor King Edward VI Schs, Birmingham, 1951-76 (Bailiff, 1958-59); President: Soc. of Public Teachers of Law, 1963-64; British and Irish Assoc. of Law Librarians, 1972-76; Hon. Mem., Midland and Oxford Circuit Bar Mess. *Publications:* Principles of English Law and the Constitution, 1939; Constitutional and Administrative Law, 6th edn (with P. Jackson), 1978; Leading Cases in Constitutional and Administrative Law, 4th edn, 1973; A First Book of English Law, 7th edn (with A. H. Hudson), 1977; Reform of the Constitution, 1970; Shakespeare and the Lawyers, 1972; contributions to various legal periodicals. *Address:* 24 Heaton Drive, Edgbaston, Birmingham B15 3LW. *T:* 021-454 2042; Easter Cottage, Clee St Margaret, Salop.

PHILLIPS, Prof. Owen Martin, FRS 1968; Decker Professor of Science and Engineering, Johns Hopkins University, since 1975; *b* 30 Dec. 1930; *s* of Richard Keith Phillips and Madeline Lofts; *m* 1953, Merle Winifred Simons; two *s* two *d. Educ:* University of Sydney; Trinity Coll., Cambridge Univ. ICI Fellow, Cambridge, 1955-57; Fellow, St John's Coll., Cambridge, 1957-60; Asst Prof., 1957-60, Assoc. Prof., 1960-63, Johns Hopkins Univ.; Asst Director of Research, Cambridge, 1961-64; Prof. of Geophysical Mechanics, Johns Hopkins Univ., 1963-68, of Geophysics, 1968-75. Assoc. Editor Jl of Fluid Mechanics, 1964-; Mem. Council, Nat. Center of Atmospheric Research, Boulder, Colorado, 1964-68; US Nat. Cttee Global Atmospheric Research Project, 1968. Mem.-at-large, Amer. Meteorol. Soc. Publications Commn, 1971-75; Sec., Bd of Trustees, Chesapeake Res. Consortium, 1973-74 (Trustee, 1972-75). Adams Prize, Univ. of Cambridge, 1965; Sverdrup Gold Medal, Amer. Metereol. Soc., 1975. *Publications:* The Dynamics of the Upper Ocean, 1966, 3rd edn 1976; Russian edn 1968; The Heart of the Earth, 1968, Italian edns 1970, 1975; various scientific papers in Jl Fluid Mechanics, Proc. Cambridge Philos. Soc., Jl Marine Research, Proc. Royal Society, Deep Sea Research, Journal Geophys. Research. *Address:* 23 Merrymount Road, Baltimore, Maryland 21210, USA. *T:* 433-7195. *Clubs:* Johns Hopkins (Baltimore), Hamilton Street (Baltimore); Quissett Yacht (Mass.)

PHILLIPS, Patrick Laurence; Joint Managing-Director (Director, 1938) of Ernest Brown & Phillips Ltd, proprietors of the Leicester Galleries, London, since 1960; *b* 1 July 1912; *e s* of late Cecil Laurence Phillips, co-founder of the Leicester Galleries, 1902, and Eileen Christina (*née* Slattery); *m* 1945, Margaret Elinor, *d* of late Ernest Lewin Chapman; two *s. Educ:* Stonyhurst. Art studies in Paris and in Museums of Europe. Joined Leicester Galleries, 1931. Served War, 8th Army, in Western Desert and Italy, 1940-45; Staff Officer, HQ, AA Command, 1945-46. Organizer of Festival Exhibition "Henry Moore at King's Lynn", held throughout the town, 1964. Specialist in 19th and 20th century British and French pictures, drawings, prints, sculpture and the work of Australian artists. *Recreations:* the Arts, travel, walking. *Address:* 164 Coleherne Court, SW5. *T:* 01-373 0304; Brandon House, Horn Hill, Dartmouth. *Club:* Dartmouth Yacht.

PHILLIPS, Sir Raymond; see Phillips, Sir J. R.

PHILLIPS, Reginald Arthur, CMG 1965; OBE 1951; Deputy Director-General, British Council, 1966-73, retired; *b* 31 Jan. 1913; *y s* of late James and Catherine Ann Phillips, Tredegar, Mon; *m* 1939, Doris Tate, *d* of William and Angelina Tate, São Paulo, Brazil; one *s* two *d. Educ:* Tredegar Grammar Sch.; Balliol Coll., Oxford (MA). Asst Master, St Paul's School, Brazil, 1936; Lecturer, Anglo-Brazilian Cultural Society, 1937-39. War of 1939-45: Intelligence Corps (Major), 1940-46. British Council: Latin America Dept, 1947; Home Div., 1948-54; Colonies Dept, 1954-57; Controller, Commonwealth Div., 1957-59; Controller, Finance Div., 1959-62; Assistant Director-General, 1962-66. *Recreations:* golf, walking, television, gardening. *Address:* 76 Chiltley Way, Liphook, Hants. *T:* Liphook 722610. *Club:* Athenæum.

PHILLIPS, Surgeon Rear-Adm. Rex Philip, CB 1972; OBE 1963; Medical Officer-in-Charge, Royal Naval Hospital, Plymouth, 1969-72, retired; *b* 17 May 1913; 2nd *s* of William John Phillips, late Consultant Anaesthetist at Royal Victoria Infirmary, Newcastle upon Tyne, and Nora Graham Phillips; *m* 1939, Gill Foley; two *s. Educ:* Epsom Coll.; Coll. of Med., Newcastle upon Tyne, Univ. of Durham (now Univ. of Newcastle upon Tyne). Qual. MB, BS 1937; Ho. Surg., Ingham Infirmary, S Shields, 1938. Joined RN, 1939; served War of 1939-45: HMS Rochester, 1939-41; Royal Marines, 1941-43; HMS Simba, 1943-45. HMS Excellent, 1945-47; qual. Dip. in Ophthalmology (London), 1948; HMS Implacable, Fleet MO,

1949-51; Specialist in Ophthalmology: HMS Ganges, 1951-53; Central Air Med. Bd, 1953-55; RN Hosp., Malta (Senior), 1955-57; Admty Adv. in Ophth. to Med. Dir-Gen., 1957-65; Surg. Captain 1963; SMO, RN Hosp., Malta, 1965-68; Staff MO to Flag Officer Submarines, 1968-69. QHS 1969-72. CStJ 1970. *Recreations:* golf, bridge. *Address:* Langstone House, Langstone Village, Havant, Hants. *T:* Havant 4668. *Club:* Royal Western Yacht (Plymouth).

PHILLIPS, Robin; Artistic Director, Stratford Festival Theatre, National Theatre of Canada, since 1974; *b* 28 Feb. 1942; *s* of James William Phillips and Ellen Anne (*née* Barfoot). *Educ:* Midhurst Grammar School, Sussex. Trained as director, actor and designer, Bristol Old Vic Co.; first appearance, Bristol, as Mr Puff in The Critic, 1959; Associate Dir, Bristol Old Vic, 1960-61; played at Lyric, Hammersmith, 1961, Chichester Fest., 1962, and with Oxford Playhouse Co., 1964. Asst Dir, Timon of Athens and Hamlet, Royal Shakespeare Co., Stratford upon Avon, 1965; Dir or Associate Dir, 1966-69: Hampstead, Exeter, (Thorndike) Leatherhead; Directed: Tiny Alice, RSC, Aldwych, 1970; Abelard and Heloise, Wyndhams and Broadway; The Two Gentlemen of Verona, Stratford and Aldwych, 1970; Caesar and Cleopatra and Dear Antoine, Chichester, 1971; Miss Julie, for RCS (also directed film); played Dubidat in The Doctor's Dilemma and directed The Lady's Not for Burning and The Beggar's Opera, Chichester, 1972. Formed Company Theatre and apptd Artistic Dir, Greenwich Th., 1973: plays directed include: The Three Sisters, Rosmerholm, Zorba. Artistic Dir, Stratford Festival, Canada, 1974-; prodns in 1975 season incl.: The Two Gentlemen of Verona and The Comedy of Errors (both also Nat. tour), Measure for Measure, Trumpets and Drums and The Importance of Being Earnest. *Films* , as actor: Decline and Fall, David Copperfield (title part), Tales from the Crypt. *TV:* Wilfred Desert in The Forsyte Saga, Constantin in The Seagull. *Address:* 151 Douglas Street, Stratford, Ontario, Canada. *T:* 519-271-4040.

PHILLIPS, Sir Robin Francis, 3rd Bt, *cr* 1912; *b* 29 July 1940; *s* of Sir Lionel Francis Phillips, 2nd Bt, and Camilla Mary, *er d* of late Hugh Parker, 22 Chapel Street, Belgrave Square, SW1; *S* father, 1944. *Educ:* Aiglon Coll., Switzerland. *Heir:* none. *Address:* 12 Manson Mews, Queen's Gate, SW7.

PHILLIPS, Sydney William Charles, CB 1955; Second Civil Service Commissioner, 1968-70, a part-time Commissioner, 1970-72; *b* 1 Dec. 1908; *s* of late Frederick Charles and Elizabeth Phillips; *m* 1932, Phyllis, *d* of late James Spence; two *s. Educ:* Bridport Grammar Sch.; University College, London. Administrative Asst, University College, Hull, 1932-37; Asst Registrar, Liverpool Univ., 1937-45; seconded to Min. of Works, 1941-43; Min. of Town and Country Planning, 1943-51 (Principal Private Sec. to Minister, 1943-44); Asst Sec., 1944; Under-Sec., Min. of Housing and Local Govt, 1952-68, Dir of Establishments, 1963-68. Fellow, UCL, 1969. *Recreations:* walking and gardening. *Address:* Innisfree, Higher Drive, Purley, Surrey. *T:* 01-660 8617. *Club:* Royal Commonwealth Society.

PHILLPOTTS, Christopher Louis George, CMG 1957; HM Diplomatic Service, retired; *b* 23 April 1915; *s* of Admiral Edward Montgomery Phillpotts, CB, and Violet Selina (*née* Cockburn); *m* 1942, Vivien Chanter-Bowden; one *s* one *d. Educ:* Royal Naval Coll., Dartmouth. Served in Royal Navy, 1932-43 (despatches twice). Joined Foreign Office, Nov. 1943. Appointed Vice-Consul, Malmö, March 1945; transferred Foreign Office, July 1945; Copenhagen, 3rd Secretary, 1947; 2nd Secretary, 1949; Foreign Office, 1951; Athens, 1st Secretary, 1953; Counsellor HM Embassy, Paris, 1957. Transferred Foreign Office, April 1962; Counsellor, Washington, 1964-66; Foreign and Commonwealth Office, 1966-70. *Recreation:* theatre. *Address:* 27 Merrick Square, SE1. *T:* 01-407 5995. *Clubs:* White's, Pratt's, Army and Navy.

PHILLPOTTS, (Mary) Adelaide Eden, (Mrs Nicholas Ross); writer; *b* Ealing, Middlesex; *d* of late Eden Phillpotts; *m* 1951, Nicholas Ross. *Publications:* novels: The Friend, 1923; Lodgers in London, 1926; Tomek, the Sculptor, 1927; A Marriage, 1928; The Atoning Years, 1929; Yellow Sands, 1930; The Youth of Jacob Ackner, 1931; The Founder of Shandon, 1932; The Growing World, 1934; Onward Journey, 1936; Broken Allegiance, 1937; What's Happened to Rankin?, 1938; The Gallant Heart, 1939; The Round of Life, 1940; Laugh with Me, 1941; Our Little Town, 1942; From Jane to John, 1943; The Adventurers, 1944; The Lodestar, 1946; The Fosterling, 1949; Stubborn Earth, 1951; plays: Arachne, 1920; Savitri the Faithful, 1923; Camillus and the Schoolmaster, 1923; Akhnaton, 1926; (with Eden Phillpotts) Yellow Sands, 1926; Laugh With Me, 1938; poetry: Illyrion, and other Poems, 1916; A Song of

Man, 1959; *travel:* Panorama of the World, 1969; *miscellaneous:* Man, a Fable, 1922; (selected with Nicholas Ross) Letters to Nicholas Ross from J. C. Powys (ed A. Uphill), 1971; A Wild Flower Wreath, 1975. *Address:* Cobblestones, Kilkhampton, Bude, Cornwall.

PHILO, Gordon Charles George, CMG 1970; MC 1944; HM Diplomatic Service; Foreign and Commonwealth Office since 1969; *b* 8 Jan. 1920; *s* of Charles Gilbert Philo and Nellie Philo (*née* Pinnock); *m* 1952, Mavis (Vicky) Ella, *d* of John Ford Galsworthy and Sybel Victoria Galsworthy (*née* Strachan). *Educ:* Haberdashers' Aske's Hampstead Sch.; Wadham Coll., Oxford. Methuen Scholar in Modern History, Wadham Coll., 1938. Served War, HM Forces, 1940-46: Royal West African Frontier Force, 1942-43; Airborne Forces, Normandy and Europe, 1944-45; India 1945-46. Alexander Korda Scholar, The Sorbonne, 1948-49; Lectr in Modern History, Wadham Coll., 1949-50; Foundn Mem., St Antony's Coll., Oxford, 1950-51. Foreign Office, 1951; Russian course, Christ's Coll., Cambridge, 1952-53; Istanbul, Third Sec., 1954-57; Ankara, Second Sec., 1957-58; FO, 1958-63; Kuala Lumpur, First Sec., 1963-67; FO, 1968; Consul-Gen., Hanoi, 1968-69. Kesatria Mangku Negara (Hon.), Order of Malaysia, 1968. *Recreations:* travel, writing. *Address:* 10 Abercorn Close, NW8. *T:* 01-286 9597. *Club:* Athenæum.

PHILP, Lieut-Colonel Robert, MC, TD; DL; *b* 12 July 1896; *s* of Major J. Philp, TD, JP; *m* 1924, Jane Black Adamson; one *d.* *Educ:* Dollar Academy. Served War 1914-18 (France), 1939-45 (India and Burma). Hon. Sheriff, Clackmannanshire, 1962-, DL 1959; Vice-Lieutenant, County of Clackmannan, 1966-73. *Address:* 1 Castle Park, Tulliallan, Kincardine, Alloa, Clackmannanshire.

PHILPOT, Oliver Lawrence Spurling, MC 1944; DFC 1941; Managing Director, Remploy Ltd, since 1974; *b* Vancouver, BC, Canada, 6 March 1913; *s* of Lawrence Benjamin Philpot, London, and Catherine Barbara (*née* Spurling), Bedford; *m* 1st, 1938 (marr. diss. 1951); one *s* two *d*; 2nd, 1954, Rosl Widhalm, BA Hons History, PhD (Lond.), Vienna; one *s* one *d.* *Educ:* Queen Mary Sch., N Vancouver; Aymestrey Court, Worcester; Radley Coll.; Worcester Coll., Oxford (BA Hons PPE). RAFVR: Pilot, 42 Torpedo/Bomber Sqdn, RAF Coastal Comd, 1940; shot down off Norway, 1941; 5 prison camps, Germany and Poland; escaped to Sweden and Scotland, as 3rd man in Wooden Horse, from Stalag Luft III at Sagan, Silesia, 1943; Sen. Scientific Officer, Air Min., 1944 (wrote 33 RAF Stations Manpower Survey, 1944). Management Trainee, Unilever Ltd, 1934; Asst (commercial) Sec., Unilever Home Margarine Exec., 1936; Exec., Maypole Dairy Ltd, 1946; Chm., Trufood Ltd, 1948; Office Manager, Unilever House, EC4, 1950; Gen. Manager (admin.), T. Walls & Sons Ltd, 1951; Coast-to-Coast Lecture Tour in N America on own book, Stolen Journey, with Peat Agency, Canadian Clubs and USAAF, 1952; Dir, Arthur Woollacott & Rappings Ltd, 1953; Chm. and Man. Dir, Spirella Co. of Great Britain Ltd, 1956; Man. Dir, Venesta (later Aluminium) Foils Ltd, 1959; Exec., Union International Ltd, 1962 (also Dep. Chm. and Chief Exec., Fropax Eskimo Food Ltd, 1965-67), i/c Lonsdale & Thompson Ltd, John Layton Ltd, Merseyside Food Products Ltd, Union Distribution Co. Ltd, Weddel Pharmaceuticals Ltd, John Gardner (Printers) Ltd, and Union Internat. Res. Centre. Chairman: Royal Air Forces Escaping Soc., and RAFES Charitable Fund, 2 terms, 1963-69. Fights local environmental battles. *Publication:* Stolen Journey, 1950 (5th edn 1951,repr. 1970; Swedish, Norwegian and Amer. edns, 1951-52; paperback 1954, repr. 4 times, 1962-66). *Recreations:* the river; talking and walking; idling; listening to sermons; reading Financial Times and obituaries in Lancet; films; following the political scene. *Address:* 30 Abingdon Villas, Kensington, W8 6BX. *T:* 01-937 6013. *Clubs:* London Rowing, Ends of the Earth, Society of Authors, United Oxford & Cambridge University, Institute of Directors, Goldfish, RAF Escaping Society; Worcester College Society (London and Oxford).

PHILPOTT, Air Vice-Marshal Peter Theodore, CB 1966; CBE 1954 (OBE 1945); Director of Service Intelligence, Ministry of Defence, 1968-70, retired; *b* 20 March 1915; *s* of late Rev. and Mrs R. G. K. F. Philpott, Worcester; *m* 1942, Marie, *d* of Charles Griffin, Malvern; two *d.* *Educ:* Malvern Coll.; RAF Coll., Cranwell, 1933; No. 31 Sqn, India, 1936-41; Staff Coll., Quetta, 1941; Directorate of Op. Trg., Air Ministry, 1942-44; OC, RAF, Horsham St Faith, 1945-46; JSSC, 1947; HQ, Fighter Command, 1948-51; OC, RAF Deversoir, 1952-54; DD Policy, Air Ministry, 1954-56; IDC Student, 1957; Director of Policy and Plans, Air Ministry, 1958-61; Senior RAF Directing Staff, Imperial Defence Coll., 1961-63; AOC No. 23 Group, Flying Training Comd, 1963-65; Head of British Defence Liaison Staff,

Canberra, 1965-68. *Address:* c/o Lloyds Bank Ltd (Cox's and King's Branch), 6 Pall Mall, SW1. *Club:* Royal Air Force.

PHILPS, Dr Frank Richard, MBE 1946; retired; Consultant in Exfoliative Cytology, University College Hospital, WC1, 1960-73; Director, Joint Royal Free and University College Hospitals, Department of Cytology, 1972-73; *b* 9 March 1914; *s* of Francis John Philps and Matilda Ann Philps (*née* Healey); *m* 1941, Emma L. F. M. Schmidt; two *s* one *d.* *Educ:* Christ's Hospital, Horsham, Sussex. MRCS, LRCP, 1939; MB, BS, 1939; DPH 1947; MD London, 1952; FRCPath, 1966; Fellow, International Academy of Cytology, 1967. RAF Medical Service, 1940-46. Junior Hospital Appointments, UCH, 1950-54; Consultant Pathologist, Eastbourne, 1954-64; Research Asst, UCH, 1955-60. Hon. Cons. in Cytology, Royal Free Hosp., 1972-73. Producer, with wife, Wild Life Series of Educational Nature Films and films on pottery making, for Educational Foundation for Visual Aids; BBC Nature Film Prize, 1963; Council for Nature Film Prize, 1966. *Publications:* A Short Manual of Respiratory Cytology, 1964; Watching Wild Life, 1968. Papers on Cytology to several medical journals, 1954-67. *Recreations:* living in the country; watching wild animals and filming them. *Address:* Woodlands, Sydenham Wood, Lewdown, Okehampton EX20 4PP. *T:* Chillaton 347.

PHIPPS, family name of **Marquess of Normanby.**

PHIPPS, Colin Barry, PhD; JP; MP (Lab) Dudley West since 1974; Chairman, Dr Colin Phipps and Partners Ltd; *b* 23 July 1934; *s* of Edgar Reeves Phipps and Winifred Elsie Phipps (*née* Carroll); *m* 1956, Marion May Phipps (*née* Lawrey); two *s* two *d.* *Educ:* Townfield Elem. Sch., Hayes, Mddx; Acton County; Swansea Grammar; University Coll. London; Birmingham Univ. BSc, 1st cl. Hons Geol. London 1955; PhD, Geol. Birm. 1957. Royal Dutch/Shell Geologist: Holland, Venezuela, USA, 1957-64; Consultant Petroleum Geologist, 1964-. Contested (Lab), Walthamstow East, 1969. FGS 1956, FInstPet 1972. *Publications:* contrib.: Qly Jl Geol. Soc., Geol. Mag., Geol. Jl, etc. *Recreations:* swimming, reading, collecting English water colours. *Address:* Mathon Court, Mathon, Malvern WR13 5NZ. *T:* Malvern 5606. *Club:* Reform.

PHIPPS, John Constantine; Metropolitan Magistrate, 1959-75; *b* 19 Jan. 1910; *er s* of Sir Edmund Phipps, CB, and Margaret Percy, *d* of late Dame Jessie Phipps, DBE; *m* 1st, 1945, Priscilla Russell Cooke (*d* 1947); 2nd, 1949, Sheila (formerly Dilke; *née* Seeds) (from whom he obtained a divorce 1965); two *d*; 3rd, 1965, Hermione Deedes. *Educ:* Winchester Coll.; Trinity Coll., Oxford. Called to Bar, Middle Temple, 1933. RE (TA) 1938; War Office, 1940; Intelligence Corps, Captain, 1941, Major, 1943; Personal Asst to Lord Justice Lawrence (later 1st Baron Oaksey), President of International Military Tribunal, Nuremburg, 1945-46. County of London Sessions: Prosecuting Counsel to Post Office, 1951-53, Junior Counsel to the Crown in Appeals, 1953-59, Prosecuting Counsel to the Crown, 1958-59; Recorder of Gravesend, 1957-59. *Address:* St Giles, Burwash, Etchingham, East Sussex TN19 7HT. *T:* Burwash 882031. *Club:* Army and Navy.

PHIPPS, Vice-Adm. Sir Peter, KBE 1964 (CBE 1962); DSC 1941 (Bar 1943); VRD 1945; retired, 1965; *b* 7 June 1909; *m* 1937, Jean Hutton; two *s* one *d.* *Educ:* Sumner Primary School; Christchurch Boys' High School. Joined staff of National Bank of NZ Ltd, 1927. Joined RNZNVR as Ord. Seaman, 1928; Sub-Lieut, 1930; Lieut, 1933. Served War of 1939-45 (American Navy Cross, 1943). Transferred to RNZN as Commander, 1945; Captain, 1952; Rear-Admiral, 1960. Chief of Naval Staff, NZ Naval Board, 1960-63; Chief of Defence Staff, New Zealand, 1963-65; Vice-Adm. 1964, retired 1965. *Recreations:* yachting, fishing, herpetology. *Address:* 126 Motuhara Road, Plimmerton, New Zealand. *T:* Plimmerton 331240. *Clubs:* Naval; Wellington (Wellington, NZ).

PHIPPS, Rt. Rev. Simon Wilton; *see* Lincoln, Bishop of.

PHIRI, Hon. Amock Israel; Minister for the North Western Province, Government of Zambia, 1974-75; *b* 25 Oct. 1932; *m* 1967, Jennifer M. Phiri; five *c.* *Educ:* Chewa Native Authority; Chisali River Sch.; Munali Secondary Sch. (Sen. Cambridge Sch. Cert.); by private corresp. ('A' Levels); Univ. of Hamburg, W Germany (MA in Sociology, 1960-66); Special Course in Regional Planning (Feb.-Aug. 1967). With Rhokana Corp. as Industrial PRO, 1957-59; Mem. staff, LOCCUM Evangelic Acad., 1959-60; Lectr in Sociology, Univ. of Zambia, Oct. 1967-Mar. 1969; MP, Parliament of Zambia, Nov. 1968-; Sec., Economic Cttee of Central Cttee of the Party, Nov. 1968-Aug. 1969; Chm. Public Accounts Cttee, 1969; Member: Manpower Cttee, 1969-70; Parly Cttee looking into Parly Affairs, 1969-70;

Zambianization and Training Cttee for Civil Service, 1970. Minister of State: Min. of National Guidance, Mar.-Dec. 1969; Min. of Information, Broadcasting and Tourism, Jan.-Oct. 1970; High Comr in London, and concurrently Ambassador to the Holy See, 1970-74. *Address:* PO Box 100, Solweze, Zambia.

PIAGET, Jean; Professor of Child Psychology, Geneva University, since 1929; Director, International Centre of Genetic Epistemology, Geneva, since 1955; *b* Neuchâtel, 9 Aug. 1896; *s* of Prof. Arthur Piaget; *m* ; three *c. Educ:* Neuchâtel, Zürich and Paris Univ. Dr ès Sc. naturelles, Neuchâtel, 1918. Chef de travaux, Institut J. J. Rousseau, Geneva, 1921-25; Prof. of Psychology, Sociology and Philosophy of Science, Univ. of Neuchâtel, 1925-29; Prof. of History of Scientific Thought, Geneva Univ., 1929-39; Dir, Institut universitaire des Sciences de l'Education, Geneva, 1933-71; Professor of: Psychology and Sociology, Univ. of Lausanne, 1938-51; Sociology, Geneva Univ., 1939-52; Experimental Psychology, Geneva Univ., 1940-71; Genetic Psychology, Sorbonne, 1952-63. Dir, Internat. Bureau of Educn, Geneva, 1929-67; formerly: Pres., Swiss Commission UNESCO; Co-Dir, Dept of Educn UNESCO; Mem., Exec. Council UNESCO. Established, with the help of the Rockefeller Foundn and Swiss Nat. Foundn for Scientific Res., Internat. Centre of Genetic Epistemology, Geneva Univ., 1955. Formerly President: Swiss Soc. of Psychology; Assoc. de Psychologie scientifique de langue française; Internat. Union of Scientific Psychology, 1954-57; Mem., 20 Academic Socs. Co-Editor: Revue Suisse de Psychologie; Archives de Psychologie, Geneva; Enfance, Paris; Acta Psychologica, Amsterdam; Methodos, Milan; Synthese, Dordrecht/Holland; Dialectica, Neuchâtel and Paris; Linguistic Inquiry, Cambridge/Mass. Dr *hc* Harvard Univ.; Hon. ScD Cambridge; 24 other Hon. Degrees; 7 Scientific Prizes. *Publications:* Recherche, 1918; Le Langage et la Pensée chez l'enfant, 1923 (Eng. trans. 1926); Le Jugement et le raisonnement chez l'enfant, 1924 (Eng. trans. 1928); La Représentation du monde chez l'enfant 1926 (Eng. trans. 1929); La Causalité physique chez l'enfant, 1927 (Eng. Trans. 1930); Le Jugement moral chez l'enfant, (and Eng. trans.), 1932; La Naissance de l'intelligence chez l'enfant, 1936 (Eng. trans. 1952); La Construction du réel chez l'enfant, 1937 (Eng. trans. 1954); (with A. Szeminska) La Genèse du nombre chez l'enfant, 1941 (Eng. trans. 1952); Classes, relations et nombres, 1942; Développement des quantités physiques chez l'enfant (Eng. trans. 1974); La Formation du symbole chez l'enfant, 1946 (Eng. trans. 1951); Le Développement de la notion de temps chez l'enfant, 1946 (Eng. trans. 1969); Les Notions de mouvement et de vitesse chez l'enfant, 1946 (Eng. trans. 1970); La Psychologie de l'intelligence, 1947 (Eng. trans. 1950); (with B. Inhelder) La Représentation de l'espace chez l'enfant, 1948 (Eng. trans. 1956); (with B. Inhelder and A. Szeminska) La Géométrie spontanée de l'enfant, 1948 (Eng. trans. 1960); Traité de logique, 1949; Introduction à l'épistémologie génétique, 1950; (with B. Inhelder) La Genèse de l'idée de hasard chez l'enfant, 1951; Essai sur les transformations des opérations logiques, 1952; Logic and Psychology, 1953; (with B. Inhelder) De la Logique de l'enfant à la logique de l'adolescent, 1955 (Eng. trans. 1958); La Genèse des structures logiques élémentaires, classifications et Sériations, 1959 (Eng. trans. 1964); Les Mécanismes perceptifs, 1961 (Eng. trans. 1969); Six Etudes de psychologie, 1964 (Eng. trans. 1967); Etudes sociologiques, 1965; Sagesse et illusion de la philosophie, 1965 (Eng. trans. 1971); (with B. Inhelder) L'Image mentale chez l'enfant, 1966 (Eng. trans. 1971); (with B. Inhelder) Psychologie de l'enfant, 1966 (Eng. trans. 1969); Biologie et connaissance, 1967 (Eng. trans. 1971); On the development of memory and identity, 1968; Logique et connaissance scientifique, 1967; Genetic Epistemology, 1970; Le Structuralisme, 1968 (Eng. trans. 1970); (with B. Inhelder and H. Sinclair-de Zwart) Mémoire et intelligence, 1968 (Eng. trans. 1973); Psychologie et pédagogie, 1969 (Eng. trans. 1970); L'Epistémologie génétique (and Eng. trans.), 1970; Psychologie et épistémologie, 1970 (Psychology and Epistemology, 1971); Epistémologie des sciences de l'homme, 1972; Où va l'éducation?, 1972 (Eng. trans. 1973); Problèmes de psychologie génétique, 1972 (Eng. trans. 1973); La Prise de conscience, 1974 (Eng. trans. 1977); Adaptation vitale et psychologie de l'intelligence, 1974; Réussir et comprendre, 1974; L'équilibration des structures cognitives; (ed) Etudes d'épistémologie génétique, 1957- (30 vols by 1973); (ed with P. Fraisse) Traité de psychologie expérimentale, 1963-65; and 500 publications in scientific periodicals. *Address:* Centre d'Epistémologie Génétique, l'Université, 1211 Geneva 4, Switzerland.

PICACHY, His Eminence Lawrence Trevor, Cardinal; *see* Calcutta, Archbishop of, (RC).

PICCARD, Dr Jacques; scientist; President, Foundation for the Study and Preservation of Seas and Lakes; *b* Belgium, 1922; Swiss Citizen; *s* of late Prof. Auguste Piccard (explorer of the stratosphere, in lighter-than-air craft, and of the ocean depths, in vehicles of his own design); *m* 1953, Marie Claude (*née* Maillard); two *s* one *d. Educ:* Brussels; Switzerland. Grad., Univ. of Geneva, 1946; Dip. from Grad. Inst. of Internat. Studies. Asst Prof., Univ. of Geneva, 1946-48. With his father, he participated in design and operation of the first deep diving vessels, which they named the bathyscaph (deep ship); this vessel, like its successor, operated independently of a mother ship; they first constructed the FNRS-2 (later turned over to the French Navy) then the Trieste (ultimately purchased by US Navy); Dr J. Piccard piloted the Trieste on 65 successive dives (the last, 23 Jan. 1960, was the record-breaking descent to 35,800 feet in the Marianas Trench, off Guam in the Pacific Ocean). He built in 1963, the mesoscaph Auguste Piccard, the first civilian submarine, which made, in 1964-65, over 1,100 dives carrying 33,000 people into the depths of Lake Geneva; built (with Grumman) 2nd mesoscaph, Ben Franklin, and in 1969 made 1.500 miles/30 days drift dive in Gulf Stream. Founded: Fondation pour l'Etude et la Protection de la Mer et des Lacs, 1966; Institut International d'Ecologie, 1972. Hon. doctorate in Science, Amer. Internat. Coll., Springfield, Mass, 1962; Hon. DSc, Hofstra Univ., 1970. Holds Distinguished Public Service Award, etc. *Publications:* The Sun beneath the Sea, 1971; technical papers and a popularized account (trans. many langs) of the Trieste, Seven Miles Down (with Robert S. Dietz). *Address:* (home) 19 avenue de l'Avenir, 1012 Lausanne, Switzerland. *T:* (021) 28 80 83; (office) Institut International d'Ecologie, 1096 Cully, Switzerland. *T:* 021. 992565.

PICKARD, Sir Cyril (Stanley), KCMG 1966 (CMG 1964); HM Diplomatic Service, retired; British High Commissioner in Nigeria, 1971-74; *b* 18 Sept. 1917; *s* of G. W. Pickard and Edith Pickard (*née* Humphrey), Sydenham; *m* 1941, Helen Elizabeth Strawson; three *s* one *d* (and one *s* decd). *Educ:* Alleyn's Sch., Dulwich; New Coll. Oxford. 1st Class Hons Modern History, 1939. Asst Principal, Home Office, 1939. War of 1939-45: Royal Artillery, 1940-41, Captain; appointment in Office of Minister of State, Cairo, 1941-44 Principal, 1943; with UNRRA in Middle East and Germany, 1944-45; transf. to Commonwealth Relations Office, 1948; Office of UK High Comr in India, New Delhi, 1950; Local Asst Sec., Office of UK High Comr, Canberra, 1952-55; Commonwealth Relations Office, Head of South Asian Dept, 1955-58; Deputy High Commissioner for the UK in New Zealand, 1958-61; Asst Under Sec. of State, CRO, 1962-66 (Acting High Commissioner in Cyprus, 1964); British High Comr, Pakistan, 1966-71. *Recreation:* gardening. *Address:* Sommer House, Oak Lane, Sevenoaks, Kent.

PICKARD, Prof. Huia Masters, FDSRCS; Professor of Conservative Dentistry, University of London, 1963-74, now Emeritus; *b* 25 March 1909; *o s* of late Ernest Pickard and Sophie Elizabeth Robins; *m* 1945, Daphne Evelyn, *d* of Hugh F. Marriott; two *d. Educ:* Latymer Sch.; Royal Dental Hosp. of London Sch. of Dental Surgery; Charing Cross Hosp. MRCS, LRCP, FDSRCS. Private dental practice with H. Sumner Moore and E. W. Fish, pre-1940; EMS, East Grinstead, 1939. Served War, in RAMC, 8th Army (despatches), 1940-45. Dental practice and teaching, 1945; Dir, Dept of Conservative Dentistry, Royal Dental Hosp., and Consultant in Dental Surgery, 1955; Reader in Conservative Dentistry, London Univ., 1957-63; Dir of Dept of Restorative Dentistry, Royal Dental Hosp., 1965-74. Mem. Bd of Governors, St George's Hosp., 1969; First Pres., British Soc. for Restorative Dentistry, 1969; Pres., Odontological Section of Royal Soc. Med., 1971; Examr for Univs of London, Newcastle, Glasgow, Birmingham, Wales; also RCS. *Publications:* Manual of Operative Dentistry (4th edn), 1976; contribs: Dental Record, Brit. Dental Jl, Internat. Dental Jl. *Recreations:* gardening, sailing. *Address:* The Nuttery, Newnham, Daventry, Northamptonshire. *T:* Daventry 3561. *Club:* Army and Navy.

PICKARD, Rt. Rev. Stanley Chapman, CBE 1968; Assistant Bishop of Johannesburg since 1968; Rector of St John's, Belgravia, Diocese of Johannesburg, since 1972; Chaplain to Anglicans of Jeppe Boys High School, since 1972; *b* 4 July 1910; *s* of John Chapman and Louisa Mary Pickard, Gloucester; unmarried. *Educ:* Grammar Sch., Birmingham. Studied pharmacy, 1928-32. Dorchester Theological College, 1933-36; Deacon, 1937; Priest, 1938; Curate St Catherine's, New Cross, SE14, 1937-39; joined UMCA, 1939; Kota Kota, Nyasaland, 1939-40; Likoma Island, Nyasaland, 1940-48; Archdeacon of Msumba, Portuguese East Africa, 1949-58; Bishop of Lebombo, 1958-68; Provincial Exec. Officer, Province of S Africa, 1968-71. *Recreations:* walking, bridge. *Address:* St John's Rectory, 170 Park Street, Belgravia, Johannesburg, South Africa.

PICKAVANCE, Thomas Gerald, CBE 1965; MA, PhD; FRS 1976; Fellow, St Cross College, Oxford, since 1967; *b* 19 October 1915; *s* of William and Ethel Pickavance, Lancashire; *m* 1943, Alice Isobel (*née* Boulton); two *s* one *d. Educ:* Cowley School, St Helens; Univ. of Liverpool. BSc (Hons Phys) 1937; PhD 1940. Research Physicist, Tube Alloys Project, 1941-46; Lecturer in Physics, University of Liverpool, 1943-46; Atomic Energy Research Establishment, Harwell: Head of Cyclotron Group, 1946-54; Head of Accelerator Group, 1954-57; Deputy Head of General Physics Division, 1955-57; Dir, Rutherford High Energy Lab., SRC, 1957-69; Dir of Nuclear Physics, SRC, 1969-72. Chm., European Cttee for Future Accelerators, 1970-71. Hon. DSc, City Univ., 1969. *Publications:* papers and articles in learned journals on nuclear physics and particle accelerators. *Recreations:* motoring, travel, photography. *Address:* 3 Kingston Close, Abingdon, Oxon OX14 1ES. *T:* Abingdon 23934.

PICKEN, Dr Laurence Ernest Rowland, FBA 1973; Emeritus Fellow of Jesus College, Cambridge, since 1944; *b* 1909. *Educ:* Oldknow Road and Waverley Road, Birmingham; Trinity Coll., Cambridge. BA 1931; PhD 1935; ScD 1952. Asst Dir of Research (Zoology), Cambridge Univ., 1946-66; Asst Dir of Research (Oriental Music), Cambridge Univ., 1966-76. FBA; FIBiol. *Publications:* The Organization of Cells and Other Organisms, 1960; Folk Musical Instruments of Turkey, 1975; Editor, Musica Asiatica, 1977; contribs to many learned jls. *Address:* Jesus College, Cambridge.

PICKERILL, Dame Cecily (Mary Wise), DBE 1977 (OBE 1958); Retired Surgeon; *b* 9 Feb. 1903; *d* of Percy Wise Clarkson and Margaret Ann Clarkson; *m* 1934, Henry Percy Pickerill, CBE, MD, MDS (*d* 1956); one *d. Educ:* Diocesan High School for Girls, Auckland, NZ; Otago Univ. Medical School, Dunedin, NZ (MB, ChB). House Surg., Dunedin Hosp., 1926; Asst Plastic Surgeon in Sydney, Aust., 1927-35; Specialist Plastic Surgeon, Wellington, NZ, 1935-68; retired, 1968. Licencee, with late husband, and owner of Bassam Hosp., Lower Hutt, NZ—a "Rooming-In" hospital for mother nursing of infants and small children with congenital defects requiring plastic surgery. *Publications:* contribs to medical and nursing journals. *Recreations:* gardening, fishing, camping, nature conservation. *Address:* Beech Dale, 50 Blue Mountains Road, Silverstream, New Zealand. *T:* Upper Hutt 84542.

PICKERING, Sir Edward (Davies), Kt 1977; Vice-Chairman, Press Council, since 1977; *b* 4 May 1912; 3rd *s* of George and Louie Pickering; *m* 1st, 1936, Margaret Soutter (marr. diss., 1947); one *d*; 2nd, 1955, Rosemary Whitton; two *s* one *d. Educ:* Middlesbrough High Sch. Chief Sub-Editor Daily Mail, 1939. Served Royal Artillery 1940-44; Staff of Supreme Headquarters Allied Expeditionary Force, 1944-45. Managing Editor: Daily Mail, 1947-49; Daily Express, 1951-57; Editor, Daily Express, 1957-62; Dir, Beaverbrook Newspapers, 1956-64; Editorial Dir, The Daily Mirror Newspapers Ltd, 1964-68, Chm., 1968-70; Director: Scottish Daily Record and Sunday Mail Ltd, 1966-69; IPC, 1966-75; Chairman: International Publishing Corporation Newspaper Div., 1968-70; IPC Magazines, 1970-74; Mirror Group Newspapers, 1975-77. Member Press Council, 1964-69, 1970-. Treasurer, Fédération Internationale de la Presse Periodique, 1971-75; Chm. Council, Commonwealth Press Union, 1977-. *Address:* The Press Council, 1 Salisbury Square, EC4. *Club:* Garrick.

PICKERING, Ven. Fred; Archdeacon of Hampstead, since 1974; *b* 18 Nov. 1919; *s* of Arthur and Elizabeth Pickering; *m* 1948, Mabel Constance Threlfall; one *s* one *d. Educ:* Preston Grammar Sch.; St Peter's Coll., Oxford; St Aidan's Theol Coll., Birkenhead. BA 1941 (PPE), MA 1945. Curate: St Andrew's, Leyland, 1943-46; St Mary's, Islington, 1946-48; Organising Sec. for Church Pastoral Aid Soc. in NE England, 1948-51; Vicar: All Saints, Burton-on-Trent, 1951-56; St John's, Carlisle, 1956-63; St Cuthbert's, Wood Green, 1963-74; Rural Dean of East Haringey, 1968-73; Exam. Chaplain to Bp of Edmonton, 1973-. *Address:* 35 Fox Lane, N13 4AD. *T:* 01-886 2680. *Clubs:* Sion College, Wood Green Rotary.

PICKERING, Frederick Derwent, CBE 1974; Vice-Chairman, Executive Council of the Association of County Councils, since 1976; County Councillor, Berkshire, since 1961; *b* 28 Nov. 1909; *s* of Frederick Owen Pickering and Emma Pickering; *m* 1935, Marjorie Champion (*née* Shotter), JP; one *s. Educ:* Bedford House Sch., Oxford. Employed in industry, 1927-43; Sudan CS, 1943-55; company dir, 1955-63. County Alderman, Berks, 1967-74; Chm., Berks CC, 1973-77. Hon. DLitt Reading, 1976. *Recreations:* cricket (now as spectator), politics (Pres., Reading South Conservative Assoc.). *Address:* 5 Scotswood, Devenish Road, Sunningdale, Berks SL5 9QP. *T:* Ascot 24884.

PICKERING, Frederick Pickering, PhD (Breslau); Professor of German, University of Reading, 1953-74, now Emeritus; *b* Bradford, Yorkshire, 10 March 1909; *s* of late F. W. Pickering and Martha (*née* Pickering); *m* 1939, Florence Joan Anderson. *Educ:* Grange High School, Bradford; Leeds University (BA). Gilchrist Travelling Studentship; Germanic languages and literature at Breslau University (PhD). Lektor in English, 1931-32; Asst Lectr and Lectr in German, Univ. of Manchester, 1932-41. Bletchley Park (Hut 3), 1941-45. Head of German Dept, Univ. of Sheffield, 1945-53; Dean of the Faculty of Letters, Univ. of Reading, 1957-60. Goethe Medal, Goethe Inst., Munich, 1975. *Publications:* Medieval language, literature and art: Christi Leiden in einer Vision geschaut, 1952, an edn; Augustinus oder Boethius?, 2 vols, 1967, 1976; University German, 1968; Literatur und darstellende Kunst im Mittelalter, 1968 (trans. as Literature and Art in the Middle Ages, 1970); The Anglo-Norman Text of the Holkham Bible Picture Book, 1971; articles and reviews in English and German learned journals. *Recreations:* anything but reading. *Address:* 1 Arborfield Court, Arborfield Cross, Berks RG2 9JS. *T:* Reading 760350.

PICKERING, Sir George White, Kt 1957; FRS 1960; MD, FRCP; Master of Pembroke College, Oxford, 1968-74; Hon. Fellow, 1974; *b* 26 June 1904; *s* of George and Ann Pickering, Whalton, Northumberland; *m* 1930, Mary Carola, *y d* of late Sir A. C. Seward, FRS; one *s* three *d. Educ:* Dulwich College; Pembroke College, Cambridge (Scholar); St Thomas' Hospital (Scholar). 1st Class Honours Nat. Sci. Tripos, Pts I, 1925 and II, 1926; MB 1930; MD 1955; FRCP 1938. Formerly Asst in Dept of Clinical Res. and Lectr in Cardio-vascular Pathology, UCH, and Mem., Scientific Staff MRC; Herzstein Lectr, Stanford Univ. and Univ. of California, 1938; Sims British Commonwealth Travelling Prof., 1949; subsequently Vis. Prof. in many American and Canadian Univs. Member: UGC, 1944-54; MRC and Clinical Res. Bd, 1954-58; Prof. of Medicine, Univ. of London and Dir of Medical Clinic, St Mary's Hosp., London, 1939-56; Regius Prof. of Medicine, Oxford Univ., Student of Christ Church, Master of God's House in Ewelme, and Physician to the United Oxford Hospitals, 1956-Dec. 1968; Pro-Vice-Chancellor, Oxford Univ., 1967-69; Emeritus Student of Christ Church, 1969, Hon. Student 1977. Member: Lord Chancellor's Cttee on Legal Educn, 1967-71; Council for Scientific Policy, 1968-71; Trustee: Beit Memorial Fellowship; Ciba Foundation. Pres. BMA, 1963-64. Stouffer Prize (jtly), 1970. Hon. degrees: DSc: Durham, 1957, Dartmouth (US), 1960, Hull, 1972; ScD, Trinity Coll., Dublin, 1962; MD: Ghent, 1948, Siena, 1965, Univ. W Aust., 1965; LLD: Manchester, 1964, Nottingham, 1965; DUniv York, 1969. Hon. Fellow: Pembroke College, Cambridge, 1959; Pembroke College, Oxford, 1974; American College of Physicians; American Medical Association; RCP Edinburgh; RCP Ireland; Acad. of Medicine of Mexico; Hon. FRSM; Hon. Member: Assoc. of American Physicians; American Gastro-enterological Assoc.; Swedish Medical Soc.; Australian Med. Assoc.; Corresp. Mem., Deutschen Gesellschaft für Innere Medizin, 1970; Membre correspondant étranger, Soc. Med. des Hôpitaux de Paris; Foreign Hon. Member: Amer. Academy of Arts and Sciences; Czechoslovakian Med. Soc.; Hellenic Cardiac Soc.; Royal Belgian Acad. of Medicine; Danish Soc. for Internal Medicine; Foreign Associate, Amer. Nat. Acad. of Sciences, 1970. *Publications:* High Blood Pressure, 1955 (2nd edn, 1968); The Nature of Essential Hypertension, 1961; The Challenge to Education, 1967; Hypertension: Causes, Consequences and Management, 1970; Creative Malady, 1974; Papers relating to vascular disease, high blood pressure, peptic ulcer, headache and education. *Recreations:* gardening, fishing. *Address:* 5 Horwood Close, Headington, Oxford. *T:* Oxford 64260. *Club:* Athenæum.

PICKERING, Herbert Kitchener; Agent-General in London, Government of Province of Alberta, since Nov. 1973; *b* 9 Feb. 1915; *s* of Herbert Pickering, Hull, and Ethel Bowman, Carlisle; *m* 1963, Florence Marion Carr; two *s* two *d. Educ:* Montreal; Bishop's Univ. (Business Admin); Cornell Univ. (Hotel Admin); Michigan State Univ. (Hotel and Business Admin). Canadian National Railways: Gen. Passenger Traffic Dept, Montreal, 1930; various cities in Canada and US; served War of 1939-45, RCAF; returned to CNR; assisted in creation and management of Maple Leaf Tour Dept, 1953-59; created Sales Dept for Canadian National Hotels in Western Canada and then for System, 1960-67; Man., Bessborough Hotel, Saskatoon, 1968; Gen. Man., Jasper Park Lodge, until 1973. *Recreations:* golf, ski-ing, swimming, philately. *Address:* 37 Hill Street, W1 7FD. *T:* 01-499 3061, (home) 01-491 3588. *Clubs:* Lansdowne, Les Ambassadeurs, Curzon House, Vanity Fair, Canada.

PICKERING, Ian George Walker, VRD (with clasp) 1952; MD; FRCP 1972; Consultant in forensic psychiatry, special hospitals,

Department of Health and Social Security, since 1976; b 24 Nov. 1915; e s of Geo. W. Pickering, Bradford, Yorks; m 1948, Jean (d 1975), 2nd d of John Bell Lowthian, MC and Bar; one s one d. Educ: Bradford Grammar Sch.; Leeds Univ. MB, ChB 1939; MD 1947; MRCP 1966; FRCPsych 1971; FFCM 1972. Various hosp. appts, 1939 and 1946-47. RNVR, 1939-46: at sea and appts RN Hosps, Plymouth and Sydney, NSW. Surgeon Lt-Comdr RNR, retd list, 1965. HM Prison Service, 1947; Senior MO, HM Prison and Borstal, Durham, 1955-63. Nuffield Travelling Fellow, 1961-62. Dir, Prison Med. Services and Inspector of Retreats for Inebriates, 1963-76; Mem. Prisons Bd, Home Office, 1967-76; Pres., British Acad. of Forensic Sciences, 1969-70; Vice-President: 2nd Internat. Congress of Social Psychiatry, London, 1969; British Assoc. of Social Psychiatry; Oxford Postgrad. Fellowship in Psychiatry, 1966-76; Soc. for Study of Addiction, 1967-74 (Vice-Chm.); Member, Executive Councils: Med. Council on Alcoholism, 1967-76; N of England Medico-Legal Soc., Newcastle upon Tyne, 1960-63. Officier de Jurade and Vigneron (hc), St Emilion, Aquitaine; Hon. Mem., Prichard Soc., Bristol. Publications: articles in professional journals. Recreations: travel, music, wine. Address: Rampton Hospital, Retford, Notts DN22 0PD. T: Retford 84321; (home) Drift House, Ockham Road North, East Horsley, Surrey KT24 6NU. Clubs: Royal Automobile, Naval.

PICKERING, John Robertson; His Honour Judge Pickering; a Circuit Judge, since 1972; b 8 Jan. 1925; s of late J. W. H. Pickering and Sarah Lilian Pickering (née Dixon); m 1951, Hilde (widow of E. M. Wright); one s two step s. Educ: Winchester; Magdalene Coll., Cambridge. Degree in Classics (wartime) and Law, MA. Served War, Lieut RNVR, Russia, Europe and Far East, 1942-47. Called to Bar, Inner Temple, 1949. Subseq. with Nat. Coal Bd and Dyson Bell & Co (Parliamentary Agents). Mem. Parliamentary Bar. Dep. Chm. of Pneumoconiosis, Byssinosis and Miscellaneous Diseases Benefit Bd, and Workmen's Compensation (Supplementation) Bd, 1970; apptd Dep. Chm. NE London Quarter Sessions, 1971. Address: 35 Eaton Terrace, SW1. T: 01-730 4271. Club: MCC.

PICKERING, Richard Edward Ingram; a Recorder of the Crown Court, since 1977; b 16 Aug. 1929; s of Richard and Dorothy Pickering; m 1962, Jean Margaret Eley; two s. Educ: Birkenhead Sch.; Magdalene Coll., Cambridge (MA). Called to the Bar, Lincoln's Inn, 1953; has practised on Northern Circuit, 1955-. Recreations: beagling, gardening, reading. Address: Trelyon, Croft Drive, Caldy, Wirral L48 2JN. T: 051-625 7043; 54 Castle Street, Liverpool L2 7LQ. Club: Athenæum (Liverpool).

PICKERING, Hon. Wilfred Francis; Hon. Mr Justice Pickering; Justice of Appeal of the Supreme Court of Hong Kong, since 1976; barrister-at-law (formerly solicitor); b 4 Dec. 1915; o s of late Wilfred Clayton Pickering and Catherine Pickering (née Pender); m 1939, Dorothy Adamson; two d (one s decd). Educ: Panton Coll.; Victoria Univ. of Manchester (LLB triple prizeman). Admitted to the Rolls, solicitor, 1938; called to Bar, Gray's Inn, 1963. Served War, RAF, 1940-46 (Flt Lt). Head of German Courts Dept, Land Niedersachsen, 1946-51; Mem., Supreme Restitution Court (internat.), 1951-55. Stipendiary Magistrate, Hong Kong, 1955-57; Chm., Cttee of Review, and Pres., Tenancy Tribunal, Hong Kong, 1957-60; Actg District Judge, 1960-62; District Judge, 1962; Judicial Comr, State of Brunei, 1967; Judge of Supreme Court, Hong Kong, 1970. Recreations: swimming, walking. Address: Supreme Court, Hong Kong. Clubs: Royal Over-Seas League; Hong Kong, LRC (Hong Kong).

PICKETT, Thomas, CBE 1972; Senior Regional Chairman, North West Area, Industrial Tribunals (England and Wales), since 1975 (Chairman for Manchester, 1972); b 22 November 1912; s of John Joseph Pickett and Caroline Pickett (née Brunt); m 1940, Winifred Irene Buckley, yr d of late Benjamin Buckley; no c. Educ: Glossop Grammar School; London University (LLB). Barrister-at-Law, Lincoln's Inn; called to Bar, 1948. Served in Army, 1939-50, retiring with permanent rank of Major. Dep. Asst Dir of Army Legal Services, 1948; Dist Magistrate, Gold Coast, 1950; Resident Magistrate, Northern Rhodesia 1955; Sen. Res. Magistrate, 1956; Acting Puisne Judge, 1960; Puisne Judge, High Courts of Northern Rhodesia, 1961-64; Zambia, 1964-69; Justice of Appeal, 1969-71; Acting Chief Justice, 1970, Judge President, Court of Appeal, 1971, Zambia. Chairman: Tribunal on Detainees, 1967; Electoral Commn (Supervisory); Delimitation Commn for Zambia, 1968; Referendum Commn, 1969; Local Govt Commn, 1970. Recreations: walking, swimming. Address: Oakmere, Chester Road, Mere, Cheshire. T: Bucklow Hill 830040. Club: Royal Over-Seas League.

PICKFORD, Frank; Under-Secretary, General Manpower Division, Department of Employment, 1970-72, retired; b 26 Oct. 1917; s of late Edwin Pickford, Bulwell, Nottingham; m 1944, May Talbot; two s. Educ: Nottingham High Sch.; St John's Coll., Cambridge. Entered Min. of Labour, 1939; Asst Private Sec. to Minister of Labour, 1941-43; Dir, London Office, Internat. Labour Office, 1951-56; Sec., NEDC, 1962-64; Under-Sec., Ministry of Labour, 1964; Asst Under-Sec. of State, Dept of Employment and Productivity, 1968-70. Address: 64 Westbere Road, NW2. T: 01-435 1207.

PICKFORD, Prof. (Lillian) Mary, DSc; FRS 1966; Special Professor of Endocrinology, University of Nottingham, since 1973; Professor, Department of Physiology, University of Edinburgh, 1966-72 (Reader in Physiology, 1952-66); retired 1972, now Emeritus Professor; b 14 Aug. 1902; d of Herbert Arthur Pickford and Lillian Alice Minnie Wintle. Educ: Wycombe Abbey Sch.; Bedford and University Colls, Univ. of London. BSc (1st cl., Gen.) 1924; BSc (2nd cl., Physiology Special) 1925; MSc (Physiology) 1926; MRCS, LRCP 1933; DSc London 1951. House Physician and Casualty Officer, Stafford Gen. Infirmary, 1935; Jun. Beit Memorial Research Fellow, 1936-39; Lectr, Dept of Physiology, Univ. of Edinburgh, 1939; Personal Chair, Dept of Physiology, Univ. of Edinburgh, 1966. Fellow, University Coll., London, 1968-. Publications: The Central Role of Hormones, 1969; papers in Jl Physiology, British Jl Pharmacology, Jl Endocrinology. Recreations: walking, travel, painting. Address: The Hall, King Sterndale, near Buxton, Derbyshire.

PICKFORD, Mary; actress; sometime partner in three producing companies in Hollywood: Comet, Triangle and Artists Alliance, and part owner, with others, of United Artists Corporation; sold holdings in United Artists, 1956; b Toronto, Canada, 8 April 1893 (family name Smith); mother a character actress; m 1st, Owen Moore (divorced, 1919); 2nd, 1920, Douglas Fairbanks (divorced, 1935); 3rd, 1937, Charles Buddy Rogers; one adopted s one adopted d. Debut on stage at 5; first marked success was in motion pictures, in Hearts Adrift; returned to stage in A Good Little Devil and Warrens of Virginia. Returned to motion pictures as star; best known pictures: Tess of the Storm Country, Stella Maris, Daddy Long Legs, Pollyanna, Rebecca of Sunny Brook Farm, Poor Little Rich Girl, Little Lord Fauntleroy, My Best Girl, etc.; also talking pictures Coquette (Academy of Motion Picture Arts and Sciences award), Taming of the Shrew, Kiki and Secrets. Mem. Bd Directors, Thomas Alva Edison Foundation; Mem. Edison Pioneers; Director, American Society for the Aged, Inc. Apptd Mem. Nat. Advisory Cttee for White House Conf. on Aging, 1959. Holds several awards both American and foreign, for public and political service and for war work. Holds Hon. Degrees. Publications: Why not try God?, 1934; The Demi Widow, 1935; My Rendezvous With Life, 1935; Sunshine and Shadow, 1956; many magazine articles. Address: 9350 Wilshire Boulevard, Beverly Hills, Calif 90212, USA.

PICKFORD, Prof. Mary; see Pickford, Prof. L. M.

PICKFORD, Prof. Ralph William; Professor of Psychology in the University of Glasgow, 1955-73, now Emeritus; b 11 Feb. 1903; s of William Pickford and Evelyn May Flower; m 1st, 1933, Alexis Susan Macquisten (d 1971); 2nd, 1971, Laura Ruth Bowyer. Educ: Bournemouth School and Municipal Coll.; Emmanuel Coll., Cambridge. Emmanuel College: Exhibitioner, 1924, Sen. Schol. and Internal Research Student, 1927; BA 1927, MA 1930, PhD 1932. Goldsmiths' Company's Exhibitioner, 1925; Moral Sciences Tripos, First Class, 1927. Lecturer in Psychology and Acting Head of Dept, Aberdeen Univ., 1929. Asst in Psychology Dept, 1930, Lectr, 1935, Sen. Lectr and Acting Head of Psychology Dept 1947, Glasgow Univ. DLitt (Glasgow) 1947. Hon. Psychotherapist Notre Dame Child Guidance Clinic, 1947-, and Davidson Clinic, Glasgow, 1952-. First Pres., Experimental Psychology Group; Chm. and then Hon. Sec. Scottish Br. Brit. Psychological Soc.; Pres. Sect. J Brit. Assoc., 1958. Vice-Pres., Internat. Assoc. of Empirical Aesthetics; Hon. Mem. Soc. Française d'Esthétique; Mem., Council of Soc. Internat. de Psychopathologie de l'Expression; Hon. Pres., Scottish Assoc. for Art and Psychopathology. FBPsS. Publications: Individual Differences in Colour Vision, 1951; The Analysis of an Obsessional, 1954; (with R. Kherumian), Hérédité et Fréquence des Dyschromatopsies, 1959; (with G. M. Wyburn and R. J. Hirst), The Human Senses and Perception, 1963; Pickford Projective Pictures, 1963; Studies in Psychiatric Art, 1967; Psychology and Visual Aesthetics, 1972; Monograph: The Psychology of Cultural Change in Painting, 1943; many articles on Experimental, Social and Clinical Psychology, and the Psychology of Art. Recreations: painting, gardening, music. Address: 34 Morven Road, Bearsden, Glasgow G61 3BX. T: 041-942 5386.

PICKLES, James; His Honour Judge Pickles; a Circuit Judge, since 1976; *b* 18 March 1925; *s* of Arthur Pickles, OBE, JP and Gladys Pickles; *m* 1948, Sheila Ratcliffe; two *s* one *d. Educ:* Worksop Coll.; Leeds Univ. (LLB); Christ Church, Oxford (MA). Called to Bar, Inner Temple, 1948 (Philip Teichman Scholar); practised at Bradford, 1949-76; a Recorder of the Crown Court, 1972-76. Councillor, Brighouse Borough Council, 1956-62. Contested (L) Brighouse and Spenborough, 1964. Author of various radio plays. *Recreations:* squash, tennis, languages. *Address:* Hazelwood, Halifax, W Yorks. *Club:* Queen's Sports (Halifax).

PICKLES, Wilfred, OBE 1950; Radio Actor; *b* 13 Oct. 1904; *s* of Fred Pickles and Margaret Catterall; *m* 1930, Mabel Myerscough; *o s* decd. *Educ:* Parkinson Lane Sch., Halifax, Yorks. First broadcast, 1927, in Children's Hour; became regular broadcaster from the North; apptd N Regional Announcer, 1938, News Reader in London, 1942. First broadcast of Have a Go series, 1946. First Appearance on West End Stage The Gay Dog (comedy), Piccadilly Theatre, in 1952; first film, The Gay Dog, 1954; Television Series, Ask Pickles, 1954; Ride a Cock Horse, Comedy, Blackpool Season, 1957; Billy Liar (film), 1963; The Family Way (film), 1966. *Publications:* Between You and Me (autobiography), 1949; Personal Choice (poetry anthology), 1950; Sometime Never (Reminiscences), 1951; Ne'er forget the people (Portraits of the new Elizabethans), 1953; My North Countrie (anthology of North Country poems, prose, rhymes, jingles and stories), 1954; For Your Delight (anthology of poetry), 1960. *Recreations:* tennis, golf. *Address:* 19 Courcels, Arundel Street, Brighton, East Sussex. *T:* 680613.

PICKTHORN, Sir Charles (William Richards), 2nd Bt *cr* 1959; Director, J. Henry Schroder Wagg & Co. Ltd, since 1971; *b* 3 March 1927; *s* of Rt Hon. Sir Kenneth William Murray Pickthorn, 1st Bt, and of Nancy Catherine Lewis, *d* of late Lewis Matthew Richards; *S* father, 1975; *m* 1951, Helen Antonia, *o d* of late Sir James Mann, KCVO; one *s* two *d. Educ:* Eton; Corpus Christi Coll., Cambridge (Major Schol., BA). Served RNVR, 1945-48. Called to the Bar, Middle Temple, 1952. Joined J. Henry Schroder Wagg & Co. Ltd, 1959. *Recreations:* sailing, reading. *Heir: s* James Francis Mann Pickthorn, *b* 18 Feb. 1955. *Address:* Manor House, Nunney, near Frome, Somerset. *T:* Nunney 574; 3 Hobury Street, SW10. *T:* 01-352 2795. *Club:* Carlton.

PICKUP, Ronald Alfred; actor; *b* 7 June 1940; *s* of Eric and Daisy Pickup; *m* 1964, Lans Traverse, USA; one *s* one *d. Educ:* King's Sch., Chester; Leeds Univ. (BA); Royal Academy of Dramatic Art. Repertory, Leicester, 1964; Royal Court, 1964 and 1965-66; National Theatre, 1965, 1966-73, 1977: appearances include: Rosalind, in all-male As You Like It, 1967; Richard II, 1972; Edmund, in Long Day's Journey into Night, 1971; Cassius, in Julius Caesar, 1977; Philip Madras, in The Madras House, 1977; Norman, in Norman Conquests; Play, Royal Court, 1976; *films:* Three Sisters, 1969; Day of the Jackal, 1972; Joseph Andrews, 1976; TV appearances: Dragon's Opponent, 1973; Jennie, 1974; Fight Against Slavery; The Philanthropist, Ghost Trio, 1977; Dominic Ayres in The Discretion of Dominic Ayres, 1977, etc. *Recreations:* listening to music, walking, painting.

PICOT, Jacques M. C. G.; *see* Georges-Picot.

PICTON, Jacob Glyndwr, (Glyn Picton), CBE 1972; Senior Lecturer in Industrial Economics, University of Birmingham, since 1947; *b* Aberdare, 28 Feb. 1912; *s* of David Picton; *m* 1939, Rhiannon Mary James (Merch Megan), LRAM, ARCM; one *s* one *d. Educ:* Aberdare Boys' County Sch.; Birmingham Univ. (MCom). Chance Bros Ltd, 1933-47, Asst Sec. 1945-47. Pres., W Midland Rent Assessment Panel, 1965-72 (Chm. Cttee 1973-); Governor, United Birmingham Hosps, 1953-74; Chm., Children's Hosp., 1956-66; Teaching Hosps Rep. Professional and Techn. Whitley Council, 1955-61; Mem., Birmingham Regional Hosp. Bd, 1958-74 (Vice-Chm. 1971-74); Mem., NHS Nat. Staff Cttee, 1964-73 (Vice-Chm. 1968-73); Chm., Birmingham Hosp. Region Staff Cttee, 1964-74; Vice-Chm., W Mids RHA, 1973-; Vice-Chm., NHS Nat. Staff Cttee (Admin. and Clerical), 1973-; NHS Nat. Assessor (Admin), 1973. Chm., Birmingham Industrial Therapy Assoc. Ltd, 1965- and W Bromwich Industrial Therapy Assoc. Ltd, 1969-; Indep. Mem., Estate Agents Council, 1967-69; Chm. of Wages Councils, 1953-; Dep. Chm., Commn of Inquiry concerning Sugar Confectionery and Food Preserving Wages Council, 1961; Chm., Commn of Inquiry concerning Licensed Residential Estabts and Restaurants Wages Council, 1963-64; sole Comr of Inquiry into S Wales Coalfield Dispute, 1965; Dep. Chm., Commn of Inquiry concerning Industrial and Staff Canteens Wages Council, 1975; Independent Arbitrator, Lock Industry,

1976-. *Publications:* various articles and official reports. *Recreations:* music, gardening, Pembrokeshire history. *Address:* 54 Chesterwood Road, Kings Heath, Birmingham B13 0QE. *T:* 021-444 3959.

PIERCE, Francis William, MA (Belfast and Dublin); Hughes Professor of Spanish, University of Sheffield, since 1953; Dean of the Faculty of Arts, 1964-67; *b* 21 Sept. 1915; *s* of late Robert Pierce, JP and Catherine Ismay Pierce; *m* 1944, Mary Charlotte Una, *o d* of late Rev. J. C. Black, Asyut, Upper Egypt; three *s. Educ:* Royal Belfast Academical Institution; Queen's University, Belfast. BA, 1st Cl. Hons, Spanish studies, QUB, 1938; Postgrad. Schol., Columbia Univ., New York, 1938-39; MA, QUB, 1939; Asst Lectr in Spanish, Univ. of Liverpool, 1939-40. Dep. to Prof. of Spanish, TCD, 1940-45; MA *jure officii,* Univ. of Dublin, 1943; Hughes Lectr in Spanish, Univ. of Sheffield, 1946. Visiting Professor: Brown Univ., Providence, RI, 1968; Case Western Reserve Univ., Cleveland, O, 1968. President: Anglo-Catalan Soc., 1955-57; Assoc. of Hispanists of GB and Ireland, 1971-73. *Publications:* The Heroic Poem of the Spanish Golden Age: Selections, chosen with Introduction and Notes, 1947 (Oxford and New York); Hispanic Studies: Review and Revision, 1954; (ed) Hispanic Studies in Honour of I. González Llubera, 1959; La poesía épica del siglo de oro, 1961 (Madrid), 2nd edn 1968; The Historie of Aravcana, transcribed with introd. and notes, 1964; (ed with C. A. Jones) Actas del Primer Congreso Internacional de Hispanistas, 1964; (ed) Two Cervantes Short Novels, 1970, 2nd edn 1976; (ed) La Cristiada by Diego de Hojeda, 1971; (ed) Luís de Camões: Os Lusiadas, 1973; Amadís de Gaula, 1976; articles and reviews in Hispanic Review, Mod. Language Review, Bulletin of Hispanic Studies, Bulletin Hispanique, Ocidente, Estudis Romànics, Quaderni Ibero-Americani. *Address:* 16 Taptonville Crescent, Sheffield S10 5BP. *T:* Sheffield 664239.

PIERCE, Hugh Humphrey; Assistant Controller, Staff Administration, BBC, since 1974; *b* 13 Oct. 1931; *s* of Dr Gwilym Pierce, Abercynon, Glam; *m* 1958, Rachel Margaret Procter; two *s. Educ:* Clifton; King's Coll., Univ. of London. LLB Hons 1954; Pres. Faculty of Laws Soc.; Pres. Union. Called to Bar, Lincoln's Inn, 1955. Diploma Personnel Management, 1962; MIPM 1963. Army Service in Intell. Corps (Cyprus), 1955-57; Kodak Ltd, legal and personnel work, 1957-63; joined BBC, 1963, personnel and industrial relations; Admin. Officer, Local Radio, 1967-68; Local Radio Develt Manager, 1968-69; General Manager, Local Radio, 1970-74. Member: Justice; Amnesty; NACRO; Council, Howard League. *Recreations:* Arsenal Football Club, violin playing. *Address:* 68 Priory Gardens, Highgate, N6. *T:* 01-348 1737.

PIERCE, Rt. Rev. Reginald James, Hon. DD (Winnipeg), 1947; *b* 1909; *s* of James Reginald Pierce and Clara (*née* Whitehand) Plymouth; *m* 1932, Ivy Bell, *d* of Edward and Lucy Jackson, Saskatoon, Canada; one *d. Educ:* University of Saskatchewan (BA 1931); Emmanuel Coll., Saskatoon (LTh 1932); Univ. of London (BD 1942). Deacon, 1932; priest, 1934; Curate of Colinton, 1932-33; Priest-in-charge, 1933-34; Rector and Rural Dean of Grande Prairie, 1934-38; Rector of South Saanich, 1938-41; Rector of St Barnabas, Calgary, 1941-43; Canon of St John's Cathedral, Winnipeg, and Warden of St John's Coll., 1943-50; Priest-in-charge of St Barnabas, Winnipeg, 1946-50; Bishop of Athabasca, 1950-74; Acting Rector: All Saints, Victoria, BC, 1975-76; St David's, Victoria, BC, 1976-. Examining Chaplain: to Bishop of Athabasca, 1935-38; to Archbishop of Rupertsland, 1943-50. *Address:* 209-25 Government Street, Victoria, BC V8V 2K4, Canada.

PIERCE-GOULDING, Lt-Col Terence Leslie Crawford, MBE 1943; CD; Secretary, Commonwealth Press Union, since Oct. 1970; *b* 2 March 1918; *o s* of late Rev. Edward Pierce-Goulding and Christina; *m* 1964, Catherine Yvonne, *d* of John Welsh, Dunedin, NZ; one *s* one *d. Educ:* public and private schs, Edmonton, Alta. Enlisted British Army, 1940, 2nd Lieut Mddx Regt (DCO); Capt. Loyal Edmonton Regt, 1941-42; Staff Coll., 1943; GS03 (Ops), Canadian Planning Staff and HQ 1st Canadian Army, 1943-44; GSO2 (PR), HQ 21 Army Gp and BAOR, 1945-46; Sen. PRO, Central Comd HQ, 1947-48; Adviser to Perm. Canadian Delegn to UN, 1948-50; regtl and staff appts, Royal Canadian Regt and Army HQ, 1950-60; Chief Logistics Officer, UN Emergency Force (Middle East), 1962-63; Dir of Sen. Appts (Army), Canadian Forces HQ, 1963-66; Sen. Admin. Officer, Canadian Defence Liaison Staff (London), 1966-69, retd 1969. Canadian Internat. Development Agency, 1969-70. *Recreations:* golf, travel, photography, literature. *Address:* 20 Hill Rise, NW11. *T:* 01-455 2306. *Clubs:* Pathfinders, Army and Navy.

PIERCY, family name of Baron Piercy.

PIERCY, 2nd Baron, *cr* 1945, of Burford; **Nicholas Pelham Piercy**; *b* 23 June 1918; *s* of 1st Baron Piercy, CBE; *S* father, 1966; *m* 1944, Oonagh Lavinia Baylay; two *s* three *d*. *Educ*: Eton; King's Coll., Cambridge (BA 1940, MA 1944). Lieut (A) RNVR (Fleet Air Arm), 1940; retd 1946. *Heir*: *s* Hon James William Piercy, *b* 19 Jan. 1946. *Address*: The Old Rectory, Elford, Tamworth, Staffs. *T*: Harlaston 233. *Club*: United Oxford & Cambridge University.

PIERCY, Hon. Joanna Elizabeth; *see* Turner, Hon. J. E.

PIERCY, Hon. Penelope Katherine, CBE 1968; Under-Secretary, Ministry of Technology, 1965-68; *b* 15 Apr. 1916; *d* of 1st Baron Piercy, CBE. *Educ*: St Paul's Girls' School; Somerville College, Oxford. War of 1939-45, various appointments, Military Intelligence. Foreign Office, 1945-47; Economist, Colonial Development Corp., 1948-54; Department of Scientific and Industrial Research, 1955-65 (Sen. Prin. Scientific Officer, 1960). CIMechE. *Address*: Southside, Hinton Martell, Wimborne, Dorset.

PIERRE, Abbé; (Henri Antoine Grouès); French priest; Founder of the Companions of Emmaüs; *b* Lyon, 5 Aug. 1912; 5th *c* of Antoine Grouès, Soyeux. *Educ*: Collège des Jésuites, Lyon. Entered Capuchin Monastery, 1930; studied at Capuchin seminary, Crest, Drôme, and Faculté de Théologie, Lyon. Secular priest, St Joseph Basilica, Grenoble. Served war of 1939-45 (Chevalier de la Légion d'Honneur, Croix de Guerre, Médaille de la Résistance); Alsatian and Alpine fronts; Vicar of the Cathedral, Grenoble; assumed name of Abbé Pierre and joined resistance movement, 1942; Chaplain of French Navy at Casablanca, 1944; of whole Free French Navy, 1945. Elected (Indep.) to 1st Constituent Assembly of 4th French Republic, 1945; elected as candidate of Mouvement Républicain Populaire to 2nd Constituent Assembly; re-elected 1946; contested (Indep.), 1951. Président de l'Exécutif du Mouvement Universel pour une Confédération Mondiale, 1947-51. Founded the Companions of Emmaüs, a movement to provide a roof for the "sanslogis" of Paris. *Publications*: 23 Mois de Vie Clandestine; L'Abbé Pierre vous Parle; Vers l'Homme; Feuilles Eparses. *Address*: 2 Avenue de la Liberté, Charenton-Val de Marne, France. *T*: 368.62.44.

PIERRE, Sir (Joseph) Henry, Kt 1957; FRCS; Consultant Surgeon, General Hospital, Port of Spain, Trinidad, WI, since 1950; Hon. Surgeon, Caura Tuberculosis Sanatorium, Trinidad; Hon. Surgeon, Mental Hospital, Trinidad; *b* 28 Oct. 1904; *s* of Charles Henry and Carmen M. Pierre; *m* 1939; one *s*; *m* 1962, Marjorie Boös; one *s*. *Educ*: Queen's Royal College, Trinidad. WI; St Bartholomew's Hosp., London; London Univ.; Royal Coll. of Surgeons, Edinburgh. Qualified in medicine, 1931; Casualty House Physician, St Bartholomew's Hosp., 1931; junior MO, Trinidad Medical Service, 1932; FRCSE 1939; FRCS 1959; Medical Officer, Grade A, 1945; Sen. Officer Surgeon, Gen. Hosp., San Fernando, 1945; Pres., Trinidad and Tobago Red Cross Soc.; Fellow Internat. Coll. of Surgeons, USA. Navy Meritorious Public Service Citation from US Govt, 1957. Coronation Medal, 1953. *Recreations*: photography, golf, yachting, tennis, horticulture. *Address*: Mira flores, 4 River Road, Maracas Valley, St Joseph, Trinidad, West Indies. *T*: 662-3094. *Clubs*: Royal Commonwealth Society (West Indian); Yacht, Union, Country, St Andrew's Golf, (Hon. mem.) Pointe-a-Pierre, UBOT (Trinidad, WI).

PIERS, Sir Charles Robert Fitzmaurice, 10th Bt, *cr* 1660; Lt-Comdr RCNVR; *b* 30 Aug. 1903; *s* of Sir Charles Piers, 9th Bt, and Hester Constance (Stella) (*d* 1936), *e d* of late S. R. Brewis of Ibstone House, Ibstone; *S* father, 1945; *m* 1936, Ann Blanche Scott (*d* 1975), *o d* of late Capt. Thomas Ferguson (The Royal Highlanders); one *s* one *d*. *Educ*: RN Colleges, Osborne and Dartmouth. Served European War, 1939-45. *Heir*: *s* James Desmond Piers, *b* 24 July 1947. *Address*: Duncan, British Columbia, Canada.

PIERSON, Warren Lee; Chairman, All America Cable and Radio; Director: Vertientes-Camaguey Sugar Co., Cuba; Molybdenum Corporation of America; The Commercial Cable Co.; ITT World Communications Inc.; Twin Fair, Inc., etc; *b* Princeton, Minn, 29 Aug. 1896; *s* of Louis W. and Hilda Pearson Pierson; *m* 1927, Eleanor Mehnert; no *c*. *Educ*: Univ. of California (AB); Harvard Univ. (LLB). Pres. and Gen. Counsel, Export-Import Bank, 1936-45; Special Counsel, Reconstruction Finance Corp., 1933-34; Mem. Nat. Emergency Council, 1934-36; Adviser to US Delegation: at 3rd meeting, Consultation of Ministers, Amer. Republics, Rio de Janeiro, 1942; at UN Monetary Conf., Bretton Woods NH, 1944; at Inter-American

Conf. on Problems of War and Peace, Mexico City, 1945. US Member of Tripartite Commission on German Debts, 1951-53; Pres., International Chamber of Commerce, 1955. Has several Orders of foreign countries. *Address*: (office) 320 Park Avenue, New York, NY 10022. *T*: Plaza 2-6000; Further Lane, East Hampton, Long Island. *T*: (516) 324-1066. *Clubs*: Brook (New York); Maidstone, Devon Yacht (Long Island).

PIGGOTT, Maj.-Gen. Francis James Claude, CB 1963; CBE 1961; DSO 1945; *b* Tokyo, Japan, 11 Oct. 1910; *s* of late Maj.-Gen. F. S. G. Piggott, CB, DSO; *m* 1940, Muriel Joan, *d* of late Wilfred E. Cottam, Rotherham, Yorks; one *s* one *d*. *Educ*: Cheltenham; RMC Sandhurst. 2nd Lieut The Queen's Royal Regt, 1931; Language Officer, Japan, 1935-37; Captain, 1939; served 1939-45 in France (despatches), New Zealand, India and Burma (DSO); in Japan, UK and Egypt (OBE and Bt Lt-Col), 1946-52; attended 1st Course, Joint Services Staff Coll., 1947; Lt-Col comdg 1st Bn The Queen's Royal Regt, 1952, BAOR and Malaya; Colonel, War Office, 1954; Comd 161 Infantry Bde (TA), 1956; Dep. Director of Military Intelligence, War Office (Brigadier), 1958; Major-General, 1961; Assistant Chief of Staff (Intelligence), SHAPE, 1961-64; retired, 1964; served in Civil Service (Security), 1965-75. Col, The Queen's Royal Surrey Regt, 1964-66; Dep. Col (Surrey) The Queen's Regt, 1967-69. *Recreations*: cricket and foreign travel. *Address*: 30 Queen's Road, Frinton, Essex. *T*: Frinton 5425. *Clubs*: Army and Navy, Free Foresters.

PIGGOTT, Lester Keith, OBE 1975; Champion Jockey for ninth time at end of British Flat racing season of 1971 (also in 1960 and yearly since 1964); *b* 5 Nov. 1935; *s* of Keith Piggott and Iris Rickaby; *m* 1960, Susan Armstrong; two *d*. Selection of races won: the Derby (8 times): 1954 (on Never Say Die); 1957 (on Crepello); 1960 (on St Paddy); 1968 (on Sir Ivor); 1970 (on Nijinsky); 1972 (on Roberto); 1976 (on Empery); 1977 (on The Minstrel); St Leger (7 times); in 1975 equalled record of 21 classic victories. In several seasons since 1955 he has ridden well over 100 winners a year, in this country alone; rode 3,000th winner in Britain, 27 July 1974; rides frequently in France; won Prix de l'Arc de Triomphe on Rheingold, 1973, on Alleged, 1977. Won Washington, DC, International on Sir Ivor, 1968 (first time since 1922 an English Derby winner raced in USA), and on Karabas, 1969. *Recreations*: swimming, water skiing, golf. *Address*: Florizel, Newmarket, Suffolk. *T*: Newmarket 2584.

PIGGOTT, Prof. Stuart, CBE 1972; FBA 1953; Abercromby Professor of Prehistoric Archæology, University of Edinburgh, 1946-77; *b* 28 May 1910; *s* of G. H. O. Piggott. *Educ*: Churchers Coll., Petersfield; St John's Coll., Oxford. On staff on Royal Commn on Ancient Monuments (Wales), 1929-34; Asst Dir of Avebury excavations, 1934-38; from 1939 in ranks and later as Intelligence Officer in Army in charge of military air photograph interpretation, South-East Asia. Conducted archæological excavations in southern England and carried out research on European prehistory up to 1942; in India, 1942-45; studied Oriental prehistory. Hon. DLittHum, Columbia, 1954. Fellow of Royal Soc. of Edinburgh, and of Soc. of Antiquaries; Mem. German Archæolog. Inst., 1953; Hon. Mem. Royal Irish Acad., 1956; Foreign Hon. Member American Academy of Arts and Sciences, 1960; advisory editor, Antiquity. Trustee, British Museum, 1968-74. Travelled in Europe and Asia. *Publications*: Some Ancient Cities of India, 1946; Fire Among the Ruins, 1948; British Prehistory, 1949; William Stukeley: an XVIII Century Antiquary, 1950; Prehistoric India, 1950; A Picture Book of Ancient British Art (with G. E. Daniel), 1951; Neolithic Cultures of British Isles, 1954; Scotland before History, 1958; Approach to Archæology, 1959; (ed) The Dawn of Civilization, 1961; The West Kennet Long Barrow, 1962; Ancient Europe, 1965; Prehistoric Societies (with J. G. D. Clark), 1965; The Druids, 1968; Introduction to Camden's Britannia of 1695, 1971; (ed jtly) France Before the Romans, 1974; Ruins in a Landscape, 1977; numerous technical papers in archæological jls. *Recreations*: reading, cooking, travel. *Address*: The Cottage, West Challon, Wantage, Oxon. *Club*: United Oxford & Cambridge University.

PIGOT, Brig.-Gen. Sir Robert, 6th Bt, of Patshull, *cr* 1764; DSO 1916; MC; Brevet Lieutenant Colonel Rifle Brigade, retired; *b* 3 May 1882; *s* of Sir G. Pigot, 5th Bt, and Alice, *d* of Sir James Thompson Mackenzie, 1st Bt, of Glen Muick; *S* father, 1934; *m* 1913, Norah Beatrice Oakley, *y d* of C. Reginald Hargreaves, Remenham, Bucks; three *d*. Served European War 1914-18 (despatches, DSO, MC, Bt Maj., Bt Lieut-Col); Flying Officer RAFVR, 1939; resigned commn with rank of Wing Comdr, 1944. *Publication*: Twenty-five Years' Big-Game Hunting, 1928. *Heir*: *n* Maj.-Gen. Robert Anthony Pigot, *qv*. *Address*: Yarlington Lodge, Wincanton, Somerset.

PIGOT, Maj.-Gen. Robert Anthony, CB 1964; OBE 1959; *b* 6 July 1915; *s* of late George Douglas Hugh Pigot and Hersey Elizabeth Pigot; *heir-pres.* to Brig.-Gen. Sir Robert Pigot, 6th Bt, *qv*; *m* 1942, Honor (*d* 1966), *d* of late Capt. Wilfred St Martin Gibbon; one *s* one *d*; *m* 1968, Sarah Anne Colville, *e d* of Mr David and Lady Joan Colville, The Old Vicarage, Dorton; one *s* one *d*. *Educ:* Stowe Sch. Commissioned into the Royal Marines, 1934; served War of 1939-45 (despatches): Regimental service in RM Div. and Special Service Group; Staff appts in 3rd Commando Brigade in SE Asia; psc 1943-44; Directing Staff, Staff Coll., Camberley, 1946-47; Min. of Defence, 1953-54; Standing Group, NATO, Washington, 1954-57; Dep. Standing Gp Rep. with North Atlantic Council, Paris, 1958-59; Chief of Staff, Royal Marines, 1960-64; retd, Dec. 1964. Man. Director, Bone Brothers Ltd, 1964-66; Director: John Brown Plastics Machinery Ltd, 1965-66; Executive Appointments Ltd, 1968-70. *Recreations:* field sports and yachting. *Address:* Yew Tree Lodge, Bembridge, Isle of Wight. *Clubs:* Royal Yacht Squadron; Bembridge Sailing.

PIGOT, Thomas Herbert, QC 1967; **His Honour Judge Pigot;** a Circuit Judge, since 1972; Deputy Senior Judge (non-resident), Sovereign Base Area, Cyprus; *b* 19 May 1921; *e s* of late Thomas Pigot and of Martha Ann Pigot; *m* 1950, Zena Marguerite, *yr d* of late Tom and Dorothy Gladys Wall; three *d*. *Educ:* Manchester Gram. Sch. (Schol.); Brasenose Coll., Oxford (Somerset Schol.). BA (1st cl. hons Jurisprudence) 1941; MA 1946; BCL 1947. Commissioned Welch Regt, 1942; served N Africa with Royal Lincs Regt; wounded and taken prisoner, 1943; released, 1945. Called to Bar, Inner Temple, 1947; practised in Liverpool on Northern Circuit until 1967. Mem., Bar Council, 1970. *Recreations:* golf, fell walking, watching Rugby football (both codes). *Address:* (home) 55 Westbourne Road, Birkdale, Southport, Lancs. *T:* Southport 67398; (London) Flat 8, Hawcroft Court, 19/21 York Street, W1. *T:* 01-935 7606; (professional) 2 Pump Court, Temple, EC4. *T:* 01-353 3106/7540. *Clubs:* United Oxford & Cambridge University, White Elephant; Vincent's (Oxford); Athenæum (Liverpool); Royal Birkdale Golf.

PIGOTT, Major Sir Berkeley, 4th Bt, *cr* 1808; *b* 29 May 1894; *s* of Charles Berkeley, *e s* of 3rd Bt and Fanny Ada, *d* of Rev. W. P. Pigott; *S* grandfather, 1911; *m* 1919, Christabel (*d* 1974), *d* of late Rev. F. H. Bowden-Smith, of Careys, Brockenhurst, Hants; one *s* two *d*. Served European War, 1914-18; Adjutant Ceylon Mounted Rifles and Ceylon Planters' Rifle Corps, 1924-28; retired pay, 1930; President, The National Pony Society, 1948; Chairman County Polo Association, 1948; Verderer of the New Forest, 1955-68; Chairman National Pony Society, 1961-62. *Heir: s* Berkeley Henry Sebastian Pigott [*b* 24 June 1925; *m* 1954, Jean, *d* of J. W. Balls, Surlingham, Norfolk; two *s* one *d*]. *Address:* 86 Admirals Walk, Bournemouth.

PIGOTT, Rt. Rev. Harold Grant, CBE 1969; *b* 20 Aug. 1894; *s* of Robert and Rosalind Pigott. *Educ:* Antigua Gram. Sch.; Codrington Coll., Barbados. BA 1916, MA 1918. Head Master Parry Sch., Barbados and Curate St Lucy, 1917-21. St Vincent: Curate, Cath., 1921; then Rector of Barrouallie, 1921-26, and of Calliaqua, 1926-33. Archdeacon of St Vincent and St Lucia, 1929-45; Canon of Cath. St Vincent, 1929-62, and Rector of Georgetown, 1933-37, Grenada. Rector: St Andrew, 1937-45, St George, 1945-62; Archdeacon of Grenada, 1945-62. Bishop of Windward Islands, 1962-69. Coronation Medal, 1953. *Publication:* Daily Meditations on the Lenten Epistles, 1939. *Address:* c/o PO Box 128, Sion Hill, St Vincent, Windward Islands.

PIGOTT, Air Vice-Marshal Michael Joseph, CBE 1956; Director of Dental Services, RAF, 1954-58; retired, 1958; *b* 16 May 1904; *m* 1938, Ethel Norah, *d* of Alfred Sutherland Blackman; one *d*. *Educ:* Blackrock College, Dublin; Nat. Univ. of Ireland; Nat. Dental Hosp. of Ireland. BDS 1925; FDSRCS 1948. Joined RAF 1930. Served War of 1939-45, Bomber Command; Inspecting Dental Officer: MEAF, 1945-48, Flying Trng Comd, 1948-49, Tech. Trng Comd, 1949-50; Principal Dental Officer, Home Comd 1950-54; Air Vice-Marshal, 1955. QHDS, 1950-58. *Address:* 18 Duck Street, Cerne Abbas, Dorchester, Dorset DT2 7LA. *T:* Cerne Abbas 538.

PIGOTT-BROWN, Sir William Brian, 3rd Bt, *cr* 1902; *b* 20 Jan. 1941; *s* of Sir John Pigott-Brown, 2nd Bt (killed in action, 1942) and Helen (who *m* 1948, Capt. Charles Raymond Radclyffe), *o d* of Major Gilbert Egerton Cotton, Priestland, Tarporley, Cheshire; *S* father, 1942. *Heir:* none. *Address:* Orchard House, Aston Upthorpe, Oxfordshire; 25 Chapel Street, SW1.

PIHL, Brig. Hon. Dame Mary Mackenzie, (Fru Mary Pihl), DBE 1970 (MBE 1958); Director, Women's Royal Army Corps, 1967-Aug. 1970, retired; *b* 3 Feb. 1916; *d* of Sir John Anderson, later 1st Viscount Waverley, PC, GCB, OM, GCSI, GCIE, FRS, and Christina Mackenzie Anderson; *m* 1973, Frithjof Pihl. *Educ:* Sutton High Sch.; Villa Brillantmont, Lausanne. Joined Auxiliary Territorial Service, 1941; transferred to Women's Royal Army Corps, 1949. Hon. ADC to the Queen, 1967-70. *Address:* Engø, 3145 Tjøme, Norway. *Club:* English-Speaking Union.

PIKE, Baroness *cr* 1974 (Life Peer), of Melton, Leics; **Irene Mervyn Parnicott Pike;** Chairman, Women's Royal Voluntary Service, since 1974; *b* 16 Sept. 1918; *d* of I. S. Pike, Company Director, Okehampton, Devonshire. *Educ:* Hunmanby Hall; Reading University. BA Hons Economics and Psychology, 1941. Served WAAF, 1941-46. Mem., WRCC, 1955-57. Contested (C): Pontefract, 1951; Leek, Staffordshire, 1955. MP (C) Melton, Leics, Dec. 1956-Feb. 1974; Assistant Postmaster-General, 1959-63; Joint Parliamentary Under-Secretary of State, Home Office, 1963-64. Chm., Economic Models Ltd; Director: Watts, Blake, Bearne & Co. Ltd; Dunderdale Investments. Chm., IBA Gen. Adv. Council, 1974-. *Recreations:* gardening, walking. *Address:* 25 Chester Row, SW1; Hownam, near Kelso, Roxburgh.

PIKE, Andrew Hamilton, CMG 1956; OBE 1945; Minister for Lands and Mineral Resources, Tanganyika, 1957-59, retired; *b* 26 August 1903; *s* of late Canon William Pike, Thurles, Co. Tipperary; *m* 1951, Catherine Provan Cathcart, *y d* of late Prof. E. P. Cathcart, CBE; four *s*. *Educ:* The Abbey, Tipperary; Trinity College, Dublin; University College, Oxford. Tanganyika: Administrative Officer (Cadet), 1927; Asst Dist Officer, 1930; Dist Officer, 1938; Dep. Provincial Comr, 1947; Provincial Comr, 1948; Senior Provincial Comr, 1951; Member for Lands and Mines, 1953. President Tanganyika Society, 1954-57; Member Editorial Board of "Tanganyika Notes and Records", until 1959. *Recreation:* golf. *Address:* Blatchfeld, Blackheath, near Guildford, Surrey. *T:* Bramley 2358. *See also Rt Rev. St J. S. Pike, Sir Theodore Pike, Rt Rev. V. J. Pike.*

PIKE, Air Cdre James Maitland Nicholson, CB 1963; DSO 1942; DFC 1941; RAF, retired; with Ministry of Defence, since 1969; *b* 8 Feb. 1916; *s* of late Frank Pike, Glendarary, Achill Island, Co. Mayo, Eire, and Daphne (*née* Kenyon Stow), Worcester; *m* 1st, 1942; one *d*; 2nd, 1955, Amber Pauline Bettesworth Hellard; one *s* one step *d*; 3rd, 1972, Dorothy May Dawson (*née* Holland); one step *d*. *Educ:* Stowe; RAF Coll., Cranwell. Commnd 1937; War Service: Aden, Middle East, UK (Coastal Command), Malta and Azores. Directing staff, RAF Staff Coll., 1945-47; Group Capt. 1955; Comd RAF Station, St Mawgan and RAF Station, Kinloss, 1955-57; SASO, RAF Malta, 1958-60; Air Cdre 1961; AOC, RAF Gibraltar, 1961-62; Imperial Defence College, 1963; Air Cdre Intelligence (B), Ministry of Defence, 1964; Dir of Security, RAF, 1965-69. *Recreations:* shooting, fishing. *Address:* Glendarary, Christmas Common, Watlington, Oxford.

PIKE, Michael Edmund; HM Diplomatic Service; Counsellor, Washington, since 1975; *b* 4 Oct. 1931; *s* of Henry Pike and Eleanor Pike; *m* 1962, Catherine (*née* Lim); one *s* two *d*. *Educ:* Wimbledon Coll.; London Sch. of Econs and Polit. Science; Brasenose Coll., Oxford (MA 1956). Service in HM Armed Forces, 1950-52. Editor, Cherwell, Oxford Univ., 1954; part-time News Reporter, Sunday Express, 1954-55; Feature Writer and Film Critic, Surrey Comet, 1955-56; joined HM Foreign (now Diplomatic) Service, 1956; Third Secretary: FO, 1956-57; Seoul, 1957-59; Second Secretary: Office of Comr Gen. for Singapore and SE Asia, 1960-62; Seoul, 1962-64; FO, 1964-68; First Sec., Warsaw, 1968-70; FCO, 1970-73; First Sec., Washington, 1973-75. Pres., Union of Catholic Students of GB, 1955-56. *Recreations:* reading, mild jogging, contemplating Greenwich. *Address:* c/o Foreign and Commonwealth Office, SW1; 5 Crooms Hill, Greenwich, SE10 8ER. *T:* 01-858 7716.

PIKE, Sir Philip Ernest Housden, Kt 1969; Chief Justice of Swaziland, 1970-72, retired; *b* 6 March 1914; *s* of Rev. Ernest Benjamin Pike and Dora Case Pike (*née* Lillie); *m* 2nd, 1959, Millicent Locke Staples; one *s* one *d* of 1st marriage. *Educ:* De Carteret School, and Munro Coll., Jamaica; Middle Temple, London. Barrister at Law, 1938. Crown Counsel, Jamaica, 1947-49; Legal Draftsman, Kenya, 1949-52; Solicitor General, Uganda, 1952-58; QC (Uganda) 1953; Attorney General, Sarawak, 1958-65; QC (Sarawak) 1958; Chief Justice, High Court in Borneo, 1965-68; Judge, High Court of Malawi, 1969-70, Actg Chief Justice, 1970. Coronation Medal, 1953. PNBS-Sarawak, 1965; Malaysia Commemorative Medal, 1967; PMN Malaysia 1968. *Recreations:* golf, photography. *Address:* c/o Barclay's National Bank Ltd, Adderley Street, Cape Town, South Africa.

PIKE, Rt. Rev. St John Surridge; DD *jure dig* 1958; an Assistant Bishop, Diocese of Guildford, since 1963; Vicar of Holy Trinity, Botleys and Lyne, and Christ Church, Longcross (in plurality), since 1971; *b* 27 Dec. 1909; *s* of late Rev. Canon William Pike, Thurles, Co. Tipperary; *m* 1958, Clare, *d* of William Henry Jones; one *s* one *d* (and one *s* decd). *Educ:* The Abbey, Tipperary; Bishop Foy School, Waterford; Trinity Coll., Dublin (MA). Deacon, 1932; Priest, 1934; Curate of Taney, 1932-37; Head of Southern Church Mission, Ballymacarrett, Belfast, 1937-47; SPG Missionary, Diocese of Gambia, 1947-52; Rector of St George's, Belfast, 1952-57; Commissary for Gambia in N Ireland, 1954-57; Bishop of Gambia and the Rio Pongas, 1958-63; Vicar of St Mary the Virgin, Ewshot, 1963-71. *Address:* The Vicarage, Lyne and Longcross, Chertsey, Surrey. *T:* Ottershaw 3551.

PIKE, Sir Theodore (Ouseley), KCMG 1956 (CMG 1953); *b* 1904; 3rd *s* of late Canon W. Pike, Thurles, Co. Tipperary; *m* 1934, Violet F., *d* of late Sir William Robinson, DL, JP; two *s* one *d. Educ:* The Abbey, Tipperary; Trinity Coll., Dublin; University Coll., Oxford. Colonial Administrative Service, Tanganyika, 1928-53. Governor, Somaliland Protectorate, 1953; Governor and Commander-in-Chief, Somaliland Protectorate, 1954-59. Hon. LLD (Dublin). *Address:* c/o Grindlay's Bank, 23 Fenchurch Street, EC3.

PIKE, Marshal of the Royal Air Force Sir Thomas (Geoffrey), GCB 1961 (KCB 1955; CB 1946); CBE 1944; DFC 1942 and Bar, 1942; DL; Deputy Supreme Allied Commander, Europe, 1964-67; *b* 29 June 1906; *s* of late Capt. S. R. Pike, RA; *m* 1930, Kathleen Althea, *e d* of Maj. H. Elwell; one *s* two *d. Educ:* Bedford School; RAF Coll., Cranwell. Joined RAF, 1923. Served War of 1939-45, Directorate of Organisation, Air Ministry; commanded a Fighter Squadron, 1941; Desert Air Force, 1943-45; AOC No 11 Group Fighter Command, 1950-51; DCS, HQ Air Forces Central Europe, 1951-53; Deputy Chief of the Air Staff, Dec. 1953-July 1956; Air Officer Commanding-in-Chief, Fighter Command, July 1956-Dec. 1959; Chief of the Air Staff, 1960-63. Squadron Leader, 1937; Group Captain, 1941; Air Commodore, 1944; Air Vice-Marshal, 1950; Air Marshal, 1955; Air Chief Marshal, 1957; Marshal of the RAF, 1962. DL Essex, 1973. Officer Legion of Merit (USA). *Address:* Little Wynters, Hastingwood, Harlow, Essex.
See also Lt-Gen. Sir William Pike.

PIKE, Rt. Rev. Victor Joseph, CB 1953; CBE 1950 (OBE 1944); DD (*hc*) 1955; *b* 1 July 1907; *s* of late Canon William Pike, Thurles, Co. Tipperary, and Mrs William Pike (*née* Surridge); *m* 1937, Dorothea Elizabeth Frend, *d* of late Capt. W. R. Frend, Sherwood Foresters; one *s* two *d. Educ:* Bishop Foy School, Waterford; Trinity College, Dublin, BA 1930; MA 1935 (Hon. DD 1955). Curate, Dundrum, Co. Dublin, 1930-32; CF 4th Class, Aldershot, Gibraltar, RMA Woolwich, 1932-39; Senior Chaplain, 43rd Div., 11th Armoured Div., 1940-42; DACG, 5th Corps, CMF, 1942-44; ACG, 8th Army, 1945 (despatches); DCG, MELF, 1946; ACG, Western Command, 1947-49; ACG, BAOR, 1950-51; Chaplain-General to the Forces, 1951-60 (with title of Archdeacon, 1958-60); Prebend of Fordington with Writhlington in Salisbury Cathedral, 1960; Bishop Suffragan of Sherborne, 1960-76. Hon. Canon of Canterbury, 1951-60; QHC, 1948-53; Chaplain to the Queen, Nov. 1953-June 1960. *Recreation:* Rugby. *Address:* 53 The Close, Salisbury, Wilts. *T:* Salisbury 5766. *Club:* Cavalry and Guards.
See also A . H . Pike, Rt Rev . St J . S . Pike, Sir Theodore Pike.

PIKE, Lt-Gen. Sir William (Gregory Huddleston), KCB 1961 (CB 1956); CBE 1952; DSO 1943; Chief Commander, St John Ambulance, 1969-75; *b* 24 June 1905; *s* of late Captain Sydney Royston Pike, RA, and Sarah Elizabeth Pike (*née* Huddleston); *m* 1939, Josephine Margaret, *er d* of late Maj.-Gen. R. H. D. Tompson, CB, CMG, DSO, and Mrs B. D. Tompson; one *s* two *d. Educ:* Bedford School; Marlborough Coll.; RMA Woolwich. Lieutenant RA, 20th and 24th Field Brigades, RA and "A" Field Brigade, Indian Artillery, 1925-36; Staff College, Camberley, 1937-38; Command and Staff Appointments in UK, France and Belgium, North Africa, USA and Far East, 1939-50; CRA, 1st Commonwealth Div., Korea, 1951-52; idc 1953; Director of Staff Duties, War Office, 1954-57; Chief of Staff, Far East Land Forces, Oct. 1957-60; Vice-Chief of the Imperial General Staff, 1960-63; Col Comdt RA, 1962-70. Lieutenant of HM Tower of London, 1963-66; Commissioner-in-Chief, St John Ambulance Brigade, 1967-73. Jt Hon. Pres., Anglo-Korean Society, 1963-69. Hon. Col 277 (Argyll and Sutherland Highlanders) Regt RA (TA), 1960-67; Hon. Col Lowland Regt RA (T), 1967-70. Member Honourable Artillery Company; Governor, Lucas-Tooth Boy's Gymnasium; Chm., Lord Mayor Treloar Trust; Corps of Commissionaires, 1964 (Mem.

Administrative Bd). Officer, US Legion of Merit, 1953. GCStJ 1976. *Recreations:* field sports and gardening. *Address:* Ganwells, Bentley, Hants; Rhos-y-Bayvil, Velindre, Crymych, Dyfed.
See also Marshal of the Royal Air Force Sir Thomas Pike.

PILCHER, Sir (Charlie) Dennis, Kt 1974; CBE 1968; FRICS; Chairman, Commission for the New Towns, since 1971; Consultant, late Senior Partner (Partner 1930), Graves, Son & Pilcher (Chartered Surveyors); Director, Save and Prosper Group Ltd, since 1970; *b* 2 July 1906; *s* of Charlie Edwin Pilcher, Fareham, Hants; *m* 1929, Mary Allison Aumonier, *d* of William Aumonier, London; two *d. Educ:* Claysmore Sch. Served War: Major, RA (despatches, Normandy), 1940-45. Hemel Hempstead Development Corp., 1949-56; Bracknell Development Corp., 1956-71 (Chm. 1968-71). Pres., RICS, 1963-64; Mem., Milner Holland Cttee on London Housing, 1963-64; Vice-Pres., London Rent Assessment Panel, 1966-70; Adviser to Business Rents Directorate of DoE, 1973. *Recreations:* opera, golf, fishing. *Address:* Brambles, Batts Lane, Mare Hill, Pulborough, West Sussex. *T:* Pulborough 2126. *Club:* Garrick.

PILCHER, Sir John (Arthur), GCMG 1973 (KCMG 1966; CMG 1957); HM Diplomatic Service, retired; Director, Foreign & Colonial Investment Trust, since 1973; Chairman: Brazil Fund, since 1975; Fleming Japan Fund, SA, since 1976; Adviser on Far Eastern Affairs, Robert Fleming & Co., since 1973; *b* 16 May 1912; *s* of late Lt-Col A. J. Pilcher; *m* 1942, Delia Margaret Taylor; one *d. Educ:* Shrewsbury; Clare Coll., Cambridge; France, Austria and Italy. Served in Japan, 1936-39; China, 1939-41; Ministry of Information and Foreign Office, 1941-48; Italy, 1948-51; Foreign Office, 1951-54; Spain (Counsellor, Madrid), 1954-59; Philippines (Ambassador), 1959-63; Assistant Under-Secretary, Foreign Office, 1963-65; Ambassador to: Austria, 1965-67; Japan, 1967-72. Member: Standing Commn on Museums and Galleries, 1973-; Cttee, Soc. for Protection of Ancient Buildings, 1974-; Treasure Trove Reviewing Cttee, 1977-. Grand Cross (Gold) Austrian Decoration of Honour, 1966; Order of the Rising Sun, First Class, Japan, 1971; Grand Official of Order of Merit of the Italian Republic, 1977. *Address:* 33 The Terrace, SW13. *T:* 01-876 9710. *Club:* Brooks's.

PILCHER, Robin Sturtevant, MS, FRCS, FRCP; Emeritus Professor of Surgery, University of London; Professor of Surgery and Director of the Surgical Unit, University College Hospital, London, 1938-67; *b* 22 June 1902; *s* of Thorold and Helena Pilcher; *m* 1929, Mabel Pearks; one *s* one *d. Educ:* St Paul's Sch.; University Coll., London. Fellow University Coll., London. *Publications:* various surgical papers. *Address:* Swanbourne, 21 Church End, Haddenham, Bucks. *T:* Haddenham 291048.

PILDITCH, Sir Richard (Edward), 4th Bt, *cr* 1929; *b* 8 Sept. 1926; *s* of Sir Philip Harold Pilditch, 2nd Bt, and Frances Isabella, *d* of J. G. Weeks, JP, Bedlington, Northumberland; *S* brother (Sir Philip John Frederick Pilditch, 3rd Bt) 1954; *m* 1950, Pauline Elizabeth Smith; one *s* one *d. Educ:* Charterhouse. Served War of 1939-45, with Royal Navy, in India and Ceylon, 1944-45. *Recreations:* shooting, fishing. *Heir:* *s* John Richard Pilditch, *b* 24 Sept. 1955. *Address:* 4 Fishermans Bank, Mudeford, Christchurch, Hants.

PILE, Colonel Sir Frederick (Devereux), 3rd Bt *cr* 1900; MC 1945; *b* 10 Dec. 1915; *s* of Gen. Sir Frederick Alfred Pile, 2nd Bt, GCB, DSO, MC; *S* father, 1976; *m* 1940, Pamela, *d* of late Philip Henstock; two *d. Educ:* Weymouth; RMC, Sandhurst. Joined Royal Tank Regt, 1935; served War of 1939-45, Egypt and NW Europe; commanded Leeds Rifles, 1955-56; Colonel GS, BJSM, Washington, DC, 1957-60; Commander, RAC Driving and Maintenance School, 1960-62. Secretary, Royal Soldiers' Daughters' School, 1965-71. *Recreations:* fishing, cricket, travelling. *Heir:* *b* John Devereux Pile, *qv. Address:* Harriet House, Sedlescombe, Battle, Sussex. *T:* Sedlescombe 240. *Club:* MCC.

PILE, John Devereux; Chairman, Imperial Group Ltd, since 1975 (Group Chief Executive, 1973-75; Member, Group Policy Committee, since 1971; Director, since 1967); *b* 5 June 1918; 2nd *s* of Gen. Sir Frederick A. Pile, 2nd Bt, GCB, DSO, MC, and Lady Ferguson; *b* and *heir-pres* : to Sir Frederick Devereux Pile, 3rd Bt, *qv*; *m* 1946, Katharine Mary Shafe; two *s* two *d. Educ:* Weymouth Coll., Dorset; Trinity Coll., Cambridge (MA). Service with RA, 1939-46 (Major). Joined Imperial Tobacco Group, 1946; Manager, W. D. & H. O. Wills and Wm Clarke & Son, Dublin, 1956-59; Chairman: Robert Sinclair Ltd, 1960-64; Churchmans, 1964-67; Chm. and Man. Dir, W. D. & H. O. Wills, 1968-71; Dep. Chm., Imperial Tobacco Gp Ltd, 1971-73;

Dir, Nat. West. Bank, 1977-. Member: Council, BIM, 1973-(FBIM 1971); Council, CBI, 1975-; Council, Industry for Management Educn, 1975-. Governor, London Graduate Sch. of Business Studies, 1976-. Freeman of City of London. *Address:* Munstead, Godalming, Surrey. *T:* Godalming 4716.

PILE, Sir William (Dennis), KCB 1971 (CB 1968); MBE 1944; Chairman, Board of Inland Revenue, since 1976; *b* 1 Dec. 1919; *s* of James Edward Pile and Jean Elizabeth Pile; *m* 1st, 1939, Brenda Skinner (marr. diss. 1947); 2nd, 1948, Joan Marguerite Crafter; one *s* two *d. Educ:* Royal Masonic School; St Catharine's College, Cambridge. Served Border Regt, 1940-45. Ministry of Education, 1947-50, 1951-66; Cabinet Office, 1950; Asst Under-Sec. of State: Dept of Education and Science, 1962; Ministry of Health, 1966; Dep. Under-Sec. of State, Home Office, 1967-70; Director-General, Prison Service, 1969-70; Permanent Under-Sec. of State, DES, 1970-76. *Address:* The Manor House, Riverhead, near Sevenoaks, Kent. *T:* Sevenoaks 54498. *Clubs:* United Oxford & Cambridge University; Hawks (Cambridge).

PILKINGTON, family name of **Baron Pilkington.**

PILKINGTON, Baron, *cr* 1968 (Life Peer), of St Helens; **Harry (William Henry) Pilkington,** Kt 1953; Chairman, Pilkington Brothers Ltd, 1949-73, non-executive Director, since 1973; Chancellor of Loughborough University of Technology since 1966; Vice Lord-Lieutenant, Merseyside, since 1974; *b* 19 April 1905; *e s* of Richard Austin Pilkington and Hon. Hope (*née* Cozens-Hardy); *m* 1930, Rosamond Margaret Rowan (*d* 1953); one *s* one *d* (and one *d* decd); *m* 1961, Mrs Mavis Wilding. *Educ:* Rugby; Magdalene Coll., Cambridge. Director of the Bank of England, 1955-72. President: Federation of British Industries, 1953-55; Council of European Industrial Federations, 1954-57; Court of British Shippers' Council, 1971-74; Chairman: Royal Commn to consider pay of Doctors and Dentists, 1957-60; Cttee on Broadcasting, 1960-62; National Advisory Council for Education for Industry and Commerce, 1956-66; Econ. Develt Cttee for the Chemical Industry, 1967-72; NW Management Centre, 1974-76; NW Regional Sports and Recreations Council, 1976-; Mem. Council Manchester Business Sch., 1964-72; President: Assoc. of Technical Institutions, 1966-68; British Plastics Fedn, 1972-74. DL Lancs, 1968. Hon. FIOB 1974. Hon. LLD: Manchester, 1959; Liverpool, 1963; Hon. DSc Loughborough, 1966; Hon. DCL Kent, 1968. Freeman, St Helens, 1968. *Recreations:* walking, gardening, tennis, cycling. *Address:* Windle Hall, St Helens, Lancs. *T:* 23423. *Club:* United Oxford & Cambridge University.

PILKINGTON, Sir Alastair; *see* Pilkington, Sir L. A. B.

PILKINGTON, Charles Vere; retired as Chairman, Sotheby & Co.; *b* 11 Jan. 1905; *e s* of Charles Carlisle Pilkington and Emilia (*née* Lloyd); *m* 1936, Honor Chedworth (*d* 1961), *y d* of first and last Baron Kylsant; one *s. Educ:* Eton; Christ Church, Oxford, (MA). Dir, Sotheby & Co., Fine Art Auctioneers, 1927-58, Chm. 1953-58. Member of Council, Royal Musical Assoc., 1952-58; Member Business Cttee Musica Britannica. *Recreation:* music (harpsichord). *Address:* Casal da Nora, Colares, Portugal. *T:* 2990.253. *Clubs:* Travellers'; Eça de Queiroz.

PILKINGTON, Rev. Canon Evan Matthias, MA; Chaplain to the Queen since 1969; Canon Residentiary of St Paul's Cathedral since 1976; *b* 27 Dec. 1916; *s* of Rev. Matthias Pilkington; *m* 1946, Elsie (*née* Lashley); four *s. Educ:* Worksop Coll.; Keble Coll., Oxford; Cuddesdon Theol. College. Curate of: Bottesford and Ashby, Scunthorpe, 1940; Holy Trinity, Southall, 1942; St John the Divine, Kennington, 1944; Vicar of: East Kirkby and Miningsby, Lincs, 1946; Holy Trinity, Upper Tooting, 1952; Kingston upon Thames, 1961; Canon Residentiary, Bristol Cathedral, 1968-76. *Recreations:* walking, lettering. *Address:* 3 Amen Court, EC4M 7BU.

PILKINGTON, Godfrey; *see* Pilkington, R. G.

PILKINGTON, Lawrence Herbert Austin, CBE 1964; JP; Director, Pilkington Brothers Ltd, since 1935; *b* 13 Oct. 1911; 2nd *s* of Richard Austin and Hon. Hope Pilkington; *m* 1936, Norah Holden, Whitby, Ont., Canada; two *d. Educ:* Bromsgrove School; Magdalene College, Cambridge. Volunteer with Grenfell Mission, 1933-34. Joined Pilkington Brothers Limited, 1935. Chairman: Glass Delegacy, 1949-54; Glass Industry Research Assoc., 1954-58; British Coal Utilisation Research Assoc., 1963-68; Soc. of Acoustic Technology, 1963-; Member: Building Research Board, 1958-62; Wilson Cttee on Noise, 1960-63; Adv. Council on R&D for Fuel and Power, 1973-75. President, Soc. of Glass Technology, 1960-64. JP Lancs 1942. Hon. LLD Sheffield, 1956; Hon. DSc Salford, 1970.

Publications: mainly on glass in various technical jls. *Recreations:* sailing, climbing, amateur radio, shooting. *Address:* Coppice End, Colborne Road, St Peter Port, Guernsey, CI. *Club:* Royal Dee Yacht.

PILKINGTON, Sir Lionel Alexander Bethune, (Sir Alastair), Kt 1970; FRS 1969; Chairman of Pilkington Brothers Ltd, St Helens, since 1973 (Executive Director, 1955-71; Deputy Chairman, 1971-73); a Director of Bank of England, since 1974; Director, British Petroleum, since 1976; *b* 7 Jan. 1920; *yr s* of late Col L. G. Pilkington and of Mrs L. G. Pilkington, Newbury, Berks; *m* 1945, Patricia Nicholls (*née* Elliott) (*d* 1977); one *s* one *d. Educ:* Sherborne School; Trinity Coll., Cambridge. War service, 1939-46. Joined Pilkington Brothers Ltd, Glass Manufacturers, St Helens, 1947; Production Manager and Asst Works Manager, Doncaster, 1949-51; Head Office, 1952; Sub-Director, 1953. Member: Central Adv. Council for Science and Technology, 1970-; SRC, 1972-; British Railways Bd, 1973-76; Court of Governors, Administrative Staff Coll., 1973-; Council, Liverpool Univ.; Royal Liverpool Philharmonic Soc. Hon. FUMIST, 1969; Hon. Fellow, Imperial Coll., 1974. FBIM 1971. Hon. DTech: Loughborough, 1968; CNAA, 1976; Hon. DEng Liverpool, 1971. Toledo Glass and Ceramic Award, 1963; Mullard Medal, Royal Soc., 1968; John Scott Medal, 1969; Wilhelm Exner Medal, 1970. *Recreations:* gardening, sailing, music. *Address:* The Crossways, View Road, Rainhill, Prescot, Lancs L35 0LS. *T:* 051-426 4228.

PILKINGTON, Rev. Canon Peter; Headmaster, King's School, Canterbury, since 1975; Hon. Canon of Canterbury Cathedral, since 1975; *b* 5 Sept. 1933; *s* of Frank and Doris Pilkington; *m* 1966, Helen, *d* of Charles and Maria Wilson; two *d. Educ:* Dame Allans Sch., Newcastle upon Tyne; Jesus Coll., Cambridge. BA 1955, MA 1958. Schoolmaster, St Joseph's Coll., Chidya, Tanganyika, 1955-57; ordained 1959; Curate in Bakewell, Derbs, 1959-62; Schoolmaster, Eton College, 1962-75, Master in College, 1965-75. *Recreations:* walking, gardening. *Address:* 14 The Precincts, Canterbury, Kent. *T:* Canterbury 62963. *Club:* Athenæum.

PILKINGTON, (Richard) Godfrey; Partner and Director, Piccadilly Gallery, since 1953; *b* 8 Nov. 1918; *e s* of Col Guy R. Pilkington, DSO and Margery (*née* Frost); *m* 1950, Evelyn Edith (Eve) Vincent; two *s* two *d. Educ:* Clifton; Trinity Coll., Cambridge (MA). Lieut, RA, N Africa and Central Mediterranean, 1940-46. Joined Frost & Reed, art dealers, 1947; edited Pictures and Prints, 1951-60; founded Piccadilly Gallery, 1953. Master, Fine Art Trade Guild, 1964-66; Chm., Soc. of London Art Dealers, 1974-77. *Publications:* numerous exhibn catalogues. *Recreations:* walking, boating, tennis, golf. *Address:* 45 Barons Court Road, W14 9DZ. *Clubs:* Athenæum, Hurlingham.

PILKINGTON, Dr Roger Windle; Author; *b* 17 Jan. 1915; 3rd *s* of Richard Austin Pilkington and Hon. Hope (*née* Cozens-Hardy); *m* 1937, Theodora Miriam Jaboor; one *s* one *d* ; *m* 1973, Fru Ingrid Geijer, Stockholm. *Educ:* Rugby; Freiburg, Germany; Magdalene Coll., Cambridge (MA, PhD). Research, genetics, 1937; Chm., London Missionary Soc., 1962; Chm. of Trustees, Homerton Coll., Cambridge, 1962; Chm. of Govs, Hall Sch., 1962; jt author, Sex and Morality Report, Brit. Council of Churches, 1966; Vice-Pres., River Thames Soc., 1967; Master, Glass Sellers' Co., 1967. *Publications:* Males and Females, 1948; Stringer's Folly, Biology, Man and God, Sons and Daughters, 1951; How Your Life Began, 1953; Revelation Through Science, 1954; Jan's Treasure, In the Beginning, 1955; Thames Waters, The Facts of Life, 1956; Small Boat Through Belgium, The Chesterfield Gold, The Great South Sea, The Ways of the Sea, 1957; The Missing Panel, 1958; Small Boat Through Holland, Robert Boyle: Father of Chemistry, How Boats Go Uphill, 1959; Small Boat to the Skagerrak, World Without End, The Dahlia's Cargo, Don John's Ducats, 1960; Small Boat to Sweden, Small Boat to Alsace, The Ways of the Air, Who's Who and Why, 1961; Small Boat to Bavaria, Nepomuk of the River, Boats Overland, How Boats are Navigated, 1962; The River, (with Noel Streatfeild) Confirmation and After, Facts of Life for Parents, Small Boat to Germany, The Eisenbart Mystery, 1963; Heavens Alive, Small Boat Through France, 1964; Small Boat in Southern France, Glass, 1965; Small Boat on the Thames, The Boy from Stink Alley, 1966; Small Boat on the Meuse, Small Boat to Luxembourg, 1967; Small Boat on the Moselle, 1968; Small Boat to Elsinore, 1968; Small Boat in Northern Germany, 1969; Small Boat on the Lower Rhine, 1970; Small Boat on the Upper Rhine, 1971; Waterways in Europe, 1972; The Ormering Tide, 1974; The Face in the River, 1976; contribs to Guardian, Daily Telegraph, Times, Family Doctor, Yachting World, etc. *Recreations:* inland waterways, walking. *Address:* La Maîson du

Côti, Mont Arthur, St Aubin, Jersey, Channel Islands. *T:* Jersey Central 43760.

PILKINGTON, Sir Thomas Henry Milborne-Swinnerton-, 14th Bt, *cr* 1635; Director, Thos & James Harrison Ltd, since 1963; Chairman, Charente Steamship Co. Ltd, since 1977; *b* 10 Mar. 1934; *s* of Sir Arthur W. Milborne-Swinnerton-Pilkington, 13th Bt and Elizabeth Mary (she *m* 1950, A. Burke), *d* of late Major J. F. Harrison, King's Walden Bury, Hitchin; *S* father 1952; *m* 1961, Susan, *e d* of N. S. R. Adamson, Durban, South Africa; one *s* two *d. Educ:* Eton College. *Recreations:* golf, cricket, racing. *Heir: s* Richard Arthur Milborne-Swinnerton-Pilkington, *b* 4 Sept. 1964. *Address:* King's Walden Bury, Hitchin, Herts. *Club:* White's.
See also Sir J. L. Armytage, Bt.

PILL, Malcolm Thomas; a Recorder of the Crown Court, since 1976; *b* 11 March 1938; *s* of Reginald Thomas Pill and Anne Pill (*née* Wright); *m* 1966, Roisin Pill (*née* Riordan); two *s* one *d. Educ:* Whitchurch Grammar Sch.; Trinity Coll., Cambridge. MA, LLB, Dip. Hague Acad. of Internat. Law. Served RA, 1956-58; Glamorgan Yeomanry (TA), 1958-67. Called to Bar, Gray's Inn, 1962; Wales and Chester Circuit, 1963. 3rd Sec., Foreign Office, 1963-64. Chm., UNA (Wales) Trust, 1969-77; Chm., Welsh Centre for Internat. Affairs, 1973-76. *Address:* 9 Westbourne Crescent, Whitchurch, Cardiff CF4 2BL. *T:* Cardiff 65961. *Clubs:* Royal Commonwealth Society; Cardiff and County (Cardiff).

PILLAI, Sir (Narayana) Raghavan, KCIE 1946 (CIE 1939); CBE 1937; Padma Vibhushan, 1960; *b* 24 July 1898; *s* of M. C. Narayana Pillai, Trivandrum, S India; *m* 1928, Edith Minnie Arthurs (*d* 1976); two *s. Educ:* Madras Univ.; Trinity Hall, Cambridge (schol.). BA (Madras) 1st Cl. English, 1918; Natural Sciences Tripos Pt 1 (Cambridge), 1st Cl., 1921; Law Tripos Pt 2, 1st Cl., 1922; ICS 1921; various appointments under the Government of Central Provinces and the Government of India. Secretary General, Ministry of External Affairs, New Delhi, 1952-60. Hon. DLitt Kerala University, 1953. Hon. Fellow, Trinity Hall, Cambridge, 1970. *Recreation:* walking. *Address:* 1022 St James's Court, SW1. *Clubs:* Oriental; Gymkhana (New Delhi).

PILLAR, Rear-Adm. William Thomas, CEng, FIMechE, FIMarE; Assistant Chief of Fleet Support, since 1977; *b* 24 Feb. 1924; *s* of William Pillar and Lily Pillar; *m* 1946, Ursula Ransley; three *s* one *d. Educ:* Blundells Sch., Tiverton; RNEC. FIMechE 1969, FIMarE 1972. Entered RN, 1942; HMS Illustrious, 1946-48; staff RNEC, 1948-51; HMS Alert, 1951-53; HM Dockyard, Gibraltar, 1954-57; HMS Corunna, 1957-59; BEO, HMS Lochinvar, 1959-61; staff of C-in-C, SASA, Cape Town, 1961-64; HMS Tiger, 1964-65; staff of Dir of Naval Officer Appts (Eng), 1965-67; sowc 1967; Naval Ship Prodn Overseer, Scotland and NI, 1967-69; IDC 1970; Asst Dir, DG Ships, 1971-73; Captain RNEC, 1973-75; Port Adm., Rosyth, 1976-77. Comdr 1958; Captain 1966; Rear-Adm. 1976. *Recreations:* sailing, rough gardening and fixing things. *Address:* c/o 21 South Embankment, Dartmouth. *T:* Dartmouth 3203. *Club:* Royal Naval Sailing Association (Portsmouth).

PIM, Captain Sir Richard (Pike), KBE 1960; Kt 1945; VRD; DL; Inspector-General, Royal Ulster Constabulary, retired; National Governor for Northern Ireland, BBC, 1962-67; Member of Council, Winston Churchill Memorial Trust, 1965-69; Member, Ulster Transport Authority, 1962-64, retired; *b* Dunmurry, Co. Antrim, 1900; *yr s* of late Cecil Pim; *m* 1925, Marjorie Angel, 3rd *d* of late John ff. Young, Dungiven, Londonderry; two *s. Educ:* Lancing Coll., Sussex; Trinity College, Dublin. Served in RNVR in European War, 1914-18; Royal Irish Constabulary, 1921. Appointed to Civil Service, N Ireland, 1922; Asst Secretary, Ministry of Home Affairs (N Ireland), 1935; Staff of Prime Minister, Northern Ireland, 1938; in charge of Mr Churchill's War Room at Admiralty, 1939, and later of Map Room at Downing St; Capt. RNVR. North African Campaign (despatches). DL City of Belfast, 1957. Order of Crown of Yugoslavia; Legion of Merit, USA. *Address:* Mullagh, Killyleagh, Co. Down, Northern Ireland. *T:* Killyleagh 267. *Club:* Ulster (Belfast).

PINAY, Antoine; Médiateur, French Republic, 1973-74; leather manufacturer; *b* Department of the Rhône, 30 Dec. 1891. *Educ:* Marist Fathers' Sch., St-Chamond. Joined a tannery business there; became Mayor, 1929; later became gen. councillor, Dept of the Loire (Pres. 1949-). Was returned to Chamber of Deputies, 1936, Ind. Radical party; Senator, 1938; elected to 2nd Constituent Assembly, 1946; then to 1st Nat. Assembly; re-elected to Nat. Assembly as an associate of Ind. Republican group; Sec. of State for Economic Affairs, Sept. 1948-Oct. 1949;

in·several successive ministries, July 1950-Feb. 1952, he was Minister of Public Works, Transportation, and Tourism; Prime Minister of France, March-Dec. 1952; Minister of Foreign Affairs, 1955-56; Minister of Finance and Economic Affairs, 1958-60. Served European War, 1914-18, in artillery as non-commmnd officer (Croix de Guerre, Médaille Militaire). *Address:* route du Coin, 42400 Saint-Chamond, France.

PINCHER, (Henry) Chapman; Assistant Editor, Daily Express, and Chief Defence Correspondent, Beaverbrook Newspapers; *b* Ambala, India, 29 March 1914; *s* of Maj. Richard Chapman Pincher, E Surrey Regt, and Helen (*née* Foster), Pontefract; *m* 1965, Constance Wolstenholme; one *s* one *d* (by previous *m*). *Educ:* Darlington Gram. Sch.; King's Coll., London; Inst. Educn; Mil. Coll. of Science. Carter Medallist, London, 1934; BSc (hons Botany, Zoology), 1935. Staff Liverpool Inst., 1936-40. Joined Royal Armoured Corps, 1940; Techn SO, Rocket Div., Min. of Supply, 1943-46; Defence, Science and Medical Editor, Daily Express, 1946-73. Granada Award, Journalist of the Year, 1964; Reporter of the Decade, 1966. *Publications:* Breeding of Farm Animals, 1946; A Study of Fishes, 1947; Into the Atomic Age, 1947; Spotlight on Animals, 1950; Evolution, 1950; (with Bernard Wicksteed) It's Fun Finding Out, 1950; Sleep, and how to get more of it, 1954; Sex in Our Time, 1973; *novels:* Not with a Bang, 1965; The Giantkiller, 1967; The Penthouse Conspirators, 1970; The Skeleton at the Villa Wolkonsky, 1975; The Eye of the Tornado, 1976; The Four Horses, 1978; original researches in genetics, numerous articles in scientific and agricultural jls. *Recreations:* fishing, shooting, natural history, country life; ferreting in Whitehall and bolting politicians. *Address:* Lowerhouse Farm, Ewhurst, Surrey.

PINCKNEY, Charles Percy, FRCP; Hon. Consulting Physician to: Pædiatric Department, St George's Hospital, SW1; Heritage Craft Schools and Hospitals, Chailey, Sussex; Windsor Group Hospitals, Windsor, Berks; *b* 28 April 1901; *er s* of late W. P. Pinckney, Dir of Rubber Cos; *m* 1934, Norah Manisty Boucher; one *s* one *d. Educ:* Radley College; Clare College, Cambridge (MA, MB, BCH). Qualified St George's Hospital, SW1. MRCS, LRCP 1925; FRCP 1941. Held various resident appointments St George's Hospital. Physician to King George Hospital, Ilford, 1931-59. *Publications:* articles in BMJ, Archives of Diseases in Children, and Medical Press, 1940-50. *Recreations:* tennis and ski-ing. *Address:* (private) 76 Albert Hall Mansions, SW7. *T:* 01-589 9351. *Club:* Hurlingham.

PINCOTT, Leslie Rundell; Managing Director, Esso Petroleum Co. Ltd, since 1970; *b* 27 March 1923; *s* of Hubert George Pincott and Gertrude Elizabeth Rundell; *m* 1944, Mary Mae Tuffin; two *s* one *d. Educ:* Mercers' Sch., Holborn. Served War, Royal Navy, 1942-46. Broads Paterson & Co., 1946-50; joined Esso Petroleum Co. Ltd, 1950; Comptroller, 1958-61; Asst Gen. Manager (Marketing), 1961-65; Dir and Gen. Manager, Cleveland Petroleum Co. Ltd, 1966-68; Standard Oil Co. (NJ): Exec. Asst to Pres., and later, to Chm., 1968-70; Director: Esso Pension Trust Ltd, 1970-; Esso Teoranta, 1971-; Remploy Ltd, 1975-. Pres., District Heating Assoc., 1971-. Mem., BR Adv. Bd (Southern), 1977-. FCA, FInstMSM. *Recreation:* tennis. *Address:* 132 Woodsford Square, Kensington, W14 8DT. *Club:* Hurlingham.

PINDLING, Rt. Hon. Lynden Oscar, PC 1976; Prime Minister and Minister of Economic Affairs of the Commonwealth of the Bahama Islands, since 1969; *b* 22 March 1930; *s* of Arnold Franklin and Viola Pindling; *m* 1956, Marguerite McKenzie; two *s* two *d. Educ:* Western Senior Sch., Nassau Govt High Sch.; London Univ. (LLB 1952; LLD 1970). Called to the Bar, Middle Temple, 1953. Practised as Lawyer, 1952-67. Parly Leader of Progressive Liberal Party, 1956; elected to Bahamas House of Assembly, 1956, re-elected 1962, 1967, and 1968. Worked for human rights and self-determination in the Bahamas; Mem., several delegns to Colonial Office, 1956-66; took part in Constitutional Conf., May 1963; Leader of Opposition, 1964; Mem., Delegns to UN Special Cttee of Twenty-four, 1965, 1966; Premier of the Bahamas and Minister of Tourism and Development, 1967; led Bahamian Delegn to Constitutional Conf., London, 1968; to Independence Conf., 1972 (first Prime Minister after Independence). Chm., Commonwealth Parly Assoc., 1968. *Recreations:* swimming, boating, travel. *Address:* Office of the Prime Minister, Rawson Square, Nassau, Bahamas.

PINE, John Bradley; *b* 2 Dec. 1913; *yr s* of late Percival William Pine and Maud Mary Pine (*née* Bradley); *m* 1st, 1945, Elizabeth Mary (Jayne) Hallett (*d* 1948); one *s*; 2nd, 1952, Ann Carney; one *s. Educ:* Douai School. Asst Solicitor, GWR, Eng., 1935-39; Mil. Service, 1939-45; a Sen. Prosecutor, CCG, 1945-47; Resident Magistrate and Crown Counsel, N Rhodesia, 1947-49;

Called to Bar, 1950; Asst Attorney Gen., Gibraltar, 1949-54; QC (Bermuda), 1955; Attorney Gen., Bermuda, 1955-57; Actg Governor of Bermuda, 1956; QC (Nyasaland), 1958; Solicitor Gen., Nyasaland, 1958-60; Minister of Justice and Attorney Gen., Nyasaland, 1960-62, when replaced by an Elected Minister under self-governing Constitution; Legal Adviser to Governor of Nyasaland, July 1963, until Independence, July 1964; Parly Draftsman, Govt of N Ireland, 1965-66; Sec., Ulster Tourist Develt Assoc., 1967; antique business, 1968-70. *Address:* c/o Lloyds Bank Ltd, Taunton, Som.

PINE, Leslie Gilbert; Author and Lecturer; Managing Editor, International Who's Who of the Arab World, 1975-76; Editor, The National Message, since 1977 (Assistant Editor, 1975-77); *b* 22 Dec. 1907; *s* of Henry Moorshead Pine, Bristol, and Lilian Grace (*née* Beswetherick); *m* 1948, Grace V. Griffin; one *s. Educ:* Tellisford House Sch., Bristol; South-West London Coll., Barnes; London Univ. (BA). Asst Editor, Burke's Landed Gentry, 1935; subseq. Editor of Burke's Peerage and Landed Gentry and other reference books and then Managing Editor, The Shooting Times, 1960-64, and Shooting Times Library, 1962-64 (resigned as unable to agree with blood sports). Director L. & G. Pine & Co. Ltd, 1964-69. Censorship and Air Min., 1940; Min. of Labour, 1941; RAF 1942; Sqn Ldr 1945-46; served in N Africa, Italy, Greece and India (Intel. Branch). Barrister-at-Law, Inner Temple, 1953; Freeman, City of London, Liveryman of the Glaziers' Company, 1954. Prospective Parly Candidate (C) Bristol Central, 1956; contested seat, 1959; re-adopted, 1960; resigned and joined Liberal Party, 1962; Prospective Parly Candidate (L), S Croydon, 1963, resigned candidature, June 1964, disagreeing profoundly with Liberalism. Dioc. Lay Reader, London, 1939, Canterbury, 1961, St Edmundsbury and Ipswich, 1975; received into Catholic Church, 1964; reconciled to C of E, 1971. Corr. Mem. Inst. Internacional de Genealogica y Heraldica (Madrid) and of Gen. Socs in Belgium, Chile and Brazil; Gov., St And. Sch., S Croydon, 1960-64. FSA Scot., 1940; MJI, 1947 (Mem. Council, 1953-61); FJI 1957; Associate, Zool. Soc., London, 1961; FRSA 1961; Soc. of Authors, 1965; Augustan Soc., 1967; FRGS 1969; FRAS 1970. Member: RUSI; Royal Soc. St George. Has given over 700 lectures in Gt Britain, Ireland, Holland and USA, also series of tutorial lectures under WEA and Further Educn. *Publications:* The Stuarts of Traquair, 1940; The House of Wavell, 1948; The Middle Sea, 1950, new edn, 1972; The Story of Heraldry, 1952 (4th edn 1968, Japan, USA); Trace Your Ancestors, 1953; The Golden Book of the Coronation, 1953; They Came with The Conqueror, 1954; The Story of the Peerage, 1956; Tales of the British Aristocracy, 1956; The House of Constantine, 1957; Teach Yourself Heraldry and Genealogy, 1957, 5th (enlarged) edn 1975; The Twilight of Monarchy, 1958; A Guide to Titles, 1959; Princes of Wales, 1959, new edn, 1970; American Origins, 1960, 1968; Your Family Tree, 1962; Ramshackledom, A Critical Appraisal of the Establishment, 1962; Heirs of the Conqueror, 1965; Heraldry, Ancestry and Titles, Questions and Answers, 1965; The Story of Surnames, 1965; After Their Blood, 1966; Tradition and Custom in Modern Britain, 1967; The Genealogist's Encyclopedia (USA and UK), 1969; The Story of Titles, 1969; International Heraldry, 1970; The Highland Clans, 1972; Sons of the Conqueror, 1972; The New Extinct Peerage, 1972; The History of Hunting, 1973; Compleat Family Historian, 1977; (contrib.) Encyclopedia Britannica, 1974. *Recreations:* reading, walking, gardening, travel, motoring; contributes articles to press. *Address:* Hall Lodge Cottage, Brettenham, Ipswich, Suffolk IP7 7QP. *T:* Rattlesden 402. *Clubs:* Press, Wig and Pen.

PINEAU, Christian Paul Francis, Officier Légion d'Honneur; Compagnon de la Libération; Croix de Guerre (French); Médaille de la Résistance (Rosette); French Statesman and Writer; *b* Chaumont (Haute-Marne), 14 Oct. 1904; *m* 1962, Mlle Blanche Bloys; one *d* (and five *s* one *d* of previous marriages). Minister of Food and Supplies, June-Nov. 1945; General Rapporteur to Budget Commission 1945-46; Chm. Nat. Assembly Finance Commn, 1946-47; Minister of Public Works, Transport, and Tourism (Schuman Cabinet), 1947-48, also (Marie Cabinet) July-Aug. 1948, also (Queuille Cabinet), Sept. 1948, also (Bidault Cabinet), Oct. 1949; Minister of Finance and Economic Affairs (Schuman Cabinet), Aug. 1946; Chm. Nat. Defence Credits Control Commn, 1951-55; Designated Premier, Feb. 1955; Minister for Foreign Affairs, Feb. 1956-June 1957. Holds GCMG (Hon.) Great Britain, and numerous other foreign decorations. *Publications: books for children:* Contes de je ne sais quand; Plume et le saumon; L'Ourse aux pattons verts; Cornerousse le Mystérieux; Histoires de la forêt de Bercé; La Planète aux enfants perdus; La Marelle et le ballon; La Bête à bêtises; *other publications;* The SNCF and French Transport; Mon cher député; La simple verité; L'escalier des ombres; economic and financial articles; contrib. to various papers. *Address:* 55 rue Vaneau, 75507 Paris, France.

PING, Aubrey Charles, FCIT; Industrial and Transport Consultant, since 1970; *b* 2 Dec. 1905; *s* of Thomas Walton Ping, Middleton Cheney, Oxon, and Hester Louisa (*née* Barden), Banbury, Oxon; *m* 1936, Constance, 2nd *d* of John and Rose Bryant, Finchley; three *s. Educ:* Manor Lane LCC School; Brockley County School. Railway clerk and official, 1922-43; various hon. Trade Union offices, 1926-43; broadcasting to French Transport Workers, 1941-43. Served War of 1939-45, Captain, Allied Commission, Italy, 1944; Major Exec. Officer and Chief Operations Branch, Allied Commission, Italy, 1945, Lt-Col Asst Director, Rome European Central Inland Transport Organisation, 1946; special purposes asst to Continental Supt, British Rlys (Southern), 1947; Lecturer, International Transport, Southern Railway Training College, 1947-49. International Transport Consultant, Central Engineering Co. Ltd, 1951-70; Chairman: Air Terminals Ltd, 1958-69; British Air Services Ltd, 1966-69; Dep. Chm., BEA Helicopters Ltd, 1967-70. Director: Gibraltar Airways, 1952-70; Cyprus Airways, 1953-58; Jersey Airlines Development Corporation, 1961; Cambrian Airways, 1963-69; BKS Air Transport, 1964-69; Schreiner BEA Helicopters NV, 1968-70; HTS Management Holdings and HTS Management Consultants, 1970-72. Mem. Bd, BEA, 1949-70; Chm. Jt Council for Civil Aviation, 1956. Dep. Chm., Airways Housing Trust, 1965-70; Chm. BEA Housing Assoc. and BEA Silver Wing Club, 1957-69. MInst Traffic Administration, 1953; FCIT 1955. *Recreations:* reading, gardening, writing. *Address:* 903 London Road, Loudwater, Bucks. *Club:* Special Forces.

PINK, Ralph Bonner, CBE 1961; VRD 1951; JP; MP (C) Portsmouth South since 1966; *b* 30 Sept. 1912; *s* of Frank Pink and Helen Mary (*née* Mumby); *m* 1939, Marguerite Nora Bannar-Martin; one *s* one *d. Educ:* Oundle School. Portsmouth City Council, 1948-; Lord Mayor of Portsmouth, 1961-62; JP for City of Portsmouth, 1950. Knight of Order of Dannebrog (Denmark). *Recreation:* yachting. *Address:* House of Commons, SW1A 0AA. *Club:* Royal Naval and Royal Albert Yacht (Portsmouth).

PINKER, George Douglas, FRCS(Ed), FRCOG; Surgeon-Gynaecologist to the Queen, since 1973; Consulting Gynaecological Surgeon and Obstetrician, St Mary's Hospital, Paddington and Samaritan Hospital, since 1958; Consulting Gynaecological Surgeon, Middlesex and Soho Hospitals, since 1969; Consultant Gynæcologist, King Edward VII Hospital for Officers, since 1974; *b* 6 Dec. 1924; *s* of late Ronald Douglas Pinker and of Queenie Elizabeth Pinker (*née* Dix); *m* Dorothy Emma (*née* Russell); three *s* one *d* (incl. twin *s* and *d*). *Educ:* Reading Sch.; St Mary's Hosp., London Univ. MB BS London 1947; DObst 1949; MRCOG 1954; FRCS(Ed) 1957; FRCOG 1964. Late Cons. Gyn. Surg., Bolingbroke Hosp., and Res. Off., Nuffield Dept of Obst., Radcliffe Infirmary, Oxford; late Cons. Gyn. Surg., Queen Charlotte's Hosp. Arthur Wilson Orator and Turnbull Scholar, and Hon. Consultant Obstetrican and Gynaecologist, Royal Women's Hosp., Melbourne, 1972. Examiner in Obst. and Gynae.: Univs of Cambridge, Dundee, London, and FRCS Edinburgh; formerly also in RCOG, and Univs of Birmingham, Glasgow and Dublin. Hon. Treasurer, RCOG, 1970. Mem., Blair Bell Research Soc.; FRSocMed. *Publications:* (all jtly) Ten Teachers Diseases of Women, 1964; Ten Teachers Obstetrics, 1966; A Short Textbook of Obstetrics and Gynaecology, 1967. *Recreations:* music, gardening, sailing, skiing, fell walking. *Address:* 96 Harley Street, W1N 1AF. *T:* 01-935 2292; Medley, Kingston Hill, Kingston-on-Thames, Surrey KT2 7IU. *Club:* Bath.

PINKER, Rev. Martin Wallis, OBE 1957; Member, Minister's Advisory Council (Canada) on Treatment of Offenders, 1959-73, retired (Chairman, 1959-73); Chairman, Ontario Training Schools Advisory Board, 1958-63; (first) General Secretary, National Association of Discharged Prisoners' Aid Societies Inc., 1936-58; Director, Men's Division, Central After-Care Association, 1948-58; *b* 11 April 1893; 2nd *s* of late Douglas Collyer Pinker and of Amelia Jane Wallis, Reading; *m* 1922, Lilian Hannah, *o d* of late Frederick and Betsy Eccles, Blackpool; one *s* one *d. Educ:* private study; Hartley Victoria Coll., Manchester. After training for business career, served European War, 1914-18, as Lieut Lancs Fus., India. Entered Primitive Methodist Ministry: ordained, 1922; served in London, Gravesend and Lymm (Cheshire) 1924-29; released from pastoral work, 1929, to become Organising Sec. of Discharged Prisoners' Aid Soc. at Strangeways Prison, Manchester. Mem. Jt Cttee to review work of Discharged Prisoners' Aid Socs (Maxwell Cttee), 1951; Internat. Prisoners' Aid Assoc. (Vice-Pres. 1951, Pres., 1954). Visited Germany at request of UN High Commn for Refugees, 1952. Has attended meetings of Congress of Correction, in USA and Canada; Founding Hon. Sec. Commonwealth Assoc. of Prisoners' Aid

Societies. *Address:* 88 Don River Boulevard, Willowdale, Ontario M2N 2M9, Canada. *Club:* Empire (Canada).

PINKERTON, Prof. John Henry McKnight; Professor of Midwifery and Gynæcology, Queen's University, Belfast, since 1963; Gynæcologist: Royal Victoria Hospital, Belfast; Ulster Hospital for Women and Children; Surgeon, Royal Maternity Hospital, Belfast; *b* 5 June 1920; *s* of late William R. and Eva Pinkerton; *m* 1947, Florence McKinstry, MB, BCh, BAO; four *s. Educ:* Royal Belfast Academical Institution; Queen's Univ., Belfast. Hyndman Univ. Entrance Scholar, 1939; MB, BCh, BAO Hons; Magrath Scholar in Obstetrics and Gynæcology, 1943. Active service in HM Ships as Surg.-Lt, RNVR, 1945-47. MD 1948; MRCOG 1949; FRCOG 1960; FZS 1960; FRCPI 1977. Sen. Lectr in Obstetrics and Gynæcology, University Coll. of the West Indies, and Consultant Obstetrician and Gynæcologist to University Coll. Hosp. of the West Indies, 1953-59; Rockefeller Research Fellow at Harvard Medical Sch., 1956-57; Prof. of Obstetrics and Gynæcology, Univ. of London, at Queen Charlotte's and Chelsea Hosps and the Inst. of Obstetrics and Gynæcology, 1959-63; Obstetric Surgeon to Queen Charlotte's Hosp.; Surgeon to Chelsea Hosp. for Women. *Publications:* various papers on obstetrical and gynæcological subjects. *Address:* Department of Midwifery and Gynæcology, The Institute of Clinical Science, Grosvenor Road, Belfast BT12 6BJ. *T:* Belfast 40503.

PINNELL, Leonard George, CIE 1938; *b* 10 June 1896; *s* of Charles John Pinnell and Clara Matilda Wills; *m* 1924, Margaret Blake (*d* 1976), *d* of Dr C. F. Coxwell; two *s. Educ:* City of London School; Balliol Coll., Oxford (Exhibitioner). Served European War, 1915-18, 10th Bedfordshire Regt, later Machine Gun Corps, Salonica; British Military Mission to USA (1917) and France; entered Indian Civil Service, 1920; served in Bengal, Survey and Settlement, Chief Manager Dacca Nawab Estate, and Districts; Private Sec. to the Governor of Bengal, 1935; Sec. to the Governor, 1937-40 and 1945; Supervisor ICS Training, 1940-42; Acting PSV 1942; Dir Civil Supplies, Bengal, 1942; Comr Chittagong and Presidency Divs, 1943-44; Principal Officers' Training Course, 1944-45; Develt Comr and *ex officio* Addl Chief Sec., 1946; Chief Admin Officer Industrial and Commercial Finance Corp. Ltd, 1948-51; advisory mission to Greece, 1951; Domestic Bursar, St John's Coll., Oxford, 1953-60. *Address:* 26 Headbourne Worthy House, Winchester, Hants SO23 7JG. *T:* Winchester 881631. *Club:* East India, Devonshire, Sports and Public Schools.

PINNINGTON, Geoffrey Charles; Editor, Sunday People, since 1972; *b* 21 March 1919; *s* of Charles and Beatrice Pinnington; *m* 1941, Beryl, *d* of Edward and Lilian Clark; two *d. Educ:* Harrow County Sch.; Rock Ferry High Sch., Birkenhead; King's Coll., Univ. of London. Served War as Air Navigator, RAF Bomber and Middle East Commands, 1940-45 (Sqdn Ldr, 1943). On staff of (successively): Middlesex Independent; Kensington Post (Editor); Daily Herald: Dep. News Editor, 1955; Northern Editor, 1957; Dep. Editor, 1958; Daily Mirror: Night Editor, 1961, Assistant Editor, 1964, Dep. Editor, 1968; Dir, Mirror Group Newspapers, 1976-. *Recreations:* his family, travel, reading, theatre and the arts, amateur cine-photography. *Address:* Sunday People, 9 New Fetter Lane, EC4A 1AR. *T:* 01-353 0246.

PINSENT, Roger Philip; HM Diplomatic Service, retired; *b* 30 Dec. 1916; *s* of late Sidney Hume Pinsent; *m* 1941, Suzanne Smalley; one *s* two *d. Educ:* Downside Sch.; Lausanne, London and Grenoble Univs. London Univ. French Scholar, 1938; BA Hons London, 1940. HM Forces, 1940-46; HM Diplomatic Service, May 1946; 1st Sec., HM Legation, Havana, 1948-50; HM Consul, Tangier, 1950-52; 1st Sec., HM Embassy, Madrid, 1952-53; FO, 1953-56; 1st Sec., Head of Chancery, HM Embassy, Lima (Chargé d'Affaires, 1958, 1959), 1956-59; Dep. Head of UK Delegation to the European Communities, Luxembourg, 1959-63; HM Ambassador to Nicaragua, 1963-67; Counsellor (Commercial), Ankara, 1967-70; Consul-Gen., São Paulo, 1970-73. Mem., Inst. of Linguists, 1976. *Recreations:* music, photography, golf. *Address:* c/o Foreign and Commonwealth Office, King Charles Street, SW1A 2AH. *T:* 01-839 8866; Cranfield Cottage, Maugersbury, Stow-on-the-Wold, Glos GL54 1HR. *T:* Stow-on-the-Wold 30992. *Clubs:* Canning; Managua Cricket (Managua); Golf Club Grand Ducal, Luxembourg; Broadway Golf; Stow on the Wold RFC.

PINSENT, Sir Roy, 2nd Bt, *cr* 1938; *b* 22 July 1883; *e s* of Sir Richard Alfred Pinsent, 1st Bt, and Laura Proctor (*d* 1931), *d* of Thomas Ryland; *S* father, 1948; *m* 1918, Mary Tirzah (*d* 1951), *d* of Dr Edward Geoffrey Walls, Spilsby, Lincs; two *s* one *d. Educ:* Marlborough; University College, Oxford (BA). Admitted Solicitor, 1909; served European War, 1916-19, Lieut,

RE. *Heir: s* Christopher Roy Pinsent [*b* 2 Aug. 1922; *m* 1951, Susan Mary, *d* of John Norton Scorer, Fotheringhay; one *s* two *d*]. *Address:* 5 St George's Square, SW1. *T:* 01-828 7282.

PINSON, Barry, QC 1973; *b* 18 Dec. 1925; *s* of Thomas Alfred Pinson and Alice Cicily Pinson; *m* 1st, 1950, Miriam Mary (marr. diss. 1976); one *s* one *d*; 2nd, 1977, Anne Kathleen Golby. *Educ:* King Edward's Sch., Birmingham; Univ. of Birmingham. LLB Hons 1945. Fellow Inst. Taxation. Mil. Service, 1944-47. Called to Bar, Gray's Inn, 1949. *Publication:* Revenue Law, 1962, 11th edn 1977. *Recreations:* music, photography. *Address:* 11 New Square, Lincoln's Inn, WC2. *T:* 01-242 3981.

PINTER, Harold, CBE 1966; actor, playwright and director; Associate Director, National Theatre, since 1973; *b* 10 Oct. 1930; *s* of J. Pinter; *m* 1956, Vivien Merchant, *qv*; one *s. Educ:* Hackney Downs Grammar Sch. Actor (mainly repertory), 1949-57. Directed: Exiles, Mermaid, 1970; Butley, 1971; Butley (film), 1973; Next of Kin, Nat. Theatre, 1974; Otherwise Engaged, Queen's, 1975, NY 1977. Shakespeare Prize, Hamburg, 1970; Austrian State Prize for European Literature, 1973. Hon. DLitt: Reading, 1970; Birmingham, 1971; Glasgow, 1974; East Anglia, 1974. *Plays:* The Room, The Birthday Party (filmed, 1968), The Dumb Waiter, 1957; A Slight Ache, (radio) 1958, (stage) 1961; A Night Out (radio), A Night Out (television), The Caretaker (filmed, 1963), 1950; Night School (television), 1960; The Dwarfs (radio), 1960, (stage), 1963; The Collection (television), 1961, (stage), 1962; The Lover (television, stage), 1963 (Italia Prize for TV); Tea Party (television), 1964; The Homecoming, 1964; Landscape (radio), 1968, (stage), 1969; Silence (stage), 1969; Old Times (stage), 1971; Monologue (television), 1972; No Man's Land (stage), 1975. *Screenplays:* The Caretaker, The Servant, 1962; The Pumpkin Eater, 1963; The Quiller Memorandum, 1966; Accident, 1967; The Birthday Party, 1968; The Go-Between, 1969; Langrishe Go-Down, 1970; A la Recherche du Temps Perdu, 1972; The Last Tycoon, 1974. *Publications:* The Caretaker, 1960; The Birthday Party, and other plays, 1960; A Slight Ache, 1961; The Collection, 1963; The Lover, 1963; The Homecoming, 1965; Tea Party, and, The Basement, 1967; Mac, 1968; Jt Editor, New Poems 1967, 1968; Landscape, and, Silence, 1969; Five Screenplays, 1971; Old Times, 1971; No Man's Land, 1975. *Recreations:* drinking and cricket. *Address:* c/o ACTAC Ltd, 16 Cadogan Lane, SW1.

PIPER, Bright Harold, (Peter Piper); Director and Chief Executive, Lloyds Bank Group, since 1973; *b* 22 Sept. 1918; 2nd *s* of Robert Harold Piper; *m* 1945, Marjorie Joyce, 2nd *d* of Captain George Arthur; one *s* one *d. Educ:* Maidstone Grammar School. Served with RN, 1939-46. Entered Lloyds Bank, 1935: Asst Gen. Man., 1963; Jt Gen. Man., 1965; Asst Chief Gen. Man., 1968; Dep. Chief Gen. Man., 1970; Chief Gen. Man., 1973. Freeman, City of London; Liveryman, Spectacle Makers' Company. *Recreation:* sailing. *Address:* Blagdon House, Hampton Wick, Kingston upon Thames, Surrey. *T:* 01-977 2458. *Clubs:* Bath, Overseas Bankers, Australia.

PIPER, David Towry, CBE 1969; MA, FSA; FRSL; Director, Ashmolean Museum, Oxford, since 1973; Fellow of Worcester College, Oxford, since 1973; *b* 21 July 1918; *s* of late Prof. S. H. Piper; *m* 1945, Anne Horatia Richmond; one *s* three *d. Educ:* Clifton Coll.; St Catharine's Coll., Cambridge. Served War of 1939-45: Indian Army (9th Jat Regt); Japanese prisoner-of-war, 1942-45. National Portrait Gallery: Asst-Keeper, 1946-64; Dir, Keeper and Sec., 1964-67; Dir and Marlay Curator, Fitzwilliam Museum, Cambridge, 1967-73; Fellow, Christ's College, Cambridge, 1967-73. Slade Prof. of Fine Art, Oxford, 1966-67. Clark Lectr, Cambridge, 1977-78. Mem., Royal Fine Art Commn, 1970-. Trustee: Paul Mellon Foundn for British Art, 1969-70; Pilgrim Trust, 1973-. *Publications:* The English Face, 1957; Catalogue of the 17th Century Portraits in the National Portrait Gallery, 1963; The Royal College of Physicians; Portraits (ed G. Wolstenholme), 1964; (ed) Enjoying Paintings, 1964; The Companion Guide to London, 1964; Shades, 1970; London, 1971; (ed) The Genius of British Painting, 1975; The Treasures of Oxford, 1977; *novels* (as Peter Towry) *include:* It's Warm Inside, 1953; Trial by Battle, 1959. *Address:* c/o Ashmolean Museum, Beaumont Street, Oxford. *Club:* Athenæum.

PIPER, John Egerton Christmas, CH 1972; painter and writer; Member of the Oxford Diocesan Advisory Committee, since 1950; Royal Fine Art Commission, since 1959; *b* 13 Dec. 1903; *s* of late C. A. Piper, Solicitor; *m* 1935, Mary Myfanwy Evans; two *s* two *d. Educ:* Epsom Coll.; Royal College of Art. Paintings, drawings, exhibited in London since 1925; Pictures bought by Tate Gallery, Contemporary Art Society, Victoria and Albert Museum, etc.; Series of watercolours of Windsor Castle commissioned by the Queen, 1941-42; windows for nave of Eton College Chapel commissioned 1958; windows and interior design, Nuffield College Chapel, Oxford, completed, 1961; window, Coventry Cathedral, completed, 1962; windows for King George VI Memorial Chapel, Windsor, 1969. Designed Tapestry for High Altar, Chichester Cathedral, 1966, and for Civic Hall, Newcastle upon Tyne. Designer for opera and ballet; a Trustee: Tate Gallery, 1946-53, 1954-61, 1968-74; National Gallery, 1967-74, 1975-; Arts Council art panel, 1952-57. Hon. ARIBA, 1957, Hon FRIBA 1971; Hon. ARCA 1959; Hon. DLitt: Leicester, 1960; Oxford, 1966. *Publications:* Wind in the Trees (poems), 1921; 'Shell Guide' to Oxfordshire, 1938; Brighton Aquatints, 1939; British Romantic Painters, 1942; Buildings and Prospects, 1949; (ed with John Betjeman) Buckinghamshire Architectural Guide, 1948; Berkshire Architectural Guide, 1949; (illus.) The Castles on the Ground by J. M. Richards, 1973; (jtly) Lincolnshire Churches, 1976. *Relevant publications:* John Piper: Paintings, Drawings and Theatre Designs, 1932-54 (arr. S. John Woods), 1955. *Address:* Fawley Bottom Farmhouse, near Henley-on-Thames, Oxon. *Club:* Athenæum.

PIPER, Peter; *see* Piper, Bright Harold.

PIPER, Air Marshal Sir Tim, (Thomas William), KBE 1968; CB 1964; AFC 1941; *b* 11 Oct. 1911; *s* of late Thomas Edward Piper, Ackleton Hall, Worfield, Shropshire; *m* 1947, Betty Bedford, *d* of late William Bedford Mitchell, Irwin, Western Australia; no *c. Educ:* Trent College. Joined RAF, 1936; served War of 1939-45, in Bomber Command (UK) (despatches thrice); pow, 1941-45; OC, RAF Schwechat, Austria, 1946-47, Germany (Berlin Air Lift), 1948-49, Middle East, 1950-53; OC, RAF Dishforth, 1953-55; Group Captain, Plans, Transport Command, 1955-58; Director of Operational Requirements, Air Ministry, 1958-60; Chief of Staff, Near East Command, 1960-62; AOC No 38 Group, RAF, 1962-64; Comdt, RAF Staff Coll., 1965-66; UK Mem., Permanent Military Deputies Group, Central Treaty Organisation, 1966-68; retd, 1968. Group Capt., 1953; Air Cdre, 1959; Air Vice-Marshal, 1960; Air Marshal, 1966; psa, 1947; jssc, 1950. *Recreations:* shooting, fishing. *Address:* Chirton Cottage, Chirton, Devizes, Wilts. *T:* Chirton 289. *Clubs:* Army and Navy, Royal Air Force.

PIPKIN, (Charles Harry) Broughton, CBE 1973; Chairman, BICC Ltd, since 1977; *b* 29 Nov. 1913; *er s* of late Charles Pipkin and Charlotte Phyllis (*née* Viney), Lewisham; *m* 1941, Viola, *yr d* of Albert and Florence Byatt, Market Harborough; one *s* one *d. Educ:* Christ's Coll., Blackheath; Faraday House. CEng, FIEE; FBIM. Various appts with BICC, 1936-73, Dep. Chm. and Chief Exec., 1973-77. War service, 1940-46: Major REME, 14th Army (despatches). President: British Non-ferrous Metals Fedn, 1965-66; Electric Cable Makers' Fedn, 1967-68; BEAMA, 1975-76. *Recreations:* travel, reading, racing. *Address:* Avonhurst, 76 Camden Park Road, Chislehurst, Kent. *T:* 01-467 4875; The Old Manor House, Bledington, Kingham, Oxon. *T:* Kingham 447. *Club:* City Livery.

PIPPARD, Prof. Sir (Alfred) Brian, Kt 1975; FRS 1956; Cavendish Professor of Physics, University of Cambridge, since 1971; *b* 7 Sept. 1920; *s* of late Prof. A. J. S. Pippard; *m* 1955, Charlotte Frances Dyer; three *d. Educ:* Clifton Coll.; Clare Coll., Cambridge (Hon. Fellow 1973). BA (Cantab) 1941, MA 1945. PhD 1949; ScD 1966. Scientific Officer, Radar Research and Development Establishment, Great Malvern, 1941-45; Stokes Student, Pembroke Coll., Cambridge, 1945-46; Demonstrator in Physics, University of Cambridge, 1946; Lecturer in Physics, 1950; Reader in Physics, 1959-60; John Humphrey Plummer Prof. of Physics, 1960-71; Pres., Clare Hall, Cambridge, 1966-73. Visiting Prof., Institute for the Study of Metals, University of Chicago, 1955-56. Fellow of Clare Coll., Cambridge, 1947-66. Cherwell-Simon Memorial Lectr, Oxford, 1968-69. Pres., Inst. of Physics, 1974-76. Hughes Medal of the Royal Soc., 1959; Holweck Medal, 1961; Dannie-Heineman Prize, 1969; Guthrie Prize, 1970. *Publications:* Elements of Classical Thermodynamics, 1957; Dynamics of Conduction Electrons, 1962; Forces and Particles, 1972; papers in Proc. Royal Soc., etc. *Recreation:* music. *Address:* 30 Porson Road, Cambridge.

PIRATIN, Philip; *b* 15 May 1907; *m* 1929, Celia Fund; one *s* two *d. Educ:* Davenant Foundation Sch., London, E1. Was a Member of Stepney Borough Council, 1937-49; MP (Com) Mile End Division of Stepney, 1945-50.

PIRBHAI, Count Sir Eboo; *see* Eboo Pirbhai.

PIRIE, Air Chief Marshal Sir George Clark, KCB 1951 (CB 1943); KBE 1946 (CBE 1942); MC; DFC; LLD; RAF retired,

formerly a Barrister-at-law; *b* 28 July 1896; *m* 1926, Dora Kennedy; one *s* one *d.* Served European War, 1914-18; Deputy Director Operations, Air Ministry, 1936-37; Air Attaché, Washington, 1937-40; Middle East, 1941-43; Director-General Organisation, Air Ministry, 1943-45; Allied Air Commander-in-Chief, SE Asia, 1946-47; Inspector-General, RAF, 1948; Member, Air Council for Supply and Organisation, 1948-50; Head of Air Force Staff, British Joint Services Mission to US, 1950-51; retired RAF, 1951. Chairman, Air League of the British Empire, 1955-58. *Address:* 38 Albemarle, Wimbledon Parkside, SW19 5NP. *Club:* Royal Air Force.

PIRIE, Group Captain Gordon Hamish, CBE 1946; DL; JP; Alderman, City of Westminster, since 1963 (Councillor, 1949; Mayor, 1959-60; Leader of Council, 1961-69; Lord Mayor, 1974-75); *b* 10 Feb. 1918; *s* of Harold Victor Campbell Pirie and Irene Gordon Hogarth; *m* 1953, Margaret Joan Bomford (*d* 1972); no *c. Educ:* Eton (scholar); RAF Coll., Cranwell. Permanent Commission, RAF, 1938. Served War of 1939-45: Dir of Ops, RNZAF, Atlantic and Pacific (despatches, CBE); retired as Group Captain, 1946. Comr No 1 (POW) Dist SJAB, 1960-69; Comdr St John Ambulance, London, 1969-75; Chm., St John Council for London, 1975-. A Governor of Westminster Sch.; Vice-Pres., Engineering Industries Assoc., 1966-69; Mem., Council of Royal Albert Hall; a Trustee, RAF Museum; Vice-Chm., London Boroughs Assoc., 1968-71; Vice-Pres., European Conf. of Local Authorities, 1974-75, 1977-; Mem. Solicitors Disciplinary Tribunal. Contested (LNat&U) Dundee West, 1955. DL, JP Co. of London, 1962; Chm., S Westminster PSD, 1974-77. Liveryman, Worshipful Company of Girdlers. KStJ 1969. Comdr, Legion of Honour, 1960; Comdr, Cross of Merit, SMO Malta, 1971. JSM Malaysia, 1974. *Recreations:* motoring, bird-watching. *Address:* Cottage Row, Tarrant Gunville, Blandford, Dorset DT11 8JJ. *T:* Tarrant Hinton 212. *Clubs:* Carlton, Royal Air Force.

PIRIE, Henry Ward; journalist and broadcaster; Sheriff (formerly Sheriff-Substitute) of Lanarkshire at Glasgow, 1955-74; *b* 13 Feb. 1922; *o surv. s* of late William Pirie, Merchant, Leith; *m* 1948, Jean Marion, *y d* of late Frank Jardine, sometime President of RCS of Edinburgh; four *s. Educ:* Watson's Coll., Edinburgh; Edinburgh Univ. MA 1944; LLB 1947. Served with Royal Scots; commnd Indian Army, 1944; Lieut, Bombay Grenadiers, 1944-46. Called to Scottish Bar, 1947. Sheriff-Substitute of Lanarkshire at Airdrie, 1954-55. OStJ 1967. *Recreations:* curling, golf, bridge. *Address:* 16 Poplar Drive, Lenzie, Kirkintilloch, Dunbartonshire. *T:* Kirkintilloch 2494.

PIRIE, Mrs John; *see* Shaw, Anne Gillespie.

PIRIE, Norman Wingate, FRS 1949; *b* 1 July 1907; *yr s* of late Sir George Pirie, painter, Torrance, Stirlingshire; *m* 1931, Antoinette Patey; one *s. Educ:* Emmanuel Coll., Cambridge. Demonstrator in Biochemical Laboratory, Cambridge, 1932-40; Virus Physiologist, 1940-46, Head of Biochemistry Dept, 1947-73, Rothamsted Experimental Station, Harpenden. Visiting Professor: Reading Univ.; Indian Statistical Inst., Calcutta, 1971-. Copley Medal, 1971; Rank Prize for Nutrition, 1976. *Publications:* scientific papers on various aspects of Biochemistry but especially on separation and properties of macromolecules; articles on viruses, the origins of life, biochemical engineering, and the need for greatly extended research on food production and contraception. *Recreation:* politics. *Address:* Rothamsted Experimental Station, Harpenden, Herts. *T:* Harpenden 63133.

PIRIE, Psyche; Editor of Homes and Gardens (IPC Magazines), since 1968; *b* 6 Feb. 1918; *d* of late George Quarmby; *m* 1940, James Mansergh Pirie; one *d. Educ:* Kensington High Sch.; Chelsea Sch. of Art. Air Ministry, 1940-44. Teaching, Ealing Sch. of Art and Willesden Sch. of Art, 1944-46; Indep. Interior Designer, 1946-56; Furnishing Editor, Homes and Gardens, 1956-68. *Recreations:* conversation, cinema, theatre, junk shops; or doing absolutely nothing. *Address:* 9 Lansdowne Walk, W11. *T:* 01-727 5294.

PIRIE-GORDON of Buthlaw, Christopher Martin, CMG 1967; OBE 1949; HM Diplomatic Service, retired; *b* 28 Sept. 1911; *er s* late Harry Pirie-Gordon of Buthlaw, OBE, DSC, and Mabel Alicia, *d* of late George Earle Buckle, sometime Editor of The Times; unmarried; *S* father as 14th Laird of Buthlaw, 1969. *Educ:* Harrow; Magdalen Coll., Oxford. Palestine Admin Service, 1935; First Secretary and Consul, British Legation, Amman, 1946 (on secondment from Colonial Service); resigned, 1949; a Secretary to Order of St John of Jerusalem, 1950-51; entered Foreign Service, 1951; Asst Political Agent, Kuwait, 1952; Political Agent, Trucial States at Dubai, 1953; Eastern Dept, FO, 1955; Chargé d'Affaires, the Yemen, 1958; Consul,

Innsbruck, 1960; Consul, Florence, and Consul-General, San Marino, 1963-70, retired 1970. Mem., Queen's Body Guard for Scotland, The Royal Co. of Archers. Lay Administrator, Dio. of Gibraltar, 1971-. CStJ 1967. Order of Merit, Italy, 1973. *Recreations:* dining, wining and talking. *Address:* Via Palestro 3, Florence, Italy. *T:* Florence 29.87.59. *Club:* Athenæum.

PIRZADA, Syed Sharifuddin, SPk; Attorney-General of Pakistan, 1965-66, and 1968-71; *b* 12 June 1923; *s* of Syed Vilayat Ali Pirzada; *m* 1960; two *s* two *d. Educ:* University of Bombay. LLB 1945. Secretary, Provincial Muslim League, 1946; Managing Editor, Morning Herald, 1946; Prof., Sind Muslim Law Coll., 1947-55; Advocate: Bombay High Court, 1946; Sind Chief Court, 1947; West Pakistan High Court, 1955; Supreme Court of Pakistan, 1961; Senior Advocate Supreme Court of Pakistan; Foreign Minister of Pakistan, 1966-68. Represented Pakistan: before International Tribunal on Rann of Kutch, 1965; before Internat. Ct of Justice regarding Namibia, SW Africa, 1971; Pakistan Chief Counsel before ICAO Montreal in complaint concerning overflights over Indian territory; Leader of Pakistan Delegations to Commonwealth Conf. and General Assembly of UN, 1966; Mem., UN Sub-Commn on Prevention of Discrimination and Protection of Minorities, 1972-. Hon. Advisor, Constitutional Commn, 1960; Chairman, Pakistan Company Law Commn, 1961-62; Mem., Internat. River Cttee, 1961-; President: Pakistan Br., Internat. Law Assoc.; Karachi Bar Assoc., 1964; Pakistan Bar Council, 1966; Institute of International Affairs. Sitara-e-Pakistan, 1964. *Publications:* Evolution of Pakistan, 1963; Fundamental Rights and Constitutional Remedies in Pakistan, 1966; Foundations of Pakistan, vol. I, 1969, vol. II, 1970. *Recreation:* bridge. *Address:* C-37, KDA Scheme No 1, Habib Ibrahim Rahimtoola Road, Karachi, Pakistan. *Clubs:* Sind (Karachi); Karachi Boat, Karachi Gymkhana.

PITBLADO, Sir David (Bruce), KCB 1967 (CB 1955); CVO 1953; Comptroller and Auditor-General, 1971-76; *b* 18 Aug. 1912; *o s* of Robert Bruce and Mary Jane Pitblado; *m* 1941, Edith, *yr d* of Captain J. T. and Mrs Rees Evans, Cardigan; one *s* one *d. Educ:* Strand Sch.; Emmanuel Coll., Cambridge (Hon. Fellow 1972); Middle Temple. Entered Dominions Office, 1935; Asst Private Secretary to Secretary of State, 1937-39; served in War Cabinet Office, 1942; transferred to Treasury, 1942; Under-Secretary, Treasury, 1949; Principal Private Secretary to the Prime Minister (Mr Clement Attlee, Mr Winston Churchill, and Sir Anthony Eden), 1951-56; Third Secretary, Treasury, 1960; Economic Minister and Head of Treasury Delegation, Washington, and Executive Dir for the UK, Internat. Monetary Fund and Internat. Bank for Reconstruction and Development, 1961-63; Permanent Sec., Min. of Power, 1966-69, Permanent Sec. (Industry), Min. of Technology, 1969-70; Second Permanent Sec., Civil Service Dept, 1970-71. Victoria County Histories Cttee. Companion Inst. of Fuel. *Address:* 23 Cadogan Street, SW3; Pengoitan, Borth, Dyfed. *Club:* Athenæum.

PITCHER, Desmond Henry, CEng, FIEE, FBCS; Managing Director, Leyland Truck & Bus, since Oct. 1976; *b* 23 March 1935; *s* of George Charles and Alice Marion Pitcher; *m* 1961, Patricia (*née* Ainsworth) (marr. diss. 1973); twin *d. Educ:* Liverpool Coll. of Technology. MIEEE (USA). A. V. Roe & Co., Develt Engr, 1955; Automatic Telephone and Elec. Co. (now Plessey), Systems Engr, 1958; Univac Remington Rand (now Sperry Rand Ltd), Systems Engr, 1961; Sperry Univac: Dir, Systems, 1966; Managing Dir, 1971; Vice-Pres., 1974; Director: British Leyland Ltd; Bus Manufrs Holdings Ltd (Chm.); Sperry Rand Ltd (Dep. Chm.); Truck & Bus (Eire) Ltd (Chm.). *Publication:* Institution of Electrical Engineers Faraday Lectures, 1974-75. *Recreations:* golf, music. *Address:* Hawthorne House, Park Avenue, Mossley Hill, Liverpool L18 8BT. *T:* 051-724 1308. *Clubs:* Royal Automobile; Royal Liverpool Golf; Camberley Heath Golf.

PITCHFORD; *see* Watkins-Pitchford.

PITCHFORD, Charles Neville; His Honour Judge Pitchford; a Circuit Judge, since 1972. Called to the Bar, Middle Temple, 1948. *Address:* Old Vicarage, Taliaris, Llandeilo, Dyfed.

PITCHFORD, John Hereward, CBE 1971; President, Ricardo & Co. Engineers (1927) Ltd, Consulting Engineers, since 1976 (Chairman, 1962-76); *b* 30 Aug. 1904; *s* of John Pitchford and Elizabeth Anne Wilson; *m* 1930, Teresa Agnes Mary Pensotti; one *s* two *d. Educ:* Brighton Coll.; Christ's Coll., Cambridge (MA). CEng, FIMechE (Pres. 1962). Ricardo & Co. Engineers (1927) Ltd: Test Shop Asst, 1926; Asst Research Engr, 1929; Personal Asst to Man. Dir, 1935; Gen. Man., 1939; Dir and Gen. Man., 1941; Man. and Jt Techn. Dir, 1947; Chm. and Man. Dir, 1962; Chm. and Jt Man. Dir, 1965; Chm., 1967. Pres.,

Fédération Internationale des Sociétés d'Ingénieurs des Techniques de l'Automobile, 1961-63; Chm., Navy Dept Fuels and Lubricants Adv. Cttee, 1964-71. Hon. Mem., Associazione Tecnica Automobile, 1958. *Publications:* papers on all aspects of internal combustion engine. *Recreations:* music, sailing. *Address:* Byeways, Ditchling, East Sussex. *T:* Hassocks 2177. *Clubs:* Athenæum, Royal Automobile.

PITCHFORTH, Harry; General Manager, Home Grown Cereals Authority, since 1974; *b* 17 Jan. 1917; *s* of John William Pitchforth and Alice Hollas; *m* 1941, Edna May Blakebrough; one *s* one *d. Educ:* Heath Sch., Halifax; Queen's Coll., Oxford. 1st class Hons, School of Modern History, Oxford, 1939. Served War, 1940-45, Captain, RASC, and later Education Officer, 5 Guards Brigade. Ministry of Food, 1945; Principal Private Secretary, to Minister, Major G. Lloyd-George, 1952-54; seconded to National Coal Board, 1955-58; Ministry of Agriculture, Fisheries and Food: Regional Controller, 1957-61; Director of Establishments and Organisation, 1961-65; Under-Sec., HM Treasury, 1965-67; Controller of HM Stationery Office and the Queen's Printer of Acts of Parliament, 1967-69; Chief Executive, Metropolitan Water Bd, 1969-74. *Recreations:* tennis, badminton, music. *Address:* 93 George V Avenue, Pinner, Mddx. *T:* 01-863 1229.

PITCHFORTH, (Roland) Vivian, RA 1953 (ARA 1942); RWS; ARCA (London); *b* 23 April 1895; *s* of Joseph Pitchforth, Wakefield; *m* 1932, Brenda Matthews (*d* 1977). *Educ:* Wakefield Grammar Sch. Studied art at Wakefield and Leeds Schools of Art and Royal College of Art. Pictures in Public Collections: Tate Gallery, Aberdeen, Southport, Stoke, Preston, Rochdale, Salford, Bradford, Wakefield, Leeds, Liverpool, Manchester, Helsinki, Sydney Art Gallery, Australia, Hamilton Art Gallery, NZ; Night Transport in possession of Tate Gallery bought by Chantrey Bequest. One man exhibitions: Coolings, Lefevre, Redfern, Leicester and Wildenstein's Galleries, also in S Africa, 1946. Exhibited at New York Fair, Pittsburgh, Chicago, Canada, Australia, Warsaw, Brussels, Paris, Sweden, and most provincial Galleries in England. Official War Artist to Ministry of Information and later to the Admiralty. *Recreation:* billiards. *Address:* Flat 17, 7 Elm Park Gardens, SW10. *Clubs:* Chelsea Arts, RA.

PITFIELD, (Peter) Michael, QC (Can.); Clerk of the Privy Council and Secretary to the Cabinet, Canada, since 1975; *b* Montreal, 18 June 1937; *s* of Ward Chipman Pitfield and Grace Edith (*née* MacDougall); *m* 1971, Nancy Snow; one *s* one *d. Educ:* Lower Canada Coll., Montreal; Sedbergh Sch., Montebello; St Lawrence Univ. (BASc); McGill Univ. (BCL); Univ. of Ottawa (DESD). Lieut, RCNR. Read Law with Mathewson Lafleur & Brown, Montreal (associated with firm, 1958-59); called to Quebec Bar, 1962; QC (Fed.) 1972; Admin. Asst to Minister of Justice and Attorney-Gen. of Canada, 1962-65; Sec. and Exec. Dir, Royal Commn on Pubns, Ottawa, 1961-62; Attaché to Gov.-Gen. of Canada, 1962-65; Sec. and Res. Supervisor of Royal Commn on Taxation, 1963-66; entered Privy Council Office and Cabinet Secretariat of Govt of Canada, 1965; Asst Sec. to Cabinet, 1967; Dep. Sec. to Cabinet (Plans), and Dep. Clerk to Council, 1969; Dep. Minister, Consumer and Corporate Affairs, 1973. Fellow, Harvard Univ., 1974. Member: Canadian, Quebec and Montreal Bar Assocs; Can. Inst. of Public Admin; Can. Hist. Assoc.; Can. Polit. Sci. Assoc.; Amer. Soc. Polit. and Social Sci.; Internat. Commn of Jurists; Beta Theta Pi. *Recreations:* squash, ski-ing, reading. *Address:* (home) 305 Thorold Road, Ottawa, Ont, Canada; 9432 Gouin Boulevard W, Montreal, Quebec, Canada; (office) Langevin Block, Wellington Street, Ottawa, Ont, Canada. *Clubs:* Rideau, University (Montreal).

PITMAN, Edwin James George, BSc, MA, FAA; Emeritus Professor of Mathematics, University of Tasmania (Professor, 1926; retired, Dec. 1962); *b* Melbourne, 29 Oct. 1897; of English parents; *s* of late Edwin Edward Major Pitman and Ann Ungley Pitman; *m* 1932, Edith Elinor Josephine, *y d* of late William Nevin Tatlow Hurst; two *s* two *d. Educ:* South Melbourne Coll.; Ormond Coll., University of Melbourne. Enlisted Australian Imperial Forces, 1918; returned from abroad, 1919; BA with First Class Honours, Dixson scholarship and Wyselaskie scholarship in Mathematics; acting-Professor of Mathematics at Canterbury Coll., University of New Zealand, 1922-23; Tutor in Mathematics and Physics at Trinity Coll. and Ormond Coll., University of Melbourne, 1924-25; Visiting Prof. of Mathematical Statistics at Columbia Univ., NY, Univ. of N Carolina, and Princeton Univ., 1948-49; Visiting Prof. of Statistics: Stanford Univ., Stanford, California, 1957; Johns Hopkins Univ., Baltimore, 1963-64. Fellow, Inst. Math. Statistics, 1948; FAA 1954; Vice-Pres., 1960; Mem. International Statistical Institute, 1956; Pres., Australian

Mathematical Soc., 1958-59; Hon. Fellow, Royal Statistical Soc., 1965; Hon. Life Mem. Statistical Soc. of Australia, 1966. *Address:* 301 Davey Street, Hobart, Tasmania 7000, Australia.

PITMAN, Sir Hubert, Kt 1961; OBE 1953; Member of Lloyd's since 1926; Chairman, H. Pitman & Co. Ltd, London, EC; *b* 19 Aug. 1901; *yr s* of W. H. Pitman, JP, sometime one of HM's Lieutenants for the City of London; unmarried. *Educ:* Repton. Member, Corporation of London, 1929-54; one of HM's Lieutenants for City of London, 1950-; Member LCC (Cities of London and Westminster), 1955-58; Alderman, 1954-63 (Sheriff, 1959-60) City of London. OStJ. Comdr Etoile Noire, France. *Recreation:* country. *Address:* 57 Porchester Terrace, W2. *T:* 01-262 6593; Danemore Park, Speldhurst, Kent. *T:* Langton 2829; 19 Leadenhall Street, EC3. *T:* 01-626 8078. *Club:* Carlton.

PITMAN, Sir (Isaac) James, KBE 1961; MA; Charter Pro-Chancellor, Bath University; Vice-President: British and Foreign School Society; British Association for Commercial and Industrial Education; Member, National Union of Teachers; Proponent of Initial Teaching Alphabet, and its designer, for the better teaching of reading; *b* London, 14 Aug. 1901; *e s* of late Ernest Pitman; *g s* of late Sir Isaac Pitman; *m* 1927, Hon. Margaret Beaufort Lawson-Johnston (Order of Mercy), 2nd *d* of 1st Baron Luke of Pavenham; three *s* one *d. Educ:* Eton; Christ Church, Oxford, 2nd Class Hons Mod. Hist. Played Rugby football for Oxford v Cambridge, 1921, for England v Scotland, 1922; ran for Oxford v Cambridge, 1922; skied for Oxford v Cambridge, 1922; won Middle Weight Public Schools Boxing, 1919. Bursar, Duke of York's and King's Camp, 1933-39. Chairman, Sir Isaac Pitman and Sons Ltd, 1934-66. RAF 1940-43, Acting Sqdn Leader; Director of Bank of England, 1941-45; HM Treasury, Director of Organisation and Methods, 1943-45. MP (C) Bath, 1945-64. Formerly: Chm., Royal Soc. of Teachers; Chm. of Council, Initial Teaching Alphabet Foundn; Mem. Cttee, London Univ. Inst. of Education and Nat. Foundn for Educational Res. (which conducted comparative researches into reasons for reading failure in earliest stages of learning); Mem., Cttee advising Public Trustee under Will of late George Bernard Shaw in carrying out his wishes for design and publication of a proposed British alphabet). Hon. Pres., Parly Group for World Govt; Vice-Pres., Inst. of Administrative Management, 1965-69; Mem. Council, St. Dunstan's. Hon. DLittHum Hofstra, NY; Hon. DLitt: Strathclyde and Bath. *Address:* 58 Chelsea Park Gardens, SW3 6AE. *T:* 01-352 7004; Holme Wood, Chisbridge, Marlow, Bucks. *T:* High Wycombe 881260. *Clubs:* Carlton; Harlequins.

PITOI, Sir Sere, Kt 1977; CBE; MACE; *b* Kapa Village, SE of Port Moresby, 1936. *Educ:* Birmingham Univ., UK; Queensland Univ. Certif. in teaching Sogeri; Certif. in Headmasters and Educnl Admin. (Birm.); Diagnostic Teaching and Remedial Educn, Queensland Univ. Held a number of teaching and admin. posts, 1955-68, in Port Moresby, the Gulf district of Papua, Eastern Highlands, New Britain. Apptd a District Inspector of Schools, 1968. Chm., Public Service Bd, Papua New Guinea, 1970 (original Mem., 1969); lately Chm., Public Services Commn, Papua New Guinea (as the Bd is now known). Fellow, PNG Inst. of Management. *Address:* c/o PO Box 6029, Boroko, Port Moresby, Papua New Guinea.

PITT, family name of **Baron Pitt of Hampstead.**

PITT OF HAMPSTEAD, Baron *cr* 1975 (Life Peer), of Hampstead, in Greater London and in Grenada; **David Thomas Pitt,** TC 1976; MB, ChB Edinburgh, DCH London; JP; Member, for Hackney, Greater London Council (Deputy Chairman, 1969-70; Chairman, 1974-75), 1964-77 (LCC 1961); Chairman, Community Relations Commission, 1977 (Deputy Chairman, 1968-77); General Practitioner, London, since 1947; *b* St David's, Grenada, WI, 3 Oct. 1913; *m* 1943, Dorothy Elaine Alleyne; one *s* two *d. Educ:* St David's RC Sch., Grenada, WI; Grenada Boys' Secondary Sch.; Edinburgh Univ. First Junior Pres., Student Rep. Council, Edinburgh Univ., 1936-37. Dist. Med. Officer, St Vincent, WI, 1938-39; Ho. Phys., San Fernando Hosp., Trinidad, 1939-41; GP, San Fernando, 1941-47; Mem. of San Fernando BC, 1941-47; Dep. Mayor, San Fernando, 1946-47; Pres., West Indian Nat. Party (Trinidad), 1943-47. Mem. Nat. Cttee for Commonwealth Immigrants, 1965-67; Chm., Campaign Against Racial Discrimination, 1965; Mem., Standing Adv. Council on Race Relations, 1977-. Mem. (part time), PO Bd, 1975. JP 1966. Contested (Lab): Hampstead, 1959; Clapham (Wandsworth), 1970. Hon. DSc Univ. of West Indies; Hon. DLitt Bradford; Hon. LLD Bristol. *Recreations:* reading, watching television, watching cricket, listening to music, theatre. *Address:* 6 Heath Drive, NW3. *T:* 01-435 7532. *Clubs:* Royal Commonwealth Society (West Indian), MCC.

PITT, Barrie (William Edward); author and editor of military histories; *b* Galway, 7 July 1918; *y s* of John Pitt and Ethel May Pitt (*née* Pennell); *m* 1st, 1943, Phyllis Kate (*née* Edwards); one *s* (decd); 2nd, 1953, Sonia Deirdre (*née* Hoskins) (marr. diss., 1971). *Educ:* Portsmouth Southern Grammar Sch. Bank Clerk, 1935. Served War of 1939-45, in Army. Surveyor, 1946. Began writing, 1954. Information Officer, Atomic Energy Authority, 1961; Historical Consultant to BBC Series, The Great War, 1963; Editor, Purnell's History of the Second World War, 1964; Editor-in-Chief: Ballantine's Illustrated History of World War 2, 1967 (US Book Series); Ballantine's Illustrated History of the Violent Century, 1971; Editor: Purnell's History of the First World War, 1969; British History Illustrated, 1974. *Publications:* The Edge of Battle, 1958; Zeebrugge, St George's Day, 1918, 1958; Coronel and Falkland, 1960; 1918 The Last Act, 1962; The Battle of the Atlantic, 1977; contrib. to: Encyclopaedia Britannica; The Sunday Times. *Recreations:* golf, travel. *Address:* Merryfield House, Ilton, near Ilminster, Somerset TA19 9EX. *Club:* Savage.

PITT, Mgr George Edward, CBE 1965; Parish Priest, St Joseph's, Wroughton, Wilts, since 1969; *b* 10 Oct. 1916; *s* of Francis Pitt and Anna Christina Oviedo. *Educ:* St Brendan's Coll., Bristol; Ven. English College, Rome. Priest, 1939; worked in Diocese of Clifton, 1940-43; joined Royal Navy as Chaplain, 1943; Principal Roman Catholic Chaplain, RN, 1963-69. Nominated a Domestic Prelate, 1963. *Recreation:* music. *Address:* 14 Wharf Road, Wroughton, Swindon, Wilts SN4 9LB. *T:* 812330. *Club:* Army and Navy.

PITT, Prof. Harry Raymond, FRS 1957; BA, PhD; Vice-Chancellor, Reading University, since 1964; *b* 3 June 1914; *s* of H. Pitt; *m* 1940, Clemency Catherine, *d* of H. C. E. Jacoby, MIEE; four *s. Educ:* King Edward's Sch., Stourbridge; Peterhouse, Cambridge. Bye-Fellow, Peterhouse, Cambridge, 1936-39; Choate Memorial Fellow, Harvard Univ., 1937-38; Univ. of Aberdeen, 1939-42. Air Min. and Min. of Aircraft Production, 1942-45. Prof. of Mathematics, Queen's Univ., Belfast, 1945-50; Deputy Vice-Chancellor, Univ. of Nottingham, 1959-62; Prof. of Pure Mathematics, Univ. of Nottingham, 1950-64. Visiting Prof., Yale Univ., 1962-63. Chm., Universities Central Council on Admissions, 1975-. Hon. LLD: Aberdeen 1970; Nottingham 1970. *Publications:* Tauberian Theorems, 1957; Measure, Integration and Probability, 1963; mathematical papers in scientific journals. *Address:* The University, Reading, Berks.

PITT, Terence John; *b* Willenhall, Staffs, 2 March 1937. *Educ:* Queen Mary's Sch., Walsall; Univ. of Aston, Birmingham. Head of Labour Party Research Department, 1965-74; Special Adviser to Lord President of the Council, 1974. *Publication:* contrib. Nuclear Power Technology (ed Pearson), 1963. *Recreation:* politics. *Address:* 75 Addison Road, W14. *T:* 01-603 3264.

PITT, William Augustus Fitzgerald Lane F.; *see* Fox-Pitt.

PITT-RIVERS, Dr Rosalind Venetia, FRS 1954; *b* 4 March 1907; *d* of late Hon. Anthony Morton Henley, CMG, DSO, and of Hon. Sylvia Laura Henley (*née* Stanley); *m* 1931, Captain George Henry Lane Fox Pitt-Rivers (*d* 1966); one *s. Educ:* Notting Hill High Sch.; Bedford Coll., University of London. MSc London 1931; PhD London, 1939. Head, Chemistry Division, Nat. Inst. for Medical Research, 1969-72. *Publications:* The Thyroid Hormones, 1959; The Chemistry of Thyroid Diseases, 1960; (with W. R. Trotter) The Thyroid Gland, 1964. *Address:* 23A Lyndhurst Road, Hampstead, NW3 5NX.

PITTAM, Robert Raymond; Assistant Under-Secretary of State, Home Office, since 1972; *b* 14 June 1919; *e s* of Rev. R. G. Pittam and Elsie Emma Pittam (*née* Sale); *m* 1946, Gwendoline Lilian Brown; one *s* one *d. Educ:* Bootle Grammar Sch.; Pembroke Coll., Cambridge. MA; 1st Cl. Law Tripos. War of 1939-45: temp. Civil Servant, and service in RAOC, 1940-46. Home Office, 1946-66: Private Sec. to Home Secretary, 1955-57; Asst Sec., 1957; HM Treasury, 1966-68; CSD, 1968-72. *Recreations:* cricket, reading. *Address:* 32 Northampton Road, Croydon CR0 7HT. *T:* 01-654 6073. *Clubs:* United Oxford & Cambridge University, Civil Service.

PITTER, Ruth, CLit 1974; poetess; *b* Ilford, Essex, 7 Nov. 1897; *d* of George Pitter, Elementary Schoolmaster. *Educ:* Elementary Sch.; Coborn Sch., Bow, E. Heinemann Foundation Award, 1954; Queen's Medal for Poetry, 1955. *Publications:* First Poems, 1920; First and Second Poems, 1927; Persephone in Hades (privately printed), 1931; A Mad Lady's Garland, 1934; A Trophy of Arms, 1936 (Hawthornden Prize, 1937); The Spirit Watches, 1939; The Rude Potato, 1941; The Bridge, 1945; Pitter on Cats, 1946; Urania, 1951; The Ermine, 1953; Still By Choice, 1966; Poems 1926-66, 1968; End of Drought, 1975. *Recreation:* gardening. *Address:* 71 Chilton Road, Long Crendon, near Aylesbury, Bucks. *T:* Long Crendon 208 373.

PITTOM, L(ois) Audrey; Under Secretary, Health and Safety Executive, Department of Employment, since 1975; *b* 4 July 1918; *d* of Thomas Pittom and Hylda (*née* Ashby). *Educ:* Laurels Sch., Wroxall Abbey, Warwick; St Anne's Coll., Oxford (BA Hons). Inspector of Factories, 1945; Superintending Inspector, Nottingham, 1967; Dep. Chief Inspector of Factories, 1970. *Recreations:* gardening, sight-seeing in Europe. *Address:* 1 Rectory Lane, Barby, Rugby, Warwicks. *T:* Rugby 890424.

PITTS, Sir Cyril (Alfred), Kt 1968; General Manager, International Coordination, ICI Ltd, since 1968; Chairman, ICI (Export) Ltd; Director, ICI Americas Ltd; Deputy Chairman, Ozalid Group Holdings Ltd, 1975-77; *b* 21 March 1916; *m* 1942, Barbara; two *s* one *d. Educ:* St Olave's; Jesus Coll., Cambridge. Chairman of ICI Companies in India, 1964-68; President, Bengal Chamber of Commerce and Industry, 1967-68; President, Associated Chambers of Commerce and Industry of India, 1967-68. Councillor, RIIA; Mem., Bd of Management, London Sch. of Hygiene and Tropical Medicine. *Address:* 11 Queensmead, St John's Wood Park, NW8. *T:* 01-586 0871. *Clubs:* Oriental, Bengal (Calcutta).

PITTS, William Ewart, CBE 1963; QPM 1956; Chief Constable, Derbyshire County Police, 1953-67; *b* 18 Sept. 1900; *s* of William Pitts and Albenia Elizabeth (*née* Nicholls), Swansea; *m* 1923, Doris, *d* of Herbert Whiteley, Wakefield, Yorks; one *d. Educ:* Rowsley, Derbyshire. Served European War, Royal Navy, 1914-18. Liverpool City Police: Constable to Chief Superintendent, 1919-49; Bootle County Borough Police, Chief Constable, 1949-53. *Recreations:* golf, fishing, swimming. *Address:* Burre Close Cottage, Station Road, Bakewell, Derbyshire. *T:* Bakewell 2600.

PITTS CRICK, R.; *see* Crick, Ronald P.

PITTS-TUCKER, Robert St John, CBE 1975; *b* 24 June 1909; *e s* of Walter Greame Pitts-Tucker, Solicitor, and Frances Elsie Wallace; *m* 1942, Joan Margery, *d* of Frank Furnivall, Civil Engineer, India, and Louisa Cameron Lees; three *s* one *d. Educ:* Haileybury (Schol.); Clare Coll., Cambridge (Schol.). 1st cl. Class. Tripos, Pts I and II, 1930 and 1931. Asst Master, Shrewsbury Sch., 1931-44; Headmaster, Pocklington Sch., 1945-66; Dep. Sec. to HMC and HMA, 1966-69, Sec., 1970-74. Mem., House of Laity, Church Assembly, 1956-70; St Albans diocese: Reader; Vice-Pres. of Synod, 1976-; Member: ER Yorks Educn Cttee, 1946-66; Herts Educn Cttee, 1974-; Vice-Chm., Yorks Rural Community Council, 1949-65; Mem., Secondary Schools Examination Council, 1954-57. Governor: Mill Hill Sch.; Haileybury; St George's, Harpenden; Mem., GBA Exec. Cttee, 1975. *Recreations:* tennis, country walks, listening to music, gardening. *Address:* 59 Kings Road, Berkhamsted, Herts. *Clubs:* Royal Commonwealth Society, Hellenic Society, East India, Devonshire, Sports and Public Schools.

PIX WESTON, John; *see* Weston, J. P.

PIXLEY, Sir Neville (Drake), Kt 1976; MBE 1944; VRD 1941; company director; *b* 21 Sept. 1905; *s* of Arthur and Florence Pixley; *m* 1938, Lorna, *d* of Llewellyn Stephens; three *d. Educ:* C of E Grammar Sch., Brisbane. FCIT. Served RANR, 1920-63; War Service, Comd Corvettes, 1939-46 (Comdr 1945). Macdonald, Hamilton & Co. (P&O agents), 1922-59, Managing Partner, 1949-59; Chm., P&O Lines of Australia, 1960-70; Director: Burns Philp & Co. Ltd, 1962-; Mauri Brothers & Thomson Ltd, 1970-77; NSW Bd of Advice, Nat. Bank of Australasia Ltd, 1970-77; Chm. Australian Cttee, Lloyd's Register of Shipping. ADC to King George VI and to the Queen, 1951-54. Receiver-Gen., Order of St John in Australia, 1963-; KStJ 1963. Chm., Royal Humane Soc. of NSW. *Recreation:* tennis. *Address:* Koiyong, 335 New South Head Road, Double Bay, Sydney, NSW 2028, Australia. *T:* 3262676. *Clubs:* Union, Australian, Imperial Service (Sydney); Queensland (Qld); Melbourne (Melbourne).
See also N. S. Pixley.

PIXLEY, Norman Stewart, CMG 1970; MBE 1941; VRD 1927; retired company director; Dean of the Consular Corps of Queensland since 1965; Hon. Consul for the Netherlands, 1948-72; *b* Brisbane, 3 May 1898; 2nd *s* of Arthur and Florence Pixley; *m* 1931, Grace Josephine, *d* of Arthur and Grace Spencer; twin *s* one *d. Educ:* Bowen House Sch.; Brisbane Grammar School. Served in RANR, 1913-46; Comdr, RANR, retd. Councillor, National Trust of Queensland; Pres., Qld Lawn

Tennis Assoc., 1948-52; Pres., Brisbane Chamber of Commerce, 1952-53; Leader of Aust. Delegn to British Commonwealth Chambers of Commerce Conf., 1951; founded Qld Div. of Navy League, 1953 (Pres. until 1969). FRHistSoc Qld 1965 (Pres. 1968-). Kt, Order of Orange Nassau, 1964. *Publications:* papers on Australian history in Jl of Royal Hist. Soc. Qld, etc. *Recreations:* tennis, yachting, golf. *Address:* 147 Sherwood Road, Toowong, Brisbane, Queensland 4066, Australia. *T:* 701150. *Clubs:* Queensland, United Service, Royal Queensland Yacht Squadron, Tattersalls, Indooroopilly Golf (all Qld).
See also Sir Neville Pixley.

PIZEY, Admiral Sir (Charles Thomas) Mark, GBE 1957 (KBE 1953); CB 1942; DSO 1942; idc; RN retired; DL; *b* 1899; *s* of late Rev. C. E. Pizey, Mark and Huntspill, Somerset; *m* Phyllis, *d* of Alfred D'Angibau; two *d.* Served European War, 1914-18, Midshipman, Revenge, 1916-18; Lieut, 1920; HMS Danae Special Service Squadron World Cruise, 1921-22; Flag Lieut to Vice-Admiral Sir Howard Kelly, 2nd in command Mediterranean Fleet, 1929-30; Destroyer Commands Mediterranean and Home Fleets, 1930-39; War of 1939-45: Captain, 1939; Commanded HMS Ausonia, Atlantic Patrol and Convoys, 1939-40. Captain (D) 21st Destoyer Flotilla in HMS Campbell, Nore Command, Channel and North Sea Operations, 1940-42 (CB, DSO, despatches twice); commanded HMS Tyne and Chief Staff Officer to Rear-Admiral Destroyers, Home Fleet, Russian convoys, 1942-43 (bar to DSO); Director of Operations (Home) Admiralty Naval Staff, 1944-45; Chief of Staff to C-in-C Home Fleet, 1946; Imperial Defence Coll., 1947; Rear-Admiral, 1948; Chief of UK Services Liaison Staff, Australia, 1948-49; Flag Officer Commanding First Cruiser Squadron, 1950-51; Vice-Admiral, 1951; Chief of Naval Staff and Commander-in-Chief, Indian Navy, 1951-55; Admiral, 1954; Commander-in-Chief, Plymouth, 1955-58, retired. DL County of Somerset, 1962. *Address:* 1 St Ann's Drive, Burnham on Sea, Somerset.

PLACE, Rear-Adm. (Basil Charles) Godfrey, VC 1944; CB 1970; DSC 1943; Lay Observer, since 1975; *b* 19 July 1921; *s* of late Major C. G. M. Place, DSO, MC, and late Mrs Place; *m* 1943, Althea Annington, *d* of late Harry Tickler, Grimsby; one *s* two *d. Educ:* The Grange, Folkestone; RNC, Dartmouth. Midshipman, 1939; 10th and 12th submarine flotillas, 1941-43; Lieut, 1942; Comdr, 1952; HMS Glory (801 Sqn), 1952-53; Comdg HMS Tumult, 1955-56; Exec. Officer, HMS Theseus, 1956-57; HMS Corunna, 1957-58; Captain, 1958; Chief SO to Flag Officer Aircraft Carriers, 1958-60; Deputy Director of Air Warfare, 1960-62; HMS Rothesay and Captain (D), 25th Escort Squadron, 1962-63; HMS Ganges, 1963-65; HMS Albion, 1966-67; Adm. Comdg Reserves, and Dir-Gen., Naval Recruiting, 1968-70. Chm., VC and GC Assoc., 1971-. Polish Cross of Valour, 1941. *Address:* 87 Bishop's Mansions, SW6; The Old Bakery, Corton Denham, Sherborne, Dorset.

PLAIDY, Jean; *see* Hibbert, Eleanor.

PLANT, Sir Arnold, Kt 1947; Economist; Emeritus Professor, University of London; *b* London, 29 April 1898; 2nd *s* of late William C. Plant, FLA; *m* 1925, Edith Render, BA, London; two *s. Educ:* Strand Sch.; London School of Economics, University of London. Gerstenberg Scholar in Economics and Political Science, 1921; Bachelor of Commerce, 1922; BSc (Econ.), 1923; previously in engineering; Professor of Commerce and Dean of the Faculty of Commerce in the University of Cape Town, 1924-30 (Hon. LLD, 1968); Professor of Commerce in the University of London, at London School of Economics, 1930-65 (Hon. Fellow, 1967). Vice-Pres., Council, Royal Economic Society; Mem., Cinematograph Films Council, 1938-69; Chairman: Industrial Injuries Advisory Council, 1955-67; Advertising Standards Authority, 1962-65; Colonial Social Science Research Council, 1955-62; Member, Overseas Research Council, 1959-64; Organiser for Ministry of Information, and first Director of Wartime Social Survey, 1940; Chairman, National Service Deferment Cttee for the Cinematograph Industry, Ministry of Labour, 1942-45; temporary civil servant, 1940-46 as Adviser to Ministerial Chairman of Interdepartmental Materials Cttee and Central Priority Cttee under Production Council (1940), Production Executive (1941), Min. of Production (1942-45), and on special duties in Cabinet Office, 1945-46; Member: BoT Cttee on a Central Institute of Management, 1945-46; Min. of Works Cttee on Distribution of Building Materials, 1946; Min. of Education Cttee on Commercial Education, 1946; Board of Trade Cttee on Film Distribution, 1949 (Chm.); Monopolies and Restrictive Practices Commission, 1953-56; Chm., Min. of Agriculture Cttee on Fowl Pest Policy, 1960-62. *Publications:* contributor to: London Essays in Economics in honour of Edwin Cannan, 1927; Tariffs: the Case Examined, 1931; Cambridge History of British

Empire (South Africa Volume, 1936); Some Modern Business Problems (editor), 1937; The Population Problem, 1938; Selected Economic Essays and Addresses, 1974; the scientific economic journals. *Address:* 19 Wildwood Road, NW11. *T:* 01-455 2863.

PLANT, Cyril Thomas Howe, CBE 1975 (OBE 1965); Vice Chairman, British Waterways Board, since 1977; Member, Monopolies and Mergers Commission, since 1975; *b* Leek, Staffs, 27 Aug. 1910; *s* of late Sidney Plant and late Rose Edna Plant; *m* 1931, Gladys Mayers; two *s* one *d. Educ:* Leek High School. Entered Post Office, 1927; Inland Revenue, 1934; Inland Revenue Staff Federation: Asst Sec., 1944; Gen. Sec., 1960-76; Chm. of Post Office and Civil Service Sanatorium Soc., 1950-75; Mem. General Council TUC, 1964-76 (Mem. Economic, Internat. Cttees TUC, Adviser to UK Workers' Deleg. ILO, 1965-); Chm., TUC, 1976; Mem. Exec. Cttee, Public Service International, 1960-77; Mem., NE Metrop. Hosp. Bd, 1965-68; UK Workers' Mem. of ILO Governing Body, Nov. 1969-77. Member: Community Relations Commn, 1974-77; Race Relations Bd, 1976-77; Chm., NI Standing Adv. Commn on Human Rights, 1976-; Chm. of Governors, Ruskin Coll., Oxford, 1967-; Treas., London Trades Council, 1952-74; Mem., Civil Service Nat. Whitley Council, 1948-76; Mem., Inland Revenue Departmental Whitley Council, 1938-76 (Chm. 1958-76); Treas., Workers' Educational Assoc., 1969-; Chm. British Productivity Council, 1972-77. A Dir, LOB, 1977-. *Recreations:* horse racing, international activity. *Address:* Longridge, 19 Montacute Road, Lewes, East Sussex. *T:* Lewes 2556. *Club:* English-Speaking Union.

PLASKETT, Maj.-Gen. Frederick Joseph, MBE 1966; Director of Movements (Army), since 1975; *b* 23 Oct. 1926; *s* of Frederick Joseph Plaskett and Grace Mary Plaskett; *m* 1950, Heather (*née* Kington); four *d. Educ:* Wallasey; Chelsea Polytechnic. Commnd infantry, 1946; RASC, 1951; RCT, 1965; regimental and staff appts, India, Korea, Nigeria, Malaya, Germany and UK; Student, Staff Coll., Camberley, 1958; Jt Services Staff Coll., 1964; Instr, Staff Coll., Camberley, 1966-68; Admin. Staff Coll., Henley, 1969; RCDS, 1975. *Recreations:* shooting, fishing, sailing, gardening. *Address:* c/o National Westminster Bank Ltd, Minster Street, Salisbury, Wilts. *Club:* Army and Navy.

PLASKETT, Harry Hemley, FRS 1936; MA (Oxon); Savilian Professor of Astronomy, Oxford, 1932-60, now Emeritus; *b* Toronto, 5 July 1893; *s* of John Stanley Plaskett, Victoria; *m* 1921, Edith Alice, *d* of John James Smith, barrister, Ottawa; one *s* one *d. Educ:* Ottawa Collegiate; Toronto Univ. (BA). Served CFA, France, 1917-18; Astronomer, Dominion Astrophysical Observatory, Victoria, 1919-27; Professor of Astrophysics, Harvard, 1928-32. Served anti-aircraft battery, 1939-40, and worked on experimental navigation for MAP, 1940-44 inc. Gold Medal, Royal Astronomical Society, 1963. Hon. LLD St Andrews, 1961. *Publications:* Papers on observational astrophysics in various journals and observatory publications. *Address:* 48 Blenheim Drive, Oxford OX2 8DQ.

PLASTOW, David Arnold Stuart; Group Managing Director, Rolls-Royce Motors Ltd, since June 1974; *b* Grimsby, 9 May 1932; *s* of James Stuart Plastow and Marie Plastow; *m* 1954, Barbara Ann May; one *s* one *d. Educ:* Culford Sch., Bury St Edmunds. Apprentice, Vauxhall Motors Ltd, 1950; joined Rolls-Royce Ltd, Motor Car Div., Crewe, Sept. 1958; apptd Marketing Dir, Motor Car Div., 1967; Managing Director: Motor Car Div., 1971; Rolls-Royce Motors Ltd, 1972. Dir, Vickers Ltd, 1975-. Vice-Pres., Inst. of Motor Industry; President: SMMT, 1976-77, 1977-78 (formerly Vice-Pres.); Motor Industry Res. Assoc., 1977-; Chm., Grand Council, Motor and Cycle Trades Benevolent Fund. Patron, Coll. of Aeronautical and Automobile Engrg. FBIM. Governor, Culford Sch. Pres., Crewe Alexandra FC; Vice-Pres., Cheshire Scouts Assoc. Young Business Man of the Year Award, The Guardian, 1976. *Recreation:* golf. *Address:* Rolls Royce Motors Ltd, Crewe, Cheshire CW1 3PL. *T:* Crewe 55155.

PLATT, family name of **Baron Platt.**

PLATT, Baron, *cr* 1967 (Life Peer), of Grindleford; **Robert Platt,** 1st Bt, *cr* 1959; MSc (Manchester); MD (Sheffield); FRCP; Professor of Medicine, Manchester University, and Physician, Royal Infirmary, Manchester, 1945-65; President of the Royal College of Physicians, 1957-62; *b* London, 16 April 1900; *s* of William Platt and Susan Jane Willis; *m* 1st, 1922, Margaret Irene Cannon, MB, ChB, DPM (marr. diss. 1974); one *s* two *d*; 2nd, 1974, Sylvia Jean Haggard (*née* Caveley), ARCM (viola). *Educ:* private schools; Sheffield Univ. Physician, Royal Infirmary, Sheffield, 1931-45; Lt-Col, 1941-44, Brig., 1944-45,

RAMC. Editor Quarterly Jl of Medicine, 1948-58. Member: Medical Research Council, 1953-57; Central Health Services Council; Cttee of Hallé Concerts Soc., 1947-53; Council Royal Manchester Coll. of Music; Medical Research Soc.; Chm., Clinical Research Board of Medical Research Council, 1964-67; Member: Medical Advisory Board, RAF; Royal Commn on Medical Educn, 1965; Pres., Eugenics Soc., 1965-68; Vice-President: British Assoc. Adv. Science, 1962; Family Planning Assoc., 1971- (Pres, 1968-71); Nat. Soc. for the Abolition of Cruel Sports, 1972-; Chm., Manchester Chamber Concerts Soc., 1952-65; Membre d'honneur de la Société de Pathologie Rénale; Hon. Member: Assoc. of Physicans; The Renal Assoc.; Assoc. of American Physicians; Hon. FACP; Hon. FRCGP; Hon. FRSocMed; Hon. Fellow, Manchester Med. Soc.; Hon. FRACP; Hon. FRCPsych; Mem. Soc. of Authors; Membre Correspondant étranger, Soc. Med. des Hôpitaux de Paris; Hon. Freeman, Worshipful Co. *of Barbers; Fellow-Commoner, Christ's Coll., Cambridge. Lectures: Lumleian, RCP, London, 1952; Doyne Memorial, Oxford, 1956; Watson Smith, RCP Edinburgh, 1958; Galton, London, 1961; Lilly, Amer. Coll. Physicians, 1961; Linacre, St John's Coll., Cambridge, 1963; Arthur Hall, Sheffield, 1965; Wiltshire, London, 1965; Oslerian Orator, 1963; Rock Carling Fellow, 1963; Harveian Orator, RCP, 1967. Hon. LLD: Sheffield, 1959; Belfast, 1959; Manchester, 1969; Hon. MD Bristol, 1959. *Publications:* Nephritis and Allied Diseases, 1934; Private and Controversial, 1972; numerous papers to Quarterly Journal of Med., Clinical Science, etc., mostly on renal disease and genetics. *Recreations:* talking with Sylvia; String Quartet playing ('cello). *Heir:* (to father's Btcy) *s* Hon. Peter Platt, Prof. of Music at Univ. of Sydney (previously at Otago Univ., NZ) [*b* 6 July 1924; *m* 1948, Jean Halliday Brentnall; one *s* two *d*]. *Address:* 53 Heathside, Hinchley Wood, Esher, Surrey KT10 9TD. *T:* 01-398 1732.

PLATT, Prof. Desmond Christopher Martin; Professor of the History of Latin America, University of Oxford, Fellow of St Antony's College and Director, Centre of Latin American Studies, since 1972; *b* 11 Nov. 1934; *s* of J. W. Platt, CBE; *m* 1958, Sarah Elizabeth Russell; no *c. Educ:* Collyer's Sch., Horsham; Balliol Coll., Oxford; Stanford Univ.; St Antony's Coll., Oxford. BA 1st cl. Hist. 1958, MA, DPhil 1962, Oxon; FRHistS. Asst Principal, Min. of Aviation, 1960-61; Asst Lectr, Edinburgh Univ., 1961-62; Lectr, Exeter Univ., 1962-68; Fellow, Queens' Coll., Cambridge and Univ. Lectr in Latin American History, 1969-72; Dir, Centre of Latin Amer. Studies, Univ. of Cambridge, 1971-72; Chm., Soc. for Latin American Studies, 1973-75. *Publications:* Finance, Trade and Politics in British Foreign Policy 1815-1914, 1968; The Cinderella Service: British Consuls since 1825, 1971; Latin America and British Trade 1806-1914, 1972; (ed) Business Imperialism: an inquiry based on British experience in Latin America before 1930, 1977. *Address:* Brill House, Brill, Aylesbury, Bucks. *T:* Brill 206.

PLATT, Sir Harry, 1st Bt, *cr* 1958; Kt 1948; MD (Victoria), MS (London), FRCS; Hon. FACS; Hon. FRCS (Canada); Hon. FRCSE; Hon. FDS; President, National Fund for Research into Crippling Diseases, since 1970; Hon. President, International Federation of Surgical Colleges (Pres., 1958-66); President: Royal College of Surgeons, 1954-57; Central Council for the Disabled, 1969; Emeritus Professor of Orthopædic Surgery, University of Manchester; Hon. President, Société Internationale de Chirurgie Orthopédique et de Traumatologie; formerly Consultant Adviser: Ministry of Health, 1940-63; Ministry of Labour, 1952-64; Member: Central Health Services Council, 1948-57; Council English-Speaking Union; The Pilgrims; *b* Thornham, Lancashire, 7 Oct. 1886; *e s* of Ernest Platt; *m* 1916, Gertrude Sarah, 2nd *d* of Richard Turney; one *s* four *d. Educ:* Victoria Univ. of Manchester. University Gold Medal. MB, BS (London), 1909; Gold Medal for thesis MD (Vic), 1921; Hunterian Prof. of Surgery and Pathology, RCS, 1921; post-graduate study in USA, 1913-14 (Boston, New York, etc.); Pres. (1934-35) British Orthopædic Association; Captain RAMC (TF), 1915-19; Surgeon in charge of Special Military Surgical Centre (Orthopædic Hospital), Manchester. Hon. Degrees: DM Berne, 1954; Dr, Univ. of Paris, 1966; LLD: Univs of Manchester, 1955, Liverpool, 1955, Belfast, 1955, Leeds, 1965. KStJ 1972. *Publications:* monographs and articles on orthopædic surgery, medical education, hospital organisation, etc. *Recreations:* music, travel. *Heir:* *s* F(rank) Lindsey Platt, Barrister-at-Law [*b* 16 Jan. 1919; *m* 1951, Johanna Laenger]. *Address:* 14 Rusholme Gardens, Platt Lane, Manchester M14 5LS; 11 Lorne Street, Manchester M13 0EZ. *T:* 061-273 3433, 061-224 2427. *Clubs:* Travellers', Royal Automobile; St James's (Manchester).
See also Sir F. J. W. Williams, Bt.

PLATT, Kenneth Harry, CBE 1966 (MBE 1944); Secretary, Institution of Mechanical Engineers, 1961-76, Secretary

Emeritus, 1977; *b* 14 March 1909; *m* 1956, Janet Heather Walters; one *d. Educ:* Shrewsbury School; Glasgow Univ. (BSc in Mech. Eng.). Lecturer, School of Mines, Treforest, 1936-38; Prof. of Mech. Engineering, Benares, India, 1938-39. War Service, RAOC and REME (Major), 1939-45. HM Inspectorate of Schools, 1946-48; Educn and Personnel Manager, Brush Elec. Eng. Co. Ltd, 1949-52; Instn of Mechanical Engineers, 1952-76; Dep. Secretary, 1955. *Address:* Highlands, The Spinning Walk, Shere, Surrey. *T:* Shere 2563.

PLATT, Rev. William James; General Secretary, British and Foreign Bible Society, 1948-60; Consultant, 1960-61; retired, 1961; *b* 2 May 1893; *s* of James and Mary Platt; *m* 1921, Hilda Waterhouse (*d* 1975); one *d. Educ:* Rivington Grammar School; Didsbury Theological College, Manchester. Methodist Missionary in West Africa, 1916-30; Chairman and General Superintendent, Methodist District of French West Africa, 1925-30; joined Bible Society Staff as Secretary for Equatorial Africa, 1930; since 1948 has travelled extensively as General Secretary of Bible Society. Chairman of Council, United Bible Societies, 1954-57. Hon. DD, Knox College, Toronto, Canada, 1954. Officer of the Order of Orange Nassau, 1954; Commander, National Order of the Ivory Coast Republic, 1964. *Publications:* An African Prophet; From Fetish to Faith; Whose World?; Three Women in Central Asia; articles in religious and missionary publications. *Address:* Flat 8, Dewstraw, 147 Lent Rise Road, Burnham, Bucks. *Club:* Royal Commonwealth Society.

PLATTS-MILLS, John Faithful Fortescue, QC 1964; Barrister-at-Law; *b* 4 Oct. 1906; *s* of John F. W. Mills and Dr Daisy Platts-Mills, Karori, Wellington, NZ; *m* 1936, Janet Katherine Cree; six *s. Educ:* Nelson College and Victoria University, NZ; Balliol College, Oxford (Rhodes Scholar). LLM (NZ), MA, BCL Oxon. MP (Lab) Finsbury, 1945-48, (Ind Lab) 1948-50. Pilot Officer, RAF, 1940; "Bevin Boy", 1944; collier, 1945. Bencher, Inner Temple, 1970. *Address:* Cloisters, Temple, EC4. *T:* 01-583 9526; New House, Uckfield, East Sussex. *T:* Buxted 3238. *Clubs:* Athenæum; Vincent's (Oxford); Hampshire (Winchester); Leander.

PLATZER, Dr Wilfried, Gold Cross of Commander, Order of Merit (Austria), 1968; Hon. GCVO 1969; Ambassador of Austria to the Court of St James's 1970-74; *b* 5 April 1909; *s* of Karl Platzer and Paula (*née* Rochelt); *m* 1939, Edith von Donat; one *s* one *d. Educ:* Univ. of Vienna; Foreign Service College. Dr of Law. Attaché, Austr. Legation, Berlin, 1933-34; Austr. Min. for Foreign Affairs, Economic Section: Attaché, 1935-38; Counsellor, 1946-49; Counsellor, Austr. Embassy, Washington, 1950-54; Minister, and Head of Economic Section, Austr. Min. for Foreign Affairs, 1954-58; Ambassador, Washington, 1958-65; Head of Econ. Section, Min. for For. Affairs, 1965-67; Sec.-Gen. for For. Affairs, 1967-70. Grand Cross of: German Order of Merit, 1969; Cedar of Lebanon, 1968; Grand Officer's Cross: Order of St Olav, Norway, 1967; Order of White Elephant, Thailand, 1967; Menelik Order of Ethiopia, 1954; Comdr, Legion d'Honneur, 1957. *Recreation:* reading. *Address:* Formanek Gasse 40, Vienna 1190, Austria. *Club:* Wiener Rennverein (Vienna).

PLAXTON, Ven. Cecil Andrew; Archdeacon of Wiltshire, 1951-74, now Archdeacon Emeritus of the Diocese of Salisbury; *b* 1902; *s* of Rev. J. W. Plaxton, Wells and Langport, Somerset; *m* 1929, Eleanor Joan Elisabeth Sowerby; one *s* one *d. Educ:* Magdalen College School, Oxford; St Edmund Hall, Oxford; Cuddesdon Theological College. BA 1924, MA 1928, Oxford; Deacon, 1926; Priest, 1927; Curate of Chard, 1926-28; Curate of St Martin, Salisbury, 1928-32; Vicar of Southbroom, Wilts, 1932-37; Vicar of Holy Trinity, Weymouth, 1937-51; Rural Dean of Weymouth, 1941-51; Rector of Pewsey, 1951-65; Canon of Salisbury and Prebend of Netheravon, 1949. Officiating Chaplain to the Forces, 1932-51. *Recreations:* archæology and travelling, music. *Address:* St Edmund's Way, Potterne Road, Devizes, Wilts. *T:* Devizes 3391.

PLAYER, Denis Sydney, CBE 1967; Hon. President, Newall Engineering Group, 1973 (Chairman 1962-73; Deputy Chairman, 1955); Chairman, Newall Machine Tool Co. Ltd, 1964-73; *b* 13 Nov. 1913; *s* of Sydney Player and Minnie Emma Rowe; *m* 1940, Phyllis Ethel Holmes Brown (*d* 1975); three *d. Educ:* England; Worcester Acad., Mass. Apprenticed to Newall Engrg Co. Ltd, 1930; spent a year with Federal Produce Corp., RI, before rejoining Newall Engrg on Sales side; Man. Dir, Optical Measuring Tools, 1940; formed Sales Div. for whole of Newall Engrg Gp, 1945. Joined Royal Artillery, 1939; invalided out, 1940. CEng, FIProdE, FRSA. High Sheriff of Rutland, 1970-71. *Recreations:* yachting, fishing, shooting. *Address:* Sundial Cottage, 3 Digby Drive, North Luffenham, near

Oakham, Rutland, Leics. *T:* North Luffenham 239; Casa La Paz, Cala-en-Porte, Menorca, Balearic Islands, Spain. *Clubs:* Royal Automobile; Royal Ocean Racing, Royal Burnham Yacht.

PLAYFAIR, Sir Edward (Wilder), KCB 1957 (CB 1949); Director: National Westminster Bank Ltd; Glaxo Holdings Ltd; Tunnel Holdings Ltd; Equity and Law Life Assurance Society Ltd; *b* 17 May 1909; *s* of late Dr Ernest Playfair; *m* 1949, Dr Mary Lois Rae; three *d. Educ:* Eton; King's Coll., Cambridge. Inland Revenue, 1931-34; HM Treasury, 1934-46 and 1947-56 (Control Office for Germany and Austria, 1946-47); Permanent Under-Secretary of State for War, 1956-59; Permanent Sec., Ministry of Defence, 1960-61. Chairman, International Computers and Tabulators Ltd, 1961-65. Governor, Imperial Coll. of Science and Technology, 1958- (Fellow, 1972); College Cttee of UCL, 1961- (Hon. Fellow, UCL, 1969); Chm., National Gallery, 1972-74 (Trustee, 1967-74). Hon. FBCS. *Address:* 12 The Vale, Chelsea, SW3 6AH. *T:* 01-352 4671. *Club:* Brooks's.

PLAYFORD, Hon. Sir Thomas, GCMG 1957; Premier, Treasurer and Minister of Immigration of S Australia, Nov. 1938-March 1965; Minister of Industry and Employment, 1946-53; Leader of the Opposition, 1965-66; MP, South Australia, 1933-66; *b* 5 July 1896; *o s* of T. Playford, Norton's Summit, SA; *gs* of late Hon. T. Playford, sometime Premier of S Australia; *m* 1928, Lorna Beaman, *e d* of F. S. Clark; one *s* two *d. Educ:* Norton Summit Public School. Engaged in primary production (fruit grower); served European War 27th Bn AIF obtaining a Commission; entered SA Parliament, 1933, as one of representatives for District of Murray; representative for Gumeracha District, 1938-68; Member of Liberal Country Party; Commissioner of Crown Lands, Minister of Repatriation and Irrigation, March 1938; succeeded Hon. R. L. Butler as Leader of Liberal Country Party, 1938. *Recreation:* horticulture. *Address:* Norton Summit, SA 5136, Australia.

PLEASENCE, Donald; actor; *b* 5 Oct. 1919; *s* of late Thomas Stanley and of Alice Pleasence; *m* 1st, 1940, Miriam Raymond; two *d*; 2nd, 1959, Josephine Crombie (marr. diss. 1970); two *d*; 3rd, 1970, Meira Shore; one *d. Educ:* The Grammar School, Ecclesfield, Yorkshire. Made first stage appearance at the Playhouse Theatre, Jersey, CI, May 1939; first London appearance, Twelfth Night, Arts Theatre, 1942. Served with RAF, 1942-46 (Flt Lieut); shot down and taken prisoner, 1944. Returned to stage in The Brothers Karamazov, Lyric, Hammersmith, 1946; Huis Clos, Arts Theatre; Birmingham Repertory Theatre, 1948-50; Bristol Old Vic, 1951; Right Side Up, and Saint's Day, Arts Theatre, 1951; Ziegfeld Theatre, New York (with L. Olivier Co.), 1951; played in own play, Ebb Tide, Edinburgh Festival and Royal Court Theatre, 1952; Stratford-on-Avon season, 1953. *Other London Appearances:* Hobson's Choice, 1952; Antony and Cleopatra, 1953; The Rules of the Game, 1955; The Lark, 1956; Misalliance, 1957; Restless Heart, 1960; The Caretaker, London, 1960, New York, 1961; Poor Bitos, London and New York; The Man in the Glass Booth, St Martin's, 1967 (London Variety Award for Stage Actor of the Year, 1968), New York, 1968-69; Tea Party, The Basement, London, 1970; Wise Child, NY, 1972. Many television appearances. Named Actor of the Year, 1958. *Films include:* The Beachcomber, Heart of a Child, Manuela, The Great Escape, Doctor Crippen, The Caretaker, The Greatest Story Ever Told, The Hallelujah Trail, Fantastic Voyage, Cul-de-Sac, The Night of the Generals, Eye of the Devil, Will Penny, The Mad Woman of Chaillot, Sleep is Lovely, Arthur! Arthur?, THX 1138, Outback, Soldier Blue, The Pied Piper, The Jerusalem File, Kidnapped, Innocent Bystanders, Death Line, Henry VIII, Wedding in White, The Rainbow Boys, Malachi's Cove, Mutations, Tales From Beyond the Grave, The Black Windmill, Escape to Witch Mountain, I Don't Want to be Born, Journey Into Fear, Hearts of the West, Trial by Combat, The Last Tycoon, The Passover Plot, The Eagle has Landed, Golden Rod, The Devil's Men. *Recreation:* talking too much. *Address:* 11 Strand on the Green, W4. *Clubs:* Royal Automobile, White Elephant.

PLEASS, Sir Clement (John), KCMG 1955 (CMG 1950); KCVO 1956; KBE 1953; MA; retired as Governor; *b* 19 November 1901; *s* of J. W. A. Pleass, Tiverton, Devon; *m* 1927, Sybil, *d* of Alwyn Child, Gerrard's Cross; one *s. Educ:* Royal Masonic School; Selwyn College, Cambridge. Joined Colonial Administrative Service, Jan. 1924; served in Nigeria, 1924-56. Lieut-Governor, 1952-54, Governor, 1954-56, Eastern Region of Nigeria. Formerly Mem., Colonial Development Corporation. *Recreation:* golf. *Address:* Higher Barton, Malborough, near Kingsbridge, S Devon. *Club:* Royal Commonwealth Society.

PLENDERLEITH, Harold James, CBE 1959; MC 1918; BSc, PhD; FRSE; FBA 1973; FSA; FMA; Director, International Centre for the Study of the Preservation and Restoration of Cultural Property (created by UNESCO), 1959-71, now Emeritus; Keeper, Research Laboratory, British Museum, WC1, 1949-59; Member of Hon. Scientific Advisory Cttee, Nat. Gallery, since 1935; Chairman, 1944-58; Vice-Pres. of International Institute for the Conservation of Museum Objects, 1958 (Pres., 1965-67, Hon Fellow, 1971); Member, Directory Board of Museum Laboratories Cttee, International Council of Museums; b 19 Sept. 1898; s of Robert James Plenderleith, FEIS; m 1926, Elizabeth K. S. Smyth. Educ: Dundee Harris Acad.; St Andrews Univ. Professor of Chemistry, Royal Academy of Arts, London, 1936-58. Hon. Treas. Internat. Inst. for Conservation of Museum Objects, 1950-58. Rhind Lecturer (Edinburgh) 1954. Gold Medal, Society of Antiquaries of London, 1964; Gold Medal, Univ. of Young Nam, Tae Gu, Korea, 1970; Bronze Medal, UNESCO, 1971; Conservation Service Award, US Dept of the Interior, 1976. Hon. LLD St Andrews. Publications: The Preservation of Antiquities, 1934; The Conservation of Prints, Drawings and Manuscripts, 1937; The Preservation of Leather Bookbindings, 1946; The Conservation of Antiquities and Works of Art, 1956 (2nd edn with A. E. A. Werner, 1971); papers on allied subjects and on technical examinations of museum specimens in museum and scientific journals. Recreations: art and music. Address: Riverside, 17 Rockfield Crescent, Dundee DD2 1JF. T: Dundee 641552. Club: Athenæum.

PLENDERLEITH, Thomas Donald, RE 1961 (ARE 1951); Senior Art Master, St Nicholas Grammar School, Northwood, since 1956; b 11 March 1921; s of James Plenderleith and Georgina Ellis; m 1949, Joyce Rogers; one s. Educ: St Clement Danes; Ealing Sch. of Art; Hornsey Sch. of Art. Pilot, Bomber Command, RAF, 1941-46. Art Master, Pinner County Grammar Sch., 1948-56. Art Teacher's Diploma, 1947. Recreations: cricket, badminton. Address: 46 Sylvia Avenue, Hatch End, Mddx. T: 01-428 5019.

PLEVEN, René Jean; French Statesman; Compagnon de la Libération, 1943; Commandeur du Mérite Maritime, 1945; Député des Côtes-du-Nord, 1945-73; Président du Conseil Général des Côtes-du-Nord, 1949; Président du Conseil Régional de Bretagne, 1974; b 15 April 1901; s of Colonel Jules Pleven; m 1924, Anne Bompard (d 1966); two d. Educ: Faculté de Droit de Paris (LLD); Ecole Libre des Sciences Politiques. Company Director. Deputy chief of French Air Mission to USA, 1939. French National Committee and Comité Français de Libération Nationale (Finances, Colonies, Foreign Affairs), 1941-44; Minister: of Colonies (Provisional Government), 1944; of Finances, 1944-46; of Defence, Nov. 1949 and 1952-54; Président du Conseil, July 1950, Aug. 1951-Jan. 1952; Vice-Président du Conseil, Feb. 1951; Ministre des Affaires Etrangères, 1958; Délégué à l'Assemblée parlementaire européenne, and Chm., Liberal Gp of this Assembly, 1956-69; Ministre de la Justice, et Garde des Sceaux, 1969-73. Grand Officer Order of Leopold, 1945; Grand Cross: Le Million d'éléphants, 1949; Etoile Polaire, 1950; Orange-Nassau, 1950; Dannebrog, 1950; Nicham Alaouite, 1950; Vietnam, 1951; Order of Merit of the Republic of Italy, 1972; National Order of Ivory Coast, 1972; Order of Central African Republic, 1972; Hon GBE, 1972. Publications: Les Ouvriers de l'agriculture anglaise depuis la guerre, 1925; Avenir de la Bretagne, 1962. Recreation: fishing. Address: 12 rue Chateaubriand, Dinan (Côtes-du-Nord), France.

PLEYDELL-BOUVERIE, family name of **Earl of Radnor.**

PLIATZKY, Sir Leo, KCB 1977 (CB 1972); Permanent Secretary, Department of Trade, since 1977; b 1919; m 1948, Marian Jean Elias; one s one d. Educ: Manchester Grammar Sch.; City of London Sch.; Corpus Christi Coll., Oxford. First Cl. Classical Honour Mods, 1939. Served in RAOC and REME, 1940-45 (despatches). First Cl. Philosophy, Politics and Economics, 1946. Research Sec., Fabian Soc., 1946-47; Min. of Food, 1947-50; HM Treasury, 1950-77; Under-Sec., 1967; Dep. Sec., 1971; Second Permanent Sec., 1976. Address: 27 River Court, Upper Ground, SE1. T: 01-928 3667; 76 Pier Avenue, Southwold, Suffolk.

PLIMMER, Sir Clifford (Ulric), KBE 1967; Chairman: New Zealand Breweries Ltd; DRG(NZ) Ltd; Haywrights Ltd; Swift (NZ) Co. Ltd; United Dominions Corporation Finance Ltd; b 25 July 1905; s of late Arthur Bloomfield Plimmer and Jessie Elizabeth (née Townsend); m 1935, Letha May (née Port); three s (and one s decd). Educ: Scots Coll., Wellington; Victoria Univ. of Wellington. Office Junior, 1922, Wright, Stephenson & Co. Ltd (stock and station agents, woolbrokers, gen. merchants,

manufrs, car dealers, insurance agents, etc), retired as Chm. and Man. Dir, 1970. Director: Cable Price Downer Ltd; Dunlop (NZ) Ltd; AMP Society; McKechnie Bros. (NZ) Ltd; NZ Farmers' Fertilizer Co. Ltd. Owns and operates a number of sheep and cattle farms in New Zealand. Chm., Inst. of Dirs (NZ Div.); Nat. Patron, Intellectually Handicapped Children's Soc. Inc.; Member: Dr Barnardos in NZ; Wellington Med. Res. Foundn. Address: PO Box 106, Wellington, New Zealand. T: 63-590. Clubs: Wellington, Wellesley (Wellington); Northern, (Auckland); Hutt (Lower Hutt, NZ).

PLIMSOLL, Sir James, Kt 1962; CBE 1956; Australian Ambassador to Belgium, Luxembourg, and the European Communities, ince 1977; b Sydney, New South Wales, 25 April 1917; s of late James E. and Jessie Plimsoll; unmarried. Educ: Sydney High School; University of Sydney. Economic Department, Bank of New South Wales, 1938-42; Australian Army, 1942-47. Australian Delegation, Far Eastern Commission, 1945-48; Australian Representative, United Nations Commission for the Unification and Rehabilitation of Korea, 1950-52; Assistant Secretary, Department of External Affairs, Canberra, 1953-59; Australian Permanent Representative at the United Nations, 1959-63; Australian High Commissioner to India and Ambassador to Nepal, 1963-65; Secretary of Dept of External Affairs, Australia, 1965-70; Australian Ambassador to USA, 1970-74, to the USSR and Mongolia, 1974-77. Address: Australian Embassy, 52 Avenue des Arts, 1040 Brussels, Belgium. T: 5113997.

PLOURDE, Most Rev. Joseph Aurèle; see Ottawa, Archbishop of, (RC).

PLOUVIEZ, Peter William; General Secretary, British Actors' Equity Association, since 1974; b 30 July 1931; s of Charles and Emma Plouviez; m 1958, Nairne Cardew; two d. Educ: Sir George Monoux Grammar Sch.; Hastings Grammar Sch. Greater London Organiser, NUBE, 1955-60; Asst Sec., Equity, 1960, Asst Gen. Sec., Equity, 1964. Contested (Lab), St Marylebone bye-election, 1963; Councillor, St Pancras, 1962-65. Chm., Radio and Television Safeguards Cttee, 1974-; Sec., Fedn of Theatre Unions, 1974-; Vice-Chm., Confedn of Entertainment Unions, 1974-; Mem., Cinematograph Films Council, 1974-; Trustee, Theatres Trust, 1977-. Recreations: supporting (half-heartedly) Leyton Orient FC, playing geriatric tennis. Address: 8 Harley Street, W1. T: 01-636 6367. Club: Gerry's.

PLOW, Maj.-Gen. the Hon. Edward Chester, CBE 1945; DSO 1944; CD 1950; DCL; Hon. DScMil; Canadian Army (Retired); b St Albans, Vermont, 28 September 1904; s of late John Plow and Hortense Harlow Plow (née Locklin); m 1937, Mary Nichols, d of late Thomas E. G. Lynch and M. Edith Lynch (née Nichols), Digby, NS; one d. Educ: Montreal schools; RMC Kingston. Commnd in RCHA, 1925; served in Canada and UK until 1939. Served War of 1939-45 (despatches twice): Italy and NW Europe; Artillery Staff Officer and Comdr; during latter part of War was Senior Artillery Officer, Canadian Army. Following the War served in various appts in Germany, Canada and the UK, and was GOC Eastern Command, Canada, 1950-58. Lieut-Governor of the Province of Nova Scotia, 1958-63. Dir, Canadian Imperial Bank of Commerce, 1963-74. Member Board of Governors: Izaak Walton Killam Hosp. for Children, Halifax; Canadian Corps of Commissionaires. Life Mem., Royal Canadian Artillery Assoc. Patron, St John Ambulance Assoc. KStJ; Comdr, Order of Orange Nassau (Netherlands). Anglican. Address: Locklands, RR1, Brockville, Ont, Canada. Clubs: Brockville Country; Halifax Saraguay (Halifax).

PLOWDEN, family name of **Baron Plowden.**

PLOWDEN, Baron, cr 1959, of Plowden (Life Peer); **Edwin Noel Plowden,** KCB 1951; KBE 1946; Chairman, Equity Capital for Industry Ltd, since 1976; Chairman, Police Complaints Board, since 1976; President of Tube Investments Ltd, since 1976 (Chairman, 1963-76); Director: Commercial Union Assurance Co. Ltd; National Westminster Bank Ltd, 1960-77; Hon. Fellow, Pembroke College, Cambridge, 1958; b 6 Jan. 1907; 4th s of late Roger H. Plowden; m 1933, Bridget Horatia (see Lady Plowden); two s two d. Educ: Switzerland; Pembroke College, Cambridge. Temporary Civil Servant Ministry of Economic Warfare, 1939-40; Ministry of Aircraft Production, 1940-46; Chief Executive, and Member of Aircraft Supply Council, 1945-46; Vice-Chairman Temporary Council Cttee of NATO, 1951-52; Chief Planning Officer and Chairman of Economic Planning Board, 1947-53. Adviser on Atomic Energy Organization, 1953-54; Chairman, Atomic Energy Authority, 1954-59; Visiting Fellow, Nuffield College, 1956-64; Chm. Cttee of Enquiry: Treasury control of Public Expenditure, 1959-61; organisation of Representational Services Overseas, 1963-64; Aircraft

Industry, 1964-65; Structure of Electricity Supply Industry in England and Wales, 1974-; into CBI's aims and organisation, 1974-75; Mem., Ford European Adv. Council. CBI: Chm., Companies Cttee; Vice-Chm., Pres.'s Cttee. Pres., London Graduate Sch. of Business Studies, 1977- (Chm. 1964-76); Chm., Standing Adv. Cttee on Pay of Higher Civil Service, 1968-70; Member: Civil Service Coll. Adv. Council, 1970-76; Engineering Industries Council, 1976-. Hon. DSc: Pennsylvania State Univ., 1958; Univ. of Aston, 1972; Hon DLitt, Loughborough, 1976. *Address:* Martels Manor, Dunmow, Essex. *T:* Great Dunmow 2141; 7 Cottesmore Gardens, W8. *T:* 01-937 4238.
See also W. J. L. Plowden.

PLOWDEN, Lady, (Bridget Horatia), DBE 1972; Chairman, Independent Broadcasting Authority, since 1975; 2nd *d* of late Admiral Sir H. W. Richmond, KCB, and of Lady Richmond (Elsa, *née* Bell); *m* 1933, Baron Plowden, *qv*; two *s* two *d*. *Educ:* Downe House. Dir, Trust Houses Forte Ltd, 1961-72. Chairman: Central Advisory Council for Education (England), 1963-66; Working Ladies Guild; Professional Classes Aid Council; Adv. Cttee for Educn of Romany and other travellers; Metropolitan Architectural Consortium for Educn; a Governor and Vice-Chm., BBC, 1970-75; Mem., Nat. Theatre Bd, 1976-. Mem., Houghton Inquiry into Pay of Teachers, 1974; Chm. of Governors: Philippa Fawcett Coll. of Educn, 1967-76; Robert Montefiore Comp. Sch., 1968-; Co-opted Mem., Educn Cttee, ILEA, 1967-73; Vice-Chm., ILEA Schools Sub-Cttee, 1967-70; President: Pre-School Playgps Assoc., 1972-; Harding House Assoc. JP Inner London Area Juvenile Panel, 1962-71. Hon. LLD: Leicester, 1968; Reading, 1970; London, 1976; Hon DLitt Loughborough, 1976; DUniv Open, 1974. Hon. Fellow, College of Preceptors, 1973. *Address:* Martels Manor, Dunmow, Essex. *T:* Great Dunmow 2141; 7 Cottesmore Gardens, W8. *T:* 01-937 4238.
See also W. J. L. Plowden.

PLOWDEN, William Julius Lowthian, PhD; Under-Secretary, Department of Industry, since 1977; *b* 7 Feb. 1935; *s* of Lord and Lady Plowden, *qqv*; *m* 1960, Veronica Gascoigne; two *s* two *d*. *Educ:* Eton; King's Coll., Cambridge (BA, PhD); Univ. of Calif, Berkeley. Staff Writer, Economist, 1959-60; BoT, 1960-65; Lectr in Govt, LSE, 1965-71; Central Policy Review Staff (Under Secretary), Cabinet Office, 1971-77. Hon. Prof., Dept of Politics, Univ. of Warwick, 1977-. *Publication:* The Motor Car and Politics in Britain, 1971. *Address:* 49 Stockwell Park Road, SW9. *T:* 01-274 4535.

PLOWMAN, Sir (John) Anthony, Kt 1961; Judge of the High Court of Justice (Chancery Division), 1961-76, Vice-Chancellor, 1974-76; *b* 27 Dec. 1905; *e s* of late John Tharp Plowman (solicitor); *m* 1933, Vernon, 3rd *d* of late A. O. Graham, Versailles; three *d*. *Educ:* Highgate School; Gonville and Caius Coll., Cambridge. Solicitors Final (John Mackrell Prize), 1927; LLB London, 1927; LLB Cantab (1st Cl.), 1929; LLM Cantab 1956. Called to Bar, Lincoln's Inn, 1931 (Tancred and Cholmeley studentships; Buchanan Prize); QC 1954; Bencher of Lincoln's Inn, 1961. Served, 1940-45, Squadron-Leader, RAF. Member of General Council of the Bar, 1956-60. *Address:* Lane End, Bucks.

PLOWRIGHT, David Ernest; Controller of Programmes since 1969 and Joint Managing Director since 1976, Granada Television Ltd; *b* 11 Dec. 1930; *s* of William Ernest Plowright and Daisy Margaret Plowright; *m* 1953, Brenda Mary (*née* Key); one *s* two *d*. *Educ:* Scunthorpe Grammar Sch.; on local weekly newspaper and during National Service, Germany. Reporter, Scunthorpe Star, 1950; freelance corresp. and sports writer, 1952; Reporter, Feature Writer and briefly Equestrian Corresp., Yorkshire Post, 1954; Granada Television: News Editor, 1957; Producer, Current Affairs, 1960; Exec. Prod., Scene at 6.30, 1964; Exec. Prod., World in Action, 1966; Head of Current Affairs, 1968; Dir, 1968. *Recreations:* television, theatre, watching sport and messing about in a boat. *Address:* Granada TV Ltd, Manchester M60 9EA. *T:* 061-832 7211; Granada TV, 36 Golden Square, W1. *T:* 01-734 8080.
See also J. A. Plowright.

PLOWRIGHT, Joan Ann, (The Lady Olivier), CBE 1970; Leading actress with the National Theatre, 1963-74; Member of the RADA Council; *b* 28 Oct. 1929; *d* of William Ernest Plowright and Daisy Margaret (*née* Burton); *m* 1st, 1953, Roger Gage (marr. diss.); 2nd, 1961, (as Sir Laurence Olivier) Baron Olivier, *qv*; one *s* two *d*. *Educ:* Scunthorpe Grammar School; Laban Art of Movement Studio; Old Vic Theatre School. First stage appearance in If Four Walls Told, Croydon Rep. Theatre, 1948; Bristol Old Vic and Mem. Old Vic Co., S Africa tour, 1952; first London appearance in The Duenna, Westminster, 1954; Moby Dick, Duke of York's, 1955; season of leading parts,

Nottingham Playhouse, 1955-56; English Stage Co., Royal Court, 1956; The Crucible, Don Juan, The Death of Satan, Cards of Identity, The Good Woman of Setzuan, The Country Wife (transferred to Adelphi, 1957); The Chairs, The Making of Moo, Royal Court, 1957; The Entertainer, Palace, 1957; The Chairs, The Lesson, Phoenix, NY, 1958; The Entertainer, Royale, NY, 1958; The Chairs, The Lesson, Major Barbara, Royal Court, 1958; Hook, Line and Sinker, Piccadilly, 1958; Roots, Royal Court, Duke of York's, 1959; Rhinoceros, Royal Court, 1960; A Taste of Honey, Lyceum, NY, 1960 (Best Actress Tony Award); Rosmersholm, Greenwich, 1973; Saturday, Sunday, Monday, Queen's, 1974-75; The Sea Gull, Lyric, 1975; The Bed Before Yesterday, Lyric, 1975 (Variety Club of GB Award, 1977); Chichester Festival: Uncle Vanya, The Chances, 1962; St Joan (Best Actress Evening Standard Award), Uncle Vanya, 1963; The Doctor's Dilemma, the Taming of the Shrew, 1972; National Theatre: St Joan, Uncle Vanya, Hobson's Choice, opening season, 1963; The Master Builder, 1964; Much Ado About Nothing, 1967, 1968; Three Sisters, 1967, 1968; Tartuffe, 1967, 1968; The Advertisement, 1968; Love's Labour's Lost, 1968; The Merchant of Venice, 1970; A Woman Killed With Kindness, 1971; The Rules of the Game, 1971; Eden End, 1974. Directed, Rites, 1969; produced, The Travails of Sancho Panza, 1969. *Films include:* Moby Dick, The Entertainer, Three Sisters, The Merchant of Venice, Equus. Appears on TV; Daphne Laureola, 1976. *Recreations:* reading, music, entertaining. *Address:* c/o LOP Ltd, 33-34 Chancery Lane, WC2A 1EN. *T:* 01-836 7932.
See also D. E. Plowright.

PLOWRIGHT, Prof. Walter, CMG 1974; FRCVS 1977; Professor of Veterinary Microbiology and Parasitology, Royal Veterinary College, London, since 1971; *b* 20 July 1923; 2nd *s* of Jonathan and Mahala Plowright, Holbeach, Lincs; *m* 1959, Dorothy Joy (*née* Bell). *Educ:* Moulton and Spalding Grammar Schs; Royal Veterinary Coll., London. MRCVS 1944; DVSc (Pret.) 1964. Commissioned, RAVC, 1945-48; Colonial Service, 1950-64; Animal Virus Research Inst., Pirbright, 1964-71 (seconded E Africa, 1966-71). J. T. Edwards Memorial Prize, 1964; R. B. Bennett Commonwealth Prize of RSA, 1972. *Publications:* numerous contribs to scientific jls relating to virus diseases of animals. *Recreations:* gardening, travel. *Address:* Springwood, Prey Heath Road, Woking, Surrey GU22 0RN. *T:* Worplesdon 2131.

PLUGGE, Capt. Leonard Frank, BSc; FRAS; Politician, Scientist, Writer, Inventor, Painter and Sculptor; Hon. Colonel RE 29th (Kent) Cadet Bn; *b* London; *o s* of Frank Plugge, Brighton; *m* Gertrude Ann, *o d* of Frederick Rowland, Muckleston, Kensington, and Muckleston, Shropshire; one *s* (one *s* and one *d* decd). *Educ:* at Dulwich; University Coll., London (BSc); Univ. of Brussels (Ingénieurs des Mines). Mem., Accademia di Belle Arti, Rome and Academy of Sciences, NY. Served European War, Lieut RNVR; Capt. RAF; Inter-Allied Aeronautical Commission of Control in Berlin; Aeronautical Delegate Spa Conference; Commission of Aeronautical Control, Paris; National Physical Laboratory, Teddington; Owens College, Manchester; Royal Aircraft Establishment, Farnborough; Imperial College of Science, South Kensington; Department of Scientific Research of Air Ministry; with Underground Railways Group of Companies; former MP (C) Chatham division of Rochester; Chairman Parliamentary Science Committee; Hon. Sec. Inter-Parliamentary Union; President International Broadcasting Club; Chairman, International Broadcasting Co., London, Imperial Broadcasting Corp., New York, and International Broadcasting Co., Toronto, Canada; created Army network, Radio International, first Radio programme for the British Expeditionary Forces in France. General Committee Radio Society of Great Britain; invented Radio two-way Telephone in Car, Television Glasses, Stereoscopic Cinematograph, Plugge Patent Auto Circuit; Member, Société Astronomique de France; Chevalier of the Légion d'Honneur; Commander of Dragon of Annam. *Publications:* Royal Aeronautical Society's Glossary of Aeronautical Terms (French Translation); contributions on Travel and Radio to publications all over the world. *Recreations:* ice skating, yachting (yacht, My Lennyann, Cannes), golf, tennis.

PLUM, Patrick; see McConville, M. A.

PLUMB, Sir (Charles) Henry, Kt 1973; DL; President of the National Farmers Union, since 1970; Chairman, British Agricultural Council, since 1975; *b* 27 March 1925; *s* of Charles and Louise Plumb; *m* 1947, Marjorie Dorothy Dunn; one *s* two *d*. *Educ:* King Edward VI School, Nuneaton. National Farmers Union: Member Council, 1959; Vice-President, 1964, 1965; Deputy-President, 1966, 1967, 1968, 1969. Mem., Duke of

Northumberland's Cttee of Enquiry on Foot and Mouth Disease, 1967-68; Pres., Warwickshire County Fedn of Young Farmers' Clubs, 1974- (Pres., Nat. Fedn of YFC); Member: Council, CBI; Council, Animal Health Trust; Liveryman, Farmers' Co.; Pres., Royal Agric. Soc. of England, 1977; Hon. Pres., Ayrshire Cattle Soc.; Past Pres., Comité des Organisations Professionels Agricoles de la CEE (COPA). FRSA 1970; FRAgS 1974. DL Warwick 1977. *Recreations:* shooting, tennis. *Address:* Southfields Farm, Coleshill, Birmingham B46 3EJ. *T:* Coleshill 63133; Agriculture House, Knightsbridge, SW1X 7NJ. *Clubs:* Farmers'; Coleshill Rotary (Hon. Member).

PLUMB, Sir Henry; see Plumb, Sir C. H.

PLUMB, John Harold; FBA 1968; historian; Professor of Modern English History, University of Cambridge, 1966-74; *b* 20 Aug. 1911; 3rd *s* of late James Plumb, Leicester. *Educ:* Alderman Newton's Sch., Leicester; University Coll., Leicester; Christ's Coll., Cambridge. BA London, 1st Class Hons History, 1933; PhD Cambridge, 1936; LittD Cambridge, 1957. Ehrman Research Fellow, King's Coll., Cambridge, 1939-46; FO, 1940-45; Fellow of Christ's Coll., 1946-, Steward, 1948-50, Tutor, 1950-59. Vice-Master, 1964-68. Univ. Lectr in History, 1946-62; Reader in Modern English History, 1962-65; Chm. of History Faculty, 1966-68, Univ. of Cambridge. Trustee of National Portrait Gallery, 1961-; Syndic of the Fitzwilliam Museum, 1960-77; Member: Wine Standards Bd, 1973-75; Council, British Acad., 1977-. FRHistS; FSA; FRSL 1969. Visiting Prof., Columbia Univ., 1960; Distinguished Vis. Prof., NYC Univ., 1971-72, 1976; Cecil and Ida Green Honors Chair, Texas Christian Univ., 1974; Lectures: Ford's, Oxford Univ., 1965-66; Saposnekov, City College, NY, 1968; Guy Stanton Ford, Univ. of Minnesota, 1969; Stenton, Reading, 1972; George Rogers Clark, Soc. of the Cincinnati. Hon. For. Mem., Amer. Acad. for Arts and Sciences, 1970. Hon. DLitt: Leicester, 1968; East Anglia, 1973; Bowdoin Coll., 1974. Editor, History of Human Society, 1959-; European Advisory Editor to American Heritage Co. Historical Adviser, Penguin Books, 1960-. *Publications:* England in the Eighteenth Century, 1950; West African Explorers (with C. Howard), 1952; Chatham, 1953; (ed) Studies in Social History, 1955; Sir Robert Walpole, Vol. I, 1956, Vol. II, 1960, both vols repr. 1972; The First Four Georges, 1956; The Renaissance, 1961; Men and Places, 1962; Crisis in the Humanities, 1964; The Growth of Political Stability in England, 1675-1725, 1967; Death of the Past, 1969; In the Light of History, 1972; The Commercialisation of Leisure, 1974; Royal Heritage, 1977; *contrib. to:* Man versus Society in Eighteenth Century Britain, 1968; Churchill Revised, 1969 (Churchill, the historian); *Festschrift:* Historical Perspectives: Essays in Honour of J. H. Plumb, 1974. *Address:* Christ's College, Cambridge. *T:* 67641; The Old Rectory, Westhorpe, Stowmarket, Suffolk. *T:* Bacton 235. *Clubs:* Brooks's, Beefsteak; Century Association (NY).

PLUMBE, William John Conway, CB 1971; HM Chief Inspector of Factories, 1967-71; *b* 17 Mar. 1910; *s* of Charles Conway Plumbe and Lilian Plumbe (*née* Lynham); *m* 1938, Margaret, *y d* of A. E. Paine, Sevenoaks; three *d. Educ:* King Edward VII, Sheffield; Sevenoaks School; Imperial College, London University. BSc, ACGI. Appointed HM Inspector of Factories, 1935. Service in HM Forces, 1943-46. HM Superintending Inspector of Factories, 1960-63; HM Deputy Chief Inspector of Factories, 1963-67. *Recreations:* gardening, country walking. *Address:* Woodmans, Fishpond, Wooton Fitzpaine, near Bridport, Dorset. *T:* Hawkchurch 253.

PLUMLEY, Rev. Prof. Jack Martin; Herbert Thompson Professor of Egyptology, University of Cambridge, 1957-77; *b* 2 Sept. 1910; *e s* of Arthur Henry Plumley and Lily Plumley (*née* Martin); *m* 1938, Gwendolen Alice Darling; three *s. Educ:* Merchant Taylors' Sch., London; St John's Coll., Durham (BA, Univ. Hebrew Schol., MLitt); King's Coll., Cambridge (MA). Deacon 1933; Priest 1934; Curacies, 1933-41; Vicar of Christ Church, Hoxton, 1942-45, of St Paul's, Tottenham, 1945-47; Rector and Vicar of All Saints', Milton, Cambridge, 1948-57. Associate Lectr in Coptic, Univ. of Cambridge, 1949-57; Fellow Selwyn Coll., 1957. Mem. Council of Senate, Cambridge, 1965-70. Dir of excavations on behalf of Egypt Exploration Soc. at Qasr Ibrim, Nubia, 1963, 1964, 1966, 1969, 1972, 1974, 1976; Chm., British Cttee of Internat. Critical Greek New Testament Project, 1963-. FSA 1966; Fellow, Inst. of Coptic Studies, United Egyptian Repub., 1966; Corresp. Mem., German Inst. of Archaeology, 1966. *Recreations:* music, rowing, photography, travel. *Address:* Selwyn College, Cambridge; 13 Lyndewode Road, Cambridge. *T:* Cambridge 50328.

PLUMMER, Alfred, BLitt Oxon; MSc (Econ.) London; MA, LLD Dublin; Hon. Librarian to the Worshipful Company of

Weavers; *b* London, 2 Nov. 1896; *o s* of Alfred Plummer; *m* 1st, 1919, Minnie D. Goodey; 2nd, 1973, Elsie Evelyn May Fellingham. *Educ:* Christ Church Sch., Brondesbury. Univ. training in Economics, Law and History at Trinity Coll., Dublin, London Univ. (London Sch. of Economics) and Oriel Coll., Oxford; enlisted in Honourable Artillery Company, 9 June 1915; active service in France, 1916-17; Lecturer in the Dept of Commerce in University Coll., Southampton, 1920-25; Vice-Principal of Ruskin Coll., Oxford, 1925-37; Head of Dept of Economics and Social Studies, City of Birmingham Commercial Coll., 1937-38; Head of Dept of Commerce, Languages and Social Studies, SW Essex Technical Coll., 1938-43; Vice-Principal of SW Essex Technical Coll. and Headmaster of the County Technical Sch., 1944-45; Dir, Forest Training Coll., 1945-49; Inspector of Further Education, LCC, 1949-60; Staff Inspector, 1960-63. *Publications:* Exercises in Economics, 1929; Labour's Path to Power, 1929; The World in Agony-An Economic Diagnosis, 1932; The Witney Blanket Industry, 1934; International Combines in Modern Industry, 1934; New British Industries in the 20th Century, 1937; Raw Materials or War Materials?, 1937; (with Richard Early) The Blanket Makers, 1669-1969, a history of Charles Early and Marriott (Witney) Ltd, 1969; Bronterre: a political biography of Bronterre O'Brien, 1971; The London Weavers' Company, 1600-1970, 1972; various articles; contributor to the Encyclopædia of the Social Sciences. *Address:* Warmington, Black Heath, Wenhaston, Suffolk.

PLUMMER, (Arthur) Christopher (Orme), CC (Canada) 1968; actor; *b* Toronto, 13 Dec. 1929; *m* 1st, 1956, Tammy Lee Grimes; one *d*; 2nd, 1962, Patricia Audrey Lewis (marr. diss. 1966); 3rd, 1970, Elaine Regina Taylor. *Educ:* public and private schs, Montreal. French and English radio, Canada, 1949-52; Ottawa Rep. Theatre; Broadway: Starcross Story, 1951-52; Home is the Hero, 1953; The Dark is Light Enough, 1954 (Theatre World Award); The Lark, 1955; J. B., 1958 (Tony nomination); Arturo Ui, 1963; Royal Hunt of the Sun, 1965-66; Stratford, Conn, 1955: Mark Antony, Ferdinand; leading actor, Stratford Festival, Canada, 1956-67: Henry V, The Bastard, Hamlet, Leontes, Mercutio, Macbeth, Cyrano de Bergerac, Benedic, Aguecheek, Antony; Royal Shakespeare Co., Stratford-on-Avon, 1961-62: Benedic, Richard III; London debut as Henry II in Becket, Aldwych and Globe, 1961 (Evening Standard Best Actor Award, 1961); National Theatre, 1971-72: Amphytrion 38, Danton's Death; Broadway musical, Cyrano, 1973 (Outer Critics Circle Award, Best Actor in a Musical); The Good Doctor, NY, 1974. *Films:* Stage-Struck, 1956; Across the Everglades, 1957; The Fall of the Roman Empire, 1963; The Sound of Music, 1964; Daisy Clover, 1964; Triple Cross, 1966; Oedipus Rex, 1967; The Battle of Britain, 1968; Royal Hunt of the Sun, 1969; The Pyx, 1973; The Man Who Would Be King, 1975; Aces High, 1976. TV appearances, Britain, Denmark, and major N American networks, incl. Hamlet at Elsinore, BBC and Danish TV, 1964 (4 Emmy Award nominations). *Recreations:* tennis, ski-ing, piano. *Address:* c/o Stanley, Gorrie, Whitson & Co., 9 Cavendish Square, W1M 0DU. *T:* 01-580 6363. *Clubs:* Hurlingham; Players (New York).

PLUMMER, Sir (Arthur) Desmond (Herne), Kt 1971; TD 1950; JP; DL; Chairman, Horserace Betting Levy Board, since 1974; *b* 25 May 1914; *s* of Arthur Herne Plummer and Janet (*née* McCormick); *m* 1941, Pat Holloway; one *d. Educ:* Hurstpierpoint Coll.; Coll. of Estate Management. Served 1939-46, Royal Engineers. Member: TA Sports Bd, 1953-; London Electricity Consultative Council, 1955-66; St Marylebone Borough Council, 1952-65 (Mayor, 1958-59); LCC, for St Marylebone, 1960-65; Inner London Educn Authority, 1964-76. Greater London Council: Mem. for Cities of London and Westminster, 1964-73, for St Marylebone, 1973-76; Leader of Opposition, 1966-67 and 1973-74; Leader of Council, 1967-73. Member: South Bank Theatre Board, 1967-74; Standing Conf. on SE Planning, 1967-74; Transport Co-ordinating Council for London, 1967-69; Local Authorities Conditions of Service Adv. Bd, 1967-71; Exec. Cttee, British Section of Internat. Union of Local Authorities, 1967-74; St John Council for London, 1971-; Exec. Cttee, Nat. Union Cons. and Unionist Assocs, 1967-76; Chm., St Marylebone Conservative Assoc., 1965-66; Director: Portman Building Soc.; Nat. Employers' Mutual Gen. Insurance Assoc. (Dep. Chm., 1973-); Nat. Employers' Life Assurance Assoc. Member of Lloyd's. Mem. Court, Univ. of London, 1967-. Chairman: Epsom and Walton Downs Trng Grounds Man. Bd, 1974-; National Stud, 1975-; Pres., London Anglers' Assoc., 1976. Liveryman, Worshipful Co. of Tin Plateworkers. FAI 1948; FRICS 1970; FRSA 1974; Hon. FFAS 1966. JP, Co. London, 1958; DL Greater London, 1970. OStJ 1968. *Publication:* Time for Change in Greater London, 1966; Report to London, 1970; Planning and Participation, 1973. *Recreations:* swimming (Capt. Otter Swimming Club, 1952-53); gardening, relaxing. *Address:* 4 The Lane, St Johns Wood, NW8 0PN. *Clubs:* Carlton, Royal Automobile, MCC.

PLUMMER, Christopher; *see* Plummer, A. C. O.

PLUMMER, Sir Desmond; *see* Plummer, Sir A. D. H.

PLUMMER, Maj.-Gen. Leo Heathcote, CBE 1974; Chief, Joint Service Liaison Organisation, Bonn, since 1976; *b* 11 June 1923; *s* of Lt-Col Edmund Waller Plummer and Mary Dorothy Brookesmith; *m* 1955, Judyth Ann Dolby; three *d*. *Educ:* Canford Sch.; Queens' Coll., Cambridge. Commnd RA, 1943; War Service, N Africa, Sicily, Italy, 1943-45 (mentioned in despatches, 1945); Adjt, TA, 1947-49; Staff Coll., Camberley, 1952, Directing Staff, 1961-63; Comdt, Sudan Staff Coll., 1963-65; CO, 20 Heavy Regt, 1965-67; Col, Gen. Staff, MoD, 1967; Brig., 1967; Comdr, 1st Artillery Bde, 1967-70; Dep. Dir Manning (Army), 1971-74; Asst Chief of Staff Ops, HQ Northern Army Gp, 1974-76. ADC to HM The Queen, 1974-76. *Recreation:* gardening. *Address:* Tanners, Mount Ephraim Lane, Cranbrook, Kent. *T:* Cranbrook 2046. *Club:* Army and Navy.

PLUMMER, Norman Swift, MD, FRCP; retired as Senior Physician, and Physician in charge of Chest Clinic, Charing Cross Hospital (1935-73); as Physician to London Chest Hospital (1947-73), to Bromley Hospital (1948-72), to Edenbridge Hospital (1946-72); *b* 10 June 1907; *s* of late Walter James Plummer and late Marianne Evelyn Clarence; *m* 1939, Helen Niven Wilson; one *s* three *d*. *Educ:* Kingswood Coll., Grahamstown; Guy's Hosp., Univ. of London; Amsterdam. Gold Medal in Medicine (Guy's), 1930; MD (London) 1933; FRCP 1941. Clin. Asst, Asst Ho. Surg., Out-Patient Officer, Ho. Phys. and Medical Registrar, Guy's Hosp., 1930-32; Post-Graduate Student, Kliniek Prof. Snapper, Amsterdam, 1932-33; Medical Registrar, Charing Cross Hosp., 1933-35. Examr in Materia Medica, Soc. of Apothecaries of London, 1947-50; Lectr and Examr in Medicine, Univ. of London; Examr in Med., Conjt Bd, and MRCP. In RAMC, 1941-46; Brig. RAMC, Cons. Phys. to MEF. Royal Coll. of Physicians: Mem. Council 1965, Censor 1966, Senior Censor and Vice-Pres., 1970. Member: Association of Physicians; Thoracic Society; Fellow American Coll. of Chest Physicians. *Publications:* contributed to British Encyclopædia of Medical Practice, 2nd edn, 1952. Various medical papers on fungal and other diseases especially on Aspergillosis in Thorax, 1952. *Address:* 118 Harley Street, W1. *T:* 01-486 2494; Jesmond, Goring Road, Steyning, West Sussex BN4 3GF. *T:* Steyning 814174.

PLUMMER, Peter Edward; Deputy Director, Department for National Savings, since 1972; *b* 4 Nov. 1919; *s* of Arthur William John and Ethel May Plummer; *m* 1949, Pauline Wheelwright; one *s* one *d*. *Educ:* Watford Grammar Sch. Customs and Excise, 1936-38; Dept for National Savings, 1938-. Served War, REME, 1941-46. Seconded National Giro, 1970-71. Principal, 1956; Assistant Sec., 1964; Under-Sec., 1972. *Recreations:* gardening, photography. *Address:* St Bernard's, Finch Lane, Bushey, Herts. *T:* 01-950 1205.

PLUMPTON, Alan, BSc, CEng, FIEE, FRSA; JP; Chairman, London Electricity Board, since Oct. 1976; *b* 24 Nov. 1926; *s* of late John Plumpton and of Doris Plumpton; *m* 1950, Audrey Smith; one *s* one *d*. *Educ:* Sunderland Technical Sch.; Durham Univ. (BSc Elec. Eng). Pupil Engr, Sunderland Corp. Elec. Undertaking, 1942; various engrg and commercial appts, NEEB, 1948-61; Dist Manager, E Monmouthshire Dist, S Wales Electricity Bd, 1961-64. Admin. Staff Coll., Henley, 1963; Dep. Chief Commercial Engr, S Wales Elec. Bd, 1964-67; Chief Commercial Engr, S Wales Elec. Bd, 1967-72; Dep. Chm., London Elec. Bd, 1972-76. JP Mon, 1971. *Recreations:* golf, gardening. *Address:* Lockhill, Stubbs Wood, Amersham, Bucks HP6 6EX. *T:* Amersham 3791. *Club:* Harewood Downs Golf.

PLUMPTRE, family name of Baron Fitzwalter.

PLUMTREE, Air Vice-Marshal Eric, CB 1974; OBE 1946; DFC 1940; Co-ordinator of Anglo-American Relations, Ministry of Defence (Air), since 1977; Director: Aviation Furnishings Ltd, since 1976; Beakes Design Consultancy, since 1976; *b* 9 March 1919; *s* of William Plumtree, Plumbley Farm, Mosborough, Derbys, and Minnie Plumtree (*née* Wheatley); *m* 1942, Dorothy Patricia (*née* Lyall); two *s* (and one *s* decd). *Educ:* Eckington Grammar Sch. Served War of 1939-45: No 53 Army Co-op. Sqdn, 1940-41; No 241 FR Sqdn, 1942; OC No 169 FR Sqdn, 1943; Chief Instr, No 41, OTU, 1944; HQ, Fighter Command, 1945; Staff Coll., Haifa, 1946; Personal Staff Officer to C-in-C, MEAF, 1947-49; OC, No 54 (F) Sqdn, 1949-52; PSO to Chief of Air Staff, 1953-56; OC Flying Wing, Oldenburg, 1957-58; OC,

Admin. Wing, Jever, 1958; JSSC, Latimer, 1959; OC, RAF Leuchars, 1959-61; Dep. Dir, Joint Planning Staff, 1962-63; IDC, 1964; Air Adviser to UK High Comr and Head of BDLS (Air), Ottawa, 1965-67; Air Cdre 1966; Dir, Air Plans, MoD (Air), 1968-69; AOC 22 Group RAF, 1970-71; Air Vice-Marshal 1971; Comdr, Southern Maritime Air Region, 1971-73; Economy Project Officer (RAF), MoD, 1973-74. Mem. Council, Adingly Coll., 1976-. *Recreations:* gardening, most sports. *Address:* Wings Cottage, Ditchling, Sussex. *T:* Hassocks 5539. *Club:* Royal Air Force.

PLUNKET, family name of Baron Plunket.

PLUNKET, 8th Baron *cr* 1827; **Robin Rathmore Plunket;** *b* 3 Dec. 1925; *s* of 6th Baron Plunket (*d* 1938) and Dorothé Mabel (*d* 1938), *d* of late Joseph Lewis and widow of Captain Jack Barnato, RAF; *S* brother, 1975; *m* 1951, Jennifer, *d* of late Bailey Southwell, Olivenhoutpoort, S. Africa. *Educ:* Eton. Formerly Captain, Rifle Brigade. *Heir: b* Hon. Shaun Albert Frederick Sheridan Plunket [*b* 5 April 1931; *m* 1961, Judith Ann, *e d* of late G. P. Power; one *s* one *d*]. *Address:* Rathmore, Melsetter, Rhodesia; 39 Lansdowne Gardens, SW8.

PLUNKET GREENE, Mrs Alexander; *see* Quant, Mary.

PLUNKETT, family name of Baron Dunsany, of Earl of Fingall, and of Baron Louth.

PLUNKETT, Brig. James Joseph, CBE 1945; Colonel Commandant, Royal Army Veterinary Corps, 1953-59; *b* 1893; *m* 1951, Mrs Rachel Kelly, *d* of Eustace H. Bent, Lelant, Cornwall. *Educ:* Royal Dick Veterinary College. Commissioned, 1914; continuous military service. Director Army Veterinary and Remount Services, 1947-51; retired pay, 1951. *Recreation:* hunting. *Address:* Templeshanbo, near Enniscorthy, Co. Wexford, Eire. *Club:* Naval and Military.

PLURENDEN, Baron *cr* 1975 (Life Peer), of Plurenden Manor, Kent; **Rudy Sternberg,** Kt 1970; Chairman, Sterling Group of Companies; President, British Agricultural Export Council (Chairman, 1968-75); *b* 17 April 1917; *s* of George Sternberg, Germany, and Paula (*née* Michel); *m* 1951, Dorothée Monica, *d* of Major Robert Bateman Prust, OBE, Vancouver; two *d*. *Educ:* in Germany. Freeman, City of London, 1960; Liveryman, Worshipful Company: of Farmers, 1963; of Horners, 1960. *Recreations:* farming, yachting. *Address:* 79b Elizabeth Street, SW1; Plurenden Manor, High Halden, Kent. *Club:* City Livery.

PLYMOUTH, 3rd Earl of, *cr* 1905; **Other Robert Ivor Windsor-Clive;** Viscount Windsor (UK 1905); 15th Baron Windsor (England, *cr* 1529); DL; FRSA 1953; *b* 9 October 1923; *e s* of 2nd Earl and Lady Irene Charteris, *d* of 11th Earl of Wemyss; *S* father, 1943; *m* 1950, Caroline Helen, *o d* of Edward Rice, Dane Court, Eastry, Kent; three *s* one *d*. *Educ:* Eton. Mem., Standing Commn on Museums and Galleries, 1972-. DL County of Salop, 1961. *Heir: s* Viscount Windsor, *qv*. *Address:* Oakly Park, Ludlow, Salop.

See also Dr Alan Glyn.

PLYMOUTH, Bishop of, (RC), since 1955; **Rt. Rev. Cyril Edward Restieaux;** *b* 25 Feb. 1910; *s* of Joseph and Edith Restieaux. *Educ:* English Coll., Rome; Gregorian University. Ordained, 1932; Curate at Nottingham, 1933; Parish Priest at Matlock, 1936; Hon. Canon of Nottingham, 1948; Vicar-General of Nottingham, 1951; Provost and Domestic Prelate to HH Pope Pius XII, 1955. *Address:* Vescourt, Hartley Road, Plymouth PL3 5LR.

PLYMOUTH, Suffragan Bishop of, since 1972; **Rt. Rev. Richard Fox Cartwright;** *b* 10 Nov. 1913; *s* of late Rev. George Frederick Cartwright, Vicar of Plumstead, and Constance Margaret Cartwright (*née* Clark); *m* 1947, Rosemary Magdalen, *d* of Francis Evelyn Bray, Woodham Grange, Surrey; one *s* three *d*. *Educ:* The King's School, Canterbury; Pembroke Coll., Cambridge (BA 1935, MA 1939); Cuddesdon Theological Coll. Deacon, 1936; Priest, 1937; Curate, St Anselm, Kennington Cross, 1936-40; Priest-in-Charge, Lower Kingswood, 1940-45; Vicar, St Andrew, Surbiton, 1945-52; Proctor in Convocation, 1950-52; Vicar of St Mary Redcliffe, Bristol (with Temple from 1956 and St John Bedminster from 1965), 1952-72; Hon. Canon of Bristol, 1960-72. Sub-Chaplain, Order of St John, 1957-; Dir, Ecclesiastical Insurance Office Ltd, 1964-. Hon. DD Univ. of the South, Tennessee, 1969. *Recreations:* fly-fishing, gardening. *Address:* Bishop's Lodge, Yelverton, South Devon. *T:* Yelverton 2308. *Clubs:* Army and Navy; Royal Western Yacht (Plymouth).

PLYMOUTH, Archdeacon of; see Matthews, Ven. F. A. J.

POCHIN, Sir Edward (Eric), Kt 1975; CBE 1959; MA, MD, FRCP; b 22 Sept. 1909; s of Charles Davenport Pochin; m 1940, Constance M. J., d of T. H. Tilly; one s one d. Educ: Repton; St John's Coll., Cambridge. Natural Science Tripos, Part I, 1st 1930, Part II (Physiology) 1st, 1931; Michael Foster Student, Strathcona Student, 1931-32; MA 1935; Gifford-Edmunds Prize, 1940; MD 1945; FRCP 1946. Mem. of Scientific Staff of MRC, 1941; Dir, Dept of Clinical Research, UCH Med. Sch., 1946-74. Horton Smith Prize, 1945. Member: International Commn on Radiological Protection, 1959-74 (Chm. 1962-69); Nat. Radiological Protection Bd; WHO Expert Adv. Panel on Radiation; Physiological Soc., Assoc. of Physicians, Internat. Radiation Protection Assoc.; British Inst. of Radiology; Hon. Member: Royal Coll. of Radiologists; British Radiological Protection Assoc.; Nippon Soc. Radiologica; British Nuclear Med. Soc. UK Representative, UN Scientific Cttee on Effects of Atomic Radiation. Mem. ICA. Publications: articles on thyroid disease, radiation protection and other medical subjects in scientific journals. Recreation: trivial painting. Address: c/o National Radiological Protection Board, Harwell, Didcot, Oxon. Clubs: Athenæum, Oriental.

POCOCK, Carmichael Charles Peter, (Michael Pocock), CBE 1967; Chairman: Shell Transport and Trading Co., since 1976; Committee of Managing Directors, Royal Dutch/Shell Group, since 1977; b 25 March 1920; s of late Lt-Col Joseph Albert Pocock; m 1943, Nina Alice Hilary (née Hearn); one s two d. Educ: Rossall School; Keble Coll., Oxford. Joined Royal Dutch/Shell Group in 1946 and served in Venezuela and London. Pres., Compania Shell de Venezuela, 1964; Regional Co-ordinator, East and Australasia, 1968; Man. Dir, Royal Dutch/Shell Gp of Cos, 1970. Chm., Council of Industry for Management Education, 1972-; Mem. Council, BIM, 1975-; Chm., London Graduate Sch. of Business Studies, 1976-. Recreations: sailing and mountain walking. Address: Shell Centre, SE1. T: 01-934 5866. Club: Buck's.

POCOCK, Air Vice-Marshal Donald Arthur, CBE 1975 (OBE 1957); General Manager, Iran, British Aircraft Corporation Guided Weapons Division, since 1976; b 5 July 1920; s of late A. Pocock and of E. Broad; m 1947, Dorothy Monica Griffiths; two s three d. Educ: Crouch End. Served War of 1939-45: commissioned, 1941; Middle East, 1941-48. Transport Command, 1948-50; commanded RAF Regt Sqdn, 1950-52; Staff Coll., 1953; Staff Officer, HQ 2nd Allied TAF, 1954-57; comd RAF Regt Wing, 1957-58; MoD, 1958-59; HQ Allied Air Forces Central Europe, 1959-62; Sen. Ground Defence SO, NEAF, 1962-63; MoD, 1963-66; Sen. Ground Defence SO, FEAF, 1966-68; ADC to the Queen, 1967; Commandant, RAF Catterick, 1968-69; Dir of Ground Defence, 1970-73; Comdt-Gen. RAF Regt, 1973-75. Recreations: shooting, equitation. Address: British Aircraft Corporation Guided Weapons Division, PO Box 12/1182, Tehran, Iran; Brincliffe, Dence Park, Herne Bay, Kent. T: Herne Bay 4773. Club: Royal Air Force.

POCOCK, Hugh Shellshear; formerly: Director, Associated Iliffe Press Ltd; Chairman of Iliffe Electrical Publications Ltd; Managing Editor, The Electrical Review; (formerly Editor) of The Wireless World; retired Dec. 1962; b 6 May 1894; 3rd s of late Lexden Lewis Pocock, artist; m 1920, Mayda, d of late Serab Sévian. Educ: Privately. Served European War, 1914-18: commissioned RE, 1915; served in Egypt, Mesopotamia, Persia, on wireless and intelligence work with rank of Capt. (despatches). Assisted in organisation of first short wave amateur transatlantic tests, 1921-22; organised first transatlantic broadcasting trials, 1923; proposed Empire Broadcasting on short wave in 1926, and urged its adoption in face of BBC opposition. Promoted and organised the National Wireless Register of technical personnel 1938, under Service auspices; CEng, FIEE; Life Senior Member of the Institute of Electrical and Electronics Engineers; Member of Honour, Union Internationale de la Presse Radiotechnique et Electronique. Publications: numerous articles relating to radio and electrical progress, technical and general. Recreations: genealogy and local history research. Address: 103 Boydell Court, St Johns Wood, NW8 6NH.

POCOCK, Kenneth Walter; b 20 June 1913; s of Walter Dunsdon Pocock and Emily Marion Pocock; m 1939, Anne Tidmarsh; one s one d. Educ: Canford School. United Dairies (London) Ltd, 1930; Armed Forces, 1942-46; Man. Dir, Edinburgh and Dumfriesshire Dairy Co. Ltd, 1946; Dir, United Dairies Ltd, 1948; Pres., Scottish Milk Trade Fedn, 1956-59; Dir, Unigate Ltd, 1959; Man. Dir, Unigate Ltd and United Dairies Ltd, 1963; Chm. of Milk Div., Unigate Ltd, 1968; Dep. Chm., Unigate Ltd,

1970-75; Pres., Unigate Long Service Corps, 1971-. Governor, Nat. Dairymen's Benevolent Instn. Recreations: motoring, shooting, photography, gardening. Address: Round Coppice, Denham Road, Iver Heath, Bucks SL0 0PH. T: Denham 3140.

POCOCK, Michael; see Pocock, C. C. P.

POCOCK, Most Rev. Philip F.; see Toronto, Archbishop of, (RC).

PODMORE, Ian Laing; Chief Executive, Sheffield City Council, since 1974; b 6 Oct. 1933; s of Harry Samuel Podmore and Annie Marion (née Laing); m 1961, Kathleen Margaret (née Langton); one s one d. Educ: Birkenhead School. Admitted Solicitor 1960. Asst Solicitor, Wallasey County Borough, 1960-63; Sen. Asst Solicitor, Southport Co. Borough, 1963-66; Deputy Town Clerk: Southport, 1966-70; Sheffield, 1970-74. Recreations: philately, gardening, watching football. Address: Town Hall, Sheffield S1 2HH. T: Sheffield 734000; 55 Devonshire Road, Sheffield S17 3NU. T: Sheffield 367654.

POETT, Gen. Sir (Joseph Howard) Nigel, KCB 1959 (CB 1952); DSO and Bar, 1945; idc; psc; b 20 Aug. 1907; s of late Maj.-General J. H. Poett, CB, CMG, CBE; m 1937, Julia, d of E. J. Herrick, Hawkes Bay, NZ; two s one d. Educ: Downside; RMC Sandhurst. 2nd Lieut, DLI, 1927; Operations, NW Frontier, 1930-31; Adjt 2nd Bn DLI, 1934-37; GSO2, 2nd Div., 1940; GSO1, War Office, 1941-42; Comd 11th Bn DLI, 1942-43; Comdr, 5th Parachute Bde, 1943-46; served North-West Europe, 1944-45; Far East, 1945-46; Director of Plans, War Office, 1946-48; idc 1948; Dep.-Commander, British Military Mission, Greece, 1949; Maj.-General, 1951; Chief of Staff, FARELF, 1950-52; GOC 3rd Infantry Division, Middle East Land Forces, 1952-54; Dir of Military Operations, War Office, 1954-56; Commandant, Staff Coll., Camberley, 1957-58; Lt-Gen., 1958; General Officer Commanding-in-Chief, Southern Command, 1958-61; Commander-in-Chief, Far East Land Forces, 1961-63; General, 1962. Colonel, The Durham Light Infantry, 1956-65. Dir, British Productivity Council, 1966-71. Silver Star, USA. Address: Swaynes Mead, Great Durnford, Salisbury, Wilts. Club: Army and Navy.

POITIER, Sidney; actor, film and stage; b Miami, Florida, 20 Feb. 1924; s of Reginald Poitier and Evelyn (née Outten); m 1950, Juanita Hardy; three d. Educ: private tutors; Western Senior High Sch., Nassau; Governor's High Sch., Nassau. Served War of 1941-45 with 1267th Medical Detachment, United States Army. Started acting with American Negro Theatre, 1946. Plays include: Anna Lucasta, Broadway, 1948; A Raisin in the Sun, Broadway, 1959; films include: Cry, the Beloved Country, 1952; Red Ball Express, 1952; Go, Man, Go, 1954; Blackboard Jungle, 1955; Goodbye, My Lady, 1956; Edge of the City, 1957; Band of Angels, 1957; Something of Value, 1957; The Mark of the Hawk, 1958; The Defiant Ones, 1958 (Silver Bear Award, Berlin Film Festival, and New York Critics Award, 1958); Porgy and Bess, 1959; A Raisin in the Sun, 1960; Paris Blues, 1960; Lilies of the Field, 1963 (award for Best Actor of 1963, Motion Picture Academy of Arts and Sciences); The Bedford Incident, 1965; The Slender Thread, 1966; A Patch of Blue, 1966; Duel at Diablo, 1966; To Sir With Love, 1967; In the Heat of the Night, 1967; Guess Who's Coming to Dinner, 1968; For Love of Ivy, 1968; They Call Me Mister Tibbs, 1971; The Organization, 1971; (and directed) Buck and the Preacher, 1972; A Warm December, 1973; The Wilby Conspiracy, 1975; Let's Do It Again, 1976.

POLAK, Cornelia Julia, OBE 1964 (MBE 1956); HM Diplomatic Service, retired; b 2 Dec. 1908; d of late Solomon Polak and late Georgina Polak (née Pozner). Foreign Office, 1925-38; Asst Archivist, British Embassy, Paris, 1938-40; Foreign Office, 1940-47; Vice-Consul, Bergen, 1947-49; Consul, Washington, 1949-51; Foreign Office, 1951-55; Consul, Paris, 1955-57; Consul, Brussels, 1957-60; Foreign Office, 1960-63; Head of Treaty and Nationality Department, Foreign Office, 1963-67; Consul General, Geneva, 1967-69, retired; re-employed at FCO, 1969-70. Address: 24 Belsize Court, NW3.

POLAND, Rear-Admiral Allan, CBE 1943; DSO 1918; RN, retired; b 1888; s of William Poland, Blackheath; m 1912, Phyllis (d 1968), d of Dr R. A. Weston, Portsmouth; one d (and one s lost in HMS Thetis, 1939). Entered Navy, 1903; served in submarines and in command of submarine flotillas, 1910-37; Senior Naval Officer, Persian Gulf, 1937-39; Commodore Commanding East Indies Station, 1938 and 1939; ADC to the King, 1939; Commodore Commanding 9th Cruiser Squadron, 1939-40; Chief of Staff to Commander-in-Chief America and West Indies, 1940-42; Senior British Naval Officer Western Atlantic (Acting Vice-Admiral), 1942; Rear-Admiral,

Alexandria, 1942-45; Naval Assistant to Director of Sea Transport, 1945-47. Grand Officer, Order of Humayun (Persia); Kt Comdr Order of Phœnix (Greece). *Address:* 35 Chiltley Way, Liphook, Hants. *T:* Liphook 722359.

POLAND, Rear-Adm. Edmund Nicholas, CB 1967; CBE 1962; Director: Scottish Association for the Care and Resettlement of Offenders, since 1975; People at Risk Aid Trust (Scotland), since 1976; has various business interests in Scotland; *b* 19 Feb. 1917; 2nd *s* of late Major Raymond A. Poland, RMLI; *m* 1941, Pauline Ruth Margaret Pechell; three *s* one *d* (and one *d* decd). *Educ:* Royal Naval Coll., Dartmouth. Served at sea during Abyssinian and Palestine crises, Spanish Civil War; War of 1939-45: convoy duties, Norwegian waters; Motor Torpedo Boats, Channel and Mediterranean; Torpedo Specialist, 1943; Staff Officer Ops to Naval Force Comdr, Burma; Sqdn T. Officer, HMS Royalist; HMS Hornet, 1946; Flotilla Torpedo and Anti-Submarine Officer of Third Submarine Flotilla, HMS Montclare; Air Warfare Div., Admiralty, 1950; British Naval Staff, Washington, 1953; jssc 1955; Directorate of Tactics and Ship Requirements, Admiralty; comd RN Air Station, Abbotsinch, 1956; Nato Standing Gp, Washington; Director of Under Sea Warfare (Naval), Ministry of Defence, 1962; Chief of Staff to C-in-C Home Fleet, 1965-68; retired. Commander, 1950; Capt., 1956; Rear-Adm., 1965. *Recreations:* golf, fishing. *Address:* Langlawhill, Broughton by Biggar, Lanarkshire ML12 6HL. *T:* Skirling 282. *Clubs:* New (Edinburgh); Hon. Company of Edinburgh Golfers.
See also R. D. Poland.

POLAND, Richard Domville, CB 1973; *b* 22 Oct. 1914; *er s* of late Major R. A. Poland, RMLI, and late Mrs F. O. Bayly-Jones; *m* 1948, Rosalind Frances, *y d* of late Surgeon-Captain H. C. Devas; one *s* one *d*. *Educ:* RN Coll., Dartmouth. Traffic Trainee, Imperial Airways, 1932; Traffic Clerk, British Continental Airways and North Eastern Airways, 1934-39. Ops Officer, Air Ministry, Civil Aviation Dept, 1939; Civil Aviation Dept Rep., W Africa, 1942-44; Private Secretary to Minister of Civil Aviation, 1944-48; Principal, 1946; Asst Secretary, 1953; Shipping Attaché, British Embassy, Washington, DC, 1957-60; Under-Secretary: Min. of Transport, 1964-70; DoE, 1970-74. *Address:* Downs House, Blunden Lane, Yalding, Kent ME18 6JD. *T:* Hunton 337.
See also Rear-Admiral E. N. Poland.

POLANI, Prof. Paul Emanuel, MD, DCH; FRCP; FRS 1973; Prince Philip Professor of Pædiatric Research in the University of London, and Director of Pædiatric Research Unit, Guy's Hospital Medical School, London, since Oct. 1960; Children's Physician and Geneticist to Guy's Hospital; Geneticist, Italian Hospital; *b* 1 Jan. 1914; first *s* of Enrico Polani and Elsa Zennaro; *m* 1944, Nina Ester Sullam; no *c*. *Educ:* Trieste, Siena and Pisa (Italy). MD (Pisa) 1938; MRCP (London) 1948; FRCP (London) 1961. National Birthday Trust Fund Fellow in Pædiatric Research, 1948; Assistant to Director, Dept of Child Health, Guy's Hospital Medical School, 1950; Research Physician on Cerebral Palsy and Director, Medical Research Unit, National Spastic Society, 1955; Consultant to WHO (Regional Office for Europe) on Pregnancy Wastage, 1959; Consultant, Nat. Inst. Neurol. Disease and Blindness, Nat. Inst. of Health, USA, 1959-. *Publications:* chapters in books on genetics, mental deficiency, psychiatry and pædiatrics; papers on genetics, congenital malformations and neurological disorders of children. *Recreations:* reading, riding, ski-ing. *Address:* Little Meadow, West Clandon, Surrey. *T:* Guildford 222436. *Club:* Athenæum.

POLANYI, Prof. John Charles, OC 1974; FRS 1971; FRSC 1966; University Professor, since 1974 and Professor of Chemistry, University of Toronto, since 1962; *b* 23 Jan. 1929; *m* 1958, Anne Ferrar Davidson; one *s* one *d*. *Educ:* Manchester Grammar Sch.; Victoria Univ., Manchester (BSc, PhD, DSc). Research Fellow: Nat. Research Council, Ottawa, 1952-54; Princeton Univ., 1954-56; Univ. of Toronto: Lectr, 1956; Asst Prof., 1957-60; Assoc. Prof., 1960-62. Sloan Foundn Fellow, 1959-63; Guggenheim Meml Fellow, 1970-71. Marlow Medal, Faraday Soc., 1963; Steacie Prize for Natural Sciences, 1965; Chem. Inst. Canada Medal, 1976 (Noranda Award, 1967); Chem. Soc. Award, 1970. Hon. For. Mem., Amer. Acad. of Arts and Sciences, 1976; Henry Marshall Tory Medal, RSC, 1977. Lectures: Centennial, Chem. Soc., 1965; Ohio State Univ., 1969 (and Mack Award); Reilly, Univ. of Notre Dame, 1970; Harkins Meml, Univ. of Chicago, 1971; Purves, McGill Univ., 1971; Killam Meml Schol., 1974, 1975; F. J. Toole, Univ. of New Brunswick, 1974; Philips, Haverford Coll., 1974; Kistiakowsky, Harvard Univ., 1975; Camille and Henry Dreyfus, Kansas, 1975; J. W. T. Spinks, Saskatchewan, 1976; Laird, Western Ontario, 1976. Hon. DSc: Waterloo, 1970; Memorial, 1976;

McMaster, 1977; Trent, 1977. *Film:* Concept in Reaction Dynamics, 1970. *Publications:* papers in scientific jls, articles on control of armaments. *Address:* 3 Rosedale Road, Toronto M4W 2P1, Canada.

POLE; see Chandos-Pole.

POLE, Col Sir John (Gawen) Carew, 12th Bt *cr* 1628; DSO 1944; TD; JP; Lord-Lieutenant of Cornwall, 1962-77; Member of the Prince of Wales's Council, 1952-68; Member, Jockey Club (incorporating National Hunt Committee), since 1969; Steward, National Hunt Committee, 1953-56; Member, Garden Society; *b* 4 March 1902; *e s* of late Lt.-Gen. Sir Reginald Pole-Carew, KCB, of Antony, Cornwall, and Lady Beatrice Pole-Carew, *er d* of 3rd Marquess of Ormonde; *S* kinsman, 1926; *m* 1928, Cynthia Mary, OBE 1959 (*d* 1977), *o d* of Walter Burns, North Mymms Park, Hatfield; one *s* two *d*. *Educ:* Eton; RMC, Sandhurst. Coldstream Guards, 1923-39; ADC to Commander-in-Chief in India, 1924-25; Comptroller to Governor-General, Union of S. Africa, 1935-36; Palestine, 1936; commanded 5th Bn Duke of Cornwall's LI (TA), 1939-43; commanded 2nd Bn Devonshire Regt, 1944; Colonel, Second Army, 1944-45; Normandy, France, Belgium, Holland, Germany, 1944-45 (despatches, immediate DSO); raised and commanded post-war TA Bn, 4/5 Bn, DCLI, 1946-47; Hon. Col, 4/5 Bn DCLI (TA), 1958-60; Hon. Col DCLI (TA), 1960-67. Director: Lloyd's Bank, 1956-72 (Chm., Devon and Cornwall Cttee, 1956-72); English China Clays Ltd, 1969-73; Keith Prowse, 1969; Vice-Chm., Westward Television Ltd, 1960-72. Member: Central Transport Consultative Cttee for Great Britain, 1948-54; SW Electricity Consultative Council, 1949-52 (Vice-Chairman, 1951-52); Western Area Board, British Transport Commission, 1955-61. JP 1939, DL 1947, CA 1954-66, Cornwall; High Sheriff, Cornwall, 1947-48; Vice-Lt, Cornwall, 1950-62; Chairman Cornwall County Council, 1952-63. A Gentleman of HM Bodyguard of the Honourable Corps of Gentlemen-at-Arms, 1950-72, Standard Bearer, 1968-72. Prime Warden Worshipful Company of Fishmongers, 1969-70. KStJ 1972. *Recreations:* gardening, shooting, travel. *Heir:* *s* (John) Richard (Walter Reginald) Carew Pole [*b* 2 Dec. 1938; *m* 1st, 1966, Hon. Victoria Lever (marr. diss. 1974), *d* of 3rd Viscount Leverhulme, *qv*; 2nd, 1974, Mary, *d* of Lt-Col Ronald Dawnay; two *s*]. *Address:* Antony House, Torpoint, Cornwall PL11 2QA. *T:* Plymouth 812406. *Clubs:* Army and Navy, Pratt's, MCC.

POLE, Sir Peter Van Notten, 5th Bt, *cr* 1791; FASA; ACIS; accountant; *b* 6 Nov. 1921; *s* of late Arthur Chandos Pole and Marjorie, *d* of late Charles Hargrave, Glen Forrest, W Australia; *S* kinsman, 1948; *m* 1949, Jean Emily, *d* of late Charles Douglas Stone, Borden, WA; one *s* one *d*. *Educ:* Guildford Grammar Sch. *Heir:* *s* Peter John Chandos Pole [*b* 27 April 1952; *m* 1973, Suzanne Norah, BAppSc (MT), *d* of Harold Raymond and Gwendoline Maude Hughes]. *Address:* 12 Lothian Street, Floreat Park, Western Australia 6014.

POLKINGHORNE, Prof. John Charlton, FRS 1974; Professor of Mathematical Physics, University of Cambridge, since 1968; *b* 16 Oct. 1930; *s* of George Baulkwill Polkinghorne and Dorothy Evelyn Polkinghorne (née Charlton); *m* 1955, Ruth Isobel Martin; two *s* one *d*. *Educ:* Elmhurst Grammar Sch.; Perse Sch.; Trinity Coll., Cambridge (MA 1956; PhD 1955; ScD 1974). Fellow, Trinity Coll., Cambridge, 1954-; Commonwealth Fund Fellow, California Institute of Technology, 1955-56; Lecturer in Mathematical Physics, Univ. of Edinburgh, 1956-58; Lecturer in Applied Mathematics, Univ. of Cambridge, 1958-65, Reader in Theoretical Physics, 1965-68. Mem. SRC, 1975-. Chm. of Governors, Perse Sch., 1972-. Licensed Reader, Diocese of Ely, 1975. *Publications:* (jointly) The Analytic S-Matrix, 1966; many articles on elementary particle physics in learned journals. *Recreation:* gardening. *Address:* 22 Rutherford Road, Cambridge. *T:* Trumpington 3321.

POLLARD, Maj.-Gen. (Charles) Barry; Chief Engineer, British Army of the Rhine, since 1976; *b* 20 April 1927; *s* of Leonard Charles Pollard and Rose Constance (née Fletcher); *m* 1954, Mary Heyes; three *d*. *Educ:* Ardingly Coll.; Selwyn Coll., Cambridge. Commnd, Corps of RE, 1947; served in ME, Korea and UK, 1947-58; Student, Staff Coll., Camberley, 1958; GSO 2 (Trng), HQ Eastern Comd, 1959-61; Liaison Officer, Ecole du Genie, France, 1961-63; OC 5 Field Sqdn, 1963-65; JSSC, 1965; Mil. Attaché to DCOS, Allied Forces Central Europe, 1966; GSO 1 MoD, 1967; GSO 1 (DS), Staff Coll., Camberley, 1968; CRE 3 Div., 1969-71; Col GS 3 Div., 1971-72; CRE 1st British Corps, 1972-74; RCDS, 1975. *Recreations:* sailing, golf. *Address:* Yateley, Coombe Road, Salisbury, Wilts. *Club:* Army and Navy.

POLLARD, Sir (Charles) Herbert, Kt˙1962; CBE 1957 (OBE 1946; MBE 1943); retired as City Treasurer, Kingston upon Hull, 1961; *b* 23 Oct. 1898; *s* of Charles Pollard; *m* 1922, Elsie (*d* 1970), *d* of Charles Crain; one *d*; *m* 1971, Hilda M. Levitch. *Educ:* Blackpool. City Treasurer, Kingston upon Hull, 1929-61; formerly held appointments in Finance Depts of Blackpool and Wallasey; Fellow, Inst. of Chartered Accountants; Member Council, Inst. of Municipal Treasurers and Accountants, 1944-61 (President Inst. 1952-53); Financial Adviser to Assoc. of Municipal Corporations, 1951-61; Member several cttees and working parties arranged by government departments on various aspects of education, housing, police and local authority finance; Hon. Manager, Savings Bank, Hull Area. Trustee: C. C. Grundy Trust; Hibbert Trust; John Gregson Trust; Chamberlain Trust. Life Vice-Pres., Hanover Housing Assoc.; Mem., Nat. Savings Cttee, 1946-51; Official delegate at International Confs on aspects of local government finance (including Education) in Rome and Geneva, held under auspices of International Union of Local Authorities (prepared British paper for this) and UNESCO Licentiate, London College of Music. Hon. Treas. and Member Council, General Assembly of Unitarian and Free Christian Churches, 1959-70 (President, 1956-57); Hon. Treas., British and Foreign Unitarian Assoc. Inc.; Member, St John Council for Lancs, 1962-72. OStJ 1962. *Publications:* contrib. to: Local Government Finance and to other local government journals. *Recreations:* music, theatre; membership of voluntary service organisations. *Address:* Cranleigh, Elloughton, Brough, N Humberside. *T:* Brough 667206. *Clubs:* Rotary (Past Pres., Hull and St Annes-on-Sea).

POLLARD, Geoffrey Samuel; Director of Finance, West Yorkshire Metropolitan County Council, since 1973; *b* 5 March 1926; *s* of Reginald Samuel Pollard and Kezia Mary (*née* Piper); *m* 1949, Estelle Mercia (*née* Smith); one *s* one *d*. *Educ:* Eastbourne Grammar School. IPFA, FCA. Clerical Asst, E Sussex CC, 1941-44; Accountancy Asst, Brighton Co. Borough Council, 1944-48; Techn. Asst, Tunbridge Wells Borough Council, 1948-50; Coventry County Borough Council: Sectional Accountant, 1950-52; Chief Accountant, 1952-55; Asst City Treas., 1955-57; Dep. Borough Treas., West Ham Co. Borough Council, 1957-62; Borough Treas., Swansea Co. Borough Council, 1962-68; Treas., W Glamorgan Water Bd, 1966-68; City Treas. and Jt Co-ordinator, Bradford Co. Borough Council, 1968-74. Pres., CIPFA, 1975 (Mem. Council, 1965-); Pres., Soc. of Co. Borough Treasurers, 1972-73 (Mem. Exec. Cttee, 1969-74); Mem. Exec. Cttee, Soc. of County Treasurers, 1974-; Chm., CIPFA Jt Cttee of Students Socs, 1972-73; Mem. Students Soc. Exec. Cttee, 1951-; Pres., NE Students Soc., CIPFA, 1974-75; Financial Adviser, Assoc. of Metrop. Authorities, 1974-; Mem., DoE Steering Gp on Regional Water Authorities Econ. and Financial Objectives (Jukes Cttee), 1972-74; Hon. Treas., Royal National Eisteddfod of Wales, 1964; Yorks Arts Assoc.: Hon. Treas., 1969-73; Hon. Auditor, 1973-; Hon. Treas., Bradford Arts Festival, 1969-73. Hon. Editor, Telescope (Jl of CIPFA Students), 1959-71 (Sir Harry Page Merit Award 1970). *Publications:* contrib. various financial jls. *Recreations:* classical music, cricket, football, photography. *Address:* Department of Finance, West Yorkshire Metropolitan County Council, County Hall, Wakefield, W Yorks WF1 2QN. *T:* Wakefield 67111.

POLLARD, Sir Herbert; *see* Pollard, Sir C. H.

POLLARD, Lt-Gen. Sir Reginald (George), KCVO 1970; KBE 1961 (CBE 1955); CB 1959; DSO 1942; psc; idc; retired; *b* 20 Jan. 1903; *s* of late Albert Edgar Pollard, Bathurst, NSW; *m* 1925, Daisy Ethel, *d* of late A. H. Potter, Strathfield, NSW; two *s. Educ:* Bathurst High Sch.; Royal Military Coll., Duntroon. Lieut, Aust. Staff Corps, 1924; served War of 1939-45, France, Middle East, Syria (despatches), SE Asia, SW Pacific; Lieut-Colonel, 1941; Colonel, 1942; ADC to The King, 1951, to The Queen, 1952; Brigadier, 1953; Comd Aust. Army Component, British Commonwealth Forces, Korea, 1953; Maj.-General, 1954; QMG, AMF, 1954-57; Lt-Gen., 1957; GOC, Eastern Command, Australia, 1957-60; Chief of the General Staff, Australian Army, 1960-63; retired, 1963; Hon. Colonel, 1965, Col Comdt, 1968-71, The Royal Australian Regt. Australian Secretary to The Queen, 1969; Dir-Gen., Royal Visit, 1970. *Address:* Duntroon, Wyrallah, NSW 2480, Australia. *T:* Wyrallah 288202.

POLLARD, Prof. Sidney; Professor of Economic History, University of Sheffield, since 1963; *b* 21 April 1925; *s* of Moses and Leontine Pollak; *m* 1949, Eileen Andrews; two *s* one *d*. *Educ:* London School of Economics. University of Sheffield: Knoop Fellow, 1950-52; Asst Lecturer, 1952-55; Lecturer, 1955-60; Senior Lecturer, 1960-63. *Publications:* Three Centuries of Sheffield Steel, 1954; A History of Labour in Sheffield 1850-1939, 1959; The Development of the British Economy, 1914-

1950, 1962; The Genesis of Modern Management, 1965; The Idea of Progress, 1968; (with D. W. Crossley) The Wealth of Britain, 1086-1966, 1968; (ed) The Gold Standard and Employment Policies between the Wars, 1970; (ed, with others) Aspects of Capital Investment in Great Britain, 1750-1850, 1971; (ed) The Trades Unions Commission: the Sheffield outrages, 1971; (ed with J. Salt) Robert Owen, prophet of the poor, 1971; (ed with C. Holmes) Documents of European Economic History, vol. 1, 1968, vols 2 and 3, 1972; The Economic Integration of Europe, 1815-1970, 1974; (ed with C. Holmes) Essays in the Economic and Social History of South Yorkshire, 1977; articles in learned journals in field of economics, economic history and history. *Recreations:* walking, music. *Address:* 523 Fulwood Road, Sheffield S10 3QB. *T:* 303765. *Club:* National Liberal.

POLLEN, Sir John Michael Hungerford, 7th Bt of Redenham, Hampshire, *cr* 1795; *b* 6 April 1919; *s* of late Lieut-Commander John Francis Hungerford Pollen, RN; *S* kinsman, Sir John Lancelot Hungerford Pollen, 6th Bt, 1959; *m* 1st, 1941, Angela Mary Oriana Russi (marr. diss., 1956); one *s* one *d*; 2nd, 1957, Mrs Diana Jubb. *Educ:* Downside; Merton Coll., Oxford. Served War of 1939-45 (despatches). *Heir: s* Richard John Hungerford Pollen [*b* 3 Nov. 1946; *m* 1971, Christianne, *d* of Sir Godfrey Agnew, *qv*; one *s* one *d*]. *Address:* Manor House, Rodbourne, Malmesbury, Wiltshire; Lochportain, Isle of North Uist, Outer Hebrides.

POLLEY, Denis William; Under-Secretary, Contributions Division, Department of Health and Social Security, since 1977; *b* 11 Feb. 1921; *s* of William Henry Polley and Laura Emily (*née* Eyre); *m* 1943, Joyce Stopford; two *d*. *Educ:* Baines Grammar Sch., Poulton le Fylde; Lancashire Indep. Coll., Manchester. Served War, Army, RASC (Captain), 1942-47. Entered Civil Service, 1947; Asst Comr, Nat. Savings Cttee, 1947-48; HEO, Min. of Nat. Insce, 1948; Asst Sec., Computers Div., 1969; Central Computer Agency, Civil Service Dept, 1972-75; Family Support Div., DHSS, 1975-76. *Recreations:* horticulture, exploring countryside. *Address:* Inniscarra, 19 Springfarm Road, Camelsdale, Haslemere, Surrey GU27 3RH. *T:* Haslemere 2481.

POLLINGTON, Viscount; John Christopher George Savile; *b* 16 May 1931; *s* of 7th Earl of Mexborough, *qv*; *m* 1st, 1958, Elizabeth Hariot (marr. diss. 1972), *d* of 6th Earl of Verulam; one *s* one *d*; 2nd, 1972, Mrs Catherine Joyce Vivian, *d* of J. K. Hope, *qv*; one *s* one *d*. *Address:* Arden Hall, Hawnby, York. *T:* Bilsdale 348. *Clubs:* Turf, Bath; All England Lawn Tennis and Croquet.

POLLOCK, family name of Viscount Hanworth.

POLLOCK, David Linton; *b* 7 July 1906; *yr s* of late Rev. C. A. E. Pollock, formerly President of Corpus Christi College, Cambridge, and of Mrs G. I. Pollock; *m* 1st, 1933, Lilian Diana Turner; one *s*; 2nd, 1950, Margaret Duncan Curtis-Bennett (*née* Mackintosh). *Educ:* Marlborough Coll.; Trinity Coll., Cambridge. Partner in the firm of Freshfields, 1938-51; served with HM Treasury, 1939-40; War of 1939-45, Commander RNVR (despatches). Member of British Government Economic Mission to Argentina, 1946. Member of Council, Royal Yachting Assoc., 1950-65. Former Director: S. Pearson & Son Ltd; National Westminster Bank Ltd; Vickers Ltd; Legal and General Assurance Soc. Ltd; Industrial and Commercial Finance Corp. Ltd. President, Société Civile du Vignoble de Château Latour. Member of Council, Marlborough College, 1950-71. *Recreation:* sailing. *Address:* The Old Rectory, Wiggonholt, near Pulborough, West Sussex RH20 2EL. *T:* Pulborough 2531. *Clubs:* Royal Thames Yacht; Itchenor Sailing (Sussex).

POLLOCK, Ellen Clara; actress and director; President, The Shaw Society; Professor at RADA and Webber Douglas School of Acting; *m* 1st, 1929, Lt-Col L. F. Hancock, OBE, RE (decd); one *s*; 2nd, 1945, James Proudfoot (*d* 1971). *Educ:* St Mary's College, W2; Convent of The Blessed Sacrament, Brighton. First appeared, Everyman, 1920, as page in Romeo and Juliet. Accompanied Lady Forbes-Robertson on her S. African tour, and later visited Australia as Moscovitch's leading lady. West End successes include: Hit the Deck, Hippodrome, 1927; Her First Affaire, Kingsway, and Duke of York's, 1930; The Good Companions, Her Majesty's, 1931; Too True to be Good, New, 1933; Finished Abroad, Savoy, 1934; French Salad, Westminster and Royalty, 1934; The Dominant Sex, Shaftesbury and Aldwych, 1935. Open Air Theatre: Lysistrata; As You Like It. Seasons of Shaw's plays: at Lyric, Hammersmith, 1944, and with late Sir Donald Wolfit at King's, Hammersmith, 1953; three seasons of Grand Guignol plays at The Irving and Granville,

Walham Green; Six Characters in Search of an Author, New Mayfair Theatre, 1963; Lady Frederick, Vaudeville and Duke of York's, 1969-70; Ambassador, Her Majesty's, 1971; Pygmalion, Albery, 1974; Tales from the Vienna Woods, Nat. Theatre, 1976; The Dark Lady of the Sonnets, Nat. Theatre, 1977. Has acted in numerous films and TV, inc. Forsyte Saga and The Pallisers. *Productions include:* Summer in December, Comedy Theatre, 1949; Miss Turner's Husband, St Martin's, 1949; The Third Visitor, Duke of York's, 1949; Shavings, St Martin's, 1951; Mrs Warren's Profession, Royal Court, 1956; A Matter of Choice, Arts, 1967. *Recreations:* motoring, antiques and cooking. *Address:* 9 Tedworth Square, SW3. *T:* 01-352 5082.

POLLOCK, Sir George, Kt 1959; QC 1951; Director, British Employers' Confederation, 1954-65; *b* 15 March 1901; *s* of William Mackford Pollock; *m* 1st, 1922, Doris Evelyn Main (*d* 1977); one *s* one *d*; 2nd, 1977, Mollie Van Santen. Sub-editor Daily Chronicle, 1922-28; called to Bar, Gray's Inn, 1928; Bencher, 1948. Recorder of Sudbury, 1946-51. Served Army (Special Forces) 1940-44, Egypt, N Africa, Sicily and Italy (Colonel, Gen. Staff). Member: Governing Body, ILO, 1963-69; EFTA Consultative Cttee, 1966-69; Royal Commn on Trade Unions and Employers' Organisations. *Publication:* Life of Mr Justice McCardie, 1934. *Address:* 62 Saffrons Court, Eastbourne, East Sussex.

POLLOCK, Sir George F(rederick), 5th Bt, *cr* 1866; Artist-Photographer since 1963; *b* 13 Aug. 1928; *s* of Sir (Frederick) John Pollock, 4th Bt and Alix l'Estom (*née* Soubiran); *S* father, 1963; *m* 1951, Doreen Mumford, *o d* of N. E. K. Nash, CMG; one *s* two *d*. *Educ:* Eton; Trinity Coll., Cambridge. BA 1953, MA 1957. 2nd Lieut, 17/21 Lancers, 1948-49. Admitted Solicitor, 1956. FRPS (Vice-Pres.); FRSA. Past Chm., London Salon of Photography; Hon. Mem., Photo Clubs Lausanne, Germinal (Brussels) and Johannesburg. *Publications:* contrib. articles to ski-ing and photographic journals. *Recreation:* ski-ing. *Heir: s* David Frederick Pollock, *b* 13 April 1959. *Address:* Netherwood, Stones Lane, Westcott, near Dorking, Surrey. *T:* Dorking 5447. *Clubs:* Lansdowne, Ski Club of Great Britain; DHO (Wengen).

POLLOCK, Sir George Seymour Montagu-; 4th Bt, *cr* 1872; Lieutenant-Commander, RN (retired); *b* 14 Sept. 1900; *s* of Sir Montagu Frederick Montagu-Pollock, 3rd Bt, and Margaret Angela (*d* 1959), *d* of late W. A. Bell, Pendell Court, Blechingley; *S* father, 1938; *m* 1927, Karen-Sofie, *o c* of Hans Ludvig Dedekam, of Oslo; one *s* one *d*. *Educ:* Royal Naval Colleges, Osborne and Dartmouth. Entered RN, 1913; retired, 1920; With Unilever, 1920-64. Served in RN, War of 1939-45. *Heir: s* Giles Hampden Montagu-Pollock; *b* 19 Oct. 1928; *m* 1963, Caroline Veronica, *yr d* of Richard Russell; one *s* one *d*]. *Address:* Brooke House, Swallowcliffe, near Salisbury, Wilts. *T:* Tisbury 220. *Clubs:* Army and Navy, Special Forces. *See also Sir William Montagu-Pollock.*

POLLOCK, James Huey Hamill, CMG 1946; OBE 1939; *b* 6 Aug. 1893; *s* of late William Charles Pollock; *m* 1919, Margaret Doris, OStJ (*d* 1962), *d* of late P. B. Kearns; two *s*. *Educ:* Royal School, Armagh. Served in Royal Irish Rifles, London Regt and Staff, 1914-20 (wounded, despatches); Dep. Governor, Ramallah, Palestine, 1920; Administrative Officer, Nigeria, 1923; Assistant Secretary, Nigerian Secretariat, Lagos, 1927; Administrative Officer, Palestine, 1930; District Commissioner, Haifa, 1939, Galilee, 1942, Jerusalem, 1944-48; Mem., Adv. Council, Palestine, 1939-48, and Exec. Council, 1945-48; Chief Civil Adviser to GOC British Troops in Palestine, 15 May 1948 till final withdrawal 30 June 1948. Colonial Office, 1949-52. Member, Senate of Northern Ireland, 1954-57; Deputy Speaker, 1956-57. Member Management Cttee, South Tyrone and Drumglass Hospitals, 1960-64. Lieutenant of Commandery of Ards, 1952-61. High Sheriff, Co. Tyrone, 1963. KJStJ. Commander of Order of George I of Greece, 1948. *Address:* 21 Queen Square, Bath, Avon. *Club:* Bath and County.

POLLOCK, John Denton; General Secretary, Educational Institute of Scotland, since 1975; *b* 21 April 1926; *s* of John Pollock and Elizabeth (*née* Crawford); *m* 1961, Joyce Margaret Sharpe; one *s* one *d*. *Educ:* Ayr Academy; Royal Technical Coll., Glasgow; Glasgow Univ.; Jordanhill Coll. of Education. BSc (Pure Science). FEIS 1971. Teacher, Mauchline Secondary Sch., 1951-59; Head Teacher, Kilmaurs Secondary Sch., 1959-65; Rector, Mainholm Acad., 1965-74. Chm., Scottish Labour Party, 1959 and 1971; Mem. Gen. Council, Scottish TUC, 1975-; Mem., (Annan) Cttee on Future of Broadcasting, 1974-77. *Recreation:* travel. *Address:* 52 Douglas Road, Longniddry, East Lothian, Scotland. *T:* Longniddry 52082.

POLLOCK, Martin Rivers, FRS 1962; Professor of Biology, University of Edinburgh, 1965-76, now Emeritus; *b* 10 Dec. 1914; *s* of Hamilton Rivers Pollock and Eveline Morton Pollock (*née* Bell); *m* 1941, Jean Ilsley Paradise; two *s* two *d*. *Educ:* Winchester Coll., Trinity Coll., Cambridge; University College Hospital, London. BA Cantab, 1936; Senior Scholar, Trinity Coll., Cambridge, 1936; MRCS, LRCP 1939; MB, BCh Cantab 1940. House Appointments at UCH and Brompton Hospital, 1940-41; Bacteriologist, Emergency Public Health Laboratory Service, 1941-45; seconded to work on Infective Hepatitis with MRC Unit, 1943-45; apppointment to scientific staff, Medical Research Council, under Sir Paul Fildes, FRS, 1945-; Head of Division of Bacterial Physiology, Nat. Inst. for Medical Research, Mill Hill (MRC), 1949-65. *Publications:* articles in British Journal of Experimental Pathology, Biochemical Journal, Journal of Microbiology, etc. *Recreation:* contemplating, planning and occasionally undertaking various forms of mildly adventurous travel, preferably through deserts. *Address:* Marsh Farm House, Margaret Marsh, Shaftesbury, Dorset SP7 0AZ.

POLLOCK, Adm. of the Fleet Sir Michael (Patrick), GCB 1971 (KCB 1969; CB 1966); MVO 1952; DSC 1944; Bath King of Arms, since 1976; *b* 19 Oct. 1916; *s* of late C. A. Pollock and of Mrs G. Pollock; *m* 1st, 1940, Margaret Steacy (*d* 1951), Bermuda; two *s* one *d*; 2nd, 1954, Marjory Helen Reece (*née* Bisset); one step *d*. *Educ:* RNC Dartmouth. Entered Navy, 1930; specialised in Gunnery, 1941. Served War of 1939-45 in Warspite, Vanessa, Arethusa and Norfolk, N. Atlantic, Mediterranean and Indian Ocean. Captain, Plans Div. of Admiralty and Director of Surface Weapons; comd HMS Vigo and Portsmouth Sqdn, 1958-59; comd HMS Ark Royal, 1963-64; Asst Chief of Naval Staff, 1964-66; Flag Officer Second in Command, Home Fleet, 1966-67; Flag Officer Submarines and Nato Commander Submarines, Eastern Atlantic, 1967-69; Controller of the Navy, 1970-71; Chief of Naval Staff and First Sea Lord, 1971-74; First and Principal Naval Aide-de-Camp to the Queen, 1972-74. Comdr, 1950; Capt., 1955; Rear-Adm., 1964; Vice-Adm., 1968; Adm., 1970. *Recreations:* sailing, tennis, golf, shooting, fishing, travel. *Address:* The Ivy House, Churchstoke, Montgomery, Powys SY15 6DU. *T:* Churchstoke 426. *Club:* Royal Naval and Royal Albert Yacht (Portsmouth).

POLLOCK, Sir William H. M.; *see* Montagu-Pollock.

POLLOK, Maj.-Gen. Robert Valentine, CB 1940; CBE 1919; DSO 1917; late Irish Guards; *b* 14 Feb. 1884; 4th *s* of late John Pollok of Lismany, Ballinasloe, Co. Galway; *m* 1916, Sylvia Bettina (*d* 1977), *d* of late George Fellows, Beeston Fields, Notts; one *s* died on active service, 1945. *Educ:* Eton; Royal Military Coll., Sandhurst. Joined 15th Hussars, 1903; ADC to Lieutenant-Governor, United Provinces, India, 1908-12; ADC Governor-Gen. Australia, 1913-14. Served European War, 1914-18 (CBE, DSO, despatches, four times wounded): employed Australian Forces, Gallipoli (Adjutant and Staff Captain), 1914-15; transferred Irish Guards, 1916; Acting Major, 1917; Acting Lt-Col, 1917; Lt-Col, 1926; Bt Col, 1929; Col, 1930; Maj.-Gen., 1938; commanded 1st Bn Irish Guards, 1917-18, and 1926-30; Staff Coll., 1921; Brigade Major 1st Guards Brigade, 1922-25; Officer Commanding Regt and Regimental District, 1930-31; Commander 1st Guards Brigade, 1931-35; Commandant Senior Officers' Sch., Sheerness, 1935-38; General Officer comdg Northern Ireland District, 1938-40; Comdr 43rd (Wessex) Div. (TA); retired pay, 1941; re-employed as Colonel, General Staff, 1941; reverted to retired pay, 1941. *Address:* The Bridge House, Rathkeale, Co. Limerick, Eire. *T:* Rathkeale 11. *Club:* Cavalry and Guards.

POLSON, Prof. Cyril John; Professor of Forensic Medicine, University of Leeds, 1947-69, now Emeritus Professor; *b* 1901; *s* of William Polson, MB, CM, and A. D., *d* of Thomas Parker, JP, MInstCE, FRSE; *m* 1932, Mary Watkinson Tordoff (*d* 1961); one *d*; *m* 1963, G. Mary Pullan (BSc, MB, ChB, MFCM, DObst, RCOG). *Educ:* Wrekin Coll.; Birmingham Univ. MB, ChB and MRCS, LRCP, 1924; MRCP 1926; FRCP, 1941; FRCPath, 1964; MD 1929, Birmingham. Called to the Bar, Inner Temple, 1940. Assistant Lecturer, Univ. of Manchester, 1927; Univ. of Leeds: Lecturer in Pathology, 1928; Senior Lecturer in Pathology, and Pathologist to St J. Hospital, Leeds, 1945; Hon. Member, N England Laryngological Society, 1948. Corr. Member la Société de Médecine Légale de France, 1950. Vice-President 2nd International Meeting in Forensic Medicine, NY, 1960; President: British Association in Forensic Medicine, 1962-65; British Acad. of Forensic Sciences, 1974-75; Mem., Leeds and West Riding Medico-Legal Society, 1963 (Pres. 1966); Hon. Mem., Leeds and West Riding Medico-Chirurgical Soc., 1970. *Publications:* Clinical Toxicology (with R. N. Tattersall), 2nd edn, 1969; The Scientific Aspects of Forensic

Medicine, 1969, Swedish trans., 1973; The Essentials of Forensic Medicine, 3rd edn (with D. J. Gee), 1973; The Disposal of the Dead (with T. K. Marshall), 3rd edn, 1975; papers in scientific journals devoted to pathology and forensic medicine. *Recreations:* gardening, photography. *Address:* 16 Tewit Well Road, Harrogate HG2 8JE. *T:* Harrogate 503434.

POLTIMORE, 6th Baron, *cr* 1831; **Hugh de Burgh Warwick Bampfylde**; Bt 1641; *b* 1888; *yr b* of 5th Baron Poltimore; *S* brother, 1967; *m* 1918, Margaret Mary, *d* of 4th Marquis de la Pasture; one *s* (and one *s* decd). *Educ:* Winchester; New Coll., Oxford. MA. Served East Africa, 1914-18. *Heir: g s* Mark Coplestone Bampfylde, *b* 8 June 1957. *Address:* The Ancient House, Peasenhall, Saxmundham, Suffolk. *Club:* Brooks's.

POLUNIN, Nicholas, CBE 1976; MS (Yale); MA, DPhil, DSc (Oxon); FLS; FRGS; Editor (founding) of Environmental Conservation, since 1974 (Biological Conservation, 1967-74), and of Plant Science Monographs, since 1954; Guest Professor, University of Geneva, 1959-61 and since 1975; *b* Checkendon, Oxon, 26 June 1909; *e s* of late Vladimir and Elizabeth Violet (*née* Hart) Polunin; *m* 1st, 1939, Helen Lovat Fraser (*d* 1973); one *s* ; 2nd, 1948, Helen Eugenie Campbell; two *s* one *d. Educ:* The Hall, Weybridge; Latymer Upper and privately; Oxford, Yale and Harvard Univs. Open Scholar of Christ Church, Oxford, 1928-32; First Class Hons Nat. Sci. Final Examination, Botany and Ecology; Goldsmiths' Senior Studentship for Research, 1932-33; Botanical tutor in various Oxford Colls, 1932-47; Henry Fellowship at Pierson Coll., Yale Univ., USA, 1933-34 (Sigma Xi); Departmental Demonstrator in Botany 1934-35, and Senior (Research) Scholar of New Coll., Oxford, 1934-36; Dept of Scientific and Industrial Research, Senior Research Award, 1935-38; Rolleston Memorial Prize, 1938; DSIR Special Investigator, 1938; Research Associate, Gray Herbarium, Harvard Univ., USA, 1936-37, and subs. Foreign Research Associate; Fielding Curator and Keeper of the Univ. Herbaria, Oxford, and Univ. Demonstrator and Lectr in Botany, 1939-47; Oxford Univ. Botanical Moderator, 1941-45; Macdonald Prof. of Botany, McGill Univ., Canada, 1947-52 (Visiting Prof., 1946-47); Research Fellow, Harvard Univ., 1950-53; Lectr in Plant Science and Research Associate, Yale Univ., 1953-55; Project Dir, US Air Force, 1953-55, and Consultant to US Army Corps of Engineers; formerly Sen. Research Fell. and Lectr, New Coll., Oxford; Prof. of Plant Ecology and Taxonomy, Head of Dept of Botany, and Dir of Univ. Herbarium, etc., Baghdad, Iraq, Jan. 1956-58 (revolution); Prof. of Botany and Head of Dept, Faculty of Science (which he established as Dean), Univ. of Ife, Nigeria, 1962-66 (revolutions, etc). Leverhulme Res. Award, 1941-43; Arctic Inst. Res. Fellowship, 1946-48; Guggenheim Mem. Fellowship, 1950-52. Haley Lectr, Acadia Univ., NS, 1950; Visiting Lectr and Adviser on Biology, Brandeis Univ., Waltham, Mass, 1953-54. US Order of Polaris; Marie-Victorin Medal for services to Canadian botany; FRHS. Fellow; AAAS, Arctic Inst. NA, American Geographical Soc. Member or Leader, numerous scientific expeditions from 1930, particularly in arctic or sub-arctic regions, including Spitsbergen, Lapland (3 times), Iceland, Greenland, Canadian Eastern Arctic (5 times, including discovery in 1946 of last major islands to be added to world map), Labrador-Ungava (many times), Canadian Western Arctic (including Magnetic Pole), Alaska, summer and winter flights over geographical North Pole; subsequently in Middle East and West Africa; Ford Foundation Award, Scandinavia and USSR, 1966-67. International Botanical Congresses: VII (Stockholm, 1950); VIII (Paris, 1954); X (Edinburgh, 1964); XI (Seattle, 1969, symposium chm., etc); XII (Leningrad, 1975, Conservation Section chm., etc). Chairman: Internat. Steering Cttee, and Editor of Proceedings, (1st) Internat. Conf. on Environmental Future, Finland, 1971; designated Sec.-Gen. and editor of future confs; Pres., Foundn for Environmental Conservation, 1973- (subsequently consolidated and placed under Swiss federal surveillance). *Publications:* Russian Waters, 1931; The Isle of Auks, 1932; Botany of the Canadian Eastern Arctic, vol. I, Pteridophyta and Spermatophyta, 1940; (ed) vol. II, Thallophyta and Bryophyta, 1947; vol. III, Vegetation and Ecology, 1948; Arctic Unfolding, 1949; Circumpolar Arctic Flora, 1959; Introduction to Plant Geography, 1960 (subseq. Amer. and other edns); Eléments de Géographie botanique, 1967; (ed) The Environmental Future, 1972; papers chiefly on arctic and boreal flora, phytogeography, ecology, vegetation, aerobiology, and conservation; editor of International Industry, 1943-46, and of World Crops Books, 1954-69; associate editor, Environmental Pollution, 1969-; contrib. Encyclopædia Britannica, and some 200 other scientific papers, editorials, reviews, etc, to various jls. *Recreations:* travel and exploration, nature conservation, stock-markets. *Address:* 15 chemin F.-Lehmann, 1218 Grand-Saconnex, Geneva, Switzerland. *T:* (022) 982383/84; c/o New College, Oxford. *Clubs:* Reform (life);

Harvard (life), Explorers, Torrey Botanical (New York City); Lake Placid (NY); New England Botanical (Boston); Canadian Field Naturalists' (Ottawa).
See also O. Polunin.

POLUNIN, Oleg; Assistant Master, Charterhouse School, 1938-72; *b* 28 Nov. 1914; Russian father, British mother; *m* 1943, Lorna Mary Venning; one *s* one *d. Educ:* St Paul's Sch.; Magdalen Coll., Oxford. Served War of 1939-45, Intelligence Corps. Botanical Exploration and collecting, Nepal, 1949-52; Turkey, 1954-56; Karakoram, Pakistan, 1960; Kashmir; Iraq; Lebanon; Lecturer and Guide on Hellenic cruises and other tours, often off the beaten track. Founder member, past Chairman, and Secretary, Surrey Naturalists' Trust. *Publications:* (with A. J. Huxley) Flowers of the Mediterranean, 1965; Flowers of Europe, 1969; Concise Flowers of Europe, 1972; (with B. E. Smythies) Flowers of South West Europe, 1973; (with B. Everard) Trees and Bushes of Europe, 1976. *Recreations:* travel, plant photography and collecting, pottery. *Address:* 2 Lockwood Court, Knoll Road, Godalming, Surrey.
See also N. Polunin.

POLWARTH, 10th Baron, *cr* 1690; **Henry Alexander Hepburne-Scott**, TD; DL; Vice-Lord-Lieutenant, Borders Region (Roxburgh, Ettrick and Lauderdale), since 1975; Member, Royal Company of Archers; a Scots Representative Peer, 1945-63; Chartered Accountant; *b* 17 Nov. 1916; *s* of late Hon. Walter Thomas Hepburne-Scott (*d* 1942); *S* grandfather, 1944; *m* 1st, 1943, Caroline Margaret (marr. diss. 1969), 2nd *d* of late Captain R. A. Hay, Marlefield, Roxburghshire, and Helmsley, Yorks; one *s* three *d*; 2nd, 1969, Jean, *d* of Adm. Sir Angus Cunninghame Graham, *qv*, and formerly wife of C. E. Jauncey, QC; two step *s* one step *d. Educ:* Eton Coll.; King's Coll., Cambridge. Served War of 1939-45, Captain, Lothians and Border Yeomanry. Former Partner, firm of Chiene and Tait, CA, Edinburgh; Governor, Bank of Scotland, 1966-72, Director, 1974-; Chairman: General Accident, Fire & Life Assurance Corp., 1968-72; Total Oil Marine Ltd, 1975-; Total Oil GB Ltd, 1975-; Director: ICI Ltd, 1969-72, 1974-; Weir Group Ltd, 1974-; Halliburton Co., 1974-; Canadian Pacific Ltd, 1975-; Sun Life Assurance Co. of Canada, 1975-. Minister of State, Scottish Office, 1972-74. Chm., later Pres., Scottish Council (Develt and Industry), 1955-72. Chm., Scottish Nat. Orchestra Soc., 1975-. Chancellor, Aberdeen Univ., 1966. Hon. LLD: St Andrews; Aberdeen; Hon. DLitt Heriot-Watt; DUniv Stirling. FRSE; FRSA. DL Roxburgh, 1962. *Heir: s* Master of Polwarth, *qv. Address:* Harden, Hawick, Scotland. *T:* Hawick 2069. *Clubs:* Brooks's, Pratt's; New (Edinburgh).

POLWARTH, Master of; Hon. Andrew Walter Hepburne-Scott; *b* 30 Nov. 1947; *s* and *heir* of 10th Baron Polwarth, *qv*; *m* 1971, Isabel Anna, *e d* of Maj. J. F. H. Surtees, OBE, MC; two *s. Educ:* Eton; Trinity Hall, Cambridge. *Address:* 72 Cloncurry Street, SW6.

POMEROY, family name of **Viscount Harberton.**

POMFRET, Surgeon Rear-Adm. Arnold Ashworth, CB 1957; OBE 1941; retired, 1957; *b* 1 June 1900; *s* of John and Eleanor Pomfret; *m* 1928, Carlene Blundstone; one *s* two *d. Educ:* Manchester Univ.; Postgraduate at London, Capetown and Oxford. MB, ChB (Manchester), 1922; DO (Oxon) 1934; DOMS (RCS&PEng), 1934. Senior Ophthalmic Specialist, RN. Last MO i/c Wei-Hai-Wei, 1940. Formerly Asst to MDG, 1944-45 and 1952-54. MO i/c RN Hospitals: Simonstown, 1946; Portland, 1948; Bermuda, 1950; MO i/c RN Hospital, Plymouth, and Command MO Plymouth, 1954-57. Gilbert Blane Medallist, 1934. Surgeon Comdr, 1934; Surgeon Captain, 1944; Surgeon Rear-Adm., 1954. QHS, 1954-57. CStJ 1957. *Recreations:* cricket, Association football. *Address:* Passlands, Forton, Chard, Somerset.

PONCET, André F.; *see* François-Poncet.

POND, Prof. Desmond Arthur, MA, MD, FRCP, FRCPsych; Professor of Psychiatry, University of London at The London Hospital Medical College, London, E1, since 1966; *b* 2 Sept. 1919; *o s* of Thomas Arthur and Ada Celia Pond; *m* 1945, Margaret Helen (*née* Jordan), MD; three *d. Educ:* John Lyon's, Harrow; St Olave's, SE1; Clare Coll., Cambridge; University College Hospital. Rockefeller Scholar, Duke Med. Sch., N Carolina, 1942-44; Sen. Lectr, Dept of Clin. Neurophysiology, Maudsley Hosp., and Cons. Psychiatrist, UCH, 1952-66; Goulstonian Lectr, RCP, 1961; Founder Mem., Inst. of Religion and Med., 1964; Mem., Archbishop's Gp on Divorce Law ('Putting Asunder'), 1964-66; Mem., MRC, 1968-72; H. B. Williams Vis. Prof., Australian and New Zealand Coll. of Psychiatrists, 1968; Riddell Memorial Lectr, Univ. of

Newcastle, 1971. *Publications:* Counselling in Religion and Psychiatry, 1973; various, on psychiatry and electroencephalography. *Recreations:* making music, gardens. *Address:* 5 Arlesey Close, Lytton Grove, SW15 2EX. *T:* 01-788 2903.

PONSFORD, Brian David; Counsellor, Office of United Kingdom Permanent Representative to the European Communities, since 1975; *b* 23 Dec. 1938; *s* of Herbert E. Ponsford and Kathleen W. C. (*née* Parish); *m* 1966, Erica Neumark; one *s*. *Educ:* City of London Sch.; Corpus Christi Coll., Oxford (1st Cl. Classical Mods 1958, 1st Cl. Lit. Hum. 1960). Teacher, Westminster Sch., 1960-61; Asst Principal, Min. of Housing and Local Govt, 1961-67; Asst Private Sec. to Minister, 1964-66; Private Sec. to Minister of State, 1966-67; Principal, 1967-69; Principal, Cabinet Office, 1969-71, DoE, 1971-73; Asst Sec., DoE, 1973-. *Recreations:* music, books, films. *Address:* 21 Cyprus Gardens, N3 1SP. *T:* 01-349 9640.

PONSONBY, family name of **Earl of Bessborough** and of **Barons de Mauley, Ponsonby of Shulbrede,** and **Sysonby.**

PONSONBY OF SHULBREDE, 3rd Baron *cr* 1930, of Shulbrede; **Thomas Arthur Ponsonby;** Chairman, London Tourist Board, since 1976; *b* 23 Oct. 1930; *o* surv. *s* of 2nd Baron Ponsonby of Shulbrede, and of Hon. Elizabeth Bigham, *o d* of 2nd Viscount Mersey, PC, CMG, CBE; *S* father, 1976; *m* 1st, 1956, Ursula Mary (marr. diss. 1973), *yr d* of Comdr Thomas Stanley Lane Fox-Pitt, OBE, RN; one *s* three *d*; 2nd, 1973, Maureen Estelle Campbell-Tiech, *d* of Alfred William Windsor, Reigate, Surrey. *Educ:* St Ronan's Sch.; Bryanston; Hertford Coll., Oxford. Councillor, 1956-65, Alderman, 1964-74, Royal Borough of Kensington and Chelsea; Leader, Labour Gp, 1968-73. GLC: Alderman, 1970-77; Chm. Covent Garden Cttee, 1973-75; Chm., Central Area Bd (Transport and Planning Cttees), 1973-76; Chm. of Council, 1976-77. Chairman: Greater London Citizens Advice Bureaux Service Ltd, 1977-; Age Concern Greater London, 1977-. Chm., Charity Law Reform Cttee, 1974-. Contested (Lab) Heston and Isleworth, general election, 1959. Fabian Society: Asst Gen. Sec., 1961-64; Gen. Sec., 1964-76. Pres., Galleon World Travel Assoc. Ltd, 1977-. Governor, London Sch. of Economics, 1970-. *Recreations:* eating, drinking, gardening. *Heir: s* Hon. Frederick Matthew Thomas Ponsonby, *b* 27 Oct. 1958. *Address:* 96 Vanbrugh Court, Wincott Street, SE11 4NS. *T:* 01-582 7306.

PONSONBY, Arthur Gordon; *b* 14 June 1892; 2nd *s* of late Rev. Stewart Gordon Ponsonby; *m* 1938, Jacqueline, 2nd *d* of late Karl Kirdorf, Krefeld, Germany; one *s*. *Educ:* Marlborough; Trinity College, Cambridge. Interned in Ruhleben during the war, 1914-18; joined HM Consular service in 1920. HM Chargé d'Affairs, Monrovia, 1938-40; Consul-General at Rio de Janeiro, 1947-51; retd from HM Foreign Service, 1951. *Recreation:* gardening. *Address:* 26 Upper High Street, Thame, Oxon. *Club:* Royal Commonwealth Society.

PONSONBY, Sir Ashley (Charles Gibbs), 2nd Bt *cr* 1956; MC 1945; DL; Managing Director of Schroder, Wagg & Co. Ltd and Director of other companies; *b* 21 Feb. 1921; *o s* of Col Sir Charles Edward Ponsonby, 1st Bt, TD, and of Hon. Winifred, *d* of 1st Baron Hunsdon; *S* father, 1976; *m* 1950, Lady Martha Butler, *yr d* of 6th Marquess of Ormonde, CVO, MC; four *s*. *Educ:* Eton; Balliol College, Oxford. 2nd Lieut Coldstream Guards, 1941; served war 1942-45 (North Africa and Italy, wounded); Captain 1943; on staff Bermuda Garrison, 1945-46. A Church Commissioner, 1963-. DL Oxon, 1974. *Heir: e s* Charles Ashley Ponsonby, *b* 10 June 1951. *Address:* Grim's Dyke Farm, Woodleys, Woodstock, Oxon. *T:* Woodstock 811717. *Club:* Brooks's.

PONSONBY, Myles Walter, CBE 1966; HM Diplomatic Service; Foreign and Commonwealth Office, since 1977; *b* 12 Sept. 1924; *s* of late Victor Coope Ponsonby, MC and Gladys Edith Ponsonby (*née* Walter); *m* 1951, Anne Veronica Theresa Maynard, *y d* of Brig. Francis Herbert Maynard, *qv*; one *s* two *d*. *Educ:* St Aubyn's, Rottingdean; Eton College. HM Forces (Captain, KRRC), 1942-49. Entered Foreign (subseq. Diplomatic) Service, 1951; served in: Egypt, 1951; Cyprus, 1952-53; Beirut, 1953-56; Djakarta, 1958-61; Nairobi, 1963-64; Hanoi (Consul-Gen.), 1964-65; FO, 1966-69; Rome, 1969-71; FCO, 1972-74; Ambassador to Mongolian People's Republic, 1974-77. *Recreation:* gardening. *Address:* c/o Foreign and Commonwealth Office, SW1; Springs Cottage, Bullingstone Lane, Speldhurst, Tunbridge Wells, Kent. *T:* Langton 3089. *Club:* Travellers'.

PONSONBY, Robert Noel; Controller of Music, BBC, since 1972; *b* 19 Dec. 1926; *o s* of late Noel Ponsonby, BMus, Organist

Christ Church Cathedral, Oxford, and Mary White-Thomson (now Mrs L. H. Jaques, Winchester); *m* 1957, Una Mary (marr. diss.), *er d* of W. J. Kenny; *m* 1977, Lesley Margaret Black, *o d* of G. T. Black. *Educ:* Eton; Trinity Coll., Oxford. MA Oxon., Eng. Litt. Commissioned Scots Guards, 1945-47. Organ Scholar, Trinity Coll., Oxon., 1948-50; staff of Glyndebourne Opera, 1951-55; Artistic Director of the Edinburgh International Festival, 1955-60; with Independent Television Authority, 1962-64; Gen. Administrator, Scottish Nat. Orchestra, 1964-72. Director, Commonwealth Arts Festival, Glasgow, 1965. Artistic Adviser to Internat. Arts Guild of Bahamas, 1960-72. Hon. RAM 1975. *Publication:* Short History of Oxford University Opera Club, 1950. *Recreations:* fell-walking, English and Scottish painting, music. *Address:* 4 Rosslyn Court, Ornan Road, NW3 4PU. *Clubs:* Oriental; Trinity Society.

PONTECORVO, Guido, FRS 1955; FRSE 1946; PhD (Edinburgh) 1941; DrAgr (Pisa) 1928; Honorary Consultant Geneticist, Imperial Cancer Research Fund, London, WC2; *b* Pisa, 1882, 29 Nov. 1907; *s* of Massimo Pontecorvo and Maria (*née* Maroni); *m* 1939, Leonore Freyenmuth, Frauenfeld, Switzerland; one *d*. *Educ:* Pisa (Classics). Ispettorato Agrario per la Toscana, Florence, 1931-38; Inst. of Animal Genetics, Univ. of Edinburgh, 1938-40 and 1944-45; Dept of Zoology, Univ. of Glasgow, 1941-44; Dept of Genetics, Univ. of Glasgow, 1945-68 (Prof. 1955-68); Mem. Res. Staff, Imperial Cancer Res. Fund, 1968-75. Jesup Lectr, Columbia Univ., 1956; Messenger Lectr, Cornell Univ., 1957; Visiting Prof., Albert Einstein Coll. Med., 1965, 1966; Vis. Lectr, Washington State Univ., 1967; Royal Society, Leverhulme Overseas Vis. Prof., Inst. of Biophysics, Rio de Janeiro, 1969 and Dept of Biology, Pahlavi Univ., 1974; Sloane Foundn Vis. Prof., Vermont, 1971; Visiting Professor: UCL, 1968-75; King's Coll., London, 1970-71; Biology Dept, Tehran Univ., 1975; Prof. Ospite Linceo, Scuola Normale Superiore, Pisa, 1976, 1977; L. C. Dunn Lectr, NY Blood Center, 1976. Sec., Genetical Soc., 1945-51, Vice-Pres., 1954-57, 1966-69, Pres., 1964-66; Vice-Pres., Inst. of Biology, 1969-71. For. Hon. Member: Amer. Acad. Arts and Sciences, 1958; Danish Royal Soc., 1966; Peruvian Soc. of Medical Genetics, 1969. Hon. DSc: Leicester, 1968; Camerino, 1974; East Anglia, 1974. Hansen Foundation Prize, 1961. *Publications:* Ricerche sull' economia montana dell' Appennino Toscano, 1933 (Florence); Trends in Genetic Analysis, 1958. Numerous papers in British, American, Swiss, French and Italian journals on genetics and high mountain botany. *Recreations:* mountaineering, alpine plants photography. *Address:* Flat 25, Cranfield House, 97 Southampton Row, WC1B 4HH. *T:* 01-636 9441.

PONTEFRACT, Bishop Suffragan of, since 1971; **Rt. Rev. Thomas Richard Hare;** *b* 1922; *m* 1963, Sara, *d* of Lt-Col J. E. Spedding, OBE; one *s* two *d*. *Educ:* Marlborough; Trinity Coll., Oxford; Westcott House, Cambridge. RAF, 1942-45, Curate of Haltwhistle, 1950-52; Domestic Chaplain to Bishop of Manchester, 1952-59; Canon Residentiary of Carlisle Cathedral, 1959-65; Archdeacon of Westmorland and Furness, 1965-71; Vicar of St George with St Luke, Barrow-in-Furness, 1965-69; Vicar of Winster, 1969-71. *Address:* 306 Barnsley Road, Wakefield WF2 6AX. *T:* Wakefield 256935.

PONTEFRACT, Archdeacon of; *see* Henderson, Ven. E. C.

PONTI, Signora Carlo; *see* Loren, Sophia.

PONTIN, Sir Frederick William, (Sir Fred Pontin), Kt 1976; Founder: Pontin's Ltd, 1946; Pontinental Ltd, 1963; Chairman and Joint Managing Director of Pontin's Ltd, since 1946, and Pontinental (HS) Ltd, since 1972; *b* 24 Oct. 1906; *m* Dorothy Beatrice Mortimer; one *d*. *Educ:* Sir George Monoux Grammar Sch., Walthamstow. Began career on London Stock Exchange. Catering and welfare work for Admiralty, Orkney Is, 1939-46. Acquired: Industrial Catering Bristol, 1946; Brean Sands Holiday Village, 1946. Chief Barker, Variety Club of GB (Raising £1,000,000 for charity), 1968; former Mem. Exec. Bd, Variety Club, 1968-, Pres. 1969-75, formed 15 regional cttees of club; Mem., Grand Order of Water Rats; co-opted Mem., Stars Orgn for Spastics. Mem., St John Council for Merseyside; President: Lancs Youth Club Assoc.; Blackpool Hotel and Catering Students Soc.; Prescot Band. Freeman of Christchurch, Dorset. *Recreations:* racing (owner of Specify, winner of 1971 Grand National, and Cala Mesquida, winner of 1971 Schweppes Gold Cup); connected with Walthamstow Avenue FC for many years prior to 1939-45 war; interested in all sporting activities. *Address:* c/o Pontin's Ltd, 240 Oxford Street, W1N 0BN. *T:* 01-493 1301. *Clubs:* Eccentric, Saints and Sinners, World Sporting (Vice-Chm.); The Toffs; Bristol (Bristol).

POOLE, family name of **Baron Poole**.

POOLE, 1st Baron, *cr* 1958, of Aldgate; **Oliver Brian Sanderson Poole**, PC 1963; CBE 1945; TD; Member of Lloyd's; Director, S. Pearson & Son Ltd; *b* 11 Aug. 1911; *s* of late Donald Louis Poole of Lloyd's; *m* 1st, 1933, Betty Margaret Gilkison (marr. diss., 1951); one *s* three *d* ; 2nd, 1952, Mrs Daphne Heber Percy (marr. diss., 1965); 3rd, 1966, Barbara Ann Taylor. *Educ:* Eton; Christ Church, Oxford. Life Guards, 1932-33; joined Warwickshire Yeomanry, 1934. Service in 1939-45 in Iraq, Syria, North Africa, Sicily and NW Europe (despatches thrice, MBE, OBE, CBE, US Legion of Merit, Order of Orange Nassau). MP (C) Oswestry Division of Salop, 1945-50. Conservative Party Organisation: Jt Hon. Treas., 1952-55; Chairman, 1955-57; Dep.-Chm., 1957-59; Jt Chm., May-Oct. 1963, Vice-Chm., Oct. 1963-Oct. 1964. Governor of Old Vic, 1948-63; a Trustee, Nat. Gallery, 1973-. Hon. DSc City Univ., 1970. *Heir: s* Hon. David Charles Poole, [*b* 6 Jan. 1945; *m* 1st, 1967, Fiona, *d* of John Donald, London SW6; one *s* ; 2nd, 1975, Philippa, *d* of Mark Reeve]. *Address:* 10 Holland Park, W11 3TH. *Clubs:* MCC, Buck's, Royal Yacht Squadron (Cowes). *See also Sir Hugh Munro-Lucas-Tooth, Bt.*

POOLE, Rev. **Canon Joseph Weston**; Canon Emeritus of Coventry Cathedral, since 1977; *b* 25 March 1909; *s* of Rev. S. J. Poole and Mrs Poole (*née* Weston); *m* 1945, Esmé Beatrice Mounsey; three *s* two *d*. *Educ:* St George's School, Windsor; King's School, Canterbury; Jesus Coll., Cambridge (Organ Schol. and Class. Exhibnr); Westcott House, Cambridge. Curate of St Mary-at-the-Walls, Colchester, 1933; Sub-Warden of Student Movement House, 1935; Minor Canon and Sacrist of Canterbury, 1936; Precentor of Canterbury, 1937; Rector of Merstham, Surrey, 1949; Hon. Canon of Coventry, 1958, Precentor, 1958-77; Canon Residentiary, 1963-77. ChStJ, 1974. FRSCM 1977. *Recreations:* music, literature, typography. *Address:* The Limes, Beauchamp Avenue, Royal Leamington Spa.

POOLE HUGHES, Rt. Rev. John Richard Worthington; *see* Llandaff, Bishop of.

POOLEY, Frederick Bernard, CBE 1968; PPRIBA; Controller of Planning and Transportation, Greater London Council, since 1974; *b* 18 April 1916; *s* of George Pooley and Elizabeth Pawley; *m* 1944, Hilda Olive Williams; three *d*. *Educ:* West Ham Grammar Sch.; RIBA, FRICS, FRTPI. Served war, RE, 1940-45. Deputy Borough Architect and Planning Officer, County Borough of West Ham, 1949-51; Deputy City Architect and Planning Officer, Coventry, 1951-54; County Architect and Planning Officer, Bucks, 1954-74. Major projects include: public and sch. bldg programme; scheme for public acquisition of bldgs of arch. or hist. interest for preservation and resale; new methods for assembling and servicing land; early planning work for new Milton Keynes. RIBA: Mem. Council, 1962-; Treasurer, 1972; Pres., 1973-75. *Publications:* contribs on planning, transport and architecture. *Address:* Long Ridge, Whiteleaf, Aylesbury, Bucks. *T:* Princes Risborough 6151. *Club:* Reform.

POORE, Dennis; *see* Poore, R. D.

POORE, Sir Herbert Edward, 6th Bt, *cr* 1795; *b* April 1930; *s* of Sir Edward Poore, 5th Bt, and Amelia Guliemone; *S* father 1938. *Heir: u* Nasionceno Poore [*b* 1900; *m* Juana Borda (*d* 1943); three *s* three *d*]. *Address:* Curuzu Cuatia, Corrientes, Argentine Republic.

POORE, Martin Edward Duncan, MA, PhD; FInstBiol; Scientific Director, International Union for Conservation of Nature and Natural Resources, Morges, Switzerland; *b* 25 May 1925; *s* of T. E. D. Poore and Elizabeth McMartin; *m* 1948, Judith Ursula, *d* of Lt-Gen. Sir Treffry Thompson, *qv* ; two *s*. *Educ:* Trinity Coll., Glenalmond; Edinburgh Univ.; Clare Coll., Cambridge. MA, PhD Cantab.; MA Oxon. Japanese interpreter, 1943-45. Nature Conservancy, 1953-56; Consultant Ecologist, Hunting Technical Services, 1956-59; Prof. of Botany, Univ. of Malaya, Kuala Lumpur, 1959-65; Dean of Science, Univ. of Malaya, 1964-65; Lectr, Forestry Dept, Oxford, 1965-66; Dir, Nature Conservancy, 1966-73. FRSA; FRGS. *Publications:* papers on ecology and land use in various jls and scientific periodicals. *Recreations:* hill walking, natural history, music, gardening, photography. *Address:* Evenlode, Stonesfield, Oxon. *T:* Stonesfield 246. *Club:* Athenæum.

POORE, Roger Dennistoun; Chairman and Managing Director: Norton Villiers Triumph Ltd, since 1973; The Federated Trust and Finance Corporation Ltd, since 1967; Chairman: Manganese Bronze Holdings Ltd, since 1963 (Director since 1961); The Scottish & Mercantile Investment Trust Ltd, since 1971; Director, Scottish Cities Investment Trust Ltd, since 1953; Member Lloyd's, since 1950; *b* 19 Aug. 1916; *s* of Lt-Col Roger Alvin Poore, DSO, and Lorne Margery, *d* of Major R. J. W. Dennistoun; *m* 1949, Mrs Peta Farley; one *d*. *Educ:* Eton; King's College, Cambridge (MA). Served War, Royal Air Force, 1939-46 (Wing Comdr 1944). Motor racing successes, 1947-55 (British Hill Climb Champion, 1950). Chm., Ocean Wilsons (Holdings) Ltd, 1958-76. *Recreations:* tennis, golf, bridge. *Address:* 33 Phillimore Gardens, W8. *T:* 01-937 1384.

POPA, Pretor; Order Star of Socialist Republic of Romania; Order of Labour and other medals; Ambassador of Romania to the Court of St James's, since 1973; *b* 20 April 1922; *m* Ileana Popa. *Educ:* Academy for High Commercial and Industrial Studies, Bucharest. Director, Ministry for Oil Extraction and Processing, 1950-66; Gen. Director, Ministry for Foreign Trade, 1966-70; Deputy Minister, Ministry for Foreign Trade, and Vice-Chairman at Chamber of Commerce, 1970-73. *Address:* (home) 1 Belgrave Square, SW1; (office) 4 Palace Green, Kensington, W8.

POPE, HH the; *see* Paul VI.

POPE, Andrew Lancelot, CMG 1972; CVO 1965; OBE 1959; HM Diplomatic Service, retired; *b* 27 July 1912; *m* 1st, 1938 (marr. diss.); 2nd, 1948, Ilse Migliarina; one *step d*. *Educ:* Harrow School. Served War of 1939-45 (despatches): Lieut, Royal Fusiliers, 1939; POW 1940-45. Served in Mil. Govt and Allied High Commn in Germany, 1945-56; entered Foreign (subseq. Diplomatic) Service, 1959; Counsellor, Bonn, 1962-72. Dir, Conf. Bd, NY; Dir, Gerling Global General and Reinsurance Co. Ltd; Mem., Adv. Bd, Gerling Konzern, Cologne. Order of Merit (Germany), 1965; Order of Merit (Bavaria), 1970; Order of Merit (Lower Saxony), 1972. *Recreations:* shooting, gardening. *Address:* Goldhill Grove, Lower Bourne, Farnham, Surrey. *T:* Farnham 21662.

POPE, Sir Barton; *see* Pope, Sir Sidney Barton.

POPE, Dudley Bernard Egerton; Naval historian and author; *b* 29 Dec. 1925; *s* of late Sydney Broughton Pope and late Alice Pope (*née* Meehan); *m* 1954, Kathleen Patricia Hall; one *d*. *Educ:* Ashford (Kent). Served War of 1939-45: Midshipman, MN, 1941-43 (wounded and invalided). The Evening News: naval and defence correspondent, 1944-57, Dep. Foreign Editor, 1957-59; resigned to take up full-time authorship, 1959. Counsellor, Navy Record Soc., 1964-68. In 1965 created "Lt Ramage RN" series of historical novels covering life of naval officer in Nelson's day; cruising trans-Atlantic and Caribbean in own yacht, doing naval historical research, 1965-. Hon. Mem., Mark Twain Soc., 1976. *Publications: non -fiction:* Flag 4, the Battle of Coastal Forces in the Mediterranean, 1954; The Battle of the River Plate, 1956; 73 North, 1958; England Expects, 1959; At 12 Mr Byng was Shot, 1962; The Black Ship, 1963; Guns, 1965; The Great Gamble, 1972; *fiction:* Ramage (Book Society Choice) 1965; Ramage and the Drum Beat (Book Society Alternative Choice), 1967; Ramage and the Freebooters (Book of the Month Club Alt. Choice), 1969; Governor Ramage, RN, 1973; Ramage's Prize, 1974; Ramage and the Guillotine, 1975; Ramage's Diamond, 1976; Ramage's Mutiny, 1977. *Recreations:* ocean cruising, skin-diving. *Address:* c/o Peter Janson Smith Ltd, 31 Newington Green, N16 9PU. *Club:* Royal Temple Yacht.

POPE, Sir Ernle; *see* Pope, Sir J. E.

POPE, Sir George (Reginald), Kt 1967; General Manager of The Times, 1965-67; Director: Times Newspapers Ltd, 1967-76 (Deputy General Manager during 1967); Kingsway Press Ltd; Medco Ltd; *b* 25 Mar. 1902; *s* of G. J. Pope; *m* 1930, Susie A. Hendy; one *s*. *Educ:* Clapham Parochial Sch. The Morning Post, 1916-37; The Daily Telegraph, 1937; The Times, 1937-. Treas., Methodist Press and Information Service. Pres. of the Advertising Assoc., 1962-63. Mackintosh Medal, 1953; Publicity Club of London Cup, 1961. *Recreation:* bowls. *Address:* 57 West Drive, Cheam, Surrey. *T:* 01-642 4754. *Club:* Royal Automobile.

POPE, Air Vice-Marshal John Clifford, CB 1963; CBE 1959; CEng, FIMechE; FRAeS; RAF (retired); *b* 27 April 1912; *s* of George Newcombe-Pope; *m* 1950, Christine Agnes, *d* of Alfred Hames, Chichester; one *s* two *d*. *Educ:* Tiverton Sch.; RAF Coll., Cranwell. Commnd, 1932; served with No 3 Sqdn, 1933, Nos 27 and 39, on NW Frontier, 1933-36. War of 1939-45; Comd RAF Station, Cleave, 1940-42; served in Egypt and Palestine, 1943-46; Asst Dir Research and Develt, Min. of Supply, 1947-50; Dir of Engineering, RNZAF, 1951-53; Comd RAF Station, Stoke Heath, 1954-57; Sen. Tech. Staff Officer, No

3 Gp Bomber Comd, 1957-59 and Flying Trng Comd, 1960-61; AOC and Comdt, RAF Technical College, 1961-63; Senior Technical Staff Officer, Transport Command, 1963-66. Life Vice-Pres., RAF Boxing Assoc. *Address:* Dilston, 47 Oxford Road, Stone, near Aylesbury, Bucks. *T:* Stone 467. *Club:* Royal Air Force.

POPE, Vice-Adm. Sir (John) Ernle, KCB 1976; Commander Allied Naval Forces, Southern Europe, 1974-76; *b* 22 May 1921; *s* of Comdr R. K. C. Pope, Homme House, Herefordshire. *Educ:* RN Coll., Dartmouth. Royal Navy, 1935. Served throughout War of 1939-45, in Destroyers. CO, HMS Decoy, 1962-64; Dir, Naval Equipment, 1964-66; CO, HMS Eagle, 1966-68; Flag Officer, Western Fleet Flotillas, 1969-71; C of S to C-in-C Western Fleet, 1971-74; Rear-Adm. 1969; Vice-Adm. 1972. *Recreations:* sailing, shooting. *Address:* Homme House, Much Marcle, Herefordshire. *Club:* Army and Navy.
See also Rear-Adm. M. D. Kyrle Pope.

POPE, Rev. (John) Russell; President of Methodist Conference, 1974-75; *b* 15 Aug. 1909; 3rd *s* of George and Rhoda Pope; *m* 1939, Doreen Minette Foulkes; one *s* one *d. Educ:* Canton High Sch., and Technical Coll., Cardiff; Handsworth Theological Coll., Birmingham. Manchester and Salford Mission, 1936-39; Liverpool South Circuit, 1939-44; Manchester and Salford Mission, 1944-48; Bristol Mission, 1948-57; Nottingham Mission, 1957-59; Chm., Plymouth and Exeter Methodist District, 1959-76. Preaching tours: S Africa, 1953; NSW, 1959; Bahamas, 1962; New England, 1966; two visits to Holy Land, 1964 and 1969 (second visit being Jt Leadership of Ecumenical Pilgrimage to Rome and Holy Land with Bp of Bath and Wells, and Bishop of Clifton); audience with the Pope. *Recreations:* gardening, travel. *Address:* 17 Score View, Ilfracombe, Devon. *T:* Ilfracombe 62175. *Club:* National Liberal.

POPE, Joseph Albert, DSc, PhD (Belfast), WhSc; Vice-Chancellor, University of Aston in Birmingham, since 1969; *b* 18 October 1914; *s* of Albert Henry and Mary Pope; *m* 1940, Evelyn Alice Gallagher; one *s* two *d. Educ:* School of Arts and Crafts, Cambridge; King's College, London. Apprentice, Boulton & Pauls, Norwich, 1930-35. Whitworth Scholarship, 1935. Assistant Lecturer in Engineering, Queen's Univ., Belfast, 1938-44; Assistant Lecturer in Engineering, Univ. of Manchester, 1944-45; Lecturer, then Senior Lecturer, Univ. of Sheffield, 1945-49; Professor of Mechanical Engineering, Nottingham University, 1949-60; Research Dir, Mirrlees Nat. Research Div., Stockport, 1960-69; Director: Mirrlees National Ltd, 1960-69; Tecquipment Ltd, 1960-; John Brown Ltd, 1970-; Midlands Electricity Bd, 1975-. Gen. Treasurer, British Assoc., 1975-. *Publications:* papers on the impact of metals and metal fatigue published in Proc. of Inst. of Mech. Engineers and Jl of Iron and Steel Inst. *Address:* 1 Arthur Road, Edgbaston, Birmingham B15 2UW. *T:* 021-454 7545.

POPE, Lt-Gen. (retd) Maurice Arthur, CB 1944; MC; CD; *b* Rivière du Loup, PQ, 29 Aug. 1889; *s* of late Sir Joseph Pope, KCMG, CVO, ISO, sometime Under-Secretary of State for External Affairs, Ottawa, and late Henriette Taschereau; *m* 1920, Comtesse Simonne du Monceau de Bergendal (Belgium); three *s* one *d. Educ:* Locally Ottawa; McGill University, BSc (Civil Engineering, 1911). Civil Engineer, Canadian Pacific Railway, 1911; European War, 1914-18 (MC, despatches) Cdn Battlefields Memorials Commission, Belgium and France, 1920-21; Staff College, Camberley, 1924-25; Staff Appts, Canada, 1926-31; War Office, 1931-33; Canada, 1933-35; Imperial Defence College, 1936; Sec., Chiefs of Staff Committee, Ottawa, 1938; Director Military Operations and Intelligence, Ottawa, 1939; Brigadier, General Staff, Cdn Military HQ, London, 1940; Vice-Chief of the General Staff, Ottawa, 1941; Chairman, Canadian Joint Staff Mission, Washington, DC, 1942-44; Military Staff Officer to the Prime Minister and Military Sec., Cabinet War Cttee, 1944-45; Head of Canadian Military Mission to Allied Control Council, Berlin, 1945-50; Ambassador to Belgium, 1950-53; Ambassador to Spain, 1953-56, retired. Hon. LLD. *Publication:* Soldiers and Politicians (memoirs), 1962. *Address:* 216 Manor Avenue, Ottawa, K1M 0H4, Canada.

POPE, Rear-Adm. Michael Donald K.; see Kyrle Pope.

POPE, Very Rev. Robert William, OBE 1971; Dean of Gibraltar, since 1977; *b* 20 May 1916; *s* of Rev. Jonas George Pope and Marjorie Mary Pope (*née* Coates); *m* 1940, Elizabeth Beatrice Matilda (*née* Bressey); two *s* one *d. Educ:* English College, Temuco, Chile; Harvey Grammar Sch., Folkestone; Maidstone Grammar Sch.; St Augustine's Coll., Canterbury; Durham Univ. (LTh). Deacon 1939, priest, 1940, Rochester; Curate: Holy Trinity, Gravesend, 1939-41; St Nicholas, Guildford, 1942-43; Priest in charge, Peaslake, 1943-44; Chaplain, Royal Navy, 1944-71; Vicar of Whitchurch with Tufton and Litchfield, Dio. Winchester, 1971-77. Member of Sion College. *Address:* The Deanery, 302 Main Street, Gibraltar. *T:* A 5745.

POPE, Russell; see Pope, J. R.

POPE, Sir (Sidney) Barton, Kt 1959; *b* 18 Feb. 1905; *s* of Henry Pope, Northam, W Australia; *m* 1944, Ada Lilian, *d* of late J. B. Hawkins; two *s* two *d. Educ:* Pulteney Grammar School, S Australia. President S Aust. Chamber of Manufacturers, 1947-49. Patron, SA Assoc. for Mental Health. *Recreations:* cricket, golf. *Address:* Swan Reach, SA 5354, Australia. *Club:* Naval, Military and Air Force (SA).

POPE-HENNESSY, Sir John (Wyndham), Kt 1971; CBE 1959 (MBE 1944); FBA 1955; FSA; FRSL; Consultative Chairman, Department of European Paintings, Metropolitan Museum, New York, since 1977; Professor of Fine Arts, New York University, since 1977; *b* 13 Dec. 1913; *er s* of late Major-General L. H. R. Pope-Hennessy, CB, DSO, and late Dame Una Pope-Hennessy, DBE. *Educ:* Downside School; Balliol Coll., Oxford. Joined staff of Victoria and Albert Museum, 1938. Served Air Ministry, 1939-45. Victoria and Albert Museum: Keeper, Dept of Architecture and Sculpture, 1954-66; Dir and Sec., 1967-73; Dir, British Museum, 1974-76. Slade Professor of Fine Art, Univ. of Oxford, 1956-57; Clark Professor of Art, Williams College, Mass., USA, 1961-62; Slade Professor of Fine Art, and Fellow of Peterhouse, University of Cambridge, 1964-65. Member: Arts Council, 1968-72; Ancient Momuments Bd for England, 1969-72; Dir, Royal Opera House, 1971-76. Corresponding Member: Accademia Senese degli Intronati; Bayerische Akademie der Wissenschaften; Hon. Academician, Accademia del Disegno, Florence; For. Mem., Amer. Philosophical Soc., 1974; Hon. Fellow, Pierpoint Morgan Library, 1975. Serena Medal of British Academy for Italian Studies, 1961; New York University Medal, 1965; Torch of Learning Award, Hebrew Univ., Jerusalem, 1977. Hon. LLD Aberdeen, 1972; Hon. Dr RCA, 1973. *Publications:* Giovanni di Paolo, 1937; Sassetta, 1939; Sienese Quattrocento Painting, 1947; A Sienese Codex of the Divine Comedy, 1947; The Drawings of Domenichino at Windsor Castle, 1948; A Lecture on Nicholas Hilliard, 1949; Donatello's Ascension, 1949; The Virgin with the Laughing Child, 1949; edition of the Autobiography of Benvenuto Cellini, 1949; Paolo Uccello, 1950, rev. edn, 1972; Italian Gothic Sculpture in the Victoria and Albert Museum, 1952; Fra Angelico, 1952, rev. edn, 1974; Italian Gothic Sculpture, 1955, rev. edn 1972; Italian Renaissance Sculpture, 1958, rev. edn 1971; Italian High Renaissance and Baroque Sculpture, 1963, rev. edn 1970; Catalogue of Italian Sculpture in the Victoria and Albert Museum, 1964; Renaissance Bronzes in the Kress Collection, 1965; The Portrait in the Renaissance, 1967; Essays on Italian Sculpture, 1968; Catalogue of Sculpture in the Frick Collection, 1970; Raphael (Wrightsman lectures), 1970; (with others) Westminster Abbey, 1972. Contributor, Burlington Magazine, etc. *Recreation:* music. *Address:* 1130 Park Avenue, New York, NY 10028, USA.

POPHAM, Margaret Evelyn, CBE 1953; Principal, Ladies' College, Cheltenham, Jan. 1937-July 1953; now nearly blind; *d* of Rev. B. G. Popham. *Educ:* Blackheath High School; Westfield College, London Univ., BA Hons Classics; Camb. Teachers Dip.; Ont. Teachers Certif. Classical Mistress Co. Sch., Chatham, 1919-23; Classical and Senior Mistress, Havergal College, Toronto, Canada, 1923-30; Headmistress: Ladies' College, Jersey, CI, 1930-32; Westonbirt School, 1932-37. Vice-Chm., Gabbitas-Thring Educational Trust, 1960-74; Member: Westfield College Council, 1935-66; Independent Television Authority, 1954-56; ITA Children's Committee, 1956-60; Individual Freedom Society (Executive), 1954-68 (now Vice-Pres.); Commonwealth Migration Council (Exec.), 1956-66; Conservative Commonwealth Coun., and Conservative Women's National Advisory Committee, 1954-57, and 1960-61; Canning House, 1955-65. South Kensington Conservative (Executive), 1958-62; European Union of Women (Executive), 1960-75; National Broadcasting Development Committee, 1961-63; formerly Mem., Governing Body of Girls' Sch. Exec. *Publication:* (memoirs) Boring—Never!, 1968. *Recreations:* literature and travelling; politics and Commonwealth questions. *Address:* 60 Stafford Court, W8 7DN. *T:* 01-937 2717. *Clubs:* Royal Commonwealth Society, Naval and Military.

POPJÁK, George Joseph, FRS 1961; DSc (London), MD, FRIC; Professor of Biochemistry at University of California in Los Angeles, since 1968; *b* 5 May 1914; *s* of late George and Maria Popják, Szeged, Hungary; *m* 1941, Hasel Marjorie, *d* of Duncan and Mabel Hammond, Beckenham, Kent. *Educ:* Royal Hungarian Francis Joseph University, Szeged. Demonstrator at

Department of Morbid Anatomy and Histology, University of Szeged, 1938-39; Br Council Scholar, Postgraduate Med. School of London, 1939-41; Demonstrator in Pathology, Dept of Pathology, St Thomas's Hosp. Med. School, London, 1941-43; Beit Mem. Fellow for medical research at St Thomas's Hosp. Med. School, London, 1943-47; Member scientific staff of Med. Research Council at Nat. Inst. for Med. Research, 1947-53; Director of Medical Research Council Experimental Radiopathology Research Unit, Hammersmith Hosp., 1953-62; Jt Dir, Chemical Enzymology Lab., Shell Res. Ltd, 1962-68; Assoc. Prof. in Molecular Sciences, Warwick Univ., 1965-68. Foreign member of Belgian Roy. Flemish Acad. of Science, Literature and Fine Arts, 1955; Hon. Member: Amer. Soc. of Biological Chemists, 1968; Alpha-Omega-Alpha, 1970; Mem., Amer. Acad. of Arts and Sciences, 1971. (With Dr J. W. Cornforth, FRS) CIBA Medal of Biochemical Soc., 1965 (first award); Stouffer Prize, 1967; Davy Medal, Royal Soc., 1968; Award in Lipid Chem., Amer. Oil Chem. Soc., 1977. *Publications:* Chemistry, Biochemistry and Isotopic Tracer Technique (Roy. Inst. of Chemistry monograph), 1955; articles on fat metabolism in Jl Path. Bact., Jl Physiol., Biochemical Jl, etc. *Recreations:* music, modelling and gardening. *Address:* Depts of Psychiatry and Biochemistry, University of California at Los Angeles, Center for the Health Sciences, Los Angeles, Calif 90024, USA.

POPLE, John Anthony, FRS 1961; John Christian Warner University Professor of Natural Sciences (formerly Professor of Chemical Physics), Carnegie-Mellon University, Pittsburgh, USA, since 1964; *b* 31 Oct. 1925; *e s* of Herbert Keith Pople and Mary Frances Jones, Burnham-on-Sea, Som.; *m* 1952, Joy Cynthia Bowers; three *s* one *d. Educ:* Bristol Grammar School; Cambridge University, MA, PhD. Mayhew Prize, 1948, Smith Prize, 1950, Cambridge; Fellow, Trinity College, 1951-58, Lecturer in Mathematics, 1954-58, Cambridge; Superintendent of Basic Physics Division, National Physical Laboratory, 1958-64. Marlow Medal, Faraday Society, 1958. Ford Visiting Professor, Carnegie Inst. of Technology, Pittsburgh, 1961-62. Fellow; Amer. Physical Soc., 1970; Amer. Acad. of Arts and Scis, 1971. For. Associate, Nat. Acad. of Sci., 1977. Awards from American Chemical Society: Langmuir, 1970; Harrison Howe, 1971; Gilbert Newton Lewis, 1973; Pittsburgh, 1975. *Publications:* High Resolution nuclear magnetic resonance, 1959; Approximate Molecular Orbital Theory, 1970; scientific papers on molecular physics and theoretical chemistry. *Recreations:* music, travel. *Address:* Carnegie-Mellon University, Pittsburgh, Pa 15213, USA.

POPONDETTA, Bishop of, since 1977; **Rt. Rev. George Somboba Ambo;** *b* Gona, Nov. 1925; *s* of late J. O. Ambo, Gona; *m* 1946, Marcella O., *d* of Karau; two *s* two *d. Educ:* St Aidan's College, Dogura; Newton Theological Coll., Dogura. Deacon, 1955; Priest, 1958. Curate of: Menapi, 1955-57; Dogura, 1957-58; Priest in charge of Boianai, Diocese of New Guinea, 1958-63; Missionary at Wamira, 1963-69; an Asst Bishop of Papua New Guinea, 1960 (first Papuan-born Anglican Bishop). *Publication:* St John's Gospel in Ewage. *Recreations:* reading, carpentry. *Address:* PO Box 26, Popondetta, Papua New Guinea.

POPPER, Prof. Sir Karl (Raimund), Kt 1965; PhD (Vienna), MA (New Zealand), DLit (London); FRS 1976; FBA 1958; Professor of Logic and Scientific Method in the University of London (London School of Economics and Political Science), 1949-69; Emeritus Professor, 1969; *b* Vienna, 28 July 1902; *s* of Dr Simon Siegmund Carl Popper, Barrister, of Vienna, and of Jenny Popper (*née* Schiff); *m* 1930, Josefine Anna Henninger; no *c. Educ:* University of Vienna. Senior Lecturer in Philosophy, Canterbury University College, Christchurch (Univ. of NZ), 1937-45; Reader in Logic in Univ. of London, 1945-48. William James Lecturer in Philosophy, Harvard Univ., 1950. Visiting Lecturer in Yale, Princeton, Chicago, and Emory Univs, 1950, 1956; Eleanor Rathbone Lectr, Bristol Univ., 1956; Fellow, Center for Advanced Study in the Behavioral Sciences, Stanford, Calif, 1956-57; Annual Philos. Lectr to Brit. Academy, 1960; Herbert Spencer Lectr, Oxford Univ., 1961 and 1973; Shearman Memorial Lectr, University Coll. London, 1961; Visiting Prof. of Philosophy, Univ. of California Berkeley, and Minnesota Center for Phil. of Science, 1962; Indiana University, and Farnum Lectr, Princeton Univ., 1963, Vis. Prof., Institute for Advanced Studies, Vienna, 1964. Arthur H. Compton Memorial Lectr, Washinton Univ., 1965; Vis. Prof., Denver University, 1966; Vis. Fellow, The Salk Institute for Biological Studies, 1966-67; Kenan Univ. Prof., Emory Univ., 1969; Jacob Ziskind Vis. Prof. in Philosophy and the History of Thought, Brandeis Univ., 1969; Romanes Lectr, Oxford, 1972; William Evans Vis. Prof., Otago, 1973; Vis. Erskine Fellow, Canterbury, NZ, 1973; Broadhead Meml Lectr, Canterbury, 1973; first Darwin Lectr, Darwin Coll., Cambridge, 1977. Member: Editorial Bd:

Foundations of Physics; British Jl Phil. of Science; Studi Internat. di Filosofia; Jl of Political Theory; Advisory Board: Medical Hypotheses; The Monist; Co-Editor: Ratio; Studies in the Foundations Methodology and Philosophy of Science; Methodology and Science; Rechtstheorie; Schriftenreihe Erfahrung und Denken; Library of Exact Philosophy; Ed. Correspond., Dialectica. Chairman, Phil. of Science Group, 1951-53; President The Aristotelian Soc., 1958-59; President British Society for the Phil. of Science, 1959-61; Mem. Council, Assoc. for Symb. Logic, 1951-55; corr. de l'Institut de France, 1974; Fellow, Internat. Acad. for Philos. of Science, 1948; Associate Mem., Acad. Royale de Belgique, 1976; Hon. Mem., RSNZ, 1965; Foreign Hon. Mem., American Acad. of Arts and Sciences, 1966; Hon. Member, Harvard Chapter of Phi Beta Kappa, 1964. Hon. Fellow, LSE, 1972. Hon. LLD Chicago and Denver; Hon. DLitt: Warwick; Canterbury, NZ; Salford; City. Prize of the City of Vienna for 'Geisteswissenschaften' (mental and moral sciences) 1965; James Scott Prize, RSE, 1970; Sonning Prize, 1973; Univ. of Copenhagen, 1973; Lippincott Award, Amer. Pol. Sci. Assoc., 1976. Grand Decoration of Honour in Gold (Austria), 1976. *Publications:* (trans into nineteen languages): Logik der Forschung, 1934, 1966, 6th edn 1976; The Open Society and Its Enemies, 1945, 5th edn, rev. 1966, 11th impr. 1977; The Poverty of Historicism, 1957, 9th impr. 1976; The Logic of Scientific Discovery, 1959, 9th impr. 1977; On the Sources of Knowledge and of Ignorance, 1961; Conjectures and Refutations, 1963, 6th impr. 1976; Of Clouds and Clocks, 1966; Objective Knowledge, 1972, 4th impr. 1975; Unended Quest: An Intellectual Autobiography, 1976, 3rd impr. 1977; (with Sir John Eccles) The Self and Its Brain, 1977; contribs to: learned jls; anthologies; Philosophy of Karl Popper; Library of Living Philosophers (ed P.A. Schilpp), 1974. *Recreation:* music. *Address:* Fallowfield, Manor Close, Manor Road, Penn, Buckinghamshire HP10 8HZ. *T:* Penn 2126.

POPPLEWELL, Oliver Bury, QC 1969; a Recorder of the Crown Court, since 1972; *b* 15 Aug. 1927; *s* of Frank and Nina Popplewell; *m* 1954, Catharine Margaret Storey; four *s* (and one *s* decd). *Educ:* Charterhouse (Schol.); Queens' Coll., Cambridge (Class. exhibnr). BA 1950; LLB 1951. CUCC, 1949-51. Called to the Bar, 1951. Recorder, Burton-on-Trent, 1970-71; Dep. Chm., Oxon QS, 1970-71. Chm. and Indep. Mem., Wages Councils; Mem. Cttee, MCC, 1971-74, 1976-. *Recreations:* sailing, cricket, tennis. *Address:* 2 Crown Office Row, Temple, EC4. *T:* 01-353 9337; Lime Tree Farm, Chartridge, Bucks. *T:* The Lee 356. *Clubs:* MCC; Hawks (Cambridge), Blakeney Sailing.

PORBANDAR, Maharaja of, Lt-Col HH Maharaja Rana Saheb, Shri Sir Natwarsinhji Bhavsinhji, KCSI 1929; *b* 30 June 1901; *s* of HH the Rana Saheb Shri Bhavsinhji Bahadur of Porbandar; *m* 1st, 1920, Princess Rupaliba, MBE (*d* 1943), *d* of late Thakore Saheb of Limbdi, KCSI, KCIE; 2nd, 1954, Anantkunver. *Educ:* Rajkumar College, Rajkot; stood first in the Diploma Examination of the Chiefs' Colleges in 1918. Offically received by HH the Pope, at the Vatican, 1922. Captained first All-India Cricket Team which toured England 1932. Orchestral works published: 42 compositions (as N. Porbandar). *Publications:* Introspect, 1950; Values Reviewed, 1952; Three Essays, 1954; From the Flow of Life, 1967; India's Problems, 1970. *Recreations:* music, painting and writing. *Address:* Porbandar, Saurashtra, India; Firgrove, Ootacamund, S India.

PORCHER, Michael Somerville, CMG 1962; OBE 1960; Secretary (Operations Division), Royal National Life-Boat Institution, since 1964; *b* 9 March 1921; *s* of late Geoffrey Lionel Porcher and Marjorie Fownes Porcher (*née* Somerville); *m* 1955, Mary Lorraine Porcher (*née* Tweedy); two *s. Educ:* Cheltenham College; St Edmund Hall, Oxford. Military Service, 1941-42. Joined Colonial Admin. Service: Sierra Leone; Cadet, 1942; Asst Dist, Comr, 1945; Dist Comr, 1951; British Guiana: Dep. Colonial Sec., 1952; Governor's Sec. and Clerk Exec. Council, 1953; Dep. Chief Sec., 1956. British Honduras: Colonial Secretary, 1960; Chief Secretary, 1961; retired, 1964. *Recreations:* fishing, shooting, sailing, riding. *Address:* Bladon, Worth Matravers, near Swanage, Dorset.

PORCHESTER, Lord; Henry George Reginald Molyneux Herbert, KBE 1976; DL; *b* 19 Jan. 1924; *o s* of 6th Earl of Carnarvon, *qv*; *m* 1956, Jean Margaret, *e d* of Hon. Oliver Wallop, Big Horn, Sheridan Co., Wyoming, USA; two *s* one *d.* Late Lieut RHG; retired pay, 1947. Hon Col, Hampshire Fortress Regt, RE (TA) 1963-67, retaining rank of Hon. Col. Racing Manager to the Queen, 1969-. Chm., South East Economic Planning Council, 1971-. Chairman: Game Research Assoc., 1960-67 (Vice-Pres., 1967-); Stallion Adv. Cttee to Betting Levy Bd, 1974-; Pres., Thoroughbred Breeders' Assoc., 1969-74 (Chm. 1964-66). Member: Hampshire Agriculture

Exec. Cttee, 1955-65; Nature Conservancy, 1963-66; Sports Council, 1965-70 (Chm., Planning Cttee, 1965-70); Forestry Commission, 1967-70; President: Amateur Riders' Assoc., 1969-75; Hampshire County Cricket Club, 1966-68; Mem., Jockey Club, 1964- (Chm., Race Planning Cttee, 1967-). CC Hants, 1954; County Alderman, 1965-74; Vice-Chm. County Council, 1971-74, Chm., New County Council, 1973-77; Vice-Chm., CC Assoc., 1972-74 (Chm. Planning Cttee, 1968-74); Member: Basingstoke Town Develt Jt Cttee, 1960-73; Andover Town Develt Jt Cttee, 1960-65. Verderer of the New Forest, 1961-65. DL Hants 1965. *Address:* Milford Lake House, Burghclere, Newbury, Berks RG16 9EL. *T:* Highclere 253387. *Clubs:* White's, Portland.
See also Earl of Portsmouth.

PORRITT, family name of **Baron Porritt.**

PORRITT, Baron *cr* 1973 (Life Peer), of Wanganui, NZ, and of Hampstead; **Arthur Espie Porritt,** GCMG 1967 (KCMG 1950); GCVO 1970 (KCVO 1957); CBE 1945 (OBE 1943); Bt 1963; Chairman: African Medical and Research Foundation, since 1973; Arthritis and Rheumatism Council, since 1973; Royal Masonic Hospital, since 1973; *b* 10 Aug. 1900; *e s* of late E. E. Porritt, VD, MD, FRCS, Wanganui, New Zealand; *m* 1st, 1926, Mary Frances Wynne, *d* of William Bond; 2nd, 1946, Kathleen Mary, 2nd *d* of late A. S. Peck and of Mrs Windley, Spalding, Lincs; two *s* one *d. Educ:* Wanganui Collegiate School, NZ; Otago University, NZ; Magdalen College, Oxford (Rhodes Scholar); St Mary's Hospital, London. MA Oxon.; MCh Oxon. Surgeon: St Mary's Hosp.; Hosp. of St John and St Elizabeth; King Edward VII Hosp. for Officers; Royal Masonic Hosp.; Consulting Surgeon: Princess Louise Kensington Hosp. for Children; Paddington Hosps; Royal Chelsea Hosp.; Civil Consulting Surgeon to the Army, 1954-67, Emeritus, 1971; Brigadier, RAMC, 21 Army Group; Surgeon-in-Ordinary to the Duke of York; Surgeon to HM Household; a Surgeon to King George VI, 1946-52; Sergeant-Surgeon to the Queen, 1952-67; Governor-General of New Zealand, 1967-72. Dir, Sterling Winthrop and Sterling Europa. Chairman: Medical Advisory Cttee, Ministry of Overseas Develt; Medical Services Review Cttee, 1958; Red Cross Comr for NZ in UK; Chapter-Gen., Order of St John; Hunterian Soc., 1934-39 (Past Pres.); President: RCS, 1960-63; BMA, 1960-61; RSM, 1966-67; Assoc. of Surgeons of Gt Britain and Ireland; Med. Council on Alcoholism; Med. Commn on Accident Prevention; Company of Veteran Motorists; Past Master, Soc. of Apothecaries, 1964-66; Vice-Pres., Royal Commonwealth Soc.; Pres., OUAC, 1925-26; holder of 100 yards and 220 yards hurdles records at Oxford and 100 yards Oxford v. Cambridge (9 9/10 seconds); represented Oxford in Athletics, 1923-26; Finalist, Olympic 100 metres (Bronze Medallist), Paris, 1924; Captain NZ Olympic Team, Paris, 1924, Amsterdam, 1928, Manager Berlin, 1936; Mem., Internat. Olympic Cttee, British Olympic Council; Vice-Pres., British Empire and Commonwealth Games Federation. FRCS (Eng.); Fellow: Amer. Surgical Assoc.; Amer. Soc. of Clinical Surgery; French Acad. of Surgery; Hon. FRACS; Hon. FRCS (Ed.); Hon. FACS; Hon. FRCS (Glas.); Hon. FRCS (Can.); Hon. FCS (SAf); Hon. FRCS (I); Hon. FRCP; Hon. FRACP; Hon FRCOG; Hon. Fellow, Magdalen College, Oxford, 1961. BMA Gold Medal, 1964. Hon. LLD: St Andrews; Birmingham; New Zealand; Otago. Hon. MD Bristol; Hon. DSc Oxon. Legion of Merit (USA); KStJ. *Publications:* Athletics (with D. G. A. Lowe), 1929; Essentials of Modern Surgery (with R. M. Handfield-Jones), 1938, 6th edn 1956; various surgical articles in medical jls. *Recreations:* riding, golf, swimming; formerly athletics and Rugby football. *Heir* (to baronetcy only): *s* Hon. Jonathon Espie Porritt, *b* 6 July 1950. *Address:* 57 Hamilton Terrace, NW8. *Club:* Buck's.

PORT ELIZABETH, Bishop of, since 1975; **Rt. Rev. Bruce Read Evans;** *b* 10 Nov. 1929; *s* of Roy Leslie and Lilia Evans; *m* 1955, Joan Vanda Erlangsen; two *s* one *d. Educ:* King Edward Sch., Johannesburg; Univ. of the Witwatersrand, Johannesburg; Oak Hill Theological Coll., London. ACIS 1952; director of companies, 1952-54. Ordained into CofE, Southwark, 1957; Curate, Holy Trinity, Redhill, Surrey, 1957-59; Senior Curate, St Paul's, Portman Square, W1, and Chaplain to West End Business Houses in London, 1959-61; Curate-in-Charge: St Luke's, Diep River, Cape, 1962; Christ Church, Kenilworth, Cape, 1963-69; Rector of St John's, Wynberg, Cape, 1969-75. *Recreations:* formerly boxing and hockey; now painting. *Address:* Bishop's House, 14 Buckingham Road, Port Elizabeth 6001, South Africa. *T:* 33-1949. *Clubs:* Port Elizabeth, Rotary (Port Elizabeth).

PORT ELIZABETH, Assistant Bishop of; *see* Cowdry, Rt Rev. R. W. F.

PORT OF SPAIN, Archbishop of, since 1968; **Most Rev. Anthony Pantin,** CSSp; *b* 27 Aug. 1929; *s* of Julian and Agnes Pantin, both of Trinidad. *Educ:* Sacred Heart Private Sch., Belmont Boys' Intermediate Sch., St Mary's Coll., Port of Spain; Seminary of Philosophy, Montreal; Holy Ghost Missionary Coll., Dublin. Ordained Dublin, 1955; Guadeloupe, French West Indies, 1956-59; Fatima College, Port of Spain, 1959-64; Superior, St Mary's Coll., Port of Spain, 1965-68. Mem., Vatican Secretariat for Christian Unity, 1971-. *Address:* Archbishop's House, 27 Maraval Road, Port of Spain, Trinidad. *T:* 21103.

PORTAL, family name of **Baroness Portal of Hungerford.**

PORTAL OF HUNGERFORD, Baroness (2nd in line), *cr* 1945; **Rosemary Ann Portal;** *b* 12 May 1923; *d* of 1st Viscount Portal of Hungerford, KG, GCB, OM, DSO, MC, and Joan Margaret, *y d* of Sir Charles Glynn Welby, 5th Bt; *S* to barony of father, 1971. Formerly Section Officer, WAAF. *Heir: sister* Hon. Mavis Elizabeth Alouette Portal, *b* 13 June 1926. *Address:* West Ashling House, Chichester, West Sussex.

PORTAL, Sir Francis Spencer, 5th Bt, *cr* 1901; DL; President, Portals Holdings Ltd; *b* 27 June 1903; *s* of 4th Bt and late Mary, *d* of late Colonel William Mure, Caldwell, Ayrshire; *S* father, 1955; *m* 1st, 1930, Rowena (*d* 1948), *d* of late Paul Selby, Johannesburg; two *d*; 2nd, 1950, Jane Mary, *d* of late Albert Henry Williams, OBE, Flint House, Langston, Havant, Hants, and of Mrs E. G. Selwyn, The Quinton, Shawford, Hants; two *s* one *d. Educ:* Winchester; Christ Church, Oxford; McGill Univ., Montreal. Served War of 1939-45, Captain, late Welsh Guards, Guards Armoured Division (Croix de Guerre, 2nd Class Belgium). Chm., YMCA Nat. Commn, 1968; Mem., Bishop's Council, Diocese of Winchester. Master, Worshipful Co. of Clothworkers, 1970. High Sheriff of Hampshire, 1963, DL Hants, 1967-. *Recreations:* miscellaneous. *Heir: s* Jonathan Francis Portal, *b* 13 Jan. 1953. *Address:* Burley Wood, Ashe, near Basingstoke, Hants RG25 3AG. *T:* Basingstoke 770269.

PORTAL, Admiral Sir Reginald Henry, KCB, *cr* 1949 (CB 1946); DSC 1916; *b* 6 Sept. 1894; *s* of late Edward Robert Portal, JP; DL; *m* 1926, Helen, *d* of late Frederick Anderson; two *s* two *d.* Served European War, 1914-19, with RN and RNAS (DSC); War of 1939-45 (despatches, CB); comd HMS York, 1939-41; HMS Royal Sovereign, 1941-42; Asst Chief of Naval Staff (Air), 1943-44; ADC to the King, 1943; Flag Officer Naval Air Stations (Australia), 1945; Naval representative on Joint Chiefs of Staff Cttee (Australia), 1946-47; Flag Officer, Air (Home), 1947-51; retired, 1951. *Address:* Savernake, Marlborough, Wilts.

PORTARLINGTON, 7th Earl of, *cr* 1785; **George Lionel Yuill Seymour Dawson-Damer;** Baron Dawson 1770; Viscount Carlow 1776; *b* 10 Aug. 1938; *er s* of Air Commodore Viscount Carlow (killed on active service, 1944) and Peggy (who *m* 2nd, 1945, Peter Nugent; she *d* 1963), *yr d* of late Charles Cambie; *S* grandfather, 1959; *m* 1961, Davina, *e d* of Sir Edward Windley, KCMG, KCVO; three *s* one *d. Educ:* Eton. Page of Honour to the Queen, 1953-55. Director: G. S. Yuill & Co. Ltd, Sydney, 1964; Cold Storage Holdings Ltd, London, 1965; Queensland Trading Holding Co. Ltd, Brisbane, 1967; Australian Stock Breeders Co. Ltd, Brisbane, 1966. *Heir: s* Viscount Carlow, *qv. Recreations:* fishing, ski-ing, books. *Address:* 19 Coolong Road, Vaucluse, NSW 2030, Australia. *T:* Sydney 337-3013. *Club:* Union (Sydney).

PORTEOUS, Alexander James Dow, MA; Sydney Jones Professor of Education, University of Liverpool, 1954-63 (Professor of Education, 1938-54); retired Sept. 1963, now Professor Emeritus; Temporary Professor of Moral Philosophy, University of Edinburgh, 1963-64; *b* 22 July 1896; *s* of late John Dow Porteous, MA, former Rector of Knox Memorial Institute, Haddington, and Agnes Paton Walker; *m* 1926, Eliza Murray Dalziel (*d* 1972), MA (Hons Edinburgh), *e d* of late George Ross, Solicitor, Inverness; three *s* two *d* (and one *s* decd). *Educ:* Knox Memorial Institute, Haddington; Universities of Edinburgh and Oxford (Bible Clerk, Oriel College); Moray House Provincial Training College for Teachers, Edinburgh. Served in Army 1916-19, first with the Royal Scots; gazetted 2nd Lieut to the Royal Scots Fusiliers June 1918 and spent seven months on active service in France with the 11th Battalion; MA (Edinburgh) with First Class Honours in Classics, 1921 (Rhind Classical Scholarship, 1920, Guthrie Classical Fellowship, 1922); Ferguson Scholar in Classics, 1922; First Class in Literae Humaniores, Oxford, 1923; MA 1928; First Class Honours in Mental Philosophy (after Graduation) at Edinburgh University, and Diploma in Education, 1924; Shaw Fellow in Mental Philosophy in the University of Edinburgh, 1924-29; Assistant Lecturer in the Department of Logic and Metaphysics,

Edinburgh University, 1924-26; Professor of Philosophy at Smith College, Northampton, Mass., USA, 1926-30; Associate Professor of Moral Philosophy, McGill University, Montreal, Canada, 1930-31; Professor, 1931-32; Lecturer in Ancient Philosophy, Edinburgh University, 1932-37; Reader, 1937-38. *Publications:* reviews and papers in philosophical journals. *Recreations:* swimming, golf. *Address:* 8 Osmaston Road, Prenton, Birkenhead, Merseyside. *T:* 051-608 3749. *Club:* Athenæum (Liverpool).

PORTEOUS, Christopher, MA; Headmaster of Eltham College, since 1959; *b* 2 April 1921; *e s* of late Rev. Gilbert Porteous; *m* 1944, Amy Clunis, *d* of Theodore J. Biggs; one *s* three *d. Educ:* Nottingham High Sch. (Foundation Scholar); Emmanuel Coll., Cambridge (Senior Scholar). First Classes, with distinction, in Classical Tripos. Master of Classical Sixth, Mill Hill Sch., 1947-55; Asst Director, HM Civil Service Commission, 1955-59. *Recreations:* travel, the countryside. *Address:* Headmaster's House, Eltham College, SE9.

PORTEOUS, Rev. Norman Walker, MA Edinburgh et Oxon, BD Edinburgh, DD St Andrews; *b* Haddington, 9 Sept. 1898; *yr s* of late John Dow Porteous, MA, formerly Rector of Knox Memorial Inst, Haddington, and Agnes Paton Walker; *m* 1929, May Hadwen, *y d* of late John Cook Robertson, Kirkcaldy; three *s* three *d. Educ:* Knox Memorial Institute, Haddington; Universities of Edinburgh, Oxford (Trinity College), Berlin, Tübingen and Münster; New Coll., Edinburgh. MA Edinburgh with 1st Class Honours in Classics; MA Oxon with 1st Class in Literæ Humaniores; BD Edinburgh with distinction in Old Testament; 1st Bursar at Edinburgh University, 1916; C. B. Black Scholar in New Testament Greek, 1920; John Edward Baxter Scholar in Classics, 1923; Ferguson Scholar in Classics, 1923; Senior Cunningham Fellow at New College and Kerr Travelling Scholar, 1927; served in army, 1917-19, commissioned 2nd Lieut, March 1918, served overseas with 13th Royal Scots; Ordained to Ministry of United Free Church of Scotland, 1929; Minister of Crossgates Church, 1929-31; Regius Professor of Hebrew and Oriental Languages in the University of St Andrews, 1931-35; Professor of Old Testament Language, Literature and Theology in the University of Edinburgh, 1935-37; Prof. of Hebrew and Semitic Languages, Univ. of Edinburgh, 1937-68; Principal of New Coll., and Dean of Faculty of Divinity, Univ. of Edinburgh, 1964-68; retd, 1968; now Emeritus Professor. Hon. DD St Andrews, 1944; Lectures: Stone, Princeton Theological Seminary, 1953; Montague Burton, Leeds, 1974. President, Soc. for Old Testament Study, 1954. *Publications:* Das Alte Testament Deutsch 23: Das Danielbuch 1962 (English edition, 1965); Living the Mystery: Collected Essays, 1967; Old Testament and History, 5 lectures in Annual of Swedish Theological Inst., vol. VIII, 1970-71; contributions to: Theologische Aufsätze Karl Barth zum 50 Geburtstag, 1936; Record and Revelation, 1938; The Old Testament and Modern Study, 1951; Peake's Commentary on the Bible, 1962. *Address:* 3 Hermitage Gardens, Edinburgh EH10 6DL. *T:* 031-447 4632.

PORTEOUS, Colonel Patrick Anthony, VC 1942; RA, retired 1970; *b* 1 Jan. 1918; *s* of late Brig.-General C. McL. Porteous, 9th Ghurkas, and late Mrs Porteous, Fleet, Hampshire; *m* 1943, Lois Mary (*d* 1953), *d* of late Maj.-General Sir H. E. Roome, KCIE; one *s* one *d; m* 1955, Deirdre, *d* of late Eric King; three *d. Educ:* Wellington Coll.; Royal Military Acad., Woolwich. BEF France, Sept. 1939-May 1940, with 6th AA Regt, RA; Dieppe, Aug. 1942 (VC); No 4 Commando, Dec. 1940-Oct. 1944; BLA June-Sept. 1944; 1st Airborne Div. Dec. 1944-July 1945; 6th Airborne Div., July 1945-March 1946; Staff Coll., Camberley, May-Nov. 1946; 16 Airborne Div. TA, Jan. 1947-Feb. 1948; 33 Airborne Lt Regt, RA, Feb. 1948-April 1949; No 1 Regular Commission Board, 1949; Instructor, RMA, Sandhurst, July 1950-July 1953; GHQ, Far East Land Forces, Singapore, Sept. 1953-July 1955; 1st Singapore Regt, RA, July-Dec. 1955; 14 Field Regt, RA, 1956-58; RAF Staff Coll., Jan. 1958-Dec. 1958; AMS, HQ Southern Comd, 1959-60; Colonel Junior Leaders Regt, RA, 1960-63; Colonel, General Staff War Office, later Ministry of Defence, 1963-66; Comdr Rheindahlen Garrison, 1966-69. *Recreation:* sailing. *Address:* Flat 1, Binderton House, Lavant, near Chichester, West Sussex.

PORTER, Alastair Robert Wilson; Secretary and Registrar, Royal College of Veterinary Surgeons, since 1966; barrister; *b* 28 Sept. 1928; *s* of late James and Olivia Porter (*née* Duncan); *m* 1954, Jennifer Mary Priaulx Forman; two *s* one *d. Educ:* Irvine Royal Academy; Glasgow Academy; Merton Coll., Oxford (MA). Called to Bar, Gray's Inn, 1952. Resident Magistrate, N Rhodesia, 1954; Registrar of High Court of N Rhodesia, 1961; Permanent Secretary: Min. of Justice, N Rhodesia, 1964; Min. of Justice, Govt of Republic of Zambia, Oct. 1964. Secretary-Gen.,

Fedn (formerly Liaison Cttee) of Veterinarians of the EEC, 1973-. *Publications:* Magistrates' Handbook, 1964 (N Rhodesia); An Anatomy of Veterinary Europe (with others), 1972; contributor to Veterinary Annual, 1970-76; papers on aspects of veterinary jurisprudence and implications of membership of EEC (for veterinary profession) in Veterinary Record and other veterinary jls. *Recreations:* squash, tennis, swimming. *Address:* 4 Savill Road, Lindfield, West Sussex. *T:* Lindfield 2001. *Club:* Caledonian.

PORTER, Alfred Ernest, CSI 1947; CIE 1942; *b* 2 Nov. 1896; *s* of F. L. Porter; *m* 1929, Nancy Florence (decd), *d* of late E. L. Melly; two *s. Educ:* Manchester Grammar Sch.; Corpus Christi Coll., Oxford. Manchester Regt, 1915; Machine Gun Corps, 1916; Indian Civil Service, 1922-48. *Address:* The Old Hall, Chawleigh, Chulmleigh, Devon EX18 7HH. *T:* Chulmleigh 280.

PORTER, Sir Andrew M. H.; *see* Horsbrugh-Porter.

PORTER, Prof. Arthur, MSc, PhD (Manchester); FIEE; FRSC 1970; Professor of Industrial Engineering, and Chairman of Department, University of Toronto, Toronto, 1961-76, now Emeritus Professor; *b* 8 Dec. 1910; *s* of late John William Porter and Mary Anne Harris; *m* 1941, Phyllis Patricia Dixon; one *s. Educ:* The Grammar Sch., Ulverston; University of Manchester. Asst Lecturer, University of Manchester, 1936-37; Commonwealth Fund Fellow, Massachusetts Inst. of Technology, USA, 1937-39; Scientific Officer, Admiralty, 1939-45; Principal Scientific Officer, National Physical Laboratory, 1946; Prof. of Instrument Technology, Royal Military Coll. of Science, 1946-49; Head, Research Division, Ferranti Electric Ltd, Toronto, Canada, 1949-55; Professor of Light Electrical Engineering, Imperial College of Science and Technology, University of London, 1955-58; Dean of the College of Engineering, Saskatchewan Univ., Saskatoon, 1958; Acting Dir, Centre for Culture and Technology, Toronto Univ., 1967-68; Academic Comr, Univ. of W Ontario, 1969-71. Chairman: Canadian Environmental Adv. Council, 1972-75; Ontario Royal Commn on Electric Power Planning, 1975-. *Publications:* An Introduction to Servomechanisms, 1950; Cybernetics Simplified, 1969; Towards a Community University, 1971; articles in Trans. Royal Society, Proc. Royal Society, Phil. Mag., Proc. Inst. Mech. Eng, Proc. IEE, Nature, etc. *Recreations:* landscape architecture, energy conservation. *Address:* Watendlath, Belfountain, Ontario L0N 1B0, Canada. *T:* (519) 927-5323; Royal Commission on Electric Power Planning, 14 Carlton Street, Toronto, Ont M5B 1K5, Canada. *Clubs:* Arts and Letters, Royal Canadian Yacht (both Toronto).

PORTER, Arthur Thomas, MA, PhD; Vice-Chancellor, University of Sierra Leone, Freetown, Sierra Leone, since 1974; *b* 26 Jan. 1924; *m* 1953, Rigmor Sondergaard (*née* Rasmussen); one *s* one *d. Educ:* Fourah Bay Coll. (BA Dunelm); Cambridge Univ. (BA (Hist Tripos), MA); Boston Univ. (PhD). Asst. Dept of Social Anthropology, Edinburgh Univ., UK, 1951-52. Prof. of History and Head of Dept of Hist., also Dir of Inst. of African Studies, Fourah Bay Coll., 1963-64; Principal, University Coll., Nairobi, Univ. of E Africa, 1964-70; UNESCO Field Staff Officer; Educl Planning Adviser, Min. of Educn, Kenya, 1970-74. Hon. LHD Boston 1969; Hon. LLD Royal Univ. of Malta 1969. Phi Beta Kappa 1972. *Publications:* Creoledom, a Study of the Development of Freetown Society, 1963; contribs to The Times, Africa, African Affairs. *Recreation:* photography. *Address:* University of Sierra Leone, Private Mail Bag, Freetown, Sierra Leone, West Africa. *T:* 26859.

PORTER, Rt. Rev. David Brownfield; *b* 10 May 1906; *s* of Sydney Lawrence Porter and Edith Alice Porter; *m* 1936, Violet Margaret Eliot (*d* 1956); one *s*; *m* 1961, Mrs Pamela Cecil (*née* Lightfoot) (*d* 1974), *widow* of Neil McNeill. *Educ:* Hertford Coll., Oxford. Curate of St Augustine's, Leeds, 1929; Tutor of Wycliffe Hall, Oxford, 1931; Chaplain, 1933; Chaplain of Wadham Coll., Oxford, 1934; Vicar of All Saints', Highfield, Oxford, 1935; Vicar of Darlington, 1943; Rector of St John's, Princes Street, Edinburgh, 1947-61; Dean of Edinburgh, 1954-61; Bishop Suffragan of Aston, 1962-72. Select Preacher, Oxford Univ., 1964. *Recreations:* fishing and painting. *Address:* Silver Leys, Brockhampton, near Cheltenham.

PORTER, Dorothea Noelle Naomi, (Thea Porter); Managing Director, Thea Porter Decorations Ltd, since 1967; *b* 24 Dec. 1927; *d* of Rev. Dr M. S. Seale and Renée Seale; *m* 1953, Robert S. Porter (marr. diss. 1967); one *d. Educ:* Lycée français, Damascus; Fernhill Manor; Royal Holloway Coll., London Univ. Embassy wife, Beirut; painter; designer of interiors, clothes and fabrics, 1964-. *Recreations:* cooking, travelling, collecting antique Islamic fabrics and objets; consulting clairvoyants. *Address:* (shop) 8 Greek Street, W1. *T:* 01-437 0781. *Club:* Colony Room.

PORTER, Eric (Richard); actor; *b* London, 8 April 1928; *s* of Richard John Porter and Phoebe Elizabeth (*née* Spall). *Educ:* LCC and Wimbledon Technical College. First professional appearance with Shakespeare Memorial Theatre Company, Arts, Cambridge, 1945; first appearance on London stage as Dunois' Page in Saint Joan with the travelling repertory company, King's, Hammersmith, 1946; Birmingham Repertory Theatre, 1948-50; under contract to H. M. Tennant, Ltd, 1951-53. *Plays include:* The Silver Box, Lyric, Hammersmith, 1951; The Three Sisters, Aldwych, 1951; Thor, With Angels, Lyric, Hammersmith, 1951; title role in Noah, Whitehall, 1951; The Same Sky, Lyric, Hammersmith, 1952; Under the Sycamore Tree, Aldwych, 1952; season at Lyric, Hammersmith, directed by John Gielgud, 1953-plays: Richard II, The Way of the World, Venice Preserved; with Bristol Old Vic Company, 1954, and again 1955-56; parts included title roles in King Lear, Uncle Vanya, Volpone; with Old Vic Company, 1954-55: parts included Jacques in As You Like It, title role in Henry IV, Bolingbroke in Richard II, Christopher Sly in The Taming of the Shrew; Romanoff and Juliet, Piccadilly, 1956; A Man of Distinction, Edinburgh Festival and Princes, 1957; Time and Again, British tour with the Lunts, 1957, and New York in The Visit, 1958; The Coast of Coromandel, English tour, 1959; Rosmersholm, Royal Court, 1959, Comedy, 1960. (Evening Standard Drama Award as Best Actor of 1959); under contract to Royal Shakespeare Company, 1960-65; parts: Malvolio in Twelfth Night, Stratford, 1960, Aldwych, 1961; Duke in The Two Gentlemen of Verona, Stratford, 1960; Leontes in The Winter's Tale, Stratford, 1960; Ulysses in Troilus and Cressida, Stratford, 1960; Ferdinand in The Duchess of Malfi, Stratford, 1960, Aldwych, 1961; Lord Chamberlain in Ondine, Aldwych, 1961; Buckingham in Richard III, Stratford, 1961; title role in Becket, Aldwych, 1961, Globe, 1962; title role in Macbeth, Stratford, 1962; Iachimo in Cymbeline, Stratford, 1962; Pope Pius XII in The Representative, Aldwych, 1963. Stratford Season, 1964; Bolingbroke in Richard II; Henry IV in Henry IV Parts I and II; Chorus in Henry V; Richmond in Richard III; Stratford Season, 1965: Barabas in The Jew of Malta; Shylock in The Merchant of Venice; Chorus in Henry V, Aldwych, 1965; Ossip in The Government Inspector, Aldwych, 1966; Stratford Season, 1968; Lear in King Lear; Faustus in Dr Faustus (US tour, 1969); Paul Thomsen in My Little Boy-My Big Girl (also directed), Fortune, 1969; The Protagonist, Brighton, 1971; Peter Pan, Coliseum, 1971; Malvolio, inaugural season, St George's Elizabethan Theatre, 1976. *Films:* The Fall of the Roman Empire, 1964; The Pumpkin Eater, 1964; The Heroes of Telemark, 1965; Kaleidoscope, 1966; The Lost Continent, 1968; Hands of the Ripper, Nicholas and Alexandra, Antony and Cleopatra, 1971; Hitler: the last ten days, 1973; The Day of the Jackal, 1973; The Belstone Fox, 1973; Callan, 1974; Hennessy, 1975. Has also appeared many times on television, including Soames Forsyte in The Forsyte Saga, BBC (Best Actor Award, Guild of TV Producers and Directors, 1967), and Karenin, in Anna Karenina, BBC, 1977. *Recreations:* walking, swimming. *Address:* c/o London Management, 235 Regent Street, W1R 7AG. *Club:* Buckstone.

PORTER, Prof. Sir George, Kt 1972; FRS 1960; BSc (Leeds); MA, PhD, ScD, (Cambridge); FRIC; Director of the Royal Institution of Great Britain, and Fullerian Professor of Chemistry, since 1966; Honorary Professor of Physical Chemistry, University of Kent at Canterbury, since 1966; Visiting Professor, Department of Chemistry, University College, London, since 1967; *b* 6 Dec. 1920; *o s* of late John Smith Porter and of Alice Ann Porter, Stainforth, Yorks; *m* 1949, Stella Jean Brooke, *o d* of late G. A. Brooke, Leeds, Kent, and late Mrs J. Brooke; two *s*. *Educ:* Thorne Grammar Sch,.; Leeds Univ.; Emmanuel Coll., Cambridge. Ackroyd Scholar, Leeds Univ., 1938-41. Served RNVR in Western Approaches and Mediterranean, 1941-45. Cambridge: Demonstrator in Physical Chemistry, 1949-52, Fellow of Emmanuel Coll., 1952-54; Hon. Fellow, 1967; Asst Director of Research in Physical Chemistry, 1952-54. Asst Director of British Rayon Research Assoc., 1954-55. Prof. of Physical Chemistry, 1955-63, Firth Prof. of Chemistry, 1963-66, Univ. of Sheffield; Prof. of Chemistry, Royal Institution, 1963-66. Member: various cttees of DSIR and SRC, 1962-68; ARC, 1964-66; Open Univ. Council, 1969-75; Science Mus. Adv. Council, 1970-73; Council and Science Bd, SRC, 1976-; President: Chemical Soc., 1970-72 (Pres. Faraday Div., 1973-74); Comité Internat. de photobiologie, 1968-72; Nat. Assoc. for Gifted Children, 1975-; Hon. Member: NY Acad. of Sciences, 1968; Leopoldina Acad., 1970; For. Associate, Nat. Acad. of Sciences, 1974; Corresp. Mem., Göttingen Acad. of Sciences, 1974; Mem. Pontifical Acad. of Sciences, 1974. Lectures: Tilden, 1958; Remsen Meml, Amer. Chem. Soc., 1962; Liversidge, 1970; Theodor Förster Meml, 1975; Geoffrey Frew, Aust. Acad. of Sci. (also Geoffrey Frew Fellow), 1976; Robbins, USA, 1976; Pahlavi, Iran, 1977.

Trustee, British Museum, 1972-74. Hon. Fellow, Inst. of Patentees and Inventors, 1970; Hon DSc: Utah, 1968; Sheffield, 1968; East Anglia, 1970; Durham, 1970; Leeds, 1971; Leicester, 1971; Heriot-Watt, 1971; City, 1971; Manchester, 1972; St Andrews, 1972; London, 1972; Kent, 1973; Oxon, 1974; DUniv. Surrey, 1970. Fairchild Dist. Scholar, California Inst. of Technology, 1974. Corday-Morgan Medal, Chem. Soc., 1955; Nobel Prize (Jt) for Chemistry, 1967; Silvanus Thompson Medal, 1969; Davy Medal of Royal Soc., 1971; Kalinga Prize, 1977. *Publications:* Chemistry for the Modern World, 1962; scientific papers in Proc. Royal Society, Trans. Faraday Society, etc. TV Series: Laws of Disorder, 1965-66; Time Machines, 1969-70; Natural History of a Sunbeam, 1976-77. *Recreation:* sailing. *Address:* The Royal Institution, 21 Albemarle Street, W1X 4BS. *T:* 01-409 2992. *Club:* Athenæum.

PORTER, Prof. Helen Kemp, FRS 1956; DSc; FRIC; Emeritus Professor, University of London; Hon. Fellow, Bedford College, since 1975; Scientific Adviser to the Secretary, Agricultural Research Council, 1971-72, retired (Second Secretary, 1969-71); Fellow, Imperial College of Science and Technology, 1966; *b* 10 Nov. 1899; *d* of George Kemp Archbold and Caroline E. B. Archbold (*née* Whitehead); *m* 1937, William George Porter, MD, MRCP (decd); *m* 1962, Arthur St George Huggett, FRS, DSc, MB, BS (*d* 1968). *Educ:* Clifton High School for Girls, Bristol; University of London, Research Assistant, Food Investigation Board, 1922-32; DSc London, 1932. On staff of Research Institute of Plant Physiology, Imperial Coll., 1932-59; Reader in Enzymology, University of London, Imperial College of Science and Technology, 1957-59; Prof. of Plant Physiology, Imperial Coll. of Science and Technology, London Univ., 1959-64; Dir, ARC Unit of Plant Physiology, 1959-64. Hon. ARCS 1964. *Publications:* contributions to Annals of Botany, Biochemical Journal, Journal of Experimental Botany, etc. *Recreation:* needlework. *Address:* 49e Beaumont Street, W1N 1RE. *T:* 01-935 5862.

PORTER, Ivor Forsyth, CMG 1963; OBE 1944; HM Diplomatic Service, retired; now Director, Atlantic Region, Research Department, Foreign and Commonwealth Office; *b* 12 Nov. 1913; *s* of Herbert and Evelyn Porter; *m* 1951, Ann, *o d* of late Dr John Speares (marr. diss., 1961); *m* 1961, Katerina, *o c* of A. T. Cholerton; one *s* one *d*. *Educ:* Barrow Grammar Sch.; Leeds Univ. (BA, PhD). Lecturer at Bucharest Univ., 1939-40; Temp. Secretary, at Bucharest Legation, 1940-41; Raiding Forces, 1941-45 (Major). Joined Foreign (subseq. Diplomatic) Service, May 1946, as 2nd Secretary in Sen. Branch; 1st Secretary 1948; transferred to Washington, 1951; Foreign Office, 1953; UK Delegation to NATO Paris as Counsellor and Head of Chancery, 1956; Nicosia, 1959 (Deputy Head UK Mission), Deputy High Commissioner, 1961-62; Cyprus; Permanent Rep. to Council of Europe, Strasbourg, 1962-65 (with personal rank of Minister); Dep. High Commissioner, Eastern India, 1965-66; Ambassador, UK Delegn to Geneva Disarmament Conf., 1968-71 (Minister, 1967-68); Ambassador to Senegal, Guinea, Mali and Mauritania, 1971-73. *Publication:* The Think Trap, 1972. *Recreations:* writing, walking. *Address:* 17 Redcliffe Road, SW10. *Club:* Travellers'.

PORTER, Maj.-General John Edmund L.; *see* Leech-Porter.

PORTER, Katherine Anne; author, lecturer and teacher to students of writing, in Colleges and Universities in USA, Mexico and Europe; *b* Texas, USA, 15 May 1890, family American (originating in Virginia) since 1648; *d* of Harrison Boone Porter, born in Kentucky, and Mary Alice Jones, Texas; *m* 1933, Eugene Dove Pressly (divorced); *m* 1938, Albert Russel Erskine, jun. (divorced); no *c*. *Educ:* private schools for girls in Louisiana and Texas. Guggenheim Foundn Fellowship, 1931-38; Gold Medal, Soc. for the Libraries of NY Univ., 1940; Fellow of Library of Congress, 1944 (Fellow of Regional American Literature). Lectr to students of writing, Stanford Univ., California, 1948-49; Vice-Pres., Nat. Inst. of Arts and Letters, NY, 1950; guest lectr on Literature, Spring Semester, Univ. of Chicago, 1951; one of reps of American Lit. to Internat. Festival of the Arts, Paris, 1952; Vis. Lectr in Contemporary Poetry, Univ. of Michigan, 1953-54; Fulbright Grant, Vis. Lectr, Univ. of Liège, 1954-55; Writer-in-residence, First Semester, Univ. of Virginia, 1958-59; Glasgow Prof., Second Semester, Washington and Lee Univ., Va, 1959; Ewing Lecturer, University of California, Los Angeles (UCPA), 1960; Dept State grants (USIA) Lecturer on American Literature, Mexico, 1960, 1964; first Regents' Lectr, Univ. of California, Riverside, 1961. Appointed by President Lyndon B. Johnson as Member Commn on Presidential Scholars, 1964. Poetry Consultant, Library of Congress, 1965-70. Hon. DLit Woman's Coll., Univ. of North Carolina, 1949; Hon. DLitt Hum, Univ. of Michigan, 1954; Hon. DLitt: Smith Coll., 1958, Maryville Coll., 1968; Sladmore

Coll., 1976; Howard Payne Univ., 1976; Hon. DHL, Univ. of Maryland, 1966; Hon. Phi Beta Kappa, Univ. of Maryland, 1966. Doctor of Fine Arts, La Salle Coll. Emerson-Thoreau Bronze Medal for Service to Literature, American Academy of Arts and Sciences, 1962; Nat. Book Award for Fiction, 1966; Pulitzer Prize for Fiction, 1966; Gold Medal for Literature, National Inst. of Arts and Letters, 1967; Edgar Allan Poe Award Mystery Writers of America, 1972. *Publications: books:* Flowering Judas, 1930; Pale Horse, Pale Rider, 1939; The Leaning Tower, 1944; Ship of Fools, 1962; Collected Stories, 1965; A Christmas Story, 1967; *essays:* The Days Before, 1952; Collected Essays and Occasional Writings, 1969; *history:* The Never-Ending Wrong, 1976; *translations:* Katherine Anne Porter's Old French Song Book, Paris, 1933; The Itching Parrot (from the Spanish), 1942. *Recreations:* old music, medieval history, reading, cookery; growing camellias, roses, irises. *Address:* Apt 1517, 6100 Westchester Park Drive, College Park, Md 20740, USA.

PORTER, Keith Ridley Douglas, MBE 1944; FRCP, FFCM, DPH, LDSRCS; Regional Medical Officer, SE Thames Regional Health Authority, since 1973; *b* 27 March 1913; *s* of Douglas David Porter and Olive Lucia (*née* Deck); *m* 1939, Elsie Grace, *d* of Captain Hartley Holmes, OBE, RA, and Elsie (*née* Walker); two *s* one *d*. *Educ:* Monkton Combe Sch., Bath; Guy's Hosp. Served War of 1939-45 (despatches twice, MBE). Sen. Admin. MO: N Ireland Hosp. Authority, 1964-69; SE Metrop. Regional Hosp. Bd, 1969-73. Council Member: London Sch. of Hygiene, 1970-75; Guy's Hosp. Med. Sch., 1971-75; Mem., Council for Professions Supp. to Medicine, 1971-75. Fellow, WHO, 1963. Mem. Court, Kent Univ., 1977-. *Publication:* (jtly) Challenges for Change, 1971. *Recreations:* gardening, swimming, travel. *Address:* Knowle Orchard, Cuckfield, Sussex RH17 5ES. *T:* Haywards Heath 54088.

PORTER, Leslie; Chairman, Tesco Stores (Holdings) Ltd, since 1973 (Deputy Chairman and Managing Director, 1972-73); *b* 10 July 1920; *s* of Henry Alfred and Jane Porter; *m* 1949, Shirley Cohen; one *s* one *d*. *Educ:* Holloway County Sch. Joined family textile business (J. Porter & Co), 1938. Served War: Techn. Quartermaster Sergt, 1st Bn The Rangers, KRRC, in Egypt, Greece, Crete, Libya, Tunisia, Algeria, Italy, 1939-46. Re-joined J. Porter & Co, 1946; became Managing Dir, 1955. Joined Tesco Stores (Holdings) Ltd: Dir, 1959; Asst Managing Dir, 1964; Dep. Chm., 1970. Member of Lloyd's, 1964- (John Poland syndicate). Pres., Inst. of Grocery Distribution, 1977. Dep. Chm., Bd of Governors, Tel Aviv Univ. Mem. President's Council, Hong Kong Baptist Coll. Hon. PhD (Business Management), Tel Aviv Univ., 1973. *Recreations:* golf, yachting, bridge. *Address:* 19 Chelwood House, Gloucester Square, W2 2SY. *T:* 01-262 2911. *Clubs:* City Livery; Dyrham Park County (Barnet, Herts); Coombe Hill Golf (Kingston Hill, Surrey).

PORTER, Air Marshal Sir (Melvin) Kenneth (Drowley), KCB 1967 (CB 1959); CBE 1945 (OBE 1942); educational and industrial consultant since 1974; *b* 19 Nov. 1912; *s* of late Edward Ernest Porter and late Helen Porter; *m* 1940, Elena, *d* of F. W. Sinclair; two *s* one *d*. *Educ:* No. 1 School of Technical Training, Halton; RAF Coll., Cranwell. Aircraft apprentice, RAF Halton; cadetship to RAF Coll., Cranwell; commissioned, 1932; Army Co-operation Sqdn, Fleet Air Arm, 1933-36, as PO and FO; specialised on Signals, 1936-37, Flt-Lieut; Sqdn Leader, 1939. Served War of 1939-45 (despatches thrice, OBE, CBE); Chief Signals Officer, Balloon Command, 1939; DCSO and CSO, HQ No. 11 Group, 1940-42; Temp. Wing Comdr, 1941; CSO, HQ 2nd TAF, 1943-45; Temp Gp Captain, 1943; Actg Air Commodore, 1944-45; CSO, HQ Bomber Command, 1945; Air Min. Tech. Plans, 1946-47, Gp Captain, 1946; Member Directing Staff, RAF Staff Coll., Andover, 1947-49; Senior Tech. Staff Officer, HQ No. 205 Group, 1950-52; Comdg Nos 1 and 2 Air Signallers Schools, 1952-54; CSO HQ 2nd ATAF, 1954-55; CSO, HQ Fighter Command, Actg Air Commodore, 1955-58, Air Cdr, 1958; Student Imperial Defence Coll., 1959; Commandant of No 4 School of Technical Training, RAF St Athan, Glamorgan, and Air Officer Wales, 1960-61; Actg Air Vice-Marshal, 1961; Air Vice-Marshal, 1962; Director-General: Ground Training, 1961-63; of Signals (Air), Ministry of Defence, 1964-66; AOC-in-C, Maintenance Command, 1966-70; Hd of RAF Engineer Branch, 1968-70; Actg Air Marshal, 1966; Air Marshal, 1967. Dir of Tech. Educn Projects, UC Cardiff, 1970-74. Governor, Bryanston Sch., 1972. CEng 1966; FIEE; FRAeS; FBIM; FInstProdE. Officer, Legion of Merit (US), 1945. *Recreation:* reading. *Address:* c/o Lloyds Bank Ltd, Redland Branch, 163 Whiteladies Road, Clifton, Bristol BS8 8RW.

PORTER, Hon. Sir Murray (Victor), Kt 1970; Agent-General for Victoria in London, 1970-76; *b* 20 Dec. 1909; *s* of late V. Porter, Pt Pirie, SA; *m* 1932, Edith Alice Johnston, *d* of late C. A. Johnston; two *d*. *Educ:* Brighton (Victoria) Grammar Sch., Australia. Served War, 2nd AIF, 1941-45. MLA (Liberal) Sandringham, Victoria, 1955-70; Govt Whip, 1955-56; Asst Minister, 1956-58; Minister for: Forests, 1958-59; Local Govt, 1959-64; Public Works, 1964-70. *Recreations:* golf, swmming. *Address:* 29 Reid Street, Beaumaris, Victoria 3193, Australia. *Clubs:* East India, Sports and Public Schools; Royal Wimbledon Golf; Melbourne Cricket, Royal Melbourne Golf, Royal Automobile Club of Victoria.

PORTER, Peter Neville Frederick; freelance writer, poet; *b* Brisbane, 16 Feb. 1929; *s* of William Ronald Porter and Marion Main; *m* 1961, Jannice Henry (*d* 1974); no *c*. *Educ:* Church of England Grammar Sch., Brisbane; Toowoomba Grammar Sch. Worked as journalist in Brisbane before coming to England in 1951; clerk, bookseller and advertising writer, before becoming full-time poet, journalist, reviewer and broadcaster in 1968. Chief work done in poetry and English literature. *Publications:* Once Bitten, Twice Bitten, 1961; Penguin Modern Poets No 2, 1962; Poems, Ancient and Modern, 1964; A Porter Folio, 1969; The Last of England, 1970; Preaching to the Converted, 1972; Living in a Calm Country, 1975; (trans.) After Martial, 1972; (with Arthur Boyd) Jonah, 1973; (with Arthur Boyd) The Lady and the Unicorn, 1975; (jt ed) New Poetry 1, 1975. *Recreations:* buying records and listening to music; travelling in Italy. *Address:* 42 Cleveland Square, W2. *T:* 01-262 4289.

PORTER, Raymond Alfred James; *b* 14 Oct. 1896; *o s* of Philip and Alice Porter; *m* 1922, Nellie, er *d* of George Edward Loveland; no *c*. *Educ:* Reigate Grammar Sch. Entered Lloyd's, 1912, Under-writing Member, 1934. Served European War, 1914-19, in Queen's Royal (West Surrey) Regt. Member, Cttee of Lloyd's, 1950-53, 1955-58, 1960-63 (Deputy Chairman of Lloyd's, 1961); Member, Cttee, Lloyd's Underwriters' Assoc., 1945-65 (Chairman, 1949-54, 1962); Chairman Joint Hull Cttee, 1958 and 1959. Member: Local Govt Management Cttee, 1964-67; Godstone RDC, 1946-60 and 1962-69 (Chairman, 1952-54); Surrey CC, 1955-58. *Address:* Mashobra, Limpsfield, Oxted, Surrey. *T:* Oxted 2509.

PORTER, Rt. Rev. Robert George; *see* Murray, Bishop of The.

PORTER, Robert Stanley, CB 1972; OBE 1959; Director-General, Economic Planning, Ministry of Overseas Development, since 1969; *b* 17 Sept. 1924; *s* of S. R. Porter; *m* 1st, 1953, Dorothea Naomi (marr. diss. 1967), *d* of Rev. Morris Seale; one *d*; 2nd, 1967, Julia Karen, *d* of Edmund A. Davies. *Educ:* St Clement Danes, Holborn Estate, Grammar Sch.; New Coll., Oxford. Research Economist, US Economic Cooperation Administration Special Mission to the UK, 1949; British Middle East Development Division: Asst Statistical Adviser, Cairo, 1951; Statistical Adviser and Economist, Beirut, 1955; Min. of Overseas Development: Dir, Geographical Div., Economic Planning Staff, 1965; Dep. Dir-Gen. of Economic Planning, 1967. *Publications:* articles in Oxford Economic Papers, Kyklos, Review of Income and Wealth. *Recreations:* music, theatre. *Address:* 82A Ashley Gardens, Thirleby Road, SW1. *T:* 01-834 8613. *Club:* Athenæum.

PORTER, Rt. Hon. Sir Robert (Wilson), Kt 1971; PC (NI) 1969; QC (NI) 1965; *b* 23 Dec. 1923; *s* of late Joseph Wilson Porter and late Letitia Mary (*née* Wasson); *m* 1953, Margaret Adelaide, *y d* of late F. W. Lynas; one *s* one *d* (and one *d* decd). *Educ:* Model Sch. and Foyle Coll., Londonderry; Queen's Univ., Belfast. RAFVR, 1943-46; Royal Artillery (TA), 1950-56. Foundation Schol., Queen's Univ., 1947 and 1948; LLB 1949. Called to Bar of N Ireland, 1950. Lecturer in Contract and Sale of Goods, Queen's Univ., 1950-51; Jun. Crown Counsel, Co. Londonderry, 1960-63, Co. Down, 1964-65; Counsel to Attorney-General for N Ireland, 1963-64 and 1965; Vice-Chairman, 1959-61, Chairman, 1961-66, War Pensions Appeal Tribunal for N Ireland. MP (U) Queen's Univ. of Belfast, 1966-69, Lagan Valley, 1969-73, Parlt of N Ireland; Minister of Health and Social Services, N Ireland, 1969; Parly Sec., Min. of Home Affairs, 1969; Minister of Home Affairs, Govt of NI, 1969-70. *Recreations:* gardening, golf. *Address:* Ardkeen, Marlborough Park North, Belfast, N Ireland BT9 6HL. *T:* 666761. *Clubs:* Royal Air Force; Ulster (Belfast).

PORTER, Prof. Rodney Robert, FRS 1964; Whitley Professor of Biochemistry, and Fellow, Trinity College, University of Oxford, since 1967; *b* 8 Oct. 1917; *s* of Joseph L. and Isobel M. Porter; *m* 1948, Julia Frances New; two *s* three *d*. *Educ:* Grammar Sch., Ashton-in-Makerfield; Liverpool and Cambridge Universities. Scientific Staff at Nat. Inst. for Medical

Research, Mill Hill, NW7, 1949-60; Pfizer Prof. of Immunology, St Mary's Hospital Medical Sch., London Univ., 1960-67. Mem., MRC, 1970-74. Linacre Lectr, Cambridge Univ., 1975; Gowland Hopkins Meml Lectr, Biochem. Soc., 1977. Award of Merit, Gairdner Foundn, 1966; Ciba Medal, Biochemical Soc., 1967; Karl Landsteiner Meml Award, Amer. Assoc. of Blood Banks, 1968; (jtly) Nobel Prize for Medicine or Physiology, 1972; Royal Medal, Royal Soc., 1973. Hon. Member: Amer. Soc. of Biological Chemists, 1968; Amer. Assoc. of Immunologists, 1973; Hon. Foreign Mem., Amer. Acad. of Arts and Sciences, 1968; Foreign Associate, Amer. Nat. Acad. of Scis, 1972. Hon. FRCP, 1974; Hon. FRSE, 1976; Hon. FIBiol, 1977. Hon. DSc: Liverpool, 1973; Hull, 1974; St Andrews, 1976; Dr *hc* Vrije Univ., Brussels, 1974. *Publications:* papers in Biochemical Journal and other learned journals. *Recreations:* walking, fishing. *Address:* Downhill Farm, Witney, Oxon.

PORTER, Thea; see Porter, D. N. N.

PORTER, Walter Stanley, TD 1950; MA (Cantab); Headmaster of Framlingham College, 1955-71; *b* 28 Sept. 1909; *s* of late Walter Porter, Rugby; *m* 1937, Doreen, *o d* of B. Haynes, Rugby; one *d. Educ:* Rugby Sch.; Gonville and Caius Coll., Cambridge. Assistant Master and Officer Commanding Training Corps, Trent Coll., 1933-36; Felsted Sch., 1936-43; Radley Coll., 1944-55. FRSA 1968. *Recreations:* travel, amateur dramatics; formerly Rugby football, hockey. *Address:* The Hermitage, 29 Cumberland Street, Woodbridge, Suffolk. *T:* Woodbridge 2340.

PORTERFIELD, Dr James Stuart; Reader in Bacteriology, Sir William Dunn School of Pathology, Oxford University, and Senior Research Fellow, Wadham College, Oxford, since 1977; Secretary and Vice-President, Royal Institution, since 1973; *b* 17 Jan. 1924; *yr s* of late Dr Samuel Porterfield and Mrs Lilian Porterfield, Widnes, Lancs. and Portstewart, Co. Londonderry, NI; *m* 1950, Betty Mary Burch; one *s* one *d. Educ:* Wade Deacon Grammar Sch., Widnes; King's Sch., Chester; Liverpool Univ. MB, ChB 1947, MD 1949. Asst Lectr in Bacteriology, Univ. of Liverpool, 1947-49; Bacteriologist and Virologist, Common Cold Res. Unit, Salisbury, Wilts, 1949-51; Pathologist, RAF Inst. of Pathology and Tropical Med., Halton, Aylesbury, Bucks, 1952-53; seconded to W African Council for Med. Res. Labs, Lagos, Nigeria, 1953-57; Mem. Scientific Staff, Nat. Inst. for Med. Res., Mill Hill, 1949-77 (Virologist, 1957-77); WHO Regional Ref. Centre for Arthropod-borne Viruses, 1961-65; WHO Collaborating Lab., 1965-; Ref. Expert on Arboviruses, Public Health Lab. Service, 1967-76. Chm., Arbovirus Study Gp, Internat. Cttee for Nomenclature of Viruses, 1968-; Meetings Sec., Soc. for General Microbiology, 1972-77; Councillor, Royal Soc. for Tropical Med. and Hygiene, 1973-76. *Publications:* contribs to medical and scientific jls. *Recreations:* fell-walking, gardening. *Address:* Sir William Dunn School of Pathology, South Parks Road, Oxford OX1 3QX.

PORTLAND, 8th Duke of, *cr* 1716; **Ferdinand William Cavendish-Bentinck,** KBE 1956; CMG 1941; Earl of Portland, Viscount Woodstock, Baron Cirencester, 1689; Marquess of Titchfield, 1716; Baron Bolsover, 1880; Member: East African Production and Supply Council; East African Advisory Council on Agriculture, Animal Industry and Forestry; East African Agricultural, Forestry and Veterinary Research Organisations Committee; Chairman and Founder of Kenya Association, 1932; *b* 4 July 1889; *s* of (William George) Frederick Cavendish-Bentinck (*d* 1948) (*g g s* of 3rd Duke) and Ruth Mary St Maur (*d* 1953); *S* kinsman, 1977; *m* 1st, 1912, Wentworth Frances Hope-Johnstone (marr. diss.); 2nd, 1950, Gwyneth, MBE, *widow* of Colonel D. A. J. Bowie, RA. *Educ:* Eton; RMC, Sandhurst; Germany. Late 60th Rifles (KRRC); served Malta, India and European War, 1914-18 (severely wounded, despatches); GSO War Office; Company Comdr, and later Asst Adjutant RMC, Sandhurst; worked for Vickers Ltd on Continent with HQ Brussels, 1923-24; Private Secretary to Governor of Uganda, 1925-27; Hon. Secretary Kenya Convention of Associations, 1930. Member for Agriculture and Natural Resources in Kenya Government, 1945-55; Speaker of Kenya Legislative Council, 1955-60 (MLC, and MEC, Kenya, 1934-60). Chairman: Tanganyika League and African Defence Federation, 1938; Agricultural Production and Settlement Board, Kenya, 1939-45; Timber Controller for East Africa, 1940-45; Member of East African Civil Defence and Supply Council, 1940-45; a Delegate to Delhi Conference, 1940; contested South Kensington, 1922; Member of many Commissions and Select Cttees. Officier de la Couronne (Belgium). *Publications:* articles on African subjects. *Heir: b* Victor Frederick William Cavendish-Bentinck, *qv*. *Clubs:* Turf, Bath, Beefsteak; Muthaiga (Nairobi).

PORTLOCK, Rear-Admiral Ronald Etridge, CB 1961; OBE 1947; DL; retired; *b* London, 28 June 1908; *o s* of late Henry and Doris Portlock; *m* 1939, Angela, *d* of late Gerard Kirke Smith; no *c. Educ:* Royal Naval Coll., Dartmouth. Naval Cadet, 1922; Midshipman, 1926; Lieut-Commander, 1938; Commander, 1943; Captain, 1949; Rear-Admiral 1959. Served War of 1939-45 in HMS Ark Royal and King George V as Lieut-Commander; Admiralty as Commander. Post-war Mine Clearance in Far East, 1946-47; Captain, HM Underwater Detection Establishment, 1950-52; Chief of Staff to C-in-C, The Nore, 1953-54; in comd HMS Newfoundland, and Flag Captain to Flag Officer; Second in Command Far East Station, 1955-56; Director of Underwater Weapons, Admiralty, 1957-58; Chief of Staff to the Commander-in-Chief, Far East Station, 1959-61, retired, 1961. ADC to the Queen, 1958. Chairman, Assoc. of Retired Naval Officers, 1965-67. DL Greater London, 1967. Royal Swedish Order of the Swords, 1954. *Address:* 1 Swan Court, Chelsea, SW3. *T:* 01-352 4390. *Club:* Royal Automobile.

PORTMAN, family name of Viscount Portman.

PORTMAN, 9th Viscount, *cr* 1873; **Edward Henry Berkeley Portman;** Baron 1873; *b* 22 April 1934; *s* of late Hon. Michael Berkeley Portman (*d* 1959) (*yr s* of 7th Viscount), and June Charles (*d* 1947); *S* uncle, 1967; *m* 1st, 1956, Rosemary Farris (marr. diss., 1965); one *s* one *d*; 2nd, 1966, Penelope Allin; four *s. Educ:* Canford; Royal Agricultural College. Farmer. *Recreations:* shooting, fishing, music. *Heir: s* Hon. Christopher Edward Berkeley Portman, *b* 30 July 1958. *Address:* Clock Mill, Clifford, Herefordshire. *T:* Clifford 235. *Club:* White's.

PORTSMOUTH, 9th Earl of, *cr* 1743; **Gerard Vernon Wallop;** Viscount Lymington, Baron Wallop, 1720; Hereditary Bailiff of Burley, New Forest; Vice-Chairman, East Africa Natural Resources Research Council, since 1963; *b* 16 May 1898; *e s* of 8th Earl and Marguerite (*d* 1938), *d* of S. J. Walker, Kentucky; *S* father 1943; *m* 1st, 1920, Mary Lawrence (who obtained a divorce, 1936, and *m* 2nd, 1938, E. J. B. How), *d* of W. K. Post, Bayport, Long Island; one *s* one *d*; 2nd, 1936, Bridget, *o d* of late Captain P. B. Crohan, Royal Navy, Owipen Manor, Glos; one *s* two *d*. Served European War, 1916-19; MP (U) Basingstoke Division of Hants, 1929-34; Member of the Milk Marketing Board, July 1933; Vice-Chairman Hampshire War Agric. Cttee, 1939-47; Vice-President and Chairman Country Landowners Assoc., 1947-48. President, Electors Union, Kenya, 1953-55; MLC Kenya (Corporate Member for Agric.), 1957-60; Vice-Chairman, East African Natural Resources Research Council, 1963-. *Publications:* Git le Cœur, 1928; Ich Dien; The Tory Path, 1931; Horn, Hoof and Corn, 1932; Famine in England, 1938; Alternative to Death, 1943; British Farm Stock, 1950; A Knot of Roots (autobiog.), 1965. *Heir: s* Viscount Lymington, *qv*. *Address:* c/o Farleigh Wallop, Basingstoke, Hants *Clubs:* Buck's; Muthaiga Country (Nairobi).
See also Viscount Chelsea, Lord Rupert Nevill, Lord Porchester.

PORTSMOUTH, Bishop of, since 1975; **Rt. Rev. Archibald Ronald McDonald Gordon;** *b* 19 March 1927; *s* of late Sir Archibald Gordon, CMG, and late Dorothy Katharine Gordon, Bridge House, Gerrards Cross, Bucks. *Educ:* Rugby Sch.; Balliol Coll., Oxford (Organ Schol., MA 1950); Cuddesdon Theol. Coll. Deacon 1952; Priest 1953; Curate of Stepney, 1952-55; Chaplain, Cuddesdon Coll., 1955-59; Vicar of St Peter, Birmingham, 1959-67; Res. Canon, Birmingham Cathedral, 1967-71; Vicar of University Church of St Mary the Virgin with St Cross and St Peter in the East, Oxford, 1971-75. Fellow of St Cross Coll., Oxford, 1975. Mem., Church Assembly and General Synod, and Proctor in Convocation, 1965-71; Chm., ACCM, 1976-. *Address:* Bishopswood, Fareham, Hants PO14 1NU.

PORTSMOUTH, Bishop of, (RC), since 1976; **Rt. Rev. Anthony Joseph Emery;** *b* Burton-on-Trent, 17 May 1918. Ordained 1953. Auxiliary Bishop of Birmingham (Titular Bishop of Tamallula), 1968-76. Chm. Catholic Education Council. *Address:* Bishop's House, Edinburgh Road, Portsmouth PO1 3HG.

PORTSMOUTH, Archdeacon of; see Scruby, Ven. R. V.

PORTSMOUTH, Provost of; see Nott, Very Rev. M. J.

PORTWAY, Col Donald, CBE 1957; TD; DL; JP; MA; FICE; Hon. MIMI; Dean, Faculty of Engineering and Professor of Mechanical Engineering, University of Khartoum, 1957-61, retired; Hon. Fellow: Downing College, Cambridge; St Catharine's College, Cambridge; Emeritus Fellow Trumbull College, Yale University, USA; *b* 28 June 1887; *s* of late Ald. H.

H. Portway, JP, Halstead, Essex; *m* 1919, Sophia Maud Grace, *niece* and adopted *d* of late J. A. Bezant, JP, Mettingham, Suffolk; one *d. Educ:* Felsted Sch.; Downing Coll., Cambridge (Senior Scholar). 1st Class Hons Mech. Sci. Tripos; Research in Mechanical Engineering, Cambridge Univ., 1911; Asst Master at RN Coll., Dartmouth, 1912; BEF 1914, 2nd Lieut to Major, RE; Fellow of St Catharine's Coll., Cambridge, and Lecturer in Engineering Dept, Cambridge Univ., 1919, subsequently Tutor, Senior Tutor and President of St Catharine's Coll., 14 years Proctor or Motor Proctor. Master of St Catharine's Coll., 1946-57. BEF 1939, as Bt Lieut-Colonel, RE (despatches), subsequently Colonel, General Staff. Army Cadet Comdt for Cambridgeshire and Isle of Ely, 1945-51; Sector Comdr, Home Guard, 1951-54. Joint Hon. Colonel University OTC Cambridge, 1950-57. *Publications:* Examples in Elementary Engineering, 1937; Science and Mechanization in Land Warfare, 1938; Military Science To-day, 1940; Talks to Future Officers, 1941; The Quest of Leadership, 1945; Korea, the Land of Morning Calm, 1953; Militant Don, 1963; Memoirs of an Academic Old Contemptible, 1971. *Recreations:* swimming, gardening; formerly winner 4 years running of Inter-Varsity Middleweights. *Address:* 33 Millington Road, Cambridge. *Clubs:* Royal Automobile; Hawks (Cambridge).

POSKITT, Frederick Richard, CBE 1962; *b* 15 Aug. 1900; *s* of Frederick Hardy Poskitt and Kate Penlington Spencer; *m* 1936, Margaret Embree, *e d* of Cecil E. Turner, Woolton, Liverpool; two *s* one *d. Educ:* Kilburn Grammar Sch.; Downing Coll., Cambridge. Asst Master, Colchester Royal Grammar Sch., 1921-25; Head of History Dept, Manchester Grammar Sch., 1926-33; Headmaster, Bolton Sch., 1933-66; Dir, Nat. Teachers' Coll., Kampala, Uganda, 1966-71. Founder Mem., Fifty-One Soc. (BBC), 1951-60; Mem., Chief Scout's Adv. Panel, 1943-49; Chairman: SE Lancs County Scout Council, 1943-60; Bolton Lads Club, 1944-53; Pres., Bolton Br., Historical Assoc., 1933-66. *Recreation:* travel. *Address:* 11 Hedge End, Hensington Gate, Woodstock, Oxon OX7 1NP. *T:* Woodstock 811590. *Club:* Royal Commonwealth Society.

POSKITT, Prof. Trevor John, DSc, PhD; Professor of Civil Engineering, Queen Mary College, University of London, since 1972; *b* 26 May 1934; *s* of late William Albert Poskitt, Worthing, and of Mrs D. M. Poskitt, Lincoln; *m* 1968, Gillian Mary, *d* of L. S. Martin, MBE, Romiley, Cheshire; one *s. Educ:* Corby Technical Sch.; Huddersfield Technical Coll.; Univ. of Leeds; Univ. of Cambridge. HND (Mech. Eng.); BSc Leeds, PhD Cambridge, DSc Manchester; FICE, FiStructE. Apprentice Engineer to Thos. Broadbent & Sons, Huddersfield, 1949-53; Graduate Assistant, English Electric Co. Ltd, 1958-60; Whitworth Fellow, 1960-63; Lectr, 1963-71, Senior Lectr, 1971-72, in Civil Engineering, Univ. of Manchester. *Publications:* numerous on civil engineering topics. *Recreations:* tennis, music. *Address:* Queen Mary College, Mile End Road, E1 4NS. *T:* 01-980 4811.

POSNER, Michael Vivian; Fellow and Director of Studies in Economics, Pembroke College, Cambridge, since 1960; Reader in Economics, University of Cambridge, since 1975; a Member, British Railways Board, since 1976; *b* 25 Aug. 1931; *s* of Jack Posner; *m* 1953, Rebecca (*née* Reynolds); one *s* one *d. Educ:* Whitgift Sch.; Balliol Coll., Oxford. Research Officer, Oxford Inst. of Statistics, 1953-57; Asst Lecturer, then Lecturer in Economics, 1958-75; Chm., Faculty Bd of Economics, Cambridge, 1974-75. Vis. Prof., Brookings Instn, Washington, 1971-72. Director of Economics, Ministry of Power, 1966-67; Economic Adviser to Treasury, 1967-69; Economic Consultant to Treasury, 1969-71; Consultant to IMF, 1971-72; Energy Adviser, NEDO, 1973-74; Econ. Adviser, Dept of Energy, 1974-75; Dep. Chief Econ. Adviser, HM Treasury, 1975-76. Mem., Adv. Council for Energy Conservation, 1974-. *Publications:* (co-author) Italian Public Enterprise, 1966; Fuel Policy: a study in applied economics, 1973; (ed) Resource Allocation in the Public Sector, 1977; books and articles on economics. *Recreation:* country life. *Address:* Pembroke College, Cambridge. *T:* Cambridge 52241; Okyamie, Bulmer, York. *T:* Whitwell-on-the-Hill 269. *Club:* United Oxford & Cambridge University.

POSNETT, Richard Neil, CMG 1976; OBE 1963; HM Diplomatic Service; Dependent Territories Adviser, Foreign and Commonwealth Office, 1977; *b* 19 July 1919; *s* of Rev. Charles Walker Posnett, K-i-H, Medak, S India and Phyllis (*née* Barker); *m* 1st; two *s* one *d*; 2nd, 1959, Shirley Margaret Hudson; two *s* one *d. Educ:* Kingswood; St John's Coll., Cambridge. BA 1940, MA 1947. Called to the Bar, Gray's Inn, 1951. HM Colonial Administrative Service in Uganda, 1941; Chm., Uganda Olympic Cttee, 1956; Colonial Office, London, 1958; Judicial Adviser, Buganda, 1960; Perm. Sec. for External Affairs, Uganda, 1962; Perm. Sec. for Trade and Industry, 1963;

joined Foreign (subseq. Diplomatic) Service, 1964; FO, 1964; served on UK Mission to UN, NY, 1967-70; briefly HM Comr in Anguilla, 1969; Head of W Indian Dept, FCO, 1970-71; Governor and C-in-C of Belize, 1972-76; Special Mission to Ocean Island, 1977. Mem., RIIA. KStJ 1972. *Address:* Timbers, Northway, Godalming, Surrey. *T:* Godalming 6869. *Clubs:* Ski Club of Great Britain, Royal Commonwealth Society, Achilles.

POSNETTE, Prof. Adrian Frank, CBE 1976; FRS 1971; Director, East Malling Research Station, Kent, since Dec. 1972 (Deputy Director, 1969-72, and Head of Plant Pathology Section, 1957-72); *b* 11 Jan. 1914; *e s* of late Frank William Posnette and Edith (*née* Webber), Cheltenham; *m* 1937, Isabelle, *d* of Dr Montgomery La Roche, New York; one *s* two *d. Educ:* Cheltenham Grammar Sch.; Christ's Coll., Cambridge. MA, ScD Cantab; PhD London; AICTA Trinidad; FIBiol. Research at Imperial Coll. of Tropical Agriculture, Trinidad, 1936-37; Colonial Agric. Service, Gold Coast, 1937; Head of Botany and Plant Pathology Dept, W African Cacao Research Inst., 1944; research at East Malling Research Stn, 1949-. Vis. Prof. in Plant Sciences, Wye Coll., Univ. of London, 1971-. *Publications:* Virus Diseases of Apples and Pears, 1963; numerous research papers in Annals of Applied Biology, Jl of Horticultural Science, Nature, Tropical Agriculture. *Recreations:* ornithology, sailing, gardening. *Address:* Walnut Tree, East Sutton, Maidstone, Kent. *T:* Sutton Valence 3282. *Clubs:* Farmers'; Hawks (Cambridge); Helford River Sailing.

POST, Col Kenneth Graham, CBE 1945; TD; *b* 21 Jan. 1908; *s* of Donnell Post and Hon. Mrs Post; *m* 1st, 1944, Stephanie Bonté Wood (marr. diss., 1963); one *s* two *d*; 2nd, 1963, Diane Allen; two *s. Educ:* Winchester; Magdalen, Oxford. London Stock Exchange, 1929-37; 2nd Lieut, RA (TA) 1937; Norway, 1940; War Office, 1941-42; Ministry of Supply, 1944-44; Ministry of Works, 1945-47; Ministry of Housing, 1956-57; Ministry of Defence, 1957-59. Member Corby New Town Development Corporation, 1955-62; Director, Civic Trust, 1957-63. *Address:* Walland House, Brookland, Romney Marsh, Kent. *T:* Brookland 379. *Club:* Pratt's.

POSTAN, Michael, FBA 1959; Professor of Economic History, 1938-65 (now Emeritus) and Fellow of Peterhouse, 1935-65 (now Hon. Fellow), Cambridge; Head of Section in MEW, 1939-42; the Official Historian of Munitions at the Offices of the War Cabinet since 1942; *b* Sept. 1899; *s* of Efim and Elena Postan, Tighina, Bessarabia; *m* 1937, Eileen Power (*d* 1940); *m* 1944, Lady Cynthia Rosalie Keppel, 2nd *d* of 9th Earl of Albemarle, *qv*; two *s.* Lecturer in History in University College (University of London), 1927-31; Lecturer in Economic History at London School of Economics, 1931-35, Hon. Fellow, 1974; Lecturer in Economic History in University of Cambridge, 1935-38. Hon. President, Internat. Economic History Assoc. Hon. DLitt. *Publications:* (with Eileen Power) Studies in English Trade in the Fifteenth Century, 1933, new edn 1951; Historical Method in Social Science, 1939; British War Production, 1952; (with E. E. Rich) Cambridge Economic History of Europe, vol. 2, Trade and Industry in the Middle Ages, 1952; The Famulus, 1954; (with D. Hay and J. D. Scott) Design and Development of Weapons: studies in government and organisation, 1964; An Economic History of Western Europe, 1945-64, 1967; Fact and Relevance; essays in historical method, 1971; The Medieval Economy and Society, 1973; Essays on Medieval Agriculture and the Medieval Economy, 1973; Medieval Trade and Finance, 1973; edited: Cambridge Economic History of Europe, vol 1, The Agrarian Life of the Middle Ages, 2nd edn 1966; (with H. J. Habakkuk) vol. 6, The Industrial Revolutions and After, 1966; also numerous articles and essays in learned publications. *Address:* 2 Sylvester Road, Cambridge; Penrallt Goch, Ffestiniog, Gwynedd. *Club:* United Oxford & Cambridge University.

POSTGATE, Prof. John Raymond, FRS 1977; FInstBiol; Assistant Director, ARC Unit of Nitrogen Fixation, since 1963, and Professor of Microbiology, University of Sussex, since 1965; *b* 24 June 1922; *s* of Raymond William Postgate and Daisy Postgate (*née* Lansbury); *m* 1948, Mary Stewart; three *d. Educ:* Woodstock Sch.; Golders Green; Kingsbury County Sch., Mddx; Balliol Coll., Oxford. BA, MA, DPhil, DSc. Research in chemical microbiology: with D. D. Woods on action of sulfonamide drugs, 1946-48, with K. R. Butlin on sulphate-reducing bacteria, 1948-59. Research on bacterial death, 1959-63, incl. Visiting Prof., Univ. of Illinois, 1962-63, working on sulphate-reducing bacteria. Visiting Prof., Oregon State Univ., 1977-78. *Publications:* Microbes and Man (Pelican), 1969, 2nd edn 1976; Biological Nitrogen Fixation, 1972; Nitrogen Fixation, 1978. A Plain Man's Guide to Jazz, 1973; ed, 3 scientific symposia; regular columnist in Jazz Monthly, 1952-72; reviewer for Gramophone, 1965-; numerous scientific papers in microbiol/biochem. jls; many record reviews and articles on jazz. *Recreations:* listening to jazz and attempting to play it. *Address:* 1 Houndean Rise, Lewes, Sussex BN7 1EG. *T:* Lewes 2675.

POSTGATE, Richmond Seymour, MA; FCP; Consultant, education and broadcasting; *b* 31 Dec. 1908; *s* of Prof. J. P. Postgate, LittD, FBA, Classical Scholar, and Edith Postgate; *m* 1949, Audrey Winifred Jones; one *s* two *d. Educ:* St George's Sch., Harpenden, Herts; Clare Coll., Cambridge. Editorial staff of Manchester Guardian newspaper; teaching in Public and Elementary Schools; County LEA Administration; RAFVR. In BBC: Head of School Broadcasting, etc; Director-General, Nigerian Broadcasting Corporation, 1959-61; Controller, Educnl Broadcasting, BBC, 1965-71. FCP 1973. *Recreation:* walking. *Address:* 40 Clarendon Road, W11 3AD.

POSTILL, Ronald, TD 1943; MA; Tutor for admissions, Millfield School; *b* 7 Feb. 1907; *er s* of late Harry Postill, Bridlington, Yorks, and S. Elizabeth Postill; *m* 1st, 1932, Nathalie Grace (marr. diss. 1938); one *d* ; 2nd, 1939, Yvonne D. P. Ebdy; one *s. Educ:* Bridlington Sch.; Trinity Coll., Cambridge. Open Exhibitioner in Natural Sciences; BA 1928; MA 1944. Asst Master: Aldenham Sch., 1928-30; Tonbridge Sch., 1930-39 and 1945; Headmaster, Victoria Coll., Jersey, 1946-67; Tutor, Millfield Sch., 1967. Commissioned TA General List, 1928; comd Tonbridge Sch. OTC 1938-39; served War of 1939-45, Royal Signals; Comdt Royal Signals OCTU, 1944-45. King Haakon VII Liberty Cross (Norway), 1945. *Recreations:* criticising cricket (played for Hertfordshire, 1930-34); crosswords and cryptic puzzles. *Address:* Lavender Cottage, Charlton Adam, Somerton, Som. *T:* Charlton Mackrell 328.

POTEZ, Andrew Louis; Special Commissioner of Income Tax, since 1977; *b* 23 June 1920; *s* of Marcel Potez and Geraldine (*née* Mackenzie); *m* 1948, June Rosemary, *d* of Sydney Avila; three *s* . *Educ:* Ampleforth Coll.; Oriel Coll., Oxford (BA). Called to the Bar, Middle Temple, 1948. Served War, Army, 1940-46 (Burma Star; Temp. Major). Office of Solicitor of Inalnd Revenue, 1949-55; Legal Adviser, C&A Modes Ltd, 1955-60; Schweppes Ltd, 1960-69 (Legal Manager; Sec., Schweppes Overseas; dir of gp cos); in practice at the Bar, 1969-76. *Recreations:* living in Dedham Vale, ecumenism. *Address:* Knights Manor, Dedham, Colchester, Essex. *T:* Colchester 323355; 95 Campden Hill Towers, Notting Hill Gate, W11. *T:* 01-727 1678.

POTT, Sir Leslie, KBE 1962 (CBE 1957); *b* 4 July 1903; *s* of Charles Groves Pott; *m* 1937, Norma, *d* of Captain Kynaston Lyons-Montgomery, Jersey; one *s. Educ:* Manchester Grammar Sch.; Gonville and Caius Coll., Cambridge (Open Scholar). Entered Levant Consular Service, 1924; served at Casablanca, Damascus and Beirut, 1926-29; Moscow and Leningrad, 1930-35; Foreign Office, 1936-37; Piraeus and Athens, 1938-40; Consul at Baghdad, 1940-43; Foreign Office, 1943-45; Consul at Alexandria, 1946-47. Consul-General at Tabriz, 1947-50; Deputy High Commissioner for the UK at Bombay, 1950-52; Consul-General at Istanbul, 1952-55; at Marseilles, 1955-61, also to Monaco, 1957-61. Retired from HM Diplomatic Service, 1962. *Address:* Becking Spring, Hudnall Common, near Berkhamsted, Herts HP4 1QJ. *T:* Little Gaddesden 3409.

POTTER, Arthur Kingscote, CMG 1957; CBE 1946; *b* 7 April 1905; *s* of late Richard Ellis Potter, Ridgewood, Almondsbury, Glos and Harriott Isabel (*née* Kingscote, of Kingscote, Glos); *m* 1950, Hilda, *d* of late W. A. Butterfield, OBE; one *d. Educ:* Charterhouse; New Coll., Oxford (BA). Entered Indian CS, 1928; posted to Burma; District Comr, 1934; Financial Adviser, Army in Burma, 1942 (despatches); Finance Secretary, Government of Burma, 1942-43; Financial Adviser (Brigadier), 11th Army Group, 1943, and Allied Land Forces, South-East Asia, 1943-44; Chief Financial Officer (Brig.), Military Administration of Burma, 1944-47; HM Treasury Representative in India, Pakistan and Burma, 1947-50; Asst Secretary, HM Treasury, 1950-56; Counsellor, UK Delegation to NATO, Paris, 1956-65. *Address:* c/o National Westminster Bank Ltd, 208 Piccadilly, W1A 2DG.

POTTER, Dennis (Christopher George); playwright, author and journalist (freelance since 1964); *b* 17 May 1935; *e s* of Walter and Margaret Potter; *m* 1959, Margaret Morgan; one *s* two *d. Educ:* Bell's Grammar Sch., Coleford, Glos; St Clement Danes Grammar Sch.; New Coll., Oxford. Editor, Isis, 1958; BA (Hons) in PPE Oxon, 1959. BBC TV (current affairs), 1959-61; Daily Herald, feature writer, then TV critic, 1961-64; contested (Lab) East Herts, 1964; Leader writer, The Sun, Sept.-Oct. 1964, then resigned. First television play, 1965. *Television plays:* Vote Vote Vote for Nigel Barton (also at Bristol Old Vic, 1968); Stand Up Nigel Barton; Where the Buffalo Roam; A Beast with Two Backs; Son of Man; Traitor; Paper Roses; Casanova; Follow the Yellow Brick Road; Only Make Believe; Joe's Ark; Schmoedipus; (adapted from novel by Angus Wilson) Late Call, 1975; Double Dare, 1976; Where Adam Stood, 1976. *Publications:* The Glittering Coffin, 1960; The Changing Forest, 1962; *plays:* The Nigel Barton Plays (paperback, 1968); Son of Man, 1970; *novel:* Hide and Seek, 1973. *Recreations:* nothing unusual, *ie* the usual personal pleasures, sought with immoderate fervour. *Address:* Morecambe Lodge, Duxmere, Ross-on-Wye, Herefordshire. *T:* Ross-on-Wye 3199.

POTTER, Donald Charles, QC 1972; *b* 24 May 1922; *s* of late Charles Potter, Shortlands, Kent. *Educ:* St Dunstan's Coll.; London Sch. of Economics. RAC (Westminster Dragoons), 1942-46 (Lieut). LLB London 1947; called to Bar, Middle Temple, 1948. Asst Lectr in Law, LSE, 1947-49; practised at Bar, 1950-. *Publication:* (with H. H. Monroe) Tax Planning with Precedents, 1954. *Recreations:* farming, travel, theatre, reading. *Address:* 37 Tufton Street, SW1P 3QL. *Club:* Garrick.

POTTER, Douglas Charles Loftus; His Honour Judge Potter; a Circuit Judge (formerly Judge of County Courts), since 1959; *b* 17 Dec. 1903; *s* of John Charles Potter, solicitor, Putney, and Caroline Annette Tidy Potter (*née* Onslow); *m* 1934, Margaret Isabel, *d* of Dr William Savile Henderson, Liverpool; one *d. Educ:* Radley; Trinity Coll., Oxford (MA). Rowed in winning crew, Ladies' Plate, Henley Regatta, 1923; Half-blue, OUAC, 3 miles, 1925. Barrister, Inner Temple, 1928; SE Circuit, Herts and Essex Sessions. Served War of 1939-45 in RAFVR, 1940-45. Judge of County Courts, 1959-71, Willesden, Croydon and Kingston upon Thames. *Publications:* The Law Relating to Garages and Car Parks, 1939; The National Insurance Act, 1946, 1946. *Recreations:* walking, travel, reading, music, gardening. *Club:* Royal Automobile.

POTTER, Francis Malcolm; a Recorder of the Crown Court, since 1974; *b* 28 July 1932; *s* of Francis Martin Potter and Zilpah Jane Potter; *m* 1970, Bertha Villamil; one *s* one *d. Educ:* Rugby Sch.; Jesus Coll., Oxford. Called to Bar, Lincoln's Inn, 1956. *Recreation:* visual art. *Address:* 5 Fountain Court, Steelhouse Lane, Birmingham B4 6DR. *T:* 021-236 5771.

POTTER, George Richard, CBE 1977; MA, PhD (Cambridge), FRHistS, FSA; retired as Professor of Medieval History, University of Sheffield, 1965; Emeritus Professor, since 1965; Hon. Research Fellow, 1973-75; Temporary Professor, University of Warwick, 1968-69; *b* 6 Aug. 1900; *e s* of George Potter, Norwich; *m* 1927, Rachel, *y d* of M. Leon, Salisbury, Rhodesia; one *s* one *d. Educ:* King Edward VI Sch., Norwich; St John's Coll., Cambridge; Head of Department of History, University College, Leicester, 1925-27; Lecturer in Medieval History, Queen's Univ. of Belfast, 1927-31; Prof. of Modern History, Univ. of Sheffield, 1931; Dean of the Faculty of Arts, 1939-42; External examiner for a number of Universities; Member Royal Commission on Historical Manuscripts; Vice-Chairman Universities Council for Adult Education, 1938-64; President, Historical Association, 1961-64. Cultural Attaché, British Embassy, Bonn, 1955-57. H. C. Lea Visiting Prof., University of Pennsylvania, 1966-67, 1967-68. Fellow, Newberry Lib., Chicago, 1974; Professorial Fellow, Univ. of Wales, 1976. Served with Royal Naval Volunteer Reserve, 1918-19. *Publications:* Sir Thomas More, 1925; The Autobiography of Ousâma, 1929; (with Bonjour and Offler) Short History of Switzerland, 1952; Zwingli, 1976; contribution to Cambridge Medieval History; advisory editor and contributor to Chambers's Encyclopædia; editor of New Cambridge Modern History, Vol. I, Renaissance; various articles. *Recreations:* walking, travel. *Address:* 11 Derwent Lane, Hathersage, Sheffield S30 1AS. *T:* Hope Valley 50428.

POTTER, Sir Ian; see Potter, Sir W. I.

POTTER, Maj.-Gen. Sir John, KBE 1968 (CBE 1963; OBE 1951); CB 1966; Chairman, Traffic Commissioners and Licensing Authority, Western Traffic Area, since 1973; *b* 18 April 1913; *s* of late Major Benjamin Henry Potter, OBE, MC; *m* 1st, 1943, Vivienne Madge (*d* 1973), *d* of late Captain Henry D'Arcy Medlicott Cooke; one *s* one *d* ; 2nd, 1974, Mrs D. Ella Purkis; one step *s* one step *d* . Served War of 1939-45. Major-General, 1962; Colonel Comdt: RAOC, 1965-69; RCT, 1968-73. Director of Supplies and Transport, 1963-65; Transport Officer in Chief (Army), 1965-66; Dir of Movements (Army), MoD, 1966-68; retired. *Address:* Orchard Cottage, The Orchard, Freshford, Bath, Avon.

POTTER, (Joseph) Raymond (Lynden); Chairman, Halifax Building Society, since 1974; *b* 21 April 1916; *s* of Rev. Henry

Lynden and Mabel Boulton Potter; *m* 1939, Daphne Marguerite, *d* of Sir Crawford Douglas-Jones, CMG; three *s* one *d*. *Educ:* Haileybury Coll.; Clare Coll., Cambridge (MA). War Service, 1939-46, Queen's Own Royal W Kent Regt, England and Middle East; GSO2 Staff Duties, GHQ, MEF; AQMG War Office. Sec., Royal Inst. of Internat. Affairs, 1947-51; joined Halifax Building Soc., 1951; Gen. Man. 1956; Chief Gen. Man., 1960-74; Dir, 1968-. Member: Board, Warrington New Town Develt Corp., 1969-; Wakefield Diocesan Bd of Finance, 1960-. Patron, Friends of Wakefield Cathedral. Mem. Council, Building Socs Assoc. (Chm., 1975-77). Life Governor, Haileybury Coll. *Recreation:* hill walking. *Address:* 1 Prince's Gate, Halifax, W Yorks HX3 0EH. *T:* Halifax 61017. *Club:* Hawks (Cambridge).

POTTER, Mrs Mary; Artist; *b* 9 April 1900; *d* of John Arthur and Kathleen Mary Attenborough; *m* 1927, Stephen Potter, (marr. diss. 1955; he *d* 1969); two *s*. *Educ:* Private Sch.; Slade Sch. (Scholar). Paintings exhibited in London and provinces since 1921. One-man shows: Bloomsbury Gallery, 1931; Redfern Gallery, 1934 and 1949; Tooth's Gallery, 1939 and 1946; Leicester Gallery, 1951, 1953, 1954, 1957, 1961, 1963; New Art Centre, 1967, 1969, 1972, 1974, 1976. Retrospective Exhibition, Whitechapel Art Gallery, 1964. Pictures bought by the Tate Gallery, Arts Council, Manchester City Art Gallery, Contemporary Art Society, etc; and galleries in New York and Canada, and Australia. *Address:* Red Studio, Aldeburgh, Suffolk. *T:* Aldeburgh 2081.

POTTER, Air Marshal Sir Patrick B. L.; see Lee Potter.

POTTER, Rev. Philip Alford; General Secretary, World Council of Churches, since Nov. 1972; *b* 19 Aug. 1921; *s* of Clement Potter and Violet Peters, Roseau, Dominica, Windward Is, WI; *m* 1956, Ethel Olive Doreen Cousins, Jamaica, WI. *Educ:* Dominica Grammar Sch.; United Theological Coll., Jamaica; London Univ. BD, MTh. Methodist Minister. Overseas Sec., British SCM, 1948-50; Superintendent, Cap Haitien Circuit, Methodist Church, Haiti, 1950-54; Sec., later Dir, Youth Dept, WCC, 1954-60; Sec. for WI and W Africa, Methodist Missionary Society, London, 1961-66; Dir, Commn on World Mission and Evangelism, and Associate Gen. Sec., WCC, 1967-72. Mem., then Chm., Youth Dept Cttee, WCC, 1948-54; Chm., World Student Christian Fedn, 1960-68. Editor: Internat. Review of Mission, 1967-72; Ecumenical Rev., 1972-. Hon. Doctor of Theology: Hamburg Univ., Germany, 1971; Geneva, 1976; Theol Inst. of Rumanian Orthodox Church, 1977; Hon. LLD W Indies, 1974. *Publications:* (with Prof. Hendrik Berkhof) Key Words of the Gospel, 1964; chapter in Explosives Lateinamerika (ed by T. Tschuy), 1969; essays in various symposia; contrib. various jls, incl. Ecumenical Rev., Internat. Rev. of Mission, Student World. *Recreations:* swimming, hiking, music, geology. *Address:* World Council of Churches, 150 Route de Ferney, 1211 Geneva 20, Switzerland. *T:* 33 34 00.

POTTER, Raymond; see Potter, J. R. L.

POTTER, Ronald Stanley James; Director of Social Services, Surrey County Council, since 1970; *b* 29 April 1921; *e s* of late Stanley Potter and Gertrude Mary Keable, Chelmsford; *m* 1954, Ann (Louisa Eleanor) Burnett; one *s* one *d*. *Educ:* King Edward VI Grammar Sch., Chelmsford. MISW. Territorial Army, 1939, War Service, 1939-47; commnd RA, 1942; Captain 1946. Area Welfare Officer, Essex CC, 1953-61; Dep. Co. Welfare Officer, Lindsey CC, 1962; County Welfare Officer: Lindsey CC, 1962-64; Herts CC, 1964-70. Dir, Watford Sheltered Workshop Ltd, 1964-70; Mem. Cttee of Enquiry into Voluntary Workers in Social Services, 1966-69; Dir, Industrial Advisers to Blind Ltd, 1969-74; Chm, SE Regional Assoc. for Deaf, 1976- (Vice-Chm., 1968-76); Member: Council of Management, RNID, 1968-71, 1976-; Nat. Jt Council for Workshops for the Blind, 1970-; Adv. Council, Nat. Corp. for Care of Old People, 1974-; Local Authorities Adv. Cttee on Conditions of Service of Blind Workers, 1974-; Exec. Council, RNIB, 1975-; Dir, Remploy Ltd, 1974-. *Recreations:* walking, swimming, caravanning. *Address:* Surrey House, 34 Eden Street, Kingston upon Thames, Surrey. *T:* 01-549 6111.

POTTER, Maj.-Gen. Sir Wilfrid John; see Potter, Maj.-Gen. Sir John.

POTTER, Sir (William) Ian, Kt 1962; Stockbroker, Melbourne, Australia; *b* 25 Aug. 1902; *s* of James William Potter and Maria Louisa (*née* McWhinnie); *m* 1955; two *d*. *Educ:* University of Sydney. Economist to Federal Treas., 1935-36; Commonwealth Rep. Rural Debt Adjustment Cttee, 1936; founded Ian Potter & Co., 1937; Principal Partner, 1937-67. Served RANVR, 1939-44. Member: Cttee Stock Exchange of Melbourne, 1945-62;

Melbourne University Council, 1947-71; Commonwealth Immigration Planning Council, 1956-62; Victorian Arts Centre Building Cttee, 1960-. President, Australian Elizabethan Theatre Trust, 1964-66, Chairman, 1968-; Vice-Pres., Howard Florey Inst., Melbourne. *Publications:* contrib. articles on financial and economic subjects to learned journals and press. *Recreations:* yachting, tennis, golfing. *Address:* 30 Sargood Street, Toorak, Victoria 3142, Australia. *T:* 24 4308. *Clubs:* Melbourne, Australian, Royal Melbourne Golf (Melbourne); The Links (NY).

POTTINGER, (William) George; *b* 11 June 1916; *e s* of late Rev. William Pottinger, MA, Orkney, and Janet Woodcock; *m* 1946, Margaret Rutherfurd Clark McGregor; one *s*. *Educ:* George Watson's; High School of Glasgow; Edinburgh Univ.; Heidelberg; Queens' Coll., Cambridge (Major Scholar). Entered Scottish Home Dept, as Assistant Principal, 1939. Served War of 1939-45, RFA; France, N Africa, Italy (despatches), Lieut-Col RA. Principal, 1945; Private Secretary to successive Secretaries of State for Scotland, 1950-52; Asst Secretary, Scottish Home Dept, 1952; Secretary, Royal Commn on Scottish Affairs, 1952-54; Under-Secretary: Scottish Home Dept, 1959-62; Scottish Home and Health Dept, 1962-63; Scottish Development Dept, 1963-64; Scottish Office, 1964-68; Dept of Agriculture and Fisheries for Scotland, 1968-71; Secretary, Dept of Agriculture and Fisheries for Scotland, 1971. *Publications:* The Winning Counter, 1971; Muirfield and the Honourable Company, 1972; St Moritz: an Alpine caprice, 1972; papers and reviews. *Recreations:* squash rackets, golf and fishing.

POTTLE, Frederick Albert, BA Colby, MA, PhD Yale, Hon. LittD Colby, Rutgers, Hon. LHD Northwestern; Hon. LLD Glasgow; Sterling Professor of English, and Fellow Emeritus of Davenport College, Yale University; Public Orator, Yale University, 1942 and 1946; *b* Lovell, Maine, 3 Aug. 1897; *y s* of late Fred Leroy Pottle and Annette Wardwell Kemp; *m* 1920, Marion Isabel Starbird, Oxford, Maine; two *s*. *Educ:* Colby Coll. (*Summa cum laude*); Yale (John Addison Porter Prize). Served as private in Evacuation Hospital No 8, AEF, 1918-19; formerly Assistant Professor of English, University of New Hampshire; Editor of the Private Papers of James Boswell (succeeding the late Geoffrey Scott); Hon. member of Johnson Club; Vice-Pres., Johnson Soc., London; Pres., Johnson Soc., Lichfield, 1974; Trustee: General Theological Seminary, 1947-68; Colby Coll., 1932-59, 1966-; Messenger Lecturer, Cornell Univ., 1941; Member of Joint Commission on Holy Matrimony of the Episcopal Church, 1940-46; Guggenheim Fellow, 1945-46, 1952-53; Chancellor Academy of American Poets, 1951-71; Chairman of Editorial Cttee of Yale Editions of Private Papers of James Boswell, 1949-; Member Provinciaal Utrechtsch Genootschap van Kunsten en Wetenschappen, 1953-; Member American Academy of Arts and Sciences, 1957-; FIAL, 1958-; Member, American Philosophical Society, 1960. Wilbur Lucius Cross Medal, Yale, 1967; William Clyde DeVane Medal, Yale, 1969; Lewis Prize, Amer. Philosophical Soc., 1975. *Publications:* Shelley and Browning, 1923; A New Portrait of James Boswell (with Chauncey B. Tinker), 1927; The Literary Career of James Boswell, 1929; Stretchers, the Story of a Hospital on the Western Front, 1929; The Private Papers of James Boswell: A Catalogue (with Marion S. Pottle), 1931; Vols 7-18 of The Private Papers of James Boswell, 1930-34; Boswell's Journal of a Tour to the Hebrides, from the Original Manuscript (with Charles H. Bennett), 1936, revised edition, 1963; Index to the Private Papers of James Boswell (with Joseph Foladare, John P. Kirby and others), 1937; Boswell and the Girl from Botany Bay, 1937; The Idiom of Poetry, 1941, revised and enlarged edition, 1946; James Boswell, the Earlier Years, 1966; editions of Boswell's *journals:* Boswell's London Journal (1762-63), 1950; Boswell in Holland (1763-64), 1952; Boswell on the Grand Tour: Germany and Switzerland (1764), 1953; Boswell on the Grand Tour: Italy, Corsica and France, 1765 (with Frank Brady), 1955; Boswell in Search of a Wife, 1766-1769 (with Frank Brady), 1956; Boswell for the Defence, 1769-1774 (with William K. Wimsatt), 1959; Boswell: The Ominous Years, 1774-1776 (with Charles Ryskamp), 1963; Boswell in Extremes, 1776-1778 (with Charles McC. Weis), 1970; Boswell, Laird of Auchinleck, 1778-1782 (with Joseph W. Reed), 1977; various articles. *Recreation:* gardening. *Address:* 35 Edgehill Road, New Haven, Conn 06511, USA. *Clubs:* Elizabethan (New Haven); Grolier, Ends of the Earth (New York).

POTTS, Archie; Under-Secretary, and Director of Scientific and Technical Intelligence, Ministry of Defence, 1964-74; *b* 28 Dec. 1914; *s* of late Mr and Mrs A. Potts, Newcastle upon Tyne; *m* 1951, Winifred Joan Bishop, MBE, *d* of late Mr and Mrs Reginald Bishop; two *s*. *Educ:* University of Durham. BSc (Hons) Physics, 1935. Research in Spectroscopy, King's Coll., University of Durham, 1936-39. War of 1939-45: Operational

Research in Radar and Allied Fields, Fighter Command, and N Africa and Italy, 1939-45; Hon. Sqdn Leader, RAFVR, 1943-45. Chief Research Officer, Fighter Command, 1946-51; Defence Research Staff, Min. of Defence, 1951-53; Scientific Adviser, Allied Air Forces Central Europe, 1954-56; Asst Scientific Adviser, Air Ministry, 1957; Dep. Director for Atomic Energy, Jt Intell. Bureau, 1957-63. FInstP 1945. *Recreation:* listening to music. *Address:* 3 The Keir, West Side, SW19 4UG. *T:* 01-946 7077. *Club:* Royal Air Force.

POTTS, Prof. Edward Logan Johnston, MSc; Professor of Mining, Department of Mining Engineering, University of Newcastle upon Tyne, since 1951; *b* Niddrie, Midlothian, 22 Jan. 1915; *s* of Samuel Potts; *m* 1940, Edith Mary, *d* of A. Hayton, Scarborough; one *s* one *d*. *Educ:* Coatbridge Grammar Sch., Lanarkshire; Gosforth Grammar Sch., Newcastle upon Tyne; King's Coll., University of Durham. BSc (dist.) 1939, 1st Class Hons (Dunelm) 1940; 1st Class Colliery Manager's Certif., 1941; MSc (Dunelm) 1945. Apprentice Mine Surveyor, Hazlerigg & Burradon Coal Co., Ltd, 1931-34. Asst to Chief Surveyor, Charlaw & Sacriston Collieries Co. Ltd, 1934-36; Certificated Mine Surveyor, 1936; Apprentice Mining Engineer, Wallsend & Hebburn Coal Co. Ltd, 1936-40; Cons. Mining Engineer, Northumberland, Durham, N Staffs; Surveyor to Northern "A" Regional cttee; prepared report on Northumberland and Cumberland Reserves and output, 1944; Reader in Mining, King's Coll., University of Durham, 1947; Mining Adviser: Northumberland Coal Owners' Assoc., 1947; Mickley Associated Collieries, 1949-51; Peterlee Development Corp. on mining subsidence, 1947-72; Adviser to Kolar Gold Fields, S India, rock bursts in deep mining, 1955-70; Mem., Coal Res. Commn, EEC, 1972-. President, N of England Inst. Mining and Mech. Engineering, 1957-58. Consultant, Rock Mechanics, ICI Mond Div., Cleveland Potash Ltd, etc. Research on rock mechanics, etc; co-designer Dunelm circular fluorescent mine lighting unit, hydraulic coal plough. *Publications:* (jointly) Horizon Mining, 1953; papers on ventilation, mine lighting, strata control in Trans. Inst. Mining Eng., British Assoc. and other journals. *Recreations:* athletics, motoring. *Address:* University of Newcastle upon Tyne, Newcastle upon Tyne NE1 7RU. *T:* Newcastle 28511; 4 Montagu Avenue, Gosforth, Newcastle upon Tyne NE3 4HX. *T:* Newcastle 852171.

POTTS, Francis Humphrey, QC 1971; a Recorder of the Crown Court, since 1972; *b* 18 Aug. 1931; *er s* of late Francis William Potts and Elizabeth Hannah Potts (*née* Humphrey); *m* 1971, Philippa Margaret Campbell, *d* of the late J. C. H. Le B. Croke; two *s*; two step-*s*. *Educ:* Royal Grammar Sch., Newcastle upon Tyne; St Catherine's Society, Oxford. BA 1953, BCL 1954, MA 1957. Barrister-at-Law, Lincoln's Inn, 1955 (Tancred Student, 1953; Cholmeley Scholar, 1954); North Eastern Circuit, 1955. *Address:* 11 King's Bench Walk, Temple, EC4. *T:* 01-353 3337. *Club:* Reform.

POTTS, Kenneth Hampson; Chief Executive, Leeds City Council, since 1973; *b* 29 Sept. 1921; *s* of late James Potts and Martha Ann Potts; *m* 1945, Joan Daphne Wilson; two *s*. *Educ:* Manchester Grammar Sch.; Liverpool Univ. (LLB Hons). Solicitor. Captain, RA, 1942-46. Deputy Town Clerk, Leeds, 1965; Chief Management and Legal Officer, Leeds, 1969. Member: Yorks and Humberside Economic Planning Council; Data Protection Cttee, 1976-. *Recreations:* golf, theatre, music, reading. *Address:* Tall Pines Court, 6 Sandmoor Lane, Alwoodley, Leeds LS17 7EA. *T:* Leeds 686666.

POTTS, Thomas Edmund, ERD 1957; Company Director; *b* 23 March 1908; *s* of late T. E. Potts, Leeds; *m* 1932, Phyllis Margaret, *d* of late J. S. Gebbie, Douglas, Isle of Man; one *s*. *Educ:* Leeds Modern School. Joined The British Oxygen Co. Ltd, 1928. Commissioned RE, Supp. R of O, 1938; served War of 1939-45, Madras Sappers and Miners in India, Eritrea, Western Desert, Tunisia, with 4th and 5th Indian Divs (despatches; Major); CRE 31st Indian Armoured Div., 9th Army (Lt-Col). Rejoined British Oxygen Co. Ltd, London, 1945; Managing Director, African Oxygen Ltd, Johannesburg, 1947; Director, British Oxygen Co. Ltd, 1955; Managing Director, The British Oxygen Co. Ltd, 1958-63; Pres. South African Instn of Welding, 1951; Vice-Pres., Inst. of Welding, 1963-64. *Recreation:* golf. *Address:* Budds Oak, Primrose Lane, Holyport, Berks. *T:* Maidenhead 26887. *Clubs:* Bath; Rand (Johannesburg); Temple Golf.

POUNCEY, Denys Duncan Rivers, MA, MusB Cantab; FRCO; Organist and Master of the Choristers, Wells Cathedral, 1936-70; Conductor of Wells Cathedral Oratorio Chorus and Orchestra, 1946-66; Hon. Diocesan Choirmaster Bath and Wells Choral Association, 1946-70; *b* 23 Dec. 1906; *s* of late Rev. George Ernest Pouncey and late Madeline Mary Roberts; *m*

1937, Evelyn Cottier. *Educ:* Marlborough College; Queens' College, Cambridge. Asst to Dr Cyril Rootham, Organist and Choirmaster of St John's Coll., Cambridge, 1928-34; Organist and Choirmaster St Matthew's, Northampton, 1934-36; Founder Conductor of Northampton Bach Choir. *Address:* Longstring, 23 Ash Lane, Wells, Somerset. *T:* Wells 73200.
See also P . M . R . Pouncey.

POUNCEY, Philip Michael Rivers, MA; FBA 1975; a Director of Sothebys, since 1966; Hon. Keeper of Italian Drawings, Fitzwilliam Museum, since 1975; *b* 15 Feb. 1910; *s* of Rev. George Ernest Pouncey and Madeline Mary Roberts; *m* 1937, Myril Gros; two *d*. *Educ:* Marlborough; Queens' Coll., Cambridge (MA). Hon. Attaché, Fitzwilliam Museum, 1931-33; Assistant, National Gall., London, 1934-45; Asst Keeper, 1945-54, Dep. Keeper, 1954-66, British Museum; Visiting Professor: Columbia Univ., NY, 1958; Inst. of Fine Arts, New York Univ., 1965. *Publications:* Catalogues of Italian Drawings in the British Museum: (with A. E. Popham) XIV-XV Centuries, 1950; (with J. A. Gere) Raphael and his Circle, 1962; Lotto disegnatore, 1965; articles in Burlington Magazine, etc. *Recreation:* travel in Italy and France. *Address:* 5 Addison Gardens, W14 8BG.
See also D . D . R . Pouncey.

POUND, Sir Derek Allen, 4th Bt, *cr* 1905; *b* 7 April 1920; *o s* of Sir Allen Leslie Pound, 3rd Bt, LLB, late sole member of legal firm of Pound & Pound, of Egham, and 1st wife, Margery (who obtained a divorce, 1925), 2nd *d* of Stephen G. Hayworth, Clapton Common; *m* 1942, Joan Amy, *d* of James Woodthorpe, Boston, Lincs; one *s* one *d*. *Educ:* Shrewsbury. Lieutenant Royal Artillery, 1941; transferred to Essex Regiment; released from Service, 1946. *Heir: s* John David Pound, [*b* 1 Nov. 1946; *m* 1968, Heather Frances O'Brien, *o d* of Harry Jackson Dean; one *s*]. *Address:* 37 Great Cumberland Place, W1.

POUNDER, Rafton John; Secretary, Northern Ireland Bankers' Association, since 1977; *b* 13 May 1933; *s* of Cuthbert C. Pounder, Gefion, Ballynahatty, Shaw's Bridge, Belfast; *m* 1959, Valerie Isobel, *d* of late Robert Stewart, MBE, Cherryvalley, Belfast; one *s* one *d*. *Educ:* Charterhouse; Christ's College, Cambridge. Qualified as a Chartered Accountant, 1959. Chm. Cambridge Univ. Cons. and Unionist Assoc., 1954; Ulster rep. on Young Cons. and Unionist Nat. Adv. Cttee, 1960-63; Hon. Mem., Ulster Young Unionist Council, 1963; Member: UK delegn (C) to Assembly of Council of Europe, and to Assembly of WEU, 1965-68; UK Delegn to European Parlt, Strasbourg, 1973-74; Exec. Cttee, Nat. Union of Cons. and Unionist Assocs, 1967-72; Exec. Cttee, Ulster Unionist Council, 1967-73. MP (UU) Belfast S, Oct. 1963-Feb. 1974; Mem., House of Commons Select Cttee on Public Accounts, 1970-73; Vice-Chm., Cons. Parly Party's Technology Cttee, 1970; PPS to Minister for Industry, 1970-71. Mem. CPA Delegn to: Jamaica and Cayman Is, Nov. 1966; Malawi, Sept. 1968. Hon. Secretary: Ulster Unionist Parly Party at Westminster, 1964-67; Cons. Parly Party's Power Cttee, 1969-70. Pres., Ulster Soc. for Prevention of Cruelty to Animals, 1968-74. Dir, Progressive Building Soc., 1968-77. Lay Member, General Synod of the Church of Ireland, 1966-. *Recreations:* golf, reading, music, sailing. *Address:* 29 Coastguard Lane, Orloch, Groomsport, Co. Down.

POUNDS, Maj.-Gen. Edgar George Derek, CB 1975; Chief Executive, British Friesian Cattle Society, since 1976; *b* 13 Oct. 1922; *s* of Edgar Henry Pounds, MBE, MSM, and Caroline Beatrice Pounds; *m* 1944, Barbara Winifred May Evans; one *s* one *d*. *Educ:* Reading Sch. War of 1939-45: enlisted, RM, 1940 (King's Badge, trng); HMS Kent, 1941-42 (Atlantic); commissioned as Reg. Off., Sept. 1942 (sword for dist., trng); HMS Berwick, 1943-44 (Atlantic and Russia). Co. Comdr, RM, 1945-51: Far East, Palestine, Malta, UK (Sniping Wing), Korea (US Bronze Star, 1950); Captain 1952. Instr, RM Officers' Trng Wing, UK, 1952-54; Adjt, 45 Commando, RM, 1954-57, Malta, Cyprus (despatches); Suez; RAF Staff Coll., Bracknell, 1958; Staff Captain, Dept of CGRM, London, 1959-60; Major 1960; Amphibious Ops Officer, HMS Bulwark, 1961-62, Kuwait, Aden, E Africa, Borneo; Corps Drafting Off., UK, 1962-64; 40 Commando RM: 2nd in Comd, 1964-65, Borneo, and CO, 1966-67, Borneo and Far East; CO, 43 Commando, RM, 1967-68, UK based; GSO1 Dept CGRM, 1969-70; Col 1970; Naval Staff, MoD, 1970-72; Comdt Commando Trng Centre, RM, 1972-73; Actg Maj.-Gen. 1973; Maj.-Gen., RM, 1974; Comdt Commanding Commando Forces, RM, 1973-76, retired. *Publications:* articles on strategy, amphibious warfare, and tactics, in professional jls. *Recreations:* hunting, target rifle shooting, boating, reading. *Address:* Langdon, Burtons Way, Chalfont St Giles, Bucks. *Clubs:* Army and Navy, Farmers'.

POUT, Harry Wilfrid, OBE 1959; CEng, FIEE; Deputy Controller, Air Systems D, Ministry of Defence, since 1975; *b* 11

April 1920; British; *m* 1949, Margaret Elizabeth (*née* Nelson); three *d. Educ:* East Ham Grammar Sch.; Imperial Coll., London. BSc (Eng); ACGI 1940. RN Scientific Service, 1940; Admty Signal Estab. (later Admty Signal and Radar Estab.), 1940-54; Dept of Operational Research, Admty, 1954-59; idc 1959; Head of Guided Weapon Projects, Admty, 1960-65; Asst Chief Scientific Adviser (Projects), MoD, 1965-69; Dir, Admiralty Surface Weapons Estabt, 1969-72; Dep Controller, Guided Weapons, MoD, 1973; Dep. Controller Guided Weapons and Electronics, MoD, 1973-75. FCGI 1972. *Publications:* (jtly) The New Scientists, 1971; classified books; contribs to jls of IEE, RAeS, RUSI, etc. *Recreations:* mountaineering, gardening and do-it-yourself activities, amateur geology. *Address:* Oakmead, Fox Corner, Worplesdon, near Guildford, Surrey. *T:* Worplesdon 2223.

POWDITCH, Alan (Cecil Robert), MC 1944; JP; District Administrator, NW District, Kensington and Chelsea and Westminster Area Health Authority, 1974-77, retired; *b* 14 April 1912; *s* of Cecil John and Annis Maudie Powditch; *m* 1942, Barbara Leggat; one *s* one *d. Educ:* Mercers School. Entered Hospital Service, 1933; Accountant, St Mary's Hospital, W2, 1938. Served War of 1939-45, with 51st Royal Tank Regt, 1941-46. Dep. House Governor, St Mary's Hospital, 1947-50, Sec. to Bd of Governors, 1950-74. Mem. Nat. Staff Cttee (Min. of Health) 1964-72; Chm., Juvenile Panel, Gore Div., 1973-76. JP Co. Middlesex 1965. *Recreations:* golf; interested in gardening when necessary. *Address:* Brentmore, Cygnet Close, Northwood, Mddx HA6 2TA.

POWELL; see Baden-Powell.

POWELL, Anthony Dymoke; CBE 1956; *b* 21 Dec. 1905; *o s* of late Lt-Col P. L. W. Powell, CBE, DSO; *m* 1934, Lady Violet Pakenham, 3rd *d* of 5th Earl of Longford, KP; two *s. Educ:* Eton; Balliol College, Oxford, MA; Hon. Fellow, 1974. Served War of 1939-45, Welch Regt and Intelligence Corps, Major. A Trustee, National Portrait Gallery, 1962-76. Hon. Mem., Amer. Acad. of Arts and Letters, 1977. Hon. DLitt: Sussex, 1971; Leicester, 1976; Kent, 1976. Orders of: the White Lion, (Czechoslovakia); the Oaken Crown and Croix de Guerre (Luxembourg); Leopold II (Belgium). *Publications:* Afternoon Men, 1931; Venusberg, 1932; From a View to a Death, 1933; Agents and Patients, 1936; What's become of Waring, 1939; John Aubrey and His Friends, 1948; Selections from John Aubrey, 1949; A Question of Upbringing, 1951 (first vol. of Music of Time series which follow); A Buyer's Market, 1952; The Acceptance World, 1955; At Lady Molly's, 1957 (James Tait Black Memorial Prize); Casanova's Chinese Restaurant, 1960; The Kindly Ones, 1962; The Valley of Bones, 1964; The Soldier's Art, 1966; The Military Philosophers, 1968; Books do Furnish a Room, 1971; Temporary Kings, 1973 (W. H. Smith Prize, 1974); Hearing Secret Harmonies, 1975; *memoirs:* Infants of the Spring (first vol. of To Keep the Ball Rolling), 1976; Messengers of Day, 1978; *plays:* Afternoon Men (adapted by Riccardo Aragno), Arts Theatre Club, 1963; The Garden God, 1971; The Rest I'll Whistle, 1971. *Address:* The Chantry, near Frome, Somerset. *T:* Nunney 314. *Clubs:* Travellers', Pratt's.

POWELL, Sir Arnold Joseph Philip; see Powell, Sir Philip.

POWELL, Arthur Barrington, CMG 1967; Executive Director, Welsh Development Agency, since 1976; *b* 24 April 1918; *er s* of late Thomas and Dorothy Powell, Maesteg, Glam; *m* 1945, Jane, *d* of late Gen. Sir George Weir, KCB, CMG, DSO; four *s* one *d. Educ:* Cowbridge; Jesus Coll. Oxford. Indian Civil Service, 1939-47; served in Province of Bihar. Asst Princ., Min. of Fuel and Power, 1947; Princ. Private Sec. to Minister, 1949-51; Asst Sec., 1955; Petroleum Div., 1957-68; Petroleum Attaché, HM Embassy, Washington, 1962-64; Gas Div., 1968-72; Reg. Finance Div., DoI, 1972-76. *Address:* Croesllanfro House, Rogerstone, Gwent. *Club:* United Oxford & Cambridge University.

POWELL, Arthur Geoffrey; Director, Strategic Plan for the South East, 1976 (Under-Secretary, Department of the Environment, 1975-76); *b* 22 Dec. 1915; *s* of late Dudley and Emma Powell; *m* 1947, Albertine Susan Muller; one *s* one *d. Educ:* Mundella, Nottingham; University Coll., Nottingham. BA London (External) 1937. Demonstrator, Dept of Geography, University Coll., Nottingham, 1938-40. Served with Royal Engineers, Intelligence Corps and Army Educn Corps, Middle East, 1940-46 (despatches). Research Dept, Min. of Town and Country Planning, et seq, 1946-61; Principal Technical Officer, Local Govt Commn for England, 1961-65; Principal Planner, Min. of Housing and Local Govt, 1965-68; Asst Chief Planner, Min. of Housing and Local Govt and DoE, 1968-74; Dep. Chief Planner, DoE, 1974-75; Under-Secretary

(Regional Dir, Eastern), DoE, 1975-76. *Recreations:* travel, fell walking, photography, music. *Address:* 3 Lorne Court, Putney Hill, SW15 6RX. *T:* 01-789 6980.

POWELL, David; *b* 1914; *s* of Edward Churton Powell and Margaret (*née* Nesfield); *m* 1941, Joan Boileau (Henderson); one *s* four *d. Educ:* Charterhouse. Served 1939-46: Lt, Kent Yeomanry RA; Captain and Major on Staff. Qualifed as Chartered Accountant, 1939, admitted, 1943; in practice, 1946-47; joined Booker McConnell Ltd, 1947; Finance Dir, 1952; Dep. Chm. 1957; Man. Dir, 1966; Chm. and Chief Exec., 1967, retired 1971; Chm., Bookers Shopkeeping Holdings, 1956-63. Mem., West India Cttee. *Recreations:* stalking, golf, English water-colours, gardening, reading. *Address:* The Cottage, 20 Coldharbour Lane, Hildenborough, Kent. *T:* Hildenborough 833103. *Club:* Travellers'.

POWELL, Dewi Watkin, JP; His Honour Judge Watkin Powell; a Circuit Judge, since 1972; *b* Aberdare, 29 July 1920; *o s* of W. H. Powell, AMICE and of M. A. Powell, Radyr, Glam; *m* 1951, Alice, *e d* of William and Mary Williams, Nantmor, Caerns; one *d. Educ:* Penarth Grammar Sch.; Jesus Coll., Oxford (MA). Called to Bar, Inner Temple, 1949. Dep. Chm., Merioneth and Cardigan QS, 1966-71; Dep. Recorder of Cardiff, Birkenhead, Merthyr Tydfil and Swansea, 1965-71; Junior, Wales and Chester Circuit, 1968; Liaison Judge for Dyfed; Vice-Pres., South and Mid Glamorgan branch of Magistrates' Assoc. Mem. Exec. Cttee, Plaid Cymru, 1943-55, Chm., Constitutional Cttee, 1967-71; Mem. Council, Hon. Soc. of Cymmrodorion, 1965-. Member: Court, Univ. of Wales; Court and Council, Univ. Coll. of Wales, Aberystwyth; Welsh Council of Social Services; Magistrates Courts and Probation and After-Care Cttees for Co. of Dyfed. JP Dyfed. *Recreations:* gardening, reading, theology, Welsh history and literature. *Address:* Crown Court, Law Courts, Cathays Park, Cardiff.

POWELL, Edward, CBE 1973; Hon. President, Chloride Group Ltd (Chairman, 1965-74); *b* 10 June 1907; *s* of Edward Churton Powell and Margaret Nesfield; *m* 1941, Patricia Florence (*née* Harris); one *s* one *d. Educ:* Shrewsbury School. Captain, Royal Marines, 1941-45. Solicitor in private practice until 1941; joined Chloride Electrical Storage Co. Ltd (now Chloride Group Ltd), 1941; Man. Dir, 1962-72. Pres., British Electrical and Allied Manufacturers' Assoc. Ltd, 1973-75. *Recreations:* landscape gardening, fishing. *Address:* Little Orchard, Mayfield, East Sussex. *T:* Mayfield 3441.

POWELL, (Elizabeth) Dilys, CBE 1974; FRSL; TV Film Critic of The Sunday Times (Film Critic, 1939-74); *yr d* of late Thomas and Mary Powell; *m* 1st, 1926, Humfry Payne, later Director of the British School of Archæology at Athens (*d* 1936); 2nd, 1943, Leonard Russell (*d* 1974); no *c. Educ:* Bournemouth High School; Somerville College, Oxford. Editorial Staff, Sunday Times, 1928-31 and 1936-41. Lived and travelled extensively in Greece, 1931-36. Member: Bd of Governors of British Film Institute, 1948-52; Independent Television Authority, 1954-57; Cinematograph Films Council, 1965-69; President, Classical Association, 1966-67. *Publications:* Descent from Parnassus, 1934; Remember Greece, 1941; The Traveller's Journey is Done, 1943; Coco, 1952; An Affair of the Heart, 1957; The Villa Ariadne, 1973. *Address:* 14 Albion Street, Hyde Park, W2. *T:* 01-723 9807.

POWELL, Rt. Hon. Enoch; see Powell, Rt Hon. J. E.

POWELL, Francis Turner, MBE 1945; a Deputy Chairman, Stock Exchange, since 1976 (Member, Stock Exchange Council, since 1963); Partner, Laing & Cruickshank (incorporating Powell Popham Dawes & Co.), Stockbrokers, since 1939; *b* 15 April 1914; *s* of Francis Arthur and Dorothy May Powell; *m* 1940, Joan Audrey Bartlett; one *s* one *d. Educ:* Lancing College. Served War, Queen's Royal Regt (TA), 1939-45 (Major). *Recreations:* golf, gardening. *Address:* Tanglewood, Oak Grange Road, West Clandon, Surrey. *T:* Guildford 222698.

POWELL, Harry Allan Rose, (Tim Powell), MBE 1944; TD 1973; Chairman and Managing Director, Massey-Ferguson Holdings Ltd, since 1970; Chairman: Massey-Ferguson (UK) Ltd, since 1971; Massey-Ferguson (Export) Ltd, since 1970; Director: Holland and Holland Holdings Ltd; W. J. Jeffrey Ltd; Massey-Ferguson companies in France, Germany, Italy, Switzerland; *b* 15 Feb. 1912; *er s* of late William Allan Powell and Marjorie (*née* Mitchell); *m* 1936, Elizabeth North Hickley; two *d. Educ:* Winchester; Pembroke Coll., Cambridge (MA). Joined Corn Products Ltd, 1934. Commissioned Hertfordshire Yeomanry, 1938; Staff Coll., 1942; War Office 1942; Joint Planning Staff, 1943; seconded to War Cabinet Secretariat, 1943-44; Head of Secretariat, Supreme Allied Commander,

South East Asia, 1944-45 (Col). Mitchells & Butlers Ltd, 1946-49 (Jt Gen. Manager, 1947); Gallaher Ltd, 1949-52 (Gen. Manager, Northern Ireland, 1951). Joined Harry Ferguson Ltd, 1952; Asst to President, Massey-Ferguson Ltd, Canada, 1959; Managing Dir, Massey-Ferguson Holdings Ltd, 1962; Chm., 1970. British Inst. of Management: Fellow, 1963; Mem. Council, 1970-; Board of Fellows, 1966-; Vice-Chm., 1970-; Chm., Internat. Management Adv. Council, 1970-. Governor, St Thomas' Hosp., 1971-74; Pres., European Cttee of Assocs of Manufrs of Farm Machinery, 1972-73. *Recreations:* fishing, shooting, skiing, arguing. *Address:* Ready Token, near Cirencester, Glos. *T:* Bibury 219; 12 Shafto Mews, Cadogan Square, SW1. *T:* 01-235 2707. *Clubs:* Bucks, Bath, MCC; York (Toronto).

POWELL, Herbert Marcus, FRS 1953; BSc, MA; Professor of Chemical Crystallography, Oxford University, 1964-74, now Emeritus; *Educ:* St John's College, Oxford. MA Oxon 1931. Reader in Chemical Crystallography in the University of Oxford, 1944-64; Fellow of Hertford College, Oxford, 1963-74, Emeritus Fellow, 1974. *Address:* 46 Davenant Road, Oxford.

POWELL, Rt. Hon. (John) Enoch, PC 1960; MBE 1943; MA (Cantab); MP (UU) South Down, since Oct. 1974; *b* 16 June 1912; *s* of Albert Enoch Powell and Ellen Mary Breese; *m* 1952, Margaret Pamela (*née* Wilson); two *d.* *Educ:* King Edwards, Birmingham; Trinity College, Cambridge. Craven Scholar, 1931; First Chancellor's Classical Medallist; Porson Prizeman; Browne Medallist, 1932; BA (Cantab); Craven Travelling Student, 1933; Fellow of Trinity College, Cambridge, 1934-38; MA (Cantab) 1937; Professor of Greek in the University of Sydney, NSW, 1937-39; Pte and L/Cpl R Warwickshire Regt, 1939-40; 2nd Lieut General List, 1940; Captain, General Staff, 1940-41; Major, General Staff, 1941; Lieut-Col, GS, 1942; Col, GS, 1944; Brig. 1944; Dipl. OAS. MP (C) Wolverhampton SW, 1950-Feb. 1974; Parly Sec., Ministry of Housing and Local Government, Dec. 1955-Jan. 1957; Financial Secretary to the Treasury, 1957-58; Minister of Health, July 1960-Oct. 1963. *Publications:* The Rendel Harris Papyri, 1936; First Poems, 1937; A Lexicon to Herodotus, 1938; The History of Herodotus, 1939; Casting-off, and other poems, 1939; Herodotus, Book VIII, 1939; Llyfr Blegywryd, 1942; Thucydidis Historia, 1942; Herodotus (translation), 1949; Dancer's End and The Wedding Gift (poems), 1951, repr. 1976; The Social Services; Needs and Means, 1952; (jointly) One Nation, 1950; Change is our Ally, 1954; Biography of a Nation (with Angus Maude), 1955, 2nd edn 1970; Great Parliamentary Occasions, 1960; Saving in a Free Society, 1960; A Nation not Afraid, 1965; Medicine and Politics, 1966, rev. edn 1976; The House of Lords in the Middle Ages (with Keith Wallis), 1968; Freedom and Reality, 1969; Common Market: the case against, 1971; Still to Decide, 1972; Common Market: renegotiate or come out, 1973; No Easy Answers, 1973; Wrestling with the Angel, 1977; numerous political pamphlets. *Address:* 33 South Eaton Place, SW1. *T:* 01-730 0988.

POWELL, Air Vice-Marshal John Frederick, OBE 1956; Warden and Director of Studies, Moor Park College, 1972-77; *b* 12 June 1915; *y s* of Rev. Morgan Powell, Limpley Stoke, Bath; *m* 1939, Geraldine Ysolda, *e d* of late Sir John Fitzgerald Moylan, CB, CBE; four *s.* *Educ:* Lancing; King's Coll., Cambridge (MA). Joined RAF Educnl Service at No 1 Sch. of Techn Trng, 1937; Junior Lectr, RAF College, 1938-39; RAFVR (Admin. and Special Duties) ops room duties, Coastal Comd, 1939-45 (despatches); RAF Educn Br., 1946; Sen. Instructor in History, RAF Coll., 1946-49; RAF Staff Coll., 1950; Air Min., 1951-53; Sen. Tutor, RAF Coll., 1953-59; Educn Staff, HQ, FEAF, 1959-62; Min. of Def., 1962-64; Comd Educn Off., HQ Bomber Comd, 1964-66; OC, RAF Sch. of Educn, 1966-67; Dir of Educational Services, RAF, 1967-72; Air Commodore, 1967; Air Vice-Marshal, 1968. *Recreations:* beagling, choral music, tennis, squash. *Address:* Old Post Office, Northington, near Alresford, Hants. *T:* Alresford 2221. *Club:* Royal Air Force.

POWELL, Lewis Franklin, Jr; Associate Justice of US Supreme Court, since Dec. 1971; *b* Suffolk, Va, USA, 19 Sept. 1907; *s* of Lewis Franklin Powell and Mary Lewis (*née* Gwathmey); *m* 1936, Josephine Pierce Rucker; one *s* three *d.* *Educ:* McGuire's Univ. Sch., Richmond, Va; Washington and Lee Univ., Lexington, Va (BS *magnum cum laude,* LLB); Harvard Law Sch. (LLM). Admitted to practice, Bar of Virginia, 1931; subseq. practised law; partner in firm of Hunton, Williams, Gay, Powell and Gibson, in Richmond, 1938-71. Served War, May 1942-Feb. 1946, USAAF, overseas, to rank Col; subseq. Col. US Reserve. Legion of Merit and Bronze Star (US), also Croix de Guerre with Palms (France). Member: Nat. Commn on Law Enforcement and Admin of Justice, 1965-67; Blue Ribbon

Defence Panel, 1969-70. Chairman or Dir of companies. Past Chm., Richmond Public Sch. Bd, etc; Trustee: Colonial Williamsburg Inc. (also Exec. and Gen. Council); Richmond Meml Hosp.; Washington and Lee Univ., etc. Mem., Amer. Bar Assoc. (Pres. 1964-65); Fellow, Amer. Bar Foundn (Pres. 1969-71); Pres. or Mem. various Bar Assocs and other legal and social instns; Hon. Bencher, Lincoln's Inn. Holds several hon. degrees. Phi Beta Kappa, Phi Delta Phi, Omiaran Delta Kappa, Phi Kappa Sigma. Is a Democrat. *Publications:* contribs to legal periodicals, etc. *Address:* (office) 1003 Electric Building, Richmond, Va 23219, USA; (home) 1238 Rothesay Road, Richmond, Va 23221, USA. *Clubs:* Century, University (NYC); Commonwealth, Country Club of Virginia (Richmond, Va).

POWELL, Prof. Michael James David; John Humphrey Plummer Professor of Applied Numerical Analysis, University of Cambridge, since 1976; *b* 29 July 1936; *s* of William James David Powell and Beatrice Margaret (*née* Page); *m* 1959, Caroline Mary Henderson; one *s* two *d.* *Educ:* Eastbourne Coll.; Peterhouse, Cambridge (Schol.; BA 1959). Mathematician at Atomic Energy Research Estabt, Harwell, 1959-76; special merit research appt to banded level, 1969, and to senior level, 1975. *Publications:* papers on numerical mathematics, especially approximation and optimization calculations. *Recreations:* canals, golf, walking. *Address:* 134 Milton Road, Cambridge.

POWELL, Michael L., FRGS; film director; *b* Bekesbourne, near Canterbury, Kent, 30 Sept. 1905; *s* of Thomas William Powell and Mabel, *d* of Frederick Corbett, Worcester; *m* 1943, Frances, *d* of Dr J. J. Reidy, JP, MD; two *s.* *Educ:* King's Sch., Canterbury; Dulwich Coll. Joined National Provincial Bank, 1922; Metro-Goldwyn-Mayer film co., 1925, making Mare Nostrum, in the Mediterranean, with Rex Ingram as Dir; various capacities on 2 subseq. Ingram films: Somerset Maugham's The Magician and Robert Hichens' The Garden of Allah; was brought to Elstree, 1928, by the painter and film director, Harry Lachman; worked on 3 Hitchcock silent films, incl. script of Blackmail (later made into talking film). Travelled in Albania; wrote scripts for films of Caste and 77 Park Lane; given chance to direct by Jerry Jackson, 1931; dir Two Crowded Hours and Rynox (both melodramas of 40 mins); went on to make a dozen short features, incl. 4 for Michael Balcon at Shepherd's Bush Studios, incl. The Fire Raisers and The Red Ensign (both orig. stories by Jackson and Powell); wrote and dir The Edge of the World, on Foula, Shetland, 1936 (prod. Joe Rock); travelled in Burma, up the Chindwin; given a contract by Alexander Korda, 1938; met Emeric Pressburger, together wrote and then dir The Spy in Black, and Contraband; co-dir, Thief of Bagdad and The Lion has Wings; prod. and dir 49th Parallel (from orig. story by Pressburger); formed The Archers Company and together wrote, prod. and dir 16 films, incl. Colonel Blimp, I Know Where I'm Going, A Matter of Life and Death, Black Narcissus, The Red Shoes, all for J. Arthur Rank; returned to Korda, 1948, to make 4 films, incl. The Small Back Room and Tales of Hoffman; returned to Rank for The Battle of the River Plate (The Archers' second Royal Perf. film) and Ill Met By Moonlight; also made Rosalinda (film of Fledermaus) at Elstree; The Archers Company then broke up; since then has dir Honeymoon, Peeping Tom, The Queen's Guards, Bluebeard's Castle (Bartók opera); The Sorcerer's Apprentice (ballet film); film (for Children's Film Foundn) from a story and script by Pressburger, The Boy Who Turned Yellow; They're a Weird Mob (Aust.); Age of Consent (Aust.). *In the theatre:* prod. and dir (Hemingway's) The Fifth Column, 1945; (Jan de Hartog's) The Skipper Next to God, 1947; (James Forsyth's) Heloise, 1951; (Raymond Massey's) Hanging Judge, 1955. TV Series (several episodes): Espionage and The Defenders, for Herbert Brodkin. *Publications:* 200,000 Feet on Foula; Graf Spee; A Waiting Game, 1975. *Recreation:* leaning on gates. *Clubs:* Savile, Royal Automobile.

POWELL, Dame Muriel, DBE 1968 (CBE 1962); Chief Nursing Officer, Scottish Home and Health Department, 1970-76; *b* 30 Oct. 1914; *d* of late Wallace George Powell and late Anne Elizabeth Powell, Cinderford, Glos. *Educ:* East Dean Grammar Sch., Cinderford; St George's Hosp., London. SRN 1937; SCM 1939; Sister Tutor Dipl., Battersea Coll. of Techn., 1941; Dipl. in Nursing, London Univ., 1942. Formerly: Ward Sister and Night Sister, St George's Hosp.; Sister, Co. Maternity Hosp., Postlip Hall, Glos. (War Emerg. Hosp.); District Nurse, Glos; Sister Tutor, Ipswich Borough Gen. Hosp.; Princ. Tutor, Manchester Royal Infirmary; Matron, St George's Hosp. London, 1947-70. Pres., Assoc. of Hosp. Matrons, 1958-63; Pres., Nat. Assoc. of State Enrolled Nurses, 1965-67; Dep. Pres., Royal Coll. of Nursing, 1963-64. Mem., Central Health Services Coun.; Chm., Standing Nursing Adv. Cttee, Min. of Health, 1958-69. *Publication:* Patients are People, 1975. *Recreation:* music. *Address:* Quay House, Newnham-on-Severn, Glos GL14 1BH. *T:* Newnham 510.

POWELL, Prof. Percival Hugh, MA, DLitt, Dr Phil.; Professor of German, Indiana University, since 1970; *b* 4 Sept. 1912; 3rd *s* of late Thomas Powell and late Marie Sophia Roeser; *m* 1944, Dorothy Mavis Pattison (*née* Donald) (marr. diss. 1964); two *s* one adopted *d*; *m* 1966, Mary Kathleen (*née* Wilson); one *s*. *Educ:* University College, Cardiff; Univs of Rostock, Zürich, Bonn. 1st Class Hons German (Wales), 1933; Univ. Teachers' Diploma in Education, 1934; MA (Wales) Dist. 1936; Research Fellow of Univ. of Wales, 1936-38; Modern Languages Master, Towyn School, 1934-36; Dr Phil. (Rostock) 1938; Lektor in English, Univ. of Bonn, 1938-39; Asst Lectr, Univ. Coll., Cardiff, 1939-40; War Service, 1940-46 (Capt. Intelligence Corps); Lecturer in German, Univ. Coll., Leicester, 1946, Head of Department of German, 1954; Prof. of German, Univ. of Leicester, 1958-69. Barclay Acheson Prof. of Internat. Studies at Macalester Coll., Minn., USA, 1965-66. DLitt (Wales) 1962. British Academy award, 1963; Fritz Thyssen Foundation Award, 1964; Leverhulme Trust Award, 1968. *Publications:* Pierre Corneilles Dramen in Deutschen Bearbeitungen, 1939; critical editions of dramas of Andreas Gryphius, 1955-72; critical edn of J. G. Schoch's Comœdia vom Studentenleben, 1976; articles and reviews in English and foreign literary jls. *Recreation:* music. *Address:* Department of Germanic Languages, Ballantine Hall, Indiana University, Bloomington, Indiana 47401, USA.

POWELL, Sir Philip, Kt 1975; OBE 1957; ARA 1972; FRIBA; Partner of Powell and Moya, Architects, since 1946, and Powell, Moya and Partners, since 1976; *b* 15 March 1921; *yr s* of late Canon A. C. Powell and late Mary Winnifred (*née* Walker), Epsom and Chichester; *m* 1953, Philippa, *d* of Lt-Col C. C. Eccles, Tunbridge Wells; one *s* one *d*. *Educ:* Epsom Coll.; AA Sch. of Architecture (Hons Diploma). *Works include:* Churchill Gdns flats, Westminster, 1948-62 (won in open competition); houses and flats at Gospel Oak, St Pancras, 1954 and Vauxhall Park, Lambeth, 1972; houses at: Chichester, 1950; Toys Hill, 1954; Oxshott, 1954; Baughurst, Hants, 1954; Skylon for Fest. of Britain, 1951 (won in open competition); British Pavilion, Expo 70, Osaka, Japan, 1970; Mayfield Sch., Putney, 1955; Plumstead Manor Sch., Woolwich, 1970; Dining Rooms at Bath Acad. of Art, Corsham, 1970, and Eton Coll., 1974; extensions, Brasenose Coll., Oxford, 1961, and Corpus Christi Coll., Oxford, 1969; picture gall. and undergrad. rooms, Christ Church, Oxford, 1967; Wolfson Coll., Oxford, 1974; Cripps Building, St John's Coll., Cambridge, 1967; new buildings, Queens' Coll., Cambridge, 1976; Chichester Fest. Theatre, 1962; Swimming Baths, Putney, 1967; Mental Hosp. extensions at Fairmile, nr Wallingford, 1957 and Borocourt, nr Henley-on-Thames, 1964; Hosps at Swindon, Slough, High Wycombe, Wythenshawe and Woolwich; Museum of London, 1976. Has won numerous medals and awards for architectural work, inc. Royal Gold Medal for Architecture, RIBA, 1974. Mem. Royal Fine Art Commn, 1969-. *Recreations:* travel, listening to music. *Address:* 16 The Little Boltons, SW10 9LP. *T:* 01-373 8620; 21 Upper Cheyne Row, SW3. *T:* 01-351 3881.

POWELL, Major Sir Richard George Douglas, 3rd Bt, *cr* 1897; MC 1944, Bar 1945; Welsh Guards; Director: Bovis Ltd; Pierson, Heldring & Pierson (UK) Ltd; Russell Garratt Ltd; Cornwall Daborn Garratt Ltd; BUPA Medical Centre Ltd; The TH inc. Group (UK) Ltd; *b* 14 Nov. 1909; *o s* of Sir Douglas Powell, 2nd Bart, and Albinia Muriel, *e d* of W. F. Powell of Sharow Hall, Ripon; *S* father, 1932; *m* 1933, Elizabeth Josephine, *o d* of late Lt-Col O. R. McMullen, CMG; one *s* two *d*. *Educ:* Eton College. Served War of 1939-45 (MC and Bar). Croix Militaire 1st Class (Belgium), 1945; Assistant Military Attaché, British Embassy, Brussels, 1945-48. Dir-Gen., Inst. of Directors, 1954-74. *Heir:* s Nicholas Folliott Douglas Powell [*b* 17 July 1935; *m* 1960, Daphne Jean, *yr d* of Major and Mrs George Errington, Monkton Ranch, Figtree, Southern Rhodesia; one *s* one *d*]. *Address:* Mackney, Brightwell-cum-Sotwell, Oxon OX10 0SJ. *T:* Wallingford 37245. *Clubs:* Cavalry and Guards, Buck's.

POWELL, Sir Richard (Royle), GCB 1967 (KCB 1961; CB 1951); KBE 1954; CMG 1946; Deputy Chairman, Permanent Committee on Invisible Exports, 1968-76; Chairman, Alusuisse (UK) Ltd and subsidiary companies, since 1969; *b* 30 July 1909; *er s* of Ernest Hartley and Florence Powell; unmarried. *Educ:* Queen Mary's Grammar Sch., Walsall; Sidney Sussex Coll., Cambridge (Hon. Fellow, 1972). Entered Civil Service, 1931 and apptd to Admiralty; Private Sec. to First Lord, 1934-37; Member of British Admiralty Technical Mission, Canada, and of British Merchant Shipbuilding Mission, and later of British Merchant Shipping Mission in USA, 1940-44; Civil Adviser to Commander-in-Chief, British Pacific Fleet, 1944-45; Under-Secretary, Ministry of Defence, 1946-48. Dep. Sec., Admiralty, 1948-50; Dep. Sec., Min. of Defence, 1950-56; Permanent Secretary, Board of Trade, 1960-68 (Min. of Defence, 1956-59). Director: Philip Hill Investment Trust; Hill Samuel Gp; GEC; Whessoe Ltd, 1968-; Wilkinson Match Ltd (formerly British Match Corporation), 1971-; Sandoz Gp of Cos, 1972-; Clerical, Medical and General Life Assurance Soc., 1972-; National Nuclear Corp., 1973-; BPB Industries Ltd, 1973-. Pres., Inst. for Fiscal Studies, 1970-. *Address:* 56 Montagu Square, W1. *T:* 01-262 0911. *Club:* Athenæum.

POWELL, Robert Lane B.; *see* Bayne-Powell.

POWELL, Robert William; Headmaster of Sherborne, 1950-70; retired; *b* 29 October 1909; *s* of late William Powell and Agnes Emma Powell; *m* 1938, Charity Rosamond Collard; one *s*. *Educ:* Bristol Grammar School; Christ Church, Oxford. Assistant Master, Repton, May-Dec. 1934; Assistant Master, Charterhouse, 1935. Served War of 1939-45, 1940-45. Housemaster of Gownboys, Charterhouse, 1946-50. *Recreations:* fishing, music. *Address:* Manor Farm House, Child Okeford, near Blandford, Dorset. *T:* Child Okeford 648.

POWELL, Roger, OBE 1976; bookbinder; *b* 17 May 1896; *er s* of late Oswald Byrom Powell and Winifred Marion Powell (*née* Cobb); *m* 1924, Rita Glanville, *y d* of late Frank and Katherine F. Harvey; one *s* twin *d*. *Educ:* Bedales Sch. Served European War, 1914-18: Hampshire Regt, Palestine, 1917; Flt Lt, RAF, Egypt, 1918. Poultry farming, 1921-30; studied bookbinding at LCC Central Sch., 1930-31; joined Douglas Cockerell & Son, bookbinders, 1935; Partner, 1936; opened own bindery at Froxfield, 1947. Member: Art Workers' Guild; Double Crown Club; Red Rose Guild. Has repaired and bound many early manuscripts, incunabula and other early printed books including: for Winchester (both Coll. and Cathedral); for TCD, The Book of Kells, 1953; The Book of Durrow, The Book of Armagh, The Book of Dimma (in accommod. Brit. Mus.), 1954-57; for Lichfield Cath., The St Chad Gospels, 1961-62; for RIA, The Book of Lecan, Lebor na hUidre, Leabhar Breac, The Book of Fermoy, 1968-74; for Durham Cathedral, The A. II. 17 Gospels, 1976. Tooled Memorial Bindings, incl: WVS Roll of Honour, Civilian War Dead, 1939-45, in Westminster Abbey. Rolls of Honour: for RMA Sandhurst and Woolwich; Coastal Command, RAF; S Africa, India, Pakistan. Other tooled bindings, in: Brit. Mus., Victoria and Albert Mus.; in Libraries: (Bodleian, Oxford; Pierpont Morgan; Syracuse Univ.; Grolier Club, New York; Newberry, Chicago), and in private collections in Britain, Ireland and USA. Visited, to advise on book-conservation: Iceland, 1965; Florence, 1966; Portugal, 1967. Hon. For. Corresp. Mem., Grolier Club, NY. Hon. MA Dublin, 1961. *Publications:* various contribs to The Library; Scriptorium, Brussels; Eriu, Dublin, 1956-69. *Recreations:* cricket, singing, 'finding out', photography, amateur operatics and dramatics, organic cultivations, bee-keeping, golf. *Address:* The Slade, Froxfield, Petersfield, Hants GU32 1EB. *T:* Hawkley 229.

POWELL, Tim; *see* Powell, H. A. R.

POWELL, Victor George Edward; Senior Partner, Victor G. Powell Associates, Management Consultants, since 1963; Senior Adviser, International Labour Organisation; Director, Mosscare Housing Association Ltd, since 1974; *b* London, 1 Jan. 1929; *s* of George Richard Powell and Kate Hughes Powell, London; *m* 1956, Patricia Copeland Allen; three *s* one *d*. *Educ:* Beckenham Grammar Sch.; Univs of Durham and Manchester. BA 1st cl. hons Econs 1954, MA Econ. Studies 1957, Dunelm; PhD Manchester 1963. RN Engrg Apprentice, 1944-48. Central Work Study Dept, ICI, London, 1954-56; Chief Work Study Engr, Ind Coope Ltd, 1956-58; Lectr in Industrial Administration, Manchester Univ., 1959, Hon. Lectr 1959-63; Asst Gen. Manager, Louis C. Edwards & Sons Ltd, 1959-63; Chm., Food Production & Processing Ltd, 1971-74. Gen. Sec., 1970-72, Dir, 1972-73, War on Want. Associate Mem., BIM, 1957; Mem. Inst. Management Consultants, 1968. *Publications:* Economics of Plant Investment and Replacement Decisions, 1964; Techniques for Improving Distribution Management, 1968; Warehousing, 1976; various articles. *Recreations:* music, walking. *Address:* Inglewood, Coppice Lane, Disley, Stockport, Cheshire SK12 2LT. *T:* Disley 2011. *Club:* Royal Commonwealth Society.

POWELL-COTTON, Christopher, CMG 1961; MBE 1951; MC 1945; JP; Uganda CS, retired; *b* 23 Feb. 1918; *s* of Major P. H. G. Powell-Cotton and Mrs H. B. Powell-Cotton (*née* Slater); unmarried. *Educ:* Harrow School; Trinity College, Cambridge. Army Service, 1939-45: commissioned Buffs, 1940; seconded KAR, Oct. 1940; T/Major, 1943. Apptd to Uganda Administration, 1940, and released for Mil. Service. District Commissioner, 1950; Provincial Commissioner, 1955; Minister of Security and External Relations, 1961. Landowner in SE Kent. Dir, Powell-Cotton Museum of Nat. History and Ethnography. *Address:* Quex Park, Birchington, Kent. *T:* Thanet 41836. *Club:* MCC.

POWELL-JONES, John Ernest, CMG 1974; HM Diplomatic Service; Ambassador to Senegal, Guinea, Mali, Mauritania and Guinea-Bissau, since 1976, to Cape Verde, since 1977; *b* 14 April 1925; *s* of late W. J. Powell-Jones; *m* 1st, 1949, Ann Murray (marr. diss. 1967); two *s* one *d*; 2nd, 1968, Pamela Sale. *Educ:* Charterhouse; University Coll., Oxford. Served with Rifle Bde, 1943-46. HM Foreign (now Diplomatic) Service, 1949; 3rd Sec. and Vice-Consul, Bogota, 1950-52; Eastern and later Levant Dept, FO, 1952-55; 2nd, later 1st Sec., Athens, 1955-59; News Dept, FO, 1959-60; 1st Sec., Leopoldville, 1961-62; UN Dept, FO, 1963-67; ndc Canada 1967-68; Counsellor, Political Adviser's Office, Singapore, 1968-69; Counsellor and Consul-General, Athens, 1970-73; Ambassador at Phnom Penh, 1973-75; RCDS 1975. *Recreations:* gardening, lawn tennis. *Address:* c/o Foreign and Commonwealth Office, SW1; Gaston Gate, Cranleigh, Surrey. *T:* Cranleigh 4313. *Club:* Travellers'.

POWER, Vice-Adm. Sir Arthur (Mackenzie), KCB 1974; MBE 1952; Secretary to the Senate of the Inns of Court and the Bar, since 1975; *b* 18 June 1921; *s* of Admiral of the Fleet Sir Arthur Power, GCB, GBE, CVO; *m* 1949, Marcia Helen Gell; two *s* one *d*. *Educ:* Rugby. Royal Navy, 1938; served War of 1939-45 and Korean War; specialised in gunnery; Captain, 1959; ADC to the Queen, 1968; Rear-Admiral, 1968; Adm. Supt, Portsmouth, 1968-71; Flag Officer, Spithead, 1969-71; Vice-Adm., 1971; Flag Officer Flotillas, Western Fleet, 1971-72; Flag Officer, First Flotilla, 1972-73; Flag Officer Plymouth, Port Adm. Devonport, Cmdr Central Sub Area, E Atlantic, and Cmdr Plymouth Sub Area, Channel, 1973-75. *Address:* Gunnsmead, South Road, Liphook, Hants. *Club:* Army and Navy.
See also M . G . Power.

POWER, Mrs Brian St Quentin; *see* Stack, (Ann) Prunella.

POWER, Sir John (Patrick McLannahan), 3rd Bt, *cr* 1924, of Newlands Manor; Chairman, Arthur Beale Ltd, London; *b* 16 March 1928; *s* of Sir Ivan McLannahan Cecil Power, 2nd Baronet, and Nancy Hilary, *d* of late Reverend J. W. Griffiths, Wentworth, Virginia Water; *m* 1st, 1957, Melanie (marr. diss. 1967), *d* of Hon. Alastair Erskine, Glenfintaig House, Spean Bridge, Inverness-shire; two *s* one *d*; 2nd, 1970, Tracey (marr. diss. 1974), *d* of George Cooper, Amberley Place, Amberley, Sussex. *Educ:* Pangbourne Coll. Served RN, 1946-48, The Cunard Steamship Co. Ltd, London, 1945-58. *Recreations:* sailing, painting. *Heir:* *s* Alastair John Cecil Power, *b* 15 Aug. 1958. *Address:* Ashwick House, Dulverton, Somerset. *T:* Dulverton 488. *Clubs:* Arts, Royal Ocean Racing, Royal London Yacht; Royal Naval Sailing Association; Island Sailing.
See also Lord Cardross.

POWER, Adm. (retd) Sir Manley (Laurence), KCB 1958 (CB 1955); CBE 1943 (OBE 1940); DSO 1944, Bar 1945; DL; *b* 10 Jan. 1904; *s* of Adm. Sir Laurence E. Power, KCB, CVO; *m* 1930, Barbara Alice Mary Topham; one *s* one *d*. *Educ:* RN Colleges, Osborne and Dartmouth. Naval Cadet, 1917; Midshipman, 1921; Sub-Lt 1924; Lt 1926; Lt-Comdr 1934; Comdr 1939; Capt. 1943; Rear-Adm. 1953; Vice-Adm. 1956; Admiral, 1960. Deputy Chief of Naval Staff, and Fifth Sea Lord, 1957-59; Commander-in-Chief, Portsmouth, Allied C-in-C, Channel, and C-in-C, Home Station (Designate), 1959-61; retired, 1961. CC, Isle of Wight, 1964-74. DL, Hampshire, 1965-74, Isle of Wight, 1974. Officer of Legion of Merit (US); Croix de Guerre avec Palme (France). *Address:* Norton Cottage, Yarmouth, Isle of Wight. *T:* Yarmouth 760401.

POWER, Michael George; Under Secretary, Civl Service Department, since 1977; *b* 2 April 1924; *s* of Admiral of the Fleet Sir Arthur Power, GCB, GBE, CVO, and Amy Isabel (*née* Bingham); *m* 1954, Kathleen Maeve (*née* McCaul); one *s* two *d* and two step *d*. *Educ:* Rugby Sch.; Corpus Christi Coll., Cambridge. Served War, Rifle Bde, 1942-46 (Captain); ME Centre of Arab Studies (Jerusalem), 1946-47; Colonial Admin. Service, 1947-63: District Officer: Kenya, 1948-53; Malaya, 1953-57; Kenya, 1957-63; Admiralty, 1963; Asst Sec., MoD, 1969; Asst Under-Sec. of State, MoD, 1973-77. *Recreations:* sailing, golf, gardening. *Address:* Wancom Way, Puttenham Heath Road, Compton, Guildford. *T:* Guildford 810470.
See also Sir A . M . Power.

POWERSCOURT, 10th Viscount *cr* 1743; **Mervyn Niall Wingfield;** Baron Wingfield, 1743; Baron Powerscourt (UK), 1885; *b* 3 Sept. 1935; *s* of 9th Viscount Powerscourt and of Sheila Claude, *d* of late Lt-Col Claude Beddington; *S* father, 1973; *m*

1962, Wendy Ann Pauline (marr. diss. 1974), *d* of R. C. G. Slazenger; one *s* one *d*. *Educ:* Stowe; Trinity Coll., Cambridge. Formerly Irish Guards. *Heir:* *s* Hon. Mervyn Anthony Wingfield, *b* 21 Aug. 1963.
See also Sir H. R. H. Langrishe, Bt.

POWIS, 6th Earl of, *cr* 1804; **Christian Victor Charles Herbert;** Baron Clive (Ire.), 1762; Baron Clive, 1794; Viscount Clive, Baron Herbert, Baron Powis, 1804; *b* 28 May 1904; 2nd *s* of Colonel Edward William Herbert, CB (*d* 1924) (*g s* of 2nd Earl of Powis) and Beatrice Anne (*d* 1928), *d* of Sir Hedworth Williamson, 8th Bt; *S* brother, 1974. *Educ:* Oundle; Trinity Coll., Cambridge (BA); University Coll., London. Barrister, Inner Temple, 1932; Private Secretary to: Governor and C-in-C, British Honduras, 1947-55; Governor of British Guiana, 1955-64. Served War of 1939-45 with RAOC, UK and India; Major, 1943. *Heir:* *cousin* George William Herbert [*b* 4 June 1925; *m* 1949, Hon. Katharine Odeyne de Grey, *d* of ' 8th Baron Walsingham, DSO, OBE; four *s* two adopted *d*]. *Address:* Powis Castle, Welshpool, N Wales. *T:* 3360. *Clubs:* Brooks's, MCC.

POWLES, Sir Guy (Richardson), KBE 1961; CMG 1954; ED 1944; first Ombudsman of New Zealand, 1962-75, Chief Ombudsman, 1975-77; *b* 5 April 1905; *s* of late Colonel C. G. Powles, CMG, DSO, New Zealand Staff Corps; *m* 1931, Eileen, *d* of A. J. Nicholls; two *s*. *Educ:* Wellington Coll., NZ; Victoria Univ. (LLB). Barrister, Supreme Court, New Zealand, 1929; served War of 1939-45 with NZ Military Forces, to rank of Colonel; Counsellor, NZ Legation, Washington, DC, USA, 1946-48; High Comr, Western Samoa, 1949-60, for NZ in India, 1960-62, Ceylon, 1960-62, and Ambassador of NZ to Nepal, 1960-62. President, NZ Inst. of Internat. Affairs, 1967-71. NZ Comr, Commn of the Churches on Internat. Affairs, World Council of Churches, 1971-; Comr, Internat. Commn of Jurists, Geneva, 1975-. Race Relations Conciliator, 1971-73. Patron: Amnesty International (NZ); NZ-India Soc.; Environmental Defence Soc. Hon. LLD Victoria Univ. of Wellington, 1969. *Publications:* articles and speeches on international affairs, administrative law and race relations. *Address:* 34 Wesley Road, Wellington, NZ.

POWLETT; *see* Orde-Powlett.

POWLETT, Vice-Admiral Sir Peveril B. R. W. W.; *see* William-Powlett.

POWLETT, Rear-Adm. Philip Frederick, CB 1961; DSO 1941 (and Bar 1942); DSC 1941; DL; retired; Secretary, Friends of Norwich Cathedral; *b* 13 Nov. 1906; *s* of late Vice-Admiral F. A. Powlett, CBE; *m* 1935, Frances Elizabeth Sykes (*née* Elwell); two *s* one *d*. *Educ:* Osborne and Dartmouth. War of 1939-45 (DSC, DSO and Bar; Polish Cross of Valour, 1942); in command of destroyers and corvettes, Shearwater, Blankney, Cassandra. Deputy Director of Naval Air Organisation and Training, 1950; Senior Officer, Reserve Fleet, Clyde, 1952-53; Captain (F), 6th Frigate Squadron, 1954-55; Director (RN), Joint Anti-Submarine School, and Senior Naval Officer, Northern Ireland, 1956-58; Flag Officer and Admiral Superintendent, Gibraltar, 1959-62; retired, 1962. DL Norfolk, 1974. *Address:* The Mill House, Lyng, Norwich, Norfolk, NR9 5QZ.

POWNALL, Henry Charles; Third Senior Prosecuting Counsel to the Crown at the Central Criminal Court, since 1974; a Recorder of the Crown Court, since 1972; *b* 25 Feb. 1927; *e s* of late John Cecil Glossop Pownall, CB, and of Margaret Nina Pownall (*née* Jesson); *m* 1955, Sarah Bettine, *d* of Major John Deverell; one *s* one *d* (and one *d* decd). *Educ:* Rugby Sch.; Trinity Coll., Cambridge; BA 1950, MA 1963; LLB 1951. Served War, Royal Navy, 1945-48. Called to Bar, Inner Temple; Master of the Bench, 1976; joined South-Eastern Circuit, 1954. Junior Prosecuting Counsel to the Crown at the Central Criminal Court, 1964-71; Fourth Sen. 1971. Mem. Cttee: Orders and Medals Research Soc., 1961-69, and 1970- (Pres., 1971-75); Nat. Benevolent Instn, 1964-. *Publication:* Korean Campaign Medals, 1950-53, 1957. *Recreations:* travel; medals and medal ribbons. *Address:* 69 Eaton Terrace, SW1W 8TN; 2 Harcourt Buildings, Temple, EC4Y 9DB. *T:* 01-353 2112. *Clubs:* United Oxford & Cambridge University, Pratt's; Hurlingham.

POWNALL, Leslie Leigh, MA, PhD; Chairman, NSW Planning and Environment Commission, 1974-77, retired; *b* 1 Nov. 1921; *y s* of A. de S. Pownall, Wanganui, New Zealand; *m* 1943, Judith, *d* of late Harold Whittaker, Palmerston North. *Educ:* Palmerston North Boys' High Sch.; Victoria University College, University of Canterbury, University of Wisconsin. Asst Master, Christchurch Boys' High Sch., 1941-46; Lecturer in Geography: Christchurch Teachers' Coll., 1946-47; Ardmore Teachers'

Coll., 1948-49; Auckland University College, 1949-51; Senior Lecturer in Geography, 1951-60, Prof. of Geography, 1960-61, Vice-Chancellor and Rector, 1961-66, University of Canterbury; Clerk of the University Senate, Univ. of London, 1966-74. Consultant, Inter-University Council for Higher Educn Overseas, London, 1963; Consultant to Chm. of Working Party on Higher Educn in E Africa, 1968-69. Member Meeting, Council on World Tensions on Social and Economic Development (S Asia and Pacific), Kuala Lumpur, Malaysia, 1964; Member, Central Governing Body, City Parochial Foundation, London, 1967-74 (Mem., Grants Sub-Cttee; Chm., Finance and Gen. Purposes Cttee); Governor, Internat. Students Trust, London, 1967-74. *Publications:* New Zealand, 1951 (New York); geographic contrib. in academic journals of America, Netherlands and New Zealand. *Recreations:* music, literature. *Address:* Box 3927, GPO, Sydney, NSW 2001, Australia. *Clubs:* Canterbury, University (Christchurch, NZ).

POWYS, family name of **Baron Lilford.**

POYNTER, (Frederick) Noel (Lawrence), BA, PhD, FLA, FRSL; Director, Wellcome Institute of History of Medicine, 1964-73; *b* 24 Dec. 1908; *s* of late H. W. Poynter; *m* 1st, 1939, Kate L. R. Marder (*d* 1966); no *c*; 2nd, 1968, Mrs Dodie Barry (*née* McClellan). *Educ:* King's and Univ. Coll., University of London. Asst Librarian, Wellcome Hist. Med. Lib., 1930; Chief Librarian, 1954. RAF, 1941-46. Founder Member, 1958, Fac. of Hist. of Medicine, Society of Apothecaries of London, Chm., 1971- (Hon. Sec. 1958-71); Member, Council, Bibliographical Society, 1960-64, 1965-72; President: Internat. Acad. of Hist. of Med., 1962-70; British Society of Hist. of Med., 1971-; XXIII Internat. Congress, Hist. of Med., London, 1972; Gideon Delaune Lecturer, Society of Apothecaries, 1964. Has given Memorial lectures, in USA; Hon. Lecturer in History of Medicine, University of British Columbia, 1966-; Henry Cohen Lecturer in Medicine, University of Jerusalem, 1968, Univ. of Liverpool, 1973; Vicary Lectr, RCS, 1973; Annual Orator, Med. Soc. London, 1974. Hon. Member, Royal Society of Medicine (Hist. Section); also Hon. Member various foreign societies, Fellow, Internat. Acads of the Hist. of Science, Medicine and Pharmacy; Hon. DLitt, California; Hon. MD Kiel; Hon. Fellow: Huguenot Society of London; Medical Society of London. *Publications:* Selected Writings of William Clowes (1544-1604), 1948; A Seventeenth Century Doctor and his Patients: John Symcotts (joint), 1951; Bibliography, some Achievements and Prospects, 1961; A Short History of Medicine (joint), 1961; The Journal of James Yonge (1647-1721), 1963; Gideon Delaune and his Family Circle, 1965; The Evolution of Medical Education in Britain, 1966; Medicine and Culture, 1968; Medicine and Man, 1971. Ed. several medical works; Ed., Medical History (quarterly) also Current Work in the History of Medicine (quarterly); also numerous articles in periodicals. *Recreations:* painting, chamber music, French literature. *Address:* 46600 Montvalent, Lot, France. *Club:* Athenæum.

POYNTON, Sir (Arthur) Hilton, GCMG 1964 (KCMG 1949; CMG 1946); *b* 20 April 1905; *y s* of late Arthur Blackburne Poynton, formerly Master of University College, Oxford; *m* 1946, Elisabeth Joan, *d* of late Rev. Edmund Williams; two *s* one *d*. *Educ:* Marlborough Coll.; Brasenose Coll., Oxford (Hon. Fellow 1964). Entered Civil Service, Department of Scientific and Industrial Research, 1927; transferred to Colonial Office, 1929; Private Secretary to Minister of Supply and Minister of Production 1941-43; reverted to Colonial Office, 1943; Permanent Under-Secretary of State, CO, 1959-66. Mem. Governing Body, SPCK, 1967-72. Mem., Ct of Governors, London Sch. Hygiene and Tropical Med., 1965-; Treas., Soc. Promotion Roman Studies, 1967-76; Dir, Overseas Branch, St John Ambulance, 1968-75. KStJ 1968. *Recreations:* music, travel. *Address:* Craigmillar, 47 Stanhope Road, Croydon CR0 5NS. *T:* 01-688 3729. *Club:* Athenæum.

POYNTON, (John) Orde, CMG 1961; MD; Consulting Bibliographer, University of Melbourne, 1962-74; Fellow of Graduate House, University of Melbourne; *b* 9 April 1906; *o s* of Frederick John Poynton, MD, FRCP, and Alice Constance, *d* of Sir John William Powlett Campbell-Orde, 3rd Bt, of Kilmory; *m* 1965, Lola, *widow* of Group Captain T. S. Horry, DFC, AFC. *Educ:* Marlborough Coll.; Gonville and Caius Coll., Cambridge; Charing Cross Hospital (Univ. Schol. 1927-30). MA, MD (Cambridge); MRCS, LRCP; Horton-Smith prize, University of Cambridge, 1940. Sen. Resident MO, Charing Cross Hosp., 1932-33; Health Officer, Fed. Malay States, 1936-37; Res. Officer Inst. for Med. Research, FMS, 1937-38, Pathologist, 1938-46; Pathologist, Inst. of Med. and Veterinary Science, S Australia, 1948-50, Director, 1950-61. Hon. LLD Melbourne; Hon. MD Adelaide. *Publications:* monographs and papers relating to medicine and bibliography. *Recreation:*

bibliognostics. *Address:* 8 Seymour Avenue, Mount Eliza, Victoria 3930, Australia. *Club:* MCC.

PRAGNELL, Anthony William, OBE 1960; DFC 1944; Deputy Director-General, Independent Broadcasting Authority (formerly Independent Television Authority), since 1961; *b* 15 Feb. 1921; *s* of William Hendley Pragnell and Silvia Pragnell; *m* 1955, Teresa Mary, *d* of Leo and Anne Monaghan, Maidstone; one *s* one *d*. *Educ:* Cardinal Vaughan Sch., London. Asst Examiner, Estate Duty Office, 1939. Joined RAF as aircrew cadet, 1942; Navigator, Bomber Command, one tour of ops with 166 Squadron; second tour with 109 Squadron (Pathfinder Force), 1943-46. Examiner, Estate Duty Office, 1946. LLB London Univ., 1949. Asst Principal, General Post Office, 1950; Asst Secretary, ITA, 1954; Secretary, ITA, 1955. *Recreations:* reading, music. *Address:* Ashley, Grassy Lane, Sevenoaks, Kent. *T:* Sevenoaks 51463. *Club:* Royal Air Force.

PRAIN, Alexander Moncur, CBE 1964; Sheriff-Substitute: of Perth and Angus at Perth, 1946-71; of Lanarkshire at Airdrie, 1943-46; *b* Longforgan, Perthshire, 19 Feb. 1908; 2nd *s* of A. M. Prain, JP, and Mary Stuart Whytock; *m* 1936, Florence Margaret Robertson; one *s*. *Educ:* Merchiston Castle; Edinburgh Academy; Edinburgh Univ. Called to Scottish Bar, 1932; Army, 1940-43, Major, RAC. *Recreations:* fishing, reading. *Address:* Castellar, Crieff, Perthshire.

PRAIN, John Murray, DSO 1940; OBE 1956; TD 1943 (two Bars); DL; *b* 17 Dec. 1902; *e s* of late James Prain, Hon. LLD St Andrews University, of Kincaple by St Andrews, Fife, and late Victoria Eleanor Murray; *m* 1934, Lorina Helen Elspeth, *o d* of late Colonel P. G. M. Skene, OBE, DL, of Halyards and Pitlour, Fife; one *s* one *d*. *Educ:* Charterhouse; Clare Coll., Cambridge, BA 1924. Chm., James Prain & Sons Ltd, Dundee, 1945-56; Vice-Chm., Caird (Dundee) Ltd, 1956-64; Director: Alliance Trust Co. Ltd, 1946-73; 2nd Alliance Trust Co. Ltd, 1946-73; Tayside Floorcloth Co. Ltd, 1946-69; The Scottish Life Assurance Co. Ltd, 1949-72; Royal Bank of Scotland, 1955-71; William Halley & Sons Ltd; Member Scottish Committee, Industrial and Commercial Finance Corporation, 1946-55; Chairman: Jute Importers Association, 1947-49; Assoc. of Jute Spinners and Manufacturers, 1950-52; Dundee District Cttee, Scottish Board for Industry, 1948-62. Member, Jute Working Party, 1946-48; part-time Member Scottish Gas Board, 1952-56; Member Employers' Panel Industrial Disputes Tribunal, 1952-59. Member: Employers' Panel, Industrial Court, 1959-71; Industrial Arbitration Bd, 1971-72. DL for County of Fife, 1958; Served in War of 1939-45, Fife and Forfar Yeomanry (wounded, despatches, DSO); GSO(2), 1943-44; Lt-Col (AQ) RAC, OCTU, RMC Sandhurst, 1944-45; Member Queen's Body Guard for Scotland, Royal Company of Archers; Hon. President, Fife and Kinross Area Council, Royal British Legion (Scotland). *Address:* Mugdrum, Newburgh, Fife KY14 6EH. *T:* Newburgh, Fife 367. *Clubs:* Cavalry and Guards; New (Edinburgh); Royal and Ancient (St Andrews).

PRAIN, Sir Ronald (Lindsay), Kt 1956; OBE 1946; Chief Executive, 1943-68, Chairman, 1950-72, RST international group of companies; Director: Foseco Minsep Ltd; Minerals Separation Ltd; Monks Investment Trust Ltd; Pan-Holding SA; Selection Trust Ltd, and other companies; *b* Iquiqui, Chile, 3 Sept. 1907; *s* of Arthur Lindsay Prain and Amy Prain (*née* Watson); *m* 1938, Esther Pansy, *d* of late Norman Brownrigg, Haslemere; two *s*. *Educ:* Cheltenham Coll. Controller (Ministry of Supply): Diamond Die and Tool Control, 1940-45; Quartz Crystal Control, 1943-45. First Chairman: Agricultural Research Council of Rhodesia & Nyasaland, 1959-63; Merchant Bank of Central Africa Ltd, 1956-66; Merchant Bank (Zambia) Ltd, 1966-72; Director: Metal Market & Exchange Co. Ltd, 1943-65; San Francisco Mines of Mexico Ltd, 1944-68; Internat. Nickel Co. of Canada Ltd, 1951-72; Wankie Colliery Co. Ltd, 1953-63; Barclays Bank International, 1971-77. Chairman, Council of Commonwealth Mining & Metallurgical Institutions, 1961-74; President, British Overseas Mining Assoc., 1952; President, Inst. of Metals, 1960-61; Mem. Council, Overseas Develt Inst.; Hon. Pres., Copper Develt Assoc.; Hon. Member: Metals Soc.; Amer. Inst. of Min. & Metall. Engrs. Trustee, Inst. for Archaeo-Metallurgical Studies; Pres. Council, Cheltenham College. ANKH Award, Copper Club, New York, 1964; Gold Medal, 1968, and Hon. Fellow, Instn of Mining and Metallurgy; Platinum Medal, Inst. of Metals, 1969. *Publications:* Selected Papers (4 Vols); Copper: the anatomy of an industry, 1975 (Japanese trans. 1976). *Recreations:* cricket, real tennis, travel. *Address:* Waverley, St George's Hill, Weybridge, Surrey KT13 0QJ. *T:* Weybridge 42776; 43 Cadogan Square, SW1X 0HX. *T:* 01-235 4900. *Clubs:* Brooks's, White's, MCC.

PRAIN, Vyvyen Alice; retired as Principal, Princess Helena College, Temple Dinsley, Herts, 1935-July 1958; *b* 11 Oct 1895; *d* of Hunter Douglas Prain and Ellen Flora Davis. *Educ:* Edinburgh Ladies' Coll.; Edinburgh Univ. Graduated MA (Hons) in History (second class) in 1918, having gained the Gladstone Memorial Prize for History and Political Economy, and three class medals; Trained for teaching at Cambridge Training Coll., and gained a First Class Teacher's Certificate in 1919; History Mistress at Princess Helena Coll., Ealing, 1919-24; History and Economics at Wycombe Abbey Sch., 1924-29; Principal of the Ladies' Coll., Guernsey, 1929-35. *Recreations:* needlework, reading, travelling. *Address:* Halesworth, Suffolk.

PRANKERD, Prof. Thomas Arthur John, FRCP; Professor of Clinical Haematology, since 1965, Dean, 1972, University College Hospital Medical School; Hon. Consultant Physician: University College Hospital, since 1965; Whittington Hospital, since 1974; *b* 11 Sept. 1924; *s* of H. A. Prankerd, Barrister-at-Law, and J. D. Shorthose; *m* 1950, Margaret Vera Harrison Cripps; three *s* one *d. Educ:* Charterhouse Sch.; St Bartholomew's Hospital Med. Sch. MD (London) Gold Medal 1949; FRCP 1962. Jnr med. appts, St Bart's and University Coll. Hosp., 1947-60. Major, RAMC, 1948-50. Univ. Travelling Fellow, USA, 1953-54; Consultant Physician, University Coll. Hosp., 1960-65. Goulstonian Lectr, RCP, 1963; Examr, RCP, and various univs. Vis. Prof., Univ. of Perth, WA, 1972. *Publications:* The Red Cell, 1961; Haematology in Medical Practice, 1968; articles in med. jls. *Recreations:* fishing, gardening, music. *Address:* Reeves Lodge, High Road, Chipstead, Surrey. *T:* Downland 55383.

PRASADA, Krishna, CIE 1943; JP; ICS retired; Director-General, Posts and Telegraphs, New Delhi, 1945-53; *b* 4 Aug. 1894; *s* of Pandit Het Ram, CIE; *m* 1911, Bishan Devi (*d* 1950); three *s. Educ:* Bareilly; New Coll., Oxford. Joined ICS 1921; Joint Magistrate and subsequently a District Magistrate in UP. Services borrowed by Government of India in 1934, when he was appointed as Postmaster-General. Led Government of India deputations to International Tele-communications Conference, Cairo, 1938, Buenos Aires, 1952, and to International Postal Congress, Paris, 1947. Retired, 1954. Director, Rotary International, 1961-63. *Recreation:* tennis, Oxford Tennis Blue (1921) and played for India in the Davis Cup in 1927 and 1932. Won All India Tennis Championships. *Address:* D/152, East of Kailash, New Delhi 24, India.

PRATLEY, Clive William; Under-Secretary, Lord Chancellor's Department (Circuit Administrator, Midland and Oxford Circuit), since 1976; *b* 23 Jan. 1929; *s* of F. W. Pratley and late Minnie Pratley (*née* Hood); *m* 1962, Eva, *d* of Nils and Kerstin Kellgren, Stockholm; one *s* one *d. Educ:* in Yorkshire and at Sandhurst; and after retirement from Army, at Univs of Stockholm, 1961-62, and Hull, 1962-65 (LLB Hons). Commissioned into Royal Tank Regt, 1949; Adjt, 2nd Royal Tank Regt, 1959-61; retired from active list, 1961; T&AVR (2RTR), 1966-67. Entered Administrative Class of Home Civil Service as Principal, 1966; Lord Chancellor's Department: Sen. Principal, 1971; Asst Sec., 1974; Courts Administrator, NE Circuit, 1971-73; Dep. Circuit Administrator, Midland and Oxford Circuit, 1974-75. *Recreations:* horses, birds, the countryside, badminton, boats, music. *Address:* 101 Carpenter Road, Edgbaston, Birmingham B15 2JU. *T:* 021-455 9000. *Club:* Army and Navy.

PRATT, family name of **Marquess Camden.**

PRATT, Arthur Geoffrey; Chairman, South Eastern Gas Region (formerly South Eastern Gas Board), since 1972; *b* 19 Aug. 1922; *s* of William Pratt, Willington, Co. Durham; *m* 1946, Ethel Luck; two *s* twin *d. Educ:* King James I Grammar Sch., Bishop Auckland. CEng, FIGasE. Joined E Mids Gas Bd, 1951: Chief Engr, 1964; Dir of Engrg, 1967; Dep. Chm., S Eastern Gas Bd, 1970. Pres., IGasE, 1974-75. *Recreations:* golf, squash, swimming, bridge. *Address:* c/o South Eastern Gas Region, Katharine Street, Croydon CR9 1JU. *T:* 01-688 4466.

PRATT, His Honour Hugh MacDonald; a Circuit Judge (formerly County Court Judge) 1947-72; *b* 15 Sept. 1900; *o c* of late Sir John William Pratt; *m* 1928, Ingeborg, *e d* of late Consul Johannes Sundför, MBE, Haugesund, Norway; one *s. Educ:* Hillhead High Sch., Glasgow; Aske's Haberdashers' Sch., London; Balliol Coll., Oxford. Called to Bar, Inner Temple, 1924; practised London and Western Circuit; member General Council of the Bar; President, Hardwicke Society; contested Drake Div. of Plymouth, 1929; Dep. President War Damage (Valuation Appeals) Panel, 1946. Chairman, Devon Quarter Sessions, 1958-64. Hon. LLD Exeter, 1972. *Publications:* English trans. of Professor Axel Möller's International Law

(Vol. I, 1931, Vol. II, 1935); trans. of various articles in Norwegian, Danish and Swedish on commercial and international law. *Recreations:* reading, gardening. *Address:* Portland Lodge, Pennsylvania, Exeter. *T:* Exeter 72859.

PRATT, Very Rev. John Francis, MA; Provost of Southwell, since 1970; Priest-in-charge, Edingley with Halam, since 1975; *s* of late Rev. J. W. J. Pratt, Churchill, Somerset; *m* 1939, Norah Elizabeth, *y d* of late F. W. Corfield, Sandford, Somerset; two *d. Educ:* Keble Coll., Oxford; Wells Theological Coll. Priest, 1937. CF, 1st KSLI, 1941-46; (despatches, 1943); SCF, Cyprus, 1946. Vicar of: Rastrick, 1946-49; Wendover, 1949-59; Reading S Mary's (with All Saints, S Saviour's, S Mark's and S Matthew's), 1959-61; Vicar of Chilton with Dorton, 1961-70; Archdeacon of Buckingham, 1961-70. RD of Wendover, 1955-59; Chaplain to High Sheriff of Bucks, 1956, 1962; Examining Chaplain to Bishop of Southwell, 1971-. *Address:* The Residence, Southwell, Notts. *T:* Southwell 812593.

PRATT, Michael John, QC 1976; a Recorder of the Crown Court, since 1974; *b* 23 May 1933; *o s* of W. Brownlow Pratt; *m* 1960, Elizabeth Jean Hendry; two *s* three *d. Educ:* West House Sch., Edgbaston; Malvern Coll. LLB (Birmingham). Army service, 2nd Lieut, 3rd Carabiniers (Prince of Wales's Dragoon Guards); Staff Captain. Called to the Bar (Middle Temple), 1954. *Recreations:* music, theatre, sport generally. *Address:* South Hill, 170 Oak Tree Lane, Bournville, Birmingham B30 1TX. *T:* 021-472 2213. *Clubs:* Cavalry and Guards; Birmingham Conservative.

PRATT, Rev. Ronald Arthur Frederick; *b* 27 Aug. 1886; *s* of Charles Robert and Florence Maria Pratt; *m* 1925, Margaret Elam; no *c. Educ:* Tonbridge Sch.; Gonville and Caius Coll., Cambridge. Curate of Emmanuel, West Hampstead, 1910-13; of St Matthew's, Bethnal Green, E2, 1913-21; Chaplain RN (temp.), 1917-19; Vicar of Ossington, Newark on Trent, 1921-23; Vicar of St John, Long Eaton, Derbyshire, 1923-32; Vicar of St Barnabas, Derby, 1932-35; Archdeacon of Belize, British Honduras, CA, 1935-46; Licentiate to Officiate Dio. Canterbury, 1947-62. Missionary work in the Diocese of British Honduras, 1930-31. *Address:* 173 Old Dover Road, Canterbury, Kent. *T:* Canterbury 62702.

PRAWER, Prof. Siegbert Salomon; Taylor Professor of German Language and Literature, University of Oxford, since 1969; Fellow of The Queen's College, Oxford, since 1969; *b* 15 Feb. 1925; *s* of Marcus and Eleonora Prawer; *m* 1949, Helga Alice (*née* Schaefer); one *s* two *d.* (and one *s* decd). *Educ:* King Henry VIII Sch., Coventry; Jesus Coll. (Schol.) and Christ's Coll., Cambridge. Charles Oldham Shakespeare Scholar, 1945, MA 1950, LittD 1962, Cantab; PhD Birmingham, 1953; MA 1969, DLitt 1969, Oxon. Adelaide Stoll Res. Student, Christ's Coll., Cambridge, 1947-48; Asst Lecturer, Lecturer, Sen. Lecturer, University of Birmingham, 1948-63; Prof. of German, Westfield Coll., London Univ., 1964-69. Visiting Professor: City Coll., NY, 1956-57; University of Chicago, 1963-64; Harvard Univ., 1968; Hamburg Univ., 1969; Univ. of Calif., Irvine, 1975; Otago Univ., 1976. Resident Fellow: Knox Coll., Dunedin, 1976; Pittsburgh Univ., 1977. Hon. Director, London Univ. Inst. of Germanic Studies, 1966-68. Goethe Medal, 1973. Co-editor: Oxford German Studies, 1971-75; Anglica Germanica, 1973-. *Publications:* German Lyric Poetry, 1952; Mörike und seine Leser, 1960; Heine's Buch der Lieder: A Critical Study, 1960; Heine: The Tragic Satirist, 1962; The Penguin Book of Lieder, 1964; The Uncanny in Literature (inaug. lect.), 1965; (ed, with R. H. Thomas and L. W. Forster). Essays in German Language, Culture and Society, 1969; (ed) The Romantic Period in Germany, 1970; Heine's Shakespeare, a Study in Contexts (inaug. lect.), 1970; (ed) Seventeen Modern German Poets, 1971; Comparative Literary Studies: an Introduction, 1973; Karl Marx and World Literature, 1976; articles on German, English and comparative literature in many specialist periodicals and symposia. *Recreation:* theatre-going. *Address:* Taylor Institution, Oxford.
See also Mrs R. P. Jhabvala.

PRAWER JHABVALA, Mrs Ruth; *see* Jhabvala.

PRAZ, Mario, KBE (Hon.) 1962; Grand'Ufficiale della Repubblica italiana 1972; LittD Florence, Dr Juris Rome; Hon. LittD Cambridge University, 1957; Professor of English Language and Literature, University of Rome, 1934-66, Professor Emerito, 1966; British Academy Gold Medallist for Anglo-Italian Studies, 1935; Italian Gold Medal, for cultural merits, 1958; national member of the Accademia dei Lincei; Hon. Member, Modern Language Association of America, 1954; *b* Rome 1896; *s* of Luciano Praz and Giulia Testa Di Marsciano; *m* 1934, Vivyan (marr. diss. 1947), *d* of late Leonora Eyles, and *step-d* of late D. L. Murray; one *d. Educ:* Rome; Florence. Came to England in 1923 to qualify for the title of *libero docente* in English Literature, which eventually he obtained in 1925; worked in the British Museum, 1923; Senior Lecturer in Italian at Liverpool Univ., 1924-32; Professor of Italian Studies at Manchester Univ., 1932-34; co-editor of La Cultura; editor of English Miscellany (Rome). Hon. LittD: Aix-Marseille Univ., 1964; Paris Univ. (Sorbonne), 1967; Uppsala Univ., 1977. *Publications:* I Saggi di Elia di Carlo Lamb, 1924; La Fortuna di Byron in Inghilterra, 1925; Poeti inglesi dell' Ottocento, 1925; Secentismo e Marinismo in Inghilterra, 1925; Machiavelli and the Elizabethans (British Academy Annual Italian Lecture), 1928; Penisola Pentagonale, 1928 (translated into English with the title Unromantic Spain, 1929); The Italian Element in English, 1929; La Carne, la Morte e il Diavolo nella Letteratura Romantica, 1930 (translated into English with the title The Romantic Agony, 1933); Studi sul concettismo, 1934 (translated into English as Studies in Seventeenth-century Imagery, 1939, 2nd vol., 1948; revised enlarged edition in one vol., 1964; Part II Addenda et Corrigenda, 1975); Antologia della letteratura inglese, 1936; Storia della letteratura inglese, 1937 (new rev. enlarged edition, 1960); Studi e svaghi inglesi, 1937; Gusto neoclassico, 1940 (3rd edn, 1974; translated into English as On Neoclassicism, 1968); Machiavelli in Inghilterra ed altri saggi, 1942 (rev. enlarged edition, 1962); Viaggio in Grecia, 1943; Fiori freschi, 1943; Ricerche anglo-italiane, 1944; La filosofia dell' arredamento, 1945 (rev. enlarged edition, 1964, in English as An Illustrated History of Interior Decoration, 1964); Motivi e figure, 1945; Prospettiva della letteratura inglese, 1947; Antologia delle letterature straniere, 1947; Cronache letterarie anglo-sassoni, Vols I, II, 1951, III, IV, 1966; Il Libro della poesia inglese, 1951; La Casa della Fama, Saggi di letteratura e d'arte, 1952; Lettrice notturna, 1952; La crisi dell'eroe nel romanzo vittoriano, 1952 (translated into English with the title The Hero in Eclipse in Victorian Fiction, 1956); Viaggi in Occidente, 1955; The Flaming Heart, Essays on Crashaw, Machiavelli, and other studies of the relations between Italian and English Literature, 1958; La Casa della Vita, 1958 (translated into English as The House of Life, 1964); Bellezza e bizzarria, 1960; I Volti del tempo, 1964; Panopticon Romano, 1967; Caleidoscopio shakespeariano, 1969; Mnemosyne: the parallel between literature and the visual arts, 1970; Scene di conversazione, 1970 (translated into English as Conversation Pieces: a survey of the intimate group portrait in Europe and America, 1971); Il patto col serpente, paralipomeni a La Carne, La Morte e il Diavolo nella Lett. Romantica, 1972; Il giardino dei sensi, studi sul manierismo e il barocco, 1975; Introduction to G. B. Piranesi, Le Carceri, 1975; translations of Shakespeare's Measure for Measure and Troilus and Cressida, 1939, and of other works (by W. Pater, J. Austen, etc); general editor of standard Italian prose translation of Shakespeare's plays, 1943-47 and of Teatro elisabettiano, 1948; editor: works of Lorenzo Magalotti, 1945; D'Annunzio's selected works, 1966; contributions to literary and philological periodicals, both Italian and English. *Recreations:* travelling, Empire furniture. *Address:* Via Zanardelli 1, Rome, Italy.

PREBBLE, John Edward Curtis, FRSL; Writer; *b* 23 June 1915; *o s* of late John William Prebble, Petty Officer, RN, and Florence (*née* Wood); *m* 1936, Betty, *d* of late Ernest Golby; two *s* one *d. Educ:* Sutherland Public Sch., Saskatchewan; Latymer Upper Sch., London. Entered journalism, 1934; in ranks with RA, 1940-45; Sergeant-reporter with No 1 British Army Newspaper Unit (Hamburg), 1945-46; reporter, columnist and feature-writer for British newspapers and magazines, 1946-60; novelist, historian, film-writer and author of many plays and dramatised documentaries for BBC TV. *Publications: novels:* Where the Sea Breaks, 1944; The Edge of Darkness, 1948; Age Without Pity, 1950; The Mather Story, 1954; The Brute Streets, 1954; The Buffalo Soldiers, 1959; *short stories:* My Great Aunt Appearing Day, 1958; Spanish Stirrup, 1972; *biography:* (with J. A. Jordan) Mongaso, 1956; *history:* The High Girders, 1956; Culloden, 1961; The Highland Clearances, 1963; Glencoe, 1966; The Darien Disaster, 1968; The Lion in the North, 1971; Mutiny: Highland Regiments in Revolt, 1975. *Recreation:* serendipity. *Address:* Shaw Coign, Alcocks Lane, Burgh Heath, Surrey. *T:* Burgh Heath 55954. *Club:* Press.

PRELOG, Prof. Dr Vladimir; Professor of Organic Chemistry, Swiss Federal Institute of Technology, 1950-76; *b* 23 July 1906; *m* 1933, Kamila Vitek; one *s. Educ:* Inst. of Technology, Prague. Chemist, Prague, 1929-34; Lecturer and Professor, University of Zagreb, 1935-41. Privatdozent, Swiss Federal Inst. of Technology, Zürich, 1941; Associate Professor, 1947. Mem. Bd, CIBA-GEIGY Ltd, Basel. Vis. Prof. of Chemistry, Univ. of Cambridge, 1974. Mem. Leopoldina, Halle/Saale, 1963; Hon. Member: American Acad. of Arts and Sciences, 1960; Chem. Society, 1960; Nat. Acad. of Sciences, Washington, 1961; Royal

Irish Acad., Dublin, 1971; Foreign Member: Royal Society, 1962; Acad. of Sciences, USSR, 1966; Acad. dei Lincei, Roma 1965; Istituto Lombardo, Milano, 1964; Royal Danish Acad. of Sciences, 1971; Amer. Philosophical Soc. Philadelphia, 1976. Dr *hc* Universities of: Zagreb, 1954; Liverpool, 1963; Paris, 1963; Bruxelles, 1969. Hon. DSc: Cambridge, 1969; Manchester, 1977. Davy Medal, Royal Society, 1967; A. W. Hofmann Medal, Gesell. deutscher Chem., 1967; Marcel Benoist Prize, 1965; Roger Adams Award, 1969; (jtly) Nobel Prize for Chemistry, 1975. *Publications:* numerous scientific papers, mainly in Helvetica chimica acta. *Address:* (office) Laboratorium für organische Chemie der ETH-Z, Universitätsstrasse 16, CH-8092 Zürich, Switzerland; (home) Bellariastr. 41, 8038 Zürich. *T:* CH 01 457802.

PREM, Dr Dhani Ram; Padmashri, 1977; Chairman, Federation of Indian organisations (UK), since 1976; Founder-President, Asian Standing Conference, since 1973; Member, Liberal Party National Council, since 1973; Deputy Chairman, Joint Council for Welfare of Immigrants, since 1972; *b* 26 Sept. 1904; *s* of Jamna Das and Dalo Devi; *m* 1928, Ratan Prem; one *d . Educ:* National Univs, Delhi and Banaras, India; Edinburgh Univ.; King's Coll. Hosp. Med. Sch.; Sch. of Tropical Med., London. MRCS, LRCP, DTM&H. Called to Bar, Middle Temple, London. Gandhi Movement (imprisoned), 1921; Sec., Indian Nat. Congress, Aligarh, India, 1923; Editor, Chand, Allahabad, India, 1931; Lectr, Nat. Med. Coll., Bombay, 1932; Mem., Birmingham CC, 1946; Mem. Nat. Cttee for Commonwealth Immigrants, 1965. Chm., Commonwealth Welfare Council, Midlands, 1965; Vice-Chm., Community Relns Council, Birm., 1968; Mem., PEP Adv. Cttee, 1973; Pres., W Midlands Indian Council; Hon. Dir, Indian Adv. Council; Trustee, Uganda Asian Relief Trust, 1973; Contested (L), Coventry SE, Feb. 1974; Dir, Indian Adv. Council, 1975; Mem., Gandhi Centenary Cttee (UK), 1970; Mem., BBC Radio Council, 1970. Scenario writer and Dir of Indian films, Bombay, 1932-38. *Publications:* Heart of a Fallen Woman (novel), 1931, 2nd edn 1939; Darling (play), 1932; Vallari (short stories), 1933; Joan of Arc, 1934; Reawakening of Russia, 1934; Injection Therapy, 1937, 2nd edn 1938; Indian National Congress, 1942; Colour and British Politics, 1965, 2nd edn 1966. *Recreations:* reading detective novels, cine photography, being with children; Chm. Asian Music Circle, 1966. *Address:* 213 Worlds End Lane, Birmingham B32 2RX. *T:* 021-422 4167 and 01-656 9159. *Club:* (Pres. 1964) Indian Social (Birmingham).

PREMINGER, Otto (Ludwig); Producer-Director since 1928; *b* 5 Dec. 1906; *m* 1960, Hope Preminger (*née* Bryce); two *s* one *d* (one *s* one *d* are twins). *Educ:* University of Vienna (LLD). Associate Professor, Yale Univ., 1938-41. *Films:* Margin for Error, 1942; A Royal Scandal, 1944; Laura, 1944; Fallen Angel, 1945; Centennial Summer, 1945; Forever Amber, 1947; Daisy Kenyon, 1948; That Lady in Ermine, 1948; The Fan, 1949; Whirlpool, 1949; Where the Sidewalk Ends, 1950; The 13th Letter, 1950; Angel Face, 1952; The Moon is Blue, 1953; The River of No Return, 1953; Carmen Jones, 1954; Court Martial of Billy Mitchell, 1955; The Man with the Golden Arm, 1955; Saint Joan, 1957; Bonjour Tristesse, 1958; Porgy and Bess, 1959; Anatomy of a Murder, 1959; Exodus, 1960; Advise and Consent, 1961; The Cardinal, 1963; In Harm's Way, 1965; Bunny Lake is Missing, 1965; Hurry Sundown, 1967; Skidoo, 1968; Tell Me that You Love Me, Julie Moon, 1970; Such Good Friends, 1972; Rosebud, 1974; *plays include:* (director) Libel, Broadway, 1936; (prod. and dir) Outward Bound, Broadway, 1938; (leading rôle and director) Margin for Error, Broadway, 1939; (prod. and dir) My Dear Children, 1940; Beverley Hills, 1940; Cue for Passion, 1940; The More the Merrier, 1941; In Time to Come, 1941; Four Twelves are 48, 1951; A Modern Primitive, 1951; (prod. and dir) The Moon is Blue, Broadway, 1951; The Trial, 1953; This is Goggle, 1958; (prod. and dir) Critic's Choice, Broadway, 1960; Full Circle, Broadway, 1973. *Publication:* Preminger: an autobiography, 1977. *Recreation:* art collector. *Address:* 711 Fifth Avenue, NYC, NY 10022, USA. *T:* 838-6100.

PRENDERGAST, (Christopher) Anthony; Chairman, Location of Offices Bureau, since 1971; Chairman, Dolphin Square Trust Ltd, since 1967; an Underwriting Member of Lloyd's; *b* 4 May 1931; *s* of Maurice Prendergast, AINA, and Winifred Mary Prendergast, Falmouth; *m* 1959, Simone Ruth Laski, OStJ, JP; one *s. Educ:* Falmouth Grammar School. Westminster City Council: Mem., 1959; Chm. Housing Cttee, 1962-65; Chm. Health Cttee, 1965-68; Lord Mayor and Dep. High Steward of Westminster, 1968-69; Governor, Westminster Sch., 1974-; Chm. Town Planning Cttee, 1972-75; Additional Mem., GLC (Covent Garden Cttee), 1971-75; Mem., London Boroughs Trng Cttee, 1965-68; Mem., Docklands Develt Cttee, 1974. *Recreations:* fishing, shooting, photography. *Address:* 51 Sutherland Street, SW1V 4JX. *T:* 01-821 7653. *Clubs:* Carlton, Irish.

PRENDERGAST, Sir John (Vincent), KBE 1977 (CBE 1960); CMG 1968; GM 1955; retired; lately Deputy Commissioner and Director of Operations, Independent Commission Against Corruption, Hong Kong; *b* 11 Feb. 1912; *y s* of late John and Margaret Prendergast; *m* 1943, Enid Sonia, *yr d* of Percy Speed; one *s* one *d. Educ:* in Ireland; London Univ. (External). Local Government, London, 1930-39. War Service, 1939-46 (Major). Asst District Comr, Palestine Administration, 1946-47; Colonial Police Service, Palestine and Gold Coast, 1947-52; seconded Army, Canal Zone, on special duties, 1952-53; Colonial Police Service, Kenya, 1953-58 (Director of Intelligence and Security, 1955-58); Chief of Intelligence, Cyprus, 1958-60; Director, Special Branch, Hong Kong (retired as Dep. Comr of Police), 1960-66. Director of Intelligence, Aden, 1966-67. Colonial Police Medal, 1955; QPM 1963. *Recreations:* golf, gardening, racing. *Address:* Driftwood, Willesley, Tetbury, Glos. *Clubs:* East India, Devonshire, Sports and Public Schools, Special Forces; Nairobi (Nairobi); Hong Kong, Royal Hong Kong Jockey (Hong Kong); Malta Racing (Malta).

PRENTICE, Hubert Archibald John, CEng; FInstP; Counsellor (Science and Technology), British Embassy, Tokyo, since 1975; *b* 5 Feb. 1920; *s* of Charles Herbert Prentice and Rose Prentice; *m* 1947, Sylvia Doreen Elias; one *s. Educ:* Woolwich Polytechnic, London; Salford Univ. (BSc, MSc). CEng; MRAeS 1962; FInstP 1967. Min. of Supply, 1939-56; R&D posts, res. estabts and prodn, MoD, 1956-60; Space Dept, RAE, Min. of Aviation, 1960-67; Head, Road User Characteristics Res., 1967-70, and Head, Driver Aids and Abilities Res., 1970-72, MoT; Head, Road User Dynamics Res., DoE, 1972-75. *Recreations:* walking, climbing. *Address:* British Embassy, Tokyo, Japan. *T:* 04-261-7056.

PRENTICE, Rt. Hon. Reginald Ernest; PC; JP; MP (C) Newham North East, since Oct. 1977 (MP (Lab) Newham North East, 1974-Oct. 1977, East Ham North, May 1957-1974); *b* 16 July 1923; *s* of Ernest George and Elizabeth Prentice; *m* 1948, Joan Godwin; one *d. Educ:* Whitgift Sch.; London School of Economics. Temporary Civil Servant, 1940-42; RA, 1942-46; commissioned 1943; served in Italy and Austria, 1944-46. Student at LSE, 1946-49. BSc (Econ). Member staff of Transport and General Workers' Union, Asst to Legal Secretary; in charge of Union's Advice and Service Bureau, 1950-57; Minister of State, Department of Education and Science, 1964-66; Minister of Public Building and Works, 1966-67; Minister of Overseas Develt, 1967-69; Opposition Spokesman on Employment, 1972-74; Sec. of State for Educn and Science, 1974-75; Minister for Overseas Develt, 1975-76. Alderman, GLC, 1970-71. JP County Borough of Croydon, 1961. *Publication:* (jt) Social Welfare and the Citizen, 1957. *Recreations:* walking, swimming, gardening. *Address:* 5 Hollingsworth Road, Croydon CR0 5RP. *Clubs:* Reform; Addington Palace Golf.

PRENTICE, Hon. Sir William (Thomas), Kt 1977; MBE 1945; Deputy Chief Justice, Papua New Guinea, since 1975; *b* 1 June 1919; *s* of Claud Stanley and Pauline Prentice; *m* 1946, Mary Elizabeth, *d* of F. B. Dignam; three *s* one *d. Educ:* St Joseph's College, Hunters Hill; Sydney Univ. (BA, LLB). AIF, Middle East and New Guinea, 2-33 Inf. Bn and Staff Captain 25 Aust. Inf. Bde, Owen Stanleys and Lae Ramu campaigns; Staff Course, Duntroon, 1944; Staff Captain, 7 Aust. Inf. Bde, Bougainville campaign, 1944-45. Resumed law studies, 1946; admitted Bar, NSW, 1947; Judge, Supreme Court, PNG, 1970; Senior Puisne Judge, 1975; Deputy Chief Justice on independence, PNG. *Recreations:* bush walking, swimming, reading. *Address:* Supreme Court, PO Box 7018, Boroko, Port Moresby, Papua New Guinea. *Clubs:* Tattersall's, NSW Leagues (Sydney).

PRENTICE, Dame Winifred (Eva), DBE 1977 (OBE 1972); SRN; President, Royal College of Nursing, 1972-76; *b* 2 Dec. 1910; *d* of Percy John Prentice and Anna Eva Prentice. *Educ:* Northgate Sch. for Girls, Ipswich; E Suffolk and Ipswich Hosp. (SRN); W Mddx Hosp. (SCM Pt I); Queen Elizabeth Coll., London Univ. (RNT); Dip. in Nursing, London Univ. Ward Sister: E Suffolk and Ipswich Hosp., 1936-39; Essex County Hosp., 1941-43; Nurse Tutor, King's Lynn Hosp., 1944-46; Principal Tutor, Stracathro Hosp., Brechin, Angus, 1947-61, Matron, 1961-72. *Publications:* articles in Nursing Times and Nursing Mirror. *Recreations:* music, amateur dramatics, gardening. *Address:* Marleish, 4 Duke Street, Brechin, Angus. *T:* Brechin 2606. *Club:* VAD Ladies.

PRESCOTT, James Arthur, CBE 1947; FRS 1951; DSc; retired; Director, Waite Agricultural Research Institute, 1938-55; Professor of Agricultural Chemistry, University of Adelaide, 1924-55, Emeritus Professor since 1956; *b* 7 Oct. 1890; *e s* of Joseph Arthur Prescott, Bolton, Lancs; *m* 1915, Elsie Mason, Accrington, Lancs; one *s. Educ:* Ecole Littré, Lille; Accrington Grammar Sch.; Manchester Univ.; Leipzig Univ. Rothamsted Experimental Station; Chief Chemist and Superintendent of Field Experiments, Bahtim Experimental Station, Sultanic Agricultural Society of Egypt, 1916-24; Chief, Division of Soils, Commonwealth Council for Scientific and Industrial Research, 1929-47. Mem. Council and Scientific Adviser, Australian Wine Research Inst., 1954-69. Hon. DAgSc Melbourne, 1956. Hon. Member, Internat. Society of Soil Science, 1964. (Foundn) FAA 1954. *Publications:* various scientific, chiefly on soils, climatology and principles of crop production. *Address:* 6 Kinross Lodge, 2 Netherby Avenue, Netherby, SA 5062, Australia.

PRESCOTT, John Leslie; MP (Lab) Kingston upon Hull (East), since 1970; *b* 31 May 1938; *s* of John Herbert Prescott, JP, and Phyllis Prescott; *m* 1961, Pauline Tilston; two *s. Educ:* Ellesmere Port Secondary Modern Sch.; WEA; Ruskin Coll., Oxford (DipEcon/Pol Oxon); Correspondence Courses; Hull Univ. (BSc Econ). Trainee Chef, 1953-55; Steward, Passenger Lines, Merchant Navy, 1955-63; Ruskin Coll., Oxford, 1963-65; Recruitment Officer, General and Municipal Workers Union (temp.), 1965; Hull Univ., 1965-68. Contested (Lab) Southport, 1966; Full-time Official, National Union of Seamen, 1968-70. Member: Select Cttee Nationalized Industries, 1973-; Council of Europe, 1972-75; European Parlt, 1975-; Leader, Lab Party delegn to European Parlt, 1976-77; PPS to Sec. of State for Trade, 1974-76. *Publication:* Not Wanted on Voyage, 1966. *Address:* 39 Gorsedale, Sutton Park, Hull, N Humberside. *T:* 825461.

PRESCOTT, Sir Mark, 3rd Bt, *cr* 1938, of Godmanchester; Racehorse Trainer, in Newmarket; *b* 3 March 1948; *s* of late Major W. R. Stanley Prescott (MP for Darwen Div., 1943-51; 2nd *s* of Colonel Sir William Prescott, 1st Bt) and of Gwendolen (who *m* 2nd, 1952, Daniel Orme (*d* 1972)), *o c* of late Leonard Aldridge, CBE; *S* uncle, Sir Richard Stanley Prescott, 2nd Bt, 1965. *Educ:* Harrow. *Address:* Heath House, Moulton Road, Newmarket, Suffolk. *T:* Newmarket 2117. *Club:* Subscription Rooms (Newmarket).

PRESCOTT, Sir Stanley (Lewis), Kt 1965; OBE 1957; MSc (Manchester); Chairman, Board of Management, Royal Perth Hospital, since 1976 (Member since 1955, Deputy Chairman, 1972-76); Member Senate, Murdoch University, 1973-76; *b* 21 March 1910; *s* of J. Prescott, JP, Tetbury, Glos, England; *m* 1937, Monica M., *d* of Rev. H. A. Job; two *s* two *d. Educ:* Tetbury Grammar Sch.; University of Manchester; Lancashire College. Wild Prizeman in Pharmacology, University of Manchester, 1934. Professor of Physiology, Cheeloo Univ., Tsinan, North China, 1936. Commissioned Royal Australian Air Force, 1941; Sqdn Leader, and appointed CO, No 1 Flying Personnel Research Unit, 1943-46. Master of Ormond Coll., Univ. of Melbourne, Australia, 1946-53; Vice-Chancellor, Univ. of W Australia, 1953-70. Chm., Aust. Vice-Chancellors' Cttee, 1964-65. Mem., Aitken Commn on University of Malaya, 1957; Chm., Commn on Nanyang Univ., Singapore, 1959; Commonwealth Consultant on Inter-University Council for Higher Education Overseas, 1960-70. Hon. LLD Western Australia. *Address:* 31 Esplanade Court, The Esplanade, South Perth, Western Australia 6151. *T:* 67-6963.

PRESS, John Bryant, FRSL; author and poet; Regional Director, British Council, Oxford, since 1972; *b* 11 Jan. 1920; *s* of late Edward Kenneth Press and of Gladys (*née* Cooper); *m* 1947, Janet Crompton; one *s* one *d. Educ:* King Edward VI Sch., Norwich; Corpus Christi Coll., Cambridge, 1938-40 and 1945-46. Served War of 1939-45: RA, 1940-45. British Council: Athens, 1946-47; Salonika, 1947-50; Madras, 1950-51; Colombo, 1951-52; Birmingham, 1952-54; Cambridge, 1955-62; London, 1962-65; Paris, 1966-71 (also Asst Cultural Attaché, British Embassy). Gave George Elliston Poetry Foundation Lectures at Univ. of Cincinnati, 1962. FRSL 1959. *Publications:* The Fire and the Fountain, 1955; Uncertainties, 1956; (ed) Poetic Heritage, 1957; The Chequer'd Shade, 1958 (RSL Heinemann Award); Andrew Marvell, 1958; Guy Fawkes Night, 1959; Herrick, 1961; Rule and Energy, 1963; Louis MacNeice, 1964; (ed) Palgrave's Golden Treasury, Book V, 1964; A Map of Modern English Verse, 1969; The Lengthening Shadows, 1971; John Betjeman, 1974; Spring at St Clair, 1974; Nine Aspects of Paris, 1975; (with Edward Lowbury and Michael Riviere) Troika, 1977; Libretto, new version of Bluebeard's Castle, for Michael Powell's colour television film of Bartok's opera, 1963. *Recreations:* travel (especially in France), theatre, opera, concerts, cinema; architecture and visual arts; watching football and cricket. *Address:* c/o British Council, 1 Beaumont Place, Oxford.

PRESS, Dr Robert, CB 1972; CBE 1962; Deputy Secretary, Science and Technology, Cabinet Office, 1974-76, retired; Adviser in the Cabinet Office since 1976; *b* 22 Feb. 1915; *s* of William J. Press; *m* 1946, Honor Elizabeth Tapp; no *c. Educ:* Regent House Secondary Sch., Co. Down; Queen's Univ., Belfast; Trinity Coll., Dublin Univ. BSc 1936, MSc 1937 QUB; PhD 1949 Dublin. Physicist: War Dept Research, UK, 1941-43, and in India, 1944-46; on Staff of Scientific Adviser, Army Council, 1946-48; in Dept of Atomic Energy, Min. of Supply, 1948-51. Attaché at HM Embassy, Washington, 1951-55; MoD, 1955-58; Mem. British Delegn to Conf. for Discontinuance of Nuclear Tests, 1958-59. Dep. Chief Scientific Officer, MoD, 1960-62, Chief Scientific Officer, 1962; Asst Chief Scientific Adviser (Nuclear), MoD, 1963-66; Chief Scientific Officer, Cabinet Office, 1967-71; Dep. Sec., Cabinet Office, 1971-74; Dep. to Chief Scientific Adviser to HM Govt, 1971-74. Hon. Sec., Inst. of Physics, 1966-76; Foundn Mem., Council of European Physical Soc., 1969-72; Board Mem., Council of Science and Technology Insts, 1976-. FPhysS 1950, FInstP 1961, FRSA 1967 (Mem. Council, 1971-76). *Publications:* Papers in: Nature, and Proc. Royal Soc., 1938, 1941; Scientific Proc. Royal Dublin Soc., 1939; Irish Jl of Med. Science, 1941. *Address:* 8 Ardross Avenue, Northwood, Mddx. *T:* Northwood 23707. *Club:* Army and Navy.

PRESSBURGER, Emeric; Author, Film Producer; *b* 5 Dec. 1902; one *d. Educ:* Universities of Prague and Stuttgart. Journalist in Hungary and Germany, author and writer of films in Berlin and Paris; came to England in 1935; formed jointly with Michael Powell, The Archers Film Producing Company, and Vega Productions Ltd, and made the following films: Spy in Black, 1938; 49th Parallel, 1940; One of our Aircraft is Missing, 1941; Colonel Blimp, 1942; I Know Where I'm Going, 1944; A Matter of Life and Death, 1945; Black Narcissus, 1946; The Red Shoes, 1947; Small Back Room, 1948; Gone to Earth, 1949; The Tales of Hoffmann, 1951; Oh Rosalinda!!, 1955; The Battle of the River Plate, 1956; Ill Met by Moonlight, 1956. Wrote, produced, and directed first film Twice Upon a Time, 1952; wrote and produced Miracle in Soho, 1957; wrote The Boy who Turned Yellow (film). *Publications:* Killing a Mouse on Sunday (novel), 1961; The Glass Pearls (novel), 1966. *Recreations:* music, travel, and sports. *Address:* c/o Barclays Bank, 27 Regent Street, SW1.

PRESSMAN, Mrs J. J.; *see* Colbert, Claudette.

PREST, Prof. Alan Richmond; Professor of Economics (with special reference to the Public Sector), London School of Economics, since 1970; *b* 1 March 1919; *s* of F. and E. A. Prest; *m* 1945, Pauline Chasey Noble; two *s* one *d. Educ:* Archbishop Holgate's Sch., York; Clare Coll., Cambridge; Christ's Coll., Cambridge. Res. Worker, Dept of Applied Economics, Cambridge, 1946-48; Rockefeller Fellow, USA, 1948-49; University Lecturer, Cambridge, 1949-64; Fellow, Christ's Coll., Cambridge, 1950-64; Tutor, 1954-55, Bursar, 1955-64, Christ's Coll.; Prof. of Economics and Public Finance, 1964-68, and Stanley Jevons Prof. of Political Economy, 1968-70, University of Manchester. Visiting Professor: Columbia Univ., New York, 1961-62; Univ. of Pittsburgh, 1969; ANU, 1971. Vis. Fellow, ANU, 1977. Mem., Royal Commn on Civil Liability and Compensation for Personal Injury, 1973-. President, Section F, British Association, 1967; Mem., Departmental Cttee on Liquor Licensing, 1971-72. Treasurer, Royal Economic Soc., 1971-75. *Publications:* War Economics of Primary Producing Countries, 1948; The National Income of Nigeria, 1950-51, (with I. G. Stewart), 1953; Consumers' Expenditure in the UK, 1900-19, 1954; Fiscal Survey of the British Caribbean, 1957; Public Finance in Theory and Practice, 1960; Public Finance in Under-Developed Countries, 1962; (ed) The UK Economy, 1966; (ed) Public Sector Economics, 1968; Transport Economics in Developing Countries, 1969; (with N. A. Barr and S. R. James) Self-Assessment for Income Tax, 1977; papers in various professional journals. *Address:* 21 Leeward Gardens, Wimbledon Hill, SW19. *T:* 01-947 4492. *Club:* United Oxford & Cambridge University.

PRESTON; *see* Campbell-Preston.

PRESTON, family name of **Viscount Gormanston.**

PRESTON, Aston Zachariah, JP; Vice-Chancellor, University of the West Indies, since 1974; *b* 16 April 1925; *s* of Zachariah and Caroline Preston; *m* 1954, Barbara Marie (*née* Mordecai); two *s* one *d. Educ:* Univ. of London (LLB); FCA, FCCA, FCIS, FREconS. University of the West Indies: Bursar, 1956; Pro-Vice-Chancellor, 1969. Mem., Bd of Governors, Univ. of Guyana, 1967; Financial Adviser to E Africa, S Africa, Zambia and S Pacific Govts on univ. financing and develt, 1968; Chm.,

Shortwood Teachers' Coll., Jamaica, 1970-77. Chairman: Public Passenger Transport Bd of Control, Jamaica, 1972-74; Jamaica Omnibus Services Ltd, 1974-77; Sole Comr of Enquiries into two railway accidents, 1973; Chm., Inst. of Internat. Relations, Trinidad, 1974; Pres., Public Accounting Bd, Jamaica, 1975; Chm., PAHO Caribbean Epidemiology Centre, Trinidad, 1975-. JP Jamaica, 1957. *Recreations:* reading, music, bridge. *Address:* Vice-Chancellor's House, University of the West Indies, Kingston, Jamaica. *T:* 92-70736.

PRESTON, (Frederick) Leslie, FRIBA; AADip; formerly Senior Partner in firm of Easton Robertson Preston and Partners, Architects; *b* 27 Nov. 1903; *m* 1927, Rita Lillian, *d* of late T. H. J. Washbourne; one *d. Educ:* Dulwich Coll.; Architectural Association Sch., London. Henry Jarvis Student, 1924; joined firm of Easton & Robertson, 1925, and engaged on: in London: Royal Horticultural Society's New Hall; Royal Bank of Canada; Metropolitan Water Board's Laboratories; in Cambridge: reconstruction of Old Library; Zoological laboratories; School of Anatomy; Gonville and Caius new buildings; in New York: British Pavilion, World's Fair, 1939. Hon. Citizen of City of New York, 1939. Served War of 1939-45, RAF, Wing Comdr, Airfield Construction Branch (despatches). *Principal works:* laboratories for Brewing Industry Research Foundation; laboratories for Coal Research Establishment, NCB, Cheltenham; Bank of England, Bristol; offices for Lloyds Bank, Plymouth; Birmingham; plans for development of Reading University: Faculty of Letters, Library, Windsor Hall, Depts of Physics and Sedimentology, Dept of Mathematics. Applied Physical Science Building, Palmer Building, Whiteknights House, Students Union, Animal Biology and Plant Sciences Buildings; additions to St Patrick's Hall and to Depts of Horticulture and Dairying, Reading Univ.; Buildings for Dulwich Coll.; office building for Salters' Co., London; Laboratories and Aquarium for Marine Biological Association, Plymouth; offices for Friends' Provident & Century Life Office, Dorking; Research Laboratories for Messrs Arthur Guinness Son & Co. (Park Royal) Ltd; University of Keele, Library; Midland Hotel, Manchester, alterations; University of Kent at Canterbury, Chemistry Laboratories, Biology Laboratories, Physics 11; Bank of England Printing Works Extension, Debden; Eagle Star Insurance Head Office, City; Plans for Aquarium, Rangoon Zoological Gardens. Member of RIBA Practice Cttee, 1951-55; Member Council of Architects' Registration Council of the UK, 1954-60. Governor of Westminster Technical College, 1957-67. Hon. DLitt, Reading, 1964. *Address:* Wichenford, Ashtead, Surrey. *Clubs:* Athenæum, Reform.

PRESTON, Geoffrey Averill; Under-Secretary (Legal), Department of Trade, since 1975; *b* 19 May 1924; *s* of George and Winifred Preston; *m* 1953, Catherine Wright. *Educ:* St Marylebone Grammar Sch. Barrister-at-Law. Served, RNVR, 1942-46. Called to Bar, Gray's Inn, 1950. Treasury Solicitor's Dept, 1952-71; Solicitor's Department: Dept of Environment, 1971-74; Dept of Trade, 1974-. *Recreations:* gardening, carpentry, chess. *Address:* Ledsham, Glaziers Lane, Normandy, Surrey. *T:* Normandy (Surrey) 2250.

PRESTON, Prof. Joseph Henry; Professor of Fluid Mechanics, University of Liverpool, 1955-76, now Emeritus; Fellow, Queen Mary College, London, since Dec. 1959; *b* 1 March 1911; *s* of William and Jean Preston, Penruddock, Cumberland; *m* 1938, Ethel Noble, Bampton, Westmorland; one *s* one *d. Educ:* Queen Elizabeth Grammar Sch., Penrith, Cumberland; Queen Mary Coll., University of London. BSc Eng London 1932; 1851 Industrial Bursary, for practical training at Short Bros Ltd, Rochester, 1932-34; PhD (Aeronautics) London 1936; Asst Lecturer, Imperial Coll., 1936-38; Officer, Aero Division, National Physical Laboratory, Teddington, 1938-46; Lecturer in Aeronautics, Cambridge Univ., 1946-54 (MA Cantab); Reader in Engineering, at Cambridge, 1955. FRAeS. *Publications:* contributor to Phil. Mag.; Journal Royal Aero. Society; Engineer; Engineering; Aero. Engineer; Aero. Quarterly; Journal of Mechanics and Applied Maths; Reports and Memoranda of the Stationery Office. *Recreation:* mountaineering. *Address:* 2 Croome Drive, West Kirby, Wirral L48 8AH. *Club:* Wayfarers (Liverpool).

PRESTON, Sir Kenneth (Huson), Kt 1959; President, Stone-Platt Industries Ltd, since 1968; *b* 19 May 1901; *e s* of late Sir Walter Preston, Tetbury, Glos; *m* 1922, Beryl Wilmot, *d* of Sir William Wilkinson; one *s* one *d. Educ:* Rugby; Trinity Coll., Oxford. Dir, J. Stone & Co, 1925; Chm. Platt Bros, 1946; Chm. Stone-Platt Industries, 1958; Dir, Midland Bank Ltd, 1945-76. Mem. S Area Bd, BR. Mem. British Olympic Yachting team, 1936 and 1952, Captain 1960. *Recreations:* yachting, hunting. *Address:* Ilsom Farm, Tetbury, Gloucestershire. *T:* Tetbury

52348. *Clubs:* Royal Yacht Squadron (Vice-Cdre, 1965-71); Thames Yacht (Vice-Cdre, 1953-56).

PRESTON, Leslie; *see* Preston, F. L.

PRESTON, Myles Park; HM Diplomatic Service; Deputy Governor, Solomon Islands, since 1977; *b* 4 April 1927; *s* of Robert and Marie Preston; *m* 1951, Ann Munro Betten; one *s* one *d*. *Educ:* Sudley Road Council Sch.; Liverpool Inst. High Sch.; Clare Coll., Cambridge. Instructor Lieut, RN, 1948-51; Asst Principal, Admty, 1951-53; CRO, 1953-54; 2nd Sec., British High Commn, New Delhi, 1954-56; 1st Sec., CRO, 1956-59; 1st Sec., Governor-General's Office and British High Commn, Lagos, 1959-62; CRO, 1962-64; 1st Sec., British High Commn, Kampala, 1964-67; Commonwealth Office and FCO, 1967-69; Counsellor and Consul-Gen., Djakarta, 1969-72; Canadian Nat. Defence Coll., 1972-73; FCO, 1973-77. *Address:* 1 Duke Humphrey Road, Blackheath, SE3 0TU. *T:* 01-852 9039. *Club:* Travellers'.

PRESTON, Peter John; Editor, The Guardian, since 1975; *b* 23 May 1938; *s* of John Whittle Preston and Kathlyn (*née* Chell); *m* 1962, Jean Mary Burrell; two *s* two *d*. *Educ:* Loughborough Grammar Sch.; St John's Coll., Oxford (MA EngLit). Editorial trainee, Liverpool Daily Post, 1960-63; Guardian: Political Reporter, 1963-64; Education Correspondent, 1965-66; Diary Editor, 1966-68; Features Editor, 1968-72; Production Editor, 1972-75. *Recreations:* football, films; four children. *Address:* The Guardian, 119-141 Farringdon Road, EC1.

PRESTON, Peter Sansome, CB 1973; Permanent Secretary, Ministry of Overseas Development, since 1976; *b* Nottingham, 18 Jan. 1922; *s* of Charles Guy Preston, Solicitor; *m* 1951, Marjory Harrison; two *s* three *d*. *Educ:* Nottingham High School. War Service, RAF, 1942-46; Board of Trade: Exec. Officer, 1947; Higher Exec. Off., 1950; Asst Principal, 1951; Principal, 1953; Trade Comr, New Delhi, 1959; Asst Sec., 1964; idc 1968; Under-Sec., BoT later DTI, 1969-72; Dep. Sec., Dept of Trade, 1972-76. Mem., BOTB, 1975-76. *Publications:* several one-act plays. *Address:* 5 Greville Park Avenue, Ashtead, Surrey. *T:* Ashtead 72099.

PRESTON, Prof. Reginald Dawson, FRS 1954; retired; Professor of Plant Biophysics, 1952-73, now Professor Emeritus; Head, Astbury Department of Biophysics, 1962-73, University of Leeds; Chairman, School of Biological Sciences, 1970-73; Dean of the Faculty of Science, 1955-58; *b* 21 July 1908; *s* of late Walter C. Preston, builder, and late Eliza Preston; *m* 1935, Sarah J. Pollard (decd); two *d* (one *s* decd); *m* 1963, Dr Eva Frei. *Educ:* Leeds University; Cornell University, USA. BSc (Hons Physics, Class I), 1929; PhD (Botany), 1931; 1851 Exhibition Fellowship, 1932-35; Rockefeller Foundation Fellowship, 1935-36. Lecturer, Botany Dept, Univ. of Leeds, 1936-46; Sen. Lectr, 1946-49; Reader, 1949-53. Vis. Prof. of Botany, Imperial Coll., London, 1976. Mem. NY Acad. Sci., 1960. DSc 1943; FInstP 1944; FLS 1958; FIWSc 1960; FIAWS 1973. Editor, Proc. Leeds Phil. Soc. Sci. Sec., 1950-74. *Publications:* Molecular Architecture of Plant Cell Walls, 1952; Physical Biology of Plant Cell Walls, 1974; about 180 articles in Proc. Roy. Soc., Nature, Ann. Bot., Biochem. Biophys Acta, Jl Exp. Bot., etc. Editor, Advances in Botanical Research; Associate Editor, Jl Exp. Bot. *Recreations:* walking, climbing, music. *Address:* 117 St Anne's Road, Leeds, West Yorks LS6 3NZ. *T:* 785248.

PRESTON, Sir Ronald (Douglas Hildebrand), 7th Bt *cr* 1815; country landowner and journalist; *b* 9 Oct. 1916; *s* of Sir Thomas Hildebrand Preston, 6th Bt, OBE, and of Ella Henrietta, *d* of F. von Schickendantz; *S* father, 1976; *m* 1st, 1954, Smilya Stefanovic (marr. diss.); 2nd, 1972, Pauleen Jane, *d* of late Paul Lurcott. *Educ:* Westminster School; Trinity Coll., Cambridge (Hons History and Economics, MA); Ecole des Sciences Politiques, Paris. Served War, 1940-46, in Intelligence Corps, reaching rank of Major: Western Desert, Middle East, Italy, Austria, Allied Control Commn, Bulgaria. Reuter's Correspondent, Belgrade, Yugoslavia, 1948-53; The Times Correspondent: Vienna and E Europe, 1953-60; Tokyo and Far East, 1960-63. HM Diplomatic Service, 1963-76; retired, 1976. *Recreations:* shooting, tennis, picture frame making. *Heir:* cousing Philip Charles Henry Hulton Preston, *b* 31 Aug. 1946. *Address:* Beeston Hall, Beeston St Lawrence, Norwich NR12 8YS. *T:* Horning 771. *Clubs:* Travellers; Norfolk (Norwich); Tokyo (Tokyo).

PRESTON, Rev. Prof. Ronald Haydn; Professor of Social and Pastoral Theology in the University of Manchester, since 1970; *b* 12 March 1913; *o s* of Haydn and Eleanor Jane Preston; *m* 1948, Edith Mary Lindley; one *s* two *d*. *Educ:* London School of Economics, University of London; St Catherine's Society,

Oxford. BSc (Econ.) 1935, Cl. II, Div. I; Industrial Secretary of Student Christian Movement, 1935-38; BA Cl. I Theology, 1940; MA 1944; MA Manchester 1974; Curate, St John, Park, Sheffield, 1940-43; Study Secretary, Student Christian Movement, 1943-48; Warden of St Anselm Hall, University of Manchester, 1948-63; Lectr in Christian Ethics, Univ. of Manchester, 1948-70; Examining Chaplain: to Bishop of Manchester, 1948-; to Bishop of Sheffield, 1971-; Canon Residentiary of Manchester Cathedral, 1957-71, Sub-Dean 1970-71, Hon. Canon 1971-. *Publications:* (jointly) Christians in Society, 1939; (jointly) The Revelation of St John the Divine, 1949; Technology and Social Justice, 1971; (ed) Industrial Conflicts and their Place in Modern Society, 1974; (ed) Perspectives on Strikes, 1975; (ed) Theology and Change, 1975; (ed) The Student Movement, 1943-48; reviews, etc. in The Guardian, Theology, etc. *Address:* 28 Rathen Road, Manchester M20 9GH. *T:* 061-445 3847.

PRESTON, Col Rupert Lionel, CBE 1945; Vice-Chairman, Royal Aero Club, 1970; Secretary-General, Royal Aero Club of the United Kingdom, 1945-63; *b* 1 Nov. 1902; *s* of late Admiral Sir Lionel Preston, KCB; *m* 1932, Jean Mary (*d* 1976), *d* of late F. B. Pitcairn and of Mrs Pitcairn; no *c*. *Educ:* Cheltenham College. Coldstream Guards, 1924-45. Assistant Provost Marshal, London, 1938-40; 11 Group RAF Defence Officer, 1940-43; comd RAF Regt 83 Group RAF, 1943-45 (despatches, 1945). Mem. Council Air Registration Boards, 1946-65; Vice-Pres. Fédération Aeronautique Internationale, 1961-64; AFRAeS; Vice-Patron, Guards Flying Club; Hon. Member Soc. of Licensed Aeronautical Engineers. Silver Medal of Royal Aero Club, 1964. Specialist in 17th century Seascape paintings of the Netherlands. *Publications:* How to become an Air Pilot, 1930, 7 edns; 17th Century Seascape: paintings of the Netherlands, 1974. *Address:* 1 St Olaves Court, St Petersburgh Place, W2. *T:* 01-727 9878 and 01-930 1794. *Clubs:* Cavalry and Guards; Aero Club de France; Wings (New York).

PRESTON, Simon John; Organist and Lecturer in Music, Christ Church, Oxford, since 1970; *b* 4 Aug. 1938. *Educ:* Canford Sch.; King's Coll., Cambridge (Dr Mann Organ Student). BA 1961, MusB 1962, MA 1964. ARCM, FRAM, Hon. FRCO. Sub Organist, Westminster Abbey, 1962-67; Acting Organist, St Albans Abbey, 1967-68; Conductor, Oxford Bach Choir, 1971-74. Edison Award, 1971. *Recreations:* croquet, cinema. *Address:* Christ Church, Oxford. *T:* Oxford 42335. *Club:* Athenæum.

PRESTT, Arthur Miller, QC 1970; JP; **His Honour Judge Prestt;** a Circuit Judge (formerly Judge of County Courts), since 1971; *b* 23 April 1925; *s* of Arthur Prestt, Wigan; *m* 1949, Jill Mary, *d* of late Graham Dawbarn, CBE, FRIBA, FRAeS, and of Olive Topham; one *s* one *d*. *Educ:* Bootham Sch., York; Trinity Hall, Cambridge (MA). Served 13th Bn Parachute Regt, BLA and Far East; Major Legal Staff, Singapore, 1947-48. Called to Bar, Middle Temple, 1949. Mental Health Review Tribunal, 1963-70; Dep. Chm., Cumberland QS, 1966-69, Chm., 1970-71. Has held various appts in Scout Assoc.: Chm. SW Lancs Assoc., 1968-74; Chm., Bispham Hall Scout Council, 1974-76; Pres., Chorley and District Scout Council, 1976-; Silver Acorn, 1970. JP Cumberland, 1966. 5 years Medal, Ampleforth Hospitalite, 1976. *Address:* Glebe House, Eccleston, Chorley, Lancs PR7 6LY. *T:* Eccleston (Lancs) 451397.

PRESTWOOD, Viscount; John Richard Attlee; *b* 3 Oct. 1956; *s* and *heir* of 2nd Earl Attlee, qv.

PRETORIA, Bishop of, since 1975; **Rt. Rev. Michael Nuttall;** *b* 3 April 1934; *s* of Neville and Lucy Nuttall; *m* 1959, Dorris Marion Meyer; two *s* one *d*. *Educ:* Maritzburg Coll. (matric. 1951); Univ. of Natal (BA 1955); Rhodes Univ. (BA Hons in History 1956). MA (Cantab), MA, DipEd (Oxon), BD Hons (London). Teacher at Westville High Sch., Natal, 1958; Lectr in History, Rhodes Univ., 1959-62; Theological Student, St Paul's Coll., Grahamstown, 1963-64; ordained deacon, 1964, priest 1965; Assistant Priest, Cathedral of St Michael and St George, Grahamstown, 1965-68; Lectr in Ecclesiastical History, Rhodes Univ., 1969-74; Dean of Grahamstown, 1975. *Publications:* a chapter on Raymond Raynes in Better Than They Knew, Volume 2 (ed R. M. de Villiers); articles in Dictionary of S African Biography. *Recreations:* walking, tennis, trout fishing. *Address:* 264 Celliers Street, Muckleneuk, Pretoria, S Africa. *T:* 44-3163.

PRETYMAN, Sir Walter (Frederick), KBE 1972; President, Usina Santa Cruz: *b* 17 Oct. 1901; *s* of Rt Hon. E. G. Pretyman and Lady Beatrice Pretyman; *m* 1st, 1929, Margaret Cunningham (*d* 1942); one *d*; 2nd, 1947, Vera de Sa Sotto Maior; two *s*. *Educ:* Eton; Magdalen Coll., Oxford. From 1923 onwards, industrial and agricultural activities in Brasil. Served

War, with RAFVR, 1943-45; despatches, 1946; retd with rank of Sqdn Ldr. *Recreations:* fishing, shooting. *Address:* 90 Rua Mexico, Rio de Janeiro, Brazil. *T:* 232-8179. *Clubs:* White's; Gavea Golf and Country, Jockey (Rio de Janeiro).

PREVIN, André (George); conductor and composer; *b* Berlin, Germany, 6 April 1929; *s* of Jack Previn and Charlotte Epstein; *m* 1970, Mia Farrow, *qv*; three *s* (inc. twin *s*), two *d*. *Educ:* Berlin and Paris Conservatoires; private study with Pierre Monteux, Castelnuovo-Tedesco. Composer of film scores, 1950-62 (four Academy Awards). Music Dir, Houston Symphony Orchestra, 1967-69; Principal Conductor, London Symphony Orchestra, 1968-; Music Dir, Pittsburgh Symphony Orchestra, 1976-; Guest Conductor, most major orchestras, US and Europe, Covent Garden Opera, Salzburg Festival, Edinburgh Festival, Osaka Festival; Music Dir, London South Bank Summer Festival, 1972-74. Member: Composers Guild of GB; Amer. Composers League; Dramatists League. Recording artist. Principal compositions: Cello Concerto; Guitar Concerto; Wind Quintet; Serenades for Violin; piano preludes; Symphony for Strings; overtures. Annual series of TV specials for BBC. *Publication:* Music Face to Face, 1971; *relevant publication:* André Previn, by Edward Greenfield, 1973. *Address:* c/o London Symphony Orchestra, 1 Montague Street, WC1. *Clubs:* Garrick, Savile.

PREVOST, Captain Sir George James Augustine, 5th Bt, *cr* 1805; *b* 16 Jan. 1910; *s* of Sir Charles Thomas Keble Prevost, 4th Bart, and Beatrice Mary (*d* 1973), *o d* of Rev. J. A. Burrow of Tunstall, Kirkby Lonsdale; *S* father, 1939; *m* 1st, 1935, Muriel Emily (*d* 1939), *d* of late Lewis William Oram; one *s* one *d*; 2nd, 1940, Phyllis Catherine Mattock (from whom he obtained a divorce, 1949); 3rd, 1952, Patricia Betty Porter, Harpenden, Herts; two *s*. *Educ:* Repton. *Heir: s* Christopher Gerald Prevost [*b* 25 July 1935; *m* 1964, Dolores Nelly, *o d* of Dezo Hoffman; one *s* one *d*]. *Address:* 12 Chiltern Road, Pinner, Mddx.

PRICA, Srdja; Member: Council of the Federation of Yugoslavia, since 1972; Council for Foreign Affairs of the Presidency of the Republic of Yugoslavia, since 1971; *b* 20 Sept. 1905; *m* 1956, Vukica Tomanovič-Prica. *Educ:* University of Zagreb, Yugoslavia. Newspaperman until 1946; Director of Department, Foreign Office, Belgrade, 1947-49; Asst Min., FO, Belgrade, 1949-51; Ambassador of Yugoslavia, Paris, 1951-55; Under-Sec. of State for Foreign Affairs, Belgrade, 1955-60; Ambassador: to Court of St James's, 1960-65; to Italy, 1967-71; to Malta, 1968-72. Grand Officier, Légion d'Honneur (France); Egyptian, Italian, Swedish, Austrian and Greek Orders. *Address:* c/o Council of the Federation of Yugoslavia, Belgrade, Yugoslavia.

PRICE, Prof. Albert Thomas, DSc; FRAS; Professor of Applied Mathematics, University of Exeter (previously the University College of the South-West) 1952-68, now Emeritus; *b* 30 Jan. 1903; *e s* of Albert Thomas Price and Marie Lavinia (*née* Light); *m* 1947, Rose Ann Waterman; no *c*. *Educ:* Monmouth Sch.; Manchester University. Asst in Pure Mathematics, QUB, 1925-26; Asst Lecturer, 1926-30, Lecturer, 1930-46, and Asst Professor and Univ. Reader in Applied Mathematics, 1946-51, Imperial Coll. of Science and Technology, London; Professor and Head of Mathematics Dept, Roy. Technical Coll., Glasgow, 1951-52. Consultant to Admiralty, 1942-45. Guest investigator at Dept of Terrestrial Magnetism, Carnegie Instn, Washington, and at Inst. of Geophysics, Univ. of Calif, Los Angeles, 1952; Dean, Faculty of Science, Exeter Univ., 1954-58; Research Fellow, Univ. of Exeter, 1968-69. Internat. Geophysical Year Research Associate, Nat. Acad. of Sciences, Washington, DC, 1961-62. Consultant, Rand Corporation, Santa Monica, 1963. Chairman, Commn IV Internat. Assoc. Geomagnetism and Aeronomy, 1964-68; Member: Council of Royal Astronomical Soc., 1956-60; National Cttee for Geomagnetism and Aeronomy, 1946-; National Advisory Council on Education for Industry and Commerce, 1957-65; Regional Council for Further Educn for the South-West, 1953-65. Gold Medal, Royal Astronomical Soc., 1969. *Publications:* papers on applied mathematics and geomagnetism in Philosophical Transactions and Proc. Royal Soc., Proc. London Maths Soc., Quarterly Jl Mech. and Applied Maths, etc. *Recreation:* gardening. *Address:* 14 Corinium Gate, Cirencester, Glos. *T:* Cirencester 4271.

PRICE, Sir A(rchibald) Grenfell, Kt 1963; CMG 1933; DLitt (Adelaide), MA (Oxon); FRGS; MHR for Boothby, S Australia, 1941-43; Master, St Mark's College, University of Adelaide, 1925-57; University Lecturer in Geography, 1949-57; *b* Adelaide, 28 Jan. 1892; *s* of Henry Archibald Price, Banker, and Elizabeth Jane Price; *m* Kitty Pauline, *d* of C. W. Hayward, Solicitor, Adelaide; two *s* one *d*. *Educ:* St Peter's College, Adelaide, Magdalen College, Oxford. Housemaster St Peter's College, Adelaide, 1922-24; Member of Council, University of

Adelaide, 1926-63; Macrossan Lecturer, University of Queensland, 1930; Chairman of Emergency Committee of S Australia, 1931-32; Research Fellowship, Rockefeller Foundation, 1932-33; Chm. SA Libraries Inquiry, 1936; Chm. Adv. Bd, Commonwealth Literary Fund, 1952-71; Hon. Sec. Australian Humanities Research Council, 1956-59, Hon. Treasurer, 1959-71; Chm. Council, Nat. Library of Australia, 1960-71; Cttee for Libraries, Austr. Adv. Cttee for Unesco, 1964-71. *Publications:* Causal Geography of World, 1918; South Australians and their Environment, 1921; The Foundation and Settlement of South Australia, 1924; (with Sir D. Stamp) Longmans' Geography of the World (Australasian edition), 1928; Founders and Pioneers of South Australia, 1929; History and Problems of Northern Territory, Australia, 1930; White Settlers in the Tropics, 1939; Australia Comes of Age, 1945; White Settlers and Native Peoples, 1949, repr. 1973; The Explorations of Captain James Cook in the Pacific (New York), 1957 and 1958, repr. 1969; The Winning of Australian Antarctica: Sir Douglas Mawson's BANZARE Voyages 1929-30, 1962; The Western Invasions of the Pacific and its Continents, 1963; The Importance of Disease in History (Syme Oration, RACS), 1964; The Challenge of New Guinea: Australian Aid to Papuan Progress, 1965; A History of St Mark's College, University of Adelaide, 1967; The Skies Remember: the story of Ross and Keith Smith, 1969; Island Continent: aspects of the historical geography of Australia and its territories, 1972; ed, The Humanities in Australia, 1959; contributed to Cambridge History of the British Empire. *Recreation:* fishing. *Address:* 33 Buxton Street, North Adelaide, SA 5006, Australia; University House, Canberra. *Clubs:* Adelaide (SA), Commonwealth (Canberra); Australasian Pioneers (Sydney).

PRICE, Arnold Justin, QC 1976; a Recorder of the Crown Court, since 1972; Adjudicator, Immigration Appeals, since 1970; *b* 16 Aug. 1919; *s* of late Sydney Walter Price, LLB, Solicitor, and Sophia Price (*née* Marks); *m* 1948, Ruth Corinne, *d* of Ralph and Dorothy Marks; four *d*. *Educ:* St Christopher's Sch., Liverpool; Kingsmead Sch., Meols; Liverpool Coll.; Liverpool Univ. Bd of Legal Studies. Served War, Royal Engrs, 42nd Inf. Div. TA (invalided), later 2nd Lieut Royal Corps Mil. Police, 42nd Inf. Div. TA. Called to Bar, Middle Temple, 1952; practised Wales and Chester Circuit; Resident Magistrate, Nyasaland, 1955; Magistrate, N Nigeria, 1957; Actg Chief Magistrate and Judge, High Court N Nigeria, 1957-60; returned to practice, Wales and Chester Circuit, 1960; Northern Circuit, 1969. CC Chester, 1963-68. *Publications:* articles on politics, agriculture and legal subjects. *Recreations:* sailing, fishing, the countryside, walking, literature. *Address:* Grosvenor House, Kirby Park, West Kirby, Cheshire. *T:* 051-625 6431; 13 Castle Street, Liverpool. *T:* 051-236 5072; 2 Pump Court, Temple, EC4. *T:* 01-353 3106. *Clubs:* Athenæum (Liverpool); Royal Yachting Assoc.

PRICE, (Arthur) Leolin, QC 1968; *b* 11 May 1924; 3rd *s* of late Evan Price and Ceridwen Price (*née* Price), Hawkhurst, Kent; *m* 1963, Hon. Rosalind Helen Penrose Lewis, *er d* of 1st Baron Brecon, PC, and of Mabel, Baroness Brecon, CBE, JP; two *s* two *d*. *Educ:* Judd Sch., Tonbridge; Keble Coll., Oxford (Schol.; MA). War service, 1943-46 with Army: Capt., RA; Adjt, Indian Mountain Artillery Trng Centre and Depot, Ambala, Punjab, 1946. Treas., Oxford Union, 1948; Pres., Oxford Univ. Conserv. Assoc., 1948. Tutor (part-time), Keble Coll., Oxford, 1951-59. Called to Bar, Middle Temple, 1949; Bencher, 1970-; Barrister of Lincoln's Inn, 1959. QC Bahamas, 1969. Member: Editorial Cttee, Modern Law Review, 1954-65; Bar Council Law Reform Cttee, 1969-75; Exec. Cttee, Soc. of Cons. Lawyers, 1971-; Cttee of Management, Inst. of Child Health, 1972- (Chm., 1976-). Governor, Gt Ormond St Hosp. for Sick Children, 1972-; Mem., Falkland Islands Cttee, 1972-. Governor, Christ Coll., Brecon, 1977-. *Publications:* articles and notes in legal jls. *Address:* 32 Hampstead Grove, NW3 6SR. *T:* 01-435 9843; 10 Old Square, Lincoln's Inn, WC2A 3SU. *T:* 01-405 0758; Mrs Price's Cottage, Cross Oak, Talybont-on-Usk, Brecon LD3 7UQ. *T:* Talybont-on-Usk 248. *Club:* Carlton.
See also V. W. C. Price.

PRICE, Aubrey Joseph; *b* 29 October 1899; *s* of Joseph and Louise Price; *m* Margaret, *y d* of Capt. J. Roberton Harvey, RN; one *s* (and one *s* decd). *Educ:* City of Oxford School; Jesus College, Oxford (Ewelme Exhibitioner, Honours School of Nat. Science). House-master, Denstone Coll.; Sen. Science Master, Berkhamsted Sch.; Officer Commanding OTC; Headmaster, St Peter's Sch., York; Headmaster: Wellington School, Somerset, 1938-45; Royal Hospital Sch., Holbrook, 1945-47; Principal, Wymondham Training College, Norfolk, 1947-50; Warden, London Univ. Goldsmiths' Coll., 1950-53; Principal, Chester College, 1953-65, retd. Lieut Royal Naval Air Service, 1917-19.

Address: 19 Durland Close, New Milton, Hants BH25 6NJ. *T:* New Milton 616950.

PRICE, (Benjamin) Terence; Secretary-General, Uranium Institute, since 1974; *b* 7 January 1921; *er s* of Benjamin and Nellie Price; *m* 1947, Jean Stella Vidal; one *s* one *d. Educ:* Crypt School, Gloucester; Queens' College, Cambridge (Scholar). Naval electronics res. in UK and Far East, 1942-46; joined Atomic Energy Research Establishment, Harwell (Nuclear Physics Division), 1947; transferred to Atomic Energy Establishment, Winfrith, as Head of Reactor Development Division, 1959; Chief Scientific Officer, Ministry of Defence, 1960-63; Assistant Chief Scientific Adviser (Studies), Ministry of Defence, 1963-65; Director, Defence Operational Analysis Establishment, MoD, 1965-68; Chief Scientific Adviser, Min. of Transport, 1968-70; Dir of Planning and Development, Vickers Ltd, 1971-73. Chm., NEDO Mechanical Handling Sector Working Party, 1976-. *Publication:* (with K. T. Spinney and C. C. Horton) Radiation Shielding, 1957. *Recreations:* flying, skiing, making music. *Address:* Seers Bough, Wilton Lane, Jordans, Buckinghamshire. *T:* Chalfont St Giles 4589. *Club:* Athenæum.

PRICE, Byron, KBE (Hon.) 1948; Medal for Merit, US, 1946; *b* Topeka, Indiana, 25 March 1891; *s* of John Price and Emaline Barnes; *m* 1920, Priscilla Alden; no *c. Educ:* Wabash College (AB). In newspaper work, 1909; exec. news editor Associated Press, 1937-41, actg gen. man., 1939; US Dir of Censorship, Dec. 1941-Nov. 1945; on special mission to Germany as personal rep. of President Truman, 1945. Vice-Pres. Motion Picture Assoc. of America; Chm. Bd Assoc. Motion Picture Producers; Pres. Central Casting Corp.; 1st Vice-Pres. Educnl Film Research Inst.; Dir Hollywood Coordinating Cttee, 1946-47; Assistant Secretary-Gen., Administrative and Financial Services, United Nations, 1947-54; retired 1954. Served as 1st Lt, later Capt., Inf., US Army, 1917-19. Special Pulitzer citation for creation and administration of press and broadcasting censorship codes, 1944; Director General, Press Congress of the World, Columbia, Mo., 1959. Mem., Indiana Acad., 1976. Holds several hon. degrees. *Address:* 27 Larkspur, Hendersonville, NC, USA. *Clubs:* National Press, Gridiron (Washington).

PRICE, Rear-Adm. Cecil Ernest, AFC 1953; Deputy Assistant Chief of Staff (Operations), SHAPE, since 1976; *b* 29 Oct. 1921; *s* of Ernest C. Price and Phyllis M. Price; *m* 1946, Megan Morgan; one *s* one *d. Educ:* Bungay Grammar Sch. Joined Royal Navy, 1941; served as Pilot in several aircraft carriers, 1942-46; completed Empire Test Pilot School, and Test Flying, Boscombe Down, 1948-52; CO 813 Sqdn, 1953-54; Comdr 1956; CO Naval Test Sqdn, Boscombe Down, 1956-58; British Navy Staff, Washington, 1959-61; Captain 1966; idc 1970; Director: Naval Air Warfare, 1971-72; Naval Operational Requirements, 1972-73; CO RNAS, Culdrose, 1973-75; Rear-Adm. 1976. *Recreations:* golf, fishing, gardening. *Address:* DACOS (OPS), SHAPE, Belgium, BFPO 26; (home) Low Farm, Mendham, Harleston, Norfolk. *T:* Harleston 852676.

PRICE, Maj.-Gen. Cedric Rhys, CB 1951; CBE 1945 (OBE 1943); Principal Staff Officer to Secretary of State for Commonwealth Relations, 1959-64; ADC to the Queen, 1954-57; *b* 13 June 1905; *o s* of late Colonel Sir Rhys H. Price, KBE, CMG, Highlands, Purley Downs; *m* 1935, Rosamund, *e d* of late Arthur W. Clifford, Dursley, Glos; two *d. Educ:* Wellington College; RMA Woolwich; Trinity College, Cambridge. Commissioned Royal Engineers, 1925; served in India, 1932-38; Staff College, 1938-39; Military Assistant Secretary, offices of War Cabinet, 1940-46; Secretary, British Joint Services Mission, Washington, USA, 1946-48; Secretary, Chiefs of Staff Cttee, Ministry of Defence, 1948-50; student, Imperial Defence College, SW1, 1951; Chief of Staff to Chairman of British Joint Services Mission, Washington, 1952-54; Brigadier, General Staff, Eastern Command, 1955-56; Director of Military Intelligence, War Office, 1956-59. *Recreations:* golf, tennis, riding. *Address:* Furze Field Cottage, Hoe Lane, Peaslake, Guildford, Surrey. *T:* Dorking 730586. *Club:* Army and Navy.

PRICE, Sir Charles (Keith Napier) Rugge-, 9th Bt *cr* 1804; Section Head, Special Projects, Domtar Ltd; *b* 7 August, 1936; *s* of Lt-Col Sir Charles James Napier Rugge-Price, 8th Bt, and of Lady (Maeve Marguerite) Rugge-Price (née de la Peña); *S* father, 1966; *m* 1965, Jacqueline Mary (née Loranger); two *s. Educ:* Middleton College, Eire. 5th Regt Royal Horse Artillery, Germany and Wales, 1954-59. Actuarial Dept, William Mercers Ltd, Canada, 1959-60; Alexander and Alexander Services Ltd, Montreal, Canada, 1960-67; with Domtar Ltd, 1968-. *Heir: s* James Keith Peter Rugge-Price, *b* 8 April 1967.

PRICE, Christopher; MP (Lab) Lewisham West, since Feb. 1974; *b* 26 Jan. 1932; *s* of Stanley Price; *m* 1956, Annie Grierson Ross; two *s* one *d. Educ:* Leeds Grammar School; Queen's College, Oxford. Sec., Oxford Univ. Labour Club, 1953; Chm., Nat. Assoc. of Labour Student Organisations, 1955-56. Sheffield City Councillor, 1962-66; Dep. Chm., Sheffield Educn Cttee, 1963-66. MP (Lab) Perry Barr Division of Birmingham, 1966-70; PPS to Secretary of State for Education and Science, 1966-67 and 1975-76. Mem., European Parlt, 1977-. Chm., Council, Nat. Youth Bureaux, 1977-. Editor, New Education, 1967-68; Educn corresp., New Statesman, 1969-74. *Publications:* (Contrib.) A Radical Future, 1967; Crisis in the Classroom, 1968; (ed) Your Child and School, 1968; Which Way?, 1969. *Recreation:* throwing pots. *Address:* House of Commons, SW1. *T:* 01-219 3437.

PRICE, Maj.-Gen. David; *see* Price, Maj.-Gen. M. D.

PRICE, David (Ernest Campbell), MP (C) Eastleigh Division of Hampshire, since 1955; *b* 20 Nov. 1924; *o s* of Major Villiers Price; *m* 1960, Rosemary Eugénie Evelyn, *o d* of late Cyril F. Johnston, OBE; one *d. Educ:* Eton; Trinity College, Cambridge; Yale University, USA; Rosebery Schol., Eton; Open History Schol., Trinity College, Cambridge. Served with 1st Battalion Scots Guards, CMF; subsequently Staff Captain (Intelligence) HQ, 56 London Div., Trieste, 1942-46. Trin. Coll., Cambridge, BA Hons, MA. Pres. Cambridge Union; Vice-Pres. Fedn of Univ. Conservative and Unionist Assocs, 1946-48; Henry Fellow of Yale Univ., USA, 1948-49. Industrial Consultant. Held various appts in Imperial Chemical Industries Ltd, 1949-62. Parly Sec., Board of Trade, 1962-64; Opposition Front-Bench spokesman on Science and Technology, 1964-70; Vice Pres., Parly and Scientific Cttee, 1975- (Vice-Chm., 1965-70, Chm., 1973-75); Public Accounts Cttee, 1974-75; Parly Sec., Min. of Technology, June-Oct. 1970; Parly Sec., Min. of Aviation Supply, 1970-71; Parly Under-Sec. of State, Aerospace, DTI, 1971-72. British Representative to Consultative Assembly of the Council of Europe, 1958-61. Director: Assoc. British Maltsters, 1966-70; T. W. Downs Ltd, 1973-; Aberdeen Cold Storage Co. Ltd. Gen. Cons. to IWM, 1973-; Cons. to Union International Ltd. Governor, Middlesex Hospital, 1956-60. *Recreations:* swimming, walking, wine, cooking. *Address:* 36 Sloane Court West, SW3. *T:* 01-730 3326; Lepe House, Exbury, Southampton. *Club:* Beefsteak.

PRICE, David William T.; *see* Tudor Price.

PRICE, (Edith) Mary, CBE 1956; Senior Land Registrar, HM Land Registry, 1953-58; *b* 14 Nov. 1897; *d* of late William Arthur Price and Edith Octavia, *d* of late William Smoult Playfair. *Educ:* Central Newcastle High School; Girton College, Cambridge. Post-Graduate Scholar, Bryn-Mawr College, Pennsylvania, USA, 1919-20; Social and Police Work in Boston and Detroit, USA, 1920-22. Called to the Bar, 1924; Member of the Inner Temple. *Address:* Penridge, Blewbury, Oxfordshire. *Club:* Voluntary Aid Detachment Ladies'.

PRICE, Eric Hardiman Mockford; Under Secretary, Economics and Statistics Division, Departments of Industry, Trade and Consumer Protection, since 1977; *b* 14 Nov. 1931; *s* of Frederick Hardiman Price and Florence Nellie Hannah Price (née Mockford); *m* 1963, Diana Teresa Mary Stanley Robinson; one *s* three *d. Educ:* St Marylebone Grammar Sch.; Christ's Coll., Cambridge. Econs Tripos, 1955; MA 1958. FREconS, 1956; FSS 1958. Supply Dept, Esso Petroleum Co. Ltd, 1955-56; Economist: Central Electricity Authority, 1956-57; Electricity Council, 1957-58; British Iron & Steel Fedn, 1958-62; Chief Economist, Port of London Authority, 1962-67; Sen. Econ. Adviser, Min. of Transport, 1966-69; Chief Econ. Adviser, Min. of Transport, 1969-71; Dir of Econs, 1971-75, Dir of Econs and Stats, 1975-76, DoE. Member: Soc. of Business Economists, 1961; Northern Regional Strategy Steering Gp, 1976-77. *Publications:* various articles in learned jls on transport economics, investment, public sector industries and regional planning. *Recreations:* tennis, squash, history. *Address:* Ranelagh, Russell Road, Moor Park, Northwood, Mddx. *Club:* Moor Park Golf.

PRICE, Sir Frank (Leslie), Kt 1966; DL; Senior Partner, Comprehensive Development Associates, since 1968; Chairman, British Waterways Board, since 1968; *b* 26 July 1922; *s* of G. F. Price; *m* 1944, Maisie Edna, *d* of Albert Davis, Handsworth; one *s. Educ:* St Matthias Church Sch., Birmingham; Vittoria Street Arts Sch. Elected to Birmingham City Council, 1949; Alderman, 1958-74; Lord Mayor, 1964-65. Director: BOS Shipping & Forwarding Ltd, 1976-; Kings Ferry Wharf Ltd, 1976-. Member: Council, Town and Country Planning Assoc., 1958-; W Midlands Economic Planning Council, 1965-72;

London Transport Exec. Planning Bd, 1973-; Nat. Water Council, 1975-. Founder/Chm., Midlands Art Centre for Young People, 1960-71; Chairman: W Midlands Sports Council, 1965-69; Telford Development Corporation, 1968-71. Chm., Minister of Transport's Cttee on Roads in W Midlands Conurbation, 1956-57; Mem., Minister of Transport's Cttee of Inquiry into Major Ports, 1961. Livery Co. of Basketmakers. Fellow, Soc. of Valuers and Auctioneers; FCIT. FRSA. DL West Midlands, 1977. Freeman, City of London. *Publications:* various pamphlets and articles on planning and transport, etc. *Recreations:* painting, inland cruising. *Address:* New Oxford House, 16 Waterloo Road, Birmingham B2 5UG. *Club:* Reform.

PRICE, Geoffrey Alan; County Treasurer, Hampshire County Council, since 1977. IPFA, MBIM. *Address:* The Castle, Winchester SO23 8UJ. *T:* Winchester 4411.

PRICE, George Cadle; Premier of Belize, since 1964; *b* 15 Jan. 1919; *s* of William Cadle Price and Irene Cecilia Escalante de Price. *Educ:* Holy Redeemer Primary Sch., Belize City; St John's Coll., Belize City. Private Sec. to late Robert S. Turton; entered politics, 1944; City Councillor, 1947-65 (Mayor of Belize City several times); founding Mem., People's United Party, 1950; Party Sec., 1950-56, Leader, 1956-; elected to National Assembly, 1954; under 1961 Ministerial System, led People's United Party to 100% victory at polls and became First Minister; under 1964 Self-Govt Constitution, title changed to Premier; has led delegns to Central American and Caribbean countries; spearheaded internationalization of Belize problem at internat. forums; addressed UN's Fourth Cttee, 1975, paving way for overwhelming victory at UN when majority of nations voted in favour of Belize's right to self-determination and territorial integrity. *Address:* Office of the Premier, Belmopan, Belize.

PRICE, Gwilym Ivor; Chairman and Managing Director, Unigate Ltd, 1960-70; Chairman and Managing Director, United Dairies Ltd, 1959-70; *b* 2 Oct. 1899; *s* of late Sir William Price; *m* 1st, 1927, Nancye Freeman (*d* 1957); two *s*; 2nd, 1958, Margaret Ryrie Greaves. *Educ:* St Paul's School; Magdalene College, Cambridge. Served European War, 1914-18 in Army; commissioned. Director of United Dairies Ltd, 1931; Managing Director, 1936. *Address:* Ryrie Cottage, Coleshill, Bucks.

PRICE, Prof. Harold Louis; Professor of Mathematics for Applied Science, University of Leeds, since 1968; *b* 3 Sept. 1917; *s* of Reuben Price and Annie Boltsa; *m* 1941, Gertrude Halpern; two *d*. *Educ:* Manchester Grammar Sch.; Sidney Sussex Coll., Cambridge; Univ. of Leeds. MA Cantab; MSc (distinction), PhD Leeds; FRAeS; FIMA. Mathematician, Rotol Airscrews Ltd, 1939-40; Aerodynamicist, Blackburn Aircraft, 1940-45; Research Mathematician, Sperry Gyroscope Co., 1945-46; Univ. of Leeds: Lectr in Applied Maths, 1946-60; Sen. Lectr, 1960-64; Prof. of Maths, 1964-68; Chm., Sch. of Mathematics, 1970-73. *Publications:* research papers on aircraft dynamics, etc. *Address:* 11 West Park Place, Leeds LS8 2EY. *T:* Leeds 664212.

PRICE, Henry Alfred, CBE 1962; Managing Director, Grove Paper Co. Ltd; *b* 3 January 1911; *s* of James Wm and Louisa Rebecca Price; *m* 1938, Ivy May Trimmer; one *s* one *d*. *Educ:* Holloway County School. Joined paper trade, 1927. Member LCC, 1946-52; MP (C) West Lewisham, 1950-64. *Recreations:* music and sport. *Address:* 22 Cator Road, Sydenham, SE26. *T:* 01-778 3838.

PRICE, Henry Habberley, FBA 1943; MA, BSc; Professor Emeritus, University of Oxford, and Honorary Fellow of New College; *b* 1899; *s* of H. H. Price; unmarried. *Educ:* Winchester College; New College, Oxford (Scholar). Served in Royal Air Force, 1917-19; 1st Class in Lit. Hum. 1921; Fellow of Magdalen College, 1922-24; Assistant lecturer at Liverpool University, 1922-23; Fellow and Lecturer in Philosophy at Trin. Coll., 1924-35; Univ. Lectr in Philosophy, 1932-35; Wykeham Prof. of Logic, and Fell. New Coll., 1935-59. Pres. of Soc. for Psychical Research, 1939-40 and 1960-61. Visiting Professor at Princeton University, USA, 1948; Gifford Lecturer, Aberdeen University, 1959-60; Flint Visiting Prof., Univ. of California, Los Angeles, 1962; Boutwood Lecturer, Cambridge, 1965; Sarum Lectr, Oxford, 1970-71. Hon. DLitt, Dublin, 1953; Hon. LLD, St Andrews, 1954; Hon DLitt, Univ. of Wales, 1964. *Publications:* Perception, 1932, repr. 1973; Hume's Theory of the External World, 1940; Thinking and Experience, 1953; Belief (Gifford Lectures), 1969; Essays in the Philosophy of Religion, 1972; articles in Proc. Aristotelian Society and other philosophical periodicals. *Recreations:* aviation, painting and ornithology. Founder-member of Oxford University and City Gliding Club. *Address:* Hillside, 69 Jack Straw's Lane, Oxford. *T:* Oxford 66985.

PRICE, Captain Henry Ryan; racehorse trainer, since 1937; *b* 16 Aug. 1912; *m* 1946, Dorothy Audrey Dale; two *s* one *d*. Served War of 1939-45, 6th Commandos (N Staffs) (MC). Big races won include: Grand National, Champion Hurdle, Schweppes Gold Trophy (four times), Oaks Stakes, St Leger Stakes. *Recreations:* shooting, fishing, work. *Address:* Soldiers Field, Findon, Sussex BN14 0SH. *T:* Findon 2388.

PRICE, Very Rev. Hilary Martin Connop; Rector and Provost of Chelmsford 1967-77; *b* 1912; *s* of late Rev. Connop Lewis Price and late Shirley (*née* Lewis); *m* 1939, Dorothea (*née* Beaty-Pownall); one *s* two *d*. *Educ:* Cheltenham Coll.; Queens' Coll., Cambridge (MA); Ridley Hall, Cambridge. Asst Curate, St Peter's, Hersham, Surrey, 1936-40; Sen. Chaplain, Portsmouth Cathedral, 1940-41; Asst Curate, Holy Trinity, Cambridge, 1941-46; Chaplain, RAFVR, 1943-46; Vicar, St Gabriel's, Bishopwearmouth, 1946-56; Rector and Rural Dean, Newcastle-under-Lyme, 1956-67. Prebendary of Lichfield, 1964-67. Proctor in Convocation: of York for Durham Dio., 1954-56; of Canterbury for Lichfield Dio., 1962-67. Mem., General Synod, 1970-75. *Address:* 98 St James Street, Shaftesbury, Dorset.

PRICE, Comdr Hugh Perceval, DSO 1940; OBE 1945; RN retired; Hydrographic Surveyor; *b* 19 May 1901; *s* of late Lt-Col Ivon Henry Price, DSO, LLD, Asst Insp.-Gen., Royal Irish Constabulary, and May Emily Kinahan; *m* 1925, Annie Grant Berry; one *s* one *d*. *Educ:* Monkstown Park School, Co. Dublin; Chesterfield School, Birr; RN Colleges, Osborne and Dartmouth. Entered RNC Osborne, 1915; HMS King George V, 1917; joined Surveying Service in 1925; employed on escort work and Hydrographic duties during war of 1939-45; retired list, 1946. *Recreation:* fishing. *Address:* 55 Tudor Avenue, Worcester Park, Surrey. *T:* 01-337 8966.

PRICE, Sir (James) Robert, KBE 1976; FAA 1959; Chairman of the Executive, Commonwealth Scientific and Industrial Research Organization, 1970-77; *b* 25 March 1912; *s* of Edgar James Price and Mary Katherine Price (*née* Hughes); *m* 1940, Joyce Ethel (*née* Brooke); one *s* two *d*. *Educ:* St Peter's Coll., Adelaide; Univ. of Adelaide (BSc Hons, MSc, DSc); Univ. of Oxford (DPhil). Head, Chemistry Section, John Innes Horticultural Inst., London, 1937-40; (UK) Min. of Supply, 1941-45; Div. of Industrial Chemistry, Council for Scientific and Industrial Research (CSIR), Australia, from 1945; CSIRO: Officer-in-Charge, Organic Chem. Section, 1960, subseq. Chief of Div. of Organic Chem.; Mem., Executive, 1966. Pres., Royal Aust. Chemical Inst., 1963-64. *Publications:* numerous scientific papers in learned jls. *Recreations:* squash; growing Australian native plants. *Address:* Yangoora, 2 Ocean View Avenue, Red Hill South, Victoria 3936, Australia. *Club:* Melbourne (Melb.).

PRICE, John Lister Willis, CVO 1965; Director, Merseyside County Council's London Office, since 1973; *b* 25 July 1915; *s* of Canon John Willis Price, Croughton, Brackley, Northants; *m* 1940, Frances Holland (marr. diss.); one *s* one *d*. *Educ:* Bradfield; New College, Oxford. Military Service, 1940-46 (despatches). Joined Foreign Office News Dept, 1946; apptd First Secretary, Paris, 1950; transf. to FO, 1952; to Sofia, 1956; FO, 1959; Counsellor, Head of British Information Services, Bonn, 1962-66; IDC 1967; seconded as Dir of Information, NATO, 1967-72. *Recreations:* ski-ing, hill walking. *Address:* 21 Sheffield Terrace, W8. *Clubs:* Savile, Ski Club of Gt Britain.

PRICE, J(ohn) Maurice, QC 1976; *b* 4 May 1922; second *s* of Edward Samuel Price and Hilda M. Price, JP; *m* 1945, Mary, *d* of Dr Horace Gibson, DSO and bar, Perth, WA; two *s*. *Educ:* Grove Park Sch., Wrexham; Trinity Coll., Cambridge (MA). Served in Royal Navy, 1941-46 (Submarines, 1943-46), Lieut RNVR. Called to Bar, Gray's Inn, 1949 (Holt Scholar, Holker Sen. Scholar); Mem., Senate of Inns of Court and the Bar, 1975-. *Recreations:* fishing, opera. *Address:* Bowzell Place, Weald, Sevenoaks, Kent TN14 6NF. *T:* Weald 262; (chambers) 2 New Square, Lincoln's Inn, WC2A 3RU. *T:* 01-242 6201. *Club:* Flyfishers'.

PRICE, John Playfair; *b* 4 July 1905; *s* of William Arthur Price and Edith Octavia Playfair; *m* 1932, Alice Elizabeth Kendall, Boston, Mass; two *d*. *Educ:* Gresham School; New College, Oxford. Hon. Exhib., New Coll., Oxford; Pres. Oxford Union Society. Diplomatic and Consular posts at Peking, Nanking, Tientsin, Canton, Chinkiang, Harbin (Manchuria), Katmandu (Nepal), Gangtok (Sikkim), Los Angeles, Kansas City, Tunis, Tangier, Lisbon, Santiago (Chile), and Geneva. Additional Judge, China, 1933-37; Foreign Office, 1938; 1st Secretary of Embassy, 1943; Consul-General for Khorasan, Sistan and Persian Baluchistan, 1948; retired from Foreign Service, 1950. Civil Service and Foreign Service Selection and Final Selection

Boards, 1950; Dir and Chm. of Exec., Central African Rhodes Centenary Exhibition, 1951-52; British Council, 1959-61. *Address:* 16 Lea Combe, Axminster, Devon.

PRICE, Leolin; see Price, A. L.

PRICE, Leontyne; Opera Prima Donna (Soprano); United States. *Educ:* Public Schools, Laurel, Mississippi; Central State College, Wilberforce, Ohio. Four Saints, 1952; Porgy and Bess, 1952-54. Operatic Debut on TV, 1955, as Tosca; Concerts in America, England, Australia, Europe. Operatic debut as Madame Lidouine in Dialogues of Carmelites, San Francisco, 1957; Covent Garden, Verona Arena, Vienna Staatsoper, 1958; five roles, inc. Leonora in Il Trovatore, Madame Butterfly, Donna Anna in Don Giovanni, Metropolitan, 1960-61; Salzburg debut singing soprano lead in Missa Solemnis, 1959; Aida in Aida, Liu in Turandot, La Scala, 1960; opened season at Metropolitan in 1961 as Minnie in Fanciulla del West; opened new Metropolitan Opera House, 1966, as Cleopatra in world premiere of Samuel Barber's Antony and Cleopatra; debut Teatre Dell'Opera, Rome, in Aida, 1967; debut Paris Opera, in Aida, 1968; debut Teatro Colon, Buenos Aires, as Leonora in Il Trovatore, 1969; opened season at Metropolitan Opera, in Aida, 1969. Has appeared on TV. Numerous recordings. Fellow, Amer. Acad. of Arts and Sciences. Hon. Dr of Music: Howard Univ., Washington, DC, 1962; Central State Coll., Wilberforce, Ohio, 1968; Hon. DHL, Dartmouth Univ., 1962; Hon. Dr of Humanities, Rust Coll., Holly Springs, Miss, 1968; Hon. Dr of Humane Letters, Fordham Univ., New York, 1969. Hon. Mem. Bd of Dirs, Campfire Girls, 1966. Presidential Medal of Freedom, 1966; Spingarn Medal, NAACP, 1965. Order of Merit (Italy), 1966. *Recreations:* cooking, dancing, shopping for clothes, etc, antiques for homes in Rome and New York. *Address:* 1133 Broadway (Suite 603), New York City, NY 10010, USA. *T:* Chelsea 3-0476.

PRICE, Sir Leslie Victor, Kt 1976; OBE 1971; General President of The Queensland Graingrowers Association; Member of the Australian Wheat Board; *m* Lorna Collins; one *s* two *d*. *Address:* 5 Starkey Court, Toowoomba, Queensland 4350, Australia.

PRICE, (Llewelyn) Ralph, CBE 1972; Chairman: Honeywell, since 1971; Honeywell Information Systems, since 1971; ML Holdings Ltd, since 1976; Vice-President, Honeywell Inc., USA; *b* 23 Oct. 1912; *s* of late L. D. Price, schoolmaster, and late Lena (*née* Dixon); *m* 1939, Vera Patricia Harrison; one *s* two *d*. *Educ:* Quarry Bank Sch., Liverpool. Chartered Accountant, 1935; Sec. to Honeywell Ltd, 1936; Cost Investigator, Min. of Supply, 1943-46; private practice, 1946; Dir of Manufacturing (Scotland), Honeywell Ltd, 1947; Financial Dir, Honeywell, UK and Europe, 1957; Dir, Computer Div., Honeywell, 1960; Managing Dir, Honeywell Ltd, 1965, Chm. 1971; Director: CII-Honeywell Bull, France; HB Network Information Services, France; Mem., Econ. Develt Cttee for Electronics Indust., NEDO; Pres., British Industrial, Measuring & Control Apparatus Manufrs Assoc., 1971-76; Board Dir, Amer. Chamber of Commerce (UK). FBIM; Companion, Chartered Inst. Measurement and Control. *Recreations:* golf, bridge, music. *Address:* Nascot, Pinkneys Drive, Pinkneys Green, Maidenhead, Berks. *T:* Maidenhead 28270. *Clubs:* Royal Automobile; Temple Golf (Maidenhead).

PRICE, Margaret Berenice; opera singer; *b* 13 April 1941. *Educ:* Pontllanfraith Secondary Sch.; Trinity Coll. of Music, London. Debut as Cherubino in Marriage of Figaro, Welsh Nat. Opera Co., 1962; debut, in same rôle, at Royal Opera House, Covent Garden, 1963; has subseq. sung many principal rôles at Glyndebourne, San Francisco Opera Co., Cologne Opera House, Munich State Opera, Hamburg State Opera, Vienna State Opera, Lyric Opera, Chicago, Paris Opera; La Scala, Milan; Metropolitan Opera House, NY. BBC recitals and concerts, also TV appearances. Has made recordings. Hon. FTCL. *Recreations:* cooking, driving, reading. *Address:* c/o Harrison/Parrott Ltd, 22 Hillgate Street, W8.

PRICE, Mary; see Price, E. M.

PRICE, Maj.-Gen. (Maurice) David, CB 1970; OBE 1956; *b* 13 Feb. 1915; *s* of Edward Allan Price and Edna Marion Price (*née* Turner); *m* 1st, 1938, Ella Lacy (*d* 1971), *d* of late H. L. Day; two *s* two *d*; 2nd, 1972, Mrs Olga Marion Oclee. *Educ:* Marlborough; RMA, Woolwich. 2nd Lt R Signals, 1935; Vice-Quartermaster-Gen., MoD (Army), 1967-70, retired. Col Comdt, Royal Corps of Signals, 1967-74. *Recreation:* fishing. *Address:* The Cross, Chilmark, Salisbury, Wiltshire. *T:* Teffont 212. *Club:* Army and Navy.

PRICE, Sir Norman (Charles), KCB 1975 (CB 1969); Chairman, Board of Inland Revenue, 1973-76 (Deputy Chairman, 1968-73); *b* 5 Jan. 1915; *s* of Charles William and Ethel Mary Price; *m* 1940, Kathleen Beatrice (*née* Elston); two *d*. *Educ:* Plaistow Grammar School. Entered Civil Service as Executive Officer, Customs and Excise, 1933; Inspector of Taxes, Inland Revenue, 1939; Secretaries' Office, Inland Revenue, 1951; Board of Inland Revenue, 1965. *Recreations:* music, history. *Address:* 604 Mountjoy House, Barbican, EC2Y 8BP. *T:* 01-628 0369.

PRICE, Norman Stewart, CMG 1959; OBE 1946; *b* 9 Aug. 1907; *s* of late Lt-Col Ivon Henry Price, DSO, LLD, Asst Inspr-Gen., RIC, and May Emily (*née* Kinahan), Greystones, Ireland; *m* 1933, Rosalind Evelyn Noelle (*née* Ormsby) (*d* 1973); two *d*. *Educ:* Portora Royal School, Enniskillen; Exeter Sch.; Trinity Coll., Dublin; Queens Coll., Oxford. LLB 1929, BA Hons 1930. Cadet, Northern Rhodesia, 1930, District Officer, 1932, Provincial Comr, Northern Rhodesia, 1951-59; retired, 1959. Coronation Medal, 1953. *Recreations:* gardening; Captain Dublin University Harriers and Athletic Club, 1928-29; Half-Blue Oxford University Cross Country, 1929. *Address:* Overton Rise, 6 Wavell Road, Highlands, Salisbury, Rhodesia. *T:* Salisbury 46350.

PRICE, Peter S.; see Stanley Price.

PRICE, Ralph; see Price, L. R.

PRICE, Sir Robert; see Price, Sir J. R.

PRICE, Sir Robert (John) G.; see Green-Price.

PRICE, Very Rev. Robert Peel; Chaplain to the Queen, 1957-61; *b* 18 Sept. 1905. *Educ:* Dover College; Wadham College, Oxford (MA); Wells Theological College. Deacon, 1930; Priest, 1931; Curate of: Wimbledon, 1930-34; St Martin, Knowle, 1934-40; Cheam (in charge of St Oswald's), 1940-42; St Peter's, Bournemouth, 1942-45; Vicar of Christchurch with Mudeford, Diocese of Winchester, 1945-61; Hon. Canon of Winchester, 1950-61; Dean of Hereford, 1961-68, now Emeritus; Priest-in-charge, St Swithun's, Bournemouth, 1968-71. *Address:* c/o Lloyds Bank Ltd, Lansdowne, Bournemouth, Dorset.

PRICE, Brig. Rollo Edward Crwys, CBE 1967; DSO 1961; *b* 6 April 1916; *s* of Eardley Edward Carnac Price, CIE; *m* 1945, Diana Budden; three *d*. *Educ:* Canford; RMC Sandhurst. Commissioned 2nd Lt in S Wales Borderers, 1936; War Service, Middle East and Italy, 1939-45; Lt-Col and seconded for service with Queen's Own Nigeria Regt, 1959-61; Col 1962; Comdr 160 Inf. Bde, 1964-67; Brig. 1966; Comdr, British Troops, Malta, 1968-69, retired. *Address:* Elsford, Netherton, near Yeovil, Somerset. *T:* Yetminster 377. *Clubs:* Naval and Military; Cardiff and County.

PRICE, Sir Rose (Francis), 6th Bt, *cr* 1815; *b* 15 March 1910; *e s* of Sir Francis Price, 5th Bt, and Marjorie (*d* 1955), *d* of Sir W. Russell Russell, Hawkes Bay, NZ; *S* father, 1949; *m* 1949, Kathleen June, *yr d* of Norman W. Hutchinson, Melbourne, Australia; two *s*. *Educ:* Wellington; Trinity College, Cambridge. BA 1931. Served War of 1939-45, Captain 4/11th Sikh Regt, 1940-45. *Heir: s* Francis Caradoc Rose Price [*b* 9 Sept. 1950; *m* 1975, Marguerite, *d* of R. S. Trussler; two *d*]. *Address:* Netherwood, Grays Park Road, Stoke Poges, Bucks. *See also L. Scott-Bowden.*

PRICE, Roy Kenneth; Under-Secretary (Legal), in office of HM Treasury Solicitor, since 1972; *b* 16 May 1916; *s* of Ernest Price and Margaret Chapman Price (*née* Scott); *m* 1948, Martha (*née* Dannhauser); one *s* one *d*. *Educ:* Eltham Coll. Qualified as Solicitor, 1937. Town Clerk, Borough of Pembroke, and Clerk to Castlemartin Justices, 1939-40. Served War, Army, 1940-46. Officer in Charge, Legal Aid (Welfare), Northern Command, 1946 (Lt-Col). Joined HM Treasury Solicitor, as Legal Asst, 1946; Sen. Legal Asst, 1950; Asst Solicitor, 1962. Chm., Richmond Assoc., Nat. Trust. *Recreations:* Marriage Guidance Counsellor, gardening, theatre, visual arts, travel. *Address:* 6 Old Palace Lane, Richmond, Surrey. *T:* (home) 01-940 6685; (work) 01-233 5312. ext. 197. *Club:* Law Society.

PRICE, Terence; see Price, B. T.

PRICE, Brig. Thomas Reginald, DSO 1917; MC; *b* Woburn Sands, 15 Sept. 1894; *s* of Rev. T. J. Price, BA; *m* 1st, 1931, Christian Farquharson Gordon (*d* 1960), *yr d* of James Leask and Mrs M. E. Fraser; 2nd, 1969, Gwendolen, *e d* of E. S. Wicks. *Educ:* Kingswood School, Bath. Special Reserve Com. Northants Regt, 1915; Lt regular army, 1916; Captain 1923; Major, 1935; Lt-Col 1941; Brig. 1941; Royal Tank Corps, 1917;

served in France, 1915-18 (DSO, MC 1917, bar to MC 1918, despatches thrice, wounded Loos, 1915. Somme, 1917, and German advance, 1918); in Nigeria, 1921-32; Lt-Col Commanding 1st Bn Nigeria Regiment, 1931-32; served War of 1939-45: Commandant Gold Coast, 1940; Commanded 31st Tank Bde, 1941-42; Commanded 1st Tank Bde, 1942-44; Brig. General Staff, Washington, 1945-48. *Recreations:* all outdoor games and sports. *Address:* Old Timbers, Dora's Green Lane, Dippenhall, Farnham, Surrey. *Club:* Naval and Military.

PRICE, Mrs Vincent; *see* Browne, C. E.

PRICE, Vivian William Cecil, QC 1972; *b* 14 April 1926; 4th *s* of late Evan Price, Hawkhurst, Kent; *m* 1961, Elizabeth Anne, *o c* of late Arthur and Georgina Rawlins; three *s* two *d. Educ:* Judd Sch., Tonbridge, Kent: Trinity Coll., Cambridge (BA); Balliol Coll., Oxford (BA). Royal Navy, 1946-49, Instructor Lieut. Called to the Bar: Middle Temple, 1954; Hong Kong, 1975. Sec., Lord Denning's Cttee on Legal Educn for Students from Africa, 1960; Junior Counsel (Patents) to the Board of Trade, 1967-72; Mem., Patents Procedure Cttee, 1973. Deputy High Court Judge (Chancery Division), 1975. *Address:* Redwall Farmhouse, Linton, Kent. *T:* Maidstone 43682; New Court, Temple, EC4. *T:* 01-353 1769; *Telex:* 8811554 NEWCT G. *Clubs:* Travellers', Arts.
See also A. L. Price.

PRICE, Walter Robert; Chairman and Managing Director, Vauxhall Motors Ltd, Luton, since 1974; *b* 26 Feb. 1926; *m* 1951, Mary Alice Hubbard; one *s* three *d. Educ:* Wesleyan Univ., Middletown, Conn, USA (BA). Managing Director: General Motors Suisse, Bienne, Switzerland, 1967; General Motors Continental, Antwerp, Belgium, 1970; General Motors South African (Pty) Ltd, Port Elizabeth, S Africa, 1971. *Recreations:* tennis, squash, golf. *Address:* Vauxhall Motors Ltd, Kimpton Road, Luton LU2 0SY.

PRICE, Willard; explorer, naturalist, author; *b* Peterboro, Ontario, Canada, 28 July 1887; *s* of Albert Price, and Estella Martin; *m* 1st, 1914, Eugenia Reeve (*d* 1929), Willoughby, Ohio; one *s*; 2nd, 1932, Mary Selden, New York. To United States, 1901; BA, Western Reserve Univ., Cleveland, Ohio, 1909; studied New York School of Philanthropy, 1911-12; MA, Columbia University, 1914; studied Journalism New York Univ. and Columbia; editorial staff, The Survey, New York, 1912-13; editorial secretary Board of Foreign Missions, Methodist Episcopal Church, 1915-19; editor World Outlook; manager of publication of Everyland and La Nueva Democracia; director periodical department of Interchurch World Movement and supervising editor various class and travel publications; travel in 140 countries, particularly on expeditions for National Geographic Society and American Museum of Natural History, 1920-67. *Publications: books:* Ancient Peoples at New Tasks; The Negro Around the World; Study of American Influence in the Orient; Pacific Adventure; Rip Tide in the South Seas; Where Are You Going, Japan?; Children of the Rising Sun; Japan Reaches Out; Barbarian (a novel); Japan Rides the Tiger; Japan's Islands of Mystery; The Son of Heaven; Key to Japan; Roving South; Tropic Adventure; Amazon Adventure; I Cannot Rest from Travel; The Amazing Amazon; Journey by Junk; Underwater Adventure; Adventures in Paradise; Volcano Adventure; Innocents in Britain; Whale Adventure; Incredible Africa; African Adventure; The Amazing Mississippi; Elephant Adventure; Rivers I Have Known; America's Paradise Lost; Safari Adventure; Lion Adventure; Gorilla Adventure; Odd Way Round the World; Diving Adventure; The Japanese Miracle; Cannibal Adventure; contrib. to Spectator, Daily Telegraph, Saturday Evening Post, Encyc. Brit., etc. *Address:* 814-N Via Alhambra, Laguna Hills, Calif 92653, USA.

PRICE, Prof. William Charles, FRS 1959; Wheatstone Professor of Physics, University of London, at King's College, 1955-76, now Emeritus; *b* 1 April 1909; *s* of Richard Price and Florence Margaret (*née* Charles); *m* 1939, Nest Myra Davies; one *s* one *d. Educ:* Swansea Grammar Sch.; University of Wales (Swansea); Johns Hopkins University, Baltimore; Trinity Coll., Cambridge, BSc (Wales) 1930; Commonwealth Fellow, 1932; PhD (Johns Hopkins), 1934; Cambridge: Senior 1851 Exhibitioner, 1935, University Demonstrator, 1937-43, PhD (Cantab) 1937. Prize Fellow, Trinity Coll., 1938; ScD (Cantab) 1949; Meldola Medal of Inst. of Chem., 1938; Senior Spectroscopist, ICI (Billingham Div.), 1943-48; Research Associate, University of Chicago, 1946-47; Reader in Physics, University of London (King's Coll.) 1948. FKC 1970. FRIC 1944; FIP 1950. Co-editor, British Bulletin of Spectroscopy, 1950-. Hon. DSc Wales, 1970. *Publications:* research and review articles on physics and chemistry in scientific journals. *Address:* 38 Cross Way, Petts Wood, Kent. *T:* 01-662 8815.

PRICE, William Frederick Barry, OBE 1977; HM Diplomatic Service; HM Consul-General, Rotterdam, since 1973; *b* 12 Feb. 1925; *s* of William Thomas and Vera Price; *m* 1948, Lorraine Elisabeth Suzanne Hoather; three *s* two *d. Educ:* Worcester Royal Grammar Sch.; St Paul's Training Coll., Cheltenham. Served War: Armed Forces, 1944-47: commissioned Royal Warwicks, 1945; demobilised, 1947. Primary Sch. Teacher, 1948. Joined Bd of Trade, 1950; Asst Trade Comr: in Delhi, 1954; in Nairobi, 1957; Trade Commissioner, Accra, 1963; transferred to HM Diplomatic Service, 1966; 1st Sec., Sofia, 1967; seconded to East European Trade Council, 1971. *Recreation:* bridge. *Address:* c/o Foreign and Commonwealth Office, SW1. *Clubs:* English-Speaking Union; Maas (Rotterdam).

PRICE, William George, MP (Lab) Rugby Division of Warwickshire, since 1966; Parliamentary Secretary, Privy Council Office, since Oct. 1974; *b* 15 June 1934; *s* of George and Lillian Price; *m* 1963, Joy Thomas; two *s. Educ:* Forest of Dene Technical Coll.; Gloucester Technical Coll. Staff Journalist: Three Forest Newspapers, Cinderford, until 1959; Coventry Evening Telegraph, 1959-62; Birmingham Post & Mail, 1962-66. PPS: to Sec. of State for Educn and Science, 1968-70; to Dep. Leader, Labour Party, 1972-74; Parly Sec., ODM, March-Oct. 1974. *Recreation:* sport. *Address:* The Old Oak House, Flecknoe, near Rugby. *T:* Rugby 890310.

PRICE, William Thomas, CBE 1960; MC 1917; BSc; Principal, Harper Adams Agricultural College, Shropshire, 1946-62, retired 1962; *b* 15 Nov. 1895; *m* 1923, Fanny Louise (*d* 1964), *d* of Philip T. Dale, Stafford; no *c* ; *m* 1965, Mrs Beryl E. Drew, *d* of T. W. Tayler, Northleach, Glos. *Educ:* Christ Coll., London; Reading Univ. Served European War, 1915-18, Royal Warwickshire Regt, RFC and RAF with rank of Captain. Lecturer in Dairy Husbandry, Staffordshire Farm Institute, 1920-22; Lecturer in Estate Management, Harper Adams Agricultural Coll., 1922-24; Wiltshire County Council: Lecturer in Agriculture, 1924-26; Organiser of Agricultural Education, 1926-46. Chief Exec. Officer, Wilts WAEC, 1939-46. President Shropshire and W Midland Agric. Society, 1963. David Black Award, 1961 (for greatest contrib. to British pig industry). Lecturer and broadcaster on agriculture. *Publications:* Wiltshire Agricultural Advisory Reports, 1939; The Housing of the Pig, 1953. Editor, The Pig, 1961; various articles on agricultural subjects. *Recreations:* fishing and travel. *Address:* Hambledon House, Park Road, Leamington Spa, Warwicks. *T:* Leamington Spa 24709.

PRICE EVANS, David Alan; *see* Evans.

PRICE HOLMES, Eric Montagu; *see* Holmes, E. M. P.

PRICE-WHITE, Lt-Col David Archibald, TD 1945; solicitor; Principal, Price White & Co., Solicitors, Colwyn Bay; *b* 5 Sept. 1906; *s* of Price Foulkes White and Charlotte Bell. *Educ:* Friars School; University College of North Wales. Admitted Solicitor (Hons), 1932; practised Solicitor, Bangor, 1933-39. Joined TA (RA), 1928; served 1939-45, France 1940, Middle East, Sicily, Italy, East Africa. MP (C) Caernarvon Boroughs, 1945-50. *Address:* Dolanog, Pwllycrochan Avenue, Colwyn Bay, N Wales. *T:* Colwyn Bay 30758.

PRICHARD, Sir Montague (Illtyd), Kt 1972; CBE 1965; MC 1944; retired March 1975 as Chairman and Chief Executive Perkins Engines Group Ltd, Peterborough, and various subsidiaries; Member, Council of Advisors, AMF Inc., White Plains, New York; Director: Polysius Ltd; Tozer, Kemsley & Millbourn (Holdings) Ltd; Brown Brothers Corporation Ltd; Turner Manufacturing Co.; *b* 26 Sept. 1915; *s* of late George Montague Prichard; *m* 1942, Kathleen Georgana Hamill; two *s* one *d. Educ:* Felsted Sch., Essex. Served War of 1939-45 (despatches thrice, MC): Royal Engineers: Somaliland, India, Burma, Malaya and Far East, Lt-Col as CRE 20 Indian Division. R. A. Lister & Co. Ltd, 1952; F. Perkins Ltd: Personal Asst to Man. Director, 1953; Director of Engineering, 1954; Dep. Man. Dir, 1956; Jt Man. Dir, 1958; Man. Dir and Chm., 1959. Member: British Productivity Council; BNEC, 1965-72; Founder Chairman: Nat. Marketing Council, 1963; British Industry Roads Campaign. Vice-Pres., SMMT, 1966-70; Pres., Motor Industry Res. Assoc., 1972-74. FInstMSM. *Address:* Monte Kay, Mijas, Malaga, Spain. *T:* Mijas (Malaga) 84. *Club:* East India, Devonshire, Sports and Public Schools.

PRICHARD, Air Commodore Richard Julian Paget, CB 1963; CBE 1958; DFC 1942; AFC 1941; *b* 4 Oct. 1915; *o s* of Major W. O. Prichard, 24th Regt; unmarried. *Educ:* Harrow; St Catharine's Coll., Cambridge. Entered RAF, 1937; Air Armament Sch., Eastchurch and Manby, 1937-39; Flying

Instructor, South Cerney, 1939-41; No. 21 (LB) Squadron, 1942-43; Staff Coll. (psa), 1943; AEAF, 1943-45; Chief Intelligence Officer, Burma and FEAF, 1946-47; Chief Flying Instructor, RAF Coll., Cranwell, 1947-49; Ministry of Defence, 1949-52; Instructor, RAF Staff Coll., 1953-55; Station Comdr, RAF Tengah, Singapore, 1956-58. IDC, 1959; Director Air Plans, Air Ministry, 1960-63; AOC No 13 Scottish Sector, Fighter Command, 1963-64; AOC Northern Sector of Fighter Command, 1965-66; retired, 1966. US Legion of Merit, 1944. *Recreations:* tennis, fishing. *Address:* c/o Lloyds Bank Ltd, 6 Pall Mall, SW1Y 5NH. *Club:* Royal Air Force.

PRICHARD-JONES, Sir John, 2nd Bt, *cr* 1910; Captain, Reserve of Officers; *b* 20 Jan. 1913; *s* of 1st Bt and Marie, *y d* of late Charles Read; *S* father, 1917; *m* 1937, Heather, (from whom he obtained a divorce, 1950), *er d* of late Sir Walter Nugent, 4th Bt; one *s*; *m* 1959, Helen Marie Thérèse, *e d* of J. F. Liddy, 20 Laurence Street, Drogheda; one *d. Educ:* Eton; Christ Church, Oxford (BA Hons; MA). Called to Bar, Gray's Inn, 1936. *Heir: s* David John Walter Prichard-Jones, BA (Hons) Oxon, *b* 14 March 1943. *Address:* Allenswood House, Lucan, Co. Dublin.

PRICKETT, Air Chief Marshal Sir Thomas (Other), KCB 1965 (CB 1957); DSO 1943; DFC 1942; RAF retired; *b* 31 July 1913; *s* of late E. G. Prickett; *m* 1942, Elizabeth Gratian, *d* of late William Galbally, Laguna Beach, Calif, USA; one *s* one *d. Educ:* Stubbington House Sch.; Haileybury Coll. Joined RAF, 1937; commanded RAF Tangmere, 1949-51; Group Captain operations, HQ Middle East Air Force, 1951-54; commanded RAF Jever, 1954-55; attended Imperial Defence Coll., 1956; Chief of Staff Air Task Force, 1956; Director of Policy, Air Ministry, 1957-58; SASO, HQ No 1 Group, 1958-60; ACAS (Ops) Air Ministry, 1960-63; ACAS (Policy and Planning) Air Ministry, 1963-64; AOC-in-C, NEAF, Comdr British Forces in Cyprus, and Administrator, Sovereign Base Area, 1964-66; AOC-in-C, RAF Air Support Command, 1967-68; Air Mem. for Supply and Organisation, MoD, 1968-70. *Recreations:* polo, sailing, golf. *Address:* 3 Grange House, Aldwick Grange, Bognor, Sussex. *Club:* Royal Air Force.

PRICKMAN, Air Cdre Thomas Bain, CB 1953; CBE 1945; *b* 1902; *m* 1st, Ethel Serica (*d* 1949), *d* of John Cubbon, Douglas, IOM; 2nd, 1952, Dorothy (who *m* 1946, Group Captain F. C. Read, *d* 1949), *d* of John Charles Clarke, *Educ:* Blundell's Sch. Joined RAF, 1923. Served War of 1939-45, with Fighter Command; RAF Liaison staff in Australia, 1946-48; AOA, Home Command, 1950-54; retired, 1954. *Address:* Well Cottage, New Pond Hill, Cross-in-Hand, East Sussex.

PRIDDLE, Robert John; Under Secretary, and Head of Continental Shelf (Participation) Division, Department of Energy, since 1977; *b* 9 Sept. 1938; *s* of Albert Leslie Priddle and Alberta Edith Priddle; *m* 1962, Janice Elizabeth Gorham; two *s*. *Educ:* King's Coll. Sch., Wimbledon; Peterhouse, Cambridge (MA). Asst Principal, Min. of Aviation, 1960, Principal 1965; Private Sec. to Minister for Aerospace, 1971-73; Asst Sec., DTI, 1973, and Dept of Energy, 1974. *Publication:* Victoriana, 1959 (2nd edn 1963). *Address:* 12 St Johns Avenue, Ewell, Surrey.

PRIDEAUX, Sir Humphrey (Povah Treverbian), Kt 1971; OBE 1945; Chairman, Brooke Bond Liebig Ltd, since 1972 (Director, 1968; Deputy Chairman, 1969-71); President, The London Life Association Ltd, since 1973 (Director, 1964; Vice-President, 1965-72); Vice-Chairman, W. H. Smith & Son Ltd, since 1977 (Director, 1969-77); Chairman, Lord Wandsworth Foundation, since 1966; *b* 13 Dec. 1915; 3rd *s* of Walter Treverbian Prideaux and Marion Fenn (*née* Arbuthnot); *m* 1939, Cynthia, *er d* of Lt-Col H. Birch Reynardson, CMG; four *s*. *Educ:* St Aubyns, Rottingdean; Eton; Trinity Coll., Oxford (MA). Commissioned 3rd Carabiniers (Prince of Wales's Dragoon Guards) 1936; DAQMG Guards Armd Div., 1941; Instructor, Staff Coll., 1942; AQMG 21 Army Gp, 1943; AA QMG Guards Armd Div., 1944; Joint Planning Staff, War Office, 1945; Naval Staff Coll., 1948; Commandant School of Administration, 1948; Chiefs of Staff Secretariat, 1950; retired, 1953. Director, NAAFI, 1956-73 (Man. Dir, 1961-65; Chm., 1963-73). *Recreation:* riding. *Address:* Summers Farm, Long Sutton, Basingstoke, Hants. *T:* Long Sutton 295. *Club:* Cavalry and Guards.
See also Sir J. F. Prideaux, W. A. Prideaux.

PRIDEAUX, Sir John (Francis), Kt 1974; OBE 1945; DL; Director: National Westminster Bank Ltd (Chairman, 1971-77); International Westminster Bank Ltd (Chairman, 1969-77); Arbuthnot Latham Holdings Ltd (Chairman, 1969-74); *b* 30 Dec. 1911; 2nd *s* of Walter Treverbian Prideaux and Marion Fenn (*née* Arbuthnot); *m* 1934, Joan, *er d* of late Captain Gordon Hargreaves Brown, MC, and Lady Pigott Brown; two *s*

one *d. Educ:* St Aubyns, Rottingdean; Eton. Joined Arbuthnot Latham & Co. Ltd, Merchant Bankers, 1930. Middlesex Yeomanry, 1933; served War of 1939-45, Colonel Q, 2nd Army, 1944. Mem., London Adv. Bd, Bank of NSW, 1948-74; Director: Westminster Bank Ltd, later National Westminster Bank Ltd, 1955-; Westminster Foreign Bank Ltd, later Internat. Westminster Bank Ltd, 1955-. Chm., Cttee of London Clearing Bankers, 1974-76; Vice-Pres., British Bankers' Assoc., 1972-77. Pres., Inst. of Bankers, 1974-76. Dep. Chm., Commonwealth Develt Corp., 1960-70. Mem., Lambeth, Southwark and Lewisham AHA(T); Treasurer and Chm., Bd of Governors, St Thomas' Hosp., 1964-74. Prime Warden, Goldsmiths' Company, 1972. DL Surrey 1976. Legion of Merit, USA, 1945. *Address:* Elderslie, Ockley, Surrey. *T:* Dorking 711263. *Clubs:* Brooks's, Overseas Bankers (Pres. 1976-77).
See also Sir H. P. T. Prideaux, W. A. Prideaux.

PRIDEAUX, Walter Arbuthnot, CBE 1973; MC 1945; TD 1948; Chairman, City Parochial Foundation; *b* 4 Jan. 1910; *e s* of Walter Treverbian Prideaux and Marion Fenn (*née* Arbuthnot); *m* 1937, Anne, *d* of Francis Stewart Cokayne; two *s* two *d. Educ:* Eton; Trinity Coll., Cambridge. Solicitor, 1934. Assistant Clerk of the Goldsmiths' Company, 1939-53, Clerk 1953-75. Kent Yeomanry, 1936-48. *Recreation:* rowed for Cambridge, 1930, 1931. *Address:* Saykers, Rusper, Horsham, West Sussex RH12 4RF. *T:* Rusper 331.
See also Sir H. P. T. Prideaux, Sir J. F. Prideaux.

PRIDEAUX-BRUNE, Sir Humphrey Ingelram, KBE 1943 (OBE 1931); CMG 1938; *b* 16 Nov. 1886; *m* 1920, Adah Louisa Anne (*d* 1947), *d* of late W. Montague Pollard-Urquhart, Castle Pollard, Co. Westmeath. *Educ:* Marlborough; University Coll., Oxford. Student Interpreter in China, 1911; one of HM Consuls in China, 1931; acting Chinese Counsellor, British Embassy, China, 1938-39; China Relations Officer in India, 1943; retired, 1945. *Address:* Compton House Nursing Home, Lindfield, West Sussex.

PRIDHAM, Brian Robert; Counsellor, British Embassy, Khartoum, since 1976; *b* 22 Feb. 1934; *s* of Reginald Buller Pridham and Emily Pridham (*née* Winser); *m* 1954, Fay Coles; three *s*. *Educ:* Hele's Sch., Exeter. RWAFF (Nigeria Regt), 1952-54; Foreign Office, 1954-57; MECAS, 1957-59; Bahrain, 1959; Vice-Consul, Muscat, 1959-62; Foreign Office, 1962-64; 2nd Sec., Algiers, 1964-66; 1st Sec., 1966-67; Foreign Office, 1967-70; Head of Chancery: La Paz, 1970-73; Abu Dhabi, 1973-75; Dir of MECAS, Shemlan, Lebanon, 1975-76. *Recreations:* sailing, old roses. *Address:* c/o Foreign and Commonwealth Office, King Charles Street, SW1A 2AH.

PRIDHAM, Kenneth Robert Comyn, CMG 1976; HM Diplomatic Service; Assistant Under Secretary of State, Foreign and Commonwealth Office, since 1974; *b* 28 July 1922; *s* of late Colonel G. R. Pridham, CBE, DSO, and Mignonne, *d* of late Charles Cumming, ICS; *m* 1965, Ann Rosalind, *d* of late E. Gilbert Woodward, Metropolitan Magistrate, and of Mrs Woodward. *Educ:* Winchester; Oriel Coll., Oxford. Lieut, 60th Rifles, 1942-46; served North Africa, Italy, Middle East (despatches). Entered Foreign (subseq. Diplomatic) Service, 1946; served at Berlin, Washington, Belgrade and Khartoum, and at the Foreign Office; Counsellor: Copenhagen, 1968-72; FCO, 1972-74. *Address:* c/o Foreign and Commonwealth Office, SW1. *Club:* Travellers'.

PRIDIE, Sir Eric (Denholm), KCMG 1953 (CMG 1941); DSO 1918; OBE 1931; MB, BS, London, MRCS, FRCP; Chief Medical Officer, Colonial Office, 1948-58, retired; *b* 10 Jan. 1896; *s* of Dr John Francis and Florence Pridie. *Educ:* St Bees Sch.; University of Liverpool. Served European War, 1914-18; France, 1915-16; Mesopotamia, 1917-18, with 6th and 7th Battalions King's Own Royal (Lancaster) Regt; Captain, 1917 (despatches, wounded, DSO); joined Sudan Med. Service, 1924; served in Kassala and Blue Nile Provinces; Asst Director, 1930; Director Sudan Medical Service, 1933-45; Member of Governor General's Council, 1934-45; President Central Board Public Health, Sudan, 1933-45, and Chairman School Council, Kitchener School of Medicine, 1933-45; Brigadier, Royal Army Medical Corps; DDMS Troops, Sudan and Eritrea, Middle East Forces, 1940-43 (despatches twice); Health Counsellor, British Embassy, Cairo, 1945-49, and Health Adviser British Middle East Office, 1946-49. Order of Nile 3rd Class. *Clubs:* Athenæum, Royal Commonwealth Society.

PRIESTLEY, Dr Charles Henry Brian, AO; FAA 1954; FRS 1967; Chairman for Environmental Physics Research, CSIRO, Australia, since 1971 (Chief of Division of Meteorological Physics, 1946-71); *b* 8 July 1915; *s* of late T. G. Priestley; *m* 1946, Constance, *d* of H. Tweedy; one *s* two *d. Educ:* Mill Hill

Sch.; St John's Coll., Cambridge. Served in Meteorological Office, Air Ministry, 1939-46; subseq. with CSIRO, Australia. MA (Cantab) 1942, ScD (Cantab) 1953. David Syme Prize, University of Melbourne, 1956. Member Exec. Cttee, International Assoc. of Meteorology, 1954-60, Vice-Pres., 1967-75; Vice-Pres., Australian Acad. of Science, 1959-60; Mem., Adv. Cttee, World Meteorological Organisation, 1964-68 (Chm., 1967; Internat. Met. Orgn Prize, 1973). FRMetSoc (Buchan Prize, 1950 and Symons Medal, 1967, of Society); FInstP. Rossby Medal, Amer. Met. Soc., 1975. *Publications:* Turbulent Transfer in the Lower Atmosphere, 1959; about 60 papers in scientific journals. *Recreation:* golf. *Address:* Flat 2, 862 Malvern Road, Armadale, Vic 3143, Australia.

PRIESTLEY, Sir Gerald William, KCIE 1946 (CIE 1943); *b* 12 Nov. 1888; *s* of James Henry Priestley; *m* 1919, Isobel Macleod Millar (*d* 1958); four *d*; *m* 1959, Evelyn May Ledward, Kloof. *Educ:* West Monmouthshire Sch., Pontypool; Trinity Coll., Cambridge. Entered ICS, 1912, in Madras; investigated Upper Bhavani and Tunga-bhadra Irrigation Projects, 1926 and 1934; Commissioner of Coorg, 1927; Member Board of Revenue, 1939; Chief Secretary to the Government of Madras, 1942; Adviser to Governor of Madras, 1945; retired, 1947. *Address:* 7 Park Lane, Kloof, Natal, South Africa.

PRIESTLEY, John Boynton, OM 1977; MA, LittD; LLD; DLitt; Author; *b* Bradford, 1894; *s* of Jonathan Priestley, schoolmaster; *m* Jacquetta Hawkes, *qv*; one *s* four *d* by previous marriages. *Educ:* Bradford; Trinity Hall, Cambridge. Served with Duke of Wellington's and Devon Regts, 1914-19. UK Delegate to UNESCO Conferences, 1946-47; Chairman of International Theatre Conf.: Paris, 1947, Prague, 1948; Chairman British Theatre Conf., 1948; President International Theatre Institute, 1949; Member of the National Theatre Board, 1966-67. Freeman, City of Bradford, 1973. *Publications:* Brief Diversions, 1922; Papers from Lilliput, 1922; I for One, 1923; Figures in Modern Literature, 1924; The English Comic Characters, 1925; George Meredith (English Men of Letters), 1926; Talking, 1926; Adam in Moonshine, 1927; Open House, 1927; Peacock (English Men of Letters), 1927; Benighted, 1927; The English Novel, 1927; Apes and Angels, 1928; English Humour, 1928; The Good Companions, 1929 (dramatised with E. Knoblock, 1931); The Balconinny, 1929; Town Major of Miraucourt; Angel Pavement, 1930; Self-Selected Essays, 1932; Dangerous Corner, play, 1932; Faraway, 1932; Wonder Hero, 1933, The Roundabout, play, 1933; Laburnum Grove, play, 1933; English Journey, 1934; Eden End, 1934; Duet in Floodlight, play, 1935; Cornelius, play, 1935; Bees on the Boat Deck, play, 1936; They Walk in the City, 1936; Midnight on the Desert, 1937; Time and the Conways, play, 1937; I Have Been Here Before, play, 1937; People at Sea, play, 1937; The Doomsday Men, 1938; Music at Night, play, 1938; When We Are Married, play, 1938; Johnson Over Jordan, play, 1939; Rain upon Godshill, 1939; Let the People Sing, 1939; The Long Mirror, play, 1940; Postscripts, 1940; Out of the People, 1941; Goodnight, Children, play, 1942; Black-Out in Gretley, 1942; They Came to a City, play, 1943; Daylight on Saturday, 1943; The Man-Power Story, 1943; British Women go to War, 1943; Desert Highway, play, 1943; How Are They At Home?, play, 1944; Three Men in New Suits, 1945; An Inspector Calls, Ever Since Paradise, plays, 1946; The Secret Dream; Bright Day, 1946; Arts under Socialism; Theatre Outlook; Jenny Villiers; The Linden Tree, play, 1947; Home is Tomorrow, play, 1948; Summer Day's Dream, play, 1949; libretto, The Olympians, opera, 1948; Delight (essays), 1949; libretto, Last Holiday (film), 1950; Festival at Farbridge, 1951; (with Jacquetta Hawkes) Dragon's Mouth, play, 1952; The Other Place, 1953; The Magicians; Low Notes on a High Level, 1954; Mr Kettle and Mrs Moon, play, 1955; Journey Down a Rainbow (with Jacquetta Hawkes), 1955; The Glass Cage, play, 1957; Thoughts in the Wilderness, 1957; The Art of the Dramatist, 1957; Topside or the Future of England, 1958; Literature and Western Man, 1960; Saturn Over The Water, 1961; The Thirty-First of June, 1961; Charles Dickens: A Pictorial Biography, 1961; The Shapes of Sleep, 1962; Margin Released, 1962; A Severed Head (with Iris Murdoch), play, 1963; Sir Michael and Sir George, 1964; Man and Time, 1964; Lost Empires, 1965; The Moment-And Other Pieces (essays), 1966; Salt is Leaving, 1966; It's an Old Country, 1967; Trumpets Over the Sea, 1968; The Image Men, Vol. I, Out of Town, 1968, Vol. II, London End, 1968; Essays of Five Decades, ed Susan Cooper, 1969; The Prince of Pleasure and his Regency, 1969; The Edwardians, 1970; Snoggle, 1971; Victoria's Heyday, 1972; Over the Long High Wall, 1972; The English, 1973; Outcries and Asides (essays), 1974; A Visit to New Zealand, 1974; The Carfitt Crisis, 1975; Particular Pleasures, 1975; Found, Lost, Found, or the English Way of Life, 1976; The Happy Dream, 1976; English Humour, 1976; Instead of the Trees (autobiog.), 1977. *Relevant publications:* J. B. Priestley: An Informal Study

of His Work, by David Hughes, 1959; J. B. Priestley: the Dramatist, by Gareth Lloyd Evans, 1964; J. B. Priestley: portrait of an author, by Susan Cooper, 1970, etc. *Address:* Albany, Piccadilly, W1; Alveston, Warwickshire.
See also Air Marshal Sir P. G. Wykeham.

PRIESTLEY, Mrs J. B.; *see* Hawkes, Jacquetta.

PRIMROSE, family name of **Earl of Rosebery.**

PRIMROSE, Sir John Ure, 3rd Bt, *cr* 1903, of Redholme; farming in the Argentine; *b* 15 April 1908; *er s* of Sir William Louis Primrose, 2nd Bt, and Elizabeth Caroline (*d* 1951), *d* of Hugh Dunsmuir, Glasgow; *S* father, 1953; *m* Enid, *d* of James Evans Sladen, British Columbia; one *s. Educ:* Rugby; Sandhurst. Lieut, QO Cameron Highlanders, 1928-33. *Heir: s* Alasdair Neil Primrose [*b* 11 Dec. 1935; *m* 1958, Elaine Noreen, *d* of E. C. Lowndes, Buenos Aires; two *s* two *d. Educ:* St George's College, Buenos Aires]. *Address:* Puerto Victoria, Alto Parana, Misiones, Argentina.

PRIMROSE, William, CBE 1952; FGSM (Hon.); Viola Soloist; *b* 23 Aug. 1904; *s* of late John Primrose and of Margaret Primrose, both of Glasgow; *m* 1st, 1928, Dorothy (*d* 1951), *d* of John Friend of Exeter; two *d*; *m* 2nd, 1952, Alice Virginia French, Davenport, Iowa. *Educ:* Guildhall School of Music, London; privately with Eugen Ysaye, Brussels. Violist with London String Quartet, 1930-35; First Violist with NBC Orchestra, New York, under Toscanini, 1937-42; since then exclusively as soloist. Professor, Viola and Chamber Music, Curtis Institute of Music, Philadelphia, 1940-50. Has toured extensively in US, Canada, Central and S America, Great Britain, Western Europe and Israel. *Recreations:* chess, cricket and reading. *Club:* Savage.

PRINCE, Prof. Frank Templeton, MA (Oxon); Professor of English, University of the West Indies, Mona, Jamaica, since 1975; *b* Kimberley, South Africa, 13 Sept. 1912; 2nd *s* of late H. Prince and Margaret Templeton (*née* Hetherington); *m* 1943, Pauline Elizabeth, *d* of late H. F. Bush; two *d. Educ:* Christian Brothers' Coll., Kimberley, South Africa; Balliol Coll., Oxford. Visiting Fellow, Graduate Coll., Princeton, NJ, 1935-36. Study Groups Department, Chatham House, 1937-40. Served Army, Intelligence Corps, 1940-46. Department of English, 1946-57, Prof. of English, 1957-74, Southampton Univ. Visiting Fellow, All Souls Coll., 1968-69. Clark Lectr, Cambridge, 1972-73. *Publications:* Poems, 1938; Soldiers Bathing (poems), 1954; The Italian Element in Milton's Verse, 1954; The Doors of Stone (poems), 1963; Memoirs in Oxford (verse), 1970; Drypoints of the Hasidim (verse), 1975; contrib. to Review of English Studies. *Recreations:* music, etc. *Address:* 32 Brookvale Road, Southampton. *T:* Southampton 555457; c/o University of the West Indies, Mona, Kingston, Jamaica.

PRINCE, Maj.-Gen. Hugh Anthony, CBE 1960; retired as Chief, Military Planning Office, SEATO, Bangkok; *b* 11 Aug. 1911; *s* of H. T. Prince, FRCS, LRCP; *m* 1st, 1938, Elizabeth (*d* 1959), *d* of Dr Walter Bapty, Victoria, BC; two *s*; 2nd, 1959, Claude-Andrée, *d* of André Romanet, Château-de-Tholot, Beaujeu, Rhône; one *s. Educ:* Eastbourne Coll.; RMC, Sandhurst. Commissioned, 1931; served in 6th Gurkha Rifles until 1947; The King's Regt (Liverpool), 1947. *Recreations:* golf, gardening, antiques. *Address:* 13200 Raphèle-les-Arles, France. *T:* 98.46.93.

PRINCE, Leslie Barnett, CBE 1973; MA; FCA; Director of Public Companies; *b* 27 May 1901; *s* of Sir Alexander William Prince, KBE, and Lady Prince (*née* Edith Jonas); *m* 1924, Norah Millie, *d* of Eliot Lewis, JP; one *s* two *d. Educ:* Clifton Coll.; Magdalene Coll., Cambridge (MA). Chartered Accountant; FCA 1930; London Chest Hospital Board, 1937-48; Hospital for Diseases of the Chest, Board of Management, 1948-61. Joint Chairman of Jewish Refugees Cttee, 1939-43; Hon. Director of Accounts, ROF, Ministry of Supply, 1944-46. Member Court of Common Council, City of London, 1950-; Chairman: Rates Finance Cttee, 1957-65; Coal and Corn and Finance Cttee, Corporation of London, 1967; Coal, Corn and Rates Finance Cttee, 1968-70; Real Estate Cttee, 1970-; Chief Commoner, City Lands and Bridge House Estates Cttee, 1971. Sheriff of City of London, 1954-55; Chm., London Court of Arbitration, 1974. Member Council: Metropolitan Hospital Sunday Fund, 1951-; Royal Veterinary Coll., 1971-. Deputy of Ward of Bishopsgate, 1970. Master, Worshipful Co. of Farriers, 1955-56. President: United Wards Club, 1957; Bishopsgate Ward Club, 1958. Pres., Old Cliftonian Soc., 1973-75 (Hon. Treas., 1934-73). Companion of Star of Ethiopia, 1954; Commandeur Léopold II, 1963; Order of Sacred Treasure (Japan), 1972; Order of Stor (Afghanistan), 1972. *Recreation:*

knitting. *Address:* 21 Cadogan Gardens, SW3. *T:* 01-730 0515. *Clubs:* Gresham, City Livery (Treasurer, 1966-72, and 1974-, Pres., 1973-74).

PRINCE-SMITH, Sir (William) Richard, 4th Bt, *cr* 1911; Landowner; *b* 27 Dec. 1928; *s* of Sir William Prince-Smith, 3rd Bt, OBE, MC, and Marjorie, Lady Prince-Smith (*d* 1970); *S* father, 1964; *m* 1st, 1955, Margaret Ann Carter; one *s* one *d*; 2nd, 1975, Ann Christina Faulds. *Educ:* Charterhouse; Clare Coll., Cambridge (MA). BA (Agric.) 1951. *Recreations:* music, photography, yachting. *Heir: s* James William Prince-Smith, *b* 2 July 1959. *Address:* Augres House, Trinity, Jersey.

PRING, David Andrew Michael, MC 1943; Clerk of Committees, House of Commons, since 1976; *b* 6 Dec. 1922; *s* of late Captain John Arthur Pring and Gladys Pring; *m* 1962, Susan Brakspear, Henley-on-Thames; one *s* one *d*. *Educ:* King's Sch., Rochester; Magdalene Coll., Cambridge (MA). Served Royal Engineers, N Africa, Sicily, Italy, Austria, 1941-46; attached staff Governor-General, Canada, 1946. A Clerk of the House of Commons, 1948-. *Publications:* various, incl. (with Kenneth Bradshaw) Parliament and Congress, 1972. *Recreation:* living in the country. *Address:* Bushy Platt, Stanford Dingley, Berks RG7 6DY. *T:* Woolhampton 2585. *Club:* Athenæum.

PRINGLE, Air Marshal Sir Charles (Norman Seton), KBE 1973 (CBE 1967); MA, CEng, FRAeS; Senior Executive, Rolls Royce Ltd, since 1976; Director, Hunting Engineering Ltd, since 1976; *b* 6 June 1919; *s* of late Seton Pringle, OBE, FRCSI, Dublin; *m* 1946, Margaret, *d* of late B. Sharp, Baildon, Yorkshire; one *s*. *Educ:* Repton; St John's Coll., Cambridge. Commissioned, RAF, 1941; served India and Ceylon, 1942-46. Air Ministry, 1946-48; RAE, Farnborough, 1949-50; attached to USAF, 1950-52; appts in UK, 1952-60; STSO No 3 Group, Bomber Comd, 1960-62, and Air Forces Middle East, 1962-64; Comdt RAF St Athan and Air Officer Wales, 1964-66; MoD, 1967; IDC, 1968. Dir-Gen. of Engineering (RAF) MoD, 1969-70; Air Officer Engineering, Strike Command, 1970-73; Dir-Gen. Engineering (RAF), 1973; Controller, Engrg and Supply (RAF), 1973-76. Pres., RAeS, 1975-76; Vice-Chm., 1976-77, Chm., 1977-78, CEI. *Recreations:* photography, ornithology, motor sport. *Address:* 8 Strangways Terrace, W14 8NE. *T:* 01-602 3356. *Clubs:* Royal Air Force, Bucks.

PRINGLE, John Martin Douglas; *b* 1912; *s* of late J. Douglas Pringle, Hawick, Scotland; *m* 1936, Celia, *d* of E. A. Carroll; one *s* two *d*. *Educ:* Shrewsbury Sch.; Lincoln Coll., Oxford. First Class Literae Humaniores, 1934. Editorial Staff of Manchester Guardian, 1934-39. Served War of 1939-45 with King's Own Scottish Borderers, 1940-44; Assistant Editor, Manchester Guardian, 1944-48; Special Writer on The Times, 1948-52; Editor of The Sydney Morning Herald, 1952-57; Deputy Editor of The Observer, 1958-63; Managing Editor, Canberra Times, 1964-65; Editor, Sydney Morning Herald, 1965-70. *Publications:* China Struggles for Unity, 1938; Australian Accent, 1958; Australian Painting Today, 1963; On Second Thoughts, 1971; Have Pen, Will Travel, 1973; The Last Shenachie, 1976. *Address:* 27 Bayview Street, McMahon's Point, N Sydney, NSW 2060, Australia.

PRINGLE, John William Sutton, MBE 1945; FRS 1954; ScD 1955; Linacre Professor of Zoology, Oxford, and Fellow of Merton College, Oxford, since 1961; *b* 22 July 1912; *e s* of late John Pringle, MD, Manchester, and of Dorothy Emily (*née* Beney); *m* 1946, Beatrice Laura Wilson (*née* Gilbert-Carter); one *s* two *d*. *Educ:* Winchester Coll.; King's Coll., Cambridge (MA). University Demonstrator in Zoology, 1937-39; University Lecturer, 1945-59; Fellow of King's Coll., Cambridge, 1938-45; Telecommunications Research Establishment, 1939-44; Ministry of War Transport, 1944-45; Fellow of Peterhouse, Cambridge, 1945-61, Emeritus Fellow, Oct. 1961-. Senior Tutor, 1948-57; Senior Bursar, 1957-59; Librarian, 1959-61; Reader in Experimental Cytology, Cambridge, 1959-61. Pres., Soc. for Experimental Biol., 1977-. American Medal of Freedom, 1945. *Publications:* Insect Flight, 1957; (ed) Biology and the Human Sciences, 1972; papers in Journal of Experimental Biology, Journal of Physiology, Philos. Trans. Royal Society. *Recreations:* gliding, canals, bee-keeping. *Address:* 437 Banbury Road, Oxford OX2 8ED. *T:* 58470.

PRINGLE, Dr Mia Lilly Kellmer, CBE 1975; Director, National Children's Bureau, since 1963; *d* of late Samuel and late Sophie Kellmer; *m* 1946, William Joseph Sommerville Pringle, BSc (*d* 1962); *m* 1969, William Leonard Hooper, MA Oxon. *Educ:* schools in Vienna; Birkbeck Coll., University of London. BA (Hons) 1944; Dip. Educ. Psychol. 1945; Fellowship, London Child Guidance Training Centre, 1945; PhD (Psych.) 1950. Teaching in Primary Schools, Middx and Herts, 1940-44; Educ.

and Clin. Psychologist, Herts Child Guidance Service, 1945-50; University of Birmingham: Lecturer in Educ. Psych., 1950-54; Dep. Head, Dept of Child Study, 1954-63; Senior Lecturer in Educ. Psych., 1960-63. Member: Birmingham Educ. Cttee, 1957-63; Home Sec.'s Adv. Council on Child Care, 1966-72; Consultative Panel for Social Develt, ODM, 1968-71; Sec. of State's Adv. Cttee on Handicapped Children, 1971-; Bd of Governors, Hosp. for Sick Children, Gt Ormond Street, 1969-; Research Consultant: on play needs, to Min. of Housing and Local Govt, 1968-73; UN Research Inst. for Social Develt, 1967-69; co-opted Mem., Islington Social Services Cttee, 1972; Mem., Personal Social Services Council, 1973- (Chm. Study Gp on A Future for Intermediate Treatment, report published 1977). Hon. DSc Bradford, 1972. Hon. Fellow, Manchester Polytechnic; Hon. FCP. Hon. Mem., British Paediatric Assoc. FBPsS; FRSocMed; FRSA. *Publications:* The Emotional and Social Adjustment of Physically Handicapped Children, 1964; Deprivation and Education, 1965; Investment in Children (ed), 1965; Social Learning and its Measurement, 1966; Adoption-Facts and Fallacies, 1966; Caring for Children (ed), 1968; Able Misfits, 1970; The Needs of Children, 1974; co-author: 11,000 Seven-Year-Olds, 1966; Four Years On, 1967; Residential Child Care-Facts and Fallacies, 1967; Foster Care-Facts and Fallacies, 1967; The Community's Children, 1967; Directory of National, Voluntary Children's Organisations, 1968; The Challenge of Thalidomide, 1970; Living with Handicap, 1970; Born Illegitimate, 1971; Growing Up Adopted, 1972; Advances in Educational Psychology, vol. 2, 1973; Early Child Care and Education, 1975; Controversial Issues in Child Development, 1977; papers in journals of psychology, education and child care. *Recreations:* tennis, music, theatre-going, walking, cooking. *Address:* (home) 68 Wimpole Street, W1; (office) 8 Wakley Street, EC1. *T:* 01-278 9441/7. *Club:* Royal Over-Seas League.

PRINGLE, Dr Robert William, OBE 1967; BSc, PhD; FRSE; FRSC; President, Nuclear Enterprises Ltd, Edinburgh, since 1976; *b* 2 May 1920; *s* of late Robert Pringle and late Lillias Dalgleish Hair; *m* 1948, Carol Stokes; three *s* one *d*. *Educ:* George Heriot's Sch., Edinburgh; Edinburgh Univ. (Vans Dunlop Scholar in Natural Philosophy); Lecturer, Natural Philosophy, Edinburgh, 1945; Associate Professor of Physics, Manitoba, 1949; Prof. and Chairman of Physics, Manitoba, 1953-56. Chm. and Man. Dir, Nuclear Enterprises Ltd, 1956-76 (Queen's Award to Industry, 1966); Dir, N Sea Assets Ltd, 1977-. Member: Scottish Council, CBI (Cttee), 1966-72; University Court, Edinburgh Univ., 1967-75; Scottish Univs Industry Liaison Cttee, 1968-75; Bd, Edinburgh Univ. Centre for Industrial Liaison and Consultancy, 1968-; Bd, Royal Observatory (Edinburgh), 1968-; Council, SRC, 1972-76; Bd, Astronomy, Space and Radio (SRC), 1970-72; Bd, Nuclear Physics (SRC), 1972-76; Economic Council for Scotland, 1971-75; Bd, Scottish Sch. Business Studies, 1972-; Press Cttee, Edinburgh Univ., 1977-; Trustee: Scottish Hospitals Endowments Res. Trust, 1974-; Scottish Trust for the Physically Disabled, 1977-. Hon. Adviser, Nat. Museum of Antiquities of Scotland, 1969. FInstP 1948; Fellow, American Inst. Physics, 1950; FRSC 1955; FRSE 1964; Hon. Fellow, Royal Scottish Soc. Arts, 1972. *Publications:* papers on nuclear spectroscopy and nuclear geophysics in UK and US scientific journals. *Recreations:* golf, book-collecting, Rugby (Edinburgh, Edinburgh and Glasgow, Rest of Scotland, 1945-48). *Address:* Westridge, 91 Ravelston Dykes, Edinburgh EH12 6EY. *T:* 031-337 2891. *Clubs:* English-Speaking Union; Royal Society (Edinburgh); Murrayfield; Bruntisfield.

PRINGLE, Maj.-Gen. Sir Steuart (Robert), 10th Bt, *cr* 1683, Stichill, Roxburghshire; Major-General Royal Marines Commando Forces, since 1978; *b* 21 July 1928; *s* of Sir Norman H. Pringle, 9th Bt and Lady (Oonagh) Pringle (*née* Curran) (*d* 1975); *S* father, 1961; *m* 1953, Jacqueline Marie Gladwell; two *s* two *d*. *Educ:* Sherborne. Royal Marines: 2nd Lieut, 1946; Lieut, 1949; RM Officers' Signal Course, 1956; Captain, 1957; 40 Commando, 1957-59; Chief Instructor, Signal Trng Wing, RM, 1959-61; 3 Commando, 1961-64; RN Staff Course, 1964; Major, 1964; Defence Planning Staff, MoD, 1964-66; Chief Signal Officer, RM, 1966-69; 40 Commando, Far East, 1969-71; sowc 1971; Lt-Col, 1971; CO 45 Commando Gp., 1971-74; HQ Commando Forces 1974-77; Col, 1975; Student, RCDS, 1977; Maj.-Gen., 1978. *Heir: s* Simon Robert Pringle, *b* 6 Jan. 1959. *Address:* 76 South Croxted Road, Dulwich, SE21.

PRIOR, Ven. Christopher, CB 1968; Archdeacon of Portsmouth, 1969-77, Archdeacon Emeritus since 1977; *b* 2 July 1912; *s* of late Ven. W. H. Prior; *m* 1945, Althea Stafford (*née* Coode); two *d*. *Educ:* King's Coll., Taunton; Keble Coll., Oxford; Cuddesdon Coll. Curate of Hornsea, 1938-41; Chaplain RN from 1941, Chaplain of the Fleet, 1966-69. Served in: HMS Royal Arthur, 1941; HMHS Maine, 1941-43; HMS Scylla, 1943-44; HMS Owl,

1944-46; various ships, 1946-58; Britannia RNC, Dartmouth, 1958-61; HMS Blake, 1961-62; HM Dockyard, Portsmouth, 1963-66; QHC, 1966-69. *Recreations:* golf, walking. *Address:* Ponies End, West Melbury, Shaftesbury, Dorset. *T:* Fontmell Magna 239.

PRIOR, Rt. Hon. James Michael Leathes, PC 1970; MP (C) Lowestoft Division of Suffolk since Oct. 1959; Farmer and Land Agent in Norfolk and Suffolk since 1951; *b* 11 Oct. 1927; 2nd *s* of late C. B. L. and A. S. M. Prior, Norwich; *m* 1954, Jane Primrose Gifford, 2nd *d* of late Air Vice-Marshal O. G. Lywood, CB, CBE; three *s* one *d. Educ:* Charterhouse; Pembroke College, Cambridge. 1st class degree in Estate Management, 1950; commissioned in Royal Norfolk Regt, 1946; served in India and Germany. PPS to Pres. of Bd of Trade, 1963, to Minister of Power, 1963-64, to Mr Edward Heath, Leader of the Opposition, 1965-70; Minister of Agriculture, Fisheries and Food, 1970-72; Lord Pres. of Council and Leader of House of Commons, 1972-74. A Dep. Chm., Cons. Party, 1972-74 (Vice-Chm., 1965); Opposition front bench spokesman on Employment, 1974-. Chm. Aston Boats Ltd, 1968-70; Director: F. Lambert and Sons Ltd, 1958-70; IDC Group, 1968-70, 1974-; United Biscuits (Holdings) Ltd, 1974-; Norwich Union Adv. Bd, 1974-; Avon Cosmetics Ltd, 1975-; Consultant: Trust Houses Forte, 1974-; Nickerson Gp, 1975-. *Recreations:* cricket, tennis, golf, gardening. *Address:* Old Hall, Brampton, Beccles, Suffolk. *T:* Brampton 278; 36 Morpeth Mansions, SW1. *T:* 01-834 5543. *Clubs:* MCC; Butterflies Cricket.

PRIOR, Peter James; Chairman, H. P. Bulmer Ltd, since 1973; Director, British Sugar Corporation, since 1969; *b* 1 Sept. 1919; *s* of Percy Prior; *m* 1957, Prinia Mary, *d* of late R. E. Moreau, Berrick Prior, Oxon; two *s. Educ:* Royal Grammar Sch., High Wycombe; London Univ. BSc(Econ). FCA, FIMC, FBIM. Joined ranks, later commnd Royal Berks Regt, 1939; Intell. Corps, 1944-46 (Captain) (Croix-de-Guerre 1944). Company Sec., Saunders-Roe (Anglesey) Ltd, 1948; Consultant, Urwick, Orr & Partners, 1951; Financial Dir, International Chemical Co., 1956; Financial Dir, British Aluminium Co., 1961; Man. Dir, H. P. Bulmer Ltd, 1966. Member: English Tourist Bd, 1969-75; Midlands Electricity Bd, 1973-; Mem. Council, Brit. Inst. of Management; Chm., Enquiry into Potato Processing Industry, 1971. Chm. Trustees, Leadership Trust, 1975. *Publications:* Leadership is not a Bowler Hat, 1977; articles on management and leadership. *Recreations:* free-fall parachuting (Vice-Chm. Hereford Parachute Club); flying, motor-cycling, restoration of locomotive King George V. *Address:* Rathays, Sutton Saint Nicholas, Herefordshire HR1 3AY. *T:* Sutton Saint Nicholas 313. *Clubs:* Army and Navy, Special Forces; Hereford Farmers.

PRIOR, William Johnson, CEng, FIEE; Member: Electricity Council, since 1976; National Coal Board, since 1977; *b* 28 Jan. 1924; *s* of Ernest Stanley and Lilian Prior; *m* 1945, Mariel (*née* Irving); two *s* one *d. Educ:* Goole and Barnsley Grammar Schs. Barugh, Mexborough, Stuart Street (Manchester) and Stockport Power Stations, 1944-52; Keadby, 1952-56, Supt, 1954-56; Supt, Berkeley, 1957-58; Supt, Hinkley Point Generating Station, 1959-66; CEGB and predecessors: Asst Reg. Dir (Generation), NW Region, 1967-70; Dir (Generation), SW Region, 1970-72; Dir-Gen., SE Region, 1972-76. *Recreation:* country walking. *Address:* Searchwood, Bishop's Down Park Road, Tunbridge Wells, Kent. *T:* Tunbridge Wells 25256.

PRIOR-PALMER, Brig. Sir Otho (Leslie), Kt 1959; DSO 1945; *b* 28 Oct. 1897; *s* of late Spunner Prior-Palmer, County Sligo, Ireland, and Merrion Square, Dublin, and Anne Leslie Gason. Kilteelagh, Co. Tipperary; *m* 1940, Sheila Mary Weller Poley (OBE 1958), Boxted Hall, Bury St Edmunds; one *s* two *d* (and one *d* by previous marr.); *m* 1964, Elizabeth, *d* of late Harold Henderson; two *s. Educ:* Wellington; RMC, Sandhurst. Commissioned 9th Lancers, 1916; commanded 2nd Northamptonshire Yeo., 1940-42; comd 30th Armoured Brigade, Mar.-Aug. 1942; 29th Armoured Brigade, 1942-43; 7th Armoured Brigade, 1943-45 (DSO); commanded latter during Italian Campaign; retd pay 1946, hon. rank of Brig. MP (C) Worthing Div. W Sussex, 1945-50, Worthing, 1950-64. Vice-Chm. Conservative Members' Defence Cttee, 1958-59; Past Chm. NATO Parliamentarians Defence Cttee. *Recreations:* skiing, sailing, all field sports, fishing. *Address:* Grange, Honiton, Devon. *T:* Broadhembury 377. *Clubs:* Royal Yacht Squadron (Cowes); Pratt's.

PRITCHARD, family name of **Baron Pritchard.**

PRITCHARD, Baron *cr* 1975 (Life Peer), of West Haddon, Northamptonshire; **Derek Wilbraham Pritchard;** Kt 1968; DL; President, Abeyfield Society, since 1970; Vice-President:

Institute of Export; Wine and Spirit Association of Great Britain; *b* 8 June 1910; *s* of Frank Wheelton Pritchard and Ethel Annie Pritchard (*née* Cheetham); *m* 1941, Denise Arfor Pritchard (*née* Huntbach); two *d. Educ:* Clifton College, Bristol. Took over family business of E. Halliday & Son, Ltd, 1929. Called up in TA and served War of 1939-45; demob. as Col and joined Bd of E. K. Cole, Ltd, 1946. Joined Ind Coope Ltd, as Man. Dir of Grants of St James's Ltd, Wine Merchants, 1949. Director: Ind Coope Ltd, 1951; Ind Coope Tetley Ansell Ltd on merger of those companies, 1961; Allied Breweries Ltd (Chm., 1968-70); Allied Breweries Investments Ltd; Guardian Assurance Ltd; Guardian Royal Exchange Assurance Ltd; George Sandeman Sons & Co. Ltd; J. & W. Nicholson & Co. Ltd; Midland Bank Ltd; Samuel Montagu Ltd; Rothmans of Pall Mall (Australia) Ltd; Rothmans of Pall Mall (Canada) Ltd; Rothmans of Singapore Ltd; Rothmans of Pall Mall (Malaysia) Behad; Rothmans Group Services Ltd; Carreras (Jamaica) Ltd; Paterson, Zochonis & Co. Ltd; Chairman: Carreras Ltd, 1970-72; Rothmans International, 1972-75; Dorchester Hotel, 1976-. Dep. Chm., BNEC, 1965-66, Chm. 1966-68. Pres., Inst. of Directors, 1968-74. DL Northants, 1974. *Recreations:* farming, fox hunting (Pytchley). *Address:* West Haddon Hall, Northampton NN6 1AU. *T:* West Haddon 210.

PRITCHARD, Arthur Alan; on secondment from Ministry of Defence as Deputy Secretary, Northern Ireland Office, since 1976; *b* 3 March 1922; *s* of Arthur Henry Standfast Pritchard and Sarah Bessie Myra Pritchard (*née* Little); *m* 1949, Betty Rona Nevard (*née* Little); two *s* one *d. Educ:* Wanstead High Sch., Essex. Joined Board of Trade, 1939. RAF Pilot, 1941-46. RAFVR, 1947-52. Joined Admiralty, 1952; Asst Sec., 1964; attended Royal College of Defence Studies, 1972; Asst Under-Sec. of State, Naval Personnel and Op. Requirements, MoD, 1972-76. *Recreations:* sailing, walking. *Address:* Stormont Castle, Belfast BT4 3ST. *Clubs:* Royal Air Force; Lilliput Sailing (Poole).

PRITCHARD, Sir Asa Hubert, Kt 1965; Merchant, retired; President, Asa H. Pritchard Ltd, Nassau; *b* 1 Aug. 1891; *s* of William Edward Pritchard, Bahamas; *m* 1915, Maud Pauline Pyfrom. *Educ:* Queen's College, Bahamas. MHA, Bahamas, 1925-62; Deputy Speaker, 1942-46; Speaker, 1946-62. Member: Board of Education, 1930-35; Electricity Board, 1940-46; Chm., Bahamas Develt Bd, 1946. *Address:* Breezy Ridge, PO Box 6218 ES, Nassau, Bahamas.

PRITCHARD, Sir Fred Eills, Kt 1947; MBE 1942; Director, Inns of Court School of Law, 1958-68; *b* 23 June 1899; *s* of late Fred Pritchard, Liverpool; *m* 1931, Mabel Celia, *d* of late F. W. Gaskin, Liverpool; one *d. Educ:* Shrewsbury Sch.; Liverpool Univ. (LLM); Middle Temple; called to Bar, Middle Temple, 1923; practised on Northern Circuit in Liverpool, 1923-37; KC 1937; commission in RMA, 1917-19; commission in Royal Artillery, 1939; Major, and Deputy Judge Advocate, 1939-42; Lt-Col and Assistant Judge Advocate-General, 1942-45; Judge of the Salford Hundred Court of Record, 1944-47; Judge of Queen's Bench Division of High Court of Justice, 1947-53, resigned; Master of the Bench of the Middle Temple since 1946, Treasurer, 1964; Hon. Bencher, Gray's Inn, 1965-; Churchwarden St John's, St John's Wood, 1945-73; Mem. of House of Laity in National Assembly of Church of England, 1955-60; Mem. Bd, Church Army, 1956-76; Chairman Appellate Tribunal for Conscientious Objectors under Nat. Service Act 1948, 1956-71; Chm. Cttee on the Rating of Charities, 1958-59; Chm. Special Grants Cttee, 1960-72; Mem. (apptd by LCJ), Governing Body Shrewsbury School, 1960-68 (Chm., 1960-68). A Church Commissioner, 1959-68; a Comr apptd by Min. of Aviation, Civil Aviation (Licensing) Regulations, 1960. Pres., Bar Musical Soc., 1977-. Hon. LLD Liverpool, 1956. *Publication:* The Common Calendar: a notebook on Criminal Law for Circuiteers. *Address:* 3 Pump Court, Temple, EC4Y 7AJ. *T:* 01-353 4962; 14 Chichester Court, Rustington, West Sussex. *T:* Rustington 6002. *Clubs:* Constitutional; Middlesex County Cricket.

PRITCHARD, Frederick Hugh Dalzel, CBE 1961; Secretary-General, British Red Cross Society, 1951-70; *b* 26 Aug. 1905; *e s* of Gerald William and Alice Bayes Pritchard (*née* Dalzel), Richmond, Surrey; *m* 1935, Rosamond Wright Marshall; two *d. Educ:* Charterhouse School; Oriel College, Oxford. Admitted Solicitor, 1931. Partner in Pritchard Sons Partington & Holland, solicitors, London, 1933. Legal Adviser, War Organisation of British Red Cross Soc. and Order of St John, 1940. Exec. Asst to Vice-Chm., British Red Cross Soc., 1948. OStJ 1942. *Address:* Denver, Bulstrode Way, Gerrards Cross, Bucks. *T:* Gerrards Cross 83483.

PRITCHARD, Rear-Adm. Gwynedd Idris; Flag Officer Sea Training, Portland, Dorset, since Nov. 1976; *b* 18 June 1924; *s* of Cyril Idris Pritchard and Lily Pritchard; *m* 1975, Mary Thérèsa (*née* Curtin); three *s* (by previous marriage). *Educ:* Wyggeston Sch., Leicester. MNI, MBIM. Joined Royal Navy, 1942; Sub-Lieut 1944; Lieut 1946; Lt-Comdr 1954; Comdr 1959; Captain 1967; Rear-Adm. 1976. *Recreations:* riding, caravanning. *Address:* Rodney House, Castletown, Portland, Dorset.

PRITCHARD, Hugh Wentworth, CBE 1969; Partner in Messrs Sharpe Pritchard & Co., Solicitors and Parliamentary Agents, Westminster; Member of Council of Law Society, 1947-66; *b* 15 March 1903; *s* of late Sir Harry G. Pritchard; *m* 1934, Barbara Stableforth; two *s. Educ:* Charterhouse; Balliol College, Oxford. Admitted a solicitor, 1927; partner in Sharpe Pritchard & Co., 1928. Pres. Soc. of Parliamentary Agents, 1952-55; Member: Statute Law Committee, 1954; Committee on Administrative Tribunals and Enquiries, 1955; Council on Tribunals, 1958-70. Lay Reader, 1947. Served War of 1939-45, in England, France, Belgium and Germany; joined The Queen's as a private; commissioned in RAOC, attaining rank of Lt-Col. *Recreation:* golf. *Address:* Barton, Great Woodcote Drive, Purley, Surrey CR2 3PL. *T:* 01-660 9029.

PRITCHARD, Prof. John Joseph, DM, MA; FRCS; Professor of Anatomy in The Queen's University, Belfast, and Consultant in Anatomy to Northern Ireland Hospitals Authority, and Eastern Area Board, since 1952; *b* 9 Feb. 1916; *s* of Leonard Charles and Isobel Violet Pritchard, Adelaide, SA; *m* 1940, Muriel Rachel Edmunds; three *s* one *d. Educ:* St Peter's College, Adelaide; St Mark's College (University of Adelaide); Magdalen College, Oxford; St Bartholomew's Hospital, London. Rhodes Scholar, SA, 1934; BSc Adelaide, 1934; BA Hons Oxford, 1936; MRCS, LRCP 1940; MA Oxon, BM, BCh Oxon, 1940; DM Oxon, 1951; FRCS 1964. Ho. Phys., Mill Hill Emergency Hosp. and St Bartholomew's Hosp.; Demonstrator in Anatomy, University Coll., London, 1940; Asst Lectr, Lecturer, then Reader in Anatomy at St Mary's Hosp. Med. School, University of London, 1941-52. Pres., Anatomical Society of Great Britain and Ireland, 1967-69. Visiting Professor of Anatomy, Univ. of Illinois, 1965-66. Chm. NI Br., Multiple Sclerosis Soc., 1975-. Fellow, British Assoc. of Orthopaedic Surgeons, 1973. Editor, Jl of Anatomy, 1973-. *Publications:* articles on placental structure and function and bone growth and repair, chiefly in Jl of Anatomy, London. *Recreation:* country cottaging. *Address:* 75 Osborne Park, Belfast, Northern Ireland. *T:* 667206.

PRITCHARD, John Michael, CBE 1962; Chief Conductor, Cologne Opera, since 1978; *b* 5 Feb. 1921; *s* of Albert Edward Pritchard and Amy Edith Shaylor. *Educ:* Sir George Monoux School, London; privately. Conductor: Derby String Orchestra, 1943-51; Music Staff, Glyndebourne Opera, 1947, Chorus master, 1949; Conductor, Jacques Orchestra, 1950-52; Asst to Fritz Busch, Vittorio Gui, 1950-51; Conductor Glyndebourne Festivals, 1952-77; Conductor and Musical Director, Royal Liverpool Philharmonic Orchestra, 1957-63; Musical Director, London Philharmonic Orchestra, 1962-66; Principal Conductor, 1967-77, and Musical Director, 1969-77, Glyndebourne Opera; Guest Conductor: Vienna State Opera, 1952-53, 1964-65; Covent Garden Opera, 1952-77; Edinburgh Internat. Festivals, opera and symphony concerts 1951-55, 1960, 1961, 1962, 1963; Aix-en-Provence Festival, 1963; Frankfurt Radio Orchestra, 1953; Cologne Radio Orchestra, 1953; Vienna Symphony Orchestra, 1953-55; Berlin Festival, 1954, 1964; Zürich Radio Orchestra, 1955, 1961; Santa Cecilia Orchestra, Rome, 1958, 1972; Orchestre Nationale, Brussels, 1958, 1965-67; Cracow Philharmonic Orch., 1961; Basel, Winterthur Orch., 1961, 1969; RIAS Orchestra, Berlin, 1961, 1966; Royal Philharmonic Soc., London, 1959, 1961, 1963, 1964, 1965, 1966, 1970, 1974; Wexford Festival, 1959, 1961; Oslo Philharmonic Orch., 1960, 1961, 1966, 1975; Pittsburgh Symphony Orch., 1963, 1964, and San Francisco Symphony, 1964; BBC Promenade Concerts, annually since 1960; tour of Switzerland, 1962, 1966; of Australia, 1962; of Germany, 1963, 1966; with BBC Symph. Orch., 1968; tour of Jugoslavia, 1968; Georges Enesco Festival, Bucharest, 1964; Lausanne Festival, 1964; Berlin Philharmonic, 1964; New York Opera Assoc., 1964; Société Philharmonique, Brussels, 1965, 1967; Helsinki Philharmonic, 1966; Salzburg Festival, 1966; Teatro Colon, Buenos Aires, 1966; RAI Symphony Orch., Turin, 1967; Sjaellands Symphony Orch., Copenhagen, 1967-70; SABC Orchestra, Johannesburg, 1967-70; Scandinavian Tour, Glyndebourne Opera, 1967; Teatro San Carlo, Naples, 1969-70; Danish Radio Symph., 1968; Palermo Sinfonia, 1968; Munich State Opera, 1968-69; Athens Festival, 1968-70; Leipzig Gewandhaus, 1968-70; Dresden Staatskapelle, 1968-70, 1972; Berlin Radio, 1968-70, 1972; Chicago Lyric Opera, 1969, 1975, 1977; Florence Maggio Musicale, 1977; Zürich Tonhalle, 1977-78; London Philharmonic Tours: Far East, 1969; USA, 1971; Hong Kong and China, 1973; New Philharmonia Orch., Osaka, Tokyo, 1970; San Francisco Opera, 1970, 1973-74, 1976, 1977; Geneva Opera, 1971, 1974; Metropolitan Opera, NY, 1971, 1973-74, 1977; Yomiuri Nippon Orch., Tokyo, 1972; English Chamber Orch. Tour, Latin America, 1972; Australian Opera, Sydney, 1974, 1977; Cologne Opera, 1975, 1976, 1977-78; Philadelphia Orch., 1975, 1976, 1978. Shakespeare Prize, Hamburg, 1975. *Recreations:* good food and wine, theatre. *Address:* Carters Corner Place, near Hailsham, East Sussex. *Club:* Spanish.

PRITCHARD, Sir Neil, KCMG 1962 (CMG 1952); HM Diplomatic Service, retired; Ambassador in Bangkok, 1967-70; *b* 14 January 1911; *s* of late Joseph and Lillian Pritchard; *m* 1943, Mary Burroughes, Pretoria, S Africa; one *s. Educ:* Liverpool Coll.; Worcester Coll., Oxford. Dominions Office, 1933; Private Secretary to Permanent Under-Sec., 1936-38; Assistant Secretary, Rhodesia-Nyasaland Royal Commission, 1938; Secretary, Office of UK High Commissioner, Pretoria, 1941-45; Principal Secretary, Office of UK Representative, Dublin, 1948-49; Assistant Under-Secretary of State, Commonwealth Relations Office, 1951-54; Dep. UK High Commissioner: Canada, 1954-57; Australia, 1957-60; Actg Dep. Under-Sec. of State, CRO, 1961; British High Comr in Tanganyika, 1961-63; Deputy Under-Secretary of State, Commonwealth Office (formerly CRO), 1963-67. *Recreation:* golf. *Address:* Little Garth, Daglingworth, Cirencester, Glos GL7 7AQ.

PRITCHETT, Sir Victor (Sawdon), Kt 1975; CBE 1968; FRSL; Author and Critic; *b* 16 Dec. 1900; *s* of Sawdon Pritchett and Beatrice Martin; *m* Dorothy, *d* of Richard Samuel Roberts, Welshpool, Montgomeryshire; one *s* one *d. Educ:* Alleyn's School. Dir of New Statesman and Nation. Christian Gauss Lectr, Princeton Univ., 1953; Beckman Prof., Univ. California, Berkeley, 1962; Writer-in-Residence, Smith Coll., Mass, 1966; Vis. Professor: Brandeis Univ., Mass; Columbia Univ.; Clark Lectr, 1969. Foreign Member: Amer. Acad. and Inst., 1971; Amer. Acad. Arts and Sciences, 1971. President: English Pen Club, 1971; Internat. PEN, 1974-76; Soc. of Authors, 1977-. Hon. LittD Leeds, 1972. *Publications:* Marching Spain, 1928; Clare Drummer, 1929; The Spanish Virgin, 1930; Shirley Sanz, 1932; Nothing Like Leather, 1935; Dead Man Leading, 1937; You Make Your Own Life, 1938; In My Good Books, 1942; It May Never Happen, 1946; The Living Novel, 1946; Why Do I Write?, 1948; Mr Beluncle, 1951; Books in General, 1953; The Spanish Temper, 1954; Collected Stories, 1956; When My Girl Comes Home, 1961; London Perceived, 1962; The Key to My Heart, 1963; Foreign Faces, 1964; New York Proclaimed, 1965; The Working Novelist, 1965; Dublin: A Portrait, 1967; A Cab at the Door (RSL Award), 1968; Blind Love, 1969; George Meredith and English Comedy, 1970; Midnight Oil, 1971; Balzac, 1973; The Camberwell Beauty, 1974; The Gentle Barbarian, 1977. *Address:* 12 Regent's Park Terrace, NW1. *Clubs:* Savile, Beefsteak.

PRITTIE, family name of **Baron Dunalley.**

PRITTIE, Hon. Terence Cornelius Farmer, MBE 1945; Editor, Britain and Israel, since 1970; *b* 15 Dec. 1913; *yr s* of 5th Baron Dunalley, DSO; *m* 1946, Laura Dundas; two *s. Educ:* Cheam Sch.; Stowe; Christ Church, Oxford (MA). Butler Exhibn for Modern History, 1934. Served Rifle Bde, 1938-45 (despatches, Calais, 1940); POW, Germany, escaped 6 times (MBE). Staff, Manchester Guardian, 1945-70: Cricket Corresp., 1946; Chief Corresp. in Germany, 1946-63; Diplomatic Corresp., 1963-70. Federal Cross of Merit of West Germany, 1971. *Publications:* South to Freedom, 1946; Mainly Middlesex, 1947; (with John Kay) Second Innings, 1947; Lancashire Hot-Pot, 1948; A History of Middlesex Cricket, 1951; Germany Divided, 1960; Germany (Life Magazine World Series), 1963; Germans Against Hitler, 1964; Israel: Miracle in the Desert, 1967; Eshkol, the Man and the Nation, 1969; Adenauer: A Study in Fortitude, 1972; (with Otto Loeb) Wines of the Moselle, 1972; Willy Brandt, 1974; Through Irish Eyes, 1977; The Economic War against the Jews, 1977. *Recreations:* cricket, shooting, real tennis, lawn tennis. *Address:* 9 Blithfield Street, W8 6RH. *T:* 01-937 0164. *Clubs:* Travellers', MCC, Burke, Greenjackets.
See also Baron Dunalley.

PROBERT, Rhys Price; CB 1972; Director, Royal Aircraft Establishment, since 1973; *b* 28 May 1921; *s* of late Reverend Thomas and Margaret Jane Probert; *m* 1947, Carolyn Cleasby, Lancaster, NH, USA; three *s* one *d. Educ:* Jones' West Monmouth School; St Catharine's College, Cambridge. Royal Aircraft Establishment, 1942-44; Power Jets (Research and Development) Ltd, 1944-46; Applied Physics Laboratory, Johns Hopkins Univ., 1946-47; National Gas Turbine Establishment, 1947-63 (Dep. Dir, 1957); Director-General of Scientific

Research/Air, Min. of Aviation, 1963-68; Dep. Controller of Aircraft A, Min. of Technology, later MoD, 1968-72. *Publications:* contribs to various scientific and technical jls. *Recreations:* squash, reading. *Address:* Fourways, Avenue Road, Farnborough, Hants. *Clubs:* Athenæum; Leander (Henley).
See also F. Walley.

PROBY, Major Sir Richard George, 1st Bt *cr* 1952; MC 1917; landowner and farmer; Vice-Lieutenant of Huntingdonshire, 1957-66; *b* 21 July 1886; *s* of late Col D. J. Proby, Elton, and of Lady Margaret Proby (*née* Hely Hutchinson), *d* of 4th Earl of Donoughmore, PC; *m* 1st, 1911, Betty Monica (*d* 1967), *d* of late A. Hallam Murray; two *s* three *d* (and one *s* decd); 2nd, 1972, Mrs Yvonne Harris. *Educ:* Eton; Royal Military Acad., Woolwich. Lieutenant RFA, 1906-10; Captain Essex Yeomanry, 1913; Major 1919; served European War, 1914-19 (MC). Private sec. to Lord Ailwyn, 1st Chm. Agricultural Wages Bd, 1918. Chm. Hunts War Agric. Exec. Cttee, 1939, liaison officer to Min. of Agriculture, 1941-44 and 1952-55. Chm. Country Landowners' Assoc., 1943-46, Pres., 1947-51; an hon. Vice-Pres. Land Agents' Soc.; Mem. Coun. RASE; Chm. Forestry Cttee of Gt Britain, 1959; Chm. Eastern Provincial Area Conservative Assoc., 1938, Pres. 1960; Chm. Ex. Cttee of National Union of Conservative and Unionist Associations, 1943; Chm. National Union, 1946; Pres. National Union, 1958. Chm. Real Estate Panel of Eton College, 1952. Member Wilson Agricultural Reorganisation Cttee, 1955; JP Hunts; CC for Hunts; DL Hunts, 1952; High Sheriff, Hunts, Cambs, and the Isle of Ely, 1953; Pres. Roy. Forestry Society of England, Wales and Northern Ireland, 1955; Chm. Timber Growers Organization of England and Wales, 1959-, Pres. 1961; Mem. Exec. of Irish Landowners' Convention; Bledisloe Gold Medal for distinguished service to Agriculture, 1967. *Publications:* articles and letters on agricultural and forestry matters contributed to the Times, the Quarterly Review, etc. *Recreations:* riding, travelling, forestry. *Heir: s* Captain Peter Proby [*b* 4 Dec. 1911; *m* 1944, Blanche Harrison, *o d* of Lt-Col Henry Harrison Cripps, DSO; one *s* three *d* (and one *s* decd)]. *Address:* The Dial House, Elton, Peterborough. *T:* Elton 572. *Clubs:* Travellers', Constitutional, Roxburghe.
See also Baron Inglewood, J. C. Moberly.

PROBYN, Air Commodore Harold Melsome, CB 1944; CBE 1943; DSO 1917; *b* 8 Dec. 1891; *s* of late William Probyn; *m* 1920, Marjory (*d* 1961), *d* of late Francis Evance Savory. Served European War, 1914-17 (despatches, DSO); commanded: 208 (AC) Squadron, Egypt; No 2 (AC), Squadron, Manston; 25 (Fighter) Squadron at Hawkinge; RAF School of Photography, 1932; No 22 Group, RAF, 1932-34; Senior Personnel Staff Officer, Middle East, Cairo, 1934-35; Senior Engineer Staff Officer, Middle East, Cairo, 1935-37; No 12 (Fighter) Group Royal Air Force, Hucknall, Notts, 1937; served War of 1939-45 (despatches); SASO, No 11 Fighter Group, Uxbridge, 1939-40; commanded RAF Station, Cranwell, 1940-44; retired, 1944. *Recreations:* flying, fishing, golf. *Address:* PO Box 93, Nyeri, Kenya. *T:* 2248. *Clubs:* Naval and Military; Nairobi (Kenya).

PROCKTOR, Patrick; painter since 1962; *b* 12 March 1936; 2nd *s* of Eric Christopher Procktor and Barbara Winifred (*née* Hopkins); *m* 1973, Kirsten Bo (*née* Andersen); one *s*. *Educ:* Highgate; Slade Sch. (Diploma). Many one-man exhibns, Redfern Gallery, from 1963. *Publications:* One Window in Venice, 1974; Coleridge's Rime of the Ancient Mariner (new illustrated edn), 1976. *Recreation:* Russian ballet. *Address:* 26 Manchester Street, W1M 5PG. *T:* 01-486 1763.

PROCTER, Evelyn Emma Stefanos, MA; *b* 6 June 1897; *y d* of late Harold and Ada Louisa Procter. *Educ:* Cheltenham Ladies' College; Somerville College, Oxford. Hons Mod. Hist. Cl. 1, 1918; Mary Somerville Research Fellow, Somerville College, 1921-25; Tutor in History (1925) and Fellow of St Hugh's College, Oxford, 1926-46; University Lecturer in Medieval European History, 1933-39; Norman Maccoll Lecturer, University of Cambridge, 1948-49; Principal, St Hugh's College, Oxford, 1946-62, retd. Hon. Fell. St Hugh's College, Oxford, 1962. Chevalier de la Légion d'Honneur. *Publications:* Alfonso X of Castile; Patron of Literature and Learning, 1951; contributor to: Oxford Essays in Medieval History, presented to H. E. Salter, 1934; Homenaje a Rubió i Lluch, 1936; articles in Transactions of Royal Historical Society, Revue Hispanique, English Historical Review and Modern Language Review. *Recreation:* water-colour sketching. *Address:* Little Newland, Eynsham, Oxford OX8 1LD. *T:* Oxford 881394.

PROCTER, Norma; Contralto Singer; *b* Cleethorpes, Lincolnshire, 1928. Studied under Roy Henderson and Alec Redshaw. Made first London appearance at Southwark Cathedral; debut at Covent Garden, in Gluck's Orpheus, 1961. Has sung at major British music and European festivals. Numerous concerts and recitals throughout Europe; frequent broadcasts in Britain, Holland and Germany; has made many recordings. Hon. RAM 1974. *Address:* 194 Clee Road, Grimsby, Lincolnshire; c/o Ibbs & Tillett Ltd, 124 Wigmore Street, W1.

PROCTER-GREGG, Humphrey, CBE 1971; Emeritus Professor; *b* Kirkby Lonsdale, 31 July 1895; *s* of Oliver Procter-Gregg, JP, and Florence Annie (*née* Hoare). *Educ:* King William's College; Peterhouse, Cambridge (Hist. and Organ Schol.); Royal College of Music (Opera Schol. and studentship to La Scala, Milan). MusB, MA. Hon. ARCM, FRCM. Became opera manager to Royal Coll. of Music, and stage-manager and/or producer to the Covent Garden, BNOC, and Carl Rosa Opera companies, also to Royal Manchester College of Music and BBC Opera Section; Dir, Carl Rosa Opera Company, 1958, Touring Opera, 1958. Professor of Music, University of Manchester, 1954-62, retired. Dir, London Opera Centre, 1962-63. Compositions include violin, viola, oboe, horn and clarinet sonatas, pianoforte music, songs and translations of operas. *Publication:* Sir Thomas Beecham: impresario and conductor, 1973, reissued, 1976, as Beecham Remembered. *Recreation:* painting. *Address:* 3 Oakland, Windermere, Cumbria LA23 1AR.

PROCTOR, Sir Dennis; see Proctor, Sir P. D.

PROCTOR, Sir (George) Philip, KBE 1971 (CBE 1961); *b* 8 June 1902; *s* of late C. A. Proctor; *m* 1st, 1926, Mary Turney (*d* 1939), *d* of late K. W. Monsarrat; one *s* two *d*; 2nd, 1939, Hilary Frances, *d* of late F. S. Clark; one *s* two *d*. *Educ:* Cheltenham Coll., Liverpool Univ. (BEng). Joined Dunlop Gp, 1927; Manager, Dunlop (NZ) Ltd, 1936-41 (Chm. and Man. Dir, 1945-65); Dir, Gear Meat Co Ltd. Chm., NZ Industrial Design Council, 1967-; Mem., Prison Parole Bd, 1964-; Chm., NZ Heart Foundn, 1968-; Nat. Co-ordinator and Chm., Duke of Edinburgh Award in NZ, 1963-69. KStJ 1976. *Recreation:* flyfishing. *Address:* Flat 5, Landscape Apartments, 123 Austin Street, Wellington 1, New Zealand. *Clubs:* Royal Automobile, Wellington (New Zealand).

PROCTOR, Ian Douglas Ben, RDI 1969; FSIAD 1969; FRSA 1972; Chairman, Ian Proctor Metal Masts Ltd, since 1959; freelance industrial designer since 1950; *b* 12 July 1918; *s* of Douglas McIntyre Proctor and Mary Albina Louise Proctor (*née* Tredwen); *m* 1943, Elizabeth Anne Gifford Lywood, *d* of Air Vice-Marshal O. G. Lywood, CB, CBE; three *s* one *d*. *Educ:* Gresham's Sch., Holt; London University. RAFVR (Flying Officer), 1941-47. Man. Dir, Gosport Yacht Co., 1947-48; Joint Editor Yachtsman Magazine, 1948-50; Daily Telegraph Yachting Correspondent, 1950-64. Yachtsman of the Year, 1965; Council of Industrial Design Award, 1967; Design Council Award, 1977. *Publications:* Racing Dinghy Handling, 1948; Racing Dinghy Maintenance, 1949; Sailing: Wind and Current, 1950; Boats for Sailing, 1968; Sailing Strategy, 1977. *Recreation:* sailing. *Address:* Fenmead, Brook Avenue, Warsash, Southampton; Ferry House, Duncannon, Stoke Gabriel, near Totnes, Devon. *Clubs:* Nash House; Hayling Island Sailing, Warsash Sailing, Hamble River Sailing, Aldenham Sailing.

PROCTOR, Ven. Jesse Heighton, MA (London); Archdeacon of Warwick, 1958-74, now Emeritus; Vicar of Sherbourne, Warwick, 1958-69; *b* 26 May 1908; *s* of Thomas and Sophia Proctor, Melton Mowbray; *m* 1938, Helena Mary Wood, *d* of John Thomas and Jessie Wood, Melton Mowbray; one *s* two *d*. *Educ:* County Grammar Sch. of King Edward VII, Melton Mowbray; Coll. of St Mark and St John, Chelsea, Univ. of London; St Andrew's Theological Training House, Whittlesford. Asst Master, Winterbourne Sch., Croydon, 1929-32; Sen. History Master, Melton Mowbray Gram. Sch., 1932-35; Deacon 1935, Priest 1936; Chap. and Tutor, St Andrew's, Whittlesford, 1935-38; Curate, St Philip's, Leicester, 1938-39; Vicar, Glen Parva and South Wigston, and Chap., Glen Parva Barracks, Leicester, 1939-46; Precentor of Coventry Cath., 1946-58; Hon. Canon of Coventry, 1947; Chaplain, Gulson Hosp., 1953-58; Sen. Examining Chap. to Bishop of Coventry, 1947-65; Canon Theologian of Coventry, 1954-59; Vice-Pres. CMS. Governor: Univ. of Warwick, 1966-68; City of Coventry Coll. of Educn, 1966-70. Barnabas of Coventry Evening Telegraph, 1955-75. *Publications:* contrib. to Neville Gorton (SPCK), 1957. *Recreations:* study of theology and history; the countryside. *Address:* Dilkusha, Bank Crescent, Ledbury, Herefordshire HR8 1AA. *T:* Ledbury 2241.

PROCTOR, Sir Philip; see Proctor, Sir G. P.

PROCTOR, Sir (Philip) Dennis, KCB 1959 (CB 1946); *b* 1 Sept. 1905; *s* of late Sir Philip Proctor, KBE; *m* 1st, 1936, Dorothy Varda (*d* 1951); no *c*; 2nd, 1953, Barbara, *d* of Sir Ronald Adam, Bt, *qv*; two *s* one *d. Educ:* Falconbury; Harrow; King's Coll., Cambridge. MA, 1929; entered Min. of Health, 1929; transferred to Treasury, 1930; Third Secretary, HM Treasury, 1948-50; resigned from Civil Service; joined the firm of A. P. Moller, Copenhagen, 1950; Man. Dir, The Maersk Company Ltd, 1951-53; re-entered Civil Service, 1953; Dep. Sec., Min. of Transport and Civil Aviation, 1953-58; Permanent Sec., Min. of Power, 1958-65. Dir, Williams Hudson Ltd, 1966-71. Trustee of Tate Gallery, 1952; Chairman of the Tate Gallery, 1953-59. Hon. Fellow, King's Coll., Cambridge, 1968. *Publications:* Hannibal's March in History, 1971; Autobiography of G. Lowes Dickinson, 1973. *Address:* 43 Canonbury Square, N1. *T:* 01-226 4676.

PROCTOR-BEAUCHAMP, Sir Christopher Radstock P.; *see* Beauchamp.

PROFUMO, John Dennis, CBE 1975 (OBE (mil.) 1944); 5th Baron of the late United Kingdom of Italy; *b* 30 Jan. 1915; *e s* of late Baron Albert Profumo, KC; *m* 1954, Valerie Hobson, *qv*; one *s. Educ:* Harrow; Brasenose College, Oxford. Chief of Staff UK Mission in Japan, 1945. MP (C) Kettering Division, Northamptonshire, 1940-45; MP (C) Stratford-on-Avon Division of Warwickshire, 1950-63; Joint Parliamentary Secretary, Ministry of Transport and Civil Aviation, Nov. 1952-Jan. 1957; Parliamentary Under-Secretary of State for the Colonies, 1957-58; Parliamentary Under-Sec. of State, Foreign Affairs, Nov. 1958-Jan. 1959; Minister of State for Foreign Affairs, 1959-60; Secretary of State for War, July 1960-June 1963. Dir, Provident Life Assoc. of London, 1975-. Mem., Bd of Visitors, HM Prison, Grendon, 1968-75. 1st Northamptonshire Yeomanry, 1939 (despatches). *Recreations:* shooting, cinematography. *Heir: s b* 30 Oct. 1955. *Club:* Boodle's.
See also Baron Balfour of Inchrye.

PROKHOROV, Prof. Alexander Mikhailovich; Physicist and Deputy Director, P. N. Lebedev Institute of Physics, Academy of Sciences of the USSR, Moscow; Editor-in-Chief, Bolshaya Sovetskaya Encyclopedia Publishing House, since 1970; *b* Atherton, Australia, 11 July 1916; *s* of Mikhail Prokhorov; *m* 1941, Galina Alexeyevna (*née* Shelepina); one *s. Educ:* Leningrad State University; Lebedev Inst. of Physics. Corresp. Mem., Academy of Sciences of the USSR (Department of General Physics and Astronomy), 1960-66, Full Mem., 1966-, Mem. Presidial Body, 1970, Academician-Secretary, 1973-. Professor, Moscow University, 1958-. Hon. Professor: Delhi Univ.; Bucharest Univ., 1971; Hon. Member: Amer. Acad. of Arts and Sciences, 1972; Acad. of Sciences of Hungary, 1976; Acad. of Sciences, German Democratic Republic, 1977. Member, Communist Party of the Soviet Union, 1950-. Awarded Lenin Prize, 1959; Nobel Prize for Physics (jointly with Prof. N. G. Basov and Prof. C. H. Townes), 1964. *Publications:* contributions on non-linear oscillations, radiospectroscopy and quantum radio-physics. *Address:* P. N. Lebedev Institute of Physics, Academy of Sciences of the USSR, 53 Lenin Prospekt, Moscow, USSR.

PROKHOROVA, Violetta; *see* Elvin, V.

PROKOSCH, Frederic; Writer; *b* 17 May 1908; *s* of Eduard (Professor of Linguistics, Yale University) and Mathilde Prokosch. *Educ:* Yale University (PhD, 1933); King's College, Cambridge. Educated as a child in Wisconsin, Texas, Munich, Austria; travelled extensively all his life; research work in Chaucerian MSS, 1933-38 (PhD Dissertation: The Chaucerian Apocrypha). *Publications:* The Asiatics (novel), 1935; The Assassins (poems), 1936; The Seven Who Fled (novel), 1937; The Carnival (poems), 1938; Night of the Poor (novel), 1939; Death at Sea (poems), 1940; The Skies of Europe (novel), 1942; The Conspirators (novel), 1943; Some Poems of Hölderlin, 1943; Chosen Poems, 1944; Age of Thunder (novel), 1945; The Idols of the Cave (novel), 1946; The Medea of Euripides, 1947; The Sonnets of Louise Labé, 1947; Storm and Echo (novel), 1948; Nine Days to Mukalla (novel), 1953; A Tale for Midnight (novel), 1955; A Ballad of Love (novel), 1960; The Seven Sisters (novel), 1962; The Dark Dancer (novel), 1964; The Wreck of the Cassandra (novel), 1966; The Missolonghi Manuscript (novel), 1968; America, My Wilderness (novel), 1972. *Recreations:* squash racquets (Champion of France, 1938, 1939, Champion of Sweden, 1944), lawn tennis (Champion of Mallorca). *Address:* Ma Trouvaille, 06 Plan de Grasse, France. *Clubs:* Pitt (Cambridge); Yale (New York); France-Amérique (Paris).

PROLE, Lozania; *see* Bloom, Ursula.

PROOPS, Mrs Marjorie, OBE 1969; journalist; *d* of Alfred and Martha Rayle; *m* 1935; one *s. Educ:* Dalston Secondary Sch. Daily Mirror, 1939-45; Daily Herald, 1945-54; Daily Mirror, 1954-. Broadcaster, Television, 1960-. Member: Royal Commn on Gambling, 1976-; Council for One Parent Families. Woman Journalist of the Year, 1969. *Publications:* Pride, Prejudice & Proops, 1975; Dear Marje, 1976. *Address:* 9 Sherwood Close, SW13.

PROPHET, Prof. Arthur Shelley, DDS; DpBact; FDSRCS; FFDRCSI; Professor of Dental Surgery, University of London, since 1956, and Dean, University College Hospital Medical School, since 1977; *b* 11 Jan. 1918; *s* of Eric Prophet and Mabel Wightman; *m* 1942, Vivienne Mary Bell; two *s. Educ:* Sedbergh School; University of Manchester. BDS Hons (Preston Prize and Medal), 1940; Diploma in Bacteriology (Manchester), 1948; DDS (Manchester) 1950; FDSRCS 1958; FFDRCS Ireland, 1964. Served in Royal Naval Volunteer Reserve (Dental Branch), 1941-46; Nuffield Dental Fellow, 1946-48; Lecturer in Dental Bacteriology, University of Manchester, 1948-54; Lecturer in Dental Surgery, QUB, 1954-56; Dir of Dental Studies, 1956-74, Dean of Dental Studies, 1974-77, UCH Dental Sch. Charles Tomes Lectr, RCS, 1977. Rep. of University of London on Gen. Dental Council, 1964-. Elected Mem. Bd, Faculty of Dental Surgery, RCS, 1964- (Vice-Dean, 1972-73); Member: Cttee of Management, Inst. of Dental Surgery, 1963-; Dental Sub-Cttee, UGC, 1968-; Bd of Governors, UCH, 1957-74; Camden and Islington AHA(T), 1974-. WHO Consultant, 1966; Consultant Dental Advr, DHSS, 1977-. *Publications:* contrib. to medical and dental journals. *Recreation:* golf. *Address:* 40 Ollards Grove, Loughton, Essex. *T:* 01-508 3566.

PROPPER, Arthur, CMG 1965; MBE 1945; *b* 3 Aug. 1910; 2nd *s* of late I. Propper; *m* 1941, Erica Mayer; one *d. Educ:* Owen's Sch.; Peterhouse, Cambridge (schol.). 1st class, Hist. Tripos, Pt 2. With W. S. Crawford Ltd (Advertising Agents), 1933-38, and the J. Walter Thompson Co. Ltd, 1939; Min. of Economic Warfare, 1940; transf. to Min. of Food, 1946 (subseq. to Min. of Agric., Fisheries and Food); established in Home Civil Service, 1949; Asst Sec., 1952; Mem. UK Delegn at Common Market negotiations, with rank of Under-Sec., 1962-63; seconded to Foreign Office, 1963; Counsellor (Agric.), UK Delegn to the European Communities, Brussels, and HM Embassy, Bonn, 1963-64; Under-Sec., Min. of Agriculture, Fisheries and Food, 1964-70; Common Mkt Advr, Unigate Ltd, 1970-73; Sec., Food Panel, Price Commn, 1973-76. *Recreations:* the theatre, music, buying books, visiting Scotland. *Address:* 3 Hill House, Stanmore Hill, Mddx. *T:* 01-954 1242. *Club:* United Oxford & Cambridge University.

PROSSER, (Albert) Russell (Garness), CMG 1967; MBE 1953; Adviser, Social Development, Ministry of Overseas Development, since 1967; *b* 8 April 1915; *s* of late Thomas Prosser; *m* 1957, Ruth Avalon Moore; one *s* (and one *s* decd). *Educ:* Godlys Sch.; London Sch. of Economics. Principal, Sch. of Social Welfare, Accra, 1947; Dep. Sec., Uganda, 1959; Permanent Secretary, Uganda, 1962; Adviser, Social Development, Kenya, 1963. Alternate UK delegate, UN Social Develt Commn, 1965-72, UK delegate, 1973-. Associate Mem., Inst. of Develt Studies, Univ. of Sussex; External Examr Rural Develt, Univ. of Reading. Editor, Clare Market Review, 1939-40. FRSA 1974. Golden Medallion, Belgian Govt, 1962. *Recreations:* angling, gardening. *Address:* 18b Wray Park Road, Reigate, Surrey. *T:* Reigate 42792.

PROSSER, (Elvet) John; a Recorder of the Crown Court, since 1972; Part-time Chairman of Industrial Tribunals, since 1975; *b* 10 July 1932; *s* of David and Hannah Prosser; *m* 1957, Mary Louise Cowdry; two *d. Educ:* Pontypridd Grammar Sch.; King's Coll., London Univ. LLB 2nd cl. hons 1955. Called to Bar, Gray's Inn, 1956. *Recreations:* watching cricket and television. *Address:* Hillcroft, Mill Road, Lisvane, Cardiff CF4 5XJ. *T:* Cardiff 752380. *Club:* Cardiff and County (Cardiff).

PROSSER, Raymond Frederick, CB 1973; MC 1942; Deputy Secretary, Department of Industry, since 1974; *b* 12 Sept. 1919; *s* of Frederick Charles Prosser and Jane Prosser (*née* Lawless); *m* 1949, Fay Newmarch Holmes; two *s* three *d. Educ:* Wimbledon Coll.; The Queen's Coll., Oxford (1938-39 and 1946). Served Royal Artillery (Field), 1939-45 (MC, despatches): service in Egypt, Libya, India and Burma; Temp. Major. Asst Principal, Min. of Civil Aviation, 1947; Sec., Air Transport Advisory Council, 1952-57; Private Sec. to Minister of Transport and Civil Aviation, 1959, and to Minister of Aviation, 1959-61; Counsellor (Civil Aviation), HM Embassy, Washington, DC, 1965-68; Under-Sec., Marine Div., BoT, later DTI, 1968-72; Deputy Sec., DTI, 1972-. Dir, European Investment Bank, 1973-. *Address:* Juniper House, Shalford Common, Shalford, Guildford, Surrey. *T:* Guildford 66498.

PROSSER, Russell; see Prosser, A. R. G.

PROSSER, Thomas Vivian, CBE 1963; Chairman, T.V. Prosser & Son (Estates) Ltd; Consultant Director, Proteus-Bygging Ltd; *b* 25 April 1908; *er s* of T. V. Prosser, Liverpool; *m* 1935, Florence Minnie (Billie), 2nd *d* of W. J. Boulton, Highworth, Wilts; one *s* one *d. Educ:* Old Swan Technical Institute (now West Derby High School); College of Technology, Liverpool. Pupil of A. E. Cuddy, LRIBA, Architect, 1924. Founder, Chm. and Man. Dir, Nat Building Agency, 1964-67. Formerly: President, Liverpool Regional Fedn of Building Trades Employers, 1956; Pres., Nat. Fedn of Building Trades Employers, 1959-60. *Recreations:* gardening, reading. *Address:* 21 Aughton, Collingbourne Kingston, near Marlborough, Wilts. *Club:* Lyceum.

PROSSER, William David, QC (Scotland) 1974; *b* 23 Nov. 1934; *yr s* of David G. Prosser, MC, WS, Edinburgh; *m* 1964, Vanessa, *er d* of Sir William O'Brien Lindsay, KBE, Nairobi; two *s* two *d. Educ:* Edinburgh Academy; Corpus Christi Coll., Oxford (MA); Edinburgh Univ. (LLB). Advocate, 1962; Standing Junior Counsel, Scottish Develt Dept, 1965-69; Standing Junior Counsel in Scotland, Board of Inland Revenue, 1969-74. Mem., Scottish Cttee, Council on Tribunals, 1977-. *Address:* 7 Randolph Crescent, Edinburgh EH3 7TH. *T:* 031-225 2709; Netherfoodie, Dairsie, Fife. *T:* Balmullo 438. *Clubs:* New, Scottish Arts (Edinburgh).

PROUD, Air Cdre Harold John Granville Ellis, CBE 1946; *b* 23 Aug. 1906; *s* of late Ralph Henry Proud, Glasgow; *m* 1927, Jenefer Angela Margaret, *d* of late Lt-Col J. Bruce, OBE, 19th Lancers; two *d.* HAC (Inf.), 1924-26; commissioned RAF, pilot, 1926; Staff Coll., 1936; served in: Mediterranean (FAA), 1928; India, 1937 and 1942; Singapore, 1949; AOC 67 (NI) Gp and Senior Air Force Officer N Ire., 1951-54; Provost Marshal and Chief of Air Force Police, 1954; retired 1956; in business, 1957-71; now domiciled in Switzerland; Mem. Council, British Residents Assoc. of Switzerland, 1973-77, Pres., 1974-75. *Address:* Appt 10, Les Libellules, 1837 Chateau d'Oex, Switzerland. *T:* (029) 46223.

PROUDFOOT, Bruce; see Proudfoot, V. B.

PROUDFOOT, Bruce Falconer; Publicity Officer, Ulster Savings Committee, 1963-69; Editor, Northern Whig and Belfast Post, 1943-63; *b* 1903; 2nd *s* of G. A. Proudfoot, Edinburgh; *m* 1928, Cecilia, *er d* of V. T. T. Thompson, Newcastle on Tyne; twin *s. Educ:* Edinburgh Education Authority's Primary and Secondary Schools. Served with Edinburgh Evening Dispatch, Galloway Gazette (Newton-Stewart) and Newcastle Daily Chronicle before joining Northern Whig, 1925. *Recreation:* golf. *Address:* 10 Ophir Gardens, Belfast BT15 5EP. *T:* 776368.
   See also *V . B . Proudfoot .*

PROUDFOOT, (George) Wilfred; owner, self-service stores; consultant in distribution; *b* 19 December 1921; *m* 1950, Margaret Mary, *d* of Percy Clifford Jackson, Pontefract, Yorks; two *s* one *d. Educ:* Crook Council Sch.; Scarborough Coll. Served War of 1939-45, NCO Fitter in RAF, 1940-46. Served Scarborough Town Council, 1950-58 (Chm. Health Cttee, 1952-58). MP (C) Cleveland Division of Yorkshire, Oct. 1959-Sept. 1964; PPS to Minister of State, Board of Trade, Apr.-July 1962, to Minister of Housing and Local Govt and Minister for Welsh Affairs (Rt Hon. Sir Keith Joseph, Bt, MP), 1962-64; MP (C) Brighouse and Spenborough, 1970-Feb. 1974; Minister of State, Dept of Employment, 1970; contested (C) Brighouse and Spenborough, Oct. 1974. Man. Dir, Radio 270, 1965-. *Publication:* The Two Factor Nation, or How to make the people rich, 1977. *Recreations:* reading, photography, caravanning, travel, walking, skiing. *Address:* 278 Scalby Road, Scarborough, North Yorkshire. *T:* Scarborough 67027. *Club:* Constitutional.

PROUDFOOT, Prof. (Vincent) Bruce, FSA 1963; Professor of Geography, University of St Andrews, since 1974; *b* 24 Sept. 1930; *s* of Bruce Falconer Proudfoot, *qv; m* 1961, Edwina Valmai Windram Field; two *s. Educ:* Royal Belfast Academical Instn; Queen's Univ., Belfast (BA, PhD). Research Officer, Nuffield Quaternary Research Unit, QUB, 1954-58; Lectr in Geography, QUB, 1958-59, Durham Univ., 1959-67; Tutor, 1960-63, Librarian, 1963-65, Hatfield Coll., Durham; Visiting Fellow, Univ. of Auckland, NZ, 1966; Associate Prof., 1967-70, Prof., 1970-74, Univ. of Alberta, Edmonton, Canada; Acting Chm., Dept of Geography, Univ. of Alberta, 1970-71; Co-ordinator, Socio-Economic Opportunity Studies, and Staff Consultant, Alberta Human Resources Research Council, 1971-72. Lister Lectr, BAAS, 1964; Commonwealth Visiting Fellow, Australia, 1966. *Publications:* The Downpatrick Gold Find,

1955; (with R. G. Ironside *et al*) Frontier Settlement Studies, 1974; numerous papers in geographical, archaeological and soils jls. *Recreation:* gardening. *Address:* Westgate, Wardlaw Gardens, St Andrews, Scotland KY16 9DW. *T:* St Andrews 3293.

PROUDFOOT, Wilfred; see Proudfoot, G. W.

PRUDE, Mrs Walter F.; see de Mille, Agnes George.

PRUNTY, Prof. Francis Thomas Garnet, FRCP; Professor of Chemical Pathology, University of London, at St Thomas's Hospital Medical School, 1954-75, now Emeritus; Honorary Consulting Physician, St Thomas' Hospital; *b* 5 Jan. 1910; *s* of Frank Hugh Prunty, and Una Elizah Newnham (*née* Marsden); *m* 1933, Rita Hepburn Stobbs (marr. diss. 1971); one *s* one *d*; *m* 1972, Jean Margaret Maxwell-Moore. *Educ:* St Paul's Sch.; Trinity Coll., Cambridge; St Thomas's Hospital Medical Sch. Senior Scholar, Trinity Coll., 1932; MA, Cambridge, 1936; MB, BChir, 1940; MD, 1944; Raymond Horton-Smith Prize, Cambridge, 1944; FRCP 1950. Research Fellow in Medicine, Harvard, USA, 1946-47; Asst in Medicine, Peter Bent Brigham Hospital, Boston, 1946-47; Rockefeller Travelling Fellow, 1946-47; Humphrey Rolleston Lecturer, RCP, 1956; Late Examr, Univ. of London. Late President: Section of Endocrinology, Royal Society Med.; International Society of Endocrinology. Life Governor, Imperial Cancer Research Fund (late Mem. Council); Hon. Member: Soc. for Endocrinology; British Nuclear Medicine Soc.; Sociedad Medica de Occidente (Guatemala); Romanian Soc. of Endocrinology; Emeritus Mem., Biochemical Soc. *Publications:* The Chemistry and Treatment of Adrenocortical Diseases, 1964; A Laboratory Manual of Chemical Pathology (jointly), 1959; various articles in Medical and Biochemical journals. *Recreations:* travel, sailing. *Address:* Pheasants Walk, Beaulieu, Hants SO4 7YJ. *Club:* Royal Thames Yacht.

PRYCE, Maurice Henry Lecorney, FRS 1951; Professor of Physics, University of British Columbia, since 1968; *b* 24 Jan. 1913; *e s* of William John Pryce and Hortense Lecorney; *m* 1939, Susanne Margarete Born (marr. diss., 1959); one *s* three *d*; *m* 1961, Freda Mary Kinsey. *Educ:* Royal Grammar Sch., Guildford; Trinity Coll., Cambridge. Commonwealth Fund Fellow at Princeton, NJ, USA, 1935-37; Fellow of Trinity Coll., Cambridge, and Faculty Asst Lecturer, University of Cambridge, 1937-39; Reader in Theoretical Physics, University of Liverpool, 1939-45. Engaged on Radar research with Admiralty Signal Establishment, 1941-44, and on Atomic Energy Research with National Research Council of Canada, Montreal, 1944-45. University Lecturer in Mathematics and Fellow of Trinity Coll., Cambridge, 1945-46; Wykeham Professor of Physics, University of Oxford, 1946-54; Henry Overton Wills Professor of Physics, University of Bristol, 1954-64; Prof. of Physics, University of Southern California, 1964-68. Visiting Professor: Princeton Univ., NJ, USA, 1950-51; Duke Univ., NC, USA, 1958; Univ. of Sussex, 1976-77. *Publications:* various on Theoretical Physics, in learned journals. *Recreations:* lawn tennis, badminton. *Address:* Physics Department, University of British Columbia, Vancouver V6T 1W5, Canada. *Club:* Athenæum.

PRYCE, Dr Roy; Director, Directorate General for Information, Commission of the European Communities, since 1973; *b* 4 Oct. 1928; *s* of Thomas and Madeleine Pryce; *m* 1954, Sheila Rose, *d* of Rt Hon. James Griffiths, CH; three *d. Educ:* Grammar Sch., Burton-on-Trent; Emmanuel Coll., Cambridge (MA, PhD). MA Oxon. Research Fellow: Emmanuel Coll., Cambridge, 1953-55; St Antony's Coll., Oxford, 1955-57; Head of London Information Office of High Authority of European Coal and Steel Community, 1957-60; Head of London Inf. Office, Jt Inf. Service of European Communities, 1960-64; Rockefeller Foundn Res. Fellow, 1964-65; Dir, Centre for Contemp. European Studies, Univ. of Sussex, 1965-73. Vis. Professorial Fellow, Centre for Contemporary European Studies, Univ. of Sussex, 1973-; Vis. Prof., Coll. of Europe, Bruges, 1965-72. *Publications:* The Italian Local Elections 1956, 1957; The Political Future of the European Community, 1962; (with John Pinder) Europe After de Gaulle, 1969, German and Ital. edns 1970; The Politics of the European Community, 1973; contrib. Encyl. Brit., Jl Common Market Studies, etc. *Recreations:* gardening, collecting water colours and prints. *Address:* Commission of the European Communities, 200 rue de la Loi, 1040 Brussels, Belgium. *T:* Brussels 735.00.40. *Club:* Europe House.

PRYCE-JONES, Alan Payan, TD; book critic; author and journalist; *b* 18 Nov. 1908; *s* of late Colonel Henry Morris Pryce-Jones, CB; *m* 1934, Thérèse (*d* 1953), *d* of late Baron Fould-Springer and of Mrs Frank Wooster, Paris; one *s*; *m* 1968, Mrs

Mary Jean Kempner Thorne (*d* 1969), *d* of late Daniel Kempner. *Educ:* Eton; Magdalen Coll., Oxford. Formerly Asst Editor, The London Mercury, 1928-32; subseq. Times Literary Supplement; Editor, Times Literary Supplement, 1948-59; Book critic: New York Herald Tribune, 1963-66; World Journal Tribune, 1967-68; Newsday, 1969-71. Trustee, National Portrait Gallery, 1950-61; Director, Old Vic Trust, 1950-61; Member Council, Royal College of Music, 1956-61; Program Associate, The Humanities and Arts Program, Ford Foundation, NY, 1961-63. Served War of 1939-45, France, Italy, Austria; Lieut-Colonel, 1945. *Publications:* The Spring Journey, 1931; People in the South, 1932; Beethoven, 1933; 27 Poems, 1935; Private Opinion, 1936; Nelson, an opera, 1954; Vanity Fair, a musical play (with Robin Miller and Julian Slade), 1962. *Recreations:* music, travelling. *Address:* 46 John Street, Newport, RI 02340, USA. *Clubs:* Travellers', Garrick, Beefsteak, Pratt's, MCC; Knickerbocker, Century (New York); Artillery (Galveston, Texas).

PRYDE, James Richmond Northridge, CBE 1944; formerly General Manager of Poonmudi Tea and Rubber Co. Ltd, retired 1956; *b* 14 Aug. 1894; *s* of James Oliphant and Bessie Anne Pryde, Leighinmohr, Ballymena, N Ireland; *m* 1921, Katharine (*d* 1973), *d* of T. M. McNeil, St John's, Newfoundland; three *s* one *d. Educ:* St Bees Sch., Cumberland. Planting (entirely) since 1912. President, United Planters' Assoc. of Southern India, 1940-44.

PRYKE, Sir David Dudley, 3rd Bt *cr* 1926; *b* 16 July 1912; *s* of Sir William Robert Dudley Pryke, 2nd Bt; *S* father 1959; *m* 1945, Doreen Winifred, *er d* of late Ralph Bernard Wilkins; two *d. Educ:* St Lawrence Coll., Ramsgate. Member, Common Council, Queenhithe Ward, 1960; Liveryman Turners' Company, 1961. *Heir: b* William Dudley Pryke [*b* 18 Nov. 1914; *m* 1940, Lucy Irene, *d* of late Frank Madgett; one *s* one *d*]. *Address:* Flatholme, Brabant Road, North Fambridge, Chelmsford, Essex. *T:* Maldon 740227.

PRYOR, Norman Selwyn; *b* 1896; *s* of Selwyn Robert Pryor, Plaw Hatch, Bishop's Stortford, Hertfordshire; *m* 1927, Nancy Mary, *d* of Kingsmill Henry Power, Sandpit Hall, Chobham, Surrey; two *d* (and one *d* decd). *Educ:* Eton; Trinity Coll., Cambridge. Served European War, 1914-19; Lieut, RFA (TF), 1916; Captain, 1918. DL 1956-68, JP, 1932-68, Essex; High Sheriff of Essex for 1957. *Address:* Manuden House, Manuden, Bishop's Stortford, Herts. *T:* Stansted 3282. *Club:* Oriental.
See also W. D. Gibson.

PRYOR, Prof. Robert Nelson, CEng, FIMM, FICE, FIMinE; Professor of Mining, Royal School of Mines, Imperial College London, since 1968; *b* 19 July 1921; *s* of Thomas Pryor and Esperanza Nelson; *m* 1945, Patricia Aloysia McMahon; three *s* one *d. Educ:* Oundle Sch.; Imperial Coll. (Royal Sch. of Mines) (BSc). Ingeniero Jefe de Minas, Cia Española de Minas de Rio Tinto, Spain, 1955; Mining Engr, Head Office, RTZ, 1960; Gen. Man., Rio Tinto Patiño, SA, Spain, 1966. Mem. Bd, CEI, 1975; Vice-Pres., Instn of Mining and Metallurgy, 1975. *Publications:* Trans Instn of Mining and Metallurgy. *Address:* Royal School of Mines, Imperial College of Science and Technology, SW7 2AZ. *T:* 01-589 5111 (ext. 1500).

PRYS JONES, David; *see* Jones, D. P.

PUCKEY, Sir Walter (Charles). *Address:* Silverdale, Beech Drive, Kingswood, Surrey.

PUDNER, Anthony Serle, MBE 1952; Director, Engineering, Cable & Wireless Ltd, 1969-74; *b* 10 Jan. 1917; *s* of late Engr Captain W. H. Pudner, RN, and late Betty Macfarlane; *m* 1952, Jonie Johnson; one *s* one *d. Educ:* Imperial Service College. Joined Cable & Wireless Ltd, 1934; foreign service, 1938-60: Bermuda, CS Cable Enterprise, Greece, Haifa, Korea, Hong Kong, West Indies; Engr-in-Chief, 1965; Director: E African External Telecommunications Co., 1969; Trinidad & Tobago External Telecommunications Co., 1970. CEng; FIEE; FIERE (Vice-Pres. 1969); MIEEE; FRSA. *Recreations:* music, tennis. *Address:* Bass Point House, The Lizard, Cornwall.

PUDNEY, John Sleigh; Poet, fiction writer, dramatist and journalist; *b* 19 Jan. 1909; *o s* of H. W. Pudney, farmer, and Mabel Elizabeth, *d* of H. C. Sleigh; *m* 1934, Crystal (marr. diss., 1955; she *m* 1955, L. R. Hale), *d* of Sir Alan Herbert; one *s* two *d*; *m* 1955, Monica Forbes Curtis, *d* of J. Grant Forbes. *Educ:* Gresham's Sch., Holt. Producer and writer on staff of BBC, 1934-37; Correspondent of News Chronicle, 1937-41; RAF, 1941-45. Book Critic Daily Express, 1947-48; Literary Editor, News Review, 1948-50; Director of Putnams, publishers, 1953-63. Contested (Lab) Sevenoaks Division, 1945. *Publications:*

verse: Ten Summers, 1944; Selected Poems, 1945; Sixpenny Songs, 1953; Collected Poems, 1957; The Trampoline, 1959; Spill Out, 1967; Spandrels, 1969; Take This Orange, 1971; Selected Poems, 1973; For Johnny (War Poems), 1976; Living in a One-Sided House, 1976; *collected stories:* It Breathed down my Neck, 1946; The Europeans, 1949; *novels:* Jacobson's Ladder, 1938; Estuary, 1947; Shuffley Wanderers, 1949; The Accomplice, 1950; Hero of a Summer's Day, 1951; The Net, 1952; A Ring for Luck, 1953; Trespass in the Sun, 1957; Thin Air, 1961; The Long Time Growing Up, 1971; *non-fiction:* The Green Grass Grew All Round, 1942; Who Only England Know, 1943; World Still There, 1945; The Thomas Cook Story, 1953; The Smallest Room, 1954; Six Great Aviators, 1955; The Seven Skies, 1955; Home and Away (autobiographical), 1960; A Pride of Unicorns, 1960; Bristol Fashion, 1960; The Camel, a monograph, 1964; The Golden Age of Steam, 1966; Suez, De Lesseps' Canal, 1968; Crossing London's River, 1972; Brunel and his World, 1973; London's Docks, 1975; Lewis Carroll and his World, 1976; *official:* The Air Battle of Malta, 1944; Atlantic Bridge, 1945; Laboratory of the Air, 1948; also books for boys and girls; *film scripts, etc.:* script writer for Travel Royal, 1952; Elizabeth is Queen, 1953; Welcome The Queen, 1954; May Wedding, 1960; joint author of screen play, Conflict of Wings, 1954; The Stolen Airliner, 1955; Blue Peter, 1955; The Concord, 1966; Mission of Fear, 1966; Ted, TV play, 1972; The Little Giant, musical play, 1972; Thomas Cook & Son, BBC TV documentary, 1978. *Recreation:* bonfires. *Address:* 4 Macartney House, Chesterfield Walk, SE10 8HJ. *T:* 01-858 0482.

PUGH, Harold Valentine, CBE 1964; Chairman, Northern Ireland Joint Electricity Authority, 1967-70, retired; *b* 18 Oct. 1899; *s* of Henry John Valentine Pugh and Martha (*née* Bott); *m* 1934, Elizabeth Mary (*née* Harwood); two *s* one *d. Educ:* The High Sch., Murree, India; Manchester College of Technology. Trained Metropolitan-Vickers (asst engineer erection, 1925-30). Chief Engineer, Cory Bros, 1930-35; Deputy Superintendent and later Superintendent, Upper Boat Power Station, 1935-43; Generation Engineer, South Wales Power Company, 1943-44; Deputy Chief Engineer, Manchester Corporation Electricity Dept, 1944-48; Controller, British Electricity Authority, South Wales Division, 1948; Controller, British (later Central) Electricity Authority, London Division, 1951; Chairman: Eastern Electricity Board, 1957-63; South-Eastern Electricity Board, 1963-66. Director: Aberdare Holdings, 1966-70. AMCT; FIEE; MIMechE. *Recreations:* gardening, golf. *Address:* Clontaff, Doggetts Wood Lane, Chalfont St Giles, Bucks. *T:* Little Chalfont 2330.

PUGH, Sir Idwal (Vaughan), KCB 1972 (CB 1967); Parliamentary Commissioner for Administration, since 1976; Health Service Commissioner for England, Wales and Scotland, since 1976; *b* 10 Feb. 1918; *s* of late Rhys Pugh and Elizabeth Pugh; *m* 1946, Mair Lewis; one *s* one *d. Educ:* Cowbridge Grammar Sch.; St John's Coll., Oxford. Army Service, 1940-46. Entered Min. of Civil Aviation, 1946; Alternate UK Rep. at International Civil Aviation Organisation, Montreal, 1950-53; Asst Secretary, 1956; Civil Air Attaché, Washington, 1957-59; Under Secretary, Min. of Transport, 1959; Min. of Housing and Local Govt, 1961; Dep. Sec., Min. of Housing and Local Govt, 1966-69; Permanent Sec., Welsh Office, 1969-71; Second Permanent Sec., DoE, 1971-76. *Recreations:* golf, walking, piano. *Address:* 801 Raleigh House, Dolphin Square, SW1; Nant-y-Garreg, Bontddu, Gwynedd. *Club:* Brooks's.

PUGH, John Arthur, OBE 1968; HM Diplomatic Service; British High Commissioner to Seychelles, since 1976; *b* 17 July 1920; *er s* of late Thomas Pugh and Dorothy Baker Pugh; unmarried. *Educ:* Brecon Grammar Sch.; Bristol Univ. RN, 1941-45. Home CS, 1950-54; Gold Coast Admin. Service, 1955-58; Adviser to Ghana Govt, 1958-60; First Sec., British High Commn, Lagos, 1962-65; First Sec. (Economic), Bangkok, and British Perm. Rep. to Economic Commn for Asia and Far East, 1965-68; British Dep. High Comr, Ibadan, 1971-73; Diplomatic Service Inspector, 1973-76. *Recreations:* Oriental ceramics, anthropology, the sea. *Address:* c/o Foreign and Commonwealth Office, SW1; Pennybrin, Hay on Wye, Hereford. *T:* Hay on Wye 695. *Club:* Royal Commonwealth Society.

PUGH, John Stanley; Editor, Liverpool Daily Post, since 1969; *b* 9 Dec. 1927; *s* of John Albert and Winifred Lloyd Pugh; *m* 1953, Kathleen Mary; two *s* one *d. Educ:* Wallasey Grammar School. *Recreation:* golf. *Address:* 26 Westwood Road, Noctorum, Birkenhead, Merseyside. *Club:* Royal Liverpool (Hoylake).

PUGH, Leslie Mervyn; Stipendiary Magistrate for Liverpool, 1965-76, and for Merseyside, 1974-76; *b* 19 Nov. 1905; *s* of late Joseph and Harriette Pugh; *m* 1931, Elizabeth Gwladys

Newcombe; two *d. Educ:* Wellington (Somerset). Admitted to Roll of Solicitors, 1928; Clerk: to Gower (Glam), RDC, 1931-40; to Swansea Justices, 1940-46; to Sheffield City Justices, 1946-57; to Hallamshire (WR), Justices, 1947-57; Stipendiary Magistrate, Huddersfield, 1957-65. President Justices' Clerks' Society, 1955-56; Member: Home Office Probation Advisory and Training Board, 1953-62; Departmental Cttee on Summary Trial of Minor Offences, 1954-55. Chm., Liverpool City Justices, 1971-76. *Publications:* Matrimonial Proceedings before Magistrates. *Recreations:* walking, gardening. *Address:* 17 St George's Road, Formby, near Liverpool L37 3HH. *T:* Formby 73426. *Club:* Athenæum (Liverpool).

PUGH, Prof. Leslie Penrhys, CBE 1962; MA (Cantab); BSc (London), FRCVS; Emeritus Professor, Cambridge University; Professor of Veterinary Clinical Studies, Cambridge, 1951-63; Life Fellow of Magdalene Coll., Cambridge; Member, Agricultural Research Council, 1952-57; President, Royal College of Veterinary Surgeons, 1956; *b* 19 Dec. 1895; *s* of David Pugh and Emily Epton Hornby; *m* 1st, 1918, Paula Storie (*d* 1930); one *s* two *d*; 2nd, 1933, Betty Chandley; one *s* one *d. Educ:* Tonbridge; Royal Veterinary Coll.; London Univ. MRCVS 1917, BSc (London) 1917. FRCVS, 1923. General Practitioner in West Kent, 1919-50; Deputy Assistant Director of Veterinary Services (44th Home Counties Division TA), 1927; Major, 1927; Divisional Commandant Kent Special Constabulary (Sevenoaks Division), 1949. *Publication:* From Farriery to Veterinary Medicine, 1962. *Recreation:* gardening. *Address:* 69 South Cliff, Bexhill-on-Sea, East Sussex. *T:* Bexhill 212047.
See also P. D. Storie-Pugh.

PUGH, Maj.-Gen. Lewis (Owain), CB 1957; CBE 1952; DSO 1945 (2 Bars, 1945, 1946); Indian Police Medal, 1940; JP; Colonel, 2 King Edward VII's Own Goorkhas (The Sirmoor Rifles), 1956-69; Representative Colonel Brigade of Gurkhas, 1958-69; Hon. Colonel: 4th Battalion, 1961-71, 3rd (Volunteer) Battalion, 1971-72, The Royal Welch Fusiliers; Vice-Lieutenant, Cardiganshire, 1961-72; *b* 18 May 1907; *s* of late Major H. O. Pugh, DSO, DL; *m* 1941, Wanda, *d* of F. F. Kendzior, Kington Langley, Wilts; two *d. Educ:* Wellington Coll.; RMA, Woolwich. Commissioned RA, 1927; RHA 1934; Royal Indian Artillery, 1940; seconded Indian Police, 1936; Staff Coll., Quetta, 1940; North West Frontier, India, 1933. Served War of 1939-45: North West Frontier, India, 1940; Burma, 1942-45 (Special Service Forces, 1942-43) (despatches); Netherlands East Indies, 1946; Malaya, 1950-52 (despatches), and 1956-57. Commander: 33 Indian Inf. Bde, 1945; 49 Indian Inf. Bde, 1946; 26th Gurkha Inf. Bde, 1949-52; Dep. Director, Military Operations, WO, 1953; IDC, 1955; Chief of Staff, GHQ, Far East, 1956-57; GOC 53 Welsh Inf. Div. (TA), and Mid West District, 1958-61; retired, 1961. Col, 1951; Brig., 1955; Maj.-Gen., 1957. Vice-President: Royal British Legion, Cards; Council for Protection of Rural Wales; President, ACF Recreational Cttee, Wales Area; formerly member: Council, Nat. Library of Wales; Council, Nat. Museum of Wales; Governing Body of the Church in Wales; Welsh Programme Advisory Cttee, ITA. Chairman: Merioneth and Montgomery Bi-County Cttee, 1961-72; N Wales Sub-Assoc., T&AVR; Vice-Chm., T&AVR Assoc., Wales and Monmouth, 1969-72. KStJ; Seneschal of Priory of Hosp. of St John in Wales. Dato (1st Class), The Most Blessed Order of Stia Negara, Brunei. JP 1961, DL 1961, High Sheriff 1964, Cardiganshire. *Recreations:* farming, polo, fishing. *Address:* Cymerau, Machynlleth, Powys, Wales. *T:* Glandyfi 230. *Club:* Naval and Military.

PUGH, Lionel Roger Price, CBE 1975; VRD 1953; DL; Director, Bridon Ltd, since 1973; *b* 9 May 1916; *s* of late Henry George Pugh, Cardiff; *m* 1942, Joyce Norma Nash; one *s* one *d. Educ:* Clifton. FCA. Supply Officer, RNVR, 1938-60; war service mainly in Mediterranean, 1939-46. With Deloitte & Co., 1933-47; joined Guest Keen & Bladwins Iron & Steel Co. Ltd, 1947; Dir 1955; Man. Dir 1960; Chm. 1962; Jt Man. Dir, GKN Steel, 1964. Dir, Product Co-ordination, British Steel Corp., 1967; Dep. Commercial Man. Dir, 1969; Man. Dir, Ops and Supplies, 1970; Mem., Corporate Finance and Planning, 1972; Exec. Mem., 1972-77. Pres., Iron and Steel Inst., 1973; Hon. Member: American Iron and Steel Inst. 1973; Metals Soc., 1976. Mem., Civil Aviation Council for Wales, 1962-66; part-time Mem., S Wales Electricity Bd, 1963-67. DL S Glamorgan (formerly Glamorgan), 1963. Gold Cross of Merit (Poland), 1942. *Address:* Brook Cottage, Bournes Green, Oakridge, Glos. *T:* Bisley 554. *Clubs:* Naval and Military; Royal Porthcawl Golf.

PUGH, Surg. Rear-Adm. Patterson David Gordon, OBE 1968; QHS 1975; Surgeon Rear-Admiral (Naval Hospitals), since 1975; *b* 19 Dec. 1920; *o s* of late W. T. Gordon Pugh, MD, FRCS, and Elaine V. A. Pugh (*née* Hobson); *m* 1st, 1948,

Margaret Sheena Fraser; three *s* one *d*; 2nd, 1967, Eleanor Margery Jones; one *s* one *d. Educ:* Lancing Coll.; Jesus Coll., Cambridge; Middlesex Hosp. Med. Sch. MA (Cantab), MB, BChir; FRCS, LRCP. Ho. Surg., North Middlesex Hosp., 1944. RNVR, 1945; served, HMS Glasgow and HMS Jamaica, 1945-47; perm. commn, 1950; served, HMS Narvik, 1952, HMS Warrior, 1956; Consultant in Orthopaedics, RN Hospitals: Malta, 1960; Haslar, 1962; Plymouth, 1968; Sen. MO (Admin.), RN Hosp., Plymouth, 1973; MO i/c, RN Hosp., Malta, 1974-75. Surg. Comdr 1961; Surg. Captain 1969; Surg. Rear-Adm. 1975. Fellow, British Orthopaedic Assoc.; Mem., South-West Orthopaedic Club; FRSA; Mem. RSM; Member: Soc. of Authors; West Country Writers' Assoc.; Osler Club of London. CStJ 1976. *Publications:* Practical Nursing, 16th edn 1945, to 21st edn 1969; Nelson and his Surgeons, 1968; Staffordshire Portrait Figures and Allied Subjects of the Victorian Era, 1970; Naval Ceramics, 1971; Heraldic China Mementos of the First World War, 1972. *Recreations:* walking, gardening, ceramics. *Address:* Royal Naval Hospital, Haslar, Gosport, Hants PO12 2AA. *T:* Portsmouth 22351; Heath Lodge, Drakewalls, Gunnislake, Cornwall. *T:* Gunnislake 832-100.

PUGH, Peter David S.; *see* Storie-Pugh.

PUGH, Prof. Ralph Bernard, MA Oxon; DLit London; FSA; Professor of English History in the University of London, 1968-77, now Emeritus; Supernumerary Fellow of St Edmund Hall, Oxford, since 1959 (Lecturer in Administrative History, 1952-59); *b* 1 Aug. 1910; *o c* of Bernard Carr and Mabel Elizabeth Pugh, Sutton, Surrey; unmarried. *Educ:* St Paul's Sch.; Queen's Coll., Oxford. 1st Class Hons, Modern History, 1932 (BA). Asst Keeper of Public Records, 2nd Cl. 1934, 1st Cl. 1946; Dominions Office, 1940-46, Acting Principal, 1941-46. Member, Institute for Advanced Study, Princeton, NJ, 1963-64, 1969-70; Raleigh Lectr, British Acad., 1973; Fellow, Folger Shakespeare Lib., Washington, DC, 1973. Wiltshire Archaeological and Nat. History Society: President, 1950-51, 1953-55; Vice-President, 1955-; Wiltshire Records Society (until 1967 Records Br. of Wilts Archaeological and Nat. History Society): Hon. Secretary and Editor, 1937-53; Chairman, 1953-67; President, 1967-; Vice-President: Selden Society, 1966-69; Nat. Trust Council, 1967-75. Editor, Victoria History of Counties of England, 1949-77. *Publications:* (ed) Abstracts of Feet of Fines for Wiltshire, Edw. I and II, 1929; (ed) Calendar of Antrobus Deeds, 1947; How to Write a Parish History, 1954; The Crown Estate, 1960; Records of the Colonial and Dominions Offices (PRO Handbooks), 1964; Itinerant Justices in English History, 1967; Imprisonment in Medieval England, 1968; (ed) Court Rolls of the Wiltshire Manors of Adam de Stratton, 1970; (ed) Calendar of London Trailbaston Trials, 1976 for 1975; articles in Victoria County History, Cambridge History of the British Empire and in learned periodicals. *Recreation:* sight-seeing. *Address:* 67 Southwood Park, N6. *T:* 01-340 5661. *Club:* Reform.

PUGH, Roger Courtenay Beckwith, MD; Pathologist to St Peter's Hospitals and the Institute of Urology, London, since 1955; *b* 23 July 1917; *y s* of late Dr Robert Pugh, Talgarth, Breconshire, and of late Margaret Louise Pugh (*née* Gough); *m* 1942, Winifred Dorothy, *yr d* of late Alfred Cooper and of Margaret Cooper (*née* Evans); one *s* one *d. Educ:* Gresham's Sch., Holt; St Mary's Hospital (University of London). MRCS, LRCP 1940; MB, BS, 1941; MD 1948; MCPath. 1964; FRCPath. 1967. House Surgeon, St Mary's Hospital and Sector Hospitals, 1940-42; War Service in RAF (Mediterranean theatre), 1942-46, Sqdn Leader; Registrar, Department of Pathology, St Mary's Hospital, 1946-48; Asst Pathologist and Lecturer in Pathology, St Mary's Hospital, 1948-51; Asst Morbid Anatomist, The Hospital for Sick Children, Great Ormond Street, 1951-54. Erasmus Wilson Demonstrator, RCS, 1959, 1961; Member: Board of Governors, St Peter's Hospitals; Pathological Society of Great Britain and Ireland; Assoc. of Clin. Pathologists; Internat. Society of Urology; Internat. Acad. of Pathology (former Pres., British Div.); Assoc. Member British Assoc. of Urological Surgeons; FRSocMed (former Pres., Sect. of Urology). *Publications:* (ed) Pathology of the Testis, 1976; various contributions to Pathological, Urological and Paediatric Journals. *Recreations:* gardening, photography. *Address:* 19 Manor Way, Beckenham, Kent. *T:* 01-658 6294.

PUGH, Rev. Canon T(homas) Jenkin, TD 1946; Chaplain to the Queen, 1962-73; *b* 15 Nov. 1903; seventh *s* of Rees and Margaret Ann Pugh; *m* 1932, Marjorie Window (*d* 1970). *Educ:* Universities of Wales and London. Ordained, 1931. Vicar of Acton and Little Waldingfield, Suffolk. Chaplain, TA, with BEF, France, 1939-40; Far East, 1941-45; New Zealand, 1945-46; Sen. Chaplain in Butlin Organisation, on staff of Archbishop of Canterbury, 1947-71. Canon of Lincoln Cathedral and Prebendary of Bedford Minor, 1955; Canon Emeritus, 1977.

Dir, Archbishop's Mission to Holiday Camps and Caravan Sites, 1969-71. MA Lambeth 1959. Member, Governing Body of the Church in Wales. *Recreation:* fishing. *Address:* Modwenna, Criccieth, N Wales. *T:* 2808. *Club:* Reform.

PUGH, William David, CBE 1965; FIM; FBIM; FIWM; JP; Deputy Chairman, English Steel Corporation Ltd, 1965-70 (Managing Director, 1955-65); Director of Personnel, British Steel Corporation (Midland Group), 1967-70; *b* 21 Nov. 1904; *s* of late Sir Arthur and Lady Pugh; *m* 1936, Mary Dorothea Barber; one *d. Educ:* Regent Street Polytechnic; Sheffield Univ. Joined Research Dept, Vickers Ltd, Sheffield, 1926, Director, Vickers Ltd, 1962-67; Chairman: The Darlington Forge Ltd, 1957-66; Taylor Bros & Co. Ltd, 1959-66; Director: (and alternate Chairman), Firth Vickers Stainless Steels Ltd, 1948-67; High Speed Steel Alloys Ltd, 1953-68; Industrial Training Council Service, 1960-67; British Iron and Steel Corp. Ltd, 1962-67; Sheffield Boy Scouts Holdings Ltd, 1965-; Sheffield Centre for Environmental Research Ltd; Crucible Theatre Trust Ltd. Associate of Metallurgy (Sheffield University; Mappin Medallist). Hon. DMet (Sheffield), 1966. *Recreations:* gardening, golf, reading. *Address:* Freebirch Cottage, Eastmoor, Chesterfield, Derbyshire S42 7DQ. *T:* Baslow 3153. *Club:* Sheffield (Sheffield).

PUGH, Rt. Rev. William Edward Augustus; *see* Penrith, Bishop Suffragan of.

PUGSLEY, Sir Alfred Grenvile, Kt 1956; OBE 1944; FRS 1952; DSc; Professor of Civil Engineering, University of Bristol, 1944-68, now Emeritus; Pro-Vice-Chancellor, 1961-64; *b* May 1903; *s* of H. W. Pugsley, BA, FLS, London; *m* 1928, Kathleen M. Warner (*d* 1974); no *c. Educ:* Rutlish Sch.; London Univ. Civil Engineering Apprenticeship at Royal Arsenal, Woolwich, 1923-26; Technical Officer, at the Royal Airship Works, Cardington, 1926-31; Member scientific and technical staff at Royal Aircraft Establishment, Farnborough, 1931-45, being Head of Structural and Mechanical Engineering Dept there, 1941-45. Visiting Lecturer on aircraft structures at Imperial Coll., London, 1938-40. Chairman of Aeronautical Research Council, 1952-57; President, Institution of Structural Engineers, 1957-58; Member: Advisory Council on Scientific Policy, 1956-59; Tribunal of Inquiry on Ronan Point, 1968; Member of various scientific and professional institutions and cttees; a Vice-Pres., ICE, 1971-73. Hon. FRAeS, 1963; Hon. DSc Belfast, 1965; Hon. DUniv. Surrey, 1968. Structural Engineers' Gold Medal, 1968. *Publications:* The Theory of Suspension Bridges, 1957 (2nd edn 1968); The Safety of Structures, 1966; (ed and contrib.) The Works of Isambard Kingdom Brunel, 1976; numerous Reports and Memoranda of Aeronautical Research Council; papers in scientific journals and publications of professional engineering bodies; articles and reviews in engineering press. *Address:* 4 Harley Court, Clifton Down, Bristol BS8 3JU. *Club:* Athenæum.

PUGSLEY, Rear-Admiral Anthony Follett, CB 1944; DSO 1943; retired; *b* 7 Dec. 1901; *e s* of late J. Follett Pugsley, Whitefield, Wiveliscombe, Somerset; *m* 1931, Barbara, *d* of late J. Byam Shaw; one *s. Educ:* RN Colleges, Osborne and Dartmouth. Midshipman, 1918; Commander, 1936; Captain, 1942; Rear-Admiral, 1952; retired, 1954. Served European War from May 1918; on Upper Yangtse, 1925-27, and in command HM Ships P.40, Antelope and Westcott, 1933-36; during War of 1939-45, in command HM Ships Javelin, Fearless, Paladin; Captain (D) 14th Flotilla, Jervis (despatches thrice, DSO and bar, Greek War Cross); took part in Normandy landing, 1944 (2nd bar to DSO); Naval Force Commander in assault on Walcheren, 1944 (CB); Captain (D) 19th Flotilla (Far East), 1945-46; Directing Staff, Senior Officers War Course, 1947-48; Naval Officer in charge, Londonderry and Director (RN) Joint Anti-Submarine School, 1948-50; in command HMS Warrior, 1951; Flag Officer, Malayan Area, Dec. 1951-Nov. 1953. *Publication:* Destroyer Man, 1957. *Address:* Javelin, Milverton, Somerset. *T:* Milverton 355.

PULLAN, John Marshall, MChir, FRCS; Surgeon: St Thomas' Hospital, London; Bolingbroke Hospital, London; Royal Masonic Hospital, London; King Edward VII Hospital; *b* 1 Aug. 1915; *e s* of late William Greaves Pullan and of Kathleen, *d* of Alfred Marshall, Otley, Yorkshire; *m* 1940, Leila Diana, *d* of H. C. Craven-Veitch, Surgeon; one *s* three *d. Educ:* Shrewsbury; King's Coll., Cambridge; St Thomas' Hospital, London. MA Cantab (1st Cl. Nat. Sc. Tripos) 1937; MB, BChir 1940; FRCS, 1942; MChir 1945. Teacher in Surgery, Univ. of London; Examiner in Surgery, Univs of: London, 1956; Cambridge. Member: Court of Examiners, RCS, 1964; Board of Governors, St Thomas' Hospital. *Publications:* Section on Diseases of the Liver, Gall Bladder and Bile Ducts, in Textbook of British

Surgery, ed Sir Henry Souttar, 1956; articles in surgical journals. *Address:* Palings, Warboys Road, Kingston Hill, Surrey. *T:* 01-546 5310; 3 Upper Wimpole Street, W1. *T:* 01-935 5873. *Clubs:* White's, Flyfishers', Boodle's.

PULLAR, Hubert Norman, CBE 1964; MA; HM Diplomatic Service, retired; *b* 26 Dec. 1914; *y s* of late William Laurence and Christine Ellen Pullar, formerly of Uplands, Bridge-of-Allan, Stirlingshire; *m* 1943, Helen Alice La Fontaine; one *s* one *d. Educ:* Trin. Coll., Glenalmond; Trin. Coll., Oxford. Entered HM Consular Service, 1938. Served in Turkey, 1938-42; USA, 1943-46; Persia, 1946-48; Morocco, 1949-52; Foreign Office, 1952-54; Finland, 1954-56; Syria, 1956; Iraq, 1957-59; Antwerp, 1960-64; HM Consul-General, Jerusalem, 1964-67; Foreign Office, 1967-68; Consul-General, Durban, 1968-71. Order of Ouissam Alouite, Morocco, 1952. CStJ 1966. Coronation Medal, 1953. *Recreations:* golf, motoring, travel. *Address:* Camelot, Ringles Cross, Uckfield, East Sussex. *T:* Uckfield 2159.

PULLÉE, Ernest Edward, CBE 1967; ARCA, ASIA, FSAE, NEAC; Chief Officer, National Council for Diplomas in Art and Design, 1967-74; retired; *b* 9 Feb. 1907; *s* of Ernest and Caroline Elizabeth Pullée; *m* 1933, Margaret Fisher, ARCA, NEAC; one *s. Educ:* St Martin's Sch., Dover; Royal Coll. of Art, London. Principal: Gloucester Coll. of Art, 1934-39; Portsmouth Coll. of Art, 1939-45; Leeds Coll. of Art, 1945-56; Leicester Coll. of Art and Design, 1956-67. Pres., Nat. Soc. for Art Educn, 1945, 1959; Chm., Assoc. of Art Instns, 1959; Mem., Nat. Adv. Coun. for Art Educn, 1959; Mem., Nat. Coun. for Diplomas in Art and Design, 1961. Hon. DA (Manchester), 1961. *Publications:* contribs to professional and academic jls. *Recreation:* travel. *Address:* 29 The Ryde, Hatfield, Herts. *T:* Hatfield 67937. *Club:* Chelsea Arts.

PULLEIN-THOMPSON, Denis; *see* Cannan, D.

PULLEN, William Reginald James, CVO 1975 (MVO 1966); LLB; FCIS; JP; Receiver-General, since 1959, Chapter Clerk since 1963 and Registrar since 1964, Westminster Abbey; *b* 17 Feb. 1922; *er s* of late William Pullen and Lillian Pullen (*née* Chinn), Falmouth; *m* 1948, Doreen Angela Hebron; two *d. Educ:* Falmouth Gram. School; King's College, London; private study. Served War of 1939-45; Flt Lt, RAFVR (admin and special duties) SE Asia. Asst to Chief Accountant, Westminster Abbey, 1947; Dep. Registrar, 1951; Sec. Westminster Abbey Appeal, 1953. Westminster City Council, 1962-65; a Chm., Inner London Juvenile Ct. Freeman, Worshipful Co. of Wax Chandlers. OStJ 1969. *Publication:* contrib. A House of Kings, 1966. *Recreations:* reading, walking, cooking. *Address:* 4b Dean's Yard, Westminster, SW1. *T:* 01-222 4023. *Clubs:* Royal Air Force, MCC.

PULLEYBLANK, Prof. Edwin George, PhD; Professor of Chinese, University of British Columbia, since 1966; *b* Calgary, Alberta, 7 Aug. 1922; *s* of W. G. E. Pulleyblank, Calgary; *m* 1945, Winona Ruth Relyea, Arnprior, Ont; one *s* two *d. Educ:* Central High School, Calgary; University of Alberta; University of London. BA Hons Classics, Univ. of Alberta, 1942; Nat. Research Council of Canada, 1943-46. School of Oriental and African Studies, Univ. of London: Chinese Govt Schol., 1946; Lectr in Classical Chinese, 1948; PhD in Classical Chinese, 1951; Lectr in Far Eastern History, 1952; Professor of Chinese, University of Cambridge, 1953; Head, Dept of Asian Studies, Univ. of British Columbia, 1968-75. Fellow of Downing Coll., Cambridge, 1955. *Publications:* The Background of the Rebellion of An Lu-Shan; articles in Asia Major, Bulletin of School of Oriental and African Studies, etc. *Address:* Department of Asian Studies, University of British Columbia, Vancouver 8, BC, Canada.

PULLICINO, Dr Anthony Alfred; *b* 14 March 1917; *s* of late Sir Philip Pullicino; *m* 1944, Edith Baker; three *s* two *d. Educ:* St Aloysius Coll., Malta; Royal Univ. of Malta; Melbourne University. BA 1939, LLD 1943, Malta; LLB Melbourne 1963. Served in Royal Malta Artillery, 1944-45 (Lieut). MLA Malta, 1951-55 (Speaker, 1951-52). Mem. Council, CPA, attending sessions in London 1952, Nairobi 1953. Practised as Solicitor, Melbourne, 1963-65; High Comr for Malta in Canberra, 1965-69; High Comr in London and Ambassador of Malta to USSR, 1970-71. *Recreation:* golf. *Address:* 191/4 Tower Road, Sliema, Malta. *Club:* Casino Maltese (Malta).

PULLING, Martin John Langley, CBE 1958 (OBE 1954); *b* 30 May 1906; *o s* of late Rev. Augustine J. Pulling and Dorothea Fremlin Key; *m* 1939, Yvonne Limborgh, Antwerp, Belgium; no *c. Educ:* Marlborough College; King's College, Cambridge (Scholar). Mech. Scis. Tripos, BA 1928; MA 1943. Various posts in radio industry, 1929-34; joined BBC Engrg Div., 1934; retired as Dep. Dir of Engrg, 1967. Was Chm. of Technical Cttee (of European Broadcasting Union) responsible for development of "Eurovision" from its inception in 1952 until 1962. Chairman: The Ferrograph Co., 1968-72; Rendar Instruments Ltd, 1968-72. FIEE 1967 (MIEE 1945, AMIEE 1935); Chm., Electronics and Communications Section, IEE, 1959-60; Mem. Council, IEE, 1963-66; MITE 1966; Hon. FBKS. *Address:* 6 Cadogan House, 93 Sloane Street, SW1X 9PD. *T:* 01-235 1739. *Clubs:* Hurlingham, MCC.

PULLINGER, Sir (Francis) Alan, Kt 1977; CBE 1970; Chairman, Haden Carrier Ltd, since 1961; *b* 22 May 1913; *s* of William Pullinger; *m* 1st, 1946, Felicity Charmian Gotch Hobson (decd); two *s* one *d*; 2nd, 1966, Jacqueline Louise Anne Durin. *Educ:* Marlborough Coll.; Balliol Coll., Oxford (MA). Pres., IHVE, 1972-73; Hon. FCIBS, 1977. *Recreations:* mountaineering, sailing, beagling. *Address:* Barnhorn, Meadway, Berkhamsted, Herts. *T:* Berkhamsted 3206. *Clubs:* Alpine, Travellers'.

PULVERTAFT, Prof. Robert James Valentine, OBE 1944; MD Cantab; FRCP; FRCPath; Emeritus Professor of Clinical Pathology, University of London (Professor, 1950-62); Visiting Professor of Pathology, Makerere University College; Visiting Professor of Pathology, University of Ibadan, W Nigeria; President Association of Clinical Pathologists, 1953; Director of Laboratories, Westminster Hospital, until 1962; Lieutenant-Colonel RAMC, 1943, serving Middle East Forces; subsequently Assistant Director of Pathology, Northern Command and MEF; lately Hon. Consultant in Pathology to the Army at Home; *b* 14 Feb. 1897; *s* of Rev. T. J. Pulvertaft and B. C. Denroche; *m* E. L. M. Costello; one *s* two *d*. *Educ:* Westminster School; Trinity College, Cambridge (Classical Scholar); St Thomas' Hosp. Lt 3rd Royal Sussex 1915-19; served with 4th Royal Sussex (Palestine); seconded to RFC as observer (Palestine) and pilot in 205 Squadron RAF (France); Senior Exhibitioner and Scholar, Nat. Science, Trinity College Cantab. 2nd class Part II Tripos Nat. Science (Physiology); Entrance University Scholar St Thomas' Hospital; Asst Bacteriologist, VD Dept St Thomas' Hospital; Pathologist to Units, St Thomas' Hosp., 1923-32; Plimmer Research Fellow in Pathology, 1929-32; EMS Sept.-Nov. 1939; National Institute Medical Research, 1939-40. Examiner in Pathology, Univs of Cambridge, Oxford, London, Trinity College, Dublin, National University of Ireland, Liverpool University; also for the Conjoint Board and Royal Army Medical Coll. Hon. FRSM 1972. *Publications:* Studies on Malignant Disease in Nigeria by Tissue Culture; various papers on bacteriology and pathology, particularly in relation to the study of living cells by cinemicrography. *Address:* Hedges, Stour Row, Dorset.

PUMPHREY, Sir (John) Laurence, KCMG 1973 (CMG 1963); HM Diplomatic Service; Ambassador to Pakistan (formerly High Commissioner), 1971-76; *b* 22 July 1916; *s* of late Charles Ernest Pumphrey and Iris Mary (*née* Moberly-Bell); *m* 1945, Jean, *e d* of Sir Walter Buchanan Riddell, 12th Bt; four *s* one *d*. *Educ:* Winchester; New College, Oxford. Served War of 1939-45 in Army. Foreign Service from 1945. Head of Establishment and Organisation Department, Foreign Office, 1955-60; Counsellor, Staff of British Commissioner-General for SE Asia, Singapore, 1960-63; Counsellor, HM Embassy, Belgrade, 1963-65; Deputy High Commissioner, Nairobi, 1965-67; British High Comr, Zambia, 1967-71. Military Cross, 3rd Class (Greece), 1941. *Address:* Caistron, Thropton, Morpeth, Northumberland NE65 7LG.

PUNGAN, Vasile; Counsellor to the President of the Socialist Republic of Romania on Economic Affairs, since 1973; *b* 2 Nov. 1926; *m* 1952, Liliana Nità (*d* 1973); one *d*. *Educ:* Inst. of Econs, Bucharest. Dr in Econ. Scis and Univ. Prof.; Dean of Faculty, Agronomical Inst., Bucharest, 1954; Gen. Dir, Min. of Agric. and Forestry, 1955-58; Counsellor, Romanian Embassy, Washington, 1959-62; Dir and Mem. College, Min. of Foreign Affairs, 1963-66; Ambassador of Socialist Republic of Romania to Court of St James's, 1966-72. Mem., Central Cttee of Romanian Communist Party, 1972 (Alternate Mem. 1969); Mem., Grand National Assembly, 1975. Holds orders and medals of Socialist Republic of Romania and several foreign countries. *Address:* State Council, Bucharest, Romania.

PURCELL, Denis; see Purcell, J. D.

PURCELL, Prof. Edward Mills, PhD; Gerhard Gade University Professor, Harvard University, since 1960; *b* 30 Aug. 1912; *s* of Edward A. Purcell and Mary Elizabeth Mills; *m* 1937, Beth C. Busser; two *s*. *Educ:* Purdue University; Harvard University. PhD Harvard, 1938; Instructor in Physics, Harvard, 1938-40;

Radiation Laboratory, Mass. Inst. of Technology, 1940-45; Associate Professor of Physics, Harvard, 1945-49; Professor of Physics, 1949-60. Senior Fellow, Society of Fellows, Harvard, 1950-71. (Jointly) Nobel Prize in Physics, 1952. Hon. DEng Purdue, 1953; Hon. DSci Washington Univ., St Louis, 1963. *Publications:* Principles of Microwave Circuits, 1948; Physics for Students of Science and Engineering, 1952; Electricity and Magnetism, 1965. Papers in Physical Review, Astrophys. Jl. *Address:* 5 Wright Street, Cambridge, Mass, USA. *T:* 547-9317.

PURCELL, (John) Denis; Metropolitan Magistrate, Clerkenwell Magistrates' Court, since 1963; *b* 7 Dec. 1913; *s* of John Poyntz Purcell and Dorothy Branston, Newark; *m* 1951, Pauline Mary, *e d* of Rev. Hiram Craven, Painswick, Glos; two *s*. *Educ:* Marlborough; Wadham College, Oxford. Called to Bar, Gray's Inn, 1938; SE Circuit; Sussex QS. Served War of 1939-45: commnd from HAC, 1939, to Shropshire Yeo., 1940; ADC to GOC-in-C, Western Command, 1941; Staff Capt., Western Command; GSO3, Italy; DAAG, HQ British Troops, Palestine. Actg Dep. Chm., London QS, 1962. *Recreations:* back-yard gardening, racing. *Address:* 1 Cheltenham Terrace, SW3. *T:* 01-730 2896.

PURCELL, Rev. Canon William Ernest; author and broadcaster; Residentiary Canon of Worcester Cathedral, 1966-76; *b* 25 May 1909; *s* of Will and Gwladys Purcell; *m* 1939, Margaret Clegg; two *s* one *d*. *Educ:* Keble Coll., Oxford (MA); Univ. of Wales (BA); Queens Coll., Birmingham. Curate: St. John's Church, Keighley, 1938; Dover Parish Church, 1939-43; Vicar: St. Peter's, Maidstone, 1944-47; Sutton Valence, 1947-53; Chaplain, HM Borstal Instn, East Sutton, 1947-53; Religious Broadcasting Organiser, BBC Midlands, 1953-66. *Publications:* These Thy Gods, 1950; Pilgrim's Programme, 1957; Onward Christian Soldier (biog. of S. Baring Gould), 1957; A Plain Man Looks At Himself, 1962; Woodbine Willie (biog. of G. Studdert Kennedy), 1962; This Is My Story, 1963; The Plain Man Looks At The Commandments, 1966; Fisher of Lambeth (biog. of Archbp of Canterbury), 1969; Portrait of Soper (biog. of Lord Soper), 1972; British Police in a Changing Society, 1974. *Address:* Eversley House, Stretton on Fosse, near Moreton in Marsh, Glos. *T:* Shipston on Stour 61732. *Club:* National Liberal.

PURCELL, Ven. William Henry Samuel, MA; Archdeacon of Dorking, since 1968; *b* 22 Jan. 1912; *m* 1941, Kathleen Clough, Leeds; one *s* (and one *s* decd). *Educ:* King Edward VI School, Norwich; Fitzwilliam House, Cambridge (MA). Asst Curate, St Michael's, Headingley, Leeds, 1937; Minor Canon of Ripon Cathedral, 1940; Vicar: St Matthew, Holbeck, Leeds, 1943; St Matthew, Chapel Allerton, Leeds, 1947; St Martin's, Epsom, 1963. Rural Dean of Epsom, 1965. Hon. Canon of Ripon Cathedral, 1962; Hon. Canon of Guildford Cathedral, 1968. *Recreations:* walking, travel. *Address:* 4 Orchardleigh, St Nicholas Hill, Leatherhead, Surrey. *T:* Leatherhead 75708.

PURCHAS, Hon. Sir Francis (Brooks), Kt 1974; Hon. Mr Justice Purchas; a Judge of the High Court of Justice, Family Division, since 1974; Presiding Judge, South Eastern Circuit, since 1977; *b* 19 June 1919; *s* of late Captain Francis Purchas, 5th Royal Irish Lancers and late Millicent Purchas (*née* Brooks); *m* 1942, Patricia Mona Kathleen, *d* of Lieut Milburn, Canada; two *s*. *Educ:* Summerfields Sch., Oxford; Marlborough Coll.; Trinity Coll., Cambridge. Served RE, 1940-46: North Africa, 1943 (despatches); Hon. Lt-Col retd (Africa Star, Italy Star, 1939-45 Medal; Defence Medal). Allied Mil. Commission, Vienna. Called to Bar, Inner Temple, 1948, QC 1965, Bencher, 1972; practised at Bar, 1948-74; Leader, SE Circuit, 1972. Dep. Chm., E Sussex QS, 1966-71; Recorder of Canterbury, 1969-71 (Hon. Recorder of Canterbury, 1972-74); Recorder of the Crown Court, 1972-74; Comr, Central Criminal Court, 1970-71. Mem., Bar Council, 1966-68, 1969-71, 1972-74. Mem. of Livery, Worshipful Co. of Broderers, 1962. *Recreations:* shooting, golf, fishing. *Address:* Parkhurst House, near Haslemere, Surrey GU27 3BY. *T:* North Chapel 280; 1 Mitre Court Buildings, Temple, EC4Y 7BS. *T:* 01-353 5124. *Club:* Hawks (Cambridge).

PURDEN, Roma Laurette, (Laurie Purden; Mrs J. K. Kotch), MBE 1973; journalist and writer; *b* 30 Sept. 1928; *d* of George Cecil Arnold Purden and Constance Mary Sheppard; *m* 1957, John Keith Kotch; two *d*. *Educ:* Harecroft Sch., Tunbridge Wells. Fiction Editor, Home Notes, 1948-51; Asst Editor, Home Notes, 1951-52; Asst Editor, Woman's Own, 1952; Sen. Asst Editor, Girl, 1952-54; Editor of: Housewife, 1954-57; Home, 1957-62; House Beautiful, 1963-65; Good Housekeeping, 1965-73; Editor-in-Chief, Good Housekeeping, and Womancraft, 1973-77. *Address:* 11 Abbey Gardens, NW8 9AS.

PURDIE, Cora Gwendolyn Jean, (Wendy); see Campbell-Purdie.

PURDON, Maj.-Gen. Corran William Brooke, CBE 1970; MC 1945; British Aircraft Corporation, since 1977; *b* 4 May 1921; *s* of Maj.-Gen. William Brooke Purdon, DSO, OBE, MC, KHS, and Dorothy Myrtle Coates; *m* 1945, Maureen Patricia, *d* of Major J. F. Petrie; two *s* one *d. Educ:* Rokeby, Wimbledon; Campbell Coll., Belfast; RMC Sandhurst. MBIM. Commnd into Royal Ulster Rifles, 1939; service with Army Commandos, France and Germany, 1940-45; 1st Bn RU Rifles, Palestine, 1945-46; GHQ MELF, 1949-51; psc 1955; Staff, Malayan Emergency, 1956-58; Co. Comdr, 1 RU Rifles, Cyprus Emergency, 1958; CO, 1st Bn RU Rifles, BAOR and Borneo War, 1962-64; GSO1 and Chief Instructor, Sch. of Infantry, Warminster, 1965-67; Comdr, Sultan's Armed Forces, Oman, and Dir of Ops, Dhofar War, 1967-70 (Sultan's Bravery Medal, 1968 and Distinguished Service Medal for Gallantry, 1969, Oman); Comdt, Sch. of Infantry, Warminster, 1970-72; GOC, NW Dist, 1972-74; GOC NELF, 1974-76, retired. Hon. Col, Queen's Univ. Belfast OTC, 1975-. Pres., Army Gymnastic Union, 1973-76. CStJ 1976. *Publications:* articles in British Army Review and Infantryman. *Recreations:* physical training, swimming, collecting military pictures and military commemorative plates. *Address:* Farley Cottage, West Street, Reigate, Surrey. *T:* Reigate 447706. *Club:* Army and Navy.

PURDY, Robert John, CMG 1963; OBE 1954; Bursar, Gresham's School, Holt, since 1965; retired from HM Overseas Civil Service, 1963; *b* 2 March 1916; 2nd *s* of late Lt-Col T. W. Purdy, Woodgate House, Aylsham, Norfolk; *m* 1957, Elizabeth (*née* Sharp); two *s* one *d. Educ:* Haileybury College; Jesus College, Cambridge (BA). Served 1940-46 with 81 West African Division Reconnaissance Regt, 3rd and 4th Burma Campaigns (despatches, Major). Appointed to Colonial Administrative Service, Northern Nigeria, 1939; promoted Resident, 1956; Senior Resident, Staff Grade, 1957. Resident, Adamawa Province, 1956; Senior Resident, Plateau Province, 1958-61; Senior Resident, Sokoto Province, 1961-63, retd. *Recreations:* shooting, fishing, gardening. *Address:* Spratt's Green House, Aylsham, Norwich NR11 6TX. *T:* Aylsham 2147.

PURSEGLOVE, John William, CMG 1973; Tropical Crops Specialist, Overseas Development Administration at East Malling Research Station, Kent, 1967-75; *b* 11 Aug. 1912; *s* of late Robert and Kate Purseglove; *m* 1947, Phyllis Agnes Adèle, *d* of late George and Mary Turner, Falkland Is; one *s* one *d. Educ:* Lady Manners Sch., Bakewell; Manchester Univ. (BSc Hons Botany); Gonville and Caius Coll, Cambridge; Imperial Coll. of Tropical Agriculture, Trinidad (AICTA). Agricultural and Sen. Agricl Officer, Uganda, 1936-52; Lectr in Tropical Agriculture, Univ. of Cambridge, 1952-54; Dir, Botanic Gardens, Singapore, 1954-57; Prof. of Botany, Imperial Coll. of Tropical Agriculture and Univ. of the West Indies, Trinidad, 1957-67. Pres., Assoc. for Tropical Biology, 1962-65. FLS 1944; FIBiol 1970. *Publications:* Tobacco in Uganda, 1951; Tropical Crops, Dicotyledons, 2 vols, 1968; Tropical Crops, Monocotyledons, 2 vols, 1972; papers on land use, ethnobotany, etc, in scientific jls and symposia vols. *Recreations:* gardening, natural history. *Address:* Walnut Trees, Sissinghurst, Cranbrook, Kent TN17 2JL. *T:* Sissinghurst 236.

PURSEY, Comdr Harry; RN, retired; Journalist and Lecturer; *b* 1891; *e s* of late G. Pursey, Sidmouth, Devon. *Educ:* elementary school; Royal Hosp. School, Greenwich (Navy's orphanage). Joined Navy as seaman boy, HMS Impregnable, Devonport, 1907, and first naval officer from lower deck to become MP. Specialised in torpedo and mining. Served European War, 1914-18, Dover Patrol, Grand Fleet, HMS Revenge (Battle of Jutland), Eastern Mediterranean (despatches). Commissioned 1917. Black Sea and Turkish operations, 1919-20; Mad Mullah campaign, Somaliland, 1920 (Africa General Service Medal and clasp); Mesopotamia, 1920. Serving in HMS Eagle when Spanish trans-Atlantic flying-boat salved in mid-Atlantic, 1929. HMS Hood, 1931-33; retired list, 1936. Press correspondent in Spain during Civil War, 1937. Ministry of Information National Speaker, 1940-41. MP (Lab) Hull East, 1945-70. Contributed to The Times, Brassey's Naval Annual, British, Dominion and American Press. *Address:* 43 Farnaby Road, Shortlands, Bromley, Kent. *T:* 01-460 0361.

PURSSELL, Anthony John Richard; Managing Director, Arthur Guinness Son & Co. Ltd, since 1975; *b* 5 July 1926; *m* 1952, Ann Margaret Batchelor; two *s* one *d. Educ:* Oriel Coll., Oxford (BA Hons Chemistry). Apptd Managing Director: Arthur Guinness Son & Co. (Park Royal) Ltd, 1968; Arthur Guinness Son & Co. (Dublin) Ltd, 1973. *Recreations:* travel, golf, sailing, books. *Address:* c/o Arthur Guinness Son & Co. Ltd, 10 Albemarle Street, W1X 4AJ. *Club:* Leander (Henley).

PURVES, James Grant, CMG 1971; HM Diplomatic Service, retired; *b* 15 May 1911; *s* of Alexander Murray and Elizabeth Purves; *m* 1947, Mary Tinsley; three *s* one *d. Educ:* Universities of St Andrews and Freiburg-im-Breisgau. Research, 1933-35; Market Research, 1935-36; Secretary, Central Council for Health Education, 1936-39; German Section, BBC, 1939-45. 1st Secretary, Foreign Service: in Berne, Warsaw, Tel Aviv, Bangkok; Consul in Luanda, Lille, Johannesburg; Counsellor, HM Embassy, Berne, 1965-67; HM Consul-General, Hamburg, 1967-71. *Recreations:* swimming, travel. *Address:* Long Roof, Walberswick, Southwold, Suffolk. *T:* Southwold 2242. *Clubs:* Royal Automobile; Anglo-German (Hamburg); Grande Société (Berne).

PUSACK, George Williams, MS; Chairman and Chief Executive, Mobil Oil Co. Ltd, since 1976; *b* 26 Sept. 1920; *s* of George F. Pusack and Winifred (*née* Williams); *m* 1942, Marian Preston; two *s* one *d. Educ:* Univ. of Michigan; Univ. of Pennsylvania. BSE (AeroEng), BSE (Eng.Math), MS (MechEng). Aero Engr, US Navy, 1942-45; Corporal, US Air Force, 1945-46; Mobil Oil Corp: Tech. Service and Research Manager, USA, 1946-53; Product Engrg Manager, USA, 1953-59; International Supply Manager, USA, 1959-69; Vice-Pres., N Amer. Div., USA, 1969-73; Regional Exec., Mobil Europe, London, 1973-76. Teacher, layreader, vestryman and warden of Episcopal Church. *Recreations:* golf, travel. *Address:* 5 Cornwall House, Cornwall Gardens, SW7 4AE. *T:* 01-937 4275. *Clubs:* RAC, Highgate Golf; Pinehurst Country (Pinehurst, NC); Echo Lake Golf (Westfield, NJ).

PUSEY, Nathan Marsh, PhD; President Emeritus, Harvard University; *b* Council Bluffs, Iowa, 4 April 1907; *s* of John Marsh Pusey and Rosa Pusey (*née* Drake); *m* 1936, Anne Woodward; two *s* one *d. Educ:* Harvard University, USA. AB 1928, AM 1932, PhD, 1937. Assistant, Harvard, 1933-34; Sophomore tutor, Lawrence Coll., 1935-38; Asst Prof., history and literature, Scripps Coll., Claremont, Calif., 1938-40; Wesleyan Univ.: Asst Prof., Classics, 1940-43, Assoc. Prof., 1943-44; President: Lawrence Coll., Appleton, Wisconsin, 1944-53; Harvard Univ., 1953-71; Andrew Mellon Foundn, 1971-75. Holds many hon. degrees from Universities and colleges in USA and other countries. Officier de la Légion d'Honneur, 1958. *Publication:* The Age of the Scholar, 1963. *Address:* 200 East 66th Street, New York, NY 10021, USA.

PUSINELLI, Miss Doris, RI 1934; PS; Artist, of British birth. *Recreations:* painting, writing. *Address:* Crede House, Bosham, Sussex. *T:* Bosham 2294.

PUSINELLI, Frederick Nigel Molière, CMG 1966; OBE 1963; MC 1940; HM Overseas Civil Service, retired; *b* 28 April 1919; second *s* of S. Jacques and T. May Pusinelli, Frettenham, Norfolk and Fowey, Cornwall; *m* 1941, Joan Mary Chaloner, *d* of Cuthbert B. and Mildred H. Smith, Cromer, Norfolk and Bexhill-on-Sea, Sussex; one *s* one *d. Educ:* Aldenham School; Pembroke College, Cambridge (BA Hons in law). Commissioned RA 1939; served BEF, 1940; India/Burma, 1942-45; Major, 1942; Staff College, Quetta, 1945. Administrative officer, Gilbert and Ellice Islands Colony, 1946-57. Transferred to Aden, 1958; Dep. Financial Sec. and frequently Actg Financial Sec. till 1962; Director of Establishments, 1962-68, and Assistant High Commissioner, 1963-68, Aden and Federation of South Arabia. Member E African Currency Board, 1960-62. Salaries Commissioner various territories in West Indies, 1968-70. Mem., Chichester Harbour Conservancy; Hon. Secretary: RYA Southern Region; Chichester Harbour Fedn of sailing clubs and yachting orgns. *Publication:* Report on Census of Population of Gilbert and Ellice Islands Colony, 1947. *Recreation:* dinghy racing. *Address:* Routledge Cottage, Westbourne, Emsworth, Hants. *T:* Emsworth 2915. *Clubs:* Royal Commonwealth Society; Royal Yachting Assoc., Cambridge University Cruising, Emsworth Sailing.

PUTT, S(amuel) Gorley, OBE 1966; MA; Fellow and Senior Tutor, Christ's College, Cambridge, since 1968; Vice-President, English Association, since 1972 (Chairman, Executive Council, 1964-72); *b* 9 June 1913; *o c* of late Poole Putt and late Ellen Blake Gorley, Brixham. *Educ:* Torquay Grammar School; Christ's College, Cambridge; Yale University. 1st Class English Tripos Pts I and II, MA 1937, Cambridge; Commonwealth Fund Fellow, MA 1936, Yale. BBC Talks Dept, 1936-38; Warden and Sec., Appts Cttee, Queen's Univ. of Belfast, 1939-40; RNVR, 1940-46, Lieut-Comdr; Warden and Tutor to Overseas Students and Director International Summer School, Univ. Coll., Exeter, 1946-49; Warden of Harkness House, 1949-68 and Director, Div. of International Fellowships, The Commonwealth Fund, 1966-68. Visiting Professor: Univ. of

Massachusetts, 1968; Univ. of the South, Sewanee, 1976. Member: English-Speaking Union, London Cttee, 1952-57; UK-US Educational Commn: Travel Grants Cttee, 1955-64; Cttee of Management, Inst. of US Studies, London Univ., 1965-69. Contested (L) Torquay, 1945. FRSL 1952. *Publications:* Men Dressed As Seamen, 1943; View from Atlantis, 1955; (ed) Cousins and Strangers, 1956; Coastline, 1959; Scholars of the Heart, 1962; (ed) Essays and Studies, 1963; A Reader's Guide to Henry James, 1966; Ginger Hot i' the Mouth, 1976. *Address:* Christ's College, Cambridge. *T:* Cambridge 67641. *Club:* Athenæum.

PUTTICK, Richard George; Chairman, Taylor Woodrow Ltd, since 1974; *b* Kingston, Surrey, 16 March 1916; *e s* of late George Frederick Puttick and Dorothea (*née* Bowerman); *m* 1943, Betty Grace Folbigg; two *s. Educ:* St Mark's, Teddington. Joined Taylor Woodrow Construction Ltd, 1940 (the Taylor Woodrow Group's largest contracting subsidiary co.); Dir, 1955; Asst Managing Dir, 1968; Dir, Taylor Woodrow Ltd, 1969; Jt Dep. Chm., 1972. Mem. Council, CBI, July 1967-Dec. 1969; Pres., NW Mddx Branch, BIM. FIOB; FBIM; FRSA; Fellow, Faculty of Building. Liveryman, Worshipful Co. of Joiners and Ceilers. Vice-Pres., Mddx Assoc. of Boys' Clubs. *Recreations:* music, reading, gardening, supporting sports. *Address:* (home) Woodlawn, Hanger Hill, Weybridge, Surrey; (office) 10 Park Street, W1Y 4DD. *T:* 01-499 8871. *Clubs:* No 10; Surrey County Cricket.

PYATT, Rt. Rev. William Allan; *see* Christchurch, Bishop of.

PYBUS, William Michael; Partner, Herbert Oppenheimer, Nathan & Vandyk, Solicitors, since 1953; Chairman: A.A.H. Ltd, since 1968; British Fuel Co., since 1968; *b* 7 May 1923; *s* of Sydney James Pybus and Evelyn Mary Pybus; *m* 1959, Elizabeth Janet Whitley; two *s* two *d. Educ:* Bedford Sch.; New College, Oxford (MA). Served War 1942-46: commissioned 1st King's Dragoon Guards; Lieut attached XIth Hussars in Normandy (wounded); King's Dragoon Guards, Egypt, Palestine, Syria, Lebanon. Admitted Solicitor (Hons), 1950. Chairman: Inter-Continental Fuels Ltd, 1975-; R. B. Tyler (Ware) Ltd, 1974-77; R. B. Tyler Group Ltd, 1977-; Chemists Holdings Ltd, 1976-; Director: National Westminster Bank (Outer London Region), 1977-; Siebe Gorman Holdings Ltd, 1972-; Coal Trade Benevolent Assoc., 1969-; Cornhill Insurance Co. Ltd, 1977-. Part-time Member: British Railways (London Midland) Bd, 1974; British Railways (Midlands and West) Bd, 1975-77; Chm., BR Adv. Bd (Midlands and N Western), 1977-. Pres., Coal Industry Soc., 1976-. Master, Pattenmakers' Co, 1972-73. FBIM, FInstM. *Recreation:* fishing. *Address:* 20 Copthall Avenue, EC2R 7JH. *T:* 01-628 9611; Beades, Old Malden Lane, Worcester Park, Surrey. *T:* 01-337 1496. *Clubs:* Cavalry and Guards, City University (Chm.), MCC.

PYE, Prof. Norman; Professor of Geography, since 1954, University of Leicester (Pro-Vice-Chancellor, 1963-66); Dean, Faculty of Science, 1957-60; *b* 2 Nov. 1913; *s* of John Whittaker Pye and Hilda Constance (*née* Platt); *m* 1940, Isabella Jane (*née* Currie); two *s. Educ:* Wigan Grammar School; Manchester University. Manchester University: BA Hons Geography Class I, 1935, Diploma in Education Class I, 1936. Asst Lecturer in Geography, Manchester Univ., 1936-37 and 1938-46; Mem., Cambridge Univ. Spitzbergen Expedn, 1938. Seconded to Hydrographic Dept, Admiralty, for War Service, 1940-46. Lecturer in Geography, 1946-53, Sen. Lecturer, 1953-54, Manchester Univ. Vis. Prof., Univ. of Alberta, Edmonton, 1973 and 1974; External Examnr: Univ. of E Africa, 1964-67; Univ. of Guyana, 1974-. Editor, "Geography". Member Corby Development Corp., 1965-. Governor, Up Holland Grammar Sch., 1953-74; Member: Northants CC Educn Cttee, 1956-74; Court, Nottingham Univ. 1964-; Standing Conf. on Univ. Entrance, 1966-; Schools Council, 1967-. Member: Council, RMetS, 1953-56; Council, Inst. of Brit. Geographers, 1954, 1955; Council, RGS, 1967-70; Council for Urban Studies Centres, 1974-; Brit. Nat. Cttee for Geography, 1970-75. *Publications:* Leicester and its Region (ed and contrib.), 1972; research papers and articles in learned journals. *Recreations:* travel, oenology, music, gardening, walking. *Address:* 127 Spencefield Lane, Evington, Leicester. *T:* Thurnby 5167. *Club:* Geographical.

PYKE, David Alan, MD, FRCP; Physician-in-charge, Diabetic Department, King's College Hospital, London, since 1971; *b* 16 May 1921; *s* of Geoffrey and Margaret Pyke; *m* 1948, Janet, *d* of Dr J. Gough Stewart; one *s* two *d. Educ:* Leighton Park Sch., Reading; Cambridge Univ.; University Coll. Hosp. Med. Sch., London. MD Cantab; FRCP. Junior med. appts in London and Oxford, 1945-59. Service in RAMC, 1946-48. Apptd to staff of King's Coll. Hosp., 1959. Hon. Sec.: Assoc. of Physicians of GB

and Ire., 1968-73; Royal Soc. of Med., 1972-74. Registrar, Royal Coll. of Physicians of London, 1975-. *Publications:* (jt ed) Clinical Diabetes and its Biochemical Basis, 1968; (ed) Clinics in Endocrinology and Metabolism, Vol. 1, No 3, 1972; (jtly) Diabetes and its Management, 1973, 2nd edn 1975; articles in med. and sci. jls. *Recreations:* golf, opera. *Address:* 17 College Road, SE21 7BG. *T:* 01-693 2313.

PYKE, Magnus, PhD, FRIC, FRSE, FInst Biol; Secretary and Chairman of Council, British Association for the Advancement of Science, 1973-77; *b* 29 Dec. 1908; *s* of Robert Bond Pyke and Clara Hannah Pyke (*née* Lewis); *m* 1937, Dorothea Mina Vaughan; one *s* one *d. Educ:* St Paul's Sch., London; McGill Univ., Montreal; University Coll. London. BSc, PhD. Scientific Adviser's Div., Min. of Food, London, 1941-45; Nutritional Adviser, Allied Commn for Austria, Vienna, 1945-46; Principal Scientific Officer (Nutrition), Min. of Food, London, 1946-48; Distillers Co. Ltd: Dep. Manager, Yeast Research Outstation, 1949-55; Manager, Glenochil Research Station, 1955-73. Member: (Vice-Pres.) Soc. for Analytical Chemistry, 1959-61; Council, Royal Inst. of Chemistry, 1953-56, 1962-65; Council, Royal Soc. of Edinburgh, 1961-64; Council, Soc. of Chemical Industry, 1967-69; (Chm.) Scottish Section, Nutrition Soc., 1954-55; (Vice-Pres.) Assoc. for Liberal Education, 1964-; (Pres.) Inst. of Food Science and Technology of the UK, 1969-71; (Pres.) Section X, British Association, 1965, Council, 1968-77. Participated in Don't Ask Me, Yorkshire TV, 1974-. FInstBiol (Mem. Council, Scottish Sect., 1959-62); Hon. Fellow Australian IFST, 1973. DUniv Stirling, 1974; Hon. DSc Lancaster 1976. Pye Colour TV Award: the most promising newcomer to television, 1975. *Publications:* Manual of Nutrition, 1945; Industrial Nutrition, 1950; Townsman's Food, 1952; Automation, Its Purpose and Future, 1956; Nothing Like Science, 1957; Slaves Unaware, 1959; The Boundaries of Science, 1961; Nutrition, 1962; The Science Myth, 1962; Food Science and Technology, 1964; The Science Century, 1967; Food and Society, 1968; Man and Food, 1970; Synthetic Food, 1970; Technological Eating, 1972; Catering Science and Technology, 1973; Success in Nutrition, 1975; Butter-side Up, 1976. *Recreation:* he writes a page a day and savours the consequences. *Address:* 3 St Peter's Villas, W6 9BQ. *T:* 01-748 9920. *Club:* Savage.

PYKE-LEES, Walter Kinnear; Registrar, General Medical Council, 1951-70; *b* 17 Dec. 1909; *m* 1944, Joan Warburton, *d* of G. F. Stebbing, FRCS, FFR, and Margaret Warburton Stebbing; two *d. Educ:* Liverpool College; Wadham College, Oxford. Clerk of the Council's Dept, LCC, 1933-37; Asst Sec., GMC, 1937; seconded to HM Treasury, 1940-45; Asst Sec., GMC, 1945-51. Lectr, Extra-Mural Dept, Univ. of London, 1972-. Mem. Exec. Cttee, English Assoc., 1950-62. Mem. Council, Britain-Burma Soc., 1968-77. *Publications:* History and Present Work of the General Medical Council, 1958; as *Peter Leyland:* The Naked Mountain (verse), 1951; The English Association Book of Verse (anthology, with M. Alderton Pink), 1953. *Recreations:* golf, travel. *Address:* 7 Burghley Road, Wimbledon, SW19. *T:* 01-946 5727.

PYLE, Cyril Alfred; Head Master, South East London School, since 1970; *s* of Alfred John Pyle and Nellie Blanche Pyle; *m* 1940, Jean Alice Cotten; one *s* one *d. Educ:* Shooters Hill Grammar Sch.; Univ. of London, Goldsmiths' Coll. Dep. Headmaster, Woolwich Polytechnic Secondary Sch., 1940-66; Headmaster, Bow Sch., 1966-70. Pres., London Teachers' Assoc., 1962; Chm., Council for Educnl Advance, 1964-76; Sec., Conference of London Comprehensive School Heads. *Recreations:* Rotary Club, motoring, gardening. *Address:* Barleyfields, Hartlip, Sittingbourne, Kent ME9 7TH. *T:* Newington 842719.

PYM, Rt. Hon. Francis Leslie, PC 1970; MC 1945; DL; MP (C) Cambridgeshire since 1961; *b* 13 Feb. 1922; *s* of late Leslie Ruthven Pym, MP, and Iris, *d* of Charles Orde; *m* 1949, Valerie Fortune Daglish; two *s* two *d. Educ:* Eton; Magdalene Coll., Cambridge. Served War of 1939-45 (despatches, 1944 and 1945, MC): 9th Lancers, 1942-46; African and Italian campaigns. Contested (C) Rhondda West, 1959. Asst Govt Whip (unpaid), Oct. 1962-64; Opposition Whip, 1964-67; Opposition Dep. Chief Whip, 1967-70; Parly Sec. to the Treasury and Govt Chief Whip, 1970-73; Sec. of State for NI, 1973-74; Opposition spokesman on: agriculture, 1974-75 and 1976; HofC affairs and devolution, 1976-. Mem. Herefordshire County Council, 1958-61. DL Cambs, 1973. *Address:* Everton Park, Sandy, Beds. *T:* Sandy 80376. *Clubs:* Buck's, Carlton, Cavalry and Guards.

PYMAN, Lancelot Frank Lee, CMG 1961; HM Diplomatic Service, retired; *b* 8 August 1910; *s* of late Dr F. L. Pyman, FRS, and of Mrs I. C. Pyman; *m* 1936, Sarah Woods Gamble. *Educ:*

Dover College; King's College, Cambridge (Exhibitioner). Entered Levant Consular Service, 1933; various posts in Persia, 1933-38; Consul, Cernauti, Roumania, 1939-40; Vice-Consul, Beirut, Lebanon, 1940-41. Served with HM Forces in Levant States, 1941. Asst Oriental Secretary, HM Embassy, Tehran, Dec. 1941-44; Foreign Office, 1944-48; Consul, St Louis, Missouri, Dec. 1948-49; Oriental Counsellor, Tehran, Dec. 1949-Sept. 1952; Counsellor, British Embassy, Rio de Janeiro, 1952-53; Consul-General, Tetuan, 1953-56; Counsellor, British Embassy, Rabat, 1956-57; HM Consul-General: Zagreb, 1957-61; Basra, March-Dec. 1961; Ambassador to the Somali Republic, 1961-63; Consul-General, San Francisco, 1963-66. *Recreations:* listening to music, tennis, golf. *Address:* c/o Foreign and Commonwealth Office, SW1.

PYRAH, Prof. Leslie Norman, CBE 1963; retired as Senior Consultant Surgeon, Department of Urology, Leeds General Infirmary (1950-64); Hon. Director, Medical Research Council Unit, Leeds General Infirmary, 1956-64; Professor of Urological Surgery, Leeds University, 1956-64, now emeritus; *b* 11 April 1899; *s* of Arthur Pyrah; *m* 1934, Mary Christopher Batley; one *s* one *d* (and one *s* decd). *Educ:* University of Leeds; School of Medicine, Leeds. Hon. Asst Surgeon, Leeds Gen. Infirmary, 1934; Hon. Consultant Surgeon, Dewsbury Infirmary, Leeds Public Dispensary, Goole Hosp., and Lecturer in Surgery, Univ. of Leeds, 1934; Hon. Cons. Surgeon, St James' Hosp., Leeds, 1941; Surgeon with charge of Out-patients, Leeds Infirmary, 1944; Weild Lectr, Royal Faculty Physicians and Surgeons, Glasgow, 1955; Ramon Guiteras Lectr, Amer. Urological Assoc., Pittsburgh, USA, 1957; Pres., Section of Urology, Royal Soc. Med., 1958; Litchfield Lectr, Univ. of Oxford, 1959; Hunterian Orator, RCS, 1969. Chm., Specialist Adv. Cttee in Urology, Jt Royal Colls of Surgeons of GB and Ireland, 1968-72. Pres., British Assoc. of Urological Surgeons, 1961, 1962; Pres. Leeds and W Riding Medico-Chirurgical Soc., 1959. Mem. Council (elected), Royal College of Surgeons of England, 1960-68. Hon. Mem. Soc. Belge de Chirurgie, 1958; Corresponding Member: Amer. Assoc. of Genito-Urinary Surgeons, 1962; Amer. Soc. of Pelvic Surgeons, 1962; Australasian Soc. of Urology, 1963. St Peter's Medal (British Assoc. of Urological Surgeons) for outstanding contributions to urology, 1959; Honorary Medal, RCS, 1975. DSc (*hc*) Leeds, 1965. *Publications:* numerous, in British Journal of Surgery, British Journal of Urology, Proc. Royal Soc. Med., Lancet, BMJ. Contrib. British Surgical Progress, 1956. *Recreations:* tennis, music. *Address:* Fieldhead, Weetwood Lane, Leeds LS16 5NP. *T:* 52777; (consulting rooms) 27 Clarendon Road, Leeds LS16 5NP. *Club:* Athenæum.

PYTCHES, Rt. Rev. George Edward David; Vicar of St Andrew's, Chorley Wood, Rickmansworth, since 1977; *b* 9 Jan. 1931; 9th *c* and 6th *s* of late Rev. Thomas Arthur Pytches and late Eirene Mildred Pytches (*née* Welldon); *m* 1958, Mary Trevisick; four *d*. *Educ:* Old Buckenham Hall, Norfolk; Framlingham Coll., Suffolk; Univ. of Bristol (BA); Trinity Coll., Bristol. Deacon 1955, priest 1956; Asst Curate, St Ebbe's, Oxford, 1955-58; Asst Curate, Holy Trinity, Wallington, 1958-59; Missionary Priest in Chol Chol, Chile, 1959-62; in Valparaiso, Chile, 1962-68; Rural Dean, Valparaiso, 1966-70; Asst Bishop of Diocese of Chile, Bolivia and Peru, 1970-72; Vicar General of Diocese, 1971-72; Bishop in Chile, Bolivia and Peru, 1972-77. *Recreations:* collecting semi-precious stones, table tennis. *Address:* The Vicarage, Quickley Lane, Chorley Wood, Rickmansworth, Herts.

Q

QUANT, Mary, (Mrs A. Plunket Greene), OBE 1966; RDI 1969; Director of Mary Quant Group of companies since 1955; *b* 11 Feb. 1934; *d* of Jack and Mildred Quant; *m* 1957, Alexander Plunket Greene; one *s*. *Educ:* 13 schools; Goldsmiths' College of Art. Fashion Designer. Mem., Design Council, 1971-. Member: British/USA Bicentennial Liaison Cttee, 1973-; Adv. Council, V&A Museum, 1976-. Exhibition, Mary Quant's London, London Museum, 1973-74. Maison Blanche Rex Award (US), 1964; Sunday Times Internat. Award, 1964; Piavola d'Oro Award (Italy), 1966; Annual Design Medal, Inst. of Industrial Artists and Designers, 1966. FSIA 1967. *Publication:* Quant by Quant, 1966. *Address:* 3 Ives Street, SW3. *T:* 01-584 8781.

QU'APPELLE, Bishop of, since 1977; **Rt. Rev. Michael Geoffrey Peers;** *b* 31 July 1934; *s* of Geoffrey Hugh Peers and Dorothy

Enid Mantle; *m* 1963, Dorothy Elizabeth Bradley; two *s* one *d*. *Educ:* University of British Columbia (BA Hons); Universität Heidelberg (Zert. Dolm.-Interpreter's Certificate); Trinity Coll., Toronto (LTh). Deacon 1959, priest 1960; Curate: St Thomas', Ottawa, 1959-61; Trinity, Ottawa, 1961-65; University Chaplain, Diocese of Ottawa, 1961-66; Rector: St Bede's, Winnipeg, 1966-72; St Martin's, Winnipeg, with St Paul's Middlechurch, 1972-74; Archdeacon of Winnipeg, 1969-74; Rector, St Paul's Cathedral, Regina, 1974-77; Dean of Qu'Appelle, 1974-77. *Address:* 1701 College Avenue, Regina, Saskatchewan S4P 1B8, Canada. *T:* 306-527-8606.

QUARMBY, David Anthony, PhD; FCIT; Member: London Transport Executive, since 1975; South East Economic Planning Council, since 1977; *b* 22 July 1941; *s* of Frank Reginald and Dorothy Margaret Quarmby; *m* 1968, Hilmary Hunter; four *d*. *Educ:* Shrewsbury Sch.; King's Coll., Cambridge (BA); Leeds Univ. (PhD, Dip. Industrial Management). Asst Lectr, then Lectr, Dept of Management Studies, Leeds Univ., 1963; Economic Adviser, Economic Planning Directorate, Min. of Transport, 1966; Dir of Operational Research, London Transport Exec., 1970; Chief Commercial and Planning Officer, LTE, 1974. *Publications:* Factors Affecting Commuter Travel Behaviour (PhD Thesis, Leeds), 1967; contribs to Jl of Transport Economics and Policy, Regional Studies, and to books on transport, economics and operational research. *Recreations:* music, singing. *Address:* 13 Shooters Hill Road, Blackheath, SE3 7AR. *T:* 01-858 7371.

QUARRELL, Prof. Arthur George, ARCS, DSc, PhD (London); Professor of Metallurgy, Sheffield University, 1950-76; *b* 30 Oct. 1910; *m* 1934, Rose Amy Atkins; one *s* (and two *s* decd). *Educ:* College Secondary School, Swindon; Imperial College of Science and Technology. University of Sheffield, Department of Metallurgy: Assistant Lecturer, 1937-39; Lecturer, 1940-45. British Non-Ferrous Metals Research Association: Senior Metallurgist, Oct. 1945-March 1946; Research Manager, March 1946-Sept. 1950; Prof. of Physical Metallurgy, Sheffield Univ., 1950-55; Dean of the Faculty of Metallurgy, 1950-55, 1962-64. Pro-Vice-Chancellor of Sheffield Univ., 1958-62. Warden of Sorby Hall, Sheffield Univ., 1963-71. Pres., Instn of Metallurgists, 1970-72. *Publications:* Physical Examination of Metals, 1940, 2nd edn 1961; Papers in Proc. Roy. Soc., Proc. Phys Soc., Jl Inst. Metals, Jl Iron and Steel Inst. *Recreations:* gardening and other manual activities. *Address:* 38 Endcliffe Grove Avenue, Sheffield S10 3EJ. *T:* 665857.

QUARREN EVANS, John Kerr; a Recorder of the Crown Court, since 1974; Partner in T. S. Edwards & Son, Solicitors, Newport, Gwent, since 1971; *b* 4 July 1926; *s* of late Hubert Royston Quarren Evans and of Violet Soule Quarren Evans; *m* 1958, Janet Shaw Lawson; one *s* one *d*. *Educ:* King Edward VIII Sch., Coventry; Cardiff High Sch.; Trinity Hall, Cambridge, 1948-51 (MA, LLB). 21st Glam. (Cardiff) Bn Home Guard, 1943-44; enlisted, Grenadier Gds, 1944; commnd Royal Welch Fusiliers, 1946; att. 2nd Bn The Welch Regt, Burma, 1946-47; Captain 1947. Articled to late C. James Hardwicke, Cardiff, 1951-53. Admitted solicitor, 1953; Partner, Lyndon Moore & Co., Newport, 1954-71; Clerk to Gen. Comrs of Income Tax, Dinas Powis Div., 1960-; Chm., Newport Nat. Ins. Local Tribunal, 1968-71. Dep. Circuit Judge, 1973; Recorder, Wales and Chester Circuit, 1974. *Recreations:* golf, fishing, music. *Address:* Draycot, Stow Park Crescent, Newport, Gwent NPT 4HD. *T:* Newport 66317. *Club:* Newport Golf.

QUARTANO, Ralph Nicholas, CEng, MIChemE; Chief Executive, The Post Office Staff Superannuation Fund, since 1974; *b* 3 Aug. 1927; *s* of late Charles and Vivienne Mary Quartano; *m* 1954, Cornelia Johanna de Gunst; two *d*. *Educ:* Sherborne Sch.; Pembroke Coll., Cambridge (MA). Bataafsche Petroleum Mij, 1952-58; The Lummus Co, 1958-59; Temple Press, 1959-65; Man. Director: Heywood Temple Industrial Publications, 1965-68; Engineering Chemical and Marine Press, 1968-70. The Post Office, 1971-; Sen. Dir, Central Finance, 1973-74; Trustee, Heitman Canadian Realty Investors, 1976-. Sloan Fellow of London Business School. *Address:* 9 Oakcroft Road, SE13 7ED. *T:* 01-852 1607.

QUARTERMAINE, Sir Allan (Stephen), Kt 1956; CBE 1943; MC; BSc; FICE; *b* 9 November 1888; *s* of late Charles Stephen Quartermaine; *m* 1914, Gladys E. H. Siddons (*d* 1956); one *s*. *Educ:* University College, London (Hons Graduate, Chadwick Scholar, and Fellow). Hertfordshire CC, Surveyor's Department; Tees Side Bridge and Engineering Works; Great Western Railway; Royal Engineers, Egypt and Palestine, 1915-19 (despatches, MC); Commanded No. 1 Bridging Company, RE, SR, 1925; Director-General, Aircraft Production Factories, 1940; Chief Engineer, Great Western Railway and Western

Region, British Railways, 1940-51; President Institution of Civil Engineers, 1951-52; Mem. Departmental Cttee on Coastal Flooding, 1953-54; Mem. Royal Fine Art Commission, 1954-60; Chm. Council for Codes of Practice, British Standards Institution, 1954-58; Mem. Hydraulics Research Board, DSIR, 1954-58. Hon. Member Institution of Royal Engineers; Chm. Civil Engineering Scholarship Trust, 1958-64. *Address:* 53 Westminster Gardens, SW1P 4JG. *T:* 01-834 2143. *Club:* Athenæum.

QUASTEL, Juda Hirsch, CC (Canada) 1970; FRS 1940; DSc London; PhD Cantab; ARCS London; FRIC; FRSC; Professor of Neurochemistry, University of British Columbia, Canada, since 1966; *b* 2 Oct. 1899; *e s* of late Jonas and Flora Quastel, Sheffield, Yorks; *m* 1st, 1931, Henrietta Jungman, MA (*d* 1973); two *s* one *d*; 2nd, 1975, Shulamit Ricardo. *Educ:* Central Secondary School, Sheffield; Imperial College of Science, London University; Trinity College, Cambridge. Commenced research in biochemistry in Cambridge University, Oct. 1921; awarded Senior Studentship by Royal Commissioners for Exhibition of 1851, 1923; Demonstrator and lecturer in biochemistry, Cambridge Univ. 1923; Fellow of Trinity College, Cambridge, 1924; Meldola Medallist 1927; Beit Memorial Research Fellow, 1928; Director of Research, Cardiff City Mental Hospital, 1929-41; Rockefeller Foundation Fellow, 1936; Director of ARC Unit of Soil Metabolism, 1941-47; Prof. of Biochemistry, McGill Univ., Montreal, 1947-66; Director: McGill-Montreal Gen. Hosp. Research Inst., 1947-65; McGill Unit of Cell Metabolism, 1965-66. Member of Council of Royal Institute of Chemistry, 1944-47; Member: Water Pollution Research Board, 1944-47; Bd of Governors, Hebrew Univ., Jerusalem, 1950; Pres., Montreal Physiological Soc., 1950; Pres. Canadian Biochemical Soc., 1963; Canadian Microbiological Soc. Award, 1965; Flavelle Medal, RSC, 1974; Gairdner Internat. Award for Med. Res., 1974. Member, British, Can. and Amer. scientific societies; Consultant, Montreal General Hosp.; Mem. Staff, Vancouver Gen. Hosp. Leeuwenhoek Lectr, Royal Society, 1954; Bryan Priestman Lectr, Univ. New Brunswick, 1956; Kearney Foundation Lectr, Univ. Calif, 1958; Seventh Jubilee Lectr, Biochemical Soc. UK, 1974; Royal Society Leverhulme Visiting Professor, in India, 1965-66; Vis. Prof., Nat. Hospital for Nervous Diseases (Neurology Dept), London, 1976-77. Fellow: NY Academy of Science, 1954; Amer. Assoc. for Advancement of Science, 1964. Hon. Fellow: Japanese Pharmacological Soc., 1963; Canadian Microbiological Soc., 1965; N Pacific Soc. of Neurology and Psychiatry, 1966. Hon. Mem., Biochemical Soc. UK, 1973. Hon. DSc McGill, 1969; Hon. PhD Jerusalem, 1970. *Publications:* since 1923 mainly on subjects of biochemical interest; author and co-editor: Neurochemistry, 1955- (1963); Methods in Medical Research, Vol. 9, 1961; Chemistry of Brain Metabolism, 1962; Metabolic Inhibitors, vol. 1, 1963, vol. 2, 1964, vol. 3, 1972, vol. 4, 1973. *Address:* Neurochemistry Division, Psychiatry Department, University of British Columbia, Vancouver V6T 1W5, BC, Canada.

QUAYLE, (John) Anthony, CBE 1952; Actor; *b* 7 September 1913; *s* of Arthur Quayle and Esther Quayle (*née* Overton); *m* 1947, Dorothy Hyson; one *s* two *d*. *Educ:* Rugby. First appeared on stage, 1931; acted in various London productions between then and 1939, including several appearances at Old Vic; also acted in New York. Served War of 1939-45, Royal Artillery. After 1945 became play-producer as well as actor, being responsible for production of Crime and Punishment, The Relapse, Harvey, Who is Sylvia. Director, Shakespeare Memorial Theatre, 1948-56, where he has produced The Winter's Tale, Troilus and Cressida, Macbeth, Julius Caesar; King Lear (with John Gielgud), Richard II, Henry IV, Part I (with John Kidd), Henry V, Othello and Measure for Measure. Among parts played at Stratford are: The Bastard, Petruchio, Claudius, Iago, Hector in Troilus and Cressida; Henry VIII, 1949; Antony and Henry VIII, 1950; Falstaff in Henry IV, Parts I and II, 1951; Coriolanus; Mosca in Volpone, 1952; Othello, Bottom in a Midsummer Night's Dream, Pandarus in Troilus and Cressida, 1954; Falstaff in The Merry Wives of Windsor; Aaron in Titus Andronicus, 1955. Took Shakespeare Memorial Theatre Company to Australia, 1949, 1953. Played Tamburlaine, New York, 1956; acted in A View from the Bridge, Comedy Theatre, 1956; Made a tour of Europe in Titus Andronicus, 1957; directed and acted in The Firstborn, New York, 1958; acted in: Long Day's Journey into Night, Edinburgh Festival and London, 1958; Look After Lulu!, Royal Court, 1959; Chin-Chin, Wyndham's, 1960; The Right Honourable Gentleman, Her Majesty's, 1964; Incident at Vichy, Phœnix, 1966; Galileo, New York, 1967; Halfway Up The Tree, New York, 1967; Sleuth, St Martin's, 1970, NY, 1970-71; The Idiot, National Theatre, 1970; The Headhunters, Washington, 1974; Old World, RSC, 1976-77. Directed: Lady Windermere's

Fan, 1967; Tiger at the Gates, New York, 1968; Harvey, Prince of Wales, 1975; Rip Van Winkle, Washington, 1976. *Films:* Saraband for Dead Lovers, Hamlet, Oh Rosalinda, Battle of the River Plate, The Wrong Man, Woman in a Dressing Gown, The Man Who Wouldn't Talk, Ice Cold in Alex, Serious Charge, Tarzan's Greatest Adventure, The Challenge, The Guns of Navarone, HMS Defiant, Lawrence of Arabia, The Fall of the Roman Empire, Operation Crossbow, A Study in Terror, Incompreso, MacKenna's Gold, Before Winter Comes, Anne of the Thousand Days, Bequest to the Nation, The Tamarind Seed, Moses the Lawgiver, Great Expectations, 21 Hours in Munich, The Eagle has Landed. *Publications:* Eight Hours from England, 1945; On Such a Night, 1947. *Address:* 49B Elystan Place, SW3 3JY.

QUEBEC, Cardinal Archbishop of, since 1965; **His Eminence Cardinal Maurice Roy,** CC (Canada) 1971; DD (Laval), DPh (Inst. Angelicum); Archbishop of Quebec since 1947; Primate of Canada since 1956; elevated to the Sacred College of Cardinals and given titular church of Our Lady of the Blessed Sacrament and the Holy Canadian Martyrs, 1965; *b* 25 Jan. 1905; *s* of late Ferdinand Roy. *Educ:* Seminary of Quebec and Laval Univ., Quebec; Collegium Angelicum, Rome; Institut catholique and Sorbonne, Paris. Priest, 1927; Professor of: Dogmatic Theology, 1930-35; Apologetics, 1935-36; Sacramentary Theology, 1936-39; Students' Chaplain, 1936-37. Hon. Capt.-Chaplain Royal 22nd Regt 1939; Hon. Major and Chief Chaplain Canadian Base Units at Aldershot, 1941; Hon. Lt-Col, Chaplain HQ First Cdn Corps (England and Italy), 1941; Sicily and Italy Campaigns, 1943; Hon. Col, Asst Prin. Chaplain 1st Cdn Army, 1944; France, Belgium, Germany, Holland campaigns, 1944-45 (despatches). Rector Grand Seminary of Quebec, 1945; Bishop of Three-Rivers, 1946; Bishop Ordinary to Cdn Armed Forces (Military Vicar), 1946. Central Commission preparatory to Council Vatican II, June 1962; Council Vatican II Commission on Sacred Theology, Dec. 1962; Sacred Congregations of the Council and of Seminaries and Universities, 1965; Chairman: Concilium De Laicis; Pontifical Commission, Justitia et Pax, Rome. OBE, 1945; Chevalier of the Legion of Honour, 1947; Commander of the Order of Leopold and Croix de Guerre with palm, 1948; Commander of the Order of Orange Nassau, Holland, 1949; Knight Grand Cross, Equestrian Order to the Holy Sepulchre of Jerusalem, 1965; Bailiff Grand Cross of Honour and Devotion, Sovereign Order of Malta, 1965. *Address:* Archevêché de Québec, Case postale 459, Québec G1R 4R6, Canada.

QUEBEC, Bishop of, since 1977; **Rt. Rev. Allen Goodings;** Dean of Holy Trinity Cathedral, Quebec; *b* Barrow-in-Furness, Lancs, 7 May 1925; *s* of late Thomas Jackson Goodings and Ada Tate; *m* 1959, Joanne Talbot; one *s* one *d*. *Educ:* Sir George Williams Univ. (BA); McGill Univ. (BD); Diocesan Theological Coll., Montreal (LTh). Studied engineering and worked for Vickers Armstrongs (Britain) and Canadian Vickers (Montreal); studied in Montreal and ordained into Ministry of Anglican Church of Canada, 1959. Chaplain, Canadian Grenadier Guards, Montreal, 1966-69. Played Rugby Union (capped for Lancashire, 1947/8), including County Championship). *Recreations:* skiing, tennis, squash, cycling. *Address:* 29 Rue des Jardins, Quebec, PQ G1R 4L5, Canada. *T:* 694-9329. *Clubs:* Cercle Universitaire (Quebec); Mess (Royale 22nd Regiment, Quebec).

QUEEN, Ellery; *see* Dannay, Frederic.

QUEENSBERRY, 12th Marquess of, *cr* 1682; **David Harrington Angus Douglas;** late Royal Horse Guards; Viscount Drumlanrig and Baron Douglas, 1628; Earl of Queensberry, 1633; Bt (Nova Scotia), 1668; Professor of Ceramics, Royal College of Art, since 1959; President, Design and Industries Association, since 1976; *b* 19 Dec. 1929; *s* of 11th Marquess of Queensberry and late Cathleen Mann; *S* father, 1954; *m* 1st, 1956, Mrs Ann Radford; two *d*; 2nd, 1969, Alexandra, *d* of Guy Wyndham Sich; two *s* one *d*. *Educ:* Eton. *Heir:* *s* Viscount Drumlanrig, *qv*.

QUEENSLAND, NORTH, Bishop of, since 1971; **Rt. Rev. Hurtle John Lewis;** *b* 2 Jan. 1926; *s* of late Hurtle John Lewis and late Hilda Lewis. *Educ:* Prince Alfred Coll.; London Univ. (BD). ThL of ACT. Royal Australian Navy, 1943-46; Student, St Michael's House, S Aust., 1946-51; Member, SSM, 1951-; Provincial Australia, SSM, 1962-68; Prior, Kobe Priory, Japan, 1969-71. *Recreations:* rowing, horse riding. *Address:* Box 1244, Townsville, Queensland 4810, Australia. *T:* 71-2297.

QUEGUINER, Jean; Légion d'Honneur, 1970; Deputy Secretary-General, Inter-Governmental Maritime Consultative Organization (IMCO), since 1968; *b* 2 June 1921; *s* of Etienne Queguiner and Anne Trehin; *m* 1952, Marguerite Gaillard; one *s*

one d. *Educ:* Lycée Buffon, Collège Stanislas and Faculté de Droit, Paris; Coll. of Administration of Maritime Affairs, St Malo. Docteur en Droit (maritime), Bordeaux. Head of Maritime Dist of Caen, 1953; Dep. Head of Coll. of Admin. of Maritime Affairs, 1955; Head of Safety of Navigation Section, 1963; Vice-Chm. of Maritime Safety Cttee of Inter-Govtl Maritime Consultative Organization, 1965-68. *Publications:* Législation et réglementation maritime, 1955; Le code de la mer, 1965; La croisière cotière, 1967; Le code fluvial à l'usage des plaisanciers, 1970. *Recreation:* sailing. *Address:* (office) 101-104 Piccadilly, W1. *T:* 01-499 9040; (home) 32 Melton Court, Old Brompton Road, SW7. *Club:* Royal Automobile.

QUÉNET, Hon. Sir Vincent (Ernest), Kt 1962; Judge President of Appellate Division, High Court of Rhodesia, 1964-70, retired; *b* 14 Dec. 1906; *y s* of George Alfred Quénet, Worcester, CP, SA; *m* 1938, Gabrielle, *d* of Hon. Norman Price; three *s*. *Educ:* Worcester High Sch.; University of Cape Town. Advocate of Supreme Court of SA and Barrister-at-law, Middle Temple. Practised at Johannesburg Bar, QC; Judge of: High Court of S Rhodesia, 1952-61; Fed. Supreme Court, Federation of Rhodesia and Nyasaland, 1961-64. *Address:* Tiger Valley, Borrowdale, Salisbury, Rhodesia. *T:* 8872813. *Clubs:* Rand (Johannesburg); Salisbury (Rhodesia).

QUENINGTON, Viscount; Michael Henry Hicks Beach; *b* 7 Feb. 1950; *s* and *heir* of 2nd Earl St Aldwyn, *qv*. *Educ:* Eton; Christ Church, Oxford. MA. *Address:* Williamstrip Park, Cirencester, Glos; 13 Upper Belgrave Street, SW1.

QUENNELL, Joan Mary, MBE 1958; JP; *b* 23 Dec. 1923; *o c* of late Walter Quennell, Dangstein, Rogate. *Educ:* Dunhurst and Bedales Schools. War Service, WLA and BRCS. Vice-Chairman, Horsham Division Cons. Assoc., 1949 (Chairman, 1958-61); W Sussex CC, 1951-61. Served on Finance, Local Government, Selection and Education Cttees, etc; also as Governor various schools and colleges; Governor, Crawley Coll., Further Education, 1956-69; Member: Southern Reg. Council for Further Education, 1959-61; Reg. Adv. Council, Technological Education (London and Home Counties), 1959-61. MP (C) Petersfield, 1960-Sept. 1974; PPS to the Minister of Transport, 1962-64; Member: Select Cttee on Public Accounts, 1970-74; Speaker's Panel of Temporary Chairmen of House of Commons, 1970-74; Cttee of Selection, House of Commons, 1970-74; Select Cttee on European Secondary Legislation, 1973-74. JP W Sussex, 1959-. *Recreations:* swimming, reading, gardening, fishing. *Address:* Dangstein, Rogate, near Petersfield, Hants.

QUENNELL, Peter, CBE 1973; *b* March 1905; *s* of late Marjorie and C. H. B. Quennell. *Educ:* Berkhamsted Grammar Sch.; Balliol Coll., Oxford. Editor, History To-day; edited The Cornhill Magazine, 1944-51. *Publications:* Poems, 1926; Baudelaire and the Symbolists, 1929, 2nd edn 1954; A Superficial Journey through Tokyo and Peking, 1932, 2nd edn 1934; Sympathy, and Other Stories, 1933; Byron, 1934; Byron: the years of fame, 1935, 3rd edn 1967; Victorian Panorama: a survey of life and fashion from contemporary photographs, 1937; Caroline of England, 1939; Byron in Italy, 1941; Four Portraits, 1945, 2nd edn 1965; John Ruskin, 1949; The Singular Preference, 1952; Spring in Sicily, 1952; Hogarth's Progress, 1955; The Sign of the Fish, 1960; Shakespeare: the poet and his background, 1964; Alexander Pope: the education of Genius 1688-1728, 1968; Romantic England, 1970; Casanova in London and other essays, 1971; Samuel Johnson: his friends and enemies, 1972; The Marble Foot (autobiog.), 1976; *edited:* Aspects of Seventeenth Century Verse, 1933, 2nd edn 1936; The Private Letters of Princess Lieven to Prince Metternich, 1820-1826, 1948; Byron: selected letters and journals, 1949; H. Mayhew, Mayhew's Characters, 1951; Diversions of History, 1954; H. Mayhew, Mayhew's London, 1954; George Borrow, The Bible in Spain, 1959; H. Mayhew, London's Underworld, 1960; G. G. N. Byron, Lord Byron, Byronic Thoughts, 1960; H. de Montherlant, Selected Essays, 1960; W. Hickey, Memoirs, 1960; T. Moore, The Journal of Thomas Moore, 1964; H. Mayhew, Mayhew's Characters, 1967; Marcel Proust, 1871-1922: a centenary volume, 1971; (with H. Johnson) A History of English Literature, 1973. *Address:* 26 Cheyne Row, SW3. *Club:* White's.

QUEREJAZU CALVO, Roberto; Cross of the Chaco and Award of Military Merit (Bolivia); Bolivian Ambassador to the Court of St James's 1966-70, and to the Court of The Hague, 1966-70; *b* 24 Nov. 1913; *m* 1944, Dorothy Lewis; one *s* one d. *Educ:* Sucre Univ., Bolivia. Director of Minister's Cabinet, Legal Dept, and Political Dept, Bolivian Foreign Service, 1939-42; First Secretary, Embassy in Brazil, 1943; Secretary-General, Bolivian Delegn to UN, 1946; Bolivian Embassy, London: Counsellor, 1947; Chargé d'Affaires, 1948-52; Bolivian Rep.: to UN

Conference on Tin, 1951; to Interamerican Conference for De-Nuclearization of Latin America, Mexico, 1964; Bolivian Delegate: XX UN General Assembly, 1965; 2nd Interamerican Conference Extraord., Rio de Janeiro, 1965; Under-Secretary of State for Foreign Affairs, Bolivia, 1966. Holds foreign awards. *Publications:* Masamaclay (History of Chaco War), 1966; Bolivia and the English, 1973; Llallagua: History of a mountain, 1976; Guano, Salitre, Sangre, History of the Pacific War, 1978. *Address:* Casilla 39, Cochabamba, Bolivia.

QUICK, Anthony Oliver Hebert; Headmaster of Bradfield College since 1971; *b* 26 May 1924; *er s* of late Canon O. C. Quick, sometime Regius Prof. of Divinity at Oxford, and Mrs F. W. Quick; *m* 1955, Éva Jean, *er d* of late W. C. Sellar and of Mrs Hope Sellar; three *s* one d. *Educ:* Shrewsbury Sch.; Corpus Christi Coll., Oxford; Sch. of Oriental and African Studies, Univ. of London (Govt Schol.). 2nd cl. hons Mod. History, Oxford. Lieut, RNVR, serving mainly on East Indies Stn, 1943-46. Asst Master, Charterhouse, 1949-61; Headmaster, Rendcomb Coll., Cirencester, 1961-71. *Publications:* (jtly) Britain 1714-1851, 1961; Britain 1851-1945, 1967; Twentieth Century Britain, 1968. *Recreations:* walking, gardening, sailing, fishing. *Address:* Crossways, Bradfield, Reading, Berks. *T:* Bradfield 203. *Club:* Naval.

QUICK SMITH, George William, CBE 1959; Chief Executive, latterly Vice-Chairman, and Member of National Freight Corporation, 1968-71; *b* 23 Aug. 1905; *s* of George Windsor Smith and Maud Edith (*née* Quick); *m* 1934, Ida Muriel Tinkler; no *c. Educ:* Univ. of London (LLB). Barrister-at-law, Inner Temple. FCIS; FCIT (past Vice-Pres.). Various positions in shipping, 1922-35; Sec. of various assocs and Mem. of joint negotiating and other bodies connected with road transport; British employers deleg. to various internat. confs including ILO, 1935-48; First Legal Adviser and Sec. and later Mem. of Board of British Road Services, 1948-59; Adviser on Special Projects, British Transport Commn, 1959-62; Chief Sec. and Chief Exec. of Transport Holding Co., 1962-71. Dir various road haulage cos; Mem., Transport Tribunal, 1973-; Trustee various transport benevolent funds; Master of Carmen's Co., 1967-68; Freeman of City of London. Churchwarden, All Saints Margaret Street, London, 1960-77. Mem. Governing Body, SPCK, 1967-75 (Vice-Pres., 1976-). Hon. Mem., Road Haulage Assoc., 1971. *Publications:* various books and papers on road transport and road transport law; Commentary on Transport Act 1947. *Recreations:* reading, writing, and the arts. *Address:* 6 Martello Towers, Canford Cliffs, Poole, Dorset BH13 7HX. *T:* Canford Cliffs 708127. *Club:* Royal Motor Yacht (Poole).

QUIGLEY, Hugh, MA; Economist and Farmer; *b* Stirling, 6 Aug. 1895; *e s* of James and Catherine Quigley, Stirling, afterwards Lanark; *m* Marion Sommerville (*d* 1974), *y d* of Joseph Dyer, Kilbank, Lanark; one *s* one d. *Educ:* Lanark Grammar Sch.; Glasgow Univ.; Naples Univ.; Munich Univ. War Service, 1915-18; MA, 1st Class Hons in French, German, Italian, Glasgow Univ., 1919; Carnegie Research Fellow in Modern Languages, 1919-21; Economist in Research Department of Metropolitan-Vickers Electrical Company, 1922-24; Head of Economic and Statistical Department of the British Electrical and Allied Manufacturers' Assoc., 1924-30; Chief Statistical Officer, Central Electricity Board, 1931-43. *Publications:* Lombardy, Tyrol, and the Trentino, 1925; The Land of the Rhone, 1927; Passchendaele and the Somme, 1928 (revised edn, 1965); Lanarkshire in Prose and Verse, 1929; Electrical Power and National Progress, 1925; Towards Industrial Recovery, 1927; Republican Germany (with R. T. Clark), 1928 (repr. 1968); German History from 1900 to 1931 (chap. in German Studies ed. Jethro Bithell), 1932; Part translator of R. Liefmann: Cartels, Concerns and Trusts, 1932; Power Resources of the World (for World Power Conference), 1929; Combines and Trusts in the Electrical Industry, 1927; The Electrical Industry of Great Britain, 1929; (both for the British Electrical and Allied Manufacturers' Association); Housing and Slum Clearance in London (with I. Goldie), 1934; Italian Criticism in the 18th Century; The Influence of English Philosophy and the Development of Aesthetics, based on Imagination; Antonio Conti (chapter in Mélanges Hauvette); The Highlands of Scotland, 1936; A Plan for the Highlands, 1936; End Monopoly Exploitation, 1941; New Forest Orchard, 1947; A Small Community, 1970; Melchet, 1971. *Recreation:* forestry. *Address:* Melchet Park, Romsey, Hants.

QUIGLEY, William George Henry, PhD; Permanent Secretary, Department of Commerce, Northern Ireland, since 1976; *b* 26 Nov. 1929; *s* of William George Cunningham Quigley and Sarah Hanson Martin; *m* 1971, Moyra Alice Munn, LLB. *Educ:* Ballymena Academy; Queen's Univ., Belfast, BA (1st Cl. Hons), 1951; PhD, 1955. Apptd Asst Principal, Northern Ireland Civil

Service, 1955. Permanent Sec., Dept of Manpower Services, NI, 1974-76. Chairman: Review Body on Industrial Relns in NI, 1971-74; Review Team on Economic and Industrial Strategy for NI, 1976. *Publication:* (ed with E. F. D. Roberts) Registrum Iohannis Mey: The Register of John Mey, Archbishop of Armagh, 1443-1456, 1972. *Recreations:* historical research, reading, music. *Address:* 22 Knockmore Park, Bangor, Co. Down, Northern Ireland. *T:* Bangor 63622.

QUILL, Colonel Raymond Humphrey, CBE 1947; DSO 1947; MVO (4th Class) 1934; Colonel (retired), Royal Marines; *b* 4 May 1897; *s* of late Maj.-General Richard Henry Quill, CB, MD; unmarried. *Educ:* Wellington Coll.; Cheltenham. Joined Royal Marines, 1914. Served European War, 1914-19. Major, RM, 1934; Lieut-Colonel, 1943; Colonel, 1944. Served War of 1939-45. ADC to the King, 1948-50; retired, 1950. Legion of Merit, USA, 1948. Fellow, British Horological Institute, 1954-. *Publication:* John Harrison: the man who found Longitude, 1967. *Recreations:* athletics, fishing, horology. *Address:* 104 Marsham Court, Westminster, SW1. *T:* 01-828 3730. *Clubs:* Boodle's, Royal Thames Yacht, Royal Automobile.

QUILLEY, Denis Clifford; actor; *b* 26 Dec. 1927; *s* of Clifford Charles Quilley and Ada Winifred (*née* Stanley); *m* 1949, Stella Chapman; one *s* two *d*. *Educ:* Bancroft's, Woodford, Essex. First appearance, Birmingham Rep. Theatre, 1945; played at Globe, London, also Phoenix, 1950; Old Vic and Young Vic Cos, 1950-51: parts included: Fabian in Twelfth Night (on tour, Italy), Gratiano in Merchant of Venice; Revue, Airs on a Shoe String (exceeded 700 perfs), Royal Court, 1953; first leading rôle in West End as Geoffrey Morris in Wild Thyme, Duke of York's, 1955; subseq. parts incl.: Tom Wilson in Grab Me a Gondola (over 600 perfs), Lyric; Captain Brassbound, and Orlando, Bristol Old Vic; Candide, Saville; Benedick in Much Ado about Nothing, Open Air Th.; Archie Rice in The Entertainer, Nottingham Playhouse; Krogstad in A Doll's House, Greenwich; Privates on Parade, Aldwych, 1977; Nat. Theatre, 1971-: Aufidius (Coriolanus); Macbeth; Bolingbroke (Richard II); Caliban (The Tempest); Lopakin (Cherry Orchard); Jamie (Long Day's Journey into Night); Claudius (Hamlet); Hector (Troilus and Cressida); Bajazeth (Tamburlaine); Morell (Candida), Albery Theatre, 1977. Has played in NY, Melbourne and Sydney. *Films:* Life at the Top, Anne of the Thousand Days, Murder on the Orient Express. *TV* plays and series: incl.: Merchant of Venice, The Father, Henry IV (Pirandello), Murder in the Cathedral, Time Slip, Contrabandits (Aust.), Clayhanger. *Recreations:* playing the piano, flute and cello, walking. *Address:* 22 Willow Road, Hampstead, NW3. *T:* 01-435 5976.

QUILTER, Sir Anthony (Raymond Leopold Cuthbert), 4th Bt, *cr* 1897; landowner since 1959; *b* 25 March 1937; *s* of Sir (John) Raymond (Cuthbert) Quilter, 3rd Bt and Margery Marianne (*née* Cooke); *S* father 1959; *m* 1964, Mary Elise, *er d* of late Colonel Brian (Sherlock) Gooch, DSO, TD; one *s* one *d*. *Educ:* Harrow. Is engaged in farming. *Recreations:* shooting, golf. *Heir:* *s* Guy Raymond Cuthbert Quilter, *b* 13 April 1967. *Address:* The Applehouse, Methersgate, Sutton, Woodbridge, Suffolk. *T:* Woodbridge 2016.

QUIN; *see* Wyndham-Quin.

QUIN, Rt. Rev. George Alderson; *see* Down and Dromore, Bishop of.

QUINCE, Peter; *see* Thompson, John W. McW.

QUINE, Prof. Willard Van Orman; American author; Professor of Philosophy, since 1948, and Edgar Pierce Professor of Philosophy, since 1956, Harvard University; *b* Akron, Ohio, 25 June 1908; *s* of Cloyd Robert and Hattie Van Orman Quine; *m* 1st, 1930, Naomi Clayton; two *d*; 2nd, 1948, Marjorie Boynton; one *s* one *d*. *Educ:* Oberlin Coll., Ohio (AB); Harvard Univ. (AM, PhD). Harvard: Sheldon Travelling Fellow, 1932-33 (Vienna, Prague, Warsaw); Jun. Fellow, Society of Fellows, 1933-36 (Sen. Fellow, 1949-, Chairman, 1957-58); Instructor and Tutor in Philosophy, 1936-41; Assoc. Professor of Philosophy, 1941-48; Chairman, Dept of Philosophy, 1952-53. Visiting Professor, Universidade de São Paulo, Brazil, 1942. Lieut, then Lieut-Commander, USNR, active duty, 1942-46. Consulting editor, Journal of Symbolic Logic, 1936-52; Vice-President, Association for Symbolic Logic, 1938-40; President, 1953-55; Vice-President, Eastern Division, American Philosophical Assoc., 1950; President, 1957; Corres. Fellow, British Academy, 1959-. FAAAS, 1945- (Councillor, 1950-53); American Philosophical Society, 1957- (Councillor, 1966-); Nat. Acad. of Sciences, 1977-; Acad. Internat. de Philosophie de Science, 1960; Instituto Brasileiro de Filosofia, 1963-; Trustee,

Institute for Unity of Science, 1949-; Syndic, Harvard University Press: 1951-53; 1954-56, 1959-60, 1962-66. George Eastman Visiting Prof., Oxford Univ., 1953-54; Vis. Professor: Univ. of Tokyo, 1959; Rockefeller Univ., 1968; Collège de France, 1969. A. T. Shearman Lecturer, University of London, 1954; Gavin David Young Lectr in Philosophy, Univ. of Adelaide, 1959; John Dewey Lectr, Columbia Univ., 1968; Paul Carus Lectr, Amer. Philos. Assoc., 1971; Hägerström Lectr, Uppsala, 1973. Member Institute for Advanced Study, Princeton, USA, 1956-57. Fellow: Centre for Advanced Study in the Behavioural Sciences, Palo Alto, California, 1958-59; Centre for Advanced Studies, Wesleyan Univ., Conn, 1965; Sir Henry Saville Fellow, Merton Coll., Oxford, 1973-74. Hon. degrees: MA Oxon, 1953; DLitt Oxon, 1970; LittD: Oberlin, 1955; Akron, 1965; Washington, 1966; Temple, 1970; LLD Ohio State, 1957; Dèsl Lille, 1965; LHD Chicago, 1967. N. M. Butler Gold Medal, 1970. *Publications:* A System of Logistic, 1934; Mathematical Logic, 1940, rev. edn 1951; Elementary Logic, 1941, rev. edn 1965; O sentido da nova logica, 1944 (São Paulo); Methods of Logic, 1950, rev. edn 1972; From a Logical Point of View, 1953, rev. edn 1961; Word and Object, 1960; Set Theory and its Logic, 1963, revised edn 1969; Ways of Paradox and Other Essays, 1966; Selected Logic Papers, 1966; Ontological Relativity and Other Essays, 1969; Philosophy of Logic, 1970; (with J. S. Ullian) The Web of Belief, 1970; The Roots of Reference, 1974; contribs to Journal of Symbolic Logic; Journal of Philosophy; Philosophical Review; Mind; Rivista di Filosofia; Scientific American; NY Review of Books; Library of Living Philosophers. *Recreation:* travel. *Address:* 38 Chestnut Street, Boston, Mass 02108, USA. *T:* 723-6754.

QUINLAN, Maj.-Gen. Henry, CB 1960; *b* 5 Jan. 1906; *s* of Dr Denis Quinlan, LRCP, LRCS (Edinburgh), of Castletownroche, Co. Cork; *m* 1936, Euphemia Nancy, *d* of John Tallents Wynyard Brooke of Shanghai, and Altrincham, Cheshire; two *s* two *d*. *Educ:* Clongowes Wood Coll., Sallins, Co. Kildare. BDS 1926; FFD RCS (I) 1964. Royal Army Dental Corps; Lieut, 1927; Captain, Dec. 1930; Major, 1937; Lieut-Colonel, Dec. 1947; Colonel, 1953; Maj.-General, Oct. 1958; Director Army Dental Service, 1958-63; QHDS 1954-64, retired; Colonel Comdt Royal Army Dental Corps, 1964-71. Officer OStJ 1958. *Address:* Whitebridge, Redlands Lane, Crondall, Hants. *T:* Crondall 239.

QUINLAN, Michael Edward; Deputy Under-Secretary of State, Ministry of Defence, since 1977; *b* 11 Aug. 1930; *s* of Gerald and Roseanne Quinlan, Wimbledon; *m* 1965, Margaret Mary Finlay; two *s* two *d*. *Educ:* Wimbledon Coll.; Merton Coll., Oxford. 1st Cl. Hon. Mods, 1st Cl. LittHum. RAF, 1952-54. Asst Principal, Air Ministry, 1954; Private Sec. to Parly Under-Sec. of State for Air, 1956-58; Principal, Air Min., 1958; Private Sec. to Chief of Air Staff, 1962-65; Asst Sec., MoD, 1968; Defence Counsellor, UK Delegn to NATO, 1970-73; Under-Sec., Cabinet Office, 1974-77. *Recreations:* cricket, squash, listening to music. *Address:* 117 Ridgway, Wimbledon SW19 4RE. *T:* 01-947 4879. *Club:* Royal Air Force.

QUINN, Prof. David Beers, DLit (QUB), PhD (London), MRIA, FRHistS; Andrew Geddes and John Rankin Professor of Modern History, University of Liverpool, 1957-76; *b* 24 April 1909; *o s* of late David Quinn, Omagh and Belfast, and Albertina Devine, Cork; *m* 1937, Alison Moffat Robertson, MA, *d* of late John Ireland Robertson, Edinburgh; two *s* one *d*. *Educ:* Clara (Offaly) No. 2 National Sch.; Royal Belfast Academical Institution; Queen's Univ., Belfast; King's Coll., University of London. University Schol., QUB, 1928-31 (1st Class Hons in Medieval and Modern History, 1931); PhD London, 1934. Asst Lecturer, 1934, and Lecturer, 1937, University College, Southampton; Lecturer in History, QUB, 1939-44; seconded to BBC European Service, 1943; Prof. of History, University College, Swansea, 1944-57; DLit (QUB), 1958. Secretary, Ulster Society for Irish Historical Studies, 1939-44; Member: Council of Hakluyt Society, 1950-54, 1957-60 (Vice-President, 1960-); Council of Royal Historical Society, 1951-55, 1956-60 (Vice-President, 1964-68); Fellow, Folger Shakespeare Lib. (Washington, DC), 1957, 1959, 1963-64; Leverhulme Res. Fellow, 1963; British Council Visiting Scholar, NZ, 1967; Hungary, 1972; Harrison Vis. Prof., Coll. of William and Mary, Williamsburg, Va, 1969-70; Vis. Prof., St Mary's Coll., St Mary's City, Md, 1976-78. Hon. DLitt: Newfoundland, 1964; New Univ. of Ulster, 1975. *Publications:* The Port Books or Petty Customs Accounts of Southampton for the Reign of Edward IV, 2 vols, 1937-38; The Voyages and Colonising Enterprises of Sir Humphrey Gilbert, 2 vols, 1940; Raleigh and the British Empire, 1947; The Roanoke Voyages, 1584-90, 2 vols, 1955; (with Paul Hulton) The American Drawings of John White, 1577-1590, 1964; (with R. A. Skelton) R. Hakluyt's Principall Navigations (1589), 1965; The Elizabethans and the

Irish, 1966; Richard Hakluyt, Editor, 1967; North American Discovery, 1971; (with W. P. Cumming and R. A. Skelton) The Discovery of North America, 1972; (with N. M. Cheshire) The New Found Land of Stephen Parmenius, 1972; (with A. M. Quinn) Virginia Voyages from Hakluyt, 1973; England and the Discovery of America 1481-1620, 1974; The Hakluyt Handbook, 2 vols, 1974; (with W. P. Cumming, S. E. Hillier and G. Williams) The Exploration of North America, 1630-1776, 1974; The Last Voyage of Thomas Cavendish, 1975; North America from First Discovery to Early Settlements, 1977; contribs on Irish history and the discovery and settlement of N. America in historical journals. *Address:* 9 Knowsley Road, Cressington Park, Liverpool L19 0PF. *T:* 051-427 2041.

QUINN, James Charles Frederick; film producer and exhibitor; *b* 23 Aug. 1919; *m* 1942, Hannah, 2nd *d* of Rev. R. M. Gwynn, BD (Sen. Fellow and Vice-Provost, TCD), and Dr Eileen Gwynn; one *s* one *d*. *Educ:* Shrewsbury Sch.; TCD (Classical Exhibnr); Christ Church, Oxford (MA; Dip. in Econ. and Polit. Sci.). Served War: 1st Bn Irish Guards, N Africa and Italy; Intell. Officer, 1943-44; Adjt, 3rd Bn, NW Europe, 1945; British Army Staff, France, and Town Major, Paris, 1945-46. Courtaulds Ltd, 1949-55. Dir, BFI, 1955-64: National Film Theatre built, London Film Festival inaugurated, and 1st Univ. Lectureship in Film Studies in UK estabd at Slade Sch. of Fine Art, University Coll., London. Council of Europe Fellowship, 1966. Director: Contemporary Cinemas Ltd (Paris Pullman), 1966-; Minema Ltd, 1975-. Chairman: Internat. Short Film Conf., 1971-; National Panel for Film Festivals, 1974-. Member: Gen. Adv. Council, BBC, 1960-64; Bd, Gardner Arts Centre, Sussex Univ., 1968-71. Trustee: Imperial War Museum, 1968-; Grierson Meml Trust, 1975-. Invited to stand by New Ulster Movement as Indep. Unionist Parly candidate, S Down, 1968. Foreign Leader Award, US State Dept, 1962. Films: co-producer, Herostratus, 1966; Producer, Overlord, 1975. Silver Bear Award, Berlin Internat. Film Festival, 1975; Special Award, London Evening News British Film Awards, 1976. *Publications:* Outside London, 1965; The Film and Television as an Aspect of European Culture, 1968; contrib. Chambers's Encyclopaedia (cinema), 1956-59. *Recreations:* lawn tennis, squash racquets; formerly Eton Fives (winner with late L. M. Minford, Public Schools Compettiton, 1938). *Address:* 7 Tregunter Road, SW10. *T:* 01-373 7354; Crescent Cottage, 108 Marine Parade, Brighton, E Sussex. *T:* Brighton 67888. *Clubs:* Cavalry and Guards; Vincent's (Oxford).

QUINNELL, Air Commodore John Charles, CB 1943; DFC 1918; *b* 7 Jan. 1891; *er s* of late John B. Quinnell, Edenburn, Gortatlea, Co. Kerry, Ireland; *m* 1923, Atwell (*d* 1945), *d* of late James McFarlane, Fifeshire, Scotland; no *c*; *m* 1948, Mildred Joan (*d* 1976), widow of Major Cyril Drummond, Cadland Fawley, Southampton, and *d* of late Horace Humphreys. *Educ:* Royal Sch., Dungannon, Co. Tyrone. Commissioned RA 1914; seconded RFC 1915; transferred RAF, 1918. Served European War, 1914-19 (despatches, DFC); RAF Staff Coll., 1924; Imperial Defence Coll., 1929; AOC No 6 Auxiliary Group, 1935-38, and of No 6 Group 1939; Senior Air Staff Officer, Advanced Air Striking Force, 1939-40 (despatches); AOC a Group, RAF, 1942; retired, 1945. Pres., Solent Cruising and Racing Assoc., 1947-; Chm., Solent Area Sailing Adv. Cttee. *Recreations:* shooting, yachting. *Address:* Nelson's Place, Fawley, Southampton, Hants. *T:* Fawley, Hants 891002. *Clubs:* Turf, Royal Thames Yacht; Royal Yacht Squadron.

QUINTON, Anthony Meredith, FBA 1977; President of Trinity College, Oxford, from Aug. 1978; *b* 25 March 1925; *s* of Richard Frith Quinton, Surgeon Captain, RN, and Gwenllyan Letitia Quinton; *m* 1952, Marcelle Wegier; one *s* one *d*. *Educ:* Stowe Sch.; Christ Church, Oxford (St Cyres Scholar; BA 1st Cl. Hons PPE 1948). Served War, RAF, 1943-46: flying officer and navigator. Fellow: All Souls Coll., Oxford, 1949-55; New Coll., Oxford, 1955-78. Delegate, OUP, 1970-76. Vis. Professor: Swarthmore Coll., Pa, 1960; Stnford Univ., Calif, 1964; New Sch. for Social Res., New York, 1976-77. Lecturer: Dawes Hicks, British Acad., 1971; Gregynog, Univ. of Wales, Aberystwyth, 1973; T. S. Eliot, Univ. of Kent, Canterbury, 1976. Pres., Aristotelian Soc., 1975-76. Governor, Stowe Sch., 1963- (Chm. Governors, 1969-75); Fellow, Winchester Coll., 1970-. *Publications:* Political Philosophy (ed), 1967; The Nature of Things, 1973; Utilitarian Ethics, 1973; (trans.) K. Ajdukiewicz (with H. Skolimowski) Problems and Theories of Philosophy, 1973; The Politics of Imperfection, 1978; Thoughts and Thinkers, 1978. *Recreations:* sedentary pursuits. *Address:* Savile House, Mansfield Road, Oxford. *T:* Oxford 42888; (from Aug. 1978) President's Lodgings, Trinity College, Oxford.

QUIRK, Prof. (Charles) Randolph, CBE 1974; MA, PhD, DLit (London); Fil.Dr (Lund and Uppsala); FBA 1975; Quain

Professor of English Language and Literature, University College, London, since 1968; Fellow of University College London; *b* 12 July 1920; *s* of late Thomas and Amy Randolph Quirk, Lambfell, Isle of Man; *m* 1946, Jean, *d* of Ellis Gauntlett Williams; two *s*. *Educ:* Cronk y Voddy Sch.; Douglas High Sch., IOM; University College, London. Served RAF, 1940-45; Lecturer in English, University College, London, 1947-54; Commonwealth Fund Fellow, Yale Univ. and University of Michigan, 1951-52; Reader in English Language and Literature, University of Durham, 1954-58; Professor of English Language in the University of Durham, 1958-60; Professor of English Language in the University of London, 1960-68; Special University Lectures, London, 1960; Director: University of London, Summer School of English, 1962-67; Survey of English Usage, 1959-; Member: Senate, Univ. of London, 1970- (Chm., Acad. Council, 1972-75); Ct, Univ. of London, 1972-75; Admin. Board, British Inst. in Paris; Chairman: Cttee of Enquiry into Speech Therapy Services; British Council English Cttee, 1976-; Mem., BBC Archives Cttee, 1975-. For. Fellow, Royal Belgian Acad. of Scis, 1975. Hon. FCST; Hon. FIL. Jubilee Medal, Inst. of Linguists, 1973. *Publications:* The Concessive Relation in Old English Poetry, 1954; Studies in Communication (with A. J. Ayer and others), 1955; An Old English Grammar (with C. L. Wrenn), 1955, revised edn, 1958; Charles Dickens and Appropriate Language, 1959; The Teaching of English (with A. H. Smith), 1959, revised edn, 1964; The Study of the Mother-Tongue, 1961; The Use of English (with Supplements by A. C. Gimson and J. Warburg), 1962, enlarged edn, 1968; Prosodic and Paralinguistic Features in English (with D. Crystal), 1964; A Common Language (with A. H. Marckwardt), 1964; Investigating Linguistic Acceptability (with J. Svartvik), 1966; Essays on the English Language—Mediaeval and Modern, 1968; (with S. Greenbaum) Elicitation Experiments in English, 1970; (with S. Greenbaum, G. Leech, J. Svartvik) A Grammar of Contemporary English, 1972; The English Language and Images of Matter, 1972; (with S. Greenbaum) A University Grammar of English, 1973; The Linguist and the English Language, 1974; (with V. Adams, D. Davy) Old English Literature: a practical introduction, 1975; contrib. to: Proc. 8th Internat. Congress of Linguists, 1958; Language and Society (Festschrift for Arthur M. Jensen), 1961; Proc. 9th International Congress of Linguists, 1962; English Teaching Abroad and the British Universities (ed G. Bullough), 1961; Dictionaries and that Dictionary (ed J. H. Sledd and W. R. Ebbitt), 1962; World Book Encyclopædia Dictionary (ed C. L. Barnhart), 1963; Early English and Norse Studies (Festschrift for A. H. Smith), 1963; (ed Lady Birkenhead) Essays by Divers Hands, 1969; Essays and Studies, 1970; Charles Dickens (ed S. Wall), 1970; A New Companion to Shakespeare Studies, 1971; Linguistics at Large, 1971; papers in linguistic and literary journals. *Address:* University College, Gower Street, WC1. *T:* 01-387 7050. *Club:* Athenæum.

QUIRK, John Stanton S.; *see* Shirley-Quirk.

QVIST, Dame Frances; *see* Gardner, Dame Frances.

QVIST, George, FRCS; Surgeon, Royal Free Hospital, since 1946, Willesden General Hospital, since 1956, Royal National Throat, Nose and Ear Hospital, since 1950; *b* 13 April 1910; *s* of Emil and Emily Qvist; *m* 1958, Dame Frances Gardner, *qv*. *Educ:* Quintin Sch.; Univ. Coll. Hosp. MB, BS Lond., 1933; FRCS 1934. Surgical Registrar, Royal Free Hospital, 1939-41; Surgeon Emergency Medical Service, 1941-44; Surgical Specialist and O/C Surgical Division, Lieutenant-Colonel RAMC, 1944-46. Member of Council, RCS; Member of Court of Examiners, RCS, 1951-57; Past President, Hunterian Society. Fellow, UCL, 1975. *Publications:* Surgical Diagnosis, 1977; various papers on surgical subjects. *Address:* 72 Harley Street, W1. *T:* 01-580 5265; Fitzroy Lodge, Fitzroy Park, Highgate, N6. *T:* 01-340 5873.

R

RABAUL, Archbishop of, (RC), since 1966, also Metropolitan; Most Rev. **John Hoehne,** MSc, DD; *b* Herbern, Germany, 12 Aug. 1910; *s* of M. Hoehne, Herbern. *Educ:* Germany. Dir, Native Seminary, 1939-45; Parish Priest, Namatanai, New Ireland, 1945-49; Dir, St Mary's, Vuvu, 1949-50; Dir, Kininigunan, 1951-56; Manager General of Catholic Mission, Vunapope, 1956-63; Vicar Apostolic from 1963. Grosses Verdienstkreuz, Federal Republic of Germany. *Publications:*

contribs to Zeitschrift für Neue Missionswissenschaft. *Recreation:* native psychology. *Address:* Archbishop's House, PO Box 414, Rabaul, Papua and New Guinea.

RABBI, The Chief; *see* Jakobovits, Rabbi Dr Immanuel.

RABI, Prof. Isidor Isaac, PhD; University Professor Emeritus, Columbia University, NY; Member: Naval Research Advisory Committee, since 1952; (US Member) Science Committee of United Nations, since 1954; (US Member) Science Committee of NATO, since 1958; General Advisory Committee, Arms Control and Disarmament Agency since 1962; Consultant: to General Advisory Committee, Atomic Energy Commission, since 1956 (Chairman, 1952-56, Member, since 1946); to Department of State, since 1958; etc; *b* Rymanov, Austria, 29 July 1898; *s* of David and Scheindel Rabi; *m* Helen Newmark; two *d. Educ:* Cornell University (BChem 1919); Columbia University (PhD, 1927). Lecturer, Physics, Columbia University, New York, 1929; then various posts, there, 1930-50, when Higgins Professor of Physics until 1964, University Professor, 1964-67. Associate Director, Radiation Laboratory, Massachusetts Institute of Technology, Cambridge, Mass, 1940-45. Mem., National Academy of Sciences; Fellow, American Physics Soc. (Pres., 1950-51). Holds numerous honorary doctorates; awarded medals and prizes, 1939 onwards, including Nobel prize in physics, 1944, Atoms for Peace Award (jointly), 1967. *Publications:* My Life and Times as a Physicist, 1960; communications to The Physical Review, 1927-; contrib. to scientific jls on magnetism, quantum mechanics, nuclear physics, and molecular beams. *Recreations:* the theatre, travel, walking. *Address:* 450 Riverside Drive, New York City, NY 10027, USA. *Clubs:* Athenæum (London); Cosmos (Washington); Century Association (New York).

RABIN, Prof. Brian Robert; Professor of Biochemistry and Head of Department of Biochemistry, University College, London, since 1970; *b* 4 Nov. 1927; *s* of Emanuel and Sophia Rabin, both British; *m* 1954; one *s* one *d. Educ:* Latymer Sch., Edmonton; University Coll., London. BSc 1951, MSc 1952, PhD 1956. University College, London: Asst Lectr, 1954-57; Lectr, 1957-63; Reader, 1963-67; Prof. of Enzymology, 1967-70. Rockefeller Fellow, Univ. of California, 1956-57. *Publications:* numerous in Biochem. Jl, European Jl of Biochem., Nature, Proc. Nat. Acad. Sciences US, etc. *Recreations:* travel, listening to music, carpentry. *Address:* 34 Grangewood, Potters Bar, Herts. *T:* Potters Bar 54576. *Club:* Athenæum.

RABORN, Vice-Adm. William Francis, Jr, DSM 1960; President, W. F. Raborn Company Inc., McLean, Virginia, since 1966; *b* Decatur, Texas, 8 June 1905; *s* of William Francis, Sr, and Mrs Cornelia V. Raborn (*née* Moore); *m* 1955, Mildred T. Terrill; one *s* one *d. Educ:* US Naval Acad., Annapolis, Md (BS); Naval War Coll., Newport, RI. Ensign, USN, 1928; Naval Aviator, 1934; Sea duty, 1928-40; Aviation Gunnery Sch., 1940-42; Exec. Off., USS Hancock, 1943-45; Chief Staff Comdr Task Force 77, W Pacific, 1945-47; Ops Off. Comdr for Air W Coast, 1947-49; R & D Guided Missiles, 1949-50; Guided Missile Div., Office of Naval Ops, 1952-54; CO, USS Bennington, 1954-55; Asst Chief of Staff to C-in-C, Atlantic Fleet, 1955; Dir, Office of Special Projects, Polaris program, 1955; Dep. Chief, Naval Ops (Develt), 1962; retd from USN, 1963; Vice-Pres., Program management Aerojet Gen. Corp., Azusa, Calif, 1963-65; Director of Central Intelligence, USA, 1965-66; Industrial Consultant, Aerojet Gen. Corp. Silver Star, 1945; Bronze Star Medal, 1951; Commendation Medal, 1954; National Security Medal, 1966. *Address:* (home and business) 1606 Crestwood Lane, McLean, Virginia 22101, USA. *Clubs:* Army-Navy, Metropolitan (Washington, DC); Burning Tree (Bethesda, Md); Canyon Country (Palm Springs, Calif).

RABUKAWAQA, Sir Josua Rasilau, KBE 1977 (CBE 1974; MBE 1968); MVO 1970; (first) High Commissioner for Fiji in London, 1970-76; *b* 2 Dec. 1917; *s* of Dr Aisea Rasilau and Adi Mereoni Dimaicakau, Bau, Fiji; *m* 1944, Mei Tolanivutu; three *s* two *d. Educ:* Suva Methodist Boys' Sch.; Queen Victoria Sch.; Teachers' Trng Coll., Auckland. Diploma in Public and Social Admin. 1958. Teaching in schools throughout Fiji, 1938-52; Co-operatives Inspector, 1952. Joined Fiji Mil. Forces, 1953; attached Gloucester Regt at Warminster Sch. of Infantry and Support Weapons Wing, Netheravon; comd Mortar Platoon, Malaya, 1954-55. Subseq. Econ. Develt Officer, Fiji, 1957; District Officer, Fiji Admin. Service, 1961; Comr, Central Div., 1968. MLC, Fiji, 1964-66; Delegate, Constitutional Conf., London, 1965. Active worker for Scouts, Red Cross and Methodist Church Choir. Formed Phoenix Choir. Compiled manual of singing in Fijian language, 1956, and guide for Fijian pronunciation for use by Fiji Broadcasting Commn, 1967; Chm., Fijian Adv. Cttee of Fiji Broadcasting Commn, 1965-70; Chm.

Bd of Examrs for High Standard Fijian and Interpreters Exams, 1965-70; Mem., Housing Authority; Mem., Educn Adv. Council. *Recreations:* cricket, Rugby football (toured NZ as player/manager for Fiji, 1967). *Address:* 6 Vunivivi Hill, Nausori, Fiji. *Clubs:* Royal Commonwealth Society; Defence, Union (Fiji).

RABY, Sir Victor Harry, KBE 1956; CB 1948; MC; Deputy Under-Secretary of State, Department of the Permanent Under-Secretary of State for Air, 1946-57, retired December 1957; *b* 1897; *s* of Harry Raby, Menheniot, Cornwall; *m* 1921, Dorothy Alys, *d* of Rodney Buzzard, Ditchling, Sussex; one *s. Educ:* Grey College, Bloemfontein, S Africa. Served European War, 1914-19, with London Regt (MC). *Address:* The Red House, Fordens Lane, Holcombe, Dawlish, Devon. *Club:* Royal Automobile.

RACE, Robert Russell, CBE 1970; FRS 1952; PhD Cantab, MRCS, FRCP; FRCPath; Director, Medical Research Council Blood Group Unit, Lister Institute, SW1, 1946-73; *b* 28 Nov. 1907; *e s* of late Joseph Dawson Race and late May Race (*née* Tweddle), Kensington; *m* 1st, 1938, Margaret Monica (*d* 1955), *d* of late J. R. C. Rotton, MVO; three *d*; 2nd, 1956, Ruth Ann Sanger, *qv. Educ:* St Paul's School; St Bartholomew's Hosp.; Trinity Hall, Cambridge. Asst Pathologist, Hosp. for Consumption and Diseases of the Chest, Brompton, 1935-37; Asst Serologist, Galton Laboratory, UCL, 1937-39; Asst Dir then Dir, Galton Laboratory Serum Unit, at Dept of Pathology, Cambridge, 1939-46. Mem., Deutsche Akademie der Naturforscher Leopoldina, 1973. Hon. MD: Univ. of Paris, 1965; Univ. of Turku, 1970. Oliver Memorial Award for Blood Transfusion, 1948; Carlos J. Finlay Medal, Republic of Cuba, 1955; Landsteiner Memorial Award, USA, jtly with Ruth Sanger, 1957; Oehlecker Medal, Deutsche Gesellschaft für Bluttransfusion, 1970; Philip Levine Award, USA, jtly with Ruth Sanger, 1970; Conway Evans Prize, Royal Soc. and RCP, 1972; Gairdner Foundn Award, Canada, jtly with Ruth Sanger, 1972. Hon. Fellow, RSM, 1974. Kruis van Verdienst, Netherlands Red Cross, 1959. *Publications:* (with Ruth Sanger) Blood Groups in Man, 1950, 6th edn, 1975; many papers in genetical and medical journals. *Address:* 22 Vicarage Road, East Sheen, SW14 8RU. *T:* 01-876 1508.

RACE, Ruth Ann; *see* Sanger, Dr R. A.

RACE, Steve, (Stephen Russell Race); broadcaster and musician; *b* Lincoln, 1 April 1921; *s* of Russell Tinniswood Race and Robina Race (*née* Hurley); *m* 1st, Marjorie Clair Lang (*d* 1969); one *d*; 2nd, Léonie Rebecca Govier Mather. *Educ:* Lincoln Sch.; Royal Academy of Music. ARAM 1968. Served War, RAF, 1941-46; free-lance pianist, arranger and composer, 1946-55; Light Music Adviser to Associated-Rediffusion Ltd, 1955-60; conductor for many TV series incl. Tony Hancock, Peter Sellers, Alfred Marks and Dickie Henderson Shows. Appearances in radio and TV shows include: My Music, Many A Slip, Music Now, Any Questions, There Goes That Song Again, Major Minor, I Hear Music, Outlook. Dep. Chm., Performing Right Society Ltd. Mem. Council, Royal Albert Hall. Governor, Purcell Sch. for Young Musicians. FRSA 1975. *Principal compositions:* Nicola (Ivor Novello Award); Faraway Music; The Pied Piper; incidental music for Richard The Third, Cyrano de Bergerac, Twelfth Night (BBC); Cantatas: Song of King David; Song of Praise; misc. works incl. ITV advertising sound-tracks (Venice Award, 1962; Cannes Award, 1963); film scores include: Black Friday, Calling Paul Temple, Three Roads to Rome, Against The Tide, Land of Three Rivers. *Recreations:* genealogy, looking at paintings, watching soccer, the open air. *Address:* Martins End Lane, Great Missenden, Bucks HP16 9HS. *T:* Great Missenden 4443.

RACZYNSKI, Count Edward, Dr Juris; Hon. President, The Polish Institute and Sikorski Museum; Chairman, Polish Cultural Foundation, since 1970; *b* 19 Dec. 1891; *s* of Count Edouard Raczynski and Countess Rose Potocka; *m* 1st, 1925, Joyous (*d* 1930), *d* of Sir Arthur Basil Markham, 1st Bt, and Lucy, CBE, *d* of Captain A. B. Cunningham, late RA; 2nd, 1932, Cecile (*d* 1962), *d* of Edward Jaroszynski and Wanda Countess Sierakowska; three *d. Educ:* Universities of Krakow and Leipzig; London School of Economics and Political Science. Entered Polish Ministry of Foreign Affairs, 1919; served in Copenhagen, London, and Warsaw; Delegate to Disarmament Conference, Geneva, 1932-34; Polish Minister accredited to the League of Nations, 1932-34; Polish Ambassador to the Court of St James's, 1934-45; Acting Polish Minister for Foreign Affairs, 1941-42; Minister of State in charge of Foreign Affairs, Cabinet of Gen. Sikorski, 1942-43; Chief Polish Rep. on Interim Treasury Cttee for Polish Questions, 1945-47; Hon. Chief Polish Adviser, Ministry of Labour and National Service, 1952-Dec. 1956; Chairman: Polish Research Centre, London, 1940-67; The

Polish Institute and Sikorski Museum, 1966-76. Grand Officier of the Order of Polonia Restituta, Grand Cross of the Crown of Rumania, etc. *Publications:* In Allied London: Diary 1939-45 (in Polish); In Allied London: (Wartime Diaries), (in English), 1963; Rogalin and its Inhabitants (in Polish), 1963; Pani Róża (in Polish), 1969; Book of Verse (in Polish), 1960; Memoirs of Viridianne Fiszer (translated from French to Polish), 1975; From Narcyz Kulikowski to Winston Churchill (in Polish), 1976. *Recreations:* tennis, golf, skating, ski-ing. *Address:* 8 Lennox Gardens, SW1; 5 Krakowskie Przedmieście, Warsaw, Poland.

RADCLIFFE, Hugh John Reginald Joseph, MBE 1944; Chairman, Dun and Bradstreet Ltd, 1974-76; *b* 3 March 1911; 2nd *s* of Sir Everard Radcliffe, 5th Bt; *m* 1937, Marie Therese, *d* of late Maj.-Gen. Sir Cecil Pereira, KCB, CMG; five *s* one *d.* *Educ:* Downside. Dep. Chm., London Stock Exchange, 1967-70. Kt Comdr St Silvester (Papal), 1965. *Address:* The White House, Stoke, Andover, Hants.
See also Sir S . E . Radcliffe , Bt .

RADCLIFFE, Sir Sebastian Everard, 7th Bt *cr* 1813; *b* 8 June 1972; *s* of Sir Joseph Benedict Everard Henry Radcliffe, 6th Bt, MC and of Marcia Anne Helen, *y d* of Major David Turville Constable Maxwell, Bosworth Hall, Husbands Bosworth, Rugby; *S* father, 1975. *Heir:* uncle Hugh John Reginald Joseph Radcliffe, *qv*. *Address:* Le Château de Cheseaux, 1033 Cheseaux, Vaud, Switzerland.

RADCLYFFE, Sir Charles E. M.; see Mott-Radclyffe.

RADFORD, Courtenay Arthur Ralegh, FBA 1956; *b* 7 Nov. 1900; *o s* of late Arthur Lock and Ada M. Radford; unmarried. *Educ:* St George's School, Harpenden; Exeter College, Oxford. BA 1921; MA 1937; Inspector of Ancient Monuments in Wales and Monmouthshire, 1929-34; Director of the British School at Rome, 1936-39; Member of Royal Commission on Ancient Monuments in Wales and Monmouthshire, 1935-46; Member of Royal Commission on Historical Monuments (England), 1953-76; supervised excavations at Tintagel, Ditchley, Castle Dore, the Hurlers, Whithorn, Glastonbury, Birsay and elsewhere; FSA 1928 (Vice-Pres. 1954-58; Gold Medal, 1972); FRHistS 1930; President: Prehistoric Soc., 1954-58; Roy. Archæological Inst., 1960-63; Cambrian Archæological Assoc., 1961; Soc. of Medieval Archæology, 1969-71. Hon. DLitt Glasgow, 1963; Univ. of Wales, 1963; Exeter, 1973; *Publications:* Reports on the Excavations at Tintagel, Ditchley, Whithorn, etc.; various articles on archæological subjects. *Address:* Culmcott, Uffculme, Devon EX15 3AT. *Club:* Athenæum.

RADFORD, Air Cdre Dudley Spencer, CB 1957; DSO 1944; DFC 1940; AFC 1943; *b* 21 Sept. 1910; *s* of late John Francis Radford and of Alice Radford; *m* 1943, Pamela Biddulph Corr (*née* Padley); two *d.* *Educ:* Bedford School. Pilot training, 1932; No III Fighter Sqdn, 1933-35; trained as flying instructor, 1936, instructional duties, 1936-38; Asst Adjt No 600 City of London Sqdn, 1938; Adjutant No 616 S Riding Sqdn, 1939; OC No 8 Sqdn, Aden, 1940-41; Chief Instructor: No 1 Flying Instructors' School, 1942; No 3 Advanced Flying Unit, 1943; OC No 10 Bomber Sqdn, 1944; RN Staff College course, 1944-45; Group Capt. Trng, HQ Transport Comd, 1945-46; Officer Comdg: RAF Spitalgate, 1947; RAF Wittering, 1948; RAF Liaison Officer, S Rhodesian Govt, 1949-50; Dep. Dir Postings, Air Ministry, 1951-53; idc 1954; Dir of Tactical and Air Transport Ops, 1955-56; Commandant, Central Reconnaissance Establishment, 1957-59; retired 1959. Officer, Order of Leopold (Belgium), 1947. *Address:* New Road Cottage, Prestbury, Cheshire.

RADFORD, Joseph; Assistant Public Trustee, since 1975; *b* 7 April 1918; *s* of Thomas Radford and Elizabeth Ann Radford (*née* Sanders); *m* 1976, Rosemary Ellen Murphy. *Educ:* Herbert Strutt, Belper; Nottingham Univ. Admitted solicitor, 1940. First Cl. Hons, Law Soc. Intermediate, 1937; Dist., Law Soc. Final, 1940. Served War, 1940-47, RA; 41st (5th North Staffordshire) RA; 1st Maritime Regt, RA; Staff, MELF (Major). Joined Public Trustee Office, 1949; Chief Admin. Officer, 1973-75. *Address:* c/o Public Trustee Office, Kingsway, WC2B 6JX. *T:* 01-405 4300.

RADFORD, Robert Edwin; Deputy Secretary and Principal Finance Officer, Department of Health and Social Security, since 1977; *b* 1 April 1921; *s* of late Richard James Radford and late May Eleanor Radford (*née* Briant); *m* 1945, Eleanor Margaret, *d* of late John Idwal Jones; one *s* one *d.* *Educ:* Royal Grammar Sch., Guildford. Board of Educn, 1938. Served War, Lieut, RNVR, 1940-46. Colonial Office: Asst Principal, 1947; Private Sec. to Permanent Under-Sec. of State for the Colonies,

1950-51; Principal, 1951; First Sec., UK Commn, Singapore, 1961-63; Asst Sec., Dept of Techn. Co-op., 1963; transferred to ODM, 1964; Counsellor, British Embassy, Washington, and UK Alternate Exec. Dir, IBRD, 1965-67; Under Secretary: FCO (ODA), 1973; DHSS, 1974-76. *Recreations:* walking, reading. *Address:* Highfield, Nether Mount, Guildford, Surrey GU2 5LL. *T:* Guildford 61822.

RADFORD, Sir Ronald (Walter), KCB 1976 (CB 1971); MBE 1947; Secretary-General, Customs Co-operation Council, from Sept. 1978; *b* 28 Feb. 1916; *er s* of late George Leonard Radford and Ethel Mary Radford; *m* 1949, Jean Alison Dunlop Strange; one *s* one *d.* *Educ:* Southend-on-Sea High Sch.; St John's Coll., Cambridge (Schol., Wrangler, MA). Joined ICS, 1939; Dist Magistrate and Collector, Shahabad, Bihar, 1945; on leave, prep. to retirement from ICS, 1947; Admin. Class, Home CS, and posted to HM Customs and Excise, 1947; Asst Sec., 1953; Comr, 1965; Dep. Chm., 1970; Chm., 1973-77. Chm., Civil Service and PO Lifeboat Fund, 1977-; Mem. Management Cttee, RNLI, 1977-. *Address:* 4 Thomas Close, Brentwood, Essex CM15 8BS. *T:* Brentwood 211567; 40 rue Washington, Brussels, Belgium. *Clubs:* Reform, Civil Service, City Livery; MCC.

RADICE, Edward Albert, CBE 1946; *b* 2 Jan. 1907; *s* of C. A. Radice, ICS and Alice Effie (*née* Murray), DSc (Econ); *m* 1936, Joan Keeling; one *s* one *d.* *Educ:* Winchester Coll.; Magdalen Coll., Oxford. DPhil, Oxford. Commonwealth Fund Fellow, Columbia Univ., New York, 1933-35; Assistant Professor of Economics, Wesleyan University, Middletown, Conn., 1937-39; League of Nations Secretariat, 1939; Ministry of Economic Warfare, 1940-44; HM Foreign Service, 1945-53; Min. of Defence, 1953-70 (Dir of Economic Intelligence, 1966-70); Senior Research Fellow, St Antony's Coll., Oxford, 1970-73. *Publications:* (jt) An American Experiment, 1936; Fundamental Issues in the United States, 1936; Savings in Great Britain, 1922-35, 1939; contribs to Econometrica, Oxford Economic Papers, Economic History Review. *Address:* 2 Talbot Road, Oxford. *T:* Oxford 55573.
See also I. de L. Radice.

RADICE, Fulke Rosavo, CBE 1959; MA; late Vice-Director International Bureau of Universal Postal Union (1946-58); *b* Naples, 8 Feb. 1888; British subject; *s* of Albert Hampden Radice, Thistleborough, NI and Adelaide Anna Teresa (*née* Visetti); *m* 1917, Katharine Stella Mary Speck (*d* 1974) *d* of late Canon J. H. Speck and Mrs Speck (*née* Dalrymple); two *s* (and one *s* killed fighting in French Maquis, 1944). *Educ:* Bedford School (Scholar); Brasenose Coll., Oxford (open scholarship in History; 2nd Cl. Hons Mods (classical), 1909; 1st Cl. Mod. History, 1911). Home Civil Service, 1911; Secretary's Office, Gen. Post Office, 1911-46. Head of Brit. Secretariat of Universal Postal Union Congress, 1929, Head of Congress Secretariat at UPU Congresses, 1947, 1952, 1957. Served European War, 1914-18, in France, Salonica, Egypt, Italy; War of 1939-45 in Home Guard. *Publications:* articles in Nineteenth Century and After, and in History. *Recreations:* rifle shooting (Oxford half blue, Oxford long range; English XX, 1909, 1910; King's Prize at Bisley, gold and silver medals, 1910; record score); Rugby football; ski-ing; freemasonry; historical studies. *Address:* 32 Jersey Avenue, Cheltenham, Glos GL52 2SZ; c/o Coutts & Co., 440 Strand, WC2. *Club:* Bath.

RADICE, Giles Heneage; MP (Lab) Chester-le-Street, since March 1973; *b* 4 Oct. 1936. *Educ:* Magdalen Coll., Oxford. Head of Researach Dept, General and Municipal Workers' Union (GMWU), 1966-73. *Publications:* Democratic Socialism, 1965; (edited jointly) More Power to People, 1968; (co-author) Will Thorne, 1974. *Recreations:* reading, tennis. *Address:* 40 Inverness Street, NW1.

RADICE, Italo de Lisle, CB 1969; Vice Chairman, National Savings Committee, since 1976; Director, Central Trustee Savings Bank Ltd, since 1976; *b* 2 March 1911; *s* of Charles Albert Radice, ICS, and Alice Effie (*née* Murray); *m* 1935, Betty Dawson; three *s* (and one *d* decd). *Educ:* Blundell's School; Magdalen College, Oxford (demy). 1st Cl. Hons Classical Mods, 2nd Cl. Lit Hum, 2nd Cl. PPE. Admitted Solicitor, 1938; Public Trustee Office, 1939; Military Government East and North Africa, Italy, and Germany, 1941-46; Treasury, 1946, Under-Secretary, 1961-68; Sec. and Comptroller General, Nat. Debt Office, 1969-76. *Recreation:* opera going. *Address:* 65 Cholmeley Crescent, N6. *T:* 01-348 4122; Old Post Office, Berrick Salome, Oxford.
See also E. A. Radice.

RADJI, Parviz Camran; diplomat; Ambassador of Iran to the Court of St James's, since 1976; *b* 1936. *Educ:* Trinity Hall, Cambridge (MA Econs). National Iranian Oil Co., 1959-62;

Private Sec. to Minister of Foreign Affairs, 1962-65; Private Sec. to Prime Minister, subseq. Personal Asst, 1965-72; Special Adviser to Prime Minister, 1972-76. *Address:* (home) 26 Princes Gate, SW7; (office) 16 Princes Gate, SW7.

RADLEY-SMITH, Eric John, MS; FRCS; Surgeon: Royal Free Hospital, London; Brentford Hospital; Epsom Hospital; Neurosurgeon, Royal National Throat, Nose and Ear Hospital. *Educ:* Paston; King's College, London; King's College Hospital. MB, BS (Hons, Distinction in Medicine, Surgery, Forensic Medicine and Hygiene), 1933; MS, London, 1936; LRCP, 1933; FRCS 1935 (MRCS 1933). Served War of 1939-45, Wing Comdr i/c Surgical Div. RAFVR. Formerly: Surgical Registrar, King's Coll. Hosp.; House Surgeon, National Hosp. for Nervous Diseases, Queen Square. Examnr in Surgery, Univs of London and West Indies. Mem. Court, RCS. Mem. Assoc. of British Neurosurgeons; Fellow, Assoc. of Surgeons of Great Britain. *Publications:* papers in medical journals. *Recreations:* football and farming. *Address:* Browns Farm, Ramsdell, Basingstoke, Hants. *T:* Tadley 4314.

RADNOR, 8th Earl of, *cr* 1765; **Jacob Pleydell-Bouverie;** Bt 1713-14; Viscount Folkestone, Baron Longford, 1747; Baron Pleydell-Bouverie, 1765; *b* 10 Nov. 1927; *e s* of 7th Earl of Radnor, KG, KCVO, and Helen Olivia, *d* of late Charles R. W. Adeane, CB; *S* father, 1968; *m* 1st, 1953, Anne (marr. diss. 1962), *d* of Donald Seth-Smith, Njoro, Kenya and Whitsbury Cross, near Fordingbridge, Hants; two *s*; 2nd, 1963, Margaret Robin, *d* of late Robin Fleming, Catter House, Drymen; four *d*. *Educ:* Harrow; Trinity Coll., Cambridge (BA Agriculture). *Heir:* *s* Viscount Folkestone, *qv*. *Address:* Longford Castle, Salisbury, Wilts. *T:* Salisbury 29732.

RADO, Prof. Richard; Professor of Pure Mathematics, University of Reading, 1954-71, Emeritus since 1971; Canadian Commonwealth Fellow, University of Waterloo, Ontario, 1971-72; *b* 28 April 1906; 2nd *s* of Leopold Rado, Berlin; *m* 1933, Luise, *e d* of Hermann Zadek, Berlin; one *s*. *Educ:* University of Berlin (DPhil); University of Göttingen; University of Cambridge (PhD). Lecturer, Sheffield Univ., 1936-47; Reader, King's College, Univ. of London, 1947-54. Vis. Prof., Calgary, Alberta, 1973. London Mathematical Society: Mem. of Council, 1948-57; Hon. Sec., 1953-54; Vice-President, 1954-56. FIMA. Sen. Berwick Prize, London Mathematical Soc., 1972. *Publications:* articles in various journals on topics in pure mathematics; *relevant publication:* Festschrift: Studies in Pure Mathematics, ed Prof. L. Mirsky, 1971. *Recreations:* music, reading, walking. *Address:* 14 Glebe Road, Reading RG2 7AG. *T:* 81281.

RADZINOWICZ, Sir Leon, Kt 1970; MA, LLD; FBA 1973; Fellow of Trinity College, Cambridge, since 1948; Wolfson Professor of Criminology, University of Cambridge, 1959-73, and Director of the Institute of Criminology, 1960-72; Associate Fellow, Silliman College, Yale, since 1966; Adjunct Professor of Law and Criminology, Columbia Law School, since 1966; *b* Poland, 15 Aug. 1906; *m* 1933, Irene Szereszewski (marr. diss., 1955); *m* 1958, Mary Ann, *d* of Gen. Nevins, Gettysburg, Pa, USA; one *s* one *d*; naturalised British subject, 1947. *Educ:* Warsaw, Paris, Geneva and Rome. University of Paris, 1924-25; Licencié en Droit, Univ. of Geneva, 1927; Doctor of Law, Rome, 1928; LLD Cambridge, 1951. Lectr, Univ. of Geneva, 1928-31; Doctor of Law, Cracow, 1929; Reported on working of penal system in Belgium, 1930; Lectr, Free Univ. of Warsaw, 1932, and Asst Prof., 1936. Came to England on behalf of Polish Ministry of Justice to report on working of English penal system, 1938; Asst Dir of Research, Univ. of Cambridge, 1946-49; Dir, Dept of Criminal Science, Univ. of Cambridge, 1949-59; Walter E. Meyer Research Prof. of Law, Yale Law Sch., 1962-63; Vis. Prof. and Carpentier Lectr, Columbia Law Sch., Visiting Professor: Virginia Law School, 1968-; Univ. of Pennsylvania, 1970-73; Rutgers Univ., 1970-; Visitor, Princeton Inst. for Advanced Study, 1975. Mem., Conseil de Direction de l'Assoc. Intern. de Droit Pénal, Paris, 1947-; Vice-Pres. Internat. Soc. of Social Defence, 1956-; Head of Social Defence Section, UN, New York, 1947-48. Mem. Roy. Commission on Capital Punishment, 1949-53; Mem. Advisory Council on the Treatment of Offenders, Home Office, 1950-63; Jt Chm., Second UN Congress on Crime, 1955; Chm. Sub-Cttee on Maximum Security in Prisons, 1967-68; Mem. Advisory Coun. on the Penal System, 1966-; Pres. Brit. Acad. of Forensic Sciences, 1960-61; Vice-Pres., 1961-; First Chm. Council of Europe Sci. Cttee, Problems of Crime, 1963-70; Mem. Royal Commn on Penal System in Eng. and Wales, 1964-66; Consultant, President's Nat. Commn on Violence, Washington, 1968-69; Hon. Vice-Chm., Fifth UN Congress on Crime, Geneva, 1975. Hon. LLD Leicester, 1965. For. Hon. Mem., Amer. Acad. of Arts and Sciences, 1973; Hon. For. Mem., Aust. Acad. Forensic Scis,

1973. Coronation Medal, 1953. Chevalier de l'Ordre de Léopold, Belgium, 1930. James Barr Ames Prize and Medal, Faculty of Harvard Law School, 1950; Bruce Smith Sr award, Amer. Acad. Criminal Justice Sciences, 1976; Sellin-Glueck Award, Amer. Assoc. of Criminology, 1976. *Publications:* Sir James Fitzjames Stephen (Selden Soc. Lect.), 1957; In Search of Criminology, 1961 (Italian edn 1965; French edn 1965; Spanish edn 1971); The Need for Criminology, 1965; Ideology and Crime (Carpentier Lectures), 1966, (Italian edn 1968); The Dangerous Offender (Frank Newsam Memorial Lecture), 1968; Editor: History of English Criminal Law, Vol. I, 1948 (under auspices of Pilgrim Trust), Vols II and III, 1956, Vol. IV, 1968 (under auspices of Rockefeller Foundation); (ed with Prof. M. E. Wolfgang) Crime and Justice, 3 vols, 1971, 2nd edn 1977; (with Joan King) The Growth of Crime, 1977; (with Dr R. Hood) Criminology and the Administration of Criminal Justice: a Bibliography (Joseph L. Andrews Award, Amer. Assoc. of Law Libraries 1977), 1976; English Studies in Criminal Science, now Cambridge Studies in Criminology, 35 vols; numerous articles in English and foreign periodicals. *Address:* 21 Cranmer Road, Cambridge. *T:* 56867; Trinity College, Cambridge. *Club:* Athenæum.

RAE, Sir Alexander (Montgomery) Wilson, KCMG 1960 (CMG 1945); MD; Chief MO Colonial Office, 1958-60; *b* 31 Jan. 1896; *s* of late Rev. Robert Rae and Kate Wilson; *m* 1924, Elizabeth Harper, MB, ChB, DPH; one *d*. *Educ:* George Heriot's School; Univ. of Edinburgh. MB, ChB 1921; MD 1929; Resident Medical Officer, North Wales Sanatorium, 1922; West African Medical Staff, 1924-45; Senior Medical Officer, Gambia, 1935-37; Deputy Director of Medical Services, Gold Coast, 1938; Deputy Director of Medical Services, Nigeria, 1939; Deputy Medical Adviser to Secretary of State for the Colonies, 1944. Lieut, Scottish Horse and Imperial Camel Corps, 1914-18. Retired, 1960. *Address:* Field House, Ramsey, Isle of Man. *T:* Ramsey 813414.

RAE, Charles Robert Angus; Under-Secretary, Ministry of Overseas Development, since 1975; *b* 20 Feb. 1922; *s* of Charles E. L. Rae and Gladys M. Horsfall; *m* 1948, Philippa Neild; one *s* two *d*. *Educ:* Eton Coll.; Trinity Coll., Cambridge; London Sch. of Slavonic Studies. BA (Hons History) Cantab, 1945, MA 1948. War service in N Russia, RNVR, 1943-45. Foreign Office, 1947, service in Rome, 1950-54, Mexico City, 1957-59, Moscow, 1959-60; Private Sec. to Parly Under-Sec., 1954-57; seconded to Dept of Technical Co-operation on its formation, 1961; transf. to ODM as Asst Sec., 1964. Chm., Chelsham and Farleigh Parish Council, 1974-. *Recreations:* walking, gardening. *Address:* Henley House, Chelsham, Warlingham, Surrey CR3 9PA. *T:* Upper Warlingham 4268.

RAE, John Malcolm, MA, PhD; Headmaster of Westminster School, since 1970; *b* 20 March 1931; *s* of Dr L. John Rae, radiologist, London Hospital, and late Blodwen Rae; *m* 1955, Daphné Ray Simpson, *d* of John Phimester Simpson; two *s* four *d*. *Educ:* Bishop's Stortford Coll.; Sidney Sussex Coll., Cambridge. MA Cantab 1958; PhD 1965. 2nd Lieut Royal Fusiliers, 1950-51. Asst Master, Harrow School, 1955-66; Dept of War Studies, King's Coll., London, 1962-65; Headmaster, Taunton School, 1966-70. Member Council: Westminster Med. Sch.; Nat. Cttee for Electoral Reform. Chm., HMC, 1977. JP Middlesex, 1961-66. *Publications:* The Custard Boys, 1960; (jtly, film) Reach for Glory (UN Award); Conscience and Politics, 1970; The Golden Crucifix, 1974; The Treasure of Westminster Abbey, 1975; Christmas is Coming, 1976; Return to the Winter Palace, 1977. *Recreations:* writing, swimming, children, cinema. *Address:* 17 Dean's Yard, SW1. *T:* 01-222 6904. *Clubs:* Athenæum; Hawks (Cambridge).

RAE, Robert Wright; Civil Service, retired; Clerk to the General Commissioners of Income Tax, Bromley and Blackheath Divisions, since 1977; *b* 27 March 1914; *s* of Walter Rae and Rachel Scott; *m* 1945, Joan McKenzie (*d* 1966); two *s*. *Educ:* George Heriot's Sch., Edinburgh; Edinburgh Univ. MA 1st cl. hons. Asst Inspector of Taxes, 1936; Dep. Chief Inspector of Taxes, 1973-75; Dir Personnel, Inland Revenue, 1975-77. *Recreations:* gardening, walking. *Address:* Oak Lodge, Blackbrook Lane, Bickley, Bromley BR1 2LP. *T:* 01-467 2377.

RAE, Air Vice-Marshal Ronald Arthur R.; *see* Ramsay Rae.

RAE, Hon. Sir Wallace (Alexander Ramsay), Kt 1976; Agent-General for Queensland, in London, since 1974; grazier, Australia; *b* 31 March 1914; *s* of George Ramsay Rae and Alice Ramsay Rae. *Educ:* Lindfield, Australia. Served War: RAAF Coastal Command, 1939; Pilot, Flt Lt, UK, then OC Test Flight, Amberley, Qld. Mem., Legislative Assembly (Nat. Party of Australia) for Gregory, Qld, 1957-74; Minister for: Local

Govt and Electricity, 1969-74; Lands and Forestry, Qld, 1974. Founder Pres., Pony Club Assoc. of Queensland. *Recreations:* show hacks, golf, bowls. *Address:* Flat 7, 5 Carlton Gardens, SW1Y 5AD. *Clubs:* Surrey County Cricket, East India, Devonshire, Sports and Public Schools, Royal Air Force; United Services, Tattersall's (Brisbane); Longreach (Longreach).
See also Air Vice-Marshal R . A . Ramsay Rae .

RAE SMITH, David Douglas, CBE 1976; MC 1946; MA; FCA; Senior Partner, Deloitte & Co., Chartered Accountants, since 1973 (Partner, 1954); *b* 15 Nov. 1919; *s* of Sir Alan Rae Smith, KBE, and Lady (Mabel Grace) Rae Smith; *m* 1947, Margaret Alison Watson; three *s* one *d*. *Educ:* Radley Coll.; Christ Church, Oxford (MA). FCA 1959. Served War, RA, 1939-46: ME, N Africa and NW Europe; Captain; MC and mentioned in despatches. Chartered accountant, 1950. Hon. Treasurer, RIIA, 1961-. Member: Licensed Dealers Tribunal, 1974-; Council, Radley Coll., 1966- (Chm., 1976-). *Recreations:* horse racing, golf, travel. *Address:* Oakdale, Crockham Hill, Edenbridge, Kent. *T:* Crockham Hill 220. *Club:* Gresham.

RAEBURN, David Antony; Headmaster of Whitgift School, Croydon, since 1970; *b* 22 May 1927; *e s* of late Walter Augustus Leopold Raeburn, QC; *m* 1961, Mary Faith, *d* of Arthur Hubbard, Salisbury, Rhodesia; two *s* one *d*. *Educ:* Charterhouse; Christ Church, Oxford (Schol., MA). 1st cl. hons Hon. Mods, 2nd in Greats. Nat. Service, 1949-51: Temp. Captain, RAEC. Asst Master: Bristol Grammar Sch., 1951-54; Bradfield Coll., 1955-58 (prod. Greek Play, 1955 and 1958); Senior Classics Master, Alleyn's Sch., Dulwich, 1958-62; Headmaster, Beckenham and Penge Grammar Sch., 1963-70 (school's name changed to Langley Park School for Boys, Beckenham in 1969). Chm. Classics Cttee, Schs Council, 1974-. FRSA 1969. *Publications:* articles on Greek play production. *Recreation:* play production. *Address:* Haling Cottage, 76 Brighton Road, South Croydon, CR2 6AB. *T:* 01-688 8114.

RAEBURN, Prof. John Ross, CBE 1972; BSc (Agric.), PhD, MS; FRSE; FIBiol; Strathcona-Fordyce Professor of Agriculture, Aberdeen University, since 1959; Principal, North of Scotland College of Agriculture, since 1963; *b* 20 Nov. 1912; *s* of late Charles Raeburn and Margaret (*née* Ross); *m* 1941, Mary, *o d* of Alfred and Kathrine Roberts; one *s* three *d*. *Educ:* Manchester Grammar School; Edinburgh and Cornell Universities. Professor of Agricultural Economics, Nanking University, 1936-37; Research Officer, Oxford University, 1938-39; Ministry of Food Divisional statistician, 1939-41, Head Agricultural Plans Branch, 1941-46; Senior research officer, Oxford University, 1946-49; Reader in Agricultural Economics, London University, 1949-59. Visiting Professor, Cornell, 1950. Consultant to UN. Member: Agricultural Mission to Yugoslavia, 1951; Mission of Enquiry into Rubber Industry, Malaya, 1954; Colonial Economic Research Committee, 1949-61; Scottish Agricultural Improvement Council, 1960-71; Scottish Agricultural Develt Council, 1971-76; Verdon-Smith Committee, 1962-64; Council, Scottish Agricultural Colls, 1974-. Hon. MA Oxford, 1946. FRSE 1961; FIBiol 1968. Vice-President, International Association of Agricultural Economists, 1964-70; President, Agric. Econ. Society, 1966-67. *Publications:* Preliminary economic survey of the Northern Territories of the Gold Coast, 1950; (jtly) Problems in the mechanisation of native agriculture in tropical African Territories, 1950; research bulletins and contributions to agricultural economic journals. *Recreations:* gardening, travel. *Address:* School of Agriculture, Aberdeen.

RAEBURN, Michael Edward Norman; (4th Bt, *cr* 1923, but does not use the title); *b* 12 Nov. 1954; *s* of Sir Edward Alfred Raeburn, 3rd Bt, and of Joan, *d* of Frederick Hill; *S* father, 1977. *Heir: kinsman* Maj.-Gen. William Digby Manifold Raeburn, *qv* . *Address:* Four Ways, Turners Green, Wadhurst, E Sussex.

RAEBURN, Maj.-Gen. William Digby Manifold, CB 1966; DSO 1945; MBE 1941; Major and Resident Governor, HM Tower of London, and Keeper of the Jewel House, since 1971; *b* 6 Aug. 1915; *s* of late Sir Ernest Manifold Raeburn, KBE, and of Lady Raeburn; *m* 1960, Adeline Margaret (*née* Pryor). *Educ:* Winchester; Magdalene College, Cambridge (MA). Commnd into Scots Guards, 1936; comd 2nd Bn Scots Guards, 1953; Lieut-Col Comdg Scots Guards, 1958; Comdr, 1st Guards Bde Group, 1959; Comdr, 51st Infty Bde Group, 1960; Director of Combat Development (Army), 1963-65; Chief of Staff to C-in-C, Allied Forces, N Europe, 1965-68; Chief Instructor (Army), Imperial Defence College, 1968-70. Freeman of City of London, 1972. *Recreations:* ski-ing, shooting, sailing. *Address:* Queen's House, HM Tower of London, EC3. *Clubs:* White's, Pratt's; Royal Yacht Squadron.

RAFAEL, Gideon; Senior Adviser to Minister for Foreign Affairs of Israel, since 1977; Israeli Ambassador to the Court of St James's, 1973-77, and Ambassador (non-resident) to Ireland, 1975-77; *b* Berlin, 5 March 1913; *s* of Max Rafael; *m* 1940, Nurit Weissberg; one *s* one *d*. *Educ:* Berlin Univ. Went to Israel, 1934; Member, kibbutz, 1934-43; Jewish Agency Polit. Dept, 1943; in charge of prep. of Jewish case for JA Polit. Dept, Nuremberg War Crimes Trial, 1945-46; Member: JA Commn to Anglo-American Commn of Enquiry, 1946, and of JA Mission to UN Special Commn for Palestine, 1947; Israel Perm. Deleg. to UN, 1951-52; Alt. Rep. to UN, 1953; Rep. at UN Gen. Assemblies, 1947-66; Counsellor in charge of ME and UN Affairs, Min. for Foreign Affairs, 1953-57. Ambassador to Belgium and Luxembourg, 1957-60, and to the European Economic Community, 1959. Head, Israel Delegn to 2nd Geneva Conf. on Maritime Law, 1960; Dep. Dir-Gen., Min. of Foreign Affairs, 1960-65; Perm. Rep. to UN and Internat. Organizations in Geneva, Sept. 1965-April 1966; Special Ambassador and Adviser to Foreign Minister, 1966-67; Perm. Rep. to UN, 1967; Dir-Gen., Min. for Foreign Affairs, 1967-71; Head, Israel Delegn to UNCTAD III, 1972; Sen. Polit. Adviser, Foreign Ministry, 1972-73. *Publications:* articles on foreign affairs in Israel and internat. periodicals. *Address:* Ministry for Foreign Affairs, Jerusalem, Israel.

RAGG, Rt. Rev. Theodore David Butler; *see* Huron, Bishop of.

RAGLAN, 5th Baron, *cr* 1852; **FitzRoy John Somerset;** JP; DL; Chairman, Cwmbran Development Corporation, since 1970; *b* 8 Nov. 1927; *er s* of 4th Baron and Hon. Julia Hamilton, CStJ (*d* 1971), *d* of 11th Baron Belhaven and Stenton, CIE; *S* father, 1964; *m* 1973, Alice Baily, *yr d* of Peter Baily, Great Whittington, Northumberland. *Educ:* Westminster; Magdalen College, Oxford; Royal Agricultural College, Cirencester. Captain, Welsh Guards, RARO. Crown Estate Comr, 1970-74. Mem., Cttee of Managers, UK Housing Assoc. Ltd. Pres., Pre Retirement Assoc., 1970-. JP 1958, DL 1971, Gwent (formerly Monmouthshire). *Heir: b* Hon. Geoffrey Somerset [*b* 29 Aug. 1932; *m* 1956, Caroline Rachel, *d* of Col E. R. Hill, *qv* ; one *s* two *d*]. *Address:* Cefntilla Court, Usk, Gwent. *T:* Usk 2050. *Clubs:* Beefsteak, Bugatti Owners, Vintage Sports Car; Usk Farmers'.

RAHIMTOOLA, Sir Fazal Ibrahim, Kt 1946; CIE 1939; MLC; BA; JP; Director: Ahmedabad Advance Mill, Ltd; Tata Power Co. Ltd; Tata Iron & Steel Co., Ltd; Bharat Line, Ltd (Chairman); The Swadeshi Mills, Ltd; Overseas Communications Service (Government of India); New Swadeshi Sugar Mills Ltd; Sultania Cotton Manufacturing Co., Ltd; Dhrangadhra Chemical Works Ltd; Fazalbhai Ibrahim & Co. Prvt Ltd; *b* 21 Oct. 1895; *s* of late Sir Ibrahim Rahimtoola, GBE, KCSI; *m* 1920, Jainabai, *d* of Alimahomed Fazalbhoy. *Educ:* St Xavier's High Sch. and Coll., Bombay; Poona Law Coll. (1st LLB). Mem., Bombay Municipal Corp., 1919-30; Trustee, Bombay Port Trust, 1921-36. Appt by Govt of India on Govt Securities Cttee; Rep. of Bombay Municipal Corp. on BB & CI Rly Advisory Council till 1930; Sec. Indian Imperial Citizenship Assoc.; Mem. Standing Finance Cttee for Railways, Rly Bd; Mem. Haj Inquiry Cttee, 1929; Chm. Reception Cttee of Bombay Presidency Muslim Educ. Conf.; Pres. Urdu Newspapers Assoc.; Rep. Bombay Govt on Cttee of the Sir Harcourt Butler Technological Inst., to advise Govt of UP; Mem. Central Broadcasting Advisory Council till 1930; Mem. Standing Cttee for Haj; Elected Mem., Central Legislative Assembly, 1925-30; appt Actg Pres., Indian Tariff Bd, 1932; Pres. Indian Tariff Bd, 1935; Elected MLA, 1937. Conducted several enquiries, 1930-38, as Mem. and Pres., Indian Tariff Board. Chairman or Mem. numerous Bombay Cttees both during War of 1939-45 and later. Delegate to Indian States on Eastern Group Conf.; Mem. War Risk Insurance Claims Cttee, Govt of India; Mem. Central Food Council and its Standing Cttee; Director, National War Front; Mem. Post-War reconstruction Cttee for Agricultural Research; Chm. Indian Fisheries Cttee; Mem. Price-Fixation Cttee of Govt of India; Mem. Gregory Foodgrains Policy Cttee; Mem. Industrial Policy Cttee (Planning Dept); Mem. All-India Council for Technical Educn; Mem. Nat. Commn for India and its Science Sub-Commn (Unesco); Elected Mem. Bombay Leg. Council, 1948; Sheriff of Bombay, 1950; Deleg. to Unesco Conf., Florence, 1950; Deleg. Internat. Engineering Confs, New Delhi, 1951; Deleg. Symposium for Utilisation of Industrial Wastes; Chm. Deep-sea Fisheries Station, Bombay, Govt of India; Mem. Central Exec. Cttee, Tuberculosis Assoc. of India; Deleg. Govt of India on Fourth Commonwealth TB and Health Conf., London, 1955; Chm., Cttee of Hosts, 38th Internat. Eucharistic Congress. Mem. East India Assoc., London; FRSA. Late Hon. Magistrate. Hon. Consul-Gen. for Thailand in Bombay. Jubilee and Coronation Medals. *Address:* Ismail Buildings, Hornby Road, Fort, Bombay, India. *Clubs:* (Pres.) Matheran, Poona

(India).
See also H. I. Rahimtoola.

RAHIMTOOLA, Habib Ibrahim, BA, LLB, FRPS (Gt Br.); Chairman: Pakistan Red Cross, 1970-73; Pakistan Government Shipping Rates Advisory Board, 1959-71; Diplomatist, Pakistan; *b* 10 March 1912; *s* of late Sir Ibrahim Rahimtoola, GBE, KCSI, CIE, and Lady Kulsum Rahimtoola (*née* Mitha); *m* Zubeida, *d* of Sir Sultan Chinoy; two *s* one *d. Educ:* St Xavier's School and College and Govt Law Coll., Bombay. High Commissioner for Pakistan in London, 1947-52; Ambassador for Pakistan to France, 1952-53; Governor of Sind Province, 1953-54, of Punjab Province, June-Nov. 1954; Minister for Commerce, Central Govt, Nov. 1954-Aug. 1955; Minister for Commerce and Industries, 1955-56. President: Fed. of Muslim Chambers of Commerce and Industry, New Delhi, 1947-48; Bombay Provincial Muslim Chamber of Commerce, 1944-47; Bombay Provincial Muslim League Parly Board for Local Bodies, 1945-47; Young Men's Muslim Association, 1946-47; Bombay Muslim Students' Union, 1946-47-48. Director, Rotary Club, 1944-46; Chairman Membership Committee, 1945-46, Classification Cttee, 1944-45; Member: Govt of India Food Delegation to UK and USA, 1946; Govt of India Policy Cttee on Shipping; Govt of Bombay Housing Panel; Civil Aviation Conference, Govt of India, 1947; Cttee on Trade Policy, Govt of India, 1947; Indian Delegation to Internat. Trade and Employment Conference, Geneva, 1947; alternate Leader Indian Delegation Special Cereals Conference, Paris, 1947; Delegate or Leader of Pakistan Delegations: Inter-Allied Reparations Agency, Brussels, 1947-48-49-50-51; FAO, Geneva, 1947; Dollar Talks, London, 1947; Internat. Trade and Employment Conf., Geneva, 1947; Freedom of Information Conf., Geneva, 1948; Safety of Life at Sea (1948), and Sterling Balance (1948, 1949, 1950, 1951) Confs, London; Prime Ministers' Conferences, London, 1948, 1949, 1951; Foreign Ministers' Conference, Ceylon, 1950; ILO, 1950; Commonwealth Finance Ministers' Conf., 1948-52; SE Asia Conf. on Colombo Plan, 1950; Commonwealth Talks on Japanese Peace Treaty, London, 1950; General Agreement on Tariffs and Trade Conf., 1950-52; Supply Ministers' Conf., London, 1951; UNESCO, Paris, 1953; Afro-Asian Conf., Bandung, 1955; Leader Pakistan Trade Delegation to Brit. E Africa, 1956; Leader, Flood Control Conf., New Delhi, 1956; Chm. Karachi Development Authority, 1958-60; Chm. Water Co-ordination Council, 1958-60. Chm., or Dir, numerous companies. Internat. Counsellor, Lions Internat.; Chairman: Karachi Race Club Ltd, 1958-70 (Pres., 1970-71); Pak-Japan Cultural Assoc., 1959-. District Governor 305W, Lions International, 1964-67. FRSA; FRPS. Order of Sacred Treasure, Japan. *Recreations:* photography, horse racing, golf, tennis. *Address:* Bandenawaz Ltd, Standard Insurance House, I.I. Chundrigar Rd, PO Box 4792, Karachi 2, Pakistan. *T:* 221267; Kulib, KDA 1, Habib I. Rahimtoola Road, Karachi 8. *T:* 412125. *Clubs:* MCC, Royal Automobile; Sind, Boat, Gymkhana (Karachi); Willingdon (Bombay).
See also Sir F. I. Rahimtoola.

RAHMAN, Shaikh Abdur, HPk 1957; Chief Justice Supreme Court of Pakistan, 1st March-4th June 1968, retired; *b* 4 June 1903; *s* of Sh. Ghulam Ali; *m* 1934, Mumtaz Jehan Mohammad Deen; three *s* one *d. Educ:* Punjab Univ. (MA); Oxford Univ. (BA Hons). Entered ICS 1928; served as Asst Comr, Sub-divl Officer, and then as Dist and Sessions Judge in various Districts of Punjab, up to May 1945; Legal Remembrancer and Sec. Legislative Dept, Punjab, up to May 1946; Judge, High Court, Lahore, May 1946; Mem., Bengal Boundary Commn at partition of India and Pakistan, 1947; Custodian of Evacuee Properties, 1947-51; Vice-Chancellor, Punjab Univ., 1950-51; Chief Justice: Lahore High Court, 1954; High Court of W Pakistan, 1955; Judge Supreme Court of Pakistan, 1958. Chairman Agartala case Special Tribunal (latter part), 1968; finally retd Feb. 1969. Dir, Inst. of Islamic Culture, Lahore; Chm., Bd for Advancement of Literature, Punjab, Lahore; Vice-Chm., Bazoni Iqbal Lahore. Holds hon. doctorates. *Publications:* Tarjuman-i-Asrar (trans. into Urdu verse of Sir Mohammad Iqbal's Persian, Asrari-Khudi), 1952; Hadith-i-Dil (collection of addresses in Urdu), 1963; Safar (collection of original poems in Urdu), 1964; Punishment of Apostasy in Islam, 1972. *Recreations:* writing and participation in cultural activities. *Address:* 65 Main Gulberg, Lahore, Pakistan. *T:* Lahore 80109. *Club:* Gymkhana (Lahore).

RAHMAN PUTRA, Tunku (Prince) Abdul; *see* Abdul Rahman Putra.

RAIKES, Sir (Henry) Victor (Alpin MacKinnon), KBE 1953; *b* 19 Jan. 1901; *s* of late H. St John Raikes, CBE, KC; *m* 1940, Audrey Elizabeth Joyce, *o d* of A. P. Wilson, Repton; two *d.*

Educ: Westminster School; Trinity Coll., Cambridge (BA). Called to Bar, Inner Temple, 1924; contested (C) Ilkeston Division of Derbyshire, 1924 and 1929; MP (C) SE Essex, 1931-45; MP (C) Wavertree Division of Liverpool, 1945-50, Garston Division of Liverpool, 1950-57 (Ind C 1957). Chm., Monday Club, 1975-. Flight Lieut RAFVR, 1940-42. JP Derbyshire, 1927. Kt of Malta, Order of St John of Jerusalem, 1970. *Address:* 8 Gledhow Gardens, SW5. *Clubs:* Carlton, MCC.

RAIKES, Vice-Adm. Sir Iwan (Geoffrey), KCB 1976; CBE 1967; DSC 1943; Flag Officer Submarines, and Commander Submarines, Eastern Atlantic Area, 1974-76; retired 1977; *b* 21 April 1921; *s* of Adm. Sir Robert Henry Taunton Raikes, KCB, CVO, DSO, and Lady (Ida Guinevere) Raikes; *m* 1947, Cecilia Primrose Hunt; one *s* one *d. Educ:* RNC Dartmouth. Entered Royal Navy, 1935; specialised in Submarines, 1941; Comdr, 1952; Captain, 1960; Rear-Adm., 1970; Naval Sec., 1970-72; Vice-Adm., 1973; Flag Officer, First Flotilla, 1973-74. *Recreations:* shooting, fishing, sailing, skiing, tennis. *Address:* Aberyscir Court, Brecon, Powys. *Club:* Naval and Military.

RAIKES, Sir Victor; *see* Raikes, Sir H. V. A. M.

RAILTON, Brig. Dame Mary, DBE 1956 (CBE 1953); *b* 28 May 1906; *d* of late James and Margery Railton. *Educ:* privately. Joined FANY, 1938; commissioned in ATS, 1940; WRAC 1949; Director WRAC, 1954-57; Deputy Controller Commandant, 1961-67. *Address:* 1 Frogmore Cottages, Great Bedwyn, Marlborough, Wilts.

RAILTON, Dame Ruth, DBE 1966 (OBE 1954); Founder and Musical Director of the National Youth Orchestra and National Junior Music School, 1947-65; Professor, Chopin Conservatoire, Warsaw, since 1960; *b* 14 Dec. 1915; *m* 1962, Cecil Harmsworth King, *qv. Educ:* St Mary's School, Wantage; Royal Academy of Music, London. Director of Music or Choral work for many schools and societies, 1937-49; Adjudicator, Fedn of Music Festivals, 1946-74; Governor, Royal Ballet School, 1966-74. Hon. Prof., Conservatoire of Azores, 1972. FRAM 1956; Hon. RMCM 1959; Hon. FRCM 1965; Hon. FTCL 1969. Hon. LLD Aberdeen Univ., 1960. *Recreations:* interested in everything. *Address:* The Pavilion, Greenfield Park, Dublin 4. *T:* Dublin 695870.

RAINBIRD, George Meadus; Deputy Chairman of Thomson Publications Ltd, since 1973, Director, since 1969; author and publisher; *b* 22 May 1905; *s* of Leonard Rainbird and Sarah (*née* Meadus); *m* 1st, 1926, Eva Warner (marr. diss.); one *s* two *d*; 2nd, 1939, Joyce Trinder (*d* 1970); two *s* one *d*; 3rd, 1972, Lena Wickman. *Educ:* local grammar school. Founded publishing house, George Rainbird Ltd, 1951; acquired Zaehnsdorf Ltd and Wigmore Bindery Ltd, 1954-56; merged with Thomson Organization, 1965. Chairman: Thos Nelson & Sons Ltd, 1970-75; George Rainbird Ltd, 1970-75; Rainbird Reference Books Ltd, 1970-75; Sphere Books Ltd, 1970-75; Michael Joseph Ltd, 1970-75; Westerham Press Ltd, 1972-75; Dir, Hamish Hamilton Ltd. Chm., International Wine and Food Soc., 1964-72. *Publications:* Escape to Sunshine, 1952; A Pocket Book of Wine, 1963, (with Ronald Searle) repr. as The Subtle Alchemist, 1973; Sherry and the Wines of Spain, 1966. *Recreations:* books, gardens and wine. *Address:* Whichford House, Shipston-on-Stour, Warwicks. *T:* Long Compton 285; A15 Albany, W1. *T:* 01-734 0143. *Clubs:* Brooks's, Saintsbury.

RAINBOW, James Conrad Douglas; Chief Education Officer, Lancashire, since 1974; *b* 25 Sept. 1926; *s* of Jack Conrad Rainbow and Winifred Edna (*née* Mears); *m* 1974, Kathleen Margaret (*née* Holmes); one *s* one *d. Educ:* William Ellis Sch., Highgate; Selwyn Coll., Cambridge (MA). Asst Master, St Paul's Sch., London, 1951-60; HM Inspector of Schools, 1960-69; Dep. Chief Educn Officer, Lancashire, 1969-74. Member: Court and Council Univ. of Lancaster; Governing Body, Centre for Educational Disadvantage. *Publications:* various articles in educnl jls. *Recreations:* rowing (now as an observer), music, reading. *Address:* 145 Inner Promenade, St Annes on Sea, Lancs. *T:* St Annes 721491. *Clubs:* Royal Commonwealth Society; Leander.

RAINE, (Harcourt) Neale; Chairman, Technician Education Council, since 1976; *b* 5 May 1923; *s* of late Harold Raine and Gertrude Maude Healey; *m* 1947, Eileen Daphne, *d* of A. A. Hooper; one *s. Educ:* Dulwich and London. MSc (Eng) London; CEng, MICE, FIMC. Various appts as professional civil engr, 1947-52; Industrial Management Consultant with Production Engrg Ltd, 1953-59; Jt Man. Dir, Mycalex & TIM Ltd, 1959-63; Chief Exec., Car Div., Wilmot Breedon Ltd, 1963; Management Consultancy in assoc. with Production Engrg Ltd, 1964-65; Dep. Man. Dir, 1965, later Chm. and Man. Dir, Brico Engrg Ltd

(Associated Engrg Gp); Chm., Coventry Radiator & Presswork Co. Ltd (Associated Engrg Gp), 1968-70; Man. Dir, Alfred Herbert Ltd, 1970-75. Dir, Associated Engineering Ltd and Man.-Dir of Gen. Div., 1968-70. Pres., Coventry and District Engrg Employers' Assoc., 1975-77 (Dep. Pres., 1973-75); Governor, Lanchester Polytechnic, Coventry and Rugby, 1970-. *Address:* Penn Lea, The Avenue, Charlton Kings, Cheltenham, Glos. *T:* Cheltenham 26185.

RAINE, Kathleen Jessie, (Mrs Madge), FRSL; poet; *b* 1908; *o d* of late George Raine, schoolmaster, and Jessie Raine; *m* Charles Madge (marr. diss.); one *s* one *d. Educ:* Girton College, Cambridge. Hon. DLitt Leicester, 1974. *Publications:* Stone and Flower, 1943; Living in Time, 1946; The Pythoness, 1949; The Year One, 1952; Collected Poems, 1956; The Hollow Hill (poems), 1965; Defending Ancient Springs (criticism), 1967; Blake and Tradition (Andrew Mellon Lectures, Washington, 1962), Princeton 1968, London 1969; (with George Mills Harper) Selected Writings of Thomas Taylor the Platonist, Princeton and London, 1969; William Blake, 1970; The Lost Country (verse), 1971 (W. H. Smith & Son Award, 1972); On a Deserted Shore (verse), 1973; Yeats, the Tarot and The Golden Dawn (criticism), 1973; Faces of Day and Night, 1973; Farewell Happy Fields (autobiog.), 1973; Death in Life and Life in Death (criticism), 1974; The Land Unknown (autobiog.), 1975; The Oval Portrait (verse), 1977; The Lion's Mouth (autobiography), 1977; contributions to literary journals. *Address:* 47 Paultons Square, SW3. *Club:* Pen.

RAINE, Neale; *see* Raine, H. N.

RAINER, Luise; Actress; *b* Vienna, 12 Jan.; *d* of Heinz Rainer; *m* 1937, Clifford Odets, (*d* 1963) (from whom she obtained a divorce, 1940); *m* 1945, Robert, *s* of late John Knittel; one *d. Educ:* Austria, France, Switzerland and Italy. Started stage career at age of sixteen under Max Reinhardt in Berlin; later was discovered by Metro-Goldwyn-Mayer talent scout in Vienna; came to Hollywood; appeared in Escapade; starred in The Great Ziegfeld, The Good Earth, Emperor's Candlesticks, Big City, Toy Wife (Frou Frou); received Motion Picture Academy of Arts and Sciences Award for the best feminine performance in 1936 and 1937. *Recreation:* mountain climbing. *Address:* 34 Eaton Mews North, SW1. *T:* 01-235 4263.

RAINEY, Dr Reginald Charles, FRS 1975; Senior Principal Scientific Officer, Centre for Overseas Pest Research, Ministry of Overseas Development (formerly Anti-Locust Research Centre), since 1958; *b* 18 June 1913; *s* of Charles Albert Rainey and Ethel May Rainey; *m* 1943, Margaret Tasman; three *s* (one *d* decd). *Educ:* Purbrook Park County High Sch., Hants; Imperial Coll. of Science and Technology (ARCS); London Sch. of Hygiene and Trop. Med. DSc London; FIBiol. Res. biologist, Empire Cotton Growing Corp., Transvaal, 1938-40 and 1946-49; Meteorological Officer, S African Air Force, S and E Africa and ME, 1940-46; Sen. Entomologist, Desert Locust Survey, E Africa High Commn (res. and develt work on use of meteorology and aircraft in forecasting and control of desert locust invasions), 1949-58; i/c FAO Desert Locust Inf. Service (desert locust forecasting, with co-operation and support of countries concerned, in Africa and Asia), 1960-67; res. and develt work on use of meteorology and aircraft in forecasting and control of other insect pests, with co-operation and support of E African Agric. and Forestry Res. Org., Sudan Gezira Bd, Canadian Forestry Service and Agricl Aviation Res. Unit (Ciba-Geigy Ltd), Cranfield Coll. of Aeronautics, 1967-. Fitzroy Prize, Royal Meteorological Soc., 1971. *Publications:* Meteorology and the Migration of Desert Locusts. 1963; (ed) Insect Flight, 1975; papers in sci. jls. *Recreations:* flying (PPL 1934-69); small boats. *Address:* Elmslea, Old Risborough Road, Stoke Mandeville, Bucks. *T:* Stoke Mandeville 2493.

RAINS, Prof. Anthony John Harding, MS, FRCS; Professor of Surgery in the University of London at Charing Cross Hospital Medical School, since Oct. 1959; Hon. Surgeon Charing Cross Hospital; Hon. Consultant Surgeon to the Army; *b* 5 Nov. 1920; *s* of late Dr Robert Harding Rains and Mrs Florence Harding Rains; *m* 1943, Mary Adelaide Lillywhite; three *d. Educ:* Christ's Hospital School, Horsham; St Mary's Hospital, London. MB, BS London, MRCS, LRCP 1943. Ho. Surg. and Ho. Phys. St Mary's, 1943. RAF, 1944-47. Ex-Service Registrar to Mr Handfield-Jones and Lord Porritt, 1947-48. FRCS 1948; Res. Surgical Officer, Bedford County Hosp., 1948-50; Lectr in Surgery, Univ. of Birmingham, 1950-54, Sen. Lectr, 1955-59. MS (London) 1952. Hon. Consulting Surgeon, United Birmingham Hospitals, 1954-59. Dean, Inst. of Basic Med. Scis; Chm., Med. Commn on Accident Prevention. Mem. Council and Mem. Court of Examiners, RCS. Sir Arthur Keith medal, RCS. Editor, Annals of RCS. *Publications:* Gallstones: Causes

and Treatment; Urgencies and Emergencies for Nurses; (ed with Dr P. B. Kunkler) The Treatment of Cancer in Clinical Practice; (ed) Bailey and Love's Short Practice of Surgery; Edward Jenner and Vaccination; articles on the surgery of the gall bladder, on the formation of gall stones, inguinal hernia and arterial disease. *Recreations:* music, country garden, painting. *Address:* Charing Cross Hospital Medical School, Fulham Palace Road, W6 8RF. *T:* 01-748 2050; The Old Rectory, Walton on the Hill, Tadworth, Surrey KT20 7RZ. *T:* Tadworth 2840.

RAINSFORD, Surg. Rear-Adm. (retd) Seymour Grome, CB 1955; FRCPath 1964; Research Fellow in Hæmophilia, Wessex Regional Hospital Board, 1967; *b* 24 April 1900; *s* of Frederick Edward Rainsford, MD, Palmerstown Hse, Co. Dublin; *m* 1st, 1929, Violet Helen (*née* Thomas) (decd); 2nd, 1972, Caroline Mary Herschel (*née* Hill). *Educ:* St Columba's College, Co. Dublin; Trinity College, Dublin. MD 1932; ScD 1939; DPH 1937; FRCPath 1964; FRCP 1977. Joined RN as Surg. Lieut, 1922. North Persian Forces Memorial Medal, for research on Mediterranean Fever, 1933; Gilbert Blane Gold Medal for research on Typhoid Fever, 1938; Chadwick Gold Medal and Prize for research on typhoid vaccine and on blood transfusion in the Royal Navy, 1939. Surgeon Rear-Adm. 1952; Deputy Medical Director-General of the Royal Navy, 1952-55. Chevalier de la Légion d'Honneur, 1948; CStJ 1955. *Publications:* papers on typhoid fever and other tropical diseases, haematology, blood transfusion and physiological problems concerned in diving and submarine escape, in Jl Hygiene, Lancet, BMJ and Journal RN Med. Serv. *Recreations:* shooting, golf. *Address:* Applegate, Frith End, near Bordon, Hants. *Club:* Army and Navy.

RAINWATER, Prof. (Leo) James; Professor of Physics, Columbia University, New York, since 1952; *b* 9 Dec. 1917; *s* of Leo Jasper Rainwater and Edna Eliza (*née* Teague); *m* 1942, Emma Louise Smith; three *s. Educ:* California Inst. of Technol.; Columbia Univ., NY (BS, MA, PhD). Asst in Physics, 1939-42, Instr 1946-47, Asst Prof. 1947-49, Assoc. Prof., 1949-52, Columbia Univ.; Scientist, OSRD and Manhattan Project, 1942-46; Dir, Nevis Cyclotron Lab., 1951-53 and 1956-61; scientific and US naval research and research contracts with Atomic Energy Commn and Nat. Science Foundn, 1947-. Fellow: Amer. Phys. Soc.; AAAS; IEEE; NY Acad. of Science; Member: Nat. Acad of Scis, Optical Soc. of Amer. Ernest Orlando Lawrence Physics Award, US Atomic Energy Commn, 1973; (jtly) Nobel Prize for Physics, 1975. *Recreations:* classical music, environmental problems, astronomy. *Publications:* numerous articles in Phys. Review 46, and other professional jls. *Address:* Physics Department, Columbia University, New York, NY 10027. *T:* 918-LYI-8100; (home) 342 Mt Hope Boulevard, Hastings-on-Hudson, NY 10706, USA. *T:* 914-GR8-1368.

RAIS, Tan Sri Abdul J.; *see* Jamil Rais.

RAISMAN, Sir (Abraham) Jeremy, GCMG 1959; GCIE 1945 (CIE 1934); KCSI 1941 (CSI 1938); Kt 1939; Commonwealth Trust Ltd; *b* 19 March 1892; *m* 1925, Renée Mary Kelly; two *s. Educ:* Leeds High School and University; Pembroke College, Oxford. MA (1st Class Mods 1st Lit Hum); John Locke Scholar in Moral Philosophy, 1915; joined ICS 1916; served in Bihar and Orissa till 1922; Customs Department Bombay and Calcutta, 1922-28; Commissioner of Income-Tax, Punjab and NWFP, 1928-31; Joint Secretary, Commerce Department, Government of India, 1931-34; Member Central Board of Revenue, 1934; Director, Reserve Bank of India, 1938; Secretary, Finance Dept, 1938-39; Finance Member of Govt of India, 1939-45; and Vice-President, Govr-Genl's Executive Council, 1944. Chairman, British Indian delegation to International Monetary Conference, Bretton Woods, USA, June-July 1944; retired from India, 1945; led UK Treasury Mission to India and Pakistan, Jan.-Feb. 1948; adviser to Govt of Pakistan on distribution of Central and Provincial revenues, Nov.-Dec. 1951; Chairman: Fiscal Commn for Federation of Rhodesia and Nyasaland, 1952; Nigeria Fiscal Commn, 1957-58; Economic and Fiscal Commn for East Africa, 1960-61. Comr, Public Works Loans Board, 1947, Chairman, 1948-70. Vice-Chm., Lloyds Bank Ltd, 1947-53, Dep.-Chm., 1953-63. Hon. LLD Leeds. Hon. Fellow of Pembroke College, Oxford. *Address:* Fieldhead, Shamley Green, Surrey. *T:* Bramley 3128. *Clubs:* Athenæum, Reform.

RAISON, Dr John Charles Anthony, MA, MD; Chief Scientific Officer (Under-Secretary), Scientific Services, Department of Health, since 1974; *b* 13 May 1926; *s* of late Cyril A. Raison, FRCS, Edgbaston, Birmingham, and of Ceres Raison; *m* 1951, Rosemary, *d* of Edgar H. Padmore, MC, Edgbaston, and Marjorie Padmore; one *s* two *d. Educ:* Malvern Coll.; Trinity Hall, Cambridge; Birmingham Univ. MA, MD; MFCM. Consultant Clinical Physiologist in Cardiac Surgery,

Birmingham Reg. Hosp. Bd, 1962; Hon. Associate Consultant Clinical Physiologist, United Birmingham Hosps, 1963; Sen. Physiologist, Dir of Clinical Res. and Chief Planner, Heart Research Inst., Presbyterian-Pacific Medical Center, San Francisco, 1966; Vis. Consultant, Civic Hosps, Lisbon (Gulbenkian Foundn), 1962; Arris and Gale Lectr, RCS, 1965. Councillor, Southam RDC, 1955-59. Fellow Royal Soc. Med. Mem., Thoracic Soc. *Publications:* chapters in books, and papers in medical jls on open-heart surgery, extracorporeal circulation, intensive care, and computers in medicine. *Recreations:* sailing, theatre, thoroughbred breeding and racing. *Address:* Oaklea Paddock, Bramshott, near Liphook, Hants GU30 7RF. *T:* Liphook 722543.

RAISON, Timothy Hugh Francis; MP (C) Aylesbury since 1970; *b* 3 Nov. 1929; *s* of Maxwell and late Celia Raison; *m* 1956, Veldes Julia Charrington; one *s* three *d. Educ:* Dragon Sch., Oxford; Eton (King's Schol.); Christ Church, Oxford (Open History Schol.). Editorial Staff: Picture Post, 1953-56; New Scientist, 1956-61; Editor: Crossbow, 1958-60; New Society, 1962-68. Member: Youth Service Develt Council, 1960-63; Central Adv. Council for Educn, 1963-66; Adv. Cttee on Drug Dependence, 1966-70; Home Office Adv, Council on Penal System, 1970-74; (co-opted) Inner London Educn Authority Educn Cttee, 1967-70; Richmond upon Thames Council, 1967-71. PPS to Sec. of State for N Ireland, 1972-73; Parly Under-Sec. of State, DES, 1973-74; Opposition spokesman on the Environment, 1975-76. Sen. Fellow, Centre for Studies in Soc. Policy, 1974-77; Consultant, Selection Trust, 1977-. Nansen Medal (for share in originating World Refugee Year), 1960. *Publications:* Why Conservative?, 1964; (ed) Youth in New Society, 1966; (ed) Founding Fathers of Social Science, 1969; various political pamphlets. *Recreation:* golf. *Address:* 2 Mill Hill Road, Barnes, SW13. *T:* 01-876 2840. *Clubs:* Beefsteak, MCC.

RAITZ, Vladimir Gavrilovich; Managing Director, Medallion Holidays, since 1976; *b* 23 May 1922; *s* of Dr Gavril Raitz and Cecilia Raitz; *m* 1954, Helen Antonia (*née* Corkrey); three *d. Educ:* Mill Hill Sch.; London University. BSc(Econ.), Econ. History, 1942. British United Press, 1942-43; Reuters, 1943-48; Chm., Horizon Holidays, 1949-74. Member: NEDC for Hotels and Catering Industry, 1968-74; Cinematograph Films Council, 1969-74; Ct of Governors, LSE, 1971-. Cavaliere Ufficiale, Order of Merit (Italy), 1971. *Recreations:* reading, ski-ing. *Address:* 53 St John's Avenue, SW15. *T:* 01-788 1728. *Club:* Reform.

RAJ, Prof. Kakkadan Nandanath; Fellow, Centre for Development Studies, Trivandrum, Kerala State, since 1973; *b* 13 May 1924; *s* of K. N. Gopalan and Karthiayani Gopalan; *m* 1957, Dr Sarasamma Narayanan; two *s. Educ:* Madras Christian Coll., Tambaram (BA (Hons), MA, in Economics); London Sch. of Economics (PhD (Econ). Asst Editor, Associated Newspapers of Ceylon, Nov. 1947-July 1948; Research Officer, Dept of Research, Reserve Bank of India, Aug. 1948-Feb. 1950; Asst Chief, Economic Div., Planning Commn, Govt of India, 1950-53; Prof. of Economics, Delhi Sch. of Economics, Univ. of Delhi, 1953-73 (Vice-Chancellor, Univ. of Delhi, 1969-70; Nat. Fellow in Economics, 1971-73). Visiting Prof., Johns Hopkins Univ., Jan.-June, 1958; Vis. Fellow, Nuffield Coll., Oxford, Jan.-June, 1960; Corresp. Fellow, British Academy, 1972. Hon. Fellow, Amer. Economic Assoc. *Publications:* The Monetary Policy of the Reserve Bank of India, 1948; Employment Aspects of Planning in Underdeveloped Economies, 1956; Some Economic Aspects of the Bhakra-Nangal Project, 1960; Indian Economic Growth-Performance and Prospects, 1964; India, Pakistan and China-Economic Growth and Outlook, 1966; Investment in Livestock in Agrarian Economies, 1969; also articles in Economic Weekly, Economic and Political Weekly, Indian Economic Review, Oxford Economic Papers. *Address:* Nandavan, Dalavakunnu, Kumarapuram, Trivandrum 695011, Kerala State, India. *T:* (home) 62409, (office) 8881-8884.

RAJAH, Arumugam Ponnu; Lawyer, in practice in Singapore, since 1973; *b* Negri Sembilan, Malaysia, 23 July 1911; *m* Vijaya Lakshmi; one *s* one *d. Educ:* St Paul's Inst., Seremban; Raffles Instn, Singapore; Oxford Univ. (BA). Barrister-at-law, Lincoln's Inn. City Councillor, Singapore: nominated, 1947-49; elected, 1949-57; MLA, Singapore, 1959-66, Speaker, 1964-66; first High Comr for Singapore to UK, 1966-71; High Comr to Australia, 1971-73. Mem. Bd of Trustees, Singapore Improvement Trust, 1949-57; Mem., Raffles Coll. Coun. and Univ. of Malaya Coun., 1955-63; Chm., Public Accounts Cttee of Legislative Assembly, 1959-63. *Address:* c/o Ministry of Foreign Affairs, Singapore.

RAKE, Alfred Mordey, CBE 1953; *b* 27 March 1906; *s* of Dr H. V. Rake, Fordingbridge, Hants; *m* 1st, 1930, Gwendolen (*d*

1944), *d* of late Edward Craig-Hall, Hove, Sussex; three *s*; 2nd, 1947, Jean Mary, *d* of late F. G. Kingsland, Thornton Heath, Surrey; two *d. Educ:* King's School, Canterbury; Corpus Christi College, Cambridge. 1st Cl. Hons Classical Tripos Pt 1, 1927; Cauldwell Scholar, 1927; 1st Cl. Hons (with distinction) Classical Tripos Pt II, 1928; Asst Principal, Min. of Transport, 1930; Private Sec. to Parliamentary Sec., 1935; Principal, 1936; Asst Sec., 1941; transferred to Min. of Fuel and Power, 1946; Under Secretary, 1955; retired, 1966. *Recreation:* gardening. *Address:* The White House, Whimple, Devon. *T:* Whimple 822560.

RALEIGH, Nigel Hugh C.; *see* Curtis-Raleigh.

RALLI, Sir Godfrey (Victor), 3rd Bt, *cr* 1912; TD; *b* 9 Sept. 1915; *s* of Sir Strati Ralli, 2nd Bt, MC; *S* father 1964; *m* 1st, 1937, Nora Margaret Forman (marriage dissolved, 1947); one *s* two *d*; 2nd, 1949, Jean, *er d* of late Keith Barlow. *Educ:* Eton. Joined Ralli Bros Ltd, 1936. Served War of 1939-45 (despatches), Captain, Berkshire Yeomanry RA. Director and Vice-Chairman, Ralli Bros Ltd, 1946-62; Chm., Greater London Fund for the Blind. *Recreations:* fishing, golf. *Heir: s* David Charles Ralli [*b* 5 April 1946; *m* 1975, Jacqueline Cecilia, *d* of David Smith]. *Address:* Great Walton, Eastry, Sandwich, Kent. *T:* Eastry 355. *Clubs:* White's, Flyfishers'.

RALPH, Ronald Seton, MRCS, LRCP, DPH; retired; late Consultant Pathologist Battersea and Putney Group of Hospitals; Hon. Pathologist, Eltham and Mottingham Cottage Hospital; *b* Saugor, India, 22 July 1895; *s* of late Col A. C. Ralph, DSO; *m* 1918, Marjorie, *d* of late Dr Joseph Bott, Richmond, Surrey; one *s. Educ:* Dover College; Guy's Hospital. Late Director of Clinical Research Assoc. Laboratories; late Clinical Pathologist, St John's Hospital, Lewisham, SE13; late Assistant Bacteriologist, Guy's Hospital, and late Physician in Charge of Diseases of the Skin, St John's Hospital, SE13. *Publications:* various on medical subjects in Lancet, Medical World, and Journal of Clinical Research. *Address:* Cotswold, Haywards Heath, West Sussex. *T:* Haywards Heath 3446.

RALPHS, Sir (Frederick) Lincoln, Kt 1973; PhD; Chief Education Officer, for Norfolk, 1950-74; Chairman of Schools Council, 1972-75; Hon. General Secretary, British Association, since 1973; Chairman of Board, Homerton College, Cambridge, since 1970; *b* 17 Feb. 1909; *s* of Frederick and Elizabeth Anne Ralphs; *m* 1938, Enid Mary Cowlin; one *s* two *d. Educ:* Firth Park Grammar Sch.; Univ. of Sheffield. MSc, PhD, LLB, DipEd, FCP. Leader, Univs debating team to USA, 1933; Past Pres.: Student Union, Sheffield, 1934; NUS, 1935-37; Internat. Confedn of Students (Vice Pres., 1935-37, Pres. 1937-38). Dep. Regional Officer for London and SE, MOI, 1942. Town Trustee Research Fellow, Univ. of Sheffield, 1936-38; Teacher and Lectr, 1938-; Life Vice-Pres., Assoc. of Educn Cttees. Pres., Nat. Adv. Council on Educn for Industry and Commerce. Vice-Pres., WEA, 1967-. Past Pres.: County Educn Officers Soc.; Assoc. of Chief Educn Officers; Educn Section of British Assoc.; Nat. Sunday Sch. Union. Chm. Governors, Culford Sch. DUniv Surrey, 1975; Hon. DSc Lancaster, 1976. Gold Medal, Phys. Educn, Paris, 1935; Officier d'Académie, Paris. *Publications:* Young Minds for Old, 1938; many articles in various jls. *Recreations:* gardening, travel. *Address:* Jesselton, 218 Unthank Road, Norwich, Norfolk. *T:* Norwich 53382. *Club:* English-Speaking Union.

RAM, Jaglivan; Minister of Defence, India, since 1977; *b* Arrah, Bihar, 5 April 1908; *m* 1935, Indrani Devi; one *s* one *d. Educ:* Banaras Hindu Univ.; Calcutta Univ. (BSc). Appeared before Hammond Commn, 1936; started Agricl Lab. Movement in Bihar and formed Bihar Provincial Khet Mazdoor (Agricl Lab.) Sabha, 1937; Parly Sec., Bihar Govt, 1937-39; jailed in 1940 and 1942 and released in Oct. 1943 on med. grounds; Vice-Pres., Bihar Br. of All India TUC, 1940-46; Sec., Bihar Provincial Congress Cttee, 1940-46; Labour Minister of interim Govt, Sept. 1946-May 1952; appeared before Cabinet Mission, 1946, as accredited leader of Scheduled Castes and rep. their case. Leader, Indian Delegn to ILO Conf., Geneva, 1947; Chm., Preparatory Asia Regional Conf. of ILO, Oct.-Nov. 1947; Leader, Indian Delegn to 33rd Session of ILO Conf. 1950 (Chm. Conf.); Communication Minister, Govt of India, 1952-56; Minister for: Transport and Railway, Dec. 1956-Apr. 1957; Railways, 1957-62; Transport and Communications, 1962-63; Labour, Employment and Rehabilitation, 1966 (AN); Leader, Indian Delegn to Asian Labour Ministers' Conf., Manila, 1966; Minister of Food, Agriculture, Community Develt and Co-op., 1967-70 (also charge Min. of Labour, Employment and Rehabilitation, Nov. 1969-1970); Minister of Defence, 1970-74; Minister of Agriculture and Irrigation, 1974-77. Leader, Indian Delegns: FAO Conf., Rome, 1967, 1974; World Food Congress,

The Hague, 1970, Khartoum, 1974. Mem. Exec. Cttee, Hindustan Mazdoor Sewak Sangh, 1947-; Pres., All India Congress Cttee, 1969-71 (Mem. Cttee, 1940-77, and of its Central Parly Bd, 1950-77); Chm., Reception Cttee, 67th Session, Indian Nat. Congress, Patna, 1962; Member: Disciplinary Action Cttee of Congress Working Cttee (since constituted, to 1977); All India Congress Working Cttee, 1948-77; Central Election Cttee, 1951-56, 1961; Gen. Body, AICC, 1973-77; Gandhi Smarak Nidhi; Chairman: Central Campaign Cttee, AICC, 1974-77; Panchayati Raj Cell, AICC, 1974-77. Formed Congress for Democracy Party, Feb. 1977. Chm., Indian Inst. of Public Admin, 1974-75; Mem. Governing Bodies, several colls and educnl instns. Trustee, Nehru Memorial Trust, etc. Past Pres. of several Trades Unions. Hon. Dr of Sciences Vikram Univ., Ujjain. *Address:* 6 Krishna Menon Marg, New Delhi 110011, India. *T:* 376555.

RAM CHANDRA, CIE 1933; MBE 1919; MA (Punjab); MA (Cantab); a Trustee of The Tribune (English daily newspaper in Chandigarh), 1949-76, President of Board of Trustees, 1967-76; *b* 1 March 1889; *m* 1917; one *s* one *d. Educ:* Government College, Lahore (Fuller Exhibitioner); Panjab Univ. (MA English 1907; MA 1st class, Mathematics, 1908); Trinity College, Cambridge (Senior Scholar and Wrangler, b star, 1913); Govt of India Bd of Examrs Cert. of High Proficiency in Persian, 1915; Degree of Honour in Urdu, 1921. Assistant Professor of Mathematics, Government College, Lahore, 1908-10; joined ICS, 1913; served in Punjab as Assistant Commissioner in various districts; Colonisation Officer, 1915; Under-Secretary, 1919-21; Settlement Officer, 1921-25; Director of Land Records, 1924; Deputy Commissioner, 1925; Secretary to Punjab Government, Transferred Department, 1926-27; Home Secretary to Punjab Government, 1928; Deputy Secretary to Govt of India, Department of Education, Health, and Lands, 1928; Joint Secretary, 1932; Secretary, 1935; Member Council of State, 1935; Member, Punjab Legislative Council, 1936; Finance Secretary to Punjab Govt, 1936-37; Commissioner, 1938-39; Sec. to Punjab Govt, Medical and Local Govt Depts, 1939-41; Chief Controller of Imports, India, 1941-44; Leader of Indian Delegation to Egypt for Cotton Conference, 1943; Secretary to Government of India, Commerce Dept, 1944-45; Secretary to Govt of India, Defence Dept, 1945-46; Financial Comr, Punjab, 1946-48; Chairman, Punjab (India) Public Service Commission, 1948-53; Mem., Punjab Legislative Council (elected by Graduates' Constituency), 1954-60; Fellow of Panjab Univ., Chandigarh, 1947-68, Syndic, 1949-64; Syndic and Fellow, Punjabi Univ., Patiala, 1962-72. Chief Comr, Scouts and Guides, Punjab, 1955-68. *Recreation:* gardening. *Address:* Forest Hill, Simla 2, India. *T:* 2129.

RAMACHANDRAN, Prof. Gopalasamudram Narayana, FRS 1977; Professor of Biophysics, Indian Institute of Science, since 1970; part-time Professor of Biophysics, University of Chicago, since 1967; *b* 8 Oct. 1922; *s* of G. R. Narayana Iyer and Lakshmi Ammal; *m* 1945, Rajalakshmi Sankaran; two *s* one *d. Educ:* Maharaja's Coll., Ernakulam, Cochin; Indian Inst. of Science; Univ. of Madras (MA, MSc, DSc); Univ. of Cambridge (PhD). Lectr in Physics, Indian Inst. of Science, 1946-47, Asst Prof., 1949-52; 1851 Exbhn Scholar, Univ. of Cambridge, 1947-49; Prof., Univ. of Madras, 1952-70 (Dean, Faculty of Science, 1964-67). Dir, Univ. Grants Commn Centre of Advanced Study in Biophysics, 1962-70; Member: Physical Res. Cttee, Science, 1959-; Nat. Cttee for Biophysics, 1961-; Bd of Sci. and Ind. Res., India, 1962-65; Council, Internat. Union of Pure and Applied Biophysics, 1969-72; Commn on Macromolecular Biophysics, 1969; Chm., Nat. Cttee for Crystallography, 1963-70; Senior Vis. Prof., Univ. of Michigan, 1965-66; Jawaharlal Nehru Fellow, 1968-70. Fellow, Indian Acad. of Sciences, 1950 (Mem. Council, 1953-70; Sec., 1956-58; Vice-Pres., 1962-64); Fellow, Nat. Inst. of Sciences, 1963; FRSA 1971. Hon. Mem., Amer. Soc. of Biological Chem., 1965; Hon. Foreign Mem., Amer. Acad. of Arts and Scis. Bhatnagar Meml Prize, 1961; Watumull Prize, 1964; John Arthur Wilson Award, 1967; Ramanujan Medal, 1971; Maghnad Saha Medal, 1971. Editor: Current Science, 1950-58; Jl Indian Inst. of Sci., 1973-; Member Editorial Board: Jl Molecular Biol., 1959-66; Biochimica et Biophysica Acta, 1965-72; Indian Jl Pure and Applied Physics, 1963-; Internat Jl Peptide and Protein Res., 1969-; Indian Jl Biochem. and Biophys., 1970-; Biopolymers, 1973-. *Publications:* Crystal Optics, in Handbuch der Physik, vol. 25; Molecular Structure of Collagen, in Internat. Review of Connective Tissue Research, vol. 1; Conformation of Polypeptides and Proteins, in Advances in Protein Chemistry, vol. 23; Conformation Polypeptide Chains, in Annual Reviews in Biochemistry, vol. 39; Fourier Methods in Crystallography, 1970; (ed) Advanced Methods of Crystallography; (ed) Aspects of Protein Structure; (ed) Treatise on Collagen, 2 vols, 1967; (ed) Conformation of Biopolymers, vols 1 and 2, 1967; (ed) Crystallography and Crystal Perfection;

(ed) Biochemistry of Collagen. *Recreations:* Indian and Western music; detective fiction. *Address:* Molecular Biophysics Unit, Indian Institute of Science, Bangalore 560012, India. *T:* Bangalore 34411.

RAMAGE, Captain Cecil Beresford, MC; *b* 17 Jan. 1895; *o s* of John Walker Ramage, Edinburgh; *m* 1921, Cathleen Nesbitt, *qv* ; one *s* one *d. Educ:* Edinburgh Academy; Pembroke College, Oxford (open Classical Scholar); President Oxford Union Society; commissioned in the Royal Scots, 1914; served Gallipoli, Egypt, Palestine, until 1919 (despatches, Order of the Nile); contested Newcastle upon Tyne, General Election, 1922; MP (L) Newcastle upon Tyne (West Division), 1923-24; contested Southport, 1929. Barrister-at-Law, Middle Temple, 1921; subseq. Oxford Circuit. *Recreations:* golf, tennis.

RAMAGE, (James) Granville (William), CMG 1975; HM Diplomatic Service, retired; *b* 19 Nov. 1919; *s* of late Rev. George Granville Ramage and Helen Marion (*née* Middlemass); *m* 1947, Eileen Mary Smith; one *s* two *d. Educ:* Glasgow Acad.; Glasgow University. Served in HM Forces, 1940-46 (despatches). Entered HM Foreign Service, 1947; seconded for service at Bombay, 1947-49; transf. to Foreign Office, 1950; First Sec. and Consul at Manila, 1952-56; South-East Asia Dept, FO, 1956-58; HM Consul at Atlanta, Ga, 1958-62; Gen. Dept, FO, 1962-63; HM Consul-General, Tangier, 1963-67; High Comr in The Gambia, 1968-71; Ambassador, People's Democratic Republic of Yemen, 1972-75; Consul General at Boston, Massachusetts, 1975-77. *Recreations:* music, photography, golf. *Address:* 4 Merton Hall Road, Wimbledon, SW19 3PP. *T:* 01-542 5492.

RAMBAHADUR LIMBU, Lieutenant, VC 1966; *b* Nov. 1939; *s* of late Tekbir Limbu; *m* 1st, 1960, Tikamaya Limbuni (*d* 1966); two *s* ; 2nd, 1967, Purnimaya Limbuni; two *s.* Army Cert. of Educn 1st cl. Enlisted 10th Princess Mary's Own Gurkha Rifles, 1957; served on ops in Borneo (VC); promoted Sergeant, 1971; WOII, 1976; commissioned, 1977. *Recreations:* football, volleyball, badminton, basketball. *Address:* c/o VC and GC Association, Room 04, Archway Block South, Old Admiralty Building, Whitehall, SW1; 10th PMO Gurkha Rifles, C Company, Gallipoli Lines BFPO 1, Hong Kong. *Clubs:* VC and GC Association, Royal Society of St George (England).

RAMBERT, Dame Marie, (Dame Marie Dukes), DBE 1962 (CBE 1953); Founder and Director of Ballet Rambert; Director, Mercury Theatre Trust Ltd; lecturer and teacher; *b* Warsaw, 1888; British; *m* 1918, Ashley Dukes, playwright (*d* 1959); two *d. Educ:* Warsaw, Paris. Studied with Jaques Dalcroze and Enrico Cecchetti; Member of Diaghilev's Ballets Russes, 1912-13; opened Rambert School of Ballet, 1920; Founder and Director of Ballet Rambert, 1926, reformed as Modern Dance Company 1966; produced first ballet, Tragedy of Fashion, by Frederick Ashton, 1926; first season of Ballet Rambert (guest artist, Tamara Karsavina) at Lyric Theatre, Hammersmith, 1930; Ballet Club at Mercury Theatre founded 1930; 50th Birthday performance, Sadler's Wells, 15th June 1976. Fellow, Royal Acad. of Dancing, Vice-Pres. 1972. Member: Grand Council, Imperial Soc. of Teachers of Dancing; Inst. of Dirs. Jupiter recording, On Ballet (with Karsavina), 1960. Radio and Television personality. Queen Elizabeth Coronation Award, Royal Acad. of Dancing, 1956; Diploma of Associateship, College of Art, Manchester, 1960; FRSA 1963; Hon. DLitt Univ. of Sussex, 1964. Jubilee Medal, 1977; Légion d'Honneur, 1957. *Publications:* (trans.) Ulanova: Her Childhood and Schooldays, 1962; Quicksilver: an autobiography-Marie Rambert, 1972; *relevant publications:* Sixteen Years of Ballet Rambert, by Lionel Bradley, 1946; Dancers of Mercury: The Story of Ballet Rambert, by Mary Clarke, 1962; 50 years of Ballet Rambert, 1926-76, ed Anya Sainsbury, Clement Crisp, Peter Williams, 1976. *Recreation:* reading. *Address:* Mercury Theatre Trust Ltd, 94 Chiswick High Road, W4. *T:* 01-995 4246.

RAMELSON, Baruch, (Bert); National Industrial Organiser, Communist Party of Great Britain, since 1965; *b* 22 March 1910; *s* of Jacob and Liuba Mendelson; *m* 1st, 1939, Marion Jessop (*d* 1967); 2nd, 1970, Joan Dorothy Smith; one step *s* two step *d. Educ:* Univ. of Alberta. 1st cl. hons LLB. Barrister and Solicitor, Edmonton, Alta, 1934-35; Internat. Bde, Mackenzie-Pappinard Bn, Spanish Civil War, 1937-39; Adjt, Canadian Bn of Internat. Bde; Tank Driver, Royal Tank Corps, 1941; captured, Tobruk, 1941; escaped Prison Camp, Italy, 1943; OCTU, Catterick, 1944-45, commnd RA 1945; served in India, 1945-46 (Actg Staff Captain Legal). Communist Party: full-time Sec., Leeds, 1946-53; Sec., Yorks, 1953-65; Mem. Nat. Exec., 1953-; Mem. Polit. Cttee, 1954-. *Publications:* various pamphlets and booklets; contrib. Communist (Moscow), Marxism Today, World Marxist

Review. *Recreations:* travel, reading. *Address:* 160A Conisborough Crescent, Catford, SE6 2SF. *T:* 01-698 0738.

RAMGOOLAM, Rt. Hon. Sir Seewoosagur, PC 1971; Kt 1965; LRCP, MRCS; MLA (Lab) for Pamplemousses-Triolet, 1959, re-elected 1967 and 1976; Prime Minister of Mauritius, since 1965; also Minister: for External Affairs, since 1968; for Defence and Internal Security and Information and Broadcasting, since 1969; Leader of the House, since 1960; *b* 1900; *m* ; one *s* one *d. Educ:* Royal Coll., Curepipe; University Coll. (Fellow, 1971) and University Coll. Hosp., London. Municipal Councillor, 1940-53, 1956-60; Deputy Mayor of Port Louis, 1956; Mayor of Port Louis, 1958; entered Legislative Council, 1940; MLC, Pamplemousse-Rivière du Rempart, 1948, re-elected 1953; Mem., Executive Council, 1948; Liaison Officer for Education, 1951-56; Ministerial Secretary to the Treasury, 1958-60; Chief Minister, 1961-65, and Minister of Finance, 1960-72. Chm., Organisation of African Unity, 1976-77. Chm., Bd of Dirs, Advance. Pres., Indian Cultural Assoc. Editor, Indian Cultural Review. Grand Croix de l'Ordre National de la République Malagasy, 1969; Médaille de l'Assemblée Nationale française, 1971; Grand Croix, Ordre National de Lion (Senegal), 1973; Grand Croix de l'Ordre du Mérite (Central African Republic), 1973; Grand Croix National de Benin, 1973; Grand Officier de la Légion d'honneur (France), 1973. UN Prize for Outstanding Achievements in the field of Human Rights, 1973. Dr in Law *hc*, New Delhi. 1st Hon. Mem., African Psychiatric Assoc., 1970. *Recreations:* art and literature. *Address:* 85 Desforges Street, Port Louis, Mauritius. *T:* 20460.

RAMIN, Mme Manfred; *see* Cotrubas, I.

RAMPHAL, Sir Shridath Surendranath, Kt 1970; CMG 1966; QC (Guyana) 1965, SC 1966; Secretary-General of the Commonwealth, since 1975; *m. Educ:* King's Coll., London (LLM 1952), FKC, 1975. Called to the Bar, Gray's Inn, 1951. Colonial Legal Probationer, 1951; Arden and Atkin Prize, 1952. Crown Counsel, British Guiana, 1953-54; Asst to Attorney-Gen., 1954-56; Legal Draftsman, 1956-58; First Legal Draftsman, West Indies, 1958-59; Solicitor-Gen., British Guiana, 1959-61; Asst Attorney-Gen., West Indies, 1961-62, Attorney-Gen., Guyana, 1965-73; Minister of State for External Affairs, Guyana, 1966-72; Foreign Minister, Guyana, 1972-75; Mem., National Assembly, Guyana, 1965-75. Member: Hon. Adv. Cttee, Center for Internat. Studies, NY Univ., 1966-; Internat. Commn of Jurists, 1970-; Bd, Vienna Inst. of Develt, 1973; Internat. Hon. Cttee, Dag Hammarskjold Foundn, 1977; Governing Body, Inst. Develt Studies, Univ. of Sussex, 1977-. Hon. LLD: Panjab, 1975; Southampton, 1976. *Publications:* contrib. various political and legal jls incl. International and Comparative Law Qly, Caribbean Qly, Public Law, Guyana Jl, Round Table, Foreign Policy. *Address:* Commonwealth Secretariat, Marlborough House, Pall Mall, SW1Y 5HX. *Clubs:* Athenæum, Royal Automobile, Travellers'.

RAMPTON, Sir Jack (Leslie), KCB 1973 (CB 1969); Permanent Under-Secretary of State, Department of Energy, since 1974; *b* 10 July 1920; *s* of late Leonard Wilfrid Rampton and of Sylvia (*née* Davies); *m* 1950, Eileen Joan (*née* Hart); one *s* one *d. Educ:* Tonbridge Sch.; Trinity Coll., Oxford. Treasury, 1941; Asst Priv. Sec. to successive Chancellors of the Exchequer, 1942-43; Priv. Sec. to Financial Sec., 1945-46; Economic and Financial Adv. to Comr-Gen. for SE Asia and to British High Comr, Malaya, 1959-61; Under-Secretary, HM Treasury, 1964-68; Dep. Sec., Min. of Technology (formerly Min. of Power), 1968-70; Dep. Sec., DTI, 1970-72; Second Permanent Sec. and Sec. (Industrial Develt), DTI, 1972-74. FBIM. *Recreations:* gardening, games, photography, travel; Oxford Squash V (Capt.) 1939-40; Authentic, 1940. *Address:* 17 The Ridgeway, Tonbridge, Kent. *T:* Tonbridge 352117. *Clubs:* Athenæum; Vincent's (Oxford).

RAMSAY, family name of Earl of Dalhousie.

RAMSAY, Lord; James Hubert Ramsay; *b* 17 Jan. 1948; *er s* and heir of 16th Earl of Dalhousie, *qv*; *m* 1973, Marilyn, *yr d* of Major David Butter, *qv*; two *d. Educ:* Ampleforth. 2nd Bn Coldstream Guards, commnd 1968-71, RARO 1971. *Address:* Brechin Castle, Brechin; 7A Vicarage Gate, W8. *Clubs:* Turf, White's.

RAMSAY, Sir Alexander William Burnett, 7th Bt, *cr* 1806, of Balmain (also *heir-pres* to Btcy of Burnett, *cr* 1626 (Nova Scotia), of Leys, Kincardineshire, which became dormant, 1959, on death of Sir Alexander Edwin Burnett of Leys, and was not claimed by Sir Alexander Burnett Ramsay, 6th Bt, of Balmain); *b* 4 Aug. 1938; *s* of Sir Alexander Burnett Ramsay, 6th Bt and Isabel Ellice, *e d* of late William Whitney, Woodstock, New South Wales; *S* father, 1965; *m* 1963, Neryl Eileen, *d* of J. C. Smith Thornton, Trangie, NSW; two *s*. *Heir:* *s* Alexander David Ramsay, *b* 20 Aug. 1966. *Address:* 30 Brian Street, Balgownie, NSW 2519, Australia.

RAMSAY, Arthur; *see* Ramsay, James A.

RAMSAY, Clyde Archibald, CMG 1969; MBE 1960; JP (Barbados); Chief Establishments Officer, 1962-72, and Head of the Civil Service, 1967-72, Barbados; *b* 8 April 1914; *s* of late Alan C. and Wilhelmina Ramsay; *m* 1943, Thelma Ione, *d* of Alfred and Rowena Pragnell; two *s. Educ:* Combermere Secondary Sch., Barbados. Joined Civil Service, 1932; Asst Auditor-Gen., 1957; Local Govt Comr, Chief Registering Officer and Supervisor of Elections, 1959; Chief Establishments Officer and Chm. of Whitley Council, Barbados, 1962. Vice-Pres., Barbados Boy Scouts' Assoc. JP 1961. *Recreation:* swimming.

RAMSAY, Henry Thomas, CBE 1960; Director, Safety in Mines Research Establishment, Ministry of Technology (formerly Ministry of Power), Sheffield, 1954-70, retired; *b* 7 Dec. 1907; *s* of Henry Thomas and Florence Emily Ramsay, Gravesend, Kent; *m* 1953, Dora Gwenllian Burgoyne Davies; one *s* one *d. Educ:* Gravesend Junior Techn. Sch.; thereafter by evening study. On scientific staff, Research Labs, GEC, 1928-48; RAE, 1948-54. Chartered engineer; FInstP; FIMinE; Pres., Midland Inst. Mining Engrs, 1970-71. *Publications:* contrib. to: trans of Instn of Electrical Engrs; Jl of Inst. of Mining Engrs; other technical jls. *Recreations:* gardening, horses. *Address:* Well Farm, Lower Ansford, Castle Cary, Somerset.

RAMSAY, J(ames) Arthur, MBE 1945; FRS 1955; Fellow of Queens' College, Cambridge, 1934-76; Professor of Comparative Physiology, University of Cambridge, 1969-76, now Emeritus Professor (Reader, 1959); *b* 6 Sept. 1909; *s* of late David Ramsay and Isabella Rae Ramsay (*née* Garvie), Maybole, Ayrshire; *m* 1939, Helen Amelie, *d* of late Oscar Dickson, Stockholm; one *s* one *d. Educ:* Fettes College; Gonville and Caius College, Cambridge. University Demonstrator and Fellow of Queens', 1934. Major RA Coast and Anti-Aircraft Defence Experimental Establishment, 1939-45. Joint Editor, Journal of Experimental Biology, 1952-74. *Publications:* Physiological Approach to the Lower Animals, 1952; The Experimental Basis of Modern Biology, 1965; A Guide to Thermodynamics, 1972; papers in Jl of Experimental Biology. *Recreations:* mountaineering, ski-ing. *Address:* The Boxer's Croft, Abriachan, Inverness-shire. *T:* Dochgarroch 269.

RAMSAY, Cdre Sir James (Maxwell), Kt 1976; CBE 1966; DSC 1952; Governor of Queensland, since 1977; *b* 27 Aug. 1916; *s* of William Ramsay and Mary Ramsay; *m* 1945, Janet Burley; one *s* three *d. Educ:* Hutchins Sch., Hobart; RAN Coll., Jervis Bay. RAN, 1930-72: Naval Representative, London, 1964-65; NOIC, Western Australia, 1968-72; Lieut-Governor of Western Australia, 1974-77. State Pres., Australia-Britain Soc., 1972; Vice Pres., Red Cross Soc., 1974. KStJ 1977. Legion of Merit, US, 1952. *Recreations:* golf, yachting, fishing. *Address:* Government House, Brisbane, Qld 4001, Australia. *Club:* Weld.

RAMSAY, Prof. John Graham, FRS 1973; Professor of Geology, Eidgenössische Technische Hochschule and University of Zürich, since 1977; *b* 17 June 1931; *s* of Robert William Ramsay and Kathleen May Ramsay; *m* 1st, 1952, Sylvia Hiorns (marr. diss. 1957); 2nd, 1960, Christine Marden; three *d* (and one *d* decd). *Educ:* Edmonton County Grammar Sch.; Imperial Coll., London. PhD, DIC, BSc, ARCS, FGS. Musician, Corps of Royal Engineers, 1955-57; academic staff Imperial Coll., London, 1957-73: Prof. of Geology, 1966-73; Prof. of Earth Sciences, Leeds Univ., 1973-76. Vice-Pres., Société Géologique de France, 1973. *Publication:* Folding and Fracturing of Rocks, 1967. *Recreations:* chamber music, mountaineering, ski-ing. *Address:* Eidgenössische Technische Hochschule Zürich, ETH Zentrum, CH 8092 Zürich, Switzerland.

RAMSAY, Sir Neis Alexander, 12th Bt of Bamff, *cr* 1666; Farmer since 1953; Landowner and Farmer since 1959; *b* 4 Oct. 1909; *s* of Sir James Douglas Ramsay, 11th Bt, MVO, TD, JP; *S* father 1959; *m* 1st, 1940, Edith Alix Ross Hayes (marriage dissolved, 1950), *d* of C. F. Hayes, Linksfield, Johannesburg; 2nd, 1952, Rachel Leanore Beatrice Drummond, *d* of late Colonel C. B. Urmstom, Glenmorven; no *c. Educ:* Winchester; Trinity College, Cambridge. 2nd Lt Gordon Highlanders, 1933-34; British South African Police, 1934-35; Lieutenant, South African Engineer Corps, 1939-45; Mining in South Africa, 1936-50; Returned to UK, 1950. *Recreations:* shooting and golf. *Heir:* none. *Address:* Bamff, Alyth, Perthshire. *T:* Alyth 382. *Clubs:* New (Edinburgh); Royal Perth Golfing Society (Perth).

RAMSAY, Norman James Gemmill; Sheriff of South Strathclyde, Dumfries and Galloway at Kircudbright and Stranraer (formerly Dumfries and Galloway, Western Division), since 1971; *b* 26 Aug. 1916; *s* of late James Ramsay and late Mrs Christina Emma Ramsay; *m* 1952, Rachael Mary Berkeley Cox, *d* of late Sir Herbert Charles Fahie Cox; two *s. Educ:* Merchiston Castle Sch.; Edinburgh Univ. (MA, LLB). Writer to the Signet, 1939; Advocate, Scotland, 1956. War Service, RN, 1940-46; Lt (S), RNVR. Colonial Legal Service, Northern Rhodesia: Administrator-General, 1947; Resident Magistrate, 1956; Sen. Resident Magistrate, 1958; Puisne Judge of High Court, Zambia, 1964-68. Mem., Victoria Falls Trust, 1950-58. *Address:* Mill of Borgue, Kirkcudbright.

RAMSAY, Patrick George Alexander; Controller, Programme Services, BBC Television Service, since 1972; *b* 14 April 1926; *yr s* of late Rt Rev. Ronald Erskine Ramsay, sometime Bishop of Malmesbury, and of Winifred Constance Ramsay (*née* Partridge); *m* 1948, Hope Seymour Dorothy, *y d* of late Rt Rev. Algernon Markham, sometime Bishop of Grantham, and Winifred Edith Markham (*née* Barne); two *s. Educ:* Marlborough Coll.; Jesus Coll., Cambridge (MA). Served War, Royal Navy (Fleet Air Arm), 1944-46. Joined BBC as Report Writer, Eastern European Desk, Monitoring Service, 1949; Liaison Officer, US Foreign Broadcasts Information Service, Cyprus, 1951-52; Asst, Appts Dept, 1953-56; Sen. Admin. Asst, External Broadcasting, 1956-58; Admin. Officer News and Head of News Administration, 1958-64; Planning Manager, Television Programme Planning, 1964-66; Asst Controller; Programme Services, 1966-69; Programme Planning, 1969-72. Dir, Windsor Festival Soc., 1973-76. Councillor and Alderman, Royal Borough of New Windsor, 1962-67; Chm., Windsor and Eton Soc., 1971-76. FRSA. *Recreations:* fellwalking, gardening, foreign travel, history, looking in junk shops, thwarting bureaucrats. *Address:* Englefield Green House, Surrey. *T:* Egham 2122. *Club:* English-Speaking Union.

RAMSAY, Thomas Anderson; Regional Medical Officer, West Midlands Regional Health Authority, since 1976; *b* 9 Feb. 1920; *s* of David Mitchell Ramsay and Ruth Bramfitt Ramsay; *m* 1949, Margaret Lilian Leggat Donald; one *s* two *d. Educ:* Glasgow Univ. BSc, MB, ChB. FRCSGlas; FFCM; FRSH 1966. Surg. Lieut, RNVR, 1945-47. Various posts in general and clinical hospital practice (mainly paediatric and orthopaedic surg.), 1943-56; Asst, later Dep. Sen. Admin. Med. Officer, NI Hospitals Authority, 1957-58; Dep. Sen., later Sen. Admin. Med. Officer, NE Metropolitan Reg. Hospital Bd, 1958-72; Post-Grad. Dean and Prof. of Post-Grad. Med., Univ. of Aberdeen, 1972-76; Dir of Post-Grad. Med. Educn, NE Region (Scotland), 1972-76. Vis. Prof. of Health Services Admin, London Sch. of Hygiene and Tropical Medicine, 1971-72. Mem. Bd, Faculty of Community Medicine, 1972-. Governor, London Hosp., 1965-72. *Publications:* several papers in learned jls regarding post-graduate medical educn and community medicine. *Recreations:* travel, photography. *Address:* 66 Woodbourne, Augustus Road, Edgbaston, Birmingham B15 3PJ. *T:* 021-454 7127.

RAMSAY, Sir Thomas (Meek), Kt 1972; CMG 1965; Chairman: The Kiwi International Company Ltd, Melbourne, since 1967; joined The Kiwi Polish Co. Pty Ltd, Melbourne, 1926, Managing Director, 1956-72 (Joint Managing Director, 1945); *b* Essendon, Victoria, 24 Nov. 1907; *s* of late William Ramsay, Scotland; *m* 1941, Catherine Anne, *d* of late Sir William Richardson, Adelaide, SA; four *s* one *d. Educ:* Malvern Grammar; Scotch Coll.; Melbourne Univ. (BSc). CMF, 1940-41 (Lieut); Asst Controller, Min. of Munitions, 1941-45. Chairman: Norwich Union Life Insurance Soc. (Aust. Bd), 1968-; Industrial Design Council of Australia, 1969-76; ANZAC Fellowship Selection Cttee, 1971-; Director: Australian Consolidated Industries Ltd Group; Collie (Aust.) Ltd Group; Alex Harvey Industries Group, NZ. President: Associated Chambers of Manufrs of Australia, 1962-63; Victorian Chamber of Manufrs, 1962-64; Member: Victoria Promotion Cttee; Selection Cttee (Industrial) Sir Winston Churchill Fellowships. FRHistS of Queensland, 1964; FRHistS of Victoria, 1965; FAIM; FSAScot. *Recreations:* gardening, golf, Australian historical research. *Address:* 23 Airlie Street, South Yarra, Victoria 3141, Australia. *T:* 26 1751. *Clubs:* Oriental (London); Athenæum, Australian, Melbourne (Melbourne); Commonwealth (Canberra).

RAMSAY-FAIRFAX-LUCY, Sir Edmund J. W. H. C.; *see* Fairfax-Lucy.

RAMSAY RAE, Air Vice-Marshal Ronald Arthur, CB 1960; OBE 1947; National Playing Fields Association, 1963-71; *b* 9 Oct. 1910; *s* of late George Ramsay Rae, Lindfield, NSW, and

Alice Ramsay Rae (*née* Haselden); *m* 1939, Rosemary Gough Howell, *d* of late Charles Gough Howell, KC, Attorney General, Singapore; one *s* one *d. Educ:* Sydney, New South Wales, Australia. Served Australian Citizen Force and then as Cadet, RAAF, at Point Cook, 1930-31; transf. to RAF, 1932; flying duties in UK and Middle East with Nos 33 and 142 Sqdns until 1936; Advanced Armament Course; Armament officer in Far East, 1938-42; then Comdr RAF Tengah, Singapore; POW, 1943-45; Gp Captain in comd Central Gunnery Sch., Leconfield, Yorks, 1946; despatches, 1946. RAF Staff Coll., Andover, 1948; Dep. Dir Organisation (Estabt), Middle East; in comd RAF North Luffenham and then RAF Oakington (206 Advanced Flying Sch.); Commandant, Aircraft and Armament Exptl Estabt, Boscombe Down, 1955-57; Dep. Air Sec., Air Min., 1957-59; AOC No 224 Group, RAF, 1959-62, retd. AFRAeS 1956. *Recreations:* cricket, golf, tennis, winter sports (Cresta Run and ski-ing). *Address:* Commonwealth Bank of Australia, Strand, WC2; Little Wakestone, Bedham, Fittleworth, W Sussex. *Club:* Royal Air Force.
See also Hon . Sir Wallace A . R . Rae.

RAMSBOTHAM, family name of **Viscount Soulbury.**

RAMSBOTHAM, Rt. Rev. John Alexander; *b* 25 Feb. 1906; *s* of late Rev. Alexander Ramsbotham and of late Margaret Emily Ramsbotham; *m* 1933, Eirian Morgan Owen; three *s* two *d. Educ:* Haileybury College; Corpus Christi College, Cambridge; Wells Theological College. Travelling Secretary, 1929-30, Missionary Secretary, 1930-33, Student Christian Movement; Chaplain, 1933-34. Vice-Principal, 1934-36, Wells Theol. Coll.; Priest-Vicar Wells Cathedral, 1933-36; Warden, College of the Ascension, Selly Oak, 1936-40; Rector of Ordsall, Notts, 1941-42; Vicar of St George's, Jesmond, Newcastle on Tyne, 1942-50; Bishop Suffragan of Jarrow, 1950-58, also Archdeacon of Auckland and Canon of Durham; Bishop of Wakefield, 1958-67; Asst Bishop, Dio. Newcastle, 1968-76. *Publication:* Belief in Christ and the Christian Community, 1949. *Recreation:* music. *Address:* 13 Hextol Terrace, Hexham, Northumberland NE46 2DF. *T:* Hexham 2607.

RAMSBOTHAM, Hon. Sir Peter (Edward), GCVO 1976; KCMG 1972 (CMG 1964); HM Diplomatic Service; Governor and C-in-C of Bermuda, since 1977; *b* 8 Oct. 1919; *yr s* of 1st Viscount Soulbury, PC, GCMG, GCVO, OBE, MC; *b* and *heir pres.* to 2nd Viscount Soulbury, *qv*; *m* 1941, Frances Blomfield; two *s* one *d. Educ:* Eton College; Magdalen College, Oxford. HM Forces, 1943-46 (Croix de Guerre, 1945). Control Office for Germany and Austria from 1947; Regional Political Officer in Hamburg; entered Foreign Service, Oct. 1948; Political Division of Allied Control Commission, Berlin, Nov. 1948; transferred to Foreign Office, 1950; 1st Secretary, 1950; transferred to UK delegation, New York, 1953; Foreign Office, 1957; Counsellor, 1961; Head of Chancery, British Embassy, Paris, 1963-67; Foreign Office, 1967-69; High Comr, Nicosia, 1969-71; Ambassador to Iran, 1971-74; Ambassador to the United States, 1974-77. KStJ 1976. *Address:* Government House, Hamilton, Bermuda; East Lane, Ovington, near Alresford, Hants. *Club:* Garrick.

RAMSBURY, Bishop Suffragan of, since 1974; **Rt. Rev. John Robert Geoffrey Neale,** AKC; Archdeacon of Wilts and Hon. Canon of Salisbury Cathedral since 1974; *b* 21 Sept. 1926; *s* of Geoffrey Brockman Neale and late Stella Beatrice (*née* Wild). *Educ:* Felsted Sch.; King's Coll., London Univ. Served War of 1939-45: Lieut RA; Army, 1944-48. Business, G. B. Neale & Co Ltd, EC2, 1948-51. King's Coll. London, 1951-55 (Jelf Prize, 1954). Deacon, 1955, priest, 1956; Curate, St Peter, St Helier, Dio. Southwark, 1955-58. Chaplain, Ardingly Coll., Sx, 1958-63; Recruitment Sec., CACTM (ACCM), 1963-67; Archbishops' Rep. for ordination candidates, 1967-68; Canon Missioner, Dio. Guildford, Hon. Canon of Guildford Cath. and Rector of Hascombe, Surrey, 1968-74. *Publication:* Ember Prayer (SPCK), 1965. *Recreation:* horticulture. *Address:* Chittoe Vicarage, Bromham, Chippenham, Wilts. *T:* Bromham 651. *Club:* Royal Commonwealth Society.

RAMSDEN, Caryl Oliver Imbert, CMG 1965; CVO 1966; Pro-Principal (Administration), University College at Buckingham, since 1975; *b* 4 April 1915; *s* of late Lt-Col J. V. Ramsden; *m* 1945, Anne, *d* of late Sir Charles Wickham, KCMG, KBE, DSO; one *s. Educ:* Eton; New Coll., Oxford. Served in Royal Regiment of Artillery, 1937-49; Assistant Military Attaché, Bucharest, 1947-49. Entered HM Foreign Service, 1949, retired 1967; Private Secretary to Prime Minister, 1957; Consul-General, Hanover, 1957-59; Counsellor, Rio de Janeiro, 1959; acted as Chargé d'Affaires, 1960; Counsellor, Brussels 1962. Commander of the Star of Ethiopia, 1954; Commander, Order of Leopold, 1966. *Recreation:* golf. *Address:* The Old Brewery, Helperby, York YO6 2NS. *Club:* Cavalry and Guards.

RAMSDEN, Sir Geoffrey Charles Frescheville, Kt 1948; CIE 1942; *b* 21 April 1893; *s* of Colonel H. F. S. Ramsden, CBE, and Hon. Edwyna Fiennes, *d* of 17th Lord Saye and Sele, DL, JP, CC; *m* 1930, Margaret Lovell (*d* 1976), *d* of late Rev. J. Robinson; no *c. Educ:* Haileybury College; Sidney Sussex Coll., Cambridge (MA). Served in the Army, 1914-19; Capt. 1st Bn Royal Sussex Regt, NW Frontier (India) 1915-19; joined ICS 1920; Secretary Indian Tariff Board, 1923-25; Deputy Commissioner of Jubbulpore, 1926 and 1931-34, and of various other Districts; Commissioner, Jubbulpore Div., 1936 and 1941-44, and Chhatisgarh Div., 1937-40; Development Adviser to Governor, 1945; Financial Comr CP and Berar, 1941-45 and 1946-47; retd, 1948. *Recreations:* travel, photography, tennis and fishing. *Address:* Fynescourt, Grayshott, Hindhead, Surrey. *T:* Hindhead 4499. *Club:* Royal Over-Seas League.

RAMSDEN, Sir Geoffrey William P., Bt; *see* Pennington-Ramsden.

RAMSDEN, Prof. Herbert, MA, Dr en Filosofía y Letras; Professor of Spanish Language and Literature, University of Manchester, since 1961; *b* 20 April 1927; *s* of Herbert and Ann Ramsden; *m* 1953, Joyce Robina Hall, SRN, ONC, CMB; three *s* (incl. twin *s*) twin *d. Educ:* Sale Grammar Sch.; Univs of Manchester, Strasbourg, Madrid and Sorbonne. National Service, Inf. and Intell. Corps, 1949-51 (commnd). Travel, study and research abroad (Kemsley Travelling Fellow, etc), 1951-54; Univ. of Manchester: Asst Lectr in Spanish, 1954-57; Lectr in Spanish, 1957-61; Chm. of MA Cttee, 1964-65; Pres., Philological Club, 1966-68. *Publications:* An Essential Course in Modern Spanish, 1959; Weak-Pronoun Position in the Early Romance Languages, 1963; (ed with critical study) Azorín, La ruta de Don Quijote, 1966; Angel Ganivet's Idearium español: A Critical Study, 1967; The Spanish Generation of 1898, 1974; The 1898 Movement in Spain, 1974; articles in Bulletin of Hispanic Studies, Modern Language Review, Modern Languages, etc. *Recreations:* family, hill-walking, foreign travel. *Address:* Grove House, Grove Lane, Cheadle Hulme, Cheshire. *T:* 061-439 4306.

RAMSDEN, Rt. Hon. James Edward, PC 1963; Director; Prudential Assurance Co. Ltd, since 1972 (Deputy Chairman, since 1976); *b* 1 Nov. 1923; *s* of Capt. Edward Ramsden, MC, and late Geraldine Ramsden, OBE, Breckamore Hall, Ripon; *m* 1949, Juliet Barbara Anne, *y d* of late Col Sir Charles Ponsonby, 1st Bt, TD, and of Hon. Lady Ponsonby, *d* of 1st Baron Hunsdon; three *s* two *d. Educ:* Eton; Trinity College, Oxford (MA). Commissioned 1942; served North-West Europe with Rifle Brigade, 1944-45. MP (C) Harrogate, WR Yorks, March 1954-Feb. 1974; PPS to Home Secretary, Nov. 1959-Oct. 1960; Under-Sec. and Financial Sec., War Office, Oct. 1960-Oct. 1963; Sec. of State for War, 1963-64; Minister of Defence for the Army, April-Oct. 1964. Director: UK Board, Colonial Mutual Life Assurance Society, 1966-72; Standard Telephones and Cables, 1971; London Clinic, 1973. Mem., Historic Buildings Council for England, 1971-72. *Address:* Old Sleningford Hall, near Ripon, North Yorks. *T:* Ripon 85229. *Clubs:* Brooks's, Pratt's.

RAMSEY OF CANTERBURY, Baron *cr* 1974 (Life Peer), of Canterbury; **Rt. Rev. and Rt. Hon. Arthur Michael Ramsey,** PC 1956; Royal Victorian Chain, 1974; MA, BD; Hon. Fellow: Magdalene College, Cambridge, since 1952; Merton College, Oxford, since 1974; Keble College, Oxford, since 1975; *b* 14 Nov. 1904; *s* of late Arthur Stanley Ramsey, Fellow and sometime President of Magdalene Coll., Cambridge; *m* 1942, Joan, *d* of Lieut-Colonel F. A. C. Hamilton. *Educ:* Repton; Magdalene Coll., Cambridge (Scholar); Cuddesdon. 2nd Class, Classical Tripos, 1925; 1st Class, Theological Tripos, 1927; President of Cambridge Union, 1926; ordained, 1928; curate of Liverpool Parish Church, 1928-30; subwarden of Lincoln Theological Coll., 1930-36; Lecturer of Boston Parish Church, 1936-38; Vicar of S Benedict, Cambridge, 1939-40; Canon of Durham Cathedral and Professor of Divinity in Univ. of Durham, 1940-50; Regius Professor of Divinity, Univ. of Cambridge, and Fellow of Magdalene Coll., 1950-52; Canon and Prebendary in Lincoln Cathedral, 1951-52; Bishop of Durham, 1952-56; Archbishop of York, 1956-61; Archbishop of Canterbury, 1961-74. Examining Chaplain to Bishop of Chester, 1932-39, to Bishop of Durham, 1940-50, and to Bishop of Lincoln, 1951-52; Select Preacher, Cambridge 1934, 1940, 1948, 1959, 1964, Oxford, 1945-46; Hulsean Preacher, Cambridge, 1969-70. Hon. Master of the Bench, Inner Temple, 1962. A President of World Council of Churches, 1961-68. Trustee, British Museum, 1963-69. Hon. degrees include: Hon. DD: Durham, 1951; Leeds, Edinburgh, Cambridge, Hull, 1957; Manchester, 1961; London, 1962; Hon. DCL: Oxford, 1960; Kent, 1966; Hon. DLitt Keele, 1967, and a number from Universities overseas. *Publications:* The Gospel and the Catholic

Church, 1936; The Resurrection of Christ, 1945; The Glory of God and the Transfiguration of Christ, 1949; F. D. Maurice and the Conflicts of Modern Theology, 1951; Durham Essays and Addresses, 1956; From Gore to Temple, 1960; Introducing the Christian Faith, 1961; Canterbury Essays and Addresses, 1964; Sacred and Secular, 1965; God, Christ and the World, 1969; (with Cardinal Svenens) The Future of the Christian Church, 1971; The Christian Priest Today, 1972; Canterbury Pilgrim, 1974; Holy Spirit, 1977. *Recreation:* walking. *Address:* 50 South Street, Durham DH1 XQP. *T:* Durham 62934.

RAMSEY, Sir Alfred (Ernest), Kt 1967; Director: Sadler & Sons, since 1974; Gola Sports, since 1975; *b* Dagenham, 1920; *m* 1951, Victoria Phyllis Answorth, *d* of William Welch. *Educ:* Becontree Heath School. Started playing for Southampton and was an International with them; transferred to Tottenham Hotspur, 1949; with Spurs (right back), 1949-51; they won the 2nd and 1st Division titles in successive seasons. Manager of Ipswich Town Football Club, which rose from 3rd Division to Championship of the League, 1955-63; Manager, FA World Cup Team, 1963-74. Played 31 times for England. Dir, Birmingham City, 1976-. *Address:* 41 Valley Road, Ipswich, Suffolk.

RAMSEY, Rt. Rev. Kenneth Venner; an Assistant Bishop, Diocese of Manchester, since 1975; *b* 26 Jan. 1909; *s* of James Ernest and Laura Rebecca Ramsey, Southsea, Hants; unmarried. *Educ:* Portsmouth Grammar Sch.; University Coll., Oxford; Manchester Univ. Curate of St Matthew, Stretford, 1933-35; Vice-Prin., Egerton Hall, Manchester, and Lectr in Christian Ethics, Manchester Univ., 1935-38; Vice-Prin., Bishop Wilson Coll., Isle of Man, 1938-39; Prin., Egerton Hall, Manchester, 1939-41; Vicar of St Paul, Peel, Little Hulton, Lancs, 1941-48; Rector of Emmanuel Church, Didsbury, Manchester, 1948-55; Hon. Canon, Manchester Cathedral, 1950-53; Proctor in Convocation and mem. Church Assembly, 1950-55; Rural Dean of Heaton, 1950-53; Bishop Suffragan of Hulme, 1953-75. *Address:* 41 Bradwell Drive, Heald Green, Cheadle, Cheshire SK8 3BX. *T:* 061-437 8612.

RAMSEY, Leonard Gerald Gwynne; Editor of The Connoisseur, 1951-72; *b* 17 March 1913; *s* of late L. B. Ramsey, London Stock Exchange; *m* 1941, Dorothy Elizabeth, *y d* of late W. J. McMillan, Belfast; one *s* one *d. Educ:* Radley College. Commissioned Oxfordshire and Buckinghamshire Light Infantry (T), 1938; invalided out of Army, 1944; on General Staff, War Office, 1941-44, and other staff appointments. Public Relations Officer, The National Trust, 1946-49; Press Officer at Board of Trade and Colonial Office, 1950-51. Member of several Committees associated with ecclesiastical art and charitable matters. FSA 1949. *Publications:* (ed) The Connoisseur Encyclopædia of Antiques, 5 vols, 1954-60; (ed. with Ralph Edwards) The Connoisseur Period Guides, 6 vols, 1956-59; Montague Dawson, marine artist, a biography, 1967; (ed with Helen Comstock) The Connoisseur's Guide to Antique Furniture, 1969. *Recreations:* historic buildings, works of art, gardening. *Address:* Church Cottage, Cockfield, Bury St Edmunds, Suffolk IP30 0LA.

RAMSEY, Prof. Norman Foster; Higgins Professor of Physics, Harvard University, since 1947; Chairman: Harvard Nuclear Physics Committee, 1948-60; Harvard Society of Fellows, since 1962; *b* 27 Aug. 1915; *s* of Brig.-Gen. and Mrs Norman F. Ramsey; *m* 1940, Elinor Stedman Jameson; four *d. Educ:* Columbia Univ.; Cambridge Univ. (England). Carnegie Fellow, Carnegie Instn of Washington, 1939-40; Assoc., Univ. of Ill, 1940-42; Asst Prof., Columbia Univ., 1942-45; Research Assoc., MIT Radiation Laboratory, 1940-43; Cons. to Nat. Defense Research Cttee, 1940-45; Expert Consultant to Sec. of War, 1942-45; Grp Leader and Assoc. Div. Head, Los Alamos Lab. of Atomic Energy Project, 1943-45; Chief Scientist of Atomic Energy Lab. at Tinian, 1945; Assoc. Prof., Columbia Univ., 1945-47; Head of Physics Dept, Brookhaven Nat. Lab., 1946-47; Assoc. Prof., Harvard Univ., 1947-50; John Simon Guggenheim Fell., Oxford Univ., 1953-54; George Eastman Vis. Prof., Oxford Univ., 1973-74. Dir Harvard Nuclear Lab., 1948-50, 1952; Science Adviser, NATO 1958-59; Fell. Amer. Phys. Soc. and Amer. Acad. of Arts and Sciences; Nat. Acad. of Sciences; Amer. Philos. Soc.; Sigma Xi; Phi Beta Kappa. Bd of Directors, Varian Associates, 1964-66; Bd of Trustees: Associated Univs; Brookhaven Nat. Lab., 1952-55; Carnegie Endowment for Internat. Peace; Univ. Research Assoc. (Pres., 1966-); Air Force Sci. Adv. Bd, 1948-54; Dept of Defense Panel on Atomic Energy, 1953-59; Bd of Editors of Review of Modern Physics, 1953-56; Chm. Exec. Cttee for Camb. Electron Accelerator, 1956-63; Coun. Amer. Phys. Soc., 1956-60 (Vice-Pres., 1977). Gen. Adv. Cttee, Atomic Energy Commn, 1960-72. Chm., High Energy Accelerator Panel of President's Sci. Adv. Cttee and AEC, 1963. Presidential Certificate of Merit, 1947; E. O.

Lawrence Award, 1960; Davisson-Germer Prize, 1974. Hon. MA Harvard, 1947; Hon. ScD Cambridge, 1953; Hon. DSc: Case Western Reserve, 1968; Middlebury Coll., 1969; MA Oxford, 1973. *Publications:* Experimental Nuclear Physics, 1952; Nuclear Moments, 1953; Molecular Beams, 1956; Quick Calculus, 1965; and numerous articles in Physical Review and other scientific jls. *Recreations:* tennis, ski-ing, walking, sailing, etc. *Address:* 55 Scott Road, Belmont, Mass 02178, USA. *T:* Ivanhoe 4.35.53, Belmont. *Club:* Authors' (London).

RAMSEY, Robert John, CBE 1977; Director of Industrial Relations, Ford Motor Company Ltd, since 1973; *b* 16 Aug. 1921; *m* 1949, Arlette Ikor; one *s* one *d*. *Educ:* Royal Liberty Sch., Romford. Joined Ford Motor Co. Ltd, as student, 1937. Served War of 1939-45: RAF Air Crew, Flt-Lt, 1942-46; POW, 1944-45. Rejoined Ford Motor Co. Ltd, 1946; Industrial Relations Manager, 1958; Dir of Labour Relations, 1969-73. Mem., CRE, 1977-. CIPM 1977. *Recreations:* reading, theatre, hill walking, boating. *Address:* 47 Eastwood Road, Leigh-on-Sea, Essex.

RAMSEY, Waldo Emerson W.; *see* Waldron-Ramsey.

RANASINHA, Sir Arthur (Godwin), Kt 1954; CMG 1949; CBE 1948; diplomat and civil servant, Sri Lanka; *b* 24 June 1898; *s* of W. P. Ranasinha, Proctor and Notary, Oriental Scholar, and Mary Ann (*née* de Alwis); *m* 1921, Annette Hilda (*d* 1968), *d* of Mudalyar de Alwis, Negombo, Ceylon; two *d* (one *s* decd). *Educ:* S Thomas' College, Colombo; Trinity Hall, Cambridge. Ceylon University, Scholar, 1917; ICS, 1920. BA (Hons in History) London, 1920. Entered Ceylon Civil Service, 1921; Police Magistrate: Point Pedro, 1923; Balapitiya, 1923; Jaffna, 1926. District Judge: Avisawella, 1928; Badulla, 1930; Asst Govt Agent, Colombo, 1932; Sec. to Minister for Agriculture and Lands, 1933; Public Trustee, 1936; Custodian of Enemy Property, 1939; Superintendent of Census, 1944; Sec. to Leader of State Council on political mission to London, 1945; Commissioner of Lands, 1946; Permanent Secretary, Min. of Agriculture and Lands, 1947-50; Secretary to the Cabinet and Deputy Secretary, Treasury, 1950-51; Permanent Secretary, Ministry of Finance, Secretary to Treasury and Secretary to Cabinet, 1951-54; Governor: Central Bank of Ceylon, 1954-59; for Ceylon, IMF, 1954-59; Ambassador for Ceylon in Italy and Greece, 1959-61; Chairman: Standing Cttee, Consultative Cttee, Colombo Plan, 1950; Finance Cttee, FAO, 1961; People's Bank Commn, 1965-66; Taxation Commn, 1966-67; Tea Commn, 1967-68. Knight Grand Cross, Order of Merit of the Italian Republic, 1961. *Publications:* General Report on Census of Ceylon, 1946, 1950; Memories and Musings, 1972. *Recreations:* chess, racing, tennis, etc. *Address:* 99/1 Rosmead Place, Colombo 7, Sri Lanka. *T:* Colombo 92067.

RANCHHODLAL, Sir Chinubhai Madhowlal, 2nd Bt, *cr* 1913; *b* 18 April 1906; *s* of 1st Bt and Sulochana, *d* of Chunilal Khushalrai; *S* father, 1916; *m* 1924, Tanumati, *d* of Jhaverilal Bulakhiram Mehta of Ahmedabad; three *s*. Father was first member of Hindu community to receive a baronetcy. *Heir: s* Udayan, [*b* 25 July 1929; *m* 1953, Muneera Khodadad Fozdar; one *s* two *d*]. *Address:* Shantikunj, PO, Shahibag, Ahmedabad, Bombay, India. *T:* 2061. *TA:* Shantikunj. *Club:* Willingdon (Bombay).

RANDALL, Rev. Edmund Laurence; Warden, St Barnabas' Theological College, since 1964; *b* 2 June 1920; *s* of Robert Leonard Randall and Grace Annie Randall (*née* Young); unmarried. *Educ:* Dulwich College; Corpus Christi College, Cambridge. BA 1941. MA 1947. Served War, 1940-45, with Royal Artillery (AA). Corpus Christi Coll., 1938-40 and 1945-47. Wells Theological College, 1947-49. Deacon, 1949; Priest, 1950. Assistant Curate at St Luke's, Bournemouth, 1949-52; Fellow of Selwyn College, Cambridge, 1952-57; Chaplain, 1953-57; Residentiary Canon of Ely and Principal of Ely Theological Coll., 1957-59; Chaplain, St Francis Theological Coll., Brisbane, 1960-64. *Recreations:* travel, motoring, *Address:* St Barnabas' Theological College, Belair, South Australia 5052, Australia. *Club:* Naval, Military and Air Force, South Australia.

RANDALL, Sir John (Turton), Kt 1962; FRS 1946; FInstP; DSc (Manchester); Emeritus Professor of Biophysics in the University of London, King's College; Honorary Professor in the University of Edinburgh; FKC 1960; *b* 23 March 1905; *o s* of late Sidney and Hannah Cawley Randall; *m* 1928, Doris Duckworth; one *s*. *Educ:* Univ. of Manchester (Graduate Res. Schol. and Prizeman, 1925; MSc 1926, DSc 1938). Res. physicist, Res. Lab of GEC Ltd, 1926-37; Warren Res. Fellow of Royal Soc. 1937-43; Hon. Mem. of the staff, Univ. of Birmingham, 1940-43; res. in Univ. of Birmingham for Admiralty, 1939-43, jt inventor (with H. A. H. Boot) of cavity

magnetron; Temp. Lectr in Cavendish Laboratory, Cambridge, 1943-44; Prof. of Natural Philosophy, United Coll. of St Salvator and St Leonard, Univ. of St Andrews, 1944-46; Wheatstone Prof. of Physics, 1946-61, Prof. of Biophysics, 1961-70, Univ. of London (King's Coll.); Dir, MRC Biophysics Research Unit, 1947-70; Chm., Sch. of Biological Sciences, KCL, 1963-69. Lectr, Rockefeller Inst. for Med. Res., NY, 1956-67; Gregynog Lectr, UCW Aberystwyth, 1958; Vis. Prof. of Biophysics, Yale Univ., 1960. Awarded (with H. A. H. Boot) Thomas Gray Meml Prize of Royal Soc. of Arts (1943) for discovery of the cavity magnetron. Duddell Medallist, Physical Soc. of London, 1945; Hughes Medallist, Royal Soc. 1946; John Price Wetherill Medal of Franklin Inst. of State of Pennsylvania, 1958; John Scott Award, City of Philadelphia, 1959. FRSE 1972. *Publications:* The Diffraction of X-rays by Amorphous Solids, Liquids and Gases, 1934; (Editor) The Nature and Structure of Collagen, 1953; (Jt Editor) Progress in Biophysics, 1950-55; papers in various scientific journals on structure in glasses and liquids, the luminescence of solids, the cavity magnetron; and, since 1946, the biophysics of connective tissues, problems of fine structure, the morphogenesis of cellular organelles and neutron and x-ray scattering of biological molecules and structures. *Address:* Department of Zoology, University of Edinburgh, West Mains Road, Edinburgh EH9 3JT; 16 Kevock Road, Lasswade EH18 1HT. *Club:* Athenæum.

RANDALL, John William, CBE 1963; Hon. President, The Dickinson Robinson Group Ltd, since 1968 (Chairman, 1966-68); Chairman, John Dickinson & Co. Ltd, 1955-68; Hon. President, The Dickinson Robinson Group Africa (Pty) Ltd; *b* 20 May 1891; *s* of late John T. and late Ellen A. Randall; *m* 1921, Lillian Anne Reeves (*d* 1973); no *c*; *m* 1977, Elma Cruise. *Educ:* Hemel Hempstead Church of England School. John Dickinson & Co. Ltd: Secretary, 1928; Financial Director, 1936; Managing Director, 1945. *Recreation:* farming. *Address:* Hawridge Court, Chesham, Bucks. *T:* Cholesbury 240.

RANDALL, Michael Bennett; Senior Managing Editor, The Sunday Times; *b* 12 Aug. 1919. *Educ:* St Peter's, Seaford; Canford. Asst Editor, Sunday Chronicle, 1952-53; Editor, Sunday Graphic, 1953; Asst Editor, Daily Mirror, 1953-56; Asst Editor, News Chronicle, 1956-57; Asst Editor, Daily Mail, 1957-61; Deputy Editor, Daily Mail, 1961-63; Editor, Daily Mail, 1963-66; Man. Editor (News), The Sunday Times, 1967-72. *Address:* Keepers, Chailey, Sussex.*T:* Newick 3168.

RANDALL, Sir Richard (John), Kt 1964; BEcon; ACIS; Secretary to the Treasury, Commonwealth of Australia, 1966-71; *b* 13 Oct. 1906; *s* of G. Randall, Birkdale, Queensland; *m* 1945, Nora Barry, *d* of T. J. Clyne; two *s* one *d*. *Educ:* Wynnum High School; University of Sydney (BEcon, 1st cl. hons). Carnegie Research Scholar, Sydney University, 1937; Research Officer, Premier's Office, Sydney, 1937-39; Commonwealth Treasury, 1940. Served with AIF, 1941-45. *Recreations:* golf, fishing. *Address:* 5 Throsby Crescent, Narrabundah, Canberra, ACT 2604, Australia. *Clubs:* Royal Canberra Golf, Commonwealth (Canberra).

RANDALL, Terence George, CBE 1959 (OBE 1946); Deputy Clerk of the LCC, 1947-65, Children's Officer, 1962-65, retired; *b* 5 May 1904; *s* of George Arthur and Kate Amelia Randall; *m* 1928, Ivy Diana Allen (*d* 1973); two *s*. *Educ:* St Bonaventure's Grammar School, Forest Gate; City of London School; Birkbeck College, London University. BA 1927. Entered clerical staff of London County Council, 1921; promoted to administrative grade, 1926. Was concerned with all sides of the Council's work, especially with housing, town planning, civil defence, staff management, the coordination of work involving several departments, and latterly child care. *Recreations:* reading, gardening. *Address:* 9 Willow Close, Hutton, Essex. *T:* Brentwood 1242.

RANDELL, John Bulmer; Physician for Psychological Medicine, Charing Cross Hospital, since 1949; *b* 25 Aug. 1918; 2nd *s* of Percy G. Randell and Katie E. Bulmer; *m* 1944, Margaret Davies; one *d*. *Educ:* The College, Penarth; Welsh Nat. School of Medicine. BSc (Wales) 1938; MB, BCh (Wales) 1941; MD 1960. MO, Cefn Coed Hosp., 1941; MO, Sully Hosp., 1941-42; Temp. Surg. Lieut, RNVR, 1942-46; DPM 1945. First Asst MO, York Clinic, Guy's Hosp., 1946-48; MRCP 1947; FRCP 1964; FRCPsych 1971; Psychotherapist, St George's Hosp., 1948-51; Asst Psychiatrist, St Thomas' Hosp., 1949-59. *Recreations:* golf and photography. *Address:* 118 Harley Street, W1. *T:* 01-486 2494. *Clubs:* Savile, Royal Automobile.

RANDLE, Prof. Philip John; Professor of Clinical Biochemistry, University of Oxford, since 1975; Fellow of Hertford College, Oxford, since 1975; *b* 16 July 1926; *s* of Alfred John and Nora

Anne Randle; *m* 1952, Elizabeth Ann Harrison; three *d* (one *s* decd). *Educ:* Sidney Sussex Coll., Cambridge (MA, PhD, MD); UCH, London. FRCP. Univ. Lectr, Biochem., Cambridge, 1955-64; Res. Fellow, Sidney Sussex Coll., 1954-57; Fellow of Trinity Hall, 1957-64; Prof. of Biochem., Univ. of Bristol, 1964-75. *Publications:* contrib. med. and sci. jls. *Recreations:* bricklaying, swimming. *Address:* Radcliffe Infirmary, Oxford OX2 6HE. *T:* Oxford 49891. *Club:* Savage.

RANDOLPH, Cyril George; *b* 26 June 1899; *s* of late Felton Randolph; *m* 1927, Betty Dixey; one *d*. *Educ:* Christ's Hospital. A Man. Dir, Glyn, Mills & Co., 1941-64; Chairman: Sun Life Assurance Society, 1953-71 (Director, 1943-71); General Funds Investment Trust, 1965-73 (Director, 1964-); Household & General Insurance Co. Ltd, 1965-71. Almoner, Christ's Hospital. *Recreation:* golf. *Address:* 3 Castle Court, Castle Hill, Farnham, Surrey. *Clubs:* Brooks's; New Zealand Golf (West Byfleet); Aldeburgh.
See also Ven. T. B. Randolph.

RANDOLPH, Denys, CEng, MRAeS, FIProdE, FBIM; Chairman: Wilkinson Match Ltd, since 1976; Wilkinson Sword Ltd, since 1972; Institute of Directors, since 1976; *b* 6 Feb. 1926; *s* of Harry Beckham Randolph and Margaret Isabel Randolph; *m* 1951, Marjorie Hales; two *d*. *Educ:* St Paul's School; Queen's Univ., Belfast (BSc). Served Royal Engineers, 1944-48 (Captain). Queen's Univ., Belfast, 1948-52; post-grad. apprenticeship, Short Bros & Harland, 1952-55; Wilkinson Sword Ltd: Prod. Engr/Prod. Dir, Graviner Div., 1955-66; Man. Dir, Hand Tools Div., 1966-69; Chm., Graviner Div., 1969-. Director, Duport Ltd, 1975-. Master, Worshipful Co. of Scientific Instrument Makers, 1977; Liveryman, Worshipful Co. of Cutlers, 1977. Member: Bd of Fellows, BIM, 1977; Bd, Management Research Gp, BIM; Council, CBI; Industrial Panel, Duke of Edinburgh's Award Scheme. Governor, Henley Admin. Staff Coll. FRSA (Manufactures and Commerce). *Publication:* From Rapiers to Razor Blades—The Development of the Light Metals Industry (paper, RSA). *Recreations:* yachting, golf. *Address:* The Cottages, Rush Court, Wallingford OX10 8LJ. *T:* Wallingford 36586. *Clubs:* Army and Navy, City Livery, Little Ship.

RANDOLPH, John Hugh Edward; His Honour Judge Randolph; a Circuit Judge, since 1972; *b* 14 Oct. 1913; *s* of late Charles Edward Randolph and Phyllis Randolph; *m* 1959, Anna Marjorie (*née* Thomson). *Educ:* Bradford Grammar Sch.; Leeds University. RAF, 1940-46. Called to Bar, Middle Temple, 1946; practised on NE Circuit until 1965; Stipendiary Magistrate of Leeds, 1965-71. Deputy Chairman: E Riding QS, 1958-63; W Riding QS, 1963-71. *Recreation:* golf. *Address:* 39 Park Square, Leeds LS1 2NU. *T:* Leeds 26633. *Club:* Leeds (Leeds).

RANDOLPH, Michael Richard Spencer; Editor since 1957, Director since 1967, British Reader's Digest; *b* 2 Jan. 1925; *s* of late Leslie Richard Randolph and late Gladys (*née* Keen); *m* 1952, Jenefer Scawen Blunt; two *s* two *d*. *Educ:* Merchant Taylors' Sch.; New Rochelle High Sch., NY, USA; Queen's Coll., Oxford. Served RNVR, Intell. Staff Eastern Fleet, 1944-46, Sub-Lieut. Editorial staff, Amalgamated Press, 1948-52; Odham's Press, 1952-56; Reader's Digest, 1956-; Dir, Reader's Digest Films Ltd, 1973-. Mem., Press Council, 1975-. Chm., Reader's Digest Pension Trustees Ltd, 1975-; Chm., Soc. of Magazine Editors, 1973; Dir, Navy internat. magazine, 1971-; Mem. Council, British Atlantic Cttee, 1970-; Mem. Council, Action on Smoking and Health, 1977. *Recreations:* country life, dinghy sailing, reading. *Address:* The Cloth Hall, Smarden, Kent TN27 8QB. *Club:* Savile.

RANDOLPH, Ven. Thomas Berkeley; Archdeacon of Hereford, 1959-70, Archdeacon Emeritus, since 1970; Canon Residentiary of Hereford Cathedral, 1961-70; *b* 15 March 1904; *s* of Felton George Randolph, Barrister-at-law, and Emily Margaret Randolph, Chichester, Sx; *m* 1935, Margaret, *d* of Rev. H. C. R. F. Jenner, Vennwood, Hereford and Wenvoe, Glam; two *s* one *d*. *Educ:* Christ's Hospital; Queen's College, Oxford (Scholar). BA (2nd Class Theology) 1927; MA 1932; Cuddesdon Coll., 1927; Curate of St Mary's, Portsea, 1928-33; Chaplain (Eccles. Est.) St Paul's Cathedral, Calcutta, 1934-37; Vicar of Eastleigh, 1938-46; Vicar of St Mary the Virgin with All Saints, St Saviour's, St Mark's and St Matthew's, Reading, 1946-59. Proctor in Convocation for the Diocese of Oxford, 1950-55; Hon. Canon of Christ Church, Oxford, 1957-59; Vicar of Wellington, Hereford, 1959-61. *Recreation:* golf. *Address:* 14 Heatherwood, Midhurst, West Sussex. *T:* Midhurst 2765.
See also C. G. Randolph.

RANDRUP, Michael; with Military Aircraft Division, BAC Warton; *b* 20 April 1913; *s* of Soeren Revsgaard and Alexandra Randrup, Skive, Denmark; *m* 1941, Betty Perry (*d* 1949); one *s* one *d*; *m* 1954, Florence May Dryden. *Educ:* King's School, Canterbury; Chelsea College of Aeronautics. Learned to fly, 1934; RAF, 1940-46; OC Engine Research Flight RAE, 1945; Chief Test Pilot, D. Napier & Son Ltd, 1946-60; Manager, British Aircraft Corporation, Saudi Arabia, 1966-73. Aircraft Altitude World Record, 1957; Britannia Trophy, 1958; Derry Richards Meml Trophy, 1958. *Address:* 10 Fairlawn Road, Lytham, Lancs.

RANFURLY, 6th Earl of, *cr* 1831; **Thomas Daniel Knox,** KCMG 1955; Baron Welles, 1781; Viscount Northland, 1791; Baron Ranfurly (UK) 1826; Chairman: Colonial Mutual Life Assurance Soc. Ltd (London Board); Madame Tussauds Ltd; Inchcape Insurance Holdings Ltd; Director: Inchcape & Co. Ltd; a Member of Lloyd's, since 1947; *b* 29 May 1913; *s* of late Viscount Northland (killed in action, 1915) and Hilda, *d* of late Sir Daniel Cooper, 2nd Bt; *S* grandfather 1933; *m* 1939, Hermione, *e d* of late G. R. P. Llewellyn, Baglan Hall, Monmouth Road, Abergavenny, Mon; one *d*. *Educ:* Eton; Trinity Coll., Cambridge. ADC to Gov.-Gen. of Australia, 1936-38; served European War of 1939-45 (prisoner). Governor and C-in-C, Bahamas, 1953-56. Chairman London Scout Council, 1957-65; Chief Scout's Commissioner, Greater London, 1965-. President, Shaftesbury Homes and "Arethusa" Training Ship, 1959-; Chairman: Bd of Governors, London Clinic, 1973-; Ranfurly Library Service Ltd. Steward, Jockey Club, 1973-75. *Heir: kinsman* Gerald François Needham Knox [*b* 4 Jan. 1929; *m* 1955, Rosemary, *o d* of late Air Vice-Marshal Felton Vesey Holt, CMG, DSO; two *s* two *d*]. *Address:* Great Pednor, Chesham, Bucks. *T:* Gt Missenden 2155. *Clubs:* White's; Jockey (Newmarket).

RANGER, Douglas, FRCS; Otolaryngologist, The Middlesex Hospital, since 1950; Dean, The Middlesex Hospital Medical School, since 1974; *b* 5 Oct. 1916; *s* of William and Hatton Thomasina Ranger; *m* 1943, Betty, *d* of Captain Sydney Harold Draper and Elsie Draper; two *s*. *Educ:* Church of England Grammar Sch., Brisbane; The Middlesex Hosp. Med. Sch. MB BS 1941, FRCS 1943. Surgical Registrar, The Mddx Hosp., 1942-44. Served War, Temp. Maj. RAMC and Surgical Specialist, 1945-48 (SEAC and MELF). Otolaryngologist, Mount Vernon Hosp., 1958-74; Hon. Sec., Brit. Assoc. of Otolaryngologists, 1965-71. RCS: Mem. Court of Examiners, 1966-72; Mem. Council, 1967-72; Pres., Assoc. of Head and Neck Oncologists of GB, 1974-77. Civil Consultant in Otolaryngology, RAF, 1965-. Dir, Ferens Inst. of Otolaryngology, 1965-; Cons. Adviser in Otolaryngology, DHSS, 1971-. *Publications:* papers and lectures on otolaryngological subjects, esp. with ref. to malignant disease. *Address:* 40 Gordon Avenue, Stanmore, Mddx HA7 3QH. *T:* 01-954 2121; 44 Wimpole Street, W1M 7DG. *T:* 01-935 3332.

RANK, Sir Benjamin (Keith), Kt 1972; CMG 1955; MS, FRCS; FRACS; FACS; Consulting Plastic Surgeon, Royal Melbourne Hospital, Repatriation Department, Victoria Eye and Ear Hospital, Queen Victoria Hospital, etc, and in Tasmania; Surgeon in charge Reparative Surgery, Peter MacCallum Clinic, Melbourne; *b* 14 Jan. 1911; *s* of Wreghitt Rank and Bessie Rank (*née* Smith); *m* 1938, Barbara Lyle Facy; one *s* three *d*. *Educ:* Scotch College, Melbourne; Ormond College, University of Melbourne. MB, BS Melbourne, 1934; Resident Medical Officer, Royal Melbourne Hospital, 1935-36; MS (Melb.), 1937; MRCS, LRCP 1938; Resident Surgical Officer, London County Council, 1938-39 (St James' Hospital, Balham); FRCS 1938; Assistant Plastic Surgeon (EMS) at Hill End (Bart's), 1939-40; AAMC, 1940-45; Officer i/c AIF Plastic Surgery Unit in Egypt, and later at Heidelberg Military Hospital, Victoria, Australia (Lt-Col); Hon. Plastic Surgeon, Royal Melbourne Hosp., 1946-66. Carnegie Fellow, 1947. Member: Dental Board of Victoria 1949-73, Joske Orator 1974; BMA State Council, 1950-60; Chm. Exec. Cttee, RACS (Pres., 1966-68); Chm., Cttee of Management, Victorian Plastic Surgery Unit (Preston Hosp.), 1966-; Mem. Bd of Management, Royal Melbourne Hosp., 1971-; Mem. Council, International House, Univ. of Melbourne. Mem., Motor Accident Bd, Victoria. Sir Arthur Sims Commonwealth Travelling Prof., RCS, 1958; Moynihan Lectr, 1972; Vis. Prof., Harvard Med. Sch., 1976. Syme Orator, RACS, 1976; Stawell Orator, 1977. 87th Mem., James IV Assoc. of Surgeons; Pres., British Assoc. of Plastic Surgeons, 1965. Pres., 5th Internat. Congress of Plastic Surgery, Melbourne, 1971. FRACS 1943; Hon. FACST 1952; Hon. FRCS Canada; Hon. FRCSE 1973; Hon. FACS. Hon. DSc Punjabi Univ., 1970; Hon. Member: Société Française de Chirurgie Plastique; Indian Association of Surgeons. *Publications:* (jointly) Surgery of Repair as applied to Hand Injuries, 1953. Papers in British, American and Australian Surgical Jls. *Recreations:* golf, gardening. *Address:* Mill Hill, Vine Street, Heidelberg, Victoria

3084, Australia. *Clubs:* Melbourne (Melbourne); Tasmanian (Hobart); Peninsula Golf.

RANK, Joseph McArthur; Chairman, Ranks Hovis McDougall Ltd, since 1969; *b* 24 April 1918; *s* of late Rowland Rank and of Margaret McArthur; *m* 1946, Hon. Moira (who *m* 1940, Peter Anthony Stanley Woodwark, killed in action, 1943; one *d*), *d* of 3rd Baron Southborough, *qv*; one *s* one *d*. *Educ:* Loretto. Joined Mark Mayhew Ltd, 1936. Served RAF, 1940-46. Personal Pilot to Air C-in-C, SEAC, 1945; Jt Man. Dir, Joseph Rank Ltd, 1955-65; Dep. Chm. and Chief Exec., Ranks Hovis McDougall Ltd, 1965-69, Chm., 1969-. Pres., Nat. Assoc. of British and Irish Millers, 1957-58. Chm., Millers Mutual Assoc., 1969-; Chm. Council, British Nutrition Foundation, 1968-69; Dir, Royal Alexandra and Albert Sch., 1952-, Chm., Governing Body, 1975-; Friend of the Royal Coll. of Physicians, 1967-; Council, Royal Warrant Holders Assoc., 1968-71. Mem., Shrievalty Assoc., 1974. First High Sheriff of East Sussex, 1974. *Recreations:* boating, travelling. *Address:* Landhurst, Hartfield, East Sussex. *T:* Hartfield 293. *Clubs:* Royal Air Force; Sussex.

RANKEILLOUR, 4th Baron *cr* 1932, of Buxted; **Peter St Thomas More Henry Hope;** *b* 29 May 1935; *s* of 3rd Baron Rankeillour and Mary Sibyl, *d* of late Col Wilfrid Ricardo, DSO; *S* father, 1967; unmarried. *Educ:* Ampleforth College; privately. *Recreations:* hunting, shooting, genealogy, boating; agricultural machinery inventor. *Heir: cousin* Michael Richard Hope [*b* 21 Oct. 1940; *m* 1964, Elizabeth Rosemary, *e d* of Col F. H. Fuller; one *s* two *d*]. *Address:* Achaderry House, Roy Bridge, West Inverness-shire. *T:* Spean Bridge 206.

RANKIN, Andrew, QC 1968; a Recorder of the Crown Court, since 1972; *b* 3 Aug. 1924; *s* of William Locke Rankin and Mary Ann McArdle, Edinburgh; *m* 1st, 1944, Winifred (marr. diss. 1963), *d* of Frank McAdam, Edinburgh; two *s* two *d* (and one *s* decd); 2nd, 1964, Veronica, *d* of George Aloysius Martin, Liverpool. *Educ:* Royal High Sch., Edinburgh; Univ. of Edinburgh; Downing Coll., Cambridge. Served War of 1939-45 (Gen. Service Medal, 1939-45 Star): Sub-Lt, RNVR, 1943. BL (Edin.) 1946; BA, 1st cl. hons Law Tripos (Cantab), 1948. Royal Commonwealth Soc. Medal, 1942; Cecil Peace Prize, 1946; Lord Justice Holker Exhibn, Gray's Inn, 1947-50; Lord Justice Holker Schol., Gray's Inn, 1950-53; Univ. Blue, Edin., 1943 and 1946 and Camb., 1948. Lectr in Law, Univ. of Liverpool, 1948-52. Called to Bar, Gray's Inn, 1950. *Publications:* (ed, 4th edn) Levie's Law of Bankruptcy in Scotland, 1950; various articles in UK and foreign legal jls. *Recreations:* swimming, travel by sea, racing (both codes), watching soccer (especially Liverpool FC). *Address:* Chelwood, Pine Walks, Prenton, Cheshire. *T:* 051-608 2987; 69 Cliffords Inn, EC4. *T:* 01-405 2932; 2 Hare Court, Temple, EC4. *T:* 01-353 0076.

RANKIN, Dame Annabelle (Jane Mary), DBE 1957; Australian High Commissioner, New Zealand, 1971-75; *b* Brisbane; *d* of Mrs A. Rankin, Brisbane, and late Col C. D. W. Rankin, former Qld MLA for many years and sometime Minister for Railways; unmarried. *Educ:* Childers and Howard State Schools, Queensland; Glennie Memorial School, Toowoomba, Queensland. Clerk in Trustee Company; State Sec., Queensland Girl Guides' Assoc. War Service: YWCA Assistant Commissioner for Queensland, attached to Australian Women's Services, 1943-46. Appointed Organiser, Junior Red Cross, Queensland, 1946. First Queensland woman to enter Federal Parliament; Senator for Queensland, 1946-71; Mem., of Public Works Cttee, 1950; Govt Whip, Senate, 1951-66; Minister of Housing, 1966-71. Mem., Parly Standing Cttee on Broadcasting, 1947; Whip of Senate Opposition, 1947; Vice-Pres, Liberal Party of Australia, Queensland Div., 1949; Mem., Australian delegn to Commonwealth Parly Assoc. Conf., Ottawa, 1952. Represented Austr. Govt at Independence Celebrations, Mauritius, 1968. *Recreations:* motoring, reading. *Address:* 79 Captain Cook Parade, Deception Bay, Qld, Australia. *Clubs:* Moreton, Lyceum (Brisbane).

RANKIN, Sir Hugh (Charles Rhys), 3rd Bt, *cr* 1898; FSAScot 1948; Representative to District Council Perth CC (Eastern District), 1949, Perth CC 1950; Councillor for Boro' of Rattray and Blairgowrie, 1949; joined RASC as 2nd Lieut, May 1940, at age of 41 years; Captain 1940-45, India; sheep farming and is a judge of sheep at prominent shows; formerly Senior Vice-President of the Western Islamic Association; a former Vice-President of Scottish National Liberal Association; has lived during the reigns of six sovereigns; *b* 8 Aug. 1899; *er s* of Sir Reginald Rankin, 2nd Bt, and Hon. Nest Rice (*d* 1943), 2nd *d* of 6th Baron Dynevor; changed his names by Scotch law in July 1946 to above; *S* father, 1931; *m* 1932, Helen Margaret (*d* 1945), *e d* of Sir Charles Stewart, KBE, 1st Public Trustee, and *widow* of Capt. Colin Campbell, Scots Guards; *m* 1946, Robina Kelly,

FSA (Scot.), Cordon Bleu (Edin.), Crieff, Perthshire. *Educ:* Harrow. Served in 1st Royal Dragoon Guards in Sinn Feinn Campaign, 1920-22; ex-Pres. Clun Forest Sheep Breeders Assoc., 1928, and their representative to National Sheep Breeders Association that year; whole-time 'piece-work' shearer, in W Australia, covering area between Bunbury and Broome, 1929-31; in 1938 was a representative on committee of British sheep breeders in London appointed to petition Government *re* sheep industry. Runner-up All Britain Sheep Judging Competition (6,000 entrants), 1962. A writer on agricultural stock; expert on Highland problems; was Brit. Rep., 1937, to 1st all European Muslim Congress at Geneva; a practising Non-Theistic Theravada Buddhist since 1944, and performed Holy Buddhist Pilgrimage, Nov. 1944, the 2nd Britisher to do so; Vice-Pres. World's Buddhist Assoc., 1945. Joined Labour Party 1939 and holds extreme political views; is a Dominion Home Ruler for Scotland, member Scottish National Party; joined Scottish Communist Party, 1945; Welsh Republican Nationalist and Welsh speaker. Mem. Roy. Inst. and Roy. Soc. of Arts; is Hereditary Piper of the Clan Maclaine. News of the World Kt of the Road (for courtesy in motor driving). Broadsword Champion of British Army (Cavalry), 1921. *Publications:* articles in agricultural publications, etc. *Recreations:* golf (holds an amateur record amongst golfers of Gt Britain in having played on 382 separate courses of UK and Eire), shooting, coarse fishing, hunting, motoring, cycling on mountain tracks to tops of British mountains (Pres. Rough Stuff Cycling Assoc., 1956); study of ancient track ways; bowls, tennis, archæology (wife and himself are only persons who have crawled under dwarf fir forest for last ½ mile of most northerly known section of any Roman road in Europe, terminating opposite end of Kirriemuir Golf Course), study of domestic animals, speaking on politics, especially *re* Scottish Home Rule and Highland problems. *Heir: nephew* Ian Niall Rankin [*b* 19 Dec. 1932; *s* of Arthur Niall Talbot Rankin and of Lady Jean Rankin, *qv*; *m* 1959, Alexandra, *o d* of Adm. Sir Laurence Durlacher, *qv*; one *s* one *d*]. *Address:* c/o The Flat, Priorsgate, Priorsfield, Godalming, Surrey. *Club:* Royal and Ancient Golf (St Andrews).

RANKIN, James Deans, PhD; Chief Inspector, Cruelty to Animals Act (1876), Home Office, since 1976; *b* 17 Jan. 1918; *s* of late Andrew Christian Fleming Rankin and Catherine Sutherland (*née* Russell); *m* 1950, Hilary Jacqueline Bradshaw; two *d*. *Educ:* Hamilton Acad.; Glasgow Veterinary Coll. (PhD Microbiology). MRCVS. Gen. practice, 1941; Res. Officer, Min. of Agriculture and Fisheries, 1942; Principal Res. Officer, ARC, 1952; Inspector, Home Office, 1969. *Publications:* scientific contribs in standard works and in med. and veterinary jls. *Recreations:* golf, DIY. *Address:* Home Office, 50 Queen Anne's Gate, SW1H 9AT. *T:* 01-213 6269. *Club:* Farmers'.

RANKIN, Lady Jean (Margaret), DCVO 1969 (CVO 1957); Woman of the Bedchamber to Queen Elizabeth The Queen Mother, since 1947; *b* 15 Aug. 1905; *d* of 12th Earl of Stair; *m* 1931, Niall Rankin (*d* 1965), *s* of Sir Reginald Rankin, 2nd Bt; two *s*. Governor, Thomas Coram Foundation. Order of Orange-Nassau, Netherlands, 1950. *Address:* House of Treshnish, Calgary, Isle of Mull. *T:* Dervaig 249; 3 Catherine Wheel Yard, SW1.

See also Sir Hugh C. R. Rankin, Bt.

RANKIN, John Mitchell, QC 1969; a Recorder of the Crown Court, since 1977; *b* 20 April 1924; *yr s* of late Very Rev. Provost H. M. Rankin, St Ninian's Cathedral, Perth, Scotland; *m* 1949, Heather Hope, *o d* of late H. K. Cox, Snaigow, Perthshire; two *s* two *d*. *Educ:* Trinity Coll., Glenalmond; Keble Coll., Oxford. Served in Royal Navy, 1942-46 (Lt RNVR, 1945). BA Oxon 1949; MA 1975; called to Bar, Middle Temple, 1950; Bencher, 1975. Dir, Norland Nursery Training Coll., Ltd. Dep. Chm., Local Govt Boundary Commn for England, 1972. Mem., Wine Standards Bd of Vintners' Co., 1973. *Recreations:* painting and graphic arts. *Address:* Carpmael Building, Temple, EC4. *T:* 01-353 5537. *Club:* Travellers'.

RANKIN, Prof. Robert Alexander, MA, PhD, ScD; Professor of Mathematics, since 1954, and Clerk of Senate, since 1971, Glasgow University; *b* 27 Oct. 1915; *s* of late Rev. Prof. Oliver Shaw Rankin, DD, and late Olivia Teresa Shaw; *m* 1942, Mary Ferrier Llewellyn, *d* of late W. M. Llewellyn and late K. F. Llewellyn, JP; one *s* three *d*. *Educ:* Fettes; Clare Coll., Cambridge. Wrangler, 1936; Fellow of Clare College, 1939-51; Vis. Fellow, Clare Hall, 1971. Ministry of Supply (work on rockets), 1940-45; Faculty Asst Lecturer, Cambridge Univ., 1945-48; Univ. Lecturer, Cambridge, 1948-51; Asst Tutor, Clare Coll., 1947-51; Praelector, Clare Coll., 1949-51; Mason Professor of Pure Mathematics at Birmingham University, 1951-54. Mathematical Sec. and Editor of Proceedings of Cambridge

Philosophical Soc., 1947-51; Hon. Pres. Glasgow Gaelic Soc., 1957-; Pres. Edinburgh Mathematical Soc., 1957-58; Mem., Special Cttee, Advisory Coun. on Educn in Scotland, 1959-61; Vis. Prof., Indiana Univ., 1963-64; Vice-Pres. Roy. Soc. of Edinburgh, 1960-63; Vice-Pres., Scottish Gaelic Texts Soc., 1967-; Founder Mem., and Chm., Scottish Mathematical Council, 1967-73; Chm., Clyde Estuary Amenity Council, 1969-. Keith Prize, RSE, 1961-63. *Publications:* Matematicheskaya Teorija Dvizhenija Neupravljaemykh Raket, 1951; An Introduction to Mathematical Analysis, 1963; The Modular Group and its Subgroups, 1969; Modular Forms and Functions, 1977; papers on the Theory of Numbers, Theory of Functions, Rocket Ballistics and Gaelic Subjects in various journals. *Recreations:* hill-walking; Gaelic studies; organ music. *Address:* 10 The University, Glasgow G12 8QG. *T:* 041-339 2641; Cromla Cottage, Corrie, Isle of Arran.

RANKINE, Sir John (Dalzell), KCMG 1954 (CMG 1947); KCVO 1956; *b* 8 June 1907; *o s* of late Sir Richard Rankine, KCMG; *m* 1939, Janet Grace (*d* 1976), *d* of Major R. L. Austin, Clifton, Bristol; one *d. Educ:* Christ's College, Christchurch, New Zealand; Exeter College, Oxford. BA 1930; entered Colonial Administration Service as Cadet, Uganda, 1931; Asst Sec. East African Governor's Conference, 1939; First Asst Sec., 1942; Asst Colonial Sec., Fiji, 1942; Colonial Sec., Barbados, 1945; Chief Secretary, Kenya, 1947-51; Chairman, Development and Reconstruction Authority. British Resident, Zanzibar, 1952-54; administered Govts of Barbados and Kenya on various occasions; Governor, Western Region, Nigeria, 1954-60. KStJ 1958. Brilliant Star of Zanzibar (1st Class), 1954. *Recreations:* tennis, squash, golf. *Address:* Wyncote, Coggins Mill Lane, Mayfield, East Sussex. *T:* Mayfield 3254. *Clubs:* Athenæum, MCC, Queen's.

RANKING, Robert Duncan; His Honour Judge Ranking; a Circuit Judge (formerly County Court Judge), since 1968; *b* 24 Oct. 1915; *yr s* of Dr R. M. Ranking, Tunbridge Wells, Kent; *m* 1949, Evelyn Mary Tagart (*née* Walker); one *d. Educ:* Cheltenham Coll.; Pembroke Coll., Cambridge (MA). Called to Bar, 1939. Served in Queen's Own Royal W Kent Regt, 1939-46. Dep. Chm. E Sussex QS, 1962-71; Dep. Chm., Agricultural Land Tribunal (S Eastern Area), 1963. *Address:* 2 Hungershall Park, Tunbridge Wells, Kent. *T:* 27551.

RANNIE, Prof. Ian; FRCPath 1964; FIBiol 1964; Professor of Pathology (Dental School), University of Newcastle upon Tyne, since 1960; *b* 29 Oct. 1915; *o s* of James Rannie, MA, and Nicholas Denniston McMeekan; *m* 1943, Flora Welch; two *s. Educ:* Ayr Academy; Glasgow University. BSc (Glas), 1935; MB, ChB (Glas), 1938; BSc Hons Pathology and Bacteriology (Glas), 1939; Hutcheson Research Schol. (Pathology), 1940. Assistant to Professor of Bacteriology, Glasgow, 1940-41; Lecturer in Pathology, 1942-60, King's College, Univ. of Durham. Consultant Pathologist, United Newcastle upon Tyne Hospitals, 1948-. Pres., International Soc. of Geographical Pathology, 1969-72; Vice-Pres., Internat. Union of Angiology. Hon. Mem., Hungarian Arteriosclerosis Res. Soc. *Publications:* papers on various subjects in medical journals. *Recreation:* golf. *Address:* 5 Osborne Villas, Newcastle upon Tyne NE2 1JU. *T:* 813163. *Club:* East India, Devonshire, Sports and Public Schools.

RANSOM, Charles Frederick George, CMG 1956; OBE 1950; an Historian, Historical Branch of Cabinet Office, since 1972; Director of the Centre for Contemporary European Studies, University of Sussex, 1973-74, Fellow of the Centre since 1968; *b* 9 July 1911; *s* of late Charles Edward Ransom and Elizabeth Ransom, Harrow, Middlesex; *m* 1943, Eileen Mary Emily, *d* of late Rt Rev. A. I. Greaves, Bishop Suffragan of Grimsby, DD; two *s* one *d. Educ:* Harrow CGS; University College, London (Ricardo Scholar, 1933-35). Schoolmaster and Univ. Extra-Mural Lecturer, 1936-40. Served in UK and Italy, York and Lancaster Regt (Major), 1940-46. FO 1946; First Sec., HM Embassy, Rome, 1958-61; FO Supernumerary Fellow, St Antony's Coll., Oxford, 1966-67. *Publications:* The European Community and Eastern Europe, 1973; articles on European affairs. *Recreations:* music, literature, gardening. *Address:* Ladyfield, Etchingham, East Sussex. *T:* 216.

RANSOME, Prof. Sir Gordon (Arthur), KBE 1972 (CBE 1962); FRCP; Professor Emeritus of Medicine, University of Singapore, since 1972; late Senior Consultant to General Hospital, Singapore; Senior Consultant to Singapore AntiTuberculosis Association, since 1947; Hon. Consultant Physician to the Sultan of Kelantan; *b* 6 May 1910; *s* of late Rev. Maurice John Ransome, St John's Coll., Cambridge, and Rector of Pulverbatch, Salop; *m* 1st, 1940, Eryl Arundel; one *d*; 2nd, 1955, Daphne Mary, *d* of Col Lawrence George Beach, RE; two

s one *d. Educ:* Dauntsey's Sch.; London University; St Bartholomew's Hosp.; Charing Cross Hosp.; London Sch. of Tropical Medicine. MRCS, LRCP 1933; MRCP 1935; FRCP 1947. War of 1939-45: Lt-Col, IMS; Adv. in Med., 12th Army; Adv. in Neurology, SEAC; Staff Officer, British Mil. Admin (Malaya), 1945 (despatches twice). Hon. Consultant to Army, Far East, 1947-71, and to ANZUK Hosp., 1971. Formerly: Sen. Med. Registrar, Charing Cross Hosp.; Chief Asst Med., Royal Westminster Ophthalmic Hosp.; Associate Prof. of Med., King Edward VII Coll. Med., Singapore; Prof. Clin. Med. and Prof. Med., Univ. of Malaya, Singapore; Prof. Med., Univ. of Singapore, Acad. Med. (AM), Singapore, 1957, Hon. AM 1977; Hon. MD 1969; Meritorious Service Medal, PJG, Singapore, 1967; Datoship by Sultan of Kelantan, DJMK (Order of the Life of the Throne), 1969; SPMJ, 1973; Datuk; Grand Comdr, Order of the Throne, Johore. *Publications:* contribs to scientific jls. *Recreations:* shooting, fly fishing, history. *Address:* The Grove, New Radnor, near Presteigne, Powys. *T:* New Radnor 276. *Clubs:* Royal Over-Seas League; Tanglin (Singapore).

RANSOME, Maj.-Gen. Robert St George Tyldesley, CB 1946; CBE 1944; MC 1940; *b* 22 June 1903; *s* of Dr A. S. Ransome; *m* 1947, Kathleen, *widow* of Brig. C. Leslie-Smith, IA. *Educ:* Winchester Coll.; Royal Military College, Sandhurst. Joined Royal Fusiliers, 1924; Instructor, Royal Military College, Sandhurst, 1935-37; Staff College, 1938-39; BEF 1939-40 (despatches, MC); Instructor, Senior Staff College, 1940; served in Mediterranean, Middle East, 1941-43; commanded 11th Battalion Royal Fusiliers, 1942. Visited Middle East, Quebec, S Africa, Yalta, Potsdam, Italy, France, etc, 1943-45; Vice-QMG to the Forces (Maj.-Gen.), 1946; idc 1947; BGS, GHQ Far East, 1948; Comdr Scottish Beach Bde (TA), 1950; Malaya, 1950 (despatches); Services Adviser, UK High Commission, Germany, 1954-55; Chief (Maj.-Gen.), Jt Services Liaison Organisation, BAOR, 1955-58, retd. Deputy Colonel, Royal Fusiliers, 1962-63. Chm., Royal Fusiliers' Old Comrades Assoc., 1960-76. *Recreations:* gardening, shooting, military history. *Address:* Wilford Cottage, Melton, Suffolk. *Clubs:* Army and Navy, MCC.

RAO, Calyampudi Radhakrishna, FRS 1967; Jawaharlal Nehru Professor, Indian Statistical Institute, since 1976; Director, Research and Training School, Indian Statistical Institute 1964-76, and Secretary, 1972-76; *b* 10 Sept. 1920; *s* of C. D. Naidu and A. Laksmikantamma; *m* 1948, C. Bhargavi Rao; one *s* one *d. Educ:* Andhra Univ. (MA, 1st Class Maths); Calcutta Univ. (MA, 1st Class Statistics; Gold Medal); PhD, ScD, Cambridge (Hon. Fellow, King's Coll., Cambridge, 1975). Superintending Statistician, Indian Statistical Institute, 1943-49; Professor and Head of Division of Theoretical Research and Training, Indian Statistical Institute, 1949-64. Co-editor, Sankhya, Indian Jl of Statistics, 1964-72, Editor, 1972-. Member, Internat. Statistical Inst., 1951 (Mem. Statistical Educn Cttee, 1958-; Treasurer, 1962-65; Pres.-elect, 1975-77, Pres., 1977-79); Chm., Indian Nat. Cttee for Statistics, 1962-; Pres., Biometric Soc., 1974. Fellow: Indian Nat. Sci. Acad., 1953 (Vice-Pres., 1973, 1974); Inst. of Math. Statistics, USA, 1958 (Pres., 1976-77); Amer. Statistical Assoc., 1972; Econometric Soc., 1973; Indian Acad. of Sciences. Hon. Fellow: Royal Stat. Soc., 1969; Amer. Acad. of Arts and Sciences, 1975. Shanti Swarup Bhatnagar Memorial Award, 1963; Guy Medal in Silver, Royal Stat. Soc., 1965; Padma Bhushan, 1968; Meghnad Saha Gold Medal, 1969. Hon. DSc: Andhra; Leningrad; Athens; Osmania; Hon. DLitt Delhi. *Publications:* (with Mahalanobis and Majumdar) Anthropometric Survey of the United Provinces, 1941, a statistical study, 1949; Advanced Statistical Methods in Biometric Research, 1952; (with Mukherjee and Trevor) The Ancient Inhabitants of Jebal Moya, 1955; (with Majumdar) Bengal Anthropometric Survey, 1945, a statistical study, 1959; Linear Statistical Inference and its Applications, 1965; (with A. Matthai and S. K. Mitra) Formulae and Tables for Statistical Work, 1966; Computers and the Future of Human Society, 1968; (with S. K. Mitra) The Generalised Inverse of Matrices and its Applications, 1971; (with A. M. Kagan and Yu. V. Linnik) Characterization Problems of Mathematical Statistics, 1973. *Address:* Indian Statistical Institute, 7 S.J.S. Sansanwal Marg, New Delhi 110029, India. *T:* (office) 651384; (home) 690113.

RAPALLO, Rt. Rev. Edward; *see* Gibraltar, Bishop of, (RC).

RAPER, Vice-Adm. Sir (Robert) George, KCB 1971 (CB 1968); Director-General, Ships, 1968-May 1974; Chief Naval Engineer Officer, 1968-74; *b* 27 Aug. 1915; *s* of Major Robert George Raper and Ida Jean (*née* MacAdam Smith); *m* 1940, Frances Joan St John (*née* Phillips); one *s* two *d. Educ:* RNC Dartmouth; RN Engineering College, Keyham; Advanced Engineering Course RNC Greenwich. Sen. Engineer, HMS Edinburgh, 1940 until ship was sunk, 1942 (despatches); Turbine Research Section, Admiralty, 1942-45; Engineer Officer, HMS Broadsword, Battleaxe, Crossbow, 1945-47; Comdr, 1947; Engineer-in-Chief's Dept, Admiralty, 1948-51; Engr Officer, HMS Birmingham, 1952-54; lent to RCN, 1954; Technical Sec. to Engineer-in-Chief of the Fleet, 1955-57; Capt. 1957; IDC 1958; in command HMS Caledonia, 1959-61; Dep. Dir of Marine Engineering, Admiralty, 1961-63; CSO (T) to Flag Officer Sea Training, 1963-65; Dir, Marine Engineering, MoD (Navy Dept), 1966-67. FRINA; FIMechE; FIMarE (Pres. 1972); FRSA. *Recreations:* carpentry, walking. *Address:* Hollytree Farm, Moorlinch, near Bridgwater, Somerset. *T:* Ashcott 510. *Club:* Naval and Military.

RAPHAEL, Chaim, CBE 1965 (OBE 1951); Research Fellow, University of Sussex, since 1969; *b* Middlesbrough, 14 July 1908; *s* of Rev. David Rabinovitch and Rachel Rabinovitch (name changed by deed poll 1936); *m* 1934, Diana Rose (marr. diss. 1964); one *s* one *d*. *Educ:* Portsmouth Grammar Sch.; University Coll., Oxford (scholar). PPE 1930. James Mew Post-Grad. Schol. in Hebrew, 1931. Kennicott Fellowship, 1933-36. Cowley Lectr in Post-Biblical Hebrew, 1932-39. Liaison Officer for Internment Camps: UK 1940; Canada 1941. Adviser, British Information Services, NY, 1942-45; Dir (Economics), 1945-57; Dep. Head of Information Div., HM Treasury, 1957-59; Head of Information Division: HM Treasury, 1959-68; Civil Service Dept, 1968-69. *Publications:* Memoirs of a Special Case, 1962; The Walls of Jerusalem, 1968; A Feast of History, 1972; A Coat of Many Colours, 1978; *novels:* (under pseudonym Jocelyn Davey): The Undoubted Deed, 1956; The Naked Villany, 1958; A Touch of Stagefright, 1960; A Killing in Hats, 1964; A Treasury Alarm, 1976. *Recreation:* America. *Address:* 27 Langdale Road, Hove, East Sussex. *T:* Brighton 70563. *Clubs:* Reform, Jack's.

RAPHAEL, Prof. David Daiches, MA, DPhil; Academic Director of Associated Studies and Professor of Philosophy, Imperial College, University of London, since 1973; *b* 25 Jan. 1916; 2nd *s* of late Jacob Raphael and late Sarah Warshawsky, Liverpool; *m* 1942, Sylvia, *er d* of late Rabbi Dr Salis Daiches and of Flora Levin, Edinburgh; two *d*. *Educ:* Liverpool Collegiate School; University College, Oxford (scholar). 1st Class, Classical Moderations, 1936; Hall-Houghton Junior Septuagint Prizeman, 1937; 1st Class, Literae Humaniores, 1938; Robinson Senior Scholar of Oriel College, Oxford, 1938-40; Passmore Edwards Scholar, 1939. Served in Army, 1940-41. Temporary Assistant Principal, Ministry of Labour and National Service, 1941-44; temp. Principal, 1944-46. Professor of Philosophy, University of Otago, Dunedin, NZ, 1946-49; Lecturer in Moral Philosophy, Univ. of Glasgow, 1949-51; Senior Lecturer, 1951-60; Edward Caird Prof. of Political and Social Philosophy, Univ. of Glasgow, 1960-70; Prof. of Philosophy, Univ. of Reading, 1970-73. Visiting Professor of Philosophy, Hamilton Coll., Clinton, NY (under Chauncey S. Truax Foundation), and Univ. of Southern California, 1959; Mahlon Powell Lectr, Indiana Univ., 1959; Vis. Fellow, All Souls Coll., Oxford, 1967-68. Independent Member: Cttee on Teaching Profession in Scotland (Wheatley Cttee), 1961-63; Scottish Agricultural Wages Board, 1962-; Agricultural Wages Bd for England and Wales, 1972-. Mem. Academic Adv. Cttee, Heriot-Watt Univ., Edinburgh, 1964-71; Mem. Cttee on Distribution of Teachers in Scotland (Roberts Cttee), 1965-66; Independent Member Police Advisory Board for Scotland, 1965-70; Member Social Sciences Adv. Cttee, UK Nat. Commission, UNESCO, 1966-74; Vice-Pres., Internat. Assoc. Philosophy of Law and Social Philosophy, 1971-; Pres., Aristotelian Soc., 1974-75. Academic Mem., Bd of Governors, Hebrew Univ. of Jerusalem, 1969-. *Publications:* The Moral Sense, 1947; Edition of Richard Price's Review of Morals, 1948; Moral Judgement, 1955; The Paradox of Tragedy, 1960; Political Theory and the Rights of Man, 1967; British Moralists 1650-1800, 1969; Problems of Political Philosophy, 1970; (ed jtly) Adam Smith's Theory of Moral Sentiments, 1976; Hobbes: Morals and Politics, 1977; (ed jtly) Adam Smith's Lectures on Jurisprudence, 1977; articles in jls of philosophy and of political studies. *Address:* Imperial College of Science and Technology, SW7 2AZ.

RAPHAEL, Frederic Michael; author; *b* 14 Aug. 1931; *s* of Cedric Michael Raphael and Irene Rose Mauser; *m* 1955, Sylvia Betty Glatt; two *s* one *d*. *Educ:* Charterhouse; St John's Coll., Cambridge (MA (Hons)). FRSL 1964. *Publications: novels:* Obbligato, 1956; The Earlsdon Way, 1958; The Limits of Love, 1960; A Wild Surmise, 1961; The Graduate Wife, 1962; The Trouble with England, 1962; Lindmann, 1963; Orchestra and Beginners, 1967; Like Men Betrayed, 1970; Who Were You With Last Night?, 1971; April, June and November, 1972; Richard's Things, 1973; California Time, 1975; The Glittering Prizes, 1976; *biography:* Somerset Maugham and his World,

1977; *essays:* (ed) Bookmarks, 1975; *screenplays:* Nothing but the Best, 1964; Darling, 1965 (Academy Award); Two For The Road, 1967; Far From the Madding Crowd, 1967; A Severed Head, 1972; Daisy Miller, 1974; The Glittering Prizes, 1976 (sequence of television plays) (Writer of the Year 1976, Royal TV Soc.); Rogue Male, 1976; Roses, Roses..., 1978; *translations:* Poems of Catullus, 1976; The Oresteia, 1978. *Recreation:* tennis. *Address:* The Wick, Langham, Colchester, Essex CO4 5PE.

RAPHAEL, Prof. Ralph Alexander, FRS 1962; PhD (London), DSc (London); FRSE; ARCS; DIC; FRIC; Fellow of Christ's College, and Professor of Organic Chemistry, Cambridge University, since June 1972; *b* 1 Jan. 1921; *s* of Jack Raphael; *m* 1944, Prudence Marguerite Anne, *d* of Col P. J. Gaffikin, MC, MD; one *s* one *d*. *Educ:* Wesley College, Dublin; Tottenham County School; Imperial College of Science and Technology. Chemist, May & Baker Ltd, 1943-46. ICI Research Fellow, Univ. of London, 1946-49; Lecturer in Organic Chemistry, Univ. of Glasgow, 1949-54; Professor of Organic Chemistry, Queen's University, Belfast, 1954-57; Regius Prof. of Chemistry, Glasgow Univ., 1957-72. Meldola Medallist, Royal Institute of Chemistry, 1948; Tilden Lectr, Chem. Soc., 1960, Corday-Morgan Vis. Lectr, 1963; Roy. Soc. Vis. Prof., 1967; Pedler Lectr, Chem. Soc., 1973. Vice-Pres. Chemical Soc., 1967-70; Mem., Academic Adv. Bd, Warwick Univ. Chem. Soc. Ciba-Geigy Award for Synthetic Chemistry, 1975. *Publications:* Chemistry of Carbon Compounds, Vol. IIA, 1953; Acetylenic Compounds in Organic Synthesis, 1955; papers in Journal of Chemical Society. *Recreations:* music, bridge. *Address:* University Chemical Laboratory, Lensfield Road, Cambridge CB2 1EW. *T:* Cambridge 66499; 4 Ivy Field, High Street, Barton, Cambs. *Club:* Athenæum.

RAPHOE, Bishop of, (RC), since 1965; Most Rev. Anthony C. MacFeely; *b* 4 Feb. 1909. *Educ:* St Columb's Coll., Londonderry; St Patrick's Coll., Maynooth; Irish Coll., Rome. Priest, 1932; Prof., St Columb's Coll., Oct. 1934; Pres., St Columb's Coll., 1950; Parish Priest, Strabane, Co. Tyrone, 1959-65. *Recreation:* walking. *Address:* Ard Eunan, Letterkenny, Co. Donegal, Ireland. *T:* Letterkenny 349.

RAPP, Sir Thomas (Cecil), KBE 1950; CMG 1945; MC; *b* Saltburn-by-the-Sea, 1893; *m* 1922, Dorothy, *d* of John Clarke; one *d* (and one *d* decd). *Educ:* Coatham School; Sidney Sussex College, Cambridge. Served European War (Duke of Wellington's Regiment TF), 1914-18, retiring with rank of Major; an assistant in Levant Consular Service, 1919; Acting Vice-Consul, Port Said, 1920; Vice-Consul, Cairo, 1922; Rabat, 1927; Consul, Sofia, 1931; Moscow, 1932; Zagreb, 1936; Consul-General at Zagreb, Jugoslavia, 1939-41. Captured by German armed forces and interned in Germany, 1941-43; Consul-General, Tabriz, 1943-44; Salonica, 1944-45; Minister to Albania (did not proceed), 1946; Deputy head and subsequently head of British Economic Mission to Greece, 1946-47; Ambassador to Mexico, 1947-50; Head of British Middle East Office, Cairo, 1950-53. *Recreation:* walking. *Address:* York Cottage, Sandgate, Kent. *T:* Folkestone 38594.

RASCH, Sir Richard Guy Carne, 3rd Bt, *cr* 1903; a Member of HM Body Guard, Honourable Corps of Gentlemen-at-Arms, since 1968; *b* 10 Oct. 1918; *s* of Brigadier G. E. C. Rasch, CVO, DSO (*d* 1955); *S* uncle, 1963; *m* 1st, 1947, Anne Mary, *d* of late Major J. H. Dent-Brocklehurst; one *s* one *d*; 2nd, 1961, Fiona Mary, *d* of Robert Douglas Shaw. *Educ:* Eton; RMC, Sandhurst. Major, late Grenadier Guards. Served War of 1939-45; retired, 1951. *Recreations:* shooting, fishing. *Heir:* *s* Simon Anthony Carne Rasch [*b* 26 Feb. 1948. *Educ:* Eton; Royal Agric. Coll., Cirencester]. *Address:* 30 Ovington Square, SW3. *T:* 01-589 9973; The Manor House, Lower Woodford, near Salisbury, Wilts. *Clubs:* White's, Cavalry and Guards.

RASH, Mrs D. E. A.; *see* Wallace, Doreen.

RASHLEIGH, Sir Harry (Evelyn Battie), 5th Bt, *cr* 1831; *b* 17 May 1923; *er s* of late Captain Harry Rashleigh, JP (3rd *s* of 3rd Bt) and Jane Henrietta, *d* of late E. W. Rashleigh, Stoketon, Saltash, Cornwall; *S* kinsman 1951; *m* 1954, Honora Elizabeth Sneyd, *d* of G. S. Sneyd, The Watch House, Downderry, Cornwall; one *s* three *d*. *Educ:* Wellington Sch., Som. Served War of 1939-45, Westminster Dragoons, 1941-45; 79th Armoured Div. Experimental Wing, 1945-46. Mechanical Engineer with John Mowlem & Co. Ltd, UK, 1947-48; John Mowlem & Co. Ltd, Tanganyika, East Africa, 1948-50; Earth Moving & Construction Ltd., Tanganyika, East Africa, 1948-51, 1954-65. Farmer. *Recreations:* shooting, sailing. *Heir:* *s* Richard Harry Rashleigh, *b* 8 July 1958. *Address:* Stowford Grange, Lewdown, near Okehampton, Devon. *T:* Lewdown 237. *Club:* Royal Fowey Yacht.

RASHLEIGH BELCHER, John; *see* Belcher, J. R.

RASMINSKY, Louis, CC (Canada), 1968; CBE 1946; Governor, Bank of Canada, 1961-73; *b* 1 Feb. 1908; *s* of David and Etta Rasminsky; *m* 1930, Lyla Rotenberg; one *s* one *d. Educ:* University of Toronto; London School of Economics. Financial Section, League of Nations, 1930-39; Chairman, Foreign Exchange Control Board, Canada, 1940-51; Deputy Governor, Bank of Canada, 1956-61. Executive Director: IMF, 1946-62; International Bank, 1950-62; Alternate Governor for Canada, IMF, 1969-73. Chm., Bd of Governors, Internat. Develt Res. Centre, 1973-. Hon. Fellow, LSE, 1960. Hon. LLD: Univ. of Toronto, 1953; Yeshiva Univ., 1965; Queen's Univ., 1967; Bishop's Univ., 1968; McMaster Univ., 1969; Trent Univ., 1972; Concordia Univ., 1975; Hon. DHL Hebrew Union Coll., 1963. Outstanding Achievement Award of Public Service of Canada, 1968; Vanier Medal, Inst. of Public Admin, 1974. *Recreations:* golf, fishing. *Address:* 440 Roxborough Road, Rockcliffe Park, Ottawa, Ont, Canada. *T:* 749-7704. *Clubs:* Cercle Universitaire d'Ottawa (Ottawa); Five Lakes Fishing (Wakefield, PQ).

RASMUSSEN, Prof. Steen Eller; architect; Professor of Architecture, Royal Academy of Fine Arts, Copenhagen, 1938-68; *b* Copenhagen, 9 Feb. 1898; *s* of General Eiler Rasmussen; *m* 1934, Karen Margrete Schrøder; two *d. Educ:* Metropolitanskolen; Royal Academy of Fine Arts, Copenhagen. Three first prizes in town planning competitions, 1919. Mem. Danish Roy. Acad. of Fine Arts, 1922; Lecturer at Architectural Sch. of the Academy, 1924; Architect to Municipal Town Planning Office, Copenhagen, 1932-38. Pres. Copenhagen Regional Planning Cttee, 1945-58. Visiting Professor in USA: Massachusetts Inst. of Technology, 1953, Yale, 1954, Philadelphia, 1958, Berkeley, 1959. Lethaby Professor, Roy. College of Art, London, 1958. Designed: Tingbjerg Housing Estate, Copenhagen, 1953-; Schools, Town Hall. Hon. Corr. Member: RIBA London, Bavarian Acad. of Fine Arts, 1958; American Institute of Architects, 1962; Hon. Royal Designer for Industry, London, 1947; Hon. Dr: Technische Hochschule Munich; Univ. of Lund. *Publications:* London, the Unique City, 1937; Towns and Buildings, 1951; Experiencing Architecture, 1959. *Recreation:* to doze in a chair thinking of future books. *Address:* Dreyersvej 9, 2960 Rungsted Kyst, Denmark. *T:* 01863510.

RASUL, Syed Alay; Hon. Chairman, Federation of Bangladesh Associations, UK, since 1974; Hon. Secretary, General Standing Conference of Asian Organisations, UK, since 1970; Senior Community Relations Officer, Sheffield, since 1967; *b* 1 Feb. 1931; *s* of late Syed Ahmed Rasul and Khodeja Rasul; *m* 1956, Kamrunnessa Rasul; three *s* one *d* (and one *d* decd). *Educ:* Univ. of Aligarh, India (BA 1950); Univ. of Dacca, Bangladesh (MA 1953); Univ. of Manchester (Dipls: Adult Educn and Community Development 1963, Social Admin. 1964); High Wycombe Coll. of Technology. NEBSS Cert., 1974; UN and Govt of Pakistan Cert. of Merit in Community Develt, 1956. Manpower Survey Officer, Pakistan Govt, 1955; E Pakistan Government: Social Welfare Organiser, 1956-60; Divl Welfare Organiser, 1960-62; Exec. Sec., Pakistan Welfare and Inf. Centre, Manchester, 1964-67. Hon. Vice-Chm., UK Immigrants Advisory Service, 1975; Convenor, EEC Migrant Workers Forum. *Publications:* 6 special brochures; weekly column in Janomot. *Recreations:* billiards, music; visiting places and meeting people. *Address:* 2 Marchwood Road, Sheffield S6 5LD. *T:* Sheffield 349506.

RATCLIFFE, Frederick William, MA, PhD; JP; University Librarian since 1965, also Director, Rylands University Library, since 1972, Manchester University; *b* 28 May 1927; *y s* of late Sydney and Dora Ratcliffe, Leek, Staffs; *m* 1952, Joyce Brierley; two *s* one *d. Educ:* Leek High Sch., Staffs; Manchester Univ. MA, PhD. Manchester University: Graduate Res. Scholarship, 1951; Res. Studentship in Arts, 1952; Asst Cataloguer and Cataloguer, 1954-62; Sub-Librarian, Glasgow Univ., 1962-63; Dep. Librarian, Univ. of Newcastle upon Tyne, 1963-65. Trustee, St Deiniol's Library, Hawarden, 1975-. Hon. Lectr in Historical Bibliography, Manchester Univ., 1970-. JP Stockport, 1972. *Publications:* many articles in learned journals. *Recreations:* book collecting, hand printing, cricket. *Address:* Light Alders Farm, Light Alders Lane, Disley, Cheshire SK12 2LW. *T:* Disley 2234.

RATCLIFFE, John Ashworth, CB 1965; CBE 1959 (OBE 1947); FRS 1951; MA; Director of Radio and Space Research Station, Slough, Oct. 1960-Feb. 1966; *b* 12 Dec. 1902; *s* of H. H. Ratcliffe, Rawtenstall, Lancs; *m* 1930, Nora Disley; two *d. Educ:* Giggleswick School; Sidney Sussex College, Cambridge. Taught Physics at Cambridge and Research in Radio Wave Propagation, 1924-60; Reader in Physics, Cambridge

University, 1947-60; Fellow of Sidney Sussex College, 1927-60, Hon. Fellow 1962. President: Physical Society, 1959-60; Section A, British Association, 1964; Chairman, Electronics Board, IEE, 1962-63; Vice-Pres., IEE, 1963-66, Pres., 1966. FIEEE. Hon. FInstP. War Service with Telecommunications Research Establishment (TRE), Malvern. Hon. FIEE; Hon. Pres., URSI. Faraday Medal (IEE), 1966; Royal Medal (Roy. Soc.), 1966; Guthrie Medal (Inst. Physics), 1971; Gold Medal (RAS), 1976. *Publications:* numerous papers in scientific journals on Radio Wave Propagation. *Address:* 193 Huntingdon Road, Cambridge CB3 0DL.

RATCLIFFE, Reginald, CB 1959; MBE 1943; Chief Executive, Machine Tool Division, Staveley Industries, 1965-68, retired; *b* 8 Jan. 1908; *s* of Elias Ratcliffe, Birkenhead; *m* 1933, Vera George; one *s* one *d. Educ:* Liverpool Univ. BEng 1930. MEng 1933; Carlton Stitt Medallist, 1930. Entered Royal Arsenal, Woolwich, as Technical Assistant, 1930; Royal Ordnance Factory, Nottingham, 1938; Dir of Instrument Production, Min. of Supply, 1954; Royal Ordnance Factories: Dep. Controller 1956-59; Controller 1959-64; Deputy Master General of the Ordnance (Production) 1964. President, Institution of Production Engineers, 1963-65. *Publications:* various contributions to technical journals. *Recreations:* tennis, swimming. *Address:* 43 Martins Drive, Ferndown, Dorset BH22 9SG. *T:* Ferndown 4081.

RATHBONE, John Francis Warre, CBE 1966; TD 1950; Secretary of National Trust for Places of Historic Interest or Natural Beauty, 1949-68; President, London Centre of the National Trust, since 1968; *b* 18 July 1909; *e s* of Francis Warre Rathbone and Edith Bertha Hampshire, Allerton Beeches, Liverpool. *Educ:* Marlborough; New College, Oxford. Solicitor, 1934. Served War of 1939-45; AA Comd and staff (Col 1945). Dir Ministry of Justice Control Branch, CCG (British Element), 1946-49. Member Bd of Governors, UCH, 1968-74. Mem. Management Cttee, Mutual Households Assoc. Ltd; Vice-Chm., S Camden Community Health Council, 1977-. *Recreations:* music, travel. *Address:* 15 Furlong Road, N7 8LS. *T:* 01-607 4854. *Club:* Travellers'.

RATHBONE, John Rankin, (Tim Rathbone); MP (C) Lewes since Feb. 1974; *b* 17 March 1933; *s* of J. R. Rathbone, MP (killed in action 1940) and Lady Wright (*see* Beatrice Wright); *m* 1960, Margarita Sanchez y Sanchez; two *s* one *d. Educ:* Eton; Christ Church, Oxford; Harvard Business School. 2nd Lieut KRRC, 1951-53. Robert Benson Lonsdale & Co., Merchant Bankers, 1956-58; Trainee to Vice-Pres., Ogilvy & Mather Inc., NY, 1958-66; Chief Publicity and Public Relations Officer, Conservative Central Office, 1966-68; Dir, Charles Barker ABH International, 1968-; Dep. Chm., Ayer Barker Hegemann Ltd, 1973- (Man. Dir 1970-73). Mem., Nat. Cttee for Electoral Reform. *Recreation:* family. *Address:* 30 Farringdon Street, EC4 4EA. *T:* 01-236 3011; Goldstrow Farm, Newick, Piltdown, Uckfield, Sussex. *Clubs:* Brooks's; Sussex; Society of Sussex Downsmen.

RATHBONE, Very Rev. Norman Stanley; Dean of Hereford since 1969; *b* 8 Sept. 1914; *er s* of Stanley George and Helen Rathbone; *m* 1952, Christine Olive Gooderson; three *s* two *d. Educ:* Lawrence Sheriff Sch., Rugby; Christ's Coll., Cambridge; Westcott House, Cambridge. BA 1936, MA 1939. St Mary Magdalen's, Coventry: Curate, 1938; Vicar, 1945; Canon Theologian, Coventry Cathedral, 1954; Canon Residentiary and Chancellor, Lincoln Cathedral, 1959. *Address:* The Deanery, Hereford. *T:* Hereford 2525.

RATHBONE, Philip Richardson; Secretary, Royal Town Planning Institute, 1960-75; *b* 21 May 1913; *s* of Herbert R. Rathbone, sometime Lord Mayor of Liverpool, and Winifred Richardson Evans, Wimbledon; *m* 1940, Angela, *d* of Captain A. B. de Beer, Liverpool; one *s* two *d. Educ:* Clifton Coll., Bristol; University Coll., Oxford. BA Hons Mod. History 1934. Sec., Housing Centre, London, 1935-39. Army, King's Regt, Liverpool; Personnel Selection, WO, 1939-45 (Major). Principal, Min. of Town and Country Planning, 1945-53; Sec., Royal Instn of Chartered Surveyors (Scotland), 1953-60. *Publication:* Paradise Merton: The Story of Nelson and the Hamiltons at Merton Place, 1973. *Recreations:* photography, writing, Lady Hamilton. *Address:* 19 Raymond Road, SW19 4AD. *T:* 01-946 2478.

RATHBONE, Tim; *see* Rathbone, J. R.

RATHCAVAN, 1st Baron, *cr* 1953, of The Braid, Co. Antrim; **(Robert William) Hugh O'Neill,** Bt, *cr* 1929, PC (Ireland 1921, Northern Ireland 1922, Gt Brit. 1937); Hon. LLD, Queen's University Belfast; HM Lieutenant for County Antrim, 1949-59;

b 8 June 1883; *o surv. s* of 2nd Baron O'Neill; *m* 1909, Sylvia (*d* 1972), *d* of Walter A. Sandeman of Morden House, Royston; three *s. Educ:* Eton; New Coll., Oxford, BA. Bar, Inner Temple, 1909; contested Stockport, 1906; MP (UU) Mid-Antrim, 1915-22, Co. Antrim, 1922-50, North Antrim, 1950-52; MP for County Antrim in the Parliament of Northern Ireland, 1921-29; first Speaker of the House of Commons of Northern Ireland, 1921-29; Chairman Cons Private Members' (1922) Committee, 1935-39; Parl. Under-Sec. of State for India and for Burma, 1939-40; late Lt North of Ireland Imperial Yeomanry; late Captain Royal Irish Rifles and Major (general list); served in European War, 1915-18, France and Palestine. *Recreations:* shooting, fishing. *Heir: s* Rt Hon. Phelim Robert Hugh O'Neill, *qv. Address:* Cleggan Lodge, Ballymena, Co. Antrim. *T:* Aughafatten 209; 28 Queen's Gate Gardens, SW7. *T:* 01-584 0358. *Clubs:* Carlton; Ulster (Belfast).
See also Hon. Sir Con D. W. O'Neill.

RATHCREEDAN, 2nd Baron, *cr* 1916; **Charles Patrick Norton**, TD; *b* 26 Nov. 1905; *er s* of 1st Baron and Marguerite Cecil (*d* 1955), *d* of Sir Charles Huntington, 1st Bart, MP; *S* father, 1930; *m* 1946, Ann Pauline, *er d* of late Surgeon Capt. William Bastian, RN; two *s* one *d. Educ:* Wellington Coll.; Lincoln Coll., Oxford, MA. Called to Bar, Inner Temple, 1931; admitted Solicitor, 1936; Major 4th Battalion Oxford and Buckinghamshire Light Inf., TA; served France, 1940; prisoner of war, 1940-45. Master, Founders' Co., 1970. *Recreations:* tennis, golf. *Heir: s* Hon. Christopher John Norton, *b* 3 June 1949. *Address:* Church Field, Fawley, Henley-on-Thames, Oxon. *T:* Henley 4160. *Clubs:* Farmers'; Leander.

RATHDONNELL, 5th Baron, *cr* 1868; **Thomas Benjamin McClintock Bunbury;** Lieutenant, RN; *b* 17 Sept. 1938; *o s* of William, 4th Baron Rathdonnell and Pamela, *e d* of late John Malcolm Drew; *S* father 1959; *m* 1965, Jessica Harriet, *d* of George Gilbert Butler, Scatorish, Bennettsbridge, Co. Kilkenny; three *s. Educ:* Charterhouse; Royal Naval College, Dartmouth. *Heir: s* Hon. William Leopold McClintock Bunbury, *b* 6 July 1966. *Address:* Lisvanagh, Rathvilly, County Carlow, Ireland. *T:* Carlow 55104.

RATTEE, Donald Keith, QC 1977; *b* 9 March 1937; *s* of Charles Ronald and Dorothy Rattee; *m* 1964, Diana Mary Howl; four *d . Educ:* Clacton-on-Sea County High School; Trinity Hall, Cambridge (MA, LLB). Called to Bar, Lincoln's Inn, 1962; Second Junior Counsel to the Inland Revenue (Chancery), 1972-77. *Recreations:* tennis, squash, gardening. *Address:* 29 Shirley Avenue, Cheam, Surrey. *T:* 01-642 3062; 7 New Square, Lincoln's Inn, WC2. *T:* 01-405 1266. *Club:* Sutton Tennis and Squash (Sutton, Surrey).

RATTER, John, CBE 1945 (OBE 1944); ERD 1953; Railway Adviser, World Bank, Washington DC, 1970-74; *b* 15 May 1908; *s* of George Dempster Ratter, South Shields; *m* 1937, Eileen Cail, Knaresborough, Yorkshire; two *s* one *d. Educ:* St Peters School, York; Durham University. BSc; MICE. Various appointments as civil engineer with London and North Eastern Railway and London Passenger Transport Board, 1929-39; War of 1939-45: served with Royal Engineers, France, Africa and Italy, and in War Office; Deputy Director of Transportation, CMF, with rank of Colonel. Various appointments with LNE Railway and LPTB and Railway Exec., 1945-53; Chief Civil Engineer, British Transport Commission, 1953-54; Technical Adviser, BTC, 1954-58; Member: BTC, 1958-62. British Railways Board, 1963-70. Pres., Internat. Union of Railways, 1960-62. Legion of Merit (USA), 1944; Légion d'Honneur (France), 1963; Order of Merit, German Federal Republic, 1968; Comdr, Order of Leopod II, Belgium, 1969.

RATTERAY, Hon. Sir George Oswald, Kt 1975; CBE 1968; Commission Merchant and Wholesaler; President, Legislative Council of Bermuda; Chairman, Bermuda Library Committee; *b* Somerset, Bermuda, 30 Sept 1903; *m* 1927, Kate Cecilia Louise (*née* Trott); two *s* one *d . Educ:* Hunty Sch., Sandys Parish, Bermuda; DipEd (external), Bennett Coll., England. Missionary, N Rhodesia (now Zambia), 1932-39; MCP Sandys North, 1953-68; Chm., Treatment of Offenders Commn; Govt Spokesman on Prisons; Mem., Bd of Immigration, 1956-60; Mem., Delegn to London for Constitutional Changes, 1966. Founder, Proprietor and Manager, Ratteray's Commission Agency. *Address:* Mutende, Sound View Road, Somerset, Bermuda; King Street, Hamilton, Bermuda.

RATTIGAN, Sir Terence (Mervyn), Kt 1971; CBE 1958; *b* 10 June 1911; unmarried. *Educ:* Harrow (Scholar); Trinity College, Oxford (Scholar in Modern History). Playwright. First Episode, Comedy, London, 1934, and New York; French without Tears,

Criterion, London, 1936, and New York; After the Dance, St James's, London, 1939; Flare Path, Apollo, London, 1942, and New York; While the Sun Shines, London, 1943, and New York; Love in Idleness, Lyric, London, 1944; (O Mistress Mine, New York, 1945); The Winslow Boy, Lyric, 1946, and USA, 1947, New, 1970; Playbill (The Browning Version and Harlequinade), Phoenix, 1948, New York, 1949; Adventure Story, St James's, 1949; French Without Tears (revived), Vaudeville, 1949; Who is Sylvia?, Criterion, 1950; The Deep Blue Sea, Duchess, 1952, New York, 1952, Guildford, 1971; The Sleeping Prince, Phoenix, 1953, New York, 1956, St Martin's, 1968; Separate Tables, St James's, 1954, New York, 1956; Variation on a Theme, Globe, 1958; Ross, Haymarket, 1960, New York, 1961; Man and Boy, Queen's, 1963, New York, 1963; A Bequest to the Nation, Haymarket, 1970; In Praise of Love, Duchess, 1973, New York, 1975; Cause Célèbre, Her Majesty's, 1977. *Films:* French without Tears, Quiet Wedding, The Day will Dawn, Uncensored, Way To The Stars, Journey Together, While The Sun Shines, The Winslow Boy, The Browning Version, The Sound Barrier, The Final Test, The Deep Blue Sea, The Prince and the Showgirl, Separate Tables; The VIP's; The Yellow Rolls-Royce; Conduct Unbecoming; A Bequest to the Nation; *television films:* High Summer, The Final Test, Heart to Heart, Nelson; *radio play:* Cause Célèbre. *Publications:* above plays. *Recreation:* watching cricket. *Address:* c/o Dr Jan Van Loewen Ltd, 81-83 Shaftesbury Avenue, W1. *Clubs:* Royal and Ancient; MCC.

RAU, Santha Rama; free-lance writer since 1945; English teacher at Sarah Lawrence College, Bronxville, NY, since 1971; *b* Madras, India, 24 Jan. 1923; *d* of late Sir Benegal Rama Rau, CIE; *m* 1st, 1952, Faubion Bowers (marr. diss. 1966); one *s*; 2nd, Gurdon W. Wattles. *Educ:* St Paul's Girls' School, London, England; Wellesley College, Mass., USA. Feature writer for the Office of War Information, New York, USA, during vacations from college, 1942-45. Hon. doctorate: Bates College, USA, 1961; Russell Sage College, 1965; Phi Beta Kappa, Wellesley College, 1960. *Publications:* Home to India, 1945; East of Home, 1950; This is India, 1953; Remember the House, 1955; View to the South-East, 1957; My Russian Journey, 1959; A Passage to India (dramatization), 1962; Gifts of Passage, 1962; The Adventuress, 1971; Cooking of India, 1971 (2 vols). Many articles and short stories in New Yorker, Art News, Horizon, Saturday Evening Post, Reader's Digest, etc. *Address:* 522 East 89th Street, New York, NY 10028, USA; 10D Mafatlal Park, Bhulabhai Desai Road, Bombay 26, India.

RAVEN, John Armstrong; Chief Executive and Vice-Chairman, Simplification of International Trade Procedures Board, since 1974 (Director, SITPRO Board, 1970-72); *b* 23 April 1920; *s* of late John Colbeck Raven; *m* 1st, 1945, Megan (*d* 1963), *d* of late Idwal Humphreys; one *s* one *d*; 2nd, 1965, Joy, *d* of late Alan Chancellor Nesbitt, of Lincoln's Inn; one step *d. Educ:* High Sch., Cardiff; Downing Coll., Cambridge (MA). Called to Bar, Gray's Inn, 1955. Dir, British Coal Exporters' Fedn, 1947-68; Section Head, Nat. Economic Develt Office, 1968-70; Dir-Gen., Assoc. of British Chambers of Commerce, 1972-74. *Publications:* regular contrib. to Daily Telegraph. *Recreation:* worrying. *Address:* 6 Farrance Court, Tunbridge Wells, Kent. *T:* Tunbridge Wells 24769. *Club:* Reform.

RAVEN, Rear-Adm. John Stanley, CB 1964; BSc, FIEE; *b* 5 Oct. 1910; *s* of Frederick William Raven; *m* 1935, Nancy, *d* of William Harold Murdoch; three *s. Educ:* Huddersfield College; Leeds University (BSc). Temp. RNVR Commission, 1939; transferred to RN, 1946; retired, 1965. *Recreation:* painting. *Address:* East Garth, School Lane, Collingham, Yorks.

RAVEN, Dame Kathleen, (Dame Kathleen Annie Ingram), DBE 1968; SRN 1936; SCM 1938; Chief Nursing Officer in the Department of Health and Social Security (formerly Ministry of Health), 1958-72; *b* 9 Nov. 1910; *o d* of late Fredric William Raven and late Annie Williams Mason; *m* 1959, Prof. John Thornton Ingram, MD, FRCP (*d* 1972). *Educ:* Ulverston Grammar School; privately; St Bartholomew's Hosp., London; City of London Maternity Hospital. St Bartholomew's Hospital: Night Superintendent, Ward Sister, Administrative Sister, Assistant Matron, 1936-49; Matron, Gen. Infirmary, Leeds, 1949-57; Dep. Chief Nursing Officer, Min. of Health, 1957-58. Mem. Gen. Nursing Council for England and Wales, 1950-57; Mem. Council and Chm. Yorkshire Br., Roy. Coll. of Nursing, 1950-57; Mem. Central Area Advisory Bd for Secondary Education, Leeds, 1953-57; Area Nursing Officer, Order of St John, 1953-57; Mem. Exec. Cttee Assoc. of Hospital Matrons for England and Wales, 1955-57; Mem. Advisory Cttee for Sister Tutor's Diploma, Univ. of Hull, 1955-57; Internal Examr for Diploma of Nursing, Univ. of Leeds, 1950-57; Member: Area Nurse Trg Cttee, 1951-57; Area Cttee Nat. Hosp. Service

Reserve, 1950-57; Central Health Services Council, 1957-58; Council and Nursing Advisory Bd, British Red Cross Soc., 1958-72; Cttee of St John Ambulance Assoc., 1958-72; National Florence Nightingale Memorial Cttee of Great Britain and Northern Ireland, 1958-72; WHO Expert Advisory Panel on Nursing, 1961-; a Vice-Pres., Royal Coll. of Nursing, 1972-. Civil Service Comr, 1972-. Nursing Adviser, Allied Med. Gp, 1974-. FRSA 1970. Officer (Sister) Order of St John, 1963. *Recreations:* painting, reading, travel. *Address:* Jesmond, Burcott, Wing, Leighton Buzzard, Bedfordshire. *T:* Wing 244; 29 Harley Street, W1. *T:* 01-580 3765. *Club:* Royal Commonwealth Society.
See also R. W. Raven.

RAVEN, Ronald William, OBE 1946; TD; FRCS 1931; Consulting Surgeon, Westminster Hospital and Royal Marsden Hospital, since 1969; Surgeon, French Hospital, London, since 1936; Cons. Surgeon (General Surgeon) Eversfield Chest Hospital since 1937; Cons. Surgeon Star and Garter Home for Disabled Sailors, Soldiers and Airmen since 1948; *b* 28 July 1904; *e s* of late Fredric William Raven and Annie Williams Mason, Coniston, Lancs. *Educ:* Ulverston Grammar School; St Bartholomew's Hospital Medical College, Univ. of London. St Bart's Hosp.: gained various prizes and surgical schol.; resident surgical appts, 1928-29; Demonstrator in Pathology, St Bart's Hosp., 1929-31; Registrar Statistics Nat. Radium Commn, 1931-34; jun. surgical appts, 1931-35; Asst Surg. Gordon Hosp., 1935; Asst Surg. Roy. Cancer Hosp., 1939-46, Surg. 1946-62; Jt Lectr in Surgery, Westminster Med. Sch., Univ. of London, 1951-69; Surgeon, Westminster (Gordon) Hosp., 1947-69; Sen. Surgeon, Royal Marsden Hosp. and Inst. of Cancer Research, Royal Cancer Hosp., 1962-69. Lectures: Arris and Gale, 1933; Erasmus Wilson, 1935, 1946 and 1947; Bradshaw, RCS, 1975; Hunterian Prof., 1948, RCS; Fellow Assoc. of Surg. of GB; Mem., Internat. Soc. of Surgery; FRSM (PP, Section of Proctology, PP, Section of Oncology); Mem. Council, 1968-76; Mem. Court of Patrons, 1976-, RCS; Pres., British Assoc. of Surgical Oncology, 1973-; Past Pres., Assoc. of Head and Neck Oncologists of GB; Chm. Council and late Chm. Exec. Cttee Marie Curie Meml Foundn; Chm. Joint Nat. Cancer Survey Cttee; Vice-Pres. and Chm., Council of Epsom Coll., 1954-; late Chm., Conjoint Cttee; late Mem. Bd of Governors Royal Marsden Hosp.; formerly Mem. Council of Queen's Institute of District Nursing; Mem. (late Chm.), Cttee of Management Med. Insurance Agency; Formerly Mem. Council, Imperial Cancer Res. Fund. Surg. EMS, 1939; joined RAMC, 1941, and served in N Africa, Italy and Malta (mentioned); o/c Surg. Div. (Lt-Col); and o/c Gen. Hosp. (Col), 1946; Lt-Col RAMC (TA); o/c Surg. Div. Gen. Hosp., 1947; Col RAMC (TA); o/c No 57 (Middlesex) General Hospital (TA), 1953-59; Colonel TARO, 1959-62; Hon. Colonel RAMC. OStJ 1946. Hon. Professor National Univ. of Colombia, 1949; Hon. MD Cartagena, 1949; Corr. For. Member: Soc. of Head and Neck Surgeons of USA; Roman Surg. Soc.; Soc. Surg. of Bogotá; Société de Chirurgie de Lyon; Member: Nat. Acad. Med. of Colombia; NY Acad. of Sciences; Soc. of Surgeons of Colombia; Italian Soc. Thoracic Surg.; Czechoslovak Soc. of J. E. Purkyne; Lectures: Malcolm Morris Meml, 1954; Blair Bell Meml, 1960; Elizabeth Matthai Endowment, Madras Univ., 1965; First W. Emory Burnett Honor, Temple Univ., USA, 1966; Edith A. Ward Meml, 1966; Gerald Townsley Meml, 1974. Vis. Prof. of Surgery, Ein-Shams University, Cairo, 1961. Surgical missions to: Colombia, 1949; Saudi Arabia, 1961, 1962, 1975, 1976. Chevalier de la Légion d'Honneur, 1952. *Publications:* Treatment of Shock, 1942; Surgical Care, 1942, 2nd edn 1952; Cancer in General Practice (jointly), 1952; Surgical Instruments and Appliances (jointly), 1952; War Wounds and Injuries (jt editor and contrib.). 1940; chapters on Shock and Malignant Disease in Encyclopædia British Medical Practice, 1952, 1955, 1962-69, and Medical Progress, 1970-71; Handbook on Cancer for Nurses and Health Visitors, 1953; Cancer and Allied Diseases, 1955; contrib. chapters in Operative Surgery (Rob and Rodney Smith), 1956-57; Editor and contrib. Cancer (7 vols), 1957-60; Cancer of the Pharynx, Larynx and Oesophagus and its Surgical Treatment, 1958; (ed) Cancer Progress, 1960 and 1963; (ed jtly) The Prevention of Cancer, 1967; (ed) Modern Trends in Oncology 1, part 1, Research Progress, part 2, Clinical Progress, 1973; Editor and contrib. The Dying Patient, 1975; papers on surgical subjects, especially relating to Cancer in British and foreign journals. *Recreations:* philately (medallist Internat. Stamp Exhibn, London, 1950), music, ceramics and pictures, travel. *Address:* 29 Harley Street, W1. *T:* 01-580 3765; Manor Lodge, Wingrave, Aylesbury, Bucks. *T:* Aston Abbots 287; Meadow View, Coniston, Lancs. *Club:* MCC.
See also Dame Kathleen Raven.

RAVEN, Simon (Arthur Noël); author, critic and dramatist since 1957; *b* 28 Dec. 1927; *s* of Arthur Godart Raven and Esther Kate Raven (*née* Christmas); *m* 1951, Susan Mandeville Kilner (marriage dissolved); one *s.* *Educ:* Charterhouse; King's Coll., Cambridge (MA). Research, 1951-52; regular commn, King's Shropshire Light Inf., 1953-57 (Capt.): served in Kenya; resigned, 1957. Member, Horatian Society. *Publications: novels:* The Feathers of Death, 1959; Brother Cain, 1959; Doctors Wear Scarlet, 1960; Close of Play, 1962; The Alms for Oblivion sequence: The Rich Pay Late, 1964; Friends in Low Places, 1965; The Sabre Squadron, 1966; Fielding Gray, 1967; The Judas Boy, 1968; Places Where They Sing, 1970; Sound the Retreat, 1971; Come like Shadows, 1972; Bring Forth the Body, 1974; The Survivors, 1976; *short stories:* The Fortunes of Fingel, 1976; *general:* The English Gentleman, 1961; Boys Will be Boys, 1963; Royal Foundation and Other Plays, 1965; contribs to Observer, Spectator, Punch, etc. *Plays and dramatisations for broadcasting:* BBC TV: Royal Foundation, 1961; The Scapegoat, 1964; Sir Jocelyn, 1965; Huxley's Point Counter-Point, 1968; Trollope's The Way We Live Now, 1969; The Pallisers, a serial in 26 episodes based on the six Palliser novels of Anthony Trollope, 1974, repeated 1976; Iris Murdoch's An Unofficial Rose, 1975; ABC TV: The Gaming Book, 1965; BBC Radio: Triad, a trilogy loosely based on Thucydides' History of the Peloponnesian War, 1965-68, repeated 1972. *Recreations:* cricket, travel, reading. *Address:* c/o Blond & Briggs Ltd, 12 Caroline Place, W2. *Clubs:* Reform; MCC, Butterflies Cricket, Trog's Cricket.

RAVENSDALE, 3rd Baron *cr* 1911; **Nicholas Mosley,** MC 1944; *b* 25 June 1923; *e s* of Sir Oswald Mosley, 6th Bt, *qv,* and late Lady Cynthia Mosley; is *heir* to father's baronetcy; *S* to Aunt's Barony, 1966; *m* 1st, 1947, Rosemary Laura Salmond (marr. diss. 1974); three *s* one *d*; 2nd, 1974, Mrs Verity Bailey; one *s*. *Educ:* Eton; Balliol College, Oxford. Served in the Rifle Brigade, Captain, 1942-46. *Publications:* (as Nicholas Mosley): Spaces of the Dark, 1951; The Rainbearers, 1955; Corruption, 1957; African Switchback, 1958; The Life of Raymond Raynes, 1961; Meeting Place, 1962; Accident, 1964; Experience and Religion, 1964; Assassins, 1966; Impossible Object, 1968; Natalie Natalia, 1971; The Assassination of Trotsky, 1972; Julian Grenfell: His Life and the Times of his Death, 1888-1915, 1976. *Heir: s* Hon. Shaun Nicholas Mosley, *b* 5 August 1949. *Address* Church Row Studios, 21A Heath Street, NW3. *T:* 01-435 8222.

RAVENSDALE, Thomas Corney, CMG 1951; retired; *b* 17 Feb. 1905; *s* of late Henry Ravensdale and late Lilian (*née* Corney); *m* (marriage dissolved): two *s*; *m* 1965, Mme Antoine Watteau (*née* Ricard). *Educ:* Royal Masonic Sch., Bushey, Herts; St Catharine's Coll., Cambridge. Acting Vice-Consul, Smyrna, 1928; 3rd Secretary, British Embassy, Ankara, 1929-34; 2nd Asst Oriental Sec., The Residency, Cairo, 1934-37; Vice-Consul, Bagdad, 1937-42; 1st Asst Oriental Sec., Brit. Embassy, Cairo, 1942-47; Oriental Counsellor, Cairo, 1948-51; Political Adviser, British Residency, Benghazi, 1951; Couns., Brit. Embassy in Libya, 1952-55; Ambassador to Dominican Republic, 1955-58; Insp. Foreign Service Establishments, 1958-60; Ambassador to the Republics of Dahomey, Niger, Upper Volta and the Ivory Coast, 1960-63. *Recreation:* gardening. *Address:* The Cottage, 13 rue de Penthièvre, Petit Andely, 27700 Les Andelys, France. *T:* 54-16-38 Les Andelys (Eure). *Club:* Athenæum.

RAVENSWORTH, 8th Baron *cr* 1821; **Arthur Waller Liddell,** Bt 1642; JP; Radio Engineer, British Broadcasting Corporation, 1944; *b* 25 July 1924; *s* of late Hon. Cyril Arthur Liddell (2nd *s* of 5th Baron) and Dorothy L., *d* of William Brown, Slinfold, Sussex; *S* cousin 1950; *m* 1950, Wendy, *d* of J. S. Bell, Cookham, Berks; one *s* one *d*. *Educ:* Harrow. JP Northumberland, 1959. *Heir: s* Hon. Thomas Arthur Hamish Liddell, *b* 27 Oct. 1954. *Address:* Eslington Park, Whittingham, Alnwick, Northumberland. *T:* Whittingham 239.

RAWBONE, Rear-Adm. Alfred Raymond, CB 1976; AFC 1951; Deputy Assistant Chief of Staff Operations, SHAPE, 1974-75; *b* 19 April 1923; *s* of A. Rawbone and Mrs E. D. Rawbone (*née* Wall); *m* 1943, Iris Alicia (*née* Willshaw); one *s* one *d*. *Educ:* Saltley Grammar Sch., Birmingham. Joined RN, 1942; 809 Sqdn War Service, 1943; CO 736 Sqdn, 1953; CO 897 Sqdn, 1955; CO Loch Killisport, 1959-60; Comdr (Air) Lossiemouth and HMS Ark Royal, 1961-63; Chief Staff Officer to Flag Officer Naval Air Comd, 1965-67; CO HMS Dido, 1968-69; CO RNAS Yeovilton, 1970-72; CO HMS Kent, 1972-73. Comdr 1958; Captain 1964; Rear-Adm. 1974. *Address:* Halstock Leigh, Halstock, near Yeovil, Somerset.

RAWCLIFFE, Prof. Gordon Hindle, MA, DSc; FRS 1972; FIEE; FIEEE; consulting electrical engineer; Professor of Electrical Engineering, University of Bristol, 1944-75, now Emeritus; *b* Sheffield, 2 June 1910; *e s* of late Rev. J. Hindle Rawcliffe, Gloucester; *m* 1st, Stella Morgan (marriage dissolved); two *d*;

2nd, 1952, Sheila Mary Wicks, MA Oxon; two *d. Educ:* St Edmund's School, Canterbury; Keble College, Oxford, Hon. Fellow 1976. 1st Class Hons Engineering Science, 1932. Metropolitan-Vickers Electrical Co. Ltd, Manchester (now GEC Ltd), 1932-37; Lecturer in Electrical Engineering, University of Liverpool, 1937-41; Head of Electrical Engineering Department, Robert Gordon's Technical College, Aberdeen, and Lecturer-in-charge of Electrical Engineering, Univ. of Aberdeen, 1941-44. Instn of Electrical Engineers: Chairman Western Centre, 1956-57; Council, 1956-58, 1966-69; Utilization Section Committee, 1960-62; Power Divisional Board, 1963-65, and 1969-72; Hunter Meml Lecture, 1970; Vice-Pres., 1972-75. Many patents and inventions relating to Electrical Machinery, including multi-speed P.A.M. induction motor. Mem., several official cttees on electrical machinery. Consultant to: GEC Machines Ltd; Brush Electrical Eng. Co. Ltd, 1955-69; Lancashire Dynamo Co. Ltd, 1958-67; Westinghouse Electric Corp., E Pittsburgh, USA; Lawrence-Scott & Electromotors; Parsons-Peebles and other organisations. Lecture and Consulting tours in USA, 1961, 1967, 1970, 1972, 1974, Canada, 1961, 1971, Hungary, 1962, Turkey, 1963, Australia and NZ, 1964, Japan and Far East, 1965, S Africa (Bernard Price Meml Lecture), 1965, Czechoslovakia, 1966, Far East, Australia, 1967, Middle and Far East, 1968, Bulgaria and Poland, 1968, Germany, 1969, Italy, 1971, 1975, France, 1972, 1976. Lectures: Marcus Greenhorne, Univ. of Aberdeen, 1976; Clifford Patterson, Royal Soc., 1977. Hon. DTech Loughborough, 1974; Hon. DSc Bath, 1976. *Publications:* numerous papers in Proceedings of Institution of Electrical Engineers (Premiums 1938, 1940, 1956, 1963, 1964, 1966) and other scientific and technical jls, etc. *Recreations:* exploring the West of England; travel, reading and music. *Address:* 28 Upper Belgrave Road, Clifton, Bristol BS8 2XL. *T:* Bristol 37940. *Club:* Athenæum.

RAWDEN-SMITH, Rupert Rawden; Metropolitan Stipendiary Magistrate since 1967; *b* 24 Sept. 1912; *s* of late Dr Hoyland Smith; *m* 1941, Mollie Snow; one *s* one *d. Educ:* Rossall School; King's College, London University (LLB). Barrister, Middle Temple, 1939; Recorder of Sunderland, 1961-67. *Recreations:* gardening, travel. *Address:* 97 Church Road, Wimbledon, SW19. *T:* 01-946 4325.

RAWES, Francis Roderick, MBE 1944; MA; Headmaster of St Edmund's School, Canterbury, 1964-Aug. 1978; *b* 28 Jan. 1916; *e s* of late Prescott Rawes and Susanna May Dockery; *m* 1940, Dorothy Joyce, *d* of E. M. Hundley, Oswestry; two *s* one *d. Educ:* Charterhouse; St Edmund Hall, Oxford. Served in Intelligence Corps, 1940-46; GSO3(I) 13 Corps; GSO1 (I) HQ 15 Army Group and MI14 WO. Asst Master at Westminster School, 1938-40 and 1946-64; Housemaster, 1947-64. Mem. Council, Friends of Canterbury Cathedral. *Address:* (until Aug. 1978) St Edmund's School, Canterbury, Kent. *T:* Canterbury 64496; Peyton House, Chipping Campden, Glos.

RAWLEY, Alan David, QC 1977; a Recorder of the Crown Court, since 1972; *b* 28 Sept. 1934; *er s* of late Cecil David Rawley and of Theresa Rawley (*née* Pack); *m* 1964, Ione Jane Ellis; two *s* one *d. Educ:* Wimbledon Coll.; Brasenose Coll., Oxford. Nat. Service, 1956-58; commnd Royal Tank Regt. Called to the Bar, Middle Temple, 1958. Dep. Chairman, Cornwall Quarter Sessions, 1971. *Address:* Lamb Building, Temple, EC4. *T:* 01-353 6381. *Clubs:* Garrick; Exeter and County (Exeter); Hampshire (Winchester).

RAWLINGS, Margaret, (Lady Barlow); Actress; *b* Osaka, Japan, 5 June 1906; *d* of Rev. G. W. Rawlings and Lilian Boddington; *m* 1st, 1927, Gabriel Toyne, actor (marr. diss. 1938); no *c*; 2nd, 1942, Robert Barlow (knighted 1943; *d* 1976); one *d. Educ:* Oxford High School for Girls; Lady Margaret Hall, Oxford. Left Oxford after one year, and joined the Macdona Players Bernard Shaw Repertory Company on tour, 1927; played Jennifer in the Doctor's Dilemma and many other parts; toured Canada with Maurice Colbourne, 1929; First London engagement Bianca Capello in The Venetian at Little Theatre in 1931, followed by New York; played Elizabeth Barrett Browning, in The Barretts of Wimpole Street in Australia and New Zealand; Oscar Wilde's Salome at Gate Theatre; Liza Kingdom, The Old Folks at Home, Queen's; Mary Fitton in This Side Idolatry, Lyric; Jean in The Greeks had a word for it, Liza Doolittle in Pygmalion and Ann in Man and Superman, Cambridge Theatre, 1935; Katie O'Shea in Parnell, Ethel Barrymore Theatre, New York 1935, later at New, London; Lady Macbeth for OUDS 1936; Mary and Lily in Black Limelight, St James's and Duke of York's, 1937-38; Helen in Trojan Women, Karen Selby in The Flashing Stream, Lyric, 1938-39, and in New York; Revival of Liza in Pygmalion, Haymarket, 1939; You of all People, Apollo, 1939; A House in the Square, St Martin's, 1940; Mrs Dearth in

Dear Brutus, 1941-42; Gwendolen Fairfax in the Importance of Being Earnest, Royal Command Perf., Haymarket, 1946; Titania in Purcell's Fairy Queen, Covent Garden, 1946; Vittoria Corombona in Webster's The White Devil, Duchess, 1947; Marceline in Jean-Jacques Bernard's The Unquiet Spirit, Arts, 1949; Germaine in A Woman in Love, tour and Embassy, 1949; The Purple Fig Tree, Piccadilly, 1950; Lady Macbeth, Arts, 1950; Spring at Marino, Arts, 1951; Zabina in Tamburlaine, Old Vic, 1951-52; Lysistrata in The Apple Cart, Haymarket, 1953; Countess in The Dark is Light Enough, Salisbury and Windsor Repertory, 1955; Paulina and Mistress Ford, Old Vic, 1955-56; Title Rôle in Racine's Phèdre, Theatre in the Round, London and tour, 1957-58; Sappho in Sappho, Lyceum, Edinburgh, 1961; Ask Me No More, Windsor, 1962; Title role in Racine's Phèdre, Cambridge Arts, 1963; Ella Rentheim in John Gabriel Borkman, Duchess, 1963; Jocasta in Œdipus, Playhouse (Nottingham), 1964; Gertrude in Hamlet, Ludlow Festival, 1965; Madame Torpe in Torpe's Hotel, Yvonne Arnaud Theatre, Guildford, 1965; Mrs Bridgenorth, in Getting Married, Strand, 1967; Carlotta, in A Song at Twilight, Windsor, 1968; Cats Play, Greenwich, 1973; Mixed Economy, King's Head Islington, 1977. *Films:* Roman Holiday; Beautiful Stranger; No Road Back; Hands of the Ripper. *Television:* Criss Cross Quiz; Somerset Maugham Hour; Sunday Break; Compact; Maigret; Planemakers; solo performance, Black Limelight, Armchair Theatre, 1969; Wives and Daughters, 1971. Innumerable broadcasts, incl. We Beg to Differ, and, Brains Trust; poetry recitals; recordings of: Keats, Gerard Manley Hopkins, Alice in Wonderland; (Marlowe Soc.) King Lear, Pericles; New English Bible Gospels. *Publication:* (Trans.) Racine's Phèdre, 1961, (US, 1962). *Recreation:* poetry. *Address:* Rocketer, Wendover, Bucks. *T:* Wendover 622234. *Club:* Arts Theatre.

RAWLINS, Colin Guy Champion, OBE 1965; DFC 1941; Director of Zoos, Zoological Society of London, since 1966; *b* 5 June 1919; *s* of R. S. C. Rawlins and Yvonne Blanche Andrews; *m* 1946, Rosemary Jensen; two *s* one *d. Educ:* Prince of Wales Sch., Nairobi; Charterhouse; Queen's Coll., Oxford (BA). Served with RAF, 1939-46: Bomber Comd, NW Europe; POW, 1941-45; Sqdn-Leader. HM Overseas Civil Service, 1946-66: Administrative Officer, Northern Rhodesia (later Zambia); appointments at Headquarters and in field; Provincial Commissioner, Resident Secretary. Mem., Pearce Commn on Rhodesian Opinion, 1972. Vice-Pres., Internat. Union of Dirs of Zool. Gardens. FCIS 1967. *Recreations:* aviation, most outdoor sports, current affairs. *Address:* c/o Zoological Society of London, Regent's Park, NW1; Birchgrove, Earl Howe Road, Holmer Green, Bucks.

RAWLINS, Surg. Vice-Adm. (Actg) John Stuart Pepys, OBE 1960 (MBE 1956); QHP; Medical Director-General (Navy), since 1977; *b* 12 May 1922; *s* of Col S. W. H. Rawlins, CB, CMG, DSO and Dorothy Pepys Cockerell; *m* 1944, Diana Colbeck; one *s* three *d. Educ:* Wellington Coll.; University Coll., Oxford; St Bartholomew's Hospital. BM, BCh 1945; MA, MRCP, FFCM, FRAeS. Surg. Lieut RNVR, HMS Triumph, 1947; Surg. Lieut RN, RAF Inst. Aviation Med., 1951; RN Physiol Lab., 1957; Surg. Comdr RAF Inst., Aviation Med., 1961; HMS Ark Royal, 1964; US Navy Medical Research Inst., 1967; Surg. Captain 1969; Surg. Cdre, Dir of Health and Research (Naval), 1973; Surg. Rear-Adm. 1975; Dean of Naval Medicine and MO i/c, Inst. of Naval Medicine, 1975-77; actg Surg. Vice-Adm. 1977. QHP 1975. Mem. Underseas Med. Soc.; Founder-Mem. European Underseas Biomed. Soc.; Mem. Aerospace Med. Soc.; FRAeS 1973; FRSM. Erroll-Eldridge Prize 1967; Sec. of US Navy's Commendation 1971; Gilbert Blane Medal 1971; Tuttle Mem. Award 1973; Chadwick Medal and Prize 1975. *Publications:* papers in fields of aviation and diving medicine. *Recreations:* diving, fishing, stalking, riding. *Address:* Wey House, Standford Lane, Headley, Bordon, Hants GU35 8RH. *T:* Bordon 2830. *Club:* Vincent's (Oxford).

RAWLINSON, Sir Anthony Henry John, 5th Bt *cr* 1891; fashion photographer; *b* 1 May 1936; *s* of Sir Alfred Frederick Rawlinson, 4th Bt and of Bessie Ford Taylor, *d* of Frank Raymond Emmatt, Harrogate; *S* father, 1969; *m* 1960, Penelope Byng Noel (marr. diss. 1967), 2nd *d* of Rear-Adm. G. J. B. Noel, RN; one *s* one *d*; 2nd, 1967, Pauline Strickland (marr. diss. 1976), *d* of J. H. Hardy, Sydney; one *s*; 3rd, 1977, Helen Leone, *d* of T. M. Kennedy, Scotland. *Educ:* Millfield School. *Heir:* s Alexander Noel Rawlinson, *b* 15 July 1964. *Address:* Heath Farm, Guist, near Dereham, Norfolk. *Club:* Clermont.

RAWLINSON, Anthony Keith, CB 1975; Second Permanent Secretary, HM Treasury, since 1977; *b* 5 March 1926; *s* of late Alfred Edward John Rawlinson, Bishop of Derby 1936-59, and Mildred Ansley Rawlinson (*née* Ellis); *m* 1956, Mary Hill; three *s. Educ:* Maidwell Hall; Eton; Christ Church, Oxford. Eton:

King's Schol., 1939, Newcastle Schol., 1944, Captain of Sch. 1944; Christ Church, Open Schol. (classics), 1944. Gren. Gds (Lieut), 1944-47. Oxford: 1st Cl. Honour Mods (classics), 1949, 2nd Cl. Lit. Hum., 1951. Entered Civil Service by open competition as Asst Principal, 1951; Min. of Labour and Nat. Service, 1951-53; transferred to Treasury, 1953; Principal, 1955; seconded to Atomic Energy Authority as Private Sec. to Chairman, 1958-60; returned to Treasury, 1960: Asst Sec., 1963; Under-Sec., 1968; Dep. Sec., 1972; Econ. Minister and Head of UK Treasury and Supply Delegn, Washington, and UK Exec. Dir, IMF and IBRD, 1972-75; Department of Industry: Dep. Sec., 1975-76; Second Permanent Sec., 1976-77. *Publications:* articles and reviews in mountaineering jls. Editor, Climbers' Club Jl, 1955-59. *Recreation:* mountaineering (Pres. OU Mountaineering Club, 1949-50). *Address:* 105 Corringham Road, NW11 7DL. *T:* 01-458 3402. *Clubs:* United Oxford & Cambridge University, Alpine (Hon. Sec., 1963-66, Vice-Pres., 1972-73).

RAWLINSON, Rt. Hon. Sir Peter (Anthony Grayson), PC 1964; Kt 1962; QC 1959; QC (NI) 1972; MP (C) Epsom and Ewell, since 1974 (Surrey, Epsom, 1955-74); *b* 26 June 1919; *o* surv. s of Lt-Col A. R. Rawlinson, OBE, and Ailsa Grayson Rawlinson; *m* 1st, 1940, Haidee Kavanagh; three *d*; 2nd, 1954, Elaine Dominguez, Newport, Rhode Island, USA; two *s* one *d. Educ:* Downside; Christ's Coll., Cambridge (Exhibitioner 1938). Officer Cadet Sandhurst, 1939; served in Irish Guards, 1940-46; N Africa, 1943 (despatches); demobilized with rank of Major, 1946. Called to Bar, Inner Temple, 1946, Bencher, 1962; called to Bar, Northern Ireland, 1972. Contested (C) Hackney South, 1951. Recorder of Salisbury, 1961-62; Solicitor-General, July 1962-Oct. 1964; Opposition Spokesman: for Law, 1964-65, 1968-70; for Broadcasting, 1965; Attorney-General, 1970-74; Attorney-General for NI, 1972-74; Recorder of Kingston upon Thames, 1975-; Leader, Western Circuit, 1975-. Vice-Chm., Cons. Parly Legal Cttee, 1966; Chm., Parly Legal Cttee, 1967-70. Member of Council, Justice, 1960-62, 1964; Trustee of Amnesty, 1960-62; Member, Bar Council, 1966-68; Mem. Senate, Inns of Court, 1968, Vice-Chm., 1974; Vice-Chm., Bar, 1974-75; Chairman: Bar Professional Conduct Cttee, 1974-75; of the Bar and of the Senate, 1975-76. Hon. Fellow, Amer. Coll. of Trial Lawyers, 1973; Hon. Mem., Amer. Bar Assoc., 1976. SMO Malta. *Recreations:* the theatre and painting. *Address:* 12 King's Bench Walk, Temple, EC4. *T:* 01-353 5892/6. *Clubs:* White's, Pratt's, MCC.

RAWSON, Christopher Selwyn Priestley; Chairman and Managing Director, Christopher Rawson Ltd; an Underwriting Member of Lloyds; *b* 25 March 1928; *e s* of late Comdr Selwyn Gerald Caygill Rawson, OBE, RN (retd) and of Dr Doris Rawson, MB, ChB (*née* Brown); *m* 1959, Rosemary Ann Focke; two *d. Educ:* The Elms Sch., Colwall, near Malvern, Worcs; The Nautical College, Pangbourne, Berks. Navigating Apprentice, Merchant Service, T. & J. Brocklebank Ltd, 1945-48. Sheriff of the City of London, 1961-62; Member of Court of Common Council (Ward of Bread Street), 1963-72; Alderman, City of London, (Ward of Lime Street), 1972-. Chairman: Governors, The Elms Sch., Colwall, near Malvern, Worcs, 1965-; Port and City of London Health Cttee, 1967-70; Billingsgate and Leadenhall Mkt Cttee, 1972-75. Silver Medal for Woollen and Worsted Raw Materials, City and Guilds of London Institute, 1951; Livery of Clothworkers Company, 1952; Freeman, Company of Watermen and Lightermen, 1966, Mem. Ct of Assts, 1974. ATI 1953; AIMarE 1962. *Recreations:* shooting, sailing. *Address:* 56 Ovington Street, SW3. *T:* 01-589 3136; Clarence House, Arthur Street, EC4. *T:* 01-623 9436. *Clubs:* Royal Thames Yacht, Royal Corinthian Yacht, Royal Automobile, City Livery.

RAWSON, Maj.-Gen. Geoffrey Grahame, CB 1941; OBE; MC; *b* 2 Dec. 1887; *s* of Edward Creswell Rawson, ICS, and Marion Duffield; *m* 1919, Ella Cane (*d* 1967); one *s* (and one *s* decd). *Educ:* Cheltenham Coll.; RMA Woolwich. Commissioned Royal Engineers, 1908; transferred Royal Corps of Signals, 1920; DAAG War Office, 1921; Chief Instructor School of Signals, 1932; Deputy Director Staff Duties, War Office, 1937; Director of Signals, War Office, 1941; Inspector of Signals, 1942; Colonel Comdt Royal Signals, 1944-50. Lt-Col, Royal Signals, 1928; Colonel, 1931; Brigadier, 1937; Major-General, 1941; served European War, 1914-18, with BEF in France and in Salonika (Brevet Major, Legion of Honour 5th Class, OBE, MC, despatches five times); ADC to the King, 1938-41; retired pay, 1944. *Address:* 15 Collingham Road, SW5.

RAY, Hon. Ajit Nath; Chief Justice of India, Supreme Court of India, 1973-77; *b* Calcutta, 29 Jan. 1912; *s* of Sati Nath Ray and Kali Kumari Debi; *m* 1944, Himani Mukherjee; one *s. Educ:* Presidency Coll., Calcutta; Hindu Coll., Calcutta Univ.

(Foundn Schol., MA); Oriel College, Oxford (MA). Called to Bar, Gray's Inn, 1939; practised at Calcutta High Court, 1940-57; Judge, Calcutta High Court, 1957-69; Judge, Supreme Court of India, 1969-73. Pres., Governing Body, Presidency Coll., Calcutta, 1959-70; Vice-Pres., Asiatic Soc., 1965-67 (Hon. Treas. 1962-65); President: Internat. Law Assoc., 1975- (Pres. Indian Br., 1973-); Indian Law Inst., New Delhi, 1973-; Soc. for Welfare of Blind, Narendrapur; Life Mem., Samsad Visva-Bharati. *Address:* 5 Krishna Menon Marg, New Delhi 110011, India. *T:* New Delhi 37 29 22, 375439; 15 Panditia Place, Calcutta 700029. *T:* Calcutta 475213. *Club:* Calcutta (Calcutta).

RAY, Rt. Rev. Chandu; Co-ordinating Officer for Asian Evangelism since 1969; *b* 14 April 1912; Pakistani parentage; *m* Anita Joy (*née* Meggitt); two *s* three *d. Educ:* D. J. Sind Coll., Karachi; Bishop's Coll., Calcutta. Bursar, Bishop Cotton Sch., Simla. Deacon, 1943; Priest, 1943. Vicar, St Philip's Church, Hyderabad, 1944; Sec., British and Foreign Bible Soc. in Pakistan, 1948; Canon of Lahore Cathedral, 1954; Archdeacon of Karachi, 1956; Asst Bishop of Lahore and Bishop in Karachi, 1957; first Bishop of Karachi, 1963-69. Hon. Dr of Sacred Theology, Wycliff, Toronto; Hon. Dr of Divinity, Huron, London. *Publications:* (trans) Old Testament in Sindhi Language, 1954; (revised 2nd edn) New Testament in Sindhi, 1955. *Recreations:* hockey, cricket, tennis. *Address:* 164 Duchess Avenue, Singapore 10. *T:* 674550 and 372938.

RAY, Cyril; *b* 16 March 1908; *e s* of Albert Benson Ray (who changed the family name from Rotenberg, 1913), and Rita Ray; *m* 1953, Elizabeth Mary, JP, *o d* of late Rev. H. C. Brocklehurst; one *s. Educ:* elementary sch., Bury, Lancs; Manchester Gr. Sch. (schol.); Jesus Coll., Oxford (open schol.). Manchester Guardian and BBC war correspondent: 5th Destroyer Flotilla, 1940; N African Landings, 1942; 8th Army, Italy (despatches); US 82nd Airborne Div., and 3rd Army, 1944-45. UNESCO missions, Italy, Greece, East, Central and S Africa, 1945-50. Sunday Times, 1949-56 (Moscow Correspondent, 1950-52); Asst Editor, The Spectator, 1958-62; Wine Correspondent: The Director, 1958-76; The Observer, 1959-73; Editorial Council, later Chief Consltnt, The Good Food Guide, 1968-74; Founder and President, Circle of Wine Writers; Trustee, Albany, 1967-. Much occasional broadcasting, 1940-62 (The Critics, 1958-62), Southern TV, 1958-59. Hon. Life Mem., NUJ. Freeman, City of London; Liveryman, Fan-Makers Co. Vice-Chm., Cranbrook Labour Party. Cavaliere dell'Ordine al Merito della Repubblica Italiana, 1972; Chevalier du Mérite Agricole, 1974. *Publications:* (ed) Scenes and Characters from Surtees, 1948; From Algiers to Austria: The History of 78 Division, 1952; The Pageant of London, 1958; Merry England, 1960; Regiment of the Line: The Story of the Lancashire Fusiliers, 1963; (ed) The Gourmet's Companion, 1963; (ed) Morton Shand's Book of French Wines, 1964; (ed) Best Murder Stories, 1965; The Wines of Italy, 1966 (Bologna Trophy, 1967); In a Glass Lightly, 1967; Lafite: The Story of Château Lafite-Rothschild, 1968. Editor, The Compleat Imbiber, 1956-71 (Wine and Food Soc.'s first André Simon Prize, 1964); Bollinger: the story of a champagne, 1971; Cognac, 1973; Mouton: the story of Mouton-Rothschild, 1974; (with Elizabeth Ray) Wine with Food, 1975; The Wines of France, 1976; The Wines of Germany, 1977; The Complete Book of Spirits and Liqueurs, 1977. *Recreation:* riding. *Address:* Albany, Piccadilly, W1. *T:* 01-734 0270. *Clubs:* Athenæum, Brooks's, Buck's, MCC, Special Forces.

RAY, Frederick Ivor, CB 1958; CBE 1953; BSc (Eng); FIEE; Telecommunications Consultant; *b* 18 Jan. 1899; *s* of Frederick Pedder Ray; *m* 1923, Katherine (*d* 1968), *d* of Hubert Abdy Fellowes, Newbury; two *s. Educ:* Royal British Orphan Sch.; Bournemouth School; Faraday House Electrical Engineering College. Served European War, 1917-19, RE. Entered GPO Engineering Dept, 1922; Sectional Engineer, 1932-35; Telephone Manager, Scotland West, 1935-39; Telecommunications Controller, NW Region, 1939; Controller Telephones, London, 1940-44; Assistant Secretary, 1944-48; Regional Director, London, 1948-56; Director of Inland Telecommunications, 1956-61; Director, International Press Communications Committee, 1965-67; Commonwealth Press Union Adviser on Telecommunications, 1963-67. *Recreations:* fishing, caravanning, golf. *Address:* 22A Edward Road, Bromley, Kent. *T:* 01-464 3859.

RAY, Gordon Norton; President of the John Simon Guggenheim Memorial Foundation, since 1963; *b* New York City, 8 Sept. 1915; *s* of Jesse Gordon and Jessie Norton Ray; unmarried. *Educ:* University of Indiana (AM); Harvard Univ. (AM, PhD). Instructor in English, Harvard, 1940-42; Guggenheim Fellow, 1941-42, 1946, 1956-57. Lt, US Navy, serving aboard aircraft carriers Belleau Wood and Boxer, Pacific, 1942-46; Professor of English, 1946-60, Head of Dept, 1950-57, Vice-President and

Provost, 1957-60, University of Illinois. Associate Secretary General, Guggenheim Foundn, 1960-61; Sec.-Gen., 1961-63. Rockefeller Fellow, 1948-49; Member US Educational Commn in UK, which established Fulbright program, 1948-49. Lowell Lectures, Boston, 1950; Berg Professor, New York Univ. 1952-53; Professor of English, 1962-. Advisor in literature, Houghton Mifflin Co., 1953-71. Member Commission on Trends in Education, Mod. Lang. Assoc., 1953-59, Trustee 1966-; Mem. Council, Smithsonian Instn, 1968-, Chm. 1970-; Dir and Treasurer, Amer. Council of Learned Socs, 1973-. Advisory Bd, Guggenheim Foundation, 1959-60, Trustee, 1963-; Trustee: Pierpont Morgan Library, 1970-; Rosenbach Foundn, 1972-; New York Public Library, 1975-. Hon. LittD: Monmouth Coll., 1959; Syracuse, 1961; Duke, 1965; Illinois, 1968; Northwestern, 1974; Hon. LLD: New York, 1961; Tulane, 1963; California, 1968; Columbia, 1969; South California, 1974; Hon. LHD, Indiana, 1964. FRSL 1948. Fellow, Amer. Acad. of Arts and Sciences, 1962. *Publications:* Letters and Private Papers of Thackeray, 4 vols, 1945-46; The Buried Life, 1952; Thackeray: The Uses of Adversity, 1955; Henry James and H. G. Wells, 1958; Thackeray: The Age of Wisdom, 1958; H. G. Wells and Rebecca West, 1974; The Illustrator and the Book in England from 1790 to 1914, 1976, etc; contrib. to magazines and learned jls. *Recreations:* book-collecting, travel. *Address:* 25 Sutton Place South, New York, NY 10022, USA. *Clubs:* Athenæum (London); Harvard, Grolier (President, 1965-69), Century (New York).

RAY, Philip Bicknell, CMG 1969; Ministry of Defence 1946-76, retired; *b* 10 July 1917; *s* of late Basil Ray and Clare (*née* Everett); *m* 1946, Bridget Mary Robertson (decd); two *s* one *d.* *Educ:* Felsted Sch.; Selwyn Coll., Cambridge (MA). Indian Police, 1939-46. *Address:* The Cottage, Little Shoddesden, Andover, Hants.

RAY, Satyajit; Padma Shree, 1957; Padma Bhushan, 1964; Padma Bibhushan, 1976; Indian film producer and film director since 1953; *b* 2 May 1921; *s* of late Sukumar and Suprabha Ray (*née* Das); *m* 1949, Bijoya (*née* Das); one *s.* *Educ:* Ballygunge Govt School; Presidency College, Calcutta. Joined British advertising firm, D. J. Keymer & Co., as visualiser, 1943; Art Director, 1950. In 1952, started first feature film, Pather Panchali, finished in 1955 (Cannes Special Award, 1956, San Francisco, best film, 1957). Left advertising for whole-time film-making, 1956. Other films: Aparajito, 1957 (Venice Grand Prix, 1957, San Francisco, best direction); Jalsaghar, 1958; Devi, 1959; Apur Sansar, 1959 (Selznick Award and Sutherland Trophy 1960); Teen Kanya (Two Daughters), 1961; Kanchanjangha, 1962; Mahanagar, 1963; Charulata, 1964; The Coward and The Holy Man (Kapurush-O-Mahapurush), 1965; The Hero (Nayak), 1965; Goopy Gyne and Bagha Byne, 1969; Days and Nights in the Forest, 1970; Pratidwandi (The Adversary), 1970; Company Limited, 1971; Distant Thunder, 1973 (Golden Bear, Berlin Film Festival, 1973); The Golden Fortress, 1974; The Middleman, 1975; The Chess Players, 1977. Founded first Film Society in Calcutta, 1947. Composes background music for own films. *Publications:* Our Films, Their Films, 1976; film articles in Sight and Sound, Sequence; (Editor, 1961-) children's magazine Sandesh, with contributions of stories, poems. *Recreations:* listening to Indian and Western classical music, and reading science-fiction. *Address:* Flat 8, 1-1 Bishop Lefroy Road, Calcutta 20, India. *T:* 44-8747.

RAY, Ted; Theatrical and BBC Entertainer; *s* of Chas Olden, comedian, and of Margaret Ellen Kenyon; *m* 1933, Dorothy Sybil Stevens; two *s.* *Educ:* Liverpool Collegiate School. Became successively clerk, ship's steward and dance band violinist. First stage appearance, Palace Theatre, Prescot, Lancs, 1927. First London appearance, London Music Hall, Shoreditch, 1930. Toured South Africa thrice; Royal Command Performances: London Palladium, 1948; London Coliseum, 1949; Empire, Leicester Sq., 1950; London Palladium, 1952. Interested in theatre charities (King Water Rat, 1949 and 1950). Began 1st radio series, Ray's a Laugh, 1949; Resident MC of BBC Calling All Forces, 1950. Television: The Ted Ray Show, BBC, 1955; I Object, Jackanory; Jokers Wild, 1969-70. *Films:* Meet Me To-night, 1952; Escape by Night, 1953; My Wife's Family, 1956; The Crowning Touch, 1957; Carry on Teacher, 1959; Please Turn Over, 1959. *Publications:* Autobiography: Raising the Laughs, 1952; My Turn Next, 1963; Golf—My Slice of Life, 1972. *Recreations:* golf, swimming, motoring, boxing. *Address:* 30 Broad Walk, N21. *Clubs:* Crews Hill Golf; Temple Golf.

RAYLEIGH, 5th Baron *cr* 1821; **John Arthur Strutt;** *b* 12 April 1908; *e s* of 4th Baron Rayleigh, FRS, and late Mary Hilda, 2nd *d* of 4th Earl of Leitrim; *S* father 1947; *m* 1934, Ursula Mary, *o d* of Lieut-Colonel R. H. R. Brocklebank, DSO and Charlotte Carissima, *o d* of General Sir Bindon Blood, GCB, GCVO.

Educ: Eton; Trinity College, Cambridge. *Heir: b* Hon. Charles Richard Strutt, *qv. Address:* Terling Place, Chelmsford, Essex. *T:* Terling 235; 01-453 3235.

RAYMER, Michael Robert, OBE 1951; Assistant Secretary, Royal Hospital, Chelsea, since 1975; *b* 22 July 1917; *surv. s* of Rev. W. H. Raymer, MA; *m* 1948, Joyce Marion Scott; two *s* one *d. Educ:* Marlborough College (Foundation Scholar); Jesus College, Cambridge (Rustat Schol.). BA (Hons) 1939. Administrative Officer, Nigeria, 1940-49 and 1952-55. Served in Royal W African Frontier Force, 1940-43. Colonial Sec. to Govt of the Falkland Islands, 1949-52; Prin. Estab. Officer, N Nigeria, 1954; Controller of Organisation and Establishments, to Government of Fiji, 1955-62; retired, 1962; Principal, MoD, 1962-75. *Recreation:* gardening. *Address:* Light Horse Court, The Royal Hospital, Chelsea, SW3; The Tithe House, Peaseland Green, Elsing, Dereham, Norfolk.

RAYMOND, Sir Stanley (Edward), Kt 1967; FCIT; FBIM; *b* 10 Aug. 1913; *s* of late Frederick George and Lilian Grace Raymond; *m* 1938, Enid, *d* of Capt. S. A. Buley, Polruan-by-Fowey; one *s. Educ:* Orphanage; Grammar Sch., Hampton, Mx. Entered Civil Service, 1930. Asst Sec., Soc. of Civil Servants, 1939-45. War service in Royal Artillery, 1942-45; Lieutenant-Colonel on demobilisation. London Passenger Transport Board, 1946; British Road Services, 1947; BTC, 1955; Director of Establishment and Staff, 1956; Chief Commercial Manager, Scottish Region, British Railways, 1957 and Asst Gen. Manager, 1959; Traffic Adviser, BTC, 1961; Chm. Western Railway Board, and General Manager, Western Region, British Railways, 1962-63; Member, 1963, a Vice-Chm., 1964-65, and Chm., 1965-67, British Railways Bd. Chairman: Horserace Betting Levy Bd, 1972-74; Gaming Bd for GB, 1968-77. *Recreation:* walking. *Address:* 26 Cavendish House, Brighton, Sussex.

RAYMOND, William Francis, FRIC; Deputy Chief Scientist, Ministry of Agriculture, Fisheries and Food, since 1972; *b* 25 Feb. 1922; *m* 1949, Amy Elizabeth Kelk; three *s* one *d. Educ:* Bristol Grammar Sch.; The Queen's Coll., Oxford (MA). Research Officer, MRC, 1943-45; Head of Animal Science Div. and later Asst Dir, Grassland Research Inst., Hurley, 1945-72. Sec., 8th Internat. Grassland Congress, 1960; Pres., Brit. Grassland Soc., 1974-75. *Publications:* (with Shepperson and Waltham) Forage Conservation and Feeding, 1972, 2nd edn 1975; over 120 papers in scientific jls. *Recreation:* gardening. *Address:* High Walls, Pinkneys Drive, Maidenhead, Berks SL6 6QD. *T:* Maidenhead 26660. *Club:* Farmers'.

RAYMONT, Prof. John Edwin George; Professor of Biological Oceanography, University of Southampton, since 1964; Deputy Vice-Chancellor, 1966-68; *b* 6 April 1915; *s* of Walter and Ellen Raymont; *m* 1945, Joan Katharine Brigit Sloan; one *s* two *d. Educ:* Hele's School and University College, Exeter. First Class Hons London External Degree in Zoology, 1936. Henry Fellow, Harvard Univ., USA, 1937-38. AM Harvard 1938; DSc Univ. of Exeter, 1960. Assistant Lecturer in Zoology, University College, Exeter, 1938-39; Lecturer in Zoology, University of Edinburgh, 1939-46; Prof. of Zoology, Univ. of Southampton, 1946-64. Mem. Wessex Regional Hosp. Bd, 1959-74; Chm. Planning and Development Cttee, 1959-74; Southampton Univ. HMC, 1959-74; Vice-Chm., Hants Area AHA, 1974-. Fellow, Indian Acad. of Sciences. *Publications:* Plankton and Productivity in the Oceans, 1963; on physiology of copepods, marine fish cultivation and marine benthos in Proc. Roy. Soc. of Edin., Biological Bulletin, Jl of Marine Biolog. Assoc., Limnol. and Oceanogr., Int. Revue ges. Hydrobiol., Deep-Sea Research, etc. *Address:* 246 Woodlands Road, Southampton.

RAYNE, family name of Baron Rayne.

RAYNE, Baron *cr* 1976 (Life Peer), of Prince's Meadow in Greater London; **Max Rayne,** Kt 1969; Chairman, London Merchant Securities Ltd, since 1960; *b* 8 Feb. 1918; *er s* of Phillip and Deborah Rayne; *m* 1st, 1941, Margaret Marco (marr. diss., 1960); one *s* two *d*; 2nd, 1965, Lady Jane Antonia Frances Vane-Tempest-Stewart, *er d* of 8th Marquess of Londonderry; two *s* two *d. Educ:* Central Foundation Sch. and University Coll., London. Served RAF 1940-45. Dir, Carlton Industries Ltd, 1960-, and other companies. Governor: St Thomas' Hosp., 1962-74 (Special Trustee, 1974-); Royal Ballet Sch., 1966-; Yehudi Menuhin Sch., 1966-; Malvern Coll., 1966-; Centre for Environmental Studies, 1967-73; Member: Gen. Council, King Edward VII's Hosp. Fund for London, 1966-; Council, St Thomas's Hospital Medical School, 1965-; Hon. Vice-Pres., Jewish Welfare Bd, 1966-; Chairman: London Festival Ballet Trust, 1967-75; Nat. Theatre Board, 1971-; Founder Patron, The Rayne Foundation, 1962-. Hon. Fellow:

Darwin Coll., Cambridge, 1966; University Coll., London, 1966; LSE 1974; Hon. FRCPsych, 1977. Hon. LLD London, 1968. Chevalier Légion d'Honneur, 1973. *Address:* 100 George Street, W1. *T:* 01-935 3555.

RAYNE, Edward, CVO 1977; Chairman and Managing Director of H. & M. Rayne Ltd, since 1951; Director, Debenhams Ltd, since 1975; President, Debenhams Inc., since 1976; Executive Chairman, Rayne-Delman Shoes Inc., since 1972 (President, 1961-72); *b* 19 Aug. 1922; *s* of Joseph Edward Rayne and Meta Elizabeth Reddish (American); *m* 1952, Phyllis Cort; two *s.* *Educ:* Harrow. Member: Export Council for Europe, 1962-71; European Trade Cttee, 1972-; Bd of Governors, Genesco Inc., 1967-73. Chm., Incorp. Soc. of London Fashion Designers, 1960-; Pres., Royal Warrant Holders' Assoc., 1964, Hon. Treas. 1974-; President: British Footwear Manufacturers' Fedn, 1965; British Boot and Shoe Instn, 1972-. FRSA 1971. Harper's Bazaar Trophy, 1963. *Recreations:* golf and bridge. *Address:* 15 Grosvenor Square, W1. *T:* 01-493 2871. *Clubs:* White's, Portland; Travellers' (Paris).

RAYNER, Bryan Roy; Under-Secretary, Department of Health and Social Security, since 1975; *b* 29 Jan. 1932; *s* of Harold and Florence Rayner; *m* 1957, Eleanora Whittaker; one *d.* *Educ:* Stationers' Company's School, N8. Clerical Officer, Customs and Excise, 1948; Asst Private Sec. to Minister of Health, 1960-62; Principal, 1965; Asst Sec., 1970. Member, Social Science Research Council, 1976-. *Address:* 6 Lawrie Lane, Lindfield, Sussex RH16 2SG. *T:* Lindfield 3484.

RAYNER, Sir Derek George, Kt 1973; Joint Managing Director, Marks & Spencer Ltd, since 1973; *b* 30 March 1926; *o s* of George William Rayner and Hilda Jane (*née* Rant); unmarried. *Educ:* City Coll., Norwich; Selwyn Coll., Cambridge. Fellow, Inst. Purchasing and Supply, 1970. Nat. Service, commnd RAF Regt, 1946-48. Joined Marks & Spencer, 1953; Dir, 1967. Special Adviser to HM Govt, 1970; Chief Exec., Procurement Executive, MoD, 1971-72. Mem., UK Permanent Security Commn, 1977-. Member: Design Council, 1973-75; Council RCA, 1973-76. *Recreations:* music, food, travel. *Address:* Michael House, Baker Street, W1. *Club:* Turf.

RAYNER, Most Rev. Keith; see Adelaide, Archbishop of.

RAYNER, Neville, JP, FRSA; Underwriting Member of Lloyd's, since 1963; General Commissioner of Income Tax, since 1965; Rating and Compensation Valuer, since 1936; *b* 1914; *m* 1941, Elsie Mary (*née* Lindley); two *s* (adopted). *Educ:* Emanuel Sch., SW11. Commd RAFVR(T), 1941-45. Mem., Court of Common Council, City of London, 1960-; Sheriff of London, 1971-72. Former Mem., LCC and Wandsworth Borough Council. Director, Bedford Building Soc. Parish Clerk, Priory Church of St Bartholomew-the-Great, Smithfield; Liveryman: Painter Stainers Co.; Basketmakers Co. (Asst); Glovers' Co. (Warden); Playing Card Makers Co.; Co. of Parish Clerks. JP, Inner London, 1959; Dep. Chm., Greater London (SW) Valuation Appeals Court, 1950-; Pres., Greater London Council Br., Royal British Legion, 1962-; Pres., London Ratepayers' Alliance; Vice-Pres., Nat. Union of Ratepayers. FRVA, FSVA, FIArb. Past Pres., Farringdon Ward Club. Member: Magistrates Assoc.; Magic Circle; Council, Gardeners' Royal Benevolent Soc.; Council, City of London Branch, Royal Soc. St George; Luxembourg Soc.; Sheriff's Soc. Order of Sacred Treasure (Japan), 1972; Star of Afghanistan, 1972; Comdr, Order of Orange-Nassau (Holland), 1972; Couronne de Chêne (Luxembourg), 1972; Ecomienda de la Orden del Merito Civil (Spain), 1975. *Recreations:* magic, travel, carpentry. *Address:* Old Selsfield, Turners Hill, West Sussex RH10 4PS. *T:* Copthorne 715203; 1 Montpelier Mews, SW7 1HB. *T:* 01-589 3939. *Clubs:* Guildhall, United Wards (Past Pres.), City Livery (Council), Pilgrims, Press, Anglo-Spanish.

RAYNHAM, Viscount; Charles George Townshend; *b* 26 Sept. 1945; *s* and *heir* of 7th Marquess Townshend, *qv; m* 1975, Hermione, *d* of Lt-Cdr R. M. D. Ponsonby and Mrs Dorothy Ponsonby; one *s.* *Educ:* Eton. *Address:* Raynham Hall, Fakenham, Norfolk. *T:* Fakenham 2133. *Club:* White's.

RAYNOR, Prof. Geoffrey Vincent, FRS 1959; MA, DPhil, DSc Oxon; Professor of Physical Metallurgy, University of Birmingham, since 1954; *b* 2 Oct. 1913; *y s* of late Alfred Ernest Raynor, Nottingham; *m* 1943, Emily Jean, *er d* of late Dr Geo. F. Brockless, London; three *s.* *Educ:* Nottingham High School; Keble Coll., Oxford, 1st cl. Hons, School of Natural Science (Chemistry), 1936, Hon. Fellow, 1972. Research Assistant, Oxford University, 1936; Departmental Demonstrator in Inorganic Chemistry, 1937-45; DSIR Senior Research Award, 1938-41. Metallurgical research for Ministry of Supply and Ministry of Aircraft Production, 1939-45; University of Birmingham: ICI Research Fellow, 1945-47; Beilby Memorial Award, 1947; Reader in Theoretical Metallurgy, 1947-49; Prof. of Metal Physics, 1949-54; Prof. of Physical Metallurgy, 1954-55; Feeney Prof. of Physical Metallurgy, and Head of Dept of Physical Metallurgy and Science of Materials, 1955-69; Dean, Faculty of Science and Engineering, 1966-69; Dep. Principal, 1969-73. Royal Soc. Leverhulme Vis. Prof., Witwatersrand Univ., 1974; Vis. Prof., Univ. of NSW, 1975. Vice-President: Inst. of Metals, 1953-56; Instn of Metallurgists, 1963-66, 1977; President: Birmingham Metallurgical Assoc., 1965-66; Keble Assoc., 1974. Walter Rosenhain Medal of Inst. of Metals, 1951; Visiting Professor of Metallurgy, Chicago University, 1951-52. Fellow New York Acad. of Science, 1961. Battelle Visiting Prof. Ohio State Univ., 1962. Heyn Medal of Deutsche Gesellschaft für Metallkunde, 1956. Member several metallurgical research committees. *Publications:* Introduction to the Electron Theory of Metals, Inst. of Metals monograph and report series, No 4, 1947; contrib. to Butterworth's scientific publications: Progress in Metal Physics, 1949, and Metals Reference Book, 1949; The Structure of Metals and Alloys (with W. Hume-Rothery), 1954; The Physical Metallurgy of Magnesium and its Alloys, 1959; scientific papers on theory of metals and alloys in Proc. Royal Soc., Philosophical Mag., Trans. Faraday Soc., and metallurgical journals. *Recreations:* rowing and sculling. *Address:* 94 Gillhurst Road, Harborne, Birmingham B17 8PA. *T:* 021-429 3176.

RAZZALL, Leonard Humphrey; a Master of the Supreme Court (Taxing) since 1954; *b* 13 Nov. 1912; *s* of Horace Razzall and Sarah Thompson, Scarborough; *m* 1st, 1936, Muriel (*d* 1968), *yr d* of late Pearson Knowles; two *s;* 2nd, 1975, Mary Elmore, *widow* of David Farrant Bland. *Educ:* Scarborough High Sch. Admitted solicitor, 1935; founded firm Humphrey Razzall & Co., 1938. Served in Royal Marines, 1941-46, Staff Captain. Contested (L) Scarborough and Whitby Division, 1945. *Recreations:* travel, cricket, book-collecting. *Address:* 10 Glentham Gardens, Lonsdale Road, SW13. *T:* 01-748 5733. *Clubs:* National Liberal, English-Speaking Union.

REA, family name of **Baron Rea.**

REA, 2nd Baron, *cr* 1937, of Eskdale; **Philip Russell Rea,** PC 1962; OBE 1946; MA; DL; JP; 2nd Bt, *cr* 1935; a Deputy Speaker, House of Lords; merchant banker, company director; Underwriter at Lloyd's; *b* London, 7 Feb. 1900; *e s* of 1st Baron Rea of Eskdale and Evelyn (*d* 1930), *d* of J. J. Muirhead; *S* father, 1948; *m* 1922, Lorna Smith (*see* Lorna Rea); one *d* (one *s* decd). *Educ:* Westminster; Christ Church, Oxford; Grenoble Univ. Grenadier Guards, 1918-19; served War of 1939-45: KRRC, attached Special Forces in Britain, France, N Africa, Malta, Egypt and Italy, 1940-46 (Lt-Col; despatches; OBE). FO, 1946-50; Chief Liberal Whip, House of Lords, 1950-55; Dep. Lord Chm. of Cttees, 1950-60; Dep. Lord Speaker, 1950-; Liberal Leader, House of Lords, 1955-67; Pres., Liberal Party, 1955. Leader, British Parly Delegn to Burma and Indonesia, 1954; UK Deleg. to Council of Europe, Strasbourg, 1957; Mem. Parly Delegn to USA, and to Hong Kong and Ceylon, 1958. Member: Cumberland Develt Council, 1950-60; BBC Adv. Council, 1957-62; Political Honours Scrutiny Cttee, 1962-76; Lord Chancellor's Adv. Cttee, Inner London; Outward Bound Trust Council. President: Fell Dales Assoc., 1950-60; Elizabethan Club, 1965-66. Pres., Nat. Liberal Club, 1966-. Governor, Westminster Sch. DL Cumberland, 1955, Greater London, 1966-76; JP Cumberland, 1950-66; JP London, 1966-. Officer, Order of Crown (Belgium); Chevalier, Legion of Honour, and Croix de Guerre with palm (France); Grand Commandeur, Ordre de Mérite (France). Hon. Adm. Louisiana, USA. *Heir: n* John Nicolas Rea, MD [*b* 6 June 1928; *m* 1951, Elizabeth Anne, *d* of late W. H. Robinson; four *s*]. *Address:* 5 St John's House, 30 Smith Square, SW1. *T:* 01-222 4040. *Clubs:* Garrick, Grillions, Special Forces (Pres. 1955), National Liberal (Pres.).

See also Sir M. J. S. Clapham.

REA, James Taylor, CMG 1958; HM Overseas Civil Service, retired; *b* 19 Oct. 1907; *s* of Rev. Martin Rea, Presbyterian Minister, and Mary Rea (*née* Fisher); *m* 1934, Catharine, *d* of Dr W. H. Bleakney, Whitman College, Walla Walla, Washington, USA; one *s* one *d.* *Educ:* Royal School, Dungannon; Queen's University, Belfast (BA); St John's College, Cambridge (MA). HM Colonial Administrative Service (now known as HM Overseas Civil Service) serving throughout in Malaya and Singapore, 1931-58; Principal offices held: Asst Sec., Chinese Affairs, Fedn of Malaya, 1948; Dep. Comr for Labour, Fedn of Malaya, 1949; Dep. Malayan Establishment Officer, 1950; Dep. Pres., 1952-55, Pres., 1955-58, City Council, Singapore. Retired, 1958. Chairman: Hotel Grants Adv. Cttee,

NI, 1963-75; NI Training Exec., 1972-75; Down District Cttee, Eastern Health and Social Services Bd, 1974-; Mem., NI Housing Trust, 1959-71, Vice Chm., 1970-71. Indep. Mem.: Catering Wages Council, N Ireland, 1965; Retail Bespoke Tailoring Wages Council, 1965-; Laundry Wages Council, 1965-; Shirtmaking Wages Council, 1965. Nominated Member General Dental Council, under Dentist Act, 1957, Nov. 1961. Mem. Downpatrick HMC, 1966-73, Chm., 1971-73. *Address:* Craigduff, Downpatrick, N Ireland. *T:* Seaforde 258.

REA, Lorna; (The Lady Rea); Writer; *b* Glasgow, 12 June 1897; *d* of late Lewis O. Smith, merchant; *m* 1922, Philip Russell Rea (*see* Baron Rea); one *d* (one *s* decd). *Educ:* St James's, West Malvern; Newnham College, Cambridge (Hons). WVS (London Region), 1940-45. *Publications:* Six Mrs Greenes, Rachel Moon, The Happy Prisoner, First Night, The Armada, Six and Seven, and other publications. *Address:* 5 St John's House, Smith Square, Westminster, SW1. *T:* 01-222 6106.

READ, Prof. Alan Ernest Alfred, MD, FRCP; Professor of Medicine and Director of Medical Professorial Unit, University of Bristol, since 1969; *b* 15 Nov. 1926; *s* of Ernest Read and Annie Lydia; *m* 1952, Enid Malein; one *s* two *d*. *Educ:* Wembley County Sch.; St Mary's Hosp. Med. Sch., London. House Phys., St Mary's Hosp., 1950; Med. Registrar, Royal Masonic Hosp., 1951; Mil. Service Med. Specialist, Trieste, 1952-54; Registrar and Sen. Registrar, Central Mddx and Hammersmith Hosps, 1954-60; Lectr in Medicine and Cons. Phys., University of Bristol, 1961, Reader in Medicine, 1966; Associate Prof. of Medicine, Univ. of Rochester, USA, 1967. *Publications:* Clinical Apprentice (jtly), 1948 (4th edn 1971); (jtly) Basic Gastroenterology, 1965 (2nd edn 1974); (jtly) Modern Medicine, 1975. *Recreations:* boating, fishing. *Address:* Riverbank, 77 Nore Road, Portishead, Bristol BS20 9JZ.

READ, Gen. Sir Antony; *see* Read, Gen. Sir J. A. J.

READ, Air Marshal Sir Charles (Frederick), KBE 1976 (CBE 1964); CB 1972; DFC 1942; AFC 1958; Chief of the Air Staff, RAAF, 1972-75, retired; *b* Sydney, NSW, 9 Oct. 1918; *s* of J. F. Read, Bristol, England; *m* 1946, Betty E., *d* of A. V. Bradshaw; three *s*. *Educ:* Sydney Grammar Sch. Former posts include: OC, RAAF Base, Point Cook, Vic, 1965-68; OC, RAAF, Richmond, NSW, 1968-70; Dep. Chief of Air Staff, 1969-72. *Recreation:* yachting. *Address:* 2007 Pittwater Road, Bayview, NSW 2104, Australia. *T:* 997-1686.

READ, Rev. David Haxton Carswell, MA, DD; Minister of Madison Avenue Presbyterian Church, New York City, USA, since 1956; regular broadcaster on National Radio Pulpit; *b* Cupar, Fife, 2 Jan. 1910; *s* of John Alexander Read and Catherine Haxton Carswell; *m* 1936, Dorothy Florence Patricia Gilbert; one *s*. *Educ:* Daniel Stewart's College, Edinburgh. Edinburgh Univ.; Univs of Montpellier, Strasbourg, Paris, and Marburg; New Coll., Edinburgh. MA Edin. (first class Hons in Lit.) 1932; BD (dist. in Dogmatics) 1936. Ordained Minister of the Church of Scotland, 1936; Minister of Coldstream West Church, 1936-39. CF, 1939-45 (despatches; POW, 1940-45, Germany). Minister of Greenbank Parish, Edinburgh, 1939-49; first Chaplain, Univ. of Edinburgh, 1949-55; Chaplain to the Queen in Scotland, 1952-55. Mem., Bd of Preachers, Harvard Univ.; Pres., Men's Cttee, Japan Internat. Christian Univ., etc. Guest Lectr and Preacher in USA, Scotland, Canada, Australia. TV Series, Pulpit and People. Hon. DD: Edinburgh, 1956; Yale, 1959; Lafayette Coll., 1965; Hope Coll., 1969; Hon. LHD: Hobart Coll., 1972; Trinity Univ., 1972; Hon. LittD Coll. of Wooster, 1966. *Publications:* The Spirit of Life, 1939; The Church to Come (trans. from German), 1939; Prisoners' Quest, Lectures on Christian doctrine in a POW Camp, 1944; The Communication of The Gospel, Warrack Lectures, 1952; The Christian Faith, 1955 (NY 1956); I am Persuaded, 1961 (NY 1962); Sons of Anak, 1964 (NY); God's Mobile Family, 1966 (NY); Whose God is Dead?, 1966 (Cin); Holy Common Sense, 1966 (Tenn); The Pattern of Christ, 1967 (NY); The Presence of Christ, 1968 (NJ); Christian Ethics, 1968 (NY 1969); Virginia Woolfe Meets Charlie Brown, 1968 (Mich); Giants Cut Down To Size, 1970; Religion Without Wrappings, 1970; Overheard, 1971; Curious Christians, 1972; Sent from God, 1974; Good News in the Letters of Paul, 1975; Evangelism... Who Needs It?, 1977; articles and sermons in Atlantic Monthly, Scottish Jl of Theology, Expository Times, etc. *Recreations:* languages; drama; travel, especially in France. *Address:* 1165 Fifth Avenue, New York, NY 10029, USA. *Club:* The Century (New York).

READ, Gen. Sir (John) Antony (Jervis), GCB 1972 (KCB 1967; CB 1965); CBE 1959 (OBE 1957); DSO 1945; MC 1941; Governor of Royal Hospital, Chelsea, since 1975; *b* 10 Sept. 1913; *e s* of late John Dale Read, Heathfield, Sussex; *m* 1947,

Sheila, *e d* of late F. G. C. Morris, London, NW8; three *d*. *Educ:* Winchester; Sandhurst. Commissioned Oxford and Bucks Lt Inf., 1934; seconded to Gold Coast Regt, RWAFF, 1936; comd 81 (WA) Div. Reconnaissance Regt, 1943; comd 1 Gambia Regt, 1944; war service Kenya, Abyssinia, Somaliland, Burma; DAMS, War Office, 1947-49; Company Comd RMA Sandhurst, 1949-52; AA&QMG 11 Armd Div., 1953-54; comd 1 Oxford and Bucks Lt Inf., 1955-57; comd 3 Inf. Bde Gp, 1957-59; Comdt School of Infantry, 1959-62; GOC Northumbrian Area and 50 (Northumbrian) Division (TA), 1962-64; Vice-Quarter-Master-General, Min. of Defence, 1964-66; GOC-in-C, Western Comd, 1966-69; Quartermaster-General, 1969-72; Comdt, Royal Coll. of Defence Studies, 1973. ADC (Gen.) to the Queen, 1971-73. Colonel Commandant: Army Catering Corps, 1966-76; The Light Division, 1968-73; Small Arms School Corps, 1969-74. President: TA Rifle Assoc.; Ex-Services Fellowship Centres, 1975-; Chm., ACF Assoc., 1973-. Chm. of Governors, Royal Sch. for Daughters of Officers of the Army, 1975- (Governor, 1966-); St Edward's Sch., Oxford, 1972; Special Comr, Duke of York's Royal Mil. Sch., 1974. FBIM 1972. *Address:* Governor's Apartments, Royal Hospital, Chelsea, SW3 4SR; Brackles, Little Chesterton, near Bicester, Oxon. *T:* Bicester 2189. *Clubs:* Beefsteak, Army and Navy.

READ, Sir John (Emms), Kt 1976; FCA 1947; Chairman, since 1974, Chief Executive, since 1969, EMI Group of Companies (Deputy Chairman, 1973-74); *b* 29 March 1918; *s* of late William Emms Read and of Daysie Elizabeth (*née* Cooper); *m* 1942, Dorothy Millicent Berry; two *s*. *Educ:* Brighton, Hove and Sussex Grammar Sch. Served Royal Navy, 1939-46 (rank of Comdr (S) RNVR); Admiral's Secretary: to Asst Chief of Naval Staff, Admty, 1942-45; to Brit. Admty Technical Mission, Ottawa, Canada, 1945-46. Ford Motor Co. Ltd, 1946-64 (Admin. Staff Coll., Henley, 1952), Dir of Sales, 1961-64; Dir, Electric and Musical Industries Ltd, 1965-. Director: Dunlop Holdings Ltd; Thames Television Ltd; Capitol Industries-EMI Inc.; EMI Australia Ltd; Pathé Marconi EMI, France; Toshiba/EMI, Japan. Chm., EDC for Electronics Industry, 1977-. Member: (part time), PO Bd, 1975; Engineering Industries Council, 1975-; BOTB, 1976-; Armed Forces Pay Review Body, 1976-; Nat. Electronics Council, 1977-; Groupe des Présidents des Grandes Enterprises Européennes, 1977-. Member: Court Brunel Univ., 1969; RN Film Corp., 1975-; Governor, Admin. Staff Coll., Henley, 1974. FBIM 1974; CompIERE 1974; FRSA 1974. *Recreations:* music, arts, sports. *Address:* 21 Roedean Crescent, Brighton. *Club:* MCC.

READ, Lt-Gen. Sir John (Hugh Sherlock), KCB 1972; OBE 1944; retired; Adviser, West Africa Committee, since 1975; *b* 6 Sept. 1917; *s* of late Group Captain John Victor Read, Blunham, Bedfordshire, and Chacewater, Cornwall, and Elizabeth Hannah (*née* Link); *m* 1942, Mary Monica Wulfhilde Curtis, *d* of late Henry Curtis, Spofforth, Yorks, and Harrogate; two *s* one *d*. *Educ:* Bedford School; RMA Woolwich; Magdalene Coll., Cambridge. BA (Cantab.) 1939. MA (Cantab.) 1944. Commissioned 2nd Lt RE, 1937. Served UK, France, Belgium, Egypt, Palestine, Greece, Austria at regimental duty and on staff, 1939-45, and UK, Austria, Germany, Hong Kong, 1945-57; GSO1, Singapore Base Dist, 1957; CO, Training Regt, RE, 1959; IDC, 1962; Min. of Defence (War Office), 1963; Comdr, Training Bde, RE, 1963; Asst Comdt, RMA, 1966-68; Director of Military Operations, MoD, 1968-70; ACDS (Policy), MoD, 1970-71; Dir, Internat. Mil. Staff, HQ, NATO, Brussels, 1971-75. Col Comdt, Corps of Royal Engineers, 1972-. *Recreations:* fishing, shooting, gardening. *Address:* Fullbrook Farm, Elstead, Surrey. *T:* Elstead 3312; Flat 4, Church Close, Church Street, Kensington, W8. *T:* 01-937 1863. *Clubs:* Flyfishers', Travellers'.

READ, Leonard Ernest, (Nipper), QPM 1976; National Co-Ordinator of Regional Crime Squads for England and Wales, 1972-76, retired; *b* 31 March 1925; *m* 1951, Marion Alexandra Millar; one *d*. *Educ:* elementary schools. Worked at Players Tobacco factory, Nottingham, 1939-43; Petty Officer, RN, 1943-46; joined Metropolitan Police, 1947; served in all ranks of CID; Det. Chief Supt on Murder Squad, 1967; Asst Chief Constable, Notts Combined Constabulary, 1970. *Recreations:* cine photography, collecting club ties. *Address:* 24 Ellesmere Road, West Bridgford, Nottingham. *T:* Nottingham 233684.

READ, Lionel Frank, QC 1973; a Recorder of the Crown Court, since 1974; *b* 7 Sept. 1929; *s* of F. W. C. Read and Lilian Chatwin; *m* 1956, Shirley Greenhalgh; two *s* one *d*. *Educ:* Oundle Sch.; St John's Coll., Cambridge (BA Hons). Called to Bar, Gray's Inn, 1954. *Recreations:* golf, gardening. *Address:* Cedarwood, Church Road, Ham Common, Surrey. *T:* 01-940 5247.

READ, Prof. Margaret (Helen), CBE 1949; MA (Cantab), PhD (London); *b* 5 Aug. 1889; *d* of Mabyn Read, MD, Worcester, and Isabel Margaret Lawford. *Educ:* Roedean School, Brighton; Newnham College, Cambridge. Social work in India, 1919-24; lecturing on international affairs in Gt Britain and USA, 1924-30; LSE, student of anthropology and occasional lecturer, 1930-34; Research Fellow, Internat. African Inst. and field work in N Rhodesia and Nyasaland, 1934-39; Asst Lecturer, LSE, 1937-40; Univ. of London Inst. of Educ., Prof. and Head of Dept of Educ. in Tropical Areas, 1940-55; Prof. of Educ., Univ. Coll., Ibadan, Nigeria, 1955-56; occasional Consultant to WHO, 1956-62; Consultant to Milbank Memorial Fund, New York, 1964, 1965, 1966, 1967, 1968, 1969. Vis. Prof., Cornell Univ., 1951-52, Northwestern Univ., 1955, Michigan State Univ., 1960, Yale Univ. Medical School, 1965, 1966, 1967, 1968. *Publications:* Indian Peasant Uprooted, 1931; Africans and their Schools, 1953; Education and Social Change in Tropical Areas, 1955; The Ngoni of Nyasaland, 1956; Children of their Fathers, 1959; Culture, Health and Disease, 1966; articles in Africa, Bantu Studies, Journal of Applied Anthropology, Annals of the American Academy, etc. *Recreations:* gardening, music. *Address:* 9 Paradise Walk, Chelsea, SW3. *T:* 01-352 0528.

READ, Piers Paul, FRSL; author; *b* 7 March 1941; 3rd *s* of Sir Herbert Read, DSO, MC and Margaret Read, Stonegrave, York; *m* 1967, Emily Albertine, *o d* of Evelyn Basil Boothby, *qv*; one *s* one *d*. *Educ:* Ampleforth Coll.; St John's Coll., Cambridge (MA). Artist-in-residence, Ford Foundn, Berlin, 1963-64; Sub-Editor, Times Literary Supplement, 1965; Harkness Fellow, Commonwealth Fund, NY, 1967-68. Member: Council, Inst. of Contemporary Arts, 1971-75; Cttee of Management, Soc. of Authors, 1973-76; Literature Panel, Arts Council, 1975. TV plays: Coincidence, 1968; The House on Highbury Hill, 1972; The Childhood Friend, 1974; radio play: The Family Firm, 1970. *Publications:* novels: Game in Heaven with Tussy Marx, 1966; The Junkers, 1968 (Sir Geoffrey Faber Meml Prize); Monk Dawson, 1969 (Hawthornden Prize and Somerset Maugham Award); The Professor's Daughter, 1971; The Upstart, 1973; Polonaise, 1976; *non-fiction:* Alive, 1974. *Address:* Old Byland Hall, Helmsley, York. *Club:* Beefsteak.

READ, Simon Holcombe Jervis, CBE 1977; MC 1944; HM Diplomatic Service, retired 1977; Secretary, Game Farmers' Association, since 1977; *b* 7 Feb. 1922; *s* of John Dale Read and Evelyn Constance Read (*née* Bowen); *m* 1st, 1946, Bridget Elizabeth Dawson (marr. diss. 1959); two *s* one *d*; 2nd, 1960, Coelestine von der Marwitz. *Educ:* Winchester Coll. Served War: Private soldier, Essex Regt, 1940; commissioned 10th Baloch Regt, 1941; SOE and Detachment 101 (US Army), 1942, in Burma; service in Burma, Malaya, Thailand, Cambodia, Indo-China, China. Joined FCO, 1946; 3rd/2nd Sec., Singapore, Thailand, 1946-50; 1st Secretary: Hongkong, 1952-54; Iran, 1954-59; Berlin, 1959-64; UK, 1964-77. *Publication:* provisional check list of Birds of Iran (Teheran Univ.), 1958. *Recreations:* ornithology, shooting, gardening. *Address:* Walnut Tree Farm, Charing, Ashford, Kent TN27 0ED. *T:* Charing 2561. *Club:* Special Forces.

READE, Sir Clyde Nixon, 12th Bt *cr* 1661; *b* 1906; *s* of Sir George Reade, 10th Bt; *S* brother, Sir John Reade, 11th Bt, 1958; *m* 1st, 1930, Trilby (*d* 1958), *d* of Charles McCarthy; 2nd, 1960, Alice Martha Asher; five *step d.* Is a Royal Arch Mason. *Address:* 408 East Columbia Street, Mason, Michigan, USA.

READER, (William Henry) Ralph, CBE 1957 (MBE 1942); theatrical producer, author, composer and actor; Producer, Scout Gang Show, 1942-74; *b* 25 May 1903; *s* of William Henry and Emma Reader, Crewkerne, Somerset. *Educ:* Crewkerne; Cardiff. Started as clerk in office in Sussex; went to Ireland with same firm; returned to England; went to America to study for the stage; appeared in numerous productions, then took up producing; after 6 years returned to London to produce shows there; in 1928 appeared in Good News at Carlton Theatre, Haymarket; has produced nine Drury Lane productions, including Jack and the Beanstalk 1936, Rise and Shine 1937, three Ivor Novello shows; also about six shows at the London Hippodrome including Yes Madam and Please Teacher; starred in The Gang Show Film, also in Limelight with Anna Neagle; appeared with The Gang at the London Palladium in the Royal Command Variety Performance, produced Daily Express Pageant, Albert Hall, London, Battle for Freedom; Hearts of Oak Naval Pageant for Daily Express, 1945; British Legion Festival of Remembrance, annually, 1944-; RAF Pageant, Per Ardua Ad Astra, 1945, all at Albert Hall, London; produced Wings for Air Council, 1947; produced Out of the Blue, June 1947, season show, Grand, Blackpool; appeared in The Gang Show, Stoll Theatre. Produced (with all star cast) Pilgrim's Progress, Covent Garden, 1948, also in 1969. Was Officer in charge of RAF Gang Shows (official RAF entertainment units). Instituted Nat. Light Opera Company, 1950. Appeared in film Derby Day; took first entertainment to the Troops in Malaya; appeared in Meet the Gang. Produced Coronation Pageant, Royal Albert Hall, Pageant of Nursing, Royal Festival Hall, Centenary Rally of YMCA Sports de Paris, Rotary Pageant, Royal Albert Hall; Produced Wild Grows the Heather, London Hippodrome, 1956; produced Voyage of the Venturer, Youth Festival, English Ranger Pageant, Royal Albert Hall, 1956; appeared Royal Command Performance, 1957; prod. 1st Amer. Gang Show, Chicago, 1958; prod. Lord Mayor's Show, 1958; wrote music, book and lyrics of Summer Holiday, musical play, prod. Scarborough Open Air Theatre, 1960; Produced Gang Show in US, 1958, 1959, 1960, 1961; prod. World Refugee Finale, Albert Hall, 1960; wrote play, The Hill, prod. 1960; appd in Here Comes the Gang, touring Gt Britain, 1961; appeared in: Royal Command Perf., London Palladium, 1937, 1957, 1964; The Story of Mike, 1961; wrote and produced 4 One-Act Plays (We Present), 1962; staged ensembles for film, The Lonely Stage, 1962; prod. Burma Reunion, also The Voyage of the Venturer (wrote book and music), Royal Albert Hall, 1962; prod. Flying High for ITV 1962; wrote and appd in All for the Boys, London, 1963; prod. El Alamein Re-union, Royal Albert Hall, 1963; wrote play, Happy Family, also played lead, 1964; prod. and appd in Babes in the Wood, 1968; carol concert for SOS, Festival Hall, 1974; prod. and appd in Cinderella, 1973; produced at Royal Albert Hall: Dr Barnardo Centenary, 1966; The Old Contemptibles; Leclerc Reunion, 1972; 30th annual Festival of Remembrance, 1972; Jewish Lads Brigade Display, 1972 (140th perf. at RAH); Burmah Reunion, 1974; A Night with the Stars, 1974; personal appearance tour, NZ, Singapore and Hong Kong, 1976. Writer and producer: yearly editions of the Gang Show; The Pathfinders, Toronto, 1965; musical play, You can't go wrong if you're right, 1967; Next Door, 1971; Look Wide, Look Wider, Nat. Conf., LA, 1972; Holme from Holme, 1974. Toured with Ralph Reader and The Stars of Tomorrow, 1972. Appears on BBC TV, Radio, ITV, US and Canadian TV. Compèred Radio Series "Startime", also, for Overseas BBC, "A Star Remembers". Subject of This Is Your Life, 1967. Illuminated Address from State of Illinois, for Services to Boyhood throughout the World, 1964. Life Member, Boy Scouts of America. Universal Declaration of Human Rights Medal, 1975; Bronze Wolf, World Scouting highest award, 1976. *Publications:* Good Turns; The Road to Where; Gang Show Music and Sketches; Music and Book of Boy Scout, performed at Albert Hall; More Sketches: Great Oaks, Oh Scouting is a Boy, The Wingate Patrol; We'll Live Forever; The Story of Mike; Leave it to Pete; The Gang Show Story; All for the Boys; *autobiography:* It's been terrific; Ralph Reader Remembers, 1974. *Recreations:* motoring, writing, football. *Address:* Round Corners, 2 Sherrock Gardens, Hendon, NW4.

READER HARRIS, Dame (Muriel) Diana, DBE 1972; Headmistress, Sherborne School for Girls, Dorset, 1950-75; President, Church Missionary Society, since 1969 (Member since 1953, Chairman 1960-63, Executive Committee); *b* Hong Kong, 11 Oct. 1912; *er d* of late Montgomery Reader Harris. *Educ:* Sherborne School for Girls; University of London (external student). BA 1st Class Honours (English), 1934. Asst Mistress, Sherborne School for Girls, 1934, and House Mistress, 1938. Organised Public Schools and Clubs Camps for Girls, 1937-39; in charge of group evacuated from Sherborne to Canada, 1940; joined staff of National Association of Girls' Clubs, 1943; Chm. Christian Consultative Cttee Nat. Assoc. of Mixed Clubs and Girls' Clubs, 1952-68, Vice-Pres., 1968; Chm. Outward Bound Girls' Courses, 1954-59; Mem. Council, Outward Bound Trust, 1956-64. Member: Women's Consultative Cttee, Min. of Labour, 1958-77; Women's Nat. Commn, 1976-. Member: Dorset Educn Cttee, 1952-70; Exec. Cttee, Assoc. of Headmistresses, 1953-58, 1960 (Pres., 1964-66); Pres., Assoc. of Headmistresses of Boarding Schs, 1960-62; Member: Cttee on Agricl Colls, Min. of Agric., 1961-64; Schs Council, 1966-75. Member: Archbishop's Council on Evangelism, 1966-68; Panel on Broadcasting, Synod of C of E, 1975-; Bd, Christian Aid, 1976-; Council, Conf. of British Missionary Socs, 1976-. King George's Jubilee Trust: Mem., Standing Res. and Adv. Cttee, 1949; Mem., Admin. Council, 1955-67; Member: Council, 1951-62, Exec. and Council, 1976-, Nat. Youth Orch. of GB; ITA, 1956-60. Governor: Greycoat Hosp., 1944-48; Godolphin Sch., Salisbury, 1975-; St Michael's Sch., Limpsfield, 1975-. FRSA 1964 (Mem. Council, RSA, 1975-). Hon. FCP 1975. *Address:* 11 Denny Crescent, SE11 4UY. *T:* 01-735 4400. *Club:* English-Speaking Union.

READHEAD, James (Templeman), 3rd Bt, *cr* 1922 (but discontinued style of Sir and the use of his title, 1965); Lieutenant late King's Own Yorkshire Light Infantry, TA; *b* 12 Feb. 1910; *s* of late Stanley Readhead, Stanhope House, Westoe,

South Shields, and late Hilda Maud, d of Thomas John Templeman, Weymouth, Dorset; S uncle, 1940; m 1946, Hilda Rosemary, o d of George Henry Hudson, The Manor, Hatfield, nr Doncaster, Yorks; one d. Educ: Repton School. Electrical Engineer, retired. Recreations: various.

READING, 3rd Marquess of, cr 1926; **Michael Alfred Rufus Isaacs,** MBE 1945; MC 1940; Earl of Reading, cr 1917; Viscount Erleigh, cr 1917; Viscount Reading, cr 1916; Baron, cr 1914; Member of The Stock Exchange since 1953; b 8 March 1916; o s of 2nd Marquess of Reading, PC, GCMG, CBE, MC, TD, QC, and Eva Violet, CBE (d 1973), d of 1st Baron Melchett, PC, FRS; S father 1960; m 1941, Margot Irene, yr d of late Percy Duke, OBE; three s one d. Educ: Eton; Balliol College, Oxford. Served 1939-46, Queen's Bays and Staff (Major). Heir: s Viscount Erleigh, qv. Address: The Old Prebendal House, Shipton-under-Wychwood, Oxfordshire OX7 6BQ. T: Shipton-under-Wychwood 830210; Flat 1, 28/29 Ormonde Gate, SW3. T: 01-332 5602. Club: City of London.
See also Baron Zuckerman, Sir Ivo Thomson, Bt.

READING, Suffragan Bishop of, since 1972; **Rt. Rev. Eric Wild;** b 6 Nov. 1914; s of R. E. and E. S. Wild; m 1946, Frances Moyra, d of late Archibald and Alice Reynolds; one s one d. Educ: Manchester Grammar School; Keble College, Oxford. Ordained deacon 1937, priest 1938, Liverpool Cathedral; Curate, St Anne, Stanley, 1937-40; Curate, St James, Haydock, 1940-42; Chaplain, RNVR, 1942-46; Vicar, St George, Wigan, 1946-52; Vicar, All Saints, Hindley, 1952-59; Director of Religious Education, Dio. Peterborough, 1959-62; Rector, Cranford with Grafton Underwood, 1959-62; Canon of Peterborough, 1961, Emeritus, 1962; Gen. Sec. of National Society and Secretary of C of E Schools Council, 1962-67; Rector of Milton, 1967-72; Archdeacon of Berks, 1967-73. Publications: articles in periodicals; reviews, etc. Recreations: gardening and walking. Address: The Well House, Upper Basildon, Reading, Berks. T: Upper Basildon 378. Club: Army and Navy.

READING, Joseph Lewis, CMG 1963; Consultant to Vocational Guidance Association; b 5 Aug. 1907; s of J. W. Reading, New Malden, Surrey; m 1934, Dorothy Elaine, d of Reginald Fitch, Esher and London Stock Exchange; three s one d. Educ: King's College School, Wimbledon; London University, BSc (Eng.) 1929; ACGI 1929. Entered Civil Service as Consular Cadet in Dept of Overseas Trade, 1932; British Embassy, Washington, 1938-39; Principal, Min. of Economic Warfare, 1939-44; Asst Secretary, Min. of Production, 1944-45; Board of Trade, 1945-64; Director, British Industries' Fair, 1952-55; Establishment Officer (Overseas), 1955-63; Economic Adviser to British High Comr and Senior British Trade Comr in NZ, 1963-67. Sec., Internat. Freight Movement EDC, NEDO, 1970-76. Recreations: gardening, fishing. Address: Forest Gate, Bourton, Gillingham, Dorset. T: Bourton (Dorset) 233.

READMAN, Maj.-Gen. Edgar Platt, CBE 1942 (OBE 1939); TD 1939; RAOC Retd; retired as Managing Director English Steel Corporation Tool Co., Manchester, 1958; b 12 Aug. 1893; s of Ernest W. Readman, Sheffield; m 1919, May, d of Marriot Stillwell, Leeds; one d. Educ: Sheffield Central School. Served European War, 1914-19, with Tank Corps; transferred RAOC, 1923, TA; Lt-Col 1934; Brigadier, 1940; Subs. Major-General, 1944; retired, 1951. Returned to industry, 1945. Address: Cedarcroft, Blackford Hill, Henley-in-Arden, Warwickshire.

READWIN, Edgar Seeley, CBE 1971; retired; b 7 Nov. 1915; s of Ernest Readwin, Master Mariner and Edith Elizabeth Readwin; m 1940, Lesley Margaret (née Barker); two s one d. Educ: Bracondale Sch., Norwich. FCA. Articled Clerk, Harman & Gowen, Norwich, 1932-37; Asst Auditor, Bengal & North Western Railway, 1938-40; commnd service 14th Punjab Regt, 1941-45, PoW Far East, Singapore, Siam-Burma Railway, 1942-45; Indian Railway Accounts Service, 1945-49. Booker Group of Companies in Guyana: Asst to Accounts Controller, 1950; Finance Dir, 1951-56; Dep. Chm., 1956-62; Chm., 1962-71. Dir, West Indies Sugar Assoc., 1962-71; Finance Dir, Indonesia Sugar Study, 1971-72; Chm., Minvielle & Chastenet Ltd, St Lucia, 1973-76. Hon. Treas., Guyana Lawn Tennis Assoc., 1951-67, Pres., 1968-70, Hon. Life Vice-Pres., 1971-. Recreations: lawn tennis, golf, squash, gardening, chess, bridge. Address: Lane End Farmhouse, Ancton Lane, Middleton-on-Sea, Sussex. T: Middleton-on-Sea 2131. Clubs: Queen's, Royal Commonwealth Society (West Indian); Middleton-on-Sea Sports; Littlehampton Golf; Cap Estate Golf (St Lucia).

REARDON-SMITH, Sir William; see Smith.

REASON, Dr Richard Edmund, OBE 1967; FRS 1971; lately Consultant, Rank Taylor-Hobson. Vis. Research Fellow, Department of Mechanical Engineering, UMIST, 1976-. Address: 5 Manor Road, Great Bowden, Leicestershire. T: Market Harborough 3219.

REAY, 14th Lord, cr 1628, of Reay, Caithness; **Hugh William Mackay;** Bt of Nova Scotia, 1627; Baron Mackay of Ophemert and Zennewijnen, Holland; Chief of Clan Mackay; Member, British Delegation to European Parliament, Strasbourg, since 1973; Vice-Chairman, European Conservative Group; b 19 July 1937; s of 13th Lord Reay and Charlotte Mary Younger; S father, 1963; m 1964, Hon. Annabel Thérèse Fraser, y d of 17th Baron Lovat, qv; two s one d. Educ: Eton; Christ Church. Heir: s the Master of Reay, qv. Address: House of Lords, SW1.

REAY, Master of; Aeneas Simon Mackay, b 20 March 1965; s and heir of 14th Lord Reay, qv.

REAY, Basil; see Reay, S. B.

REAY, Maj.-Gen. Hubert Alan John, QHP, FRCP, FRCP(Edin); Postgraduate Dean and Commandant, Royal Army Medical College, Millbank, since 1977; b 19 March 1925; s of Rev. John Reay; m 1960, Ferelith Haslewood Deane; two s two d (and one s decd). Educ: Lancing College; Edinburgh Univ. MB, FRCP, FRCP(Edin), DCH. Field Medical Services, Malayan Campaign, 1949; Exchange Physician, Brooke Hosp., San Antonio, Texas, 1957; Command Consultant Paediatrician: Far East, 1962; BAOR, 1965; Consultant Adviser in Paediatrics, MoD (Army), 1968. Hon. Out-patient Consultant, Great Ormond Street Hosp., 1975; Sec., Paediatric Section, RSocMed, 1977. Publications: paediatric articles in med. jls. Recreations: bird watching, walking, gardening. Address: 5 Atterbury Street, SW1P 4RJ. T: 01-821 7086.

REAY, (Stanley) Basil, OBE 1957; Secretary, The Lawn Tennis Association, 1948-73; Secretary General, The International Lawn Tennis Federation and the Davis Cup Competition, 1973-76 (Hon. Secretary, 1948-73); Wing Comdr, RAFVR; b 2 Feb. 1909; s of Robert and Maud Reay (née Cox), Stockton on Tees; m 1935, Beatrice Levene; one s one d. Educ: Queen Elizabeth Grammar School, Hexham; St John's College. Schoolmaster in England, 1929-32; Min. of Education, Egypt, 1932-39. Chairman Inter-Services Language Training Cttee, 1945-47. Served RAF, 1939-47, chiefly in ME (Wing Comdr, 1944). Commandeur, Ordre de Merite Sportif (France), 1960. Recreations: travel and sports. Address: Molende, Molember Road, East Molesey, Surrey. Clubs: Royal Automobile, RAF Reserves; All England (Wimbledon); International Lawn Tennis Clubs of Great Britain, USA, France, Italy, Sweden, Denmark, Australia, Argentina, Belgium.

REBBECK, Dr Denis, CBE 1952; MA, MSc, PhD, BLitt; DL, JP; CEng, FICE, FIMechE, FRINA, FIMarE, FCIT; b 22 Jan. 1914; er s of late Sir Frederick Ernest Rebbeck, KBE; m 1938, Rosamond Annette Kathleen, e d of late Henry Jameson, Bangor, Co. Down; four s. Educ: Campbell Coll., Belfast; Pembroke Coll., Cambridge. BA (Hons) Mech. Sciences Tripos, 1935; MA (Cantab) 1939; MA (Dublin) 1945; BLitt (Dublin) 1946; MSc (Belfast) 1946; PhD (Belfast) 1950; Part-time Postgrad. Research. Harland & Wolff, Ltd: Director, 1946-70; Dep. Man. Director, 1953; Man. Dir, 1962-70; Chm., 1965-66. Chm., 1972-, Dir, 1950-, Iron Trades Employers' Insurance Association Ltd and Iron Trades Mutual Insurance Co. Ltd (Vice-Chm., 1969-72); Director: Belships Co. Ltd, 1970-76 (Chm., 1972-76); Colvilles Ltd, 1963-67; Brown Brothers & Co. Ltd, 1967-68; Shipbuilding Corporation Ltd, 1963-73; National Commercial Bank of Scotland Ltd, 1965-69; Royal Bank of Scotland Ltd, 1969-; John Kelly Ltd, 1968- (Dep. Chm., 1968; Chm., 1969-); Howdens Ltd, 1977-; Norman Canning Ltd, 1977-; C. A. Investments Ltd (Chm.), 1977-; National Shipbuilders Security, Ltd, 1952-58. Special Consultant, Swan Hunter Group Ltd, 1970-. Belfast Harbour Commissioner, 1962-. Member Research Council, and Chairman, Design Main Committee, British Ship Research Association, 1965-73; Pres., Shipbuilding Employers' Fedn, 1962-63; Past Chm. Warship Gp., Shipbuilding Conf.; NI Economic Council, 1965-70; Lloyd's Register of Shipping General Cttee, 1962- and Technical Cttee, 1964-76; Management Board, Engineering Employers Fedn, 1963-75; Council, RINA, 1964-72; Council for Scientific R&D in NI, 1948-59; Member Inst. of Engineers and Shipbuilders in Scotland; Past Chm. and Trustee, Belfast Savings Bank; Cambridge Univ. Engineers' Assoc.; Science Masters' Assoc. (Pres. NI Branch, 1954-55); NI Grammar Schools Careers Assoc. (Pres., 1964-65); Life Mem. Brit. Assoc. for the Advancement of Science; National Playing Fields Assoc. (NI Exec. Cttee); Chm., Adv. Cttee on Marine Pilotage, 1977-;

Member: Drummond Technical Investigation Cttee, 1955-56; Lord Coleraine's Committee to enquire into Youth Employment Services in NI, 1957-58; Sir John Lockwood's Cttee on Univ. and Higher Techn. Educn in Northern Ireland, 1963-64; Queen's Univ., Better Equipment Fund Exec. Cttee; Vice-Pres. of Belfast Savings Council; Visitor, Linen Industry Research Assoc., DSIR, 1954-57; President: Belfast Assoc. of Engineers, 1947-48; NI Society of Incorporated Secretaries, 1955-70; Glencraig Curative Schools, NI, 1953-70; Disabled Drivers Assoc., NI Gp; Vice-Pres., World Ship Soc., 1956-; Past Mem. Council IMechE; IMarE; Chm. NI Assoc., ICE, 1952-53. Third Warden, Worshipful Company of Shipwrights. Vice-Pres., Queen's Univ. Guild, 1951-65; Board Governors Campbell Coll., Belfast, 1952-60 (Vice-Chm. 1957-60); Member of Court, New Univ. of Ulster. Mem., T&AFA for Belfast, 1947-65; Dep.-Chm. NI Festival of Britain, 1948-51; papers read before British Association, ICE, etc; Akroyd Stuart Award, IMarE, 1943. JP County Borough of Belfast, 1949; DL County of the City of Belfast, 1960. *Recreation:* sailing. *Address:* The White House, Craigavad, Holywood, County Down, N Ireland BT18 0HE. *T:* Holywood 2294. *Clubs:* Royal Yacht Squadron, Royal Automobile, City Livery, Den Norske; Cambridge Union; Shippingklubben (Oslo); Royal Norwegian Yacht; Royal North of Ireland Yacht (Cultra, Co. Down).

REBBECK, Rear-Admiral Sir (Leopold) Edward, KBE 1956; CB 1954; retired; *b* 26 July 1901; *s* of Edward Wise Rebbeck, Bournemouth; *m* Clara Margaret Allen, *e d* of R. G. Coombe, Ceylon; two *s* two *d. Educ:* Pembroke Lodge; Royal Naval Colls Osborne and Dartmouth. Served European War in HMS Erin; HM Yacht Victoria and Albert, 1932-35; War of 1939-45; HMS Birmingham, and as Assistant Naval Attaché, USA. Commanding Officer, RN Air Station Anthorn, 1946; Fleet Engineer Officer to C in C Mediterranean, 1949. ADC to King George VI, 1951-52; ADC to the Queen, 1952; Rear-Admiral Reserve Aircraft, 1952-55, retired. Vickers Group, 1956-66. Mem., Soc. Naval Architects and Marine Engineers (New York). *Recreations:* golf, motoring. *Address:* Stubb Hill House, Iping, near Midhurst, West Sussex. *T:* Milland 238. *Clubs:* Army and Navy, Royal Automobile.

RECKITT, Lt-Col Basil Norman; TD 1946; Director, Reckitt and Colman Ltd, retired 1972 (Chairman, 1966-70); *b* 12 Aug. 1905; *s* of Frank Norman Reckitt, Architect, and Beatrice Margaret Hewett; *m* 1st, 1928, Virginia Carre-Smith (*d* 1961); three *d*; 2nd, 1966, Mary Holmes (*née* Peirce), widow of Paul Holmes, Malham Tarn, near Settle. *Educ:* Uppingham; King's Coll., Cambridge (MA). Joined Reckitt & Sons Ltd, 1927; Dir, Reckitt & Colman Ltd, 1938. 2nd Lieut, 62nd HAA Regt (TA), 1939; Bde Major, 39th AA Brigade, 1940; CO 141 HAA (M) Regt, 1942; Military Government, Germany, 1944-45. Chm. Council, and Pro-Chancellor, Hull Univ., 1971-. Sheriff of Hull, 1970-71. Hon. LLD, Hull University, 1967. *Publications:* History of Reckitt & Sons Ltd, 1951; Charles I and Hull, 1952; The Lindley Affair, 1972. *Recreations:* riding and walking. *Address:* Haverbrack, Milnthorpe, Cumbria. *T:* Milnthorpe 3142.

REDCLIFFE-MAUD, family name of **Baron Redcliffe-Maud.**

REDCLIFFE-MAUD, Baron *cr* 1967 (Life Peer), of City and County of Bristol; **John Primatt Redcliffe Redcliffe-Maud,** GCB 1955 (KCB 1946); CBE 1942; Master of University College, Oxford, 1963-76; *b* 3 Feb. 1906; *yr s* of late John Primatt Maud, Bishop of Kensington, and late Elizabeth Diana Furse; *m* 1932, Jean, *yr d* of late J. B. Hamilton, Melrose; one *s* two *d. Educ:* Eton (King's Scholar); New College, Oxford (Open Classical Scholar); Harvard College, USA. Henry P. Davison Scholar from Oxford Univ. to Harvard College, 1928-29; AB Harvard, 1929; Junior Research Fellow, 1929, University College, Oxford; Fellow and Dean, 1932-39; Rhodes Travelling Fellowship to Africa, 1932; University Lecturer in Politics, 1938-39; Councillor Oxford City, 1930-36; invited by Johannesburg City Council to write municipal history of city; Tutor to Colonial Administrative Services Course, Oxford, 1937-39; Master of Birkbeck College, University of London, 1939-43; Deputy Secretary, later Second Secretary, Ministry of Food, 1941-44; Second Secretary, Office of the Minister of Reconstruction, 1944-45; Secretary, Office of Lord President of the Council, 1945; Permanent Secretary, Ministry of Education, 1945-52; Mem. Economic Planning Board; Permanent Secretary, Ministry of Fuel and Power, 1952-59; British Ambassador in South Africa, 1961-63 (High Commissioner, 1959-61), and High Commissioner for Basutoland, Bechuanaland Protectorate and Swaziland, 1959-63. High Bailiff of Westminster, 1967-. UK deleg. to Confs on Food and Agric., Hot Springs, 1943, UNRRA, Atlantic City, 1943, and UNESCO, 1946, 1947, 1948, 1949, 1950 (President Executive Board, 1949-50). Chm., Council, Royal Coll. of Music, 1965-73.

Chairman: Local Govt Management Cttee, 1964-67; Royal Commn on Local Govt in England, 1966-69; Prime Minister's Cttee on Local Govt Rules of Conduct, 1973-74. President: Royal Inst. of Public Administration, 1969; British Diabetic Assoc., 1977. Hon. Fellow: New Coll., Oxford, 1964; University Coll., Oxford, 1976; Fellow, Eton Coll., 1964-76. For. Associate, Venezuelan Acad. of Scis, 1973. Hon. LLD: Witwatersrand, 1960; Natal, 1963; Leeds, 1967; Nottingham, 1968; Hon. DSocSc Birmingham, 1968. Sen. Fell., RCA, 1961; FRCM, 1964; Associate Fellow, Jonathan Edwards Coll., Yale, 1968. *Publications:* English Local Government, 1932; City Government: The Johannesburg Experiment, 1938; Chapter in Oxford and the Groups, 1934; Chapter in Personal Ethics, 1935; Johannesburg and the Art of Self-Government, 1937; Chapter in Education in a Changing World, 1951; English Local Government Reformed, 1974; Support for the Arts in England and Wales, 1976. *Address:* 221 Woodstock Road, Oxford. *T:* Oxford 55354. *Clubs:* Savile; Eton Ramblers.
See also Hon. H. J. H. Maud.

REDDAWAY, Arthur Frederick John, CMG 1959; OBE 1957; Director-General, Arab-British Centre, London; *b* 12 April 1916; *s* of Arthur Joseph Reddaway, Chartered Accountant, and Thirza May King; *m* 1945, Anthoula, *d* of Dr Christodoulos Papaioannou, Nicosia; two *s. Educ:* County High School, Ilford; University of Reading. Colonial Administrative Service, Cyprus, 1938; Imperial Defence College, 1954; Administrative Sec., Cyprus, 1957-60; Dep. Comr-General, UNRWA for Palestine Refugees, 1960-68. *Address:* 19 Woodsyre, Sydenham Hill, SE26. *Club:* East India, Sports and Public Schools, Royal Commonwealth Society.

REDDAWAY, (George Frank) Norman, CBE 1965 (MBE 1946); HM Diplomatic Service; Ambassador to Poland, since 1974; *b* 2 May 1918; *s* of late William Fiddian Reddaway and late Kate Waterland Reddaway (*née* Sills); *m* 1944, Jean Brett; two *s* three *d. Educ:* Oundle School; King's College, Cambridge. Scholar Modern Langs, 1935; 1st Class Hons Mod. Langs Tripos Parts 1 and 2, 1937 and 1939. Served in Army, 1939-46; psc Camberley, 1944. Foreign Office, 1946; Private Sec. to Parly Under Sec. of State, 1947-49; Rome, 1949; Ottawa, 1952; Foreign Office, 1955; Imperial Defence College, 1960; Beirut, 1961; Counsellor, Office of the Political Adviser to the C-in-C, Far East, Singapore, 1965-66; Counsellor (Commercial), Khartoum, 1967-69; Asst Under-Sec. of State, FCO, 1970-74. *Recreations:* gardening, family history. *Address:* c/o Foreign and Commonwealth Office, SW1. *Club:* United Oxford & Cambridge University.

REDDAWAY, William Brian, CBE 1971; FBA 1967; Professor of Political Economy, University of Cambridge, since 1969; Fellow of Clare College, Cambridge, since 1938; Economic Adviser to CBI, since 1972; *b* 8 Jan. 1913; *s* of late William Fiddian Reddaway and late Kate Waterland Reddaway (*née* Sills); *m* 1938, Barbara Augusta Bennett; three *s* one *d. Educ:* Oundle Sch.; King's Coll., Cambridge; Maj. schol. natural science; 1st cl. Maths tripos, part I, 1st cl. 1st div. Economics tripos, part II; Adam Smith Prize; MA. Assistant, Bank of England, 1934-35; Research Fellow in Economics, University of Melbourne, 1936-37; Statistics Division, Board of Trade (final rank Chief Statistician), 1940-47; University Lectr in Economics, 1939-55, Reader in Applied Economics, 1957-65, Dir of Dept of Applied Economics, 1955-69, Univ. of Cambridge. Economic Adviser to OEEC, 1951-52; Visiting Economist, Center for International Studies, New Delhi, 1959-60; Vis. Lectr, Economic Develt Inst. (Washington), 1966-67; Consultant, Harvard Develt Adv. Service (in Ghana), 1967; Vis. Prof., Bangladesh Inst. of Develt Studies, 1974-75. Member: Royal Commn on the Press, 1961-62; NBPI, 1967-71; Chm., Inquiry into Consulting Engineering Firms' Costs and Earnings, 1971-72. Editor, Economic Jl, 1971-76. *Publications:* Russian Financial System, 1935; Economics of a Declining Population, 1939; (with C. F. Carter, Richard Stone) Measurement of Production Movements, 1948; The Development of the Indian Economy, 1962; Effects of UK Direct Investment Overseas, Interim Report, 1967, Final Report, 1968; Effects of the Selective Employment Tax, First Report, 1970, Final Report, 1973; articles in numerous economic journals. *Recreations:* skating, squash, walking. *Address:* 4 Adams Road, Cambridge. *T:* 50041.

REDDICK, Ven. Percy George, MA Oxon; Archdeacon of Bristol, 1950-67; Canon Residentiary, Bristol Cathedral, 1955-62; Hon. Canon, 1962-67, now Emeritus; *b* 9 November 1896; *s* of Henry Reddick and Elisabeth (*née* Powell); *m* 1st, 1922, Edith Annie Cropper, one *d*; 2nd, 1944, Elsie Maud Thomas. *Educ:* St Edmund Hall and Wycliffe Hall, Oxford. Served European War, King's Royal Rifles, 1915-17 (General Service and Victory Medal); invalided. Oxford, 1919-23. Curate: St Michael's,

Southfields, 1923-25; Holy Trinity, Sydenham, 1925-30; Vicar: St Saviour, Herne Hill, 1930-40; Downend, 1940-43; Diocesan Secretary, Bristol, 1943-50; Chaplain to Bishop of Bristol and Diocesan Chaplain, 1943-50; Hon. Canon Bristol Cathedral, 1946-50; Examining Chaplain to Bishop of Bristol. *Recreation:* woodwork. *Address:* Cowlin House, 26 Pembroke Road, Bristol BS8 3BB.

REDDISH, Sir Halford (Walter Lupton), Kt 1958; FCA; Chairman and Chief Executive, The Rugby Portland Cement Co. Ltd and subsidiary companies, 1933-76; Director: Granada Group Ltd; Meldrum Investment Trust Ltd; Warburg Investment Management Ltd; Underwriting Member of Lloyd's; Patron, Rugby Conservative Association; Member of Council, Imp. Soc. of Knights Bachelor; Freeman of the City of London in the Livery of the Pattenmakers; *b* 15 Aug. 1898; *s* of Henry Lupton Reddish; *m* Valerie (*d* 1971), *e d* of Arthur Grosart Lehman Smith, MRCS, LRCP. *Educ:* Rugby School. Served European War, 1914-18. Gold Medallist and Inst. Prizeman, Inst. Chartered Accountants, 1920. Hon. FRCP, 1977. *Recreations:* business, chess. *Address:* Welton House, near Daventry, Northants. *T:* Daventry 2525; Dorchester Hotel, W1. *T:* 01-629 8888; (office) Rugby. *T:* Rugby 2244. *Club:* Carlton.

REDDISH, Prof. Vincent Cartledge, OBE 1974; Regius Professor of Astronomy in Edinburgh University, Director of the Royal Observatory, Edinburgh, and Astronomer Royal for Scotland, since 1975; *b* 28 April 1926; *s* of William H. M. Reddish and Evelyn Reddish; *m* 1951, Elizabeth Waltho; two *s*. *Educ:* Wigan Techn. Coll.; London Univ. BSc Hons, PhD, DSc. Lectr in Astronomy, Edinburgh Univ., 1954; Lectr in Radio Astronomy, Manchester Univ., 1959; Royal Observatory, Edinburgh: Principal Scientific Officer, 1962; Sen. Principal Sci. Off., 1966; Dep. Chief Sci. Off., 1974. *Publications:* Evolution of the Galaxies, 1967; The Physics of Stellar Interiors, 1974; numerous sci. papers in Monthly Notices RAS, Nature and other jls. *Recreations:* hill walking, ornithology, do-it-yourself. *Address:* Royal Observatory, Edinburgh EH9 3HJ. *T:* 031-667 3321.

REDESDALE, 5th Baron, *cr* 1902; **Clement Napier Bertram Mitford;** Vice President, Corporate Communications Europe, Chase Manhattan Bank NA; *b* 28 Oct. 1932; *o s* of late Hon. E. R. B. O. Freeman-Mitford, 5th *s* of 1st Baron; *S* uncle, 1963; *m* 1958, Sarah Georgina Cranston Todd; one *s* six *d*. *Educ:* Eton. DipCAM. Joined Colin Turner (London) Ltd, 1953; joined Erwin Wasey (Advertising), 1955, Associate Director, 1960-64. Pres., Guild of Cleaners and Launderers, 1968-70. Chm., Nat. Council of Royal Soc. of St George, 1970-75, Pres., 1975-. Governor, Yehudi Menuhin Sch., 1973-. *Heir: s* Hon. Rupert Bertram Mitford, *b* 18 July 1967. *Address:* 2 St Mark's Square, NW1 7TP. *T:* 01-722 1965. *Club:* Lansdowne.

REDFEARN, Sir Herbert, Kt 1973; JP; DL; wire and wire goods manufacturer; Chairman, Siddall & Hilton Ltd, and all subsidiary companies, since 1972; *b* 26 Sept. 1915; *s* of Harry Reginald and Annie Elizabeth Redfearn; *m* 1942, Doris Vickerman, *y d* of Joseph Vickerman and Sarah Elizabeth Vickerman; one *s* one *d*. *Educ:* local council and technical schs. Brighouse: Borough Council, 1943-74; Alderman of Borough, 1953-74; Mayor, 1967. Chm., Brighouse and Spenborough Conservative Constituency Assoc., 1961-66, Pres., 1966-; Treas., Yorks Provincial Area Council of Conservative and Unionist Assoc., 1966-70, Chm., 1971-76. Member: Conservative Party Bd of Finance, 1966-70; Nat. Union Exec. Cttee, 1966-; Cons. and Unionist Agents': Examination Bd, 1970-; Superannuation Fund Management Cttee, 1972-; Vice-Chm., Nat. Union of Cons. and Unionist Assocs, 1976. JP W Yorks, 1956; DL W Yorks, 1977. *Recreations:* freemasonry, gardening. *Address:* Ash Lea, Woodhouse Lane, Brighouse, West Yorkshire. *Club:* Junior Carlton.

REDFERN, Sir (Arthur) Shuldham, KCVO 1939; CMG 1945; *b* 13 June 1895; *er s* of Dr J. J. Redfern; *m* 1925, Ruth Marion Grimshaw (*d* 1972); one *s*. *Educ:* Winchester; Trinity College, Cambridge. Served European War, 1914-19, Major Royal Flying Corps and RAF, 1918; joined Sudan Political Service, 1920; successively Assistant District Commissioner in Provinces of Khartoum, Darfur, Blue Nile; Dep. Governor of Blue Nile Province, 1927; Assistant Civil Secretary, Khartoum, 1929; Commissioner Port Sudan, 1932; Governor Kassala Province, 1934; Secretary to Governor-General of Canada, 1935-45; British Council, 1947-51. CStJ; Officer of Order of the Nile, 1925. *Publications:* articles in Canadian papers. *Recreations:* music, painting. *Address:* 32 Sheffield Terrace, W8. *T:* 01-229 1323. *Club:* Athenæum.

REDFERN, Philip; Deputy Director, Office of Population, Censuses and Surveys, since 1970; *b* 14 Dec. 1922; *m* 1951, Gwendoline Mary Phillips; three *d*. *Educ:* Bemrose Sch., Derby; St John's Coll., Cambridge. Wrangler, Mathematical Tripos, Cambridge, 1942. Asst Statistician, Central Statistical Office, 1947; Chief Statistician, Min. of Education, 1960; Dir of Statistics and Jt Head of Planning Branch, Dept of Educn and Science, 1967. *Address:* Northanger Cottage, Bookhurst Hill, Cranleigh, Surrey.

REDFERN, Sir Shuldham; *see* Redfern, Sir A. S.

REDFORD, Donald Kirkman; Chairman since 1972 and Managing Director since 1970, The Manchester Ship Canal Company; *b* 18 Feb. 1919; *er s* of T. J. and S. A. Redford; *m* 1942, Mabel (*née* Wilkinson), Humberstone, Lincs; one *s* one *d*. *Educ:* Culford Sch.; King's Coll., Univ. of London (LLB). Served, 1937-39, and War until 1945, in RAFVR (retd as Wing Comdr). Practice at the Bar until end of 1946, when joined The Manchester Ship Canal Company, with which Company has since remained; Director: Bridgewater Estates Ltd; Manchester Dry Docks Ltd. Chairman, Nat. Assoc. of Port Employers, 1972-74; Dep. Chm., British Ports Assoc., 1973-74, Chm. 1974-. *Recreations:* reading, history, sailing, golf. *Address:* North Cotes, 8 Harrod Drive, Birkdale, Southport. *T:* Southport 67406; The Manchester Ship Canal Co., Ship Canal House, King Street, Manchester M2 4WX. *T:* 061-872 2411. *Clubs:* Oriental; St James's (Manchester).

REDGRAVE, Lynn; actress; *b* 8 March 1943; *d* of Sir Michael Redgrave, *qv*, and of Rachel Kempson, actress; *m* 1967, John Clark; one *s* one *d*. *Educ:* Queensgate Sch.; Central Sch. of Speech and Drama. Nat. Theatre of GB, 1963-66 (Tulip Tree, Mother Courage, Andorra, Hay Fever, etc); Black Comedy, Broadway 1967; The Two of Us, Slag, Zoo Zoo Widdershins Zoo, Born Yesterday, London 1968-71; A Better Place, Dublin 1972; My Fat Friend, Knock Knock, Mrs Warren's Profession, Broadway 1973-76; The Two of Us, California Suite, Hellzapoppin, US tours 1976-77; Saint Joan, Chicago and NY 1977. *Films include:* Tom Jones, Girl with Green Eyes, Georgy Girl (NY Film Critics, Golden Globe and IFIDA awards, Academy nomination Best Actress), Deadly Affair, Smashing Time, Virgin Soldiers, Last of the Mobile Hotshots, Every Little Crook and Nanny, National Health, Happy Hooker, Everything You Always Wanted to Know about Sex, The Big Bus. Co-host of nationally televised talk-show, Not For Women Only, in USA. *Recreations:* cooking, gardening. *Address:* 205 West 57 Street, New York, NY 10019, USA. *T:* (212) 489-0597.

REDGRAVE, Sir Michael (Scudamore), Kt 1959; CBE 1952; Actor; *b* 20 March 1908; *s* of G. E. ("Roy") Redgrave, actor, and Margaret Scudamore, actress; *m* 1935, Rachel Kempson; one *s* two *d*. *Educ:* Clifton Coll.; Magdalene Coll., Cambridge. MA; formerly modern language master Cranleigh Sch. Liverpool Repertory Theatre, 1934-36; Country Wife, As You Like It, Hamlet, etc, Old Vic Season, 1936-37; Richard II, School for Scandal, Three Sisters, Queen's Theatre, 1937-38; White Guard, Twelfth Night, Phœnix Theatre, 1938-39; Family Reunion, Westminster Theatre, 1939; Beggar's Opera, Haymarket Theatre, 1940; Thunder Rock, Globe Theatre, 1940; The Duke in Darkness, St James's Theatre, 1942; A Month in the Country, Parisienne, St James's Theatre, 1943; Uncle Harry, Garrick Theatre, 1944; Jacobowsky and the Colonel, Piccadilly, 1945; Macbeth, Aldwych, 1947; Macbeth, National Theatre, New York, 1948; The Father, Embassy, 1948, and Duchess, 1949; A Woman in Love, Embassy, 1949; Love's Labour's Lost, She Stoops to Conquer, A Month in the Country, Hamlet, with Old Vic Theatre Co., New, 1949-50; played Hamlet at Switzerland and Holland Festivals, also at Kronborg Castle, Elsinore, 1950; Richard II, Henry IV Parts 1 and 2, Henry V, The Tempest, Memorial Theatre, Stratford-on-Avon, 1951; solo performance of Shakespeare, Holland Festival, 1951; Winter Journey, St James's, 1952; Rockefeller Foundation Lecturer, Bristol Univ., 1952; Shylock, Antony and King Lear, Stratford-on-Avon, 1953; Antony, Princes, 1953, and Amsterdam, Brussels and Paris, 1954; Tiger at the Gates, Apollo, 1955, and Plymouth, New York, 1955; Theodore Spencer Memorial Lecturer, Harvard Univ., 1956; The Sleeping Prince, Coronet, New York, 1956; A Touch of the Sun, Saville, 1958; Hamlet and Benedick, Stratford-on-Avon, 1958; played Hamlet with Shakespeare Memorial Theatre Co., in Russia, 1958; The Aspern Papers, Queen's, 1959; The Tiger and the Horse, Queen's, 1960; solo performances of Shakespeare and of Hans Andersen, Bath Festival, 1961; The Complaisant Lover, Barrymore, NY, 1961; Uncle Vanya, Chichester Festival, 1962; Out of Bounds, Wyndham's, 1962; Uncle Vanya, Chichester Festival, 1963; joined National Theatre, 1963 (first production, Oct. 1963); Claudius in Hamlet; Uncle Vanya, Hobson's Choice,

The Master Builder; A Month in the Country, Y. Arnaud and Cambridge Theatres, also Samson Agonistes (YA), 1965; The Old Boys, Mermaid, 1971; A Voyage Round My Father, Haymarket, Canada and Australia, 1972-73; The Hollow Crown, and Pleasure and Repentance, US 1973, 1974, World Tour, 1975; Shakespeare's People, S African tour, 1975; South America and Eastern Canada Tour, 1976; Denmark, British Columbia, NZ, US tours, 1977; *films:* The Lady Vanishes, The Stars Look Down, Kipps, Jeannie, Thunder Rock, The Way to the Stars, Dead of Night, The Captive Heart, The Man Within, Fame is the Spur, Mourning Becomes Electra, The Browning Version, The Importance of being Earnest, The Green Scarf, Dam Busters, The Night My Number Came Up, Confidential Report, 1984, Time without Pity, The Happy Road, The Quiet American, Shake Hands with the Devil, Wreck of the Mary Deare; No, my darling daughter!, The Innocents, The Loneliness of the Long-Distance Runner, Young Cassidy, The Hill, The Heroes of Telemark, Oh What a Lovely War!, The Battle of Britain, Goodbye Mr Chips, Connecting Rooms, The Go-Between, Nicholas and Alexandra. Producer: Werther, Glyndebourne, 1966, 1969; La Bohème, Glyndebourne, 1967. Joined Royal Navy, 1941; discharged on medical grounds, 1942. President, English-Speaking Board; President, Questors Theatre; Director of Festival, Yvonne Arnaud Theatre, Guildford, 1965. FRSA; Hon. DLitt (Bristol), 1966. Commander Order of Dannebrog, 1955. *Publications:* The Seventh Man (play), 1936; Actor's Ways and Means, 1953; Mask or Face, 1958; The Aspern Papers (play), 1959; The Mountebank's Tale (novel), 1959; Circus Boy (play), 1963. *Relevant Publication:* Michael Redgrave, Actor, by Richard Findlater, 1956. *Address:* c/o Hutton Management Ltd, 194 Old Brompton Road, SW1 1RW.
See also Lynn Redgrave, Vanessa Redgrave.

REDGRAVE, Maj.-Gen. Roy Michael Frederick, MC 1945; Commander, British Forces, Hong Kong, since 1978; *b* 16 Sept. 1925; *s* of late Robin Roy Redgrave and Michelene Jean Capsa; *m* 1953, Caroline Margaret Valerie, *d* of Major Arthur Wellesley; two *s*. *Educ:* Sherborne Sch. Served War of 1939-45: enlisted Trooper, Royal Horse Guards, 1943; Lieut, 1st Household Cavalry Regt, NW Europe, 1944-45. GSO III Intell., HQ Rhine Army, 1950; Canadian Army Staff Coll., 1955; GSO II Ops HQ, London Dist, 1956; Recce, Sqdn Ldr, Cyprus, 1959 (despatches); Mil. Assistant to Dep. SACEUR, Paris, 1960-62; JSSC 1962; Comd Household Cavalry Regt (Mounted), 1963-64; Comd Royal Horse Guards (The Blues), 1965-67; AAG PS12, MgD, 1967-68; Chief of Staff, HQ 2nd Div., 1968-70; Comdr, Royal Armoured Corps, 3rd Div., 1970-72; Nat. Defence Coll., Canada, 1973; Comdt Royal Armoured Corps Centre, 1974-75; British Comdt, Berlin, 1975-78. *Recreations:* walking, archaeology, philately. *Address:* Hong Kong, British Forces Post Office 1; c/o Lloyds Bank, Wareham, Dorset BH20 4LX. *Club:* Cavalry and Guards.

REDGRAVE, Vanessa, CBE 1967; Actress since 1957; *b* 30 Jan. 1937; *d* of Sir Michael Redgrave, *qv*; *m* 1962, Tony Richardson, *qv* (marr. diss., 1967); two *d*. *Educ:* Queensgate School; Central School of Speech and Drama. Frinton Summer Repertory, 1957; Touch of the Sun, Saville, 1958; Midsummer Night's Dream, Stratford, 1959; Look on Tempests, 1960; The Tiger and the Horse, 1960; Lady from the Sea, 1960; Royal Shakespeare Theatre Company: As You Like It, 1961, Taming of the Shrew, 1961, Cymbeline, 1962; The Seagull, 1964; The Prime of Miss Jean Brodie, Wyndham's, 1966; Daniel Deronda, 1969; Cato Street, 1971; The Threepenny Opera, Prince of Wales, 1972; Twelfth Night, Shaw Theatre, 1972; Antony and Cleopatra, Bankside Globe, 1973; Design for Living, Phoenix, 1973; Macbeth, LA, 1974; Lady from the Sea, NY, 1976. *Films:* Morgan-A Suitable Case for Treatment, 1966 (Cannes Fest. Award, Best Actress 1966); The Sailor from Gibraltar, 1967; Blow-Up, 1967; Camelot, 1967; Red White and Zero, 1967; Charge of the Light Brigade, 1968; Isadora, 1968; A Quiet Place in the Country, 1968; The Seagull, 1969; Drop-Out, 1970; La Vacanza, 1970; The Trojan Women, 1971; The Devils, 1971; Mary, Queen of Scots, 1972; Murder on the Orient Express, 1974; Out of Season, 1975; Seven Per Cent Solution, 1975; Julia, 1976. Has appeared on TV. *Publication:* Pussies and Tigers (anthology of writings of school children), 1963.

REDGROVE, Peter William; poet; Resident Author, Falmouth School of Art, since 1966; *b* 2 Jan. 1932; *s* of Gordon James Redgrove and Nancy Lena Cestrilli-Bell. *Educ:* Taunton Sch.; Queens' Coll., Cambridge. Scientific journalist and copywriter, 1954-61; Visiting Poet, Buffalo Univ., NY, 1961-62; Gregory Fellow in Poetry, Leeds Univ., 1962-65; study with John Layard, 1968-69. O'Connor Prof. of Literature, Colgate Univ., NY, 1974-75. George Rylands' Verse-speaking Prize, 1954; Fulbright Award, 1961; Poetry Book Society Choices, 1961 and

1966; Arts Council Awards, 1969, 1970, 1973, 1975; Guardian Fiction Prize, 1973. *Publications: poetry:* The Collector, 1960; The Nature of Cold Weather, 1961; At the White Monument, 1963; The Force, 1966; Penguin Modern Poets 11, 1968; Work in Progress, 1969; Dr Faust's Sea-Spiral Spirit, 1972; Three Pieces for Voices, 1972; The Hermaphrodite Album (with Penelope Shuttle), 1973; Sons of My Skin: Selected Poems, 1975; From Every Chink of the Ark, 1977; Ten Poems, 1977; *novels:* In the Country of the Skin, 1973; The Terrors of Dr Treviles (with Penelope Shuttle), 1974; The Glass Cottage, 1976; The God of Glass, 1978; *plays:* Miss Carstairs Dressed for Blooding, 1976; *psychology:* The Wise Wound (with Penelope Shuttle), 1978. *Recreations:* work; photography; judo (1st Kyu Judo: Otani and Brit. Judo Assoc.). *Address:* c/o Anthony Sheil Associates, 2/3 Morwell Street, WC1B 3AR. *T:* 01-636 2901. *Club:* Authors'.

REDINGTON, Frank Mitchell, MA, FIA; Chief Actuary, Prudential Assurance Co. Ltd, 1950-68, Director since 1968; *b* 10 May 1906; *e s* of late William David and Lily Redington; *m* 1938, Katie Marianne Rosenfeld; one *s* one *d*. *Educ:* Liverpool Institute; Magdalene College, Cambridge (MA). Entered Prudential, 1928; FIA 1934; Chairman, Life Offices Association, 1956-57; President, Institute of Actuaries, 1958-60 (Gold Medal of Inst., 1968). *Publications:* contributions to Jl of Inst. of Actuaries and foreign actuarial journals. *Address:* 10 Rose Walk, St Albans, Herts. *T:* St Albans 54722.

REDMAN, Maj.-Gen. Denis Arthur Kay, CB 1963; OBE 1942; Colonel Commandant, REME, 1963-68; Director, Electrical and Mechanical Engineering, War Office, 1960-63, retd; *b* 8 April 1910; *s* of late Brig. A. S. Redman, CB; *m* 1943, Penelope, *d* of A. S. Kay; one *s* one *d*. *Educ:* Wellington Coll.; London Univ. BSc (Eng) 1st class Hons (London); FCGI, MIMechE, AMIEE. Commissioned in RAOC, 1934; served in Middle East, 1936-43; transferred to REME, 1942; Temp. Brig., 1944; DDME 1st Corps, 1951; Comdt REME Training Centre 1957-59. Graduate of Staff Coll., Joint Services Staff Coll. and Imperial Defence Coll. *Recreations:* normal. *Address:* Caerleon, 8 Murdoch Road, Wokingham, Berks. *T:* Wokingham 780084. *Club:* Army and Navy.

REDMAN, Lt-Gen. Sir Harold, KCB 1953 (CB 1947); CBE 1944; *b* 25 August 1899; *s* of late A. E. Redman, Shawford, Winchester; *m* 1st, 1947, Patricia Mary (*d* 1951), *d* of late Brig. John Leslie Weston, CBE, DSO; one *d*; 2nd, 1953, Barbara Ann, *d* of late J. R. Wharton, Haffield, nr Ledbury; one *s* one *d*. *Educ:* Farnham; RMA, Woolwich. Commissioned into R Artillery, 1917; served in France and Germany, 1918 (BWM, VM); Waziristan, 1923-24 (NWF medal); Staff College, Camberley, 1929-30; transferred to KOYLI 1929; GSO 3 War Office, 1932-34; Bt Major, 1935; Brigade Major (3rd Division), 1934-36; GSO 2 Senior Officer School, 1937-38; GSO 2 Staff College, 1938-39; Bt Lt-Col 1939; War Cabinet Secretariat, 1939-40; Col 1942; Comd 7 Bn KOYLI 1940-41; Comd 151 (DLI) Infantry Bde Feb.-Dec. 1941; BGS Eighth Army, 1941-42; Comd 10 Ind. Motor Bde 1942-43; Secretary Combined Chiefs of Staff (Brig.), 1943-44; Deputy Commander French Forces of the Interior (Maj.-Gen.), Aug.-Sept. 1944; SHAEF Mission to French High Command, 1944-45; Head British Military Mission (France), 1945-46; CGS, ALFSEA, 1946-48; Director of Military Operations, War Office, 1948-51; Principal Staff Officer to Deputy Supreme Allied Commander, Europe, 1951-52; Vice-Chief of the Imperial General Staff, 1952-55; Governor and Commander-in-Chief, Gibraltar, 1955-58, retired. Director and Secretary The Wolfson Foundation, 1958-67. Col KOYLI, 1950-60. *Recreation:* gardening. *Address:* Stair House, West Lulworth, Dorset. *T:* West Lulworth 257.

REDMAN, Maurice; Chairman, Scottish Region, British Gas Corporation, since 1974; *b* 30 Aug. 1922; *s* of Herbert Redman and Olive (*née* Dyson); *m* 1960, Dorothy (*née* Appleton); two *d*. *Educ:* Hulme Grammar Sch., Oldham; Manchester Univ. BSc(Tech), 1st cl. Hons. Joined staff of Co. Borough of Oldham Gas Dept, 1943; Asst, later Dep. Production Engr, North Western Gas Bd, 1951; Chief Develt Engr, NW Gas Bd, 1957; Chief Engr, Southern Gas Bd, 1966; Dir of Engrg, Southern Gas Bd, 1970; Dep. Chm., Scottish Gas Bd, 1970; Regional Dep. Chm., Scottish Region, British Gas Corp., 1973. *Publications:* papers to Instn of Gas Engrs, Inst. of Fuel, Czechoslovak Internat. Gasification Symposium, etc. *Recreations:* gardening, music, photography. *Address:* c/o Scottish Gas, Granton House, 340 West Granton Road, Edinburgh EH5 1YB. *T:* 031-552 6271.

REDMAN, Sydney, CB 1961; Director-General, Timber Trade Federation, since 1973; *b* 12 Feb. 1914; *s* of John Barritt Redman and Ann Meech; *m* 1939, Barbara Mary Grey; one *s*

two *d. Educ:* Manchester Gram. Sch.; Corpus Christi Coll., Oxford. Principal Private Sec. to Secretary of State for War, 1942-44. Asst Under-Sec. of State: War Office, 1957-63; Ministry of Defence, 1963-64; Dep. Under-Sec. of State, MoD, 1964-73. *Address:* Littlehurst, Birch Avenue, Haywards Heath, West Sussex. *T:* Haywards Heath 413738.

REDMAYNE, family name of **Baron Redmayne.**

REDMAYNE, Baron *cr* 1966 (Life Peer), of Rushcliffe; **Martin Redmayne;** Bt *cr* 1964; PC 1959; DSO 1944; DL; Deputy Chairman, House of Fraser Ltd; Director, The Boots Co.; Chairman, 1971-76, Deputy Chairman, 1976-77, Retail Consortium; *b* 16 Nov. 1910; *s* of Leonard Redmayne; *m* 1933, Anne Griffiths; one *s. Educ:* Radley. Commanded 14th Bn The Sherwood Foresters, Italy, 1943; formed and commanded 66 Inf. Bde, 1944-45; Hon. Brig., 1945. MP (C) Rushcliffe Div. of Notts, 1950-66. A Govt Whip, 1951; A Lord Comr of the Treasury, 1953-59; Dep. Govt Chief Whip, 1955-59; Parly Sec. to Treasury and Govt Chief Whip, Oct. 1959-64; Opposition Chief Whip, Oct.-Nov. 1964. Chm., N American Adv. Gp, BOTB, 1972-76. JP Nottingham, 1946-66; DL Notts, 1954. *Recreations:* golf, fishing. *Heir:* (to Baronetcy only): *s* Hon. Nicholas Redmayne [*b* 1 Feb. 1938; *m* 1963, Ann Saunders (marr. diss. 1976); one *s* one *d*]. *Address:* 27 Hans Place, SW1X 0JY. *T:* 01-584 1525. *Club:* Buck's.

REDMOND, James, FIEE; Director of Engineering, BBC, since 1968; *b* 8 Nov. 1918; *s* of Patrick and Marion Redmond; *m* 1942, Joan Morris; one *s* one *d. Educ:* Graeme High Sch., Falkirk. Radio Officer, Merchant Navy, 1935-37 and 1939-45; BBC Television, Alexandra Palace, 1937-39; BBC: Installation Engr, 1949; Supt Engr Television Recording, 1960; Sen. Supt Engr TV, 1963; Asst Dir of Engrg, 1967. Pres., Soc. of Electronic and Radio Technicians, 1970-75; Vice-Pres., 1973-76, Dep. Pres., 1977-, IEE. *Recreation:* golf. *Address:* 43 Cholmeley Crescent, Highgate, N6. *T:* 01-340 1611. *Club:* Athenæum.

REDMOND, Robert Spencer, TD 1953; Director and Chief Executive, National Federation of Clay Industries, since 1976; *b* 10 Sept. 1919; *m* 1949, Marjorie Helen Heyes; one *s. Educ:* Liverpool Coll. Served War, Army, 1939-46: commissioned The Liverpool Scottish, 1938; transferred, RASC, 1941; Middle East, Junior Staff Sch., 1943; DAQMG, HQ Special Ops (Mediterranean), 1943-45; released, rank of Major, 1946. Conservative Agent, 1947-56 (Wigan, 1947-49, Knutsford, 1949-56). Managing Dir, Heyes & Co. Ltd, Wigan, 1956-66; Ashley Associates Ltd: Commercial Manager, 1966-69; Managing Dir, 1969-70; Dir, 1970-72. Dir, Manchester Chamber of Commerce, 1969-74. MP (C) Bolton West, 1970-Sept. 1974; Vice-Chm., Cons. Parly Employment Cttee, 1972-74 (Sec., 1971-72). Pres., Alderley Edge British Legion, 1968-76; Chm. (and Founder), NW Export Club, 1958-60. *Publication:* formerly contrib. to The Director, Manchester Evening News, Bolton Evening News, FBI Review. *Address:* Ballytrent, White Edge Drive, Baslow, Bakewell, Derbyshire. *T:* Baslow 3228. *Club:* Special Forces.

REDPATH, John Thomas, CB 1969; MBE 1944; FRIBA; architect in private practice, since 1977; *b* 24 Jan. 1915; *m* 1st, 1939, Kate (*née* Francis) (*d* 1949); one *d*; 2nd, 1949, Claesina (*née* van der Vlerk); three *s* one *d. Educ:* Price's Sch.; Southern Coll. of Art. Served with RE, 1940-47. Asst Architect: Kent CC, 1936-38; Oxford City Coun., 1938-40; Princ. Asst Architect, Herts, CC, 1948-55; Dep. County Architect, Somerset CC, 1955-59; Chief Architect (Abroad), War Office, 1959-63; MPBW later DoE: Dir of Development, 1963-67; Dir Gen. of Research and Development, 1967-71; Dir Gen. of Develt, 1971-72; Dep. Ch. Exec., Property Services Agency, 1972-75; Man. Dir, Millbank Technical Services Educn Ltd, 1975-77. *Publications:* various articles in architectural jls. *Recreation:* golf. *Address:* Pines Edge, Sandy Lane, Cobham, Surrey. *Club:* Arts.

REDSHAW, Sir Leonard, Kt 1972; Director and Chairman, Vickers Offshore Engineering Group, since 1975, and Vickers Oceanics Ltd, since 1972; Assistant Managing Director, Vickers Ltd, and Chairman, Vickers Ltd Shipbuilding Group, 1967-76; *b* 15 April 1911; *s* of late Joseph Stanley Redshaw, Naval Architect; *m* 1939, Joan Mary, *d* of Wm White, London; one *s* one *d. Educ:* Barrow Grammar Sch.; Univ. of Liverpool. 1st cl. Hons degree in naval architecture; 1851 Roy. Comr's exhibn post grad. Schol., Master's degree. Joined the Management Staff of Vickers-Armstrongs, 1936; Asst to Shipbuilding Manager, 1950; Special Dir, 1953; when Vickers-Armstrongs (Shipbuilders) Ltd was formed he was apptd Shipbuilding Gen. Man. of Yards at Barrow-in-Furness and Newcastle, 1955; Dir, Vickers-Armstrongs (Shipbuilders) Ltd, 1956, Deputy

Managing Director, 1961; Builders' Chief Polaris Exec., 1963; Man. Dir, Vickers Ltd Shipbuilding Group, 1964; Special Dir, Vickers Ltd, 1965; Dir, Vickers Ltd, 1967; Chairman: Vickers Ltd Shipbuilding Group, 1967-76; Slingsby Sailplanes, 1969; Brown Brothers & Co. Ltd, 1973; Director: Rolls Royce & Associates, Ltd, Derby, 1966; Shipbuilding Corp. Ltd, 1970-72; Brown Bros & Co. Ltd, 1970; Fillite (Runcorn) Ltd, 1971; Silica Fillers Ltd, 1971; Cockatoo Docks & Eng. Co. Pty Ltd, 1972-76. Jt Chm., Tech. Cttee, Lloyd's Register of Shipping and Mem., Lloyd's General Cttee. Mem., Nat. Defence Industries Council, 1971; Chairman: Assoc. W European Shipbuilders, 1972-73; Warshipbuilders Cttee; President: Shipbuilders and Repairers Nat. Assoc., 1971-72; Inst. of Welding, 1963-65 (Mem. Council). FRINA; FInstW. *Publications:* British Shipbuilding-Welding, 1947; Application of Welding to Ship Construction, 1962. *Recreations:* gliding, fishing. *Address:* Netherclose, Ireleth, Askam-in-Furness, Cumbria LA16 7EZ. *T:* Dalton-in-Furness 62529.

REDSHAW, Emeritus Prof. Seymour Cunningham, DSc (Wales), PhD (London), FICE, FIStructE, FRAeS; Beale Professor and Head of Civil Engineering Department, University of Birmingham, 1950-69; Dean of Faculty of Science, 1955-57; Member of Aeronautical Research Council, 1955; a Governor of Coll. of Aeronautics, 1951-69; *b* 20 March 1906; *s* of Walter James Redshaw and Edith Marion Cunningham; *m* 1935, Mary Elizabeth Jarrold; three *s. Educ:* Blundell's School; University of Wales. Technical Assistant, Bristol Aeroplane Co. Ltd, 1927-31; Asst Designer General Aircraft Ltd, 1931-32; Member of Staff: Imperial College, London, 1933-35; Building Research Station, 1936-40; Boulton Paul Aircraft Ltd, 1940-50: Chief Engineer, 1945; Director, 1949. Mem. Adv. Cttee on Building Research, 1965-67; Mem. Council, Univ. of Aston, 1966-67; Chm., Acad. Adv. Cttee, and Mem. Council, Univ. of Bath, 1966. Hon. DSc: Bath, 1966; Cranfield, 1976. *Publications:* numerous papers in scientific and engineering journals. *Address:* 32 Newport Street, Brewood, Staffs. *T:* Brewood 850274.

REDWOOD, Sir Peter (Boverton), 3rd Bt *cr* 1911; Major, King's Own Scottish Borderers; *b* 1 Dec. 1937; *o s* of Sir Thomas Boverton Redwood, 2nd Bt, TD, and of Ruth Mary Redwood (*née* Creighton, now Blair); *S* father, 1974; *m* 1964, Gilian, *o d* of John Lee Waddington Wood, Limuru, Kenya; three *d. Educ:* Gordonstoun. National Service, 1956-58; commissioned into Seaforth Highlanders; regular commn, 1959, KOSB. *Heir:* half-*b* Robert Boverton Redwood, *b* 24 June 1953. *Address:* c/o National Westminster Bank Ltd, Thames House, Millbank, SW1. *Club:* Army and Navy.

REECE, Sir Alan; *see* Reece, Sir L. A.

REECE, Courtenay Walton; Puisne Judge, Hong Kong, 1952-61, retired; *b* 4 Dec. 1899; 3rd *s* of H. Walter Reece, KC (Barbados); *m* 1927, Rosa U. E. Parker (*d* 1956); two *d. Educ:* Harrison College and Codrington College, Barbados; Jesus College, Oxford (BA). Called to Bar, Middle Temple, 1925; Police Magistrate, Barbados, 1926; Registrar, Barbados, 1931; Magistrate, Nigeria, 1938; Crown Counsel, Nigeria, 1939; Senior Crown Counsel, Nigeria, 1946; Puisne Judge, Nigeria, 1949. *Recreations:* motor-boating, swimming, carpentry, fishing. *Address:* 108 Macdonnell Road, 7th Floor, Hong Kong. *T:* 5-231705. *Club:* Royal Hong Kong Jockey.

REECE, Sir Gerald, KCMG 1950; CBE 1943 (OBE 1937); DL; Chairman of Managers, Loaningdale Approved School, 1968-76; *b* 10 Jan. 1897; *s* of Edward Mackintosh Reece; *m* 1936, Alys Isabel Wingfield, *d* of Dr H. E. H. Tracy; one *s* two *d* (and one *s* decd). *Educ:* Rugby School. Commissioned Sherwood Foresters, 1915; served France and Belgium (wounded thrice). Solicitor Sup. Court, England, 1921; entered Kenya Administrative Service, 1925; seconded as HBM's Consul for Southern Ethiopia, 1934; Senior Political Officer, Borana Province of Ethiopia, 1941; Officer in Charge, Northern Frontier of Kenya, 1939-45; Provincial Commissioner, Kenya, 1945-48; Military Governor, British Somaliland, 1948; Governor and Commander-in-Chief, Somaliland Protectorate, 1948-53. Scottish Chm., Howard League for Penal Reform, 1961-73. Chairman: Scottish Soc. for Prevention of Vivisection, 1973-; St Andrews Animal Fund, 1974-. Hon. Sheriff, E Lothian, 1962-73; DL, E Lothian, 1971-. *Address:* Bolton Old Manse, near Haddington, East Lothian. *T:* Gifford 351.

REECE, Sir (Louis) Alan, Kt 1964; CMG 1963; *b* 1906; *s* of Claud Austin Reece; *m* 1941, Erna Irmgard Meyer. *Educ:* Queen's Royal Coll., Trinidad. Secretary to the Cabinet and Permanent Secretary to the Prime Minister, Trinidad and Tobago, 1961-63, retd. Chm., Elections and Boundaries

Commn; former Chairman: Trinidad and Tobago Electricity Commn; Industrial Develt Corp. *Address:* c/o 4 Hayes Street, St Clair, Port of Spain, Trinidad.

REED, Adrian Harbottle; HM Diplomatic Service; Consul-General, Munich, since 1973; *b* 5 Jan. 1921; *s* of Harbottle Reed, MBE, FRIBA, and Winifred Reed (*née* Rowland); *m* 1st, 1947, Doris Davidson Duthie (marr. diss. 1975); one *s* one *d*; 2nd, 1975, Maria-Louise, *d* of Dr and Mrs A. J. Boekelman, Zeist, Netherlands. *Educ:* Hele's Sch., Exeter; Emmanuel Coll., Cambridge. Royal Artillery, 1941-47. India Office, 1947; Commonwealth Relations Office, 1947; served in UK High Commission: Pakistan, 1948-50; Fedn of Rhodesia and Nyasaland, 1953-56; British Embassy, Dublin, 1960-62; Commonwealth Office, 1962-68; Counsellor (Commercial), and Consul-Gen., Helsinki, 1968-70; Economic Counsellor, Pretoria, 1971-73. *Address:* c/o Foreign and Commonwealth Office, SW1.

REED, David; Public Affairs Manager, Hewlett-Packard, since 1975; *b* 24 April 1945; *s* of Wilfred Reed and Elsie Swindon; *m* 1973, Susan Garrett, MA Oxon, MScEcon. *Educ:* West Hartlepool Grammar Sch. Journalist: Northern Echo, 1963-64; Imperial Chemical Industries, 1964-65; Public Relations Officer: NE Development Council, 1966-68; Vickers Ltd, 1968-70. MP (Lab) Sedgefield, Co. Durham, 1970-Feb. 1974. *Publications:* many articles in national newspapers and other jls, on regional and consumer affairs. *Recreations:* many and varied. *Address:* 37 Damer Gardens, Henley-on-Thames, Oxon RG9 1HX. *T:* Henley 3777.

REED, Edward John; Clerk to the Clothworkers' Company of the City of London since 1963; *b* 2 Sept. 1913; *o c* of late Edward Reed; *m* 1939, Rita Isabel Venus Cheston-Porter; one *s* one *d*. *Educ:* St Paul's School. Admitted Solicitor, 1938. Territorial Service with HAC; commnd 1940; served BEF and BAOR with 63 (WR) Medium Regt RA; Capt. 1942. Clerk to Governors of Mary Datchelor Girls' Sch., 1963; Chm. of Metropolitan Society for the Blind and Indigent Blind Visiting Society, 1965; Vice-Pres., N London District, St John Ambulance, 1969. CStJ 1968. Chevalier, Order of Leopold with Palm, and Croix de Guerre with Palm, Belgium, 1944. *Recreations:* sailing, photography. *Address:* Clothworkers' Hall, Dunster Court, Mincing Lane, EC3. *T:* 01-623 7041.

REED, Henry; poet, radio-dramatist, translator; *b* 22 Feb. 1914; *s* of late Henry Reed and late Mary Ann Ball; unmarried. *Educ:* King Edward VI Sch., Aston, Birmingham; Birmingham Univ. (BA 1st cl. Hons Lang. and Lit., 1934; Charles Grant Robertson Scholar, 1934; MA 1936). From then on, verse and journalism. Taught for a year before call-up in 1941; served (or rather *studied*) in Army, 1941-42; transf. to Naval Intelligence, FO, 1942-45; released VJ day, 1945; recalled to Army, 1945; did not go, 1945; matter silently dropped, 1945. During war continued to write and publish verse and book-reviews; began occasional broadcasting; began writing radio-plays, 1946 (Premio della Radio Italiana, 1953), and doing much translation from Italian and French. Academic appts at Univ. of Washington, Seattle: Vis. Prof. of Poetry, winter quarter 1964; Asst Prof. of English, 1965-66; Vis. Prof. of Poetry, winter quarter 1967. *Publications:* A Map of Verona (poems), 1946, enl. edn NY 1947; Moby Dick (radio-version in prose and verse of Melville's novel), 1947; The Novel since 1939 (British Council booklet), 1947; The Lessons of the War (poems), 1970; Hilda Tablet and others, 1971; The Streets of Pompeii and other plays for radio, 1971; The Auction Sale and other poems, 1977. Numerous published translations include: Paride Rombi: Perdu and his Father (novel), 1954; Ugo Betti: Three Plays (with foreword), 1956, NY 1958; Ugo Betti: Crime on Goat Island, 1961 (staged NY 1960); Dino Buzzati: Larger than Life (novel), 1962; Balzac: Père Goriot, NY 1962; Balzac: Eugénie Grandet, NY 1964; Natalia Ginzburg: The Advertisement (play), 1969 (Nat. Theatre 1969). *Address:* c/o Messrs Jonathan Cape Ltd, 30 Bedford Square, WC1.

REED, Jane Barbara; Editor, Woman's Own, since 1970; 2nd *d* of William and late Gwendoline Reed, Letchworth, Herts. *Educ:* Royal Masonic Sch.; sundry further educational establishments. Worked on numerous magazines, both living and dead; returned to Woman's Own, 1965; Asst Editor, 1967. *Publication:* Girl About Town, 1964. *Address:* Woman's Own, King's Reach Tower, Stamford Street, SE1; (home) Fulham, London.

REED, Laurance Douglas; *b* 4 Dec. 1937; *s* of Douglas Austin Reed and late Mary Ellen Reed (*née* Philpott). *Educ:* Gresham's Sch., Holt; University Coll., Oxford (MA). Nat. Service, RN, 1956-58; worked and studied on Continent (Brussels, Bruges, Leyden, Luxembourg, Strasbourg, Paris, Rome, Bologna, Geneva), 1963-66; Public Sector Research Unit, 1967-69. MP

(C) Bolton East, 1970-Feb. 1974; PPS to Chancellor of Duchy of Lancaster, 1973-74. Jt Sec., Parly and Scientific Cttee, 1971-74; Member: Soc. for Underwater Technology; Select Cttee on Science and Technology, 1971-74. Vice-Pres., Solent Protection Soc. *Publications:* Europe in a Shrinking World, 1967; An Ocean of Waste, 1972; Political Consequences of North Sea Oil, 1973. *Recreations:* gardening, painting. *Address:* Water-Flag House, Isle of Soay, Inverness-shire. *T:* Soay 4. *Club:* Carlton.

REED, Michael, CB 1962; *b* 7 July 1912; *s* of late Richard and Winifred Reed; *m* 1st, 1939, Marcia Jackson; two *d*; 2nd, 1950, Hermione Jeanne, *d* of Dr P. Roux, Kimberley, SA; one *s* one *d*. *Educ:* Christ's Hospital; Jesus College, Cambridge. Entered Ministry of Health, 1935; Private Secretary to Minister, 1942-45; Under-Secretary, Ministry of Health, 1956-58, Cabinet Office, 1958-61, Ministry of Health, 1961-63; Registrar General, 1963-72 and Dir, Office of Population Censuses and Surveys, 1970-72. *Address:* Welgemeend, Firgrove, Cape, South Africa.

REED, Sir Nigel (Vernon), Kt 1970; CBE 1967 (MBE (mil.) 1945); TD 1950; Chief Justice of the Northern States of Nigeria, 1968-75; *b* 31 Oct. 1913; *s* of Vernon Herbert Reed, formerly MP and MLC New Zealand, and of Eila Mabel Reed; *m* 1945, Ellen Elizabeth Langstaff; one *s* two *d*. *Educ:* Wanganui Collegiate School, NZ; Victoria University College, NZ; Jesus College, Cambridge. LLB (NZ) and LLB (Cantab). Called to the Bar, Lincoln's Inn, 1939. Military Service, 1939-45, Lt-Col 1944. Appointed to Colonial Legal Service, 1946; Magistrate, Nigeria, 1946; Chief Magistrate, Nigeria, 1951; Chief Registrar, High Court of the Northern Region of Nigeria, 1955; Judge, High Court of the Northern Region of Nigeria, 1956; Sen. Puisne Judge, High Court of Northern Nigeria, 1964. *Address:* Old Farm Cottage, Corton, Warminster, Wilts.

REED, Philip Dunham; Corporation Director; *b* Milwaukee, Wisconsin, 16 Nov. 1899; *s* of William Dennis Reed and Virginia Brandreth Dunham; *m* 1921, Mabel Mayhew Smith; one *s* one *d*. *Educ:* University of Wisconsin (BS in Electrical Engineering); Fordham Univ. (LLB). Hon. LLD, Union Coll. and Brooklyn Poly. Inst., Hon. DEng Rensslaer Poly. Inst.; Hon. Dr of Commercial Science, New York Univ. 1950; Hon. Dr of Laws, Univ. of Wisconsin, 1950. Swarthmore Coll., 1954. With General Electric Co. (Law Dept), 1926-; Asst to Pres. and Dir, 1937-39; Chm. of Bd, 1940; resigned Chairmanship Dec. 1942 to continue war work in England; re-elected Chm. of Bd, 1945-58; Chm., Finance Cttee, General Electric Co., NY, 1945-59, Director Emeritus, 1968-. Chm. of Board: of Internat. General Electric Company, 1945 until merger with parent co., 1952; Federal Reserve Bank of NY, 1960-65. Director: American Express Co.; American Express Internat. Banking Corp., 1958-72; US Financial, 1970-72; Otis Elevator Company, 1958-72; Kraftco Corp., 1958-70; Scott Paper Co., 1958-66; Metropolitan Life Insurance Co., 1940-73; Tiffany & Co., 1956-; Bigelow-Sanford Inc., 1959-74; Bankers Trust Co., 1966-72; Cowles Communications Inc., 1972-; Metropolitan Opera Assoc. Inc., 1945-53; Mem. Business Advisory Council for Dept of Commerce, 1940- (Vice-Chm. 1951-52); US Adv. Commn on Information, 1948-61; Member: Executive Commn, Payroll Savings Adv. Cttee for US Treasury Dept, 1946-56; Dir, Council on Foreign Relations, 1946-69; Trustee: Carnegie Endowment for Internat. Peace, 1945-53; Cttee for Economic Development (and Member Research and Policy Cttee); Member of the Visiting Cttee, Graduate School of Business Admin., Harvard Univ., 1940-60; Director, Ford Foundation Fund for Advancement of Education, 1951-53; Consultant to US Deleg., San Francisco Conf. on World Organization; Chm. US Associates (now US Council), Internat. Chamber of Commerce, 1945-Jan. 1948; mem. Exec. Cttee, US Council, ICC; Hon. Pres. Internat. Chamber of Commerce (Pres., 1949-51); Chm. US Side of Anglo-American Productivity Council, 1948-52; Vice-Chm. Eisenhower Exchange Fellowships, 1953-; Chm. Finance Cttee, 1955-56. Mem. President's Cttee on Information Activities Abroad, 1960; Mem. Cttee on the Univ. and World Affairs (Ford Foundn), 1960; Trustee of Kress Foundn, 1960-65. Entered War work, 1941, with Office of Production Management, Washington, and its successor the War Production Board (Chief of Bureau of Industry Branches responsible for organising and converting peacetime industries to war production). Went to London, July 1942, as Deputy Chief of Economic Mission headed by W. Averell Harriman; Chief of Mission for Economic Affairs, London, with rank of Minister, Oct. 1943-31 Dec. 1944. Special Ambassador to Mexico, 1958. President's Certificate of Merit Award, 1947; Comdr Légion d'Honneur (France), 1951 (Officer, 1947). *Address:* 375 Park Avenue, New York, NY 10022, USA; (home) Rye, NY. *Clubs:* University, The Links (NY City); Apawamis (Rye, NY); Blind Brook (Port Chester, NY); Augusta National Golf (Augusta, Ga); Bohemian (San Francisco); Mill Reef (Antigua, WI).

REED, Sir Reginald Charles, Kt 1971; CBE 1967; Governing Director (previously Managing Director), Patrick Operations Pty Ltd, since 1971; Chairman: Glebe Island Terminals Pty Ltd; Opal Maritime Agencies Pty, Ltd; Deputy Chairman, Australian National Line; Director: J. Meloy Ltd; Universal Charterers Pty Ltd; Sims Consolidated Ltd; *b* 26 Sept. 1909; *s* of Reginald Paul and Emily Christina Reed; *m* 1934, May Moore; one *s. Educ:* Greenwich Public Sch., Australia. Associated with James Patrick & Co. Pty Ltd, and Patrick Stevedoring Co., 1930-; Commonwealth Govt appt, Australian Stevedoring Industry Authority, 1949-56; Chm., Australian Shipbuilding Bd, 1966. *Recreations:* surfing, reading, riding. *Address:* 11 Montah Avenue, Killara, NSW 2071, Australia. *T:* 498-2734. *Clubs:* Australia (London); Australian, American National, Royal Sydney Yacht Squadron (all in Sydney).

REED, Stanley William; Director, British Film Institute, 1964-72, Consultant on Regional Development, 1972-76; *b* 21 Jan. 1911; *s* of Sidney James Reed and Ellen Maria Patient; *m* 1937, Alicia Mary Chapman; three *d. Educ:* Stratford Grammar Sch.; Coll. of St Mark and St John, Chelsea. Teacher in E London schools, 1931-39. In charge of school evacuation parties, 1939-45. Teacher and Visual Aids Officer, West Ham Education Cttee, 1939-50. British Film Institute: Educn Officer, 1952-56; Sec., 1956-64. *Publications:* The Cinema, 1952; How Films are Made, 1955; A Guide to Good Viewing, 1961. Neighbourhood 15 (film, also Dir). *Recreations:* opera and exploring London's suburbs. *Address:* 54 Felstead Road, Wanstead, E11. *T:* 01-989 6021.

REED, Most Rev. Thomas Thornton, MA, DLitt, ThD; *b* Eastwood, South Australia, 9 Sept. 1902; *s* of Alfred Ernest Reed, Avoca, Vic; *m* 1932, Audrey Airlie, *d* of Major Harry Lort Spencer Balfour-Ogilvy, MBE, DCM, Tannadice, Renmark, South Australia; two *d* (and one *d* decd). *Educ:* Collegiate Sch. of St Peter, Adelaide; Trinity College, University of Melbourne (Hon. Schol., BA, MA); St Barnabas' Theol. Coll., Adelaide. ThL, ATC, 1st cl. hons. Fred Johns Schol. for Biography, Univ. of Adelaide, 1950. Deacon, 1926; Priest, 1927; Curate, St Augustine's, Unley, 1926-28; Priest in Charge, Berri Mission, 1928-29; Resident Tutor, St Mark's Coll., Univ. of Adelaide, and Area Padre, Toc H, 1929-31; Asst Chaplain, Melbourne Grammar Sch., 1932-36; Rector, St Michael's, Henley Beach, 1936-44; Rector, St Theodore's, Rose Park, 1944-54; Chaplain, Australian Mil. Forces, 1939-57; Chaplain, AIF with HQ, New Guinea Force, 1944-45; Asst Tutor, St Barnabas' Coll., 1940-46; Senior Chaplain, RAAChD, HQ, C Command, South Australia, 1953-56; Editor, Adelaide Church Guardian, 1940-44; Rural Dean, Western Suburbs, 1944; Priest Comr, Adelaide Dio. Centenary, 1947; Canon of Adelaide, 1947-49; Archdeacon of Adelaide, 1949-53; Dean of Adelaide, 1953-57; Bishop of Adelaide, 1957-73; Archbishop of Adelaide, and Metropolitan of S Australia, 1973-75. Pres., Toc H, S Aust., 1960; Pres., St Mark's Coll., Univ. of Adelaide, 1961-74, Hon. Fellow, 1973. Hon. ThD, Australian Coll., of Theology, 1955; DLitt, Univ. of Adelaide, 1954. Chaplain and Sub Prelate of Venerable Order of St John of Jerusalem, 1965. *Publications:* Henry Kendall: A Critical Appreciation, 1960; Sonnets and Songs, 1962; (ed) The Poetical Works of Henry Kendall, 1966; A History of the Cathedral Church of St Peter, Adelaide, 1969. *Recreations:* golf, research on Australian literature, heraldry, and genealogy. *Address:* 44 Jeffcott Street, North Adelaide, SA 5006, Australia. *T:* 2674841; PO Box 130, North Adelaide, SA 5006, Australia. *Clubs:* Adelaide, Naval, Military and Air Force, Royal Adelaide Golf (Adelaide).

REEDY, Norris John; Editor, The Birmingham Post, since 1974; *b* 1934; *s* of John Reedy; *m* 1964, Sheila Campbell McGregor; one *d. Educ:* Chorlton High Sch., Manchester; Univ. of Sheffield. Sheffield Telegraph, 1956; Sunday Times, 1961; Lancashire Evening Telegraph, 1962; Guardian, 1964; Birmingham Post: Features Editor, 1964; Sen. Asst Editor, 1968; Dep. Editor, 1973. *Recreations:* astronomy, natural history, riding, photography. *Address:* The Old Manor, Rowington, near Warwick. *T:* Lapworth 3129.

REEKIE, Henry Enfield; Headmaster of Felsted School, 1951-68; *b* Hayfield, Derbyshire, 17 Oct. 1907; *s* of John Albert Reekie and Edith Dowson; *m* 1936, Pauline Rosalind, *d* of Eric W. Seeman; one *s* three *d. Educ:* Oundle; Clare College, Cambridge. Asst Master, Felsted School, 1929, Housemaster, 1933, Senior Science Master, 1945; Headmaster, St Bees School, 1946. *Recreations:* ski-ing, gardening, travel. *Address:* Tarn House, Mark Cross, Crowborough, East Sussex. *T:* Mayfield 3100. *Club:* East India, Devonshire, Sports and Public Schools.

REES, Arthur Morgan, CBE 1974 (OBE 1963); QPM 1970; DL; Chief Constable of Staffordshire, 1964-77; *b* 20 Nov. 1912; *s* of

Thomas and Jane Rees, The Limes, Llangadog; *m* 1943, Dorothy Webb; one *d. Educ:* Llandovery Coll.; St Catharine's Coll., Cambridge. BA 1935, MA 1939. Metropolitan Police, 1935-41; RAF (Pilot), 1941-46 (Subst. Sqdn Ldr; Actg Wing Comdr); Metropolitan Police, 1946-57; Chief Constable, Denbighshire, 1957-64. Chm., Midlands Sports Adv. Cttee; Chm., Queen's Silver Jubilee Appeal, 1976-; Mem., King George's Jubilee Trust Council, 1973-; Pres., Martial Arts Commn; Trustee and Board of Governors, Llandovery College. DL Staffs, 1967. CStJ 1969. *Recreations:* former Rugby International for Wales (14 caps), Cambridge Rugby Blue, 1933 and 1934; Chairman: Crawshays Welsh Rugby XV, 1970. *Address:* The Old Vicarage, Ellenhall, Stafford. *T:* (office) Stafford 57717 and 55530. *Clubs:* Royal Air Force; Hawks (Cambridge).

REES, Brian, MA Cantab; Headmaster, Charterhouse, since 1973; *b* 20 Aug. 1929; *s* of late Frederick T. Rees; *m* 1959, Julia, *d* of Sir Robert Birley, *qv*; two *s* three *d. Educ:* Bede Grammar Sch., Sunderland; Trinity Coll., Cambridge (Scholar). 1st cl. Historical Tripos, Part I, 1951; Part II, 1952. Eton College: Asst Master, 1952-65; Housemaster, 1963-65; Headmaster, Merchant Taylors' Sch., 1965-73. Pres., Conference for Independent Further Education, 1973. Mem. Council, UC of Buckingham, 1973-; Chm., Tormead Sch. Council. *Recreations:* music, painting. *Address:* Charterhouse, Godalming, Surrey. *T:* Godalming 22589. *Clubs:* Athenæum, Savile.

REES, Brinley Roderick, MA Oxon, PhD Wales; Principal, Saint David's University College, Lampeter, since 1975; *b* 27 Dec. 1919; *s* of John David Rees and Mary Ann (*née* Roderick); *m* 1951, Zena Muriel Stella Mayall; two *s. Educ:* Christ Coll., Brecon; Merton Coll., Oxford (Postmaster). 1st Cl., Class. Hons Mods and Hon. Mention, Craven and Ireland Schols, 1946. Welch Regt, 1940-45. Asst Classics Master, Christ Coll., Brecon, 1947; Cardiff High Sch., 1947-48; Asst Lectr in Classics, University Coll. of Wales Aberystwyth, 1948-49; Lectr 1949-56; Sen. Lectr in Greek, Univ. of Manchester, 1956-58; UC Cardiff: Prof. of Greek, 1958-70; Dean of Faculty of Arts, 1963-65; Dean of Students, 1967-68; Univ. of Birmingham: Prof. of Greek, 1970-75; Dean of Faculty of Arts, 1973-75. Governor, Christ College, Brecon, 1961-72. Hon. Secretary, Classical Association, 1963-69, Vice-Pres., 1969-. *Publications:* The Merton Papyri, Vol. II (with H. I. Bell and J. W. B. Barns), 1959; The Use of Greek, 1961; Papyri from Hermopolis and other Byzantine Documents, 1964; (with M. E. Jervis) Lampas: a new approach to Greek, 1970; Classics: an outline for intending students, 1970; Aristotle's Theory and Milton's Practice, 1972; articles and reviews in various classical and other jls. *Address:* St David's University College, Lampeter SA48 7ED. *T:* Lampeter 422351.

REES, Prof. Charles Wayne, DSc; FRS 1974; FRIC; Heath Harrison Professor of Organic Chemistry, University of Liverpool, 1977-78 (Professor of Organic Chemistry, 1969-77); Hofmann Professor of Organic Chemistry, Imperial College, London, from Oct. 1978; *b* 15 Oct. 1927; *s* of Percival Charles Rees and Daisy Alice Beck; *m* 1953, Patricia Mary Francis; three *s. Educ:* Farnham Grammar Sch.; University Coll., Southampton (BSc, PhD). Lectr in Organic Chem.: Birkbeck Coll., Univ. of London, 1955-57; King's Coll., Univ. of London, 1957-63, Reader, 1963-65; Prof. of Organic Chem., Univ. of Leicester, 1965-69. Visiting Prof., Univ. of Würzburg, 1968; Tilden Lectr, Chemical Soc., 1973-74. *Publications:* Organic Reaction Mechanism (8 annual vols), 1965-72; Carbenes, Nitrenes, Arynes, 1969; about 200 research papers and reviews, mostly in jls of Chemical Soc. *Recreations:* music, wine. *Address:* (until Oct. 1978) Robert Robinson Laboratories, University of Liverpool, PO Box 147, Liverpool L69 3BX. *T:* 051-709 6022; (from Oct. 1978) Department of Chemistry, Imperial College of Science and Technology, South Kensington, SW7 2AY.

REES, Hon. Sir (Charles William) Stanley, Kt 1962; TD 1949; DL; **Hon. Mr Justice Rees;** Judge of High Court of Justice, Family Division (formerly Probate, Divorce and Admiralty Division), since 1962; *b* 30 Nov. 1907; *s* of Dr David Charles Rees, MRCS, LRCP, and Myrtle May (*née* Dolley); *m* 1934, Jean Isabel Munro Wheildon; one *s. Educ:* St Andrew's College, Grahamstown, S Africa; University College, Oxford. BA, BCL (Oxon). Called to the Bar, 1931; Bencher, Inner Temple, 1962. 2nd Lt 99th Regt AA RA (London Welsh), 1939; JAG's office in Home Commands, 1940-43; Lt-Col in charge JAG's Branch, HQ Palestine Command, 1944-45; released from military service as Hon. Lt-Col, 1945. QC 1957; Recorder of Croydon, 1961-62; Commissioner of Assize, Stafford, Dec. 1961; Dep. Chm., 1959-64, Chm., 1964-71, E Sussex QS. DL E Sussex (formerly Sussex), 1968. Member Governing Body, Brighton College. *Recreations:* walking, gardening. *Address:* Royal Courts of Justice, Strand,

WC2; Lark Rise, Lyoth Lane, Lindfield, Sussex. *Club:* United Oxford & Cambridge University.
See also Harland Rees.

REES, Prof. David, FRS 1968; Professor of Pure Mathematics, University of Exeter, since 1958; *b* 29 May 1918; *s* of David and Florence Gertrude Rees; *m* 1952, Joan Sybil Cushen; four *d. Educ:* King Henry VIII Grammar School, Abergavenny; Sidney Sussex College, Cambridge. Manchester University: Assistant Lecturer, 1945-46, Lecturer, 1946-49; Cambridge University: Lecturer, 1949-58; Fellow of Downing College, Cambridge, 1950-58, Hon. Fellow, 1970-. *Publications:* papers on Algebraic topics in British and foreign mathematical journals. *Recreations:* reading and listening to music. *Address:* 6 Hillcrest Park, Exeter EX4 4SH. *T:* Exeter 59398.

REES, David Morgan, CBE 1956; CEng; JP; *b* 29 March 1904; *s* of late Rees Rees, JP, Pencoed, Glam.; *m* 1935, Marjorie Griffith; one *s* one *d. Educ:* Llandovery Coll.; Birmingham University. Mining Engineer, qualified Birmingham University. Mining in Wales, 1930-36; Agent, BA Colliery, 1936-46. Area General Manager, East Midlands Division, 1947-52; Chairman South Western Division, National Coal Board, 1952-61. Mem., Council for Wales and Mon., 1953-56. Commander (Brother), Order of St John. JP Newcastle, Ogmore, and Bridgend, Glam. *Address:* Tynewydd, Abergolech, Dyfed. *T:* Talley 443. *Clubs:* Cardiff and County (Cardiff); Royal Porthcawl Golf (Porthcawl).

REES, Dame Dorothy (Mary), DBE 1975 (CBE 1964); Member, Central Training Council, 1964-67; *b* 1898; widow. *Educ:* Elementary and Secondary Schools. Formerly: school teacher; Member of Barry Borough Council. Alderman of Glamorgan CC; former Mem. Nat. Advisory Committee for National Insurance; Member: Joint Education Committee for Wales (Chm., Technical Educn Sub-Cttee); Welsh Teaching Hospitals Board. Liaison Officer, Ministry of Food, during War of 1939-45. MP (Lab) Barry Division of Glamorganshire, 1950-51; formerly Parliamentary Private Secretary to the Minister of National Insurance. *Address:* Mor-Hafren, 341 Barry Road, Barry, S Glam.

REES, Dr (Florence) Gwendolen, FRS 1971; FIBiol; a Professor of Zoology, University of Wales, at University College of Wales, Aberystwyth, 1971-73, now Emeritus; *b* 3 July 1906; *yr d* of late E. and E. A. Rees; unmarried. *Educ:* Girls' Grammar Sch., Aberdare; UCW Cardiff. BSc 1927; PhD 1930; DSc 1942. FIBiol 1971. UCW, Aberystwyth: Lectr in Zoology, 1930-46; Sen. Lectr, 1946-66; Reader, 1966-71. Vis. Scientist, Univ. of Ghana, 1961. Research grants from Royal Soc., SRC, Shell Grants Cttee, Nat. Research Council, USA. Hon. Member: Amer. Soc. of Parasitologists, 1975; British Soc. for Parasitology, 1976. *Publications:* numerous papers on parasitology (helminthology) in scientific jls. *Recreations:* riding, amateur dramatics, the arts. *Address:* Grey Mist, North Road, Aberystwyth, Dyfed. *T:* Aberystwyth 612389.

REES, Prof. Garnet; Professor of French, since 1957, Pro-Vice-Chancellor, 1972-74, University of Hull; *b* 15 March 1912; *o s* of William Garnet and Mabel Rees; *m* 1941, Dilys, *o d* of Robert and Ellen Hughes; two *d. Educ:* Pontardawe Grammar School; University College of Wales, Aberystwyth; University of Paris. BA (Wales), 1934; MA (Wales), 1937; Docteur de l'Université de Paris, 1940; Fellow of Univ. of Wales, 1937-39; Asst Lecturer in French, Univ. Coll., Aberystwyth, 1939-40. Served War of 1939-45, in Roy. Regt of Artillery (Captain, Instructor in Gunnery), 1940-45. Lecturer in French, Univ. of Southampton, 1945-46; Sen. Lecturer in French, Univ. Coll., Swansea, 1946-57. Officier des Palmes Académiques (France), 1961. Chevalier de la Légion d'Honneur, 1967. *Publications:* Remy de Gourmont, 1940; Guillaume Apollinaire, Alcools, 1975; Baudelaire, Sartre and Camus: lectures and commentaries, 1976; articles on modern French literature and bibliography in learned journals. *Recreations:* gardening and motoring. *Address:* The University of Hull, Hull HU6 7RX; 88 Newland Park, Hull. *T:* 444110.

REES, Geraint; *see* Rees, R. G.

REES, Goronwy; *see* Rees, Morgan Goronwy.

REES, Gwendolen; *see* Rees, F. G.

REES, Harland, MA, MCh, FRCS; Hon. Consultant Urological Surgeon, King's College Hospital; Hon. Consultant Surgeon and Urological Surgeon, Royal Free Hospital; *b* 21 Sept. 1909; *yr s* of Dr David Charles Rees, MRCS, LRCP, and Myrtle May (*née* Dolley); *m* 1950, Helen Marie Tarver; two *s* (one *d* decd). *Educ:*

St Andrew's Coll., Grahamstown, S Africa; University Coll., Oxford; Charing Cross Hospital. Rhodes Scholar, Oxford University. Served RAMC, 1942-46; OC Surgical Div. 53, Indian General Hospital. Adviser in Surgery, Siam (Thailand). Examiner in Surgery, University of Cambridge, 1963-73. *Publications:* articles and chapters in various books and journals, 1952-63. *Recreations:* walking, cultivation of trees; Rugby football, Oxford *v* Cambridge, 1932-33. *Address:* Clinic Seven, Royal Free Hospital, Pond Street, NW3. *T:* 01-794 0050; Kensworth Gorse, Kensworth, near Dunstable, Beds. *T:* Whipsnade 872411. *Club:* Vincent's (Oxford).
See also Hon. Sir C. W. S. Rees.

REES, Haydn; *see* Rees, T. M. H.

REES, Prof. Hubert, DFC 1945; PhD, DSc; FRS 1976; Professor of Agricultural Botany, University College of Wales, Aberystwyth, since 1968; *b* 2 Oct. 1923; *s* of Owen Rees and Tugela Rees, Llangennech, Carmarthenshire; *m* 1946, Mavis Hill; two *s* two *d. Educ:* Llandovery and Llanelli Grammar Schs; University Coll. of Wales, Aberystwyth (BSc). PhD, DSc Birmingham. Served RAF, 1942-46. Student, Aberystwyth, 1946-50; Lectr in Cytology, Univ. of Birmingham, 1950-58; Sen. Lectr in Agric. Botany, University Coll. of Wales, Aberystwyth, 1958, Reader 1966. *Publications:* Chromosome Genetics, 1977; articles on genetic control of chromosomes and on evolutionary changes in chromosome organisation. *Recreation:* fishing. *Address:* Irfon, Llanbadarn Road, Aberystwyth, Dyfed. *T:* Aberystwyth 3668.

REES, Hugh; *see* Rees, J. E. H.

REES, Hugh Francis E.; *see* Ellis-Rees.

REES, (John Edward) Hugh; Chartered Surveyor, Chartered Auctioneer and Estate Agent; *b* 8 Jan. 1928; *s* of David Emlyn Rees, The Mirador, Swansea; *m* 1961, Jill Dian Milo-Jones; two *s. Educ:* Parc Wern School, Glanmor School, Swansea; Bromsgrove School. Served in Army (commissioned RA), 1946-48. MP (C) Swansea, West Division, Oct. 1959-64; PPS to Parliamentary Sec. for Housing and Local Govt and to Minister of State, Board of Trade, 1961; Assistant Government Whip, 1962-64. UK Rep., Econ. and Soc. Cttee, EEC, 1973-. Mem., Welsh Lang. Council. Governor, Nat, Mus. of Wales. FRICS, FAI, FRVA. *Address:* Sherwood, 35 Caswell Road, Newton, Mumbles, Swansea, W Glamorgan.

REES, Very Rev. John Ivor; Dean of Bangor, since 1976; *b* 19 Feb. 1926; *o s* of David Morgan Rees and Cecilia Perrott Rees; *m* 1954, Beverley Richards; three *s. Educ:* Llanelli Gram. Sch.; University Coll. of Wales (BA 1950); Westcott House, Cambridge. Served RN, Coastal Forces and British Pacific Fleet, 1943-47. Deacon 1952, priest 1953, Dio. St David's; Curate: Fishguard, 1952-55; Llangathen, 1955-57; Priest-in-Charge, Uzmaston, 1957-59; Vicar: Slebech and Uzmaston, 1959-65; Llangollen, 1965-74; Rural Dean of Llangollen, 1970-74; Rector of Wrexham, 1974-76; Canon of St Asaph, 1975-76; Chaplain, Order of St John for County of Clwyd, 1974-76, County of Gwynedd, 1976-. SBStJ 1975. *Publication:* Monograph—The Parish of Llangollen and its Churches, 1971. *Recreations:* music and good light reading. *Address:* The Deanery, Bangor, Gwynedd LL57 1LH. *T:* Bangor 51693.

REES, Rev. Canon Leslie Lloyd; Chaplain General of Prisons, Home Office Prison Department, since 1962; Chaplain to the Queen, since 1971; *b* 14 April 1919; *s* of Rees Thomas and Elizabeth Rees; *m* 1944, Rosamond Smith; two *s. Educ:* Pontardawe Grammar Sch.; Kelham Theological College. Asst Curate, St Saviour, Roath, 1942; Asst Chaplain, HM Prison, Cardiff, 1942; Chaplain, HM Prison: Durham, 1945; Dartmoor, 1948; Vicar of Princetown, 1948; Chaplain, HM Prison, Winchester, 1955. Hon. Canon of Canterbury, 1966-. Freeman, City of London. *Recreations:* music, brass bands. *Address:* 18 Hubert Road, St Cross, Winchester, Hants. *T:* (home) Winchester 4064 (office) 01-828 9848.

REES, Llewellyn; *see* Rees, (Walter) L.

REES, Prof. Martin John; Plumian Professor of Astronomy and Experimental Philosophy, Cambridge University, since 1973; Fellow of King's College, since 1973 (and 1969-72); Director, Institute of Astronomy, since 1977; *b* 23 June 1942; *s* of Reginald J. and Joan Rees. *Educ:* Shrewsbury Sch.; Trinity Coll., Cambridge (Exhibnr and Sen. Schol.). MA, PhD (Cantab). Research Fellow, Jesus Coll., Cambridge, 1967-69; Research Associate, California Inst. of Technology, 1967-68 and 1971; Mem., Inst. for Advanced Study, Princeton, 1969-70; Visiting Prof., Harvard Univ., 1972; Prof., Univ. of Sussex,

1972-73. For. Hon. Mem., Amer. Acad. of Arts and Sciences, 1975. *Publications:* mainly articles and reviews in scientific jls. *Address:* c/o King's College, Cambridge. *T:* Cambridge 50411; (office) Cambridge 62204.

REES, Rt. Hon. Merlyn, PC 1974; MP (Lab) South Leeds since June 1963; Home Secretary, since 1976; *b* Cilfynydd, South Wales, 18 Dec. 1920; *s* of late L. D. and E. M. Rees; *m* 1949, Colleen Faith (*née* Cleveley); three *s. Educ:* Elementary Schools, S Wales and Wembley, Middx; Harrow Weald Grammar School; Goldsmiths' Coll., Univ. of London; London School of Economics; London Univ. Institute of Education. Nottingham Univ. Air Sqdn; Served RAF, 1941-46; demobilised as Sqdn Ldr. Teacher in Economics and History, Harrow Weald Grammar School, 1949-60. Organised Festival of Labour, 1960-62. Lecturer in Economics, Luton Coll. of Technology, 1962-63; contested (Lab) Harrow East, Gen. Elections 1955 and 1959 and by-election, 1959; PPS to Chancellor of the Exchequer, 1964; Parly Under-Sec. of State, MoD (Army), 1965-66; MoD (RAF), 1966-68; Home Office, 1968-70; Mem., Shadow Cabinet, 1972-74; Opposition spokesman on NI affairs, 1972-74; Sec. of State for NI, 1974-76. Mem., Cttee to examine operation of Section 2 of Official Secrets Act, 1971. *Publication:* The Public Sector in the Mixed Economy, 1973. *Recreation:* reading. *Address:* House of Commons, SW1. *Club:* Reform.

REES, (Morgan) Goronwy; *b* 29 Nov. 1909; *yr s* of Rev. Richard Jenkyn Rees and Apphia Mary James; *m* 1940, Margaret Ewing Morris; three *s* two *d. Educ:* High School for Boys, Cardiff; New Coll., Oxford. Fellow of All Souls, 1931; Leader Writer, The Manchester Guardian, 1932; Asst Editor, The Spectator, 1936. War of 1939-45: Gunner, 90 Field Regt RA, 1939; commissioned Royal Welch Fusiliers, 1940. Director of a firm of general engineers and coppersmiths, 1946. Estates Bursar, All Souls College, Oxford, 1951. Principal, University College of Wales, Aberystwyth, 1953-57. *Publications:* The Multi-Millionaires: Six Studies in Wealth, 1961; The Rhine; St Michael: a history of Marks & Spencer, 1969; A Chapter of Accidents, 1972; Brief Encounters, 1974; *novels:* A Summer Flood, 1932; A Bridge to Divide Them, 1937; Where No Wounds Were; *translations:* (with Stephen Spender) Danton's Death, by Georg Büchner, 1939; Conversations with Kafka, 1939, new edn, 1971; *reminiscences:* A Bundle of Sensations, 1960; The Great Slump, 1970; (ed) McVicar By Himself, 1974. *Address:* 40 Pyrmont Road, Strand-on-the-Green, W4. *T:* 01-994 0855.

REES, Peter Magnall; Under-Secretary, Department of Industry, since 1974; *b* 17 March 1921; *s* of late Edward Saunders Rees and of Gertrude Rees (*née* Magnall); *m* 1949, Moya Mildred Carroll. *Educ:* Manchester Grammar Sch.; Jesus Coll., Oxford. Served War, RA, 1941-46 (SE Asia, 1942-45). HM Overseas Service, Nigeria, 1948; Dep. Govt Statistician, Kenya, 1956; Dir of Economics and Statistics, Kenya, 1961; HM Treasury, 1964; Chief Statistician, 1966; Under-Sec., DTI later Dept of Industry, 1973-. *Publications:* articles in statistical jls. *Recreations:* choral singing, music, studying architecture. *Address:* Fiddlers Green, West Clandon, Guildford, Surrey GU4 7TL. *T:* Guildford 222311. *Club:* Royal Commonwealth Society.

REES, Peter Wynford Innes, QC 1969; MP (C) Dover and Deal, since 1974 (Dover, 1970-74); *b* 9 Dec. 1926; *s* of late Maj.-Gen. T. W. Rees, Indian Army, Goytre Hall, Abergavenny; *m* 1969, Mrs Anthea Wendell, *d* of Major H. J. M. Hyslop, late Argyll and Sutherland Highlanders. *Educ:* Stowe; Christ Church, Oxford. Served Scots Guards, 1945-48. Called to the Bar, 1953, Bencher, Inner Temple, 1976; Oxford Circuit. Contested (C): Abertillery, 1964 and 1965; Liverpool, West Derby, 1966. PPS to Solicitor General, 1972. *Address:* 39 Headfort Place, SW1; Goytre Hall, Abergavenny, Gwent; 5 Church Street, St Clement's, Sandwich, Kent. *Club:* Boodle's.

REES, Richard Geraint; His Honour Judge Geraint Rees; a Circuit Judge (formerly Deputy Chairman, Inner London Sessions), since 1971; *b* 5 May 1907; *s* of Rev. Richard Jenkyn Rees, MA, and Apphia Mary Rees, Aberystwyth; *m* 1st, 1938, Mary Davies; one *s*; 2nd, 1950, Margaret Grotrian; one *d. Educ:* Cardiff High School; University College of Wales, Aberystwyth; St John's College, Cambridge. LLB 1st Cl. Hons, University Coll. of Wales, 1929, BA 1st Cl. Parts I and II Law Tripos, 1930 and 1931; Barrister, Inner Temple, 1932 (Certificate of Honour). Practised on S Wales Circuit, 1934-39. Commissioned Welsh Guards, Nov. 1939; DAAG London Dist, 1943-44; Assistant Director Army Welfare Services, Lt-Col, British Army Staff, Paris, 1944-45; Despatches, Bronze Star (USA), 1946. Practised in London and on Wales and Chester Circuit, 1946-56; Metropolitan Stipendiary Magistrate, 1956-71. *Recreation:* gardening. *Address:* Fellside, 23 Heath Road, Weybridge, Surrey. *T:* Weybridge 42230.

REES, Hon. Sir Stanley; *see* Rees, Hon. Sir C. W. S.

REES, (Thomas Morgan) Haydn, CBE 1975; DL; Chairman, Welsh National Water Development Authority, since 1977; Member: National Water Council, since 1977; Water Space Amenity Commission, since 1977; *b* 22 May 1915; *y s* of late Thomas Rees and Mary Rees, Gorseinon, Swansea; *m* 1941, Marion, *y d* of A. B. Beer, Mumbles, Swansea; one *d. Educ:* Swansea Business Coll. Served War, 1939-45. Admitted solicitor, 1946; Sen. Asst Solicitor, Caernarvonshire CC, 1947; Flints County Council, 1948-65: Dep. Clerk, Dep. Clerk of the Peace, Police Authority, Magistrates Courts Cttee, and of Probation Cttee; 1966-74: Chief Exec.; Clerk of Peace (until office abolished, 1971); Clerk, Flints Police Authority (until merger with N Wales Police Authority, 1967); Clerk of Probation, Magistrates Courts, and of Justices Adv. Cttees; Clerk to Lieutenancy; Chief Exec., Clwydd CC, and Clerk, Magistrates Courts Cttee, 1974-77; Clerk to Lieutenance and of Justices Adv. Cttee, Clwyd, 1974-77. Clerk: N Wales Police Authority, 1967-77; Theatr Clwyd Governors, 1974-77. Secretary: Welsh Counties Cttee, 1968-77; (Corresp.) Rep. Body (Ombudsman) Cttee for Wales, 1974-77. Asst Comr, Royal Commn on Constitution, 1969-73. Chm., New Jobs Team, Shotton Steelworks, 1977-; Vice-Chm., N Wales Arts Assoc. Member: Lord Chancellor's Circuit Cttee for Wales and Chester Circuit, 1972-77; Welsh Council; Welsh Arts Council; Gorsedd, Royal National Eisteddfod for Wales; Prince of Wales Cttee. Vice-Pres., Inst. of Dirs, Wales Branch. DL Flints 1969, Clwyd 1974. *Recreations:* the arts, golf. *Address:* Cefn Bryn, Gwernaffield Road, Mold, Clwyd CH7 1RQ. *T:* Mold 2421. *Clubs:* National Liberal, Number Ten; Mold Golf.

REES, (Walter) Llewellyn, MA; Actor and Theatre Administrator; Director, Travelling Playhouse Ltd; Honorary President of International Theatre Institute since 1951; *b* 18 June 1901; *s* of Walter Francis Rees and Mary Gwendoline Naden; *m* 1961, Madeleine Newbury; one *s* one *d. Educ:* King Edward's School, Birmingham; Keble College, Oxford. Private Tutor, 1923-26; studied at RADA, 1926-28; Actor, 1928-40; Gen. Sec. of British Actors' Equity Assoc., 1940-46; Jt Secretary: London Theatre Council, 1940-46, Prov. Theatre Council, 1942-46; Sec. of Fed. of Theatre Unions, 1944-46; Governor of the Old Vic, 1945-47; Drama Director, Arts Council of Great Britain, 1947-49; Administrator of the Old Vic, 1949-51; Administrator of Arts Theatre, 1951-52; General Administrator, Donald Wolfit's Company, 1952-58; Chairman Executive Committee of International Theatre Institute, 1948-51; Hon. Counsellor to Council of Repertory Theatres, 1951-. Returned to West End Stage, 1956, as Bishop of Buenos Aires in The Strong are Lonely, Theatre Royal, Haymarket; Olmeda in The Master of Santiago, Lyric Theatre, Hammersmith, 1957; Polonius in Hamlet, Bristol Old Vic, 1958; Dean of College in My Friend Judas, Arts Theatre, 1959; Mr Brandy in Settled out of Court, Strand Theatre, 1960-61; Justice Worthy in Lock Up Your Daughters, Mermaid Theatre and Her Majesty's, 1962-63; Sir Henry James in the Right Honourable Gentleman, Her Majesty's, 1964-65; Father Ambrose in The Servants and the Snow, Greenwich, 1970; Duncan in Macbeth, Greenwich, 1971. Many film and television appearances. *Recreation:* travel. *Address:* 30 Ullswater Road, Barnes, SW13 9PN.

REES, Professor William; Emeritus Professor of the History of Wales and Head of Department of History at University College, Cardiff; *b* 14 Dec. 1887; *s* of Daniel and Margaret Rees; *m* 1914, Agnes Price; no *c. Educ:* Brecon County School; Univ. Coll., Cardiff; LSE, University of London. BA Hons (Wales), 1909; MA (Wales), 1914; DScEcon (London), 1920; Hon. DLitt (Wales), 1969; FSA; FRHistS; formerly Vice-Principal and Mem. of Council; formerly Fellow of Univ. of Wales and Prof. of the History of Wales and Head of the Department of History, University College, Cardiff; O'Donnell Lecturer in Celtic Studies, Univ. of Wales, 1957 and Univ. of Oxford, 1959-60; President: Cambrian Archæological Assoc., 1960-61; Cardiff Naturalists' Soc., 1949-50; Member Acad. Bd and Board of Celtic Studies, University of Wales; former Mem. Ancient Monuments Board for Wales; Member of Court and Council: National Museum of Wales; Welsh Folk Museum; Mem. Court, Nat. Library of Wales; Editor S Wales and Monmouth Record Soc.; Mem. various Editorial Boards; former Mem. Exec., Standing Conference of Local History. Chairman Exec., Welsh National Council of UNA, 1945-56. Mem., UNESCO Nat. Co-operating Body for the Social Sciences, 1952-62. KStJ 1963. *Publications:* South Wales and the March, a Social and Agrarian Study, 1924, repr. 1974; The Making of Europe; Historical Map of South Wales and the Border in the Fourteenth Century, 1933; An Historical Atlas of Wales, 1951, repr. 1972; Caerphilly Castle (repr. 1974); The Union of England and Wales; The Order of St John of Jerusalem; The Charters of Newport (Mon),

The Duchy of Lancaster Lordships in Wales, 1954; A Breviat of Glamorgan, 1954; Cardiff, A History of the City, 1962, repr. 1969; Survivals of Ancient Celtic Custom in Mediæval England, in, Angles and Britons, 1963; The Black Death in Wales, in, Essays in Mediæval History, 1968; Industry before the Industrial Revolution, 2 vols, 1968; Ancient Petitions relating to Wales, 1975; contributor to Dictionary of National Biography, Encyclopædia Britannica, Encyclopedia Americana, and Chambers's Encyclopædia; numerous papers, cartographical and bibliographical studies. List of published works in Mediæval Lordship of Brecon, Brecknock Museum, Brecon, 1968. *Address:* 2 Park Road, Penarth, S Glam CF6 2BD. *T:* Penarth 701465.

REES, William Linford Llewelyn, FRCP; PRCPsych; Professor of Psychiatry, St Bartholomew's Hospital Medical College, University of London, since 1966; Physician in charge of Department of Psychological Medicine, St Bartholomew's Hospital, since 1959; Lecturer in Psychological Medicine, St Bartholomew's Medical College, since 1958; Recognised Clinical Teacher in Mental Diseases, Institute of Psychiatry, University of London, since 1956; Chairman, University of London Teachers of Psychiatry Committee; *b* 24 Oct. 1914; *e s* of late Edward Parry Rees and Mary Rees, Llanelly, Carmathenshire; *m* 1940, Catherine, *y d* of late David Thomas, and of Angharad Thomas, Alltwen, Glam; two *s* two *d. Educ:* Llanelly Grammar School; University Coll., Cardiff; Welsh Nat. Sch. of Medicine; The Maudsley Hosp.; Univ. of London. BSc 1935; MB, BCh 1938; DPM 1940; MRCP 1942; MD 1943; FRCP 1950; FRCPsych 1971 (Pres., 1975-). David Hepburn Medal and Alfred Hughes Medal in Anatomy, 1935; John Maclean Medal and Prize in Obstetrics and Gynaecology, 1937, etc. Specialist, EMS, 1942; Dep. Med. Supt, Mill Hill Emergency Hosp., 1945; Asst Physician and Postgrad. Teacher in Clinical Psychiatry, The Maudsley Hosp., 1946; Dep. Physician Supt, Whitchurch Hosp., 1947; Regional Psychiatrist for Wales and Mon, 1948; Consultant Physician, The Bethlem Royal Hosp. and The Maudsley Hosp., 1954-66. Civilian Advisor in Psychiatry to RAF. WHO Consultant to Sri Lanka, 1973. Hon. Consultant, Royal Sch. for Deaf Children. Lectures to Univs and Learned Socs in Europe, USA, Asia, Australia and S America. Examiner: Diploma Psychological Medicine, RCP, 1964-69; MRCP, RCP, RCPE and RCPGlas, 1969-; MB and DPM, Univ. of Leeds, 1969-. President: Soc. for Psychosomatic Research, 1957-58; BMA, 1978-. Vice-President: Section of Psychiatry, RSM, 1968 (Pres. 1971-72); Royal Coll. of Psychiatrists, 1972-75 (Chm., E Anglian Region). Treasurer, World Psychiatric Assoc., 1966-. Member: Clinical Psychiatry Cttee, MRC, 1959-; Council, Royal Medio-Psychological Assoc. (Chm., Research and Clinical Section, 1957-63); Soc. for Study of Human Biology; Asthma Research Council; Cttee on Safety of Medicines (also Toxicity and Clinical Trials Sub-Cttee), 1971-; Psychological Medicine Group, BMA, 1967-; Bd of Advanced Med. Studies, Univ. of London, 1966-69; Higher Degrees Cttee, Univ. of London; Acad. Council Standing Sub-Cttee in Medicine, Univ. of London; Cttee of Management, Inst. of Psychiatry, Maudsley Hosp., 1968-; Council and Exec. Cttee, St Bartholomew's Hosp. Med. Coll., 1972-; Jt Policy Cttee, QMC, St Bartholomew's Hosp. and London Hosp., 1973-; Cttee on Review of Medicines (Chm., Psychotropic Drugs Sub-Cttee); Central Health Services Council; Standing Medical Adv. Cttee; Jt Consultants Cttee; Conference of Presidents of Royal Colls. Founder Mem., Internat. Coll. of Neuro-psychopharmacology. Hon. Mem. Learned Socs in USA, Sweden, Venezuela, East Germany and Australia. FRSM; Fellow: Eugenics Soc.; and Vice-Pres., Internat. Coll. of Psychosomatic Medicine, 1973; Distinguished Fellow, Amer. Psychiatric Assoc., 1968; Hon. Fellow: Eastern Psychoanalytic Assoc., USA; Amer. Coll. Psychiatrists; Hon. Mem., Biological Psychiatry Assoc., USA. Governor, The Bethlem Royal Hosp. and The Maudsley Hosp. Co-Editor, Jl of Psychosomatic Research. Liveryman: Barber Surgeons; Apothecaries. *Publications:* (with Eysenck and Himmelweit) Dimensions of Personality, 1947; Short Textbook of Psychiatry, 1967. Chapters in: Modern Treatment in General Practice, 1947; Recent Progress in Psychiatry, 1950; Schizophrenia: Somatic Aspects, 1957; Psychoendocrinology, 1958; Recent Progress in Psychosomatic Research, 1960; Stress and Psychiatric Disorders, 1960. Papers in: Nature, BMJ, Jl of Mental Sci., Jl of Psychosomatic Research, Eugenics Review, etc. Contribs to Med. Annual, 1958-68. *Recreations:* swimming, photography, amusing grandchildren. *Address:* Penbryn, 62 Oakwood Avenue, Purley, Surrey. *T:* 01-660 8575. *Club:* Athenæum.

REES-DAVIES, William Rupert, QC 1973; MP (C) Thanet West, since 1974 (Isle of Thanet, March 1953-1974); Barrister-at-law; *b* 19 Nov. 1916; *o s* of late Sir William Rees-Davies, KC, DL, JP, formerly Chief Justice of Hong Kong and Liberal MP for Pembroke and of late Lady Rees-Davies; *m* 1959, Jane, *d* of Mr and Mrs Henry Mander; two *d. Educ:* Eton; Trinity Coll., Cambridge; Eton Soc., Eton XI, 1934-35; Eton Victor Ludorum; Cambridge Cricket XI, 1938; Honours in History and Law. Called to Bar, Inner Temple, 1939. Commissioned HM Welsh Guards, 1939; served War of 1939-45 (discharged disabled with loss of arm, 1943). Contested (C) South Nottingham in 1950 and 1951. Chm., British-Greek Parly Gp. *Recreations:* collecting pictures and antiques. *Address:* 6 Victoria Square, SW1. *T:* 01-828 3357. *Clubs:* MCC; Hawks, University Pitt (Cambridge).

REES-JONES, Geoffrey Rippon, MA Oxon; Principal, King William's College, Isle of Man, since 1958; *b* 8 July 1914; *er s* of W. Rees-Jones, BA, Ipswich; *m* 1950, Unity Margaret McConnell, *d* of Major P. M. Sanders, Hampstead; one *s* one *d. Educ:* Ipswich School (scholar); University College, Oxford (open scholar). Assistant Master, Eastbourne College, 1936-38, Marlborough College, 1938-54 (Housemaster, C2, 1946-54); Headmaster, Bembridge School, 1954-58; served War mainly in Commandos, 1940-45; Commandant, Commando Mountain Warfare School, 1943; Staff College, Camberley, 1944 (sc); Brigade Major, 4 Commando Bde, 1944-45 (despatches). *Recreations:* sailing, cricket, golf, fives; Oxford Rugby 'blue', 1933-35, Wales XV, 1934-36. *Address:* King William's College, Isle of Man. *T:* Castletown 2551.

REES-MOGG, William; Editor of The Times since 1967; Director of The Times Ltd, since 1968; Member, Executive Board, Times Newspapers Ltd, since 1968; *b* 14 July 1928; *s* of late Edmund Fletcher Rees-Mogg and Beatrice Rees-Mogg (*née* Warren), Temple Cloud, Somerset; *m* 1962, Gillian Shakespeare Morris, *d* of T. R. Morris; two *s* two *d. Educ:* Charterhouse; Balliol Coll., Oxford (Brackenbury Scholar). President, Oxford Union, 1951. Financial Times, 1952-60, Chief Leader Writer, 1955-60; Asst Editor, 1957-60; Sunday Times, City Editor, 1960-61; Political and Economic Editor, 1961-63; Deputy Editor, 1964-67. Contested (C) Chester-le-Street, Co. Durham, By-election 1956; General Election, 1959. Treasurer, Institute of Journalists, 1960-63, 1966-68, Pres., 1963-64; Vice-Chm. Cons. Party's Nat. Advisory Cttee on Political Education, 1961-63. Vis. Fellow, Nuffield Coll., Oxford, 1968-72. Hon. LLD Bath, 1977. *Publications:* The Reigning Error: the crisis of world inflation, 1974; An Humbler Heaven, 1977. *Recreation:* book collecting. *Address:* 3 Smith Square, SW1; Ston Easton Park, near Bath. *Club:* Garrick.

REES-REYNOLDS, Col Alan Randall, CBE 1945; TD; DL; company director; *b* 24 Feb. 1909; *yr s* of Charles and Adelaide Rees-Reynolds, Woking; *m* 1936, Ruth, *y d* of late Frederick and Anne Hardy, Fittleworth; one *d* (and one *s* decd). *Educ:* Sherborne. Solicitor, 1931. HAC, 1928-31, rejoined 1938; commnd 2nd Lieut 2/5 Queens Royal Regt TA, 1939; Middle East, Western Desert, Libya, Egypt and Italy, 1940-45; Lt-Col 1942; Col 1944; Dep. Provost Marshal British Troops in Egypt, 1942-43; Provost Marshal Allied Armies in Italy, 1943-44 and Central Mediterranean Forces, 1944-45 (despatches 1944). Partner, Joynson-Hicks & Co., until 1965; Exec. Dep. Chm., Pollard Bearings Ltd, 1965-70. Mem. Court, Univ. of Surrey. Deputy and Under Sheriff of Surrey, 1956-66, High Sheriff 1970; DL Surrey, 1970. Hon. Deputy Sheriff Middlesex County, Massachusetts, 1969-. Governor, St Catherine's Sch., Bramley; Mem. Council, Cranleigh and Bramley Schs. *Recreations:* people, working for the tax gatherer, shooting, fishing. *Address:* Priors Gate, Godalming, Surrey. *T:* Guildford 810391. *Clubs:* Boodle's, Garrick.

REES-THOMAS, William, CB 1950; MD (London); FRCP (England); DPM (Cantab); Medical Senior Commissioner Board of Control, 1932, retired; *b* Bailea, Senny, Breconshire, S Wales, 15 June 1887; *m* 1st, 1917, Muriel (*decd*), *o d* of Rev. F. Hodgson Jones; one *s* one *d*; 2nd, 1948, Ruth Darwin, CBE (*d* 1972). *Educ:* County School, Brecon; Cardiff University; Charing Cross Hospital. MB, BS (hons) London, 1909; MD (London), 1910; MRCP 1913; FRCP, 1933; DPM (Cantab), 1914; Alfred Sheen Prize, 1906; Alfred Hughes Memorial Medal, 1907; Llewelyn Prize, 1909; Murchison Scholar (RCP), 1912; Gaskell Prize and Gold Medal, 1913; Certificate Psychiatry Royal Medico Psychological Association; Distinguished Psychiatry RCP; Fellow Royal Society of Medicine; Member BMA and Royal Medico-Psychological Association; late House Physician Charing Cross Hospital; Deputy Superintendent East Sussex Mental Hospital; Medical Superintendent Rampton State Institution; KHP, 1944-47. *Publications:* various. *Recreations:* golf, photography. *Address:* 20 Haleswood, Four Wents, Cobham, Surrey. *T:* Cobham 2240.

REES-WILLIAMS, family name of **Baron Ogmore.**

REESE, Surg. Rear-Adm. John Mansel, CB 1962; OBE 1953; *b* 3 July 1906; *s* of late Dr D. W. Reese, and late Mrs A. M. Reese; *m* 1946, Beryl (*née* Dunn) (*d* 1973); two *d* (and one *s* decd). *Educ:* Epsom Coll.; St Mary's Hosp. Med. Sch., London University. MRCS, LRCP 1930; DPH 1934. Entered Royal Navy, Jan. 1931; Naval Medical Officer of Health, Orkney and Shetland Comd, 1942-44; Naval MOH, Ceylon, 1944-46; Admiralty, 1947-53; Medical Officer-in-Charge RN Hospital, Plymouth, 1960-63; QHP 1960-63. Surgeon Comdr, 1943; Surgeon Captain, 1954; Surgeon Rear-Adm., 1960; retd 1963. FRSTM&H. Sir Gilbert Blane Gold Medal, 1939. Member Gray's Inn, 1953. CStJ 1961. *Address:* c/o Lloyds Bank Ltd, 263 Tottenham Court Road, W1.

REESE, (John) Terence; bridge expert, author and journalist; *b* 28 Aug. 1913; *s* of John and Anne Reese; *m* 1970, Alwyn Sherrington. *Educ:* Bilton Grange; Bradfield Coll. (top scholar); New Coll., Oxford (top class. scholar). Worked at Harrods, 1935-36; left to follow career as bridge expert and journalist. Edited various bridge magazines, became bridge correspondent of the Evening News, 1948 and of the Observer, 1950. Winner of numerous British, European and World Championships. *Publications:* The Elements of Contract, 1938; Reese on Play, 1948; The Expert Game, 1958; Play Bridge with Reese, 1960; Story of an Accusation, 1966; Precision Bidding and Precision Play, 1972; Play These Hands With Me, 1976; Bridge at the Top (autobiog.), 1977; *with Albert Dormer:* The Acol System Today, 1961; The Play of the Cards, 1967; Bridge for Tournament Players, 1969; The Complete Book of Bridge, 1973; and many others. *Recreations:* golf, snooker, backgammon. *Address:* 18a Woods Mews, Park Lane, W1. *T:* 01-629 5553. *Clubs:* Clermont, Crockford's, Eccentric; Berkshire Golf.

REEVE, Rt. Rev. (Arthur) Stretton, DD (Lambeth), 1953; DD (Leeds), 1956; *b* 11 June 1907; *s* of Rev. Arthur and Mrs Violet Inez Reeve; *m* 1936, Flora Montgomerie (*née* McNeill); one *s* two *d*. *Educ:* Brighton Coll. (Exhibitioner); Selwyn Coll., Cambridge (Scholar); Westcott House, Cambridge, 1st class Theological Tripos, 1928, 2nd class Theological Tripos, 1929; BA 1929, MA 1933; rowed in Cambridge Univ. crew, 1930. Curate of Putney, 1930-32; Domestic Chaplain to Bishop of Winchester and Joint Hon. Secretary, Winchester Diocesan Council of Youth, 1932-36; Vicar of Highfield, Southampton, 1936-43; Vicar of Leeds, 1943-53; Rural Dean of Leeds, 1943-53; Proctor in Convocation for Diocese of Ripon, 1945-53; Hon. Canon of Ripon Cathedral, 1947-53; Chaplain to the Queen, 1952-53 (to King George VI, 1945-52); Bishop of Lichfield, 1953-74. Hon. Fellow, Selwyn Coll., Cambridge, 1955-; Hon. DLitt Keele, 1975. *Address:* 25 Huntington Green, Ashford Carbonell, Ludlow, Salop SY8 4DN. *T:* Richards Castle 209. *Club:* Leander (Henley on Thames).

REEVE, Hon. Sir (Charles) Trevor, Kt 1973; **Hon. Mr Justice Reeve;** a Judge of the High Court of Justice, Family Division, since 1973; *b* 4 July 1915; *o s* of William George Reeve and Elsie (*née* Bowring), Wokingham; *m* 1941, Marjorie, *d* of Charles Evelyn Browne, Eccles, Lancs. *Educ:* Winchester College; Trinity College, Oxford. Commissioned 10th Royal Hussars (PWO) 1940; served BEF, CMF (Major) 1940-44 (despatches); Staff College, Camberley, 1945. Called to Bar (Inner Temple), 1946; Bencher, 1965; QC 1965; Mem., Bar Council, 1950-54; County Court Judge, 1968; Circuit Judge, 1972. Mem., Appeals Tribunal for E Africa in respect of Commonwealth Immigration Act, 1968. *Recreations:* golf, dancing. *Address:* 95 Abingdon Road, Kensington, W8 6QU. *T:* 01-937 7530. *Clubs:* Garrick; Royal North Devon Golf (Westward Ho!); Sunningdale Golf.

REEVE, James Ernest; HM Diplomatic Service; Consul-General, Zürich and Principality of Liechtenstein, since 1975; *b* 8 June 1926; *s* of Ernest and Anthea Reeve; *m* 1947, Lillian Irene Watkins; one *s* one *d*. *Educ:* Bishops Stortford Coll. Vice-Consul, Ahwaz and Khorramshahr, Iran, 1949-51; UN General Assembly, Paris, 1951; Asst Private Sec. to Rt Hon. Selwyn Lloyd, Foreign Office, 1951-53; 2nd Secretary: Brit. Embassy, Washington, 1953-57; Brit. Embassy, Bangkok, 1957-59; FO, 1959-61; HM Consul, Frankfurt, 1961-65; 1st Secretary: Brit. Embassy in Libya, 1965-69; Brit. Embassy, Budapest, 1970-72; Chargé d'Affaires, Budapest, 1972; Counsellor (Commercial), East Berlin, 1973-75. *Recreations:* theatre, tennis, travel. *Address:* c/o Foreign and Commonwealth Office, SW1; 20 Glenmore House, Richmond Hill, Surrey. *T:* 01-940 4781. *Club:* Royal Automobile.

REEVE, Major-General John Talbot Wentworth, CB 1946; CBE 1941; DSO 1919; *b* 1891; *e s* of Charles Sydney Wentworth Reeve; *m* 1st, 1919, Sybil Alice (*d* 1949), 4th *d* of Sir George Agnew, 2nd Bt; one *d* (one *s* killed in North Africa, June 1942); 2nd, 1950, Mrs Marjorie Frances Wagstaff (*see* Mrs M. F.

Reeve). *Educ:* Eton; Royal Military College, Sandhurst. Served European War, 1914-19 (despatches, DSO); commanded 1st Bn The Rifle Brigade, 1936-38; Commander Hong Kong Infantry Brigade, 1938-41; DAG Home Forces, 1942-43; Commander Sussex District, 1943-44; DAG, MEF, 1944-46; retd pay, 1946. *Address:* Livermere Lodge, near Bury St Edmunds, Suffolk. *T:* Honington 376. *Club:* Army and Navy.

REEVE, Mrs Marjorie Frances Wentworth, CBE 1944; TD 1950; JP; *d* of late Charles Fry, Bedford; *m* 1st, Lieutenant-Commander J. K. Laughton, Royal Navy (*d* 1925); one *s*; 2nd, Major-General C. M. Wagstaff, CB, CMG, CIE, DSO (*d* 1934); 3rd, 1950, Major-General J. T. Wentworth Reeve, *qv*. Joined ATS, 1938; served with BEF, and in Middle East and BAOR; late Controller ATS. Was i/c Public Welfare Section of Control Commission for Germany (BE); Principal in Board of Trade (Overseas) till 1950; Swedish Red Cross Medal in Silver, 1950; County Director, BRCS, 1953-57; Dep. Pres. Suffolk BRCS, 1957, Hon. Vice-Pres., 1977. Badge of Honour (2nd Class) BRCS, 1970. JP (W Suffolk), 1954. *Address:* Livermere Lodge, near Bury St Edmunds, Suffolk. *T:* Honington 376. *Club:* Army and Navy.

REEVE, Rt. Rev. Stretton; *see* Reeve, Rt Rev. A. S.

REEVE, Hon. Sir Trevor; *see* Reeve, Hon. Sir C. T.

REEVES, Rt. Rev. Ambrose; *see* Reeves, Rt Rev. R. A.

REEVES, James, MA; FRSL; free-lance author, editor and broadcaster since 1952; *b* 1 July 1909; *er s* of Albert John and Ethel Mary Reeves; *m* 1936, Mary (*née* Phillips) (*d* 1966); one *s* two *d*. *Educ:* Stowe; Cambridge. Schoolmaster and lectr in teachers' training colleges, 1933-52. *Publications:* The Wandering Moon, 1950; The Blackbird in the Lilac, 1952; English Fables and Fairy Stories, 1954; Pigeons and Princesses, 1956; The Critical Sense, 1956; Prefabulous Animiles, 1957; Mulbridge Manor, 1958; Teaching Poetry, 1958; The Idiom of the People, 1958; Exploits of Don Quixote, 1959; The Everlasting Circle, 1960; Collected Poems, 1960; A Short History of English Poetry, 1961; Ragged Robin, 1961, repr. 1972; Fables from Æsop, 1961; (ed) A Golden Land, 1958; (ed) Great English Essays, 1961; (ed) Penguin Book of Georgian Poetry, 1962; Sailor Rumbelow and Britannia, 1962; The Strange Light, 1964; Three Tall Tales, 1964; The Questioning Tiger (poems), 1964; The Pillar-Box Thieves, 1965; Understanding Poetry, 1965; (ed) Cassell Book of English Poetry, 1965; The Road to a Kingdom, 1965; The Secret Shoemakers, 1966; Selected Poems, 1967; The Cold Flame, 1967; (ed jtly) A New Canon of English Poetry, 1967; Rhyming Will, 1967; (ed jtly) Homage to Trumbull Stickney, 1968; The Trojan Horse, 1968; (ed) The Christmas Book, 1968, repr. 1972; (ed) One's None, 1968; Subsong, 1969; Poems, 1969; Commitment to Poetry, 1969; Heroes and Monsters, 1969; The Angel and the Donkey, 1969; Mr Horrox and the Gratch, 1969; (ed) The Poets and Their Critics, Vol. III, 1969; (ed jtly) Selected Poems of Andrew Marvell, 1969; (jtly) Inside Poetry, 1970; (ed) Chaucer: lyric and allegory, 1970; Maeldun the Voyager, 1971; How to Write Poems for Children, 1971; How the Moon Began, 1971; The Path of Gold, 1972; Poems and Paraphrases, 1972; (ed) Complete English Poems of Thomas Gray, 1973; (ed) A Vein of Mockery, 1973; The Voyage of Odysseus, 1973; The Forbidden Forest, 1973; Complete Poems for Children, 1973; The Lion That Flew, 1974; Collected Poems 1929-1974, 1974; Two Greedy Bears, 1974; (ed) Five Late Romantic Poets, 1974; More Prefabulous Animiles, 1975; The Shadow of the Hawk, 1975; The Reputation and Writing of Alexander Pope, 1976; The Springtime Book, 1976; The Ballad, 1976; The Clever Mouse, 1976; Quest and Conquest, 1976; Arcadian Ballads, 1977; The Autumn Book, 1977. *Recreations:* music, Venice. *Address:* Flints, Rotten Row, Lewes, East Sussex. *T:* Lewes 2579.

REEVES, Marjorie Ethel, MA (Oxon), PhD (London), DLitt (Oxon); FRHistS; FBA 1974; Vice-Principal, St Anne's College, Oxford, 1951-62, 1964-67; *b* 17 July 1905; *d* of Robert J. W. Reeves and Edith Saffery Whitaker. *Educ:* The High School for Girls, Trowbridge, Wilts; St Hugh's Coll., Oxford; Westfield Coll., London. Asst Mistress, Roan School, Greenwich, 1927-29; Research Fellow, Westfield Coll., London, 1929-31; Lecturer, St Gabriel's Trng Coll., London, 1931-38; Tutor, later Fellow of St Anne's College, 1938-72, Hon. Fellow, 1973. Member: Central Advisory Council, Min. of Educn, 1947-61; Academic Planning Bd, Univ. of Kent; Academic Advisory Cttee, University of Surrey; formerly Member: Educn Council, ITA; British Council of Churches; School Broadcasting Council. *Publications:* Growing Up in a Modern Society, 1946; (ed, with L. Tondelli, B. Hirsch-Reich) Il Libro delle Figure dell'Abate

Gioachino da Fiore, 1953; Three Questions in Higher Education (Hazen Foundation, USA), 1955; Moral Education in a Changing Society (ed W. Niblett), 1963; ed, Eighteen Plus: Unity and Diversity in Higher Education, 1965; The Influence of Prophecy in the later Middle Ages: a study in Joachimism, 1969; Higher Education: demand and response (ed W. R. Niblett), 1969; (with B. Hirsch-Reich) The Figurae of Joachim of Fiore, 1972; Joachim of Fiore and the Prophetic Future, 1976; Then and There Series: The Medieval Town, 1954, The Medieval Village, 1954, Elizabethan Court, 1956, The Medieval Monastery, 1957, The Norman Conquest, 1958, Alfred and the Danes, 1959; The Medieval Castle, 1960, Elizabethan Citizen, 1961; A Medieval King Governs, 1971; contributions on history in Speculum, Medieval and Renaissance Studies, Sophia, Recherches de Théologie, etc, and on education in Times Educational Supplement, New Era, etc. *Recreations:* music, gardening, bird-watching. *Address:* 38 Norham Road, Oxford. *T:* Oxford 57039. *Club:* University Women's.

REEVES, Rt. Rev. Paul Alfred; *see* Waiapu, Bishop of.

REEVES, Philip Thomas Langford, RSA 1976 (ARSA 1971); artist in etching and other mediums; Senior Lecturer, Glasgow School of Art, since 1973; *b* 7 July 1931; *s* of Herbert Reeves and Lilian; *m* 1964, Christine MacLaren; one *d*. *Educ:* Naunton Park Sch., Cheltenham. Student, Cheltenham Sch. of Art, 1947-49. Army service, 4th/7th Royal Dragoon Guards, Middle East, 1949-51. RCA, 1951-54 (ARCA 1st Cl.); Lectr, Glasgow Sch. of Art, 1954-73. Associate, Royal Soc. of Painter Etchers, 1954, Fellow 1964; RSW 1962. Works in permanent collections: Arts Council; Gall. of Modern Art, Edinburgh; Glasgow Art Gall.; Glasgow Univ. Print Collection; Manchester City Art Gall.; Royal Scottish Acad.; Aberdeen Art Gall.; Paisley Art Gall.; Inverness Art Gall.; Milngavie Art Gall.; Dept of the Environment. *Recreation:* walking. *Address:* 13 Hamilton Drive, Glasgow G12 8DN. *Club:* Traverse (Edinburgh).

.. **REEVES, Rt. Rev. (Richard) Ambrose;** Assistant Bishop in the Diocese of Chichester, since 1966; *b* 6 Dec. 1899; *m* 1931, Ada Margaret van Ryssen; one *s* two *d* (and one *s* decd). *Educ:* Sidney Sussex Coll., Cambridge. 2nd class Historical Tripos, Part I, 1923, BA (2nd class Moral Science Tripos, Part II), 1924, MA 1943. College of the Resurrection, Mirfield, 1924; Gen. Th. Seminary, New York, 1926. Deacon, 1926; Priest, 1927; Curate of St Albans, Golders Green, 1926-31; Rector of St Margaret, Leven, 1931-35; licensed to officiate in the Diocese of Gibraltar and permission to officiate in the Diocese of London (N and C Eur.), 1935-37; Vicar of St James Haydock, 1937-42; Rector of St Nicholas City and Dio. Liverpool, 1942-49; Canon of Liverpool Cathedral, 1944-49; Proctor in Convocation, Liverpool, 1945-49; Bishop of Johannesburg, 1949-61; Assistant Bishop of London, 1962-66; Priest in Charge of St Michael's, Lewes, 1966-68, Rector, 1968-72. General Secretary, Student Christian Movement of Great Britain and Ireland, 1962-65; Secretary, World Student Christian Federation, Geneva, 1935-37. Sub-Prelate Ven. Order of St John of Jerusalem, 1953; STD, Theological Seminary, NY, 1954, Pres., Anti-Apartheid Movement, 1970-. Fellow, Ancient Monuments Soc., 1957; Hon. Fellow, Sidney Sussex Coll., Cambridge, 1960. Hon. DLitt Sussex, 1975. *Publications:* Shooting at Sharpeville: the Agony of South Africa, 1960; South Africa-Yesterday and Tomorrow, 1962; Let the facts speak (Christian Action), 1962; Calvary Now, 1965. *Address:* Whitefriars, Church Street, Shoreham-by-Sea, East Sussex BN4 5DQ. *T:* Shoreham 62555.

REFSHAUGE, Maj.-Gen. Sir William (Dudley), Kt 1966; CBE 1959 (OBE 1944); ED 1965; Secretary-General, World Medical Association, 1973-75; 3 April 1913; *s* of late F. C. Refshauge, Melbourne; *m* 1942, Helen Elizabeth, *d* of late R. E. Allwright, Tasmania; four *s* one *d*. *Educ:* Hampton High Sch.; Scotch Coll., Melbourne; Melbourne University. MB, BS (Melbourne) 1938; FRCOG 1961; FRACS 1962; FRACP 1963; Hon. FRSH 1967; FACMA 1967. Served with AIF, 1939-46; Lt-Col, RAAMC (despatches four times). Medical Supt, Royal Women's Hosp., Melbourne, 1948-51; Col, and Dep. DGAMS, Aust., 1951-55; Maj.-Gen., and DGAMS, Aust., 1955-60; QHP, 1955-64. Commonwealth Dir-Gen. of Health, Australia, 1960-73. Chairman: Council, Aust. Coll. of Nursing, 1958-60 (Chm. Educn Cttee, 1951-58); Nat. Health and MRC, 1960-; Nat. Fitness Council, 1960-; Nat. Tuberculosis Adv. Council, 1960-; Prog. and Budget Cttee, 15th World Health Assembly, 1962; Admin., Fin. and Legal Cttee 19th World Health Assembly; Pres., 24th Assembly, 1971; Exec. Bd, WHO, 1969-70. Member: Council, Aust. Red Cross Soc., 1954-60; Mem. Nat. Blood Transfusion Cttee, ARCS 1955-60; Nat. Trustee, Returned Services League Aust., 1961-73; Mem. Bd of Management, Canberra Grammar Sch., 1963-68. *Publications:* contribs to Australian Med. Jl, NZ Med. Jl, etc. *Recreations:* bowls,

gardening. *Address:* PO Box 1561, Canberra, ACT 2601, Australia. *Clubs:* Royal Society of Medicine (London); Melbourne, Naval and Military, Cricket (Melbourne); University (Sydney); Commonwealth (Canberra); Bowling (Canberra).

REGAN, Charles Maurice; Under-Secretary, Department of Health and Social Security, since 1972; *b* 31 Oct. 1925; *m* 1961, Susan (*née* Littmann) (*d* 1972); one *s* one *d*. *Educ:* London Sch. of Economics and Political Science (BSc(Econ)). Academic research, 1950-52. Asst Principal, Min. of National Insurance, 1952; Principal Private Sec. to Minister of Pensions and National Insurance, 1962-64; Asst Sec., 1964; Treasury/Civil Service Dept, 1967-70. *Recreations:* theatre, travel. *Address:* 35 Crediton Hill, NW6 1HS. *T:* 01-794 6404.

REGAN, Hon. Gerald Augustine, QC (Can.); MLA; Premier of Nova Scotia since Oct. 1970; lawyer; *b* Windsor, NS, 13 Feb. 1928; *s* of Walter E. Regan and Rose M. Greene; *m* 1956, A. Carole, *d* of John H. Harrison; three *s* three *d*. *Educ:* Windsor Academy; St Mary's and Dalhousie Univs, Canada; Dalhousie Law Sch. (LLB). Called to Bar of Nova Scotia, 1954; QC (Can.) 1970. Formerly practising lawyer. Liberal candidate in Provincial gen. elecs, 1956 and 1960, and in Fed. gen. elec., 1962. Mem. for Halifax, NS, 1963; Leader, Liberal Party of Nova Scotia, 1965-; MLA for Halifax-Needham, Provincial gen. elec., 1967, re-elected, 1970. Mem., NS Barristers Soc.; Chm. Exec. Cttee, Commonwealth Parly Assoc., 1973-76; Mem., Canadian Delegn, UN, 1965. *Recreations:* tennis, ski-ing. *Address:* Province House, Halifax, Nova Scotia, Canada. *T:* 424-4119; (home) Shore Drive, Bedford, Nova Scotia, Canada. *Club:* Halifax (Halifax, NS).

REGINA, Archbishop of, (RC), since 1973; **Most Rev. Charles A. Halpin;** *b* 30 Aug. 1930; *s* of John S. Halpin and Marie Anne Gervais. *Educ:* St Boniface Coll. (BA); St Boniface Seminary (BTh); Gregorian Univ., Rome (JCL). Priest, 1956; Vice-Chancellor of Archdiocese of Winnipeg and Secretary to Archbishop, 1960; Officialis of Archdiocesan Matrimonial Tribunal, 1962; Chaplain to the Holy Father with title of Monsignor, 1969; ordained Bishop, Nov. 1973; installed as Archbishop of Regina, Dec. 1973. *Address:* 2522 Retallack Street, Regina, Saskatchewan, Canada S4T 2L3. *T:* (306) 522-9150.

REHNQUIST, Hon. William H.; Associate Justice, Supreme Court of the United States, since 1972; *b* 1 Oct. 1924; *s* of William Benjamin and Margery Peck Rehnquist; *m* 1953, Natalie Cornell; one *s* two *d*. *Educ:* Stanford and Harvard Univs. BA, MA 1948, LLB 1952, Stanford; MA Harvard 1949. Law Clerk for Mr Justice Robert H. Jackson, 1952-53; Partner, Phoenix, Ariz: Evans, Kitchell & Jenckes, 1953-55; Ragan & Rehnquist, 1956-57; Cunningham, Carson & Messenger, 1957-60; Powers & Rehnquist, 1960-69; Asst Attorney-Gen., Office of Legal Counsel, Dept of Justice, 1969-72. Phi Beta Kappa; Order of the Coif. *Publications:* contrib. US News and World Report, Jl of Amer. Bar Assoc., Arizona Law Review. *Recreations:* swimming, tennis, reading, hiking. *Address:* Supreme Court of the United States, Washington, DC 20543, USA. *Club:* National Lawyers (Washington, DC).

REICHENBACH, Henry-Béat de F.; *see* de Fischer-Reichenbach.

REICHSTEIN, Prof. Tadeus, Dr ing chem; Ordentlicher Professor, Head of Department of Organic Chemistry, University of Basel, 1946-60, now Emeritus; *b* Wloclawek, Poland, 20 July 1897; *s* of Isidor Reichstein and Gustava Brockmann; *m* 1927, Henriette Louise Quarles van Ufford; one *d*. *Educ:* Oberrealschule and Eidgenössische Technische Hochschule, Department of Chemistry, Zürich. Assistant, ETH, Zürich, 1922-34; professor of organic chemistry, ETH, Zürich, 1934; head of department of pharmacy, University of Basel, 1938. Dr *hc* Sorbonne, Paris, 1947, Basel 1951, Geneva, 1967, ETH, Zürich, 1967, Abidjan 1967, London 1968, Leeds 1970; Marcel Benoît Prize, 1948; (jointly) Nobel Prize for Medicine, 1950; Cameron Prize, 1951; Foreign Member Royal Society, 1952; Copley Medal, Royal Soc., 1968; Dale Medal, Soc. for Endocrinology, 1975. *Publications:* numerous papers. *Recreations:* swimmer, skier, devoted gardener, mountain-climber. *Address:* Institut für Organische Chemie der Universität, St Johanns-Ring 19, CH 4056 Basel, Switzerland. *T:* (061) 44 90 90.

REID, Sir Alexander (James), 3rd Bt *cr* 1897; JP; DL; *b* 6 Dec. 1932; *s* of Sir Edward James Reid, 2nd Bt, KBE, and of Tatiana, *d* of Col Alexander Fenoult, formerly of Russian Imperial Guard; *S* father, 1972; *m* 1955, Michaela Ann, *d* of Olaf Kier, *qv*; one *s* three *d*. *Educ:* Eton; Magdalene Coll., Cambridge. Nat. Certificate Agriculture (NCA). 2nd Lieut, 1st Bn Gordon Highlanders, 1951; served Malaya; Captain, 3rd Bn Gordon Highlanders (TA), retired 1964. Director: Ellon Castle Estates Co. Ltd, 1965-; Cristina Securities Ltd, 1970-; Quantock Veal Ltd, 1974-; Bellinger Bros Ltd, 1975-; Kingston Agricultural Services Ltd, 1977-. Governor, Heath Mount Prep. Sch., Hertford, 1970, Chm., 1976. JP Cambridgeshire and Isle of Ely, 1971, DL 1973. *Recreations:* shooting, flying, golf. *Heir: s* Charles Edward James Reid, *b* 24 June 1956. *Address:* Kingston Wood Manor, Arrington, Royston, Herts. *T:* Caxton 231. *Club:* Caledonian.

REID, Archibald Cameron, CMG 1963; CVO 1970; Deputy High Commissioner in the Kingdom of Tonga, 1970-71; *b* 7 Aug. 1915; *s* of William Reid; *m* 1941, Joan Raymond Charlton; two *s* two *d*. *Educ:* Fettes; Queen's College, Cambridge. Apptd Admin. Officer, Class II, in Colony of Fiji, 1938; Admin. Officer, Class I, 1954; British Agent and Consul, Tonga, 1957-59; Sec. for Fijian Affairs, 1959-65; British Comr and Consul, Tonga, 1965-70. *Recreations:* hill walking, painting, golf. *Address:* 2a Ramsay Garden, Edinburgh EH1 2NA. *T:* 031-225 6541.

REID, Charles William, BSc (Econ); ASAA; *b* 29 May 1895; *s* of Charles and Ada Reid; *m* 1924, Gladys Ellen Edith Dudley; two *d*. *Educ:* Latymer Upper School; Holloway County School; University of London. War Office, 1914; Queen's Westminster Rifles, 1915-19 (served overseas, wounded twice). Exchequer and Audit Department, 1919-38; Exports Credit Guarantee Dept, 1938-39; Ministry of Supply, 1939-40; Ministry of Supply Mission, USA, 1940-46, Director of Requirements and Secretary-General; Ministry of Supply, Overseas Disposals, 1946-48; Dep. Financial Adviser. Control Commn, Germany, 1948-50; Min. of Works, Comptroller of Accounts, 1950-54; Under-Secretary for Finance, 1954-56; retired, 1956. Incorporated Accountant, 1926. Medal of Freedom (USA), 1947. *Recreations:* travel and sports. Athletics purple, Univ. of London; represented Great Britain in first athletics match with France, 1921. *Address:* Pynes, Edington, Bridgwater TA7 9LD. *T:* Chilton Polden 772320.

REID, Desmond Arthur; *b* 6 Feb. 1918; *s* of late Col Percy Lester Reid, CBE, DL, and late Mrs Katharine Marjorie Elizabeth Reid; *m* 1939, Anne, *d* of late Major J. B. Paget and late Mrs J. B. Paget, London SW7; one *s*. *Educ:* Eton. Joined Lloyd's, 1936, Member 1939. SRO, Irish Guards, 1939 (wounded in Normandy, 1944; Major). Returned Lloyd's, 1946. Chairman: R. K. Harrison & Co. Ltd, 1947-; Yeoman Investment Trust Ltd; Young Companies Investment Trust; Prudential Unit Trust Managers Ltd; Prudential Pensions Ltd; Director: Drayton Premier Investment Trust Ltd; Edger Investments Ltd; Estate Duties Investment Trust Ltd; General Consolidated Investment Trust Ltd; London & St Lawrence Investment Co. Ltd; Moorgate Investment Co. Ltd; Practical Investment Co. Ltd; Prudential Assurance Co Ltd, 1960- (Dep. Chm., 1968-72); Selection Croissance; Pan Holding SA. Managing Trustee, Irish Guards Common Investment Fund, 1970-. Mem., Lloyd's Investment Cttee, 1971- (Chm. 1974-). Governor: Royal Ballet, 1973-; Royal Ballet School, 1974-. Councillor, Chelsea Bor. Council, 1945-52 (Chm. Finance Cttee, 1950-52). Chm., Inst. of Obstetrics and Gynæcology; Vice-Pres., Insurance Inst. of London; Mem., The Livery of Merchant Taylors. *Recreations:* shooting, gardening, ballet. *Address:* 3 Belgrave Place, SW1. *T:* 01-235 6507; Burmans, Ripe, Sussex. *T:* Ripe 271. *Clubs:* White's, City of London (Chm., 1977), MCC; Travellers' (Paris).

REID, Dougal Gordon; HM Diplomatic Service; Counsellor, and Head of Chancery, British High Commission, New Delhi, since 1977; *b* 31 Dec. 1925; *e s* of late Douglas Reid and Catherine Jean (*née* Lowson); *m* 1950, Georgina Elizabeth Johnston; one *s* (and one *s* decd). *Educ:* Sedbergh Sch.; Trinity Hall, Cambridge; LSE. Served in Royal Marines, 1944-46. Cadet, Colonial Admin. Service (later HMOCS), Sierra Leone, 1949; District Comr 1956; retd as Perm. Sec., Min. of Natural Resources, 1962. Arthur Guinness Son & Co. Ltd, 1962-63. Entered CRO, 1963; 1st Sec., Accra, 1964-65; Commonwealth Office, 1966; Accra, 1966-68 (concurrently Lomé, 1967-68); Seoul, 1968-71; FCO, 1971-74; Counsellor (Commercial) and Consul-General, Kinshasa (and concurrently at Brazzaville, Bujumbura and Kigali), 1974-77. *Recreations:* golf, tennis, music, watching sport. *Address:* c/o Foreign and Commonwealth Office, SW1A 2AL. *Clubs:* Travellers', Royal Commonwealth Society, MCC.

REID, George Newlands; MP (SNP) Stirlingshire East and Clackmannan, since Feb. 1974; freelance broadcaster and journalist since 1972; *b* 4 June 1939; *s* of George Reid, company director, and Margaret Forsyth; *m* 1968, Daphne Ann MacColl; two *d*. *Educ:* Tullibody Sch.; Dollar Academy; Univ. of St Andrews (MA Hons). Pres., Students' Representative Council. Features Writer, Scottish Daily Express, 1962; Reporter, Scottish Television, 1964; Producer, Granada Television, 1965; Head of News and Current Affairs (Scottish Television), 1968. Member, Select Committee on: Assistance to Private Members, 1975-76; Direct Elections to European Assembly, 1976-77; Mem., British Parly Delegn to Council of Europe and WEU, 1977-. Dir, Scottish Council Res. Inst., 1974-. *Address:* 11 Drysdale Street, Alloa, Clackmannanshire FK10 1JL. *T:* Alloa 6485. *Club:* Caledonian.

REID, Hon. Sir George Oswald, Kt 1972; QC (Vic) 1971; Attorney-General, Victoria, Australia, 1967-73; Barrister and Solicitor; *b* Hawthorn, Vic, 22 July 1903; *s* of late George Watson Reid and Lillias Margaret Reid (*née* Easton); *m* 1st, 1930, Beatrix Waring McCay, LLM (*d* 1972), *d* of Lt-Gen. Hon. Sir James McCay; one *d* ; 2nd, 1973, Dorothy, *d* of late C. W. F. Ruttledge. *Educ:* Camberwell Grammar Sch. and Scotch Coll., Melbourne; Melbourne Univ. (LLB). Admitted to practice as Barrister and Solicitor, Supreme Ct of Vic., 1926. Has practised as Solicitor in Melbourne, 1929-. Served War, RAAF, 1940-46, Wing Comdr. MLA (Liberal) for Box Hill, 1947-52, and 1955-73. Government of Victoria: Minister without Portfolio, 1955-56; Minister of Labour and Industry and Electrical Undertakings, 1956-65; Minister: for Fuel and Power, 1965-67; of Immigration, 1967-70; Chief Secretary, March 9-Apr. 27, 1971. *Recreations:* bowls, golf, reading. *Address:* Nilja, Alexander Road, Warrandyte, Vic 3113, Australia. *Clubs:* Melbourne, Savage, Melbourne Cricket (Melbourne); Royal Automobile (Victoria).

REID, Air Vice-Marshal Sir (George) Ranald Macfarlane, KCB, *cr* 1945 (CB 1941); DSO 1919; MC and bar; Extra Gentleman Usher to the Queen, 1959; Gentleman Usher to the Queen, 1952 (formerly to King George VI, 1952); *s* of late George Macfarlane Reid, Queensland and Prestwick; *m* 1934, Leslie Livermore Washburne, *d* of late Hamilton Wright, Washington, DC, USA, and *g d* of Senator William Washburne; one *s* one *d*. *Educ:* Routenburn; Malvern Coll. Regular Officer, 1914-46 in: 4th (SR) Argyll and Sutherland Highlanders; 2nd Black Watch; RFC and RAF. Served European War, 1914-18 (wounded, despatches, MC and Bar, DSO); Egypt, 1919-21; Sudan, 1927-29; RAF Staff Coll., 1930; Imperial Defence Coll., 1932; Air Attaché, British Embassy, Washington, 1933-35; AOC Halton, 1936-38; Air Officer Commanding British Forces, Aden, 1938-41; Air Officer Administration Flying Training Command; AOC 54 Group; AOC West Africa, 1944-45; retired from Royal Air Force, 1946. *Address:* c/o Lloyds Bank Ltd, 6 Pall Mall, SW1. *Clubs:* Royal Air Force; Weld (Perth, Western Australia).

REID, George Smith; retired; Sheriff (formerly Sheriff-Substitute) of Ayr and Bute, later South Strathclyde, Dumfries and Galloway, at Ayr, 1948-76; *b* 29 Feb. 1904; *yr s* of John Mitchell Reid, manufacturer, Glasgow; *m* 1935, Marion Liddell Boyd; two *s* two *d*. *Educ:* Hutchesons' Grammar School, Glasgow; Glasgow University. MA 1925, LLB 1927. Called to Scottish Bar, 1935. *Recreation:* swimming. *Address:* 10 Wheatfield Road, Ayr. *T:* 67858.

REID, Very Rev. George Thomson Henderson, MC 1945; Minister of West Church of St Andrews, Aberdeen, 1955-75; Chaplain to the Queen in Scotland, since 1969; *b* 31 March 1910; *s* of Rev. David Reid, DD; *m* 1938, Anne Guilland Watt, *d* of late Principal Very Rev. Hugh Watt, DD, Edinburgh; three *s* one *d*. *Educ:* George Watson's Boys' Coll.; Univ. of Edinburgh. MA 1932, BD 1935, Edinburgh. Served as Chaplain to 3rd Bn Scots Guards, 1940-45, Sen. Chaplain to 15th (S) Div., 1945. Minister at: Port Seton, E Lothian, 1935-38; Juniper Green, Edinburgh, 1938-49; Claremont Church, Glasgow, 1949-55. Moderator of the General Assembly of the Church of Scotland, 1973-74. Hon. DD Aberdeen, 1969. *Recreations:* golf, bird-watching, painting. *Address:* 33 Westgarth Avenue, Colinton, Edinburgh.

REID, Graham Livingstone; Director of Manpower Intelligence and Planning, Manpower Services Commission, since 1975; *b* 30 June 1937; *s* of late William L. Reid and of Louise M. Reid; *m* 1973, Eileen M. Loudfoot. *Educ:* Univ. of St Andrews (MA); Queen's Univ., Kingston, Canada (MA). Dept of Social and Economic Res., Univ. of Glasgow: Asst Lectr in Applied Economics, 1960, Lectr 1963, Sen. Lectr 1968, Reader 1971; Sen. Econ. Adviser and Head of Econs and Statistics Unit, Scottish Office, 1973. Vis. Associate Prof., Mich State Univ., 1967; Vis. Res. Fellow, Queen's Univ., Canada, 1969. *Publications:* Fringe Benefits, Labour Costs and Social Security (ed with D. J. Robertson), 1965; (with K. J. Allen) Nationalised

Industries, 1970 (3rd edn 1975); (with L. C. Hunter and D. Boddy) Labour Problems of Technological Change, 1970; (with K. J. Allen and D. J. Harris) The Nationalised Fuel Industries, 1973; contrib. to Econ. Jl, Brit. Jl of Indust. Relations, Scot. Jl of Polit. Econ., Indust & Lab. Relns Rev. *Recreations:* golf, music. *Address:* 15 Allison Grove, SE21 7ER. *T:* 01-693 8252. *Club:* Royal Commonwealth Society.

REID, (Harold) Martin (Smith); HM Diplomatic Service; Head of Central and Southern African Department, Foreign and Commonwealth Office, since 1974; *b* 27 Aug. 1928; *s* of late Marcus Reid and late Winifred Mary Reid (*née* Stephens); *m* 1956, Jane Elizabeth Harwood; one *s* three *d. Educ:* Merchant Taylors' Sch.; Brasenose Coll., Oxford. Entered HM Foreign Service, 1953; served in: FO, 1953-54; Paris, 1954-57; Rangoon, 1958-61; FO, 1961-65; Georgetown, 1965-68; Bucharest, 1968-70; Dep. High Comr, Malawi, 1970-73; Private Sec. to successive Secs of State for NI, 1973-74. *Recreations:* painting and drawing; chess. *Address:* c/o Foreign and Commonwealth Office, SW1; 43 Carson Road, SE21 8HT. *T:* 01-670 6151. *Club:* United Oxford & Cambridge University.
See also M . H . M . Reid .

REID, Sir Hugh, 3rd Bt *cr* 1922; farmer, and company director since 1961; *b* 27 Nov. 1933; *s* of Sir Douglas Neilson Reid, 2nd Bt, and of Margaret Brighton Young, *d* of Robert Young Maxtone, MBE, JP; *S* father, 1971. *Educ:* Loretto. Royal Air Force, 1952-56; Flying Officer RAFVR (Training Branch). *Recreations:* skiing, travel. *Heir:* none. *Address:* Auchterarder House, Auchterarder, Perthshire.

REID, James, OBE (mil.) 1968; VRD 1967; Director, Investments and Loans, Commission of European Communities, 1973-76; *b* 23 Nov. 1921; *s* of William Reid, MBE, and Dora Louisa Reid (*née* Smith); *m* 1949, Margaret James; two *d. Educ:* City of London Sch.; Emmanuel Coll., Cambridge (MA). Served War, RN: RNVR (Sub. Lieut), 1942-45. Served RNVR and RNR (Comdr), 1953-72. Entered Northern Ireland Civil Service, 1948 (Asst Principal); Min. of Finance, 1948-61 and 1963-73; Min. of Commerce, 1961-63; Principal, 1953; Asst Sec., 1963; Sen. Asst Sec., 1971; Dep. Sec., 1972. *Recreations:* reading, music. *Address:* 6 Avenue Guillaume, Luxembourg. *Club:* United Oxford & Cambridge University.

REID, John, CB 1967; Chief Veterinary Officer, Ministry of Agriculture, Fisheries and Food, 1965-70; *b* 14 May 1906; *s* of late John and Jessie Jamieson Reid, Callander, Perthshire; *m* 1933, Molly Russell; one *d. Educ:* McLaren High Sch., Callander; Royal (Dick) Veterinary Coll., Edinburgh. FRCVS 1971; DVSM 1931. Asst Veterinary Officer, Midlothian County Council, 1931; Asst Veterinary Officer, Cumberland County Council, 1932; Ministry of Agriculture and Fisheries: Divisional Veterinary Officer, 1938; Superintending Veterinary Officer, 1952; Ministry of Agriculture, Fisheries and Food: Regional Veterinary Officer, 1958; Deputy Chief Veterinary Officer, 1960; Director of Veterinary Field Services, 1963. Mem. ARC, 1965-70. Vice-Chm., FAO European Commn for Control of Foot-and-Mouth Disease, 1967-70; Member: Cttee of Inquiry into Veterinary Profession, 1971-75; Scientific Authority for Animals, DoE, 1976-. *Recreations:* gardening, bird watching. *Address:* Owl's Green Cottage, Dennington, Woodbridge, Suffolk IP13 8BY. *T:* Badingham 205. *Club:* Farmers'.

REID, Dr. John James Andrew, CB 1975; TD; MD, FRCP, FRCPE; Chief Medical Officer, Scottish Home and Health Department, since 1977; Hon. Consultant in Community Medicine to the Army, since 1972; *b* 21 Jan. 1925; *s* of Alexander Scott Reid and Mary Cullen Reid (*née* Andrew); *m* 1949, Marjorie Reid (*née* Crumpton), MB, ChB; one *s* four *d. Educ:* Bell-Baxter Sch.; Univ. of St Andrews. BSc 1944; MB, ChB 1947; DPH 1952; MD 1961; FRCP (Edin.) 1970; FRCP 1971; FFCM 1972. Lt-Col RAMC (TA). Hospital, Army (Nat. Service) and junior Public Health posts, 1947-55; Lectr in Public Health and Social Medicine, Univ. of St Andrews, 1955-59; Dep. County MOH, Northamptonshire, 1959-62; County MOH, Northamptonshire, 1962-67; County MOH, Buckinghamshire, 1967-72; Dep. Chief MO, DHSS, 1972-77. Member: GMC (Crown Nominee), 1973-; Council for Post-grad. Med. Educn, 1973-; Exec. Bd, WHO; Formerly: WHO Fellow; Mem., Standing Med. Adv. Cttee, DHSS; Chm., Jt Sub-Cttee on Health and Welfare Services for People with Epilepsy; Vice-Chm. of Council, Queen's Inst. of District Nursing; Mem., Working Party on Medical Administrators. Vis. Prof. in Health Services Admin, London Sch. of Hygiene and Tropical Medicine, 1973-77. *Publications:* papers on medical care, public health, diabetes, epilepsy, etc, in BMJ, Lancet, etc. *Address:* St Andrew's House, Edinburgh EH1 3DE.

REID, John Kelman Sutherland, CBE 1970; TD 1961; Professor of Christian Dogmatics, 1961-70, of Systematic Theology 1970-76, University of Aberdeen; *b* 31 March 1910; *y s* of late Reverend Dr David Reid, Calcutta and Leith, and of late Mrs G. T. Reid (*née* Stuart); *m* 1950, Margaret Winifrid Brookes. *Educ:* George Watson's Boys' College, Edinburgh; Universities of Edinburgh (MA and BD), Heidelberg, Marburg, Basel, and Strasbourg. MA 1st Cl. Hons Philosophy, 1933. Prof. of Philosophy in Scottish Church Coll., Univ. of Calcutta, 1935-37; BD (dist. in Theol.), 1938, and Cunningham Fellow. Ordained into Church of Scotland and inducted into Parish of Craigmillar Park, Edinburgh, 1939. CF, chiefly with Parachute Regt, 1942-46. Jt Ed. Scot. Jl Theol. since inception, 1947; Hon. Sec. Jt Cttee on New Translation of the Bible, 1949-; Prof. of Theology and Head of Department of Theology, University of Leeds, 1952-61. Hon. DD (Edinburgh), 1957. *Publications:* The Authority of Scripture, 1957; Our Life in Christ, 1963; Christian Apologetics, 1969. Translation of: Oscar Cullmann's The Earliest Christian Confessions, 1949; Baptism in the New Testament, 1952; Calvin's Theological Treatises, ed and trans. 1954; Jean Bosc's The Kingly Office of the Lord Jesus Christ, 1959; Calvin's Concerning the Eternal Pre-destination of God, ed and trans., 1961. *Address:* 1 Camus Park, Fairmilehead, Edinburgh. *Club:* Mortonhall Golf (Edinburgh).

REID, Rt. Rev. John Robert; Assistant Bishop, Diocese of Sydney, NSW, since 1972; *b* 15 July 1928; *s* of John and Edna Reid; *m* 1955, Alison Gertrude Dunn; two *s* four *d. Educ:* Melbourne Univ. (BA); Moore Coll., Sydney (ThL). Deacon 1955, Priest 1955; Curate, Manly, 1955-56; Rector, Christ Church, Gladesville, NSW, 1956-69; Archdeacon of Cumberland, NSW, 1969-72. *Recreation:* walking. *Address:* 33 Fairfax Road, Bellevue Hill, NSW 2023, Australia. *T:* 36-3320.

REID, Sir John (Thyne), Kt 1974; CMG 1971; Director, Johns Perry; *b* 15 Oct. 1903; *s* of Andrew Reid and Margaret (*née* Thyne), both born in Scotland; *m* 1929, Gladys Violet Boyd Scott, Glasgow; one *s* three *d. Educ:* King's Sch., Parramatta, NSW; Edinburgh Academy, Scotland. Mem., 1961-72, Vice-Chm., 1968-72, Australian Broadcasting Commn. Mem. Council, Victorian Coll. of the Arts. Hon. LLD Melbourne, 1977; Hon. DASc VIC, 1977. *Recreation:* bowls. *Address:* 4 St George's Court, 290 Cotham Road, Kew, Vic 3101, Australia. *T:* 80 4759. *Clubs:* Caledonian (London); Australian (Melbourne and Sydney); Rotary (Melbourne).

REID, Louis Arnaud, MA, PhD, DLitt; Professor Emeritus of Philosophy of Education, Institute of Education, London University, (Professor 1947-62); *b* Ellon, Aberdeenshire; *s* of late Rev. A. H. Reid and late Margaret C. Miller; *m* 1920, Gladys Kate, *y d* of late W. H. Bignold; two *s* ; *m* 1957, Frances Mary Holt, *d* of Denys Horton; two *step d. Educ:* Aberdeen Grammar School; Leys Sch., Camb.; University of Edinburgh. Studied engineering, 1913; RE 1914; discharged, 1915; 1st Cl. Hons in Mental Philosophy, 1919; medallist, English Essays; University verse prizeman; Cousin prizeman in Fine Art; medallist in Moral Philosophy; Bruce of Grangehill and Falkland prizeman in Advanced Metaphysics; Vans Dunlop scholar in Moral Philosophy; Lord Rector's prizeman; Hamilton Philosophical Fellow; Mrs Foster Watson Memorial Prizeman; Lecturer in Philosophy in University College, Aberystwyth, 1919-26; Visiting Professor Stanford University, California, 1927; Independent Lecturer in Philosophy University of Liverpool, 1926-32; Prof. of Philosophy Armstrong Coll. (now Univ. of Newcastle upon Tyne), 1932-47. Visiting Prof., Univ. of British Columbia, 1951; Vis. Prof. of Philosophy, Univ. of Oregon, 1962-63; Vis. Prof., Chinese Univ. of Hong Kong, 1966-67. Ext. Examiner, Univs of Liverpool, Sheffield, Leeds, Edinburgh, Aberdeen, Glasgow, London, Warwick, Leicester, W Indies, Hong Kong. Pres., Philosophy of Educn Soc. of GB. *Publications:* Knowledge and Truth, An Epistemological Essay, 1923; A Study in Aesthetics, 1931; Creative Morality, 1936; Preface to Faith, 1939; The Rediscovery of Belief, 1945; Ways of Knowledge and Experience, 1960; Philosophy and Education, 1961; Meaning in the Arts, 1970; articles in Mind, Hibbert Journal, Proceedings of the Aristotelian Society, Times Ed. Supp., etc. *Address:* 50 Rotherwick Road, NW11. *T:* 01-455 6850. *Clubs:* Athenæum, PEN.

REID, Prof. Lynne McArthur; Professor of Experimental Pathology, Institute of Diseases of the Chest (Cardiothoracic Institute 1973), University of London, 1967-76; Hon. Lecturer, University College Medical School, 1971-76; Hon. Consultant, Experimental Pathology, Brompton Hospital, 1963-76; Dean, Cardiothoracic Institute (British Postgraduate Medical Federation), 1973-76; S. Burt Wolbach Professor of Pathology, Harvard Medical School, since 1976; Chairman, Department of Pathology, Children's Hospital Medical Center, Boston, since

1976; b Melbourne, 12 Nov. 1923; er d of Robert Muir Reid and Violet Annie Reid (née McArthur). Educ: Wimbledon Girls' Sch. (GPDST); Janet Clarke Hall, Trinity Coll., Melbourne Univ.; Royal Melbourne Hosp. MB, BS Melb. 1946; MRACP 1950; MRCP 1951; FRACP, MRCPath (Foundn Mem.) 1964; FRCPath 1966; FRCP 1969; MD Melb. 1969. House Staff, Royal Melb. Hosp., 1946-49; Res. Fellow, Nat. Health and MRC, Royal Melb. Hosp. and Eliza Hall, 1949-51; Res. Asst, Inst. Diseases of Chest, 1951-55; Sen. Lectr founding Res. Dept of Path., Inst. Diseases of Chest, 1955; Reader in Exper. Path., London Univ., 1964; 1st Hastings Vis. Prof. in Path., Univ. of California, 1965; Holme Lectr, UC Med. Sch., 1969; Walker-Ames Prof., Univ. of Washington, 1971; Mem. Fleischner Soc., 1971; 1st Hon. Fellow, Canadian Thoracic Soc., 1973; Chm., Cystic Fibrosis Res. Trust, 1974 (Mem. Med. Adv. Cttee 1964); Royal Soc. Medicine (Sect. Pathology): Vice-Pres. 1974; Standing Liaison Cttee on Sci. Aspects of Smoking and Health, 1971; Commn of European Cttees (Industrial Safety and Medicine), 1972; Mem. Bd of Governors, Nat. Heart and Chest Hosps, 1974; Manager, Royal Instn of Gt Britain, 1973 (Vice-Pres. 1974); Mem. Gov. Body, British Postgrad. Med. Fedn, 1974. Publications: The Pathology of Emphysema, 1967; numerous papers in sci. jls. Recreations: music, travel, reading. Address: 75 Montrose Court, Princes Gate, SW7; Children's Hospital Medical Center, Harvard Medical School, 300 Longwood Avenue, Boston, Mass 02115, USA. Club: University Women's.

REID, Malcolm Herbert Marcus; Under Secretary, Department of Industry, since 1974; b 2 March 1927; s of late Marcus Reid and Winifred Stephens; m 1st, 1956, Eleanor (d 1974), d of late H. G. Evans, MC; four s; 2nd, 1975, Daphne, e d of Sir John Griffin, qv. Educ: Merchant Taylors' Sch.; St John's Coll., Oxford. Served in Navy, 1945-48 and in RNVR, 1949-53. Entered Board of Trade, 1951; Private Secretary to Permanent Secretary, 1954-57; Trade Comr in Ottawa, 1957-60; Board of Trade, 1960-63; Private Secretary to successive Prime Ministers, 1963-66; Commercial Counsellor, Madrid, 1967-71; Asst Sec., DTI, 1972-74. Recreation: National Hunt racing. Address: 71 Thurleigh Road, SW12 8UA. T: 01-675 1172; Collins Cottage, Duton Hill, Essex. T: Great Easton 462. Club: United Oxford & Cambridge University.
See also H . M . S . Reid .

REID, Martin; see Reid, H. M. S.

REID, May, CBE 1920; b Bombay, 1 May 1882; e d of late Edward Jervis Reid. Educ: privately; Bedford College. Assistant and Acting County Secretary, London Branch British Red Cross Society, 1914-23; Secretary to Lord Queenborough, 1923-28; Assistant Sec. National Christian Council of India, 1932-41. Address: 4 Bywater Street, SW3. T: 01-589 3270.

REID, Sir Norman (Robert), Kt 1970; DA (Edinburgh); FMA; FIIC; Director, the Tate Gallery, since 1964; b 27 December 1915; o s of Edward Daniel Reid and Blanche, d of Richard Drouet; m 1941, Jean Lindsay Bertram; one s one d. Educ: Wilson's Grammar School; Edinburgh Coll. of Art; Edinburgh Univ. Served War of 1939-46, Major, Argyll and Sutherland Highlanders. Joined staff of Tate Gallery, 1946; Deputy Director, 1954; Keeper, 1959. Fellow, International Institute for Conservation (IIC) (Secretary General, 1963-65; Vice-Chm., 1966); British Rep. Internat. Committee on Museums and Galleries of Modern Art, 1963-; President, Penwith Society of Arts; Member: Council, Friends of the Tate Gall., 1958- (Founder Mem.); Arts Council Art Panel, 1964-74; Inst. of Contemporary Arts Adv. Panel, 1965-; Contemporary Art Soc. Cttee, 1965-72, 1973-77; "Paintings in Hospitals" Adv. Cttee, 1965-69; British Council Fine Arts Cttee, 1965-77 (Chm. 1968-75); Culture Adv. Cttee of UK Nat. Commn for Unesco, 1966-70; Univ. of London, Bd of Studies in History of Art, 1968; Cttee, The Rome Centre, 1969-77 (Pres. 1975-77); Adv. Council, Paul Mellon Centre, 1971-; Council of Management, Inst. of Contemp. Prints, 1972-; Council, RCA, 1974-77. Mem. Bd, Burlington Magazine, 1971-75. Hon. LittD East Anglia, 1970. Officer of the Mexican Order of the Aztec Eagle. Address: The Tate Gallery, Millbank, SW1. T: 01-828 1212; 50 Brabourne Rise, Park Langley, Beckenham, Kent. T: 01-650 7088.

REID, Patrick Robert, MBE 1940; MC 1943; Managing Director, Kem Estates Ltd; b 13 Nov. 1910; s of John Reid, CIE, ICS, and Alice Mabel Daniell; m 1943, Jane Cabot (marr. diss. 1966); three s two d; m 1977, Mrs Mary Stewart Cunliffe-Lister. Educ: Clongowes Wood College, Co. Kildare; Wimbledon College; King's College, London University. BSc (London) 1932; AMICE, 1936; Pupilage, Sir Alex Gibb & Partners, 1934-37. Served War of 1939-45, BEF, France, Capt. RASC 2nd Div., Ammunition Officer, 1939-40; POW Germany, 1940-42; Asst

Mil. Attaché, Berne, 1943-46; First Sec. (Commercial), British Embassy, Ankara, 1946-49; Chief Administrator, OEEC, Paris, 1949-52. Prospective Parly Candidate (C) Dartford and Erith, 1953-55. Director, Richard Costain (Projects) Ltd, 1959-62; Dir, Richard Costain (Middle East) Ltd, 1959-62. W. S. Atkins & Partners, Consulting Engineers, 1962-63. Publications: The Colditz Story, 1953; The Latter Days, 1955 (omnibus edn of the two, as Colditz, 1962); (with Sir Olaf Caroe and Sir Thomas Rapp) From Nile to Indus, 1960; Winged Diplomat, 1962; Economic Survey Northern Nigeria, 1962; My Favourite Escape Stories, 1975. Recreations: ski-ing, yachting, gardening. Address: The Well House, Eastbourne Road, Uckfield, East Sussex. Club: Lansdowne.

REID, Maj.-Gen. Peter Daer; Director, Royal Armoured Corps, since 1976; b 5 Aug. 1925; s of Col S. D. Reid and Dorothy Hungerford (née Jackson); m 1958, Catherine Fleetwood (née Boodle); two s two d. Educ: Cheltenham College; Wadham Coll., Oxford. Commissioned into Coldstream Guards, 1945; transferred Royal Dragoons, 1947; served: Germany, Egypt, Malaya, Gibraltar, Morocco; Staff Coll., 1959; Comdg Officer, The Royal Dragoons, 1965-68; student, Royal College of Defence Studies, 1973; Commander RAC, 3rd Div., 1974-76. Recreations: sailing, skiing, fishing, bird watching. Address: The Old Vicarage, Idmiston, near Salisbury, Wilts SP4 0AT. T: Idmiston 610312. Clubs: Royal Western Yacht; Parkstone Yacht; Kandahar Ski.

REID, Philip; see under Ingrams, R. R.

REID, Air Vice-Marshal Sir Ranald; see Reid, Sir G. R. M.

REID, Robert, QC (Scotland) 1961; Sheriff Principal, Glasgow and Strathkelvin, since 1977; b 5 Sept. 1922; s of late Robert Reid and of Mary Forsyth, Inverness; m 1946, Sheila Stuart Fraser (d 1951); m 1962, Jane (late Lynch or Thomson); one s. Educ: Inverness Royal Academy; Edinburgh University (BL). Passed Advocate, 1949. Sheriff Principal: Ayr and Bute, 1973-75; South Strathclyde, Dumfries and Galloway, 1975-77. Sen. Counsel to Sec. of State under Private Legislation Procedure (Scotland) Act, 1971-75. Pres., Industrial Tribunals for Scotland, 1965-71. Dir, Royal Lyceum Theatre Co. Ltd, Edinburgh. Recreations: poetry, gardening. Address: 33 Regent Terrace, Edinburgh. T: 031-556 1783. Clubs: Arts, Edinburgh University Staff (Edinburgh).

REID, Robert Basil, FCIT; Executive Member for Marketing, British Railways Board, since 1977; b 7 Feb. 1921; s of Sir Robert Niel Reid, KCSI, KCIE, ICS and Lady (A.H.) Reid (née Disney); m 1951, Isobel Jean McLachlan (d 1976); one s one d. Educ: Malvern Coll.; Brasenose Coll., Oxford (MA). Commnd Royal Tank Regt, 1941, Captain 1945. Traffic Apprentice, LNER, 1947; Goods Agent, York, 1958; Asst Dist Goods Manager, Glasgow, 1960, Dist Passenger Man., 1961, Divl Commercial Man., 1963; Planning Man., Scottish Region, 1967; Divl Man., Doncaster, 1968; Dep. Gen. Man., Eastern Region, York, 1972; Gen. Manager, Southern Reg., BR, 1974-76. Dir, British Transport Hotels Ltd. MBIM. Recreations: golf, sailing, shooting. Address: 23 Edgehill Road, Purley, Surrey CR2 2ND. T: 01-660 5429. Club: Naval and Military.

REID, Dr Robert Douglas; b 6 Sept. 1898; s of John and Maud Helen Reid; unmarried. Educ: Wells Cathedral School; St John's College, Oxford (DPhil); Bristol University (BSc). Army 1917-19, Somerset Light Infantry in Flanders and Ireland; Assistant Master at Downside School, 1923-24; Canford School, 1924-28; Housemaster at Worksop College, 1928-33; Headmaster Kings School, Taunton, 1933-37. Somerset County Council, 1958-66; High Constable and Dep. Mayor, City of Wells. Publications: Cathedral Church of St Andrew at Wells; Diary of Mary Yeoman; Notes on Practical Chemistry; A Concise General Science, 1949. Recreations: archæology, lawn tennis. Address: 8 Chamberlain Street, Wells, Somerset. T: 72494.

REID, Thomas Bertram Wallace, MA (Oxon), MA, LLB (Dublin), MA (Manchester), L ès L (Montpellier); Officier des Palmes académiques; Professor Emeritus, University of Oxford, and Emeritus Fellow of Trinity College, Oxford; b 10 July 1901; e s of late Thomas E. Reid, MBE, JP, Little Castledillon, Armagh; m 1942, Joyce M. H. Smalley; one s. Educ: Armagh Royal School; Trinity Coll., Dublin. Foundation Scholar, Hutchinson Stewart Literary Scholar, First Senior Moderator in Modern Literature, Prizeman in Old French and Provençal, Irish, and Law. Lecteur d'Anglais, Univ. of Montpellier, 1924-26; Asst Master, Frome County School, 1926-29; Assistant Lecturer in French, University of Manchester, 1929-35; Lecturer, 1935-45; Prof. of Romance Philology, 1945-58; Dean of the Faculty of Arts, 1950-51; Pro-Vice-Chancellor, 1957-58;

Prof. of the Romance Languages, Univ. of Oxford, and Fellow, Trinity Coll., Oxford, 1958-68. Vis. Prof., Univ. of Toronto, 1969-70. Pres., Anglo-Norman Text Society, 1962-. *Publications:* (ed) The Yvain of Chrestien de Troyes, 1942; (ed) Twelve Fabliaux, 1958; Historical Philology and Linguistic Science, 1960; The Romance of Horn by Thomas, ed. M. K. Pope, Vol. II (revised and completed), 1964; The Tristran of Beroul: a textual commentary, 1972; articles and reviews on linguistic subjects in Modern Lang. Review, Medium Aevum, French Studies, etc. *Address:* 37 Blandford Avenue, Oxford. *T:* Oxford 58112.

REID, Whitelaw; President and Director, Reid Enterprises; *b* 26 July 1913; *s* of late Ogden Reid and Mrs Ogden Reid; *m* 1st, 1948, Joan Brandon (marr. diss., 1959); two *s*; 2nd, 1959, Elizabeth Ann Brooks; one *s* one *d. Educ:* Lincoln Sch., NYC; St Paul's Sch., Concord, New Hampshire; Yale Univ. (BA). New York Herald Tribune: in various departments, 1938-40; foreign correspondent, England, 1940; Assistant to Editor, 1946; Editor (and Pres., 1953-55), 1947-55; Chm. of Bd, 1955-58; Director, 1946-65; Pres., Herald Tribune Fresh Air Fund, 1946-62, Dir 1962-. Served War of 1939-45, 1st Lieut, USNR. Pres., Reid Foundation; formerly Dir, Farfield Foundn; Director: Freedom House; Korean Soc. Inc.; Golden's Bridge Hounds Inc., 1970-. Chm., NY State Cttee on Public Employee Security Procedure, 1956-57. Member: Nat. Commn for Unesco, 1955-60; President's Citizen Advisers on the Mutual Security Program, 1956-57; Yale Alumni Board (Vice-Chm., 1962-64), Yale Univ. Council (Chm., Publications Cttee, 1965-70); Council on Foreign Relations; Nat. Inst. of Social Sciences. District Comr, Purchase Pony Club, 1964-70; Pres., New York State Horse Council (formerly Empire State Horsemen's Assoc.). Fellow, Pearson Coll., Yale, 1949-. *Address:* (home and office) Reid Enterprises, Ophir Farm, Purchase, New York 10577, USA. *Clubs:* Century, Overseas Press, Silurians, Pilgrims, Amateur Ski (New York); Metropolitan (Washington); St Regis Yacht; Manursing Is; Windham Mountain.

REID, Flight Lt William, VC 1943; National Cattle and Sheep Adviser (based at Spillers Farm Feeds Ltd, Remington House, 65 Holborn Viaduct, EC1A 2FH), Spillers Ltd, since 1959; Agriculture Adviser, The MacRobert Trust, Douneside, Tarland, Aberdeenshire, from 1950; *b* 21 Dec. 1921; *s* of late William Reid, Baillieston, Glasgow; *m* 1952, Violet Gallagher, 11 Dryburgh Gdns, Glasgow, NW1; one *s* one *d. Educ:* Coatbridge Secondary Sch.; Glasgow Univ.; West of Scotland Coll. of Agriculture. Student of Metallurgy, Sept. 1940; BSc (Agric.), 1949; Post-Graduate World Travelling Scholarship for 6 months, to study Agric. and Installations in India, Australia, NZ, USA and Canada, 1949-50. Joined RAF 1941; trained in Lancaster, Calif, USA. Won VC during a trip to Düsseldorf, 3 Nov. 1943, when member of 61 Squadron; pilot RAFVR, 617 Squadron (prisoner); demobilised, 1946; recalled to RAF for 3 months, Dec. 1951. Joined RAFVR, commissioned Jan. 1949, 103 Reserve Centre, Perth. *Recreations:* golf, shooting, fishing, etc. *Address:* Morven, 68 Upper Hall Park, Berkhamsted, Herts. *T:* Berkhamsted 2541. *Club:* Royal Air Force Reserves.

REID, Sir William, Kt 1972; CBE 1962; PhD, DSc; Chairman, Northern Economic Planning Council, 1970-73; *b* 20 June 1906; *o s* of late Sir Charles Carlow Reid; *m* 1935, Sheila Janette Christiana Davidson; one *s* one *d. Educ:* Dollar Acad.; Dunfermline High School. Early underground practical experience in coal mining attached to The Fife Coal Co. Ltd, and in the Ruhr and US. BSc (Mining and Metallurgy) 1929, and PhD (Mining) 1933, Univ. of Edinburgh. Held various mining appointments with The Fife Coal Co. Ltd, 1922-42; apptd Gen. Works Manager and Dir, 1942. Leader of Ministry of Fuel and Power Technical Mission to the Ruhr Coalfield, 1945; apptd in the Scottish Div. Nat. Coal Board, Prod. Dir, 1947, Deputy Chairman, 1950, Chairman, 1952; Board Member for Production, NCB, 1955-57; Chm., Durham Div., NCB, 1957-63; Chm., Northumberland and Durham Div., NCB, 1964-67, Regional Chm., 1967-69. Leader of NCB Technical Mission to coalfields of Soviet Union, 1956. Chm., Northern Regional Marketing Cttee, 1966. Mem., N Reg. Econ. Planning Council, 1965. Chairman: Northern Brick Co., 1968-71; Associated Heat Services (N) Ltd, 1968-71; Chm., Victor Products (Wallsend) Ltd, 1972-77; Chm., Council, Univ. of Durham, 1972. President: Mining Inst. of Scotland, 1951-52; IMinE, 1956-57. Hon. DCL Durham, 1970. *Publications:* numerous papers related to industry, particularly coal mining. *Recreation:* golf. *Address:* Norwood, Picktree Village, Chester-le-Street, Co. Durham. *T:* Chester-le-Street 882260.

REID, William, FSA; FMA; Director, National Army Museum, since 1970; *b* Glasgow, 8 Nov. 1926; *o s* of Colin Colquhoun Reid and Mary Evelyn Bingham; *m* 1958, Nina Frances

Brigden. *Educ:* Glasgow and Oxford. Commnd RAF Regt, 1946-48. Joined staff of Armouries, Tower of London, 1956. Organising Sec., 3rd Internat. Congress of Museums of Arms and Military History, London, Glasgow and Edinburgh, 1963; Sec.-Gen., Internat. Assoc. of Museums of Arms and Military History, 1969-; Mem., British Nat. Cttee, ICOM, 1973-. Fellow, Soc. of Antiquaries, 1965 (Mem. Council, 1975-76); Fellow, Museums Assoc., 1974. Trustee, Royal Armoured Corps Tank Museum, 1970-. *Publications:* The Lore of Arms, 1976 (also trans. French, German, Danish and Swedish); contribs to Connoisseur, Guildhall Miscellany, Jl of Arms and Armour Soc. and other British and foreign jls. *Recreations:* the study of armour and arms, music, ornithology. *Address:* 66 Ennerdale Road, Richmond, Surrey. *T:* 01-940 0904. *Club:* Athenæum.

REID, William Kennedy; Under-Secretary, Department of Education and Science, since 1974; Accountant-General, since 1976; *b* 15 Feb. 1931; 3rd *s* of late James and Elspet Reid; *m* 1959, Ann, *d* of Rev. Donald Campbell; two *s* one *d. Educ:* Robert Gordon's Coll.; George Watson's Coll.; Univ. of Edinburgh; Trinity Coll., Cambridge. MA 1st cl. Classics Edinburgh, 1952; BA 1st cl. Class. Tripos Pt II Cantab 1956. Ferguson scholar 1952; Craven scholar 1956. Nat. service, 1952-54. Min. of Educn, 1956; Asst Private Sec. to Minister, 1958-60; Cabinet Office, 1964; Private Sec. to Sec. of Cabinet, 1965-67; Asst Sec., DES, 1967; Secretary: Council for Scientific Policy, 1967-72. *Address:* The Wing, Portman Park, Tonbridge, Kent TN9 1LW. *T:* Tonbridge 355789.

REID-ADAM, Randle, CBE 1953 (OBE 1947); *b* 16 Jan. 1912; *s* of late James and of Helen Reid-Adam; *m* 1942, Rita Audrey Carty; two *d. Educ:* Oundle; Trinity Hall, Cambridge. Appointed to Department of Overseas Trade, 1933. Commercial Secretary, British Embassy, Washington, 1940. Served in Foreign Service posts at Cairo, New York, Cologne, Stockholm, San Francisco and Panama; retired 1964. *Address:* Thuya, Draycott, near Moreton-in-Marsh, Glos.

REIDHAVEN, Viscount, (Master of Seafield); James Andrew Ogilvie-Grant; *b* 30 Nov. 1963; *s* and *heir* of Earl of Seafield, *qv*.

REIDY, Joseph Patrick Irwin, FRCS; Consulting Plastic Surgeon, retired: Westminster Hospital, 1948-72; Stoke Mandeville Hospital, Bucks, 1951-72 (Director, Plastic Surgery, 1957-72); Oldchurch Hospital, Romford, 1946-72; Consulting Plastic Surgeon (Hon.), St Paul's Hospital, WC, 1959-72; *b* 30 October 1907; 2nd *s* of late Dr Jerome J. Reidy, JP, MD, Co. Limerick and London and of Alderman Mrs F. W. Reidy, JP (*née* Dawson), Castle Dawson, Co. Derry; *m* 1943, Anne (*d* 1970), *e d* of late T. Johnson, and of late Mrs T. Johnson, County Durham; three *d*; *m* 1972, Freda M. Clout (*née* Lowe), Gosfield Hall, Essex. *Educ:* Stonyhurst College, Lancs; St John's Coll., Cambridge; London Hospital. MA (Nat. Sci. Trip.) (Cantab); MD, BCh (Cantab); FRCS. Casualty Officer and Ho. Phys., Poplar Hosp., 1932; Ho. Surg. and Casualty Officer, London Hosp., 1933; Ho. Surg., Leicester Roy. Inf., 1934; General Practitioner, 1934-37. Surgeon H. Div., Metropolitan Police, 1934-37. Hon. Dem. of Anatomy, Med. Sch., Middx Hosp., 1938; Civilian Surg., RAF Hosp., Halton, Bucks, 1939; Res. Surg. Officer; EMS, Albert Dock Hosp., 1939-40; EMS, St Andrew's Hosp., Billericay, 1940-42; Chief Asst, Plastic Surgery, St Thomas' Hosp., 1943-48. Cons. Plastic Surgeon, Essex Co. Hosp., Colchester, 1943-46; Senior Grade Surgeon, Plastic Surg. Unit, Min. of Pensions: Stoke Mandeville Hosp., Bucks, 1942-51; Queen Mary's Hosp., Roehampton, 1942-51. Consulting Plastic Surgeon: Middlesex CC, 1944-48; Nelson Hosp., Kingston, 1948-50; Metropolitan ENT Hosp., 1948-50; West Middlesex Hosp.; Lord Mayor Treloar Hosp., Alton, 1953-56. Hon. Chief MO, Amateur Boxing Association, 1948; Hon. Secretary and Treas. United Hospitals Rugby Football Club, 1957-62. Liveryman Soc. of Apothecaries; BMA; Freeman of City of London; FRSocMed; FMedSoc Lond.; Fellow Hunterian Soc.; Pres., Chiltern Medical Soc., 1958-60; Pres., Brit. Assoc. of Plastic Surgeons, 1962. Member British Assoc. of Surgeons. Hunterian Professor, RCS 1957, 1968. Member, Brit. Acad. of Forensic Sciences; Lecturer, London Univ., 1952; Purkinje Medal, Czechoslovak Acad. of Sciences, 1965. *Publications:* contrib. since 1944 to: Proc. Roy. Soc. Med., Medical Press, West London Medico-Chirurgical Journal, British Journal of Plastic Surgery, BMJ, Medical History 2nd World War, Monograph Plastic Surgery and Physiotherapy, Annals RCS, etc. *Recreations:* gardening, sailing, fishing. *Address:* 5 Salisbury Terrace, Baltimore, Co. Cork, Ireland. *T:* Baltimore 75. *Club:* Royal Over-Seas League.

REIGATE, Baron *cr* 1970 (Life Peer), of Outwood, Surrey; **John Kenyon Vaughan-Morgan;** Bt 1960; PC 1961; *b* 2 Feb. 1905; *yr s* of late Sir Kenyon Vaughan-Morgan, DL, OBE, MP and late

Lady Vaughan-Morgan; *m* 1940, Emily, *d* of late Mr and Mrs W. Redmond Cross, New York City; two *d. Educ:* Eton; Christ Church, Oxford. Mem. Chelsea Borough Council, 1928; Member of London County Council for Chelsea, 1946-52; Chm. East Fulham Conservative and Unionist Assoc., 1935-38 (Pres. 1945); MP (C) Reigate Div. of Surrey, 1950-70. Parly Sec., Min. of Health, 1957; Minister of State, BoT, 1957-59. Dir, Morgan Crucible Co. Ltd, now retired. Chm. Bd of Govs, Westminster Hosp., 1963-74 (Mem., 1960). Pres., Royal Philanthropic Sch., Redhill. Dep. Chm., South Westminster Justices, now retired. Mem., Court of Assistants, Merchant Taylors Co. (Master 1970). Hon. Freeman, Borough of Reigate, 1971. Served War of 1939-45; Welsh Guards, 1940; GSO2, War Office; GSO1, HQ 21 Army Group (despatches). *Address:* 36 Eaton Square, SW1. *T:* 01-235 6506. *Clubs:* Brooks's, Hurlingham.

REILLY, Sir (D'Arcy) Patrick, GCMG 1968 (KCMG 1957; CMG 1949); OBE 1942; Chairman: Banque Nationale de Paris Ltd (formerly British and French Bank), since 1969; *b* 17 March 1909; *s* of late Sir D'Arcy Reilly, Indian Civil Service; *m* 1938, Rachel Mary, *d* of late Brigadier-General Sir Percy Sykes, KCIE, CB, CMG; two *d. Educ:* Winchester; New Coll., Oxford. (1st class Hon. Mods, 1930, Lit Hum 1932), Hon. Fellow 1972. Laming Travelling Fellow, Queen's College, 1932; Fellow of All Souls College, 1932-39, 1969-; Diplomatic Service, 1933; Third Secretary, Tehran, 1935-38; Ministry of Economic Warfare, 1939-42; First Secretary, Algiers, 1943; Paris, 1944; Athens, 1945. Counsellor, HM Foreign Service, 1947; Counsellor at Athens, 1947-48; Imperial Defence College, 1949; Assistant Under-Secretary of State, Foreign Office, 1950-53; Minister in Paris, 1953-56; Dep. Under-Sec. of State, Foreign Office, Oct. 1956; Ambassador to the USSR, 1957-60; Dep. Under-Sec. of State, Foreign Office, 1960-64; Official Head of UK Delegation to UN Conference on Trade and Development, 1964; Ambassador to France, 1965-68. Pres., 1972-75, Vice-Pres., 1975-, London Chamber of Commerce and Industry. Chairman: London Chamber of Commerce Standing Cttee for Common Market countries, 1969-72; Overseas Policy Cttee, Assoc. of British Chambers of Commerce, 1970-72; London Univ. Management Cttee, British Inst. in Paris; Council, Bedford Coll., London Univ., 1970-75. *Address:* Hampden Cottage, Ramsden, Oxford OX7 3AU. *T:* Ramsden 348. *Club:* Athenæum.

REILLY, Noel Marcus Prowse, CMG 1958; MA Cantab; BSc(Econ), PhD London; Deputy Head of UK Treasury Delegation, Washington, and Alternate Director for the UK, International Bank for Reconstruction and Development, International Finance Corporation and International Development Association, 1962-65, retired; *b* 31 Dec. 1902; *s* of late Frederick Reilly and late Ellen Prowse; *m* 1st, 1927, Dolores Albra Pratten (marr. diss., 1963); one *s* one *d*; 2nd, 1963, Dorothy Alma Rainsford. *Educ:* University Coll. Sch.; Gonville and Caius College, Cambridge. Schoolmaster, Boston, Massachusetts, USA, 1924; business in New Zealand, 1926, England, 1928; Secretary, Area Cttee for National Fitness for Oxon, Bucks, and Berks, 1938; Press Censor, Ministry of Information, 1939; Principal, HM Treasury, 1946; 1st Cl. Hons Economics, London, 1946; Economic Counsellor, Persian Gulf, 1953-59; Financial Counsellor, HM Embassy, Washington, 1960-65. *Publication:* The Key to Prosperity, 1931. *Recreations:* ski-ing, sailing, canoeing. *Address:* North Sandwich, New Hampshire 03259, USA.

REILLY, Sir Patrick; *see* Reilly, Sir D. P.

REILLY, Sir Paul, Kt 1967; Director: Conran Associates; The Building Trades Exhibition Ltd; Chairman, Race International Design Ltd; part-time Consultant on design matters, Courtaulds Ltd; Director, Design Council (formerly Council of Industrial Design), 1960-77; *b* 29 May 1912; *s* of late Prof. Sir Charles Reilly, formerly Head of Liverpool Sch. of Architecture; *m* 1st, 1939, Pamela Wentworth Foster; one *d*; 2nd, 1952, Annette Stockwell. *Educ:* Winchester; Hertford College, Oxford; London School of Economics. Salesman and Sales Manager, Venesta Ltd, 1934-36; Leader Page Editor and Features Editor, News Chronicle, 1936-40. RAC, 1940; RNVR 1941-45. Editorial Staff, Modern Plastics, New York, 1946; Co-Editor, British Plastics Encyclopædia, 1947; Chief Information Officer, Council of Industrial Design, 1948; Deputy Director, 1954. Member: Council, Royal Society of Arts, 1959-62, 1963-70; Council, BTA, 1960-70; Council, RCA 1963-; BBC General Advisory Council, 1964-70; BNEC, 1966-70; British Railways Bd Design Panel, 1966-; Environment Panel, 1977-; GLC Historic Buildings Cttee, 1967-; Post Office Stamp Adv. Cttee, 1967-, Design Adv. Cttee, 1970-; British Council Fine Arts Adv. Cttee, 1970-; Conseil Supérieur de la Création Esthétique Industrielle (France), 1971-73; Adv. Council of Science Policy Foundn,

1971-; British Crafts Centre Bd, 1972-77; Nat. Theatre Design Adv. Cttee, 1974-; Royal Fine Art Commn, 1976-; Crafts Advisory Cttee, 1977- (Chief Exec., 1971-77). Chm., Building Conservation Assoc., 1977-. President: Soc. of Designer-Craftsmen, 1976-; Assoc. of Art Institutions, 1977-. Governor: Hammersmith Coll. of Art and Building, 1948-67; Central Sch. of Art and Design, 1953-74; Camberwell Sch. of Art and Design, 1967-77; City of Birmingham Polytechnic, 1970-77. Mem., Ct of Governors, LSE, 1975-. Hon. FSIA, 1959; Hon. FRIBA, 1965; Sen. Fellow, RCA, 1972; Hon. Assoc. Manchester Coll. of Art, 1963; Hon. Member, Art Workers Guild, 1961; Hon. Corresponding Mem., Svenskaslöjdforeningen, 1956. Hon. DSc Loughborough, 1977. Comdr, Royal Order of Vasa (Sweden), 1961. Bicentenary Medal, RSA, 1963. *Publication:* An Introduction to Regency Architecture (Art and Technics), 1948. *Recreation:* looking at buildings. *Address:* 3 Alexander Place, SW7 2SG. *T:* 01-589 4031. *Clubs:* Athenæum, Arts.

REINDORP, Rt. Rev. G. E.; *see* Salisbury, Bishop of.

REINERS, William Joseph; Director of Research Policy, Departments of the Environment and Transport, since 1977; *b* 19 May 1923; *s* of late William and Hannah Reiners; *m* 1952, Catharine Anne Palmer; three *s* one *d. Educ:* Liverpool Collegiate Sch.; Liverpool Univ. RAE Farnborough, 1944-46; Min. of Works, 1946-50; Head, Building Operations and Economics Div., Building Research Station, 1950-63; Dir of Research and Information, MPBW, 1963-71; Dir of Research Requirements, DoE, 1971-77. *Publications:* various on building operations and economics. *Address:* Valais, Berks Hill, Chorleywood, Herts. *T:* Chorleywood 3293.

REINHARDT, Max; Joint Chairman, Chatto, Bodley Head and Jonathan Cape Ltd, since 1973; Managing Director, Bodley Head Group of Publishers, since 1957; Chairman, Max Reinhardt Ltd and HFL (Publishers) Ltd, since 1948; *b* 30 Nov. 1915; *s* of Ernest Reinhardt and Frieda Reinhardt (*née* Darr); *m* 1st, 1947, Margaret Leighton, CBE (marr. diss. 1955; she *d* 1976); 2nd, 1957, Joan, *d* of Carlisle and Dorothy MacDonald, New York City; two *d. Educ:* English High Sch. for Boys, Istanbul; Ecole des Hautes Etudes Commerciales, Paris; London School of Economics. Acquired HFL (Publishers) Ltd, 1947; founded Max Reinhardt Ltd, 1948, which bought: The Bodley Head Ltd, 1956; Putnam & Co. and Bowes & Bowes, 1963. Mem. Council: Publishers' Assoc., 1963-69; Royal Academy of Dramatic Art, 1965-. *Recreations:* squash racquets, tennis, swimming, bridge. *Address:* 16 Pelham Crescent, SW7 2NR. *T:* 01-589 5527. *Clubs:* Savile, Beefsteak, Garrick, Hurlingham, Royal Automobile.

REISS, Sir John (Anthony Ewart), Kt 1967; BEM 1941; Chairman of Associated Portland Cement Manufacturers Ltd, 1957-74; *b* 8 April 1909; *m* 1st, 1938, Marie Ambrosine Phillpotts; one *s* one *d*; 2nd, 1951, Elizabeth Booth-Jones (*née* MacEwan); two *d. Educ:* Eton. Cotton, Banking, Insurance, 1928-34. Joined Associated Portland Cement Manufacturers, 1934; Dir, 1946; Managing Director, 1948. Chairman: Foundn for Business Responsibilities; British Empire Migration Council; Aims for Freedom and Enterprise (formerly Aims of Industry), 1967-; Hon. Treasurer, British Empire Cancer Campaign. *Recreations:* shooting, cricket. *Address:* The Clachan, Newtonairds, near Dumfries. *T:* Dunscore 34. *Club:* Buck's.

REISS, John Henry, OBE 1972; British Ambassador to Liberia, 1973-78; *b* 26 March 1918; *s* of late Rev. Leopold Reiss and Dora Lillian (*née* Twisden-Bedford); *m* 1943, Dora Lily (*née* York); one *s* two *d. Educ:* Bradfield Coll.; St Thomas' Hosp. Served War, Army, 1939-42. Kenya Govt, 1945-59; Dir of Information, 1954-59; Commonwealth Office, 1959; Dir of Information Services: Johannesburg, 1961-63; Wellington, New Zealand, 1963-65. Foreign and Commonwealth Office, 1966-69; Dep. British Govt Representative, Antigua/St Kitts, 1969-73. *Recreations:* golf, tennis, bridge. *Address:* 2 Cumberland Court, Oaks Drive, Colchester, Essex. *Club:* Royal Over-Seas League.

REISZ, Karel; film director; *b* 21 July 1926; *s* of Joseph Reisz and Frederika; *m* 1963, Betsy Blair; three *s. Educ:* Leighton Park Sch., Reading; Emmanuel Coll., Cambridge (BA). Formerly: co-ed with Lindsay Anderson, film magazine, Sequence; worked for BFI; first Programme Dir, National Film Theatre. Co-directed, with Tony Richardson, Momma Don't Allow, 1956; produced: Every Day Except Christmas, 1957; This Sporting Life, 1960; directed: We Are the Lambeth Boys, 1958; Saturday Night and Sunday Morning, 1959; Night Must Fall, 1963; Morgan, a Suitable Case for Treatment, 1965; Isadora, 1967; The Gambler, 1975; Dog Soldiers, 1977. *Publication:* The Technique of Film Editing (also ed), 1953. *Address:* c/o Film Contracts, 2 Lower James Street, Golden Square, W1.

REITH, Barony of (*cr* 1940); title disclaimed by 2nd Baron; *see under* Reith, Christopher John.

REITH, Christopher John; farmer; *b* 27 May 1928; *s* of 1st Baron Reith, KT, PC, GCVO, GBE, CB, TD, of Stonehaven, and Muriel Katharine, *y d* of late John Lynch Odhams; *S* father, 1971, as 2nd Baron Reith, but disclaimed his peerage for life, 1972; *m* 1969, Penelope Margaret Ann, *er d* of late H. R. Morris; one *s* one *d*. *Educ*: Eton; Worcester College, Oxford (MA Agriculture). Served in Royal Navy, 1946-48; farming thereafter. *Recreations:* fishing, gardening, forestry. *Heir (to disclaimed peerage):* s Hon. James Harry John Reith, *b* 2 June 1971. *Address:* Whitebank Farm, Methven, Perthshire. *T:* Methven 333.

REITH, Douglas, QC (Scotland) 1957; a National Insurance Commissioner, since 1960; *b* 29 June 1919; *s* of William Reith and Jessie McAllan; *m* 1949, Elizabeth Archer Stewart; one *s* one *d*. *Educ*: Aberdeen Grammar School; Aberdeen University (MA, LLB). Became Member of Faculty of Advocates in Scotland, 1946. Served in Royal Signals, 1939-46. Standing Junior Counsel in Scotland to Customs and Excise, 1949-51; Advocate-Depute, Crown Office, Scotland, 1953-57; Pres., Pensions Appeal Tribunal (Scotland), 1958-64; Chm., Nat. Health Service Tribunal (Scotland), 1963-65. *Address:* 11 Heriot Row, Edinburgh EH3 6HP. *T:* 031-556 6966. *Club:* New (Edinburgh).

REITLINGER, Gerald Roberts, BLitt; Writer on contemporary history and the history of art; Editor and publisher of Drawing and Design, 1927-29; *b* London, 2 March 1900; 3rd *s* of Albert Reitlinger; *m* 1945; one *d*. *Educ*: Westminster School; Christ Church, Oxford. Studied art, Slade School and Westminster School of Art; exhibited paintings at New English Art Club; London Group, British Artists exhibitions; National Society, etc; directed with Professor D. Talbot Rice, Oxford Univ. Expedition to Hira, Iraq, 1931-32; served RA, 1939-41; lectr to HM Forces, 1942-45. *Publications:* A Tower of Skulls, 1932; South of the Clouds, 1939; The Final Solution, 1953 (rev. edn, 1967); The SS, Alibi of a Nation, 1956; The House built on Sand; Conflicts of German policy in Russia, 1939-45, 1960; The Economics of Taste: vol. 1, The Rise and Fall of Picture Prices 1760-1960, 1961; vol. 2, The Rise and Fall of Objets d'Art Prices since 1750, 1963; vol. 3, The Art Market in the 1960s, 1970; book reviews and articles, Daily Telegraph, Observer, Commentary, Connoisseur, Antiques Year Book, Financial Times, New York Times, etc; numerous archæological monographs in Iraq; Ars Islamica, Royal Central Asian Society Journal, The Burlington Magazine, Ars Orientalis, OCS Bulletin, etc. *Address:* Woodgate House, Beckley, Rye, East Sussex. *Club:* Savile.

RELPH, Michael Leighton George; film producer, director, designer, writer; *s* of late George Relph and Deborah Relph (later Harker); *m* 1st, 1939, Doris Gosden (marr. diss.); one *s*; 2nd, 1950, Maria Barry; one *d*. *Educ*: Bembridge Sch. Stage designer, 1940-50: West-end prodns include: Indoor Fireworks; The Doctor's Dilemma; Up and Doing; Watch on the Rhine; The Man Who Came to Dinner; Frieda; Saloon Bar; Old Acquaintance; Quiet Week-end; Heartbreak House; Relative Values; A Month in the Country; The Last of Summer; Love in Idleness; The White Carnation; The Petrified Forest; The Banbury Nose; They Came to a City. Began film career as apprentice, then Asst Art Dir, Gaumont British Studios; Art Dir, Warner Brothers Studios; Art Dir, Ealing Studios, 1942-45: prodns include: The Bells Go Down; Dead of Night; Champagne Charley; Nicholas Nickleby; Saraband for Dead Lovers (nominated Hollywood Oscar); Associate Producer to Michael Balcon, 1945; subseq. Producer with Basil Dearden as Dir until Dearden's death, 1972: prodns include: The Captive Heart; Kind Hearts and Coronets; The Blue Lamp (Best British Film Award, Brit. Film Acad.); Frieda; Saraband for Dead Lovers; I Believe in You (co-author); The Ship that Died of Shame; The Rainbow Jacket; The Square Ring; The Gentle Gunman; Cage of Gold; Pool of London. Director: Davy, 1957; Rockets Galore, 1958; Producer: Violent Playground; Sapphire (Best British Film Award, Brit. Film Acad.); All Night Long; The Smallest Show on Earth. Founder Dir, Allied Film Makers: produced: League of Gentlemen; Victim; Man in the Moon (co-author); Life for Ruth. Director: The Mind Benders; Woman of Straw (co-author); Masquerade (co-author); The Assassination Bureau (also author and designer); The Man Who Haunted Himself. Chm., Film Prodn Assoc. of GB, 1971-76; Mem., Cinematograph Films Council, 1971-76; Governor, BFI (also Chm., Prodn Bd). *Recreations:* reading, theatre going, painting. *Address:* The Lodge, Kingstown Street, Fitzroy Road, NW1 8JP. *T:* 01-586 0249.

REMEZ, Aharon; Chairman, Airports Authority Board, Israel, since 1977; *b* 8 May 1919; *m* 1952, Rita (*née* Levy); one *s* three *d*. *Educ*: Herzliah Grammar Sch., Tel Aviv. Volunteered for service with RAF, and served as fighter pilot in Gt Brit. and in European theatre of war; after end of war with British Occupation forces in Germany. Mem., kibbutz Kfar Blum, 1947-. Dir Planning and of Ops and subseq. Chief of Staff, and C-in-C Israel Air Force (rank Brig.-Gen.), 1948-51; Head of Min. of Defence Purchasing Mission, USA, 1951-53; Aviation Adviser to Minister of Def., 1953-54; Mem. Bd of Dirs, Solel Boneh Ltd, and Exec. Dir, Koor Industries Ltd, 1954-59; MP (Israel Lab Party) for Mapai, 1956-57; Admin. Dir, Weizmann Inst. of Science, Rehovot, 1959-60. Dir, Internat. Co-op. Dept, Min. for Foreign Affairs, Jerusalem, 1960; Adviser on Internat. Co-operation to Min. for Foreign Affairs, also Consultant to OECD, 1964-65; Ambassador of Israel to the Court of St James's, 1965-70. Dir Gen., Israel Ports Authority, 1970-77. Chm., Nat. Council for Civil Aviation, 1960-. *Recreations:* handicrafts, sculpture. *Address:* 8 San Martin Street, The Cottages, Jerusalem, Israel.

REMNANT, family name of **Baron Remnant**.

REMNANT, 3rd Baron *cr* 1928, of Wenhaston; **James Wogan Remnant,** Bt 1917; FCA; Managing Director, Touche, Remnant & Co.; *b* 23 October 1930; *s* of 2nd Baron and of Dowager Lady Remnant; *S* father, 1967; *m* 1953, Serena Jane Loehnis, *o d* of Sir Clive Loehnis, *qv*; three *s* one *d*. *Educ*: Eton. Partner, Touche Ross & Co., 1958-70; Director: Australia and New Zealand Banking Group (Dep. Chm.); National Provident Institution; Ultramar Ltd; Union Discount Co. of London (Dep. Chm.); Atlas Electric & General Trust, United Dominions Trust; Standard Trust (Chm.), and other cos. A Church Comr, 1976-. Hon. Treasurer, The Queen's Silver Jubilee Appeal Council, 1976-. FCA 1955. *Heir:* s Hon. Philip John Remnant [*b* 20 December 1954; *m* 1977, Caroline Elizabeth Clare, *yr d* of late Godfrey H. R. Cavendish]. *Address:* Bear Place, Hare Hatch, Reading RG10 9XR.

RENALS, Sir Stanley, 4th Bt, *cr* 1895; formerly in the Merchant Navy; *b* 20 May 1923; 2nd *s* of Sir James Herbert Renals, 2nd Bt; *S* brother, Sir Herbert Renals, 3rd Bt, 1961; *m* 1957, Maria Dolores Rodriguez Pinto, *d* of late José Rodriguez Ruiz; one *s*. *Educ*: City of London Freemen's School. *Heir:* s Stanley Michael Renals, *b* 14 January 1958. *Address:* 47 Baden Road, Brighton, East Sussex BN2 4DP. *T:* Brighton 682734.

RENAUD, Madeleine, (Mme Jean-Louis Barrault); Officier de la Légion d'Honneur; actress; formed Madeleine Renaud-Jean-Louis Barrault Company, 1946, Co-director and player leading parts; *b* Paris, 21 Feb. 1903; *d* of Prof. Jean Renaud; *m* 1940, Jean-Louis Barrault, *qv*. *Educ*: Lycée Racine; Conservatoire de Paris (Ier Prix de Comédie). Pensionnaire, Comédie Française, 1921-46. Has appeared in classical and modern plays, and in films. Commandeur des Arts et Lettres. *Publications:* novels, short stories, plays. *Address:* 18 Avenue du Président Wilson, Paris 16e, France.

RENAULT, Mary, (pseudonym of **Mary Challans**); *b* 4 Sept. 1905; *er d* of late Dr Frank Challans, and of Clementine Mary Newsome Challans (*née* Baxter). *Educ*: Clifton High School, Bristol; St Hugh's Coll. Oxford (MA Oxon). Radcliffe Infirmary, Oxford. Completed nursing training in 1937; returned to nursing, 1939, until end of War. FRSL 1959. *Publications:* Purposes of Love, 1939; Kind Are Her Answers, 1940; The Friendly Young Ladies, 1944; Return to Night, 1946; North Face, 1948; The Charioteer, 1953; The Last of the Wine, 1956; The King Must Die, 1958; The Bull from the Sea, 1962; The Lion in the Gateway (for children), 1964; The Mask of Apollo, 1966; Fire from Heaven, 1970 (Silver Pen Award 1971); The Persian Boy, 1972; The Nature of Alexander (biography), 1975; contrib. TLS. *Recreations:* conversation and dogs. *Address:* 3 Atholl Road, Camps Bay, Cape Town 8001, South Africa.

RENDALL, Archibald, OBE 1967; HM Consul General, Lille, France, since 1977; *b* 10 Aug. 1921; *s* of late James Henry Rendall; *m* 1951, Sheila Catherine (*née* Martin); one *d*. *Educ*: Broughton Sch., Edinburgh. Inland Revenue Dept, 1938; served in RN, 1941-46; joined Foreign (subseq. Diplomatic) Service, 1948; Vice-Consul, Monrovia, 1948-49; Vice-Consul and 2nd Sec., Baghdad, 1950-54; FO, 1954-57; 1st Sec. (Commercial), Beirut, 1957-60; Consul (Commercial), New York, 1960-65; 1st Sec. (Commercial), Bucharest, 1965-68; FCO, 1969-72; Consul-Gen., St Louis, 1972-77. *Address:* c/o Foreign and Commonwealth Office, SW1A 2AH.

RENDALL, Peter Godfrey; Headmaster, Bembridge School, Isle of Wight, 1959-74; Clerk to Burford Parish Council; *b* 25 April 1909; *s* of Godfrey A. H. Rendall and Mary Whishaw Rendall (*née* Wilson); *m* 1944, Ann McKnight Kauffer; two *s* one *d*. *Educ:* Rugby School; Corpus Christi College, Oxford. Assistant Master: Felsted School, Essex, 1931-34; Upper Canada College, Toronto, 1934-35; Felsted School, Essex, 1935-43. Served War of 1939-45, RAF, 1943-46, Flight-Lieut. Second Master, St Bees School, Cumberland, 1946-48; Headmaster Achimota School, Gold Coast, 1949-54; Assistant Master, Lancing College, 1954-59. Coronation Medal, 1953. *Recreations:* reading, gardening, carpentry, painting. *Address:* Chippings, The Hill, Burford, Oxon. *Clubs:* Royal Commonwealth Society; Oxford Union Society.

RENDALL, Philip Stanley, MBE 1964; DL; retired as Managing Director of Courtaulds Ltd (1943-61), and as Deputy Chairman (1949-61); *b* 7 July 1895; *s* of late Dr Stanley Rendall and Claire Louise Rendall; *m* 1923, Louise Gwendoline, 2nd *d* of James Calcott; two *d*. *Educ:* Shrewsbury. Served European War, 1914-18, in France. Joined Courtaulds Ltd, 1920; Director, 1937. Chairman, Lustre Fibres Limited, 1946-57; formerly Chairman, British Nylon Spinners Ltd, Chairman, British Celanese Ltd, 1960-61 (Vice-Chm., 1957-60). High Sheriff of Warwickshire, 1949-50. Commandant, Warwickshire Special Constabulary, retired. DL Co. Warwick, 1967. Chevalier de la Légion d'Honneur, 1957. *Recreations:* golf, tennis. *Address:* 47 Kenilworth Road, Leamington Spa. *T:* Leamington Spa 24682. *Club:* Leamington Tennis Court (Leamington).

RENDEL, Sir George William, KCMG 1943 (CMG 1932); *b* 1889; *y s* of George Wightwick Rendel, Civil Engineer and Professional Civil Lord of the Admiralty; *m* 1914, Geraldine, OBE 1943 (*d* 1965), *d* of Gerald Beresford FitzGerald; two *s* one *d* (and one *d* decd). *Educ:* Downside; Queen's College, Oxford (Classical scholar, 1st Class, Mod. Hist. 1911). Entered Diplomatic Service, 1913; served in Berlin, Athens, Rome, Lisbon and Madrid; Head of the Eastern Department, Foreign Office, 1930-38; HM Envoy Extraordinary and Minister Plenipotentiary to Bulgaria, 1938-41; British Minister and (later) Ambassador to the Yugoslav Govt in London, 1941-43; Employed in Foreign Office and UK Representative on European Cttee of UNRRA, 1944-47; attended UNRRA Confs, Atlantic City, Montreal, Geneva, etc; UK Representative for Refugee questions on Econ. and Social Council of UN and on various other confs and UN Cttees in London, New York, Geneva, Lausanne, etc, 1945-47; British Ambassador to Belgium, 1947-50 (also Minister to Luxembourg, 1947-49); Chief United Kingdom Delegate on Austrian Treaty Commission in Vienna, 1947, and for negotiation of Treaty of Brussels, 1948; Montreux Straits Conference, 1936; crossed Arabia from the Persian Gulf to Red Sea (with Lady Rendel), visiting Hasa and Riyadh at the invitation of King Ibn Saud, 1937; negotiated agreement with Italy on Red Sea and Middle East, March 1938; visited the Belgian Congo, officially (with Lady Rendel), returning via East Africa, 1948. Retired on pension, 1950. Re-employed by the Foreign Office as Leader of UK Deleg. to Internat. High-frequency Broadcasting Conf., Rapallo, 1950, and as UK Mem. (and Chm.) of Tripartite Commn on German Debts, 1951-53; Chm. Commission on Constitutional Development in Singapore, 1953-54; UK Mem. of Saar Referendum Commission, 1955; Special Ambassador to Lima and La Paz for inaugurations of Presidents of Peru and Bolivia, 1956. Re-employed by the Foreign Office in connection with the Anglo-Egyptian Financial Agreement, 1959-64. Chm., Singer & Friedlander Ltd, 1957-68. *Publication:* The Sword and the Olive; Recollections of Diplomacy and the Foreign Service, 1913-54, 1957. *Recreations:* travelling, sketching, music. *Address:* Flat 5, 24 Lennox Gardens, SW1. *Club:* Travellers'.

RENDELL, Sir William, Kt 1967; General Manager, Commonwealth Development Corporation, 1953-73, retired; *b* 25 Jan. 1908; *s* of William Reginald Rendell and Hon. Janet Marion Rendell; *m* 1950, Annie Henriette Maria (*née* Thorsen). *Educ:* Winchester; Trinity Coll., Cambridge. FCA. Partner, Whinney Murray & Co., 1947-52. Mem., PLA. *Recreations:* shooting, fishing, gardening. *Address:* 10 Montpelier Place, SW7. *T:* 01-584 8232.

RENDLE, Peter Critchfield; Under-Secretary (Housing), Scottish Development Department, since 1973; *b* Truro, 31 July 1919; *s* of late Martyn Rendle and Florence Rendle (*née* Critchfield); *m* 1944, Helen Barbara Moyes; three *s*. *Educ:* Queen Elizabeth's Sch., Hartlebury. Clerical Officer, Min. of Transport, 1936. Served War, Royal Navy, ordinary seaman, 1940; RNVR: Sub-Lt, 1941-46. Min. of Transport, 1946-49; Min. of Town and Country Planning, 1949; Dept of Health for Scotland, 1950-59 (Sec., Guest Cttee on Bldg Legislation in

Scotland); Scottish Home and Health Dept, 1959-63; Scottish Educn Dept, 1963-72; Scottish Home and Health Dept, 1972-73; Scottish Development Dept, 1973. *Recreations:* umpiring for hockey (Scottish Hockey Assoc.: Umpire, 1963-65; Selector, 1965-70; Vice-Pres., 1972-74); taking photographs, gardening. *Address:* St Clair, 159 Granton Road, Edinburgh EH5 3NL. *T:* 031-552 3396.

RENDLESHAM, 8th Baron, *cr* 1806; **Charles Anthony Hugh Thellusson;** Royal Corps of Signals; *b* 15 March 1915; *s* of Lt-Col Hon. Hugh Edmund Thellusson, DSO (3rd *s* of 5th Baron); *S* uncle, 1943; *m* 1st, 1940, Margaret Elizabeth (who obtained a divorce, 1947; she *m* 1962, Patrick P. C. Barthropp) *d* of Lt-Col Robin Rome, Monk's Hall, Glemsford; one *d*; 2nd, 1947, Clare, *d* of Lt-Col D. H. G. McCririck; one *s* three *d*. *Educ:* Eton. *Heir:* *s* Hon. Charles William Brooke Thellusson, *b* 10 Jan. 1954. *Address:* 28 Walham Grove, SW6.
See also Sir William Goring, Bt.

RENFREW, Prof. (Andrew) Colin; Professor of Archaeology, University of Southampton, since 1972; *b* 25 July 1937; *s* of Archibald Renfrew and Helena Douglas Renfrew (*née* Savage); *m* 1965, Jane Margaret, *d* of Ven. Walter F. Ewbank, *qv*; two *s* one *d*. *Educ:* St Albans Sch.; St John's Coll., Cambridge (Exhibr) British Sch. of Archaeology, Athens. Pt I Nat. Scis Tripos 1960; BA 1st cl. hons Archaeol. and Anthrop. Tripos 1962; MA 1964; PhD 1965; ScD 1976. Pres., Cambridge Union Soc., 1961; Sir Joseph Larmor Award 1961. Nat. Service, Flying Officer (Signals), RAF, 1956-58. Res. Fellow, St John's Coll., Cambridge, 1965; Bulgarian Govt Schol., 1966; Univ. of Sheffield: Lectr in Prehistory and Archaeol., 1965-70; Sen. Lectr, 1970-72; Reader, 1972. Vis. Lectr, Univ. of Calif at Los Angeles, 1967. Contested (C) Sheffield Brightside, 1968; Vice-Chm., Sheffield Brightside Conserv. Assoc., 1968-72. Member: Ancient Monuments Bd for England, 1974-; Royal Commn on Historical Monuments (England), 1977-; Trustee, Antiquity Trust, 1974-; Chm., Hants Archaeol Cttee, 1974-; Dalrymple Lectr in Archaeol., Univ. of Glasgow, 1975; George Grant MacCusay Lectr, Harvard, 1977. Excavations: Saliagos near Antiparos, 1964-65; Sitagroi, Macedonia, 1968-70; Phylakopi in Melos, 1974-76; Quanterness, Orkney, 1972-74; Maes Howe, 1973-74; Ring of Brodgar, 1974; Liddle Farm, 1973-74. FSA 1968; FSAScot 1970. *Publications:* (with J. D. Evans) Excavations at Saliagos near Antiparos, 1968; The Emergence of Civilisation, 1972; (ed) The Explanation of Culture Change, 1973; Before Civilisation, 1973; (ed) British Prehistory, a New Outline, 1974; articles in archaeol jls. *Recreations:* modern art, numismatics, travel. *Address:* 17 Malcolm Close, Chandlers Ford, Hants. *T:* Chandlers Ford 2102. *Club:* United Oxford & Cambridge University.

RENFREW, Rt. Rev. Charles McDonald; Titular Bishop of Abula and Auxiliary to the Archbishop of Glasgow, (RC), since 1977; Vicar General of Archdiocese of Glasgow, since 1974; *b* 21 June 1929; *s* of Alexander Renfrew and Mary (*née* Dougherty). *Educ:* St Aloysius College, Glasgow; Scots College, Rome. PhL, STL (Gregorian). Ordained Rome, 1953; Assistant at Immaculate Conception, Glasgow, 1953-56; Professor and Procurator, Blairs Coll., Aberdeen, 1956-61; First Rector and founder of St Vincent's Coll., Langbank, 1961-74. Sound and television broadcasts for BBC and STV. *Publications:* St Vincent's Prayer Book, 1971; pamphlets and articles in newspapers and magazines. *Recreation:* music, especially grand and light opera. *Address:* St Joseph's, 38 Mansionhouse Road, Glasgow G41 3DN. *T:* 041-649 2228.

RENFREY, Rt. Rev. Lionel Edward William; Dean of Adelaide, since 1966; Assistant Bishop of Adelaide, since 1969; *b* Adelaide, SA, 26 March 1916; *s* of late Alfred Cyril Marinus Renfrey and Catherine Elizabeth Rose Frerichs (*née* Dickson); *m* 1948, Joan Anne, *d* of Donald Smith, Cooke's Plains, SA; one *s* five *d*. *Educ:* Unley High School; St Mark's Coll., Univ. of Adelaide; St Barnabas' Theological Coll., Adelaide. BA (First Cl. Hons English), ThL (ACT) (Second Cl. Hons). Deacon 1940, priest 1941, Dio. Adelaide; Curate, St Cuthbert's, Prospect, 1940-43; Mission Chaplain, Mid Yorke Peninsula, 1943-44; Warden, Brotherhood of St John Baptist, 1944-47; Priest-in-charge, Berri-Barmera, 1948-50; Kensington Gardens, 1950-57; Rector, St James', Mile End, 1957-63; Rural Dean, Western Suburbs, 1962-63; Organising Chaplain, Bishop's Home Mission Soc., 1963-66; Editor, Adelaide Church Guardian, 1961-66; Archdeacon of Adelaide, 1965-66; Examining Chaplain to Bishop of Adelaide, 1965-; Administrator (sede vacante), Diocese of Adelaide, 1974-75. SBStJ 1969. *Publications:* Father Wise: a Memoir, 1950; Short History of St Barnabas' Theological College, 1965. *Recreations:* reading, golf, motoring. *Address:* 40 Pennington Terrace, North Adelaide, S Australia 5006. *T:* 2672597. *Club:* Royal Adelaide Golf.

RENNELL, 2nd Baron, *cr* 1933, of Rodd, Herefordshire; **Francis James Rennell Rodd,** KBE 1944; CB 1943; JP; MA (Oxon); retired as Director, Morgan, Grenfell & Co., and other public bodies; *b* 25 Oct. 1895; *e s* of 1st Baron and Lilias (*d* 1951), *d* of J. A. Guthrie, Craigie, Forfar; *S* father, 1941; *m* 1928, Mary Constance Vivian, *d* of 1st Baron Bicester; four *d. Educ:* Eton; Balliol Coll., Oxford. Served in RFA in France, 1914-15; Intelligence Officer in Italy, 1916; Staff Officer in Libya, Egypt, Sinai, Palestine, and Syria, 1917-18 (despatches, Italian Order of St Maurice and Lazarus); entered Diplomatic Service, 1919; served in Rome, Sofia, where was Chargé d'Affaires, and Foreign Office; resigned, 1924; Stock Exchange, 1926-28; Bank of England, 1929-32; Manager, Bank for International Settlements, 1930-31. Served 1939-44 (despatches, CB, KBE); Major-General, Civil Affairs Administration in Middle East, E Africa, and Italy. Visiting Fellow, Nuffield Coll., Oxford, 1947-59. Exploration in S Sahara during 1922 and 1927, for which RGS awarded Cuthbert Peake Grant and Founder's Medal, 1929. Mem. Bd, BOAC, 1954-65. President, RGS, 1945-48; Hon. Vice-Pres. and Hon. Mem., RGS; Mem. Council, Brit. School in Rome; Mem. Council, British Association for Advancement of Science; Conservative. DL 1948, Vice-Lieutenant 1957-73, Herefordshire. Hon. LLD (Manchester), 1962. *Publications:* People of the Veil; General William Eaton; British Military Administration of African Territories, 1940-45; Valley on the March; and articles in periodicals. *Recreations:* geography and farming. *Heir: nephew* (John Adrian) Tremayne Rodd [*b* 28 June 1935; *m* 1977, Phyllis, *d* of T. D. Neill]. *Address:* 23 Great Winchester Street, EC2; The Rodd, near Presteigne, Powys. *T:* Presteigne 362. *Club:* Beefsteak.
See also Baroness Emmet of Amberley.

RENNERT, Guenther, Dr jur; Opera and Theatre Producer; Director, Bavarian State Opera, Munich, since 1967; *b* 1 April 1911; *m* 1956, Elisabeth Rennert (*née* Abegg); one *s* three *d. Educ:* Germany. Asst Prod., films, operas and plays, 1933-35; Producer in Frankfurt, 1935-37; Wuppertal, 1937-39; Head Producer: Charlottenburg Opera House, 1942-45, Munich, 1945-46; Dir of Opera and Dir State Opera House, Hamburg, 1946-56; Artistic Counsellor and Head of Production of Glyndebourne Festival Opera, 1959-67. Productions (Opera): Mozart, Wagner, Verdi, Rossini, Britten, Berg, Stravinski; Productions at: Salzburg Festival, 1948-; Edinburgh Festival, 1952-; Glyndebourne Festival, 1959-; New York Metropolitan Opera; Metropolitan National Company; San Francisco; London (Covent Garden); Hamburg; Stuttgart; Milan (Scala), 1954-; Munich (Staatsoper), 1962-. Prodns (Theatre): Shakespeare, O'Neill, Gogol, Schehade, Giraudoux, Brecht, MacLeish, Frisch, Hauptmann; Prodns in: Vienna (Burg Theater); Berlin (Schillertheater); Stuttgart (Staatstheater). Mem., Akademie der Künste, Berlin, 1961-. Brahms-Medaille, Hamburg, 1956; Decoration of Honour for Science and the Arts, Austria, 1970; Federal Republic of Germany, 1972; Bavaria, 1973. *Publications:* Bearbeitungen der Opern: Iphigenia in Aulis (Gluck), 1960; Der Türke in Italien (Rossini); Die Liebesprobe (Rossini), 1962; Jephta (Handel), 1958; Verlobung im Kloster (Prokoviev), 1962; translations of Puccini and Rossini; Opernarbeit, 1974. *Address:* 8033 Krailling, Schwalbenweg 11a, Germany. *Club:* Rotary.

RENNIE, Alexander Allan, QPM 1971; Chief Constable, West Mercia Constabulary, since 1975; *b* 13 June 1917; *s* of Charles Rennie and Susan Parsons Rennie; *m* 1941, Lucy Brunt; one *s* one *d. Educ:* Ellon Acad., Aberdeenshire. Armed Services, 1941-45: commnd 30 Corps Royal Northumberland Fusiliers; active service in Europe (mentioned in despatches, 1945). Joined Durham County Constab., 1937; Chief Supt, 1963; Dep. Chief Constable, Shropshire, 1963-67; Dir, Sen. Comd Course, Police Coll., Bramshill, 1967-69; Asst Chief Constable, West Mercia, 1969-72, Dep. Chief Constable, 1973-75. OStJ 1975. *Recreations:* golf, hill walking. *Address:* Green Acres, Tibberton, Droitwich, Worcs. *T:* Spetchley 204.

RENNIE, Sir Alfred (Baillie), Kt 1960; formerly a Federal Justice of the West Indies Federation (1958-62); *b* 18 March 1896; *s* of James Malcolm and Mary Jane Rennie; *m* 1925, Patricia Margaret O'Gorman; one *s* two *d. Educ:* Wolmer's School, Kingston, Jamaica; King's College, London. Lieut, British West Indies Regt, 1916-19. Called to the Bar, 1922; practised in Jamaica and Bermuda, 1922-29; Clerk of the Courts, Jamaica, 1929-33; Resident Magistrate, 1933-34; Crown Solicitor, 1934-49; Judge of Supreme Court of Jamaica, 1949-58. *Recreation:* shooting. *Address:* 24 Waterloo Road, Kingston 10, Jamaica.

RENNIE, Archibald Louden; Secretary, Scottish Home and Health Department, since 1977; *b* 4 June 1924; *s* of John and Isabella Rennie; *m* 1950, Kathleen Harkess; four *s. Educ:* Madras Coll.; St Andrews University. Experimental Officer, Mine Design Dept, Admty, 1944-47; Dept of Health for Scotland, 1947-62; Private Sec. to Sec. of State for Scotland, 1962-63; Asst Sec., Scottish Home and Health Dept, 1963-69; Registrar Gen. for Scotland, 1969-73; Under-Sec., Scottish Office, 1973-77. *Recreations:* Scottish literature, sailing, gardening. *Address:* 24 Mayfield Terrace, Edinburgh EH9 1RZ. *T:* 031-667 1359. *Club:* Scottish Arts (Edinburgh).

RENNIE, Compton Alexander, CMG 1969; Nuclear Energy Consultant since 1968; *b* 12 Dec. 1915; *s* of George Malcolm Rennie, Southampton; *m* 1941, Marjorie Dorothy Pearson; no *c. Educ:* Sutton Valence Sch., Kent; Sidney Sussex Coll., Cambridge. Radar Officer, TRE, Malvern, 1940-45. Atomic Energy Research Estabt, Harwell, 1945-59: Overseas Liaison Officer, 1955; Dep. Head, Reactor Div., 1957; Head, High Temperature Reactor Div., 1958; Atomic Energy Estabt, Winfrith, Dorset, and Chief Exec. of OECD High Temperature Reactor Project (Dragon Project), 1959-68; Dir, Nuclear Power and Reactors Div., Internat. Atomic Energy Agency, Vienna, 1970-72. Ford Foundn Atoms for Peace Award, 1969. *Recreations:* golf, sailing, gardening. *Address:* 33 Stowell Crescent, Wareham, Dorset. *T:* Wareham 2671.

RENNIE, Sir Gilbert (McCall), GBE 1954; KCMG 1949 (CMG 1941); Kt 1946; MC; MA, Hon. LLD (Glasgow); *b* 24 Sept 1895; *yr s* of late John Rennie; *m* 1929, Jean Marcella Huggins; two *s* one *d. Educ:* Stirling High School; Glasgow Univ. Served European War, 1915-19, KOSB, Capt.; Ceylon Civil Service, 1920-37; Financial Sec., Gold Coast, 1937-39; Chief Secretary, Kenya, 1939-47; Governor and C-in-C Northern Rhodesia, 1948-54; High Comr in UK for Fedn of Rhodesia and Nyasaland, 1954-61. Chm., Commonwealth Econ. Cttee, 1957 and 1958; Chm., UK Cttee for Freedom from Hunger Campaign, 1965-; Joint Treasurer, Royal Society of Arts, 1965-70. KStJ. *Recreations:* gardening, fishing, golf. *Address:* 7 Beech Hill, Hadley Wood, Barnet, Herts EN4 0JN. *Club:* Royal Commonwealth Society.

RENNIE, James Douglas Milne; Parliamentary Counsel, Civil Service Department, since 1976; *b* 2 Nov. 1931; *s* of Douglas Frederick Milne Rennie and Margaret Wilson Fleming Rennie (*née* Keanie); *m* 1962, Patricia Margaret Calhoun Watson; one *s* one *d. Educ:* Charterhouse; New Coll., Oxford (Schol.). 1st cl. Hon. Mods 1953; 2nd cl. Lit. Hum. 1955; 2nd cl. Jurisprudence 1957; MA. Called to Bar, Lincoln's Inn, 1958 (Cholmeley Schol.). Asst Lectr, UCW Aberystwyth, 1957; practised at Chancery Bar, 1958-65; Asst Parly Counsel, HM Treasury, 1965; Sen. Asst Parly Counsel, 1972; Dep. Parly Counsel, 1973-75. *Recreations:* opera, travel. *Address:* 46 Holland Park, W11 3RS. *T:* 01-727 5000; Old Tythe House, Happisburgh, Norfolk. *T:* Walcot 380.

RENNIE, John Chalmers; Town Clerk of Aberdeen, 1946-68; *b* 16 April 1907; *s* of late John Chalmers Rennie, Pharmacist, Wishaw; *m* 1937, Georgina Stoddart, *d* of late Henry Bell, Engineer and Ironfounder, Wishaw; one *s. Educ:* University of Glasgow. Town Clerk Depute, Motherwell and Wishaw, 1929-43; Town Clerk Depute, Aberdeen, 1943-46. *Recreations:* motoring, do-it-yourself. *Address:* 34 Morningfield Road, Aberdeen. *T:* Aberdeen 36904.

RENNIE, Sir John (Ogilvy), KCMG 1967 (CMG 1956); Deputy Under-Secretary of State, Foreign and Commonwealth Office, 1967-74; *b* 13 Jan. 1914; *o s* of late Charles Ogilvy Rennie and Agnes Annette Paton; *m* 1938, Anne-Marie Celine Monica Godat (*d* 1964); one *s*; *m* 1966, Mrs Jennifer Margaret Rycroft; two *s. Educ:* Wellington College; Balliol College, Oxford. Kenyon & Eckhardt Inc., New York, 1935-39; Vice-Consul, Baltimore, 1940; British Press Service, New York, 1941; British Information Services, 1942-46; Foreign Office, 1946-49; First Secretary (Commercial) HM Embassy, Washington, 1949-51; First Secretary HM Embassy, Warsaw, 1951-53; Counsellor, Foreign Office, 1953; Head of Information Research Dept, FO, 1953-58; Minister (Commercial), British Embassy: Buenos Aires, 1958-60; Washington, 1960-63; Asst Under Sec. of State, FO, 1964-65; on loan to Civil Service Commission during 1966. *Recreations:* electronics, painting (Exhibitor RA, 1930, 1931; Paris Salon, 1932). *Clubs:* Bath, Brooks's.

RENNIE, Sir John Shaw, GCMG 1968 (KCMG 1962; CMG 1958); OBE 1955; Commissioner-General, United Nations Relief and Works Agency for Palestine Refugees, 1971-77 (Deputy Commissioner-General, 1968-71); *b* 12 Jan. 1917; *s* of late John Shaw Rennie, Saskatoon, Sask, Canada; *m* 1946, Mary Winifred Macalpine Robertson; one *s. Educ:* Hillhead High School; Glasgow University; Balliol College, Oxford. Cadet, Tanganyika, 1940; Asst District Officer, 1942; District Officer,

1949; Deputy Colonial Secretary, Mauritius, 1951; British Resident Comr, New Hebrides, 1955-62; Governor and C-in-C of Mauritius, 1962-March 1968, Governor-General, March-Aug. 1968. Hon. LLD Glasgow, 1972. *Address:* via Roma 33, 06050 Collazzone (PG), Italy; 26 College Cross, N1. *Club:* Royal Commonwealth Society.

RENOIR, Jean; Chevalier de la Légion d'Honneur; Croix de Guerre; Commandeur de l'Ordre des Arts et Lettres; Film director, producer and writer, since 1924, and Stage, since 1953; *b* Paris, 15 Sept. 1894; *s* of Pierre Auguste Renoir, painter, and Aline (*née* Charigot); *m* 1944, Dido Freire; one *s* (by previous marriage). *Educ:* Sainte-Croix College, Neuilly; The University, Aix-en-Provence. Served War of 1914-18 (Croix de Guerre), Cavalry Officer and Air Force Pilot. Served one semester as Regents' Professor, University of California, Berkeley, USA, 1960. Subsequently concerned with ceramics, Motion pictures, and stage (directed, Shakespeare's Julius Caesar at Arles, 1954; author and dir, Orvet, French adaptation Clifford Odets Le Grand Couteau). Numerous films including: La Chienne; La Bête Humaine; La Grande Illusion (one of 12 best films of all times, Brussels Fair, 1958); La Règle du Jeu; The Southerner; The River; The Golden Coach; French Can-Can; Elena et Les Hommes; Le Testament du Dr Cordelier; Le Déjeuner sur l'Herbe, Le Caporal Epinglé, 1962; Le petit théâtre de Jean Renoir, 1969. Louis Delluc Prize, 1937; NY Critics award, 1941; Golden Lion awards, 1937, 1946, 1951; Golden Laurel Trophy, 1958; Osella d'oro, Venice, 1968; Grand Prix de l'Académie du Cinéma, 1956; Acad. of Motion Picture Arts and Sciences Special Award for lifetime achievement, 1974. Hon. Dr of Fine Arts, Univ. of California, 1963; Fellow American Acad. of Arts and Sciences, 1964; Sociétaire, Soc. des Auteurs et Compositeurs Dramatiques; Mem., Federazione Internazionale dei Cavalieri del Cinema; Hon. Mem. Royal Acad. of Arts; Hon. Dr RCA 1971. *Publications:* Orvet, 1953; Renoir, My Father, 1962 (Prix Charles Blanc, Académie Française 1963); The Notebooks of Captain Georges, 1966; My Life and My Films, 1974. *Recreation:* Art collector. *Address:* 1273 Leona Drive, Beverly Hills, Calif 90210, USA.

RENOWDEN, Very Rev. Charles Raymond; Dean of St Asaph since 1971; *b* 27 Oct. 1923; *s* of Rev. Canon Charles Renowden; *m* 1951, Ruth Cecil Mary Collis; one *s* two *d. Educ:* Llandysil Grammar Sch.; St David's Univ. Coll., Lampeter; Selwyn Coll., Cambridge. BA (Hons Philosophy, cl. I), Lampeter; BA, MA (Hons Theology, cl. I), Cambridge. Served War, Army, Intelligence Corps, in India and Japan, 1944-47. Cambridge Ordination Course; Deacon, 1951, Priest, 1952, Wales. Asst Curate, Hubberston, Milford Haven, 1951-55. St David's Univ. Coll., Lampeter: Lectr in Philosophy and Theology, 1955-57; Head of Dept of Philosophy, 1957-69; Sen. Lectr in Philosophy and Theology, 1969-71. *Publications:* (monograph) The Idea of Unity, 1965; New Patterns of Ministry, 1973; The Rôle of a Cathedral Today and Tomorrow, 1974; contributor to: Theology, The Modern Churchman, Church Quarterly Review, Trivium, Province. *Recreations:* music, gardening, ornithology. *Address:* The Deanery, St Asaph, Clwyd. *T:* St Asaph 583597.

RENSHAW, Sir Charles Maurice Bine, 3rd Bt *cr* 1903; *b* 7 Oct. 1912; *s* of Sir (Charles) Stephen (Bine) Renshaw, 2nd Bt and of Edith Mary, *d* of Rear-Adm. Sir Edward Chichester, 9th Bt, CB, CMG; *S* father, 1976; *m* 1942, Isabel Bassett (marr. diss. 1947), *d* of late Rev. John L. T. Popkin; one *s* one *d* (and one *s* decd). *Educ:* Eton. Served as Flying Officer, RAF (invalided). *Heir: s* John David Renshaw [*b* 9 Oct. 1945; *m* 1970, Jennifer, *d* of Group Captain F. Murray, RAF]. *Address:* Tam-na-Marghaidh, Balquhidder, Perthshire.

RENTON, Rt. Hon. Sir David (Lockhart-Mure), PC 1962; KBE 1964; TD; QC 1954; MA; BCL; DL; MP (Nat L), 1945-50, (Nat L and C), 1950-68, (C) since 1968, Huntingdonshire; *b* 12 Aug. 1908; *s* of late Dr Maurice Waugh Renton, The Bridge House, Dartford, Kent, and Eszma Olivia, *d* of late Allen Walter Borman, Alexandria; *m* 1947, Claire Cicely, *y d* of late Walter Duncan; three *d. Educ:* Stubbington; Oundle; University College, Oxford. BA (Hons Jurisprudence), 1930; BCL, 1931; MA. Called to Bar, Lincoln's Inn, 1933; South-Eastern Circuit; elected to General Council of the Bar, 1939; Bencher, Lincoln's Inn, 1962. Commnd RE (TA), 1938; transferred to RA 1940; served throughout War of 1939-45; Capt. 1941; Major, 1943; served in Middle East, 1942-45. Parly Sec., Min. of Fuel and Power, 1955-57, Ministry of Power, 1957-58; Joint Parly Under-Sec. of State, Home Office, 1958-61; Minister of State, Home Office, 1961-62; Chm., Select Cttee for Revision of Standing Orders, House of Commons, 1963 and 1970; Mem., Cttee of Privileges, 1973-. Recorder of Rochester, 1963-68, of Guildford, 1968-71; Vice-Chm., Council of Legal Educn, 1968-70, 1971-73. Member: Senate of Inns of Court, 1967-69, 1970-71, 1975-;

Commn on the Constitution, 1971-73; Chm., Cttee on Preparation of Legislation, 1973-75. Hon. Treasurer, Nat. Soc. for Mentally Handicapped Children, 1976-. Pres., Conservation Soc., 1970-71. DL Huntingdonshire, 1962, Huntingdon and Peterborough, 1964, Cambs, 1974. *Recreations:* outdoor sports and games, gardening. *Address:* Moat House, Abbots Ripton, Huntingdon. *T:* Abbots Ripton 227; 22 Old Square, Lincoln's Inn, WC2. *T:* 01-242 8986. 5 King's Bench Walk, Temple, EC4. *T:* 01-353 2882/4. *Clubs:* Carlton, Pratt's.

RENTON, Ronald Timothy; MP (C) Mid-Sussex since Feb. 1974; *b* 28 May 1932; *yr s* of R. K. D. Renton, CBE, and Mrs Renton, MBE; *m* 1960, Alice Fergusson of Kilkerran, Ayrshire; two *s* three *d. Educ:* Eton Coll. (King's Schol.); Magdalen Coll., Oxford (Roberts Gawen Schol.). First cl. degree in History, MA Oxon. Joined C. Tennant Sons & Co. Ltd, London, 1954; with Tennants' subsidiaries in Canada, 1957-62; Dir, C. Tennant Sons & Co. Ltd and Managing Dir of Tennant Trading Ltd, 1964-73; Director: Silvermines Ltd, 1967-; Australia & New Zealand Banking Group, 1967-76; J. H. Vavasseur & Co. Ltd, 1971-74. Mem., Select Cttee on Nationalised Industries, 1974-; Vice-Chm., Cons. Parly Trade Cttee, 1974-. Contested (C) Sheffield Park Div., 1970. *Publications:* articles in: Statist, Financial Times, Bankers' Magazine, Contemporary Rev., The Times *et al. Recreations:* gardening, tennis, growing trees. *Address:* Mount Harry House, Offham, Lewes, E Sussex. *T:* Lewes 4456. *Clubs:* Brooks's, Coningsby.

RENWICK, family name of **Baron Renwick.**

RENWICK, 2nd Baron *cr* 1964, of Coombe; **Harry Andrew Renwick;** Bt 1927; Partner, W. Greenwell & Co., Stockbrokers; *b* 10 Oct. 1935; *s* of 1st Baron Renwick, KBE, and of Mrs John Ormiston, Miserden House, Stroud, *er d* of late Major Harold Parkes, Alveston, Stratford-on-Avon; *S* father, 1973; *m* 1965, Susan Jane, *d* of late Captain Kenneth S. B. Lucking and of Mrs Moir P. Stormonth-Darling, Lednathie, Glen Prosen, Angus; two *s. Educ:* Eton. Grenadier Guards (National Service), 1955-56. *Heir: s* Hon. Robert James Renwick, *b* 19 Aug. 1966. *Address:* 8 Lyall Street, SW1. *Clubs:* White's, Turf.

RENWICK, George Russell, MA; Headmaster, Dover College, 1934-54, retired; *b* 7 Aug. 1901; *s* of George Edward Renwick and Helen Isabella Russell; *m* 1927, Isabella Alice Watkins; one *s* three *d. Educ:* Charterhouse; New College, Oxford. Assistant Master, Stowe School, 1924-25; Charterhouse, 1926-34; OUAC 1923, 1924; British Olympic Team, 1924. Councillor, Dover Borough Council, 1946-50. *Address:* The Old Parsonage, Sidlesham, near Chichester. *Club:* (former Commodore) Royal Cinque Ports Yacht (Dover).

RENWICK, Sir John, Kt 1968; JP; Consultant with Renwick & Co., Solicitors, Eckington; *b* 16 Nov. 1901; *s* of James David and Mary Beatrice Renwick; *m* 1933, Margaret Rachel, *d* of Alfred Stanley and Rachel Fawcett; one *s* one *d. Educ:* King Edward VII School, Sheffield; Sidney Sussex College, Cambridge (MA, LLB). Admitted a Solicitor, 1927, practising, since, at Eckington, near Sheffield. Mem. Council, Law Society, 1949-72 (Pres. 1967-68); Chm., Trustee Savings Banks Inspection Cttee, 1954-76; Trustee, Sheffield Savings Bank, 1948- (Chm., 1972); Sheffield Town Trustee, 1971. Hon. LLD Sheffield, 1968. *Recreations:* walking, gardening and carpentry. *Address:* Saint Cross, Ridgeway, near Sheffield. *T:* Eckington (Derbyshire) 3114. *Club:* Sheffield (Sheffield).

RENWICK, Sir Richard Eustace, 4th Bt *cr* 1921; *b* 13 Jan. 1938; *er s* of Sir Eustace Deuchar Renwick, 3rd Bt, and of Diana Mary, *e d* of Colonel Bernard Cruddas, DSO; *S* father, 1973; *m* 1966, Caroline Anne, *er d* of Major Rupert Milburn; three *s. Educ:* Eton. *Heir: s* Charles Richard Renwick, *b* 10 April 1967. *Address:* Whalton House, Whalton, Morpeth, Northumberland. *T:* Whalton 383. *Club:* Northern Counties (Newcastle).

REPORTER, Sir Shapoor (Ardeshirji), KBE 1973 (OBE 1969); Consultant on Economic and Political Matters concerning Iran, since 1962; *b* 26 Feb. 1921; *s* of Ardeshirji Reporter and Shirin Reporter; *m* 1952, Assia Alexandra; one *s* one *d. Educ:* Zoroastrian Public Sch., Teheran; matriculated in Bombay (specially designed course in Political Science under Cambridge Univ. Tutors, UK). PRO, British Legation, Teheran, 1941-43; in charge of Persian Unit of All India Radio, New Delhi, 1943-45; Teaching English, Imperial Staff Coll., Teheran, 1945-48; Political Adviser, US Embassy, Teheran, 1948-54; Free-lance Correspondent, 1954-62; Economic Consultant to major British interests in Iran, 1962-73. *Publications:* English-Persian Phrases, 1945 (Delhi); Dictionary of English-Persian Idioms, 1956 (Teheran); Dictionary of Persian-English Idioms, 1972 (Teheran Univ.). *Recreations:* tennis, walking, travelling.

Address: 65 Zartosht Street, Teheran, Iran. *T:* 621706. *Club:* Bath.

REPTON, Bishop Suffragan of, since 1977; **Rt. Rev. Stephen Edmund Verney,** MBE 1945; *b* 17 April 1919; 2nd *s* of late Sir Harry Verney, 4th Bt, DSO and Lady Rachel Verney (*née* Bruce); *m* 1947, Priscilla Avice Sophie Scwerdt (*d* 1974); one *s* three *d*. *Educ:* Harrow School; Balliol College, Oxford (MA). Curate of Gedling, Nottingham, 1950; Priest-in-charge and then first Vicar, St Francis, Clifton, Nottingham, 1952; Vicar of Leamington Hastings and Diocesan Missioner, Dio. Coventry, 1958; Canon Residentiary, Coventry Cathedral, 1964; Canon of Windsor, 1970. *Publications:* Fire in Coventry, 1964; People and Cities, 1969; Into the New Age, 1976. *Recreations:* conversation and aloneness; music, gardening, travel. *Address:* Repton House, Lea, Matlock, Derbys DE4 5JP. *Club:* English-Speaking Union.
See also L. J. Verney, Sir R. B. Verney, Bt.

RESTIEAUX, Rt. Rev. Cyril Edward; see Plymouth, Bishop of, (RC).

RESTON, Clifford Arthur; Principal Chief Clerk, Inner London Magistrates Courts, and Clerk to the Committee of Magistrates for Inner London, since 1976; *b* 29 Aug. 1928; *s* of Percival and Ethel May Reston; *m* 1955, Joyce Doreen (*née* Birch); two *s* one *d*. *Educ:* Liverpool Institute School; King's College, Univ. of London (LLB). Called to the Bar, Middle Temple, 1955. Inland Revenue, 1945-46, 1947-57. Served in RAF, 1946-47. Metropolitan Magistrates Courts (which became Inner London Courts in 1965): Dep. Chief Clerk, 1957-63; Chief Clerk, 1963, serving at North London Court until 1966; Chief Clerk (Training), 1966-70; Chief Clerk, Tower Bridge, 1970-71; Sen. Chief Clerk, Marylebone, 1971-76. *Recreations:* gardening, dog-walking, music. *Address:* c/o Inner London Magistrates Courts, 3rd Floor, NW Wing, Bush House, Aldwych, WC2. *T:* 01-836 9331; Four Winds, Hacketts Lane, Pyrford, Woking, Surrey. *T:* Byfleet 41511.

REUTER, Prof. Gerd Edzard Harry, MA Cantab; Professor of Mathematics, Imperial College of Science and Technology, London, since 1965; *b* 21 Nov. 1921; *s* of Ernst Rudolf Johannes Reuter and Gertrud Charlotte Reuter (*née* Scholz); *m* 1945, Eileen Grace Legard; one *s* three *d*. *Educ:* The Leys School and Trinity College, Cambridge. Mem. of Dept of Mathematics, Univ. of Manchester, 1946-58; Professor of Pure Mathematics, Univ. of Durham, 1959-65. *Publications:* Elementary Differential Equations and Operators, 1958; articles in various mathematical and scientific jls. *Address:* Department of Mathematics, Imperial College of Science and Technology, SW7.

REVANS, Sir John, Kt 1977; CBE 1967 (MBE 1943); retired; *b* 7 June 1911; *s* of Thomas William Revans, MINA and Ethel Amelia Revans; *m* 1936, Eileen Parkhurst Mitchell; two *d*. *Educ:* Middlesex Hosp. Med. Sch.; London Univ. DCH 1946; FRCP 1969. Served War of 1939-45 (despatches 1941): Col Indian Med. Service, 1936-47, retd. Sen. Admin. MO, Wessex RHB, 1959-73; Regional MO, Wessex RHA, 1973-76. Hon. LLD Southampton, 1970. Hon. FRCGP 1974. OStJ 1946. *Recreation:* sailing (RYA/DTI Yachtmaster (Offshore)). *Address:* The Triangle, Durley, Southampton SO3 2AJ. *T:* Durley 348. *Club:* Little Ship.
See also Prof. R. W. Revans.

REVANS, Prof. Reginald William, PhD; MIMinE; Founder, Action Learning Trust, 1977; *b* 14 May 1907; *s* of Thomas William Revans, Principal Ship Surveyor, Board of Trade; *m* 1st, 1932, Annida Aquist, Gothenburg (marriage dissolved, 1947); three *d*; 2nd, 1955, Norah Mary Merritt, Chelmsford; one *s*. *Educ:* Battersea Grammar School; University Coll., London; Emmanuel Coll., Cambridge. BSc London, PhD Cantab. Commonwealth Fund Fellow, Univ. of Michigan, 1930-32; Research Fellow, Emmanuel Coll., Cambridge, 1932-35; Dep. Chief Education Officer, Essex CC, 1935-45; Dir of Education, Mining Assoc. of Gt Britain, 1945-47 and NCB, 1947-50; Research on management of coalmines, 1950-55; Prof., Industrial Admin., Univ. of Manchester, 1955-65; Res. Fellow, Guy's Hosp. Med. Sch., 1965-68; External Prof., Management Studies, Leeds Univ., 1976-. Dist. Vis. Scholar, Southern Methodist Univ., USA, 1972. Hon. DSc Bath, 1969. Chevalier, Order of Leopold, Belgium, 1971. *Publications:* Report on Education for Mining Industry, 1945; Education of the Young Worker, 1949; Standards for Morale, 1964; Science and the Manager, 1965; The Theory and Practice of Management, 1965; Developing Effective Managers, 1971; (ed) Hospitals, Communication, Choice and Change, 1972; Workers' Attitudes and Motivation (OECD Report), 1972; Childhood and

Maturity, 1973; Action Learning in Hospitals, 1976; various in professional magazines upon application of analytical methods to understanding of industrial morale. *Recreations:* British Olympic Team, 1928; holder of Cambridge undergraduate long jump record, 1929-62. *Address:* 8 Higher Downs, Altrincham, Cheshire. *Club:* National Liberal.
See also Sir J. Revans.

REVELSTOKE, 4th Baron *cr* 1885; **Rupert Baring;** *b* 8 Feb. 1911; *o s* of 3rd Baron and Maude (*d* 1922), *d* of late Pierre Lorillard; *S* father, 1934; *m* 1934, Flora (who obtained a divorce 1944), 2nd *d* of 1st Baron Hesketh; two *s*. *Educ:* Eton. 2nd Lt Royal Armoured Corps (TA). *Heir: s* Hon. John Baring, *b* 2 Dec. 1934. *Address:* Lambay Island, Rush, Co. Dublin, Ireland.

REVERDIN, Prof. Olivier, DrLitt; Professor of Greek, University of Geneva, since 1958; Member, Consultative Assembly of Council of Europe, 1963-74 (President, 1969-72); Deputy (Liberal) for Geneva, Swiss National Council, 1955-71; Council of States (Senate), since 1971; *b* 15 July 1913; *m* 1936, Renée Chaponnière; two *s* one *d*. *Educ:* Geneva, Paris and Athens. LicLitt 1935. Foreign Mem., French Sch. of Archaeology, Athens, 1936-38; Attaché Swiss Legation, Service of Foreign Interests, Rome, 1941-43; Privatdocent of Greek, Univ. of Geneva, 1945-57; Parly Redactor, 1945-54; Chief Editor 1954-59, Manager 1954-67, Pres., 1972-, Journal de Genève. Mem. 1963-, Pres. 1968-, Swiss National Research Council; Mem., Swiss Science Council; Pres., Fondation Hardt pour l'étude de l'antiquité classique, Geneva, 1959-; Vice-Pres., European Science Foundn, 1974-. *Publications:* La religion de la cité platonicienne, 1945; La guerre du Sonderbund, 1947; La Crète, berceau de la civilisation occidentale, 1960; Connaissance de la Suisse, 1966. *Address:* 8 rue des Granges, 1204 Geneva, Switzerland. *T:* 022-21-51-91.

REVIE, Donald, OBE; National Team Coach, United Arab Emirates Football Association, since 1977; *b* 10 July 1927; *m* 1949, Elsie May Leonard Duncan; one *s* one *d*. *Educ:* Archibald Secondary Modern Sch., Middlesbrough, Yorks. Professional footballer with Leicester, Hull, Manchester City, Sunderland, and Leeds United, 1945-61; Player-Manager, then Manager, Leeds United Football Club, 1961-74; Manager of England Team, FA, 1974-77. *Publication:* Soccer's Happy Wanderer, 1955. *Recreations:* golf, reading. *Address:* UAE Football Association, Dubai, United Arab Emirates.

REVINGTON, Air Commodore Arthur Pethick, CB 1950; CBE 1945 (OBE 1940); retired; *b* 24 June 1901; *s* of late Cdr G. A. Revington, RN; *m* 1946, Joan, widow of Cuthbert William Prideaux Selby. *Educ:* Plymouth College; RAF College, Cranwell. Served War of 1939-45 (despatches thrice); AOC No 4 Gp, 1946-47; AOC No 47 Gp, 1948-50; Sen. Air Liaison Officer, United Kingdom Service Liaison Staff, Canada, 1950-53; retired 1954. *Address:* Trescoll, Newton Ferrers, South Devon. *T:* Newton Ferrers 872465. *Clubs:* Royal Air Force; Royal Western Yacht; Royal Air Force Yacht.

REX, Prof. John Arderne; Professor of Sociology, University of Warwick, since 1970; *b* 5 March 1925; *s* of Frederick Edward George Rex and Winifred Natalie Rex; *m* 1st, 1949, Pamela Margaret Rutherford (marr. diss. 1963); two *d*; 2nd, 1965, Margaret Ellen Biggs; two *s*. *Educ:* Grey Institute High Sch. and Rhodes University Coll., Port Elizabeth, S Africa. BA (S Africa), PhD (Leeds). Served War, Royal Navy (Able Seaman), 1943-45. Graduated, 1948; Lecturer: Univ. of Leeds, 1949-62; Birmingham, 1962-64; Prof. of Social Theory and Institutions, Durham, 1964-70. Vis. Prof., Univ. of Toronto, 1974-75. *Publications:* Key Problems of Sociological Theory, 1961; (with Robert Moore) Race Community and Conflict, 1967, 2nd edn 1973; Race Relations in Sociological Theory, 1970; Discovering Sociology, 1973; Race, Colonialism and the City, 1974; (ed) Approaches to Sociology, 1974; Sociology and the Demystification of the Modern World, 1974. *Recreations:* politics, race relations work. *Address:* University of Warwick, Coventry CV4 7AL. *T:* Coventry 24011.

REY, Jean; Leader, Parti pour la Réforme et la Liberté de Wallonie, since 1976; *b* Liège, 15 July 1902; *s* of Arnold Rey, Protestant Pastor; *m*; four *c*. *Educ:* Athénée and Univ. of Liège (Dr of Law). Advocate, Court of Appeal, Liège, 1926-58; Served War of 1939-45 (Croix de Guerre, Commem. Medal); POW, Germany, 1940-45. Councillor, Liège, 1935-58; Mem. for Liège, Chamber of Deputies, 1939-58; founder Mem., Entente Libérale Wallone; Minister of Reconstruction, 1949-50; Minister of Economic Affairs, 1954-58; Mem. EEC, 1958-67, Pres. 1967-70. Delegate; 3rd Gen. Assembly, UN, Paris, 1948; 1st Assembly, 1949 and 5th Assembly, 1953, Council of Europe; Mem., Commn to study European Problems, 1952. President: Court of

Arbitration, Internat. Chamber of Commerce, 1972-; Internat. European Movement, 1974-. Dir, Philips Electrical Gp, 1970-; President: Sofina, 1971-; Papeteries de Belgique. Hon. DCL, Oxon, 1968; Dr *hc* Harvard. Grand Cross, Order of the Crown; Grand Officer, Order of Leopold; Grand Cross, Order of Orange Nassau; Grand Cordon, Order of Lion of Finland; Comdr, Order of Crown of Oak, and many other high national distinctions. *Address:* 235 rue de la Loi, 1040 Brussels, Belgium.

REYES, Narciso G., Bintang Mahaputera, 1964; Order of Diplomatic Service Merit, 1972; Philippine Permanent Representative to the United Nations, since 1970; *b* Manila, 6 Feb. 1914; *m. Educ:* Univ. of Sto Tomas (AB). Mem., English Faculty, Univ. of Sto Tomas, 1935-36; Assoc. Ed., Philippines Commonweal, 1935-41; Nat. Language Faculty, Ateneo de Manila, 1939-41; Assoc. Ed., Manila Post, 1945-47; Assoc. News Ed., Evening News, Manila, 1947-48; Man. Ed., Philippine Newspaper Guild Organ, 1947-48; various advisory and UN posts, 1948-; Dir, Philippine Information Agency, 1954-55; Minister-Counsellor, Bangkok, 1956; Public Relations Dir, SEATO, 1956-58; Minister, later Amb., Burma, 1958-62; Ambassador to: Indonesia, 1962-67; London, Stockholm, Oslo, Copenhagen, 1967-70. Mem. various delegns and missions, incl. sessions of UN; Philippine Rep. to UN Commn for Social Devt, 1967-72 (Vice-Chm., 1967; Chm., 1968); Special UN Rep. on Social Develt, 1968; Rep. to UN Human Rights Commn, 1970-72; Chairman: UNICEF Exec. Bd, 1972-74; UN Gen. Assembly Finance and Economic Cttee, 1971; Pres., UNDP Governing Council; Vice-Pres., UN Environment Governing Council. Outstanding Alumnus, Univ. of Sto Tomas, 1969. Dr of Laws (*hc*), Philippine Women's Univ., 1977. *Publications:* essays, poems and short stories. *Address:* 556 Fifth Avenue, New York, NY 10036, USA.

REYNOLDS, Alan Lowe, CMG 1957; OBE 1951; retired; *b* 19 Aug. 1897; *m* 1925, Hilda Quinn; two *s. Educ:* Milton School, S Rhodesia. S Rhodesian Govt Service, 1915-57; Magistrate in various places; Secretary for Justice and Defence, S Rhodesia, 1948; Secretary for Justice, Internal Affairs and Housing, S Rhodesia, 1953-57. *Recreations:* fishing, golf. *Address:* 7 Falmouth Road, Alexandra Park, Salisbury, Rhodesia. *Club:* Royal Salisbury Golf (Salisbury, Rhodesia).

REYNOLDS, Alan (Munro); painter, maker of reliefs, and printmaker; *b* 27 April 1926; *m* 1957, Vona Darby. *Educ:* Woolwich Polytechnic Art School; Royal College of Art (Scholarship and Medal). One man exhibitions: Redfern Gall., London, 1952, 1953, 1954, 1956, 1960, 1962, 1964, 1966, 1970, 1972, 1974; Durlacher Gall., New York, 1954, 1959; Leicester Galleries, London, 1958; Aldeburgh, Suffolk, 1965; Arnolfini Gall., Bristol, 1971 (graphics). Work in exhibitions: Carnegie (Pittsburgh) Internat., USA, 1952, 1955, 1958, 1961; Internat. Exhibn, Rome, (awarded one of the three equal prizes), subsequently Musée d'Art Moderne, Paris, and Brussels; British Council Exhibn, Oslo and Copenhagen, 1956; Redfern Gall., 1971; Spectrum, Arts Council of GB, 1971. Works acquired by: Tate Gall.; V&A; National Galleries of: S Aust.; Felton Bequest, Vic., Aust.; NZ; Canada; City Art Galleries of: Birmingham; Bristol; Manchester; Wakefield; Mus. of Modern Art, NY; Contemporary Art Soc.; British Council; Arts Council of GB; Rothschild Foundn; The Graves Art Gall., Sheffield; Nottingham Castle Mus.; Fitzwilliam Mus., Cambridge; Mus. of Modern Art, São Paulo, Brazil; Leeds Art Gall.; Toledo Art Gall., Ohio, USA; Barnes Foundn, USA; Oriel Coll., Oxford; Warwick Univ.; Mus. and Art Galls, Brighton and Plymouth; Texas Univ., Austin, USA. CoID Award, 1965; Arts Council of GB Purchase Award, 1967. *Relevant Publication:* The Painter, Alan Reynolds, by J. P. Hodin, 1962. *Address:* Briar Cottage, High Street, Cranbrook, Kent.

REYNOLDS, Col Alan Randall R.; *see* Rees-Reynolds.

REYNOLDS, (Arthur) Graham; Keeper of the Department of Prints and Drawings, 1961-74 (of Engraving, Illustration and Design, 1959-61), and of Paintings, Victoria and Albert Museum, 1959-74; *b* Highgate, 10 Jan. 1914; *o s* of late Arthur T. Reynolds and Eva Mullins; *m* 1943, Daphne, *d* of late Thomas Dent, Huddersfield. *Educ:* Highgate School; Queens' College, Cambridge. Joined staff of Victoria and Albert Museum, 1937. Seconded to Ministry of Home Security, 1939-45. Trustee, William Morris Gallery, Walthamstow, 1972-75. *Publications:* Twentieth Century Drawings, 1946; Nicholas Hilliard and Isaac Oliver, 1947, 2nd edn, 1971; Van Gogh, 1947; Nineteenth Century Drawings, 1949; Thomas Bewick, 1949; An Introduction to English Water-Colour Painting, 1950; Gastronomic Pleasures, 1950; Elizabethan and Jacobean Costume, 1951; English Portrait Miniatures, 1952; Painters of the Victorian Scene, 1953; Catalogue of the Constable

Collection, Victoria and Albert Museum, 1960, rev. edn, 1973; Constable, the Natural Painter, 1965; Victorian Painting, 1966; Turner, 1969; A Concise History of Water Colour Painting, 1972. Editor of series English Masters of Black and White. Contributions to Burlington Magazine, Apollo, etc. *Address:* The Old Manse, Bradfield St George, Bury St Edmunds, Suffolk. *T:* Sicklesmere 610. *Club:* Athenæum.

REYNOLDS, Barbara, MA Cantab; BA (Hons), PhD London; author, lexicographer; Reader in Italian Studies, University of Nottingham, since 1969; *b* 13 June 1914; *d* of late Alfred Charles Reynolds; *m* 1939, Prof. Lewis Thorpe (*d* 1977); one *s* one *d. Educ:* St Paul's Girls' Sch.; UCL. Asst Lectr in Italian, LSE 1937-40. Chief Exec. and Gen. Editor, The Cambridge Italian Dictionary, 1948-; Mem. Coun. Senate, Cambridge Univ., 1961-62. University Lecturer in Italian Literature and Language, Cambridge, 1945-62 (Faculty Assistant Lecturer, 1940-45); Warden of Willoughby Hall, Univ. of Nottingham, 1963-69; Reader in Italian, Univ. of Nottingham, 1966-69. Vis. Prof., Univ. of Calif., Berkeley, 1974-75. Hon. Reader in Italian, Univ. of Warwick, 1975-. Hon. Mem., Lucy Cavendish Coll., Cambridge. FRSA. Silver medal for Services to Italian culture (Italian Govt), 1964; Edmund Gardner Prize, 1964; Silver Medal for service to Anglo-Veneto Cultural relations, Prov. Admin of Vicenza, 1971. *Publications:* (with K. T. Butler) Tredici Novelle Moderne, 1947; The Linguistic Writings of Alessandro Manzoni: a Textual and Chronological Reconstruction, 1950; rev. edn with introd., Dante and the Early Astronomers, by M. A. Orr, 1956; The Cambridge Italian Dictionary, Vol. I, Italian-English, 1962; (with Dorothy L. Sayers) Paradise: a translation into English triple rhyme, from the Italian of Dante Alighieri, 1962; (with Lewis Thorpe) Guido Farina, Painter of Verona, 1967; La Vita Nuova (Poems of Youth); trans. of Dante's Vita Nuova, 1969; Concise Cambridge Italian Dictionary, 1975; Orlando Furioso, trans. into rhymed octaves of Ariosto's epic, Vol. I, 1975 (Internat. Literary Prize, Monselice, Italy, 1976) Vol. II, 1977; numerous articles on Italian literature in learned jls. *Address:* 26 Parkside, Wollaton Vale, Nottingham NG8 2NN. *T:* Nottingham 255114. *Club:* University Women's.

REYNOLDS, Sir David James, 3rd Bt, *cr* 1923; Member of Lloyds Insurance; *b* 26 Jan. 1924; *er s* of Sir John Francis Roskell Reynolds, 2nd Bt, MBE, JP and Milicent (*d* 1931), *d* of late Major James Orr-Ewing and late Lady Margaret Orr-Ewing; *S* father 1956; *m* 1966, Charlotte Baumgartner; one *s* two *d. Educ:* Downside. Active service in Army, 1942-47, Italy, etc; on demobilisation, Captain 15/19 Hussars. *Recreation:* sport. *Heir: s* James Francis Reynolds, *b* 10 July 1971. *Address:* Blanche Pierre House, St Lawrence, Jersey, CI.

REYNOLDS, Doris Livesey, (Mrs Arthur Holmes), DSc, FRSE, FGS; Honorary Research Fellow, Bedford College, since 1962; *b* 1 July 1899; *d* of Alfred Reynolds and Louisa Margaret Livesey; *m* 1939, Arthur Holmes, FRS (*d* 1965). *Educ:* Palmer's School, Grays, Essex; Bedford College, London University. Assistant in Geology, Queen's Univ., Belfast, 1921-26; Dem. in Geology, Bedford Coll., London Univ., 1927-31; Lectr in Petrology, University Coll., London Univ., 1931-33; Lectr in Petrology, Durham Colls, Durham Univ., 1933-43. Hon. Research Fellow of the University of Edinburgh, 1943-62. Leverhulme Fellowship to investigate the geology of the Slieve Gullion volcano, 1946-48. Lyell Medallist, Geological Soc., London, 1960. *Publications:* Elements of Physical Geology, 1969; Revision for 3rd edn of Holmes Principles of Physical Geology, 1977; on the origin of granite and allied subjects in Quart. Journ. Geol Soc., Proc. Roy. Irish Acad., Roy. Soc. of Edin., Geological Magazine, etc. *Address:* 7 Tandridge Road, Hove, E Sussex.

REYNOLDS, Eric Vincent, TD 1948; MA; Headmaster of Stowe, 1949-58, retired; *b* 30 April 1904; *o s* of late Arthur John and Lily Reynolds; unmarried. *Educ:* Haileybury College; St John's College, Cambridge. Modern and Mediæval languages Tripos, Parts 1 and 2; Lector in English at University of Leipzig, 1926-27; MA 1930. Assistant Master: Rugby School, 1927-31; Upper Canada College, Toronto, 1931-32; Rugby School, 1932-49 (Housemaster, 1944-49). CO, Rugby School JTC, 1938-44. *Recreations:* ski-ing and mountaineering. *Address:* 48 Lemsford Road, St Albans, Herts. *T:* 53599.

REYNOLDS, Eva Mary Barbara; *see* Reynolds, Barbara.

REYNOLDS, Frank Arrowsmith, OBE 1974; LLB; HM Diplomatic Service, retired; *b* 30 March 1916; *s* of late Sydney Edward Clyde Reynolds and Bessie (*née* Foster); *m* 1938, Joan Marion Lockyer; one *s* two *d. Educ:* Addey and Stanhope Sch.; London University. Army, 1941-46 (Lieut, RE). District

Officer, Tanganyika, 1950; Commonwealth Relations Office, 1962-63; First Secretary, Bombay, 1964-67; CO, later FCO, 1967-69; Consul-Gen., Seville, 1969-71; Head of Chancery, Maseru, 1971-75. *Recreations:* music, sailing, photography. *Address:* Generalisimo 34D 8A, Sanlucar de Barrameda, Spain. *Club:* Royal Bombay Yacht; Nautico de Sanlucar de Barrameda.

REYNOLDS, Graham; see Reynolds, A. G.

REYNOLDS, Guy Edwin K.; see King-Reynolds.

REYNOLDS, Maj-Gen. Jack Raymond, CB 1971; OBE 1945; ERD 1948; Director-General, British Equestrian Federation, since 1975; *b* 10 June 1916; *s* of Walter Reynolds and Evelyn Marion (*née* Burrows); *m* 1940, Joan Howe Taylor; one *s* one *d. Educ:* Haberdashers' Aske's. Student Apprentice, AEC Ltd, 1934. Commissioned RASC (SR), 1936. Served War of 1939-45, France, Middle East and Italy (despatches). CRASC 7th Armoured Div., 1955-57; GSO 1 War Office, 1958-60; Col GS; UK Delegn to NATO Standing Group, Washington, DC, 1960-62; DDST, Southern Command, 1962-64; Commandant, RASC Training Centre, 1964-65; Imperial Defence College, 1966; Dep. Quarter-Master-General, BAOR, 1967-68; Dir of Movements (Army), MoD, 1968-71, retired. Col Comdt, Royal Corps of Transport, 1972-. Dir-Gen., BHS, 1971-75. FCIT. *Recreation:* shooting. *Address:* Old Mill House, Hellidon, near Daventry, Northants. *Club:* Army and Navy.

REYNOLDS, James; Judge of the High Court, Eastern Region of Nigeria, 1956-63; *b* Belfast, May, 1908; *yr s* of late James Reynolds and late Agnes Forde (*née* Cully); *m* 1946, Alexandra Mary Erskine Strain; two *s* two *d. Educ:* Belfast Roy. Acad.; Queen's Univ., Belfast. Called to Bar of N Ire., 1931; practised at N Ire Bar, 1931-40. Colonial Legal Service as Crown Counsel in Hong Kong, 1940. Prisoner-of-war in Japanese hands, 1941-45. Returned to Hong Kong, 1946; apptd District Judge, 1953. Chairman: Local Tribunal under Nat. Insce Acts, 1964; Industrial Tribunal, 1969. *Address:* 10 Church Road, Helen's Bay, Co. Down, Northern Ireland.

REYNOLDS, Peter William John, CBE 1975; Group Managing Director, Ranks Hovis McDougall Ltd, since 1972; *b* 10 Sept. 1929; *s* of Harry and Gladys Victoria Reynolds; *m* 1955, Barbara Anne (*née* Johnson); two *s. Educ:* Haileybury Coll., Herts. National Service, 2nd Lieut, RA, 1948-50. Unilever Ltd, 1950-70: Trainee; Managing Dir, then Chm., Walls (Meat & Handy Foods) Ltd. Asst Gp Managing Dir, Ranks Hovis McDougall Ltd, 1971. *Recreations:* squash, tennis, gardening. *Address:* The White House, Beamond End, Amersham, Bucks. *T:* Holmer Green 3248. *Clubs:* Naval and Military, Farmers'.

REYNOLDS, Richard S., Jr; Honorary Chairman of the Board, Reynolds Metals Co., USA (Director, since 1936; Chairman, 1963-76; President, 1971-75); Chairman, Board and Executive Committee, Robertshaw Controls Co.; former Director: British Aluminium Ltd; Reynolds TI Aluminium Ltd; Central National Bank, Richmond, Va; *b* Winston-Salem, NC, 27 May 1908; *e s* of R. S. and Louise Parham Reynolds; *m* 1933, Virginia Sargeant; one *s. Educ:* Davidson College; Wharton School of Finance, Univ. of Pennsylvania (BS). Became Mem. New York Stock Exchange, 1930, and with two partners, formed banking firm of Reynolds & Co. which he left, 1938, to join Reynolds Metals Co. as asst to the President. He served as treasurer of Reynolds, 1938-44; Vice-Pres. and Treasurer, 1944-48; President, 1948-63; Chm. and Pres., 1963-75. Member: Business Council; Bd of Univ. of Richmond; Trustee Emeritus, Univ. of Pennsylvania. Hon. Mem., Amer. Inst. of Architects. *Recreation:* fox hunting (formerly master of hounds, Deep Run Hunt Club). *Address:* Reynolds Metals Company, 6601 West Broad Street, Richmond, Va, USA. *T:* 281-2148. *Clubs:* Buck's; Commonwealth, Country Club of Virginia (Richmond, Va); Farmington Country Club; Brook, Jockey (New York); Metropolitan (Washington).

REYNOLDS, Major-General Roger Clayton, CB 1944; OBE 1941; MC 1916; *b* 26 Jan. 1895; *s* of late Lewis William Reynolds and Fanny Matilda Clayton; *m* 1st, 1918, Marjorie Grace McVeagh (*d* 1938); one *s* one *d*; 2nd, 1952, Mrs August Oddleifson, Rochester, New York, USA. *Educ:* Bradfield College; RMA, Woolwich. 1st Commission RA, Aug. 1914; served European War, 1914-18 (MC, 1914 Star); Staff College, Camberley, 1928-29; Staff Captain Delhi Independent Brigade, 1931; DAAG, AHQ, India, 1932-36; GSO 1 War Office, 1939-40; AA Brigade Comd 1941-42; comd 3rd AA Group, Bristol, 1942-44; Comd 1 AA Group London, 1944-47; retired pay, 1948. *Recreations:* Bradfield College 1st XI Soccer, cricket; RMA, 1st XI Soccer; Staff College 1st team hockey, tennis. *Address:* The Old Orchard, Avon, New York State 14414, USA. *Club:* Army and Navy.

REYNOLDS, Seymour John Romer, MA, MB, BChir (Cambridge) 1936; MRCS, LRCP, 1935; DMRE 1938; Physician to Radiological Department, Charing Cross Hospital, 1945-76; Consultant Radiologist: Kingston Hospital Group, 1948-73; New Victoria Hospital, Kingston-upon-Thames; *b* 26 April 1911; *s* of late Russell J. Reynolds, CBE, FRCP; *m* 1939, Margaret Stuart McCombie; one *s. Educ:* Westminster School; Trinity Coll., Cambridge; Charing Cross Hosp. Med. School. Formerly: House Surgeon, House Physician and Clin. Asst at Charing Cross Hosp.; Univ. Demonstrator in Anatomy, Cambridge Univ., 1937; Radiologist: Victoria Hosp., Kingston-upon-Thames, 1939; Prince of Wales Gen. Hosp., Tottenham, 1939; Highlands Hosp.; Hackney Hosp.; Epsom Hosp. 1943; Queen Mary's Hosp., Roehampton, 1946. Dean of Charing Cross Hosp. Med. Sch., 1962-76. Mem. Bd of Governors, Charing Cross Hosp., 1962-74; Mem., Ealing, Hammersmith and Hounslow AHA, 1974-76. *Recreations:* gardening, visiting art galleries. *Address:* Camelot, Renfrew Road, Kingston Hill, Surrey. *T:* 01-942 3808.

REYNOLDS, William Oliver, OBE 1973 (MBE 1944); Chairman, Derek Crouch Construction Co., since 1976; *b* 2 Nov. 1915; *s* of Edgar Ernest Reynolds and Elizabeth Wilson Biesterfield; *m* 1944, Eleanor Gill; two *s. Educ:* Royal Grammar Sch., Newcastle upon Tyne. LNER Traffic apprentice, 1936. Served War, with Royal Engineers, 1940-46: despatches, 1942 and 1944; Lt-Col, 1944. Lt-Col, Engineer and Railway Staff Corps, RE (T&AVR IV), 1971-. Divisional Manager, London Midland, BR, 1960; Asst Gen. Manager, Scottish Region, 1964; Chief Operating Manager, BR Bd, 1968; Exec. Dir, BR Bd, 1969; Gen. Manager, Eastern Region, British Rail, 1973-76. Mem., Adv. Council, Science Mus. 1975-. FCIT. *Recreations:* fishing, golf, gardening. *Address:* Oak House, Follifoot, Harrogate, N Yorks. *Club:* Oriental.

REYNOLDS, William Vaughan; Principal, St Marylebone Literary Institute, 1965-70, retired; *b* 10 May 1908; *yr s* of late William Reynolds, MBE, editor of The Midland Daily Telegraph; *m* 1932, Gertrude Mabel, *yr d* of late Arthur Charles Flint; four *s. Educ:* King Henry VIII School, Coventry; St Edmund Hall, Oxford. First class in Final Hons School of Eng. Lang. and Lit., 1930; BLitt, 1931; MA 1934; Senior Exhibitioner, St Edmund Hall, 1930-31. Assistant Lecturer in English Literature, University of Sheffield, 1931-34; Lecturer, 1934-41. Deputy Regional Officer, Ministry of Information (NE Region), 1941-45; Sec., East and West Ridings Industrial Publicity Cttee, 1943-45. Joined staff of The Birmingham Post as Leader-writer and Editorial Asst, 1945; served in London office, 1949; Editor, 1950-64, retired. Mem. British Cttee, Internat. Press Inst., 1952-64; Pres., Rotary Club of Birmingham, 1962-63; Mem., Church Information Adv. Cttee, 1966-72. *Publications:* Selections from Johnson, 1935; articles contributed to The Review of English Studies and to Notes and Queries; literary and dramatic reviews in various periodicals and newspapers. Has broadcast frequently in Gt Britain and US. *Recreations:* motoring, cats, theatre going, and reading. *Address:* Retraitée, West Lane, Dolton, Winkleigh, Devon EX19 8QU. *T:* Dolton 358. *Club:* Athenæum.

RHEA, Alexander Dodson, III; *b* 10 May 1919; *s* of Alexander D. Rhea, Jr and Annie Rhea; *m* 1945, Suzanne Menocal; one *s. Educ:* Princeton Univ. BA Econs and Social Instns. Active service as Lt-Comdr USNR, 1941-45. Vice-Pres., Govt Employees Ins. Corp., Washington, DC, 1946-48; Treas. and Man. Dir, General Motors de Venezuela, Caracas, 1949-55; Vice-Pres., General Motors Overseas Corp., 1960-68; Regional Gp Dir, NY, 1960-66, Staff Man., 1966-67, General Motors Overseas Operations; Chm. and Man. Dir, General Motors-Holden's, Melbourne, 1968-70; Chm. and Man. Dir., Vauxhall Motors Ltd, 1970-74; Chm., General Motors Corp. European Adv. Council, 1974-77; Exec. Vice-Pres. and Dir, General Motors Overseas Corp., 1974-77. *Recreations:* reading, golf. *Address:* 2132 Hidden Creek Road, Westover Hills, Fort Worth, Texas 76107, USA. *Clubs:* Knickerbocker, Metropolitan, Princeton, Colony (New York); Fort Worth,, River Crest Country, Century II (Fort Worth, Texas); Melbourne (Melbourne).

RHIND, Donald, CMG 1962; OBE 1947; retired 1970; *b* 26 September 1899; *er s* of late Thomas Rhind, MRCS, LRCP; *m* 1939, Annemarie Eugenia Ludovica von Ferrari und Brunnerfeld; one *s* one *d. Educ:* Aldenham School; Bristol University (BSc). Economic Botanist, Burma, 1923-45; Civil Affairs Service, Burma (Lieutenant-Colonel), 1945; Senior Economic Botanist, Burma, 1946-47; Director of Agriculture, Ceylon, 1947-50; Secretary for Agriculture and Forestry Research, West Africa, 1951-53; Secretary for Colonial Agricultural Research, 1953-61; Adviser on Agricultural

Research, Department of Technical Co-operation, 1961-64; Min. of Overseas Development, 1964-67; Agricultural Research Coordinator, SEATO, 1968-69. FLS, FIBiol. *Publications:* The Grasses of Burma, 1945; numerous scientific papers on tropical agriculture. *Address:* 1 The Briars, Upper Richmond Road, Putney, SW15. *T:* 01-788 9512.

RHINE, Prof. Joseph Banks, PhD; Executive Director of Foundation for Research on the Nature of Man, Durham, NC, USA, since 1964; *b* 29 September 1895; *m* 1920, Louisa Ella Weckesser; one *s* three *d. Educ:* Ohio Northern; Wooster; Univ. of Chicago. Research, Plant Physiology, Boyce Thompson Inst., 1923-24; Instructor, Plant Physiology, Botany Dept, West Virginia Univ., 1924-26; Duke University: Instructor, Philosophy and Psychology, 1928; Asst Prof., Psychol., 1930; Assoc. Prof., Psychol., 1934, Professor, 1937-50. *Publications:* Extrasensory Perception, 1934; New Frontiers of the Mind, 1937; (co-author) Extrasensory Perception After Sixty Years, 1940; The Reach of the Mind, 1947; New World of the Mind, 1953; (co-author) Parapsychology, Frontier Science of the Mind, 1957; Parapsychology, From Duke to FRNM, 1965; (co-ed) Parapsychology Today, 1968; (ed) Progress in Parapsychology, 1970. *Recreations:* music, nature, and family life. *Address:* Box 6847, College Station, Durham, NC 27708, USA.

RHODES, family name of **Baron Rhodes.**

RHODES, Baron *cr* 1964, of Saddleworth (Life Peer); **Hervey Rhodes,** KG 1972; PC 1969; DFC and Bar; DL; *b* 12 August 1895; *s* of John Eastwood and Elizabeth Ann Rhodes; *m* 1925, Ann Bradbury; two *d. Educ:* Greenfield, St Mary's Elementary Sch.; Huddersfield Technical College (Fellow, Huddersfield Polytechnic, 1976). Woollen worker pre-1914; joined King's Own Royal Lancs, 1914, commissioned, seconded to Flying Corps (wounded, DFC and Bar). Discharged from Hospital, 1921. Commenced business as woollen manufacturer. Served on Local Authority. Chairman of Urban District Council, 1944-45. Chairman, Saddleworth War Charities. Commanded 36th West Riding Bn Home Guard. Contested Royton Division of Lancs, 1945; MP (Lab) Ashton-under-Lyne, 1945-64; PPS, Min. of Pensions, 1948; Parliamentary Secretary, Board of Trade, 1950-51, 1964-67. Lord Lieutenant of Lancaster, 1968-71; DL Lancs, 1971. Freedom of Borough of Ashton-under-Lyne, 1965, and of Saddleworth, Yorks. KStJ 1969. Hon. DTech Bradford, 1966; Hon LLD Manchester, 1971. *Address:* Cribbstones, Delph, near Oldham, Lancs. *T:* Saddleworth 4500.

RHODES, Rev. Canon Cecil; Canon Residentiary of St Edmundsbury Cathedral, since Oct. 1964; *b* Preston, Lancs, 5 Oct. 1910; *s* of James Rhodes; *m* 1940, Gladys, *d* of H. B. Farlie; one *s* two *d. Educ:* Preston Gram. Sch.; St Peter's Hall, Oxford; Wycliffe Hall, Oxford (MA). Deacon, 1936. Priest, 1937. Curate, St Stephen, Selly Hill, Birmingham, 1936-38; Asst Editor and Youth Sec., The Pathfinder, 1938-40; Jt Editor, Light and Life Publications, 1941-44; Diocesan Chaplain-in-charge, St Mary, Pype Hayes, Birmingham, 1940-44; Vicar: St Luke, Tunbridge Wells, 1944-49; St Augustine, Edgbaston, Birmingham, 1949-64; Birmingham Diocesan Adviser for Stewardship, 1960-64; Hon. Canon of Birmingham, 1961-64. Diocesan Dir of Lay Training, Di⸗ese of St Edmundsbury and Ipswich, 1968-74; Chm., Diocesan Information Cttee, 1968-76. Founder and Editor, Church News, 1946-; Jt Editor, The Pilgrim, C of E youth magazine, 1949-50; regular contributor to The Birmingham Post, 1950-64; East Anglian Daily Times, 1970-. *Recreations:* writing, books, travel. *Address:* Abbey Precincts, Bury St Edmunds, Suffolk. *T:* Bury St Edmunds 3530.

RHODES, Rev. Clifford Oswald, MA Oxon; Rector of Somerton, Oxfordshire, since 1958; also Priest-in-charge, Upper Heyford, Lower Heyford and Rousham, since 1976; *b* 12 April 1911; *s* of Rev. Edward Rhodes; *m* 1941, Elizabeth, *e d* of H. R. Bowden; one *s* three *d. Educ:* The Grange Grammar Sch., Bradford; St Peter's Coll., Oxford. Journalism, 1934-37; Wycliffe Hall, Oxford, 1937-38; Curate, St Luke's Church, Wythenshawe, Manchester, 1938-40; CF 1940-45; Editor of the Record, 1946-49. Hon. Chaplain, St Bride's, Fleet Street, 1952-; Lectr, St Margaret's, Lothbury, EC2, 1954-. Licence to preach, from Oxford Univ., 1957. Editor of the Church of England Newspaper, 1949-59; Director and Secretary, the Modern Churchmen's Union, 1954-60; Editor of Business, 1960-63; Account Executive, Gilbert McAllister and Partners Ltd, public relations consultants, 1963-65. Editorial Director, Harcourt Kitchin and Partners Ltd, 1964-72. *Publications:* The New Church in the New Age, 1958; Musical Instruments and the Orchestra, 1968; The Awful Boss's Book, 1968; (ed) Authority in a Changing Society, 1969; The Necessity for Love: the history of interpersonal relations, 1972; contrib. to many newspapers and periodicals and learned jls. *Recreations:* the arts and country

life. *Address:* The Rectory, Somerton, Oxfordshire OX5 4NF. *T:* Fritwell 255.

RHODES, Sir John (Christopher Douglas), 4th Bt, *cr* 1919; *b* 24 May 1946; *s* of Sir Christopher Rhodes, 3rd Bt, and of Mary Florence, *d* of late Dr Douglas Wardleworth; *S* father, 1964. *Heir: b* Michael Philip James Rhodes [*b* 3 April 1948; *m* 1973, Susan, *d* of Patrick Roney-Dougal].

RHODES, John Ivor McKinnon, CMG 1971; Member, United Nations Committee on Contributions, 1966-71, and since 1975; *b* 6 March 1914; *s* of late Joseph Thomas Rhodes and late Hilda (*née* McKinnon); *m* 1939, Eden Annetta (*née* Clark); one *s* one *d. Educ:* Leeds Modern School. Exec. Officer, WO, 1933; Financial Adviser's Office, HQ British Forces in Palestine, 1938; Major 1940; Asst Comd Sec., Southern Comd, 1944; Financial Adviser, London District, 1946; Principal 1947, Asst Sec. 1959, HM Treasury; Minister, UK Mission to UN, 1966-74. Mem., UN Pension Board, 1966-71; Chm., UN Adv. Cttee on Admin. and Budgetary Questions, 1971-74. *Recreations:* gardening, playing the electronic organ. *Address:* Quintins, Watersfield, Sussex. *T:* Bury 634. *Club:* Royal Commonwealth Society.

RHODES, Marion, RE 1953 (ARE 1941); etcher, painter in water colour and oils; *b* Huddersfield, Yorks, 1907; *d* of Samuel Rhodes and Mary Jane Mallinson. *Educ:* Greenhead High School, Huddersfield; Huddersfield Art School; Leeds College of Art; The Central School of Arts and Crafts, London. Art Teachers' Certificate (Univ. of Oxford), 1930; teaching posts, 1930-67; pt-time lecturer in Art at Berridge House Training Coll., 1947-55. SGA 1936, Hon. Life Mem., 1969; FRSA 1944; Member, Manchester Acad. of Fine Art, 1955; Paris Salon: Honourable Mention, 1952; Bronze Medal, 1956; Silver Medal 1961; Gold Medal, 1967. Exhibited from 1934 at: Royal Academy, Royal Scottish Academy, Mall Gall., The Paris Salon, Walker Art Gall., Towner Art Gall., Atkinson Art Gall., Southport, Brighton, Bradford, Leeds, Manchester and other provincial Art Galls, also USA and S Africa. Etching of Jordans' Hostel and drawing of The Meeting House purchased by Contemporary Art Soc. and presented to British Museum; other works in the Print Room, BM; work also purchased by Bradford Corp. Art Gall., Brighouse Art Gall., Huddersfield Art Gall., Stoke-on-Trent Educn Cttee's Loan Scheme, and South London (Camberwell) Library Committee; works reproduced. Fellow, Ancient Monuments Soc.; Associate, Artistes Français, 1971; Hon. Mem., Tommasso Campanella Acad., Rome (Silver Medal, 1970). Cert. of Merit, Dictionary of Internat. Biography, 1972. *Recreations:* gardening and geology. *Address:* 2 Goodwyn Avenue, Mill Hill, NW7 3RG. *T:* 01-959 2280. *Club:* English-Speaking Union.

RHODES, Peregrine Alexander, CMG 1976; HM Diplomatic Service; on secondment as Under Secretary, Cabinet Office, since 1975; *b* 14 May 1925; *s* of Cyril Edmunds Rhodes and Elizabeth Jocelyn Rhodes; *m* 1st, 1951, Jane Marion Hassell (marr. diss.); two *s* one *d* ; 2nd, 1969, Margaret Rosemary Page. *Educ:* Winchester Coll.; New Coll., Oxford. Served with Coldstream Guards, 1944-47. Joined FO, 1950; 2nd Sec., Rangoon, 1953-56; Private Sec. to Minister of State, 1956-59; 1st Sec., Vienna, 1959-62; 1st Sec., Helsinki, 1962-65; FCO, 1965-68, Counsellor 1967; Inst. for Study of Internat. Organisation, Sussex Univ., 1968-69; Counsellor: Rome, 1970-73; E Berlin, 1973-75. *Recreations:* photography, reading. *Address:* c/o Cabinet Office, Whitehall, SW1. *Club:* Travellers'.

RHODES, Philip, FRCS, FRCOG, FACMA; Postgraduate Dean and Director, Regional Postgraduate Institute for Medicine and Dentistry, Newcastle University, since 1977; *b* 2 May 1922; *s* of Sydney Rhodes, Dore, Sheffield; *m* 1946, Mary Elizabeth Worley, Barrowden, Rutland; three *s* two *d. Educ:* King Edward VII Sch., Sheffield; Clare Coll., Cambridge; St Thomas's Hospital Medical School. BA(Cantab) 1943, MB, BChir(Cantab) 1946; FRCS 1953; MRCOG 1956; FRCOG 1964; FACMA 1976. Major RAMC, 1948-50. Medical appointments held in St Thomas' Hosp., Folkestone, Harrogate, Chelsea Hosp. for Women, Queen Charlotte's Hosp., 1946-58; Consultant Obstetric Physician, St Thomas' Hosp., 1958-63; Prof. of Obstetrics and Gynæcol., St Thomas's Hosp. Med. Sch., Univ. of London, 1964-74, Dean, 1968-74; Dean, Faculty of Medicine, Univ. of Adelaide, 1975-77. Governor: Dulwich College, 1966-74; St Thomas' Hosp., 1969-74; Pembroke Sch., Adelaide, 1976-77. Member: SW Metropolitan Regional Hosp. Board, 1967-74; SE Thames Reg. Health Authority, 1974. Mem. Steering Cttee of DHSS on management of NHS, 1971-72. Mem., Adv. Cttee, Nat. Inst. of Medical Hist., Australia, 1976. *Publications:* Fluid Balance in Obstetrics, 1960; Introduction to Gynæcology and Obstetrics, 1967; Reproductive Physiology for Medical Students, 1969; Woman: A Biological Study, 1969; The

Value of Medicine, 1976; Dr John Leake's Hospital, 1978; articles in Jl of Obstetrics and Gynæcology of the British Empire, Lancet, Brit. Med. Jl, Med. Jl of Australia. *Recreations:* reading, gardening, photography, anthropology, sociology. *Address:* Postgraduate Institute, Medical School, The University, Newcastle upon Tyne NE1 7RH.

RHODES, Reginald Paul; Chairman, Southern Gas Region, since 1975; *b* 10 April 1918; *s* of Edwin Rhodes and Dorothy Lena Molyneux; *m* 1940, Margaret Frances Fish; two *s* three *d* . *Educ:* Merchant Taylors Sch., Northwood. Joined Gas Light & Coke Co., 1937; North Thames Gas, 1948 (Dep. Chm., 1972). Member, Co. of Pikemen, Honourable Artillery Company. FIGasE. *Recreations:* music, gardening. *Address:* Tidebrook Lodge, Royden Lane, Boldre, near Lymington, Hants SO4 8PE. *T:* Brockenhurst 2399.

RHODES, Stephen, OBE 1969; solicitor; Secretary, Association of District Councils, since 1973; *b* 19 Jan. 1918; *s* of late Edward Hugh Rhodes, CBE, and Helen Edith Laurie Patricia Rhodes; *m* 1958, Jane, *d* of late Norman S. Bradley, Sydney, Aust.; one *s* two *d* . *Educ:* St Paul's Sch.; Law Society's Sch. of Law. LLB (London). Articled to Sir Cecil Oakes, CBE, Clerk of East Suffolk CC; admitted solicitor, 1941. Served RAF, 1939-46: commnd 1941; Sqdn-Ldr, 1944 (despatches). Asst Solicitor, East Suffolk CC, 1946-47; Sen. Asst Solicitor, Norfolk CC, 1947-49; Asst Sec., County Councils Assoc., 1949-59; Secretary, Rural District Councils Assoc., 1959-73; Jt Sec., Internat. Union of Local Authorities, 1975-. Mem., Health Educn Council, 1968-74; Jt Sec., Standing Adv. Cttee on Local Authorities and the Theatre, 1975-; Hon. Sec., Southwark Soc. for Mentally Handicapped Children, 1965-. *Address:* (office) 25 Buckingham Gate, SW1E 6LE. *T:* 01-828 7931; (home) 9 Hitherwood Drive, College Road, SE19 1XA. *T:* 01-670 7520. *Clubs:* National Liberal, English-Speaking Union.

RHODES, Zandra Lindsey, DesRCA; RDI; Managing Director, Zandra Rhodes (UK) Ltd and Zandra Rhodes (Shops) Ltd, since 1975; *b* 19 Sept. 1940; *d* of Albert James Rhodes and Beatrice Ellen (*née* Twigg). *Educ:* Medway Technical Sch. for Girls, Chatham; Medway Coll. of Art; Royal Coll. of Art (DesRCA 1965). RDI 1976. With Alexander MacIntyre, set up print factory and studio, 1965; sold designs (and converted them on to cloth) to Foale and Tuffin and Roger Nelson; formed partnership with Sylvia Ayton and began producing dresses using her own prints, 1966; opened Fulham Road Clothes Shop, designing dresses as well as prints, first in partnership, 1967-68, then (Fulham Road shop closed) alone, producing first clothes range in which she revolutionised use of prints in clothes by cutting round patterns to make shapes never before used; took collection to USA, 1969; sold to Fortnum and Mason, London, through Anne Knight, 1969, then to Piero de Monzi, 1971; began building up name and business in USA (known for her annual spectacular Fantasy Shows); also started designing in jersey and revolutionised its treatment with lettuce edges and seams on the outside; with Anne Knight and Ronnie Stirling founded Zandra Rhodes (UK) Ltd and Zandra Rhodes (Shops) Ltd, opening first shop in London, 1975; others opened in Bloomingdales NY, Marshall Field, Chicago, and Harrods, London, 1976; first collection of sheets and pillowcases, for Wamsutta, USA, 1976, of Lingerie, made in US, launched 1977. *Recreations:* travelling, drawing. *Address:* (studio) 64 Porchester Road, W2. *T:* (business) 01-602 1929.

RHODES JAMES, Robert Vidal; MP (C) Cambridge, since Dec. 1976; *b* 10 April 1933; *y s* of late Lieut-Col W. R. James, OBE, MC; *m* 1956, Angela Margaret Robertson, *er d* of late R. M. Robertson; four *d* . *Educ:* private schs in India; Sedbergh Sch.; Worcester Coll., Oxford. Asst Clerk, House of Commons, 1955-61; Senior Clerk, 1961-64. Fellow of All Souls Coll., Oxford, 1965-68; Dir, Inst. for Study of Internat. Organisation, Univ. of Sussex, 1968-73; Principal Officer, Exec. Office of Sec.-Gen. of UN, 1973-76. Kratter Prof. of European History, Stanford Univ., Calif., 1968. Consultant to UN Conf. on Human Environment, 1971-72; UK Mem., UN Sub-Commn on Prevention of Discrimination and Protection of Minorities, 1972-73. FRSL 1964; NATO Fellow, 1965; FRHistS 1973; Professorial Fellow, Univ. of Sussex, 1973. *Publications:* Lord Randolph Churchill, 1959; An Introduction to the House of Commons, 1961 (John Llewelyn Rhys Memorial Prize); Rosebery, 1963 (Royal Society Lit. Award); Gallipoli, 1965; Standardization and Production of Military Equipment in NATO, 1967; Churchill: a study in failure, 1900-39, 1970; Ambitions and Realities: British politics 1964-70, 1972; Victor Cazalet: a portrait, 1976; The British Revolution 1880-1939, vol. I, 1976, vol. II, 1977. (ed) Chips: The Diaries of Sir Henry Channon, 1967; (ed) Memoirs of a Conservative: J. C. C. Davidson's Memoirs and Papers, 1969; (ed) The Czechoslovak

Crisis 1968, 1969; (ed) The Complete Speeches of Sir Winston Churchill, 1897-1963, 1974; contrib. to: Suez Ten Years After, 1967; Essays From Divers Hands, 1967; Churchill: four faces and the man, 1969; International Administration, 1971; The Prime Ministers, vol. II, 1975. *Address:* The Watermill, Hildersham, Cambridge CB1 6BS. *Clubs:* Travellers'; Century (New York).

RHYL, Baron *cr* 1970 (Life Peer), of Holywell, Southampton; **(Evelyn) Nigel (Chetwode) Birch,** PC 1955; OBE 1945; *b* 1906; *s* of late Gen. Sir Noel Birch, GBE, KCB, KCMG, 11 Kensington Gore, SW7; *m* 1950, Hon. Esmé Glyn, *d* of 4th Baron Wolverton. *Educ:* Eton. Partner in Cohen Laming Hoare until May 1939 when retired to study politics. Territorial Army officer before the war. Served War of 1939-45 in KRRC and on Gen. Staff; Lt-Col 1944; served in Great Britain and Italy. MP (C) Flintshire, 1945-50, West Flint, 1950-70; Parly Under-Sec. of State, Air Ministry, 1951-52; Parliamentary Sec., Ministry of Defence, 1952-54; Minister of Works, Oct. 1954-Dec. 1955; Sec. of State for Air, Dec. 1955-17 Jan. 1957; Economic Sec. to the Treasury, 1957-58, resigned. Pres., Johnson Soc., Lichfield, 1966. *Publication:* The Conservative Party, 1949. *Recreations:* reading history; gardening; shooting; fishing. *Address:* 73 Ashley Gardens, SW1; Holywell House, Swanmore, Hants. *Clubs:* Pratt's, White's.

RHYMES, Rev. Canon Douglas Alfred; Canon Residentiary and Librarian, Southwark Cathedral, 1962-69, Hon. Canon, since 1969; Parish Priest of Woldingham, since 1976; Tutor, Southwark Ordination Course; *b* 26 March 1914; *s* of Peter Alfred and Jessie Rhymes; unmarried. *Educ:* King Edward VI School, Birmingham; Birmingham Univ.; Ripon Hall Theological College, Oxford. BA (2nd Cl. Hons 1st Div.) Philosophy 1939. Asst Curate, Dovercourt, Essex, 1940-43; Chaplain to the Forces, 1943-46; Asst Curate, Romford, Essex (in charge of St George's, Romford and St Thomas', Noak Hill), 1946-49; Priest-in-charge, Ascension, Chelmsford, 1949-50; Sacrist, Southwark Cathedral, 1950-54; Vicar, All Saints, New Eltham, SE9, 1954-62; Director of Lay Training, Diocese of Southwark, 1962-68; Vicar of St Giles, Camberwell, 1968-76. Proctor in Convocation and Mem. of Gen. Synod, 1975-. *Publications:* (part author) Crisis Booklets, Christianity and Communism, 1952; Layman's Church, 1963; No New Morality, 1964; Prayer in the Secular City, 1967; Through Prayer to Reality, 1974. *Recreations:* theatre, conversation, country walks. *Address:* The Rectory, Woldingham, Surrey. *T:* 01-905 2192.

RHYS, family name of **Baron Dynevor.**

RHYS, Jean, (Mrs Jean Hamer); writer; *b* 24 Aug. 1894; *d* of Dr Rees Williams, Roseau, Dominica and Mrs Rees Williams (*née* Lockhart); *m* ; one *d* ; *m* 3rd, 1947, Max Hamer. *Educ:* The Convent, Roseau, Dominica; RADA. Left England, 1919; began to write in Paris, helped and encouraged by friends; subseq. returned to London. FRSL 1966. *Publications:* The Left Bank, 1927; Quartet, 1928 (as Postures, New York); After leaving Mr Mackenzie, 1930; Voyage in the Dark, 1934; Good Morning Midnight, 1939; Wide Sargasso Sea, 1966 (RSL Award, 1966; W. H. Smith Annual Literary Award, 1966; Arts Council Bursary, 1967); Tigers are Better Looking, 1967; Sleep It Off Lady (short stories), 1976. *Address:* 6 Landboat Bungalows, Cheriton Fitzpaine, Crediton, Devon EX17 4HA.

RHYS, Keidrych; poet and writer; editor (founder) of magazine Wales, 1937-60; *b* Bethlehem, Llandilo, 26 Dec. 1915; *m* 1st, 1939, Lynette Roberts, poet and novelist, of Buenos Aires; one *s* one *d* ; 2nd, 1956, Eva Smith; one *s*. *Educ:* Bethlehem; Llangadog; Llandovery Grammar Sch., etc. Literary and other journalism, London, etc, 1935. Served in Army (London Welsh AA) (1939-45 medals); with Ministry of Information, London, 1943-44; War Correspondent (France, Belgium, Holland, Germany), 1944-45. Public Relations Consultant, various charities and organisations, 1950-54; Welsh columnist and correspondent, The People, 1954-60; London Editor, Poetry London-New York, 1956-60; Editor, Druid Books, Publishers. Arts Council Award in Literature, 1969-70; with Lyrebird Press, with Tambimuttu, 1972-. Vice-President International Musical Festival and Eisteddfod; Executive Committee (writers' group); Chairman Friends of Wales Soc.; Vice-Pres. Carmarthen Arts Club; Carmarthenshire County Drama Cttee and Rural Community Council. *Publications:* The Van Pool and other poems, 1941; Poems from the Forces, 1942; More Poems from the Forces, 1943; Modern Welsh Poetry, 1945; Angry Prayers, 1952; The Expatriates, 1964; Poems; Contributor to: Wales, Times Lit. Supp., New Statesman, anthologies, and to European and American jls. *Recreations:* Welsh National affairs, lecturing, theatre. *Address:* 40 Heath Street, NW3. *T:* 01-794 2970. *Club:* Press.

RHYS WILLIAMS, Sir Brandon (Meredith), 2nd Bt, *cr* 1918; MP (C) Kensington, since 1974 (Kensington South, March 1968-1974); Member, British Delegation to European Parliament, Strasbourg, since 1973; *b* 14 Nov. 1927; *s* of Sir Rhys Rhys Williams, 1st Bt, DSO, QC, and Lady (Juliet) Rhys Williams, DBE (*d* 1964); *S* father, 1955; *m* 1961, Caroline Susan, *e d* of L. A. Foster, Greatham Manor, Pulborough, Sussex; one *s* two *d. Educ:* Eton. Served in Welsh Guards, 1946-48 (Lt). Contested (C) Pontypridd Parly Div., 1959, and Ebbw Vale Div., 1960 and 1964. Consultant, Management Selection Ltd, 1963-71; formerly with ICI Ltd. Asst Dir, Spastics Soc., 1962-63. Vice-Chm., European Parlt Economic and Monetary Affairs Cttee (Rapporteur, Econ. and Monetary Union); Mem., Soc. Affairs and Employment Cttee. *Publications:* The New Social Contract, 1967; More Power to the Shareholder?, 1969; Redistributing Income in a Free Society, 1969. *Heir: s* Gareth Ludovic Emrys Rhys Williams, *b* 9 Nov. 1961. *Address:* 32 Rawlings Street, SW3. *T:* 01-584 0636; Miskin Manor, Pontyclun, Mid Glamorgan. *T:* Llantrisant 224204. *Clubs:* White's, Pratt's; Cardiff and County (Cardiff).

RIABOUCHINSKA, Tatiana, (Mme Lichine); Ballerina of Russian Ballet; *b* 23 May 1916; *d* of Michael P. Riabouchinsky, Moscow (Banker), and Tatiana Riabouchinska (*d* 1935), Dancer of Moscow Imperial School of Dance; *m* 1942, David Lichine (*d* 1972); one *d. Educ:* Cour Fénelon, Paris. Trained first by her mother; then by Volinine (dancer of the Moscow Imperial Grand Theatre); then by Mathilde Kchesinska. First appeared as child dancer with Balieff's Chauve Souris in London, 1931; joined new Russian Ballet (de-Basil), 1932, and danced with them in nearly all countries of Western Europe, Australia and N and S America. Contribution to books on dancing by: Andre Levinson, Arnold L. Haskell, Irving Deakin, Rayner Heppenstall, Kay Ambrose, Prince Peter Lieven, Cyril W. Beaumont, Cyril Brahms, Adrian Stokes, A. V. Coton, Ninette de Valois, etc. *Address:* 965 Oakmont Drive, Los Angeles, Calif 90049, USA.

RIALL, Air Cdre Arthur Bookey, CBE 1956 (OBE 1953); RAF Regiment, retired; General Secretary, National Rifle Association, since 1968; *b* 7 Dec. 1911; *o s* of Major M. B. Riall, OBE, and Mrs S. M. Riall (*née* Lefroy); *m* 1950, Pamela Patricia Hewitt; five *s* one *d. Educ:* Charterhouse; RMC, Sandhurst. Commissioned E Yorks Regt, 1932; served in India with 1st Bn until 1939 when posted as Instr to Small Arms Sch.; Staff Coll., 1941; staff appts until Home posting, 1944; served 2nd Bn NW Europe (wounded, despatches); seconded to RAF in Iraq, for service with Iraq Levies, 1947; transf. RAF Regt, 1948; Chief Instr, RAF Regt Depot, 1951-53; commanded RAF levies, until their disbandment, 1953-55 and RAF Regt Depot, Catterick, 1955-59; Staff appts in UK and Cyprus, 1959-61; Air Cdre, 1963; apptd Dir of Ground Defence, RAF, 1963; retd Dec. 1966, and joined staff of NRA. *Recreations:* hunting (Master, Royal Exodus Hunt, until disbandment in 1955), target rifle shooting (rep. GB, Ireland and RAF), ornithology (Vice-Pres., RAF Ornith. Soc.). *Address:* Hill House, Ewshot, Farnham, Surrey. *Club:* Naval and Military.

RIBBANS, Prof. Geoffrey Wilfrid, MA; Gilmour Professor of Spanish, University of Liverpool, since 1963, and Dean, Faculty of Arts, since 1977; Editor, Bulletin of Hispanic Studies, since 1964; *b* 15 April 1927; *o s* of late Wilfrid Henry Ribbans and Rose Matilda Burton; *m* 1956, Magdalena Cumming (*née* Willmann), Cologne; one *s* two *d. Educ:* Sir George Monoux Grammar Sch., Walthamstow; King's Coll., Univ. of London. BA Hons Spanish 1st cl., 1948; Univ. of London Postgrad. Studentship; MA 1953. Asst Lectr, Queen's Univ., Belfast, 1951-52; Asst, St Salvator's Coll., Univ. of St Andrews, 1952-53; Univ. of Sheffield: Asst Lectr, 1953-55; Lectr, 1955-61; Sen. Lectr, 1961-63. First Director, Centre for Latin-American Studies, Univ. of Liverpool, 1966-70; Andrew Mellon Vis. Prof., Univ. of Pittsburgh, 1970-71; Leverhulme Res. Fellow, 1975. Vice-Pres., Internat. Assoc. of Hispanists, 1974; Pres., Anglo-Catalan Soc., 1976; Dir, Liverpool Playhouse, 1974-. Hon. Fellow, Inst. of Linguists, 1972. *Publications:* Catalunya i València vistes pels viatgers anglesos del segle XVIIIè, 1955; Niebla y Soledad: aspectos de Unamuno y Machado, 1971; ed, Soledades, Galerias, otros poemas, by Antonio Machado, 1975; Antonio Machado (1875-1939): poetry and integrity, 1975; B. Pérez Galdós: Fortunata y Jacinta, a critical guide, 1977; numerous articles on Spanish literature in specialised publications. *Recreations:* travel, fine art. *Address:* The Knowle, 18 Pine Walks, Prenton, Birkenhead, Merseyside L42 8NE. *T:* 051-608 3909.

RICE; *see* Spring Rice, family name of Baron Monteagle of Brandon.

RICE, Maj.-Gen. Desmond Hind Garrett, CBE 1976; Director of Manning, since 1977; *b* 1 Dec. 1924; *s* of Arthur Garrett Rice and Alice Constance (*née* Henman); *m* 1954, Denise Ann (*née* Ravenscroft); one *d. Educ:* Marlborough College. Commissioned into The Queen's Bays, 1944; psc 1954; 1st The Queen's Dragoon Guards, 1958; jssc 1963; First Comdg Officer, The Royal Yeomanry, 1967-69; Col GS 4 Div., 1970-73; BGS (MO) MoD, 1973-75; rcds 1976. *Recreations:* field sports, skiing, gardening. *Address:* Fairway, Malacca Farm, West Clandon, Surrey. *T:* Guildford 222677. *Club:* Cavalry and Guards.

RICE, George Ritchie, CMG 1947; OBE 1927; *b* 31 July 1881; *s* of late John Norman Rice; *m* 1911, Elvina, *d* of late Charles Moore, Messing, Essex; one *d; m* 1956, Helen Woodman, Bexhill. *Educ:* Wilson's School; King's College, London. Civil Service; War Office, 1899; trans. to Army Accounts Dept, 1905; Chief Accountant, 1926; Financial Adviser, GOC China, 1927-29; GOC Egypt, 1934-35; GOC Palestine, 1936; joined Ministry of Supply, 1939; Director of Clothing and Textiles, 1939-43; Dep. Director-Gen. Equipment and Stores, 1943-45; Director-Gen. Disposals Mission, Middle East, 1945-46; Ministry of Supply, Special Representative for S Africa, 1946-47; Ministry of Supply, Director of Sales, Hamburg, 1947-50; retired from Civil Service, 1950. *Address:* 4 Chiltern Court, Sutherland Avenue, Bexhill-on-Sea, East Sussex. *T:* Bexhill-on-Sea 210489. *Club:* National.

RICE, Peter D.; *see* Davis-Rice.

RICE, Roderick Alexander, FACCA; Executive Director, Cable & Wireless Ltd, since 1965; *b* 7 April 1922; *s* of Samuel Richard Rice and Katrine Alice Rice; *m* 1965, Monica McClean; three *s. Educ:* Brockley County Grammar Sch. Cable & Wireless Ltd: Asst Chief Accountant, 1959; Dep. Chief Accountant, 1961; Chief Accountant, 1962; Executive Director, 1965. Jordan Star of Independence, 1965. *Recreations:* bowls, cricket, gardening. *Address:* 10 Beverley Close, Camberley, Surrey. *T:* Camberley 26731. *Clubs:* Royal Commonwealth Institute; (Chairman) Exiles (Richmond).

RICE, Timothy Miles Bindon; writer and broadcaster; *b* 10 Nov. 1944; *s* of Hugh Gordon Rice and Joan Odette Rice; *m* 1974, Jane Artereta McIntosh; one *s* one *d. Educ:* Lancing Coll. EMI Records, 1966-68; Norrie Paramor Org., 1968-69. Lyrics for musicals (with music by Andrew Lloyd Webber): Joseph and the amazing technicolour dreamcoat, 1968 (rev. 1973); Jesus Christ Superstar, 1970; Evita 1976. *Publications:* Heartaches Cricketers' Almanac, 1975-; (with Jo Rice) Guinness Book of British Hit Singles, 1977; (with Andrew Lloyd Webber), Evita, 1978. *Recreations:* cricket, history of popular music. *Address:* 118 Wardour Street, W1V 4BT. *T:* 01-437 3224. *Club:* MCC.

RICE, Wilfred Eric, CBE 1948 (OBE 1942); Chairman and Life Governing Director, Rice & Son Ltd, building contractors; *b* 25 May 1898; *s* of late Sir Frederick Gill Rice, one-time MP for Harwich, Essex; *m* 1923, Vera Lillian Lampard, MBE, 1944, *d* of late W. B. Lampard. *Educ:* Dulwich College. Served European War, 1914-18, Lieut 3rd London Regt (severely wounded). Entered family business of Rice & Son Ltd, 1919. Past President: London Master Builders Assoc., 1942-43; London Rotary Club, 1944-45. Chairman: Hotel and Catering Trades Advisory Cttee (Min. of Labour), 1947-60; Disabled Persons Advisory Cttee, Brixton, 1948-59; Local Employment Cttee, Brixton, 1935-47; West London Road Safety Cttee, 1946-62; Deputy Chm. Westminster Bench, 1957-67. JP London since 1943. Member Conscientious Objectors Tribunal, 1941-44. Master, Worshipful Company of Innholders; Liveryman, Worshipful Company of Paviors. Mayor of the City of Westminster, 1950-51. Comdr Royal Order of Dannebrog (Denmark); Officer of Order of Orange Nassau (Holland), 1950. *Address:* 3 Buckingham Gate, SW1. *T:* 01-834 2831; 10 The Beach, Walmer, Kent. *T:* Deal 5516.

RICE-JONES, His Honour Benjamin Rowland, BA, LLB Hons Cambridge; retired as County Court Judge, Circuit No 56 (1952-60); *b* 19 June 1888; *s* of J. E. and E. H. Rice-Jones; *m* 1916, Nancy (*d* 1966), *d* of H. Shelmerdine; one *d. Educ:* Temple Grove Sch.; Clifton Coll.; Christ's College, Cambridge. Called to Bar, Inner Temple, 1912 (Certificate of Honour); joined Northern Circuit. Assistant Judge at the Liverpool Court of Passage; Judge, Circuit No. 12, 1945-52. Served in HM Forces, 1914-19, Inns of Court OTC, 2/2 Lancs Battery RGA, TF, 1/1 West Riding Battery RGA TF (wounded at Ypres). *Address:* Kinross, West Hill Lane, Budleigh Salterton, Devon. *T:* 3214.

RICE-OXLEY, James Keith; Director: General Council of British Shipping, since 1975; International Shipping Federation, since 1970; *b* 15 Aug. 1920; *o s* of late Montague Keith Rice-Oxley and Margery Hyacinth Rice-Oxley (*née* Burrell), Kensington; *m* 1949, Barbara, *yr d* of late Frederick Parsons, Gerrards Cross; two *d. Educ:* Marlborough Coll.; Trinity Coll., Oxford (MA). Served War of 1939-45: Wiltshire Regt; GSO III, HQ 3 Corps; GSO II, HQ Land Forces, Greece (despatches). Joined Shipping Fedn, 1947 (Gen. Manager, 1962; Dir, 1965). Chm., Nat. Sea Training Trust; Vice-Chm., Merchant Navy Trg Bd; Mem. Nat. Maritime Bd; Mem., HMS Conway Trust; Shipowner Mem., Merchant Navy Welfare Bd; Mem. Council, King George's Fund for Sailors; Mem. various cttees of CBI; Shipowners' Chm. and British Shipowners' Rep. on Jt Maritime Commn of ILO; Chm., Shipowners' Gp at Internat. Labour (Maritime) Confs, 1969, 1970, 1975-. *Recreations:* squash, tennis, water-skiing. *Address:* Magpies, Lynx Hill, East Horsley, Surrey. *T:* East Horsley 2298.

RICH, Sir Almeric (Frederic Conness), 6th Bt, *cr* 1791; *b* 9 Feb. 1897; *o s* of Sir Almeric E. F. Rich, 5th Bt, and Louise (*d* 1932), *d* of Hon. John Conness, Mattapan, Mass, USA; *S* father 1948. Lt RGA, 1914-19. HM Borstal Service, 1932-61. *Address:* c/o National Westminster Bank Ltd, 1 St James's Square, SW1. *Club:* Phyllis Court (Henley-on-Thames).

RICH, Prof. Edwin Ernest, MA; LittD; Vere Harmsworth Professor of Naval and Imperial History, Cambridge, 1951-70; Master of St Catharine's College, Cambridge, 1957-73 (Fellow, 1930-73, now Emeritus); Hon. Fellow: Trumbull College, Yale; Selwyn College, Cambridge; Worcester College, Oxford; *b* 4 August 1904; *s* of George Edwin and Rose Rich, Brislington, Bristol; *m* 1934, Adele (*d* 1975), *d* of Laurence Blades; one *d. Educ:* Colston's School, Bristol; Selwyn College, Cambridge. *Publications:* Staple Courts of Bristol, 1931; Ordinances of the Merchants of the Staple, 1935; The Hudson's Bay Company, 1670-1870, 1958-59; Gen. Ed. Hudson's Bay Record Soc., 1937-60; Montreal and the Fur Trade, 1966; The Fur Trade and the Northwest, 1967. *Recreations:* caravanning, golf. *Address:* Stryp Lynch, Heydon, S Cambs.

RICH, Jacob Morris, MA, LLB; Secretary, South African Jewish Board of Deputies, 1939-74; Associate Secretary, Co-ordinating Board of Jewish Organisations for Consultation with Economic and Social Council of UN; *b* Longton, Stoke-on-Trent, 4 March 1897; *m* 1940, Sylvia Linken; two *d. Educ:* Hanley High School; Fitzwilliam Hall, Cambridge. Served in Palestine with Jewish Battalions of the Royal Fusiliers during European War; Secretary to the Board of Deputies of British Jews, 1926-31; Secretary of the Joint Foreign Committee of the Board of Deputies of British Jews and the Anglo-Jewish Association, 1930-31; Hon. Secretary Jewish Historical Society of England, 1924-31; Editor, The Jewish Chronicle, 1931-36. *Address:* 17 Campbell Rd, Parktown West, Johannesburg, S Africa.

RICH, John Rowland; HM Diplomatic Service; Commercial Counsellor, Bonn, since 1974; *b* 29 June 1928; *s* of Rowland William Rich, *qv*; *m* 1956, Rosemary Ann, *yr d* of late Bertram Evan Williams, Ferndown, Dorset; two *s* one *d. Educ:* Sedbergh; Clare Coll., Cambridge (Foundn Exhibnr 1948). BA 1949, MA 1954. HM Forces, 1949-51; FO, 1951-53; 3rd, later 2nd Sec., Addis Ababa, 1953-56; 2nd, later 1st Sec., Stockholm, 1956-59; FO, 1959-63; 1st Sec. (Economic) and Head of Chancery, Bahrain (Political Residency), 1963-66; FCO, 1966-69; Counsellor and Head of Chancery, Prague, 1969-72; Diplomatic Service Inspector, 1972-74. *Recreations:* motoring, walking, gardening, tennis. *Address:* c/o Foreign and Commonwealth Office, SW1; 23 Embercourt Road, Thames Ditton, Surrey KT7 0LH. *T:* 01-398 1205. *Club:* Travellers'.

RICH, Rowland William; Principal, City of Leeds Training College, 1933-63; *b* 1901; *s* of William Henry Rich of Weston-super-Mare; *m* 1926, Phyllis Mary, *e d* of Charles Linstead Chambers of Southgate; one *s* one *d. Educ:* Brighton Grammar School; University College, London; London Day Training College, BA (Hons English), 1921, Teachers' Diploma, 1922, MA (Education), 1925; PhD 1934; English master and housemaster, Newport (Essex) Grammar School, 1922-25; Lecturer in Education, University of Durham (Durham Division), 1925-30; Professor of Education, University College, Hull, 1930-33; Tutor to extra-mural tutorial classes (WEA) in English Literature, Social History and Psychology; Vice-Chairman, Association of Tutors in Adult Education, 1931-33; President Training College Association, 1938; Chairman, Association of Teachers in Colleges and Departments of Education, 1946; Member National Advisory Council on Training and Supply of Teachers, 1950-56. *Publications:* The Training of Teachers in the Nineteenth Century, 1933; The Teacher in a Planned Society, 1949; contributor to Adult Education in Practice, 1934, Britain Today, 1943, Education in

Britain, 1944. *Recreations:* gardening, walking. *Address:* 65 Cheriton Road, Winchester, Hants. *T:* Winchester 3654.
See also J. R. Rich.

RICHARD, Cliff; singer, actor; *b* 14 Oct. 1940; *s* of Rodger Webb and Dorothy Webb. *Educ:* Riversmead Sch., Cheshunt. Awarded 7 Gold Discs for records: Living Doll, 1959; The Young Ones, 1962; Bachelor Boy, 1962; Lucky Lips, 1963; Congratulations, 1968; Power to all Our Friends, 1973; Devil Woman, 1976; also 25 Silver Discs. Films: Serious Charge, 1959; Expresso Bongo, 1960; The Young Ones, 1962; Summer Holiday, 1963; Wonderful Life, 1964; Finders Keepers, 1966; Two a Penny, 1968; His Land, 1970; Take Me High, 1973. Own TV series, ATV and BBC; rep. and variety seasons. Top Box Office Star of GB, 1962-63 and 1963-64. *Publications:* Questions, 1970; The Way I See It, 1972; The Way I See It Now, 1975; Which One's Cliff, 1977. *Recreations:* swimming, badminton. *Address:* c/o Peter Gormley, 16 Harley House, Marylebone Road, NW1 4PZ. *T:* 01-486 4182.

RICHARD, Ivor Seward, QC 1971; Barrister-at-Law; United Kingdom Permanent Representative to the United Nations, since 1974; Chairman, The Rhodesia Conference, Geneva, 1976; *b* 30 May 1932; *s* of Seward Thomas Richard, mining and electrical engineer, and Isabella Irene Richard; *m* 1962, Alison Mary Imrie; one *s* one *d* (and one *s* by former marriage). *Educ:* St Michael's Sch., Bryn, Llanelly; Cheltenham Coll.; Pembroke Coll. (Wightwick Scholar), Oxford. BA Oxon (Jurisprudence) 1953; MA 1970; called to Bar, 1955. Practised in chambers, London, 1955-74. Parly Candidate, S Kensington, 1959; MP (Lab) Barons Court, 1964-Feb. 1974. Delegate: Assembly, Council of Europe, 1965-68; Western European Union, 1965-68; Vice-Chm., Legal Cttee, Council of Europe, 1966-67; PPS, Sec. of State for Defence, 1966-69; Parly Under-Sec. (Army), Min. of Defence, 1969-70; Opposition Spokesman, Broadcasting, Posts and Telecommunications, 1970-71; Dep. Spokesman, Foreign Affairs, 1971-74. Member: Fabian Society; Society of Labour Lawyers; Inst. of Strategic Studies; Royal Inst. of Internat. Affairs. *Publications:* (jt) Europe or the Open Sea, 1971; articles in various political jls. *Recreations:* playing piano, watching football matches (Chelsea), talking. *Address:* United Kingdom Mission to the United Nations, 845 Third Avenue, New York, NY 10022, USA; 47 Burntwood Grange Road, SW18. *T:* 01-870 1473.

RICHARDS, family name of **Baron Milverton.**

RICHARDS, Archibald Banks, CA; Senior Partner, Touche Ross & Co., Chartered Accountants, Edinburgh, since 1969; *b* 29 March 1911; *s* of late Charles Richards and Margaret Pollock Richards; *m* 1941, Edith Janet Sinclair; one *s* one *d. Educ:* Daniel Stewart's Coll., Edinburgh. Partner, A. T. Niven & Co., Chartered Accountants, Edinburgh, 1934-69, Touche Ross & Co., 1969-. Inst. of Chartered Accountants of Scotland: Mem., 1934; Mem. Council, 1968-73; Vice Pres., 1974-76; Pres., 1976-77. *Address:* (office) 15 Melville Street, Edinburgh EH3 7PQ. *T:* 031-225 6834; (home) 7 Midmar Gardens, Edinburgh EH10 6DY. *T:* 031-447 1942. *Clubs:* New, Caledonian (Edinburgh).

RICHARDS, Audrey Isabel, CBE 1955; FBA 1967; Hon. Fellow, Newnham College, Cambridge (Fellow, 1956); Smuts Reader in Anthropology, Cambridge University, 1961-67; *b* 1899. *Educ:* Downe House Sch.; Newnham Coll., Cambridge (MA); PhD (Lond.). Field work: in Northern Rhodesia, 1930-31, 1933-34, 1957; in Northern Transvaal, 1939-40; in Uganda, 1950-55. Lecturer in Social Anthropology, London School of Economics, 1931-33; 1935-37; Reader in Social Anthropology, London Univ. 1946-50; Director, East African Institute of Social Research, Makerere College, Kampala, Uganda, 1950-56; Dir, Centre for African Studies, Cambridge University, 1956-67. Member: Colonial Res. Cttee, 1944-47; Colonial Social Science Res. Council, 1944-50 and 1956-62; Committee for scientific research in Africa South of Sahara, 1954-55. President: Royal Anthropological Institute, 1959-61; African Studies Assoc., 1964-65. Overseas Fellow, American Acad. of Arts and Sciences, 1974. *Publications:* Hunger and Work in a Savage Tribe, 1932; Land, Labour and Diet in N Rhodesia, 1939; (ed) Economic Development and Tribal Change, 1954 (2nd edn, 1975); Chisungu, a study of girls' initiation ceremonies in N Rhodesia, 1956; (ed) East African Chiefs, 1960; The Changing Structure of a Ganda Village, 1966; The Multi-Cultural States of East Africa, 1969; (with A. Keyser) Councils in Action, 1971; (ed) Subsistence to Commercial Farming in Buganda, 1973; (with Jean Robin) Some Elmdon Families, 1974; papers in Africa, African Studies and African Affairs. *Address:* Crawley Cottage, Elmdon, Saffron Walden, Essex. *Club:* Royal Commonwealth Society.

RICHARDS, Bertrand; see Richards, E. B. B.

RICHARDS, Sir Brooks; see Richards, Sir F. B.

RICHARDS, Charles Anthony Langdon, CMG 1958; *b* 18 April 1911; *s* of T. L. Richards, Bristol, Musician; *m* 1937, Mary Edith Warren-Codrington; two *s. Educ:* Clifton Coll.; Brasenose Coll., Oxford. Appointed Colonial CS, Uganda, 1934; Major, 7th King's African Rifles, 1939-41: duties in Mauritius, 1941-46; District Officer, Uganda, 1946-50; Commissioner for Social Development, Tanganyika, 1950-53; Commissioner for Community Development, Uganda, 1953-54; Resident, Buganda, Oct. 1954-60; Minister of Local Government, Uganda, 1960-61. *Recreation:* gardening. *Address:* The Wall House, Oak Drive, Highworth, Wilts SN6 7BP.

RICHARDS, Rev. Canon Daniel; Residentiary Canon of Llandaff Cathedral since 1949; Priest-in-charge of Merthyr Mawr and Ewenny, since 1968; *b* 13 February 1892; *s* of John and Elizabeth Richards; *m* 1919, Hilda Roberts; one *s* (and one *s* killed 1944). *Educ:* St David's College, Lampeter, Cards. LD 1915, Mathews Scholar, 1928-29, BA and BD 1929; Curate of St Mary's Church, Court Henry, Carms, 1915-18; Curate of St Mary's Church, Burry Port, Carms, 1918-24; Rector of Llangeitho, Cards, 1924-31; Vicar of: Llangynwyd with Maesteg, 1931-66; Grouped Parish of Troedyrhiw Garth, Maesteg, 1950-60; Precentor of Llandaff Cathedral, 1961-67; SPCK Hon. Group Secretary for Dioceses of St David's, Swansea and Brecon, Llandaff and Monmouth, 1966-. Fellow of Philosophical Society of England, 1942. *Publications:* Honest to Self (autobiog.), 1971; History of the Lampeter Society, 1972. *Address:* Llandre, 26 Brynteg Avenue, Bridgend, Mid Glamorgan. *T:* Bridgend 5117.

RICHARDS, Denis Edward; HM Diplomatic Service; Consul-General, Philadelphia, since 1974; *b* 25 May 1923; *m* 1947, Nancy Beryl Brown; two *d. Educ:* Wilson's Grammar Sch., London; St Peter's Coll., Oxford. Lieut RNVR, 1941-46; Colonial Service (HMOCS), 1948-60: District Admin. and Min. of Finance, Ghana (Gold Coast); HM Diplomatic Service, 1960-: CRO, 1960; Karachi, 1961-63; FO (News Dept), 1964-68; Brussels (NATO), 1969; Brussels (UK Negotiating Delegn), 1970-72; Counsellor, Kinshasa, 1972-74. *Recreations:* music, amateur dramatics. *Address:* British Consulate General, 12 South 12th Street, Philadelphia, Pa 19107, USA. *Clubs:* Philadelphia, Franklin Inn (Philadelphia).

RICHARDS, Denis George; author; *b* 10 Sept. 1910; *s* of late George Richards and Frances Amelia Gosland; *m* 1940, Barbara, *d* of J. H. Smethurst, Heaton, Bolton; four *d. Educ:* Owen's Sch.; Trinity Hall, Cambridge (Scholar). BA 1931 (1st Cl. in both Parts of Historical Tripos); MA 1935; Asst Master, Manchester Grammar School, 1931-39; Senior History and English Master, Bradfield Coll., 1939-41; Narrator in Air Ministry Historical Branch, writing confidential studies on various aspects of the air war, 1942-43; Sen. Narrator, 1943-47; Hon. Sqdn Ldr RAFVR, 1943-47; engaged in writing, under Air Min. auspices, an official History of the Royal Air Force in the Second World War, 1947-49; was established in Admin. Civil Service, Principal, Department of Permanent Under Secretary of State for Air, 1949-50; Principal, Morley College, 1950-65; Longman Fellow in Univ. of Sussex, 1965-68. Chm., Women's League of Health and Beauty; Chm. of Governors, Purcell Sch. for Young Musicians. *Publications:* An Illustrated History of Modern Europe, 1938; Modern Europe (1919-39 section for revised edn of work by Sydney Herbert), 1940; (with J. W. Hunt) An Illustrated History of Modern Britain, 1950; (with late Hilary St G. Saunders) Royal Air Force 1939-45-an officially commissioned history in 3 volumes, 1953-54 (awarded C. P. Robertson Memorial Trophy, 1954); (with J. Evan Cruikshank) The Modern Age, 1955; Britain under the Tudors and Stuarts, 1958; Offspring of the Vic: a History of Morley College, 1958; (with Anthony Quick) Britain 1714-1851, 1961; (with J. A. Bolton) Britain and the Ancient World, 1963; (with Anthony Quick) Britain, 1851-1945, 1967; (with Anthony Quick) Twentieth Century Britain, 1968; (with A. W. Ellis) Medieval Britain, 1973; Portal of Hungerford, 1977. *Recreations:* music, pictures, golf, travel in the more civilized parts of Europe, the lighter tasks in the garden. *Address:* 16 Broadlands Road, N6. *T:* 01-340 5259. *Clubs:* Arts, Garrick, PEN.
See also W. P. Shovelton.

RICHARDS, Edgar Lynton, (Tony Richards), CBE 1971 (MBE 1954); MC 1944, Bar 1945; TD 1953; Partner, Moy, Vandervell & Co., since 1973; Member, Monopolies and Mergers Commission (formerly Monopolies Commission); *b* 21 April 1912; *s* of late Thomas Edgar Richards, ARIBA, MICE, and Enid Marie (*née* Thomas); *m* 1937, Barbara Lebus; three *s* one *d.*

Educ: Harrow. Served War of 1939-45. *Address:* Bury House, Heydon, Cambs.

RICHARDS, (Edmund) Bertrand (Bamford); His Honour Judge Bertrand Richards; a Circuit Judge since 1972; *b* 14 Feb. 1913; *s* of Rev. Edmund Milo Richards, Llewesog Hall, Denbigh; *m* 1966, Jane, *widow* of Edward Stephen Porter. *Educ:* Lancing Coll.; Corpus Christi Coll., Oxford. Served War, RA, 1940-46. Called to Bar, Inner Temple, 1941. Dep. Chm., Denbighshire QS, 1964-71. Hon. Recorder of Ipswich, 1975. *Address:* Melton Hall, near Woodbridge, Suffolk. *T:* Woodbridge 4215. *Club:* Carlton.

RICHARDS, Hon. Sir Edward (Trenton), Kt 1970; CBE 1967; Premier of Bermuda, 1972-75 (Leader, 1971; Deputy Leader, 1968-71); MP 1948; *b* 4 Oct. 1908; 2nd *s* of late George A. Richards and Millicent Richards, British Guiana; *m* 1940, Madree Elizabeth Williams; one *s* two *d. Educ:* Collegiate Sch.; Queen's Coll., Guyana; Middle Temple. Secondary School-teacher, 1930-43; called to Bar, 1946. Elected to House of Assembly, Bermuda, 1948; served numerous Select Cttees of Parliament; served on Commns; Member, Exec. Council (now Cabinet), 1963-; Mem. of Govt responsible for Immigration, Labour and Soc. Security, 1968-71. Served on many Govt Boards; Chairman: Public Transportation Board; Transport Control Board. Bermuda Representative: CPA Confs, Lagos, 1962, Kuala Lumpur, 1971; Guyana's Independence Celebrations, 1966, Bahamas Independence Celebrations, 1973; Mem., Constitution Conf., 1966; Leader Bermuda Delegn, ILO Confs Geneva, 1969-71. Magistrate, 1958. Chm., Berkeley Educational Soc., 1956-72. Hon. Life Vice-Pres., Bermuda Football Assoc. Hon. LLD, Wilberforce, USA, 1960. *Recreations:* music, reading, walking. *Address:* Wilton, Keith Hall Road, Warwick East, Bermuda. *T:* 2-3645. *Clubs:* Somerset Cricket, Warwick Workman's, Blue Waters Anglers (Bermuda); Royal Hamilton Amateur Dinghy.

RICHARDS, Prof. Elfyn John, OBE 1958; FRAeS; FIMechE; Research Professor, Southampton University, and Acoustical Consultant, since 1975; *b* Barry, Glamorgan, South Wales, 28 Dec. 1914; *s* of Edward James Richards, Barry, schoolmaster, and of Catherine Richards; *m* 1941, Eluned Gwenddydd Jones, Aberporth, Cardigan; three *d. Educ:* Barry County School; Univ. Coll. of Wales, Aberystwyth (BSc); St John's Coll., Cambridge (MA). DSc (Wales), 1959. Research Asst, Bristol Aeroplane Company, 1938-39; Scientific Officer, National Physical Laboratory, Teddington, 1939-45, and Secretary, various Aeronautical Research Council sub-cttees; Chief Aerodynamicist and Asst Chief-Designer, Vickers Armstrong, Ltd, Weybridge, 1945-50; Prof. of Aeronautical Engineering, 1950-64, and Dir, Inst. of Sound and Vibration Research, 1963-67, Univ. of Southampton, also Aeronautical Engineering Consultant; Vice-Chancellor, Loughborough Univ., 1967-75. Member: SRC, 1970-74; Noise Adv. Council; Noise Research Council, ARC, 1968-71; Construction Research and Adv. Council, 1968-71; Inland Transport and Develt Council, 1968-71; Gen. Adv. Council of BBC (Chm. Midlands Adv. Council, 1968-71); Cttee of Scientific Advisory Council; Wilson Cttee on Problems of Noise; Planning and Transport Res. Adv. Council, 1971-. Chm., Univs Council for Adult Educn; President: British Acoustical Soc., 1968-70; Soc. of Environmental Engrs, 1971-73. Mem. Leics CC. Hon. LLD Wales, 1973; Hon. DSc Southampton, 1973; Hon DTech Loughborough, 1975. Taylor Gold Medal, RAeS, 1949; James Watt Medal, ICE, 1963; Silver Medal, RSA, 1971. *Publications:* many reports and memoranda of Aeronautical Research Council; articles and lectures in Roy. Aeronautical Soc. *Recreations:* swimming, walking. *Address:* 10 Glen Eyre Road, Southampton.

RICHARDS, Sir (Francis) Brooks, KCMG 1976 (CMG 1963); DSC and Bar, 1943; HM Diplomatic Service; HM Ambassador to Greece, since 1974; *b* 18 July 1918; *s* of Francis Bartlett Richards; *m* 1941, Hazel Myfanwy, *d* of Lt-Col Stanley Price Williams, CIE; one *s* one *d. Educ:* Stowe School; Magdalene College, Cambridge. Served with RN, 1939-44 (Lieut-Comdr RNVR). HM Embassy: Paris, 1944-48; Athens, 1952-54; First Sec. and Head of Chancery, Political Residency, Persian Gulf, 1954-57; Assistant Private Secretary to Foreign Secretary, 1958-59; Counsellor (Information), HM Embassy, Paris, 1959-64; Head of Information Policy Dept, 1964-65, and of Jt Inf. Policy and Guidance Dept, FO/CRO, 1965-66; seconded to Cabinet Office, 1966-68; HM Minister, Bonn, 1969-71; HM Ambassador, Saigon, 1972-74. Chevalier, Légion d'Honneur and Croix de Guerre (France), 1944. *Recreations:* sailing, gardening. *Address:* c/o Foreign and Commonwealth Office, SW1; The Ranger's House, Farnham, Surrey. *T:* Farnham (Sy) 6764. *Clubs:* Travellers', Royal Ocean Racing.

RICHARDS, Frank Roydon, MA, BMus Oxon; Hon. LLD Glasgow; retired as Rector of Glasgow Academy (1932-59); *b* 16 Jan. 1899; *s* of Frank Herbert Richards and Edith Alice Phillips; *m* 1927, Nancy Warry; one *s* two *d* (and one *s* decd). *Educ:* Christ's Hosp.; Queen's Coll., Oxford (Scholar). 1st Class Classical Mods 1920, 2nd Class Literae Humaniores, 1922; Asst Master Glasgow Acad., 1922-24; Grecians Tutor, Christ's Hosp., 1924-28; Headmaster, Bridlington School, 1928-32; 2nd Lt RGA (SR) BEF France, 1918; OTC Lieut 1919; Capt. 1925. *Recreation:* music. *Address:* 21 Learmonth Court, Edinburgh EH4 1PB. *T:* 031-332 2068.

RICHARDS, Maj.-Gen. George Warren, CB 1945; CBE 1944; DSO 1942, Bar, 1943; MC 1918; DL; *b* 4 July 1898; *s* of late John Richards, Llewynderw Hall, Welshpool; *m* 1930, Gwen Laird; two *d*. *Educ:* Oswestry; Sandhurst; commissioned into RW Fus., 1916; attached to MGC, 1917; Tank Corps, 1920. Retired from Army, 1949. DL Monmouthshire, 1965. *Address:* Trewarren, Llandewi Rhydderch, near Abergavenny, Gwent.

RICHARDS, Sir Gordon, Kt 1953; Racing Manager, since 1970 (Jockey, retired 1954, then Trainer, 1955-70); *b* 5 May 1904; *s* of Nathan Richards; *m*; two *s*. Started life as a clerk; went as a stable apprentice to Mr Martin G. Hartigan, 1919; has headed the list of winning jockeys, 1925, 1927-29, 1931-33, 1938-40, 1942; 259 winners in 1933, breaking Fred Archer's record; passed Archer's record total of 2,749 winners, 26 April 1943; passed own record with 269 winners, 1947; rode 4000th winner 4 May 1950; broke world record with 4,500 winners 17 July 1952; final total, 4,970. Won the 1953 Derby on Pinza. Hon. Member, Jockey Club, 1970. *Publication:* My Story, 1955. *Recreations:* shooting, watching football. *Address:* Duff House, Kintbury, Berks.

RICHARDS, Very Rev. Gwynfryn; Dean of Bangor, 1962-71; Archdeacon of Bangor, 1957-62; Rector of Llandudno, 1956-62; *b* 10 Sept. 1902; *er s* of Joshua and Elizabeth Ann Richards, Nantyffyllon, Glam; *m* 1935, Margery Phyllis Evans; one *s* one *d*. *Educ:* Universities of Wales, Oxford and Boston. Scholar, Univ. Coll., Cardiff, 1918-21; BSc (Wales), 1921; Jesus Coll., Oxford, 1921-23; Certificate, School of Geography, Oxford, 1922; BA 1st Cl. Hons School of Natural Science, 1923; MA 1928. In industry (USA), 1923-25. Boston Univ. Sch. of Theology, 1926-28; STB First Cl., 1928; Scholar and Travelling Fellow, 1928-29; Oxford, 1928-29; St Michael's Coll., Llandaff, 1929-30; deacon, 1930; priest, 1931. Curate of: Llanrhos, 1930-34; Aberystwyth, St Michael, 1934-38; Rector of Llanllyfni, 1938-49; Vicar of Conway with Gyffin, 1949-56. Canon of Bangor Cathedral, 1943-62, Treas., 1943-57; Examining Chaplain to Bp of Bangor, 1944-71; Rural Dean of Arllechwedd, 1953-57. Pantyfedwen Lectr, Univ. Coll., Aberystwyth, 1967. *Publications:* Ffurfiau Ordeinio Holl Eglwysi Cymru, 1943; Yr Hen Fam, 1952; Ein Hymraniadau Annedwydd, 1963; Gwir a Diogel Obaith, 1972; Ar Lawer Trywydd, 1973; contrib. to Journal of the Historical Society of the Church in Wales, Nat. Library of Wales Jl, Trans of Caenarvonshire Hist. Soc. *Recreations:* gardening, photography, local history. *Address:* Llain Werdd, Llandegfan, Menai Bridge, Gwynedd LL59 5LY. *T:* Menai Bridge 713429.

RICHARDS, Brigadier Hugh Upton, CBE 1943; DSO 1944; *b* 1894; *s* of J. Richards; *m* Florence Matilda (*d* 1964), *d* of J. McLeod; one *s*; *m* 1966, Mrs Irene Mary Olver, *widow* of Cecil Paul Olver. Served European War, 1914-19, with Worcestershire Regiment; Lieutenant, 1917; Captain, 1931; Bt Major, 1934; Major, 1936; transfd West Yorkshire Regt, 1936; Lt-Col 1939; Col 1942; Brig. 1940; commanded 4 Bn Nigeria Regt 1933-34, Sierra Leone Bn 1939, and 3 (West African) Inf. Bde, 1940-44. Campaign Palestine, 1936 and 1938 and Burma. *Address:* 50 Britannia Square, Worcester. *Club:* Army and Navy.

RICHARDS, Ivor Armstrong, CH 1964; MA; LittD; University Professor (Emeritus, 1963), Harvard University, Cambridge, Massachusetts, USA (Professor 1944); Fellow of Magdalene College, Cambridge, 1926, Hon. Fellow, 1964; *b* 26 Feb. 1893; *s* of late W. Armstrong Richards, Sandbach, Cheshire; *m* 1926, Dorothy Eleanor, *e d* of John J. Pilley. *Educ:* Clifton; Magdalene College, Cambridge. Class I, Moral Sciences Tripos, Part I, 1915; MA, LittD Cambridge. College Lecturer in English and Moral Sciences, 1922; Visiting Professor Tsing Hua University, Peking, 1929-30; Visiting Lecturer, Harvard University, 1931; Director, The Orthological Institute (Basic English) of China, 1936-38. Hon. LittD Harvard, 1944; Hon. LLD Cambridge, 1977. Corresponding Fellow of the British Academy, 1959. Loines Poetry Award, 1962; Emerson-Thoreau Medal, Amer. Acad. of Arts and Sciences, 1970. *Publications:* Foundations of Aesthetics (with C. K. Ogden and James Wood), 1921; The

Meaning of Meaning (with C. K. Ogden), 1923; Principles of Literary Criticism, 1924; Science and Poetry, 1925; Practical Criticism, 1929; Mencius on the Mind, 193 ; Coleridge On Imagination, 1934; Interpretation in Teaching, 1938; How to Read a Page, 1942; The Republic of Plato (a simplified version), 1942; Basic English and its Uses, 1943; Speculative Instruments, 1955; Goodbye Earth and other Poems, 1958; The Screens and other Poems, 1960; Tomorrow Morning, Faustus!, 1962; Why So, Socrates?, 1963; So Much Nearer: Essays Toward a World English, 1968; Design for Escape: World Education through Modern Media, 1968; Poetries & Sciences, 1970; Internal Colloquies, 1972; Beyond, 1974; Poetries: their media and ends, 1974; Complementarities, Uncollected Papers (ed J. P. Russo), 1975. *Recreations:* mountaineering, travel. *Address:* Magdalene College, Cambridge. *Club:* Alpine.

RICHARDS, James Alan; Agent-General for Western Australia in London, since 1975; *b* 8 Oct. 1913; *s* of James Percival Richards and Alice Pearl Richards (*née* Bullock), Adelaide; *m* 1939, Mabel Joyce, *d* of R. H. Cooper, Riverton, S Austr.; three *s* one *d*. *Educ:* Unley High Sch.; Coll. of Business Admin, Univ. of Hawaii. Served War of 1939-45, 2nd AIF. Ampol Petroleum Ltd, 1946-75: Sales Man., South Australia, 1952-53; State Man., Western Australia, 1954-75. *Recreation:* bowls. *Address:* Western Australia House, 115 Strand, WC2R 0AJ. *T:* 01-240 2881. *Clubs:* West Australian (Perth); Western Australian Cricket Association.

RICHARDS, Sir James (Maude), Kt 1972; CBE 1959; architectural writer, critic and historian; Editor, Architectural Review, 1937-71; Editor, Architects' Journal, 1947-49 (editorial board, 1949-61); Architectural Correspondent, The Times, 1947-71; *b* 13 Aug. 1907; 2nd *s* of late Louis Saurin Richards and Lucy Denes (*née* Clarence); *m* 1st, 1936 Margaret (marr. diss., 1948), *d* of late David Angus; (one *s* decd) one *d*; 2nd, 1954, Kathleen Margaret (Kit), *widow* of late Morland Lewis and 2nd *d* of late Henry Bryan Godfrey-Faussett-Osborne, Queendown Warren, Sittingbourne, Kent; one *s* decd. *Educ:* Gresham's School, Holt; AA School of Architecture. ARIBA, AADipl 1930. Studied and practised architecture in Canada and USA, 1930-31; London and Dublin, 1931-32; Asst Editor, The Architects' Jl, 1933; The Architectural Review, 1935; Editor, Publications Div., 1942, Director of Publications, Middle East, Cairo, 1943-46, MOI; Gen. Editor, The Architectural Press, 1946. Hoffman Wood Prof. of Architecture, Leeds Univ., 1957-59. Editor, European Heritage, 1973-75. Member: exec. cttee Modern Architectural Research Gp, 1946-54; AA Council, 1948-51, 1958-61, 1973-74; Advisory Council, Inst. of Contemporary Arts, 1947-68; Architecture Council, Festival of Britain, 1949-51; British Cttee, Internat. Union of Architects, 1950-66; Royal Fine Art Commn, 1951-66; Fine Art Cttee, Brit. Council, 1954-; Council of Industrial Design, 1955-61; Min. of Transport (Worboys) Cttee on traffic signs, 1962-63; Chm., Arts Council inquiry into provision for the arts in Ireland, 1974-76. World Soc. of Ekistics, 1965-; Council, Victorian Soc., 1965-; Vice-Pres. Nat. Council on Inland Transport, 1963-. Broadcaster, television and sound (regular member, BBC Critics panel, 1948-68). FRSA 1970; Hon. AILA, 1955. Chevalier (First Class), Order of White Rose of Finland, 1960; Gold Medal, Mexican Institute of Architects, 1963; Bicentenary Medal, RSA, 1971. *Publications:* Miniature History of the English House, 1938; (with late Eric Ravilious) High Street, 1938; Introduction to Modern Architecture, 1940, new edn 1970 (trans. seven langs); (with John Summerson) The Bombed Buildings of Britain, 1942; Edward Bawden, 1946; The Castles on the Ground, 1946, new enl. edn 1973; The Functional Tradition in Early Industrial Buildings, 1958; (ed) New Building in the Commonwealth, 1961; An Architectural Journey in Japan, 1963; Guide to Finnish Architecture, 1966 A Critic's View, 1970; (ed, with Nikolaus Pevsner) The Anti-Rationalists, 1972; Planning and Redevelopment in London's Entertainment Area, 1973 (Arts Council report); Architecture, 1974; (ed) Who's Who in Architecture: from 1400 to the present day, 1977. *Recreations:* travel and topography. *Address:* 29 Fawcett Street, SW10. *T:* 01-352 9874. *Club:* Athenæum.

RICHARDS, John Arthur; Under-Secretary, Department of Education and Science, since 1973; *b* 23 June 1918; *s* of late Alderman A. J. Richards and Mrs Annie Richards, Dulwich; *m* 1946, Sheelagh, *d* of late Patrick McWalter and Katherine McWalter, Balla, Co. Mayo; two *s* one *d*. *Educ:* Brockley Sch.; King's Coll., London. BA, AKC, Dip. in Educn. Hon. Sec., King's Coll. Union Soc., 1939. Served War: Captain RA; Directorate of Personnel Selection, War Office, 1945-46. Temp. Third Sec., Foreign Office, 1946; Staff, Hackney Downs Grammar Sch., 1948; Ministry of Education Asst Principal and Principal, 1949 (Jt Sec., Secondary Schs Examinations Council, 1956-57); Asst Sec. (also Dept of Educn and Science), 1963-73.

Mem., Catholic Union of GB. *Publications:* occasional verse and contribs to journals. *Recreations:* walking, writing verse. *Address:* 121 Norfolk Avenue, Sanderstead, Surrey CR2 8BY. *T:* 01-657 1275.

RICHARDS, Lt-Gen. John Charles Chisholm; Commandant General, Royal Marines, since 1977; *b* 21 Feb. 1927; *s* of Charles C. Richards and Alice Milner; *m* 1953, Audrey Hidson; two *s* one *d*. *Educ:* Worksop Coll., Notts. MBIM. Joined Royal Marines, 1945; commnd 1946; 45 Commando, Malaya, 1950-52; HMS Birmingham, 1955-56; Canadian Army Staff Coll. (student), 1959-61; 43 Commando, 1962-63; DAQMG, DCGRM and naval staff, 1963-64; DS, Staff Coll., Camberley, 1965-67; 45 Commando: Aden, 1967; CO, 1968-69; GSO1 Plymouth Gp, 1969; CO 42 Commando, 1970-72; Chief of Staff, Brit. Def. Staff, Washington DC, UN Deleg., and Mem. Mil. Staff Cttee, 1972-74; Comdr 3 Commando Bde, 1975-76. *Recreations:* golf, gardening. *Address:* 20 Merrick Square, SE1 4JB. *T:* 01-407 1966.

RICHARDS, John Deacon, ARSA 1974; RIBA, FRIAS; architect; Partner in Robert Matthew, Johnson-Marshall and Partners, since 1964; *b* 7 May 1931; *s* of William John Richards and late Ethel Richards; *m* 1958, Margaret Brown; one *s* three *d*. *Educ:* Geelong Grammar Sch., Vic; Cranleigh Sch.; Architect. Assoc. Sch. of Arch., London (Dipl. 1954). RIBA 1955; FRIAS 1968. NCB, 1954; RE, 1955-57; joined Robert Matthew and Johnson Marshall, 1957. Buildings include: Stirling Univ., 1965-; Royal Commonwealth Pool, Edinburgh, 1970; airport terminals, Edinburgh and Aberdeen, 1977. Mem., Royal Fine Art Commn for Scotland, 1975-. Hon. DUniv Stirling, 1976. Gold Medallist, RSA, 1972. *Recreation:* sailing. *Address:* 57 Northumberland Street, Edinburgh EH3 6JQ. *T:* 031-556 3210. *Club:* Royal Forth Yacht (Edinburgh).

RICHARDS, Rt. Rev. John Richards, DD (Lambeth); President, St David's University College, Lampeter, 1971-77; *b* 3 March 1901; *s* of Thomas and Elizabeth Richards, Llanbadarn, Fawr, Aberystwyth; *m* 1929, Katherine Mary, *d* of W. E. and M. Hodgkinson, Inglewood, St Michael's, Tenterden; one *s* one *d*. *Educ:* Ardwyn School, Aberystwyth; Univ. College of Wales; St Michael's College Llandaff. BA 1922 (2nd Cl. Hons Mod. Langs); MA 1955; DD 1956. Deacon, 1924; priest, 1925; Curate of Pembrey w Burry Post, 1924-27; CMS missionary in Iran, 1927-45, at Shiraz, 1927-36, at Yezd, 1938-42, at Isfahan, 1942-45; Archdeacon in Iran, 1937-45. Mem. of Near East Christian Council, 1932-38; Hon. CF, Paiforce, 1942-45; Vicar of Skewen, 1945-52, Vicar of St Catherine, Pontypridd, 1952-54; Canon of St Andrew in Llandaff Cathedral, 1949-54; Dean of Bangor, 1955-56; Vicar of St James', Bangor, and Canon of Bangor Cathedral, 1954-55; Bishop of St David's, 1956-March 1971. Pantyfedwen Lectr, UC Swansea, 1972. Mem. of Governing Body of the Church in Wales, 1948-71. Chaplain and Sub-Prelate, Order of St John, 1961. Hon. LLD Wales, 1971. *Publications:* The Religion of the Baha'is, 1932; The Open Road in Persia, 1932; Baha'ism, 1965; Under His Banner, 1973; Jesus: Son of God and Son of Man, 1974. *Address:* Lluest Wen, Llanbadarn Road, Aberystwyth SY23 1EY.

RICHARDS, Michael; Chairman of Wood Hall Trust Ltd since 1950; Director, Samuel Montagu & Co. Ltd, since 1959; *b* 4 Oct. 1915; *s* of Frank Richards and Jenny Charlotte (*née* Levinsen); *m* 1942, Lucy Helen Quirey; three *d*. *Educ:* Roundhay High Sch., Leeds; Leeds Univ. (LLB). Solicitor, 1936. Partner, Ashurst, Morris Crisp & Co., Solicitors, City of London, 1936-54; Chm. and Man. Dir, Hart, Son & Co. Ltd, Merchant Bankers, 1954-60. *Recreations:* work, farming, collecting works of art. *Address:* Wood Hall, Shenley, Radlett, Herts. *T:* Radlett 6624; 1 St James's Street, SW1. *T:* 01-930 7703. *Club:* American National (Sydney).

RICHARDS, Sir Norman (Grantham Lewis), Kt 1977; OBE 1945; QC 1955; **His Honour Judge Norman Richards;** a Circuit Judge (formerly an Official Referee of the Supreme Court), since 1963; *b* 29 Dec. 1905; *s* of L. M. Richards and Gertrude E. Richards; *m* 1930, Helen Nina Colls; one *d*. *Educ:* Charterhouse; Trinity College, Cambridge. Called to Bar, Inner Temple, 1928, Master of the Bench, 1961. Wales and Chester Circuit. Served War of 1939-45 (despatches twice, OBE). Recorder of Merthyr Tydfil, 1960-63; Dep. Chm., Mddx QS, 1962-65. Pres., HM Council of Circuit Judges, 1973. *Recreations:* golf, cricket. *Address:* 35 Ormonde Gate, Chelsea, SW3. *T:* 01-352 7874. *Clubs:* Brooks's, Portland, MCC.

RICHARDS, Prof. Owain Westmacott, FRS 1959; MA, DSc (Oxford); Professor of Zoology and Applied Entomology, Imperial College, London, 1953-67, now Emeritus; Fellow of Imperial College, 1969; *b* 31 Dec. 1901; 2nd *s* of H. M. Richards,

MD; *m* 1st, 1931, Maud Jessie (*d* 1970), *d* of Eng. Capt. C. M. Norris, RN; two *d*; 2nd, 1972, Joyce Elinor Benson (*née* McLuckie). *Educ:* Hereford Cathedral School; Brasenose College, Oxford. Exhibitioner, 1920, and Senior Hulme Schol., Brasenose Coll.; Christopher Welch Schol., Oxford Univ., 1924. Research Asst, Dept of Entomology, Imperial College, 1927; Lecturer, 1930; Reader, 1937. Hon. Mem. Société Entomologique d'Egypte; Hon. Fellow, Royal Entomological Soc. of London; Hon. Member: Nederlandsche Entomologische Vereeniging; British Ecological Soc.; Accademia Nazionale Italiana di Entomologia. *Publications:* The Variations of Animals in Nature (with G. C. Robson), 1936; The Social Insects, 1953; Imms' General Textbook of Entomology, 9th edn (with R. G. Davies), 1957. *Recreation:* entomology. *Address:* 89 St Stephen's Road, Ealing, W13 8JA.

RICHARDS, Raymond, MA, FSA, FRHistS; Past Chairman, Ancient Monuments Society; Trustee: Historic Churches Preservation Trust; Historic Cheshire Churches Preservation Trust; Friends of Ancient English Churches; *b* Macclesfield, 19 July 1906; *er s* of late Thomas Edward Richards and Lucy Mary, *d* of late William Kersall Gatley, Gatley, Cheshire; *m* 1940, Monica, *y d* of late John Relf, Liverpool and Brightling, Sussex; two *s*. Chairman: Cheshire Cttee, Nat. Register of Archives (Historical Manuscripts Commission); Southport Repertory Company, in Association with Arts Council of Gt Britain, 1948-51; Past President, Macclesfield and District Field Club. Member: Chester Diocesan Faculties Advisory Committee; Central Council for Care of Churches, 1948-58; Parochial Church Libraries Sub-Cttee, 1950-51; House of Laity, Church Assembly; Patron, Living and Manor of Gawsworth, Cheshire. Mem., Court of Keele University. Hon. MA Liverpool, 1948. *Publications:* Old Cheshire Churches, 1947, rev. edn 1973; St Winifred's Chapel, Holywell, 1948; High Legh Chapels, 1950; The Lesser Chapels of Cheshire, Part 1, 1951; Part 2, 1953; The Manor of Gawsworth, 1955, rev. edn 1974. *Recreation:* yachting. *Address:* Gawsworth Hall, Gawsworth, Cheshire. *T:* North Rode 456. *Clubs:* Athenæum; Athenæum (Liverpool); Royal Mersey Yacht; Dublin University (Dublin).

RICHARDS, Sir Rex (Edward), Kt 1977; DSc Oxon 1970; FRS 1959; FRIC; Warden of Merton College, Oxford, since 1969; Vice-Chancellor, Oxford University, since 1977; *b* 28 Oct. 1922; *s* of H. W. and E. N. Richards; *m* 1948, Eva Edith Vago; two *d*. *Educ:* Colyton Grammar School, Devon; St John's College, Oxford. Senior Demy, Magdalen College, Oxford, 1946; MA; DPhil; Fellow, Lincoln College, Oxford, 1947-64, Hon. Fellow, 1968; Research Fellow, Harvard University, 1955; Dr Lee's Prof. of Chemistry, Oxford, 1964-70; Fellow Exeter College, 1964-69; Hon. Fellow, St John's Coll., Oxford, 1968; Associate Fellow, Morse Coll., Yale, 1974-79. Member: Chemical Society Council, 1957; Faraday Society Council, 1963; Royal Soc. Council, 1973-75. Tilden Lectr, 1962. Corday-Morgan Medal of Chemical Soc., 1954; Davy Medal, Royal Soc., 1976; Award in Theoretical Chemistry and Spectroscopy, Chem. Soc., 1977. FRIC 1970. Hon. DSc: East Anglia, 1971; Exeter, 1975; Hon. LLD Dundee, 1977. *Publications:* various contributions to scientific journals. *Recreation:* contemporary art. *Address:* Warden's Lodgings, Merton College, Oxford. *T:* Oxford 49651.

RICHARDS, Rt. Rev. Ronald Edwin, MA, ThD (*jure dig*); *b* Ballarat, Vic., 25 Oct. 1908; *s* of Edward and Margaret Elizabeth Richards, Ballarat; *m* 1937, Nancy, *d* of W. E. Lloyd Green; one *d*. *Educ:* Ballarat High Sch.; Trinity Coll., Melbourne Univ. BA 2nd Cl Hons Phil., 1932, MA 1937; Asst Master, Ballarat C of E Gram. Sch., 1926, Malvern C of E Gram. Sch., 1927-28; deacon, 1932; priest, 1933; Curate of Rokewood, 1932-33, Priest-in-charge, 1934; Priest-in-charge, Lismore, 1934-41 and 1945-46; Chaplain AIF, 1941-45; Vicar of Warrnambool, 1946-50; Archdeacon of Ballarat, and Examining Chapl. to Bp of Ballarat, 1950-57; Vicar-Gen., 1952-57; Bishop of Bendigo, 1957-74. *Address:* Madron, 119 Dare Street, Ocean Grove, Victoria 3226, Australia. *Club:* Naval and Military (Melbourne).

RICHARDS, Tony; *see* Richards, E. L.

RICHARDS, William James, CBE 1971; QPM 1964; Chief Constable of Greater Manchester, since 1974 (Manchester and Salford, 1968-74); *b* 1915; *m* 1940, Beryl Ferrier, *d* of Henry Cornforth. *Educ:* Lawrence Coll., Birmingham. Dir of Studies, Dept of Law, Police Coll., Ryton-on-Dunsmore, 1958-59; Dep. Chief Constable, Manchester, 1959-66; Chief Constable, Manchester, 1966-68. OStJ. Hon. MA 1977. *Address:* Freshways, 24 Cecil Avenue, Sale, Cheshire.

RICHARDSON, Alexander Stewart, CBE 1943; BSc; *b* 17 May 1897; *e s* of late Alexander Stewart Richardson and Susan Hamilton Horsburgh; *m* 1931, Kathleen Margaret, *o d* of late

Angus McColl, Inverness; one s one d. *Educ:* Edinburgh University. Military Service, 1916-19; Agricultural Officer, Tanganyika Territory, 1924; Senior Agricultural Officer, 1930; Deputy Director of Agriculture, Uganda, 1937; Director of Agriculture, Nyasaland, 1940-44; MLC 1940; Chairman Supply Board and Controller of Essential Supplies and Prices, 1941 and 1942; Controller of Production and Food, 1943. Member of Executive and Legislative Councils; Officer in general charge of Supplies, Prices and Distribution of Commodities; Uganda Govt Rep. on East African Production and Supply Council; Leader of East African Cotton deleg. to New Delhi, India, 1946; retired, 1947; Director of Agriculture, Uganda, 1944-47. *Recreations:* golf, shooting, fishing. *Address:* 24 Drummond Road, Inverness IV2 4NF. *T:* 33497.

RICHARDSON, Councillor Arthur; *b* 31 Jan. 1897; *s* of Thomas and Annie Eliza Richardson; unmarried. *Educ:* St Mary's Church of England School, Hull. With Messrs Rank Ltd, Flourmillers, Hull, 1912-29; business on own account as Licensee of Public House. Member: Hull Board of Guardians, 1922-30; elected Hull City Council, 1929; Alderman 1946, retired 1949; elected Councillor again, 1949-70, 1971-76, retired; Lord Mayor of Kingston-upon-Hull, and Admiral of the Humber, 1953-54. Coronation Medal, 1953. *Recreations:* swimming, politics. *Address:* 79 Auckland House, Porter Street, Kingston upon Hull HU1 2SR.

RICHARDSON, Gen. Sir Charles (Leslie), GCB 1967 (KCB 1962; CB 1957); CBE 1945; DSO 1943; Chief Royal Engineer, since 1972; *s* of late Lieutenant-Colonel C. W. Richardson, RA, and Mrs Richardson; *m* 1947, Audrey Styles (*née* Jorgensen); one *s* two *d. Educ:* Wellington College; Royal Military Acad., Woolwich (King's Medal); Cambridge Univ. (BA). Commissioned Royal Engineers, 1928; Exhibitioner, Clare College, Cambridge, 1930, 1st Cl. Hons Mech Sciences Tripos. Served France and Belgium, 1939-40; GSO1 Plans HQ, Eighth Army, 1942; BGS Eighth Army, 1943; Deputy Chief of Staff Fifth US Army, 1943; BGS Plans, 21st Army Group, 1944; Brigade Commander, 1953-54; Commandant, Royal Military College of Science, 1955-58; General Officer Commanding Singapore District, 1958-60; Director of Combat Development, War Office, 1960-61; Director-General of Military Training, 1961-63; General Officer Commanding-in-Chief, Northern Command, 1963-65. Quartermaster General to the Forces, 1965-66; Master-General of the Ordnance, 1966-71; ADC (General) to the Queen, 1967-70. Legion of Merit (US), 1944. Col Comdt, RAOC, 1967-71. *Address:* The Stables, Betchworth, Surrey RH3 7AA. *Club:* Army and Navy.

RICHARDSON, Brigadier (Retd) Charles Walter Philipps, DSO and Bar 1945; *b* 8 Jan. 1905; *s* of W. J. Richardson and E. C. Philipps; *m* 1st, 1932, Joan Kathleen Constance Lang (from whom he obtained a divorce, 1946); one *s*; 2nd, 1946, Hon. Mrs Averil Diana Going; one *s. Educ:* RNC Osborne and Dartmouth; RMC Sandhurst. 2nd Lieut KOSB, 1924; served in Egypt, China and India; Bde Maj. 52nd (Lowland) Div., 1942; Comdr 6th Bn KOSB 15th (Scottish) Div., 1944-46; Colonel 1946; Comdt, Tactical Wing, School of Infantry, Warminster, 1947-48; GSO(1) Singapore District, 1948-49; Deputy Comdt Malay Regt, 1949; Dir Amphibious Warfare Trg, 1951; Comdr 158 Inf. Bde (TA), 1952; Brig. 1952; Dep. Comdr Lowland District, 1955-57. Retired 1957. Order of Leopold and Belgian Croix de Guerre, 1945. *Recreations:* shooting, fishing. *Address:* Quintans, Steventon, Hants. *T:* Dummer 473. *Club:* Army and Navy.

RICHARDSON, David; Secretary, Advisory, Conciliation and Arbitration Service, since 1977; *b* 24 April 1928; *s* of Harold George Richardson and Madeleine Raphaële Richardson (*née* Lebret); *m* 1951, Frances Joan Pring; three *s* one *d. Educ:* Wimbledon Coll.; King's Coll., London (BA Hons). Served in RAF, 1949. With Unilever, 1951. Inland Revenue, 1953; Min. of Labour: Asst Principal, 1956; Principal, 1960; Sec., Construction Industry Training Bd, 1964; Asst Sec., Min. of Labour, 1967; Chm., Central Youth Employment Exec., 1969; attended Royal Coll. of Defence Studies, 1971; Under Sec., Incomes Div., Dept of Employment, 1972; Dir, Safety and Gen. Gp, Health and Safety Exec., 1975-77. *Recreations:* music, walking, landscape gardening. *Address:* 183 Banstead Road, Carshalton, Surrey. *T:* 01-642 1052. *Club:* Army and Navy.

RICHARDSON, Sir Egerton (Rudolf), OJ 1975; Kt 1968; CMG 1959; Government Adviser on International Affairs, Jamaica, 1971-74; retired; *b* 15 Aug. 1912; *s* of James Neil Richardson and Doris Adel (*née* Burton); *m* (wid of 1966); one *s* one *d. Educ:* Calabar High School, Kingston, Jamaica; Oxford University. Entered Civil Service, 1933; Secretary Land Policy Co-ordinating Committee, 1943-53; Permanent Sec., Min. of Agric.

and Lands, 1953-54; Under-Sec. Finance, 1954-56; on secondment, CO, London, 1953-54; Financial Secretary, Jamaica, 1956-62; Ambassador: and Permanent Representative at UN, 1962-67; to USA, 1967-72; to Mexico, 1967-75; Permanent Sec., Min. of the Public Service, 1973-75; Mem., Nat. Bauxite Commn, 1972-75. *Recreations:* swimming, golf, astronomy. *Address:* PO Box 244, Kingston 6, Jamaica.

RICHARDSON, Elliot Lee; Ambassador-at-large and Special Representative of the US President to the Law of the Sea Conference, since 1977; *b* 20 July 1920; *s* of Dr Edward P. and Clara Lee Richardson; *m* 1952, Anne F. Hazard; two *s* one *d. Educ:* Harvard Coll.; Harvard Law Sch. BA 1941, LLB 1947, *cum laude.* Served with US Army, 1942-45 (Lieut): litter-bearer platoon ldr, 4th Inf. Div., Normandy Landing (Bronze Star, Purple Heart). Law clerk, 1947-49; Assoc., Ropes, Gray, Best, Coolidge and Rugg, lawyers, Boston, 1949-53 and 1955-56; Asst to Senator Saltonstall, Washington, 1953 and 1954; Asst Sec. for Legislation of Dept of Health, Educn and Welfare, 1957-59 (Actg Sec., April-July 1958); US Attorney for Massachusetts, 1959-61; Special Asst to Attorney General of US, 1961; Partner, Ropes & Gray, 1961-62 and 1963-64; Lieut Governor of Mass, 1964; Attorney General of Mass, 1966; Under Sec. of State, 1969-70; Sec. of Health, Educn and Welfare, 1970-73; Sec. of Defense, Jan.-May 1973; Attorney General of US, May-Oct. 1973, resigned; Ambassador to UK, 1975-76; Sec. of Commerce, 1976-77. Fellow, Woodrow Wilson Internat. Center for Scholars, 1973-74. Holds numerous hon. degrees. *Publications:* The Creative Balance, 1976; numerous articles on law, social services and govt policy. *Address:* 1100 Crest Lane, Mclean, Va 22101, USA.

RICHARDSON, Sir Eric; *see* Richardson, Sir J. E.

RICHARDSON, Sir Frank; *see* Richardson, Sir (H.) Frank.

RICHARDSON, Maj.-Gen. Frank McLean, CB 1960; DSO 1941; OBE 1945; MD; Director Medical Services, BAOR, 1956-61; *b* 3 March 1904; *s* of late Col Hugh Richardson, DSO, and of Elizabeth Richardson; *m* 1944, Sylvia Innes, *d* of Col S. A. Innes, DSO; two *s* one *d. Educ:* Glenalmond; Edinburgh Univ. MB, ChB 1926. MD 1938. Joined RAMC, 1927; Captain 1930; Major 1936; Lt-Col 1945; Col 1949; Brig. 1956; Maj.-Gen. 1957. Honorary Surgeon to the Queen, 1957-61. Hon. Col 51 (H) Div. Dist RAMC, TA, 1963-67. *Publications:* Napoleon: Bisexual Emperor, 1972; Napoleon's Death: An Inquest, 1974. *Address:* c/o Williams & Glyn's Bank Ltd, Kirkland House, SW1; 10 Barnton Avenue West, Edinburgh EH4 6DE.

RICHARDSON, Prof. Frederick Denys, FRS 1968; BSc, PhD, DSc; FIM; FIMM; FIChemE; Professor Emeritus and Senior Research Fellow, Department of Metallurgy, Imperial College of Science and Technology, London University, since 1976; *b* 17 Sept. 1913; *y s* of late Charles Willerton Richardson, Bombay; *m* 1942, Irene Mary, *o d* of late George E. Austin, Birkdale; two *s. Educ:* privately; University College, London (Fellow, 1971); Princeton University, USA. Commonwealth Fund Fellow, 1937-39; RNVR 1939-46; Commander, 1942; Deputy Director Miscellaneous Weapon Development, Admiralty, 1943-46; Superintending Chemist, British Iron and Steel Research Association, 1946-50; Nuffield Fellow and Director Nuffield Research Group, Imperial College, 1950-57; Prof. of Extraction Metallurgy, Imperial Coll., 1957-76. Member: Council, Iron and Steel Inst., 1962-74; InstnMM, 1961- (Pres., 1975-76); Metals Soc., 1974-; Charter Fellow, Metallurgical Soc.; American Inst. of Mining and Metallurgical Engineers, 1963. Sir George Beilby Memorial Award for researches on the thermodynamics of high temperature systems, 1956; Bessemer Gold Medal of Iron and Steel Inst. for contribs to kinetics and thermodynamics of metallurgical processes, 1968. Howe, Hatfield, May, Wernher and AIME Extractive Metallurgy and Yukawa Lectures, 1964-73. Hon. Member: Japanese Iron and Steel Inst.; Ingénieurs de Liège; Foreign Associate, Nat. Acad. of Engrg, USA, 1976. Hon. DIng, Technische Hochschule, Aachen; Hon. Dr, Liège. Gold Medal, InstnMM, 1973; Gold Medal, Amer. Soc. of Metals, 1975; Tunner Medal, Verein Eisenhütte Osterreich, 1976; Grande Medaille, Soc. Française de Métallurgie, 1977. *Publications:* The Physical Chemistry of Melts in Metallurgy, 1974; papers on chemical and metallurgical research in scientific jls. *Recreations:* riding, fishing, gardening. *Address:* Imperial College, Prince Consort Road, SW7. *Club:* Royal Automobile.

RICHARDSON, George Barclay; Fellow of St John's College, Oxford, since 1951; Secretary to the Delegates and Chief Executive of the Oxford University Press, since 1974; *b* 19 Sept. 1924; *s* of George and Christina Richardson; *m* 1957, Isabel Alison Chalk; two *s. Educ:* Aberdeen Central Secondary Sch. and other schs in Scotland; Aberdeen Univ.; Corpus Christi

Coll., Oxford. BSc Physics and Maths, 1944 (Aberdeen); MA (Oxon) PPE 1949. Admty Scientific Res. Dept, 1944; Lieut, RNVR, 1945. Intell. Officer, HQ Intell. Div. BAOR, 1946-47; Third Sec., HM Foreign Service, 1949; Student, Nuffield Coll., Oxford, 1950; University Reader in Economics, 1969-73. Economic Advr, UKAEA, 1968-74. Member: Economic Develt Cttee for Electrical Engineering Industry, 1964-73; Monopolies Commn, 1969-74; Royal Commn on Environmental Pollution, 1973-74. Deleg., Oxford Univ. Press, 1971-74. *Publications:* Information and Investment, 1960; Economic Theory, 1964; articles in academic jls. *Address:* Cutts End, Cumnor, Oxford. *Club:* United Oxford & Cambridge University.

RICHARDSON, George Taylor; President, James Richardson & Sons, Limited, Winnipeg, Canada, since 1966 (Vice-President 1954); Senior Partner, Richardson Securities of Canada, since 1947; Governor, Hudson's Bay Co., since 1970; *b* 22 Sept. 1924; *s* of late James Armstrong Richardson and Muriel (*née* Sprague); *m* 1948, Tannis Maree Thorlakson; two *s* two *d. Educ:* Grosvenor Sch. and Ravenscourt Sch. Winnipeg; Univ. of Manitoba (BComm). Joined family firm of James Richardson & Sons Ltd, 1946. Chm., Pioneer Grain Co. Ltd; Chm., James Richardson & Sons Overseas Ltd, London, and Chm./Dir of other cos owned by James Richardson & Sons Ltd; Vice-Pres. and Mem., Exec. Cttee, Canadian Imperial Bank of Commerce; Director: Inco Ltd; Hudson's Bay Oil & Gas Co. Ltd. Hon. Dr of Laws, Univ. of Manitoba, 1969. *Recreations:* hunting, helicopter flying. *Address:* (business) James Richardson & Sons, Limited, Richardson Building, One Lombard Place, Winnipeg R3B 0Y1, Manitoba, Canada. *T:* 988-5811. *Clubs:* Manitoba, St Charles, Winnipeg Winter (Winnipeg); Vancouver (Vancouver, BC); Royal Lake of the Woods Yacht (Ont.).

RICHARDSON, Sir George Wigham, 3rd Bt *cr* 1929; Underwriting Member of Lloyd's; President, Wigham Poland Ltd, and Director of other companies; *b* 12 April 1895; 2nd *s* of Sir Philip Wigham Richardson, 1st Bt; *S* brother, 1973; *m* 1st, 1923, Adela Nancy (marr. diss., 1937), *d* of late A. O. Davies; 2nd, 1944, Barbara, *d* of late Harry Clements Ansell, Sutton Coldfield; three *d. Educ:* Rugby School. Served European War in Flanders and France, 1915-18, and with Army of Occupation in Germany, 1918-19 (despatches). Prime Warden of Worshipful Company of Shipwrights, 1943. *Address:* H3 Albany, W1. *T:* 01-734 1861; Old Manor House, Benenden, Kent. *T:* Benenden 570. *Clubs:* Carlton, Constitutional, City of London.

RICHARDSON, Rt. Hon. Gordon (William Humphreys), PC 1976; MBE 1944; Governor, Bank of England, since 1973, Member, Court of the Bank of England, since 1967; *b* 25 Nov. 1915; *er s* of John Robert and Nellie Richardson; *m* 1941, Margaret Alison, *er d* of Canon H. R. L. Sheppard; one *s* one *d. Educ:* Nottingham High School; Gonville and Caius College, Cambridge (BA, LLB). Commnd S Notts Hussars Yeomanry, 1939; Staff Coll., Camberley, 1941; served until 1946. Called to Bar, Gray's Inn, 1946 (Hon. Bencher, 1973); Mem. Bar Council, 1951-55; ceased practice at Bar, Aug. 1955. Industrial and Commercial Finance Corp. Ltd, 1955-57; Director: J. Henry Schroder & Co., 1957; Lloyds Bank Ltd, 1960-67 (Vice-Chm., 1962-66); Legal and General Assurance Soc., Ltd, 1956-70 (Vice-Chm. 1959-70); Director: Rolls Royce (1971) Ltd, 1971-73; ICI Ltd, 1972-73; Chairman: J. Henry Schroder Wagg & Co. Ltd, 1962-72; Schroders Ltd, 1966-73; Schroders Inc. (NY), 1968-73. Chm., Industrial Develt Adv. Bd, 1972-73. Mem. Company Law Amendment Committee (Jenkins Committee), 1959-62; Chm. Cttee on Turnover Taxation, 1963. Member: Court of London University, 1962-65; NEDC, 1971-73; Trustee, National Gallery, 1971-73. One of HM Lieutenants, City of London, 1974-. Hon. Fellow, Wolfson Coll., Cambridge, 1977. Hon. DSc City Univ., 1976. *Address:* Bank of England, EC2R 8AH. *T:* 01-601 4444. *Club:* Brooks's.
See also Sir John Riddell, Bt.

RICHARDSON, Graham Edmund; Rector, Dollar Academy, Clackmannanshire, 1962-75; *b* 16 July 1913; *s* of H. W. Richardson, BSc, MIEE, AMIMechE, Studland, Dorset; *m* 1939, Eileen Cynthia, *d* of Lewis Beesly, FRCSE, Brightwalton, Newbury, Berks; one *s* one *d. Educ:* Tonbridge School; Strasbourg University; Queen's College, Oxford. Asst Master, Fettes College, Edinburgh, 1935-55; Housemaster, 1946-55; Headmaster, Melville College, Edinburgh, 1955-62. Mem., Scottish Adv. Cttee, IBA, 1968-73. *Address:* Sunnyholme, Studland, Dorset.

RICHARDSON, Prof. Harold Owen Wilson, DSc, PhD; FRSE; Hildred Carlile Professor of Physics, Bedford College, University of London, 1956-73, now Emeritus; *b* 1907; *e s* of late Sir Owen Richardson; *m* 1st, 1930, Jean Rosemary Campbell

(marr. diss., 1940); one *d* ; 2nd, 1955, Sylvia Camroux Topsfield. *Educ:* University College School; King's College, London. BSc (London); PhD (Cantab); DSc (Edinburgh). Research student, Cavendish Lab., Cambridge (Trinity Coll.), 1928-30; part-time Demonstrator at King's Coll., London, 1930-31; Demonstrator, Bedford Coll., London, 1931-35; Asst Lectr, Univ. of Leeds, 1935-36; Asst Lecturer and Lecturer, Univ. of Liverpool, 1936-46; Experimental Officer, Projectile Development Establishment, Min. of Supply, 1940-42; Lecturer in Natural Philosophy, Univ. of Edinburgh, 1946-51, Reader, 1951-52; Prof. of Physics, Univ. of Exeter, 1952-56. Warden of Reed Hall, Univ. Coll. of the South-West, 1953-55. Regional Scientific Adviser to the Home Office, 1953-56. *Publications:* papers on radioactivity, the magnetic focusing of electrons and the design of magnets. *Address:* 57 Dartmouth Park Hill, NW5.

RICHARDSON, Sir Henry; *see* Richardson, Sir J. H. S.

RICHARDSON, Sir (H.) Frank, Kt 1953; *b* 1901; *s* of William Thomas and Louisa Jane Richardson; *m* 1949, Marjorie Amy Hislop; four *s* two *d. Educ:* All Saints Gram. Sch., St Kilda, Vict.; Univ. of Tasmania, Australia. Deputy Chairman: Business Board, Defence Department, Commonwealth of Australia, 1941-47; Commonwealth Disposals Commission, Australia, 1944-49. Past Chairman of various Department Stores, etc., in Australia; now Director of Proprietary companies. Life Governor, Retail Traders Assoc. of Victoria. Mem. Council, The Australian National University, 1953-76. *Recreations:* tennis, golf. *Address:* 40 Heyington Place, Toorak, Victoria 3142, Australia. *T:* 20.40.30. *Club:* Athenæum (Melbourne, Australia).

RICHARDSON, Horace Vincent, OBE 1968; HM Diplomatic Service, retired; *b* 28 Oct. 1913; *s* of late Arthur John Alfred Richardson and Mrs Margaret Helena Jane Richardson (*née* Hooson); *m* 1942, Margery Tebbutt; two *s* one *d* (and one *d* decd). *Educ:* Abergele Grammar Sch.; King's Coll., London (LLB). Served with Army, 1940-45. LCC, 1931-35; Supreme Court of Judicature, 1935-47; FO, 1947-48; British Vice-Consul, Shanghai, 1948-50; Washington, 1950-53; 2nd Sec., Rome, 1953-56; FO, 1956-61; Consul, Philadelphia, 1961-63; FO, 1963-66; Consul, Cairo, 1966-68; 1st Sec., Washington, 1968-70; Head of Nationality and Treaty Dept, FCO, 1970-73. Rep. HM Govt at 9th and 10th Sessions of Hague Conf. of Private Internat. Law. *Recreations:* golf, gardening, tennis. *Address:* 34 Friern Barnet Lane, N11. *T:* 01-368 1983. *Clubs:* Civil Service; Turf (Cairo); Highgate Golf.

RICHARDSON, Hugh Edward, CIE 1947; OBE 1944; *b* 22 Dec. 1905; *s* of Hugh Richardson, DSO, MD, and Elizabeth, *née* McLean; *m* 1951, Huldah Rennie (*née* Walker). *Educ:* Trinity College, Glenalmond; Keble College, Oxford. Entered Indian Civil Service, 1930; SDO, Tamluk, Midnapore Dist, Bengal, 1932-34; entered Foreign and Political Service of Govt of India, 1934; APA Loralai, Baluchistan, 1934-35; British Trade Agent, Gyantse, and O-in-C British Mission, Lhasa, 1936-40; service in NWFP, 1940-42; 1st Sec. Indian Agency-General in China, Chungking, 1942-43; Dep. Sec. to Govt of India, EA Dept, 1944-45; British Trade Agent, Gyantse, and O-in-C, British Mission, Lhasa, 1946-47; Indian Trade Agent, Gyantse and Officer-in-charge, Indian Mission, Lhasa, 1947-50. Retd from ICS, 1950. *Publications:* Tibet and its History, 1962; (with D. L. Snellgrove) A Cultural History of Tibet, 1968. *Recreation:* golf. *Address:* c/o Grindlay's Bank Ltd, 13 St James's Square, SW1. *Club:* Royal and Ancient Golf (St Andrews).

RICHARDSON, Ian; actor; *b* 7 April 1934; *s* of John Richardson and Margaret Drummond; *m* 1961, Maroussia Frank; two *s. Educ:* Tynecastle; Edinburgh; Univ. of Glasgow. Studied for stage at Coll. of Dramatic Art, Glasgow (James Bridie Gold Medal, 1957). FRSAMD. Joined Birmingham Repertory Theatre Co. 1958 (leading parts incl. Hamlet); joined Shakespeare Meml Theatre Co. (later RSC), 1960; rôles, Stratford and Aldwych, 1960-: Arragon in Merchant of Venice; Sir Andrew Aguecheek, 1960; Malatesti in Duchess of Malfi, 1960; Oberon in A Midsummer Night's Dream, 1961; Tranio in Taming of the Shrew, 1961; the Doctor in The Representative, 1963; Edmund in King Lear, 1964; Antipholus of Ephesus in Comedy of Errors, 1964; Herald and Marat in Marat/Sade, 1964, 1965; Ithamore, The Jew of Malta, 1964; Ford, Merry Wives of Windsor, 1964, 1966, 1969; Antipholus of Syracuse in Comedy of Errors, 1965; Chorus, Henry V, 1965; Vindice, The Revengers Tragedy, 1965, 1969; Coriolanus, 1966; Bertram, All's Well That Ends Well, 1966; Malcolm, Macbeth, 1966; Cassius, Julius Caesar, 1968; Pericles, 1969; Angelo, Measure for Measure, 1970; Buckingham, Richard III, 1970; Proteus, Two Gentlemen of Verona, 1970; Prospero, The Tempest, 1970; Richard II/Bolingbroke, Richard II, 1973; Berowne, Love's

Labour's Lost, 1973; Iachimo, Cymbeline, 1974; Shalimov, Summer Folk, 1974; Ford, Merry Wives of Windsor, 1975; Richard III, 1975; tours with RSC: Europe and USSR, NY, 1964; NY, 1965; USSR, 1966; Japan, 1970; NY, 1974, 1975; Tom Wrench in musical Trelawny, Sadler's Wells, 1971-72; Professor Higgins, My Fair Lady, Broadway, 1976; Jack Tanner, in Man and Superman, and Doctor in The Millionairess, Shaw Festival Theatre, Niagara, Ont. *Films:* Captain Fitzroy in The Darwin Adventure, 1971; Priest in Man of la Mancha, 1972. Anthony Beavis in BBC TV serial Eyeless in Gaza, 1971. FRSAM, 1971. *Recreations:* music, exploring churches and castles. *Address:* c/o London Management, Regent House, 235-241 Regent Street, W1. *T:* 01-734 4192. *Club:* Garrick.

RICHARDSON, Hon. James Armstrong, PC (Can.); MP (L) for Winnipeg South; *b* Winnipeg, Manitoba, 28 March 1922; *s* of James Armstrong Richardson and Muriel Sprague; *m* 1949, Shirley Anne, *d* of John R. Rooper, Shamley Green, Surrey, England; two *s* three *d*. *Educ:* St John's, Ravenscourt, Winnipeg; Queen's Univ., Kingston, Ont. (BA). Pilot with No 10 BR Sqdn, before entering family firm of James Richardson & Sons, Ltd, Winnipeg, Oct. 1945; he was Chm. and Chief Exec. Officer of this company, but resigned to enter public life, 1968. MP (L), June 1968 (re-elected, Oct. 1972, July 1974); Minister without Portfolio, Canadian Federal Cabinet, July 1968; Minister of Supply and Services, May 1969; Minister of Nat. Defence, 1972-76; resigned from Federal Cabinet over constitutional language issue, Oct. 1976. *Address:* (home) 5209 Roblin Boulevard, Winnipeg, Manitoba, Canada, R3R 0G8; (office) House of Commons, Ottawa, Canada.
See also G. T. Richardson.

RICHARDSON, Joanna, MA Oxon; FRSL; author; *o d* of Frederick Richardson and Charlotte Elsa (*née* Benjamin). *Educ:* The Downs School, Seaford; St Anne's College, Oxford. Mem. Council, Royal Soc. of Literature, 1961-. *Publications:* Fanny Brawne: a biography, 1952; Rachel, 1956; Théophile Gautier: his Life and Times, 1958; Sarah Bernhardt, 1959; Edward FitzGerald, 1960; The Disastrous Marriage: a Study of George IV and Caroline of Brunswick, 1960; My Dearest Uncle: a Life of Leopold, First King of the Belgians, 1961; (ed) FitzGerald: Selected Works, 1962; The Pre-Eminent Victorian: a study of Tennyson, 1962; The Everlasting Spell: a study of Keats and his Friends, 1963; (ed) Essays by Divers Hands (trans. Royal Soc. Lit.), 1963; introd. to Victor Hugo: Choses Vues (The Oxford Lib. of French Classics), 1964; Edward Lear, 1965; George IV: a Portrait, 1966; Creevey and Greville, 1967; Princess Mathilde, 1969; The Bohemians, 1969; Verlaine, 1971; La Vie Parisienne, 1852-1870, 1971; Enid Starkie, 1973; (ed) Verlaine, (poems in trans.), 1974; Stendhal: a critical biography, 1974; ed and trans., Baudelaire, Poems, 1975; Victor Hugo, 1976; Sarah Bernhardt and Her World, 1977; Victoria and Albert: a study of a marriage, 1977; Emile Zola, 1978. Contributor, BBC. Has also written for The Times, The Times Literary Supplement, Sunday Times, Spectator, New Statesman, New York Times Book Review, The Washington Post, French Studies, Modern Language Review, Keats-Shelley Memorial Bulletin, etc. *Recreations:* antique-collecting, sketching. *Address:* 55 Flask Walk, NW3. *T:* 01-435 5156.

RICHARDSON, Rt. Rev. John; Assistant Bishop of Andaman and Nicobar Islands (Bishop of Car Nicobar), 1966-77; of Car Nicobarese parentage; *m* 1st, 1913; one *s* two *d* (and two *s* one *d* decd); 2nd, 1942; one *s* two *d* (and one *d* decd). *Educ:* SPG Mission Sch., Mandalay, Upper Burma. Leader of the Nicobarese; teacher and catechist, Car Nicobar, 1912; acted as hon. third class Magistrate, Conservator of Port, 1920-33; Assistant Bishop and Commissary to Bishop and Metropolitan of Calcutta (Bishop of Nicobar Islands), 1950-66. Nominated member of House of Parliament, New Delhi, India, by the President, 1952. Hon. DD, Serampore Coll., 1965. Padma Shri Madel, India, 1965. *Recreations:* formerly: walking, cycling and fishing. *Address:* Mus, Car Nicobar, Port Blair, Andaman and Nicobar Islands.

RICHARDSON, John David Benbow, MC 1942, and Bar 1943; Vice-President, Northern Rent Assessment Panel, since 1968; *b* 6 April 1919; *s* of His Honour Judge Thomas Richardson, OBE, and Winifred Ernestine (*née* Templer); *m* 1946, Kathleen Mildred (*née* Price-Turner); four *s*. *Educ:* Harrow; Clare Coll., Cambridge. Called to Bar, Middle Temple, 1947. Served War of 1939-45, as Captain in King's Dragoon Guards (wounded; MC and Bar). ADC to Governor of South Australia (Lt-Gen. Sir Willoughby Norrie, later Lord Norrie), 1946-47. Dep. Chm., Durham County Quarter Sessions, 1964-71, and Recorder, 1972-73. Mem., Police Complaints Bd, 1977-. *Recreations:* fishing, gardening, golf. *Address:* Cliffe Lodge, Corbridge,

Northumberland. *T:* Corbridge 2101. *Clubs:* MCC; York County Stand; Northern Counties (Newcastle upon Tyne).

RICHARDSON, Sir (John) Eric, Kt 1967; CBE 1962; PhD, BEng, CEng, FIEE, MIMechE, FBHI, FPS; FRSA; Director, The Polytechnic of Central London, 1969-70; *b* 30 June 1905; *e surv. s* of late William and Mary Elizabeth Richardson, Birkenhead; *m* 1941, Alice May, *d* of H. M. Wilson, Hull; one *s* two *d* (and one *d* decd). *Educ:* Birkenhead Higher Elementary Sch.; Liverpool Univ. BEng 1st Cl. Hons, 1931, PhD 1933, Liverpool. Chief Lectr in Electrical Engineering, 1933-37, Head of Engineering Dept, 1937-41, Hull Municipal Technical Coll.; Principal: Oldham Municipal Technical Coll., 1942-44; Royal Technical Coll., Salford, 1944-47; Northampton Polytechnic, London, EC1, 1947-56; Dir Nat. Coll. of Horology and Instrument Technology, 1947-56; Dir of Educn, Regent Street Polytechnic, W1, 1957-69. Hon. Sec., Assoc. of Technical Insts, 1957-67, Chm., 1967-68; Pres. Assoc. of Principals of Technical Instns, 1961-62; Dep. Chm., Council for Overseas Colls of Arts, Science and Technology, 1949-62; Member: Council for Tech. Educn and Trng in Overseas Countries, 1962-73 (Chm. Technical Educn Cttee, 1971-73); and Vice-Chm. Council and Cttees, London and Home Counties Regional Adv. Council for Technol Educn, 1972-; Chm., Adv. Cttee on Educn for Management, 1961-66; Member: Governing Council of Nigerian Coll. of Art, Science and Technology, 1953-61; Council, Univ. Coll., Nairobi, 1961-70; Provisional Council, Univ. of East Africa, 1961-63; Governing Body, College of Aeronautics, Cranfield, 1956-59; Council of British Horological Institute, 1951-; Gen. Optical Council, 1959- (Chm., 1975-); Science and Technol Cttee of CNAA, 1965-71; Electrical Engrg Bd of CNAA (Chm.); Industrial Trg Bd for Electricity Supply Industry, 1965-71; Univ. and Polytechnic Grants Cttee, Hong Kong, 1972-77; Council, RSA, 1968- (Chm. Exams Cttee, 1969-, Hon. Treasurer, 1974); Council and Exec. Cttee, Leprosy Mission, 1970- (Chm., 1974-); Council and Exec. Cttee, City and Guilds of London Inst., 1969- (Chm. Policy and Overseas Cttees; Vice-Chm. Technical Educn Cttee; Jt Hon. Sec., 1970-); Chm., Ealing Civic Soc., 1972-76. Chairman: Africa Evangelical Fellowship (SAGM), 1950-70; Nat. Young Life Campaign, 1949-64; Council, Inter-Varsity Fellowship of Evangelical Unions, 1966-69; Pres., Crusaders Union, 1972-; Chm., Governors of London Bible Coll., 1970-77; Chm., Governors, Clarendon Sch., Abergele, 1971-75. *Publications:* paper in IEE Jl (Instn Prize); various papers on higher technological education in UK and Nigeria. *Recreations:* gardening, photography. *Address:* 73 Delamere Road, Ealing, W5 3JP. *T:* 01-567 1588.

RICHARDSON, John Eric, MS; FRCS; Surgeon: The London Hospital since 1949; The Royal Masonic Hospital since 1960; King Edward VII's Hospital for Officers since 1960; Prince of Wales Hospital, Tottenham, N15, 1958-65; Consultant Surgeon to the Navy; *b* Loughborough, 24 February 1916; *s* of late C. G. Richardson, MD, FRCS; *m* 1943, Elisabeth Jean, *d* of late Rev. John Webster; one *s* one *d*. *Educ:* Clifton College; London Hospital. MB, BS London (Hons and Distinction, Pathology), 1939; MRCS, LRCP 1939. Andrew Clarke Prize, London Hosp., 1939. Resident Appointments, London Hospital and Poplar Hospital, 1939-41; Surgeon Lieut RNVR (Surgical Specialist), 1941-46; Surgical Registrar, London Hosp., 1946-47; Rockefeller Travelling Fellow, 1947-48; Research Fellow in Surgery, Harvard Univ., 1947-48; Fellow in Clinical Surgery, Massachusetts Gen. Hosp., Boston, Mass, 1947-48. Surgeon, St Andrews Hosp., Dollis Hill, 1965-73. Hunterian Prof., RCS, 1953; Lettsomian Lectr, Med. Soc. of London, 1973. Pres., Med. Soc. of London, 1974-75. Examr in Surgery to Soc. of Apothecaries, London, 1959-67 and Univ. of London, 1962-63, 1965-66. *Publications:* contrib. to Lancet and BMJ on gastro-enterology and endocrine disease. *Address:* 90 Harley Street, W1 1AF. *T:* 01-935 2186; 10 Middle Field, NW8 6NE. *T:* 01-722 1101; Allen's Barn, Swinbrook, Oxon OX8 4EA. *T:* Burford 2456.

RICHARDSON, Ven. John Farquhar, MA; Archdeacon of Derby, 1952-73, now Emeritus; Chaplain to The Queen, 1952-76; First Residentiary Canon of Derby Cathedral 1954-73; *b* 23 April 1905; 2nd *s* of late William Henry Richardson and Gertrude Richardson (*née* Walker); *m* 1936, Elizabeth Mary, *d* of Henry Roy Dean; one *s* two *d*. *Educ:* Winchester; Trinity Hall, Cambridge; Westcott House, Cambridge. Curate of Holy Trinity, Cambridge, 1929-32; Chaplain of Repton School, 1932-35; Curate of St Martin-in-the-Fields, 1935-36; Vicar of Christ Church, Hampstead, 1936-41; Rector of Bishopwearmouth, 1941-52; Rural Dean of Wearmouth, 1947-52. Proctor in Convocation, 1950-52; Hon. Canon of Durham, 1951-52. *Recreation:* golf. *Address:* 474 Kedleston Road, Derby DE3 2NE. *T:* Derby 59135. *Clubs:* Royal Automobile; Jesters; Hawks (Cambridge).

RICHARDSON, John Flint; Chairman of Tyne and Wear County Council, 1976-77; *b* 5 May 1906; *s* of Robert Flint Richardson and Jane Lavinia; *m* 1932, Alexandra Graham; two *s*. *Educ*: Cone Street, South Shields. Councillor, 1938, Alderman, 1954, Mayor, 1960-61, South Shields; Freeman, South Shields, 1973. *Recreations*: serving people, reading. *Address*: 16 Forster Avenue, South Shields, Tyne and Wear NE34 6NL. *T*: South Shields 5784.

RICHARDSON, Sir (John) Henry (Swain), Kt 1941; Former Director: Yule Catto & Co. Ltd, East India Merchants; The Chartered Bank; *b* 18 June 1889; *o s* of late John Richardson, Ashford, Kent; *m* 1920, Olga, 2nd *d* of George John Stavridi, of Geneva and Calcutta; one *d*. Served European War, 1914-19, in Mesopotamia and India with 5th Buffs and XIth Rajputs; Senior Deputy Chairman, Andrew Yule & Co. Ltd, 1936-41; Vice-Pres. Bengal Chamber of Commerce, 1939, and Pres., 1940; Pres. Associated Chambers of Commerce of India, 1940, Member, Council of State, Govt of India, 1939-41; Member, Legislative Assembly, Govt of India, and Leader, European Group, 1942-45. *Recreation*: music. *Address*: Fairlawn, Hall Place Drive, Queen's Road, Weybridge, Surrey. *Club*: Oriental.

RICHARDSON, Sir John (Samuel), 1st Bt, *cr* 1963; Kt 1960; MVO 1943; MD, FRCP; President, General Medical Council, since 1973; Hon. Consulting Physician: St Thomas' Hospital; King Edward VII's Hospital for Officers; Consultant Emeritus to the Army; Consulting Physician: Metropolitan Police, since 1957; London Transport Board, since 1964; *b* 16 June 1910; *s* of Major John Watson Richardson, solicitor, and Elizabeth Blakeney, *d* of Sir Samuel Roberts, 1st Bt, both of Sheffield; *m* 1933, Sybil Angela Stephanie, *d* of A. Ronald Trist, Stanmore, and late Mrs Trist; two *d*. *Educ*: Charterhouse; Trinity Coll., Cambridge. MB BChir 1936, MD 1940; MRCP 1937, FRCP 1948. Major, RAMC (temp.), 1939; Lt-Col, RAMC (temp.), 1942. 1st asst, Med. Professorial Unit, St Thomas's Hosp., 1946; Physician to St Thomas's Hosp., 1947-75. President: Internat. Soc. of Internal Medicine, 1966-70 (Hon. Pres. 1970); Royal Soc. of Medicine, 1969-71 (Hon. Librarian, 1957-63; Pres., Med. Educn Sect., 1967-68); BMA, 1970-71; 2nd Congress, Assoc. Européenne de Médicine Interne d'Ensemble, Bad-Godesberg, 1973 (Hon. Mem. 1974); Vice-President: Med. Soc. of London, 1961-63; Royal Coll. of Nursing, 1972-; Assoc. for the Study of Med. Educn, 1974-; Chairman: Jt Consultants Cttee, 1967-72; Council for Postgrad. Med. Educn in England and Wales, 1972-; Medico-Pharmaceutical Forum, 1973-76; Armed Forces Med. Adv. Bd, MoD, 1975-. Mem., Bd of Governors, St Thomas's Hosp., 1953-59, 1964-74. Mem. Ct, Soc. of Apothecaries, 1960- (Master, 1971-72). Lectures: Lettsomian, Med. Soc. of London, 1963; Scott Heron, Royal Victoria Hosp., Belfast, 1969; Maudsley, RCPsych, 1971; Wilkinson Meml, Inst. of Dental Surgeons, London Univ., 1976. Hon. Fellow: Swedish Soc. Med. Scis, 1970; RSocMed 1973; Heberden Soc., 1973; Osler Club of London, 1973; Hon. FPS, 1974; Hon. FRCPE 1975; Hon. FRCPI 1975; Hon. FFCM 1977. CStJ 1970. Hon. Bencher, Gray's Inn, 1974. Hon. DSc NUI, 1975. Editor-in-Chief, British Encyclopaedia of Medical Practice, 1970-74. *Publications*: The Practice of Medicine, 2nd edn 1960; Connective Tissue Disorders, 1963; Anticoagulant Prophylaxis and Treatment (jointly), 1965. *Heir*: none. *Address*: Flat 9, Weymouth House, 84 Hallam Street, W1N 5LS. *T*: 01-580 0709; Windcutter, Lee, near Ilfracombe, North Devon EX34 8LW. *T*: Ilfracombe 63198.

RICHARDSON, Josephine; MP (Lab) Barking, since Feb. 1974; *b* 28 Aug. 1923; *d* of J. J. Richardson. *Educ*: Southend-on-Sea High School for Girls. Vice-Chairperson: Parly Cttee, ASTMS; Campaign for Nuclear Disarmament; Mem., Exec. Council, Nat. Council for Civil Liberties; Secretary: Keep Left Gp; Bevan Gp; Tribune Gp, 1948-. *Recreations*: politics, cooking. *Address* House of Commons, SW1A 0AA. *T*: 01-219 5028.

RICHARDSON, Kenneth Albert; Fifth Senior Prosecuting Counsel to the Crown, since 1973; *b* 28 July 1926; *s* of Albert Robert Richardson and Ida Elizabeth Richardson (*née* Williams); *m* 1956, Dr Eileen Mary O'Cleary, Galway; two *s* one *d* (and one *s* decd). *Educ*: Ruthin Sch.; Merton Coll., Oxford. MA (in English and Jurisprudence). Called to the Bar, Middle Temple, 1952 (Harmsworth Scholar; Bencher, 1975). Commissioned RWF, 1945 (attached 8th Punjab Regt). Apptd Junior Prosecuting Counsel to the Crown, 1967. Mem., Bar Council, 1972; Senate of the Inns and Bar, 1974. *Recreations*: skiing, golf, sailing, music. *Address*: Queen Elizabeth Building, Temple, EC4. *Clubs*: Ski Club of Great Britain; Blackheath FC; Vincent's (Oxford).

RICHARDSON, Prof. Leopold John Dixon, OBE 1965; MA; Professor (Hon.) of Classical Literature, TCD, 1963; Member,

Royal Irish Academy, 1965; retired as Professor of Greek, University College, Cardiff, 1946-58; Research Associate (Hon.) University College, London, 1964-66; Hon. Secretary, Classical Association, 1943-63; *b* 3 Aug. 1893; *o s* of late William Hamilton Irwin Richardson and late Sara Ann Dagg; *m* 1925, Frances Petticrew Patton (*d* 1955); two *d*. *Educ*: The High School, Dublin; Trinity College, Dublin. Classical Sizarship, Classical Foundn Schol.; Sen. Moderatorship with Gold Medal in Classics and in Mental and Moral Science, and Univ. Studentship in Classics, 1916; Vice-Chancellor's Prizeman, Greek Prose, Greek Verse, Latin Verse; Berkeley, Tyrrell and Vice-Chancellor's Medallist; Ferrar, William Roberts, Hebrew and Sanskrit Prizeman; Fellowship Prizeman, 1929. MA 1920; MA (Wales) 1942. Member of Council: Philological Soc., 1944-50; Roman Soc., 1949-52; Hellenic Soc., 1955-58. Editor: Proc. of Classical Assoc., 1948-63; Studies in Mycenaean Inscriptions and Dialect, 1959-73. Asst to Prof. of Greek, Queen's Univ., Belfast, 1922-23; Dep. Prof., 1923-24; Lectr in Latin, Univ. Coll., Cardiff, 1925-46. *Publications*: Ta Indika, 1929; various articles in English, Irish and foreign learned journals. *Address*: 1 Howell's Crescent, Llandaff, Glam. *T*: Cardiff 561078; 75 Wellington Road, Dublin 4. *T*: 689542.

RICHARDSON, Sir Leslie Lewis, 2nd Bt, *cr* 1924; Director of Companies; *b* 14 August 1915; *s* of Sir Lewis Richardson, 1st Bart, CBE, head of the firm of L. Richardson & Co. of London, Port Elizabeth, New York and Boston, and Phoebe, *o d* of Isaac Isaacs; *S* father 1934; *m* 1946, Joy Patricia, twin *d* of P. J. Rillstone, Johannesburg; two *s* one *d*. *Educ*: Harrow, Served with South African Artillery, 1940-44, in the Union and North Africa. *Heir*: *s* Anthony Lewis Richardson, *b* 5 Aug. 1950. *Address*: Old Vineyard, Constantia, Cape Town, 7800, South Africa. *T*: Cape Town 741176.

RICHARDSON, Group Captain Michael Oborne, RAF, retired; *b* Holmfirth, Yorks, 13 May 1908; *s* of Rev. Canon G. L. Richardson, MA, BD, and Edith Maria (*née* Ellison); *m* 1935, Nellie Marguerita, *d* of Walter Ross Somervell, Elizavetgrad, Russia; one *s* one *d*. *Educ*: Lancing Coll.; Keble Coll., Oxford; Guy's Hospital. BA 1929; MRCS, LRCP 1938; DPH 1955; MA Oxon 1963; DPhysMed 1964. Oxford House, Bethnal Green, 1930. Commissioned RAF, 1939; served at Kenley; War Service included HQ Fighter Comd (Unit), S Africa, Western Desert, Malta, Sicily, Italy (despatches). Post-war service in Germany and Aden and comdt various hosps and Medical Rehabilitation Units; Commandant, Star and Garter Home for Disabled Sailors, Soldiers and Airmen, 1967-73. OStJ 1965. *Recreation*: the countryside. *Address*: 10 North Street, Tywardreath, Par, Cornwall. *T*: Par 3519. *Clubs*: Royal Air Force; Webbe.

RICHARDSON, Sir Ralph David, Kt 1947; Actor; President, National Youth Theatre, since 1959; *b* Cheltenham, Glos, 19 Dec. 1902; *s* of Arthur Richardson and Lydia Russell; *m* 1st, 1924, Muriel Hewitt (*d* 1942); no *c*; 2nd, 1944, Meriel Forbes-Robertson; one *s*. *Educ*: Xaverian Coll., Brighton; privately. Made his first appearance on the stage at Brighton, 1921; toured in the Provinces in Shakespeare Repertory for four years; joined the Birmingham Repertory Theatre in 1925; first London appearance in 1926 at the Haymarket Theatre as Arthur Varwell in Yellow Sands; season of plays at the Court Theatre in 1928; toured in South Africa in 1929; from 1930 to 1932 played two seasons at the Old Vic and two seasons at the Malvern summer theatre; Too True To Be Good at the New Theatre and For Services Rendered at the Queen's in 1933, followed by Wild Decembers and Sheppey; Eden End and Cornelius at the Duchess Theatre in 1935, and played Mercutio in Romeo and Juliet in the USA in 1936; Promise, Bees on the Boatdeck and The Amazing Dr Clitterhouse, until 1937; in 1938, The Midsummer Night's Dream and Othello at the Old Vic; Johnson over Jordan, Sept. 1939, joined Fleet Air Arm as Sub/Lieut RNVR; Lieut (A) RNVR 1940; Lt-Comdr RNVR 1941. Released from Naval Service, June 1944, to act for and direct Drama of Old Vic Theatre Company; Old Vic 1st Season, 1944-45: played Peer Gynt, Bluntschli in Arms and the Man, Uncle Vanya, Henry VII in Richard the Third, toured Germany and visited Comédie Française in Paris. Old Vic 2nd season, 1945-46: played Falstaff in Henry IV, parts 1 and 2, Bluntschli in Arms and the Man, Tiresias in Oedipus Rex, Lord Burleigh in The Critic. Visited New York for six weeks' season. Old Vic 3rd Season, 1946-47: played Cyrano in Cyrano de Bergerac, the Inspector in An Inspector Calls, Face in The Alchemist, produced Richard II (playing Gaunt); Dr Sloper in The Heiress, Haymarket, 1949; David Preston in Home at Seven, Wyndham's 1950; Vershinin in Three Sisters, Aldwych, 1951; Stratford-on-Avon Season, 1952; Macbeth, Volpone, The Tempest; The White Carnation (playing John Greenwood), Globe, 1953; A Day by the Sea, Haymarket, 1954; Sleeping Prince and Separate Tables, Australian and New Zealand Tour, 1955; The Waltz of the Toreadors (New York), 1957; Flowering Cherry, Haymarket, 1958; The Complaisant Lover, Globe, 1959; The Last Joke, 1960; The School for Scandal, Haymarket and US Tour, 1962; Six Characters in search of an Author, May Fair, 1963; The Merchant of Venice and A Midsummer Night's Dream, South American and European Tour, 1964; Carving a Statue, Haymarket, 1964; You Never Can Tell, 1966; The Rivals, 1966, 1967; Merchant of Venice, 1967; What the Butler Saw, 1969; Home, London, 1970 (Evening Standard Best Actor Award), NY, 1971; West of Suez, 1971; Lloyd George Knew My Father, 1972-73 (Austr. tour 1973); John Gabriel Borkman, National, 1975; No Man's Land, National, 1975, NY 1976; The Kingfisher, Lyric, 1977; *films:* made his first film, The Ghoul, in 1933; other films include: Things to Come; The Man Who Could Work Miracles; Bulldog Drummond; South Riding; Divorce of Lady X; The Citadel; Four Feathers; Q Planes; Night of the Fire; The Silver Fleet; The Volunteer; School for Secrets; Anna Karenina, The Fallen Idol, The Heiress (Hollywood); Outcast of the Islands; Home at Seven; The Holly and the Ivy; The Sound Barrier; The Passionate Stranger; Oscar Wilde; Exodus; Spartacus; Long Day's Journey into Night; Woman of Straw; Dr Zhivago, 1965; The Wrong Box, 1966; Gordon of Khartoum, 1966; Twelfth Night, 1968; Battle of Britain, 1968; Oh! What a Lovely War, 1968; The Bed-Sitting Room, 1968; The Looking-Glass War, 1968; Mr Micawber in David Copperfield, 1969; A Run on Gold, 1969; Gingerbread House, 1971; Lady Caroline Lamb, 1972; Alice's Adventures in Wonderland, 1972; Eagle in a Cage, 1973; A Doll's House, 1973; O Lucky Man, 1973; Rollerball, 1975. Hon. DLitt Oxon, 1969. Order of St Olaf (Norway), 1950. *Publications:* articles in magazines and newspapers. *Recreations:* drawing, tennis. *Address:* 1 Chester Terrace, Regent's Park, NW1. *Clubs:* Athenæum, Beefsteak, Savile.

RICHARDSON, Robert Augustus; HM Chief Inspector of Schools, Department of Education and Science, 1968-72; *b* 2 Aug. 1912; *s* of late Ferdinand Augustus Richardson and Muriel Emma Richardson; *m* 1936, Elizabeth Gertrude Williamson; one *d. Educ:* Royal College of Art. Schoolmaster, 1934; Headmaster, Sidcup School of Art, 1937. Served in Royal Navy, 1941-46. Principal: Folkestone Sch. of Art, 1946; Maidstone Coll. of Art, 1948. Dept of Education and Science: HM Inspector of Schools, 1958; HM Staff Inspector, 1966. ARCA 1934. *Recreations:* theatre, music. *Address:* 68 Highfield Drive, Hurstpierpoint, West Sussex. *T:* Hurstpierpoint 832186.

RICHARDSON, Rev. Canon Robert Douglas, DD, BLitt, MA; *b* 26 February 1893; *er s* of late Frederick Richardson; *m* 1929, Professor Linetta P. de Castelvecchio (*d* 1975). *Educ:* Hertford College and Ripon Hall, Oxford. Served European War, 1914-18, in RN; Curate of Stourport-on-Severn; Succentor of Birmingham Cathedral; Vicar of Four Oaks and Vicar of Harborne; Select Preacher, Cambridge University; sometime External Lectr in Biblical Studies to Univ. of Birmingham; Examining Chaplain to Bishop of Birmingham, 1932-53; Canon Emeritus of Birmingham Cathedral; Principal of Ripon Hall, Oxford, 1948-52; Rector of Boyton with Sherrington, 1952-67. *Publications:* The Conflict of Ideals in the Church of England, 1923; The Gospel of Modernism, 1933; Sectional Editor of Webster's Dictionary (1934 edn); A Revised Order of Holy Communion, 1936. Christian Belief and Practice, 1940. A Further Inquiry into Eucharistic Origins (in the English edn of Lietzmann's Mass and Lord's Supper), publ. in fascicles, 1953-; The Psalms as Christian Prayers and Praises, 1960; article on Luke and the Eucharistic Tradition, in Studia Evangelica, 1957, in The Gospels Reconsidered, 1960; contrib. to various Theological Jls. *Address:* Corton Parva, near Warminster, Wilts. *T:* Codford St Mary 286.

RICHARDSON, Maj.-Gen. Robert Francis, CBE 1975 (OBE 1971; MBE 1965); General Officer Commanding Berlin (British Sector), since Jan. 1978; *b* 2 March 1929; *s* of late Robert Buchan Richardson and Anne (*née* Smith); *m* 1956, Maureen Anne Robinson; three *s* one *d. Educ:* George Heriot's Sch., Edinburgh; RMA Sandhurst. Commnd into The Royal Scots, 1949; served in BAOR, Korea, and Middle East with 1st Bn The Royal Scots until 1960; Defence Services Staff Coll., India, 1960-61; psc 1961; GSO II MO4, MoD, 1961-64; jssc 1964; Brigade Major Aden Bde, 1967 (Despatches); GSO II ACDS (Ops), MoD, 1968-69; CO 1st Bn The Royal Scots, 1969-71; Col Gen. Staff, Staff Coll. Camberley, 1971-74; Comdr 39 Infantry Bde, Northern Ireland, 1974-75; Deputy Adjutant General, HQ BAOR, 1975-78. *Recreations:* golf and other outdoor sports. *Address:* c/o Lloyds Bank Ltd, Cox's and King's Branch, 6 Pall Mall, SW1. *Club:* Royal Scots (Edinburgh).

RICHARDSON, Ronald Frederick, CBE 1973 (MBE 1945); Deputy Chairman, Electricity Council, 1972-76; Member, Price

Commission, since 1977; *b* 1913; *s* of Albert F. Richardson and Elizabeth Jane (*née* Sayer); *m* 1946, Anne Elizabeth McArdle; two *s. Educ:* Coopers' Company's School; Northampton Engineering Inst.; Polytechnic Inst.; Administrative Staff College. Served War of 1939-45: Major, Field Park Company RE, 1942-46. Callenders Cables, 1929-36; Central London Electricity, 1936-39, 1946-48; London Electricity Board, 1948-52; British Electricity Authority, 1952-57; South Western Electricity Board, 1957-63; Chm., North Western Electricity Board, 1964-71. Chm., Nat. Inspection Council for Electrical Installation Contracting, 1969-70; Dep. Chm., NW Regional Council, CBI, 1971; Member: North West Economic Planning Council, 1965-70; Adv. Council on Energy Conservation, 1974-76; (part-time): NCB, 1975-; Electricity Council, 1976. Member: Court of Manchester Univ., 1969-71; Council, 1970-71, Court, 1970-, Salford Univ.; Governor, William Temple Coll., 1971-74. *Recreations:* music, the open air. *Address:* 22 Frank Dixon Way, Dulwich, SE21 7ET. *Club:* Athenæum.

RICHARDSON, Sir Simon Alaisdair S.; *see* Stewart-Richardson.

RICHARDSON, Maj.-Gen. Thomas Anthony, CB 1976; MBE 1960; Defence and Military Adviser, India, 1974-77, retired; *b* 9 Aug. 1922; *s* of late Maj.-Gen. T. W. Richardson, Eaton Cottage, Unthank Road, Norwich, and late Mrs J. H. Boothby, Camberley; *m* 1945, Katharine Joanna Ruxton Roberts, Woodland Place, Bath; one *s* one *d. Educ:* Wellington Coll., Berks. ptsc, psc, pl, ph, p. War of 1939-45: enlisted, Feb. 1941; commissioned, RA, March 1942; Essex Yeomanry (France and Germany), 1942-45; Air Observation Post, 1945-46. Tech. Staff/G Staff, 1949-52, 1954-55, 1959-60, 1963-64; Regt duty, 1942-45, 1952-54, 1957-58, 1961-62. Instr, Mil. Coll. Science, 1955-56; CO, 7th Para, RHA, 1965-67; CRA, 2 Div., 1967-69; Dir, Operational Requirements (Army), 1969-71; Dir, Army Aviation, 1971-74. MRAeS; MBIM. *Recreations:* sailing, skiing, fishing, shooting. *Address:* c/o Lloyds Bank Ltd, Norwich NR2 1LZ; 12 Lauriston Road, Wimbledon, SW19. *Club:* Army and Navy.

RICHARDSON, Tony; Director, Woodfall Film Productions Ltd, since 1958; *b* 5 June 1928; *s* of Clarence Albert and Elsie Evans Richardson; *m* 1962, Vanessa Redgrave, *qv* (marr. diss., 1967); two *d. Educ:* Wadham College, Oxford. *Plays* directed or produced: Look Back in Anger; The Chairs; Pericles and Othello (Stratford); The Entertainer; Semi-Detached; Luther; The Seagull; St Joan of the Stockyards; Hamlet; The Threepenny Opera, Prince of Wales, 1972; I Claudius, Queen's, 1972; Antony and Cleopatra, Bankside Globe, 1973. *Films* directed or produced: Look Back in Anger, 1958; The Entertainer, 1959; Saturday Night and Sunday Morning (prod.), 1960; Taste of Honey, 1961; The Loneliness of the Long Distance Runner (prod. and dir.), 1962; Tom Jones (dir.), 1962; Girl with Green Eyes (prod.), 1964; The Loved One (prod.), 1965; Mademoiselle (dir.), 1965; The Sailor from Gibraltar (dir.), 1965; Red and Blue (dir.) 1966; The Charge of the Light Brigade (dir.), 1968; Laughter in the Dark (dir.), 1969; Hamlet (dir.), 1969; Ned Kelly (dir.), 1969; A Delicate Balance, 1972; Dead Cert, 1974; Joseph Andrews, 1977. *Recreations:* directing plays and films. *Address:* c/o 23 Albermarle Street, W1.

RICHARDSON, William Eric, CEng, FIEE, FBIM; Chairman, South Wales Electricity Board, 1968-77; Member, Electricity Council, 1968-77; *b* 21 May 1915; *o s* of William Pryor and Elizabeth Jane Richardson, Hove, Sussex; *m* (she *d* 1975); one *s* ; *m* 1976, Barbara Mary Leech. *Educ:* Royal Masonic Sch., Bushey. Engineer with Brighton Corp., 1934-37; Southampton Corp., 1937-39; Norwich Corp., 1939-46; Distribution Engr with Newport (Mon) Corp., 1946-48; Area Engr with S Wales Electricity Bd, 1948-57; Area Manager, 1957-65; Chief Commercial Engr, 1965-67; Dep. Chm., 1967-68. *Recreations:* sailing, golf, gardening. *Address:* Beaumont, 92 Allt-yr-yn Avenue, Newport, Gwent. *T:* Newport (Gwent) 64388.

RICHARDSON, Sir William (Robert), Kt 1967; Chief Executive Officer, Cooperative Press Ltd, 1967-74; *b* 16 Jan. 1909; *s* of Thomas and Constance Margaret Richardson; *m* 1932, Gladys Gillians; one *s* two *d. Educ:* various public elem. schs, Newcastle upon Tyne; evening classes; Cooperative College. Editor, Cooperative News, 1938; Editor, Reynolds News, later changed name to Sunday Citizen, 1942-67, when paper closed. Mem. Post Office Users' Nat. Council, 1969-. *Publication:* The CWS in War and Peace 1938-1976, 1977. *Recreation:* reading. *Address:* 6 Alders Road, Disley, Cheshire. *T:* Disley 3758.

RICHARDSON, William Rowson, CMG 1948; formerly Under-Secretary, Ministry of Education; *b* 1 Jan. 1892; *s* of George and Maria Richardson, Leeds; *m* 1922, Margaret Hadfield, *d* of late

J. N. Marsden, Lisbon; one *s* (one *d* decd). Chevalier 1st Class Order of St Olaf, 1948. *Address:* Lark Rise, Stonards Brow, Shamley Green, Nr Guildford. *T:* Bramley 2114.

RICHARDSON-BUNBURY, Sir (Richard David) Michael, *see* Bunbury.

RICHES, Sir Derek (Martin Hurry), KCMG 1963 (CMG 1958); Ambassador to Lebanon, 1963-67, retired; *b* 26 July 1912; *s* of late Claud Riches and Flora Martin; *m* 1942 Helen Barkley Hayes, Poughkeepsie, NY, USA; one *d. Educ:* University College School; University College, London. Appointed Probationer Vice-Consul, Beirut, Dec. 1934. Subsequently promoted and held various appts, Ethiopia and Cairo; Foreign Office, 1944; promoted one of HM Consuls serving in FO, 1945. Kabul, 1948 (in charge, 1948 and 1949); Consul at Jedda, 1951 (Chargé d'Affaires, 1952); Officer Grade 6, Branch A, Foreign Service and apptd Trade Comr, Khartoum, 1953. Attached to Imperial Defence College, 1955; returned to Foreign Office, 1955; Counsellor in the Foreign Office, Head of Eastern Department, 1955; British Ambassador in Libya, 1959-61; British Ambassador to the Congo, 1961-63. *Address:* 48 The Avenue, Kew Gardens, Surrey.

RICHES, Sir Eric (William), Kt 1958; MC; MS (London), FRCS; Emeritus Surgeon and Urologist to Middlesex Hospital; Hon. Consultant Urologist to Hospital of St John and St Elizabeth; formerly Consulting Urologist to the Army and to Ministry of Pensions Spinal Injury Centre; Urologist, St Andrew's Hospital, Dollis Hill; lately Urologist, Royal Masonic Hospital; Hon. Curator, Historical Surgical Instruments Collection, Royal College of Surgeons, 1962; *b* Alford, Lincolnshire, 29 July 1897; *s* of William Riches; *m* 1st, 1927, Annie M. S. (*d* 1952), *d* of late Dr A. T. Brand, Driffield, E Yorks; two *d* ; 2nd, 1954, Susan Elizabeth Ann, *d* of Lt-Col L. H. Kitton, MBE, MC; one *d. Educ:* Christ's Hospital; Middlesex Hospital. Served European War, 10th Lincoln and 11th Suffolk Regt, Capt. and Adjutant (MC); Senior Broderip Scholar and Lyell Gold Medallist, Middlesex Hospital, 1925. Past Vice-President, Royal College of Surgeons, Member of Court of Examiners, 1940-46; Hunterian Professor 1938 and 1942, Jacksonian Prizeman, 1942; Bradshaw Lecturer, 1962; Gordon-Taylor Lecturer, 1967. Hon. Fellow Royal Society of Medicine, 1966, lately Hon. Librarian, ex-President Clinical Section, Section of Urology, and Section of Surgery. Past-President Medical Society of London; Lettsomian Lecturer, 1958, Orator, 1970; Senior Fellow Association of Surgeons of Great Britain and Ireland; Past President Hunterian Society, Orator, 1967; Vice-President, Internat. Soc. of Urology (Pres. XIII Congress, 1964); Hon. Fellow and Past Pres. of British Assoc. of Urological Surgeons; St Peters medallist, 1964; Member Association Française d'Urologie; Honorary Member: Urological Society of Australasia; Canadian Urological Assoc.; Swedish Urological Soc.; American Urological Assoc.; American Assoc. of Genito-Urinary Surgeons; Ramon Guitéras Lectr, 1963; Hon. Associate Mem. French Academy of Surgery, 1961; Emeritus Mem. Internat. Soc. of Surgery; Past Treas. British Journal of Surgery; Past Chm., Ed. Cttee, British Jl of Urology; Mem. of Biological and Medical Cttee, Royal Commission on Population. Visiting Professor, Urol.: University of Texas and State University of New York, 1965; Visiting Professor and Balfour Lecturer, University of Toronto, 1966. Treasurer, Christ's Hospital, and Chm., Council of Almoners, 1970-76. *Publications:* Modern Trends in Urology, Series 1, 1953, Series 2, 1960, Series 3, 1969; Tumours of the Kidney and Ureter, 1964; various articles on Surgery and Urology in Scientific journals; contributor to Text Book of Urology, British Surgical Practice, and to Encyclopædia of Urology. *Recreations:* golf, music, photography. *Address:* 22 Weymouth Street, W1N 3FA. *T:* 01-580 4800.

RICHES, General Sir Ian (Hurry), KCB 1960 (CB 1959); DSO 1945; *b* 27 Sept. 1908; *s* of C. W. H. Riches; *m* 1936, Winifred Eleanor Layton; two *s. Educ:* Univ. Coll. Sch., London. Joined Royal Marines, 1927; Major, 1946; Lt-Colonel, 1949; Colonel, 1953; Maj.-Gen., 1957; Lt-Gen. 1959; General 1961. Maj.-Gen., RM, Portsmouth Group, 1957-59; Commandant-General, Royal Marines, 1959-62; Regional Dir of Civil Defence, 1964-68; Representative Col Comdt, 1967-68. *Address:* Leith House, Old Hillside Road, Winchester, Hants.

RICHES, Rt. Rev. Kenneth, DD, STD; Assistant Bishop of Louisiana, USA, 1976-77; *b* 20 Sept. 1908; *s* of Capt. A. G. Riches; *m* 1942, Kathleen Mary Dixon, JP 1964; two *s* one *d. Educ:* Royal Gram. Sch., Colchester; Corpus Christi Coll., Cambridge. Curate of St Mary's, Portsea, 1932-35; St John's, East Dulwich, 1935-36; Chaplain and Librarian, Sidney Sussex Coll., Cambridge, 1936-42; Examining Chaplain to Bishops of Bradford and Wakefield, 1936; Editorial Sec., Cambridgeshire

Syllabus, 1935; Editor, Cambridge Review, 1941-42; Rector of Bredfield with Boulge, Suffolk, and Dir of Service Ordination Candidates, 1942-45; Principal of Cuddesdon Theological Coll., Oxford, and Vicar of Cuddesdon, 1945-52; Hon. Canon of Portsmouth Cathedral, 1950-52; Bishop Suffragan of Dorchester, Archdeacon of Oxford and Canon of Christ Church, 1952-56; Bishop of Lincoln, 1956-74. Select Preacher: University of Cambridge, 1941, 1948, 1961, and 1963; University of Oxford, 1954-55. Mem. Archbishops' Commission on Training for the Ministry, 1942; Sec. of Theol. Commn on the Church of Faith and Order Movement. Visiting Lecturer the General Theological Seminary, New York, 1956 and 1962. Hon. Fellow: Sidney Sussex Coll., Cambridge, 1958; Lincoln Coll., Oxford, 1975; Corpus Christi Coll., Cambridge, 1975. Chm., Central Advisory Council for the Ministry, 1959-65. *Recreations:* gardening, antiques, and country life. *Address:* Little Dingle, Dunwich, Saxmundham, Suffolk. *T:* Westleton 316. *Club:* Royal Automobile.

RICHLER, Mordecai; author; *b* 27 Jan. 1931; *s* of late Moses Isaac Richler and Lily Rosenberg; *m* 1960, Florence Wood; three *s* two *d. Educ:* Sir George Williams Univ., Montreal (left without degree). Writer-in-residence, Sir George Williams Univ., 1968-69; Vis. Prof., English Dept, Carleton Univ., Ottawa, 1972-74. Edit. Bd, Book-of-the-Month Club, NY. Canada Council Senior Arts Fellowship, 1960; Guggenheim Fellowship, Creative Writing, 1961; Governor-General's Award for Literature, 1969 and 1972; Paris Review Humour Prize, 1969. *Publications:* novels: The Acrobats, 1954; A Choice of Enemies, 1955; Son of a Smaller Hero, 1957; The Apprenticeship of Duddy Kravitz, 1959, repr. 1972 (filmed, Golden Bear Award, Berlin Film Fest., 1974; Writers Guild of America Annual Award, 1974; Academy Award nomination, 1974); The Incomparable Atuk, 1963; Cocksure, 1968; St Urbain's Horseman, 1971; *essays:* Hunting Tigers Under Glass, 1969; Shovelling Trouble, 1973; *autobiography:* The Street, 1972; *children's book:* Jacob Two-Two Meets the Hooded Fang, 1975; contrib. Encounter, Commentary, New York Review of Books, etc. *Recreations:* poker, snooker. *Address:* 218 Edgehill Road, Westmount 217, Que., Canada. *T:* 514-488-4774.

RICHMAN, Stella; Chairman, White Elephant Club Ltd, since 1951; Managing Director, Stella Richman Productions Ltd (Independent Television Production Co.), since 1972; *b* 9 Nov. 1922; *d* of Jacob Richman and Leoni Richman; *m* 1st, Alec Clunes; 2nd, 1953, Victor Brusa (*d* 1965); one *s* one *d. Educ:* Clapton County Secondary Sch. for Girls. Started TV career at ATV, running Script Dept 1960; created and produced Love Story, 1963; joined Rediffusion, 1964: produced The Hidden Truth, and Blackmail; Exec. Head of Series (prod The Informer); Exec. Prod., award-winning Man of Our Times and Half Hour Story; prod first 6 plays, Company of Five, for newly formed London Weekend Television, 1968; Man. Dir, London Weekend Internat., 1969, and Controller of Programmes, London Weekend Television, 1970-71 (first woman to sit on bd of a television co.); partnership with David Frost to form Stella Richman Productions, 1972: resp. for Miss Nightingale, Jennie Churchill, Clayhanger, Bill Brand, Fathers and Families, Just William. *Publication:* The White Elephant Cook Book, 1973. *Recreations:* reading, doing absolutely nothing. *Address:* 1 Audley House, 9 North Audley Street, W1Y 1WF. *T:* 01-499 3163. *Clubs:* White Elephant (owner), White Elephant on the River (owner).

RICHMOND, 9th Duke of, *cr* 1675, **and GORDON,** 4th Duke of, *cr* 1876; **Frederick Charles Gordon-Lennox;** Earl of March, Baron Settrington, Duke of Lennox, Earl of Darnley, Baron Methuen, 1675; Earl of Kinrara, 1876; Duke d'Aubigny (France), 1683-84; Hereditary Constable of Inverness Castle; Flight Lieut, RAFVR; *b* 5 Feb. 1904; *o* surv. *s* of 8th Duke and Hilda, DBE, *d* of late Henry Arthur Brassey, Preston Hall, Kent; *S* father, 1935; *m* 1927, Elizabeth Grace, *y d* of late Rev. T. W. Hudson; two *s. Educ:* Eton; Christ Church, Oxford. *Heir:* *s* Earl of March, qv. *Address:* Carne's Seat, Goodwood, Chichester, W Sussex; 29 Hyde Park Street, W2.
    See also Sir Alastair Coats, Bt, Lord N. C. Gordon Lennox, C. G. Vyner.

RICHMOND, Archdeacon of; *see* Burbridge, Ven. J. P.

RICHMOND, Sir Alan (James), Kt 1969; Principal, Strode College, since 1972; *b* 12 Oct. 1919. Trained and employed Engineering Industry, 1938-45; London Univ., BSc(Eng) 1945, PhD 1954; Lecturer, Battersea Polytechnic, 1946-55; Head of Engineering Dept, Welsh Coll. of Advanced Technology, 1955-58; Principal, Lanchester College of Technology, Coventry, 1959-69; Director, Lanchester Polytechnic, 1970-71. FIMechE. Hon. DSc CNAA, 1972. *Publications:* (with W. J. Peck)

Applied Thermodynamics Problems for Engineers, 1950; Problems in Heat Engines, 1957; various reviews and articles. *Recreations:* gardening, reading. *Address:* Strode College, Church Road, Street, Somerset. *Club:* Royal Commonwealth Society.

RICHMOND, Rt. Hon. Sir Clifford (Parris), PC 1973; KBE 1977; Kt 1972; **Rt. Hon. 'Mr Justice Richmond;** Judge of the Court of Appeal of New Zealand since 1972, President, since 1976; *b* 23 June 1914; *s* of Howard Parris Richmond, QC, and Elsie Wilhelmina (*née* MacTavish); *m* 1938, Valerie Jean Hamilton; two *s* one *d. Educ:* Wanganui Collegiate Sch.; Victoria and Auckland Univs. LLM (1st cl. Hons). Served War of 1939-45: 4 Field Regt 2NZEF, North Africa and Italy, 1942-45 (despatches, 1944). Partner, legal firm, Buddle Richmond & Co., Auckland, 1946-60. Judge of the Supreme Court of New Zealand, 1960-71. *Recreations:* golf, fishing. *Address:* 21 McFarlane Street, Mount Victoria, Wellington, New Zealand. *T:* 846-974. *Club:* Wellington (NZ).

RICHMOND, Rev. Canon Francis Henry Arthur, MA; Warden, Lincoln Theological College, and Canon and Prebendary of Lincoln Cathedral, since 1977; *b* 6 Jan. 1936; *s* of Frank and Lena Richmond; *m* 1966, Caroline Mary Berent; two *s* one *d. Educ:* Portora Royal School, Enniskillen; Trinity Coll., Dublin (MA); Univ. of Strasbourg (BTh); Linacre House, Oxford (BLitt); Wycliffe Hall, Oxford. Deacon, 1963; Priest, 1964; Asst Curate, Woodlands, Doncaster, 1963-66; Sir Henry Stephenson Research Fellow, Sheffield Univ. and Chaplain, Sheffield Cathedral, 1966-69; Vicar, St George's, Sheffield, 1969-77. Anglican Chaplain to Sheffield Univ. and Mem. Sheffield Chaplaincy for Higher Education, 1974-77. *Recreations:* listening to classical music, playing piano, reading, theatre, walking. *Address:* Lincoln Theological College, The Bishop's Hostel, Lincoln LN1 3BP. *T:* Lincoln 25879.

RICHMOND, Prof. John, MD, FRCPE, FRCP; Sir George Franklin Professor of Medicine, University of Sheffield, since 1973; *b* 30 May 1926; *er s* of late Hugh Richmond (Principal, Doncaster Tech. Coll., 1947-52), and Janet Hyslop Brown; *m* 1951, Jenny Nicol, 2nd *d* of T. Nicol; two *s* one *d. Educ:* Doncaster Grammar Sch.; Univ. of Edinburgh. MB, ChB 1948; MD 1963. FRCPE 1963, FRCP 1970. House Officer, in Edinburgh hosps and Northants, 1948-49, 1952-54; RAMC, Military Mission to Ethiopia, Captain 1st Bn King's African Rifles, N Rhodesia, 1949-50; Rural Gen. Practice, Galloway, Scotland, 1950-52; Res. Fellow, Meml Sloan Kettering Cancer Center, New York, 1958-59; Sen. Lectr, later Reader in Medicine, Univ. of Edinburgh, 1963-73. Visiting Prof. of Medicine: Univ. of Florida, 1968; Makerere Univ. Med. Sch., Uganda, 1971. High Constables of Edinburgh, 1961-70. *Publications:* Mem. Edit. Bd and contribs, A Companion to Medical Studies, ed R. Passmore and J. S. Robson, vols I-III, 1968-1974; contribs: Davidson's Principles and Practice of Medicine, 11th edn ed J. G. Macleod, 1974; Abdominal Operations, 6th edn ed Rodney Maingot, 1974; (jtly) The Spleen, 1973; papers in med. jls mainly on haematology and oncology. *Recreations:* gardening, photography, travel. *Address:* Stumper Lea, 42 Stumperlowe Hall Road, Sheffield S10 3QS. *T:* Sheffield 301395.

RICHMOND, Sir John (Christopher Blake), KCMG 1963 (CMG 1959); retired; *b* 7 September 1909; *s* of E. T. Richmond, FRIBA, and M. M. Richmond (*née* Lubbock); *m* 1939, D. M. L. Galbraith; two *s* three *d. Educ:* Lancing College; Hertford College, Oxford; University College, London. Various archaeological expeditions, 1931-36; HM Office of Works, 1937-39; served War, Middle East, 1939-46; Dept of Antiquities, Palestine Govt, 1946-47; HM Diplomatic Service, Baghdad, 1947; Foreign Office, 1951; Counsellor, British Embassy, Amman, 1953-55; HM Consul-General, Houston, Texas, 1955-58; Foreign Office, 1958-59; Counsellor, British Property Commission, Cairo, 1959; HM Ambassador to Kuwait, 1961-63 (Political Agent, Kuwait, 1959-61); Supernumerary Fellow of St Antony's College, Oxford, 1963-64; Ambassador to Sudan, 1965-66; Lectr, Modern Near East History, Sch. of Oriental Studies, Univ. of Durham, 1966-74. *Address:* 20 The Avenue, Durham City DH1 4ED.

RICHMOND, Sir John (Frederick), 2nd Bt, *cr* 1929; *b* 12 Aug. 1924; *s* of Sir Frederick Henry Richmond, 1st Bt (formerly Chm. Debenham's Ltd and Harvey Nichols & Co. Ltd), and Dorothy Agnes, *d* of Frances Joseph Sheppard; *S* father 1953; *m* 1965, Mrs Anne Moreen Bentley; one *d. Educ:* Eton; Jesus Coll., Cambridge. Lt 10th Roy. Hussars; seconded Provost br., 1944-47. *Address:* Shimpling Park Farm, Bury St Edmunds, Suffolk. *Club:* Cavalry.

RICHMOND, Prof. Mark Henry, MRCPath; Professor of Bacteriology, University of Bristol, since 1968; *b* 1 Feb. 1931; *s* of Harold Sylvester Richmond and Dorothy Plaistowe Richmond; *m* 1958, Shirley Jean Townrow; one *s* two *d. Educ:* Epsom College; Clare Coll., Cambridge. BA, PhD, ScD. Scientific Staff, MRC, 1958-65; Reader in Molecular Biology, Univ. of Edinburgh, 1965-68. *Publications:* several in microbiology and biochemistry jls. *Recreation:* hill-walking. *Address:* 117 Eastfield Road, Westbury on Trym, Bristol BS9 4AN. *T:* Bristol 628227.

RICHMOND, Vice-Adm. Sir Maxwell, KBE 1957 (OBE 1940); CB 1954; DSO 1942; RN retired; *b* 19 Oct. 1900; *e s* of Robert Richardson Richmond and Bernadette Richmond (*née* Farrell); *m* 1929, Jessie Messervy Craig; one *s* three *d* (and one *s* decd). *Educ:* New Zealand State Schools; Westminster. Cadet Royal Navy 1918; Lieutenant 1922; specialised navigation; held various (N) posts, 1926-36. Comdr 1936; HMS Hostile in Comd, 1936-38; Staff Coll., 1939; HMS Basilisk in Comd, 1939-40; Dover Patrol, Norway and Dunkirk; Operations, Admty, 1940-41; HMS Bulldog as Sen. Officer Escort Gp, 1942, Atlantic and Russian Convoys; Capt. 1942; Chief Staff Officer to Cdre, Londonderry, 1943; HMS Milne as Capt. (D) 3rd Dest. Flot., 1944-46; Home Fleet, Russian Convoys and Flank Force, Mediterranean; Asst Chief of Supplies, Admty, 1946-48; Naval Liaison Officer, Wellington, NZ, 1948-50; Sen. Naval Officer, N Ire., 1951; Rear-Adm. 1952; Deputy Chief of Naval Personnel (Training), 1952-55; Flag Officer (Air), Mediterranean, and Flag Officer Second-in-Command, Mediterranean Fleet, 1955-Oct. 1956. Order of the Red Banner (Russian) 1942; Croix de Guerre (French) 1945. *Recreations:* sailing and tramping. *Address:* No 4 Rural Delivery, Whangarei, New Zealand. *Club:* Naval and Military.

RICHNELL, Donovan Thomas, CBE 1973; Director General, British Library Reference Division, since 1974; *b* 3 Aug. 1911; *o s* of Thomas Hodgson Richnell and Constance Margaret Richnell (*née* Allen); *m* 1957, Renée Norma Hilton; one *s* one *d. Educ:* St Paul's School; Corpus Christi Coll., Cambridge; University Coll., London (Fellow 1975). BA, FLA. Library Asst, Royal Soc. Med., 1934-35; Asst Librarian, Nat. Library of Scotland, 1935-46; Sub-Librarian, Royal Soc. Med., 1946-49; Dep. Librarian, London Univ. Library, 1949-60; Librarian, Univ. of Reading, 1960-67; Dir, and Goldsmiths' Librarian, Univ. of London Library, 1967-74. Sec. to Regional Comr for Civil Defence, Scotland, 1939-40. Royal Navy, 1942-46; Lieut (sp.) RNVR. Detached service with US Army X Corps, New Guinea and Philippines, 1944-45 (US Bronze Star, Philippines campaign, 1945). Library Association: Mem. Council, 1962-; President 1970; Hon. Sec., U and R Section, 1961-65; National and University Libraries Committee: Chm., 1962-66; Aslib: Mem. Council, 1951-75; Hon. Sec., 1957-63, 1973-75; Chm. of Council, 1968-70. Member: Library Adv. Council for England, 1966-71, 1974-; Nat. Central Library Exec. Cttee, 1964-73; British Library Organising Cttee, 1971-73; Adv. Cttee for Scientific and Technical Information, 1970-74; British Library Bd, 1974-; Chm., Standing Conf. of Nat. and Univ. Libraries, 1973-75. Hon. DLitt Loughborough, 1977. *Publications:* various articles. *Recreations:* music, theatre. *Address:* 2 Queen Anne's Gardens, Bedford Park, W4.

RICHTER, Prof. Burton; Professor of Physics, Stanford University, USA, since 1967; *b* 22 March 1931; *s* of Abraham Richter and Fannie Pollack; *m* 1960, Laurose Becker; one *s* one *d. Educ:* Massachusetts Inst. of Technology. BS 1952, PhD (Physics) 1956. Stanford University: Research Associate, Physics, High Energy Physics Lab., 1956-60; Asst Prof., 1960-63; Associate Prof., 1963-67; full Prof., 1967. E. O. Lawrence Award, 1975; Nobel Prize for Physics (jointly), 1976. *Publications:* over 80 articles in various scientific journals. *Address:* Stanford Linear Accelerator Center, PO Box 4349, Stanford University, Stanford, California 94305, USA.

RICHTER, Hon. Sir Harold, Kt 1971; Minister for Local Government and Conservation, Queensland, 1963-69; MLA for Somerset, Queensland, 1957-72; *b* 17 Jan. 1906; *s* of F. Richter; *m* 1933, Gladys, *d* of A. James; two *s* two *d. Educ:* Ipswich Gram. Sch., Qld. Minister for Public Works and Local Govt, Qld, 1961-63. Chairman: Boonah Shire Council, 1943-47; Boonah Show Soc., 1944-57. Vice-Pres., 1951-55, Pres., 1956-60, Queensland Div. Australian Country Party. *Recreation:* bowls. *Address:* 20 Wills Street, Coorparoo, Brisbane, Qld 4000, Australia. *Club:* Brisbane.

RICHTER, Sviatoslav; Hero of Socialist Labour, 1975; pianist; *b* Zhitomir, Ukraine, 20 March 1915; *m* Nina Dorliak. *Educ:* Moscow State Conservatoire. Gave first piano recital at age of nineteen and began to give concerts on a wide scale in 1942.

Appeared at the Royal Albert Hall and the Royal Festival Hall, London, 1961; Royal Festival Hall, 1963, 1966, 1977. Was recently awarded Lenin Prize, and also holds the title of "Peoples' Artist of the USSR"; Order of Lenin, 1965. *Recreations:* walking, ski-ing and painting. *Address:* c/o Victor Hochhauser Ltd, 4 Holland Park Avenue, W11.

RICKARDS, Oscar Stanley Norman, CBE 1945; Grand Officer in the Order of Orange-Nassau, 1947; Haakon VII Liberty Cross, 1947; Director of Victualling, Admiralty, 1941-58; *b* 14 Nov. 1893; *s* of Thomas Rickards and Laura Rose Short; *m* 1925, Sylvia Annie Dean; one *d. Educ:* University College School, Hampstead. Joined Admiralty, 1913. *Address:* Little Thresholds, Hawkshill Way, Esher, Surrey. *T:* 64914.

RICKETT, Sir Denis Hubert Fletcher, KCMG 1956 (CMG 1947); CB 1951; Director: Schroder International, since 1974; De La Rue Co., since 1974; Adviser, J. Henry Schroder Wagg & Co., since 1974; *b* 27 July 1907; *s* of late Hubert Cecil Rickett, OBE, JP; *m* 1946, Ruth Pauline (MB, BS, MRCS, LRCP), *d* of late William Anderson Armstrong, JP; two *s* one *d. Educ:* Rugby School; Balliol College, Oxford. Fellow of All Souls College, Oxford, 1929-49. Joined staff of Economic Advisory Council, 1931; Offices of War Cabinet, 1939; Principal Private Secretary to Right Honourable Oliver Lyttelton, when Minister of Production, 1943-45; Personal Assistant (for work on Atomic Energy) to Rt Hon. Sir John Anderson, when Chancellor of the Exchequer, 1945; transferred to Treasury, 1947; Principal Private Secretary to the Rt Hon. C. R. Attlee, when Prime Minister, 1950-51; Economic Minister, British Embassy, Washington, and Head of UK Treasury and Supply Delegation, 1951-54; Third Secretary, HM Treasury, 1955-60, Second Secretary, 1960-68. Vice-Pres., IBRD, 1968-74. *Recreation:* music. *Address:* The Maltings, Ugley, near Bishops Stortford, Herts. *T:* Rickling 261. *Clubs:* Athenæum, Brooks's.

RICKETT, Dr Raymond Mildmay Wilson, BSc, PhD, CChem, FRIC; Director, Middlesex Polytechnic, since 1972; *b* 17 March 1927; *s* of Mildmay Louis Rickett and Winifred Georgina Rickett; *m* 1958, Naomi Nishida; one *s* two *d. Educ:* Faversham Grammar Sch.; Medway Coll. of Technology (BSc London); Illinois Inst. of Technology (PhD). Royal Navy, 1946-48; Medway Coll. of Technology, 1953-55; Illinois Inst. of Technology, 1955-59; Plymouth Coll. of Technology, 1959; Lectr, Liverpool Coll. of Technology, 1960-62; Senr Lectr/Principal Lectr, West Ham Coll. of Technology, 1962-64; Head of Dept, Wolverhampton Coll. of Technology, 1965-66; Vice-Principal, Sir John Cass Coll., 1967-69; Vice-Provost, City of London Polytechnic, 1969-72. British Rep., UNESCO Adv. Cttee, European Centre for Higher Educn; Member: Inter-Univ. Council for Higher Educn Overseas; Working Gp, Management of Higher Educn (Oakes Cttee); Chm., Acad. Affairs Bd, Cttee of Dirs of Polytechnics. FRSA. Governor, Live Music Now. *Publications:* Experimental in Physical Chemistry (jtly), 1962, new edn 1968; 2 chapters in The Use of the Chemical Literature, 1962, new edn 1969; articles on Polytechnics in the national press and contribs to learned jls. *Recreations:* cricket, theatregoing, opera. *Address:* Principal's Lodge, Trent Park, Cockfosters Road, Barnet, Herts EN4 0PS. *T:* 01-449 9012.

RICKETTS, Maj.-Gen. Abdy Henry Gough, CBE 1952; DSO 1945; DL; *b* 8 Dec. 1905; *s* of Lt-Col P. E. Ricketts, DSO, MVO, and L. C. Ricketts (née Morant); *m* 1932, Joan Warre, *d* of E. T. Close, Camberley; one *s* one *d. Educ:* Winchester. Sandhurst, 1924; Durham LI, 1925; Shanghai Defence Force, 1927; NW Frontier, India (medal and clasp), 1930; Burma "Chindit" campaign, 1944-45; Gen. Service Medal and clasp, Malaya, 1950; comd British Brigade, Korea, 1952; Comdr (temp. Maj.-Gen.), Cyprus District, 1955-56. Col, Durham LI, 1965-68; Dep. Col, The Light Infantry (Durham), 1968-70. DL Somerset, 1968. Officer, Legion of Merit (USA), 1953. *Address:* The Old Rectory, Pylle, Shepton Mallet, Som. *T:* Ditcheat 248. *Club:* Army and Navy.

RICKETTS, Michael Rodney, MA; Headmaster, Sutton Valence School, since Sept. 1967; *b* 29 Sept. 1923; *er s* of late Rt Rev. C. M. Ricketts, Bishop of Dunwich, and of Mrs Ricketts; *m* 1958, Judith Anne Caroline Corry; two *s* two *d. Educ:* Sherborne; Trinity Coll., Oxford. Served War of 1939-45: in 8th Army with 60th Rifles, 1942-47. Trinity Coll., Oxford, 1947-50; Asst Master and Housemaster, Bradfield Coll., 1950-67. *Recreations:* cricket, shooting, country activities. *Address:* Headmaster's House, Sutton Valence School, near Maidstone, Kent. *T:* Sutton Valence 2281. *Clubs:* East India, Devonshire, Sports and Public Schools, MCC.

RICKETTS, Sir Robert (Cornwallis Gerald St Leger), 7th Bt, *cr* 1828; retired Solicitor; *b* 8 Nov. 1917; *s* of Sir Claude Albert

Frederick Ricketts, 6th Bt, and Lilian Helen Gwendoline (*d* 1955), *o d* of Arthur M. Hill, late 5th Fusiliers; *S* father 1937; *m* 1945, Anne Theresa, *d* of late Rt Hon. Sir Richard Stafford Cripps, PC, CH, FRS, QC; two *s* two *d. Educ:* Haileybury; Magdalene College, Cambridge (2nd Cl. Hons in History and Law, BA 1939, MA 1943). Served War of 1939-45 (Captain, Devon Regiment); Personal Assistant to Chief of Staff, Gibraltar, 1942-45; ADC to Lieutenant-Governor of Jersey, 1945-46. Formerly Partner in Wellington and Clifford. FRSA. Hon. Citizen, Mobile, USA, 1970. *Heir: s* Robert Tristram Ricketts [*b* 17 April 1946; *m* 1969, Ann, *yr d* of E. W. C. Lewis, *qv*; one *s* one *d*]. *Address:* Forwood House, Minchinhampton, Glos. *TA* and *T:* Brimscombe 2160.

RICKFORD, Richard Braithwaite Keevil, MD (London), BS, FRCS, FRCOG; Physician in charge, Obstetric Department, St Thomas' Hospital, London, since 1946; Surgeon, Chelsea Hospital for Women, since 1950; Gynæcologist, Oxted Hospitals, since 1952; Dean, Institute of Obstetrics and Gynaecology; *b* 1 June 1914; *e s* of late L. T. R. Rickford; *m* 1939, Dorothy, *d* of late Thomas Lathan; three *s* (and one *s* decd). *Educ:* Weymouth College; University of London. Various surgical, obstetric and gynæcological appointments at Norfolk and Norwich Hospital and St Thomas' Hospital. Examiner to: Universities of London, Cambridge and Glasgow; Royal Coll. of Obstetricians and Gynæcologists; Conjoint Board; Central Midwives Board. *Publications:* contributions to medical journals. *Recreations:* winter sports, sailing. *Address:* 100 Harley Street, W1. *T:* 01-935 8422; 25 Stormont Road, Highgate, N6. *T:* 01-340 9700. *Club:* Royal Dart Yacht (Kingswear, Devon).

RICKS, Prof. Christopher Bruce, FBA 1975; Professor of English, University of Cambridge, since 1975; *b* 18 Sept. 1933; *s* of James Bruce Ricks and Gabrielle Roszak; *m* 1956, Kirsten Jensen (marr. diss.); two *s* two *d. Educ:* King Alfred's Sch., Wantage; Balliol Coll., Oxford. 2nd Lieut, Green Howards, 1952. BA 1956, BLitt 1958, MA 1960, Oxon. Andrew Bradley Jun. Res. Fellow, Balliol Coll., Oxford, 1957; Fellow of Worcester Coll., Oxford, 1958-68; Prof. of English, Bristol Univ., 1968-75. Visiting Professor: Berkeley and Stanford, 1965; Smith Coll., 1967; Harvard, 1971; Wesleyan, 1974; Brandeis, 1977. A Vice-Pres., Tennyson Soc. Co-editor, Essays in Criticism. *Publications:* Milton's Grand Style, 1963; (ed) The Poems of Tennyson, 1969; Tennyson, 1972; Keats and Embarrassment, 1974. *Address:* Christ's College, Cambridge; Gorse Cottage, High Street, Little Eversden, Cambs. *T:* Comberton 2350; Lasborough Cottage, Lasborough Park, near Tetbury, Glos. *T:* Leighterton 252.

RICKS, Sir John (Plowman), Kt 1964; Solicitor to the Post Office, 1953-72; *b* 3 April 1910; *s* of late James Young Ricks; *m* 1st, 1936, May Celia (*d* 1975), *d* of late Robert William Chubb; three *s*; 2nd, 1976, Mrs Doreen Ilsley. *Educ:* Christ's Hosp.; Jesus Coll., Oxford. Admitted Solicitor, 1935; entered Post Office Solicitor's Department, 1935; Assistant Solicitor, Post Office, 1951. *Address:* 8 Sunset View, Barnet, Herts. *T:* 01-449 6114.

RIDDELL, Sir John (Charles Buchanan), 13th Bt, *cr* 1628; Chartered Accountant; with First Boston (Europe) Ltd, since 1972, Director since 1975; Director, United Kingdom Provident Institution, since 1975; *b* 3 Jan. 1934; *o s* of Sir Walter Buchanan Riddell, 12th Bt, and Hon. Rachel Beatrice Lyttelton (*d* 1965), *y d* of 8th Viscount Cobham; *S* father 1934; *m* 1969, Sarah, *o d* of Rt Hon. Gordon Richardson, *qv*; two *s. Educ:* Eton; Christ Church, Oxford. Contested (C): Durham NW, Feb. 1974; Sunderland S, Oct. 1974. *Heir: s* Walter John Buchanan, *b* 10 June 1974. *Address:* Hepple, Morpeth, Northumberland. *TA:* Hepple; 31 Woodsford Square W14. *Club:* Beefsteak.
See also Sir J. L. Pumphrey.

RIDDELL-WEBSTER, John Alexander, MC 1943; Deputy Managing Director, BP Oil Ltd, since 1976; *b* 17 July 1921; *s* of Gen. Sir Thomas Riddell-Webster, GCB, DSO; *m* 1960, Ruth, *d* of late S. P. L. A. Lithgow; two *s* one *d. Educ:* Harrow; Pembroke Coll., Cambridge. Seaforth Highlanders (Major), 1940-46. Joined Anglo-Iranian Oil Co., 1946; served in Iran, Iraq, Bahrain, Aden; Vice-Pres. Marketing, BP Canada, 1959; Dir, Shell-Mex and BP, 1965, Man. Dir, Marketing, 1971-75. Member of Council: Advertising Assoc.; Inc. Soc. of British Advertisers; for Vehicle Servicing and Repair (Chm., 1975); Royal Warrent Holders' Assoc.; British Road Fedn; Pres., Oil Industries Club. FBIM. *Recreations:* shooting, fishing, gardening. *Address:* Fewells, Fuller Street, Fairstead, Chelmsford, Essex. *T:* Great Leighs 440. *Club:* Perth Golfing Society.

RIDDELSDELL, Dame Mildred, DCB 1972; CBE 1958; Second Permanent Secretary, Department of Health and Social Security, 1971-73; (Deputy Secretary, 1966-71); *b* 1 Dec. 1913; 2nd *d* of Rev. H. J. Riddelsdell. *Educ:* St Mary's Hall, Brighton; Bedford Coll., London. Entered Min. of Labour, 1936; Asst Sec., Min. of National Insurance, 1945; Under Secretary, 1950; On loan to United Nations, 1953-56; Secretary, National Incomes Commission, 1962-65; Ministry of Pensions and National Insurance, 1965, Social Security, 1966. Chm., CS Retirement Fellowship, 1974-77. *Recreation:* gardening. *Address:* 26A New Yatt Road, Witney, Oxon.

RIDDLE, Hugh Joseph, (Huseph), RP 1960; Artist; Portrait Painter; *b* 24 May 1912; *s* of late Hugh Howard Riddle and late Christine Simons Brown; *m* 1936, Joan Claudia Johnson; one *s* two *d*. *Educ:* Harrow; Magdalen, Oxford; Slade School of Art; Byam Shaw School of Art and others. *Recreations:* sailing, skiing, swimming, tennis, golf. *Address:* 18 Boulevard Verdi, Domaine du château de Tournon, Montauroux 83710, France.

RIDDOCH, John Haddow, CMG 1963; Under-Secretary, Board of Trade, 1966-69, retired; *b* 4 Feb. 1909; *s* of Joseph Riddoch, Gourock, Renfrewshire; *m* 1st, 1938, Isobel W. Russell (*d* 1972); one *s* two *d*; 2nd, 1975, Margaret C. McKimmie. *Educ:* Greenock Acad.; Glasgow Univ. Entered Inland Revenue Dept (Inspectorate of Taxes), 1932; Asst Principal in Air Ministry (Dept of Civil Aviation), 1939; Principal, 1942; Asst Sec., Min. of Civil Aviation, 1945; Under-Sec., Min. of Transport and Civil Aviation, 1957, Min. of Aviation, 1959; United Kingdom Representative on the Council of the ICAO, 1957-62 (First Vice-Pres. of Council, 1961-62); Under-Sec., Min. of Aviation, 1962-66. *Recreations:* music, bowls, gardening. *Address:* 10 The Fairway, New Barnet, Herts EN5 1HN.

RIDEALGH, Mrs Mabel; General Secretary of Women's Co-operative Guild, 1953-63; Member, Women's Advisory Committee, British Standards Institute, 1953-63; *b* 11 Aug. 1898; *d* of M. A. Jewitt, Wallsend-on-Tyne, Northumberland; *m* 1919, Leonard, *s* of W. R. Ridealgh, Sunderland, Durham; one *s* one *d*. National Pres. Women's Co-op. Guild, 1941-42; Hon. Regional Organiser Bd of Trade (Make-do and Mend), 1942-44; MP (Lab) Ilford North, 1945-50. *Address:* 2 Eastwood Rd, Goodmayes, Ilford, Essex. *T:* 01-599 8960.

RIDEOUT, Prof. Roger William; Professor of Labour Law, University College, London, since 1973; *b* 9 Jan. 1935; *s* of Sidney and Hilda Rideout; *m* 1959, Marjorie Roberts (marr. diss. 1976); one *d*. *Educ:* Bedford School; University Coll., London (LLB, PhD). Called to the Bar, Gray's Inn, 1964. National Service, 1958-60; 2nd Lt RAEC, Educn Officer, 1st Bn Coldstream Guards. Lecturer: Univ. of Sheffield, 1960-63; Univ. of Bristol, 1963-64. University Coll., London: Sen. Lectr, 1964-65; Reader, 1965-73; Dean of Faculty of Laws, 1975-77. Dep. Chm., Central Arbitration Cttee. Chairman, Industrial Law Society, 1977-. *Publications:* The Right to Membership of a Trade Union, 1962; The Practice and Procedure of the NIRC, 1973; Trade Unions and the Law, 1973; Principles of Labour Law, 1972 (2nd edn, 1976); (ed, with Lord Lloyd of Hampstead) Current Legal Problems. *Recreations:* fishing, gardening. *Address:* 63 Wood Lane, Highgate, N6 5UD. *T:* 01-340 1694.

RIDGE, Anthony Hubert; Director-General, International Bureau, Universal Postal Union, Bern, 1973-74 (Deputy Director-General, 1964-73); *b* 5 Oct. 1913; *s* of Timothy Leopold Ridge and Magdalen (*née* Hernig); *m* 1938, Marjory Joan Sage; three *s* one *d*. *Educ:* Christ's Hospital; Jesus College, Cambridge. Asst Principal in GPO and Ministry of Home Security, 1937-42; Principal in Ministry of Home Security and GPO, 1942-47; Principal Private Sec. to PMG, Secretary to Post Office Board, 1947-49; Dep. Regional Director, London Postal Region, 1949-51; Asst Secretary, mainly in international Postal Service, 1951-60; Director of Clerical Mechanization and Buildings, and Member of Post Office Board, GPO, 1960-63. Governor, Christ's Hosp. *Recreations:* music, languages, transport, gardening. *Address:* Staple, Postling, Hythe, Kent. *T:* Lyminge 862315. *Clubs:* Christ's Hospital, United Oxford & Cambridge University, Cambridge Society.

RIDGERS, John Nalton Sharpe; Deputy Chairman and Treasurer, Lloyd's Register of Shipping, since 1973; Director: London Trust Co. Ltd, since 1963; Smit International (UK) Ltd, since 1974; Arbuthnot Insurance Services Ltd, since 1974; Danae Investment Trust Ltd, since 1975; *b* 10 June 1910; 4th *c* and *o s* of Sharpe Ridgers; *m* 1936, Barbara Mary, *o d* of Robert Cobb; five *d*. *Educ:* Wellington College. Entered Lloyd's, 1928; underwriting member, 1932. Member Cttee Lloyd's Underwriters' Association, 1951-61, 1964-69, Chm. 1961; Member Joint Hull Cttee, 1957-69, Dep. Chm., 1968, Chm.,

1969. Mem. Cttee of Lloyd's, 1957-60, 1962-65, Dep. Chm., 1962, Chm., 1963. *Recreations:* rackets, squash and lawn tennis. *Address:* Watlynge, Dyants Lane, Bitchet Green, near Sevenoaks, Kent. *T:* Sevenoaks 61353.

RIDGWAY, Gen. Matthew Bunker, DSC (with Oak Leaf Cluster); DSM (with 3rd Oak Leaf Cluster); Silver Star (with Oak Leaf Cluster); Legion of Merit; Bronze Star Medal (with Oak Leaf Cluster); Purple Heart; Hon. KCB 1955 (Hon. CB 1945); Chairman of The Mellon Institute of Industrial Research 1955-60, retired; *b* 3 March 1895; *s* of Thomas Ridgway and Ruth Starbuck Bunker; *m* 1930; one *d*; *m* 1947, Mary Anthony; (one *s* decd). *Educ:* United States Military Academy, 1913-17. Inf. School (Company Officers' Course), 1924-25; Mem. Am. Electoral Commn, Nicaragua, 1927-28; Mem. Commn on Bolivian-Paraguayan boundary dispute, 1929; Inf. School (Advanced Course), 1929-30; Liaison Officer to Govt in Philippine Is, Tech. Adviser to Gov.-Gen., 1932-33; Comd and Gen. Staff School, 1933-35; Asst Chief of Staff, 6th Corps Area, 1935-36; Dep. Chief of Staff, Second Army, 1936; Army War College, 1936-37; Assistant Chief of Staff, Fourth Army, 1937-39; accompanied Gen. Marshall on special mission to Brazil, 1939; War Plans Div., War Department Gen. Staff, 1939-42; Asst Div. Comdr, 82nd Inf. Div., 1942; Comdr 1942; Comdg Gen. 82nd Airborne Div., Sicily, Italy, Normandy, 1942-44; Comdr 18th Airborne Corps, Belgium, France, Germany, 1944-45; Comdr Luzon Area Command, 1945; Comdr Medit. Theater, and Dep. Supreme Allied Comdr, Medit., 1945-46; Senior US Army Member Military Staff Cttee, UN, 1946-48; Chm. Inter-Am. Defense Bd, 1946-48; C-in-C Caribbean Command, 1948-49; Dep. Army Chief of Staff for Admin., 1949-50 (and Chm. Inter-Am. Defense Bd, 1950); Comdg Gen. Eighth Army in Korea, 1950-51; Comdr UN Comd in Far East, C-in-C of Far East Comd and Supreme Comdr for Allied Powers in Japan, 1951-52; Supreme Allied Comdr, Europe, 1952-53; Chief of Staff, United States Army, 1953-55, retired. Holds many American and foreign decorations. *Address:* 918 W Waldheim Road, Fox Chapel, Pittsburgh, Pa 15215, USA.

RIDING, George A., MA; Headmaster, Aldenham School, 1933-July 1949; *b* 1 April 1888; *s* of Daniel A. Riding and Anne Deighton; *m* Aideen Maud, *d* of T. W. Rolleston, *g d* of late Rev. Stopford Brooke; two *s*. *Educ:* Manchester Grammar School (Scholar); University of Manchester (MA Hons English Language and Literature); New College, Oxford, 1st Class Honours, Modern Languages (French and German), 1921, Heath Harrison Travelling Scholarship, 1920; President, Oxford University French Club, 1920; Assistant Master: Penarth County Sch., 1909-14; Mill Hill School, 1914-15; Rugby School, 1921-28 (Sixth Form Master); served with Northumberland Fusiliers (wounded); Registrar, King's Lancashire Military Convalescent Hospital, 1917-18; Captain in Rugby School OTC; Headmaster, Warwick School, 1928-33. Member of House of Laity, Church Assembly, 1944. Member of Council, Inc. Assoc. of Head Masters, 1942-44. Foundation Member of Hispanic Council. Member School Broadcasting Council, 1947-58; Chairman Secondary Programmes Committee, 1947-54. Chairman: Cornwall Modern Churchmen's Union, 1950; Truro Divisional Liberal Association, 1950-51; Cornwall Liberal Council, 1950; Minack Theatre Society, 1960-66; E Cornwall Society for the Mentally Handicapped, 1960-66. Carried out (with headmaster of Fettes Coll.) survey of pre-service educn in Pakistan, 1951. *Publications:* Blackie's Longer French Texts; Les Trois Mousquetaires; La Bête dans les Neiges; Moral Foundations of Citizenship; contrib. to Naval Review, Spectator. *Address:* Colona, Port Mellon, Mevagissey, St Austell, Cornwall PL26 6PH. *T:* Mevagissey 3440.

RIDING, Laura, (Mrs Schuyler B. Jackson); *b* New York City, 16 Jan. 1901; American mother and naturalised (Austrian-born) father (Nathaniel S. Reichenthal); *m* 1941, Schuyler B. Jackson (*d* 1968) (American writer; poetry-editor of Time, 1938-43). *Educ:* American public schools; Cornell University. First published poems in American poetry magazines; member of group of Southern poets, The Fugitives; went to England in 1926, remaining abroad until 1939; engaging in writing and allied activities, seeking a single terminology of truth to supersede our confused terminological diversity (*eg*, as Editor of Epilogue, a critical miscellany); was co-operator of Seizin Press, first author of A Survey of Modernist Poetry (Robert Graves, collaborator), 1927; devoted herself to helping other poets with their work. Has since renounced poetry as humanly inadequate and concentrated on direct linguistic handling of truth-problem, studying ways to intensify people's consciousness of word-meanings; working long with husband on a book in which the principles of language and the principles of definition are brought into relation, which she has now completed, under the title Rational Meaning: A New Foundation for the Definition of

Words (publishing arrangements pending). Mark Rothko Appreciation Award, 1971; Guggenheim Fellowship award, 1973. *Publications include:* (as Laura Riding, until 1941, thereafter as Laura (Riding) Jackson) individual books of poems (10), from 1926; Contemporaries and Snobs, 1928; Anarchism Is Not Enough, 1928; Experts are Puzzled, 1930; Progress of Stories, 1935; Trojan Ending, 1937; The World and Ourselves, 1938; Collected Poems, 1938; Lives of Wives, 1939; The Telling (a personal evangel-complete magazine publication, Chelsea, USA), 1967, enl. edn in book form, UK 1972, USA 1973; Selected Poems: in five sets, 1970, USA 1973; Writings of 50 Years—Author's Miscellany, entire biannual issue, Chelsea (USA), autumn 1976; contribs to magazines. *Address:* Box 35, Wabasso, Florida 32970, USA.

RIDLER, Anne (Barbara); author; *b* 30 July 1912; *o d* of late H. C. Bradby, housemaster of Rugby School, and Violet Milford; *m* 1938, Vivian Ridler, *qv*; two *s* two *d*. *Educ:* Downe House School; King's College, London; and in Florence and Rome. *Publications: poems:* Poems, 1939; A Dream Observed, 1941; The Nine Bright Shiners, 1943; The Golden Bird, 1951; A Matter of Life and Death, 1959; Selected Poems (New York), 1961; Some Time After, 1972; *plays:* Cain, 1943; The Shadow Factory, 1946; Henry Bly and other plays, 1950; The Trial of Thomas Cranmer, 1956; Who is my Neighbour?, 1963; The Jesse Tree (libretto), 1972; The King of the Golden River (libretto), 1975; *translations:* Italian opera libretti: Rosinda, 1973; Orfeo, 1975; Eritrea, 1975; *biography:* Olive Willis and Downe House, 1967; *Editor:* Shakespeare Criticism, 1919-35; A Little Book of Modern Verse, 1941; Best Ghost Stories, 1945; Supplement to Faber Book of Modern Verse, 1951; The Image of the City and other essays by Charles Williams, 1958; Shakespeare Criticism 1935-60, 1963; Poems of James Thomson, 1963; Thomas Traherne, 1966; (with Christopher Bradby) Best Stories of Church and Clergy, 1966; Poems of George Darley, 1977. *Recreations:* music; the theatre; the cinema. *Address:* 14 Stanley Road, Oxford.

RIDLER, Vivian Hughes, CBE 1971; MA Oxon 1958 (by decree; Corpus Christi College); Printer to the University of Oxford, 1958 until Sept. 1978; *b* 2 Oct. 1913; *s* of Bertram Hughes Ridler and Elizabeth Emmeline (*née* Best); *m* 1938, Anne Barbara Bradby (*see* A. B. Ridler); two *s* two *d*. *Educ:* Bristol Gram. Sch. Appren. E. S. & A. Robinson, Ltd, 1931-36. Works Manager University Press, Oxford, 1948; Assistant Printer, 1949-58. Pres., British Federation of Master Printers, 1968-69. Professorial Fellow, St Edmund Hall, 1966. *Recreations:* printing, theatre, cinema, cinematography. *Address:* 14 Stanley Road, Oxford. *T:* Oxford 47595.

RIDLEY, family name of **Viscount Ridley.**

RIDLEY, 4th Viscount, *cr* 1900; **Matthew White Ridley,** TD 1960; DL; Baron Wensleydale, *cr* 1900; Bt 1756; *b* 29 July 1925; *e s* of 3rd Viscount Ridley; *S* father, 1964; *m* 1953, Lady Anne Lumley, 3rd *d* of 11th Earl of Scarbrough, KG, PC, GCSI, GCIE, GCVO; one *s* three *d*. *Educ:* Eton; Balliol College, Oxford. Captain, Coldstream Guards, 1946; Bt-Col Northumberland Hussars (TA). Pres., North Eastern Housing Assoc. Ltd; Director: Northern Rock Building Society; Tyne Tees Television; Barclays Bank (NE) Ltd. Pres., British Deer Soc., 1970-73. Mem., Layfield Cttee of Enquiry into Local Govt Finance, 1974-. JP 1957, CC 1958, CA 1963, DL 1968, Northumberland; Chm., Northumberland CC, 1967-74, Chm., new Northumberland CC, 1974-. *Heir: s* Hon. Matthew White Ridley, *b* 7 Feb. 1958. *Address:* Blagdon, Seaton Burn, Northumberland. *T:* Stannington 236. *Clubs:* Turf, Pratts; Northern Counties (Newcastle upon Tyne).
See also Hon. Nicholas Ridley.

RIDLEY, Arnold; dramatic author, actor, and producer; *b* Bath, 7 January 1896; *s* of late William Robert Ridley and Rosa Morrish; *m* Althea Parker; one *s*. *Educ:* Bristol University. Formerly a schoolmaster; enlisted, 1915; served in ranks; was severely wounded, Somme, 1916, and discharged 1917; rejoined HM Forces Oct. 1939, served on PR Staff with acting rank of Major BEF, France, 1939-40; joined Birmingham Repertory Company, 1918, and played various parts for several seasons; later with: Plymouth Repertory Company; White Rose Players, Harrogate; Oxford Repertory Theatre Company; original Walter Gabriel in stage version of The Archers; frequent appearances on Television (Harry Crane in BBC series Starr and Co.; The Vicar in Crossroads; Private Godfrey in Dad's Army); also radio: Doughy Hood in The Archers; Crocks, 1960; The Tides of Chance, 1967; author of the following produced plays: The Brass God, 1921; The Ghost Train, 1925; The Burnett Mystery, 1926; The God o' Mud, 1926; The Wrecker (with Bernard Merivale), 1927; Keepers of Youth, 1929; The Flying Fool (with Merivale), 1929; Third Time Lucky, 1929; Recipe for Murder, 1932; Headline, 1934; Half-a-Crown (with Douglas Furber), 1934; Glory Be, 1934; Needs Must, 1938; Out Goes She (with Merivale), 1939; Peril at End House (with Agatha Christie), 1940; Happy Holiday (with Eric Maschwitz), 1954; Tabitha (with Mary Cathcart Borer), 1955; The Running Man (with Anthony Armstrong), 1955; Murder Happens, 1945; Easy Money, 1947; Trifles Light as Air (with St Vincent Troubridge), 1949; East of Ludgate Hill, 1950; The Dark ·Corridor (with Richard Reich), 1950; Beggar My Neighbour, 1951; You, My Guests!, 1956; Shadows on the Sand (with Borer), 1956; Geranium, 1957; Bellamy (with Anthony Armstrong), 1959; High Fidelity (with Cedric Wallis), 1964; Festive Board, 1970; The Ghost Train, revived 1976; prod the following plays: Sunshine House, Little Theatre 1933; Rude Awakening, Shilling Theatre, 1934; Flood Tide, Phœnix Theatre, 1938; Producer, Malvern Company, 1942-44. Wrote and directed film Royal Eagle, 1935; other films include: East of Ludgate Hill, 1935; Blind Justice, 1935; The Last Chance, 1936; The Seven Sinners, 1936. *Publications:* Keepers of Youth, 1929; various short stories and articles. *Recreations:* Rugby football and cricket; takes active interest in Bath Rugby Club, served as hon. match sec. several years and elected President 1950-52, and Life Member, 1963. *Address:* c/o Hughes Massie & Co., 69 Great Russell Street, WC1. *Clubs:* Savage, Dramatists'.

RIDLEY, Dame Betty; *see* Ridley, Dame M. B.

RIDLEY, Edward Alexander Keane, CB 1963; Principal Assistant Solicitor, Treasury Solicitor's Department, 1956-69, retired; *b* 16 April 1904; *s* of late Major Edward Keane Ridley, Dudswell House, near Berkhamsted, Herts, and late Ethel Janet Ridley, *d* of Alexander Forbes Tweedie; unmarried. *Educ:* Wellington College; Keble College, Oxford. Admitted Solicitor, 1928. Entered Treasury Solicitor's Department, 1934. *Publicatipn:* Wind Instruments of European Art Music, 1975. *Recreation:* music. *Address:* c/o Coutts & Co., 440 Strand, WC2.

RIDLEY, Jasper Godwin; author; *b* 25 May 1920; *s* of Geoffrey Ridley and Ursula (*née* King); *m* 1949, Vera, *d* of Emil Pollak; two *s* one *d*. *Educ:* Felcourt Sch.; Sorbonne, Paris; Magdalen Coll., Oxford. Certif. of Honour, Bar Finals. Called to Bar, Inner Temple, 1945. St Pancras Borough Council, 1945-49. Pres., Hardwicke Soc., 1954-55. Contested (Lab) Winchester, 1955; Westbury, 1959. Has written many radio scripts on historical subjects. FRSL 1963. *Publications:* Nicholas Ridley, 1957; The Law of Carriage of Goods, 1957; Thomas Cranmer, 1962; John Knox, 1968; Lord Palmerston, 1970 (James Tait Black Meml Prize, 1970); Mary Tudor, 1973; Garibaldi, 1974; The Roundheads, 1976. *Recreations:* walking, tennis, chess. *Address:* The Strakes, West Hoathly, East Grinstead, West Sussex. *T:* Sharpthorne 810481.

RIDLEY, Dame (Mildred) Betty, DBE 1975; MA (Lambeth) 1958; Third Church Estates Commissioner, since 1972; a Church Commissioner, since 1959; *b* 10 Sept. 1909; *d* of late Rt Rev. Henry Mosley, sometime Bishop of Southwell; *m* 1929, Rev. Michael Ridley (*d* 1953), Rector of Finchley; three *s* one *d*. *Educ:* North London Collegiate School; Cheltenham Ladies' College. Member: General Synod of Church of England, 1970-, and its Standing Cttee, 1971-; Central Board of Finance, 1955-; Vice-Pres. British Council of Churches, 1954-56. *Recreations:* walking, gardening. *Address:* Little Dickers, Hannington, Basingstoke, Hants. *T:* Basingstoke 298191.

RIDLEY, Hon. Nicholas, MICE; MP (C) Cirencester and Tewkesbury Division of Gloucestershire since Oct. 1959; *b* 17 Feb. 1929; *yr s* of 3rd Viscount Ridley, CBE, TD; *m* 1950, Hon. Clayre Campbell (marr. diss. 1974), 2nd *d* of 4th Baron Stratheden and Campbell, *qv*; three *d*. *Educ:* Eton; Balliol College, Oxford. Civil Engineering Contractor, Brims & Co. Ltd, Newcastle upon Tyne, 1950-59, Director, 1954-70; Director: Heenan Group Ltd, 1961-68; Ausonia Finance, 1973-; Marshall Andrew Ltd, 1975. Contested (C) Blyth, Gen. Election, 1955; PPS to Minister of Education, 1962-64; Delegate to Council of Europe and WEU, 1962-66; Parly Sec., Min. of Technology, June-Oct. 1970; Parly Under-Sec. of State, DTI, 1970-72. Mem., Royal Commn on Historical Manuscripts, 1967-. *Recreations:* painting, architecture and fishing. *Address:* Old Rectory, Naunton, Cheltenham, Glos. *T:* Guiting Power 252; 50 Warwick Square, SW1. *T:* 01-828 1816.

RIDLEY, Nicholas Harold Lloyd, MD, FRCS; Hon. Consultant Surgeon, Moorfields Eye Hospital, 1971 (Surgeon, 1938-71); Hon. Consultant Surgeon, Ophthalmic Department, St Thomas' Hospital, 1971 (Ophthalmic Surgeon, 1946-71); *b* 10 July 1906; *s* of late N. C. Ridley, MB (London), FRCS, Royal Navy retired,

Leicester; *m* 1941, Elisabeth Jane, *d* of late H. B. Wetherill, CIE; two *s* one *d. Educ:* Charterhouse; Pembroke Coll., Cambridge; St Thomas' Hospital, London. MB 1931, MD 1946, Cambridge; FRCS 1932. Late Hon. Ophthalmic Surgeon, Royal Buckinghamshire Hospital, Temp. Major RAMC. Hon. Cons. in Ophthalmology to Min. of Defence (Army), 1964-71; late Vice-Pres., Ophthalmological Soc. of UK; Member: Oxford Ophthalmological Congress; Advisory Panel, WHO, 1966-71; Hon. Fellow International College of Surgeons, Chicago, 1952; Hon. Member: Peruvian Ophthalmic Society, 1957. Ophthalmological Society of Australia, 1963; Hon. Member, Irish Ophthalmological Society. *Publications:* Monograph on Ocular Onchocerciasis; numerous contrib. in textbooks and medical journals on intraocular acrylic lens surgery and other subjects. *Recreation:* fly-fishing. *Address:* 53 Harley Street, W1. *T:* 01-580 1077. *Club:* Flyfishers'.

RIDLEY, Philip Waller, CBE 1969; Deputy Secretary, Department of Industry, since 1975; *b* 25 March 1921; *s* of Basil White Ridley and Frida (*née* Gutknecht); *m* 1942, Foye Robins; two *s* one *d. Educ:* Lewes County Grammar Sch.; Trinity Coll., Cambridge. Intelligence Corps, 1941-47 (Major); German Section, FO, 1948-51; Min. of Supply, 1951-55; BoT, 1955-56 and 1960-66; Atomic Energy Office, 1956-60; Counsellor (Commercial), British Embassy, Washington, 1966-70; Under-Sec., Dept of Industry, 1971-75. *Recreations:* music, gardening, ski-ing, sailing. *Address:* Old Chimneys, Plumpton Green, Lewes, East Sussex. *T:* Plumpton 890342.

RIDLEY, Sir Sidney, Kt 1953; Emeritus Fellow, St John's College, Oxford, 1969 (Fellow, 1962); Indian Civil Service, retired; *b* 26 March 1902; *s* of John William and Elizabeth Janet Ridley; *m* 1929, Dorothy Hoole; three *d. Educ:* Lancaster Royal Grammar Sch.; Sidney Sussex Coll., Cambridge. MA Cantab, MA Oxon. Joined ICS, 1926; Finance Secretary, Govt of Sind, 1936; Secretary to the Agent-General for India in South Africa, 1936-40; Chief Secretary, Govt of Sind, 1946; Commissioner: Northern Division, Ahmedabad, 1946; Central Div., Poona, 1947; Revenue Commissioner in Sind and Secretary to Government, 1947-54. Representative of W Africa Cttee in Ghana, Sierra Leone and the Gambia, 1957-60; Domestic Bursar, St John's Coll., Oxford, 1960-68. *Recreation:* golf. *Address:* Lambrook Cottage, Waytown, Bridport, Dorset. *Club:* East India, Devonshire, Sports and Public Schools.

RIDLEY, Rear-Adm. William Terence Colborne, CB 1968; OBE 1954; Admiral Superintendent/Port Admiral, Rosyth, 1966-72; Chairman, Ex-Services Mental Welfare Society, since 1973; *b* 9 March 1915; *s* of late Capt. W. H. W. Ridley, RN and late Vera Constance (*née* Walker); *m* 1938, Barbara Allen; one *s. Educ:* Emsworth House; RNC, Dartmouth (Robert Roxburgh Prize); RNEC, Keyham. HMS Exeter, 1936; HMS Valiant, 1939; HMS Firedrake, 1940 (despatches twice); E-in-C Dept Admty, 1941; HMS Indefatigable, 1944; Admty Fuel Experimental Stn, 1947; Seaslug Project Officer, RAE Farnborough, 1950; HMS Ark Royal, 1956; E-in-C Dept Admty, Dreadnought Project Team, 1958; CO, RNEC, 1962; Staff of C-in-C Portsmouth, 1964. Lt-Comdr 1944; Comdr 1947; Capt. 1957; Rear-Adm. 1966. *Recreations:* gardening, botany, caravanning, do-it-yourself. *Address:* The Green, Brompton Ralph, Taunton, Somerset. *T:* Wiveliscombe 23305.

RIDSDALE, Julian Errington, CBE 1977; MP (C) Harwich Division of Essex, since Feb. 1954; *b* 8 June 1915; *m* 1942, Victoire Evelyn Patricia Bennett; one *d. Educ:* Tonbridge; Sandhurst. 2nd Lieutenant, Royal Norfolk Regiment, 1935; attached British Embassy, Tokyo, 1938-39; served War of 1939-45: Royal Norfolk Regt, Royal Scots, and Somerset Light Infantry; GSO3, Far Eastern Sect., War Office, 1941; GSO2, Joint Staff Mission, Washington, 1944-45; retired from Army with rank of Major, 1946. Contested SW Islington (C), LCC, 1949, N Paddington (C), Gen. Elec., 1951. PPS to Parly Under-Sec. of State for Colonies, 1957-58; PPS to Minister of State for Foreign Affairs, 1958-60; Parly Under-Sec. of State: for Air and Vice-President of the Air Council, 1962-64; for Defence for the Royal Air Force, Ministry of Defence, April-Oct. 1964. Chm., British Japanese Parly Group, 1964-; Vice-Chm., UN Parly Assoc., 1966-; Mem., Select Cttee of Public Accounts, 1970-74. Mem. Trilateral Commn, EEC, USA and Japan, 1973-. Chm., Japan Soc., London, 1976- Master, Skinners' Co., 1970-71. Order of the Sacred Treasure, Japan. *Recreations:* tennis, chess, gardening, travelling, and sailing. *Address:* 12 The Boltons, SW10. *T:* 01-373 6159; Fiddan, St Osyth, Essex. *T:* St Osyth 367. *Clubs:* Carlton, MCC, Hurlingham; Frinton Tennis.

RIE, Lucie, OBE 1968; studio potter since 1927; *b* 16 March 1902; *d* of Prof. Dr Benjamin and Gisela Gomperz. *Educ:* Vienna Gymnasium (matriculate); Arts and Crafts School. Pottery

workshop: Vienna, 1927; London, 1939. Hon. Doctor, Royal College of Art, 1969. *Address:* 18 Albion Mews, W2 2BA. *T:* 01-723 0938.

RIEGER, Sir Clarence (Oscar Ferrero), Kt 1969; CBE 1965; FRACS, FRCSE; *b* 23 Nov. 1897; *s* of Oscar Paul Philip and Sarina Rieger; *m* 1923, Bessie Eileen, *d* of Charles Ernest Main; two *s* one *d. Educ:* Adelaide High Sch.; Univ. of Adelaide. MBBS Adelaide 1919; FRCSE 1932; FRACS 1957. Served War of 1939-45: Major, AAMC, AIF. Adelaide Children's Hospital: Hon. Surgeon, 1939; Hon. Cons. Surg., 1958; Pres. and Chm. Bd, 1958-. Member: Branch Council, BMA, 1946-61 (Pres., 1949-51); Med. Bd of SA, 1952-70; Fed. Council BMA, 1950-61; Fed. Council AMA, 1962-64 (Vice-Pres., 1964-67); President: First Aust. Med. Congress, 1962; AMA, 1967-70; BMA, 1968. FAMA, 1964; FBMA 1970; Hon. FACMA, 1970. Gold Medal, AMA, 1969. Hon. LLD Aberdeen, 1969. *Publications:* contrib. (1950-) to: Med. Jl Aust., BMJ, NZ Med. Jl. *Recreation:* painting. *Address:* 52 Brougham Place, North Adelaide, South Australia 5006. *Clubs:* Adelaide; Kooyonga Golf (Lockleys).

RIFKIND, Malcolm Leslie; MP (C) Edinburgh, Pentlands, since Feb. 1974; *b* 21 June 1946; *yr s* of E. Rifkind, Edinburgh; *m* 1970, Edith Amalia Rifkind (*née* Steinberg); one *s* one *d. Educ:* George Watson's Coll.; Edinburgh Univ. LLB, MSc. Lectured at Univ. of Rhodesia, 1967-68. Called to Scottish Bar, 1970. Contested (C) Edinburgh, Central, 1970. Opposition front-bench spokesman on Scottish Affairs, 1975-76; Chm., Scottish Cons. Devolution Cttee, 1976; Mem., Select Cttee on Europ. Secondary Legislation, 1975-76; Hon. Pres., Scottish Young Conservatives, 1975-76; Hon. Sec., Fedn of Cons. Students, 1977-. *Address:* 8 Old Church Lane, Duddingston Village, Edinburgh. *T:* 031-661 4716.

RIGBY, Herbert Cecil, DFC 1943, and Bar 1944; a Recorder of the Crown Court, Wales and Chester Circuit, since Dec. 1972; Senior Partner, H. P. & H. C. Rigby, Solicitors, Sandbach, Cheshire; *b* 2 April 1917; *s* of Captain Herbert Parrot Rigby, TD; *m* 1st, 1939, Ethel Muriel Horton; two *d*; 2nd, 1949, Florence Rita Scotts; one *s. Educ:* Sandbach Sch.; Ellesmere Coll.; Liverpool Univ. (Law Faculty). Articled R. S. Rigby, Winsford, Law Intermediate, 1937-39. Commissioned, 7th Cheshire Regt, 1937. Served War: Expeditionary Force, France, 1939; evacuated, Dunkirk, 1940; transfer to RAF, 1941; Wings, 11 Gp, Hornchurch (Spitfires), 1942; Landing, N Africa, 1942; commanded 222 Sqdn, Invasion of France, 1944-45 (Bt Militaire de Pilote D'Avion, 1945); demobilised, 1946. Commanded 610 City of Chester Auxiliary Sqdn, 1947-49. Articled R. A. Burrows of Gibson & Weldon, London, 1946-47; Law Final, and admitted solicitor, 1947; Partner, H. P. and H. C. Rigby, 1947-. Mem., Parish and Dist Councils, 1949-74 (Chm. Congleton RDC, 1959-60); Governor, Sandbach Indep. Sch., 1950- (Chm., 1955-); Pres. Sandbach British Legion and United Services Club, 1952-; Area Representative: SSAFA, 1952-; Officers Assoc., 1955-. Member: Cheshire Brine Compensation Bd, 1952-74 (Chm. 1969-74); Cheshire CC, 1955-69; (Chm.) S Cheshire Hosp. Management Cttee, 1963-74; Runcorn New Town Corp., 1964- (Dep. Chm., 1974-). *Recreations:* fishing, golf, boating, gardening; formerly: Rugby football, also cricket (Cheshire County and Cheshire Gentlemen). *Address:* Shelbourne, New Platt Lane, Cranage, *via* Crewe, Cheshire. *Club:* North Wales Cruising (Conway).

RIGBY, Lt-Col Sir (Hugh) John (Macbeth), 2nd Bt, *cr* 1929; ERD and 2 clasps; Director, Executors of James Mills Ltd; *b* 1 Sept 1914; *s* of Sir Hugh Mallinson Rigby, 1st Bt, and Flora (*d* 1970), *d* of Norman Macbeth; *S* father, 1944; *m* 1946, Mary Patricia Erskine Leacock; four *s. Educ:* Rugby; Magdalene Coll., Cambridge. Lt-Col RCT, retd, 1967. *Heir: s* Anthony John Rigby, *b* 3 Oct. 1946. *Address:* Ridgehill, Sutton, near Macclesfield, Cheshire. *T:* Sutton 2353.

RIGBY, Sir Ivo (Charles Clayton), Kt 1964; President, Court of Appeal, Brunel, since 1973; a Metropolitan Stipendiary Magistrate, since 1976; a Recorder of the Crown Court, since 1975; *b* 2 June 1911; *s* of late James Philip Clayton Rigby and late Elisabeth Mary Corbett; *m* 1st, 1938, Agnes Bothway; 2nd, Kathleen Nancy, *d* of late Dr W. E. Jones, CMG; no *c. Educ:* Magdalen College School, Oxford. Called to the Bar (Inner Temple), 1932; Magistrate, Gambia, 1935-38; Chief Magistrate, Crown Counsel, and President of a District Court, Palestine, 1938-48; Assistant Judge, Nyasaland, 1948-54; President of Sessions Court, Malaya, 1954-55; Puisne Judge, Malaya, 1956-61; Senior Puisne Judge, Hong Kong, 1961-70; Chief Justice of Hong Kong and of Brunei, 1970-73. *Publications:* The Law Reports of Nyasaland, 1934-1952. *Recreations:* squash, cricket and bridge. *Address:* 8 More's Garden, Cheyne Walk, SW3. *T:* 01-352 0120. *Clubs:* Bath, East India, Devonshire, Sports and Public Schools, MCC; Hong Kong.

RIGBY, Sir John; *see* Rigby, Sir H. J. M.

RIGBY, Norman Leslie; Director, Spillers Ltd, since 1970, Divisional Managing Director, since 1977; *b* 27 June 1920; *s* of Leslie Rigby and Elsie Lester Wright; *m* 1950, Mary Josephine Calderhead; two *d* (one *s* decd). *Educ:* Cowley Sch., St Helens. Served RAF, 1939-45, War Intell. Officer to Free French Air Force. Management Trainee, Simon Engineering Group, 1946-48; Marketing Exec., Procter & Gamble Ltd, 1948-55; Marketing Dir, Macleans Ltd (Beecham Group), 1955-59; Nabisco Ltd: Marketing Dir 1959; Man. Dir 1960; Vice-Chm. 1962; Chm. 1964; Industrial Adviser, 1968-70, Co-ordinator of Industrial Advisers, HM Govt, 1969-70. FBIM. *Recreations:* gardening, tennis, golf. *Address:* 38 West Common Way, Harpenden, Herts. *T:* Harpenden 5448.

RIGBY, Reginald Francis, TD 1950 and Clasp 1952; a Recorder of the Crown Court, since 1977; Partner, Rigby, Rowley Cooper & Co., Solicitors, Newcastle-under-Lyme; *b* Rudyard, Staffs, 22 June 1919; *s* of Reginald Rigby, FRIBA, FRICS, and Beatrice May Rigby, *d* of John Frederick Green, Woodbridge, Suffolk; *m* 1949, Joan Edwina, *d* of Samuel E. M. Simpson, Newcastle-under-Lyme, and of Dorothy C. Simpson; two *s*. *Educ:* Manchester Grammar Sch.; Victoria Univ., Manchester. Solicitor, 1947, Hons; John Peacock and George Hadfield Prizeman, Law Society Art Prize, 1962. Served War: commissioned 2nd Lieut 41 Bn, Royal Tank Corps, TA, 1939; served AFV Sch.; volunteered for maritime service: Captain in RASC motor boat companies in home coastal waters, India, Burma, Malaya and its Archipelago; demob. 1946; Major, QORR, The Staffordshire Yeomanry. Mem., Market Drayton RDC, 1966-71; Chm., Woore Parish Council; Hon. Sec., North Staffs Forces Help Soc.; Mem., Staffs War Pensions Cttee; Member: 1745 Assoc. and Mil. Hist. Soc.; Staffordshire Record Soc.; Lancs and Cheshire Record Soc.; Lancs and Cheshire Hist. Soc.; Cheetham Soc.; Lancs Parish Register Soc.; Pres., Uttoxeter Flyfishing Club; Trustee, Birdsgrove Flyfishing Club, Ashbourne. Member, Military and Hospitaller Order of St Lazarus of Jerusalem. *Recreations:* fishing, shooting. *Address:* The Rookery, Woore, Salop CW3 9RG. *T:* Pipe Gate 414. *Club:* Flyfishers'.

RIGG, Diana; actress; *b* Doncaster, Yorks, 20 July 1938; *d* of Louis Rigg and Beryl Helliwell; *m* 1973, Menachen Gueffen (marr. diss. 1976). *Educ:* Fulneck Girls' Sch., Pudsey. Trained for the stage at Royal Academy of Dramatic Art. First appearance on stage in RADA prod. in York Festival, at Theatre Royal, York, summer, 1957 (Natella Abashwili in The Caucasian Chalk Circle); after appearing in repertory in Chesterfield and in York she joined the Royal Shakespeare Company, Stratford-upon-Avon, 1959; first appearance in London, Aldwych Theatre, 1961 (2nd Ondine and Violanta in Ondine); at same theatre, in repertory (The Devils, Becket, The Taming of the Shrew), 1961; (The Art of Seduction), 1962; Royal Shakespeare, Stratford-upon-Avon, Apr. 1962 (Helena in A Midsummer Night's Dream, Bianca in The Taming of the Shrew, Lady Macduff in Macbeth, Adriana in The Comedy of Errors, Cordelia in King Lear); subseq. appeared in the last production at the Aldwych, Dec. 1962, followed by Adriana in The Comedy of Errors and Monica Stettler in The Physicists, 1963. Toured the provinces, spring, 1963, in A Midsummer Night's Dream; subseq. appeared at the Royal Shakespeare, Stratford, and at the Aldwych, in Comedy of Errors, Dec. 1963; again played Cordelia in King Lear, 1964, prior to touring with both plays for the British Council, in Europe, the USSR, and the US; during this tour she first appeared in New York (State Theatre), 1964, in same plays; Viola in Twelfth Night, Stratford, June 1966; Heloise in Abelard and Heloise, Wyndham's, 1970, also at the Atkinson, New York, 1971; joined The National Theatre, 1972: in Jumpers, 'Tis Pity She's a Whore and Lady Macbeth in Macbeth, 1972; The Misanthrope, 1973, Washington and NY, 1975; Pygmalion, Albery, 1974; Phaedra Britannica, 1975; *films include:* Assassination Bureau, On Her Majesty's Secret Service, Julius Caesar, The Hospital, Theatre of Blood. First appeared on television, 1964, as Adriana, in The Comedy of Errors; subseq. in The Avengers, Married Alive, The House of Brede (US), A Little Night Music, Three Piece Suite, and others. *Recreations:* reading and trying to get organized. *Address:* c/o John Redway and Associates Ltd, 5-11 Mortimer Street, W1N 7RH.

RIGNEY, Howard Ernest; Counsellor, HM Diplomatic Service; Head of Migration and Visa Department, Foreign and Commonwealth Office, since 1973; *b* 22 June 1922; *o s* of late Wilbert Ernest and Minnie Rigney; *m* 1950, Margaret Grayling Benn; one *s*. *Educ:* Univs of Western Ontario, Toronto and Paris. BA Western Ont. 1945, MA Toronto 1947. Lectr, Univ. of British Columbia, 1946-48; grad. studies, Paris Univ., 1948-50; COI, 1953-56; CRO, 1956; Regional Information Officer, Dacca, 1957-60, Montreal, 1960-63; CRO, 1963-65; FO/CO, 1965-67; Consul (Information), Chicago, 1967-69; Dep. Consul-Gen., Chicago, 1969-71; Head of Chancery and Consul, Rangoon, 1971-73. Hon DLitt, Winston Churchill Coll., Ill, 1971. *Recreations:* opera, book-collecting, gardening. *Address:* c/o Foreign and Commonwealth Office, SW1A 2AL.

RILEY, Bridget Louise, CBE 1972; Artist; *b* 24 April 1931; *d* of John Riley and late Louise (*née* Gladstone). *Educ:* Cheltenham Ladies' College; Goldsmiths' School of Art; Royal College of Art. ARCA 1955. AICA critics Prize, 1963; Stuyvesant Bursary, 1964. Mem., RSA. One-man shows: London, 1962, 1963, 1969, 1971 (retrospective, at Hayward Gall.), 1976; New York, Los Angeles, 1965; New York, 1967, 1975; Hanover, 1970; Turin, Dusseldorf, Berne, Prague, 1971; Basle, 1975. Exhibited in group shows: England, France, Israel, America, Germany, Italy. Represented Britain: Paris Biennale, 1965; Venice Biennale, 1968 (awarded Chief internat. painting prize). Public collections include: Tate Gallery, Victoria and Albert Museum, Arts Council, British Council, Museum of Modern Art, New York, Museum of Modern Art, Pasadena, Ferens Art Gallery, Hull, Allbright Knox, Buffalo, USA, Museum of Contemporary Art, Chicago, Ulster Museum, Ireland, Stedelijk Museum, Berne Kunsthalle. Hon. LLD Manchester, 1976.

RILEY, Harry Lister, DSc, ARCS, DIC, FRIC; Consultant; *b* 7 Sept. 1899; *s* of late Arthur Riley, Keighley, Yorks; *m* 1924, Marion, *o c* of David Belfield; two *s* one *d*. *Educ:* The Grammar School, Keighley; Imperial College of Science and Technology (Royal College of Science). Served with 9th Bn KOYLI, 1917-19. Beit Scientific Research Fellow, 1921-23; Demonstrator, and later Lecturer in Chemistry at the Royal College of Science, South Kensington, SW7, 1923-32; Professor of Inorganic and Physical Chemistry, King's Coll. (Univ. of Durham), Newcastle on Tyne, 1932-47; Hon. Secretary and Dir of Research to the Northern Coke Research Committee; Jubilee Memorial Lecturer, Society of Chemical Industry, 1938-39; Director of Chemical Research and Development, United Steel Companies Ltd, 1947-64; Dir of carbonization research, Nat. Coal Board, 1947. *Publications:* various research publications in The Journal of the Chemical Society, the Philosophical Magazine, the Geological Magazine, and the Proceedings of the Royal Society, etc. *Recreation:* golf. *Address:* 12 Willow Place, Ponteland, Newcastle upon Tyne NE20 9RL.

RILEY, Norman Denbigh, CBE 1952; Keeper, Department of Entomology, British Museum (Natural History), 1932-Nov. 1955; retired; *b* 1890; *m* 1920, Edith Vaughan; one *s* one *d*. *Educ:* Dulwich College. Demonstrator in Entomology, Imperial College of Science, 1911; entered Museum, 1911. Served as Captain in ASC and The Queens in France, 1914-19 (despatches). Fellow Royal Entomological Society of London (Vice-Pres. 1929, 1940; Treas., 1939-40; Sec., 1926-29, 1941-51; Pres., 1951-52). *Publications:* Field Guide to Butterflies of Britain and Europe (with Lionel Higgins), 1970; Field Guide to Butterflies of the West Indies, 1975; numerous papers on Lepidoptera. *Address:* 7 McKay Road, Wimbledon, SW20.

RILEY, Ralph, FRS 1967; DSc; Director, Plant Breeding Institute, Cambridge, since 1971; Special Professor of Botany, University of Nottingham, since 1970; *b* 23 Oct. 1924; *y c* of Ralph and Clara Riley; *m* 1949, Joan Elizabeth Norrington; two *d*. *Educ:* Audenshaw Gram. Sch.; Univ. of Sheffield. Infantry Soldier, 1943-47; Univ. of Sheffield, 1947-52; Research worker, Plant Breeding Inst., Cambridge, 1952-; Head of Cytogenetics Dept, 1954-72; National Research Council/Nuffield Foundn Lectr at Canadian Univs, 1966; Fellow of Wolfson Coll., Cambridge. William Bate Hardy Prize, Cambridge Phil. Soc., 1969. Sir Henry Tizard Meml Lectr, 1973. Pres., Genetical Soc., 1973-75; Mem. Bd, Internat. Rice Research Inst. Philippines, 1973-; Sec., Internat. Genetics Fedn, 1973-. Woodhull Lectr, Royal Instn, 1976. For. Fellow, Indian Nat. Sci. Acad., 1976. *Publications:* scientific papers and articles on genetics of chromosome behaviour, plant cytogenetics and evolution and breeding of crop plants especially wheat. *Address:* 2 High Street, Little Shelford, Cambridge. *T:* Shelford 3845.

RIMBAULT, Brig. Geoffrey Acworth, CBE 1954; DSO 1945; MC 1936; DL; Director, Army Sport Control Board, 1961-73; *b* 17 April 1908; *s* of late Arthur Henry Rimbault, London; *m* 1933, Joan, *d* of late Thomas Hallet-Fry, Beckenham, Kent; one *s*. *Educ:* Dulwich College. 2nd Lieut, The Loyal Regt (N Lancs), 1930; served: India, Waziristan, 1931-36; Palestine, 1937; Staff Coll., Camberley; N Africa, Anzio, Italy and Palestine, 1939-46; Chief Instructor, RMA Sandhurst, 1950-51; Chief of Staff, E Africa, 1952-54; comd 131 Inf. Bde, 1955-57; comd Aldershot Garrison, 1958-61. Colonel, The Loyal Regt, 1959-70.

Liveryman, Mercers' Co., 1961, Master, 1970-71. DL Surrey, 1971. *Recreations:* cricket, tennis, golf, shooting. *Address:* Manor Cottage, Smithbrook, Cranleigh, Surrey. *T:* Cranleigh 3018. *Clubs:* Army and Navy, MCC.

RIMINGTON, Claude, FRS 1954, MA, PhD Cantab, DSc London; Emeritus Professor of Chemical Pathology, University of London; Head of Department of Chemical Pathology, University College Hospital Medical School, 1945-67; *b* 17 Nov. 1902; *s* of George Garthwaite Rimington, Newcastle-on-Tyne; *m* 1929, Soffi, *d* of Clemet Andersen, Askeröy, Lyngör, Norway; one *d*. *Educ:* Emmanuel College, Cambridge. Benn W. Levy Research Scholar, Univ. of Cambridge, 1926-28; Biochemist, Wool Industries Research Association, Leeds, 1928-30; Empire Marketing Board Senior Research Fellow, then Scientific Research Officer, Division of Veterinary Services, Govt of Union of South Africa, at Onderstepoort Veterinary Research Laboratory, Pretoria, 1931-37; Biochemist, National Institute for Medical Research, Medical Research Council, London, 1937-45. Hon. FRCP Edinburgh, 1967; Hon. Mem. Brit. Assoc. of Dermatology, 1967. Graham Gold Medal, Univ. of London, 1967. *Publications:* (with A. Goldberg), Diseases of Porphyrin Metabolism, 1962; numerous biochemical and scientific papers. *Recreations:* sailing, languages, Scandinavian literature. *Address:* Askerøy, Per Vestra Sandøy 4915, Norway.

RIMMER, Prof. Frederick William, MA (Cantab), BMus (Dunelm); FRCO; Gardiner Professor of Music, University of Glasgow, since 1966, and Director of Scottish Music Archive since 1968; Organ Recitalist; *b* 21 Feb. 1914; 2nd *s* of William Rimmer and Amy Graham McMillan, Liverpool; *m* 1941, Joan Doreen, *d* of Major Alexander Hume Graham and Beatrice Cecilia Myles; two *s* one *d*. *Educ:* Quarry Bank High Sch., Liverpool. FRCO (Harding Prize), 1934; BMus (Dunelm), 1939. Served War: 11th Bn, The Lancashire Fusiliers, Middle East, 1941-45 (Maj. 1944). Selwyn Coll., Cambridge (Organ Scholar), 1946-48; Sen. Lectr in Music, Homerton Coll., Cambridge, 1948-51; Cramb Lectr in Music, Univ. of Glasgow, 1951-56; Sen. Lectr, 1956-66, and Organist to the Univ., 1954-66. Henrietta Harvey Vis. Prof., Memorial Univ. of Newfoundland, 1977. A Dir of Scottish Opera, 1966-; Chm., BBC's Scottish Music Adv. Cttee, 1972-77; Mem., Music Adv. Cttee, British Council, 1973-. Special Award for services to contemp. music in Scotland, Composers' Guild of GB, 1975. *Publications:* contrib. to: A History of Scottish Music, 1973; articles on 20th century music, in: Tempo; Music Review; Organists' Review; compositions for solo organ: Five Preludes on Scottish Psalm Tunes, Pastorale and Toccata, Invenzione e Passacaglia Capricciosa; anthems for choir and organ: Sing we merrily; Christus natus est alleluia; O Lord, we beseech thee; Five carols of the Nativity. *Recreations:* reading and gardening. *Address:* 62 Oakfield Avenue, Glasgow G12 8LS. *T:* 041-334 1217.

RING, Prof. James; Professor of Physics, Imperial College of Science and Technology, since 1967; *b* 22 Aug. 1927; *s* of James and Florence Ring; *m* 1949, Patricia, *d* of Major H. J. Smith, MBE; two *s*. *Educ:* Univ. of Manchester (BSc, PhD). FInstP, FRAS. Reader in Spectrometry, Univ. of Manchester, 1957; Prof. of Applied Physics, Hull Univ., 1962. Mem., IBA, 1974-. *Publications:* numerous papers and articles in learned jls. *Address:* 8 Riverview Gardens, Barnes, SW13.

RING, Sir Lindsay (Roberts), GBE 1975; JP; Chairman, Ring & Brymer (Birchs) Ltd; Lord Mayor of London for 1975-76; *b* 1 May 1914; *y s* of George Arthur Ring and Helen Rhoda Mason Ring (*née* Stedman); *m* 1940, Hazel Doris, *d* of A. Trevor Nichols, CBE; two *s* one *d*. *Educ:* Dulwich Coll.; Mecklenburg, Germany. Served 1939-45, Europe and Middle East, Major RASC. Underwriting Member of Lloyd's, 1964. Fellow, Hotel and Catering Inst.; Chm., Hotel and Catering Trades Benevolent Assoc., 1962-71; Member: Bd of Verge of Royal Palaces; Gaming Bd for GB, 1977-; NI Develt Agency. Chancellor, City Univ., 1975-76. Governor, Farringtons Sch. Hon. Treasurer, Church Army Housing. Freeman, City of London, 1935; Mem. Court of Assistants, Armourers' and Brasiers' Co., Master 1972; Common Councilman, City of London (Ward of Bishopsgate), 1964-68; Alderman (Ward of Vintry), 1968; Sheriff, City of London, 1967-68; HM Lieut for City of London; JP Inner London, 1964. Hon. Col, 151 (Greater London) Regt, RCT(V). Hon. Burgess, Borough of Coleraine, NI. KStJ 1976. FCIS 1976. Hon. DSc City Univ., 1976; Hon. DLitt Ulster, 1976. Comdr, Legion of Honour, 1976; Order of Rio Branca (Brazil), 1976. *Address:* Chalvedune, Wilderness Road, Chislehurst, Kent, BR7 5EY. *T:* 01-467 3199. *Club:* City Livery.

RINGADOO, Hon. Sir Veerasamy, Kt 1975; Officier de l'Ordre National Malgache 1969; Minister of Finance, Mauritius, since 1968; *b* 1920; *s* of Nagaya Ringadoo; *m* 1954, Lydie

Vadamootoo; one *s* one *d*. *Educ:* Port Louis Grammar Sch.; LSE Eng. (LLB); Hon. Fellow, 1976. Called to Bar, 1949; Municipal Councillor, 1956; MLC for Moka-Flacq, 1951-67; Minister: Labour and Social Scurity, 1959-64; Education, 1964-67; Agriculture and Natural Resources, 1967-68; attended London Constitutional Conf., 1965; first MLA (Lab) for Quartier Militaire and Moka, 1967, re-elected 1976. Governor, IMF; Chm., Bd of Governors, African Development Bank and African Development Fund, 1977-78. Hon LLD Mauritius, 1976. *Address:* Ministry of Finance, Port Louis, Mauritius. *T:* 2-5331.

RINGROSE, Prof. John Robert, FRS 1977; FRSE; Professor of Pure Mathematics, University of Newcastle upon Tyne, since 1964; *b* 21 Dec. 1932; *s* of Albert Frederick Ringrose and Elsie Lilian Ringrose (*née* Roberts); *m* 1956, Jean Margaret Bates; three *s*. *Educ:* Buckhurst Hill County High School, Chigwell, Essex; St John's Coll., Cambridge (MA, PhD). Lecturer in Mathematics: King's Coll., Newcastle upon Tyne, 1957-61; Univ. of Cambridge (also Fellow of St John's Coll.), 1961-63; Sen. Lectr in Mathematics, Univ. of Newcastle upon Tyne, 1963-64. *Publications:* Compact Non-self-adjoint Operators, 1971; mathematical papers in various research jls. *Address:* School of Mathematics, The University, Newcastle upon Tyne NE1 7RU. *T:* 28511.

RINGWOOD, Prof. Alfred Edward, FAA 1966; FRS 1972; Professor of Geochemistry, Australian National University, since 1967; *b* 19 April 1930; *s* of Alfred Edward Ringwood and Wilhelmena Grace Bruce Ringwood (*née* Robertson); *m* 1960, Gun Ivor Karlsson, Halsingborg, Sweden; one *s* one *d*. *Educ:* Hawthorn Central Sch., Melbourne; Geelong Grammar Sch.; Melbourne Univ. BSc 1950, MSc 1953, PhD 1956, Melbourne. Research Fellow, Geochemistry, Harvard Univ., 1957-58; Australian National Univ.: Sen. Res. Fellow, 1959; Sen. Fellow, 1960; Personal Prof., 1963. William Smith Lectr, Geol Soc. of London, 1973; Vernadsky Lectr. USSR Acad of Scis, 1975; Centenary Lectr and Medallist, Chem. Soc., London, 1977. Commonwealth and Foreign Mem., Geol. Soc., London, 1967; Fellow, Amer. Geophysical Union, 1969; Vice-Pres., Australian Acad. of Science, 1971. For. Associate, Nat. Acad. of Scis of Amer., 1975; Hon. Mem., All-Union Mineralog. Soc., USSR, 1976. Mineralogical Soc. of America Award, 1967; Britannica Australia Award for Science, 1969; Rosentiel Award, Miami Univ., 1971; Werner Medaille, German Mineralogical Soc., 1972; Bowie Medal, American Geophysical Union, 1974; Day Medal, Geological Soc. of America, 1974; Mueller Medal, Aust. and NZ Assoc. for Advancement of Sci., 1975. *Publications:* Composition and Petrology of the Earth's Mantle, 1975; numerous papers in learned jls dealing with nature of earth's interior, phase transformations under high pressures, origin and evolution of earth, moon, planets and meteorites. *Recreations:* music, travel. *Address:* 3 Vancouver Street, Red Hill, Canberra, ACT 2603, Australia. *T:* Canberra 95-9929.

RINK, George Arnold, QC 1956; Bencher of Lincoln's Inn; *b* 21 April 1902; *s* of late M. Rink; *m* 1949, Dr Margaret Joan Suttill, *qv*. *Educ:* Charterhouse; University College, Oxford. 1st Cl. Hon. Mods, and Lit. Hum.; BCL; MA; half-blue for fencing. Barrister, Lincoln's Inn, 1926; Civil Service, 1939-44. Chm., Licensed Dealers' Tribunal, 1968-76. Mem., Senate, Inns of Court, 1973-74. Trustee of Charterhouse in Southwark, 1948-66. Member Board of Governors, Royal Free Hospital, 1955-64, Middlesex Hospital, 1964-70. Member, Advisory Council, Science Policy Foundation, 1966-. Vice-Pres., Bar Musical Soc., 1977-. *Publications:* articles in professional journals. *Recreations:* music, reading, winter-sports, swimming, walking. *Address:* 17 Old Buildings, Lincoln's Inn, WC2. *T:* 01-405 5017; 173 Oakwood Court, W14. *T:* 01-602 2143. *Club:* Athenæum.

RINK, Margaret Joan; *see* Suttill, Dr. M. J.

RIPLEY, Sir Hugh, 4th Bt, *cr* 1880; Director, John Walker & Sons Ltd, Scotch Whisky Distillers; *b* 26 May 1916; *s* of Sir Henry William Alfred Ripley, 3rd Bt, and Dorothy (*d* 1964), *e d* of late Robert William Daker Harley; *S* father 1956; *m* 1st, 1946, Dorothy Mary Dunlop Bruce-Jones (marr. diss. 1971); one *s* one *d*; 2nd, 1972, Susan, *d* of W. Parker, Leics; one *d*. *Educ:* Eton. Served in Africa and Italy with 1st Bn KSLI (despatches twice, American Silver Star); retired regular Major. *Recreations:* golf, fishing, shooting. *Heir:* *s* William Hugh Ripley, *b* 13 April 1950. *Address:* 20 Abingdon Villas, W8; The Oak, Bedstone, Bucknell, Salop. *Club:* Boodle's.

RIPLEY, Sydney William Leonard, DL; Member, Greater London Council (Kingston-upon-Thames Borough), since 1964; Chairman, Open Spaces and Recreation Committee, since 1977; *b* 17 July 1909; *o s* of late Leonard Ripley; *m* 1st, 1934, Doris

Emily (from whom he obtained a divorce, 1966), d of late William Gray; one s two d; 2nd, 1972, Mrs Pida Polkinghorne. *Educ:* King's School, Canterbury; London. Served War of 1939-45, with RAF, Flight-Lieut (despatches). Contested (C) Ipswich, 1950, Watford, 1951; Chairman Malden and Coombe Conservative Assoc., 1938-49, Pres., 1950-; Vice-Pres., Kingston Division, 1955-. Formerly Chairman Leonard Ripley and Co. Ltd and other printing and outdoor advertising companies, resigned 1973. Member, Malden and Coombe Borough Council, 1938-48, formerly Chm. Finance Cttee; DL Surrey 1960; DL Greater London, 1966; JP 1959-69, CC 1946, CA 1955, Surrey (Chairman, Finance Cttee, 1962-64); Vice-Chm. Surrey CC, 1956-59; Chm. General Purposes Cttee, 1952-59; Chm. Surrey County Council, 1959-62; Mem., Surrey Jt Standing Cttee, 1959-65; County Council rep. on Metrop. Water Bd, 1956-65; County Councils Assoc., 1958-65; Surrey T&AFA, 1959-65; Governor Westminster Hosp., 1963-65; Jt Dep. Leader, Cons. Opposition, GLC, 1964-66; GLC rep. on Surrey T&AFA, 1965-68; London Tourist Board, 1965-68; Thames Water Authority, 1975-. Chm., SW Regional Hosp. Bd, 1963-65. Freeman, City of London. *Recreations:* golf, swimming, tennis. *Address:* 12 South Audley Street, WI. *Clubs:* Brooks's, Carlton.

RIPON, Bishop of, since 1977; **Rt. Rev. David Nigel de Lorentz Young;** b 2 Sept. 1931; s of late Brig. K. de L. Young, CIE, MC; m 1967, Jane Havill Collison; three s one d. *Educ:* Wellington Coll.; Balliol Coll., Oxford (MA). Director, Dept of Buddhist Studies, Theological Coll. of Lanka, 1964; Lecturer in Comparative Religion, Manchester Univ., 1967; Vicar of Burwell, Cambridge, 1970-75; Archdeacon of Huntingdon, 1975-77; Vicar of Great with Little and Steeple Gidding, 1975-77; Rector of Hemingford Abbots, 1977; Hon. Canon of Ely Cathedral, 1975-77. *Publications:* contribs to Religious Studies. *Recreations:* tennis, sailing. *Address:* Bishop Mount, Ripon, N Yorks HG4 5DP.

RIPON, Dean of; *see* Le Grice, Very Rev. F. E.

RIPPENGAL, Derek; Counsel to Chairman of Committees, House of Lords, since 1977; b 8 Sept. 1928; s of William Thomas Rippengal and Margaret Mary Rippengal (*née* Parry); m 1963, Elizabeth Melrose (d 1973); one s one d. *Educ:* Hampton Grammar Sch.; St Catharine's Coll., Cambridge (MA). Called to Bar, Middle Temple, 1953 (Harmsworth schol.). Entered Treasury Solicitor's Office, 1958, after Chancery Bar and univ. posts; Sen. Legal Asst, 1961; Asst Treasury Solicitor, 1967; Principal Asst Treasury Solicitor, 1971; Solicitor to DTI, 1972-73; Dep. Parly Counsel, 1973-74, Parly Counsel, 1974-76, Law Commn. *Recreations:* music, fishing. *Address:* 16 Blacketts Wood Drive, Chorleywood, Herts. *T:* Chorleywood 2131. *Club:* Athenæum.

RIPPON, Rt. Hon. (Aubrey) Geoffrey (Frederick), PC 1962; QC 1964; MP (C) Hexham, since 1966; Leader, Conservative Group, European Parliament, since 1977; b 28 May 1924; o s of late A. E. S. Rippon; m 1946, Ann Leyland, d of Donald Yorke, MC, Prenton, Birkenhead, Cheshire; one s three d. *Educ:* King's College, Taunton; Brasenose College, Oxford (Hulme Open Exhibitioner; MA), Hon. Fellow, 1972. Secretary and Librarian of the Oxford Union, 1942; Pres. Oxford University Conservative Assoc., 1942; Chm., Federation of University Conservative Associations, 1943. Called to the Bar, Middle Temple, 1948 (Robert Garraway Rice Pupillage Prizeman). Member Surbiton Borough Council, 1945-54; Alderman, 1949-54; Mayor, 1951-52; Member: LCC (Chelsea), 1952-61 (Leader of Conserv. Party on LCC, 1957-59); Court, Univ. of London, 1958-; Dep. Chm., British Section of the Council of European Municipalities; President: British Sect., European League for Economic Co-operation; The Enterprise Assoc.; London Mayors' Assoc., 1968-71; Surrey Mayors' Assoc., 1974-76; Admiral of the Manx Herring Fleet, 1971-74. Chm. Conservative National Advisory Committee on Local Government, 1957-59, Pres., 1972-74; Vice-Pres., Council of Europe's Local Government Conference, 1957 and 1958; Contested (C) Shoreditch and Finsbury, General Elections, 1950 and 1951; MP (C) Norwich South, 1955-64. PPS, Min. of Housing and Local Govt, 1956-57, Min. of Defence, 1957-59; Parly Sec., Min. of Aviation, 1959-61; Jt Parly Sec., Min. of Housing and Local Govt, Oct. 1961-July 1962; Minister of Public Building and Works, 1962-64 (Cabinet, 1963-64); Chief Opposition Spokesman on housing, local govt and law, 1966-68, on defence, 1968-70; Minister of Technology, 1970; Chancellor of the Duchy of Lancaster, 1970-72; Sec. of State for the Environment, 1972-74; Chief Opposition Spokesman on Foreign and Commonwealth Affairs, 1974-. Leader, Cons. Party Delegn to Council of Europe and WEU, 1967-70. Chm., Dun and Bradstreet Ltd, 1976-; formerly: Chm., Holland, Hannen & Cubitts; Dep. Chm., Drake & Gorham; Director: Fairey Co.

Ltd; Bristol Aeroplane Co.; Hotung Estates. *Publications:* (Co-author) Forward from Victory, 1943; The Rent Act, 1957; various pamphlets and articles on foreign affairs, local government and legal subjects. *Recreations:* watching cricket, travel. *Address:* Ellwood House, Barrasford, Hexham, Northumberland; 21 Caroline Terrace, SW1; 2 Paper Buildings, Temple, EC4. *T:* 01-353 5835. *Clubs:* Whites, Pratt's, MCC; Northern Conservative and Unionist (Newcastle upon Tyne).

RISHBETH, John, ScD; FRS 1974; Reader in Plant Pathology, University of Cambridge, since 1973; b 10 July 1918; e s of late Prof. Oswald Henry Theodore Rishbeth and Kathleen (*née* Haddon), Cambridge; m 1946, Barbara Sadler; one s one d. *Educ:* St Lawrence Coll., Ramsgate; Christ's Coll., Cambridge. MA, PhD, ScD (Cantab). Frank Smart Prize, 1940, and Studentship, 1944, 1946, in Botany. Chemist, Royal Ordnance Factories, 1940-43; Bacteriologist, Scientific Adviser's Div., Min. of Food, 1943-45; Demonstrator in Botany, Univ. of Cambridge, 1947-49; Plant Pathologist, West Indian Banana Research Scheme, 1950-52; Lectr in Botany, Univ. of Cambridge, 1953-73. Visiting Prof. in Forest Pathology, N Carolina State Univ., 1967. Hon. Dr.agro, Royal Veterinary and Agricl Univ., Copenhagen, 1976. *Publications:* papers on: root diseases, especially of trees, caused by fungi; biological control. *Recreations:* hill walking, tennis. *Address:* 36 Wingate Way, Cambridge CB2 2HD. *T:* Trumpington 3298. *Club:* Hawks (Cambridge).

RISK, Thomas Neilson; Partner, Maclay Murray & Spens, Solicitors, Glasgow and Edinburgh, since 1950; b 13 Sept. 1922; s of late Ralph Risk, CBE, MC, and of Margaret Nelson Robertson; m 1949, Suzanne Eiloart; four s. *Educ:* Kelvinside Academy; Glasgow Univ. Flight Lieut, RAF, 1941-46; RAFVR, 1946-53. Director: Standard Life Assurance Co. (Chm., 1969-77); Bank of Scotland (Dep. Governor, 1977-); British Linen Bank (Governor, 1977-); Bank of Scotland Finance Co. Ltd (Chm., 1973-); Howden Group Ltd; Merchants Trust Ltd; Mine Safety Appliances Co. Ltd. Mem., Scottish Industrial Develt Bd, 1972-75. Trustee, Hamilton Bequest. *Recreations:* shooting, golf. *Address:* 24 Boclair Crescent, Bearsden, Glasgow. *T:* 041-942 0392. *Clubs:* Royal Air Force; Western (Glasgow); Royal and Ancient (St Andrews).

RISK, William Symington, CA; Chairman: Martin-Black Ltd; Alexander Cross (Seeds) Ltd; Robert Edgar & Sons Ltd; Fleming & Ferguson Ltd; Mayflower Carpets Ltd; Director: Anglo Scottish Investment Trust; Block, Grey & Block Ltd; Brengreen Ltd; Hambros Industrial Management Ltd; Tectonic (Electronics) Ltd; Queen Charlotte's Hospital; b 15 Sept. 1909; er s of late William Risk and Agnes Hetherington Symington, Glasgow; m 1937, Isobel Brown McLay; one s one d. *Educ:* Glasgow Academy; Glasgow Univ.; Edinburgh Univ. (BCom). FCMA 1944, JDipMA 1969. Cost Accountant and Deptl Manager, Penmaenmawr & Welsh Granite Co. Ltd, 1936. Served War, with Admiralty, on torpedo production at RN Torpedo Factory, at Greenock and elsewhere, 1940-45. Partner, Robson, Morrow & Co., 1945-53; Managing Director: H. W. Nevill Ltd (Nevill's Bread), 1953; Aerated Bread Co. Ltd, 1956; Chm., The London Multiple Bakers' Alliance, 1958-59; Regional Dir for Southern England, British Bakeries Ltd, 1960; Industrial Consultant, Hambros Bank Ltd, 1963. Inst. of Chartered Accountants of Scotland: Mem. Exam. Bd, 1951-55; Mem. Council, 1963-68; Pres., 1974-75; Jt Dip. in Management Accounting Services, and First Chm. of Bd, 1966; Inst. of Cost and Management Accountants: Mem. Council, 1952-70; Pres. of Inst., 1960-61; Gold Medal of Inst., for services to the Inst. and the profession, 1965. Mem. Bd of Governors, Queen Charlotte's Hosp., 1970. *Publications:* many technical papers on Accountancy and Management subjects; papers to internat. Congress of Accountants (London, 1952, Paris, 1967). *Recreations:* golf, hill walking, badminton, gardening, reading. *Address:* Fenmore, Copperkins Lane, Amersham, Buckinghamshire HP6 5RA. *T:* Amersham 5172. *Clubs:* Caledonian, Oriental.

RISSON, Maj.-Gen. Sir Robert Joseph Henry, Kt 1970; CB 1958; CBE 1945 (OBE 1942); DSO 1942; ED 1948; Chairman Melbourne and Metropolitan Tramways Board, 1949-70; Chairman, National Fitness Council of Victoria, 1961-71; b 20 April 1901; s of late Robert Risson; m 1934, Gwendolyn, d of late C. A. Spurgin; no c. *Educ:* Gatton High Sch.; Univ. of Queensland. BE (Civil); FICE; FIEAust; FCIT; FAIM. Served AIF, War of 1939-45: GOC 3 Div. (Australian), 1953-56; Citizen Military Forces Member Australian Military Board, 1957-58. Chief Commissioner, Boy Scouts, Victoria, 1958-63; Pres., Instn Engineers, Australia, 1962-63. OStJ 1966. *Address:* 39 Somers Street, Burwood, Victoria 3125, Australia. *Clubs:* Australian (Melbourne); Naval and Military (Melbourne); United Service (Brisbane).

RITCHARD, Cyril; actor; *b* Sydney, NSW, 1 Dec. 1898; *s* of Herbert Trimnell-Ritchard and Margaret (*née* Collins); *m* Madge Elliott (*d* 1955), actress. *Educ:* St Aloysius College, Sydney, New South Wales; Sydney University. Various light comedy parts, 1917-24; went to USA, 1924; first appearance on London stage in Bubbly (revival), Duke of York's, 1925; in various productions, 1925-31, including Charlot's Revue and the Co-Optimists of 1930; Australia, 1932-36; returned to England, 1936; played the leading part in Nine Sharp (Revue), Little, 1938-39; The Little Review, Little, 1939; produced The New Ambassadors' Revue, Ambassadors', 1941; appeared in Big Top, His Majesty's, 1942; The Importance of Being Earnest (Algernon Moncrieffe), Phœnix, 1942; The Merry Widow (Prince Danilo), His Majesty's, 1943, on tour abroad for the Forces, 1943-44, Coliseum, 1944; Gay Rosalinda, Palace, 1945; returned to Australia, taking various parts at Theatre Royal, Sydney, 1946; Love for Love (Tattle), New York, 1947; The Relapse (Sir Novelty Fashion), Lyric, Hammersmith, Dec. 1947, Phœnix, Jan. 1948, and in USA 1950. Since 1948 has directed and played in USA, London, etc. Recent successes include: The Millionairess (Adrian Blenderbland), New, and in New York, 1952; High Spirits, London Hippodrome, 1953; Captain Hook in Musical of Peter Pan, Winter Garden, New York, 1954; (directed) Tales of Hoffman, New York Metropolitan Opera, 1955; Eisenstein in Rosalinda, Civic Light Opera Co., Los Angeles and San Francisco, 1956; (directed and played Don Andres) Offenbach's La Perichole, Metropolitan Opera House, New York, 1956; (directed) Reluctant Debutante, Henry Miller Theatre, New York, 1956; (directed and played in) Visit to a Small Planet (Kreton), Booth Theatre, New York, 1957; (directed) new versions of The Marriage of Figaro and Gypsy Baron, Metropolitan Opera, 1958-59; (directed and starred in) The Pleasure of his Company, USA, 1958-60, touring Australia, 1960; (directed and starred in) The Happiest Girl in the World, New York, 1961; The Roar of the Greasepaint-the Smell of the Crowd, New York, 1965; appeared in Half a Sixpence (film), 1967; (directed and played in) Midsummer Night's Dream, Stratford, Connecticut, 1967; (directed and played Gen. Burgoyne) The Devil's Disciple, Stratford, Conn., 1969, and Hartke Theatre, Catholic Univ., Washington, 1970; (narrated) Facade (Sitwell-Walton), Ottawa Symphony, Canada, 1970; (narrated) Peter and the Wolf, Balanchine Ballet, NY City Centre, 1970, and Lancaster, Ohio, 1971; Metropolitan Opera, NY: (directed) Contes d'Hoffmann, 1971; (directed and played Don Andres) La Perichole, 1971, and tour 1971; (directed and played Pogo Poole) The Pleasure of his Company, 1971; Osgood in Sugar, Majestic Theatre, NY 1972-73. Starred in Romulus, Music Box Theater, New York; and in revival of La Perichole, Metropolitan Opera House; played Phineas Fogg in musical version of Around the World in 80 days, St Louis Municipal Opera and Kansas City Starlight Theater. Has also appeared in films and starred in several TV spectaculars. *Address:* 135 Central Park West, New York City, USA.

RITCHESON, Prof. Charles Ray; Lovell Distinguished Professor of History, University of Southern California, since 1977; *b* 26 Feb. 1925; *s* of Charles Frederick and Jewell Ida Ritcheson; *m* 1st, 1953, Shirley Spackman (marr. diss. 1963); two *s*; 2nd, 1965, Alice Luethi; three *s*. *Educ:* Univs of Harvard, Zürich, Oklahoma and Oxford. DPhil (Oxon). Prof. and Chm. of History, Kenyon Coll., 1953-65; Chm. and Dir, Graduate Studies, Southern Methodist Univ., 1965-70; Lovell Prof. of History, Univ. of Southern Calif., 1971-74; Cultural Attaché, US Embassy, 1974-77. Member: Board of Dirs, Amer. Friends of Covent Garden; Adv. Council, Ditchley Foundn. Hon. DLitt Leicester, 1976. *Publications:* British Politics and the American Revolution, 1954; Aftermath of Revolution: British policy toward the United States 1783-1795, 1969 (paperback, 1971); The American Revolution: the Anglo-American relation, 1969; (with E. Wright) A Tug of Loyalties, 1971. *Recreations:* horseback riding, swimming, opera. *Address:* 471 South Bristol Avenue, Los Angeles, Calif 90047, USA. *T:* (213)828-0926. *Clubs:* Athenæum, Beefsteak, Garrick.

RITCHIE, family name of **Baron Ritchie of Dundee.**

RITCHIE OF DUNDEE, 4th Baron *cr* 1905; **Colin Neville Ower Ritchie;** *b* 9 July 1908; 3rd *s* of 2nd Baron Ritchie of Dundee and Sarah Ruth (*d* 1950), 4th *d* of L. J. Jennings, MP; *S* brother, 1975; *m* 1943, Anne Petronill, *d* of H. C. Burra, Rye. *Educ:* Down House, Rottingdean; Trinity Coll., Oxford (BA 1929). Formerly Headmaster of Brickwall School, Northiam, Sussex. *Heir:* *b* Hon. (Harold) Malcolm Ritchie [*b* 29 Aug. 1919; *m* 1948, Anne, *d* of late Col Charles George Johnstone, MC, Durban; one *s* one *d*]. *Address:* 5 Fairmeadow, Rye Hill, Rye, Sussex. *Clubs:* All England Lawn Tennis, International Lawn Tennis of GB, Rye Golf.

RITCHIE, Albert Edgar, CC 1975; Canadian Ambassador to the Republic of Ireland, since 1976; *b* 20 Dec. 1916; *m* ; two *s* two *d*. *Educ:* Mount Allison Univ., New Brunswick (BA 1938); Queen's College, Oxford (Rhodes Scholar, 1940; BA). Deputy Under-Secretary of State for External Affairs, Canada, 1964-66; Canadian Ambassador to USA, 1966-70; Under-Sec. of State for External Affairs, Canada, 1970-74; Special Advisor to Privy Council Office, Canada, 1974-76. Hon. LLD: Mount Allison Univ., 1966; St Thomas Univ., 1968. *Address:* Canadian Embassy, 4th Floor, 65-68 St Stephen's Green, Dublin 2, Ireland; 16 Carlyle Avenue, Ottawa K1S 4Y3, Ont, Canada. *Club:* Rideau (Ottawa).

RITCHIE, Alexander James Otway; Deputy Chairman, Grindlays Bank Ltd, since 1977; Chairman, Union Discount Co. of London Ltd, since 1970; *b* 5 May 1928; *s* of Charles Henry Ritchie and Marjorie Alice Ritchie (*née* Stewart); *m* 1953, Joanna Willink Fletcher; two *s* one *d*. *Educ:* Stowe; St John's Coll., Cambridge (MA). Joined Glyn, Mills and Co., 1951 (Dir, 1964); Exec. Dir, Williams & Glyn's Bank, 1970; resigned Williams & Glyn's Bank, 1977, for present post. Mem., London Cttee, Ottoman Bank, 1966-; Mem., Export Guarantees Adv. Council. *Recreation:* inland waterways. *Address:* Thornfield House, Vine Road, SW13 0NE. *T:* 01-876 4450. *Club:* Boodle's.

RITCHIE, Anthony Elliot, MA, BSc, MD; FRSE; Secretary and Treasurer, Carnegie Trust for the Universities of Scotland, since 1969; *b* 30 March 1915; *s* of late Prof. James Ritchie; *m* 1941, Elizabeth Lambie Knox, MB, ChB, *y d* of John Knox, Dunfermline; one *s* three *d*. *Educ:* Edinburgh Academy; Aberdeen and Edinburgh Universities. MA (Aber), 1933; BSc 1936, with Hunter Memorial Prize. MB, ChB (Edin.) 1940. Carnegie Research Scholar, Physiology Dept, Edin. Univ., 1940-41; Asst Lectr 1941; Lectr 1942. Ellis Prize in Physiology, 1941; Gunning Victoria Jubilee Prize, 1943; MD (Edin.) with Gold Medal Thesis, 1945; senior lecturer grade, 1946. Lecturer in Electrotherapy, Edin. Royal Infirmary, 1943-48, 1972-; Chandos Prof. of Physiology, Univ. of St Andrews, 1948-69; Dean, Faculty of Science, 1961-66. Hon. Physiologist Gogarburn Nerve Injuries Hospital, 1941-46; Honeyman Gillespie Lecturer, 1944; Hon. Consultant in Electrotherapy, Scot. E Regional Hospital Board, 1950-69; Fellow Royal Soc. of Edinburgh, 1951 (Council RSE 1957-60; Secretary to Ordinary Meetings, 1960-65, Vice-President, 1965-66 and 1976-; General Secretary, 1966-76); Scientific Adviser, Civil Defence, 1961-77; Adv. Cttee on Med. Research, Scotland, 1961-, Vice-Chm., 1967-69; Chairman: Scottish Cttee on Science Educn, 1970-; Blood Transfusion Adv. Gp, 1970-; Scottish Universities Entrance Bd, 1963-69; St Leonard's Sch., St Andrews, 1968-69; Mem., British Library Bd, 1973-; Trustee, Nat. Library of Scotland. Mem., Cttee of Inquiry into Teachers' Pay. Examiner, Chartered Soc. of Physiotherapy, Pharmaceutical Soc. of Great Britain, and RCSE. RAMC (TA) commission, 1942-44. Hon. FCSP, 1970. Hon. DSc St Andrews, 1972. *Publications:* (with J. Lenman) Clinical Electromyography, 1976; medical and scientific papers on nerve injury diagnosis and medical electronics. *Recreations:* reading, mountaineering, motor cars. *Address:* 12 Ravelston Park, Edinburgh EH4 3DX. *T:* 031-332 6560. *Clubs:* Caledonian; New (Edinburgh).

RITCHIE, Charles Stewart Almon, CC 1972; *b* 23 Sept. 1906; *s* of William Bruce Almon Ritchie, KC and Lilian Constance Harriette Ritchie (*née* Stewart), both of Halifax, Nova Scotia; *m* 1948, Sylvia Catherine Beatrice Smellie; no *c*. *Educ:* University of King's College; Ecole Libre des Sciences Politiques, Paris. BA, MA Oxford 1929, MA Harvard, 1930. Joined Dept of External Affairs, 3rd Sec. Ottawa, 1934; 3rd Sec., Washington, 1936; 2nd Sec., London, 1939; 1st Sec., London, 1943; 1st Sec., Ottawa, 1945; Counsellor, Paris, 1947; Asst Under-Secretary of State for External Affairs, Ottawa, 1950, Deputy Under-Secretary of State for External Affairs, 1952; Ambassador to Federal Republic of Germany, Bonn, and Head of Military Mission, Berlin, 1954; Permanent Rep. to UN, New York 1958; Ambassador of Canada to the United States, 1962; Ambassador and Permanent Representative of Canada to the North Atlantic Council, 1966-67; Canadian High Comr in London, 1967-71; Special Adviser to Privy Council, Canada, 1971-73. Hon. DCL, Univ. of King's College, Halifax, NS; Hon. Fellow, Pembroke College, Oxford. *Publication:* The Siren years: undiplomatic diaries 1937-1945, 1974. *Address:* Apt 10, 216 Metcalfe Street, Ottawa, Canada. *Clubs:* Brooks's, Beefsteak, Travellers'.

RITCHIE, Sir Douglas; see Ritchie, Sir J. D.

RITCHIE, Rear-Adm. George Stephen, CB 1967; DSC 1942; President, Directing Committee, International Hydrographic Bureau, Monaco, since 1972; *b* 30 Oct. 1914; *s* of Sir (John) Douglas Ritchie, *qv*; *m* 1942, Mrs Disa Elizabeth Smith (*née*

Beveridge); three *s* one *d. Educ:* RNC, Dartmouth. Joined RN Surveying Service, 1936; attached Eighth Army, 1942-43; served in HM Survey Ship Scott for invasion of Europe, 1944; comd HMS Challenger on scientific voyage round world, 1950-51; comd HM New Zealand Survey Ship Lachlan and NZ Surveying Service, 1953-56; comd HM Surveying Ship Dalrymple, Persian Gulf, 1959; comd HM Surveying Ship Vidal, West Indies and Western Europe, 1963-65; ADC to the Queen, 1965; Hydrographer of the Navy, 1966-71; Vis. Research Fellow, Southampton Univ., 1971-72. Founder's Medal, RGS, 1972; Prix Manley-Bendall, Académie de Marine, Paris, 1977. *Publications:* Challenger, 1957; The Admiralty Chart, 1967; papers on navigation and oceanography in various jls, including Developments in British Hydrography since days of Captain Cook (RSA Silver Medal, 1970). *Recreations:* writing, painting, gardening, hunting. *Address:* St James, Avenue Princesse Alice, Monte-Carlo, Monaco. *Clubs:* Reform; Monte Carlo (Pres. 1976-).

RITCHIE, Harry Parker, CMG 1966; *b* 3 June, 1919; *s* of W. S. Ritchie; *m* 1949, Mary Grace, *née* Foster; two *s. Educ:* Royal Belfast Academical Institution; Queen's University, Belfast. Served War of 1939-45 (Captain). Administrative Cadet, Bechuanaland Protectorate, 1946; Swaziland, 1948; District Officer, 1953; seconded to Office of High Commissioner, as Assistant Secretary, 1954; Deputy Financial Secretary, Fiji, 1957, Financial Secretary, 1962-67, Minister of Finance, 1967-70; Secretary for Finance, Papua New Guinea, 1971-74. Financial and Econ. Consultant to Papua New Guinea Govt, 1974-75; Consultant on Civil Service Salaries to Govt of Tonga (report pubd 1976), to Govt of Seychelles (report pubd 1977). *Recreations:* gardening, reading. *Address:* 6 Mill Rise, Mill Lane, Bourton, Dorset. *Club:* Royal Over-Seas League.

RITCHIE, Horace David; Professor of Surgery, University of London, and Director of the Surgical Unit at The London Hospital, since 1964; *b* 24 Sept. 1920; *m*; three *s. Educ:* Universities of Glasgow, Cambridge and Edinburgh. *Publications:* contribs to various scientific journals. *Address:* 129 Burbage Road, Dulwich Village, SE21.

RITCHIE, Sir James Edward Thomson, 2nd Bt, *cr* 1918 (2nd creation); TD 1943 (2 clasps); FRSA; Chairman M. W. Hardy & Co. Ltd; Director, Wm Ritchie & Son (Textiles) Ltd; Member Court of Assistants, Merchant Taylors' Co. (Master, 1963-64); *b* 16 June 1902; *s* of 1st Baronet and Ada Bevan, *d* of late Edward ap Rees Bryant; *S* father, 1937; *m* 1st, 1928, Esme Phyllis (*d* 1939), *o d* of late J. M. Oldham, Ormidale, Ascot; 2nd, 1936, Rosemary, *yr d* of late Col. Henry Streatfeild, DSO, TD; two *d. Educ:* Rugby; The Queen's Coll., Oxford. Joined Inns of Court Regt, 1936; commissioned, 1938; served 1939-45 (CMF 1944-45), various staff and regimental appts; Lt-Col 1945; re-commissioned, 1949, to command 44 (Home Counties) Div. Provost Co. RCMP (TA); retired 1953. Co-opted Mem. Kent TA&AFA (Mem. General Purposes Cttee), 1953-68. Chm., Chatwood-Milner (formerly Milners Safe Co. Ltd), 1937-70; Director: Caledonian Insurance Co. (London Bd), 1951-67; Guardian Assurance Co. Ltd (Local London Bd, 1967-71). Pres., Royal British Legion, Ashford (Kent) Br., 1952-75; Patron, Ashford and Dist Caledonian Society; Chm. Finance and General Purposes Cttee and joint Hon. Treas., London School of Hygiene and Tropical Medicine, Univ. of London, 1951-61; co-opted Mem. Bd of Management and Finance and Gen. Purposes Cttee, 1964-67. *Heir: half-b* William Peter Emerton Ritchie, *b* 1918. *Address:* Kirkbank House, High Halden, Ashford, Kent TN26 2JD. *T:* Ashford 85249. *Club:* Army and Navy.

RITCHIE, (James) Martin; Chairman, British Enkalon Ltd, since 1975; Director: Vickers Ltd; Sun Alliance and London Insurance Ltd; Haymills Holdings Ltd; *b* 29 May 1917; *s* of late Sir James Ritchie, CBE and Lady Ritchie (*née* Gemmell); *m* 1939, Noreen Mary Louise Johnston; three *s. Educ:* Strathallan Sch., Perthshire. Joined Andrew Ritchie & Son Ltd, Glasgow, corrugated fibre container manufrs, 1934; Dir, 1938. TA Officer, 1938; served War of 1939-45: HAA Regt; Capt. 1941; psc 1943; DAA&QMG, MEF, Middle East, 1944-45 (Maj.). Rejoined Andrew Ritchie & Son Ltd, then part of Eburite Organisation; Man. Dir, 1950; Gen. Man., Bowater-Eburite Ltd, on merger with Bowater Organisation, 1956; Bowater Paper Corp. Ltd: Dir, 1959; Man. Dir, 1964; Dep. Chm. and Man. Dir, 1967; Chm. 1969-72. FBIM 1971; FRSA 1971. *Recreations:* golf, fishing. *Address:* The Court House, Fulmer, Bucks. *T:* Fulmer 2585. *Clubs:* Denham Golf; Costa Brava Golf (Santa Cristina de Aro, Spain).

RITCHIE, James Walter, MC; a Managing Director, Inchcape & Co. Ltd, since 1975; *b* 12 Jan. 1920; *s* of Sir Adam Ritchie; *m*

1951, Penelope June (*née* Forbes); two *s* two *d. Educ:* Ampleforth Coll.; Clare Coll., Cambridge. Gordon Highlanders, 1941-46. Smith Mackenzie & Co. Ltd, and Mackenzie (Kenya) Ltd, Nairobi, 1946-71; Dir, Inchcape & Co. Ltd, 1972-75. *Recreations:* hunting, fishing, golf. *Address:* Lockeridge Down, Lockeridge, near Marlborough, Wilts. *T:* Lockeridge 244. *Clubs:* City of London, Oriental.

RITCHIE, John, MBE 1944; Master of the Supreme Court of Judicature (Queen's Bench Division) since 1960; *b* 7 Feb. 1913; *e s* of W. Tod Ritchie, JP, Rector of Hutchesons' Grammar School, Glasgow; *m* 1936, Nora Gwendolen Margaret, *yr d* of Sir Frederic G. Kenyon, GBE, KCB, FBA; one *s* two *d. Educ:* Glasgow Academy; Magdalen College, Oxford. BA 1935; MA 1948. Called to the Bar, Middle Temple, 1935; practised in London and on South-Eastern Circuit, 1935-60; Recorder of King's Lynn, 1956-58. Served War of 1939-45 (MBE, Belgian Croix de Guerre, despatches twice): BEF 1940; BLA 1944-45; private, Royal Fusiliers, 1939; commissioned Queen's Own Cameron Highlanders, 1940; Major, 1942. Belgian Croix de Guerre, 1944. *Recreations:* cricket; tennis; painting; rose-growing; wine-tasting. *Address:* Kirkstead, Godstone, Surrey. *T:* Godstone 2335; Royal Courts of Justice, Strand, WC2. *T:* 01-405 7641. *Club:* Caledonian.

RITCHIE, Sir (John) Douglas, Kt 1941; MC; *b* 28 Nov. 1885; *s* of John Walker Ritchie, Collieston, Aberdeenshire, and Mary Southern; *m* 1913, Margaret Stephen, OBE 1946, JP, Officer of the Order of Orange-Nassau (*d* 1976), *d* of James Allan, Methlick, Aberdeenshire; one *s. Educ:* Manchester Grammar School; Manchester Univ. Served European War in France in 4th Gordon Highlanders and Tank Corps (MC); Town Clerk of Burnley, 1920-23; Solicitor to the Port of London Authority, 1923-26; Solicitor and Secretary to the Port of London Authority, 1927-38; Deputy General Manager, 1938; Gen. Manager, 1938-46; Vice-Chm., Port of London Authority, 1946-55. Mem. Aberdeen County Council, 1955-65; Pres., Dock and Harbour Authorities Assoc., 1954-56; Pres. of Burns Club of London, 1934-35; Chief Executive of London Port Emergency Cttee, 1939-46; Member of Inland Transport War Council; Col. Engineer and Railway Staff Corps RE (TA). *Recreations:* sailing, fishing. *Address:* Collieston, Aberdeenshire. *T:* Collieston 216.

See also Rear-Adm. G. S. Ritchie.

RITCHIE, Prof. J(oseph) Murdoch, PhD, DSc; FRS 1976; Eugene Higgins Professor of Pharmacology, since 1968, and Director, Division of Biological Sciences, since 1975, Yale University; *b* 10 June 1925; *s* of Alexander Farquharson Ritchie and Agnes Jane (*née* Bremner); *m* 1951, Brenda Rachel (*née* Bigland); one *s* one *d. Educ:* Aberdeen Central Secondary Sch.; Aberdeen Univ. (BSc Maths); UCL (BSc Physiol., PhD, DSc). MInstP. Res. in Radar, Telecommunications Res. Estabt, Malvern, 1944-46; University Coll. London: Hon. Res. Asst, Biophysics Res. Unit, 1946-49; Lectr in Physiol., 1949-51; Mem. staff, Nat. Inst. for Med. Res., Mill Hill, 1951-55; Asst Prof. of Pharmacology, 1956-57, Associate Prof., 1958-63 and Prof., 1963-68, Albert Einstein Coll. of Medicine, NY; Overseas Fellow, Churchill Coll., Cambridge, 1964-65; Chm., Dept of Pharmacol., Yale Univ., 1968-74. Hon. MA Yale, 1968. *Publications:* papers on nerve and muscle physiol. and biophysics in Jl of Physiol. *Recreations:* skiing, chess. *Address:* 47 Deepwood Drive, Hamden, Conn 06517, USA. *T:* (home) (203) 777-0420; (office) (203) 436-3617. *Club:* Yale (NYC).

RITCHIE, Kenneth Gordon, CMG 1968; HM Diplomatic Service, retired; *b* 19 Aug. 1921; *s* of Walter Ritchie, Arbroath; *m* 1951, Esme Stronsa Nash. *Educ:* Arbroath High Sch.; St Andrews Univ. (MA). Joined FO, 1944; Embassy, Ankara, 1944-47; Foreign Office, 1947-49; Khorramshahr, 1949-50; Tehran, 1950-52; Djakarta, 1952-55; Foreign Office, 1955-57; Peking, 1957-62; Santiago, 1962-64; Elisabethville, 1965-66; Dep. High Commissioner, Lusaka, 1966-67; High Commissioner, Guyana, 1967-70; Head of Perm. Under-Sec.'s Dept, FCO, 1970-73; High Comr, Malawi, 1973-77. *Recreations:* cinephotography, model railways. *Address:* Dalforbie, North Esk Road, Edzell, Angus.

RITCHIE, Margaret Claire; Headmistress of Queenswood School, since 1972; *b* 18 Sept. 1937; *d* of Roderick M. Ritchie, Edinburgh. *Educ:* Leeds Girls' High Sch.; Univ. of Leeds (BSc). Postgraduate Certificate in Education, Univ. of London. Asst Mistress, St Leonards Sch., St Andrews, 1960-64; Head of Science Dept, Wycombe Abbey Sch., High Wycombe, 1964-71. *Address:* Queenswood, Hatfield, Herts AL9 6NS. *T:* Potters Bar 52262.

RITCHIE, Martin; see Ritchie, J. M.

RITCHIE, Gen. Sir Neil Methuen, GBE 1951 (KBE 1945; CBE 1940); KCB 1947 (CB 1944); DSO 1917; MC 1918; retired; Director: Electra Investments (Can.) Ltd; Tanqueray Gordon & Co. (Can.) Ltd; *b* 29 July 1897; 2nd *s* of late Dugald Ritchie of Restholme, Liss, Hants; *m* 1937, Catherine, *d* of James A. Minnes, Kingston, Ontario; one *s* one *d. Educ:* Lancing; RMC, Sandhurst. 2nd Lieut The Black Watch, 1914; Lieutenant 1915; Capt. 1917; Bt Major, 1933; Major, 1934; Bt Lt-Col 1936; Lt-Col The King's Own Royal Regt 1938; Col 1939; Brigadier 1939; Acting Maj.-General 1940; Temp. Major-General 1941; Maj.-Gen. 1943; Temp. Lt-Gen. 1944; Lt-Gen. 1945; General 1947; served European War, 1914-19; France, 1915; Mesopotamia, 1916-17; Palestine, 1918 (despatches, DSO, MC); Palestine, 1938-39 (despatches); Gen. Staff Officer, 3rd Grade, War Office, 1923-27; Staff College, Camberley, 1929-30; GSO2, Northern Command, India, 1933-37; GSO1, 1939; Brigadier, General Staff, 1939; Comdr 51st Highland Division, 1940-41; Deputy Chief of Staff Middle East, 1941; Commander of 8th Army, Libya, acting rank of Lieut-General, 1941; Comd 52nd Lowland Division, 1942-43; Comd 12 Corps BLA, 1944-45; GOC-in-C Scottish Command and Governor of Edinburgh Castle, 1945-47; C-in-C, Far East Land Forces, 1947-49; Commander British Army Staff, Washington, and Military Member of Joint Services Mission 1950-51; ADC General to the King, 1948-51; retired pay, 1951. Colonel, The Black Watch (Royal Highland Regiment), 1950-52. Queen's Body Guard for Scotland. Dir Emeritus, Mercantile & General Re-insurance Co. of Canada Ltd. Virtuti Militari (Poland), 1942; Comdr Legion of Honour, Croix de Guerre (France), 1945; Kt Comdr Orange Nassau (Holland), 1945; Comdr Order of Merit (USA), 1945. KStJ 1963. *Address:* RR2, Claremont, Ontario L0H 1E0, Canada. *T:* (416) 294-1001. *Clubs:* Caledonian, I Zingari, Free Foresters; York (Toronto).

RITCHIE, Major-General Walter Henry Dennison, CB 1953; CBE 1944 (OBE 1940); Life President, Earls Court & Olympia Ltd, 1974 (Chairman, Earls Court Ltd, 1967, Earls Court & Olympia Ltd, 1973); *b* 28 April 1901; *s* of Henry Montague Ritchie, Perth; *m* 1930, Gladys Stella, *d* of William Craven, Southsea; one *s* one *d. Educ:* St John's Coll., Southsea. 2nd Lieut RASC, 1925; served War of 1939-45, in France, N Africa, Italy; Maj. 1939; Brig. 1943; Maj.-Gen. 1953; Director of Quartering, War Office, 1953-54; Director of Supplies and Transport, War Office, 1954-57; retired. Col Comdt, RASC, 1959-64; Hon. Col 101 AER Regt, RCT, 1965-67. Freeman, City of London, 1962. Officer Legion of Merit, USA 1945. *Club:* Army and Navy.

RITCHIE-CALDER; family name of **Baron Ritchie-Calder.**

RITCHIE-CALDER, Baron, *cr* 1966, of Balmashannar (Life Peer); **Peter Ritchie Ritchie-Calder,** CBE 1945; MA (Edinburgh) 1961; author and journalist; Senior Fellow, Center for the Study of Democratic Institutions, Santa Barbara, California, 1972-75; *b* 1 July 1906; *s* of David Lindsay Calder and Georgina Ritchie, Forfar, Angus; *m* 1927, Mabel Jane Forbes, *d* of Dr David McKail, Glasgow; three *s* two *d. Educ:* Forfar Academy. Police court reporter, Dundee Courier (1922), D. C. Thomson Press (London office, 1924, Glasgow, 1925), Daily News (1926-30), Daily Chronicle (1930), Daily Herald (1930-41). Author, scientific, social and political journalist and broadcaster (radio and television). Science Editor, News Chronicle, 1945-56. Dept of FO, 1941-45; Editorial Staff, New Statesman, 1945-58; Montague Burton Professor of International Relations, Edinburgh University, 1961-67. Chm., Metrication Bd, 1969-72. Vis Prof., Heriot-Watt Univ., 1973-; Charles Beard lectr, Ruskin College, Oxford, 1957; Bentwich Lectr, Hebrew Univ., 1973; Brodetsky Lectr, Leeds Univ. 1973. Member Council British Association, Pres. Section X, 1955; Fell. Amer. Assoc. for Advancement of Science; Fabian Executive; Secretary of H. G. Wells' Debate, and Viscount Sankey Cttee, on New Declaration of the Rights of Man, 1940; Mem. British delegn to Unesco (Paris, 1946, Mexico City, 1947, 1966, 1968); special adviser at FAO Famine Conf. (Washington, 1946); Desert survey for Unesco, 1950; chief, special UN Mission to SE Asia, 1951; Mission (UN auspices) to Arctic, 1955; Member UN Secretariat, at Peaceful Uses of Atomic Energy Confs, 1955 and 1958, and Member WHO group on mental aspects of Atomic Energy, 1957; Consultant-Editor, UN Science and Technology Conference, Geneva, 1963; Chm. Chicago University study group on Radiation in the Environment, 1960; Special UN Mission to Congo, 1960; 2nd UN Mission to SE Asia, 1962. Associate, Center for the Study of Democratic Institutions, California, 1965; Chairman Association of British Science Writers, 1949-55. President: Mental Health Film Council; National Peace Council; British Sub-Aqua Club, 1971-74; Fellow of World Academy of Arts and

Science; Danforth Foundation Lecturer, USA, 1965. UK Commn for WHO; UK Commn for Unesco; Cons., OXFAM; Vice-Pres. Workers' Educational Assoc., 1958-68; Member: Gen. Council, Open Univ., 1969-; Community Relations Commn, 1968-70; Council, Internat. Ocean Inst., 1970-; Consultant, US Librarian of Congress, 1976. DUniv Open, 1975; DSc York, Ont, 1976. Kalinga Internat. Award for science writing, 1960; Victor Gollanz Award for service to humanity, 1969; New York Library Jubilee Medal, 1961; WHO Med. Soc. Medal, 1974. *Publications:* Birth of the Future, 1934; Conquest of Suffering, 1935; Roving Commission, 1935; Lesson of London, 1941; Carry on, London, 1941; Start Planning Britain Now, 1941; Men against the Desert, 1951; Profile of Science, 1951; The Lamp is Lit, 1951; Men against Ignorance, 1953 (UNESCO); Men Against the Jungle, 1954; Science in Our Lives, 1954 (USA); Science Makes Sense, 1955; Men against the Frozen North, 1957; Magic to Medicine, 1958; Medicine and Man, 1958; Ten Steps Forward: The Story of WHO, 1958; The Hand of Life: The Story of the Weizmann Institute, 1959; The Inheritors, 1960; Agony of the Congo, 1961; Life-Savers, 1961; Common Sense about a Starving World, 1962; Living with the Atom, 1962; World of Opportunity (for United Nations), 1963; Two-Way Passage, 1964; The Evolution of the Machine, 1968; Man and the Cosmos, 1968; Leonardo and the Age of the Eye, 1970; How Long have we got?, 1972; The Pollution of the Mediterranean, 1972. *Recreation:* carpentry. *Address:* 1 Randolph Place, Edinburgh EH3 7TQ. *T:* 031-225 5565. *Clubs:* Savile; Scottish Arts, University Staff (Edinburgh); Century (New York).

See also N. D. R. Calder.

RITSON, Sir Edward Herbert, KBE 1950; CB 1945; LLB; *b* 1892; *s* of late Edward E. Ritson, Liverpool; *m* 1922, Norah, *d* of David Halley, Broughty Ferry; one *s. Educ:* Liverpool Institute; London Univ. Entered Civil Service, 1910; Deputy Chairman, Board of Inland Revenue, 1949-57. *Address:* The Small House, Dinton, Salisbury, Wilts. *T:* Teffont 209.

RITSON, Muriel; CBE 1936; Controller (Scot.) (retd), Ministry of National Insurance; *b* 1885; *d* of John Fletcher Ritson and Agnes Jane Catto. *Educ:* Greenock Academy; Germany. Social Worker and Rent Collector, Glasgow Workman's Dwgs Coy. Ltd, 1908-11; Secretary Women's Friendly Society of Scotland, 1911-19; Member Scottish Board of Health, 1919-29; Controller Health and Pensions Insurance, Department of Health, Scotland, 1929-45. Member Ryan Committee of Enquiry into Health Insurance; Committee on Admission of Women to Diplomatic and Consular Service; Beveridge Comm. on Social Insurance. *Address:* 8 Eton Terrace, Edinburgh.

RIVERDALE, 2nd Baron, *cr* 1935; **Robert Arthur Balfour,** Bt 1929; DL; President, Balfour Darwins Ltd, 1969-75 (Chairman, 1961-69); *b* Sheffield, 1 Sept. 1901; *er s* of 1st Baron Riverdale, GBE; *S* father, 1957; *m* 1st, 1926, Nancy Marguerite (*d* 1928), *d* of late Rear-Adm. Mark Rundle, DSO; one *s*; 2nd, 1933, Christian Mary, *er d* of late Major Rowland Hill; one *s* one *d. Educ:* Aysgarth; Oundle. Served with RNVR, 1940-45, attaining rank of Lt-Comdr. Joined Arthur Balfour & Co. Ltd, 1918; Dir, 1924; Man. Dir, 1949; Chm. and Man. Dir, 1957-61; Exec. Chm. 1961-69. Director: National Provincial Bank, Main Central Bd, 1964-69 (Local Bd, 1949-69); National Westminster Bank, E Region, 1969-71; Light Trades House Ltd, 1956-65; Yorkshire Television, 1967-73. The Association of British Chambers of Commerce: Mem. Exec. Council, 1950-; Vice-Pres., 1952-54; Dep. Pres., 1954-57; Pres., 1957-58; Chm., Overseas Cttee, 1953-57. President: Nat. Fedn of Engineers' Tool Manufacturers, 1951-57 (Hon. Vice-Pres., 1957-; Representative on Gauge and Tool Adv. Council, 1946-64); Sheffield Chamber of Commerce, 1950 (Jt Hon. Sec., 1957-); Milling Cutter and Reamer Trade Assoc., 1936-54 (Vice-Pres., 1954-57); Twist Drill Traders' Assoc., 1946-55; Chm., British Council, Aust. Assoc. of British Manufacturers, 1954-57 (Vice-Chm., 1957-65; Hon. Mem., 1965-); Member: Management and Tech. Cttee, High Speed Steel Assoc., 1947-65; British Nat. Cttee of Internat. Chamber of Commerce Adv. Cttee, 1957-58; Nat. Production Adv. Cttee, 1957-58; Consultative Cttee for Industry, 1957-58; Standing Cttee, Crucible and High Speed Steel Conf., 1951-64; Western Hemisphere Exports Council (formerly Dollar Exports Council), 1957-61; Governor, Sheffield Savings Bank, 1948-58 (Patron, 1968-); Master Cutler, 1946; Trustee, Sheffield Town Trust, 1958-; Town Collector, Sheffield, 1974-; Guardian of Standard of Wrought Plate within City of Sheffield, 1948-; Belgian Consul for Sheffield area, 1945-. JP, City of Sheffield, 1950-66 (Pres., S Yorks Br. Magistrates' Assoc., 1971-); DL, S Yorks (formerly WR Yorks and City and County of York), 1959-. Pres., Derwent Fly Fishing Club. Is a Churchman and a Conservative. Chevalier of Order of the Crown, Belgium, 1956; La Médaille Civique de première classe; Officier de l'Ordre de

Leopold II, 1971. *Recreations:* yachting, yacht designing, shooting, stalking, fishing. *Heir: s* Hon. Mark Robin Balfour [*b* 16 July 1927; *m* 1959, Susan Ann, *e d* of R. P. Phillips, Sandygate, Sheffield; one *s* two *d*. *Educ:* Aysgarth; Trinity College School, Ontario. Company Director]. *Address:* Ropes, Grindleford, via Sheffield. *T:* Hope Valley 30408. *Clubs:* Bath, Royal Cruising; Sheffield (Sheffield).

RIVERINA, Bishop of, since 1971; **Rt. Rev. Barry Russell Hunter;** *b* Brisbane, Queensland, 15 Aug. 1927; *s* of late John Hunter; *m* 1961, Dorothy Nancy, *d* of B. P. Sanders, Brisbane; three *d*. *Educ:* Toowoomba Grammar Sch.; St Francis' Theological Coll., Brisbane; Univ. of Queensland (BA,ThL). Assistant Curate, St Matthew's, Sherwood, 1953-56; Member, Bush Brotherhood of St Paul, Cunnamulla, Queensland, 1956-61; Rector, St Cecilia's, Chinchilla, 1961-66; Rector, St Gabriel's, Biloela, 1966-71; Archdeacon of the East, Diocese of Rockhampton, 1969-71. *Recreation:* music. *Address:* Bishop's Lodge, 127 Audley Street, Narrandera, NSW 2700. *T:* Narrandera 59 1177. *Club:* Griffith Aero (Griffith).

RIVERS, Alfred Peter, FCA, FCIS; Chairman, Hovis-McDougall Ltd, 1965-71 (Deputy Chairman and Managing Director, 1957-65); *b* 7 April 1906; *s* of late Peter McKay Rivers and Grace Skinner; *m* 1934, Louise, *d* of late Charles Masters; one *s* one *d*. *Educ:* Addiscombe New Coll. and privately. Director: Norwich Union Insurance Group (London Board), 1964; Ranks Hovis McDougall Ltd, 1962-71. Member: UK Adv. Council on Education for Management, 1961-65; Council, Chartered Inst. of Secretaries, 1957-73 (Pres., 1970); Bd of Governors, King's Coll. Hosp., 1958-74; Economics and Business Studies Bd, Council for Nat. Acad. Awards, 1965-69; NEDC for Food Manufacturing Industry, 1968-71; Council, Chest and Heart Assoc., 1968-. Chairman: Fitton Trust, 1958-; Nat. Appeal Cttee, Shaftesbury Soc., 1962-68; Appeals and Public Relations Cttee, Voluntary Research Trust of King's Coll. Hosp. and Med. Sch., 1962-; Triad Trust, 1967-; Flour Adv. Bureau, 1968-71. Trustee, Southwark Rehearsal Hall Trust, 1973-; Special Trustee, King's Coll. Hosp., 1974-; Mem. Council: London Philharmonic Orchestra, 1971-76 (Vice-Chm., 1972-); King's Coll. Hosp. Med. Sch., 1973-76. *Recreations:* music and humour. *Address:* Elmcourt, Sutton Lane, Banstead, Surrey. *T:* Burgh Heath 56363.

RIVERS, Georgia; *see* Clark, Marjorie.

RIVERS, Mrs Rosalind V.; *see* Pitt-Rivers.

RIVETT-CARNAC, Rev. Sir (Thomas) Nicholas, 8th Bt *cr* 1836; Priest-in-charge, St Mark's, Kennington Oval, SE11; *b* 3 June 1927; *s* of Vice-Admiral James William Rivett-Carnac, CB, CBE, DSC (2nd *s* of 6th Bt) (*d* 1970), and of Isla Nesta Rivett-Carnac (*d* 1974), *d* of Harry Officer Blackwood; *S* uncle, 1972. *Educ:* Marlborough College. Scots Guards, 1945-55. Probation Service, 1957-59. Ordained, 1962. *Heir: b* Miles James Rivett-Carnac, Commander, RN [*b* 7 Feb. 1933; *m* 1958, April Sally, *d* of late Major Arthur Andrew Sidney Villar; two *s* one *d*]. *Address:* St Mark's Vicarage, Kennington Oval, SE11. *T:* 01-735 1801.

RIVETT-DRAKE, Brig. Dame Jean (Elizabeth), DBE 1964 (MBE 1947); JP; Member, Hove Borough Council, since 1966; Mayor of Hove, 1977-78; Lay Member, Press Council, since 1973; Director, Women's Royal Army Corps, 1961-64, retd; *b* 13 July 1909; *d* of Comdr Bertram Gregory Drake and of late Dora Rivett-Drake. *Educ:* St Mary's Hall, Brighton; Paris; Royal Academy of Music (LRAM piano). Served War of 1939-45 (despatches, 1946); driver, 1st London Motor Transport Co., Women's Transport Service (FANY), 1940; commnd ATS, 1942; served with BLA and 3 Port Staging Camp, Calais, 1945-47. Comdt Warr. Offrs' and Non-Commnd Offrs' Sch., 1947-48; Dep. Pres. No 10 Regular Commns Bd, 1948-49; Asst Dep. Dir: Home Counties Dist, 1949-52; London Dist, 1952-54; Far ELF, 1954-56; Dep. Dir: WO, 1957-60; Eastern Comd, 1960-61. Hon. ADC to the Queen, 1961-64. Mem., East Sussex CC, 1973-77 (Mem. Educn and Social Services Cttees, AHA). JP 1966. *Address:* 87 Hove Park Road, Hove, East Sussex BN3 6LN. *T:* Brighton 505839; c/o Barclays Bank Ltd, 92 Church Road, Hove, East Sussex. *Club:* English-Speaking Union.

RIX, Brian Norman Roger, CBE 1977; actor-manager, since 1948; Director and Theatre Controller, Cooney-Marsh Group, since 1976; *b* 27 Jan. 1924; *s* of late Herbert and Fanny Rix; *m* 1949, Elspet Jeans Macgregor-Gray; two *s* two *d*. *Educ:* Bootham Sch., York. Stage career: joined Donald Wolfit, 1942; first West End appearance, Sebastian in Twelfth Night, St James's, 1943; White Rose Players, Harrogate, 1943-44. Served War of 1939-45, RAF and Bevin Boy. Became actor-manager,

1948; ran repertory cos at Ilkley, Bridlington and Margate, 1948-50; toured Reluctant Heroes and brought to Whitehall Theatre, 1950-54; Dry Rot, 1954-58; Simple Spymen, 1958-61; One For the Pot, 1961-64; Chase Me Comrade, 1964-66; went to Garrick Theatre, 1967, with repertoire of farce: Stand By Your Bedouin; Uproar in the House; Let Sleeping Wives Lie; after 6 months went over to latter, only, which ran till 1969; then followed: She's Done It Again, 1969-70; Don't Just Lie There, Say Something!, 1971-73 (filmed 1973); New Theatre, Cardiff, Robinson Crusoe, 1973; Cambridge Theatre, A Bit Between The Teeth, 1974; Fringe Benefits, Whitehall Theatre, 1976. Entered films, 1951: subsequently made eleven, including Reluctant Heroes, 1951, Dry Rot, 1956. BBC, TV contract to present farces on TV, 1956-72; first ITV series Men of Affairs, 1973; A Roof Over My Head, BBC TV series, 1977. *Publication:* My Farce from My Elbow: an autobiography, 1975. *Recreations:* cricket, amateur radio (G2DQU). *Address:* 3 St Mary's Grove, Barnes Common, SW13. *T:* 01-785 9626. *Clubs:* Lord's Taverners' (Pres. 1970), MCC; Leander (Hon. Mem.).

RIX, Sir John, Kt 1977; MBE 1955; Chairman and Chief Executive, Vosper Thornycroft (UK) Ltd, since 1970; Chairman, Keith Nelson & Co. Ltd, since 1970; Director, David Brown-Vosper (Offshore) Ltd, since 1974; *b* 1917; *s* of Reginald Arthur Rix; *m* 1943, Sylvia Gene Howe; two *s* one *d*. *Educ:* Southampton Univ. Mem. Inst. of Naval Architects; MIMarE. Student apprentice in shipbuilding, John I. Thornycroft & Co. Ltd, 1934-37; Vosper Ltd: Techn. Dept, 1937; Works Dept, 1940-45; Shipyard Man., 1945-50; Commercial Man., 1950-55; Gen. Man., 1955-63. *Recreations:* sailing, tennis, walking. *Address:* Lower Baybridge House, Owslebury, Winchester, Hants. *T:* Owslebury 306. *Clubs:* Royal Thames Yacht, Island Sailing.

RIZZELLO, Michael Gaspard, OBE 1977; President, Royal Society of British Sculptors; sculptor and coin designer; *b* 2 April 1926; *s* of Arthur Rizzello and Maria Rizzello (*née* D'Angelo); *m* 1950, Sheila Semple Maguire; one *d*. *Educ:* Oratory Central Boys Sch., SW3; Royal College of Art. Military Service, 1944-48; served in India and Far East; commissioned 1945. Major Travelling Scholarship (Sculpture) and Drawing Prize, RCA, 1950. ARCA 1950; ARBS 1955; FRBS 1961; PRBS 1976. Pres., Soc. of Portrait Sculptors, 1968. Governor, Fedn of British Artists, 1968. Prix de Rome (Sculpture), 1951. Sir Otto Beit Medal for Sculpture, 1961. Sculptor: National Memorial to David Lloyd George, Cardiff; Official Medals for Investiture of HRH Prince of Wales, 1969; 900th Anniversary of Westminster Abbey, 1965; Churchill Centenary Trust, 1974. Designer and Sculptor of coinages for over 30 countries. *Recreation:* people. *Address:* Melrose Studio, 7 Melrose Road, SW18 1ND. *T:* 01-870 8561.

ROACH, Harry Robert, MA Cantab; Headmaster, Hymers College, Hull, 1951-71; *b* 4 Sept. 1906; *m* 1943, Blanche Hortense Sinner; one *s* one *d*. *Educ:* St Olave's Grammar School, London; Clare College, Cambridge. Assistant Master: Aldenham School, 1928-38; King's School, Canterbury, 1938-42; Eton College, 1945-46; Head Master, King Edward VI Grammar School, Five Ways, Birmingham, 1946-51. Served War of 1939-45, in Intelligence Corps, 1942-45. *Publication:* Six Plays of Racine, 1951. *Recreations:* reading and acting. *Address:* 26 St Nicholas Drive, Hornsea, North Humberside.

ROADS, Dr Christopher Herbert; Deputy Director General, Imperial War Museum, since 1964; *b* 3 Jan. 1934; *s* of late Herbert Clifford Roads and of Vera Iris Roads; *m* 1976, Charlotte Alicia Dorothy Mary Lothian. *Educ:* Cambridge and County Sch.; Trinity Hall, Cambridge (MA; PhD 1961). Adviser to WO on Disposal of Amnesty Arms, 1961-62; Keeper of Dept of Records, Imperial War Museum, 1962-70. Founder and Dir, Cambridge Coral/Starfish Res. Gp, 1968-; Chm., Coral Conservation Trust, 1972-; President: Cataloguing Commn, Internat. Films and TV Council, 1970-; Historical Breechloading Small Arms Assoc., 1973-; Vice President: World Expeditionary Assoc., 1971-; Duxford Aviation Soc., 1974-. Member Council: Scientific Exploration Soc., 1971-; Cambridge Univ. Rifle Assoc., 1955-. Trustee, HMS Belfast Trust, 1970-. Adjt, English VIII, 1964-. Churchill Fellowship, 1970. *Publications:* The British Soldier's Firearm, 1850-1864, 1964; (jtly) New Studies on the Crown of Thorns Starfish, 1970; The Story of the Gun, 1977. *Recreations:* rifle shooting, marine and submarine exploration, hovercrafting, motorcycling, cine and still photography. *Address:* 60 Shelford Road, Trumpington, Cambridge. *T:* Trumpington 3176 or 2132. *Clubs:* United Oxford & Cambridge University; Hawks (Cambridge).

ROADS, Peter George; Regional Medical Officer, South West Thames Regional Health Authority, since 1973; *b* 14 Nov. 1917;

s of Frank George Roads and Mary Dee Hill (née Bury); m 1949, Evelyn Clara (née Daniel); one s one d. Educ: Bedford Sch.; Univ. of London (St Mary's Hosp. Med. Sch.); Hon. Society of Inner Temple. MD (London); FFCM, Royal Colls of Physicians. Served War, in China, 1944-46. MRC, Pneumoconiosis Unit, 1949-50; Dep. MOH, etc, City and Co. of Bristol, 1956-59; MOH, Principal Sch. Med. Officer and Port Med. Officer for City and Port of Portsmouth, 1959-73; Med. Referee to Portchester Crematorium, 1959-73. Mem., Central Midwives Bd, 1964-76; Adviser on Health Services, Assoc. of Municipal Corporations, 1966-74. FRSocMed; Fellow, Soc. of Community Medicine. Publications: Care of Elderly in Portsmouth, 1970; Medical Importance of Open Air Recreation (Proc. 1st Internat. Congress on Leisure and Touring), 1966. Recreations: open air, walking, forestry, riding, ski-ing, history, touring. Address: 14 Oakhill Court, Edge Hill, SW19. T: 01-946 7770; c/o Shanklin 2627.

ROARK, Helen Wills; b California, 1905; d of Dr Clarence A. Wills (surgeon) and Catherine A. Wills; m 1st, 1929, Frederick Schander Moody (marr. diss. 1937); 2nd, 1939, Aidan Roark. Educ: Anna Head School, Berkeley, California; University of California; Phi Beta Kappa (Scholarship Society). Publications: three books on tennis; Mystery Book, 1939; articles in various magazines and periodicals. Recreations: American Lawn Tennis Championship, 1923-24-25-27-28-29 and 1931; English Lawn Tennis Championship, 1927-28-29-30-32-33-35-38; French, 1927-28-29-30; has held exhibitions of drawing and paintings at Cooling Galleries, London, 1929 (drawings); Grand Central Art Galleries, New York, 1930 (drawings), 1936 (flower paintings in oil); Berheim-Jenne Galleries, Paris, 1932 (etchings). Clubs: All England Lawn Tennis; Colony, West Side Lawn Tennis (New York); Burlingame Country (California).

ROB, Prof. Charles Granville, MC 1943; Chairman, Department of Surgery, University of Rochester School of Medicine and Professor of Surgery, University of Rochester, New York, since 1960; b 4 May 1913; s of Joseph William Rob, OBE, MD; m 1941, Mary Dorothy Elaine Beazley; two s two d. Educ: Oundle School; Cambridge Univ.; St Thomas's Hospital. FRCS 1939; MChir Cantab, 1941. Lt-Col RAMC Surgeon, St Thomas' Hospital, 1948; Professor of Surgery, London University, 1950-60; formerly Surgeon and Director ot the Surgical Professorial Unit, St Mary's Hospital; Consultant Vascular Surgeon to the Army. Publications: various surgical. Recreations: mountaineering. ski-ing. Address: 260 Crittenden Boulevard, Rochester 20, NY, USA. Club: Alpine.

ROBARTS, Basil; Director, since 1964 and Chief General Manager, 1963-75, Norwich Union Insurance Group; b 13 Jan. 1915; s of late Henry Ernest Robarts and Beatrice Katie (née Stevens); m 1941, Sheila Margaret Cooper Thwaites; one s one d. Educ: Gresham's Sch., Holt. Served Army, 1939-45 (Lt-Col, RA). Joined Norwich Union Life Insce Soc., 1934; Gen. Man. and Actuary, 1953. Director: Scottish Union & Nat. Insce Co., Co., 1959; Norwich Union Life and Fire Insce Socs, 1964; Maritime Insce Co., 1968. Institute of Actuaries: Fellow (FIA), 1939; Treas., 1965-67; Gen. Commissioner of Income Tax, 1958-; Chm., British Insce Assoc., 1969-71. Recreations: tennis, sailing, music. Address: 466B Unthank Road, Norwich. T: Norwich 51135. Club: Naval and Military.

ROBARTS, David John; Director of Robert Fleming & Co. Ltd, 1944-76; Director of other companies; Chairman, Committee of London Clearing Bankers and President, British Bankers' Association, 1956-60 and 1968-70; b 1906; e s of Capt. Gerald Robarts; m 1951, Pauline Mary, d of Colonel Francis Follett, and widow of Clive Stoddart; three s one d. Educ: Eton; Magdalen College, Oxford. Dir, National Westminster Bank Ltd, to 1976 (Chm., 1969-71; Chm., National Provincial Bank Ltd, 1954-68). Church Commissioner, 1957-65. High Sheriff of Buckinghamshire, 1963. Address: 7 Smith Square, Westminster, SW1. T: 01-222 2428; Lillingstone House, Buckingham. T: Lillingstone Dayrell 202. Club: Pratt's.

ROBARTS, Eric Kirkby; b 20 Jan. 1908; s of Charles Martin Robarts and Flora Robarts (née Kirkby); m 1930, Iris Lucy Swan; five d. Educ: Bishops Stortford Coll.; Herts Inst. of Agriculture. Ran family business, C. M. Robarts & Son, until Aug. 1942. Joined Express Dairy Co. Ltd, 1942: Dir, 1947-74; Man. Dir, 1960-74; Dep. Chm., 1966; Chm., 1967-74. FRSA; FBIM. Recreations: hunting, shooting. Address: Frithcote, Watford Road, Northwood, Middx. T: Northwood 22533. Club: Farmers'.

ROBATHAN, Rev. Canon Frederick Norman, OBE 1945; MA; Hon. CF (1st Cl.); Canon Emeritus of Ely Cathedral, since 1960; b 4 Jan. 1896; s of Reverend Thomas Frederick and Edith Jane

Robathan, St Andrew's College, Gorakpur, India; m 1st, 1922, Renée Wells (d 1972) (JP 1947-53); one s (and one s decd); 2nd, 1972, Ruth Elizabeth Emma Corfe, 3rd d of late Canon E. C. Corfe and Mrs Emma Corfe. Educ: King's School, Chester; Dean Close Sch., Cheltenham; St Edmund Hall, Oxford (MA); Wycliffe Hall, Oxford. Served as Commissioned Officer, European War, 1914-19 (campaign medals), France, 1915-16. Ordained, 1921; Curate, Quarry Bank, Staffs, 1921; Priest Vicar, Truro Cathedral, 1923-25; Priest Vicar, Lincoln Cathedral, 1925-28; Chaplain HM Prison, Lincoln, 1926-28; Minor Canon and Sacrist and Junior Cardinal, St Paul's Cathedral, 1928-34; Chaplain Guy's Hosp., 1932-33; Minor Canon, Westminster Abbey, 1934-37, and Chaplain, Westminster Hospital; Rector of Hackney, 1937-45, and Chaplain East London Hospital, CF, RARO, 1923. War of 1939-45 (campaign medals); BEF 1940; Evacuation, Dunkirk, 1940; Sen. Chaplain 43 Div., 1941; Army Technical Sch., Arborfield, 1941; Sen. Chaplain Royal Garrison Church, Aldershot, 1942; Dep. Asst Chaplain-Gen. 12th Corps, 1943; Asst Chaplain-Gen. 21 Army Grp., 1944; Normandy Landings, 1944 (despatches). Vicar of Brighton, Sussex and Canon and Prebendary of Waltham in Chichester Cathedral, 1945-53; Canon Residentiary and Treasurer, Ely Cathedral, 1953-59; Vicar of Cardington, Bedford, 1959. Sen. Chaplain Army Cadet Force, Cambs, 1954-59. Councillor, Bedford RDC, 1960. Chaplain to High Sheriff of Beds., 1962; Rector of Charleton with Buckland tout Saints, Kingsbridge, S Devon, 1962-66. Hon. Priest Vicar, Truro Cathedral, 1967. Coronation Medal, 1937. Recreations: rowing, hockey, cricket, antiquaries. Address: Myrtle Court, Mevagissey, Cornwall. T: Mevagissey 2233.

ROBB, Prof. James Christie; Professor of Physical Chemistry, University of Birmingham, since 1957; b 23 April 1924; s of James M. Robb, Rocklands, The House of Daviot, Inverurie, Aberdeenshire; m 1951, Joyce Irene Morley; three d. Educ: Daviot School; Inverurie Academy; Aberdeen University. BSc Hons, 1945, PhD, 1948, Aberdeen; DSIR Senior Research Award, 1948-50. ICI Fellow, Birmingham Univ., 1950-51; on Birmingham Univ. staff, 1951-. DSc, Birmingham, 1954. Publications: scientific contrib. to Proc. Royal Soc., Trans. Faraday Soc., etc. Recreations: motoring, photography. Address: 42 School Road, Moseley, Birmingham B13 9SN. T: 021-449 2610.

ROBB, Michael Antony Moyse, CMG 1961; Deputy Director, Central Bureau for Educational Visits and Exchanges, 1970-72; b Cairo, Egypt, 3 April 1914; s of late George Robb (Ministry of Education, Cairo, and later représentative of Messrs Macmillan); m 1943, Brenda Patience Shankland (widow, née Robinson); two step s one s one d. Educ: Malvern College; Germany, France, Spain. Passed into Consular Service, 1936; Probationer Vice-Consul, British Consulate-General, New York, Nov. 1936; confirmed as Vice-Consul, 1939; HBM Vice-Consul, Miami, Fla, 1941; Acting Consul, Atlanta, in 1943 and 1944. Served in Foreign Office, 1945-Dec. 1947; Foreign Service Officer Grade 7, 1945; First Secretary (Information), at British Embassy, The Hague, 1948; Counsellor (Information), at British High Commission, later British Embassy, Bonn, 1951; Foreign Service Officer Grade 6, 1953; Counsellor, British Embassy, Rio de Janeiro, 1955-59; Foreign Service Inspector, Foreign Office, 1959-61; Minister (Information) at British Embassy, Washington, 1961-65; Minister, British Embassy, Pretoria, 1965-69. Address: 26 Pattison Road, NW2. T: 01-435 5689.

ROBB, William, NDA, FRSE; b 1885; e s of late William Robb, Rochsolloch, Airdrie; m 1924, Agnes Logan, e d of late Archibald Steel, Prestwick, Ayrshire; two d. Educ: Airdrie Academy; West of Scotland Agricultural College, Glasgow. Assist, Agriculture Department, The University of St Andrews, 1913-16 and 1919-20; War Service, Royal Engineers, 1916-19; Assistant Director, Scottish Society for Research in Plant Breeding, 1921-25; Director of Research, 1925-50, retired. Recreation: gardening. Address: 24 Downie Terrace, Edinburgh EH12 7AU.

ROBBE-GRILLET, Alain, literary consultant, writer and cinéaste; Editions de Minuit, Paris, since 1955; b 18 Aug. 1922; s of Gaston Robbe-Grillet and Yvonne Canu; m 1957, Catherine Rstakian. Educ: Lycée Buffon, Paris; Lycée St Louis, Paris; Institut National Agronomique, Paris. Engineer: Institut National de la Statistique, 1945-49; Institut des Fruits et Agrumes Coloniaux, 1949-51. Films: L'Immortelle, 1963; Trans-Europ-Express, 1967; L'Homme qui ment, 1968; L'Eden et après, 1970; Glissements progressifs du plaisir, 1974; Le jeu avec le feu, 1975. Publications: Les Gommes, 1953 (The Erasers, 1966); Le Voyeur, 1955 (The Voyeur, 1959); La Jalousie, 1957 (Jealousy, 1960); Dans le labyrinthe, 1959 (In the Labyrinth, 1967); L'Année dernière à Marienbad, 1961 (Last Year in

Marienbad, 1962); Instantanés, 1962 (Snapshots, and, Towards a New Novel, 1965); L'Immortelle, 1963 (The Immortal One, 1971); Pour un nouveau roman, 1964; La Maison de rendezvous, 1965; Projet pour une révolution à New York, 1970 (Project for a Revolution in New York, 1972); Glissements progressifs du plaisir, 1974; Le Jeu avec le feu, 1975; Topologie d'une cité fantôme, 1976; La Belle captive, 1976. *Address:* 18 Boulevard Maillot, 92 Neuilly-sur-Seine, France. *T:* 722 31.22.

ROBBINS, family name of **Baron Robbins.**

ROBBINS, Baron *cr* 1959 (Life Peer), of Clare Market; **Lionel Charles Robbins,** CH 1968; CB 1944; FBA 1942; MA Oxon, BSc (Econ.); First Chancellor of Stirling University, since 1968; *b* 22 Nov. 1898; *e s* of late Rowland Richard Robbins, CBE; *m* 1924, Iris Elizabeth, *d* of late A. G. Gardiner; one *s* one *d. Educ:* Southall County Sch.; Univ. Coll., London; London School of Economics. Served European War, 1916-19 (RFA); Lecturer New College, Oxford, 1924; Lecturer London School of Economics, 1925-27; Fellow and Lecturer New College, Oxford, 1927-29; Professor of Economics in the University of London, at London School of Economics, 1929-61; Chm., Financial Times, 1961-70. Chm., Cttee on Higher Education, 1961-64; Mem., Court of Governors, London School of Economics, (Chm., 1968-74). Director of the Economic Section of Offices of the War Cabinet, 1941-45; President of Royal Economic Society, 1954-55. Trustee: National Gallery, 1952-59, 1960-67, 1967-74; Tate Gall., 1953-59, 1962-67; Dir Royal Opera House, Covent Garden; Mem. Planning Board for Univ. of York; President British Academy, 1962-67. Member: Accademia dei Lincei, Rome; American Philosophical Society; American Acad. of Arts and Sciences; Foreign Associate, National Acad. of Education, America. Hon. DLitt (Dunelm, Exeter, Strathclyde, Sheffield, Heriot-Watt); Hon. LHD (Columbia); Hon. LLD (Cantab, Leicester, Strasbourg, CNAA); Hon. Dr of Laws, Calif; Hon. Doutor en Ciências Econòmicas e Financeiras Universidade Técnica de Lisboa; Hon. DSc (Econ.) London; Hon. DUniv: York; Stirling; Hon. Dr, RCA; Hon. DHL Pennsylvania; Hon. Fellow: Univ. Coll. London; Manchester Coll. of Science and Technology; LSE; London Grad. Sch. of Business Studies. *Publications:* An Essay on the Nature and Significance of Economic Science; The Great Depression; Economic Planning and International Order; The Economic Basis of Class Conflict and other Essays in Political Economy; The Economic Causes of War; The Economic Problem in Peace and War, 1947; The Theory of Economic Policy in English Classical Political Economy, 1952; The Economist in the Twentieth Century and other Lectures in Political Economy, 1954; Robert Torrens and the Evolution of Classical Economics; Politics and Economics, 1963; The University in the Modern World, 1966; The Theory of Economic Development in the History of Economic Thought, 1968; The Evolution of Modern Economic Theory, 1970; Autobiography of an Economist, 1971; Money, Trade and International Relations, 1971; Political Economy Past and Present: a review of leading theories of economic policy, 1976; articles in Economic Jl, Economica, Lloyds Bank Review, etc. *Address:* 10 Meadway Close, NW11.

ROBBINS, Edgar Carmichael, CBE 1957; Legal Adviser to The British Broadcasting Corporation, 1959-74; *b* 22 March 1911; *s* of John Haldeman Robbins; *m* 1936, Alice Eugenia, *d* of Rev. Herbert Norman Nash; two *s* two *d. Educ:* Westminster Sch.; London Univ. (LLB). Admitted a solicitor, 1933. Employed by The British Broadcasting Corporation, 1934-74; Solicitor to the BBC 1945-59. Clerk, City of London Solicitors' Company, 1976-. *Publications:* William Paston, Justice, 1932; The Cursed Norfolk Justice, 1936. *Address:* 30 Royal Avenue, Chelsea, SW3. *T:* 01-730 5767. *Club:* Athenæum.

ROBBINS, Prof. Frederick C., MD; Bronze Star (US Army), 1945; Professor of Pediatrics, Case Western Reserve University School of Medicine, Cleveland, since 1952, Dean of the School, since 1966; *b* 25 Aug. 1916; *s* of William J. Robbins and Christine Chapman Robbins; *m* 1948, Alice Havemeyer Northrop; two *d. Educ:* University of Missouri (AB); University of Missouri Medical School (BS); Harvard Medical School (MD). US Army, 1942-46; rank on discharge, Major. Various posts in the Children's Hospital, Boston, from 1940, finishing as Chief Resident in Medicine, 1948; Sen. Fellow in Virus Diseases, National Research Council, 1948-50; Research Fellow in Pediatrics, Harvard Med. Sch., 1948-50; Instr in Ped., 1950-51, Associate in Ped., 1951-52, at Harvard Medical School; Dir, Department of Pediatrics, Cleveland Metropolitan General Hospital, 1952-66. Associate Research Div. of Infectious Diseases, the Children's Medical Center, Boston, 1950-52; Research Fellow in Ped., the Boston Lying-in Hospital, Boston, Mass, 1950-52; Asst to Children's Medical Service, Mass Gen. Hosp., Boston, 1950-52. Visiting Scientist, Donner Lab., Univ.

of California, 1963-64. President: Soc. for Pediatric Research, 1961-62; Amer. Pediatric Soc., 1973-74. Member: Nat. Acad. of Sciences, 1972 (Co-Chm., Forum on Human Experimentation, 1974); Amer. Philosophical Soc., 1972; Adv. Cttee, Office of Technol. Assessment for Congress, 1973. First Mead Johnson Award, 1953; Nobel Prize in Physiology and Medicine, 1954; Award for Distinguished Achievement (Modern Medicine), 1963; Med. Mutual Honor Award for 1969. Hon. Dr of Science: John Carroll University, 1955; Univ. of Missouri, 1958; Hon. Dr of Laws, Univ. of New Mexico, 1968. *Publications:* numerous in various jls, primarily on subject of viruses and infectious diseases. *Recreations:* music, tennis, sailing. *Address:* 2467 Guilford Road, Cleveland Heights, Ohio 44118, USA. *T:* 321-0885; (office) Case Western Reserve University School of Medicine, 2119 Abington Road, Cleveland, Ohio 44106, USA. *T:* 216 368-2820.

ROBBINS, Harold; writer; *m* Grace; one *d. Educ:* New York. Formerly sugar exporter, film publicist, film impresario, etc. *Publications:* The Dream Merchants, 1949; 79 Park Avenue, 1955; A Stone for Danny Fisher, 1955; Never Leave Me, 1956; Never Love a Stranger, 1958; Stiletto, 1960; The Carpetbaggers, 1961; Where Love Has Gone, 1964; The Adventurers, 1966; The Inheritors, 1969; The Betsy, 1971; The Adventurers, 1973; The Pirate, 1974; The Lonely Lady, 1976; Dreams Die First, 1977. *Address:* c/o New English Library, Barnard's Inn, Holborn, EC1N 2JR.

ROBBINS, Jerome; Choreographer; Associate Artistic Director, New York City Ballet, since 1949; Director, Ballets: USA, since 1958; *b* New York, 11 Oct. 1918; *s* of Harry and Lena Robbins. *Educ:* Woodrow Wilson High School, Weehawken, NJ; New York University. Studied ballet with Antony Tudor and Eugene Loring, and Modern, Spanish and oriental dance. First stage experience with Sandor-Sorel Dance Center, New York, 1937; dancer in chorus of American musicals, 1938-40; Theatre Ballet, 1940-44 (soloist 1941), London season, 1946; formed own company, Ballets: USA, 1958. Handel Medallion, NYC, 1976. Chevalier, Order of Arts and Letters (France), 1964. Best known ballets include: Fancy Free; Interplay; Age of Anxiety; The Cage; Afternoon of a Faun; The Concert; NY Export, Op. Jazz; Moves; Les Noces; Dances at a Gathering; The Goldberg Variations; Watermill; Concerto in G major. Has created choreography for musicals including: On the Town, 1945; High Button Shoes, 1947 (Tony Award); Call Me Madam, 1950; The King and I, 1951; Peter Pan, 1954 (also conceived and dir.); Bells Are Ringing, 1956; West Side Story, 1957 (Tony Award; 2 Academy Awards, 1961); Gypsy, 1959 (also dir.); Funny Girl, 1964; Fiddler on the Roof, 1964 (also dir.) (won 2 Tony Awards, 1965). *Address:* c/o New York City Ballet, New York State Theater, Lincoln Center, New York, NY 10023, USA.

ROBBINS, John Dennis, OBE 1945; TD 1950; FCA; Chairman, Gulf Public Relations (Europe) Ltd, since 1977; *b* 28 July 1915; *s* of Duncan Ross Robbins and Harriette Winifred Robbins (*née* Goodyear); *m* 1942, Joan Mary Mason; one *s* two *d. Educ:* Aldenham School. Commnd Mddx Regt (DCO), 2nd Lieut 1939, Captain 1940, Major 1941, Lt-Col 1944; served N Africa, Italy, Palestine (OBE, despatches twice); retd as Lt-Col 1946. Partner, Kay Keeping & Co., Chartered Accountants, 1946-49; joined British Metal Corp. Ltd, 1950; Dir and Gen. Man., 1952; a Man. Dir, 1963. Amalgamated Metal Corp. Ltd: Dir 1965; Chief Exec. 1971; Exec. Dep. Chm., 1972, Chm., 1975-77; Mem. London Bd of Advice, National Bank of Australasia; Dir, Smith & Nephew Associated Cos; Dir, Norddeutsche Affinerie Hamburg; Mem., Copper Develt Council. *Recreations:* gardening, shooting, fly-fishing. *Address:* Inworth Hall, Kelvedon, Colchester, Essex. *T:* Kelvedon 70318. *Club:* Gresham.

ROBBINS, Dr Raymond Frank; Director, Plymouth Polytechnic, since 1974; *b* 15 Feb. 1928; *s* of Harold and Elsie Robbins; *m* 1955, Eirian Meredith Edwards; two *d. Educ:* Grove Park Grammar Sch., Wrexham; UCW Aberystwyth. PhD 1954; FRIC 1962. Research Chemist, Monsanto Chemicals Ltd, 1954-55; Research Fellow, Univ. of Exeter, 1955-56; Lectr, Nottingham Coll. of Technology, 1956-59; Sen. Lectr, Hatfield Coll. of Technology, 1960-61; Head of Dept of Chem. Sciences, Hatfield Polytechnic, 1961-70; Dep. Dir, Plymouth Polytechnic, 1970-74. *Publications:* papers on organic chemistry in chem. jls, various reviews and articles in sci. and educnl press. *Recreations:* hill walking, sailing. *Address:* 3 Windermere Crescent, Plymouth PL6 5HX. *T:* Plymouth 776522.

ROBBINS, (Richard) Michael, CBE 1976; Managing Director, Railways, London Transport Executive, since 1971 (Member, London Transport Board/Executive, since 1965); *b* 7 Sept. 1915; *er s* of late Alfred Gordon Robbins and Josephine, *d* of R. L.

Capell, Northampton; *m* 1939, Rose Margaret Elspeth, *er d* of late Sir Robert Reid Bannatyne, CB, Lindfield, Sussex; one *s* two *d. Educ:* Westminster Sch. (King's Schol.); Christ Church, Oxford (Westminster Schol.; MA); Univ. of Vienna. Joined London Passenger Transport Board, 1939. War service, RE (Transportation), 1939-46: Persia and Iraq, 1941-43; GHQ, MEF, 1943-44; Major, AML (Greece), 1944-45. Rejoined London Transport, 1946; Sec. to Chm., 1947-50; Sec., London Transp. Exec., 1950-55; Sec. and Chief Public Relations Off., 1955-60; Chief Commercial and Pub. Rel. Off., 1960-65. Pres., Inst. of Transport, 1975-76 (Mem. Council, 1957-60 and 1962-64; Chm., Metrop. Sect., 1962-63; Chm., Educn and Trg Cttee, 1969-72; Vice-Pres., 1972-75); Pres., Omnibus Soc., 1965; Chairman: Middx Victoria County History Council, 1963-76; Middx Local History Council, 1958-65; Internat. Metrop. Rlys Cttee, Internat. Union of Public Transport, 1976-; Mem. Council, British Archæol. Assoc., 1957-60; President: London and Middx Archæol. Soc., 1965-71 (Mem. Council, 1951-56 and 1960-65); Greater London Industrial Archæol. Soc., 1969-; Rly Students Assoc., 1967-68; St Marylebone Soc., 1971-74. Dunhill lectr on industrial design, Australia, 1974. FSA 1957 (Mem. Council, 1965-67, 1970-71; Treasurer, 1971-). Governor, Museum of London, 1968-; Trustee, London Museum, 1970-75. *Publications:* The North London Railway, 1937; 190 in Persia, 1951; The Isle of Wight Railways, 1953; Middlesex, 1953; (ed) Middlesex Parish Churches, 1955; The Railway Age, 1962; (with T. C. Barker) History of London Transport, vol. 1, 1963, vol. 2, 1974; George and Robert Stephenson, 1966; Points and Signals, 1967; Joint Editor, Journal of Transport History, 1953-65; contribs to transport and historical jls. *Recreations:* exploring cities and suburbs; travelling abroad and in branch railway trains; concert-going. *Address:* 7 Courthope Villas, Wimbledon, SW19 4EH. *T:* 01-946 7308.

ROBBINS, Brig. (Hon.) Thomas, CB 1945; CBE 1945; MC 1918; Croix de Guerre (France) 1918; *m* 1955, Clare, *widow* of Lt-Col Malcolm Gordon Douglas, OBE, DSO, MC, HAC. Served European War, 1914-19, with Liverpool Scottish, BEF, 1914, and 6(T) Bn Lancashire Fusiliers; seconded to Intelligence Corps. Intelligence Officer 62 (WR) Division, France and Germany, 1917-19 (despatches thrice); Captain RARO, 1919; War of 1939-45, asst Comdt Intelligence Training Centre and Politico-Military Course, Cambridge; British Army Staff, Washington, DC, and Military Intelligence Training Centre, US Army, Camp Ritchie, Md (Col GSOI), 1942; First Comdt Civil Affairs Staff Centre, Wimbledon; Brigadier, 1943; Chief Staff Officer for Civil Affairs, HQ 21 Army Group, 1943-45; served in NW Europe, 1944-45; retired, 1945. British Commercial Commissioner and 2nd Commercial Secretary, HBM Embassy, Berlin, 1919-20. Freeman and Vintner, City of London, 1946. Officer Legion of Merit (USA); Officier Légion d'Honneur (France); Commander Order of the Cross, Leopold II (Belgium); Citoyen d'Honneur de la Commune de Cornac, Lot, 1966; and, with his wife Clare, enrolled Citoyens d'Honneur de la Commune de Loubressac, 1976. *Address:* Loubressac, 46130 Bretenoux, Lot, France.

ROBENS, family name of Baron Robens of Woldingham.

ROBENS OF WOLDINGHAM, Baron *cr* 1961, of Woldingham (Life Peer); **Alfred Robens,** PC 1951; Chairman: Vickers Ltd, since 1971; MLH Consultants, since 1971; Johnson Matthey & Co. Ltd, since 1971; St Regis International since 1976; a Director: Bank of England, since 1966; Times Newspapers Ltd, since 1967; Trust Houses Forte Ltd, since 1971; Chairman, Engineering Industries Council, since 1976; *b* 18 Dec. 1910; *s* of George and Edith Robens; *m* 1937, Eva, *d* of Fred and Elizabeth Powell. *Educ:* Manchester Secondary Sch. Official of Union of Distributive and Allied Workers, 1935-45; Manchester City Councillor, 1942-45. MP (Lab) Wansbeck Div. of Northumberland, 1945-50, and for Blyth, 1950-60. Parliamentary Private Secretary to Minister of Transport, 1945-47; Parliamentary Secretary, Ministry of Fuel and Power, 1947-51; Minister of Labour and National Service, April-Oct. 1951. Chm., National Coal Bd, 1961-71. Chm. Foundation on Automation and Employment, 1962; Member: NEDC, 1962-71; Royal Commn on Trade Unions and Employers' Assocs, 1965-68. President: Advertising Assoc., 1963-68; Incorporated Soc. of British Advertisers, 1973-76; Chairman: Jt Steering Cttee for Malta, 1967; Jt Econ. Mission to Malta, 1967. Member: Council of Manchester Business School, 1964- (Dep. Chm., 1964-70; Chm., 1970); Court of Governors, LSE, 1965; Chancellor, Univ. of Surrey, 1966-77. Governor, Queen Elizabeth Training Coll. for the Disabled, 1951-; Chairman: Bd of Govs, Guy's Hosp., 1965-74; Guy's Hosp. Medical and Dental Sch., 1974-; Cttee on Safety and Health of people at their place of work, 1970-72; Fellow, Manchester Coll. of Science and Technology, 1965-; Hon. FRCR, 1975. Hon. DCL: Univ. of Newcastle upon Tyne,

1964; Manchester Univ., 1974; Hon. LLD: Leicester, 1966; London, 1971. Hon. MInstM, 1968; Hon. FIOB, 1974. Mackintosh Medal, Advertising Assoc., 1970; Albert Medal, RSA, 1977. *Publications:* Engineering and Economic Progress, 1965; Industry and Government, 1970; Human Engineering, 1970; Ten Year Stint, 1972; sundry articles to magazines, journals and newspapers. *Recreation:* gardening. *Address:* Walton Manor, Walton-on-the-Hill, Surrey. *Club:* Reform.

ROBERGE, Guy, QC (Can.); Vice-President, Canadian Transport Commission, Ottawa, since 1971; *b* 26 Jan. 1915; *s* of P. A. Roberge and Irène Duchesneau; *m* 1957, Marie Raymond; one *s* one *d. Educ:* Laval Univ., Quebec. Called to Bar, 1937; Mem., Quebec Legislative Assembly, 1944-48; Mem., Restrictive Trade Practices Commn of Canada, 1955-57; Chm. and Chief Exec. Officer, Nat. Film Bd of Canada, 1957-66; Agent-General for Govt of PQ in UK, 1966-71. Hon. DCL, Bishop's Univ., 1967; Hon. docteur d'université, Laval Univ., 1975. *Address:* Canadian Transport Commission, 275 Slater Street, Ottawa, Canada, K1A 0N9. *T:* 996-4672; (home) 415 Wood Avenue, Ottawa, Ontario. *Clubs:* Quebec Garrison (Quebec City); Rideau (Ottawa).

ROBERTHALL, family name of Baron Roberthall.

ROBERTHALL, Baron *cr* 1969 (Life Peer), of Silverspur, Queensland, and Trenance, Cornwall; **Robert Lowe Roberthall,** KCMG 1954; CB 1950; MA; Principal Hertford College, Oxford, 1964-67, Hon. Fellow since 1969; Member of Economic Planning Board, 1947-61; *b* New South Wales, 6 March 1901; *s* of late Edgar Hall and Rose Helen, *d* of A. K. Cullen; changed surname to Roberthall by deed poll, 1969; *m* 1932, Laura Margaret (marr. diss. 1968), *d* of G. E. Linfoot; two *d* ; *m* 1968, Perilla Thyme, *d* of late Sir Richard Southwell, FRS. *Educ:* Ipswich, Qld; Univ. of Queensland; Magdalen College, Oxford. BEng, Queensland, 1922; Rhodes Scholar, 1923-26 (First in Modern Greats, 1926); Lecturer in Economics, Trinity College, 1926-47; Fellow, 1927-50; Hon. Fellow, 1958; Junior Dean, 1927; Dean, 1933-38; Bursar, 1938-39; Proproctor, 1933; Ministry of Supply, 1939-46; British Raw Materials Mission, Washington, 1942-44; Adviser, Board of Trade, 1946-47; Director Economic Section, Cabinet Office, 1947-53; Economic Adviser to HM Government, 1953-61; Advisory Dir, Unilever, 1961-71; advr to Tube Investments, 1961-76. Fellow of Nuffield College, 1938-47, Visiting Fellow, 1961-64. Mem. of Economic and Employment Commn UN, 1946-49; Chm., OEEC Gp of Economic Experts, 1955-61; UK Mem., Commonwealth Economic Cttee, 1961-67; Mem., (Franks) Commn of Inquiry into Oxford Univ., 1964-66; Chm. Exec. Cttee, NIESR, 1962-70; Chm. Select Cttee on Commodity Prices, 1976-77. Vice-Pres. Royal Economic Society (Hon. Secretary, 1948-58; President, 1958-60); Pres., Soc. of Business Economists, 1968-73, Hon. Fellow, 1973. Rede Lecturer, Cambridge University, 1962. Hon. DSc, University of Queensland. *Publications:* Earning and Spending, 1934; The Economic System in a Socialist State, 1936; various articles, etc on economics. *Recreations:* walking, gardening. *Address:* 7a Carey Mansions, Rutherford Street, SW1. *T:* 01-834 7041; Quarry, Trenance, Newquay, Cornwall. *T:* St Mawgan 242. *Club:* Travellers'.

ROBERTS; *see* Goronwy-Roberts.

ROBERTS, family name of Baron Clwyd.

ROBERTS, Albert, JP; DL; MP (Lab) Normanton Division of West Riding of Yorkshire since 1951; *b* 14 May 1908; *s* of Albert Roberts and Annie Roberts (*née* Ward); *m* 1932, Alice Ashton; one *s* one *d. Educ:* Woodlesford School; Normanton and Whitwood Technical College, Yorks. Safety Board, Mines Inspector, 1941-51. Vice-Chm., Anglo-Spanish Parly Cttee; Chm., Anglo-South Korean Parly Group; Exec. Mem., British Group, Inter-Parly Union, 1967-. Exec. Mem., Yorkshire Area Heart Foundn. JP 1946, DL 1967, W Yorks. Order of Isabela la Catolica (Spain), 1967. *Recreations:* cricket, bowls. *Address:* Cordoba, 14 Aberford Road, Oulton-Woodlesford, near Leeds. *T:* Leeds 822303.

ROBERTS, Dr Albert, MSc, PhD; MIMinE, MIMM, AMInstCE, FGS, CEng; Head of Department of Mining Engineering, University of Nevada, 1969-75, retired 1975; *b* 25 April 1911; British; *m* 1938, May Taberner; two *s* one *d. Educ:* Wigan Mining and Techn. College. Mining Engr, Wigan Coal Corp., 1931-35, 1938-40; Ashanti Goldfields Corp., 1935-38; Lectr: Sunderland Techn. Coll., 1940-45; Nottingham Univ., 1945-55; Sheffield Univ., 1955; Dir, Postgraduate Sch. of Mining, Sheffield Univ., 1956-69. Ed., Internat. Jl of Rock Mechanics and Mining Sciences, 1964-68. *Publications:* Geological Structures, 1946; Underground Lighting, 1959; Mine

Ventilation, 1959; Mineral Processing, 1965; Geotechnology, 1977. *Recreations:* gardening, photography, music, fishing. *Address:* The Garth, Bull Bay, Gwynedd. *T:* Amlwch 830612.

ROBERTS, Angus Thomas; Director of Litigation and Prosecution, Post Office Solicitor's Office (formerly Principal Assistant Solicitor to General Post Office), 1965-74; *b* 28 March 1913; *s* of late Edward Roberts and late Margaret (*née* Murray); *m* 1940, Frances Monica, *d* of late Frederick and late Agnes Bertha Cane; two *s. Educ:* Felsted School. Admitted Solicitor, 1936. Entered Post Office Solicitor's Dept, 1939. Served in Royal Navy, 1941-46 (Lieut, RNVR). Asst Solicitor to GPO, 1951. *Recreations:* golf, fishing, gardening. *Address:* Caen Cottage, Helmsdale, Sutherland, Scotland. *T:* Helmsdale 277. *Clubs:* Helmsdale Golf, Brora Golf.

ROBERTS, Ann Clwyd; see Clwyd, Ann.

ROBERTS, Arthur Loten, OBE 1971; Emeritus Professor, formerly Livesey Professor of Coal Gas and Fuel Industries, 1947-71, and Chairman of the Houldsworth School of Applied Science, 1956-70, University of Leeds; Pro-Vice-Chancellor, 1967-69; *b* 1 April 1906; *s* of Arthur James Roberts, Hull, and Alice Maude Loten, Hornsea, E Yorks; *m* 1941, Katherine Mary Hargrove; one *s* one *d. Educ:* Christ's Hospital; Univ. of Leeds. BSc 1928, PhD 1930, Assistant Lecturer, Lecturer, Senior Lecturer, Leeds Univ. Part-time mem. North-Eastern Area Gas Board, 1950-71; Mem. Gas Corp. Res. Cttee (formerly Gas Council Research Cttee), 1951-; Hon. Sec. Advisory Research Cttee of Gas Council and University, 1947-71; Chairman Joint Refractories Cttee of British Ceramic Research Assoc. and the Gas Corporation; Pres. British Ceramic Society, 1957-58; Member of Technology Sub-Cttee, UGC, 1960-69. FRIC, FInstF, Hon. Fellow Inst. Ceram., Hon. FInstGasE, Hon. FIChemE. *Publications:* numerous contributions to chemical, ceramic and fuel jls. *Recreations:* painting, pianoforte, garden. *Address:* Hillside, 6 King's Road, Bramhope, Leeds, W Yorks. *T:* Leeds 674977.

ROBERTS, Prof. Benjamin Charles, MA Oxon; Professor of Industrial Relations, London School of Economics, University of London, since 1962; *b* 1 Aug. 1917; *s* of Walter Whitfield Roberts and Mabel Frances Roberts; *m* 1945, Veronica Lilian Vine-Lott; two *s. Educ:* LSE; New Coll., Oxford. Research Student, Nuffield Coll., Oxford, 1948-49; Part-time Lectr, Ruskin Coll., Oxford, 1948-49; London Sch. of Economics: Lectr in Trade Union Studies, 1949-56; Reader in Industrial Relations, 1956-62; Mem. Ct of Govs, 1964-69. Vis. Prof: Princeton Univ., 1958; MIT 1959; Univ. of Calif., Berkeley, 1965. Assoc., Internat. Inst. of Labour Studies, Geneva, 1966; Mem. Council: Inst. Manpower Studies; Foundn for Automation and Employment; Mem., British-N American Cttee; Mem., Nat. Reference Tribunal of Coal Mining Industry, 1970-. Editor, British Jl of Industrial Relations, 1963-. Pres., British Univs Industrial Relations Assoc., 1965-68; Pres., Internat. Industrial Relations Assoc., 1967-73. Consultant to EEC, 1976-77. *Publications:* Trade Unions in the New Era, 1947; Trade Union Government and Administration in Great Britain, 1956; National Wages Policy in War and Peace, 1958; The Trades Union Congress, 1868-1921, 1958; Trade Unions in a Free Society, 1959; (ed) Industrial Relations: Contemporary Problems and Perspectives, 1962; Labour in the Tropical Territories of the Commonwealth, 1964; (ed) Manpower Planning and Employment Trends 1966; (with L. Greyfié de Bellecombe) Collective Bargaining in African Countries, 1967; (ed) Industrial Relations: Contemporary Issues, 1968; (with John Lovell) A Short History of the TUC, 1968; (with R. O. Clarke and D. J. Fatchet) Workers' Participation in Management in Britain, 1972; (with R. Loveridge and J. Gennard) Reluctant Militants: a study of industrial technicians, 1972; also Evidence to Royal Commn on Trade Unions, 1966, and Report to ILO on Labour and Automation: Manpower Adjustment Programmes in the United Kingdom, 1967. *Address:* 28 Temple Fortune Lane, NW11. *T:* 01-458 1421. *Club:* Reform.

ROBERTS, Bertie; Director, Department of the Environment (Property Services Agency), since 1971, Regional Director, Germany, since 1976; *b* 4 June 1919; *y s* of late Thomas and Louisa Roberts, Blaengarw, S Wales; *m* 1st, 1946, Dr Peggy Clark; one *s*; 2nd, 1962, Catherine Matthew. *Educ:* Garw Grammar School. Entered Civil Service (Office of Works), 1936; HM Forces, 1942-46, Captain RAOC; Comptroller of Accounts, MPBW, 1963; Dir of Computer Services, 1967; Dir Organisation and Methods, 1969; Dir, Estate Management Overseas, 1971-76. *Recreations:* travel; Rotarian (Rotary Club of Dulwich). *Address:* Property Services Agency, HQ British Forces Germany, BFPO 40. *T:* 02161 45011; Fairmount, Hollington Park Road, St Leonards on Sea, E Sussex.

ROBERTS, Brian Birley, CMG 1969; PhD; Research Associate, Scott Polar Research Institute, Cambridge (half-time), since 1960 (Research Fellow (half-time), 1946-60); *b* 23 Oct. 1912; *y s* of late Charles Michael Roberts, MB, BS; unmarried. *Educ:* Uppingham Sch.; Emmanuel Coll., Cambridge. MA 1934, PhD 1940. Leader, Cambridge Expedns to Iceland, 1932, and E Greenland, 1933; Mem., British Graham Land Expedn, 1934-37 (Polar Medal, 1940); Special adviser on cold climate equipment to Controller of Ordnance Services, WO, 1940-41; Bruce Memorial Prize of RSE, of Royal Phys. Soc. Edinburgh and RSGS, 1940; Admty, NID, 1941-43; Jt Editor, Polar Record, 1942-75; FO Res. Dept, 1944-68 (half-time 1946-68); FO Latin America Dept (half-time), 1968-75. Co-founder and Editor, Jl of Glaciology, 1947; Back Award of RGS, 1948; Mem., Op. Lyon, Canadian Arctic, 1949; Mem. Norwegian-British-Swedish Antarctic Expedn, 1950-51; exch. visit to USSR Arctic orgs, 1956; UK Deleg. to Wash. Antarctic Conf., 1959, and subseq. Antarctic Treaty Consultative Meetings: Canberra, 1961; Buenos Aires, 1962; Brussels, 1964; Santiago, 1966; Paris, 1968; Tokyo, 1970; Wellington, 1972; Oslo, 1975; Official UK Observer with US Op. Deep Freeze, 1960-61; UK Deleg. to Conf. on Conservation of Antarctic Seals, 1972. President: Antarctic Club, 1963-64; Arctic Club, 1972-73; Mem. French Expedn to sub-Antarctic islands in S Indian Ocean, 1964. Fellow of Churchill Coll., Cambridge, 1965. Founder's Medal, RGS, 1976. *Publications:* Iceland papers, 1939; Handbook on clothing and equipment required in cold climates, 1941; Organization of polar information, 1960; (ed jtly) Illustrated glossary of snow and ice, 1966; (ed) Edward Wilson's Birds of the Antarctic, 1967; The Arctic Ocean, 1971; numerous papers in scientific periodicals. *Recreations:* ornithology, glaciology, small islands. *Address:* 41 Causewayside, Fen Causeway, Cambridge. *T:* Cambridge 55506.

ROBERTS, Brian Richard; Editor, The Sunday Telegraph, 1966-76 (Managing Editor, 1961-66); *b* 16 Sept. 1906; *e s* of late Robert Lewis Roberts, CBE; *m* 1935, Elisabeth Franziska Dora, *er d* of late Dr Leo Zuntz; one adopted *s. Educ:* Merchant Taylors' Sch.; St John's Coll., Oxford (MA); Hon. Fellow 1975. Editorial staff, Oxford Mail, 1930-33; Daily Mail, 1933-38 (Night Editor, 1936-38); Joined The Daily Telegraph, 1939 (Night Editor, 1944-57, Chief Asst Editor 1957-60). Pres., Inst. of Journalists, 1954-55; Pres., Guild of Agricultural Journalists, 1976; Mem. Governing Body, Northern Polytechnic, London, 1946-71 (Chm. 1956-71); Mem., Ct of Governors, Polytechnic of N London, 1971-, Chm., 1971-74 (Chm., Formation Cttee, 1970-71); Chm. of Council, Assoc. of Colls for Further and Higher Educn (formerly Assoc. of Technical Instns), 1964-65, Hon. Treasurer, 1967-77. Gold Medal, Inst. of Journalists, 1971; special award, National Press Awards, 1974; Queen's Jubilee Medal, 1977. *Recreation:* agriculture. *Address:* Old Foxhunt Manor, Waldron, near Heathfield, Sussex TN21 0RU. *T:* Horam Road 2618. *Club:* United Oxford & Cambridge University.
See also C. H. Roberts and Rev. R. L. Roberts.

ROBERTS, Sir Bryan Clieve, KCMG 1973 (CMG 1964); QC; JP; Secretary of Commissions, since 1977; *b* 22 March 1923; *s* of late Herbert Roberts, MA, and of Doris Evelyn Clieve; *m* 1st, 1958, Pamela Dorothy (marr. diss. 1975), *d* of late Major Charles Knight; 2nd, 1976, Brigitte Patricia Reilly-Morrison. *Educ:* Whitgift School; Magdalen Coll., Oxford (BA Hons). Served War of 1939-45: commissioned in RA and RHA, 1941-46; active service in Normandy, Belgium, Holland and Germany, 1944-45. Called to Bar, Gray's Inn, 1950; in chambers in Temple, 1950-51; Treasury Solicitor's Dept, 1951-53. Crown Counsel, N Rhodesia, 1953-60; Dir of Public Prosecutions, N Rhodesia, 1960-61; Nyasaland: Solicitor-Gen. and Perm. Sec. to Min. of Justice, 1961; Solicitor-General, 1961-64; Minister of Justice, 1962-63; Mem., Nyasaland Legislative Council, 1961-63; Attorney-Gen. of Malawi, 1964-72; Perm. Sec. to Office of the President, Sec. to the Cabinet, and Head of Malawi Civil Service, 1965-72; Chairman: Malawi Army Council; Nat. Security and Intell. Cttee; Nat. Develt and Planning Cttee, 1966-72. Lord Chancellor's Office, 1973-. JP South Westminster, 1975. Officer of the Order of Menelik II of Ethiopia, 1965; Comdr. Nat. Order of Republic of Malagasy, 1969. *Address:* 16 Ansdell Terrace, W8. *Club:* Royal Commonwealth Society.

ROBERTS, Rear-Adm. Cedric Kenelm; CB 1970; DSO 1952; *b* 19 April 1918; *s* of F. A. Roberts; *m* 1940, Audrey, *d* of T. M. Elias; four *s. Educ:* King Edward's Sch., Birmingham. Joined RN as Naval Airman 2nd Cl., 1940; commnd Temp. Sub-Lt (A), RNVR, 1940; sunk in HMS Manchester, 1942, Malta Convoy; interned in Sahara; released, Nov. 1942; Personal Pilot to Vice-Adm. Sir Arthur Lyster, 1943; HMS Trumpeter, Russian Convoys, 1944; perm. commn as Lt RN, HMS Vindex, Pacific, 1945; CO 813 Sqdn, 1948; Naval Staff Coll., 1949; CO 767 Sqdn,

1950-51; CO 825 Sqdn, 1951-52; CO, RNAS Eglinton, 1958-59; Chief Staff Officer: FONFT, 1959-61; FOAC, 1961-62; Capt., HMS Osprey, 1962-64; Capt., RNAS Culdrose, 1964-65; Chief Staff Officer (Ops), Far East Fleet, 1966-67; Flag Officer, Naval Flying Training, 1968-71; retired 1971. Comdr 1952; Capt. 1958; Rear-Adm. 1968. *Recreations:* cider and home-made wine making and drinking. *Address:* Hambush Farm, Baltonsborough, Somerset. *T:* Baltonsborough 343.

ROBERTS, Charles Stuart; CMG 1975; HM Diplomatic Service; High Commissioner in Barbados, since 1973; *b* 24 May 1918; *s* of late Charles William Roberts and of Dorothy Roberts; *m* 1946, Margaret Ethel Jones; one *s* two *d. Educ:* Merchant Taylors' School. Entered Colonial Office, 1936. Naval Service (Lieut RNVR), 1940-46. Economic and Financial Adviser, Leeward Is, 1955-57; transferred to HM Diplomatic Service (Counsellor), 1966; British Govt Representative, W Indies Associated States, 1967-70; Head of Caribbean Dept, FCO, 1970-73. *Recreations:* chess, crosswords. *Address:* c/o Foreign and Commonwealth Office, SW1. *Clubs:* MCC; Royal Commonwealth Society (West Indian).

ROBERTS, Colin Henderson, CBE 1973; FBA 1947; Secretary to Delegates of Oxford University Press, 1954-74; Fellow of St John's College, Oxford, 1934-76, Hon. Fellow, 1976; *b* 8 June 1909; *s* of late Robert Lewis Roberts, CBE; *m* 1947, Alison Muriel, *d* of Reginald Haynes and Phyllis Irene Barrow; one *d. Educ:* Merchant Taylors' School; St John's College, Oxford (MA). 1st Cl., Hon. Class. Mods, 1929; 1st Cl., Lit. hum. 1931; Sen. Schol., St John's Coll., 1931-34; Craven Univ. Fellow, 1932-34. Studied Berlin Univ., 1932; Univ. of Michigan, Near East Research (Egypt), 1932-34; Dept of Foreign Office, 1939-45. Lecturer in Classics, St John's College, Oxford, 1939-53; tutor, 1946-53; University Lecturer in Papyrology, 1937-48; Reader, 1948-53. Delegate of Oxford Univ. Press, 1946-53; FBA 1947; Visiting Mem. of Inst. for Advanced Study, Princeton, NJ, 1951-52; Sandars Reader in Bibliography, University of Cambridge, 1960-61. Schweich Lectr, British Acad., 1977. Hon. DLitt Oxon. 1975. *Publications:* An Unpublished Fragment of the Fourth Gospel, 1935; Catalogue of the Greek Papyri in the Rylands Library, Manchester, Vol. III, 1938, Vol. IV (with E. G. Turner), 1952; part editor of the Oxyrhynchus Papyri, Parts XVIII-XX, 1941-52 and XXII, 1954; The Antinoopolis Papyri, 1950; The Merton Papyri (with H. I. Bell), 1948; The Codex, 1955; The Greek Bookhand, 1955. *Recreation:* gardening. *Address:* Appleton House, near Abingdon, Oxon.
See also B. R. Roberts and Rev. R. L. Roberts.

ROBERTS, Cyril Alfred, CBE 1947 (MBE 1944); *b* 4 June 1908; *s* of late A. W. Roberts; *m* 1932, Christine Annabel Kitson, *d* of late Hon. E. C. Kitson, Leeds; three *s* one *d. Educ:* Eton; Trinity Coll., Oxford. Called to the Bar, 1932, and practised until 1939. Served War of 1939-45, HM Forces, 1939-46; France, 1940; Western Desert, 1941-42; Instructor, Staff Coll., Haifa, 1943; War Office, Army Council Secretariat, 1943-45; Brigadier AG Co-ordination, 1945-46. Asst Sec., NCB, 1946-47, Under-Sec. 1947-51, Sec., 1951-59; Member of the Board, 1960-67. Dir, later Dep. Chm., Woodall-Duckham Gp Ltd, 1968-73. Chm., Inst. of Cardiology, 1967-72; Mem. Bd of Governors, Brompton Hosp., Chm. House Cttee, Nat. Heart Hosp., 1973-76. Adviser to Minister of Defence on Resettlement from the Forces, 1968-70; Mem., Armed Forces Pay Review Bd, 1971-. FBIM. Mem., Chichester District Council, 1973-. *Address:* Bury Gate House, Pulborough, West Sussex. *T:* Bury 440.

ROBERTS, David Arthur, CMG 1975; HM Diplomatic Service; Ambassador to the United Arab Emirates, since 1977; *b* 8 Aug. 1924; *s* of late Rev. T. A. Roberts and Mrs T. A. Roberts; *m* 1st, 1951, Nicole Marie Fay (*d* 1965); two *d* ; 2nd, 1968, Hazel Faith Arnot. *Educ:* Hereford Cathedral Sch.; Jesus Coll., Oxford (Scholar; BA). Served RAC, 1943-46. HM Foreign Service, Dec. 1947. Served: Baghdad, 1948-49; Tokyo, 1949-51; FO, 1951-53; Alexandria, 1953-55; Khartoum, 1955-58; FO, 1958-60; Dakar, 1960-61 (Chargé d'Affairs at Bamako and at Lomé during same period); FO, 1962-63; Damascus, 1963-66; Political Agent in the Trucial States, Dubai, 1966-68; Head of Accommodation Dept, FCO, 1968-71; High Comr in Barbados, 1971-73; Ambassador to Syria, 1973-76; High Comr in Sierra Leone, 1976-77. *Address:* c/o Foreign and Commonwealth Office, SW1; 15 Basingbourne Close, Fleet, Hampshire. *Club:* Reform.
See also M . H . A . Roberts .

ROBERTS, Rt. Rev. (David) John; Abbot of Downside, since 1974; *b* 31 March 1919; *s* of Albert Edward and Elizabeth Minnith Roberts. *Educ:* Downside School; Trinity Coll., Cambridge (MA). Royal Sussex Regt, Oct. 1939-Nov. 1945 (POW Germany, May 1940-April 1945). Entered monastery, Feb. 1946; ordained, 1951. House Master, Downside School,

1953-62; Novice Master, 1962-66; Prior 1966-74. *Address:* Downside Abbey, Stratton-on-the-Fosse, Bath BA3 4RH.

ROBERTS, Dr Denis; *see* Roberts, Dr E. F. D.

ROBERTS, Denis Edwin, CBE 1974 (MBE 1945); Managing Director, Posts, Post Office, since 1977; *b* 6 Jan. 1917; *s* of late Edwin Roberts and of Alice G. Roberts; *m* 1940, Edith (*née* Whitehead); two *s. Educ:* Holgate Grammar Sch., Barnsley. Served War of 1939-45, Royal Signals, France, N Africa, Italy and Austria. Entered Post Office, Barnsley, 1933; Asst Traffic Supt, Leeds Telephone Area, 1939; Asst Postal Controller II and I Postal Hdqtrs and Home Counties Region, 1947-62; Controller London Postal Region, 1962-69; Dep. Regional Dir, London Postal Region, 1969-71; Dir Postal Ops, 1971-75; Sen. Dir, Postal Services, 1975-77. *Address:* 302 Gilbert House, Barbican, EC2Y 8BD. *T:* 01-638 0881.

ROBERTS, Sir Denys (Tudor Emil), KBE 1975 (CBE 1970; OBE 1960); QC (Gibraltar 1960, Hong Kong 1964); Chief Secretary of Hong Kong since 1973; *b* 19 Jan. 1923; *s* of William David and Dorothy Elizabeth Roberts; (marriage dissolved); one *s* one *d*). *Educ:* Aldenham; Wadham Coll., Oxford, 1942 and 1946-49 (MA 1948, BCL 1949); served with Royal Artillery, 1943-46, France, Belgium, Holland, Germany, India (Captain); English Bar, 1950-53; Crown Counsel, Nyasaland, 1953-59; Attorney-General, Gibraltar, 1960-62; Solicitor-General, Hong Kong, 1962-66; Attorney-General, Hong Kong, 1966-73. *Publications:* Smuggler's Circuit, 1954; Beds and Roses, 1956; The Elwood Wager, 1958; The Bones of the Wajingas, 1960; How to Dispense with Lawyers, 1964. *Recreations:* cricket, writing. *Address:* Colonial Secretariat, Hong Kong; High Point, Beaucroft Lane, Colehill, Wimborne, Dorset. *Clubs:* MCC; Hong Kong (Hong Kong).

ROBERTS, Rev. Canon Edward Eric, JP; Canon Residentiary, Vice-Provost of Southwell Cathedral and Personal Chaplain to the Bishop of Southwell, since 1968; Canon, 1964; Ecumenical Officer, diocese of Southwell, since 1973; *b* 29 April 1911; *o s* of late Edward Thomas Roberts and Mrs Charlotte Roberts, Liverpool; *m* 1938, Sybil Mary (*née* Curren); two *d. Educ:* Univ. of Liverpool; St Augustine's Coll., Canterbury. Youth Officer: City of Oxford LEA, 1938-43; Wallasey CB, LEA, 1943-44; Training Officer, Church of England Youth Council, 1944-52; Southwell Diocesan Director: of Further Educn, 1952-61; of Educn, 1961-68. JP, City of Nottingham, 1958-. *Recreation:* photography. *Address:* 13 Farthingate Close, Southwell, Notts. *T:* Southwell 812295.

ROBERTS, Dr (Edward Frederick) Denis; Librarian, National Library of Scotland, since 1970; *b* 16 June 1927; *s* of Herbert Roberts and Jane Spottiswoode Roberts (*née* Wilkinson); *m* 1954, Irene Mary Beatrice (*née* Richardson); one *s* one *d. Educ:* Royal Belfast Academical Institution; Queen's University of Belfast. BA (1st cl. Hons Modern History) 1951; PhD 1955. Research Assistant, Dept of History, Queen's Univ. of Belfast, 1951-55; National Library of Scotland: Asst Keeper, Dept of Manuscripts, 1955-66; Secretary of the Library, 1966-67; Librarian, Trinity College Dublin, 1967-70; Hon. Prof., Univ. of Edinburgh, 1975. *Publication:* (with W. G. H. Quigley) Registrum Iohannis Mey: The Register of John Mey, Archbishop of Armagh, 1443-1456, 1972. *Address:* 6 Oswald Court, Edinburgh EH9 2HY. *T:* 031-667 9473. *Club:* New (Edinburgh).

ROBERTS, Rt. Rev. Edward James Keymer; *b* 18 April 1908; *s* of Rev. Arthur Henry Roberts; *m* 1941, Dorothy Frances, *d* of Canon Edwin David Bowser, Deal; three *s* one *d. Educ:* Marlborough; Corpus Christi Coll., Cambridge; Cuddesdon Theological Coll. BA 2nd class Theological Tripos, 1930; MA 1935; DD (*hc*) Cambridge, 1965. FRSCM 1977. Deacon, 1931; priest, 1932; Curate of All Saints, Margaret Street, 1931-35; Vice-Principal Cuddesdon Coll., 1935-39; Examining Chaplain to Bishop of Portsmouth and Commissary, Johannesburg, 1936-39; Vicar of St Matthew, Southsea, 1940-45; Curate-in-charge of St Bartholomew, Southsea, 1941-45; Examining Chaplain to Bishop of Portsmouth, 1942-56; Proctor in Convocation, Portsmouth, 1944-49; Commissary, Northern Rhodesia, 1946-51; Hon. Canon of Portsmouth, 1947-49; Archdeacon of Isle of Wight, Vicar of Brading, Rector of Yaverland, 1949-52; Archdeacon of Portsmouth, 1952-56; Suffragan Bishop of Malmesbury, 1956-62; Examining Chaplain to Bishop of Bristol, 1959-62; Suffragan Bishop of Kensington, 1962-64; Bishop of Ely, 1964-77. Hon. Fellow, Corpus Christi Coll., Cambridge, 1964-. Select Preacher, University of Cambridge, 1966. *Recreation:* shoe cleaning. *Address:* Garden House, Tyne Hall, Bembridge, IoW. *T:* Bembridge 2645.

ROBERTS, Eirlys Rhiwen Cadwaladr, CBE 1977 (OBE 1971); Deputy Director, Consumers' Association (Which?), 1973-77 (Head of Research and Editorial Division, 1958-73); Chief Executive (part-time), Bureau of European Consumer Organisations, since 1973; *b* 3 Jan. 1911; *d* of Dr Ellis James Roberts and Jane Tennant Macaulay; *m* 1941, John Cullen (marr. diss.); no *c. Educ:* Clapham High School; Girton College, Cambridge. BA (Hons) Classics. Sub-editor in Amalgamated Press; Military, then Political Intelligence, 1943-44 and 1944-45; Public Relations in UNRRA, Albanian Mission, 1945-47; Information Division of the Treasury, 1947-57. Mem., Royal Commn on the Press, 1974-77. Trustee, Res. Inst. for Consumer Affairs, 1976-; Mem., Economic and Social Cttee of EEC, 1973-. *Publication:* Consumers, 1966. *Recreations:* climbing, ice-skating, reading detective novels. *Address:* 8 Lloyd Square, WC1. *T:* 01-837 2492.

ROBERTS, Emrys, CBE 1976 (MBE 1946); Chairman, Development Board for Rural Wales, since 1977; Director: Cambrian & General Securities Ltd, since 1974; Filtrasol Ltd, since 1974; *b* 22 Sept. 1910; *s* of late Owen Owens Roberts and of Mary Grace Williams, both of Caernarvon; *m* 1948, Anna Elisabeth Tudor; one *s* one *d. Educ:* Caernarvon; Aberystwyth; Gonville and Caius Coll., Cambridge; Geneva. MA (Cantab); LLB (Wales); 1st Class, Parts I and II, Law Tripos, Cambridge, 1933; 1st Class Hons, University of Wales, 1931, S. T. Evans Prize; Solicitor, 1936, 1st Class Hons, Clements Inn Prize. Squadron Leader RAF, 1941-45 (MBE). Barrister, Gray's Inn, 1944. MP (L) for Merioneth, 1945-51; Member of Parliamentary Delegations to Yugoslavia, Germany, Rumania, and Sweden; Representative at Council of Europe, 1950 and 1951. Dir, Tootal Broadhurst Lee Co. Ltd, 1958-63; Gp Sec. and Legal Adviser, English Sewing Cotton Co. Ltd and English Calico Ltd, 1963-72; Director: English Calico Ltd and Tootal Ltd, 1970-75; Raysil Ltd, Van Allan Ltd, and Yates Duxbury Ltd, to 1974. Chm., Mid-Wales Develt Corp., 1968-77; Mem., Welsh Develt Agency, 1977-. Mem. Court and Council, Univ. Coll. of Wales, Aberystwyth, 1972-; Chm. of Council, Nat. Eisteddfod of Wales, 1964-67, and Hon. Counsel, 1957-74; Vice-Pres. Hon. Soc. of Cymmrodorion. *Publications:* (jointly) The Law of Restrictive Trade Practices and Monopolies. *Address:* Dwy Dderwen, Glyn Garth, Menai Bridge, Gwynedd LL59 5NP. *T:* Menai Bridge 712793.

ROBERTS, Rt. Rev. Eric Matthias; *see* St David's, Bishop of.

ROBERTS, Major-General Frank Crowther, VC 1918; DSO 1915; OBE 1921; MC 1917; *b* 2 June 1891; *s* of Rev. Frank Roberts, Vicar of St John, Southall; *m* 1932, Winifred Margaret, *y d* of John Downing Wragg. *Educ:* St Lawrence College; RMC. Commissioned Worcestershire Regt, 1911, Lieut 1914, Captain 1915; served with 1st Bn Worcs Regt, War of 1914-18, in France and Belgium; wounded three times, despatches five times, VC, DSO, MC; OC 1st Bn, 1917-18 (acting Lt-Col); attached Egyptian Army, Sudan, 1919-20 (Brevet Major 1919; despatches; Gold Medal of Order of Mohammed Ali; Sudan Medal and Clasp, Aliab Dinka); Egypt, 1923-24; Brigade Major, Rhine Army, 1925-26; GSO2 South China, 1926-28; transf. to Royal Warwickshire Regt, 1927, Major; Iraq, 1930-32 (GSO1; Brevet Lt-Col, Brevet Col; Iraq Medal); GSO2 N Ireland Dist., 1935-36; Lt-Col 1936; Local Brig., S Command, India, 1937; Brigade Comdr, Poona, 1938-May 1939; Maj.-Gen. 1939; Comdr, 48th (S Midland) Div., TA, June-Oct. 1939, retired Dec. 1939. *Address:* Four Winds, Bretby, near Burton-on-Trent DE15 0QF. *T:* Burton-on-Trent 217358.

ROBERTS, Sir Frank (Kenyon), GCMG 1963 (KCMG 1953); CMG 1946); GCVO 1965; Advisory Director of Unilever; Director, Dunlop Holdings Ltd; President: British Atlantic Committee, since 1968; European Atlantic Group, since 1973 (Chairman, 1970-73); Vice-President, Atlantic Treaty Association, since 1973 (President, 1969-73); *b* Buenos Aires, 27 Oct. 1907; *s* of Henry George Roberts, Preston, and Gertrude Kenyon, Blackburn; *m* 1937, Celeste Leila Beatrix, *d* of late Sir Said Shoucair Pasha, Cairo, Financial Adviser to Sudan Government; no *c. Educ:* Bedales; Rugby; Trinity College, Cambridge (Scholar). Entered Foreign Office, 1930; served HM Embassy, Paris, 1932-35 and at HM Embassy, Cairo, 1935-37; Foreign Office, 1937-45; Chargé d'Affaires to Czechoslovak Govt, 1943; British Minister in Moscow, 1945-47; Principal Private Secretary to Secretary of State for Foreign Affairs, 1947-49; Deputy High Commr (UK) in India, 1949-51; Deputy-Under Secretary of State, Foreign Office, 1951-54; HM Ambassador to Yugoslavia, 1954-57; United Kingdom Permanent Representative on the North Atlantic Council, 1957-60; Ambassador: to the USSR, 1960-62; to the Federal Republic of Germany, 1963-68. Vice-Pres., German Chamber of Commerce in UK, 1974- (Pres., 1971-74). Mem., FCO Review Cttee on Overseas Representation, 1968-69. Grand Cross, German Order of Merit, 1965. *Address:* 25 Kensington Court Gardens, W8. *Clubs:* Brooks's, Royal Automobile.

ROBERTS, Geoffrey Frank Ingleson; Member for Production and Supply, British Gas Corporation (formerly The Gas Council), since 1972; *b* 9 May 1926; *s* of late Arthur and Laura Roberts; *m* 1949, Veronica, *d* of late Captain J. Busby, Hartlepool; two *d. Educ:* Cathedral Sch., and High Sch. for Boys, Hereford; Leeds Univ. (BSc hons). FIGasE, MInstF. Pupil engr, Gas Light & Coke Co., and North Thames Gas Bd, 1947-50; North Thames Gas Board: Asst Engr, 1950-59; Stn Engr, Slough, 1959-61; Dept. Stn Engr, Southall Stn, 1961-66; Group Engr, Slough Group, 1966-68; Dep. Dir (Ops) Gas Council, 1968-71. *Recreations:* gardening, reading. *Address:* Berry Hill, Deepdene Drive, Dorking, Surrey. *T:* Dorking 4795.

ROBERTS, Air Cdre Sir Geoffrey Newland, Kt 1973; CBE 1946; AFC 1942; FRAeS; Company Director; *b* Inglewood, Taranaki, New Zealand, 8 Dec. 1906; *s* of Charles Oxford Roberts, England, and Hilda Marion Newland, New Zealand; *m* 1934, Phyllis Hamilton Bird; one *s* one *d. Educ:* New Plymouth Boys' High Sch., New Plymouth, Taranaki, NZ. In commerce, NZ, 1924-28; RAF, England/India, 1928-34; commerce, UK, 1935-36; commerce, NZ, 1936-39. Served War: RNZAF, NZ and Pacific (final rank Air Cdre), 1939-46. Air New Zealand, General Manager, 1946-58; Dir, 1958-65; Chm., 1965-75. Director: NZ National Airways Corp., 1958-75; Air Pacific, 1962-75; NZ Breweries Ltd, 1962; Montana Wines Ltd, 1969; NZ Mutual Fund Ltd, 1971. US Legion of Merit, 1945. *Recreations:* formerly: mountaineering, Rugby football, etc; now: farming with son, and commerce generally. *Address:* Puketiro, No 2: RD, Wellsford, North Auckland, New Zealand. *T:* Wellsford 4311. *Clubs:* Northern, Auckland (Auckland, NZ); Rotary (Wellsford, NZ).

ROBERTS, Brig. Sir Geoffrey P. H.; *see* Hardy-Roberts.

ROBERTS, George Charles L.; *see* Lloyd-Roberts.

ROBERTS, Maj.-Gen. George Philip Bradley, CB 1945; DSO 1942; MC 1941; late RTR; *b* 5 Nov. 1906; *m* 1936, Désirée, *d* of Major A. B. Godfray, Jersey; two *s* two *d. Educ:* Marlborough; RMC, Sandhurst. 2nd Lieut Royal Tank Corps, 1926; served War of 1939-45 (MC, DSO and two Bars, CB, despatches thrice); Officier Légion d'Honneur; Croix de Guerre avec palmes. Adjt 6 RTR 1939; DAQMG 7th Armed Div., Bde Maj. 4th Armed Bde, GSO II 7th Armed Div., AQMG 30 Corps, CO 3 RTR 1939-41; Comd 22nd Armed Bde, Comd 26th Armed Bde, Comd 30th Armed Bde, 1941-43; Commander 11th Armoured Div., 1943-46; Comdr 7th Armoured Div., 1947-48; Dir, Royal Armoured Corps, War Office, 1948-49; retired pay, 1949. Hon. Col Kent and County of London Yeomanry Squadron, The Royal Yeomanry Regt, T&AVR, 1963-70. JP County of Kent, 1960-70. *Address:* Se Serra Mitjana, Calonge, Majorca; c/o Williams & Glyn's Bank Ltd, Kirkland House, Whitehall, SW1. *Club:* Army and Navy.

ROBERTS, Sir Gilbert, Kt 1965; FRS 1965; BScEng; Consultant, Freeman, Fox and Partners, since 1969; *b* 18 Feb. 1899; *s* of Henry William Roberts; *m* 1925, Elizabeth Nada Hora; two *d. Educ:* City and Guilds Coll., London. Flt-Lt 73 Sqdn RFC, 1917-18. Asst to Sir Ralph Freeman on design of Sydney Harbour Bridge; in bridge dept of Dorman Long and Co. Ltd, 1926-35; worked on design of numerous bridges, develt of welded constrn and Chromador high tensile structural steel; joined Sir William Arrol & Co. Ltd, Glasgow: in charge of constrn and develt, 1936; Dir and Chief Engnr, 1945; joined Freeman, Fox and Partners as partner responsible for design of Severn Bridge on behalf of jt consg engrs, 1949; designed Forth Road Bridge for same consultants; invented and patented design of present Severn Bridge. Designer of: Auckland Harbour Bridge; Volta Bridge, Ghana; new Maidenhead Bridge and others; also radio-telescopes for CSIRO (Aust.) and NRC (Can.). Inventor of 500-ton Goliath Crane designed for Babcock's power station work; designer of other welded crane structures. FInstW; FICE; FIStrucE; Fell., AmSocCE; Fell., Imperial College; FCGI, Telford Gold Medal, ICE, 1967; Royal Medal, Royal Soc., 1968; James Watt Medal, ICE, 1969; MacRobert Award, 1969; Churchill Gold Medal, Soc. of Engrs, 1970. *Publications:* numerous papers and articles on engineering subjects. *Address:* 42 Wynnstay Gardens, Allen Street, W8. *Club:* Athenæum.

ROBERTS, Capt. Gilbert Howland, CBE 1944; RD 1964; Royal Navy (retired); *b* 11 Oct. 1900; *s* of Colonel Sir Howland Roberts, 12th Baronet, and Elizabeth Marie La Roche; *m* 1930 (marriage dissolved); one *s* one *d*; *m* 1947, Jean Winifred

Warren; one *d. Educ:* Westminster; Royal Naval Colleges, Osborne and Dartmouth. Served European War, 1916-18; specialised in gunnery, 1922; Medal of Royal Humane Society, 1922; Submarine X One, 1926; Commander, 1935; Staff of HM Tactical School, 1935-36; command HMS Fearless, 1937-38; invalided, 1938; rejoined Royal Navy, 1940; served since in HMS Excellent and on Staff of C-in-C Western Approaches as Director Tactical School (CBE, Comdr Order of Polonia Restituta); Captain, 1942. Commodore Royal Norwegian Navy, Naval Assistant to Norwegian Naval C-in-C, 1946-47 (1st class Comdr, Order of St Olaf; Officer, Legion of Honour); lent Royal Canadian Navy for duty and lecture tour, 1955; Comd HMS Vivid, RNR, 1956-64 (RD 1964). Lees-Knowles Lecturer, Military History, Cambridge Univ., 1951. CC Devon, 1957; Alderman, Torbay County Borough, 1967-74. *Recreation:* gardening. *Address:* Little Priors, Watcome, Torquay. *T:* 38919.

ROBERTS, Glynn S.; *see* Silyn Roberts.

ROBERTS, Gwilym Edffrwd; MP (Lab) Cannock, since Feb. 1974; *b* 7 Aug. 1928; *s* of William and Jane Ann Roberts; *m* 1954, Mair Griffiths; no *c. Educ:* Brynrefail Gram. Sch.; UCW (Bangor). Industrial Management, 1952-57; Lecturer (Polytechnic and University), 1957-66, 1970-74. MP (Lab) South Bedfordshire, 1966-70. Industrial Consultant, Economic Forecasting, Market and Operational Research, 1957-. Mem. Council, Inst. of Statisticians; Editor, Inst. of Statisticians Newsletter. *Recreations:* cricket, table tennis, journalism. *Address:* 60 Swasedale Road, Luton, Beds. *T:* 53893; 8 Main Road, Brereton, Rugeley, Staffs. *T:* Rugeley 3601.

ROBERTS, Rev. Harold, PhD (Cambridge); Principal, Richmond College, Surrey (University of London), 1955-68; Chair of Systematic Theology and Philosophy of Religion, Richmond College, 1940-68; President of the Methodist Conference, 1957; *b* Ashley, Cheshire; *s* of E. J. and A. Roberts; *m* 1st, 1926, Edna Tydvil Thomas, BA (*d* 1964); 2nd, 1972, Myra Stevenson Johnson, BA. *Educ:* Hulme Gram. Sch., Manchester; Univ. Coll., Bangor; Wesley House and Jesus College, Cambridge. BA 1st Class Hons Philosophy 1920, MA 1921, Univ. Coll., Bangor. Asst Tutor, Wesley House, Camb., 1924-26; Minister: Liverpool (Waterloo), 1926-29; Oxford, 1929-34; Chair of Systematic Theology and Philosophy of Religion, Wesley College, Headingley, 1934-40; Minister, Ipswich (Museum St), 1941-45. Univ. of London: Member of Senate, 1951-59, Dean of Faculty of Theology, 1953-56; Examiner in Theology, Univ. of London, Queen's Univ., Belfast, Univ. of Wales, etc. Cato Lecturer, Australia, 1950; Fernley-Hartley Lecturer, 1954; Tipple Lecturer, Drew Univ., USA, 1956. Member of Central Cttee World Council of Churches, 1954-62; Pres. of World Methodist Coun., 1956-61; Jt Chm., Anglican-Methodist Unity Commn, 1967; Select Preacher, Univ. of Cambridge, 1958. Hon. DD Trinity College, Dublin, 1961. *Publications:* part-author: The Doctrine of the Holy Spirit, 1938; The Message and Mission of Methodism (Ed.), 1945; Jesus and the Kingdom of God, 1955; Anglican-Methodist Conversations, 1963. *Address:* Wincote, 32 Byng Road, Tunbridge Wells, Kent. *T:* 21945. *Club:* Athenæum.

ROBERTS, Sir Harold (Charles West), Kt 1953; **CBE** 1948; **MC** 1916; *b* 23 May 1892; *s* of T. B. and Elizabeth Roberts, Stoke-on-Trent; *m* Alice May, *d* of A. T. Bourne, Trentham, Staffs; no *c. Educ:* Newcastle School; Birmingham University. Trained as a mining engineer in North Staffordshire. Served European War, in France and Italy, Middlesex Regiment, 1916-18; in India, Indian Army, 1918-19. BSc 1921. HM Inspector of Mines, 1922; senior Inspector, 1936; Chief Inspector of Training, Ministry of Fuel and Power, 1943; Deputy Chief Inspector of Mines, 1945; HM Chief Inspector of Mines, 1951-58, retired. *Recreations:* golf and walking. *Address:* 30 Greys Close, Cavendish, Suffolk.

ROBERTS, (Herbert) John, CMG 1965; MP Zambia, 1964-69 (Nat. Progress Party, 1964-66, Ind., 1967-69); *b* 22 Nov. 1919; *m* 1946, Margaret Pollard; three *s* one *d. Educ:* Holy Trinity, Weymouth; Milton, Bulawayo. Served War of 1939-45; Somaliland, Ethiopia, Burma. Elected MLC, 1954; Leader of Northern Rhodesia United Federal Party, 1959-63; Founder of National Progress Party, 1963; Min. of Labour and Mines, 1959-61; Leader of Opposition (NR), 1961-64; Leader of Opposition (Zambia), 1964-65; disbanded Nat. Progress Party, 1966. *Address:* Chanyanya Ranch, PO Box 2037, Lusaka, Zambia.

ROBERTS, Hugh Eifion Pritchard, QC 1971; **His Honour Judge Eifion Roberts;** a Circuit Judge, since 1977; *b* 22 Nov. 1927; *er s* of late Rev. and Mrs E. P. Roberts, Anglesey; *m* 1958, Buddug Williams; one *s* two *d. Educ:* Beaumaris Grammar Sch.; University Coll. of Wales, Aberystwyth (LLB); Exeter Coll., Oxford (BCL). Called to Bar, Gray's Inn, 1953; practised as a

Junior Counsel on Wales and Chester Circuit, Sept. 1953-April 1971. Dep. Chairman: Anglesey QS, 1966-71; Denbighshire QS, 1970-71; a Recorder of the Crown Court, 1972-77. Formerly Asst Parly Boundary Comr for Wales; Mem. for Wales of the Crawford Cttee on Broadcasting Coverage. *Recreation:* gardening. *Address:* Maes-y-Rhedyn, Gresford Road, Llay, Wrexham, Clwyd. *T:* Gresford 2292. *Club:* National Liberal.

ROBERTS, (Ieuan) Wyn (Pritchard); MP (C) Conway since 1970; *b* 10 July 1930; *s* of late Rev. E. P. Roberts and Margaret Ann; *m* 1956, Enid Grace Williams; three *s. Educ:* Harrow; University Coll., Oxford. Sub-editor, Liverpool Daily Post, 1952-54; News Asst, BBC, 1954-57; TWW Ltd: News, Special Events and Welsh Language Programmes Producer, 1957-59; Production Controller, 1959-60; Exec. Producer, 1960-68; Welsh Controller, 1964-68; Programme Exec., Harlech TV, 1969. PPS to Sec. of State for Wales, 1970-74. Opposition Front-Bench Spokesman on Welsh Affairs, 1974-75, 1976-. Mem. of Gorsedd, Royal National Eisteddfod of Wales, 1966. Member, Court of Governors: Nat. Library of Wales; Nat. Museum of Wales; University Coll. of Wales, Aberystwyth, 1970-. *Recreation:* gardening. *Address:* Tan y Gwalia, Conway, Gwynedd. *T:* Tyn y Groes 371. *Clubs:* Savile; Cardiff and County (Cardiff).

ROBERTS, Dame Jean, DBE 1962; JP; DL; *m* 1922, Cameron Roberts (decd), Headmaster of Albert Senior Secondary Sch., Springburn; one *d. Educ:* Albert Sch.; Whitehill Sch. Taught at Bishopstreet School and later in a special school for handicapped children. Representative of Kingston Ward in Corp. of City of Glasgow from Nov. 1929-May 1966; DL 1964, JP 1934, Glasgow; Sen. Magistrate; held the following posts as first woman to do so: Convener of Electrical Cttee; Dep. Chm. of Corporation; Leader of the Labour Group; City Treasurer; Lord Provost of the City of Glasgow and Lord Lieut of the county of the City of Glasgow, 1960-63. Chm., Cumbernauld Develt Corp., 1965-72. Chm., Scottish National Orchestra Society, 1970-75; Member: Scottish Arts Council, 1963; Arts Council of Gt Britain, 1965-68. Since 1930: apptd by Secretary of State for Scotland to serve on many Advisory Cttees dealing with Local Govt, Social and Economic matters in Scotland. Hon. LLD Glasgow, 1977. Order of St Olav, 1962. *Recreations:* music and public service. *Address:* 35 Beechwood Drive, Glasgow W1. *T:* 041-334 1930.

ROBERTS, John; *see* Roberts, H. J.

ROBERTS, John Alexander Fraser, CBE 1965; **FRS** 1963; **MA** Cantab; MD, DSc (Edinburgh); FRCP; FRCPsych; Geneticist, Paediatric Research Unit, Guy's Hospital Medical School, SE1, 1964; Hon. Clinical Geneticist, Guy's Hospital; Consultant in Medical Genetics to Royal Eastern Counties Hospital, Colchester; *b* 8 Sept. 1899; *er s* of late Robert Henry Roberts, Foxhall, Denbigh, and late Elizabeth Mary; *m* 1st, 1941, Doris, *y d* of late Herbert and Kate Hare; two *d*; 2nd, 1975, Margaret, *d* of Dorothy and late Sydney Ralph. *Educ:* Denbigh Gram. Sch.; privately; Gonville and Caius Coll., Cambridge; Univs of Edinburgh, Wales and Bristol. 2nd Lieut Royal Welch Fusiliers, 1918-19; War of 1939-45: Surgeon-Comdr RNVR and Cons. in Med. Statistics, RN, 1942-46. Research Asst, Inst. of Animal Genetics, Univ. of Edinburgh, 1928-31; Biologist, Wool Industries Research Assoc., 1928-31; Macaulay Research Fellow, Univ. of Edinburgh, 1931-33; Dir, Burden Mental Research Dept, Stoke Park Colony, Bristol, 1933-57; Lectr in Med. Genetics, London School of Hygiene and Trop. Med., 1946-57; Dir, Clinical Genetics Research Unit (MRC), Inst. of Child Health, Univ. of London, and Hon. Consultant in Med. Genetics, The Hospital for Sick Children, Gt Ormond St, 1957-64. President: Royal Anthropological Inst. of Gt Britain and Ire., 1957-59; Biometric Society (British Region), 1960-62; Section of Epidemiology and Preventive Medicine, RSM, 1960-62, Lectures: Charles West, RCP, 1961; Leonard Parsons, Univ. of Birmingham, 1963; Donald Paterson, Univ. of British Columbia (and Vis. Prof.), 1967; Lumleian, RCP, 1971. Ballantyne Prize, RCPE 1976. *Publications:* An Introduction to Medical Genetics, 1940, 6th edn 1973; papers in medical, biological and genetical journals. *Recreation:* mountain walks. *Address:* 10 Aspley Road, Wandsworth, SW18. *T:* 01-874 4826; Foxhall, Denbigh. *Club:* Athenæum.

ROBERTS, John Arthur, CEng, FIEE; Under-Secretary, Department of Energy, 1974-77; *b* 21 Dec. 1917; *s* of late John Richard and Emily Roberts; *m* 1944, Winifred Wilks Scott (*d* 1976); two *s* one *d. Educ:* Liverpool Institute; Liverpool Univ. (BEng). Apprentice, Metropolitan-Vickers Electrical Co Ltd, 1939. Served War, Royal Signals, 1940-46, Major. Sen. Lectr, Applied Science, RMA, Sandhurst, 1947-49; SSO and PSO, RAE, Farnborough, 1949-59; Head, Control and Computers

Section, Applications Br., Central Electricity Generating Bd, 1959-62; Project Ldr, Automatic Control, CEGB, 1962-67; DCSO, Min. of Tech. and DTI, 1967-72; Under-Sec., DTI, 1972-74. *Address:* 15 Gorsehill Lane, Virginia Water, Surrey. *T:* Wentworth 2457.

ROBERTS, John Eric, DSc (Leeds), FInstP; Emeritus Professor of Physics, University of London, 1969; Physicist to Middlesex Hospital, W1, 1946-69; Consultant Adviser in Physics, Department of Health and Social Security, 1960-71; *b* Leeds, 1907; *e s* of late James J. Roberts, Normanton, Yorks; *m* Sarah, *o d* of late Thomas Raybould, Normanton, Yorks; two *d. Educ:* Normanton Grammar School; University of Leeds (Brown Scholar). BSc (Physics Hons), Leeds, 1928; Univ. Research Scholar, PhD 1930; Research Assistant in Physics, University of Leeds, 1930; Assistant Physicist, Royal Cancer Hospital, 1932; Senior Asst Physicist, Middlesex Hosp., 1937; Joel Prof. of Physics Applied to Medicine, Univ. of London, 1946-69; Regional Adviser, ME, Internat. Atomic Energy Agency, 1963-64. FInstP. 1938; DSc (Leeds), 1944. Pres., British Inst. of Radiology, 1951-52; Pres. Hospital Physicists Assoc., 1950-51; Editor, Physics in Medicine and Biology, 1956-60; Editor, British Jl of Radiology, 1964-67. Hon. Mem., Royal Coll. of Radiologists. *Publications:* Nuclear War and Peace, 1956; scientific papers in various journals. *Address:* Windrush, Malthouse Lane, Ludham, Great Yarmouth, Norfolk NR29 5QL. *T:* St Benets 459.

ROBERTS, Air Vice-Marshal John Frederick, CB 1967; CBE 1960 (OBE 1954); with Deloitte & Co., Chartered Accountants, Swansea, since 1969; *b* 24 Feb. 1913; *y s* of late W. J. Roberts, Pontardawe; *m* 1st, 1942, Mary Winifred (*d* 1968), *d* of late J. E. Newns; one *s*; 2nd, 1976, Mrs P. J. Hull, *d* of A. Stiles. *Educ:* Pontardawe Gram. Sch., Glam. Chartered Accountant, 1936. Joined RAF, 1938; service in Middle East, 1942-45; Mem. Directing Staff, RAF Staff Coll., Bracknell, 1954-56; SASO, RAF Record Office, 1958-60; Dep. Comptroller, Allied Forces Central Europe, 1960-62; Stn Comdr RAF Uxbridge, 1963; Dir of Personal Services I, Min. of Def. (Air), 1964-65; Dir-Gen. of Ground Training (RAF), 1966-68; retd, 1968. *Recreations:* cricket, golf, cabinet-making. *Address:* Cefneithrym, 1 Lon Cadog, Sketty, Swansea SA2 0TS. *T:* Swansea 23-763. *Clubs:* Royal Air Force, MCC.

ROBERTS, John Lewis; Assistant Under-Secretary of State (Personnel), Ministry of Defence (Air), since 1977; *b* 21 April 1928; *s* of Thomas Hubert and Meudwen Roberts; *m* 1952, Maureen Jocelyn (*née* Moriarty); two *s. Educ:* Pontardawe Grammar Sch.; Trinity Hall, Cambridge. BA (Hons) History. Joined Min. of Civil Aviation, 1950; Private Sec. to the Parly Sec., 1953; Principal: in Railways, then in Sea Transport; branches of MoT and Civil Aviation, 1954-59; Civil Air Attaché, Bonn Embassy, 1959-62; Defence Supply Counsellor, Paris Embassy, 1966-69; Asst Sec., Internat. Policy Div., MoD, 1971-74; Asst Under-Sec. of State (Air), MoD PE, 1974-76, (Sales), 1976-77. *Recreations:* angling, sailing. *Address:* 23 Mount Ararat Road, Richmond, Surrey TW10 6PQ. *T:* 01-940 1035. *Club:* Fly Fishers'.

ROBERTS, John Morris; Fellow and Tutor, Merton College, Oxford, since 1953; Acting Warden, Merton College, Oxford, since 1977; *b* 14 April 1928; *s* of late Edward Henry Roberts and late Dorothy Julia Roberts, Bath, Som.; *m* 1964, Judith Cecilia Mary, *e d* of late Rev. James Armitage and Monica Armitage; one *s* two *d. Educ:* Taunton Sch.; Keble Coll., Oxford (Schol.). National Service, 1949-50; Prize Fell., Magdalen Coll., Oxford, 1951-53; Commonwealth Fund Fell., Princeton and Yale, 1953-54; Sen. Proctor, Merton Coll., 1967-68, acting Warden, 1969-70, 1977-. Mem., Inst. for Advanced Study, Princeton, 1960-61; Vis. Prof., Univ. of S Carolina, 1961; Sec. of Harmsworth Trust, 1962-68; Mem., Gen. Cttee, Royal Literary Fund, 1975-. Editor, English Historical Review, 1967-77. *Publications:* French Revolution Documents, 1966; Europe 1880-1945, 1967; The Mythology of the Secret Societies, 1972; The Paris Commune from the Right, 1973; Revolution and Improvement: the Western World 1775-1847, 1976; History of the World, 1976; The Great French Revolution, 1978; (Gen. Editor) Purnell's History of the 20th Century; articles and reviews in learned jls. *Recreation:* music. *Address:* Merton College, Oxford. *Club:* United Oxford & Cambridge University.

ROBERTS, Rear-Adm. John Oliver, CB 1976; Flag Officer, Naval Air Command, 1976-78; *b* 4 April 1924; *er s* of J. V. and M. C. Roberts; *m* 1st, 1950, Lady Hermione Mary Morton Stuart (marr. diss. 1960; she *d* 1969); one *d*; 2nd, 1963, Honor Marigold Gordon Gray; one *s* one *d. Educ:* RN Coll., Dartmouth. Served War: Midshipman, HM Ships Renown and Tartar, 1941-43; Sub-Lt, HMS Serapis, 1943-44; Lieut, 1945;

Pilot Trg, 1944-46. HMS Triumph, 1947-49; RNAS, Lossiemouth, 1949-51; Flag-Lt to FOGT, 1952; Lt-Comdr, 1953; HMAS Vengeance and Sydney, 1953-54; RNVR, Southern Air Div., 1954-56; CO, No 803 Sqdn, HMS Eagle, 1957-58; Comdr, 1958; RNAS, Brawdy, 1958-60; CO, HMS St Bride's Bay, 1960-61; Naval Staff, 1962-64; Captain, 1964; CSO, Flag Officer Aircraft Carriers, 1964-66; CO, HMS Galatea, 1966-68; Naval Staff, 1968-70; CO, HMS Ark Royal, 1971-72; Rear-Adm., 1972; Flag Officer Sea Training, 1972-74; COS to C-in-C Fleet, 1974-76. *Recreations:* Rugby football, cricket, athletics, sailing, skiing. *Address:* 52 Southleigh Road, Havant, Hants. *T:* Havant 4904. *Club:* East India, Devonshire, Sports and Public Schools.

ROBERTS, Dr Lewis Edward John; Director, Atomic Energy Research Establishment, Harwell, since 1975; *b* 31 Jan. 1922; *s* of William Edward Roberts and Lilian Lewis Roberts; *m* 1947, Eleanor Mary Luscombe; one *s*. *Educ:* Swansea Grammar Sch.; Jesus Coll., Oxford (MA, DPhil). Clarendon Laboratory, Oxford, 1944; Scientific Officer, Chalk River Res. Estabt, Ont, Canada, 1946-47; AERE, Harwell, 1947, Principal Scientific Officer, 1952; Commonwealth Fund Fellow, Univ. of Calif, Berkeley, 1954-55; Dep. Head, Chemistry Div., 1966, Asst Dir, 1967, AERE. *Publications:* papers in qly revs and in Jl Chem. Soc., Jl Inorganic and Nuclear Chem., and IAEA pubns. *Recreations:* reading, gardening. *Address:* Atomic Energy Research Establishment, Harwell, Didcot, Oxon. *T:* Abingdon 24141.

ROBERTS, Prof. Michael, FBA 1960; Director, Institute for Social and Economic Research, Rhodes University, 1974-76; Professor of Modern History, The Queen's University, Belfast, 1954-73; Dean of the Faculty of Arts, 1957-60; *b* 21 May 1908; *s* of Arthur Roberts and Hannah Elizabeth Landless; *m* 1941, Ann McKinnon Morton; one *d. Educ:* Brighton Coll.; Worcester Coll., Oxford. Gladstone Meml Prizeman, 1931; A. M. P. Read Scholar (Oxford), 1932. Procter Vis. Fell., Princeton Univ., USA, 1931-32; Lectr, Merton Coll., Oxford, 1932-34; DPhil, Oxford, 1935; Prof. of Modern History, Rhodes Univ., S Africa, 1935-53. Lieut, SA Int. Corps, 1942-44. British Council Representative, Stockholm, 1944-46. Public Orator, Rhodes Univ., 1951-53; Hugh Le May Vis. Fellow, Rhodes Univ., 1960-61; Lectures: A. L. Smith, Balliol Coll., Oxford, 1962; Enid Muir Meml, Univ. of Newcastle upon Tyne, 1965; Creighton in History, Univ. of London, 1965; Stenton, Univ. of Reading, 1969; James Ford special, Oxford Univ., 1973; Wiles, QUB, 1977. Hon. Fellow, Worcester Coll., Oxford, 1966; Vis. Fellow, All Souls Coll., Oxford, 1968-69; Leverhulme Faculty Fellow in European Studies, 1973. MRIA 1968. For. Member: Roy. Swedish Acad. of Letters, History and Antiquities; Royal Swedish Academy of Science; Hon. Mem. Samfundet för utgivande av handskrifter rörande Skandinaviens historia. FRHistS; Fil dr (*hc*) (Stockholm), 1960; Hon. DLit QUB, 1977. Chevalier, Order of North Star (Sweden), 1954. *Publications:* The Whig Party, 1807-1812, 1939; (with A. E. G. Trollip) The South African Opposition, 1939-1945, 1947; Gustavus Adolphus: A History of Sweden, 1611-1632, Vol. I, 1953, Vol. II, 1958; Essays in Swedish History, 1967; The Early Vasas: A History of Sweden 1523-1611, 1968; Sweden as a Great Power 1611-1697, 1968; Sverige och Europa, 1969; Gustav Vasa, 1970; Gustavus Adolphus and the Rise of Sweden, 1973; (ed) Sweden's Age of Greatness, 1973; Macartney in Russia, 1974; trans. from Swedish of works by Nils Ahnlund, F. G. Bengtsson, Gunnar Wennerberg (Gluntarne), Birger Sjöberg (Fridas bok); articles in EHR, History, Historical Jl; Past and Present; South African Archives Yearbook, etc. *Recreation:* music. *Address:* 38 Somerset Street, Grahamstown, CP, South Africa. *T:* Grahamstown 4855.

ROBERTS, Michael (Hilary Arthur); MP (C) Cardiff North West, since 1974 (Cardiff North, 1970-74); *b* 1927; *s* of Rev. T. A. Roberts (formerly Rector of Neath); *m* 1952, Eileen Jean Evans; two *s* one *d. Educ:* Neath Grammar School; Cardiff University College. First Headmaster of the Bishop of Llandaff High School, 1963-70. An Opposition Whip, 1974-. *Address:* Ashgrove Farm, Whitchurch, Cardiff.

ROBERTS, Norman Stafford, MA, DPA; Headmaster, Taunton School, since Sept. 1970; *b* 15 Feb. 1926; *s* of late Walter S. Roberts, LLM and Florence E. Roberts (*née* Phythian), Calderstones, Liverpool; *m* 1965, Beatrice, *o d* of late George and Winifred Best, Donaghadee, Co. Down; one *s* two *d. Educ:* Quarry Bank High Sch., Liverpool; Hertford Coll., Oxford (Open Exhibnr, History). Served in RA, Egypt and Palestine, 1945-47 (Lieut). 2nd cl. hons PPE 1950; DipEd Oxford 1951; DPA London 1951. Asst Master, Berkhamsted Junior Sch., 1951-55; House Master, Sixth Form Master, Berkhamsted Sch., 1955-59; Walter Hines Page Scholar to USA, 1959; Senior

History Master, CO CCF (Hon. Major 1965), Monkton Combe Sch., 1959-65, Housemaster 1962-65; Schoolmaster Student, Merton Coll., Oxford, 1964; Headmaster, Sexey's Sch., Bruton, 1965-70. *Recreations:* foreign travel, bridge, hockey, tennis. *Address:* The Gables, Private Road, Staplegrove, Taunton, Somerset. *T:* Taunton 2588. *Club:* East India, Devonshire, Sports and Public Schools.

ROBERTS, Gen. Sir Ouvry Lindfield, GCB 1953 (KCB 1952; CB 1946); KBE 1950 (CBE 1944); DSO 1941; President of Grosvenor Laing (BC) Limited (Canada), 1955-60; formerly Director: Grosvenor/Laing (BC) Ltd; Grosvenor/Laing (Langley Park) Ltd; Grosvenor International Ltd; Redhill Investment Corporation Ltd; Macdonald Buchanan Properties Ltd; *b* 3 April 1898; *m* 1924, Elsie Nora Eileen Webster (*d* 1955); two *s*; *m* 1955, Joyce Mary Segar, *yr d* of Eric W. Scorer, OBE, Coombe Hurst, Lincoln; two *s* one *d. Educ:* Cheltenham College; Royal Military Academy, Woolwich; King's Coll., Cambridge (MA). RE, commissioned 1917; Comdg 23 Ind. Div., 1943-45; Comdg 34 Ind. Corps, 1945; Vice-Adjutant-Gen. War Office, 1945-47; GOC Northern Ireland District, 1948-49; GOC-in-C Southern Command, 1949-52; Quarter-master-General to the Forces, 1952-55; ADC General to the Queen, 1952-55; Colonel Commandant, Corps of Royal Engineers, 1952-62. Administrative Officer, Univ. of BC, 1961-68. *Recreations:* cricket (Army, Quidnunc); hockey (Cambridge, Army, Wales). *Address:* Upper Field House, 105 Church Way, Iffley, Oxford. *T:* Oxford 779351. *Clubs:* Oriental, MCC.

ROBERTS, Percy Charles; Chairman and Chief Executive, Mirror Group Newspapers Ltd, since 1977; *b* 30 July 1920; *s* of late Herbert Bramwell Roberts and Alice (*née* Lang); *m* 1946, Constance Teresa Violet Butler; two *s. Educ:* Brighton Hove and Sussex Grammar Sch. Reporter, Sussex Daily News, 1936-39. Served War of 1939-45: Sussex Yeomanry, in France and ME (Captain). Sub-Editor, Egyptian Mail, Cairo, 1946; Reporter, Mid-East Mail, Palestine, 1947; Sub-Editor: Sussex Daily News, 1948; Liverpool Daily Post, 1949; Editor, Nigerian Citizen, 1949-51; Editorial Adviser, Gen. Manager, Managing Dir, Nigerian Daily Times, 1951-60; Managing Dir, Mirror Gp Newspapers in Caribbean, 1960-62; Gen. Manager, Mirror Newspapers in Manchester, 1962-66; Dir, 1964-, Managing Dir, 1966-, Daily Mirror Newspapers Ltd; Vice-Chm., West of England Newspapers Ltd, 1965-69; Managing Dir, IPC Newspapers Ltd, 1968-75; Dir, Scottish Daily Record & Sunday Mail Ltd, 1969-74; Chm., Overseas Newspapers Ltd, 1969-75; Dep. Chm. and Chief Exec., Mirror Gp Newspapers Ltd, 1975-77. Dir, Reed Publishing Holdings Ltd, 1975-; Mem., Reed Internat. UK Cttee, 1975-. Mem., CBI Employment Policy Cttee, 1975. *Recreation:* boating. *Address:* 5 Albion Close, W2 2AT; Merrick House, Weston-under-Penyard, near Ross-on-Wye, Herefordshire HR9 7PG. *Clubs:* Arts, Royal Automobile.

ROBERTS, Sir Peter Geoffrey, 3rd Bt, *cr* 1919; *b* 23 June 1912; *yr* and *o* surv. *s* of Sir Samuel Roberts, 2nd Bt and Gladys Mary (*d* 1966), *d* of W. E. Dring, MD, Tenterden, Kent; *S* father 1955; *m* 1939, Judith Randell Hempson; one *s* four *d. Educ:* Harrow; Trinity College, Cambridge. Barr.-at-Law, Inner Temple, 1935. Maj. Coldstream Guards. MP (C) Ecclesall Div. of Sheffield, 1945-50; (C-L) Heeley Div. of Sheffield, 1950-66. Chairman: Newton Chambers & Co., Ltd, 1954-72; Curzonia Knitwear Ltd; The Wombwell Investment Co. Ltd; Hadfields Ltd, 1961-67; Director: Wellman Engineering Corp. Ltd (Chm., 1952-72); Guardian Royal Exchange Assurance Ltd; Williams & Glyn's Bank Ltd. Past Chm., Conservative Members' Committee on Fuel and Power; Past Pres., Soc. of British Gas Industries (Pres., 1963). Master Cutler, Sheffield, 1957. High Sheriff of Hallamshire, 1970-71. Hon. Freeman, 1970, Town Collector, 1971-74, Sheffield. *Publication:* Coal Act, 1938. *Heir: s* Samuel Roberts [*b* 16 April 1948; *m* 1977, Georgina, *yr d* of David Cory]. *Address:* 11 Mount Street, W1Y 5RA. *T:* 01-499 4242; Stubbin House, Carsick Hill Road, Sheffield, S Yorkshire S10 3LU. *T:* Sheffield 302700; Cockley Cley Hall, Swaffham, Norfolk. *T:* Swaffham 21308. *Clubs:* Carlton, Brooks's; Sheffield (Sheffield).

ROBERTS, Lieut-Comdr Peter Scawen Watkinson, VC 1942; DSC 1942; RN retired; *b* 28 July 1917; *yr s* of George Watkinson Roberts, 82 King William Street, EC4; *m* 1940, Brigid Victoria, *yr d* of S. J. Lethbridge, Plymouth; one *s* one *d. Educ:* King's School, Canterbury. Entered Royal Navy, 1935; Sub-Lieut 1938; Lieut 1940; Lt-Comdr 1947. HMS Shropshire, 1936-38; Submarines, Sept. 1939; HMS: Tribune, 1940; Thrasher, 1941; Beagle, 1941-42; Vernon, 1943-45; Black Prince, 1945-46; Defiance, 1946-48; Eagle, 1948; Gorregan, 1950; Apollo, 1952; Cardigan Bay, 1953; Dingley, 1955; Vernon, 1956 (HM Underwater Countermeasures and Weapons Estabt, 1957); Drake, 1959. Retired list, 1962. *Address:* The Coach House,

Membland, Newton Ferrers, S Devon. *T:* Newton Ferrers 346. *Clubs:* Royal Burnham Yacht (Burnham-on-Crouch); Royal Naval Sailing Association.

ROBERTS, Rachel; actress; *b* 20 Sept. 1927; *d* of Rev. Richard Rhys Roberts, BA, OCF and Rachel Ann Jones; *m* 1st, 1955, Alan Dobie (marr. diss. 1960); 2nd, 1962, Rex Harrison (marr. diss. 1971). *Educ:* Univ. of Wales (BA); Royal Acad. of Dramatic Art (Dipl.). Stratford Meml Theatre, 1951-52; Old Vic, 1954-55; Bristol Old Vic, 1956; cabaret; Oh My Papa, Garrick; Maggie May, Adelphi; Blithe Spirit, NY; Platonov, Royal Court (Clarence Derivent Award); Alpha Beta, Apollo, 1972; films: Saturday Night and Sunday Morning (British Film Acad. Award for Best Actress), 1960; This Sporting Life (British Film Acad. Award for Best Actress), 1962; O Lucky Man!, 1973; The Belstone Fox, 1973; Murder on the Orient Express, 1974; films, TV and theatre, America, 1970-72. *Recreations:* reading, writing, people and cats. *Address:* c/o ICM, 22 Grafton Street, W1. *T:* 01-629 8080.

ROBERTS, Richard (David Hallam); Headmaster, Wycliffe College, Stonehouse, since 1967; *b* 27 July 1931; *s* of Arthur Hallam Roberts, Barrister-at-law, sometime Attorney-General, Zanzibar, and Ruvé Constance Jessie Roberts; *m* 1960, Wendy Ewen Mount; three *s. Educ:* King's Sch., Canterbury; Jesus Coll., Cambridge. Commissioned into RA 6th Field Regt, 1952. Asst Master, King's Sch., Canterbury, 1956; Housemaster, 1957; Head of Modern Language Dept, 1961; Senior Housemaster, 1965. *Address:* The Headmaster's House, Wycliffe College, Stonehouse, Glos GL10 2JQ.

ROBERTS, Rear-Adm. Richard Douglas, CB 1971; CEng; FIMechE; Rear-Admiral Engineering on staff Flag Officer Naval Air Command, 1969-72; *b* 7 Nov. 1916; *s* of Rear-Adm. E. W. Roberts and Mrs R. E. Roberts (*née* Cox); *m* 1943, Mary Norma Wright; one *s* one *d. Educ:* RNC Dartmouth; RNEC Keyham. Frobisher, 1934; RNEC Keyham, 1935-38 (qual. Marine Eng); HM Ships: Kent, 1938-40; Exeter, 1941; Bermuda, 1942; Mauritius, 1943-45; RNEC Manadon, 1945 (qual. Aero Eng); RNAY Donibristle, 1946 (AMIMechE); RNAS Worthy Down, 1947; RNAS Yeovilton, 1948-49; Staff of Rear-Adm. Reserve Aircraft, 1949-50; Comdr, 1950; RN Staff Coll., 1951; RNAY Fleetlands, 1952-53 (Production Man.); HMS Newfoundland, 1954-56 (Engr Officer); Engr-in-Chief's Dept, Bath, 1956-60; Captain 1960; RNAY Belfast, 1961-62 (Supt); idc, 1963 (MIMechE); Dir, Fleet Maintenance, 1964-66; Dir, Naval Officer Appts (E), 1966-68; Rear-Adm. 1969. MBIM 1967. *Recreations:* sailing (RNSA, 1936), fishing; light railways; Chairman, Axe Vale Conservation Cttee. *Club:* Army and Navy.

ROBERTS, Robert Evan, CBE 1976; National General Secretary, National Council of YMCAs, 1965-75; *b* 16 July 1912; *s* of late Robert Thomas Roberts, Llanilar, Denbighshire; *m* 1939, Rhoda, *d* of late William Driver, Burnley, Lancs; one *s* one *d. Educ:* Cilcain, Flintshire; Liverpool. YMCA: Asst Sec.: Central YMCA Liverpool, 1933; Hornsey (N London), 1935; Asst Div. Sec., Lancs/Cheshire, 1937; Div. Sec., NW Div., 1939; Dep. Dir, YMCA Welfare Services, NW Europe, 1944-46 (despatches); Mem. 21st Army Gp, Council of Voluntary Welfare Work, 1944-46. Nat. Sec., Ireland, 1946; Sec., Personnel Dept, Nat. Council of YMCAs, London, 1948; Nat. Sec., Nat. Council of YMCAs, Wales, 1956-65; Hon. Sec/Treasurer, Assoc. of Secs of YMCAs of Gt Brit. and Ireland, 1963-65; Dep. Chm., Welsh Standing Conf. of Nat. Vol. Youth Orgs. 1963-65. Past Member: Welsh Nat. Council of Social Service; Welsh Jt Educn Cttee; Nat. Inst. of Adult Educn. Member: Nat. Council of Social Service, 1965-75; Brit. Council of Churches (and its Exec.), 1965-74; Council of Voluntary Welfare Work, 1965-75; World Council of YMCAs (and its Finance Cttee), 1965-75; Vice-Pres., Welsh Nat. Council of YMCAs, 1975; Mem. Exec. Cttee, Age Concern, Cumbria, 1976-; Chairman: Age Concern, S Lakeland, 1977-; Job Creation Programme, Barrow and S Lakeland, 1976-; Exec. Mem., SE Lakeland Community Health Council, 1977. Trustee, Framlington Trust, 1973-. Fellow, Royal Commonwealth Soc., 1974-. Silver Jubilee Medal, 1977. *Recreations:* fell-walking, gardening. *Address:* Haford, Lumley Road, Kendal, Cumbria LA9 5HT. *T:* Kendal 24887.

ROBERTS, Rev. Roger Lewis, CVO 1973; MA Oxon; Chaplain, the Queen's Chapel of the Savoy, and Chaplain of the Royal Victorian Order, 1961-73; Chaplain to the Queen, since 1969; *b* 3 Aug. 1911; 3rd *s* of late Robert Lewis Roberts, CBE; *m* 1935, Katie Agnes Mary Perryman; one *s. Educ:* Highgate School; Exeter College, Oxford. 1st Class Hon. Mods, 1931; 1st Class Lit. Hum., 1933; Charles Oldham Prize, 1933; BA 1933; MA 1938; Sixth Form Master, The Liverpool Institute, 1933-34; Sixth Form Master, Rugby School, 1934-40; enlisted RRA, 1940; Army Educational Corps, 1941-43 (Major). Headmaster,

Blundell's Sch., 1943-47; Deacon, Exeter, 1946; Priest, St Albans, 1948; Assistant Priest, Cathedral and Abbey Church of St Alban, 1948-49. Vicar of Sharnbrook, Bedfordshire, 1949-54. Vicar of the Guild Church of All Hallows, London Wall, 1954-58, of St Botolph without Aldersgate, 1958-61. Warden, The Church of England Men's Society, 1957-61 (Gen. Sec. 1954-57, Vice-Pres. 1962-). Member of editorial staff, The Church Times, 1950-76 (Editor, 1960-68). Chaplain: Instn of Electrical Engineers, 1961-73; Worshipful Co. of Glaziers, 1967-. *Recreation:* walking. *Address:* 97 Corringham Road, Golders Green, NW11. *T:* 01-455 2118. *Club:* United Oxford & Cambridge University.
See also *B. R. Roberts and C. H. Roberts.*

ROBERTS, Shelagh Marjorie; Industrial Relations Consultant since 1956; Member, Greater London Council, since 1970, and Leader, Planning and Communications Policy Committee, since 1977; Member, Port of London Authority, since 1976; *b* 13 Oct. 1924; *d* of Glyn Roberts, Ystalyfera. *Educ:* St Wyburn Sch., Birkdale, Lancs. Member: Kensington Borough Council, 1953-71; Bd of Basildon Development Corp., 1971-75; Occupational Pensions Bd, 1973-; Race Relations Bd, 1973-77; Panel of Industrial Tribunals, 1973-; Chm., National Women's Advisory Cttee of Conservative Party, 1972-75; Chm., Nat. Union of Conservative Party, 1976-. *Publications:* (co-author) Fair Share for the Fair Sex, 1969; More Help for the Cities, 1974. *Recreation:* enjoying the sun and fresh air. *Address:* 23 Dovehouse Street, Chelsea, SW3 6JY. *T:* 01-352 3711. *Club:* Hurlingham.

ROBERTS, Thomas Arnold, OBE 1962; TD 1947; FRICS; a Church Commissioner, since 1973; Chartered Surveyor; former Senior Partner, Richard Ellis, Chartered Surveyors, London, EC3; *b* 5 Nov. 1911; *s* of Sidney Herbert Roberts, Liverpool; *m* Kathleen Audrey Robertshaw. *Educ:* Bedford Sch. Joined Westminster Dragoons, 1932; transf. to Royal Signals, 1938. Served War, in N Africa and Italy, 1942-44. Partnership in Richard Ellis & Son, Chartered Surveyors, 1946. Surrey TA Assoc., 1950-72 (Chm., 1956-60); Hon. Col: 381 Lt Regt (TA), 1957-61; Surrey Yeomanry, 1961-68. Property Adviser to Electricity Council, 1957-73. A Governor of Cranleigh Sch., 1960-73 (Chm., 1965-72). DL Surrey, 1958-73. *Recreations:* vintage and sporting motor vehicles, travel. *Address:* Purslow Hall, Clunbury, Craven Arms, Salop. *T:* Little Brampton 205. *Clubs:* Athenæum, Naval and Military.

ROBERTS, Col Sir Thomas Langdon Howland, 6th Bt, of Glassenbury and Brightfieldstown, Co. Cork, *cr* 1809 (claimant to 13th Baronetcy *cr* 1620); CBE 1964; DL; Roy. Artillery (retd); late King's Regt, and VIth KAR; Hon. Colonel 499 (M) HAA Regiment RA (TA), 1949; Actg Col Comdr, No 4 Sector, County of London Home Guard, 1952-56; Commandant County of London ACF, 1956-63; *b* 18 June 1898; *s* of 12th Bt and Elizabeth Marie (*d* 1949), *d* of late W. T. La Roche, MD, New Jersey, USA; *S* father, 1917; *m* 1930, Evelyn Margaret, *o d* of late H. Fielding-Hall, Burma Commission; two *s* one *d*. *Educ:* Westminster School; RMA, Woolwich. Capt. 1928; Major, 1938; Lt-Col 1941. President, County of Kent SS&AFA, 1964-72; Hon. Col, SE London Bde, ACF, 1964-; Vice-Chm., Royal Cambridge Home for Soldiers' Widows, 1961-68; Hon. Sec., Royal Artillery Officers' Sports Fund, 1951-; Hon. Treas., Guild of St Helena, 1958-74; Hon. Treas., Officers' Families Fund, 1964-67. Pres., Kent County Small Bore Rifle Assoc., 1971-. DL, County of London (Wandsworth), 1962-. *Recreations:* sailing, shooting, riding, stamp collecting. *Heir: s* Gilbert Howland Rookehurst Roberts, Lt TARO, BA Cambridge [*b* 31 May 1934; *m* 1958, Ines, *o d* of late A. Labunski; one *s* one *d*]. *Address:* Furzebank, Shorne Ridgeway, near Gravesend, Kent. *Clubs:* Army and Navy; RA Yacht; RE Yacht.

ROBERTS, Thomas Somerville, Chairman, Milford Haven Conservancy Board, since 1976; Deputy Chairman, Welsh Development Agency, since 1976; *b* Ruabon, N Wales, 10 Dec. 1911; *s* of Joseph Richard Roberts, Rhosllanerchrugog and Lily Agnes (*née* Caldwell); *m* 1st, 1938, Ruth Moira Teasdale; two *s*; 2nd, 1950, Margaret Peggy Anderson, Sunderland. *Educ:* Roath Park Elem. Sch., Cardiff; Cardiff High Sch.; Balliol Coll., Oxford (Domus Exhibnr). Traffic Apprentice, LNER, 1933; Docks Manager, Middlesbrough and Hartlepool, 1949; Chief Docks Manager: Hull, 1959; S Wales, 1962; Port Dir, S Wales Ports, 1970-75. Chm., S Wales Port Employers, 1962-75; Member: Nat. Jt Council for Port Transport Industry, 1962-75; Nat. Dock Labour Bd, 1970-75; Race Relations Bd, 1968-76. Dir, Develt Corp. for Wales, 1965-. Member: Council, University Coll., Cardiff (Chm. Finance Cttee); Council, Univ. of Wales Inst. of Science and Technol.; Pwyllgor Tywysog Cymru (Prince of Wales' Cttee), 1977-; Exec. Cttee, Welsh Environment Foundn, 1977-. JP City of Cardiff, 1966.

Recreation: TV. *Address:* Marcross Lodge, 9 Ely Road, Llandaff, Cardiff CF5 2JE. *T:* Cardiff 561153. *Club:* Cardiff and County (Cardiff).

ROBERTS, Sir Walter St Clair Howland, KCMG, *cr* 1951 (CMG 1937); MC; *b* 14 Dec. 1893; *m* 1st, 1924, Helen Cecil Ronayne (*d* 1951), *o c* of late Colonel A. W. Weekes, DSO, OBE, RE; 2nd, Cecily (*d* 1964), widow of H. E. Ormond. *Educ:* Winchester; Brasenose Coll., Oxford. Prisoner of War, 1914-16; served with RFA, 1917-19 (MC). Entered Foreign Office, 1919; Head of Western Europe Dept, 1936-39, and POW Dept, 1941-45; Ambassador to Peru, 1945-48; Minister to Roumania, 1949-51; Minister to Holy See, 1951-53. OStJ 1974. *Address:* Leaton Lodge, Bomere Heath, Salop.

ROBERTS, Wilfrid, JP; *b* 28 Aug. 1900; *s* of Charles and Lady Cecilia Roberts, Boothby, Brampton, Cumberland; *m* 1928, Anne Constance Jennings; three *d*. *Educ:* Gresham School; Balliol College, Oxford. MP (L) North Cumberland, 1935-50; joined Labour Party, July 1956. *Address:* Boothby, Brampton, Cumbria.

ROBERTS, William; RA 1966 (ARA 1958); artist; member of the London Group; *b* London, 1895. *Educ:* St Martin's School of Art; Slade School, London University. Worked at Omega Workshops under Roger Fry before 1914-18 War. Joined Vorticist Gp, 1914 (started by Wyndham Lewis). London Group, 1915. Official War Artist during European War, 1914-18 and War of 1939-45. Three paintings acquired by the Tate Gallery. Retrospective Exhibition, Tate Gallery, 1965; Exhibition, d'Offay Couper Gallery, 1969; Retrospective Exhibition, Hamet Gallery, 1971. *Address:* 14 St Marks Crescent, NW1.

ROBERTS, Sir William (James Denby), 3rd Bt *cr* 1909; *b* 10 Aug. 1936; *s* of Sir James Denby Roberts, 2nd Bt, OBE, and of Irene Charlotte D'Orsey, *yr d* of late William Dunn, MB, CM; *S* father, 1973. *Educ:* Rugby; Royal Agricultural Coll., Cirencester. MRAC, ARICS. Farms at Strathallan Castle, and Combwell Priory, Flimwell, Wadhurst, Sussex. Owner, Strathallan Aircraft Collection. *Recreations:* swimming and flying. *Heir: b* Andrew Denby Roberts, *b* 21 May 1938. *Address:* Strathallan Castle, Auchterarder, Perthshire. *T:* Auchterarder 2131.

ROBERTS, Col William Quincey, CVO 1977; CBE 1958 (OBE 1952); DSO 1944 (Bar, 1945); MVO 1955; TD; JP; DL; Land Steward, Duchy of Cornwall, since 1948; *b* 5 Aug. 1912; *s* of late C. M. Roberts, MVO, Woodland Place, Bathwick Hill, Bath; *m* 1938, Janet Finnimore Hughes, *d* of late G. E. Hughes, Bath; three *d*. *Educ:* Tonbridge School. Asst Land Steward, Duchy of Cornwall, 1933. Commissioned Somerset LI (TA), 1933; Captain 1939; Major 1940; 2 i/c 6th Bn, 1942; served NW Europe, 1944-45; 2 i/c 4 Som. LI 1944; Lt-Col 1944; Comdr, 5 Bn Wilts Regt, 1944, 4 Bn Dorset Regt, 1944-45, and 4 Bn Somerset LI, 1947-52; Bt-Col 1952; Col 1954; Dep.-Comdr 130 Inf. Bde (TA), 1953-58. ADC to the Queen, 1956-61. Hon. Col: The Somerset Light Infantry, 1960-67; Somerset Yeomanry and Light Infantry, 1967-71; 1st Wessex Volunteers, T&AVR, 1970-75; 6th Bn LI (Volunteers), 1972-77 (Dep. Hon. Col, 1971-72). JP Avon, formerly Somerset, 1949; DL 1958; High Sheriff, 1969-70. Hon. Show Dir, Bath and West Southern Counties Soc., 1957-. Fellow Land Agents' Soc., 1947. *Recreations:* all field sports. *Address:* Stonewalls, Newton St Loe, near Bath, Avon. *T:* Saltford 3646. *Clubs:* Army and Navy; Bath and County (Bath).

ROBERTS, Wyn; see Roberts, I. W. P.

ROBERTS-JONES, Ivor, CBE 1975; RA 1973 (ARA 1969); sculptor; Teacher of sculpture, Goldsmiths' College School of Art; *b* 2 Nov. 1913; *s* of William and Florence Robert-Jones; *m* 1940, Monica Florence Booth; one *d* (one *s* decd). *Educ:* Oswestry Grammar Sch.; Worksop Coll.; Goldsmiths' Coll. Art Sch.; Royal Academy Schs. Served in RA, 1939-46; active service in Arakan, Burma. One-man Exhibition of Sculpture, Beaux Arts Gall., 1957. Works purchased by: Tate Gallery; Arts Council of Gt Brit.; Welsh Arts Council; Beaverbrook Foundation, New Brunswick; Nat. Mus. of Wales. Public commissions: Winston Churchill, Parliament Square; Augustus John Memorial, Fordingbridge; Saint Francis, Lady Chapel, Ardleigh, Essex; Apsley Cherry Garrard, Wheathampstead; Winston Churchill, Oslo, commissioned 1975, etc. Exhibited at: The John Moore, Leicester Galls, Royal Academy, Arts Council travelling exhibitions, etc. Work is in many private collections. Best known portraits include: Paul Claudel, Somerset Maugham, Yehudi Menuhin, The Duke of Edinburgh. *Publications:* poetry published in Welsh Review, Poets of the

Forties, etc. Sculpture illustr. in British Art since 1900 by John Rothenstein; British Sculptors, 1947; Architectural Review, etc. *Recreation:* sailing. *Address:* 31 St James's Gardens, W11. *T:* 01-603 9614. *Club:* Cruising Association.

ROBERTS-WRAY, Sir Kenneth Owen, GCMG 1960 (KCMG 1949; CMG 1946); QC 1959; Legal Adviser, Commonwealth Relations Office (Dominions Office until 1947) and Colonial Office, 1945-60, retired; *b* 6 June 1899; *s* of late Captain Thomas Henry Roberts-Wray, CB, OBE, VD, RNVR, sometime ADC to King George V, and late Florence Grace Roberts-Wray; *m* 1st, 1927, Joan Tremayne Waring (*d* 1961); three *s*; 2nd, 1965, Lady (Mary Howard) Williams, *widow* of Sir Ernest Williams, JP. *Educ:* University Tutorial Coll.; RMA, Woolwich; Merton College, Oxford (1st Class Hons School of Jurisprudence). 2/Lt RA 1918; Lieutenant, 1919; retired on account of wounds, 1920. Called to Bar 1924 (Certificate of Honour); Professional Legal Clerk, Min. of Health, 1926; Asst Chief Clerk, 1929; 2nd Asst Legal Adviser, Dominions Office and Colonial Office, 1931; Asst Legal Adviser, 1943. Chairman: Law Officers Conf., WI, 1944; Judicial Advisers Confs, Uganda, 1953, Nigeria, 1956. Acting Attorney-Gen., Gibraltar, Jan.-June 1969. DCL Oxon, 1967; Hon. LLD Birmingham, 1968. *Publications:* part author of The Law of Collisions on Land, 1925; (Contrib.) Changing Law in Developing Countries (ed Anderson), 1963; Commonwealth and Colonial Law, 1966; articles on Colonial Law in legal publications. *Recreations:* golf, photography. *Address:* The Old Golf House, Forest Row, East Sussex. *T:* Forest Row 2588; 5 King's Bench Walk, Temple, EC4. *T:* 01-353 2882/2884. *Clubs:* United Oxford & Cambridge University; Royal Ashdown Forest Golf.

ROBERTSON, family name of **Baron Robertson of Oakridge.**

ROBERTSON OF OAKRIDGE, 2nd Baron *cr* 1961; **William Ronald Robertson;** Bt 1919; Member of the London Stock Exchange, since 1973; *b* 8 Dec. 1930; *s* of General Lord Robertson of Oakridge, GCB, GBE, KCMG, KCVO, DSO, MC, and of Edith, *d* of late J. B. Macindoe; *S* father, 1974; *m* 1972, Celia Jane, *d* of William R. Elworthy; one *s*. *Educ:* Hilton Coll., Natal; Charterhouse; Staff Coll., Camberley (psc). Served The Royal Scots Greys, 1949-69. Mem. Salters' Co. *Heir: s* Hon. William Brian Elworthy Robertson, *b* 15 Nov. 1975. *Club:* Anglo-German Association.

ROBERTSON, Hon. Lord; Ian Macdonald Robertson, TD 1946; a Senator of the College of Justice in Scotland (with judicial title of Lord Robertson) since 1966; *b* 30 Oct. 1912; *s* of late James Robertson and Margaret Eva Wilson, Broughty Ferry, Angus, and Edinburgh; *m* 1938, Anna Love Glen, *d* of late Judge James Fulton Glen, Tampa, Florida, USA; one *s* two *d*. *Educ:* Merchiston Castle School; Balliol College, Oxford; Edinburgh University. BA Oxford (Mod. Greats), 1934; LLB Edinburgh 1937; Vans Dunlop Schol. in Law, Edinburgh 1937. Member Faculty of Advocates, 1939; Advocate-Depute, 1949-51; QC (Scot.), 1954; Sheriff of Ayr and Bute, 1961-66; Sheriff of Perth and Angus, 1966. Chairman: Medical Appeals Tribunal, 1957-63; Scottish Jt Council for Teachers' Salaries, 1965; Scottish Valuation Adv. Council, 1977; Member Court of Session Rules Council; External Examiner in law subjects, Aberdeen, Glasgow, Edinburgh and St Andrews Universities; Member Committee on Conflicts of Jurisdiction affecting Children, 1958; Governor of Merchiston Castle School, 1954, Chm., 1970; Assessor on Court of Edinburgh Univ., 1967. Chairman: Edinburgh Centre of Rural Economy; Edinburgh Centre for Tropical Veterinary Medicine; Jt Cttee, Edinburgh Sch. of Agriculture. Served War of 1939-45, 8th Bn The Royal Scots (The Royal Regt); commd 1939; SO (Capt.), 44th Lowland Brigade (15th Scottish Division), Normandy and NW Europe (despatches). *Publication:* From Normandy to the Baltic, 1945. *Recreation:* golf. *Address:* 13 Moray Place, Edinburgh EH3 6DT. *T:* 031-225 6637. *Clubs:* New, Honourable Company of Edinburgh Golfers (Captain 1970-72).
See also Sir James W. Robertson.

ROBERTSON, Alan, OBE 1965; FRS 1964; BA; DSc; Deputy Chief Scientific Officer, ARC Unit of Animal Genetics, Edinburgh; *b* 21 Feb. 1920; *s* of late John Mouat Robertson and Annie Grace; *m* 1947, Margaret Sidney, *y d* of late Maurice Bernheim; two *s* one *d*. *Educ:* Liverpool Institute; Gonville and Caius College, Cambridge. Operational Research Section, Coastal Command, RAF, 1943-46. ARC Unit of Animal Genetics, Edinburgh, 1947-. Hon. Prof., Edinburgh Univ., 1967. Hon. Dr rer nat Univ. of Hohenheim, 1968. Gold Medal, Royal Agric. Soc., 1958. *Publications:* papers in scientific jls. *Recreations:* gardening, tennis. *Address:* 47 Braid Road, Edinburgh EH10 6AW. *T:* 031-447 4239. *Club:* Farmers'.

ROBERTSON, Alan Murray; Director: Motherwell Bridge (Holdings) Ltd; Scrimgeour Hardcastle (Holdings) Ltd; formerly Managing Director, BP Oil Ltd, and a Director, BP Trading Ltd; *b* 19 Dec. 1914; *s* of late Dr James R. Robertson; *m* 1st; one *s* two *d*; 2nd, Judith-Anne, *d* of late Robert Russell, Glasgow. *Educ:* St Anselm's Bakewell; Malvern; Pembroke Coll., Cambridge (MA). Joined Anglo-Iranian Oil Co., 1937 in Paris; served 1939-46 in RTR and RASC, Middle East and Italian Campaigns (despatches, Major); Anglo-Iranian representative in France, 1949-53; Gen. Man., Scottish Oils & Shell-Mex Ltd, 1955-56; Man. Dir, National Benzole Co. Ltd, 1957-63; Exec. Vice-Pres., BP Oil Corp., New York, 1968-70. *Recreations:* travel, fishing, gardening. *Address:* Shepherds Cottage, Shipton-under-Wychwood, Oxon. *Club:* Caledonian.

ROBERTSON, Alec; *see* Robertson, A. T. P.

ROBERTSON, Prof. Sir Alexander, Kt 1970; CBE 1963; Professor of Tropical Animal Health, University of Edinburgh, since 1971; Director: Veterinary Field Station, since 1968; Centre for Tropical Veterinary Medicine, Edinburgh University, since 1971; *b* 3 Feb. 1908; *m* 1936, Janet McKinlay; two *d*. *Educ:* Stonehaven Mackie Acad.; Aberdeen University; and Royal (Dick) Veterinary College, Edinburgh. MA Aberdeen, 1929; BSc Aberdeen, 1930; PhD Edinburgh, 1940; MRCVS, 1934. Demonstrator in Anatomy, Royal (Dick) Veterinary College, Edinburgh, 1934; Vet. Inspector, Min. of Agriculture, 1935-37; Sen. Lectr in Physiology, 1938-44, Prof. of Vet. Hygiene, 1944-53, William Dick Prof. of Animal Health, 1953-71, Director, 1957-63, Royal (Dick) School of Veterinary Studies, Univ. of Edinburgh; Dean of Faculty of Vet. Medicine, Univ. of Edinburgh, 1964-70. Exec. Officer for Scotland, Farm Livestock Emergency Service, 1942-47. FRSE, 1945; FRIC, 1946; FRSH, 1950; FRZSScot, 1952; Mem. Departmental Cttee on Foot and Mouth Disease, 1952-54; Pres. Brit. Vet. Assoc., 1954-55; Vice-Pres. Roy. Zoological Soc. of Scotland, 1959-; Mem. Governing Body, Animal Virus Research Inst., Pirbright, 1954-62; Member: Council Royal Coll. of Veterinary Surgeons, 1957-(Treasurer, 1964-67; Vice-Pres., 1967-68, 1969-70; Pres., 1968-69); Artificial Insemination Adv. Cttee for Scotland, 1958-65; ARC Tech. Adv. Cttee on Nutrient Requirements, 1959-; Departmental Cttee of Inquiry into Fowl Pest, 1960-61; Governing Body Rowett Research Institute, 1962-; ARC Adv. Cttee on Meat Research, 1968-73; Trustee, Internat. Laboratory for Res. in Animal Diseases, 1973-; Chairman: Sci. Adv. Panel, Pig Industry Develt Authority, 1962-68; Research Adv. Cttee, Meat and Livestock Commn, 1969-73; Vet. Adv. Panel, British Council, 1971-; Member: FAO/WHO Expert Panel on Veterinary Educn, 1962-; East African Natural Resources Research Council, 1963-; Cttee of Inquiry into Veterinary Profession, 1971-75; Council, RSE, 1963-65, Vice-Pres., 1969-72; Inter Univ. Council, 1973-75. Hon. FRCVS, 1970. Hon. Mem., World Veterinary Assoc., 1975. Hon. LLD Aberdeen, 1971; Hon. DVSc Melbourne, 1973. *Publications:* (ed) International Encyclopædia of Veterinary Medicine; numerous articles in veterinary and other scientific journals. *Recreations:* gardening, motoring, hill climbing. *Address:* 205 Mayfield Road, Edinburgh EH9 3BD. *T:* 031-667 1242. *Clubs:* Caledonian; New (Edinburgh).

ROBERTSON, Alexander Thomas Parke, (Alec Robertson), MBE 1972; FRAM, 1945; *b* 3 June 1892; *s* of J. R. S. Robertson, MD, and Elizabeth Macrory. *Educ:* Bradfield College, Berks; Royal Academy of Music. Began professional career as organist of Frensham Parish Church, 1914; Farnham Parish Church, 1914. Served European War, 1914-18, commissioned Hampshire Regt 1914; went to India, 1914, Palestine, for active service, 1917. Joined The Gramophone Co. (His Master's Voice) in 1920 to develop educational use of the gramophone by means of lectures, building up repertoire, etc.; head of this Education Dept, 1925. Went to Rome to study theology, church music, etc., at Collegio Beda, 1930. Joined BBC in Gramophone Dept, 1940, Music Dept, 1941, finally Talks Dept, 1944; Specialist Talks Producer (Music), British Broadcasting Corporation, 1944-53; retired, 1953; besides organising output of music talks, became well known as a broadcaster. An authority on plainchant and early church music; writer, lecturer, and adjudicator. *Publications:* The Interpretation of Plainchant, 1937; Dvořák, 1945; Contrasts, Arts and Religion, 1947; Sacred Music, 1950; More than Music (autobiography), 1961; Catholic Church Music, 1961; Schubert's Songs (in symposium), 1946; (ed) Chamber Music (Pelican), 1956; Jt Ed., Pelican History of Music in 3 vols, 1961-66; Requiem, 1967; Church Cantatas of J. S. Bach, 1972; contrib. to Chambers's Encyc., Grove's Dictionary of Music and Musicians (1954 edn), and to musical and other journals. *Address:* The Platt, Apsley Farm, Pulborough, West Sussex. *T:* Coolham 359.

ROBERTSON, Prof. Anne Strachan, DLitt; FRSE; FSA, FSAScot; Titular Professor of Roman Archaeology, Glasgow University, 1974-75, retired; *d* of John Anderson Robertson and Margaret Purden. *Educ:* Hillhead High Sch.; Glasgow High Sch. for Girls; Glasgow Univ. (MA, DLitt); London Univ. (MA). FRSE 1975; FMA 1958; FRNS 1937; FSA 1958; FSAScot 1941. Glasgow University: Dalrymple Lectr in Archaeol., 1939; Under-Keeper, Hunterian Museum and Curator, Hunter Coin Cabinet, 1952; Reader in Roman Archaeol., Keeper of Cultural Collections and of Hunter Coin Cabinet, Hunterian Museum, 1964; Keeper of Roman Collections and of Hunter Coin Cabinet, 1974. Silver Medal, RNS, 1964; Silver Huntington Medal, Amer. Numismatic Soc., 1970. *Publications:* An Antonine Fort: Golden Hill, Duntocher, 1957; The Antonine Wall, 1960 (5th edn 1973); Sylloge of Anglo-Saxon Coins in the Hunter Coin Cabinet, 1961; Catalogue of Roman Imperial Coins in the Hunter Coin Cabinet: Vol. 1, 1962; Vol. 2, 1971; Vol. 3, 1977; Vol. 4, 1978; The Roman Fort at Castledykes, 1964; Birrens (Blatobulgium), 1975; contrib. to Britannia, Numismatic Chron., Proc. Soc. of Antiquaries of Scotland. *Recreations:* reading, writing, photography, walking. *Address:* Flat 7, 60 Partickhill Road, Glasgow G11 5AB. *T:* 041-339 6198.

ROBERTSON, Bryan Charles Francis, OBE 1961; Author, Broadcasting and Television, etc; regular contributor to The Spectator; *b* 1 April 1925; *yr s* of A. F. Robertson and Ellen Dorothy Black; unmarried. *Educ:* Battersea Grammar School. Worked and studied in France and Germany, 1947-48; Director: Heffer Gallery, Cambridge, 1949-51; Whitechapel Art Gallery, London, 1952-68. Mem. Arts Council Art Panel, 1958-61; Mem. Contemporary Art Soc. Cttee, 1958-73. US Embassy Grant to visit United States, 1956; Lectr on art, Royal Ballet School, 1958; Ford Foundn Grant for research for writing, 1961; British Council Lecture Tour, SE Asia and Australian State Galleries, 1960. Dir, State Univ. of NY Museum, 1971. Since 1953 has organized major exhibitions at Whitechapel, including Turner, Hepworth, Moore, Stubbs, John Martin, Rowlandson and Gillray, Bellotto, Mondrian, de Stäel, Nolan, Davie, Smith, Malevich, Pollock, Richards, Australian Painting, Rothko, Tobey, Vaughan, Guston, Poliakof, Caro, Medley, etc. *Publications:* Jackson Pollock, a monograph, 1960; Sidney Nolan, a monograph, 1961; (with Sir Kenneth Clark and Colin MacInnes) Robert Motherwell, a monograph, 1964; Pollock, 1971; (with H. Tatlock Miller) Loudon Sainthill, 1973; contribs (art criticism) to London Magazine, Art News (US), Spectator, New Statesman, Twentieth Century, Listener, Cambridge Review, Museums Jl, etc.

ROBERTSON, Catherine Christian, MA; Headmistress of George Watson's Ladies' College, 1926-45; *b* 10 Dec. 1886; *d* of late Alexander Robertson, Perth, and Mary Macfarlane Duncan, Edinburgh. *Educ:* privately; Perth Academy; University of Edinburgh. Graduated in Arts, with Hons in English Literature and Language, Class II, 1910; Cherwell Hall, Oxford; Diploma of Education, 1911; George Scott Travelling Scholar, 1911. Head of the English Department, Edinburgh Ladies' Coll., 1919-26; travel in America as Chautauqua Scholar of the English-Speaking Union (first Scotswoman to hold this award), 1925. President, Association of Headmistresses, Scottish Branch, 1941-42; Vice-Chairman of Council, Girls' Training Corps, Scotland, 1942. *Recreations:* walking, foreign travel, music. *Address:* c/o Mrs Wylie, 14 Muirhall Terrace, Perth.

ROBERTSON, Maj.-Gen. Cecil Bruce, CB 1948; CBE 1946; MC 1918; DL; JP; *b* 8 March 1897; *er s* of late W. Bruce Robertson, 26 Kensington Palace Gdns, London, W, and of Mrs Bruce Robertson; *m* 1925, Sheila Mary, *d* of late Brig.-Gen. F. A. MacFarlan, CB; two *s* one *d*. *Educ:* Cheltenham; RMC Sandhurst. Commnd 2nd Lt The Argyll and Sutherland Highlanders, 1914. GSO2 HQ1 Corps, 1939-40; GSO1, 45 Div., 1940-41; Bde Commander 44 Div., 1941-42; DD of O (O) War Office, 1943; Director of Combined Operations (Military), 1943-45; BGS Southern Command, 1945-47; Chief of Staff Southern Command, 1947-48. Temp. Major-Gen., 1947; retired, 1948. DL Devon, 1954; JP 1955. *Address:* The Glebe House, Chudleigh, Devon. *T:* Chudleigh 2223. *Club:* Army and Navy.

ROBERTSON, Prof. Charles Martin; FBA 1967; Lincoln Professor of Classical Archaeology and Art, University of Oxford, 1961-Sept. 1978; Fellow of Lincoln College; *b* 11 Sept. 1911; *s* of late Professor Donald Struan Robertson, FBA, FSA, and Petica Coursolles Jones; *m* 1942, Theodosia Cecil Spring Rice; four *s* two *d*. *Educ:* Leys School, Cambridge; Trinity College, Cambridge. BA Cambridge, 1934, MA 1947; student at British School of Archaeology, Athens, 1934-36; Asst Keeper, Dept of Greek and Roman Antiquities, British Museum, 1936-48 (released for service, War of 1939-45, 1940-46); Yates Professor of Classical Art and Archaeology in the Univ. of London (Univ. Coll.), 1948-61. Corresp. Mem., German Archaeological Inst., 1953; Ordinary Mem., 1953; Chm., Man. Cttee, British School at Athens, 1958-68. Mem., Inst. for Advanced Study, Princeton, 1968-69. *Publications:* Why Study Greek Art? (Inaugural Lecture), 1949; Greek Painting, 1959; The Visual Arts of the Greeks (in The Greeks), 1962; Between Archaeology and Art History (Inaugural Lecture), 1963; Crooked Connections (poems), 1970; indexes and editorial work in late Sir John Beazley's Paralipomena, 1971; For Rachel (poems), 1972; A History of Greek Art, 1975; (with Alison Frantz) The Parthenon Frieze, 1975; A Hot Bath at Bedtime (poems), 1977; articles, notes and reviews since 1935, in British and foreign periodicals. *Address:* The Clockhouse, Sheepstead, Abingdon OX13 6QG. *T:* Frilford Heath 390605.

ROBERTSON, Charles Robert Suttie; Member, Management Committee of The Distillers Company Ltd, since 1970; chartered accountant; *b* 23 Nov. 1920; *s* of late David Young McLellan Robertson and Doris May Beaumont; *m* 1949, Shona MacGregor Riddel, *d* of Robert Riddel, MC, and Phyllis Mary Stewart; one *s*. *Educ:* Dollar Academy. Joined DCL group, 1949; appointed: Managing Director, Scottish Malt Distillers, 1960; Sec., DCL, 1966, Finance Director, 1967. *Recreations:* hill walking, golf. *Address:* 30 Murrayfield Road, Edinburgh EH12 6ER. *T:* 031-337 7786. *Club:* Army and Navy.

ROBERTSON, David Lars Manwaring; Director: Kleinwort, Benson Ltd, since 1955; Kleinwort, Benson, Lonsdale Ltd; *b* 29 Jan. 1917; *m* 1939, Pamela Lauderdale Meares; three *s*. *Educ:* Rugby; University Coll., Oxford. Man. Dir, Charterhouse Finance Corp. Ltd, 1945-55; joined Kleinwort, Sons & Co. Ltd, 1955. Dep. Chm., Kleinwort, Benson Inc., NY, 1971-; Chairman: MK Electric Holdings Ltd; MK Electric Ltd; Insulators Ltd, 1975-; Provident Mutual Life Assurance Assoc., 1973-; Provident Mutual Managed Pensions Funds Ltd, 1974-; Director: Berry Bros and Rudd; Kleinwort Benson Investment Trust Ltd; Pres., Kleinwort Benson (Geneva) SA, 1975. *Recreations:* skiing, golf, tennis, shooting. *Address:* Kleinwort, Benson Ltd, 20 Fenchurch Street, EC3P 3DB; Ketches, Newick, near Lewes, East Sussex. *Clubs:* Boodle's, MCC.

ROBERTSON, Donald Buchanan, QC (Scot.) 1973; *b* 29 March 1932; *s* of Donald Robertson, yachtbuilder, Sandbank, Argyll, and Jean Dunsmore Buchanan; *m* 1st, 1955, Louise Charlotte, *d* of Dr J. Linthorst-Homan; one *s* one *d*; 2nd, 1965, Daphne Jean Black Kincaid, *d* of Rev. R. B. Kincaid. *Educ:* Dunoon Grammar Sch.; Glasgow Univ. (LLB). Admitted Solicitor, 1954; Royal Air Force (National Service), 1954-56. Passed Advocate, 1960; Standing Junior to Registrar of Restrictive Practices, 1970-73. Member: Sheriff Court Rules Council, 1972-76; Royal Commn on Legal Services in Scotland, 1976-. *Recreations:* shooting, numismatics, riding. *Address:* 6 Great Stuart Street, Edinburgh EH3 6AW. *T:* 031-225 1729; Cranshaws Castle, By Duns, Berwickshire. *T:* Longformacus 268. *Club:* New (Edinburgh).

ROBERTSON, Douglas William, CMG 1947; DSO 1918; MC 1918; *b* 30 Nov. 1898; 2nd surv. *s* of late Rev. J. A. Robertson, MA; *m* 1924, Mary Eagland (*d* 1968), *y d* of late W. E. Longbottom, Adelaide; no *c*. *Educ:* George Watson's College, Edinburgh. 2nd Lt KRRC, 1917; France, 1918 (wounded, MC, DSO, despatches); Administrative Service, Uganda, 1921-50; Resident of Buganda, 1945; Secretary for African Affairs, Uganda, 1947-50, retired, 1950. *Address:* 3a Ravelston Park, Edinburgh EH4 3DX. *Clubs:* East India, Devonshire, Sports and Public Schools; New (Edinburgh).

ROBERTSON, Eric Desmond, OBE 1964; Controller, English Services, BBC External Services, and Deputy to Managing Director, External Broadcasting, 1973-74; *b* 5 Oct. 1914; *s* of late Major Frank George Watt Robertson, Indian Army, and Amy Robertson (*née* Davidson); *m* 1943, Aileen Margaret Broadhead; two *s*. *Educ:* Aberdeen Grammar Sch.; Univ. of Aberdeen. BSc (Forestry) 1934, BSc 1936, Hunter Meml Prize, 1936. Scientific Adviser, Guthrie & Co. Ltd, Malaya, 1938-39; Malayan Forest Service, Asst Conservator, 1939-40. War of 1939-45: Malaya Command, on special duty, 1940-41. Producer, Malaya Broadcasting Corp., 1941-42; Special Officer, Far Eastern Broadcasting, All India Radio, 1942-45; Malay Editor, BBC, 1945-46; Far Eastern Service Organiser, BBC, 1946-49; Asst Head of Far Eastern Service, BBC, 1949-52; Head of Far Eastern Service, BBC, 1952-58; Head of Asian Services, BBC, 1958-64; Asst Controller, Overseas Services, BBC, 1964-70; Controller, Overseas Services, BBC, 1970-73. *Address:* 26 Noel Road, Islington, N1 8HA. *T:* 01-359 9765.

ROBERTSON, Francis Calder F.; see Ford Robertson.

ROBERTSON, George Paterson; Executive Director, National and Commercial Banking Group Ltd, 1969-73; b 28 March 1911; 2nd s of Alexander Paterson Robertson and Helen Allan Guthrie; m 1941, Mary Martin Crichton; one d (one s decd). Educ: Allan Glen's Sch., Glasgow. Commissioned RAF Accountant Branch, 1940-46; Cashier and Gen. Manager, The Royal Bank of Scotland, 1965-68; Director: The Royal Bank of Scotland, 1967-68; Glyn Mills & Co., 1965-68; Williams Deacon's Bank Ltd, 1965-68; Scottish Agricultural Securities Corp. Ltd, 1965-68. Pres., Inst. of Bankers in Scotland, 1967-69; Vice-Pres., British Bankers' Assoc., 1968-69; Past Hon. Treasurer: Earl Haig Fund (Scotland), 1965-68; Officers' Assoc. (Scottish Br.), 1965-68; Scottish Veterans' Garden City Assoc. Inc., 1965-68. Address: 3 Kings Court, Beckenham, Kent. T: 01-650 5414.

ROBERTSON, (Harold) Rocke, CC (Canada) 1969; MD, CM, FRCS(C), FRCSE, FACS, FRSC; Principal and Vice-Chancellor of McGill University, 1962-70; b 4 Aug. 1912; s of Harold Bruce Robertson and Helen McGregor Rogers; m 1937, Beatrice Roslyn Arnold; three s one d. Educ: St Michael's Sch., Victoria, BC; Ecole Nouvelle, Switzerland; Brentwood College, Victoria, BC; McGill University. Montreal Gen. Hospital: rotating, 1936; pathology, 1937-38; Clin. Asst in Surg., Roy. Infirmary, Edinburgh, 1938-39; Demonstr in Anat., Middx Hosp. Med. Sch., 1939; Jun. Asst in Surg., Montreal Gen. Hosp., 1939-40; Chief of Surgery: Shaughnessy Hosp., DVA, Vancouver, 1945-59 (Prof. of Surg., Univ. of BC, 1950-59); Vancouver Gen. Hosp., 1950-59; Montreal Gen. Hosp., 1959-62 (Prof. of Surg., McGill University, 1959-62). Mem. Nat. Research Coun., 1964. Director: Bell Telephone Co. of Canada, 1965-; Ralston Purina Canada, 1973. Hon. DCL, Bishop's Univ., 1963; Hon. LLD: Manitoba, 1964; Toronto, 1964; Victoria, 1964; Glasgow, 1965; Michigan, 1967; Dartmouth, 1967; Sir George Williams, 1970; McGill, 1970; Hon. DSc: Brit. Columbia, 1964; Memorial, 1968; Jefferson Med. Coll., 1969; Dr de l'Univ., Montreal, 1965. FRSA 1963. Publications: article on wounds, Encyclopædia Britannica; numerous contribs to scientific journals and text books. Recreations: tennis, fishing, gardening, golf. Address: RR2, Mountain, Ontario K0E 1S0, Canada. T: 613-989-2967. Club: Rideau (Ottawa).

ROBERTSON of Brackla, Maj.-Gen. Ian Argyll, CB 1968; MBE 1947; MA; DL; Representative in Scotland of Messrs Spink & Son, 1969-76; Chairman, Royal British Legion, Scotland, 1974-77 (Vice-Chairman, 1971-74); b 17 July 1913; 2nd s of John Argyll Robertson and Sarah Lilian Pitt Healing; m 1939, Marjorie Violet Isobel Duncan; two d. Educ: Winchester Coll.; Trinity Coll., Oxford. Commnd Seaforth Highlanders, 1934; Brigade Major: 152 Highland Bde, 1943; 231 Infantry Bde, 1944; GSO2, Staff College, Camberley, 1944-45; AAG, 15 Indian Corps, 1945-46; GSO1, 51 Highland Div., 1952-54; Comdg 1st Bn Seaforth Highlanders, 1954-57; Comdg Support Weapons Wing, 1957-59; Comdg 127 (East Lancs) Inf. Bde, TA, 1959-61; Nat. Defence College, Delhi, 1962-63; Comdg School of Infantry, 1963-64; Commanding 51st Highland Division, 1964-66; Director of Army Equipment Policy, Ministry of Defence, 1966-68; retd. Mem. Council, Nat. Trust for Scotland, 1972-75. DL Nairn 1973. Recreations: various in a minor way. Address: Brackla House, Nairn. T: Cawdor 220. Clubs: Army and Navy, MCC; Vincent's (Oxford).

ROBERTSON, Rear-Adm. Ian George William, CB 1974; DSC 1944; Scoutreach Resources Organiser, Scout Association, since 1976; b 21 Oct. 1922; s of W. H. Robertson, MC, and late Mrs A. M. Robertson; m 1947, Barbara Irène Holdsworth; one s one d. Educ: Radley College. Joined RNVR, 1941; qual. Pilot; Sub-Lt 1943; air strike ops against enemy shipping and attacks against German battleship Tirpitz, 1944 (DSC); Lieut, RN, 1945; flying and instructional appts, 1944-53; Comdr (Air): RNAS Culdrose, 1956; HMS Albion, 1958; in comd: HMS Keppel, 1960; HMS Mohawk, 1963; RNAS Culdrose, 1965; HMS Eagle, 1970; Admiral Comdg Reserves, 1972-74; retd 1974. Comdr 1954; Captain 1963; Rear-Adm. 1972; idc 1968. Dir-Gen., Navy League, 1975-76. Recreations: golf, sailing. Address: 30 Hesper Mews, SW5 0HH. T: 01-373 0869. Clubs: Naval; Royal Mid-Surrey Golf.

ROBERTSON, Ian (Gow), MA Oxon; Keeper of Western Art, Ashmolean Museum, Oxford, and of Hope Collection of Engraved Portraits, and Fellow of Worcester College, Oxford, 1962-68; b Killearn, Stirlingshire, 20 Sept. 1910; er s of John Gow Robertson and Margaret Stewart. Educ: The King's School, Canterbury. Studied art at continental centres, in US and in public and private collections in UK. Assistant Keeper in Dept of Fine Art, Ashmolean Museum, 1931. Ministry of Home

Security, 1939-41; served in Royal Navy, 1941-46. Senior Assistant Keeper, Ashmolean Museum, 1949. Recreations: gardening, listening to music. Address: 15 Gledhow Gardens, SW5. Club: Naval.

ROBERTSON, Ian Macbeth, CB 1976; MVO 1956; Under-Secretary, Scottish Education Department, 1966-78; b 1 Feb. 1918; s of late Sheriff-Substitute J. A. T. Robertson; m 1947, Anne Stewart Marshall. Educ: Melville College; Edinburgh University. Served War of 1939-45 in Middle East and Italy; Royal Artillery and London Scottish, Captain. Entered Dept of Health for Scotland, 1946. Private Secretary to Minister of State, Scottish Office, 1951-52 and to Secretary of State for Scotland, 1952-55. Asst Secretary, Dept of Health for Scotland, 1955; Assistant Under-Secretary of State, Scottish Office, 1963-64; Under-Secretary, Scottish Development Department, 1964-65. Address: 8 Middleby Street, Edinburgh EH9 1TD. T: 031-667 3999. Clubs: Naval and Military; New (Edinburgh).

ROBERTSON, Ian Macdonald; see Robertson, Hon. Lord.

ROBERTSON, James, CBE 1969; MA; FRCM; Hon. FTCL; Hon. GSM; Hon. RAM; Director, London Opera Centre, 1964-77, Consultant, 1977-78; b 17 June 1912; s of Ainslie John Robertson and Phyllis Mary Roughton; m 1949, Rachel June Fraser; two s. Educ: Winchester College; Trinity College, Cambridge; Conservatorium, Leipzig; Royal College of Music, London. On musical staff, Glyndebourne Opera, 1937-39; Conductor, Carl Rosa Opera, Co., 1938-39; Conductor, Canadian Broadcasting Corp., 1939-40; Air Ministry, 1940-42; RAFVR (Intelligence), 1942-46. Director, Sadler's Wells Opera Company, 1946-54; Conductor of National Orchestra of New Zealand Broadcasting Service, Sept. 1954-Nov. 1957. Conductor, Touring Opera, 1958; Adviser on Opera, Théâtre de la Monnaie, Brussels, 1960-61; Artistic and Musical Director, New Zealand Opera Co., 1962-63. Recreation: languages. Address: Ty Helyg, Llwynmawr, Pontfadog, Llangollen, Clwyd LL20 7BG.

ROBERTSON, Maj.-Gen. James Alexander Rowland, CB 1958; CBE 1956 (OBE 1949; MBE 1942); DSO 1944 (Bar 1945); DL; Administrative Official, National Canine Defence League, since 1969; b 23 March 1910; s of Colonel James Currie Robertson, CIE, CMG, CBE, IMS, and Catherine Rowland Jones; m 1st, 1949, Ann Madeline Tosswill (d 1949); 2nd, Joan Wills (née Abercromby), widow of R. L. Wills, CBE, MC. Educ: Aysgarth School; Epsom College, RMC, Sandhurst. Commissioned 2 Lieutenant IA, 1930, attached 1st KOYLI; posted 6th Gurkha Rifles, 1931; Instructor Sch. of Physical Training, 1936-37; Staff Coll., Quetta, July-Dec. 1941; Bde Major 1 (Maymyo) Bde, Jan.-June, 1942; Bde Major, 106 1 Inf. Bde, 1942-44; Comdr 1/7 Gurkha Rifles, 1944-45; Comdr 48 Ind. Inf. Bde, 1945-47; GSO 1, Instr Staff Coll., Quetta, June-Nov., 1947; Comdr 1/6th Gurkha Rifles, 1947-48; GSO 1 Gurkha Planning Staff, March-June, 1948; GSO 1 Malaya comd, June-Nov. 1948; BGS 1948-49. GSO 1, War Office, 1950-52; Col GS, 1 Corps, Germany, 1952-54; Comdr 51 Indep. Bde, 1955-57; Commander 17 Gurkha Division Overseas Commonwealth Land Forces, and Maj.-Gen. Brigade of Gurkhas, 1958-61; GOC Land Forces, Middle East Command, 1961-63; Gurkha Liaison Officer, War Office, 1963-64, retd. Personnel Dir, NAAFI, 1964-69. Colonel, 6th Queen Elizabeth's Own Gurkha Rifles, 1961-69; Chm. Gurkha Brigade Assoc., 1968. DL Greater London, 1977. Recreations: fishing and an outdoor life. Club: Army and Navy.

ROBERTSON, Sir James (Anderson), Kt 1968; CBE 1963 (OBE 1949; MBE 1942); QPM 1961; b Glasgow, 8 April 1906; s of James Robertson, East Haugh, Pitlochry, Perthshire and later of Glasgow, and Mary Rankin Anderson, Glasgow; m 1942, Janet Lorraine Gilfillan Macfarlane, Largs, Ayrshire; two s one d. Educ: Provanside Sch., Glasgow and Glasgow Univ. BL 1936. Chief Constable of Glasgow, 1960-71. Chairman: Scotland Cttee, Nat. Children's Home; Glasgow Standing Conf. of Voluntary Youth Organisations; Hon. President: Glasgow Bn Boys' Brigade. OStJ 1964. Recreations: golf and gardening. Address: 3 Kirklee Road, Glasgow G12 0RL. T: 041-339 4400.

ROBERTSON, James Cassels; Lord-Lieutenant of Dunbartonshire, since 1975; Director, William Robertson Shipowners Ltd, Glasgow, since 1949; Chairman: Robertson Research Holdings Ltd, since 1971; Tharsis Sulphur and Copper Co. Ltd; b 19 May 1921; yr s of late William Francis Robertson and of Harriett Willis Cassels; m 1947, Joan, er d of late Lt-Comdr E. Kirkpatrick-Crockett, RN, and of Leila Bootiman; two s one d. Educ: Winchester. Served in RNVR, 1940-46. DL Dunbartonshire, 1965; Vice-Lieutenant, Dunbartonshire, 1968-75. Mem., Queen's Body Guard for Scotland, Royal Co. of Archers. Chm., Scottish and Ulster Area, British Shipping Fedn,

1968-73; Deacon, Incorporation of Hammermen of Glasgow, 1971. Chairman: Scottish Council, King George's Fund for Sailors, 1972-; Bd of Governors, Glasgow Coll. of Nautical Studies, 1969-75; Glasgow Veteran Seafarers Assoc., 1962-. OStJ. *Recreation:* yachting. *Address:* Cromalt, Helensburgh, Dunbartonshire. *T:* Helensburgh 6111. *Clubs:* Royal Thames Yacht; Royal Yacht Squadron (Cowes); Royal Northern Yacht (Rhu) (Cdre 1964-70).

ROBERTSON, James Geddes, CMG 1961; formerly Under-Secretary, Department of the Environment, and Chairman, Northern Economic Planning Board, 1965-71, retired 1971; *b* 29 Nov. 1910; *s* of late Captain A. M. Robertson, Portsoy, Banffshire; *m* 1939, Marion Mitchell Black; one *s* one *d. Educ:* Fordyce Academy, Banffshire; George Watson's College, Edinburgh; Edinburgh University. Kitchener Schol., 1928-32, MA 1st cl. Hons History (Edinburgh), 1932. Entered Ministry of Labour as Third Class Officer, 1933; Principal, 1943; on exchange to Commonwealth Dept of Labour and Nat. Service, Australia, 1947-49; Asst Sec., Min of Labour, 1956; Member of Government Delegations to Governing Body and Conference of ILO, 1956-60, and Social Cttee, Council of Europe, 1953-61; Safety and Health Dept, 1961-63; Training Department, Ministry of Labour, 1963-65. Member: Industrial Tribunals Panel, 1971-73; Northern Rent Scrutiny Bd, 1973-74; Rent Assessment Panel for Scotland, 1975-. Served War of 1939-45, RAF 1942-45. *Address:* 12a Abbotsford Crescent, Edinburgh EH10 5DY. *T:* 031-447 4675.

ROBERTSON, Maj.-Gen. James Howden, CB 1974; Director, Army Dental Service, 1970-74; *b* 16 Oct. 1915; *s* of John and Marion Robertson, Glasgow and Creetown; *m* 1942, Muriel Edna, *d* of Alfred Jefferies, Elgin; two *s* one *d. Educ:* White Hill Sch., Glasgow; Glasgow Dental Hospital. LDS, RFPS(G) 1939; FDS, RCSE 1957. Lieut, Army Dental Corps, 1939; Captain 1940; Major 1943; Lt-Col 1954; Col 1962; Brig. 1967; Maj.-Gen. 1970. Served in UK and Norway, 1939-44, Europe, 1944-50; Senior Specialist in Dental Surgery, 1957; Middle East, 1958-61; Consultant, CMH Aldershot, 1962-67; Consulting Dental Surgeon to the Army, 1967-70. Col Comdt, RADC, 1975-. QHDS, 1967-74. Pres., Oral Surgery Club of GB, 1975-76. OStJ 1969. *Publications:* various articles in medical and dental jls on oral and maxillo-facial surgery. *Recreations:* wildfowling, fishing, gardening. *Address:* Struan, Hethfelton Hollow, East Stoke, Dorset. *T:* Bindon Abbey 462272.

ROBERTSON, Mrs James Hugh; *see* Mueller, A. E.

ROBERTSON, Rev. Canon James Smith; Canon Emeritus, Zambia, 1965; Secretary, United Society for the Propagation of the Gospel, since 1973; *b* 4 Sept. 1917; *s* of Stuart Robertson and Elizabeth Mann Smith, Forfar; *m* 1950, Margaret Isabel Mina Mounsey; one *d. Educ:* Glasgow Univ.; Edinburgh Theol Coll.; London Univ. MA Glasgow 1938; PCE London 1953. Curate, St Salvador's, Edinburgh, 1940-45; Mission Priest, UMCA, N Rhodesia, 1945-50; St Mark's Coll., Mapanza, 1950-55; Chalimbana Trng Coll., Lusaka, 1955-65, Principal 1958-65; Head, Educn Dept, Bede Coll., Durham, 1965-68; Sec., Church Colls of Educn, Gen. Synod Bd of Educn, 1968-73. *Publications:* (contrib.) Education in South Africa, 1970; (contrib.) The Training of Teachers, 1972; (contrib.) Values and Moral Development in Higher Education, 1974. *Recreations:* music, electronics, philosophy. *Address:* 5 Fitzwilliam Avenue, Kew Gardens, Richmond, Surrey. *T:* 01-940 8574.

ROBERTSON, Sir James (Wilson), KT 1965; GCMG 1957 (KCMG 1953); GCVO 1956; KBE 1948 (MBE 1931); *b* 27 Oct. 1899; *e s* of late James Robertson, Broughty Ferry, Angus and Edinburgh, and late Mrs Robertson, Gleniyon, Spylaw Bank Road, Colinton, Midlothian; *m* 1926, Nancy, *er d* of H. S. Walker, Huddersfield; one *s* one *d. Educ:* Merchiston Castle School, Edinburgh; Balliol College, Oxford. BA 1922, MA 1930; Honorary Fellow of Balliol, 1953. Oxford University Rugby XV, 1921. Officer Cadet, 1918-19; 2nd Lieutenant, Black Watch, 1919; entered Sudan Political Service, 1922; Assistant Dist Commissioner and Dist Comr, 1922-36. Jebel Aulia compensation commission, 1936. Sub-Governor White Nile Province, 1937; Dep. Governor Gezira Province, 1939; actg Governor Gezira Province, 1940-41. Asst Civil Secretary, 1941; Deputy Civil Secretary, 1942; Civil Secretary Sudan Government, 1945-53; Chairman British Guiana Constitutional Commission, 1953-54; Director, Uganda Co. Ltd, 1954-55 and 1961-69; Governor-General and Commander-in-Chief of Federation of Nigeria, 1955-60 (first Governor-General and Commander-in-Chief of the Independent Federation of Nigeria, Oct.-Nov. 1960). Comr to examine the question of Kenya Coastal Strip, Oct. 1961. Dir, Barclays Bank DCO, 1961-71. Chairman: Commonwealth Inst., 1961-68; Central Coun. Roy.

Over-Seas League, 1962-67; Sudan British Pensioners' Assoc., 1961-67; Coun. for Aid to African Students, 1961-76; Pres. Overseas Service Pensioners' Assoc., 1961-71; Pres. Britain-Nigeria Assoc., 1961-; a Governor, Queen Mary Coll., Univ. of London, 1961-74; Mem. Council, Royal Commonwealth Society for the Blind; Deputy Chairman, Nat. Cttee for Commonwealth Immigrants, 1965-68. Hon. LLD Leeds University, 1961. FRSA 1964. Wellcome Medal, Royal African Society, 1961. Order of the Nile, 4th Class, 1934. KStJ 1955. *Publication:* Transition in Africa—Memoirs, 1974. *Address:* The Old Bakehouse, Cholsey, near Wallingford, Oxon. *T:* Cholsey 651234; Douglas Cottage, Killichonan, Rannoch Station, Perthshire. *T:* Bridge of Gaur 242. *Club:* Athenæum.
See also Hon. Lord Robertson.

ROBERTSON, John; MP (SLP) Paisley since 1976 (MP (Lab), 1961-76); *b* 3 Feb. 1913; *s* of William Robertson; *m* 1939 (marr. diss. 1977); two *s* three *d*; *m* 1977, June Robertson. *Educ:* elementary and secondary schools. Formerly District Secretary and Assistant Divisional Organizer of the Amalgamated Engineering Union, West of Scotland. Mem., Lanarkshire County Council, Motherwell and Wishaw Town Council, 1946-52. Member of Labour Party, 1943-; contested (Lab) Scotstoun Division of Glasgow, General Election, Oct. 1951; elected for Paisley, 1961. Among the founders of the Scottish Labour Party, Jan. 1976. *Recreations:* politics, painting, bowling and Trade Union. *Address:* 7 Finlas Avenue, Ayr. *T:* Alloway 42150.

ROBERTSON, Maj.-Gen. John Carnegie, Director of Army Legal Services, Ministry of Defence, 1973-76; *b* 24 Nov. 1917. *Educ:* Cheltenham Coll.; RMC, Sandhurst. Served War of 1939-45: Officer in Gloucestershire Regt (PoW, Germany, 1940). Called to the Bar, Gray's Inn, 1949. Joined Judge Advocate's Dept, 1948; served subseq. in Middle East, BAOR, East Africa and the Far East. Dep. Dir, Army Legal Services, HQ, BAOR, 1971-73. *Recreation:* golf. *Address:* Berry House, Nuffield, Henley-on-Thames, Oxon. *T:* Nettlebed 740.

ROBERTSON, John Monteath, CBE 1962; FRS 1945; FRIC, FInstP, FRSE; MA, PhD, DSc (Glasgow); Gardiner Professor of Chemistry, University of Glasgow, 1942-70, now Professor Emeritus; Director of Laboratories, 1955-70; *b* 24 July 1900; *s* of William Robertson and Jane Monteath, of Nether Fordun, Auchterarder; *m* 1930, Stella Kennard Nairn, MA; two *s* one *d. Educ:* Perth Academy; Glasgow University. Commonwealth Fellow, USA, 1928; Member staff of Davy Faraday Laboratory of Royal Institution, 1930; Senior Lecturer in Physical Chemistry, University of Sheffield, 1939; Scientific Adviser (Chemical) to Bomber Command, 1941; Hon. Scientific Adviser to RAF, 1942. George Fisher Baker Lecturer, Cornell Univ., USA, 1951; Visiting Prof., Univ. of California, Berkeley, USA, 1958. Member, University Grants Committee, 1960-65; President, Chemical Society, 1962-64. Davy Medal, Royal Soc., 1960; Longstaff Medal, Chemical Society, 1966. Corresp. Member Turin Academy of Sciences, 1962. Hon. LLD Aberdeen, 1963; Hon. DSc Strathclyde, 1970; Paracelsus Medal, Swiss Chem. Soc., 1971. *Publications:* Organic Crystals and Molecules, 1953; papers and articles on chemical, physical, and X-ray diffraction subjects in Proc. Royal Soc., Jl of Chem. Soc., etc. *Address:* 42 Bailie Drive, Bearsden, Glasgow G61 3AH. *T:* 041-942 2640. *Club:* Athenæum.

ROBERTSON, John Windeler; Partner, Wedd Durlacher Mordaunt; Deputy Chairman, Stock Exchange, since 1976; *b* 9 May 1934; *s* of John Bruce Robertson and Evelyn Windeler Robertson; *m* 1959, Jennifer-Ann Gourdou; one *s* one *d. Educ:* Winchester Coll. National Service, RNVR, 1953-55. Joined Wedd Jefferson & Co. (Members of Stock Exchange), 1955; Partner, 1961; Shareholder, Wedd Durlacher Mordaunt, 1968; Director, Wedd Durlacher Mordaunt Ltd, 1974; a Managing Partner, Wedd Durlacher Mordaunt, 1976. *Recreations:* golf, deer stalking. *Address:* Grayshurst, Haslemere, Surrey. *T:* Haslemere 2822. *Club:* City of London.

ROBERTSON, Lewis, CBE 1969; Deputy Chairman and Chief Executive, Scottish Development Agency, 1976 (Member, since 1975); Director, Scottish and Newcastle Breweries Ltd, since 1975; *b* 28 Nov. 1922; *s* of John Farquharson Robertson and Margaret Arthur; *m* 1950, Elspeth Badenoch; three *s* one *d. Educ:* Trinity Coll., Glenalmond. Accountancy training; RAF Intelligence; Industrialist. Chm., 1968-70, and Man. Dir, 1965-70, Scott & Robertson Ltd. Chief Executive, 1971-76, and Dep. Chm., 1973-76, Grampian Holdings Ltd. Chm. Eastern Regional Hosp. Bd (Scotland), 1960-70; Trustee (Exec. Cttee), Carnegie Trust for Univs of Scotland, 1963-; Mem. General Synod, Episcopal Church of Scotland, 1963- (Chm. Policy Cttee, 1974-76); Mem. (Sainsbury) Cttee of Enquiry, Pharmaceutical Industry, 1965-67; Mem. of Court (Finance Convener), Univ. of

Dundee, 1967-70; Mem. Monopolies and Mergers Commn, 1969-76; Mem., Arts Council of GB and Chm., Scottish Arts Council, 1970-71. FBIM 1976. Hon. LLD, Dundee, 1971. *Recreations:* music, literature, food, Italy. *Address:* The Blair, Blairlogie, Stirling FK9 5PX. *T:* Alva 61473. *Clubs:* Caledonian; New (Edinburgh).

ROBERTSON, Commandant Dame Nancy (Margaret), DBE 1957 (CBE 1953; OBE 1946); retired as Director of Women's Royal Naval Service (Dec. 1954-April 1958); *b* 1 March 1909; *er d* of Rev. William Cowper Robertson and Jessie Katharine (*née* McGregor). *Educ:* Esdaile School, Edinburgh; Paris. Secretarial work, London and Paris, 1928-39; WRNS, 1939. *Recreations:* needlework, gardening. *Address:* Rose Cottage, Buckland Common, Tring, Herts. *T:* Cholesbury 354.

ROBERTSON, Prof. Noel Farnie, BSc Edinburgh; MA Cantab; PhD Edinburgh; FRSE; Professor of Agriculture and Rural Economy, University of Edinburgh, and Principal, East of Scotland College of Agriculture, since 1969; *b* 24 Dec. 1923; *o s* of James Robertson and Catherine Landles Robertson (*née* Brown); *m* 1948, Doreen Colina Gardner; two *s* two *d. Educ:* Trinity Academy, Edinburgh; University of Edinburgh; Trinity College, Cambridge. Plant Pathologist, West African Cacao Research Institute, 1946-48; Lecturer in Botany, University of Cambridge, 1948-59; Prof. of Botany, Univ. of Hull, 1959-69. Mem. Horticulture Bd, ARC/DAFS/MAFF Jt Cons. Org. for Res. and Develt in Agric. and Food, 1973-. Pres., British Mycol Soc., 1965. Governor: Scottish Horticultural Res. Inst., 1973; Plant Breeding Inst., 1966-; Macaulay Inst. for Soil Res., 1970-. *Address:* Boghall Farmhouse, Biggar Road, Edinburgh EH10 7DX. *T:* 031-445 3194. *Club:* Farmers'.

ROBERTSON, Patrick Allan Pearson, CMG 1956; *b* 11 Aug. 1913; *s* of A. N. McI. Robertson; *m* 1st, 1939, Penelope Margaret Gaskell (*d* 1966); one *s* two *d*; 2nd, 1975, Lady Stewart-Richardson. *Educ:* Sedbergh School; King's College, Cambridge. Cadet, Tanganyika, 1936; Asst Dist Officer, 1938; Clerk of Exec. and Legislative Councils, 1945-46; Dist Officer, 1948; Principal Asst Sec., 1949; Financial Sec., 1951; Asst Sec., Colonial Office, 1956-57; Chief Sec., Zanzibar, 1958; Civil Sec., Zanzibar, 1961-64; Deputy British Resident, Zanzibar, 1963-64; retired, 1964. Associate Member, Commonwealth Parliamentary Association. Freeman, City of London. *Recreations:* golf, tennis, fishing. *Address:* Lynedale, Longcross, Chertsey, Surrey. *T:* Ottershaw 2329. *Club:* Royal Commonwealth Society.
See also Sir Simon Stewart -Richardson , Bt .

ROBERTSON, Robert, CBE 1967; JP; Member, Convention of Scottish Local Authorities, since 1975; *b* 15 Aug. 1909; *s* of late Rev. William Robertson, MA; *m* 1938, Jean, *d* of late James Moffatt, MA, Invermay, Broomhill, Glasgow; one *s* one *d. Educ:* Forres Academy; Royal Technical Coll., Glasgow. Civil Engr, retd 1969. Mem., Eastwood Dist Council, 1952-58; Chm., Renfrewshire Educn Cttee, 1962-73; Mem., Strathclyde Regional Council, 1974-; Convener, Renfrewshire County Council, 1973-75 (Mem., 1958). Chm., Sec. of State's Cttee on Supply and Trng of Teachers for Further Educn, 1962-; Chm., Nat. Cttee for Inservice Trng of Teachers, 1965-. Mem. Scottish Council for: Research in Educn, 1962-; Commercial Admin. and Profl Educn, 1960-69; Development of Industry, 1973-75. Chm., Sch. of Further Educn for training of teachers in Scotland, 1969-. Governor: Jordanhill Coll. of Educn, 1966; Watt Memorial and Reid Kerr Colls, 1966-75. Member: Scottish Nat. School Camps Assoc., 1975-; Scottish Assoc. of Young Farmers' Clubs, 1975-. Fellow, Educnl Inst. of Scotland (FEIS), at Stirling Univ., 1970; Hon. Warden, Co. of Renfrew, Ont., Canada, 1970. JP Renfrewshire, 1958. *Publications:* Robertson Report on: The Training of Teachers in Further Education (HMSO), 1965. *Recreations:* fishing, painting. *Address:* Castlehill, Newton Mearns, Renfrewshire. *T:* 041-639 3089; Castlehill, Maybole, Ayrshire. *Clubs:* RNVR (Scotland); SV Carrick (Glasgow).

ROBERTSON, Ronald Foote, MD, FRCP, FRCPEdin; President, Royal College of Physicians of Edinburgh, since 1976; *b* 27 Dec. 1920; *s* of Thomas Robertson and Mary Foote; *m* 1949, Dorothy Tweedy Wilkinson; two *d* (and one *d* decd). *Educ:* Perth Acad.; Univ. of Edinburgh. MB, ChB (Hons) 1945; MD (High Commendation) 1953; FRCPEdin. 1952; FRCP London 1969. Consultant Physician: Leith Hosp., 1959-74; Deaconess Hosp., 1958-; Royal Infirmary of Edinburgh, 1975-. Sec., RCPEdin., 1958-63; Vice-Pres., 1973-76. Principal MO, Scottish Life Assce Co., 1968-. Mem., Assoc. of Phys. of Gt Britain and Ireland. Has served on numerous NHS cttees. *Publications:* several articles in scientific jls. *Recreations:* gardening, curling, fishing. *Address:* 15 Wester Coates Terrace,

Edinburgh EH12 5LR. *T:* 031-337 6377. *Club:* University Staff (Edinburgh).

ROBERTSON, Prof. Sir Rutherford (Ness), Kt 1972; CMG 1968; DSc; PhD; FRS 1961; FAA; Director, Research School of Biological Sciences, Australian National University, since Jan. 1973 (Master of University House, 1969-72); *b* 29 Sept. 1913; *o c* of Rev. J. Robertson, MA, and Josephine Robertson; *m* 1937, Mary Helen Bruce Rogerson; one *s. Educ:* St Andrew's Coll., NZ; Univ. of Sydney; St John's Coll., Cambridge (Hon. Fellow 1973). DSc Sydney 1961; FAA 1954. Sydney Univ. Science Res. Schol., 1934-35, Linnean Macleay Fell., 1935-36. Exhibn of 1851 Res. Schol., 1936-39; Res. at Botany Sch., Cambridge, in plant physiology, 1936-39, PhD 1939; Asst Lectr, later Lectr, Botany Sch., Univ. of Sydney, 1939-46; Sen. Res. Offr, later Chief Res. Offr, Div. of Food Preservation, CSIRO, 1946-59 (res. in plant physiol. and biochem.); Sydney University: jointly in charge of Plant Physiol. Unit, 1952-59, Hon. Res. Associate, 1954-59; Visiting Prof., Univ. of Calif, Los Angeles, 1958-59; Kerney Foundn Lectr, Univ. of Calif, Berkeley, 1959; Mem. Exec., CSIRO 1959-62; Prof. of Botany, Univ. of Adelaide, 1962-69, now Emeritus. Chm., Aust. Res. Grants Cttee, 1965-69; Dep. Chm., Aust. Sci. and Tech. Council, 1977-. Pres. Linnean Soc. of NSW, 1949; Hon. Sec. Austr. Nat. Res. Council, 1951-55; Pres., Australian Academy of Science, 1970-74 (Sec. Biological Sciences, 1957-58); Pres., Aust. and NZ Assoc. for the Advancement of Science, 1964-66; Corresp. Mem., Amer. Soc. of Plant Physiologists, 1953; For. Associate, US Nat. Acad. of Scis, 1962; Hon. Mem., Royal Soc. of NZ, 1971; For. Mem., Amer. Philosophical Soc., 1971; for. Hon. Mem., Amer. Acad. of Arts and Scis, 1973. Hon. DSc: Tasmania, 1965; Monash 1970; Hon ScD Cambridge, 1969. Clarke Meml Medal, Royal Soc. of NSW, 1955; Farrer Meml Medal, 1963; ANZAAS Medal, 1968; Mueller Medal, 1970. *Publications:* (with G. E. Briggs, FRS, and A. B. Hope) Electrolytes and Plant Cells, 1961; Protons, Electrons, Phosphorylation and Active Transport, 1968; various scientific papers on plant physiology and biochemistry. *Recreations:* riding, water colours. *Address:* Research School of Biological Sciences, Australian National University, Box 475, PO Canberra City, ACT 2601, Australia. *Clubs:* Adelaide (Adelaide); Commonwealth (Canberra).

ROBERTSON, Air Cdre William Duncan, CBE 1968; Royal Air Force, retired; Senior Air Staff Officer, HQ 38 Group, Royal Air Force, 1975-77; *b* 24 June 1922; *s* of William and Helen Robertson, Aberdeen; *m* 1st, 1952, Doreen Mary (*d* 1963), *d* of late Comdr G. A. C. Sharp, DSC, RN (retd); one *s* one *d*; 2nd, 1968, Ute, *d* of late Dr R. Koenig, Wesel, West Germany; one *d. Educ:* Robert Gordon's Coll., Aberdeen. Sqdn Comdr, No 207 Sqdn, 1959-61. Gp Dir, RAF Staff Coll., 1962-65; Station Comdr, RAF Wildenrath, 1965-67; Dep. Dir, Administrative Plans, 1967; Dir of Ops (Plans), 1968; Dir of Ops Air Defence and Overseas, 1969-71; RCDS, 1971-72; SASO RAF Germany, 1972-74; SASO 46 Group, 1975. *Recreations:* golf, tennis. *Address:* Culter Lodge, Milltimber, Aberdeenshire. *Club:* Royal Air Force.

ROBERTSON, William Walter Samuel, CBE 1957 (OBE 1950); *b* 3 July 1906; *s* of W. H. A. and A. M. Robertson (*née* Lane); *m* 1935, Kathleen Elizabeth Chawner East; one *s* two *d. Educ:* Bedford School; King's College, London. BSc (Eng.) First Class Hons, 1926. Apprenticeship to W. H. A. Robertson & Co. Ltd (Director, 1929) and to Torrington Mfg Co., USA, 1926-28. Regional Controller and Chm. of North Midland Regional Bd for Production, 1943-45; Chairman, Eastern Regional Bd for Industry, 1949-64 (Vice-Chm., 1945-49); Member Advisory Committee, Revolving Fund for Industry, 1955-58. MIMechE, 1943. High Sheriff of Bedfordshire, 1963. Governor, St Felix School, Southwold; Mem., Harpur Trust. *Recreations:* rowing, golf. *Address:* Oakley House, Oakley, Beds. *T:* Oakley 2895. *Clubs:* Caledonian; Leander (Henley-on-Thames).

ROBEY, Douglas John Brett, CMG 1960; HM Diplomatic Service, retired; *b* 7 Aug. 1914; *s* of late E. J. B. and Margaret Robey; *m* 1943, Elizabeth, *d* of late Col David D. Barrett, US Army; two *s* one *d. Educ:* Cranleigh School; St John's College, Oxford; Ecole des Sciences Politiques, Paris. BA (History); Editor of The Cherwell. Joined HM Foreign Service, 1937. Served in China, USA, Paris, Berlin, Baghdad; Consul-Gen., Chicago, 1966-69; Ambassador and Permanent UK Representative, Council of Europe, Strasbourg, 1969-74. *Publication:* The Innovator, 1945. *Recreations:* reading, writing, and the Niebelung Ring. *Address:* Allan Down House, Rotherfield, East Sussex. *T:* Rotherfield 2329. *Club:* Cercle Européen de Strasbourg (Hon. Life Pres.).

ROBEY, Edward George Haydon, BA, LLB; Barrister-at-Law; a Metropolitan Magistrate, 1954-72; *s* of late Sir George Robey,

CBE, and his first wife, the late Ethel Haydon; *m* 1942, Denise, *d* of late Denis Williams, Virginia Water. *Educ:* Westminster School; Jesus Coll., Cambridge. Called to Bar, Inner Temple, 1925; professional staff of Director of Public Prosecutions, 1932-50; apptd to Attorney-General's Executive for prosecution of the Major War Criminals at Nuremberg, 1945. *Publication:* The Jester and the Court, 1976. *Recreation:* music. *Address:* 11 Shrewsbury House, Cheyne Walk, SW3. *T:* 01-352 2403. *Club:* Garrick.

ROBICHAUD, Most Rev. Norbert; former Archbishop of Moncton; *b* Saint Charles, Kent. Co., NB, 1 April 1905; *s* of Marcel F. Robichaud and Nathalie Robichaud (*née* Gallant). *Educ:* St Ann's Coll., Church Point, NS; Holy Heart Seminary, Halifax, NS. Pontifical Inst. Angelicum, Rome, 1938; DPh St Joseph's Univ., 1943; Doctorate in Arts, Univ. of Montreal, 1946. Archbishop of Moncton, 1942-72. *Address:* 2144 Vallée Lourdes, CP 1500, Bathurst, NB, Canada. *T:* 506-546-3316.

ROBIN, Dr Gordon de Quetteville; Director, Scott Polar Research Institute, University of Cambridge, since 1958; Fellow since 1964 and Vice-Master since 1974, Darwin College, Cambridge; *b* Melbourne, 17 Jan. 1921; *s* of Reginald James Robin and Emily Mabel Robin; *m* 1953, Jean Margaret Fortt, Bath; two *d. Educ:* Wesley Coll., Melbourne; Melbourne Univ. ScD Cantab, MSc Melbourne, PhD Birmingham; FInstP. War service, RANVR: anti-submarine, 1942-44; submarine, RN, 1944-45 (Lieut). Physics Dept, Birmingham Univ.: research student, lectr, ICI Research Fellow, 1945-56; Sen. Fellow, Geophysics Dept, ANU, 1957-58. Meteorologist and Officer i/c Signy Is, South Orkneys, with Falkland Is Dependencies Survey, 1947-48; Physicist and Sen. British Mem. of Norwegian-British-Swedish Antarctic Expedn, 1949-52 (made first effective measurements of Antarctic ice thickness); further researches in Antarctic in 1959, 1967, 1969, 1974, and in Arctic, 1964, 1966, 1973; Sec., 1958-70, Pres., 1970-74, and Hon. Mem., Scientific Cttee on Antarctic Research of Internat. Council of Scientific Unions. Kongens Fortjensmedalje, Norway, 1952; Back Grant, RGS, 1953; Bruce Medal, RSE, 1953; Polar Medal, 1956; Patrons Medal, RGS, 1974. *Publications:* scientific reports of Norwegian-British-Swedish Antarctic Expedition (Glaciology III, 1958; Upper Winds, 1972); (ed) Annals of the IGY, Vol. 41, Glaciology, 1967; papers and articles on polar glaciology in scientific jls. *Recreations:* travel, walking. *Address:* 10 Melbourne Place, Cambridge CB1 1EQ. *T:* Cambridge 58463.

ROBIN, Ian (Gibson), FRCS; *b* 22 May 1909; *s* of Dr Arthur Robin, Edinburgh, and Elizabeth Parker; *m* 1939, Shelagh Marian, *d* of late Colonel C. M. Croft; one *s* two *d. Educ:* Merchiston Castle School; Clare College, Cambridge. MA, MB, BCh Cantab 1933; LRCP 1933; FRCS 1935. Guy's Hosp.; late House Phys.; Sen. Science Schol., 1930; Treasurer's Gold Medals in Clinical Surgery and Medicine, 1933; Arthur Durham Travelling Schol., 1933; Charles Oldham Prize in Ophthalmology, 1933; Registrar and Chief Clin. Asst, ENT Dept, 1935-36; late Consulting ENT Surgeon: Royal Chest Hosp., 1939-44; Royal Northern Hosp., 1937-74; St Mary's Hosp., Paddington, 1948-74; Princess Louise (Kensington) Hosp. for Children, 1948-69; Paddington Green Children's Hosp., 1969-74; Surgeon EMS, Sector III London Area, 1939-45. Late Vice-Chm., Royal Nat. Institute for the Deaf. Member Hunterian Soc.; Council of Nat. Deaf Children's Soc.; Past Pres., Brit. Assoc. of Otolaryngologists, 1971-72; Past Pres., Laryng. Section, RSM, 1967-68; Vice-Pres., Otolog. Section, RSM, 1967-68, 1969; late Examiner for DLO of RCS of England. Lectures: Yearsley, 1968; Jobson Horne, 1969. Mem., Royal Water-Colour Soc. *Publications:* (jt) Diseases of Ear, Nose and Throat (Synopsis Series), 1957; papers in various med. treatises, jls, etc. *Recreations:* golf, gardening, sketching; formerly athletics and Rugby. *Address:* Stowe House, 3 North End, Hampstead, NW3. *T:* 01-458 2292; 86 Harley Street, W1. *T:* 01-580 3625. *Clubs:* Hawks (Cambridge); Achilles (Great Britain); Hampstead Golf.

ROBINS, Mrs Denise; *b* Whitehall Court, SW1; *m* 1st, 1918; three *d*; 2nd, 1939, Lt-Col R. O'Neill Pearson. *Educ:* Staten Island, USA; Convent, Upper Norwood, SE. Entered Dundee Courier Office, Dundee, 1914; became a Free Lance writer, and published numerous serials and short stories; first novel published in 1924. *Publications:* 169 books including House of the 7th Cross, The Noble One, Khamsin, Dark Corridor, etc.; *historical novels:* Gold for the Gay Masters, Dance in the Dust, etc; *autobiography:* Stranger Than Fiction. *Recreations:* music, books, travel. *Address:* 15 Oathall Road, Haywards Heath, Sussex RH16 3EG. *T:* Haywards Heath 50580.

ROBINS, Malcolm Owen; a Director, Science Research Council, since 1972; *b* 25 Feb. 1918; *s* of late Owen Wilfred Robins and

Amelia Ada (*née* Wheelwright); *m* 1944, Frances Mary, *d* of late William and Frances Hand; one *s* one *d. Educ:* King Edward's Sch., Stourbridge; The Queen's Coll., Oxford (Open Scholar in Science). MA (Oxon) 1943. On scientific staff of Royal Aircraft Establishment, 1940-57; a Div. Supt in Guided Weapons Dept, RAE, 1955-57; Asst Dir, Guided Weapons, Min. of Supply, London, 1957-58; UK Project Manager for jt UK/USA Space Research programme, and hon. Research Associate, University Coll. London, 1958-62; a Dep. Chief Scientific Officer and Head of Space Research Management Unit, Office of Minister for Science (later Dept of Educn and Science), 1962-65; Head of Astronomy, Space and Radio Div., SRC, 1965-68; a Research Planning post in Min. of Technology (later Dept of Trade and Industry), 1968-72. Vis. Prof., University Coll., London, 1974-77. FInstP 1945; FRAS 1974. *Publications:* papers on space research in scientific jls. *Recreation:* gardening. *Address:* Wychbury, Gorse Lane, Farnham, Surrey. *T:* Farnham 4886. *Club:* Athenæum.

ROBINS, Prof. Robert Henry; Professor of General Linguistics, University of London, since 1966; Head of Department of Phonetics and Linguistics, School of Oriental and African Studies, University of London, since 1970; *b* 1 July 1921; *s* of John Norman Robins, medical practitioner, and Muriel Winifred (*née* Porter); *m* 1953, Sheila Marie Fynn. *Educ:* Tonbridge Sch.; New Coll., Oxford, 1940-41 and 1945-48, MA 1948; DLit London 1968. Lectr in Linguistics, Sch. of Oriental and African Studies, London, 1948-55; Reader in General Linguistics, Univ. of London, 1955-65. Research Fellow, Univ. of California, 1951; Vis. Professor: Washington, 1963; Hawaii, 1968; Minnesota, 1971; Florida, 1975. Hon. Sec., Philological Soc., 1961-; British Representative, CIPL, 1970-. *Publications:* Ancient and Mediaeval Grammatical Theory in Europe, 1951; The Yurok Language, 1958; General Linguistics: an introductory survey, 1964; A Short History of Linguistics, 1967; Diversions of Bloomsbury, 1970; Ideen und Problemgeschichte der Sprachwissenschaft, 1973; articles in Language, TPS, BSOAS, Lingua, Foundations of Language, Man, etc. *Recreations:* gardening, travel. *Address:* 65 Dome Hill, Caterham, Surrey. *T:* Caterham 43778. *Club:* Royal Commonwealth Society.

ROBINS, William Edward Charles; Metropolitan Stipendiary Magistrate since 1971; solicitor; *b* 13 March 1924; *s* of late E. T. and late L. R. Robins; *m* 1946, Jean Elizabeth, *yr d* of Bruce and Flora Forsyth, Carlyle, Saskatchewan, Canada; one *s* one *d. Educ:* St Alban's Sch. Served War: commissioned as Navigator, RAF, 1943-47. Admitted as a Solicitor, 1948; joined Metropolitan Magistrates' Courts' service, 1950; Dep. Chief Clerk, 1951-60; Chief Clerk, 1960-67; Sen. Chief Clerk, Thames Petty Sessional Div., 1968-71. Sec., London Magistrates' Clerks' Assoc., 1953-60 (Chm. 1965-71). Member, Home Office working parties, on: Magistrates' Courts' Rules; Legal Aid; Motor Vehicle Licences; Fines and Maintenance Orders Enforcement, 1968-71; Member: Lord Chancellor's Sub-Cttee on Magistrates' Courts' Rules, 1969-70; Adv. Council on Misuse of Drugs, 1973-. Fellow Commoner, Corpus Christi Coll., Cambridge, Michaelmas 1975. *Recreations:* touring off the beaten track, music, theatre. *Address:* Bow Street Magistrates' Court, WC2.

ROBINSON, family name of **Baron Martonmere.**

ROBINSON, Sir Albert (Edward Phineas), Kt 1962; Chairman: Johannesburg Consolidated Investment Company, since 1971; Rustenburg Platinum Mines, since 1971; *b* 30 December 1915; *s* of late Charles Phineas Robinson (formerly MP Durban, S Africa) and of late Mabel V. Robinson; *m* 1st, 1944, Mary Judith Bertish (*d* 1973); four *d*; 2nd, 1975, Mrs M. L. Royston-Pigott. *Educ:* Durban High School; Universities of Stellenbosch, London, Cambridge and Leiden; MA (Cantab). Barrister, Lincoln's Inn. Served War of 1939-45, in Imperial Light Horse, Western Desert, N Africa, 1940-43. Member Johannesburg City Council, 1945-48 (Leader United Party in Council, 1946-47); MP (United Party), S African Parl., 1947-53; became permanent resident in Rhodesia, 1953. Director: Anglo American Corp. of SA Ltd; Anglo American Corp., Rhodesia Ltd; Founders Bldg Soc.; Director (in Rhodesia) of Bd of Standard Bank, and (in SA) of Standard Bank Investment Corp.; Director, in Rhodesia and South Africa, of various Mining, Financial and Industrial Companies. Chm. Central African Airways Corp., 1957-61. Member, Monckton Commission, 1960; High Commissioner in the UK for the Federation of Rhodesia and Nyasaland, 1961-63. *Recreations:* people, music and conversation. *Address:* Rumbavu Park, PO Box 2341, Salisbury, Rhodesia; (office) PO Box 590, Johannesburg, South Africa. *Clubs:* Carlton (London); Salisbury (Salisbury, Rhodesia); City (Capetown).

ROBINSON, Maj.-Gen. Alfred Eryk, CB 1949; DSO 1940; JP; DL; *b* 19 Sept. 1894; *s* of late A. H. Robinson, JP, Derwent House, West Ayton, Scarborough; *m* 1942, Ailison Campbell, *d* of late P. C. Low, Dowrich House, Sandford, Crediton, and widow of Major S. H. Birchall Wood, R Deccan Horse. *Educ:* RMC, Sandhurst. Joined Green Howards, Aug. 1914; Lieut-Colonel, 1st Bn Green Howards, 1939; Col 1942; Temp. Maj.-Gen. 1943; retired, 1948. Colonel, The Green Howards, 1949-59. N Riding of Yorkshire: DL, 1952, JP 1953. *Address:* Derwent House, East Ayton, Scarborough, N Yorks. *T:* West Ayton 2130.

ROBINSON, Arthur Alexander; computer consultant; Director of Computing, University of Wales Institute of Science and Technology, since 1976; *b* 5 Aug. 1924; *o s* of Arthur Robinson and Elizabeth (*née* Thompson); *m* 1956, Sylvia Joyce Wagstaff; two *s* one *d. Educ:* Epsom Coll.; Clare Coll., Cambridge (MA); Univ. of Manchester (PhD). English Electric Co. Ltd, 1944; Ferranti Ltd, 1950; Dir and Gen. Man., Univ. of London Atlas Computing Service, 1962; Dir, Univ. of London Computer Centre, 1968; Dir, National Computing Centre Ltd, 1969-74. *Publications:* papers in Proc. IEE. *Recreation:* gardening. *Address:* Lodge Close, Pendoglan, Cowbridge, S Glamorgan.

ROBINSON, Arthur Napoleon Raymond; MHR for Tobago East; Chairman, Democratic Action Congress, Trinidad and Tobago, since 1971; *b* 16 Dec. 1926; *s* of late James Alexander Andrew Robinson, Headmaster, and Emily Isabella Robinson; *m* 1961, Patricia Rawlins; one *s* one *d. Educ:* Bishop's High Sch., Tobago; St John's Coll., Oxford. LLB (London); MA (PPE) Oxon. Called to Bar, Inner Temple; in practice, 1956-61. Treas., People's Nat. Movt (governing Party) 1956; Mem. Federal Parlt, 1958; Mem. for Tobago East, 1961; Minister of Finance, 1961-66; Dep. Political Leader of Party, 1966; Actg Prime Minister (during his absence), April and Aug. 1967; Minister of External Affairs, Trinidad and Tobago, 1967-68. Member: Legal Commn on US Leased Areas under 1941 Agreement, 1959; Industrial Develt Corp., 1960; Council, Univ. of West Indies, 1960-62. Consultant, Foundn for establishment of an Internat. Criminal Court, 1972-75, Exec. Dir, 1976-77. Dist. Internat. Criminal Lawyer Award, Internat. Law Commn, 1977. *Publications:* The New Frontier and the New Africa, 1961; Fiscal Reform in Trinidad and Tobago, 1966; The Path of Progress, 1967; The Teacher and Nationalism, 1967; The Mechanics of Independence, 1971; articles and addresses. *Address:* 21 Ellerslie Park, Maraval, Trinidad.

ROBINSON, Sir Austin; see Robinson, Sir E. A. G.

ROBINSON, Basil William; retired; *b* 20 June 1912; *o c* of William Robinson and Rebecca Frances Mabel, *d* of Rev. George Gilbanks; *m* 1st, 1945, Ailsa Mary Stewart (*d* 1954); 2nd, 1958, Oriel Hermione Steel; one *s* one *d. Educ:* Winchester (Exhibitioner); CCC Oxford. BA 1935; MA, BLitt, 1938. Asst Keeper, Victoria and Albert Museum, 1939. Min. of Home Security, 1939-40. Served as Capt., 2nd Punjab Regt, India, Burma, Malaya, 1943-46. Deputy Keeper, V&A Museum, 1954, Keeper, Dept of Metalwork, 1966-72, Keeper Emeritus, 1972-76. Pres., Royal Asiatic Soc., 1970-73; Vice-Pres., Arms and Armour Soc., 1953; Hon. Pres., Tô-ken Soc. of Great Britain, 1967. FSA 1974. *Publications:* A Primer of Japanese Sword-blades, 1955; Persian Miniatures, 1957; Japanese Landscape Prints of the 19th Century, 1957; A Descriptive Catalogue of the Persian Paintings in the Bodleian Library, 1958; Kuniyoshi, 1961; The Arts of the Japanese Sword, 1961, 2nd edn, 1971; Persian Drawings, 1965; part-author, vols 2 and 3, Catalogue of Persian MSS and Miniatures in the Chester Beatty Library, 3 vols, 1958-62; Persian Miniature Painting, 1967; Persian Paintings in the India Office Library, 1976; (ed. and jt author) Islamic painting in the Keir Collection, 1976; numerous booklets, articles and reviews on Persian and Japanese art. *Recreations:* catch singing (founder and Chairman, Aldrich Catch Club); cats. *Address:* 41 Redcliffe Gardens, SW10 9JH. *T:* 01-352 1290. *Club:* Hurlingham.

ROBINSON, Air Vice-Marshal Bruce, CB 1968; CBE 1953; Air Officer Commanding No 24 Gp, RAF, 1965-67; retired, 1967; *b* 19 Jan. 1912; *s* of late Dr G. Burton Robinson, Cannington, Somerset; *m* 1940, Elizabeth Ann Compton, *d* of Air Commodore D. F. Lucking; one *s* one *d. Educ:* King's School, Bruton. Commissioned in SR of O, The Somerset Light Infty, 1931-33; Commissioned in RAF, 1933; No 16 (Army Co-op. Sqdn), 1934-37; Specialist Engineer course, 1937-39. Served War of 1939-45: Technical duties in Fighter and Bomber Commands, UK Senior Technical Staff Officer, Rhodesian Air Training Group, 1946-48; on loan to Indian Air Force (Director of Technical Services), 1951-53; Commandant, No 1 Radio School, RAF Locking, 1953-55; Sen. RAF Officer at Wright Patterson Air Force Base, Dayton, Ohio, 1958-60; Commandant No 1 Sch. of Technical Training, RAF Halton, Bucks, 1961-63. Director of RAF Aircraft Development, Min. of Aviation, 1963-65. *Recreations:* golf, sailing, painting, writing. *Address:* Bent Hollow, Bromeswell, Woodbridge, Suffolk. *T:* Eyke 295.

ROBINSON, Rt. Rev. Christopher James Gossage, MA; *b* 10 June 1903; *s* of late Canon Albert Gossage Robinson; unmarried. *Educ:* Marlborough, Christ's Coll., Cambridge. Lecturer at St Stephen's Coll., Delhi, 1926-29; Deacon, 1929; Priest, 1930; Curate St Mary's, Portsea, 1929-31; Asst Priest, St James, Delhi, 1931-32; Vicar of St James, and Chaplain of Delhi, 1932-42; Vicar of St Thomas, New Delhi, 1942-45; Hon. Canon of Lahore Cathedral, 1944-47; Bishop of Lucknow, 1947-62; Bishop of Bombay, 1962-70. Member Cambridge Brotherhood of the Ascension, Delhi, since 1931. *Address:* Brotherhood House, 7 Court Lane, Delhi 110-054, India. *Club:* Royal Commonwealth Society.

See also Sir E . A . G . Robinson .

ROBINSON, Christopher John; Organist and Master of the Choristers, St George's Chapel, Windsor Castle, since 1974; *b* 20 April 1936; *s* of late John Robinson, Malvern, Worcs; *m* 1962, Shirley Ann, *d* of H. F. Churchman, Sawston, Cambs; one *s* one *d. Educ:* St Michael's Coll., Tenbury; Rugby; Christ Church, Oxford. MA, BMus, FRCO. Assistant Organist of Christ Church, Oxford, 1955-58; Assistant Organist of New College, Oxford, 1957-58; Music Master at Oundle School, 1959-62; Assistant Organist of Worcester Cathedral, 1962-63; Organist and Master of Choristers, Worcester Cathedral, 1963-74. Conductor: City of Birmingham Choir, 1963-; Oxford Bach Choir, 1977-; Leith Hill Musical Festival, 1977-. *Recreations:* watching cricket, motoring. *Address:* 23 The Cloisters, Windsor Castle, Berks.

ROBINSON, Mrs Clare; see Panter-Downes, M. P.

ROBINSON, Clifton Eugene Bancroft, OBE 1973; JP; Deputy-Chairman, Commission for Racial Equality, since 1977; *b* 5 Oct. 1926; *s* of Theodore Emanuel and Lafrance Robinson; *m* (marr. diss.); one *s* three *d; m* 1977, Margaret Ann Ennever. *Educ:* Kingston Technical Coll., Jamaica; Birmingham Univ.; Leicester Univ.; Lancaster Coll. of Educn. BA, DipEd. Served War, RAF, 1944-49. Teacher: Mellor Sch., Leicester, 1951-61; i/c Special Educn Unit, St Peter's Sch., Leicester, 1961-64; Dep. Headteacher, Charnwood Sch., Leicester, 1964-68; Headteacher: St Peter's Sch., Leicester, 1968-70; Uplands Sch., Leicester, 1970-77. JP 1974. *Recreations:* music (mainly classical), walking; when there is time, gardening. *Address:* Stable End Cottage, The Manor House, Newton Harcourt, Leicestershire LE8 0ST.

ROBINSON, Derek; Fellow of Magdalen College, Oxford, since 1969; Senior Research Officer, Oxford Institute of Economics and Statistics; Chairman, Social Science Research Council, since 1975; *b* 9 Feb. 1932; *s* of Benjamin and Mary Robinson; *m* 1956, Jean Evelyn (*née* Lynch); one *s* one *d. Educ:* Barnsley Holgate Grammar Sch.; Ruskin Coll., Oxford; Lincoln Coll., Oxford. MA (Oxon), DipEcPolSci (Oxon). Civil Service, 1948-55. Sheffield Univ., 1959-60; Senior Research Officer, Oxford Inst. of Economics and Statistics, 1961-. Economic Adviser, Nat. Bd for Prices and Incomes, 1965-67; Sen. Economic Adviser, Dept of Employment and Productivity, 1968-70; Dep. Chm., Pay Bd, 1973-74; Chairman: Oxfordshire and S Bucks Dist Manpower Cttee, 1975-; Cttee of Inquiry into the remuneration of members of local authorities, 1977. *Publications:* Non-Wage Incomes and Prices Policy, 1966; Wage Drift, Fringe Benefits and Manpower Distribution, 1968; Workers' Negotiated Savings Plans for Capital Formation, 1970; (ed) Local Labour Markets and Wage Structures, 1970; Prices and Incomes Policy: the Austrian Experience (with H. Suppanz), 1972; Incomes Policy and Capital Sharing in Europe, 1973; (with J. Vincens) Research into Labour Market Behaviour, 1974; contributor to Bulletin of Oxford Univ. Inst. of Economics and Statistics; Industrial Relations Jl, etc. *Address:* 56 Lonsdale Road, Oxford. *T:* Oxford 52276. *Club:* Reform.

ROBINSON, Rt. Rev. Donald William Bradley; Assistant Bishop, Diocese of Sydney (Bishop in Parramatta), since 1973; *b* 9 Nov. 1922; *s* of Rev. Richard Bradley Robinson and Gertrude Marston Robinson (*née* Ross); *m* 1949, Marie Elizabeth Taubman; three *s* one *d. Educ:* Sydney Church of England Gram. Sch.; Univ. of Sydney (BA); Queens' Coll., Cambridge (MA). Australian Army, 1941-45, Lieut Intell. Corps, 1944. Deacon 1950, Sydney; priest 1951; Curate, Manly, NSW, 1950-52; St Philip's, Sydney, 1952-53; Lecturer: Moore Coll., 1952- (Vice-Principal, 1959-72); Sydney Univ., 1964-. *Address:* 5 Keith Place, Baulkham Hills, NSW 2153, Australia. *T:* (02) 639 4752.

ROBINSON, Sir Dove-Myer, Kt 1970; JP; Mayor of Auckland, New Zealand, 1959-65, and since 1968; *b* Sheffield, 15 June 1901; 6th *c* of Moss Robinson and Ida Robinson (*née* Brown); of Jewish race; *m* 1st, Bettine Williams; 2nd, Thelma Ruth Thompson; one *s* five *d. Educ:* primary schools in Sheffield, Manchester, London and Devonport (Auckland, NZ). Mem., Auckland City Council, 1952-59; Chm., Auckland Metropolitan Drainage Bd, 1953-55; Chm., Auckland Airport Cttee, 1959-61; Mem., Auckland Univ. Council, 1952-; Chm., Auckland Regional Authority, 1963-65, Mem., 1963-; Chm.-Chm. Rapid Transit Cttee, 1968-74; Vice-Pres., NZ Municipal Assoc., 1959-65, 1968-; President: Auckland Rugby League, 1964-; NZ Anti-Fluoridation Soc., 1954-; Auckland Festival Soc., 1959-65, 1968-, Hon. Fellow 1974. Fellow, NZ Inst. of Management; Mem., Inst. Water Pollution Control, etc; MRSH. OStJ 1972. *Publications:* Utilization of Town and Country Wastes, Garbage and Sewage, 1946; Passenger Transport in Auckland, 1969; numerous leaflets and pubns on Pollution, Conservation, Fluoridation, Nutrition, Local and Regional Govt, Town Planning, Rapid Transit, etc. *Recreations:* golf, fishing, boating, photography, motoring, local government. *Address:* (private) 12a Aldred Road, Remuera, Auckland 5, New Zealand. *T:* 503-693; (office) Auckland City Council Civic Administration Building, Civic Square, Auckland. *T:* 74650. *Clubs:* Remuera Golf, Rugby League, etc (Auckland, NZ).

ROBINSON, Prof. Sir (Edward) Austin (Gossage), Kt 1975; CMG 1947; OBE 1944; FBA 1955; Emeritus Professor of Economics, Cambridge University since 1966 (Professor, 1950-65); Fellow of Sidney Sussex College, Cambridge, since 1931; Secretary of Royal Economic Society, 1945-70; Joint Editor of Economic Journal, 1944-70; *b* 20 Nov. 1897; *s* of late Rev. Canon Albert Gossage Robinson; *m* 1926, Joan (*see* Prof. J. V. Robinson), *d* of late Major-General Sir Frederick Maurice, KCMG, CB; two *d. Educ:* Marlborough College (Scholar); Christ's College, Cambridge (Scholar). BA 1921; MA 1923; RNAS and RAF (Pilot), 1917-19; Fellow of Corpus Christi Coll., Cambridge, 1923-26; Tutor to HH The Maharaja of Gwalior, 1926-28; University Lecturer, Cambridge, 1929-49; Asst Editor of Economic Journal, 1934, Joint Editor, 1944-70; Member of Economic Section, War Cabinet Office, 1939-42; Economic Adviser and Head of Programmes Division, Ministry of Production, 1942-45; Member of British Reparations Mission, Moscow and Berlin, 1945; Economic Adviser to Board of Trade, 1946; returned to Cambridge, Sept. 1946. Mem. of Economic Planning Staff, 1947-48; Treasurer of International Economic Association, 1950-59, President 1959-62; Mem. Council, DSIR, 1954-59; Dir of Economics, Min. of Power, 1967-68. Chairman: Council Nat. Inst. of Economic and Social Research, 1949-62; European Energy Advisory Commn, OEEC, 1957-60; Exec. Cttee, Overseas Develt Inst. *Publications:* The Structure of Competitive Industry, 1931; Monopoly, 1941; Economic Consequences of the Size of Nations, 1960; Economic Development of Africa South of the Sahara, 1964; Problems in Economic Development, 1965; The Economics of Education (with J. E. Vaizey), 1966; Backward Areas in Advanced Countries, 1969; Economic Development in South Asia, 1970; (ed jtly) The Economic Development of Bangladesh within a Socialist Framework, 1974; contributor to: Modern Industry and the African, 1933; Lord Hailey's African Survey, 1938; articles in Economic Journal, etc. *Address:* Sidney Sussex College, Cambridge; 62 Grange Road, Cambridge. *T:* Cambridge 57548. *Club:* Reform.
See also Rt. Rev. C. J. G. Robinson.

ROBINSON, Hon. Sir (Ernest) Stanley, Kt 1969; CBE 1966; President of the Barbados Senate, 1966-73 (Member, 1964-73); sugar planter; *b* 18 Jan. 1905; *s* of Samuel Stanley Robinson and Hannah Eliza Robinson; *m* 1926, Annie Carmen Yearwood; one *s* two *d. Educ:* Harrison Coll., Barbados; Warwick Sch., England; St John's Coll., Cambridge. MHA Barbados, 1928-32, 1937-46; MLC, 1952-64; Mem. Barbados Privy Council, 1968. Founder Mem., Barbados Sugar Producers Assoc.; Dir, West Indies Sugar Assoc.; Chm., Plantations Ltd, Bridgetown, Barbados; Director: Foursquare Sugar Estates Ltd; Foursquare Factory Ltd; Constant Estates Ltd; Barbados Light & Power Co. *Recreations:* swimming, shooting. *Address:* Constant Estates Ltd, St George, Barbados, West Indies. *Club:* Barbados Yacht.

ROBINSON, Forbes; Principal Artist (Bass), Royal Opera House, Covent Garden, since 1954; *b* Macclesfield, 21 May 1926; *s* of Wilfred and Gertrude Robinson; *m* 1952, Marion Stubbs; two *d. Educ:* King's Sch., Macclesfield. St Paul's Coll., Cheltenham (teacher's trg), 1943-46. Capt. in RAEC, 1946-48. Loughborough Coll. (Hons Dipl., Phys. Educn), 1949-50; La Scuola di Canto (Scala, Milan), 1952-53. Promenade Debut, 1957. Guest artist with Dublin, Handel, Sadler's Wells, Scottish and Welsh National Opera Cos. Has sung at Festivals at

Aldeburgh, Barcelona, Edinburgh, Holland, Leeds, Lucerne, Portugal and Schwetzingen. Has also sung in Argentina, Belgium, Denmark, France, Germany, Luxembourg, Sweden, and USA. First British singer to sing Don Giovanni at Royal Opera House, Covent Garden, for 100 years. Awarded Opera Medal for 1963, for creating King Priam (Tippett). *Recreations:* walking, swimming. *Address:* 225 Princes Gardens, W3. *T:* 01-992 5498. *Club:* Savage.

ROBINSON, Frank Arnold, DSc, CChem, FRIC; Director of Twyford Laboratories Ltd & Twyford Pharmaceutical Services Ltd, retired; Director of other subsidiary companies of Arthur Guinness Son & Co. Ltd, since 1960; *b* 3 Dec. 1907; *s* of Frank Robinson and Edith Robinson (*née* Jagger); *m* 1st, 1930, Margaret Olive Jones; two *s*; 2nd, 1958, Beth Clarence Smith. *Educ:* Elland Grammar Sch.; Univ. of Manchester (James Gaskill Scholar); BSc Tech (Hons) 1929, MSc Tech 1930, DSc 1958; Univ. of London LLB (Hons.) 1940. Laboratory of Govt Chemist, 1930-33; Research Chemist, Glaxo Laboratories Ltd, Greenford, 1933-45; Manager, Distillers Co. Research Labs, Epsom, 1945-48; Dir of Research, Allen & Hanburys Ltd, Ware, 1948-60. FRIC 1940. Hon. Professorial Fellow, University Coll., Cardiff, 1967-72; Hon. DSc: Bath, 1968; Salford, 1972. Chm., Biochemical Soc., 1946, and Treas., 1952-62; Pres., Section I (Biomedical) of British Assoc. for the Advancement of Science, 1972-73; Mem., British National Cttee for Biochemistry, 1973-; President: Royal Inst. Chem., 1972-74 (Vice-Pres., 1961-63, 1970-72); Chemical Soc., 1975-76; 12th Congress of Assoc. Internat. d'Expertise Chimique, Cambridge, 1972; Mem., UNESCO Cttee on status of scientific researchers, 1974; Chairman: Council, Science and Technology Insts Ltd, 1975-76; Council for Environmental Science and Engineering, 1975-. *Publications:* Principles and Practice of Chromatography, 1941; The Vitamin B Complex, 1951; Antibiotics, 1951; Vitamin Co-Factors of Enzyme Systems, 1966; Chemists and the Law, 1967; research papers and reviews in scientific jls. *Recreations:* gardening, archæology. *Address:* Gilpins, 1 Cowpers Way, Tewin Wood, Welwyn, Herts. *T:* Bulls Green 288.

ROBINSON, Geoffrey; MP (Lab) Coventry North-West, since March 1976; *b* 25 May 1938; *s* of Robert Norman Robinson and Dorothy Jane Robinson (*née* Skelly); *m* 1967, Marie Elena Giorgio; one *d. Educ:* Emanuel School; Cambridge and Yale Univs. Labour Party Research Assistant, 1965-68; Senior Executive, Industrial Reorganisation Corporation, 1968-70; Financial Controller, British Leyland, 1971-72; Managing Director, Leyland Innocenti, Milan, 1972-73; Chief Executive, Jaguar Cars, Coventry, 1973-75. *Recreations:* reading, squash. *Address:* House of Commons, SW1A 0AA. *T:* 01-491 4207.

ROBINSON, Sir George (Gilmour), Kt 1955; *b* 30 Aug. 1894; *s* of George Thomas Robinson and Ada Violet Gallier; *m* 1942, Muriel Alice Fry. *Educ:* Repton; Trinity College, Oxford. (MA). Served European War, 1914-19. Called to Bar, 1924, and practised. Resident Magistrate, Kenya, 1930-38; Puisne Judge, Northern Rhodesia, 1938-46; Puisne Judge, Nigeria, 1947-52; Chief Justice, Zanzibar, 1952-55; retired 1955. *Recreations:* shooting, golf. *Address:* The Old House, Southwold, Suffolk. *T:* 2374.

ROBINSON, Gleeson Edward, CB 1945; MC; LLD (London); Hon. Captain, RFA; *s* of Rev. John Robinson, Dudley; *m* 1945, Frances Elizabeth (*d* 1966), *widow* of P. J. Horsley. *Educ:* King Edward's Sch., Birmingham; London University. Solicitor, London, 1904-15; Royal Field Artillery, 1915-19, served in France (despatches, MC and Bar); Barrister-at-Law, Middle Temple, 1920; Secretary of Clearing Office (Enemy Debts), 1920-25; British Member of Anglo-German Mixed Arbitral Tribunal established under Treaty of Versailles, 1925-30; Traffic Comr (Metropolitan Area), 1931-46; Chm. Road Rail Traffic Appeal Tribunal, 1946-49. *Publication:* Public Authorities and Legal Liability. *Recreations:* golf, fishing. *Address:* La Falaise, Noirmont Lane, Ouaisne, Jersey, CI. *T:* Central 41461.

ROBINSON, Mrs Gower; *see* Bloom, Ursula.

ROBINSON, Sir Harold (Ernest), Kt 1955; company director, Trinidad and Tobago; Member of Trinidad and Tobago Senate, 1971-76; *b* 9 Oct. 1905; *s* of Ernest Augustus Robinson and Henrietta Mabel (*née* Fitt); *m* 1929, Clarice Graeme (*née* Yearwood); two *s* three *d. Educ:* Lancing; Stowe; Magdalene Coll., Cambridge. Joined Staff of Usine St Madeleine Sugar Estate Ltd, San Fernando, Trinidad, 1927; joined staff of Woodford Lodge Estates Ltd, 1929, Man. Dir, 1944-61. President: Agricultural Soc. of Trinidad and Tobago; British Caribbean Citrus Assoc.; Chm., Sugar Industry Control Bd; Vice-Pres., West India Cttee. MLC, 1946-61. *Recreations:* flying, fishing, horticulture. *Address:* c/o 17-19 Edward Street,

Port of Spain, Trinidad, WI. *T:* 62-51482. *Club:* Union (Port of Spain, Trinidad).

ROBINSON, Harold George Robert, OBE 1961; CEng, MIEE; a Deputy Director, Royal Aircraft Establishment, since 1976; *b* 2 April 1924; *s* of Harold Arthur Robinson and Winifred Margaret (*née* Ballard); *m* 1955, Sonja (*née* Lapthorn); two *s. Educ:* Portsmouth Northern Grammar Sch.; Imperial Coll., London Univ.; California Inst. of Technology. WhSch 1944; BSc 1948; FCGI 1970. Joined RAE as Scientific Officer, 1948; Head of Satellite Launcher Div., Space Dept, RAE, 1961; Head of Avionics Dept, RAE, 1965-69; Head of Research Planning Div., Min. of Technology, 1969-71; Dir Gen., Aerospace Assessment and Res., DTI, 1971-74; Under-Sec., Space and Air Res., DoI, 1974-76. Pres., Astronautics Commn, FAI, 1969-70. Bronze Medal, RAeS, 1961; Paul Tissandier Diploma, FAI, 1971. *Publications:* various scientific and technical papers, contribs to books, primarily on rocket and space research. *Recreations:* sailing, riding, painting. *Address:* 39 Crosby Hill Drive, Camberley, Surrey. *T:* Camberley 23771.

ROBINSON, Prof. Joan Violet, FBA 1958; Professor of Economics, University of Cambridge, 1965-71, retired 1973; *b* 31 Oct. 1903; *d* of late Major-General Sir Frederick Maurice, KCMG, CB; *m* 1926, Sir E. A. G. Robinson, *qv*; two *d. Educ:* St Paul's Girls' School, London; Girton Coll., Cambridge. Economics Tripos, 1925; Faculty Asst Lectr in Economics, Cambridge Univ., 1931; Univ. Lectr, 1937; Reader, 1949. *Publications:* Economics of Imperfect Competition, 1933; Essays in the Theory of Employment, 1937; Introduction to the Theory of Employment, 1937; Essay on Marxian Economics, 1942; Collected Economic Papers, Vol. I, 1951; The Rate of Interest and Other Essays, 1952; The Accumulation of Capital, 1956; Collected Economic Papers, Vol. II, 1960; Essays in The Theory of Economic Growth, 1963; Economic Philosophy, 1963; Collected Economic Papers, Vol. III, 1965; Economics: An Awkward Corner, 1966; The Cultural Revolution in China, 1969; Freedom and Necessity, 1970; Economic Heresies, 1971; (ed) After Keynes, 1973; (with John Eatwell) Introduction to Modern Economics, 1973; Collected Economic Papers, Vol. IV, 1973; articles, etc in Economic Journal, etc. *Address:* 62 Grange Road, Cambridge. *T:* 57548.

ROBINSON, John Armstrong, CMG 1969; HM Diplomatic Service; Ambassador to Algeria, since 1974; *b* 18 Dec. 1925; *m* 1952, Marianne Berger; one *s* one *d.* HM Forces, 1944-46; Foreign Office, 1949-50; Second Secretary, Delhi, 1950-52; Foreign Office, 1952-53; Helsinki, 1953-56; Second later First Secretary, Paris, 1956-58; Foreign Office, 1958-61; First Secretary in UK Delegation to European Communities, Brussels, 1962-67; Counsellor, Foreign Office, 1967; Head of European Economic Integration Dept, FCO, 1968-70; appointed Member of team of nine officials for negotiations on British entry into the Common Market, Brussels, 1970-71; Asst Under-Sec. of State, FCO, 1971-73. *Address:* c/o Foreign and Commonwealth Office, SW1.

ROBINSON, Rt. Rev. John Arthur Thomas, MA, BD, DD, PhD; Lecturer in Theology, Trinity College, Cambridge, since 1969; Fellow, and Dean of Chapel, Trinity College, since 1969; also Assistant Bishop, Diocese of Southwark, since 1969; *b* 15 June 1919; *s* of Reverend Canon Arthur William Robinson, DD and Mary Beatrice Robinson; *m* 1947, Ruth (*née* Grace); one *s* three *d. Educ:* Marlborough College; Jesus and Trinity Colleges, Cambridge; Westcott House, Cambridge. BA 1942 (1st class Theology); MA 1945; PhD 1946; BD 1962; DD 1968. Curate of St Matthew, Moorfields, Bristol, 1945-48; Chaplain, Wells Theological College, 1948-51; Fellow and Dean, Clare College, Cambridge, 1951-59; Assistant Lecturer in Divinity, Cambridge University, 1953-54; Lecturer in Divinity, 1954-59; Bishop Suffragan of Woolwich, 1959-69. Examining Chaplain to Archbishop of Canterbury, 1953-59; Six Preacher, Canterbury Cathedral, 1958-68; Proctor in Convocation, Diocese of Southwark, 1960-70. Vis. Prof. and Noble Lectr, Harvard, 1955; Vis. Prof.: Union Theological Seminary, Richmond, VA, 1958; Univ. of South Africa, Pretoria, 1975; Univ. of Witwatersrand, 1977; Lectures: Reinicker, Va Seminary, 1958; Purdy, Hartford Seminary, Conn, 1964; Thorp, Cornell University, 1964; Lilley, Wabash Coll., Indiana, 1966; West, Stanford Univ., 1966; Hulsean, Cambridge, 1970; Nelson, Lancaster Univ., 1971; Owen Evans, University Coll. of Aberystwyth, 1971; Carnahan, Union Theological Seminary, Buenos Aires, 1971; Teape, Delhi, Madras and Calcutta, 1977-78. *Publications:* In the End God, 1950 (rev. edn, 1968); The Body, 1952; Jesus and His Coming, 1957; On Being the Church in the World, 1960, rev. edn 1969; Christ Comes In, 1960; Liturgy Coming to Life, 1960; Twelve New Testament Studies, 1962; Honest to God, 1963; Christian Morals Today, 1964; The New Reformation?, 1965; But That I

Can't Believe!, 1967; Exploration into God, 1967; Christian Freedom in a Permissive Society, 1970; The Difference in Being a Christian Today, 1972; The Human Face of God, 1973; Redating the New Testament, 1976; Can We Trust the New Testament?, 1977; *contrib . to:* Christian Faith and Communist Faith, 1953; Becoming a Christian, 1954; The Historic Episcopate, 1954; Jesus Christ, History, Interpretation and Faith, 1956; New Ways with the Ministry, 1960; Bishops, 1961; The Interpreter's Dictionary of the Bible (article: Resurrection in the NT), 1962; Layman's Church, 1963; The Roads Converge, 1963; The Honest to God Debate, 1963; The Authorship and Integrity of the New Testament, 1965; The Restless Church, 1966; Theologians of our Time, 1966; Theological Freedom and Social Responsibility, 1967; Sermons from Great St Mary's, 1968; The Christian Priesthood, 1970; More Sermons from Great St Mary's, 1971; Theological Crossings, 1971; Christ, Faith and History, 1972; To God be the Glory, 1973; Christ and Spirit in the New Testament, 1973; articles in learned journals, mainly on New Testament subjects. *Address:* Trinity College, Cambridge CB2 1TQ. *T:* Cambridge 58201.

ROBINSON, Sir John Beverley, 7th Bt, *cr* 1854; *b* 3 Oct. 1913; *s* of Sir John Beverley Robinson, 6th Bt, and Constance Marie (*d* 1977), *d* of Robert W. Pentecost; *S* father 1954. *Heir:* kinsman Christopher Philipse Robinson [*b* 10 Nov. 1938; *m* 1962, Barbara Judith, *d* of Richard Duncan; two *s* (and one *s* decd)]. *Address:* 435 Leinster Street, Apt 7, Woodstock, Ont, Canada.

ROBINSON, Sir John (Edgar), Kt 1958; Chairman Frederic Robinson Ltd and associated companies since 1933; *b* 20 March 1895; *s* of William Robinson, Stockport and Wilmslow and Priscilla (*née* Needham); *m* 1926, Gwendolen Harriet May, *d* of Sydney Herbert Evans, London; three *s. Educ:* Stockport Grammar School; Manchester University (LLB). Qualified as Solicitor, 1918; entered family business of Frederic Robinson, Ltd, 1918. President Stockport Chamber of Commerce, 1947. Held various offices in Conservative Party, 1945-75; Chairman Knutsford Division Conservative Assoc., 1949-52, Deputy President, 1952-71, President, 1971-75. *Recreation:* sailing. *Address:* Wellfield, Dean Row, Wilmslow, Cheshire. *T:* Wilmslow 23384.

ROBINSON, John Foster, CBE 1968; TD; DL; Honorary Vice-President, The Dickinson Robinson Group Ltd (Chairman, 1968-74; Deputy Chairman 1966); *b* 2 Feb. 1909; *s* of late Sir Foster Gotch Robinson; *m* 1935, Margaret Eve Hannah Paterson (*d* 1977); two *s* two *d. Educ:* Harrow; Christ Church, Oxford. Dir, E..S. & A. Robinson Ltd, 1943, Jt Man. Dir 1948; Chm., E. S. & A. Robinson (Holdings) Ltd, 1961; Director: Eagle Star Insurance Co. Ltd, 1968; National Westminster Bank Ltd (Mem., SW Regional Bd, 1969-76); Bristol & West Building Soc., 1973-. DL Glos 1972; High Sheriff, Avon, 1975. *Recreations:* shooting, fishing, golf. *Address:* St George's Hill, Easton-in-Gordano, Bristol BS20 0PX. *T:* Pill 2108. *Clubs:* Portland, Houghton; Clifton, Bristol, Constitutional (Bristol).

ROBINSON, Sir John (James Michael Laud), 11th Bt *cr* 1660; Director of Research, Crang & Ostiguy, Montreal, Canada; *b* 19 Jan. 1943; *s* of Michael Frederick Laud Robinson (*d* 1971) and Elizabeth (*née* Bridge); *S* grandfather, 1975; *m* 1968, Gayle Elizabeth (*née* Keyes); two *s . Educ:* Eton; Trinity Coll., Dublin (MA, Economics and Political Science). Chartered Financial Analyst. *Heir: s* Mark Christopher Michael Villiers Robinson, *b* 23 April 1972. *Address:* Cranford, Kettering, Northants; 20802 Lakeshore Road, Baie d'Urfé, Quebec, Canada. *T:* (514) 457 6795.

ROBINSON, Rev. Canon Joseph, MTh, FKC; Canon Residentiary, Canterbury Cathedral, since 1968, Treasurer, since 1972, Librarian, 1968-73; Examining Chaplain to the Archbishop of Canterbury, since 1968; *b* 23 Feb. 1927; *er s* of Thomas and Maggie Robinson; *m* 1953, Anne Antrobus; two *s* two *d. Educ:* Upholland Grammar Sch., Lancs; King's Coll., London. BD (1st cl. Hons); AKC (1st cl.) 1951; MTh 1958; FKC 1973. Deacon, 1952; Priest, 1953; Curate, All Hallows, Tottenham, 1952-55; Minor Canon of St Paul's Cathedral, 1956-68; Sacrist, 1958-68; Lectr in Hebrew and Old Testament Studies, King's Coll., London, 1959-68. Golden Lectr, 1963; St Antholin Lectr, 1964-67. Chaplain, Worshipful Co. of Cutlers, 1963-; Sub Chaplain, Order of St John of Jerusalem, 1965-. *Publications:* The Cambridge Bible Commentary on 1 Kings, 1972, 2 Kings, 1976; articles in: Church Quarterly Review, Expository Times, Church Times; many reviews in various jls. *Recreations:* reading, gardening. *Address:* 15 The Precincts, Canterbury, Kent. *T:* Canterbury 61954. *Club:* Athenæum.

ROBINSON, Kathleen Marian, (Mrs Vincent F. Sherry; Kathleen M. Sherry); FRCS, FRCOG, MD; Obstetrician, and

Gynæcologist, Royal Free Hospital since 1946; Obstetrician, Queen Charlotte's Hospital, since 1946; *b* 25 May 1911; *d* of late James Robinson and Ruth Robinson (*née* Edmeston); *m* 1946, Vincent Francis Sherry; one *s* two *d*. *Educ:* Penrhos College, Colwyn Bay; Royal Free Hospital School of Medicine, London University. MB, BS, 1936; MRCS, LRCP 1936; MD London 1940; FRCS 1940; MRCOG 1941; FRCOG 1953. House Surgeon: Royal Free Hospital; Samaritan Hospital, Royal Marsden Hospital, Queen Charlotte's Hospital. Resident Obstetrician, Queen Charlotte's Hospital. Recognised Teacher of the London University. FRSM; FRHS. *Publications:* contributor to Queen Charlotte's Text Book of Obstetrics, also to Practical Motherhood and Parentcraft. *Recreations:* gardening, cooking, travel. *Address:* 17 Herondale Avenue, Wandsworth Common, SW18. *T:* 01-874 8588; 97 Harley Street, W1. *T:* 01-935 5077.

ROBINSON, Rt. Hon. Kenneth, PC 1964; FCIT; Chairman: London Transport Executive, since 1975; Arts Council of Great Britain, since 1977; *b* Warrington, Lancs, 19 March 1911; *s* of late Clarence Robinson, MRCS, LRCP; *m* 1941, Helen Elizabeth Edwards; one *d*. *Educ:* Oundle Sch. Insurance Broker at Lloyd's, 1927-40. Served War of 1939-45, RN 1941-46; Ord. Seaman, 1941; commissioned, 1942; Lieut-Comdr RNVR, 1944; served Home Fleet, Mediterranean, Far East and Pacific. Company Secretary, 1946-69. MP (Lab) St Pancras N, 1949-70; Asst Whip (unpaid), 1950-51, an Opposition Whip, 1951-54; Minister of Health, 1964-68; Minister for Planning and Land, Min. of Housing and Local Govt, 1968-69; Dir, Social Policy, 1970-72, Man. Dir (Personnel and Social Policy Div.), 1972-74, British Steel Corp. Chm. of English National Opera, 1972-77. *Publications:* Wilkie Collins, a Biography, 1951; Policy for Mental Health, 1958; Patterns of Care, 1961; Look at Parliament, 1962; *Recreations:* looking at paintings, reading, listening to music. *Address:* 55 Broadway, SW1; 12 Grove Terrace, NW5.

ROBINSON, Kenneth Dean, MA Oxon; Headmaster, Bradford Grammar School, 1963-74; *b* 9 March 1909; *s* of late Rev. Arthur Edward and late Mary Edith Robinson; *m* 1936, Marjorie Belle Carter, Bradford, Yorks; two *s* two *d*. *Educ:* Bradford Grammar Sch.; Corpus Christi Coll., Oxford (Scholar). Classical Honour Mods Class I, Litt Hum. Class II. Sixth Form Classical Master, St Edmund's, Canterbury, 1932-34; Head of Classical Dept, Wellington College, Berks, 1934-41; Intelligence Corps, 1941-45; Asst to Director of Education, Shire Hall, Reading, Berks, 1945-46; Headmaster, Birkenhead Sch., Cheshire, 1946-63. Classics panel Secondary Sch. Examinations Council, 1948-50; Pres. Liverpool Br., Class. Assoc., 1958; Council, IAHM, 1949-53; HMC Cttee, 1956-60; Chm. NW Div., HMC, 1958-59; Chm. Direct Grant Cttee, HMC, 1958-59, Mem., 1967-70; Chm., NE Div., HMC, 1971-72; Chm. Op. Res. Sect. Div. XII, IAHM, 1952-60; Chm. Div. XII, IAHM, 1961-62; Mem. Council, 1962-63. Governor, Giggleswick Sch., 1974-. Chm., Leeds/Bradford Branch, Nat. Assoc. for Gifted Children. *Publications:* (with R. L. Chambers) Septimus: a First Latin Reader, 1936; The Latin Way, 1947. *Recreations:* gardening, chess, painting, canals, country. *Address:* Lane House, Cowling, near Keighley, West Yorks BD22 0LX. *T:* Crosshills 34487.

ROBINSON, Kenneth Ernest, CBE 1971; MA, FRHistS; *b* 9 March 1914; *o s* of late Ernest and Isabel Robinson, Plumstead, Kent; *m* 1938, Stephanie, *o d* of late William Wilson, Westminster; one *s* one *d*. *Educ:* Monoux Grammar School, Walthamstow; Hertford College, Oxford (Scholar, 1st Cl. PPE; 1st Cl. Mod. Hist.; Beit Senior Schol. in Colonial History); London School of Economics. Colonial Office, 1936; Asst Sec. 1946; resigned 1948. Fellow of Nuffield Coll., and Reader in Commonwealth Govt, Oxford, 1948-57; Director of the Institute of Commonwealth Studies and Professor of Commonwealth Affairs, Univ. of London, 1957-65; Vice-Chancellor, Univ. of Hong Kong, 1965-72; Hallsworth Res. Fellow, Univ. of Manchester, 1972-74; Dir, Commonwealth Studies Resources Survey, Univ. of London, 1974-76. Leverhulme Research Fellow, 1952-53; Visiting Lecturer, School of Advanced International Studies, Johns Hopkins Univ., USA, 1954; Carnegie Travel Grant, East, Central and South Africa, 1960; Reid Lecturer, Acadia Univ., 1963; Visiting Professor, Duke Univ., NC, 1963. Editor, Journal of Commonwealth Political Studies, 1961-65; Special Commonwealth Award (Min. of Overseas Development), 1965. Member: (part-time) Directing Staff, Civil Service Selection Board, 1951-56, and of Assessor Panel, 1973-; Colonial Economic Research Committee, 1949-62; Colonial Social Science Research Council, 1958-62; Inter-Univ. Council for Higher Educn Overseas, 1973-; Mem. Council: Overseas Development Institute, 1960-65; Royal Inst. of Internat. Affairs, 1962-65; Internat. African Inst., 1960-65;

African Studies Assoc., UK, 1963-65; Assoc. of Commonwealth Univs, 1967-68; Hong Kong Management Assoc., 1965-72; Chinese Univ. of Hong Kong, 1965-72; Univ. of Cape Coast, 1972-74; Royal Commonwealth Soc., 1974-; Life Mem. Ct, Univ. of Hong Kong, 1972. Governor, LSE, 1959-65. Corresp. Mem., Académie des Sciences d'Outre-Mer, Paris. Hon. LLD Chinese Univ. of Hong Kong, 1969; Hon. DLitt, Univ. of Hong Kong, 1972. JP Hong Kong, 1967-72. *Publications:* (with W. J. M. Mackenzie) Five Elections in Africa, 1960; (with A. F. Madden) Essays in Imperial Government presented to Margery Perham, 1963; The Dilemmas of Trusteeship, 1965; (with W. B. Hamilton & C. D. Goodwin) A Decade of the Commonwealth 1955-64 (USA), 1966. Contrib. to Africa Today (USA), 1955; Africa in the Modern World (USA), 1955; University Cooperation and Asian Development (USA), 1967; L'Europe du XIXe et du XXe Siècle, Vol. 7 (Italy), 1968; papers in learned jls. *Address:* 10 St Augustine's Road, NW1. *T:* 01-485 1198; The Old Rectory, Church Westcote, Oxon. *T:* Shipton under Wychwood 830586. *Clubs:* Royal Commonwealth Society; Hong Kong.

ROBINSON, Lee Fisher; Chief Executive and Deputy Chairman, Turriff Construction Corporation Ltd, since 1970; Consultant, International Management Consultants, since 1972; *b* 17 July 1923; *m* 1st, 1944, Zelda Isobel Fisher; three *d*; 2nd, 1976, June Edna Hopkins. *Educ:* Howard Sch.; Cardiff Tech. College. CEng, MIArb. Royal Engrs, Sappers and Miners, IE, 1942-45. Man. Dir, Power Gas Corp. Ltd, 1944; Turriff Const. Corp. Ltd, HBM (BCC), 1963; Director: Davy-Ashmore Ltd, 1970; Combustion Systems (NRDC), 1972; Redwood Internat. (UK) Ltd, 1972; Altech SA, 1976-; Protech SA, 1976-; Altech of Canada, 1976-; Banks Gowerton, 1976-; Hawke Ltd, 1976-; BCS Ltd, 1976-; Charterhouse Strategic Development Ltd, 1976- (Gp Indust. Adviser, Charterhouse Gp). Chm., Warren Spring Adv. Bd; Mem. Adv. Council for Technology, 1968-69. *Publications:* Cost and Financing of Fertiliser Projects in India, 1967; various articles. *Recreations:* badminton, sailing. *Address:* Flat 3, Athenaeum Hall, Vale-of-Health, NW3 1AP. *Clubs:* East India, Devonshire, Sports and Public Schools, Wig and Pen.

ROBINSON, Leonard Keith; County Chief Executive, Hampshire County Council, since 1974; Clerk of Lieutenancy since 1974; *b* 2 July 1920; *s* of Cuthbert Lawrence Robinson and Hilda Robinson; *m* 1948, Susan May Tomkinson; two *s* two *d*. *Educ:* Queen Elizabeth's Grammar Sch., Blackburn; Victoria Univ. of Manchester (LLB). Solicitor. RAFVR, 1940-46 (Navigator, Sqdn-Ldr). Asst Solicitor, City and County of Bristol, 1948-55; Dep. Town Clerk, Birkenhead Co. Borough Council, 1955-56; Town Clerk, Stoke-on-Trent City Council, 1966-73. Member: W Mids Econ. Planning Council, 1967-73; Central Cttee for Reclamation of Derelict Land, 1971-74; Quality Assce Council, BSI, 1973-; Job Creation Programme Action Cttee for SE London, 1976-; Chm., Assoc. of County Chief Execs, 1975-77. *Publications:* contrib. local govt and legal jls. *Recreations:* cricket, theatre, cine photography, gardening. *Address:* Byewood, Hocombe Road, Chandler's Ford, Hampshire SO5 1SL. *Clubs:* National Liberal, MCC.

ROBINSON, Lloyd; *see* Robinson, T. L.

ROBINSON, Group Captain Marcus, CB 1956; AFC 1942 and Bar 1944; DL; Chairman: Robinson, Dunn & Co. Ltd since 1966 (Director since 1939); RD (Chemicals & Wood Processes) Ltd, since 1973 (Director, since 1946); Director: Thomson & Balfour Ltd since 1966; Temple Builders Market Ltd, since 1973; Timber Preservation (Aberdeen) Ltd, since 1975; *b* 27 May 1912; *s* of Wilson and Eileen Robinson; *m* 1st, 1941, Mrs Mary Playfair (marr. diss. 1951); 2nd, 1953, Mrs Joan E. G. O. Weatherlake (*née* Carter); one *s* one *d*. *Educ:* Rossall. Commissioned AAF, 602 Sqdn, 1934; Squadron Ldr, 1940, commanding 616 Squadron; Wing Comdr, 1943; Group Capt., 1945; re-formed 602 Squadron, 1947; Member Air Advisory Council, Air Ministry, 1952-56; Chairman Glasgow TA and AFA, 1953-56; Chairman Glasgow Rating Valuation Appeals Cttee, 1963-74 (Dep. Chm., 1958-63). Chm. Earl Haig Fund, Scotland, 1974-. DL Glasgow, 1955. *Recreations:* ski-ing, sailing. *Clubs:* Western (Glasgow), Royal Northern Yacht (Rhu).

ROBINSON, Sir Niall B. L.; *see* Lynch-Robinson.

ROBINSON, Nigel Francis Maltby; Metropolitan Stipendiary Magistrate since 1962; *b* 5 Nov. 1906; *s* of Francis George Robinson, OBE, Ilkeston, Derbyshire; *m* 1933, Flora, *d* of John McKay, Sutton, Surrey. *Educ:* Lancing; Hertford College, Oxford (MA, BCL). Called to Bar, Middle Temple, 1928; Practised Midland Circuit, 1928-62. Served Royal Artillery, 1940-45. JP and Dep. Chairman, Quarter Sessions for

Derbyshire, 1958-64; JP and Dep. Chm., Nottinghamshire Quarter Sessions, 1961-66. *Address:* 42 Parkside, Vanbrugh Fields, SE3 7QG. *Clubs:* Flyfishers'; Nottingham and Nottinghamshire United Services.

ROBINSON, Rev. Prof. Norman Hamilton Galloway, MA (Glasgow); BD (Edinburgh); DLitt (Glasgow); DD (Edinburgh); Professor of Divinity and Systematic Theology in the University of St Andrews; *b* 7 October 1912; *e s* of late George Robinson and late Barbara Fraser, Troon, Ayrshire; *m* 1936, Mary Elizabeth, *o d* of Christopher Johnston, Portrush; two *s* two *d. Educ:* Ayr Academy; Universities of Glasgow, Oxford and Edinburgh. Minister of: Sandsting Parish Church, Shetland, 1939-43; South Church, Fraserburgh, Aberdeenshire, 1943-48; High Kirk of Rothesay, 1948-54; Prof. of Divinity and Dean of Faculty, Rhodes Univ., Grahamstown, SA, 1954-56; Prof. of Systematic Theology, 1956-67, of Divinity and Systematic Theology, 1967-, Univ. of St Andrews. Dean of Faculty of Divinity, Univ. of St Andrews, 1958-62; Examiner in Divinity, Universities of: Natal, 1954-55, South Africa, 1954-56, Aberdeen, 1960-62, Edinburgh, 1962-65, Newcastle upon Tyne, 1965-67, Glasgow, 1967-71, QUB, 1971-73, Durham, 1974-76; Wales, 1975-. Special Lectr in Christian Ethics: Assembly's Coll., Belfast, 1960-61; Univ. Coll. of North Wales, Bangor, 1975; Guest Lecturer: Institute of Theology, Princeton Theol Seminary, USA, 1966; Graduate Summer Session, Anglican Theol and Union Colls, Vancouver, Canada, 1966. Mem., Ct of Univ. of St Andrews, 1971-75. Gov. of Strathallan School. *Publications:* Faith and Duty, 1950; The Claim of Morality, 1952; Christ and Conscience, 1956; The Groundwork of Christian Ethics, 1971; contribs to: Theologians of Our Time, 1966; Dictionary of Christian Theology, 1969; Talk of God, 1969; Preface to Christian Studies, 1971; Sprachlogik des Glaubens, 1974; articles and reviews in Philosophy, The Philosophical Quarterly, Theology, The Expository Times, Hibbert Jl, Scottish Journal of Theology, Religious Studies, etc. *Recreation:* golf. *Address:* Byculla, 10 Trinity Place, St Andrews, Fife KY16 8SG. *T:* 2531.

ROBINSON, Oliver John; Editor, Good Housekeeping, 1947-65, Editor-in-Chief, 1965-67; *b* 7 April 1908; *s* of late W. Heath and Josephine Constance Robinson; *m* 1933, Evelyn Anne Laidler. *Educ:* Cranleigh Sch. Art Editor, Good Housekeeping, 1930; Art Editor, Nash's, 1933. Temporary commission, Queen's Royal Regt, 1941; Camouflage Development and Training Centre, 1942; Staff Officer, War Office, 1944. *Address:* 92 Charlbert Court, Eamont Street, NW8 7DA. *T:* 01-722 0723. *Club:* Savage.

ROBINSON, Peter; Chairman and Chief Executive, British Printing Corporation, since 1976; *b* 18 Jan. 1922; *s* of Harold Robinson and Jane Elizabeth Robinson; *m* Lesley Anne, step-*d* of Major J. M. May, TD; two *s* two *d. Educ:* Prince Henry's Sch., Otley; Leeds Coll. of Technology (Diploma in Printing). Mem., Inst. of Printing; FBIM. Management Trainee, 1940-41; flying duties, RAFVR, 1942-46; Leeds Coll. of Technol., 1946-49; Asst Manager, Robinson & Sons Ltd, Chesterfield, 1949-53; Works Dir and Man. Dir, Taylowe Ltd, 1953-62; Dir, Hazell Sun, 1964; Dir, British Printing Corp., 1966, Man. Dir, 1969-75; Dir, Tootal Ltd. Council Mem., PIRA. *Recreations:* military history, cricket, golf. *Address:* Well End Lodge, Bourne End, Bucks. *T:* Bourne End 20187.

ROBINSON, Peter Damian; Circuit Administrator, South Eastern Circuit (Lord Chancellor's Department), since 1974; *b* 11 July 1926; *s* of late John Robinson and Jill Clegg (*née* Easten); *m* 1956, Mary Katinka Bonner, Peterborough; two *d. Educ:* Corby Sch., Sunderland; Lincoln Coll., Oxford. MA. Royal Marines, 1944-46. Called to Bar, Middle Temple, 1951; Clerk of Assize, NE Circuit, 1959-70; Administrator, NE Circuit, 1970-74. Member, Home Office Departmental Cttee on Legal Aid in Criminal Proceedings (the Widgery Cttee), 1964-66. *Recreations:* beagling, reading and the countryside. *Address:* Thanet House, 232 Strand, WC2R 1DA. *T:* 01-353 8060.

ROBINSON, Philip Henry; Director, J. Henry Schroder Wagg & Co. Ltd, since 1966; Executive Vice-President, Schroder International Ltd, since 1977 (Director, since 1973); *b* 4 Jan. 1926; *s* of Arthur Robinson and Frances M. Robinson; *m* 1959, Helen Wharton; one *s* one *d. Educ:* Lincoln Sch.; Jesus Coll., Cambridge (Exhibr, MA); Sch. of Oriental and African Studies, London Univ.; NY Univ. Graduate Sch. of Business Admin. Member, Gray's Inn. Served with RN, 1944-47; N. M. Rothschild & Sons, 1950-54; Actg Sec., British Newfoundland Corp., Montreal, 1954-56; Asst Vice-Pres., J. Henry Schroder Banking Corp., NY, 1956-61; J. Henry Schroder Wagg & Co. Ltd, 1961; Director: J. Henry Schroder Wagg & Co. Ltd, 1966; Siemens Ltd, 1967; Schroders & Chartered Ltd Hong Kong,

1971. Managing Trustee, Municipal Mutual Insurance Ltd, 1977-. Mem., NCB, 1973-77. *Publications:* contrib. Investor's Chronicle. *Recreations:* music, walking. *Address:* 16 Smith Street, SW3. *T:* 01-730 4978. *Club:* Annabel's.

ROBINSON, Robert Henry; writer and broadcaster; *b* 17 Dec. 1927; *o s* of Ernest Redfern Robinson and Johanna Hogan; *m* 1958, Josephine Mary Richard; one *s* two *d. Educ:* Raynes Park Grammar Sch.; Exeter Coll., Oxford (MA). Editor of Isis, 1950. TV columnist, Sunday Chronicle, 1952; film and theatre columnist, Sunday Graphic, and radio critic, Sunday Times, 1956; editor Atticus, Sunday Times, 1960; weekly column, Private View, Sunday Times, 1962; film critic, Sunday Telegraph, 1965. Writer and presenter of TV programmes: Picture Parade, 1959; Points of View, 1961; Divided We Stand, 1964; The Look of the Week, 1966; Reason to Believe?, The Fifties, 1969; Chm., Call My Bluff, Ask The Family, 1967; The Book Programme, 1974; contribs Panorama, Monitor, Meeting Point, etc; presenter of: BBC radio current affairs programme Today, 1971-74; Vital Statistics, 1974; Chm., Brain of Britain, 1973-; Chm., Stop the Week, 1974. Radio Personality of the Year, Radio Industries Club, 1973. Chm., Whitbread Literary Prize, 1975. *Publications:* (ed) Poetry from Oxford, 1951; Landscape with Dead Dons, 1956; Inside Robert Robinson (essays), 1965; (contrib.) To Nevill Coghill from Friends, 1966; The Conspiracy, 1968; contrib. New Statesman, Spectator, Punch, Observer, Listener, etc. *Address:* 16 Cheyne Row, SW3; Laurel Cottage, Buckland St Mary, Somerset. *Club:* Savile.

ROBINSON, Prof. Ronald Edward, CBE 1970; DFC 1944; Beit Professor of the History of the British Commonwealth, and Fellow of Balliol College, Oxford University, since 1971; *b* 3 Sept. 1920; *e s* of William Edward and Ada Theresa Robinson, Clapham; *m* 1948, Alice Josephine Denny; two *s* two *d. Educ:* Battersea Grammar Sch.; St John's Coll., Cambridge. Major Scholar in History, St John's Coll., 1939; BA 1946, PhD 1949, Cantab. F/Lt, 58 Bomber Sqn, RAF, 1942-45. Research Officer, African Studies Branch, Colonial Office, 1947-49; Lectr in History, 1953-66, Smuts Reader in History of the British Commonwealth, 1966-71, Univ. of Cambridge; Chm., Faculty Bd of Modern Hist., 1974-76; Tutor 1961-66, Fellow 1949-71, St John's Coll., Cambridge. Inst. for Advanced Studies, Princeton, 1959-60. Mem., Bridges Cttee on Trng in Public Administration, 1961-62; Chm., Cambridge Confs on Problems of Developing Countries, 1961-70. *Publications:* Africa and the Victorians, 1961; Developing the Third World, 1971; articles in Cambridge History of the British Empire, Vol. III, 1959, and The New Cambridge Modern History, Vol. XI, 1963; reports on Problems of Developing Countries, 1963-71; articles and reviews in learned jls. *Recreations:* room cricket, tennis. *Address:* Balliol College, Oxford. *Clubs:* Royal Commonwealth Society; Hawks (Cambridge).

ROBINSON, Stanford, OBE 1972; Orchestral, Choral and Opera Conductor; Lecturer on conducting and kindred musical subjects; *b* Leeds, 5 July 1904; *s* of James Percy and Carrie Robinson; *m* Lorely Dyer; one *d. Educ:* Stationers' Company's School; Royal College of Music, London, and abroad. British Broadcasting Corporation, 1924-66; Chorus Master until 1932, during which time formed the BBC choral activities in London, including the BBC Singers, the Choral Society, and the BBC Chorus; during the period also conducted the Wireless Orchestra extensively in all kinds of programmes, symphonic and otherwise; Conductor of BBC Theatre Orchestra, 1932-46; Music Dir Variety Dept, 1932-36; Dir Music Productions, producing and conducting all studio performances of opera besides operetta and other musical feature programmes, 1936-46; Opera Director and Associate Conductor of the BBC Symphony Orchestra, 1946-49; Conductor Opera Orch. and Opera Organiser, BBC, 1949-52. Toured Australia and New Zealand, conducting ABC and NZBC orchestras in numerous cities, 1966-67; Chief Conductor, Queensland Symphony Orchestra, 1968-69. Hon. ARCM; Hon. GSM. *Publications:* Orchestral Music, Brass Band Music, part songs, choral arrangements and songs. *Recreations:* gardening, photography. *Address:* 3 Belmont Court, Belmont, Dyke Road, Brighton BN1 3TX. *T:* Brighton 202272.

ROBINSON, Sir Stanley; see Robinson, Sir E. S.

ROBINSON, Stanley Scott, MBE 1944; TD 1950; Sheriff of Grampian, Highland and Islands (formerly Inverness (including Western Isles), Ross, Cromarty, Moray and Nairn); *b* 27 March 1913; *s* of late William Scott Robinson, Engineer, and of Christina Douglas Robinson; *m* 1937, Helen Annan Hardie; three *s. Educ:* Boroughmuir Sch., Edinburgh; Edinburgh Univ. Admitted as solicitor, 1935; Solicitor in the Supreme Courts. Commissioned in TA, 1935. Served War: France and Belgium,

1939-40, Captain RA; France, Holland and Germany, 1944-45 (despatches twice); Major, RA, 1943; Lt-Col, 1948. Solicitor in gen. practice in Montrose, Angus, 1935-72 (except during war service). Hon. Sheriff of Perth and Angus, 1970-72. Mem. Council of Law Society of Scotland, 1963-72 (Vice-Pres., 1971-72); Dean, Soc. of Solicitors of Angus, 1970-72. *Publications:* contribs to Jl of Law Society of Scotland. *Recreations:* golf, bowling, military history. *Address:* Flat 3, Drumallin, Drummond Road, Inverness. *T:* Inverness 33488. *Club:* Highland (Inverness).

ROBINSON, Stephen Joseph, OBE 1971; FRS 1976; CEng, FIEE; Product Director, MEL Equipment Co. Ltd, since 1973; *b* 6 Aug. 1931; *s* of Joseph Allan Robinson and Ethel (*née* Bunting); *m* 1957, Monica Mabs Scott; one *s* one *d. Educ:* Sebright Sch., Wolverley; Jesus Coll., Cambridge (MA Natural Sciences). RAF, 1950-51. Mullard Res. Labs, 1954-72; MEL Equipment Co. Ltd, 1972-. *Recreations:* sailing, ski-ing. *Address:* Greenfields, Carlton Road, South Godstone, Surrey. *T:* South Godstone 3310.

ROBINSON, Sydney Allen; General President, National Union of Boot and Shoe Operatives, 1947-70, retired; Member: Monopolies and Mergers Commission, since 1966; TUC-CBI Conciliation Panel, since 1972; *b* 13 Aug. 1905; *m* 1940, Grace Mary Lack; one *s* one *d. Educ:* Clophill Elementary School, Bedfordshire. National Union of Boot and Shoe Operatives: Full-time Branch Officer, 1939; National Organiser, 1947; Assistant General Secretary, 1949. Mem., Panel of Inquiry into Beef Supplies and Prices, 1973. *Recreations:* gardening, adult education. *Address:* 45 Fourth Avenue, Wellingborough, Northants. *T:* Wellingborough 2956.

ROBINSON, Thomas Lloyd, TD; Chairman, The Dickinson Robinson Group Ltd, 1974-77 (Deputy Chairman, 1968); *b* 21 Dec. 1912; *s* of late Thomas Rosser Robinson and Rebe Francis-Watkins; *m* 1939, Pamela Rosemary Foster; one *s* two *d. Educ:* Wycliffe Coll. Served War, 1939-45: Royal Warwickshire Regt, 61 Div., and SHAEF; Staff Coll., Camberley. Director, E. S. & A. Robinson Ltd, 1952; Jt Managing Dir, 1958; Dep. Chm., E. S. & A. Robinson (Holdings) Ltd, 1963; Director: Legal & General Assurance Soc. Ltd, 1970; West of England Trust Ltd, 1973; Van Leer Groep Stichting, Holland; Chm., Legal & General Western Advisory Bd, 1972; Chm., Council of Governors, Wycliffe Coll., 1971. *Recreations:* travel, antiques, golf, formerly cricket and rugby football. *Address:* Lechlade, 23 Druid Stoke Avenue, Stoke Bishop, Bristol BS9 1DB. *T:* Bristol 681957. *Clubs:* Bath, Army & Navy, MCC; Royal and Ancient (St Andrews).

ROBINSON, Sir Wilfred (Henry Frederick), 3rd Bt, *cr* 1908; Vice-Principal, Diocesan College School, Rondebosch, South Africa; *b* 24 Dec. 1917; *s* of Wilfred Henry Robinson (*d* 1922) (3rd *s* of 1st Bt), and Eileen (*d* 1963), *d* of Frederick St Leger, Claremont, SA; *S* uncle, Sir Joseph Benjamin Robinson, 2nd Bt, 1954; *m* 1946, Margaret Alison Kathleen, *d* of late Frank Mellish, MC, Bergendal, Gansbaai, Cape Province, SA; one *s* two *d. Educ:* Diocesan Coll., Rondebosch; St John's Coll., Cambridge, MA 1944. Served War of 1939-45, Devonshire Regt and Parachute Regt, Major. *Heir: s* Peter Frank Robinson, *b* 1949. *Address:* c/o Coutts & Co., 162 Brompton Road, SW3 1HW.

ROBINSON, Maj.-Gen. William Arthur, CB 1964; OBE 1944; MA; MD; retired; *b* 2 March 1908; *s* of late Sir William Robinson, DL, JP; *m* 1934, Sheela, *d* of J. R. Yarr, Newbury, Berks; two *s. Educ:* Wesley College and Trinity College, Dublin. MA, MD, 1934. MRCGP 1961. Commissioned RAMC, 1931; served in Egypt and Sudan, 1932-37; Instructor and MO Army Gas School, 1938-41; Adviser in Chemical Warfare, 1941-43; Comd 200 Fd Ambulance (Egypt, Sicily and NW Europe), 1943-44; ADMS: 3 (Brit.) Inf. Div., NW Europe, 1945-46; Lt-Col Assistant Director-General Army Medical Dept (AMD1) War Office, 1946-49; jssc 1949; OC Hospital, E Africa, 1950-51; ADMS HQ Cyrenaica Dist (Colonel, ADMS 1 Bn Div., 1951-52, ADG (AMD1), War Office, 1952-54; DDMS Malta, 1954-57; Commandant, Depot and TE RAMC, 1958-60; Major-General, 1960; Deputy Director-General, Army Medical Services, 1960-61; DDMS Southern Command, 1961; DMS, Far East Land Forces, 1963-65; QHS, 1960-65. Col Comdt, RAMC, 1966-. *Recreations:* cross-country running (sen. colours); sailing, hockey, golf. *Address:* Lechlade, Horton Heath, Eastleigh, Hants.

ROBINSON, Rt. Rev. William James; see Ottawa, Bishop of.

ROBLES, Marisa, (Mrs Christopher Hyde-Smith); harpist; Professor of Harp: Madrid Conservatoire, since 1958; Royal College of Music, since 1971; *b* 4 May 1937; *d* of Cristobal Robles and Maria Bonilla; *m* 1968, Christopher Hyde-Smith; two *s* one *d. Educ:* Madrid National Sch.; Madrid Conservatoire. Recitals in Europe, Africa and America; soloist with major internat. orchestras. Hon. Royal Madrid Conservatoire 1958; Hon. RCM 1973. *Recreations:* theatre, indoor plants, family life in general. *Address:* 38 Luttrell Avenue, Putney, SW15 6PE. *T:* 01-788 3753. *Club:* Anglo-Spanish.

ROBOROUGH, 2nd Baron, *cr* 1938, of Maristow; **Massey Henry Edgcumbe Lopes;** Bt, *cr* 1805; JP; Brevet Major Reserve of Officers Royal Scots Greys; Lord-Lieutenant of Devon, since 1958; *b* 4 Oct. 1903; *o s* of 1st Baron and Lady Albertha Louisa Florence Edgcumbe (*d* 1941), *d* of 4th Earl of Mount Edgcumbe; *S* father 1938; *m* 1936, Helen, *o d* of late Colonel E. A. F. Dawson, Launde Abbey, Leicestershire; two *s* (and one *d* decd). *Educ:* Eton Coll.; Christ Church, Oxford (BA). Served in Royal Scots Greys, 1925-38; served again 1939-45 (wounded). ADC to Earl of Clarendon, when Governor of Union of South Africa, 1936-37. CA Devon, 1956-74; DL 1946; Vice-Lieutenant of Devon, 1951; Member of Duchy of Cornwall Council, 1958-68; High Steward of Barnstaple. Chairman: Dartmoor National Park, 1965-74; SW Devon Div. Educn Cttee, 1954-74; Devon Outward Bound, 1967-75. Hon. Col, Devon Army Cadet Force, 1967-. Hon. LLD Exeter, 1969. KStJ. *Heir: s* Hon. Henry Massey Lopes [*b* 2 Feb. 1940; *m* 1968, Robyn, *é d* of John Bromwich, Melbourne, Aust.; two *s* one *d*]. *Address:* Bickham House, Roborough, Plymouth, Devon. *T:* Yelverton 478. *Club:* Cavalry and Guards.
See also Baron Carnock.

ROBSON, family name of **Baroness Robson of Kiddington.**

ROBSON OF KIDDINGTON, Baroness *cr* 1974 (Life Peer), of Kiddington; **Inga-Stina Robson,** JP; Chairman, South-West Thames Regional Health Authority, since 1974; *b* 20 Aug. 1919; *d* of Erik R. Arvidsson and Lilly A. Arvidsson (*née* Danielson); *m* 1940, Lawrence W. Robson, *qv;* one *s* two *d. Educ:* Stockholm, Sweden. Swedish Foreign Office, 1939-40; Min. of Information, 1942-43. Contested (L) Eye Div., 1955 and 1959, Gloucester City, 1964 and 1966. President: Women's Liberal Fedn, 1968-69 and 1969-70; Liberal Party Org., 1970-71; Chm., Liberal Party Environment Panel, 1971-77. Chairman: Bd of Governors, Queen Charlotte's and Chelsea Hosps, 1970-; Midwife Teachers Training Coll.; Member: Cttee of Management, Inst. of Obst. and Gynaecology; Bd of Governors, University Coll. Hosp., 1966-74; Council, Surrey Univ., 1974. JP Oxfordshire, 1955. *Recreations:* sailing, skiing. *Address:* Kiddington Hall, Woodstock, Oxon.

ROBSON, Air Vice-Marshal Adam Henry, CB 1949; OBE 1938; MC; MSc; PhD; RAF retd; *b* 3 Aug. 1892; *s* of J. Robson, Low Fell, Co. Durham; *m* 1917, Vera Mary, *d* of late Robert Purvis, Solicitor, South Shields; two *s. Educ:* Armstrong College, Newcastle upon Tyne; King's College, University of London. Asst Sec., Dorset County Educ. Cttee, 1920-23; Entered RAF Educational Service in 1923; Dir of Educational Services, RAF, 1944-52. Mem. Exec. Cttee and Coun., Nat. Inst. of Adult Educn, 1947-52; Mem. Exec. Cttee and Coun. Nat. Foundn of Educl Research, 1947-52; Mem. Governing Body, Sch. of Oriental and African Studies, London Univ., 1948-52; Director, Hungarian Students Resettlement, World Univ. Service, London, 1957-58. Mem., Hampshire County Youth Adv. Cttee, 1961-67. Served in Durham Light Infantry, 1914-19 (MC and bar, despatches, wounded thrice). *Address:* Wey Cottage, Bentley, Farnham, Surrey. *T:* Bentley 2264.
See also J. A. Robson.

ROBSON, Brian Ewart; Assistant Under-Secretary of State, Ministry of Defence, since 1976; *b* 25 July 1926; 2nd *s* of late Walter Ewart Robson and Lily Robson; *m* 1962, Cynthia Margaret, *o d* of late William James Scott, Recife, Brazil; two *d. Educ:* Steyning Grammar Sch.; Varndean Sch., Brighton; The Queen's Coll., Oxford (BA Hons). Joined Army, 1944; commissioned Royal Sussex Regt, 1945; attached to Indian Army (Kumaon Regt), 1945-47; demobilised, 1948. Oxford, 1948-50; entered Admin. class, Home Civil Service, 1950; Asst Private Sec. to Sec. of State for Air, 1953-55; Principal, 1955; Asst Sec., 1965; Imperial Defence Coll., 1970; Ecole Nationale d'Administration, Paris, 1975. *Publications:* Swords of the British Army: the regulation patterns 1788-1914, 1975; numerous articles in learned jls on weapons and military history. *Recreations:* military history, cricket, travel. *Address:* 17 Woodlands, Hove, Sussex BN3 6TJ. *T:* Hove 505803. *Club:* Athenæum.

ROBSON, His Honour Denis Hicks, QC 1955; a County Court Judge, later a Circuit Judge, 1957-72; *b* 7 Jan. 1904; *s* of late Robert Robson, ISO, and Helen Julia, *d* of late James J. Hicks, KCSG; *m* 1931, Mary Grace (*d* 1947), *e d* of late Sir William Orpen, KBE; one *s* one *d*; *m* 1960, Hon. Elizabeth (*widow* of John Cockburn Millar), *d* of late Lord Atkin, PC. *Educ:* Douai School; Trinity Hall, Cambridge. Called to the Bar, Inner Temple, 1927; North Eastern Circuit. War of 1939-45, commissioned in RASC, 1940; Military Department of Judge Advocate General's Office, 1942-45; Major, 1944; Recorder of Doncaster, 1950-53; Recorder of Middlesbrough, 1953-57; Chm., Northamptonshire QS, 1970-71, Vice-Chm., 1960-70. *Address:* Glendalough, Caragh Lake, Co. Kerry, Ireland.

ROBSON, Donald; Chairman, Guinness Mahon & Co. Ltd, since 1976; *b* 29 Oct. 1910; *s* of Herbert William and Ida Robson; *m* 1956, Doreen Elizabeth Buzzel; two *s*. *Educ:* Malton Grammar Sch. BCom; FIB. Westminster Bank Ltd, 1927-67 (to Jt Gen. Manager, 1960); Internat. Commercial Bank Ltd, Managing Dir, 1967-76. *Recreations:* French, reading. *Address:* 32 St Mary at Hill, EC3R 8DH. *T:* 01-623 9333.

ROBSON, Dame Flora, DBE 1960; *b* South Shields, 28 March 1902; *d* of David Mather Robson and Eliza McKenzie. Royal Academy of Dramatic Art (Bronze medal). Hon. DLitt: Oxon, 1974, Durham, Wales; Hon. DLit London, 1971; Hon. Fellow: St Anne's Coll., Oxford, 1975; Sunderland Polytechnic, 1975; Order of Finland's White Rose and Finland's Lion. First appearance on stage, 1921; in All God's Chillun, 1933; Old Vic Season, 1934; Touchwood and Mary Read, Dragoon and Pirate; Close Quarters, 1935; Mary Tudor, 1936; Lady Brooke in Autumn, St Martin's Theatre; Thérèse Raquin in Guilty, Lyric Theatre, Hammersmith, 1944; Man about the House, Piccadilly; Message from Margaret, Duchess; Lady Macbeth, New York, 1948; Captain Brassbound's Conversion (Shaw), Lyric Hammersmith, 1948; Alicia Christie in Black Chiffon, Westminster, 1949; Paulina in The Winter's Tale, Phœnix, 1951; Miss Giddens in The Innocents, Her Majesty's, 1952; Sister Agatha in The Return, Duchess, 1953; Rachel in No Escape; Sarah in A Kind of Folly, Duchess, 1955; Mrs Smith in Suspect, Royal Court, 1955; Janet Holt in The House by the Lake, Duke of York's, 1956-58; Mrs Alving in Ghosts, Old Vic, 1958; Miss Tina in The Aspern Papers, Queen's, 1959; and tour, S Africa, 1960; Grace Rouarte in Time and Yellow Roses, St Martin's, 1961; Miss Moffat in The Corn is Green, in S Africa, S Rhodesia and at Flora Robson Playhouse, Newcastle upon Tyne, 1962; tour, Close Quarters, 1963; Mrs Borkman in John Gabriel Borkman, Duchess, 1962; The Trojan Women, Edinburgh Festival, 1966; tour, Brother and Sister; Miss Prism in The Importance of Being Earnest, Haymarket, 1968; Ring Round The Moon, 1969; The Old Ladies, 1969. *Films:* Empress Elizabeth of Russia in Catherine the Great, 1933; Queen Elizabeth in Fire Over England; Mrs Blair in Farewell Again; Ellen Dean in Wuthering Heights; Mary Rider in Poison Pen; Ftata Teeta in Cæsar and Cleopatra; Sister Phillippa in Black Narcissus; Nell Dawson, MP, in Frieda; Countess Von Platen in Saraband for Dead Lovers; Mary Rackham in Tall Headlines; Melita in Malta Story; The Nurse in Romeo and Juliet; Donna McKenzie in High Tide at Noon; Mrs Haggard in The Gipsy and the Gentleman; Olivia in Innocent Sinners; The Empress of China in 55 Days at Peking; Miss Gilchrist in Murder at the Gallop; Young Cassidy; Guns at Batasi; Those Magnificent Men in their Flying Machines; Seven Women; The Shuttered Room; Cry in the Wind; Eye of the Devil; Fragment of Fear; The Cellar; The Beloved; Alice in Wonderland. BBC TV series: Heidi, 1974; A Legacy, 1975; Mr Lollipop, 1976; The Shrimp and the Anemone, 1977. *Publication:* (contrib.) My Drama School, 1977. *Relevant Publication:* Flora Robson by Janet Dunbar, 1960. *Address:* 7 Wykeham Terrace, Brighton, E Sussex BN1 3FF.

ROBSON, Vice-Adm. (retd) Sir Geoffrey; *see* Robson, Vice-Adm. Sir W. G. A.

ROBSON, Prof. Sir Hugh (Norwood), Kt 1974; MB, ChB, FRCP, FRCPEd, FRACP, FRSE; Principal, University of Edinburgh, since 1974; *b* 18 Oct. 1917; *s* of late Hugh and Elizabeth Robson; *m* 1942, Alice Eleanor, *o d* of late A. McD Livingstone, CIE, MC, MA, BSc, and Gladys Livingstone, Berkhamsted, Herts; one *s* two *d*. *Educ:* Dumfries Academy; University of Edinburgh. Surg.-Lieut RNVR, Western Approaches, Normandy, Arakan, Malaya, 1942-46. Clinical Tutor, Royal Infirmary, Edinburgh, 1946; Lecturer, Dept of Medicine, Univ. of Edinburgh, 1947-50; Sen. Lectr, Dept of Medicine, Univ. of Aberdeen, 1950-53; Prof. of Medicine, Univ. of Adelaide, S Australia, 1953-65, Prof. Emeritus, 1965; Vice-Chancellor, Univ. of Sheffield, 1966-74. Member: Nat. Health and Med. Research Council of Australia, 1957-65; New Guinea Med. Research Council, 1962-65; Australian Drug Evaluation Cttee, 1963-65; Inter-Univ. Council for Higher Educn Overseas, 1967-; Special Steels Div. Adv. Bd, BSC, 1970-72; UN Univ. Founding Cttee, 1973; Chairman: Central Cttee on Postgraduate Med. Educn, GB, 1968-70 (Mem. 1967); Council for Postgraduate Med. Educn in England and Wales, 1970-72; Adv. Council on the Misuse of Drugs, 1971-76; Cttee of Vice-Chancellors and Principals of Univs of UK, 1972-74 (Vice-Chm., 1970-71); British Cttee of Award for Harkness Fellowships (Commonwealth Fund), 1974-77 (Mem., 1968-); Scottish Health Service Planning Council, 1974-; Mem., Northwick Park Adv. Cttee, 1971-76; Trustee, Nuffield Provincial Hosps Trust, 1966-. FRSA. Hon. DSc Philadelphia; Hon. LLD Sheffield; Hon. FRCSE; Hon. Fellow Sheffield Polytechnic. *Publications:* papers on hæmatological and other subjects in Brit., Amer. and Aust. med. jls. *Recreations:* reading, carpentry and golf. *Address:* Principal's Office, University of Edinburgh, Old College, South Bridge, Edinburgh EH8 9YL. *Clubs:* Caledonian; New (Edinburgh).

ROBSON, Professor Emeritus James, MA, DLitt (Glasgow), DD (Hon. St Andrews); MA (Hon. Manchester); *b* 1890; *s* of Rev. Charles Robson; *m* 1919, Annie, *d* of John Cunningham, Dunblane; one *s* one *d*. *Educ:* Inverness Royal Acad.; Stirling High School; Glasgow University; Trinity College, Glasgow. Assistant to Hebrew Professor, Glasgow Univ., 1915-16. Served with YMCA in Mesopotamia and India, 1916-18. Lecturer in English, Forman Christian College, Lahore, 1918-19; Missionary at Sheikh Othman, Aden, 1919-26; Minister at Shandon, Dunbartonshire, 1926-28; Lecturer in Arabic, 1928-48, Reader in Arabic, 1948-49, Glasgow Univ.; Prof. of Arabic, the Univ. of Manchester, 1949-58; Recording Secretary, Glasgow University Oriental Soc., 1931-49; Secretary, 1959-68. External Examiner for Hons Degree: Manchester, 1933-36, 1942-45, 1961-64; Edinburgh, 1945-47, 1952-54, 1961-63; St Andrews, 1957-60; Aberdeen, 1960-62; Glasgow, 1960, 1962; London, 1955-66; and for PhD on occasion at Cambridge, Melbourne, etc. Hon. Fellow, British Soc. for Middle Eastern Studies. *Publications:* Ion Keith-Falconer of Arabia, 1923; Christ in Islam, 1929; Tracts on listening to Music, 1938; Ancient Arabian Musical Instruments, 1938; An introduction to the science of Tradition, 1953; Mishkât al-masâbîh (trans and notes), 4 vols, 1963-65; ed and wrote Islam section in A Dictionary of Comparative Religion, 1970; articles in learned journals. *Recreation:* gardening. *Address:* 17 Woodlands Drive, Glasgow G4 9EQ. *T:* 041-332 4088.

ROBSON, Prof. James Gordon, CBE 1977; MB, ChB; FRCS; Professor of Anaesthetics, University of London, Royal Postgraduate Medical School, since 1964; Hon. Consultant, Hammersmith Hospital, since 1964; Consultant Adviser in Anaesthetics to Department of Health and Social Security, since 1975; *b* Stirling, Scot., 18 March 1921; *o s* of late James Cyril Robson and Freda Elizabeth Howard; *m* 1945, Dr Martha Graham Kennedy (*d* 1975); one *s*. *Educ:* High Sch. of Stirling; Univ. of Glasgow. FRCS 1977. RAMC, 1945-48 (Captain). Sen. Registrar in Anaesthesia, Western Inf., Glasgow, 1948-52; First Asst, Dept of Anaesthetics, Univ. of Durham, 1952-54; Cons. Anaesth., Royal Inf., Edinburgh, 1954-56; Wellcome Res. Prof. of Anaesth., McGill Univ., Montreal, 1956-64. Mem. Bd of Faculty of Anaesthetists, RCS, 1968- (Dean of Faculty, 1973-76); Mem. Council, RCS, 1973- (a Vice-Pres., 1977); Chm., Jt Cttee on Higher Trng of Anaesthetists, 1973-76; Member: AHA, Ealing, Hammersmith and Hounslow, 1974-77 (NW Met. RHB, 1971-74); Chief Scientists' Res. Cttee and Panel on Med. Res., DHSS, 1973-77; Neurosciences Bd, MRC, 1974-; Clin. Res. Bd, MRC (Chm. Grants Cttee II), 1969-71; Mem. Council, RPMS (Vice-Chm. Academic Bd, 1973-; Chm. 1976-); Mem., Rock Carling Fellowship Panel, 1976-; Vice-Chm., Jt Consultants' Cttee, 1974-; Special Trustee, Hammersmith Hosp., 1974-; Examiner, Primary FFARCS, 1967-73; Mem. Editorial Bd and Cons. Ed, British Jl of Anaesthesia, 1965-; Mem. Edit. Bd, Psychopharmacology. Mem. Council, Assoc. of Anaesths of GB and Ire., 1973-; Member: Physiol. Soc., 1966-; RSocMed; Hon. Mem., Assoc. of Univ. Anaesths (USA), 1963-; Sir Arthur Sims Commonwealth Trav. Prof., 1968; Visiting Prof. to many med. centres, USA and Canada; Wesley Bourne Lectr, McGill Univ., 1965. Joseph Clover Medal and Dudley Buxton Prize, Fac. of Anaesths, RCS, 1972; Hon. FFARACS 1968. *Publications:* on neurophysiol., anaesthesia, pain and central nervous system mechanisms of respiration, in learned jls. *Recreations:* practice of anaesthesia; golf, wet fly fishing. *Address:* Department of Anaesthetics, Royal Postgraduate Medical School, Ducane Road, W12 0HS. *T:* 01-743 2030 (ext. 264). *Clubs:* Council of Royal College of Surgeons, Denham Golf.

ROBSON, James Jeavons, CBE 1972; FICE; MIStructE; FIArb; Secretary for the Environment, Hong Kong, 1973-76; Member of Legislative Council, Hong Kong, 1969-76; *b* 4 July 1918; *m* 1945, Avis Metcalfe; one *s*. *Educ:* Constantine Coll., Middlesbrough. MICE 1948, FICE 1958; MIStructE 1946; FIArb 1969. War Service, RM, 1942-46 (Captain). Engrg Trng, Messrs Dorman Long & Co. and ICI, 1936-41; joined Colonial Engrg Service and posted to PWD, Hong Kong, 1946; Dir of Public Works, 1969. Mem. Council, ICE, 1967; Telford Premium (for paper, Overall Planning in Hong Kong), ICE, 1971. *Publications:* articles on civil engineering in Jl ICE. *Recreations:* golf, racing, gardening. *Address:* Labéjan, 32300 Mirande, France. *Clubs:* Oriental; Hong Kong, Royal Hong Kong Jockey, Royal Hong Kong Golf.

ROBSON, John Adam; HM Diplomatic Service; Counsellor and Consul-General, Oslo, since 1976; *b* 16 April 1930; *yr s* of Air Vice-Marshal Adam Henry Robson, *qv*; *m* 1958, Maureen Molly, *er d* of E. H. S. Bullen, Edgware; three *d*. *Educ:* Charterhouse; Gonville and Caius Coll., Cambridge (Major Scholar). BA 1952, MA 1955, PhD 1958. Fellow, Gonville and Caius Coll., 1954-58; Asst Lectr, University Coll. London, 1958-60. HM Foreign Service (later Diplomatic Service), 1961; Second Sec., British Embassy, Bonn, 1962-64; Second, later First, Secretary, Lima, 1964-66; First Sec., British High Commn, Madras, 1966-69; Asst Head, Latin American Dept, FCO, 1969-73; Head of Chancery, Lusaka, 1973-74; RCDS, 1975. *Publications:* Wyclif and the Oxford Schools, 1961; articles in historical jls. *Address:* c/o Foreign and Commonwealth Office, Whitehall, SW1.

ROBSON, Prof. John Michael; Professor of Pharmacology, Guy's Hospital Medical School, London University, 1950-68, now Emeritus; *b* 13 Dec. 1900; *m* 1930, Sarah Benjamin. *Educ:* Leeds Central High School; Leeds University. Qualified MB, ChB, 1925; MD, 1930; DSc, 1932. Lecturer in Pharmacology, Edinburgh University, 1934; Reader in Pharmacology, Guy's Hospital Medical School, 1946. *Publications:* Recent Advances in Sex and Reproductive Physiology, 1934 (2nd edn 1940, 3rd edn 1947); Chapter in Endocrine in Theory and Practice, 1937; Chapter in The Practice of Endocrinology, 1948; (with C. A. Keele) Recent Advances in Pharmacology, 1950, 2nd edn 1956, 3rd edn (with S. Stacey) 1962, 4th edn, 1968; papers in British Journal of Pharmacol., Journal Physiol., Lancet, British Medical Journal, etc. *Recreations:* bridge, detective stories. *Address:* 2 Brunel House, Cheyne Walk, SW10. *T:* 01-352 8473.

ROBSON, Sir Kenneth, Kt 1968; CBE 1959; FRCP; Hon. Consultant Physician: St George's Hospital, SW1; Brompton Hospital, SW3; King Edward VII Hospital for Officers; King Edward VII Hospital, Midhurst; Confederation Life Insurance Co.; *b* 1909; *y s* of late John Ajmer and Katherine Robson. *Educ:* Bradfield; Christ's College, Cambridge; Middlesex Hospital. Davis and Cree Prizes in Medicine; 2nd Broderip Schol., 1933; qualified, 1933; Resident Posts and Registrarships at Middlesex and Brompton Hospitals. MA, MD, BChir Cantab; MRCP 1935, FRCP 1943; FRCPE 1975. Goulstonian Lectr, RCP, 1944; Examr, 1949-57; Censor, 1959; Registrar, 1961-75. Examr in Med.: Univs Camb., London, Durham. RAFVR Med. Br., 1938; whole time service, 1939-46; Wing Comdr-in-charge of Med. Divs at hosps in England and India; Air Cdre, Consultant-in-Medicine to RAF in India and Far East; Civil Consultant in Medicine, RAF, 1949-77; Hon. Air Cdre, RAF Central Medical Estab., 1977. Toured Medical Estabs for HM Colonial Office in N Caribbean Is and Br Honduras, 1959; Visitor for RCP and RCS to Medical Faculty, Univ. of Khartoum, 1963; RCP Visitor, Australia and New Zealand, 1965, 1975, S Africa, 1969. Chm., Jt Consultants Cttee, 1972-74; Member: Deptl Cttee on Radiological Protection; Defence Med. Services Inquiry Cttee. Mem. Assoc. of Physicians and of Thoracic Society (President 1965; Secretary 1947-60); Hon. Fellow: Amer. Coll. of Physicians; S African Coll. of Physicians; Hon. FRCPI; Hon. FRACP. *Publications:* contributions to text books and various scientific jls mostly in connection with the chest. *Recreation:* pottering about. *Address:* 34 Sydney Street, SW3. *T:* 01-352 3852; Tatham's, Danehill, East Sussex. *Clubs:* Athenæum, Royal Air Force; Crowborough Golf.

ROBSON, Lawrence Fendick; Member, Electricity Council, 1972-76; *b* 23 Jan. 1916; *s* of (William) Bertram Robson and Annie (*née* Fendick); *m* 1945, Lorna Winifred Jagger, Shafton, Yorks; two *s* one *d*. *Educ:* Rotherham Grammar Sch.; Clare Coll., Cambridge (BA). FIEE. North Eastern Electric Supply Co. Ltd, 1937; Royal Corps of Signals, 1939-45; various positions with NE and London Electricity Bds, 1948-65; Commercial Adviser, Electricity Council, 1965-72. *Recreations:* music, open air. *Address:* Millers Hill, Priestman's Lane, Thornton Dale, N Yorks.

ROBSON, Lawrence William, FCA, FCMA, JDipMA; Senior Partner, Robson, Rhodes & Co., 186 City Road, EC1, 1927-75; *b* 8 Aug. 1904; *e s* of late Michael William Robson and of Jane Robson, Norton-on-Tees, Co. Durham; *m* 1940, Inga-Stina Arvidsson (now Baroness Robson of Kiddington, *qv*); one *s* two *d*. *Educ:* Stockton Grammar School. Financial Adviser, UNRRA, 1944-46, and IRO, 1946; Chm. of several engineering cos; Member: Lloyd's; London Transport Executive, 1969-75; Council, Inst. of Chartered Accountants in England and Wales, 1949-69; Anglo-Amer. Productivity Team, 1949; Liberal Party Organisation (Pres., 1953-54); Herbert Cttee of Inquiry into efficiency and organisation of elect. supply industry, 1954-56; Economic Policy Cttee, FBI, 1956-62; Britain in Europe Cttee (Chm. 1958-64); Adv. Cttee on Censuses of Production, 1961-67; British Nat. Cttee of Internat. Council on Combustion Engines (Chm., 1966-); Council, BIM, 1961-71; Council, Inst. Fiscal Studies, 1970-; Anglo-Swedish Soc. (Chm.); European Atlantic Gp (Vice-Pres., 1969-); Council of European Movement, 1969-. Pres., Inst. Cost and Works Accountants, 1950-51; Liveryman, Worshipful Cos of Farmers, Painter-Stainers and Shipwrights. Fellow, Woodard Foundn. *Publications:* papers on accountancy, management, political and economic subjects. *Recreations:* ski-ing, cricket, sailing and shooting. *Address:* Kiddington Hall, Woodstock, Oxon. *T:* Enstone 398. *Club:* Boodle's.

ROBSON, Nigel John; Chairman, Grindlays Bank Ltd, since 1977 (Director, since 1969; Deputy Chairman, 1975-76); Director, Arbuthnot Latham Holdings Ltd, and of other companies; *b* 25 Dec. 1926; *s* of late Col the Hon. Harold Burge Robson, TD, DL, JP, Pinewood Hill, Wormley, Surrey, and Iris Robson (*née* Abel Smith); *m* 1957, Anne Gladstone, *yr d* of late Stephen Deiniol Gladstone and late Clair Gladstone, Edenbridge, Kent; three *s*. *Educ:* Eton. Grenadier Guards, 1945-48. Joined Arbuthnot Latham & Co Ltd, Merchant Bankers, 1949, a Director, 1953, Chm., 1969-75. *Recreations:* tennis, walking, music. *Address:* Pinewood Hill, Wormley, Godalming, Surrey. *Club:* Brooks's.

ROBSON, Sir Thomas (Buston), Kt 1954; MBE 1919; FCA; Partner in Price Waterhouse & Co., Chartered Accountants, 1934-66; Chairman, Renold Ltd, 1967-72; *b* Newcastle upon Tyne, 4 Jan. 1896; *s* of late Thomas Robson, Langholm, Dumfriesshire, and Newcastle upon Tyne; *m* 1936, Roberta Cecilia Helen, *d* of late Rev. Archibald Fleming, DD, St Columba's Church of Scotland, Pont St, SW1; two *d*. *Educ:* Rutherford College, Newcastle upon Tyne; Armstrong Collge, University of Durham. BA Hons, Modern History, 1920; MA 1923. Served European War, 1914-18, with British Salonika Force in Macedonia; Captain RGA; MBE, despatches 1919; articled with Sisson & Allden, Chartered Accountants, Newcastle upon Tyne, 1920; W. B. Peat gold medal in final examination of Inst. Chartered Accountants in England and Wales, 1922; joined staff of Price Waterhouse & Co., London, 1923; ACA, 1923, FCA, 1939; Mem. Council of Inst., 1941-66 (Vice-Pres. 1951-52; Pres., 1952-53); rep. Inst. at overseas mtgs of accountants; FCA (Ont.); CA (Rhodesia). Member: Committee on Amendment of Census of Production Act, Bd of Trade, 1945; Central Valuation Bd for Coal Industry, 1947; Accountancy Advisory Cttee on Companies Act, Bd of Trade, 1948-68 (Chm. 1955-68); Cttee of Inquiry into London Transport Exec., Min. of Transport and Civil Aviation, 1953; Chm. Cttees of Inquiry into Coal Distribution Costs, Min. of Fuel and Power, 1956 and Min. of Commerce, N Ireland, 1956; Mem. Advisory Cttee on Replacement of the "Queen" ships, Min. of Transport and Civil Aviation, 1959; Chm. Economic Development Cttee for Paper and Board Industry under National Economic Development Council, 1964-67. Vice-Pres. Union Européenne des Experts Comptables, Economiques et Financiers, 1963-64; Mem. Transport Tribunal, 1963-69. *Publications:* Garnsey's Holding Companies and their Published Accounts, 3rd edn, 1936; The Construction of Consolidated Accounts, 1936; Consolidated and other Group Accounts, 1st edn, 1946, 4th edn, 1969; numerous papers and addresses on professional subjects. *Recreations:* walking and reading; for many years an active worker in Boy Scout movement (Vice-Pres., Gr London Central Scout Council). *Address:* 23 Brompton Square, SW3 2AD. *T:* 01-589 6553. *Club:* Athenæum.

ROBSON, William Alexander; Professor Emeritus of Public Administration in the University of London (London School of Economics and Political Science) (Professor, 1947-62); Barrister-at-law; Hon. Fellow, London Sch. of Economics; *b* 14 July 1895; *s* of late J. Robson; *m* 1929, Juliette Alvin, *qv*; two *s* one *d*. *Educ:* Univ. of London (London School of Economics and Political Science); BSc (Economics) First Class Honours, 1922; PhD 1924; LLM 1928. Served European War, 1914-18, as

Lieutenant on active service in Royal Flying Corps and RAF; called to Bar, Lincoln's Inn, 1922; Lecturer at the London School of Economics from 1926; Reader in Administrative Law, 1933-46; Visiting Professor, University of Chicago, 1933, University of N Carolina, 1951, University of Patna, 1953, and other Indian Univs, Univ. of California, Berkeley, 1957; Indian Institute of Public Administration, 1960; Internat. Christian Univ., Tokyo, 1969. Principal, Mines Department, 1940-42; Ministry of Fuel and Power, 1942-43; Asst Sec., Air Ministry, 1943-45; Ministry of Civil Aviation, 1945; Member: Council, Town and Country Planning Assoc.; Deptl Cttee on Admin. of Greater London Plan; Cttee on Training in Public Administration for Overseas Countries; Vice-President: Royal Inst. of Public Admin; Political Studies Assoc. Pres., Internat. Political Science Assoc., 1950-53. Chairman, Gr London Gp, LSE. Noranda Lectr, Expo 1967. Founder, 1930, Joint Editor, 1930-75, Chm. Editorial Bd, 1975-, The Political Quarterly. Consultant to Govts of Lebanon, Nigeria, Turkey, Tokyo Metropol. Govt, UNICEF and State Commn for New York City Charter Reform. Hon. Fellow, Jt Univ. Council for Social and Public Administration. Docteur de l'Univ. (hc); Lille, 1953; Grenoble, 1955; Paris, 1955; Algiers, 1959; Hon. DLitt: Dunelm, 1963; Manchester, 1964; Hon. DSocSci, Birmingham, 1970. Publications: From Patronage to Proficiency in the Public Service, 1922; The Relation of Wealth to Welfare, 1924; Justice and Administrative Law, 1928; Civilisation and the Growth of Law, 1935; The Town Councillor (with C. R. Attlee), 1925; contributor to London Essays in Economics, 1927; Modern Theories of Law, 1938; The Development of Local Government, 1931; The Law of Local Government Audit, 1930; A Century of Municipal Progress (contributor and Joint Editor), 1935; The British Civil Servant, (contributor and editor), 1937; Public Enterprise (contributor and editor), 1937; The Government and Misgovernment of London, 1939; The British System of Government, 1940; Social Security (contributor and editor), 1943; Planning and Performance, 1943; Population and the People, 1945; British Government since 1918 (contributor), 1950; Problems of Nationalised Industry, 1952; The Teaching of Political Science (Unesco), 1954; (ed jtly) Great Cities of the World, 1955, repr. 1973; The Civil Service in Britain and France, 1956; Nationalised Industry and Public Ownership, 1960; The Governors and the Governed, 1964; The Heart of Greater London, 1965; Local Government in Crisis, 1966; Politics and Government at Home and Abroad, 1967; (ed with B. Crick) Protest and Discontent, 1970; (ed) The Political Quarterly in the Thirties, 1971; (ed) Man and the Social Sciences, 1972; (ed with B. Crick) Taxation Policy, 1973; Welfare State and Welfare Society, 1976. Editor, Politics Section, Hutchinson University Library. Recreations: walking and swimming. Address: 48 Lanchester Road, N6. T: 01-883 1331. Clubs: Athenæum, Campden Hill Tennis.

ROBSON, Vice-Adm. Sir (William) Geoffrey (Arthur), KBE 1956; CB 1953; DSO 1940 (Bar 1941); DSC 1941; Lieutenant-Governor and Commander-in-Chief of Guernsey, 1958-64; b 10 March 1902; s of Major John Robson; m 1st, 1925, Sylvia Margaret Forrester (d 1968); one s; 2nd, 1969, Elizabeth Kathleen, widow of Lt-Col V. H. Holt. Educ: RN Colleges, Osborne and Dartmouth. Midshipman, HMS Malaya, 1918; served in Destroyers, 1922-37. Commanded Rowena, 1934; Wren, 1935-36; RN Staff Course, 1937; RAF Staff Course, 1938. Served War of 1939-45 (despatches thrice, DSO and Bar, DSC): Comd HMS Kandahar, 1939-41; Combined Operations, 1942-43; Commanded the 26th Destroyer Flotilla, 1944, in HMS Hardy; Captain of Coastal Forces (Nore), 1945; HMS Superb in command, 1945-47; Comd HMS Ganges, 1948-50; President of Admiralty Interview Board, 1950-51; Flag Officer (Flotillas), Home Fleet, 1951-53; Flag Officer, Scotland, 1952-56; Commander-in-Chief, South Atlantic, 1956-58; retd, 1958. Commander of the Order of St Olav (Norway). Recreations: shooting, fishing, and golf. Address: Amat, Ardgay, Ross-shire; Le Paradou, Forest, Guernsey. Club: Army and Navy.

ROBSON, William Michael; Deputy Chairman: The Standard Bank Ltd, since 1965 (Director, since 1960); The Chartered Bank, since 1974; Standard and Chartered Banking Group Ltd, since 1974 (Director, since 1970); Director: Booker McConnell Ltd, since 1955; Antony Gibbs (Insurance Holdings), since 1976; Member of Lloyd's, since 1938; b 31 Dec. 1912; e s of late Col the Hon. Harold Burge Robson, TD, DL, JP, Pinewood Hill, Witley, Surrey and late Ysolt Robson (née Leroy-Lewis); m 1st, 1939, Audrey Isobel Wales (d 1964), d of late Maj. William Dick, Low Gosforth Hall, Northumberland; two s one d; 2nd, 1965, Frances Mary Wyville, d of late James Anderson Ramage Dawson, Balado House, Kinross, and widow of Andrew Alexander Nigel Buchanan (he d 1960). Educ: Eton; New College, Oxford. Served War of 1939-45: with Grenadier Guards (Maj. 1944), England and Europe BAOR. A Vice-Chm.,

Victoria League for Commonwealth Friendship, 1962-65. Director: British South Africa Co., 1961-66 (Vice-Chm., Jt East & Central African Bd, 1956-63); Antony Gibbs & Sons (Insurance) Ltd, 1946-48, 1973-76; Chm., Standard Bank Finance & Develt Corp. Ltd, 1966-73; Mem., BNEC, Africa, 1965- (Dep. Chm., 1970-71). High Sheriff of Kent, 1970. Liveryman, Vintners Co., 1953. Mem. Council of The Shrievalty Assoc., 1971-76. Address: 28 Smith Terrace, Chelsea, SW3. T: 01-352 2177; Hales Place, Tenterden, Kent. T: Tenterden 2932. Clubs: Brooks's, MCC, Overseas Bankers'.

ROBSON-SCOTT, Prof. William Douglas, MA Oxon, DrPhil Vienna; Hon. Director, Institute of Germanic Studies, 1968-73; b 9 Aug. 1901; s of late Thomas William Robson-Scott and Florence Jane (née Lang); m 1947, Elaine Davies; one d. Educ: Rugby Sch.; University Coll., Oxford; Univs of Berlin and Vienna. 1st cl. hons English, Oxon, 1923. Lektor, Univ. of Berlin, 1933-37; seconded to War Office, 1939-45; Birkbeck Coll., Univ. of London: Lectr in German, 1939-61; Reader, 1961-66; Prof. of German Language and Literature, 1966-68, Emer. Prof. 1968. Publications: German Travellers in England 1400-1800, 1953; The Literary Background of the Gothic Revival in Germany, 1965; Goethe and the Visual Arts, 1967; German Romanticism and the Visual Arts, 1970; Goethe and the Art of the Netherlands, 1971; various translations including: (with E. Robson-Scott) Sigmund Freud and Lou Andreas-Salomé: Letters, 1972; various articles in learned jls. Recreations: hill-walking, travel. Address: 19 Dorset Square, NW1. T: 01-262 2877; Southdean Lodge, Hawick, Roxburghshire. T: Bonchester Bridge 656.

ROCH, John Ormond, QC 1976; a Recorder of the Crown Court since 1975; b 19 April 1934; s of Frederick Ormond Roch and Vera Elizabeth (née Chamberlain); m 1967, Anne Elizabeth Greany; three d. Educ: Wrekin Coll.; Clare Coll., Cambridge (BA, LLB). Called to Bar, Gray's Inn, 1961. Recreations: sailing, golf, music. Address: 82 Heath Park Avenue, Cardiff CF4 3RJ. T: Cardiff 754031. Clubs: Pembrokeshire Yacht, Dale Yacht, Cardiff Golf (Cardiff).

ROCH, Muriel Elizabeth Sutcliffe, BA; Headmistress, School of S Mary and S Anne, Abbots Bromley, Staffs, 1953-77; b 7 Sept. 1916; d of late Rev. Sydney John Roch, MA Cantab, Pembroke and Manchester. Educ: Manchester High Sch.; Bedford Coll., London; Hughes Hall, Cambridge. Teaching appointments at: Devonport High School, 1939-41; Lady Manners, Bakewell, 1941-44; Howells School, Denbigh, 1944-47; Talbot Heath, Bournemouth, 1947-53. Recreations: music, travel. Address: Northdown Cottage, Lamphey, Dyfed. T: Lamphey 2577.

ROCHDALE, 1st Viscount cr 1960; 2nd Baron 1913; **John Durival Kemp**, OBE 1945; TD; DL; Deputy Chairman, Williams & Glyn's Bank Ltd, 1973-77 (Director since 1970); Director, National and Commercial Banking Group Ltd, 1971-77; President, North West Industrial Development Association; b 5 June 1906; s of 1st Baron and Lady Beatrice Egerton, 3rd d of 3rd Earl of Ellesmere; S father, 1945; m 1931, Elinor Dorothea Pease (CBE 1964; JP); one s (one d decd). Educ: Eton; Trin. Coll., Cambridge. Hons degree Nat. Science Tripos. Served War of 1939-45 (despatches); attached USA forces in Pacific with rank of Col, 1944; Temp. Brig., 1945. Hon. Col 251 (Westmorland and Cumberland Yeomanry) Field Regiment, RA, TA, late 851 (W&CY) Field Bty, RA, 1959-67. Chairman: Kelsall & Kemp Ltd, 1952-71; Harland & Wolff, 1971-75; Dep. Chm., West Riding Worsted & Woollen Mills, 1969-72; Director: Consett Iron Co. Ltd, 1957-67; Williams Deacon's Bank Ltd, 1960-70. President National Union of Manufacturers, 1953-56; Member, Dollar Exports Council, 1953-61; Western Hemisphere Exports Council, 1961-64; a Gov. of the BBC 1954-59; Pres., British Legion, NW Area, 1955-61; Mem. Central Transport Consultative Cttee for GB, 1953-57; Chairman: Docks and Harbours Committee of Inquiry, 1961; Cotton Board, 1957-62; National Ports Council, 1963-67; Cttee of Inquiry into Shipping, 1967-70. DL Cumberland, 1948. Heir: s Hon. St John Durival Kemp [b 15 Jan. 1938; m 1st, 1960, Serena Jane Clark-Hall (marr. diss. 1974); two s two d; 2nd, 1976, Elizabeth Anderton]. Address: Lingholm, Keswick, Cumbria. T: Keswick 72003. Club: Lansdowne.
See also Sir John D. Barlow, Sir V. B. J. Seely, Duke of Sutherland.

ROCHDALE, Archdeacon of; see Fielding, Ven. H.O.

ROCHE, family name of Baron Fermoy.

ROCHE, Sir David (O'Grady), 5th Bt cr 1838; ACA; Manager, Samuel Montagu & Co. Ltd; b 21 Sept. 1947; s of Sir Standish O'Grady Roche, 4th Bt, DSO, and of Evelyn Laura, d of Major

William Andon; *S* father, 1977; *m* 1971, Hon. (Helen) Alexandra Briscoe Frewen, *d* of 3rd Viscount Selby; one *s* (and one *s* decd). *Educ:* Wellington Coll., Berks; Trinity Coll., Dublin. Qualified as Chartered Accountant with Peat, Marwick, Mitchell & Co., 1974. Freeman of the City of London. *Heir: s* David Alexander O'Grady Roche, *b* 28 Jan. 1976. *Address:* 36 Coniger Road, SW6. *T:* 01-736 0382. *Clubs:* Buck's; Kildare Street and University (Dublin).

ROCHE, Frederick Lloyd; General Manager, Milton Keynes Development Corporation, since 1971; *b* 11 March 1931; *s* of John Francis Roche and Margaret Roche; *m* 1955, Sheila Lindsay; one *s* one *d*. *Educ:* Regent Street Polytechnic. DipArch, ARIBA. Architect (Schools), City of Coventry, 1958-62; Principal Develt Architect, Midlands Housing Consortium, 1962-64; Chief Architect and Planning Officer, Runcorn Develt Corp., 1964-70. Member: Environmental Bd, 1975-; British Urban Development Unit, 1976-; Town and Country Planning Council, 1977-. *Publications:* numerous technical articles. *Recreations:* new towns, sport, reading, people. *Address:* Milton Keynes Development Corporation, Wavendon Tower, Wavendon, Milton Keynes MK17 8LX. *T:* Milton Keynes 74000.

ROCHE, James Michael; Director: General Motors Corporation; Pepsico Inc.; Chicago Board of Trade; New York Stock Exchange; *b* 16 Dec. 1906; *s* of Thomas E. and Gertrude Agnes (Buel) Roche; *m* 1929, Louise McMillan; two *s* one *d*. *Educ:* LaSalle Univ., Chicago. Statistician, Cadillac Motor Car Div., Chicago Sales and Service Br., 1927; Asst to Chicago Br. Man., Cadillac, 1928; Asst Regional Business Man., NY, Cadillac, 1931; Asst Man., Cadillac Business Management Dept, Detroit, 1933; Man., Nat. Business Management, Cadillac, 1935; Dir of Personnel, Cadillac, 1943; Dir of Personnel and Public Relations, Cadillac, 1949; Gen. Sales Man., Cadillac, 1950; Gen. Man. of Cadillac, 1957; General Motors Corporation: Vice-Pres., 1957; Vice-Pres., Distribution Staff, 1960; Exec. Vice-Pres., 1962; Pres. and Chief Operating Off., 1965; Chm. and Chief Exec. Officer, 1967-71. Hon. Dr of Laws: John Carrol Univ., Ohio, 1963; Fordham Univ., NY, 1966; Michigan State Univ., 1968; Eastern Michigan Univ., 1969; Hon. Dr of Science, Judson Coll., Ill, 1965; Hon. Dr of Commercial Science Niagara Univ., 1972. Kt of Malta (Amer. Chapter), 1951. *Recreations:* music, reading, fishing. *Address:* 425 Dunston Road, Bloomfield Hills, Michigan 48013, USA. *Clubs:* Detroit, Economic (Detroit); Links, University, Economic (NY); Detroit Athletic, Orchard Lake Country, Bloomfield Hills Country.

ROCHE, Hon. Thomas Gabriel, QC 1955; Recorder of the City of Worcester, 1959-71; *b* 1909; *yr s* of late Baron Roche, PC. *Educ:* Rugby; Wadham Coll., Oxford. Called to the Bar, Inner Temple, 1932. Served War of 1939-45 (Lt-Col 1944, despatches). Church Commissioner, 1961-65; Member, Monopolies Commission, 1966-69. *Address:* Chadlington, Oxford. *Club:* United Oxford & Cambridge University.

ROCHESTER, 2nd Baron, of the 4th creation, *cr* 1931, of Rochester in the County of Kent; **Foster Charles Lowry Lamb;** Pro-Chancellor, University of Keele, since 1976; *b* 7 June 1916; *s* of 1st Baron Rochester, CMG, and Rosa Dorothea, *y d* of late W. J. Hurst, JP, Drumaness, County Down; *S* father 1955; *m* 1942, Mary Carlisle, *yr d* of T. B. Wheeler, CBE, Hartford, Cheshire; two *s* one *d* (and one *d* decd). *Educ:* Mill Hill; Jesus College, Cambridge. Served War of 1939-45: Captain 23rd Hussars; France, 1944. Personnel Manager, Mond Div., ICI Ltd, 1964-72. Chairman: Cheshire Scout Assoc.; Governors of Chester Coll., 1974; Vale Royal Dist Manpower Cttee, 1975-. *Heir: s* Hon. David Charles Lamb [*b* 8 Sept. 1944; *m* 1969, Jacqueline Stamp; two *s*. *Educ:* Shrewsbury Sch.; Univ. of Sussex]. *Address:* The Hollies, Hartford, Northwich, Cheshire. *T:* Northwich 74733. *Club:* Reform.
See also Hon. K. H. L. Lamb.

ROCHESTER, Bishop of, since 1961; **Rt. Rev. Richard David Say,** DD (Lambeth) 1961; High Almoner to HM the Queen, since 1970; *b* 4 Oct. 1914; *s* of Commander Richard Say, OBE, RNVR, and Kathleen Mary (*née* Wildy); *m* 1943, Irene Frances (JP), *e d* of Seaburne and Frances Rayner, Exeter; one *s* two *d* (and one *s* decd). *Educ:* University Coll. Sch.; Christ's College, Cambridge (MA); Ridley Hall, Cambridge. Ordained deacon, 1939; priest, 1940. Curate of Croydon Parish Church, 1939-43; Curate of St Martin-in-the-Fields, London, 1943-50; Asst Sec. Church of England Youth Council, 1942-44; Gen. Sec., 1944-47; Gen. Sec. British Council of Churches, 1947-55; Church of England delegate to World Council of Churches, 1948, 1954 and 1961. Select Preacher, University of Cambridge, 1954 and University of Oxford, 1963; Rector of Bishop's Hatfield, 1955-61; Hon. Canon of St Albans, 1957-61. Domestic Chaplain to

Marquess of Salisbury and Chaplain of Welfield Hospital, 1955-61; Hon. Chaplain of The Pilgrims, 1968-. Entered House of Lords, 1969. Chaplain and Sub-Prelate, Order of St John. Freeman of City of London, 1953. Hon. Mem., Smeatonian Soc., 1977. *Recreations:* sailing and travel. *Address:* Bishopscourt, Rochester ME1 1TS. *T:* Medway 42721. *Club:* United Oxford & Cambridge University.

ROCHESTER, Archdeacon of; *see* Palmer, Ven. D. G.

ROCHESTER, Prof. George Dixon, FRS 1958; FInstP; Professor of Physics, University of Durham, 1955-73, now Professor Emeritus; *b* 4 Feb. 1908; *s* of Thomas and Ellen Rochester; *m* 1938, Idaline, *o d* of Rev. J. B. Bayliffe; one *s* one *d*. *Educ:* Wallsend Grammar School; Universities of Durham, Stockholm and California. BSc, MSc, PhD (Dunelm). Earl Grey Memorial Scholar, Armstrong College, Durham University, 1926-29; Earl Grey Fellow, at Stockholm Univ., 1934-35; Commonwealth Fund Fellow at California Univ., 1935-37; Manchester University: Asst Lectr, 1937-46; Lectr, 1946-49; Sen. Lectr, 1949-53; Reader, 1953-55. Scientific Adviser in Civil Defence for NW Region, 1952-55. C. V. Boys Prizeman of the Physical Society of London, 1956; Symons Memorial Lecturer of the Royal Meteorological Soc., 1962. Member: Council CNAA, 1964-74; Council, British Assoc. for Advancement of Science, 1971-72; Council, Royal Soc., 1972-74; Chm., NE Branch, Inst. of Physics, 1972-74. Second Pro-Vice-Chancellor, Univ. of Durham, 1967-69, Pro-Vice-Chancellor, 1969-70. Hon. DSc: Newcastle upon Tyne, 1973; CNAA, 1975. *Publications:* (with J. G. Wilson) Cloud Chamber Photographs of the Cosmic Radiation, 1952; scientific papers on cosmic rays and spectroscopy. *Recreations:* gardening, travel. *Address:* 18 Dryburn Road, Durham DH1 5AJ. *T:* Durham 64796.

ROCHETA, Dr Manuel Farrajota; Military Order of Christ of Portugal; Ambassador for Portugal in Madrid, 1968-74, retired; *b* 6 Aug. 1906; *s* of Manuel and Rosa Rocheta; *m* 1933, Maria Luiza Belmarco Rocheta; one *d*. *Educ:* Lisbon University. Entered Diplomatic Service, 1931; Assistant Consul Hamburg, 1934; Consul Copenhagen, 1935-39; First Sec. and Chargé d'Affaires *ai*, Bucarest, 1943-45; First Sec. and Chargé d'Affaires *ai*, Dublin, 1945; First Secretary, Washington, 1946, Counsellor, 1947, Minister-Counsellor, 1950 (Chargé d'Affaires, 1 Nov. 1946-31 March 1947 and 11 Feb. 1950-6 June 1950); Asst Dir-Gen. of Political Dept, Foreign Affairs Ministry, Lisbon, 1951; Minister-Plen. and Dir-Gen. of Political Dept, Foreign Ministry, Lisbon, 1954; Minister in Bonn, 1956, Ambassador, 1956-58; Ambassador: to Rio de Janeiro, 1958-61; to the Court of St James's, 1961-68. Doctor in Law, Univ. of Bahia, Brazil. Knight Grand Cross of Royal Victorian Order, Gt Brit. (Hon. GCVO) 1955, and holds Grand Cross of several foreign orders. *Recreations:* walking and swimming. *Address:* c/o Ministry of Foreign Affairs, Lisbon, Portugal.

ROCHFORD, James Donald Henry; Admiralty Registrar of the Supreme Court, since 1973; Barrister-at-Law; *b* 8 July 1921; *e s* of Leonard Henry Rochford, DSC, DFC; *m* 1953, Elizabeth Mary Beverley Robinson, *d* of late Lt-Col B. B. Robinson, DSO; two *s* one *d*. *Educ:* Douai Sch., Woolhampton, Berks. Served War: Royal Navy and RNVR, 1940-47. Called to Bar, Inner Temple, 1951. *Recreation:* messing about in boats. *Address:* Studland, Stockcroft Road, Balcombe, West Sussex. *T:* Balcombe 321.

ROCHFORT, Sir C. C. B.; *see* Boyd-Rochfort.

ROCKE, John Roy Mansfield; Vice-Chairman, J. Bibby & Sons; Director, Czarnikow Group; *b* 13 April 1918; *s* of late Frederick Gilbert Rocke and late Mary Susan Rocke; *m* 1948, Pauline Diane Berry; no *c*. *Educ:* Charterhouse; Trinity Coll., Cambridge (BA). War Service, Grenadier Guards, 1940-46 (Maj.). Orme & Eykyn (Stockbrokers), 1946-50; Booker McConnell Ltd, 1950-70, Dir, 1954, Vice-Chm., 1962-70. Mem., BNEC, and Chm., BNEC (Caribbean), 1965-68; Chm., Nat. Econ. Development Cttee for the Food Manufacturing Industry, 1967-71. *Address:* 22 Bruton Street, W1. *T:* 01-629 3393; Pendomer Manor, Pendomer, near Yeovil, Somerset.

ROCKEFELLER, David; banker; *b* New York City, 12 June 1915; *s* of John Davison and Abby Greene (Aldrich) Rockefeller; *m* 1940, Margaret, *d* of Francis Sims McGrath, Mount Kisco, NY; two *s* four *d*. *Educ:* Lincoln School of Columbia University's Teachers College; Harvard Univ. (BS); London School of Economics; Univ. of Chicago (PhD). Asst Regional Dir, US Office of Defense Health and Welfare Services, 1941. Served in US Army, N Africa and France, 1942-45 (Captain). Joined Chase National Bank, NYC, 1946; Asst Manager, Foreign Dept, 1946-47; Asst Cashier, 1947-48; Second

Vice-Pres., 1948-49; Vice-Pres., 1949-51; Senior Vice-Pres., 1951-55; Exec. Vice-Pres., Chase Manhattan Bank (formed by merging Chase Nat. Bank and Bank of Manhattan Co.), 1955-57; Dir, 1955-; Vice-Chm., 1957-61; Pres. and Chm., Exec. Cttee, 1961-69; Chm., Chase Internat. Investment Corp., 1961-. Trustee: Rockefeller Brothers Fund Inc. (Vice-Chm., 1968-); Rockefeller Family Fund; Univ. of Chicago, 1947-62, Life Trustee, 1966; Carnegie Endowment for Internat. Peace, 1947-60; John F. Kennedy Library; Council of the Americas (Chm., 1965-70); Chairman: Council on Foreign Relations; Downtown-Lower Manhattan Assoc., Inc.; Bd of Trustees: Museum of Modern Art; Rockefeller Univ.; Director: Internat. Exec. Service Corps (Chm., 1964-68); NY Clearing House; Rockefeller Center Inc.; Center for Inter-Amer. Relations (Chm., 1966-70); Overseas Devlt Council; Member: The Business Council; Steering Cttee, Nat. Urban Coalition; Conf. Bd, Sen. Exec. Council; Fed. Adv. Bd for 2nd Fed. Reserve Dist; Hon. Mem., Commn on White House Fellows, 1964-65. Director: Morningside Heights, 1947-70 (Pres., 1947-57, Chm., 1957-65); Internat. House, NY, 1940-63; Equitable Life Assce Soc. of US, 1960-65; B. F. Goodrich Co., 1956-64. Member: Harvard Coll. Bd of Overseers, 1954-60, 1962-68; Urban Develt Corp., NY State, Business Adv. Council, 1968-72; US Adv. Cttee on reform of Internat. Monetary System, 1973-. World Brotherhood Award, Jewish Theol Seminary, 1953; Gold Medal, Nat. Inst. Social Sciences, 1967; NYC Planning Medal, Amer. Inst. Architects, 1968; C. Walter Nichols Award, NY Univ., 1970; Reg. Planning Assoc. Award, 1971. Hon. LLD: Columbia Univ., 1954; Bowdoin Coll., 1958; Jewish Theol Seminary, 1958; Williams Coll., 1966; Wagner Coll., 1967; Harvard, 1969; Pace Coll., 1970; St John's Univ., 1971. Holds civic awards and numerous foreign orders, incl. Officer, Legion of Honour, 1955. *Publications:* Unused Resources and Economic Waste, 1940; Creative Management in Banking, 1964. *Recreation:* sailing. *Address:* 1 Chase Manhattan Plaza, New York, NY 10015, USA. *Clubs:* Century, Harvard, Knickerbocker, Links, University (New York); New York Yacht.
See also John D. Rockefeller, L. S. Rockefeller, N. A. Rockefeller.

ROCKEFELLER, James Stillman; Director, First National City Trust Co. (Bahamas) Ltd; Vice-President and Director, Indian Spring Land Co.; Director: Pan-American World Airways; Cranston (RI) Print Works Co.; *b* New York, 8 June 1902; *s* of William Goodsell Rockefeller and Elsie (*née* Stillman); *m* 1925, Nancy Carnegie; two *s* two *d. Educ:* Yale University (BA). With Brown Bros & Co., NYC, 1924-30; joined National City Bank of New York (later First Nat. City Bank), 1930; Asst Cashier, 1931; Asst Vice-Pres. 1933; Vice-Pres., 1940-48; Sen. Vice-Pres., 1948-52; Exec. Vice-Pres., 1952; Pres. and Director, 1952-59; Chairman, 1959-67. Rep. Greenwich (Conn.) Town Meeting, 1933-42. Served as Lieutenant-Colonel in US Army, 1942-46. Member Board of Managers, Memorial Hospital for Cancer and Allied Diseases, NY; Trustee of Estate of William Rockefeller; Trustee American Museum of National History. *Address:* First National City Bank, 399 Park Avenue, New York, NY 10022, USA. *Clubs:* Links, Down Town Assoc., Union League, University (New York); Metropolitan (Washington, DC); Field (Greenwich, Conn).

ROCKEFELLER, John Davison, 3rd, OBE (Hon.) 1948; Hon. Chairman, Rockefeller Foundation, (Chairman, 1952-71, Trustee, 1931-71); Chairman, Commission on Population Growth and the American Future, 1970-72; *b* 21 March 1906; *s* of late John Davison Rockefeller, Jr, FRS, and Abby Greene Aldrich; *m* 1932, Blanchette Ferry Hooker; one *s* three *d. Educ:* Loomis School, Windsor, Conn.; Princeton Univ., Princeton, NJ (BS). Lt-Comdr, USNR, working with Combined Civil Affairs Cttee and State-War-Navy Co-ordinating Cttee, 1942-45. Consultant to the Dulles Mission to Japan on Peace Settlement, 1951; Adviser, US Delegation, Japanese Peace Treaty Conf., San Francisco, 1951. Established Rockefeller Public Service Awards, 1952. Chairman: Nat. Policy Panel on World Population and Quality of Human Develt; Population Council (founder); Greater New York Fund Campaign, 1949; Agricultural Development Council (founder); Asia Soc. (founder); Japan Soc. (Pres. 1952-70); President: The JDR 3rd Fund (founder); Amer. Youth Hostels, 1948-51. Trustee: Rockefeller Brothers Fund (Pres., 1940-56; Chm., Performing Arts Panel, 1963-65); Rockefeller Family Fund, 1967-; Princeton Univ. (emeritus); United Negro College Fund (Hon. Chm., 1965-69; Chm., Nat. Council, 1958-65); Colonial Williamsburg Inc., 1934-54 (Chm., 1939-53); Educational Broadcasting Corp., 1962-64; General Education Bd, 1932-71 (Chm., 1952-71); Internat. House, NYC, 1930-49; Lincoln Center for the Performing Arts (Hon. Chm., Chm., 1961-70); Riverside Church, 1930-49, now Hon. Trustee; Rockefeller Inst. (now Rockefeller Univ.), 1932-49. Director: Phelps Meml Hosp., 1935-68; Foreign Policy Assoc., 1954-61;

NY Life Ins. Co., 1949-59; Rockefeller Center Inc., 1932-63. Special Tony Award, American Theater Wing, 1960; Lasker Award in Planned Parenthood, 1961; Gold Baton Award, Amer. Symphony Orch. League, 1963; Handel Medallion, NYC, 1964; Silver Plaque, Fedn of Jewish Philanthropies of NY, 1964; Presidential Citation, 1967 (for Rockefeller Public Service Awards); Margaret Sanger Award for Public Service in Family Planning, 1967; Gold Medal, Nat. Inst. of Social Sciences, 1967; Soc. for the Family of Man Award, Protestant Council, 1968. Grand Cordon, Order of Sacred Treasure, Japan, 1954; Most Noble Order of the Crown of Thailand, 1st cl, 1960; Order of Sikatuna, Philippines, 1967; Grand Cordon, Order of Rising Sun, Japan, 1968. *Recreations:* riding, golf, sailing. *Address:* 30 Rockefeller Plaza, New York City 10020. *Clubs:* Century Association, University (New York); Metropolitan (Washington, DC).
See also David Rockefeller, L. S. Rockefeller, N. A. Rockefeller.

ROCKEFELLER, Laurance Spelman, OBE (Hon.) 1971; conservationist and business executive; Director, Rockefeller Center Inc. (Chairman, 1953-56, 1958-66); *b* New York, 26 May 1910; *s* of John Davison Rockefeller, Jr, FRS and Abby Greene Aldrich; *m* 1934, Mary French; one *s* three *d. Educ:* Lincoln School of Teachers College; Princeton University (BA). War service, Lt-Comdr, USNR, 1942-45. Chairman: Citizens' Adv. Cttee on Environmental Quality; Meml Sloan-Kettering Cancer Center; NY Zool Soc.; Caneel Bay Plantation Inc.; New York State Council of Parks and Recreation; Rockefeller Bros Fund; President: Amer. Conservation Assoc.; Jackson Hole Preserve, Inc.; Palisades Interstate Park Commn; Charter Trustee: Princeton Univ.; Alfred P. Sloan Foundn; Sealantic Fund; Greenacre Foundn; Nat. Geog. Soc.; NY State Bd for Historic Preservation; Nat. Park Foundn; Life Mem., Mass Inst. of Technology; Dir, Community Blood Council of Gtr NY; Mem., Nat. Cancer Adv. Bd; Chairman: Outdoor Recreation Resources Review Commn, 1958-65; Hudson River Valley Commn, 1956-66; 1965 White House Conf. on Nat. Beauty; Delegate UN Conf. on Human Environment, 1972. Holds numerous awards, medals and hon. degrees. Comdr, Royal Order of the Lion, Belgium, 1950; US Medal of Freedom, 1969. *Address:* Room 5600, 30 Rockefeller Plaza, New York, NY 10020, USA. *Clubs:* Boone and Crockett, River, Princeton, Downtown Association, Brook, New York Yacht, Links, Knickerbocker (New York City); Cosmos, Metropolitan (Washington, DC).
See also David Rockefeller, John D. Rockefeller, N. A. Rockefeller.

ROCKEFELLER, Nelson Aldrich; Vice-President of the United States of America, 1974-77; *b* 8 July 1908; *s* of late John D. Rockefeller, Jr, and Abby Greene Aldrich; *m* 1st, 1930, Mary Todhunter Clark (marr. diss. 1962); two *s* two *d* (and one *s* decd); 2nd, 1963, Margaretta Fitler Murphy; two *s. Educ:* Dartmouth College (AB). Rockefeller Center, Inc.: Director, 1931-58; Pres., 1938-45, 1948-51; Chm., 1945-53 and 1956-58; Rockefeller Brothers Fund, Inc.: Pres., 1956-58; Trustee, 1940-; Museum of Modern Art (NY City): Pres., 1939-41, 1946-53; Chm., 1957-58; Trustee, 1932-. Co-ordinator of Inter-American Affairs, 1940-44; Asst Sec. of State, for Amer. Republic's Affairs, 1944-45; Chairman: Internat. Basic Economy Corp., 1958 (Pres., 1947-53, 1956-58, Dir, 1947-53, 1956-58); Internat. Develt Adv. Bd, 1950-51; Govt Affairs Foundn Inc., 1953-58 (founder); Mem., President's Advisory Cttee on Govt Organization, 1953-58; Under Secretary, Department of Health, Education and Welfare, USA, 1953-54; Special Assistant to the President, USA, 1954-55. Governor, New York State, 1958-Dec. 1973, resigned. Mem. President's Adv. Commn on Intergovernmental Relations, 1965-69. Museum of Primitive Art (NY City): Founder and Pres., 1954-, Trustee, 1954-. Holds numerous awards and medals incl. Gold Medal, Nat. Inst. of Social Sciences, 1967. Holds various Hon. Degrees in Law and Humane Letters, Awards (US) incl. Medal of Freedom, 1977, also Foreign Orders. Citation by Nat. Conf. of Christians and Jews for work in field of human relations, 1948; Thomas F. Cunningham Award for contrib. toward betterment of Inter-American Relations, 1964. *Publications:* The Future of Federalism, 1962; Unity, Freedom and Peace, 1968; Our Environment Can Be Saved, 1970. *Address:* Pocantico Hills, North Tarrytown, NY 10591, USA. *Clubs:* Century Association, Dartmouth (NY); Cosmos (Washington, DC).
See also David Rockefeller, John D. Rockefeller, L. S. Rockefeller.

ROCKHAMPTON, Bishop of, since 1971; **Rt. Rev. John Basil Rowland Grindrod;** *b* 14 Dec. 1919; *s* of Edward Basil and Dorothy Gladys Grindrod; *m* 1949, Ailsa W., *d* of G. Newman; two *d. Educ:* Repton School; Queen's College, Oxford; Lincoln

Theological College. BA 1949; MA 1953. Deacon, 1951; Priest, 1952, Manchester. Curate: St Michael's, Hulme, 1951-54; Bundaberg, Qld, 1954-56; Rector: All Souls, Ancoats, Manchester, 1956-60; Emerald, Qld, 1960-61; St Barnabas, N Rockhampton, Qld, 1961-65; Archdeacon of Rockhampton, Qld, 1960-65; Vicar, Christ Church, S Yarra, Vic, 1965-66; Bishop of Riverina, NSW, 1966-71. *Address:* Lis Escop, 12 Athelstane Street, Rockhampton, Queensland 4700, Australia.

ROCKLEY, 3rd Baron *cr* 1934; **James Hugh Cecil;** Director, Kleinwort Benson Ltd, since 1970; *b* 5 April 1934; *s* of 2nd Baron Rockley, and of Anne Margaret, *d* of late Adm. Hon. Sir Herbert Meade-Featherstonhaugh, GCVO, CB, DSO; *S* father, 1976; *m* 1958, Lady Sarah Primrose Beatrix, *e d* of 7th Earl Cadogan, *qv*; one *s* two *d*. *Educ:* Eton; New Coll., Oxford. Wood Gundy & Co. Ltd, 1957-62; Kleinwort Benson Ltd, 1963-. *Heir: s* Hon. Anthony Robert Cecil, *b* 29 July 1961. *Address:* Lytchett Heath, Poole, Dorset. *T:* Lytchett Minster 2228.

ROCKSAVAGE, Earl of; **David George Philip Cholmondeley;** *b* 27 June 1960; *s* and *heir* of 6th Marquess of Cholmondeley, *qv*.

RODD, family name of **Baron Rennell.**

RODDAN, **Gilbert** **McMicking,** CMG 1957; Deputy Agricultural Adviser, Department of Technical Co-operation, 1961 (to Secretary of State for Colonies, 1956); retired 1965; *b* 13 May 1906; *m* 1934, Olive Mary Wetherill; two *d*. *Educ:* Dumfries Academy; Glasgow and Oxford Universities; Imperial College of Tropical Agriculture, Trinidad. Colonial Service, 1930-56. *Address:* Wayland, Edinburgh Road, Peebles. *Club:* Royal Commonwealth Society.

RODEN, 9th Earl of, *cr* 1771; **Robert William Jocelyn;** Baron Newport, 1743; Viscount Jocelyn, 1755; a baronet of England, 1665; Captain Royal Navy; retired; *b* 4 Dec. 1909; *S* father 1956; *m* 1937, Clodagh, *d* of late Edward Kennedy, Bishopscourt, Co. Kildare; three *s*. Retired 1960. *Heir: s* Viscount Jocelyn, *qv*. *Address:* Bryansford, Co. Down. *T:* Newcastle 23469.

RODERICK, **Caerwyn Eifion;** MP (Lab) Brecon and Radnor since 1970; *b* 15 July 1927; *m* 1952, Eirlys Mary Lewis; one *s* two *d*. *Educ:* Maes-y-Dderwen County Sch., Ystradgynlais; University Coll. of North Wales, Bangor. Asst Master, Caterham Sch., Surrey, 1949-52; Sen. Master, Chartesey Sch., LCC, 1952-54; Sen. Maths Master, Boys' Grammar Sch., Brecon, 1954-57; Method Study Engineer, NCB, 1957-60; Sen. Maths Master, Hartridge High Sch., Newport, Mon, 1960-69; Lecturer, Coll. of Educn, Cardiff, 1969-70. PPS to Rt Hon. Michael Foot; Mem., Public Accounts Cttee. *Address:* House of Commons, SW1; 29 Charlotte Square, Rhiwbina, Cardiff. *T:* Cardiff 68269.

RODERICK, **Rev.** **Charles Edward Morys;** Chaplain to the Queen since 1962; Rector of Longparish and Hurstbourne Priors, since 1971; *b* 18 June 1910; *s* of Edward Thomas and Marion Petronella Roderick; *m* 1940, Betty Margaret Arrowsmith; two *s*. *Educ:* Christ's College, Brecon; Trinity College, Oxford (MA). Schoolmaster, 1932-38; training for ordination, 1938-39; ordained, 1939; Curate, St Luke's Parish Church of Chelsea, 1939-46; Chaplain to the Forces, 1940-45; Rector of Denham, Bucks, 1946-53. Vicar of St Michael's, Chester Square, London, 1953-71. HCF. *Address:* Longparish Rectory, Andover, Hants. *T:* Longparish 215.

RODGER, **Prof. Alec, (Thomas Alexander),** MA Cantab, FBPsS; Professor of Occupational Psychology, University of London, 1960-75 (Reader in Psychology, 1948-60); now Emeritus Professor; Director, Manpower Analysis and Planning Ltd, since 1971; *b* 22 Nov. 1907; *e s* of late T. Ritchie Rodger, OBE; unmarried. *Educ:* Scarborough College; Gonville and Caius College, Cambridge (Yatman Exhibitioner). Nat. Inst. Industrial Psychology, 1929-47 (Head of Vocational Guidance Dept 1936-47; concurrently Psychologist, WO, 1940-41, and Senior Psychologist to the Admlty, 1941-47). (Estab.) Sen. Psychologist to Admlty, 1947-48, and first Member of Civil Service Psychologist Class. Mem. Psychology Cttee, MRC, 1946-56; Mem. Human Factors Panel, Govt Cttee on Industrial Productivity, 1948-51; Editor, Occupational Psychology, 1948-68; Adviser, Min. of Labour, 1948-68; Chm. Working Party on Personnel Selection Methods, Min. of Defence, 1950-51; Mem., Min. of Health's Adv. Cttee for Management Efficiency in the NHS, 1964-66. Vis. Lectr, Dept of Engrg Prodn, Univ. of Birmingham, 1951-68; Nuffield Res. Fellow, 1974-75. Chm., Psychology Bd, CNAA, 1968-73. Gen. Sec., British Psychological Soc., 1948-54, Pres. 1957-58; Pres. Section J. British Association, 1955; Founder-Dir, MSL Group, 1956-70.

Fellow, Amer. Psychological Association, 1968. *Publications:* A Borstal Experiment in Vocational Guidance, 1937; Occupational Versatility and Planned Procrastination, 1961; Seventh C. S. Myers Memorial Lecture, 1970; (with P. Cavanagh) OECD Report on Occupational Guidance, 1970; (with T. Morgan and D. Guest) The Industrial Training Officer, 1971; contrib. to Chambers's Encyclopædia; The Study of Society; Current Trends in British Psychology; Society, Problems and Methods of Study; Educational and Occupational Selection in West Africa; Readings in Psychology; Recruitment Handbook; and to various periodicals. *Recreations:* music, motoring abroad. *Address:* 3 Prior Bolton Street, N1. *Club:* Royal Automobile.

RODGER, **Allan George,** OBE 1944; Under-Secretary, Scottish Education Department, 1959-63, retired; *b* Kirkcaldy, 7 Jan. 1902; *s* of Allan Rodger, Schoolmaster, and Annie Venters; *m* 1930, Barbara Melville Simpson; one *s* one *d*. *Educ:* Pathhead Primary School, Kirkcaldy; Kirkcaldy High School; Edinburgh University (MA (Hons) Maths, BSc, MEd, Dip Geog). Teacher, Viewforth School, Kirkcaldy, 1926-29; Lecturer, Moray House Training Coll. and Univ. Dept of Educ. (Edinburgh), 1929-35; HM Inspector of Schools, 1935-45, with special duties in regard to geography, special schools, and training colleges (seconded to special administrative duties in Education Dept, 1939-45); Asst Secretary, Scottish Educ. Dept, 1945-59. Served on Educational Commission for Govts of Uganda and Kenya, 1961. Chairman of various Govt Cttees on Scottish Educ. matters. *Publications:* contrib. to Jl of Educational Psychology and other educational journals. *Recreations:* reading, music, gardening. *Address:* 72 Duddingston Road West, Edinburgh EH15 3PT. *T:* 031-661 1746.

RODGER, **Rt. Rev. Patrick Campbell;** see Manchester, Bishop of.

RODGER, **Thomas Ferguson,** CBE 1967; FRCPGlas, FRCPEd, FRCPsych; Professor of Psychological Medicine, University of Glasgow, 1948-73; Consulting Psychiatrist, Western Infirmary and Southern General Hospital, Glasgow; Hon. Consulting Psychiatrist to the Army in Scotland; External Examiner, Edinburgh and Leeds Universities; *b* 4 Nov. 1907; *m* 1934, Jean Chalmers; two *s* one *d*. *Educ:* North Kelvinside School, Glasgow; Glasgow University. BSc, 1927; MB, ChB, with Commendation, 1929; MRCP Ed., 1939; FRCP Ed., 1947, Glas. 1962; FRFPSG 1958; FBPsS; FRCPsych, 1971, Hon. Fellow 1972. Past Pres., Royal Medico-Psychological Assoc. Asst, Dept of Psychiatry, Johns Hopkins Univ., Baltimore, 1931-32; Dep. Superintendent, Glasgow Roy. Mental Hosp., and Assistant Lecturer in Psychiatry, Glasgow Univ., 1933-40; War of 1939-45: Specialist in Psychiatry, RAMC, 1940-44; Consultant in Psychiatry, Army Medical Services, SEAC and India, 1944-45; Commissioner, General Board of Control for Scotland, 1945-48. *Publications:* (jointly) Notes on Psychological Medicine, 1962; Psychology in Relation to Medicine, 1963; articles in medical journals on psychiatric subjects. *Address:* 25 Campbell Drive, Bearsden, Glasgow. *T:* 041-942 3101.

RODGERS, **Mrs Barbara Noel,** OBE 1975; Hon. Fellow, Centre for Studies in Social Policy, since 1973; *b* 1912; *d* of F. S. Stancliffe, Wilmslow, Cheshire; *m* 1950, Brian Rodgers; no *c*. *Educ:* Wycombe Abbey Sch.; (Exhibitioner) Somerville Coll., Oxford (MA). Social work and travel, 1935-39; Jt appt with Manch. and Salford Council of Social Service and Manchester Univ. (practical work Tutor and special Lectr), 1939-45. Lectr 1945, Sen. Lectr, 1955, and Reader, 1965-73, Manchester Univ.; Teaching Fellowship in Grad. Sch. of Social Work, Toronto Univ., 1948-49. Member: various wages councils, 1950-; National Assistance Bd, 1965; Supplementary Benefits Commn, 1966-76; Industrial Tribunal Panel; Adv. Cttee on Rent Rebates and Rent Allowances. Served and serving on numerous voluntary welfare organisations. *Publications:* (co-author) Till We Build Again, 1948; (with Julia Dixon) Portrait of Social Work, 1960; A Follow Up Study of Manchester Social Administration Students, 1940-60, 1963; Careers of Social Studies Graduates, 1964; (co-author) Comparative Social Administration, 1968; (with June Stevenson) A New Portrait of Social Work, 1973; chapter on Comparative Studies in Social Administration, in Foundations of Social Administration (ed H. Heisler), 1977; numerous articles in learned jls mainly on social security and social services in America, France and Canada. *Recreations:* walking, bird watching, travel. *Address:* The Old Vicarage, Goostrey, Crewe, Cheshire. *T:* Holmes Chapel 2397.

RODGERS, **George;** MP (Lab) Chorley since Feb. 1974; *b* 7 Nov. 1925; *s* of George and Lettitia Georgina Rodgers; *m* 1952, Joan, *d* of James Patrick and Elizabeth Graham; one *s* two *d*. *Educ:* St Margaret's and Holy Trinity, Liverpool; St Michael's, Sylvester,

Rupert Road and Longview, Huyton. Co-operative Soc., Whiston, Lancs, 1939-43. Served War, RN, 1943-46 (War Medals, France, Germany Star). White's, Engrs, Widnes, 1946-50; with Civil Engineers: Eave's, Blackpool, 1950-53; Costain, Liverpool, 1953-54; Brit. Insulated Callender Cables, 1954-74. Mem., Huyton UDC, 1964-74 (Chm., Educn Cttee, 1969-73; Chm., Local Authority, 1973-74); Mem. Liverpool Regional Hosp. Bd, 1967-74; Chm., NW Region Labour MPs. *Recreations:* cycling, political history, amateur boxing (spectator). *Address:* 32 Willoughby Road, Huyton, Liverpool L14 6XB. *T:* 051-489 1913. *Club:* Labour (Huyton).

RODGERS, Gerald Fleming; *b* 22 Sept. 1917; *s* of Thomas Fleming Rodgers and Mary Elizabeth (*née* Gillespie); *m* 1965, Helen Lucy, *y d* of late Dr Wall, Coleshill; two *s*. *Educ:* Rugby; Queens' Coll., Cambridge. Served War of 1939-45, Army, 1939-46. Foreign (subseq. Diplomatic) Service, 1947; served at: Jedda, 1947-49; British Middle East Office, Cairo and Fayid, 1949-53; FO, 1953-59; Peking, 1959-61; UK Delegation to OECD, 1961-64; Djakarta, 1964-65; Counsellor, Paris, 1965-67. *Address:* Laurelcroft, North Street, Kilsby, Rugby, Warwickshire. *T:* Crick 822314.

RODGERS, Prof. Harold William, OBE 1943; FRCS 1933; Professor of Surgery and Head of Division of Hospital Care, University of Ife, Nigeria, 1974-77, retired; *b* 1 Dec. 1907; *s* of Major R. T. Rodgers; *m* 1938, Margaret Boycott; one *s* three *d*. *Educ:* King's College School; St Bartholomew's Hospital. St Bartholomew's Hospital: House Surgeon, Demonstrator in Anatomy, Chief Asst, Casualty Surgeon, Senior Asst Surgeon. Served War of 1939-45, RAMC, North Africa, Italy, France; Hon. Lieut-Col. Prof. of Surgery, Queen's Univ. of Belfast, 1947-73, Professor Emeritus, 1973. Nuffield Medical Visitor to African Territories; WHO Vis. Prof. to India; Fellow Roy. Institute of International Affairs; Vice-Pres. Intervarsity Fellowship; FRC Soc.; Past Pres., Section of Surgery, RSM; Past President: British Society of Gastro-enterology; Christian Medical Fellowship; British Surgical Research Soc.; Past Chairman, Ct of Examiners of RCS; President: YMCA (Belfast); Hibernian CMS. District Surgeon, St John's Ambulance Brigade. OStJ 1968. *Publications:* Gastroscopy, 1937; general articles in surgical and medical journals. *Recreations:* painting, travel. *Address:* 47 Fordington Road, N6.

RODGERS, Sir John (Charles), 1st Bt, *cr* 1964; DL; MP (C) Sevenoaks Division of Kent since 1950; *b* 5 Oct. 1906; *o s* of Charles and Maud Mary Rodgers; *m* Betsy, JP, East Sussex, *y d* of Francis W. Aikin-Sneath, JP, and of Louisa, *d* of Col W. Langworthy Baker; two *s*. *Educ:* St Peter's, York; Ecole des Roches, France; Keble College, Oxford (scholar). MA. Sub-Warden, Mary Ward Settlement, 1929; Lectr and Administrative Asst, Univ. of Hull, 1930; FO, 1939 and 1944-45; Special Mission to Portugal, December 1945; Dir, Commercial Relations Div., MOI, 1939-41; Dir, Post-War Export Trade Develt, Dept of Overseas Trade, 1941-42; Dep. Head Industrial Inf. Div., Min. of Production, 1942-44; Foundation Gov. of Administrative Staff Coll.; Exec. Council Member, Foundation for Management Education, 1959-; BBC General Advisory Council, 1946-52; Hon. Secretary Smuts Memorial Committee, 1953; Chm. Cttee on Litter in Royal Parks, 1954; Exec. Cttee of British Council, 1957-58; Governor, British Film Institute, 1958; Member Tucker Cttee on Proceedings before Examining Justices, 1957; Leader, Parliamentary Panel, and on Exec. and Coun., Inst. of Dirs, 1955-58; Vice-Chm. Exec. Cttee Political and Economic Planning (PEP), 1962-68; Exec. London Library, 1963-71; PPS to Rt Hon. Viscount Eccles (at Ministries of Works, Education and Board of Trade), 1951-57; Parliamentary Sec., Bd of Trade, and Minister co-ordinating plans for regional development and employment, 1958-60. UK Delegate and Leader of the Conservatives to Parly Assembly, Council of Europe, and Vice-Pres., WEU, 1969-; Chm., Independent Gp, Council of Europe, 1974-; Vice-Pres., European League for Econ. Co-operation, 1970-. Pres., Centre Européen de Documentation et Information, 1963-66. Dep. Chm., J. Walter Thompson Co. Ltd, 1931-70; Vice-Chm., Cocoa Merchants Ltd; Chm., British Market Research Bureau Ltd, 1933-54; Dir other companies; President: Inst. of Practitioners in Advertising, 1967-69; Soc. for Individual Freedom, 1970-73; Inst. of Statisticians, 1971-; Master, Worshipful Company of Masons, 1968-69; Freeman of the City of London. DL Kent 1973. FBIM; FSS; FIS; FRSA. Knight Grand Cross, Order of Civil Merit (Spain), 1965; Grand Cross of Liechtenstein, 1970; Comdr, Order of Dom Infante Henrique, Portugal, 1972. *Publications:* Mary Ward Settlement: a history, 1930; The Old Public Schools of England, 1938; The English Woodland, 1941; (jtly) Industry looks at the New Order, 1941; English Rivers, 1948; (jtly) One Nation, 1950; York, 1951; (ed) Thomas Gray, 1953; (jtly) Change is our Ally, 1954; (jtly)

Capitalism-Strength and Stress, 1958; One Nation at Work, 1976. *Recreations:* travel, theatre. *Heir: s* John Fairlie Tobias Rodgers, *b* 2 July 1940. *Address:* 72 Berkeley House, Hay Hill, W1. *T:* 01-629 5220; The Dower House, Groombridge, Kent. *T:* 213; House of Commons, SW1. *Clubs:* Brooks's, Pratt's, Royal Thames Yacht.

RODGERS, Richard; American composer and producer; *b* New York, 28 June 1902; *m* 1930, Dorothy Feiner; two *d*. *Educ:* Columbia University; Institute of Musical Art, New York. Musical scores include: Lido Lady (London) 1926; One Dam Thing After Another (London) 1927; Evergreen (London) 1930; America's Sweetheart, 1931; Jumbo, 1935; On Your Toes, 1936; Babes in Arms, 1937; I'd Rather Be Right, 1937; I Married An Angel, 1938; The Boys From Syracuse, 1938; Too Many Girls, 1939; Higher and Higher, 1940; Pal Joey, 1940; Oklahoma, 1943 (Pulitzer Award, 1944); Carousel, 1945; Allegro, 1947. Wrote music for: Love Me Tonight (film); Ghost Town (ballet), 1939; State Fair (film), 1945. Co-producer: By Jupiter, 1942 (wrote music); I Remember Mama, 1944; Annie Get Your Gun, Happy Birthday, 1946; John Loves Mary, Show Boat, 1947; South Pacific, 1949 (wrote score) (Pulitzer Prize, 1950); The Happy Time, 1950; wrote scores for: The King and I, 1951; Pipe Dream, 1955; Flower Drum Song, 1958; The Sound of Music, 1959; No Strings, 1962 (and produced); Do I Hear a Waltz?, 1965; Two By Two, 1970; Rex, 1976. TV series: Churchill, The Valiant Years; Victory at Sea; TV Specials; Cinderella, 1957; Androcles and the Lion, 1967. President Dramatists' Guild, 1943-47. Member: Authors League of America; Nat. Assoc. for Amer. Composers and Conductors; Nat. Inst. of Arts and Letters. Hon. Degrees: Drury Coll., 1949; Columbia, 1954; Univ. of Massachusetts, 1954; Univ. of Bridgeport, 1962; Univ. of Maryland, 1962; Hamilton Coll., 1965; Brandeis Univ., 1965; Fairfield Univ., 1968; New York Univ., 1971; New England Conservatory of Music, 1976. *Address:* c/o Rodgers & Hammerstein, 598 Madison Avenue, New York, NY 10022, USA.

RODGERS, Rt. Hon. William Thomas, PC 1975; MP (Lab) Teesside, Stockton, since 1974 (Stockton-on-Tees, 1962-74); Secretary of State for Transport, since 1976; *b* 28 Oct. 1928; *s* of William Arthur and Gertrude Helen Rodgers; *m* 1955, Silvia, *d* of Hirsch Szulman; three *d*. *Educ:* Sudley Road Council Sch.; Quarry Bank High School, Liverpool; Magdalen College, Oxford. General Secretary, Fabian Society, 1953-60. Contested (Lab) Bristol West, March 1957; Parly Under-Sec. of State: Dept of Econ. Affairs, 1964-67, Foreign Office, 1967-68; Leader, UK delegn to Council of Europe and Assembly of WEU, 1967-68; Minister of State: BoT, 1968-69; Treasury, 1969-70; MoD, 1974-76. Chm., Expenditure Cttee on Trade and Industry, 1971-74. Borough Councillor, St Marylebone, 1958-62. *Publications:* Hugh Gaitskell, 1906-1963 (ed), 1964; (jt) The People into Parliament, 1966; pamphlets, etc. *Address:* 48 Patshull Road, NW5. *T:* 01-485 9997.

RODNEY, family name of **Baron Rodney.**

RODNEY, 9th Baron *cr* 1782; **John Francis Rodney;** Bt 1764; Marketing Director, Vacuumatic Ltd, since 1959; *b* 28 June 1920; *s* of 8th Lord Rodney and Lady Marjorie Lowther (*d* 1968), *d* of 6th Earl of Lonsdale; *S* father, 1973; *m* 1952, Régine, *d* of late Chevalier Pangaert d'Opdorp, Belgium, and the Baronne Pangaert d'Opdorp; one *s* one *d*. *Educ:* Stowe Sch., Buckingham; McGill Univ., Montreal. Served War of 1939-45 with Commandos, Burma, 1943-45 (despatches). Worked with Rootes Ltd, 1946-52, firstly as Executive Trainee, becoming Director of Rootes, Switzerland. With Vacuumatic Ltd (a member of Portals gp), 1952-: firstly Sales Manager, then Marketing Director. Chm., British Printing Machinery Assoc., 1976-. *Recreations:* sailing, shooting, gardening, travelling round the world (not all recreation). *Heir: s* Hon. George Brydges Rodney, *b* 3 Jan. 1953. *Address:* 38 Pembroke Road, W8. *T:* 01-602 4391; Brizes Park, Kelvedon Hatch, Brentwood, Essex. *T:* Coxtie Green 72139. *Clubs:* White's; Island Sailing (Cowes).

RODRIGUES, Sir Alberto, Kt 1966; CBE 1964 (OBE 1960); MBE (mil.) 1948); General Medical Practitioner, Hong Kong; Senior Unofficial Member Executive Council 1964-74; Pro-Chancellor and Chairman of Executive Council, University of Hong Kong; *b* 5 November 1911; *s* of late Luiz Gonzaga Rodrigues and late Giovanina Remedios; *m* 1940, Cynthia Maria da Silva; one *s* two *d*. *Educ:* St Joseph's College and University of Hong Kong. MBBS Univ. of Hong Kong, 1934; Post graduate work, London and Lisbon, 1935-36; Medical Practitioner, 1937-40; also Medical Officer in Hong Kong Defence Force. POW, 1940-45. Medical Practitioner, 1945-50; Post graduate work, New York, 1951-52; Resident, Winnipeg

Maternity Hosp. (Canada), 1952-53; General Medical Practitioner, 1953-. Member: Urban Council (Hong Kong), 1940-41; 1947-50; Legislative Council, 1953-60; Executive Council, 1960-74. Med. Superintendent, St Paul's Hospital, 1953-. Director: Jardine Securities, 1969-; Lap Heng Co. Ltd, 1970-; Hill & Shanghai Hotels Ltd, 1969-; Peak Tramways Co. Ltd, 1971-; Li & Fung Ltd, 1973; Hill Antenna and Engineering Co. Ltd, 1972-; Computer Data (Hill) Ltd, 1973-; Hill Commercial Broadcasting Co. Ltd, 1974-; Hong Kong and Shanghai Banking Corporation, 1974-. Officer, Ordem de Cristo (Portugal), 1949; Chevalier, Légion d'Honneur (France), 1962; Knight Grand Cross, Order of St Sylvester (Vatican), 1966. *Recreations:* cricket, hockey, tennis, swimming, badminton. *Address:* St Paul's Hospital Annexe, Causeway Bay, Hong Kong. *T:* 760017. *Clubs:* Hong Kong, Royal Hong Kong Jockey, Hong Kong Country, Lusitano, Recreio (all Hong Kong).

ROE, Frederic Gordon, FSA, FRHistS; *b* 24 Sept. 1894; *s* of late Fred Roe, RI, RBC, and Letitia Mabel, *e d* of Sydney W. Lee; *m* 1921, Eleanor Beatrice, *o d* of late Cecil Reginald Grundy; one *d. Educ:* Westminster School; in Art under his father, and at the Chelsea School of Art. Joined The Connoisseur, 1913; Art Critic, 1919; Assistant Editor, 1921-32; Acting-Editor, March-June 1926; Editor, 1933; Director, Connoisseur Ltd, 1931-34; Gunner, 1212 Battery, RFA, 1917-19; Art Critic, Daily Mail, 1920 (resigned 1921); Member, Junior Art Workers' Guild, 1920-23; restored to Westminster Abbey Muniments Wren's Original designs for the restoration of the Abbey, 1927; Hon. Member Society of Pewter Collectors, 1933-; Art Critic, The Artist, 1935-36; ARP Warden (and higher grades), 1940-45; Odhams Press Book Dept, 1943-44. FRSA 1968. *Publications:* Henry Bright of the Norwich School, 1920; Charles Bentley, 1921; Dictator of the Royal Academy (Joseph Farington, RA), 1921; David Cox, 1924-original MS of this book is in the National Museum of Wales, Cardiff; Sporting Prints of the 18th and early 19th centuries, 1927; The Life and Times of King Edward the Eighth, 1937; Coronation Cavalcade, 1937; Catalogue of Paintings in the Nettlefold Collection (with C. R. Grundy), 1937-38; Etty and the Nude (with W. Gaunt), 1943; The Nude from Cranach to Etty and beyond, 1944; The Bronze Cross, 1945; Cox the Master, 1946; English Period Furniture, 1946; Rowlandson, 1947; Sea Painters of Britain, 1947-48; Old English Furniture, 1948; Clarence below the Basement (for children), 1948; English Cottage Furniture, 1949, 2nd edn, 1950, rev. edn., 1961; Britain's Birthright, 1950; Victorian Furniture, 1952; Windsor Chairs, 1953; The Victorian Child, 1959; The Georgian Child, 1961; The British Museum's Pictures (with J. R. F. Thompson), 1961; Home Furnishing with Antiques, 1965; Victorian Corners, 1968; Women in Profile: a study in Silhouette, 1970; The Hillingford Saga, 1975; Fred Roe, RI, his life and art (with a catalogue), 1977; much work in over 70 vols of The Connoisseur; also British Racehorse, Concise Encyclopædia of Antiques, etc. *Recreations:* walking, reading, genealogical research. *Address:* 19 Vallance Road, Alexandra Park, N22 4UD. *T:* 01-888 4029.

ROE, Air Marshal Sir Rex David, KCB 1977 (CB 1974); AFC; Air Officer Commanding-in-Chief, RAF Support Command, since 1977; *b* 1925; *m* 1948, Helen Sophie (*née* Nairn); one *s* two *d. Educ:* City of London Sch.; London University. Joined RAF 1943; trained in Canada; served with Metropolitan Fighter Sector, No 11 Group, 203 Sqn, 1950-51; Sch. of Maritime Reconnaissance, 1951-53; Central Flying School and Flying Training Units, 1953-55; Commanded RNZAF Central Flying School, 1956-58; RAF Staff College, 1959; Commanded No 204 Sqn, 1960-62; College of Air Warfare, 1962-64; SASO No 18 (Maritime) Gp, 1964-67; Stn Comdr RAF Syerston, 1967-69; Director of Flying Trng, 1969-71; RCDS, 1971; Deputy Controller Aircraft (C), MoD (Procurement Executive), 1972-74; SASO HQ Near East Air Force, 1972-76; AOC-in-C Training Comd, 1976-77. *Recreations:* reading, Rugby football. *Address:* Water Meadows, Brampton, Huntingdon, Cambs. *Club:* Royal Air Force.

ROEBUCK, Roy Delville; Barrister-at-law; *b* Manchester, 25 Sept. 1929; *m* 1957, Dr Mary Ogilvy Adams; one *s. Educ:* various newspapers. Called to the Bar, Gray's Inn, 1964. Served RAF, 1948-50 (National Service). Journalist, 1950-66. MP (Lab) Harrow East, 1966-70. Contested (Lab) Altrincham and Sale, 1964 and Feb. 1965; Leek, Feb. 1974. *Recreations:* ski-ing, music. *Address:* 15 Old Forge Close, Stanmore, Mddx. *T:* 01-954 2251; 6 Gray's Inn Square, WC1. *T:* 01-242 9228.

ROEG, Nicolas Jack; film director; *b* 15 Aug. 1928; *s* of Jack Roeg and Gertrude Silk; *m* 1957, Susan, *d* of Major F. W. Stephen, MC; four *s. Educ:* Mercers Sch. Original story of Prize of Arms; Cinematographer: The Caretaker; Masque of the Red Death; Nothing But the Best; Petulia; A Funny Thing Happened on the Way to the Forum; Fahrenheit 451; Far From the Madding Crowd, etc; 2nd Unit Director and Cinematographer: Judith; Lawrence of Arabia; Co-Dir, Performance; Director: Walkabout; Don't Look Now; The Man who Fell to Earth. *Address:* Flat E, 2 Oxford and Cambridge Mansions, Old Marylebone Road, NW1. *T:* 01-262 8612.

ROFFEY, Harry Norman, CMG 1971; Assistant Secretary, Department of Health and Social Security, 1954-72, retired; *b* 2 March 1911; *s* of Henry Roffey and Ella Leggatt; *m* 1964, Florence Dickie; no *c. Educ:* Brighton Grammar Sch.; St Catharine's Coll., Cambridge (BA Hons, MA); Inst. of Education, London Univ. (Teacher's Dip.). Teaching (languages), 1935-40. Air Ministry and Foreign Office, 1940-45 (left as Wing Comdr); Min. of Health (Principal), 1946-54; Dept of Health and Social Security, 1954-72 (as Asst Sec. i/c Internat. Affairs, on the Health side). *Recreations:* foreign travel, music, etc. *Address:* 2 Sunnyside Place, Wimbledon, SW19 4SJ. *T:* 01-946 4991.

ROGAN, Rev. William Henry; Chaplain to the Queen, since 1966; *b* 1908; *s* of late Rev. John Rogan and Christian Ann McGhie; *m* 1940, Norah Violet Henderson, Helensburgh; one *s* two *d. Educ:* Royal High Sch. of Edinburgh; Univ. of Edinburgh. MA 1928; BD 1931. Asst, St Cuthbert's Parish Church, Edinburgh, 1930-32; Minister: Whithorn Parish, 1932; St Bride's Parish, Helensburgh, 1936-50; Paisley Abbey, 1950-69; Humbie, East Lothian, 1969-74. Supt, Church of Scotland Huts and Canteens in Orkney and Shetland, 1941-42; Army Chaplain, 1943-46. Select Preacher: Glasgow Univ., 1960-65; Aberdeen Univ., 1959-66; St Andrews Univ., 1959; Convener, Church of Scotland Youth Cttee, 1965-70. Founder and formerly Chm., Soc. of Friends of Paisley Abbey. Pres., Scottish Church Soc., 1977-78. Hon. DD Edinburgh, 1963. *Recreation:* angling. *Address:* Mid Latch, Gifford, East Lothian. *T:* Gifford 367.

ROGERS, Rt. Rev. Alan Francis Bright, MA; an Hon. Assistant Bishop of Peterborough, since 1975; *b* 12 Sept. 1907; *s* of Thomas and Alice Rogers, London, W9; *m* 1932, Millicent Boarder; two *s. Educ:* Westminster City Sch.; King's Coll., London; Leeds Univ.; Bishop's Coll., Cheshunt. Curate of St Stephen's, Shepherds Bush, 1930-32; Holy Trinity, Twickenham, 1932-34; Civil Chaplain, Mauritius, 1934-49; Archdeacon of Mauritius, 1946-49; Commissary to Bishop of Mauritius, 1949-59; Vicar of Twickenham, 1949-54; Proctor in Convocation, 1951-59; Vicar of Hampstead, 1954-59; Rural Dean of Hampstead, 1955-59; Bishop of Mauritius, 1959-66; Suffragan Bishop of Fulham, 1966-70; Suffragan Bishop of Edmonton, 1970-75. MA Lambeth 1959. *Recreations:* walking, light music. *Address:* 2 Collswell Lane, Blakesley, near Towcester, Northants NN12 8RB. *T:* Blakesley 502. *Club:* Royal Commonwealth Society.

ROGERS, Surgeon Rear-Adm. (D) Brian Frederick; Director of Naval Dental Service, since 1977; *b* 27 Feb. 1923; *s* of Frederick Reginald Rogers and Rosa Jane Rogers; *m* 1946, Mavis Elizabeth (*née* Scott); one *s* two *d. Educ:* Rock Ferry High Sch.; Liverpool Univ. (LDS 1945). House Surgeon, Liverpool Dental Hosp., 1945; joined RNVR, 1946; transf. to RN, 1954; served HMS Ocean, 1954-56 and HMS Eagle, 1964-66; Fleet Dental Surg. on staff of C-in-C Fleet, 1974-77; Comd Dental Surg. to C-in-C Naval Home Comd, 1977. *Recreations:* European touring, photography, DIY. *Address:* 22 Trerieve, Downderry, Torpoint, Cornwall PL11 3LY. *T:* Downderry 526; 1 Burton Lodge, Portinscale Road, Putney, SW15 2HT. *T:* 01-870 2120.

ROGERS, Prof. C(laude) Ambrose, FRS 1959; Astor Professor of Mathematics, University College, London, since 1958; *b* 1 Nov. 1920; *s* of late Sir Leonard Rogers, KCSI, CIE, FRS; *m* 1952, Mrs J. M. Gordon, widow of W. G. Gordon, and *d* of F. W. G. North; two *d. Educ:* Berkhamsted School; University Coll., London; Birkbeck Coll., London. BSc, PhD, DSc (London, 1941, 1949, 1952). Experimental officer, Ministry of Supply, 1940-45; lecturer and reader, University College, London, 1946-54; Prof. of Pure Mathematics, Univ. of Birmingham, 1954-58. Pres., London Mathematical Soc., 1970-72. *Publications:* Packing and Covering, 1964; Hausdorff Measures, 1970; articles in various mathematical journals. *Recreation:* string figures. *Address:* Department of Mathematics, University College, WC1E 6BT; 8 Grey Close, NW11 6QG. *T:* 01-455 8027.

ROGERS, Claude Maurice, OBE 1959; painter; Member of the London Group (President, 1952-65); Professor of Fine Art, Reading University, 1963-72, Professor Emeritus, since 1972; Fellow, University College, London; *b* 24 Jan. 1907; *e c* of late David de Sola Rogers, LDS, RCS; *m* 1937, Elsie, *e d* of late

Jethro Few, Kingston, Jamaica; one *s. Educ:* St Paul's; Slade Sch. of Fine Art, London University. With Victor Pasmore and William Coldstream founded School of Drawing and Painting, 316 Euston Rd, 1937-39. Royal Engineer, 1941-43 (Corporal). Lectr, Slade Sch. of Fine Arts, London Univ., 1955-63. Member: Arts Panel, Arts Council of GB, 1957-63; Nat. Council for Diplomas in Art and Design, and Chm., Fine Art Panel, 1961-69. Exhibitions: one-man exhibns: London Artists' Assoc., 1933; Leicester Galls, 1940, 1947, 1954, 1960; Fischer Fine Arts, 1975; Exhibitor UNESCO Exhib., Paris, 1946; Carnegie Internat., 1936 and 1950; with British Council in America, Canada, etc.; with Arts Council (Four Contemporary British Painters, The Euston Road School and some others, Sixty Pictures for '51, British Painting, 1974, etc); retrospective Exhibitions: Newcastle, Manchester, Bristol, Leicester, etc, 1955; (Drawings and Paintings, 1927-73) Whitechapel Art Gall., Birmingham, Reading, Southampton, Sheffield, etc, 1973; represented in Tate Gallery, British Museum, Print Room, Victoria and Albert Museum, Ashmolean Museum, Fitzwilliam Museum; Commonwealth galleries. Works also acquired by: Chantry Bequest, Contemporary Art Society. *Address:* 36 Southwood Lane, Highgate, N6. *T:* 01-348 1997; The Old Rectory, Somerton, near Bury St Edmunds, Suffolk. *T:* Hawkedon 231.

ROGERS, Ven. David Arthur; Vicar of Sedbergh, Cautley and Garsdale, since 1959; also Archdeacon of Craven, since 1977; *b* 12 March 1921; *s* of Rev. Canon Thomas Godfrey Rogers and Doris Mary Cleaver Rogers (*née* Steele); *m* 1951, Joan Malkin; one *s* three *d. Educ:* Saint Edward's School, Oxford (scholar); Christ's College, Cambridge (exhibitioner). BA 1947, MA 1952. War service with Green Howards and RAC, 1940-45; Christ's Coll. and Ridley Hall, Cambridge, 1945-49; Asst Curate, St George's, Stockport, 1949-53; Rector, St Peter's, Levenshulme, Manchester, 1953-59; Rural Dean of Sedbergh and then of Ewecross, 1959-77; Hon. Canon of Bradford Cathedral, 1967. *Address:* The Vicarage, Sedbergh, Cumbria LA10 5SQ. *T:* Sedbergh 20283.

ROGERS, Rev. Edward; General Secretary, Methodist Division of Social Responsibility (formerly Christian Citizenship Department), 1950-75; *b* 4 Jan. 1909; *s* of Capt. E. E. Rogers, Fleetwood; *m* 1937, Edith May, *o d* of A. L. Sutton, Plaistow. *Educ:* Baines's Poulton-Le-Fylde Grammar School; Manchester University. Kitchener Scholar, Shuttleworth Scholar, Hulme Hall, Manchester. MA (Econ. and Pol.) 1931; Hartley Coll.; BD, 1933. Methodist Circuit Minister: East London Mission, Bakewell, Birmingham (Sutton Park), Southport, 1933-50. Lectures: Fernley, 1951; Ainslie, 1952; Beckly, 1957; Peake 1971. Organising Director, Methodist Relief Fund, 1953-75; Chairman, Inter-Church Aid and Refugee Service, British Council of Churches, 1960-64; Pres., Methodist Conf., 1960; Moderator, Free Church Federal Council, 1968; Vice-Pres., British Council of Churches, 1971-74. Chairman: Standing Commn on Migration, 1964-70; Churches Cttee on Gambling Legislation, 1967-73; Exec. Council, UK Immigrants Adv. Service, 1970-; Community and Race Relations Unit, 1971-75; AVEC Board, 1977-; Select Committee on Cruelty to Animals, 1963. *Publications:* First Easter, 1948; A Commentary on Communism, 1951; Programme for Peace, 1954; God's Business, 1957; That They Might Have Life, 1958; The Christian Approach to the Communist, 1959; Church Government, 1964; Living Standards, 1964; Law, Morality and Gospel, 1969; Search for Security, 1973; Plundered Planet, 1973; Money, 1976; Thinking About Human Rights, 1977. *Recreations:* travel, indiscriminate reading. *Address:* 6 Green Court Gardens, Croydon, Surrey CR0 7LH. *T:* 01-654 5573.

ROGERS, Eric William Evan, DSc(Eng); FRAeS; Head, Aerodynamics, Structures and Materials Group of Departments, Royal Aircraft Establishment, Farnborough, Hants, since 1974; *b* 12 April 1925; *o s* of W. P. Rogers, Southgate, N London; *m* 1950, Dorothy Joyce Loveless; two *s* one *d. Educ:* Southgate County Grammar Sch.; Imperial Coll. London. FCGI, DIC. Aerodynamics Div., NPL, 1945-70 (Head of Hypersonic Research, 1961); Aerodynamics Dept, RAE, 1970 (Head, 1973). Member: various Cttees of Royal Aeronautical Soc. and of Aeronautical Research Council; Governor, Kennington Sch. *Publications:* various papers on high-speed aerodynamics and on industrial aerodynamics, in ARC (R and M series), RAeS jls and elsewhere. *Recreations:* music, philately. *Address:* 64 Thetford Road, New Malden, Surrey. *T:* 01-942 7452.

ROGERS, Ven. Evan James Gwyn; Archdeacon of Doncaster since 1967; *b* 14 Jan. 1914; *s* of John Morgan Rogers and Margaret Rogers; *m* 1943, Eleanor Mabel, *d* of Capt. J. H. Evans; one *s* one *d. Educ:* St David's, Lampeter; Wycliffe Hall, Oxford. Vicar: Hamer, 1943; St Catharine's, Wigan, 1947;

Diocesan Missioner, Dio. Liverpool, 1953; Hon. Chaplain to Bp of Liverpool, 1953; Hon. Canon, Liverpool Cathedral, 1957; Vicar of Coniston Cold, 1960; Dir of Educn, Dio. Bradford, 1960; Exam. Chaplain to Bp of Sheffield, 1963; Vice-Chm. Standing Conf., WR Educn Cttee, 1963; Hon. Canon of Bradford, 1964. *Publications:* Do This in Remembrance, 1950; Dr Barnardo, 1951; (with Canon F. L. M. Bennett) A Communion Book, 1951; contrib. to West Riding New Agreed Syllabus, 1966. *Address:* St David's, 1a Spring Lane, Sprotborough, Doncaster. *T:* Doncaster 854005.

ROGERS, Frank J.; Chairman, East Midland Allied Press, since 1973 (Director, since 1971); Director, Plessey New Jersey Inc.; Adviser on Corporate Affairs, The Plessey Co. Ltd; *b* 24 Feb. 1920; *s* of Percy Rogers, Stoke-on-Trent; *m* 1949; two *d. Educ:* Wolstanton Grammar School. Journalist, 1937-49; Military Service, 1940-46; Gen. Man., Nigerian Daily Times, 1949-52; Manager, Argus, Melbourne, 1952-55; Man. Dir, Overseas Newspapers, 1958-60; Dir, Daily Mirror, 1960-65; Man. Dir, IPC, 1965-70. Chm., Nat. Newspaper Steering Gp, 1970-72; Dir, Newspaper Publishers Assoc., 1971-73. Mem. Council and Chm., Exec. Cttee, Industrial Soc. *Recreations:* motoring, golf. *Address:* Greensleeves, Loudwater Drive, Rickmansworth, Herts. *T:* Rickmansworth 75358; (during week) 86 Pier House, Cheyne Walk, SW3. *T:* 01-352 9339. *Club:* Reform.

ROGERS, George Henry Roland, CBE 1965; *b* 1906; *m* ; one *s* one *d. Educ:* Willesden Elementary School; Middlesex CC Schools. A railway clerk. Member Wembley Borough Council, 1937-41. Served War of 1939-45, Royal Corps of Signals, 1942. MP (Lab) North Kensington, 1945-70; Chairman, London Group of Labour Members, 1949-54; Opposition London Whip, 1954-64; a Lord Commissioner of the Treasury, October 1964-January 1966. PPS to Min. of Supply, 1947-49 and to Minister of State for Foreign Affairs, 1950; Delegate to UN Assembly 1950; Delegate to Council of Europe and Western European Union, 1961-63. Hon. Sec. Parliamentary Painting Group, 1950-70. *Address:* Flat 15, 72 Bournemouth Road, Poole, Dorset.

ROGERS, George Theodore; Under-Secretary, Department of Trade, since 1974; *b* 26 Feb. 1919; *s* of George James and Margaret Lilian Rogers; *m* 1944, Mary Katherine Stedman; three *s* two *d. Educ:* Portsmouth Grammar Sch.; Keble Coll., Oxford (Open Schol. in Classics). Served War, Indian Infy, Burma, 1939-45. Resumed univ. educn (PPE), 1945-48; NATO Defence Coll., 1953-54. Min. of Supply/Min. of Aviation, 1948-65; Univ. Grants Cttee, 1965-68; Min. of Technology, 1968-70; DTI, 1970-74; Under-Sec., 1973. *Recreation:* gardening. *Address:* 39 Sandy Lane, Cheam, Surrey SM2 7PQ. *T:* 01-642 6428.

ROGERS, Henry Augustus, OBE 1976 (MBE 1967); HM Diplomatic Service; British Consul-General, Brisbane, Australia, since 1976; *b* 11 Dec. 1918; *s* of Henry Augustus Rogers and Evelyn Mary Rogers (*née* Casey); *m* 1947, Margaret May Stainsby; three *s. Educ:* The Fox Sch.; West Kensington Central Sch., London, W. Junior clerk with Solicitors, Wedlake Letts & Birds, Temple, prior to war. Joined RNVR, 1938; served war, 1939-45. Joined Foreign Office, 1945; Buenos Aires, 1946; Havana, 1953; Vice-Consul, Guatemala City, 1954; Vice-Consul (Comm.), Los Angeles, 1958; Second Sec. (Comm.), Belgrade, 1961; FO, 1963; Second Sec., Kaduna, 1965; First Sec., Head of Chancery and Consul, Tegucigalpa, 1967; FCO, 1971. *Recreations:* studying the arts, classical literature and modern history, painting (the Impressionists), music. *Address:* c/o Foreign and Commonwealth Office, SW1; 11 Devonshire Close, Amersham, Bucks HP6 5JG. *T:* Amersham 3874. *Club:* Royal Commonwealth Society.

ROGERS, Hugh Charles Innes, MA, FIMechE; Chairman, Avon Rubber Co., since 1968; Vice-Chairman, Bristol and West Building Society; *b* 2 November 1904; *s* of late Hugh Innes Rogers, OBE, MIEE; *m* 1930, Iris Monica Seymour; one *s* three *d. Educ:* Marlborough; Clare College, Cambridge. Brecknell Munro & Rogers, 1926-31 (Chairman and Jt Man. Dir, 1931-41); SW Reg. Controller, Min. of Supply, 1941; SW Reg. Controller, Min. of Production and Chm. of Regional Bd, 1942-44; Dep. Controller (Production) in Admiralty, 1944-46. Imperial Tobacco Co. Ltd, Bristol: Chief Engr, 1948; Dir, 1949-67; a Dep. Chm., 1964-67; Dir, British American Tobacco Co., 1964-67. Member Bristol University Council, 1938, Chm., 1968-72. Chairman: SW Regional Housing Bd, 1952-53; SW Regional Council, FBI, 1954. High Sheriff of Avon, 1974. Hon. LLD Bristol, 1971; Hon. DSc Bath, 1971. *Recreations:* sailing, shooting, tennis, farming. *Address:* Beach House, Bitton, near Bristol BS15 6NP. *T:* Bitton 3127.

ROGERS, John Michael Thomas; barrister-at-law; a Recorder of the Crown Court, since 1976; *b* 13 May 1938; *s* of Harold Stuart Rogers and Sarah Joan Roberts; *m* 1971, Jennifer Ruth Platt. *Educ:* Rydal Sch.; Birkenhead Sch.; Fitzwilliam House, Cambridge (MA, LLB). Schoolmaster, 1962-64; called to Bar, Gray's Inn, 1963. *Recreations:* farming, gardening. *Address:* Hengoed, Ruthin, Clwyd LL15 2DE. *T:* Ruthin 3849; 40 King Street, Chester CH1 2AH. *T:* Chester 23886. *Clubs:* Pragmatists (Wirral); Ruthin Rugby Football.

ROGERS, Air Vice-Marshal John Robson, CBE 1971; Director-General of Organisation (RAF), since 1977; *b* 11 Jan. 1928; *s* of B. R. Rogers; *m* 1955, Gytha Elspeth Campbell; two *s* two *d*. *Educ:* Brentwood Sch.; No 1 Radio Sch., Cranwell; Royal Air Force Coll., Cranwell. OC 56(F) Sqdn, 1960-61; Gp Captain, 1967; OC RAF Coningsby, 1967-69; Air Commodore, 1971; Dir of Operational Requirements (RAF), 1971-73; Dep. Comdt, RAF Coll., 1973-75; RCDS, 1976; Air Vice-Marshal, 1977. *Address:* c/o Lloyds Bank Ltd, 27 High Street, Colchester, Essex. *Club:* Royal Air Force.

ROGERS, John Willis, QC 1975; a Recorder of the Crown Court, since 1974; *b* 7 Nov. 1929; *s* of late Reginald John Rogers and late Joan Daisy Alexandra Rogers (*née* Willis); *m* 1952, Sheila Elizabeth Cann; one *s* one *d*. *Educ:* Sevenoaks Sch.; Fitzwilliam House, Cambridge (MA). Called to Bar, Lincoln's Inn, 1955 (Cholmeley Schol.). 1st Prosecuting Counsel to Inland Revenue, SE Circuit, 1969-75. *Recreations:* cricket, gardening, change ringing. *Address:* Carpmael Building, Temple, EC4Y 7AT. *T:* 01-353 5537. *Clubs:* Garrick, MCC, Band of Brothers.

ROGERS, Martin Hartley Guy; HM Diplomatic Service; British High Commissioner in The Gambia, since 1975; *b* 11 June 1925; *s* of late Rev. Canon T. Guy Rogers and Marguerite Inez Rogers; *m* 1959, Jean Beresford Chinn; one *s* three *d*. *Educ:* Marlborough Coll.; Jesus Coll., Cambridge. CRO, 1949; 2nd Sec., Karachi, 1951-53; CRO, 1953-56 and 1958-60; seconded to Govt of Fedn of Nigeria, 1956-57; ndc 1960-61; 1st Sec., Ottawa, 1961-62; Adviser to Jamaican Min. of External Affairs, 1963; CRO, later Commonwealth Office, 1963-68; Dep. High Comr, Bombay, 1968-71, Kaduna, 1972-75. *Recreations:* golf, tennis. *Address:* c/o Foreign and Commonwealth Office, SW1. *Club:* United Oxford & Cambridge University.

ROGERS, Martin John Wyndham; Headmaster of Malvern College since 1971; *b* 9 April 1931; *s* of John Frederick Rogers and Grace Mary Rogers; *m* 1957, Jane Cook; two *s* one *d*. *Educ:* Oundle Sch.; Heidelberg Univ.; Trinity Hall, Cambridge (MA). Henry Wiggin & Co., 1953-55; Westminster School: Asst Master, 1955-60; Sen. Chemistry Master, 1960-64; Housemaster, 1964-66; Under Master and Master of the Queen's Scholars, 1967-71. Seconded as Nuffield Research Fellow (O-level Chemistry Project), 1962-64; Salter's Company Fellow, Dept of Chemical Engrg and Chemical Technology, Imperial Coll., London, 1969. *Publications:* John Dalton and the Atomic Theory, 1965; Chemistry and Energy, 1968; (Editor) Foreground Chemistry Series, 1968; Gas Syringe Experiments, 1970; (co-author) Chemistry: facts, patterns and principles, 1972. *Address:* Headmaster's House, Malvern College, Worcs. *T:* Malvern 4472.

ROGERS, Maurice Arthur Thorold; Secretary, Royal Institution, 1968-73; Joint Head, Head Office Research and Development Department, ICI, 1962-72; *b* 8 June 1911; *s* of A. G. L. Rogers; *g s* of Prof. J. E. Thorold Rogers; *m* 1947, Margaret Joan (*née* Craven); one *s* two *d*. *Educ:* Dragon Sch.; Westminster Sch.; University Coll., London. 1st Class hons BSc (Chem.) UCL 1932, PhD (Chem.) 1934. Chemist, ICI Dyestuffs Div., 1934-45; Head of Academic Relations Dept, 1946-58; Head of Head Office Research Dept, ICI, 1958-62. *Publications:* numerous papers in: Jl of Chem. Soc.; Nature; etc. *Recreations:* climbing, gardening, china restoration, conservation of countryside. *Address:* Mount Skippet, Ramsden, Oxford OX7 3AP. *T:* Ramsden 253.

ROGERS, Murray Rowland Fletcher; Member, Courts of Appeal for the Seychelles, St Helena, The Falkland Islands Colony and Dependencies, and the British Antarctic Territory, 1965-75; *b* 13 Sept. 1899; *s* of Geoffrey Pearson and Adeline Maud Rogers; *m* 1924, Dorothy Lilian Bardsley (*d* 1950); one *s* (one *d* decd). *Educ:* St Edward's School; RMC, Sandhurst; 2nd Lieut 8th Hussars, 1918-21; Liverpool Univ. (BA 1924). Schoolmaster until 1929; called to Bar, Gray's Inn, 1929; Northern Circuit until 1937; Magistrate, Nigeria, 1937-42; Chief Magistrate, Palestine, 1942-47; District Judge, Malaya, 1947-49; President Sessions Court, Malaya, 1949-52; Judge of Supreme Court, Sarawak, N Borneo and Brunei, 1952-63, retd. *Publication:* Law Reports of the Seychelles Court of Appeal, vol 1, 1965-76, 1976.

Address: Flat 10, 2 Mountview Road, N4. *Clubs:* Athenæum; Artists' (Liverpool).

ROGERS, Prof. Neville William, DLit London; FRSL; Professor of English, Ohio University, since 1964; *b* 5 Jan. 1908; *s* of Leonard George and Carrie Elizabeth Rogers (*née* Jennings). *Educ:* Rossall Sch.; Birkbeck Coll., London; studied French, Italian, Spanish and German privately abroad. BA Gen. 1932, BA Hons cl. II Classics, 1934, London; Phi Beta Kappa, Lambda Chapter of Ohio, 1974. Intell. Officer, RAF, Middle East and Italy, 1942-46. Asst Master, various prep. schs, 1927-32; Headmaster, Wellesley Sch., Croydon, 1932-34; Asst Master: King Edward VI Sch., Stafford, 1935-39; St Marylebone Grammar Sch., 1939-52; Leverhulme Fellow at Oxford, working on Shelley MSS, 1952-55; Sen. Res. Fellow and Lectr, Univ. of Birmingham, 1956-62; Vis. Professor: Michigan, 1959; Washington, St Louis, UCLA, 1960; Brandeis, 1962-64; Grant-in-Aid, American Council of Learned Socs for Res. in England, 1974; has lectured at many US and French univs. Has broadcast in English, Italian and French. Mem., Kennedy Scott's Philharmonic Choir, 1933-39; Founder Mem., London Philharmonic Choir (Vice-Chm. 1947-48); Mem. Cttee: British-Italian Soc., 1947-; Keats Shelley Memorial Assoc., 1946-. *Publications:* Keats, Shelley and Rome, 1949 (4th edn 1970); Shelley at Work, 1956 (2nd edn 1968); (ed with Archibald Colquhoun) Italian Regional Tales of the Nineteenth Century, 1961; (ed) The Esdaile Poems, 1966; (ed and annotated) Selected Poetry of Shelley, 1968; (ed) Complete Poetical Works of Percy Bysshe Shelley (Oxford English Texts, 4 vols), Vol I, 1802-1813, 1972, Vol. II, 1814-1817, 1975; contribs to Encycl. Britannica, Times Lit. Supp., Times Educnl Supp., Twentieth Century, Review of English Studies, Mod. Lang. Review, Keats-Shelley Memorial Bulletin, Keats-Shelley Jl, Book Collector, Ulisse, Il Ponte, Ohio Review. *Recreations:* literature, languages, music, travel. *Address:* 22 Clavering Avenue, SW13. *T:* 01-748 1358; Ohio University, Athens, Ohio, USA. *Clubs:* National Liberal, Authors'.

ROGERS, Maj.-Gen. Norman A. C.; *see* Coxwell-Rogers.

ROGERS, Maj.-Gen. Norman Charles, FRCS 1949; Clinical Superintendent, since 1975, and Consultant, since 1973, Accident and Emergency Department, Guy's Hospital; *b* 14 Oct. 1916; *s* of Wing Comdr Charles William Rogers, RAF, and Edith Minnie Rogers (*née* Weaver); *m* 1954, Pamela Marion (*née* Rose); two *s* one *d*. *Educ:* Imperial Service Coll.; St Bartholomew's Hosp. MB, BS London; MRCS, LRCP 1939. Emergency Commn, Lieut RAMC, Oct. 1939; 131 Field Amb. RAMC, Dunkirk (despatches); RMO, 4th Royal Tank Regt, N Africa, 1941-42; Italy, 1942-43 (POW); RMO 1st Black Watch, NW Europe, 1944-45 (wounded, despatches twice). Ho. Surg., St Bartholomew's Hosp., 1946-47; Registrar (Surgical) Appts, Norwich, 1948-52; Sen. Registrar Appts, Birmingham, 1952-56; granted permanent commn, RAMC, 1956; surgical appts in mil. hospitals: Chester, Dhekelia (Cyprus), Catterick, Iserlohn (BAOR), 1956-67; Command Consultant Surgeon, BAOR, 1967-69; Dir, Army Surgery, 1969-73. QHS, 1969-73. *Publications:* contribs on surgical subjects. *Address:* 31 Merrick Square, SE1. *T:* 01-407 3774.

ROGERS, Mrs P. E.; *see* Box, B. E.

ROGERS, Paul; actor; *b* Plympton, Devon, 22 March 1917; *s* of Edwin and Dulcie Myrtle Rogers; *m* 1st, 1939, Jocelyn Wynne (marr. diss. 1955); two *s*; 2nd, 1955, Rosalind Boxall; two *d*. *Educ:* Newton Abbot Grammar School, Devon. Michael Chekhov Theatre Studio, 1936-38. First appearance on stage as Charles Dickens in Bird's Eye of Valour, Scala, 1938; Stratford-upon-Avon Shakespeare Memorial Theatre, 1939; Concert Party and Colchester Rep. Co. until 1940. Served Royal Navy, 1940-46. Colchester Rep. Co. and Arts Council Tour and London Season, Tess of the D'Urbervilles, 1946-47; Bristol Old Vic, 1947-49; London Old Vic (incl. tour S Africa and Southern Rhodesia), 1949-53; also at Edinburgh, London and in USA, 1954-57; London, 1958; tour to Moscow, Leningrad and Warsaw, 1960. Roles with Old Vic include numerous Shakespearean leads. Other parts include: Sir Claude Mulhammer in The Confidential Clerk, Edinburgh Festival and Lyric, London, 1953; Lord Claverton in The Elder Statesman, Edinburgh Fest. and Cambridge Theatre, London, 1958; Mr Fox in Mr Fox of Venice, Piccadilly, 1959; Johnny Condell in One More River, Duke of York's and Westminster, 1959; Nickles in JB, Phœnix, 1961; Reginald Kinsale in Photo Finish, Saville, 1962; The Seagull, Queen's, 1964; Season of Goodwill, Queen's, 1964; The Homecoming, Aldwych, 1965; Timon of Athens, Stratford-upon-Avon, 1965; The Government Inspector, Aldwych, 1966; Henry IV, Stratford-upon-Avon, 1966; Max in The Homecoming, New York, 1967 (Tony Award and Whitbread Anglo-American Award); Plaza Suite, Lyric, 1969; The Happy Apple, Apollo, 1970; Sleuth, St Martin's, 1970, NY, 1971; Othello, Nat. Theatre Co., Old Vic, 1974; Heartbreak House, Nat. Theatre, 1975; The Marrying of Ann Leete, Aldwych, 1975; The Return of A. J. Raffles, Aldwych, 1975; The Zykovs, Aldwych, 1976; Volpone, The Madras House, National Theatre, 1977. Appears in films and television. *Publication:* a Preface to Folio Soc. edition of Shakespeare's Love's Labour's Lost, 1959. *Recreations:* gardening, carpentry, books. *Address:* 9 Hillside Gardens, Highgate, N6. *T:* 01-340 2656. *Club:* Naval.

ROGERS, Rev. Percival Hallewell, MBE 1945; Assistant Priest, Trinity Episcopal Church, New Orleans, since 1976; *b* 13 Sept. 1912; *m* 1940, Annie Mary Stuart, 2nd *d* of Lt-Col James Morwood; two *s* one *d*. *Educ:* Brentwood School; St Edmund Hall, Oxford. BA Class II, Hons English, Oxford, 1935; Diploma in Education, 1936; MA 1946. Two terms of teaching, Westminster School; Master in charge of English, Haileybury, 1936; served War, 1940-45 (despatches twice, MBE): RA, Major; DAA QMG; Bishop's College, Cheshunt, 1946; ordained, 1947; Asst Chaplain and English Master, Haileybury, 1947; Chaplain and English Master, 1949; Headmaster, Portora Royal Sch., Enniskillen, 1954-73; student, Internat. Acad. for Continuous Educn, Cheltenham, 1973-74; Chaplain, Gresham's Sch., Holt, 1974-75; Dean, Internat. Acad. for Continuous Educn, 1975-76. *Publications:* The Needs of the Whole Man, Systematics, 1971; Editor and contrib. to A Guide to Divinity Teaching (SPCK), 1962. *Address:* 18 Rosa Park, New Orleans, Louisiana 70115, USA. *Clubs:* East India, Devonshire, Sports and Public Schools; Friendly Brothers (Dublin).

ROGERS, Sir Philip, GCB 1975 (KCB 1970; CB 1965); CMG 1952; Chairman: Outward Bound Trust, since 1976; Board of Management, London School of Hygiene and Tropical Medicine, since 1977; Universities Superannuation Scheme, since 1977; *b* 19 Aug. 1914; *s* of William Edward and Sarah Jane Rogers; *m* 1940, Heather Mavis Gordon; one *s* one *d*. *Educ:* William Hulme's Grammar School, Manchester; Emmanuel Coll., Cambridge. Apptd to administrative class of Home Civil Service, as an Asst Principal in Colonial Office, 1936; seconded to be Private Secretary to Governor of Jamaica, Jan.-Dec. 1939; Asst Secretary, Colonial Office, 1946-53; Assistant Under-Secretary of State, Colonial Office, 1953-61; Under-Secretary, Department of Technical Co-operation, 1961-64; Dep. Sec. of Cabinet, 1964-67; Third Secretary, Treasury, 1967-68; Dep. Secretary, 1968-69, Second Permanent Secretary, 1969-70, Civil Service Dept; Permanent Secretary, DHSS, 1970-75. *Recreation:* gardening. *Address:* Orchard House, Wargrave, Berks RG10 8DE. *T:* Wargrave 2760. *Club:* East India, Devonshire, Sports and Public Schools.

ROGERS, Sir Philip (James), Kt 1961; CBE 1952; Chairman, Tobacco Research Council, 1963-71; *b* 1908; *s* of late James Henry Rogers; *m* 1939, Brenda Mary Sharp, CBE, *d* of late Ernest Thompson Sharp. *Educ:* Blundell's Sch. Served War (RWAFF and Intell. Corps), 1940-44. MLC, Nigeria, 1947-51; MLC, Kenya, 1957-62; Elected Representative, Kenya, East African Legislative Assembly, 1962 and 1963. President: Nig. Chamber of Commerce, 1948 and 1950 (Vice-Pres. 1947 and 1949); Nairobi Chamber of Commerce, 1957 (Vice-Pres. 1956); AAA of Nig., 1951; Dir, Nig. Elec. Corp., 1951; Governor, Nig. Coll. of Technology, 1951; Member: Nig. Reconstr. Cttee, Rd Transport Bd, 1948-51; Central Council Red Cross Soc. of W Africa, 1950-51; Trades Adv. Cttee, Nig., 1950 and 1951-; Wages Adv. Bd, Kenya, 1955-61; EA Industrial Council, 1954-63; EA Air Licensing Appeals Trib., 1958-60; EA Air Adv. Council, 1956-60; Kenya Road Authority, 1957-61; Provl Council, Univ. of E Africa, 1961-63; Gov. Council, Roy. Tech. Coll. of E Africa, 1957-58 (Chm. 1958/59/60). Chairman: East African Tobacco Co. Ltd, 1951-63; Rift Valley Cigarette Co. Ltd, 1956-63; EA Rd Fedn, 1954-56; Kenya Cttee on Study and Trg in USA, 1958-63; Bd of Govs, Coll. of Social Studies, 1960-63; Nairobi Special Loans Cttee, 1960-63; Af. Teachers' Service Bd, 1956-63; Council, Royal College (now University Coll., Nairobi), 1961-63; Fedn of Sussex Amenity Socs, 1968-; Trustee, Outward Bound Trust of Kenya, 1959-63; Rep. of Assoc. Chambers of Commerce & Indust. of Eastern Africa; Mem. of Industrial Tribunals, England and Wales, 1966-. Governor, Plumpton Agric. Coll., 1967-. Member: E Sussex Educn Cttee, 1969-; Finance Cttee, UCL, 1972-; Indep. Schools Careers Orgn, 1972-; Chairman: Fedn of Sussex Amenity Socs, 1968-; Age Concern, East Sussex, 1974-. *Address:* Brislands, Newick, East Sussex. *T:* Newick 2210.

ROGERS, Thomas Edward, CMG 1960; MBE 1945; HM Diplomatic Service, retired; *b* 28 Dec. 1912; *s* of T. E. Rogers and Lucy Jane Browne; *m* 1950, Eileen Mary, *d* of R. J.

Speechley; no *c. Educ:* Bedford Sch.; Emmanuel Coll., Cambridge (Exhibnr); School of Oriental Studies, London. Selected for Indian Civil Service, 1936, and for Indian Political Service, 1941. Served in Bengal, 1937-41; in Persia and Persian Gulf, 1941-45; Political Agent, Quetta, 1947. Entered Foreign Service, 1948: FO, 1948-50; Bogota, 1950-53; jssc, 1953-54; Coun. (Comm.), Madrid, 1954-58; Coun. (Econ.), Belgrade, 1958-62; Minister (Econ.), Buenos Aires, 1963-65; Dep. UK High Comr, Canada, 1966-70, Actg High Comr, 1967-68; Ambassador to Colombia, 1970-73. Grand Cross of St Carlos, Colombia, 1974. *Recreation:* travel. *Address:* Chintens, Firway, Grayshott, Hants. *Club:* United Oxford & Cambridge University.

ROGERS, Thomas Gordon Parry; Director of Personnel, The Plessey Co. Ltd, since 1974; Director: The Plessey Co.; Plessey Pension Trust; Plessey GmbH; ICL; *b* 7 Aug. 1924; *s* of Victor Francis Rogers and Ella (*née* May); *m* 1st, 1947, Pamela Mary (*née* Greene) (marr. diss. 1973); one *s* seven *d*; 2nd, 1973, Patricia Juliet (*née* Curtis); one *s*. *Educ:* West Hartlepool Grammar Sch.; St Edmund Hall, Oxford. MA; CIPM, FBIM, AMIPR. Proctor and Gamble Ltd, 1948-54; Mars Ltd, 1954-56; Hardy Spicer Ltd, 1956-61; IBM United Kingdom Ltd, 1961-74. Chairman: Adv. Cttee on Charitable Fund Raising, NCSS, 1970-76; Exec. Cttee, Inst. of Manpower Studies; Pres., Inst. of Personnel Management, 1975-77; Member: Council of Careers Research Adv. Centre, 1968-; Council and Exec., Industrial Participation Assoc., 1972-; CBI/BIM Panel on Management Educn, 1968-; Council and Exec., IMS, 1968-; Oxford Univ. Appts Cttee, 1972-. Associate Lectr, SW London Coll., 1969-. *Publications:* The Recruitment and Training of Graduates, 1970; contribs to: The Director's Handbook, Management and the Working Environment, and various newspapers and jls. *Recreations:* birdwatching, golf, tennis. *Address:* 138 Park Road, Chiswick, W4 3HP. *T:* 01-994 1594. *Clubs:* Savile, Royal Wimbledon Golf.

ROGERS, William Pierce; Partner, law firm of Royall, Koegel, Rogers and Wells, 1961-69, and since 1973, when renamed Rogers & Wells; *b* 23 June 1913; *s* of Harrison A. and Myra Beswick Rogers; *m* 1937, Adele Langston; three *s* one *d*. *Educ:* Canton High School, Canton, New York; Colgate University; Cornell Law School. Law firm of Cadwalader, Wickersham and Taft, NY City, 1937; an asst District Attorney in NY County, 1938; US Navy, 1942-46; Dist Attorney's Office in New York, 1946; Chief Counsel, Senate Investigating Cttee, 1947; Counsel, Senate Permanent Investigating Cttee, 1949; law firm of Dwight, Royall, Harris, Koegel and Caskey, offices in New York and Washington, 1950; Dep. Attorney-General, 1953; Attorney-General of the US, 1957-61; Secretary of State, USA, 1969-73. Holds several hon. degrees in Law, from Univs and Colls in the USA, 1956-60. Mem. Bar Assocs in the USA. US Representative: to 20th Session of UN General Assembly, 1965; on UN Ad Hoc Cttee on SW Africa, 1967; Mem., President's Commn on Law Enforcement and Administration of Justice, 1965-67. *Recreations:* golf, tennis, swimming. *Address:* 7007 Glenbrook Road, Bethesda, Md 20014, USA; 870 United Nations Plaza, New York, NY 10017. *Clubs:* Metropolitan (Washington); Burning Tree (Bethesda); The Recess, Racquet and Tennis, The Sky (NYC); Chevy Chase (Chevy Chase).

ROGERSON, John; Part-time Inspector, Department of the Environment, 1973-75; *b* 9 March 1917; *s* of late Walter John Lancashire Rogerson and Anne Marion Rogerson; *m* 1972, Audrey, *d* of late Adrian Maitland-Heriot and Dorothy Maitland-Heriot. *Educ:* Tonbridge Sch.; St John's Coll., Oxford (BA). Served War, 2nd Lieut, later Captain, Royal Norfolk Regt, 1940-46. Principal: Min. of Town and Country Planning, 1947-49; HM Treasury, 1949-51; Min. of Housing and Local Govt (later Dept of the Environment), 1951-73; Asst Sec., 1955; Under-Sec., 1963; retd 1973. *Recreations:* botany, archaeology, mycophagy. *Address:* 95 Ridgmount Gardens, WC1E 7AZ. *T:* 01-636 0433.

ROGG, Lionel; organist and composer; Professor of Organ and Counterpoint, Geneva Conservatoire de Musique, since 1961; *b* 1936; *m* Claudine Effront; three *s*. *Educ:* Conservatoire de Musique, Geneva (1st prize for piano and organ). Records include works by Alain, Buxtehude, Couperin and Martin; also complete works of J. S. Bach (Grand Prix du Disque, 1970, for The Art of the Fugue). *Compositions:* Acclamations, 1964; Chorale Preludes, 1971; Partita, 1975. *Publication:* Eléments de Contrepoint, 1969. *Address:* Conservatoire de Musique, Place Neuve, Geneva, Switzerland; 38A route de Troinex, 1227 Carouge, Geneva, Switzerland.

ROIJEN, Jan Herman Van; Grand Cross, Order of Orange Nassau; Commander, Order of the Netherlands Lion;

Netherlands Ambassador to the United Kingdom, 1964-70; Netherlands Ambassador to the Icelandic Republic, 1964-70; Netherlands Permanent Representative to Council of Western European Union, 1964-70; *b* Istanbul, 10 April 1905; *s* of Jan Herman van Roijen (sometime Netherlands Min. to USA), and (American-born) Albertina Winthrop van Roijen; *m* 1934, Anne Snouck Hurgronje; two *s* two *d*. *Educ:* Univ. of Utrecht. Doctor in Law, 1929. Joined Foreign Service, 1930; Attaché to Neths Legn, Washington, 1930-32; Min. of For. Affairs, 1933-36; Sec. to Neths Legn, Tokyo, 1936-39; Chief of Polit. Div. of Min. of For. Affairs, 1939. Jailed during German occupation; escaped to London, 1944. Minister without Portfolio, 1945; Minister for For. Affairs, March-July 1946; Asst Deleg. and Deleg. to UN Conf. and Assemblies, 1945-48; Ambassador to Canada, 1947-50. Leader, Neths Delegn to bring about Netherlands-Indonesian Round Table Conf., Batavia, 1949; Dep. Leader, Neths Delegn at Round Table Conf., The Hague, 1949. Ambassador to the United States, 1950-64. Leader, Neths Delegn in negotiations with Indonesia about W New Guinea, Middleburg (Va.) and New York, 1962. Holds several hon. doctorates in Laws, of Univs and Colls in USA; Gr. Cross, Order of Oak Crown, Luxembourg; Gr. Cross, Order of Falcon, Iceland; Comdr, Order of British Empire (CBE); Comdr, Order of Holy Treasure, Japan. *Recreations:* reading, theatre, golf. *Address:* Stoephoutflat, Stoeplaan 11, Wassenaar, Netherlands. *Clubs:* Turf, Beefsteak; Century Assoc. (NY); De Haagsche (The Hague).

ROKISON, Kenneth Stuart, QC 1976; *b* 13 April 1937; *s* of Frank Edward and Kitty Winifred Rokison; *m* 1973, Rosalind Julia (*née* Mitchell); two *d*. *Educ:* Whitgift School, Croydon; Magdalene College, Cambridge (BA 1960). Called to the Bar, Gray's Inn, 1961. *Recreations:* acting, theatre, watching cricket and Rugby football. *Address:* Ashcroft Farm, Gadbrook, Betchworth, Surrey. *T:* Dawes Green 244.

ROLAND, Nicholas; *see* Walmsley, Arnold Robert.

ROLFE, Rear-Adm. (Retd) Henry Cuthbert Norris, CB 1959; *b* 1908; *s* of Benedict Hugh Rolfe, MA Oxon; *m* 1931, Mary Monica Fox; one *s* two *d*. *Educ:* Pangbourne Nautical College. Joined Royal Navy, 1925. Served War of 1939-45: HMS Hermes, 1939; South-East Asia, 1944; Staff of Director of Air Warfare, Admiralty, 1947; Commanded HMS Veryan Bay, 1948; service with Royal Canadian Navy, 1949; Commanded HMS Vengeance, 1952; Commanded RN Air Station, Culdrose, 1952; Commanded HMS Centaur, 1954-56; Commanded RN Air Station, Ford, 1956-57; Asst Chief of Naval Staff (Warfare) 1957-60; Regional Director, Northern Region, Commonwealth Graves Commission, 1961-64, retd. Naval ADC to the Queen, 1957; Rear-Admiral, 1957. Liveryman, Worshipful Company of Coachmakers and Coach Harnessmakers, 1962. *Address:* 85 High Street, Market Lavington, Wiltshire.

ROLFE, Hume B.; *see* Boggis-Rolfe.

ROLL, family name of Baron Roll of Ipsden.

ROLL OF IPSDEN, Baron *cr* 1977 (Life Peer), of Ipsden in the County of Oxfordshire; **Eric Roll,** KCMG 1962 (CMG 1949); CB 1956; Director of the Bank of England, 1968-77; Chancellor, University of Southampton, since 1974; Chairman: S. G. Warburg & Co. Ltd, since 1974 (Deputy Chairman, 1967-74); Mercury Securities Ltd, since 1974; *b* 1 Dec. 1907; *yr s* of Mathias and Fany Roll; *m* 1934, Winifred, *o d* of Elliott and Sophia Taylor; two *d*. *Educ:* on the Continent; Univ. of Birmingham. BCom 1928; PhD 1930; Gladstone Memorial Prize, 1928; Univ. Research Scholarship, 1929. Prof. of Economics and Commerce, Univ. Coll. of Hull, 1935-46 (leave of absence 1939-46). Special Rockefeller Foundation Fellow, USA, 1939-41. Member, later Dep. Head, British Food Mission to N America, 1941-46; UK Dep. Member and UK Exec. Officer, Combined Food Board, Washington, until 1946; Asst Sec., Ministry of Food, 1946-47; Under-Secretary, HM Treasury (Central Economic Planning Staff), 1948; Minister, UK Delegation to OEEC, 1949. Deputy Head, United Kingdom Delegation to North Atlantic Treaty Organization, Paris, 1952; Under Secretary Ministry of Agriculture, Fisheries and Food, 1953-57; Executive Dir, International Sugar Council, 1957-59; Chm., United Nations Sugar Conf., 1958; Deputy Secretary, Ministry of Agriculture, Fisheries and Food, 1959-61; Deputy Leader, UK Delegation for negotiations with the European Economic Community, 1961-63; Economic Minister and Head of UK Treasury Delegation, Washington, 1963-64, also Exec. Dir for the UK International Monetary Fund and International Bank for Reconstruction and Development; Permanent Under-Sec. of State, Dept of Economic Affairs, 1964-66. Chm., subseq. Hon. Chm., Book Development Council, 1967-. Independent

Mem., NEDC, 1971-. Dir, Times Newspapers Ltd, 1967-; also other Directorships. Hon. DSc Hull, 1967; Hon. DSocSci Birmingham, 1967; Hon. LLD Southampton, 1974. *Publications:* An Early Experiment in Industrial Organization, 1930; Spotlight on Germany, 1933; About Money, 1934; Elements of Economic Theory, 1935; Organized Labour (collaborated), 1938; The British Commonwealth at War (collaborated), 1943; A History of Economic Thought, 1954, new edn, 1973; The Combined Food Board, 1957; The World After Keynes, 1968; articles in Economic Jl, Economica, American Economic Review, etc. *Recreation:* reading. *Address:* D2 Albany, Piccadilly, W1. *Clubs:* Athenæum, Brooks's.

ROLL, Rev. Sir James (William Cecil), 4th Bt, *cr* 1921; Vicar of St John's, Becontree, since 1958; *b* 1 June 1912; *s* of Sir Cecil Ernest Roll, 3rd Bt, and Mildred Kate (*d* 1926), *d* of William Wells, Snaresbrook; *S* father, 1938; unmarried. *Educ:* Chigwell School, Essex; Pembroke College, Oxford; Chichester Theological College. Deacon, 1937. Curate East Ham Parish Church, 1944-58. *Heir:* none. *Address:* St John's Vicarage, 34 Castle Road, Dagenham, Essex. *T:* 01-592 5409.

ROLLO, family name of **Baron Rollo.**

ROLLO, 13th Baron, *cr* 1651; **Eric John Stapylton Rollo;** Baron Dunning, 1869; JP; *b* 3 Dec. 1915; *s* of 12th Baron and Helen Maud (*d* 1928), *o c* of Frederick Chetwynd Stapylton of Hatton Hill, Windlesham, Surrey; *S* father, 1947; *m* 1938, Suzanne Hatton; two *s* one *d*. *Educ:* Eton. Served War of 1939-45, Grenadier Guards, retiring with rank of Captain. JP Perthshire, 1962. *Heir: s* Master of Rollo, *qv. Address:* Pitcairns, Dunning, Perthshire. *T:* Dunning 202.

ROLLO, Master of; Hon. David Eric Howard Rollo; *b* 31 March 1943; *s* and *heir* of 13th Baron Rollo, *qv*; *m* 1971, Felicity Anne Christian, *o d* of Lt-Comdr J. B. Lamb; two *s*. *Educ:* Eton. Captain Grenadier Guards. *Address:* 20 Draycott Avenue, SW3. *Clubs:* Cavalry and Guards, Turf.

ROLO, Cyril Felix, CMG 1975; OBE 1959; HM Diplomatic Service, retired; *b* 13 Feb. 1918; *s* of late I. J. Rolo and Linda (*née* Suares); *m* 1948, Marie Luise Christine (*née* Baeurle); one *s*. *Educ:* Charterhouse; Oriel Coll., Oxford (BA). Served with Armed Forces, 1940-46 (Major): Oxf. and Bucks LI, later on Gen. Staff; Western Desert, E Africa, Italy, Austria. Joined HM Foreign (subseq. Diplomatic) Service, 1946: Allied Commn for Austria, 1947-48; 2nd Sec., Rome, 1948-50; Political Adviser's Office, Berlin, 1950-52; FO, 1952-57; 1st Sec., Vienna, 1957-62; FO (subseq. FCO), 1962-76; Counsellor, 1971. *Recreations:* travel, golf, reading. *Address:* 32 Roxburghe Mansion, Kensington Court, W8 5BH. *T:* 01-927 4696;·2 Queen's Street, Bloxham, Oxon. *Clubs:* Travellers'; Sunningdale Golf.

ROLPH, C. H.; *see* Hewitt, Cecil R.

ROMAIN, Roderick Jessel Anidjar; Metropolitan Magistrate, since 1972; a Deputy Circuit Judge, since 1975; *b* 2 Dec. 1916; *s* of late Artom A. Romain and Winifred (*née* Rodrigues); *m* 1947, Miriam, *d* of late Semtob Sequerra; one *s* one *d*. *Educ:* Malvern Coll.; Sidney Sussex Coll., Cambridge (MA(Hons)). Called to the Bar, Middle Temple, 1939. Commissioned from HAC to 27th Field Regt, RA, 1940. Served War of 1939-45; France and Belgium, also N Africa and Italy, JAG Staff, 1943-45; JA at Neuengamme War Crimes Trial. Admitted a Solicitor, 1949, in practice as Partner, in Freke Palmer, Romain & Gassman, until 1972; recalled to Bar, Middle Temple, 1973. *Recreations:* golf, gardening. *Address:* 43 Lyndale Avenue, NW2 2QB. *T:* 01-435 5913. *Clubs:* Garrick; Royal Eastbourne.

ROMANES, Professor George John, CBE 1971; PhD; Professor of Anatomy, Edinburgh University since 1954; *b* 2 Dec. 1916; *s* of George Romanes, BSc, AMICE, and Isabella Elizabeth Burn Smith; *m* 1945, Muriel Grace Adam, Edinburgh; four *d*. *Educ:* Edinburgh Academy; Christ's College, Cambridge (BA, PhD); Edinburgh University (MB, ChB). Marmaduke Sheild Scholar in Human Anatomy, 1938-40; Demonstrator in Anatomy, Cambridge, 1939; Beit Memorial Fellow for Medical Research, Cambridge, 1944-46; Lectr in Neuroanatomy, Edinburgh, 1946; Prof. of Anatomy, Edinburgh, 1954. Commonwealth Fund Fell., Columbia Univ., NY, 1949-50. Chm., Bd of Management, Edinburgh Royal Infirmary, 1959-74. Mem. Anatomical Soc. of Gt Brit. and Ireland; Mem. Amer. Assoc. of Anatomists; Assoc. Mem. Amer. Neurological Assoc. FRSE 1955; FRCSE 1958. *Publications:* (ed) Cunningham's Textbook and Manuals of Anatomy; various papers on the anatomy and development of the nervous system in Jl of Anatomy and Jl of Comparative Neurology. *Recreations:* angling and curling. *Address:* 197 Colinton Road, Edinburgh EH14 1BJ. *T:* 031-443 1101.

ROME, Maj.-Gen. Francis David, CB 1955; CMG 1959; CBE 1949; DSO 1944; retired; *b* 11 Sept. 1905; *er s* of late Francis James Rome; *m* 1936, Sybil Parry, 2nd *d* of late Lieut-Colonel Henry Carden, DCLI; no *c. Educ:* Cheltenham Coll.; RMC, Sandhurst. Commander: 111 Indian Infantry Brigade, Special Force, SEAC, 1944-45 (DSO); 3rd Parachute Bde, 1946-47; 1st Parachute Bde, 1947-48 (CBE). Served War of 1939-45, France, 1939-40, SEAC, 1943-45; Palestine, 1946-48; Malaya, 1950-51; General Officer Commanding, 16th Airborne Division (Territorial Army), 1953-56; General Officer Commanding, Berlin (British Sector), 1956-59. Colonel, The Royal Fusiliers, 1954-59. *Recreations:* shooting, fishing. *Address:* Ferne Down, Ham, Marlborough, Wilts SN8 3RB. *T:* Inkpen 341. *Club:* Army and Navy.

ROMER, Mark Lemon Robert; a Metropolitan Stipendiary Magistrate since 1972; *b* 12 July 1927; *s* of late Rt Hon. Sir Charles Romer, OBE, and Hon. Lady Romer; *m* 1953, Philippa Maynard Tomson; one *s* two *d. Educ:* Bryanston; Trinity Hall, Cambridge (BA, LLB). Called to Bar, Lincoln's Inn, 1952; practised privately until 1958 when joined Govt Legal Service. *Recreations:* bird-watching, reading, music. *Address:* The Old Vicarage, Braughing, Ware, Herts. *T:* Ware 821434.

ROMILLY, family name of **Baron Romilly.**

ROMILLY, 4th Baron, *cr* 1865; **William Gaspard Guy Romilly,** Hon. MA Oxon 1943; *b* 8 March 1899; *o c* of 3rd Baron and Violet Edith, *o sister* of Sir Philip H. B. Grey Egerton, 12th Bt, and *niece* of Lord Londesborough; *S* father, 1905; *m* 1st, 1929, Hon. Diana Joan Sackville-West (marriage dissolved, 1944), *o d* of 4th Baron Sackville, KBE; 2nd, 1944, Dora (*d* 1960), *d* of late Reginald Morris; 3rd, 1966, Elizabeth, *widow* of Capt. Lionel Cecil, and *er d* of late Charles M. Clover. *Educ:* Eton; Sandhurst. Coldstream Guards, 1917-23; served in France in European War; Reserve of Officers, 1923. Rejoined Coldstream Guards, September 1939; served until 1945 and granted honorary rank of Major. Member of Malborough and Ramsbury Rural District Council, 1949-74 (Chairman, 1964-67). *Heir:* none. *Address:* Bridge House, Chilton Foliat, near Hungerford, Berks. *T:* Hungerford 2328.

ROMNEY, 7th Earl of, *cr* 1801; **Michael Henry Marsham;** Bt 1663; Baron of Romney, 1716; Viscount Marsham, 1801; *b* 22 Nov. 1910; *s* of Lt-Col the Hon. Reginald Marsham Marsham, OBE (*d* 1922) (2nd *s* of 4th Earl) and Dora Hermione (*d* 1923), *d* of late Charles North; *S* cousin, 1975; *m* 1939, Frances Aileen, *o d* of late Lt-Col James Russell Landale, IA. *Educ:* Sherborne. Served War of 1939-45, Major RA. *Heir: cousin* Julian Charles Marsham, *b* 28 March 1948. *Address:* Wensum Farm, West Rudham, King's Lynn, Norfolk. *T:* East Rudham 249.

RONALD, Mrs Edmund; *see* Templeton, Mrs Edith.

RONALDS, Andrew John, CBE 1961 (OBE 1951); *b* 4 Feb. 1897; *s* of General John Romanenko and Mary (*née* Drentenl); *m* 1918, Nathalie (*d* 1975), *d* of General Nicolas Woronow and Catherine (*née* Genishta); no *c. Educ:* Imperial Corps of Pages, St Petersburg. Served European War, 1914-18, with Russian Army, 4th Guards Rifles, Imperial Family's Own (twice wounded, Major); attached British Mil. Mission in S Russia, 1919-20; served at British Vice-Consulate, Dubrovnik, 1926-29. Entered British Consular Service, 1936, established in Foreign Service, 1947; served at Belgrade, Sarajevo, Split (captured by enemy forces, 1941), Lisbon, Lourenço Marques, Athens, Naples, Venice, Beira and Bilbao; Consul General at Tananarive, Madagascar, 1956; Ambassador to Malagasy Republic (Madagascar), 1960-61; retired August 1961. On special service with Armed Forces in ME and Central Mediterranean, 1943-45 (despatches). Imperial Order of St George, 4th Class (Russia). *Recreations:* music, walking. *Address:* c/o Barclays National Bank Ltd, PO Box 471, East London 5200, South Africa. *Clubs:* Civil Service; Società Dell'Unione (Venice).

RONALDSHAY, Earl of; Lawrence Mark Dundas; *b* 28 Dec. 1937; *e s* of 3rd Marquess of Zetland, *qv*; *m* 1964, Susan, 2nd *d* of Guy Chamberlin, Shefford House, Great Shefford, and late Mrs Chamberlin; two *s* two *d. Educ:* Harrow School; Christ's College, Cambridge. Late 2nd Lieut, Grenadier Guards. *Heir: s* Lord Dundas, *qv. Address:* Hill House, Cheriton, Alresford, Hampshire. *T:* Bramdean 377.

ROOK, Prof. John Allan Fynes, FRSE, FRIC, FIBiol; Director, Hannah Research Institute, Ayr; Hannah Professor of Animal Nutrition, University of Glasgow, since 1971; *b* 1 May 1926; *s* of Edward Fynes Rook and Annie Rook; *m* 1952, Marion Horsburgh Millar; two *s* one *d. Educ:* Scarborough Boys' High Sch.; University College of Wales, Aberystwyth. BSc, DSc (Wales); PhD (Glasgow). National Institute for Research in Dairying, Shinfield, Berks, 1954-65; Prof. of Agricultural Chemistry, Univ. of Leeds, 1965-70. *Publications:* numerous articles in British Jl of Nutrition, Jl of Dairy Research, etc. *Recreations:* gardening, golf; shutting doors and switching off lights after other members of the family. *Address:* 37 Dunure Road, Ayr, Scotland. *T:* Alloway 41933. *Club:* Farmers'.

ROOKE, Daphne Marie; author; *b* 6 March 1914; *d* of Robert Pizzey and Marie Knevitt; *m* 1937, Irvin Rooke; one *d. Educ:* Durban, S Africa. *Publications:* A Grove of Fever Trees, 1950; Mittee, 1951; Ratoons; The South African Twins, 1953; The Australian Twins, 1954; Wizards' Country; The New Zealand Twins, 1957; Beti, 1959; A Lover for Estelle, 1961; The Greyling, 1962; Diamond Jo, 1965; Boy on the Mountain, 1969; Double Ex!, 1970; Margaretha de la Porte, 1974; A Horse of his Own, 1976. *Recreation:* bushwalking. *Address:* Bardouroka, NSW 2315, Australia.

ROOKE, Sir Denis (Eric), Kt 1977; CBE 1970; BSc (Eng.); Chairman, British Gas Corporation (formerly The Gas Council), since 1976 (Deputy Chairman, 1972-76); *b* 2 April 1924; *yr s* of F. G. Rooke; *m* 1949, Elizabeth Brenda, *d* of D. D. Evans, Ystradgynlais, Brecon; one *d. Educ:* Westminster City Sch.; Addey and Stanhope Sch.; University Coll., London (Fellow, 1972). Served with REME, UK and India, 1944-49 (Major). Joined staff of S Eastern Gas Bd as Asst Mechanical Engr in coal-tar by-products works, 1949; Dep. Man. of works, 1954; seconded to N Thames Gas Bd, 1957, for work in UK and USA on liquefied natural gas; mem. technical team which sailed in Methane Pioneer on first voyage bringing liquefied natural gas to UK, 1959; S Eastern Gas Bd's Development Engr, 1959; Development Engr, Gas Council, 1960; Mem. for Production and Supplies, 1966-71. Member: Adv. Council for R&D, 1972-77; Adv. Council for Energy Conservation, 1974-77; Offshore Energy Technology Bd, 1975-; British National Oil Corp., 1976-; NEDC, 1976-; Energy Commn, 1977. Pres., IGasE, 1975. *Publications:* papers to Instn of Gas Engrs, World Power Conf., World Petroleum Conf., etc. *Recreations:* photography, listening to music. *Address:* 23 Hardy Road, Blackheath, SE3. *Clubs:* Athenæum, English-Speaking Union.

ROOKE, Giles Hugh, TD 1963; a Recorder of the Crown Court, since 1975; *b* 28 Oct. 1930; *s* of late Charles Eustace Rooke, CMG, and Irene Phyllis Rooke; *m* 1968, Anne Bernadette Seymour, *d* of His Honour Judge Perrett, *qv*; two *s* one *d. Educ:* Stowe; Exeter Coll., Oxford (MA). Kent Yeomanry, 1951-61, Kent and County of London Yeomanry, 1961-65 (TA), Major. Called to Bar, Lincoln's Inn, 1957; practised SE Circuit, 1957-. *Address:* St Stephen's Cottage, Bridge, Canterbury CT4 5AH. *T:* Bridge 830298. *Club:* Junior Carlton.

ROOKE, James Smith, CMG 1961; OBE 1949; Chief Executive, British Overseas Trade Board, 1972-75; HM Diplomatic Service, retired; now company director; *b* 6 July 1916; *s* of Joseph Nelson Rooke and Adeline Mounser (*née* Woodgate); *m* 1938, Maria Theresa Rebrec, Vienna; one *s* two *d. Educ:* Workington Grammar Sch.; University College, London; Vienna Univ. Apptd to Dept of Overseas Trade, 1938. Military service, 1940-45, KRRC and AEC. Second Secretary (Commercial), British Embassy, Bogotá, 1946; UK Delegation to ITO Conf., Havana, 1947; Dep. UK Commercial Rep., Frankfurt, 1948; First Secretary (Commercial), British Embassy, Rome, 1951; Consul (Commercial), Milan, 1954; Deputy Consul-General (Commercial), New York, 1955-59; HM Counsellor (Commercial) British Embassy, Berne, 1959-63, Rome, 1963-66; Minister (Commercial), British High Commn, Canberra, 1966-68; Minister (Economic), British Embassy, Paris, 1968-72. *Recreations:* climbing, tennis, ski-ing. *Address:* 18 Wedderburn Road, NW3. *Club:* East India, Devonshire, Sports and Public Schools.

ROOKER, Jeffrey William, CEng; MP (Lab) Birmingham, Perry Barr, since 1974; *b* 5 June 1941; *m* 1972, Angela. *Educ:* Handsworth Tech. Sch.; Handsworth Tech. Coll.; Warwick Univ. (MA); Aston Univ. (BScEng). CEng, MIProdE, Grad. IMechE; AMBIM. Apprentice toolmaker, King's Heath Engrg Co. Ltd, Birmingham, 1957-63; student apprentice, BLMC, 1963-64; Asst to Works Manager, Geo. Salter & Co., West Bromwich, 1964-65; Assembly Manager, 1965-67; Prodn Manager, Rola Celestion Ltd, Thames Ditton and Ipswich, 1967-70; Industrial Relations and Safety Officer, Metro-Cammell, Birmingham, 1971; Lectr, Lanchester Polytechnic, Coventry, 1972-74. Mem. Council, Instn of Prodn Engrs, 1975-. *Recreation:* full-time MP. *Address:* 14 Spiral Court, Wheelwright Road, Birmingham B24 8NU. *T:* 021-350 6186.

ROOM, Thomas Gerald, FRS 1941; Professor of Mathematics, Sydney University, 1935-68, now Emeritus; *b* 10 Nov. 1902; 2nd *s* of E. W. Room, OBE, JP; *m* 1937, Jessie, *d* of C. F. Bannerman; one *s* two *d. Educ:* Alleyn's School; St John's Coll., Cambridge (ScD). Asst Lectr, Liverpool University, 1925; Fellow of St John's College, Cambridge, 1927-29; Lecturer in Mathematics, Cambridge University, 1929-34; Visiting Prof. of Mathematics: Univ. of Washington, 1948; Univ. of Tennessee, 1949; Univ. of Sussex, 1966; Westfield Coll., Univ. of London, 1969-70; Open Univ., 1971-73. Fellow Sydney University Senate and Dean of Faculty of Science, 1952-56, 1960-65. Member Inst. for Advanced Study, Princeton, NJ, 1949 and 1957-58; Vis. Lectr, Univ. of Princeton, 1958. Pres., Austr. Mathematical Soc., 1960-62. *Publications:* Geometry of Determinantal Loci, 1939; The Sorting Process, 1966; A Background to Geometry, 1967; Miniquaternion Geometry, 1970. *Address:* High Walden, St Ives, NSW 2075, Australia. *T:* (Sydney) 449-5743.

ROOME, Rear-Admiral Henry Stewart, CBE 1949; *b* 7 May 1896; *s* of late Eng. Rear-Adm. G. W. Roome, CBE; *m* 1921, Aileen D. M. L., *d* of Comdr C. T. Scott, RIM; two *s* one *d. Educ:* RN Colleges; Osborne, Dartmouth, Keyham. Midshipman, HMS Bellerophon, 1913; acting Sub-Lt 1915. Served European War in Grand Fleet Destroyers, 1916-18 (despatches); Lieut, 1917; RN Coll., Keyham, 1918; Lieut (E) 1919; Comdr (E), 1928; Capt. (E), 1940. ADC to the King, 1946-47; Rear-Adm. (E), 1947. Served War of 1939-45, HM Dockyards, Devonport and Sheerness; and at Admiralty; Manager Engineering Department, HM Dockyard, Portsmouth, 1945-50; retired, 1950. *Address:* Moorlands, Moorland Avenue, Barton-on-Sea, Hants.

ROOME, Maj.-Gen. Oliver McCrea, CBE 1973; *b* 9 March 1921; *s* of late Maj.-Gen. Sir Horace Roome, KCIE, CB, CBE, MC, DL, late Royal Engineers; *m* 1947, Isobel Anstis, *d* of Rev. A. B. Jordan; two *s* one *d. Educ:* Wellington Coll. Commissioned in Royal Engineers, 1940. Served War: UK, Western Desert, Sicily, Italy, 1939-45. Various appts, UK, Far and Middle East, Berlin, 1946-68; IDC, 1969; Director of Army Recruiting, 1970-73; Chief, Jt Services Liaison Organisation, Bonn, 1973-76; retired. County Comr, Scouts, Isle of Wight, 1977-. *Recreations:* sailing, maritime and military history. *Address:* Lloyds Bank Ltd, 6 Pall Mall, SW1. *Clubs:* Royal Ocean Racing, Royal Cruising, Army and Navy.

ROOT, Frederick James, CB 1952; Deputy Secretary, Ministry of Public Building and Works (previously Ministry of Works), 1959-66; *b* 2 July 1906; *s* of late Alan and Elizabeth A. Root; *m* 1941, Margaret Eleanor Barbour, *d* of late Dr G. F. Barbour Simpson, Edinburgh; two *d. Educ:* Christ's Hosp.; Merton Coll., Oxford. Entered Civil Service, 1928; Private Secretary to successive First Commissioners of Works, 1933-37, and to successive Ministers of Works, 1940-43. *Address:* Halland, Pathfields Close, Haslemere, Surrey GU27 2BL. *T:* Haslemere 3750. *Club:* Athenæum.

ROOT, Rev. Prof. Howard Eugene; Professor of Theology, University of Southampton, since 1966; *b* 13 April 1926; *s* of late Howard Root and Flora Hoskins; *m* 1952, Celia, *e* *d* of late Col R. T. Holland, CBE, DSO, MC; two *s* two *d. Educ:* Univ. of Southern California; St Catherine's Coll. and Magdalen Coll., Oxford; Ripon Hall, Oxford. BA S Calif 1945; BA Oxon 1951; MA Oxon 1970; MA Cantab 1953. Teaching Fellow, 1945-47; Instructor, American Univ., Cairo, 1947-49; Sen. Demy, Magdalen Coll., Oxford, and Liddon Student, 1952-53. Deacon, 1953; Priest, 1954. Curate of Trumpington, 1953; Asst Lectr in Divinity, Cambridge, 1953-57; Lectr, 1957-65; Fellow, Emmanuel Coll., Cambridge, 1954-65, Chaplain, 1954-56, Dean, 1956-65. Wilde Lectr Oxford Univ., 1957-60; Senior Denyer and Johnson Scholar, Oxford, 1963-64; Bampton Lectr, Univ. of Oxford, 1972. Exam. Chaplain to Bishops of Southwark, Bristol and Winchester; Official Anglican Observer at Second Vatican Council, 1963-65; Consultant, Lambeth Conf., 1968. Chm., Archbishops' Commn on Marriage, 1968-71; Member: Academic Council, Ecumenical Inst., Jerusalem, 1966-; Anglican-RC Preparatory Commn, 1967-68; Archbishops' Commn on Christian Doctrine, 1967-74; Anglican-Roman Catholic Internat. Commn, 1969-. Hon. Chaplain, Winchester Cathedral, 1966-67; Canon Theologian of Winchester, 1967-. Mem., BBC Central Religious Adv. Cttee, 1971-75. Jt Editor, Jl of Theol Studies, 1969-74. *Recreations:* music, silence. *Address:* Department of Theology, The University, Southampton SO9 5NH. *T:* 559122.

ROOTES, family name of **Baron Rootes.**

ROOTES, 2nd Baron *cr* 1959; **William Geoffrey Rootes;** Chairman, 1967-73, Chrysler United Kingdom (lately Rootes

Motors Ltd); *b* 14 June 1917; *er* *s* of 1st Baron Rootes, GBE; *S* father, 1964; *m* 1946, Marian, *widow* of Wing Comdr J. H. Slater, AFC, and *d* of late Lt-Col H. R. Hayter, DSO; one *s* one *d. Educ:* Harrow; Christ Church, Oxford. Served War of 1939-45 in RASC (France, E Africa, Western Desert, Libya, Tunisia and Italy), demobilised, Actg Major, 1946. Rejoined Rootes Group, 1946: Man. Dir, 1962-67; Dep. Chm., 1965-67; Chm. 1967-70. Director: Rank Hovis McDougall, 1973-; Joseph Lucas Industries Ltd, 1973-. Pres., Motor & Cycle Trades Benevolent Fund, 1968-70. Member: Nat. Adv. Council, Motor Manufrg Industry, 1964-71; Nat. Economic Development Cttee, Motor Manufacturing Industry, 1968-73; BNEC (Chm., American Cttee, 1969-71); Council, CBI, 1967-74, Europe Cttee CBI, 1972-76; Council, Inst. of Dirs, 1953-; Council, Warwick Univ., 1968-74 (Chm., Careers Adv. Bd); Hon. Officer, 1958-62, Chm. Exec. Cttee, 1972-73, Pres., 1960-61, SMMT; President: Motor Ind. Research Assoc., 1970-71; Inst. of Motor Industry, 1973-75. Chm., Game Conservancy, 1975-. FBIM; FRSA. County Pres., St John Ambulance, Berks. *Recreations:* shooting, tennis, ski-ing. *Heir:* *s* Hon. Nicholas Geoffrey Rootes, *b* 12 July 1951. *Address:* North Standen House, Hungerford, Berks RG17 0QZ; Glenalmond House, Glenalmond, Perthshire. *Clubs:* Brooks's, Buck's, Flyfishers'.

ROOTES, Sir Reginald (Claud), Kt 1946; *b* 20 Oct. 1896; *s* of late William and Jane Rootes; *m* 1st, 1922, Ruth Joyce, *d* of late Harding Bensted; one *s*; 2nd, 1938, Nancy Norris, *d* of late J. C. Beadle. *Educ:* Cranbrook Sch., Kent, Civil Service, Admiralty, 1915-18. Pres. Society of Motor Manufacturers and Traders, 1945-46, Dep. Pres., 1946-50; Past Pres. Motor Industry Research Assoc. *Recreations:* various. *Address:* Polla House, Hothfield, Ashford, Kent. *T:* Ashford 21495. *Club:* Buck's.

ROOTHAM, Jasper St John, MA; *b* 21 Nov. 1910; *s* of Dr Cyril Bradley and Rosamond Margaret Rootham; *m* 1944, Joan McClelland; one *s* one *d. Educ:* Tonbridge Sch. (Judd Schol.); St John's Coll., Cambridge (Maj. Schol.). 1st cl. Class. Tripos Pts I and II. Entered Civil Service, 1933; Min. of Agric., 1933-34; CO, 1934-36; Treasury, 1936-38; Pte Sec. to Prime Minister, 1938-39; Treasury, 1939-40; resigned to join Army, 1940; served Middle East, Balkans, Germany (despatches); demobilized, 1946 (Col); entered Bank of England as Actg Asst Adviser, 1946; Adviser to Governor, 1957; Chief of Overseas Dept, 1962; Asst to Governor, 1964; retd, 1967. Man. Dir, Lazard Bros & Co. Ltd, 1967-75; Dir, Agricultural Mortgage Corp., 1967-77 (Dep. Chm., 1973-77); Director: British Sugar Corp.; Stanley Miller Holdings, Newcastle. *Publications:* Miss Fire, 1946; Demi-Paradise, 1960; Verses 1928-72, 1972; The Celestial City and Other Poems, 1975. *Recreations:* music, country life. *Address:* Crag House, Wall, Hexham, Northumberland NE46 4HA. *T:* Humshaugh 276. *Clubs:* Overseas Bankers'; Northern Counties (Newcastle upon Tyne).

ROOTS, Paul John; Employee Relations Director, Ford Motor Co. Ltd, since 1974; Lecturer in Industrial Relations; *b* 16 Oct. 1929; *s* of John Earl and Helen Roots; *m* 1951, Anna Theresa Pateman; two *s* two *d. Educ:* Dormers Wells Sch.; London Sch. of Economics. Cert. in Personnel Admin. MIPM. RN, 1947-54: service in Korean War. Personnel Officer, Brush Gp, 1955; Labour Officer, UKAEA, 1956, Labour Manager, 1959; Ford Motor Co. Ltd: Personnel Manager, Halewood, 1962; Forward Planning Manager, 1966; Labour Relations Manager, 1969. Member: Employee Rel. Cttee, IPM, 1973-; CBI Sub-Cttee on European Social Affairs, 1973-. *Publications:* articles in personnel management jls. *Recreations:* riding, theatre, music. *Address:* Low Waters, The Ridge, Little Baddow, Chelmsford, Essex. *T:* Danbury 3269.

ROPER; *see* Trevor-Roper.

ROPER, Captain Edward Gregson, CBE 1959; DSO 1942; DSC; Capt. RN retd; *b* 12 April 1910; *s* of late John Gregson Roper, OBE; *m* 1933, Sylvia, *d* of E. F. L. Hopkins; one *d. Educ:* Oundle. Joined Royal Navy, 1928; served War of 1939-45 (DSC, DSO): Comd HMS Velox, 1940-42; Impulsive, 1942-43; Comdr, 1943; Comd 18th Destroyer Flotilla, 1944-45. Captain, 1950; Comd HMS Ocean, 1955-56; Royal Naval College, Greenwich, 1956-59; retired, 1959. *Address:* Polmayne, Rock, Cornwall.

ROPER, Maj.-Gen. Henry Ernest, CB 1976; BSc(Eng), CEng, MIERE; Assistant Chief of Staff (Operational Requirements), Ministry of Defence, since 1975; *b* 6 April 1923; *s* of late Ernest Roper and Lydia (*née* Hayward); *m* 1950, Beryl Claire (*née* Jennings); one *s* one *d. Educ:* Queen Mary's Grammar Sch., Walsall; Worcester Coll., Oxford; RMCS, Shrivenham. Commnd Royal Signals, 1942; served War: UK, NW Europe, SEAC, 1941-45; FE, UK, BAOR, 1946-58; ptsc 1952; HQ 51 Independ. Inf. Bde, Cyprus, 1958-59; DS, RMCS, 1959-62; 7th

Signal Regt, BAOR, 1962-64; Comd, 30th Signal Regt, 1964-66; Asst Mil. Sec., MoD, 1966-67; Col, GS Army Signals Equipment, 1967-68; Dir, Proj. Mallard, Min. of Tech., 1968-71; RCDS, 1971-72; CSO, BAOR, 1972-75. *Recreations:* all ball games, athletics (Chm., Army Athletic Assoc.), radio controlled model aircraft. *Address:* c/o Midland Bank Ltd, The Bridge, Walsall, Staffs WS1 1LN. *Club:* Army and Navy.

ROPER, John Charles Abercromby, CMG 1969; MC; HM Diplomatic Service, retired; *b* 8 June 1915; *s* of late Charles Roper, MD, and of Mrs Roper; *m* 1st, 1945, Valerie Armstrong-MacDonnell (marr. diss.); two *d*; 2nd, 1960, Kathryn, *d* of late Edgar Bibas, New York. *Educ:* Harrow; Universities of Cambridge and Princeton (Commonwealth Fellow). Served 1939-46, Scots Guards and Special Forces, Major (MC). HM Diplomatic Service, 1946; Athens, 1947-51; Foreign Office, 1951-54; Washington, 1954-59. Seconded to Min. of Defence and apptd Dep. Commandant (Civil) of NATO Defence College, Paris, 1960-62; Asst Sec., Cabinet Office, 1962-64; Counsellor, UK Delegn to OECD, 1964-70; Ambassador to Luxembourg, 1970-75. *Address:* Cavallini, Paganico, Provincia di Grosseto, Italy; Island of Hydra, Greece. *Clubs:* Bath, Special Forces.

ROPER, John (Francis Hodgess); MP (Lab and Co-op) Farnworth since 1970; *b* 10 Sept. 1935; *e s* of Rev. Frederick Mabor Hodgess Roper and Ellen Frances (*née* Brockway); *m* 1959, Valerie Hope, *er d* of late Rt Hon. L. John Edwards, PC, OBE, MP, and Mrs D. M. Edwards; one *d*. *Educ:* William Hulme's Grammar Sch., Manchester; Reading Sch.; Magdalen Coll., Oxford; Univ. of Chicago. Nat. Service, commnd RNVR, 1954-56; studied PPE, Oxford, 1956-59 (Pres. UN Student Assoc., 1957; organised Univ. referendum on Nuclear Disarmament); Harkness Fellow, Commonwealth Fund, 1959-61; Research Fellow in Economic Statistics, Univ. of Manchester, 1961; Asst Lectr in Econs, 1962-64, Lectr 1964-70, Faculty Tutor 1968-70. Contested (Lab) High Peak (Derbs), 1964. Sec., Anglo-Benelux Parly Gp, 1974-; Vice-Chm., Anglo-German Parly Gp, 1974-; Chm., British-Atlantic Gp of Young Politicians, 1974-75. Council of Europe: Consultant, 1965-66; Mem., Consultative Assembly, 1973-; Vice-Chm., Ctttee on Culture and Educn, 1974-; Mem., WEU, 1973-. Chm., Labour Cttee for Europe, 1976-; Vice-Chm., GB East Europe Centre, 1974-. Research Adviser (part-time), DEA in NW, 1967-69. Director: Co-op. Wholesale Soc., 1969-74; Co-op Insurance Soc., 1973-74. Pres., Gen. Council, UNA, 1972-; Mem. Council, Inst. of Fiscal Studies, 1975-; Mem. Gen. Adv. Council, IBA, 1974-. Vice-Pres., Manchester Statistical Soc., 1971-. Trustee, Hist. of Parlt Trust, 1974-. *Publications:* (with Lloyd Harrison) Towards Regional Co-operatives, 1967; The Teaching of Economics at University Level, 1970; articles and reviews in Co-operative jls and Manchester School. *Recreations:* reading, travel. *Address:* House of Commons, SW1. *Clubs:* Farnworth and Kearsley Labour (Kearsley, Lancs).

ROPER, Robert Burnell; Chief Land Registrar, since 1975 (Deputy Chief Land Registrar, 1973-75); *b* 23 Nov. 1921; *s* of Allen George and Winifred Roper; *m* 1948, Mary Brookes; two *s*. *Educ:* King's College Sch., Wimbledon; King's Coll., London. LLB (Hons) 1941. Called to Bar, Gray's Inn, 1948. Served War, RAF, 1942-46. Miners' Welfare Commn, 1946-48; Nat. Coal Bd, 1948-49; Treasury Solicitor's Dept, 1949-50; HM Land Registry, 1950-. *Publications:* (Ruoff and Roper) The Law and Practice of Registered Conveyancing, 3rd edn, 1972; Consulting Editor on Land Registration matters for Encyclopaedia of Forms and Precedents (4th edn). *Recreations:* golf, squash racquets. *Address:* 22 Hood Road, West Wimbledon, SW20 0SR. *T:* 01-946 5508. *Club:* University Vandals RFC (Walton-on-Thames).

ROPER-CURZON, family name of **Baron Teynham**.

ROPNER, Sir John (Bruce Woollacott), 2nd Bt *cr* 1952; Director, Ropner Holdings Ltd; *b* 16 April 1937; *s* of Sir Leonard Ropner, 1st Bt, MC, TD, and of Esmé, *y d* of late Bruce Robertson; *S* father, 1977; *m* 1st, 1961, Anne Melicent (marr. diss. 1970), *d* of late Sir Ralph Delmé-Radcliffe; two *d*; 2nd, 1970, Auriol, *d* of Captain Graham Lawrie Mackeson-Sandbach, Caerllo, Llangernyw; two *d*. *Educ:* Eton; St Paul's School, USA. *Address:* Park House, Bedale, Yorks.

ROPNER, John Raymond; Director, Ropner Holdings Ltd, and other companies; *b* 8 May 1903; *s* of William Ropner; *m* 1928, Joan Redhead; two *s* one *d*. *Educ:* Harrow; Clare College, Cambridge (BAEcon 1925). Durham Heavy Bde, RA (TA), 1922-28; joined Sir R. Ropner & Co. Ltd, 1925; Ministry of War Transport, North Western Europe, 1944-45. High Sheriff of Durham, 1958. Member, Shipping Advisory Panel, 1962. Order of Oranje-Nassau, 1947. *Recreations:* gardening, fishing; formerly golf (Cambridge blue, 1925). *Address:* Middleton Lodge, Middleton Tyas, Richmond, Yorks. *T:* Barton (Yorks) 212. *Club:* Bath.

ROPNER, Sir Robert Douglas, 4th Bt, *cr* 1904; *b* 1 Dec. 1921; *o s* of Sir (E. H. O.) Robert Ropner, 3rd Bt; *S* father, 1962; *m* 1943, Patricia Kathleen, *d* of W. E. Scofield, W. Malling, Kent; one *s* one *d*. *Educ:* Harrow. Formerly Captain, RA. *Heir: s* Robert Clinton Ropner, *b* 6 Feb. 1949.

ROSCOE, Edward John Townsend; Director, Willis Faber & Dumas Ltd, 1957-73 (Chairman, 1967-71); *b* 21 March 1913; *o s* of late Edward Gawne Roscoe and Mary Frances Roscoe, Clifton Manor, Warwicks; *m* 1st, 1940, Jean Mary Todd; one *s* two *d*; 2nd, 1974, Jennifer Helen, *yr d* of J. R. Fawcus; two *s*. *Educ:* West Downs, Winchester; Marlborough Coll.; Trinity Coll., Oxford. BA, PPE. Joined Sedgwick Collins & Co., Lloyds Brokers, 1934; War Service, 1939-46; joined Willis Faber & Dumas Ltd, 1949; Underwriting Member of Lloyds, 1945. *Recreations:* foxhunting, tennis, swimming. *Address:* West Penthouse, Parkside, Knightsbridge, SW1. *T:* 01-235 8899. *Clubs:* Boodle's, City of London.

ROSCOE, Air Cdre Peter Henry, CB 1967; FCA; *b* 1912. Dept of Air Member for Personnel, 1963-67; Dir of Personnel (Ground) Min. of Defence (RAF), 1966; retired 1967. *Address:* Fairhaven, Tan-y-Bryn Road, Holyhead, Gwynedd.

ROSE, Sir Alec (Richard), Kt 1968; *b* 13 July 1908; *s* of Ambrose Rose; *m* 1st, 1931, Barbara Kathleen (*née* Baldwin); two *s* two *d*; 2nd, 1960, Dorothy Mabel (*née* Walker). *Educ:* Simon Langton Boys School, Canterbury. Farming in Canada, 1928-30; Haulage Contractor, 1930-39; served RNVR, 1939-45; Market Gardener, 1945-57; Fruit Merchant, 1957-71. President: British Junior Exploration Soc., 1969-; British Wildlife Soc., 1970-. Member: Fruiterers Co.; Worshipful Co. of Basketmakers; Worshipful Co. of Shipwrights. Hon. Life Governor, RNLI, 1975-. Freedom of Portsmouth, 1968. Blue Water Medal, Cruising Club of America, 1969. *Publication:* My Lively Lady, 1968. *Recreation:* sailing (inc. circumnavigation of world, 1968). *Address:* Woodlands Cottage, Eastleigh Road, Havant, Hants. *T:* Havant 77124. *Clubs:* City Livery; Portsmouth County, Royal Naval and Royal Albert Yacht (Portsmouth); Royal Yacht Squadron, Royal Naval Sailing Assoc.; Eastney Cruising Assoc.

ROSE, Bernard William George, MusB Cantab 1938, MA Oxon, Cantab, DMus Oxon 1955, FRCO; Fellow, Organist, Informator Choristarum, Magdalen College, Oxford, since 1957, Vice-President, 1973 and 1974; University Lecturer in Music since 1950; Choragus in the University, 1958-63; *b* Little Hallingbury, Herts, 9 May 1916; *s* of William and Jessie Rose; *m* 1939, Molly Daphne, JP, 5th *d* of D. G. Marshall, MBE, Cambridge; three *s*. *Educ:* Salisbury Cathedral Sch.; Royal Coll. of Music; St Catharine's Coll., Cambridge. Organ Scholar, St Catharine's, Cambridge, 1935-39; Stewart of Rannoch Scholar in Sacred Music, Cambridge, 1935-39; Organist, and Conductor of the Eaglesfield Musical Soc., The Queen's Coll., Oxford, 1939-57, Fellow, 1949. Served with 4th Co. of London Yeomanry (Sharpshooters), 1941-44, Adjutant 1942 (PoW 1943-44). Conductor, Oxford Orchestra Soc., 1971-74. Mem. Council, Royal Coll. of Organists (Pres. 1974-76). *Publications:* contrib. Proc. Roy. Mus. Assoc.; various church music compositions and edns of church music; edns of Anthems of Thomas Tomkins; (ed) Early English Church Music, Vols 5, 9 and 14; Hallische Händel Ausgabe, 'Susanna'; General Editor, Novello Church Music. Reviews in Music and Letters, articles in Musical Times. *Recreation:* carpentry. *Address:* Appleton Manor, near Abingdon, Oxon. *T:* Cumnor 2919.

ROSE, Christine Brooke; see Brooke-Rose.

ROSE, Christopher Dudley Roger, QC 1974; *b* 10 Feb. 1937; *s* of Roger Rose and Hilda Rose, Morecambe; *m* 1964, Judith, *d* of late George and Charlotte Brand, Didsbury; one *s* one *d*. *Educ:* Morecambe Grammar Sch.; Repton; Leeds Univ.; Wadham Coll., Oxford. LLB and Hughes Prize, Leeds, 1957; 1st cl. hons BCL 1959, Eldon Scholar 1960, Oxon. Lectr in Law, Wadham Coll., Oxford, 1959-60; called to Bar, Middle Temple, 1960; Bigelow Teaching Fellow, Law Sch., Univ. of Chicago, 1960-61; Harmsworth Scholar, 1961; joined Northern Circuit, 1961. *Recreations:* playing the piano, listening to music, golf, travel. *Address:* 5 Essex Court, Temple, EC4Y 9AH. *T:* 01-353 4356. *Clubs:* Big Four (Manchester); Wilmslow Golf.

ROSE, Clifford Alan, FCIT, MIPM; Member (Personnel), British Railways Board, since 1977; *b* 31 Aug. 1929; *s* of Francis

William and Edith May Rose; *m* 1953, Maureen (*née* Wallen); one *d*. *Educ:* Royal Grammar Sch., High Wycombe. Joined GWR as booking clerk, 1944; served in London area, West Country and S Wales; Divl Movements Manager, Cardiff, 1966; Asst Divl Manager, 1968. Movements Manager, Southern Region, 1968; Divl Manager, first of S Western, then S Eastern Div., 1970; Chief Personnel Officer of Southern Region, 1972; Exec. Dir, Personnel, BRB, 1975. OStJ 1975. *Recreations:* cricket, Rugby (watching, now), gardening, walking. *Address:* 45 Durleston Park Drive, Great Bookham, Surrey KT23 4AJ. *T:* Bookham 52705. *Club:* MCC.

ROSE, Sir Clive (Martin), KCMG 1976 (CMG 1967); HM Diplomatic Service; Deputy Secretary, Cabinet Office, since 1976; *b* 15 Sept. 1921; *s* of late Rt. Rev. Alfred Carey Wollaston Rose; *m* 1946, Elisabeth Mackenzie, *d* of late Rev. Cyril Lewis, Gilston; two *s* three *d*. *Educ:* Marlborough College; Christ Church, Oxford. Rifle Bde, 1941-46 (Maj.; despatches): served in Europe, 1944-45; India, 1945; Iraq, 1945-46. Commonwealth Relations Office, 1948; Office of Deputy High Comr, Madras, 1948-49; Foreign Office, 1950-53; UK High Commn, Germany, 1953-54; British Embassy, Bonn, 1955; FO, 1956-59; 1st Sec. and HM Consul, Montevideo, 1959-62; FO, 1962-65; Commercial Counsellor, Paris, 1965-67; Imp. Defence Coll., 1968; Counsellor, British Embassy, Washington, 1969-71; Asst Under-Sec. of State, FCO, 1971-73; Head, British Delegn to Negotiations on Mutual Reduction of Forces and Armaments and Associated Measures in Central Europe, 1973-76. *Address:* c/o Foreign and Commonwealth Office, SW1. *Club:* Army and Navy.

See also Adm. Sir A. M. Lewis.

ROSE, (Edward) Michael, CMG 1955; Director and Secretary, East Africa and Mauritius Association, since 1969; Chairman, International Department, British Council of Churches, since 1974; *b* 18 Oct. 1913; *s* of Frank Atcherley Rose and Marian Elizabeth Darling Harris; unmarried. *Educ:* Rugby; St John's College, Cambridge. Entered Diplomatic Service, 1937; served Oslo 1940, Algiers, 1944, Copenhagen 1945-48; Deputy to GOC British Sector of Berlin, 1952-55; Counsellor, Foreign Office, 1955-60; Minister, Bonn, 1960-63; Ambassador to the Congo (Leopoldville), 1963-65; Asst Under-Sec., Foreign Office, 1965-67; Dep. Sec., Cabinet Office, 1967-68. Fellow, Center for Internat. Affairs, Harvard Univ., 1958-59. *Recreations:* golf, gardening. *Address:* 2 Godfrey Street, SW3; Ovington Grange, Clare, Suffolk. *Club:* National Liberal.

ROSE, Eliot Joseph Benn (Jim Rose); Chairman, since 1973 and Chief Executive, since 1976, Penguin Books; Chairman, Viking-Penguin, since 1975; *b* 7 June 1909; *s* of late Colonel E. A. Rose, CBE, and Dula, *e d* of Eliot Lewis, JP; *m* 1946, Susan Pamela Gibson; one *s* one *d*. *Educ:* Rugby; New College, Oxford. Served War of 1939-45, RAF, Wing-Comdr. Literary Editor, The Observer, 1948-51; Director: International Press Institute, Zürich, 1951-62; Survey of Race Relations in Britain, 1963-69; Editorial Dir, Westminster Press Ltd, 1970-74. Chm., Inter-Action Trust. Sidney Ball Meml Lectr, Oxford, 1970. Legion of Merit (US). *Publication:* Colour and Citizenship, 1969. *Address:* 37 Pembroke Square, W8. *T:* 01-937 3772. *Clubs:* Bath, Garrick.

ROSE, Sir Francis Cyril, 4th Bt, *cr* 1872; Painter and Author; *b* 18 Sept. 1909; *e s* of 3rd Bt and Laetitia, *d* of late Comte Rouy de Labadesse; *S* father, 1915; *m* 1st, 1943, Frederica Dorothy Violet (marr. diss. 1966), *d* of late General Sir Frederick Carrington, KCB, KCMG; 2nd, 1967, Mrs Beryl Davis (marr. diss.), widow of Squadron Leader Basil Montefiore Davis, RAF. *Educ:* St Anthony's Preparatory School, Eastbourne; Beaumont College. Served War of 1939-45; RAF 1940-42 (invalided out). Artistic Adviser Edinburgh Tapestry Co. Ltd, 1948-50; Artistic Consultant Roosen Silks Ltd. Exhibns: Paris, 1933, New York, Chicago and London, 1934; Petit Palace, Paris, 1938 (official show); represented British Modern Art (with Group), Salon d'Automne, Paris, 1939; Reid and Lefevre, London, 1944; Exhibition of Paintings organised by US Army (441st Troop Carrier Group) Gallery Pierre Colle, Paris, Feb. 1945; Wallpaper designs, History of Wallpaper Exhibition, Suffolk Gallery, London, 1945; Cotton Board Flower Painting Exhibition, Manchester, 1945; Redfern Gallery, London, 1945; Associated American Artists, NY, 1947; Gimpel Fils, London, 1949 and 1952; Passedoit Gallery, NY, 1950; Gallery Pierre Colle, Paris, 1950; Molton Gallery, 1961; Preston Gallery, Bolton, Lancs, 1964; Upper Grosvenor Galleries, 1967; retrospective exhibition, GLC London Gall. and Royal Pavilion, Brighton, 1966. Costumes and Scenery for Cupid and Psyche Ballet at Sadler's Wells, 1939; for La Peri, ballet given by Serge Lifar, Monte Carlo ballets, 1946; sets for Trigon, Arts Theatre, 1964. Textile designs for the Cotton Board, 1944; Artistic adviser for 1947-48, Mount Row Prints Ltd. *Publications:* The

White Cow and other Chinese Tales, 1945; The Shadowy Pine Tree, 1945; Your Home, 1946. Illustrations; The World is Round, 1939, Paris France, 1940, by Gertrude Stein; Gertrude Stein's First Reader, and 3 plays, Maurice Fridberg, 1946; Autobiography: Saying Life, 1961; Drinking at Home, 1964; Gertrude Stein and Painting, 1968. *Heir: cousin,* Sir Julian Rose, Bt, *qv*.

ROSE, Francis Leslie, OBE 1949; FRS 1957; PhD; DSc; FRIC; Consultant, Imperial Chemical Industries Ltd (formerly Research Manager, Pharmaceuticals Division) and Home Office Forensic Services; Hon. Fellow and formerly Hon. Reader in Organic Chemistry, University of Manchester Institute of Science and Technology; *b* 27 June 1909; *s* of late Frederick William and Elizabeth Ann Rose Lincoln; *m* 1935, Ailsa Buckley; one *s*. *Educ:* City Sch., Lincoln; Univ. of Nottingham. BSc (London) Hons Chemistry, 1930; PhD (Lond.) 1934; DSc (Nottingham) 1950; research chemist ICI Ltd, 1932; gold medallist, Society of Apothecaries, 1948; Tilden Lecture, Chem. Soc., 1951; Medal, Soc. of Chem. Industry, 1975; Royal Soc. Leverhulme Medal, 1975. Former Mem., Court of Governors, Manchester University and Court of Governors, Univ. of Manchester Inst. of Science and Technology. Hon. Fellow, Manchester Polytechnic. *Publications:* numerous scientific papers on chemotherapeutic themes, mainly in Jl of Chem. Soc., Brit. Jl of Pharmacol., Biochem. Jl, etc. *Recreations:* music, in particular the organ; sailing. *Address:* 26 Queensway, Heald Green, Cheadle, Cheshire. *T:* 061-437 2876. *Club:* Athenæum.

ROSE, Gerald Gershon, PhD; CChem, FRIC; Director, Thornton Research Centre, Shell Research Ltd, since 1975; *b* 4 May 1921; *m* 1945, Olive Sylvia; one *s* two *d*. *Educ:* Hendon County Grammar Sch.; Imperial Coll. of Science and Technology (BSc, ARCS, DIC, PhD). Joined Shell Group, 1944; served in refineries, Stanlow, Trinidad, Singapore and South Africa; General Manager, Shell/BP South Africa Petroleum Refineries, 1963; Manufacturing and Supply Director, Shell/BP Service Co., 1968; Manager, Teesport Refinery, 1971. *Recreations:* golf, tennis, gardening. *Address:* The Tithe Barn, Great Barrow, Chester, Cheshire CH3 7HW. *T:* Tarvin 40623.

ROSE, Prof. Harold Bertram; Group Economic Adviser, Barclays Bank Ltd, since 1975; Professor of Finance, London Graduate School of Business Studies, since 1965 (Esmée Fairbairn Chair until 1975, then part-time); *b* 9 Aug. 1923; *s* of late Isaac Rose and Rose Rose (*née* Barnett); *m* 1st, 1949, Valerie Frances Anne Chubb (marr. diss. 1974); three *s* one *d*; 2nd, 1974, Diana Mary Campbell Scarlett; one *d*. *Educ:* Davenant Foundn Sch.; LSE (BCom). Served with RA in Britain, India and Burma, 1942-45 (Captain). Head of Econ. Intell. Dept, Prudential Assce Co., Ltd, 1948-58; Sen. Lectr, then Reader, in Business Finance, LSE, 1958-65; Member: Council, Consumers' Assoc., 1958-63; Central Adv. Council on Primary Educn (Plowden Cttee), 1963-65; Business Studies Cttee, SSRC, 1967-68, and Univ. Grants Cttee, 1968-69; Reserve Pension Bd, 1973-75. Dir, Abbey National Building Soc., 1975-. *Publications:* The Economic Background to Investment, 1959; Disclosure in Company Accounts, 1963; Management Education in the 1970's, 1970; various papers in econ. and financial jls. *Recreations:* music, tennis, running. *Address:* 33 Dartmouth Park Avenue, NW5. *T:* 01-485 7315. *Club:* Reform.

ROSE, Dame Hilda Nora; *see* Lloyd, Dame H. N.

ROSE, Jack, CMG 1963; MBE 1954; DFC 1942; Secretary, Salmon and Trout Association, ince 1975; *b* 18 Jan. 1917; *s* of late Charles Thomas Rose; *m* 1st, 1940, Margaret Valerie (*d* 1966), 2nd *d* of late Alec Stuart Budd; two *s*; 2nd, 1967, Beryl Elizabeth, 4th *d* of late A. S. Budd. *Educ:* Shooters Hill School; London University. Served RAF, 1938-46 (Wing Commander); in fighter, fighter/bomber and rocket firing sqdns; France, 1940; Battle of Britain, 1944; Burma, 1944-45. Joined Colonial Administrative Service, N Rhodesia, 1947; Private Secretary to Governor of Northern Rhodesia, 1950-53; seconded to Colonial Office, 1954-56; Administrative posts, Northern Rhodesia, 1956-60; Administrator, Cayman Islands (seconded), 1960-63; Assistant to Governor, British Guiana, 1963-64 (Actg Governor and Dep. Governor for periods). Member: Professional and Technical 'A' Whitley Council for Health Services, 1965-75 (Chm., 1973-75); Gen. Whitley Council for Health Services, 1973-75. Sec., Chartered Soc. of Physiotherapy, 1965-75. *Recreations:* gardening, Rugby football, fishing. *Address:* Oakhill, Church Road, Stone Street, Sevenoaks, Kent. *T:* Sevenoaks 61791. *Clubs:* Royal Air Force, Royal Air Force Reserves.

ROSE, Jim; *see* Rose, E. J. B.

ROSE, Sir Julian (Day), 4th Bt *cr* 1909; *b* 3 March 1947; 3rd and *o surv. s* of Sir Charles Henry Rose, 3rd Bt and of Phoebe, *d* of 2nd Baron Phillimore (*d* 1947); *S* father, 1966. *Educ:* Stanbridge School. *Address:* Hardwick House, Whitchurch-on-Thames, Oxfordshire.
See also Sir Francis Rose, Bt.

ROSE, Michael; *see* Rose, Edward Michael.

ROSE, Morris James Alexander, DFC 1945; Sheriff of Grampian, Highland and Islands (formerly Aberdeen, Kincardine and Banff) at Aberdeen and Stonehaven since 1968; *b* 21 Feb. 1923; *er s* of late Alexander Alistair Rose, Glasgow, and Eileen May McClure, *d* of late James Howe McClure, Glasgow; *m* 1953, Jennifer Jane Moncrieff, *yr d* of late William Wallace Moncrieff, Troon; one *s* one *d. Educ:* Kelvinside Academy; Uppingham Sch.; Glasgow Univ. Served with RAFVR, 1941-46. Admitted to Faculty of Advocates, 1952. *Recreation:* golf. *Address:* Sheriff's Chambers, Aberdeen AB9 1AP.

ROSE, Paul (Bernard); MP (Lab) Blackley Division of Manchester since 1964; *b* 26 Dec. 1935; *s* of Arthur and Norah Rose; *m* 1957, Eve Marie-Thérèse; two *s* one *d. Educ:* Bury Gram. Sch.; Manchester Univ.; Gray's Inn. LLB (Hons) Manch., 1956; Barrister-at-Law, 1957. Legal and Secretarial Dept, Co-op. Union Ltd, 1957-60; Lectureship, Dept of Liberal Studies, Royal Coll. of Advanced Technology, Salford, 1961-63; Barrister-at-Law, practising on SE circuit. PPS to Minister of Transport, 1967-68; Opposition Front Bench Spokesman, Dept of Employment, 1970-72. Chairman: NW Regional Sports Council, 1966-68; Parly Labour Home Office Group, 1968-70; Parly Labour Employment Group, 1974-; Campaign for Democracy in Ulster, 1965-73. Delegate to Council of Europe and WEU, 1968-69; Vice-Chm., Labour Cttee for Europe. Mem., Commn on Electoral Reform, 1975-. *Publications:* Handbook to Industrial and Provident Societies Act, 1960; Guide to Weights and Measures, 1965; The Manchester Martyrs, 1970; (jt) A History of the Fenian Movement in Britain, 1972; contrib. to many periodicals on political and legal topics. *Recreations:* sport, theatre. *Address:* House of Commons, SW1.

ROSE, Captain Sir Philip (Humphrey Vivian), 3rd Bt, *cr* 1874; RA, enlisted 1939; *g s* of Sir Philip Rose, Rayners, Penn, 2nd Bt (whom he succeeded in 1919), and *s* of late Capt. Philip Vivian Rose, 3rd Batt. Oxfords. Light Infantry, and Maude Winifred, 2nd *d* of William Gillilan, 6 Palace Gate, W8; *b* 16 Mar. 1903; *m* 1927, Joan, *yr d* of late Dr Martin Richardson; (one *s* killed in aircraft accident at Downside on 15 May 1943) two *d. Heir:* cousin , David Lancaster Rose [*b* 17 Feb. 1934; *m* 1965, Dorothy Whitehead; one *s*]. *Address:* Rayners Cottage, High Street, Great Missenden, Bucks. *T:* Great Missenden 3401.
See also A. F. Waley.

ROSE, Reginald L. S.; *see* Smith-Rose.

ROSE, Prof. Richard; Professor of Politics, University of Strathclyde, since 1966; Director, Centre for Study of Public Policy, since 1976; *b* 9 April 1933; *o s* of Charles Imse and Mary Conely Rose, St Louis, Mo, USA; *m* 1956, Rosemary J., *o d* of late James Kenny, Whitstable, Kent; two *s* one *d. Educ:* Clayton High Sch., Mo; Johns Hopkins Univ., BA (Distinction, Phi Beta Kappa) comparative drama, 1953; London Sch. of Economics, 1953-54; Oxford University, 1957-60, DPhil (Lincoln and Nuffield Colls). Political public relations, Mississippi Valley, 1954-55; Reporter, St Louis Post-Dispatch, 1955-57; Lecturer in Govt, Univ. of Manchester, 1961-66. Dir, ISSC, European Summer Sch., 1973. Election Correspondent, The Times, 1964-. Pres., Scottish Political Studies Assoc., 1967, 1972. Psephologist, Indep. Television News, 1970-; Sec., Cttee on Political Sociology, Internat. Sociological Assoc., 1970-; Member: Cttee, European Consortium for Political Res., 1970-; US/UK Fulbright Commn, 1971-75; Eisenhower Fellowship Programme, 1971. Guggenheim Foundn Fellow, 1974; Vis. Scholar, Woodrow Wilson Internat. Centre, Washington DC, 1974; Vis. Scholar, Brookings Inst., Washington DC, 1976; Vis. Prof., European Univ. Inst., Florence, 1977, 1978. BBC Radio 3: Man of Action, 1974. Liaison Officer, British Politics Gp, 1974-; Convenor, Work Gp on UK Politics, Political Science Assoc., 1976-; Mem. Council, Internat. Political Science Assoc., 1976-. *Publications:* The British General Election of 1959 (with D. E. Butler), 1960; Must Labour Lose? (with Mark Abrams) 1960; Politics in England, 1964, 2nd edn, Politics in England Today, 1974; (ed) Studies in British Politics, 1966, 2nd edn 1969, 3rd edn 1976; Influencing Voters, 1967; (ed) Policy Making in Britain, 1969; People in Politics, 1970; (ed, with M. Dogan) European Politics, 1971; Governing Without Consensus: an

Irish perspective, 1971; (with T. Mackie) International Almanack of Electoral History, 1974; (ed) Electoral Behaviour: a comparative handbook, 1974; (ed) Lessons from America, 1974; The Problem of Party Government, 1974; (ed) The Management of Urban Change in Britain and Germany, 1974; Northern Ireland: a time of choice, 1976; Managing Presidential Objectives, 1976; (ed) The Dynamics of Public Policy, 1976; (ed, with D. Kavanagh) New Trends in British Politics, 1977; What is Governing: Purpose and Policy in Washington, 1978; (ed, with G. Hermet and A. Rouquié) Elections without Choice, 1978; contribs to academic journals in Europe and America; broadcasts on British, Irish and American politics. *Recreations:* architecture (historical, Britain; modern, America), music, writing. *Address:* Department of Politics, McCance Building, Richmond Street, Glasgow G1 1XQ. *T:* 041-552 4400; Bennochy, 1 East Abercromby Street, Helensburgh, Dunbartonshire G84 75P. *T:* Helensburgh 2164; 7430 Byron Place, Clayton, St Louis County, Mo 63105, USA. *Club:* Reform.

ROSE, (Thomas) Stuart, CBE 1974; FSIA; Design Adviser, The Post Office, 1968-76; *b* 2 Oct. 1911; *s* of Thomas and Nellie Rose; *m* 1940, Dorothea Winifred, *d* of F. G. Ebsworth, Petrograd; two *d. Educ:* Choral Scholar, Magdalen College Sch., Oxford; Central Sch. of Arts and Crafts. Designer, Crawfords Advertising, 1934-39; free-lance graphics designer and typographer, 1946-68; Typographer, Cement and Concrete Assoc., 1946-51; Print Consultant, Fedn of British Industries, 1947-68; Art Editor, Design Magazine, 1947-53; Typographic Adviser to Postmaster General, 1962-68; Associate, Design Research Unit, industrial design partnership, 1964-68. Member: Industrial Design Cttee, FBI, 1948-65 (Chm. 1965-68); CoID Stamp Adv. Cttee, 1960-62; Post Office Stamp Adv. Cttee, 1968-77. Mem., Soc. of Industrial Artists and Designers, 1936, Pres. 1965. Governor, Central Sch. of Art and Design, 1965-74 (Vice-Chm., 1971-74). FRSA 1970. Phillips Gold Medal for Stamp Design, 1974. *Recreations:* drawing, music, the country. *Address:* 25 Balcombe Street, NW1 6HE. *T:* 01-262 8242; Ladyland, Good Easter, Essex. *T:* Good Easter 365. *Club:* Arts.

ROSE, Wilfred Andrew; Ambassador of Trinidad and Tobago to Brazil, 1969-72; *b* 4 Oct. 1916; *s* of James Emmanuel Rose and Eleanora Rose; *m* 1944, Pamphylia Marcano; one *s. Educ:* Tranquility Boys' Intermediate Sch.; Queen's Royal Coll.; Imperial Coll. of Tropical Agriculture, Trinidad (DipAgr); Coll. of Estate Management, London; London University. Agric. Technologist, Food Control Dept, during War of 1939-45. Subseq. Cane Farmers' Superintendent; Estate Manager; Housing Manager, Planning and Housing Commission, Trinidad and Tobago. Editor, Jl of Agricl Soc. of Trinidad and Tobago. Member: Roy. Soc. of Health; Agricl Soc. of Trinidad and Tobago (Life); W India Cttee; Chartered Auctioneers' and Estate Agents' Inst. (Associate). West Indies National Party; People's National Movement (several cttees). Chm., Commn of Enquiry on Road Passenger Transport. Elected Member for St Ann's, Trinidad, Federal Elections of the West Indies, 1958. Minister of Communications and Works, Federal Govt, West Indies, 1958-62 (twice acted as Dep. Prime Minister); High Commissioner for Trinidad and Tobago: in Canada, 1962-64; in UK, 1964-69, Ambassador to EEC, 1965-69, and Ambassador to UN Agencies, Europe, and Permanent Representative to GATT, 1965-68; led West Indies delegn to various confs; Rep. of Govt, frequently abroad. Chm., Commonwealth Rhodesia Sanctions Cttee, 1968-69; Vice-Chm., UNCTAD II, New Delhi, 1968; Member: Commonwealth Telecommunications Bd, 1964-68; Commonwealth Telecommunications Council, 1968. Freeman, City of London, 1967. *Publications:* articles on agriculture in the Trinidad Press, 1942-45. *Recreations:* agriculture, horse-riding, golf. *Address:* 15 Charlotte Street, Port of Spain, Trinidad. *Clubs:* Royal Commonwealth Society (West Indian); Travellers' (both in London); Gávea Golf and Country (Rio de Janeiro).

ROSE-MILLER, Brig. G. P.; *see* Miller.

ROSEBERY, 7th Earl of, *cr* 1703; **Neil Archibald Primrose,** DL; Bt 1651; Viscount of Rosebery, Baron Primrose and Dalmeny, 1700; Viscount of Inverkeithing, Baron Dalmeny and Primrose, 1703; Baron Rosebery (UK), 1828; Earl of Midlothian, Viscount Mentmore, Baron Epsom, 1911; *b* 11 Feb. 1929; *o surv. s* of 6th Earl of Rosebery, KT, PC, DSO, MC, and of Eva Isabel Marian (Eva Countess of Rosebery, DBE), *d* of 2nd Baron Aberdare; *S* father, 1974; *m* 1955, Alison Mary Deirdre, *d* of Ronald W. Reid, 19 Lexden Road, Colchester, Essex; one *s* four *d. Educ:* Stowe; New Coll., Oxford. DL Midlothian, 1960. *Heir: s* Lord Dalmeny, *qv. Address:* Dalmeny House, South Queensferry, West Lothian.

ROSEHILL, Lord; David John MacRae Carnegie; *b* 3 Nov. 1954; *s* and *heir* of 13th Earl of Northesk, *qv*.

ROSEN, Charles; pianist; Professor of Music, State University of New York at Stony Brook; *b* New York, 5 May 1927; *s* of Irvin Rosen and Anita Gerber. *Educ:* studied piano with Mr and Mrs Moriz Rosenthal; Princeton Univ. (PhD). Début, NY, 1951. His many recordings include: first complete recording of Debussy Etudes, 1951; late keyboard works of Bach, 1969; last six Beethoven Sonatas, 1970; also works by Liszt, Elliott Carter, Boulez, etc. Hon. MusD Trinity Coll., Dublin, 1976. *Publications:* The Classical Style, 1971; Schoenberg, 1976. *Recreations:* music, books. *Address:* c/o Basil Douglas Ltd, 8 St George's Terrace, NW1 8XJ. *T:* 01-722 7142.

ROSEN, Rabbi Jeremy, MA; Headmaster, Carmel College, since 1971; *b* 11 Sept. 1942; *s* of Rabbi Kopul Rosen and Bella Rosen; *m* 1971, Vera Giuditta Zippel; one *s* one *d*. *Educ:* Carmel Coll.; Pembroke Coll., Cambridge (MA); Mir Academy, Jerusalem. Minister, Bulawayo Hebrew Congregation, Rhodesia, 1966; Minister, Giffnock Hebrew Congregation, Scotland, 1968-71. *Address:* Mongewell Park, Wallingford, Oxon OX10 8BT. *T:* Wallingford 37505.

ROSENBERG HOFFMAN, Anna; *see* Hoffman, Anna Rosenberg.

ROSENBLUM, Prof. Robert; Professor of Fine Arts, New York University, USA, since 1966; *b* 24 July 1927. *Educ:* Queens Coll., Flushing, NY (BA); Yale Univ. (MA); New York Univ. (PhD); Oxford Univ. (MA). Prof. of Art and Archaeology, Princeton Univ., USA, 1956-66; Slade Prof. of Fine Arts, Oxford Univ., 1971-72. *Publications:* Cubism and Twentieth-Century Art, 1960; Transformations in Late Eighteenth Century Art, 1967; Jean-Auguste-Dominique Ingres, 1967; Frank Stella, 1971; Modern Painting and the Northern Romantic Tradition: Friedrich to Rothko, 1975; articles in learned jls: Art Bulletin; Burlington Magazine; Jl of the Warburg and Courtauld Institutes; La Revue de l'Art, etc. *Address:* c/o Institute of Fine Arts, 1 East 78 Street, New York, NY 10021, USA. *T:* (212)-YU8-5550.

ROSENBROCK, Prof. Howard Harry, DSc, CEng; FRS 1976; FIEE, FIChemE; FInstMC; Professor of Control Engineering, since 1966, Vice-Principal, since 1977, University of Manchester Institute of Science and Technology, (UMIST); *b* 16 Dec. 1920; *s* of Henry Frederick Rosenbrock and Harriett Emily (*née* Gleed); *m* 1950, Cathryn June (*née* Press); one *s* one *d*. *Educ:* Slough Grammar Sch.; University Coll. London. BSc, PhD. Served War, RAFVR, 1941-46. GEC, 1947-48; Electrical Research Assoc., 1949-51; John Brown & Co., 1951-54; Constructors John Brown Ltd, 1954-62 (latterly Research Manager); ADR, Cambridge Univ., 1962-66. Mem. Council, IEE, 1966-70, Vice-Pres., 1977-; Pres., Inst. of Measurement and Control, 1972-73; Member: Computer Bd, 1972-76; SRC Engineering Bd, 1976-. *Publications:* (with C. Storey) Computational Techniques for Chemical Engineers, 1966; (with C. Storey) Mathematics of Dynamical Systems, 1970; State-space and Multivariable Theory, 1970; Computer-aided Control System Design, 1974; contribs Proc. IEE, Trans IChemE, Proc. IEEE, Automatica, Internat. Jl Control, etc. *Recreations:* microscopy, photography, 17th and 18th Century literature. *Address:* Manor Lodge, Mill Lane, Cheadle, Cheshire. *T:* 061-428 7482. *Club:* Chemical.

ROSENFELD, Alfred John; Under-Secretary and Principal Finance Officer, Department of Transport, since 1976; *b* 27 Feb. 1922; *s* of late Ernest Rosenfeld and late Annie Jeanette Rosenfeld (*née* Samson); *m* 1955, Mary Elisabeth (*née* Prudence); two *s* one *d*. *Educ:* Leyton County High Sch. Entered Public Trustee Office, 1938. Served War, Fleet Air Arm, 1942-46. Min. of Civil Aviation, 1947 (later, Min. of Transport, and Dept of Environment); Private Sec. to Jt Parliamentary Sec., 1958-59; Asst Sec., 1967; Under-Sec., 1972. *Recreations:* chess, bridge, gardening. *Address:* 33 Elmfield Road, Chingford, E4 7HT. *T:* 01-529 8160.

ROSENHEAD, Prof. Louis, CBE 1954; FRS 1946; DSc (Leeds); PhD (Cantab.); Professor of Applied Mathematics, The University, Liverpool, 1933-73, now Professor Emeritus; formerly Fellow of St John's College, Cambridge; *b* 1 Jan. 1906; *s* of Abraham Rosenhead and Helen Nelson; *m* 1932, Esther Brostoff; two *s*. *Educ:* Leeds Central High School; The University of Leeds; St John's College, Cambridge (Strathcona Research Student); The University of Göttingen. BSc (Leeds 1st Class Hons); PhD (Leeds); Senior Research Student of the Dept of Scientific and Industrial Research, 1929; PhD (Cantab) 1930; DSc (Leeds) 1935; Senior Research Student of Royal Exhibition of 1851; Lecturer, Applied Mathematics at the University

College of Swansea, 1931-33. Temporarily attached Min. of Supply, 1940-45. Mem. of various Govt Scientific Cttees, 1939-75. Pro-Vice-Chancellor, 1961-65, Public Orator, 1968-72, University of Liverpool. *Publications:* Index of Mathematical Tables, 2nd edn 1962 (part-author); Compressible Airflow; Tables, 1952 (part-author); Compressible Airflow: Graphs, 1954 (part-author); Laminar Boundary Layers, 1963 (editor); Scientific Publications in the Proceedings of the Royal Society, Proceedings of the Cambridge Philosophical Society, Monthly Notices of the Royal Astronomical Society, etc. *Address:* 30 Wheatcroft Road, Liverpool L18 9UF. *T:* 051-427 6033.

ROSENTHAL, Erwin Isak Jacob, LittD, DrPhil, MA; Reader in Oriental Studies, University of Cambridge, 1959-71, now Emeritus Reader; Fellow of Pembroke College, 1962-71, now Emeritus Fellow; *b* 18 Sept. 1904; *y s* of Moses and Amalie Rosenthal; *m* 1933, Elizabeth Charlotte Marx; one *s* one *d*. *Educ:* Heilbronn; Universities of Heidelberg, Munich, Berlin. Goldsmid Lectr in Hebrew, Lectr in North-Semitic Epigraphy, Head of Dept of Hebrew, University Coll., Univ. of London, 1933-36; Special Lectr, Semitic Langs and Lits, Univ. of Manchester, 1936-44, Nat. Service: RASC, 1944-45; attached FO, 1945; German Sect., FO, 1946-48. Lectr, Central Advisory Coun. for Educn, HM Forces, 1940-44; Tutor, Adult Educn, Univ. Tutorial Class, WEA, London, 1946-48 (Part-time); Univ. Lectr in Hebrew, Cambridge, 1948-59. Vis. Professor: Columbia Univ., 1967-68; El Colegio de Mexico, 1968; Leverhulme ·Emeritus Fellow, 1974, 1975. Pres., British Assoc. for Jewish Studies, 1977. *Publications:* Ibn Khalduns Gedanken über den Staat, 1932; Law and Religion (Vol. 3 Judaism and Christianity), 1938 (ed and contrib.); Saadya Studies, 1943 (ed and contrib.); Averroes' Commentary on Plato's Republic, 1956, 1966, 1969 (ed and trans.); Political Thought in Medieval Islam, 1958, 1962, 1968 (Spanish trans., 1967; Japanese trans., 1970); Griechisches Erbe in der jüdischen Religionsphilosophie des Mittelalters, 1960; Judaism and Islam, 1961; Islam in the Modern National State, 1965; (ed) Judaism section, in Religion in the Middle East, 1969; Studia Semitica (I: Jewish Themes; II: Islamic Themes), 1971; articles in learned jls; Festschriften. *Recreations:* music, walking, travelling. *Address:* Pembroke College and 199 Chesterton Road, Cambridge. *T:* 57648.

ROSENTHAL, Harold David; Editor of Opera since 1953; Lecturer and Broadcaster since 1950; *b* 30 Sept. 1917; *s* of Israel Victor Rosenthal and Leah Samuels; *m* 1944, Lillah Phyllis Weiner; one *s* one *d*. *Educ:* City of London School; University College, London (BA); Inst. of Education, London. Asst Editor, Opera, 1950-53; Archivist, Royal Opera House, Covent Garden, 1950-56. Member: Arts Council Patrons of Music Fund Cttee, 1960-; Council, Friends of Covent Garden, 1962-; Chairman, Music Section, Critics' Circle of Gt Britain, 1965-67. *Publications:* Sopranos of Today, 1956; Two Centuries of Opera at Covent Garden, 1958; A Concise Oxford Dictionary of Opera (with John Warrack), 1964, paperback edn, 1972, rev. and enl. edn, 1978; Great Singers of Today, 1966; Mapleson Memoires (ed and annotated), 1966; The Opera Bedside Book, 1965; Opera at Covent Garden, 1967; Covent Garden, 1976. *Recreations:* travel, food; collecting playbills, prints, programmes, etc. *Address:* 6 Woodland Rise, N10 3UH. *T:* 01-883 4415.

ROSEVEARE, Sir Martin (Pearson), Kt 1946; Hon. Fellow of St John's College, Cambridge, since 1952; *b* 24 April 1898; *s* of late Canon R. P. Roseveare, late Vicar of Lewisham; *m* 1921, Edith Mary Pearse (marr. diss., 1958; she *d* 1975); one *s* three *d* (and one *d* decd); *m* 1958, Olivia Margaret Montgomery. *Educ:* Marlborough College; St John's College, Cambridge (scholar). Maths Tripos, Part I, Class 1, 1919; Part II wrangler (b), 1921; Schoolmaster, Repton School, 1921-23; Haileybury College, 1923-26; Board of Education, HM Inspector of Schools, 1927; Staff Inspector of Mathematics, 1939. Lent to Ministry of Information, 1939, Ministry of Food, 1939-44 and 1946 (acting Assistant Sec., 1940, acting Principal Assistant Sec. 1942); Senior Chief Inspector, Ministry of Education, 1944-57, retired; Headmaster Mzuzu School, Nyasaland, 1957-63; Principal, Soche Hill College, Malawi, 1964-67; Schoolmaster, Marymount School, Mzuzu, Malawi, 1967-70. Served European War, RFA, Lt 1916-19, France, Belgium, Italy (wounded, despatches). *Recreations:* hockey, camping. *Address:* Box 29, Mzuzu, Malawi.

ROSEVEARE, Robert William, CBE 1977; Secretary, since 1967, Managing Director, Policy Co-ordination, since 1973, British Steel Corporation; *b* Mandalay, Burma, 23 Aug. 1924; *s* of late William Leonard Roseveare, MC and of Marjory C. Roseveare; *m* 1954, Patricia Elizabeth, *d* of Guy L. Thompson, FRCS, Scarborough; one *s* three *d*. *Educ:* Gresham's Sch., Holt; St John's Coll., Cambridge (MA). Served in Fleet Air Arm, 1943-46. Home Civil Service, Admin. Class, 1949. Asst Private

Sec. to Minister of Power, 1952-54; Prin., 1954; seconded to Cabinet Office, 1958-60; British Embassy, Washington, 1960-62; Asst Sec., Min. of Power, 1964. Special Asst to Chm. of Organising Cttee for British Steel Corporation (Lord Melchett), 1966; seconded to British Steel Corporation on its formation, 1967; Dir, Admin. Services, 1969; Man. Dir, Corporate Administration, 1971. *Recreations:* walking, bird-watching, sailing, singing. *Address:* Elm Tree Cottage, Ox Lane, Harpenden, Herts. *T:* Harpenden 3071.

ROSIER, Air Chief Marshal Sir Frederick (Ernest), GCB 1972 (KCB 1966; CB 1961); CBE 1955 (OBE 1943); DSO 1942; RAF, retired; Director-in-Charge, British Aircraft Corporation Ltd, Saudi Arabia, 1977; *b* 13 Oct. 1915; *s* of E. G. Rosier; *m* 1939, Hettie Denise Blackwell; three *s* one *d. Educ:* Grove Park School, Wrexham. Commissioned RAF, 1935; 43 (F) Sqdn, 1936-39. Served War of 1939-45 in France, UK, Western Desert and Europe. OC Horsham St Faith, 1947; exchange duties with USAF, 1948-50; Instructor at Jt Services Staff College, 1950-52; Gp Capt. Operations at Central Fighter Establishment, 1952-54; Gp Capt. Plans at Fighter Command, 1955-56; ADC to the Queen, 1956-58; idc 1957; Director of Joint Plans, Air Ministry, 1958; Chm. Joint Planning Staff, 1959-61; AOC Air Forces Middle East, 1961-63; Senior Air Staff Officer, HQ Transport Command, 1964-66; Air Officer C-in-C, RAF, Fighter Command, 1966-68; UK Mem., Permanent Military Deputies Group, Central Treaty Organisation, Ankara, 1968-70; Dep. C-in-C, Allied Forces Central Europe, 1970-73. Air ADC to the Queen, 1972-73. Mil. Advr and Dir, British Aircraft Corp. (Preston) Ltd, 1973-77. Commander, Order of Orange Nassau, 1947. *Address:* Flat 286, Latymer Court, Hammersmith, W6. *Club:* Royal Air Force.

ROSIER, Rt. Rev. Stanley Bruce; *see* Willochra, Bishop of.

ROSKELL, Prof. John Smith, MA, DPhil; FBA 1968; Professor of Medieval History, University of Manchester, since 1962; *b* Norden, Rochdale, 2 July 1913; *s* of late John Edmund and of Lucy A. Roskell; *m* 1942, Evelyn Liddle; one *s* one *d. Educ:* Rochdale Municipal Secondary School; Accrington Grammar Sch.; University of Manchester; Balliol College, Oxford. Asst Lecturer in History, Manchester University, 1938; Lecturer, 1945; Senior Lecturer, 1950-52; Professor of Medieval History, University of Nottingham, 1952-62. President: Lancashire Parish Register Soc., 1962; Chetham Soc., 1972. Royal Navy, 1940-45; Lieut RNVR, 1942-45. *Publications:* The Knights of the Shire of the County Palatine of Lancaster (1377-1460), Chetham Society, 1937; The Commons in the Parliament of 1422, 1954; The Commons and their Speakers in English Parliaments, 1376-1523, 1965; (ed with F. Taylor) Gesta Henrici Quinti, 1976; articles in English Historical Review, Bulletin of the Institute of Historical Research, etc. *Recreation:* cricket. *Address:* 42 Barcheston Road, Cheadle, Cheshire. *T:* 061-428 4630.

ROSKILL, Sir Ashton (Wentworth), Kt 1967; QC 1949; MA Oxon; Chairman, Monopolies and Mergers Commission (formerly Monopolies Commission), 1965-75 (Part-time Member, 1960-65); *b* 1 Jan. 1902; *e s* of late John Roskill, KC, and Sybil Mary Wentworth, *d* of late Ashton Dilke, MP; *m* 1st, 1932, Violet Willoughby (*d* 1964), *d* of late Charles W. Waddington, CIE; one *s* one *d* ; 2nd, 1965, Phyllis Sydney, *y d* of late Sydney Burney, CBE. *Educ:* Winchester; Exeter Coll., Oxford (Schol.), 1st class hons Modern History, 1923; Barrister-at-Law, Inner Temple, 1925, Certificate of Honour, Council of Legal Education. Attached War Office, Intelligence Staff, 1940-45, Bencher, Inner Temple, 1958. Chm., Barristers Benevolent Assoc., 1968-. *Address:* 8 King's Bench Walk, Temple, EC4. *T:* 01-353 2734; Cox's Newtown, Newbury, Berks. *T:* Newbury 40328. *Club:* Reform.
See also Sir E . W . Roskill , O . W . Roskill , Captain S . W . Roskill .

ROSKILL, Rt. Hon. Sir Eustace Wentworth, PC 1971; Kt 1962; DL; Rt. Hon. Lord Justice Roskill; a Lord Justice of Appeal, since 1971; *b* 6 Feb. 1911; *y s* of late John Roskill, KC and of late Sybil Mary Wentworth, *d* of Ashton Wentworth Dilke, MP; *m* 1947, Elisabeth Wallace Jackson, 3rd *d* of late Thomas Frame Jackson, Buenos Aires; one *s* two *d. Educ:* Winchester College (exhibnr); Exeter Coll., Oxford (exhibnr). 1st Cl. hons, Hon. Sch. of Mod. Hist. Oxford, BA 1932; MA 1936. Harmsworth Law Schol. Middle Temple, 1932; called to Bar, Middle Temple, 1933 (Bencher 1961). Worked at Ministries of Shipping and War Transport, 1939-45. QC 1953. Dep. Chm. Hants QS, 1951-60, Chm. 1960-71; Comr of Assize (Birmingham), 1961; Judge of the High Court of Justice, Queen's Bench Division, 1962-71. Vice-Chm., Parole Bd., 1967-69; Chm., Commn on Third London Airport, 1968-70. Chm., Average Adjusters Assoc.,

1977-78. Pres., Senate of Four Inns of Court, 1972-74; Hon. Mem., 1974; Life Mem., Canadian Bar Assoc., 1974. Hon. Fellow, Exeter College, Oxford, 1963. Hampshire: JP 1950; DL 1972. *Recreations:* music, swimming, gardening. *Address:* Heatherfield, Newtown, Newbury, Berks RG15 9DB. *T:* Newbury 40606; New Court, Temple, EC4. *T:* 01-353 8870; Royal Courts of Justice, Strand, WC2A 2LL. *Club:* Reform.
See also Sir Patrick Dean, Sir A. W. Roskill, O. W. Roskill, Captain S. W. Roskill.

ROSKILL, Oliver Wentworth, FRIC, CEng, CChem, FInstChemE, CIMechE, FInstF, FBIM, FIMC; Senior Partner, O. W. Roskill Industrial Consultants, 1930-74; Chairman: O. W. Roskill & Co (Reports) Ltd, 1957-74; Roskill Information Services Ltd, 1971-74; *b* 28 April 1906; *s* of John Roskill, KC, and Sibyl Mary Wentworth, *d* of Ashton Wentworth Dilke, MP. *Educ:* Oundle Sch.; Lincoln Coll., Oxford (scholar). MA, BSc (Oxon) (1st Cl. Hons). Captain, Oxford Univ. Rugby Fives Club, 1927. Imperial Chemical Industries Ltd, 1928-30. Min. of Economic Warfare, Dep. Head, Enemy Countries Intell., 1939-41. Mem. Exec. Cttee of Political and Economic Planning, 1931, Vice-Pres., 1975; Founder Mem. Council, British Inst. of Management, 1947-53 (Chm. Inf. and Research Cttee); Mem. British Nat. Export Council, Caribbean Cttee, 1965-69; Mem. Council, Inst. of Management Consultants, 1963-74 (Pres., 1970-71). Consultant on industrial development projects to Govts of Iran, Pakistan, Malta and others. *Publications:* Founder and part author of 'Who Owns Whom' series of directories; author of monographs on economics of metals and minerals (incl. tungsten, titanium, chromium, fluorspar); contributor to many jls of learned societies (incl. Inst. Fuel, RIBA, Town Planning Inst.). *Recreations:* mountain walking, playing chamber music, choral singing, real tennis, gardening. *Address:* The Priory, Beech Hill, Reading, Berks. *T:* Reading 883146. *Clubs:* Brooks's; Woodmen of Arden; Hampton Court Tennis, Holyport Tennis, Hatfield Tennis.
See also Sir A. W. Roskill, Sir E. W. Roskill, Captain S. W. Roskill.

ROSKILL, Captain Stephen Wentworth, CBE 1971; DSC 1944; MA Cantab; LittD Cantab 1971; FBA 1971; FRHistS; late RN; Fellow of Churchill College, Cambridge, 1961, Life Fellow, 1970; *b* 1 Aug. 1903; *s* of late John Henry Roskill, KC, and Sybil Mary Dilke, *d* of Ashton Wentworth Dilke, MP; *m* 1930, Elizabeth, *d* of Henry Van den Bergh; four *s* three *d. Educ:* RN Colleges, Osborne and Dartmouth. RN, 1917-48; Gunnery Specialist, 1928; Commander, 1938; Captain, 1944. Served at sea as Commander HMS Warspite, 1939; Naval Staff, 1939-41; Commander and Captain, HMNZS Leander, 1941-44; Senior Observer, Bikini Atomic Bomb Trials, 1946; Dep. Director of Naval Intelligence, 1946-48; invalided, 1948; Cabinet Office, Official Naval Historian, 1949-60. Officer Legion of Merit (USA). Lees Knowles Lecturer, Cambridge, 1961; Distinguished Visitor Lecturer, US Naval Academy, Annapolis, 1965; Richmond Lecturer, Cambridge, 1967; Leverhulme Res. Fellow, National Maritime Museum, 1974. Navy Records Society: Councillor, 1956-66, and 1968-70; Vice-Pres., 1966-68, 1970, Hon. Life Vice-Pres., 1976. Hon. LittD Leeds, 1975. Chesney Gold Medal, RUSI, 1975. *Publications:* The War at Sea (official history), Vol. I, 1954, Vol. II, 1957; HMS Warspite, 1957; The Secret Capture, 1959; The War at Sea, Vol. III, Part I, 1960; The Navy at War, 1960; the War at Sea, Vol. III, Part II, 1961; The Strategy of Sea Power, 1962; A Merchant Fleet in War, 1962; The Art of Leadership, 1964; Naval Policy between the Wars, Vol. I, 1968, Vol. II, 1976; Documents relating to the Naval Air Service 1908-1918, 1969; Hankey, Man of Secrets, Vol. 1, 1877-1918, 1970, Vol. 2, 1919-1931, 1972; Vol. 3, 1931-63, 1974; numerous contribs to learned jls. *Recreations:* all country pursuits, painting. *Address:* Frostlake Cottage, Malting Lane, Cambridge. *T:* 54705. *Club:* Travellers'.
See also Sir A. W. Roskill, Sir E. W. Roskill, O. W. Roskill.

ROSOMAN, Leonard Henry, RA 1969 (ARA 1960); FSA; Tutor, Royal College of Art, since 1957; *b* 27 Oct. 1913; *s* of Henry Rosoman; *m* 1963, Jocelyn (marr. diss. 1969), *d* of Bertie Rickards, Melbourne, Australia. *Educ:* Deacons Sch., Peterborough; Durham Univ. Teacher of Drawing and Painting, Reimann Sch. of Art, London, 1938-39; Official War Artist to Admiralty, 1943-45; Teacher: Camberwell Sch. of Art, London, 1947-48; (Mural Painting) Edinburgh Coll. of Art, 1948-56; Chelsea School of Art, 1956-57; Tutor, Royal Coll. of Art, 1957-. One Man Shows: St George's Gallery, London, 1946 and 1949; Roland, Browse and Delbanco Gallery, London, 1954, 1957, 1959, 1965 and 1969. Works bought by: HM Govt, Arts Council, British Council, York Art Gall., Contemporary Art Soc., Adelaide Art Gallery, V&A Museum. Executed large mural paintings for: Festival of Britain, 1951; British Pavilion, Brussels World Fair, 1958; Harewood House, 1959. FSIA; Hon.

ARCA. *Recreation:* travelling as much as possible. *Address:* 7 Pembroke Studios, Pembroke Gardens, W8. *T:* 01-603 3638.

ROSPIGLIOSI, family name of **Earl of Newburgh.**

ROSS, Hon. Lord; Donald MacArthur Ross; a Senator of the College of Justice, Scotland, and Lord of Session, since 1977; *b* 29 March 1927; *s* of late John Ross, solicitor, Dundee; *m* 1958, Dorothy Margaret, *d* of late William Annand, Kirriemuir; two *d*. *Educ:* Dundee High School; Edinburgh University. MA (Edinburgh) 1947; LLB with distinction (Edinburgh) 1951. National Service with The Black Watch (RHR), 2nd Lt, 1947-49. Territorial Service, 1949-56, Captain. Advocate, 1952; QC (Scotland) 1964; Vice-Dean, Faculty of Advocates of Scotland, 1967-73; Dean, 1973-76; Standing Junior Counsel in Scotland to: Min. of Labour and Nat. Service, 1959-62; Scottish Development Dept (Highways), 1962-64; Junior Legal Assessor to Edinburgh Burgh and Dean of Guild Courts, 1958-64; Sheriff Principal of Ayr and Bute, 1972-73. Member: Scottish Cttee of Council on Tribunals, 1970-76; Cttee on Privacy, 1970. *Recreation:* gardening. *Address:* 33 Lauder Road, Edinburgh EH9 2JG. *T:* 031-667 5731. *Club:* New (Edinburgh).

ROSS, Bishop of, (RC); *see under* Cork, Bishop of, (RC).

ROSS, Alan; author, publisher and journalist; Editor of London Magazine; Managing Director, London Magazine Editions (Publishers); *b* Calcutta, 6 May 1922; *o s* of John Brackenridge Ross, CBE and Clare, *d* of Captain Patrick Fitzpatrick, Indian Army; *m* 1949, Jennifer, *d* of Sir Geoffrey Fry, 1st and last Bt, KCB, CVO; one *s*. *Educ:* Haileybury; St John's College, Oxford. RN 1942-47; general service, Arctic and North Seas, 1942-44; Asst Staff Officer, Intelligence, 16th Destroyer Flotilla, 1944; on staff of Flag Officer, Western Germany, 1945, and Interpreter to British Naval Commander-in-Chief, Germany, 1946. British Council, 1947-50; on staff of The Observer 1950-71. Toured Australia as correspondent, with MCC, 1954-55, 1962-63; toured South Africa, 1956-57, 1964-65; toured West Indies, 1960, 1968. Atlantic Award for Literature (Rockefeller Foundation), 1946. FRSL 1971. *Publications:* The Derelict Day, 1947; Time Was Away, 1948; The Forties, 1950; The Gulf of Pleasure, 1951; Poetry 1945-50, 1951; The Bandit on the Billiard Table, 1954 (revised edition South to Sardinia, 1960); Something of the Sea, 1954; Australia 55, 1956; Abroad (ed), 1957; Cape Summer and the Australians in England, 1957; To Whom It May Concern, 1958; The Onion Man, 1959; Through the Caribbean, 1960; The Cricketer's Companion (ed), 1960; Danger on Glass Island, 1960; African Negatives, 1962; Australia 63, 1963; West Indies at Lord's, 1963; North from Sicily, 1965; Poems 1942-67, 1968; Tropical Ice, 1972; The Taj Express, 1973; (ed) London Magazine Stories 1-10, 1964-76; (ed) Living in London, 1974; Open Sea, 1975; (ed) Selected Poems of Lawrence Durrell, 1977; several trans and introductions; contrib. to various jls in England and America. *Recreations:* travel, sport (played cricket and squash for Oxford University and Royal Navy), collecting pictures, racing. *Address:* Clayton Manor, near Hassocks, Sussex. *T:* Hassocks 3666. *Clubs:* Garrick, MCC; Vincent's (Oxford).

ROSS, Alan Strode Campbell, MA Oxon, MA Birmingham; Professor of Linguistics, University of Birmingham, 1951-74 (Professor of English Language, 1948-51); *b* 1 February 1907; *er s* of late Archibald Campbell Carne Ross, Penzance and Brecon, and Millicent Strode Cobham; *m* 1933, Elizabeth Stefanyja (*d* 1973), *yr d* of late Bronislas Olszewski, Warsaw; one *s*. *Educ:* Lindisfarne, Blackheath; Naish House, Burnham-on-Sea; Malvern College; Christ College, Brecon. Henry Skynner Scholarship in Astronomy, Balliol College, Oxford, 1925; First Class Hons School of English Lang and Lit., Oxford, 1929; Asst Lecturer in English Lang., Leeds Univ., 1929. Lecturer, 1936. Foreign Office, 1940-45. Lecturer in English Lang., Univ. of Birmingham, 1946, Reader, 1947. Corresp. member of Suomalais-ugrilainen Seura. Liveryman, Grocers' Company. *Publications:* The Dream of the Rood (with B. Dickins), 1934; Studies in the Accidence of the Lindisfarne Gospels, 1937; The Numeral-Signs of the Mohenjo-daro Script, 1938; The Terfinnas and Beormas of Ohthere, 1940; Ginger, 1952; Urs Graf edn of the Lindisfarne Gospels (with others), 1956-60; Etymology, 1958; Essentials of German Grammar, 1963; (with F. G. Healey) Patience Napoléon, 1963; (with A. W. Moverley) The Pitcairnese Language, 1964; Essentials of English Grammar, 1964; (with N. F. C. Owen) I. I. Revzin, Models of Language (translated from Russian), 1966; Arts v. Science (ed), 1967; (ed) What are U, 1969; (ed jtly) The Durham Ritual, 1969; How to pronounce it, 1970; Don't Say It, 1973; articles in Acta Philologica Scandinavica, Archivum Linguisticum, Biometrika, Englische Studien, Finnisch-ugrische Forschungen, Indogermanische Forschungen, Geographical Journal, Journal

English and Germanic Philology, Journal Roy. Statistical Soc., Mathematical Gazette, Moderna Sprak, Mod. Lang. Notes, Mod. Lang. Rev., Nature, Neuphilologische Mitteilungen; Studia germanica; Zeitschrift für vergleichende Sprachforschung. Noblesse Oblige (ed. N. Mitford); Saga-Book of Viking Soc., Trans of Philological Soc., etc. Part-ed Leeds Studies in English (I-VI); Ed. English Philological Studies. *Recreations:* land-rovering, stamp-collecting, patience, croquet. *Address:* 37 Phoenix Way, Southwick, Sussex BN4 4HP. *T:* Brighton 595027.

ROSS, Sir Alexander, Kt 1971; Chairman, United Dominions Trust Ltd, 1963-74 (Director, 1955; Vice-Chairman, 1962); Deputy Chairman, Eagle Star Insurance Co. Ltd; Chairman, Australia and New Zealand Banking Group Ltd, 1970-75; Director: Whitbread Investment Trust Ltd, since 1972; British Australian Investment Trust Ltd, since 1975; Power Components Ltd, since 1976; *b* 2 Sept. 1907; *s* of late William Alexander Ross and of Kathleen Ross; *m* 1933, Nora Bethia Burgess (*d* 1974); two *s* two *d*; *m* 1975, Cynthia Alice Barton. *Educ:* Mount Albert Gram. Sch.; Auckland University Coll., Auckland, NZ. Joined Nat. Bank of NZ, 1927, and Reserve Bank of NZ on its establishment in 1934; Dep. Gov., 1948-55. Rep. NZ on numerous occasions overseas, including Sterling Area Conf. in Australia, 1954. Rep. NZ in rowing, at Empire Games, 1930; managed NZ team to Empire Games, Vancouver, 1954; NZ rowing selector for Olympic and Empire Games; Chairman: British Commonwealth Games Fedn, 1968-; Cttee for Exports to NZ, 1965-67; East European Trade Council, 1967-69; Vice-Pres., British Export Houses Assoc., 1968-71; Member: BNEC, 1965-69; NRDC, 1966-74; New Zealand Soc. (Past Pres.); Cttee of Directors, Royal Caledonian Schools, 1964-69; Council, Dominion Students' Hall Trust. Pres., Fellowship of the Motor Industry, 1971-73. A past Governor, English Speaking Union; Central Council, Royal Over-Seas League. *Recreation:* walking. *Address:* 36 Fairacres, Roehampton Lane, SW15. *T:* 01-876 3802. *Club:* Brooks's.

ROSS, Alfred William, OBE 1955; MA, MIEE; Technical and Operational Research Consultant; Deputy Chief Scientist (Navy), Ministry of Defence, 1972-74; *b* 13 Sept. 1914; *m* 1946, Margaret Elizabeth Wilson; three *d*. *Educ:* King Edward VI School, Stourbridge; Christ's Coll., Cambridge. Joined HM Signal Sch., Portsmouth, 1936. Worked on Radar during War at Admiralty Signal and Radar Establishment. Defence Research Policy Staff, Ministry of Defence, 1946-47; Chief Superintendent, Army Operational Research Group, 1951-56. Director, Naval Physical Research, MoD, 1956-68; Chief of Naval Research, MoD, 1968-72. *Publications:* scientific papers on radar, electronics and operational research. *Recreation:* golf. *Address:* 336 Fir Tree Road, Epsom Downs, Surrey KT17 3NW. *T:* Burgh Heath 56774. *Club:* Walton Heath Golf.

ROSS, Prof. Allan Dawson, BSc, PhD (Edinburgh), CEng, FICE, FRSE; Consulting Engineer, advising, in particular, on concrete structures for nuclear power stations; Professor of Civil Engineering at University of London, King's College, 1946-71, Professor Emeritus since 1971; *b* 22 Feb. 1909; 4th *s* of Robert and Anne Ross, Dublin; *m* 1935, Isabel Goodburn; one *d*. *Educ:* Peebles High School; University of Edinburgh. Bursar of The Royal Commission for the Exhibition of 1851. Held civil engineering appointments in road and railway construction, 1929-32; Assistant to late Prof. Sir T. Hudson Beare, Univ. of Edinburgh, 1932-34; Education Officer, Air Ministry, 1934-35; Lecturer in Civil and Mechanical Engineering, University of London, King's College, 1935-46. *Publications:* numerous papers published in journals of learned and technical institutions. *Address:* 7 Old Farm Avenue, Colinton, Edinburgh EH13 0QQ.

ROSS, Sir Archibald (David Manisty), KCMG 1961 (CMG 1953); HM Diplomatic Service, retired; Chairman: Alfa-Laval Co.; Saab (Great Britain); Scania (Great Britain), since 1972; Datasaab, since 1975; *b* 12 Oct. 1911; *s* of late J. A. Ross, Indian Civil Service, and Dorothea, *e d* of late G. Eldon Manisty, Bengal Civil Service; *m* 1939, Mary Melville, *d* of Melville Macfadyen; one *s* one *d* (and one *s* decd). *Educ:* Winchester; New College, Oxford (MA). 1st Class Hon. Mods 1932, Lit. Hum. 1934; Gaisford Greek Verse Prize, 1932; Laming Travelling Fellow, Queen's College, 1934-35. Diplomatic Service, 1936; Berlin, 1939, Stockholm, 1939-44; Foreign Office, 1944-47, Tehran, 1947-50; Counsellor, Foreign Office, 1950-53; HM Minister, Rome, 1953-56; Assistant Under Secretary of State for Foreign Affairs, 1956-60; Ambassador to Portugal, 1961-66; Ambassador to Sweden, 1966-71. *Address:* 17 Ennismore Gardens, SW7. *Clubs:* Travellers'; Leander.

ROSS, Hon. Sir Bruce; see Ross, Hon. Sir D. B.

ROSS, (Claud) Richard, CB 1973; MA; a Deputy Secretary, Central Policy Review Staff, Cabinet Office, since 1971; *b* 24 March 1924; *o s* of late Claud Frederick Ross and Frances Muriel Ross, Steyning, Sussex; *m* 1954, Leslie Beatrice, *d* of Oliver Arnell and late Dr H. M. Arnell, Kitale, Kenya; two *d. Educ:* Ardingly Coll.; Hertford Coll., Oxford (Open Schol., Mod. Hist.). Served in Royal Engineers, 1942-47. 1st cl. PPE, 1950. Fellow of Hertford Coll., 1951-63; Lectr in Economics, Oxford Univ., 1951-52 and 1955-63; Economic Section, HM Treasury, 1952-55; Junior Proctor, Oxford Univ., 1958-59; Bursar, Hertford Coll., 1959-63; Prof. of Economics and Dean of Social Studies, Univ. of East Anglia, 1963-69 (Pro-Vice-Chancellor, 1964-68); Consultant, OECD, Paris, 1969-71. Adviser, Bankers' Mission to India and Pakistan, 1960. Represented HM Treasury on OECD Working Party on Policies for Economic Growth, 1961-68. Leader, British Economic Mission to Tanzania, 1965; Member: East Anglia Economic Planning Council, 1966-69 (Dep. Chm., 1967-69); Jt Mission for Malta, 1967. *Publications:* Financial and Physical Problems of Development in the Gold Coast (with D. Seers), 1952; articles on economics. *Address:* 2a Oliver's Wharf, 64 Wapping High Street, E1.

ROSS, Donald MacArthur; see Ross, Hon. Lord.

ROSS, Donald Nixon, FRCS; consultant cardiac surgeon; *b* 4 Oct. 1922; *m* 1956, Dorothy Curtis; one *d. Educ:* Boys' High Sch., Kimberley, S Africa; Univ. of Capetown (BSc, MB, ChB 1st Cl. Hons, 1946). FRCS 1949; FACC 1973; FACS 1976. Sen. Registrar in Thoracic Surgery, Bristol, 1952; Guy's Hospital: Res. Fellow, 1953; Sen. Thoracic Registrar, 1954; Cons. Thoracic Surg., 1958; Cons. Surg., National Heart Hosp., 1963, Sen. Surg., 1967; Dir, Dept of Surgery, Inst. of Cardiology, 1970. Order of Cedar of Lebanon, 1975. *Publications:* A Surgeon's Guide to Cardiac Diagnosis, 1962; (jtly) Medical and Surgical Cardiology, 1968; (jtly) Biological Tissue in Heart Valve Replacement, 1972; contrib. BMJ, Lancet, Proc. RSM, Annals Royal Coll. Surg., Amer. Jl Cardiol. *Recreations:* horseriding, gardening. *Address:* 2 Chester Place, Regent's Park, NW1. *T:* 01-935 6191. *Clubs:* Garrick; Kimberley (SA).

ROSS, Hon. Sir (Dudley) Bruce, Kt 1962; retired; *b* 21 May 1892; *s* of William Alexander Ross and Annie Isabella Ross, Adelaide, S Australia; *m* 1st, 1920, Margaret Eleanor Waterhouse (decd); one *s* three *d* ; 2nd, 1954, Agnes Jessie Linklater. *Educ:* Queen's School, St Peter's College and University of Adelaide, S Australia. LLB (Adelaide) 1914. KC 1945. Judge of Supreme Court of S Australia, 1952-62. Pres. Law Society of S Australia, 1948-49; Vice-Pres., Law Council of Australia, 1948-49; Chancellor, Dioceses of Adelaide and Willochra, 1944-69; Grand Master, Grand Lodge of SA, 1959-64; Member Council of Governors, St Peter's Coll., Adelaide, 1948-60; Pres. Church of England Boys' Home, 1943-73; Pres., Kindergarten Union of SA, 1962-73. Served European War, 1914-18, with 5th Division, AIF. *Recreation:* bowls. *Address:* 19 Sherbourne Road, Medindie Gardens, SA 5081, Australia. *T:* 442178. *Club:* Adelaide.

ROSS, Rear-Adm. George Campbell, CB 1952; CBE 1945; FRGS; CEng, MIMechE; AFRAeS; retired; *b* 9 Aug. 1900; *s* of late Sir Archibald Ross, KBE; *m* 1st, 1929, Alice Behrens; 2nd, 1950, Lucia Boer (marr. diss. 1969); two *d* ; 3rd, 1975, Manolita Harris. *Educ:* Royal Naval Colleges, Osborne and Dartmouth. Served European War, 1914-18, Home Fleet. Engineering Courses at RN College, Greenwich, and RNE College, Keyham, 1919-21; HMS Hawkins, Flagship China Station, 1921-24; RNE Coll., Lecturer in Marine Engineering, 1924-27; HMS Effingham, Flagship East Indies Station, 1927-29; HM Dockyard, Chatham, 1929-31; HMS Rodney, 1931-33; Comdr 1933; Asst Naval Attaché, Embassy, Tokyo, 1933-36; HMS Manchester, 1937-39; Engineer-in-Chief's Dept, Admiralty, 1939-41; HMS Nelson, 1941-43 (Staff Engineer Officer to Flag Officer, Force "H", Malta Convoy, N Africa and Sicily); Capt. 1943; Aircraft Maintenance and Repair Dept, Admiralty, 1943-47; ADC to the King, 1948-49; Chief of Staff to Rear-Admiral Reserve Aircraft, 1948-49; Rear-Adm. (E) 1949; Director of Aircraft Maintenance and Repair, Admiralty, 1949-53; retd, Oct. 1953. Joined Hawker Siddeley group, Nov. 1953, and retd Sept. 1965. Consultant to Grievson Grant, Stockbrokers, and other cos. Chairman, Combined Services Winter Sports Assoc., 1951-67. Freedom and Livery of Worshipful Company of Carmen. *Recreations:* fishing, travel, painting, writing. *Address:* 11 Redcliffe Close, Old Brompton Road, SW5. *T:* 01-373 0609. *Club:* Hurlingham.

ROSS, James, QC 1966; **His Honour Judge Ross;** a Circuit Judge (formerly a Judge of County Courts), since 1971; *b* 22 March 1913; *s* of John Stuart Ross, FRCSE; *m* 1939, Clare Margaret, *d* of Alderman Robert Cort-Cox, Stratford-on-Avon; one *d. Educ:* Glenalmond; Exeter Coll., Oxford. BA Oxon 1934. Admitted Solicitor, 1938; called to Bar, Gray's Inn, 1945. Legal Member, Mental Health Review Tribunal, Birmingham Region, 1962; Deputy Chairman, Agricultural Land Tribunal, East Midland Area, 1963; Dep. Chm. QS, Parts of Lindsey, 1968-71; Recorder of Coventry, 1968-71; Mem., Parole Bd, 1974-76. *Recreation:* sailing. *Address:* 2 Dr Johnson's Buildings, Temple, EC4. *T:* 01-353 5371. *Clubs:* Bar Yacht, Royal Yachting Association.

ROSS, James Alexander, MBE (mil.) 1944; MD, FRCSEd, FRCSGlas; Vice-President, International Federation of Surgical Colleges, since 1975; *b* 25 June 1911; *s* of James McMath Ross and Bessie Hopper Flint; *m* 1940, Catherine Elizabeth, *d* of Clark Booth Curtis; one *s* three *d . Educ:* Merchiston Castle Sch.; Edinburgh Univ. MB ChB Ed 1934, MD Ed 1947; FRCSEd 1938, FRCSGlas 1965. Served War: RAMC, 1939-45: France, ME, Europe; then Lt-Col RAMC, RARO, 1953-55. Surgeon, Leith Hosp., 1946-61, and Royal Infirmary, Edinburgh, 1947-61; Surgeon, Eastern Gen. Hosp., 1961-76 and Edenhall Hosp., 1970-76. Hon. Sec., Royal Coll. of Surgeons of Edinburgh, 1960-68; Vice-Pres., 1971-73; Pres., RCSEd, 1973-76. Hon. Cons. Surgeon to Army in Scotland, 1970-76; Guthrie Medallist, RAMC, 1976; McCombe Lectr, 1977. Hon. FRCSI, 1976; Hon. FRACS, 1977; Hon. Fellow: Pakistan Coll., P and S, 1976; Sri Lanka Coll. of Surgeons, 1976; Hong Kong Surgical Soc., 1976. *Publications:* Memoirs of an Army Surgeon, 1948; (jtly) Manual of Surgical Anatomy, 1964; (jtly) Behaviour of the Human Ureter, in Health and Disease, 1972. *Recreations:* walking, swimming, watching cricket. *Address:* 5 Newbattle Terrace, Edinburgh EH10 4RU. *T:* 031-447 2292. *Club:* Caledonian.

ROSS, Sir James Paterson, 1st Bt, *cr* 1960; KCVO 1949; Surgeon to the Queen, 1952-64, retd; Professor of Surgery, University of London, 1935-60, Emeritus Professor, 1960; Director, British Post-graduate Medical Federation, 1960-66; Consulting Surgeon, St Bartholomew's Hospital; President Royal College of Surgeons of England, 1957-60; *b* 26 May 1895; *s* of James Ross and May Paterson; *m* 1924, Marjorie Burton Townsend; two *s. Educ:* Christ's College, Finchley; St Bartholomew's Hospital Medical College (Entrance Scholarship in Science). Treasurer's Prize and Junior Scholarship Anatomy and Physiology, St Bartholomew's, 1914; Sergeant RAMC(T), 1914-15; Temp. Surgeon Lieutenant, Royal Navy, 1917-19; Gold Medal, University of London MB Examination, 1920; FRCS(Eng.), 1922. Associate in Surgery (Neurological Clinic) Peter Bent Brigham Hospital, Boston, USA, 1923; MS London, 1928; Jacksonian Prize Essay, Hunterian Prof., Royal College of Surgeons; Examiner in Surgery, Universities of London, Edinburgh, Glasgow, Belfast, Wales, Manchester, Bristol and Aberdeen. Sims Commonwealth Travelling Prof., 1957. FACS (Hon.), 1953, FRACS (Hon.), 1957. LLD (Hon.), Glasgow, 1957; FRCSEd (Hon.), 1959; FFR (Hon.) 1959; FRCSGlas. (Hon.) 1959; FDS (Hon.) 1964. *Publications:* The Surgery of the Sympathetic Nervous System (with G. E. Gask), 1934; (Jt Editor) British Surgical Practice (with Sir E. Rock Carling), 1947; several papers on surgical subjects in Medical Press. *Heir:* *s* James Keith Ross, RD, MS, FRCS [*b* 9 May 1927; *m* 1956, Jaqueline Annella Clarke; one *s* three *d*]. *Address:* Flat H, 14 John Spencer Square, Canonbury, N1 2LZ. *T:* 01-359 1122.

ROSS, Leonard Q.; see Rosten, L. C.

ROSS, Lewis Nathan, CMG 1974; FCA; Chartered Accountant (Fellow) in Public Practice, since 1932; company director, New Zealand; *b* 7 March 1911; *e s* of Robert and Raie Ross; *m* 1937, Ella Myrtle Burns, Melbourne, Australia; two *s* one *d. Educ:* Auckland Grammar Sch.; Univ. of Auckland. Commenced practice as CA, founding firm now known as Ross, Melville, Bridgman & Co, 1932; withdrew from partnership in 1965 to practise as consultant. Pres., Associated Chambers of Commerce of NZ, 1955-56; Chm., Govt Cttee: on PAYE taxation, 1964; to review all aspects of Central Govt Taxation in NZ, 1966-67. Pres., NZ Soc. of Accountants, 1972-73. Director: Bank of NZ (Chm.); NZ Ins. Co. Ltd (Chm.); NZ Forest Products Ltd; L. D. Nathan & Co Ltd; Rex Consolidated Ltd (Chm.); Mainline Corporation of NZ Ltd (Chm.); and other public and private cos. *Publications:* Taxation—Principles, Purpose and Incidence, 1964 (rev. edn 1973); Finance for Business, 1964; Accounting Problems that arise from Business Combinations, 1973; articles in Accountants' Jl and other business pubns. *Recreations:* bowls, contract bridge. *Address:* (private) 11 Rewiti Street, Orakei, Auckland, New Zealand. *T:* 547-449; (business) PO Box 881, Auckland, New Zealand. *T:* 364-485. *Club:* Northern (Auckland).

ROSS, Malcolm Keir; Headmaster of Crown Woods School, London, 1957-71; *b* 8 June 1910; *m* 1937, Isabel Munkley; two *d. Educ:* Grangefield Grammar Sch., Stockton-on-Tees; Keble Coll., Oxford. Schoolmaster: Gordonstoun, 1933-34; Haverfordwest Grammar Sch., 1934-36; Bromley Grammar Sch., 1936-40; war service with RAF, 1940-45; Warden of Village Coll., Sawston, Cambs, 1945-57. Mem., Cttee of Enquiry into conditions of service life for young servicemen, 1969. Governor, Rachel McMillan Coll. of Education. Book reviewer for The Times Educational Supplement. FRSA. *Recreations:* gardening, reading. *Address:* The Pheasantry, North Sydmonton, Newbury, Berks RG15 8JN.

ROSS, Rear-Admiral Maurice James, CB 1962; DSC 1940; retired; *b* 31 Oct. 1908; *s* of Basil James Ross and Avis Mary (*née* Wilkinson); *m* 1946, Helen Matheson McCall; one *d. Educ:* Charterhouse. Entered Royal Navy, 1927; Lieut, 1931; Lieut-Comdr, 1939; Comdr, 1943; Captain, 1951; Rear-Adm., 1960. Specialised in gunnery, 1935; served War of 1939-45, in HM Ships Somali and Cleopatra, at HMS Excellent, and Admiralty; comd HMS Hart on Far East Station, 1947-48; subsequently held appointments at Admiralty, Singapore, and Washington: Director of Tactical, Ship Requirements and Staff Duties Div., Naval Staff, 1958-59; Assistant Chief of Naval Staff (Warfare), 1960-63. *Address:* Monk's Cottage, Leaveland, Faversham, Kent. *T:* Challock 227.

ROSS, Mrs Nicholas; see Phillpotts, M. Adelaide Eden.

ROSS, Norman Stilliard; Assistant Under-Secretary of State, Fire Department, Home Office, since 1976; *b* 10 April 1919; *s* of late James Ross and Mary Jane Elizabeth Ross; *m* 1946, Sarah Cahill; one *s* two *d. Educ:* Solihull Sch., Warwickshire; Birmingham Univ. (BA). Served in local govt, City of Birmingham, 1935-39. War service, Army, RAMC and RAOC, in France, Belgium, Kenya, Ceylon, Burma and India, 1939-46 (despatches, France and Belgium, 1940). Asst Principal, Min. of Fuel and Power, 1949; Home Office, 1950; Asst Private Sec. to Sec. of State, 1950-52; Principal, 1952; Asst Sec., 1963; Asst Under-Sec. of State, 1976. *Recreations:* walking, music, reading. *Address:* 27 Detillens Lane, Limpsfield, Oxted, Surrey RH8 0DH. *T:* Oxted 2579.

ROSS, Richard; see Ross, C. R.

ROSS, Robert, MA, FLS; Keeper of Botany, British Museum (Natural History), 1966-77; *b* 14 Aug. 1912; *e s* of Robert Ross, Pinner, Middx; *m* 1939, Margaret Helen Steadman; one *s* three *d. Educ:* St Paul's Sch.; St John's Coll., Cambridge. Asst Keeper, British Museum (Natural History), 1936; Principal Scientific Officer, 1950; Deputy Keeper, 1962. Royal Microscopical Society: Hon. Librarian, 1947-51; Hon. Editor, 1953-71; Vice-Pres., 1959-60. Administrator of Finances, Internat. Assoc. of Plant Taxonomy, 1964-69; Sec., Gen. Cttee for Plant Nomenclature, 1964-69, Chm., 1969-. President: British Phycological Soc., 1969-71; Quekett Microscopical Club, 1974-76. *Publications:* various papers in scientific jls on botanical subjects. *Recreations:* morris dancing (Bagman, Morris Ring of England, 1946-50); walking; gardening. *Address:* The Garden House, Evesbatch, Bishop's Frome, Worcester. *T:* Bosbury 366.

ROSS, Comdr Ronald Douglas, RN; Clerk to the Worshipful Company of Vintners, since 1969; *b* 30 July 1920; *o s* of Captain James Ross, FRGS, Scottish Horse of Chengtu, Szechwan Province, China; *m* 1952, Elizabeth Mary, *er d* of Canon S. J. S. Groves; one *d. Educ:* Cargilfield; Sedbergh; RN Staff Coll. Joined Accountant Br. of RN and went to sea, 1937; war service in HM Ships Exeter, Devonshire and Tartar. Called to Bar, Middle Temple, 1950; pupil in Treasury Counsel Chambers, 1951; called to the Bar, Supreme Court of Hong Kong, 1963; officiated frequently as Judge Advocate; Admiralty Prize Medal for Naval History, 1957; retired list, 1967. Mem., Wine Standards Bd, 1973. Chevalier du Sacavin d'Anjou, 1974; Citizen and Vintner, 1975. *Publications:* contribs to The Times, Scotsman, New York Times, Investors' Chronicle, Brassey's Naval Annual, etc. *Recreations:* reading, writing, golf. *Address:* Black Swan House, Kennet Wharf Lane, EC4. *T:* 01-236 1863.

ROSS, Stanley Graham, DSO 1918; MC; BA, MD (McGill), FRCP; *b* Dundas, Ontario, Canada, 29 April 1888; *e s* of late James Ross, MD, and Beatrice Dudgeon Graham; *m* 1930, Jean Lesley, *d* of late Arthur L. Drummond, Montreal, Canada; three *s* one *d. Educ:* Hamilton Collegiate Institute; McGill University. Resident Physician Royal Victoria Hospital 1913-14; served overseas 1915-19 CEF (despatches twice, DSO, MC, 1914-15 star, two medals); Major in CAMC 1917; post-graduate work in London 1919-20, in the Johns Hopkins Hospital, Baltimore, 1920-22; Member of the American Pediatric Society; Member of the Canadian Pediatric Society. *Address:* 65 Rosemount Crescent, Westmount, Montreal 217, Canada. *Club:* University (Montreal).

ROSS, Stephen Sherlock, FRICS; MP (L) Isle of Wight, since Feb. 1974; *b* 6 July 1926; *s* of Reginald Sherlock Ross and Florence Beryl (*née* Weston); *m* 1949, Brenda Marie Hughes; two *s* two *d. Educ:* Bedford Sch. Served War of 1939-45, RN, 1944-48. Articled Nock & Joseland, Kidderminster, 1948-51; Assistant: Heywood & Sons, Stone, Staffs, 1951-53; Sir Francis Pittis & Son, Newport, IoW, 1953-57 (Partner, 1958-73). County Councillor, IoW CC, 1967-74 (Chm. Policy and Resources Cttee, 1973-74; Chm., Library Cttee, 1970-74). *Recreations:* cricket; antique porcelain collector. *Address:* 47 Quay Street, Newport, Isle of Wight PO30 5BA. *T:* Newport 2215. *Clubs:* National Liberal; Isle of Wight County (Newport).

ROSS, Mrs Thomas A.; see Runge, N. C.

ROSS, Col. Walter John Macdonald, CB 1958; OBE 1955; MC 1946; TD 1946 and 2 Bars; JP; Landed Proprietor and Farmer; Lord-Lieutenant, Dumfries and Galloway Region, District of Stewartry, since 1977; *b* 1914; *s* of late Major Robert Ross of Ledgowan, Ross-shire, and Marion, *d* of late Walter Macfarlane, DL, JP; *m* 1940, Josephine May, 2nd *d* of late Malcolm Cross, and of late Evelyn Cross of Earlston House, Borgue; two *s* one *d. Educ:* Loretto. Commissioned RA (TA), 1935. Served War of 1939-45, UK and NW Europe. Comd 5 KOSB (TA), 1951-55; Deputy Comd 157 (L) Inf. Bde, 1955-59. Underwriting Member of Lloyd's. DL 1960 and JP 1958, Stewartry of Kirkcudbright. Royal Humane Society Parchment for Saving Life, 1963. Member of Royal Company of Archers, Queen's Body Guard for Scotland. Formerly County Councillor (Vice-Convener), Stewartry of Kirkcudbright. Hon. FEIS, 1974. *Recreations:* shooting, fishing. *Address:* Netherhall, Bridge-of-Dee, Kirkcudbrightshire DG7 2AA. *T:* Bridge-of-Dee 208. *Clubs:* New (Edinburgh); Western (Glasgow).

ROSS, Rt. Hon. William, PC 1964; MBE (mil.) 1945; MA; MP (Lab) Kilmarnock Division Ayr and Bute since 1946; *b* 7 April 1911; *s* of W. Ross, Ayr; *m* 1948, Elizabeth Jane Elma Aitkenhead, Ayr; two *d. Educ:* Ayr Academy; Glasgow University. MA 1932; Schoolmaster. Served War of 1939-45, HLI, R Signals, Major; India, SACSEA. Contested Ayr Burgh, General Election, 1945. Secretary of State for Scotland, 1964-70, 1974-76; Opposition spokesman on Scottish Affairs, 1970-74; Mem., Labour Parly Cttee, 1970-. FEIS 1971. Hon. LLD: St Andrews, 1967; Strathclyde, 1969. *Recreation:* golf. *Address:* House of Commons, SW1; 10 Chapelpark Road, Ayr. *T:* Ayr 65673.

ROSS, William; MP (UU) Londonderry, since Feb. 1974; *b* 4 Feb. 1936; *m* 1974, Christine; one *s. Recreations:* fishing, shooting. *Address:* Hillquarter, Turmeel, Dungiven, Northern Ireland. *T:* Dungiven 428. *Club:* Northern Counties (Londonderry).

ROSS-MUNRO, Colin William Gordon, QC 1972; *b* 12 Feb. 1928; *s* of late William Ross-Munro and of Adela Chirgwin; *m* 1958, Janice Jill Pedrana; one step *d. Educ:* Lycée Français de Londres; Harrow Sch.; King's Coll., Cambridge. Served in Scots Guards and in Army Education Corps. Called to the Bar, Middle Temple, 1951. *Recreations:* tennis and travel. *Address:* (home) 1 Ralston Street, Chelsea, SW3; 2 Hare Court, Temple EC4Y 7BH.

ROSS TAYLOR, Walter; Assistant Public Trustee, 1971-73; *b* 5 Aug. 1912; *er s* of late Walter and Frances Ross Taylor; *m* 1939, Vera Julia, *y d* of Col Mackenzie Churchill, Cheltenham; two *s* one *d. Educ:* Repton Sch.; Trinity Coll., Oxford (BA). Called to Bar, 1934. Enlisted Princess Louise's Kensington Regt TA, 1938; served War of 1939-45 (despatches, 1945; Captain): commnd Suffolk Regt, 1940; transf. to RAC, 1941; served with 142 Regt RAC in N Africa, and subseq. on staff of Special Ops (Mediterranean). Entered Public Trustee Office, 1938: Chief Administrative Officer, 1966. *Recreations:* travelling, walking. *Address:* Little Court, 13 Courtmoor Avenue, Fleet, Hants.

ROSS WILLIAMSON, Hugh, FRSL; Writer; *b* 1901; *e s* of late Rev. Hugh Ross Williamson and Grace Winifred Walker; *m* 1941, Margaret Joan Cox; one *s* one *d.* Asst Editor, The Yorkshire Post, 1925-30; Editor of The Bookman, 1930-34; Acting Editor of the Strand Magazine, 1934-35; Director of London General Press, 1936-42, and 1968-. Anglican Priest, 1943-55; reconciled to Catholic Church, 1955. *Publications:* The Poetry of T. S. Eliot, 1932; John Hampden, 1933; King James I, 1936; Who is for Liberty?, 1939; George Villiers, Duke of Buckingham, 1940; AD 33, 1941; Captain Thomas Schofield, 1942; Charles and Cromwell, 1946; The Arrow and the Sword,

1947; The Silver Bowl, 1948; Four Stuart Portraits, 1949; The Seven Christian Virtues, 1949; The Gunpowder Plot, 1951; Sir Walter Ralegh, 1951; Jeremy Taylor, 1952; Canterbury Cathedral, 1953; The Ancient Capital, 1953; Historical Whodunits, 1955; James by the Grace of God-, 1955; The Great Prayer, 1955; The Walled Garden (autobiography), 1956; The Day they killed the King, 1957; Enigmas of History, 1957; Beginning of the English Reformation, 1957; The Sisters, 1958; The Challenge of Bernadette, 1958; The Day Shakespeare Died, 1962; Sixty Saints of Christendom, 1960; A Wicked Pack of Cards, 1961; The Flowering Hawthorn, 1962; Guy Fawkes, 1964; The Butt of Malmsey, 1967; The Marriage made in Blood, 1968; A Matter of Martyrdom, 1969; The Cardinal in Exile, 1969; The Cardinal in England, 1970; The Florentine Woman, 1970; The Last of The Valois, 1971; Paris is worth a Mass, 1971; Kind Kit, 1972; Catherine de Medici, 1973; Lorenzo the Magnificent, 1974; Historical Enigmas, 1974; Letter to Julia, 1975; The Princess a Nun!, 1978. *Plays:* In a Glass Darkly, 1932; Rose and Glove, 1934; The Seven Deadly Virtues, 1935; Monsieur Moi, 1935; Various Heavens, 1936; Mr Gladstone, 1937; Paul, a Bond-slave, 1945; Queen Elizabeth, 1946; Odds beyond Arithmetic, 1947; Fool's Paradise, 1949; The Cardinal's Learning, 1950; Gunpowder, Treason and Plot, 1951; Diamond cut Diamond, 1952; His Eminence of England, 1953; The Mime of Bernadette, 1958; Test of Truth, 1958; Heart of Bruce, 1959; Teresa of Avila, 1961; (with Ian Burford) Quartet for Lovers, 1962; Pavane for a Dead Infanta, 1968. *Club:* Savage.

ROSSE, 6th Earl of, *cr* 1806; **Laurence Michael Harvey Parsons,** KBE 1974 (MBE (mil.) 1945); MRIA, FSA (London and Ireland); Bt 1677; Baron Oxmantown, 1792; Pro-Chancellor of University of Dublin since 1965 (Vice-Chancellor, 1949-65); Chairman: London Prudential Investment Trust, 1956-76; New Hibernia Investment Trust; Birr Fabrics; *b* 28 Sept. 1906; *s* of 5th Earl and Lois, *d* of Sir Cecil Lister-Kaye, 4th Bart, and Lady Beatrice Lister-Kaye (she *m* 2nd, 5th Viscount de Vesci); *S* father, 1918; *m* 1935, Anne, *o d* of Lt-Col Leonard Messel, OBE, Nymans, Staplefield, Sussex; two *s. Educ:* Eton; Christ Church, Oxford (MA). Chairman: Standing Commission on Museums and Galleries; Properties Cttee; Internat. Dendrology Soc.; Dep. Chm., National Trust, 1961-76; Trustee, Historic Churches Preservation Trust. President: Friends of the National Collections of Ireland; Ancient Monuments Society; Irish Architectural Records Association; Royal Hortic. Soc. of Ireland, 1959-69; Adelaide Hospital; Furniture History Soc.; Georgian Group (Chm., 1946-68); Member: Arts Council of Ireland, 1953-74; Nat. Monuments Adv. Council of Ireland; Adv. Council, Victoria and Albert Museum and Science Museum; Min. of Transport Trunk Roads Adv. Cttee, 1956-74. Pres., London Soc. FRAS; FRSA; Hon FRIBA; Hon. LLD (Dublin and Belfast). Served War of 1939-45 (MBE). *Publication:* (with Colonel E. R. Hill) The Story of the Guards Armoured Division, 1941-45, 1956. *Heir: s* Lord Oxmantown, *qv. Address:* Womersley Park, Doncaster, S Yorks. *T:* Wentbridge 282; 18 Stafford Terrace, W8. *T:* 01-937 5857; Birr Castle, Co. Offaly. *T:* Birr 23. *Clubs:* Brooks's, Royal Automobile; Royal Irish Automobile, Kildare Street and University (Dublin).
See also Earl of Snowdon.

ROSSER, Sir Melvyn (Wynne), Kt 1974; Partner in Deloitte & Co., Chartered Accountants; Chairman, Welsh Council, since 1971; Director: British Steel Corporation, since 1972; Wales and Marches Telecommunications Board, since 1970; Development Corporation for Wales; Welsh Regional Council, CBI; *b* 11 Nov. 1926; *s* of late David John and of Anita Rosser; *m* 1957, Margaret; one *s* two *d. Educ:* Glanmor Sch., Swansea; Bishop Gore Grammar Sch., Swansea. Chartered Accountant, qual. 1949; joined staff Deloitte & Co., Swansea, 1950, Partner 1961; practised in Swansea, 1961-68, in Cardiff, 1968-. Member: Welsh Econ. Council, 1965-68; Welsh Council, 1968-71; Dir, National Bus Co., 1969-72. Mem., Royal Commn on Standards of Conduct in Public Life, 1974-. Vice-Pres., UCW, Aberystwyth, 1977-. Mem. Gorsedd of Bards, Royal Nat. Eisteddfod of Wales. *Recreations:* music, gardening. *Address:* Corlan, 53 Birchgrove Road, Lonlas, Swansea SA7 9JR. *T:* Swansea 812286. *Clubs:* Reform; Cardiff and County (Cardiff).

ROSSETTI, Harold Ford, CB 1959; *b* 19 Feb. 1909; *s* of Gabriel Arthur Madox Rossetti and Dora Brandreth Lewis; *m* 1933, Joan, *er d* of Rev. G. H. Holley; two *s* one *d. Educ:* Bolton School; Gonville and Caius College, Cambridge. Administrative Civil Servant, 1932-69; Customs and Excise Dept, 1932-34; Min. of Labour, 1934-51; OEEC, Paris, 1951-55; Min. of Labour, 1955-63; Dept of Educn and Science, 1963-69; Director, London Office, ILO, 1970-75. *Publication:* The Darkling Plain (novel), 1936. *Address:* 30 Castle Street, Framlingham, Suffolk. *T:* Framlingham 723586.

ROSSI, Hugh Alexis Louis; MP (C) Haringey, Hornsey, since 1974 (Hornsey, 1966-74); *b* 21 June 1927; *m* 1955, Philomena Elizabeth Jennings; one *s* four *d. Educ:* Finchley Catholic Gram. Sch.; King's Coll., Univ. of London (LLB). Solicitor with Hons, 1950; consultant in London practice. Member: Hornsey Borough Coun., 1956-65; Haringey Council, 1965-68; Middlesex CC, 1961-65. Govt Whip, Oct. 1970-April 1972; Europe Whip, Oct. 1971-1973; a Lord Comr, HM Treasury, 1972-74; Parly Under-Sec. of State, DoE, 1974; opposition spokesman on housing and land, 1974-. Dep. Leader, UK Delegn to Council of Europe and WEU, 1972-73 (Mem., 1970-73). Knight of Holy Sepulchre, 1966. *Publications:* Guide to the Rent Act, 1974; Guide to Community Land Act, 1975; Guide to Rent (Agriculture) Act, 1976. *Address:* 24 Wilton Place, SW1.

ROSSITER, John Frederick; Agent-General for Victoria, in London, since 1976; *b* 17 Dec. 1913; *s* of James and Sarah Rossiter; *m* 1939, Joan Durrant Stewart; one *s* two *d. Educ:* Melbourne Univ. (BA 1937). Senior Lecturer in English, Royal Melbourne Inst. of Technology, 1946-55; MLA (Lib.), Brighton, Vic., 1955; Minister of Labour and Industry; Minister of Health; Chief Secretary, 1964-76. *Recreation:* golf. *Address:* 11 Kingston House, Knightsbridge, SW1. *Clubs:* Wig and Pen, United Oxford & Cambridge University, Les Ambassadeurs; Naval and Military (Melbourne), Royal Melbourne Golf, Barman Heads Golf, Melbourne CC; Royal Wimbledon Golf.

ROSSITER, Leonard; actor; *b* 21 Oct. 1926; *s* of John Rossiter and Elizabeth Rossiter; *m* 1972, Gillian Raine; one *d. Educ:* Liverpool Collegiate Secondary Sch. Entered theatre, 1954; 1st London appearance, Free As Air, Savoy, 1958; Broadway début, Semi-Detached, 1963. London appearances include: Volpone, Garrick, 1967; (title role) The Resistible Rise of Arturo Ui, Savile, 1969 (Edinburgh Festival, 1968; London Critics' Best Actor Award and Variety Club's Best Actor Award, 1969); The Heretic, Duke of York's, 1970; The Caretaker, Mermaid, 1972; The Banana Box, Hampstead Theatre Club and Apollo, 1973; Old Vic, 1976. Film and television appearances. *Recreations:* squash, wine. *Address:* 13 Billing Road, SW10. *Club:* Hurlingham.

ROSSLYN, 6th Earl of, *cr* 1801; **Antony Hugh Francis Harry St Clair-Erskine;** Bt 1666; Baron Loughborough, 1795; Captain King's Royal Rifle Corps; underwriting member of Lloyd's; Director of R. F. Kershaw Ltd; *b* 18 May 1917; *s* of late Lord Loughborough (*d* 1929) and Sheila (who obtained a divorce, 1926, and *m* 2nd, 1928, Sir John Milbanke, 11th Bt, 3rd, 1954, Prince Dimitri of Russia; she *d* 1969), *o d* of Harry Chisholm, Australia; *S* grandfather, 1939; *m* 1955, Athenais De Mortemart (marriage dissolved, 1962), *o d* of late Duc De Vivonne and Mme M. V. Ollivier, La Ferme Ste Barbe, Arcangues, BP, France; one *s* one *d. Educ:* Eton; Magdalen Coll., Oxford. Served with GHQ Liaison Regt (Phantom) and attached to 3rd Canadian Infantry Division (despatches). Member: Mental Health Research Fund; Pinewood Hosp. House Cttee (Windsor Group), 1952-57. A Governor, Ludgrove Sch. Trust Ltd. *Heir: s* Lord Loughborough, *qv. Address:* Stonerwood Park, Petersfield, Hants. *T:* Petersfield 3433. *Clubs:* White's, Royal Automobile, MCC; New (Edinburgh); Royal and Ancient (St Andrews); Travellers' (Paris).

ROSSMORE, 7th Baron, *cr* 1796; **William Warner Westenra;** *b* 14 Feb. 1931; *o s* of 6th Baron and of Dolores Cecil, *d* of late Lieut-Col James Alban Wilson, DSO, West Burton, Yorks; *S* father, 1958. *Educ:* Eton; Trinity Coll., Cambridge (BA). 2nd Lieut, Somerset LI. *Heir:* none. *Address:* Rossmore Park, Co. Monaghan, Eire. *T:* Monaghan 47.

ROST, Peter Lewis; MP (C) Derbyshire South-East, since 1970; Member, London Stock Exchange; *b* 19 Sept. 1930; *s* of Frederick Rosenstiel and Elisabeth Merz; *m* 1961, Hilary Mayo; two *s* two *d. Educ:* various primary schs; Aylesbury Grammar Sch. National Service, RAF, 1948-50; Birmingham Univ. (BA Hons Geog.), 1950-53. Investment Analyst and Financial Journalist with Investors Chronicle, 1953-58; firstly Investment Advisor, 1958, and then, 1962, Mem. London Stock Exchange and Partner with present firm. Secretary: Cons. Parly Trade and Industry Cttee, 1971-73; Cons. Parly Energy Cttee, 1974-; Mem., Select Cttee on Sci. and Technol. (Energy Resources). Treasurer, Anglo-German Parly Gp, 1974-. *Recreations:* tennis, ski-ing, gardening, antique map collecting. *Address:* Norcott Court, Berkhamsted, Herts. *T:* Berkhamsted 6123.

ROSTAL, Professor Max, CBE 1977; Professor at the Guildhall School of Music, London, 1944-58; Professor of the Master-Class, State Academy of Music, Cologne, since 1957; Professor of the Master-Class, Conservatoire, Berne, Switzerland, since 1958; *b* 7 Aug. 1905; *m* 1946, Karoline T. J. (*née* Reichsedle von

Hohenblum-Simitsch); two *d. Educ:* State Acad., Vienna (Prof. Rosé); State Academy, Berlin (Prof. Flesch). Concert artist since age of 6; gave concerts in all parts of the world; at age of 23 Assistant to Prof. Flesch; Professor at State Academy of Music, Berlin, 1928-33. Lived in London, 1934-58; now residing in Switzerland. Has made various recordings for HMV, Decca, Argo, Concert Hall Soc., and Deutsche Grammophon Companies. FGSM 1945. Silver Medal, State Acad. of Music, Cologne, 1965; Bundesverdienstkreuz 1st Class, German Federal Govt, 1968; Music Award, City of Berne, Switzerland, 1972. *Publications:* many compositions, transcriptions, arrangements, editions. *Recreations:* motoring, photography, reading. *Address:* Chalet Pro Musica, Ausserschwand, CH-3715 Adelboden, Switzerland. *T:* (0)33-732233.

ROSTEN, Leo C., (pseudonym: **Leonard Q. Ross**); author and social scientist; *b* 11 April 1908; *s* of Samuel C. and Ida F. Rosten; *m* 1st, 1935, Priscilla Ann Mead (decd); one *s* two *d*; 2nd, 1960, Gertrude Zimmerman. *Educ:* University of Chicago (PhD); London School of Economics (Hon. Fellow, 1975). Research Assistant, Political Science Dept, Univ. of Chicago, 1933-35; Fellow, Social Science Research Council, 1934-36; Grants from Rockefeller Foundation and Carnegie Corporation, 1938-40. Dir, Motion Picture Research Project, 1939-41. Spec. Consultant, Nat. Defense Advisory Commn, Washington, 1939; Chief, Motion Picture Div., Office of Facts and Figures, Washington, 1941-42; Dep. Dir, Office of War Information, Washington, 1942-45; Special Consultant, Sec. of War, Washington, 1945; special mission to France, Germany, England, 1945. Faculty Associate, Columbia Univ., 1953-; Lectr in Political Science, Yale Univ., 1955, New School for Social Research, NY, 1959. Ford Vis. Prof. in Pol. Sci., Univ. of California (Berkeley), USA, 1960-61. Wrote film screenplays: Sleep, My Love; The Velvet Touch; Walk East on Beacon; The Dark Corner, etc. Member: Amer. Acad. of Political and Social Science; Amer. Assoc. for Advancement of Science; Nat. Acad. of Lit. and the Arts; Authors League of America; Authors Guild of America; Educnl Policies Cttee of Nat. Educnl Assoc. Phi Beta Kappa, 1929; Freedom Foundation's Award, 1955; George Polk Meml Award, 1955; Distinguished Alumnus Award, Univ. of Chicago, 1970. Hon. DHL Univ. of Rochester, 1973. *Publications:* The Education of H*y*m*a*n K*a*p*l*a*n, 1937; The Washington Correspondents, 1937; The Strangest Places, 1939; Hollywood: The Movie Colony, The Movie Makers, 1941; The Dark Corner, 1945; Guide To The Religions of America (Ed.), 1957; The Return of H*y*m*a*n K*a*p*l*a*n 1959; Captain Newman, MD, 1961; The Story Behind the Painting, 1961; The Many Worlds of Leo Rosten; The Leo Rosten Bedside Book, 1965; A Most Private Intrigue, 1967; The Joys of Yiddish, 1968; A Trumpet for Reason, 1970; People I have Loved, Known or Admired, 1970; Rome Wasn't Burned in a Day, 1971; Leo Rosten's Treasury of Jewish Quotations, 1973; Dear "Herm", 1974; (ed) The Look Book, 1975; The 3.10 to Anywhere, 1976; O Kaplan! My Kaplan!, 1976; contrib. learned journals. *Recreations:* photography; travel. *Address:* c/o Stanley Senior Associates, 70 Pine Street, NYC, USA. *Clubs:* Savile, Reform, Garrick (London); Cosmos (Washington), Chaos (New York).

ROSTOW, Prof. Eugene Victor; Sterling Professor of Law, Yale University; *b* 25 Aug. 1913; *s* of Victor A. and Lillian H. Rostow; *m* 1933, Edna B. Greenberg; two *s* one *d. Educ:* Yale Coll.; King's Coll., Cambridge (LLD 1962); Yale Law Sch. Practised law, New York, 1937-38; Yale Law Faculty, 1938-. Asst to Asst Sec. of State Acheson, 1942-44; Asst to Exec. Sec., Econ. Commn for Europe, UN, Geneva, 1949-50; Dean of Yale Law Sch., 1955-65; Under-Sec. of State for Political Affairs, 1966-69. Pres., Atlantic Treaty Assoc., 1973-76. Pitt Prof., Cambridge, 1959-60; Eastman Prof., Oxford, 1970-71. Dir, American Jewish Cttee, 1972-74. Hon. LLD Boston, 1976. Chevalier, Legion of Honour (France), 1960; Grand Cross, Order of the Crown (Belgium), 1969. *Publications:* A National Policy for the Oil Industry, 1948; Planning for Freedom, 1959; The Sovereign Prerogative, 1962; Law, Power and the Pursuit of Peace, 1968; (ed) Is Law Dead?, 1971; Peace in the Balance, 1972; The Ideal in Law, 1977; contribs to legal and economic jls. *Address:* 208 St Ronan Street, New Haven, Conn 06511, USA. *T:* 203-776-3906; Peru, Vermont 05152, USA. *T:* 802-824-6627. *Clubs:* Century (New York); Elizabethan, Lawn (New Haven). *See also W. W. Rostow.*

ROSTOW, Walt Whitman; Professor of Economics and of History, University of Texas at Austin, Texas, since 1969; *b* 7 Oct. 1916; 2nd *s* of Victor and Lillian Rostow; *m* 1947, Elspeth, *o d* of Milton J. and Harriet Vaughan Davies; one *s* one *d. Educ:* Yale (BA 1936; PhD 1940); Oxford (Rhodes Scholar). Social Science Research Council Fellow, 1939-40; Instructor, Columbia Univ., 1940-41; Office Strategic Services, 1941-45 (Army of the United States, 1943-45, Major; Legion of Merit;

Hon. OBE); Assistant Chief Division German-Austrian Economic Affairs, Department of State, 1945-46; Harmsworth Professor American History, Oxford, 1946-47; Special Assistant to Executive Secretary, Economic Commission for Europe, 1947-49; Pitt Professor of American History, Cambridge, 1949-50; Professor of Economic History, Massachusetts Institute of Technology, 1950-61. Deputy Special Assistant to the President (USA) for National Security Affairs, Jan. 1961-Dec. 1961; Counselor and Chairman, Policy Planning Council, Department of State, 1961-66; US Mem., Inter-Amer. Cttee on Alliance for Progress, 1964-66; Special Assistant to the President, The White House, 1966-69. Member: Royal Economic Society, England; American Academy of Arts and Sciences, 1957. Hon. LLD: Carnegie Inst. of Tech., Pittsburgh, 1962; Univ. Miami, 1965; Univ. Notre Dame, 1966; Middlebury Coll., 1967. Presidential Medal of Freedom, with distinction, 1969. *Publications:* The American Diplomatic Revolution, 1947; Essays on the British Economy of the Nineteenth Century, 1948; The Process of Economic Growth, 1952; (with A. D. Gayer and A. J. Schwartz) The Growth and Fluctuation of the British Economy, 1790-1850, 1953, 1975; (with A. Levin and others) The Dynamics of Soviet Society, 1953; (with others) The Prospects for Communist China, 1954; (with R. W. Hatch) An American Policy in Asia, 1955; (with M. F. Millikan) A Proposal: Key to An Effective Foreign Policy, 1957; The Stages of Economic Growth, 1960, 2nd edn 1971; The United States in the World Arena, 1960; The Economics of Take-off into Sustained Growth (ed), 1963; View from the Seventh Floor, 1964; A Design for Asian Development, 1965; Politics and the Stages of Growth, 1971; The Diffusion of Power, 1972; How It All Began: origins of the modern economy, 1975; various articles contributed to: The Economist, Economic Journal, Economic History Review, Journal of Econ. History, American Econ. Review, etc. *Address:* 1 Wild Wind Point, Austin, Texas 78746, USA. *Clubs:* Elizabethan (New Haven, Conn, USA); Cosmos (Washington, DC). *See also E. V. Rostow.*

ROSTRON, Sir Frank, Kt 1967; MBE 1954; FIEE; Director, Ferranti Ltd, Hollinwood, Lancs, 1958-68; *b* 11 Sept. 1900; *s* of late Samuel Ernest and Martha Rostron, Oldham; *m* 1929, Helen Jodrell Owen; one *s* one *d. Educ:* Oldham High Sch.; Manchester Coll. of Tech. Ferranti Ltd, 1917-68. Served War of 1939-45: Electrical Engineer Officer, RAF; released with rank of Squadron Leader. President, Manchester Chamber of Commerce, 1956 and 1957. Director: National and Vulcan Boiler and General Insurance Co. Ltd, 1961-70; Aron Meters Ltd, 1961-68; McKechnie Brothers Ltd, 1966-71. Chairman: Cotton Board, 1963-67 (Independent Member, 1959); Cotton and Allied Textiles Industry Training Board, 1966-67; Textile Council, 1967-68. *Address:* 5 Brocklehurst Drive, Prestbury, Macclesfield, Cheshire SK10 4JD. *T:* Prestbury 49577.

ROSTROPOVICH, Mstislav; 'cellist; Music Director and Conductor, National Symphony Orchestra, Washington, since 1977; *b* 1927; *m* Galina Vishnevskaya, *qv*; two *d. Educ:* State Conservatoire, Moscow. Has played in many concerts in Russia and abroad from 1942; first performance of Shostakovich's 'cello concerto (dedicated to him), Edinburgh Festival, 1960. Series of concerts with London Symphony Orchestra under Gennadi Rozhdestvensky, Festival Hall, 1965 (Gold Medal); first perf. Britten's third cello suite, Aldeburgh, 1974. An Artistic Dir, Aldeburgh Festival, 1977-. Mem. Union of Soviet Composers, 1950-. Lenin Prize, 1964. Hon. MusD: St Andrews, 1968; Cambridge, 1975; Harvard, 1976; Yale, 1976. *Address:* c/o Edgar Vincent Associates, 156 East 52nd Street, New York, NY 10022, USA.

ROTBLAT, Prof. Joseph, CBE 1965; MA, DSc (Warsaw); PhD (Liverpool); DSc (London); FInstP; Professor of Physics in the University of London, at St Bartholomew's Hospital Medical College, 1950-76, now Emeritus; Physicist to St Bartholomew's Hospital, 1950-76; *b* 4 Nov. 1908; *e s* of late Z. Rotblat, Warsaw. *Educ:* University of Warsaw, Poland. Research Fellow of Radiological Laboratory of Scientific Society of Warsaw, 1933-39; Asst Director of Atomic Physics Institute of Free Univ. of Poland, 1937-39; Oliver Lodge Fellow of Univ. of Liverpool, 1939-40; Lecturer and afterwards Senior Lecturer in Dept of Physics, Liverpool Univ., 1940-49; Director of Research in nuclear physics at Liverpool Univ., 1945-49; work on atomic energy at Liverpool Univ. and Los Alamos, New Mexico. Treasurer, St Bartholomew's Hosp. Med. Coll., 1974-76; Vice-Dean, Faculty of Sci., London Univ., 1974-76. Mem., Adv. Cttee on Med. Res., WHO, 1972-75. Ed., Physics in Medicine and Biol., 1960-72. Sec.-Gen., Pugwash Confs on Science and World Affairs, 1957-73. Pres., Hosp. Physicists' Assoc, 1969-70; Pres., British Inst. of Radiology, 1971-72. Mem. Governing Body of Stockholm Internat. Peace Res. Inst., 1966-71. Pres., Internat. Youth Sci. Fortnight, 1972-74. Vis. Prof. of Internat.

Relations, Univ. of Edinburgh, 1975-76. Member, Polish Academy of Sciences, 1966; Hon. For. Mem., Amer. Acad. of Arts and Sciences, 1972. Hon. DSc Bradford, 1973. *Publications:* Progress in Nuclear Physics, 1950; (with Chadwick) Radio-activity and Radioactive Substances, 1953; Atomic Energy, a Survey, 1954; Atoms and the Universe, 1956; Science and World Affairs, 1962; Aspects of Medical Physics, 1966; Pugwash, the First Ten Years, 1967; Scientists in the Quest for Peace, 1972; Nuclear Reactors: to breed or not to breed, 1977; papers on nuclear physics and radiation biology in Proceedings of Royal Society, Radiation Research, Nature, etc. *Recreations:* recorded music, travel. *Address:* 8 Asmara Road, West Hampstead, NW2 3ST. *T:* 01-435 1471. *Club:* Athenæum.

ROTH, Andrew; Political Correspondent, Manchester Evening News, since 1972; Director, Parliamentary Profiles, since 1955; *b* NY, 23 April 1919; *s* of Emil and Bertha Roth; *m* 1949, Mathilda Ann Friederich; one *s* one *d*. *Educ:* City Coll. of NY (BSS); Columbia Univ. (MA); Harvard Univ. Reader, City Coll., 1939; Res. Associate, Inst. of Pacific Relations, 1940; US Naval Intell., 1941-45 (Lieut, SG); Editorial Writer, The Nation, 1945-46; Foreign Corresp., Toronto Star Weekly, 1946-50; London Corresp., France Observateur, Sekai, Singapore Standard, 1950-60. *Publications:* Japan Strikes South, 1941; French Interests and Policies in the Far East, 1942; Dilemma in Japan, 1945 (UK 1946); The Business Background of Members of Parliament, 1959, 1963, 1965, 1967, 1972, 1975; The MPs' Chart, 1967, 1971, 1975, 1976; Enoch Powell: Tory Tribune, 1970; Can Parliament Decide..., 1971; Heath and the Heathmen, 1972; Lord on the Board, 1972; The Prime Ministers, Vol. II (Heath chapter), 1975; Sir Harold Wilson: Yorkshire Walter Mitty, 1977. *Recreations:* tennis, sketching/caricaturing. *Address:* 34 Somali Road, NW2 3RL. *T:* 01-435 6673; 26 Palace Chambers, Bridge Street, SW1 2JT. *T:* 01-930 2677. *Club:* Brondesbury Cricket and Tennis.

ROTH, Prof. Klaus Friedrich, FRS 1960; Professor of Pure Mathematics (Theory of Numbers) at Imperial College of Science and Technology, since 1966; *b* 29 Oct. 1925; *s* of late Dr Franz Roth and Mathilde Roth (*née* Liebrecht); *m* 1955, Melek Khairy, BSc, PhD. *Educ:* St Paul's Sch.; Peterhouse, Cambridge; Univ. College, London. BA (Cambridge, 1945); MSc, PhD (London, 1948, 1950). Asst Master, Gordonstoun School, 1945-46. Member of Dept of Mathematics, University College, London, 1948-66; title of Professor in the University of London conferred 1961. Visiting Lecturer, 1956-57, Vis. Prof., 1965-66, at Mass Inst. of Techn., USA. Fields Medal awarded at International Congress of Mathematicians, 1958. Foreign Hon. Mem., Amer. Acad. of Arts and Sciences, 1966. *Publications:* papers in various mathematical jls. *Recreations:* chess, cinema. *Address:* Department of Mathematics, Imperial College, Queen's Gate, SW7 5HH; 24 Burnsall Street, SW3 3ST. *T:* 01-352 1363.

ROTH, Prof. Sir Martin, Kt 1972; MD (London); FRCP; DPM; Professor of Psychiatry, New Addenbrooke's Hospital, University of Cambridge, since March 1977; Fellow, Trinity College, Cambridge; *b* 6 Nov. 1917; *s* of Samuel Simon and late Regina Roth; *m* 1945, Constance Heller; three *d*. *Educ:* University of London, St Mary's Hospital. Formerly: Senior Registrar, Maida Vale, and Maudsley Hosps; Physician, Crichton Royal Hosp., Dumfries; Director of Clinical Research, Graylingwell Hosp.; Prof. of Psychological Medicine, Univ. of Newcastle upon Tyne, 1956-77. Visiting Assistant Professor, in the Department of Psychiatry, McGill University, Montreal, 1954; Consultant, WHO Expert Cttee on Mental Health Problems of Ageing and the Aged, 1958; Member: Med. Cons. Cttee, Nuffield Provincial Hosp. Trust, 1962; Central Health Services Council, Standing Med. Adv. Cttee, Standing Mental Health Adv. Cttee, DHSS, 1966-75; Scientific Adv. Cttee, CIBA Foundn, 1970-. Mayne Vis. Prof., Univ. of Queensland, 1968; Albert Sterne Vis. Prof., Univ. of Indiana, 1976. Adolf Meyer Lectr, Amer. Psychiatric Assoc., 1971. Pres., Section of Psychiatry, RSM, 1968-69; Member: MRC, 1964-68; Clinical Research Board, MRC, 1964-70; Hon. Dir, MRC Group for study of relationship between functional and organic mental disorders, 1962-67. Co-Editor, British Jl of Psychiatry, 1967. FRCPsych (Foundn Fellow; Pres., 1971-75); Distinguished Fellow, Amer. Psychiatric Assoc., 1972; Hon. FRCPGlas. Corresp. Mem., Deutsche Gesellschaft für Psychiatrie und Nervenheilkunde; Hon. Member: Société Royale de Médecine Mentale de Belgique; Canadian Psychiatric Assoc., 1972. Hon. Fellow: Amer. Coll. Neuropsychopharmacology; Australian and New Zealand College of Psychiatry. Hon. ScD Trinity College, Dublin, 1977. *Publications:* (with Mayer-Gross and Slater) Clinical Psychiatry, 1954, (with Slater) 3rd edn 1969; Studies in the Classification of Affective Disorders, 1977; papers on psychiatric aspects of ageing, depressive illness,

schizophrenia, in various psychiatric and medical journals. *Recreations:* music, literature, conversation, travel. *Address:* Department of Psychiatry, New Addenbrooke's Hospital, University of Cambridge. *Club:* Athenæum.

ROTH, Air Commodore Victor Henry Batten, CB 1959; CBE 1949; RAF, retd; *b* 7 June 1904; *s* of late Victor Roth; *m* 1948, Catherine Lang, *d* of late John McNaught Colquhoun. *Educ:* London Sch. of Economics (BCom.). Commnd into RAF, 1929; Home Aircraft Depot, 1929-31; No 2 Maintenance Unit, 1931-32; Air HQ, Iraq, 1933; Aircraft Depot, Iraq, 1934; No 2 Maintenance Unit, 1935; Equipt Staff, Air Min., 1935-43; OC No 312 Maintenance Unit, SEAC, 1943-44; Sen. Equipt Staff Officer, No 226 Gp, SEAC, 1944; HQ Base Air Forces, SE Asia, 1944-45; Mil. Staff Coll., Quetta, 1945-46; Dir of Administrative Plans, Air Min., and Mem., Jt Admin. Planning Staff, MoD, 1946-49; Equipt Staff, Air Min., 1949-51; Sen. Equipt Staff Officer, FEAF, 1951-52; Imperial Defence Coll., 1953; OC No 61 Maintenance Unit, 1954-55; Dir of Equipt (D), Air Min., 1955-59; Sen. Air Staff Officer, No 40 Gp, 1959-61; AOC No 40 Gp (acting Air Vice-Marshal), 1961; Comdt RAF Supply Control Centre, 1961-62; retired, Jan. 1963. King's Commendation, 1941. Member: Thingoe RDC, 1964-74 (Chm., Finance and Gen. Purposes Cttee, 1970-72); St Edmundsbury Borough Council, 1973- (Chm., Finance Sub Cttee, 1973-); Chm., Horringer-cum-Ickworth Parish Council, 1973-75, 1976-78; Mayor, Borough of St Edmundsbury, 1975-76, Dep. Mayor, 1976-77. Hon. Helper, RAF Benevolent Fund, 1963-; Trustee, Horringer Charities, 1964-; Pres., Bury St Edmunds Branch, RAFA, 1974-; Mem., Eastern Road Accident Prevention Fedn, RoSPA, 1974-; Vice Chm., Bury St Edmunds Road Safety Cttee, 1977-. Mem., Suffolk Inst. Archaeology, 1965-. Life Mem. Convocation, Univ. of London. *Address:* 1 Sharp's Green, Horringer, Bury St Edmunds, Suffolk IP29 5PP. *T:* Horringer 332. *Club:* Athenæum (Bury St Edmunds).

ROTHA, Paul, FRSA; Film Producer and Director; Author; Journalist; Managing Director, Paul Rotha Productions Ltd, since 1941; *b* London, 3 June 1907. *Educ:* Highgate School; Slade School of Art, London. Painter and designer; Art Critic to The Connoisseur, 1927-28; specialised in the production of documentary films, starting with Empire Marketing Board; has made documentary films for Unesco, The Times, Shell-Mex, Imperial Airways, Manchester Corporation, Scottish Office, National Council of Social Service, Gas Industry, Royal National Life-Boat Institution, Central Electricity Board, National Book Council, Vickers-Armstrong, Orient Line, etc, Gold Medals for Films at Venice Film Festival (1934), Brussels Film Festival (1935) and Leipsig Film Festival (1962); British Film Academy Awards, 1947 and 1952. Visited US under auspices of Rockefeller Foundation, 1937-38, to lecture on documentary films, 1953-54; Simon Senior Research Fellow, Univ. of Manchester, 1967-68; Head of Documentary at BBC Television; Arts Council Grant, 1970. Producer and/or Director: The Silent Raid (feature), Life of Adolf Hitler, World Without End (co-dir), Cradle of Genius, Cat and Mouse (feature), No Resting Place (feature), The World is Rich, The Challenge of Television (BBC), A City Speaks, Total War in Britain, Land of Promise, Children of the City, World of Plenty, Contact, To-Day We Live, Cover to Cover, The Future's in the Air, The Face of Britain, New Worlds for Old, The Fourth Estate, etc. *Publications:* The Film Till Now, 1930, new edns 1949, 1960, 1967; Celluloid; The Film To-Day, 1931; Documentary Film, 1936, new edns 1939, 1952, 1970; (with Roger Manvell) Movie Parade, 1936, new edn, 1950; (with E. Anstey and others) Shots in the Dark, 1951; (ed) Portrait of a Flying Yorkshireman, 1952; Television in the Making, 1956; Rotha on the Film, 1958; (with Basil Wright and A. Calder-Marshall) The Innocent Eye: a biography of Robert Flaherty, 1963; Documentary Diary, 1973; Richard Winnington: Film Criticism and Caricatures, 1975. *Address:* c/o John Farquharson Ltd, Bell House, Bell Yard, London WC2A 2JU.

ROTHENSTEIN, Sir John (Knewstub Maurice), Kt 1952; CBE 1948; KCSG; PhD (London); Hon. LLD (New Brunswick; St Andrews); writer; Director of the Tate Gallery, 1938-64; Hon. Fellow: Worcester College, Oxford, 1963; University College London, 1976; Member: British Council, since 1938; Advisory Committee on Decoration of Westminster Cathedral, since 1953; Council, Friends of the Tate Gallery, since 1958; President, Friends of the Bradford City Art Gallery and Museums, since 1973; *b* London, 11 July 1901; *e s* of Sir William Rothenstein and Alice Mary, *e c* of Walter John Knewstub, of Chelsea; *m* 1929, Elizabeth Kennard Whittington, 2nd *d* of Charles Judson Smith, of Lexington, Kentucky; one *d*. *Educ:* Bedales School; Worcester College, Oxford (MA); University College, London (PhD). Assistant Professor: of Art History in the University of Kentucky, 1927-28; Department of Fine Arts,

University of Pittsburgh, 1928-29; Director: City Art Gallery, Leeds, 1932-34; City Art Galleries and Ruskin Museum, Sheffield, 1933-38; Member: Executive Committee, Contemporary Art Society, 1938-65; Art Panel, Arts Council of Great Britain, 1945-52, and 1953-56. Rector, University of St Andrews, 1964-67. Visiting Professor: Dept of Fine Arts, Fordham Univ., USA, 1967-68; of History of Art, Agnes Scott Coll., Ga, USA, 1969-70; Distinguished Prof., City Univ. of NY, at Brooklyn Coll., 1971, 1972; Regents' Lectr, Univ. of Calif at Irvine, 1973. Editor, The Masters, 1965-67; Hon. Editor, Museums Jl, 1959-61. Knight Commander, Mexican Order of the Aztec Eagle, 1953. *Publications:* The Portrait Drawings of William Rothenstein, 1889-1925, 1926; Eric Gill, 1927; The Artists of the 1890's, 1928; Morning Sorrow: a novel, 1930; British Artists and the War, 1931; Nineteenth Century Painting, 1932; An Introduction to English Painting, 1933; The Life and Death of Conder, 1938; Augustus John (Phaidon British Artists), 1944; Edward Burra (Penguin Modern Painters), 1945; Manet, 1945; Modern Foreign Pictures in the Tate Gallery, 1949; Turner, 1949; London's River, 1951 (with Father Vincent Turner, SJ); Modern English Painters, vol. I, Sickert to Smith, 1952, vol. II, Lewis to Moore, 1956, vol. III, Wood to Hockney, 1973; The Tate Gallery, 1958; Turner, 1960; British Art since 1900; an Anthology, 1962; Sickert, 1961; Paul Nash, 1961; Augustus John, 1962; Matthew Smith, 1962; Turner (with Martin Butlin), 1963; Francis Bacon (with Ronald Alley), 1964; Edward Burra, 1973; Walter Greaves (with Michael Parkin), 1978; (ed) Sixteen Letters from Oscar Wilde, 1930; (ed) Stanley Spencer: correspondence and reminiscences, 1978; *autobiography:* Summer's Lease (I), 1965; Brave Day, Hideous Night (II), 1966; Time's Thievish Progress (III), 1970. *Television:* Churchill the Painter, COI, 1968; Collection and Recollection, BBC, 1968. *Address:* Beauforest House, Newington, Dorchester-on-Thames, Oxon OX9 8AG; 8 Tryon Street, Chelsea, SW3 3LH. *Clubs:* Athenæum, Chelsea Arts (Hon. Mem.).
See also Baron Dynevor.

ROTHENSTEIN, Michael, ARA 1977; Painter and print-maker; *b* 1908; *yr s* of late Sir William Rothenstein; *m* 1936, Betty Desmond Fitz-Gerald (marr. diss., 1957); one *s* one *d*; *m* 1958, Diana, 2nd *d* of late Comdr H. C. Arnold-Forster, CMG. Retrospective exhibitions: Kunstnernes Hus, Oslo, 1969; Bradford Art Gallery, 1972; ICA, 1974. Works acquired by: Museum of Modern Art and Brooklyn Museum, New York; Tate Gallery; British Museum; Victoria and Albert Museum; Library of Congress, Washington; British Council; Arts Council; museums of: Sydney; Victoria; Dallas; Boston; Cincinnati; Lugano; etc. Exhibited: Cincinnati Biennial, 1954, 1960; Ljublyana Biennial of Graphic Art, 1957, 1961, 1963; Albertina, Vienna (Prints), 1963; Internat. Triennale, Grechen, 1961, 1964, 1967; 8th Internat. Exhibition, Lugano; 4th Internat. Print Exhibn, Tokyo, 1966; Internat. Print Biennale, Cracow, 1970, 1972, 1974. Trust House Award, 1963; Gold Medal, first internat. Engraving Biennale, Buenos Aires; Prix d'Achat, Cracow Internat. Print Biennale, 1974. *Publications:* Frontiers of Printmaking, 1966; Relief Printing, 1970; Suns and Moons, 1972; Seven Colours (with Edward Lucie Smith), 1975. *Address:* Columbia House, Stisted, Braintree, Essex. *T:* Braintree 25444.

ROTHERHAM, Air Vice-Marshal John Kevitt, CB 1962; CBE 1960; Director-General (Engineering), RAF, 1967-69; retired; *b* 28 Dec. 1910; *s* of Colonel Ewan Rotherham; *m* 1st, 1936, Joan Catherine Penrose (*d* 1940); one *d*; 2nd, 1941, Margot Susan Hayter. *Educ:* Uppingham; Exeter College, Oxford. Joined RAF with Univ. perm. commn, 1933; 17 (F) Sqdn, 1934; 605 (B) Sqdn, 1936; School of Aeronautical Engineering, Henlow, 1936; post-grad. course, Imperial Coll., 1938; 43 (M) Group, 1939; Kidbrooke, 1940; MAP 1941; 41 (M) Group, 1942; HQ Flying Training Comd, 1946; exchange posting with USAF, 1947; Air Ministry, 1948; Joint Services Staff Coll., 1951; No 205 Group, Middle East, 1952; Air Ministry, 1954; seconded to Pakistan Air Force, 1957; Senior Technical Staff Officer, Transport Command, RAF, 1960-63; AOC No 24 (Training) Group, Technical Training Command, RAF, 1963-65; Senior Tech. Staff Officer, Bomber Command, 1965-67. AFRAeS 1949, FRAeS 1967. *Recreations:* sailing, ski-ing, golf. *Address:* South Meadow, Shore Road, Old Bosham, Chichester, Sussex PO18 8QL. *T:* Bosham 573346. *Clubs:* Royal Air Force; Island Sailing, Bosham Sailing.
See also R. J. S. McDowall.

ROTHERHAM, Leonard, CBE 1970; DSc; FRS 1963; CEng, FIEE, FInstF, FIM, FInstP; Vice-Chancellor, Bath University, 1969-76; *b* 31 Aug. 1913; *m* 1937, Nora Mary Thompson; one *s* two *d*. *Educ:* Strutt School, Belper; University College, London. Physicist, Brown Firth Research Laboratories, 1935-46; Head of Metallurgy Dept, RAE Farnborough, 1946-50; Dir, R&D, UKAEA, Industrial Group, Risley, 1950-58. Mem. for Research, Central Electricity Generating Bd, 1958-69; Head of Research, Electricity Supply Industry and Electricity Council, 1965-69. Chairman: Adv. Cttee for Scientific and Technical Information, 1970-74; Defence Scientific Adv. Council, 1974-. Member: Central Adv. Council for Science and Technology, 1968-70; Adv. Council for Energy Conservation, 1974-; Adv. Council for Applied R&D, 1976-. Hon. LLD Bristol, 1972; Hon. DSc Bath, 1976. Fellow UCL, 1959; Hon. Fellow, Inst. of Welding, 1965; Hon. Life Mem., American Society of Mechanical Engineers, 1963; President, Instn of Metallurgists, 1964; Inst. of Metals, 1965; Member of Council, Royal Society, 1965-66. Founder Fellow, Fellowship of Engineering, 1976. *Publications:* Creep of Metals, 1951; various scientific and technical papers; also lectures: Hatfield Memorial, 1961; Coal Science, 1961; Calvin Rice (of Amer. Soc. of Mech. Engrs), 1963; 2nd Metallurgical Engineering, Inst. of Metals, 1963. *Address:* Westhanger, Horningsham, Warminster, Wilts. *Club:* Athenæum.

ROTHERMERE, 2nd Viscount, *cr* 1919, of Hemsted; **Esmond Cecil Harmsworth,** Baron, *cr* 1914; Bt *cr* 1910; Chairman, Daily Mail and General Trust Ltd; President and Director of group finance, Associated Newspapers Ltd, since 1971 (Chairman, 1932-71); *b* 29 May 1898; *o surv s* of 1st Viscount and Mary Lilian (*d* 1937), *d* of George Wade Share; *S* father, 1940; *m* 1st, 1920, Margaret Hunam (from whom he obtained a divorce, 1938), *d* of late William Redhead; one *s* two *d*; 2nd, 1945, Lady O'Neill (marr. diss., 1952; she *m* 1952, late Ian L. Fleming), *widow* of 3rd Baron O'Neill and *e d* of Hon. Guy Charteris; 3rd, 1966, Mrs Mary Ohrstrom, *d* of Kenneth Murchison, Dallas, Texas; one *s*. *Educ:* Eton. Commission in Royal Marine Artillery, 1917; ADC to Prime Minister in Paris (Peace Conference), 1919; MP (U) Isle of Thanet, 1919-29. Mem., Adv. Council, Min. of Information, 1939; Chm., Newspaper Proprietors Assoc., 1934-61. Chancellor, Newfoundland Univ., 1952-61. DCL Bishop's University, PQ, 1954. *Recreations:* tennis and racquets. *Heir: s* Hon. Vere Harold Esmond Harmsworth, *qv*. *Address:* 11 South Audley Street, W1. *Clubs:* White's, Beefsteak.
See also Sir Neill Cooper-Key, Earl of Cromer.

ROTHERWICK, 2nd Baron *cr* 1939; **Herbert Robin Cayzer;** Bt 1924; *b* 5 Dec. 1912; *s* of 1st Baron Rotherwick; *S* father 1958; *m* 1952, Sarah-Jane, *o d* of Sir Michael Nial Slade, 6th Bt; three *s* one *d*. *Educ:* Eton; Christ Church, Oxford (BA). Supplementary Reserve Royal Scots Greys, 1938; served War of 1939-45 with them in Middle East. Deputy Chairman British & Commonwealth Shipping Co. Ltd, and Director of other and associated companies. *Heir: s* Hon. (Herbert) Robin Cayzer, Lt Life Guards (T&AVR), *b* 12 March 1954. *Address:* Cornbury Park, Charlbury, Oxfordshire. *T:* Charlbury 311; 51 Eaton Square, SW1. *Clubs:* Turf, White's.

ROTHES, 21st Earl of, *cr* before 1457; **Ian Lionel Malcolm Leslie;** Lord Leslie 1445; Baron Ballenbreich 1457; *b* 10 May 1932; *o s* of 20th Earl of Rothes and of Beryl, *o d* of J. Lionel Dugdale; *S* father, 1975; *m* 1955, Marigold, *o d* of Sir David M. Evans Bevan, 1st Bt; two *s*. *Educ:* Eton. Sub-Lt RNVR, 1953. *Heir: s* Lord Leslie, *qv*. *Address:* Tanglewood, West Tytherley, Salisbury, Wilts.

ROTHMAN, Sydney; Chairman of Rothmans Tobacco (Holdings) Ltd since 1953 (Chairman and Managing Director Rothmans Ltd 1929-53); *b* 2 December 1897; *s* of Louis and Jane Rothman; *m* 1929, Jeannette Tropp; one *s* one *d*. *Educ:* Highgate School. Joined L. Rothman & Company, 1919, Partner, 1923, Rothmans Ltd. Ministry of Supply, 1941-45. *Recreation:* golf. *Address:* c/o National Westminster Bank, 227C City Road, EC4.

ROTHNIE, Alan Keir, CMG 1967; HM Diplomatic Service; Ambassador to Switzerland, since 1976; *b* 2 May 1920; *s* of late John and Dora Rothnie, Aberdeen; *m* 1953, Anne Cadogan Harris, *d* of Euan Cadogan Harris, *qv*; two *s* one *d*. *Educ:* Montrose Acad.; St Andrews University. Served RNVR, 1939-45. Entered Diplomatic Service, Nov. 1945; Foreign Office, 1945-46; 3rd Sec., HM Legation, Vienna, 1946-48; 2nd Sec., HM Embassy, Bangkok, 1949-50; FO 1951-53; 1st Sec. HM Embassy, Madrid, 1953-55; Asst Political Agent, Kuwait, 1956-58; FO, 1958-60; Middle East Centre for Arab Studies, Shemlan, 1960-62 (Chargé d'Affaires, HM Embassy, Kuwait, 1961); Commercial Counsellor: HM Embassy, Baghdad, 1963-64; HM Embassy, Moscow, 1965-68; Consul-Gen., Chicago, 1969-72; Ambassador to Saudi Arabia, 1972-76. *Recreations:* cricket, lawn tennis, ski-ing. *Address:* c/o Foreign and Commonwealth Office, SW1A 2AH. *Clubs:* White's, MCC.

ROTHSCHILD, family name of **Baron Rothschild.**

ROTHSCHILD, 3rd Baron, *cr* 1885; **Nathaniel Mayer Victor Rothschild;** Bt 1846; GBE 1975; GM 1944; PhD; ScD; FRS 1953; Chairman, Rothschilds Continuation, since 1976; Director, N. M. Rothschild & Sons (Chairman, 1975-76); Chairman, Royal Commission on Gambling, since 1976; *b* 31 Oct. 1910; *s* of late Hon. (Nathaniel) Charles Rothschild, 2nd *s* of 1st Baron Rothschild; *S* uncle, 1937; *m* 1st, 1933, Barbara (divorced, 1946), *o d* of late St John Hutchinson, KC; one *s* two *d*; 2nd, 1946, Teresa, MBE, MA, JP, *d* of late R. J. G. Mayor, CB; one *s* two *d* (and one *s* decd). *Educ:* Harrow, Trinity Coll., Cambridge. Fellow of Trinity Coll., Cambridge, 1935-39, Hon. Fellow, 1961. War of 1939-45: Military Intelligence (despatches, American Legion of Merit, American Bronze Star). Director, BOAC, 1946-58; Chm., Agricultural Res. Council, 1948-58; Assistant Dir of Research, Dept of Zoology, Cambridge, 1950-70; Vice-Chm., Shell Research Ltd, 1961-63, Chm., 1963-70; Chm., Shell Research NV, 1967-70; Director: Shell Internationale Research Mij, 1965-70; Shell Chemicals UK Ltd, 1963-70; Shell International Gas, 1969-70; Research Co-ordinator, Royal Dutch Shell Group, 1965-70; Dir Gen. and First Perm. Under-Sec., Central Policy Review Staff, Cabinet Office, 1971-74. Dir, Slater Walker Securities Ltd, 1975-. Member: BBC General Advisory Council, 1952-56; Council for Scientific Policy, 1965-67; Central Adv. Council for Science and Technology, 1969-. Hon. Fellow: Bellairs Research Inst. of McGill Univ., Barbados, 1960; Weizmann Inst. of Science, Rehovoth, 1962; University Coll., Cambridge, 1966; Inst. of Biol., 1971; Imperial Coll., 1975. Hon. DSc: Newcastle, 1964; Manchester, 1966; Technion, Haifa, 1968; City Univ., 1972; Hon. PhD: Tel Aviv, 1971; Hebrew Univ., Jerusalem, 1975; Hon. LLD London, 1977. *Publications:* The History of Tom Jones, a changeling, 1951; The Rothschild Library, 1955, new edn, 1972; Fertilization, 1956; A Classification of Living Animals, 1961; Meditations of a Broomstick, 1977; scientific papers. *Heir: s* Hon. (Nathaniel Charles) Jacob Rothschild, *qv.*

ROTHSCHILD, Edmund Leopold de; TD; President, N. M. Rothschild & Sons, since 1975 (Partner since 1946, Senior Partner, 1960-70, Chairman, 1970-75); Chairman, Straflo Ltd; *b* 2 Jan. 1916; *s* of late Lionel Nathan de Rothschild and Marie Louise Beer; *m* 1948, Elizabeth Edith Lentner; two *s* two *d. Educ:* Harrow Sch.; Trinity Coll., Cambridge. Major, RA (TA). Served France, North Africa and Italy, 1939-46 (wounded). Dep. Chairman: Brit. Newfoundland Corp. Ltd, 1963-69; Churchill Falls (Labrador) Corp. Ltd, 1966-69. Mem., Asia Cttee, BNEC, 1970-71, Chm., 1971. Trustee, Queen's Nursing Inst.; Mem. Council, Royal Nat. Pension Fund for Nurses; Pres., Assoc. of Jewish Ex-Servicemen and Women; Jt Treasurer: Council of Christians and Jews; Friends of the Hebrew Univ. of Jerusalem. Hon. LLD, Memorial Univ. of Newfoundland, 1961. Order of the Sacred Treasure, 1st Class (Japan), 1973. *Publication:* Window on the World, 1949. *Recreations:* gardening, fishing, shooting, cine-photography, hunting butterflies. *Address:* Inchmery House, Exbury, Southampton SO4 1AE. *T:* Fawley 893145. *Clubs:* White's, Portland; Mount Royal (Montreal).
See also L. D. de Rothschild.

ROTHSCHILD, Evelyn de; Chairman, N. M. Rothschild & Sons Ltd; *b* 29 Aug. 1931; *s* of late Anthony Gustav de Rothschild; *m* 1973, Victoria Schott; one *s* one *d. Educ:* Harrow; Trinity Coll., Cambridge. Dep. Chm., Milton Keynes Development Corp., 1971-; Chm., Economist Newspaper, 1972-. *Recreations:* art, racing. *Address:* Ascott, Wing, Bucks.

ROTHSCHILD, Baron Guy (Edouard Alphonse Paul) de; Officier de la Légion d'Honneur, 1959; President: Banque Rothschild, since 1968; Société Imetal, since 1975; Director: N. M. Rothschild & Sons Ltd (non executive); Société Minière et Métallurgique de Penarroya (President, 1964-71); Francarep; Centro Asegurador SA, Madrid; New Court Securities Corp.; Rio Tinto-Zinc Corp. Ltd; Compagnie du Nord (President, Executive Committee); Rothschild Continuation; *b* 21 May 1909; *s* of late Baron Edouard de Rothschild and late Baronne de Rothschild (*née* Germaine Halphen); *m* 1st, 1937, Baronne Alix Schey de Koromla (marriage dissolved, 1956); one *s*; 2nd, 1957, Baronne Marie-Hélène de Zuylen de Nyevelt (who *m* 1st, Comte François de Nicolay); one *s* and one step *s. Educ:* Lycées Condorcet et Louis le Grand, Facultés de Droit et des Lettres (Licencié en Droit). Served War of 1939-45 (Croix de Guerre). Chevalier du Mérite Agricole, 1948. Associé de MM de Rothschild Frères, 1936-67; Pres., Compagnie du Chemin de Fer du Nord, 1949-68. Pres., Fonds Social Juif Unifié. Mem., Société d'Encouragement. *Recreation:* haras et écurie de courses, golf. *Address:* 2 rue St-Louis en l'Isle, 75004 Paris, France. *Clubs:* Nouveau Cercle, Automobile Club de France, Cercle Interallié.

ROTHSCHILD, Hon. Jacob; *see* Rothschild, Hon. N.C.J.

ROTHSCHILD, Leopold David de; Director, N. M. Rothschild & Sons Ltd, since 1970 (Partner, 1956-70); *b* 12 May 1927; *yr s* of Lionel de Rothschild and Marie Louise Beer. *Educ:* Bishops Coll. Sch., Canada; Harrow; Trinity Coll., Cambridge. Chm., Rothschild Intercontinental Bank Ltd, 1969-75; Director of Bank of England, 1970-. Chairman: English Chamber Orchestra and Music Soc. Ltd, 1963; Bach Choir, 1976; Anglo Venezuelan Soc., 1976. *Recreations:* music, sailing. *Address:* New Court, St Swithin's Lane, EC4. *T:* 01-626 4356. *Clubs:* Brooks's; Royal Yacht Squadron.
See also E. L. de Rothschild.

ROTHSCHILD, Hon. Miriam, (Hon. Mrs Miriam Lane); *b* 5 Aug. 1908; *e d* of Hon. N. C. Rothschild and Rozsika de Wertheimstein; *m* 1943, Capt. George Lane, MC (marriage dissolved, 1957); one *s* three *d* (and one *s* one *d* decd). *Educ:* home. Member: Zoological and Entomological Research Coun.; Marine Biological Assoc.; Royal Entomological Soc.; Systematics Assoc.; Soc. for Promotion of Nature Reserves, etc.; Ed., Novitates Zoologica, 1938-41; Mem., Publications Cttee, Zoological Soc.; Foreign Office, 1940-42; Trustee, British Museum of Natural History, 1967-75. Mem., Amer. Acad. of Arts and Scis. Vis. Prof. in Biology, Royal Free Hosp. Hon. Fellow, St Hugh's Coll., Oxford. Hon. DSc, Oxford. Defence Medal (1940-45). *Publications:* Catalogue Rothschild Collection of Fleas (5 vols), British Museum; (with Theresa Clay) Fleas, Flukes and Cuckoos; 200 contribs to scientific jls. *Recreation:* watching butterflies. *Address:* Ashton, Peterborough. *Clubs:* Queen's, British Ornithological, Entomological.
See also Baron Rothschild.

ROTHSCHILD, Hon. (Nathaniel Charles) Jacob; Director, N. M. Rothschild & Sons Ltd, since 1963; Chairman, Rothschild Investment Trust Ltd, since 1971; *b* 29 April 1936; *e s* and *heir* of 3rd Baron Rothschild, *qv*; *m* 1961, Serena Mary, *er d* of late Sir Philip Gordon Dunn, 2nd Bt; one *s* three *d. Educ:* Eton; Christ Church, Oxford. BA 1st cl. hons History. *Address:* PO Box 185, New Court, St Swithin's Lane, EC4P 4DU. *T:* 01-626 4356.

ROTHSCHILD, Robert, KCMG (Hon.) 1963; Grand Officier de l'Ordre de la Couronne (Belgium); Belgian Ambassador to the Court of St James's, 1973-76; *b* 16 Dec. 1911; *s* of Bernard Rothschild and Marianne von Rynveld; one *d. Educ:* Univ. of Brussels (DrRerPol). Entered Belgian Foreign Office: Brussels, 1937; Lisbon, 1942; Chungking, China, 1944; Shanghai, 1946, Washington, USA, 1950; Paris, NATO, 1952; Brussels, 1954; Ambassador to Yugoslavia, 1958; Head of Mission, Katanga, Congo, 1960; Brussels, 1960; Ambassador to: Switzerland, 1964; France, 1966. *Publication:* La Chute de Chiang Kai-Shek, 1973 (Paris). *Recreations:* gardening, travel. *Address:* 51 Avenue du Général de Gaulle, Bruxelles, Belgium. *Clubs:* Travellers'; Cercle de l'Union (Paris); Cercle Gaulois (Brussels).

ROTHSTEIN, Saul; Solicitor to the Post Office, since 1976; *b* 4 July 1920; *s* of late Simon Rothstein and late Zelda Rothstein; *m* 1949, Judith Noemi (*née* Katz); two *d. Educ:* Church Institute Sch., Bolton; Manchester Univ (LLB). Admitted solicitor, 1947. War service, RAF, 1941-46 (Flt-Lt). Entered Solicitor's Dept, General Post Office, 1949, Asst Solicitor, 1963; Director, Advisory Dept, Solicitor's Office, Post Office, 1972-76. *Recreations:* chamber music, walking, travel. *Address:* 9 Templars Crescent, Finchley, N3 3QR. *T:* 01-346 3701.

ROTHWELL, Harry, BA, PhD Cantab; Professor of History, University of Southampton, 1945-68; Emeritus, 1968; Dean of the Faculty of Arts, 1949-52; *b* 8 September 1902; *s* of Harry Rothwell and Emma Watson; *m* 1935, Martha Annabella Goedecke; two *d. Educ:* Barnsley Grammar School; Manchester University; St John's College, Cambridge. 1st Class Hons in History, Prizeman and Faulkner Fellow, Manchester, 1925; Mullinger Schol., St John's Coll., Cambridge, 1925-28; Senior Asst to Keeper of Western Manuscripts, Bodleian Library, 1928-29; Lectr in Medieval History, Univ. of Toronto, Toronto, 1929-31; Lecturer in Medieval and European History, Edinburgh Univ., 1931-45; Lieut (Sp) RNVR, 1942-45. Past Pres., Hampshire Field Club and Archæological Soc. *Publications:* The Chronicle of Walter of Guisborough, 1957; (ed) English Historical Documents 1189-1327, 1975; articles and reviews in professional journals. *Address:* Hill House, Knapp, Ampfield, near Romsey, Hants. *T:* Braishfield 88666.

ROUGIER, Richard George, QC 1972; a Recorder of the Crown Court, since 1973; *b* 12 Feb. 1932; *s* of late George Ronald Rougier, CBE, QC, and Georgette Heyer, novelist; *m* 1962, Susanna Allen Flint (*née* Whitworth); one *s. Educ:* Marlborough

Coll.; Pembroke Coll., Cambridge (Exhibr, BA). Called to Bar, Inner Temple, 1956. *Recreations:* fishing, golf, bridge. *Address:* 35 St Georges Court, Gloucester Road, SW7. *T:* 01-584 9285. *Clubs:* Garrick; Rye Golf.

ROUND, Prof. Nicholas Grenville; Stevenson Professor of Hispanic Studies, in the University of Glasgow, since 1972; *b* 6 June 1938; *s* of Isaac Eric Round and Laura Christabel (*née* Poole); *m* 1966, Ann Le Vin; one *d*. *Educ:* Boyton CP Sch., Cornwall; Launceston Coll.; Pembroke Coll., Oxford. BA (1st cl. Hons, Spanish and French) 1959; MA 1963; DPhil 1967. Lecturer in Spanish, Queen's Univ. of Belfast, 1962-71, Reader, 1971-72; Warden, Alanbrooke Hall, QUB, 1970-72. *Publications:* Unamuno: Abel Sánchez: a critical guide, 1974; contribs to: Mod. Lang. Review, Bulletin Hispanic Studies, Proc. Royal Irish Academy, etc. *Recreations:* reading, music, all aspects of Cornwall. *Address:* Department of Hispanic Studies, The University, Glasgow G12 8QQ. *T:* 041-339 8855. *Club:* (Hon. Life Mem.) Students' Union (Belfast).

ROUS, family name of **Earl of Stradbroke.**

ROUS, Sir Stanley (Ford), Kt 1949; CBE 1943; JP; Secretary of the Football Association, 1934-61 (now Hon. Vice-President); President, Fédération Internationale de Football Associations, 1961-74 (now Hon. President); *b* 25 April 1895; *s* of George Samuel and Alice Rous; *m* 1924, Adrienne Gacon (*d* 1950). *Educ:* Sir John Leman School, Beccles; St Luke's College, Exeter. Served European War, 1914-18, in France and Palestine, 272nd Brigade RFA (East Anglian); Assistant Master, Watford Grammar School, 1921-34; Member Paddington Borough Council, 1943-47; Past Pres. Paddington and Marylebone Rotary Club: Hon. Vice-Pres., Central Council for Physical Recreation, 1973- (Chm., 1945-73). JP Paddington Div., 1950. Mem. King George's Jubilee Trust, King George VI Foundation. Vice-Pres., Arts Educn Trust; Governor, St Luke's Coll., Exeter, Dir, Humphries Holdings Ltd. Liveryman Worshipful Co. of Loriners. Chevalier de l'Ordre Grand-Ducal de la Couronne de Chêne de Luxembourg; Chevalier de la Légion d'Honneur; Commendatore, Ordine Al Merito della Repubblica Italiana; Commander, Order of Ouissam Alaouite (Morocco), 1968; Grosses Verdienstkreuz des Verdienstordens der Bundesrepublik Deutschland, 1974. Hon. Mem., UEFA, 1976. *Publications:* (jtly) The Football Association Coaching Manual, 1942; Recreative Physical Exercises and Activities for Association Football and other Games Players, 1942; A History of the Laws of Association Football, 1974. *Recreation:* tennis. *Address:* 115 Ladbroke Road, W11. *T:* 01-727 4113. *Clubs:* MCC; All England Lawn Tennis and Croquet, Hurlingham.

ROUSE, Sir Anthony (Gerald Roderick), KCMG 1969 (CMG 1961); OBE 1945; HM Diplomatic Service, retired; *b* 9 April 1911; *s* of late Lt-Col Maxwell Rouse and of Mrs Rouse, Eastbourne; *m* 1935, Beatrice Catherine Ellis. *Educ:* Harrow; Heidelberg Univ. Joined HAC 1935; RA (T) 1938; 2 Lt 1940; transf. to Intelligence Corps; served MEF and CMF on staff of 3rd Corps (commendation); Lt-Col 1944. Entered Foreign Service, 1946; First Secretary (Information), Athens, 1946; Foreign Office, 1949. British Embassy, Moscow, 1952-54; Counsellor, 1955; Office of UK High Commissioner, Canberra, 1955-57; HM Inspector of Foreign Service Establishments, 1957-59; Counsellor (Information) British Embassy, Bonn, 1959-62; British Deputy Commandant, Berlin, 1962-64; HM Minister, British Embassy, Rome, 1964-66; Consul-General, New York, 1966-71. *Address:* Furzewood, Speldhurst, Kent.

ROUSE, Arthur Frederick, CMG 1949; *b* 25 Sept. 1910; *s* of late G. A. Rouse, Reading; *m* 1937, Helena, *y d* of late Rev. L. Klamborowski, Clare, Suffolk. *Educ:* Reading School; St John's College, Oxford. White Scholar of St John's, 1928; 1st Cl. Hons Classical Moderations, 1929; 2nd Cl. Literae Humaniores, 1932. Assistant Master Edinburgh Academy, 1932; entered Home Civil Service by competitive exam. starting as Asst Principal in Ministry of Labour, 1933; Private Sec. to Parl. Secretary, 1936-38; accompanied British Delegation to Internat. Labour Conf., 1936-37; Principal, Ministry of Labour, 1938, Asst Secretary, 1944; Dep. Chief, Manpower Division, CCG (British Element), 1945-46; UK Govt Rep. on various Internat. Cttees, 1946-49, including OEEC Manpower Cttee, Chairman of ILO European Manpower Cttee; Special Asst on Manpower to Dir-Gen. of ILO, 1949-50; Head of Latin American Immigration Field Office of ILO, 1950-51; Chairman of Beatrice Intensive Conservative Area Cttee, 1956; Senior Research Fellow, Univ. Coll. of Rhodesia and Nyasaland, 1957-62; Chairman, Wages Advisory Board for Nyasaland, 1960-62. Public administration and industrial consultant. *Recreations:* farming and travel. *Address:* Alicedale Farm, Beatrice, Rhodesia.

ROUSE, E(dward) Clive, MBE 1946; Medieval Archæologist; Specialist in Mural and Panel Paintings; Lecturer; *b* 15 October 1901; *s* of late Edward Foxwell Rouse (Stroud, Gloucestershire and Acton, Middlesex) and late Frances Sarah Rouse (*née* Sams). *Educ:* Gresham's School; St Martin's School of Art. On leaving school studied art and medieval antiquities, 1920-21; FSA London, 1937 (Mem. of Council, 1943-44); FRSA 1968. President: Royal Archæological Institute, 1969-72 (Vice-Pres., 1965); Bucks Archæological Soc., 1969. Liveryman, Fishmongers' Company, 1962. Hon. MA Oxon 1969. Served War of 1939-45, RAFVR (Intelligence); Flight-Lt, 1941-45; MBE for special services at Central Interpretation Unit, Medmenham. *Publications:* The Old Towns of England, 1936 (twice reprinted); Discovering Wall Paintings, 1968 (reprinted); (jointly) Guide to Buckinghamshire, 1935; contributor to: The Beauty of Britain, 1935; Collins' Guide to English Parish Churches, 1958. Papers in Archæologia, Antiquaries' Journal, Archæological Journal, and publications of many County Archæological Societies. *Recreation:* travel. *Address:* Oakfield, North Park, Gerrards Cross, Bucks. *T:* Gerrards Cross 82595.

ROUSSOS, Stavros G.; Ambassador of Greece to the Court of St James's, since 1974; *b* 1918; *m*; two *s* one *d*. *Educ:* Univ. of Lyons (LèsL); Univ. of Paris (LèsL, LèsScPol, LLD). Entered Greek Diplomatic Service as Attaché, Min. of Foreign Affairs, 1946; Mem., Greek Delegn to Gen. Assembly of UN, 1948 and 1954-55; Sec. to Permanent Mission of Greece to UN in New York, 1950; Consul, Alexandria, 1955; i/c Greek Consulate General, Cairo, 1956; Counsellor, 1959; Min. of Foreign Affairs, 1959-61; Mem., Perm. Delegn of Greece to EEC, Brussels, 1962; Perm. Rep. to EEC, 1969; Dir-Gen., Econ. and Commercial Affairs, Min. of Foreign Affairs, 1972. Grand Comdr, Order of Phoenix; Commander: Order of Belgian Crown; Order of Merit of Egypt. *Publication:* The Status of Dodecanese Islands in International Law, 1940 (Paris). *Address:* 1a Holland Park, W11 3TP.

ROUTH, Augustus Crosbie; *b* 7 Aug. 1892; *s* of late Augustus Routh, Manager of Imperial Ottoman Bank, Salonica; *m* 1917, Ethel Madeleine Martin (*d* 1973), The Steyne, Worthing; one *d* (and one *s* killed in action, 1941, one *d* decd). *Educ:* abroad; Edinburgh; LSE, London. Shipping Clerk, Consulate-General, Smyrna, 1910, Chief Clerk, 1920; General Consular Service, 1920; Acting Consul-General, Marseilles, Strasbourg, Milan, Genoa, and Monrovia at various dates: Consul at Istanbul, 1934; Actg Consul-Gen., Tripoli, 1935; Consul at Benghazi, 1936; Actg Consul-General, Marseilles, 1937; re-appointed Consul at Istanbul, 1938; Acting Consul-General, Antwerp, 1940; Chargé d'Affaires and Consul-General, Monrovia, Liberia, 1941; promoted Consul-General at Nice, France, 1944; HM Minister, Haiti, 1946-50; retired, 1950. Coronation Medal, 1937. *Address:* 16 Hailsham Road, Worthing, W Sussex. *T:* Worthing 49250.

ROUTLEDGE, Alan; Head of Communications Planning Staff, Foreign and Commonwealth Office (formerly Foreign Office) (Head, Cypher and Signals Branch, Diplomatic Wireless Service); *b* 12 May 1919; *s* of George and Rose Routledge, Wallasey, Cheshire; *m* 1949, Irene Hendry, Falkirk, Stirlingshire; one *s* (and one *s* decd). *Educ:* Liscard High Sch., Wallasey. Served Army, Cheshire (Earl of Chester's) Yeomanry, 1939-46. Control Commn for Germany, 1946-51; Diplomatic Wireless Service of FO (now Foreign and Commonwealth Office), 1951-. *Recreations:* cricket, golf, English history. *Address:* 10 St Margaret's Close, Orpington, Kent. *T:* Orpington 23900. *Clubs:* Civil Service; Knoll Country (Orpington).

ROUTLEY, Rev. Erik Reginald; Professor of Church Music, Westminster Choir College, Princeton, since 1975; *b* 31 Oct. 1917; *s* of John and Eleanor Routley; *m* 1944, Margaret Scott; two *s* one *d*. *Educ:* Lancing Coll.; Magdalen and Mansfield Colls, Oxford. BA 1940; MA 1943; BD 1946; DPhil 1952. FRSCM 1965. Ordained, 1943; Minister: Trinity Congl Church, Wednesbury, 1943-45; Dartford Congl Church, 1945-48; Mansfield Coll., Oxford: Tutor in Church History, 1948-56; Mackennal Lectr in Church History, 1956-59; Chaplain, 1949-59; Librarian and Dir of Music, 1948-59; Minister, Augustine-Bristo Congl Church, Edinburgh, 1959-67; Minister, St James's URC, Newcastle upon Tyne, 1967-74. Vis. Dir of Music, Princeton Theol Seminary, 1975. Pres., Congregational Church in England and Wales, 1970-71. Editor: Bulletin of Hymn Soc., 1948-; Studies in Church Music, 1964-. *Publications:* The Church and Music, 1950, new edn, 1967; I'll Praise my Maker, 1951; Hymns and Human Life, 1952; (with K. L. Parry) Companion to Congregational Praise, 1953; Hymns and the Faith, 1955; The Wisdom of the Fathers, 1957; The Gift of Conversion, 1957; The Organist's Guide to Congregational Praise, 1957; The Music of Christian Hymnody, 1957; The English Carol, 1958; Church Music and Theology, 1959; What is Conversion?, 1959; English Religious Dissent, 1960; Music, Sacred and Profane, 1960; The Story of Congregationalism, 1961; Creeds and Confessions, 1962; Ascent to the Cross, 1962; Beginning the Old Testament, 1962; Into a Far Country, 1962; Congregationalists and Unity, 1962; Twentieth Century Church Music, 1964; The Man for Others, 1964; Hymns Today and Tomorrow, 1964; Music Leadership in the Church (USA), 1966; Words, Music and the Church, 1967; The Musical Wesleys, 1969; Saul Among the Prophets, 1971; The Puritan Pleasures of the Detective Story, 1972; Exploring the Psalms, 1975; (ed) Westminster Praise, 1976; A Short History of English Church Music, 1977. *Recreation:* music. *Address:* Route 518, RDI, Skillman, NJ 08558, USA. *T:* (609) 921 7806.

ROW, Hon. Sir John Alfred, Kt 1974; Sugar Cane Farmer since 1926; retd as Minister for Primary Industries, Queensland, Australia, 1963-72; *b* Hamleigh, Ingham, Qld, Aust., 1 Jan. 1905; *s* of Charles Edward and Emily Harriet Row; *m* 1st, 1929, Gladys M. (decd), *d* of late H. E. Hollins; one *d*; 2nd, 1966, Irene, *d* of late F. C. Gough. *Educ:* Toowoomba Grammar Sch., Qld; Trebonne State Sch., Qld. Mem. for Hinchinbrook, Qld Legislative Assembly, 1960-72. Mem. Victoria Mill Suppliers Cttee and Herbert River Cane Growers Exec., 1932-60. Rep. Local Cane Prices Bd, 1948-60; Dir, Co-op Cane Growers Store, 1955-60; Councillor, Hinchinbrook Shire, and Rep. on Townsville Regional Electricity Bd, 1952-63; Life Mem.: Aust. Sugar Producers' Assoc.; Herbert River Pastoral and Agricultural Assoc. *Recreations:* bowls (past Pres. and Trustee of Ingham Bowls Club), gardening. *Address:* 10 Gort Street, Ingham, Queensland 4850, Australia. *T:* Ingham 761671.

ROW, Commander Sir Philip (John), KCVO 1969 (CVO 1965; MVO 1958); OBE 1944; RN Retired; an Extra Equerry to the Queen since 1969; Deputy Treasurer to the Queen, 1958-68. *Address:* Clare Lodge, Ewshot, Farnham, Surrey.

ROWALLAN, 2nd Baron, *cr* 1911; **Thomas Godfrey Polson Corbett,** KT 1957; KBE 1951; MC; TD; DL; Lieutenant-Colonel (retired) Royal Scots Fusiliers; *b* 19 Dec. 1895; *o* surv. *s* of 1st Baron and Alice Mary (*d* 1902), *o d* of John Polson, of Castle Levan, Gourock; *S* father, 1933; *m* 1918, Gwyn Mervyn (*d* 1971), *d* of J. B. Grimond, St Andrews; three *s* (and two *s* decd (one killed in action, 1944)) one *d*. *Educ:* Eton. Served European War, 1914-18: Gallipoli, Egypt, Palestine and France (wounded, MC); also France, 1940, comdg a Bn of Royal Scots Fusiliers; retired 1944. Chief Scout British Commonwealth and Empire, 1945-59. Governor, National Bank of Scotland, 1951-59; Governor of Tasmania, 1959 until April 1963. Hon. Col Roy. Tasmania Regt, 1961-63. Mem., The Pilgrims Soc. Hon. LLD, McGill Univ., 1948, Glasgow Univ., 1952, Birmingham Univ., 1957. Freeman of the City of Edinburgh, 1957. KStJ, 1959. *Heir:* *s* Captain Hon. Arthur Cameron Corbett, Royal Artillery; TA [*b* 17 Dec. 1919; *m* 1945, Eleanor Mary (marriage dissolved, 1962), *o d* of late Capt. George Boyle, The Royal Scots Fusiliers; one *s* three *d*. *Educ:* Eton]. *Address:* Rowallan, Kilmarnock, Scotland. *Club:* Brooks's.

ROWAN, Carl T.; Syndicated columnist, correspondent, Chicago Daily News; radio and TV commentator, Post-Newsweek Broadcasting; Roving Editor, Reader's Digest; *b* 11 August 1925; *s* of Thomas D. and Johnnie B. Rowan; *m* 1950, Vivien Murphy; two *s* one *d*. *Educ:* Tennessee State University; Washburn University; Oberlin Coll.; University of Minnesota. Mem. Staff of Minneapolis Tribune, 1948-61; Dept of State, 1961-63; US Ambassador to Finland, 1963-64; Director, United States Information Agency, Washington, DC, 1964-65. Hon. DLitt: Simpson Coll., 1957; Hamline Univ., 1958; Oberlin Coll., 1962; Dr of Humane Letters: Washburn Univ., 1964; Talladega Coll., 1965; St Olaf Coll., 1966; Knoxville Coll., 1966; Rhode Island Coll., 1970; Maine Univ., 1971; Dr of Laws: Howard Univ., 1964; Alfred Univ., 1964; Temple Univ., 1964; Atlanta Univ., 1965; Allegheny Coll., 1966; Colby Univ., 1968; Clark Univ., 1971; Notre Dame, 1973; Dr of Public Admin., Morgan State Coll., 1964; Dr of Letters: Wooster Coll., 1968; Drexel Inst. of Technology. *Publications:* South of Freedom, 1953; The Pitiful and the Proud, 1956; Go South to Sorrow, 1957; Wait Till Next Year, 1960. *Recreations:* tennis, golf and bowling, singing and dancing. *Address:* 3116 Fessenden Street North-West, Washington, DC 20008, USA. *Clubs:* Federal City, Indian Spring, (Washington, DC).

ROWAN-LEGG, Allan Aubrey; Vice President, Western Region: Edcom Ltd, Canada, since 1976; MSX Petrochemical Ltd, since 1977; *b* 19 May 1912; *m* 1944, Daphne M. Ker; three *d*. Dir, Vice-Pres. and Gen. Sales Man., Interlake Fuel Oil Ltd, and Interlake Steel Products, 1955-57; Pres. and Dir, Superior Propane Ltd, Northern Propane Gas Co., 1957-63; Dir, Vice-Pres. and Gen. Man., Garlock of Canada Ltd, and Yale Rubber

Mfg Co. of Canada Ltd, 1963-64; Regional Dir for Ont., Canadian Corp. for 1967 World Exhibn, 1964-67; Agent General for Ontario in UK, 1967-72; Man. Dir, Canada Permanent Mortgage Corp. and Canada Permanent Trust Co., 1973-75. Liveryman, Painter Stainers Co., 1969-. Freeman of City of London, 1969. Canada Centennial Medal. *Recreations:* yachting, golfing, swimming, curling. *Address:* 1790 Glastonbury Road, Victoria, British Columbia V8P 2H3, Canada. *Clubs:* Royal Lymington Yacht (Hants); Union, Canadian Men's, Victoria Golf, Rotary (Victoria, BC).

ROWBOTHAM, Edgar Stanley, MD, MRCP, FFARCS, DA; Retired Cons. (late Senior) Anæsthetist, Royal Free Hospital, London; *b* 8 May 1890; *s* of Dr E. J. Rowbotham and Gertrude Wootton; *m* 1915, May Levesley (*d* 1969); no *c*; *m* 1969, Beatrice Mary Howard. *Educ:* King's College, London; Charing Cross Hospital. Served European War, 1914-18, RAMC (despatches twice); served 1939-44. Bronze Star US Forces, 1945. *Publications:* Anæsthesia in Operations for Goitre, 1945; numerous in medical journals. *Recreations:* golf, sailing. *Address:* Caminho Velho da Ajuda 24, Funchal, Madeira. *T:* 2 67 18.

ROWE, Eric George, CMG 1955; *b* 30 June 1904; *s* of late Ernest Kruse Rowe; *m* 1931, Gladys Ethel, *d* of late Charles Horace Rogers, ARCA. *Educ:* Chatham House School, Ramsgate; St Edmund Hall Oxford. Assistant Master, Queen Mary's Grammar School, Walsall, 1926-27. Entered Colonial Service, Tanganyika; Administrative Officer (Cadet), 1928; Asst District Officer, 1930; District Officer, 1940; Provincial Commissioner, 1948; Senior Provincial Commissioner, 1952; Minister for Local Government and Administration, Tanganyika, 1958; Supervisor, Overseas Services Courses, Oxford, 1959-69. *Publication:* paper in Ibis. *Recreation:* ornithology. *Address:* Manor Farm, East Hanney, Oxon. *T:* West Hanney 229. *Club:* Royal Commonwealth Society.

ROWE, Henry Peter, CB 1971; First Parliamentary Counsel, since 1977; *b* 18 Aug. 1916; 3rd *s* of late Dr Richard Röhr and Olga Röhr, Vienna; *m* 1947, Patricia, *yr d* of R. W. King, London; two *s* one *d*. *Educ:* Vienna; Gonville and Caius Coll., Cambridge. War service, Pioneer Corps, RAC, Military Govt, British Troops, Berlin, 1941-46. Called to Bar, Gray's Inn, 1947. Joined Parliamentary Counsel Office, 1947; Jt Second Parly Counsel, 1973-76. Commonwealth Fund Travelling Fellowship in US, 1955; with Law Commn, 1966-68. *Recreations:* music, reading, walking. *Address:* 19 Paxton Gardens, Woking, Surrey. *T:* Byfleet 43816.

ROWE, Sir Michael (Edward), Kt 1963; CBE 1946; QC 1945; President of the Lands Tribunal, 1966-73; *b* 24 December 1901; *s* of late John Tetley Rowe, Archdeacon of Rochester; *m* 1927, Elizabeth, *d* of Basil Guy, Stonaford House, Launceston; three *d*. *Educ:* Marlborough College; Trinity College, Cambridge (MA, LLB). Barrister, Gray's Inn, 1925; Bencher, 1945; Treasurer, 1961. 2nd Lt Queen's Roy. Regt, 1940; Staff Capt. 1941; released to become Asst Sec. War Damage Commission; Deputy Secretary, 1944-45; returned to practice, Jan. 1946; Member, General Claims Tribunal, 1946; Member of Council of Royal Institution of Chartered Surveyors, 1949-60; Member, Committee Inland Waterways, 1956-58; Deputy-Chairman Local Government Commission for England, 1958-65. Former Editor, Ryde on Rating. *Recreations:* gardening. *Address:* Hunter's End, S Chailey, E Sussex.

ROWE, Norbert Edward, CBE 1944; CEng; FIMechE; Vice-President, Engineering De Havilland Aircraft of Canada, 1963-67, retired, 1967; *b* 18 June 1898; *s* of Harold Arthur and Jane Rowe, Plymouth, Devon; *m* 1929, Cecilia Brown; two *s* two *d*. *Educ:* City and Guilds (Engineering) Coll. Whitworth Exhibition, 1921; BSc Eng. London, 1st Cl. Hons, 1923; Associate of City and Guilds Institute, 1923; DIC 1924; FRAeS 1944; Air Ministry; Royal Aircraft Establishment, 1924, Junior Technical Officer, 1925; Testing Establishment, Technical Officer, 1926; Senior Technical Officer, 1937; Testing Establishment, Chief Technical Officer, 1937; Headquarters, Asst Director, 1938; Ministry of Aircraft Production Headquarters, Deputy Director, Research and Develt of Aircraft, 1940; Director of Technical Development, Ministry of Aircraft Production, 1941-45; Director-General of Technical Development, 1945-46; Controller of Research and Special Developments, British European Airways Corporation (on resignation from Civil Service), 1946-51; Technical Director Blackburn and General Aircraft Ltd, E Yorks, 1952-61; Joint Managing Director of the Blackburn Aircraft Company, 1960-61; Director, Hawker Siddeley Aviation, 1961-63. Member: Air Registration Bd, 1968; ARC, 1969-72. Fellow Inst. Aeronautical Sciences of Amer., 1953; FCGI 1954. Pres. Royal Aeronautical

Society, 1955-56, Hon. Fellow 1962. President: Helicopter Assoc. of GB, 1959-60; Whitworth Soc., 1974-75. Hon. Fellow, Canadian Aerospace Inst., 1965. *Address:* 22 Westfields Road, Mirfield, West Yorks WF14 9PW.

ROWE, Norman Francis; one of the Special Commissioners of Income Tax, 1950-73; Commissioner of Income Tax, St Marylebone Division, 1974; *b* 18 May 1908; *o s* of late Frank Rowe and Eva Eveline (*née* Metcalfe), Watford; *m* 1941, Suzanne Marian (marr. diss., 1964), *o d* of D. S. Richardson; one *s*; *m* 1965, Vittoria, *yr d* of P. Cav. Tondi; one *s*. *Educ:* Sherborne. Chartered Accountant, 1931-37, retired; re-admitted, 1977; ACA. Called to Bar, Lincoln's Inn, 1940; Mem. of Western Circuit. Served War of 1939-45 (despatches); RAF, 1940-45, serving in UK, Middle East, India, Burma and Ceylon; demobilised with rank of Squadron Leader. Freeman, City of London; Liveryman, Worshipful Co. of Glaziers and Painters of Glass. *Publications:* author of Schedule C and Profits Tax sections of Simon's Income Tax, 1st edn. *Recreations:* fishing, yachting. *Address:* 9 Old Square, Lincoln's Inn, WC2A 3SR. *T:* 01-242 5730; Via Leonardo da Vinci 286, 55049 Viareggio, Italy. *T:* 0584 30248. *Clubs:* Naval and Military, City Livery, Bar Yacht, Little Ship.

ROWE, Norman Lester, CBE 1976; FRCS, FDSRCS, FDSRCSE, FDSRCPSGlas, LRCP, LMSSA (London), HDDRCS (Edinburgh); Consultant in Oral Surgery to: Westminster Hospital; Plastic & Oral Surgery Centre, Queen Mary's Hospital, Roehampton; Civilian Consultant to the Royal Navy and the Army; Recognised Teacher in Oral Surgery, University of London; Examiner, Royal College of Surgeons, Royal College of Surgeons of Glasgow and RCSI; *b* 15 Dec. 1915; *s* of late A. W. Rowe, OBE and of L. L. Rowe; *m* 1938, Cynthia Mary Freeman; one *s* one *d*. *Educ:* Malvern College; Guy's Hospital. Gen. Practice, 1937-41; Captain RADC, 1941-46. Formerly Senior Registrar, Plastic and Jaw Injuries Unit, Hill End Hosp., St Albans, 1947, and consultant in Oral Surgery, Plastic and Oral Surgery Centre, Rooksdown House, Park Prewett, Basingstoke, 1948-59; formerly Mem., Army Med. Adv. Bd; Mem. Bd of Faculty of Dental Surgery, RCS, 1956-74; Vice-Dean, 1967; Webb-Johnson Lectr, 1967-69. Foundn Fellow, Brit. Assoc. of Oral Surgeons, Hon. Sec., 1962-68, Pres., 1969-70 (Down's Surgical Prize Medal, 1976); Fellow Internat. Assoc. of Oral Surgeons (Sec. Gen., 1968-71); Associate Mem., Brit. Assoc. of Plastic Surgeons; Member: European Assoc. for Maxillo-Facial Surgery (Pres., 1974-76); Assoc. of Head and Neck Oncol. (GB); Oral Surgery Club (GB); Academia Nacional de Medicina de Buenos Aires, Argentina; Hon. Member: Egyptian Dental Assoc.; Soc. of Amer. Oral Surgeons in Europe; Emeritus Fellow, Colegio Brasileiro de Cirurgia e Traumatologia Buco-Maxilo-Facial (Le Fort Prize Medal, 1970); Hon. Fellow: Sociedad Venezolana de Cirurgia Bucal; Finnish Soc. of Oral Surgeons; Australian and New Zealand Soc. of Oral Surgeons; Assoc. Française des Chirurgiens Maxillo-Faciaux; Soc. Royale Belge de Stomatol. et de Chirurgie Maxillo-Faciale; Deutsche Gesellschaft für Mund-Kiefer und Gesichtschirugie; Soc. of Maxillo-Facial and Oral Surgeons of S Africa. *Publications:* Fractures of the Facial Skeleton (jtly), 1955, 2nd edn, 1968; various articles in British and Foreign Medical and Dental Jls. *Address:* Brackendale, Holly Bank Road, Hook Heath, Woking, Surrey GU22 0JP. *T:* Woking 60008. *Club:* Royal Naval Medical.

ROWE, Owen John Tressider, MA; Headmaster of Epsom College, since 1970; *b* 30 July 1922; *e s* of late Harold Ridges Rowe and of Emma Eliza (*née* Matthews), Lymington, Hampshire; *m* 1946, Marcelle Ljufliny Hyde-Johnson; one *s* one *d*. *Educ:* King Edward VI School, Southampton; Exeter College, Oxford (Scholar, MA); 1st Cl. Hons in Classical Hon. Mods, 1942. Served War of 1939-45, Lieut in Roy. Hampshire Regt, 1942-45. 1st Cl. Hons in Lit Hum, Dec. 1947; Assistant Master: Royal Grammar School, Lancaster, 1948-50; Charterhouse, 1950-60 (Head of Classical Dept); Officer Comdg Charterhouse CCF, 1954-60; Headmaster of Giggleswick School, 1961-70. Governor, Welbeck College. *Recreation:* golf. *Address:* Epsom College, Epsom, Surrey. *T:* Epsom 23621. *Club:* East India, Devonshire, Sports and Public Schools.

ROWE, Prof. Peter Noël, DSc (Eng); CEng, FIChemE; Ramsay Memorial Professor of Chemical Engineering, and Head of Department, University College, London, since 1965; *b* 25 Dec. 1919; *e s* of Charles Henry Rowe and Kate Winifred (*née* Storry); *m* 1952, Pauline Garmirian; two *s*. *Educ:* Preston Grammar Sch.; Manchester Coll. of Technology; Imperial Coll., London. Princ. Scientific Officer, AERE, Harwell, 1958-65. *Publications:* scientific articles in Trans. IChemE, Chem. Eng. Science, etc. *Address:* Pamber Green, Upper Basildon, Reading, Berks. *T:* Upper Basildon 382. *Club:* Athenæum.

ROWE, Peter Whitmill, MA; Headmaster of Cranbrook School, Kent, since 1970; *b* 12 Feb. 1928; British; *s* of Gerald Whitmill Rowe, chartered accountant, one-time General Manager of Morris Commercials Co. Ltd; *m* 1952, Bridget Ann Moyle; two *s* one *d*. *Educ:* Bishop's Stortford College; St John's College, Cambridge. BA 1950; MA (Hons) 1956. VI Form History Master, Brentwood School, Essex, 1951-54; Senior History Master, Repton School, Derbys, 1954-57; Headmaster of Bishop's Stortford Coll., Herts, 1957-70. JP, Bishop's Stortford, 1968-70, Cranbrook, 1971. *Recreations:* literature, music, cricket, golf. *Address:* School House, Cranbrook, Kent TN17 3JD. *T:* Cranbrook 2163.

ROWE, Robert Stewart, CBE 1969; Director, Leeds City Art Gallery and Temple Newsam House, since 1958 (and also of Lotherton Hall since 1968); *b* 31 Dec. 1920; *s* of late James Stewart Rowe and late Mrs A. G. Gillespie; *m* 1953, Barbara Elizabeth Hamilton Baynes; one *s* two *d*. *Educ:* privately; Downing Coll., Cambridge; Richmond Sch. of Art. Asst Keeper of Art, Birmingham Museum and Art Gallery, 1950-56; Dep. Dir, Manchester City Art Galls, 1956-58. Pres., Museums Assoc., 1973-74; Mem., Fine Arts Adv. Cttee, British Council. Liveryman, Worshipful Co. of Goldsmiths. *Publications:* Adam Silver, 1965; articles in Burlington Magazine, Museums Jl, etc. *Recreations:* gardening, walking, reading. *Address:* Grove Lodge, Shadwell, Leeds LS17 8LB. *T:* Leeds 656365.

ROWELL, Sir (Herbert Babington) Robin, Kt 1952; CBE 1948; AFC 1918; late of R. & W. Hawthorn, Leslie & Co. Ltd, Hebburn-on-Tyne, (Director 1929, Chairman, 1943-65); *b* 28 May 1894; *s* of late Sir Herbert Babington Rowell, KBE, The Manor House, Newcastle on Tyne, and late Lady Mary Dobree Rowell, Redesmouth House, Bellingham, Northumberland; *m* 1924, Hilda, *d* of Oswald Dobell, Neston, Cheshire; two *d*. *Educ:* Repton. Served European War, 1914-18, with RE, RFC and RAF, 1914-19; Capt. 1916; retd 1920. Chm. of Council, British Shipbuilding Research Assoc., 1951-52; Vice-President Institution of Naval Architects; President: Shipbuilding Conference, 1948; Shipbuilding Employers' Federation, 1941-42; North East Coast Institution of Engineers and Shipbuilders, 1946-48; Chairman Tyne Shipbuilders Association, 1942-47. DL Co. Durham, 1944. Hon. DSc Dunelm. *Recreations:* shooting, golf. *Address:* Wylam Cottage, Wylam, Northumberland. *T:* Wylam 2207.

ROWETT, Geoffrey Charles; Managing Director, The Charterhouse Group Ltd, since 1974; *b* 1 Aug. 1925; *s* of Frederick Charles and Nell Rowett; *m* 1951, Joyce Eddiford; two *s*. *Educ:* Roundhay Sch., Leeds. Articled to Blackburns, Robson Coates & Co., Leeds and London. FCA, FCMA, JDipMA, FIMC, FBIM. Midland Bank Executor & Trustee Co. Ltd, 1941; Royal Navy, 1943-46; Blackburns, Robson Coates & Co., 1947; Deloitte, Plender Griffiths Annan & Co., 1952; Production-Engineering SA (Pty) Ltd, 1954; P-E Consulting Group Ltd, 1964; Thomson Newspapers Ltd, 1965; Man. Dir, Sunday Times, 1965; Dir and Gen. Manager, Times Newspapers Ltd, 1967-72; Man. Dir, Corporate Finance, BSC, 1973. Member: Bd of Governors, St Mary's Hosp. Gp, 1970-74; Council, ICMA, 1974- (Vice-Pres., 1976). *Address:* 3 Wildwood Road, NW11 6UL. *T:* 01-455 4561. *Club:* Royal Automobile.

ROWLAND, David Powys; Stipendiary Magistrate, Mid Glamorgan (formerly Merthyr Tydfil), since 1961; *b* 7 Aug. 1917; *s* of late Henry Rowland, CBE, Weston-super-Mare; *m* 1st, 1946, Joan (*d* 1958), *d* of late Group Capt. J. McCrae, MBE, Weston-super-Mare; one *s* one *d*; 2nd, 1961, Jenny, *d* of late Percival Lance, Swanage, and widow of Michael A. Forester-Bennett, Alverstoke; one *s* one *d*. (and one step-*d*). *Educ:* Cheltenham Coll.; Oriel Coll., Oxford (BA). Lieut, Royal Welch Fusiliers, 1940-46. Called to Bar, Middle Temple, 1947. Deputy Chairman: Glamorgan QS, 1961-71; Breconshire QS, 1964-71. Mem. Nat. Adv. Council on Training of Magistrates, 1964-73. *Recreations:* fly-fishing, gardening, golf. *Address:* 53 St Tydfil's Court, Merthyr Tydfil, Mid. Glam. *T:* Merthyr Tydfil 3768; 9 Whitecross Square, Cheltenham. *T:* Cheltenham 56514.

ROWLAND, Deborah Molly; Her Honour Judge Rowland; a Circuit Judge (formerly a County Court Judge) since 1971; *d* of Samuel and Hilda Rowland. *Educ:* Slade Sch. of Art; Bartlett Sch. of Architecture; Courtauld Inst of Fine Art. Diploma in Fine Art and Architecture. Called to the Bar, Lincoln's Inn, June 1950. *Publication:* Guide to Security of Tenure for Business and Professional Tenants, 1956. *Recreations:* music (Founder and Chm. Bar Musical Soc.), painting, sculpture. *Address:* Lincoln's Inn, WC2.

ROWLAND, Herbert Grimley; Chairman, South Middlesex Rent Tribunal, since 1972; *b* 10 Feb. 1905; *s* of Frank Rowland,

MRCS, LRCP, and Josephine Mary (*née* Quirke); *m* 1938, Margaret Jane Elizabeth, *yr d* of Robert Crawford Higginson and Mary Higginson; one *d. Educ:* Nautical Coll., Pangbourne; Peterhouse, Cambridge. Called to Bar, 1928; admitted Solicitor, 1933; private practice, Solicitor, 1933-40; joined Office of Solicitor of Inland Revenue, 1940; Princ. Asst Solicitor of Inland Revenue, 1961-65; Acting Solicitor of Inland Revenue, 1961; Special Commissioner of Income Tax, 1965-70. *Recreation:* golf. *Address:* 10 Hillcrest, Durlston Road, Swanage, Dorset. *T:* Swanage 3256. *Clubs:* National Liberal; Bramley Golf (Surrey); Isle of Purbeck (Swanage).

ROWLAND, Air Marshal Sir James (Anthony), KBE 1977; DFC 1944; AFC 1953; CEng, FRAeS; Chief of Air Staff, Royal Australian Air Force, since 1975; *b* 1 Nov. 1922; *s* of Louis Claude Rowland and Elsie Jean Rowland; *m* 1955, Faye Alison (*née* Doughton); one *d. Educ:* Cranbrook Sch., Sydney; St Paul's Coll., Univ. of Sydney (BE Aero). CEng, FRAeS 1969. Served War, Pilot, RAAF and RAF Bomber Comd, 1942-45. Sydney Univ., 1940-41 and 1946-47; Empire Test Pilots' Sch., Farnborough, 1949; Chief Test Pilot, RAAF R&D Unit, 1951-54; Staff Coll. and unit posts, incl. OC R&D, 1957-60; RAAF Mirage Mission, Paris, 1961-64; CO No 1 Aircraft Depot, 1966; Sen. Engr SO, Ops Comd, 1968-69; RCDS, 1971; Dir Gen., Aircraft Engrg, RAAF, 1972; Air Mem. for Technical Services, 1973. *Publications:* contribs to professional jls. *Recreations:* surfing, reading, golf. *Address:* 4 Galway Place, Deakin, ACT 2600, Australia. *T:* Canberra 65.5474. *Clubs:* United Services (Brisbane); Commonwealth (Canberra).

ROWLAND, Robert Todd, QC 1969; **His Honour Judge Rowland;** County Court Judge of Northern Ireland, since 1974; *b* 12 Jan. 1922; *yr s* of late Lt-Col Charles Rowland and Jean Rowland; *m* 1952, Kathleen, *er d* of late H. J. Busby, Lambourn, Berks; two *s. Educ:* Crossley and Porter Sch., Halifax, Yorks; Ballyclare High Sch.; Queen's Univ. of Belfast (LLB 1948). Called to Bar of N Ireland, 1949; Mem., Bar Council, 1967-72. Served 2nd Punjab Regt, IA, in India, Assam, Burma, Thailand, Malaya, 1942-46. Counsel to Attorney-Gen. for N Ireland, 1966-69; Sen. Crown Prosecutor for Co. Tyrone, 1969-72; Vice-Pres., VAT Tribunal for N Ireland, 1972-74. Served on County Court Rules Cttee, 1965-72 and 1975-; Chm., War Pensions Appeal Tribunal, 1962-72; Member: Bd of Governors, Strathearn Sch., 1969-; Legal Adv. Cttee, Gen. Synod of Church of Ireland, 1975-. *Recreations:* angling, golf. *Address:* 36 Knocklofty Park, Belfast, N Ireland BT4 3NB. *Club:* Ulster (Belfast).

ROWLANDS, Edward; MP (Lab) Merthyr Tydfil, since April 1972; Minister of State, Foreign and Commonwealth Office, since 1976; *b* 23 Jan. 1940; *e s* of W. S. Rowlands; *m* 1968, Janice Williams, Kidwelly, Carmarthenshire; two *s* one *d. Educ:* Rhondda Grammar Sch.; Wirral Grammar Sch.; King's Coll., London. BA Hons History (London) 1962. Research Asst, History of Parliament Trust, 1963-65; Lectr in Modern History and 'Govt, Welsh Coll. of Adv. Technology, 1965-. MP (Lab) Cardiff North, 1966-70; Parliamentary Under-Secretary of State: Welsh Office, 1969-70, 1974-75; FCO, 1975-76. *Recreations:* gardening, golf. *Address:* House of Commons, SW1; 5 Park Crescent, Thomastown, Merthyr Tydfil, Mid Glamorgan. *T:* Merthyr 4912.

ROWLANDS, Air Marshal Sir John (Samuel), GC 1943; KBE 1971 (OBE 1954); Assistant Principal, Sheffield Polytechnic, since 1974; *b* 23 Sept. 1915; *s* of late Samuel and Sarah Rowlands; *m* 1942, Constance Wight; two *d. Educ:* Hawarden School; University of Wales (BSc Hons). Joined RAFVR, 1939; permanent commission in RAF, 1945. British Defence Staff, Washington, 1961-63; Imperial Defence College, 1964; Royal Air Force College, Cranwell, 1965-68; First Director General of Training, RAF, 1968-70; AOC-in-C, RAF Maintenance comd, 1970-73. *Recreations:* photography, tennis, motoring. *Address:* 45 Lyndhurst Road, Sheffield S11 9BJ. *Club:* Royal Air Force.

ROWLANDS, Maldwyn Jones, FLA, FRGS; Head of Library Services (designation Librarian, until 1974), British Museum (Natural History), since 1965; *b* 7 March 1918; *s* of Thomas and Elizabeth Rowlands; *m* 1941, Sybil Elizabeth Price; two *s* one *d. Educ:* Newtown Grammar Sch., Montgomeryshire; University Coll. London. Served in Army, 1940-46: commnd 1941 (Lieut), HQ 21 Army Gp (Staff Captain), 1944-46 (C-in-C's Cert. 1945). Asst Librarian, Science Museum Library, 1946-54; Deputy Librarian: British Museum (Natural History), 1954-63; Patent Office, 1963-65. *Recreations:* old books and bindings, Welsh history and folk-lore. *Address:* 69 Downs Hill, Beckenham, Kent BR3 2HD. *T:* 01-650 9897.

ROWLANDSON, Sir (Stanley) Graham, Kt 1956; MBE 1943; JP 1944; FCA; Chairman, Rowlandson Organisation; Senior Partner, S. Graham Rowlandson & Co., Chartered Accountants; Chairman, The Finance & Industrial Trust Ltd; *b* 25 Aug. 1908; *s* of late H. Stanley Rowlandson, Claremont, Enfield, Middx; *m* 1938, Vera Elworthy, *d* of late Ernest Alfred Lane, Woodside Pk, N; two *s* one *d. Educ:* Mill Hill Sch.; Blois, France. Member, Enfield UDC, 1934-46 (Chm., 1940-42; Chm. Finance Cttee, 1937-45; Leader, Cons. Group and Council, 1937-40, 1942-45); Middlesex CC, 1942-46, 1947-51, 1959-65, CA, 1951-58, High Sheriff 1958 (Vice-Chm. Establishment Cttee 1949-51, Chm. 1951-55; Chm. Finance Cttee 1949-51, Vice-Chm. 1951-55; Dep. Leader, 1951, 1964-65; Leader, 1951-54; Vice-Chm. CC 1954-55, Chm. 1955-56; Chm. Health Cttee, 1956-58, 1961-65; Mem., Standing Jt Cttee, 1951-58, 1961-65); Mem. for Enfield, GLC, 1964-73; Chairman: Finance Cttee, GLC, 1969-73; Establishment Cttee, 1967-69 (Vice-Chm., 1977-); Member: Gen. Purposes Cttee, Supplies Cttee (Leader of Opposition), of GLC, 1964-67; Rep. on Local Govt Training Bd of GLC, 1967-70, Chm. Finance Cttee, 1967-70; Member: Local Govt Computer Centre, 1967-70; Exec. Coun. CCs Assoc., 1955-58; Local Authorities Management Services and Computer Cttee, 1969-70; Jt Hon. Treas., Middx Assoc., 1965-69, Vice-Pres., 1969-76, Pres., 1976; Vice-Chm., Home Counties N Local Govt Adv. Cttee, 1959-64; Greater London Area Local Govt Adv. Cttee, 1964-72, Dep. Chm., 1964-72; Mem., Nat. Local Govt Adv. Cttee, 1960-72; Common Councilman, City of London, for Coleman St Ward, 1961; Chm., Port and City of London Health and Welfare Cttees, 1964-67; Mem., Lord Mayor and Sheriffs Cttee, 1971. Contested (C) N Tottenham, 1937 and 1938; Chairman: Enfield W Cons. Assoc., 1949-52; Enfield Bor. Cons. Assoc., 1952-64 (Pres. 1964-72); Hon. Life Pres., N Enfield Cons. Assoc., 1972-; Nat. Union of Cons. and Unionist Assocs: Vice-Chm. Home Counties N Prov. Area, 1953-54, 1961-64; Mem. Nat. Exec. Cttee, 1964-; Mem., GP Cttee, 1972-75; Mem., Cons. Commonwealth and Overseas Council, 1972-; Mem. Finance and GP Cttee, Greater London Area, 1964- (Dep. Chm., 1964-69, and 1970-71, Chm., 1972-75); Hon. Treasurer, Primrose League, 1975-; Chm. Middx Parly and Local Govt Gps, 1953-54; Mem. Middx Exec. Council, 1951-53, 1962-63. Chm., Enfield Savings, 1940-45; Mem., Nat. Savings London Reg. Adv. Cttee, 1942-46; Mem., Admin. Council, Lord Mayor's Nat. Air Raid Distress Fund, 1940-54. Governor: Royal Nat. Orthopædic Hosp., 1948-52; Med. Coll., St Bartholomew's Hosp., 1966-; Chm., Chairmen of Reg. Hosp. Bds, 1971-74; Member: Gen. Council, King Edward's Hosp. Fund for London, 1956-; NE Met. Reg. Hosp. Bd, 1952-74 (Chm., 1956-74); Ct of Govs, London Sch. of Hygiene and Tropical Med., 1957-58; Bd of Governors: St Bartholomew's Hosp., 1957-74, London Hosp., 1960-74, Hammersmith and St Mark's Hosps, 1960-74, Moorfields Eye Hosp., 1961-; Eastman Dental Hosp., 1974-; Vice-Chm., Enfield Gp Hosp. Man. Cttees, 1948-53; Chairman: Appeals Cttee, St Antony's Hosp., Cheam, 1974; Funding Cttee, Inst. for the Study of Drug Dependence, 1976-; Member: Whitley Council for Health Services, 1957-64; Nat. Cons Council on Recruitment of Nurses and Midwives, 1963-74; Inner London Exec. Council, 1971-74; Family Practitioner Cttee, City and E London Area Health Authority, 1974-; Council of Fed. Superannuation Scheme for Nurses and Hospital Officers, 1965-74; Nat. Old People's Welfare Council, 1959-74; Adv. Council on Overseas Services Resettlement Bureau, 1968-; Finance Cttee Internat. Soc. for Rehabilitation of Disabled, 1958-67 (Chm., 1964-67; Vice-Chm, 1963-73, Chm., 1973-75, Brit. Cttee); Nat. Baby Welfare Council, 1961-63; Vice-Chm., Council for Professions supp. to Medicine, 1961- (Chm. Finance Cttee); Hon. Treasurer: UK Cttee, WHO, 1963-73; Infantile Paralysis Fellowship, 1949-52 (Chm. 1952-57); Hand Crafts Adv. Assoc. for the Disabled, 1975-; Vice-Pres., Edmonton and Enfield Br, British Diabetic Assoc., 1960; Trustee: City Parochial Foundn, 1968-74, 1977-; Westminster Philanthropic Soc., 1960-75. Mem., Management Cttee, Bridgehead Housing Assoc. Ltd, 1974-75; Chm., Stonham Housing Assoc. Ltd, 1975-; Member: Roma Housing Assoc. Ltd, 1975-; Court, Univ. of Essex, 1965-74; SE Circuit Cttee, 1972-; Governor: Mill Hill Sch., 1952-58, 1961-; London Festival Ballet Trust, 1971-73; Vice-Pres., Internat. Cultural Exchange, 1964-; Mem. Council RSA, 1966-76 (Hon. Treasurer, 1971-76); Pres., Boy Scouts Assoc., Enfield Br., 1958-77; Vice-President: London Scout Council, 1956-65; Co. of Greater London N Scout Council, 1965-71 (Pres., 1971-); Pres., Middx Table Tennis Assoc., 1957-; Mem. Council, Royal Warrant Holders' Assoc., 1958-59. Worshipful Co. of Masons: Mem. Ct of Assts; Renter Warden, 1962; Upper Warden, 1963; Master, 1964; Liveryman, Paviors' Co. (Mem., Ct of Assts, 1973-; Renter Warden, 1977). Coleman St Ward Club: Vice-Chm., 1965; Chm., 1966. *Recreations:* entertaining, racing (race-horse owner). *Address:* Salisbury House, EC2. *T:* 01-628 8566; 18 Grosvenor Square, W1. *T:* 01-449 2010; Harmer Green End,

Digswell, Herts. *T:* Welwyn 5141. *Clubs:* United and Cecil; Old Millhillians (Pres. 1965-66).

ROWLEY, Sir Charles (Robert), 7th Bt *cr* 1836; *b* 15 March 1926; *s* of Sir William Joshua Rowley, 6th Bt and Beatrice Gwendoline, *d* of Rev. Augustus George Kirby; *S* father, 1971; *m* 1952, Astrid, *d* of Sir Arthur Massey, *qv*; one *s* one *d. Educ:* Wellington. *Heir: s* Richard Charles Rowley, *b* 14 Aug. 1959. *Address:* 21 Tedworth Square, SW3; Naseby Hall, Northamptonshire.

ROWLEY, Frederick Allan, OBE 1959; MC 1945; Major (retd); HM Diplomatic Service; Counsellor, Foreign and Commonwealth Office, since Dec. 1973; *b* 27 July 1922; *m* 1951, Anne Crawley; one *s* three *d. Educ:* Haig Sch., Aldershot. Served War of 1939-45: Ranks, 8th Worcs Regt (TA), 1939-40; Emergency Commnd Officer, 5th Bn, 10th Baluch Regt (KGVO), Jacob's Rifles, Indian Army, Burma Campaign (MC), June 1941-Nov. 1948. At partition of India, granted regular commn (back-dated, 1942) in Worcestershire Regt, but retd (wounded), sub. Major. Joined HM Diplomatic Service, Nov. 1948: served (with brief periods in FO) in: Egypt; Ethiopia; Turkey; Burma; Singapore; Australia; Malaysia; FCO 1971-72; Under-Sec., N Ireland Office (on secondment), 1972-73. Joint Services Staff College (jssc), 1959. *Recreations:* cricket, golf. *Address:* 26 Clarendon Street, Pimlico, SW1. *T:* 01-828 8459. *Clubs:* Boodle's, MCC, Surrey County Cricket.

ROWLEY, John Charles, CMG 1977; Head of Middle East Development Division, Amman, Jordan, since 1971; *b* 29 Sept. 1919; *s* of John Ernest Rowley and Edith Muriel (*née* Aldridge); *m* 1st, 1945, Pamela Hilda Godfrey (marr. diss. 1971); two *d*; 2nd, 1972, Anne Patricia Dening; one *s. Educ:* Ilford; King's College, London (LLB 1948, Upper Second Cl. Hons). Inland Revenue, 1938-40. RAF, 1940-46, pilot, Flight-Lieut; Iceland, 1944 (despatches). Inland Revenue, 1946-64; Min. of Overseas Development, 1964-. *Recreations:* choral singing, sailing. *Address:* Cranford, 8A Pankridge Street, Crondall, Farnham, Surrey. *T:* Aldershot 850743.

ROWLEY, John Hewitt, CBE 1968; Controller, BBC, Wales, 1967-74; *b* 1917. *Educ:* University Coll. of N Wales, Bangor (BA); Jesus Coll., Oxford. ICS, 1939-47. Joined BBC, 1949; Asst Head, Central Estabt, 1949-53; Staff Admin. Officer (II), 1953-55; Staff Admin. Officer, 1955-56; Asst Controller, Staff Admin, 1956-60, Controller, 1960-67. CIPM. *Address:* 21 Lakeside, The Knap, Barry CF6 8ST.

ROWLEY, John Vincent d'Alessio; General Manager, Bracknell New Town Development Corporation, 1955-73; *b* 12 Sept. 1907; 2nd *s* of late Ven. Hugh Rowley, Archdeacon of Kingwilliamstown, S Africa; *m* 1st, 1936, Violet Maud (*d* 1969), *d* of S. H. Day, Grahamstown, S Africa; one *s*; 2nd, 1972, Mary Hawkesworth. *Educ:* St Andrews Coll., Grahamstown; Trinity Coll., Oxford (Rhodes Schol.). BA 1929; Oxford Univ. Rugby XV, 1929. Entered Sudan Political Service, 1930; Asst District Comr and District Comr, 1930-49; seconded Sudan Defence Force, 1940-42; Dep. Gov., Kordofan Province, 1950-52; Asst Financial Sec., 1952-53; Governor, Darfur Province, 1953-55. *Recreations:* music, gardening, golf. *Address:* The Spring, Stanford Dingley, near Bradfield, Berks. *T:* Bradfield 270. *Club:* United Oxford & Cambridge University.

ROWLEY, Sir Joshua Francis, 7th Bt, *cr* 1786; Vice-Lord-Lieutenant of Suffolk, since 1973; *b* 31 Dec. 1920; *o s* of 6th Bt and Margery Frances Bacon (*d* 1977); *S* father, 1962; *m* 1959, Hon. Celia Ella Vere Monckton, 2nd *d* of 8th Viscount Galway; one *d. Educ:* Eton; Trinity College, Cambridge. Grenadier Guards, 1940-46. Deputy Secretary, National Trust, 1952-55. Chairman: W Suffolk CC, 1971-74; Suffolk CC, 1976-; DL 1968, High Sheriff 1971, Suffolk. *Address:* The Cottage, Stoke-by-Nayland, Suffolk. *T:* Nayland 262400. *Clubs:* Boodle's, Pratt's, MCC.

ROWLEY-CONWY, family name of **Baron Langford.**

ROWLING, Rt. Hon. Wallace Edward, PC 1974; MP (Lab) for Buller, New Zealand, later for Tasman, since 1967; Prime Minister of New Zealand, 1974-75; *b* Motueka, 15 Nov. 1927; *s* of A. Rowling; *m* 1951, Glen Elna, *d* of Captain J. M. Reeves; two *s* two *d. Educ:* Nelson Coll. MA. Fulbright Schol., 1955-56. Formerly Asst Dir of Educn, NZ Army. Minister of Finance, 1972-74; Governor for New Zealand, IMF. Rep. NZ at annual meeting of ADB, Kuala Lumpur, 1974. *Recreation:* golf. *Address:* Parliament Buildings, Wellington, New Zealand; 15 Waverley Street, Richmond, New Zealand.

ROWLINSON, Prof. John Shipley, FRS 1970; BSc, MA, DPhil Oxon; FRIC; FIChemE; Dr Lee's Professor of Physical Chemistry, Oxford University, since 1974; Fellow of Exeter College, since 1974; *b* 12 May 1926; *er s* of Frank Rowlinson and Winifred Jones; *m* 1952, Nancy Gaskell; one *s* one *d. Educ:* Rossall School (Scholar); Trinity College, Oxford (Millard Scholar). Research Associate, Univ. of Wisconsin, USA, 1950-51; ICI Research Fellow, Lecturer, and Senior Lecturer in Chemistry, University of Manchester, 1951-60; Prof. of Chemical Technology, London Univ. (Imperial Coll.), 1961-73. Liversidge Lectr, Chem. Soc., 1978. Hon. Treas., Faraday Society, 1968-71; Vice-Pres., Royal Instn of GB, 1974-76; Member, Sale Borough Council, 1956-59. Meldola Medal, Roy. Inst. of Chemistry, 1954; Marlow Medal, Faraday Soc., 1957. *Publications:* Liquids and Liquid Mixtures, 1959, 1969; The Perfect Gas, 1963; Physics of Simple Liquids (joint editor), 1968; (trans. jtly) The Metric System, 1969; (jtly) Thermodynamics for Chemical Engineers, 1975; papers in scientific journals. *Recreation:* climbing. *Address:* 12 Pullens Field, Headington, Oxford OX3 0BU. *T:* Oxford 67507; Physical Chemistry Laboratory, South Parks Road, Oxford OX1 3QZ. *T:* Oxford 53324.

ROWNTREE, Sir Norman Andrew Forster, Kt 1970; CEng; FICE; Professor of Civil Engineering, University of Manchester Institute of Science and Technology, since 1975; *b* 11 March 1912; *s* of Arthur Thomas Rowntree, London, and Ethel, *d* of Andrew Forster; *m* 1939, Betty, *d* of William Arthur Thomas; two *s* one *d. Educ:* Tottenham County Sch.; London Univ. (BSc(Eng)). Consulting Engineer, 1953-64; Mem. and Dir, Water Resources Bd, 1964-73; Mem., Adv. Council for Applied R&D, 1976-. Pres., Inst. of Water Engineers, 1962-63. Vice-Pres., ICE, 1972-75, Pres. 1975-76. Vis. Prof., KCL, 1972-75; CEI Graham Clark Lectr, 1972. Hon. DSc City Univ, 1974. *Address:* Coralie, Quarry Lane, Kelsall, Tarporley, Cheshire CW6 0NJ. *T:* Kelsall 51195; University of Manchester Institute of Science and Technology, PO Box 88, Manchester M60 1QD. *Clubs:* Athenæum, St Stephen's.

ROWSE, Alfred Leslie, MA, DLitt; FBA; Fellow of All Souls College, Oxford, 1925-74; *b* St Austell, Cornwall, 4 Dec. 1903. *Educ:* Elementary and Grammar Schools, St Austell; Christ Church Oxford (Douglas Jerrold Scholar in English Literature). Fellow of the Royal Society of Literature; President of the English Association, 1952; Raleigh Lecturer, British Academy, 1957; Trevelyan Lecturer, Cambridge, 1958; Beatty Memorial Lecturer, McGill University, 1963. Pres., Shakespeare Club, Stratford-upon-Avon, 1970-71. *Publications:* Politics and the Younger Generation, 1931; Mr Keynes and the Labour Movement, 1936; Sir Richard Grenville of the Revenge, 1937; Tudor Cornwall, 1941; Poems of a Decade, 1931-41; A Cornish Childhood, 1942; The Spirit of English History, 1943; Poems Chiefly Cornish, 1944; The English Spirit: Essays in History and Literature, 1944, rev. edn 1966; West Country Stories, 1945; The Use of History, 1946; Poems of Deliverance, 1946; The End of an Epoch, 1947; The England of Elizabeth, 1950; The English Past, 1951 (rev. edn, as Times, Persons, Places, 1965); Translation and completion of Lucien Romier's History of France, 1953; The Expansion of Elizabethan England, 1955; The Early Churchills, 1956; The Later Churchills, 1958; Poems Partly American, 1958; The Elizabethans and America, 1959; St Austell: Church, Town, Parish, 1960; All Souls and Appeasement, 1961; Ralegh and the Throckmortons, 1962; William Shakespeare: A Biography, 1963; Christopher Marlowe: A Biography, 1964; A Cornishman at Oxford, 1965; Shakespeare's Southampton: Patron of Virginia, 1965; Bosworth Field and the Wars of the Roses, 1966; Poems of Cornwall and America, 1967; Cornish Stories, 1967; A Cornish Anthology, 1968; The Cornish in America, 1969; The Elizabethan Renaissance: the Life of the Society, 1971; The Elizabethan Renaissance: The Cultural Achievement, 1972; Strange Encounter (poems), 1972; The Tower of London in the History of the Nation, 1972; Westminster Abbey in the History of the Nation, 1972; Shakespeare's Sonnets: a modern edition, 1973; Shakespeare the Man, 1973; Simon Forman: Sex and Society in Shakespeare's Age, 1974; Peter the White Cat of Trenarren, 1974; Windsor Castle in the History of the Nation, 1974; (with John Betjeman) Victorian and Edwardian Cornwall, 1974; Oxford in the History of the Nation, 1975; Discoveries and Reviews, 1975; Jonathan Swift: major prophet, 1975; A Cornishman Abroad, 1976; Brown Buck: a Californian fantasy, 1976; Matthew Arnold: poet and prophet, 1976; Homosexuals in History: ambivalence in society, literature and the arts, 1977; The Heritage of Britain, 1977; Milton the Puritan: portrait of a mind, 1977; The Road to Oxford: poems, vol. 7, 1978. *Address:* Trenarren House, St Austell, Cornwall. *Club:* Athenæum.

ROWSON, Lionel Edward Aston, OBE 1955; FRS 1973; FRCVS; Director, Cambridge and District Cattle Breeders (AI Centre), since 1942; Officer in Charge, Agricultural Research Council Animal Research Station, Cambridge, since 1976; Fellow of Wolfson College, Cambridge, since 1973; *b* 28 May 1914; *s* of L. F. Rowson, LDS, and M. A. Rowson (*née* Aston); *m* 1942, Audrey Kathleen Foster; two *s* two *d*. *Educ:* King Edward VIth Sch., Stafford; Royal Veterinary Coll., London. MRCVS, FRCVS 1972; FRVC 1975. Engaged in general practice, 1939-42. Dep. Dir, ARC Unit of Reproductive Physiology and Biochemistry, 1955-76. Thomas Baxter Prize, 1956; Wooldridge Meml Lecture and Medal, 1974; Dalrymple-Champneys Cup and Medal, 1975. *Publications:* (jointly) Reproduction in Domestic Animals (ed H. H. Cole and P. T. Cupps); Mem. Editorial Bd: Jl of Reproduction and Fertility; Jl of Agricultural Science. *Recreations:* shooting, cricket, thoroughbred breeding. *Address:* The Grove, Water Lane, Histon, Cambridge. *T:* Histon 2534.

ROXBEE COX, family name of Baron Kings Norton.

ROXBURGH, Air Vice-Marshal Henry Lindsay, CBE 1966; FRCP, FRCPE; Commandant, RAF Institute of Aviation Medicine, 1969-73; retired; *b* 5 Dec. 1909; *s* of John Roxburgh, Galston, Ayrshire and Cape Town, and Edith Mary Roxburgh (*née* Smithers), Kenilworth, Cape; *m* 1944, Hermione Babington (*née* Collard); one *s* two *d*. *Educ:* George Watson's College, Edinburgh; Edinburgh University. BSc 1932; PhD 1934; MB, ChB 1940; FRCPE 1966; FRCP 1972. Medical Branch, Royal Air Force, 1941-73. Service mainly at RAF Inst. of Aviation Med.: research undertaken in various aspects of aviation physiology and related subjects; apptd Prof. in Aviation Medicine, 1966. Chairman, Aero-Space Medical Panel of Advisory Gp of Aero-Space Research and Development, Paris, 1965-67. Mem., Internat. Acad. of Aviation and Space Medicine. QHS 1971-73. FRAeS 1965. *Publications:* papers in field of aviation medicine. *Recreation:* gardening. *Address:* 11 Auderville, Alderney, CI. *Club:* Royal Air Force.

ROXBURGH, Ven. James William; Archdeacon of Colchester, since 1977; *b* 5 July 1921; *s* of James Thomas and Margaret Roxburgh; *m* 1949, Marjorie Winifred (*née* Hipkiss); one *s* one *d*. *Educ:* Whitgift School; St Catharine's Coll., Cambridge (MA); Wycliffe Hall, Oxford. Deacon 1944, priest 1945; Curate: Christ Church and Holy Trinity, Folkestone, 1944-47; Handsworth, Birmingham, 1947-50; Vicar: S Matthew, Bootle, 1950-56; Drypool, Hull, 1956-65; Barking, 1965-77. Canon of Chelmsford, 1972-. Pro-Prolocutor, Convocation of Canterbury, 1977-. Pres. Barking Rotary Club, 1976-77. *Recreations:* travel, philately. *Address:* Uplands, Powers Hall End, Witham, Essex CM8 2HE. *T:* Witham 513447.

ROXBURGH, Vice-Adm. Sir John (Charles Young), KCB 1972 (CB 1969); CBE 1967; DSO 1943; DSC 1942 (Bar, 1945); *b* 29 June 1919; *s* of Sir (Thomas) James (Young) Roxburgh, CIE; *m* 1942, Philippa, 3rd *d* of late Major C. M. Hewlett, MC; one *s* one *d*. *Educ:* RNC, Dartmouth. Naval Cadet, 1933; Midshipman, 1937; Sub-Lt 1939; Lt 1941; Lt-Comdr 1949; Comdr 1952; Capt. 1958; Rear-Adm. 1967; Vice-Adm. 1970. Served in various ships, 1937-39; joined Submarine Br., 1940; served in ops off Norway, in Bay of Biscay and Mediterranean, 1940-42; comd HM Submarines H43, United and Tapir, 1942-45 in ops in Mediterranean and off Norway; HMS Vanguard, 1948-50; comd HM Submarine Turpin, 1951-53; HMS Triumph, 1955; HMS Ark Royal, 1955-56; comd HMS Contest, 1956-58; Brit. Jt Services Mission, Wash., 1958-60; comd 3rd Submarine Sqdn and HMS Adamant, 1960-61; idc 1962; Dep. Dir of Defence Plans (Navy), MoD, 1963-65; comd HMS Eagle, 1965-67; Flag Officer: Sea Training, 1967-69; Plymouth, 1969; Submarines, and NATO Comdr Submarines, E Atlantic, 1969-72, retired 1972. Chm., Grovebell Group Ltd, 1972-75. Co. Councillor, Surrey, 1977-. *Recreations:* golf, sailing, walking, music. *Address:* Oakdene, Wood Road, Hindhead, Surrey. *T:* Hindhead 5600. *Club:* Army and Navy.

ROXBURGH, Sir Ronald Francis, Kt 1946; Judge of High Court of Justice, Chancery Division, 1946-60, retired; *b* 19 Nov. 1889; *o s* of Francis Roxburgh and Annie Gertrude Mortlock; *m* 1st, 1935, Jane Minney (*d* 1960), *yr d* of Archibald H. and Lady Frances Gordon-Duff; one *d*; 2nd, 1966, Mrs Dorothea Mary Hodge. *Educ:* Harrow; Trinity College, Cambridge. Classical Tripos Part I, Class I, Division II, 1911. Whewell International Law Scholar, 1912; called to Bar, Middle Temple, 1914; KC 1933; Bencher of Lincoln's Inn, 1937, Treasurer, 1957. *Publications:* Prisoners of War Information Bureau in London, 1915; International Conventions and Third States, 1917; The Origins of Lincoln's Inn, 1963; (ed) The Black Books of Lincoln's Inn, vol. v, 1968; edited Oppenheim's International

Law (3rd edn), 1920-21. *Recreations:* walking, travel. *Address:* 8 Old Square, Lincoln's Inn, WC2. *T:* 01-242 4748; Holman's House, Stone-in-Oxney, Tenterden, Kent. *T:* Wittersham 321.

ROXBURGHE, 10th Duke of, *cr* 1707; Guy David Innes-Ker; Baron Roxburghe 1600; Earl of Roxburghe, Baron Ker of Cessford and Cavertoun, 1616; Bt (NS) 1625; Viscount Broxmouth, Earl of Kelso, Marquess of Bowmont and Cessford, 1707; Earl Innes (UK), 1837; *b* 18 Nov. 1954; *s* of 9th Duke of Roxburghe, and of Margaret Elisabeth (who *m* 1976, Jocelyn Olaf Hambro, *qv*), *d* of late Frederick Bradshaw McConnel; *S* father, 1974; *m* 1977, Lady Jane Meriel Grosvenor, *yr d* of Duke of Westminster, *qv*. *Educ:* Eton; RMA Sandhurst (Sword of Honour, June 1974). Commnd into Royal Horse Guards/1st Dragoons, 1974; RARO 1977. *Heir: b* Lord Robert Anthony Innes-Ker, *b* 28 May 1959. *Address:* Floors Castle, Kelso.

ROXBY, John Henry M.; *see* Maude-Roxby.

ROY, Andrew Donald; Chief Economic Adviser (Under Secretary), Department of Health and Social Security, since 1976; *b* 28 June 1920; *er s* of late Donald Whatley Roy, FRCS, FRCOG, and late Beatrice Anne Roy (*née* Barstow); *m* 1947, Katherine Juliet Grove-White; one *s* two *d*. *Educ:* Malvern Coll. (Scholar); Sidney Sussex Coll., Cambridge (Scholar). Maths Trip. Pt I 1939 and Econ. Trip. Pt II 1948, Class I hons. 1939-45: served Royal Artillery, in UK, India and Burma (8 Medium Regt). Cambridge Univ.: Asst Lecturer, 1949-51; Lecturer, 1951-64; Jun. Proctor, 1956-57; Sidney Sussex Coll.: Fellow, 1951-64; Tutor, 1953-56; Sen. Tutor, 1956-62. HM Treasury: Economic Consultant, 1962; Sen. Economic Adviser, 1964; Under-Sec (Economics), 1969-72. Under-Sec., DTI, 1972-74, MoD, 1974-76. *Publications:* British Economic Statistics (with C. F. Carter), 1954; articles in economic and statistical jls. *Address:* 15 Rusholme Road, Putney, SW15 3JX. *T:* 01-789 3180. *Club:* United Oxford & Cambridge University.

ROY, Prof. Arthur Douglas, FRCS, FRCSE, FRCSGlas, FRCSI; Professor of Surgery, Queen's University of Belfast, since 1973; *b* 10 April 1925; *s* of Arthur Roy and Edith Mary (*née* Brown); *m* 1st, 1954, Monica Cecilia Mary Bowley; three *d*; 2nd, 1973, Patricia Irene McColl. *Educ:* Paisley Grammar Sch.; Univ. of Glasgow (MB, ChB, Commendation). RAMC, 1948-50; Surgical Registrar posts in Glasgow and Inverness, 1950-54; Sen. Surgical Registrar, Aylesbury and Oxford, 1954-57; Cons. Surgeon and Hon. Lectr, Western Infirmary, Glasgow, 1957-68; Foundn Prof. of Surgery, Univ. of Nairobi, 1968-72. *Publications:* Lecture Notes in Surgery: tropical supplement, 1975; various papers on gastro-enterology, endocrine surgery, tropical medicine, etc. *Recreations:* skiing, squash, gardening. *Address:* 15 Pinehill Road, Ballycairn, Lisburn, N Ireland BT27 5TU. *T:* Drumbo 217. *Club:* Royal Commonwealth Society.

ROY, Sir Asoka Kumar, Kt 1937; *b* 9 Sept. 1886; *s* of late Akshoy Kumar Roy Chaudhury of Taki and late Shoroshi Bala Roy Chaudhurani; *m* 1908, Charu Hashini, 4th *d* of late Taraprasad Roy Chaudhury; one *s* one *d*. *Educ:* Doveton College, Presidency College and Ripon College, Calcutta. MA, BL (Calcutta); Vakil, Calcutta High Court, 1908; called to Bar, Middle Temple, 1912 (First Class Honoursman at the Final Bar Examination); Standing Counsel, Bengal, 1929; twice acted as a Judge of the High Court of Calcutta; Advocate-General of Bengal, 1934-43; Law Member, Governor-General's Council, India, 1943-46. Director, Jardine Henderson Ltd and other big companies, 1950-70. *Recreations:* gardening and walking. *Address:* 3 Upper Wood Street, Calcutta, India. *Clubs:* Calcutta, Royal Calcutta Turf (Calcutta).

ROY, Ian; Assistant Under-Secretary of State, Home Office, 1963-72; *b* 2 Aug. 1912; *o s* of late John Roy and Annie Froude Marshall; *m* 1939, Betty Louise Blissett; one *s* two *d*. *Educ:* Manchester Grammar School; Peterhouse, Cambridge. Assistant Inspector of Taxes, 1935; Assistant Principal, Home Office, 1936; Private Secretary to Permanent Under-Secretary of State, 1938; to Parliamentary Under-Secretary of State, 1939-40; Asst Secretary, 1947. *Address:* Flat 47, Cholmeley Lodge, Cholmeley Park, Highgate, N6. *T:* 01-340 3143.

ROY, His Eminence Cardinal Maurice; *see* Quebec, Cardinal Archbishop of.

ROY, Maurice Paul Mary; Grand Officier, Légion d'Honneur; Professor at Ecole Polytechnique, Paris, 1947-69; Président: Committee on Space Research; International Union of Theoretical and Applied Mechanics; *b* 7 Nov. 1899; *m* 1932, Maritchu Nebout; one *s*. *Educ:* Ecole Polytechnique; Ecole Nat. Sup. des Mines. Ingénieur Général des Mines (retd); Contrôle Technique des Chemins de Fer, 1922-35; Director General:

Mechanical Industry, 1935-40; Office Nat. de la Recherche Aéronautique, 1949-62; Professor successively at French Nat. Engineering Schs (Ponts et Chaussées, Génie Rural, Aéronautique), and at Ecole Polytechnique. Membre de l'Institut (Académie des Sciences), 1949 (Pres. 1966). Foreign Member: US Nat. Acad. of Sci.; Austrian Acad. of Sci.; Hon. FRAeS. Dr *hc* Bruxelles, Aachen, Saarbrucken, Québec, Oxford. Médaille d'Or Lomonossov, USSR Acad. of Sci., 1976. *Publications:* books on Thermodynamics, Mechanics, Aviation and Propulsion; scientific and technical papers. *Recreations:* literature, golf. *Address:* 86 Avenue Niel, 75017 Paris, France. *T:* 924-0102.

ROYCE, David Nowill; Under-Secretary, CRE 3 and Export Development Divisions, Department of Trade, since 1975; *b* 10 Sept. 1920; *s* of late Bernard Royce and Ida Christine (*née* Nowill); *m* 1942, Esther Sylvia Yule; two *s* one *d*. *Educ:* Reading School; Vienna University. Served HM Forces, 1940-46. Major, Intelligence Corps, 1946; Asst Principal, Foreign Office, German Section, 1948; Foreign Service, 1949; First Secretary: Athens, 1953; Saigon, 1955; Foreign Office, 1957; Head of Chancery, Caracas, 1960; Counsellor (Commercial), Bonn, 1963; Counsellor (Commercial) and Consul-Gen., Helsinki, 1967-68; Commercial Inspector, FCO, 1969-71; Dir for Co-ordination of Export Services, DTI, 1971-73; Under-Sec., Overseas Finance and Planning Div., Dept of Trade, 1973-75. *Recreations:* tennis, swimming, sailing. *Address:* 5 Sprimont Place, SW3. *T:* 01-589 9148. *Clubs:* Travellers', Hurlingham.

ROYDEN, Sir Christopher (John), 5th Bt *cr* 1905; Partner, Spencer Thornton & Co., since 1974; *b* 26 Feb. 1937; *s* of Sir John Ledward Royden, 4th Bt, and of Dolores Catherine, *d* of late Cecil J. G. Coward; *S* father, 1976; *m* 1961, Diana Bridget, *d* of Lt-Col J. H. Goodhart, MC; two *s* one *d*. *Educ:* Winchester Coll.; Christ Church, Oxford (MA). Duncan Fox & Co. Ltd, 1960-71; Spencer Thornton & Co., 1971-. *Recreations:* fishing, shooting, gardening. *Heir: s* John Michael Joseph Royden, *b* 17 March 1965. *Address:* 9 Stanhope Gardens, SW7. *T:* 01-370 2665. *Club:* Cavalry and Guards.

ROYDS, Rev. John Caress, MA Cantab; Rector of Loddington with Cransley, since 1976; Diocesan Director of Education for Peterborough, since 1976; *b* 1920; 3rd *s* of Rev. Edward Thomas Hubert Royds, BA. *Educ:* Monkton Combe School, Bath; Queens' College, Cambridge. II 1 hons History, 1947. Military service with British and Indian Armies, 1940-46. Assistant master, Bryanston School, Dorset, 1947-61, House-master, 1951-61; Headmaster: General Wingate School, Addis Ababa, 1961-65; Uppingham Sch., 1965-75. Deacon, 1974; Priest, 1975. *Address:* Loddington Rectory, Kettering NN14 1JZ. *Club:* Royal Commonwealth Society.

ROYLE, Sir Anthony (Henry Fanshawe), KCMG 1974; MP (C) Richmond, since Oct. 1959; *b* 27 March 1927; *s* of Sir Lancelot Royle, *qv*; *m* 1957, Shirley Worthington; two *d*. *Educ:* Harrow; Sandhurst. Captain, The Life Guards (Germany, Egypt, Palestine and Transjordan), 1945-48; served with 21st Special Air Service Regt (TA), 1948-51. Parliamentary Private Secretary: to Under-Sec. of State for the Colonies, 1960; to Sec. of State for Air, 1960-62; to Minister of Aviation, 1962-64; Vice-Chm., Cons. Parly Foreign Affairs Cttee, 1965-67; Tory Opposition Whip, 1967-70; Parly Under-Sec. of State for Foreign and Commonwealth Affairs, 1970-74. Mem., Assembly of Council of Europe and WEU, 1965. Director: British Match Corp., 1969-70; Sedgwick Forbes UK Ltd, 1974-; Brooke Bond Liebig Ltd, 1974-; Wilkinson Match Ltd, 1974-. Esteemed Family Order (1st cl.), Brunei, 1975. *Address:* 47 Cadogan Place, SW1; The Chapter Manor, South Cerney, Gloucestershire. *Clubs:* Pratt's, White's.

ROYLE, Prof. Joseph Kenneth; Head of Department of Mechanical Engineering, University of Sheffield, since 1966; *b* 3 April 1924; *s* of J. Royle, Accrington, Lancs; *m* 1955, P. R. Wallwork; one *s* two *d*. *Educ:* Manchester University. Royal Aircraft Estabt, 1944-48; Manchester Univ., 1949-61; Vis. Assoc. Prof., MIT, 1961-62; Sen. Lectr, Univ. of Manchester Inst. of Science and Technology, 1962-64; Dept of Mech. Engrg, Univ. of Sheffield, 1964-. *Publications:* contribs to Proc. IMechE, etc. *Recreations:* gardening, music. *Address:* Anselm, Over Lane, Baslow, Derbyshire. *T:* Baslow 3149.

ROYLE, Mrs Julian A. C.; *see* Harwood, Elizabeth Jean.

ROYLE, Sir Lancelot (Carrington), KBE 1944; *b* 31 May 1898; *y s* of Rev. Vernon Peter Fanshawe and Eleanor Agnes Royle, Stanmore Park, Stanmore, Middlesex; *m* 1922, Barbara Rachel Haldin (*d* 1977); two *s* one *d*. *Educ:* Stanmore Park; Harrow School; RMA Woolwich. Left Woolwich, 1918; France, 113

Army Brigade, RFA, 1918; Cologne, 1918-21; Army Champion, 100 yds, 1920; resigned commission, 1921; took up appointment with Van den Berghs, Ltd, subsequently by amalgamation, Lever & Unilever, Ltd; recalled, War of 1939-45; served with 56th Heavy Battery, RA, 1940; appointed member Macharg/Royle Committee by Treasury, 1940. Gov. of Harrow School, 1947-62. Chairman: Navy, Army and Air Force Institutes, 1941-53; Allied Suppliers Ltd, 1947-58; Lipton Ltd, 1952-59; Lipton (Overseas) Ltd, 1959-63. Director: British Match Corp. Ltd, 1961-68; Bryant & May Ltd, 1961-71; Liebigs Extract of Meat Co. Ltd, 1961-68; Oxo Ltd, 1961-68. *Recreations:* athletics (Olympic Games, 1924), football, cricket. *Address:* 31 Elsworthy Road, Primrose Hill, NW3. *T:* 01-722 5445. *Club:* Army and Navy.
See also Sir A. H. F. Royle.

ROZHDESTVENSKY, Gennadi Nikolaevich; Chief Conductor, Stockholm Philharmonic Orchestra, since 1974; Chief Conductor, BBC Symphony Orchestra, from autumn 1978; *b* 1931; *m* Victoria Postnikova, concert pianist. Studied piano at Moscow Conservatoire; started conducting at 18. Conductor Bolshoi Theatre, 1956-60 (Assistant Conductor, 1951); Chief Conductor, USSR Radio and Television Symphony Orchestra, 1960-65 and 1970-74; Principal Conductor, Bolshoi Theatre, 1965-70. Guest conductor, Europe, Israel, America. Merited Artist of the RSFSR. *Recreation:* photography. *Address:* c/o Victor Hochhauser Ltd, 4 Holland Park Avenue, W11.

RUBBRA, Edmund, CBE 1960; MA Oxon, DMus; Hon. LLD Leicester; MRAM 1970; FGSM 1968; composer pianist; Professor of Composition at Guildhall School of Music, 1961-74; Senior Lecturer in Music, Oxford University, 1947-68; Fellow, Worcester College, Oxford, 1963; *b* Northampton, 23 May 1901. *Educ:* Northampton; University of Reading; Royal College of Music. Orchestral works include: ten symphonies; two overtures; Sinfonia Concertante for piano and orchestra; Concertos for piano, violin, and viola; Soliloquy for cello and small orchestra; Improvisation for Violin and orchestra; Improvisations on Virginal Pieces by Giles Farnaby; Variations for Brass Band; Brahms-Handel Variations scored for full orchestra. Opera, The Shadow. Chamber works include: Sonatas for violin and piano, cello and piano, oboe and piano; 2 Piano Trios; four string quartets; Lyric Movement for piano and string quartet; Phantasy for two violins and piano; Introduction and Fugue for piano; Eight Preludes for piano; Prelude and Fugue on a Theme by Cyril Scott for piano; Pezzo Ostinato for harp solo; Transformations for solo harp; Discourse for harp and 'cello; The Buddha Suite for flute, oboe and string trio; Meditazioni for recorder and harpsichord; Fantasia on a Theme of Machaut for recorder and string quartet; Notturno for four recorders; Passacaglia sopra Plusieurs Regrets for recorder and harpsichord; Sonatina for recorder and harpsichord; 3 works for unaccomp. violin, viola and cello. Vocal works include: 9 Motets; 7 Madrigals; Mass and Festival Gloria for double choir; 4-part Mass; 3-part Mass; Missa Brevis for 3-part treble choir and organ; The Morning Watch for choir and orchestra; The Dark Night of the Soul for Choir and orchestra; Song of the Soul for choir, strings, harp and timpani; In die et nocte canticum for choir and orchestra; Inscape for choir, strings and harp; Veni, Creator Spiritus, for Choir and Brass; 3 Psalms for low voice and piano; Advent Cantata for baritone, choir and small orchestra; Amoretti for tenor and string quartet; 5 Spenser Sonnets for tenor and string orchestra; 4 Medieval Latin Lyrics for baritone and string orchestra; The Jade Mountain, five songs for harp and voice; Magnificat and Nunc Dimittis for choir and organ; Te Deum for choir, solo, and orchestra; Cantata, in Honorem Mariae Matris Dei, for choir, boys' voices, soprano and alto soli, and orchestra; Ode to the Queen for Voice and orchestra; Tenebrae settings for unaccompanied choir; Two Sonnets by William Alabaster for voice, viola and piano; Cantata Pastorale for voice, recorder, harpsichord and cello; Autumn for 3-part female choir and piano; The Beatitudes for 3-part female choir unaccompanied; Anthems: Up O my soul; And when the Builders; Lord, with what care; This Spiritual House Almighty God shall inhabit; Blessed is He; Prayer for the Queen; 3 Greek folk songs; The Givers for 4-part unaccompanied choir; Cantata di camera Crucifixus pro nobis; Te Deum for 8-part unaccompanied choir; Lauda Sion, for unaccompanied double choir; Agnus Dei, for 4-part unaccompanied choir; Creature-Songs to Heaven, for 3-part treble voices, piano and strings; numerous songs. *Publications:* Counterpoint: A Survey; Holst: A monograph; ed Casella, The Evolution of Music, rev. and enl. edn; Collected Essays on Gustav Holst. *Address:* Lindens, Bull Lane, Gerrards Cross, Bucks SL9 8RU. *T:* Gerrards Cross 84650.

RUBENS, Bernice Ruth; writer and director of documentary films, since 1957; *b* 26 July 1928; *m* 1947, Rudi Nassauer; two *d*.

Educ: University of Wales, Cardiff (BA, Hons English). Followed teaching profession, 1950-55. American Blue Ribbon award for documentary film, Stress, 1968. *Publications:* Set on Edge, 1960; Madame Sousatzka, 1962; Mate in Three, 1965; The Elected Member, 1969 (Booker Prize, 1970); Sunday Best, 1971; Go Tell the Lemming, 1973; I Sent a Letter to my Love, 1975; The Ponsonby Post, 1977. *Recreation:* plays piano and 'cello. *Address:* 89 Greencroft Gardens, NW6 3LJ. *T:* 01-328 1415.

RUBIN, Kenneth Warnell; His Honour Judge Rubin; a Circuit Judge since 1972; *b* 8 March 1920; *s* of late Albert Reginald Rubin and late Mary Eales Rubin; *m* 1948, Jeanne Marie Louise de Wilde; one *s* two *d. Educ:* King's College Sch., Wimbledon; King's Coll., London (LLB). Served HM Forces, 1939-45. Called to Bar, Gray's Inn, 1948. *Address:* Tyrrellswood, Shere Road, West Horsley, Surrey. *T:* East Horsley 2848.

RUBINSTEIN, Arthur, Hon. KBE 1977; pianist; *b* Lodz, Poland, 28 January 1887; *m* 1932, Aniela Mlynarska; two *s* two *d. Educ:* under Joachim, Prof. Heinrich Barth, Robert Kahn and Max Bruch. Gave many concerts in Russia, Poland, Germany, Austria; made first appearance in Spain in 1915, followed by 120 concerts in Spain alone; later in Latin America, where made 13 tours; since 1924 has toured Europe extensively; again in US, 1937, and became American Citizen. Toured Far East. Since 1945, every year, has made tours in US and all Western Europe (but refused to play in Germany, 1914-). In 1961 gave 10 recitals at Carnegie Hall, New York, in 4 weeks' time, all for 10 different charities. Appeared Festival Hall, London, 1954, 1955, 1956, 1957, 1960, 1962, 1963, 1965, 1968, 1969, 1970, 1972. US Medal of Freedom, 1976; holds several foreign Orders. Doctor *hc* : Yale Univ.; Brown Univ.; North-western Univ.; Hon. Member: Acad. Santa Cecilia, Rome; Acad. of Brazil; Gold Medal, Beethoven, Roy. Phil. Society. *Publication:* My Young Years, 1973. *Address:* 22 square de l'avenue Foch, 75116 Paris, France.

RUBINSTEIN, Prof. Nicolai, FBA 1971; FRHistS; Professor of History, Westfield College, London University, since 1965; *b* 13 July 1911; *s* of Bernhard and Irene Rubinstein; *m* 1954, Ruth Kidder Olitsky. *Educ:* Univs of Berlin and Florence. LittD Florence. Lectr, UC Southampton, 1942-45; Lectr, 1945-62, Reader, 1962-65, Westfield Coll., Univ. of London. Serena Medal, British Acad., 1974. *Publications:* The Government of Florence under the Medici 1434-94, 1966; (ed) Florentine Studies: politics and society in Renaissance Florence, 1968; Gen. Editor, Letters of Lorenzo de'Medici; articles in Jl of Warburg and Courtauld Insts, Italian Studies, Archivio Storico Italiano, Rinascimento. *Address:* Department of History, Westfield College, Kidderpore Avenue, Hampstead, NW3 7ST. *T:* 01-435 7141; (home) 16 Gardnor Mansions, Church Row, NW3. *T:* 01-435 6995.

RUBNER, Ben; General Secretary, Furniture, Timber and Allied Trades Union, since 1976; *b* 30 Sept. 1921; *s* of Charles and Lily Rubner; *m* 1952, Amelia Sonia Bagnari; one *s* one *d. Educ:* Mansford Street Central Sch., Bethnal Green, E2. Apprentice cabinet maker, 1935; Mem. Cttee, Trade Union Br., 1937. Served war in armed forces, Royal Corps of Signals: N Africa, Italy, Sicily, 1941-46. Shop Steward, Sec., Chm. and Convenor, London Furniture Workers Shop Stewards Council, 1947-52; NUFTO: London Dist Cttee, 1954; Gen. Exec. Council, 1958; London Dist Organiser, 1959. Nat. Trade Organiser, 1963; Asst Gen. Sec., FTAT, 1973-76. British TUC: London Delegate, 1955-58; full-time Officer Deleg., 1974-77. *Recreations:* music (opera, light and grand), chess, table tennis. *Address:* 116 Arcadian Gardens, Wood Green, N22 5AE. *T:* 01-888 6956. *Club:* Cambridge and Bethnal Green Old Boys.

RUBYTHON, Eric Gerald; Chairman and Managing Director, Hawker Siddeley Aviation, since 1977; Member of Board, and Deputy Chief Executive of Aircraft Group, British Aerospace, since 1977; *b* 11 Feb. 1921; *s* of Reginald Rubython and Bessie Rubython; *m* 1943, Joan Ellen Mills. Joined Hawker Aircraft Ltd, 1948; Co. Sec., 1953; Exec. Dir, 1959; Dir and Gen. Man., 1960; Divl Dir and Gen. Man., Hawker Blackburn Div., 1963; Commercial Dir, Hawker Siddeley Aviation, 1965; Dir and Gen. Manager, Hawker Siddeley Aviation, 1970. *Recreations:* golf, gardening. *Address:* Brayfield, Wonersh Park, Wonersh, near Guildford, Surrey. *T:* Bramley (Surrey) 2018.

RUCK, Berta, (Mrs Oliver Onions); novelist; *b* 2 Aug. 1878; *d* of Col and Mrs A. A. Ruck; *m* 1909, Oliver Onions (George Oliver) (*d* 1961); two *s. Educ:* St Winifred's School, Bangor, Wales. Studied art at the Slade School (scholarship), and at Calorossi's, Paris. Afterwards took to writing articles and short stories, first novel published 1913. Has lectured under Adult Education for HM Forces, and has recently broadcast. TV programme Yesterday's Witness, 1970. *Publications:* over 100

books, including: His Official Fiancée; The Lad with Wings; The Girls at his Billet; Sir or Madam and many other novels, the latest being Tomboy in Lace, She Danced in the Ballet, Love and Apron-Strings, Hopeful Journey, Song of the Lark, Marriage is a Blind Date, Fantastic Holiday, The Men in Her Life, We All Have Our Secrets, Romance and a Film Star, A Wish A Day, A Smile for the Past (memoirs), Romantic after-thought, Love and A Rich Girl, Sherry and Ghosts, Runaway Lovers, Rendezvous at Zagarelli's, Shopping for a Husband, A Trickle of Welsh Blood, Asset to Wales, Ancestral Voices. *Recreations:* was an ice-breaker, and liked air travel; is now 99 but fit. *Address:* Bryntegwel, Aberdovey, Gwynedd, Wales. *T:* Aberdovey 286.

RUCKER, Sir Arthur Nevil, KCMG 1942; CB 1941; CBE 1937; Chairman of Stevenage New Town Corporation, 1962-66 (Vice-Chairman, 1956-62); *b* 20 June 1895; *o s* of late Sir Arthur Rucker, FRS, and Lady Rucker of Everington House, nr Newbury; *m* 1922, Elsie Marion Broadbent; two *s* two *d. Educ:* Marlborough; Trinity College, Cambridge. Served European War (12th Suffolk Regiment, Lieutenant), 1915-18; entered Civil Service as Assistant Principal, 1920; Private Secretary to successive Ministers of Health, 1928-36; Director of Establishments and Public Relations, Ministry of Health, 1937-39; Principal Private Secretary to Prime Minister, 1939-40; seconded for special duties, 1941, returned to Ministry of Health as Deputy Secretary, 1943; Deputy Director-General, IRO, 1948. Deputy Agent-General of the UN Korean Reconstruction Agency, 1951; Member Commonwealth War Graves Commission, 1956-69. Hon. LLD Wales, 1965. Korean Order of Diplomatic Merit, Heung-in Medal, 1974. *Address:* Manor Farm House, Yattendon, Berks. *T:* Yattendon 205. *Club:* Athenæum.

RUDDEN, James; Advisory Head Teacher on Secondary Reorganisation, ILEA, 1976-77; President: National Association of Head Teachers, 1971; London Head Teachers Association, 1969; Metropolitan Catholic Teachers Association, 1964; *b* 11 Dec. 1911; *s* of Bernard and Mary Rudden; *m* 1937, Eileen Finlay; one *s* four *d. Educ:* Carlisle Grammar Sch.; St Mary's Coll., Twickenham. BSc (Special, Geo.) (London Univ.); Teacher's Cert. (London Univ.). Asst Teacher, Carlisle, 1933-47; served War, RAF Educn Officer, 1940-45. First Head: St Cuthbert's Sec. Mod. Sch., Cleator, 1948-52; St Thomas More Sec. Mod. Sch., Tottenham, 1952-59; Bishop Thomas Grant Comprehensive Sch., Streatham, 1959-75. Chairman: London Comprehensive Head Teachers Conf., 1974-75; Southwark Diocesan Schs Commn; Governing Body of Schs Council; Adv. Council for Supply and Trng of Teachers. KSG 1969. *Publications:* numerous articles on educnl topics in Education, and in national press. *Recreations:* good music, good conversation, good wine and food. *Address:* 5 The Gorse, Rissington Road, Bourton-on-the-Water, Glos.

RUDDERHAM, Rt. Rev. Joseph Edward; *b* 17 June 1899; *s* of William Rudderham and Agnes Mary Coan. *Educ:* St Bede's Coll., Manchester; St Edmund's Coll. Old Hall, Ware; Christ's Coll., Cambridge; Ven. English Coll., Rome. Priest 1926 (by Cardinal Pompili in Rome); Curate at All Souls Church, Peterborough, 1927-32. Parish Priest, 1932-43; Administrator of Northampton Cathedral, 1943-49; Canon Penitentiary of Northampton Cathedral Chapter, 1946-49; Diocesan Inspector of Schs, 1941-49; Bishop of Clifton, 1949-74. *Address:* Nazareth House, London Road, Charlton Kings, Cheltenham, Glos GL52 6YJ. *T:* Cheltenham 56361.

RUDDLE, Lt-Col Sir (George) Kenneth (Fordham), Kt 1957; TD; DL; *b* 17 May 1903; *o s* of late George Ruddle; *m* 1930, Nancy Margaret, *er d* of late H. G. Allen, Woburn Sands, Beds; one *s* two *d* (and one *d* decd). *Educ:* Repton. Pres. and former Chm., of family brewing business, G. Ruddle & Co. Ltd; Mem., Exec. Cttee of National Union of Conservative and Unionist Assocs, 1951-62, 1964-67; Chm. E Midland area of Nat. Union of Cons. and Unionist Assocs, 1951-57. Alderman, Rutland CC; Chairman, 1958-70; DL Co. of Rutland 1938-; High Sheriff of Rutland, 1938. Former Vice-Chm., Leics and Rutland T&AFA; Pres. Rutland Horticultural Soc. *Recreations:* cricket, gardening. *Address:* Islington Lodge, Langham, Oakham, Rutland. *T:* Oakham 2944. *Clubs:* Carlton, MCC.

RUDÉ, Prof. George Frederick Elliot; Professor of History, Concordia University, Montreal, since 1970; *b* 8 Feb. 1910; *s* of Jens Essendrop Rude, Norway, and Amy Geraldine Elliot Rude, England; *m* 1940, Doreen, *d* of J. W. De la Hoyde, Dublin; no *c. Educ:* Shrewsbury Sch.; Trinity Coll., Cambridge. Dr of Letters (Adelaide), 1967. Taught at: Stowe Sch., Bucks, 1931-35; St Paul's Sch., London, 1936-49; Sir Walter St John's Sch., London, 1950-54; Holloway Sch., London, 1954-59; Univ. of Adelaide: Sen. Lectr in History, 1960-63; Prof. of History, 1964-

67; Prof. of History, Flinders Univ., SA, 1968-70; Leverhulme Vis. Prof., Univ. of Tokyo, Sept.-Nov. 1967; Vis. Prof., Univ. of Stirling, 1968. Mem., Australian Research Grants Cttee, 1969. Alexander Prize, Roy. Hist. Soc., 1955. FRHistSoc. 1957; Fellow, Australian Acad. of Humanities, 1963. *Publications:* The Crowd in the French Revolution, 1959; Wilkes and Liberty, 1962; Revolutionary Europe 1783-1815, 1964; The Crowd in History, 1964; (ed) The Eighteenth Century 1715-1815, 1965; (ed) Robespierre, 1967; (with E. J. Hobsbawm) Captain Swing, 1969; Paris and London in the 18th Century, 1970; Hanoverian London 1714-1808, 1971; Debate on Europe 1815-1850, 1972; Europe in the Eighteenth Century, 1972; Robespierre, 1975; contribs to Eng. Hist. Review, Eng. Econ. Hist. Review, Revue Historique, Past and Present, etc. *Recreations:* swimming, reading, public speaking. *Address:* Concordia University, Sir George Williams Campus, Montreal, PQ, Canada; The Oast House, Hope Farm, Beckley, Rye, Sussex.

RUDGARD, Ven. Richard Cuthbert, OBE 1944; TD 1950; Rector of Ellisfield and Farleigh Wallop, Basingstoke, 1960-74, and of Dumme, 1968-74; Archdeacon of Basingstoke and Canon of Winchester, 1958-71; now Archdeacon Emeritus; *b* 28 Dec. 1901; *e s* of Canon R. W. and Mrs E. M. Rudgard; *m* 1st, 1933, Mary M. McLean (decd); one *s*; 2nd, 1939, Maisie M. Cooke. *Educ:* Radley College; St Augustine's College, Canterbury. With Melanesian Mission, 1922-33. Assistant Priest, Heene, Worthing, 1934; Rector of Newbold Pacey with Moreton Morrell, 1936-45; Rector of Eversley, 1946-60; Rural Dean of Odiham, 1953-59. War of 1939-45 (despatches thrice); Chaplain to the Forces, TA, 1939; SCF 1st Armoured Division, 1942, N Africa; DACG 13 Corps, 1943, Sicily and Italy; Personal Chaplain to Chaplain General, 1944-46. DACG (TA) Southern Command, 1947-56. Hon. Chaplain to the Queen, 1954-56. *Recreations:* riding and tennis. *Address:* Clevedale Cottage, 22 Christchurch Road, Winchester SO23 9SS. *T:* Winchester 61419.

RUDKIN, Walter Charles; Director of Economic Intelligence, Ministry of Defence, since 1973; *b* 22 Sept. 1922; *e s* of Walter and Bertha Rudkin; *m* 1950, Hilda Mary Hope; two *s*. *Educ:* Carre's Grammar Sch., Sleaford; UC Hull. BSc (Econ) London. Served with RAF, 1942-46. Lectr, Dept of Econs and Econ. History, Univ. of Witwatersrand, 1948-52. Entered Min. of Defence, 1954; various appts, incl. Hong Kong, 1956-59; Junior Directing Staff, Imperial Defence Coll., 1962-64; Cabinet Office, 1968-71. *Recreation:* fishing. *Address:* 85 Kingsway, Petts Wood, Orpington, Kent BR5 1PW. *T:* Orpington 22603. *Club:* Royal Commonwealth Society.

RUDOE, Wulf; CB 1975; Assistant Secretary, Price Commission, since 1976; *b* 9 March 1916; *m* 1942, Ellen Trilling; one *s* one *d*. *Educ:* Central Foundation School; Peterhouse, Cambridge (Open Schol. and Research Schol.). Mathematics Tripos Pt III, 1938, Distinction. Royal Aircraft Establishment, 1939. Operational Research, RAF, 1939-45. Operational Research in Building Industry, Min. of Works, 1946-48, Principal Scientific Officer 1948; Board of Trade, Statistician 1948, Chief Statistician 1952; Dir of Statistics and Research, DHSS (formerly Min. of Health), 1966-76. Fellow Inst. of Statisticians; Mem. Council, 1962-, Hon. Treasurer, 1965-74, Vice-Pres., 1974-75 and 1976-77, Roy. Statistical Soc. *Recreations:* walking, travel, languages. *Address:* 72 North End Road, NW11. *T:* 01-455 2890.

RUE, Dr (Elsie) Rosemary, CBE 1977; Regional Medical Officer, Oxford Regional Health Authority, since 1973; *b* 14 June 1928; *d* of Harry and Daisy Laurence; divorced; two *s*. *Educ:* Sydenham High Sch.; Univ. of London; Oxford Univ. Med. School. MB, BS, FRCP, DCH, MRCPsych, FFCM. Gen. Practitioner, 1952-58; Public Health Service, 1958-65; Hospital Service, 1965-73; SAMO, Oxford RHB, 1971. *Publications:* papers on gen. practice, women in medicine, ward design, community hosps, health services, individuals requiring security. *Address:* 2 Stanton St John, Oxford. *T:* Oxford 64861.

RUEFF, Jacques, Grand' Croix de la Légion d'Honneur; Croix de Guerre (3 citations); French Economist; Member of French Academy and of Academy of Moral and Political Sciences; Chancellor of the French Institute; Member of Economic and Social Council; *b* 23 Aug. 1896; *m* 1937, Christiane Vignat; two *d*. *Educ:* Ecole Polytechnique, Paris. Inspector of Finance, 1923; Mem. Secretariat, League of Nations, 1927-30; Financial Attaché, London, 1930-34; Asst Director, later Director, Treasury, Ministry of Finance, 1934-39; Counsellor of State, 1937; Vice-Governor, Bank of France, 1939-41, resigned; Econ. Adviser to Commander-in-Chief Germany, 1945; Delegate to Reparations Commn, Moscow, and Pres., Inter-Allied Reparations Agency, 1946; Judge, Court of Justice of European

Steel and Coal Community, 1952; Judge, Court of European Communities, 1958-62; Pres., Cttee for Reform of French Financial Situation, 1958; Vice-Pres., Cttee for Removal of Economic Obstacles, 1960. Foreign Associate: Nat. Acad. of Lincei, Rome; Roy. Acad. of Sciences, Letters and Fine Arts, Belgium. Grand Cross and Grand Officer of several foreign orders. *Publications:* Des Sciences physiques au Sciences morales, 1921, new edn 1969; Theorie des Phénomènes monétaires, 1927; L'ordre social, 1946; Epître aux Dirigistes, 1949; L'âge de l'inflation, 1963; Le lancinant problème des balances de paiement, 1965; Les Dieux et les Rois, 1967; Le Péché monétaire de l'Occident, 1971; Combats pour l'ordre financier, 1972; La réforme du système monétaire international, 1973; La création du monde (comédie-ballet), 1974. *Recreation:* golf. *Address:* 51 rue de Varenne, Paris 7e, France *T:* Littré 36-01; Berville, par 27 Beuzeville. *Club:* Saint-Cloud.

RUEGGER, Paul J.; Swiss diplomat and jurist; *b* 14 August 1897; *s* of Prof. J. Ruegger; *m* 1st, 1932, Countess Isabella Salazar y Munatones (*d* 1969); 2nd, 1971, Marquise Isabella Francesca Fossi. *Educ:* College Lucerne; Univs of Lausanne, Munich, and Zürich (Doctor of Law). Attaché at Swiss Foreign Office and Sec. Swiss Advisory Cttee for League of Nations and post-war problems, 1918; Secretary of the Swiss Delegation to the League of Nations, 1920-25 (technical adviser, 1923-25); Sec. Swiss Delegation to Internat. Econ. Conf. of Genoa, 1922; Asst Prof. of Internat. Law, Univ. of Geneva, 1922-24; Legal Adviser to Swiss Delegation Conference for control of trade of arms, etc., 1925; Deputy Registrar Permanent Court of International Justice, 1926-28; Counsellor Swiss Legation in Rome, 1929-31; Head of Political Office Foreign Affairs Dept in Berne, 1931-33; 1st Counsellor of the Swiss Legation in Paris, 1933-36; Swiss Minister in Rome, 1936-42; Swiss Minister to Great Britain, 1944-48. Head of the Swiss Delegation for establishment of a Convention between Switzerland and UN on diplomatic privileges and immunities of UNO establishments in Switzerland; member of Swiss Deleg. to last League of Nations Assembly, Geneva, 1946; President Internat. Committee of Red Cross, 1948-55, Chm. 1968-; Chm. ILO Committee on Forced Labour, 1956-60. Prof. of Human Rights, Univ. of Strasbourg, 1964. Member of: Perm. Court of Arbitration; Curatorium of Acad. of Internat. Law, at The Hague; Inst. of Internat. Law; Commissions of Conciliation: between Switzerland and USA; between Switzerland and Spain; between France and the Netherlands; between Sweden and Denmark (Chm). UN Nansen Medal Award Cttee; Ambassador, 1957; Chm. Swiss Deleg. to UN Conf. on Law of the Sea, Geneva, 1958 and 1960, and to UN Confs on Diplomatic Relations and Immunities, Vienna, 1961; on Consular Relations and Immunities, Vienna, 1963; on Law of Treaties, Vienna, 1968 and 1969; Chm. Cttee of UN Atomic Energy Agency, Vienna, on Civil Liability and Internat. Responsibility for Nuclear Hazards, 1959-62; Chm. ILO Arbitral Commn, Ghana-Portugal, 1961-62; Pres., prep. UN Conf., 1964, and of conf. of plenipotentiaries, New York, on transit trade of land-locked countries, 1965; Chm., Study Gp on Labour and Trade Union Situation in Spain, 1968-69. *Publications:* The Nationality of Corporations in International Law, 1918; Terms of Civil Law in International Law, 1920; The Responsibility of States for Crimes committed on their Territory, 1923; The Practice of International Conciliation Committees, 1929; Foreign Administration as Institutional Function of Intercourse between States, 1934; The Economic Foundations of International Law, 1931; Switzerland's Economy and the British Empire, 1946; The Juridical Aspects of the Organisation of the International Red Cross, 1953; Swiss Neutrality and European Integration, 1953; Notes of the International Responsibility of States for Nuclear Hazards, in Mélanges Séféréades, 1961; Introduction to Max Huber's Denkwürdigkeiten, and book on Max Huber, 1974, etc. *Address:* Villa il Pino, 267 Via Bolognese, Florence, Italy; Palazzo Fossi, 16 Via de'Benci, Florence, Italy. *Club:* Circolo dell' Unione (Florence).

See also Baron Armstrong.

RUETE, Dr jur. Hans Hellmuth; Ambassador of the Federal Republic of Germany at the Court of St James's, since 1977; *b* 21 Dec. 1914; *s* of Prof. Dr med. Alfred E. Ruete and Margarita (*née* Bohnstedt); *m* 1948, Ruth (*née* Arfsten); one *s* two *d*. *Educ:* Univs of Kiel, Lausanne, Marburg, Tokyo (Political Science and Law). Doctor's Degree in Law. Judge at Ministry of Justice in Hesse, 1949-50; then at Federal Min. of Justice; Federal Foreign Office, 1952-; Tokyo, 1952-56; Bonn, 1956-60 (Head of Russian Desk); Center for International Affairs, Harvard Univ., 1960-61; Consul-Gen., Calcutta, 1961-64; Dept for Eastern Affairs, Bonn, 1964-70; Ambassador: Paris, 1970-72; Warsaw, 1972-77. *Publication:* Der Einfluss des abendländischen Rechts auf die Rechtsentwicklung in China und Japan, 1940. *Recreations:* music, literature, theatre. *Address:* 22 Belgrave Square, SW1X 8PZ. *T:* 01-235 5033.

RUFF, William Willis, CBE 1973; DL; Clerk of the Surrey County Council, 1952-74; Member, Parliamentary Boundary Commission for England, since 1974; *b* 22 Sept. 1914; *s* of late William Ruff, Whitby, Yorks; *m* 1939, Agnes, *d* of late Howard Nankivell; two *s. Educ:* Durham School. Served War of 1939-45: Royal Signals, North Africa and India, 1940-45; Capt., 1942; Maj., 1943. Asst Solicitor: Scarborough Corp., 1937; Heston and Isleworth Corp., 1938; Surrey County Council: Asst Solicitor, 1939; Senior Asst Solicitor, 1947; Asst Clerk, 1948; Deputy Clerk, 1951. Chm., Soc. of Clerks of Peace and of Clerks of County Councils, 1969-72. DL Surrey, 1964. *Recreations:* music and cricket. *Address:* 3 Brympton Close, Ridgeway Road, Dorking, Surrey. *T:* Dorking 2406. *Clubs:* MCC; Surrey County Cricket.

RUFFLE, Mrs Thomas; *see* Dilnot, Mary.

RUGAMBWA, HE Cardinal Laurean; *see* Dar-es-Salaam, Archbishop of, (RC).

RUGBY, 2nd Baron, *cr* 1947, of Rugby; **Alan Loader Maffey;** *b* 16 April 1913; *s* of 1st Baron Rugby, GCMG, KCB, KCVO, CSI, CIE, and Dorothy Gladys, OBE 1919 (*d* 1973), *d* of late Charles Lang Huggins, JP, Hadlow Grange, Buxted; *S* father, 1969; *m* 1947, Margaret, *d* of late Harold Bindley; four *s* two *d. Educ:* Stowe. Served War of 1939-45, RAF. Inventor, Foldgate Herd Handler (RASE Silver Award, 1974). Mem. Court of Assistants, Saddlers' Co. *Heir: s* Hon. John Richard Maffey, *b* 28 Aug. 1949. *Address:* Grove Farm, Frankton, near Rugby, Warwicks.

RUGG, Sir (Edward) Percy, Kt 1959; JP; DL; Councillor for Royal Borough of Kensington and Chelsea, Greater London Council, 1964-70; Leader of Conservative Party, on the Council, 1964-66; Chairman of Council, 1967-68; Councillor for Chelsea, LCC (Alderman, 1958-61; Leader of Conservative Party, on the LCC 1959-65); *b* 14 Jan. 1906; *s* of Albert Henry and Louise Rugg; *m* 1933, Elizabeth Frances Symes; two *s* one *d. Educ:* Leys Sch. Solicitor, 1929. Hertfordshire County Council, 1940-45. Chairman: Hertford Division Conservative Association, 1948-52; Ware Rural District Council, 1949-54; Junior Carlton Club Political Council, 1954-57; Commercial Law and International Arbitration Committee of British National Committee of International Chamber of Commerce, 1957-; Gen. Purposes Cttee, GLC, 1969-70; Heathrow Airport Consultative Cttee, 1969-70; President: East Herts Conservative Assoc., 1961-; Chelsea Conservative Assoc., 1974-. Member: London Tourist Bd, 1968-69; BTA, 1969-. JP, Herts, 1949-; DL Greater London, 1967-. Dep. Kt Pres., Hon. Soc. of Knights of Round Table; Friend, RCP, 1973-. *Recreations:* shooting, fishing. *Address:* 97 Rivermead Court, Hurlingham, SW6. *T:* 01-736 3996. *Clubs:* City Livery, Hurlingham.

RUGGE-PRICE, Sir C. K. N.; *see* Price.

RUGGLES-BRISE, Captain Guy Edward, TD, DL; Senior Partner, Brewin, Dolphin & Co., Stockbrokers; Director, The Investment Co. Ltd, since 1972; *b* 15 June 1914; *s* of late Col Sir Edward Archibald Ruggles-Brise, 1st Bt, MC, TD, DL, JP, MP, and Agatha, *e d* of J. H. Gurney, DL, JP, Keswick Hall, Norfolk; *b* and *heir pres.* of Sir John Ruggles-Brise, Bt, *qv*; *m* 1940, Elizabeth, *o d* of James Knox, Smithstone House, Kilwinning, Ayrshire; three *s. Educ:* Eton. Captain 104th (Essex Yeo.) Field Bde RHA (TA), No 7 Commando. Served War of 1939-45 (PoW). Vice-Chm., Pony Riding for the Disabled Trust, Chigwell, Essex, 1969; Hon. Financial Adviser, Riding for the Disabled Assoc., 1972. DL 1967, High Sheriff 1967, Essex. *Recreations:* field sports. *Address:* Housham Tye, Harlow, Essex. *T:* Matching 236; Ledgowan Lodge, Achnasheen, Ross-shire. *T:* Achnasheen 245; (business) Basildon House, 7 Moorgate, EC2R 6AJ. *Clubs:* Cavalry and Guards, City of London.

RUGGLES-BRISE, Col Sir John Archibald, 2nd Bt, *cr* 1935; CB 1958; OBE (mil.) 1945; TD; JP; Lord-Lieutenant of Essex, since 1958; a Pro-Chancellor, University of Essex, since 1964; *b* 13 June 1908; *er s* of Colonel Sir Edward Archibald Ruggles-Brise, 1st Bt, MC, TD, DL, JP, MP, and Agatha (*d* of J. H. Gurney, DL, JP, of Keswick Hall, Norfolk; *S* father, 1942. *Educ:* Eton. Served AA Comd, 1939-45. Member of Lloyd's. Pres., CLA, 1957-59; Church Comr 1959-64; Chm., Council of the Baronetage, 1958-63. DL 1945, JP 1946, Vice-Lieutenant, 1947, Co. Essex. Hon. Freeman of Chelmsford. Governor of Felsted and Chigwell Schools. KStJ. *Recreation:* shooting. *Heir: b* Capt. Guy Edward Ruggles-Brise, *qv. Address:* Spains Hall, Finchingfield, Essex. *T:* Great Dunmow 810266. *Club:* Carlton.

RUIZ SOLER, Antonio, (Antonio); Cross of the Order of Isabella the Catholic, 1951; Comdr Order of Civil Merit, 1964; Spanish dancer; *b* Seville, 4 November 1921. Studied at the Realito Dance Academy. First stage appearance at the age of eight; subsequently toured North and South America Southern and Western Europe, and Scandinavia. First stage appearance in Great Britain, Edinburgh Festival, 1950; London début, Cambridge Theatre, 1951. Golden Medal, Fine Arts, 1952. Formed Ballet Company, 1953; début in Generalife Theatre, Granada, presenting his Ballet in Europe, S and N America. Has also appeared in many festivals in Spain. Appearances with Ballet in London: Stoll, 1954; Palace, 1956; Coliseum, 1958; Royalty, 1960; Drury Lane, 1963; Coliseum, 1975. Gala perf. in Washington to President Kennedy, Ed Sullivan Show in New York, appearances Europe, 1963. Festivals of Spain, 1964-65; Madrid Season, 1965; N Amer. tour, 1965; Ed Sullivan Show, 1965. Appears on TV. Gold Medal, Swedish Acad. of Dancing, 1963; Medal of Min. of Information and Tourism, Madrid, 1963. *Address:* Marbella, Spain.

RUMBLE, Peter William; Under-Secretary, (Housing Directorate 'C'), Department of the Environment, since 1977; *b* 28 April 1929; *s* of Arthur Victor Rumble and Dorothy Emily (*née* Sadler); *m* 1953, Joyce Audrey Stephenson; one *s* one *d. Educ:* Harwich County High Sch.; Oriel Coll., Oxford (BA). Entered Civil Service, 1952; HM Inspector of Taxes, 1952; Principal, Min. of Housing and Local Govt, 1963; Asst Sec., Dept of the Environment, 1972. *Recreation:* music. *Address:* 11 Hillside Road, Cheam, Surrey SM2 6ET. *T:* 01-643 1752.

RUMBOLD, Sir Algernon; *see* Rumbold, Sir H. A. F.

RUMBOLD, Sir Anthony; *see* Rumbold, Sir H. A. C.

RUMBOLD, Sir (Horace) Algernon (Fraser), KCMG 1960 (CMG 1953); CIE 1947; *b* 27 Feb. 1906; *s* of late Colonel William Edwin Rumbold, CMG; *m* 1946, Margaret Adél, *d* of late Arthur Joseph Hughes, OBE; two *d. Educ:* Wellington College; Christ Church, Oxford. Assistant Principal, India Office, 1929; Private Sec. to Parliamentary Under-Secretaries of State for India, 1930-33, and to Permanent Under-Secretary of State, 1933-34; Principal, 1934; Asst Sec., 1943; transferred to Commonwealth Relations Office, 1947; Deputy High Commissioner in the Union of South Africa, 1949-53; Commonwealth Relations Office: Asst Under Sec. of State, 1954-58; Dep. Under Sec. of State, 1958-66; retired, 1966. Chm. Cttee on Inter-Territorial Questions in Central Africa, 1963; Advr, Welsh Office, 1967. Dep. Chm., Air Transport Licensing Bd, 1971-72. Mem. Governing Body, SOAS, 1965-. *Address:* Shortwoods, West Clandon, Surrey. *T:* Guildford 222757. *Club:* Travellers'.

RUMBOLD, Sir (Horace) Anthony (Claude), 10th Bt, *cr* 1779; KCMG 1962 (CMG 1953); KCVO 1969; CB 1955; HM Diplomatic Service, retired; *b* 7 March 1911; *s* of Right Hon. Sir Horace Rumbold, 9th Bt, GCB, GCMG, MVO, and Etheldred, Lady Rumbold, CBE (*d* 1964), 2nd *d* of Sir Edmund Fane, KCMG; *m* 1st, 1937, Felicity Ann (marr. diss. 1974), *yr d* of late Lt-Col F. G. Bailey and late Lady Janet Bailey, Lake House, Salisbury, Wilts; one *s* three *d*; 2nd, 1974, Mrs Pauline Graham, *d* of late Hon. David Tennant and of Hermione Baddeley, *qv. Educ:* Eton; Magdalen College, Oxford (BA). Fellow, Queen's Coll., Oxford, 1933. Third Sec. in the Foreign Office, 1935; transferred to Washington, 1937; Second Secretary, 1940; transferred to Foreign Office, 1942; served on staff of Resident Minister, Mediterranean, 1944; First Sec., 1945; transferred Prague, 1947; transferred to Foreign Office as Counsellor, 1949; transferred to Paris as Counsellor, 1951; appointed Principal Private Secretary to Foreign Secretary, 1954; Assistant Under-Secretary of State, Foreign Office, 1957; British Minister in Paris, 1960-63; Ambassador to Thailand and UK Representative on the Council of SEATO, 1965-67; Ambassador to Austria, 1967-70. Commander of the Order of St Olaf, 1955; Grand Cross of Order of Merit, Austria, 1969. *Heir: s* Henry John Sebastian Rumbold, *b* 24 Dec. 1947. *Address:* Var House, Stinsford, Dorchester, Dorset. *T:* Dorchester 2644. *Club:* Travellers'.

RUNCIE, Rt. Rev. Robert Alexander Kennedy; *see* St Albans, Bishop of.

RUNCIMAN, family name of Viscount Runciman of Doxford.

RUNCIMAN OF DOXFORD, 2nd Viscount, *cr* 1937; **Walter Leslie Runciman,** OBE 1946; AFC; DL; Bt 1906; Baron Runciman, 1933, of Shoreston; Director, Walter Runciman & Co. Ltd and other cos; *b* 26 Aug. 1900; *er s* of 1st Viscount Runciman of Doxford, PC, and Hilda (*d* 1956), MP (L) St Ives, 1928-29, *d* of J. C. Stevenson; *S* father 1949; *m* 2nd, 1932,

Katherine Schuyler, *y d* of late Wm R. Garrison, New York; one *s. Educ:* Eton (King's Scholar); Trinity College, Cambridge (Scholar). Director, 1932, Dep. Chm., 1962-71, Lloyds Bank Ltd. Chm., North of England Shipowners Association, 1931-32 and 1970-71; Chairman of Council, Armstrong College, University of Durham, 1935-37; Director-General of British Overseas Airways Corporation, 1940-43; Air Commodore and Air Attaché, Tehran, 1943-46. Pres. Chamber of Shipping of the UK, and Chm. General Council of British Shipping, 1952; Mem. Air Transport Advisory Council, 1946-54, Vice-Chm., 1951-54; President, RINA, 1951-61; Mem. Shipping Advisory Panel, 1962. Chairman: Cttee on Horticultural Marketing, 1955-56; Trustees, Nat. Maritime Museum, 1962-72; Adv. Cttee on Historic Wreck Sites, 1973-; British Hallmarking Council, 1974-. Cdre, RYS, 1968-74. Hon. Elder Brother of Trinity House. Hon. Mem., Hon. Co. of Master Mariners. DL Northumberland, 1961. Hon. DCL, Durham. *Recreations:* sailing, shooting. *Heir: s* Hon. Walter Garrison Runciman, *qv*. *Address:* 46 Abbey Lodge, Park Road, NW8; Doxford, Chathill, Northumberland. *Clubs:* Brooks's; Royal Yacht Squadron.
See also Hon. Sir Steven Runciman.

RUNCIMAN, Hon. Sir Steven; (James Cochran Stevenson), Kt 1958; FBA 1957; FSA 1964; MA; *b* 7 July 1903; 2nd *s* of 1st Viscount Runciman of Doxford, PC. *Educ:* Eton (King's Schol.); Trinity College, Cambridge (Schol.). Fellow of Trinity College, Cambridge, 1927-38 (Hon. Fellow 1965); Lecturer at the University of Cambridge, 1932-38; Press Attaché, British Legation, Sofia, 1940; British Embassy, Cairo, 1941; Professor of Byzantine Art and History in Univ. of Istanbul, 1942-45; Rep. Brit. Council in Greece, 1945-47. Lectures: Waynflete, Magdalen Coll., Oxford, 1953-54; Gifford, St Andrews, 1960-62; Birkbeck, Trinity Coll., Cambridge, 1966; Wiles, Queen's Univ., Belfast, 1968; Robb, Auckland, 1970; Regents', Los Angeles, California, 1971; Weir, Cincinnati, 1973. Alexander White Prof., Chicago, 1963. Mem. Advisory Council, Victoria and Albert Museum, 1957; Chairman: Anglo-Hellenic League, 1951-67; Nat. Trust for Greece, 1977-; Trustee: British Museum, 1960-67; Scottish Nat. Museum of Antiquities, 1972; Hon. Vice-Pres., RHistS; Vice-Pres., London Library; Chm., Scottish Ballet Adv. Council. Pres. British Inst. of Archæology at Ankara, 1960-75. For. Mem., American Philosophical Soc.; Corresp. Mem. Real Academia de Historia, Madrid. Hon. LittD Cambridge, 1955; Hon. LLD Glasgow, 1955; Hon. DLitt: Durham, 1956; St Andrews, 1969; Oxon, 1971; Birmingham, 1973; Hon. LitD London, 1966; Hon. DPhil Salonika, 1951; Hon. DD Wabash, USA, 1962; Hon. DHL Chicago, 1963. Knight Commander, Order of the Phœnix (Greece), 1961. *Publications:* The Emperor Romanus Lecapenus, 1929; The First Bulgarian Empire, 1930; Byzantine Civilization, 1933; The Medieval Manichee, 1947; A History of the Crusades, Vol. I, 1951, Vol. II, 1952, Vol. III, 1954; The Eastern Schism, 1955; The Sicilian Vespers, 1958; The White Rajahs, 1960; The Fall of Constantinople, 1453, 1965; The Great Church in Captivity, 1968; The Last Byzantine Renaissance, 1970; The Orthodox Churches and the Secular State, 1972; Byzantine Style and Civilisation, 1975; The Byzantine Theocracy, 1977; contributions to various historical journals. *Address:* Elshieshields, Lockerbie, Dumfriesshire DG11 1LY. *Club:* Athenæum.

RUNCIMAN, Hon. Walter Garrison, FBA 1975; Chairman, Walter Runciman & Co. Ltd and subsidiary companies, since 1976; Fellow, Trinity College, Cambridge, since 1971; *b* 10 Nov. 1934; *o s* and *heir* of 2nd Viscount Runciman of Doxford, *qv*; *m* 1963, Ruth, *o d* of late Joseph Hellmann and Dr Ellen Hellmann, Johannesburg; one *s* two *d*. *Educ:* Eton (Oppidan Schol.); Trinity Coll., Cambridge (Schol.; Fellow, 1959-63, 1971-). National Service, 1953-55 (2/Lt, Grenadier Guards); Harkness Fellow, 1958-60; joined Walter Runciman & Co. Ltd, 1964; part-time Reader in Sociology, Univ. of Sussex, 1967-69; Visiting Lectr in Sociology, Harvard Univ., 1970. Treas., Child Poverty Action Gp, 1972-; Mem., Social Science Research Council, 1974-. *Publications:* Plato's Later Epistemology, 1962; Social Science and Political Theory, 1963, 2nd edn 1969; Relative Deprivation and Social Justice, 1966, 2nd edn 1972; Sociology in its Place, and other essays, 1970; A Critique of Max Weber's Philosophy of Social Science, 1972; articles in academic jls. *Address:* 36 Carlton Hill, NW8 0JY. *Club:* Brooks's.

RUNCORN, Prof. Stanley Keith, FRS 1965; Professor of Physics and Head of the School of Physics, University of Newcastle upon Tyne, since 1963, and in the University of Durham (King's College), 1956-63; *b* 19 November 1922; *s* of W. H. Runcorn, Southport, Lancs; unmarried. *Educ:* King George V Sch., Southport; Gonville and Caius Coll., Cambridge. ScD 1963. Radar Research and Devel. Establishment (Min. of Supply), 1943-46; Asst Lecturer, 1946-48, and Lecturer, 1948-49, in Physics, Univ. of Manchester; Asst Dir of Research in Geophysics, Cambridge Univ., 1950-55; Research Geophysicist, Univ. of California at Los Angeles, 1952 and 1953; Fellow of Gonville and Caius Coll., Cambridge, 1948-55; Visiting Scientist, Dominion Observatory, Ottawa, 1955; Vis. Prof. of Geophysics: Cal. Inst. of Tech., 1957; Univ. of Miami, 1966; Pa State Univ., 1967; Florida State Univ., 1968; UCLA, 1975; J. Ellerton Becker Senior Visiting Fellow, Australian Academy of Science, 1963; Res. Associate, Mus. of N Arizona; Rutherford Memorial Lectr (Kenya, Tanzania and Uganda), 1970; Halley Lectr, Oxford Univ., 1972-73. Mem., Natural Environment Research Council, 1965-69. Napier Shaw Prize, Royal Met. Soc., 1959; Vetlesen Prize, 1971. Hon. DSc: Utrecht, 1969; Ghent, 1971. *Publications:* scientific papers. *Recreations:* usual. *Address:* University of Newcastle upon Tyne, Newcastle upon Tyne NE1 7RU.

RUNDALL, Sir Francis (Brian Anthony), GCMG 1968 (KCMG 1956; CMG 1951); OBE 1944; Ambassador to Japan, 1963-67; *b* 11 Sept. 1908; *s* of late Lieutenant-Colonel Charles Frank Rundall, CMG, DSO; *m* 1935, Mary, *d* of late Frank Syrett, MD; one *s* one *d*. *Educ:* Marlborough College; Peterhouse, Cambridge. Entered General Consular Service, 1930; served in Antwerp, Colon, Panama, Boston, Barcelona, Piraeus; Consul, New York, 1944; transferred Foreign Office, 1946; HM Inspector of Foreign Service Establishments, 1949-53. Chief Administrative Officer, UK High Commission in Germany during 1953; Consul-General in New York, 1953-57; Ambassador to Israel, 1957-59; Deputy Under-Secretary of State, Foreign Office, 1959-63. *Address:* Lime Tree Cottage, Church Oakley, Basingstoke, Hants. *T:* Basingstoke 780217. *Club:* Travellers'.

RUNGE, Norah Cecil, (Mrs Thomas A. Ross), OBE 1918; Alderman LCC, 1937-61; *b* London, 1884; *d* of late Lawrence Hasluck; *m* 1st, 1906, J. J. Runge (*d* 1935); one *s* one *d* (and two *s* decd); 2nd, 1939, Thomas Arthur Ross, MD, FRCP (*d* 1941). *Educ:* privately. Supt of the Soldiers' and Sailors' Free Buffet, Paddington Station, 1915-19; President of the Rotherhithe Conservative and Unionist Association, 1932-46; Vice-Chairman of Central Women's Advisory Committee of Conservative and Unionist Associations, 1941-42, of the London Conservative Union Council, 1940-47; Chm. of the London Area Women's Advisory Committee, 1938-43, Pres. 1943-45; Member of Civil Defence, Bermondsey; worked for Red Cross POW Dept., 1941-45. MP (U) Rotherhithe, 1931-35; contested Rotherhithe, 1935 and 1945. Chairman Horton Hospital Management Committee, 1948-52; Member of Board of Governors of Bethlem Royal, and Maudsley Hosp., 1948-60. Dep. Chm. LCC, 1951-52. *Address:* St John's House, Smith Square, SW1. *T:* 01-222 1563.
See also Baron Drumalbyn.

RUOFF, Theodore Burton Fox, CB 1970; CBE 1962; Chief Land Registrar, 1963-75; *b* 12 April 1910; *s* of late Percy Ruoff and late Edith Crane; *m* 1947, Marjorie Alice, *er d* of late George Mawson, Worthing; no *c*. *Educ:* Clarence School, Weston-super-Mare; King Edward VI School, Bury St Edmunds. Admitted as a solicitor, 1933; 2nd class Hons; Hertfordshire Law Society prizeman; Nuffield Fellowship in Australia and New Zealand, 1951-52; Senior Land Registrar of HM Land Registry, 1958. Member: Council, Soc. for Computers and Law Ltd, 1974; Law Society's Special Cttee on Computer Services, 1976. *Publications:* An Englishman Looks at the Torrens System, 1957; Concise Land Registration Practice, 1959; Rent charges in Registered Conveyancing, 1961; Land Registration Forms, 1962; Curtis and Ruoff's The Law and Practice of Registered Conveyancing (2nd edn, 1965); (with R. B. Roper) Ruoff and Roper's Registered Conveyancing, 1972; Searching without Tears: the Land Charges Computer, 1974; regular contribs to Australian Law Jl, Law Soc.'s Gazette, Solicitors' Jl. *Recreations:* sketching, indifferent golf, gardening. *Address:* Flat One, 83 South Hill Park, Hampstead, NW3 2SS. *T:* 01-435 8014. *Clubs:* Travellers', MCC.

RUPERT'S LAND, Metropolitan of; *see* Athabasca, Bishop of (in Supplementary Pages).

RUPERT'S LAND, Bishop of, since 1970; **Rt. Rev. Barry Valentine,** MA, BD, LTh, DD; *b* 26 Sept. 1927; *s* of Harry John Valentine and Ethel Margaret Purkiss; *m* 1952, Mary Currell Hayes; three *s* one *d*. *Educ:* Brentwood Sch.; St John's Coll., Cambridge; McGill Univ., Montreal. Curate, Christ Church Cath., Montreal, 1952; Incumbent, Chateauguay-Beauharnois, 1954; Dir, Religious Education, Dio. Montreal, 1957; Rector of St Lambert, PQ, 1961; Exec. Officer, Dio. Montreal, 1965; Dean of Montreal, 1968; Bishop Coadjutor of Rupert's Land, 1969; Chancellor, St John's Coll., Winnipeg, 1970. Hon. DD: St John's

Coll., Winnipeg, 1969; Montreal Dio. Theol Coll., 1970. *Recreations:* music, theatre, walking, reading; over-aged and bibulous cricket. *Address:* Anglican Centre, 66 St Cross Street, Winnipeg, Manitoba R2W 3X8, Canada. *T:* 204-589 4347. *Clubs:* Winnipeg Squash Racquet; Taverners Cricket.

RUPP, Rev. Prof. Ernest Gordon, MA, DD Cantab; FBA 1970; Dixie Professor of Ecclesiastical History, University of Cambridge, 1968-77, now Emeritus; Principal, Wesley House, Cambridge, 1967-74; *b* 7 Jan. 1910; *m* 1938, Marjorie Hibbard; one *s. Educ:* Owen's School, EC; King's College, London (BA); Wesley House, Cambridge; Universities of Strasbourg and Basel. Methodist Minister, Chislehurst, Kent, 1938-46; Wesley House, Cambridge, 1946-47; Richmond College, Surrey, 1947-52; Birkbeck Lectr, Trinity Coll., Cambridge, 1947; Lecturer in Divinity, Cambridge Univ., 1952-56; Prof. of Ecclesiastical History, Univ. of Manchester, 1956-67. President of the Methodist Conference, 1968-69; Mem., Central Cttee of World Council of Churches, 1969. Fellow, Emmanuel Coll., 1968; Hon. Fellow: Fitzwilliam College, 1969; King's Coll., London, 1969. Hon. DD Aberdeen; Hon. Dr Théol, Paris. *Publications:* Studies in the English Protestant Tradition, 1947; Luther's Progress to the Diet of Worms, 1951; The Righteousness of God (Luther studies), 1953; Some Makers of English Religion, 1957; The Old Reformation and the New, 1967; Patterns of Reformation, 1969; Just Men, 1977. *Address:* 42 Malcolm Place, King Street, Cambridge.

RUSBRIDGE, Brian John; Secretary, Local Authorities' Conditions of Service Advisory Board, since 1973; Secretary: to all Local Authority National Councils; Burnham Committees for Teachers; Police Council for the United Kingdom; Fire Brigades; Probation Service; Whitley Councils for New Towns Staffs and for Industrial Estates Corporations; Adviser to the States of Jersey and Guernsey; *b* 10 Sept. 1922; *s* of late Arthur John and Leonora Rusbridge, Appleton, Berks; *m* 1951, Joyce, *d* of late Joseph Young Elliott, Darlington; two *s. Educ:* Willowfield Sch., Eastbourne; Univ. of Oxford Dept of Social and Admin. Studies (Dip. Social Admin.). Served War of 1939-45, Lieut RNVR. Personnel Manager, Imperial Chemical Industries (Teesside), 1949; British Railways Board: Dir of Industrial Relations, 1963; Divisional Manager, London, 1970. Companion, Inst. of Personnel Management; Mem., Chartered Inst. of Transport. *Recreations:* walking, gardening. *Address:* 19 Beauchamp Road, East Molesey, Surrey KT8 0PA. *T:* 01-979 4952.

RUSBY, Vice-Adm. Cameron, MVO 1965; Flag Officer Scotland and Northern Ireland, since 1977; *b* 20 Feb. 1926; *s* of Captain Victor Evelyn Rusby, CBE, RN (Rtd), and Mrs Irene Margaret Rusby; *m* 1948, Marion Elizabeth Bell; two *d. Educ:* RNC, Dartmouth. Midshipman 1943; specialised in communications, 1950; CO HMS Ulster, 1958-59; Exec. Officer, HM Yacht Britannia, 1962-65; Dep. Dir, Naval Signals, 1965-68; CO HMS Tartar, 1968-69; Dep. ACOS (Plans and Policy), staff of Allied C-in-C Southern Europe, 1969-72; Sen. Naval Off., WI, 1972-74; Rear-Adm. 1974; ACDS (Ops), 1974-77; Vice-Adm. 1977. *Recreations:* sailing, equitation. *Address:* Yeoman's, Hannington, Basingstoke, Hants. *Club:* Army and Navy.

RUSBY, Norman Lloyd, MA, DM Oxon, FRCP; Consulting Physician: London Hospital since 1970 (Physician, 1946-70); London Chest Hospital since 1970 (Physician, 1936-70); King Edward VII Hospital, Midhurst; Benenden Chest Hospital (Civil Service); Civil Consultant in Diseases of the Chest to the Royal Navy; *b* 26 October 1905; *s* of Dr Edward L. M. Rusby, Streatham and Katharine Helen Rusby (née Wright); *m* 1941, Elizabeth, *e d* of F. A. Broadhead, FRIBA, Nottingham; three *s. Educ:* Lancing College; St John's College, Oxford; St Thomas's Hospital. Res. MO and Registrar, London Chest Hosp., 1934-36; Medical Registrar and Tutor, British Postgraduate Medical School, Hammersmith, 1937-39. Member Standing Advisory Committee on Tuberculosis to Min. of Health, 1940-44; Editor of Tubercle, 1938-44; RAMC Med. specialist (France and Germany), 1944-45; Officer i/c Med. Div., ME Chest Unit, 1945-46; Local Brigadier, Consulting Physician Middle East Land Forces, 1946. Nuffield visitor to East Africa, 1950, 1953. Lecturer for British Council: Poland, 1959; Malta, 1966; Nepal, India and Afghanistan, 1973. Examiner in Medicine: Univ. of London, 1951-56; Univ. of Cambridge, 1957-60; Univ. of W Indies, 1967; RCP, 1962-68. Councillor, RCP, 1964-66; Mitchell Lecturer, RCP, 1967. Mem., Attendance Allowance Bd. Member: Council, Chest, Heart and Stroke Assoc. (Vice-Chm., 1957-77); Assoc. of Physicians of Gt Britain and Ireland; Thoracic Society; Hon. Mem., Brit. Thoracic and Tuberculosis Assoc. Mem., Board of Governors: Hospitals for Diseases of the Chest, 1962-67; London Hospital, 1967-70. *Publications:* (jtly) Recent Advances in Respiratory Tuberculosis, 4th and 5th edns,

(ed jtly) 6th edn 1968; contributions to various journals, chiefly on diseases of the chest. *Address:* 80 Harley Street, W1. *T:* 01-935 2007; 21 Windmill Hill, Hampstead, NW3. *T:* 01-794 6889. *Club:* United Oxford & Cambridge University.

RUSH, Most Rev. Francis Roberts; *see* Brisbane, Archbishop of, (RC).

RUSHBROOK WILLIAMS, L. F.; *see* Williams.

RUSHBROOKE, Prof. G(eorge) Stanley, MA, PhD; FRSE; Professor of Theoretical Physics, University of Newcastle upon Tyne, since 1951; *b* 19 January 1915; *s* of George Henry Rushbrooke and Frances Isobel Rushbrooke (née Wright), Willenhall, Staffs; *m* 1949, Thelma Barbara Cox (*d* 1977). *Educ:* Wolverhampton Grammar School; St John's College, Cambridge. Schol. St John's Coll., Camb., 1933-37; Research Asst, Bristol Univ., 1938-39; Senior DSIR award and Carnegie Teaching Fellowship, 1939-44, UC Dundee, Univ. of St Andrews; Lectr in Mathematical Chemistry, The Univ., Leeds, 1944-48; Sen. Lectr in Theoretical Physics, Oxford, Univ. and Lecturer in Mathematics, University Coll., Oxford, 1948-51; Visiting Prof., Dept of Chemistry, Univ. of Oregon, USA, 1962-63; Vis. Prof. of Physics and Chemistry, Rice Univ., Houston, 1967. *Publications:* Introduction to Statistical Mechanics, 1949; research papers in scientific journals. *Address:* The University, Newcastle upon Tyne NE1 7RU.

RUSHFORD, Antony Redfern, CMG 1963; HM Diplomatic Service; Deputy Legal Adviser, Foreign and Commonwealth Office, since 1969; *b* 9 February 1922; *m* 1975, Mrs June Jeffery Wells; one step *s* one step *d. Educ:* Taunton School; Trinity College, Cambridge. RAFVR, 1943-47, Sqdn Ldr, 1946. Admitted a Solicitor, 1944 (removed from roll at own request, 1957). BA, LLB 1948; MA 1951; Student, Inner Temple, 1957. Colonial Office: Legal Asst, 1949-54; Senior Legal Assistant, 1954-60; Assistant Legal Adviser, 1960-66; Legal Counsellor, FCO (formerly CO), 1966-69. Foundn Mem. Exec. Council, Royal Commonwealth Soc. for the Blind, 1969-. *Address:* 12 Chester Row, SW1W 9JH. *T:* 01-730 2811; 9 Moorland Avenue, Barton on Sea, New Milton, Hants BH25 7DB. *T:* New Milton 615325.

RUSHTON, Frederick Alan; Director, Northern Counties Board, Legal and General Assurance Society Ltd, 1969-73; formerly Chief General Manager and Director, District Bank Ltd, Manchester; *b* 15 Feb. 1905; *s* of Frederick and Elizabeth Rushton; *m* 1931, Eirene Williams; two *s. Educ:* University Sch., Southport, Lancs. Mem. Court, Univ. of Manchester. FIB. *Recreations:* foreign travel, gardening. *Address:* Gortmore, Broadway, Hale, Cheshire. *T:* 061-980 4809.

RUSHTON, Sir Reginald (Fielding), Kt 1971; Chairman, MacRobertson Miller Airlines Ltd (MMA), since 1955; Chairman, Sydney Atkinson Motors Ltd; Director: Ansett Transport Industries Ltd, since 1969. Has given outstanding service to the community in Western Australia. Chairman: the Princess Margaret Hospital Board of Management, Perth, Western Australia; Medical Research Foundation. *Address:* MacRobertson Miller Airline Services, 194 St George's Terrace, Perth, Western Australia 6000, Australia. *T:* 21 2821 and 21 2691; (private) 50 Jutland Parade, Dalkeith, Perth, WA 6009, Australia. *T:* 86.2572.

RUSHTON, William Albert Hugh, FRS 1948; ScD, PhD, MA, MRCS, LRCP; Fellow, Trinity College, Cambridge, since 1938 (Director of Medical Studies, 1938-63); *b* 8 December 1901; *er s* of William and Alice Rushton, Harley Street and Hampstead, London; *m* 1930, Marjorie, 2nd *d* of Norman Kendrick, Cardiff; two *s* two *d. Educ:* Gresham's, Holt; Emmanuel Coll., Cambridge; University Coll. Hosp., London; Stokes Student Pembroke Coll., Cambridge, 1927; Johnson Fellow, Univ. Pennsylvania, 1929; Research Fellow, Emmanuel Coll., 1931; Lectr in Physiology, Cambridge University, 1935-53; Reader, 1953-65; Prof. of Visual Physiology, Cambridge Univ., 1966-68, Emeritus Prof., 1977. Distinguished Res. Prof. in Psychobiology, Florida State Univ., Tallahassee, 1968-76. Vis. Prof., Univ. of Sydney, 1973-74; Vis. Fellow, ANU, 1973-74. Hon. Member: American Academy of Arts and Sciences, 1963; Swedish Royal Soc., 1968; Physiological Soc., 1973. Ferrier Lectr, Royal Soc., 1962; Silliman Lectr, Yale Univ., 1966; Waynflete Lectr, Magdalen Coll., Oxford, 1968; Fogarty Internat. Scholar, NIH, USA, 1972-73. First Prentice Medallist, Amer. Acad. Optometry, 1963; Feldberg Prize, 1967; Royal Medal, Royal Soc., 1970; Proctor Medal, USA, 1971; Kenneth Craik Award, St John's Coll., Cambridge, 1973. Hon. DSc Case Western Reserve Univ., 1969. *Publications:* papers in Jl of Physiology, Proc. Roy. Soc., etc. *Recreation:* music (viola and bassoon). *Address:* Trinity College, Cambridge; Shawms, Conduit Head Road, Cambridge. *T:* 54742.

RUSK, Dean, KBE (Hon.) 1976; Professor of International Law, University of Georgia School of Law, Athens, Georgia, since 1971; *b* 9 February 1909; *s* of Robert Hugh Rusk and Frances Elizabeth Clotfelter; *m* 1937, Virginia Foisie; two *s* one *d. Educ:* Davidson College, North Carolina; St John's College, Oxford. Assoc. Prof. of Government and Dean of Faculty, Mills Coll., 1934-40; US Army, 1940-46; Special Asst to Secretary of War, 1946; US Dept of State, 1947-51; Asst Sec. of State for UN Affairs, 1949; Dep. Under Sec. of State, 1949-50; Asst Sec. of State for Far Eastern Affairs, 1950-51; Sec. of State, 1961-69; President, The Rockefeller Foundation, 1952-61, Distinguished Fellow, 1969-. Hon. Fellow, St John's Coll., Oxford, 1955. Hon. LLD: Mills Coll., Calif, 1948; Davidson Coll., 1950; Univ. of Calif, 1961; Emory Univ., Georgia, 1961; Princeton Univ., NJ, 1961; Louisiana State Univ. 1962; Amherst Coll., 1962; Columbia Univ., 1963; Harvard Univ., 1963; Rhode Island Univ., 1963; Valparaiso Univ., 1964; Williams Coll., 1964; Univ. of N Carolina, 1964; George Washington Univ., 1965; Oberlin Coll., 1965; Maryville Coll., 1965; Denver Univ., 1966; Erskine Coll., 1967. Hon. DCL Oxford, 1962; Hon. LHD: Westminster Coll., 1962; Hebrew Union Coll., 1963; Hardin-Simmons Univ., 1967. Cecil Peace Prize, 1933. Legion of Merit (Oak Leaf Cluster). *Address:* 1 Lafayette Square, 620 Hill Street, Athens, Ga 30601, USA.

RUSSELL; *see* Hamilton-Russell.

RUSSELL, family name of **Duke of Bedford, Earl Russell, Baron Ampthill, Baron de Clifford, Baron Russell of Killowen** and **Baron Russell of Liverpool.**

RUSSELL, 4th Earl *cr* 1861; **John Conrad Russell;** Viscount Amberley, 1861; *b* 16 Nov. 1921; *er s* of 3rd Earl Russell, OM, FRS, and Dora Winifred, MBE, *d* of late Sir Frederick Black, KCB; *S* father, 1970; *m* 1946, Susan Doniphan (marr. diss. 1954), *d* of late Vachel Lindsay; one *d* (and one *d* decd). *Educ:* Dartington Hall School; University of California, Los Angeles; Harvard University. Served War of 1939-45, in RNVR, 1943-46; Temp. Admin. Asst, FAO of the United Nations, Washington, DC, 1946-47; temp. Admin. Asst, HM Treasury, 1947-49. Took his seat in the House of Lords, 12 May 1976. *Heir:* half-brother Hon. Conrad Sebastian Robert Russell [*b* 15 April 1937; *m* 1962, Elizabeth Franklin, *e d* of Horace Sanders; two *s*]. *Address:* Carn Voel, Porthcurno, near Penzance, Cornwall.

RUSSELL OF KILLOWEN, Baron *cr* 1975 (Life Peer), of Killowen, Co. Down; **Charles Ritchie Russell,** PC 1962; Kt 1960; a Lord of Appeal in Ordinary, since 1975; *b* 12 Jan. 1908; *s* of Francis Xavier, Baron Russell of Killowen, Lord Chief Justice of England) and Mary Emily Ritchie (*d* of 1st Baron Ritchie of Dundee, former Chancellor of Exchequer); *m* 1933, Joan Elisabeth (*d* 1976), *d* of late Dr J. A. Torrens, MD, FRCP; two *s* one *d. Educ:* Beaumont; Oriel College, Oxford. Called to Bar, Lincoln's Inn, 1931; QC 1948; Bencher, 1952; Treasurer, 1972. Army, 1939-45; RA (Airborne) (despatches, French Croix de Guerre with star). Attorney-General to the Duchy of Cornwall, 1951-60; Judge of Chancery Division, High Court of Justice, 1960-62; a Lord Justice of Appeal, 1962-75. President, Restrictive Practices Court, 1961-62 (Member, 1960-62). *Recreation:* golf. *Address:* Orchard House, Sheepdown, Petworth, West Sussex. *T:* Petworth 42657. *Clubs:* Garrick, Beefsteak.

RUSSELL OF LIVERPOOL, 2nd Baron, *cr* 1919; **Edward Frederick Langley Russell,** CBE 1945 (OBE 1943); MC; Barrister-at-Law, Gray's Inn, 1931; *b* 10 April 1895; *o s* of Richard Henry Langley Russell and Mabel Younge; *S* grandfather, 1920; *m* 1946, Alix (*d* 1971), *o d* of Marquis de Bréviaire d'Alaincourt, and *widow* of Comte Bernard de Richard d'Ivry; *m* 1972, Mrs A. W. Brayley (*d* 1977); two *d* (one *s* decd) of previous marriages. *Educ:* Liverpool Coll.; St John's Coll., Oxford. Served European War, 1914-18 (MC and two bars); War of 1939-45 (despatches, OBE, CBE); Brig. (retd); ADJAG, BEF, 1939-40; DJAG, HQ First Army, 1942-43; Allied Force HQ, 1943-45; GHQ Middle East Forces, 1945-46; HQ BAOR, 1946-47, 1948-51; Assistant Judge Advocate General, 1951-54. Officier de la Légion d'Honneur, 1960. *Publications:* The Scourge of the Swastika, 1954; Though the Heavens Fall, 1956; The Knights of Bushido, 1958; That Reminds Me, 1959; If I forget Thee, 1960; The Royal Conscience, 1961; The Trial of Adolf Eichmann, 1962; The Tragedy of the Congo, 1962; South Africa Today-and Tomorrow?, 1963; The Knight of the Sword, 1964; Deadman's Hill, 1965; Caroline the Unhappy Queen, 1967; Return of the Swastika?, 1968; Henry of Navarre, 1969; The French Corsairs, 1970. *Heir: g s* Simon Gordon Jared Russell, *b* 30 Aug. 1952. *Address:* 53 The Drive, Hove, Sussex. *Club:* Wig and Pen.

RUSSELL, Alan; Director: Alexanders Discount Co. Ltd; IBM United Kingdom Ltd; National Westminster Bank Ltd; Yorkshire Bank Ltd; *b* 5 Dec. 1910; *s* of late Hon. Cyril Russell; *m* 1st, 1937, Grace Evelyn Moore (decd); one *d* ; 2nd, 1944, Jean Patricia, *widow* of Wing Comdr J. R. Cridland, AAF, and *d* of late Stafford Croom Johnson, JP; one step *s* one *s. Educ:* Beaumont. Served War of 1939-45, in Army, London Scottish, Lt-Col, attached US Army, Europe, 1941-45. *Address:* 23 Rutland Gate, SW7.

RUSSELL, Albert Muir Galloway, QC (Scot.) 1965; Sheriff of Grampian, Highland and Islands (formerly Aberdeen, Kincardine and Banff) at Aberdeen and Stonehaven, since 1971; *b* 26 Oct. 1925; *s* of Hon. Lord Russell; *m* 1954, Margaret Winifred, *o d* of T. McW Millar, FRCS(E), Edinburgh; two *s* two *d. Educ:* Edinburgh Academy; Wellington College; Brasenose College, Oxford. BA (Hons) Oxon, 1949; LLB (Edin.), 1951. Lieut, Scots Guards, 1944-47. Member of Faculty of Advocates, 1951-. *Recreation:* golf. *Address:* Enfield, Craigton Road, Aberdeen. *T:* Aberdeen 47160. *Club:* Royal Northern (Aberdeen).

RUSSELL, Anna; International Concert Comedienne; *b* 27 Dec. 1911; *d* of Col C. Russell-Brown, CB, DSO, RE, and Beatrice M. Tandy; single. *Educ:* St Felix School, Southwold; Royal College of Music, London. Folk singer, BBC, 1935-40; Canadian Broadcasting Corp. programmes, 1942-46; Radio interviewer, CBC, 1945-46; Debut, Town Hall, New York, as concert comedienne, 1948; Broadway show, Anna Russell and her Little Show, 1953; Towns of USA, Canada, Great Britain, Australia, New Zealand, the Orient and South Africa, 1948-60. Television, Radio Summer Theatre, USA; recordings, Columbia Masterworks. Resident in Australia, 1968-75. Mayfair Theatre, London, 1976. *Publications:* The Power of Being a Positive Stinker (NY); The Anna Russell Song Book. *Recreation:* gardening. *Address:* No 16, 1148 W Huntington Drive, Arcadia, Calif 91006, USA. *Club:* Zouta International (USA, Toronto Branch, Internat. Mem.).

RUSSELL, Sir Archibald (Edward), Kt 1972; CBE 1954; FRS 1970; Joint Chairman, Concorde Executive Committee of Directors, 1965-69; Vice-Chairman, BAC-Sud Aviation Concorde Committee, 1969-70, retired; *b* 30 May 1904; *m* ; one *s* one *d. Educ:* Fairfield Secondary Sch.; Bristol Univ. Joined Bristol Aeroplane Co. Ltd, 1926; Chief Technician, 1931; Technical Designer, 1938; Chief Engineer, 1944; Dir, 1951; Tech. Dir, 1960-66; Chm., British Aircraft Corporation, Filton Div., 1967-69 (Man. Dir, 1966-67). Wright Bros Memorial Lecture, Washington, 1949; 42nd Wilbur Wright Memorial Lecture, London, 1954; RAeS British Gold Medal, 1951; David Guggenheim Medal, 1971; Hon. DSc Bristol, 1951. CEng; FIAeS; Hon FRAeS 1967. *Publications:* papers in R&M Series of Aeronautical Research Cttee and RAeS Journal. *Address:* 2 Glendower House, Clifton Park, Bristol BS9 1BP. *T:* Bristol 39208.

RUSSELL, Rev. Arthur Colin, CMG 1957; ED; MA; *b* 1906; *e s* of late Arthur W. Russell, OBE, WS; *m* 1939, Elma (*d* 1967), *d* of late Douglas Strachan, Hon. RSA; three *d. Educ:* Harrow; Brasenose College, Oxford. Barrister-at-law, Inner Temple. Cadet, Gold Coast (now Ghana), 1929; Asst Dist Comr, 1930; Dist Comr, 1940; Judicial Adviser, 1947; Senior, 1951; Regional Officer, 1952; Permanent Sec., Min. of Education and Social Welfare, 1953; Governor's Secretary, 1954; Chief Regional Officer, Ashanti, 1955-57, retd. Trained for the Ministry, 1957-59; Ordained (Church of Scotland), 1959; Parish Minister, Aberlemno, 1959-76; retd. District Councillor, Angus District, 1977. *Publication:* Stained Glass Windows of Douglas Strachan, 1972. *Address:* Aberlemno, Forfar, Angus. *T:* Aberlemno 265. *Club:* New (Edinburgh).

RUSSELL, Audrey; *see* Russell, M. A.

RUSSELL, Barbara Winifred, MA; Headmistress, Berkhamsted School for Girls, 1950-July 1971; *b* 5 Jan. 1910; *er d* of Lionel Wilfred and Elizabeth Martin Russell. *Educ:* St Oran's School, Edinburgh; Edinburgh University; Oxford University, Dept of Education. History Mistress, Brighton and Hove High School, 1932-38; Senior History Mistress, Roedean School, 1938-49. *Recreations:* reading, gardening, travel. *Address:* 1 Beech Road, Thame, Oxon. *T:* Thame 2738. *Club:* East India, Devonshire, Sports and Public Schools.

RUSSELL, Ben Harold; Vice-President, Scientific Development Corporation, 1964-72; Chairman, SDC (GB) Ltd, 1964-72; Associate Director, The Dorchester Hotel, since 1964; Director, Cunard House Ltd, 1962-63; *o s* of late John and Clara Russell; *m* 1926, Evelyn Scotney White (*d* 1967), Melbourne, Australia; one *s*; 2nd, 1968, Elizabeth Gertrude Boor. *Educ:* privately; Christ Church, Cheltenham. Served War of 1914-18 (despatches). Entered service of Cunard Steamship Co. Ltd, 1906, Dir 1947-62, Dep. Gen. Manager, 1947-56; Director: Cunard White Star Ltd, 1947-56; Cunard House Ltd, 1962-63. Member of Board, Travel Assoc., 1946-50; Member Board British Travel and Holidays Assoc. (as rep. British Liner Cttee) on formation of Board, 1950-64, first Vice-President, 1964; Member of the London Tourist Board on formation, 1962 (Vice-Chairman, 1965, Chairman, 1966-68, Vice-President, 1968-75); Rep. International Chamber of Shipping at UN Conf. on Tourism, Rome, 1963. Member Board of Governors, University College Hospital, 1951-66; Member Whitley Councils for the Health Services (GB) Medical Council, 1953-66; Vice-President, Institute of Travel Managers; Chairman, US Sect., London Chamber of Commerce, 1964-68; Vice-Chm., Exec. Assoc. of Great Britain, 1941-43; Mem. Inst. of Directors; Liveryman, Worshipful Company of Shipwrights; Freeman, City of London. Member, The Pilgrims. FRSA. Meritorious Service Medal, 1917; Chevalier Order of Orange-Nassau, 1947. *Address:* 11A Lincoln House, Basil Street, SW3. *T:* 01-589 9157. *Clubs:* Naval and Military, Canada, Saints and Sinners, Anchorites.

RUSSELL, Brian Fitzgerald, MD, FRCP; Consulting Physician, formerly Physician, Department of Dermatology, The London Hospital (1951-69); Consulting Physician, formerly Physician, St John's Hospital for Diseases of the Skin (1947-69); formerly Civilian Consultant in Dermatology to the Royal Navy (1955-69); past Dean, Institute of Dermatology; *b* 1 Sept. 1904; *s* of Dr John Hutchinson Russell and Helen Margaret (*née* Collingwood); *m* 1932, Phyllis Daisy Woodward; three *s* one *d*. *Educ:* Merchant Taylors' School. MD (London) 1929; FRCP 1951; DPH (Eng.) 1943. Medical First Asst, London Hosp., 1930-32; general medical practice, 1933-45; Dermatologist, Prince of Wales's Hosp., Tottenham, 1946-51; Asst Physician, Dept of Dermatology St Bartholomew's Hosp., 1946-51. President: St John's Hosp. Dermatological Soc., 1958-60; Dermatological Sect., RSM, 1968-69 (Hon. Mem., 1977); Corr. Mem.: American Dermatological Soc.; Danish Dermatological Soc. *Publications:* St John's Hospital for Diseases of the Skin, 1863-1963, 1963; (with Eric Wittkower) Emotional Factors in Skin Diseases, 1953; Section on Dermatology in Price's Medicine (ed by Bodley Scott), 1973. *Recreation:* rustication. *Address:* Parsonage Farm Cottage, Arkesden, Saffron Walden, Essex CB11 4EX. *T:* Clavering 379.

RUSSELL, Cecil Anthony Francis; Director of Intelligence, Greater London Council, 1970-76; *b* 7 June 1921; *s* of late Comdr S. F. Russell, OBE, RN retd and Mrs M. E. Russell (*née* Sneyd-Kynnersley); *m* 1950, Editha May (*née* Birch); no *c*. *Educ:* Winchester Coll.; University Coll., Oxford (1940-41, 1945-47). Civil Service, 1949-70: Road Research Lab., 1949-50; Air Min., 1950-62; Dep. Statistical Adviser, Home Office, 1962-67; Head of Census Div., General Register Office, 1967-70. FSS. *Recreation:* ocean sailing. *Address:* Pagan Hill, Whiteleaf, Princes Risborough, Bucks. *T:* Princes Risborough 3655. *Club:* Cruising Association.

RUSSELL, Sir Charles Ian, 3rd Bt, *cr* 1916; partner in Charles Russell & Co., Hale Court, Lincoln's Inn, WC2; Captain, RHA (despatches); *b* 13 March 1918; *s* of Captain Sir Alec Charles Russell, 2nd Bt, and Monica (who *m* 2nd, 1942, Brig. John Victor Faviell, CBE, MC), *d* of Hon. Sir Charles Russell, 1st Bt; *S* father, 1938; *m* 1947, Rosemary, *er d* of late Sir John Prestige; one *s* one *d*. *Educ:* Beaumont College; University College, Oxford. Admitted Solicitor, 1947. *Recreation:* golf. *Heir: s* Charles Dominic Russell, *b* 28 May 1956. *Address:* 35 Coleherne Court, Little Boltons, SW5; Hidden House, Sandwich, Kent. *Clubs:* Garrick, Army and Navy; Royal St George's (Sandwich).

RUSSELL, Rev. David Syme, MA, BD, DLitt; General Secretary, Baptist Union of Great Britain and Ireland, since 1967; *b* 21 Nov. 1916; second *s* of Peter Russell and Janet Marshall Syme; *m* 1943, Marion Hamilton Campbell; one *s* one *d*. *Educ:* Scottish Baptist Coll., Glasgow; Trinity Coll., Glasgow Univ. (MA, BD, DLitt); Regent's Park Coll.; Oxford Univ. (MA, BLitt). Minister of Baptist Churches: Berwick, 1939-41; Oxford, 1943-45; Acton, 1945-53. Principal of Rawdon Coll., Leeds, and lectr in Old Testament languages and literature, 1953-64; Joint Principal of the Northern Baptist College, Manchester, 1964-67. Moderator, Free Church Federal Council, 1974-75. Mem., Central Cttee, WCC, 1968-.

Publications: Between the Testaments, 1960; Two Refugees (Ezekiel and Second Isaiah), 1962; The Method and Message of Jewish Apocalyptic, 1964; The Jews from Alexander to Herod, 1967; contrib. to Encyc. Britannica, 1963. *Recreation:* woodwork. *Address:* 33 Friars Walk, Southgate, N14 5LL. *T:* 01-368 2915.

RUSSELL, David Sturrock W.; *see* West-Russell.

RUSSELL, Donald Andrew Frank Moore, FBA 1971; Fellow and Tutor, St John's College, Oxford since 1948; *b* 13 Oct. 1920; *s* of Samuel Charles Russell (schoolmaster) and Laura Moore; *m* 1967, Joycelyne Gledhill Dickinson. *Educ:* King's College Sch., Wimbledon; Balliol Coll., Oxford (MA). Served War: Army (R Signals and Intelligence Corps), 1941-45. Craven Scholar, 1946; Lectr, Christ Church, Oxford, 1947; Fellow of St John's Coll., 1948; Dean, 1957-64; Tutor for Admissions, 1968-72. Co-editor, Classical Quarterly, 1965-70. *Publications:* Commentary on Longinus, On the Sublime, 1964; Ancient Literary Criticism (with M. Winterbottom), 1972; Plutarch, 1972; articles and reviews in classical periodicals. *Recreations:* walking, gardening. *Address:* 47 Woodstock Road, Oxford. *T:* Oxford 56135.

RUSSELL, Dorothy Stuart, MD (London); MA (Oxon); ScD (Cantab); LLD (Glasgow); DSc (McGill); FRCP; retired 1960; Director of Bernhard Baron Institute of Pathology, London Hospital; Professor of Morbid Anatomy in University of London, 1946-60, Emeritus Professor, 1960; Hon. Fellow: Girton College, Cambridge; St Hugh's College, Oxford; *b* 27 June 1895; 2nd *d* of late Philip Stuart Russell, Sydney, NSW, and Alice Louisa, *d* of William Cave. *Educ:* Perse High School for Girls, Cambridge; Girton College, Cambridge; London Hospital. Natural Sciences Tripos, Part I, Class I, 1918; Gilchrist Studentship, Girton College, 1918; Sutton Prize in Pathology and Clinical Obstetrics and Gynæcology Prize, London Hospital, 1921; Junior Beit Fellow, 1923-26, attached to Bernhard Baron Institute of Pathology, London Hospital, and subsequently with grants from Medical Research Council; Rockefeller Travelling Fellow, 1928-29, at Boston, Mass, and Montreal; Medical Research Council, Scientific Staff, 1933-46. Attached to Nuffield Dept of Surgery, Oxford, 1940-44; returned to London Hospital, Oct. 1944. John Hunter Medal and Triennial Prize, Royal College of Surgeons, 1934, for work on the kidney and the brain; Oliver-Sharpey Prize, RCP, 1968, for research. Hon. FRCPath 1973. *Publications:* Tumours of the Nervous System; papers in pathology to various journals. *Address:* Holcombe End, Westcott, Dorking, Surrey.

RUSSELL, Lt.-Gen. Sir Dudley, KBE 1950 (CBE 1944); CB 1945; DSO 1942; MC; late IA, retired; *b* 1 Dec. 1896; *m* 1929, Elizabeth, *d* of Sandys Birket Foster, New York, USA. Served Eritrea and Abyssinia, 1941 (OBE); Western Desert, 1942 (DSO); Italy, 1944-45 (CBE, CB, Commander Order of the American Legion of Merit); Chief British Adviser to Indian Army, 1948-54; retd 1954. *Address:* c/o Barclays Bank, Nassau, Bahamas.

RUSSELL, Sir (Edward) Lionel, Kt 1962; CBE 1953; *b* 8 May 1903; *s* of Edward and Kate Russell, Bristol. *Educ:* Clifton College; Christ's College, Cambridge. Lecturer in English, Univ. of Lund, Sweden, 1925-31; Assistant Master, Charterhouse, 1932-35; Asst Director of Education, Liverpool, 1935-38; Asst Education Officer, Birmingham, 1938-46; Chief Education Officer, Birmingham, 1946-68. Member: Univ. Grants Cttee, 1954-63; Council for Nat. Academic Awards, 1964-70; Nat. Cttee for Commonwealth Immigrants, 1965-68; Chairman: Inquiry into Adult Educn in England and Wales, 1969-73; Centre for Educnl Develt Overseas, 1970-74; Nat. Adv. Council on Educn for Industry and Commerce, 1975-; Youth Employment Service Training Bd, 1970-75. Pres., Assoc. of Chief Education Officers, 1955-57. Hon. ACT Birmingham, 1962; Hon. DEd CNAA, 1969; Hon. DLitt Warwick, 1974; Hon. LLD Birmingham, 1975. *Address:* 24 Tyndall's Park Road, Bristol BS8 1PY. *T:* Bristol 37121. *Club:* Athenæum.

RUSSELL, Edward Walter, CMG 1960; MA Cantab, PhD Cantab; Professor of Soil Science, Reading University, 1964-70, now Professor Emeritus; *b* Wye, Kent, 27 Oct. 1904; *e s* of late Sir (Edward) John Russell, OBE, FRS; *m* 1933, Margaret, *y d* of late Sir Hugh Calthrop Webster; one *s* two *d*. *Educ:* Oundle; Gonville and Caius College, Cambridge. Soil Physicist, Rothamsted Experimental Station, Harpenden, 1930-48; Reader in Soil Science, Oxford Univ., 1948-55; Director, East African Agriculture and Forestry Research Organisation, 1955-64. Member: Scientific Council for Africa, 1956-63; Agricultural Research Council of Central Africa, 1959-64. Pres., British Soc. of Soil Science, 1968-70. FInstP; FIBiol; FIAgrE. For. Corr. Mem., French Acad. of Agriculture, 1969. Hon. Councillor,

Consejo Superior de Investigations Cientificas, Madrid, 1970. Hon DSc Univ. of East Africa, 1970. *Publications:* 8th, 9th and 10th Editions of Soil Conditions and Plant Growth; contrib. on physics and chemistry of soils to agricultural and soil science journals. *Address:* 31 Brooklyn Drive, Emmer Green, Reading, Berks RG4 8SR. *T:* Reading 472934.

RUSSELL, Edwin John Cumming, ARBS 1969; sculptor; *b* 4 May 1939; *s* of Edwin Russell and Mary Elizabeth Russell; *m* 1964, Lorne McKean (sculptor; commnd by the Queen for her personal silver wedding gift to Prince Philip—Prince Philip riding polo pony); two *d*. *Educ:* Brighton Coll. of Art and Crafts; Royal Academy Schs (CertRAS). *Works:* Crucifix, pulpit, St Paul's Cathedral, 1964; St Catherine, Little Cloister, Westminster Abbey, 1966; St Michael, Chapel of St Michael and St George, St Paul's Cath., 1970; commnd to carve new figures on exterior of St Paul's Cath., 1971. Royal Academy Gold Medal for Sculpture, 1960. *Recreation:* philosophy. *Address:* Lethendry, Polecat Valley, Hindhead, Surrey GU26 6BE. *T:* Hindhead 5655.

RUSSELL, Evelyn Charles Sackville; Metropolitan Stipendiary Magistrate since 1961; *b* 2 Dec. 1912; *s* of late Henry Frederick Russell and late Kathleen Isabel, *d* of Richard Morphy; *m* 1939, Joan, *er d* of Harold Edward Jocelyn Camps; one *d*. *Educ:* Douai School; Château de Mesnières, Seine Maritime, France. Hon. Artillery Co., 1938. Served War of 1939-45, Royal Artillery, in UK, N Africa, Italy and Greece. Called to the Bar (Gray's Inn), 1945. *Recreations:* tennis, racing. *Address:* The Gate House, Coopersale, Epping, Essex. *T:* Epping 72568. *Club:* Garrick.

RUSSELL, Sir Frederick (Stratten), Kt 1965; CBE 1955; DSC, DFC; FRS 1938; BA Cantab; Secretary to Marine Biological Association of the United Kingdom and Director of the Plymouth Laboratory, 1945-65, retd; *b* Bridport, 3 Nov. 1897; *y s* of late William Russell, MA Oxon, Newquay, and late Lucy Binfield, *d* of Henry Newman, Liverpool; *m* 1923, Gweneth, MBE, *d* of late John and late Mary Barnhouse Moy Evans; one *s*. *Educ:* Oundle School; Gonville and Caius College, Cambridge. Served European War, RNAS and RAF, 1916-18 (DSC, DFC, French Croix de Guerre); Interallied Belgian Coast Defence Committee, 1919; Assistant Director of Fisheries Research to Government of Egypt, 1922-23; on scientific staff of Marine Biological Association's Laboratory, Plymouth, Devon, 1924-65; Great Barrier Reef Expedition, 1928-29; served War of 1939-45 as Wing Comdr on Air Staff Intelligence, 1940-45. Colonial Fisheries Advisory Cttee, 1945-61; Min. Overseas Devlt Fisheries Advisory Panel, 1961-; National Oceanographic Council, 1950-65; Chairman, Advisory Panel on biological research to Central Electricity Generating Board, 1962-75; Trustee, Nat. Maritime Museum, 1965-72; Pres. Devonshire Association, 1953. Editor, Journal of Marine Biological Association, 1945-65; Advances in Marine Biology, 1962-. Hon. LLD Glasgow, 1957; Hon. DSc: Exeter, 1960; Birmingham, 1966; Bristol, 1972. Coronation Medal. Linnean Soc. Gold Medal, 1961. Hon. Fellow, Gonville and Caius Coll., Cambridge. For. Mem. Roy. Danish Acad.; Hon. Member: Physiological Soc.; Challenger Soc.; Fisheries Soc. of British Isles. *Publications:* The Seas (with C. M. Yonge), 1928; The Medusae of the British Isles, 1953, vol. II, 1970; The Eggs and Planktonic Stages of British Marine Fishes, 1976; numerous scientific publications on biology of marine plankton invertebrates and fishes, in scientific journals, and on marine biology in Britannica Book of The Year, 1949-70. *Recreations:* angling, sketching. *Address:* Wardour, 295 Tavistock Road, Plymouth, Devon PL6 8AA. *T:* Plymouth 772887; The Laboratory, Citadel Hill, Plymouth. *T:* Plymouth 21761.

RUSSELL, Sir George Michael, 7th Bt, *cr* 1812; *b* 30 Sept. 1908; *s* of Sir Arthur Edward Ian Montagu Russell, 6th Bt, MBE and late Aileen Kerr, *y d* of Admiral Mark Robert Pechell; *S* father, 1964; *m* 1936, Joy Frances Bedford, *d* of late W. Mitchell, Irwin, Western Australia; two *d*. *Educ:* Radley, Berkshire, England. *Heir:* half-b Arthur Mervyn Russell, *b* 7 Feb. 1923.
See also Baron Broughshane.

RUSSELL, Sir Gordon; see Russell, Sir S. G.

RUSSELL, Henry Stanway; His Honour Judge Russell; a Circuit Judge (formerly County Court Judge), since 1965; *b* 27 April 1910; *s* of William Stanway Russell and Dorothy Sophia Taylor; *m* 1937, Norah Patricia Knight Tapson; two *d*. *Educ:* Haileybury College; Merton College, Oxford. Called to Bar Inner Temple, 1934; Western Circuit, 1934. 1st Derbyshire Yeomanry RAC (Lieut). Served Tunisia and Italy, 1942-44. Capt., Judge Advocate General's Dept., 1945; Dep. Chm., Cornwall QS, 1963-71. *Address:* The Manor, Hinton Bluett, Temple Cloud, near Bristol. *T:* Temple Cloud 52259.

RUSSELL, Prof. James Knox, MD; ChB; FRCOG; Professor of Obstetrics and Gynæcology, and Postgraduate Dean, University of Newcastle upon Tyne; Consulting Obstetrician, Princess Mary Maternity Hospital; Consultant Gynæcologist, Royal Victoria Infirmary, Newcastle upon Tyne, since 1956; *b* 5 Sept. 1919; *s* of James Russell, Aberdeen; *m* 1944, Cecillia V. Urquhart, MD, DCH, *o d* of Patrick Urquhart, MA; three *d*. *Educ:* Aberdeen Grammar School; University of Aberdeen. MB, ChB 1942, MD 1954, Aberdeen; MRCOG 1949; FRCOG 1958. First Assistant to Prof. of Obstetrics and Gynæcology, Univ. of Durham, 1950; Senior Lecturer in Obstetrics and Gynæcology, Univ. of Durham, 1956; Consultant Obstetrician, Princess Mary Maternity Hosp., 1956; Consultant Gynæcologist, Royal Victoria Infirmary, Newcastle upon Tyne, 1956. Hon. Obstetrician, MRC Unit on Reproduction and Growth; Examiner in Obstetrics and Gynæcology, Univs of London, Birmingham, Aberdeen, and Liverpool; Consultant in human reproduction, WHO. Served War, 1943-46, as MO in RAF, UK and Western Europe. *Publications:* various papers on obstetrical and gynæcological subjects to learned journals. *Recreations:* photography and gardening. *Address:* Newlands, Tranwell Woods, Morpeth, Northumberland NE61 6AG. *T:* Morpeth 55666. *Club:* Royal Over-Seas League.

RUSSELL, John, CBE 1975; Art critic, The New York Times, since 1974; *b* 1919; *o s* of Isaac James Russell and Harriet Elizabeth Atkins; *m* 1st, 1946, Alexandrine Apponyi (marr. diss., 1950); one *d*; 2nd, 1956, Vera Poliakoff (marr. diss., 1971); 3rd, 1975, Rosamond Bernier. *Educ:* St Paul's Sch.; Magdalen Coll., Oxford (BA). Hon. Attaché, Tate Gall., 1940-41; MOI, 1941-43; Naval Intell. Div., Admty, 1943-46. Regular contributor, The Sunday Times, 1945-, art critic, 1949-74. Mem. art panel, Arts Council, 1958-68. Organised Arts Council exhibns: Modigliani, 1964, Rouault, 1966 and Balthus, 1968 (all at Tate Gallery); Pop Art (with Suzi Gablik), 1969 (at the Hayward Gallery); organised Vuillard exhibn (Toronto, Chicago, San Francisco), 1971. Grand Medal of Honour (Austria), 1972; Officier de l'Ordre des Arts et des Lettres, 1975. *Publications:* books include: Shakespeare's Country, 1942; British Portrait Painters, 1945; Switzerland, 1950; Logan Pearsall Smith, 1950; Erich Kleiber, 1956; Paris, 1960; Seurat, 1965; Private View (with Bryan Robertson and Lord Snowdon), 1965; Max Ernst, 1967; Henry Moore, 1968; Ben Nicholson, 1969; Pop Art Redefined (with Suzi Gablik), 1969; The World of Matisse, 1970; Francis Bacon, 1971; Edouard Vuillard, 1971; The Meanings of Modern Art, 1975. *Recreations:* reading, writing, Raimund (1790-1836). *Address:* c/o The New York Times, 229 West 43rd Street, New York, NY 10036, USA. *Clubs:* Travellers'; Century, Knickerbocker (New York).

RUSSELL, Air Vice-Marshal John Bernard, CB 1964; CBE 1960 (OBE 1954); DSO 1943; UK Representative on Council of International Civil Aviation Organization, Montreal, since 1969; *b* 13 April 1916; *m* 1937, Dorothy Mary Lucas; one *s* one *d*. *Educ:* Marwood's Sch., Sandwich. Commissioned, RAF, 1935; Specialist Navigator, 1939; served War of 1939-45, 502 and 172 Squadrons and Staff appointments in Coastal Comd, 1940-44; Staff Coll., 1944; Middle East, 1944-45; Directing Staff, 1945-48; British Jt Services Mission, Washington, 1948-50; Air Ministry, 1951-54; HQ No 19 Group, 1954-57; RAF Malta, 1957-59; Director of Operations (Maritime, Navigation and Air Traffic Control), 1960-63; SASO, RAF Coastal Command, 1963-66; Controller, Nat. Air Traffic Control Services, BoT, 1966-69; retired 1969. *Recreation:* golf. *Address:* PO Box 460, International Aviation Square, 1000 Sherbrooke Street West, Montreal, Quebec H3A 2P1, Canada; 1 Stanley Road, Deal, Kent.

RUSSELL, Rt. Rev. John Keith; Assistant Bishop, Diocese of Rochester since 1965; Rector of Hever with March Beech, since 1973; *b* 4 Aug. 1916; *s* of Rev. B. Russell and A. M. Russell; *m* 1941, Doreen Glen Johnston; one *s* three *d*. *Educ:* Shrewsbury School; Christ's College, Cambridge; Ridley Hall, Cambridge. Assistant Curate, Shirley, Southampton, 1940-45; Tutor, Buwalasi College, Uganda, and Mass Literacy Field Worker, Upper Nile Diocese, 1946-48; Rural Dean, Masaba Deanery, Upper Nile Diocese, 1948-52; Education Secretary, Mbale Archdeaconry, Upper Nile Dio., 1948-55; Asst Bishop on Upper Nile, Uganda, 1955-60; Bishop of Northern Uganda, 1961-64; Vicar, King Charles the Martyr, Tunbridge Wells, 1965-73. Chm., Jt Social Responsibility Council for Canterbury and Rochester Dioceses, 1968-. *Publication:* Men without God?, 1966. *Recreations:* cricket, football, music. *Address:* The Rectory, Hever, Edenbridge, Kent.

RUSSELL, Sir John (Weir), Kt 1958; *b* 1893; *s* of Samuel Russell, ICS, and Maud Morrison (*née* Parr); *m* 1st, 1920, Lucy Ellen Mead; one *s* one *d*; 2nd, 1932, Mary Catherine Davies (*née*

Stewart). *Educ:* Winchester; New College, Oxford. European War, 1914-18; L.-Corp. King Edward's Horse, 1914; 2nd Lt, Lt, Capt., RFA. President, Oxford Union, 1920. Barrister-at-Law, Inner Temple, 1922. War of 1939-45: Major, General Staff Intelligence, War Office; Lt-Col Comdg Special Communications Unit. Chairman, London Conservative Union, 1953-55. Governor: Old Vic; Sadler's Wells; Morley Coll.; Chm., Vic-Wells Assoc.; Trustee City Parochial Foundation; Pres., Shakespearean Authorship Soc.; Pres. Fifth Army (1916-18) Old Comrades Assoc.; Chairman Osteopathic Association Clinic. Registrar Imperial Society of Knights Bachelor. *Recreations:* golf, reading, fishing. *Address:* 57 Rivermead Court, SW6. *T:* 01-736 6783; 4 Brick Court, Temple, EC4. *T:* 01-353 2725. *Clubs:* Carlton, Junior Carlton, Garrick; Hurlingham.

RUSSELL, Sir John (Wriothesley), GCVO 1968 (KCVO 1965); CMG 1958; HM Diplomatic Service, retired; Foreign Affairs Adviser, Rolls Royce Ltd; *b* 23 Aug. 1914; *s* of late Sir Thomas Russell Pasha, KBE, CMG; *m* 1945, Aliki Diplarakos, Athens, Greece; one *s* one *d. Educ:* Eton; Trinity Coll., Cambridge. Entered HM Diplomatic Service, 1937; 3rd Sec.: Foreign Office, 1937, Vienna, 1937, Foreign Office, 1938, Moscow, 1939; 2nd Sec., Washington, 1942; 1st Sec.: Warsaw, 1945, Foreign Office, 1948; First Dir-Gen., Brussels Treaty Orgn, London, 1948. Rome, 1950; Counsellor, 1953, and Dir Gen. British Information Services, New York; Counsellor, HM Embassy, Teheran, 1956-59; Foreign Office Spokesman (Head of News Dept, Foreign Office) 1959-62; Ambassador: to Ethiopia, 1962-66; to Brazil, 1966-69; to Spain, 1969-74. Joint Master, West Street Foxhounds, 1960-. Coronation Medal, 1953. Order of the Throne, Iran; Order of the Star of Ethiopia; Order of the Southern Cross, Brazil. *Address:* 80 Chester Square, SW1W 9DU. *T:* 01-730 3355; The Vine Farm, Northbourne, Kent. *T:* Deal 4794. *Clubs:* Beefsteak, White's.
See also Sir H . R . B . Boothby , Bt

RUSSELL, Ken; film director since 1958; *b* 3 July 1927. Merchant Navy, 1945; RAF, 1946-49. Ny Norsk Ballet, 1950; Garrick Players, 1951; free-lance photographer, 1951-57; Film Director, BBC, 1958-66; free-lance film director, 1966; *Films:* Elgar; Bartok; Debussy; Henri Rousseau; Isadora Duncan; Delius; Richard Strauss; French Dressing; The Billion Dollar Brain; Women in Love; The Music Lovers; The Devils; The Boy Friend; Savage Messiah; Mahler; Tommy; Lisztomania; Valentino. *Recreation:* music.

RUSSELL, Mrs Leonard; *see* Powell, (E.) Dilys.

RUSSELL, Hon. Leopold Oliver, CBE 1970 (OBE 1944); TD; Director-General, Cement and Concrete Association, 1958-77, Chairman, since 1976; Chairman, East Anglia Regional Health Authority, since 1973; *b* 26 Jan. 1907; 4th *s* of 2nd Baron Ampthill, GCSI, GCIE; *m* 1935, Rosemary Wintour (marr. diss., 1954); no *c. Educ:* Eton. Weekly newspaper publishing company, 1925-38; served War of 1939-45, 5th Battalion Beds and Herts Regiment TA; Gen. Staff appts HQ 18th Div., Eastern Command, South-Eastern Command, GHQ Home Forces, HQ 21st Army Group, and CCG; released with rank of Brigadier; Asst Sec. to Board of Trade, 1946-47; Dir, British Institute of Management, 1947-56. Member: Bd of Governors, Nat. Hosps for Nervous Diseases, 1976; E Anglian Regional Hosp. Bd, 1972-73. *Address:* 17 Onslow Square, SW7. *T:* 01-589 0891; The Old Rectory, Kettlebaston, Bildeston, Suffolk. *T:* Bildeston 740314. *Clubs:* Brooks's, Buck's, Beefsteak, Pratt's.

RUSSELL, Sir Lionel; *see* Russell, Sir E. L.

RUSSELL, Martin Guthrie, CBE 1970; Children's Division, Home Office, later Department of Health and Social Security, 1964-74; *b* 7 May 1914; *s* of William James Russell and Bessie Gertrude Meades; *m* 1951, Moira May Eynon, *d* of Capt. Richard Threlfell; one *d. Educ:* Alleyn's School; Sidney Sussex Coll., Cambridge (MA). Asst Principal, Home Office, 1937; Asst Private Sec. to Lord Privy Seal, 1942; Principal, Home Office, 1942; seconded to Treasury, 1949-51 and 1952-54; Asst Sec. 1950; Estabt Officer, 1954, Dep. Chm., 1960-64, Prison Commn. In charge of Interdepartmental Social Work Gp, 1969-70. *Recreations:* gardening, enjoying retirement. *Address:* 4 Camden Road, Sutton, Surrey SM1 2SH. *T:* 01-642 5090. *Club:* United Oxford & Cambridge University.

RUSSELL, (Muriel) Audrey, MVO 1976; Broadcaster, Radio and Television; *o d* of late John Strangman Russell and Muriel Russell (née Metcalfe), Co. Dublin; unmarried. *Educ:* privately, in England, and France. Trained Central School of Speech and Drama. First stage appearance in London in Victoria Regina, Lyric, 1937. National Fire Service, 1939-42; joined war-time staff, BBC, 1942; accredited BBC war correspondent overseas,

1944-45; news reporter, BBC 1946-51. Commentaries on State occasions have included: Princess Elizabeth's wedding; Funeral of King George VI at Windsor; the Coronation of Queen Elizabeth II in Westminster Abbey; Weddings: Princess Margaret's; Princess Alexandra's; Duke of Kent's; Princess Anne's; Funeral of Sir Winston Churchill in St Paul's; Royal Silver Wedding, 1972; Silver Jubilee, 1977. BBC Commentator, 1953-: on Commonwealth Tours of the Queen and Duke of Edinburgh to Bermuda, NZ, Australia, Uganda, Malta, Canada, Nigeria, India, Pakistan, Ghana, Sierra Leone, Tanganyika; visits of Queen Elizabeth the Queen Mother to Central and E Africa; State Visits include: Oslo, 1955; Stockholm, 1956; Lisbon, Paris, Copenhagen, USA, 1957; Amsterdam, 1958; Nepal, Iran, Italy, 1961; W Germany, 1965; Austria, 1969; France, 1972. Royal Maundy Distribution broadcasts, 1952-76; numerous TV appearances in connection with history and art. FRSA. Freeman of City of London, 1967. *Recreations:* painting in oils, and visiting art galleries. *Address:* 117 Kenilworth Court, SW15. *Club:* United Oxford & Cambridge University.

RUSSELL, Prof. Peter Edward Lionel Russell, FBA 1977; (surname formerly Wheeler); King Alfonso XIII Professor of Spanish and Director of Portuguese Studies, Oxford, since 1953; *b* 24 Oct. 1913; *er s* of Hugh Bernard Wheeler and late Rita Muriel (née Russell), Christchurch, NZ. *Educ:* Cheltenham College; Queen's College, Oxford. First Class Final Honour School of Modern Langs 1935. Lecturer of St John's College, 1937-53 and Queen's College, 1938-45. Enlisted, 1940; commissioned (Intelligence Corps) Dec. 1940; Temp. Lt-Col, 1945; specially employed in Caribbean, W Africa and SE Asia, 1942-46. Fellow of Queen's College, 1946-53, and Univ. Lectr in Spanish Studies, 1946-53; Fellow of Exeter Coll., 1953; Norman Maccoll Lectr, Cambridge, 1969. Member: Portuguese Academy of History, 1956; Real Academia de Buenas Letras, Barcelona, 1972; UGC Cttee on Latin-American Studies in British Univs, 1962-64. FRHistS. *Publications:* As Fontes de Fernão Lopes, 1941 (Coimbra); The English Intervention in Spain and Portugal in the Time of Edward III and Richard II, 1955; Prince Henry the Navigator, 1960; (with D. M. Rogers) Hispanic Manuscripts and Books in the Bodleian and Oxford College Libraries, 1962; (ed) Spain: a Companion to Spanish Studies, 1973; Temas de la Celestina y otros estudios (del Cid al Quijote), 1977; articles and reviews in Modern Language Review, Medium Aevum, Bulletin of Hispanic Studies, etc. *Recreations:* photography and travel. *Address:* 23 Belsyre Court, Woodstock Road, Oxford. *T:* Oxford 56086. *Club:* United Oxford & Cambridge University.

RUSSELL, Rt. Rev. Philip Welsford Richmond; *see* Natal, Bishop of.

RUSSELL, Richard Drew, RDI 1944; Professor of Furniture Design, Royal College of Art, 1948-64; Professor Emeritus, 1964; Consultant Industrial Designer; *b* 21 Dec. 1903; *s* of Sydney Bolton Russell and Elizabeth Russell (née Shefford); *m* 1933, Marian Pepler; two *s* one *d. Educ:* Dean Close School, Cheltenham. Trained at Architectural Association School; joined Gordon Russell Ltd, 1929, eventually becoming Director in charge of design; joined Murphy Radio Ltd as staff industrial designer, 1934; set up in private practice in London as consultant industrial designer, 1936; joined RNVR to work on camouflage of ships, 1942; resumed private practice in London as designer, 1946. FSIA, 1946; Master of Faculty, RDI, 1957-59. *Recreation:* gardens. *Address:* 39 Friars Quay, Norwich, Norfolk NR3 1ES.

RUSSELL, Ritchie; *see* Russell, W. R.

RUSSELL, Robert Christopher Hamlyn; Director, Hydraulics Research Station, Department of the Environment (formerly Ministry of Technology), since 1965; *b* Singapore, 1921; *s* of Philip Charles and Hilda Gertrude Russell; *m* 1950, Cynthia Mary Roberts; one *s* two *d. Educ:* Stowe; King's Coll., Cambridge. Asst Engineer: BTH Co., Rugby, 1944; Dunlop Rubber Co., 1946; Sen. Scientific Officer, later PSO, then SPSO, in Hydraulics Research Station, 1949-65. Visiting Prof., Univ. of Strathclyde, 1967. *Publications:* Waves and Tides, 1951; papers on civil engineering hydraulics. *Address:* 29 St Mary's Street, Wallingford, Oxfordshire. *T:* Wallingford 3323.

RUSSELL, Robert Mark, CMG 1977; HM Diplomatic Service; Counsellor, HM Embassy, Washington, since 1974, and Head of Chancery, since 1977; *b* 3 Sept. 1929; *s* of Sir Robert E. Russell, CSI, CIE; *m* 1954, Virginia Mary Rogers; two *s* two *d. Educ:* Trinity Coll., Glenalmond; Exeter Coll., Oxford (MA). Hon. Mods cl. 2, Lit. Hum. cl. 1. Royal Artillery, 1952-54; FO, 1954-56; 3rd, later 2nd Sec., HM Legation, Budapest, 1956-58; 2nd Sec., Berne, 1958-61; FO, 1961-65; 1st Sec., 1962; 1st Sec. and Head of Chancery, Kabul, 1965-67; 1st Sec., DSAO, 1967-69;

Counsellor, 1969; Dep. Head of Personnel (Ops) Dept, FCO, 1969-70; Commercial Counsellor, Bucharest, 1970-73. *Recreations:* travel, music, golf. *Address:* c/o British Embassy, 3100 Massachusetts Avenue NW, Washington, DC 20008, USA; 12 Rotherwick Road, NW11. *T:* 01-455 0115; 8 Thirlestane Road, Edinburgh EH9 1AN. *T:* 031-447 7185. *Clubs:* Royal Commonwealth Society; Cosmos (Washington, DC).

RUSSELL, Prof. **Roger Wolcott;** Vice Chancellor, and Professor of Psychobiology, Flinders University of South Australia, since 1972; *b* 30 Aug. 1914; *s* of Leonard Walker and Sadie Stanhope Russell, Worcester, Mass, USA; *m* 1945, Kathleen Sherman Fortescue; one *s* one *d. Educ:* Worcester (Mass, USA) Public Schools; Clark Univ. (Livermore Schol., Clark Fellow in Psychology); BA 1935, MA 1936; Peabody Coll. (Payne Schol.); University of Virginia (Du Pont Research Fellow); PhD 1939; DSc Univ. of London, 1954. Instructor in Psychology: Univ. of Nebraska, 1939-41, Michigan State Coll., 1941; Research Psychologist, USAF Sch. of Aviation Medicine, 1941-42; Officer USAF, 1942-46; Asst Prof. in Psychol., Univ. of Pittsburgh, 1946-47; Assoc. Prof. of Psychol., Univ. of Pittsburgh and Res. Fellow in Neurophysiol., Western Psychiatric Inst., 1947-49; Fulbright Advanced Research Schol. and Director, Animal Research Lab., Institute of Psychiatry, Univ. of London, 1949-50; Prof. of Psychology and Head of Dept of Psychol., University Coll., London 1950-57 (on leave of absence, 1956-57); Dean of Advanced Studies, Indiana Univ., 1966-67 (Prof. and Chm. Dept of Psychology, 1959-66); Vice Chancellor, Academic Affairs, and Prof. of Psycho-Biology and of Clinical Pharmacology and Therapeutics, Univ. of Calif., Irvine, 1967-72. Executive Sec. of the American Psychological Assoc., 1956-59, Board of Directors, 1963-65, Pres. Div. 1, 1968-69; Mem., USPHS Advis. Cttee in Psychopharmacology, 1957-63, 1967-70; Member: Nat. Research Coun. (USA), 1958-61, 1963-65, 1967-71; Army Sci. Adv. Panel (USA), 1958-66; Sec.-Gen. Internat. Union of Psychological Science, 1960-66 (Vice-Pres., 1966-69; Pres., 1969-72); Aust.-Amer. Educn Foundn Vis. Prof., Dept of Psychol., Univ. of Sydney, 1965-66; Vis. Erskine Fellow, Univ. of Canterbury, NZ, 1966. Member, Scientific and Professional Socs in Europe, USA, Australia. FACE 1972; FASSA 1973. Bronze Star Medal (USA), 1945. Army Commendation Medal (USA), 1946. *Publications:* (ed) Frontiers in Psychology, 1964; (ed) Frontiers in physiological Psychology, 1966; research papers on neurochemical bases of behaviour, experimental psycho-pathology, physiological, child and social psychology, psychopharmacology. *Recreations:* golf, tennis. *Address:* The Flinders University of South Australia, Bedford Park, SA 5042, Australia. *T:* Adelaide 275-3911.

RUSSELL, Sir (Sydney) **Gordon,** Kt 1955; CBE 1947; MC; RDI; FSIA; *b* London, 20 May 1892; *e s* of late S. B. Russell, Snowshill, Glos. and Elizabeth Russell; *m* 1921, Constance Elizabeth Jane Vere, *d* of late Dr F. A. V. Denning, Sligo; two *s* one *d* (and one *s* decd). *Educ:* Campden Grammar School. Served European War with Worcestershire Regiment, 1914-19 (MC). Designer, Managing Director, Gordon Russell Ltd, 1926-40, later Director (Chm., 1967-77); Partner Russell & Sons, 1919-46, later Director (Chm., 1970-76). The Lygon Arms Ltd (Broadway). Mem. Art Workers Guild, 1926, Master, 1962; RDI, 1940, Master of the Faculty, 1947-49; Member Utility Furniture Advisory Cttee and Furniture Production Cttee (Bd of Trade), 1942 and Chm. of Bd of Trade Design Panel, 1943-47; Specialist Assessor for Nat. Diploma in Design to Min. of Educ., 1938-53; served on jury of Internat. Low-Cost Furniture Competition, Museum of Modern Art, New York, 1948; Original Member Exec. Cttee, Festival of Britain, 1951; Member: Art Panel of Arts Council, 1948-53, Fine Arts Cttee of British Council, 1948-58, Council of Roy. Soc. of Arts, 1947-49 and 1951-55; Original Mem. Council of Industrial Design (now Design Council), 1944, Dir, 1947-59, Life Mem., 1960-; Member: Council, Royal Coll. of Art, 1948-51, and 1952-63; Council, Royal Sch. of Needlework, 1951-68; Design Panel, BR Bd, 1956-66; Pres., Design and Industries Assoc., 1959-62; Member: Nat. Council for Diplomas in Art and Design, 1961-68; Crafts Adv. Cttee, 1971-74. First FSIA, 1945; FRSA, 1949; First Hon. DesRCA, 1952, Senior Fellow, 1960; Hon. ARIBA, 1953, Hon. Fellow, 1965; Hon. AILA, 1955; Hon. LLD Birmingham Univ., 1960; DUniv. York, 1969. Mem. Hon. Cttee for Internat. Exhibition of architecture and industrial design, Hälsingborg, Sweden, 1955; Mem. Higher Jury, XIIth Milan Triennale Exhibition, 1960. Officer, Swedish Royal Order of the Vasa, 1954; Commander, Norwegian Royal Order of St Olav, 1957. Gold Albert Medal, RSA, 1962. *Publications:* The Story of Furniture (Puffin), 1947; The Things We See: Furniture (Penguin), 1948; Looking at Furniture, 1964; (autobiography) Designer's Trade, 1968; and articles, lectures and broadcasts on design and country life. *Recreations:* gardening and hand-work

WW—68

of many kinds. *Address:* Kingcombe, Chipping Campden, Glos. *T:* Evesham 840253. *Club:* Arts.

RUSSELL, **Thomas,** CBE 1970 (OBE 1963); Governor of the Cayman Islands, since 1974; *b* 27 May 1920; *s* of Thomas Russell, OBE, MC and Margaret Thomson Russell; *m* 1951, Andrée Irma Désfossés; one *s. Educ:* Hawick High Sch.; St Andrews Univ.; Peterhouse, Cambridge. MA St Andrews; Dip. Anthrop. Cantab. War Service, Cameronians (Scottish Rifles), 1941; 5th Bn (Scottish), Parachute Regt, 1943: served in N Africa and Italy; POW, 1944; Captain 1945; OC Parachute Trng Company, 1946. Cambridge Univ., 1946-47. Colonial Admin. Service, 1948; District Comr, British Solomon Is Protectorate, 1948; Asst Sec., Western Pacific High Commn, Fiji, 1951; District Comr, British Solomon Is Protectorate, 1954-56; seconded Colonial Office, 1956-57; Admin. Officer Class A, 1956; Dep. Financial Sec., 1962; Financial Sec., 1965; Chief Sec. to W Pacific High Commn, 1970-74. FRAI. *Publications:* monographs in Oceania, Jl of Polynesian Society. *Recreations:* anthropology, archæology. *Address:* c/o Foreign and Commonwealth Office, SW1; Government House, Grand Cayman, WI; 49 Trafalgar Court, Firgrove Hill, Farnham, Surrey. *T:* Farnham 3363. *Club:* Royal Commonwealth Society.

RUSSELL, **Thomas Patrick,** QC 1971; a Recorder, since 1972 (Recorder of Barrow-in-Furness, 1971); *b* 30 July 1926; *s* of late Sidney Arthur Russell and Elsie Russell; *m* 1951, Doreen (Janie) Ireland; two *d. Educ:* Urmston Grammar Sch.; Manchester Univ. (LLB). Served in Intelligence Corps and RASC, 1945-48. Called to Bar, Middle Temple, 1949, Northern Circuit. Prosecuting Counsel to the Post Office (Northern Circuit), 1961-70; Asst Recorder of Bolton, 1963-70. Mem., Lord Justice James Cttee on Distribution of Criminal Business, 1973-76. *Recreations:* cricket, golf. *Address:* Oakfield, 65 Crofts Bank Road, Urmston, Manchester M31 1UB. *T:* 061-748 2004.

RUSSELL, **(William) Ritchie,** CBE 1952; MD, FRCP; Consultant Neurologist: to United Oxford Hospitals, 1945-70; to Army, 1948-69; Professor of Clinical Neurology, Oxford Univ., 1966-70; retired; *b* 7 Feb. 1903; *s* of Professor William Russell, MD; *m* 1932, Jean Stuart Low; one *s* one *d. Educ:* Edinburgh Academy; Edinburgh Univ. MBChB, 1926; MD(Edin.), 1932; FRCPEd, 1933; FRCP, 1943; MA Oxon, 1946; DSc Oxon, 1955. Asst Physician, Royal Infirmary, Edinburgh, 1934; Lecturer in Neurology: University of Edinburgh, 1938; Oxford University, 1949-66. Served RAMC, 1940-45; Consultant Neurologist (Brig.), MEF, 1943. Editor of Jl of Neurol., Neurosurg, Psychiat., 1948-69. KStJ 1957. *Publications:* Poliomyelitis, 2nd edn 1956; Brain-Memory-Learning, 1959; Traumatic Aphasia, 1961; The Traumatic Amnesias, 1971; Explaining the Brain, 1975; research papers on neurological subjects in medical journals. *Address:* Flat 31, 380 Banbury Road, Oxford OX2 7PW.

RUSSELL, **William Robert;** Chairman, Australia and New Zealand Advisory Committee to British Overseas Trade Board, since 1975; *b* 6 Aug. 1913; *s* of William Andrew Russell and Mary Margaret Russell; *m* 1940, Muriel Faith Rolfe; one *s* one *d. Educ:* Wakefield Road Central, East Ham. Served War of 1939-45: Mine-Sweeping and Anti-Submarine vessels; Commissioned, 1942; appointed to command, 1943. Joined Shaw Savill & Albion Co. Ltd, 1929; Director, 1958-; Manager, 1959; General Manager, 1961; Deputy Chairman, 1966; Chm. and Man. Dir, 1968-73; Dir, Bank of New Zealand. Chairman: British Council, Australian British Trade Assoc., 1967-72 and 1975-; Council of European and Japanese Nat. Shipowners Assocs, 1969-76. *Recreations:* gardening, golf. *Address:* Westland, Uvedale Road, Limpsfield, Oxted, Surrey. *T:* Oxted 3080. *Club:* Naval.

RUSSELL SCOTT, **Charles;** see Scott, C. R.

RUSSELL-SMITH, Dame **Enid, (Mary Russell),** DBE 1953; MA; Principal of St Aidan's College, Durham University, 1963-70; Hon. part-time Lecturer in Politics since 1964; *b* 3 March 1903; *d* of late Arthur Russell-Smith, of Hartfield, Sussex. *Educ:* St Felix Sch., Southwold, Suffolk; Newnham Coll., Cambridge. Modern Languages Tripos (French and German). Entered Civil Service as Assistant Principal in Ministry of Health, 1925. Deputy Secretary, Ministry of Health, 1956-63. Co-opted Mem., Teesside (later Cleveland) Educn Cttee, 1968-75; Chairman: Sunderland Church Commn., 1971; Durham County Conservation Trust, 1973-75; St Paul's Jarrow Develt Trust, 1975-. Associate Fellow, Newnham College, 1956-72, Hon. Fellow, 1974. *Publication:* Modern Bureaucracy: the Home Civil Service, 1974. *Address:* 3 Pimlico, Durham DH1 4QW. *Club:* University Women's.

RUSSELL VICK, Arnold Oughtred; see Vick, A. O. R.

RUSSO, Sir Peter (George), Kt 1964; CBE 1953 (OBE 1939); JP; Barrister-at-Law; Minister of Housing and Economic Development, Gibraltar Council, 1964-68; *b* 1899; *s* of George Russo; *m* 1926, Margot, *d* of late John A. Imossi, Gibraltar; one *d.* Mem. various Govt bodies and cttees; Dir of several local cos; Trustee, John Mackintosh Foundation; past Chm. City Council, former Mem. Exec. Council, Gibraltar. JP Gibraltar, 1947-. *Address:* 2 Red Sands Lane, Gibraltar. *T:* Gibraltar A622. *Club:* Royal Gibraltar Yacht (past Cdre).

RUTHERFORD, Prof. Andrew; Regius (Chalmers) Professor of English Literature, University of Aberdeen, since 1968; *b* Helmsdale, Sutherland, 23 July 1929; *s* of Thomas Armstrong Rutherford and Christian P. Rutherford (*née* Russell); *m* 1953, Nancy Milroy Browning, *d* of Dr Arthur Browning, and Dr Jean G. Browning (*née* Thomson); two *s* one *d.* *Educ:* Helmsdale Sch.; George Watson's Boys' Coll.; Univ. of Edinburgh; Merton Coll., Oxford. MA Edinburgh Univ., First Cl. Hons Eng. Lang. and Lit., James Elliott Prize, and Vans Dunlop Schol., 1951; Carnegie Schol., 1953; BLitt Oxford, 1959. Commnd Seaforth Hldrs, 1952; served with Somaliland Scouts, 1952-53; 11th Bn Seaforth Hldrs (TA), 1953-58. Asst Lectr in English, Univ. of Edinburgh, 1955; Lectr, 1956-64; Vis. Assoc. Prof., Univ. of Rochester (NY), 1963; Sen. Lectr, Univ. of Aberdeen, 1964; Second Prof. of English, Univ. of Aberdeen, 1965-68. Lectures: Byron Foundn, Nottingham Univ., 1964; Chatterton, British Acad., 1965; Stevenson, Edinburgh Univ., 1967; Byron Soc., 1973. Chm., English Bd, CNAA, 1966-73. British Council lecture tours in: India, Greece, Italy, Colombia, Austria, Luxembourg. *Publications:* Byron: A Critical Study, 1961; (ed) Kipling's Mind and Art, 1964; (ed) Byron: The Critical Heritage, 1970; (ed) 20th Century Interpretations of A Passage to India, 1970; (ed) Kipling, A Sahibs' War and other stories, 1971; (ed) Kipling, Friendly Brook and other stories, 1971; articles in learned journals. *Recreation:* shooting. *Address:* Department of English, Taylor Building, King's College, Aberdeen AB9 2UB; 150 Hamilton Place, Aberdeen AB2 4BB. *T:* Aberdeen 23868.

RUTHERFORD, Herman Graham, CBE 1966; QPM 1957; DL; Chief Constable of Surrey, 1956-68; retired, 1968; *b* 3 April 1908; *m* 1940, Dorothy Weaver; three *s* one *d.* *Educ:* Grammar School, Consett, County Durham. Metropolitan Police, 1929-45; Chief Constable: of Oxfordshire, 1945-54; of Lincolnshire, 1954-56. Barrister, Gray's Inn, 1941. Served Army, Allied Military Government, 1943-45, Lt-Colonel. DL Surrey, 1968. *Recreation:* sailing. *Address:* Hankley Farm, Elstead, Surrey. *T:* Elstead 2200; Milina, Volos, Greece.

RUTHERFORD, Thomas; Chairman, North Eastern Electricity Board, since 1977; *b* 4 June 1924; *s* of Thomas and Catherine Rutherford; *m* 1950, Joyce Foreman; one *s* one *d.* *Educ:* Tynemouth High Sch.; King's Coll., Durham Univ. BSc(Hons); CEng, FIEE. Engrg Trainee, subseq. Research Engr, A Reyrolle & Co. Ltd, Hebburn-on-Tyne, 1943-49; North Eastern Electricity Bd: various engrg and commercial appts, 1949-61; Personal Asst to Chm., 1961-63; Area Commercial Engr, then Area Engr, Tees Area, 1964-69; Dep. Commercial Man., 1969-70; Commercial Man., 1970-72; Chief Engr, 1972-73; Dep. Chm., 1973-75; Chm., SE Electricity Board, 1975-77. *Recreations:* outdoors, especially mountains. *Address:* 76 Beach Road, Tynemouth, Tyne and Wear. *T:* North Shields 71775.

RUTHERFORD, Brig.-Gen. Thomas John, CBE 1945; ED; retired as National Chairman, Farm Credit Corporation (1959-63); *b* Leith, Ontario, Canada, 16 Jan. 1893; *s* of Malcolm Rutherford; *m* 1919, Helen Sibbald; three *s* one *d.* Engaged in farming at Leith, Ont.; joined Grey Regt, September 1912; proceeded overseas, 1916; served in France and Belgium with 4th Canadian Mounted Rifles (wounded, despatches); demobilised, 1919. Contested House of Commons, Grey North, 1921; Local Registrar Supreme Court and Surrogate Regist. and Sheriff, Co. Grey, 1923; Lt-Col to command Grey Regt, 1925; Col to command 22nd Cdn Inf. Bde, 1932; R of O, 1936; reverted to Major, 1939, to command a company of the Grey and Simcoe Foresters; Lt-Col to command the Grey and Simcoe Foresters (Overseas Unit), 1940; Brig. to command 1st Canadian Armoured Brigade, 1941; commanded Canadian Armoured Corps Reinforcement Units (UK) and Senior Adviser Canadian Armoured Corps, UK, 1943; Dep. Comdr, Canadian Forces, Netherlands, and Canadian Repatriation Units, UK, 1946. Dir-Gen. of Rehabn, Can., 1946; Nat. Dir, Soldier Settlement and Veterans' Land Act, 1947-62. Hon. Col, Grey and Simcoe Foresters. *Publications:* Scouts and Patrols; Production-line Farming. *Address:* RR1, Owen Sound, Ont, Canada. *Club:* Royal Canadian Military Institute.

RUTHNASWAMY, Prof. Miriadas, CIE 1930; MA Cantab; MP, Council of States, New Delhi, since 1962; *b* Madras Royapuran, 15 Aug. 1885; *s* of Rai Bahadur M. I. Ruthnaswamy, officer on old Nizam's Railway; *m* 1914, Marie Dhyrianathan; four *s* five *d.* *Educ:* St Joseph's Coll., Cuddalor; St Joseph's Coll., Trichinopoly; Nizam's Coll., Hyderabad; Madras Univ.; Downing Coll., Cambridge. Barrister-at-Law, Gray's Inn. Asst Prof. of English and History, Baroda Coll., 1913-18; Prof. of History, Pachiappa's Coll., 1918-27, Principal, 1921-27; Principal, Law Coll., Madras, 1928-30; Mem. Madras Public Services Commission, 1930-42; Vice-Chancellor, Annamalai University, 1942-48. Member: Mun. Corp., Madras, 1921-24; Madras Legisl. Council, 1922-26 (Pres. 1925-26); Indian Legsl. Assembly, 1927. Founded Catholic Union of India, 1925. Padma Bhushan Award, 1968. *Publications:* The Political Philosophy of Mr Gandhi, 1922; The Making of the State, 1935; Influences in British Administrative System, 1937; India from the Dawn, 1949; Principles and Practices of Public Administration, 1953, 1956, 1959, 1962, 1970; Principles and Practice of Foreign Policy, 1962; India after God, 1964; Agenda for India, 1972. *Recreations:* walking, conversation. *Address:* H-2 Block, Foreshore Estate, Madras 600028, India.

RUTHVEN, family name of **Earl of Gowrie.**

RUTHVEN OF CANBERRA and DIRLETON, Viscount; Patrick Leo Brer Ruthven; *b* 4 Feb. 1964; *s* and *heir* of 2nd Earl of Gowrie, *qv.*

RUTHVEN OF FREELAND, Lady, 10th in line, Scot. *cr* 1651; **Bridget Helen Monckton, (The Dowager Viscountess Monckton of Brenchley),** CBE 1947; *b* 27 July 1896; *e d* of 9th Lord Ruthven, CB, CMG, DSO and Jean Leslie (*d* 1952), *d* of Norman George Lampson; *S* father 1956; *m* 1st, 1918, 11th Earl of Carlisle (marr. diss., 1947; he *d* 1963); one *s* one *d* ; 2nd, 1947, (as Sir Walter Monckton), 1st Viscount Monckton of Brenchley, PC, GCVO, KCMG, MC, QC (*d* 1965). Joined ATS, 1938, as Sen. Comdr; promoted Controller, 1941; Dir Women's Auxilliary Corps (India), 1944-46, with rank of Sen. Controller. Governor, St George's Hosp., 1952-69; Mem. SE Metropolitan Regional Hosp. Board, 1953-71; Governor, Bethlem Royal Hosp. and the Maudsley Hosp., 1957-71; Member: St Francis and Lady Chichester Hosp. Management Cttees, 1959-68; Mid-Sussex Hosp. Management Cttee, 1965-68; Hellingley Hosp., Hailsham, 1970-71; Chm. Nat. Assoc. of Leagues of Hosp. Friends, 1962. Mem. Court, Sussex Univ. Victory Medal, 1946. *Heir:* s Earl of Carlisle, *qv.* *Address:* 113 Eaton Square, SW1.

RUTLAND, 10th Duke of, *cr* 1703; **Charles John Robert Manners,** CBE 1962; Marquess of Granby, 1703; Earl of Rutland, 1525; Baron Manners of Haddon, 1679; Baron Roos of Belvoir, 1896; Captain Grenadier Guards; Chairman, Leicestershire County Council, since 1974; *b* 28 May 1919; *e s* of 9th Duke and Kathleen, 3rd *d* of late F. J. Tennant; *S* father, 1940; *m* 1946, Anne Bairstow Cumming (marr. diss. 1956), *e d* of late Major Cumming Bell, Binham Lodge, Edgerton, Huddersfield; one *d* ; *m* 1958, Frances Helen, *d* of Charles Sweeny and of Margaret, Duchess of Argyll; two *s* one *d* (and one *s* decd). *Educ:* Eton; Trinity Coll., Cambridge. Owns 18,000 acres; minerals in Leicestershire and Derbyshire; picture gallery at Belvoir Castle. Chm., E Midlands Economic Planning Council, 1971-74. *Heir:* s Marquis of Granby, *qv.* *Address:* Belvoir Castle, Grantham; Haddon Hall, Derby.
See also Marquess of Anglesey, Sir R. G. M. Throckmorton, Bt, Earl of Wemyss.

RUTT, Rt. Rev. Cecil Richard; see St Germans, Bishop Suffragan of.

RUTTER, Prof. Arthur John; Professor of Botany since 1967 and Head of Department of Botany and Plant Technology since 1971, Imperial College, University of London; *b* 22 Nov. 1917; *s* of W. Arthur Rutter, *qv* ; *m* 1944, Betsy Rosier Stone; two *s* one *d.* *Educ:* Royal Grammar Sch., Guildford; Imperial Coll. of Science and Technology. ARCS, BSc, PhD, FIBiol. Mem., ARC team for selection of oil-seed crops and develt selective herbicides, 1940-45; Asst Lectr, Imperial Coll., 1945, Lectr 1946; Reader in Ecology, Univ. of London, 1956. Vis. Prof., Univ. of the Panjab, W Pakistan, 1960-61. *Publications:* papers, mainly in Annals of Botany, Jl of Ecology, Jl of Applied Ecology on water relations of plants and forest hydrology. *Recreations:* gardening, walking. *Address:* Fairseat, Bagshot Road, Knaphill, Woking, Surrey. *T:* Brookwood 3347.

RUTTER, John Cleverdon; His Honour Judge Rutter; a Circuit Judge, since 1972; *b* 18 Sept. 1919; 2nd *s* of late Edgar John Rutter; *m* 1951, Jill, *d* of Maxwell Duncan McIntosh; one *s* one *d.* *Educ:* Cardiff High Sch.; Univ. Coll., of SW of England,

Exeter (Open Schol.); Keble Coll., Oxford. MA Oxon; LLB London. Royal Artillery, 1940-45; commnd 1941; served overseas. Called to the Bar, Lincoln's Inn, 1948; practised Wales and Chester Circuit, 1948-66, Stipendiary Magistrate for City of Cardiff, 1966-71. A Legal Member, Mental Health Review Tribunal for Wales Region, 1960-66. An Assistant Recorder of: Cardiff, 1962-66; Merthyr Tydfil, 1962-66; Swansea, 1965-66; Dep. Chm., Glamorgan QS, 1969-71. *Recreations:* golf, reading. *Address:* Law Courts, Cardiff. *T:* Cardiff 45931.

RUTTER, Air Vice-Marshal (Retd) Norman Colpoy Simpson, CB 1965; CBE 1945; idc; jssc; psa; Sen. Tech. Staff Officer, Bomber Command, 1961-65; *b* 1909; *s* of Rufus John Rutter; *m* 1936, Irene Sophia, *d* of late Colonel A. M. Lloyd; one *s* one *d.* Air Cdre, 1957; Air Officer Commanding and Commandant of the Royal Air Force Technical College, Henlow, 1959-61. CEng, FIMechE; FRAeS. *Address:* 37 Meadow Road, Pinner, Mddx.

RUTTER, W(illiam) Arthur, CBE 1949 (OBE 1944); FRIBA; retired; *b* Cardiff, 8 Jan. 1890; *s* of William Rutter; *m* 1915, Amy, *d* of William Dyche, BA, Cardiff; one *s* three *d.* Chief Architect to the Ministry of Works, 1946-51. *Address:* 13 Manor Way, Onslow Village, Guildford, Surrey.
    See also Prof. A. J. Rutter.

RUTTLE, Henry Samuel; His Honour Judge Ruttle; a Circuit Judge (formerly Judge of County Courts), since 1959; *b* 10 Nov. 1906; *yr s* of late Michael Ruttle, Portlaw, Co. Waterford, Ireland; *m* 1943, Joyce Mayo Moriarty (*d* 1968), *yr d* of late J. O. M. Moriarty, Plymouth; one *s* two *d.* *Educ:* Wesley College, Dublin and Trinity College, Dublin. BA (Moderatorship in Legal and Political Science) and LLB, 1929; LLD 1933; MA 1950. Called to the Bar, Gray's Inn, 1933; practised in Common Law: London and Western Circuit. Served War of 1939-45: RAFVR, 1940-45; Squadron Leader. Deputy Judge Advocate Judge Advocate General's Office. Resumed practice at Bar, 1945. Member of Church Assembly, 1948-55; Mem., General Council of the Bar, 1957-59; Deputy Chairman Agricultural Land Tribunal (SW Area), 1958-59. JP, Co. Surrey, 1961. Mem., County Court Rules Cttee, 1969-. Jt Editor, The County Court Practice, 1973. *Recreations:* Rugby football (Leinster Inter-Provincial, 1927; Captain London Irish RFC, 1935-36; Middlesex County); fly-fishing. *Address:* West Lodge, West Side, Wimbledon Common, SW19.

RYAN, Arthur James, CBE 1953; Regional Director, London Postal Region, 1949-60, retired; *b* 10 Oct. 1900; *e s* of late Stephen James Ryan, Little Common, Bexhill on Sea, Sx; *m* 1926, Marjorie, *y d* of late George James Dee; two *d.* *Educ:* City of London College and privately. Clerk, Headquarters, GPO London, 1918; Asst Surveyor, GPO, Class II, 1926, Class I, 1935; served in N Wales, Eastern Counties, South Western District; Chief Superintendent, then Assistant Controller, 1936, Controller (Mails and Transport), 1941, London Postal Region; Assistant Secretary, Min. of Fuel and Power (on loan), 1941; Dep. Regional Director, London Postal Region, 1944; Member of Post Office Board, 1950. Freeman, City of London. *Recreations:* golf, gardening. *Address:* Daymer Cottage, Cooden Drive, Bexhill-on-Sea, East Sussex. *T:* Cooden 2277. *Club:* Royal Automobile.

RYAN, (Christopher) Nigel (John), CBE 1977; Vice-President, National Broadcasting Company News, America, since 1977; *b* 12 Dec. 1929; *s* of Brig. C. E. Ryan, MC, RA and Joyce Dodgson. *Educ:* Ampleforth Coll.; Queen's Coll., Oxford (BA). Joined Reuters, London, 1954; Foreign Corresp., 1957-60; joined Independent Television News, 1961, Editor, 1968-71, Editor and Chief Executive, 1971-77; freelance scriptwriter. Silver Medal, Royal Television Soc., 1970; Desmond Davis Award, 1972. *Publications:* trans. novels from French by Georges Simenon and others. *Address:* NBC Inc., 30 Rockefeller Plaza, New York, NY 10020, USA.

RYAN, Sir Derek Gerald, 3rd Bt, *cr* 1919; *b* 9 July 1922; *s* of Sir Gerald Ellis Ryan, 2nd Bt, and Hylda Winifryde Herapath; *S* father 1947; *m* 1st, 1947, Penelope Anne Hawkings (marr. diss. 1971); one *s* three *d*; 2nd, 1972, Katja, *d* of Ernst Best. *Educ:* Harrow. Served War of 1939-45. Lieut Grenadier Guards, 1941-45. *Heir: s* Derek Gerald Ryan, Junior, *b* 25 March 1954. *Address:* 6228 Eltville/Rheingau, Erbacher Strasse 12, West Germany.

RYAN, Most Rev. Dermot; see Dublin, Archbishop of, and Primate of Ireland, (RC).

RYAN, Most Rev. Hugh Edward, DD; Titular Bishop of Nigizubi, since 1967; *b* Kyabram, Victoria, 25 April 1888. *Educ:* Assumption College, Kilmore, Vic.; St Joseph's College,

Hunter's Hill, NSW; St Patrick's College, Manly, NSW; College of Propaganda, Rome. Ordained, 1916. Bishop of Townsville, 1938-67. *Address:* Villa Vincent, Gulliver Street, Hermit Park, Queensland 4812, Australia.

RYAN, James Stewart; Principal Assistant Solicitor, Department of the Environment, since 1975; *b* 9 Sept 1913; *o s* of late Philip F. Ryan and Bridget Ryan; *m* 1939, Rachel Alleyn; two *s* four *d.* *Educ:* Beaumont Coll.; Balliol Coll., Oxford (BA). Called to Bar, Inner Temple, 1939. War service, 1939-46, Oxford and Bucks Light Infantry, War Office, DAAG, Major 1944. Joined Govt Legal Service, 1946; Asst Solicitor, Min. of Housing and Local Govt, 1957, later DoE. *Address:* 28 Manor Road, Henley-on-Thames RG9 1LU. *T:* Henley-on-Thames 3345. *Club:* Leander (Henley).

RYAN, John; Management consultant and lecturer; *b* 30 April 1940; *m* 1964, Eunice Ann Edmonds; two *s.* *Educ:* Lanark Grammar School; Glasgow University. Member, National Association of Labour Student Organisations, 1958-62; formerly Youth Organiser, Lanark City Labour Party; Member, Executive Committee, North Paddington Labour Party, 1964-66. Contested (Lab) Buckinghamshire South, 1964; MP (Lab) Uxbridge, 1966-70. Member, Fabian Society, 1961; Dir, Tribune Publications Ltd, 1969-. Mem., Inst. of Marketing; Associate Member: Market Res. Soc.; BIM. *Recreations:* golf, walking.

RYAN, John Francis, FFARCS; Consulting Anæsthetist, St Thomas' Hospital; *b* 1894; *s* of John Ryan, OBE, and Ellen Rebecca Ryan; *m* 1924, Frances Emmeline Perry; three *d.* *Educ:* Merchant Taylors' School; St Thomas' Hosp. MRCS, LRCP 1917; MB, BS London 1919; DA Eng. 1939; FFARCS Eng 1949. Formerly Anæsthetist, Nat. Hosp. for Paralysed and Epileptic; Evelina Hosp. for Children. European War, 1914-18, Temp. Surg. RN; War of 1939-45, Temp. Surg. Lt-Comdr RNVR, Specialist in Anæsthetics, RN. FRSocMed; Fellow Assoc. of Anæsthetists of Gt Brit. and Ire. *Publications:* contribs to med. jls. *Recreations:* gardening, golf. *Address:* The Rookery, Burton Bradstock, Dorset. *T:* Burton Bradstock 256. *Clubs:* Naval, Lansdowne.

RYAN, Rt. Rev. Joseph Francis, DD, JCD; *b* Dundas, Ontario, 1 March 1897; *s* of Wm Ryan and Ellen Manion. *Educ:* St Mary's Sch., Hamilton; St Jerome's Coll., Kitchener; St Augustine's Seminary, Toronto; Appolinaris Univ., Rome, Italy. Ordained 1921; Asst Priest, St Mary's Cathedral, Hamilton, 1921-25; Rector, 1925; First Rector of new Cathedral of Christ the King, Hamilton, 1933; Administrator of diocese after serving several years as Chancellor; Bishop of Hamilton, 1937-73. *Address:* St Mary's Parish, 56 Mulberry Street, Hamilton, Ontario L8R 2C7, Canada.

RYAN, Nigel; see Ryan, C. N. J.

RYAN, Patrick John McNamara; a Recorder of the Crown Court, since 1972; Director of several companies since 1950; *b* 7 March 1919; *m* 1949, Vera, *d* of W. Craven-Ellis. *Educ:* Wimbledon Coll.; Beaumont Coll. Commnd in London Irish Rifles, 1939. Solicitor, 1946. Pres., W Surrey Law Soc., 1964-65; Chm. and Pres., Esher Conservative Constituency Assoc., 1962-65; Mem., SE Circuit Adv. Cttee, 1972. Mem., NW Surrey Medical Ethics Cttee, 1976. *Recreations:* woodwork; gardener's handyman; trying to find peace! *Address:* Beaumont Lodge, St George's Hill, Weybridge, Surrey. *Clubs:* Royal Automobile; St George's Hill Golf; Weybridge Golf.

RYAN PRICE, Henry; see Price, H. R.

RYBURN, Rev. Hubert James, CMG 1959; MA (Oxon and NZ), BD (Union); *b* 19 April 1897; *s* of Very Rev. Robert Middleton Ryburn and Anna Jane Steadman; *m* 1931, Jocelyn Maud Dunlop, *d* of Professor F. W. Dunlop; two *s* two *d.* *Educ:* Otago University; Oxford University; Union Theological Seminary, NY. Rhodes Scholar, 1921-24. Ordained a minister of the Presbyterian Church of New Zealand, 1926; Minister: Bay of Islands, 1926-29; St Andrews', Dunedin, 1929-41; Master of Knox College, Dunedin, 1941-63. Member: Council of Otago University, 1946-71, Chancellor, 1955-70; Senate of Univ. of NZ, 1948-61; Pro-Chancellor of Univ. of Otago, 1954-55. Hon. LLD (Otago). *Recreation:* fishing. *Address:* 15 Cornwall Street, Dunedin, NZ. *T:* 42-032.

RYCROFT, Sir Richard Newton, 7th Bt, *cr* 1784; *b* 23 Jan. 1918; *yr s* of Sir Nelson Edward Oliver Rycroft, 6th Bt, and Ethel Sylvia (*d* 1952), *d* of late Robert Nurton, Odcombe, Yeovil; *S* father 1958; *m* 1947, Ann, *d* of late Hugh Bellingham-Smith, Alfriston, Sussex, and Mrs Harvey Robarts; two *d.* *Educ:* Winchester; Christ Church, Oxford (BA). Served War of 1939-

45: Bedfordshire and Hertfordshire Regt, on special service work in Balkans (Major, despatches); Knight's Cross of Royal Order of Phœnix with Swords (Greece). *Heir: uncle* Henry Richard Rycroft, OBE, DSC, Comdr RN retd [*b* 28 Dec. 1911; *m* 1941, Penelope Gwendolen, *d* of late Lt-Col C. S. B. Evans-Lombe; one *s* three *d*]. *Address:* Winalls Wood House, Stuckton, Fordingbridge, Hampshire. *T:* Fordingbridge 2263.
See also Viscount FitzHarris.

RYDBECK, Olof; Royal Order of the Star of the North, Sweden; Ambassador of Sweden to the Court of St James's, since 1976; *b* Djursholm, 15 April 1913; *s* of Oscar Rydbeck and Signe Olson; *m* 1940, Monica Schnell; one *s* one *d*. *Educ:* Univ. of Uppsala, Sweden (BA 1934, LLB 1939). Attaché, Min. for Foreign Affairs, 1939; Berlin, 1940; Ankara, 1941; Stockholm, 1942; Second Sec., 1943; First Sec., Swedish Embassy, Washington, 1945; Bonn, 1950; Head of Press Sect., Min. for For. Affairs, 1952; Dir Gen., Swedish Broadcasting Corp., 1955-70; Perm. Rep. to UN, 1970-76; Rep. of Sweden to Security Council, 1975-76; Special Rep. of Sec. Gen. on Western Sahara, 1976. Chairman: Adv. Cttee on Outer Space Communications, UNESCO, 1966-70; Working Gp on Direct Broadcast Satellites, UN Cttee on Peaceful Uses of Outer Space, 1969-75; Cttee of Trustees, UN Trust Fund for S Africa, 1970-75; Prep. Cttee, World Food Conf., 1974; Second Cttee, 30th Gen. Assembly, 1975. Chairman: Assoc. of Royal Swedish Nat. Defence Coll., 1957-70; Internat. Broadcasting Inst., Rome, 1967-70; Hon. Pres., EBU, 1964- (Pres., 1961-64). Member: Central Cttee, Swedish Red Cross; Nat. Swedish Preparedness Commn for Psychol. Defence, 1954-70 (Vice Chm., 1962-70); Royal Swed. Acad. of Music, 1962-. Member Boards: Swed. Inst., 1953-55; Amer.-Swed. News Exchange, 1953-55; Swed. Tourist Traffic Assoc., 1953-55; Stockholm Philharmonic Soc., 1955-62; Swed. Central News Agency, 1967-70; Swed. Inst. of Internat. Affairs, 1967-. Order of: White Rose, Finland; Falcon, Iceland; Dannebrog, Denmark; Verdienstcreutz, Fed. Republic of Germany. *Recreations:* music, equitation. *Address:* Swedish Embassy, 27 Portland Place, W1. *T:* 01-499 9500.

RYDEN, Kenneth, MC and Bar 1945; Consultant Chartered Surveyor; *b* 15 Feb. 1917; *s* of Walter and Elizabeth Ryden; *m* 1950, Catherine Kershaw (*née* Wilkinson); two *s*. *Educ:* Queen Elizabeth's Grammar School, Blackburn. FRICS. Served War of 1939-45 (MC and Bar, despatches 1945): RE, attached Royal Bombay Sappers and Miners, India, Assam and Burma, 1940-46, retd (Captain). Articled pupil and prof. trng, 1936-39; Min. of Works: Estate Surveyor, 1946-47; attached UK High Commns, India and Pakistan, 1947-50; Sen. Estate Surveyor, Scotland, 1950-59. Founder and Sen. Partner, Kenneth Ryden & Partners (Chartered Surveyors) Edinburgh, Glasgow and London, 1959-74, retd, Consultant 1974-. Chm., Scottish Br. Chartered Auctioneers and Estate Agents' Institute, 1960-61; Mem., Edinburgh Valuation Appeal Cttee, 1965-75. Member Board: Housing Corp., 1972-76; Legal & General (Northern & Scottish Region); Aberdeen Hotel Co. Ltd. Master, Co. of Merchants of City of Edinburgh, 1976. *Recreations:* fishing, golf, gardening, Scottish art. *Address:* 20 Frogston Road West, Edinburgh EH10 7AR. *T:* 031-445 1732. *Clubs:* Caledonian; New (Edinburgh).

RYDER, family name of **Earl of Harrowby** and of **Baron Ryder of Eaton Hastings.**

RYDER OF EATON HASTINGS, Baron *cr* 1975 (Life Peer); of Eaton Hastings, Oxfordshire; **Sydney Thomas Franklin, (Don), Ryder,** Kt 1972; Industrial Adviser to the Government, since 1974; Chairman, National Enterprise Board, 1975-77; *b* 16 Sept. 1916; *s* of John Ryder; *m* 1950; one *s* one *d*. *Educ:* Ealing. Editor, Stock Exchange Gazette, 1950-60; Jt Man. Dir, 1960-61, Sole Man. Dir, 1961-63, Kelly Iliffe Holdings, and Associated Iliffe Press Ltd; Dir, Internat. Publishing Corp., 1963-70; Man. Dir, Reed Paper Gp, 1963-68; Chm. and Chief Executive, Reed International Ltd, 1968-75; Dir, MEPC Ltd, 1972-75. Member: British Gas Corp., 1973-; Reserve Pension Bd, 1973-; Council and Bd of Fellows, BIM, 1970-; Court and Council, Cranfield Inst. of Technology, 1970-74; Council, UK S Africa Trade Assoc., 1974-; Nat. Materials Handling Centre (Pres., 1970-); Council, Industrial Soc., 1971-; NEDC, 1976-. Vice-Pres., RoSPA, 1973-. *Recreations:* sailing, chess. *Address:* 12-18 Grosvenor Gardens, SW1W 0DW.

RYDER, Eric Charles, MA, LLB; Barrister; Professor of English Law in the University of London (University College) since 1960; *b* 28 July 1915; *er s* of late Charles Henry Ryder, solicitor, Hanley, Staffs, and of Ellen Miller; *m* 1941, Nancy Winifred Roberts; no *c*. *Educ:* Hanley High School; Gonville and Caius College, Cambridge (scholar). BA (Law Tripos Parts I and II, 1st Cl.), 1936; LLB (1st Cl.) 1937; MA 1940; Tapp Law Scholar,

Gonville and Caius College, 1937; called to Bar, Gray's Inn, 1937; practice at Chancery Bar. Ministry of Food, 1941-44; Lecturer in Law, King's College, Newcastle upon Tyne, 1944; Dean of Faculty of Law, Univ. of Durham, 1947-60; Professor of Law, Univ. of Durham (King's College), 1953-60. Practised as conveyancing counsel, Newcastle upon Tyne, 1944-53. *Publications:* Hawkins and Ryder on the Construction of Wills, 1965; contrib. to legal periodicals. *Address:* 19 Langton Ave, Whetstone, N20. *T:* 01-445 1588.

RYDER, Peter Hugh Dudley, MBE 1944; Managing Director, Thomas Tilling Ltd, 1957-68; *b* 28 April 1913; *s* of Hon. Archibald Dudley Ryder and Eleanor Frederica Fisher-Rowe; *m* 1940, Sarah Susannah Bowes-Lyon; two *s* one *d*. *Educ:* Oundle School. Provincial Newspapers Ltd, Hull and Leeds, 1930-33; Illustrated Newspapers Ltd, 1933-39; seconded from TA to Political Intell. Dept of FO, 1939-45 (Lt-Col 1944); Jt Man. Dir, Contact Publications Ltd, 1945; Man. Dir, Daimler Hire Ltd, 1950; Commercial Dir, James A. Jobling & Co. Ltd, Sunderland, 1953; Chairman: James A. Jobling & Co. Ltd, 1957-62 and 1967-68; Heinemann Gp of Publishers Ltd, 1961-68; Director: District Bank Ltd, 1961-69; Cornhill Insce Co. Ltd, 1965-68. Mem. Council, BIM, 1966-69 (Mem. Bd of Fellows, 1968-69); Mem. Bd of Govs, Ashridge Management Coll., 1968. *Recreations:* home life, many forms of sport and games. *Address:* Ballig, Kirk Michael, Isle of Man.

RYDER, Captain Robert Edward Dudley, VC 1942; RN (retired); *b* 16 Feb. 1908; *s* of late Col C. H. D. Ryder, CB, CIE, DSO; *m* 1941, Hilare Myfanwy Green-Wilkinson; one *s* one *d*. *Educ:* Hazelhurst, Frant; Cheltenham College. Entered RN 1926; commanded Yacht Tai Mo Shan, 1933-34, on passage from Hong-Kong to Dartmouth; a member of British Graham Land Expedition to the Antarctic, 1934-37, in command of the Research Yacht Penola (Polar Medal with Clasp); commanded Naval forces in attack on St Nazaire, March 1942 (VC); took part in attack on Dieppe, Aug. 1942 (despatches); retd list, 1950. MP (C) Merton and Morden, 1950-55. *Publications:* The Attack on St Nazaire, 1947; Coverplan, 1953. *Address:* c/o Lloyds Bank, Cox's & King's Branch, 6 Pall Mall, SW1.

RYDER, Susan, (Mrs G. L. Cheshire), CMG 1976; OBE 1957; Founder and Social Worker, Sue Ryder Foundation for the Sick and Disabled of all Age Groups; *b* 3 July 1923; *d* of late Charles and Elizabeth Ryder; *m* 1959, Geoffrey Leonard Cheshire, *qv*; one *s* one *d*. *Educ:* Benenden Sch., Kent. Served War of 1939-45 with FANY and with Special Ops Executive. Co-Founder, Mission for the Relief of Suffering; Trustee, Cheshire Foundn. Hon. LLD Liverpool, 1973. Holds Officer's Cross of Order of Polonia Restituta, Poland, 1965; Medal of Yugoslav Flag with Gold Wreath and Diploma, 1971; Golden Order of Merit, Polish People's Republic, 1976. *Publications:* Remembrance (annual leaflet of the Sue Ryder Foundation); And the Morrow is Theirs (autobiog.), 1975. *Address:* Sue Ryder Home, Cavendish, Suffolk CO10 8AY.

RYDGE, Sir Norman, Kt 1966; CBE 1955; Hon. President, The Greater Union Organisation Pty Ltd; Chairman: Carlton Hotel Ltd; Manly Hotels Ltd; Carlton Investments Ltd; Amalgamated Holdings Ltd; *b* 18 Oct. 1900; *s* of William Rydge and Margaret McSweeney; *m* 1950, Phoebe Caroline McEwing; three *s* (and one *s* decd). *Educ:* Fort Street High School. Hon. Life Governor: Royal Prince Alfred Hosp. (Sydney); Royal Children's Hosp. and Alfred Hosp. (Melb.); Australian Inst. of Management; Royal Life Saving Soc. of NSW. Founder of Rydge's Business Journal, 1927. *Publications:* Federal Income Tax Law; Federal Land Tax Law; The Law of Income Tax in NSW; Employers' Endowment Tax; Commonwealth Income Tax Acts; Australasian Executorship Law and Accounts; The NSW Income Tax Management Act; Australasian edition of Stevens' Mercantile Law. *Recreations:* boating, gardening. *Address:* 55 Wunulla Road, Point Piper, NSW 2027, Australia. *T:* 36-6314. *Clubs:* Tattersall's, American National, Australian Golf, Royal Motor Yacht (all Sydney).

RYDILL, Louis Joseph, OBE 1962; RCNC; Director of Ship Design and Engineering (formerly Warship Design), since 1976; *b* 16 Aug. 1922; *s* of Louis and Queenie Rydill; *m* 1949, Eva (*née* Newman); two *d*. *Educ:* HM Dockyard Sch., Devonport; RNEC Keyham; RNC Greenwich; Royal Corps of Naval Constructors. CEng, FRINA (Gold Medallist). Asst Constructor, 1946-52; Constructor, 1952-62, incl. Asst Prof. of Naval Architecture, RNC Greenwich, 1953-57; Chief Constructor, 1962-72, incl. Prof. of Naval Architecture, RNC Greenwich and UCL, 1967-72; Asst Dir Submarines, Constructive, 1972-74; Dep. Dir Submarines (Polaris), 1974-76. Hon. Res. Fellow, UCL, 1974. Silver Jubilee Medal, 1977. *Recreations:* literature, theatre, jazz and other music. *Address:* The Lodge, Entry Hill Drive, Bath, Avon. *T:* Bath 27888.

RYDON, Prof. Henry Norman, DSc, PhD (London), DPhil (Oxon), FRIC; Professor of Chemistry, University of Exeter, 1957-77, now Emeritus; Deputy Vice-Chancellor, 1973-75; Public Orator, 1976-77; *b* 24 March 1912; *o s* of late Henry William Rydon and Elizabeth Mary Anne (*née* Salmon); *m* 1st, 1937, Eleanor Alice Tattersall (*d* 1968); one *d* ; 2nd, 1968, Lovis Elna Hibbard (*née* Davies). *Educ:* Central Foundation Sch., London; Imperial Coll., London. BSc (London), 1931; PhD (London), 1933; DSc (London), 1938; DPhil (Oxon), 1939. Demonstrator in Organic Chemistry, Imperial College, London, 1933-37; Demonstrator in Chemistry, Birkbeck College, London, 1933-37; 1851 Exhibition Senior Student, Oxford University, 1937-40; Chemical Defence Experimental Station, Porton, 1940-45; Member Scientific Staff, Medical Research Council, Lister Institute, 1945-47; Reader in Organic Chemistry, Birkbeck Coll., London, 1947-49; Asst Prof. and Reader in Organic Chemistry, Imperial Coll., London, 1949-52; Professor of Chemistry and Director of the Chemical Laboratories, Manchester College of Science and Technology, 1952-57. Member Council: Chem. Society, 1947-50, 1951-52, 1954-57, 1964-67; Roy. Inst. of Chemistry, 1955-58, 1959-62, 1963-66, 1971-73; Soc. of Chemical Industry, 1961-63; Regional Scientific Adviser for Civil Defence, Home Office, 1951-52, 1955-57. Meldola Medal, Roy. Inst. of Chemistry, 1939; Harrison Memorial Prize, Chem. Soc., 1941. *Publications:* papers in Jl of Chem. Soc. and other scientific jls, 1933-. *Recreations:* travel, gardening and motoring. *Address:* Stadmans, Dunsford, Exeter, EX6 7DD. *T:* Christow 52532.

RYKWERT, Prof. Joseph, DrRCA; Professor of Art, University of Essex, since 1967; *b* 5 April 1926; *s* of Szymon Rykwert and Elizabeth Melup; *m* 1st, 1960 (marr. diss. 1967); 2nd, 1972, Anne-Marie Sandersley; one *s* one *d* . *Educ:* Charterhouse; Bartlett Sch. of Architecture; Architectural Assoc. Lectr, Hochschule für Gestaltung, Ulm, 1958; Librarian and Tutor, Royal Coll. of Art, 1961-67. Fellow, Inst. for Arch. and Urban Studies, NY, 1969-71; Sen. Fellow, Council of Humanities, Princeton Univ., 1971; Visiting Professor: Institut d'Urbanisme, Univ. of Paris, 1974-76; Princeton Univ., 1977; Andrew Mellon Vis. Prof., Cooper Union, NY, 1977. Mem. Commn, Venice Biennale, 1974-; Co-editor, Lotus, 1974-. *Publications:* The Golden House, 1947; (ed) The Ten Books of Architecture, by L. B. Alberti, 1955; The Idea of a Town, 1963, 2nd edn 1976; Church Building, 1966; On Adam's House in Paradise, 1972; (ed) Parole nel Vuoto, by A. Loos, 1972; contrib. Arch. Rev., Burlington Mag., Lotus. *Recreations:* rare. *Address:* Department of Art, University of Essex, Wivenhoe Park, Colchester, Essex CO4 3SQ. *T:* Colchester 44144. *Club:* Savile.

RYLAND, Sir (Albert) William (Cecil), Kt 1973; CB 1965; Chairman, Post Office Corporation, 1971-77; *b* 10 Nov. 1913; *s* of late A. E. Ryland, OBE; *m* 1946, Sybil, *d* of late H. C. Wookey; one *s* one *d*. *Educ:* Gosforth County Grammar School. Assistant Traffic Superintendent, GPO, 1934; Asst Surveyor, GPO, 1938. Served War of 1939-45 in Royal Engineers (Postal Section), Middle East and Central Mediterranean. Principal, GPO, 1949; Principal Private Secretary to PMG, 1954; Asst Secretary, GPO, 1955; Director of Establishments and Organisation, GPO, 1958; Director of Inland Telecommunications, GPO, 1961-65; Dep. Director-General, 1965-67; Man. Dir, Telecommunications, GPO, 1967-69; PO Corporation: Jt Dep. Chm. and Chief Exec., 1969-70; Acting Chm., 1970-71. CompIEE; FBIM; Hon. CGIA. *Address:* 13 Mill View Gardens, Croydon CR0 5HW. *T:* 01-656 4224. *Clubs:* Reform, City Livery, Royal Automobile.

RYLAND, Charles Mortimer Tollemache S.; *see* Smith-Ryland.

RYLAND, Judge John, CIE 1946; RIN (retired); Judge for British Columbia, 1969; retired; *b* 31 March 1900; *s* of late W. J. Ryland, Surbiton; *m* 1938, Lucy Lenore, *d* of J. W. Bryden, Victoria, BC; two *s*. *Educ:* King's College School; HMS Conway. *Address:* Royston, BC, Canada.

RYLAND, Sir William; *see* Ryland, Sir A. W. C.

RYLANDS, George Humphrey Wolferstan, CBE 1961; MA; Fellow of King's College, Cambridge; Sometime Dean, Bursar, College Lecturer, and Director of Studies; University Lecturer in English Literature (retd); *b* 23 October 1902; *s* of Thomas Kirkland Rylands. *Educ:* Eton (King's Scholar); King's Coll., Cambridge (Scholar). Chm. of Directors and Trustees of the Arts Theatre, Cambridge; Governor of the Old Vic; Chm. of Apollo Soc., 1946-72. Member: Cheltenham Coll. Council, 1946-76; Council of RADA. Directed Hamlet with Sir John Gielgud, 1945; LP Recordings of the Shakespeare canon and the English Poets, for the British Council. Hon. LittD Cambridge, 1976. *Publications:* Words and Poetry, 1928; Shakespeare the

Poet (in a Companion to Shakespeare Studies), 1934; Poems; The Ages of Man, a Shakespeare Anthology, 1939; Shakespeare's Poetic Energy (British Academy Lecture, 1951). *Address:* King's College, Cambridge. *T:* Cambridge 50411. *Clubs:* Athenæum, Reform.

RYLE, George Bodley, CBE 1960; *b* 4 March 1902; *y s* of late Reginald John Ryle, MD, JP, and Catherine Ryle (*née* Scott); *m* 1934, Margaret Bevan; one *s* three *d*. *Educ:* Brighton College; St Catherine's, Oxford. Entered Forestry Commission, 1924; Dep. Director Gen., 1963; retired 1965. Seconded as Divisional Officer, Home Timber Production Dept, Ministry of Supply, 1939-46; as Chief Control Officer, North German Timber Control, Control Commission for Germany, 1946-47; Conservator, Forestry Commission, 1947-54; Dir of Forestry for Wales, 1954-58; Dir of Forestry for England, 1958-63. Apptd Verderer of the New Forest, 1966. Fellow and 1973 Medallist, Inst. of Foresters. *Publications:* Forest Service, 1969; numerous in Forestry, Quarterly Journal of Forestry and Empire Forestry Review. *Recreations:* walking the hills, but now only up memory tracks; entomology. *Address:* 5 Whitby Court, Milford-on-Sea, Hants SO4 0WB.

RYLE, Kenneth Sherriff, CBE 1964; MC 1945; Secretary to the Church Commissioners for England, 1969-75; *b* 13 April 1912; *s* of Herbert Ryle, CVO, OBE; *m* 1941, Jean Margaret Watt; one *s* one *d*. *Educ:* Cheltenham Coll. Chartered Accountant, 1936; Queen Anne's Bounty, 1936-48. Served in RA, 1940-45: India, Persia, Middle East, Sicily, Italy, Germany; Captain 1944. Church Commissioners, 1948- (Dep. Sec., 1964-69). *Recreation:* golf. *Address:* 47 Albyfield, Bickley, Kent. *T:* 01-467 6319. *Clubs:* Naval and Military; Chislehurst Golf.

RYLE, Sir Martin, Kt 1966; FRS 1952; Professor of Radio Astronomy, Cambridge, since 1959; Director, Mullard Radio-Astronomy Observatory, Cambridge, since 1957; Astronomer Royal, since 1972; *b* 27 Sept. 1918; *s* of late Prof. J. A. Ryle, MD, FRCP, and Mrs Miriam Ryle (*née* Scully); *m* 1947, Ella Rowena Palmer; one *s* two *d*. *Educ:* Bradfield Coll.; Christ Church, Oxford. Telecommunications Research Establishment, 1939-45; ICI Fellowship, Cavendish Laboratory, Cambridge, 1945-48; University Lecturer in Physics, Cambridge, 1948-59. Fellowship, Trinity Coll., Cambridge, 1949-. For. Mem., Russian Academy of Sciences, 1971. Hughes Medal, 1954, Royal Medal, 1973, Royal Soc.; Gold Medal, Royal Astronomical Soc., 1964; Henry Draper Medal, Nat. Academy of Sciences (US), 1965; Nobel Prize for Physics (jtly), 1974. Hon. DSc: Strathclyde, 1968; Oxford, 1969. *Publications:* papers in: Proc. Roy. Soc., Proc. Physical Soc., Monthly Notices of Roy. Astronomical Soc. *Recreation:* sailing. *Address:* 5a Herschel Road, Cambridge. *T:* 56670.

RYLEY, Air Vice-Marshal Douglas William Robert, CB 1956; CBE 1944; retired, 1962; *b* 11 November 1905; *y s* of late Lachlan Macpherson Ryley, OBE, Ichapur, India and Palta, Bournemouth; *m* 1932, Madeline Doreen, *d* of late William Lloyd-Evans, Postlip, Glos; one *d*. *Educ:* Bedford School; RAF College, Cranwell. Commissioned in RAF 1925; India, 1929-34; Air Armament School, 1935; HQ RAF Far East, 1937; Woolwich Arsenal, 1939; UK Tech. Mission, USA, 1941; UK Tech. Mission, Canada, 1943; Ordnance Board, 1944; Superintendent EE Pendine, 1945; OC 10 S of TT, 1947; STSO No. 3 Group, 1948; AOC and Comdt, RAF Tech. Coll., Henlow, 1949; STSO HQ Coastal Comd, 1952; Dir of Armament Engineering, Air Min., 1954; Dir of Guided Weapons Engineering, Air Min., 1957; AOA, HQ Maintenance Command, 1958. *Recreations:* golf and shooting. *Address:* Foresters, Over Wallop, Stockbridge, Hants.

RYMAN, Prof. Brenda Edith, (Mrs Harry Barkley), MA, PhD; FRIC; Professor of Biochemistry, Charing Cross Hospital Medical School, University of London, since 1972, and Mistress of Girton College, Cambridge, since 1976; *b* 6 Dec. 1922; *d* of William Henry Ryman and Edith Florence Terry; *m* 1948, Dr Harry Barkley, BSc, FRCP, FRCPath; one *s* one *d*. *Educ:* Colston Girls' Sch., Bristol; Cambridge Univ. (BA, MA); Birmingham Univ. (PhD). Royal Free Hospital Medical School: Asst Lectr in Biochemistry, 1948-51; Lectr, 1952-61; Sen. Lectr, 1961-69; Reader, 1970-72. *Publications:* many scientific, in jls such as Biochem. Jl, European Jl of Biochem., FEBS Letters, Biochim. et Biophys. Acta, Advances in Enzymology, Jl of Clin. Path., Nature. *Recreations:* foreign travel, athletic pursuits, gardening. *Address:* 54 Primrose Gardens, Hampstead, NW3 4TP. *T:* 01-722 1627.

RYMAN, John; MP (Lab) Blyth, since Oct. 1974; *b* 7 Nov. 1930. *Educ:* Leighton Park; Pembroke College, Oxford. Called to the Bar, Middle Temple, 1957. Harmsworth Law Scholar.

Practising barrister, July 1957-; 2nd Prosecuting Counsel to Inland Revenue at Central Criminal Court, July 1969; 1st Prosecuting Counsel, May 1970. *Recreation:* Hunting with the Meynell. *Address:* House of Commons, SW1A 0AA.

RYMER-JONES, Brig. John Murray, CBE 1950 (OBE 1941); MC 1917, and Bar 1918; QPM 1959; retired as Assistant Commissioner Metropolitan Police (1950-59); Secretary, Drinking Fountain Association, 1959-76; Committee Member, Royal Humane Society, since 1957; *b* 12 July 1897; *s* of late John and Lilian Rymer-Jones; *m* 1930, Gertrude Alice Wobey; one *s* two *d*. *Educ:* Felsted School; RMA, Woolwich. Commissioned RFA 1916; served European War: France and Flanders, 1916-18; Army of Rhine, 1919. Ireland, 1920-21 with KORR (Lancaster); Plebiscite, Upper Silesia, 1921; HQ British Army in Egypt, 1921-25; HQ Shanghai Defence Force, 1927-28; Company Commander and Instructor, RMA, Woolwich, 1929-33; retired as Captain, RA. Joined Metropolitan Police as Chief Inspector, 1934; Superintendent, 1935; Chief Constable, 1936; Inspector-General and Brigadier commanding Palestine Police, 1943-46. Commander Metropolitan Police, 1946-50. Area Comr, St John Ambulance, North Kent, 1963-66. Commander of St John of Jerusalem, 1952; Chevalier, Légion d'Honneur, 1950; *Recreations:* talking and music. *Address:* Lion House Lodge, High Halden, Kent. *T:* High Halden 538. *Club:* Army and Navy.

RYMILL, Hon. Sir Arthur (Campbell), Kt 1954; MLC, South Australia, 1956-75; Chairman of Directors, The Bank of Adelaide, since 1953; Member of Principal Board, Australian Mutual Provident Society; Director of public companies in South Australia; *b* 8 Dec. 1907; *s* of late Arthur Graham Rymill, North Adelaide; *m* 1934, Margaret Earle, *d* of Roland Cudmore; two *d*. *Educ:* Queen's Sch. and St Peter's Coll., Adelaide; Univ. of Adelaide. Barrister and Solicitor, 1930. Mem. Adelaide City Council, 1933-38, 1946-64; Lord Mayor of Adelaide, 1950-54. Pres., S Australian Liberal and Country League, 1953-55; First Pres., Nat. Trust of S Australia; Vice-Pres., Aust. Elizabethan Theatre Trust, 1954-63; Mem., Found. Bd of Govs, Adelaide Festival of Arts; Vice-Pres., Adelaide Children's Hosp. Won Australasian Unlimited Speedboat Championship, 1933; rep. S Austr. in Australasian Polo Championships, 1938 and 1951. Served War of 1939-45, 2nd AIF: enlisted Private, 2/7th Field Regt, later commissioned. *Recreations:* farming, violin playing, golf. *Address:* 39 Jeffcott Street, North Adelaide, SA 5006, Australia. *T:* 267 2477. *Clubs:* Adelaide (Adelaide); Melbourne (Melbourne); Royal Adelaide Golf, Royal SA Yacht Squadron.

RYRIE, William Sinclair; Economic Minister and Head of UK Treasury and Supply Delegation, Washington, and UK Executive Director, IMF and IBRD, since 1975; *b* 10 Nov. 1928; *s* of Rev. Dr Frank Ryrie and Mabel Moncrieff Ryrie (*née* Watt); *m* 1st, 1953, Dorrit Klein (marr. diss. 1969); two *s* one *d*; 2nd, 1969, Christine Gray Thomson; one *s*. *Educ:* Mount Hermon Sch., Darjeeling; Heriot's Sch., Edinburgh; Edinburgh Univ. MA 1st cl. hons History, 1951. Nat. Service, 1951-53: Lieut, Intell. Corps, Malaya, 1952-53 (despatches). Colonial Office, 1953; seconded to Uganda, 1956-58; Principal 1958; transf. to Treasury, 1963; Asst Sec., internat. monetary affairs, 1966-69; Principal Private Sec. to Chancellor of Exchequer, 1969-71; Under-Sec., Public Sector Gp, HM Treasury, 1971-75. *Recreations:* hill walking, music. *Address:* 76 Kalorama Circle NW, Washington, DC 20008, USA. *Club:* Reform.

S

SABATINI, Lawrence John; Assistant Under Secretary of State, Ministry of Defence, since 1972; *b* 5 Dec. 1919; *s* of Frederick Laurence Sabatini and Elsie May Sabatini (*née* Friggens); *m* 1947, Patricia Dyson; one *s* one *d*. *Educ:* Watford Grammar School. Joined HM Office of Works, 1938. Army service, 1940-46: commnd in RTR, 1943: service in NW Europe with 5 RTR. Asst Principal, Min. of Works, 1947; Asst Private Sec. to Minister of Works, 1948-49; Principal, 1949; Principal Private Sec. to Ministers of Defence, 1958-60; Asst Sec., MoD, 1960; Defence Counsellor, UK Delegn to NATO, on secondment to Diplomatic Service, 1963-67. *Recreations:* gardening, photography, music. *Address:* 44a Batchworth Lane, Northwood, Mddx HA6 3DT. *T:* Northwood 23249.

SABBEN-CLARE, Ernest E., MA Oxon, BA London; Information Officer to University of Oxford, 1970-77; *b* 11 Aug.

1910; *s* of late Mr and Mrs J. W. Sabben-Clare; *m* 1938, Rosamond Dorothy Mary Scott; two *s* one *d*. *Educ:* Winchester Coll. (schol.); New College, Oxford (schol.). 1st cl. Mod. Hist., Oxford, 1932. Asst Master, Winchester Coll., 1932-34; Asst Dist Officer, Tanganyika, 1935-40; seconded Colonial Office, 1940-47; Lt, 10th Essex Bn Home Guard; Colonial Attaché, British Embassy, Washington, and Comr, Caribbean Commn, 1947-49; Nigerian Govt, 1950-55; Permanent Sec., Min. of Commerce, 1953-55; 1st cl. French, London Univ. (external), 1954; Asst Master, Marlborough Coll., 1955-60, Under-Master from 1957; Headmaster, Bishop Wordsworth's School, Salisbury, 1960-63; Headmaster, Leeds Grammar Sch., 1963-70. *Publication:* Editor, Wilts Archaeological and Natural History Magazine, 1956-62. *Recreations:* caravanning, gardening. *Address:* The Shambles, Yarnton Road, Cassington, Oxford OX8 1DY. *Club:* Athenæum.

SABIN, Professor Albert B.; Distinguished Research Professor of Biomedicine, Medical University of South Carolina, Charleston, SC, since 1974; Consultant: to US Army Medical Research and Development Command, since 1975; to World Health Organization, since 1969; *b* 26 Aug. 1906; *s* of Jacob Sabin and Tillie Krugman; *m* 1935, Sylvia Tregillus (*d* 1966); two *d*; *m* 1967, Jane Blach Warner (marr. diss. 1971); *m* 1972, Heloisa Dunshee de Abranches. *Educ:* New York Univ. (MD). Ho. Phys., Bellevue Hosp., NY, 1932-33; Nat. Research Council Fellow, Lister Inst., London, 1934; Rockefeller Inst. for Med. Research, NY, 1935-39; Associate Prof. of Research Pediatrics, Univ. of Cincinnati, 1939-43; active duty, US Army, 1943-46 (Legion of Merit, 1945); Prof. of Research Pediatrics, Univ. of Cincinnati Coll. of Medicine and The Children's Hosp. Research Foundn, 1946-60, Distinguished Service Prof., 1960-71, Emeritus, 1971-. Pres., Weizmann Inst. of Science, Israel, 1970-72. Fogarty Scholar, NIH, 1973. Mem. Nat. Acad. of Sciences of the USA; Fellow, Amer. Acad. of Arts and Sciences; Mem. and Hon. Mem. of various Amer. and foreign societies; Hon. Member: Royal Acad. of Med. of Belgium; British Paediatric Association. Holds hon. degrees; awards include: Feltrinelli Prize ($40,000) of Accad. Naz. dei Lincei, Rome, 1964; Lasker ($10,000) Prize for Clinical Medicine Research, 1965. Gold Medal, Royal Soc. of Health, 1969; National Medal of Science (USA), 1970; Statesman in Medicine Award (USA), 1973. Hon. FRSH London. *Publications:* numerous papers on pneumococcus infection, poliomyelitis, encephalitis, virus diseases of nervous system, toxoplasmosis, sandfly fever, dengue, other topics relating to various infectious diseases and virus-cancer relationships. *Recreations:* reading and music. *Address:* Medical University of South Carolina, Charleston, SC 29401, USA; 715 Knotty Pine Road, Charleston, SC 29412, USA.

SABIN, Howard Westcott; Legal Adviser to Associated Newspapers Ltd since 1972; *b* 19 Oct. 1916; *s* of John Howard Sabin and Octavia Roads (*née* Scruby); *m* 1st, 1942, Joan Eunice Noble (marr. diss. 1959); two *s* one *d*; 2nd, 1959, Janet Eileen Baillie. *Educ:* Shrewsbury; St John's Coll., Cambridge; MA (Hons in History and Law). Lieut, RNVR, 1939-46 (despatches 1944). Called to the Bar, Middle Temple, 1946. Dep. Chm., Bedfordshire QS, 1968-72; Assistant Recorder, Portsmouth, 1966, Bournemouth, 1967. Counsel for Post Office (Midland Circuit), 1964. *Recreations:* golf, swimming, music. *Address:* 40 Wynnstay Gardens, W8 6UT. *T:* 01-937 9247. *Clubs:* Royal Commonwealth Society; Hadley Wood Golf.

SABINE, Neville Warde, CMG 1960; CBE 1957; *b* 6 April 1910; *s* of late John William Sabine; *m* 1954, Zoë Margherita Bargna; two *d*. *Educ:* Manchester Grammar School; Brasenose College, Oxford. BA Hons. (Oxon) 1934. Colonial Service (Colonial Audit Dept) 1934; served Gold Coast, Malaya, Uganda, Leeward Islands, and N Borneo. Served War of 1939-45: Gold Coast Regt, 1939-40; Singapore RA (V), 1940-42; British Military Administration, Malaya, 1945-46. Auditor-General, Ghana, 1954-64; Secretary, Central Bd of Finance of Church of England, 1964-75. Sec., Soc. of Sussex Downsmen, 1976. *Recreations:* bridge and tennis. *Address:* 11 Windlesham Road, Brighton BN1 3AG. *T:* Brighton 732157. *Club:* Royal Commonwealth Society.

SABITI, Most Rev. Erica; *b* 1903; *m* 1934, Geraldine Kamuhigi; four *s* three *d*. *Educ:* Mbarara High Sch.; King's Coll., Budo; Makerere Coll. Teacher, 1920-25 and 1929-30; training in education, 1925-29; training for Ministry, 1931-32; ordained, 1933; Bishop of Ruwenzori, 1960-72; Bishop of Kampala, 1972-74; Archbishop of Uganda, Rwanda, Burundi and Boga Zaire, 1966-74. *Address:* PO Box 134, Mbarara, Uganda.

SACHER, Michael Moses; Vice-Chairman and Joint Managing Director, Marks & Spencer Ltd, since 1972; *b* 17 Oct. 1917; *e s* of late Harry and Miriam Sacher; *m* 1938, Audrey Glucksman;

three s two d. Educ: St Paul's Sch.; New Coll., Oxford (MA). RASC, 1940-46: served Western Desert; psc Haifa 1943; Liaison Gen. Leclerc's HQ Free French, N Africa; Allied Armies in Italy. Marks & Spencer Ltd, 1938-39 and 1946-: Alt. Dir, 1954-62; full Dir, 1962-71; Jt Man. Dir, 1971-72. Mem. Jewish Agency Exec. and Governor of Jewish Agency, 1971-; Jt Pres., Jt Israel Appeal (UK); Dir and Mem. Council, Weizmann Inst. Foundn; Vice Pres., Jewish Colonization Assoc.; Governor: Hebrew Univ. of Jerusalem; Weizmann Inst.; Reali Sch., Haifa; Vice-Pres. and Mem. Admin. Cttee, Jewish Nat. Fund for Gt Britain and Ireland (Past Pres.); Chm., Keren Hayesod Dist Trust; Director: Brit Olim Soc. Ltd, Israel; Jewish Telegraphic Agency Ltd; and Mem. Bd of Management, Jewish Nat. Fund Charitable Trust. Hon. Vice-Pres., Zionist Fedn of GB. FRSA; FRPSL. *Publications:* various philatelic monographs. *Recreation:* philately. *Address:* Michael House, Baker Street, W1A 1DN. *T:* 01-935 4422.
See also M. J. Gilbert.

SACHS, Rt. Hon. Sir Eric, PC 1966; Kt 1954; MBE 1941; TD; a Lord Justice of Appeal, 1966-73; *b* London, 23 July 1898; *o s* of late Edwin O. Sachs, FRS (Edinburgh), 5 Ulster Tce, Regent's Park; *m* 1934, Hon. Margaret, 2nd *d* of late Baron Goddard of Aldbourne, GCB; one *s* one *d*. *Educ:* Charterhouse; Christ Church, Oxford (Hon. Student, 1971). Served European War, 1917-19, Lieut RA (wounded); recommissioned as 2nd Lieut Aug. 1939; Capt. 1939; Major and DAAG 1940; Lt-Col and AAG 1941; Brig. (specially employed) 1942-45. Called to Bar, Middle Temple, 1921; KC 1938; QC 1952; Leader of the Oxford Circuit, 1952-54; Bencher, 1947, Treasurer, 1967; Recorder of Dudley, 1938-43; Recorder of Stoke-on-Trent, 1943-54; Commissioner of Assize, 1946 (Western Circuit), 1948 (S-Eastern Circuit) and 1953 (Birmingham); Special Commission to Gold Coast (Appeals from Enquiry into Customs, Supplies and Currency Control Depts). 1947; Mem. of Gen. Council of the Bar (Exec. Cttee), 1946-53; Mem. of Legal Aid Committees (Legal Aid Act, 1949), 1948-53; a Judge of the High Court of Justice, Probate, Divorce and Admiralty Div., 1954-60, Queen's Bench Div., 1960-66. Gresham Lecturer on Law, 1948-49. Brig. (late RA, TARO). *Publication:* Legal Aid, 1951. *Recreation:* travel. *Address:* Walland Oast, Wadhurst, E Sussex. *T:* 2080. *Clubs:* Army and Navy, Hurlingham.

SACKVILLE, family name of **Earl De la Warr.**

SACKVILLE, 6th Baron, *cr* 1876; **Lionel Bertrand Sackville-West;** *b* 30 May 1913; *s* of late Hon. Bertrand George Sackville-West, *y b* of 4th Baron and Eva Adela Mabel Inigo (*d* 1936), *d* of late Maj.-Gen. Inigo Richmond Jones, CB, CVO; *S* cousin, 1965; *m* 1st, 1953, Jacobine Napier (*d* 1971), *widow* of Captain John Hichens, RA, and *d* of J. R. Menzies-Wilson; five *d*; 2nd, 1974, Arlie, Lady de Guingand. *Educ:* Winchester; Magdalen Coll., Oxford. Formerly Capt. Coldstream Gds; served War, 1939-42 (POW). Member of Lloyd's, 1949. *Heir:* b Hugh Rosslyn Inigo Sackville-West, MC [b 1 Feb. 1919; m 1957, Bridget Eleanor, d of Capt. Robert Lionel Brooke Cunliffe, qv; two s three d]. *Address:* Knole, Sevenoaks, Kent.

SACKVILLE-WEST, family name of **Baron Sackville.**

SACKWOOD, Dr Mark; Regional Medical Officer, Northern Regional Health Authority, since 1973; *b* London, 18 Jan. 1926; *s* of Philip and Frances Sackwood; *m* 1953, Anne Harper Wilson; one *s* two *d*. *Educ:* King's Coll., London; Westminster Hosp. Med. School. MB, BS, FFCM, LRCP, MRCS, DPH, DRCOG. Various hosp. appts, South of England, 1949-58; mil. service, Far East, 1951-53; subseq. admin. med. appts, Middlesbrough and Newcastle upon Tyne, incl. Dep. Sen. Admin. MO with Newcastle RHB, 1968-73. *Recreations:* walking, reading, music. *Address:* 11 The Chesters, Beaumont Park, Whitley Bay, Tyne and Wear. *T:* Whitley Bay 527401.

SADAT, Mohamed Anwar El; see El-Sadat, M. A.

SADIE, Stanley (John); Music Critic on staff of The Times, since 1964; Editor: The Musical Times, since 1967; The New Grove Dictionary of Music and Musicians, since 1970; Master Musicians series, since 1976; *b* 30 Oct. 1930; *s* of David Sadie and Deborah (*née* Simons); *m* 1953, Adèle Bloom; two *s* one *d*. *Educ:* St Paul's Sch.; Gonville and Caius Coll., Cambridge Univ. (MA, PhD, MusB). Prof., Trinity Coll. of Music, London, 1957-65. Writer and broadcaster on musical subjects, circa 1955-; Editor of many edns of 18th-century music, circa 1955-. Mem. Council, Royal Musical Assoc.; Member: Internat. Musicological Soc.; American Musicological Soc.; Critics' Circle. *Publications:* Handel, 1962; Mozart, 1966; Beethoven, 1967; Handel, 1968; (with Arthur Jacobs) Pan Book of Opera/The Opera Guide, 1964, new edn 1969; Handel

Concertos, 1973; contrib.: The Musical Times, The Gramophone, Opera, Music and Letters, Musical Quarterly, Proc. Roy. Musical Assoc. *Recreations:* watching cricket, drinking (mainly coffee), bridge, reading. *Address:* 1 Carlisle Gardens, Harrow, Mddx HA3 0JX. *T:* 01-907 6515.

SADLER, John Stephen; Finance Director, John Lewis Partnership Ltd, since 1971; Member, Monopolies and Mergers Commission, since 1973; *b* 6 May 1930; *s* of Bernard and Phyllis Sadler; *m* 1952, Ella (*née* McCleery); three *s*. *Educ:* Reading Sch.; Corpus Christi Coll., Oxford (BA). Board of Trade, 1952-54; Treasury, 1954-56; Board of Trade, 1956-60; British Trade Commissioner, Lagos, Nigeria, 1960-64; Board of Trade, 1964-66. John Lewis Partnership Ltd, 1966-. *Recreations:* golf, boating, gardening. *Address:* Isomer, The Warren, Mapledurham, Reading RG4 7TQ. *T:* Reading 472684. *Club:* Winter Hill Golf.

SAGAN, Françoise, pen-name of Françoise Quoirez; authoress; *b* France, 21 June 1935; *y c* of Paul Quoirez; *m* 1958, Guy Schoeller (marr. diss. 1960); *m* 1962, Robert James Westhoff; one *s*. *Educ:* convent and private school. Published first novel at age of 18. Has written some songs and collaborated in scheme for ballet Le Rendez-vous Manqué, produced Paris and London, 1958. *Publications:* (all trans into Eng., usually French title): Bonjour Tristesse, 1954; Un Certain Sourire, 1956 (filmed, 1958); Dans un mois, dans un an, 1957 (Eng. trans Those Without Shadows, 1958); Aimez-vous Brahms.... 1959 (Eng. trans. 1960); Château en Suède (play), 1960; Les Violons, parfois... (play), 1961; La Robe Mauve de Valentine (play), 1963; Bonheur, impair et passe (play), 1964; Toxique... (tr. 1965); La Chamade, 1965 (tr. 1966) (film, 1970); Le Cheval Evanoui (play), 1966; L'Echarde, 1966; Le Garde du cœur, 1968 (tr., The Heart-Keeper, 1968); Un peu de soleil dans l'eau froide, 1969 (tr., Sunlight and Cold Water, 1971); Un piano dans l'herbe (play), 1970; Des bleus à l'âme, 1972 (tr., Scars on the Soul, 1974); Zaphorie (play), 1973; Lost Profile, 1976. *Address:* c/o Editions Flammarion, 26 rue Racine, 75006 Paris, France.

SAGITTARIUS; see Katzin, Olga.

SAINER, Leonard; Senior Partner, Titmuss, Sainer & Webb; *b* 12 Oct. 1909; *s* of Archer and Sarah Sainer. Deputy Chairman: Sears Holdings Ltd; British Shoe Corporation Ltd; Sears Engineering Ltd; Lewis Investment Trust Ltd; Selfridges Ltd; Bentley Engineering Group Ltd; Dir, First National Finance Corp Ltd; Chm., United Real Property Trust Ltd. *Address:* (business) 2 Serjeants' Inn, EC4; (home) 15 Chesterfield House, South Audley Street, W1.

SAINSBURY, family name of **Baron Sainsbury.**

SAINSBURY, Baron, *cr* 1962, of Drury Lane (Life Peer); **Alan John Sainsbury;** Joint President of J. Sainsbury Ltd, since 1967 (Chairman, 1956-67); *b* 13 Aug. 1902; *er s* of John Benjamin and Mabel Miriam Sainsbury; *m* 1st, 1925, Doreen Davan Adams (marr. diss. 1939); three *s*; 2nd, 1944, Anne Elizabeth Lewy; one *d*. *Educ:* Haileybury. Joined Grocery and Provision Firm of J. Sainsbury, Ltd (founded by his grandparents), 1921. Served on many war-time consultative committees of Ministry of Food; Member Williams' Committee on Milk Distribution, 1947-48; Member: Food Research Advisory Cttee, 1960-70 (Chm., 1965-70); NEDC Cttee for the Distributive Trades, 1964-68; Exec. Cttee, PEP, 1970-76; Chm, Cttee of Inquiry into Relationship of Pharmaceutical Industry with National Health Service, 1965-67. President: Multiple Shops' Fedn, 1963-65; The Grocers' Inst., 1963-66; Internat. Assoc. of Chain Stores, 1965-68; The Royal Inst. of Public Health and Hygiene, 1965-70; Pestalozzi Children's Village Trust, 1963-; Distributive Trades Educn and Trng Council, 1975-; a Vice-President, Assoc. of Agriculture, 1965-73; Royal Society for the Encouragement of Arts, Manufactures and Commerce, 1962-66; Mem., Court of Univ. of Essex, 1966-; Governor, City Literary Inst., 1967-69; Chairman of Trustees: Overseas Students Adv. Bureau; Uganda Asian Relief Trust, 1972-74; Vice-Pres., World Development Movement. Liberal candidate, Sudbury Div. of Suffolk, Gen. Elections of 1929, 1931 and 1935. Joined Labour Party, 1945. Hon. Fellow, Inst. of Food Sci. and Technology. *Address:* J. Sainsbury Ltd, Stamford House, Stamford Street, SE1.
See also Hon. J. D. Sainsbury, Hon. T. A. D. Sainsbury.

SAINSBURY, Edward Hardwicke; TD 1945; Solicitor and Partner, Dawson, Hart & Co., Uckfield, since 1963; District Notary Public, Uckfield, since 1965; *b* 17 Sept. 1912; *e s* of Henry Morgan Sainsbury, and *g s* of James C. Hardwicke, a pioneer of technical and other education in S Wales; *m* 1946, Ann, 2nd *d* of Kenneth Ellis, Tunbridge Wells; one *s* one *d*. *Educ:* Cardiff High School; University of S Wales and

Monmouth. Solicitor in private practice, 1935; commissioned (TA) 1936; Prosecuting Solicitor, Cardiff, 1938, Sen. Pros. Solicitor, 1939. Served War of 1939-45; Adjutant, 77th HAA Regt, 1940; comd 240 HAA Battery Gibraltar, 1944; demobilised Nov. 1945. Hong Kong: Asst Crown Solicitor, 1946; commissioner for revision of the laws of Hong Kong, 1947; magistrate, 1948; registrar, High Court, 1949; sen. magistrate, Kowloon, 1951; Barrister, Inner Temple, 1951; Land Officer and crown counsel, Hong Kong, 1952; legal draftsman, Nigeria, 1953; Principal Legal Draftsman, Fed. of Nigeria, 1958. President, Commonwealth Parliamentary Assoc., Southern Cameroons, 1959-63. Judge, High Court of Lagos, 1960-63, and of Southern Cameroons, 1961-63 (Speaker, House of Assembly, 1958-63, Chm., Public Service Commn, 1961-63, Southern Cameroons). *Publication:* (jointly) Revised Laws of Hong Kong, 1948. *Recreations:* squash (a memory), golf. *Address:* Little Gassons, Fairwarp, Uckfield, East Sussex. *T:* Nutley 2100.

SAINSBURY, Hon. Mrs John; *see* Linden, Anya.

SAINSBURY, Hon. John Davan; Chairman, J. Sainsbury Ltd, since 1969 (Vice-Chairman, 1967-69); Director, Royal Opera House, Covent Garden, since 1969; Trustee, National Gallery, since 1976; *b* 2 Nov. 1927; *e s* of Baron Sainsbury, *qv*; *m* 1963, Anya Linden, *qv*; two *s* one *d. Educ:* Stowe School; Worcester College, Oxford. Director: J. Sainsbury Ltd, 1958; The Economist, 1972-; Ashwood Educational Productions Ltd, 1974-; Royal Opera House Trust, 1974-; European Educational Research Trust, 1975. Jt Hon. Treas., European Movement, 1972-75, a Pres., 1975-. Member: Council, Retail Consortium, 1975-; Adv. Council, V&A Museum, 1976-; Nat. Cttee for Electoral Reform, 1976-; Chm., Friends of Covent Garden, 1969-. *Address:* c/o Stamford House, Stamford Street, SE1 9LL. *T:* 01-921 6000. *Club:* Garrick.
˙ *See also Hon. T. A. D. Sainsbury.*

SAINSBURY, Richard Eric, CBE 1964; consultant; *b* 15 Sept. 1909; 2nd *s* of E. A. Sainsbury and F. W. Sainsbury (*née* Hill), Trowbridge, Wilts; *m* 1936, Margaret (*née* Horne); one *s. Educ:* Lewisham School, Weston-super-Mare; Bristol University. Grad. in Engineering, 1932; time-study with J. Lucas, 1934; subseq. with various firms; Ministry of Aircraft Production, 1940, Deputy Director, 1943; Joint Services Staff College, 1947; Director Instrument and Radio Production, Ministry of Supply, 1950; Imperial Defence College, 1959; Director, Guided Weapons Production, 1960; Dir-Gen., Electronics and Weapons Prodn, Min. of Aviation, 1961-67, Min. of Technology, 1967-70, Min. of Aviation Supply, 1970-71; Dir Gen., Telecommunications, MoD, 1971-72. Dir, Aeromaritime Ltd, Hounslow, 1973-75. Coronation Medal, 1953. *Recreations:* walking, reading, skiing. *Address:* 6 Blenheim Drive, Oxford OX2 8DG. *T:* Oxford 56029.

SAINSBURY, Sir Robert, Kt 1967 (for services to the arts); Joint President, J. Sainsbury Ltd; *b* 24 Oct. 1906; *s* of late John Benjamin Sainsbury and late Mable Miriam (*née* Van den Bergh); *m* 1937, Lisa Ingeborg (*née* Van den Bergh; second cousin); one *s* two *d* (and one *d* decd). *Educ:* Haileybury Coll.; Pembroke Coll., Cambridge (MA). ACA, 1930, FCA, 1935. Joined J. Sainsbury Ltd, 1930; Dir, 1934; Jt Gen. Man., 1938; Dep. Chm., 1956; Chm. 1967; Jt Pres., 1969. Formerly Mem. Art Panel of Arts Council. Trustee, Tate Gall., 1959-73 (Vice-Chm. 1967, Chm., 1969); Mem. Vis. Cttee to Primitive Art Dept, Metropolitan Museum of Art, NY; Hon. Treasurer, Inst. of Med. Social Workers, 1948-71; Past Governor, St Thomas' Hospital. Hon. Dr RCA, 1976; Hon. DLitt East Anglia, 1977. *Address:* 5 Smith Square, SW1. *T:* 01-222 7252; The Old Vicarage, Bucklebury, Berks. *T:* Yattendon 204.

SAINSBURY, Hon. Timothy Alan Davan; MP (C) Hove, since Nov. 1973; Director, J. Sainsbury Ltd, since 1962; *b* 11 June 1932; *y s* of Baron Sainsbury, *qv*; *m* 1961, Susan Mary Mitchell; two *s* two *d. Educ:* Eton; Worcester Coll., Oxford (MA). Chm., Council for the Unit for Retail Planning Information Ltd, 1974-. Governor, Centre for Environmental Studies, 1976-. *Address:* House of Commons, SW1A 0AA.
See also Hon. J. D. Sainsbury.

SAINT, Sir (Sidney) John, Kt 1950; CMG 1946; OBE 1942; BSc, PhD (London); MSc (Reading); FRIC; Dir, Sugar Technological Laboratory, Barbados, 1949-63, retd; *b* 16 Sept. 1897; *m* 1923, Constance Elizabeth Hole; two *s* one *d. Educ:* Beaminster Grammar School; Reading University. Served with RAF, 1916-19; Salter's Research Fellow, 1920-22; Lecturer in Agricultural Chemistry, Leeds University, 1922-27; Chemist, Department of Agriculture, Barbados, 1927-37; Director of Agriculture Barbados, 1937-49; Chm., BWI Sugar Cane Breeding Station, 1937-49; Competent Authority and Controller

of Supplies, Barbados, 1939-46; Pres., Barbados Technologists Assoc., 1939-42, 1950-63; Gen. Chm., Internat. Soc. of Sugar Cane Technologists, 1950-53; Chairman: Barbados Public Service Commn, 1952-57; Barbados Development Bd, 1956-59; Interim Federal Public Service Commn, 1956-59. Pres. Museum and Hist. Soc., 1946-59. MEC, 1947-61; PC (Barbados), 1961-63. Hon. Freeman, City of Bridgetown, Barbados, 1963. *Publications:* numerous papers on soils, manuring of tropical crops and sugar technology. *Address:* Selwyn, St George's Lane, Hurstpierpoint, Sussex. *T:* Hurstpierpoint 832335.

SAINT, Dr Stafford Eric, CVO 1956; Medical Practitioner, 1931-70; *b* 13 April 1904; *s* of late Sir Wakelin Saint; *m* 1931, Isabel Mary Fulford; two *s* one *d. Educ:* King's School, Ely; The London Hospital. MRCS Eng., LRCP Lond., 1926. *Address:* 28 The Uplands, Gerrard's Cross, Bucks SL9 7JG.

ST ALBANS, 13th Duke of, *cr* 1684; **Charles Frederic Aubrey de Vere Beauclerk,** OBE 1945; Earl of Burford and Baron of Heddington, 1676; Baron Vere, 1750; Hereditary Grand Falconer of England; Hereditary Registrar, Court of Chancery; Chairman: Amalgamated Developers Group; Travelworld Olympic Ltd; Director: James Archibald Productions Ltd; Isle of Man and Overseas Estates Corp. Ltd, and other companies; *b* 16 Aug. 1915; *s* of Aubrey Topham Beauclerk and Gwendolen, *d* of late Sir Frederic Hughes; *S* kinsman, 1964; *m* 1st, Nathalie Chatham (who obtained a divorce, 1947), *d* of late P. F. Walker; one *s*; 2nd, 1947, Suzanne Marie Adele, *d* of late Emile William Fesq, Mas Mistral, Vence, AM, France; three *s* one *d. Educ:* Eton; Magdalene Coll., Cambridge (MA). Served War of 1939-45 in Infantry, Military Intelligence and Psychological Warfare; Col, Intelligence Corps. Controller Inf. Services, Allied Commn for Austria, 1946-50. Central Office of Information: Chief Books Editor, 1951-58; Chief Films Production Officer, 1958-60; Dir, Films Div., 1960-64. Pres., Fedn of Industrial Develt Assocs; Vice-Pres., Ancient Monuments Soc.; Governor General, Royal Stuart Soc. *Heir: s* Earl of Burford, *qv. Address:* St Albans, 30 Cheyne Walk, SW3. *T:* 01-352 8008. *Clubs:* Brooks's, Beefsteak.

ST ALBANS, Bishop of, since 1970; **Rt. Rev. Robert Alexander Kennedy Runcie,** MC 1945; *b* 2 Oct. 1921; *s* of Robert Dalziel Runcie and Anne Runcie; *m* 1957, Angela Rosalind, *d* of J. W. Cecil Turner; one *s* one *d. Educ:* Merchant Taylors', Crosby; Brasenose Coll., Oxford (Squire Minor Schol.); Westcott House, Cambridge. BA (1st Cl. Hons, Lit. Hum.), MA Oxon, 1948. Served Scots Guards, War of 1939-45 (MC). Deacon, 1950; Priest, 1951; Curate, All Saints, Gosforth, 1950-52; Chaplain, Westcott House, Cambridge, 1953-54; Vice-Principal, 1954-56; Fellow, Dean and Asst Tutor of Trinity Hall, Cambridge, 1956-60, Hon. Fellow 1975; Vicar of Cuddesdon and Principal of Cuddesdon Coll., 1960-69. Canon and Prebendary of Lincoln, 1969. Chm., BBC and IBA Central Religious Adv. Cttee, 1973-. Teape Lectr, St Stephen's Coll., Delhi, 1962. Select Preacher: Cambridge, 1957 and 1975, Oxford, 1959 and 1973. Anglican Chm., Anglican-Orthodox Jt Doctrinal Commn, 1973-. *Recreations:* travel, reading novels. *Address:* Abbey Gate House, St Albans, Herts AL3 4HD. *T:* St Albans 53305. *Club:* Athenæum.

ST ALBANS, Dean of; *see* Moore, Very Rev. P. C.

ST ALBANS, Archdeacon of; *see* Farmbrough, Ven. D. J.

ST ALDWYN, 2nd Earl, *cr* 1915, of Coln St Aldwyns; **Michael John Hicks Beach,** PC 1959; KBE 1964; TD 1949; DL, JP; Bt 1619; Viscount St Aldwyn, 1906; Viscount Quenington, 1915; Opposition Chief Whip, House of Lords, 1964-70 and since 1974; *b* 9 Oct. 1912; *s* of Visc. Quenington, Roy. Glos. Hussars Yeo. (*d* 1916; *o s* of 1st Earl) and Marjorie (*d* 1916), *d* of late H. Dent Brocklehurst, Sudeley Castle, Gloucs; *S* grandfather, 1916 (his father having been killed in action a week previously); *m* 1948, Diana Mary Christian, DStJ (she *m* 1st, 1939, Major Richard Patrick Pilkington Smyly, MC; marriage annulled, 1942), *o d* of late Henry C. G. and Mrs Mills; three *s. Educ:* Eton; Christ Church, Oxford. Major Royal Glos Hussars Yeomanry, 1942. Parliamentary Secretary, Ministry of Agriculture and Fisheries, 1954-58; Captain of the Honorable Corps of Gentlemen-at-Arms and Govt Chief Whip, House of Lords, 1958-64 and 1970-74. DL 1950, JP 1952, Glos. KStJ; Vice-Chancellor, Order of St John, 1969-. *Heir: s* Viscount Quenington, *qv. Address:* Williamstrip Park, Cirencester, Gloucestershire. *T:* Coln St Aldwyns 226; 13 Upper Belgrave Street, SW1. *T:* 01-235 8464. *Clubs:* Beefsteak, Pratts; Royal Yacht Squadron.
See also Sir Richard Keane, Bt.

ST ANDREWS, Earl of; George Philip Nicholas Windsor; *b* 26 June 1962; *s* of HRH the Duke of Kent and HRH the Duchess

of Kent.
See under Royal Family.

ST ANDREWS AND EDINBURGH, Archbishop of, (RC), since 1951; **His Eminence Cardinal Gordon Joseph Gray,** MA (Hon.) St Andrews; Hon. DD St Andrews, 1967; *b* 10 August 1910; 2nd *s* of Francis William and Angela Gray. *Educ:* Holy Cross Acad., Edinburgh; St John's Seminary, Wonersh. Assistant-Priest, St Andrews, 1935-41; Parish Priest, Hawick, 1941-47; Rector of Blairs College, Aberdeen (Scottish National Junior Seminary), 1947-51. Cardinal, 1969. Member Pontifical Congregation: for Evangelization of Peoples; for Divine Worship; Mem., Pontifical Commn for Social Communications. Hon. FEIS, 1970. *Address:* St Bennet's, 42 Greenhill Gardens, Edinburgh EH10 4BJ. *T:* 031-447 3337.

ST ANDREWS AND EDINBURGH, Bishop Auxiliary of, (RC); *see* Monaghan, Rt Rev. James.

ST ANDREWS, DUNKELD AND DUNBLANE, Bishop of, since 1969; **Rt. Rev. Michael Geoffrey Hare Duke;** *b* 28 Nov. 1925; *s* of late A. R. A. Hare Duke, Civil Engineer; *m* 1949, Grace Lydia Frances McKean Dodd; one *s* three *d. Educ:* Bradfield Coll.; Trinity Coll., Oxford. BA 1949, MA 1951. Sub-Lt, RNVR, 1944-46. Deacon, 1952; Priest, 1953; Curate, St John's Wood Church, 1952-56; Vicar, St Mark's, Bury, 1956-62; Pastoral Dir, Clin. Theol. Assoc., 1962-64; Vicar, St Paul's, Daybrook, and Pastoral Consultant to Clin. Theol. Assoc., 1964-69; OCF, E Midland Dist HQ, 1968-69. Mem. Editorial Bd, Contact Magazine, 1962-. *Publications:* (jointly): The Caring Church, 1963; First Aid in Counselling, 1968; Understanding the Adolescent, 1969; The Break of Glory, 1970; Freud, 1972; Good News, 1976. Contributor to: Expository Times, Blackfriars, New Christian, Church Quarterly Review, Church Times, Contact. *Address:* Bishop's House, Fairmount Road, Perth, PH2 7AP. *T:* Perth 21580.

ST ANDREWS, DUNKELD AND DUNBLANE, Dean of; *see* Irvine, Very Rev. Thomas Thurstan.

ST ARNAUD, Diocese; amalgamated with diocese of Bendigo, 1977.

ST ASAPH, Bishop of, since 1971; **Rt. Rev. Harold John Charles;** *b* 26 June 1914; *s* of Rev. David Charles and Mary Charles, Carmarthenshire; *m* 1941, Margaret Noeline; one *d. Educ:* Welsh Univ. Aberystwyth; Keble Coll., Oxford. BA Wales 1935; BA Oxford 1938, MA 1943. Curate of Abergwili, Carms, 1938-40; Bishop's Messenger, Diocese of Swansea and Brecon, 1940-48; Warden of University Church Hostel, Bangor, and Lecturer at University College, Bangor, 1948-52; Vicar of St James, Bangor, 1952-54; Canon Residentiary of Bangor, 1953-54; Warden of St Michael's Coll., Llandaff, 1954-57; Canon of Llandaff, 1956-57; Dean of St Asaph, 1957-71. ChStJ 1973. *Address:* Esgobty, St Asaph, Clwyd. *T:* 583503.

ST ASAPH, Dean of; *see* Renowden, Very Rev. C. R.

ST AUBYN, family name of **Baron St Levan.**

ST AUBYN; *see* Molesworth-St Aubyn.

ST AUBYN, Hon. John Francis Arthur, DSC 1942; DL; landowner and company director; *b* 23 Feb. 1919; *s* and *heir* of Baron St Levan *qv*; *m* 1970, Susan Maria Marcia, *d* of late Maj.-Gen. Sir John Kennedy, GCMG, KCVO, KBE, CB. *Educ:* Eton Coll.; Trinity Coll., Cambridge (BA). Admitted a Solicitor, 1948. High Sheriff of Cornwall, 1974; DL Cornwall, 1977. Pres., Cornwall Br., CPRE, 1975. FRSA 1974. *Publication:* Illustrated History of St Michael's Mount, 1974. *Recreations:* sailing, visiting historic houses. *Address:* St Michael's Mount, Marazion, Cornwall. *Clubs:* Brooks's; Royal Yacht Squadron.

ST BONIFACE, Archbishop of, (RC), since 1974; **Most Rev. Antoine Hacault,** STD; *b* Bruxelles, Manitoba, 17 Jan. 1926. *Educ:* Sainte-Marie Elem. Sch., Bruxelles; St Boniface Coll. (BA 1947); St Boniface Major Seminary; Angelicum Univ., Rome (STD 1954). Priest, 1951; Prof. of Theology, St Boniface Major Seminary, 1954-64; Auxiliary Bishop of St Boniface and Titular Bishop of Media, 1964; also Rector, St Boniface College, 1967; Bishop Coadjutor of St Boniface, 1972. Member: Vatican Secretariat for Non-Believers, 1973-; Vatican Secretariat for promoting Christian Unity, 1976-; Pastoral Team of Canadian Conf. of Catholic Bishops. Pres., Canadian Episcopal Commn for Ecumenism. *Address:* Archbishop's Residence, 151 Cathedral Avenue, St Boniface, Manitoba R2H 0H6, Canada.

SAINT BRIDES, Baron *cr* 1977 (Life Peer), of Hasguard, Dyfed; **John Morrice Cairns James,** PC 1968; GCMG 1975 (KCMG 1962; CMG 1957); CVO 1961; MBE 1944; King of Arms of the Most Distinguished Order of St Michael and St George, since 1975; *b* 30 April 1916; *s* of late Lewis Cairns James and Catherine, *d* of John Maitland Marshall; *m* 1st, 1948, Elizabeth Margaret Roper Piesse (*d* 1966); one *s* two *d*; 2nd, 1968, Mme Geneviève Sarasin. *Educ:* Bradfield; Balliol Coll., Oxford. Dominions Office, 1939; served Royal Navy and Royal Marines, 1940-45; released as Lieut-Col. Asst Sec., Office of UK High Comr in S Africa, 1946-47; Head of Defence Dept, Commonwealth Relations Office, 1949-51, and of Establishment Dept, 1951-52; Dep. High Comr for the UK, Lahore, 1952-53; attended Imperial Defence Coll., 1954; Dep. High Comr for UK in Pakistan, 1955-56; Asst Under-Sec. of State, Commonwealth Relations Office, 1957. Dep. High Comr for UK in India, 1958-61; British High Comr in Pakistan, 1961-66; Dep. Under Sec. of State, CO, 1966-68; Permanent Under-Sec. of State, CO, March-Oct. 1968; British High Commissioner: in India, 1968-71; in Australia, 1971-76. *Recreations:* walking and swimming in remote places. *Address:* Cap Saint-Pierre, 83990 Saint Tropez, France. *T:* (94) 97-14-75.

ST CLAIR, family name of **Baron Sinclair.**

ST CLAIR, Malcolm Archibald James, farmer; *b* 16 Feb. 1927; *o s* of late Maj.-Gen. George James Paul St Clair, CB, CBE, DSO and late Charlotte Theresa Orme Little; *m* 1955, Mary-Jean Rosalie Alice, *o d* of Wing-Comdr Caryl Liddell Hargreaves, Broadwood House, Sunningdale; two *s* one *d. Educ:* Eton. Served with Royal Scots Greys, 1944-48. Formerly Hon. Sec. to Sir Winston Churchill. Contested (C) Bristol South-East, 1959; MP (C) Bristol South-East, 1961-63. Lt Col Comdg, Royal Gloucestershire Hussars (TA), 1967-69. High Sheriff Glos, 1972. *Recreation:* hunting. *Address:* Upton House, Tetbury, Glos. *Clubs:* Cavalry and Guards, White's.

ST CLAIR-ERSKINE, family name of **Earl of Rosslyn.**

ST CLAIR-FORD, Capt. Sir Aubrey, 6th Bt, *cr* 1793; DSO 1942; RN, retired; *b* 29 Feb. 1904; *e s* of late Anson and Elsie St Clair-Ford; *S* cousin 1948; *m* 1945, Anne, *o d* of Harold Christopherson, Penerley Lodge, Beaulieu, Hants; one *s* one *d. Educ:* Stubbington House; RNC, Osborne and Dartmouth. Served War of 1939-45 (despatches, DSO and bar); Korean War of 1950-53 (despatches, Officer, Legion of Merit, US). *Heir: s* James Anson St Clair-Ford [*b* 16 March 1952; *m* 1977, Jennifer Margaret, *yr d* of Cdre Robin Grindle]. *Address:* Corner House, Sandle Copse, Fordingbridge, Hants. *Club:* Army and Navy.
See also Maj.-Gen. Sir Peter St Clair-Ford.

ST CLAIR-FORD, Maj.-Gen. Sir Peter, KBE 1961 (CBE 1953); CB 1954; DSO 1943 and Bar 1944; idc; psc; General Secretary of the Officers' Association, 1963-66; *b* 25 Nov. 1905; *s* of late Anson St Clair-Ford and Elsie (*née* Adams); unmarried. *Educ:* Dover College; Royal Military College, Sandhurst. Commissioned into KOYLI, 1925; Somaliland Camel Corps, 1932-39; France, 1939; Staff College, Camberley, 1940 (psc); various Staff appts, UK, 1940-43; Comd 1 Bn KOYLI, 1943-44, Italy and Palestine; Comd 3 Inf. Bde, 1944-46, Italy and Palestine; Comd 129 Inf. Bde (TA), 1947-48; BGS Southern Command (UK), 1948-49; Imperial Defence College (idc), 1950; BGS, FARELF, 1951-52; Training Adviser to Pakistan Army, 1952-54; Commander 1 Federal Division, Malaya, 1954-57; Deputy Chief of Staff, Headquarters Allied Land Forces Central Europe, 1958-60; retd, 1960. *Recreations:* golf, racing. *Address:* Cotswold Lodge, Littlestone, New Romney, Kent. *T:* New Romney 2368. *Club:* East India, Sports and Public Schools.
See also Capt. Sir Aubrey St Clair-Ford, Bt.

ST CYRES, Viscount; John Stafford Northcote; *b* 15 Feb. 1957; *s* and *heir* of 4th Earl of Iddesleigh, *qv*. *Educ:* Downside Sch.; RAC Cirencester. *Address:* Shillands House, Upton Pyne Hill, Exeter, Devon EX5 5EB.

ST DAVIDS, 2nd Viscount, *cr* 1918; **Jestyn Reginald Austen Plantagenet Philipps;** Baron Strange of Knokin, 1299; Baron Hungerford, 1426; Baron de Moleyns, 1445; Bt 1621; Baron St Davids, 1908; Founder and Patron, Pirate Club, Floating Youth Club for Boys and Girls; *b* 19 Feb. 1917; *s* of 1st Viscount and Elizabeth Frances (Baroness Strange of Knokin, Baroness Hungerford and Baroness de Moleyns), *d* of late Hon. Paulyn F. C. Rawdon-Hastings, of The Manor House, Ashby-de-la-Zouch; *S* father, 1938, and to baronies of mother, 1974; *m* 1938, Doreen Guinness (marr. diss., 1954; she *d* 1956), *o d* of Captain Arthur Jowett, Toorak, Australia; one *s* four *d*; *m* 1954, Elisabeth Joyce, *e d* of Dr E. A. Woolf, Hove, Sussex (marr. diss., 1959); *m* 1959, Evelyn Marjorie, *d* of late Dr J. E. G. Harris, Bray, Berks.

Educ: Eton; Trinity Coll., Cambridge. *Heir: s* Hon. Colwyn Jestyn John Philipps [*b* 30 Jan. 1939; *m* 1965, Augusta Victoria Correa Larrain, *d* of late Don Estantislao Correa Ugarte; two *s*]. *Address:* 15 St Mark's Crescent, Regent's Park, NW1.

ST DAVID'S, Bishop of, since 1971; **Rt. Rev. Eric Matthias Roberts;** *b* 18 Feb. 1914; *s* of Richard and Jane Roberts; *m* 1944, Nancy Jane Roberts (*née* Davies); two *s. Educ:* Friars Sch., Bangor; University Coll., Bangor; St Edmund Hall, Oxon (MA); St Michael's Coll., Llandaff. Curate, Penmaenmawr, 1938-40; Sub-Warden, St Michael's Coll., Llandaff, 1940-47; Vicar: Port Talbot, 1947-56; Roath, 1956-65; Archdeacon of Margam, 1965-71. ChStJ 1973. *Address:* Llys Esgob, Abergwili, Carmarthen, Dyfed SA31 2JG. *T:* Carmarthen 6597.

ST DAVID'S, Dean of; *see* Bowen, Very Rev. L.

ST EDMUNDSBURY and IPSWICH, Bishop of, since 1966; **Rt. Rev. Leslie Wilfrid Brown,** CBE 1965; *b* 10 June 1912; *s* of Harry and Maud Brown; *m* 1939, Annie Winifred, *d* of Hon. R. D. Megaw, Belfast; one *d. Educ:* Enfield Gram. School; London College of Divinity (London Univ.). BD 1936, MTh 1944, DD 1957. MA Cantab. hon. causa, 1953. Deacon, Curate St James' Milton, Portsmouth, 1935; priest, 1936. Missionary, CMS, 1938 to Cambridge Nicholson Instn, Kottayam, Travancore, S India. Fellow Commoner and Chaplain, Downing College, Cambridge, 1943; Kerala United Theological Seminary, Trivandrum: tutor, 1945, Principal, 1946, and from 1951. Chaplain, Jesus Coll., Cambridge and Select Preacher before Univ. of Cambridge, 1950, 1967, Oxford, 1967. Archbishop of Uganda, Rwanda and Burundi, 1961-65; Bishop of Namirembe, 1960-65 (of Uganda, 1953-60; name of diocese changed). Chm., ACCM, 1972-76. Hon. Fellow, Downing Coll., Cambridge, 1966. DD (*hc*) Trinity Coll., Toronto, 1963. Chaplain and Sub-Prelate, Order of St John, 1968. *Publications:* The Indian Christians of St Thomas, 1956; The Christian Family, 1959; God as Christians see Him, 1961; Relevant Liturgy, 1965. *Address:* Bishop's House, 4 Park Road, Ipswich IP1 3ST. *T:* Ipswich 52829. *Club:* Royal Commonwealth Society.

ST GEORGE, Air Vice-Marshal Douglas Fitzclarence, CB 1974; CBE 1971; DFC; AFC; RNZAF, retd; *b* Nelson, NZ, 7 Sept. 1919; *s* of D. St George; *m* 1953, Patrine, *d* of J. Darrow; two *s. Educ:* Auckland Grammar Sch., NZ. Served War, Royal New Zealand Air Force, 1938-45. Comdg Flying Wing, RNZAF, Ohakea, 1953-56; exchange duty, RAAF, Aust., 1956-58; Comdg Ohakea, 1958-60; Dir ops, RNZAF, 1961-63; Rep. of NZ Mil. Advisers, HQ of SEATO, Bangkok, 1963-65; AOC comdg Training Gp, 1966-67; Air Mem. for Personnel, HQ of RNZAF, 1969-70; Dep. Chief of the Air Staff, NZ, 1970-71; Chief of the Air Staff, NZ, 1971-74. *Address:* 84 Barton Road, Heretaunga, New Zealand.

ST GEORGE, Sir Robert Alan, 7th Bt, *cr* 1766; now Religious Lay Brother; *b* 20 March 1900; *s* of Sir Theophilus John St George, 6th Bt, and Florence Emma, *d* of late John Venderplank, Natal; *S* father, 1943. *Educ:* St Charles Coll., Maritzburg. Served RAF, 1918; War of 1939-45, Middle East (prisoner). *Heir: b* Rev. Denis Howard, *b* 6 Sept. 1902. *Address:* St Joseph's Scholasticate, Cedara, Natal, SA.

ST GERMANS, 9th Earl of, *cr* 1815; **Nicholas Richard Michael Eliot;** Baron Eliot, 1784; Major, Duke of Cornwall's Light Infantry; *b* 26 Jan. 1914; *er s* of 8th Earl of St Germans, KCVO, OBE, and of Helen Agnes Post (*d* 1962) (*d* of Lady Barrymore and late Arthur Post, New York, USA); *S* father 1960; *m* 1st, 1939, Helen Mary (marr. diss., 1947; she *d* 1951), *d* of late Lt-Col Charles Walter Villiers, CBE, DSO, and late Lady Kathleen Villiers; one *s* one *d*; 2nd, 1948, Mrs Margaret Eleanor Eyston (marr. diss., 1959), *o d* of late Lt-Col William Francis George Wyndham, MVO; 3rd, 1965, Mrs Mary Bridget Lotinga, *d* of late Sir Shenton Thomas and of Lady Thomas, SW7. *Educ:* Eton. Joined Duke of Cornwall's Light Infantry, 1937. Served War of 1939-45: attached Royal Armoured Corps. *Heir: s* Lord Eliot, *qv*.

See also Earl of Shelburne.

ST GERMANS, Bishop Suffragan of, since 1974; **Rt Rev. Cecil Richard Rutt,** CBE 1973; MA; Hon. Canon, St Mary's Cathedral, Truro, since 1974; *b* 27 Aug. 1925; *s* of Cecil Rutt and Mary Hare Turner; *m* 1969, Joan Mary Ford. *Educ:* Huntingdon Grammar School; Kelham Theol. Coll.; Pembroke Coll., Cambridge. RNVR, 1943-46. Deacon, 1951; Priest, 1952. Asst Curate, St George's, Cambridge, 1951-54; Dio. of Korea, 1954; Parish Priest of Anjung, 1956-58; Warden of St Bede's House Univ. Centre, Seoul, 1959-64; Rector of St Michael's Seminary, Oryu Dong, Seoul, 1964-66; Archdeacon, West Kyonggi (Dio. Seoul), 1965-66; Asst Bishop of Taejon, 1966-68;

Bishop of Taejon, 1968-74. Associate Gen. Sec., Korean Bible Soc., 1964-74; Episcopal Sec., Council of the Church of SE Asia, 1968-74; Commissary, Dio. Taejon, 1974-; Pres., Roy. Asiatic Soc., Korea Br., 1974. Interested in the Cornish language. Bard of the Gorsedd of Cornwall, Cornwhylen, 1976. Tasan Cultural Award (for writings on Korea), 1964; Hon. DLitt, Confucian Univ., Seoul, 1974. Order of Civil Merit, Peony Class (Korea), 1974. *Publications:* (ed) Songgonghoe Songga (Korean Anglican Hymnal), 1961; Korean Works and Days, 1964; P'ungnyu Han'guk (in Korean), 1965; (trans.) An Anthology of Korean Sijo, 1970; The Bamboo Grove, an introduction to Korean Sijo poetry, 1971; James Scarth Gale and his History of the Korean People, 1972; Virtuous Women, three masterpieces of traditional Korean fiction, 1974; contribs on Korean classical poetry and history to Trans. Royal Asiatic Soc. (Korea Br.) and various Korean and liturgiological publications. *Address:* 32 Falmouth Road, Truro, Cornwall TR1 2HX. *T:* Truro 3190.

ST HELENA, Bishop of, since 1973; **Rt. Rev. (George) Kenneth Giggall,** OBE 1961; *b* 15 April 1914; *s* of Arthur William and Matilda Hannah Giggall; unmarried. *Educ:* Manchester Central High Sch.; Univ. of Manchester; St Chad's Coll., Univ. of Durham. BA, DipTheol. Deacon, 1939; Priest, 1940. Curate of St Alban's Cheetwood, Dio. Manchester, 1939-41, St Elisabeth's Reddish, 1941-45; Chaplain, RN, 1945; HMS Braganza, 1945; 34th Amphibious Support Regt, RM, 1945-46; Chaplain, Sch. of Combined Ops, 1946-47; HMS: Norfolk, 1947-49; Ocean, 1949-50; Flotilla Comd Mediterranean and HMS Phoenicia, 1950-52; HMS Campania for Operation Hurricane, 1952; RNC Dartmouth, 1952-53; HMS: Centaur, 1953-56; Ceylon, 1956-58; Fisgard, 1958-60; Royal Arthur and Lectr RAF Chaplains' Sch., 1960-63; HMS: Eagle, 1963-65; Drake, 1965-69; QHC, 1967-69; Dean of Gibraltar and Officiating Chaplain, HMS Rooke and Flag Officer, Gibraltar, 1969-73. *Recreation:* music. *Address:* Bishopsholme, Island of St Helena, South Atlantic Ocean. *Clubs:* Royal Commonwealth Society, Sion College; Exiles (Ascension Island).

ST HELENS, 1st Baron *cr* 1964; **Michael Henry Colin Hughes-Young,** MC 1944; *b* 28 Oct. 1912; *s* of late Brig.-Gen. H. G. Young, CIE, DSO; *m* 1939, Elizabeth Agnes Blakiston-Houston (*d* 1956); one *s* three *d* (and *er s* decd). *Educ:* Harrow; Sandhurst. Joined Black Watch, 1932; attached French Army, 1934; seconded King's African Rifles, 1935; Abyssinian War and Invasion of Europe, 1940 and 1944 (wounded twice); retired as Lt-Col, 1947. Contested (C) St Helens, 1951; Conservative Central Office, 1948-55; MP (C) Wandsworth Central, 1955-64; PPS to Minister of State, Board of Trade, March-April 1956; Assistant Whip (unpaid), 1956-58, a Lord Commissioner of the Treasury, 1958-62, Dep. Govt Chief Whip, 1959-64, and Treasurer of HM Household, 1962-64. *Heir: s* Hon. Richard Francis Hughes-Young, *b* 4 Nov. 1945. *Address:* Marchfield, Binfield, Berks. *T:* Bracknell 3338. *Club:* Carlton.

ST JOHN, family name of **Baron St John of Bletso,** and of **Viscount Bolingbroke.**

ST JOHN OF BLETSO, 20th Baron *cr* 1558; **Andrew Beauchamp St John,** TD 1952; Bt 1660; *b* 23 Aug. 1918; 3rd *s* of Lt-Col Hon. Rowland Tudor St John (*d* 1948) (3rd *s* of 16th Baron) and Katharine Madge (*d* 1954), *d* of late Sir Frank Lockwood, QC, MP; *S* cousin, 1976; *m* 1955, Katharine von Berg; one *s. Educ:* Wellington College. Joined Bank of England, 1937. Served War of 1939-45 with Indian Army. Commanded Tower Hamlets Regt (TA), 1951-54. Emigrated to South Africa 1957, joining Syfret's Trust Company in Cape Town. *Recreations:* painting, golf. *Heir: s* Hon. Anthony Tudor St John, *b* 16 May 1957. *Address:* c/o Syfret's Trust Company Ltd, 24 Wale Street, Cape Town 8001, S Africa. *Clubs:* Naval and Military; City, Netherlands, Western Province Sports (Cape Town).

ST JOHN, Maj.-Gen. Roger Ellis Tudor, CB 1965; MC 1944; *b* Hexham on Tyne, 4 Oct. 1911; *s* of late Major B. T. St John, Craigveigh, Aboyne, Aberdeenshire; *m* 1943, Rosemary Jean Douglas Vickers, Englefield Green, Surrey; one *s* three *d. Educ:* Wellington College; RMC Sandhurst. Joined Fifth Fusiliers, 1931; served War of 1939-45 (despatches, MC), in Hong Kong, UK and NW Europe; Bde Major 11 Armoured Div., 1944-45; GSO 2 Instructor Camberley Staff Coll., 1945-46; AA and QMG 1st Division, Tripoli, 1948-50; comd 1st Bn Royal Northumberland Fusiliers, 1953-55 (despatches), Mau Mau Rebellion; AMS Mil. Secretary's Branch, War Office, 1955-57; Comdr 11 Inf. Bde Group, BAOR, 1957-60; Asst Comdt, Camberley Staff Coll., 1960-62; Comdr, British Army Staff, Military Member, British Defence Staffs, and Military Attaché, Washington, 1963-65; President, Regular Army Commissions Board, 1965-67; retired, 1967. Colonel, Royal Northumberland

Fusiliers, 1965-68. Personnel Adminr, Urwick, Orr and Partners Ltd, Management Consultants, 1967-73. *Address:* Harelaw, Gorse Hill Road, Virginia Water, Surrey. *Club:* Army and Navy.

ST JOHN PARKER, Michael, MA (Cantab); Headmaster, Abingdon School, Oxfordshire, since 1975; *b* 21 July 1941; *s* of Rev. Canon J. W. Parker; *m* 1965, Annette Monica Ugle; two *s* two *d*. *Educ:* Stamford Sch.; King's Coll., Cambridge. Asst Master: Sevenoaks Sch., 1962-63; King's Sch., Canterbury, 1963-69; Winchester Coll., 1969-75; Head of History Dept, Winchester Coll., 1970-75. *Publications:* The British Revolution—Social and Economic History 1750-1970, 1972; various pamphlets and articles. *Recreations:* old buildings, music, books. *Address:* Lacies Court, Abingdon, Oxfordshire. *T:* Abingdon 20163.

ST JOHN-STEVAS, Norman Antony Francis; MP (C) Chelmsford, since Oct. 1964; author, barrister and journalist; *b* London, 18 May 1929; *o s* of late Stephen S. Stevas, civil engineer and company director, and late Kitty St John O'Connor; unmarried. *Educ:* Ratcliffe; Fitzwilliam, Cambridge; Christ Church, Oxford; Yale. Scholar, Clothworkers Exhibnr, 1946, 1947; BA (Cambridge) (1st cl. hons in law), 1950, MA 1954; President, Cambridge Union, 1950; Whitlock Prize, 1950; MA 1952, BCL 1954 (Oxon); Sec. Oxford Union, 1952. Contested (C) Dagenham, Gen. Election, 1951; Barrister, Middle Temple, 1952; Blackstone and Harmsworth schol., 1952; Blackstone Prize, 1953. Lecturer, Southampton University, 1952-53; King's Coll., London, 1953-56, tutored in jurisprudence, Christ Church, 1953-55, and Merton, 1955-57, Oxford. Founder member, Inst. of Higher European Studies, Bolzano, 1955; PhD (Lond.) 1957; Yorke Prize, Cambridge Univ., 1957; Fellow Yale Law School, 1957; Fulbright Award, 1957; Fund for the Republic Fellow, 1958; Dr of Sc. and Law (Yale), 1960; Lecture tours of USA, 1958-68. Regents' Prof., Univ. of California at Santa Barbara, 1969. Legal Adviser to Sir Alan Herbert's Cttee on book censorship, 1954-59; joined The Economist, 1959, to edit collected works of Walter Bagehot and became legal, ecclesiastical and political correspondent. Deleg., Council of Europe and WEU, 1967-71; Parly Under-Sec. of State, DES, 1972-73; Min. of State for the Arts, DES, 1973-74; Sec., Cons. Parly Home Affairs Cttee, 1969-72; Vice-Chm., Cons. Parly N Ireland Cttee, 1972-; Mem. Executive, Cons. Parly 1922 Cttee, 1971-72 and 1974; Vice Chm., Cons. Group for Europe, 1972-75; Mem. Shadow Cabinet, 1974-, and Opposition Spokesman on Educn, Science and the Arts; Member: Cons. Nat. Adv. Cttee on Policy, 1971; Fulbright Commission, 1961; Parly Select Cttee: on Race Relations and Immigration, 1970-72; on Civil List, 1971-. Founder Mem., Christian-Social Inst. of Culture, Rome, 1969; Hon. Sec., Fedn of Cons. Students, 1971-73, Hon. Vice-Pres. 1973. Editor The Dublin (Wiseman) Review, 1961. Vice Pres., Les Amis de Napoléon III, 1974; Mem., Académie du Second Empire, 1975. Silver Jubilee Medal, 1977. Cavaliere, Order of Merit (Italian Republic), 1965. KSLJ 1963. FRSL, 1966. *Publications:* Obscenity and the Law, 1956; Walter Bagehot; Life, Death and the Law, 1961; The Right to Life, 1963; Law and Morals, 1964; The Literary Works of Walter Bagehot, vols, I, II, 1966, The Historical Works, vols III, IV, 1968, The Political Works, vols V, VI, VII, and VIII, 1974, The Economic Works, vols IX, X and XI, 1977; The Agonising Choice, 1971. Contrib. to: Critical Quarterly, Modern Law Review, Criminal Law Review, Law and Contemporary Problems, Twentieth Century, Times Lit. Supp., Dublin Review. *Recreations:* reading, talking, listening (to music), travelling, walking, appearing on television, sleeping. *Address:* 34 Montpelier Square, SW1. *T:* 01-589 3001. *Clubs:* Garrick, Pratt's.

ST JOHN WILSON, Colin Alexander; *see* Wilson.

ST JOHN'S (Newfoundland), Archbishop of, (RC), since 1951; **Most Rev. Patrick James Skinner, CJM;** *b* 1904. *Educ:* St Bonaventure's College, St John's; Holy Heart Seminary, Halifax; Eudist Seminary, Gros Pin, PQ; Laval University, Quebec. Priest, 1929; consecrated, as Auxiliary to Archbishop of St John's, Newfoundland, 1950. *Address:* Basilica Residence, Bonaventure Avenue, St John's, Newfoundland.

ST JOHN'S (South Africa), Bishop of, since 1956; **Rt. Rev. James Leo Schuster;** *b* 18 July 1912; *s* of Rev. Harold Vernon Schuster and Elsie Jane (*née* Roberton); *m* 1951, Ilse Henriette Emmy Gottschalk; three *s* two *d* (and one *s* decd). *Educ:* Lancing; Keble Coll., Oxford. Deacon, 1937; Priest, 1938; Asst Missioner, Clare Coll. Mission, Rotherhithe, 1937-38; Chaplain St Stephen's House, Oxford, 1938-40; CF (EC), 1940-46; wounded, 1942; despatches, 1943. Chaplain, St Stephen's House, Oxford, 1946-49; Principal St Bede's Coll., Umtata, 1949-56.

Address: Bishopsmead, PO Box 163, Umtata, CP, South Africa. *T:* Umtata 74.

ST JOHNSTON, Colonel Sir (Thomas) Eric, Kt 1967; CBE 1952 (OBE 1945); QPM 1958; MA Cantab; Member of Lloyd's; Director, Group 4 Total Security; Chairman, Interflow Ltd; *b* 7 Jan. 1911; *o s* of late T. G. St Johnston, Edgbaston, Warwicks; *m* 1st, 1937, Joan (marr. diss. 1969; she *d* 1974); one *s* two *d*; 2nd, 1969, Margaret Emily Jameson Till, *widow* of Lt-Col S. Jameson Till, MC. *Educ:* Bromsgrove School, Worcestershire; Corpus Christi, Cambridge. Late RA (TA), 1929-35; employed in rank of Colonel for special duties, War Office, 1943, and as Head of Public Safety Section, G5 Div., SHAEF, 1944; member staff of King's Camp, 1932 *et seq*; employed on civil staff at New Scotland Yard, 1932-35; Barrister, Middle Temple, 1934; Metropolitan Police College, 1935 (winner of Baton of Honour); Inspector, Metropolitan Police, 1936-40; Chief Constable of Oxfordshire, 1940-44, of Durham County, 1944-50, of Lancashire, 1950-67; HM Chief Inspector of Constabulary for England and Wales, 1967-70. Visited USA as guest of US Government, 1953; Visiting Lecturer, Univ. of California, 1953; Visiting Lectr to Israeli Police, 1955; British Council Lecturer in Australia and New Zealand, 1966; idc, 1957; invited by Govt of Victoria, Australia to examine and report on efficiency of Police Force in the State, 1970-71. Dir of Admin, Spencer Stuart & Associates Ltd, 1971-75. Freeman of City of London and Liveryman of Vintners' Company, 1956; Chevalier de Tastevin, 1965. Chairman, Christian Police Trust Corp. Ltd, 1954-67. Dep. Chm., Sail Training Assoc., 1968-73. Governor and Endowment Trustee, Bromsgrove School. Hon. Col 33rd (Lancs and Cheshire) Signal Regt (V), 1967-70. Hon. MA Manchester, 1961. Mem., Chapter Gen, Order of St John, 1968-69; KStJ 1966 (CStJ, 1960). Legion of Honour and Croix de Guerre (France). *Publications:* contrib. to Police periodicals in UK, and USA. *Recreations:* shooting and sailing. *Address:* Old Swan House, Great Rissington, Glos. *T:* Bourton-on-the-Water 20776. *Clubs:* Buck's, Naval and Military, MCC.

ST JOSEPH, Prof. John Kenneth Sinclair, OBE 1962; Professor of Aerial Photographic Studies, University of Cambridge, and Professorial Fellow of Selwyn College, since 1973, Vice-Master, since 1974; *b* 1912; *s* of late John D. St Joseph and of Irma Robertson (*née* Marris); *m* 1945, Daphne Margaret, *d* of late H. March, Worcester; two *s* two *d*. *Educ:* Bromsgrove Sch.; Selwyn Coll., Cambridge (Scholar). BA 1934, PhD 1937, MA 1938, LittD 1976. Harkness Scholar, 1934; Goldsmiths' Company Senior Student, 1935-37; DSIR Sen. Research Award, 1936-37; Fellow, Lectr in Natural Sciences, and Dean, Selwyn Coll., Cambridge, 1939, Tutor, 1945-62; Univ. Demonstrator in Geology, 1937-45; Operational Research, Min. of Aircraft Production, 1942-45; Univ. Lectr in Geology, 1945-48; Leverhulme Research Fellow, 1948-49; Curator in Aerial Photography at Cambridge, 1948-62; Dir in Aerial Photography, 1962-. Has undertaken aerial reconnaissance and photography, in aid of research, over the United Kingdom, Ireland, Denmark, the Netherlands and Northern France. Governor, Stratton Sch., Biggleswade, 1952-64; Hon. Corresp. Mem., German Archæological Inst., 1964; Member: Ancient Monuments Bd (England), 1969-; Royal Commn on Historical Monuments (England), 1972-; Vice-Pres., Soc. for Promotion of Roman Studies, 1975. Chatwin Meml Lectr, Birmingham, 1969; David Murray Lectr, Glasgow Univ., 1973. Cuthbert Peek Award, RGS, 1976; President's Award, Inst. of Incorporated Photographers, 1977. FGS 1937; FSAScot 1940; FSA 1944; Hon. ScD, Trinity Coll., Dublin; Hon. LLD, Dundee. *Publications:* The Pentameracea of the Oslo Region, 1939; chapters in The Roman Occupation of SW Scotland (ed S. N. Miller), 1945; Monastic Sites from the Air (with M. C. Knowles), 1952; Medieval England, an aerial survey (with M. W. Beresford), 1957; (ed) The Uses of Air Photography, 1966, 2nd rev. edn 1977; The Early Development of Irish Society (with E. R. Norman), 1970; papers in learned jls on fossil Silurian Brachiopoda, and on aerial photography and archæology, especially of Roman Britain. *Recreations:* gardening, lumbering. *Address:* Selwyn College, Cambridge CB3 9DQ. *T:* Cambridge 62381; Histon Manor, Cambridge CB4 4JJ.

ST JUST, 2nd Baron, *cr* 1935, of St Just in Penwith; **Peter George Grenfell;** *b* 22 July 1922; *s* of 1st Baron and Florence (*d* 1971), *e d* of late George W. Henderson; *s* father, 1941; *m* 1st, 1949, Leslie (marriage dissolved, 1955), *d* of late Condé Nast, New York; one *d*; 2nd, 1956, Maria Britneva; two *d*. *Educ:* Harrow. Served War, 1941-46, 60th Rifles. *Address:* 9 Gerald Road, SW1. *T:* 01-730 7621; Wilbury Park, Newton Tony, near Salisbury, Wilts. *T:* Cholderton 664. *Clubs:* White's, House of Lords Yacht.

SAINT LAURENT, Yves (Henri Donat Mathieu); couturier; *b* 1 Aug. 1936; *s* of Charles Mathieu and Lucienne-Andrée Saint Laurent. *Educ:* Lycée d'Oran. Designer for Christian Dior, 1954-60; Dir, Société Yves Saint Laurent, 1962-. Costume designer for several plays, ballets and films. *Publication:* La Vilaine Lulu, 1967. *Address:* (office) 5 avenue Marceau, 75016 Paris; (home) 55 rue de Babylone, 75007 Paris, France.

ST LEGER, family name of **Viscount Doneraile.**

ST LEONARDS, 4th Baron *cr* 1852; **John Gerard Sugden;** *b* 3 Feb. 1950; *s* of Arthur Herbert Sugden (*g g s* of 1st Baron) (*d* 1958) and of Julia Sheila, *d* of late Philip Wyatt; *S* kinsman, 1972. *Heir: uncle* Dr Edward Charles Sugden, *b* 24 July 1902.

ST LEVAN, 3rd Baron (*cr* 1887), **Francis Cecil St Aubyn,** Bt, *cr* 1866; JP; DL; late Major Gren. Guards; Colonel Home Guard; *b* 18 April 1895; *s* of late Hon. A. J. D. Stuart St Aubyn; *S* uncle 1940; *m* 1916, Hon. Clementina Gwendolen Catharine Nicolson, *o d* of 1st Baron Carnock; three *s* two *d*. *Educ:* Eton; Sandhurst. Served European War, 1914-15 (wounded); rejoined Grenadier Guards 1939-42. DL for County of Cornwall, 1961. *Heir: s* Hon. John Francis Arthur St Aubyn, *qv*. *Address:* Avallon, Green Lane, Marazion, Cornwall. *T:* 22. *Clubs:* Army and Navy; Royal Cornwall Yacht.
See also Earl Amherst.

ST OSWALD, 4th Baron, *cr* 1885; **Rowland Denys Guy Winn,** MC 1951; DL; Member, British Delegation to European Parliament, since 1973; Vice-Chairman of Central and Eastern European Commission of the European Movement; Chairman, Crabtree Denims Ltd; *b* 19 Sept. 1916; *s* of 3rd Baron St Oswald and Eva (*d* 1976), *d* of Charles Greene; *S* father 1957; *m* 1st, 1952, Laurian (from whom he obtained a divorce, 1955), *o d* of Sir Roderick Jones, KBE; 2nd, 1955, Marie Wanda, *y d* of late Sigismund Jaxa-Chamiec, Zorawia, Warsaw; no *c*. *Educ:* Stowe Sch.; Universities of Bonn and Freiburg. Reuter's Corresp. for Spain, 1935; Daily Telegraph Corresp. and War Corresp., 1936 (condemned to death, Sept. 1936); Corresp. in Middle East, 1938, in Balkans 1939. Enlisted Army, 1939; served Middle East (8th King's Royal Hussars), 1941-44; Far East, 1945 (despatches). Resided Spain, 1946-50. Volunteered to serve in Korea, 1950; 8th King's Roy. Irish Hussars, 1950-51. Contested (C) Dearne Valley Div., 1955; adopted as Conservative candidate, Pudsey Div., 1957. A Lord-in-Waiting to the Queen, 1959-62; Jt Parly Sec. to Min. of Agriculture, Fisheries and Food, 1962-64. Chairman, Mid-Yorkshire Conservative Assoc., 1965; President: W Riding of Yorks Playing Fields Assoc., 1970-; British Assoc. Industrial Editors, 1964-70; Yorks Region Nat. Soc. Mentally Handicapped Children; Yorkshire Area Young Conservatives; Ackworth, Upton, Hemsworth and Wrangbrooke Branches, British Legion; Vice-President: W Riding British Legion; Anglo-Polish Soc., 1969. Trustee and Pres., Northern Cttee of Cheshire Foundn Homes for the Sick. Pres., Soc. of Yorkshiremen in London, 1960-61; Pres. Huddersfield Branch, Coldstreamers' Assoc.; Patron of Wakefield Trinity Football Club; Pres., Yorkshire Agric. Soc., 1968. Hon. Col 150 (Northumbrian) Regt RCT (V), 1967-. DL West Riding, Yorks, 1962. Croix de Guerre and Order of Leopold (Belgium), 1951; Légion d'Honneur and Croix de Guerre (France), 1945. *Publications:* Lord Highport Dropped at Dawn, 1949; My Dear, it's Heaven, 1950; Carmela, 1954 (USA 1955). *Recreations:* the company of his wife; talking and writing to friends. *Heir: b* Capt. Hon. Derek Edward Anthony Winn [*b* 9 July 1919; *m* 1954, Denise Eileen Charlotte, *o d* of Wilfrid Haig Loyd; one *s* one *d*]. *Address:* Nostell Priory, Wakefield, W Yorks. *T:* Wakefield 862394; White Lodge, Gilston Road, SW10. *T:* 01-373 3660. *Clubs:* Cavalry and Guards, Garrick, Press, Special Forces, Beefsteak, Pratt's.

ST PAUL'S, Dean of; *see* Webster, Very Rev. A. B.

ST VINCENT, 7th Viscount (*cr* 1801); **Ronald George James Jervis;** *b* 3 May 1905; *o* surv. *s* of 6th Viscount and Marion Annie (*d* 1911), *d* of James Brown, JP, Orchard, Carluke, Scotland; *S* father, 1940; *m* 1945, Phillida, *o d* of Lt-Col R. H. Logan, Taunton; two *s* one *d*. *Educ:* Sherborne. JP Somerset, 1950-55. *Heir: s* Hon. Edward Robert James Jervis [*b* 12 May 1951; *m* 1977, Victoria Margaret, *o d* of Wilton J. Oldham, St Peter, Jersey]. *Address:* Les Charrieres, St Ouen, Jersey, CI.

ST VINCENT FERRERI, 8th Marquis of, **Alfio Testaferrata Ghâxaq** (Marquis Testaferrata); *b* 1911; *s* of Daniel Testaferrata Bonici Ghâxaq and Agnese (*d* 1941), *d* of Baroncino Nicola Galea di San Marciano; *S* father, 1945. *Educ:* Stonyhurst College, Blackburn; University Coll., Oxford. Sometime Mem., Cttee of Privileges of Maltese Nobility; Member Royal Numismatic Society; Membre de la Société suisse de Numismatique. Hereditary Knight of the Holy Roman Empire; Patrician of Rome, Messina, and Citta di Castello. *Address:* 29 Villegaignon Street, Mdina, Malta, GC. *T:* Rabat 74139. *Club:* Casino Maltese (Valletta).

SAINTONGE, Rolland A. A. C. de; *see* Chaput de Saintonge.

SAINTY, John Christopher; Reading Clerk, House of Lords, since 1974; *b* 31 Dec. 1934; *s* of Christopher Lawrence Sainty and Nancy Lee Sainty (*née* Miller); *m* 1965, Elizabeth Frances Sherlock; three *s*. *Educ:* Winchester Coll.; New Coll., Oxford (MA). FRHistS. Clerk, Parlt Office, House of Lords, 1959; seconded as Private Sec. to Leader of House and Chief Whip, House of Lords, 1963; Clerk of Journals, House of Lords, 1965; Res. Asst and Editor, Inst. of Historical Research, 1970. FSA. *Publications:* Treasury Officials 1660-1870, 1972; Officials of the Secretaries of State 1660-1782, 1973; Officials of the Boards of Trade 1660-1870, 1974; Admiralty Officials 1660-1870, 1975; Home Office Officials, 1782-1870, 1975; Colonial Office Officials 1794-1870, 1976; (with D. Dewar) Divisions in the House of Lords: an analytical list 1685-1857, 1976; articles in Eng. Hist. Rev., Bull. Inst. Hist. Research. *Address:* 22 Kelso Place, W8 5QG. *T:* 01-937 9460.

SAKHAROV, Dr Andrei Dimitrievich; Member, Academy of Sciences of USSR, since 1953; *b* 21 May 1921; *m* 2nd, 1971, Elena Bonner; one *s* one *d*. *Educ:* Moscow State Univ. Joined P. N. Lebedev Physics Inst. as physicist, 1945; worked with Dr Igor Tamm on nuclear fusion. Member: Amer. Acad. of Arts and Scis, 1969; Nat. Acad. of Scis, 1972-. Eleanor Roosevelt Peace Award, 1973; Cino del Duca Prize, 1974; Reinhold Niebuhr Prize, Chicago Univ., 1974; Nobel Peace Prize, 1975. *Publications:* Progress, Peaceful Co-existence and Intellectual Freedom, 1968; Sakharov Speaks, 1974; My Country and the World, 1975; scientific works, etc. *Address:* Academy of Sciences of USSR, Leninsky prospekt 14, Moscow, USSR.

SAKZEWSKI, Sir Albert, Kt 1973; FCA, FASA; Chairman, TAB Queensland, since 1962; Founder, Albert Sakzewski Charitable Foundation. Member Board, Queensland Division, Heart Foundn; first Treasurer, Police Youth Club; Past Pres., Aust. Amateur Billiards Assoc. *Address:* 512 Sandgate Road, Clayfield, Qld 4011, Australia.

SALAM, Professor Abdus, Sitara-i-Pakistan, 1959; FRS 1959; PhD; Professor of Theoretical Physics at the Imperial College of Science and Technology in the University of London since 1957; Director, International Centre for Theoretical Physics, Trieste, since 1964; Chairman, UN Advisory Cttee on Science and Technology; *b* 29 Jan. 1926. *Educ:* Govt Coll., Lahore, Pakistan (MA); St John's Coll., Camb. (BA, PhD). Fellow, St John's Coll., Cambridge, 1951-56 (Hon. Fellow, 1972); Professor of Mathematics, Government College, Lahore, 1951-54; Lecturer in Mathematics, University of Cambridge, 1954-56. Sci. Advr to Pres. of Pakistan, 1961-74. Has made contributions to the theory of elementary particles. Vice-Pres., IUPAP, 1972-. Fellow, Royal Swedish Acad. of Sciences, 1970; For. Mem., USSR Acad. of Scis, 1971. Hon. DSc: Panjab University, Lahore, Pakistan, 1957; Edinburgh, 1971. Hopkins Prize, Cambridge Philosophical Soc., 1957; Adams Prize, Cambridge Univ., 1958; Maxwell Medal and Prize, IPPS, 1962; Hughes Medal, Royal Society, 1964; Atoms for Peace Award, 1968; Oppenheimer Prize and Medal, 1971; Guthrie Medal and Prize, IPPS, 1976. *Address:* Imperial College of Science and Technology, Prince Consort Road, SW7; International Centre for Theoretical Physics PO Box 586, 34100 Trieste, Italy. *Club:* Athenæum.

SALAMAN, Myer Head, MD; Research Pathologist, Royal College of Surgeons, 1968-74; *b* 2 August 1902; *e s* of Redcliffe N. Salaman, MD, FRS and Nina Salaman; *m* 1926, Esther Polianowsky; one *s* three *d*. *Educ:* Clifton College; Bedales School; Trinity College, Cambridge; London Hospital Medical College. Natural Science Tripos Pts I and II, Cambridge, 1921-25; London Hosp.: Clinical training, 1927-30; House Appts, 1931-32; Research on Viruses, 1932-34, and Lister Inst. (Junior Beit Mem. Fellow) 1935-38; Cancer Research, St Bartholomew's Hosp., 1939; Asst Pathologist, Emergency Public Health Service, 1940-42; Cancer and Virus Research, Strangeways Lab., 1942-43; Temp. Major, RAMC, 1943-46. Engaged in Cancer Research at the London Hospital, 1946-48; Dir, Dept of Cancer Research, London Hosp. Med. Sch., 1948-67; engaged in Cancer Research at RCS, 1968-74. MA 1926, MD 1936 Cantab; MRCS, LRCP, 1930; Dipl. Bact. London, 1936. FRSocMed. *Publications:* papers on virus diseases, and on cancer, in Jour. Pathology and Bacteriology, Proc. Roy. Soc. (B), Brit. Jl Cancer, etc. *Recreation:* walking. *Address:* 23 Bisham Gardens, Highgate, N6. *T:* 01-340 1019. *Club:* Athenæum.
See also Prof. H. B. Barlow.

SALAS, Rafael Montinola; Executive Director (with rank of Under Secretary-General), United Nations Fund for Population Activities, since 1971 (Sen. Consultant to Administrator of UNDP, 1969; Director UNFPA, 1970), UN official responsible for 'World Population Year, 1974'; *b* Bago, Negros Occidental, Philippines, 7 Aug. 1928; *s* of Ernesto Salas and Isabel Montinola; *m* 1967, Carmelita J. Rodriguez; one *s*. *Educ:* Negros Occidental Provincial High Sch.; Coll. of Liberal Arts, Univ. of the Philippines (Associate in Arts (AA) with high honours, 1950; AB *magna cum laude*, 1953); Coll. of Law, Univ. of the Philippines (LLB *cum laude* 1953); Littauer Center of Public Admin. (MPA), Harvard Univ., 1955. PhD *hc*, DHL *hc*, LLD *hc*. Mem., Philippine Bar, 1953. Fellow on Local Govt Develt Planning, Harvard Univ., 1958-59. Professorial Lectr in: Polit. Sci. and Economics, Univ. of the Philippines, 1955-59; Economics, Grad. Sch., Far Eastern Univ., 1960-61; Law, Univ. of the Philippines, 1963-66 (Asst. Vice-Pres., 1962-63, Mem., Board of Regents, 1966-69, of the Univ.). Philippine Govt Positions: Asst to Exec. Sec., Office of the President, 1954-55; various appts, 1955-57; Exec. Sec., UNESCO Nat. Commn of the Philippines, 1957; Nat. Economic Council: Exec. Officer (with Cabinet rank), 1960-61; Exec. Dir (with Cabinet rank), 1961; Actg Chm., 1966, 1968. Special Asst: to Sec. of Agriculture and Natural Resources, 1961; to the President, on Local Govts, Office of the President, 1961. Gen. Manager, the Manila Chronicle, 1963-65; Asst to the President, Meralco Securities Corp., 1963-65. Chairman: Bd of Trustees, Govt Service Insce System, 1966; Admin. Code Revision Cttee, 1966; Nat. Cttee on Disaster Ops, 1966-69; Govt Reorganization Commn, 1968-69. Action Officer. Nat. Rice and Corn Sufficiency Programme, 1967-69 (of vital importance to "Green Revolution"); Nat. Projects Overall Co-ordinator and Action Officer, 1966-69; Exec. Sec. of Republic of the Philippines, 1966-69 (office 2nd to President in executive powers). Holds foreign Orders. *Publications:* People: an international choice, 1976; formerly one of editors of Philippine Law Jl; has contrib. articles to numerous professional jls. *Recreation:* reading. *Address:* 411 East 53rd Street, New York, NY 10022, USA.

SALE, Geoffrey Stead; Director of Studies, RMA, Sandhurst, Camberley, 1967-71; *b* 6 Aug. 1907; *s* of Frederic W. R. Sale, Solicitor, Carlisle, and Ivy I. Davidson; *m* 1938, Olivia Jean Bell-Scott (*d* 1950), Edinburgh; one *s* three *d*. *Educ:* Berkhamsted School; Lincoln College, Oxford (MA). Diploma in Education; Assistant Master and Housemaster, Fettes College, Edinburgh, 1931-46; Headmaster, King's School, Bruton, 1946-57; Headmaster, Rossall School, 1957-67. Captain TA (General List). Member, House of Laity, Church Assembly, 1960-70. FRSA 1953. *Publication:* Four Hundred Years a School (History of King's School). *Recreations:* walking, photography, writing. *Address:* Low House, Brackenthwaite, Cockermouth, Cumbria CA13 9UX. *T:* Lorton 642.

SALE, Richard; Headmaster of Brentwood School since 1966; *b* 4 Oct. 1919; *e s* of late Richard and Rachel Sale; *m* 1943, Elizabeth Thérèse Bauer; four *s* one *d*. *Educ:* Repton Sch. (Schol.); Oriel Coll., Oxford. Commissioned, KSLI, 1940; served War of 1939-45; Canada and Normandy; demobilised, rank of Major, 1946. Asst Master, Repton Sch., 1946-61; Housemaster of The Priory, 1953-61; Headmaster, Oswestry School, Shropshire, 1962-66. Member: London Univ. Examinations Cttee; Council, Football Association. Governor, Moreton Hall School. FRSA 1969. *Recreations:* cricket (Oxford Blue; Warwickshire, 1939, 1946, 1947; Derbyshire, 1949-54), golf, fives (Oxford Blue), and other games. *Address:* Roden House, Brentwood, Essex. *T:* Brentwood 228036. *Clubs:* MCC; Vincent's (Oxford).

SALES, William Henry, BSc (Econ.) Hons. London; Chairman, Yorkshire (late NE) Division of the National Coal Board, 1957-67, retired (Member, National Coal Board, 1953-57); *b* 26 April 1903. *Educ:* pit; Fircroft; London School of Economics. Miners' Welfare Scholarship. Varied career; pit; boys' clubs; WEA Lecturer; schoolmaster. Dep. Labour Director, East Midlands Division, NCB, 1947-51; Deputy Chairman, North-Western Division, 1951-53. Chm. Church of England Industrial Council, 1967-71. Hon. Fellow, LSE, 1960. *Publications:* various papers in Economic and Sociological Journals. *Address:* Handley Cross, Cantley, Doncaster, S Yorks.

SALFORD, Bishop of, (RC), since 1964; **Rt. Rev. Thomas Holland,** DSC 1944; DD (Gregorian); *b* 11 June 1908; *s* of John Holland and Mary (*née* Fletcher). *Educ:* Upholland; Valladolid; Rome. PhD Valladolid, 1929; DD Gregorian, Rome, 1936. Taught theology: Spain, 1936-42; Lisbon, 1942-43. Chaplain, RN, 1943-46; Port Chaplain, Bombay, 1946-48; CMS, 1948-56; Secretary to Apostolic Delegate, 1956-60; Coadjutor Bp of Portsmouth, 1960-64. Privy Chamberlain to the Pope, 1958. Member of Vatican Secretariat for Promoting Christian Unity,

1962-74, for Unbelievers, 1965-73. *Publication:* Great Cross, 1958. *Address:* Wardley Hall, Worsley, Manchester M28 5ND. *T:* 061-794 2825-6.

SALFORD, Auxiliary Bishop of, (RC); *see* Burke, Rt Rev. Geoffrey.

SALINGER, Jerome David; American author; *b* New York City, 1919; *m*; one *s* one *d*. *Educ:* Manhattan public schools; Military Academy, Paris. Served with 4th Infantry Division, US Army, 1942-46 (Staff Sergeant). Travelled in Europe, 1937-38. Started writing at age of 15; first story published, 1940. *Publications:* The Catcher in the Rye, 1951; For Esme-with Love and Squalor, 1953; Franny and Zooey, 1962; Raise High the Roof Beam, Carpenters and Seymour: an Introduction, 1963. *Address:* c/o Harold Ober Associates, 40 East 49th Street, New York, NY 10017, USA.

SALINGER, Pierre (Emil George); Politician, Journalist; Roving Editor, L'Express, Paris, since 1973; *b* San Francisco, 14 June 1925; *s* of Herbert and Jehanne Salinger; *m* 1st; one *s* one *d*; 2nd, 1957, Nancy Brook Joy (marr. diss., 1965); 3rd, 1965, Nicole Gillmann, Paris, France; one *s*. *Educ:* Lowell High School, San Francisco; State Coll., San Francisco; Univ. of San Francisco. Served War, 1942-45, with US Navy. With San Francisco Chronicle, 1942-55; Guest Lectr, Mills Coll., Calif, 1950-55; Press Officer, Democratic Presidential Campaign (Calif), 1952; West Coast Editor, Contributing Editor, Collier's Magazine, 1955-56; Investigator, Senate Labor Rackets Cttee, 1957-59; Press Sec. to President Kennedy (when Senator), 1959-61, and to President of the United States, 1961-64; appointed to serve as a US Senator, 4 Aug. 1964-2 Jan. 1965. Dep. Chm., Gramco (UK) Ltd, 1970-71. Trustee, Robert F. Kennedy Meml Foundn; Mem., Adv. Council, Johns Hopkins University Center, Bologna, Italy. *Publications:* articles on county jail conditions in California, 1953; A Tribute to John F. Kennedy, Encyclopedia Britannica, 1964; With Kennedy, 1966; A Tribute to Robert F. Kennedy, 1968; For the Eyes of the President Only, 1971; Je suis un Americain, 1975; La France et le Nouveau Monde, 1976. *Address:* 248 rue de Rivoli, 75001 Paris, France.

SALISBURY, 6th Marquess of, *cr* 1789; **Robert Edward Peter Cecil;** DL; Baron Cecil, 1603; Viscount Cranborne, 1604; Earl of Salisbury, 1605; Captain Grenadier Guards; High Steward of Hertford since 1972; *b* 24 Oct. 1916; *s* of 5th Marquess of Salisbury, KG, PC, FRS, and of Elizabeth Vere, e *d* of late Lord Richard Cavendish, PC, CB, CMG; *S* father, 1972; *m* 1945, Marjorie Olein (Mollie), *d* of Captain Hon. Valentine Wyndham-Quin, *qv*; five *s* one *d*. MP (C) Bournemouth West, 1950-54. Pres., Monday Club, 1974-. DL Dorset, 1974. *Heir: s* Viscount Cranborne, *qv*. *Address:* Manor House, Cranborne, Dorset; Hatfield House, Hatfield, Herts.
See also Lord David Cecil, Dowager Duchess of Devonshire, Dowager Lady Harlech.

SALISBURY, Bishop of, since 1973; **Rt. Rev. George Edmund Reindorp,** DD; *b* 19 Dec. 1911; *s* of Rev. Hector William Reindorp and Dora Lucy (*née* George), Goodmayes, Essex; *m* 1943, Alix Violet Edington, MB, ChB, *d* of Alexander Edington, MD, and Helen Edington, Durban, Natal; three *s* one *d* (and one *d* decd). *Educ:* Felsted Sch.; Trinity Coll., Cambridge; Westcott House, Cambridge. MA Cantab, 1939. Deacon, 1937; Priest, 1938; Curate, S Mary Abbots, Kensington, 1937-39; Chaplain RNVR, 1938-46; Vicar St Stephen with St John, Westminster, 1946-57. Commissary for: Bishop of Natal, 1948-61; Bishop of New Guinea, 1956-61; Provost of Southwark and Rector of St Saviour with All Hallows, Southwark, 1957-61; Bishop of Guildford, 1961-73. Mem., House of Lords, 1970. Chaplain, RCGP, 1965. Hon. DD Lambeth, 1961; DUniv Surrey, 1970. *Publications:* What about You?, 1956; No Common Task, 1957; Putting it Over: ten points for preachers, 1961; Over to You, 1964; Preaching Through the Christian Year, 1973. *Recreations:* ski-ing, radio and television; avoiding committees. *Address:* Bishop's Office, Church House, Crane Street, Salisbury, Wilts SP1 2QB. *T:* Salisbury 4031. *Clubs:* Ski Club of Great Britain, Kandahar.
See also Sir Humphrey Mynors, Bt.

SALISBURY, Dean of; *see* Evans, Very Rev. S. H.

SALISBURY (Rhodesia), Archbishop of, (RC), since 1976; **Most Rev. Patrick Chakaipa;** *b* 20 June 1932; *s* of Chakaipa and Chokutaura. *Educ:* Chishawasha Minor and Regional Major Seminary, nr Salisbury; Kutama Teachers' Coll. Ecclesiastic qualifications in Philosophy and Theology; Teacher Training Cert. Asst priest, Makumbi Mission, 1967-69; Priest-in-Charge, All Souls Mission, Mtoko, 1969-73; Episcopal Vicar, Mtoko-Mrewa Area, 1970-73; Auxiliary Bishop of Salisbury, 1973-76.

Publications: Karikoga, 1958; Pfumo reRopa, 1961; Rudo Ibofu, 1961; Garandichauya, 1963; Dzasukwa, 1967. *Recreation:* chess. *Address:* PO Box 8060, Causeway, Salisbury, Rhodesia. *T:* 792125.

SALISBURY, Sir Edward James, Kt 1946; CBE 1939; FRS 1933; DSc, Hon. LLD (Edinburgh and Glasgow); VMH; FLS; Director, Royal Botanic Gardens, Kew, 1943-56; Vice-Chairman, Agricultural Improvement Council, 1944-56; Chairman, Joint Committee of AIC and ARC, 1944-59; Mem. Cttee on Higher Agricultural Educn, 1944; Scientific Advisory Cttee to Cabinet, 1943-45; Vice-Pres. RHS; Hon. Adviser Ministry of Labour; Vice-Chm. Cttee on Colonial Agricultural Research, 1945; Fullerton Prof. of Physiology, Royal Instn, 1947-52; Leader of British Delegation to Australian Conference on Plant and Animal Nutrition, 1949; *b* 16 April 1886; *y s* of J. Wright Salisbury, of Limbrick Hall, Harpenden; *m* Mabel (*d* 1956), *d* of J. Elwin-Coles. *Educ:* University College School and University College, London. Gold Medal in Botany, BSc Hons Botany, Research Medal, Quain Student University College, DSc; Senior Lecturer East London College, 1914-18; Lecturer University College, 1918; Reader in Plant Ecology, 1924; formerly Quain Professor of Botany, Univ. of London, University Coll.; Fellow of University Coll., 1920; Vice-Pres., Royal Society, 1943, 1948-55 (Biological Secretary, 1945-55); Pres. SE Union Sci. Societies, 1932; President British Ecological Society, 1928; Pres. Herts NHS, 1922-25; Pres. Norfolk and Norwich Nat. Soc., 1931; VP Linnean Society, 1928; Pres. Section K British Association, 1937; Pres. School Nature Study Union, 1938-44; Pres. Science Masters' Association, 1955; Hon. Sec. British Ecological Soc., 1917-32; Veitchian Gold Medal, 1936; Master's Memorial Lecturer, 1937, 1962; Symonds Memorial Lecturer, 1939; Amos Memorial Lecturer, 1950; Des Vœux Lecturer, 1954; Hon. Fellow Botanical Society of Edinburgh, 1938; Fellow Queen Mary College, London University, 1938; formerly Governor: Royal Holloway College; Queen Mary Coll.; East Malling Research Station; Trustee Lawes Agricultural Trust; Chm. Commonwealth Bursaries Cttee, 1953-66; Mem. of Senate, Univ. of London, 1934-44; Mem. Univ. Grants Cttee, 1944-49; Percy Sladen Trustee, 1939-66; Member of Agricultural Research Council, 1940-44; President: Sussex Naturalists' Trust, 1961-68; Bee Research Assoc., 1964. Hon. Member: Brit. Ecological Soc., 1958; Botanical Soc. of British Isles, 1968. Hon. FInstBiol. Royal Medal of Royal Society, 1945; Hon. Freeman, Worshipful Co. of Gardeners, 1951; VMH 1953. *Publications:* numerous technical papers; article Ecology, in Encyclopædia Britannica; An Introduction to the Study of Plants, 1914, 9th edn 1928; An Introduction to the Structure and Reproduction of Plants, 1920, 2nd edn 1927; Elementary Studies in Plant Life, 1915, 8th edn 1926; Botany for Medical Students, 1921, 3rd edn 1928; The East Anglian Flora, 1933; The Living Garden, 1935, 2nd edn 1942, German edn 1936, American edn 1936; Plant Form and Function, 1938-54; The Reproductive Capacity of Plants, 1942; Flowers of the Woods, 1946; Downs and Dunes, 1952; Weeds and Aliens, 1961; The Biology of Garden Weeds, 1962. *Recreations:* walking, gardening. *Address:* Croindene, Strandway, Felpham, Bognor Regis, West Sussex PO22 7LH.

SALISBURY, Harrison Evans; Associate Editor, New York Times, since 1972 (Assistant Editor, Op-Ed Page, 1971-73); *b* 14 Nov. 1908; *s* of Percy Pritchard Salisbury and Georgiana Evans Salisbury; *m* 1st, 1933, Mary Hollis (marr. diss.); two *s*; 2nd, 1964, Charlotte Young Rand. *Educ:* Univ. of Minnesota (AB). United Press, 1930: London Manager, 1943; Foreign Editor, 1945. New York Times: Moscow Corresp., 1949-54; National Editor, 1962; Asst Man. Editor, 1964. Pres., Nat. Inst. of Arts and Letters, 1975-77. Pulitzer Prize, International Correspondence, 1955. Holds hon. doctorates. *Publications:* Russia on the Way, 1946; American in Russia, 1955; The Shook-up Generation, 1958; To Moscow-And Beyond, 1960; Moscow Journal, 1961; The Northern Palmyra Affair, 1962; A New Russia?, 1962; Russia, 1965; Orbit of China, 1967; Behind the Lines-Hanoi 1967; The Soviet Union-The 50 Years, 1967; The 900 Days, the Siege of Leningrad, 1969; The Coming War Between Russia and China, 1969; The Many Americas Shall Be One, 1971; The Eloquence of Protest: voices of the seventies, 1972; To Peking-and Beyond, 1973; The Gates of Hell, 1975; Black Night, White Snow: Russia's Revolutions 1905-1917. *Address:* Box 70, Taconic, Conn, USA. *Clubs:* Century Association (New York); National Press (Washington, DC).

SALISBURY-JONES, Maj.-Gen. Sir (Arthur) Guy, GCVO 1961 (KCVO 1953); CMG 1949; CBE 1945; MC; DL; Extra Equerry to the Queen since 1962; *b* 4 July 1896; *s* of late Arthur Thomas Salisbury-Jones; *m* Hilda, *widow* of Maj. Guy Yerburgh, Irish Guards, and *d* of Rt Hon. Sir Maurice de Bunsen, Bt, PC, GCMG, GCVO, CB; one *s* one *d. Educ:* Eton. Joined Coldstream Guards, 1915; served European War, 1914-18 (twice wounded, MC and Bar); student at Ecole Spéciale Militaire, St Cyr, 1920-21; Liaison Officer in Syria, 1924-26; Jebel Druze Campaign, 1925-26 (French Croix de Guerre); China, 1927; Staff College, 1932-34; Staff London District, 1935-38; commanded 3rd Battalion Coldstream Guards, in Palestine, 1938-39 (despatches); served in Syria, Italian Somaliland, Greece and Crete, 1939-41 (despatches); was Head of Military Mission to South Africa, 1941-44; Supreme HQ Allied Exped. Force, 1944-45; Head of British Military Mission to France and Military Attaché, Paris, 1946-49; ADC to the King, 1948-49; retired, 1949; HM Marshal of the Diplomatic Corps, 1950-61. Chm., Franco-British Soc., 1963-67. Wine Grower; Pres., English Vineyards Assoc. DL Hampshire, 1965. Order of Red Banner USSR, Order of White Lion Czechoslovakia, Grand Officier Legion of Honour, Croix de Guerre. *Publication:* So Full a Glory-A Life of Marshal de Lattre de Tassigny, 1954. *Address:* Mill Down, Hambledon, Hants. *T:* Hambledon 475. *Clubs:* Cavalry and Guards, Pratt's, Leander.
See also Baron Saye and Sele.

SALK, Jonas Edward, BS, MD; Fellow and Director, Salk Institute for Biological Studies, 1963-75, Fellow and Founding Director since 1975; Adjunct Professor of Health Sciences in Departments of Psychiatry, Community Medicine, and Medicine, University of California at San Diego, since 1970; *b* New York, 28 Oct. 1914; *s* of Daniel B. Salk; *m* 1st, 1939, Donna Lindsay (marr. diss. 1968); three *s*; 2nd, 1970, Françoise Gilot. *Educ:* NY University College of Medicine; Coll. of New York City (BS). Fellow, NY Univ. Coll. of Medicine, 1935-40; Mount Sinai Hosp., NYC, 1940-42; Nat. Research Council Fellow, Sch. of Public Health, Univ. of Michigan, 1942-43, Research Fellow in Epidemiology, 1943-44, Research Assoc., 1944-46, Asst Professor, 1946-47; Assoc. Prof. of Bacteriology and Director of Virus Research, School of Medicine, Univ. of Pittsburgh, 1947-49, Research Prof., 1949-54. Consultant in epidemic diseases to: Sec. of War, 1944-46, Sec. of Army, 1947-54; Commonwealth Professor of Experimental Medicine, 1957-62 (Professor of Preventive Med., Sch. of Med., Univ. of Pittsburgh, USA, and Chairman of the Department, 1954-57). Vis. Prof.-at-Large, Pittsburgh, 1963. Specialist in polio research; developed antipoliomyelitis vaccine, 1954. Member: Amer. Epidemiological Soc., Soc. of Amer. Bacteriologists, etc. Fellow: Amer. Public Health Assoc., Amer. Soc. for Advancement of Science. US Medal of Freedom, 1977. *Address:* 2444 Ellentown Road, La Jolla, Calif 92037, USA.

SALMON, family name of **Baron Salmon.**

SALMON, Baron *cr* 1972 (Life Peer), of Sandwich, Kent; **Cyril Barnet Salmon,** PC 1964; Kt 1957; a Lord of Appeal in Ordinary, since 1972; *b* 28 Dec. 1903; *s* of late Montagu Salmon; *m* 1st, 1929, Rencie (*d* 1942), *d* of late Sidney Gorton Vanderfelt, OBE; one *s* one *d*; 2nd, 1946, Jean, Lady Morris, *d* of late Lt-Col D. Maitland-Makgill-Crichton. *Educ:* Mill Hill; Pembroke College, Cambridge. BA 1925; called to Bar, Middle Temple, 1925; QC 1945; Bencher 1953; Treasurer, 1972. Recorder of Gravesend, 1947-57; Judge of High Court of Justice, Queen's Bench Division, 1957-64; a Lord Justice of Appeal, 1964-72. Chairman: Royal Commission on the Working of the Tribunals of Inquiry (Evidence) Act, 1921, 1966; Royal Commission on Standards of Conduct in Public Life, 1974-76. Commissioned Royal Artillery, 1940. 8th Army HQ Staff, 1943-44. JP (Kent), 1949. Commissioner of Assize, Wales and Chester Circuit, 1955. Captain of the Royal St George's, Sandwich, 1972-73. Governor of Mill Hill School. Hon. Fellow, Pembroke College, Cambridge. *Recreations:* golf, fishing. *Address:* Manwood House, Sandwich, Kent. *T:* Sandwich 2744; 57 Westminster Gardens, Marsham Street, SW1. *T:* 01-834 0961. *Clubs:* Athenæum, Brooks's.

SALMON, Brian Lawson, CBE 1972; Chairman, J. Lyons & Co. Ltd, 1972-77 (Director, 1961-77, Joint Managing Director, 1967-69, Deputy Chairman, 1969-71); *b* 30 June 1917; *s* of Julius Salmon; *m* 1946, Annette Wilson Mackay; two *s* one *d. Educ:* Grenham Hse; Malvern Coll. Chm., Cttee on Sen. Nursing Staff Structure, 1963-66. Vice-Chm., Bd of Governors, Westminster Hosp. Gp, 1963-74; Chm., Camden and Islington AHA, 1974-77. *Recreations:* theatre, ballet, food and wine. *Address:* 34 Kingston House North, Princes Gate, SW7 1LN.
See also N . L . Salmon.

SALMON, Cyril, QC 1970; **His Honour Judge Salmon;** a Circuit Judge, since 1976; *b* 27 Aug. 1924; *s* of Jack and Freda Salmon; *m* 1948, Patrice Ruth Tanchan; one *s* one *d. Educ:* Northampton Sch.; Trinity Hall, Cambridge. Chm. Debates, Cambridge Union Soc., 1944. Called to Bar, Middle Temple, 1947. A Recorder of the Crown Court, 1972-76. *Recreations:* reading history and literature. *Address:* 1 Hare Court, Temple, EC4. *T:* 01-353 5324.

SALMON, Air Vice-Marshal Sir Cyril John Roderic; *see* Salmon, Air Vice-Marshal Sir Roderic.

SALMON, Geoffrey Isidore Hamilton, CBE 1954; President, J. Lyons & Co. Ltd, 1972-77 (Chairman, 1968-72); *b* 14 Jan. 1908; *s* of Harry Salmon and Lena (*née* Gluckstein); *m* 1936, Peggy Rica (*née* Jacobs); two *s* one *d. Educ:* Malvern Coll.; Jesus Coll., Cambridge (BA). Hon. Catering Adviser to the Army, 1959-71. *Address:* 10 Stavordale Lodge, Melbury Road, W14 8LW. *T:* 01-602 3425.

SALMON, Sir Julian, Kt 1969; CBE 1957 (OBE (mil.) 1943); Chairman, Luncheon Vouchers Catering Education Trust, since 1965, Research Institute, since 1966; Director: Sweetheart Plastics Ltd, since 1969 (Chairman, 1969-72); Spey Investments Ltd, since 1969; *b* 29 Aug. 1903; *s* of late Sir Isidore Salmon, CBE, MP; *m* 1930, Anne Handelman. *Educ:* Repton; Jesus College, Cambridge. BA, LLB, 1924. Served War of 1939-45, RAFVR (Wing Comdr). Hon. Catering Adviser to the Royal Air Force, 1949-71. Dir, J. Lyons & Co. Ltd, 1938-69 (Dep. Chm., 1965-69). Chm., Hotel and Catering Ind. Trng Bd, 1966-73. Fellow, Hotel and Catering Inst., 1949-71; FHCIMA 1971-73, Hon. Fellow, 1973-. Member: Corbett Cttee on Navy, Army and Air Force Insts, 1961; Deptl Cttee on Jury Service, 1963. Member: W London Hosp. Hse Cttee, 1959-73 (Vice-Chm., 1967-73); Bd of Governors, Charing Cross Hosp., 1961-73; Cassell Hosp. Management Cttee, 1972-73. Chairman of Managers, 1953-76, Chm. of Trustees, 1972-, Finnart House, Community Home, Weybridge; Mem. Management Cttee, Mathilda and Terence Kennedy Inst. of Rheumatology, 1975-. *Address:* 54 Melbury Court, W8. *T:* 01-602 3203. *Club:* Junior Carlton.

SALMON, Dame Nancy (Marion); *see* Snagge, Dame Nancy.

SALMON, Neil Lawson; Chairman, J. Lyons & Co. Ltd, since 1977; *b* 17 Feb. 1921; *s* of Julius and Mimi Salmon; *m* 1944, Yvonne Hélène Isaacs; one *s* one *d. Educ:* Malvern Coll., Malvern; Institut Minerva, Zürich. Trainee, J. Lyons & Co. Ltd, 1938-41. Served War (Army), 1941-46. Gen. Manager, J. Lyons & Co., 1946; Chm., Glacier Foods Ltd, 1962; Dir, J. Lyons & Co., 1965; Jt Managing Dir, 1967; Gp Managing Dir, 1969; Dep. Chm. and Man. Dir, 1972. FBIM 1971. *Recreations:* opera, ballet, theatre, wine, puzzles. *Address:* Cadby Hall, W14 0PA. *T:* 01-603 2040 (ext. 2342). *Club:* Savile.
See also B . L . Salmon .

SALMON, Air Vice-Marshal Sir Roderic, KBE 1968 (OBE 1945); CB 1959; RAF; Secretary, Diocese of St Edmundsbury and Ipswich, since 1968; *b* 21 Aug. 1911; *s* of Edmund Frederick and Edna Salmon; *m* 1939, Hilda (*née* Mitchell); one *s* two adopted *d. Educ:* Howard Gardens High School, Cardiff; City of Cardiff Technical College. Commissioned in Royal Air Force, 1935; No 2 Squadron, 1936; No 70 Squadron, 1936-38; Air Ministry, Directorate of Movements, 1939-43; Second Tactical Air Force (Senior Movements Staff Officer), 1944-46 (despatches); RAF Staff College (Student), 1946; CO No 33 Maintenance Unit, 1947; No 57 Maintenance Unit, 1947-49; Member of the Directing Staff, Joint Services Staff College, 1949-51; Head of Logistics Planning, HQ Allied Air Forces, Central Europe, 1951-53; CO No 16 Maintenance Unit, 1953-54; Imperial Defence College, 1955: HQ No 40 Group (Operations Staff), 1956-59; Director of Equipment (A), Air Ministry, 1959-62; Senior Air Staff Officer, HQ Maintenance Command, 1962-64; Dir-Gen. of Equipment (RAF), MoD, 1964-68; retd. 1968. *Recreations:* gardening, fishing and tennis. *Address:* Damer Close, Little Bealings, Woodbridge, Suffolk. *T:* Kesgrave 2408.

SALMON, Sir Samuel (Isidore), Kt 1960; President, J. Lyons & Company Ltd, 1968-72 (Chairman, 1965-68); *b* 18 Oct. 1900; *s* of late Sir Isidore Salmon, CBE, DL, JP, MP, and of Lady Salmon; *m* 1937, Lallah Wendy, *d* of Alexander and Hannah Benjamin; one *s* one *d. Educ:* Bedales School, Petersfield; Jesus College, Cambridge (MA). LCC Member for Cities of London and Westminster, 1949-65; Deputy Chairman, LCC, 1959-60; (elected) GLC Mem. for City of Westminster, 1964-67; Mayor of London Borough of Hammersmith, 1968-69. Chm., Metropolitan Water Bd, 1970-. Formerly: Chm., Palace Hotel Ltd; Dir, Cadogan Investments Ltd. Governor, Regent Street Polytechnic, 1950-. *Recreations:* bridge, reading. *Address:* 14 Carlos Place, W1. *T:* 01-629 6217. *Clubs:* Carlton, 1900, Leander.

SALMON, Thomas David; Under-Secretary (Legal), Department of Industry (also advises Department of Trade), since 1974; *b* 1 Nov. 1916; *s* of late Rev. T. Salmon, N Stoneham, near Eastleigh, Hants, and late Isabel Salmon (*née* Littleton); *m* 1950, Morris Patricia Reyner Turner, *o d* of G. S. Turner and late Mrs

Turner, Ilford, Essex; one *s* two *d. Educ:* Winchester Coll.; Christ Church, Oxford (MA). Admitted solicitor, 1949. Served War of 1939-45: Captain 133 Field Regt RA (despatches). Temp. Asst Principal, Cabinet Office, 1946. Entered Treasury Solicitor's Dept, 1951; Asst Treasury Solicitor, 1965; Asst Solicitor, Bd of Trade, 1966; Asst Solicitor, Dept of Trade and Industry, 1970, Under Sec. (Legal), DTI, 1973. *Recreations:* walking, reading, gardening. *Address:* Tenures, 23 Sole Farm Road, Great Bookham, Surrey. *T:* Bookham 52837.

SALMON, Very Rev. Thomas Noel Desmond Cornwall; Dean of Christ Church, Dublin, since 1967; *b* Dublin, 5 Feb. 1913; *s* of Francis Allen Cornwall Salmon, BDS, and Emma Sophia, *d* of Dr Hamilton Jolly, Clonroche, Co. Wexford; unmarried. *Educ:* privately; Trinity College, Dublin; BA 1935, MA, BD. Deacon 1937; Priest 1938. Curate Assistant: Bangor, Co. Down, 1937-40; St James' Belfast, 1940-42; Larne, Co. Antrim, 1942-44; Clerical Vicar, Christ Church Cathedral, 1944-45; Curate Assistant, Rathfarnham, Dublin, 1945-50; Incumbent: Tullow, Carrickmines, 1950-62; St Ann, Dublin, 1962-67. Asst Lectr in Divinity School, TCD, 1945-63; Examining Chaplain to Archbishop of Dublin, 1949-. *Recreations:* in younger days Rugby football (Monkstown FC Dublin) and swimming; now walking, gardening and reading. *Address:* 13 Merlyn Park, Ballsbridge, Dublin 4. *T:* 694780.

SALMON, Col William Alexander, OBE 1956; Assistant Ecclesiastical Secretary to Lord Chancellor (appointed 1964), and to Prime Minister, since 1965; *b* 16 Nov. 1910; *o s* of late Lt-Colonel W. H. B. Salmon, late IA; *m* 1939, Jean Barbara Macmillan, *o d* of late J. V. Macmillan, DD, OBE (Bishop of Guildford, 1934-49); one *s* two *d. Educ:* Haileybury College; RMC, Sandhurst. Commissioned 2nd Lt HLI 1930; ADC to Governor of Sind, 1936-38. Served during War of 1939-45: France, 1939; Middle East, Italy, Greece, Bde Major, 1942; GSO2 HQ Aegean Force, 1943; CO, 2nd Bn Beds and Herts Regt, 1945-46. CO, 2nd Bn Royal Irish Fusiliers, 1946-47; GSO1 (Trng), HQ Scottish Command, 1947-49; Chief of Staff to Lt-Gen. Glubb Pasha, HQ Arab Legion, 1950-53; CO 1st Bn HLI, 1953-55; Col, GS (O and T Div.) SHAPE, 1957-59; AQMG (QAE2), The War Office, 1959-62; AAG (AG14), The War Office, 1962-63; retd 1963. Hashemite Order of El Istiqlal (2nd Cl.), 1953. *Recreations:* shooting, fishing, gardening. *Address:* Little Thorpe, 220 Forest Road, Tunbridge Wells, Kent TN2 5HS. *T:* Tunbridge Wells 26562. *Club:* Army and Navy.

SALOMON, Walter Hans; Chairman of Rea Brothers Ltd, Merchant Bank, since 1950; Chairman, Canal-Randolph Corporation; *b* 16 April 1906; *s* of Henry Salomon and Rena (*née* Oppenheimer); *m* 1935; one *s* one *d. Educ:* Oberreal, Eppendorf, Hamburg; Hamburg Univ. FIB. Member of Lloyd's; Member of Baltic Exchange; Founder and Treas., Young Enterprise; Vice-Pres., Cambridge Settlement; Freeman, City of London; Master, Pattenmakers' Co.; Member: Luso-Brazilian Council; Hudson Institute; Trustees, Foundn for Educn in Economics. Has lectured widely on economic and financial matters. Comdr, Southern Cross of Brazil, 1971. *Publications:* One Man's View, 1973; numerous newspaper articles. *Recreations:* yachting, ski-ing, tennis, art, bridge, snooker. *Address:* Castlemaine House, 21-22 St James's Place, SW1A 1NH. *T:* 01-493 1273. *Clubs:* Reform, City Livery, Canning House 1001, Hurlingham; Wentworth Golf; Norddeutscher Regatta-Verein Hamburg; Poole Harbour and Royal Torbay Yacht.

SALOP, Archdeacon of; *see* Austerberry, Ven. S. D.

SALT, Sir David Shirley, 5th Bt, *cr* 1869; *b* 14 June 1930; *s* of 4th Bt and Stella Houlton (*d* 1974), 2nd *d* of Richard Houlton Jackson, MRCS, LRCP, Bakewell, Derbyshire; *S* father 1953; *m* 1st, 1955, Margaret Gillian (marr. diss. 1974), *d* of H. Alwyn Lenox, 31 Markham Square, SW3; 2nd, 1975, Freda Evelyn Blows. *Educ:* Stowe. *Heir: b* Anthony Houlton Salt [*b* 15 Sept. 1931; *m* 1957, Prudence Meath Baker; four *d*]. *Address:* c/o Lloyd's Bank Ltd, 61 Moorgate, EC2.
See also Baron Glanusk .

SALT, Mrs Emmaline Juanita, CBE 1975; JP; *b* 22 Jan. 1910; *d* of Willie Southcombe Propert and Edith Mary (*née* Bacon); *m* 1934, William Edward Salt; two *d. Educ:* Colston's Girls' Sch.; Bristol Univ. (MA Econ). Bristol City Councillor, 1938-41; Member: Central Council of Probation and After-Care Cttees, 1960- (Chm., 1968-71); Home Secretary's Adv. Council for Probation and After-Care, 1961-; Chm., Avon Probation and After-Care Cttee, 1974-. Dep. Sec., SW Regional Cttee for Educn in HM Forces, 1941-45; sometime lecturer for WEA. JP Bristol, 1946-. *Recreations:* grandchildren, walking, opera, history. *Address:* 1 Heathercliffe, Goodeve Road, Sneyd Park, Bristol BS9 1PN. *T:* Bristol 681208.

SALT, George, FRS 1956; ScD; Fellow of King's College, Cambridge, since 1933; Reader in Animal Ecology, University of Cambridge, 1965-71, now Emeritus; *b* Loughborough, 12 Dec. 1903; *s* of late Walter Salt and Mary Cecilia (*née* Hulme); *m* 1939, Joyce Laing, Newnham Coll. and Stockton-on-Tees; two *s. Educ:* Crescent Heights Collegiate Inst., Calgary; Univ. of Alberta (BSc); Harvard Univ. (SM, SD); Univ. of Cambridge (PhD, ScD). National Research Fellow, Harvard Univ., 1927-28; Entomologist, Imperial Inst. Entom, 1929-31; Royal Soc. Moseley Research Student, 1932-33; Univ. Lectr in Zoology, Cambridge, 1937-65; Fellow of King's Coll., Cambridge, 1933-, Dean, 1939-45, Tutor for Advanced Students, 1945-51. Visiting Prof. Univ. of California, Berkeley, 1966. On biological expedns in NW Canada and Rocky Mts, Cuba, Republic of Colombia, E Africa, Pakistan. *Publications:* The Cellular Defence Reactions of Insects, 1970; papers in scientific jls on insect parasitism and ecology. *Recreations:* mountaineering, gardening, calligraphy and illumination. *Address:* King's College, Cambridge; 21 Barton Road, Cambridge. *T:* Cambridge 55450.

SALT, Sir (Thomas) Michael (John), 4th Bt, *cr* 1899; *b* 7 Nov. 1946; *s* of Lt-Col Sir Thomas Henry Salt, 3rd Bt, and Meriel Sophia Wilmot, *d* of late Capt. Berkeley C. W. Williams and Hon. Mrs Williams, Herringston, Dorchester; *S* father 1965; *m* 1971, Caroline, *er d* of Henry Hildyard. *Educ:* Eton. *Heir: b* Anthony William David Salt, *b* 5 Feb. 1950. *Recreations:* cricket, shooting. *Address:* Shillingstone House, Shillingstone, Dorset. *Club:* Boodle's.

SALTER, Harry Charles, DFC 1945; Director of the Financing of the Community Budget, Commission of the European Communities, since 1973; *b* 29 July 1918; *er s* of late Harry Arnold Salter and of Irene Beatrice Salter; *m* 1946, Anne Hooper; one *d. Educ:* St Albans Sch. Entered Ministry of Health, 1936. Served War, Royal Artillery, 1939-46 (despatches, DFC). Asst Sec., Min. of Health, 1963; Under-Sec., DHSS, 1971-73. *Recreations:* golf, chess, bridge. *Address:* 66c Avenue de Tervuren, 1040 Brussels. *T:* 7335713.

SALTER, Vice-Admiral Jocelyn Stuart Cambridge, CB 1954; DSO 1942 (Bar 1951); OBE 1942; *b* 24 Nov. 1901; *s* of late Henry Stuart Salter, of Messrs Lee, Bolton & Lee (Solicitors); *m* 1935, Joan (*d* 1971), *d* of late Rev. C. E. C. de Coetlogon, of the Indian Ecclesiastical Establishment; one *s* one *d. Educ:* Royal Naval Colleges, Osborne and Dartmouth. Joined Royal Navy, 1915; Midshipman, 1917; served European War in HMS Ramillies, Grand Fleet, 1917-19; Lieut 1923; Comdr 1937; Comd HMS Foresight in Force H, and in Home Fleet, 1941-42; Capt. 1942. Comd 16th Dest. Flotilla, 1944-45; Comd HMS Jamaica, 1950-51 (served with UN Fleet in Korean waters); served on staff of SHAPE, 1951; ADC, 1951; Rear-Admiral, 1952; Vice-Admiral, 1954; Flag Officer, Malta, and Admiral Superintendent HM Dockyard, Malta, 1952-54; Admiral Superintendent HM Dockyard, Portsmouth, 1954-57; retired, 1957. Mem., Court of Assistants, Haberdashers' Company, Warden, 1958, 1963, 1968, Master, 1970. Norwegian Haakon VII Liberty Cross, 1946; United States Bronze Star medal, 1950. *Address:* Folly House, Hambledon, Hampshire. *T:* Hambledon 732. *Club:* Naval and Military.

SALTER DAVIES, Roy Dicker; *see* Davies.

SALTOUN, 19th Lord, *cr* 1445, of Abernethy; **Alexander Arthur Fraser,** MC; a Representative Peer for Scotland, 1935-63; *b* 8 March 1886; *e s* of 18th Lord and Mary (*d* 1940), *o d* of Thomas Arthur Grattan-Bellew, MP; *S* father, 1933; *m* 1920, Dorothy, *e d* of Sir Charles Welby, 5th Bt; one *d* (one *s* killed in action). Late Sub-Lieutenant Forfar and Kincardine Artillery Militia: Captain, retired, 3rd Battalion Gordon Highlanders; prisoner of war, 1914-18. Grand Master Mason of Scotland, 1934-36. Formerly Vice-Convener, RNLI for Scotland, 1945-53, Convener, 1953-59. *Heiress: d* Hon. Flora Marjory Fraser [*b* 18 Oct. 1930; *m* 1956, Captain Alexander Ramsay, Grenadier Guards, *o s* of late Adm. Hon. Sir Alexander Ramsay, GCVO, KCB, DSO, and The Lady Patricia Ramsay, CI, VA; three *d*]. *Address:* Cairnbulg Castle, Fraserburgh; Cross Deep, Twickenham. *Clubs:* Athenæum; New (Edinburgh).

SALTZMAN, Charles Eskridge, OBE (Hon.) 1943; DSM 1945 (US); Legion of Merit (US) 1943: Limited Partner, Goldman, Sachs & Co. (investment banking) since 1956; *b* 19 Sept. 1903; *s* of Maj.-Gen. Charles McKinley Saltzman and Mary Saltzman (*née* Eskridge); *m* 1st, 1931, Gertrude Lamont (marr. diss.); one *s* ; 2nd, 1947, Cynthia Southall Myrick (marr. diss.); two *d* (one *s* decd). *Educ:* Cornell Univ.; US Mil. Acad.; Magdalen College,

Oxford University. BS (US Mil. Acad.); BA, MA (Rhodes Scholar) (Oxford Univ.). Served as 2nd Lt, Corps of Engrs, US Army, 1925-30; commissioned 1st Lieut, NY National Guard, 1930; Lieutenant-Colonel 1940; on active duty in US Army, 1940-46, serving overseas, 1942-46; Brigadier-General 1945; relieved from active duty, 1946; Maj.-Gen. AUS (Retd). With NY Telephone Co., 1930-35; with NY Stock Exchange, 1935-49 (Asst to Exec. Vice-Pres., later Sec. and Vice-Pres.). Asst Sec. of State, 1947-49; Partner Henry Sears & Co., 1949-56; Under-Sec. of State for Admin., 1954-55. Former Dir, A. H. Robins Co., Inc. President: English-Speaking Union of the US, 1961-66; Assoc. of Graduates, US Mil. Academy, 1974-; Mem. Pilgrims of the United States. Hon. Mem., Soc. of the Cincinnati. Member, Director, or Trustee of many boards, societies and religious, medical and educational institutions. Holds foreign decorations. *Address:* (home) 101 E 69th Street, New York, NY 10021, USA. *T:* (212) RE 4 5400; (office) 55 Broad Street, New York, NY 10004. *T:* (212) 676-8000. *Clubs:* Century Association, Recess, River, Union, University (New York); Metropolitan (Washington).

SALUSBURY-TRELAWNY, Sir J. B.; *see* Trelawny.

SAMBELL, Most Rev. Geoffrey Tremayne; *see* Perth (Australia), Archbishop of.

SAMMAN, Peter Derrick, MD, FRCP; Physician to Dermatological Department, Westminster Hospital, since 1951, and St John's Hospital for Diseases of the Skin since 1959; Consultant Dermatologist, Orpington and Sevenoaks Hospitals, since 1951; Dean, Institute of Dermatology, 1965-70; *b* 20 March 1914; *y s* of Herbert Frederick Samman and Emily Elizabeth Savage; *m* 1953, Judith Mary Kelly; three *d. Educ:* King William's Coll., IOM; Emmanual Coll., Cambridge; King's Coll. Hosp., London. BA (Nat. Scis. Tripos), 1936; MB, BChir Cantab 1939; MRCP 1946; MA, MD Cantab 1948; FRCP 1963. House Surg., King's Coll. Hosp., 1939; Sqdn Ldr, RAFVR, 1940-45; House Phys. and Registrar, King's Coll. Hosp., 1946; Sen. Dermatological Registrar and Tutor in Dermatology, United Bristol Hosps, 1947-48; Sen. Registrar, St John's Hosp. for Diseases of the Skin, 1949-50. FRSocMed; Mem. Brit. Assoc. of Dermatology; Hon. Mem., Dermatological Soc. of S Africa. *Publications:* The Nails in Disease, 1965, 2nd edn 1972; chapters in Textbook of Dermatology (ed Rook, Wilkinson and Ebling), 1968; (jtly) Tutorials in Postgraduate Medicine: Dermatology, 1977; various articles in med. jls. *Recreation:* gardening. *Address:* 18 Sutherland Avenue, Orpington, Kent. *T:* Orpington 20839.

SAMPLES, Reginald McCartney, CMG 1971; DSO 1942; OBE 1963; HM Diplomatic Service; Consul-General, Toronto, Canada, since 1974; *b* 11 Aug. 1918; *o s* of William and Jessie Samples; *m* 1947, Elsie Roberts Hide; two *s* one step *d. Educ:* Rhyl Grammar Sch.; Liverpool Univ. (BCom). Served, 1940-46; RNVR (Air Branch); torpedo action with 825 Sqn against German ships Scharnhorst, Gneisenau and Prinz Eugen in English Channel (wounded, DSO); Lieut (A). Central Office of Information (Economic Editor, Overseas Newspapers), 1947-48. CRO (Brit. Inf. Services, India), 1948; Economic Information Officer, Bombay, 1948-52; Editor-in-Chief, BIS, New Delhi, 1952; Dep.-Dir, BIS, New Delhi, 1952-56; Dir, BIS, Pakistan (Karachi), 1956-59; Dir, BIS, Canada (Ottawa), 1959-65, OBE; Counsellor (Information) to Brit. High Comr, India, and Dir, BIS, India (New Delhi), 1965-68; Asst Under-Sec. of State, Commonwealth Office, 1968; Head of British Govt Office, and Sen. British Trade Comr, Toronto, 1969. *Recreations:* tennis, golf. *Address:* c/o Foreign and Commonwealth Office, SW1. *Club:* Naval.

SAMPSON, Anthony (Terrell Seward); writer and journalist; *b* 3 Aug. 1926; *s* of Michael Sampson and Phyllis, *d* of Sir Albert Seward, FRS; *m* 1965, Sally, *d* of Dr P. G. Bentlif, Jersey, and of Mrs G. Denison-Smith, Islip, Oxon; one *s* one *d. Educ:* Westminster School; Christ Church, Oxford. Served with Royal Navy, 1944-47; Sub-Lieut, RNVR, 1946. Editor of Drum Magazine, Johannesburg, 1951-55; Editorial staff of The Observer, 1955-66, Chief American Corresp., 1973-74. Editor, The Observer Magazine, 1965-66. Associate Prof., Univ. of Vincennes, Paris, 1968-70. *Publications:* Drum, a Venture into the New Africa, 1956; The Treason Cage, 1958; Commonsense about Africa, 1960; (with S. Pienaar) South Africa: two views of Separate Development 1960; Anatomy of Britain, 1962; Anatomy of Britain Today, 1965; Macmillan: a study in ambiguity, 1967; The New Europeans, 1968; The New Anatomy of Britain, 1971; The Sovereign State: the secret history of ITT, 1973; The Seven Sisters, 1975 (Prix International de la Presse, Nice, 1976); The Arms Bazaar, 1977. *Recreation:* gardening. *Address:* 27 Ladbroke Grove, W11. *T:* 01-727 4188, 01-221

5738; 2 Valley Farm, Walberswick, Suffolk. *T:* Southwold 2080. *Clubs:* Beefsteak, Savile.

SAMUEL, family name of **Viscounts Bearsted** and **Samuel** and **Baron Samuel of Wych Cross.**

SAMUEL, 2nd Viscount, *cr* 1937, of Mount Carmel and of Toxteth, Liverpool; **Edwin Herbert Samuel,** CMG 1947; Colonial Service, retired; Principal of the Institute of Public Administration in Israel; *b* 11 Sept. 1898; *e s* of 1st Viscount Samuel, PC, GCB, OM, GBE, and Beatrice (*d* 1959), *y d* of Ellis A. Franklin; *S* father, 1963; *m* 1920, Hadassah Goor; two *s*. *Educ:* Westminster School; Balliol Coll., Oxford (BA); Commonwealth Fund Fellow, Columbia University, 1931-32. 2nd Lieut RFA and GSI, GHQ, EEF, 1917-19; District Officer: Jerusalem, Ramallah, and Jaffa, 1920-27; Assistant Secretary, Government of Palestine, 1927-30; Assistant District Comr, Galilee, 1933-34; Deputy Comr for Migration, 1934-39; Postal and Telegraph Censor, Jerusalem, 1939-42; Chief Censor and (from 1944) Press Censor, 1942-45; Director of Broadcasting, 1945-48; Visiting Professor in Middle East Govt, Dropsie College, Philadelphia, 1948-49; European Director of the Conquest of the Desert, International Exhibition, Jerusalem, 1951-53; Sen. Lectr in British Institutions, Hebrew Univ., Jerusalem, 1954-69; Visiting Lectr in Public Administration, Univ. of the Witwatersrand, 1955; Visiting Professor: in Political Science, Graduate School of Public Affairs, Albany State Univ. of New York, 1963; in Public Admin, Graduate Sch. of Public and Internat. Affairs, Pittsburgh Univ., 1970; Dept of Urban Affairs, Univ. of Miami, Fla, 1971. A Director: the Jewish Chronicle, London, 1951-70; Vallentine Mitchell (publishers), London, 1965-; Ellern Investment Corp. Ltd, Tel Aviv, 1964-; Moller Textile Corporation, Nahariya, 1965-; Adviser to the Magen David Adom (Israel Nat. Red Cross Society) on publicity and public relations, 1957-75; Mem. of Council: Anglo-Israel Assoc., London; Anglo-Jewish Assoc., London; Labour Friends of Israel, London; (British) Friends of the Hebrew University, etc. *Publications:* A Primer on Palestine, 1932; Handbook of the Jewish Communal Villages, 1938 and 1945; The Children's Community of Mishmar HaEmek, 1942; The Theory of Administration, 1947; Problems of Government in the State of Israel, 1956; British Traditions in the Administration of Israel, 1957; Anglo-Israel Relations, 1948-1968: a catalogue, 1969; Structure of Society in Israel, 1969; A Lifetime in Jerusalem: memoirs, 1970; See How They Run: the administration of venerable institutions, 1976; Israel's Immigration Cycle, 1976; A Cottage in Galilee (short stories), 1957; A Coat of Many Colours (short stories), 1960; My Friend Musa (short stories), 1963; The Cucumber King (short stories), 1965; Capt. Noah and His Ark (illustrated children's story), 1965; His Celestial Highness (short stories), 1968; The Man Who Liked Cats (short stories), 1975; (with M. Kamrat) Roots (Hebrew-English Lexicon), 1970. *Heir: s* Prof. The Hon. David Herbert Samuel, MA, PhD [*b* 8 July 1922; *m* 1st, 1950, Esther Berelowitz (marr. diss., 1957), Cape Town; one *d*; 2nd, 1960, Mrs Rinna Dafni, *d* of late Meir Grossman, Israel; one *d*]. *Address:* House of Lords, SW1; 15 Rashba Road, Jerusalem, Israel. *T:* 33871.

SAMUEL OF WYCH CROSS, Baron *cr* 1972 (Life Peer), of Wych Cross, Sussex; **Harold Samuel,** Kt 1963; FRICS; Hon. Fellow: Magdalene College, Cambridge, 1961; University College, London, 1968; Chairman: The Land Securities Investment Trust Ltd; The Central London Housing Trust for the Aged; *b* London, 23 April 1912; *s* of late Vivian and Ada Samuel; *m* 1936, Edna Nedas; two *d* (and one *d* decd). *Educ:* Mill Hill School; College of Estate Management. Member: Crown Estate Commissioners Regent St Cttee, 1963-; Land Commission, 1967-70; Special (Rebuilding) Cttee, RICS, 1962-76; Reserve Pension Bd, 1974; Covent Garden Market Authority, 1961-74. Member: Court of The City Univ.; Court of Univ. of Sussex; Court of Univ. Coll. of Swansea; Court of Patrons, RCS; a Vice-Pres., British Heart Foundation; Trustee, Mill Hill Sch.; Director, Railway Sites Ltd (British Rail), 1962-65. *Recreations:* swimming, horticulture. *Address:* 75 Avenue Road, Regent's Park, NW8 6JD; Wych Cross Place, Forest Row, East Sussex RH18 5JJ. *Club:* East India, Devonshire, Sports and Public Schools.

SAMUEL, Adrian Christopher Ian, CMG 1959; CVO 1963; Director, British Agrochemicals Association, since 1972; *b* 20 Aug. 1915; *s* of late George Christopher Samuel and Alma Richards; *m* 1942, Sheila, *er d* of late J. C. Barrett, Killiney, Co. Dublin; three *s* one *d*. *Educ:* Rugby Sch.; St John's Coll., Oxford. Entered HM Consular Service, 1938; served at Beirut, Tunis and Trieste. Served War, 1940-44, in Royal Air Force. Returned to HM Foreign Service and served at HM Embassies in Ankara, Cairo and Damascus; First Secretary, 1947; Counsellor, 1956;

Principal Private Secretary to the Secretary of State for Foreign Affairs, Oct. 1959-63; Minister at HM Embassy, Madrid, 1963-65; resigned 1965. Dir, British Chemical Engrg Contractors Assoc., 1966-69. *Recreations:* golf, shooting, sailing and reading. *Address:* The Laundry House, Handcross, near Haywards Heath, West Sussex RH17 6HQ. *T:* Handcross 717. *Clubs:* Garrick, Lansdowne.

SAMUEL, Herbert Dawkin; Director of Greenwich Hospital, Admiralty, 1959-64, retired; *b* 21 Jan. 1904; *o s* of Alfred Samuel, Llanelly; *m* 1936, Evelyn Mary, *d* of Col H. J. Barton, RE; two *s*. *Educ:* Clifton Coll.; Merton Coll., Oxford; Heidelberg University. 1st cl. Hons, Mod. Langs; Laming Fellow, Queen's Coll., Oxford, 1925-27. Entered Consular Service, 1927; Actg Vice-consul, Genoa, 1927, Paris, 1929. Asst Master: Repton School, 1930; Harrow School, 1931; Dist. Inspector, Bd of Education, 1938. Entered Admiralty as Principal, 1939; Under-Secretary, 1956. Coronation Medal, 1953. *Address:* 25 Storrs Close, Bovey Tracey, Devon TQ13 9RH.

SAMUEL, Sir Jon (Michael Glen), 5th Bt, *cr* 1898; Director, Advanced Vehicle Systems Ltd, since 1971; *b* 25 Jan. 1944; *o s* of Sir John Oliver Cecil Samuel, 4th Bt, and of Charlotte Mary, *d* of late R. H. Hoyt, Calgary, Canada; *S* father, 1962; *m* 1966, Antoinette Sandra, *d* of late Captain Antony Hewitt, RE, 2nd SAS Regt, and of Mrs K. A. H. Casson, Frith Farm, Wolverton, Hants; two *s*. *Educ:* Radley; London Univ. Dir, Enfield Automotive, 1967-70. *Recreations:* motor racing, water ski-ing. *Heir: s* Anthony John Fulton Samuel, *b* 13 Oct. 1972. *Address:* Havoc House, Beenham, Berks. *T:* Woolhampton 3623.

SAMUEL, Hon. Peter Montefiore, MC 1942; TD 1951; Banker; Deputy Chairman, Hill, Samuel Group, since 1935; Chairman: Dylon International Ltd, since 1958; Hill Samuel & Co. (Ireland) Ltd, since 1964; *b* 9 Dec. 1911; second *s* of 2nd Viscount Bearsted and Dorothea, *e d* of late E. Montefiore Micholls; *b* and *heir-pres.* to 3rd Viscount Bearsted, *qv*; *m* 1st, 1939, Deirdre du Barry (marr. diss. 1942); 2nd, 1946, Hon. Elizabeth Adelaide Pearce Serocold, *d* of late Baron Cohen, PC; two *s* one *d*. *Educ:* Eton; New College, Oxford (BA). Served Warwickshire Yeo, Middle East and Italy, 1939-45. Director: Shell Transport & Trading Co. Ltd, 1938-; Samuel Properties Ltd, 1961-; Mayborn Products Ltd (Chm.), 1946-; Trades Union Unit Trust Managers Ltd, 1961-77; Computer and Systems Engineering Ltd (Chm.), 1971-77; General Consolidated Investment Trust Ltd, 1975-. President, Norwood Home for Jewish Children, 1962-; Hon. Treas., Nat. Assoc. for Gifted Children, 1968-; Chm. Council, Royal Free Hospital of Medicine, 1973- (Mem., 1948-). *Recreations:* golf, fishing, shooting. *Address:* Flat 12, Rutland Court, SW7 1BN. Farley Hall, Farley Hill, near Reading, Berkshire RG7 1UL. *T:* Eversley 733242. *Club:* White's.

SAMUEL, Richard Christopher; HM Diplomatic Service; Head of Far Eastern Department, Foreign and Commonwealth Office, since 1976; *b* Edinburgh, 8 Aug. 1933. *Educ:* Durham Sch.; St John's Coll., Cambridge (BA). Royal Navy, 1952-54. FO, 1957-58; Warsaw, 1958-59; Rome, 1960-63; FO, 1963; Private Sec. to Parly Under-Sec. of State, 1965-68; Hong Kong, 1968-69; 1st Sec. and Head of Chancery: Singapore, 1969-71; Peking, 1971-73; Counsellor, Washington, 1973-76. *Recreations:* music, science fiction. *Address:* c/o Foreign and Commonwealth Office, SW1A 2AL; 49 St Dionis Road, SW6 4UB. *T:* 01-736 5279.

SAMUELS, Albert Edward, LLB; JP; Legal Member, London Rent Assessment Panel, 1965-73; *b* 12 May 1900; *er s* of John Samuels and Esther Stella Samuels; *m* 1934, Sadie Beatrice, BSc (Econ.); one *s*. *Educ:* Sir Walter St John's School; University of London (King's College). Admitted a Solicitor, 1921. Elected to Battersea Borough Council, 1922; Councillor, 1922-25; Alderman, 1925-31; contested LCC Election, 1925; Mem. of LCC, 1928-31, 1934-37, 1946-49 and 1952-65 (for Bermondsey); Chairman: Public Control Cttee, 1934-37, 1946-48 and 1952-55; Establishment Cttee, 1955-58, 1960-65; Jt Cttee of Members and Staff 1955-58; Interim Staff Panel, 1960-65; Chairman, LCC, 1958-59; Mem., GLC, 1964-67 (Chm. Public Health Services Cttee). Vice-Chm. Jt Cttee of LCC and QS 1934-36, 1947-48. Mem., Metropolitan Water Bd, 1925-28, 1941-46; Chm., Redhill and Netherne Gp HMC, 1968-74. Pres. Sir Walter St John's Old Boys' Assoc., 1956-57. JP (County of London) 1933. Comdr Order of Merit of Italian Republic, 1958; Kt Comdr of the Order of Merit of the Federal Republic of Germany, 1958. *Recreations:* reading, walking and golf. *Address:* The Chantry, Cronks Hill, Reigate, Surrey. *T:* 43717; 37 Harley Street, W1. *T:* 01-580 9972. *Clubs:* Athenæum, Royal Automobile.

SAMUELS, Sir Alexander, Kt 1963; CBE 1956; JP, FRSA, FCIT, MIMechE; Member, (part-time) British Waterways Board, 1966-75, and Covent Garden Market Authority, 1961-75; *b* 15 Sept. 1905. *Educ:* Elementary Sch. Mem., Shoreditch Borough Council, 1945-61; Chairman: London and Home Counties Traffic Advisory Cttee, 1946-61; Special Enquiry into London Traffic Congestion, 1951; Working Party for Car Parking, 1953; Cttee for Speed limit Enquiry, 1954; Special Survey Cttee on use of Parking Meters, 1956; London Travel Cttee, 1958; Operations Group of the Transport Co-ordinating Council for London, 1966; Dep. Chm., Nat. Road Safety Advisory Council, 1965-66; Vice-Pres., London Accident Prevention Council, 1956; Member: Departmental Cttee Road Safety, 1957-64; Adviser to the Minister of Transport on London Traffic Management, 1961-65, on Road Traffic, 1965-66. *Recreation:* golf. *Address:* Redcroft, 19 Hartsbourne Avenue, Bushey Heath, Herts. *T:* 01-950 1162. *Club:* Reform.

SAMUELS, David Jessel T.; *see* Turner-Samuels.

SAMUELS, Prof. Michael Louis; Professor of English Language, University of Glasgow, since 1959; *b* 1920; *s* of late Harry Samuels, OBE, MA, barrister-at-law, and of Céline Samuels (*née* Aronowitz), London; *m* 1950, Hilary, *d* of late Julius and Ruth Samuel, Glasgow; one *d. Educ:* St Paul's School; Balliol College, Oxford. Domus Exhibitioner in Classics, Balliol College, Oxford, 1938-40 and 1945-47; MA 1947 (First Class Hons English Lang. and Lit.). Worked for Air Ministry (Maintenance Command), 1940-45. Research Fellow, University of Birmingham, 1947-48; Assistant in English Language, University of Edinburgh, 1948-49; Lecturer in English Language, Univ. of Edinburgh, 1949-59. *Publications:* Linguistic Evolution, 1972; articles and reviews in Trans Philological Soc., Medium Aevum, Review of English Studies, Archivum Linguisticum, English Studies, English and Germanic Studies. *Address:* 4 Queen's Gate, Dowanhill, Glasgow G12 9DN. *T:* 041-334 4999.

SAMUELSON, Sir Francis Henry Bernard, 4th Bt, *cr* 1884; *b* 22 Feb. 1890; *s* of late Sir Francis (Arthur Edward) Samuelson, 3rd Bt, and Fanny Isabel (*d* 1897), *e d* of William Merritt Wright, St John, New Brunswick, Canada; *S* father, 1946; *m* 1913, Margaret Kendall, *d* of late H. Kendall Barnes; three *s* one *d* (and one *d* decd). *Educ:* Eton; Trinity College, Cambridge. *Heir:* *s* (Bernard) Michael (Francis) Samuelson [*b* 17 Jan. 1917; *m* 1952, Janet Amy, *yr d* of Lt-Comdr L. G. Elkington, Chelsea; two *s* two *d*]. *Address:* Midway House, Partridge Green, Sussex.

SAMUELSON, Prof. Paul A.; Institute Professor, Massachusetts Institute of Technology, 1966; *b* Gary, Indiana, 15 May 1915; *m* 1938, Marion Crawford; four *s* two *d. Educ:* Univs of Chicago (BS) and Harvard (MA, PhD). SSRC Predoctoral Fellow, 1935-37; Soc. of Fellows, Harvard, 1937-40; Guggenheim Fellow, 1948-49; Ford Faculty Research Fellow, 1958-59; Hoyt Vis. Fellow, Calhoun Coll., Yale, 1962; Carnegie Foundn Reflective Year, 1965-66. MIT: Asst Prof. of Econs, 1940; Assoc. Prof. of Econs, 1944; Staff Mem., Radiation Lab., 1944-45; Prof. of Econs, 1947; Prof. of Internat. Economic Relations (part-time), Fletcher Sch. of Law and Diplomacy, 1945. Consultant: to Nat. Resources Planning Bd, 1941-43; to Rand Corp., 1948-75; to US Treasury, 1945-52, 1961-; to Johnson Task Force on Sustained Prosperity, 1964; to Council of Econ. Advisers, 1960-; to Federal Reserve Bd, 1965-; to Jt Economic Council; to Congressional Budget Office. Economic Adviser to Senator, Candidate and President-elect John F. Kennedy, informal adviser to President Kennedy. Member: War Prodn Bd and Office of War Mobilization and Reconstruction, 1945; Bureau of the Budget, 1952; Adv. Bd of Nat Commn on Money and Credit, 1958-60; Research Adv. Panel to President's Nat. Goals Commn, 1959-60; Research Adv. Bd Cttee for Econ. Develt, 1960; Nat. Task Force on Econ. Educn, 1960-61; Sen. Advr, Brookings Panel on Econ. Activity. Contrib. Editor and Columnist, Newsweek. Lectures: Stamp Meml, London, 1961; Wicksell, Stockholm, 1962; Franklin, Detroit, 1962; Gerhard Colm Meml, NYC, 1971; Davidson, Univ. of New Hampshire, 1971; 12th John von Neumann, Univ. of Wisconsin, 1971; J. Willard Gibbs Lecture, Amer. Mathematical Soc., 1974. 1st Sulzbacher Distinguished Lectr, Colombia Law Sch., 1974; John Diebold Lectr, Harvard Univ., 1976. Corresp. Fellow, British Acad., 1960; Fellow: Amer. Philosoph. Soc.; Econometric Soc. (Mem. Council; Vice-Pres. 1950; Pres. 1951); Member: Amer. Acad. Arts and Sciences; Amer. Econ. Assoc. (Pres. 1961; Hon. Fellow, 1965); Phi Beta Kappa; Commn on Social Sciences (NSF), 1967-; Internat. Econ. Assoc. (Pres. 1965-68; Hon. Pres. 1968-); Nat. Acad. of Sciences, 1970-; Omicron Delta Epsilon, Bd of Trustees (Internat. Honor Soc. in Econ.). Hon. Fellow, LSE. David A. Wells Prize, Harvard, 1941; John Bates Clark Medal, Amer. Econ. Assoc., 1947; Medal of Honor, Univ. of Evansville, 1970;

Nobel Prize in Econ. Science, 1970; Albert Einstein Commemorative Award, 1971. Hon. LLD: Chicago, 1961; Oberlin, 1961; Boston Coll., 1964; Indiana, 1966; Michigan, 1967; Claremont Grad. Sch., 1970; New Hampshire, 1971; Keio, Tokyo, 1971; Harvard, 1972; Gustavas Adolphus Coll., 1974; Univ. of Southern Calif, 1975; Univ. of Rochester, 1976; Univ. of Pennsylvania, 1976; Emmanuel Coll., 1977. Hon. DLitt: Ripon Coll., 1962; Northern Michigan Univ., 1973; Hon DSc: E Anglia, 1966; Massachusetts, 1972; Rhode Is., 1972; Hon. LHD: Seton Hall, 1971; Williams Coll., 1971; D*hc* Université Catholique de Lourain, Belgium, 1976. *Publications:* Foundations of Economic Analysis, 1947; Economics, 1948, 10th edn 1976 (trans. 24 langs); (jtly) Linear Programming and Economic Analysis, 1958 (trans. French, Japanese); Readings in Economics, 1955; The Collected Scientific Papers of Paul A. Samuelson (ed J. E. Stiglitz), vols I and II, 1966, vol. III (ed R. C. Merton), 1972, vol. IV (ed H. Nagatani and K. Crowley), 1977; co-author, other books in field, papers in various jls, etc. *Recreation:* tennis. *Address:* Department of Economics, Massachusetts Institute of Technology E52-383, Cambridge, Mass 02139, USA. *T:* 617-253-3368. *Club:* Belmont Hill (Mass).

SAN VINCENZO FERRERI, Marquis of; *see* St Vincent Ferreri.

SANCHEZ-GAVITO, Vicente, GCVO (Hon.) 1973; Advisor to Minister of External Relations and to National Council of Science and Technology, since 1976; *b* 25 May 1910; *s* of Vicente Sanchez Gavito and Maria P. de Sanchez Gavito. *Educ:* Nat. Univ. of Mexico (BA); Escuela Libre de Derecho, Mexico City (LLB). Min. of External Relations, Mexico: Solicitor, Gen. Commn on Claims between USA and Mexico and at Commn on Agrarian Claims, 1935-39 (Alt. Comr for Mexico, 1937); Head, N Amer. Affairs Dept, 1939-43; Dir-Gen. of Diplomatic Service, 1947-51; Mem., UN Tribunals in Libya and Eritrea, 1951-55; Pres., Jt Honduras-Nicaraguan Commn (decision of boundary controversy, 1961); Ambassador to Organisation of Amer. States, 1959-65: Pres. Council, 1959-60; Pres. Interamerican Peace Commn, 1960-61; Mem. OAS Special Cttees visiting Central Amer. 1959, Venezuela 1960, Panama 1964; Ambassador of Mexico to Brazil, 1965-70, to London, 1970-73, to Federal Republic of Germany, 1974-75. Leader or member of numerous delegations. Order of: Southern Cross, Brazil, 1960; Liberator, Venezuela, 1962; Rio Branco, Brazil, 1970. *Recreation:* chess. *Address:* c/o Secretaria de Relaciones, Mexico DF. *Club:* University (Washington, DC).

SANCTUARY, Gerald Philip; Secretary, Professional and Public Relations, The Law Society, since 1971; *b* 22 Nov. 1930; *s* of late John Cyril Tabor Sanctuary, MD and of Maisie Toppin Sanctuary (*née* Brooks); *m* 1956, Rosemary Patricia L'Estrange, Dublin; three *s* two *d . Educ:* Bryanston Sch.; Law Soc.'s Sch. of Law. National Service Pilot, 1953-55; Asst Solicitor, Kingston, 1955-56; Partner in Hasties, Solicitors, Lincoln's Inn Fields, 1957-62; Field Sec., Nat. Marriage Guidance Council, 1963-65, Nat. Secretary 1965-69; Exec. Dir, Sex Information and Educn Council of US, 1969-71. Editor, Law Soc. series: It's Your Law, 1973-. Regular broadcaster on radio. *Publications:* Marriage Under Stress, 1968; Divorce- and After, 1970, 2nd edn 1976; Before You See a Solicitor, 1973; contrib., Moral Implications of Marriage Counseling, 1971; Vie Affective et Sexuelle, 1972. *Recreation:* amateur drama. *Address:* 100 Fishpool Street, St Albans, Herts. *T:* St Albans 65229.

SANDARS, George Edward Russell, CMG 1951; MBE 1933; *b* 19 Oct. 1901; *s* of Rev. Canon George Russell Sandars and Mary Lambart Wyld; *m* 1937, Vera Margaret Molyneux-Seel; no *c. Educ:* Winchester; New College, Oxford. Joined Sudan Political Service, 1924; Private Secretary to Governor General, 1933-37; Sudan Agent in Cairo, 1941-45; Governor of Blue Nile Province, 1948-51. Sec., Inst. of Brewing, 1951-64. *Address:* Red Cottages, Dogmersfield, near Basingstoke, Hants. *T:* Fleet 4801. *Club:* Athenæum.

SANDBACH, Prof. Francis Henry, FBA 1968; Fellow of Trinity College, Cambridge, since 1927; *b* 23 Feb. 1903; *s* of late Prof. F. E. and Ethel Sandbach; *m* 1932, Mary Warburton Mathews; one *s* one *d* (and one *s* decd). *Educ:* King Edward's Sch., Birmingham; Trinity Coll., Cambridge. Browne Schol., 1922; Craven Schol., 1923; Chancellor's Medallist, 1925; Charles Oldham Class. Schol., 1925. Asst Lectr, Manchester Univ., 1926-28; Lectr in Classics, Univ. of Cambridge, 1929-67; Brereton Reader in Classics, 1951-67; Prof. of Classics, 1967-70. Junior Proctor, 1940-41; Trinity Coll.: Lecturer in Classics, 1929-63; Tutor, 1945-52; Sen. Tutor, 1952-56. *Publications:* (some jointly): Plutarch's Moralia, vol. ix, 1961, vol. xi, 1965, vol. xv, 1969; Plutarchus Moralia, vol. vii, 1967; Menandri Reliquiae Selectae, 1972; Menander: a commentary, 1973; The

Stoics, 1975; The Comic Theatre of Greece and Rome, 1977; articles in class. jls. *Address:* 2 Hedgerley Close, Cambridge CB3 0EW. *T:* 53152.

SANDBERG, Michael Graham Ruddock, OBE 1977; JP; Chairman, The Hongkong and Shanghai Banking Corporation, Mercantile Bank Ltd, since 1977; *b* 31 May 1927; *s* of Gerald Arthur Clifford Sandberg and Ethel Marion Sandberg; *m* 1954, Carmel Mary Roseleen Donnelly; two *s* two *d*. *Educ:* St Edward's Sch., Oxford. 6th Lancers (Indian Army) and King's Dragoon Guards, 1945. Joined The Hongkong and Shanghai Banking Corp., 1949: service in Hong Kong, Japan and Singapore; Gen. Manager, 1971; Exec. Dir, 1972; Dep. Chm., 1973. JP (Hong Kong), 1972-; Steward, Royal Hong Kong Jockey Club, 1972-; Treasurer, Univ. of Hong Kong, 1977. *Recreations:* horse racing, bridge, cricket, horology. *Address:* c/o The Hongkong and Shanghai Banking Corporation, 1 Queen's Road Central, Hong Kong. *T:* 5-222011. *Clubs:* Cavalry and Guards, Junior Carlton, MCC, Surrey CCC.

SANDELSON, Neville Devonshire; MP (Lab) Hillingdon, Hayes and Harlington, since 1974 (Hayes and Harlington, June 1971-1974); Barrister-at-Law; *b* Leeds, 27 Nov. 1923; *s* of late David I. Sandelson, OBE, and Dora Sandelson, (*née* Lightman); *m* 1959, Nana Karlinski, Neuilly sur Seine, France; one *s* two *d*. *Educ:* Westminster School; Trinity College, Cambridge; MA. Called to Bar, Inner Temple, 1946; for some years director of local newspaper and book publishing cos and producer of TV documentary programmes until resuming practice at Bar, 1964. Mem. London County Council, 1952-58; junior Whip of majority group. Travelled extensively in USA, Middle East, Europe. Contested Ashford (Kent) 1950, 1951 and 1955; Beckenham (by-election) 1957; Rushcliffe 1959; Heston & Isleworth 1966; SW Leicester (by-election) 1967; Chichester 1970. Vice-Chairman: PLP Legal and Judicial Gp; PLP Home Affairs Gp; PLP Foreign and Commonwealth Gp. Promoted, as a Private Member's Bill, the Matrimonial Proceedings (Polygamous Marriages) Act, 1972. Member: Fabian Soc; General & Municipal Workers Union; Soc. of Labour Lawyers. Mem. Ct. Brunel Univ., 1975-. *Address:* 9 King's Bench Walk, Temple, EC4. *T:* 01-353 5638; House of Commons, SW1. *Club:* Reform.

SANDERS, Christopher Cavania, RA 1961 (ARA 1953); RP 1968; ARCA 1928; artist-painter; *b* near Wakefield, 25 Dec. 1905; *s* of Alfred B. Sanders; *m* 1931, Barbara L. Stubbs (ARCA 1928) (*d* 1967), *d* of Francis F. Stubbs, Isleworth and Felpham; two *s* two *d*. *Educ:* Ossett Grammar Sch.; Wakefield Sch. of Art; Leeds Coll. of Art; Royal Coll. of Art. Gold Medallist, Paris Salon, 1955. *Address:* 2 Tudor Gardens, Slough, Berks SL1 6HJ.

SANDERS, Cyril Woods, CB 1959; Lord of the Manor of Kavenham-Stoke-Wereham and Wretton in Norfolk; *b* 21 Feb. 1912; *er s* of Cyril Sturgis Sanders and Dorothy (*née* Woods); *m* 1944, Kate Emily Boyes, *qv*; one *s* three *d*. *Educ:* St Paul's Sch.; Queen's Coll., Oxford. BA Oxon 1934, Lit. Hum. Joined General Post Office as Assistant Principal, 1934; transferred to Board of Trade, 1935; retired from Dept of Trade and Industry (formerly Bd of Trade) as Under-Secretary, 1972. *Recreations:* walking, sailing, painting. *Address:* 41 Smith St, Chelsea, SW3. *T:* 01-352 8053; Giles Point, Winchelsea, Sussex; Canower, Cashel, Connemara, Eire. *Clubs:* Ski Club of Gt Britain; Island Cruising (Devon).

SANDERS, Mrs Cyril Woods; *see* Boyes, K. E. T.

SANDERS, Donald Neil; Deputy Governor and Deputy Chairman of Board, Reserve Bank of Australia, since 1975; *b* Sydney, 21 June 1927; *s* of L. G. Sanders; *m* 1952, Betty Elaine, *d* of W. B. Constance; four *s* one *d*. *Educ:* Wollongong High Sch.; Univ. of Sydney (BEc). Commonwealth Bank of Australia, 1943-60; Australian Treasury, 1956; Bank of England, 1960; Reserve Bank of Australia, 1960-: Supt, Credit Policy Div., Banking Dept, 1964-66; Dep. Manager: Banking Dept, 1966-67; Res. Dept, 1967-70; Aust. Embassy, Washington DC, 1968; Chief Manager: Securities Markets Dept, 1970-72; Banking and Finance Dept, 1972-74; Adviser and Chief Manager, Banking and Finance Dept, 1974-75. *Address:* Reserve Bank of Australia, 65 Martin Place, Sydney, NSW 2000, Australia.

SANDERS, Sir Harold (George), Kt 1963; MA, PhD; Deputy Chairman, University Grants Committee, 1964-67 (Member, 1949-55); *b* 9 Oct. 1898; *s* of W. O. Sanders, JP, Wollaston, nr Wellingborough; *m* 1923, Kathleen Penson Plunkett (*d* 1973); one *s* one *d*. *Educ:* Wellingborough School; St John's College, Cambridge. Assistant (Physiology), Animal Nutrition Inst., School of Agriculture, Cambridge, 1922-29; University Lecturer (Agriculture), Cambridge, 1929-44; Fellow, St John's College,

Cambridge, 1938-44; Executive Officer, Herts War Agricultural Executive Committee, 1941-44; Prof. of Agriculture, Reading Univ., 1945-54; Chief Scientific Adviser (Agriculture) to Ministry of Agriculture, Fisheries and Food, 1955-64. Served European War, 1917-19, 2nd Lt RFA (France). *Publications:* An Outline of British Crop Husbandry, 1939, 3rd edn, 1958; (with G. Eley) Farms of Britain, 1946. *Address:* West Croft, Elraston Road, Hexham, Northumberland; Orchard Close, Theale, Berks. *T:* Reading 302264. *Club:* Farmers'.

SANDERS, John Derek; Organist and Master of the Choristers, Gloucester Cathedral, since 1967; *b* 26 Nov. 1933; *s* of Alderman J. T. Sanders, JP, CA and Mrs E. M. Sanders (*née* Trivett); *m* 1967, Janet Ann Dawson; one *s* one *d*. *Educ:* Felsted Sch., Essex; Royal Coll. of Music; Gonville and Caius Coll., Cambridge. ARCM 1952; FRCO 1955; MusB 1956; MA 1958. Dir of Music, King's Sch., Gloucester, and Asst Organist, Gloucester Cathedral, 1958-63; Organist and Master of the Choristers, Chester Cathedral, 1964-67. Dir of Music, Cheltenham Ladies' Coll., 1968-. Conductor: Gloucestershire Symphony Orchestra, 1967-; Gloucester Choral Soc., 1967-. Conductor of Three Choirs Festival, 1968, 1971, 1974 and 1977. *Publications:* Festival Te Deum, 1962; Soliloquy for Organ, 1977. *Recreations:* gastronomy, travelling. *Address:* 7 Miller's Green, Gloucester GL1 2BN. *T:* 24764.

SANDERS, John Leslie Yorath; HM Diplomatic Service; Director of Research and Commonwealth Office, since 1976; *b* 5 May 1929; *s* of late Reginald Yorath Sanders and Gladys Elizabeth Sanders (*née* Blything); *m* 1953, Brigit Mary Lucine Altounyan; one *s* two *d*. *Educ:* Dulwich Coll. Prep. Sch.; Cranleigh School. Nat. Service in HM Forces (RA), 1948-50; entered HM Foreign Service, 1950; FO, 1950-52; MECAS, Lebanon, 1953; Damascus, 1954-55; Bahrain, 1955-56; Vice-Consul, Basra, 1956-60; Oriental Sec., Rabat, 1960-63; FO, 1964-67; 1st Sec., Beirut, 1968-70; 1st Sec. and Head of Chancery, Mexico City, 1970-73; Counsellor, Khartoum, 1973-75; Counsellor, Beirut, 1975-76. *Recreations:* sailing, music. *Address:* c/o Foreign and Commonwealth Office, SW1; Town Yeat, High Nibthwaite, Ulverston, Cumbria. *Club:* Travellers'.

SANDERS, John Reynolds M.; *see* Mayhew-Sanders, J. R.

SANDERS, Peter Basil; Director, Equal Opportunities Division, Commission for Racial Equality, since 1977; *b* 9 June 1938; *s* of Basil Alfred Horace Sanders and Ellen May Sanders (*née* Cockrell); *m* 1961, Janet Valerie (*née* Child); two *s* one *d*. *Educ:* Queen Elizabeth's Grammar Sch., Barnet; Wadham Coll., Oxford (MA, DPhil). Administrative Officer, Basutoland, 1961-66; Research in Oxford for DPhil, 1966-70; Officer, Min. of Defence, 1971-73; Race Relations Bd: Principal Conciliation Officer, 1973-74; Dep. Chief Officer, 1974-77. *Publications:* Lithoko: Sotho Praise—Poems (ed jtly and trans. with an Introd. and Notes), 1974; Moshoeshoe, Chief of the Sotho, 1975. *Address:* 34 Highfield Avenue, Headington, Oxford OX3 7LR. *T:* Oxford 61441.

SANDERS, Robert Tait, CMG 1974; HMOCS; Secretary to the Cabinet, Government of Fiji, since 1970; *b* 2 Feb. 1925; *s* of late A. S. W. Sanders and Charlotte McCulloch; *m* 1951, Barbara, *d* of G. Sutcliffe; three *s*. *Educ:* Canmore Public Sch., Dunfermline; Dunfermline High Sch.; Fettes Coll., Edinburgh; Pembroke Coll. (Major Open Classical Schol. 1943), Cambridge (John Stewart of Rannoch Schol. in Latin and Greek, 1947); London Sch. of Economics. First cl. Hons, Pts I and II of Classical Tripos, Cantab. Served War, 1943-46: Lieut, 1st Bn the Royal Scots, India and Malaya. Sir Arthur Thomson Travelling Schol., 1948; Sir William Browne Medal for Latin Epigram, 1948; MA (Cantab) 1951. Joined HM Overseas Civil Service, Fiji, as Dist Officer, 1950; Sec. to Govt of Tonga, 1956-58; Sec., Coconut Commn of Enquiry, 1963; MLC, Fiji, 1963-64; Sec. for Natural Resources, 1965-67; Actg Sec. Fijian Affairs, and Actg Chm. Native Lands and Fisheries Commn, 1967; MEC, Fiji, 1967; Sec. to Chief Minister and to Council of Ministers, 1967; apptd Sec. to Cabinet, 1970, also Sec. for Foreign Affairs, 1970-74, and Sec. for Home Affairs, 1972-74. Fiji Independence Medal, 1970. *Publications:* Interlude, in, Fiji, 1963; articles in Corona, jl of HMOCS. *Recreations:* golf, sailing, music, crosswords, scrabble. *Address:* Cabinet Office, Suva, Fiji. *T:* 211207. *Clubs:* Royal Scots (Edinburgh); Nausori Golf (Fiji).

SANDERS, Terence Robert Beaumont, CB 1950; TD; DL; Chairman, Buckland Sand and Silica Co. Ltd; *b* 2 June 1901; *yr s* of late Robert Massy Dawson Sanders, Charleville Park, Co. Cork, and Hilda Beaumont, Buckland Court, Surrey; *m* 1st, 1931, Marion (*d* 1961), *er d* of late Colonel A. W. Macdonald, DSO, Spean Bridge: five *s*; 2nd, 1965, Deborah, *y d* of late Daniel C. Donoghue of Philadelphia. *Educ:* Eton; Trinity Coll.

Cambridge. Fellow of CCC, Cambridge, 1924, Estates Bursar, 1935, Life Fellow, 1945; sometime Univ. Lectr in Engineering, Cambridge Univ. Commissioned TA, 1923, RA; Capt. 1928, Maj. 1939; Herts Yeo. 1939-42. Min. of Supply, 1944; Asst Chief Engineer, Armament Design and later Principal Dir of Tech. Development (Defence); demobilised, 1945, with rank of Colonel. Entered Scientific Civil Service, 1946, retd 1951. Engrg Advr to BSI, 1952-72, closely associated with work of Internat. Orgn for Standardization; Chm., ISO/STACO, 1964-72. Mem., S-E Gas Bd, 1961-69. Dir, GHP Gp, 1962-76. Rowed in Univ. Boat Race, 1922; won Henley Stewards' Cup, 1922, 1923, 1924; Grand, 1929; Olympic IVs, 1924; Hon. Treas., CUBC, 1928-39. FICE, FIMechE, FInstW. High Sheriff, Surrey, 1967; DL Surrey, 1967. *Publication:* Centenary History of Boat Race. *Recreations:* rowing, shooting, farming. *Address:* Slough House, Buckland, Surrey. *Clubs:* Bath, Leander.

SANDERSON OF AYOT, 2nd Baron *cr* 1960, title disclaimed by the heir, Dr Alan Lindsay Sanderson, 1971.

SANDERSON, Sir Bryan; *see* Sanderson, Sir F. P. B.

SANDERSON, Sir (Frank Philip) Bryan, 2nd Bt, *cr* 1920; Lt-Comdr RNVR; *b* 18 Feb. 1910; *s* of Sir Frank Bernard Sanderson, 1st Bt, and Amy Edith (*d* 1949), *d* of David Wing, Scarborough; *S* father 1965; *m* 1933, Annette Irene Caroline (*d* 1967), *d* of late Col Korab Laskowski, Warsaw, (*g d* of General Count de Castellaz); two *s* one *d*. *Educ:* Stowe; Pembroke College, Oxford. Served War of 1939-45 with Fleet Air Arm. A Member of Lloyd's. Former Chairman, Humber Fishing and Fish Manure Co., Hull. *Recreation:* shooting. *Heir: s* Frank Linton Sanderson [*b* 21 Nov. 1933; *m* 1961, Margaret Ann, *o d* of John C. Maxwell; two *s* three *d*]. *Address:* Lychgate Cottage, Scaynes Hill, Haywards Heath, West Sussex RH17 7NH. *Club:* Junior Carlton.

SANDERSON, George Rutherford; British Council Representative, Spain, since 1976; *b* 23 Nov. 1919; *er s* of late George Sanderson and of Edith Mary Sanderson, Blyth, Northumberland; *m* 1947, Jean Cecilia, *d* of James C. McDougall, Chesterfield, Derbyshire; two *s*. *Educ:* Blyth Grammar Sch.; Univ. of London (BA 1st Cl. Hons French and Italian). War Service, 1940-46: RA, Malta and Egypt (Major). British Council, 1949-: Actg Dir, Anglo Argentine Cultural Inst., La Plata, Argentina, 1949; Dir, Tucuman, Argentina, 1950-52; Asst Rep., Santiago, Chile, 1952-58; Dep. Area Officer, Oxford, 1958-62; Reg. Dir, and Dir Anglo Argentine Cultural Assoc., Rosario, Argentina, 1962-66; Asst Rep., Buenos Aires, 1966-69; Reg. Dir, and Dir Anglo Brazilian Cultural Soc., São Paulo, Brazil, 1969-72; Dir, Drama and Music Dept, and Dep. Controller, Arts Div., 1973; Educnl Attaché, British Embassy, Washington, 1973-76. *Recreations:* art, reading. *Address:* Leafield House, Holton, Oxford. *T:* Wheatley 2526.

SANDERSON, John Ellerslie; Under-Secretary, Department of Transport, since 1976; *b* 19 March 1922; *yr s* of late Joseph Sanderson and Daisy (*née* Beeman); *m* 1941, Joan Ethel, *y d* of H. H. Mitchell, Bromley, Kent; three *s*. *Educ:* Portsmouth Grammar Sch. Entered Civil Service in 1947 and joined Min. of Transport, 1952. On loan to Intergovernmental Maritime Consultative Organisation, 1959-61; Asst Sec., Min. of Transport, 1963; Under-Sec., Ports, DoE later Dept of Transport, 1971. *Recreations:* music, gardening. *Address:* Wavenden, Thorpe Lea Road, Egham, Surrey. *T:* Egham 3359.

SANDERSON, Captain Lancelot, CIE 1942; RIN, retired; Captain, RN Emergency List; *b* 1889; *s* of late Herbert Elsworth Sanderson; *m* 1919, Anna St John, *d* of late William Sloane; two *d*. *Educ:* HMS Worcester. Joined RIN 1911; served European War, 1914-19; Surveyor-in-Charge, Marine Survey of India, 1935-39; Naval Officer-in-Charge, Calcutta, 1939-43; Chief of Personnel, Naval Headquarters, New Delhi, 1944-45; retired 1946. *Address:* 19 Elm Grove, Saffron Walden CB10 1NA. *T:* Saffron Walden 23405.

SANDERSON, Very Rev. Roy; *see* Sanderson, Very Rev. W. R.

SANDERSON, Rt. Rev. Wilfrid Guy; *b* 17 Aug. 1905; *s* of late Wilfrid E. Sanderson; *m* 1934, Cecily Julia Mary Garratt; one *s* two *d*. *Educ:* Malvern College; Merton College, Oxford (MA). Ordained, 1931; Curate at S Farnborough, Hants, till 1934; Priest-in-charge of St Aidan's, Aldershot, 1934-37; Vicar of All Saints, Woodham, Surrey, 1937-46; Vicar of All Saints, Alton, Hants, 1946-54; Rector of Silverton, Devon, 1954-59; Archdeacon of Barnstaple, 1958-62; Rector of Shirwell, 1959-62; Suffragan Bishop of Plymouth, 1962-72. *Address:* 3 Hinton Close, Hinton St George, Somerset TA17 8SH. *T:* Crewkerne 73840.

SANDERSON, Very Rev. (William) Roy; Parish Minister at Stenton and Whittingehame, 1963-73; Extra Chaplain to the Queen in Scotland, since 1977 (Chaplain, 1965-77); *b* 23 Sept. 1907; *er s* of late Arthur Watson Sanderson, Leith, and late Ethel Catherine Watson, Dundee; *m* 1941, Annie Muriel Easton, Glasgow; three *s* two *d*. *Educ:* Cargilfield Sch.; Fettes Coll.; Oriel Coll.; Oxford; Edinburgh University. BA 1929, MA 1933, Oxon. Ordained, 1933. Asst Minister, St Giles' Cath., Edin., 1932-34; Minister: at St Andrew's, Lochgelly, 1935-39; at the Barony of Glasgow, 1939-63. Moderator: Glasgow Presbytery, 1958; Haddington and Dunbar Presbytery, 1972-74; Convener of Assembly Cttees: on Religious Instruction of Youth, 1950-55; on Deaconesses, 1956-61; Panel of Doctrine, 1960-65; on Gen. Administration, 1967-72. Convener of Business Cttee and Leader of General Assembly of the Church of Scotland, 1965-66, 1968-72. Moderator of Gen. Assembly of the Church of Scotland, May 1967-May 1968. Chm., BBC Scottish Religious Advisory Committee, 1961-71; Member Central Religious Advisory Cttee of BBC and ITA, 1961-71. Governor, Fettes Coll., Edinburgh, 1967-76. Hon. DD Glasgow, 1959. *Publication:* Responsibility (Moderatorial address), 1967. *Recreations:* golf, reading. *Address:* 1a York Road, North Berwick, East Lothian. *T:* North Berwick 2780. *Club:* Overseas (Edinburgh).

SANDFORD, 2nd Baron, *cr* 1945, of Banbury; **Rev. John Cyril Edmondson,** DSC 1942; Conservative Peer in House of Lords, since 1959; *b* 22 Dec. 1920; *e s* of 1st Baron Sandford; *S* father, 1959; *m* 1947, Catharine Mary Hunt; two *s* two *d*. *Educ:* Eton Coll.; Royal Naval Coll., Dartmouth; Westcott House, Cambridge. Served War of 1939-45: Mediterranean Fleet, 1940-41; Home Fleet, 1942; Normandy Landings, 1944 (wounded); Mediterranean Fleet, HMS Saumarez, 1946 (wounded). Staff of RN Coll., Dartmouth, 1947-49; HMS Vengeance, 1950; HMS Cleopatra, 1951-52; Staff Commander-in-Chief Far East, 1953-55; Commander of Home Fleet Flagship, HMS Tyne, 1956; retired 1956. Ordained in Church of England, 1958; Parish of St Nicholas, Harpenden, 1958-63; Exec. Chaplain to Bishop of St Albans, 1965-68. Opposition Whip, House of Lords, 1966-70; Parly Sec., Min. of Housing and Local Govt, June-Oct. 1970; Parliamentary Under-Secretary of State: DoE, 1970-73; DES, 1973-74. Chm., Cttee to review the condition and future of National Parks in England and Wales, 1971. Chairman: Hertfordshire Council of Social Service, 1966-69; Westminster Council of Social Service, 1969-70; Church Army, 1969-70; Mem., Adv. Council on Penal Reform, 1968-70. Pres., Council for Environmental Educn. Hon. Fellow, Inst. of Landscape Architects. *Heir: s* Hon. James John Mowbray Edmondson [*b* 1 July 1949; *m* 1973, Ellen Sarah, *d* of Jack Shapiro, Toronto; one *d*]. *Address:* 6 Smith Square, Westminster, SW1. *T:* 01-222 5715. *Club:* Ski Club of Gt Britain.

SANDFORD, Prof. Cedric Thomas; Professor of Political Economy, University of Bath, since 1965, and Director of Bath University Centre for Fiscal Studies, since 1974; *b* 21 Nov. 1924; *s* of Thomas Sandford and Louisa (*née* Hodge); *m* 1945, Evelyn Belch; one *s* one *d*. *Educ:* Manchester Univ. (BAEcon 1948, MAEcon 1949); London Univ. (BA History (external) 1955). Undergraduate, Manchester Univ., 1942-43 and 1946-48; RAF, 1943-46 (Pilot). Graduate Research Schol., Univ. of Manchester, 1948-49; Lectr, Burnley Municipal Coll., 1949-60; Sen. Lectr, subseq. Head of General and Social Studies Dept, Bristol Coll. of Science and Technology, 1960-65; Head of Sch. of Humanities and Social Sciences, Univ. of Bath, 1965-68 and 1971-74. Visiting Prof., Univ. of Delaware, USA, 1969. *Publications:* Taxing Inheritance and Capital Gains (Hobart Paper 32, IEA), 1965, 2nd edn 1967; Economics of Public Finance, 1969, 2nd edn 1977; Realistic Tax Reform, 1971; Taxing Personal Wealth, 1971; National Economic Planning, 1972, 2nd edn 1976; Hidden Costs of Taxation, 1973; (jtly) An Accessions Tax, 1973; (jtly) An Annual Wealth Tax, 1975; (sen. editor, and jt author) Case Studies in Economics (3 vols), 1971, 2nd edn 1977; Social Economics, 1977; numerous articles in wide range of learned jls. *Recreations:* gardening, fishing, violin-playing. *Address:* 10 Summerhill Road, Bath BA1 2UR. *T:* Bath 26049.

SANDFORD, Sir Folliott Herbert, KBE 1949; CMG 1944; Registrar of Oxford University, and Fellow, New College, Oxford, 1958-72; *b* 28 Oct. 1906; *s* of late W. C. Sandford, Barrister-at-Law; *m* 1935, Gwendoline Alexander Masters (*d* 1977); no *c*. *Educ:* Winchester; New Coll., Oxford (1st Class Greats, 1st Class Law); Geneva. Entered Air Ministry, 1930; Principal Private Secretary to successive Secretaries of State (Viscount Swinton, Sir Kingsley Wood, Sir Samuel Hoare, and Sir Archibald Sinclair), 1937-40; attached to RAF Ferry Command, Montreal, 1941-42; Secretary, Office of Resident Minister, West Africa, 1942-44; Assistant Under-Secretary of

State, Air Ministry, 1944-47; Deputy Under-Secretary of State, Air Ministry, 1947-58. Master, Skinners' Company, 1975-76. Hon. Fellow, New Coll. and Wolfson Coll., Oxford, 1972. Hon. DCL Oxon, 1973. *Address:* Damsel's Mill, Painswick, Glos. *Club:* Reform.

SANDFORD, Jeremy; writer; *b* 5 Dec. 1934; *s* of Christopher Sandford, owner/director of the Golden Cockerel Press, and Lettice Sandford, wood engraver, craft worker; *m* 1956, Nell Dunn; three *s. Educ:* Eton; Oxford. Dir, The Cyrenians; Exec., Gypsy Council; Sponsor: Shelter; The Simon Community. Editor, Romano Drom (gypsy newspaper). Screen Writers' Guild of Gt Britain Award, 1967, 1971; Prix Italia prize for TV drama, 1968; Critics Award for TV drama, 1971. *Publications:* Synthetic Fun, 1967; Cathy Come Home, 1967; Whelks and Chromium, 1968; Edna the Inebriate Woman, 1971; Down and Out in Britain, 1971; In Search of the Magic Mushrooms, 1972; Gypsies, 1973; Tomorrow's People, 1974; Prostitutes, 1975; Smiling David, 1975; Virgin of the Clearways, 1977. *Recreations:* painting, music, travel, mountain exploration, getting to know British people. *Address:* 7 Earls Court Square, SW5.

SANDFORD, Kenneth Leslie, CMG 1974; Chairman, Accident Compensation Commission (New Zealand), since 1972; *b* 14 Aug. 1915; *s* of Albert Edgar Sandford and Barbara Ivy (*née* Hill); *m* 1946, Airini Ethel Scott Sergel; one *s* one *d* (and one *d* decd). *Educ:* King's Coll., Auckland, NZ; Auckland University Coll. LLB 1938. Served War: 34 Bn (NZ), rank of Captain, 1940-45. Barrister and Solicitor, 1939-72; Crown Solicitor (Hamilton), 1950-72. *Publications:* Dead Reckoning, 1955; Dead Secret, 1957; Mark of the Lion, 1962. *Recreation:* cricket (Pres. NZ Cricket Council, 1971-73). *Address:* 10 Hillview Crescent, Paparangi, Wellington, New Zealand. *Club:* Wellington (NZ).

SANDFORD, Rear-Adm. Sefton Ronald, CB 1976; Managing Director, Dateline Channel Islands Ltd; company director; *b* 23 July 1925; *s* of Col H. R. Sandford and Mrs Faye Sandford (*née* Renouf); *m* 1st, 1950, Mary Ann Prins (*d* 1972); one *s*; 2nd, 1972, Jennifer Rachel Newell; two *d*. *Educ:* St Aubyns, Rottingdean, 1934-38; Royal Naval Coll., Dartmouth, 1939-42. Served War: went to sea, July 1942; commanded HMMTB 2017, Lieut, 1946-47; ADC to Comdr British Forces, Hong Kong (Lt-Gen. Sir Terence Airey), 1952-53; commanded HMS Teazer (rank Comdr), 1958; Staff of Imperial Defence Coll., 1963-65; comd HMS Protector, Captain, 1965-67; Naval Attaché, Moscow, 1968-70; comd HMS Devonshire, 1971-73; Flag Officer, Gibraltar, 1974-76. A Younger Brother of Trinity House, 1968. *Recreations:* cricket, sailing, fishing. *Address:* 2 St Mannelier Close, St Saviour, Jersey, Channel Islands. *T:* Jersey Central 26782. *Clubs:* Marylebone Cricket (MCC); Royal Yacht Squadron (Cowes).

SANDFORD SMITH, Richard Henry, FCIS; Chairman, Eastern Gas Region (formerly Eastern Gas Board), 1970-73; *b* 29 March 1909; *s* of late Dr H. Sandford Smith; *m* 1936, Dorothy Hewitt, *y d* of late Rev. J. F. Hewitt; one *s. Educ:* Haileybury Coll. London Stock Exchange, 1926. Qualified as Chartered Secretary and awarded Sir Ernest Clarke Prize, 1932. Joined Gas Light & Coke Co., 1932; Sec., SE Gas Corp. Ltd, 1939-49; Sec., SE Gas Bd, 1949-56 (Dep. Chm., 1956-69). Mem., Emergency Bed Service Cttee of King Edward's Hosp. Fund for London. *Recreations:* theatre, golf, gardening. *Address:* 60 The Marlowes, St John's Wood Park, NW8. *Club:* Bath.

SANDHURST, 5th Baron, *cr* 1871; **(John Edward) Terence Mansfield,** DFC 1944; Managing Director, Leslie Rankin Ltd, Jersey; *b* 4 Sept. 1920, *er s* of 4th Baron Sandhurst, OBE, and Morley Victoria (*née* Upcher; *d* 1961); *S* father 1964; *m* 1947, Janet Mary, *er d* of late John Edward Lloyd, NY, USA; one *s* one *d. Educ:* Harrow. Served RAFVR, 1939-46: Bomber Command (as Navigator and Bombing Leader): 149 Sqdn, 1941; 419 (RCAF) Sqdn, 1942; 12 Sqdn, 1943-45. 1946-55: Metropolitan Special Constabulary 'C' Div., Sergeant, 1949-52; long service medal, 1955. Hon. ADC to Lieutenant-Governor of Jersey, 1969-74. *Recreation:* golf. *Heir:* *s* Hon. Guy Rhys John Mansfield [*b* 3 March 1949; *m* 1976, Philippa, *er d* of Digby Verdon-Roe]. *Address:* Les Sapins, St Mary, Jersey, CI. *Clubs:* MCC, Pathfinder; United (Jersey).
See also Earl of Macclesfield.

SANDILANDS, family name of **Baron Torphichen.**

SANDILANDS, Sir Francis (Edwin Prescott), Kt 1976; CBE 1967; Chairman since 1972 (Vice-Chairman, 1968-72), and Director since 1965, Commercial Union Assurance Co. Ltd; *b* 11 December 1913; *s* of late Lieut-Col Prescott Sandilands,

DSO, RM, and late Gladys Baird Murton; *m* 1939, Susan Gillian Jackson; two *s. Educ:* Eton; Corpus Christi College, Cambridge (Hon. Fellow, 1975). MA 1938. Served War of 1939-45, Royal Scots Fusiliers and General Staff, UK and NW Europe (Lt-Col; despatches). Joined Ocean Accident and Guarantee Corporation Ltd, 1935, Manager, 1955; General Manager, then Chief General Manager Commercial Union Assurance Co. Ltd, 1958-72; Chairman: Royal Trust Company of Canada, 1974-; Director: Finance for Industry Ltd; ICI Ltd; Trafalgar House Ltd; Kleinwort, Benson, Lonsdale Ltd; Plessey Co. Ltd; Royal Opera House; Chairman: London Salvage Corps, 1962-63; British Insurance Assoc., 1965-67; Pres., Insurance Inst. of London, 1969-70. Chm., Govt Cttee of Enquiry on Inflation and Company Accounts, 1974-75; Cttee on Invisible Exports, 1975-; Member: BOTB, 1976-; Adv. Cttee, Queen's Award to Industry. Governor, Admin. Staff Coll., Henley. Treas., UCL. Commandeur de l'Ordre de la Couronne (Belgium), 1974. *Address:* 53 Cadogan Square, SW1. *T:* 01-235 6384; Thackers, Geldeston, near Beccles, Suffolk. *T:* Kirby Cane 226. *Club:* Brooks's.

SANDON, Viscount; Dudley Danvers Granville Coutts Ryder, TD; Chairman, International Westminster Bank Ltd, since 1977; a Deputy Chairman, National Westminster Bank Ltd, since 1971 (Director since 1968); a Managing Director, Coutts and Co. since 1949, Deputy Chairman, since 1970; Director: United Kingdom Provident Institution, since 1955 (Deputy Chairman, 1956-64); Powell Duffryn Group, since 1976; Sheepbridge Engineering Ltd, since 1977; *b* 20 Dec. 1922; *er s* of 6th Earl of Harrowby, *qv*; *m* 1949, Jeannette Rosalthé, *yr d* of late Captain Peter Johnston-Saint; one *s* one *d. Educ:* Eton. Lt-Col RA. OC 254 (City of London) Field Regt, RA (TA), 1962-64. Served War of 1939-45: 59 Inf. Div., 5 Para. Bde, in NW Europe (wounded); India and Java (political offr), 56 Armoured Div., 1941-45. Dir, National Provincial Bank, 1964-69; Chm., Olympia Group, 1971-73. Mem. Kensington Borough Council, 1950-65, Kensington and Chelsea BC 1965-71. Hon. Treasurer: Family Welfare Assoc., 1951-65; Central Council for the Care of Cripples, 1953-60; South Kensington Conservative Association, 1953-56; Pres., Wolverhampton SW Conservative and Unionist Assoc., 1959-68. General Commissioner for Income Tax, 1954-71; Mem., Lord Chancellor's Adv. Investment Cttees, for Court of Protection, 1965-77, for Public Trustee, 1974-77. Manager, Fulham and Kensington Hosp. Group, 1953-56; Chairman: Nat. Biological Standards Bd, 1973-; Inst. of Psychiatry, 1965-73; Board of Governors Bethlem Royal and Maudsley Hospitals, 1965-73; Deputy Chairman: Teaching Hospitals Assoc.; London Postgraduate Cttee, 1968-69; Member: Bd of Govs of Univ. of Keele, 1956-68; Exec. Cttee London area Conservative Assoc., 1949-50; Council, Timber Growers' Organisation, 1961-62. Pres., Staffordshire Soc., 1957-59 (Hon. Treas., 1947-51). Mem., Ct of Assts, Goldsmiths Co., 1972-. *Heir:* *s* Hon. Dudley Adrian Conroy Ryder [*b* 18 March 1951; *m* 1977, Sarah Nichola Hobhouse, *d* of late Captain Anthony Payne]. *Address:* 5 Tregunter Road, SW10. *T:* 01-373 9276; Sandon Hall, Stafford. *T:* Sandon 338; Burnt Norton, Campden, Glos.

SANDON, Frank, MA Cantab; Life Fellow, Royal Statistical Society; Fellow, Institute of Statisticians; Fellow, Institute of Mathematics, and its Applications; Associate, British Psychological Society; *b* 3 June 1890; *e s* of late Robert Sandon, HM Examiner of Patents, and Louisa Rudkins Watts; *m* 1919, Sophie (*d* 1968), 2nd *d* of late Carl Gugenheim and of late Laura Maison; no *c. Educ:* Burghley Road Board School; Owen's School, Islington (Foundation Scholar and Leaving Exhibitioner); Corpus Christi College, Cambridge (Scholar and Prizeman. Wrangler, 1912); Diploma (with distinction) in Education, Oxford, 1925; Higher Division Clerk, Home Office, 1913-19; Friends' Ambulance Unit, BEF, 1916-19; Mathematics and Form Master, Sheffield CSS, 1919-20; Roan School, 1920-21; Highgate School, 1921-23; West Ham Secondary School, 1923-29; Devonport High School for Boys, 1937-41; Head Master: Corporation Grammar School, Plymouth, 1929-37; Millom Grammar School, Millom Technical School and Millom Commercial School (Millom County Secondary School, Millom, Cumberland), 1941-50; Mathematics Master, King Edward's School, Aston, 1955-57; Edgbaston High School, 1957-58; Lordswood Technical School for Girls, 1958-59; Hon. Lectr Working Men's Coll., 1914-16; Lectr in Statistics, LCC, 1920-29; Principal, Millom Institute, 1942-50; Lectr, Coll. of Commerce, Birmingham, 1955-59; Examiner: NUJMB, 1927-29, 1932-33; London Univ., SEC, 1928-31, 1940-41; Oxford Locals and Cambridge Locals, 1938-40, 1945; Oxford and Cambridge Schools Examination Bd, 1941-47; Education Committees of LCC, 1930 and 1938, Birmingham, 1930-41, and Wiltshire, 1940; International Inst. Exams Enquiry, 1934; Civil Service Commn since 1940; Chief Examiner, Somerset, 1945-48, 1955-59; Chief Examiner, Birmingham, 1941-50; Selection

Officer, Birmingham, 1951-55; Founder-Pres. Plymouth Branch, Math. Assoc. *Publications:* mathematical, statistical, and pedagogical articles, notes, reviews, etc; Every-Day Mathematics, 1920; Wightman's Mathematical Tables, 1921; Wightman's Arithmetical Tables, 1921; miscellaneous press articles on swimming, rambling, etc. *Recreations:* swimming (CUSC, Blue, 1910-12; British team, Olympic Games, Stockholm, 1912; Hon. Rep. Plymouth and Penzance, Royal Life Saving Society), fell walking, and rambling (Gen. Cttee Holiday Fellowship; Founder Pres., Plymouth Group; Founder Treasurer, Devon and Cornwall YHA). *Address:* 726 Enterprise House, King's Head Hill, Chingford, E4 7NF. *T:* 01-524 1801.

SANDOVER, Sir (Alfred) Eric, Kt 1967; MC 1916; Chairman, Swan Portland Cement, since 1956; Director of other companies; *b* 11 Feb. 1897; *s* of Alfred Sandover, MBE, and Rosalind Sandover; *m* 1923, Kathleen Barber, OBE, *d* of Maj.-Gen. G. W. Barber, CMG, DSO; two *s* one *d. Educ:* St Peter's Coll., Adelaide. Served European War, 1914-18: E Surrey Regt; 6th Sherwood Foresters, Somme, 1916; served War of 1939-45: 44 Bn AIF and on Staff, Land HQ, Australian Army. Mem. Cttee, Employers' Fedn of Australia, 1950-; Mem. Cttee, Chamber of Commerce of Australia, 1935-; Past Pres., Hardware Assoc. of Australia; Patron, Mentally Incurable Children Assoc.; Business Adviser, Ngala Mothercraft Home, etc. Mem. Shire Coun. of Peppermint Grove for 25 years. *Recreations:* riding horses (formerly MFH West Australian Hunt Club); golf, swimming, deep-sea fishing, etc. *Address:* 29 Leake Street, Peppermint Grove, West Australia 6011. *T:* 3-2101. *Clubs:* (Past Pres.) Weld, (Past Pres.) Naval, Military and Air Force, Karrinyup Golf, West Australian Turf, WA Hunt, etc. (all Perth).

SANDREY, John Gordon, FRCS; Consultant Surgeon, St Peter's Hospital for Stone; Consultant Urologist to the Royal Navy, etc; *b* 20 May 1903; *m* 1932, Eulie Barbara Johnston; one *d. Educ:* Sydney, Australia; MB, ChM Sydney, 1926; MRCS, LRCP, 1929; FRCS 1930. Temporary Surgeon-Captain RNVR, 1940-46. Mem. de la Soc. Internat. d'Urol.; FRSocMed. Formerly Surgical Registrar, Royal Prince Alfred Hospital, Sydney, and Resident Surgical Officer, St Mark's and St Peter's Hospital. *Publications:* contributions to medical journals from 1943. *Address:* 27 Pont Street, SW1. *T:* 01-235 7494.

SANDWICH, 10th Earl of, *cr* 1660; Viscount Hinchingbrooke and Baron Montagu of St Neots, 1660 [Disclaimed his Peerages for life, 24 July 1964]; *see under* Montagu, A. V. E. P.

SANDYS, *see* Duncan-Sandys.

SANDYS, 7th Baron, *cr* 1802; **Richard Michael Oliver Hill;** DL; Landowner; *b* 21 July 1931; *o s* of late Lt-Col the Lord Sandys and of Lady Sandys; *S* father, 1961; *m* 1961, Patricia Simpson Hall, *d* of late Captain Lionel Hall, MC. *Educ:* Royal Naval College, Dartmouth. Lieutenant in The Royal Scots Greys, 1950-55. A Lord in Waiting, 1974; an Opposition Whip, 1974-. FRGS. DL Worcestershire, 1968. *Heir: cousin,* Marcus Tufton Hill, *b* 13 March 1931. *Address:* Ombersley Court, Droitwich, Worcestershire. *T:* Worcester 620220. *Club:* Cavalry and Guards.

SANER, Robert Morton; *see* Morton-Saner.

SANGER, Frederick, CBE 1963; FRS 1954; on staff of Medical Research Council since 1951; *b* 13 Aug. 1918; *s* of Frederick Sanger, MD, and Cicely Sanger; *m* 1940, M. Joan Howe; two *s* one *d. Educ:* Bryanston; St John's College, Cambridge. BA 1939; PhD 1943. From 1940, research in Biochemistry at Cambridge University; Beit Memorial Fellowship for Medical Research, 1944-51; at MRC Lab. of Molecular Biol., Cambridge, 1961-; Fellowship at King's College, Cambridge, 1954. For. Hon. Mem., Amer. Acad. of Arts and Sciences, 1958; Hon. Mem. Amer. Society of Biological Chemists, 1961; Foreign Assoc., Nat. Acad. of Sciences, 1967. Hon. DSc: Leicester, 1968; Oxon, 1970; Strasbourg, 1970. Corday-Morgan Medal and Prize, Chem. Soc., 1951; Nobel Prize for Chemistry, 1958; Alfred Benzon Prize, 1966; Royal Medal, Royal Soc., 1969; Sir Frederick Gowland Hopkins Meml Medal, 1971; Gairdner Foundation Annual Award, 1971; William Bate Hardy Prize, Cambridge Philosophical Soc., 1976; Hanbury Meml Medal, 1976. *Publications:* papers on Chemistry of Insulin and Nucleic Acid Structure in Biochemical and other journals. *Address:* 252 Hills Road, Cambridge CB2 2QE; MRC Laboratory of Molecular Biology, Hills Road, Cambridge CB2 2QH. *T:* Cambridge 48011.

SANGER, Gerald Fountaine, CBE 1954; JP; Director: Daily Mail and General Trust Ltd; British Movietonews Ltd; *b* 23 May 1898; *s* of late William Sanger, CB; *m* 1922, Margaret Hope, *d* of late G. H. Munroe, of Chessington Place, Surrey; two *s* one *d. Educ:* Shrewsbury School; Keble College, Oxford, MA. Lieut Royal Marine Artillery, 1917-19; Private Secretary to Hon. Esmond Harmsworth, 1921-29; Editor of British Movietone News, 1929-54; Admin. Dir Associated Newspapers Ltd, 1954-63. Capt. The Queen's Royal Regt, 1939; Hon. Sec., Old Salopian Club, 1942-55, Chm., 1955-57, Pres., 1963-64; Hon. Production Adviser, Conservative and Unionist Films Assoc., 1948-59; Chm., Dorking Division of Surrey Conservative and Unionist Association, 1949-52, President, 1958-63. JP Surrey, 1949. Surrey CC (Horsleys Division), 1965-74. *Recreations:* photography, study of prosody. *Address:* Willingham Cottage, Send, Surrey. *T:* Guildford 222142. *Club:* Garrick.

SANGER, Dr Ruth Ann, (Mrs R. R. Race), FRS 1972; Director, Medical Research Council Blood Group Unit, since 1973 (Member of Scientific Staff since 1946); *b* 6 June 1918; *yr d* of late Rev. Hubert Sanger and late Katharine M. R. Sanger (née Cameron), Urunga, NSW; *m* 1956, Robert Russell Race, *qv*; no *c. Educ:* Abbotsleigh, Sydney; Sydney and London Univs. BSc Sydney 1939, PhD London 1948. Scientific Staff of Red Cross Blood Transfusion Service, Sydney, 1940-46. Hon. Member: Sociedad de Hematologia del Instituto Mexicano del Seguro Social; Deutsche Gesellschaft für Bluttransfusion; Toronto Antibody Club; Norwegian Soc. of Immunohaematology. Landsteiner Memorial and Philip Levine Awards, USA (jtly with R. R. Race); Gairdner Foundn Award, Canada; Oliver Meml Award for Blood Transfusion, British Red Cross, 1973. *Publications:* (with R. R. Race) Blood Groups in Man, 1950, 6th edn, 1975; many papers in genetical and med. jls. *Address:* 22 Vicarage Road, East Sheen, SW14 8RU. *T:* 01-876 1508; MRC Blood Group Unit, Wolfson House, 4 Stephenson Way, NW1 2HE.

SANKEY, John Anthony; HM Diplomatic Service; Counsellor, The Hague, since 1975; *b* 8 June 1930; *o s* of Henry and Ivy Sankey, Plumstead, London; *m* 1958, Gwendoline Winifred Putman; two *s* two *d. Educ:* Cardinal Vaughan Sch., Kensington; Peterhouse, Cambridge (MA). 1st Singapore Regt, RA, 1952-53. Colonial Office: Asst Principal, 1953; Principal, 1958; First Sec. (Colonial Affairs) UK Mission to United Nations, 1961; Foreign Office, 1964; Dep. High Comr, Guyana, 1968; Counsellor, Singapore, 1971; NATO Defence Coll., Rome, 1973; Dep. High Comr, Malta, 1973-75. *Address:* c/o Foreign and Commonwealth Office, SW1.

SANSBURY, Rt. Rev. (Cyril) Kenneth, MA Cantab; Hon. DD (Trinity College, Wycliffe College, Toronto); Priest-in-Charge of St Mary in the Marsh, Diocese of Norwich, since 1973; Minor Canon of Norwich Cathedral, since 1974; *b* 21 Jan. 1905; *s* of late Cyril J. Sansbury; *m* 1931, Ada Ethelreda Mary, *d* of late Captain P. B. Wamsley; one *s* two *d. Educ:* St Paul's School; Peterhouse, Cambridge; Westcott House, Cambridge. 2nd cl. Classical Tripos, 1926; 1st cl. Theological Tripos, Pt I 1927 and Pt II 1928. Curate of St Peter's, Dulwich Common, 1928-31 and Wimbledon, 1931-32; SPG Missionary, Numazu, Japan, 1932-34; Prof. at Central Theological Coll. and British Chaplain at St Andrew's, Tokyo, 1934-41; Chaplain to HM Embassy, Tokyo, 1938-41; Chaplain, RCAF, 1941-45; Warden, Lincoln Theological Coll., 1945-52; Canon and Prebendary of Asgarby in Lincoln Cathedral, 1948-53; Warden, St Augustine's College, Canterbury (Central College of the Anglican Communion), 1952-61; Hon. Canon, Canterbury Cathedral, 1953-61; Bishop of Singapore and Malaya, 1961-66; Asst Bishop, dio. London, 1966-73. Commissary: to Bishop of Jamaica, 1950-61; to Bishop of Caledonia, 1953-61; Proctor in Convocation: for Lincoln, 1950-55; for Canterbury, 1955-61. Examining Chaplain: to Bishop in S Tokyo, 1935-41; to Bishop of Lincoln, 1946-53; to Bishop of Edinburgh, 1947-59; to Bishop of Bradford, 1956-61; to Archbishop of Canterbury, 1959-61. Select Preacher, Univ. of Cambridge, 1957. Gen. Sec., British Council of Churches, 1966-73. Hon. Fellow, St Augustine's College, Canterbury, 1961. *Publications:* Truth, Unity and Concord, 1967; Combating Racism, 1975. *Address:* 53 The Close, Norwich NR1 4EG. *Club:* Royal Over-Seas League.
See also Canon G. R. Sansbury.

SANSBURY, Rev. Canon Graham Rogers, MA; Rector of Grantham, 1973-77 (Vicar, 1958-73); Chaplain to the Queen since 1969; Canon of Lincoln Cathedral since 1961; *b* 4 Aug. 1909; *s* of Cyril and Sophie Sansbury; *m* 1935, Cecily (*d* 1971), *d* of Prof. Bompas Smith; one *s* one *d* (and one *d* decd); *m* 1974, Marjorie, *d* of William Buckman. *Educ:* Dulwich Coll.; Peterhouse, Cambridge; Westcott House, Cambridge. Curate: St Peter St Helier, Southwark, 1932-35; Old Malden, 1935-38; Chaplain, Kolar Gold Field, South India, 1938-44; Priest i/c St Michael's, North Hull, 1945-48; Rector of Skegness, 1948-58;

Proctor in Convocation for Lincoln Dio., 1955-; Rural Dean of Grantham, 1958-69. *Publications:* The Paul Report: A Study Guide, 1964; contrib. to The Paul Report Considered. *Recreations:* cine-photography, walking, gardening. *Address:* 5 Rock House Gardens, Radcliffe Road, Stamford, Lincs PE19 1AS. *T:* Stamford 54438. *Club:* Royal Commonwealth Society. *See also* Rt Rev. C. K. Sansbury.

SANSOM, Lt-Gen. Ernest William, CB 1943; DSO 1919; CD; *b* 18 Dec. 1890; *m* 1st, 1917, Eileen Curzon-Smith (*d* 1927); two *d*; 2nd, 1930, Lucy Aymor Waddell (*d* 1974); one *d*. *Educ:* Public schools, New Brunswick; Commercial Coll., Fredericton, NB; Univ. of Toronto; Staff Coll., Camberley, Surrey. Joined 71st York Regt, Canadian Militia, 1906; Lieut, 1907; Canadian Expeditionary Force during European War, 1914-19; Commanded 16th Canadian Machine Gun Company, 2nd Bn and 1st Bn Canadian Machine Gun Corps; Permanent Active Militia, from 1920; Organised and Commanded Royal Canadian Machine Gun Brigade until 1923; Army Staff College, Camberley, 1924-25; GSO2, Halifax, NS, 1926-27; GSO2, Defence HQ, Ottawa, 1928-30; AA and QMG, Military District No 12, 1931-34; GS01, Military District No 4, Montreal, 1935-36; Director of Military Training for Canada, 1937-39; proceeded overseas 1939 with 1st Canadian Division as AA and QMG; Commanded 2nd Inf. Bde and served as DAG at Canadian Military HQ, London, July-Nov., 1940; Commanded 3rd Canadian Div., 1940-41; 5th Canadian Armoured Division, 1941-43; 2nd Canadian Corps, 1943-44; returned to Canada, Feb. 1944, on sick leave; Inspector-General Canadian Army Overseas, Jan. 1945; retired, May 1945. Hon. ADC to Governor-General of Canada, 1948. Progressive-Conservative candidate York-Sunbury general election, June 1945 (defeated), also by-election 1947. Past President: Fredericton Soc. of St Andrew; Fredericton Br., Royal Canadian Legion; Life Mem., Canadian Rehabilitation Council for Disabled; Dir, St John Ambulance Assoc.; Hon. Vice Pres., United Empire Loyalists Assoc. of Canada. KStJ. *Recreations:* fishing, shooting and gardening. *Address:* Fredericton, New Brunswick E3B 4X3, Canada. *Club:* Fredericton Garrison (Hon. Pres.).

SANSOM, George Samuel, MC, DFC; DSc; Fellow of University College, London, since 1930; *b* London, 7 Aug. 1888; *s* of S. G. C. Sansom and Annie Sansom; *m* 1921, Dorothy Vivien (*d* 1973) *d* of Rev. F. V. Dodgson and *g d* of Gen. Sir David Scott Dodgson, KCB; three *s*. *Educ:* Wellington Coll.; University Coll, London. BSc 1911; Derby Scholar, Zoology, 1912. Planned and took part in many new difficult rock climbs in Cumberland, inc. Scafell Central Buttress, 1914. British Red Cross in Flanders, 1914; Royal Air Force Balloon Observer in France, 1915-18 (MC, DFC); ROC, 1939-45. Hon. Res. Asst, Dept of Embryology, UCL. *Recreations:* formerly rock-climbing, flying; now pistol shooting. *Address:* Kennel Moor, Godalming, Surrey. *T:* Godalming 6887. *Club:* (Hon. Mem.) Fell and Rock Climbing.

SANTA CRUZ, Marqués de, *cr* 1569; **José Fernandez Villaverde y Roca de Togores;** Grand Cross of Carlos III; Grand Cross of Isabel La Catolica; Grand Cross of Merito Naval; Knight of Calatrava; Spanish Ambassador to Court of St James's, 1958-72; Councillor of State, May, 1972; *b* 4 April 1902; *s* of Raimundo F. Villaverde, Marqués de Pozo Rubio and Angela, Marquesa de Pozo Rubio, Grandee of Spain; *m* 1942, Casilda de Silva y Fernandez de Henestrosa, Marquesa de Santa Cruz, Duquesa de San Carlos; three *s* one *d*. *Educ:* privately in Madrid; University of Madrid; New College, Oxford. Entered Diplomatic Service, 1921; Attaché: London, 1921, Rome, 1923; Secretary Legation; Vienna, 1927, Stockholm, 1933, London, 1934; Minister-Counsellor Embassy, London, 1944; Minister: Copenhagen, 1948, The Hague, 1950. Chm. Spanish Delegn, 7th Session The Hague Conf. on Private Internat. Law, 1951; Ambassador to Cairo, 1953; Under Secretary of State for Foreign Affairs, 1955. Representative of Spain on Exec. Council of Latin Union, 1955; Spanish Deleg. to 11th and 12th Gen. Assembly of UN, 1956 and 1957, Permanent Counsellor of State, 1972-; Chm. of Spanish Delegn to XLVI Conf. of Inter-Parly Union, 1957. Hon. Fellow, New College, Oxford 1959. Holds several foreign decorations. *Recreations:* riding, shooting, golf. *Heir:* s Alvaro Villaverde, Marqués del Viso; *b* 3 Nov. 1943. *Address:* San Bernardino 14, Madrid 8, Spain. *Clubs:* Beefsteak, White's; Nuevo (Madrid).

SANTA CRUZ, Victor (Rafael Andrés), GCVO (Hon.) 1965; Ambassador of Chile to the Court of St James's, 1959-70; *b* 7 May 1913; *s* of Don Gregorio Santa Cruz and Doña Matilde Serrano; *m* 1937, Doña Adriana Sutil Alcalde; two *s* two *d*. *Educ:* Stonyhurst; Instituto Nacional, Chile. Law degree, Chile, 1937; Prof. of Civil Law, in Chile, 1941; elected MP, Chilean Parliament, 1945. *Recreation:* golf. *Clubs:* White's, Turf, Beefsteak; Club de la Union (Santiago).

SANTER, Rev. Mark, MA; Principal of Westcott House, Cambridge, since 1973; *b* 29 Dec. 1936; *s* of Eric Arthur Robert Santer and Phyllis Clare Barlow; *m* 1964, Henriette Cornelia Weststrate; one *s* two *d*. *Educ:* Marlborough Coll.; Queens' Coll., Cambridge; Westcott House, Cambridge. Deacon, 1963; priest 1964; Asst Curate, Cuddesdon, 1963-67; Tutor, Cuddesdon Theological Coll., 1963-67; Fellow and Dean of Clare Coll., Cambridge, 1967-72 (and Tutor, 1968-72); Univ. Asst Lectr in Divinity, 1968-72. *Publications:* (contrib.) The Phenomenon of Christian Belief, 1970; (with M. F. Wiles) Documents in Early Christian Thought, 1975; articles in: Jl of Theological Studies; New Testament Studies; Theology. *Address:* Westcott House, Cambridge. *T:* Cambridge 50074.

SAOUMA, Edouard; Director-General of the Food and Agriculture Organization of the United Nations, Rome, since 1976; agricultural engineer and international official; *b* Beirut, Lebanon, 6 Nov. 1926; *m* Inés Forero; one *s* two *d,*. *Educ:* St Joseph's University Sch. of Engineering, Beirut; Ecole Nat. Supérieure d'Agronomie, Montpellier, France. Director: Tel Amara Agric. Sch., 1952-53; Nat. Centre for Farm Mechanization, 1954-55; Sec. Gen., Nat. Fedn of Lebanese Agronomists, 1955; Dir-Gen., Nat. Inst. for Agric. Research, 1955-62; Mem. Gov. Bd, Nat. Grains Office, 1960-62; Minister of Agric., Fisheries and Forestry, 1970. Food and Agric. Organization of UN: Dep. Regional Rep. for Asia and Far East, 1962-65; Dir, Land and Water Develt Div., 1965-75; Dir-Gen., 1976. Order of the Cedar, Lebanon; Said Akl Prize, Lebanon; Mérite Agricole, France. *Address:* Food and Agriculture Organization of the United Nations, Via delle Terme di Caracalla, Rome 00100, Italy. *T:* 5797.

SAPPER, Alan Louis Geoffrey; General Secretary, Association of Cinematograph, Television and Allied Technicians, since 1969; *b* 18 March 1931; *y s* of late Max and Kate Sapper; *m* 1959, Helen Rubens; one *s* one *d*. *Educ:* Upper Latymer Sch.; Univ. of London. Botanist, Royal Botanic Gardens, Kew, 1948-58; Asst Gen. Sec., 1958-64, Dep. Gen. Sec., 1967-69, Assoc. of Cinematograph, Television and Allied Technicians; Gen. Sec., Writers' Guild of Great Britain, 1964-67. Mem. General Council, Trades Union Congress, 1970-. President: Confedn of Entertainment Unions; Internat. Fedn of Audio-Visual Workers; Sec., Fedn of Film Unions; Treas., Fedn of Broadcasting Unions; Member: Film Industry Educn Adv. Cttee, Film Sch. Assoc.; British Copyright Council; Cinematograph Films Council; Wilson Interim Action Cttee on Film Industry, 1977-. Governor: BFI, 1974-; Hammersmith Hosp., 1965-72. Chm. League for Democracy in Greece. *Publications:* articles, short stories; stage plays, On Licence, Kith and Kin; TV play, The Return, 1961. *Recreations:* taxonomic botany, hill walking, politics and human nature. *Address:* 19 Lavington Road, West Ealing, W13 9NN. *T:* 01-567 4900. *See also* L. J. Sapper.

SAPPER, Laurence Joseph; General Secretary, Association of University Teachers, since 1969; *b* 15 Sept. 1922; *s* of late Max and Kate Sapper; *m* 1951, Rita Jeski; one *d*. *Educ:* Univ. of London (External Student). LLB. Called to Bar, Lincoln's Inn, 1950. Churchill Fellow, 1966. Min. of Agric. and Fisheries, 1939-41 and 1946-51; Educn Instructor, RAF, 1941-46; Private Sec. to Minister of Agriculture, 1948-50; Asst Sec., Instn of Professional Civil Servants, 1951-56; Dep. Gen. Sec., Post Office Engrg Union, 1956-69. Mem. Council, Brunel Univ., 1964-; Mem., NW Met. Regional Hosp. Board, 1965-71. *Publications:* Your Job and the Law, 1969; (with G. Socrates) SI Units and Metrication, 1969; papers, articles, broadcasts. *Recreations:* astronomy, writing, law reform. *Address:* 53 Wavendon Avenue, Chiswick, W4. *T:* 01-994 5197. *See also* A. L. G. Sapper.

SARAGAT, Giuseppe; President of the Italian Republic, 1964-71; a Life Senator; President, Social Democratic Party, 1975-76, and since 1976; *b* 19 Sept. 1898; *s* of Giovanni Saragat and Ernestina Stratta; *m* 1922, Giuseppina Bollani (*d* 1961); one *s* one *d*. *Educ:* University of Economic and Commercial Science, Turin. Served European War, 1915-18 (Lieut); joined Italian Socialist Party, 1924; Member, Exec. Office, Italian Socialist Party, 1925; left Italy for Vienna, Paris and south of France during fascist period, 1926-43; imprisoned by Nazi occupation authorities in Rome, escaped, 1943; Minister without portfolio, 1944; Italian Ambassador in Paris, 1945-46; Pres., Constituent Assembly, 1946; founded Italian Workers Socialist Party (later called Social Democratic Party), 1947; Deputy Prime Minister, 1947-48; Member of Parliament, 1948-64; Deputy Prime Minister and Minister of Merchant Marine, 1948; Deputy Prime Minister, 1954-57; Chm., Standing Cttee for Foreign Affairs, Chamber of Deputies, 1963; Minister of Foreign Affairs, 1963-64. Secretary,

Social Democratic Party, 1949-54, 1957-64, and in 1976. *Publications:* L'umanesimo marxista, 1944; Socialismo e libertà, 1944; Per la difesa delle classi lavoratrici, 1951; Il problema della pace, 1951; L'unità socialista, 1956; Per una politica di centrosinistra, 1960; Quaranta anni di lotta per la democrazia, 1965. *Address:* c/o Partito Socialista Democratico, Via Santa Maria in Via 12, 00187 Rome, Italy.

SARAJČIĆ, Ivo; Director, Institute for Developing Countries, since 1970; *b* 10 March 1915; *s* of Ivan and Elizabeth Sarajčić; *m* 1944, Marija Godiar; three *s. Educ:* Univ. of Philosophy, Zagreb. Participated in War of Liberation from (beginning) 1941 (Partizan Remembrance Medal); held various prominent political positions. Subsequently: Secretary, Presidium of Nat. Assembly of Croatia; Editor-in-Chief of Borba; Asst Minister of Educn; Dir of Information Office of Yugoslav Govt; MEC, Croatia; also Mem. Central Cttee of League of Communists of Croatia, Mem. Federal Assembly, Mem. Council for Foreign Affairs and Internat. Relations. Yugoslav Diplomatic Service, 1959; Ambassador to Austria, 1960-63; Asst Sec. of State for Foreign Affairs, 1963-66; Ambassador to London, 1966-70. *Address:* Institute for Developing Countries, 41000 Zagreb Ul. 8 maja 82, Yugoslavia.

SARELL, Captain Richard Iwan Alexander, DSO 1939; RN retd; *b* 22 Feb. 1909; *s* of late Philip Charles Sarell; *m* 1961, Mrs Ann Morgan (*née* Keenlyside). *Educ:* Royal Naval Coll., Dartmouth. Entered RNC Dartmouth, 1922; Comdr 1943; Capt. 1948; specialised in Gunnery, 1934; DSO for action against enemy submarines while in command of HMS Broke, 1943; despatches, 1943. Naval Attaché, Moscow and Helsinki, 1949-51; student Imperial Defence Coll., 1952; Defence Research Policy Staff, 1954; retd 1957. *Recreation:* fishing. *Address:* 43 Rivermead Court, Ranelagh Gardens, SW6 3RX. *Club:* Pratt's.

SARELL, Sir Roderick (Francis Gisbert), KCMG 1968 (CMG 1958); KCVO 1971; HM Diplomatic Service, retired; *b* 23 Jan. 1913; *y s* of late Philip Charles Sarell, HM Consular Service and of Ethel Ida Rebecca, *d* of late John Dewar Campbell; *m* 1946, Pamela Muriel, *d* of late Vivian Francis Crowther-Smith; three *s. Educ:* Ashdown House, Sussex; Radley; Magdalen College, Oxford. HM Consular Service, 1936; Vice-Consul, Persia, 1937; Italian East Africa, 1939; Iraq, 1940; 2nd Secretary, Addis Ababa, 1942; 1st Secretary, HM Foreign Service, 1946; Rome, Bucharest, 1946; Foreign Office, 1949; Acting Counsellor, 1952; Counsellor and Consul-General, Rangoon, 1953; Consul-General, Algiers, 1956-59; Head of Southern Dept, Foreign Office, 1959-61, General Dept, 1961-63; Ambassador: to Libya, 1964-69; to Turkey, 1969-73. Coronation medal, 1953. *Recreations:* swimming, ski-ing, walking. *Address:* The Litten, Hampstead Norreys, Newbury, Berks RG16 0TD. *T:* Hermitage 201274. *Clubs:* Oriental, Royal Over-Seas League; Leander.

SARGAN, Prof. John Denis; Professor of Econometrics, London School of Economics and Political Science, since 1964; *b* 23 Aug. 1924; *s* of H. and G. A. Sargan; *m* 1953, Phyllis Mary Millard; two *s* one *d. Educ:* Doncaster Grammar Sch.; St John's Coll., Cambridge. Asst. Lectr, Lectr and Reader, Leeds Univ., 1948-63; Reader, LSE, 1963-64. *Address:* 119 Highfield Way, Rickmansworth, Herts.

SARGANT, Sir (Henry) Edmund, Kt 1969; President of the Law Society, 1968-69; Partner in Radcliffes and Co., 1930-71, and Senior Partner for twenty years; *b* 24 May 1906; *s* of Rt Hon. Sir Charles Henry Sargant, Lord Justice of Appeal, and Amelia Julia Sargant, RRC; *m* 1930, Mary Kathleen Lemmey, 3rd *d* of Tom Lemmey, DD, Housemaster, subseq. Second Master, Wellington College, Berks; one *s. Educ:* Rugby School; Trinity College, Cambridge (MA). 3rd Cl. Hons Solicitors' final examination; admitted 1930. Served War of 1939-45 in RAF, Provost and Security Branch; (W Africa; Middle East; Acting Wing Comdr). Member, Council, Law Society, 1951-75; Chm., Disciplinary Cttee of Architects Registration Council, 1964, 1965, 1966. Master, Worshipful Co. of Merchant Taylors, 1954. *Recreations:* gardening, cine photography. *Address:* 1 Harley Gardens, The Boltons, SW10. *T:* 01-373 4269. *Club:* United Oxford & Cambridge University.

See also M. C. Nourse.

SARGANT, William Walters, MA, MB Cantab, FRCP, FRCPsych, DPM; Hon. Consulting Psychiatrist, St Thomas' Hospital; Physician in charge of Department of Psychological Medicine, St Thomas' Hospital, London, 1948-72; *b* 1907; *s* of Norman T. C. Sargant, Highgate; *m* 1940, Margaret Heriot Glen. *Educ:* Leys School; St John's College, Cambridge. Geraldine Harmsworth Schol., St Mary's Hosp., 1928; Asst to Medical Professorial Unit, St Mary's Hosp., 1932-34; MO and Phys., Maudsley Hosp., 1935-49; Rockefeller Travelling

Fellowship and Research Fellow, Harvard Medical Sch., USA, 1938-39; Asst Clinical Dir Sutton Emergency Hosp., 1939-47; Visiting Prof. of Neuropsychiatry, Duke Univ. Med. Sch., USA, 1947-48; Registrar Royal Medico-Psychological Assoc., 1951-71; Actg Dean, Royal Coll. of Psychiatrists, 1971; Pres., Section of Psychiatry, Royal Society of Medicine, 1956-57; Examiner in Psychological Medicine, Conjoint Board of England, 1960-63; Associate Secretary, World Psychiatric Assoc., 1961-66 (Hon. Mem., 1972). Lectures: Ernest Parsons Memorial, Amer. Soc. of Biological Psychiatry, 1964; Herman Goldham Internat., New York Coll. of Med., 1964; Watson Smith, RCP, 1966; Maudsley, RMPA, 1968; Belisle Memorial, Michigan, 1968. Taylor Manor Hosp. Award, 1971; Starkey Meml Prize, Royal Soc. of Health, 1973. *Publications:* Physical Methods of Treatment in Psychiatry, 1944, 5th edn, 1972; Battle for the Mind, 1957; The Unquiet Mind, 1967; The Mind Possessed, 1973; Various papers on psychiatric topics, in medical jls. *Recreation:* (formerly) Barbarians RFC, St Mary's Hosp. RFC (Capt.) and Middlesex Co. RFC. *Address:* 23 Harley Street, W1. *T:* 01-636 5161. *Club:* Savage.

SARGEANT, Frank Charles Douglas, CMG 1972; HM Diplomatic Service, retired 1977; *b* 7 Nov. 1917; *s* of late John Sargeant and Anna Sargeant; *m* 1946, Joan Adene Bickerton; one *s* one *d. Educ:* Lincoln; St Catharine's Coll., Cambridge. MA Cantab, Natural Sciences. Cadbury Bros. Ltd, 1939. Served War: Army, 1939-46; Lt-Col, Royal Signals. Imperial Chemical Industries Ltd, 1947-48. HM Diplomatic Service: Curacao, 1948; The Hague, 1951; Kuwait, 1954; Foreign Office, 1957 (First Sec. 1958); First Sec., Head of Chancery and Consul, Mogadishu, 1959; First Sec. (Commercial) Stockholm, 1962-66; First Sec., Head of Chancery, Colombo, and Consul for the Maldive Islands, 1967; Counsellor, 1968; Consul-General, Lubumbashi, 1968-70; Dep. High Comr, Dacca, 1970-71; Sen. Officers' War Course, RN Coll., Greenwich, 1971-72; Consul Gen., Lyons, 1972-77. *Recreations:* shooting, fishing. *Address:* c/o Lloyds Bank, Darwen, Lancs.

SARGEANT, Ven. Frank Pilkington; Archdeacon of Bradford, since 1977; *b* 12 Sept. 1932; *s* of John Stanley and Grace Sargeant; *m* 1958, Sally Jeanette McDermott; three *s* two *d. Educ:* Boston Grammar School; Durham Univ., St John's Coll. and Cranmer Hall (BA, Dip Theol); Nottingham Univ. (Diploma in Adult Education). National Service Commission, RA (20th Field Regt), 1955-57. Assistant Curate: Gainsborough Parish Church, 1958-62; Grimsby Parish Church, and Priest-in-Charge of St Martin's, Grimsby, 1962-67; Vicar of North Hykeham and Rector of South Hykeham, 1967-73; Residentiary Canon, Bradford Cathedral, 1973-77. *Recreations:* cricket, oil painting, games and simulations; special interest, adult education. *Address:* 11 Carlton Drive, Bradford BD9 4AU. *T:* Bradford 45747.

SARGEAUNT, Bertram Edward, MVO 1920; OBE 1918; FSA; Government Secretary and Treasurer, Isle of Man, 1910-44; *b* 4 Dec. 1877; *s* of late Captain F. A. Sargeaunt, Royal Navy, and Alice Caroline, *sister* of 1st Baron Fisher of Kilverstone, Admiral of the Fleet; *m* 1910, Kathleen Hamilton (*d* 1962), *e d* of late Robert Thornewill, Craythorne, Burton-on-Trent; one *d. Educ:* Bedford School. Staff, Royal United Service Institution, Whitehall, 1899-1910. Late Captain, 12th London Regiment. Officer of the Order of St John of Jerusalem. A trustee of Manx Museum, 1922-53, and a Church Commissioner for Isle of Man, 1943-53. Organised and presided at centenary luncheon held in London in 1955 for sons and daughters of those who served in the Crimean War, 1854-1856; also Golden Jubilee Luncheon held in London, 1958, for TA Officers who served as such in 1908; administered internment camps for 26,000 prisoners in the first World War and 16,000 in the Second World War. FRGS (Hon. Fellow 1976). *Publications:* The Royal Monmouthshire Militia; The Isle of Man and the Great War; The Royal Manx Fencibles; A Military History of the Isle of Man. *Address:* Ladymead, Hurstpierpoint, Sussex. *T:* Hurstpierpoint 2159.

SARGEAUNT, Henry Anthony, CB 1961; OBE 1949; Scientific Consultant, United Nations, since 1968; *b* 11 June 1907; *o s* of Lt-Col Henry Sargeaunt and Norah Ierne Carden; *m* 1939, Winifred Doris Parkinson; two *s* one *d. Educ:* Clifton Coll.; University Coll., Reading (London Univ.); Cambridge Univ. Rhodes Research Grant, 1939-42; served with HM Forces, 1944-46: France, 1944; Staff Capt. with 21 Army Group, 1944; Supt Operational Research Group (ORG) (W&E), Min. of Supply, 1946; Supt, Army ORG, 1947-50; Dep. Scientific Adviser, 1950-52, Scientific Adviser, to Army Council, 1952-55; Asst Scientific Adviser to Supreme Allied Commander in Europe, Sept. 1955-57; Dep. Science Adviser, NATO, 1958-59; re-apptd Scientific Adviser to Army Council, 1959; Dep. Chief Scientist (B), War Office, 1960-62; Chief Scientific Adviser,

Home Office, 1962-67. *Recreations:* yachting, horse-racing, bird-watching. *Address:* 4 Arnewood Court, Sway, Lymington, Hants.

SARGEAUNT, Margaret Joan, MA, BLitt; Principal of Queen Elizabeth College (formerly King's College of Household and Social Science), University of London, 1947-66; *b* 29 July 1903; *d* of Rev. William Drake Sargeaunt and Florence Thursby. *Educ:* Godolphin School, Salisbury; St Hugh's College, Oxford. First Class Hons in Eng. Lang. and Lit., 1925; Diploma in Educn with distinction, 1926; BLitt (Oxon), 1931. Asst Mistress at Wycombe Abbey School, 1926-29; Lecturer in Education, Univ. of Sheffield, 1931-37; Adviser of Women Students and Warden of Masson Hall, Univ. of Edinburgh, 1937-47. Hon. Fellow, Queen Elizabeth Coll., 1966. *Publications:* John Ford, 1935, US edn, 1966; various articles and notes (Review of English Studies). *Recreation:* walking. *Address:* The Tangle, Ibstone, High Wycombe, Bucks. *T:* Turville Heath 383.

SARGENT, Rev. Canon Alexander, MA; Archdeacon of Canterbury, 1942-68, and Canon Residentiary of Canterbury Cathedral, 1939-68; Hon. Canon, 1968, Canon Emeritus, 1974; *b* 9 May 1895; *s* of Frederick George Sargent and Florence Crundall. *Educ:* King's School, Canterbury; St Edmund Hall, Oxford; Cuddesdon Theological Coll. Deacon, 1919; Priest, 1920; Curate of St Margarets-at-Cliffe, 1919; of All Saints, Maidstone, 1921; Chaplain of Cuddesdon Theological College, 1923; Sub-Warden of St Paul's College, Grahamstown, 1927; Resident Chaplain to the Archbishop of Canterbury, 1929-39; Archdeacon of Maidstone, 1939-42; Commissary to the Bishop of Grahamstown, 1931; Six Preacher in Canterbury Cathedral, 1933; Select Preacher, Univ. of Oxford, 1949-51. *Address:* Starr's House, The Precincts, Canterbury, Kent. *T:* Canterbury 65960.

SARGENT, Sir Donald, KBE 1961; CB 1951; Chairman: Civil Service Retirement Fellowship, 1968-74; Society of Pension Consultants, since 1970; Vice-Chairman, Hospital Saving Association, since 1970; *b* 11 Dec. 1906; *s* of late S. G. Sargent; *m* 1944, Dorothy Mary, *d* of late E. Raven, CB; one *s. Educ:* King Edward's School, Birmingham; Trinity College, Cambridge. BA (Classical Tripos, 1st Cl.), 1928. Asst Principal, GPO, 1929; Private Sec. to Director General, 1935-37; Principal, 1937; Home Office, ARP Dept, 1938-41; Principal Private Secretary to PMG, 1941-44; Asst Sec., GPO, 1944; Dep. Chief Administrative Officer, CCG, 1946-47; idc, 1948; Director of Personnel and Accommodation, GPO 1949-53; Director of Postal Services, 1953-55; Deputy Director General, 1955-59; Secretary, National Assistance Bd, 1959-66; Sec., Supplementary Benefits Commn, and Dep. Sec., Min. of Social Security, 1966-68. Dir, Abbeyfield Soc., 1968-70. *Recreations:* mountaineering, sailing, music. *Address:* 1 Croham Valley Road, Croydon, Surrey. *T:* 01-657 4023. *Clubs:* United Oxford & Cambridge University; MCC.

SARGENT, Rt. Rev. Douglas Noel; *b* 19 Dec. 1907; *s* of Edwin Dowdeswell Sargent, Watford, and Charlotte Elizabeth (*née* Taylor), St Albans; *m* 1942, Imogene Grace Ward; three *s* (one *d* decd). *Educ:* Watford Grammar School; King's College, Cambridge; London College of Divinity; Union Theological Seminary, New York. Deacon, 1931; Priest, 1932; Curate of Willian, 1931-34; Missionary with CMS at Chengtu, 1934-48, and at Lingling, 1949-51; Principal of CMS Men's Training College, Blackheath, 1951-52, Chislehurst, 1952-62; Bishop Suffragan of Selby, 1962-71. *Publications:* The Making of a Missionary, 1960; jointly, The Churchman's Companion, 1964. *Recreations:* gardening, local history. *Address:* 1 Ramsey Avenue, Bishopthorpe, York.

SARGENT, Prof. Roger William Herbert; Courtaulds Professor of Chemical Engineering, Imperial College, since 1966; *b* 14 Oct. 1926; *s* of Herbert Alfred Sargent and May Elizabeth (*née* Gill); *m* 1951, Shirley Jane Levesque (*née* Spooner); two *s. Educ:* Bedford Sch.; Imperial Coll., London. BSc, ACGI, PhD, DIC; FIChemE, FIMA. Design Engineer, Société l'Air Liquide, Paris, 1951-58; Imperial College: Sen. Lectr, 1958-62; Prof. of Chem. Engrg, 1962-66; Dean, City and Guilds Coll., 1973-76; Head of Dept of Chem. Engrg and Chem. Technology, 1975-. Pres., Instn of Chem. Engrs, 1973-74. Fellow, Fellowship of Engineering, 1976; Hon. FCGI 1977. *Publications:* contrib.: Optimization and Design, 1972; Numerical Methods for Constrained Optimization, 1974; Optimization in Action, 1976; contribs to: Trans. Instn Chem. Engrs, Chem. Engrg Sci., Génie Chimique, Computer Jl, Jl of Optimization Theory and Applications, Internat. Jl of Control, Automatica, etc. *Address:* Mulberry Cottage, Sheen Road, Richmond, Surrey TW10 5AW. *T:* 01-876 9623.

SARGENT, Sir (Sidney) Donald; see Sargent, Sir Donald.

SARGINSON, Edward William; retired from Civil Service, 1976; with Confederation of British Industry; *b* 22 May 1919; *s* of Frederick William and Edith Sarginson; *m* 1944, Olive Pescod; one *s* one *d. Educ:* Barrow-in-Furness Grammar School. Entered Civil Service, War Office, 1936; served Infantry, 1939-46; Principal, Min. of Supply, 1955; Asst Sec., Min. of Aviation, 1965; Asst Under Sec. of State, MoD(PE), 1972-76. *Recreation:* hill walking. *Address:* 41 Kendall Avenue South, Sanderstead, Surrey. *T:* 01-660 4476.

SARGOOD, Richard; Trade Union Officer; retired; *b* 31 July 1888; *m* 1919, Sarah Lilian Deane; one *d. Educ:* Kennington Road LCC School; Evening Continuation School. Trade Union Official since 1919; Member Camberwell Borough Council, 1923-29; Vice-Chm. LCC, 1951-52 (Member 1934-65). Chm., Peckham Divisional Labour Party, 1932-47. MP (Lab) for West Bermondsey, 1945-50; formerly Chairman: Mental Hospitals Committee of LCC, Supplies Cttee, Parliamentary Cttee, Fire Brigade Cttee; (till 1965) Staff Appeals Committee, LCC; Camberwell Youth Employment Cttee; Vice-Chm., Finance Cttee, LCC. *Recreations:* walking, reading, keenly interested in amateur football. *Address:* 50 Lower Drive, Dawlish, Devon EX7 0AT.

SARILA, HH Maharaja Mahipal Singh, ju Deo, Maharaja of, CSI 1939; *b* 11 Sept. 1898; *m* 1919, *d* of Landlord of Basela, UP; five *s* three *d. Educ:* Daly Coll., Indore. Invested with Ruling Powers, 1919; State Delegate to the First and Second Indian Round Table Conferences, London 1931 and 1932. Late Secretary, General Council and Working Committee, Daly College, Indore. 2nd *s* succeeded, 1942, as HH Maharajadhiraja of Charkhari, UP. *Recreations:* is a keen sportsman and good tennis player and has won tournaments. *Heir: s* Raja Bahadur Narendra Singh ju deo, [Indian Ambassador to Spain. *Educ:* Mayo Coll., Ajmer, India; Magdalene Coll., Cambridge]. *Address:* Mahipal Niwas Palace, Sarila State, Bundel Khand, UP, India. *TA:* Maharaja Sarila State, India. *Clubs:* National Liberal; Delhi Gymkhana (New Delhi).

SARNOFF, Robert W.; Chairman of Board, RCA Corporation, 1970-76 (Chief Executive Officer, 1968-75); Director: Manufacturers Hanover Trust Co., 1967; New York Stock Exchange, 1972; American Home Products Corporation, 1969; American Arbitration Association, 1955; Economic Development Council of New York City, 1972; *b* 2 July 1918; *s* of late David and Lizette Hermant Sarnoff; *m* 1974, Anna Moffo; three *d* by two former *m. Educ:* Phillips Acad.; Harvard Univ. (BA). Ensign, USN, 1942, Lieut 1945. Publisher's asst, Des Moines Register and Tribune, then joined staff of Look Magazine; joined Nat. Broadcasting Co. (subsid. of RCA), 1948: Vice-Pres. 1951; Dir, 1953; Pres. and Chief Executive Officer, 1955; Chm. 1958; Dir, RCA, 1957; Chief Operating Officer, RCA, 1966 and Pres., 1966-71. Trustee or cttee member many organisations, etc. Hon. Fellow, Royal Television Soc., 1973; Fellow, Imperial Coll. of Science and Technology, 1973. Holds numerous hon. degrees and various foreign awards. *Address:* 30 Rockefeller Plaza, New York, NY 10020, USA. *T:* 598-5900.

SAROYAN, William; writer; *b* Fresno, California, 31 Aug. 1908; *s* of Armenak Saroyan (*d* 1911) and Takoohi Saroyan (*d* 1950), of Bitlis, Armenia, who emigrated to America in 1905 and 1907; *m* 1943, Carol Marcus (marriage dissolved 1949); one *s* one *d. Educ:* Fresno public schools until fifteen years of age; public libraries; movie and vaudeville theatres; streets. Began selling newspapers when seven; from that year until his twenty-second year worked at a variety of jobs; since twenty-second year has done very little but loaf and write; began to write when nine years old; writing was constantly interrupted or delayed by work; this displeased him, so he stopped working; has no intention of ever working again, as it bores him. *Religion:* living. *Party:* William Saroyan. *Publications:* The Daring Young Man on the Flying Trapeze, 1934; Inhale and Exhale, 1936; Three Times Three, 1936 (US only); The Gay and Melancholy Flux, 1936 (England only); Little Children, 1937; Love, Here Is My Hat, 1938; The Trouble with Tigers, 1938; Peace, It's Wonderful, 1939; My Heart's in the Highlands (play), 1939; The Time of Your Life (play), 1939; Love's Old Sweet Song (play), 1939; My Name is Aram, 1940; Saroyan's Fables (US only), 1941; The Beautiful People (play), 1941; Sweeney in the Trees (play), 1941; Across the Board on Tomorrow Morning (play), 1941; The Human Comedy (novel), 1943; Get Away Old Man (play), 1943; Dear Baby (stories), 1944; The Adventures of Wesley Jackson (novel), 1946; Jim Dandy, Fat Man in a Famine (play), 1947; Don't Go Away Mad (play), 1949; Sam Ego's House (play), 1949; A Decent Birth, A Happy Funeral (play), 1949; The Twin Adventures, 1950, A Novel and a Diary (US only); The Assyrian (short stories), 1950; Rock Wagram (novel), 1951; Tracy's Tiger (novel), 1952; The Laughing Matter (novel), 1953; The Bicycle Rider in Beverly Hills (memoir), 1952; Mama I Love You, 1957; The Whole Voyald (short stories), 1957; Papa You're Crazy, 1958; The Cave Dwellers (play), 1959; Sam, the Highest Jumper of Them All (play, written and directed for Theatre Workshop), 1960; Talking To You (one act play, Duke of York's), 1962; Short Drive, Sweet Chariot (autobiographical), 1964; One Day in the Afternoon of the World (novel), 1965; Not Dying, 1966; (with A. Rothstein) Look At Us, 1967; I Used to Believe I Had Forever, Now I'm Not So Sure (Short Stories), 1968; Letters from 74 Rue Taitbout, or Don't Go, But If You Must, Say Hello to Everybody, 1969; Days of Life and Death and Escape to the Moon, 1971; Places Where I've Done Time, 1973; The Tooth and My Father, 1974. *Recreation:* everything. *Address:* 2729 W Griffith Way, Fresno, Calif 93705, USA.

SARRAUTE, Nathalie; writer; *b* Ivanowo, Russia, 18 July 1902; *d* of Ilya Tcherniak and Pauline Chatounowski; *m* 1925, Raymond Sarraute; three *d. Educ:* Sorbonne; Ecole de Droit de Paris; Oxford. *Publications:* Tropismes, 1939 (trans. Tropisms, 1964); Portrait d'un inconnu, 1948 (Portrait of a Man Unknown, 1959); Martereau, 1953 (trans. 1964); L'Ere du soupçon, 1956 (The Age of Suspicion, 1964); Le Planétarium, 1959 (The Planetarium, 1962); Les Fruits d'or, 1963 (The Golden Fruits, 1965) (Prix international de Litterature, 1964); Entre la vie et la mort, 1968 (Between Life and Death, 1969); (*plays*): Le Silence, Le Mensonge, 1967 (Silence, and The Lie, 1969); Isma, 1970; C'est beau, 1973; "disent les imbéciles," 1976. *Address:* 12 avenue Pierre I de Serbie, 75116 Paris, France. *T:* 20.58.28.

SARTRE, Jean-Paul; author; *b* Paris, 21 June 1905. *Educ:* Paris; La Rochelle. Degree in Philosophy, 1930. Professor at Le Havre, French Institute at Berlin, Lycée Condorcet, Paris and Lycée Pasteur, Paris. Wrote philosophical works first, then novels and plays. Mobilised, 1939, served in Army, 1939-40, prisoner of war, 1940-41, returned from Germany and took part in resistance movement, 1941-44. Prof. of philosophy until 1944 when resigned to become founder and editor of Les Temps Modernes. Refused Nobel Prize for Literature, 1964 (saying that he had always refused to accept all official distinctions). *Publications:* Imaginaire, 1936; Imagination, 1937; Nausée, 1937; le Mur, 1938; les Mouches, Huis-Clos, l'Etre et le Néant, 1943; les Chemins de la liberté, 1944-45; Morts sans sépulture, La Putain respectueuse, 1946; The Age of Reason, 1947; Reprieve, 1947; Le Diable et le Bon Dieu, 1948; Iron in the Soul, 1950; The Psychology of Imagination, 1951; Les Mains sales, 1952; Œuvres Complètes, 1952; Nekrassov, 1953 (Edinburgh Fest., 1957); Les Sequestrés d'Altona, 1959; Critique de la Raison dialectique, 1961; Words (memoirs), 1964; Baudelaire, 1964; Saint Genet, Actor and Martyr, 1964 (Eng. trans. by B. Frechtman); Situations, 1965 (trans. B. Eisler); Literary and Philosophical Essays, 1968; The Communists and Peace, 1969; The Spectre of Stalin, 1969; L'Idiot de la famille, 1972; Politics and Literature, 1973, etc. *Address:* c/o Hamish Hamilton Ltd, 90 Great Russell Street, WC1.

SARUM, Archdeacon of; *see* Wingfield Digby, Ven. S. B.

SASKATCHEWAN, Bishop of, since 1970; **Rt. Rev. Hedley Vicars Roycraft Short;** *b* 24 Jan. 1914; *s* of Hedley Vicars Short and Martha Hallam Parke; *m* 1953, Elizabeth Frances Louise Shirley; one *s* four *d. Educ:* Trinity College, Univ. of Toronto (BA, LTh, BD). Deacon, 1943, priest, 1944, Assistant Curate St Michael and All Angels, Toronto; Junior Chaplain, Coventry Cathedral, England, 1946-47; Lecturer, Trinity Coll., Toronto, 1947-51; Dean of Residence, 1949-51; Rector, Cochrane, Ont, 1951-56; Rector, St Barnabas, St Catharines, Ont, 1956-63; Canon, Christ's Church Cathedral, Hamilton, Ont, 1962; Dean of Saskatchewan, 1963-70. Member of General Synod, 1955-; Examining Chaplain successively to Bishops of Moosonee, Niagara and Saskatchewan. Pres. Council, Coll. of Emmanuel and St Chad, Saskatoon, 1974-; Chm., Natonum Community Coll., Prince Albert, 1974-76; Chancellor, Univ. of Emmanuel Coll., 1975-. Hon. DD Trinity Coll., Toronto, 1964. *Publication:* (contrib.) Eucharistic Dimensions. *Recreations:* music, sketching, reading. *Address:* Bishopsthorpe, 427 21st Street W, Prince Albert, Saskatchewan S6V 4J5, Canada. *T:* 763-5534, (office) 763-2455.

SASKATOON, Bishop of, since Nov. 1970; **Rt. Rev. Douglas Albert Ford;** *b* 16 July 1917; *s* of Thomas George Ford and Elizabeth Eleanor (Taylor), both English; *m* 1944, Doris Ada (Elborne); two *s* one *d. Educ:* primary and secondary schs, Vancouver; Univ. of British Columbia (BA); Anglican Theological Coll. of BC (LTh); General Synod (BD). Deacon, 1941; Priest, 1942; Curate, St Mary's, Kerrisdale, 1941-42; St George's, Vancouver, 1942-44; Vicar of Strathmore, 1944-49;

Rector of: Okotoks, 1949-52; Vermilion, 1952-55; St Michael and All Angels, Calgary, 1955-62; St Augustine, Lethbridge, 1962-66; Dean and Rector, St John's Cath., Saskatoon, 1966-70. Hon. DD: Coll. of Emmanuel and St Chad, Saskatoon, 1970; Anglican Theological Coll. of BC, Vancouver, 1971. *Address:* 1104 Elliott Street, Saskatoon, Saskatchewan, Canada. *T:* 653-0890.

SATCHELL, Edward William John, CEng, FIEE, FIERE, FIMarE, RCNC; Director of Engineering (Ships), 1973-76; *b* 23 Sept. 1916; *s* of Horsey John Robert Satchell and Ethel Satchell (*née* Chandler); *m* 1941, Stella Grace Cook; one *d. Educ:* Esplanade House Sch., Southsea; Royal Dockyard Sch., Portsmouth; RNC, Greenwich. Electrical Apprentice, Portsmouth Dockyard, 1932; Probationary Asst Electrical Engr, 1936; Asst Electrical Engr, 1939; Electrical Engr, 1943; Suptg Electrical Engr, 1955. Served with British Naval Mission in USA, 1951-53. Warship Electrical Supt, Scotland, 1958-61; Dep. Admty Repair Manager, Malta, 1961-64; Dep. Elec. Engrg Manager, Devonport, 1964-66; Asst Dir of Electrical Engineering, 1966; Dep. Dir of Elec. Engrg, 1970; Head of RN Engrng Service, 1973-75; Dep. Head, RCNC (L), 1975-76; retired 1976. *Recreations:* reading, gardening, bird watching. *Address:* 6 Badminton Gardens, Bath BA1 2XS. *T:* Bath 26974.

SATO, Eisaku, Supreme Order of Grand Cordon of Chrysanthemum 1972; Member of House of Representatives, Japan; *b* 27 March 1901; *s* of Hidesuke and Moyo Sato; *m* 1926, Hiroko Sato; two *s. Educ:* Tokyo Imperial Univ. (LLB). With Ministry of Railways, Japan, 1924-47; Vice-Minister of Transportation, 1947-48; Chief Cabinet Sec., 1948-49; Minister: of Postal Service, 1951; of Telecommunications, 1951; of Posts and Telecommunications, 1951-52; of Construction, 1952-53; of Finance, 1958-60; of Int. Trade and Industry, 1961-62; of State, Dir of Science and Technology Agency and Hokkaido Develt Agency, Chm. Atomic Energy Commn, and i/c Olympic Affairs, 1963-64; Prime Minister, Nov. 1964-July 1972. Hon. Dr of Laws, Columbia Univ., NY, 1967; Nobel Peace Prize, 1974. *Publication:* (autobiog.) Today is Tomorrow's Yesterday, 1964. *Recreations:* golf, fishing. *Address:* 17-10 3-chome, Daizawa, Setagaya-Ku, Tokyo, Japan. *T:* (office) 581-4760, (home) 421-4800.

SATOW, Rear-Adm. Derek Graham, CB 1977; Deputy Director-General, Ships, Ministry of Defence, since 1976, and Chief Naval Engineer Officer, since 1977; *b* 13 June 1923; *y s* of late Graham F. H. Satow, OBE, and of Evelyn M. Satow (*née* Moore); *m* 1944, Patricia E. A. Penalig_gon; two *d. Educ:* Oakley Hall Sch.; Haileybury Coll.; Royal Naval Engineering Coll. CEng, FIMechE, FIMarE. HMS Ceylon, 1945-46; RNC, Greenwich, 1946-48; HMS Duke of York, 1948-49; RAE Farnborough, 1949-51; HMS Newcastle, 1951-53 (despatches, 1953); Naval Ordnance and Weapons Dept, Admiralty, 1953-59; Dir of Engineering, RNEC, 1959-62; HMS Tiger, 1962-64; Asst and Dep. Dir of Marine Engineering, MoD, 1964-67; IDC, 1968; Captain, RNEC, 1969-71; Dir, Naval Officer Appointments (Eng), MoD, 1971-73; Chief Staff Officer, Technical, later Engineering, to C-in-C Fleet, 1974-76. Comdr, 1955; Captain, 1964; Rear-Adm., 1973. *Address:* Ship Department, Ministry of Defence, Foxhill, Bath, Avon.

SATTERLY, Air Vice-Marshal Harold Vivian, CB 1949; CBE 1943; DFC 1941; RAF retired; Director, Grampian Travel Ltd; *b* 24 May 1907; *s* of late Ernest Satterly, Honeaworth, Devon; *m* 1935, Mary Gavin, *d* of late Col A. L. Lindesay, St Andrews, Fife; one *s* two *d. Educ:* Hele's School, Exeter; Exmouth; RAF Halton, Air Officer Comdg, 205 Group, Middle East Air Forces, 1952-54; ACAS (Operational Requirements), Air Ministry, 1954-57; Air Officer Commanding 64 (Northern) Group, 1957-59. Air Commodore, 1948; Air Vice-Marshal, 1952. Retired, 1959. *Recreations:* various.

SATTERTHWAITE, Rt. Rev. John Richard; *see* Gibraltar, Bishop of.

SATTERTHWAITE, Lt-Col Richard George, OBE 1961; Director and General Secretary, National Playing Fields Association, since 1972; *b* 8 April 1920; *s* of R. E. Satterthwaite and A. M. Elers; *m* 1949, Rosemary Ann, *d* of Gen. Sir Frank Messervy, KCSI, KBE, CB, DSO; three *s* (one *d* decd). *Educ:* Rugby Sch.; RMC Sandhurst. 2nd Lieut, 19th King George V's Own Lancers, 1939; served India, Burma, Malaya; transf. to 17th/21st Lancers, 1949; comd 17th/21st Lancers, 1959-61; retd 1962. National Playing Fields Assoc., 1969. *Recreations:* cricket, golf. *Address:* 4 Wardo Avenue, SW6. *T:* 01-731 2752. *Club:* MCC.

SAUMAREZ, family name of **Baron de Saumarez.**

SAUNDERS, Albert Edward, CMG 1975; OBE 1970; HM Diplomatic Service; Ambassador to the United Republic of Cameroon and the Republic of Equatorial Guinea, since 1975; *b* 5 June 1919; *s* of late Albert Edward and Marie Marguerite Saunders; *m* 1945, Dorothea Charlotte Mary Whittle; one *s* one *d*. *Educ:* yes. Westminster Bank Ltd, 1937. Royal Navy, 1942-45: last appt, Asst Chief Port Security Officer, Middle East. Apptd to British Embassy, Cairo, 1938 and 1945; Asst Information Officer, Tripoli, 1949; Asst Admin. Officer, Athens, 1951; Middle East Centre for Arabic Studies, 1952; Third Sec., Office of UK Trade Comr, Khartoum, 1953; Third Sec. (Information), Beirut, 1954; POMEF, Cyprus, 1956; FO, 1957; Second Sec. (Oriental), Baghdad, 1958; FO, 1959; Vice-Consul, Casablanca, 1963; Second Sec. (Oriental), Rabat, 1963; Consul, Jerusalem, 1964; First Sec., FO, 1967; Chancery, Baghdad, 1968; Head of Chancery and Consul, Rabat, 1969; Counsellor and Consul General in charge British Embassy, Dubai, 1972; Chargé d'Affaires, Abu Dhabi, 1972 and 1973; RN War Coll., Greenwich, 1974, sowc, 1975. *Recreation:* iconoclasm (20th Century). *Address:* c/o Foreign and Commonwealth Office, SW1A 2AH. *Club:* Royal Commonwealth Society.

SAUNDERS, Andrew Downing; Chief Inspector of Ancient Monuments and Historic Buildings, Department of the Environment, since 1973; *b* 22 Sept. 1931; *s* of Lionel Edward Saunders; *m* 1961, Hilary Jean (*née* Aikman); two *s* one *d*. *Educ:* Magdalen Coll. Sch., Oxford; Magdalen Coll., Oxford (MA). FSA. Joined Ancient Monuments Inspectorate, 1954; Inspector of Ancient Monuments for England, 1964. Vice-President: Cornwall Archaeol Soc.; Hendon and Dist Archaeol Soc.; Member: Adv. Cttee on Historic Wrecks; Soc. for Medieval Archaeology; Exec. Cttee, Soc. of Antiquaries; British and Exec. Cttees, Internat. Council of Monuments and Sites; Cttee for Aerial Photography, Cambridge Univ.; Cttee of Fortress Study Gp; Council for British Archaeology. *Publications:* ed jtly and contrib., Ancient Monuments and their Interpretation, 1977; articles on castles and artillery fortification in various archæological and historical jls. *Address:* 9 Somerset Road, New Barnet, Herts. *T:* 01-449 7101. *Club:* Athenæum.

SAUNDERS, Christopher Thomas, CMG 1953; Professorial Fellow, Centre for Contemporary European Studies, University of Sussex, since 1973; *b* 5 Nov. 1907; *s* of Thomas Beckenn Avening Saunders, clergyman, and Mary Theodora Slater; *m* 1947, Cornelia Jacomijntje Gielstra; one *s*. *Educ:* Craig School, Windermere; St Edward's School; Christ Church, Oxford. BA 1929; MA 1932; University of Liverpool: Social Survey of Merseyside, 1930-33; University of Manchester: Economic Research Dept, 1933-35; Joint Committee of Cotton Trade Organisations, Manchester, 1935-40; Cotton Control, 1940-44; Combined Production and Resources Board, Washington, 1944-45; Min. of Labour, 1945-47; Central Statistical Office, 1947-57; Dir, Nat. Inst. of Econ. and Social Research, 1957-64; Economist, UN Econ. Commn for Europe, 1965-72. *Publications:* Red Oxford (with M. P. Ashley), 1929; Social Survey of Merseyside (collaborated in), 1934; Seasonal Variations in Employment, 1936; articles in Economic Jl, Jl of Roy. Statistical Soc., The Manchester School. *Recreations:* walking and other forms of travel; painting. *Address:* Centre for Contemporary European Studies, University of Sussex, Brighton BN1 9RF. *Club:* Reform.

SAUNDERS, Dr Cicely Mary Strode, OBE 1967; FRCP; Medical Director, St Christopher's Hospice, since 1967; *b* 22 June 1918; *d* of Gordon Saunders and Mary Christian Knight. *Educ:* Roedean Sch.; St Anne's Coll., Oxford; St Thomas's Hosp. Med. Sch.; Nightingale Sch. of Nursing. SRN 1944; MB, BS, 1957; MA 1960 (BA (war degree) 1945). FRCP 1974 (MRCP 1968). Founded St Christopher's Hospice, 1967 (St Christopher's has been a Registered Charity since 1961 and was opened as a Hospice in 1967). Mem., MRC, 1976-. AIMSW 1947; Hon. DSc Yale, 1969; Dr of Medicine, Lambeth, 1977. *Publications:* Care of the Dying, 1960, 2nd edn 1977; various papers on terminal care. *Recreations:* music, bird watching, Polish art. *Address:* St Christopher's Hospice, 51-53 Lawrie Park Road, Sydenham, SE26 6DZ. *T:* 01-778 9252.

SAUNDERS, Prof. Derek William; Pro-Vice-Chancellor, 1973-76, Head of Department of Materials since 1969 and Professor of Polymer Physics and Engineering, since 1967, Cranfield Institute of Technology; *b* 4 Dec. 1925; *s* of Alfred and Elizabeth Hannah Saunders; *m* 1949, Mahalah Harrison; three *s* two *d*. *Educ:* Morley Grammar Sch.; Imperial Coll., Univ. of London. PhD, ARCS, FInstP, FPRI, FIM. Building Res. Stn, Garston, 1945-47; British Rubber Producers Res. Assoc., 1947-51; Royal Instn, 1951-54; British Rayon Res. Assoc., 1954-60; Sen. Lectr

1960, subseq. Reader, Cranfield Inst. of Technology. Chm. Council, Plastics Inst., 1973-75; Chm. Council, Plastics and Rubber Inst., 1975-76; Mem. Harpur Trust (Bedford Charity), 1968-. *Publications:* chapters in several books on polymeric materials; sci. papers in various learned jls. *Recreation:* sailing. *Address:* 64 De Parys Avenue, Bedford. *T:* Bedford 53869.

SAUNDERS, Henry George Boulton; Organist and Choirmaster to the Hon. Society of Benchers at Gray's Inn; Organist and Master of the Choir to the Household Division; Area Inspector of Schools, Surrey County Council, since 1962; *b* Devonport, Feb. 1914; *m* 1943, Kathleen Mary, *d* of Major S. Brandle, MC, London; one *s* two *d*. *Educ:* Grammar Sch., Kilburn; Royal Acad. of Music (Thomas Threlfall Organ Scholar). DMus Durham; BMus Durham and London; Grad. Royal Schs of Music, London, 1935; FRCO (La Fontaine prize, 1935); FRAM; Worshipful Company of Musicians Silver Medal, 1937; Organist and Choirmaster at St Saviour's, Hampstead, 1934-35; Music Master Trinity County Sch., Wood Green, 1935-46; Inspector of Secondary Schs, City of Leicester, 1946-62. *Publication:* Read and Sing, 1959. *Recreations:* gardening, riding. *Address:* Principal's Lodge, St Margaret's Drive, Twickenham, Mddx. *T:* 01-892 2009; Court Farm, Pebworth, Stratford-upon-Avon, Warwicks CV37 8XW. *T:* Pebworth 428.

SAUNDERS, Air Chief Marshal Sir Hugh (William Lumsden), GCB 1953 (KCB 1950; CB 1943); KBE 1945 (CBE 1941); MC, DFC; MM; Chairman, HM Forces Savings Committee, 1956-70; *b* 1894; *s* of Frederick William Saunders, Transvaal; *m* 1923, Phyllis Margaret, *d* of Major P. W. Mabbett, Bidborough, Kent; one *s* (and one *s* decd). *Educ:* Marist Brothers' School, Johannesburg. Served European War, 1914-19, with Witwatersrand Rifles and South African Horse; transf. RFC 1917; Group Capt. 1939; Air Commodore, 1941; temp. Air Vice-Marshal, 1942; Air Marshal, 1947; Air Chief Marshal, 1950; Chief of Air Staff, New Zealand, 1939-41; AOC, No. 11 Group, Fighter Command, 1942-44; Director-General of Postings, Air Ministry, 1944-45; Air Marshal Commanding RAF Burma, 1945-46; AOC-in-C, Bomber Command, 1947; Air Council Member for Personnel, 1947-49; Inspector-General of the RAF, 1949-50; Commander-in-Chief Air Forces Western Europe, Jan.-April 1951. Air Deputy to Supreme Allied Commander Europe, 1951-53; Special Air Adviser to Royal Danish Air Force, 1954-56; Chief Co-ordinator of Anglo-American hospitality activities in UK, 1956-59. A Vice-Chm., Nat. Savings Cttee, 1956-70. Order of Polonia Restituta, 2nd Class (Poland); Commander Order of Merit (US); Officier Légion d'Honneur (France); Grand Cross of Dannebrog (Denmark). *Address:* c/o Barclays Bank International, Goodenough House, 33 Old Broad Street, EC2. *Club:* Royal Air Force.

SAUNDERS, Sir John (Anthony Holt), Kt 1972; CBE 1970; DSO 1945; MC 1944; Chairman: Amalgamated Metal Corporation, since 1977; International Commercial Bank, since 1972; *b* 29 July 1917; *s* of late E. B. Saunders; *m* 1942, Enid Mary Durant Cassidy; two *d*. *Educ:* Bromsgrove Sch. Joined The Hongkong and Shanghai Banking Corp., 1937. War Service, 1940-45; OCTU Sandhurst (Belt of Honour); East Surrey Regt. Lived in Hong Kong 1950-72; Chm. and Chief Exec., Hongkong and Shanghai Banking Corp., 1964-72; MEC Hong Kong Govt, 1966-72. Chm. of Stewards, Royal Hong Kong Jockey Club, 1967-72; Treasurer, Univ. of Hong Kong, 1964-72; returned to UK 1972. Director: British Bank of Middle East; Rediffusion Ltd; P&OSN Co. Mem., London Cttee H&SBC. Hon. DSocSc (Hong Kong) 1969. Comdr, Order of Prince Henry the Navigator (Portugal), 1966. *Address:* 17 Hyde Park Gate, SW7. *T:* 01-589 0429; The Dairy House, Maresfield Park, Uckfield, East Sussex. *Clubs:* MCC, Oriental.

SAUNDERS, Maj.-Gen. Kenneth, OBE 1970; Paymaster in Chief and Inspector of Army Pay Services, since 1975; *b* 1 Jan. 1920; *m* 1953, Ann Lawrence Addison; one *s*. *Educ:* Lancastrian Sch., Shrewsbury. Enlisted King's Shropshire LI, 1939; commnd Royal Welch Fus., 1940; served in France, Belgium, Holland and Germany (despatches 1945); various staff appts, NW Europe and Far East, 1945-52; transf. to RAPC, 1952; Staff Paymaster: WO 1962-63; HQ Div./Malaya, 1965-67; MoD, 1967-70; Chief Paymaster: MoD, 1970-71; 1 British Corps, 1971-72; Dep. Paymaster in Chief, 1972-75. Captain 1942; Major 1945; Lt-Col 1963; Col 1970; Brig. 1972; Maj.-Gen. 1975. *Recreations:* rough fishing, travel. *Address:* 31 Prestonville Court, Dyke Road, Brighton BN1 3UG. *T:* Brighton 28866. *Club:* Army and Navy.

SAUNDERS, Sir Owen (Alfred), Kt 1965; FRS 1958; MA, DSc; Hon. FIMechE; FInstF; FInstF; FRAeS; Hon. FCGI; Life Member of ASME; Emeritus Professor of Mechanical Engineering, University of London, Imperial College (Professor,

1946; Head of Department, 1946-65; Pro-Rector, 1964-67, Acting Rector, 1966-67); Vice-Chancellor, University of London, 1967-69; *b* 24 September 1904; *s* of Alfred George Saunders and Margaret Ellen Jones, *m* 1935, Marion Isabel McKechney; one *s* two *d.*, *Educ:* Emanuel School; Birkbeck College, London; Trinity College, Cambridge (Senior Scholar). Scientific Officer, Dept of Scientific and Industrial Research, 1926; Lecturer in Applied Mathematical Physics, Imperial College, 1932; Clothworkers' Reader in Applied Thermodynamics, Univ. of London, 1937; on loan to Directorate of Turbine Engines, MAP, 1942-45. Dean, City and Guilds Coll., 1955-64. Past Pres., IMechE; Mem., ITA, 1964-69; President: British Flame Research Cttee; Section G, British Assoc., 1959; Chairman: Nuclear Safety Advisory Cttee, 1966-77; Council, Royal Holloway Coll., 1971-. Founder Fellow, Fellowship of Engineering, 1976. Hon. Mem., Japan Soc. of Mechanical Engrs; Mem., Yugoslav Acad. Hon. DSc Strathclyde, 1964. Melchett medallist, Inst. of Fuel, 1962; Max Jakob Award, ASME, 1966. *Publications:* The Calculation of Heat Transmission, 1932; An Introduction to Heat Transfer, 1950; various scientific and technical papers in Proceedings of Royal Society, Phil. Mag., Physical Society, Engineering, and the Institutions. *Recreations:* music, golf. *Address:* Oakbank, Sea Lane, Middleton, Sussex. *T:* Middleton 2966. *Club:* Athenæum.

SAUNDERS, Peter; Chairman and Managing Director: Peter Saunders Properties; Peter Saunders Ltd; Peter Saunders Theatres Ltd; Volcano Productions Ltd; Kroy Investments Ltd; Director: West End Theatre Managers Ltd; Dominfast Investments Ltd; *b* 23 Nov. 1911; *s* of Ernest and Aletta Saunders; *m* 1959, Ann Stewart (*d* 1976); no *c. Educ:* Oundle Sch.; Lausanne. Film cameraman, film director, journalist and press agent; served War of 1939-45 (Captain); started in theatrical production, 1947; has presented over 100 plays incl. The Mousetrap, which has run for more than 23 years (world's longest ever run, Dec. 1970); other major successes include: Witness for the Prosecution (London and NY); Spider's Web; The Bride and the Bachelor; The Unexpected Guest; Alfie; The Reluctant Peer; Hostile Witness; Arsenic and Old Lace; The Jockey Club Stakes; Move Over Mrs Markham. Controls St Martin's, Vaudeville and Duke of York's theatres; an original Dir, Yorkshire Television; Mem. consortium awarded London Gen. Radio Station by IBA, 1973. Vice-Pres., Actors' Benevolent Fund, 1972-; Lord Goodman's Vice-Chm., Theatre Investment Fund, 1973-; Mem. Exec. Council, Soc. of West End Theatre Managers, 1954- (Pres. 1961-62 and 1967-69); Mem. Council, Theatrical Managers' Assoc., 1958-64; Pres., Stage Golfing Soc., 1963; Pres., Stage Cricket Club, 1956-65. Silver Heart award, Variety Club of GB, 1955. *Publication:* The Mousetrap Man (autobiog.), 1972. *Recreations:* cricket, chess, music of George Gershwin, telephoning. *Address:* Vaudeville Theatre Offices, 10 Maiden Lane, WC2E 7NA. *T:* 01-240 3177.

SAUNDERS-JACOBS, Brig. John Conrad, CBE 1945; DSO 1944; Indian Army, retired; *b* 12 Nov. 1900; *s* of George Saunders-Jacobs; *m* 1930, Sylvia, *e d* of Col H. Drury Shaw, DSO; one *d. Educ:* University College, London; RMC, Sandhurst. Joined Royal Garhwal Rifles in India, 1921; Co. comd, RMC, Sandhurst, 1937-38; Bt Major, 1938; War of 1939-45: GSO1, NWF, India, 1941-42; bn, bde and actg div. comdr, Middle East, Italy and Greece, 1942-46. Staff Coll., Quetta, 1934-35; Imperial Defence Coll., London, 1946; Asst Comdt, Staff Coll., Quetta, 1947; GHQ India, Dir of Mil. Operations, Delhi, 1947; retired Indian Army, 1948. FO UK delegate to UN Special Cttee on the Balkans, 1948; Official mil. historian, Cabinet Office, 1949-50; export agent, London, 1950-53; RO II, War Office, 1954; landscape gardener, 1955-57; govt service in Mins of Defence, Aviation and Technology, 1958-71. *Recreations:* walking, gardening, current affairs. *Address:* Firlands, West Chiltington, Pulborough, West Sussex. *T:* West Chiltington 3197.

SAUVAGNARGUES, Jean Victor; Commander, Légion d'Honneur, Croix de Guerre avec palme (1939-45); French Ambassador to the Court of St James's, since 1977; *b* Paris, 2 April 1915; *s* of Edmond Sauvagnargues and Alice Caplan; *m* 1948, Lise Marie L'Evesque; two *s* two *d. Educ:* Higher Normal Sch.; Dip., Political Science Sch.; Univ. (German) (Agrégé). Attaché, Embassy, Bucharest, 1941. Served War with Free French Forces, 1943 (Army, June 1944-May 1945). Cabinet of: the High Commn, Beirut, 1943; M Massigli, 1944; Gen. de Gaulle, 1945-46; Specialist on German questions, Quai d'Orsay, 1947-55; Cabinet of M Pinay, 1955. In negotiations about the Saar, Jan.-June 1956. Ambassador to: Ethiopia, 1956-60; Tunisia, 1962-70. Director, African and Middle-Eastern Affairs, Min. of Foreign Affairs, 1960-62. Ambassador to the Federal Republic of Germany, Bonn, 1970-74; Minister for Foreign Affairs, France, 1974-76. Commander of the National Order of Merit. *Address:* 11 Kensington Palace Gardens, W8; 14 avenue Pierre 1er de Serbie, 75116 Paris.

SAUZIER, Sir (André) Guy, Kt 1973; CBE 1959; ED; General Overseas Representative of Mauritius Chamber of Agriculture, since 1959; Minister Plenipotentiary, Mauritius Mission to EEC, since 1972; *b* 20 Oct. 1910; *s* of J. Adrien Sauzier, Mauritius; *m* 1936, Thérèse, *d* of Henri Mallac; six *s* two *d. Educ:* Royal Coll., Mauritius. Served War of 1939-45; late Major, Mauritius TF. A (nominated) Member of the Legislative Council, Mauritius, 1949-57; Member, Mauritius Political Delegn to the UK, 1955; Minister of Works and Communications, 1957-59. Represented Mauritius at the Coronation, 1953. FRSA. *Address:* 64 Cadogan Place, SW1. *Clubs:* Athenæum; Cercle Royal Gaulois (Brussels).

SAVA, George; (George Alexis Milkomanovich Milkomane); Author and Consulting Surgeon; *b* 15 Oct. 1903; *s* of Col Ivan Alexandrovitch and Countess Maria Ignatiev; *nephew* of Prince Alexander Milkomanovich Milkomane; *m* 1939, Jannette Hollingdale; two *s* two *d. Educ:* Public Schools in Bulgaria and Russia. Entered Russian Imperial Naval Academy in 1913; after the Revolution studied in various medical schools, Univ. of Paris, Florence, Rome, Munich, Berlin and Bonn; domiciled in this country since 1932; further medical education at Manchester, Glasgow and Edinburgh; naturalised British subject in 1938; Research scholarships in medicine and surgery, University of Rome, Libero Docente (Professorship) of Univ. of Rome, 1954. Grand Chev. of the Crown of Bulgaria; Commendatore dell' Ordine al Merito Della Repubblica Italiana, 1961. *Publications: autobiog. medical:* The Healing Knife, 1937; Beauty from the Surgeon's Knife, 1938; A Surgeon's Destiny, 1939; Donkey's Serenade, 1940; Twice the Clock Round, 1941; A Ring at the Door, 1941; Surgeon's Symphony, 1944; They come by Appointment, 1946; The Knife Heals Again, 1948; The Way of a Surgeon, 1949; Strange Cases, 1950; A Doctor's Odyssey, 1951; Patients' Progress, 1952; A Surgeon Remembers, 1953; Surgeon Under Capricorn, 1954; The Lure of Surgery, 1955; A Surgeon at Large, 1957; Surgery and Crime, 1957; All this and Surgery too, 1958; Surgery Holds the Door, 1960; A Surgeon in Rome, 1961; A Surgeon in California, 1962; Appointments in Rome, 1963; A Surgeon in New Zealand, 1964; A Surgeon in Cyprus, 1965; A Surgeon in Australia, 1966; Sex, Surgery, People, 1967; The Gates of Heaven are Narrow, 1968; Bitter-Sweet Surgery, 1969; One Russian's Story, 1970; A Stranger in Harley Street, 1970; *political and historical books:* Rasputin Speaks, 1941; Valley of Forgotten People, 1942; The Chetniks, 1943; School for War, 1943; They Stayed in London, 1943; Russia Triumphant, 1944; A Tale of Ten Cities, 1944; War Without Guns, 1944; Caught by Revolution, 1952; *novels:* Land Fit for Heroes, 1945; Link of Two Hearts, 1945; Gissy, 1946; Call it Life, 1946; Boy in Samarkand, 1950; Flight from the Palace, 1953; Pursuit in the Desert, 1955; The Emperor Story, 1959; Punishment Deferred, 1966; Man Without Label, 1967; Alias Dr Holtzman, 1968; City of Cain, 1969; The Imperfect Surgeon, 1969; Nothing Sacred, 1970; Of Guilt Possessed, 1970; A Skeleton for My Mate, 1971; The Beloved Nemesis, 1971; On the Wings of Angels, 1972; The Sins of Andrea, 1972; Tell Your Grief Softly, 1972; Cocaine for Breakfast, 1973; Return from the Valley, 1973; Sheilah of Buckleigh Manor, 1974; Every Sweet Hath Its Sour, 1974; The Way of the Healing Knife, 1976; Mary Mary Quite Contrary, 1977; Crusader's Clinic, 1977; *as George Borodin:* Street of a Thousand Misters, 1939; Those Borgias, 1940; Visions of Contempt, 1941; Bastard Angels, 1942; This Russian Land, 1943; Peace in Nobody's Time, 1944; President Died at Noon, 1944; Red Surgeon: a biography of Maxim Murov, 1944; Soviet and Tsarist Siberia, 1944; Cradle of Splendour, the Song of Samarkand, 1945; Against the Tide, 1946; Friendly Ocean, 1946; This thing called Ballet, 1946; Book of Joanna, 1947; Pillar of Fire, 1947; Spurious Sun, 1948; One Horizon, 1948; Man of Kerioth: the story of Judas, 1949; Invitation to the Ballet, 1950; No Crown of Laurels, 1950; Austrian Concerto: a romantic life of Mozart, 1952; Charm of Ballet, 1955. *Recreations:* tennis, golf, riding, aviation. *Address:* 33 Ferncroft Avenue, NW3.

SAVAGE, Albert Walter, CMG 1954; Director-General (retired), Colonial Civil Aviation Service; *b* 12 June 1898; *s* of William Albert Savage, Wheathampstead, Herts; *m* 1923, Lilian Marie Gertrude Storch; one *s* one *d. Educ:* Northern Polytechnic, Northampton Institute and Sheffield University. Apprentice, Grahame White Flying School, 1914-16. Served European War, 1914-18, RFC, 1916 to end of war. Aeronautical Inspection Directorate, Air Ministry, UK 1921-34, India, 1934-36; seconded to Egyptian Govt as Chief Technical Inspector, Civil Aviation Dept, Cairo, 1936-46; Colonial Civil Aviation Service, 1946-; Director of Civil Aviation, W Africa, 1946-49; Director-

General of Civil Aviation, Malaya/Borneo territories, 1949-54; Civil Aviation Adviser, Government of Jordan, 1954-55; Director of Civil Aviation, Leeward and Windward Islands, 1956-60. Director of Civil Aviation, Sierra Leone, 1961-62. *Recreations:* golf, tennis and squash. *Address:* White Cottage, 29 Wrestwood Avenue, Willingdon, Eastbourne. *T:* Eastbourne 53708.

SAVAGE, Sir Alfred William Lungley, KCMG 1951 (CMG 1948); Chairman, West African Currency Board, 1956-69; *b* 5 May 1903; *y s* of late Charles Savage, Gillingham, Kent; *m* 1931, Doreen, 2nd *d* of James Hopwood, OBE, Bulawayo, Rhodesia; one *s* one *d*. *Educ:* Owens School, London. Entered Home Civil Service, 1920; Asst Treasurer, Govt of N Rhodesia, 1928; Dep. Treas., Govt of Fiji, 1935; Dep. Treas., 1939, Dep. Financial Sec., 1940, Under-Sec., 1945, Govt of Palestine; Dep. Financial Sec., Govt of Nigeria, 1946; Financial Sec., 1948; Governor and C-in-C, Barbados, 1949-53; British Guiana, 1953-55; Crown Agent for Overseas Governments, 1955-63. *Address:* 19 Caledonia Place, Clifton, Bristol BS8 4DJ.

SAVAGE, Anthony; Chief Executive, Intervention Board for Agricultural Produce, since 1972; *b* 23 Aug. 1920; *s* of late Edmund Savage and Dorothy Mary (*née* Gray); *m* 1945, Heather Mary (*née* Templeman); one *s* three *d*. *Educ:* Johnston Sch., Durham. Entered Min. of Agriculture, 1937. War Service, Royal Artillery, 1939-46: Middle East, Italy and NW Europe, 1940-46; commnd 1943. Asst Principal, MAFF, 1947; Principal, 1951; Cabinet Office, 1951-53; Asst Sec., 1961; Regional Controller, E Midland Region, 1964-69; Head of Land Drainage Div., 1969-71; Under-Sec., 1972. *Address:* 112 Powys Lane, Palmers Green, N13 4HR. *T:* 01-886 0839.

SAVAGE, Sir (Edward) Graham, Kt 1947; CB 1935; *b* 31 Aug. 1886; *s* of Edward Graham Savage and Mary Matilda Dewey; *m* 1911; two *s* one *d*. *Educ:* Upper Sheringham School; King Edward VI Middle School, Norwich; Downing College, Cambridge. Tutor Bede College, Durham; Assistant Master, St Andrew's College, Toronto; Tewfikieh School, Cairo; Lecturer, Khedivial Training College, Egypt; served R W Kent Regt Gallipoli and France, 1914-19; Assistant Master, Eton College; District Inspector, Board of Education, 1919-27; Staff Inspector for Science, 1927; Divisional Inspector NW Division, 1931-32; Chief Inspector, of Technical Schools and Colleges, 1932; Senior Chief Inspector, 1933-40. Education Officer to the LCC, 1940-51, retired. Chm. League of the Empire, 1947-62; Chm. Simplified Spelling Society, 1949-68; President Science Masters' Assoc., 1952-53; Chief Assessor to Industrial Fund for Advancement of Science Teaching in Schools, 1956; Chm., Board of Building Education, 1956-66; Mem. Council and Exec. Cttee, City and Guilds of London Institute, 1963 (Vice-Chairman, 1967-71, Vice-President, 1967-74). Hon. Fellow, Inst. of Builders, 1966. *Publication:* The Planning and Equipment of School Science Blocks, 1964. *Recreations:* walking, gardening. *Address:* Barbary, Maresfield Park, Uckfield, East Sussex. *T:* Uckfield 2586.

SAVAGE, Rt. Rev. Gordon David, MA; *b* 14 April 1915; *s* of Augustus Johnson Savage and Louisa Hannah Atkinson; *m* 1938, Eva Louise, *y d* of H. J. Jessen, Copenhagen; one *s* two *d*. *Educ:* Reading Sch.; Tyndale Hall, Bristol; St Catherine's, Oxford. MA Oxon, 1949. Was a Librarian before ordination, 1932-37; deacon, 1940, priest, 1941; Chaplain, Lecturer and Tutor, Tyndale Hall, Bristol, 1940-44; General Secretary Church Society, London, 1945-52; Curate-in-Charge of the City Church, Oxford, 1948-52; Proctor in Convocation, 1951-61; Vicar of Marston, Oxford, 1952-57; Archdeacon of Buckingham and Vicar of Whitchurch, Bucks, 1957-61; Suffragan Bishop of Buckingham, 1960-64; Bishop of Southwell, 1964-70. *Address:* c/o Barclays Bank Ltd, 92-93 High Street, Oxford OX1 4BN.

SAVAGE, Sir Graham; see Savage, Sir E. G.

SAVARESE, Signora Fernando; see Elvin, Violetta.

SAVILE, family name of **Earl of Mexborough.**

SAVILE, 3rd Baron, *cr* 1888; **George Halifax Lumley-Savile**; DL; JP; *b* 24 Jan. 1919; *s* of 2nd Baron and Esme Grace Virginia (*d* 1958), *d* of J. Wolton; *S* father, 1931. *Educ:* Eton. Served in 1939-45 War in Duke of Wellington's Regiment, and attached Lincolnshire Regiment during the Burma Campaigns. DL W Yorks, 1954. Is Patron of two livings. Owns about 18,000 acres. JP Borough of Dewsbury, 1955. OStJ. *Recreations:* music and shooting. *Heir: b* Hon. Henry Leoline Thornhill Lumley-Savile [*b* 2 Oct. 1923; *m* 1st, 1946, Presiley June (marr. diss. 1951), *o d* of Major G. H. E. Inchbald, Halebourne House, Chobham, Surrey; one *s*; 2nd, 1961, Caroline Jeffie (*d* 1970), *o d* of Peter

Clive, California, USA, and Elizabeth Clive, 58 Queens' Gate, SW7; 3rd, 1972, Margaret, *widow* of Peter Bruce; three *s* (triplets). Served War of 1939-45, in Grenadier Guards, Italy (wounded)]. *Address:* Gryce Hall, Shelley, Huddersfield. *T:* Kirkburton 2774; Walshaw, Hebden Bridge, Yorks. *T:* Hebden Bridge 2275. *Club:* Brooks's.

SAVILL, David Malcolm, QC 1969; a Recorder of the Crown Court, since 1972; *b* 18 Sept. 1930; *s* of late Lionel and of Lisbeth Savill; *m* 1955, Mary Arnott (*née* Eadie), JP, *d* of late Lady Hinchcliffe and step *d* of late Hon. Sir (George) Raymond Hinchcliffe; one *s* two *d*. *Educ:* Marlborough Coll.; Clare Coll., Cambridge. 2nd Lieut Grenadier Guards, 1949-50. BA (Hons) Cambridge, 1953. Called to the Bar, Middle Temple, 1954; Mem., Senate of Inns of Court and the Bar, 1976-; Master of the Bench, 1977; Chancellor, diocese of Bradford, 1976-. *Recreations:* cricket, golf, gardening. *Address:* The Priory, Knaresborough, North Yorks HG5 8HX. *T:* Harrogate 862309. *Clubs:* MCC; Leeds (Leeds).

SAVILL, Sir Eric (Humphrey), KCVO 1955 (CVO 1950; MVO 1938); CBE 1946; MC, MA Cantab, FRICS; Director of the Gardens, Windsor Great Park, 1959-70, retired; architect and planter of The Savill and Valley Gardens, which were begun in 1932; *b* 20 October 1895; *s* of late Sir Edwin Savill. *Educ:* Malvern Coll.; Magdalene Coll., Cambridge. At outbreak of European War joined Univ. and Public School Corps as a Private; Commissioned to Devonshire Regt 1915, Captain 1916; served in France with 8th and 2nd Bns (wounded); joined firm of Alfred Savill & Sons, chartered Surveyors, 1920; Partner, 1926. Deputy Surveyor, Windsor Parks and Woods, 1931-59; Deputy Ranger of Windsor Great Park, 1937-59; Director of Forestry to Crown Estate, 1958-62. Mem. Bd Management: Hosp. for Sick Children, Gt Ormond St, 1926-42; King Edward VII Hosp., Windsor, 1933-46; Mem. Min. of Transport Adv. Cttee on Landscape Treatment of Trunk Roads, 1954-69 (Chm., 1962-69). Gold Veitch Memorial Medal, The Royal Horticultural Society, 1963; Gold Medal, The Royal Forestry Soc. of England, Wales and Northern Ireland, 1963. *Recreations:* gardening, fishing. *Address:* The Garden House, The Great Park, Windsor. *T:* Egham 4617.

SAVILL, Colonel Kenneth Edward, CVO 1976; DSO 1945; DL; Member, HM Bodyguard of Hon. Corps of Gentlemen at Arms, 1955-76 (Lieutenant, 1973-76; Standard Bearer, 1972-73); *b* 8 August 1906; *o s* of Walter Savill, Chilton Manor, Alresford and May, *d* of Major Charles Marriott; *m* 1935, Jacqueline, *o d* of Brig. John Salusbury Hughes, MC; two *d* (and one *d* decd). *Educ:* Winchester College; RMC Sandhurst. Commissioned, 12th Royal Lancers, 1926; 1st King's Dragoon Guards, 1936; The Queen's Bays, 1947. Served War of 1939-45, France, 1939-40; N Africa and Italy, 1943-45. Comd 12th Green Howards (TA), 1943; comd 12th Royal Lancers, 1944-45; comd Queen's Bays, 1947-50; Col 1950; retd 1953. Chm., The Sunnygama Co. Ltd, 1957; Dir, Mid Southern Water Co., 1964-77. CC Hampshire, 1961-74; High Sheriff of Hampshire, 1961; DL Hampshire, 1965. Col, 1st The Queen's Dragoon Guards, 1964-68. *Address:* Chilton Manor, Alresford, Hants. *T:* Preston Candover 246. *Clubs:* Cavalry and Guards, Army and Navy.

SAVILLE, Prof. John; Professor of Economic and Social History, University of Hull, since 1972; *b* 2 April 1916; *o s* of Orestes Stamatopoulos, Volos, Greece, and Edith Vessey (name changed by deed poll to that of step-father, 1937); *m* 1943, Constance Betty Saunders; three *s* one *d*. *Educ:* Royal Liberty Sch.; London Sch. of Economics. 1st Cl. Hons BSc (Econ) 1937. Served War, RA, 1940-46; Chief Scientific Adviser's Div., Min. of Works, 1946-47; Univ. of Hull, 1947-. Mem., British Communist Party, 1934-56; Chm., Oral Hist. Soc., 1976-; Vice-Chm., Soc. for Study of Labour Hist., 1974; Mem. Exec. Cttee and Founder-Mem., Council for Academic Freedom and Democracy, 1971-; Chm., Economic and Social Hist. Cttee, Social Science Research Council, 1977-78. *Publications:* Ernest Jones, Chartist, 1952; Rural Depopulation in England and Wales 1851-1951, 1957; numerous articles; Co-Editor: (with E. P. Thompson) Reasoner and New Reasoner, 1956-59; (with Asa Briggs) Essays in Labour History, 1960, 1971, 1977; (with Ralph Miliband) Socialist Register (annual, 1964-); (with Joyce M. Bellamy) Dictionary of Labour Biography, 1972-. *Recreations:* working for socialism, looking at churches. *Address:* 152 Westbourne Avenue, Hull HU5 3HZ. *T:* Hull 43425.

SAVILLE, (Leonard) Malcolm; author; Editor of General Books, George Newnes Ltd and C. Arthur Pearson Ltd, 1957-66; *b* 21 February 1901; *s* of Ernest Vivian Saville and Fanny Ethel Hayes; *m* 1926, Dorothy May McCoy; two *s* two *d*. *Educ:* Private Schools. Has written original stories for Children's Film Foundation; seven stories adapted as serials for BBC.

Publications: books for children (as Malcolm Saville): King of Kings; Jane's Country Year; Adventure of the Lifeboat Service; Country Scrapbook for Boys and Girls; Open Air Scrapbook for Boys and Girls; Seaside Scrapbook for Boys and Girls; Coronation Gift Book; Mystery at Witchend; Seven White Gates; The Gay Dolphin Adventure; The Secret of Grey Walls; Lone Pine Five; The Elusive Grasshopper; The Neglected Mountain; Saucers Over the Moor; Wings Over Witchend; Lone Pine London; The Secret of the Gorge; Mystery Mine; Sea Witch Comes Home; Not Scarlet but Gold; Treasure at Amorys; Man with Three Fingers; Rye Royal; Strangers at Witchend; Where's My Girl?; All Summer Through; Christmas at Nettleford; Spring Comes to Nettleford; The Secret of Buzzard Scar; Redshank's Warning; Two Fair Plaits; The Sign of the Alpine Rose; The Luck of Sallowby; Strangers at Snowfell; The Ambermere Treasure; The Master of Maryknoll; The Buckinghams at Ravenswyke; The Long Passage; A Palace for the Buckinghams; The Secret of the Villa Rosa; Diamond in the Sky; Trouble at Townsend; The Riddle of the Painted Box; The Flying Fish Adventure; The Secret of the Hidden Pool; Young Johnnie Bimbo; The Fourth Key; Susan, Bill and the Wolfdog; Susan, Bill and the Ivy-clad Oak; Susan, Bill and the Vanishing Boy; Susan, Bill and the Golden Clock; Susan, Bill and the Dark Stranger; Susan, Bill and the Saucy Kate; Susan, Bill and the Brightstar Circus; Susan, Bill and the Pirates Bold; Treasure at the Mill; Four and Twenty Blackbirds (repr. as The Secret of Galleybird Pit); The Thin Grey Man; Malcolm Saville's Country Book; Malcolm Saville's Seaside Book; Three Towers in Tuscany; The Purple Valley; Dark Danger; White Fire; Power of Three; The Dagger and the Flame; Marston, Master Spy; Come to London; Strange Story; Come to Devon; Come to Cornwall; Come to Somerset; See How It Grows; Good Dog Dandy; The Roman Treasure Mystery; Eat What You Grow; Portrait of Rye. *Recreations:* walking, watching cricket, reading. *Address:* Chelsea Cottage, Winchelsea, East Sussex. *T:* Winchelsea 449. *Club:* Savage.

SAVILLE, Malcolm; *see* Saville, Leonard Malcolm.

SAVILLE, Mark Oliver, QC 1975; *b* 20 March 1936; *s* of Kenneth Vivian Saville and Olivia Sarah Frances Gray; *m* 1961, Gillian Whitworth Gray; two *s*. *Educ:* St Paul's Primary Sch., Hastings; Rye Grammar Sch.; Brasenose Coll., Oxford (BA, BCL). Nat. Service, 2nd Lieut Royal Sussex Regt, 1954-56; Oxford Univ., 1956-60 (Vinerian Schol. 1960); called to Bar, Middle Temple, 1962. *Recreation:* sailing. *Address:* 4 Essex Court, Temple, EC4Y 9AJ. *T:* 01-353 6771.

SAVIN, Lewis Herbert, MD, MS, London (University Medal in Ophthalmology), MRCP, FRCS; Fellow, King's College, London, 1953; Hunterian Professor Royal College of Surgeons of England, 1943; FRSM (Member Council Ophthalmic Section, 1943; Vice-President 1955); *b* 1901; *e s* of late Lewis Savin, MRCS, Yunnan, and of late Kate C. Savin; *m* 1931, Mary Helen, *e d* of late Walter Griffith, Wimbledon; two *s* one *d*. *Educ:* Christ's Hosp.; King's Coll., London; King's Coll. Hosp (Warneford Entrance Scholarship, Warneford and Barry Prizes). House Physician and House Surg. to the City of London Hosp. for Diseases of Heart and Lungs, 1924; 1st Assistant Medical Officer to St Marylebone Hospital, 1927; Medical Superintendent Seamen's Hospital, Greenwich, 1928; House Surgeon to Royal Eye Hospital, 1923; afterwards clinical assistant, pathologist, assistant Surgeon, Surgeon, Senior Surgeon, Royal Eye Hospital, SE1, resigning 1956. Ophthalmic Surgeon, Metropolitan Hospital, 1929-34; Consulting Ophthalmic Surgeon, Maudsley Hospital, 1937-39; Consulting Ophthalmic Surgeon to the LCC General Hospitals, 1936-48, and to Whipps Cross Hospital, 1931-47; Ophthalmologist to Horton War Hospital (Ministry of Health Emergency Medical Service), 1939-47; Consulting Ophthalmic Surgeon, King's College Hospital, 1966 (Asst Ophthalmic Surgeon, 1931; Senior Ophthalmic Surgeon, 1945-66). Hon. Secretary Ophthalmological Soc. of UK, 1937-39 (Member Council, 1939-42; Vice-President, 1957); Emeritus Lecturer in Ophthalmology, King's Coll. Hosp. Med. Sch.; Examr under Conjoint Examining Bd for DOMS Part I, 1941-46; Examiner in DO, 1949; Staff Examiner in Ophthalmology, Univ. of London, 1952. Vice-Pres. sect. of ophth. Roy. Soc. Med., 1956-57; President Faculty of Ophthalmologists, 1957. *Publications:* Medical and Ophthalmic contributions to Lancet, British Journal of Ophthalmology (The Effect of Aluminium and its Alloys on the Eye: a Report presented to Vision Committee of Medical Research Council, 1947), and Transactions of Ophthalmological Society of the United Kingdom. *Address:* 149 Eastcote Road, Pinner Mddx HA5 1EX. *T:* 01-866 1581.

SAVORY, Hubert Newman, MA, DPhil Oxon, FSA; Keeper of Archæology, National Museum of Wales, Cardiff, 1956-76; *b* 7

Aug. 1911; *s* of William Charles Newman Savory and Alice Amelia (*née* Minns); *m* 1949, Priscilla Valerie Thirkell; four *s* two *d*. *Educ:* Magdalen College Sch., Oxford; St Edmund Hall, Oxford Univ. BA Oxon 1934 (Lit. Hum. 1st Cl.); DPhil Oxon 1937; Randall MacIver Student in Iberian Archæology, 1936-38. Assistant, 1938, Asst Keeper, 1939, Dept of Archæology, National Museum of Wales. Member: Royal Commn on Ancient Monuments (Wales), 1970-; Ancient Monuments Board for Wales; Pres., Cambrian Archæological Assoc., 1975-76; Chm., Glamorgan Gwent Archæological Trust, 1975-. Conducted excavations of various Welsh cromlechs, round barrows, hill-forts, etc. Served War of 1939-45, in Army, 1940-45. *Publications:* Spain and Portugal: The Prehistory of the Iberian Peninsular, 1968; Guide Catalogue of the Early Iron Age Collections, National Museum of Wales, 1976; contrib. to Proc. of Prehistoric Soc.; Archæologia Cambrensis, etc. *Recreations:* walking, gardening. *Address:* 31 Lady Mary Road, Cardiff. *T:* Cardiff 753106.

SAVORY, Lt-Gen. Sir Reginald Arthur, KCIE 1947; CB 1944; DSO 1941; MC; psc; late Indian Army; *b* 26 July 1894; *s* of A. L. Savory, Bramham Gardens, London; *m* 1st, 1922, Myrtle Estelle Richardson (*d* 1965); no *c*; 2nd, 1969, Marie Nikolaevna McIlwraith (*née* Zurabova). *Educ:* Uppingham; Hanover; Sandhurst. First Commission, 1914; served European War, Egypt, Gallipoli (wounded, despatches, MC), Persia, Mesopotamia, Siberia; Kurdistan, 1923; Brevet Major, 1930; North-West Frontier, India, 1930 (despatches); Instructor, Indian Mil. Acad., 1932-34; Brevet Lt-Col 1934; Waziristan, 1937 (despatches); War of 1939-45, commanded 11th Indian Infantry Brigade, 1940-41, Middle East (DSO); GOC Eritrea, 1941 (despatches); Maj.-Gen. 1943; commanded 23rd Indian Div. 1942-43 (despatches); Director of Infantry (India), 1943-45; GOC Persia and Iraq, 1945-46; Lt-Gen. 1947. Adjutant-General in India, 1946-47; retired 1948. Col, Sikh Light Infantry, 1947-56. DL Somerset, 1952-60; JP Somerset, 1952-60; CC Somerset, 1952-59; County Alderman, Somerset, 1959-60; Chm. T & AFA, Somerset, 1953-59. *Publication:* His Britannic Majesty's Army in Germany, during the Seven Years War, 1966. *Address:* School Hill Cottage, Seale, Farnham, Surrey GU10 1HY. *Clubs:* Athenæum, Naval and Military.

SAVORY, Sir Reginald (Charles Frank), Kt 1972; CBE 1965; Chairman of Directors, R. Savory Ltd, Building Contractors, since 1933; *b* 27 May 1908; *s* of Frank and Margaret Savory, Auckland, NZ; *m* 1935, Fai-Ola, *o c* of Ernest Vaile, Auckland; two *d*. *Educ:* Auckland Grammar Sch. Chm., Bd of Governors, Council of Auckland Technical Institutes; Member: Auckland Harbour Bd (Chm., 1961-71); Auckland City Council, 1953-62, Drainage Bd, 1956-62, and Chamber of Commerce, 1961-71. Pres., NZ Harbours Assoc., 1963-67; Past Pres., NZ Technical Assoc.; Life Mem. (Past Pres.) NZ Builders' Fedn; FIOB (Gt Britain) 1959. *Recreations:* boating, fishing, golf, bowls; watching Rugby football. *Address:* 452 Remuera Road, Auckland 5, New Zealand. *T:* 545-428. *Clubs:* New Zealand Officers', Auckland (Auckland); Civil Service (Wellington, NZ); NZ Royal Yacht Squadron.

SAW, Prof. Ruth Lydia; Professor Emeritus in Aesthetics, University of London, 1964; *b* 1 August 1901; *d* of Samuel James and Matilda Louisa Saw (*née* Horner). *Educ:* County School for Girls, Wallington, Surrey; Bedford College, University of London. Lecturer in Philosophy, Smith Coll., Northampton, Mass., USA, 1927-34; Lecturer in Philosophy: Bedford College, 1939-44; Birkbeck College, 1939-46, Reader in Philosophy, 1946-61; Prof. of Aesthetics in Univ. of London, 1961-64, and Head of Dept of Philosophy, Birkbeck Coll. British Society of Aesthetics: Founder Mem. and Chm. Council, 1960; Vice-Pres., 1963; Pres., 1969; Pres., Aristotelian Soc., 1965. *Publications:* The Vindication of Metaphysics, 1951; Leibniz, 1954; Aesthetics, 1970; sections (William of Ockham, Leibniz), in A Critical History of Western Philosophy. Contrib. to Proc. Aristotelian Soc., Philosophy, Brit. Jl of Aesthetics. *Recreations:* gardening, the theatre; interested in illuminated manuscripts, early gardening and botany books. *Address:* 72 Grosvenor Avenue, Carshalton, Surrey. *T:* 01-647 8898. *Club:* Women's Farm and Garden.

SAWBRIDGE, Henry Raywood, CBE 1960; retired from HM Foreign Service, 1964; Deputy Director, Centre of Japanese Studies, University of Sheffield, 1964-66; *b* 1 Nov. 1907; 2nd *s* of Rev. John Edward Bridgman Sawbridge; *m* 1947, Lilian, *d* of late William Herbert Wood; one *s* one *d*. *Educ:* Eton; Trinity Coll., Oxford. Entered HM Consular Service, 1931, and served in Japan, Korea and at FO; served with Australian Forces, 1943; HM Consul-General, Yokohama, 1949; Chargé d'Affaires, Korea, 1950; HM Consul-General, Geneva, 1953; Counsellor at Foreign Office, 1960. Coronation Medal, 1953. *Recreations:*

shooting, fishing. *Address:* The Moorings, Kingsgate, Kent. *Club:* Travellers'.

SAWERS, David Richard Hall; Under-Secretary, Departments of the Environment and Transport, since 1977; *b* 23 April 1931; *s* of late Edward and of Madeline Sawers; unmarried. *Educ:* Westminster Sch.; Christ Church, Oxford (MA). Research Asst to Prof. J. Jewkes, Oxford Univ., 1954-58; Journalist, The Economist, 1959-64; Vis. Fellow, Princeton Univ., 1964-65; Econ. Adviser, Min. of Aviation and of Technology, 1966-68; Sen. Econ. Adviser, Min. of Technology, Aviation Supply, and DTI, 1968-72; Under-Sec., Depts of Industry, Trade and Prices and Consumer Protection, 1972-76. *Publications:* (with John Jewkes and Richard Stillerman) The Sources of Invention, 1958; (with Ronald Miller) The Technical Development of Modern Aviation, 1968. *Recreations:* listening to music, looking at pictures, gardening. *Address:* 26 Groveway, SW9 0AR.

SAWERS, Maj.-Gen. James Maxwell, CB 1974; MBE 1953; Managing Director, Services Kinema Corporation, since 1975; *b* 14 May 1920; *s* of late Lt-Col James Sawers, Woking, Surrey; *m* 1945, Grace, *d* of Joseph William Walker, Tynemouth; two *s* one *d. Educ:* Rugby; RMA Woolwich. 2nd Lieut, Royal Signals, 1939. Served War of 1939-45 in W Africa and Burma. Lt-Col, 1960; Brig., 1966; BGS, MoD, 1966-68; Comd Corps Royal Signals, 1st British Corps, 1968-69; attended IDC, 1970; Signal Officer in Chief, 1971-74. Col Comdt, Royal Signals, 1974-; Hon. Col, 71 (Yeomanry) Signal Regt, 1977-. psc, jssc, idc. FBIM. Member, Council, Cinema and TV Benevolent Fund; Managing Trustee: Soldiers' Widows Fund; Single Soldiers' Dependants Fund; Chm., Army Benevolent Fund Bucks Appeals Cttee. *Recreations:* sailing, skiing, gardening, golf, photography. *Address:* Holly Lodge, Keepers Lane, Hyde Heath, Amersham, Bucks. *T:* Chesham 3367. *Club:* Army and Navy.

SAWYER, Charles; Senior partner, Taft, Stettinus and Hollister, Attorneys at Law; *b* 10 Feb. 1887; *s* of Edward Milton and Caroline Butler Sawyer; *m* 1st, 1918, Margaret Sterrett Johnston (*d* 1937); three *s* two *d*; 2nd, 1942, Elizabeth L. de Veyrac. *Educ:* Oberlin College, Oberlin, Ohio (BA); University of Cincinnati (LLB). Elected to City Council, Cincinnati, Ohio, 1911; Lieut Governor of Ohio, 1932; Democratic Candidate for Governor of Ohio, 1938; Ambassador to Belgium and Minister to Luxembourg, 1944; Secretary of Commerce, 1948-53. Hon. LLD: University of Cincinnati; Bryant College; Franklin and Marshall College; Miami University; Oberlin College. Hon. JD University of Cincinnati, 1968. *Publication:* Concerns of a Conservative Democrat, 1968. *Address:* Fountain Avenue, Glendale, Ohio 45246, USA. *Clubs:* Queen City, Cincinnati Country (Cincinnati); Chevy Chase (Maryland); Everglades, Bath and Tennis (Palm Beach, Fla).

SAWYER, John Stanley, MA; FRS 1962; Director of Research, Meteorological Office, 1965-76; *b* 19 June 1916; *s* of late Arthur Stanley Sawyer and of Emily Florence Sawyer (*née* Frost), Bladon, Oxford; *m* 1951, Betty Vera Beeching (*née* Tooke), widow; one *d. Educ:* Latymer Upper Sch., Hammersmith; Jesus Coll., Cambridge. Entered Meteorological Office, 1937. Mem., NERC, 1975-. Pres., Commn for Atmospheric Sciences, World Meteorological Organisation, 1968-73 (IMO Prize, 1973); Pres., Royal Meteorological Soc., 1963-65 (Hugh Robert Mill Medal 1956, Buchan Prize 1962, Symons Medal 1971). *Publications:* Ways of the Weather, 1958; scientific papers largely in Quart. Jl Roy. Met. Soc. *Address:* Ivy Corner, Corfe, Taunton, Somerset. *T:* Blagdon Hill 612.

SAWYERR, Rev. Prof. Canon Harry Alphonso Ebun, CBE 1963 (MBE 1954); Grand Commander, Order of the Star of Africa (Liberia), 1971; Tutor, since 1974, and Vice-Principal, since 1975, Codrington College; Visiting Lecturer on West African Indigenous Religious Thought Forms, United Theological College of the West Indies, Kingston, Jamaica, and St John's Vianney, Roman Catholic Seminary, Tunapuna, Trinidad, since 1975; *b* 16 Oct. 1909; *s* of Rev. Obrien Alphonso Dandeson Sawyerr and Mrs Cleopatra Florence Omodele Sawyerr; *m* 1935, Edith Kehinde Lavinia Edwin; one *d. Educ:* Prince of Wales Sch.; Fourah Bay Coll.; St John's Coll., Durham. BA 1933; MA 1936; MEd 1940. Fourah Bay Coll.: Tutor 1933-45; Lectr 1948-52; Chaplain 1948-56; Sen. Lectr 1952-62; Vice-Principal 1956-58 and 1964-68; Prof. of Theology, 1962-74; Principal, 1968-74; Vice-Chancellor, Univ. of Sierra Leone, 1970-72 (Pro-Vice-Chancellor, 1968-70). Sec., Theological Advisers Board, Province of W Africa, 1952-58; Member: World Council of Churches Commn on Faith and Order, 1962-75; Permanent Cttee, Assoc. Internationale pour Etude des Religions Préhistoriques et Ethnologiques, 1976-. Select Preacher, UC Ibadan, 1961; Chm., Board of Teacher Trng, 1960-63; Pres.,

Milton Margai Trng (now Teachers) Coll., 1960-69; Leader, Sierra Leone Delegn to 3rd Commonwealth Educn Conf., 1964; Mem., Public Service Commn, 1968-69. Editor: Aureol Pamphlets, 1957-74; Sierra Leone Bulletin of Religion, 1962-68; Select Preacher: Fourah Bay Coll., UC Sierra Leone, 1964; Service of Re-interment of Bishop Adjayi Crowther (*ob* 1891), Christ Church Cathedral, Lagos, 1971; Univ. of Ghana, 1974; Service commemorating 150th Anniversary of Landing of 1st Bishop of Barbados, William Hart Coleridge, DD, St Michael's Cath., Barbados, 1975; Lectr, Provincial Clergy Sch., Church of the Province of WI, 1975; Leader of week of prayer for Christian Unity, Trinidad and Tobago, 1975; Conductor of Clergy Retreat, Diocese of Trinidad and Tobago, 1976, 1977. 1st Prize, Thomas Cochrane Essay Comp., 1960. Sierra Leone Independence Medal, 1961. Hon. DD Durham, 1970. *Publications:* Creative Evangelism, 1968; (with W. T. Harris) The Springs of Mende Belief and Conduct, 1968; God: Ancestor or Creator?, 1970; (contrib.) Biblical Revelation and Traditional Beliefs (ed K. Dickson and P. Ellingworth), 1969; (contrib.) Religion in a Pluralist Society (ed J. Pobee), 1976; articles in Scottish Jl of Theology, Church Quarterly, East Asia Jl of Theology, Internat. Review of Missions, Numen, Sierra Leone Bulletin of Religion, W African Jl of Educn, African Theological Jl, Caribbean Jl of Religious Studies; Caribbean Jl of African Studies. *Recreations:* motor driving, walking, gardening. *Address:* Codrington College, St John, Barbados, WI. *T:* 31330.

SAXTON, John Arthur, CBE 1973; DSc, PhD, CEng, FIEE, FInstP; Consultant, Radio Technology Department, Home Office, since 1977; Director, Appleton Laboratory (formerly Radio and Space Research Station), Science Research Council, 1966-77; Visiting Professor of Physics, University College, London, since 1968; *b* 28 June 1914; *s* of late H. and L. E. Saxton; *m* 1939, Kathleen Florence Crook, BA, JP, *d* of late Alfred H. Crook, OBE, MA; one *s* one *d. Educ:* Loughborough Grammar School; Imperial Coll., London Univ. (Royal Sch.). 1st Class Hons Phys 1935; Imperial Coll., Governors' Prize for Physics, 1935. Demonstrator Physics Dept, Imperial Coll., 1936-38; Mem. Scientific Staff, DSIR, at Nat. Phys. Laboratory, 1938-52, and at Radio Research Station, 1952-64; Dep. Dir Radio Research Station, 1960-64; Director, United Kingdom Scientific Mission, Washington, DC, USA, and Scientific Counsellor at the British Embassy there, 1964-66. Admin. Staff Coll., Henley-on-Thames, 1955; Special Lectr, Imperial Coll., 1948-58; Vis. Prof. of Elec. Engrg, Univ. Texas, 1961-62. Mem. Council, Instn of Elec. Engrs, 1949-52, 1962-64, 1966-71; Chm., Elec. Div. Bd, IEE, 1969-70. Delegate to several confs of Internat. Radio Consultative Cttee and Internat. Scientific Radio Union, 1953-; Chairman: URSI Commn II, 1966-69; CCIR Study Gp 5, 1970-. *Publications:* numerous papers in scientific jls on radio wave propagation and dielectric studies. *Address:* 106 Teddington Park Road, Teddington, Middlesex TW11 8NE. *Club:* Athenæum.

SAY, Rt. Rev. Richard David; *see* Rochester, Bishop of.

SAYCE, Roy Beavan, FRICS; Chief Surveyor, Land Service, Agricultural Development and Advisory Service, Ministry of Agriculture, Fisheries and Food, since 1977; *b* 19 July 1920; *s* of Roger Sayce, BScAgric, NDA, and Lilian Irene Sayce; *m* 1949, Barbara Sarah (*née* Leverton); two *s. Educ:* Culford; Royal Agricultural Coll. (MRAC). FRICS 1949. Univ. of London, 1938-40. Served War, Intell., RAFVR, 1940-46. Agricultural Land Service: Asst Land Comr, Chelmsford, 1949-50; Sen. Asst Land Comr, Norwich, 1950-63; Divl Land Comr, Oxford, 1963-71; Reg. Surveyor, Land Service, Agric. Develt and Adv. Service, Bristol, 1971-76. Royal Instn of Chartered Surveyors: Mem., Gen. and Divl Councils, (various times) 1970-; Divl Pres., Land Agency and Agriculture Div., 1973-74. Governor, Royal Agric. Coll., Cirencester, 1975- (Silver Medal, 1948). FRSA 1975. *Publications:* Farm Buildings, 1966; (contrib.) Walmsley's Rural Estate Management, 1969; contrib. professional jls. *Recreations:* golf, non-professional writing. *Address:* 13 Haywards Close, Wantage, Oxon OX12 7AT. *T:* Wantage 4836. *Clubs:* Farmers', Civil Service.

SAYE AND SELE, 21st Baron *cr* 1447 and 1603; **Nathaniel Thomas Allen Fiennes;** *b* 22 September 1920; *s* of Ivo Murray Twisleton-Wykeham-Fiennes, 20th Baron Saye and Sele, OBE, MC, and Hersey Cecilia Hester, *d* of late Captain Sir Thomas Dacres Butler, KCVO; *S* father, 1968; *m* 1958, Mariette Helena, *d* of Maj.-Gen. Sir Guy Salisbury-Jones, *qv*; three *s* one *d* (and one *s* decd). *Educ:* Eton; New College, Oxford. Served with Rifle Brigade, 1941-49 (despatches twice). Chartered Surveyor. Partner in firm of Laws and Fiennes. *Heir: s* Hon. Richard Ingel Fiennes, *b* 19 August 1959. *Address:* Broughton Castle, Banbury, Oxon. *T:* Banbury 2624.

See also Very Rev. Hon. O. W. Fiennes.

SAYEED, Dr Abul Fatah Akram, OBE 1976; President, Standing Conference of Asian Organizations in UK; General Secretary, Overseas Doctors Association in UK; General Medical Practitioner; *b* Bangladesh, 23 Nov. 1935; *s* of late Mokhles Ahmed, school teacher; registered British; *m* 1959, Hosne-ara Ali, *d* of M. S. Ali; two *s* one *d. Educ:* St Joseph's Sch., Khulna; Dacca Univ. MB, BS 1958. Editor, Dacca Med. Coll. Jl and Magazines, 1957-58; Lit. Sec., Students Union. Went to USA, 1960; resident in Britain from 1961. Mem. Staff, Leicester Royal Infirmary. Co-founder, Nat. Fedn of Pakistani Assocs in Gt Britain, 1962; Adviser, Nat. Cttee for Commonwealth Immigrants, 1965-68; Founder Member: Leicester Council for Community Relations, 1965; British-Bangladesh Soc.; Mem., Community Relations Commn, 1968-77; Chm., Standing Conference of Asian Orgs in UK, 1973-77 (Vice-Chm., 1970-73); Life Mem., Pakistan Soc. Mem., BBC Asian Programme Adv. Cttee. Special interest in problems of Asians; Gen. Sec., Overseas Doctors Assoc., 1975-; has done much work with disaster funds, etc. *Recreations:* gardening, photography, stamp collecting. *Address:* Ramna, 2 Mickleton Drive, Leicester LE5 6GD. *T:* Leicester 416703. *Club:* National Liberal (non-political member).

SAYER, Vice-Adm. Sir Guy (Bourchier), KBE 1959; CB 1956; DSC 1943; retired as Flag Officer Commanding Reserve Fleet (1958-59); *b* 2 January 1903; 3rd *s* of late William Feetham and late Edith Alexandra Sayer, E Finchley, London, N; *m* 1925, Sylvia Rosalind Pleadwell, *d* of late Maj.-Gen. R. C. Munday, CB, RAF, and late Mrs Olive Munday, Hartley, Plymouth, Devon; twin *s. Educ:* Cholmeley House, Highgate; RN Colleges Osborne and Dartmouth. Naval Cadet, 1916; Midshipman, 1920; Sub-Lieut, 1923; Lieut-Comdr, 1933; Comdr Dec. 1937; Capt. 1944; Rear-Adm., 1953. Vice-Controller of the Navy and Director of Naval Equipment, Admiralty, 1953-56; Flag Officer, Home Fleet Training Squadron, 1956-57; Vice-Adm. 1957; retired, 1959. *Publication:* The History of HMS Vernon, 1929. *Recreations:* estate maintenance, walking. *Address:* Old Middle Cator, Widecombe-in-the-Moor, Devon. *T:* Widecombe 228.

SAYER, Guy Mowbray, JP; Chairman: Hongkong & Shanghai Banking Corporation, 1972-77; Mercantile Bank Ltd, 1973-77; Hongkong Bank of California, San Francisco, 1972-77; Director: Mercantile Credits Ltd, Sydney, 1971-77; International Commercial Bank Ltd, London, 1969-77; *b* 18 June 1924; yr *s* of late Geoffrey Robley and Winifred Lily Sayer; *m* 1951, Marie Anne Sophie, *o d* of late Henri-Marie and Elisabeth Mertens; one *s* two *d. Educ:* Mill Mead Prep. Sch.; Shrewsbury School. FIB 1971. Royal Navy, 1942-46. Joined Honkong & Shanghai Banking Corp., 1946; service in London, China, Japan, Malaysia, Burma and Hong Kong; Gen. Man. 1969; Exec. Dir 1970; Dep. Chm. 1971. Treas., Hong Kong Univ., 1972-77. Mem., Exchange Fund Adv. Cttee, Hong Kong, 1971-77. MLC, 1973-74, MEC, 1974-77, Hong Kong. JP Hong Kong, 1971. *Recreations:* golf, walking. *Address:* 65 Cadogan Square, SW1. *T:* 01-235 2586. *Clubs:* MCC; Hong Kong, Shek O Country (Hong Kong).

SAYERS, Sir Edward (George), Kt 1965; CMG 1956; MD, Hon. DSc, FRCP, FRACP, Hon. FACP, Hon. FRCPE, FRS (NZ); DTM&H; Formerly Dean of the Medical Faculty and Professor of Therapeutics, University of Otago, New Zealand, 1959-67; *b* 10 Sept. 1902; *s* of Henry Hind Sayers; *m* 1st, 1928, Jane Lumsden, *d* of Wm Grove, MD; two *s* four *d*; 2nd, Patricia Dorothy, *d* of Gordon Coleman. *Educ:* Christ's College, Christchurch; Otago University; Otago Medical School, 1920-24; MB, ChB (NZ), 1924. House Physician, Wellington Hospital, 1925; Student and House Physician, London Sch. of Tropical Medicine, DTM&H 1926; Medical Missionary, British Solomon Is, 1927-34; MRCP 1935. Consulting Physician, Auckland (NZ), 1935-39; FRACP 1938. Served War of 1939-45, Middle East and Pacific, 1939-44; OC Medical Div. 1st NZ Gen. Hosp., Egypt and Greece; Cons. Physician NZ Forces in Pacific; OC 4 New Zealand Gen. Hosp. (Colonel); Cons. Physician, Auckland, NZ, 1945-59; Pres. RACP, 1956-58. Chm. NZ Med. Council, 1956-64; Mem. NZ Med. Research Council, 1959-67; Chm., Scientific Cttee, Nat. Heart Foundn of NZ, 1968-. Col Comdt, Royal NZMC, 1963-67. Pres., NZ Branch, BMA, 1963; Fellow Christ's College (NZ); Mem. Council, Univ. of Otago, 1959-67. FRCP 1949; Hon. FACP, 1957; Hon. FRCPE, 1960; FRS (NZ), 1961; Hon. DSc Otago, 1975. Cilento Medal for distinguished work in Pacific, 1940. Legion of Merit (USA), 1944, KStJ. *Publications:* articles in med. jls. *Recreation:* fishing. *Address:* 27A Henry Street, Maori Hill, Dunedin, New Zealand. *Club:* Fernhill (Dunedin).

SAYERS, Eric Colin, FCA; Chairman, Duport Ltd, since 1973; *b* 20 Sept. 1916; *s* of Alfred William and Emily Clara Sayers; *m* 1940, Winifred Bristow; two *d. Educ:* Acton County Grammar School. JDipMA, FBIM. Joined Duport Ltd, 1956; Director, 1962; Managing Director, 1966-75. Director: Ductile Steels Ltd, 1973-; International Timber Corp. Ltd, 1977-. Part-time Member, Midlands Electricity Board, 1973-; Member: Council of CBI (Chm. Energy Policy Cttee, 1975-); Government's Advisory Council on Energy Conservation, 1977-; Energy Commn, 1977-; Birmingham Cttee of Inst. of Directors, 1974-. Pres., Birmingham and W Midlands Soc. of Chartered Accountants, 1971-72; Inst. of Chartered Accountants in England and Wales: Council Member, 1966-; Vice-Pres., 1976; Dep. Pres., 1977. Treas., Univ. of Aston in Birmingham, 1976-. *Recreations:* golf, fishing, winemaking. *Address:* 73 Silhill Hall Road, Solihull, West Midlands B91 1JT. *T:* 021-705 3973. *Club:* Junior Carlton.

SAYERS, Prof. James, MSc, PhD Cantab; Professor of Electron Physics, University of Birmingham, 1946-72; *b* 2 Sept. 1912; *s* of late J. Sayers; *m* 1943, Diana Ailsa Joan Montgomery; two *s* one *d. Educ:* Ballymena Academy; University of Belfast; St John's College, Cambridge. Fellow of St John's College, Cambridge, 1941-46. Research for Admiralty in Univ. of Birmingham, 1939-43, on micro-wave radar; Member of British Group of Atomic Scientists transferred to work on the US Manhattan Project, 1943-45. Award by the Royal Commission on Awards to Inventors, 1949. British delegate to Internat. Scientific Radio Union, Zürich, 1950. Life Fellow, Franklin Inst. of State of Pennsylvania. John Price Wetherill Medallist, for discovery in Physical Science, 1958. *Publications:* papers in Proc. Royal Soc., Proc. Phys. Soc., and in the reports of various Internat. Scientific Conferences, on Upper Atmosphere Physics and the Physics of Ionized Gases. *Recreations:* tennis, cine-photography. *Address:* 3 Ballyweaney Road, Corkey, Ballymena, Co. Antrim, Northern Ireland. *T:* Loughgiel 232.

SAYERS, (Matthew Herbert) Patrick, OBE 1945; Major-General late RAMC (retired); MD; FRCPath; formerly Consulting Pathologist, Employment Medical Advisory Service, Department of Employment and Health and Safety Executive, 1967-75; Hon. Physician to HM The Queen, 1965-67; Director of Army Pathology and Consulting Pathologist to the Army, 1964-67; *b* 17 Jan. 1908; *s* of late Herbert John Ireland Sayers, Musician, and late Julia Alice Sayers (*née* Tabb); *m* 1935, Moira, *d* of Robert Dougall; two *s* one *d. Educ:* Whitgift School; St Thomas' Hospital, London. MRCS, LRCP 1932; MB, BS London 1933; MD London 1961; FCPath 1964. Commissioned Lieutenant RAMC, 1935; served India and Far East, 1936-46: Asst Dir of Pathology, HQ 14th Army, 1942-44; Dep. Dir of Pathology, Allied Land Forces, SE Asia, 1945. Asst Dir-Gen., War Office, 1948; OC The David Bruce Laboratories, 1949-52 and 1955-61; Asst Dir of Pathology, Middle East Land Forces, 1953-55; Editor, Journal RAMC, 1955-61; Dep. Dir of Pathology, Far East Land Forces, 1961-64. CStJ 1968. *Publications:* contribs to scientific jls on scrub typhus, immunology and industrial-medicine. *Recreations:* gardening, music, cricket, field sports. *Address:* High Trees, Walmer, Kent. *T:* Deal 63526. *Clubs:* Army and Navy; MCC.

SAYERS, Richard Sidney, FBA 1957; Emeritus Professor of Economics with special reference to Money and Banking, University of London (Cassel Professor of Economics, 1947-68); *b* 1908; *s* of S. J. Sayers; *m* 1930, Millicent Hodson; one *s* one *d. Educ:* St Catharine's Coll., Cambridge. Asst Lectr in Economics, London Sch. of Economics, 1931-35; Lectr in Economics, Exeter, Corpus Christi and Pembroke Colleges, Oxford, 1935-45; Fellow of Pembroke College, Oxford, 1939-45; Ministry of Supply, 1940-45; Economic Adviser, Cabinet Office, 1945-47. Member: Radcliffe Committee on the Working of the Monetary System, 1957-59; OECD Cttee on Fiscal Measures, 1966-68; Monopolies Commission, 1968. Pres. Section F, Brit. Assoc., 1960; Vice-Pres., Brit. Academy, 1966-67; Pres., Economic Hist. Soc., 1972-74; Vice-Pres., Royal Econ. Soc., 1973-. Hon. Fellow: St Catharine's Coll., Cambridge; LSE; Inst. of Bankers. Hon. DLitt Warwick, 1967; Hon. DCL Kent, 1967. *Publications:* Bank of England Operations, 1890-1914, 1936; Modern Banking, 1938 (7th edn 1967); American Banking System, 1948; (ed) Banking in the British Commonwealth, 1952; (jt editor with T. S. Ashton) Papers in English Monetary History, 1953; Financial Policy, 1939-45, 1956; Central Banking after Bagehot, 1957; Lloyds Bank in the History of English Banking, 1957; (ed) Banking in Western Europe, 1962; (ed) Economic Writings of James Pennington, 1963; A History of Economic Change in England, 1880-1939, 1967; Gilletts in the London Money Market, 1867-1967, 1968; The Bank of England 1891-1944, 1976.

SAYLES, Prof. George Osborne, LittD, DLitt; FBA 1962; MRIA; *b* 20 April 1901; *s* of Rev. L. P. Sayles and Margaret Brown, Glasgow; *m* 1936, Agnes, *d* of George Sutherland,

Glasgow; one s one d. Educ: Ilkeston Grammar Sch.; Glasgow Univ.; University Coll., London. Open Bursar, Ewing Gold Medallist, First Cl. Hons History, Glasgow Univ., 1923; Carnegie Res. Schol., University Coll., London, 1923-24. Asst. 1924, Lectr, 1925 and Sen. Lectr, 1934-45, in History, Glasgow Univ.; Leverhulme Res. Fellow, 1939; Professor of Modern History in the Queen's University, Belfast, 1945-53; Burnett-Fletcher Professor of History in the Univ. of Aberdeen, 1953-62; first Kenan Prof. of History, New York Univ., 1967; Vis. Prof., Louvain Univ., Belgium, 1951; Woodward Lectr, Yale Univ., USA, 1952; Fellow, Folger Library, Washington, 1960-61. Vis. Mem., Inst. for Advanced Study, Princeton, NJ, 1969. Hon. LittD Trinity Coll. Dublin. James Barr Ames Medal, Fac. of Law, Harvard Univ., 1958. Vice-Pres., Selden Soc., London, 1953. Chm. Advisory Cttee, Official War History of Northern Ireland, 1949; Member: Commission Internationale pour l'Histoire des Assemblées d'Etats; Advisory Historical Committee, Official Histories of War (Gt Brit.), 1950; Irish Manuscripts Commn, Dublin, 1949; Scottish Cttee on History of Scottish Parliament, 1937; Council of Stair Soc. (Scotland). Intelligence Officer (voluntary) to District Commissioner for Civil Defence SW Scotland, 1939-44; HG Glasgow, 12th Bn 1940. Publications: Author, Editor or Joint Editor (with H. G. Richardson) of: The Early Statutes, 1934; Rotuli Parliamentorum Anglie Hactenus Inediti, 1935; Select Cases in Court of King's Bench: under Edward I (3 vols), 1936-39; Edward II (1 vol.), 1956; Edward III (2 vols), 1958, 1965; Richard II, Henry IV, Henry V (1 vol.), 1972; Select Cases in Procedure without Writ, 1943; Parliaments and Councils of Medieval Ireland, 1947; Medieval Foundations of England, 1948, 3rd edn 1964, American edn, 1950; Irish Parliament in the Middle Ages, 1952, 2nd edn 1964; The Irish Parliament in 1782, 1954; Fleta, vol I, 1955, vol II, 1972; Parliaments and Great Councils in Medieval England, 1961; Governance of Medieval England, 1963; The Administration of Ireland, 1172-1377, 1964; Law and Legislation in Medieval England, 1966; The King's Parliament of England, 1974; articles and Reviews in Eng. Hist. Review, Scot. Hist. Review, Law Quarterly Review, Proc. RIA, etc. Recreations: travel, motoring. Address: Warren Hill, Crowborough, East Sussex. T: 61439.

SCADDING, John Guyett, MD (London), FRCP; Emeritus Professor of Medicine in the University of London; Hon. Consulting Physician, Brompton and Hammersmith Hospitals; b 30 August 1907; e s of late John William Scadding and Jessima Alice Guyett; m 1940, Mabel Pennington; one s two d. Educ: Mercers' School; Middlesex Hospital Medical School, University of London. MRCS, LRCP, 1929; MB, BS (London), 1930. Resident appts, Middx Hosp., Connaught Hosp., Walthamstow, and Brompton Hosp., 1930-35; MRCP 1932; MD (London, Univ. gold medal), 1932; First Asst, Dept of Med., Brit. Postgrad. Med. Sch., 1935; FRCP 1941; RAMC 1940-45 (Lt-Col, O i/c Med. Div.); Phys., Hammersmith Hosp., Postgrad. Med. Sch. of London, 1946-72; Physician, Brompton Hosp., 1939-72; Inst. of Diseases of the Chest: Dean, 1946-60; Dir of Studies, 1950-62; Prof. of Medicine, 1962-72; Hon. Cons. in Diseases of the Chest to the Army at Home, 1953-72 (Guthrie Medal, 1973). Visiting Professor: Univ. Oklahoma, 1963; Stanford Univ. and Univ. Colorado, 1965; McMaster Univ., 1973; Univ. Manitoba, 1974; Univ. Chicago, 1976; Dalhousie Univ., 1977. Mem. Central Health Services Council, and Standing Medical Advisory Cttee, 1954-66; Mem. Clinical Research Board, 1960-65. Royal College of Physicians: Bradshaw Lectr, 1949; Mitchell Lectr, 1960; Tudor Edwards Lectr, 1970; Lumleian Lectr, 1973; Councillor, 1949-52; Censor, 1968-70; Second Vice-Pres., 1971-72; Moxon Medal, 1975; Lettsomian Lectr, Med. Soc. of London, 1955. Editor, Thorax, 1946-59. President: British Tuberculosis Assoc., 1959-61; Section of Medicine, RSM, 1969-71; Thoracic Soc., 1971-72. Publications: Sarcoidosis, 1967; contributions to textbooks and articles, mainly on respiratory diseases, in medical journals. Recreations: music, pottering about. Address: 5 Astor Close, Kingston Hill, Kingston upon Thames, Surrey KT2 7LT. T: 01-546 7648. Club: Athenæum.

SCANLON, Hugh Parr; President, Amalgamated Union of Engineering Workers, 1968-Oct. 1978; Member: TUC General Council, since 1968; TUC Economic Committee, since 1968; Member, British Gas Corporation, since 1976; b 26 Oct. 1913; m 1943, Nora; two d. Educ: Stretford Elem. Sch.; NCLC. Apprentice, Instrument Maker, Shop Steward-Convener, AEI, Trafford Park; Divisional Organiser, AEU, Manchester, 1947-63; Member: Exec. Council, AEU, London, 1963-67; NEDC, 1971-; Metrication Bd, 1973-; NEB, 1977-; Chm., Engineering Industry Training Bd, 1975-. Vice-Pres., Internat. Metalworkers' Fedn; Pres., European Metal Workers' Fedn, 1974-. Recreations: golf, swimming, gardening. Address: 30 Crown Woods Way, Eltham, SE9. Club: Eltham Warren Golf.

SCANNELL, Vernon, FRSL; free-lance author, poet and broadcaster, since 1962; b 23 Jan. 1922. Educ: elementary schools; Leeds Univ. Served with Gordon Highlanders (51st Highland Div.), ME and Normandy, 1940-45; Leeds Univ. (reading Eng. Lit.), 1946-47; various jobs incl. English Master at Hazelwood Prep. Sch., 1955-62. Southern Arts Assoc. Writing Fellowship, 1975-76. FRSL 1960. Publications: novels: The Fight, 1953; The Wound and the Scar, 1953; The Big Chance, 1960; The Face of the Enemy, 1961; The Shadowed Place, 1961; The Dividing Night, 1962; The Big Time, 1965; The Dangerous Ones, 1970; poetry: The Masks of Love, 1960 (Heinemann Award, 1960); A Sense of Danger, 1962; (ed, with Ted Hughes and Patricia Beer) New Poems: a PEN anthology, 1962; Walking Wounded: poems 1962-65, 1968; Epithets of War: poems 1965-69, 1969; Mastering the Craft (Poets Today Series), 1970; (with J. Silkin) Pergamon Poets, No 8, 1970; Selected Poems, 1971; The Winter Man: new poems, 1973; The Apple Raid and other poems, 1974 (Cholmondeley Poetry Prize, 1974); The Loving Game, 1975 (also in paperback); Not Without Glory: poets of World War II, 1976; autobiography: The Tiger and the Rose, 1971; A Proper Gentleman, 1977. Recreations: listening to radio (mainly music), drink, boxing (as a spectator), films, reading. Address: 5 Holly Street, Rhydyfelin, Pontypridd, Glamorgan CF37 5DB. T: Pontypridd 406237.

SCARASCIA-MUGNOZZA, Carlo; Vice-President, Commission of the European Communities, 1972-77; b Rome, 19 Jan. 1920. Mem., Italian Chamber of Deputies, for Lecce-Brindisi-Taranto, 1953; Vice-Pres., Christian Democrat Parly Gp, 1958-62; Leader, Italian Delegn to UNESCO, 1962; Secretary of State: for Educn, 1962-63; for Justice, June 1963-Dec. 1963; Mem., European Parliament, 1961, Chm., Political Cttee, 1971-72.

SCARBOROUGH, Prof. Harold, CBE 1976; b 27 March 1909; British; unmarried. Educ: Bridlington School, Yorks; Edinburgh University; St Mary's Hospital Medical School; Harvard University. Clinical Tutor, Royal Infirmary of Edinburgh and Assistant, Dept of Therapeutics, Edinburgh Univ., 1933-38; Beit Memorial Research Fellow and Demonstrator in Pharmacology, Edinburgh Univ., 1938-39; Beit Memorial Research Fellow, Medical Unit, St Mary's Hosp., London, 1945-47; Rockefeller Travelling Fellow at Harvard Medical School, 1947-48; Reader in Medicine, University of Birmingham, 1949-50; Prof. of Medicine in Welsh Nat. Sch. of Medicine, Univ. of Wales, 1950-70; formerly: Dir, Med. Unit, Cardiff Royal Infirmary; Chm., Div. of Medicine, United Cardiff Hosps; Prof. of Medicine and Dean of the Faculty of Medicine, Ahmadu Bello Univ., Zaria, Nigeria, 1970-76. Publications: (part author) Textbook of Physiology and Biochemistry, 1950; papers in BMJ, Lancet, Quart. Jl Med., and other medical and scientific journals. Recreations: gardening, the theatre. Address: Id-dwejra, Iklin Road, Naxxar Road, Malta. Club: Athenæum.

SCARBROUGH, 12th Earl of, cr 1690; **Richard Aldred Lumley,** DL; Viscount Lumley (Ire.), 1628; Baron Lumley, 1681; Viscount Lumley, 1690; b 5 Dec. 1932; o s of 11th Earl of Scarbrough, KG, PC, GCSI, GCIE, GCVO, and of Katharine Isobel, Dowager Countess of Scarbrough, DCVO, d of late R. F. McEwen; S father, 1969; m 1970, Lady Elizabeth Ramsay, d of Earl of Dalhousie, qv; one s. Educ: Eton; Magdalen College, Oxford. 2nd Lt 11th Hussars, 1951-52; formerly Lt Queen's Own Yorkshire Dragoons. ADC to Governor and C-in-C, Cyprus, 1956. Hon. Col, 1st Bn The Yorkshire Volunteers, 1975-. DL S Yorks; Heir: s Viscount Lumley, qv. Address: Sandbeck Park, Maltby, Rotherham, S Yorks S66 8PF. T: Doncaster 742210. Clubs: White's, Pratt's; Jockey (Newmarket).

SCARFE, Prof. Francis Harold, CBE 1972 (OBE 1965); FRSL; author; Director, British Institute in Paris, 1959-Sept. 1978, and Professor of French in the University of London, 1965-Sept. 1978; b 18 September 1911; s of John James Scarfe and Margaret Ingham Dobson; m 1938, Margarete M. Geisler; one s. Educ: Universities of Durham, Cambridge and Paris. RAOC and RAEC, 1941-46; Lt-Col, 1945. Supervisor of Studies and Secretary, Extension Lectures Committee, University of Oxford, 1946-47; Senior Lecturer in French, University of Glasgow, 1947-59. Chevalier des Arts et Lettres. Prix de l'Ile St Louis, 1967. Publications: poetry: Inscapes, 1940; Poems and Ballads, 1941; Underworlds, 1950; criticism: Auden and After, 1942; W. H. Auden, 1949 (Monaco); The Art of Paul Valéry, 1954; La vie et l'œuvre de T. S. Eliot, 1964 (Paris); editions: Baudelaire, 1961; Chénier, 1961; André Chénier, his Life and Work, 1965; novels: Promises, 1950; Single Blessedness, 1951; Unfinished Woman, 1954; various translations. Address: 11 rue de Constantine, 75007 Paris, France. T: 555.71.99.

SCARFE, Gerald; artist; *b* 1 June 1936. *Educ:* scattered (due to chronic asthma as a child). Punch, 1960; Private Eye, 1961; Daily Mail, 1966; Sunday Times, 1967; cover artist to illustrator, Time Magazine, 1967; animation and film directing for BBC, 1969-. Has taken part in exhibitions: Grosvenor Gall., 1969 and 1970; Pavillon d'Humour, Montreal, 1967 and 1971; Expo '70, Osaka, 1970. One-man exhibitions of sculptures and lithographs: Waddell Gall., New York, 1968 and 1970; Grosvenor Gall., 1969; Vincent Price Gall., Chicago, 1969; National Portrait Gall., 1971. Animated film for BBC, Long Drawn Out Trip, 1973 (prizewinner, Zagreb). *Publications:* Gerald Scarfe's People, 1966; Indecent Exposure (ltd edn), 1973; Expletive Deleted: the life and times of Richard Nixon (ltd edn), 1974. *Recreations:* drawing, painting and sculpting. *Address:* 10 Cheyne Walk, SW3.

SCARLETT, family name of **Baron Abinger.**

SCARLETT, James Harvey Anglin; His Honour Judge Scarlett; a Circuit Judge, since 1974; *b* 27 Jan. 1924; *s* of Lt-Col James Alexander Scarlett, DSO, RA, and Muriel Scarlett, *d* of Walter Blease; unmarried. *Educ:* Shrewsbury Sch.; Christ Church, Oxford (MA). Barrister-at-law. Served War, Royal Artillery (Lieut), 1943-47. Called to the Bar, Inner Temple, 1950. A Recorder of the Crown Court, 1972-74. Malayan Civil Service, 1955-58. *Recreation:* fell walking. *Address:* 16 Eaton Road, Cressington Park, Liverpool L19 0PW. *T:* 051-427 1540. *Clubs:* Athenæum; Athenæum (Liverpool); Cumberland County (Carlisle).

SCARLETT, Hon. John Leopold Campbell, CBE 1973; Deputy to Health Service Commissioner, 1973-76; *b* 18 Dec. 1916; 2nd *s* of 7th Baron Abinger and Marjorie, 2nd *d* of John McPhillamy, Bathurst, NSW; *m* 1947, Bridget Valerie, *d* of late H. B. Crook; two *s* one *d*. *Educ:* Eton; Magdalene Coll., Cambridge (MA). Served War of 1939-45, France, Madagascar, Burma (despatches); 2nd Lieut 1940; Major 1944, RA. House Governor, London Hosp., 1962-72. *Address:* Bramblewood, Castle Walk, Wadhurst, Sussex TN5 6DB. *T:* Wadhurst 2642. *Club:* Royal Automobile.

SCARLETT, Sir Peter (William Shelley Yorke), KCMG 1958 (CMG 1949); KCVO 1955; *b* 30 March 1905; *s* of late William James Yorke Scarlett, Fyfield House, Andover; *m* 1934, Elisabeth, *d* of late Sir John Dearman Birchall, TD, MP, Cotswold Farm, Cirencester; one *s* three *d*. *Educ:* Eton; Christ Church, Oxford. Apptd to Foreign Office as a Third Secretary, 1929; Cairo, 1930; Bagdad, 1932; Lisbon, 1934; promoted a Second Secretary, 1934; acted as Chargé d'Affaires, Riga, 1937 and 1938. Attached to representative of Latvia at coronation of King George VI, 1937; Brussels, 1938; promoted actg First Sec., 1940; captured by enemy forces, 1940; returned to UK and resumed duties at Foreign Office, 1941; Paris, 1944; Allied Forces Headquarters, Caserta, 1946; Counsellor, Foreign Office, 1947; Inspector of HM Diplomatic Service Establishments, 1950; British Permanent Representative on the Council of Europe, Strasbourg, 1952; HM Ambassador to Norway, 1955; HM Minister to the Holy See, 1960-65, retired. Chairman, Cathedrals Advisory Committee, 1967-. *Address:* Rudhall, Ross-on-Wye, Herefordshire. *Club:* Junior Carlton.

SCARMAN, family name of **Baron Scarman.**

SCARMAN, Baron *cr* 1977 (Life Peer), of Quatt in the county of Salop; **Leslie George Scarman,** PC 1973; Kt 1961; OBE 1944; a Lord of Appeal in Ordinary, since 1977; *b* 29 July 1911; *s* of late George Charles and Ida Irene Scarman; *m* 1947, Ruth Clement Wright; one *s*. *Educ:* Radley College; Brasenose College, Oxford. Classical Scholar, Radley, 1925; Open Classical Scholar, Brasenose Coll., 1930; Hon. Mods 1st cl., 1932; Lit. Hum. 1st cl., 1934; Harmsworth Law Scholar, Middle Temple, 1936, Barrister, 1936; QC 1957. A Judge of the High Court of Justice, Probate, Divorce, and Admiralty Div., later Family Div., 1961-73; a Lord Justice of Appeal, 1973-77. Chairman: Law Commn, 1965-73; Council of Legal Educn, 1973-. Chm., Univ. of London Court, 1970, Dep. Chm., 1966-70; Chancellor, Univ. of Warwick, 1977-. Vice-Chm., Statute Law Cttee, 1967-. Pres., Senate of Inns of Court and Bar, 1976-77, 1977-78. Mem. Arts Council, 1968-70, 1972-73. Hon. Fellow: Brasenose College, Oxford, 1966; Imperial Coll., Univ. of London, 1975. Hon. LLD: Exeter, 1965; Glasgow, 1969; London, 1971; Keele, 1972; Freiburg, 1973; Warwick, 1974; Bristol, 1976; Manchester, 1977. RAFVR, 1940-45; Chm., Malcolm Clubs, RAF. Order of Battle Merit (Russia), 1945. *Publications:* Pattern of Law Reform, 1967; English Law—The New Dimension, 1975. *Recreations:* gardening, walking. *Address:* 12 Wellington Court, SW1X 7PL.

SCARR, John Geoffrey Fearnley; *b* 12 July 1910; 2nd *s* of late William Harcourt Scarr and Lydia (*née* Harrop); *m* 1945, Dorothy Edna Terry; two *d*. *Educ:* King's School, Ely; Trinity College, Cambridge (MA Hons, LLB). Called to the Bar, Lincoln's Inn, 1935; practised Northern Circuit and Lancashire Palatine Court. Served throughout War of 1939-45: Far East and War Office; major. Colonial Service; Resident Magistrate and Coroner, N Rhodesia, 1953; Chief Judicial Comr, Western Pacific High Commn Territories, 1959; Judge of the Supreme Court, Nassau and Bahamas, 1961-65; Acting Chief Justice on several occasions; Chancellor Dio. Nassau and the Bahamas, 1962-64; Deputy Chairman, Bahamas Constituencies Commn, 1964; Legal Staff of Law Commn, 1965-66, and of Foreign Compensation Commn, 1970-75. *Publications:* The Law and Practice of Land Registration, Northern Rhodesia Law Reports, 1949-54; contrib. to legal journals. *Recreations:* golf, music, sailing, painting. *Address:* Littlegate, Shiplake, Henley-on-Thames, Oxon. *T:* Wargrave 2201. *Club:* Royal Nassau Sailing.

SCARSDALE, 3rd Viscount *cr* 1911; **Francis John Nathaniel Curzon;** Bt (Scotland) 1636, (England) 1641; Baron Scarsdale 1761; late Captain, Scots Guards; *b* 28 July 1924; *o s* of late Hon. Francis Nathaniel Curzon, 3rd *s* of 4th Baron Scarsdale, and late Winifred Phyllis (*née* Combe); *S* cousin, 1977; *m* 1st, 1948, Solange (marr. diss. 1967, she *d* 1974), *yr d* of late Oscar Hanse, Belgium; two *s* one *d*; 2nd, 1968, Helene Gladys Frances, *o d* of late Maj. William Ferguson Thomson, Kinellar, Aberdeenshire; two *s*. *Educ:* Eton. *Recreations:* piping, photography. *Heir:* *s* Hon. Peter Ghislain Nathaniel Curzon, *b* 6 March 1949. *Address:* Weston Lodge, Kedleston, Derby. *T:* Derby 840665. *Club:* County (Derby).

SCATCHARD, Vice-Adm. John Percival, CB 1963; DSC 1941; first Bar, 1944; second Bar, 1945; *b* 5 Sept. 1910; *s* of Dr James P. Scatchard, MB, BS, Tadcaster, Yorks; *m* 1943, Edith Margaret Niven; one *d*. *Educ:* Aysgarth School, Yorkshire; RNC Dartmouth. Joined RN, 1924; served War of 1939-45, in HMS Kashmir-Garth and Termagent; Captain (D) Portsmouth, 1951-52; Captain 5th Destroyer Squadron, 1957-58; Director Naval Equipment, Admiralty, 1959-60; Commandant, Joint Services Staff College, Latimer, Bucks, 1960-62; Flag Officer, Second-in-Command, Far East Fleet, 1962-64; retd list, 1964. *Recreations:* riding, gardening, sailing. *Address:* Reachfar, Warsash, near Southampton, Hants.

SCERRI, Arthur J.; High Commissioner for Malta: in London since 1971; to Cyprus, since 1972; Ambassador to the USSR and to Iran, since 1972; *b* 31 Jan. 1921; *s* of Alfred and Carmen Lautier; *m* 1951, Ruby Howell, Wales; one *d*. *Educ:* St Albert's Coll.; St Mary's Coll.; HM Dockyard Technical College. Diplomas in Statistics, Work Study, English. Electrical Engr, HM Dockyard, Malta, 1937-50; Instrument Draughtsman in UK, 1950-71; Malta Rep. of Malta Labour Party in London, and London Corresp. of Voice of Malta, 1954-71. Took part in Integration Round Table Conf., 1956 and Independence Conf., 1963. *Publications:* various articles. *Recreations:* politics, reading, Maltese stamps. *Address:* 15 Upper Belgrave Street, SW1. *T:* 01-235 3931. *Clubs:* Travellers', Hurlingham, Royal Automobile.

SCHAEFFER, Prof. Claude Frederic Armand; Officier Légion d'Honneur, 1947; Hon. Professor, Collège de France; Member of French Academy; General Director of Archæological Expeditions of Ras Shamra Ugarit (Syria) and Enkomi Alasia (Cyprus); Member of National Council of Scientific Research; Member Higher Council of Archaeological Research, Ministry of Cultural Affairs; *b* Strasbourg, Alsace, 6 March 1898; *s* of Henri Schaeffer, industrialist, and Mme Schaeffer (*née* Wiernsberger); *m* 1924, Odile, *d* of Prof. Robert Forrer, archæologist and collector; one *s* two *d*. *Educ:* Univ. Strasbourg. Keeper: Archæological Museum, Strasbourg, 1924-33; Coin Cabinet, Univ. Strasbourg, 1926-33; Museum of Nat. Antiquities, Château de St-Germain-en-Laye, 1933-56; Fellow of St John's Coll., Oxford, 1941-45; Hon. Fellow, 1955-. Captain of Corvette, Free French Naval Forces, England, 1940-45. Director of Research, Nat. Centre of Scientific Research, 1946-54; Prof. of European Pre-history and Nat. Archæology, Ecole de Louvre, 1951-54. Vice-Pres., Commn des Fouilles et Missions Archéologiques, Min. of Foreign Affairs, 1952-69. Life Mem., Cttee of Honour, Internat. Union of Prehistoric and Protohistoric Sciences, 1964. Is Member or Hon. Mem. of a number of socs. DrLit *hc* Oxford, 1942; Dr of Law *hc* Glasgow, 1948; Gold Medal: Soc. of Antiquaries of London, 1958; Soc. of Sciences, Famagusta, 1965. Foreign Member, Royal Academy of Denmark. Hon. Citizen: Famagusta, 1970; Latakia, 1950. Holds other foreign awards. *Publications:* Les Haches néolithiques du Musée de Haguenau, 1924; Les Tertres funéraires préhistoriques dans la forêt de Haguenau, Vol. I, Les

Tumulus de l'Age du Bronze, 1926; Un Dépôt d'outils et un trésor de bronze de l'époque galloromaine, découverts à Seltz, 1927; Les Tertres funéraires préhistoriques dans la forêt de Haguenau, Vol. II, Les Tumulus de l'Age du Fer, 1930; Le Casque romain de Drusenheim, 1932; Missions en Chypre, 1936; The Cuneiform Texts of Ras Shamra-Ugarit, 1939; Ugaritica, I, 1939; Stratigraphie comparée et chronologie de l'Asie Occidentale, vol. I, 1948; Ugaritica, II, 1949; Enkomi-Alasia, I, 1952; Ugaritica, III, 1956; IV, 1962; V, 1968; VI, 1969; VII, 1978; Alasia, I, 1970; also very numerous contributions to learned journals, etc. *Recreations:* travel, exploration, mountains. *Address:* Le Castel Blanc, 16 rue Turgot, 78100 St Germain-en-Laye, France. *T:* 963.42.25; La Chaumière, Fréland, 68240 Kaysersberg, France; L'Escale, 83420 La Croix-Valmer, BP16, France. *T:* 79.62.14.

SCHAFFTER, Ernest Merill James; Secretary, Royal Aeronautical Society, since 1973 (Deputy Secretary, 1970-73); Director, Engineering Sciences Data Unit Ltd; *b* 1922; *er s* of late Dr Charles Merill Schaffter and of Bertha Grace Brownrigg, of the CMS in Isfahan, Iran; *m* 1951, Barbara Joy, *o c* of Alfred Bennett Wallis and Hilda Frances Hammond; three *d. Educ:* Trent Coll., Nottinghamshire; King's Coll., Cambridge. BA 1950, MA 1955. Served War: RAF, as Pilot with Coastal and Transport Command, Flt Lt, 1941-46. De Havilland Aircraft Co., Hatfield, as Aerodynamicist and Engr, 1950-54; Marshall's Flying Sch., Cambridge, as Engr, 1954-60; Marshall of Cambridge (Eng) Ltd, as Personal Asst to Chief Designer and later as Design Office Manager, 1960-70. MRAeS, AFCASI, AMBIM. *Address:* Royal Aeronautical Society, 4 Hamilton Place, W1V 0BQ. *T:* 01-499 3515; 43 Speldhurst Road, W4 1BX. *T:* 01-995 0708. *Club:* Royal Air Force.

SCHAPERA, Prof. Isaac, MA (Cape Town) 1925; PhD (London) 1929; DSc (London) 1939; FBA 1958; FRSSAf 1934; Emeritus Professor, University of London (London School of Economics), 1969; *b* Garies, South Africa, 23 June 1905; 3rd *s* of late Herman and Rose Schapera. *Educ:* S African Coll. Sch., Cape Town; Universities of Cape Town and London. Prof. of Social Anthropology, Univ. of Cape Town, 1935-50; Prof. of Anthropology, Univ. of London (LSE), 1950-69, now Emeritus; Hon. Fellow, 1974. Many anthropological field expeditions to Bechuanaland Protectorate, 1929-50. Chairman Association of Social Anthropologists of the British Commonwealth, 1954-57; President, Royal Anthropological Inst., 1961-63. Hon. DLitt Cape Town, 1975. *Publications:* The Khoisan Peoples of South Africa, 1930; A Handbook of Tswana Law and Custom, 1938; Married Life in an African Tribe, 1940; Native Land Tenure in the Bechuanaland Protectorate, 1943; Migrant Labour and Tribal Life, 1948; The Ethnic Composition of Tswana Tribes, 1952; The Tswana, 1953; Government and Politics in Tribal Societies, 1956; Praise Poems of Tswana Chiefs, 1965; Tribal Innovators, 1970; Rainmaking Rites of Tswana Tribes, 1971; Kinship Terminology in Jane Austen's Novels, 1977; Editor: Western Civilization and the Natives of South Africa, 1934; The Bantu-speaking Tribes of South Africa, 1937; David Livingstone's Journals and Letters, 1841-56 (6 vols), 1959-63; David Livingstone: South African Papers 1849-1853, 1974; contrib. to many learned journals. *Address:* 457 White House, Albany Street, NW1 3UP.

SCHAPIRO, Prof. Leonard Bertram, LLB; FBA 1971; Professor of Political Science, with Special Reference to Russian Studies, London School of Economics and Political Science, University of London, 1963-75; *b* Glasgow, 22 April 1908; *s* of Max Schapiro and Leah (*née* Levine); *m* 1st, 1943, Isabel Margaret (marr. diss. 1976), *d* of Don Salvador de Madariaga, *qv*; no *c*; *m* 2nd, 1976, Roma Thewes, *d* of late Dr C Sherris. *Educ:* St Paul's Sch.; University Coll., London. Fellow 1973. Called to Bar, Gray's Inn, 1932; practised at Bar, London and Western Circuit, 1932-39; BBC Monitoring Service, 1940-42; War Office, 1942-45; Intell. Div., German Control Commn, 1945-46 (Maj.); practised at Bar, 1946-55; Dept of Politics, LSE, 1955-. Chairman: Council, Inst. for Study of Conflict, 1970-; Member: Res. Bd, Inst. of Jewish Affairs; Council, Inst. for Religion and Communism. Chm., Editorial Board, Government and Opposition; Mem., Editorial Board: Soviet Survey; Soviet Jewish Affairs. For. Hon. Mem., Amer. Acad. of Arts and Sciences, 1967. *Publications:* The Origin of the Communist Autocracy, 1955; The Communist Party of the Soviet Union, 1960, 2nd edn 1970; The Government and Politics of Soviet Russia, 1965, 7th edn 1977; Rationalism and Nationalism in Russian Nineteenth Century Political Thought, 1967; trans. (with critical essay) Turgenev's Spring Torrents, 1972; Totalitarianism, 1972; numerous contribs to learned jls, symposia, Encyclopædia Britannica, etc. *Recreations:* music, travel, mediæval art. *Address:* 11 Lampard House, Maida Avenue, W2. *Club:* Reform.

SCHAPIRO, Meyer; University Professor, Columbia University, 1965-73, now Emeritus Professor; *b* Shavly, Lithuania, 23 Sept. 1904; *s* of Nathan Menahem Schapiro and Feige Edelman; *m* 1928, Dr Lillian Milgram; one *s* one *d. Educ:* Boys' High Sch., Brooklyn; Columbia University. PhD Columbia, 1929. Columbia University: Lectr, Dept of Art History and Archæology, 1928; Asst Prof., 1936; Assoc. Prof., 1948; Prof., 1952; University Prof., 1965. Visiting Lecturer: Institute of Fine Arts, NY University, 1931-36; New School for Social Research, NY, 1938-50; Vis. Prof.: Univ. of London, 1947, 1957; Univ. of Jerusalem, 1961; Messenger Lectr, Cornell Univ., 1960; Patten Lectr, Indiana Univ., 1961; Charles Eliot Norton Prof., Harvard Univ., 1966-67; Slade Prof. of Fine Art, Oxford Univ., 1968; Vis. Lectr, Collège de France, 1974. Guggenheim Fellow, 1939, 1943; Fellow: Amer. Acad. of Arts and Sciences, 1952; Inst. for Advanced Study in Behavioral Sciences, Palo Alto, 1962-63; Amer. Philosophical Soc., 1969; Mediaeval Acad., 1970; Amer. Inst. of Arts and Letters, 1976. Bd of Editors: Jl of History of Ideas; Semiotica; Dissent. Award for Distinction, Amer. Council of Learned Socs, 1960. *Publications:* The Romanesque Sculpture of Moissac, 1931; Van Gogh, 1950; Cézanne, 1952; The Parma Ildefonsus, 1964; Words and Pictures, 1973; Selected Papers, Vol I, Romanesque Art, 1976; articles in collective books and in Art Bulletin, Gazette des Beaux-Arts, Jl Warburg and Courtauld Insts, Jl History of Ideas, Jl Architectural Historians, Kritische Berichte, Amer. Jl Sociology, Partisan Review, Encounter, etc. *Address:* 279 West 4th Street, New York, NY 10014, USA.

SCHEEL, Walter; President of the Federal Republic of Germany, since 1974; *b* 8 July 1919; *m* 1969, Dr Mildred Scheel; one *s* two *d* (and one *s* of previous *m*). *Educ:* Reform Gymnasium, Solingen. Served in German Air Force, War of 1939-45. At one time head of market research organization. Mem. of Bundestag, 1953-74; Federal Minister for Economic Co-operation, 1961-Oct. 1966, Vice-President of Bundestag, 1967-69; Vice-Chancellor and Foreign Minister, 1969-74. Former Mem., Landtag North Rhine Westphalia. Chm., Free Democrats, 1968-74. *Publications:* Konturen einer neuen Welt, 1965; Reden und Interviews, 1973. *Address:* Haus des Bundespräsidenten, Bonn, German Federal Republic.

SCHERER, Prof. Jacques, DèsL; Marshal Foch Professor of French Literature, and Fellow of All Souls College, University of Oxford, since 1973; *b* 24 Feb. 1912; *s* of Maurice Scherer and Madeleine Franck; *m* 1965, Colette Bié. *Educ:* Ecole Normale Supérieure; Sorbonne Univ., Paris (Agrégé des Lettres, Docteur ès Lettres). Prof. of French Literature, Univ. of Nancy, 1946-54; Prof. of French Literature and Theatre, Sorbonne Univ., 1954-73. *Publications:* L'expression littéraire dans l'œuvre de Mallarmé, 1947; La dramaturgie classique en France, 1950; La dramaturgie de Beaumarchais, 1954; Le 'Livre' de Mallarmé, 1957; Structures de Tartuffe, 1966; Sur le Dom Juan de Molière, 1967; Le cardinal et l'orang-outang, essai sur Diderot, 1972; Théâtre du XVIIe siècle, 1975. *Address:* All Souls College, Oxford. *T:* Oxford 722251.

SCHERGER, Air Chief Marshal Sir Frederick (Rudolph Williams), KBE 1958 (CBE 1950); CB 1954; DSO 1944; AFC 1940; *b* 18 May 1904; *o s* of Frederick H. Scherger and Sarah (*née* Chamberlain), Ararat, Victoria, Australia; *m* 1929, Thelma Lilian Harricks (*d* 1974); one *d*; *m* 1975, Mrs J. Robertson. *Educ:* Ararat High School; Royal Military College, Australia. Grad. Dec. 1924; seconded to RAAF Jan. 1925; completed flying course, Dec. 1925. Various flying training and squadron appts, 1926-35; RAF Staff Coll. Course, 1935; RAF attachments, 1936; Director of Training, RAAF, 1937-40; AOC No. 10 Group, RAAF, 1943-44; AOC 1st TAF, RAAF, 1945-46; idc, 1946; Deputy Chief of Air Staff, RAAF, 1947-51; Head Australian Joint Services Staff, Washington, 1951-52; Air Officer Commanding, RAF, Malaya, 1953-54; Air Member for Personnel, RAAF, 1955-57; CAS, RAAF, 1957-61; Chairman, Chiefs of Staff, 1961-66. Chairman: Australian Nat. Airlines Commn, 1966-75; Commonwealth Aircraft Corp. Pty Ltd, 1968-74. *Recreations:* golf, shooting, motoring. *Address:* 45 Stephens Street, North Balwyn, Vic 3104, Australia. *Clubs:* Melbourne, Naval and Military (Melbourne).

SCHILD, Heinz Otto, FRS 1966; MD, PhD, DSc; FIBiol; Professor of Pharmacology, University of London, at University College, 1961-73, Emeritus Professor, 1973; *b* Fiume, 18 May 1906; *s* of Hermann Schild and Thekla (*née* Spiegel); *m* 1938, Mireille Madeleine Haquin; three *d. Educ:* Universities of Munich, Berlin and Edinburgh. MD Munich, 1931; PhD Edinburgh, 1935; DSc London, 1950. Assistant, Pharmacology Dept, Univ. of Edinburgh, 1936; Demonstrator, 1937, Lecturer, 1942, Reader, 1945, Dept of Pharmacology, University Coll., London; Dean, Faculty of Med. Sciences, University Coll., 1964-

67. Vis. Prof., NY State Univ., 1968. Mem., WHO Visiting Team of Medical Scientists to SE Asia, 1952. Examiner, Univs of Leeds, Liverpool, Oxford, Edinburgh, West Africa, West Indies, Makerere College. Schmiedeberg Plakette Deutsche Pharmak. Ges., 1977; Hon. Mem., British Pharmacol. Soc.; Sen. Mem., British Immunol. Soc.; Mem., Asthma Res. Council. *Publications:* (joint) Applied Pharmacology, 1975; papers in Journal of Physiology, British Journal of Pharmacology, Immunology, Lancet, Nature. *Recreation:* walking slowly. *Address:* Mole Ridge, St Mary's Road, Leatherhead, Surrey. *T:* Leatherhead 73773.

SCHILLER, Prof. Dr Karl; Member of Deutscher Bundestag, 1965-72; Professor of Political Economy, University of Hamburg, and Director of Institute for Foreign Trade and Overseas Economy, 1947-72; President, EDESA, since 1973; *b* 24 April 1911; *s* of Carl and Maria Schiller; *m*; one *s* three *d*. *Educ:* Univs of Kiel, Frankfurt, Berlin, Heidelberg. Research Asst, Institut für Weltwirtschaft, Kiel, 1935-39; Lectr, Univ. of Kiel, 1945-46; Rector, Univ. of Hamburg, 1956-58. Senator for Economic Affairs and Transportation, Hamburg, 1948-53; Mem., Bürgerschaft Hamburg, 1949-57; Senator for Economics, West Berlin, 1961-65; Federal Minister of Economics, 1966-71, of Economics and Finance, 1971-72. *Publications:* Sozialismus und Wettbewerb, 1955; Neueste Entwicklungen in der Theorie der Wirtschaftspolitik, 1958; Zur Wachstumsproblematik der Entwicklungsländer, 1960; Der Ökonom und die Gesellschaft, 1964; Reden zur Wirtschaft und Finanzpolitik (10 vols), 1966-72, etc. *Address:* 2 Hamburg 55, Kuulsbarg 26, West Germany.

SCHILLING, Prof. Richard Selwyn Francis, CBE 1975; MD (London); DSc (London); FRCP; FFCM; DPH; DIH; Professor of Occupational Health, London School of Hygiene and Tropical Medicine, University of London, 1960-76, now Emeritus; Director, TUC Centenary Institute of Occupational Health, 1968-76; *b* 9 Jan. 1911; *s* of late George Schilling and of Florence Louise Schilling, Kessingland, Suffolk; *m* 1937, Heather Maude Elinore Norman; one *s* two *d*. *Educ:* Epsom College; St Thomas' Hospital. Obstetric house physician, St Thomas' Hosp., 1935; house physician, Addenbrooke's Hosp., Cambridge, 1936; Asst Industrial MO, ICI (metals) Ltd, Birmingham, 1937; Medical Inspector of Factories, 1939-42. Served War of 1939-45, Captain RAMC, France and Belgium, 1939-40. Sec. Industrial Health Research Board of Med. Research Council, 1942-46; Nuffield Fellow in Industrial Health, 1946-47; Reader in Occupational Health, Univ. of Manchester, 1947-56; WHO Consultant, 1956-69. Lectures: Milroy, RCP, 1956; Mackenzie, BMA, 1956; Cantor, RSA, 1963; C.-E. A. Winslow, Yale Univ., 1963; Ernestine Henry, RCP, 1970. Former Vice-Pres., Perm. Commn, Internat. Assoc. Occupational Health. Former President: Assoc. of Industrial Medical Officers; British Occupational Hygiene Soc.; Occup. Med. Sect. of Roy. Soc. Med. Member: Committee of Inquiry into Trawler Safety, 1968; Royal Commn on Civil Liability and Compensation for Personal Injury, 1973-. Hon. FRSM 1976. FRSA 1964. *Publications:* (ed) Modern Trends in Occupational Health, 1960; (ed) Occupational Health Practice, 1973; original papers on Byssinosis (respiratory disease of textile workers) and other subjects in occupational health in BMJ, Lancet, Brit. Jl of Industrial Medicine, and foreign journals. *Recreations:* fishing, gardening, golf. *Address:* 46 Northchurch Road, N1. *T:* 01-254 4379.

SCHLESINGER, Arthur (Meier), Jr; writer; educator; Schweitzer Professor of the Humanities, City University of New York since 1966; *b* Columbus, Ohio, 15 Oct. 1917; *s* of late Arthur Meier and of Elizabeth Bancroft Schlesinger; *m* 1st, 1940, Marian Cannon (marr. diss. 1970); two *s* two *d*; 2nd, 1971, Alexandra Emmet; one *s*. *Educ:* Phillips Exeter Acad.; Harvard; Peterhouse, Cambridge. AB (Harvard), 1938; Henry Fellow, Peterhouse, Cambridge, 1938-39. Soc. of Fellows, Harvard, 1939-42; US Office of War Information, 1942-43; US Office of Strategic Services, 1943-45; US Army, 1945. Mem. Adlai Stevenson Campaign Staff, 1952, 1956. Professor of History, Harvard University, 1954-61 (Associate, 1946-54); Special Assistant to President Kennedy, 1961-63. Film Reviewer: Show, 1962-65; Vogue (US), 1966-70. Member of Jury, Cannes Film Festival, 1964. Holds Hon. Doctorates, 1950-. Mem. of numerous Socs and Instns. Pulitzer Prize: History, 1946; Biography, 1966; Nat. Inst. of Arts and Letters, Gold Medal for History, 1967. *Publications:* Orestes A. Brownson: a Pilgrim's Progress, 1939; The Age of Jackson, 1945; The Vital Center, 1949, (in UK) The Politics of Freedom, 1950; The General and the President (with R. H. Rovere), 1951; (co-editor) Harvard Guide to American History, 1954; The Age of Roosevelt: I: The Crisis of the Old Order, 1957; II: The Coming of the New Deal, 1958; III: The Politics of Upheaval, 1960; Kennedy or Nixon, 1960; The Politics of Hope, 1963; (ed

with Morton White) Paths of American Thought, 1963; A Thousand Days: John F. Kennedy in the White House, 1965; The Bitter Heritage, 1967; The Crisis of Confidence: ideas, power & violence in America, 1969; (ed with F. L. Israel) History of American Presidential Elections, 1971; The Imperial Presidency, 1973; (ed) History of US Political Parties, 1973; articles to magazines and newspapers. *Address:* (office) 33 W 42nd Street, New York City. *T:* 790-4261. *Clubs:* Century, Coffee House (New York), Federal City (Washington).

SCHLESINGER, Bernard, OBE 1946; MA, MD, FRCP; Consulting Physician to University College Hospital, Hospital for Sick Children, Great Ormond Street, and Royal Northern Hospital; originally Consulting Paediatrician to the Army; now retired; *b* 23 Nov. 1896; *s* of late Richard Schlesinger; *m* 1925, Winifred Henrietta, *d* of late H. Regensburg, London; two *s* one *d* (and two *d* decd). *Educ:* Uppingham; Emmanuel Coll., Cambridge. Served European War, 1914-18 as a Private, and in War of 1939-45, as Brigadier, Consulting Physician, NW Army and Central Command, India Command. Fell. of Assoc. of Physicians, Brit. Pædiatric Assoc. (Pres., 1953-54); Fell., Roy. Soc. of Med. (Pres., Pædiatric Sect, 1960-61). Milroy Lectr, 1938. Dawson Williams Prize, 1961. *Publications:* numerous articles and books on Diseases of Children and Researches on Rheumatism. *Recreations:* tennis, gardening. *Address:* Oliver's Cottage, Boxford, near Newbury, Berks. *T:* Boxford 206. *Club:* Anglo-Belgian.
See also J. R. Schlesinger.

SCHLESINGER, John Richard, CBE 1970; film director; Associate Director, National Theatre, since 1973; *b* 16 Feb. 1926; *s* of Bernard Schlesinger, qv. *Educ:* Uppingham; Balliol Coll., Oxford (BA). Directed: *films:* for Monitor and Tonight (BBC TV), 1958-60; Terminus, for British Transport Films, 1960; A Kind of Loving, 1961; Billy Liar, 1962-63; Darling, 1964-65; Far from the Madding Crowd, 1966-67; Midnight Cowboy, 1968-69; Sunday, Bloody Sunday, 1971; contrib. Visions of Eight, 1973; Day of the Locust, 1973; Marathon Man, 1975-76; *plays:* Timon of Athens, and Days in the Trees, for RSC, 1964-66; I and Albert, Piccadilly, 1972; Heartbreak House, 1975, and Julius Caesar, 1977, for Nat. Theatre. Soc. of TV and Film Academy Award for Best Director, also Director's Guild of America Award and an American Oscar, for Midnight Cowboy; Golden Lion Award, Venice Film Festival 1961, for Terminus; Golden Bear Award, Berlin Film Festival 1962, for A Kind of Loving; New York Critics Award, for Darling; Soc. of TV and Film Academy Award for Best Director and David di Donatello Award, for Sunday, Bloody Sunday, 1972. *Recreations:* gardening, travel, music, antiques. *Address:* c/o Michael Oliver, Berger Oliver & Co., 40 Piccadilly, W1. *T:* 01-734 7421.

SCHMIDT, Helmut H. W.; Chancellor, Federal Republic of Germany, since 1974; Member of Bundestag, 1953-62, and since 1965; *b* 23 Dec. 1918; *s* of Gustav L. and Ludovica Schmidt; *m* 1942, Hannelore Glaser; one *d*. *Educ:* Univ. of Hamburg. Diplom-Volkswirt, 1948. Manager of Transport Administration, State of Hamburg, 1949-53; Social Democratic Party: Member, 1946-; Chm., Parly Gp, 1967-69; Vice-Chm. of Party, 1968-; Senator (Minister) for Domestic Affairs in Hamburg, 1961-65; Minister of Defence, 1969-72; Minister of Finance and Econs, 1972; Minister of Finance, 1972-74. Hon LLD Newberry Coll., S Carolina, 1973. *Publications:* Defence or Retaliation, 1962; Beiträge, 1967; Balance of Power, 1971; Auf dem Fundament des Godesberger Programms, 1973; Bundestagsreden, 1975; Kontinuität und Konzentration, 1975; Als Christ in der politischen Entscheidung, 1976; (with Willy Brandt) Deutschland 1976-Zwei Sozialdemokraten im Gespräch, 1976. *Recreations:* sailing, chess, playing the organ. *Address:* Bundeskanzleramt, Adenauerallee 139, 53 Bonn 1, W Germany. *T:* 561.

SCHMOLLER, Hans Peter, RDI 1976; typographer; *b* 9 April 1916; *o c* of Dr Hans Schmoller and Marie (*née* Behrend); *m* 1st, 1947, Dorothée Wachsmuth (*d* 1948); one *d*; 2nd, 1950, Tatyana Kent; one *s*. *Educ:* Kaiser-Friedrich-Sch., Berlin-Charlottenburg. Left sch. soon after Hitler came to power, 1933; served apprenticeship as compositor, studying calligraphy and typography privately, 1933-37; Morija Printing Works, Morija, Basutoland (now Lesotho), 1938-46; Asst to Oliver Simon at Curwen Press, London, 1947-49; joined Penguin Books Ltd, as Typographer, 1949; Head of Production, 1956-76; Dir, 1960-76; Consultant, 1976-. Has served on book design juries in Britain and USA; lectured on typography in England and abroad; participated in internat. book design projects. Francis Minns Memorial Award, 1974. Gold medal, Internat. Book Design Exhibn, Leipzig, 1971. Corresp. Mem., Bund Deutscher Buchkünstler (Fed. Germany), 1965. *Publications:* Contributor to: Essays in The History of Publishing: Longman 1724-1974 (ed Asa Briggs); The Times, TLS, Penrose Annual, Signature, Imprimatur, Philobiblon; ed, The Work-Book of the Officina Bodoni of Giovanni Mardersteig (German edn), 1978. *Recreations:* collecting books and fine paper, peregrinating. *Address:* Steading, Down Place, Windsor, Berks SL4 5UG. *T:* Maidenhead 23565. *Clubs:* Arts; Double Crown (Pres. 1968-69).

SCHNEIDER, Dr William George, OC 1977; FRS 1962; FRSC 1951; President, National Research Council of Canada, Ottawa, since 1967; *b* Wolseley, Saskatchewan, 1 June 1915; *s* of Michael Schneider and Phillipina Schneider (*née* Kraushaar); *m* 1940, Jean Frances Purves; two *d. Educ:* University of Saskatchewan; McGill University; Harvard University. BSc 1937, MSc 1939, University of Saskatchewan; PhD (in physical chem.), 1941, McGill Univ. Research physicist at Woods Hole Oceanographic Inst., Woods Hole, Mass, USA, 1943-46 (US Navy Certificate of Merit, 1946). Joined Nat. Research Council, Division of Pure Chemistry, Ottawa, 1946; Vice-President (Scientific), 1965-67. Chemical Inst. of Canada Medal, 1961, Montreal Medal, 1973; Henry Marshall Tory Medal, RSC, 1969. Hon. DSc: York, 1966; Memorial, 1968; Saskatchewan, 1969; Moncton, 1969; McMaster, 1969; Laval, 1969; New Brunswick, 1970; Montreal, 1970; McGill, 1970; Acadia, 1976; Hon. LLD: Alberta, 1968; Laurentian, 1968. *Publications:* (with J. A. Pople and H. J. Bernstein) High Resolution Nuclear Magnetic Resonance, 1959; scientific papers in chemistry and physics research jls. *Recreations:* tennis, ski-ing. *Address:* National Research Council of Canada, Ottawa K1A 0R6, Canada. *T:* 993-2024.

SCHNEIDERHAN, Frau Wolfgang; *see* Seefried, Irmgard.

SCHNYDER, Félix; Ambassador of Switzerland to the United States, 1966-75; *b* 5 March 1910; Swiss; *s* of Maximilian Schnyder and Louise (*née* Steiner); *m* 1941, Sigrid Bucher; one *d. Educ:* University of Berne. Barrister, 1938; activities in private enterprise, 1938-40; joined Federal Political Dept, 1940; assigned to Swiss Legation in Moscow, 1947-49; Counsellor of Legation, Head of Swiss Delegation in Berlin, 1949-54; First Counsellor, Swiss Legation in Washington, 1954-57; Swiss Minister in Israel, 1957; Permanent Observer for Switzerland at UN in New York, 1958-61; Swiss Delegate to Technical Assistance Cttee; Swiss Delegate to Exec. Board of UNICEF (Chm. 1960); UN High Comr for Refugees, 1961-65. President: Swiss Nat. Cttee for UNESCO, 1976-; Swiss Foreign Policy Assoc., 1976-. *Recreations:* ski-ing, mountaineering, reading (history and politics), chess and bridge. *Address:* Via Navegna 25, 6648 Minusio-Locarno, Switzerland.

SCHOFIELD, Alfred, FBS; President, Leeds Permanent Building Society, since 1975; General Commissioner for Income Tax, Leeds district, since 1971; *b* 18 Feb. 1913; *s* of James Henry and Alice Schofield; *m* 1939, Kathleen Risingham; one *d. Educ:* Queen Elizabeth's Grammar Sch., Wakefield. Apptd General Manager, Leeds Permanent Bldg Soc., 1967; retd, 1973. Trustee, 1969-, Dep. Chm., 1973-, Sutton Housing Trust; Director: Leeds Bd, Royal Insce Co. Ltd, 1967-; Housing Corporation Finance Co. Ltd, 1977-. *Recreation:* orchid growing. *Address:* The Cottage, Rudding, Harrogate, N Yorks HG3 1DH. *T:* Harrogate 872037.

SCHOFIELD, Prof. Andrew Noel, MA, PhD (Cantab), MSc (Manch.); CEng, FICE; Professor of Engineering, Cambridge University, since 1974; Fellow of Churchill College, Cambridge, 1963-66 and since 1974; *b* 1 Nov. 1930; *s* of Rev. John Noel Schofield and Winifred Jane Mary (*née* Eyles); *m* 1961, Margaret Eileen Green; two *s* two *d. Educ:* Mill Hill Sch.; Christ's Coll., Cambridge. John Winbolt Prize, 1954. Asst Engr, in Malawi, with Scott Wilson Kirkpatrick and Partners, 1951. Cambridge Univ.: Demonstrator, 1955, Lectr, 1959, Dept of Engrg. Research Fellow, California Inst. of Technology, 1963-64. Univ. of Manchester Inst. of Science and Technology: Prof. of Civil Engrg, 1968; Head of Dept of Civil and Structural Engrg, 1973. Vis. Prof., Univ. of Calif at Davis, 1976. *Publications:* (with C. P. Wroth) Critical State Soil Mechanics, 1968; papers on soil mechanics and civil engrg. *Address:* 14 Hills Avenue, Cambridge CB1 4XA. *T:* Cambridge 47551.

SCHOFIELD, Bertram, CBE 1959; MA, PhD, LittD; Keeper of Manuscripts and Egerton Librarian, British Museum, 1956-61; *b* 13 June 1896; *m* 1928, Edith, *d* of Arthur William and Edith Emily Thomas; one *s* two *d. Educ:* University Sch., Southport; University of Liverpool (Charles Beard and University Fellow); Sorbonne, Ecole des Chartes and Ecole des Hautes Etudes, Paris; Emmanuel College, Cambridge (Open Research Student). Served European War, with Roy. Wilts Yeomanry, 1917-19. Asst Keeper, Dept of MSS, British Museum, 1922; Deputy-Keeper, 1947; Keeper, 1956. Seconded to Min. of Economic

Warfare, 1940-42, and for special duties with Inter-Services Intelligence and Combined Ops, HQ, 1942-44. Member: Bd of Studies in Palæography, University of London; Committee of Inst. of Historical Research, 1951-61; Council of Royal Historical Society, 1956-59; Canterbury and York Society; Vice-Pres. British Records Assoc., 1956-61; Governor: North London Collegiate School and Camden High Sch. for Girls, 1955-64. *Publications:* Muchelney Memoranda (Somerset Record Soc.), 1927; (with A. J. Collins) Legal and Manorial Formularies, 1933; The Knyvett Letters, 1949; contrib. to Musical Quarterly, Music Review, Music and Letters. British Museum Quarterly, Studies presented to Sir Hilary Jenkinson, 1957; Musik in Geschichte und Gegenwart, etc. *Recreations:* gardening and music. *Address:* 4 Farm Close, Kidlington, Oxford. *T:* Kidlington 4110.

SCHOFIELD, Vice-Adm. Brian Betham, CB 1949; CBE 1943; *b* 11 Oct. 1895; *s* of Thomas Dodgshon Schofield and Margaret Annie Bradley; *m* 1st, 1922, Doris Sibyl Ambrose (marr. diss., 1941); one *s* (and one *s* decd); 2nd, 1941, Norah Kathleen Handley (*née* Beatty) (*d* 1946); 3rd, 1946, Grace Mildred Seale; two *d. Educ:* RN Colleges, Osborne and Dartmouth. Midshipman, 1913 (Dogger Bank action); Lieut-Comdr 1925; Comdr 1931; Capt., 1938; Rear-Admiral, 1947; Vice-Adm., 1950; Naval Attaché at The Hague and Brussels, 1939-40; commanded HMS King George V, 1945-46; despatches, 1946. Retired list, 1950. King George VI Coronation medal. Officer of Legion of Merit (USA). *Publications:* The Royal Navy Today, 1960; The Russian Convoys, 1964; British Seapower, 1967; The Rescue Ships (with L. F. Martyn), 1968; The Loss of the Bismarck, 1972; The Attack on Taranto, 1973; Operation Neptune, 1974; The Arctic Convoys, 1977; Navigation and Direction, 1977. *Address:* Holme, Lower Shiplake, Henley-on-Thames, Oxon. *T:* Wargrave 2809.

SCHOFIELD, (Edward) Guy; FJI; Journalist; Director: United Newspapers Publications Ltd; United Newspapers Ltd; Sheffield Newspapers Ltd; Yorkshire Post Newspapers Ltd; *b* 10 July 1902; *s* of Frank Garside Schofield and Fanny Atkinson; *m* 1st, Norah Ellett (*d* 1935); one *d*; 2nd, Ellen Clark. *Educ:* Leeds Modern School. Leeds Mercury, 1918-25; Daily Dispatch, Manchester, 1925-27; Evening Chronicle, Manchester, 1929-30; Chief Sub-Editor, Evening Standard, London, 1931-38; Editor: Yorkshire Evening News, 1938-42; The Evening News, London, 1942-50; Daily Mail, London, 1950-55; Dir of Associated Newspapers Ltd, 1947-55. Member of Press Council, 1953-55; Chairman British Committee, International Press Institute, 1953-55; Director of Publicity, Conservative Party Headquarters, 1955-57; Deputy Editor, The Yorkshire Post, 1957-59; Editor, Weekly Post, 1960-61. *Publications:* The Purple and the Scarlet, 1959; Crime Before Calvary, 1960; In the Year 62, 1962; Why Was He Killed?, 1965; The Men that Carry the News, 1975. *Address:* Pear Tree Cottage, Sinnington, York. *Club:* National Liberal.

SCHOFIELD, Grace Florence; Regional Nursing Officer to the South West Thames Regional Health Authority; *b* 24 Feb. 1925; *d* of Percy and Matilda Schofield. *Educ:* Mayfield Sch., Putney; University College Hosp. (SRN, SCM); Univ. of London (Dip. in Nursing); Royal College of Nursing (Dip. in Nursing Admin. (Hosp.)). Asst Matron, Guy's Hosp., 1960-61; Dep. Matron, Hammersmith Hosp., 1962-66; Matron, Mount Vernon Hosp. Northwood, and Harefield Hosp., Harefield, 1966-69; Chief Nursing Officer, University Coll. Hosp., 1969-73. *Address:* Flat 24, 74 Wimbledon Park Road, SW18 5SH.

SCHOFIELD, Ivor Frederick Wentworth, CMG 1957; ED 1943; *b* 5 July 1904; *s* of Charles William and Jane Schofield; *m* 1937, Gladys May Powell. *Educ:* King's School, Worcester; Hertford Coll., Oxford. Cadet, Admin. Service, Nigeria, 1927; Resident, 1949; Administrative officer, Staff Grade, Nigeria (Western Region), 1954; Commissioner of Inland Revenue, Western Region, Nigeria, 1958; retired 1959; re-engaged on contract as Comr of Inland Rev. until Dec. 1960; Administrator of Income Tax, Southern Cameroons, 1960-61; Comr of Income Tax, The Gambia (UNO, Opex), 1964-66; Adviser on Income Tax, The Gambia (UNO), 1967-70. Served War of 1939-45: Royal West African Frontier Force, 1940-42; British Military Administration, Tripolitania, 1942-43; British Military Administration, Dodecanese (Temp. Lt-Col) 1943-45 (despatches). *Recreation:* gardening. *Address:* 10 Mountain View, Ballaugh, IoM. *T:* Sulby 493.

SCHOLEFIELD, Charles Edward, QC 1959; *b* 15 July 1902; *e s* of Edward Scholefield, Castleford, Yorks; *m* 1966, Catherine Heléne (formerly Childs), *o d* of Reginald and Marguerite Blyth; one step *s*; one step *d. Educ:* St Peter's School, York. Admitted a Solicitor, 1925; Barrister, Middle Temple, 1934; North Eastern

Circuit. Served in Royal Army Pay Corps, 1940-45; Captain, 1943-45. Chm., Council of Professions supplementary to Medicine, 1966-73. Master of the Bench of the Middle Temple, 1966. *Publications:* (ed) 11th and 12th edns, Lumley's Public Health. *Recreations:* cricket and Rugby football (watching only now); walking; Sherlock Holmes Society of London; Society of Yorkshiremen in London (Past Chairman). *Address:* Gray's Inn Chambers, Gray's Inn, WC2. *T:* 01-242 5226; 135 Surrenden Road, Brighton, East Sussex. *Club:* Reform.

SCHOLES, Alwyn Denton; Senior Puisne Judge, Hong Kong, 1970-71 (Acting Chief Justice, 1970); *b* 16 Dec. 1910; *s* of Denton Scholes and Mrs Scholes (*née* Birch); *m* 1939, Juliet Angela Ierne Pyne; one *s* four *d*. *Educ:* Cheltenham College; Selwyn College, Cambridge. Legal Tripos Parts I and II, Cantab, 1932, 1933; MA 1933. Called to the Bar, 1934; practised at the Bar in London and on Midland Circuit, 1934-38; apptd District Magistrate, Gold Coast, 1938; Acting Crown Counsel and Solicitor General, Gold Coast, 1941; apptd · Magistrate, Hong Kong, 1948; First Magistrate: Kowloon, 1949; Hong Kong, 1949. Appointed District Judge, Hong Kong, 1953, Puisne Judge, Hong Kong, 1958. Comr, Supreme Ct of State of Brunei, 1964-67, 1968-71. Pres. or Mem., Hong Kong Full Ct of Appeal, on occasions, 1949-71. Member: Sidmouth Parish Council, 1972-; Ottery Deanery Synod, 1973-. *Recreations:* golf, walking, swimming, gardening. *Address:* Western Field, Manor Road, Sidmouth, Devon EX10 8RR. *Clubs:* Royal Commonwealth Society; Sidmouth Golf.

SCHOLES, Hon. Gordon Glen Denton; MHR for Corio (Victoria), since 1967; Shadow Minister for Posts and Telecommunications, since 1976, for Primary Industry, since 1977; *b* 7 June 1931; *s* of Glen Scholes and Mary Scholes; *m* 1957, Della Kathleen Robinson; two *d*. *Educ:* various schs. Loco-engine driver, Vic Railways, 1949-67. Councillor, Geelong City, 1965-67; Pres., Geelong Trades Hall Council, 1965-66. House of Representatives: Chm. cttees, 1973-75; Speaker, 1975-76. Amateur Boxing Champion (Heavyweight), Vic, 1949. *Recreations:* golf, reading. *Address:* 11 Lascelles Avenue, Geelong West, Vic 3218, Australia. *T:* 98516.

SCHOLES, Hubert, CB 1977; Under-Secretary, Department of Industry, since 1974; *b* 22 March 1921; *s* of late Hubert Scholes and Lucy (*née* Carter); *m* 1949, Patricia Caldwell; one *s*. *Educ:* Shrewsbury Sch.; Balliol Coll., Oxford. Served RA, 1940-45. Asst Principal, Min. of Fuel and Power, 1946; Principal, 1950; Ministry of Housing and Local Govt, 1956-57; Principal Private Sec. to Minister of Power, 1959-62; Asst Sec., 1962; Under-Sec., Min. of Power, subseq. Min. of Technol., DTI and Dept of Industry, 1968-. *Address:* 5A Lancaster Avenue, Farnham, Surrey.

SCHOLES, Joseph, CB 1945; OBE 1918; *b* 4 Sept. 1889; *s* of John Scholes, Radcliffe, Lancs; *m* 1915, Edna Horrocks. *Educ:* Manchester Grammar School; Trinity College, Cambridge. Wrangler, Mathematical Tripos, 1911; entered GPO through Higher Division, 1912; Assistant Director of Vegetable Supplies, Ministry of Food, 1916-20; Postmaster-Surveyor, Glasgow, 1936; Regional Director, GPO 1939; Principal Officer to Regional Commissioner, Ministry of Home Security, 1940-43; Assistant Director-General (Personnel) GPO, 1946-49; retired. *Address:* Church Orchard, North Newton, Bridgwater, Somerset. *T:* North Petherton 662338.

SCHOLES, Mary Elizabeth, SRN; Chief Area Nursing Officer, Tayside Health Board, since 1973; *b* 8 April 1924; *d* of late John Neville Carpenter Scholes and Margaret Elizabeth (*née* Hines). *Educ:* Wyggeston Grammar Sch. for Girls, Leicester; Leicester Royal Infirmary and Children's Hosp. (SRN 1946); Guy's Hosp., London (CMB Pt I Cert. 1947); Royal Coll. of Nursing, London (Nursing Admin (Hosp.) Cert. 1962). Leicester Royal Infirmary and Children's Hospital: Staff Nurse, 1947-48; Night Sister, 1948-50; Ward Sister, 1950-56; Night Supt, 1956-58; Asst Matron, 1958-61; Asst Matron, Memorial/Brook Gen. Hosp., London, 1962-64; Matron, Dundee Royal Infirm. and Matron Designate, Ninewells Hosp., Dundee, 1964-68; Chief Nursing Officer, Bd of Management for Dundee Gen. Hosps and Bd of Man. for Ninewells and Associated Hosps, 1968-73. Pres., Scottish Assoc. of Nurse Administrators, 1973-77. Member: Scottish Bd, Royal Coll. of Nursing, 1965-70; Gen. Nursing Council for Scotland, 1966-70; Standing Nursing and Midwifery Cttee, Scotland, 1971-74 (Vice-Chm.). *Recreations:* travel, gardening, music. *Address:* Tayside Health Board, PO Box 75, Vernonholme, Riverside Drive, Dundee DD1 9NL. *T:* Dundee 645151. *Club:* Royal Commonwealth Society.

SCHOLEY, David Gerald, CBE 1976; Vice-Chairman, S. G. Warburg & Co. Ltd, Bankers, since 1973; *b* 28 June 1935; *s* of

Dudley and Lois Scholey; *m* 1960, Alexandra Beatrix, *d* of Hon. George and Fiorenza Drew, Canada; one *s* one *d*. *Educ:* Wellington Coll., Berks; Christ Church, Oxford. Joined S. G. Warburg & Co. Ltd, 1965, Dir 1967; Dir, Mercury Securities Ltd, 1969. Mem., Export Guarantees Adv. Council, 1970-75, Dep. Chm. 1974-75; Chm., Construction Exports Adv. Bd, 1975. *Address:* Heath End House, Spaniards Road, NW3 7JE. *T:* 01-455 4795. *Clubs:* Boodle's, City of London, MCC.

SCHOLEY, Robert; Member and Chief Executive, since 1973, Deputy Chairman, since 1976, British Steel Corporation; *b* 8 Oct. 1921; *s* of Harold and Eveline Scholey; *m* 1946, Joan Methley; two *d*. *Educ:* King Edward VII Sch. and Sheffield Univ. Associateship in Mech Engrg. United Steel Companies, 1947-68; British Steel Corporation: (following nationalisation) Dir, Rotherham Div., Midland Gp, 1968; Dir, Steelworks Gp, Special Steels Div., 1970; Managing Dir: Ops (London), 1972; Strip Mills Div., 1972. *Recreations:* gardening, reading, photography, camping and caravanning; history of the arts, especially painting and architecture. *Address:* The Coach House, Much Hadham, Herts. *T:* Much Hadham 2908.

SCHOLTE, Lieut-Col Frederick Lewellen, OBE (mil.) 1919; FIMechE; late RFC; retired Consulting Engineer; *b* 1890; *m* Hilda May (*d* 1969), *d* of James Gardner, Skelmorlie, Ayrshire; one *s* two *d*. *Educ:* Highgate School. *Address:* 6 Alvanley Court, Finchley Rd, NW3. *T:* 01-435 5685. *Clubs:* Royal Automobile, Royal Air Force.

SCHON, family name of **Baron Schon.**

SCHON, Baron *cr* 1976 (Life Peer), of Whitehaven, Cumbria; **Frank Schon,** Kt 1966; Chairman, National Research Development Corporation, since 1969 (Member, since 1967); *b* 18 May 1912; *o s* of Dr Frederick Schon and Henriette (*née* Nettel); *m* 1936, Gertrude Secher; two *d*. *Educ:* Rainer Gymnasium, Vienna II; University of Prague; University of Vienna (studied law externally). Co-founder: Marchon Products Ltd, 1939; Solway Chemicals Ltd, 1943; Chairman and Managing Director of both until May 1967; Director, Albright & Wilson Ltd, 1956-67; Non-executive Director: Associated Portland Cement Manufacturers Ltd, 1967-. Mem. of Council: King's College, Durham, 1959-63; University of Newcastle upon Tyne, 1963-66. Member of Court, Univ. of Newcastle upon Tyne, 1963-. Chm. Cumberland Development Council, 1964-68; Member: Northern Economic Planning Council, 1965-68; Industrial Reorganisation Corp., 1966-71; Adv. Council of Technology, 1968-70; part-time Mem., Northern Gas Bd, 1963-66. Hon. Freeman of Whitehaven, 1961. Hon. DCL Durham, 1961. *Recreations:* golf, reading. *Address:* Spaniards Field, Wildwood Rise, NW11. *T:* 01-455 3729.

SCHÖNER, Dr Josef A., GCVO (Hon.) 1966; Austrian Ambassador to the Court of St James's, 1966-70; retired; *b* 18 Feb. 1904; *s* of Andreas Schöner and Lina (*née* Eder); *m* 1965, Henriette (*née* Welz); no *c*. *Educ:* Grammar Sch., Vienna; Univ. of Vienna; Dr jur and Dr rer pol. Entered Austrian Foreign Service, 1933; Attaché, Austr. Legation, Washington, 1934; Ministry for Foreign Affairs, Vienna, 1934-38; dismissed by German authorities after Anschluss; returned to Foreign Service, 1945; Counsellor, Austr. Leg., London, 1947; Washington, 1947-50; Chief of Austr. Liaison Offices in Germany (Bonn); Envoy Extraordinary and Minister Plenipotentiary, 1952; Head, Dept of Political Affairs, Vienna, 1953-55; Secretary-General for Foreign Affairs, Vienna, 1955-58; Austr. Ambassador, Bonn, 1958-66. Holds Austrian Grand Decoration with Star in Silver, Grand Cross of foreign Orders and other decorations. *Recreations:* sailing, photography, painting and sculpture. *Address:* 13 Seilerstaette, 1010 Wien, Austria. *Club:* Union Yacht (Austria).

SCHOTZ, Benno, RSA 1937; artist-sculptor; Queen's Sculptor in Ordinary for Scotland, since 1963; *b* 1891; *s* of Jacob Schotz; *m* 1927, Milly Stelmach; one *s* one *d*. *Educ:* Pärnu, Estonia; Glasgow. BSc 1965. Head of Sculpture and Ceramics Departments, Glasgow School of Art, 1938-61. Originally studied engineering at Darmstadt and Glasgow Royal Technical Coll.; then took up sculpture; at Glasgow Art School; first one-man show in 1926 at Reid and Lefèvre's in Glasgow; second 1929; first London one-man show at the Lefèvre Galleries, 1930; one-man show in Dundee, 1935, Edinburgh, 1945, Jerusalem and Haifa Municipal Galleries, 1954-55; Edinburgh Festival, 1955; Royal Fine Art Institute Rooms, Glasgow, 1957; Exhibitions: by Arts Council of Great Britain (Scottish Cttee) in Edinburgh, Aberdeen, Dundee, Perth, Stirling, 1962; Glasgow, 1963; New Charing Cross Gall, 1968; by Scottish Arts Council, Edinburgh and Aberdeen, 1971; represented in Public Galleries in Glasgow, Edinburgh, Aberdeen, Perth, Dundee, Paisley,

Stoke-on-Trent, Belfast, Jerusalem, Tel-Aviv and New Zealand; modelled many personalities in the arts and politics; Bust of Keir Hardie in House of Commons, 1956. Has a number of carvings on buildings in Glasgow and elsewhere; sculpture groups in churches and schools; 23 foot high Group Town Centre piece in Glenrothes; statue of Rob Roy, Stirling, 1975, etc. Hon. FRIAS 1969; Hon. President: Glasgow Group, 1970; Royal Glasgow Inst. of Fine Arts, 1973. Hon. LLD Strathclyde, 1969. *Address:* 2 Kirklee Road, Glasgow G12 0TN. *T:* 041-339 9963. *Club:* Glasgow Art (Glasgow).

SCHOUVALOFF, Alexander, MA; Curator, Theatre Museum, Victoria and Albert Museum, since 1974; *b* 4 May 1934; *s* of Paul Schouvaloff (professional name Paul Sheriff) and Anna Schouvaloff (*née* Raevsky); *m* 1971, Daria Chorley; one *s*. *Educ:* Harrow Sch.; Jesus Coll., Oxford (MA). Asst Director, Edinburgh Festival, 1965-67; Dir, North West Arts Assoc., 1967-74; Director: Rochdale Festival, 1971; Chester Festival, 1973. Cross of Polonia Restituta, 1971. *Publication:* Place for the Arts, 1971. *Recreation:* skating on thin ice. *Address:* 59 Lyndhurst Grove, SE15. *T:* 01-703 3671.

SCHRAM, Emil; Chairman of Board, Peru Trust Co.; *b* Peru, Indiana, 23 November 1893; *s* of Emil Alexander Schram and Katharine Graf; *m* 1914, Mabel Miller (decd); three *s*; *m* 1971, Margaret Beauchamp Percy. *Educ:* Peru High School. Book-keeper, J. O. Cole, Peru, Ind., 1910-15; manager Hartwell Land Trust, Hillview, Ill., 1915-33; Chairman National Drainage Assoc., 1931-33; chief, drainage, levee and irrigation div., Reconstruction Finance Corp., 1933-36; Director, 1936-41; Chm., 1939-41; President, New York Stock Exchange, 1941-51; Director: Cities Service Co.; Associates Investment Co.; Home Insce Co.; Indiana National Bank; CTS Corp. Valley Farms, Inc.; Hon. Mem. Business Council. Hon. degrees: Dr of Law: New York Univ.; Univ. of Vermont; Franklin College; Indiana Univ. *Recreations:* golf and fishing. *Address:* Hillcrest, RR1, Peru, Ind 46970, USA. *T:* 473 9100. *Club:* Columbia (Indianapolis).

SCHRAM, Prof. Stuart Reynolds; Professor of Politics (with reference to China) in the University of London, School of Oriental and African Studies, since 1968; *b* Excelsior, Minn, 27 Feb. 1924; *s* of Warren R. Schram and Nada Stedman Schram; *m* 1972, Marie-Annick Lancelot. *Educ:* West High Sch., Minneapolis, Minn; Univ. of Minnesota (BA, 1944); Columbia Univ. (PhD 1954). Dir, Soviet and Chinese Section, Centre d'Etude des Relations Internationales, Fondation Nationale des Sciences Politiques, Paris, 1954-67; Head, Contemporary China Inst., SOAS, 1968-72. *Publications:* Protestantism and Politics in France, 1954; La théorie de la "révolution permanente" en Chine, 1963; The Political Thought of Mao Tse-Tung, 1963, rev. edn 1969; Le marxisme et l'Asie 1853-1964, 1965, rev. and enl. English edn 1969; Mao Tse-tung, 1966, 2nd rev. edn 1978; Authority, Participation and Cultural Change in China, 1973; *translations:* Mao Ze-dong, Une étude de l'éducation physique, 1962; Mao Tse-tung, Basic Tactics, 1966; Mao Tse-tung Unrehearsed, 1974. *Recreations:* concert- and theatre-going, walking in the country, fishing. *Address:* 4 Regal Lane, NW1.

SCHREIBER, Mrs Gaby, FSIAD; General Consultant Designer for Industry; specialist in Colour Consultancy and Interiors; Adviser on purchases of works of art; Chairman: Gaby Schreiber & Associates; Convel Ltd; *d* of Gunther George Peter Wolff; *m* Leopold Schreiber (*d* 1961). *Educ:* studied art and stage and interior design in Vienna, Florence, Berlin and Paris. Interior Design Consultant to: National Westminster Bank Ltd; Westminster Foreign Bank, Brussels, 1972-73; Chm.'s offices, GHP Gp Ltd, 1974; Pres.'s offices, Gulf Oil-Eastern Hemisphere, 1973-74; Lythe Hill Hotel, Haslemere, Surrey; Anglo-Continental Investment & Finance Co. and Continental Bankers Agents, London; Myers & Co.; Peter Robinson Ltd; David Morgan, Cardiff; W Cumberland Hosp.; Newcastle Regnl Hosp. Bd; Fine Fare Ltd (Queensway Store, Crawley); Gen. Consultant and Designer to: Cunard Steamship Co. Ltd (QE2); Zarach Ltd; Marquess of Londonderry; Crown Agents; Allen and Hanbury (Surgical Engineering) Limited; BOAC (whole fleet of aeroplanes, 1957-63); Divs of Dunlop Rubber Gp; Bartrev Gp of Cos; Hawker Siddeley Aviation Ltd (for the Queen's Flight and RAF); Rank Organisation Ltd; Semtex; Design Consultant on Plastics to Marks & Spencer Ltd. Yachts: Sir Gerard d'Erlanger; Whitney Straight, and others. Designed Exhibn Stands in Britain, Europe and USA. Member CoID, 1960-62 (Mem. Design Awards Cttee, 1961); Judge on Indep. Panel, to select Duke of Edinburgh's Prize for Elegant Design, 1960 and 1961. Fellow, Soc. of Industrial Artists and Designers (Past Chm., Consultant Designers Gp and Internat. Relations Cttee; Mem. Council; UK delegate at Gen. Assembly of Internat. Council of Soc. of Ind. Design, Venice, 1961); Mem.,

Panel of Judges for newspaper and magazine competitions on ind. design. Has broadcast and appeared on TV. *Publications:* her work has appeared in internat. books and jls on design. *Recreations:* gardening, farming, golf, paintings, drawings. *Address:* 9 Eaton Square, SW1. *T:* 01-235 4656.

SCHREIBER, Mark Shuldham; Editorial Staff of The Economist, since 1974, lobby correspondent, since 1976; *b* 11 Sept. 1931; *s* of late John Shuldham Schreiber, DL, Marlesford Hall, Suffolk and Maureen Schreiber (*née* Dent); *m* 1969, Gabriella Federica, *d* of Conte Teodoro Veglio di Castelletto Uzzone; two *d*. *Educ:* Eton; Trinity Coll., Cambridge. Nat. Service in Coldstream Guards, 1950-51. Fisons Ltd, 1957-63; Conservative Research Dept, 1963-67; Dir, Conservative Party Public Sector Research Unit, 1967-70; Special Advr to the Govt, 1970-74; Special Adviser to Leader of the Opposition, 1974-75; Member: Royal Ordnance Factories Bd, 1972-74; Govt Computer Agency Council, 1973-74. Mem., East Suffolk CC, 1968-70. *Recreation:* thinking the unthinkable. *Address:* Marlesford Hall, Woodbridge, Suffolk. *T:* Wickham Market 310; 5 Kersley Street, SW11. *Clubs:* Turf, Pratt's.

SCHRIEFFER, Prof. John Robert, PhD; Mary Amanda Wood Professor of Physics, University of Pennsylvania, since 1964 (Member Faculty, since 1962); *b* Oak Park, Ill, 31 May 1931; *s* of John Henry Schrieffer and Louise Anderson; *m* 1960, Anne Grete Thomsen; one *s* two *d*. *Educ:* MIT(BS); Univ. of Illinois (MS, PhD). Nat. Sci. Foundn Fellow, Univ. of Birmingham, and Niels Bohr Inst. for Theoretical Physics, Copenhagen, 1957-58; Asst Prof., Univ. of Chicago, 1957-59; Asst Prof., Univ. of Illinois, 1959-60, Associate Prof., 1960-62. Guggenheim Fellow, Copenhagen, 1967. Member: Nat. Acad. Scis; Amer. Acad. of Arts and Scis; Amer. Philos. Soc.; Amer. Phys Soc. Hon. ScD: Technische Hoschschule, Munich, 1968; Univ. of Geneva, 1968; Univ. of Pennsylvania, 1973; Illinois Univ., 1974; Univ. of Cincinnati, 1977. Buckley Prize, Amer. Phys Soc., 1968; Comstock Prize, Nat. Acad. Scis, 1968; (jtly) Nobel Prize for Physics, 1972; John Ericsson Medal, Amer. Soc. of Swedish Engineers, 1976. *Publications:* Theory of Superconductivity, 1964; articles on solid state physics and chemistry. *Recreations:* painting, gardening, wood working. *Address:* Department of Physics, University of Pennsylvania, Philadelphia, Pa 19104, USA; 1303 Club House Road, Gladwyne, Pa 19035, USA.

SCHRODER, Ernest Melville, CMG 1970; *b* 23 Aug. 1901; *s* of Harold Schroder and Florence L. A. Schroder (*née* Stimson); *m* 1928, Winsome Dawson; two *s* one *d*. *Educ:* Newcastle (NSW) High Sch.; Newcastle Techn. College. Chief Chemist: Kandos Cement Co., Sydney, 1927-30; Australian Cement Ltd, Geelong, 1930-44; Man. Dir, Adelaide Cement Ltd, Adelaide, 1944-68, Chm., 1970-77; Dir, Quarry Industries Ltd, retd. Pres., SA Chamber of Manufacturers, 1963-64, 1964-65; Vice-Pres., Assoc. Chamber of Manufrs of Aust., 1964-65; Pres., Cement and Concrete Assoc. of Aust., 1953-54, 1960-61; State Cttee Mem., CSIRO, 1954-71; Mem., CSIRO Adv. Council, 1955-61. FRACI; AIEAust; MAIMM; FAIM. *Recreation:* gardening. *Address:* 23 Coreega Avenue, Springfield, South Australia 5062. *T:* Adelaide 796452. *Club:* Adelaide.

SCHULTZ, Sir Leo, (Joseph Leopold), Kt 1966; OBE 1945; Member: Humberside County Council, since 1973; Kingston upon Hull District Council, since 1973; *b* 4 Feb. 1900; *s* of Solomon Schultz; *m* 1928, Kate, *d* of George Pickersgill; one *s*. *Educ:* Hull. Alderman, City of Kingston upon Hull, 1962-74. Chm., Humberside Local Govt Reorganisation Jt Cttee, 1973. *Recreation:* cricket. *Address:* 6 Newland Park, Kingston upon Hull HU5 2DW. *T:* Hull 42253.

SCHUMANN, Maurice; Chevalier de la Légion d'Honneur; Compagnon de la Libération; Croix de Guerre (1939-45); Senator from the Department of the Nord, since 1974; Member, Académie Française, since 1974; writer and broadcaster; *b* Paris, 10 April 1911; *s* of Julien Schumann and Thérèse Michel; *m* 1944, Lucie Daniel; three *d*. *Educ:* Lycées de Janson-de-Sailly and Henry IV; Faculty of Letters, Univ. of Paris (Licencié ès Lettres). Attached to l'Agence Havas in London and later Paris, 1935-39; Chief Official Broadcaster, BBC French Service, 1940-44; Liaison Officer with Allied Expeditionary Forces at end of war; Mem. Provisional Consultative Assembly, Nov. 1944-July 1945; Deputy for Nord, 1945-67 and 1968-73; Mem. Constituent Assemblies, Oct. 1945-May 1946 and June-Nov. 1946. Chm., Popular Republican Movement (MRP); Deputy of this group, 1945-73 (Pres., 1945-49; Hon. Pres., 1949-); Dep. Minister for Foreign Affairs, 1951-54; Pres., For. Affairs Cttee of Nat. Assembly, 1959; Minister of State (Prime Minister's Office), Arpil-May 1962; Minister of State, in charge of scientific res. and atomic and spacial questions, 1967-68; Minister of State for Social Affairs, 1968-69; Minister for Foreign Affairs, 1969-73.

Has been Pres. of various organisations, incl. Internat. Movement for Atlantic Union, 1966-. Hon. LLD: Cantab, 1972; St Andrews, 1974. *Publications:* Le Germanisme en marche, 1938; Mussolini, 1939; Les problèmes Ukrainiens et la paix européenne, 1939; Honneur et Patrie, 1945; Le vrai malaise des intellectuels de gauche, 1957; La Mort née de leur propre vie: essai sur Péguy, Simone Weil et Gandhi, 1974; *novels:* Le Rendezvous avec quelqu'un, 1962; Les Flots roulant au loin, 1973; La Communication, 1974; chapters in: Mazarin, 1960; Talleyrand, 1962; Clemenceau, 1974; many articles etc (under pseudonym of André Sidobre) to L'Aube (Paris daily), Le Temps présent and La Vie catholique, etc. *Address:* 53 avenue du Maréchal-Lyautey, Paris 16e, France.

SCHUSCHNIGG, Dr Kurt von; Professor, St Louis University, USA, 1948-67; *b* Riva (South Tyrol), 14 Dec. 1897; *s* of late Artur von Schuschnigg, Austrian General; *m* 1st, 1924, Herma Masera (*d* 1935); one *s*; 2nd, 1938, Countess Czernin. *Educ:* Stella Matutina College, Feldkirch; Innsbruck University. Member Austrian Parliament, 1927; Minister for Justice, 1932; Chancellor of Austria, 1934-38. *Publications:* Dreimal Oesterreich, 1937 (Farewell, Austria, 1938); Requiem in Rot-Weiss-Rot, 1945 (Zürich, Milan, New York; The Law of Peace, 1959); Im Kampf mit Hitler: die Ueberwindung der Anschussidee, 1969 (London, New York; The Brutal Takeover, 1971). *Address:* Mutters, near Innsbrück, Austria.

SCHUSTER, Sir (Felix) James (Moncrieff), 3rd Bt, *cr* 1906; OBE 1955; TD; *b* 8 January 1913; *o s* of Sir Victor Schuster, 2nd Bt, and Lucy, *d* of W. B. Skene, Pitlour-Halyards, Fife; *S* father, 1962; *m* 1937, Ragna, *er d* of late Direktor Sundø, Copenhagen; two *d. Educ:* Winchester. Served War of 1939-45, with The Rifle Brigade (Middle East and Combined Operations). Lt-Col comdg London Rifle Brigade. Rangers (RB), TA, 1952; Bt-Colonel, 1955. Hon. Col, 5th Bn Royal Green Jackets, 1970-75. *Heir:* none. *Address:* Little Swanborough, near Lewes, East Sussex. *Clubs:* Bath, Lansdowne.

SCHUSTER, Sir George Ernest, KCSI 1931; KCMG 1926; CBE 1918; MC; Vice-President, International Council, United World Colleges; *b* 1881; *s* of late Ernest Schuster, KC; *m* 1908, Hon. Gwendolen, *d* of Lord Parker of Waddington; one *s* (and one killed in action, 1941). *Educ:* Charterhouse (Scholar); New College, Oxford (Classical Exhibitioner), 1st Class in Greats, 1903. Barrister-at-Law, 1905; partner in Schuster Son & Co.; and Director of numerous companies, 1906-14; served European War, 1914-18, with QO Oxfordshire Hussars and on Staff in France; North Russia, 1919, AA and QMG, Murmansk Force, Lt-Col TF Reserve (despatches four times, MC. CBE); travelled Central Europe to report on economic conditions for Anglo-Danubian Assoc. Ltd, 1920; Chief Assist to Organiser of International Credits under League of Nations, 1921; Member of Advisory Committee to Treasury under Trade Facilities Act, 1921-22; Financial Secretary Sudan Government, 1922-27; Chairman of Advisory Committee to Colonial Secretary on East African Loans, 1926-28; Economic and Financial Adviser, Colonial Office, 1927-28; Member of East African Commission on Closer Union, 1928; Finance Mem. of Executive Council of Viceroy of India, 1928-34; Chairman of Joint Committee of Inquiry into the Anglo Argentine Meat Trade, 1935-38; Mem. of Colonial Development Advisory Cttee, 1936-38; MP (L Nat) Walsall, 1938-45; Member of Select Committee on National Expenditure, 1939-45. Member of Govt Cttee on Industrial Productivity and Chairman of Cttee's Panel on Human Relations, 1947-51; Mem. and Treas. of Medical Research Council, 1947-51; visited Malta at request of Malta Govt to advise on economic and financial policy, 1950 and 1956-57. Chm., Oxford Regional Hosp. Bd, 1951-63; Chm. Bd of Governors, United World Coll. of Atlantic, 1963-73. Mem., Oxon CC, 1952-74. Hon. DCL Oxford. *Publications:* India and Democracy, 1941; Christianity and Human Relations in Industry, 1951. *Recreations:* all country sports. *Address:* Nether Worton House, Middle Barton, Oxon OX5 4AT. *Clubs:* Athenæum, Brooks's.

SCHUSTER, Sir James; *see* Schuster, Sir F. J. M.

SCHUSTER, Rt. Rev. James Leo; *see* St John's (S Africa), Bishop of.

SCHWARTZ, George Leopold, BA, BSc (Econ.); Deputy City Editor Sunday Times, Economic Adviser Kemsley Newspapers, 1944-61; writer of Sunday Times economics column, 1961-71; *b* 10 Feb. 1891; *s* of late Adolph George Schwartz, Philadelphia; *m* 1927, Rhoda Lomax (*d* 1966). *Educ:* Varndean Sch.; St Paul's Coll., Cheltenham; London School of Economics. Teacher, LCC, 1913; Secretary London Cambridge Economic Service, 1923; Cassel Lecturer in University of London, 1929. Editor

Bankers' Magazine, 1945-54. Hon. Fellow, London School of Economics. *Publications:* (with F. W. Paish) Insurance Funds and their Investment, 1934; Bread and Circuses, 1959. Articles and pamphlets. *Recreation:* detesting government. *Address:* 28 Spencer Drive, N2. *T:* 01-455 7423. *Club:* Reform.

SCHWARZ, Rudolf; CBE 1973; Principal Guest Conductor, Northern Sinfonia Orchestra, Newcastle upon Tyne, and Bournemouth Symphony Orchestra; *b* 29 April 1905; Austrian (British subject, 1952); *m* 1950, Greta Ohlson; one *s* (and one step *d* and one *step s*). *Educ:* Vienna. Conductor, Opera House, Düsseldorf, 1923-27; Conductor, Opera House, Karlsruhe, 1927-33; Musical Director, Jewish Cultural Organisation, Berlin, 1936-41; Conductor, Bournemouth Municipal Orchestra, 1947-51; Conductor, City of Birmingham Symphony Orchestra, 1951-57; Chief Conductor of the BBC Symphony Orchestra, 1957-62; Principal Conductor, Northern Sinfonia Orchestra, Newcastle upon Tyne, 1964-73; Guest Conductor, Bergen Orchestra, Norway, 1964-71. Hon. RAM; Hon. GSM; DMus (*hc*) Newcastle upon Tyne, 1972. *Address:* 24 Wildcroft Manor, SW15 3TS.

SCHWARZ-BART, André; French writer; *b* Metz, Lorraine, France, 1928; 2nd *s* of parents from Poland; *m* Simone Schwarz-Bart. *Educ:* self-educated; Sorbonne. Joined French Resistance at 15. Has worked in a factory and in Les Halles, Paris, while writing. *Publication:* Le Dernier des Justes, 1959 (Prix Goncourt, 1959; Eng. trans., 1960); (with Simone Schwarz-Bart) Un plat de porc aux bananes vertes, 1967 (Jerusalem Prize, 1967); A Woman Named Solitude, 1973. *Address:* c/o Editions du Seuil, 27 rue Jacob, 75261 Paris Cedex 06, France.

SCHWARZENBERG, Dr Johannes Erkinger, GCVO (Hon.) 1966; Minister Plenipotentiary of Sovereign Order of Malta to Italy, since 1969; *b* 31 Jan. 1903; *m* 1931, Kathleen, Vicomtesse de Spoelberch; one *s* one *d. Educ:* Univ. of Vienna (Doctor of Law). Civil servant, Ministry of the Interior, Austria, 1928; Attaché, Federal Chancellery, Foreign Affairs, 1930; Secretary, Austrian Legation, Rome, 1933, Berlin, 1935; left diplomatic career, 1938; Director and Delegate, Internat. Cttee of Red Cross, Geneva, 1940-46; re-entered Austrian diplomatic career as Counsellor in Paris, 1946; Austrian Minister in Rome, 1948; Austrian Ambassador: in Rome, 1950; in London, 1955-66; to Holy See, 1966-68. Commander's Cross in gold, Austrian Order of Merit, 1955, Grand Cross of the Italian Order of Merit, 1955, and other decorations. *Address:* 32 via Botteghe Oscure, 00186 Rome, Italy.

SCHWARZENBERGER, Prof. Georg; Professor of International Law in the University of London, 1962-75, now Emeritus; Dean, Faculty of Laws, University College, London, 1965-67 (Vice-Dean, 1949-55 and 1963-65); Director, London Institute of World Affairs since 1943; Barrister-at-Law, Gray's Inn, since 1955; *b* 20 May 1908; *o s* of Ludwig and Ferry Schwarzenberger; *m* 1931, Suse Schwarz; one *s. Educ:* Karls-Gymnasium, Heilbronn aN; Univs of Heidelberg, Frankfurt, Berlin, Tübingen, Paris and London. Dr Jur. (Tübingen) 1930; PhD (London) 1936. Sec. London Inst. of World Affairs (formerly New Commonwealth Inst.) 1934-43; Lectr in Internat. Law and Relations, University Coll., London, 1938-45; Sub-Dean and Tutor, Faculty of Laws, 1942-49; Reader in Internat. Law, 1945-62. Co-Editor (with G. W. Keeton) of: The Library of World Affairs, 1946-; The Year Book of World Affairs, 1947-; Current Legal Problems, 1948-72. Member, Permanent Finnish-Netherlands Conciliation Commission. *Publications:* The League of Nations and World Order, 1936; Power Politics: A Study of World Society (1st edn 1941, 3rd edn 1964); International Law and Totalitarian Lawlessness, 1943; International Law as Applied by International Court and Tribunals, 1945 (Vol. I, 3rd edn 1957, Vol. II, 1968, Vol. III, 1976); A Manual of International Law, 1947 (6th edn (with E. D. Brown) 1976); The Fundamental Principles of International Law, Hague Academy of Internat. Law (Recueil, Vol. 87), 1955; The Legality of Nuclear Weapons, 1958; The Frontiers of International Law, 1962; The Inductive Approach to International Law, 1965; The Principles and Standards of International Economic Law, Hague Acad. of Internat. Law (Recueil, Vol. 117), 1966; Foreign Investments and International Law, 1969; International Law and Order, 1971; The Dynamics of International Law, 1976. *Recreations:* gardening, swimming. *Address:* 4 Bowers Way, Harpenden, Herts. *T:* Harpenden 3497.

SCHWARZKOPF, Elisabeth; Opera and Concert Singer; *b* 9 Dec. 1915; *o d* of Gymnasial-direktor Friedrich Schwarzkopf and Elisabeth (*née* Fröhlich); *m* Walter Legge. *Educ:* High School for Music, Berlin. Appears at Vienna State Opera, Royal Opera House, Covent Garden, La Scala, Milan (inc.

inauguration Piccolo Teatro della Scala, 1955), Metropolitan Opera, NY, San Francisco Opera, Bayreuth, Aix-en-Provence (first Cigale d'Or, 1974), and other internat. festivals. Made film, Der Rosenkavalier, 1962. Mem., Royal Swedish Acad. for Arts and Sciences. MusD (hc) Cambridge, 1976. Lilli Lehmann Medal, Salzburg, 1950; first Premio Orfeo d'oro, Mantua; Lily Pons Medal, Paris; Hugo Wolf Verein Medal, Vienna, 1973. Grosse Verdienstkreuz, Germany, 1974; 1st class Order of Dannebrog, Denmark. Hon. RAM. *Recreations:* music, theatre, tennis, gardening, ski-ing, mountaineering.

SCHWEITZER, Pierre-Paul; Grand Officier de la Légion d'Honneur; Croix de Guerre (1939-45); Médaille de la Résistance avec rosette; Inspecteur Général des Finances Honoraire, 1974; Chairman: Bank of America International, Luxembourg, since 1974; Banque Petrofigaz, Paris, since 1974; *b* 29 May 1912; *s* of Paul Schweitzer and Emma Munch; *m* 1941, Catherine Hatt; one *s* one *d. Educ:* Univs of Strasbourg and Paris; Ecole Libre des Sciences Politiques. Joined French Treasury as Inspecteur des Finances, 1936; Dep. Dir for Internat. Finance, French Treasury, Paris, 1946; Alternate Exec. Dir, IMF, Washington, 1947; Sec.-Gen. for European Economic Cooperation in the French Administration, Paris, 1948; Financial Counsellor, French Embassy, Washington, 1949; Director, Treasury, Paris, 1953; Dep. Governor of the Banque de France, Paris, 1960-63; Inspecteur Général des Finances, 1963; Man. Dir and Chm. Exec. Bd, IMF, 1963-73. Dir, Robeco Gp, Rotterdam, 1974-; Adv. Dir, Bank of America, NY, and Unilever NV, Rotterdam, 1974-. Hon. LLD: Yale, 1966; Harvard 1966; Leeds, 1968; New York, 1968; George Washington Univ., 1972; Wales, 1972; Williams, 1973. *Address:* 19 rue de Valois, 75001 Paris, France. *T:* 261.48.85.

SCHWINGER, Prof. Julian, AB, PhD; Professor of Physics, University of California at Los Angeles, since 1972; *b* 12 Feb. 1918; *s* of Benjamin Schwinger and Belle Schwinger (*née* Rosenfeld); *m* 1947, Clarice Carrol. *Educ:* Columbia University. Nat. Research Council Fellow, 1939-40; Research Associate, University of California at Berkeley, 1940-41; Instructor, later Assistant Professor, Purdue University, 1941-43; Member Staff: Radiation Laboratory, MIT, 1943-46; Metallurgy Laboratory, University of Chicago, 1943; Associate Professor of Physics, Harvard University, 1945-47, Prof., 1947-72, Higgins Prof. of Physics, 1966-72. Member, Board of Sponsors, Bulletin of the Atomic Scientists. Member: Nat. Acad. of Scis; Amer. Acad. of Arts and Scis; Amer. Phys. Soc.; Amer. Assoc. for Advancement of Science; NY Acad. of Sciences; Bd of Sponsors, Amer. Fedn of Scientists; Civil Liberties Union. Guggenheim Fellow, 1970. Awarded Nobel Prize for Physics (with R. Feynman and S. Tomonaga), 1965; many other awards and medals. Hon. DSc: Purdue University, 1961; Harvard, 1962; Columbia, 1966; Brandeis Univ., 1973; Gustavus Adolphus Coll., 1975; Hon. LLD City Univ. of NY, 1972. *Publications:* Quantum Electrodynamics (editor), 1958; (with D. Saxon) Discontinuities in Wave Guides, 1968; Particles and Sources, 1969; Quantum Kinematics and Dynamics, 1970; Particles, Sources and Fields, vol I, 1970, vol II, 1973. *Recreations:* tennis, swimming, ski-ing, driving, and being one of the world's worst pianists. *Address:* Department of Physics, University of California at Los Angeles, Calif 90024, USA; 10727 Stradella Court, Los Angeles, Calif 90024.

SCICLUNA, Sir Hannibal Publius, Kt 1955; MBE 1935; MA (hc Oxon, 1938); LLD (hc Malta, 1966); FSA (London, 1946, Scotland 1959); *b* 15 February 1880; *s* of late Joseph Scicluna and Carmen (*née* Galdes); *m* 1st, 1903, Amalia (*née* Lanfranco) (*d* 1947); two *s* (and one *s* decd) three *d*; 2nd, 1959, Margaret Helen Jarvis (*née* Cadzow) (*d* 1977). *Educ:* St Ignatius College; Royal Malta University. Entered Malta Civil Service, 1902; Solicitor, 1905; Secretary and Registrar of Malta University, 1913-20; Solicitor and Clerk, Crown Advocate's Office and Min. of Justice, 1916-23; Secretary to Legal Sec., Malta Imp. Govt, 1921-23; Rep. of Malta Govt Emigration Cttee in Devastated Regions, France, 1920 (Officier d'Académie, France); Mem. Antiquities Cttee, Malta, 1922; Librarian of Roy. Malta Library, 1923; Malta Rep. Internat. Cttee of Hist. Sciences, 1931; Dir Malta Museum, 1937; Dep. Comr BRCOStJ Joint War Organisation, 1940; Pres. Malta Cttee BRCS, 1952; Archivist and Librarian, Sov. Mil. Order of Malta, 1955 (Rome). Frequent delegate for Malta at internat. congresses, etc. Mem. Council, Imp. Soc. of Kts Bachelor, 1956. Hon. Life Pres., Chamber of Legal Procurators, Malta, 1972. King's Jubilee Medal, 1935; Coronation Medal, 1937. KStJ 1938; Distinguished Service Medal, OStJ; Kt Grand Cross of Magistral Grace with Riband, Order of St John of Jerusalem and of Malta, 1959; Chevalier Officier Legion Hon., 1950; Coronation Medal, 1953. Kt Grand Cross of Merit of Order of Malta, 1956; Kt Commander Order of St Gregory the Great, 1956; Kt Grand Cross Hospitaller and Military Order of St Lazarus of Jerusalem, 1967; Kt of Honour, Order of House of Lippe, 1962; Grand Cross with Riband of Constantinian Order of St George, 1963; Grand Cross, Order of St Maurice and St Lazarus, 1973; Volunteer Medical Service Medal, BRCS, 1970. *Publications:* The Archives of the SM Order of Malta, 1912; The French Occupation of Malta (1798-1800), 1923; The Order of St John of Jerusalem, 1929; The Book of Deliberations of the Venerable Tongue of England, 1949; The Church of St John in Valletta, 1955; The Order of St John of Jerusalem and Places of Interest in Malta and Gozo, 1969; numerous historical and documentary. *Recreations:* travel; formerly football (Association), riding, tennis, swimming, boating. *Address:* Samuelston, East Saltoun, Pencaitland, East Lothian. *T:* Pencaitland 340252; Villa St Martin, Malta, GC. *T:* St Paul's 73428; The Cloisters, 27 Mrabat Street, Sliema, Malta, GC. *T:* Sliema 30493. *Clubs:* Casino Maltese (Valletta); Malta Union (Sliema, Malta, GC).

SCLATER-BOOTH, family name of **Baron Basing.**

SCOBLE, (Arthur William) John; Chairman, Economic Planning Board, South West Region (Bristol), 1965-71, retired; *er s* of Arthur Scoble; *m* 1935, Constance Aveline, *d* of Samuel Robbins; three *d.* Min. of Nat. Insce, 1945-50; jssc 1950; Min. of Works, 1951-59; UN, Buenos Aires, 1960-61; Min. of Works, 1962-64; Dept of Economic Affairs, 1965-70; Dept of the Environment, 1970-71, 1972-73. Dir, Bath Preservation Trust, 1973-74. Regional Advisor, Employment Fellowship, 1975-. *Address:* Lavender Cottage, Bathampton, Bath, Avon. *T:* Bath 63259.

SCOFIELD, (David) Paul, CBE 1956; Actor; *b* 21 Jan. 1922; *s* of Edward H. and M. Scofield; *m* 1943, Joy Parker (actress); one *s* one *d. Educ:* Varndean Sch. for Boys, Brighton. Theatre training, Croydon Repertory, 1939; London Mask Theatre School, 1940. Shakespeare with ENSA, 1940-41; Birmingham Repertory Theatre, 1942; CEMA Factory tours, 1942-43; Whitehall Theatre, 1943; Birmingham Repertory, 1943-44-45; Stratford-upon-Avon, 1946-47-48. Mem., Royal Shakespeare Directorate, 1966-68. Associate Dir, Nat. Theatre, 1970-71. London theatres: Arts, 1946; Phoenix, 1947; Adventure Story, and The Seagull, St James's, 1949; Ring Round the Moon, Globe, 1950; Much Ado About Nothing, Phœnix, 1952; The River Line, Edin. Fest., Lyric (Hammersmith), Strand, 1952; John Gielgud's Company, 1952-53: Richard II, The Way of the World, Venice Preserved, etc; A Question of Fact, Piccadilly, 1953-54; Time Remembered, Lyric, Hammersmith, New Theatre, 1954-55; Hamlet, Moscow, 1955; Paul Scofield-Peter Brook Season, Phœnix Theatre, 1956; Hamlet, The Power and the Glory, Family Reunion; A Dead Secret, Piccadilly Theatre, 1957; Expresso Bongo, Saville Theatre, 1958; The Complaisant Lover, Globe Theatre, 1959; A Man For All Seasons, Globe Theatre, 1960, New York, 1961-62; Coriolanus and Love's Labour's Lost, at Shakespeare Festival Season, Stratford, Ont., 1961; King Lear: Stratford-on-Avon, Aldwych Theatre, 1962-63, Europe and US, 1964; Timon of Athens, Stratford-on-Avon, 1965; The Government Inspector, also Staircase, Aldwych, 1966; Macbeth, Stratford-on-Avon, 1967, Russia, Finland, 1967, Aldwych, 1968; The Hotel in Amsterdam, Royal Court, 1968; Uncle Vanya, Royal Court, 1970; The Captain of Kopenick, The Rules of the Game, National, 1971; Savages, Royal Court and Comedy, 1973; The Tempest, Wyndhams, 1975; Dimetos, Comedy, 1976; Volpone, The Madras House, National, 1977. *Films:* The Train, 1964; A Man for All Seasons, 1966 (from the play); Bartleby, King Lear, 1971; Scorpio, 1973; A Delicate Balance, 1974. Hon. LLD Glasgow, 1968; Hon. DLit Kent, 1973. Shakespeare prize, Hamburg, 1972. *Relevant Publication:* Paul Scofield, by J. C. Trewin, 1956. *Address:* The Gables, Balcombe, Sussex. *T:* 378.

SCOFIELD, Paul; *see* Scofield, (D.) P.

SCOLLAN, Thomas; engineer; trade union organiser for distributive workers. Former President Scottish Trade Union Congress. MP (Lab) Western Renfrew, 1945-50.

SCOONES, Major-General Sir Reginald (Laurence), KBE 1955 (OBE 1941); CB 1951; DSO 1945; late Royal Armoured Corps; Director, The Brewers' Society, 1957-69; *b* 18 Dec. 1900; *s* of late Major Fitzmaurice Scoones, Royal Fusiliers; *m* 1933, Isabella Bowie, *d* of John Nisbet, Cumbrae Isles, Scotland; one *d. Educ:* Wellington College; RMC, Sandhurst. 2nd Lt R Fus., 1920; transferred Royal Tank Corps, 1923; attd Sudan Defence Force, 1926-34; served War of 1939-45, Middle East and Burma; Lt-Col 1941; Brig. 1942; Maj.-Gen. 1950; Major-General Commanding British Troops Sudan and Commandant Sudan Defence Force, 1950-54. *Recreations:* riding, golf, tennis. *Address:* Casa Pandora, Montes da Luz, Lagos, Algarve, Portugal. *Club:* Oriental.

SCOPES, Sir Frederick, Kt 1954; Consultant, formerly Chairman, Solid Smokeless Fuels Federation; *b* 24 Feb. 1892; *o s* of Harry and Alice D. Scopes; *m* 1st, 1916, Effie Theresa (*d* 1962); two *s*; 2nd, 1964, Ellen Frederica, *d* of late Capt. H. P. Wallis, RHA (formerly Mrs Downe). *Educ:* King Edward's Schools, Camp Hill and New St, Birmingham; Corpus Christi College, Oxford (Modern History Scholar). MA. Chairman: The Stanton Ironworks Co. Ltd, 1957-62 (Man. Dir 1942-57); Chamberlin and Hill, 1961-71. President, The Joint Iron Council, 1948-54; OStJ. Liveryman, Worshipful Company of Founders. *Publication:* The Development of Corby Works, 1968. *Address:* 6 Clarendon Terrace, Brighton BN2 1FD.

SCOPES, Sir Leonard Arthur, KCVO 1961; CMG 1957; OBE 1946; *b* 19 March 1912; *s* of late Arthur Edward Scopes and Jessie Russell Hendry; *m* 1938, Brunhilde Slater Rolfe; two *s* two *d*. *Educ:* St Dunstan's College; Gonville and Caius College, Cambridge (MA). Joined HM Consular Service, 1933; Vice-Consul: Antwerp, 1933, Saigon, 1935; Canton, 1937; Acting Consul, Surabaya, 1941; Vice-Consul, Lourenço Marques, 1942; Consul, Skoplje and Ljubljana, 1945; Commercial Secretary, Bogota, 1947; Assistant in United Nations (Economic and Social) Department of Foreign Office, 1950; Counsellor, Djakarta, 1952; Foreign Service Inspector, 1954; HM Ambassador to Nepal, 1957-62; HM Ambassador to Paraguay, 1962-67; Mem., UN Jt Inspection Unit, Geneva, 1968-71. *Recreation:* retirement. *Address:* Salcombe, Devon.

SCORER, Philip Segar; a Recorder of the Crown Court, since 1976; *b* 11 March 1916; *s* of Eric W. Scorer and Maud Scorer (*née* Segar); *m* 1950, Monica Smith; one *s* three *d*. *Educ:* Repton. Admitted Solicitor, 1938; London County Council Legal Dept, 1938-40. Served War, Army (Royal Signals: War Office, SHAEF and BAS, Paris), 1940-46. Solicitors' Dept, New Scotland Yard, 1947-51; Partner in Burton & Co., Solicitors, Lincoln, 1952-; Clerk of the Peace, City of Lincoln, 1952-71; Under-Sheriff of Lincolnshire, 1954-. *Address:* Stonebow, Lincoln LN2 1DA. *T:* Lincoln 23215. *Club:* National Liberal.

SCORGIE, Mervyn Nelson; Member of Greater London Council for City of London and Westminster South, since 1973; Chairman, Industry and Employment Committee, Greater London Council, since 1977; *b* 21 Oct. 1915; 2nd *s* of late Robert Lind Scorgie and Elsie Ida Mary Scorgie. *Educ:* King Edward VI Sch., Southampton; LSE (BScEcon Hons 1946). Qual. pharmaceutical chemist, 1938. Called to the Bar, Middle Temple, 1948. Abbott Labs, Queensborough, Kent, 1949-64: Man. Dir, 1954-64. Mem. GLC, for Cities of London and Westminster, 1970-73. Vice-Chm., SE Area Provincial Council, Conservative Party, 1965-71; Chm., SE Area Cons. Polit. Centre, 1967-70; National Chm., Cons. Polit. Centre, 1972-75 (Vice-Chm., 1969-72); Pres., Faversham Cons. Assoc., 1975- (Chm., 1969-70); Vice-Chm., Cities of London and Westminster Cons. Assoc., 1972-75. Cons. Parly Candidate, Neath, 1964. Governor: Parliament Hill Sch.; Pimlico Sch.; William Ellis Sch. ILEA Rep., Sir William Boreman's Foundn of Drapers Co.; Liveryman, Fletchers Co. Freeman, City of London, 1974. *Recreations:* reading, theatre, bridge, racing. *Address:* 1018A Kings House, St James Court, Buckingham Gate, SW1E 6BT. *T:* 01-834 5455. *Clubs:* Carlton, St Stephens.

SCORRER, Aileen Mona, CBE 1953; Chief Inspector, Children's Department, Home Office, 1950-65; *b* 26 Feb. 1905; *d* of late G. H. Scorrer, Sussex, and late Mina Scorrer (*née* Drury). *Educ:* Huyton College, Liverpool; Royal Holloway College, London. *Address:* The Glade, Mead Road, Chislehurst, Kent BR7 6AD. *T:* 01-467 5370.

SCOTHORNE, Prof. Raymond John, BSc, MD Leeds; MD Chicago; FRSE; FRCSGlas; Regius Professor of Anatomy, University of Glasgow, since 1972; *b* 1920; *s* of late John Scothorne and of Lavinia Scothorne; *m* 1948, Audrey, *o d* of Rev. Selwyn Gillott, Oxford; one *s* two *d*. *Educ:* Royal Grammar School, Newcastle upon Tyne; Universities of Leeds and Chicago, BSc (Hons) 1st cl. (Leeds), 1941; MD (Chicago), Rockefeller Student, 1941-43; MB (Hons) 1st cl. (Leeds), 1944; MD (with Distinction) (Leeds), 1951. Demonstrator and Lecturer in Anatomy, 1944-50, Univ. of Leeds; Sen. Lecturer in Anatomy, 1950-60, Univ. of Glasgow; Prof., Univ. of Newcastle upon Tyne, 1960-72. Hon. Sec., Anat. Soc. of Great Britain and Ireland, 1967-71, Pres., 1971-73; Mem., Med. Sub-Cttee, UGC, 1967-76. Hon. Mem., Assoc. des Anatomistes. Struthers Prize and Gold Medal in Anatomy, Univ. of Glasgow, 1957. Anatomical Editor, Companion to Medical Studies. *Publications:* chapter on Peripheral Nervous System in Textbook of Anatomy, 2nd edn; chapters on Early Development and on the Nervous System in Companion to Medical Studies, 2nd edn; papers on embryology, histology and tissue

transplantation. *Address:* Department of Anatomy, University of Glasgow, Glasgow G12 8QQ; Southernknowe, Linlithgow, West Lothian. *T:* Linlithgow 2463.

SCOTLAND, James, CBE 1975; MA, LLB, MEd, FEIS; Principal, Aberdeen College of Education, since 1961; *b* 1917; *s* of Duncan Anderson Scotland and Mary Emmerson; *m* 1944, Jean Cowan; two *s*. *Educ:* Whitehill Sch., Glasgow; Glasgow Univ. MA 1st cl. English 1938; MA 1st cl. History, 1939; BL 1940; LLB 1943; MEd 1st cl. 1949. Commandant, Arts and Modern Studies Wing, Formation College, Central Mediterranean Forces, 1945-46. Lectr in History, Jordanhill Coll. of Educn, 1949-50; Principal Lectr in Educn, 1950-61. Member: Scottish Council for Research in Educn, 1951-55; Scottish Certificate of Education Examination Board, 1964-73; General Teaching Council for Scotland, 1965- (Chm., 1976-); Consultative Cttee on Curriculum, 1965-71; Police Advisory Council for Scotland, 1965-; Senatus, Univ. of Aberdeen, 1965-; Schools Broadcasting Council for Scotland, 1965-; Pres., Scottish Community Drama Assoc., 1964-69; Governor, Scottish Police College, 1965-; Sec., Standing Conf. on Studies in Educn, 1967-; Chm., Cttee of Principals in Scottish Colleges of Educn, 1965-67, 1971-73; Vice Chm. Jt Cttee of Colleges of Educn in Scotland, 1971-73. *Publications:* Modern Scotland, 1953; Our Law, 1955; chapter in Scottish Education Looks Ahead, 1969; The History of Scottish Education, two vols, 1970; (jointly) The Management of Innovation, 1970; chapters in The Education of Teachers, 1973, and Education in Europe, 1974; various articles in professional jls; author of many plays on stage, radio and television. *Recreations:* drama, golf. *Address:* Aberdeen College of Education, Hilton Place, Aberdeen AB9 1FA; (private) 67 Forest Road, Aberdeen AB2 4BJ. *Club:* Royal Scots (Edinburgh).

SCOTLAND, Rear-Adm. John Earl, CB 1964; DSC 1943; DL; Director, The Britain-Australia Society, since 1972; *b* 24 Aug. 1911; *s* of late Capt. W. R. Scotland, RN and Gwladys Lewis, Sydney, New South Wales; *m* 1940, Eileen Anne Studholme Brownrigg; one *s* two *d*. *Educ:* Cranbrook School, Sydney, New South Wales; Royal Naval Coll., Dartmouth. Qual. Gunnery Officer; in command HMS Modeste, 1946; Comdr 1946; in comd HMS Gravelines, 1951; Captain, 1953; in comd Gunnery School, Devonport, 1953; in comd HMS Vigilant and Dartmouth Training Sqdn, 1955 Naval Attaché, Rome, 1957; in comd HMS Lion, 1960; Rear-Adm. 1962; Flag Officer Middle East, 1962-64; Senior Naval Member, Ordnance Board, 1965-67, Pres., 1967-68. Chm., Governors, RN Scholarship Fund, 1973. DL Greater London, 1977. Officer, Order of Merit of the Republic of Italy. *Recreations:* painting, tennis, water ski-ing, golf. *Address:* 9 Tite Street, SW3. *Clubs:* Naval and Military; Royal Wimbledon Golf.

SCOTT, family name of **Earl of Eldon.**

SCOTT; *see* Hepburne-Scott, family name of Baron Polwarth.

SCOTT; *see* Montagu Douglas Scott, family name of Duke of Buccleuch.

SCOTT, Alan James; MLC, 1976; Secretary for Housing, Hong Kong, and Chairman, Hong Kong Housing Authority, since 1977; *b* 14 Jan. 1925; *s* of Harold James Scott and Phyllis Mary Barbara Scott; *m* 1st, 1958, Mary Elizabeth (*d* 1969), *d* of William Harold Victor Ireland and Ivy Elizabeth Ireland; one *s* two *d*; 2nd, 1971, Joan, *d* of Charles Harold Hall and Jennie Corinne Hall; one step *s* two step *d*. *Educ:* King's Sch., Ely; Cambridge Univ. (BA Classics and Social Anthropology). Suffolk Regt, Italy and Germany, 1952-54. HMOCS, 1958-: Fiji: Dist Officer, 1958; Estabt Officer, 1960; Registrar, Univ. of S Pacific, 1968; Controller, Organisation and Estabts, 1969; Hong Kong: Asst Financial Sec., 1971; Principal Asst Financial Sec., 1972; Sec. for Civil Service, 1973. *Recreations:* athletics (UKAAA Coach), music (Italian opera), squash. *Address:* 76 Peak Road, Hong Kong; San Pietro a Dame, Cortona, Arezzo, Italy. *Clubs:* Farmers'; Ladies Recreation (Hong Kong).

SCOTT, Prof. Alexander Whiteford, CBE 1960; Professor of Chemical Engineering, University of Strathclyde, Glasgow, 1955-71; Hon. Engineering Consultant to Ministry of Agriculture, Fisheries and Food, 1946-62; *b* 28 January 1904; *s* of Alexander Scott, Glasgow; *m* 1933, Rowena Christiana (*d* 1970), *d* of John Craig, Glasgow; one *s*. *Educ:* Royal College of Science and Technology, Glasgow. BSc, PhD, ARCST, Glasgow. Pres., Instn of Engineers and Shipbuilders in Scotland, 1975-76 and 1976-77. FIMechE, FIChemE, Hon. FIHVE. *Address:* 9 Rowallan Road, Thornliebank, Glasgow G46 7EP. *T:* 041-638 2968.

SCOTT, Anthony Douglas, TD 1972; Director of Consumer Credit, Office of Fair Trading, since 1974; *b* 6 Nov. 1933; *o s* of Douglas Ernest and Mary Gladys Scott; *m* 1962, Irene Robson; one *s* one *d. Educ:* Gateshead Central Technical Secondary Sch. Articled to Middleton & Middleton, also J. Stanley Armstrong, Chartered Accountants, Newcastle upon Tyne, 1952-57; National Service, WO Selection Bd, 1957-59; Accountant with Commercial Plastics Ltd, 1959; joined ICI Ltd (Agricl Div), 1961; seconded by ICI to Hargreaves Fertilisers Ltd, as Chief Accountant, 1966; ICI Ltd (Nobel Div.) as Asst Chief Acct, 1970; seconded by ICI to MoD as Dir-Gen. Internal Audit, 1972-74. Chm., Teesside Soc. of Chartered Accts, 1969-70; Mem. Cttee, London Chartered Accountants, 1974-. FCA, ACIS. *Recreations:* mountaineering, gardening; TA (Major, Parachute Regt (T&AVR), 1959-). *Address:* 33 Barlings Road, Harpenden, Herts. *T:* Harpenden 63067 (office) 01-242 2858.

SCOTT, Maj.-Gen. Anthony Gerald O'Carroll, CB 1951; CBE 1946 (OBE 1945); DL; *b* 22 June 1899; *s* of late Brigadier-General P. C. J. Scott, CB, and Mrs F. K. Scott (*née* Carroll); *m* 1926, Helena, *d* of Francis R. James, Hereford; one *d. Educ:* Wellington College; RMA, Woolwich. Gazetted 2nd Lt RFA, 1918; served European War, 1914-18, with Chestnut Troop, RHA; RFA, 1919-21; seconded King's African Rifles (local Capt.), 1921-26; Adjutant Beds Yeo., 1927-31; Instructor in Gunnery, School of Artillery, 1932; student Staff College, Camberley, psc, 1934-35; India, 1936; Staff Officer, RA, Western Comd, India, 1937; Instructor, Staff College, Quetta, 1938; BGS, 15 Indian Corps, Arakan, Burma, 1942 (despatches); CRA 25 Indian Div., 1943; Comdr 53 Indian Inf. Bde, 1944; BGS Eastern Comd, UK, 1945; Comd Sussex AA Bde, 1948; Commander Hamburg District, 1950-51; Commander, Singapore Base District, 1951-54; retired 1954. Vice-Pres., British Falconers' Club (Pres., 1956-66); MBOU. DL Bedfordshire, 1955; CC 1955-70. *Publications:* occasional articles in sporting papers. *Recreations:* hunting, fishing, shooting, falconry, training gun dogs, gardening. *Address:* Mill Lane, Pavenham, Bedfordshire.

SCOTT, Archibald Gifford, CIE 1942; *b* 21 April 1889; *s* of late William Gifford Scott, MB, and Caroline (*née* Strickland), Newton Abbot, Devon; *m* 1932, Kathleen, *d* of late H. J. Burton-Jones, Boulters, Maidenhead, Berks. *Educ:* Bromsgrove. King's Police Medal, 1931. Inspector-General of Police, Central Provinces and Berar, 1941-44. *Recreations:* fishing, shooting, golf. *Address:* Leigh Peverell, Doddiscombsleigh, near Exeter. *Clubs:* East India, Devonshire, Sports and Public Schools; Royal Bombay Yacht.

SCOTT, Audrey; *see* Scott, M. Audrey.

SCOTT, Bernard Francis William, CBE 1974; TD; Chairman, Lucas Industries Ltd, since 1974 (Deputy Chairman, 1969-73; Managing Director, 1972-74); Director, Lloyds Bank, since 1975; *b* Kings Norton, 19 Nov. 1914; *s* of Francis William Robert Scott and Agnes Edith Kett; *m* 1942, Charlotte Kathleen, *d* of Charles and Charlotte Laidlow, Monkseaton; one *s* two *d. Educ:* Bishop Vesey's Grammar Sch.; Epsom College. CEng, FIMechE, FBIM, FRSA. Served War of 1939-45 (despatches, 1944): mobilised as TA Officer in 45th Bn Royal Warwicks Regt, 1939; Major, RA, 1946. Joined Joseph Lucas Ltd as apprentice, 1931; Personal Asst to Oliver Lucas, 1936; Sales Dir, Joseph Lucas (Electrical) Ltd, 1947; Vice-Chm. and Gen. Man., CAV Ltd and dir of various Lucas subsids at home and abroad, 1959; Dir, Joseph Lucas (Industries) Ltd, 1968. Mem., Export Council for Europe, 1966-71; Chm., European Components Service (BNEC), 1967-71; President: Birmingham Chamber of Commerce, 1972-73 (Vice-Pres. 1970); Motor Industry Res. Assoc. Council, 1975-; Engineering Industries Council, 1975-; Vice-President: ABCC; EEF; Instn of Motor Industry, 1976; Member: Council, CBI, 1974-76; British Overseas Trade Bd, 1973-77; British Overseas Trade Adv. Council, 1975-77; Nat. Defence Industries Council, 1976-; Council, SMM&T, 1971-, Exec. Cttee, 1974, Vice-Pres., 1976. Chm., Berks Council Boys' Clubs, 1950-70; Vice-Chm., Nat. Assoc. of Boys' Clubs, 1974; Pres., Birmingham Fedn of Boys Clubs. Belgian Croix de Guerre, 1945; Chevalier, Order of Leopold with palm, 1945. *Recreations:* sailing, gardening. *Address:* Burchetts Green House, Burchetts Green, Berks. *T:* Littlewick Green 2768; 15 Westbourne Road, Edgbaston, Birmingham. *T:* 021-454 0338. *Clubs:* Royal Thames Yacht; Royal Lymington Yacht.

SCOTT, Sir (Charles) Hilary, Kt 1967; *b* Bradford, 27 March 1906; *s* of late Lieutenant-Colonel C. E. Scott and Mrs M. E. M. Scott, of Bradford; *m* 1932, Beatrice Margery, *d* of late Reverend Canon Garrad; one *s* two *d. Educ:* Sedbergh Sch. Articled with Wade & Co., Bradford. Qual. as Solicitor (Class 2 Hons) 1930;

Partner Slaughter & May, London, 1937-75. Served in RNVR, 1940-45 (Lieut-Comdr); President of the Law Society, 1966 (Mem. Council, 1948-71; Vice-Pres. 1965-66); Member: Nat. Film Finance Corp., 1948-70 (Chm. 1964-69); Jenkins Cttee on Company Law, 1959-62; Panel of Judges of The Accountant Awards for company accounts, 1961-69; London Adv. Bd of Salvation Army; Noise Adv. Council, 1971-75; Council, Royal Sch. of Church Music; Chm., Cttee on Property Bonds and Equity-linked Life Assurance, 1971-73. Trustee, Glyndebourne Arts Trust, 1961-76. Director: Tarmac Ltd, 1968-76; Equity & Law Life Assurance Society Ltd; London Board, Bank of Scotland, 1966-76. FRSA. *Recreations:* travel, music. *Address:* Knowle House, Bishop's Walk, Addington, Surrey. *T:* 01-654 3638. *Clubs:* Junior Carlton, MCC.
  See also M. Audrey Scott, G. M. C. Thornely.

SCOTT, (Charles) Peter, CMG 1964; OBE 1948; HM Diplomatic Service; Ambassador to Norway, since 1975; *b* 30 Dec. 1917; *er s* of late Rev. John Joseph Scott and late Dorothea Scott (*née* Senior); *m* 1954, Rachael, *yr d* of C. W. Lloyd Jones, *qv*; one *s* two *d. Educ:* Weymouth Coll.; Pembroke Coll., Cambridge. Indian Civil Service: Probationer, 1939; appointed to Madras Presidency, 1940; Asst Private Sec. to Viceroy, 1946-47. Entered HM Diplomatic Service, 1947, Second Sec., Tokyo, 1948; First Sec., 1949; Foreign Office, 1950; Private Sec. to Gen. Lord Ismay at NATO, Paris, 1952; First Sec., Vienna, 1954; First Sec. at British Information Services, NY, 1956; Counsellor and Consul-General, Washington, 1959; Student at IDC, 1962; Head of UK Mission to European Office of the United Nations, Geneva, 1963; Minister at HM Embassy, Rome, 1966-69; Temp. Vis. Fellow at Centre for Contemporary European Studies, Univ. of Sussex, 1969-70; Asst Under-Sec. of State, FCO, 1970-75. *Recreations:* walking, and such as offer. *Address:* c/o Foreign and Commonwealth Office, Whitehall, SW1; c/o Coutts & Co., 440 Strand, WC2. *Club:* United Oxford & Cambridge University.

SCOTT, C(harles) Russell, MA Cantab; JP; Headmaster of Cranbrook School, 1929-60; retired; *b* 8 Feb. 1898; *s* of late Russell Scott and Susanna Laetitia Worthington; *m* 1923, Irene Keightley, 2nd *d* of late Harold Rankin, JP, Rochford, Essex; three *s* one *d. Educ:* Bedales School; Haileybury Coll.; St John's Coll., Cambridge (Exhibitioner in Science). 2nd Lt RGA, 1917; BEF France with 529 Siege Battery RGA, Lieut Nov. 1918; Asst in Kent County Education Office, 1921-22; Asst Education Secretary, Cambridgeshire, 1922-27; first Hon. Secretary Cambridgeshire Festival of Music; Assistant Master Tonbridge School, 1927-29; Hon. Secretary Committee for *Music and the Community,* 1933 (the Cambridgeshire Report on the Teaching of Music); Chairman of Standing Conference for Amateur Music, 1946-63, Rural Music Schools Assoc., 1958-62, Kent Council of Social Service, 1958-73, Advisory Committee on Amateur Opera, 1948-63, Kent County Music Cttee, 1932-65, and Kent Rural Music School, 1964-67. *Recreations:* music, social work. *Address:* The Quarry, Wrotham, Kent. *T:* Fairseat 822453.

SCOTT, Ven. Claud Syms; Archdeacon of Suffolk, 1962-70, Archdeacon Emeritus, 1970; Vicar of Hoxne with Denham St John, 1962-70; *b* 31 Aug. 1901; *s* of Claud Syms and Margaret Elizabeth Scott; *m* 1930, Grace Maud Savery. *Educ:* Brentwood Sch.; Trinity Coll., Oxf. BA 1923, MA 1927. Deacon, 1926; Priest, 1927; Asst Curate, St Luke, Bedminster, 1926-30; Curate-in-charge, All Hallows Conventional District, Ipswich, 1930-38; Vicar of Exning with Landwade, 1938-54; Rural Dean of Newmarket, 1946-54; Hon. Canon of St Edmundsbury, 1953; Rector of Stradbroke with Horham and Athelington, 1954-58; Rector of St Mary Stoke, Ipswich, 1958-62; Rural Dean of Ipswich, 1958-Dec. 1961. Master, Worshipful Company of Armourers and Brasiers, 1951. *Address:* 68 Lowestoft Road, Reydon, Southwold, Suffolk. *T:* Southwold 3485.

SCOTT, Prof. Dana Stewart, FBA 1976; Professor of Mathematical Logic, Oxford University, since 1972; *b* Berkeley, Calif, 11 Oct. 1932; *m* 1959, Irene Schreier; one *d. Educ:* Univ. of Calif, Berkeley (BA); Princeton Univ. (PhD). Instructor, Univ. of Chicago, 1958-60; Asst Prof., Univ. of Calif, Berkeley, 1960-63; Associate Prof. and Prof., Stanford Univ., 1963-69; Prof., Princeton, 1969-72. Visiting Prof., Amsterdam, 1968-69. *Publications:* papers on Logic and Mathematics in technical jls. *Address:* Merton College, Oxford. *T:* Oxford 49651.

SCOTT, Sir David; *see* Scott, Sir W. D. S.

SCOTT, David; *b* 6 Sept. 1916; *er s* of late Sir Basil Scott and late Gertrude, MBE, 2nd *d* of Henry Villiers Stuart of Dromana, MP; *m* 1951, Hester Mary (MA Edinburgh; BA Oxon), *y d* of late Gilbert Ogilvy of Winton and Pencaitland; one *s* three *d.*

Educ: Stowe; New College, Oxford (MA). War Service 1939-45: Argyll and Sutherland Highlanders (SR), Reconnaissance Corps and Highland Light Infantry; T/Capt., 1941; Asst to Political Adviser for Khuzistan, Iran, 1944; Actg Vice Consul, Ahwaz, 1944-45. Clerk, House of Commons, 1946; Deputy Principal Clerk, 1962; Clerk of Standing Cttees, 1966-70; Clerk of Select Cttees, 1970-73; Clerk of Private Bills, an Examiner of Petitions for Private Bills and Taxing Officer, House of Commons, 1974-77; retired 1977. *Recreation:* fishing. *Address:* Glenaros, Aros, Isle of Mull. *T:* Aros 337. *Clubs:* Pratt's; Puffins (Edinburgh).

SCOTT, Ven. David; Archdeacon of Stow, since 1975; Vicar of Hackthorn with Cold Hanworth, since 1975; *b* 19 June 1924; *m*; two *c*. *Educ:* Trinity Hall, Cambridge (BA 1950, MA 1954); Cuddesdon Theological College. Deacon 1952, priest 1953, dio. Portsmouth; Curate of St Mark, Portsea, 1952-58; Asst Chaplain, Univ. of London, 1958-59; Priest-in-charge, Old Brumby, 1959-66; Vicar of Boston, Lincs, 1966-75; Rural Dean of Holland East, 1971-75; Canon and Prebendary of Lincoln Cathedral, 1971-; Surrogate, 1972-. *Address:* The Vicarage, Hackthorn, Lincoln LN2 3PF.

SCOTT, Sir David (Aubrey), KCMG 1974 (CMG 1966); HM Diplomatic Service; British Ambassador to South Africa, since 1976; *b* 3 Aug. 1919; *s* of late Hugh Sumner Scott and of Barbara E. Scott, JP (*née* Jackson); *m* 1941, Vera Kathleen, *d* of late Major G. H. Ibbitson, MBE, RA; two *s* one *d*. *Educ:* Charterhouse; Birmingham University. Served War of 1939-45, Royal Artillery, 1939-47; Chief Radar Adviser, British Military Mission to Egyptian Army, 1945-47, Major. Appointed to CRO, 1948; Asst Private Secretary to Secretary of State, 1949; Pretoria, 1951-53; seconded to Cabinet Office, 1954-56; Asst Sec., Malta Round Table Conf., 1955; Secretary-General, Malaya and Caribbean Constitutional Confs, 1956; Singapore, 1956-58; Asst Sec., Monckton Commn, 1960; Dep. Brit. High Comr, Fedn of Rhodesia and Nyasaland, 1961-63; Imperial Defence College, 1964; Deputy British High Commissioner in India, 1965-67; British High Comr in Uganda, and Ambassador to Rwanda (non-resident), 1967-70; Asst Under-Sec. of State, FCO, 1970-73; High Comr to New Zealand, and Governor, Pitcairn Is., 1973-75. *Recreations:* music, bird-watching. *Address:* c/o Foreign and Commonwealth Office, SW1. *Clubs:* Royal Over-Seas League; Pretoria (SA); City and Civil Service (Cape Town).

SCOTT, Sir David John Montagu Douglas, KCMG 1941 (CMG 1935); OBE 1919; *b* 7 March 1887; *s* of Adm. Lord Charles Scott, GCB; *m* 1918, Dorothy Charlotte Drummond (*d* 1965); one *s* (killed during the War, 1941); *m* 1970, Valerie Finnis, VMH, *d* of late Comdr Steriker Finnis. *Educ:* Eton; Christ Church, Oxford. Joined 3rd Batt. the Royal Scots, 1906; entered the Foreign Office, 1911; served in France, Flanders and Salonika, 1914-18 (wounded, despatches, Legion of Honour, OBE); re-joined Foreign Office, 1919; Assistant Under-Secretary of State for Foreign Affairs, 1938-44; Deputy Under-Secretary of State in the Foreign Office, 1944; retired, 1947. *Recreations:* gardening, fishing, shooting. *Address:* Boughton House, Kettering, Northants. *T:* Kettering 82279.

SCOTT, Donald; see Scott, W. D.

SCOTT, Prof. Douglas Frederick Schumacher; Professor of German in the University of Durham (late Durham Colleges), 1958-75, now Emeritus Professor; *b* Newcastle under Lyme, Staffs, 17 Sept. 1910; *o s* of Frederick Scott and Magdalena (*née* Gronbach); *m* 1942, Margaret (*d* 1972), *o d* of late Owen Gray Ellis, Beaumaris, Anglesey, and Helen (*née* Gibbs); two *d*. *Educ:* Queen Mary's Grammar School, Walsall, Staffs; Dillman-Realgymnasium Stuttgart, Germany; University of Tübingen, Göttingen (Dr phil.); University College, London (MA). Part-time Assistant, German Dept, University Coll., London, 1935-37; Lecturer in charge German Dept, Huddersfield Technical Coll., 1937-38; Lecturer in German, King's Coll., Newcastle, 1938-46; released for service with Friends' Ambulance Unit, 1940-46; Lecturer in German, King's Coll., London, 1946-49; Reader and Head of Dept of German, The Durham Colls, 1949-58. *Publications:* Some English Correspondents of Goethe, 1949; W. v. Humboldt and the Idea of a University, 1960; Luke Howard: his correspondence with Goethe and his continental journey of 1816, 1976; articles and reviews on German lit. and Anglo-German literary relations in various English and German Journals. *Recreations:* music, travel. *Address:* 6 Fieldhouse Terrace, Durham DH1 4NA. *T:* Durham 64518. *Club:* Penn.

SCOTT, Douglas Keith, (Doug Scott); President, Alpine Climbing Group, since 1976; *b* Nottingham, 29 May 1941; *s* of George Douglas Scott and Edith Joyce Scott; *m* 1962, Janice Elaine Brook; one *s* one *d*. *Educ:* Cottesmore Secondary

Modern Sch.; Mundella Grammar Sch., Nottingham; Loughborough Teachers' Trng Coll. (Teaching Certificate). Began climbing age of 12, British crag climbing, and most weekends thereafter; visited the Alps age of 16 and every year thereafter; first ascent, Tarso Teiroko, Tibest Mts, Sahara, 1965; first ascents, Cilo Dag Mts, SE Turkey, 1966; first ascent, S face Koh-i-Bandaka (22,500 ft), Hindu Kush, Afghanistan, 1967; first British ascent, Salathé Wall, El Capitain, Yosemite, 1971; 1972: Spring, Mem., European Mt Everest Expedn to SW face; Summer, first ascent, E Pillar of Mt Asgard, Baffin Island Expedn; Autumn, Mem., British Mt Everest Expedn to SW face; 1974: first ascent, Changabang; first ascent, SE spur, Pic Lenin (23,500 ft); reached summit of Mt Everest, via SW face, with Dougal Haston as Members, British Everest Expedn, 24th Sept. 1975; first Alpine ascent of S face, Mt McKinley (20,320 ft), via new route, British Direct, with Dougal Haston, 1976; first ascent, East Face Direct, Mt Kenya, 1976. Former Editor, Alpine Climbing Club Bulletin. *Publications:* Big Wall Climbing, 1974 (N America, 1974); contrib. to Alpine Jl, Amer. Alpine Jl and Mountain Magazine. *Recreations:* mountaineering; active Rugby Union player, Nottingham Moderns Rugby Football Club. *Address:* 110 Raleigh Street, Nottingham. *T:* Nottingham 703239. *Clubs:* Alpine; Alpine Climbing Group; Nottingham Climbers'.

SCOTT, Col Sir Douglas Winchester, 2nd Bt *cr* 1913; *b* 4 Feb. 1907; *s* of Admiral Sir Percy Scott, KCB, KCVO, LLD, 1st Bt, and Roma, *e d* of Sir Frederic Dixon Hartland, 1st Bt; *S* father, 1924; *m* 1933, Elizabeth Joyce, 2nd *d* of W. N. C. Grant, Lyne Place, Virginia Water, Surrey; two *s* one *d*. *Educ:* Harrow; RMC Sandhurst. Comd 3rd Hussars, 1944; Comd 9th Lancers, 1947; Hon. Col 3rd Hussars, 1955-58; Col Queen's Own Hussars, 1962-65. Treasurer Thomas Coram Foundation, 1958, Vice-Pres. 1970. *Heir: s* Anthony Percy Scott [*b* 1 May 1937; *m* 1962, Caroline Teresa Anne, *er d* of Edward Bacon; two *s* one *d*]. *Address:* Habyn Hill, Rogate, near Petersfield, Hants. *Club:* Cavalry and Guards.

SCOTT, Sir Edward Arthur Dolman, 8th Bt, *cr* 1806; resident in South Australia; *b* 14 Dec. 1905; *e s* of Sir Douglas Edward Scott, 7th Bt, and Florence Ada, *d* of W. Wilderman; *S* father 1951; *m*; one *d*. *Educ:* Reading Grammar School. *Heir: b* Douglas Francis Scott, *b* 6 Aug. 1907. *Address:* 8 Alice Street, South Plympton, SA 5038, Australia.

SCOTT, Edward Hey L.; see Laughton-Scott.

SCOTT, Most Rev. Edward Walter; Archbishop, and Primate of All Canada, since 1971; *b* Edmonton, Alberta; *s* of Tom Walter Scott and Kathleen Frances Ford; *m* 1942, Isabel Florence Brannan; one *s* three *d*. *Educ:* Univ. of British Columbia; Anglican Theological Coll. of BC. Vicar of St Peter's, Seal Cove, 1943-45; SCM Secretary, Univ. of Manitoba, 1945-59; Staff of St John's Coll., Winnipeg, 1947-48; Rector: St John the Baptist, Fort Garry, 1949-55; St Jude's, Winnipeg, 1955-60; Dir, Diocesan Council for Social Service, Diocese of Rupertsland, and Priest Dir of Indian Work, 1960-64; Associate Sec., Council for Social Service, Anglican Church of Canada, 1964-66; Bishop of Kootenay, 1966-71. Moderator of Executive and Central Cttees, WCC, 1976. Hon. DD: Anglican Theol Coll., BC; Trinity Coll., Toronto, Montreal Dio. Coll.; Wycliffe Coll., Toronto; Huron Coll., Ont.; United Theol Coll., Montreal; Hon. DCL St John's Coll., Winnipeg; Hon. STD Thorneloe Coll., Ont. *Recreation:* carpentry. *Address:* 600 Jarvis Street, Toronto, Ontario M4Y 2J6, Canada.

SCOTT, Sir Eric, Kt 1965; OBE 1958; President, The Pharmacy Guild of Australia (formerly Federated Pharmaceutical Service Guild of Australia), 1947-71; *b* 11 Dec. 1891; *s* of W. G. Scott, Hawthorn, Victoria, Aust.; *m* 1914, Eva Caroline (*d* 1968), *d* of R. J. Poulton; one *s* two *d*; *m* 1971, Peggy Vane, *d* of C. V. Lansell. *Educ:* Wesley College, Melbourne, Victoria. Pharmaceutical Chemist, 1927. State President, Federated Pharmaceutical Service Guild of Australia (Victorian Branch), 1931-47; President, Pharmaceutical Society of Victoria, 1955-60; Chm., Drug Res. Appeal Cttee, 1972; Mem., Commonwealth and State Pharmaceutical Benefits Committees under National Health Act, 1954-. Hon. Mem., Pharmaceutical Society of Great Britain, 1970. *Recreations:* golf, gardening, cooking. *Address:* Woorak, 64 Heyington Place, Toorak, Victoria 3142, Australia. *T:* 20-4883. *Clubs:* Commonwealth (Canberra); Royal Automobile of Victoria, Athenæum (Melbourne).

SCOTT, Ethleen Mary, MA; retired as Principal of St Aidan's College, University of Durham, (1961-63); *b* 25 Nov. 1896; *d* of Rev. H. R. Scott, MA, DD, and Jennie Hill Scott. *Educ:* Walthamstow Hall, Sevenoaks, Kent; Royal Holloway College, University of London. BA Hons in French, Cl. I 1919; MA (with dist.) 1923; LRAM 1919; ARCM 1942. French Mistress, Queen Elizabeth's Girls' Grammar School, Barnet, 1921-25; Lecturer in French, Royal Holloway College, 1925-28; Lecturer in French, Durham Colleges in the University of Durham, 1928-47; Principal of St Aidan's Society, 1947-61. *Recreations:* music, gardening. *Address:* Whitegates, Westbere, Canterbury, Kent.

SCOTT, Francis Clayton; *b* 6 Aug. 1881; *s* of Sir James William Scott, 1st Bt, and Anne Jane, *d* of John Haslam of Gilnow Hall, Bolton-le-Moors; *m* 1911, Gwendolen Frieda Martha (*d* 1973), *d* of late George Jager of Lingdale, Birkenhead; one *s* one *d*; *m* 1974, Elsa Marion Gatey, *widow* of Norman Gatey, Windermere, and *d* of late Edward McNaughton, The Grange, Ambleside. *Educ:* Bedales; Oriel College, Oxford (BA). Formerly Chairman of the Provincial Insurance Company Limited of Kendal and London, founded by his father. Founder and former Chairman of Brathay Hall Centre, Ambleside; High Sheriff of Westmorland, 1934. *Recreations:* shooting, fishing, yachting. *Address:* Matson Ground, Windermere, Cumbria. *T:* 3162.

SCOTT, Frank, (Francis Reginald), CC (Canada) 1967; QC (Quebec) 1961; FRSC 1947; Emeritus Professor of Law and Poet; *b* Quebec, PQ, 1 Aug. 1899; *s* of Archdeacon Frederick George and Amy Scott; *m* 1928, Marian Mildred Dale; one *s*. *Educ:* Quebec High School; Bishop's College, Lennoxville, PQ (BA 1919); Magdalen College, Oxford (Rhodes Scholar, BA 1922, BLitt 1923); McGill University, Montreal (BCL 1927). Practised law one year, then became full-time teacher, McGill Faculty of Law, 1928; Dean of Faculty, 1961-64. Vis. Professor: Toronto 1953; Michigan State Univ., 1957; French Canada Studies Program, McGill, 1967-71; Dalhousie, 1969-71. Co-founder and past-Pres., League for Social Reconstruction; Mem., Nat. Exec., Canadian Inst. of Internat. Affairs, 1935-50; Nat. Chm., Co-operative Commonwealth Fedn Party, 1942-50; Chm., Legal Research Cttee, Canadian Bar Assoc., 1954-56; Mem., Royal Commn on Bilingualism and Biculturalism, 1963-71. Delegate to British Commonwealth Labour Parties Conferences, London 1944 and Toronto 1947; adviser to Govt of Saskatchewan at Constitutional Confs, 1950 and 1960; UN Technical Assistance Resident Rep. to Burma, 1952. Chm., Canadian Writers' Conf., 1955. Co-editor: McGill Fortnightly Review, 1925-27; The Canadian Mercury, 1928; Canadian Forum, 1936-39; Preview, 1942-45; Northern Review, 1945-47. Counsel in several civil liberties cases, Supreme Court of Canada, 1956-64. Hon. For. Mem., Amer. Acad. of Arts and Sciences, 1967; Guggenheim Fellowship, 1940. Hon. degrees: Dalhousie; Manitoba; Queen's; British Columbia; Saskatchewan; Osgoode Hall; Sir George Williams; Montreal; Toronto; McGill; Laval; Windsor; Bishop's; York; Carleton. Guarantor's Prize for Poetry, Chicago, 1944; Lorne Pierce Medal, Royal Soc. of Canada, 1964; Molson Award, Canada Council, 1967. *Publications:* (*poetry*): Overture, 1945; Events and Signals, 1954; The Eye of the Needle, 1957; (trans.) Poems of Garneau and Hébert, 1962; Signature, 1964; Selected Poems, 1966; Trouvailles, 1967; The Dance is One, 1973; (trans.) Poems of French Canada, 1977; (ed, with A. J. M. Smith): New Provinces: poems of several authors, 1936; The Blasted Pine: an anthology of satire, irreverent and disrespectful verse, 1957; (*prose*): (jtly) Social Planning for Canada, 1935; Canada Today, Her National Interests and National Policy, 1938; (jtly) Democracy Needs Socialism, 1938; (jtly) Make This Your Canada, 1943; (jtly) Canada after the War, 1943; Civil Liberties and Canadian Federalism, 1959; (jtly) Quebec States Her Case, 1964; numerous articles on constitutional law and politics. *Address:* 451 Clarke Avenue, Montreal H3Y 3C5, Canada. *Clubs:* McGill Faculty, University, International PEN (all Montreal).

SCOTT, Sir George (Edward), Kt 1967; CBE 1963 (OBE 1941); KPM; Chief Constable of the West Riding Constabulary, 1959-68, and of the West Yorkshire Constabulary, 1968-69, retired; *b* 6 June 1903; *s* of late Frederick William Scott; *m* 1926, Lilian, *d* of Matthew Brown, Norwich; one *s* one *d*. *Educ:* City of Norwich School. Joined Norwich City Police, as Cadet, 1918; Dep. Chief Constable, Norwich, 1933-36; Chief Constable: Luton, 1936-44; Newcastle upon Tyne, 1944-48; Sheffield, 1948-59. President: Northern Police Convalescent Home; Northern Police Orphans Trust; Vice-Pres., Royal Life Saving Soc. King's Police Medal, 1949; KStJ 1966 (CStJ 1957). *Recreations:* golf, sailing. *Address:* White Lodge, Barham Close, Weybridge, Surrey. *Club:* St John.

SCOTT, George Edwin; author, television commentator, broadcaster, journalist; Editor of The Listener, since 1974; *b* 22 June 1925; *s* of late George Benjamin Scott and Florence Hilda

Scott; *m* 1947, Shelagh Maud Isobel Maw; two *s* one *d*. *Educ:* Middlesbrough High School; New College, Oxford. Northern Echo, 1941-42; Yorkshire Post, 1942-43; RNVR, 1943-46; New College, Oxford, 1946-48 (Founder and Editor of Oxford Viewpoint); Daily Express, 1948-53; Truth, 1953-57 (Deputy Editor, 1954; Editor, 1954-57, when ceased publication); The Economist, 1970-74. Contested (L) Middlesbrough East, March 1962, Middlesbrough West, June 1962, Wimbledon, 1964. Chm., Political Div., Liberal Party, 1962-63. Mem., Panorama team, 1958-59; Chairman/Interviewer: TWW, 1959-67; Rediffusion, 1966-68; Tyne-Tees, 1970-74; Presenter, The Editors, BBC, 1976-. *Publications:* Time and Place (auto-biographical), 1956; The RCs, 1967; Reporter Anonymous, 1968; Rise and Fall of the League of Nations, 1973; contrib. column, Liberal View, Daily Mirror, 1962-64; contribs to Punch and other jls. *Recreations:* theatre, cricket and watching others gardening. *Address:* 26 Vineyard Hill Road, Wimbledon Park, SW19 7JH. *T:* 01-946 5899. *Club:* Reform.

SCOTT, Prof. George Ian, CBE 1968; FRCSE; FRCPE; FRSE; Surgeon Oculist to the Queen in Scotland; Professor of Ophthalmology, University of Edinburgh, 1954-72, now Emeritus Professor; Ophthalmic Surgeon, Royal Infirmary, Edinburgh, 1953-72, now Hon. Ophthalmic Surgeon; *b* 15 March 1907; *s* of late George John Scott; *m* 1946, Maxine, *d* of late A. D. Vandamm; one *s*. *Educ:* Edinburgh Acad.; Univ. of Edinburgh. MA 1929; MB, ChB 1933; FRCS Edin. 1937; FRS Edin. 1954. Served War of 1939-45, RAMC; Command Ophthalmologist, Scottish Command, 1939; Mem. Advisory Ophthalmic Panel, Ministry of Supply, 1941; Consultant Ophthalmologist, MEF, 1942; Brig. RAMC, 1942. Asst Ophthalmic Surgeon, Royal Infirmary, Edinburgh, 1946; Mem. Vision Cttee, MRC, 1946; Visiting Consultant, Western General and Bangour Hosps, 1949; Consultant in Neuro-Ophthalmology to Department of Neuro-Surgery, Edinburgh, 1954. Member, International Council of Ophthalmology, 1963-70; Past President: Faculty of Ophthalmologists; RCSE; Ophthalmological Soc. of UK; Member Association of British Neurologists; FRSoc.Med. (former Vice-President Section of Ophthalmology); Hon. Col RAMC. *Publications:* papers in British Journal of Ophthalmology, Nature, Lancet, British Medical Journal, British Journal of Radiology, Proc. Roy. Soc. Med., Trans. Ophthalmological Soc., United Kingdom, and The American Journal of Ophthalmology. *Address:* 4 Moray Place, Edinburgh EH3 6DS. *T:* 031-225 6943. *Clubs:* Garrick, Army and Navy; New (Edinburgh).

SCOTT, Dr Graham Alexander; Deputy Chief Medical Officer, Scottish Home and Health Department, since 1975; *b* 26 Nov. 1927; *s* of Alexander Scott and Jessie Scott; *m* 1951, Helena Patricia Margaret Cavanagh; two *s* one *d*. *Educ:* Daniel Stewart's Coll., Edinburgh; Edinburgh Univ. (MB, ChB). MFCM, DPH. RAAMC, 1951-56 (Dep. Asst Dir, Army Health, 1st Commonwealth Div., Korea, 1953-54). Sen. Asst MO, Stirling CC, 1957-62, Dep. County MO, 1962-65; Scottish Home and Health Department: MO, 1965-68; SMO, 1968-74; PMO, 1974-75. *Recreations:* curling and walking. *Address:* 2 Garden Terrace, Easter Park Drive, Edinburgh EH4 6JR. *T:* 031-336 7025. *Club:* Royal Commonwealth Society.

SCOTT, Rev. G(uthrie) Michael; Anglican priest, Diocese of Chichester, since 1950; *b* 30 July 1907; *s* of Rev. Perceval Caleb Scott and Ethel Maud (*née* Burn); unmarried. *Educ:* King's College, Taunton; St Paul's College, Grahamstown, S Africa; Chichester Theological College. Ordained, 1930; Curate St Mary, Slaugham, Sussex, 1930-32; St Stephen's, Gloucester Rd, S Kensington, 1932-34. Domestic Chaplain to Bishop of Bombay, 1935-37; Chaplain, St Paul's Cathedral, Calcutta, 1937-38; Kasauli, 1938-39. Enlisted RAF 1940, invalided 1941. Returned to S Africa, 1943; St Alban's Coloured Mission and Chaplain St Joseph's Orphanage, Johannesburg, 1943-46; General License: Diocese of Johannesburg, 1946-50, Chichester, 1950-. In 1947 appealed to United Nations on behalf of two tribes of SW African Mandated Territory; attended sessions of General Assembly at Chiefs' request and was granted hearing by Fourth Cttee 1949, 1950 and 1955; Question referred to International Court of Justice. Took part in formation of Africa Bureau, 1952. Nagaland Peace Mission, 1964-66. Hon. Canon, St George's Cathedral, Windhoek, Namibia, 1975. Grand Companion, Order of Freedom (Zambia), 1968. Hon. STD General Theological Seminary, NY, 1972. *Publications:* Shadow over Africa, 1950; Attitude to Africa (Penguin), 1951; African Episode, 1954; Orphans' Heritage, 1958; A Time to Speak (autobiography), 1958; The Nagas in Search of Peace, 1966; Voices for Life (UN World Population Year). *Recreations:* walking, reading, sailing, theatre, etc. *Address:* c/o Lloyds Bank, 6 Pall Mall, SW1.

SCOTT, Hardiman; *see* Scott, J. P. H.

SCOTT, Sir Hilary; see Scott, Sir C. H.

SCOTT, Sir Ian Dixon, KCMG 1962 (CMG 1959); KCVO 1965; CIE 1947; *b* Inverness, 6 March 1909; *s* of late Thomas Henderson Scott, OBE, MICE, and Mary Agnes Dixon, Selkirk; *m* 1937, Hon. Anna Drusilla Lindsay, *d* of 1st Baron Lindsay of Birker, CBE, LLD; one *s* four *d. Educ:* Queen's Royal College, Trinidad; Balliol College, Oxford (MA); London School of Economics. Entered Indian Civil Service, 1932; Indian Political Service, 1935; Assistant Director of Intelligence, Peshawar, 1941; Principal, Islamia College, Peshawar, 1943; Deputy Private Secretary to the Viceroy of India, 1945-47. Dep. Dir of Personnel, John Lewis & Co. Ltd, 1948-50. Appointed to Foreign Service, 1950; First Secretary, Foreign Office, 1950-51; British Legation, Helsinki, 1952; British Embassy, Beirut, 1954; Counsellor, 1956; Chargé d'Affaires, 1956, 1957, 1958; idc 1959; Consul-General, then Ambassador to the Congo, 1960-61; Ambassador to Sudan, 1961-65, to Norway, 1965-68. Chm., Clarksons Holidays Ltd, 1972-73 (Dir, 1968-73). Chairman: Suffolk AHA, 1973-77; Council, Dr Barnardo's, 1972-; Bd of Governors, Felixstowe Coll., 1972-. *Publication:* Tumbled House, 1969. *Recreation:* sailing. *Address:* Ash House, Alde Lane, Aldeburgh, Suffolk.

SCOTT, (Jack Peter) Hardiman; Chief Assistant to Director General BBC, since 1975; *b* King's Lynn, 2 April 1920; *s* of Thomas Hardiman Scott and Dorothy Constance Smith; *m* 1st, 1942, Sheilah Stewart Roberts (marr. diss.); two *s*; 2nd, Patricia Mary (Sue) Windle. *Educ:* Grammar Sch.; privately. Northampton Chronicle and Echo series, 1939; then various provincial newspapers; Associated Press, and finally Hants and Sussex News, when began freelance broadcasting, 1948. Joined BBC; Asst News Editor Midland Region, 1950; gen. reporting staff, London, 1954; various foreign assignments, incl. Suez war; BBC's first Polit. Corresp., 1960; subseq. first Polit. Editor until 1975. *Publications:* Secret Sussex, 1949; How Shall I Vote?, 1976; *poems:* Adam and Eve and Us, 1946; When the Words are Gone, 1972; *novels:* Within the Centre, 1946; The Lonely River, 1950; Text for Murder, 1951. *Recreations:* poetry, paintings, listening to music, conservation, East Anglia. *Address:* 48 Chester Court, Albany Street, NW1 4BU. *T:* 01-935 6001; 4 Butchers Lane, Boxford, Colchester, Essex. *T:* Boxford (Suffolk) 210320.

SCOTT, Prof. James Alexander; Regional Medical Officer, Trent Regional Health Authority, since 1973; Special Professor of Health Care Planning, Nottingham University, since 1974; *b* 3 July 1931; *s* of Thomas Scott, MA Oxon and Margaret L. Scott; *m* 1957, Margaret Olive Slinger, SRN; one *s* two *d. Educ:* Doncaster Grammar Sch.; Trinity Coll., Dublin Univ. BA 1953; MB, BCh, BAO 1955; MA, MD 1965; FFCM 1974. Pathologist, Sir Patrick Dun's Hosp., Dublin, 1957-59; Registrar in Clinical Pathology, United Sheffield Hosps, 1959-61; Trainee, later Asst and Principal Asst Sen. MO, Sheffield RHB, 1961-70; Sen. Lectr in Community Medicine, Nottingham Univ., 1967-71; Sen. Admin. MO, Sheffield RHB, 1971-73. Mem. and Vice-Pres., Hospital Cttee, EEC; Mem., Public Health Lab. Service Bd. *Publications:* contrib. Lancet. *Recreations:* stamp collecting, camping. *Address:* 5 Slayleigh Lane, Sheffield S10 3RE. *T:* Sheffield 302238.

SCOTT, James Archibald, MVO 1961; Under-Secretary, Scottish Economic Planning Department, since 1976; *b* 5 March 1932; *s* of James Scott, MBE, and Agnes Bone Howie; *m* 1957, Elizabeth Agnes Joyce Buchan-Hepburn; three *s* one *d. Educ:* Dollar Acad.; Queen's Univ. of Ont.; Univ. of St Andrews (MA Hons). RAF aircrew, 1954-56. Asst Principal, CRO, 1956; served in New Delhi, 1958-62, and UK Mission to UN, New York, 1962-65; transf. to Scottish Office, 1965; Private Sec. to Sec. of State for Scotland, 1969-71; Asst Sec., Scottish Office, 1971. *Recreations:* music, golf. *Address:* 38 Queen's Crescent, Edinburgh EH9 2BA. *T:* 031-667 8417. *Club:* Travellers'.

SCOTT, J(ames) M(aurice), OBE 1945; MA; Author and explorer; *b* 13 Dec. 1906. *Educ:* Fettes College; Clare College, Cambridge. *Publications:* Gino Watkins, 1935; Land of Seals, 1949; Bright Eyes of Danger, 1950; Hudson of Hudson's Bay, 1950; Other Side of the Moon, 1950; Snowstone, 1950; Vineyards of France, 1950; Captain Smith and Pocahontas, 1953; Man Who Made Wine, 1953; Heather Mary, 1953; Seawyf and Biscuit, 1955; White Magic, 1955; Choice of Heaven, 1959; The Tea Story, 1964; The Book of Pall Mall, 1965; Dingo, 1966; The Devil You Don't, 1967; In a Beautiful Pea-Green Boat, 1968; The White Poppy, 1968; From Sea to Ocean, 1969; A Walk Along the Appenines, 1973; Boadicea, 1975. *Recreations:* mountain walking, sailing. *Address:* Thatched Cottage, Yelling, Huntingdon, Cambs.

SCOTT, James Steel, MD, FRCSEd; Professor of Obstetrics and Gynæcology, University of Leeds, since 1961; *b* 18 April 1924; *s* of late Dr Angus M. Scott and late Margaret Scott; *m* 1958, Olive Sharpe; two *s. Educ:* Glasgow Academy; University of Glasgow. MB, ChB 1946. Service in RAMC, 1946-48. MRCOG 1953. Obstetric Tutor, Liverpool University, 1954; Lecturer, 1958; Senior Lecturer, 1960. MD, FRCSEd 1959. *Publications:* contrib. to Lancet, Brit. Med. Jl, Jl of Obst. and Gynæc. of Brit. Empire, Amer. Jl of Obstetrics and Gynæcology. *Recreation:* sailing. *Address:* 24 Long Causeway, Leeds LS16 8EQ.

SCOTT, Sir James (Walter), 2nd Bt, *cr* 1962; one of HM Body Guard, Hon. Corps of Gentlemen-at-Arms, since 1977; *b* 26 Oct. 1924; *e s* of Sir Jervoise Bolitho Scott, 1st Bt, and Kathleen Isabel, *yr d* of late Godfrey Walter, Malshanger, Basingstoke; *S* father 1965; *m* 1951, Anne Constantia, *e d* of late Lt-Col Clive Austin, Roundwood, Micheldever, Hants; three *s* one *d* (and one *d* decd). *Educ:* Eton. Lt-Col The Life Guards, formerly Grenadier Guards, retired 1969. Served War of 1939-45: NW Europe, 1944-45. Palestine, 1945-46; ADC to Viceroy and Gov.-Gen. of India, 1946-48; Malaya, 1948-49; Cyprus, 1958, 1960, 1964; Malaysia, 1966. Underwriting Member of Lloyd's. Master, Mercers' Co., 1976. Councillor, Hants CC, 1973-. *Heir: s* James Jervoise Scott, *b* 12 Oct. 1952. *Address:* Rotherfield Park, Alton, Hampshire. *T:* Tisted 204. *Clubs:* Cavalry and Guards, Farmers'.

SCOTT, Sir John A. G.; see Guillum Scott.

SCOTT, John Dick; Author; *b* 26 Feb. 1917; *o s* of late Alexander Scott, OBE, and of Margaret Gourlay Allardice; *m* 1941, Helen Elisabeth, *y d* of late Sir Edmund Whittaker, FRS, and Lady Whittaker; two *s. Educ:* Stewart's Coll., Edinburgh; Edinburgh Univ. (MA, Hons History). Assistant Principal, Ministry of Aircraft Production, 1940; attached to Cabinet Office for Work on official History of the War, 1944. Literary editor of the Spectator, 1953-56; Editor, Finance and Development, 1963-74. *Publications:* The Cellar, 1947; The Margin, 1949; The Way to Glory, 1952; The End of an Old Song, 1954; (with Richard Hughes) The Administration of War Production, 1956; Life in Britain, 1956; Siemens Brothers, 1958; Vickers: A History, 1962; The Pretty Penny, 1963. *Address:* Gwyngoed Fawr, Llanddew Brefi, Tregaron, Dyfed. *Club:* Garrick.

SCOTT, Prof. John Fraser; Vice-Chancellor, La Trobe University, Melbourne, since 1977; *b* 10 Oct. 1928; *s* of Douglas Fraser Scott and Cecilia Louise Scott; *m* 1956, Dorothea Elizabeth Paton Scott; one *s* three *d. Educ:* Bristol Grammar Sch.; Trinity Coll., Cambridge. MA, FIS. Research Asst, Univ. of Sheffield, 1950-53; Asst, Univ. of Aberdeen, 1953-55; Lectr in Biometry, Univ. of Oxford, 1955-65; Univ. of Sussex: Reader in Statistics, 1965-67; Prof. of Applied Statistics, 1967-77; Pro-Vice-Chancellor, 1971-77. Reader, Church of England, 1971-77; Examining Chaplain to Bp of Chichester, 1974-77. Editor, Applied Statistics, 1971-76. *Publications:* The Comparability of Grade Standards in Mathematics, 1975; papers in JRSS, Lancet, BMJ, Chemistry and Industry, Statistician, etc. *Recreations:* wine, women and song; canals. *Address:* La Trobe University, Bundoora, Victoria 3083, Australia. *T:* 478 3122.

SCOTT, John James; HM Diplomatic Service; Counsellor, Foreign and Commonwealth Office, since 1976; *b* 4 Sept. 1924; *s* of late Col John Creagh Scott, DSO, OBE and Mary Elizabeth Marjory (*née* Murray of Polmaise); *m* 1st, Katherine Mary (*née* Bruce); twin *d*; 2nd, Heather Marguerite (*née* Douglas Brown); 3rd, June Rose (*née* Mackie); twin *s. Educ:* Radley (Schol.); Corpus Christi Coll., Cambridge (Schol.); National Inst. for Medical Research, London. War Service, Captain, Argyll and Sutherland Highlanders, 1944-47. BA 1st cl. hons Nat. Sci. Tripos, Pts I and II, 1950, MA 1953, Cantab; PhD London 1954. Senior Lectr in Chem. Pathology, St Mary's Hosp., 1955-61; Mem. Editorial Bd, Biochem. Jl, 1956-61; Mem. Cttee of Biochem. Soc., 1961; Vis. Scientist, Nat. Insts of Health, Bethesda, Md, 1961. Entered Diplomatic Service, 1961; Office of Comr Gen. for SE Asia, Singapore, 1962; Office of Political Adviser to C-in-C, Singapore, 1963; FO, 1966; Counsellor, Rio de Janeiro and Brasilia, 1971; seconded to NI Office as Asst Sec., Stormont, 1974-76. Francis Bacon Prize, Cambridge, 1950. *Publications:* papers in Biochem. Jl, Proc. Royal Soc. and other learned jls. *Recreations:* botany, photography, music. *Address:* Ashford Hill House, Brimpton Common, Reading, Berks. *T:* Tadley 4720; c/o Foreign and Commonwealth Office, SW1A 2AH. *Clubs:* Junior Carlton; Leander (Henley-on-Thames); Hawks (Cambridge).

SCOTT, Kenneth Bertram Adam; HM Diplomatic Service; Head of East European and Soviet Department, Foreign and Commonwealth Office, since 1977; *b* 23 Jan. 1931; *s* of late

Adam Scott, OBE, and Lena Kaye; *m* 1966, Gabrielle Justine (*d* 1977), *d* of R. W. Smart, Christchurch, New Zealand; one *s* one *d*. *Educ:* George Watson's Coll., Edinburgh; Edinburgh Univ. MA Hons 1952. Foreign Office, 1954; Third Sec., Moscow 1956; Second Sec., (Commercial), Bonn, 1958; FO, 1961; First Sec., Washington, 1964; Head of Chancery and Consul, Vientiane, 1968; First Sec., 1970, Counsellor and Head of Chancery, 1971-72, Moscow; Sen. Officers' War Course, RNC, Greenwich, 1973; Dep. Head, Personnel Ops Dept, FCO, 1973-75; Counsellor and Head of Chancery, Washington, 1975-77. *Address:* 17 Woodsyre, Sydenham Hill, SE26.

SCOTT, Laurence Prestwich; Chairman of the Manchester Guardian & Evening News Ltd, 1949-73; *b* 10 June 1909; *s* of John Russell and Alice Olga Scott; *m* 1939, Constance Mary Black (*d* 1969); two *s* one *d*; *m* 1970, Jessica Mary Crowther Thompson; one *s*. *Educ:* Rugby; Trinity College, Cambridge. Director, Anglia Television Ltd; Dir, Press Assoc. and Reuters, 1948-55, 1956-60. Mem., Council of Manchester University, 1946-70 (Dep. Chm., 1957-70). *Address:* Redes House, Siddington, Macclesfield, Cheshire.

SCOTT, M. Audrey; Headmistress of the Perse School for Girls, Cambridge, 1947-67, retired; *b* 22 Oct. 1904; *d* of late Lieutenant-Colonel C. E. Scott, solicitor, and Mrs M. E. M. Scott, Bradford. *Educ:* Queen Margaret's School, Scarborough (now at Escrick); Newnham College, Cambridge. Teaching at Benenden School, Kent, 1926-29; Atherley School, Southampton, 1929-31; Edgbaston Church College, 1931-40; Thornbury Grammar School, Glos, 1941-43; Headmistress, Yeovil High School, Jan. 1944-Aug. 1947. Association of Headmistresses: Exec. Cttee, 1956-62; Chm., Foreign and Commonwealth Education Cttee, 1960-62; Pres., Six Counties Branch, 1959-61. *Address:* 14 Storey's Way, Cambridge. *T:* 55030.
See also Sir Hilary Scott.

SCOTT, Rev. Michael; *see* Scott, Rev. G. M.

SCOTT, Michael, CMG 1977; MVO 1961; HM Diplomatic Service; High Commissioner in Malaŵi, since 1977; *b* 19 May 1923; *yr s* of late John Scott and of Kathleen Scott; *m* 1971, Jennifer Cameron Smith Slawikowsky. *Educ:* Dame Allan's School; Durham Univ. Durham Light Infantry, 1941; 1st Gurkha Rifles, 1943-47. Colonial Office, 1949; CRO, 1957; First Secretary, Karachi, 1958-59; Deputy High Commissioner, Peshawar, 1959-62; Counsellor and Director, British Information Services in India, New Delhi, 1963-65; FCO, 1965-68; Counsellor, British High Commn, Nicosia, 1968-72; RCDS, 1973; Ambassador to Nepal, 1974-77. *Address:* c/o Foreign and Commonwealth Office, SW1.

SCOTT, Sir Michael Fergus M.; *see* Maxwell Scott.

SCOTT, Maj.-Gen. Michael Frederick, JP; Farmer; *b* 25 Oct. 1911; *s* of Col F. W. Scott, Romsey, Hants; *m* 1961, Laila Wallis (*née* Tatchell). *Educ:* Harrow. Apprenticed as Mechanical Engr to John I. Thornycroft Co. Basingstoke, 1932-35; commnd Lieut, RAOC, 1935; transf. REME 1942. Served: India, 1938-44; Palestine, 1947-48; Germany, 1951-54; Cyprus, 1955-58. Inspector, REME, 1960-63; Commandant Technical Group, REME, 1963-65 (retd); Col Comdt, REME, 1968-73. CEng; FIMechE. JP Somerset, 1967. *Recreations:* sailing, shooting, country pursuits. *Address:* Parsonage Farm, South Barrow, Yeovil, Somerset. *T:* North Cadbury 417. *Club:* Royal Ocean Racing.

SCOTT, Most Rev. Moses Nathanael Christopher Omobiala; *see* West Africa, Archbishop of.

SCOTT, Nicholas Paul, MBE 1964; JP; MP (C) Kensington and Chelsea, Chelsea, since Oct. 1974; *b* 1933; *e s* of P. J. Scott; *m* 1964, Elizabeth Robinson (marr. diss. 1976); one *s* two *d*. *Educ:* Clapham College. Served Holborn Borough Coun., 1956-59 and 1962-65; contested (C) SW Islington, 1959 and 1964; MP (C) Paddington S, 1966-Feb. 1974; PPS to: Chancellor of the Exchequer, Rt Hon. Iain Macleod, 1970; Home Sec., Rt. Hon. Robert Carr, 1972-74; Parly Under-Sec. of State, Dept of Employment, 1974; Opposition spokesman on housing, 1974-75; Dir, London Office, European Cons. Gp in European Parlt, 1974. Nat. Chm., Young Conservatives, 1963; Vice-Chm., Conservative Parly Employment Cttee, 1967-72. Chairman: Westminster Community Relations Council, 1967-72; Paddington Churches Housing Assoc., 1970-76; British Atlantic Gp Younger Politicians, 1970-73; Nat. Pres., Tory Reform Gp. Dep. Chm., British Caribbean Assoc.; Mem. Council, Community Service Volunteers; Governor, British Inst. of Human Rights. Mem., Cttee, MCC, 1972-75. Churchwarden, St

Margaret's, Westminster, 1971-73. Man. Dir, E. Allom & Co., 1968-70; Chm., Creative Consultants Ltd, 1969-; Director: A. S. Kerswill Ltd, 1970-; Eastbourne Printers Ltd, 1970-; Juniper Studios Ltd, 1970-; Midhurst White Holdings Ltd, 1977-; Bonusplan Ltd, 1977-; Cleveland Offshore Fund Inc., 1970-; Throgmorton Securities Ltd, 1970-74; Consultant: Campbell-Johnson Ltd, 1970-; Roulston & Co. Inc., 1970-; Lombard North Central Ltd, 1971-74; Clevebourne Investments Ltd, 1974-76; Claremont Textiles Ltd, 1974-76; Procter & Gamble Ltd, 1974-; VSO, 1974-76; Council, Bank Staff Assocs, 1968-77. JP London, 1961. *Recreations:* cricket, tennis. *Address:* House of Commons, SW1A 0AA. *Club:* Turf.

SCOTT, Sir Oliver (Christopher Anderson), 3rd Bt, of Yews, Westmorland, *cr* 1909; Radiobiologist, 1954-66, Director, British Empire Cancer Campaign Research Unit in Radiobiology, 1966-69; Hon. Consultant, Institute of Cancer Research, Sutton, since 1974; *b* 6 November 1922; *s* of Sir Samuel H. Scott, 2nd Bt and Nancy Lilian (*née* Anderson); *S* father 1960; *m* 1951, Phoebe Ann Tolhurst; one *s* two *d*. *Educ:* Charterhouse; King's College, Cambridge. Clinical training at St Thomas' Hosp., 1943-46; MRCS, LRCP, 1946; MB, BCh, Cambridge, 1946; MD Cambridge, 1976; Surgeon-Lieutenant RNVR, 1947-49. Dir, Provincial Insurance Co., 1955-64. Vice-Pres., British Cancer Council, 1972- (Chm., Finance Cttee, 1970-72). High Sheriff of Westmorland, 1966. *Publications:* contributions to scientific books and journals. *Recreations:* skiing and walking. *Heir: s* Christopher James Scott, *b* 16 Jan. 1955. *Address:* 31 Kensington Square, W8. *T:* 01-937 8556. *Club:* Brooks's.

SCOTT, Oliver Lester Schreiner; Physician-in-Charge, Skin Department, Charing Cross Hospital, since 1957; Consultant Dermatologist, South West Metropolitan Regional Hospital Board, since 1951; *b* London, 16 June 1919; *s* of Ralph Lester Scott, FRCSE, and Ursula Hester Schreiner; *m* 1943, Katherine Ogle Branfoot; two *d*. *Educ:* Diocesan College, Cape Town; Trinity College, Cambridge; St Thomas's Hospital, London. MRCS, LRCP 1942; MA, MB, BChir, (Cantab) 1943; MRCP (London) 1944. FRCP 1964. Med. Specialist, RAF Med. Branch, 1943-46. Hon. Treasurer, British Assoc. of Dermatologists. Mem. Council, Royal Med. Foundn of Epsom Coll., 1953-. *Publications:* section on skin disorders in Clinical Genetics, ed A. Sorsby; medical articles in Lancet, British Journal of Dermatology, etc. *Recreation:* fishing. *Address:* 114 Harley Street, W1. *T:* 01-935 0621; South Lodge, South Side, Wimbledon Common, SW19. *T:* 01-946 6662.

SCOTT, Paul Henderson, CMG 1974; HM Diplomatic Service; Minister and Consul-General, Milan, since 1977; *b* 7 Nov. 1920; *s* of Alan Scott and Catherine Scott (*née* Henderson), Edinburgh; *m* 1953, Beatrice Celia Sharpe; one *s* one *d*. *Educ:* Royal High School, Edinburgh; Edinburgh University (MA). HM Forces, 1941-47 (Major RA). Foreign Office, 1947-53; First Secretary, Warsaw, 1953-55; First Secretary, La Paz, 1955-59; Foreign Office, 1959-62; Counsellor, Havana, 1962-64; Canadian National Defence College, 1964-65; British Deputy Commissioner General for Montreal Exhibition, 1965-67; Counsellor and Consul-General, Vienna, 1968-71; Head of British Govt Office, 1971, Consul-Gen., 1974-75, Montreal; Research Associate, IISS, 1975-76; Asst Under Sec., FO (negotiator on behalf of EEC Presidency for negotiations with USSR, Poland and East Germany), 1977. Grosse Goldene Ehrenzeichen, Austria, 1969. *Publications:* articles and book reviews esp. in Economist, Scotsman and Blackwood's. *Recreations:* ski-ing, sailing. *Address:* c/o Foreign and Commonwealth Office, SW1. *Club:* Travellers'.

SCOTT, Paul Mark, FRSL; author; *b* 25 March 1920; *y s* of Tom Scott and Frances Scott; *m* 1941, Nancy Edith Avery; two *d*. *Educ:* Winchmore Hill Collegiate Sch. FRSL 1963. Co. Sec., Falcon & Grey Walls Press, 1946-50; Dir, David Higham Associates Ltd (formerly Pearn Pollinger & Higham), 1950-60. TV and radio plays: Lines of Communication, 1951; The Alien Sky, 1954; Sahibs and Memsahibs, 1956; The Mark of the Warrior, 1959; The Bender (adapted by Jeremy Paul), 1964. *Publications: novels:* Johnnie Sahib (Eyre & Spottiswoode Literary Fellowship Award), 1952 (collected edn 1968); The Alien Sky, 1953 (collected edn 1967); A Male Child, 1956 (collected edn 1968); The Mark of the Warrior, 1958 (collected edn 1967); The Chinese Love Pavilion, 1960 (collected edn 1967); The Birds of Paradise (Book Soc. Choice), 1962 (collected edn 1967); The Bender, 1963; The Corrida at San Feliú, 1964; The Jewel in the Crown, 1966; The Day of the Scorpion, 1968; The Towers of Silence (Yorkshire Post Fiction Prize), 1971; A Division of the Spoils, 1975; The Raj Quartet (Omnibus volume of Jewel in the Crown, Day of the Scorpion, Towers of Silence, Division of the Spoils), 1976; Staying On, 1977; *poetry:* I,

Gerontius, 1941; *play:* Pillars of Salt, 1948; contrib. The Times, Country Life. *Recreations:* coarse gardening, watching local wild-life, listening to music, long-distance travel, not working during Wimbledon fortnight. *Address:* c/o David Higham Associates Ltd, 5-8 Lower John Street, Golden Square, W1R 4HA. *T:* 01-437 7888.

SCOTT, Rev. Dr Percy; Warden of Hartley Hall, Manchester, 1973-77, retired; *b* 14 Nov. 1910; *s* of Herbert and Emma Scott; *m* 1937, Christa Schleining; one *s* two *d. Educ:* Lincoln City School; London and Marburg Universities. Richmond College, London, 1931-35; Marburg, 1935-37; Minister at: Exeter, 1937-39; Stockton-on-Tees, 1939-45; Leeds, 1945-47; Tutor in Systematic Theology at Hartley Victoria College, 1947-73; Member, Faculty of Theology, Manchester Univ., 1953-, Principal, Hartley Victoria Coll., Manchester, 1959-73. *Publications:* John Wesley's Lehre von der Heiligung, 1938; (trans.) Day by Day we Magnify Thee (Luther), 1950; other translations from German; signed reviews in The Expository Times and London Quarterly; articles. *Recreation:* sport. *Address:* 53 Alexander Road, South Manchester M16 8GH. *T:* 061-226 7311. *Club:* Rotarian (Manchester South).

SCOTT, Peter; *see* Scott, C. P.

SCOTT, Peter; *see* Scott, J. P. H.

SCOTT, Sir Peter (Markham), Kt 1973; CBE 1953 (MBE 1942); DSC 1943; Artist; Chancellor, Birmingham University, since 1974; Chairman, World Wildlife Fund; Hon. Director, Wildfowl Trust; Lt-Comdr RNVR, retired; *b* 14 Sept. 1909; *s* of Captain Robert Falcon Scott, CVO, RN, and Kathleen Bruce (she *m* 2nd, 1922, Edward Hilton Young, later 1st Baron Kennet, PC, GBE, DSO, DSC, who *died* 1960; she *died* 1947); *m* 1st, 1942, Elizabeth Jane (marr. diss., 1951), *d* of David Howard; one *d*; 2nd, 1951, Philippa, *d* of late Comdr F. W. Talbot-Ponsonby, RN; one *s* one *d. Educ:* Oundle; Trinity College, Cambridge (MA); Munich State Academy; Royal Academy Schools, London. Exhibited paintings Royal Acad. since 1933; held Exhibitions of oil paintings at Ackermann's Galleries, Bond Street, also New York; specialises in bird-painting and portraits; lectures and nature feature programmes on television. Won international 14-foot Dinghy Championship for Prince of Wales Cup, 1937, 1938, and 1946. Represented Great Britain at Olympic Games, 1936 in single-handed sailing (bronze medal). Served in destroyers in Battle of Atlantic, and Light Coastal Forces in Channel, 1939-45 (despatches thrice, MBE, DSC and Bar). President: Soc. of Wildlife Artists; Glos Assoc. of Youth Clubs; Internat. Yacht Racing Union, 1955-69; Vice-President: British Gliding Assoc.; Inland Waterways Assoc.; Camping Club of Great Britain; Bristol Gliding Club; Chairman: Survival Service Commn, Internat. Union for the Conservation of Nature and Natural Resources; Fauna Preservation Society; Olympic Yachting Committee, 1947-48; Internat. Jury for Yachting, Olympic Games: 1956, Melbourne; 1960, Naples; 1964, Japan; Member Council, Boy Scout Assoc.; Winston Churchill Meml Trust. Rector, Aberdeen Univ., 1960-63. Admiral, Manx Herring Fleet, 1962-65. Explored unmapped Perry River area in Canadian Arctic, May-August 1949; Leader of ornithological expeditions to Central Highlands, Iceland, to mark wild geese, 1951, 1953; Expeditions to Australasia Galapagos Is, Seychelles and Antarctic (thrice). Gliding: International Gold Badge, 1958; International Diamond badge, 1963; National Gliding Champion, 1963; Chm., British Gliding Assoc., 1968-70. Hon. Fellow, UMIST, 1974. Hon. LLD: Exeter, 1963; Aberdeen, 1963; Birmingham, 1974; Bristol, 1975. Cherry Kearton Medal, RGS, 1967; Albert Medal, RSA, 1970; Bernard Tucker Medal, BOU, 1970; Arthur Allen Medal, Cornell Univ., 1971; Gold Medal, NY Zoological Soc., 1975. Icelandic Order of the Falcon, 1969; Commander, Dutch Order of Golden Ark, 1976; Internat. Pahlavi Environment Prize (UN), 1977. *Publications:* Morning Flight, 1935; Wild Chorus, 1938; The Battle of the Narrow Seas, 1945; Portrait Drawings, 1949; Key to Wildfowl of the World, 1949 (Coloured Key, 1958); Wild Geese and Eskimos, 1951; (with James Fisher) A Thousand Geese, 1953; (with Hugh Boyd) Wildfowl of the British Isles, 1957; The Eye of the Wind (autobiography), 1961; (with Philippa Scott) Animals in Africa, 1962; (with the Wildfowl Trust) The Swans, 1972; Fishwatchers' Guide to West Atlantic Coral Reefs, 1972; Illustrated Lord Kennet's A Bird in the Bush, Michael Bratby's Grey Goose and Through the Air, Paul Gallico's The Snow Goose, Adventures Among Birds, Handbook of British Birds, Vol. III, Jean Delacour's Waterfowl of the World. *Recreations:* exploring, bird-watching, fish-watching, yacht racing, gliding. *Address:* New Grounds, Slimbridge, Glos. *Clubs:* Savile, Royal Thames Yacht; Royal Yacht Squadron; Explorers (New York).

SCOTT, Ralph Roylance, CMG 1939; MC; MB; MRCS; LRCP; DPH; retired; *b* 10 July 1893; *o s* of late Ernest Scott, Tynemouth. *Educ:* Blundell's School; Durham University. RAMC (SR), 1914; Active Service, 1916-19; Colonial Medical Service, 1919; Director of Medical Services, Tanganyika, 1935-45. *Publications:* Introduction to the Study of Preventive Medicine, 1939; Glossary of Scientific Terms, 1929; contrib. E African Med. Jl, 1963. *Recreation:* music. *Address:* PO Karen, Nairobi, Kenya. *Club:* Nairobi.

SCOTT, Prof. Richard; Professor of General Practice, University of Edinburgh, since 1963; *b* 11 May 1914; *s* of Richard Scott and Beatrice Scott (*née* Aitken); *m* 1938, Mary Ellen Maclachlan; three *s* two *d. Educ:* Beath High Sch.; Edinburgh Univ. MB, ChB 1936; MD (with commendation) 1938; Lewis Cameron Postgrad. Prize, 1938; DPH Edin. 1946 (class medal); FRCGP 1967; MRCPE 1971; MCFP (Can) 1972. General Practice, 1936-39. War Service, 1939-46 (Lieutenant-Colonel RAMC). Lecturer in Public Health and Social Medicine, Edin. Univ., 1946; Sen. Lectr and Dir General Practice Teaching Unit, 1951; subseq. Reader in General Practice. Mem. Foundn Steering Cttee, Coll. of GPs 1951; James Mackenzie Lectr, 1964; Albert Warder Lectr, RSM, 1967. Hon. Sec. Scottish Council, RCGP, 1952-68. Consultant and Technical Advisor, WHO. *Publications:* Contrib. to scientific and medical jls. *Address:* 24 Fountainhall Road, Edinburgh EH9 2LW. *T:* 031-667 4244.

SCOTT, Richard Rashleigh Folliott, QC 1975; *b* 2 Oct. 1934; *s* of Lt-Col C. W. F. Scott, 2/9th Gurkha Rifles and Katharine Scott (*née* Rashleigh); *m* 1959, Rima Elisa, *d* of Salvador Ripoll and Blanca Korsi de Ripoll, Panama City; two *s* two *d. Educ:* Michaelhouse Coll., Natal; Univ. of Cape Town (BA); Trinity Coll., Cambridge (BA, LLB). Bigelow Fellow, Univ. of Chicago, 1958-59. Called to Bar, Inner Temple, 1959. *Recreations:* hunting, tennis, bridge; formerly Rugby (Cambridge Blue, 1957). *Address:* The Old Rectory, Foscote, Buckingham. *T:* Buckingham 3142; 11 Old Square, Lincoln's Inn, WC2. *T:* 01-405 5243.

SCOTT, Robert, CBE 1976; Director, Polytechnic, Wolverhampton, 1969-77, retired; *b* 7 July 1913; 2nd *s* of H. Scott, Westhoughton, Bolton; *m* 1940, Dorothy M. Howell; one *s* one *d. Educ:* Hindley and Abram Grammar Sch., Lancs; Univ. of Liverpool; St John's Coll., Cambridge (Wrangler; MA). BSc 1st cl. hons 1934, DipEd 1937, Liverpool; BA Cantab, 1936; FIMA. Asst Master, Newton-le-Willows Grammar Sch., 1937-41; Army and WO Staff, 1941-46; Scientific Civil Service at RMCS Shrivenham, 1946-54; Vice-Principal, Bolton Techn. Coll., 1954-57; Principal, Wolverhampton and Staffs Coll. of Technology, 1958-69. *Recreations:* motoring, reading. *Address:* 4 Wrekin Lane, The Wergs, Wolverhampton, WV6 8UL. *T:* Wolverhampton 752107.

SCOTT, Sir Robert (Heatlie), GCMG 1958 (KCMG 1954; CMG 1950); CBE 1946; JP; Lord-Lieutenant of Tweeddale (formerly of Peebleshire), since 1968; Permanent Secretary, Ministry of Defence, 1961-63, retired; *b* Peterhead, Scotland, 20 September 1905; *s* of T. H. Scott, OBE, MInstCE; *m* 1933, Rosamond Dewar Durie; one *d. Educ:* Queen's Royal College, Trinidad; New College, Oxford. Called to the Bar, Gray's Inn, 1927. Joined HM Consular Service in China, 1927; served in Peking, Shanghai, Canton, Hong Kong, Singapore; Assistant Under-Secretary of State, Foreign Office, 1950-53; Minister British Embassy, Washington, 1953-55; Commissioner-General for the UK in South-East Asia, 1955-59; Commandant, Imperial Defence College, 1960-61. JP 1968. Hon. LLD Dundee, 1972. *Address:* Lyne Station House, by Peebles, Tweeddale EH45 8NP.

SCOTT, Robin; *see* Scutt, R. H.

SCOTT, Ronald; musician; *b* 28 Jan. 1927. *Educ:* Jews' Infant Sch., Aldgate, El; Benthal Road Elementary Sch., N16; Central Foundation Sch., Cowper St, El. Musician (Tenor Saxophone), 1943-. Opened Ronnie Scott's Club, 1959. *Recreation:* motor sport. *Address:* 47 Frith Street, W1. *T:* 01-439 0747. *Club:* just his own.

SCOTT, Sir Ronald B.; *see* Bodley Scott.

SCOTT, Group Captain Roy Charles Edwin, CBE 1965; MVO 1954; AFC 1944 and Bar, 1946; Principal, College of Air Training, Hamble, since 1971; *b* 11 Jan. 1918; *s* of late John Ellis Scott, Wellington, NZ; *m* 1942, Monica, *d* of Lt-Col F. A. B. Nicoll, OBE, HM Colonial Service; two *s* one *d. Educ:* Wellington Coll., NZ; Victoria University. RNZAF, 1939 (Reserve, 1938); RAF, 1940-68: Nos 207 and 103 Sqdns, Bomber Comd, 1940-41; Flying Trng Comd, 1942; Transport

Comd, 1943; RAF Staff Coll.; OC Transport Comd Examining Unit, 1946-49; OC The Queen's Flight, 1950-53; Air Attaché, Berne, 1953-56; Dep. Dir of Air Transport Ops, MoD, 1961-64; Dep. Air Comdr, Borneo, 1964-65; retd from RAF, 1968. Dept of the Environment, 1968-71. *Recreations:* tennis, swimming, photography. *Address:* The College of Air Training, Hamble, Hants. *T:* Hamble 3001. *Club:* Royal Air Force.

SCOTT, Sheila (Christine), OBE 1968; aviator; lecturer; actress; writer; *b* 27 April 1927; *d* of Harold R. Hopkins, Worcester, and Edith Hopkins (*née* Kenward); *m* 1945, Rupert Leaman Bellamy (marr. diss. 1950). *Educ:* Alice Ottley School, Worcs. VAD, RN, 1945; acting, 1946-59, with Repertory Companies at Watford, Aldershot and Windsor; small parts in films, TV and West End Stage. Started flying, 1959; obtained British and USA commercial licences; Racing Pilot: first race won 1960 national air races (De Havilland Trophy, etc); Holder of 100 World Class Records (Aviation), incl. Round the World in class CIc and in open feminine classes; London to Capetown and Capetown to London; N Atlantic (western and eastern crossings direct); S Atlantic, Brazil to W Africa; has flown solo three times round world, including first world flight via North Pole in a light aircraft, 1971; winner of many air races; won female Light Aircraft prize, Transatlantic Air Race London-New York May 1969; won Ford Woman's Prize, London-Sydney Air Race, Dec. 1969. Founder and 1st Gov., Brit. Section, Ninety Nines Inc., 1964. Founder British Balloon and Airships Club. Life Mem. and Hon. Diploma, Academia Romana vel Sodalitis Quirinale. Silver Award of Merit, Brit. Guild of Air Pilots and Navigators, 1966, Liveryman, 1968; Isabella D'Este Award (Italy), 1966; Silver Medal, Royal Aero Club, 1967, Gold Medal, 1972; Harmon Trophy, USA, 1967; Britannia Trophy, 1968. *Publications:* I Must Fly, 1968; On Top of the World, 1973; Barefoot in the Sky, 1974. *Recreation:* sailing. *Address:* 593 Park West, W2. *T:* 01-262 7733. *Club:* Naval and Military.

SCOTT, Rev. Sidney; *see* Scott, Rev. (Walter) S.

SCOTT, Sir Terence Charles Stuart M.; *see* Morrison-Scott.

SCOTT, Prof. Thomas Frederick McNair, MA Cantab, MD Cantab, MRCS; FRCP; Professor of Paediatrics since 1974, and Co-Director of Ambulatory Paediatrics since 1975, Hahnemann Medical College and Hospital (Co-ordinator of Ambulatory Care Teaching, 1974-75); Senior Physician, The Children's Hospital of Philadelphia, 1940-69, now Physician Emeritus; *b* 18 June 1901; *e s* of Robert Frederick McNair Scott, MB, ChB (Edin.), and Alice Nystrom; *m* 1936, Mary Dwight Baker, PhD (Radcliffe), *o d* of late Clarence Dwight Baker, Wisconsin, USA; one *s* one *d.* *Educ:* Cheltenham College; Caius College, Cambridge (Scholar). Natural Science Tripos Pt I Class I, Part II (Physiology) Class II; Junior University Entrance Scholarship to St George's Hospital, 1924; Brackenbury Prize in Medicine, 1926; Qualified conjoint board, 1927; MRCP, 1928; FRCP 1953; MD (Cantab) 1938; Casualty Officer, House Surgeon, House Physn, Resident Obst. Asst, Medical Registrar, at St George's Hospital, 1927-29; House Physician Queens Hospital for Children, 1930; Research Fellow of Medicine, Harvard University, Mass, USA, 1930-31; Instructor in Pædiatrics Johns Hopkins University, Baltimore, Md, USA, 1931-34; Assistant Resident Physician at Hospital of Rockefeller Institute for Medical Research, New York, USA, working on Virus diseases, 1934-36; Assistant Physician i/c of Children's Out-patients, Lecturer in Children's Diseases, at St George's Hospital, SW1, Assistant Physician at Queens Hospital for Children, E2, 1936-38; Prof. of Pediatrics, Temple Univ. Med. Sch., Philadelphia, 1938-40; Research Prof. of Pediatrics, Univ. of Pennsylvania, 1940-66, Prof. of Paediatrics, 1966-69, now Emeritus. *Publications:* Papers on Cytology and Blood diseases, Lead poisoning in children, Virus diseases of the central nervous system, Herpetic stomatitis in children, Virus diseases of the skin. *Address:* 426 South 26th Street, Philadelphia, Pa 19146, USA; Department of Paediatrics, Hahnemann Medical College and Hospital, 230 North Broad Street, Philadelphia, Pa 19102, USA.

SCOTT, Sir Walter, 4th Bt, *cr* 1907; DL; *b* 29 July 1918; *s* of Sir Walter Scott, 3rd Bt, and Nancie Margot, *d* of S. H. March; *S* father, 1967; *m* 1945, Diana Mary, *d* of J. R. Owen; one *s* one *d.* *Educ:* Eton; Jesus College, Cambridge. Served 1st Royal Dragoons, 1939-46; Temp. Major, 1945. JP East Sussex, 1963; DL East Sussex, 1975. *Recreations:* field sports. *Heir:* *s* Walter John Scott, *b* 24 Feb. 1948. *Address:* Eckington Manor, Ripe, Lewes, East Sussex. *T:* Ripe 204. *Club:* United Oxford & Cambridge University.
   See also Duke of Hamilton and Brandon .

SCOTT, Sir Walter, Kt 1966; CMG 1960; Governing Director, W. D. Scott and Co. Pty Ltd, since 1938; *b* 10 Nov. 1903; *s* of Alexander and Selina Scott; *m* 1931, Dorothy Ada Ransom; two *s.* *Educ:* Modern School, Perth, WA. Chm., Austr. Decimal Curr. Bd, 1963-69; Industr. Design Coun., 1961-67; Productivity Coun., 1964-68. Member: Secondary Industries Commn, 1944-50; Aust. Aluminium Production Commn, 1944-52; Roy. Commn on Collinsville, 1954-55; Chairman: Motor Car Production Adv. Cttee, 1945-50; Cttee of Investigation, NSW Coal Prices, 1954; Decimal Currency Cttee, 1959-60; Australian Decimal Currency Bd, 1963-69; Australian Pharmaceutical Benefits Pricing Cttee, 1964-; Secondary Sch. Educn Standards, NSW, 1969; Australian Govt Procurement Enquiry, 1973-74. World Pres., Internat. Cttee for Scientific Management (CIOS), 1958-60. Pres., Federated Commonwealth Chamber of Commerce, 1968-70. Wallace Clark Award (for services to Internat. Management) (USA), 1957; Henry Robinson Towne Lectr, 1961; John Storey Award, 1962; Frank and Lillian Gilbreth Award, 1963; Chancellor, Internat. Acad. of Management, 1969 (Vice-Chancellor, 1965); Fellow International Academy of Management, 1961. Gold Medal, Conseil Internat. pour l'Organisation Scientifique, 1966; Leffingwell Award, 1969. *Publications:* Budgetary Control, 1937; Cost Accounting, 1944; Greater Production, 1950; Australia and the Challenge of Change, 1957. *Address:* The Anchorage, 5 Milson Road, Cremorne Point, NSW 2090, Australia. *T:* 90-7569. *Clubs:* Union, Royal Sydney Yacht Squadron, American National, Rotary (Sydney, NSW).

SCOTT, Rev. (Walter) Sidney; Clergyman (licensed to officiate Dioceses of London and Winchester since 1946, Portsmouth since 1953 and Guildford since 1958); Author and Lecturer; *b* 2 November 1900; *o s* of late Walter Samuel Scott, KC; *m* 1937, Margaret (*d* 1974), *o d* of John E. Jefferson Hogg, OBE, JP, DL, Norton House, Co. Durham; no *c.* *Educ:* St Columba's College, Dublin; Trinity College, Dublin (BA 1st Class and Respondent; MA); University of Alberta, Canada (BA); Université de Nancy, France, (D d'Univ., avec mention très honorable); Wells Theological College. Curate of Writtle, Essex, 1929-31; Precentor (1931-41) and Priest-in-Charge (1941-46) of St Peter's, Cranley Gardens, SW. British Chaplain of Ostend, 1937; High Sheriff's Chaplain, Sussex, 1940 and 1941; Mem. of Bd, American Students' Center, Paris, 1955-74. At various times temporary Chaplain of Paris, Antwerp, Dinard, Amsterdam, Oslo, etc. Pres., Royal Martyr Church Union. Trustee, Gilbert White Museum, Selborne. Officier d'Académie (France), 1939; Officier de l'Instruction Publique (France), 1949; Chevalier de la Légion d'Honneur (France), 1958; Médaille d'Honneur (Chinon) 1963; Freedom of Vaucouleurs, France, 1949, and of Chinon, France, 1969. *Publications:* Worship and Drama, 1938; Prayers and Intercessions, 1939; A War-Time Compline, 1940; Little Chelsea, 1941; The Athenians, 1943; Harriet and Mary, 1944; Shelley at Oxford, 1944; The Fantasticks, 1945; A Clowder of Cats, 1945; John Donne, 1946; Georgian Theatre, 1946; Pride of London (with Walter Scott and Joan Stevenson) 1947; Bygone Pleasures of London, 1948; (ed) New Shelley Letters, 1948; (ed) Gilbert White's Antiquities of Selborne, 1949; A Selborne Handbook, 1950; (ed) Hogg's Alexy Haimatoff, 1952; (ed) Letters of Maria Edgeworth and A. L. Barbauld, 1953; A Journal of the Terror, 1955; Green Retreats, 1955; The Trial of Joan of Arc, 1956; L'Art du Culte selon la coutume de l'Eglise d'Angleterre, 1957; (ed) Gilbert White's Natural History of Selborne, 1962; A Crusading Dean, 1967; Jeanne d'Arc: a biography, 1973. *Recreation:* book collecting. *Address:* Shortfield House, Frensham, Surrey. *T:* 2566. *Club:* Athenæum.

SCOTT, William Clifford Munro, MD; Consulting Psychiatrist, Montreal Children's Hospital, and Montreal General Hospital; *b* 11 March 1903; *o s* of late Rev. Robert Smyth Scott and late Katherine Munro Hopper; *m* 1934, Emmy Luise (marr. diss.), *er d* of late Hugo Böcking; two *s*; *m* 1970, Evelyn Freeman Fitch. *Educ:* Parkdale Collegiate, Toronto; University of Toronto. BSc (Med.), MD (Tor.), DPM (London), LMSSA. James H. Richardson Fellow, Department of Anat., 1922-24; Lectr in Anat. and Physiol., Margaret Eaton Sch. of Phys. Educ., Toronto, 1923-25; Post-Grad. Educ. in Psychiatry: Johns Hopkins Med. Sch., 1928-29; Boston Psychopathic Hosp., Harvard Univ. Med. Sch., 1929-30; Commonwealth Fund Fellow, Dept of Psychiatry, Harvard Univ., 1930-33; studied at Nat. Hosp., Queen Sq., London, 1931-32, and at Inst of Psycho-Analysis, London, 1931-33. Staff positions Maudsley Hosp., 1933-35, Cassel Hosp., 1935-38; private practice, 1938-. EMS Psychiatrist, Min. of Health, London, Sheffield and S Wales, 1939-46; Psychiatric Cons. to St Dunstan's, 1945. Mem. Cttee of Management, Inst. of Psychiatry (Univ. of London), 1951-53; Med. Dir London Clinic of Psycho-Analysis, 1947-53; Senior Psychotherapist, Bethlem Royal Hosp. and Maudsley Hosp., 1948-54; Teacher Inst. of Psychiatry (Univ. of London), 1948-

54; Associate Professor in charge of Training in Psycho-Analysis, Department of Psychiatry, McGill University, Montreal, 1954-59; Post-Grad. Teacher (Psychiatry and Psycho-Analysis), 1945-. Chm. Psychotherapy and Social Psychiatry Section, Roy. Medico-Psychological Assoc., 1952-54; Pres. Brit. Psycho-Analytical Soc., 1953-54; Mem. Bd Dirs, Inst. of Psycho-Analysis, 1947-54 (Chm. 1954); Director of Canadian Inst. of Psycho-Analysis, 1965-67. FRCPsych; FBPsS; ex-Chm. Med. Sect. and Mem. Council, Brit. Psychological Soc.; ex-Mem. Cttee Sect. Psychiatry; Roy. Soc. Med.; Amer. Psychiatric Assoc.; Vice-Pres., Psychiatric Sect., BMA, 1952 and 1955; Asst Ed. Internat. Jl Psycho-Analysis; ex-Asst Ed., Brit. Jl Med. Psychology. Mem., Montreal AAA. *Publications:* chiefly in Brit. Jl of Med. Psychol. and Internat. Jl of Psycho-Analysis. *Recreations:* people and books. *Address:* 1260 McGregor Avenue, Montreal, PQ, Canada.

SCOTT, Rear-Adm. Sir (William) David (Stewart), KBE 1977; CB 1974; Chief Polaris Executive, since 1976; *b* 5 April 1921; *y s* of Brig. H. St G. Scott, CB, DSO and Ida Christabel Trower Scott (*née* Hogg); *m* 1952, Pamela Dorothy Whitlock; one *s* two *d. Educ:* Tonbridge. Naval Cadet, 1938; comd HM Submarines: Umbra, 1944; Satyr, 1945; Andrew, 1953; Thermopylae, 1955; comd HM Ships: Gateshead, 1951; Surprise, 1960; Adamant, 1963; Fife, 1969; Chief of British Navy Staff, Washington, UK Rep. to SACLANT, and Naval Attaché to USA, 1971-73; Deputy Controller, Polaris, 1973-76; Comdr 1956; Captain 1962; Rear-Adm. 1971. *Address:* c/o Lloyds Bank Ltd, 6 Pall Mall, SW1.

SCOTT, (William) Donald, CBE 1968; MA (Oxon); BSc (Yale); *b* 22 May 1903; *s* of late Reverend William Scott and Sara Jane (*née* Platt); *m* 1928, Muriel Barbara, *d* of late Louis F. Rothschild, NYC; two *s* one *d. Educ:* Taunton Sch., Taunton; Univ. College, Oxford (open scholar); Yale University, USA (Henry P. Davison Scholar). Hercules Powder Co., USA and Rotterdam, 1926-28; British Paint & Lacquer Co., Cowley, Oxford, 1928-35; ICI Ltd: Nobel Div., 1935-41; Dyestuffs Div., 1941-43; Southern Sales Region, Dep. Regional Manager, 1943-45; Regional Manager, 1945-51; Billingham Div., Jt Man. Dir, 1951-55; Main Board Director, 1954-65. Director, 1952-60, and Chairman, 1956-60, Scottish Agricultural Industries Ltd; Chm., Home Grown Cereals Authority, 1965-68; Director: Canadian Industries Ltd, 1957-62; Glaxo Group Ltd, 1965-68; Laporte Industries Ltd, 1965-68. Mem., Western Hemisphere Exports Council, 1961-64. FRSA 1968. *Recreations:* cricket, golf. *Address:* Mabasque, Les Hauts de St Paul, 06570 St Paul de Vence, France.

SCOTT, Prof. William Douglas R.; *see* Robson-Scott.

SCOTT, Rev. W(illiam) G.; *see* Gardiner-Scott.

SCOTT, William (George), CBE 1966; ARA 1977; painter; *b* 15 Feb. 1913; *e s* of William John and Agnes Scott; *m* 1937, Hilda Mary Lucas; two *s. Educ:* Enniskillen; Belfast Sch. of Art; Roy. Acad. Schools, London. Hon. Dr RCA, 1975; Hon. DLit: Belfast, 1976; Dublin, 1977. *Exhibitions:* Leger Gall., 1942, 1944, 1946; Leicester Gall., 1948, 1951; Hanover Gall., 1953, 1956, 1961, 1963, 1965, 1967; Martha Jackson Gall., NY, 1954, 1958, 1973; Venice Biennale, 1958; VIth Sao Paulo Biennial, 1953 and 1961, Brazil; Tate Gall., 1972; Gimpel Fils Gall., 1974; Martha Jackson Gall., NY, 1974; Moos Gall., Toronto, 1975; Kasahara Gall., Japan, 1976; in British Council Exhibns in Europe; *works exhibited in:* Tate Gall.; Victoria and Albert Museum; Paris; New York; Toledo, USA; S Africa; Canada; Australia; S America. *Address:* 13 Edith Terrace, Chelsea, SW10. *T:* 01-352 8044.

SCOTT-BARRETT, Lt-Gen. Sir David (William), KBE 1976 (MBE 1956); MC 1945; GOC Scotland and Governor of Edinburgh Castle, since 1976; *b* 16 Dec. 1922; 2nd *s* of late Brig. Rev. H. Scott-Barrett, CB, CBE; *m* 1948, Marie Elise, *d* of late Norman Morris; three *s. Educ:* Westminster School. Commnd Scots Guards, 1942; served NW Europe, 3rd Armd Bn Scots Guards; GSO3 Gds Div., 1948; Co. Comdr 2nd Bn Malaya, 1951; GSO2, 1st Div., 1955; DS Camberley, 1961; Comdt Gds Depot, 1963; GSO1, 4th Div. BAOR, 1965; comd 6 Inf. Bde BAOR, 1967; idc 1970; GOC Eastern District, 1971-73; GOC Berlin, 1973-75. Col Comdt, Scottish Div., 1976-. *Address:* The White House, Littlewick Common, Knaphill, Woking, Surrey. *T:* Brookwood 4198. *Club:* Cavalry and Guards.

SCOTT-BATEY, Rowland William James, JP; Chairman, Tyne & Wear Passenger Transport Authority, since 1973; *b* 30 Dec. 1913; *s* of John Henry Scott-Batey and Eva (*née* Hepburn); *m* 1942, Jessie Macpherson Ross; one *s* three *d. Educ:* South Shields High Sch.; Durham Univ. Served War of 1939-45:

Captain, Oxford and Bucks LI. English Industrial Estates Corp., 1946-. Chairman: Newcastle City Labour Party, 1958-76; Northern Regional Council of the Labour Party, 1972-76. Councillor, Tyne & Wear CC 1973- (Chm. 1973-75). JP, Newcastle upon Tyne, 1958-. *Recreations:* watching cricket, reading. *Address:* 186 Jesmond Dene Road, Newcastle upon Tyne NE2 2NL. *T:* Newcastle 814723.

SCOTT BLAIR, George William, MA (Oxon), DSc (London); FRIC; FInstP; *b* 23 July 1902; *s* of late James and Jessie Scott Blair; *m* 1927, Margaret Florence Riddelsdell; no *c. Educ:* Charterhouse; Trinity College, Oxford. Ten years on Research Staff at Rothamsted Experimental Station; sometime Fellow on Rockefeller Foundation at University of Cornell; Head of Chemistry, later Physics Department National Institute for Research in Dairying, University of Reading, 1937-67; retired. Herbert Freundlich Medal, Deutsche Rheol. Ges., 1954; Poiseuille Gold Medal, Internat. Soc. of Biorheology, 1969; Gold Medal, Brit. Soc. of Rheology, 1970. Membre d'honneur, Groupe français de Rhéologie, 1970. *Publications:* An Introduction to Industrial Rheology, 1938; A Survey of General and Applied Rheology, 1943, 2nd edn 1949; Measurements of Mind and Matter, 1950; (ed) Foodstuffs: their Plasticity, Fluidity, and Consistency, 1953; (with Prof. M. Reiner) Agricultural Rheology, 1957; Elementary Rheology, 1969; An Introduction to Biorheology, 1974; many papers in various scientific journals, 1925 to date. *Recreations:* music, modern languages, philosophy of science. *Address:* Grist Cottage, Iffley, Oxford. *T:* Oxford 777462.

SCOTT-BOWDEN, Maj.-Gen. Logan, CBE 1972 (OBE 1964); DSO 1944; MC 1944 and Bar 1946; *b* 21 Feb. 1920; *s* of Lt-Col Jonathan Scott-Bowden, OBE, TD, and late Mary Scott-Bowden (*née* Logan); *m* 1950, Helen Jocelyn, *d* of late Major Sir Francis Caradoc Rose Price, 5th Bt, and late Marjorie Lady Price; three *s* three *d. Educ:* Malvern Coll.; RMA Woolwich. Commissioned Royal Engineers, 1939; served in War of 1939-45: Norway, 1940; Adjt, 53rd (Welsh) Div. RE, 1941; Liaison Duties in Canada and USA, 1942; Normandy Beach Reconnaissance Team (Major), 1943; OC 17 Fd Co RE, NW Europe, 1944; psc 1945; Singapore, Burma (Bde Maj. 98 Indian Inf. Bde), Palestine, Libya, 1946-51; Korea, 1953; jssc 1956; Arabia, 1958-60 (Lt-Col 1959); CRE 1st Div., BAOR, 1960; Head, UK Land Forces Planning Staff, 1963; Asst Dir, Def. Plans MoD (Col), 1964; Comd Trg Bde RE (Brig.), 1966; Nat. Defence Coll. (India), 1969; Comd Ulster Defence Regiment, 1970-71; Head of British Defence Liaison Staff, India, 1971-74, retd 1974. Col Comdt RE, 1975-. *Recreations:* riding, ski-ing, sailing, shooting and travel. *Address:* c/o Lloyds Bank Ltd, 6 Pall Mall, SW1A 2AH.

SCOTT-BROWN, Walter Graham, CVO 1945; BA (Hon. Nat. Sci. Tripos), MD, BCh Cambridge; FRCS, FRCSE; Consulting Surgeon Throat, Nose and Ear Department Royal Free Hospital and late Surgeon at Royal National Throat, Nose and Ear Hospital; late Consulting Aurist and Laryngologist at East Grinstead Cottage Hospital and at the Maxillo-facial unit; and Lecturer to University of London; late Lecturer at Royal National Hospital; Fellow Royal Society Medicine and Member Otological and Laryngological Section; Fellow Medical Society of London; engaged in consulting practice in London as oto-rhino-laryngologist; *e s* of late George A. Brown; *m* 1926, Margaret Affleck, *d* of G. K. Bannerman, High Wycombe; one *s* three *d. Educ:* Corpus Christi College, Cambridge; St Bartholomew's Hospital, London. Served European War, 1916-18 (despatches, wounded); France and Italy T Battery RHA and Captain and Adjutant 14th Brigade RHA 1918; Exhibitioner Corpus Christi College, Cambridge, 1919; Shuter Scholar St Bartholomew's Hospital, 1922; House Surgeon and Clinical Assistant in Ear, Nose and Throat Dept St Barts; Copeman Medallist for Scientific Research, Cambridge, 1932; Dorothy Temple Cross Research Fellowship (travelling), 1932, Berlin, Vienna, Stockholm, Copenhagen, etc. *Publications:* Allergic affections of the Nose, 1945; (ed and contrib.) Diseases of the Ear, Nose and Throat, 2nd edn 1965; Methods of Examination in Ear, Nose and Throat, 1953; Broncho-oesophageal fistula, Cavernous sinus thrombosis: a fatal complication of minor facial sepsis, and other scientific and clinical publications. *Recreations:* fishing, painting. *Address:* 61 Harley Street, W1. *T:* 01-580 1831; Little Down, Ropley, Hants. *T:* 2314.

See also Earl of Orkney.

SCOTT-ELLIOT, Aydua Helen, CVO 1970 (MVO 1958); FSA; retired 1970; *b* 1909; *d* of late Lewis Alexander Scott-Elliot and of Princess Eydua Odescalchi. *Educ:* St Paul's Girls' School and abroad. Temp. Asst Civilian Officer, Admty, 1941-46; Keeper of Prints and Drawings, Royal Library, Windsor Castle, 1946-69. *Publications:* articles in Burlington Magazine, Apollo, etc.

Recreation: gardening. *Address:* Shaldon, Station Road, Mayfield, East Sussex. *T:* Mayfield 2079. *Club:* University Women's.

SCOTT ELLIOT, Major-General James, CB 1954; CBE 1945 (OBE 1940); DSO 1943, Bar 1944; HM Lieutenant of the County of Dumfries, 1962-67; *b* 6 Nov. 1902; *s* of late Lt-Col W. Scott Elliot, DSO and Marie Theresa Scott Elliot (*née* Lyon); *m* 1st, 1932, Cecil Margaret Du Buisson; one *s* two *d*; 2nd, 1971, Mrs Fay Courtauld. *Educ:* Wellington College; Sandhurst. 2nd Lieut KOSB, 1923; Capt. Argyll and Sutherland Highlanders, 1936; psc 1937-38; Major, 1940; served in Egypt, China, India, Malta, Palestine. War of 1939-45: France, N Africa, Sicily, Italy; Temp. Lt-Col 1941; Temp. Brig. 1944; despatches, 1945; Germany, 1946-47; War Office, 1948-49; Maj.-Gen., 1954; GOC 51st (Highland) Division and Highland Dist, 1952-56; retd, 1956. Colonel King's Own Scottish Borderers, 1954-61. President: Dumfries and Galloway Natural History and Antiquarian Soc., 1962-65; Soc. of Antiquaries of Scotland, 1965-67; Brit. Soc. of Dowsers, 1966-75. *Address:* 43 Sheldon Avenue, N6 4JP. *Club:* Army and Navy.

SCOTT-ELLIOT, Walter Travers; *b* 9 Oct. 1895; *o s* of Wm Scott Elliot, Arkleton, Dumfriesshire, and Maude, *o c* of Robert Boyle Travers, Farsid, Co. Cork; *m* 1948, Dorothy Alice, *d* of late William Nunn, Calcutta. *Educ:* Eton. 2nd Lieut Coldstream Guards, Special Reserve, 1914; Capt. 1917; retired, 1919. Subsequently joined Bombay Company Ltd, East India Merchants; Managing Director, 1927. Served on Headquarters, Ministry of Labour, 1941-45; MP (Lab) Accrington, 1945-50; PPS to Sec. of State for War, 1946-47. *Recreations:* shooting and travelling. *Address:* 22 Richmond Court, Sloane Street, SW1. *Club:* Reform.

SCOTT-ELLIS, family name of **Baron Howard de Walden.**

SCOTT FOX, Sir (Robert) David (John), KCMG 1963 (CMG 1956); HM Diplomatic Service, retired; *b* 20 June 1910; *yr s* of late Judge John Scott Fox, KC, and late Agnes Maria Theresa, *d* of Hermann Hammer; *m* 1951, Brigitte, *d* of Pierre Taton; three *d*. *Educ:* Eton; Christ Church, Oxford; Fellow Queen's College. Entered HM Diplomatic Service, 1934. Served Berlin, 1937; Prague, 1937-39; Rio de Janeiro, 1940-44; Foreign Office, 1944-49; Counsellor at Jedda, 1949-51; Chargé d'Affaires there in 1949 and 1950; transferred to Ankara, Counsellor, 1951; Chargé d'Affaires there, 1951, 1952, 1953 and 1954; Minister (Economic and Social Affairs) to UK Delegation to UN, 1955-58; Minister to Roumania, 1959-61; Ambassador to Chile, 1961-66; Ambassador to Finland, 1966-69. Special Rep. of the Sec. of State for Foreign and Commonwealth Affairs, 1970-75. Grand Cross, Chilean Order of Merit, 1965; Order of the Finnish Lion, 1969. *Address:* 47 Eaton Terrace, SW1. *T:* 01-730 5505. *Club:* Travellers'.

SCOTT-HOPKINS, Major James Sidney Rawdon; MP (C) Derbyshire West, since Nov. 1967 (North Cornwall, 1959-66); Member, British Delegation to European Parliament, Deputy Leader, European Conservative Group, and Spokesman on Agriculture, European Parliament, since 1973; Vice-President, European Parliament, since 1976; *b* 29 Nov. 1921; *s* of late Col R. Scott-Hopkins, DSO, MC and late Mrs Scott-Hopkins; *m* 1946, Geraldine Elizabeth Mary Hargreaves; three *s* one *d*. *Educ:* Eton; Oxford. Army, 1939-50; farming, 1950-59. Joint Parliamentary Secretary, Ministry of Agriculture, Fisheries and Food, 1962-64. *Recreations:* riding, shooting. *Address:* House of Commons, SW1; 602 Nelson House, Dolphin Square, SW1. *Clubs:* Carlton, Farmers', St Stephen's.

SCOTT-JAMES, Anne Eleanor, (Lady Lancaster); journalist; *b* 5 April 1913; *d* of R. A. Scott-James and Violet Brooks; *m* 1st, 1944, Macdonald Hastings; one *s* one *d*; 2nd, 1967, Sir Osbert Lancaster, *qv*. *Educ:* St Paul's Girls' Sch.; Somerville Coll., Oxford (Class. Schol.). Editorial staff of Vogue, 1934-41; Woman's Editor, Picture Post, 1941-45; Editor, Harper's Bazaar, 1945-51; Woman's Editor, Sunday Express, 1953-57; Woman's Adviser to Beaverbrook Newspapers, 1959-60; Columnist, Daily Mail, 1960-68; freelance journalist, broadcasting, TV, 1968-. Mem. Council, RCA, 1948-51, 1954-56. *Publications:* In the Mink, 1952; Down to Earth, 1971; Sissinghurst: The Making of a Garden, 1975; (with Osbert Lancaster) The Pleasure Garden, 1977. *Recreations:* reading, gardening, travelling looking at churches and flowers. *Address:* Rose Cottage, Aldworth, Reading, Berks.

SCOTT-MALDEN, (Charles) Peter, CB 1966; Deputy Secretary, Construction, New Towns, Sport and Countryside, Department of the Environment, 1976; *b* 29 June 1918; *e s* of late Gilbert Scott Scott-Malden and of Phyllis Dorothy Scott-Malden (*née* Wilkinson); *m* 1941, Jean Honor Chamberlain Silver, *yr d* of late Lt-Col J. P. Silver, CBE, DSO, RAMC; two *s* two *d*. *Educ:* Winchester Coll. (Schol.); King's College, Cambridge (major Scholar). Entered Ministry of Transport, 1939. War of 1939-45; RAMC 1940-41; Glider Pilot Regiment, 1942-45. Min. of Transport (later DoE): Asst Sec., 1949; Under-Sec., 1959; Dep. Sec., 1968. Attended course at Imperial Defence College, 1956 (idc). *Recreations:* music, golf. *Address:* 23 Burdon Lane, Cheam, Surrey. *T:* 01-642 7086.

SCOTT-MALDEN, Air Vice-Marshal (Francis) David (Stephen), DSO 1942; DFC 1941; RAF (Retd); Department of Transport, since 1966; *b* 26 Dec. 1919; *s* of late Gilbert Scott Scott-Malden and of Phyllis Dorothy Wilkinson; *m* 1955, Anne Elizabeth Watson; two *s* two *d*. *Educ:* Winchester Coll. (Scholar; Goddard Scholar, 1938); King's Coll., Cambridge (Scholar, Sir William Browne Medal for Greek Verse, 1939). Joined Cambridge University Air Squadron, Nov. 1938; called up into RAFVR as Pilot Officer, Oct 1939; flying on operations, 1940-42, as Pilot Officer, Flight Lt, Squadron Leader, and Wing Comdr (DFC and Bar, DSO, Norwegian War Cross; Commander, Order of Orange Nassau, 1945). Visited International Youth Assembly at Washington, DC, as rep. of English Universities, and toured USA as member of United Nations delegation, Sept.-Nov. 1942. RAF Selection Board (Dep. Pres.), 1946; on staff of RAF College, 1946-48; Central Fighter Establishment, 1948; RAF Staff Coll., Bracknell, 1951; psa; RAF Flying Coll., 1954-55; pfc; Jt Planning Staff, Min. of Defence, 1955-57; Group Capt. 1958; Imperial Defence College, 1957-59; idc. Dep. Dir Plans, Air Ministry, 1959-61; Air Cdre 1962; Air Vice-Marshal, 1965. *Recreations:* shooting, fishing, sailing. *Address:* Moray House, Fairway, Merrow, Guildford, Surrey. *T:* Guildford 63311.

SCOTT-MALDEN, Peter; see Scott-Malden, C. P.

SCOTT-MILLER, Commander Ronald, VRD 1942; RNVR (Retired); *b* 1 Nov. 1904; *s* of late Colonel Walter Scott-Miller, DL; *m* 1932, Stella Louise Farquhar, *d* of late Farquhar Deuchar, Shortridge Hall, Northumberland. *Educ:* Aldro School, Eastbourne; Uppingham. Joined London Division, RNVR, as Midshipman, 1924; War of 1939-45 (despatches): HMS Dunedin, Northern Patrol, 1939; HMS London, Atlantic, Russian Convoys, 1940-43; Combined Operations, Mediterranean, NW Europe, 1943-45. Commander, 1943; retired, 1946. MP (C) King's Lynn Division of Norfolk, 1951-59; Parliamentary Private Secretary: to Financial Secretary to Treasury, Dec. 1953-July 1954; to Minister of Transport, 1954-56; to Minister of Pensions and National Insurance, 1956-59. Trustee of Uppingham School, 1954-59. Freeman of the City of London, and Liveryman of Worshipful Company of Butchers, 1926. US Legion of Merit (Legionaire), 1943. *Recreations:* shooting, sailing. *Address:* c/o Temple Gothard & Co., 33/34 Chancery Lane, WC2A 1EN. *Club:* Naval.

SCOTT-MONCRIEFF, Adm. Sir Alan (Kenneth), KCB 1955 (CB 1952); CBE 1952; DSO 1942, Bar 1943; *s* of Robert Lawrence Scott-Moncrieff and Victoria Troutbeck; *m*, 1st, 1923, Norah Doreen Vereker (*d* 1973); one *d*; 2nd, 1974, Mrs Winifred Titley. *Educ:* RN Colleges, Osborne and Dartmouth. Joined HMS Orion, as Midshipman, 1917; Comd HMS Enchantress, 1939-40; Comd HMS Faulkner, Capt. "D" 8th Flotilla, 1942-43 (despatches twice). Imperial Defence College, 1948; Comd HMS Superb, 1949; Flag Officer Comd Fifth Cruiser Sqdn, 1951-52. Korean War (CBE, despatches); Adm. Comd. Reserves, 1953-55; C-in-C, Far East Station, 1955-57. Retired, 1958. A Younger Brother of Trinity House. Mem., Victory Services Club. King Haakon Medal (Norway), 1945; Comdr Legion of Merit (US), 1952. *Address:* 7 King's Walk, Henley-on-Thames. *T:* Henley-on-Thames 2510. *Clubs:* Naval and Military; Phyllis Court (Henley-on-Thames).

SCOTT-MONCRIEFF, Joanna Constance; *b* 7 Sept. 1920; *y d* of late Rev. C. W. Scott-Moncrieff, MA, and Constance E. H. Lunn; *m* 1961, Noel John Horne Baker; one *d*. *Educ:* St Swithun's Sch., Winchester; Sorbonne, Paris. Social work, 1941; Political Warfare Executive, 1941-45; joined BBC, 1945; Deputy Editor, Woman's Hour, 1950; Editor, 1956-64; Producer, Religious Broadcasting, 1964-72. Mem., Gen. Purposes Cttee, Voluntary and Christian Service, 1972-. *Publications:* Pause for Thought, 1971; The 60 Plus Book, 1977. *Address:* Berins Hill, Ipsden, Oxon.

SCOTT-MONCRIEFF, William; Under-Secretary for Finance (Health), Department of Health and Social Security, since 1977; *b* 22 Aug. 1922; *s* of Major R. Scott-Moncrieff and Mrs R. Scott-Moncrieff; *m* 1950, Dora Rosemary Knollys; two *d*. *Educ:* Trinity Coll., Glenalmond; Emmanuel Coll., Cambridge (BA Mech. Sciences). Served RE, 1941-65 (Lt-Col); DHSS (formerly

Min. of Social Security), 1965-. *Recreations:* golf, fishing, painting. *Address:* Combe Cottage, Chiddingfold, Surrey. *T:* Wormley 2937.

SCOTT-SMITH, Catharine Mary, MA Cantab; Principal of Beechlawn Tutorial College, Oxford, 1966-71, retired; *b* 4 April 1912; *d* of Edward Montagu Scott-Smith and Catharine Lorance (*née* Garland). *Educ:* Wycombe Abbey School, Bucks; Girton College, Cambridge. Classics Mistress: St Katharine's School, Wantage, 1933-37; Godolphin School, Salisbury 1937-41; Classics Mistress and house-mistress, Headington School, Oxford, 1941-47, Second Mistress, 1946-47; Classics Mistress and house-mistress, Wycombe Abbey School, Bucks, 1947-55. Second Mistress, 1951-54; Headmistress of Westonbirt School, Tetbury, Gloucestershire, 1955-64. Member Council: Berkhamsted School for Girls; Berkhamsted School; formerly Mem. Exec. Cttee, GBGSA. Pres., Wycombe Abbey School Seniors. *Address:* Graystones, Fairlight, Hastings, East Sussex. *T:* Pett 3071. *Club:* University Women's.

SCOTT-TAGGART, John, OBE 1975; MC; Wing Commander; Barrister-at-law; *b* Bolton, Lancashire, 1897; *s* of Wm Scott-Taggart, MIMechE, consulting engineer. *Educ:* Bolton School; Technological Institutions; King's College, University of London; Law at University College, London. Specialised in radio engineering and patent work; served European War, 1914-19 (despatches, MC); Head of the Patent Department, Radio Communication Company, Ltd, 1920; founded 1922 and later became sole proprietor of the Radio Press, Ltd; served War of 1939-45 with RAF, France, 1939-40 (despatches). Staff Officer, Air Ministry, immediately responsible for all Radar training in RAF, 1940-41; Senior Technical Officer, No 73 Wing and, as such, was technically responsible for all radar stations in two-thirds of England and Wales, 1943-45 (despatches); Admiralty Signal and Radar Establishment, 1951-59. Has acted as Patent Adviser to radio concerns on both sides of the Atlantic. Has taken out numerous patents relating to valve manufacture, radio receiving and transmitting circuits, and allied matters since 1918; CEng; Fellow of the Institute of Radio Engineers; FIEE; FIMechE; FInstP; Fellow American Institute of Electrical Engineers. Cavaliere Ufficiale of Order Al Merito della Repubblica Italiana, 1962 (for services to art); OBE (for services to radio engineering), 1975. *Publications:* Textbooks: Manual of Modern Radio; Book of Practical Radio; Thermionic Tubes in Radio Telegraphy and Telephony; Elementary Textbook on Wireless Vacuum Tubes; Radio Valves and How to Use Them; Wireless Valves Simply Explained; Practical Wireless Valve Circuits, etc; Bibliography of Italian Maiolica, 1967; Italian Maiolica, 1972; Spanish Pottery and Porcelain, 1973; over five hundred articles in technical press; papers read before learned societies (twice at Brit. Assoc.). *Recreation:* collection of paintings, sculpture and ceramics. *Address:* 96 Gregories Road, Beaconsfield, Bucks.

SCOTT WHYTE, Stuart; *see* Whyte, J. S. S.

SCOTT WRIGHT, Prof. Margaret; Director and Professor of the School of Nursing, Dalhousie University, Halifax, Nova Scotia, since 1976; *b* 10 Sept. 1923; *d* of Ebenezer Wright and Margaret Greig Masson. *Educ:* Wallington County Grammar Sch.; Univ. of Edinburgh; St George's and Queen Charlotte's Hosps, London. MA Hons History, PhD and Dipl. Med. Services Admin, Edinburgh; SRN and SCM. Research Asst, Unilever Ltd, 1947-50; Staff Nurse and Sister, St George's Hosp., London, 1953-57; Boots Research Fellow in Nursing, Dept of Social Medicine, Univ. of Edinburgh, 1957-61; Rockefeller Fellow, USA, 1961-62; Deputy Matron, St George's Hosp., 1962-64; Matron, Middlesex Hosp., 1965-68; Dir, Dept of Nursing Studies, Univ. of Edinburgh, 1968-71; Prof. of Nursing Studies, Univ. of Edinburgh, 1972-76. Second Vice-Pres., Internat. Council of Nurses, 1973-77. *Publications:* Experimental Nurse Training at Glasgow Royal Infirmary, 1963; Student Nurses in Scotland, 1968. *Recreations:* walking, music, reading, travel. *Address:* Dalhousie University, Halifax, Nova Scotia, Canada. *Clubs:* University Women's; Dalhousie University.

SCOTTER, Lt-Gen. Sir William Norman Roy, KCB 1975; OBE 1965; MC 1945; Vice Chief of the General Staff, since 1975; *b* 9 Feb. 1922; *s* of Claude Norman Scotter, Carlisle, and Hilda Marie (*née* Turner); *m* 1947, Jean, *d* of Rev. D. S. Stiven, MC, DD; one *s* two *d*. *Educ:* St Bees Sch., Cumberland. Scots Guards, 1941-42; RMA Dehra Dun, 1942; commnd 7th Gurkha Rifles, 1942; served in Burma, 1944-45, 1/7th Gurkha Rifles (MC); 2nd Bn Border Regt, 1946-47, 1/2 Goorkhas Malaya, 1948-51; psc 1951; NATO Northern Flank, 1952-54; 1st Bn Border Regt, 1954-56; HQ 6 Bde, 1956-58; jssc 1959; Instructor Camberley, 1960-63; MoD, 1963-65; CO 1 King's Own Royal

Border Regt, 1965-67; Comdr 19 Inf. Bde, 1967-69; ndc 1969-70; Chief of Staff, Southern Command, 1970-72, HQ UK Land Forces, 1972; Dir, Mil. Ops, MoD, 1972-75. Col, King's Own Royal Border Regt, 1971-; Col Comdt, APTC, 1976-. MBIM. *Recreations:* ball games (Pres., Army Rugby Union, 1972-); sawing logs. *Address:* c/o Midland Bank Ltd, Court Square, Carlisle, Cumbria. *Club:* Army and Navy.

SCOULLER, (John) Alan; Assistant General Manager (Personnel, formerly Staff), Midland Bank, since 1975; *b* 23 Sept. 1929; *e s* of late Charles James Scouller and Mary Helena Scouller; *m* 1954, Angela Geneste Ambrose; two *s* five *d*. *Educ:* John Fisher Sch., Purley. Army service, Queen's Own Royal W Kent Regt, 1948-58 (Captain). Joined Unilever as management trainee, 1958; Personnel Man., Wall's Ice Cream, 1959-62; Domestos, 1963-66; Holpak, 1966-68; Commercial Plastics and Holpak, 1968-69; left Unilever to join Commn on Industrial Relations, 1969; Dir of Industrial Relations until 1973, full-time Comr, 1973-74. Mem., Employment Appeal Tribunal, 1976-. *Address:* Shortlands, 32 Sollershott West, Letchworth, Herts. *T:* Letchworth 2781.

SCOURFIELD, Edward Grismond Beaumont D.; *see* Davies-Scourfield.

SCOWEN, Sir Eric (Frank), Kt 1973; MD, DSc; FRCP, FRCS, FRCPE; FRCPath; Director, Medical Professorial Unit, 1955-75; Physician to St Bartholomew's Hospital, 1946-75; Professor of Medicine, University of London, 1961-75 (Reader in Medicine, 1938-61); Chairman, Council of Imperial Cancer Research Fund, since 1967; *b* 22 April 1910; *s* of late Frank Edward Scowen and Eleanor Betsy (*née* Barnes) (*d* 1969). *Educ:* City of London School; St Bartholomew's Hospital Medical College. St Bartholomew's Hospital: House Physician, 1931, Second Assistant, 1933, to Medical Professorial Unit; Baly Research Fell. in Clin. Med., 1933; First Asst to Med. Professorial Unit, 1935; Asst Dir of Med. Prof. Unit, and Asst Phys, 1937; Rockefeller Research Fell. to Columbia Univ., New York, 1937. Chairman: Cttee on Safety of Drugs, 1969- (Mem., 1963); British Pharmacopœia Commission, 1963-69; Cttee on Safety of Medicines, 1970-; Cttee on the Review of Medicines, 1975-; Poisons Bd (Home Office), 1976-. *Publications:* various in medical and scientific journals. *Address:* 44 Lincoln's Inn Fields, WC2A 3PX. *T:* 01-405 4480. *Club:* Athenæum.

SCRAGG, Air Vice-Marshal Sir Colin, KBE 1963 (CBE 1953; MBE 1940); CB 1960; AFC 1942, Bar to AFC 1949; retired; *b* 8 Sept. 1908; *s* of late Lt A. Scragg, KRRC; *m* 1932, Phyllis Kathleen Rayner, Southampton; one *s* two *d*. *Educ:* King Edward VI School, Southampton. No 1 (Fighter) Squadron, 1931-34; served in a succession of flying training schools, including 34 FTS Canada, until 1943; War of 1939-45, Comd No 166 (Bomber) Squadron, 1943-44 (pow, Germany). Transport Command Development Unit, 1946-49; Dep. Director, Operational Requirements, Air Min., 1950-53, Director, 1955-58; idc 1954; AOC No 23 Training Group, 1958-60; Deputy Controller Aircraft (RAF), Ministry of Aviation, 1960-64. Order of Orange Nassau (Netherlands), 1945. *Address:* Wedgwood, Pine Walk, Chilworth, Southampton. *T:* Southampton 769110.

SCREECH, Prof. Michael Andrew; Fielden Professor of French Language and Literature in the University of London, since 1971; *b* 2 May 1926; 3rd *s* of Richard John Screech, MM and Nellie Screech (*née* Maunder); *m* 1956, Ursula Anne Grace (*née* Reeve); three *s*. *Educ:* Sutton High Sch., Plymouth; University Coll. London (BA); University of Montpellier, France. DLitt (Birmingham), 1958. Other Rank, Intelligence Corps (Far East), 1944-48. Asst, UCL, 1950-51; Birmingham Univ.: Lectr, 1951-58; Sen. Lectr., 1959-61; Reader, UCL 1961-66; Vis. Prof., Univ. of Western Ontario, 1964-65; Personal Chair of French, UCL, 1966; Vis. Prof., Univ. of New York, Albany, 1968-69. Membre du Comité d'Humanisme et Renaissance, 1971. *Publications:* The Rabelaisian Marriage, 1958; L'Evangélisme de Rabelais, 1959; Tiers Livre de Pantagruel, 1964, repr. 1975; Les epistres et évangiles de Lefèvre d'Etaples, 1964; Les Regrets et autres oeuvres poëtiques (Du Bellay), 1966, repr. 1975; Marot évangélique, 1967; (contrib.) The Art of Criticism, ed P. H. Nurse, 1969; Gargantua, 1970; Le Nouveau Testament de Lefèvre d'Etaples, 1970; F. de Billon: Le Fort inexpugnable de l'Honneur du Sexe Femenin, 1970; Opuscules d'Amour par Héroët et autres divins poëtes, 1970; Amyot: Les œuvres morales et meslées de Plutarque, 1971; (contrib.) Colloquia Erasmiana Turonensia, ed J. C. Margolin, 1972; La Pantagrueline Prognostication, 1975; (contrib.) Classical Influences in Europe AD 1500-1700, ed R. A. Bolgar, 1976; articles on Renaissance and Reformation in: Bibliothèque d'Humanisme et Renaissance, Etudes rabelaisiennes, Jl of

Warburg Inst., etc. *Recreations:* walking, rose-growing, boating, puericulture. *Address:* 5 Swanston-field, Whitchurch-on-Thames RG8 7HP. *T:* Pangbourne 2513.

SCRIMGEOUR, James, CMG 1959; OBE 1944; *b* 8 June 1903; *s* of late Alexander Carron Scrimgeour and Helen May Scrimgeour (*née* Bird); *m* 1928, Winifred, *d* of late Stephen Ward Giles; one *s. Educ:* Loretto School; Clare College, Cambridge. Member of Stock Exchange, 1929-69. Auxiliary Air Force, 1938-45; Air staff, Air Ministry, 1942-45. Senior Partner, J. & A. Scrimgeour, 1949-69; Chm., Hume Holdings Ltd, 1953-75. Mem. Council of White Ensign Assoc. *Address:* 7 Princes Gate, SW7 1QL. *Clubs:* Turf; Hawks (Cambridge).

SCRIMSHAW, Frank Herbert; Deputy Director (Air), RAE, Farnborough, since 1976; *b* 25 Dec. 1917; *s* of late John Leonard Scrimshaw and Jessie Scrimshaw (*née* Sewell), Lincoln; *m* 1950, Joan Olive, *d* of Leslie Stephen Paskall, Felixstowe; one *s. Educ:* The City Sch., Lincoln; University Coll., Nottingham. BSc London. Joined Scientific Civil Service, 1939; various posts at RAE, Farnborough, and Blind Landing Experimental Unit, RAF Martlesham Heath, 1939-58; Dir of Scientific Research (Electronics), Min. of Aviation, 1959-61; RRE, Malvern: Head of Guided Weapons Group, 1961-65; Head of Mil. and Civil Systems Dept, 1965-67; Dir Gen., Electronics R&D, Min. of Technology, later MoD, 1967-72; Dep. Dir (Equipment), RAE, Farnborough, 1972-76. *Address:* Brambles, 129 Prospect Road, Farnborough, Hants. *T:* Farnborough 45742.

SCRIVENER, Anthony Frank Bertram, QC 1975; a Recorder of the Crown Court, since 1976; *b* 31 July 1935; *s* of Frank Bertram Scrivener and Edna Scrivener; *m* 1964, Irén Becze; one *s* one *d. Educ:* Kent Coll., Canterbury; University Coll. London (LLB). Called to Bar, Gray's Inn, 1958. Lectr in Law, Ghana, 1959-61; practice as Junior, 1961-75. *Recreations:* tennis, chess, cricket. *Address:* 4 Willow Dene, Uxbridge Road, Pinner, Mddx HA5 3LT. *T:* 01-868 7678; 8 New Square, Lincoln's Inn, WC2A 3QP.

SCRIVENER, Ronald Stratford, CMG 1965; HM Diplomatic Service, retired; Executive Director, British Soviet Chamber of Commerce, since 1977; *b* 29 Dec. 1919; *s* of Sir Patrick Scrivener, KCMG; *m* 1st, 1947, Elizabeth Drake-Brockman (marr. diss., 1952); 2nd, 1962, Mary Alice Olga Sofia Jane Hohler, *d* of late Squadron-Leader Robert Charlton Lane; two step-*s* two step-*d. Educ:* Westminster School; St Catharine's College, Cambridge. Served with Royal Air Force Volunteer Reserve, 1940-45. Appointed HM Diplomatic Service, Dec. 1945. Served in Berlin, Buenos Aires, Vienna, Caracas, Berne, Bangkok; Ambassador to: Panama, 1969-70; Czechoslovakia, 1971-74; Asst Under-Sec. of State, FCO, 1974-76. *Recreations:* travel, fishing. *Address:* 72 Bedford Gardens, W8. *Clubs:* White's, Anglo-Belgian.

SCRIVENOR, Sir Thomas (Vaisey), Kt 1960; CMG 1956; *b* 28 Aug. 1908; *e s* of late John Brooke Scrivenor, ISO, formerly Dir of Geological Survey, Malaya; *m* 1934, Mary Elizabeth Neatby; one *s* three *d. Educ:* King's School, Canterbury; Oriel College, Oxford (MA). Temp. Assistant Principal, Colonial Office, 1930-33; Assistant District Officer, Tanganyika, 1934-37; Assistant District Commissioner, Palestine, 1937-43; Assistant Lt-Governor, Malta, 1943-44; Principal, Colonial Office, 1944-46; Principal Asst Sec., Palestine, 1946-48; Civil Service Comr, Nigeria, 1948-53; Deputy High Commissioner for Basutoland, the Bechuanaland Protectorate, and Swaziland, 1953-60. Sec. to Exec. Council of Commonwealth Agric. Bureaux, 1961-73. *Address:* Vine Cottage, Minster Lovell, Oxon. *T:* Asthall Leigh 620.

SCROGGIE, Alan Ure Reith, CBE 1973 (OBE 1961); QPM 1968; one of HM's Inspectors of Constabulary 1963-75; *b* 1912; *s* of late Col W. R. J. Scroggie, CIE, IMS, Callander, Perthshire; *m* 1940, Shiela Catherine, *d* of late Finlay Mackenzie, Elgin, Morayshire; two *s. Educ:* Cargilfield Preparatory Sch.; Fettes Coll.; Edinburgh Univ. (BL). Joined Edinburgh City Police, 1930; Asst Chief Constable of Bucks, 1947-53; Chief Constable of Northumberland, 1953-63. OStJ 1955. *Recreations:* golf, fishing, shooting. *Address:* Fowler's Cottage, Abercrombie, by St Monan's, Fife. *Clubs:* Royal and Ancient (St Andrews); Northumberland Golf.

SCRUBY, Ven. Ronald Victor, MA; Archdeacon of Portsmouth, since 1977; *b* 23 Dec. 1919; 6th *s* of late Thomas Henry Scruby and late Florence Jane Scruby, Norwood Green, Southall, Middx; *m* 1955, Sylvia Tremayne Miles, *e d* of late Rear-Adm. Roderic B. T. Miles, Trotton, Sussex; two *s* one *d. Educ:* Southall Technical Coll.; Trinity Hall, Cambridge. Engineering Apprentice, London Transport, 1936-39. Royal Engineers, 1939-45; Capt. 1943. Trinity Hall, Cambridge, 1945-48;

Cuddesdon Coll., Oxford, 1948-50. Asst Curate, Rogate, Sussex, 1950-53; Chaplain, King Edward VII Hosp., Midhurst, 1950-53; Chaplain, Saunders-Roe, Osborne, E Cowes, 1953-58; Vicar of Eastney, Portsmouth, 1958-65; Rural Dean of Portsmouth, 1960-65; Archdeacon of the Isle of Wight, 1965-77. *Recreations:* rowing, walking. *Address:* Victoria Lodge, 36 Osborne Road, Fareham, Hants PO16 7OS. *T:* Fareham 80101.

SCRUTTON, (Thomas) Hugh, CBE 1967; *b* 8 June 1917; *s* of late Rev. Canon Tom Burton Scrutton and Lesley Hay; *m* 1st, 1941, Helen Greeves (who obtd a divorce, 1952); one *d*; 2nd, 1960, Elizabeth Quayle. *Educ:* Charterhouse; King's Coll., Cambridge (MA). Temporary Asst Keeper, Print Room, British Museum, 1946; Asst, 1947, and Director, 1948, Whitechapel Art Gallery; Director, Walker Art Gallery, Liverpool, 1952-70; Dir, Nat. Galls of Scotland, Edinburgh, 1971-77, retired. Pres., Museums Assoc., 1970-71. Hon. DLitt Liverpool, 1971. *Address:* 21 Braid Avenue, Edinburgh EH10 4SR.

SCRYMGEOUR, Lord; Alexander Henry Scrymgeour-Wedderburn; *b* 5 June 1949; *s* and *heir* of 11th Earl of Dundee, *qv. Educ:* Eton. Page of Honour to the Queen, 1964-65. *Address:* Birkhill, Cupar, Fife. *T:* Gauldry 209.

SCRYMGEOUR-WEDDERBURN, family name of **Earl of Dundee.**

SCULLARD, Geoffrey Layton, OBE 1971; HM Diplomatic Service; Counsellor (Administration) and Consul-General, HM Embassy, Washington, since 1973; *b* 5 July 1922; *s* of late William Harold Scullard and late Eleanor Mary Scullard (*née* Tomkin); *m* 1945, Catherine Margaret Pinington; three *d. Educ:* St Olave's Grammar Sch. Joined Foreign Office, 1939. Served War (RAF Signals), 1942-46. Diplomatic service at: Stockholm, Washington, Baghdad, Los Angeles, Moscow. *Recreations:* fishing, golf. *Address:* c/o Foreign and Commonwealth Office, SW1A 2AH; 9 Beech Court, Easington Place, Guildford, Surrey GU1 2EJ. *T:* Guildford 70201.

SCULLARD, Howard Hayes, FBA 1955; FSA; Professor Emeritus of Ancient History in the University of London; *b* 9 Feb. 1903; *s* of late Rev. Professor Herbert H. Scullard and Barbara Louise Scullard (*née* Dodds). *Educ:* Highgate School; St John's Coll., Cambridge (Scholar). First Class Classical Tripos Part II, 1926; Thirlwall Prize, Cambridge, 1929; MA Cambridge, PhD London, 1930. Classical Tutor, New College, London, 1926-35; Reader, 1935-59, Professor of Ancient History, 1959-70, King's College, London. A Governor of New College, London, 1930-77; Vice-Pres., Soc. for the Promotion of Roman Studies; former Mem. Council, British Acad. and of Royal Numismatic Soc.; Actg Dir, Inst. of Classical Studies, London, 1964. FKC, 1970. *Publications:* Scipio Africanus in the Second Punic War, 1930; A History of the Roman World from 753 to 146 BC, 1935, 4th edn 1978; (edited with H. E. Butler) Livy book XXX, 1939, 6th edn 1953; (Joint Editor of and contrib. to) The Oxford Classical Dictionary, 1949, Editor (with N. G. L. Hammond) of new edn, 1970; Roman Politics, 220-150 BC, 1951, 2nd edn 1973; (rev.) F. B. Marsh, A History of the Roman World from 146 to 30 BC, 1953, 3rd edn 1962; From the Gracchi to Nero, 1959, 4th edn 1976; (rev. jtly) J. C. Stobbart: The Grandeur that was Rome, 1961; (ed) Atlas of the Classical World, 1959 and Shorter Atlas of the Classical World, 1962 (Dutch, French and Spanish translations); The Etruscan Cities and Rome, 1967 (Italian translation, 1969); Scipio Africanus: Soldier and Politician, 1970; The Elephant in the Greek and Roman World, 1974; A History of Rome (rev. and rewritten edn of Prof. M. Cary's book, 1935), 1975; A Concise History of Roman Britain, 1978; (Gen. Editor of series) Aspects of Greek and Roman Life, 33 Vols to date; Annual Survey of Roman history in The Year's Work in Classical Studies, 1937-48, and of ancient history in Annual Bulletin of Historical Literature, 1949-73; articles and reviews in Journal of Roman Studies, Classical Review, Encyclopædia Britannica, etc. *Recreation:* golf. *Address:* 6 Foscote Road, Hendon, NW4. *Club:* Athenæum.

SCULLY, Vincent William Thomas, CMG 1946; United States Medal of Freedom (Bronze Palm); FCA; *b* 9 Jan. 1900; *s* of James Scully, Dist. Inspector, RIC, and Katherine Scully, New Ross, County Wexford, Ireland; *m* 1930, Sylvia, *d* of late Sir Wyly Grier; one *s. Educ:* Christian Brothers School, New Ross and Thurles, Ireland; Trinity Coll., Dublin. Chartered Accountant, Ontario, 1929; practised as Chartered Acct with Clarkson, Gordon, Dilworth and Nash, 1925-32; Director and Sec.-Treas., J. D. Woods & Co. Ltd, 1932-45; Controller and Sec. Treas., York Knitting Mills Ltd, 1932-45; Sec.-Treas, Plateau Co. Ltd (Crown Co.), 1940-41; Treas. and subsequently Pres. War Supplies, Ltd (Crown Co.), 1941-44; Pres. Victory

Aircraft Ltd (Crown Co.), 1944-45; Deputy Minister of Reconstruction and Supply and Vice-Pres., Nat. Research Council, 1945-47; Deputy Minister of National Revenue (Taxation), 1948-51; Comptroller, The Steel Company of Canada Ltd, 1951, Pres., 1957, Chief Exec. Officer, 1960, Chm. Bd, 1966, retired, 1976. *Address:* 9 Deer Park Crescent, Apt 1203, Toronto, Ontario M4V 2C4, Canada. *Clubs:* Royal Ottawa Golf (Ottawa); Toronto, York, Toronto Golf (Toronto).

SCUPHAM, John, OBE 1961; retired as Controller of Educational Broadcasting, British Broadcasting Corporation, 1963-65; *b* 7 Sept. 1904; *s* of Roger Scupham and Kate Whittingham; *m* 1932, Dorothy Lacey Clark; one *s* one *d. Educ:* Market Rasen Gram. Sch.; Emmanuel Coll., Cambridge (Scholar). BA 1st Cl., History, 1926, 1st Cl. English, 1927 (Cantab). Various teaching posts, 1927-46. Joined staff of BBC as Educn Officer, 1946; Head of Educational Broadcasting, 1954. Member, Central Advisory Council for Education (England), 1961-63; Member, Church of England Board of Education, 1960-72. President, Educational Section of British Association, 1965-66. Mem. Council, Open Univ., 1969-. DUniv, Open Univ., 1975. *Publications:* Broadcasting and the Community, 1967; The Revolution in Communications, 1970; Open Learning, 1976. *Recreations:* reading, gardening. *Address:* 26 Crabtree Lane, Harpenden, Herts. *T:* Harpenden 3223.
See also A . R . H . Glover .

SCUSE, Dennis George, MBE 1957; TD 1946; Managing Director, Dennis Scuse Ltd, PR, TV and Radio Consultants; *b* 19 May 1921; *yr s* of late Charles H. and Katherine Scuse; *m* 1948, Joyce Evelyn, *yr d* of late Frank and Frances Burt; one *s. Educ:* Park Sch., Ilford; Mercers' Sch., London. Joined Martins Bank, 1937. TA (RA), 1938; mobilised, Sept. 1939. Served War, commissioned 78th (HyAA) Regt, RA, 1940. Air Defence of Gt Britain, 1940-41; Command Entertainment Officer, Ceylon Army Comd, 1942; subseq. 65th (HyAA) Regt, in MELF and CMF, 1943-44; joined Army Broadcasting Service, CMF: commanded stations in Bari, Rome and Athens, 1945-46; demobilised, Sept. 1946. Joined Overseas Div. BBC and seconded to War Office for Forces Broadcasting Service in Benghasi and Canal Zone; Chief Programme Officer, 1947-48; Asst Dir, British Forces Network, Germany, 1949-50; Dir, 1950-57. Introduced "Two-Way Family Favourites", 1952-57; Sen. Planning Asst, BBC-TV, 1958-59; Chief Asst (Light Entertainment), BBC-TV, 1960; Chief Asst (TV), BBC New York Office, Sept. 1960; BBC Rep. in USA, July 1962; Gen. Manager, BBC-TV Enterprises, 1963-72, and BBC Radio Enterprises, 1968-72. Trident Management Ltd, 1972; Man. Dir, Trident Internat. TV Enterprises Ltd, 1972-76. *Publications:* numerous articles on broadcasting, television programme exports, etc. *Recreations:* wine making, watching television. *Address:* 246 Sheen Lane, SW14. *T:* 01-876 2372.

SCUTT, Robin Hugh, CBE 1976; Deputy Managing Director, BBC-TV, since 1977; *b* Sandgate, Kent, 24 Oct. 1920; *s* of late Rev. A. O. Scutt, MA and Freda M. Scutt (*née* Palmer); *m* 1st, 1943, Judy Watson (marr. diss. 1960); two *s* ; 2nd, 1961, Patricia A. M. Smith. *Educ:* Fonthill; Bryanston; Jesus Coll., Cambridge (MA Mod. Lang.). Served Intell. Corps, 1941-42 (invalided out). BBC Eur. Service (French Section), 1942; Senior Programme Asst., 1945; BBC TV Outside Broadcasts Producer, 1955; BBC Paris Rep., 1958; Gen. Man., Trans Europe Television, 1962; rejoined BBC TV Outside Broadcasts, 1963; Asst Head of BBC TV Presentation (BBC1), 1966; Controller: BBC Light Programme, 1967; BBC Radio 1 and 2, 1967-68; BBC 2, 1969-74; Development, BBC-TV, 1974-77. *Recreations:* music, theatre, gardening. *Address:* c/o BBC Television Service, W12; The Abbey Cottage, Cockfield, Suffolk.

SEA-LION; *see* Bennett, Captain G. M.

SEABORG, Glenn Theodore; University Professor of Chemistry, University of California, Berkeley, since 1971; *b* 19 April 1912; *s* of Herman Theodore and Selma Erickson Seaborg; *m* 1942, Helen Lucille Griggs; four *s* two *d. Educ:* Univ. of Calif, Los Angeles (BA); Univ. of Calif, Berkeley (PhD). University of California, Berkeley: Res. Associate (with Prof. Gilbert N. Lewis), Coll. of Chem., 1937-39; Instr, Dept of Chem., 1939-41; Asst Prof., 1941-45, Prof., 1945-71; Chancellor, 1958-61; Lawrence Berkeley Laboratory: Associate Dir, 1954-61, and 1972-; Dir, Nuclear Chem. Div., 1946-58, and 1972-75; Head, Plutonium Chem. Metall. Lab., Univ. of Chicago, 1942-46; Chm., US Atomic Energy Commn, 1961-71. Member, US Delegns to: 3rd (Chm.) and 4th (Chm. and Pres.) UN Internat. Confs on Peaceful Uses of Atomic Energy, Geneva, 1964 and 1971; 5-15th annual Gen. Confs of Internat. Atomic Energy Agency, 1961-71; USSR, for signing of Memorandum on Cooperation in the Field of Utilization of Atomic Energy for

Peaceful Purposes (Chm.), 1963; USSR, for signing of Limited Test Ban Treaty, 1963. Member: Nat. Council on Marine Resources and Engineering Development, 1966-71; Nat. Aeronautics and Space Council, 1961-71; Fed. Council for Science and Tech., 1961-71; Pres.'s Cttee on Manpower, 1964-69; Fed. Radiation Council, 1961-69; Nat. Sci. Bd, Nat. Sci. Foundn, 1960-61; Pres.'s Science Adv. Cttee, 1959-61; 1st Gen. Adv. Cttee, US Atomic Energy Commn, 1946-50; Commn on the Humanities, 1962-65; Scientific Adv. Bd, Robert A. Welch Foundn, 1957-; Bd of Dirs, Nat. Educnl TV and Radio Centre, 1958-64, 1967-70; Bd of Dirs, World Future Soc., 1969-; Nat. Programming Council for Public TV, 1970-72; Bd of Governors, Amer.-Swedish Hist. Foundn, 1972-; Steering Cttee, Chem. Educn Material Study (Chm.), 1959-74; Nat. Cttee on America's Goals and Resources, Nat. Planning Assoc., 1962-64; Electoral Coll. Hall of Fame for Great Americans, 1969-; Council on Foreign Relations, 1965-; Bd of Trustees: Pacific Science Centre Foundn, 1962-; Science Service, 1965- (Pres., 1966-); Amer.-Scandinavian Foundn, 1968-; Educnl Broadcasting Corp., 1970-73; Amer. Assoc. for the Advancement of Science (Pres. 1972, Chm. 1973); Amer. Chem. Soc. (Pres., 1976). Mem. and Hon. Mem., Fellow and Hon. Fellow, numerous scientific and professional socs and instns, Argentina, German Dem. Republic., German Fed. Republic, Poland, Spain, Sweden, UK, USA, USSR. Holds over 40 hon. doctorates from univs and colls. Named one of America's 10 Outstanding Young Men, 1947. Awards (1947-) include: Nobel Prize for Chemistry (jtly), 1951; Perkin Medal (Amer. Sect. Soc. Chem. Ind.), 1957; USAEC Enrico Fermi Award, 1959; Priestley Meml Award, 1960; Franklin Medal (Franklin Inst. of Philadelphia), 1963; Award in Pure Chem., 1947, Charles Lathrop Parsons Award, (Amer. Chem. Soc.), 1964; Chem. Pioneer Award, 1968, Gold Medal Award, (Am. Inst. of Chemists), 1973; Arches of Science Award (Pacific Science Centre, Seattle), 1968; Officer, French Legion of Honour, 1973. Co-discoverer of: nuclear energy source isotopes Pu-239 and U-233; elements (1940-74): 94, plutonium; 95, americium; 96, curium; 97, berkelium; 98, californium; 99, einsteinium; 100, fermium; 101, mendelevium; 102, nobelium; element 106. *Publications:* (jtly) The Chemistry of the Actinide Elements, 1958; The Transuranium Elements (Silliman Lectures), 1958; (jtly) Elements of the Universe, 1958; Man-made Transuranium Elements, 1963; (jtly) Education and the Atom, 1964; (jtly) The Nuclear Properties of the Heavy Elements, 1964; (jtly) Oppenheimer, 1969; (jtly) Man and Atom, 1971; Nuclear Milestones, 1972; contrib. numerous papers on nuclear chem. and nuclear physics, transuranium elements, high energy nuclear reactions and educn in Physical Rev., Jl Amer. Chm. Soc., Annual Rev. of Nuclear Science, etc. *Recreations:* golf, reading, hiking. *Address:* (business) Lawrence Berkeley Laboratory, University of California, Berkeley, Calif 94720, USA; (home) 1154 Glen Road, Lafayette, Calif 94549, USA. *Clubs:* Faculty (Univ. Calif, Berkeley); Commonwealth Club of California, Bohemian (San Francisco); Chemists (NY); Cosmos, University (Washington).

SEABORN, Most Rev. Robert Lowder; *see* Newfoundland, Archbishop of.

SEABORNE DAVIES, David Richard; *see* Davies, D. R. S.

SEABROOK, Air Vice-Marshal Geoffrey Leonard, CB 1965; *b* 25 Aug. 1909; *s* of late Robert Leonard Seabrook; *m* 1949, Beryl Mary (*née* Hughes); one *s* one *d. Educ:* King's Sch., Canterbury. Commissioned in RAF (Accountant Branch), 1933; served in: Middle East, 1935-43; Bomber Command, 1943-45; Transport Command, 1945-47; Iraq, 1947-49; Signals Command, 1949-51; Air Ministry Organisation and Methods, 1951-53; Home Command Group Captain Organisation, 1953-56; Far East Air Force, 1957-59; idc 1960; Director of Personnel, Air Ministry, 1961-63; Air Officer Administration, HQ, RAF Tech. Trg Comd, 1963-66; retired June 1966. Air Cdre 1961; Air Vice-Marshal, 1964. Head of Secretarial Branch, Royal Air Force, 1963-66. FCA 1957 (Associate, 1932). *Recreations:* sailing, tennis, golf. *Address:* Smugglers, Crowborough, East Sussex. *T:* Crowborough 2923. *Clubs:* Royal Air Force; Walton and Frinton Yacht.

SEABROOK, John, CMG 1970; AFC 1918; ED 1947; JP; Founder Chairman, Seabrook Fowlds Ltd, Auckland, NZ, 1919-70; Chairman, Amalgamated Pacific Industries Ltd, since 1970; *b* 6 Jan. 1896; *e s* of Albert David Seabrook and Marion May Seabrook; *m* 1926, Doreen Mary Alexina Carr, *d* of Charles Edward and Rose Louise McKenzie Carr, Auckland; one *s* one *d. Educ:* Auckland Grammar School. Served RFC, France, 1916-17; RAF, Middle East, 1918 (Captain). Returned to NZ, 1919, and founded Seabrook Fowlds Ltd. Served RNZAF, 1940-44 (Group Captain). Mem. Board of Trustees, NZ Inst. for Blind for 24 years; Dir, NZ National Airways,

1952-61; Dep. Chm., Blinded Servicemen's Trust Board; Mem., Nature Conservation Council, Wellington; Mem., Hauraki Gulf Maritime Park Board; Pres., Auckland Inst. and Museum, 1961-63. *Recreations:* yachting, gardening. *Address:* 146 Orakei Road, Remuera, Auckland 5, NZ. *T:* 52735. *Club:* Royal Air Force.

SEABROOKE, George Alfred; Director, The Polytechnic, Wolverhampton, since 1977; *b* 8 Dec. 1923; *s* of John Arthur Seabrooke and Elsie Seabrooke; *m* 1945, Evelyn Sargent; two *s*. *Educ:* Keighley Boys' Grammar Sch.; Bradford Technical Coll.; Stoke-on-Trent Tech. Coll.; King's Coll., London Univ. National Service, 1946-48. Post Office Engrg Dept, 1940-50; Estate Duty Office, Comrs of Inland Revenue, 1950-56; SW London Coll. of Commerce, 1956-60; Trent Polytechnic, Nottingham (and precursor Colls) 1960-73; Dep. Dir, NE London Polytechnic, 1974-77. *Publications:* Air Law, 1964; contrib. learned jls. *Recreations:* music, cricket, rugby. *Address:* The Polytechnic, Wolverhampton, West Midlands. *T:* Wolverhampton 27371.

SEABY, Wilfred Arthur; retired museum official; Director, Ulster Museum (previously Belfast Museum and Art Gallery), 1953-70; Numismatic Section, Department of Technology and Local History, 1970-73; *b* 16 Sept. 1910; *y s* of late Allen W. Seaby, sometime Prof. of Art, Univ. of Reading; *m* 1937, Nora, *d* of late A. E. Pecover, Reading; two *s* one *d*. *Educ:* Wycliffe College; Reading University, College of Art. Dip. Museums Assoc., 1939. Served War of 1939-45, Royal Air Force, 1940-46 (Flt-Lt). B. A. Seaby Ltd, 1927-30; Reading, Birmingham, and Taunton Museums, 1931-53. FSA 1948. Hon. MA QUB, 1971. *Recreation:* water colour painting. *Address:* 36 Ladbrook Road, Solihull, West Midlands.

SEAFIELD, 13th Earl of, *cr* 1701; **Ian Derek Francis Ogilvie-Grant;** Viscount Seafield, Baron Ogilvy of Cullen, 1698; Viscount Reidhaven, Baron Ogilvy of Deskford and Cullen, 1701; *b* 20 March 1939; *s* of Countess of Seafield (12th in line), and Derek Studley-Herbert (who assumed by deed poll, 1939, the additional surnames of Ogilvie-Grant; he *d* 1960); *S* mother, 1969; *m* 1st, 1960, Mary Dawn Mackenzie (marr. diss., 1971); *m* *d* of Henry Illingworth; two *s*; 2nd, 1971, Leila, *d* of Mahmoud Refaat, Cairo. *Educ:* Eton. *Recreations:* shooting, fishing, tennis. *Heir: s* Viscount Reidhaven, *qv*. *Address:* Old Cullen, Cullen, Banffshire. *T:* Cullen 40221; Kinveachy Forest, Boat of Garten, Inverness-shire. *T:* Boat of Garten 232. *Club:* White's.

SEAGER, family name of **Baron Leighton of Saint Mellons.**

SEAGER, Basil William, CMG 1949; OBE 1939; HM Immigration Service, retired 1970; *b* 1898; *s* of late E. J. P. Seager, Constantinople, and L. D. Seager (*née* Sellar); *m* 1944, Heather Mildred Carmichael, *d* of late Lt-Col R. C. Bell, DSO, OBE, late Central India Horse. *Educ:* abroad. Communications Department, FO, 1926; British Agency and Consulate (now HM Embassy), Jedda, Saudi Arabia, 1926-34; seconded to Aden Govt as Political Officer, 1933-34; Colonial Administrative Service as PO (Frontier Officer), 1934; Acting Political Secretary on various occasions, 1935-40; Political Officer in charge W Aden Protectorate, 1940; British Agent, Western Aden Protectorate, 1942; Chairman (ex-officio) Abyan (Cotton) Board, 1947-54; retired Colonial Administrative Service, 1954. Served European War 1914-18, 1916-22 (Captain); War of 1939-45, 1941-42 (Major). *Address:* 16 Broadwater Down, Tunbridge Wells, Kent.

SEAGER, Ven. Edward Leslie; Archdeacon of Dorset, 1955-74; Archdeacon Emeritus of Salisbury Cathedral since 1975; Canon and Prebendary of Gillingham Major since 1968; Vicar of Gillingham, Dorset, since 1946 and of Fifehead Magdalen since 1966; Rural Dean of Blackmore Vale since 1975; *b* 5 Oct. 1904; *s* of William Seager, Chaddesley Corbett, Worcs; unmarried. *Educ:* Bromsgrove Sch.; Hatfield College, Durham. Foundation Scholar, Hatfield College, 1923; BA, Jenkyn's Scholar, 1926; Diploma in Theology, 1928; MA, 1931. Deacon, 1928, priest, 1929, Newcastle upon Tyne; Chaplain, Wellington School, 1931-39. War of 1939-45, CF, 1937-46; SCF, 1942-45; DACG, 1945-46; HCF, 1946-. Rural Dean of Shaftesbury, 1951-56; Canon and Prebendary of Shipton in Salisbury Cathedral, 1954-68; Examining Chaplain to Bishop of Salisbury, 1968. Governor of Milton Abbey School, 1956-; Chairman of Governors, Gillingham School, 1959-. *Publication:* Day unto Day, 1932. *Recreations:* scouting, golf. *Address:* The Vicarage, Gillingham, Dorset SP8 4AJ. *T:* Gillingham 2435. *Club:* East India, Devonshire, Sports and Public Schools.

SEAGER, Major Ronald Frank, RA, retired; Executive Director, RSPCA, since 1971 (Secretary, 1966-71); Advisory Director,

International Society for Protection of Animals; *b* 27 May 1918; *s* of Frank Seager and Lilias K. (*née* Parr); *m* 1941, Josephine, *d* of Rev. R. M. Chadwick; one *s* one *d*. *Educ:* St Albans School. Royal Artillery (HAC), 1939; commnd, 1941; Italy, 1944-45; seconded Royal Pakistan Artillery, 1949-50; served Korean War, 1953-54; Perm. Pres. Courts Martial, Eastern Command, 1960-63. Joined RSPCA, 1963. *Recreations:* golf, gardening. *Address:* Overmead, Uplands Avenue, Barton on Sea, Hants. *T:* New Milton 611235. *Club:* Army and Navy.

SEAL, Richard Godfrey, FRCO; Organist of Salisbury Cathedral, since 1968; *b* 4 Dec. 1935; *s* of William Godfrey Seal and Shelagh Seal (*née* Bagshaw); *m* 1975, Dr Sarah Helen Hamilton. *Educ:* New Coll. Choir Sch., Oxford; Cranleigh Sch., Surrey; Christ's Coll., Cambridge (MA). FRCO 1958. Asst Organist: St Bartholomews the Great, London, 1960-61; Chichester Cathedral (and Dir of Music, Prebendal Sch.) Sussex, 1961-68. *Address:* 5 The Close, Salisbury, Wilts. *T:* Salisbury 6828. *Club:* Crudgemens (Godalming).

SEALE, Douglas (Robert); Producer (Stage); Artistic Director, Philadelphia Drama Guild, since 1974; *b* 28 Oct. 1913; *s* of Robert Henry Seale and Margaret Seale (*née* Law). *Educ:* Rutlish. Studied for stage at Royal Academy of Dramatic Art and became an actor. First appeared as Starling in The Drums Begin, Embassy, 1934; subseq. in Repertory. Served in Army, 1940-46, commissioned in Royal Signals. Joined Shakespeare Memorial Theatre Company, Stratford-on-Avon season's 1946 and 1947. From 1948 produced at Birmingham Repertory Theatre, at The Bedford, Camden Town (under Donald Wolfit), and again at Birmingham where he became Director of Productions, 1950. Later Productions include: Figaro and Fidelio, Sadler's Wells; Shaw's Caesar and Cleopatra at Birmingham Rep. Theatre, 1956 (later presented at Théâtre Sarah Bernhardt, Paris, and Old Vic). Season 1957: The Tempest, at Univ. of BC, Vancouver; King John, Stratford-on-Avon; Richard III, Old Vic; Trilogy of Henry VI, Old Vic; Season 1958; The World of the Wonderful Dark, for first Vancouver Festival; King Lear, Old Vic; Much Ado about Nothing, Stratford-on-Avon. Old Vic productions as Associate Director, 1958: Julius Caesar; Macbeth; 1959: Molière's Tartuffe; Pinero's The Magistrate; Dryden-Davenant-Purcell version of Shakespeare's The Tempest; St Joan; She Stoops to Conquer, 1960, Landscape with Figures, by Cecil Beaton, Dublin Festival, 1960: King John, Festival Theatre, Stratford, Ontario, 1960; Director of tours in Russia and Poland for Old Vic Theatre Co., 1961: prod. The Importance of Being Earnest, New York, 1962; The Comedy of Errors, Henry V, Stratford, Connecticut, 1963; Regent's Prof., Univ. of Calif. at Santa Barbara, Jan.-June 1965; Artistic Director, Center Stage, Baltimore, Maryland, USA, 1965-67; directed and acted, Meadowbrook Theater, Rochester, Mich, 1968; co-producing Director, Goodman Theater, Chicago, 1969-72 (productions incl.: Soldiers, Marching Song, Heartbreak House (Jefferson award), The Tempest, Twelfth Night, own musical adaptation of Lady Audley's Secret); directed and acted in Lady Audley's Secret, Washington and New York, 1972; Giovani, in Pirandello's Henry IV, New York, 1973; directed: King Lear, Marin Shakespeare Festival, San Francisco; Doll's House and Look Back in Anger, Cleveland, Getting Married, Newhaven, 1973; Sorin in The Seagull, Seattle, dir Too True to be Good, 1974, Caesar and Cleopatra, 1975, Shaw Festival, Ont. Has also produced for TV. Hon. DFA Washington Coll., Md, 1967.

SEALE, Sir John Henry, 5th Bt, *cr* 1838; ARIBA; *b* 3 March 1921; *s* of 4th Bt; *S* father, 1964; *m* 1953, Ray Josephine, *d* of Robert Gordon Charters, MC, Christchurch, New Zealand; one *s* one *d*. *Educ:* Eton; Christ Church, Oxford. Served War of 1939-45: Royal Artillery, North Africa and Italy; Captain, 1945. ARIBA 1951. *Heir: s* John Robert Charters Seale, *b* 17 Aug. 1954. *Address:* Slade, near Kingsbridge, South Devon. *T:* Loddiswell 226.

SEAMAN, Christopher; Principal Conductor and Artistic Director, Northern Sinfonia Orchestra, since 1974; *b* 7 March 1942; *s* of late Albert Edward Seaman and of Ethel Margery Seaman (*née* Chambers). *Educ:* Canterbury Cathedral Choir Sch.; The King's Sch., Canterbury; King's Coll., Cambridge. MA, double first cl. Hons in Music; ARCM, ARCO. Principal Timpanist, London Philharmonic Orch., 1964-68 (Mem., LPO Bd of Dirs, 1965-68); Asst Conductor, 1968-70, Principal Conductor, 1971-77, BBC Scottish Symphony Orchestra. Freelance Conductor, appearing in New Zealand, Italy and many parts of the United Kingdom, 1970-71. FGSM 1972. *Recreations:* people, reading, walking; New Testament Greek. *Address:* 4 Crown Circus, Glasgow G12 9HB. *T:* 041-339 1309.

SEAMAN, Edwin de Grey; Chairman, Edwin Seaman Farms Ltd; *b* 27 Aug. 1908; *s* of Edwin de Grey Seaman and Catherine Anne Farrow (*née* Sayer); *m* 1940, Eileen Purdy; two *d. Educ:* Glebe House Sch., Hunstanton; Cheltenham Coll., Glos. Started farming 90 acres in Norfolk, 1929; marketing Fatstock for Norfolk Farmers, 1933, and extended to importing from Canada and Ireland; imported 300 pedigree Holstein Fresian cattle from Canada and founded Canadian Holstein Fresian Association, 1946. Joined NFU, 1944; became Delegate to Nat. Council, 1949. Chm., Working Party which produced a scheme for Fatstock Scheme, 1952; (with Lord Netherthorpe) founded Fatstock Marketing Corp., 1953 (which became FMC Ltd, 1963) (Vice-Chm. 1972, Dep. Chm., 1974-75). Founded Seaman's Cream Dairies Ltd, 1963; extended to five counties and sold to Milk Marketing Bd, 1963. During War of 1939-45 was Member: Agricl Exec. Cttee; Milk Production Cttee; Special Police Auxiliary and Home Guard, also Air Training Corps (ATC). Member: Royal Agricultural Soc. of England; Royal Norfolk Agricultural Soc. *Recreations:* farming (3000 acres), fishing, shooting, and his work. *Address:* Rising Lodge, South Wootton, King's Lynn, Norfolk PE30 3PD. *T:* Kings Lynn 671079. *Clubs:* Farmers', Smithfield; Refley Society (King's Lynn).

SEAMAN, Gilbert Frederick, CMG 1967; Chairman, State Bank of South Australia, since 1963; Deputy Chairman, Electricity Trust of SA, since 1970; Trustee, Savings Bank of SA, since 1973; *b* 7 Sept. 1912; *s* of Eli S. Seaman, McLaren Vale, South Australia; *m* 1935, Avenal Essie Fong; one *s* one *d. Educ:* University of Adelaide. BEc, Associate of University of Adelaide, 1935, High School Teacher, Port Pirie and Unley, 1932-35; South Australian Public Service, 1936-41; Seconded to Commonwealth of Australia as Assistant Director of Manpower for SA, 1941-46; Economist, SA Treasury, 1946-60; Under Treasurer for SA, 1960-72. *Address:* 27 William Street, Hawthorn, SA 5062, Australia. *T:* 71-4271.

SEARCY, Philip Roy, OBE 1966; Australian Consul-General, Los Angeles, 1971-75; *b* Adelaide, South Australia, 15 April 1914; *s* of Herbert Leslie Searcy and Mary Ellen MacGregor; *m* 1946, Mary Elizabeth Gavan Duffy; four *d. Educ:* Collegiate School of St Peter, Adelaide; Adelaide University. Royal Australian Air Force, 1940; Air Operations, Europe, 1941; Prisoner of War, Germany, Nov. 1941-45. Joined Australian Govt Trade Commissioner Service, 1955; Australian Govt Trade Commissioner, Calcutta, 1956; Commercial Counsellor, Singapore, 1957; Australian Govt Senior Trade Commissioner: London, 1958-62; Tokyo, 1962-65; Hong Kong, 1966-70. *Address:* The Bridge, Gundaroo, NSW 2581, Australia. *Clubs:* Naval and Military (Melbourne); Tokyo; Shek O, Hong Kong.

SEARLE, Humphrey, CBE 1968; Composer; *b* Oxford, 26 Aug. 1915; *e s* of late Humphrey Frederic Searle and Charlotte Mathilde Mary (*née* Schlich); *m* 1st, 1949, Margaret (Lesley) Gillen Gray (*d* 1957); 2nd, 1960, Fiona Elizabeth Anne Nicholson. *Educ:* Winchester Coll.; New Coll., Oxford. Composition study at RCM, Vienna Conservatorium, and privately with Dr Anton Webern, 1937-38. Member, BBC Music Department, 1938-40. Served Gloucestershire Regiment, Intelligence Corps and General List, 1940-46. Programme producer, BBC Music Dept, 1946-48. General Secretary, International Soc. for Contemporary Music, 1947-49. Hon. Secretary, Liszt Society, 1950-62. Member Sadler's Wells Ballet Advisory Panel, 1951-57; Resident Composer, Stanford University, California, 1964-65; Prof. of Composition, Royal Coll. of Music, 1965-; Guest composer, Aspen Music Festival, Colorado, 1967; Guest Prof., Staatliche Hochschule für Musik, Karlsruhe, 1968-72; Vis. Prof., Univ. of Southern California, Los Angeles, 1976-77. Hon. ARCM, 1966, FRCM 1969. *Principal Compositions:* Gold Coast Customs (Edith Sitwell), 1949; Poem for 22 Strings, 1950; The Riverrun (James Joyce), 1951; Piano sonata, 1951; The Shadow of Cain (Edith Sitwell), 1952; Symphony No 1, 1953; Piano Concerto No 2, 1955; Noctambules, ballet, 1956; Symphony No 2, 1958; The Great Peacock, ballet, 1958; The Diary of a Madman, opera, 1958; Symphony No 3, 1960; Symphony No 4, 1962; Dualities, ballet, 1963; The Photo of the Colonel, Opera, 1964; Song of the Birds, Song of the Sun, 1964; Symphony No 5, 1964; Scherzi for Orchestra, 1964; The Canticle of the Rose (Edith Sitwell) 1965; Oxus, scena, 1967; Hamlet, opera, 1968; Sinfonietta, 1968-69; Jerusalem (Blake), choral work, 1970; Zodiac Variations, 1970; Labyrinth, 1971; Cello Fantasia, 1972; Les Fleurs du mal, song cycle, 1972; Fantasy-Toccata for organ, 1973; Kubla Khan, cantata, 1974; Five for guitar, 1974; Nocturnall (Donne), 1974; Il Penseroso e L'Allegro, 1974; Contemplations, 1975; Fantasia on British Airs, 1976; Dr Faustus, cantata, 1977; also chamber music, theatre, radio, televison, and film scores. Orchestration of Liszt, Sonata in B minor, 1962. *Publications:* The Music of Liszt,

1954 (rev. edn, 1967); Twentieth Century Counterpoint, 1954; Ballet Music, an Introduction, 1958 (rev. edn 1973); 20th Century Composers, Vol 3 (Britain and Holland), 1972; (ed) Arnold Schoenberg, Structural Functions of Harmony, 1954; (ed) Hector Berlioz: Selected Letters, 1966; *translated:* Josef Rufer, Composition with Twelve Notes, 1954; H. H. Stuckenschmidt, Arnold Schoenberg, 1959; Friedrich Wildgans, Anton Webern, 1966; Walter Kolneder, Anton Webern, 1967; H. H. Stuckenschmidt, Schoenberg, 1975; has made contributions to: Encyclopædia Britannica; Dictionary of National Biography; Grove's Dictionary of Music and Musicians; Chambers's Encyclopædia; Proceedings of the Royal Musical Association; and to various other musical publications. *Recreation:* travel. *Address:* 44 Ordnance Hill, NW8. *T:* 01-722 5182. *Club:* Savage.

SEARLE, Rear-Adm. (retd) Malcolm Walter St Leger, CB 1955; CBE 1945; *b* 23 Dec. 1900; *s* of late Sir Malcolm W. Searle, Wynberg, S Africa; *m* 1930, Betty Margaret, *d* of late Dr H. R. Crampton; one *s* two *d. Educ:* RN Colleges Osborne and Dartmouth. Entered RN 1914; served European War, 1914-19; Comdr 1936; served War of 1939-45; Capt. 1943; Commodore, RN Barracks, Portsmouth, 1951; Rear-Adm. 1952; Deputy Chief of Naval Personnel, 1953-55; retired, 1956. *Address:* Lindens, Kithurst Park, Storrington, Pulborough, West Sussex RH20 4JH.

SEARLE, Ronald William Fordham, FSIA; AGI; Artist; *b* Cambridge, 3 March 1920; *s* of late William James Searle and of Nellie Hunt; *m* 1st, Kaye Webb (marr. diss. 1967); one *s* one *d*; 2nd, 1967, Monica Koenig. *Educ:* Cambridge School of Art. Humorous work first published in Cambridge Daily News and Granta, 1935-39. Served with 287 Field Co. RE, 1939-46; captured by the Japanese at fall of Singapore, 1942; Prisoner of War in Siam and Malaya, 1942-45; Allied Force HQ Port Said Ops, 1956. Began contributing widely to nat. publications from 1946; creator of the schoolgirls of St Trinians, 1941 (abandoned them in 1953); Cartoonist to Tribune, 1949-51; to Sunday Express, 1950-51; Special feature artist, News Chronicle, 1951-53; Weekly Cartoonist, News Chronicle, 1954; Punch Theatre artist, 1949-62; Contributor, New Yorker. Designer of commemorative medals for the French Mint, since 1974; *Awards:* Art Dirs Club, Philadelphia, Medal, 1959; Nat. Cartoonists Soc. of America, Awards, 1959, 1960, 1966; Art Dirs Club, LA, Medal, 1959; Gold Medal, III Biennale Tolentino, 1965; Prix de la Critique Belge, 1968; Médaille de la ville d'Avignon, 1971; Prix d'Humour du Festival d'Avignon, 1971; Grand Prix de l'Humour noir "Grandville", 1971- Prix Internationale Charles Huard de dessin de presse, 1972. *One Man Exhibitions:* Batsford Gall., 1947; Leicester Galls, 1948, 1950, 1954, 1957; New York, 1959, 1963, 1969, 1976; Hannover, Tolentino (Italy), Stuttgart, Berlin, 1965; Bremerhaven, Basle, Linz, 1966; Galerie La Pochade, Paris, 1966, 1967, 1968, 1969, 1971; Galerie Gurlitt, Munich, 1967, 1968, 1969, 1970, 1971, 1973, 1976; Grosvenor Gall., London, Brussels, 1968; Frankfurt, 1969; Konstanz, Würzburg, 1970; Salzburg, 1971; Lausanne, Poncey, 1972; Paris, Vienna, 1973; Lausanne, 1974; Paris, 1975; Berlin, Hannover, Stuttgart, Mainz, Recklinghausen, New York, Stuttgart, Paris, 1976; Brussels, London, Paris, 1977. *Works in permanent collections:* V&A, BM, London; Bibliothèque Nat., Paris; Kunsthalle, Bremen; Wilhelm-Busch Museum, Hanover; Stadtmuseum, Munich; Art Museum, Dallas, Texas. *Films based on the characters of St Trinian's:* The Belles of St Trinian's, 1954; Blue Murder at St Trinian's, 1957; The Pure Hell of St Trinian's, 1960; The Great St Trinian's Train Robbery, 1966. *Films designed:* John Gilpin, 1951; On the Twelfth Day, 1954 (Acad. Award Nomination); Energetically Yours (USA), 1957; Germany, 1960 (for Suddeutschen RTV); The King's Breakfast, 1962; Those Magnificent Men in their Flying Machines (Animation Sequence), 1965; Monte Carlo or Bust (Animation Sequence), 1969; Scrooge (Animation Sequence), 1970; Dick Deadeye, 1975. *Publications:* Forty Drawings, 1946; Le Nouveau Ballet Anglais, 1947; Hurrah for St Trinian's!, 1948; The Female Approach, 1949; Back to the Slaughterhouse, 1951; John Gilpin, 1952; Souls in Torment, 1953; Rake's Progress, 1955; Merry England, etc, 1956; A Christmas Carol, 1961; Which Way Did He Go, 1961; Searle in the Sixties, 1964; From Frozen North to Filthy Lucre, 1964; Pardong M'sieur, 1965; Searle's Cats, 1967; The Square Egg, 1968; Take one Toad, 1968; Baron Munchausen, 1969; Hello-where did all the people go?, 1969; Hommage à Toulouse-Lautrec, 1969; Secret Sketchbook, 1970; The Addict, 1971; More Cats, 1975; Drawings from Gilbert and Sullivan, 1975; The Zoodiac, 1977; *in collaboration:* (with D. B. Wyndham Lewis) The Terror of St Trinian's, 1952; (with Geoffrey Willans) Down with Skool, 1953; How to be Topp, 1954; Whizz for Atomms, 1956; The Compleet Molesworth, 1958; The Dog's Ear Book, 1958; Back in the Jug Agane, 1959;

(with Kaye Webb) Paris Sketchbook, 1950 and 1957; Looking at London, 1953; The St Trinian's Story, 1959; Refugees 1960, 1960; (with Alex Atkinson) The Big City, 1958; USA for Beginners, 1959; Russia for Beginners, 1960; Escape from the Amazon!, 1964; (with A. Andrews & B. Richardson) Those Magnificent Men in their Flying Machines, 1965; (with Heinz Huber) Haven't We Met Before Somewhere?, 1966; (with Kildare Dobbs) The Great Fur Opera, 1970; (with Irwin Shaw) Paris! Paris!, 1977. *Address:* c/o Hope Leresche & Sayle, 11 Jubilee Place, SW3 3TE. *T:* 01-352 4311. *Club:* Garrick.

SEARS, Raymond Arthur William, QC 1975; a Recorder of the Crown Court, since 1977; *b* 10 March 1933; *s* of William Arthur and Lillian Sears; *m* 1960, Adelaide Sadler; one *s* one *d*. *Educ:* Epsom Coll.; Jesus Coll., Cambridge. BA 1956. Called to Bar, Gray's Inn, 1957. *Recreations:* watching horse-racing; gardening. *Address:* Spindles, Langley Vale Road, Epsom Downs, Epsom, Surrey. *Club:* Royal Automobile.

SEATON, Colin Robert; Circuit Administrator of Northern Circuit (Under Secretary), Lord Chancellor's Office, since Oct. 1974; Barrister-at-Law; *b* 21 Nov. 1928; 2nd *s* of late Arthur William Robert Seaton and of Helen Amelia Seaton (*née* Stone); *m* 1952, Betty (*née* Gosling); two *s*. *Educ:* Wallington County Grammar Sch. for Boys; Worcester Coll., Oxford. BA 1953; MA 1956. Royal Air Force, 1947-49. Called to Bar, Inner Temple, 1956; Schoolmaster for LCC (now GLC), 1953-57; Solicitor's Dept, Ministries of Health and Housing and Local Govt, also Dept of the Environment, 1957-71; Sec. (Master) of Nat. Industrial Relations Court, 1971-74. *Publication:* Aspects of the National Health Service Acts, 1966. *Recreations:* swimming, reading. *Address:* 57 St Michael's Avenue, Bramhall, Stockport, Cheshire SK7 2PL. *T:* 061-439 9571. *Club:* Civil Service.
See also M. J. Seaton.

SEATON, Prof. Michael John, FRS 1967; Professor of Physics, University College, London, since 1963; *b* 16 Jan. 1923; *s* of Arthur William Robert Seaton and Helen Amelia Seaton; *m* 1st, 1943, Olive May (*d* 1959), *d* of Charles Edward Singleton; one *s* one *d*; 2nd, 1960, Joy Clarice, *d* of Harry Albert Balchin; one *s*. *Educ:* Wallington Co. Sch., Surrey; University Coll., London (Fellow, 1972). BSc 1948, PhD 1951, London. Dept of Physics, UCL: Asst Lectr, 1950; Lectr, 1953; Reader, 1959; Prof., 1963. Chargé de Recherche, Institut d'Astrophysique, Paris, 1954-55; Univ. of Colorado, 1961; Fellow-Adjoint, Jt Inst. for Laboratory Astrophysics (Nat. Bureau of Standards and Univ. of Colorado), Boulder, Colo, 1964-. Dr *hc*, Observatoire de Paris. *Publications:* papers on atomic physics and astrophysics in various jls. *Address:* 51 Hall Drive, Sydenham, SE26 6XL. *T:* 01-778 7121.
See also C. R. Seaton.

SEATON, Reginald Ethelbert; Chairman, Greater London Area Sessions (inner area), 1965-69 (Chairman, London Sessions, 1959-65); retired; *b* 27 Dec. 1899; 2nd *s* of Albert Edward and Edith Gertrude Seaton; *m* 1930, Vera Wilson Barnett; one *s* three *d*. *Educ:* Epsom College; Downing College, Cambridge. BA Cantab. 1923; called to Bar, Middle Temple, 1924, Bencher, 1951; Counsel to Post Office at Central Criminal Court, 1942-43; Third Junior Prosecuting Counsel to the Crown, Central Criminal Court, 1943; Dep. Chm., E Sussex QS, 1950; Recorder of Maidstone, 1951-59; Second Senior Prosecuting Counsel to the Crown Central Criminal Court, 1954-59. *Publication:* (with R. H. Blundell) Trial of Jean Pierre Vacquier. *Recreations:* golf, gardening. *Address:* Queen Elizabeth Building, Temple, EC4. *T:* 01-353 2576; Casa Maya, 2 Rudgwick Avenue, Goring-by-Sea, Sussex. *T:* Worthing 44560.

SEBAG-MONTEFIORE, Harold Henry; Barrister-at-law; *b* 5 Dec. 1924; *e s* of late John Sebag-Montefiore and Violet, *o c* of late James Henry Solomon; *m* 1968, Harriet, *o d* of Benjamin Harrison Paley, New York; one step *d*. *Educ:* Stowe; Lower Canada Coll., Montreal; Pembroke Coll., Cambridge (MA). Served War of 1939-45, RAF. Called to Bar, Lincoln's Inn, 1951. Contested (C) North Paddington, Gen. Elec., 1959; Chm., Conservative Parly Candidates Assoc., 1960-64. Member: LCC, 1955-65; GLC, for Cities of London and Westminster, 1964-73; Chm., Arts and Recreation Cttee, 1968-73; Sports Council, 1972-74. Pres., Anglo-Jewish Assoc., 1966-71. Freeman, City of London, and Liveryman, Spectacle Makers' Co; Governor, National Theatre; Trustee, London Festival Ballet. Chevalier, Légion d'Honneur, 1973. *Publications:* book reviews and articles on Polo under *nom-de-plume* of "Marco II". *Address:* 7B Vicarage Gate, W8; 2 Paper Buildings, Temple, EC4. *T:* 01-353 5835. *Clubs:* Carlton, Hurlingham.

SEBASTIAN, Rear-Admiral (Retired) Brian Leonard Geoffrey, CB 1948; *b* 7 Feb. 1891; *s* of late Lewis Boyd Sebastian, Barrister-at-Law, and late Harriet M. Lennartson, Karlstad, Sweden; *m* 1927, Cicely Grace, *e d* of Dr F. W. Andrew, Hendon; one *d*. *Educ:* Osborne, Dartmouth and Greenwich Colleges; RN Engineering College, Keyham. Joined RN Coll., Osborne, with first term of new scheme, 1903; various appts at sea as junior officer; qualified in Engineering, 1914. Served in various ships during European War; Comdr (E) 1925; various appointments till 1936; Capt. (E) 1937; Squadron EO Home Fleet, in charge of RN Aircraft Training establishment, Newcastle-under-Lyme, and RN Eng. Coll., Keyham; Rear-Adm. (E) 1944; Deputy Head of British Admiralty Technical Mission, Ottawa; Staffs of C-in-C Rosyth and Plymouth, 1948; retired, 1948. *Address:* Flat 3, Weyside, Farnham, Surrey GU9 7RH. *T:* Farnham 22705.

SEBASTIAN, Erroll Graham, CBE 1946; DSO 1917; *b* 2 August 1892; *s* of Lewis Boyd Sebastian and Henrietta Maria Lennartson; *m* 1959, Mrs Hilda Reynolds Gardner. *Educ:* Winchester; University Coll., Oxford. Served European War, 2nd Buffs in France, Salonica, and Constantinople, 1914-19 (DSO); served in Consular Service in Siam, Roumania, Belgium, Greece; Consul-General at Athens, 1940-41; attached Minister of State's Office, Cairo, 1941-42; Consul-General at Gothenburg, 1942-44; at Antwerp, 1944-50; Consul-General at Milan, 1950-52; retired 1952. *Recreations:* needlework, music. *Address:* Bridge House, Coggeshall, Colchester, Essex.

SEBRIGHT, Sir Hugo Giles Edmund, 14th Bt, *cr* 1626; *b* 2 March 1931; *s* of Lieutenant-Colonel Sir Giles Edward Sebright, 13th Bt, CBE, and of Margery Hilda, *d* of late Admiral Sir Sydney Robert Fremantle, GCB, MVO; *S* father 1954; *m* 1st, 1952, Deirdre Ann (marr. diss. 1964), *d* of Major Vivian Lionel Slingsby Bethell, late Royal Artillery; one *s*; 2nd, 1965, Mrs Sheila Mary Howard Hervey. *Heir: s* Peter Giles Vivian Sebright, *b* 2nd Aug. 1953.

SECCOMBE, Hugh Digorie, CBE 1976; Chairman, Seccombe Marshall & Campion Ltd, 1962-77; *b* 3 June 1917; *s* of Lawrence Henry Seccombe and Norah (*née* Wood); *m* 1947, Eirene Rosemary Banister, *d* of Richard Whittow and Eirene, and *widow* of Lieut P. C. McC. Banister, DSC, RN; one *s* one *d*. *Educ:* Stowe; Sidney Sussex Coll., Cambridge (BA 1938, MA 1942). RNVR, 1939-50; retd, Lt-Comdr. Joined Seccombe Marshall & Campion, 1938; Dir, 1947. Chm., YWCA Central Club, 1971-. Fellow, Inst. of Bankers, 1964. *Recreations:* gardening, fishing, shooting, hill-walking. *Address:* Woodlands, Shamley Green, Surrey. *T:* Bramley (Surrey) 3296; Benmore Lodge, Isle of Mull, Argyllshire. *T:* Aros 351. *Clubs:* City of London, Army and Navy.

SECKER, Martin; publisher; formerly proprietor of The Unicorn Press and director of the Richards Press Ltd; *b* Kensington, 6 April 1882; *m* 1921 (marriage dissolved, 1938); one *s*; *m* 1954, Sylvia Hope Gibsone. Entered publishing trade, 1908, in office of Eveleigh Nash; started in business on his own account in the Adelphi, 1910, and published early work of Sir Compton Mackenzie, Sir Hugh Walpole, Francis Brett Young, and other prominent writers, and all the works of D. H. Lawrence from 1921 until that author's death in 1930; business reconstructed under style of Martin Secker and Warburg Ltd, 1935; severed his connection therewith in 1937. Is an authority on the literature of the 1890's. *Publication:* (privately) Letters from D. H. Lawrence 1910-1930, 1970. *Address:* Bridgefoot, Iver, Bucks. *Clubs:* none.

SECOMBE, Harry (Donald), CBE 1963; Actor, Comedian and Singer; *b* 8 Sept. 1921; *m* 1948, Myra Joan Atherton, Swansea; two *s* two *d*. *Educ:* Dynevor School, Swansea. Served with Royal Artillery, 1939-46. Windmill Theatre, 1947-48: General Variety since 1948. Appearances include: at London Palladium, 1956, 1958, 1959, 1961, 1966; in Roy. Command Perfs, 1955, 1957, 1958, 1963, 1966, 1969, 1975; (musical) Pickwick, Saville, 1963; (musical) The Four Musketeers, Drury Lane, 1967; The Plumber's Progress, Prince of Wales, 1975. Radio: Goon Show, 1949-60, and special performance of Goon Show for 50th Anniversary of BBC, 1972. Television: BBC, ITV, CBS (New York), 1950-. Films: Davy, for Ealing Films, 1957; Jetstorm, 1959; Bed-Sitting Room, 1968; Mr Bumble in Oliver!, 1968; Bjornsen in Song of Norway, 1969; Rhubarb, 1969; Doctor in Trouble, 1970; The Magnificent Seven Deadly Sins, 1971; Sunstruck, 1972. Has made recordings for HMV, 1953-54, and Philips Records, 1955-. FRSA 1971. *Publication:* Twice Brightly, 1974; Goon for Lunch, 1975. *Recreations:* film photography, literature, travel, golf, cricket. *Address:* 46 St James's Place, SW1. *T:* 01-629 2768. *Clubs:* Savage, Royal Automobile, Lord's Taverners, Variety Club of Great Britain.

SECONDÉ, Reginald Louis, CMG 1972; CVO 1968 (MVO 1957); HM Diplomatic Service; Ambassador to Romania, since

1977; *b* 28 July 1922; *s* of late Lt-Col Emile Charles Secondé and Doreen Secondé (*née* Sutherland); *m* 1951, Catherine Penelope, *d* of late Thomas Ralph Sneyd-Kynnersley and Alice Sneyd-Kynnersley; one *s* two *d*. *Educ:* Beaumont; King's Coll., Cambridge. Served, 1941-47, in Coldstream Guards: N Africa and Italy (despatches); Major. Entered Diplomatic Service, 1949; UK Delegn to the UN, New York, 1951-55; British Embassy: Lisbon, 1955-57; Cambodia, 1957-59; FO, 1959-62; British Embassy: Warsaw, 1962-64; First Secretary (Information), 1964-66, Counsellor (Political), 1966-69, Rio de Janeiro; Head of S European Dept, FCO, 1969-72; Royal Coll. of Defence Studies, 1972-73; Ambassador to Chile, 1973-76. Comdr, Order of the Southern Cross (Brazil), 1968. *Recreations:* gardening, shooting. *Address:* c/o Foreign and Commonwealth Office, SW1; Wamil Hall, near Mildenhall, Suffolk. *T:* Mildenhall 714 160. *Club:* Cavalry and Guards.

SEDDON, Sir Herbert (John), Kt 1964; CMG 1951; DM, MA Oxon, MB, BS (London University Gold Medal); FRCS; Hon. FACS; Dr *hc* Grenoble University; Hon. MD Malta; Hon. LLD Glasgow; retired; Hon. Consulting Surgeon, Royal National Orthopædic Hospital; Member MRC, 1956-59; *b* 13 July 1903; *s* of late John Seddon and Ellen Thornton, Sutton, Surrey; *m* 1931, Mary Lorene Lytle, Marquette, Mich., USA; one *s* one *d*. *Educ:* William Hulme Gram. Sch., Manchester; St Bartholomew's Hospital, London. Instructor in Surgery at the Hospital of the Univ. of Michigan, Ann Arbor, Michigan, USA, 1930, Carl Badgley Lecturer, 1963; Resident Surgeon, Country Branch of Royal National Orthopædic Hospital, London, 1931-39; Nuffield Professor of Orthopædic Surgery, University of Oxford, 1940-48; Fellow of Worcester College, 1940-48 (Hon. Fellow 1966); Director of Studies, Inst. of Orthopædics, 1948-65; Prof. of Orthopædics, Univ. of London, 1965-67; Fellow, Hon. Sec. 1940-44, Pres., 1960-61, of British Orthopædic Association; Robert Jones Medal and Association Prize, 1933; Robert Jones Lecturer, 1960 and Watson-Jones Lecturer, 1962, Royal College of Surgeons; other eponymous lectures. Hon. Mem. Brit. Pædiatric Assoc.; Corr. or Hon. Mem. of a number of foreign professional socs; Hon. FRSM 1975 (Pres., Orthopædic Section, 1948-49); Worked abroad, mainly in Africa and for HM Govt; visited East Africa as Mem. of Cttee on (EA) Univ. Needs and Priorities, 1962; Chm., MRC Working Party on Tuberculosis of the Spine, 1963-73; formerly Mem. Colonial Advisory Med. Cttee, Tropical Med. Res. Bd, and of panel of colonial medical visitors. Reader, parish of St John's, Stanmore. Lawrence Poole Prize, University of Edinburgh, 1962. Officer, Order of the Cedar of Lebanon; Mérite Libanais (first class). *Publications:* Surgical Disorders of the Peripheral Nerves, 1972, 2nd edn 1975; papers in medical journals on tuberculous disease of joints, infantile paralysis and on peripheral nerve injuries. Editor and contributor MRC special report on peripheral nerve injuries. *Recreations:* gardening, photography, painting. *Address:* Lake House, 24 Gordon Avenue, Stanmore, Mddx HA7 3QD. *T:* 01-954 0827.

SEDDON, Dr John; aeronautical consultant; *b* 29 Sept. 1915; *m* 1940, Barbara Mary Mackintosh; one *s* two *d*. *Educ:* Leeds Modern Sch.; Univ. of Leeds. BSc 1937, PhD 1939. Scientific Officer, RAE, Farnborough, 1939-55; Harkness Fund Fellow, California Inst. of Technology, 1955-56; Head of Experimental Supersonics, RAE, Farnborough, 1957-59; Supt, Tunnels II Div., RAE, Bedford, 1959-66; Dir, Scientific Research (Air), Min. of Technology, 1966-68; Dir-Gen. Research, Aircraft, MoD, 1969-75. Senior Vis. Fellow, Univ. of Bristol, 1976-77. *Publications:* papers on air intakes and other aerodynamic subjects, in ARC Reports and Memoranda Series and other scientific media. *Recreations:* music, golf. *Address:* 7 Vicarage Hill, The Bourne, Farnham, Surrey. *T:* Farnham 23680.

SEDDON, Richard Harding, PhD; RWS, ARCA; Director of Art History and Liberal Studies in the School of Design and Furniture at Buckinghamshire College of Higher Education, since 1963; painter and writer; *b* 1 May 1915; *s* of Cyril Harding Seddon; *m* 1946, Audrey Madeline Wareham. *Educ:* King Edward VII School; Roy. Coll. of Art; Univ. of Reading (PhD 1946). Demonstrator in Fine Art, Univ. of Reading, 1944; Extra-Mural Staff Tutor in Fine Art, Univ. of Birmingham, 1947; Director, Sheffield City Art Galleries, 1948-63; Curator, Ruskin Collection, 1948-63. Hon. Advisory Panel, Hereford Art Galls, 1948; Arts Council Selection Bd (Art Students Exhib.), 1947; Pres. Ludlow Art Soc., 1947-67; Hon. Member: Sheffield Soc. of Artists; Oxford Folk Art Soc.; Sheffield Photographic Soc.; Mem., Oxford Bureau for Artists in War-time, 1940; Chm. Selection Cttee, Nottingham Artists Exhibition, 1953; Guest Speaker Educational Centres Association Annual Conference, 1951; West Riding Artists Exhibition Selection Committee, 1956; Northern Young Artists Exhibition Selection Committee, 1958; Member Sheffield Univ. Court; Sheffield Diocesan

Advisory Cttee, 1948. Exhibitor at: RA; NEAC; RI; RBA; Internat. Artists; Architectural Assoc.; RIBA; National Gallery (War Artists) 1943; Leicester Galleries; Redfern Galleries. Official acquisitions: V. & A. Museum, 1939; Pilgrim Trust, 1942; Imperial War Museum (War Artists), 1943, 1956 (ten paintings); Graves Gall., Sheffield, 1943 and 1956; Atkinson Gall., Southport, 1953; Reading Art Gall., 1956; Leeds Education Cttee Collection, 1956. Extra Mural and Univ. Extension lectr on art to Univs of Oxford, Birmingham, London and Sheffield, 1948-; initiated Sheffield Conference on Nation's Art Treasures, 1958; FMA, 1951-74; Mem. Yorkshire Fed. Museums and Art Galls, 1948 (Committee 1952 and 1957, President, 1954-55, Vice-President, 1955-56); Secretary Yorks Regional Fact Finding Committee, 1959; National Art Collections Fund Rep. for Yorks, 1954-63; Hon. Adviser to Co. of Cutlers in Hallamshire, 1950-64; Dep. Chm., Sheffield Design Council for Gold, Silver and Jewelry Trades, 1960; Mem. BBC '51 Soc., 1960; Mem. Govg Council, Design and Res. Centre, 1960; Mem. Art Adv. Cttee Yorks Area Scheme for Museums and Art Galleries, 1963; Art Critic: Birmingham Post, 1963-71; Yorkshire Post, 1974-; Jl Fedn of British Artists, 1975-; Mem. Recognised Panel of London Univ. Extension Lectrs, 1964; ARWS, 1972, Mem. Council and Hon. Treasurer, 1976; RWS 1976; Hon. Mem., Mark Twain Soc., USA, 1976. War Service with RAOC Field Park, France, 1940 (King's Badge); facilities by War Office Order to make war drawings in Maginot Line, 1940. *Publications:* The Technical Methods of Paul Nash (Memorial Vol.), 1949; The Artist's Vision, 1949; The Academic Technique of Oil Painting, 1960; A Hand Uplifted (war memoirs), 1962; Art Collecting for Amateurs, 1964. Articles on fine art for Jl of Aesthetics (USA), Burlington Magazine, Apollo, The Studio, The Connoisseur, Arch. Review, The Artist, The Antique Collector and daily press; lectures on art in England and abroad; criticisms; book reviews; broadcasts. *Recreations:* the theatre and photography. *Address:* 6 Arlesey Close, Putney, SW15 2EX. *T:* 01-788 5899; Buckinghamshire College of Higher Education, High Wycombe, Bucks. *T:* High Wycombe 22141.

SEDGEMORE, Brian Charles John; MP (Lab) Luton West, since Feb. 1974; barrister-at-law; *b* 17 March 1937; *s* of Charles John Sedgemore, fisherman; *m* 1964, Mary Audrey Reece; one *s*. *Educ:* Newtown Primary Sch.; Heles Sch.; Oxford Univ. (MA). Diploma in public and social administration. Called to Bar, Middle Temple, 1966. RAF, 1956-58; Oxford, 1958-62. Administrative Class, Civil Service, Min. of Housing and Local Govt, 1962-66 (Private Sec. to R. J. Mellish, MP, then Junior Minister of Housing, 1964-66). Practising barrister, 1966-74. *Publication:* contributor to Tribune, one time contributor to Britain's top satirical magazine. *Recreation:* sleeping on the grass. *Address:* 28 Studley Road, Luton. *T:* Luton 23512; Flat 57, Belvedere Court, Upper Richmond Road, Putney, SW15. *T:* 01-789 1680.

SEDGMAN, Francis Arthur; Lawn tennis Champion: Australia, 1949, 1950; America, 1951, 1952; Wimbledon, 1952; Professional Tennis Player since 1953; Proprietor, Sedgman's Squash Centre; Director: Flex-Straw (A/Asia) Pty Ltd; Princes Hotel Pty Ltd; Peninsula Squash Courts Pty Ltd; Highmont Hotel Pty Ltd; Tennis Camps of Australia Pty Ltd; Managing Director of Isle of Wight Hotel, Cowes, Victoria, Australia; *b* Victoria, Australia, 29 Oct. 1927; *m* 1952, Jean Margaret Spence; four *d*. *Educ:* Box Hill High School, Vic, Australia. First played in the Australian Davis Cup team, 1949. With Kenneth McGregor, won the Australian, French, English and American doubles titles in the same year (1951), the only pair ever to do so. *Publication:* Winning Tennis, 1955. *Recreation:* golfing. *Address:* 28 Bolton Avenue, Hampton, Victoria 3188, Australia. *T:* 98 6341. *Clubs:* All England Tennis and Croquet; Melbourne Cricket (Melbourne); Kooyong Tennis; Grace Park Tennis; Yarra Yarra Golf; Cowes Golf; Woodlands Golf.

SEDGWICK, Mrs A. R. M.; *see* Milkina, Nina.

SEDGWICK, Patrick Cardinall Mason, CMG 1965; *b* 8 March 1911; 2nd *s* of late William Francis Mason Sedgwick, Goudhurst, Kent; *m* 1943, Beth Mannering, Thompson, *e d* of late Frederick Mannering Thompson, St Kilda, Victoria, Australia; three *s* one *d*. *Educ:* St Lawrence Coll., Ramsgate; Brasenose Coll., Oxford (BA Hons); Queens' College, Cambridge. Colonial Admin. Service: Cadet Officer, Hong Kong, 1935; seconded Malayan Civil Service, Dec. 1941-Feb. 1942; Attaché, British Embassy, Chungking, 1942-43; Hong Kong Planning Unit, CO, London, 1944-45; various Govt Posts in Hong Kong, including Principal Assistant Colonial Secretary, Estabt Officer, Chm. Urban Council, and Dir of Commerce and Industry; Comr of Labour and Mines, 1955-65; MEC and MLC, of Hong Kong up to June 1965; Dir, Hong Kong Govt Office,

London, 1965-69; Salaries Commissioner: St Helena, 1971; Falkland Islands and Mauritius, 1972. *Recreations:* sailing, gardening. *Address:* Chingley Manor, Flimwell, Sussex. *T:* Flimwell 462. *Clubs:* Bewl Bridge Sailing; Hong Kong, Royal Hong Kong Yacht (Hong Kong).

SEDOV, Leonid I.; 5 Orders of Lenin, Hero of Socialist Labour, USSR; Professor, Moscow University, since 1937; Member, USSR Academy of Sciences; *b* 14 Nov. 1907; *m* 1931, Galya Tolstova; one *s* one *d. Educ:* Moscow University. Chief Engineer, Associate Chief lab., N.E. Zhukovsky Aerohydrodynamic Inst., Moscow, 1930-47; Chief of Dept of Hydrodynamics, Moscow University, 1944; President, International Astronautical Federation, 1959-61. Hon. Member: American Academy of Arts and Sciences; Internat. Astronautical Acad.; Serbian Academy, Belgrade; Tech. Academy, Finland; Correspondent, Acad. of Sciences, Paris; Academia Leopoldina. Hon. doctorates from many foreign universities. Medal of Obert; State Prize; Chaplygin Prize; Lomonosov Prize; Lyapunov Medal. Commander de la Légion d'Honneur (France). *Publications:* Theory of Plane Flow of Liquids, 1939; Plane Problems of Hydrodynamics and Aerodynamics, 1950, 1966; Similarity and Dimensional Methods in Mechanics, 1944, 1951, 1953, 1957, 1960, 1965, 1967, 1972; Introduction into the Mechanics of Continua, 1962; Mechanics of Continuous Media, 2 vols, 1970, 1973; numerous articles. *Address:* Moscow University, Zone U, kv 84 Leninskie Gory, Moscow B-234, USSR.

SEEAR, family name of **Baroness Seear.**

SEEAR, Baroness *cr* 1971 (Life Peer), of Paddington; **Beatrice Nancy Seear;** Reader in Personnel Management, University of London, The London School of Economics; *b* 7 Aug. 1913; *d* of late Herbert Charles Seear and Beatrice Maud Catchpole. *Educ:* Croydon High Sch.; Newnham Coll., Cambridge; London Sch. of Economics and Political Science. BA (Cambridge Hist. Tripos). Personnel Officer, C. & J. Clark Ltd, shoe manufacturers, 1936-46; seconded as Mem. (pt-time), staff of Production Efficiency Bd at Min. of Aircraft Production, 1943-45; Teacher at London School of Economics, 1946-. Mem., Hansard Soc. Commn on Electoral Reform, 1975-76. Pres., BSI, 1974. Chairman: Nat. Council for the Single Woman and her Dependents; Council, Morley Coll. President: Women's Liberal Fedn, 1974; Fawcett Soc.; Mem. Council, Industrial Soc. Governor, Centre for Environmental Studies, 1972-. *Publications:* (with P. Jephcott and J. H. Smith) Married Women Working, 1962; (with V. Roberts and J. Brock) A Career for Women in Industry?, 1964; Industrial Social Services, 1964; The Position of Women in Industry, 1967; The Re-Entry of Women into Employment, 1971. *Recreations:* travel, gardening. *Address:* The Garden Flat, 44 Blomfield Road, W9. *T:* 01-286 5701. *Club:* Royal Commonwealth Society.

SEEBOHM, family name of **Baron Seebohm.**

SEEBOHM, Baron *cr* 1972 (Life Peer), of Hertford; **Frederic Seebohm,** Kt 1970; TD; Lt-Col (Retd); Director: Barclays Bank Ltd, since 1947 (Deputy Chairman, 1968-74); Barclays Bank International Ltd (formerly Barclays Bank DCO) (Vice-Chairman, 1955-59, Deputy Chairman, 1959-65, Chairman, 1965-72); Chairman: Finance Corporation for Industry, since 1974; Finance for Industry, since 1974; Industrial and Commercial Finance Corporation, since 1974; Director: Gillett Bros Discount Co. Ltd; Friends' Provident Life Office (Chairman, 1962-68); Technical Development Capital Ltd; Ship Mortgage Finance Co. Ltd; Finance for Shipping Ltd; Estate Duties Investment Trust Ltd; Equity Capital for Industry Ltd; *b* 18 Jan. 1909; *s* of late H. E. Seebohm, Poynders End, Hitchin, Herts; *m* 1932, Evangeline, *d* of late Sir Gerald Hurst, QC; one *s* two *d. Educ:* Leighton Park School; Trinity Coll., Cambridge. Joined Staff of Barclays Bank Ltd, 1929; Vice-Chm., Barclays Bank SA, 1968-73. Chairman: Joseph Rowntree Memorial Trust; London House; Seebohm Cttee on Local Authority and Allied Personal Social Services; Export Guarantees Adv. Council, 1967-72 (Dep. Chm., 1966-67); President: Age Concern; Nat. Inst. for Social Work; Royal African Soc. Member: Design Council (Chm., Finance and General Purpose Cttee); Overseas Develt Inst. (Chm., 1972-77). Governor: London School of Economics; Haileybury Imperial Service Coll., 1970; Fellow, Inst. of Bankers (Pres., 1966-68). Served with Royal Artillery, 1939-45 (despatches). High Sheriff, Herts, 1970-71. Hon. LLD Nottingham, 1970; Hon. DSc Aston, 1976. Bronze Star of America, 1945. *Recreation:* painting. *Address:* 5 Lowndes Lodge, Cadogan Place, SW1. *T:* 01-235 3076; Brook House, Dedham, near Colchester, Essex. *T:* Dedham 3372. *Clubs:* Carlton, Brooks's.

SEEFRIED, Irmgard Maria Theresia; Austrian opera and concert singer; Kammersängerin at Vienna State Opera since 1943; *b* Koengetried, Bavaria; *m* 1948, Wolfgang Schneiderhan; two *d. Educ:* Augsburg Conservatory, Germany. First engagement under von Karajan, at Aachen, Germany, 1940. Concert tours all over the world; appeared: Metropolitan Opera, New York; Covent Garden, London; La Scala, Milan; also festivals at Salzburg, Lucerne, Edinburgh, San Francisco. Recipient various Mozart Medals; Lilly-Lehmann Medal; Golden Cross of merit for Culture and Science; Decoration of Chevalier I, Denmark. Hon. Mem. Boston Symphony Orch.; Vienna Philharmonic Orch. Grosses Verdienstkreuz des Verdienstordens der Bundesrepublik Deutschland, 1968; Schubert Medal; Hugo Wolf Medal; Auszeichnung für beispielhalbe kunsterische Leistung-verliehen von AWMM-Luxemburg. *Publications:* Articles on Mozart, Bartók, Hindemith, Hugo Wolf. *Address:* Vienna State Opera, Austria.

SEELEY, Edward Alexander; President of Industrial Tribunals (England and Wales), since 1974; *b* 30 Sept. 1913; *s* of late Alexander Anthony Szilágyi and Elisabeth (*née* Knoll); *m* 1946, Patricia, *er d* of late John Howard-Kyan; one *s. Educ:* St Paul's Sch.; Jesus Coll., Cambridge. Nat. Scis Tripos, MA; rowing blue, 1935. Murex Ltd, 1936; called to Bar, Lincoln's Inn, 1951; Chm. Industrial Tribunals, 1971. *Recreation:* travel. *Address:* 54 Campden Street, W8 7EL. *T:* 01-727 8635. *Clubs:* Hurlingham; Leander (Henley-on-Thames).

SEELY, family name of **Baron Mottistone.**

SEELY, Sir Victor Basil John, 4th Bt *cr* 1896; *b* 18 May 1900; *s* of Sir Charles H. Seely, 2nd Bt; *S* to Baronetcy of brother, 1st Baron Sherwood, 1970; *m* 1st, 1922, Sybil Helen (divorced, 1931), *widow* of Sir John Shiffner, 6th Bt; one *s*; 2nd, 1931, Hon. Patience (*d* 1935), *er d* of 1st Baron Rochdale, CB, and sister of 1st Viscount Rochdale, *qv*; one *d*; 3rd, 1937, Mary Frances Margaret, *er d* of W. R. Collins, 31 Lennox Gardens, SW1; one *s* one *d. Educ:* Eton; Trinity College, Cambridge. Late Lt S Notts Yeomanry; contested (Nat L) Pontefract, 1935, (C) Derby North, 1950; War of 1939-45 Major 9th Queen's Royal Lancers DAAG 2nd Armoured Division 1940; prisoner, 1941-43, escaped; HM Legation, Berne, 1944. Dir of Cos of Drayton Corp. Ltd, 1954-72. Master of Gunmakers' Co., 1957 and 1965. *Heir: s* Nigel Edward Seely [*b* 28 July 1923; *m* 1949, Loraine, *d* of late W. W. Lindley-Travis; three *d*]. *Address:* 42 Orchard Court, Portman Square, W1. *T:* 01-935 1311. *Clubs:* White's, Beefsteak, City; Royal Solent Yacht.

SEENEY, Leslie Elon Sidney; Director General (formerly General Secretary), National Chamber of Trade, since 1971; *b* 19 Jan. 1922; *s* of Sidney Leonard and Daisy Seeney, Forest Hill; *m* 1947, Marjory Doreen Greenwood, Spalding; one *s. Educ:* St Matthews, Camberwell. RAFVR, 1941-46 (Flt Lt, Pilot). Man. Dir, family manufrg business (clothing), 1946-63, with other interests in insce and advertising. Mem., West Lewisham Chamber of Commerce, 1951, subseq. Sec. and Chm.; Delegate to Nat. Chamber of Trade, 1960; joined NCT staff, 1966. *Publications:* various articles. *Recreations:* reading, writing, travel, photography. *Address:* 16 Barn Close, Southcote, Reading, Berks. *T:* Reading 55478. *Club:* Punch.

SEENEY, Noel Conway; Commissioner of Stamp Duties, Queensland, since 1975; *b* 7 April 1926; *s* of Percy Matthew Mark Seeney and Wilhelmina Augusta Zanow; *m* 1949, Valrae Muriel Uhlmann; two *d. Educ:* Teachers' Coll., Brisbane; Univ. of Queensland (BCom). Assoc. Accountancy, Assoc. Coll. of Preceptors, London. Teacher, 1944; Dep. Principal, Secondary Sch., 1960; Principal 1964; Official Sec., Office of Agent-General for Qld in London, 1969; Agent-General for Qld in London, 1973. *Recreations:* golf, tennis. *Address:* State Government Offices, Anzac Square, Brisbane, Qld 4000. *T:* Brisbane 229-4143. *Clubs:* Tattersall's (Brisbane); Indooroopilly Golf.

SEERS, Dudley, CMG 1975; Fellow, Institute of Development Studies, University of Sussex, since 1972 (Director, 1967-72, Director MPhil course, 1975-77); *b* 11 April 1920; *s* of late George Clarence Seers and of Mabel Edith Seers (*née* Hallett); *m* 1943, Patricia Hindell; one *s* three *d. Educ:* Rugby Sch.; Pembroke Coll., Cambridge. Served Royal Navy, 1941-45. PM's Office, New Zealand Govt, 1945-46; Res. Off. (later Lectr and Sen. Lectr in Economic Statistics) Oxford Univ., 1946-53 and 1954-55; Mem. Min. of Health Cttee on Housebuilding Costs, 1949-50; Economist, UN Headqrs, 1953-54; Statistical Adviser to Barbados, Leeward and Windward Isles, 1955-57; Chief, Survey Section, UN Econ. Commn for Latin America, 1957-61; Vis. Prof., Yale Univ., 1961-63; Dir, Economic Develt Div., UN Econ. Commn for Africa, 1963-64; Leader, UN Economic Mission to Zambia, 1964; Director-General, Economic Planning

Staff, Ministry of Overseas Development, 1964-67. Also consultant for Govts of Burma, Ghana, Jamaica, Kenya, Malaysia, Malta, Portugal, Sri Lanka, Trinidad, for Internat. Bank, ILO, OECD, and for Univ. of Guyana. Member: Editorial Bd, Jl of Develt Studies; SSRC panel on N Sea Oil, 1975; OECD team on Japan's social science policy, 1975; Chm., WUS Chile Awards Cttee, 1974-; Pres., European Assoc. of Develt Insts, 1975-78. Leader, ILO Missions to Colombia, 1970, Sri Lanka, 1971. Order of Boyacá, Colombia, 1970. *Publications:* (ed) Cuba: The Economic and Social Revolution, 1964; contrib.: The Theory and Design of Economic Development (ed Adelman and Thorbecke), 1967; The Teaching of Development Economics (ed Martin and Knapp), 1967; Crisis in the Civil Service (ed Thomas), 1968; Africa and the World, 1969; Unfashionable Economics: essays in honour of Lord Balogh (ed Streeten), 1970; The Labour Government's Economic Record 1964-70 (ed Beckerman), 1972; (ed) Development in a Divided World, 1971; (ed) Crisis in Planning, 1972; contribs to: Population and its Problems (ed Parry), 1976; Employment, Income Distribution and Development Strategy, essays in honour of H. W. Singer, 1976; Statistical Needs for Development, 1977; contrib. to: North Sea Oil-the application of development theories, 1977; Sussex Essays on Dependence, 1978; Econ. Jl; Oxford Econ. Papers; Social and Econ. Studies; Jl of Development Studies; Bulletin of IDS. *Recreations:* tennis, skiing, teasing bureaucrats. *Address:* Stanmer House, Stanmer, Brighton, East Sussex. *T:* Brighton 602354; (office) Brighton 606261.

SEFTON, William Henry; Chairman: Runcorn Development Corporation, since 1974; North West Economic Planning Council, since 1975; Opposition Leader, Merseyside County Council, since 1977; *b* 5 Aug. 1915; *s* of George and Emma Sefton; *m* 1940, Phyllis Kerr. *Educ:* Duncombe Road Sch., Liverpool. Joined Liverpool CC, 1953, Leader 1964; Chm. and Leader, Merseyside CC, 1974-77. Joined Runcorn Develt Corp., 1964, Dep. Chm. 1967. *Recreations:* gardening, woodwork. *Address:* 88 Tramway Road, Liverpool L17 7AZ. *T:* 051-727 3900.

SEGAL, family name of **Baron Segal.**

SEGAL, Baron *cr* 1964, of Wytham (Life Peer); **Samuel Segal,** MRCS, LRCP; MA Oxon; Deputy Speaker, and Deputy Chairman of Committees, House of Lords, since 1973; *b* 2 April 1902; *e s* of late Professor M. H. Segal, MA; *m* 1934, Molly, *o d* of Robert J. Rolo, OBE, Alexandria, Egypt; two *d* (one *s* decd). *Educ:* Royal Grammar Sch., Newcastle upon Tyne (Scholar); Jesus Coll., Oxford (Exhibitioner); Westminster Hosp. (Scholar). Casualty Surgeon and HP Westminster Hospital; Senior Clinical Assistant, Great Ormond Street Children's Hospital. Served on various LCC Hospital Committees. Contested (Lab) Tynemouth, 1935, Aston (Birmingham) By-Election, May 1939. Joined RAFVR Medical Branch, Oct. 1939; served in Aden 1940, Western Desert 1941, Syrian Campaign 1941; attached Greek Air Force, 1941; Squadron Leader, 1942; Sen. Med. Officer RAF Naval Co-operation Group in Mediterranean, 1942; on Headquarters Staff Middle East, 1943-44; on Air Min. Med. Staff, 1944-45; travelled extensively on RAF Medical duties throughout North and East Africa, Iraq, Persian Gulf, India, etc.; Regional MO, Min. of Health, 1951-62. MP (Lab) for Preston, 1945-50; Member Parly Delegations: to Austria, 1946; to Nigeria, Cameroons, Gold Coast, Sierra Leone and Gambia, 1947; to Egypt, 1947; Hungary, 1965; Cyprus, 1965; Bahrain, Aden, 1966; Malawi, 1966 (Leader); Hong Kong, Singapore and S Vietnam, 1968; Caribbean, 1974 (Leader); UK delegate, Inter-Parly Union Conf., Tokyo 1974, London 1975. Mem. FO Mission to Persia, 1947. Chairman: Nat. Soc. for Mentally Handicapped Children, 1965-; British Assoc. for the Retarded; Council, Anglo-Israel Assoc.; Dolphin Square Tenants Assoc., 1973-77; Oxford Soc. in London; Jesus Coll. Assoc., London Branch, 1976-; Hon. Treas., Anglo-Iranian Parly Gp, 1970-; Member: Home Office Adv. Cttee on Service Parly Candidates; Council, Oxford Society; President: Oxford-Paddington Passenger Assoc.; The Haven Foundn; Vice-Pres., Music Therapy Charity Ltd; Patron, Oxford Diocesan Assoc. for the Deaf. Life Governor, Manchester Coll., Oxford, Visitor 1972; Governor, Carmel Coll. Hon. Fellow, Jesus College, Oxford, 1966. *Recreation:* getting lost. *Address:* Wytham Abbey, Oxford OX2 8QF. *T:* Oxford 47200; 208 Frobisher House, Dolphin Square, SW1V 3LL. *T:* 01-828 7172. *Clubs:* Royal Air Force, United Oxford & Cambridge University; Royal Commonwealth Society.

SEGAL, Prof. Judah Benzion, MC 1942; FBA 1968; Professor of Semitic Languages in the University of London, School of Oriental and African Studies, since 1961; *b* 21 June 1912; *s* of Prof. Moses H. Segal and Hannah Leah Segal; *m* 1946, Leah (*née* Seidemann); two *d*. *Educ:* Magdalen College School,

Oxford; St Catharine's College, Cambridge. Jarrett Schol., 1932; John Stewart of Rannoch Schol., in Hebrew, 1933; 1st Cl. Oriental Langs Tripos, 1935; Tyrwhitt Schol. and Mason Prizeman, 1936; BA (Cambridge), 1935; MA 1938. Mansel Research Exhibitioner, St John's Coll., Oxford, 1936-39; James Mew Schol., 1937; DPhil (Oxon.), 1939. Deputy Assistant Director, Public Security, Sudan Government, 1939-41; served War of 1939-45, GHQ, MEF, 1942-44, Captain; Education Officer, British Military Administration, Tripolitania, 1945-46. Head of Dept of Near and Middle East, Sch. of Oriental and African Studies, 1961-68. Dir, Jewish Chronicle Trust. Mem., Council of Christians and Jews. Freedom, City of Urfa, Turkey, 1973. *Publications:* The Diacritical Point and the Accents in Syriac, 1953; The Hebrew Passover, 1963; Edessa, 1970; articles in learned periodicals. *Recreation:* walking. *Address:* 17 Hillersdon Avenue, Edgware, Mddx. *T:* 01-958 4993.

SEGOVIA, Andres; Spanish concert-guitarist; *b* Spain 18 Feb. 1894; *m* 1962, Emilia; one *s* (and one *s* one *d* by former marr.). Brought up in Granada; has been playing the guitar since the age of ten; first came to England as a young man; has often returned on concert tours since 1952; has had many pupils and has taught at Santiago de Compostela and Academy Chigi, Siena, and other schools; has adapted works of Bach, Haydn, Mozart and other classical composers for the guitar; has had many works composed especially for him by Casella, Castelnuovo-Tedesco, De Falla, Ponce, Roussel, Tansman, Turina, Villa-Lobos and others. Hon. DMus Oxon, 1972. Gold Medal for Meritorious Work (Spain), 1967. *Publication:* An Autobiography of the years 1893-1920, 1920, 1977. *Address:* c/o Ibbs & Tillett, 124 Wigmore Street, W1.

SEGRÈ, Prof. Emilio; Grande Ufficiale, Merito della Repubblica (Italy); Professor of Physics, University of California, Berkeley, 1946-72, now Emeritus; *b* 1 Feb. 1905; *s* of Giuseppe Segrè and Amelia Treves-Segrè; *m* 1936, Elfriede Spiro (*d* 1970); one *s* two *d*; *m* 1972, Rosa Mines Segrè. *Educ:* University of Rome, Italy. Asst Prof. of Physics, Rome, 1929-35; Dir, Physics Inst., Univ. of Palermo, Italy, 1936-38; Research Associate and Lectr, Univ. of Calif., Berkeley, 1938-42; Group Leader, Los Alamos Scientific Lab., 1942-46. Hon. Prof. S Marcos Univ., Lima, 1954; Prof. of Nuclear Physics, Univ. of Rome, 1974-75. Hon. DSc Palermo, 1958; Hon. Dr Tel Aviv Univ. Nobel laureate (joint) for physics, 1959. Member: Nat. Acad. Sciences, USA, 1952; Accad. Nazionale Lincei, Roma, 1959; Heidelberg Akad. der Wissenschaften; Amer. Phil. Soc.; Amer. Acad. of Arts and Sciences; Indian Acad. of Sciences. Editor, Annual Review of Nuclear Science. *Publications:* Nuclei and Particles, 1964; Enrico Fermi, Physicist, 1970; contrib. to Physical Review, Proc. Roy. Soc. London, Nature, Nuovo Cimento. *Recreations:* mountaineering and fishing. *Address:* 36 Crest Road, Lafayette, Calif 94549, USA; Department of Physics, University of California, Berkeley, Calif 94720. *Club:* University of California Faculty (Berkeley).

SEIFERT, Robin (also known as **Richard**); JP; FRIBA; Principal R. Seifert and Partners, Architects, since 1934; *b* 25 Nov. 1910; *s* of William Seifert; *m* 1939, Josephine Jeanette Harding; two *s* one *d*. *Educ:* Central Foundation Sch., City of London; University College, London (DipArch), Fellow, 1971. Commenced architectural practice, 1934. Corps of Royal Engineers, 1940-44; Indian Army, 1944-46; Hon. Lt-Col, 1946; Certif. for Meritorious Services Home Forces, 1943. Returned to private practice, 1948. Designed: ICI Laboratories, Dyestuffs Div., Blackley, Manchester; The Times Newspapers building, Printing House Square; Centre Point, St Giles Circus; Drapers Gardens, Nat. West. Bank Tower, City; The Royal Garden Hotel, Kensington; Tolworth Towers, Surbiton; Guiness Mahon Bank, Gracechurch Street; HQ of ICT, Putney; Kellogg House, Baker Street; Dunlop House, King Street, St James's; BSC Res. Labs, Middlesbrough; Britannia Hotel; Park Tower Hotel; London Heathrow Hotel; Sobell Sports Centre; ATV Centre, Birmingham; International Press Centre; Metropolitan Police HQ, Putney; Wembley Conference Centre; Princess Grace Hospital, Marylebone Road. Member: MoT Road Safety Council, 1969 (now disbanded); Home Office Cttee of Management, Housing Assoc. for Discharged Offenders; (part-time) British Waterways Bd, 1971-74; Council, RIBA, 1971-74. FRSA 1976. Liveryman, Glaziers' Co. City of London. JP Barnet, 1969. *Recreations:* chess, violin. *Address:* Eleventrees, Milespit Hill, Mill Hill, NW7. *T:* 01-959 3397. *Clubs:* Army and Navy, City Livery, Arts.

SEKYI, Henry Van Hien; High Commissioner for Ghana in the United Kingdom, 1972-75; *b* 15 Jan. 1928; *s* of W. E. G. Sekyi, MA London, BL, and Lily Anna Sekyi (*née* Cleland); *m* 1958, Maria Joyce Sekyi (*née* Tachie-Menson); one *s* one *d*. *Educ:* Adisadel Coll., Cape Coast; Univ. of Ghana; King's Coll.,

Cambridge; LSE. BA London 1953; BA Cantab 1955. Third Sec., Second Sec., and First Sec., in succession, Ghana Embassy, Washington, DC, USA, 1958-61; First Sec., later Counsellor, Ghana Embassy, Rome, 1961-62; Director, Min. Foreign Affairs, 1962-65, in charge of Divisions of: Eastern Europe and China; Middle East and Asia; UN Affairs; Personnel and Administration; Acting Principal Sec., Min. of Foreign Affairs, 1965-66; Ghana High Comr to Australia, 1966-70; Ghana Ambassador to Italy, 1970-72. *Recreations:* classics, music, Africana and gymnastics. *Address:* c/o Ministry of Foreign Affairs, Accra, Ghana.

SELBORNE, 4th Earl of, *cr* 1882; **John Roundell Palmer,** JP; Baron Selborne, 1872; Viscount Wolmer, 1882; Treasurer, Bridewell Royal Hospital (King Edward's School, Witley), since 1972; *b* 24 March 1940; *er s* of William Matthew, Viscount Wolmer (killed on active service, 1942), and of Priscilla (who *m* 1948, Hon. Peter Legh, now 4th Baron Newton, *qv*), *d* of late Captain John Egerton-Warburton; *S* grandfather, 1971; *m* 1969, Joanna Van Antwerp, *yr d* of Evan Maitland James, *qv* ; three *s*. *Educ:* Eton; Christ Church, Oxford (MA). Vice-Chm., Apple and Pear Develt Council, 1969-73; Member: Hops Mkting Bd, 1972-; ARC, 1975-. Hampshire County Council, 1967-74. JP Hants 1971. *Heir: s* Viscount Wolmer, *qv. Address:* Temple Manor, Selborne, Alton, Hants. *T:* Bordon 3646. *Club:* Brooks's.

SELBY, 4th Viscount, *cr* 1905; **Michael Guy John Gully;** Chairman: Grosvenor Bindings Ltd; Lakeside Artists & Printers Ltd; Director: Kames Fish Farming Ltd; Clan Fish Products Ltd; Ledger Selby Ltd; Computer Time Services Ltd; Verden Properties Ltd; West Highland Quality Foods Ltd; Partner, Fisher and Co., chartered accountants; *b* 15 Aug. 1942; *s* of 3rd Viscount and of Veronica, *er d* of late J. George and of Mrs Briscoe-George; *S* father, 1959; *m* 1965, Mary Theresa, *d* of late Capt. Thomas Powell, London, SW7; one *s* one *d. Educ:* Harrow. ACA, ATII. *Recreations:* shooting, fishing, sailing. *Heir: s* Hon. Edward Thomas William Gully, *b* 21 Sept. 1967. *Address:* Ardfern House, by Lochgilphead, Argyll PA31 8QN.

SELBY, Bishop Suffragan of, since 1972; **Rt. Rev. Morris Henry St John Maddocks;** *b* 28 April 1928; *s* of Rev. Canon Morris Arthur Maddocks and Gladys Mabel Sharpe; *m* 1955, Anne Sheail; no *c. Educ:* St John's Sch., Leatherhead; Trinity Coll., Cambridge; Chichester Theological Coll. BA 1952, MA 1956, Cambridge. Ordained in St Paul's Cathedral, London, 1954. Curate: St Peter's, Ealing, 1954-55; St Andrews, Uxbridge, 1955-58; Vicar of: Weaverthorpe, Helperthorpe and Luttons Ambo, 1958-61; S Martin's on the Hill, Scarborough, 1961-71. Co-Chm., Churches' Council for Health and Healing, 1975-. *Recreations:* golf, music, gardening, painting. *Address:* Tollgarth, 100 Tadcaster Road, Dringhouses, York YO2 2LT. *T:* York 706433. *Club:* Ganton Golf (Yorkshire).

SELBY, Harry; MP (Lab) Govan Div. of Glasgow, since Feb. 1974; *b* 18 May 1913; *s* of Max Soldberg and Annie (*née* Saltman); *m* 1937, Jeannie McKearn Reid; one *s. Educ:* Queen's Park Secondary, Glasgow. Served War of 1939-45: Private, Highland Light Infantry, June 1940; Royal Corps of Signals, March 1941; released Dec. 1945. *Address:* 363 Paisley Road, Glasgow G5 8RN. *T:* 041-429 0741.

SELBY, Sir Kenneth, Kt 1970; FCMA, FCCA, FBIM, MIQ; Chairman, Bath & Portland Group Ltd, since 1969; *b* 16 Feb. 1914; *s* of Thomas William Selby; *m* 1937, Elma Gertrude, *d* of Johnstone Sleator; two *s. Educ:* High School for Boys, Worthing. Managing Director, Bath & Portland Group Ltd, 1963. Governor: Bath Inst. Medical Engineering; Wells Cathedral Sch., 1976-; Mem., Ct and Council, Chm. Council, 1975-, Pro Chancellor, 1975-, Bath Univ.; Governor, Bell Sch. of Languages, 1973-; Chm., Air Travel Reserve Fund Agency, 1975-. *Address:* Hartham Park, Corsham, Wilts. *T:* Corsham 713176. *Clubs:* Reform; Savages (Bristol).

SELBY, Ralph Walford, CMG 1961; HM Diplomatic Service, retired; *b* 20 March 1915; *e s* of late Sir Walford Selby, KCMG, CB, CVO; *m* 1947, Julianna Snell; three *d. Educ:* Eton; Christ Church, Oxford. Entered HM Diplomatic Service, Sept. 1938; served in Foreign Office until Oct. 1939. Enlisted in Army and served with Grenadier Guards, March 1940-Feb. 1945, when returned to Foreign Office; seconded to Treasury for service in India as First Secretary in Office of High Commissioner for UK, Sept. 1947; transferred to The Hague, 1950; returned to FO, 1953-56; transf. to Tokyo as Counsellor, 1956, to Copenhagen in 1958, to Djakarta in 1961, to Warsaw in 1964; Chargé d'Affaires in 1952, 1958, 1959, 1960, 1961, 1962, 1964, 1965, 1969, 1970; Consul-Gen., Boston, 1966-69; Minister, British Embassy, Rome, 1969-72; Ambassador to Norway, 1972-75. *Recreation:* sports as available. *Address:* Mengeham House, Mengham Lane, Hayling Island, Hants PO11 9JX. *Club:* Turf.

SELBY, Rear-Adm. William Halford, CB 1955; DSC 1942; *b* 29 April 1902; *s* of E. H. Selby; *m* 1926, Hilary Elizabeth Salter (*d* 1960); two *d; m* 1961, Mrs R. Milne. *Educ:* Royal Naval Colleges, Osborne and Dartmouth. Entered Royal Navy, 1916; Midshipman, HMS Royal Oak, Black Sea and Dardanelles, 1920; Sub.-Lt HMS Vendetta and HMY Victoria and Albert, 1924. Destroyers, Medit and China Station between 1927 and 1936; Naval Staff Coll., 1939; War of 1939-45: in comd HMS Wren, Mashona (despatches), Onslaught (despatches). Capt. 1943; Chief of Staff, Londonderry, 1944-45; Capt. 'D' Third Flotilla in comd HMS Saumarez, 1946-47; Dep. Dir Ops Div., Admty, 1948-50; Capt-in-Charge, Simonstown, 1950-52; Rear-Adm. 1953; Head of British Naval Mission to Greece, 1953-55; retired, 1956. *Address:* The Old Cottage, Chittoe, Chippenham, Wilts.

SELBY WRIGHT, Very Rev. Ronald (William Vernon); *see* Wright.

SELDON TRUSS, Leslie; author; *b* 1892; *s* of George Marquand Truss and Ann Blanche, *d* of Samuel Seldon, CB; *m* 1st, 1918, Gwendolen, *d* of Charles Kershaw, Cooden Mount, Sussex; one *d* ; 2nd, 1925, Kathleen Mary, *d* of Charles Hornung, of Oaklands, Hookwood, Surrey; one *s* one *d.* Lieut Scots Guards, Special Reserve, 1915-19; Major Home Guard, 1940-44. *Publications:* Gallows Bait, 1928; The Stolen Millionaire, 1929; The Man Without Pity, 1930; The Hunterstone Outrage, 1931; Turmoil at Brede, 1932; Mr Coroner Presides, 1932; They Came by Night, 1933; The Daughters of Belial, 1934; Murder Paves the Way; Escort to Danger, 1935; Draw the Blinds; Rooksmiths, 1936; The Man who Played Patience; She Could Take Care; Footsteps Behind Them, 1937; Foreign Bodies, 1938; The Disappearance of Julie Hints, 1940; Sweeter for his Going, Where's Mr Chumley?, 1949; Ladies Always Talk, 1950; Never Fight a Lady, 1951; Death of No Lady, 1952; Always Ask a Policeman, 1953; Put Out The Light, The High Wall, 1954; The Long Night, The Barberton Intrigue, 1956; The Truth About Claire Veryan, 1957; In Secret Places, 1958; The Hidden Men, 1959; One Man's Death, 1960; Seven Years Dead, 1961; A Time to Hate, 1962; Technique for Treachery, 1963; Walk a Crooked Mile, 1964; The Town That Went Sick, 1965; Eyes at the Window, 1966; The Bride That Got Away, 1967; The Hands of the Shadow, 1968; The Corpse That Got Away, 1969; under *pseudonym* of George Selmark, Murder in Silence, 1939; various short stories and serials. *Recreations:* anything but writing. *Address:* Dale Hill House, Ticehurst, Sussex. *T:* Ticehurst 251.

SELF, Hugh Michael, QC 1973; a Recorder of the Crown Court, since 1975; *b* 19 March 1921; *s* of Sir (Albert) Henry Self, KCB, KCMG, KBE; *m* 1950, Penelope Ann, *d* of John Drinkwater, and of Daisy Kennedy, *qv* ; two *d. Educ:* Lancing Coll.; Worcester Coll., Oxford (BA). Royal Navy, 1942-46, Lieut RNVR 1946. Called to Bar, Lincoln's Inn, 1951. *Recreations:* golf, walking in England, literature. *Address:* 59 Maresfield Gardens, Hampstead, NW3 5TE. *T:* 01-435 8311. *Club:* Savile. *See also Prof. P. J. O. Self.*

SELF, Prof. Peter John Otter; Professor of Public Administration, University of London, since 1963; Vice-Chairman of Executive, Town and Country Planning Association; *b* 7 June 1919; *s* of Sir (Albert) Henry Self, KCB, KCMG, KBE; *m* 1st, 1950, Diana Mary Pitt (marr. diss.); 2nd, 1959, Elaine Rosenbloom Adams; two *s. Educ:* Lancing Coll.; Balliol Coll., Oxford (MA). Editorial staff of The Economist, 1944-62; Extra-mural Lectr, London Univ., 1944-49; Lectr in Public Administration, LSE, 1948-61; Reader in Political Science, LSE, 1961-63. Dir of Studies (Administration), Civil Service Dept, 1969-70. Mem. Exec. and Coun., 1954, Vice-Chm. Exec., 1955, Chm. Exec., 1961-69, Town and Country Planning Assoc.; Mem., SE Regional Economic Planning Coun., 1966-. *Publications:* Regionalism, 1949; Cities in Flood: The Problems of Urban Growth, 1957; (with H. Storing) The State and the Farmer, 1962; Administrative Theories and Politics, 1972; Econocrats and the Policy Process, 1976; numerous articles on administration, politics and planning. *Recreations:* walking, golf, story-telling. *Address:* 43 Brim Hill, N2. *T:* 01-458 1046. *Club:* Reform. *See also H. M. Self.*

SELIGMAN, Henry, OBE 1958; PhD; President, EXEC AG, Basle; Scientific Consultant (part-time) to International Atomic Energy Agency, Vienna, since 1969; Scientific Adviser to various industries, since 1970; *b* Frankfurt am Main, 25 Feb. 1909; *s* of Milton Seligman and Marie (*née* Gans); *m* 1941, Lesley Bradley; two *s. Educ:* Liebigschule Frankfurt; Sorbonne; Universities of Lausanne and of Zürich. Staff, DSIR, Cavendish Lab., Cambridge, 1942-43. Joined British-Canadian Research Project at Montreal, 1943, Chalk River, Ontario, 1944-; Staff,

Brit. Atomic Energy Project, 1946; Head of Isotope Div., Atomic Energy Research Establishment, Harwell, UK, 1947-58; Dep. Dir Gen., Dept of Research and Isotopes, Internat. Atomic Energy Agency, Vienna, 1958-69. Editor-in-Chief, Scientific Jl. *Publications:* papers on: physical constants necessary for reactor development; waste disposal; production and uses of radioisotopes; contrib. scientific journals. *Address:* Scherpegasse 8/6/4, 1190 Vienna, Austria. *T:* Vienna 3247764.

SELIGMAN, Peter Wendel, CBE 1969; Chairman, APV Holdings Ltd, 1965-77; *b* 16 Jan. 1913; *s* of late Richard Joseph Simon Seligman and of Hilda Mary Seligman; *m* 1937, Elizabeth Lavinia Mary Wheatley; two *s* four *d*. *Educ:* King's Coll. Sch., Wimbledon; Harrow Sch.; Caius Coll., Cambridge. Joined APV Co. Ltd, as Asst to Man. Dir, 1936; appointed Dir, 1939; Man. Dir, 1947; Dep. Chm., 1961. Mem., Engineering Industries Council, 1975-77. Chm., Nat. Sale Fedn of GB, 1977-. *Recreations:* sailing, ski-ing. *Address:* Dagmar House, Birmingham Road, Cowes, IoW. *Clubs:* Athenæum, Cruising Association; Hawks (Cambridge); Island Sailing (Cowes); Kandahar Ski (Chm., 1972-77).

SELKIRK, 10th Earl of, *cr* 1646; **George Nigel Douglas-Hamilton,** KT 1976; PC 1955; GCMG 1959; GBE 1963 (OBE 1941); AFC; AE; QC(Scot.), 1959; late Gp Capt. Auxiliary Air Force; Scottish Representative Peer, 1945-63; *b* Merly, Wimborne, Dorset, 4 Jan. 1906; 2nd *s* of 13th Duke of Hamilton and Brandon; *S* to earldom of father under terms of special remainder, 1940; *m* 1949, Audrey Durell, *o d* of late Maurice Drummond-Sale-Barker and of Mrs H. S. Brooks. *Educ:* Eton; Balliol College, Oxford, MA; Edinburgh University, LLB. Admitted to Faculty of Advocates, 1935; Commanded 603 Squadron AAF, 1934-38; Member of Edinburgh Town Council, 1935-40; Commisssioner of General Board of Control (Scotland), 1936-39; Commissioner for Special Areas in Scotland, 1937-39. Served War of 1939-45 (OBE, despatches twice). A Lord-in-Waiting to the Queen, 1952-53 (to King George VI, 1951-52); Paymaster-General, Nov. 1953-Dec. 1955; Chancellor of the Duchy of Lancaster, Dec. 1955-Jan. 1957; First Lord of the Admiralty, 1957-Oct. 1959; UK Commissioner for Singapore and Comr Gen. for SE Asia, 1959-63; also UK Council Representative to SEATO, 1960-63; Chm., Cons. Commonwealth Council, 1965-72. Freeman of Hamilton. President: National Ski Fedn of Great Britain, 1964-68; Anglo-Swiss Society, 1965-70; Building Societies Assoc., 1965; Royal Soc. for Asian Affairs, 1966-76; Assoc. of Independent Unionist Peers, 1967-. Chm., Victoria League, 1971-77. Hon. Chief, Saulteaux Indians, 1967. *Heir presumptive: nephew* Alasdair Malcolm Douglas-Hamilton [*b* 10 Sept. 1939; *m* 1965, Angela Kathleen, 2nd *d* of John Molony Longley; two *s* one *d*]. *Address:* Rose Lawn Coppice, Wimborne, Dorset. *T:* Wimborne 3160; 60 Eaton Place, SW1. *T:* 01-235 6926. *Clubs:* Athenæum, Caledonian; New (Edinburgh).

SELLECK, Sir Francis Palmer, KBE 1957; Kt 1956; MC 1918; Lord Mayor, City of Melbourne, 1954-57; *b* 20 Aug. 1895; *s* of late Christopher and Emily Selleck; *m* 1923, Mollie Constance Maud Miller; one *s* one *d*. *Educ:* High School, Shepparton, Australia. Chartered Accountant; Director of Companies; Lord Mayor of Melbourne, 1954-57; Lord Mayor, Olympic Games, Melb., 1956. Served Australian Imperial Forces, Gallipoli, France, 1915-18 (despatches, MC). Served with Board of Business Administration, Australian Defence HQ, 1940-45. Chm., St Paul's Anglican Cathedral Melbourne Restoration Appeal, 1960-67. *Address:* Suite 26, 67 Queens Road, Melbourne, Vic. 3004, Australia. *T:* 51-5362; (home) 24-6780. *Club:* Naval and Military (Melbourne).

SELLERS, Rt. Hon. Sir Frederic Aked, PC 1957; Kt 1946; MC; a Lord Justice of Appeal, 1957-68; *b* 14 Jan. 1893; 3rd *s* of John Shuttleworth Sellers and Elizabeth Stuart; *m* 1917, Grace, *y d* of William Malin, JP, Derby; four *s* one *d*. *Educ:* Silcoates Sch.; Univ. of Liverpool. Served with King's (Liverpool) Regt 13th Battn 1914-18 (Capt.; MC 1916, 2 Bars 1918); HG, 1940-45; called to Bar, Gray's Inn, 1919; KC 1935; sometime Mem. Bar Council; Bencher, Gray's Inn, 1938; Treasurer, 1952; Vice-Treasurer, 1953; Northern Circuit; Recorder of Bolton, 1938-46; Judge, Queen's Bench Division, 1946-57. Mem., Standing Committee on Criminal Law Revision (Chm., 1959-69). Liberal Candidate Waterloo Div. of Lancashire, General Election, 1929, Hendon North, 1945. Chairman of Governors: Mill Hill School, 1951-68; Silcoates Sch., 1953-58. Hon. LLD Liverpool, 1956. *Address:* Highwood Lodge, Mill Hill, NW7. *T:* 01-959 3066. *Club:* Reform.
See also N. W. M. Sellers.

SELLERS, Norman William Malin, VRD; **His Honour Judge Sellers;** a Circuit Judge, since 1974; *b* 29 Aug. 1919; *e s* of Rt

Hon. Sir Frederic Sellers, *qv*; *m* 1946, Angela Laurie, *er d* of Sidney Jukes, Barnet; four *d*. *Educ:* Merchant Taylors' Sch., Crosby; Silcoates Sch., Wakefield; Hertford Coll., Oxford (MA). Officer, RNVR, 1940-65 (despatches, HMS Nelson, 1942); Lt Cdr 1953, comd HMS Mersey. Called to Bar, Gray's Inn, 1947; Northern Circuit; Asst Recorder of Blackpool, 1962-71; Recorder of Crown Court, 1972-74. Contested (L) Crosby Div. of Lancs, 1964. *Recreation:* sailing. *Address:* 71 Dowhills Road, Blundellsands, Liverpool L23 8SL. *T:* 051-924 4309. *Clubs:* Bar Yacht, West Lancashire Yacht.

SELLERS, Peter (Richard Henry), CBE 1966; Actor; *b* 8 Sept. 1925; *s* of late William Sellers and late Agnes Marks; *m* 1951, Anne Howe (marr. diss. 1964); one *s* one *d*; *m* 1964, Britt Ekland (marr. diss. 1969); one *d*; *m* 1970, Miranda (marr. diss. 1974), *d* of Richard St John Quarry, and of Lady Mancroft; *m* 1977, Lynne Frederick. *Educ:* St Aloysius Coll., Highgate. War of 1939-45 (Burma Star, etc). Began career at the Windmill Theatre, 1948. *Radio:* Ray's A Laugh (5 years); The Goon Show (9 years); *television:* Idiots Weekly; A Show Called Fred; Son of Fred; *variety:* touring, 1949-54; appeared at Palladium, 4 times; *films:* The Ladykillers, The Smallest Show on Earth, The Naked Truth, Tom Thumb, Carleton Browne of the FO, The Mouse That Roared, I'm Alright Jack, Up The Creek, Two Way Stretch, Battle of the Sexes, Never Let Go, The Millionairess, Mr Topaze (also Dir), The Running, Jumping and Standing Still Film (Prod), Only Two Can Play, The Waltz of the Toreadors, The Dock Brief, Lolita, The Wrong Arm of the Law, Heavens Above!, Dr Strangelove or How I Learned to Stop Worrying and Love the Bomb, The World of Henry Orient, The Pink Panther, Shot in the Dark, What's New Pussycat?, The Wrong Box, After the Fox, Casino Royale, The Bobo, The Party, I Love You Alice B. Toklas, The Magic Christian, Hoffman, There's a Girl in my Soup, Where Does it Hurt?, Alice's Adventures in Wonderland, The Blockhouse, The Optimists, Soft Beds—Hard Battles, The Great McGonagall, The Return of the Pink Panther, Murder by Death, The Pink Panther Strikes Again; *stage:* Brouhaha, 1958. Has made some recordings. Awards: Best Actor for 1959 (British Film Academy Award); Golden Gate Award, 1959; San Sebastian Film Award for Best British Actor, 1962; Best Actor award, Tehran Film Festival, 1973. *Recreations:* photography, cars. *Address:* Barclays Bank Ltd, 119 Waterloo Road, SE1. *Club:* Royal Automobile.

SELLORS, Patrick John Holmes, FRCS; Surgeon-Oculist to HM Household since 1974; Surgeon, King Edward VIIth Hospital for Officers, since 1975; Ophthalmic Surgeon: St George's Hospital since 1965; Croydon Eye Unit since 1970; *b* 11 Feb. 1934; *s* of Sir Thomas Holmes Sellors, *qv*; *m* 1961, Gillian Gratton Swallow; two *s* one *d*. *Educ:* Rugby Sch.; Oriel Coll., Oxford; Middlesex Hosp. Med. School. BM, BCh Oxon 1958; FRCS 1965. Registrar, Moorfields Eye Hosp., 1962-65; recognised teacher in Ophthalmology, St George's Hosp., 1966. Sec. to Ophthalmic Soc. of UK, 1970-72; Examr for Diploma of Ophthalmology, 1974-77; Mem. Council, Faculty of Ophthalmologists, 1977-; Vice-Pres., Med. Defence Union, 1977-. *Publications:* articles in BMJ and Trans OSUK. *Recreations:* gardening, golf. *Address:* 149 Harley Street, W1N 2DE. *T:* 01-935 4444.

SELLORS, Sir Thomas Holmes, Kt 1963; DM, MCh; FRCP; FRCS; Consultant Surgeon, London Chest Hospital, since 1934; Emeritus Thoracic Surgeon, Middlesex Hospital, since 1947; Consultant Surgeon, National Heart and Harefield Hospitals, since 1957; Consulting Surgeon, Aylesbury Group of Hospitals; *b* 7 April 1902; *s* of Dr T. B. Sellors; *m* 1st, Brenda Lyell (*d* 1928); 2nd, 1932, Dorothy Elizabeth Chesshire (*d* 1953); one *s* one *d*; 3rd, 1955, Marie Hobson. *Educ:* Loretto School; Oriel Coll., Oxford. Hon. Fellow 1973. BA Oxon 1923, MA 1927; MRCS, LRCP 1926; BM, BCh Oxon 1926; G. H. Hunt Travelling Scholarship, Univ. of Oxford, 1928; MCh 1931, DM 1933. Held various appts in London hosps; FRCS 1930; Member of Council, RCS, 1957-73, Vice-Pres., 1968-69, President 1969-72; FRCP 1963; Chairman of Joint Consultants Committee, 1958-67; President: Thoracic Society, 1960; Soc. of Thoracic Surgeons of Great Britain and Ireland, 1961-62; BMA, 1972; Royal Med. Benevolent Fund; Vice-Pres., Internat. Soc. Surg., 1967, 1975, Pres. Congress 1977; Chm. Council, British Heart Foundn. Surgeon to Royal Waterloo and Queen Mary's Hospitals; Regional Adviser in Thoracic Surgery, 1940-45. Hunterian Prof. RCS, 1944; Lectures: Carey Coombs, Univ. of Bristol, 1956; G. A. Gibson, RCPE, 1959; Strickland Goodall, Society Apothecaries, 1960; Entwhistle Meml and W. W. Hamburger, Chicago, 1961; St Cyre's, 1965; Grey-Turner, Internat. Soc. Surg., 1967; Gordon-Taylor, RCS, 1968; Tudor Edwards Meml, RCS, 1968; Bradshaw, RCS, 1969; Colles, RCSI, 1975. Hunterian Orator, RCS, 1973. Examiner in Surgery, Univ. of Oxford. Member: Acad. of Medicine, Rome;

Royal Acad. of Medicine, Belgium; Membre d'Honneur, Europe Cardiol. Soc.; Hon. Fellow: Amer. Coll. Surgeons, 1971; Coll. of Med., S Africa; RCSE, 1972; RCSI; Faculty of Dental Surgeons, RCS, 1974. MD (*hc*) Groningen, 1964; Hon. DSc Liverpool, 1970; Hon. MS Southampton, 1972. Médaille de la Reconnaissance Française. Officer of the Order of Carlos Finlay, Cuba. *Publications:* Surgery of the Thorax, 1933. Editor and contributor in current text books. Articles in English and foreign medical publications. *Recreations:* water-colour painting, gardening. *Address:* Spring Coppice Farm, Speen, Aylesbury, Bucks. *T:* Hampden Row 379.
See also *P . J . H . Sellors* .

SELLS, Arthur Lytton L.; *see* Lytton Sells.

SELOUS, Gerald Holgate, CBE 1946 (OBE 1929; MBE 1920); *b* 14 July 1887; *o s* of late Edmund Selous, barrister-at-law and ornithologist, and late Fanny Margaret, *d* of John Maxwell, publisher, and Mary Elizabeth Braddon, novelist; *m* Camilla, *er d* of late Jay B. Lippincott and Camilla Hare, Philadelphia, Pa; one *s.* *Educ:* Cheltenham College; Pembroke College, Cambridge; studied at Scoones, crammers for FO exams. Student Interpreter Levant Consular Service, 1908; Vice-Consul, Saffi, Morocco, 1914-24; Consul at Casablanca, Morocco, 1924-28; Consul at Basra, Iraq, 1929-32; Commercial Counsellor at Cairo, 1933-38, and at Brussels, 1938-40; served in Dept of Overseas Trade, 1940-42; Home Guard (St James's LDV Section), 1940-42; Trade Comr at Vancouver, BC, 1942-45; Counsellor (Commercial) at Berne, 1945-47. Silver Jubilee Medal, 1935; Coronation Medal, 1937. *Publications:* Appointment to Fez, 1956; various (published) economic reports. *Recreations:* archæology, natural history. *Address:* Château d'Hauteville, 1806 St Légier, Vaud, Switzerland. *T:* 021/54.11.95. *Clubs:* Travellers', Lansdowne, Royal Automobile; Grande Société (Berne).

SELSDON, 3rd Baron, *cr* 1932, of Croydon; **Malcolm McEacharn Mitchell-Thomson;** Bt 1900; banker; *b* 27 Oct. 1937; *s* of 2nd Baron Selsdon (3rd Bt, *cr* 1900), DSC; *S* father, 1963; *m* 1965, Patricia Anne, *d* of Donald Smith; one *s.* *Educ:* Winchester College. Sub-Lieut, RNVR. Deleg. to Council of Europe and WEU, 1972-. Chm., Greater London and SE Regional Council for Sport and Recreation, 1977-. *Recreations:* rackets, squash, tennis, lawn tennis, cricket, ski-ing, sailing. *Heir: s* Hon. Callum Malcolm McEacharn Mitchell-Thomson, *b* 7 Nov. 1969. *Address:* 33 Cadogan Lane, SW1. *T:* 01-235 8692. *Club:* MCC.

SELVON, Samuel Dickson; author since 1954; *b* Trinidad, West Indies, 20 May 1923; *m* 1st, 1947, Draupadi Persaud; one *d* ; 2nd, 1963, Althea Nesta Daroux; two *s* one *d.* *Educ:* Naparima College, Trinidad. Wireless Operator, 1940-45; Journalist, 1946-50; Civil Servant, 1950-53. Fellow, John Simon Guggenheim Memorial Foundn (USA), 1954 and 1968; Travelling Schol., Soc. of Authors (London), 1958; Trinidad Govt Schol., 1962. Humming Bird Medal (Trinidad), 1969. *Publications:* A Brighter Sun, 1952; An Island is a World, 1954; The Lonely Londoners, 1956; Ways of Sunlight, 1957; Turn Again Tiger, 1959; I Hear Thunder, 1963; The Housing Lark, 1965; The Plains of Caroni, 1970; Those Who Eat the Cascadura, 1972; Moses Ascending, 1975; contribs to London Magazine, New Statesman and Nation, Sunday Times, also Evergreen Review (USA). *Recreations:* tennis, swimming, gardening, cooking. *Address:* 36 Woodside Avenue, SE25.

SELWAY, Air Marshal Sir Anthony (Dunkerton), KCB 1961 (CB 1952); DFC 1940; Registrar and Secretary of the Order of the Bath, since 1968 (Gentleman Usher of the Scarlet Rod, 1964-68); *b* 20 Feb. 1909; *s* of C. J. Selway, CVO, CBE, TD; *m* 1936, Patricia Graham, *d* of Col. P. C. MacFarlane, Ballagan, Strathblane, Stirlingshire; one *s* one *d.* *Educ:* Highgate School; Cranwell. No. 1 Squadron, Tangmere, 1929; Central Flying School, 1932-34; Middle East Command, 1936-42 (despatches); Flying Trg Comd, 1942-44; Fighter Comd, 1944-45; Burma and Far East, 1945-48; Joint Services Staff Coll., 1948; Air Ministry, 1948-51; Commandant, Central Flying School, 1951-53; Air Attaché, Paris, 1953-Nov. 1955; Comdr, RAF Staff, British Joint Services Mission (USA), 1955-58; AOC No. 18 Group Coastal Command, and Air Officer, Scotland 1958-60; C-in-C FEAF, 1960-62; AOC-in-C, RAF Coastal Command, 1962-65; Group Capt. 1942; Air Cdre 1951; Air Vice-Marshal, 1955; Air Marshal, 1961; retired, 1965. *Address:* c/o Williams & Glyn's Bank Ltd, 22 Whitehall, SW1. *Clubs:* Royal Air Force, White's.

SELWYN, John Sidney Augustus, OBE 1962 (MBE 1939); HM Diplomatic Service, retired; *b* 17 Oct. 1908; *s* of Rev. A. L. H. Selwyn; *m* 1932, Cicely Georgina Armour (marr. diss.); one *s* one *d* (and one *d* decd); *m* 1952, Janette Bruce Mullin (*d* 1968);

one *s* ; *m* 1971, Sonja Fischer; one *d.* *Educ:* St Lawrence College, Ramsgate; Royal Military Coll., Sandhurst. Entered the Indian Police, 1928. Served in NWF Campaigns, 1930, 1937 and 1941. Major, 12th Frontier Force Regt, active service in Burma, 1942-46, Allied Control Commission, Germany, 1946-48. Entered Foreign Service, 1948. Served in Bucharest, Lisbon, London, Lima, Santos, Beirut; Consul-General: Berlin, 1963; Strasbourg, 1964-68; Vice-Consul, Calais, 1969-73. *Recreation:* fishing. *Address:* Erlaufstrasse 35/2/6, A-2344 Maria Enzersdorf-Südstadt, Austria. *Club:* Civil Service.

SELWYN-LLOYD, family name of **Baron Selwyn-Lloyd.**

SELWYN-LLOYD, Baron *cr* 1976 (Life Peer), of Wirral, Merseyside; **John Selwyn Brooke Selwyn-Lloyd,** PC 1951; CH 1962; CBE 1945 (OBE 1943); TD; QC 1947; DL; *b* 28 July 1904; *s* of late J. W. Lloyd, MRCS, LRCP, Hoylake, and Rodney Street, Liverpool; *m* 1951, Elizabeth Marshall (marr. diss., 1957); one *d.* *Educ:* Fettes; Magdalene Coll., Cambridge. President Cambridge Union, 1927; Barrister Gray's Inn and Northern Circuit, 1930; a Master of the Bench, Gray's Inn, 1951. Service throughout War in Army, 2nd Lieut (TA) June 1939; Captain, Jan. 1940; Major, July 1940; Lieut-Colonel, 1942; Colonel, 1943; Brigadier, 1944. Served as General Staff Officer on HQ Second Army from its formation to surrender of Germany; returned to Bar, Aug. 1945; Recorder of Wigan, 1948-51. MP (C) Wirral Div. of Cheshire, 1945-70 (when elected Speaker); MP Wirral and Speaker of the House of Commons, 1971-76; Minister of State, FO, Oct. 1951-54; Minister of Supply, Oct. 1954-April 1955; Minister of Defence, April-Dec. 1955; Secretary of State for Foreign Affairs, 1955-60; Chancellor of the Exchequer, July 1960-62; Lord Privy Seal and Leader of the House of Commons, 1963-64; Member: Commn on the Constitution, 1969-71; NEDC 1962. Director: Sun Alliance and London Insurance Ltd, 1965-71; Sun Alliance, 1962-63, 1965-71; Alliance, 1950-51, 1962-63, 1965-71; English & Caledonian Investment Co. Ltd, 1966-71; Rank Organisation Ltd, 1963, 1965-71; IDC Group Ltd, 1970-71. Produced Selwyn Lloyd Report, 1963 (for Conservative Party Organisation). President: Nat. Assoc. of Conservative Clubs, 1963-64; National Union of Conservative and Unionist Associations, 1965-66; Hansard Soc., 1971-. Chm., Young Volunteer Force Foundn, 1970-71, Pres., 1971-. Chm., Adv. Council of Task Force, 1964-; Patron: Home Farm Trust; Methodist Homes for the Aged; President: Liverpool Sch. of Tropical Medicine, 1976; British Foundn for Age Research. Dep. High Steward, Cambridge Univ., 1971-. Hon. Freeman, Borough of Ellesmere Port, 1972. DL City and County of Chester, 1963-, Merseyside, 1974-. Hon. LLD: Sheffield, 1955; Liverpool, 1957; Cambridge, 1975; Hon. DCL Oxford, 1960; Hon. Fellow, Magdalene Coll. Legion of Merit, Degree of Commander, USA, 1946. *Publication:* Mr Speaker Sir, 1976. *Address:* 7 Gray's Inn Square, WC1; Hilbre House, Macdona Drive, West Kirby, Wirral, Merseyside L48 3JD. *Clubs:* Hon. Member: Carlton, Pratt's, Constitutional, Oxford and Cambridge; Royal Liverpool Golf (Centenary Captain, 1969).

SEMEGA-JANNEH, Bocar Ousman, MBE 1954; High Commissioner for The Gambia in London and Ambassador to Western Germany, Belgium, Sweden, Switzerland, France and Austria, since 1971; *b* 21 July 1910; *s* of late Ousman Semega-Janneh, merchant and late Koumba Tunkara, The Gambia; *m* 1936, and other Muslim marriages; several *c.* *Educ:* Mohammedan Primary Sch.; Methodist Boys' High School. Air Raid Warden, Bathurst, 1939-45. Gambia Surveys Dept: Surveys Asst 1931; Surveyor 1937; Sen. Surveyor 1948; Dir 1953; retd 1966. Gambian High Comr, Senegal, 1967; Ambassador to Mauritania, Mali, Guinea and Liberia, and High Comr, Sierra Leone, 1969; rep. Gambia at Gen. Assembly of UN, 1968-; rep. at meetings of Ministers of Foreign Affairs and Heads of State and Govt of members of Organisation of African Unity, 1968-. Rep. Gambia, triennial Survey Officers' Conf., Cambridge, 1955-65. Boy Scout, 1925; District Scout-master, 1938-42; Chief Comr of Scouts, The Gambia, 1947-66 (Silver Acorn 1954). Bathurst City Council: Councillor, 1951; Dep. Chm., 1957; Chm., 1960; first Mayor 1965; resigned 1967. Vice-Pres. 1955-56, Pres. 1957-67, Gambia Football Assoc.; formerly: Mem. Kombo Rural Authority; Governor, Gambia High Sch.; Actg Mem. Gambia Oilseeds Marketing Bd; Mem. Bathurst Colony Team and Town Planning Bd; Mem. Consultative Cttee for foundation of Constitution; Mem., Mohammedan Sch. Man. Cttee. Grand Officer, Order of Merit: Senegal, 1971; Mauritania, 1971; Officer of Republic of The Gambia. *Recreations:* football, cricket, golf, lawn tennis (singles champion, Gambia, 1932-50). *Address:* Gambia High Commission, 60 Ennismore Gardens, SW7. *T:* 01-584 1242/3.

SEMENOV, Prof. Nikolai Nikolaevich; Orders of Lenin; State awards; Director, Institute of Chemical Physics of the USSR Academy of Sciences since 1931; Professor, Moscow State University; *b* 16 April 1896; *s* of a state employee; *m* Lidiya Grigorievna Scherbakova; one *s* one *d*. *Educ:* Leningrad State University. Chief of Electronic Phenomena Laboratory of Physico-Technical Institute in Leningrad, 1920; Assistant Professor and then Professor, Leningrad Polytechnic Institute, 1920-41. (Jointly) Nobel Prize for Chemistry, 1956. Foreign Mem., Royal Society, 1958-; Member: USSR Academy of Sciences, 1932-; Chem. Soc. of England, 1949-; Naturalists' Soc., Leopoldina (Halle DDR), 1959; Amer. Chem. Soc., 1976; Hon. Fellow: Indian Academy of Sciences, 1959; Hungarian Academy of Sciences, 1961; New York Academy of Sciences, 1962; Roumanian Acad. Sci., 1965; Czechoslovakian Acad. Sci., 1965; Roy. Soc. of Edinburgh, 1966; For. Associate, Nat. Acad. of Sciences (USA), 1963; Corresp. Member: Akademie der Wissenschaften, Berlin, DDR, 1966; Bulgarian Acad. of Sciences, 1969; Hon. DSc: Oxford, 1960; Bruxelles, 1962; London, 1965; Hon. DrSci: Milan, 1964; Prague, 1965; Budapest, 1965; Humboldt-Universität zu Berlin, 1973. *Publications:* several textbooks and scientific monographs, notably: Chain reactions, 1934 (Russia), 1935 (Oxford); Some Problems on Chemical Kinetics and Reactivity, 1954 (Russia), enlarged 2nd edn 1958 (Russia), (Eng. trans. 1959); Science and Community, 1973 (Russia); numerous articles in the field of chemical physics. *Address:* Vorobyevskoye chaussée 2-B, Institute of Chemical Physics, Moscow 117334, USSR.

SEMKEN, John Douglas, MC 1944; Legal Adviser to the Home Office and the Northern Ireland Office, since 1977; *b* 9 Jan. 1921; *s* of Wm R. Semken and Mrs B. R. Semken (*née* Craymer); *m* 1952, Edna Margaret, *yr d* of T. R. Poole; three *s*. *Educ:* St Albans Sch.; Pembroke Coll., Oxford (MA, BCL). Solicitor's Articled Clerk, 1938-39. Commnd in Sherwood Rangers Yeo., 1940; 1st Lieut 1941, Captain 1942, Major 1944; 8th Armd Bde, N Africa, 1942-43; Normandy beaches to Germany, 1944. Called to Bar, Lincoln's Inn, 1949; practised at Chancery Bar, 1949-54; joined Legal Adviser's Br., Home Office, 1954, Principal Asst Legal Advr, 1972-77. Silver Star Medal (USA), 1944. *Address:* 2 The Ridgeway, Mill Hill, NW7 1RS. *T:* 01-346 3092. *Clubs:* Athenæum; Lawrenny Yacht.

SEMPER, Dudley Henry; Puisne Judge, Jamaica, 1954-63, retired; *b* St Kitts, BWI, 14 Nov. 1905; *s* of late D. H. Semper, ISO, and Helen Semper; *m* 1937, Aileen Malone; one *d*. *Educ:* Antigua Grammar School; West Buckland School, North Devon. Called to Bar, Gray's Inn, 1927; practised at Bar of Leeward Islands, 1928-32; Colonial Service, 1933; Actg District Magistrate, Registrar Supreme Court, St Kitts-Nevis, 1934; District Magistrate, St Kitts-Nevis, 1935; Crown Attorney, St Kitts-Nevis, 1939; Actg Attorney General, Leeward Islands, 1943-44; Officer administering Govt of St Kitts-Nevis, intermittently 1943-44; Resident Magistrate, Jamaica, 1944. *Recreations:* shooting, fishing. *Address:* Bracebridge, 50 Cliff Road, Worlebury, Weston-super-Mare, Avon. *Club:* Royal Commonwealth Society.

SEMPILL, family name of **Lady Sempill** (*née* Forbes-Sempill).

SEMPILL, Lady (20th in line, of the Lordship *cr* 1489); **Ann Moira Sempill** (*née* Forbes-Sempill); *b* 19 March 1920; *d* of 19th Lord Sempill, AFC; *S* father, 1965; *m* 1st, 1941, Captain Eric Holt (marr. diss., 1945); one *d*; 2nd, 1948, Lt-Col Stuart Whitemore Chant, OBE, MC (who assumed by decree of Lyon Court, 1966, the additional surname of Sempill), now Chant-Sempill; two *s*. *Educ:* Austrian, German and English Convents. Served War, 1939-42 (Petty Officer, WRNS). *Heir: s* The Master of Sempill, *qv*. *Address:* 15 Onslow Court, Drayton Gardens, SW10; East Lodge, Druminnor, Rhynie, Aberdeenshire.
See also Hon. *Sir Ewan Forbes of Brux, Bt.*

SEMPILL, Master of; Hon. James William Stuart Whitemore Sempill; Regional Manager, Argus of Ayr Ltd; *b* 25 Feb. 1949; *s* and *heir* of Lady Sempill, *qv*, and of Lt-Col Stuart Whitemore Chant-Sempill; *m* 1977, Josephine Ann Edith, *e d* of J. Norman Rees, Johannesburg. *Educ:* The Oratory School; St Clare's Hall, Oxford (BA Hons History, 1971); Hertford Coll., Oxford. Joined Gallagher Ltd, 1972. *Address:* 2 Northumberland Place, Edinburgh EH3 64Q. *Clubs:* Vincent's, Carlton (Oxford).

SEMPLE, Prof. Andrew Best, CBE 1966; VRD 1953; QHP 1962; Professor of Community and Environmental Health (formerly of Public Health), University of Liverpool, 1953-77, now Professor Emeritus; Area Medical Officer (teaching), Liverpool Area Health Authority, 1974-77; *b* 3 May 1912; *m* 1941, Jean (*née* Sweet); one *d*. *Educ:* Allan Glen's School, Glasgow; Glasgow Univ. MB, ChB 1934, MD 1947, DPH 1936, Glasgow.

FFCM 1972. Various hospital appointments, 1934-38; Asst MOH and Deputy Medical Superintendent, Infectious Diseases Hosp., Portsmouth, 1938-39; Asst MOH and Asst School Medical Officer, Blackburn, 1939-47 (interrupted by War Service); Senior Asst MOH, Manchester, 1947-48; Deputy MOH, City and Port of Liverpool, 1948-53, MOH and Principal Sch. Med. Officer, 1953-74. Served War of 1939-46; Surgeon Commander, RNVR; Naval MOH, Western Approaches, Malta and Central Mediterranean. Chm. Council and Hon. Treasurer, RSH, 1963. *Publications:* various regarding infectious disease, port health, hygiene, etc. *Address:* Kelvin, 433 Woolton Road, Gateacre, Liverpool L25 4SY. *T:* 051-428 2081.

SEMPLE, Andrew Greenlees; Under Secretary, Water Directorate, Department of the Environment, since 1976; *b* 16 Jan. 1934; *s* of William Hugh Semple, *qv*; *m* 1961, Janet Elizabeth, *d* of late H. R. G. Whates and of Mrs Whates, Ludlow, Salop; one *s* one *d*. *Educ:* Winchester Coll.; St John's Coll., Cambridge (MA). Entered Min. of Transport and Civil Aviation, 1957; Private Sec. to Permanent Sec., 1960-62; Principal, 1962; Asst Sec., 1970; Private Sec. to successive Secs of State for the Environment, 1972-74. *Recreations:* squash, reading, gardening. *Address:* 83 Burbage Road, SE24 9HB. *T:* 01-274 6550. *Club:* Dulwich Squash.

SEMPLE, John Greenlees, MA, PhD, MRIA; University Professor of Mathematics, King's College, London, 1936-69, now Emeritus; *b* 10 June 1904; *s* of James Semple, 240 Ravenhill Road, Belfast; *m* 1936, Daphne Caroline, *d* of Professor F. H. Hummel, Queen's University, Belfast; one *s* one *d*. *Educ:* Royal Belfast Academical Institution; Queen's University, Belfast, MA; St John's College, Cambridge (Philip Bayliss Student); Wrangler b star, Rayleigh Prize, 1929, Fellowship of St John's College, 1931; lecturer Edinburgh University, 1929; Professor of Pure Mathematics at Queen's University, Belfast, 1930-36. *Publications:* (with L. Roth) Introduction to Algebraic Geometry, 1949; (with G. T. Kneebone) Algebraic Projective Geometry, 1952; Algebraic Curves, 1959; (with J. A. Tyrrell) Generalized Clifford Parallelism, 1971; various papers in Cambridge Philosophical Society, London Mathematical Society, Royal Irish Academy, Royal Society, London, etc. *Recreations:* reading, gardening, golf. *Address:* 3 Elm Road, Redhill, Surrey. *T:* Redhill 61142.

SEMPLE, Prof. Stephen John Greenhill, MD, FRCP; Professor of Medicine, The Middlesex Hospital Medical School, since 1970; *b* 4 Aug. 1926; *s* of late John Edward Stewart and of Janet Semple; *m* 1961, Penelope Ann, *y d* of Sir Geoffrey Aldington, *qv*; three *s*. *Educ:* Westminster; London Univ. MB, BS, 1950, MD 1952, FRCP 1968. Research Asst, St Thomas' Hosp. Med. Sch., 1952; Jun. Med. Specialist, RAMC, Malaya, 1953-55; Instr, Med. Sch., Univ. of Pennsylvania, USA, 1957-59; St Thomas' Hosp. Medical Sch.: Lectr, 1959; Sen. Lectr, 1961; Reader, 1965; Prof. in Med., 1969. *Publications:* Disorders of Respiration, 1972; articles in: Lancet, Jl Physiol. (London), Jl Applied Physiol. *Recreations:* tennis, music. *Address:* White Lodge, Claremont Park Road, Esher, Surrey. *T:* Esher 65057. *Club:* Queen's.

SEMPLE, William David Crowe; Director of Education, Lothian Region, since 1974; *b* 11 June 1933; *s* of George Crowe and Helen Davidson; *m* 1958, Margaret Bain Donald; one *s* one *d*. *Educ:* Glasgow Univ.; Jordanhill Coll. of Educn; London Univ. BSc Hons, DipEd. Educn Officer, Northern Rhodesia, 1958-64; Zambia: Dep. Chief Educn Officer, 1964-66; Chief Educn Officer, 1966-67; Actg Dir of Techn. Educn, 1967-68; Edinburgh: Asst Dir of Educn, 1968-72; Depute Dir of Educn, 1972-74. *Publications:* contrib. Scottish Geog. Magazine. *Recreations:* gardening, reading, gastronomy. *Address:* 15 Essex Park, Edinburgh EH4 6LH. *T:* 031-336 1947.

SEMPLE, Professor William Hugh, MA [Belfast and Manchester), PhD (Cambridge); Professor Emeritus, University of Manchester, since 1967; Governor of Sedbergh School, 1943-75; *b* 25 Feb. 1900; *s* of late James Semple, Belfast, Northern Ireland; *m* 1932, Hilda Madeline, *d* of late E. H. Wood, Malvern, Worcs; one *s*. *Educ:* Royal Belfast Academical Institution; Queen's University, Belfast; St John's College, Cambridge. Queen's University, Belfast: Assistant in Department of Greek, 1921-22; Senior Assistant in Department of English Literature, 1922-25; Research in Classics, St John's College, Cambridge, 1925-27. University of Reading: Lecturer in Classics, 1927-31; Reader in Latin, 1931-37; Univ. of Manchester, Professor of Latin, 1937-67. *Publications:* various articles in Classical Review; Classical Quarterly; Transactions of Cambridge Philological Soc.; Bulletin of John Rylands Library; Jl of Ecclesiastical History; (with Prof. C. R. Cheney) Selected Letters of Pope Innocent III concerning England. *Recreations:*

walking, gardening. *Address:* 3 Linden Road, Didsbury, Manchester M20 8QJ. *T:* 061-445 2558.
See also A . G . Semple .

SEN, Prof. Amartya Kumar, FBA 1977; Professor of Economics, Oxford University, since 1977; Fellow of Nuffield College, since 1977; *b* 3 Nov. 1933; *s* of late Dr Ashutosh Sen, Dacca, and of Amita Sen, Santiniketan, India. *Educ:* Calcutta Univ.; Cambridge Univ. MA, PhD. Prof. of Economics, Jadavpur Univ., Calcutta, 1956-58; Trinity Coll., Cambridge: Prize Fellow, 1957-61; Staff Fellow, 1961-63; Professor of Economics: Delhi Univ., 1963-71 (Chm., Dept of Economics, 1966-68); LSE, 1971-77. Hon. Dir, Agricultural Economics Research Centre, Delhi, 1966-68 and 1969-71. Vis. Prof.: MIT, 1960-61; Univ. of Calif. at Berkeley, 1964-65; Harvard Univ., 1968-69. Chm., UN Expert Gp Meeting on Role of Advanced Skill and Technology, New York, 1967; Fellow, Econometric Soc., 1968-; Mem. Council, Royal Economic Soc. *Publications:* Choice of Techniques: an aspect of planned economic development, 1960 (3rd edn, 1968); Growth Economics, 1970; Collective Choice and Social Welfare, 1971; On Economic Inequality, 1973; Employment, Technology and Development, 1975; articles in various jls in economics, philosophy and political science. *Address:* Nuffield College, Oxford OX1 1NF.

SEN, Shri Binay Ranjan, Padmabibhusan 1970; CIE 1944; ICS; Director-General of the United Nations Food and Agriculture Organisation, Rome, 1956-67; *b* 1 Jan. 1898; *s* of Dr K. M. Sen; *m* 1931, Chiprova Chatterjee. *Educ:* Calcutta and Oxford Universities. Secretary to Govt of Bengal, Political and Appointment Departments, and Press Officer, 1931-34; District Magistrate, Midnapore, 1937-40; Revenue Secretary to Government of Bengal, 1940-43; Director of Civil Evacuation, Bengal, 1942-43; Relief Commissioner, 1942-43; Director-General of Food, Government of India, 1943-46; Sec. to Food Dept, Govt of India, 1946; Minister of the Embassy of India, at Washington, 1947-50; Indian Ambassador to: Italy and Yugoslavia, 1950-51; US and Mexico, 1951-52; Italy and Yugoslavia, 1952-55; Japan, 1955-56. Member Indian Delegation to General Assembly of United Nations, 1947; India's Rep. to United Nations Security Council, 1947; Agriculture Sec. to Govt of India, 1948; Head of Jt Mission of FAO and ECAFE (Economic Commn for Asia and the Far East) in Far East to study Agricultural Development plans; Head of Ind. Deleg. to: ECOSOC (Economic and Social Council of the UN), 1949 and 1953; Annual Conf. of FAO, 1949, and FAO Coun., 1950, 1951, 1953. Hon. Fellow, St Catherine's Coll., Oxford. Several Hon. degrees and decorations, incl. Kt Comdr Piani Ordinis, and Kt Grand Cross Ordinis Sancti Silvetri Papae. *Address:* 14/2 Palm Avenue, Calcutta 19, India.

SEN, K. Chandra; late Indian CS; *b* 5 Oct. 1888; *s* of Durgadas Sen and Mokshada Sundari Devi; *m* 1916, Lilavati Das-Gupta; one *s* two *d. Educ:* Hindu Sch., Calcutta; Presidency College, Calcutta; Trinity Hall, Cambridge (BA in Moral Sciences Tripos, 1913). Joined Indian Civil Service, 1913; Assistant Collector, Bombay Presidency, 1913-21; service in Judicial department of Government of Bombay since 1921; acted as a puisne judge of Bombay High Court, various times 1934-38; Secretary to Government of Bombay, Legal Department and Remembrancer of Legal Affairs, 1935-37; Additional Judge of High Court, 1939-41; Judge, High Court of Bombay, 1941-48; Pres. Industrial Court, Bombay, 1948-53; Pres. Bombay Co-op, Revenue, and Sales Tax Tribunals, between 1953 and 1959; Constitutional Adviser to Govt of West Bengal and Chm., State Law Commn, 1959-64; Chm., Police Commn, W Bengal, and Mem. Hindu Religious Endowments Commn, 1960-62. *Address:* A-12, Sea Face Park, Bombay 26, India. *T:* 36-4368.

SEN, Prof. Satyendra Nath, MA, PhD (Econ) London; Vice-Chancellor, Calcutta University, since 1968; Professor of Economics since 1958; *b* April 1908. Visited UK and other parts of Europe, 1949-51; Vis. Prof., Princeton and Stanford Univs (sponsored Ford Foundn), 1962-63; subseq. Dean, Faculties of Arts and Commerce, and Head of Dept of Econs, Calcutta University. Mem. Senate, Indian Inst. of Technology, Kharagpur; Mem. Gov. Body of Research and Trng Sch., Indian Statistical Inst., Calcutta; Mem. Bd of Trustees: Indian Musuem, Calcutta; Victoria Memorial, Calcutta; Mahajati Sadan, Calcutta; Mem. Research Programmes Cttee, Planning Commn, Govt of India (Chm. East Regional Cttee); Mem. Pay Commn, Govt of W Bengal, 1967-69; Discussion Leader, Section of Medium and Longterm Credit, Internat. Conf. on Agricultural Credit, Lahore (FAO and ECAFE), 1956; Mem. Industrial Tribunal adjudicating dispute between United Bank of India Ltd and its employees, 1954-55. Mem., Nat. Co-operative Union Delhi; Vice-Pres., State Co-operative Union, W Bengal. Mem. Adv. Cttee of Vice-Chancellors, University

Grants Commn, New Delhi; Chm., UGC Cttee on salary scales of univ. and coll. teachers, 1974; Pres., Assoc. of Indian Univs, 1976; Mem., Central Adv. Commn on Educn, Govt of India, 1976. *Publications:* Central Banking in Undeveloped Money Markets, 1952; The City of Calcutta: a socio-economic survey, 1954-55 to 1957-58, 1960; The Co-operative Movement in West Bengal, 1966; (with T. Piplai) Industrial Relations in Jute Industry in West Bengal, 1968. *Address:* University of Calcutta, Senate House, Calcutta 12, India.

SENDALL, Bernard Charles, CBE 1952; Deputy Director-General, Independent Broadcasting Authority (formerly Independent Television Authority), 1955-77; *b* 30 April 1913; *s* of late William Sendall, Malvern, Worcestershire; *m* 1963, Barbara Mary, *d* of late Ambrose Coviello, DCM, FRCM. *Educ:* Magdalen College, Oxford; Harvard University. Entered Civil Service in the Admiralty, 1935; Principal Private Secretary to Minister of Information 1941-45; Controller (Home), Central Office of Information, 1946-49; Controller, Festival of Britain Office, 1949-51; Assistant Secretary, Admiralty, 1951-55. *Address:* Lynton Cottage, Watts Green, Chearsley, Bucks. *Club:* Arts.

SENDER, Ramón José; Medal of Morocco, 1924; Spanish Military Cross of Merit, 1924; writer; *b* Alcolea de Cinca, Spain, 1902; *s* of José Sender and Andrea Garcés Sender; *m* 1st, 1934, Amparo Barayón (*d* 1936); one *s* one *d* ; 2nd, 1943, Florence Hall (marr. diss., 1963). *Educ:* Colegio de la Sagrada Familia, Reus (Catalonia); Inst. de Zaragoza; Inst. de Teruel; Univ. of Madrid. Infantry Officer, Morocco, 1923-24; Editor El Sol, Madrid, 1924-31; free-lance writer, 1931-36. Major on General Staff, Spanish Republican Army, 1936-39. Prof. Spanish Lit., Amherst Coll., Mass, 1943-44; Denver Univ., 1944; Prof. of Spanish Lit., Univ. of New Mexico, 1947 (Emer. 1963). Mem. Bd of Advs, Hispanic Soc. of America; Spanish Nat. Prize of Lit., 1935; Guggenheim Fell., 1942. Speaking tour as rep. Spanish Republic, 1938; member: Ateneo governing board, sec. Ibero-American section, 1926-34; Nat. Council of Culture, Spain, 1936-39; Alliance of Intellectuals for Defense of Democracy, Spain, 1936-39. Visiting Prof., Ohio State Univ., summer 1951; Writers' Workshop, Inter Amer. Univ., San Germán, Puerto Rico, summer 1961; Vis. Prof., Univ. of Calif in Los Angeles, semester II, 1961-62; Prof., Univ. of S Calif in Los Angeles, 1964. Life FIAL, Switzerland. Hon. DLitt Univ. of New Mexico, 1968; Hon. LLD Univ. of Southern California. Hon. Citizen of Los Angeles, 1968. *Publications:* Pro Patria, 1934; Seven Red Sundays, 1935; Mr Witt among the Rebels, 1936; Counter-Attack in Spain, 1938; A Man's Place, 1940; Epitalamio del Prieto Trinidad, 1942; Dark Wedding, 1943; Chronicle of Dawn, 1944; The King and the Queen, 1948; The Sphere, 1949; The Affable Hangman, 1954; Before Noon, 1957; Los Laureles de Anselmo, 1958; Requiem for a Spanish Peasant, 1960; The Exemplary Novels of Cíbola, 1963; Carolus Rex, 1963; El Bandido Adolescente, 1965; Tres Novelas Teresianas, 1967; Comedia del Diantre y Otras Dos, 1969; Tres Ejemplos de Amor y Una Teoría, 1969; Aventura equinoccial de Lope de Aguirre, 1970; Ensayos del Otro Mundo, 1970; Nocturno de los 14, 1970; Tanit, 1970; Relatos Fronterizos, 1970; El Angel Anfibio, 1971; Las criaturas saturnianas, 1971; Don Juan en la Mancebía, 1972; La luna de los perros, 1972; En la vida de Ignacio Morel, 1972; El Extraño Señor Photynos, 1973; La antesala, 1973; El fugitivo, 1973; Tupac Amaru, 1973; Una Virgen Llama a Tu Puerta, 1973; Jubileo en el Zocalo, 1974; Las Tres Sorores, 1974; Arlene y la Gaya Ciencia, 1976; Iman, 1976; contrib. to literary and popular journals. *Recreations:* chess, tennis. *Address:* Editorial Destino, 425 Consejo de Ciento, Barcelona 9, Spain.

SENIOR, Derek; free-lance writer; *b* 4 May 1912; *s* of Oliver and Sally G. Senior; *m* 1st, 1942, Edith Frances Bentley; one *s* two *d* ; 2nd, 1959, Helen Elizabeth Mair; one *d. Educ:* six elementary schools; Manchester Grammar Sch.; Balliol Coll., Oxford (BA). Joined editorial staff of Manchester Guardian, 1937; turned free-lance, 1960. Member, Royal Commission on Local Government in England, 1966-69. Mem., Basildon Develt Corp., 1975-. Hon. MRTPI (Hon. AMTPI 1956). *Publications:* Guide to the Cambridge Plan, 1956; Your Architect, 1964; The Regional City, 1966; Memorandum of Dissent from Redcliffe-Maud Report, 1969; Skopje Resurgent, 1971; numerous planning publications. *Recreations:* gardening, arguing. *Address:* Birling House, Birling, Maidstone, Kent. *T:* West Malling 842229.

SENIOR, Sir Edward (Walters), Kt 1970; CMG 1955; Chairman, Ransome Hoffman Pollard Ltd, 1953-72; Chairman, George Senior & Sons Ltd, since 1930 (Managing Director, 1929); *b* 29 March 1902; *s* of Albert Senior; *m* 1928, Stephanie Vera Heald; one *s* one *d. Educ:* Repton School; Sheffield University. Vice-Consul for Sweden, in Sheffield, 1930; RA, TA, Major, 1938;

General Director of Alloy and Special Steels, Iron and Steel Control, 1941; Director, Steel Division of Raw Materials Mission, Washington, DC, 1942; Controller of Ball and Roller Bearings, 1944; British Iron and Steel Federation: Commercial Dir, 1949-61; Dir, 1961-62; Dir-Gen., 1962-66; retd, Dec. 1966; Exec. Chm., Derbyshire Stone Ltd, 1967-68; Dep. Chm., Tarmac Derby Ltd, 1968-71. Master of Cutlers' Company of Hallamshire in County of York, 1947; Vice-President of the Sheffield Chamber of Commerce, 1948; Chairman of Steel Re-Armament Panel, 1951. FBIM, 1971. JP Sheffield, 1937-50. *Recreations:* normal country activities. *Address:* Hollies, Church Close, Brenchley, Tonbridge, Kent TN12 7AA. *T:* Brenchley 2359. *Clubs:* Naval and Military; Sheffield (Sheffield).

SENIOR, Olive Edith, JP, SRN; Regional Nursing Officer, Trent Regional Health Authority, since Nov. 1973; *b* 26 April 1934; *d* of Harold and Doris Senior, Mansfield, Notts. *Educ:* Harlow Wood Orthopaedic Hosp., 1949-52; St George's Hosp., Hyde Park Corner, 1952-56; City Hosp., Nottingham (Pt I, CMB), 1956; Nottingham Univ. (HV Cert.), 1957. Health Visitor, Notts CC, 1958-60; St George's Hosp., London (Ward Sister), 1960-63; S Africa, June-Dec. 1963; Forest Gate Hosp., London (SCM), 1964; St Mary's Hosp., Portsmouth (Asst Matron/Night Supt), 1964-66; NE Metropolitan Regional Hosp. Bd (Management Services), 1966-71; Chief Nursing Officer, Nottingham and Dist. Hosp. Management Cttee, 1971-73. Secretary of State Fellow, 1973. JP Nottingham Guildhall, 1973. *Publication:* contrib. to Nursing Times (Determining Nursing Establishments). *Address:* Trent Regional Health Authority, Fulwood House, Old Fulwood Road, Sheffield S10 3TH. *T:* Sheffield 306511. *Club:* Nottingham Univ. (Nottingham).

SENIOR, Ronald Henry, DSO 1940, Bar 1943; TD; *b* 3 July 1904; *e s* of Lawrence Henry Senior and Emmadonna Shuttleworth, *d* of Reverend J. S. Holden, Aston-on-Trent, Derbyshire; *m* 1932, Hon. Norah Marguerite Joicey, *e d* of 2nd Baron Joicey; two *d. Educ:* Cheltenham College. Chairman, Nat. Assoc. of Port Employers, 1954-59. Joined TA 1924; served France, 1940; Middle East; Sicily, NW Europe. Hon. Rank Brigadier. *Recreation:* golf. *Address:* 110 Eaton Square, SW1. *Club:* Carlton.

SENIOR, William Hirst, CB 1964; Deputy Secretary (Agriculture), Dept of Agriculture and Fisheries for Scotland, 1958-66; *b* 24 August 1904; *o s* of Capt. Arthur Senior and Sarah G. G. Binns, Batley, Yorks; *m* 1930, Olive Kathleen, *e d* of William Henry Killick, Shawford, Hampshire; two *s* three *d. Educ:* Bradford Grammar School; Reading University. BSc London 1926; MSc Reading 1929. Research Scholar, Reading Univ., 1926-28. Joined Dept of Agriculture for Scotland, 1929; Advisory Officer on Farm Economics, 1933; Principal, 1941; Secretary of Balfour of Burleigh Cttee on Hill Sheep Farming in Scotland, 1941-44; Asst Secretary, 1946; FRSE 1947; Under-Secretary, 1958. Mem., Agricultural Research Council, 1959-66. Chairman, Scottish Agricultural Improvement Council, 1960-66; Mem., Small Industries Council for Scotland. Pres., Agricl Econs Soc., 1963-64. Governor, Rannoch Sch. *Recreations:* varied. *Address:* Manse Wood, Innerwick, Dunbar, East Lothian. *Club:* Royal Commonwealth Society.

SENOUSSI, Badreddine; Officer, Order of Ouissame Alaouite, Morocco; Ambassador of the Kingdom of Morocco to the Court of St James's, since 1977; *b* 30 March 1933; *m* 1958; three *s. Educ:* Univ. of Bordeaux, France (Lic. (MA) en Droit); Univ. Mohamed V Rabat, Morocco (Lic. ès Lettres). Counsellor, High Cherifian Tribunal, 1956; in charge of: State Min. of Public Functions, Mar. 1957; Nat. Defense Min., Mar.-Sept. 1958; Gen. Sec., Tobacco Management, Oct. 1958-Feb. 1963; Chief, Royal Cabinet, 1963-64; Under-Sec. of State for Commerce, Industry, Mines and Merchant Navy, Dec. 1964-June 1965; Under-Sec. of State for Admin. Affairs, June 1965-Feb. 1966; Post and Telecommunications Minister, Feb. 1966-Mar. 1970; Benslimane Dep., Mem. Representative Chamber, Aug. 1970; Youth, Sports and Social Affairs Minister, Mar. 1970-Aug. 1971; Ambassador of Kingdom of Morocco: in Washington, Sept 1971-Dec. 1974; in Teheran, Mar. 1974-Sept. 1976. Holds many foreign honours. *Address:* Royal Moroccan Embassy, 49 Queen's Gate Gardens, SW7 5NE. *T:* 01-584 8827. *Clubs:* Les Ambassadeurs, Mark's, White Elephant.

SENSI, His Eminence Cardinal (Giuseppe M.); *b* 27 May 1907. Ordained, 1929; Sec. of Apostolic Nunciature in Roumania, 1934-38; Secretary and Auditor of Apostolic Nunciature in Switzerland, 1938-46; Councillor of Apostolic Nunciature in Belgium, 1946-47; Chargé d'Affaires of the Holy See in Prague, 1948-49; Councillor in the Secretariat of State of His Holiness, 1949-53; Permanent Observer of the Holy See at UNESCO in Paris, 1953-55; apptd Nuncio Apostolic to Costa Rica, May 1955, and consecrated Titular Archbishop of Sardi, July 1955; Apostolic Delegate to Jerusalem, 1957; Apostolic Nuncio to Ireland, 1962-67; Apostolic Nuncio to Portugal, 1967-76; Cardinal, 1977. Hon. Mem., Accademia Cosentiria, 1976. *Address:* Piazza S Calisto 16, 00153 Rome, Italy.

SEOUL, (Korea), Bishop of, since 1965; **Rt. Rev. Paul Chun Hwan Lee,** CBE 1974; *b* 5 April 1922; unmarried. *Educ:* St Michael's Theological Seminary, Seoul; St Augustine's College, Canterbury. Deacon, 1952 (Pusan Parish); Priest, 1953 (Sangju and Choungju Parish). Director of Yonsei University, Seoul, 1960-, Chm., Bd of Trustees, 1972-, Hon. DD 1971. Chairman: Christian Council of Korea, 1966-67; Christian Literature Soc. of Korea, 1968-; Korean Bible Soc., 1972- (Vice-Pres., 1969-72); Nat. Council of Churches in Korea, 1976-. *Recreation:* reading. *Address:* 3 Chong Dong, Seoul, Korea. *T:* 75-6157.

SEPEKU, Most Rev. John; see Tanzania, Archbishop of.

SEPHTON, Ven. Arthur; Archdeacon of Craven, 1956-72; Archdeacon Emeritus, since 1972; *b* 25 March 1894; *s* of Thomas G. and Laura Sephton, Newport Pagnell; *m* 1924, Unita Catherine, *d* of E. Brookhouse Richards, JP; one *d. Educ:* Christ Church, Oxford (MA); Cuddesdon Theological College. Assistant Curate: St Mary Redcliffe, Bristol, 1921; St John, Hove, 1924; Christ Church, Harrogate, 1928; Vicar: Holmfirth, Yorks, 1929; Kirkburton, Yorks, 1933; Rector and Rural Dean of Skipton, 1943-64; Hon. Canon of Bradford, 1944. Proctor in Convocation, 1945-56. *Address:* 17 Riversway, Gargrave, Skipton, N Yorks. *T:* Gargrave 266.

SERBY, John Edward, CB 1958; CBE 1951; FRAeS; Consultant; *b* 15 March 1902; *m* 1933, Clarice Lilian (*née* Hawes); one *d. Educ:* Haberdashers' Aske's School; Emmanuel College, Cambridge (BA). Junior Scientific Officer, Admiralty, 1927-30; Scientific Officer, RAE, 1930-38; Headquarters, MAP, 1938-50; Deputy Director, Royal Aircraft Establishment, Farnborough, 1950-54; Dir-Gen. of Guided Weapons, Min. of Aviation, 1954-61. Dep. Controller Guided Weapons, Ministry of Aviation, 1961-63. *Recreation:* gardening. *Address:* Overwey, Bishopsmead, Farnham, Surrey. *T:* Farnham 3526.

SERGEANT, Maj.-Gen. Frederick Cavendish H.; see Hilton-Sergeant.

SERGENT, René Edmond, Hon. KBE 1973; Officier de la Légion d'Honneur, 1952; *b* 16 January 1904; *s* of Charles Sergent and Emma Duvernet; *m* 1931, Monique Schweisguth; three *s* three *d. Educ:* Lycée Janson-de-Sailly, Paris, France; Ecole Polytechnique. Sub-Lieut, Artillery, 1925; Assistant, Inspection Générale des Finances, 1929; Financial Controller, Nat. Socs of Aeronautical Construction, 1937; Direction du Commerce Extérieur, 1940; Pres., French Economic and Financial Deleg. to Control Commission, Berlin, 1945; Financial Attaché, French Embassy, London, 1947; Asst Sec.-Gen. for Economics and Finance, NATO, 1952; Secretary-Gen. of OEEC, Paris, 1955; Vice-Prés. Délégué, Syndicat Général de la Construction Electrique, 1960; Président, Groupement des Industries de la Construction Electrique, 1969-75. *Address:* 1 Boulevard de Beauséjour, 75016 Paris, France. *T:* 288 3031.

SERIES, Prof. George William, FRS 1971; Professor of Physics, University of Reading, since 1968; *b* 22 Feb. 1920; *s* of William Series and Alice (*née* Crosthwaite); *m* 1948, Annette (*née* Pepper); three *s* one *d. Educ:* Reading Sch.; St John's Coll., Oxford. MA 1946, DPhil 1950, DSc 1969, Oxford. Served with Friends' Ambulance Unit, 1942-46. Open Schol., Oxford, 1938; 1st cl. hons Physics, Oxford, 1947. University Demonstrator, Oxford, 1951; St Edmund Hall, Oxford: Lectr, 1953; Fellow, 1954; Emeritus Fellow, 1969. *Publication:* Spectrum of Atomic Hydrogen, 1957. *Recreation:* family. *Address:* J. J. Thomson Physical Laboratory, Whiteknights, Reading RG6 2AF. *T:* Reading 85123.

SERJEANT, Robert Bertram; Sir Thomas Adams's Professor of Arabic since 1970, and Director, Middle East Centre, since 1965, University of Cambridge; *b* 23 March 1915; *er s* of R. T. R. and A. B. Serjeant; *m* Marion Keith Serjeant (*née* Robertson), MB, ChB; one *s* one *d. Educ:* Edinburgh; Trinity Coll., Cambridge. Vans Dunlop Schol. 1935; Visit to Syria, 1935; MA 1st Cl. Hons Semitic Langs, Edinburgh Univ., 1936; PhD Cambridge 1939; Tweedie Fellow Edinburgh, 1939; Studentship, SOAS, for research in S Arabia, 1940; Governor's Commn in Aden Prot. G Guards, 1940-41. Attached Mission 106. Lectr, SOAS, 1941; Seconded to BBC Eastern Service, 1942; Editor, Arabic Listener, 1943-45; Min. of Inf., Editor Arabic pubns, 1944. Colonial Research Fell., in Hadramawt,

1947-48; Reader in Arabic, 1948; Research in S Arabia and Persian Gulf, 1953-54; in N Nigeria, Minister of Education's mission to examine instruction in Arabic, 1956; Sec. of State for Colonies' mission to examine Muslim Education in E Africa, 1957; Inter-University Council's Advisory Delegation on University of N Nigeria, 1961; Research in Trucial States, Yemen, Aden, 1963-64 and 1966; Professor of Arabic, 1955-64, Middle East Department, SOAS, University of London; Lectr in Islamic History, ME Centre, Univ. of Cambridge, 1964-66, Reader in Arabic Studies, 1966-70. Member: ME Comd Expedition to Socotra, 1967; Cambridge expedn to San'ā' and N Yemen, 1972. Corresp. Mem., Arab Acad., Cairo, 1976. Lawrence of Arabia Meml Medal, RCAS, 1974. Co-editor, Arabian Studies, 1973-. *Publications:* Cat. Arabic, Persian & Hindustani MSS in New College, Edinburgh, 1942; Materials for a History of Islamic Textiles, 1942-51; Prose and Poetry from Hadramawt, I, 1950; Saiyids of Hadramawt, 1957; Portuguese off the South Arabian Coast, 1961; The South Arabian Hunt, 1976; articles in BSOAS, JRAS, Le Muséon, Rivista d. Studi Orientali, Islamic Culture, etc. *Address:* Faculty of Oriental Studies, Sidgwick Avenue, Cambridge. *Clubs:* Royal Central Asian Society, Royal Asiatic Society.

SERKIN, Rudolf, Presidential Medal of Freedom, 1963; Director, Curtis Institute of Music, Philadelphia, Pa, 1968-76, Head of Piano Department, 1939-76; *b* 28 March 1903; *s* of Mordko Serkin and Augusta Schargel; *m* 1935, Irene Busch; two *s* four *d*. *Educ:* Vienna, Austria. Concert Pianist: Début, Vienna, 1915; USA since 1933; New York Philharmonic with Arturo Toscanini, 1936. President of Marlboro School of Music, Marlboro, Vermont. Mem., Nat. Council on the Arts, USA; Fellow, Amer. Acad. of Arts and Scis; Hon. Member: Accademia Nationale di Santa Cecilia; Verein Beethoven Haus, Bonn; Philharmonic-Symphony Soc. of NY. Dr *hc* : Curtis Inst., Philadelphia; Temple Univ., Philadelphia; Univ. of Vermont; Williams Coll., Williamstown, Mass; Oberlin Coll.; Rochester Univ.; Harvard, 1973. *Address:* RFD 3, Brattleboro, Vermont 05301, USA.

SEROTA, family name of Baroness Serota.

SEROTA, Baroness, *cr* 1967 (Life Peer), of Hampstead in Greater London; **Beatrice Serota,** JP; Chairman, Commission for Local Administration, since 1974; Member, BBC Complaints Commission, since 1975; Governor, BBC, since 1977; *b* 15 Oct. 1919; *m* 1942, Stanley Serota, BSc (Eng), FICE; one *s* one *d*. *Educ:* John Howard School; London School of Economics (BSc (Econ)); Hon. Fellow, 1976. Member: Hampstead Borough Council, 1945-49; LCC for Brixton, 1954-65 (Chm., Children's Cttee, 1958-65); GLC for Lambeth, 1964-67 (Chief Whip, Vice-Chm. ILEC). Baroness in Waiting, 1968-69; Minister of State (Health), Dept of Health and Social Security, 1969-70. Member: Adv. Council in Child Care, and Central Training Council in Child Care, 1958-68; Adv. Council on Treatment of Offenders, 1960-64; Longford Cttee on "Crime-A Challenge to us all", 1964; Royal Commn on Penal System, 1964-66; Latey Cttee on Age of Majority, 1965-67; Adv. Council on Penal System, 1966-68, 1974- (Chm., 1976); Seebohm Cttee on Organization of Local Authority Personal Social Services, 1966-68; Community Relations Commn, 1970-76. Vice-President: Nat. Council for Single Parent Families; Volunteer Centre. JP Inner London (West Central Division). Peerage conferred for services to children. *Recreations:* dressmaking, gardening, collecting shells. *Address:* 78 Fitzjohns Avenue, Hampstead, NW3.

SERPELL, Sir David Radford, KCB 1968 (CB 1962); CMG 1952; OBE 1944; Chairman, Nature Conservancy Council, 1973-77; *b* 10 Nov. 1911; 2nd *s* of Charles Robert and Elsie Leila Serpell, Plymouth; *m* 1st, Ann Dooley (marr. diss.); three *s*; 2nd, Doris Farr. *Educ:* Plymouth Coll.; Exeter Coll., Oxford; Univ. of Toulouse (DèsL); Syracuse University, USA; Fletcher School of Law and Diplomacy, USA. (Fell.) Imp. Economic Cttee, 1937-39; Min. of Food, 1939-42; Min. of Fuel and Power, 1942-45; HM Treasury, 1945 (Under-Sec.), 1954-60); Dep. Sec., MoT, 1960-63; Second Sec., BoT, 1963-66; Second Permanent Sec., 1966-68; Second Sec., Treasury, 1968; Permanent Secretary: MoT, 1968-70; DoE, 1970-72. Private Sec. to Parly Sec., Ministry of Food, 1941-42; Principal Private Sec. to Minister of Fuel and Power, 1942-45. Member: NERC, 1973-76; British Railways Bd, 1974-. *Recreations:* fishing, golf. *Address:* Dolphin Cottage, Lamberhurst, Kent. *T:* Lamberhurst 422. *Club:* United Oxford & Cambridge University.

SERVAES, Vice-Adm. Reginald Maxwell, CB 1947; CBE 1940; *b* 25 July 1893; *s* of late J. M. Servaes; *m* 1st, 1919, Hilda Edith Johnson (*d* 1956); one *s*; 2nd, 1959, Mansel, *widow* of H. V. Bond. *Educ:* Royal Naval Colleges, Osborne and Dartmouth. Sub-Lieutenant, 1914; Lieut, 1915; European War, served in

HM ships Exe, Comus and Phaeton; specialised in Gunnery, 1917; RN Staff College, 1922-23; Commander, 1928; Captain, 1935; HMS Resource, 1937; Dir of Local Defence, Admiralty, 1938-40; HMS London, 1940-42; an Assistant Chief of Naval Staff, 1943-45; ADC to King George VI, 1944-45; Rear-Adm. 1945; Rear-Admiral Commanding Second Cruiser Squadron, British Pacific Fleet, 1945-46; Flag Officer Commanding Reserve Fleet, 1947-48; retired list, 1948, Vice-Admiral. *Address:* Crocker Hill House, near Chichester, West Sussex. *T:* Halnaker 220.

SERVAN-SCHREIBER, Jean-Jacques; politician, author and journalist; Deputy for Lorraine, French National Assembly, since 1970; President, Region of Lorraine, since 1976; President, the Radical Party, since 1977; *b* Paris, 13 Feb. 1924; *s* of late Emile Servan-Schreiber, journalist, and of Denise Bressard; *m* 1960, Sabine de Fouquières; four *s*. *Educ:* Lycée Janson-de-Sailly, Paris; Lycée de Grenoble; Ecole Polytechnique. Served as fighter pilot, Free French Air Force, World War II. Diplomatic Editor of Le Monde, 1948-53; Founder and Director of weekly news-magazine, L'Express, 1953-69. Minister of Reforms, June 1974. Pres. (Founder) Fedn-nationale des anciens d'Algérie, 1958-65. Sec.-Gen., 1969-71. Holds military cross for valour. *Publications:* Lieutenant en Algérie, 1957 (Lieutenant in Algeria, 1957); Le défi américain, 1967 (The American Challenge, 1968); Le Manifeste Radical, 1970 (The Radical Alternative, 1970); Le Pouvoir Régional, 1971; Le Manifeste, 1977. *Address:* 49 boulevard de Courcelles, 75008 Paris, France.

SERVICE, Alastair Stanley Douglas; Chairman, Family Planning Association, since 1975; writer and publisher; *b* 8 May 1933; *s* of Douglas William Service and Evelyn Caroline (*née* Sharp); *m* 1959, Louisa Anne (*née* Hemming), *qv*; one *s* one *d*. *Educ:* Westminster Sch.; Queen's Coll., Oxford. Midshipman, RNR, 1952-54. Director: McKinlay, Watson and Co. Ltd, Brazil, USA and London, 1959-64 (export finance); Seeley, Service and Co. Ltd (publishers), 1965-; Municipal Journal Ltd, 1970-. Hon. Parly Officer: Abortion Law Reform Assoc., during passage of Abortion Act, 1964-67; Divorce Law Reform Union, during passage of Divorce Reform Act, 1967-69; Chm., Birth Control Campaign, during passage of NHS (Family Planning) Amendment Act, 1972, and NHS Reorganisation Act, 1973 (made vasectomy and contraception available free from NHS); involved in other parly campaigns, incl.: Town and Country Amenities Act, 1974; Children's Act, 1975; Public Lending Right for Authors; One-Parent Families. Mem. cttees, FPA, 1964-, Mem. Nat. Exec. Cttee, 1972-; Mem., Health Educn Council (Sec. of State appointee), 1976-. Mem. Cttee, Victorian Soc., 1976-. *Publications:* A Birth Control Plan for Britain (with Dr John Dunwoody and Dr Tom Stuttaford), 1972; The Benefits of Birth Control—Aberdeen's Experience, 1973; Edwardian Architecture and its Origins, 1975; Edwardian Architecture, 1977; The Architects of London, from Inigo Jones to the Present Day, 1978; articles in Arch. Rev., Arch. Assoc. Qly, Guardian, etc. *Recreations:* looking at buildings, opera, squash et al. *Address:* 75 Flask Walk, NW3. *Club:* Bath.

SERVICE, Louisa Anne, JP; Chairman, The Municipal Group of Companies, since 1976; *d* of late Henry Harold Hemming, OBE, MC, and of Alice Louisa Weaver, OBE; *m* 1959, Alastair Stanley Douglas Service, *qv*; one *s* one *d*. *Educ:* private and state schs, Canada, USA and Britain; Ecole des Sciences Politiques, Paris; St Hilda's Coll., Oxford (BA and MA, PPE). Export Dir, Ladybird Appliances Ltd, 1957-59; Municipal Journal Ltd and associated cos: Financial Dir, 1966; Dep. Chm., 1974; Chm., Merchant Printers Ltd, 1975-; Dir, Brintex Ltd, 1965-; Dir, Glass's Guides Services Ltd, 1971, Dep. Chm. 1976-. JP Inner London Juvenile Courts, 1969; Chm., Hackney Juvenile Court, 1975; a Chm., Exec. Cttee, Inner London Juvenile Courts, 1977-; Mem., working party on re-org. of London Juvenile Courts, 1975-; Vice-Chm., Paddington Probation Hostel, 1976-. Chm. Council, Mayer-Lismann Opera Workshop; Hon. Sec., Women's India Assoc. of UK, 1967-74. *Publications:* articles on a variety of subjects. *Recreations:* travel, and attractive and witty people including my family. *Address:* c/o The Municipal Journal Ltd, 178-202 Great Portland Street, W1N 6NH. *T:* 01-637 2400.
See also J . H . Hemming.

SESSFORD, Rt. Rev. George Minshull; see Moray, Ross and Caithness, Bishop of.

SETH, Prof. George; Professor of Psychology, 1958-71, Head of Department of Psychology, 1946-71, The Queen's University, Belfast; now Professor Emeritus; *b* 23 April 1905; *s* of George Seth and Jane Steven Loudon; *m* 1936, May, *er d* of John Dods, Edinburgh, and Lily Anderson; three *s* one *d*. *Educ:* Royal High School and University of Edinburgh. MA (Edin.) 1928; BEd

(Edin.) 1930; PhD (Edin.) 1933. Assistant in Psychology, Edinburgh University and University Psychological Clinic, 1930-34; Research Fellow, Yale Univ., USA, 1934-35; Lecturer in Education, University College, Cardiff, and Psychologist, Cardiff Child Guidance Clinic, 1935-46; Senior Psychologist, Welsh Board of Health, (Evacuation Service), 1941-45. Vans Dunlop Scholar (Psychology), Edinburgh, 1930-33; Rockefeller Fellow, USA, 1935-36. Fellow, British Psychological Soc., President, 1967, Vice-Pres., 1968; President, Psychology Section, British Association, 1961. Member: Psychology Bd, CNAA, 1968-75; N Ireland Council for Educnl Research. Hon. Fellow, Psychological Soc. of Ireland, 1970, Lectr 1975. *Publications:* (with Douglas Guthrie) Speech in Childhood, 1934; articles in various psychological and educational jls. *Address:* 24 Osborne Park, Belfast BT9 6SN.

SETON, Lady, (Alice Ida), CBE 1949; Group Officer, WRAF, retired; *d* of late P. C. Hodge, Port Elizabeth, South Africa; *m* 1923, Capt. Sir John Hastings Seton, 10th Bt (from whom she obtained a divorce, 1950); one *s* (*see* Sir Robert Seton, 11th Bt) one *d*. Joined WAAF as Assistant Section Officer, 1939. *Address:* 3 Maddison Close, Teddington, Mddx.

SETON, Anya, (Anya Seton Chase); Author; *b* as British subject, New York City, USA; *d* of late Ernest Thompson Seton and late Grace Gallatin Thompson Seton. *Educ:* private tutors in England. *Publications:* (in USA, UK and 20 foreign countries) My Theodosia, 1941; Dragonwyck, 1944; The Turquoise, 1946; The Hearth and the Eagle, 1948; Foxfire, 1951; Katherine, 1954; The Mistletoe and Sword (juvenile), 1956; The Winthrop Woman, 1958; Washington Irving (juvenile), 1960; Devil Water, 1962; Avalon, 1966; Green Darkness, 1972; Smouldering Fires (juvenile), 1975. *Recreations:* swimming, croquet, bridge, cooking. *Address:* Binney Lane, Old Greenwich, Conn 06870, USA. *Clubs:* (Hon.) Pen and Brush (New York); PEN.

SETON, Sir (Christopher) Bruce, 12th Bt *cr* 1663, of Abercorn; farmer; *b* 3 Oct. 1909; *s* of Charles Henry Seton (*d* 1917), and Mrs V. A. Neilson (*d* 1973), Greys, Kelvedon, Essex; *S* cousin, 1969; *m* 1939, Joyce Vivian, *e d* of late O. G. Barnard, Stowmarket; two *s* two *d*. *Educ:* Marlborough; Univ. of Cambridge (BA Agric. 1931). Farming since 1931. *Heir: s* Iain Bruce Seton [*b* 27 Aug. 1942; *m* 1963, Margaret Ann, *o d* of Walter Charles Faulkner; one *s* one *d*]. *Address:* Bay Laurel, Thorrington Road, Great Bentley, Colchester, Essex. *T:* Colchester 250723.

SETON, Sir Claud Ramsay Wilmot, Kt, *cr* 1944; MC; *b* 1888; *e s* of Rev. Andrew Ramsay Wilmot Seton and Emily Georgina, *e d* of Rev. George Edmund Walker; *m* 1933, Mary Eleanor (*d* 1965), *yr d* of Sir Francis Bennett; no *c*. *Educ:* Framlingham Coll.; Laleham, Margate; University College, London. Solicitor, 1910; Member of firm of Shelton and Co. London and Wolverhampton until outbreak of War; served European War, 1914-20 (wounded, despatches twice, MC); President of District Court, Jaffa, Palestine, 1920-26; Judicial Adviser Transjordan, 1926-31 (Order of Istiqlal second class); President District Court of Haifa, Palestine, 1931-35; Puisne Judge, Jamaica, 1935-41; Chief Justice, Nyasaland, 1941-45; Chief Justice of Fiji and Chief Judicial Commissioner for the Western Pacific, 1945-49; retired from Colonial Service, 1950. Various part-time appointments in Kenya, 1950-60. Called to Bar, Gray's Inn, 1928. *Publication:* Legislation of Transjordan, 1918-30. *Address:* 15 Eaton Mansions, Cliveden Place, SW1. *T:* 01-730 5807.

SETON, Lady, (Julia), VMH; (Julia Clements, professionally); author, speaker, international floral art judge; flower arrangement judge for RHS and National Association of Flower Arrangement Societies; *d* of late Frank Clements; *m* 1962, Sir Alexander Hay Seton, 10th Bt, of Abercorn (*d* 1963); no *c*. *Educ:* Isle of Wight; Zwicker College, Belgium. Organised and conducted first Judges' School in England at Royal Horticultural Society Halls; has since conducted many other courses for judges all over Britain. VMH, RHS, 1974. *Publications:* Fun with Flowers; Fun without Flowers; 101 Ideas for Flower Arrangement; Party Pieces; First Steps with Flowers; The Julia Clements Colour Book of Flower Arrangements; Flower Arrangements in Stately Homes; Julia Clements' Gift Book of Flower Arranging, Flowers in Praise, etc. *Address:* 122 Swan Court, SW3. *T:* 01-352 9039. *Clubs:* Women's Press, Anglo-Belge.

SETON, Sir Robert (James), 11th Bt, *cr* 1683; *b* 20 April 1926; *s* of Captain Sir John Hastings Seton, 10th Bt and Alice (*see* Lady Seton), *d* of Percy Hodge, Cape Civil Service; *S* father 1956; unmarried. *Educ:* HMS Worcester (Thames Nautical Training College). Midshipman RNVR (invalided), 1943-44. Banker,

with Hong Kong and Shanghai Banking Corpn, 1946-61 (retd). *Heir: kinsman* James Christall Seton [*b* 21 Jan. 1913; *m* 1939, Evelyn, *d* of Ray Hafer]. *Address:* c/o The British Bank of the Middle East, 99 Bishopsgate, EC2. *Club:* Tanglin (Singapore).

SETON-WATSON, Prof. George Hugh Nicholas, DLitt; FBA 1969; Professor of Russian History, School of Slavonic and East European Studies, University of London, since 1951; *b* 15 Feb. 1916; *er s* of late Prof. Robert William Seton-Watson and late Mrs Seton-Watson; *m* 1947, Mary Hope, *d* of late G. D. Rokeling, lately of Ministry of Education; three *d*. *Educ:* Winchester; New College, Oxford. DLitt Oxon, 1974. Was attached to British Legations in Roumania and Yugoslavia, 1940-41; served Special Forces GHQ, Middle East, 1941-44. Fellow and Praelector in Politics, University Coll., Oxford, 1946-51. Mem. Council, RIIA, 1952. Vis. Prof., Columbia Univ., 1957-58; Fellow, Center for Advanced Study in the Behavioural Sciences, Stanford, Calif., 1963-64; Vis. Fellow, ANU, Canberra, 1964; Visiting Professor: Indiana Univ., 1973; Washington Univ., Seattle, 1973. *Publications:* Eastern Europe between the Wars, 1945; The East European Revolution, 1950; The Decline of Imperial Russia, 1952; The Pattern of Communist Revolution, 1953; Neither War Nor Peace, 1960; The New Imperialism, 1961; Nationalism and Communism (Essays, 1946-63); The Russian Empire, 1801-1917, 1967; The "Sick Heart" of Modern Europe, 1976. *Recreations:* travel, ornithology. *Address:* 8 Burghley Road, Wimbledon Common, SW19. *T:* 01-946 0861. *Club:* Athenæum.

SETSHOGO, Boithoko Moonwa; High Commissioner of Botswana in London, since 1975; *b* Serowe, 16 June 1941; *m* 1971, Jennifer Tlalane; two *d*. *Educ:* Moeng Coll.; Univ. of Botswana, Lesotho and Swaziland (BA). District Officer, Kanye, 1969-70; First Sec., High Commn, London, 1970-72; Clerk to the Cabinet, 1972-73; Under-Sec., Min. of Commerce and Industry, 1973-75. *Address:* Botswana High Commission, 162 Buckingham Palace Road, SW1. *T:* 01-730 5216/9; (residence) 95 Platts Lane, NW3. *T:* 01-435 6807.

SETTLE, Alison, OBE 1961; *m* A. Towers Settle, barrister-at-law; one *s* one *d*. Formerly Editor of Vogue; for 22 years fashion editor of The Observer and Fashion Consultant to leading firms; regular contributor to The Lady. Member: Council of Arts and Industry; Council of Industrial Design, 1953-58; Silver Medallist, RSA. Pres. Women's Press Club, 1952-54. *Publications:* Clothes Line, 1937 (republished 1941); English Fashion (Britain in Pictures Series), 1948; Fashion as a Career, 1963; (jtly) Paris Fashion, 1972. *Address:* 6 Church Street, Steyning, West Sussex.

SETTLE, Charles Arthur, QC 1960; a Commons Commissioner, since 1974; *b* 26 April 1905; *s* of Theodore Settle; *m* 1st, 1936, Pamela (*d* 1938), *d* of F. N. Marcy; one *d*; 2nd, 1947, Jane Anne, *d* of Huw Jones. *Educ:* Marlborough College; Trinity College, Cambridge. Served War of 1939-45 (despatches, 1944). Called to Bar by Middle Temple, 1928; Master of Bench, 1966. Vice-Chm., Bar Council, 1968-70. Judge of Cts of Appeal, Jersey and Guernsey, 1971-75. *Recreation:* fishing. *Address:* 3 Thurloe Close, SW7. *T:* 01-589 8932. *Clubs:* Brooks's, Flyfishers'.

SETTRINGTON, Lord; Charles Henry Gordon-Lennox; *b* 8 Jan. 1955; *s* and *heir* of Earl of March and Kinrara, *qv*; *m* 1976, Sally, *d* of late Maurice Clayton and of Mrs Denis Irwin. *Educ:* Eton. *Address:* Goodwood House, Chichester, West Sussex.

SEUFFERT, Stanislaus, QC 1965; Special Divorce Commissioner and Deputy Judge, 1967-75; Barrister-at-Law, retired 1975; *b* Johannesburg, 17 May 1899; *e s* of late Philip Seuffert and Marie Winefride Seuffert (*née* Brennan); *m* 1st, Alice, widow of George Jackson (*née* McCarthy); 2nd, Norma (*née* Klerck), widow of Maj.-Gen. Pienaar, CB, DSO; one *s* one *d*. *Educ:* Marist Brothers, Johannesburg; Stonyhurst Coll., Lancashire. Served World War, Middx Regt, 1917. Barrister, Middle Temple, 1925, Bencher, 1970. Mem. Senate, Four Inns of Court, 1970-74. First Chm., Guild of Catholic Artists, 1929; Chm. Catholic Prisoners' Aid Soc., 1938-60; Hon. Treas. and Sec., Soc. of Our Lady of Good Counsel, 1935-58. Contested (Lab) East Grinstead, 1935; Borough Councillor, Fulham, 1934-49; Dep. Civil Def. Controller, Fulham, and Leader of Council, 1939-44; Chm. Fulham Food Control Committee, 1939-46; Mayor of Fulham 1944-45. KHS Grand Cross, 1955; Kt of Order of St Gregory (Papal), 1962. *Publications:* annotations: Matrimonial Causes Act, 1937; Local Govt Act, 1949; Adoption Act, 1950. Handbook of Matrimonial Causes. *Recreations:* playgoing, reading. *Address:* Lamb Building, Temple, EC4; 2 Gaywood Court, 42 Hawthorne Road, Bickley, Bromley BR1 2HN. *T:* 01-467 6427.

SEVER, (Eric) John; MP (Lab) Birmingham Ladywood, since Aug. 1977; *b* 1 April 1943; *s* of Eric and Clara Sever. *Educ:* Sparkhill Commercial School. Travel Executive with tour operator, 1970-77. *Recreations:* theatre, cinema, reading. *Address:* 14 Brookfield Precinct, Birmingham B18 7BU. *T:* 021-236 8057.

SEVERN, David; *see* Unwin, David Storr.

SEVERNE, Air Cdre John de Milt, MVO 1961; OBE 1968; AFC 1955; Air Commodore Flying Training, HQ RAF Support Command, RAF Brampton, since 1976; *b* 15 Aug. 1925; *s* of late Dr A. de M. Severne, Wateringbury, Kent; *m* 1951, Katharine Veronica, *d* of late Captain V. E. Kemball, RN (Retd); three *d.* *Educ:* Marlborough. MBIM. Joined RAF, 1944; Flying Instr., Cranwell, 1948; Staff Instr. and PA to Comdt CFS, 1950-53; Flt Comdr No 98 Sqdn, Germany, 1954-55; Sqdn Comdr No 26 Sqdn, Germany, 1956-57; Air Min., 1958; Equerry to Duke of Edinburgh, 1958-61; psa 1962; Chief Instr No 226 Operational Conversion Unit (Lightning), 1963-65; jssc 1965; Jt HQ, ME Comd, Aden, 1966-67; Dirg Staff, Jt Services Staff Coll., 1968; Gp Captain Organisation, HQ Strike Comd, 1968-70; Stn Comdr, RAF Kinloss, 1971-72; RCDS 1973; Comdt, Central Flying School, RAF, 1974-76. ADC to the Queen, 1972-73. Won Kings Cup Air Race, British Air Racing Champion, 1960. Pres., RAF Equitation Assoc., 1976- (Chm. 1973); Vice-Chm., Jt Services Equitation Cttee, 1976-. Chevalier, Legion of Honour, 1960; Order of Tri Shakti (Nepal), 1960. *Recreations:* flying, equitation, photography, music. *Address:* 31 Park Lane, Brampton, Huntingdon PE18 8QD. *T:* Huntingdon 55870. *Club:* Royal Air Force.

SEWARD, Sir Eric (John), KBE 1960 (CBE 1954); retired; *b* 18 May 1899; *s* of William Edwards Seward and Florence Lloyd; *m* 1924, Ella Maud, *d* of Frederick L'Estrange Wallace and Gwendoline Gilling-Lax; three *s.* *Educ:* Parkstone Sch. Served European War 1914-18 with 5th Cavalry Reserve Regt in UK. Chm. British Chamber of Commerce in the Argentine Republic, 1951-62, now Hon. Vice-President. Liveryman Worshipful Company of Butchers. *Address:* Dr G. Rawson 2420, 1636 Olivos, Prov. de Buenos Aires, Argentina.

SEWARD, William Richard, RCNC; General Manager, HM Dockyard, Portsmouth, since 1975; *b* 7 Feb. 1922; *s* of William and Gertrude Seward, Portsmouth; *m* 1946, Mary Deas Ritchie; one *d.* *Educ:* Portsmouth Dockyard Techn. Coll.; RNC Greenwich; Royal Corps of Naval Constructors. Asst Constructor, HM Dockyard, Rosyth, 1945-47; Constructor, Naval Construction Dept, Admty, 1947-58; Admty Constructor Overseer, Birkenhead, 1958-63; Chief Constructor, MoD (N), 1963-70; Prodn Man., HM Dockyard, Chatham, 1970-73, Gen. Manager, 1973-75. *Recreations:* reading, music, caravanning, walking. *Address:* HM Dockyard, Portsmouth. *T:* Portsmouth 22351 or 22465. *Club:* Civil Service.

SEWELL, Sir (John) Allan, Kt 1977; ISO 1968; Auditor-General of Queensland, Australia, since 1970; *b* 23 July 1915; *s* of George Allan Sewell and Francis Doris Sewell; *m* 1939, Thelma Edith Buchholz (decd); one *s* one *d.* *Educ:* Brisbane Grammar Sch. AASA; Associate Inst. of Chartered Secs and Administrators; Fellow Inst. of Municipal Admin. Dir of Local Govt, 1948-60; Under Treasurer of Qld, 1960-70. *Recreation:* game fishing. *Address:* 19 Howell Street, Kedron, Brisbane, Qld 4031, Australia. *T:* 59-1374. *Clubs:* Cairns Game Fishing (Cairns); Moreton Bay Game Fishing (Brisbane).

SEWELL, Thomas Robert McKie; Assistant Secretary, Ministry of Agriculture, Fisheries and Food, since 1970; UK Representative to International Wheat Council; *b* 18 Aug. 1921; *s* of O. B. Fane Sewell and late Frances M. Sewell (*née* Sharp); *m* 1955, Jennifer Mary Sandeman; two *d.* *Educ:* Eastbourne Coll.; Trinity Coll., Oxford (Schol., Heath Harrison Prize, MA); Lausanne and Stockholm Univs (Schol.). HM Forces, 1940-45 (despatches); Major. Entered Foreign Service, 1949; Second Sec., Moscow, 1950-52; FO, 1952-55; First Sec., 1954; Madrid, 1955-59; Lima, 1959-61; Chargé d'Affaires, 1960; FO, 1961-63; Counsellor and Head of Chancery, Moscow, 1964-66; Diplomatic Service Rep. at IDC, 1966; Head of Associated States, West Indies and Swaziland Depts, Commonwealth Office, 1967-68; Head of N American and Caribbean Dept, FCO, 1968-70. *Recreations:* ski-ing, inland waterways cruising. *Address:* c/o Williams & Glyn's Bank, Whitehall, SW1. *Clubs:* Travellers', Airborne.

SEXTON, Maj.-Gen. Francis Michael, (Mike Sexton), OBE 1966; Director of Military Survey, and Chief of Geographic Section of General Staff, Ministry of Defence, since 1977; *b* 15 July 1923; *s* of Timothy Sexton and Catherine Regan; *m* 1947,

Naomi, *d* of Bertram Alonzo Middleton and Dorothy May Middleton; one *s* one *d.* *Educ:* Wanstead County High Sch.; Birmingham Univ. Commnd RE, 1943; Royal Bombay Sappers and Miners, India and Burma, 1943-46; RE units, UK, Egypt and Cyprus, 1946-53; Dept of Mines and Surveys, Canada, 1953-56; Asst Dir, MoD, 1964-65; Dep. Dir, Ordnance Survey, 1966-70; Chief Geographic Officer, SHAPE, Belgium, 1970-73; Brig. (Survey) and Dep. Chief of Geographic Section of GS, 1973-77. *Recreations:* interested in most ball games; active lawn tennis and racquet ball. *Address:* Pipers Croft, Elsenwood Crescent, Camberley, Surrey. *T:* Camberley 26047.

SEYCHELLES, Bishop of, since 1973; **Rt. Rev. George Cardell Briggs;** *b* Latchford, Warrington, Cheshire, 6 Sept. 1910; *s* of George Cecil and Mary Theodora Briggs; unmarried. *Educ:* Worksop Coll., Notts; Sidney Sussex Coll., Cambridge (MA); Cuddesdon Theological Coll. Deacon 1934; priest 1935; Curate of St Alban's, Stockport, 1934-37; Missionary priest, Diocese of Masasi, Tanzania, 1937; Archdeacon of Newala and Canon of Masasi, 1955-64; Rector of St Alban's, Dar-es-Salaam, 1964-69; Warden of St Cyprian's Theological Coll., Masasi, 1969-73. *Recreations:* walking, reading, music. *Address:* PO Box 44, Victoria, Seychelles. *T:* 22712.

SEYLER, Athene, CBE 1959; Actress on the London stage; *b* London, 31 May 1889; *d* of Clara Thies and Clarence H. Seyler; *m* 1st, James Bury Sterndale-Bennett; one *d*; 2nd, Nicholas James Hannen, OBE (*d* 1972). *Educ:* Coombe Hill School; Bedford College. Gold Medallist, Royal Academy of Dramatic Art, 1908; first appearance on the stage at Kingsway Theatre, 1909; specialised in comedy acting; served on the Drama Panel of CEMA, 1943 and subsequently of the Arts Council of Great Britain. Pres. of RADA, 1950; Pres. of Theatrical Ladies' Guild. Principal successes as Madame Ranevska in The Cherry Orchard, Fanny Farrelli in Watch on the Rhine, the Duchess of Berwick in Lady Windermere's Fan, Vita Louise in Harvey, Mrs Malaprop in The Rivals, The Nurse in Romeo and Juliet. Has appeared in films, 1932-. Hon. Treasurer of British Actors Equity Association, 1944. *Publication:* The Craft of Comedy, 1944. *Recreations:* walking, talking. *Address:* Coach House, 26 Upper Mall, Hammersmith, W6.

SEYMOUR, family name of **Marquess of Hertford** and **Duke of Somerset.**

SEYMOUR, Lord; John Michael Edward Seymour, ARICS; *b* 30 Dec. 1952; *s* and *heir* of 18th Duke of Somerset, *qv.* *Educ:* Eton. *Address:* Maiden Bradley, Warminster, Wilts. *Club:* MCC.

SEYMOUR, Derek Robert Gurth, MA; Headmaster of Bloxham School since Sept. 1965; *b* 4 Sept. 1917; *s* of G. Haco Seymour; *m* 1940, Betty, *d* of late Lt-Col S. H. Little; two *s.* *Educ:* Trinity Coll., Cambridge. BA 1939; MA 1943. Head of Chemistry, Junior Housemaster, St John's School, Leatherhead, 1939-44; Asst Master, Head of Science, i/c RAF Section, CCF; Housemaster, Marlborough College, 1944-65. Seconded as Head of Chemistry and House Tutor, Cranbrook Sch., Sydney, 1951-52. Examr and Chief Examr in A and S Level Chemistry, Southern Univs Jt Bd, 1955-63. *Address:* Park Close, Bloxham, Banbury, Oxon OX15 4PS. *T:* Banbury 720321.

SEYMOUR, Sir Horace James, GCMG 1946 (KCMG 1939; CMG 1927); CVO 1936; *b* 26 Feb. 1885; *e s* of late Hugh F. Seymour; *m* 1917, Violet, *d* of late Thomas Erskine; one *s* two *d.* *Educ:* Eton; Trinity College, Cambridge. Foreign Office and Diplomatic Service, 1908; British Minister, Tehran, 1936-39; Assistant Under-Secretary of State at Foreign Office, 1939-42; Ambassador to China, 1942-46; retired, 1947. *Address:* Bratton House, Westbury, Wilts. *T:* Bratton 231.
See also Sir Ivo Stourton.

SEYMOUR, Lady Katharine, DCVO 1961 (CVO 1939); Extra Woman of the Bedchamber to Queen Elizabeth the Queen Mother since 1960 (Woman of the Bedchamber to the Queen (now Queen Elizabeth the Queen Mother), 1937-60); First Woman of the Bedchamber to Queen Mary, 1927-30 (on marriage became Extra Woman of the Bedchamber, 1930-53); *b* 25 Feb. 1900; 3rd *d* of 3rd Duke of Abercorn; *m* 1930, Sir R. H. Seymour, KCVO (*d* 1938); one *s* one *d* (and one *d* decd). *Address:* Strettington House, Chichester, West Sussex. *T:* Halnaker 265.

SEYMOUR, Lynn, CBE 1976; Ballerina; *b* Wainwright, Alberta, 8 March 1939; *d* of E. V. Springbett; *m* 1st, 1963, Colin Jones, photo-journalist (marr. diss.); 2nd, 1974, Philip Pace. *Educ:* Vancouver; Sadler's Wells Ballet School. Joined Sadler's Wells Ballet Company, 1957; Deutsche Oper, Berlin, 1966. *Roles created:* Adolescent, in The Burrow, Royal Opera House, 1958;

Bride, in Le Baiser de la Fée, 1960; Girl, in The Invitation, 1960; Young Girl, in Les Deux Pigeons, 1961; Principal, in Symphony, 1963; Principal, in Images of Love, 1964; Juliet, in Romeo and Juliet, 1964; Albertine, BBC TV, 1966; Concerto, 1966; Anastasia, 1966; Flowers, 1972; mother, in Fourth Symphony, 1977. *Other appearances include:* Danses Concertantes; Solitaire; La Fête Etrange; Sleeping Beauty; Swan Lake, Australasia, 1958-59, London, 1959; Giselle (title-role), 1960; Cinderella, London, 1961; Das Lied von der Erde, 1966; The Four Seasons, 1975; A Month in the Country, Voluntaries, 1976. *Choreography for:* Rashomon, 1976; The Court of Love, 1977. *Address:* c/o Royal Opera House, Covent Garden, WC2.

SEYMOUR, Commander Sir Michael Culme-, 5th Bt, *cr* 1809; Royal Navy (retired); *b* 26 April 1909; *o s* of Vice-Admiral Sir M. Culme-Seymour, 4th Bt, and Florence Agnes Louisa (*d* 1956), *y d* of late A. L. Nugent; *S* father, 1925; *m* 1948, Lady (Mary) Faith Nesbitt, *er d* of 9th Earl of Sandwich; one *step-d* (two *s* decd). Succeeded Rev. Wentworth Watson to the Rockingham Castle estates, 1925, and transferred them to his nephew, Cmdr L. M. M. Saunders Watson, RN, 1967; is a farmer and a landowner. ADC to Governor-General of Canada, 1933-35; served War of 1939-45 (despatches); served Imperial Defence College, 1946-47; retired from RN 1947. JP Northants, 1949; Mem. Northants CC 1948-55; DL Northants, 1958-71; High Sheriff of Northants, 1966. Bledisloe Gold Medal for Landowners, 1972. *Heir to baronetcy: cousin* John Dennis Culme-Seymour [*b* 3 Dec. 1923; *m* 1957, (Elizabeth) Jane Mackessack; one *d*]. *Address:* Wytherston, Powerstock, Bridport, Dorset. *T:* Powerstock 211. *Club:* Brooks's.

SEYMOUR, Richard, CMG 1966; CBE 1946; *b* 16 Sept. 1903; *s* of late Richard Seymour and Edith, *d* of William Hales; *m* 1940, Charlotte, *d* of Ernest Leigh; two *d. Educ:* Highgate Sch.; Christ Church, Oxford (Scholar, MA). Admitted a Solicitor, 1927; partner in firm of Rhys Roberts & Co. until 1940. Secretary, Books Commission of Conference of Allied Ministers of Education, 1942-45. Deputy Secretary-General, British Council, 1940-47, Secretary, 1947-53; Controller, Commonwealth Div., 1953-57, European Div., 1957-59; Representative in Germany, 1959-66. *Address:* The Old Manse, Staplecross, Robertsbridge, East Sussex.

SEYMOUR, Air Commodore Roland George, CB 1961; CBE 1945; RAF, retired; *b* 16 May 1905; *s* of William and Jeannie Seymour; *m* 1942, Dorothy Beatrice Hutchings; two *s. Educ:* Christ's Hospital. Pilot Officer, RAF, Jan. 1929, psc 1942; Actg Air Commodore, 1945, as Dep. to Air Officer i/c Administration, Mediterranean Allied Air Forces; Air Commodore, 1958; served in: Iraq, 1930-32; N Africa and Italy, 1942-45; Singapore, 1952-54; Deputy Assistant Chief of Staff (Logistics), Supreme HQ Allied Powers Europe, 1961-63. Legion of Merit (USA), 1946. *Address:* c/o Williams & Glyn's Bank Ltd, Lawrie House, Victoria Road, Farnborough GU15 7PA.

SEYMOUR, Rosalind; *see* Wade, R. (H.).

SEZNEC, Prof. Jean J., FBA 1960; Marshal Foch Professor of French Literature, Oxford, 1950-72; *b* 18 March 1905; *s* of Jean Seznec and Pauline Le Férec. *Educ:* Ecole Normale Supérieure, Paris. Fellow, French School of Archaeology, Rome, 1929-31; Univ. Lecturer, Cambridge, 1931-33; Prof., Lycée of Marseilles, 1933-34; Prof., French Inst., Florence, 1934-39, Asst Director, 1939; Assoc. Professor, Harvard University, 1941-46, Professor, 1946, Smith Professor of the French and Spanish Languages, 1947-50. Mary Flexner Lecturer, Bryn Mawr, 1955; Lord Northcliffe Lecturer, London, 1958; Dillon Visiting Prof., Harvard University, 1958. Mem., Adv. Council, V&A Museum, 1970-. Hon. DLitt: Harvard, 1961; St Andrews, 1972. Officier de la Légion d'Honneur, 1957; Comdr de l'Ordre National du Mérite, 1973. *Publications:* La Survivance des Dieux Antiques, 1940; L'Episode des Dieux dans la Tentation de Saint Antoine, 1940; Nouvelles Etudes sur la Tentation de Saint Antoine, 1949; Essais sur Diderot et l'Antiquité, 1958; John Martin en France, 1964; Un tableau de Paris au milieu du XVIIIe siècle, 1974; (joint) Fragonard, Drawings for Ariosto, 1945; Diderot, Salons, Vol. I, 1957, 2nd edn 1975; Vol. II, 1960; Vol. III, 1963; Vol. IV, 1967; contributions to: French Studies, Jl of Warburg and Courtauld Institutes, Romanic Review, Gazette des Beaux Arts, etc. *Address:* 1 Stanton Harcourt, Oxford.

SHACKLE, Prof. George Lennox Sharman, FBA 1967; Brunner Professor of Economic Science in the University of Liverpool, 1951-69, now Professor Emeritus; *b* 14 July 1903; *s* of Robert Walker Shackle, MA (Cambridge) and of Fanny Shackle (*née* Sharman); *m* 1939, Gertrude Courtney Susan Rowe; two *s* one *d* (and one *d* decd). *Educ:* The Perse School, Cambridge; The

London School of Economics; New College, Oxford. BA (London) 1931; Leverhulme Research Schol., 1934; PhD (Econ) (London), 1937; DPhil (Oxford), 1940. Oxford University Institute of Statistics, 1937; University of St Andrews, 1939; Admiralty and Cabinet Office; Sir Winston Churchill's Statistical Branch, 1939; Economic Section of Cabinet Secretariat, 1945; Reader in Economic Theory, Univ. of Leeds, 1950. F. de Vries Lecturer, Amsterdam, 1957; Visiting Professor: Columbia University, 1957-58; of Economics and Philosophy, Univ. of Pittsburgh, 1967; Keynes Lectr, British Acad., 1976. Mem. Council, Royal Economic Society, 1955-69; Pres., Section F, BAAS, 1966. Fellow of Econometric Society, 1960. Hon. DSc NUU, 1974. *Publications:* Expectations, Investment, and Income, 1938, 2nd edn 1968; Expectation in Economics, 1949, 2nd edn, 1952; Mathematics at the Fireside, 1952 (French edn 1967); Uncertainty in Economics and Other Reflections, 1955; Time in Economics, 1957; Economics for Pleasure, 1959, 2nd edn 1968 (paperback, 1962; also foreign editions); Decision, Order and Time in Human Affairs, 1961 (2nd edn 1969; also foreign editions); A Scheme of Economic Theory, 1965 (also Portuguese edn); The Nature of Economic Thought, 1966 (also Spanish edn); The Years of High Theory, 1967; Expectation, Enterprise and Profit, 1970 (Spanish edn 1976); Epistemics and Economics, 1973; An Economic Querist, 1973 (Spanish edn 1976); Keynesian Kaleidics, 1974; (ed and contrib.) Uncertainty and Business Decisions, 1954, 2nd edn, 1957; The Theory of General Static Equilibrium, 1957; A New Prospect of Economics, 1958; On the Nature of Business Success, 1968; articles in Chambers's Encyclopædia, 1950, 1967, Internat. Encyclopedia of the Social Sciences, 1968, and in other books; sixty or more main articles in learned jls. *Address:* Rudloe, Alde House Drive, Aldeburgh, Suffolk IP15 5EE.

SHACKLETON, family name of **Baron Shackleton.**

SHACKLETON, Baron *cr* 1958 (Life Peer), of Burley; **Edward Arthur Alexander Shackleton,** KG 1974; PC 1966; OBE 1945; Deputy Chairman, RTZ Corporation, since 1975; *b* 15 July 1911; *s* of late Sir Ernest Shackleton, CVO, OBE; *m* 1938, Betty Homan; one *s* one *d. Educ:* Radley College, Magdalen College, Oxford (MA). Surveyor, Oxford University Expedition to Sarawak, 1932; Organiser and Surveyor, Oxford University Expedition to Ellesmereland, 1934-35; Lecture tours in Europe and America; BBC talks producer, MOI. Served War of 1939-45, 1940-45; RAF Station Intelligence Officer, St Eval; Anti-U-Boat Planner and Intelligence Officer, Coastal Command; Naval and Military Intelligence, Air Ministry; Wing Cdr (despatches twice, OBE). Contested (Lab) Epsom, General Election, and Bournemouth by-election, 1945; MP (Lab), Preston (by-election), 1946-50, Preston South, 1950-55. Parliamentary Private Secretary to Minister of Supply, 1949-50; Parliamentary Private Sec. to Foreign Sec., March-Oct. 1951 (to Lord President of the Council, 1950-51); Minister of Defence for the RAF, 1964-67. Minister Without Portfolio and Deputy Leader, House of Lords, 1967-68; Lord Privy Seal, Jan.-April, 1968; Paymaster-General, April-Oct. 1968; Leader of the House of Lords, April 1968-70; Lord Privy Seal, Oct. 1968-1970; Minister in charge, Civil Service Dept, Nov. 1968-70; Opposition Leader, House of Lords, 1970-74. Vice-Pres., Parly and Scientific Cttee. Sen. Executive and Director, J. Lewis Partnership, 1955-64; Chm., RTZ Development Enterprises; Exec. Dir, 1974-75, Dep. Chm., 1975-, RTZ Corp. Ltd (Personnel/Admin). Chairman: Cttee on Oil Pollution, 1962-64; Political Honours Scrutiny Committee, 1976-; Pres., Brit. Assoc. of Industrial Editors, 1960-64; Mem. Council, Industrial Soc. Special Mission to South Arabia, 1967; Mem., BOTB, 1975-; Pres., Parly and Scientific Cttee, 1975-. Pres., ASLIB, 1963-65; Pres., Royal Geographical Society, 1971-74 (formerly Vice-Pres.); Cuthbert Peek Award (Royal Geographical Society), 1933; Ludwig Medallist (Munich Geog. Soc.), 1938. Pres., Arctic Club, 1960. FBIM. Hon. LLD Univ. of Newfoundland, 1970. *Publications:* Arctic Journeys; Nansen, the Explorer; (part-author) Borneo Jungle; articles, broadcasts, etc. on geographical and political subjects and personnel and general administration. *Address:* Long Coppice, Canford Magna, Wimborne, Dorset. *T:* Broadstone 3635.

SHACKLETON, Robert, MA, DLitt Oxon; FSA, FRSL; FBA 1966; Bodley's Librarian, Oxford, since 1966; Fellow of Brasenose College since 1946 (Professorial Fellow since 1966); *b* 25 Nov. 1919; *e s* of Albert Shackleton and Emily (*née* Sunderland); unmarried. *Educ:* Todmorden Grammar School; Oriel College, Oxford (Scholar). 1st class, Hon. School of Modern Languages, 1940. Military Service, Royal Signals, 1940-45. Candidate (L), Blackburn, Gen. Elec., 1945. Lectr, Trinity Coll., Oxford, 1946-49; Fellow, Brasenose Coll., 1946-. (Librarian, 1948-66, Sen. Dean, 1954-61, Vice-Principal, 1963-66); Lectr in French, Oxford Univ., 1949-65; Reader in French literature, Oxford Univ., 1965-66; Chm., Cttee on Oxford Univ. Libraries, 1965-66; Vis. Prof. Dept of French and Italian, Univ. of Wisconsin, 1968; Zaharoff Lectr, Oxford Univ., 1970. Delegate, Oxford Univ. Press. Corresp. Member: Acad. de Bordeaux, 1954; Acad. Montesquieu (Bordeaux), 1956; Prix Montesquieu, 1956; President, Society for French Studies, 1959-60; Member, Editorial Board: French Studies, 1960- (Gen. Ed., 1965-67); Archives internationales d'histoire des idées, 1962-. Pres., Internat. Comparative Liter. Assoc., 1964-67; Pres., Internat. Soc. for 18th Century Studies, 1975-. Hon. Member: Soc. d'Histoire Littéraire de la France; Assoc. Internat. de Bibliophilie; Australasian and Pacific Soc. for 18th Century Studies; Soc. Univ. Studi di Lingua e Letteratura Francese; For. Hon. Mem., Amer. Acad. of Arts and Sciences; Hon. For. Corresp. Mem., Grolier Club, NY. Hon. Fellow, Oriel Coll., Oxford, 1971; Hon. Professorial Fellow, UC of Wales, 1972; Assoc. Fellow, Silliman Coll., Yale Univ., 1972. Hon. Dr Univ. Bordeaux, 1966; Hon. LittD Univ. of Dublin, 1967. *Publications:* Editor: Fontenelle, Entretiens sur la pluralité des mondes, 1955; Montesquieu, a critical biography, 1961 (French translation, 1976); The Encyclopédie and the Clerks (Zaharoff lect.), 1970; (ed jtly) The Artist and Writer in France, 1975; articles in learned jls, Encyclopædia Britannica, etc. *Recreations:* book-collecting, foreign travel. *Address:* Bodleian Library, Oxford. *T:* 44675; Brasenose College, Oxford. *T:* 48641. *Clubs:* Athenæum, National Liberal; Grolier (New York); Elizabethan (Yale).

SHACKLETON, Prof. Robert Millner, BSc, PhD; FRS 1971; FGS; Professor of Geology, University of Leeds, 1962-75, now Emeritus; Director, Research Institute of African Geology, University of Leeds, 1966-75; *b* 30 Dec. 1909; *m* 1st, 1934, Gwen Isabel Harland; one *s* two *d*; 2nd, 1949, Judith Wyndham Jeffreys; one *s* one *d*. *Educ:* Sidcot School; University of Liverpool. BSc (Hons) 1931, PhD 1934, Liverpool; Beit Fellow, Imperial College, 1932-34; Chief Geologist to Whitehall Explorations Ltd in Fiji, 1935-36; on teaching staff, Imperial College, 1936-40 and 1945-48; Geologist, Mining and Geological Dept, Kenya, 1940-45; Herdman Professor of Geology, University of Liverpool, 1948-62. Royal Society Leverhulme Vis. Prof., Haile Sellassie I Univ., 1970-71. Vice-Pres., Geolog. Soc. of London, 1966. Murchison Medal, 1970. *Publications:* Mining and Geological Dept of Kenya Reports 10, 11, 12; papers in geological journals, etc. *Address:* Flat 9, Grove House Court, North Lane, Leeds LS8 2NQ. *T:* Leeds 650979.

SHACKLETON BAILEY, D. R.; *see* Bailey.

SHACKLOCK, Constance, OBE 1971; LRAM 1940; FRAM 1953; International Opera and Concert Singer; Professor, Royal Academy of Music, since 1968; *b* 16 April 1913; *e d* of Randolph and Hilda Shacklock, Nottingham; *m* 1947, Eric Mitchell (*d* 1965). *Educ:* Huntingdon Street Secondary School, Nottingham; RAM. Principal mezzo-soprano, Covent Garden, 1946-56. Outstanding rôles: Carmen, Amneris (Aida), Octavian (Der Rosenkavalier), Brangaene (Tristan und Isolde). Guest artist: Wagner Society, Holland, 1949; Berlin State Opera, 1951; Edinburgh Festival, 1954; Berlin Festival, 1956; Teatro Colon, Buenos Aires, 1956; Bolshoi Theatre, Moscow, 1957; Kirov Theatre, Leningrad, 1957; Elizabethan Theatre Trust, Sydney, 1958; Liège Opera, 1960; London production of The Sound of Music, 1961-66. *Recreations:* gardening, reading, tapestry. *Address:* Royal Academy of Music, Marylebone Road, NW1; East Dorincourt, Kingston Vale, SW15 3RN.

SHACKMAN, Prof. Ralph; Professor of Urology, University of London, at Royal Post-graduate Medical School, 1961-75; *b* 29 March 1910; *s* of David and Sophia Shackman; *m* 1940, Ida Mary Seal; no *c*. *Educ:* Grocers' Company School; St Bartholomew's Hospital Medical School. MB, BS (London) 1934; FRCS 1936. Resident Surgical Officer, Royal Infirmary, Sheffield, 1937. Served War of 1939-45, Wing-Commander Surgical Specialist, RAF. Brit. Post-Grad. Travelling Fellowship in USA, 1947-48. Sen. Lectr, Post-grad. Med. Sch., 1949; Reader in Surgery, Univ. of London, 1955; Mem. Court of Examiners, RCS, England, 1962; Member of Council: Experimental Med. and Therapeutics, Roy. Soc. Med., 1962; Sect. of Urology, Roy. Soc. Med., 1963; Brit. Assoc. of Urological Surgeons, 1964; Brit. Assoc. of Surgeons, 1965; Member, International Society of Urology, 1964. *Publications:* contrib. to medical and scientific jls. *Recreations:* gardening, carpentry. *Address:* Motts Farmhouse, Chilton Street, Clare, Suffolk. *T:* Clare 7835.

SHAFFER, Peter Levin; playwright; critic; *b* 15 May 1926; *s* of Jack Shaffer and Reka Shaffer (*née* Fredman). *Educ:* St Paul's School, London; Trinity College, Cambridge. Literary Critic, Truth, 1956-57; Music Critic, Time and Tide, 1961-62. Awards:

Evening Standard Drama Award, 1958; New York Drama Critics Circle Award (best foreign play), 1959-60. *Stage Plays:* Five Finger Exercise, prod. Comedy, London, 1958-60, and Music Box Theatre, New York, 1960-61; (double bill) The Private Ear (filmed 1966) and The Public Eye, produced, Globe, London, 1962, Morosco Theater, New York 1963 (filmed 1972); The Merry Roosters Panto (with Joan Littlewood and Theatre Workshop) prod. Wyndham's Theatre, Christmas, 1963; The Royal Hunt of the Sun, Nat. Theatre, Chichester Festival, 1964, The Old Vic, and Queen's Theatres, 1964-67, NY, 1965-66 (filmed 1969); Black Comedy, Nat. Theatre, Chichester Fest., 1965, The Old Vic and Queen's Theatres, 1965-67; as double bill with White Lies, NY, 1967, Shaw, 1976; The White Liars, Lyric, 1968; The Battle of Shrivings, Lyric, 1970; Equus, Nat. Theatre, 1973-74, NY, 1976, Albery Theatre, 1976-77 (filmed 1977). Plays produced on television and sound include: Salt Land (ITV), 1955; Balance of Terror (BBC TV), 1957; The Prodigal Father (Radio), etc. *Recreations:* music, architecture. *Address:* 18 Earls Terrace, Kensington High Street, W8. *T:* 01-602 6892.

SHAFTESBURY, 10th Earl of, *cr* 1672; **Anthony Ashley-Cooper;** Bt 1622; Baron Ashley 1661; Baron Cooper of Paulet, 1672; *b* 22 May 1938; *o s* of Major Lord Ashley (*d* 1947; *e s* of 9th Earl of Shaftesbury, KP, PC, GCVO, CBE) and of Françoise Soulier; *S* grandfather, 1961; *m* 1st, 1966, Bianca Maria (marr. diss. 1976), *o d* of late Gino de Paolis; 2nd, 1976, Christina Eva, *o d* of Ambassador Nils Montan; one *s*. *Educ:* Eton; Christchurch, Oxford. Chm., London Philharmonic Orchestra Council. Hon. Citizen, South Carolina, USA, 1967. Patron of seven livings. *Recreations:* ski-ing, music, shooting. *Heir: s* Lord Ashley, *qv*. *Address:* St Giles, Wimborne, Dorset. *T:* Cranborne 312. *Club:* Turf.

See also Viscount Head.

SHAFTESLEY, John Maurice, OBE 1956; Editor of publications, Jewish Historical Society of England, a Vice-President, 1974; a Director of The Jewish Chronicle, London, 1958-60; *b* 25 June 1901; *s* of late David Shaftesley and Nellie Rosenblum; *m* 1926, Evelyn Adler; one *d*. *Educ:* Salford Grammar Sch.; Manchester Sch. of Art; London University (BA Hons). Allied Newspapers, technical staff, 1924-26; Manchester Guardian staff, 1926-36; Lecturer, Department of Printing Technology, Manchester College of Technology, 1933-36; Assistant Editor, The Jewish Chronicle, 1937-46 (Editor 1946-58). Fellow Royal Society of Arts, 1938; President, Wingate Services Club, High Wycombe, War of 1939-45; Mem. Council, Friends of the Hebrew Univ. of Jerusalem; Chm., Zangwill Centenary Cttee, 1964, and of Israel Zangwill Fellowship; Hon. Sec., Soc. of Indexers, 1967-68, Chm., 1973-76. A Departmental Editor and contributor, Encyclopædia Judaica, 1966-72. Works include: Cumulative Index to the *Jewish Chronicle* 1841-1880, 1881-90; Cumulative Index to the *Voice of Jacob* 1841-1846; Remember the Days (ed and contributor), 1966; Lodge of Israel No 205: A History 1793-1968, 1968, etc. *Address:* 33 The Grove, Edgware, Mddx. *T:* 01-958 9006. *Clubs:* Reform, Press.

SHAKERLEY, Sir Geoffrey (Adam), 6th Bt *cr* 1838; Director, Photographic Records Ltd, since 1970; *b* 9 Dec. 1932; *s* of Sir Cyril Holland Shakerley, 5th Bt, and of Elizabeth Averil (MBE 1955), *d* of late Edward Gwynne Eardley-Wilmot; *S* father, 1970; *m* 1st, 1961, Virginia Elizabeth (*d* 1968), *d* of W. E. Maskell; two *s*; 2nd, 1972, Lady Elizabeth Georgiana, *d* of Viscount Anson and of Princess Georg of Denmark; one *d*. *Educ:* Harrow; Trinity College, Oxford. *Heir: s* Nicholas Simon Adam Shakerley, *b* 20 Dec. 1963. *Address:* 56 Ladbroke Grove, W11.

SHAKERLEY, Sir Geoffrey (Peter), Kt 1972; CBE 1964; MC 1945; TD; Vice-Lieutenant of Gloucestershire, since 1969; *b* 11 April 1906; *s* of Lieutenant-Colonel G. C. Shakerley, DSO (killed in action, 1915) and of late Mrs G. C. Shakerley (*née* Harvey); *m* 1932, Barbara Storrs Howard; two *s* two *d*. *Educ:* Wellington College; Christ Church, Oxford (MA). Served War of 1939-45, with KRRC (TA), UK, Egypt, Italy; comdg R Gloucestershire Hussars (TA), 1951-53; Dep. Comdr, 129 Inf. Bde (TA), 1954-55. Chm., Gloucestershire CC, 1955-67; Vice-Chm., County Councils Assoc., 1965, Chm. 1969. DL Glos 1953; High Sheriff of Gloucestershire, 1961. *Recreation:* golf. *Address:* The Old Barn, Sevenhampton, near Cheltenham, Glos GL54 5SW. *T:* Andoversford 402.

SHAKESPEARE, Rt. Hon. Sir Geoffrey Hithersay, PC 1945; 1st Bt, *cr* 1942; Barrister; Deputy Chairman, Abbey National Building Society, 1965-69, Director, 1943-77; *b* 1893; 2nd *s* of late Rev. J. H. Shakespeare; *m* 1st, 1926, Lady Frater (*d* 1950), of 103 Sloane St, *widow* of Comdr Sir Thomas Fisher, RN; one *s* (one *d* decd); 2nd, 1952, Elizabeth, *er d* of late Brig.-Gen. R. W. Hare, CMG, DSO. *Educ:* Highgate School; Emmanuel,

Cambridge. MA, LLB; President of the Union; served European War; Private Secretary to Rt Hon. D. Lloyd George, 1921-23; MP (NL) Wellingborough Division of Northants, 1922-23; MP (L) Norwich, 1929-31 (L Nat.), 1931-45; Lord Commissioner of the Treasury and Chief Whip Liberal Nationals, Nov. 1931-Oct. 1932; Parliamentary Secretary, Ministry of Health, 1932-36; Parliamentary Secretary to Board of Education, 1936-37; Parliamentary and Financial Secretary to the Admiralty, 1937-40; Parliamentary Secretary to Dept of Overseas Trade, April to May 1940; Parliamentary Under-Secretary of State, Dominions Office and Chairman Children's Overseas Reception Board, 1940-42; called to Bar, 1922; political journalist, 1924; Vice-Chairman, Board of Governors Westminster Hosp., 1948-63; Pres. Soc. of British Gas Industries, 1953-54; Chairman: Industrial Co-Partnership Assoc., 1958-68; Nat. Liberal Exec., 1950-51; Standing Council of the Baronetage, 1972-75. *Publication:* Let Candles be brought in (Memoirs), 1949. *Recreation:* golf. *Heir: s* William Geoffrey Shakespeare [*b* 12 Oct. 1927; *m* 1964, Susan Mary, *d* of A. D. Raffel, Colombo, Ceylon, and of Mrs S. G. Sproule, Aylesbury, Bucks; two *s*]. *Address:* Flat 6, Great Ash, Lubbock Road, Chislehurst, Kent. *T:* 01-467 5898. *Club:* Reform.
See also Sir Nigel Fisher.

SHAKESPEARE, John William Richmond, MVO 1968; HM Diplomatic Service; Head of Mexico and Caribbean Department, Foreign and Commonwealth Office, since 1977; *b* 11 June 1930; *m* 1955, Lalage Ann Mais; three *s* one *d. Educ:* Winchester; Trinity Coll., Oxford (Scholar, MA). 2nd Lieut Irish Guards, 1949-50. Lectr in English, Ecole Normale Supérieure, Paris, 1953-54; on editorial staff, Times Educational Supplement, 1955-56 and Times, 1956-59; entered Diplomatic Service, 1959; Private Sec. to Ambassador in Paris, 1959-61; FO, 1961-63; 1st Sec., Phnom-Penh, 1963-64; 1st Sec., Office of Polit. Adviser to C-in-C Far East, Singapore, 1964-66; Dir of British Information Service in Brazil, 1966-69; FCO, 1969-73; Counsellor and Consul-Gen., Buenos Aires, 1973-75; Chargé d'Affaires, Buenos Aires, 1976-77. Officer, Order of Southern Cross (Brazil), 1968. *Recreations:* tennis, sailing, gardening, sun-bathing, music (popular), poetry. *Address:* c/o Foreign and Commonwealth Office, SW1A 2AH; 40 Victoria Drive, SW19 6BG. *T:* 01-788 9103.

SHAMOYA, Leonard Hantebele; High Commissioner for Zambia, 1975-77; *b* 20 Dec. 1936; *s* of Chiyupa Shamoya and Kavumbu Shamoya; *m* 1964; two *s* three *d. Educ:* London Univ. (BA); Brunel Univ. (MTech). RCM, Zambia: Secretarial Asst, 1964-67; Personnel Officer, 1967-69; Chief Personnel Officer, 1969-75. Director: Bank of Zambia, 1964-75; Zambia Trade Fair, 1966-68 and 1970-75; Zambia Nat. Building Soc., 1974-75; Shell and BP, 1975. Mayor, City of Ndola, 1966-68 and 1970-75; Constituency Sec., UNIP, 1970-75. *Recreations:* football, sports. *Address:* c/o Ministry of Foreign Affairs, PO Box RW69, Lusaka, Zambia.

SHAND, Major Bruce Middleton Hope, MC 1940, and Bar 1942; Vice Lord Lieutenant, East Sussex, since 1974; Chairman, Ellis, Son & Vidler Ltd, Wine Merchants, London and Hastings, since 1970; *b* 22 Jan. 1917; *s* of late P. Morton Shand; *m* 1946, Rosalind Maud, *d* of 3rd Baron Ashcombe; one *s* two *d. Educ:* Rugby; RMC, Sandhurst. 2nd Lieut 12th Royal Lancers, 1937; Major 1942; wounded and PoW 1942; retd 1947. Exon, Queen's Bodyguard of the Yeoman of the Guard, 1971. Joint or Acting Master, Southdown Fox Hounds, 1956-75. DL Sussex, 1962. *Recreations:* hunting, gardening. *Address:* The Laines, Plumpton, near Lewes, East Sussex BN7 3AJ. *T:* Plumpton 890248. *Clubs:* White's, Cavalry and Guards.
See also E . R . M . Howe .

SHAND, Rt. Rev. David Hubert Warner; Vicar of St Stephen's, Mt Waverley, Diocese of Melbourne, since 1976; *b* 6 April 1921; *s* of late Rev. Canon Rupert Warner Shand and Madeleine Ethel Warner Shand; *m* 1946, Muriel Jean Horwood Bennett; one *s* three *d. Educ:* The Southport Sch., Queensland; St Francis' Theological Coll., Brisbane (ThL, 2nd Cl. Hons); Univ. of Queensland (BA, 2nd Cl. Hons). Served War, AIF, 1941-45: Lieut, 1942. St Francis' Coll., Brisbane, 1946-48. Deacon, 1948; Priest, 1949; Asst Curate, Lutwyche. Served in Parishes: Moorooka, Inglewood, Nambour, Ipswich; Org. Sec., Home Mission Fund, 1960-63; Rural Dean of Ipswich, 1963-66; Dio. of Brisbane: Chaplain CMF, 1950-57; Vicar, Christ Church, South Yarra, 1966-69; St Andrew's, Brighton, 1969-73; Rural Dean of St Kilda, 1972-73; Dio. of Melbourne: consecrated Bishop, St Paul's Cathedral, Melbourne, Nov. 1973; Bishop of St Arnaud, 1973-76 (when diocese amalgamated with that of Bendigo). *Recreation:* carpentry. *Address:* St Stephen's Vicarage, 383 High Street Road, Mt Waverley, Victoria 3149, Australia.

SHANKLAND, Sir Thomas (Murray), Kt 1960; CMG 1955; JP; Deputy-Governor, Western Region, Nigeria, 1954-57; retired; Chairman, London Board of Public Service Commission, Western Region, Nigeria, 1957-61; *b* 25 Aug. 1905; *y s* of late W. C. Shankland, MBE, Barrister-at-Law, and late E. B. Shankland; *m* 1931, Margaret Crawford Goudie; one *d. Educ:* Felsted School; Queens' College, Cambridge (BA). Administrative Officer, Class IV, Nigeria, 1929; Food and Price Controller, Nigeria, 1944-45; Director of Supplies, Nigeria, 1946-47; Secretary, Western Provinces, Nigeria, 1949; Civil Secretary, Western Region, Nigeria, 1951; Chairman, Constituency Delimitation Commn, WR Nigeria, 1959. Mem. Jt CC, Moray and Nairn, 1958-70. JP Morayshire 1960. *Recreation:* golf. *Address:* Ardlarig, Grantown-on-Spey, Morayshire. *T:* Grantown-on-Spey 2160. *Club:* East India, Devonshire, Sports and Public Schools.

SHANKS, Ernest Pattison, CBE 1975; QC (Singapore) 1958; Deputy Bailiff of Guernsey, 1973-76; *b* 11 Jan. 1911; *e s* of late Hugh P. Shanks and Mary E. Shanks; *m* 1st, 1937, Audrey E. Moore; one *s*; 2nd, 1947, Betty Katherine Battersby; two *s* one *d. Educ:* Mill Hill Sch.; Downing Coll., Cambridge (MA); Inner Temple; Staff Coll., Camberley. Called to the Bar, Inner Temple, 1936; N Eastern Circuit. SRO, Mddx Regt, 1939-44: Princess Louise's Kensington Regt, France (despatches); Sicily, Italy, 1944; Staff Coll., Camberley, 1944-46; Sen. Legal Officer, Schleswig-Holstein, Milit. Govt, Germany, 1946; Lt-Col RARO, 1946. Colonial Legal Service: Dist Judge, Trengganu, Malaya, 1946; Singapore: Dist Judge and First Magistrate, 1947; Crown Counsel and Solicitor-Gen.; Attorney-Gen. and Minister of Legal Affairs, 1957-59. HM Comptroller, Guernsey, 1960; HM Procureur, 1969. *Address:* Le Petit Mas, Clos des Fosses, St Martin's, Guernsey. *T:* Guernsey 38300. *Clubs:* Old Millhillians, Royal Commonwealth Society; Royal Channel Islands Yacht.

SHANKS, Michael James; Director: BOC International, since 1976; George Bassett (Holdings), since 1977; Royal Ordnance Factories since 1977; Henley Centre for Forecasting, Environmental Resources, since 1977; Chairman, National Consumer Council, since 1977; *b* 12 April 1927; *s* of Alan James Shanks and Margaret Lee; *m* 1st, 1953, Elizabeth Juliet Richardson (*d* 1972); three *s* one *d*; 2nd, 1973, Patricia Jaffé (*née* Aspin). *Educ:* Blundell's Sch.; Balliol Coll., Oxford (MA). Lectr in Econs, Williams Coll., Mass, 1950-51; Labour Corresp., Financial Times, 1954-57; Industrial Editor, Financial Times, 1957-64; Economic Corresp., Sunday Times, 1964-65; Industrial Adviser, DEA, 1965-66; Industrial Policy Coordinator, DEA, 1966-67; Economic Adviser, Leyland Motors, 1967-68; Dir of Marketing Services and Economic Planning, British Leyland Motor Corp., 1968-71; Chief Executive, Finance & Planning, British Oxygen, 1971-72, Dir, Group Strategy, Jan.-June 1973; Dir Gen. for Social Affairs, EEC, 1973-76. Vis. Prof., Brunel Univ., 1973-; Vis. Fellow, Univ. of Lancaster, 1969-. Hon. Treas., Fabian Soc., 1964-65; Member: Cttee of Management, Science Policy Foundn, 1968-73; Adv. Council, Business Graduates Assoc., 1968-73; Editorial Bd, Times Management Library, 1968-73; Exec. Cttee, Warwick Univ. Centre of Industrial and Business Studies, 1968-73; Wilton Park Academic Council, 1967-; Council, Soc. of Business Economists, 1968-73; Electrical Engrg EDC, 1965-73; Employment Appeal Tribunal, 1976-; Council: Soc. for Long-Range Planning, 1971-73; Foundn for Management Educn, 1971-; Centre for Studies in Soc. Policy, 1974; Inst. of Directors, 1976-. FBIM 1972. *Publications:* The Stagnant Society, 1961; (with John Lambert) Britain and the New Europe, 1962; (ed) The Lessons of Public Enterprise, 1963; The Innovators, 1967; The Quest for Growth, 1973; European Social Policy, To-day and To-morrow, 1977; pamphlets, contribs to symposia, learned jls, etc. *Recreations:* reading, gardening, travelling. *Address:* Enderley, Stony Lane, Little Kingshill, Great Missenden, Bucks. *T:* Great Missenden 2504. *Club:* Reform.

SHANKS, S(eymour) Cochrane, CBE 1958; MD, ChB; FRCP; FRCR; Consulting Radiologist to University College Hospital; late Lecturer in Radiology, University College Hospital Medical School (Dean of the Medical School, 1943-49); late Radiologist, Goldie Leigh Hosp.; late Hon. Radiologist: University College, London; Lord Mayor Treloar's Hosp., Alton; Past Adviser in Radiology to the Ministry of Health; Past Warden of Fellowship, Past President, Skinner and Knox lecturer, and Gold Medallist (1973), RCR; Member, Spens Committee on remuneration of Consultants and Specialists, 1947; Examiner in Radiology to Universities of Durham and Liverpool; Examiner in X-ray Diagnosis, 1942, and in Medicine, 1952, RCR; Examiner in Radiology, RCP, 1940-44; Fellow (Past Hon. Treas.) RSM (PP and Hon. Mem., Section of Radiology); Fellow and Lettsomian Lecturer, Medical Society of London; Hon. Fellow, Royal Inst. of Public Health and Hygiene; Hon. Mem.,

British Assoc. of Dermatologists; Senior Vice-President, 6th International Congress of Radiology, 1950; Vice-Pres. Emeritus, 7th International Congress of Radiology, Copenhagen, 1953; Past Pres., Medical Defence Union; Past Chm. Institute of Dermatology, British Post-Graduate Medical Federation; Member: British Institute of Radiology; BMA (Past Chm. Medico-legal Sub-Cttee); Distribution Cttee King Edward's Hosp. Fund, 1949-59; *b* 1893; 5th *s* of late William Shanks, JP, Barrhead, Renfrewshire, and late Catherine Cook McCallum, Leeds; *m* 1st, Edith Margaret Govan (*d* 1955); no *c*; 2nd, 1956, Chrisma Elsie Clara Govan, both *d* of late James Finlayson Govan of Glasgow. *Educ:* Glasgow Academy; Glasgow University (Burns and Asher-Asher Gold Medals); Western Infirmary, Glasgow; St Thomas's Hospital. House-Surgeon, Western Infirmary, Glasgow, 1915; Temp. Capt. RAMC, 1915-18; served with BEF in Egypt and France; late Medical Assessor, Ministry of Pensions; late Visiting Radiologist, Ministry of Pensions Hospital, Orpington; late Hon. Radiologist, St Mark's Hospital; Physician with charge of out-patients, Radiological Department, Charing Cross Hosp.; Radiologist, The Prince of Wales's Gen. Hosp. Hon. Member: Dutch Soc. of Radiology; Toronto Radiological Soc. Bose Gold Medal, Indian Radiological Soc. *Publications:* Jt Ed., Textbook of X-ray Diagnosis by British Authors; papers on Radiology in Med. Jls. *Recreations:* golf, motoring. *Address:* 11 Wimpole Street, W1. *T:* 01-580 1660, 01-580 4356; 11 Heath Rise, SW15. *T:* 01-789 3682. *Club:* Royal Wimbledon.

SHANN, Keith Charles Owen (Mick Shann), CBE 1964; Chairman, Australian Public Service Board, since 1977; *b* 22 Nov. 1917; *s* of late F. Shann, Melbourne; *m* 1944, Betty, *d* of late C. L. Evans; two *s* one *d*. *Educ:* Trinity Grammar Sch., Kew, Vic; Trinity Coll., Melbourne Univ. (BA). Commonwealth Treasury Dept, 1939; Dept of Labour and Nat. Service, 1940; joined Dept of External Affairs: 2nd Sec., UN Div., 1946; 1st Sec., Acting Counsellor i/c UN Div., 1948; Aust. Mission to UN, New York, 1949-52; Head, UN Branch, 1952-55; Head, Americas and Pacific Branch, 1955; Minister, later Ambassador, to the Philippines, 1955-59; External Affairs Officer, London, 1959-62; Ambassador to Indonesia, 1962-66; First Asst Sec., 1966-70, Dep. Sec., 1970-74, Dept of External (later Foreign) Affairs; Ambassador to Japan, 1974-77. Mem. Delegns to UN Gen. Assembly, Paris, 1948, 1951, NY 1949, 1950, 1952, 1953, 1957, 1967; Aust. Observer Bandoeng Conf., 1955; *Rapporteur*, UN Special Cttee on Hungary, 1957; Leader, Aust. Delegn to Develt Assistance Cttee of OECD, 1966-67, 1968-69. *Recreations:* golf, gardening, music. *Address:* 11 Grey Street, Deakin, Canberra 2600, Australia. *Clubs:* Commonwealth (Canberra); Melbourne Cricket, Royal Canberra Golf.

SHANNON, 9th Earl of, *cr* 1756; **Richard Bentinck Boyle;** Viscount Boyle, Baron of Castle-Martyr, 1756; Baron Carleton (GB), 1786; late Captain Irish Guards; Director, Committee of Directors of Research Associations; Director of companies; *b* 23 Oct. 1924; *o s* of 8th Earl of Shannon; S father, 1963; *m* 1st, 1947, Catherine Irene Helen (marr. diss., 1955; she *m* 1955, Greville P. Baylis), *d* of the Marquis Demetrio Imperiali di Francavilla; 2nd, 1957, Susan Margaret, *d* of late J. P. R. Hogg; one *s* two *d*. *Educ:* Eton College. Pres., Architectural Metalwork Assoc., 1966-74. Sec. and Treas., Fedn of European Industrial Co-op. Res. Orgns. *Heir: s* Viscount Boyle, *qv*. *Address:* Old Loose Court, Loose, Maidstone, Kent. *T:* Maidstone 43139. *Club:* White's.

SHANNON, Alastair; journalist; Foreign News department, Daily Telegraph and Morning Post, 1937-71; *b* Hawick, 1894; *o s* of late Rev. J. W. Shannon and Agnes, *d* of Rev. Alexander Renton; *m* 1920, Betty, *d* of Rev. A. Russell; one *s* one *d*. *Educ:* George Watson's College and University, Edinburgh. Served Flanders, 1915; Commission, Nov. 1915; Mesopotamia Relieving Force; Prisoner of War in Turkey, Apr. 1916 to Nov. 1918; joined Staff of Morning Post, 1919; Editor Madras Mail, 1921-23; rejoined Morning Post, 1924; Foreign Editor, Morning Post, 1928-37. *Publications:* Morning Knowledge, 1920; The Black Scorpion, 1926. *Address:* 1 Highpoint, Lyonsdown Road, New Barnet, Herts. *T:* 01-440 3593.

SHANNON, Godfrey Eccleston Boyd, CMG 1951; Assistant Under-Secretary of State, in the Commonwealth Office, 1956-68, retired 1968; *b* 14 Dec. 1907; *s* of late W. B. Shannon. *Educ:* Wellington; St John's College, Cambridge. Appointed to Dominions Office, 1930; visited Australia and New Zealand, as Private Sec., with 10th Duke of Devonshire, 1936; Official Sec., UK High Commissioner's Office, New Zealand, 1939-41; served on UK Delegation to various international conferences in London, Geneva, New York, Chicago and Moscow, 1944-48, to UNCTAD, 1964, and to Commonwealth Finance Ministers' meetings, Jamaica, Montreal and Trinidad, 1965-67; Deputy

United Kingdom High Commissioner in Canada, 1948-50, in Calcutta, 1952-56. Member, Cttee for Exports: to Canada, 1964-68; to Australia, 1965-68. Renter Warden, Dyers' Co., 1967-68, Prime Warden, 1968-69. *Address:* 25 Paultons Square, SW3 5AP. *T:* 01-351 1585. *Clubs:* Travellers'; Bengal (Calcutta).

SHAPCOTT, Sidney Edward, CEng, FIEE, FInstP; Director-General, Air Electronics Systems, Ministry of Defence, since 1976; *b* 20 June 1920; *s* of late Percy Thomas and Beatrice Shapcott; *m* 1943, Betty Jean Richens; two *s* one *d*. *Educ:* Hele's School, Exeter; King's College, London. BSc. Joined Air Defence Experimental Establishment, 1941; various appointments in Min. of Supply and Min. of Aviation, 1941-62; DCSO, 1963; Dir of Projects, ESRO, 1963-65; Min. of Defence, Navy Dept, 1965-75; CSO, 1968; Dep. Dir, Admiralty Surface Weapons Establishment, 1968-72; Dir, Underwater Weapon Projects, Admiralty Underwater Weapons Establishment, Portland, 1972-75. *Recreations:* travel, cinephotography. *Address:* 26 Southcote Way, Tylers Green, High Wycombe, Bucks. *T:* High Wycombe 813401.

SHAPLAND, Cyril Dee, MB, BS London, MRCP, FRCS; Ophthalmic Surgeon, 1931-67, retired; Hon. Cons. Ophthalmic Surgeon: University College Hospital, London, since 1965; Moorfields Eye Hospital, since 1964; Royal Marsden Hospital, since 1959; Teacher in Ophthalmology, University of London (UCH Medical School and Institute of Ophthalmology); *b* 22 Nov. 1899; *s* of John Dee Shapland, MD, Exmouth, Devon, and Gertrude Emma Bond, Axminster, Devon; *m* 1st, 1927, Elizabeth Stratton (*d* 1971); 2nd, 1972, Gertrude Nelson Gellatly. *Educ:* Univ. Coll.; Univ. Coll. Hospital, London. House Phys. and House Surg., UCH, 1922-23; Res. Phys., Ruthin Castle, N Wales, 1924-26; Jun. and Clin. Asst Moorfields Eye Hosp., 1927-29; 3rd, 2nd and 1st House Surg., and Sen. Res. Officer, Moorfields Eye Hosp., 1929-31; Registrar and Chief Clin. Asst, Moorfields, 1931-36; Opth. Surg. Middlesex CC, 1931-42; Ophth. Surg. to Willesden Gen. Hosp., 1932-37; Pathologist and Curator, Moorfields Eye Hosp., 1936-39, Ophth. Surg. 1938-64; Senior Ophth. Surg., UCH, 1933-65; Ophth. Surg., Royal Marsden Hosp., 1932-59; Cons. Ophth. Surg., Queen Mary's Hosp., Roehampton, 1946-61. FRSocMed; Hon. Sec., Section of Ophthalmology, RSM, 1938-42, Vice-Pres. 1952-55; Hon. Sec., Sect. of Ophthalmology, BMA, Oxford, 1936, Vice-Pres. BMA, Glasgow, 1954. War Service: part-time Ophth. Surg., EMS, 1939-42; RAMC Ophth. Specialist, Royal Victoria Hospital, Netley, 1942-44; Comd Ophthalmologist, Southern Command, Jan.-Nov. 1944; Comd Ophth., London Dist, and Ophthalmic Specialist, Millbank, 1944-46; Adviser in Ophthalmology, United Kingdom, 1945-46 (rank of Lieutenant-Colonel). Pres. UCH Old Students' Assoc., 1967-68. Liveryman of Worshipful Society of Apothecaries of London, and Freeman of City of London; Mem. Council, Ophthalmological Soc. of UK, 1945-48, Vice-Pres. 1965-68. Mem., Irish Ophth. Soc.; Membre Titulaire, Soc. Franç. d'Ophthalmologie; Hon. Member Instituto Barraquer, Barcelona, Spain; Membre d'Honneur, Club Jules Gonin, Lausanne, 1966. *Publications:* contrib. to Modern Trends in Ophthalmology, 3rd Series (ed A. Sorsby), 1955, to Operative Surgery, Vol. 8 (ed Rob and Smith), 1957, to Surgical Progress, 1960; and to The Operations of Surgery, vol. 2 (ed A. Gardham and D. R. Davies), 1969; various in British Medical Jl, Lancet, Brit. Jl Ophth., Trans. Ophth. Soc., Proc. Roy. Soc. Med., Jl of RAMC, Medical World, Medical Press, etc, since 1923. *Recreations:* fishing, photography, contract bridge. *Address:* (home) Cornerways, Orley Farm Road, Harrow-on-the-Hill, Mddx. *T:* 01-422 2450. *Clubs:* Flyfishers'; Harrow Fifty (Harrow-on-the-Hill).

SHAPLAND, Maj.-Gen. Peter Charles, CB 1977; MBE 1960; MA; Director, Volunteers Territorials and Cadets, Ministry of Defence (Army), 1974-77; *b* 14 July 1923; *s* of late F. C. Shapland, Merton Park, Surrey; *m* 1954, Joyce Barbara Shapland (*née* Peradon); two *s*. *Educ:* Rutlish Sch., Merton Park; St Catharine's Coll., Cambridge. Served War: commissioned Royal Engineers, 1944; QVO Madras Sappers and Miners, Indian Army, 1944-47. Served United Kingdom, Middle East (Canal Zone) and Cyprus, 1948-63. Attended Staff Coll., 1952; jssc, 1960. Lt-Col, 1965; comd in Aden, 1965-67; Brig., Dec. 1968; comd 30 Engineer Bde. Attended Royal Coll. of Defence Studies, 1971. Dep. Comdr and Chief of Staff, HQ SE Dist, 1972-74; Maj.-Gen. 1974. *Publications:* contribs to Royal Engineers' Jl. *Recreations:* sailing, swimming, golf. *Address:* Timbers, 7 Rosedene Gardens, Fleet, Hants. *T:* Fleet 20230. *Clubs:* Royal Ocean Racing, Lansdowne; Royal Channel Islands Yacht (Jersey), Royal Engineer Yacht (Chatham).

SHAPLAND, William Arthur; Chairman and Chief Executive, Blackwood Hodge Ltd, since 1964 (non-executive Director, 1946-55, Executive Director, 1955-64); Director, Bernard

Sunley Investment Trust Ltd, since 1948 (Deputy Chairman and Chief Executive, 1964-77); Trustee, Bernard Sunley Charitable Foundation; *b* 20 Oct. 1912; *s* of late Arthur Frederick Shapland and of Alice Maud (*née* Jackson); *m* 1943, Madeline Annie (*née* Amiss); two *d. Educ:* Tollington Sch., Muswell Hill. Incorporated Accountant, 1936; Chartered Accountant, 1946. Allan Charlesworth & Co, Chartered Accountants, London, Cambridge and Rangoon: Clerk, 1929-36; Manager, 1936-46; Partner, 1946-55. *Recreations:* golf, gardening, travel. *Address:* (home) 44 Beech Drive, N2 9NY. *T:* 01-883 5073; (office) 25 Berkeley Square, W1A 4AX. *T:* 01-629 9090.

SHARMA, Vishnu Datt; General Secretary, Joint Council for the Welfare of Immigrants, since 1975; *b* 19 Oct. 1921; *s* of Pandit Girdhari Lal Kaushik and Shrimati Ganga Devi; *m* 1960, Krishna Sharma; one *d. Educ:* High Sch. in India. Came to UK from India, 1957; worked in factories until 1967; apptd Mem. Nat. Cttee for Commonwealth Immigrants (by the Prime Minister, Rt Hon. Harold Wilson); twice elected Gen. Sec. of Indian Workers' Assoc., Southall, 1961-63 and 1965-67, Pres., 1977 and 1978; Nat. Organiser, Campaign Against Racial Discrimination (later Vice-Chm.), 1966-67; Exec. Sec., Jt Council for the Welfare of Immigrants, 1970-75. *Recreations:* cinema, watching television, sight-seeing, etc. *Address:* 43 Lady Margaret Road, Southall, Mddx UB1 2TJ. *T:* 01-571 4243.

SHARMAN, Peter William; Director since 1974 and Chief General Manager since 1975, Norwich Union Insurance Group; *b* 1 June 1924; *s* of William Charles Sharman and Olive Mabel (*née* Burl); *m* 1946, Eileen Barbara Crix; one *s* two *d. Educ:* Northgate Grammar Sch., Ipswich; Edinburgh Univ. MA 1950; FIA 1956. War service as Pilot, RAF. Joined Norwich Union Insce Gp, 1950; Gen. Man. and Actuary, 1969. Chm., Life Offices' Assoc., 1977. *Recreations:* tennis, squash, badminton, golf. *Address:* 21 Eaton Road, Norwich NR4 6PR. *T:* Norwich 51230.

SHARMAN, Thomas Charles, OBE 1960; HM Diplomatic Service, retired; *b* 12 April 1912; *s* of Thomas Sharman and Mary Ward; *m* 1935, Paulete Elisabeth Padioleau; one *d. Educ:* Long Eaton County Secondary Sch.; Clare Coll., Cambridge. HM Consular Service, 1934; Paris, 1935; Saigon, 1937; Milan, 1939; British Embassy, Lisbon, 1940, and Moscow, 1945; HM Foreign Service, 1945; Batavia, 1946; Sao Paulo, 1947; Superintending Trade Consul, New Orleans, 1949; HM Consul, Luanda, 1952, Consul (Commercial) Hamburg, 1953; Counsellor (Commercial) Lisbon, 1960; Consul-General, Atlanta, Georgia, USA, 1965-68; Consul-General, Oporto, 1968-70. *Recreations:* fell- and particularly ben-walking; foreign languages. *Address:* 103 Résidence Jeanne Hachette, 60000 Beauvais, France. *Club:* Royal Automobile.

SHARP, family name of **Baroness Sharp.**

SHARP, Baroness (Life Peer) *cr* 1966, of Hornsey; **Evelyn (Adelaide) Sharp,** GBE 1961 (DBE 1948); President, London and Quadrant Housing Trust, since 1977 (Chairman, 1973-77); *b* 25 May 1903; *d* of Reverend Charles James Sharp, Vicar of Ealing, Middlesex, to 1935. *Educ:* St Paul's Girls' School; Somerville College, Oxford. Entered Administrative Class of Home Civil Service, 1926. Perm. Sec., Min. of Housing and Local Govt, 1955-66. Mem., Independent Broadcasting Authority (formerly ITA), 1966-73. Hon. DCL Oxon, 1960; Hon. LLD: Cardiff, 1962; Manchester, 1967; Sussex, 1969. *Recreation:* pottering. *Address:* The Small House, Dinton, Salisbury, Wilts. *T:* Teffont 209. *Club:* University Women's.

SHARP, Alastair George, MBE 1945; QC 1961; DL; **His Honour Judge Sharp;** a Circuit Judge (formerly Judge of County Courts), since 1962; Chairman, Washington New Town Licensed Premises Committee, 1966; *b* 25 May 1911; *s* of late Alexander Sharp, Advocate in Aberdeen, and of late Mrs Isabella Sharp, OBE; *m* 1940, Daphne Sybil, *d* of late Maj. Harold Smithers, RGA, and late Mrs Connor; one *s* two *d. Educ:* Aberdeen Grammar School; Fettes; Clare College, Cambridge (Archdeacon Johnson Exhibitioner in Classics). BA 1933, 1st Class Hons Classical Tripos Part II, Aegrotat Part I. Boxed Cambridge Univ., 1931-32; Cambridge Union Debating Team in America, 1933. On staff of Bonar Law College, Ashridge, 1934-35; Barrister, Middle Temple, 1935; Harmsworth Law Scholar; North Eastern Circuit, 1936. Dep. Chm. of Agricultural Land Tribunal, Northern Area, 1958-62; Recorder of Rotherham, 1960-62; Dep. Chm., 1965-70, Chm., 1970-71, Durham QS. Commissioned, The Gordon Highlanders, Feb. 1939; served War of 1939-45: Staff Coll., 1943; 2nd Bn The London Scottish, 1943, Temp. Major. DL Co. Durham, 1973. *Recreations:* golf, gardening, music, Scottish dancing, fishing, shooting. *Address:* 49 South Street, Durham.

T: Durham 3706; 5 King's Bench Walk, Temple, EC4; The Old Kennels, Tomintoul, Banffshire. *Clubs:* Durham County; Bar Yacht, Brancepeth Castle Golf.
See also Baron Mackie of Benshie, *R. L. Sharp*.

SHARP, Derek Joseph; Controller, Africa and Middle East Division, British Council, since 1977; *b* 12 June 1925; *s* of Joseph Frank Sharp and Sylvia May (*née* Allen); *m* 1957, Hilda Francesca Cernigoj; two *s. Educ:* Preston Grammar School; Queen's Coll., Oxford; MA, DipEd. Lectr, British Inst., Milan, 1956-58; British Council, 1958; served Indonesia, Bristol, Bangkok, Addis Ababa, and London, 1958-71; IUC, 1971-72; Head of Planning Unit, 1972; Asst Controller, Home Div., 1972-73; Dir, Far East Dept, 1973; Dep. Controller, Asia, America and Pacific Div., 1974-75; Cultural Attaché, British Embassy, Pretoria, 1975-77. *Recreations:* history of architecture, music, tennis, visiting Italy. *Address:* 14 Grove Park Road, SE9 4QA. *T:* 01-857 1272.

SHARP, Sir Edward Herbert, 3rd Bt *cr* 1922; *b* 3 Dec. 1927; *s* of Sir Herbert Edward Sharp, 2nd Bt, and Ray Alice Mary, *d* of Frederick George Bloomfield, Ealing; *S* father 1936; *m* 1949, Beryl Kathleen, *d* of L. Simmons-Green, Shirley, Warwicks; two *s* one *d. Educ:* Haileybury. **Heir:** *s* Adrian Sharp, *b* 17 Sept. 1951. *Address:* PO Box 749, Manzini, Swaziland.

SHARP, Sir George, Kt 1976; OBE 1969; JP; Convener, Fife Regional Council, since 1974; commercial manager, since 1969; *b* 8 April 1919; *s* of Angus Sharp and Mary S. McNee; *m* 1948, Elsie May Rodger, *o d* of David Porter Rodger and Williamina S. Young; one *s. Educ:* Thornton Public Sch.; Buckhaven High Sch. Engine driver, 1962; PRO, 1962-69. Fife County Council: Mem., 1945-75; Chm., Water and Drainage Cttee, 1955-61; Chm., Finance Cttee, 1961-72; Convener, 1972-75. President: Assoc. of County Councils, 1972-75; Convention of Scottish Local Authorities, 1975-. Chairman: Kirkcaldy Dist Council, 1958-75; Fife and Kinross Water Bd, 1967-75; Forth River Purification Bd, 1955-67 and 1975-; Scottish River Purification Adv. Cttee, 1967-75. Vice-Chairman: Glenrothes Develt Corp., 1973-; Forth Road Bridge Cttee, 1972-. Member: Scottish Water Adv. Cttee, 1962-69; Cttee of Enquiry into Salmon and Trout Fishing, 1963; Scottish Valuation Adv. Cttee, 1972; Cttee of Enquiry into Local Govt Finance, 1974-76; Scottish Develt Agency, 1975-. Dir, Grampian Television, 1975-. JP Fife, 1975. *Recreation:* golf. *Address:* Strathlea, 56 Station Road, Thornton, Fife. *T:* Thornton 347.

SHARP, Lt-Col Granville Maynard, MA (Cantab); *b* 5 Jan. 1906; *s* of Walter Sharp, Cleckheaton, Yorks; *m* 1935, Margaret, *d* of Dr J. H. Vincent, Wembley Hill; two *d. Educ:* Cleckheaton Grammar School; Ashville College, Harrogate; St John's College, Cambridge, MA (Hons) (Economics). Lecturer in Economics at West Riding Technical Institutes, 1929-34; Chairman, Spenborough Housing and Town Planning Committee, 1935-40; Hon. Secretary, Spen Valley Divisional Labour Party, 1938-42; Battery Capt. 68 Anti-Tank Regt RA, 1939-42; Staff Capt. and DAQMG Belfast Area, 1942-43; Senior British Staff Officer, Economics Section, Allied Control Commission, Italy, 1943-44; Chief Economics and Supply Officer, Military Govt, Austria, 1944-45. MP (Lab) for Spen Valley Div. of West Riding of Yorks, 1945-50; PPS Min. of Civil Aviation, 1946; Chairman, Select Cttee of Estimates Sub-Cttee, 1946-48; Parliamentary Private Sec. to Minister of Works, 1947-50. Keymer Parish Councillor; CC E Sussex, 1970-74; CC W Sussex (Chm., Rts of Way Cttee); Mem., Mid-Sussex DC. *Recreations:* swimming, singing, scything, Sussex Downs. *Address:* 31 Wilmington Close, Hassocks, West Sussex. *T:* Hassocks 2294.

SHARP, Henry Sutcliffe, FRCS; Honorary Consulting Surgeon, Ear, Nose and Throat Department: Hospital for Sick Children, Great Ormond Street; Charing Cross Hospital; Putney Hospital; *b* 23 June 1910; *s* of late Alexander Sharp, CB, CMG; *m* 1st, 1948, Muiriel Oliver; two *s*; 2nd, 1964, Elizabeth Plant; one *s. Educ:* Haileybury College; Caius Coll., Cambridge; St Thomas's Hosp. BA, MB, ChB (Cantab); FRCS 1939. House Surgeon and Chief Asst, Ear, Nose and Throat Dept, St Thomas's Hosp., 1935. Major RAMC, 1940-45. FRSocMed; Member and past Hon. Sec. of Sections of Laryngology and Otology; Corresp. Mem., Excerpta Medica, Amsterdam. *Publications:* various articles concerning otolaryngology in Jl of Laryngology, Lancet, and Brit. Jl of Surgery. *Recreations:* golf, squash rackets. *Address:* 82 Wildwood Road, NW11. *T:* 01-458 3937.

SHARP, Dr John; Headmaster of Rossall School, since 1973; *b* 18 Dec. 1927; *o s* of late Alfred and May Sharp, North Ives, Oxenhope, Keighley; *m* 1950, Jean Prosser; one *s* two *d. Educ:* Boys' Grammar Sch., Keighley; Brasenose Coll., Oxford. BSc,

MA, DPhil Oxon. RAF Educn Br., 1950-52; research at Oxford, 1952-54; Asst Master, Marlborough Coll., 1954-62; Senior Chemistry Master, 1956-62; Senior Science Master, 1959-62; Headmaster, Christ Coll., Brecon, 1962-72. Co-opted Mem., Oxford and Cambridge Schools Examn Bd, 1966-74; Selected Mem., Breconshire Educn Cttee, 1966-72; Co-opted Mem., Lancs Educn Cttee, 1974-; Divisional Chm., HMC, SW 1971 and NW 1977. *Publications:* contrib. Anal. Chim. Acta. *Recreations:* fishing, photography, roses and shrubs. *Address:* The Hall, Rossall School, Fleetwood, Lancs FY7 8JW. *T:* Fleetwood 3849. *Club:* East India, Devonshire, Sports and Public Schools.

SHARP, J(ohn) M(ichael) Cartwright; Secretary of Law Commission, since 1968; *b* 11 Aug. 1918; *s* of W. H. Cartwright Sharp, KC, and Dorothy (*née* Shelton). *Educ:* Rossall Sch.; Lincoln Coll., Oxford. Royal Artillery, 1940-46. Called to Bar, Middle Temple, 1947. Lord Chancellor's Office, 1951-65; Legal Sec. to Law Officers, 1965; Asst Solicitor, Law Commn, 1966. *Recreations:* travel, reading. *Address:* 15 Bolton Gardens, SW5. *T:* 01-370 1896. *Clubs:* Beefsteak, Garrick, Reform.

SHARP, Kenneth Johnston, TD 1960; Head of the Government Accountancy Service and Accountancy Adviser to the Department of Industry, since 1975; *b* 29 Dec. 1926; *s* of Johnston Sharp and late Ann Sharp (*née* Routledge); *m* 1955, Barbara Maud Keating; one *s. Educ:* Rickerby House Sch., Carlisle; Shrewsbury Sch.; St John's Coll., Cambridge (MA). ACA 1955, FCA 1960. Partner, Armstrong, Watson & Co., Chartered Accountants, 1955-75. Indian Army, 1945-48; TA, 251st (Westmorland and Cumberland Yeo.) Field Regt RA, 1948-62; comd R Battery, 1956-59; 2nd-in-Comd, 1959-62. Inst. of Chartered Accountants: Mem. Council, 1966-; Vice-Pres., 1972-73; Dep. Pres., 1973-74; Pres., 1974-75. JP Carlisle, 1957-73. *Publications:* The Family Business and the Companies Act 1967, 1967; articles in professional accountancy press. *Recreations:* sailing, canal cruising, gardening. *Address:* Hopefield, Somerton, Somerset TA11 7NG. *T:* Somerton 72104. *Clubs:* United Oxford & Cambridge University, Royal Automobile.

SHARP, Brig. Mainwaring Cato Ensor, CBE 1945; *b* 1 March 1897; *s* of late Rev. Cato Ensor Sharp; *m* 1949, Betty Yolande Constance, *o d* of late Col M. H. Knaggs, CMG. *Educ:* Trinity College School, Port Hope; RMC, Kingston, Canada. Commissioned, 1915, 5th RI Lancers; transfd Leinster Regt 1916; S Lanc. Regt 1922. Staff College, Camberley, 1928-29; retired, 1935; Insurance Broker, 1937-39; rejoined, 1939; Lt-Col 1941; Brig. 1944. Served European War and War of 1939-45 (despatches twice). Director of Maintenance, Control Commission, Germany, 1946-51; employed by War Office, 1951-58. Croix de Guerre (France); Officer, Legion of Merit (USA). *Recreations:* golf, ornithology. *Address:* The Old Malt House, Walberton, Arundel, West Sussex. *T:* Yapton 551274.

SHARP, Margery; novelist and playwright; *m* 1938, Major G. L. Castle, RA. *Educ:* Streatham Hill High School; London University. French Honours BA. *Publications:* Rhododendron Pie; Fanfare for Tin Trumpets; The Flowering Thorn; Four Gardens; The Nymph and the Nobleman; Sophy Cassmajor; Meeting at Night (play); The Nutmeg Tree, 1937 (play: USA 1940, England 1941, filmed as Julia Misbehaves, 1948); The Stone of Chastity, 1940; Cluny Brown, 1944 (filmed 1946); Britannia Mews, 1946 (filmed 1949); The Foolish Gentlewoman, 1948 (Play, London, 1949); Lise Lillywhite, 1951; The Gipsy in the Parlour, 1953; The Tigress on the Hearth, 1955; The Eye of Love, 1957; The Rescuers, 1959; Something Light, 1960; Martha in Paris, 1962; Martha, Eric and George, 1964; The Sun in Scorpio, 1965; In Pious Memory, 1968; Rosa, 1969; The Innocents, 1971; The Faithful Servants, 1975; *books for children:* Miss Bianca, 1962; The Turret, 1964 (USA 1963); Miss Bianca in the Salt Mines, 1966; Lost at the Fair, 1967; Miss Bianca in the Orient, 1970; Miss Bianca in the Antarctic, 1971; Miss Bianca and the Bridesmaid, 1972; The Magical Cockatoo, 1974; The Children Next Door, 1974; Bernard the Brave, 1976; Summer Visits, 1977; *short stories:* The Lost Chapel Picnic, 1973. *Address:* c/o William Heinemann Ltd, 15-16 Queen Street, W1X 8BE.

SHARP, Michael Cartwright; *see* Sharp, J. M. C.

SHARP, Sir Milton Reginald, 3rd Bt, *cr* 1920; Capt. REME, TA; *b* 21 Nov. 1909; *s* of Sir Milton Sharp, 2nd Bt, and Gertrude (*d* 1940), *d* of John Earl, of London; *S* father, 1941; *m* 1951, Marie-Louise de Vignon, Paris. *Educ:* Shrewsbury; Trinity Hall, Cambridge.

SHARP, Hon. Mitchell William, PC (Can.); MP for Eglinton; Government Leader in the House of Commons, Canada, 1974-76; *b* 11 May 1911; *s* of Thomas Sharp and Elizabeth (*née* Little); *m* 1938, Daisy Boyd (decd); one *s*; *m* 1976, Jeannette Dugal. *Educ:* University of Manitoba; London School of Economics. Statistician, Sanford Evans Statistical Service, 1926-36; Economist, James Richardson & Sons Ltd, 1937-42; Officer, Canadian Dept of Finance, Ottawa, 1942-51; Director Economic Policy Division, 1947-51; Associate Deputy Minister, Canadian Dept Trade and Commerce, 1951-57; Dep. Minister, 1957-58; Minister, 1963-65; elected to Canadian House of Commons, 1963; Minister of Finance, 1965-68; Sec. of State for External Affairs, 1968-74; Pres., Privy Council, 1974-76. Vice-Pres., Brazilian Traction, Light & Power Co., Toronto, 1958-62. Hon. LLD: Univ. of Manitoba, 1965; Univ. of Western Ontario, 1977; Hon. DrSocSci Ottawa, 1970. *Recreations:* music, walking, skating. *Address:* Parliament Buildings, Ottawa, Ont, Canada. *T:* 992-1518.

SHARP, Noel Farquharson; Keeper, Department of Printed Books, British Museum, 1959-66; *b* 22 Dec. 1905; *o s* of Robert Farquharson Sharp, sometime Keeper, Department of Printed Books, British Museum; *m* 1945, Rosemarie Helen, *d* of Commander E. F. Fanning, RN; one *s* one *d. Educ:* Haileybury College; New College, Oxford. Assistant Keeper, Department of Printed Books, British Museum, 1929-52; Deputy Keeper also Superintendent of Reading Room, British Museum, 1952-59. Hon. FLA, 1968. *Address:* 1 Tudor Cottages, Hall Street, Long Melford, Suffolk CO10 9HZ. *Club:* Travellers'.

SHARP, Rear-Adm. Philip Graham, CB 1967; DSC 1942; Secretary General, The National Society for Clean Air; President: Reserve Forces Association; International Confederation of Reserve Officers; *b* 23 Nov. 1913; *e s* of late Rev. Douglas Simmonds Sharp; *m* 1940, Dilys Mary Adwyth, *er d* of late David Roberts, Welford-on-Avon, Warwicks; one *s. Educ:* Northampton Sch.; Tynemouth High Sch. Sub-Lt, RNVR, 1937; War Service in destroyers; Capt. 1956; comdg HMS Defender, 1956-58; NATO, 1958-60; Capt. of Fleet, Home Fleet, 1960-62; comdg HMS Centaur 1962-63; Cdre RN Barracks, Portsmouth, 1963-65; Rear-Adm. 1965; Flag Officer Sea Training, Portland, 1965-67; retired 1967. ADC to the Queen, 1965. *Recreations:* golf, fishing, music, model-making. *Address:* Dolphin House, Old Shoreham Road, Hove, East Sussex. *T:* Brighton 736545. *Club:* Naval and Military.

SHARP, Ven. Richard Lloyd; Archdeacon of Dorset since 1975; *b* 30 Nov. 1916; *s* of Tom and Anne Lloyd Sharp; *m* 1942, Joan Elizabeth Rhodes; two *s. Educ:* Brighton and Hove Grammar Sch.; St Edmund Hall, Oxford (MA). Curate, Holy Trinity, Weymouth, 1940-44; Vicar: St John, Portland, 1944-49; Wootton Bassett, 1949-55; St Mark, Salisbury, 1955-64; Holy Trinity, Weymouth, 1964-74; Canon of Salisbury Cathedral, 1968-. *Recreations:* local history, photography. *Address:* Archdeacon's House, Horton, Wimborne, Dorset BH21 7JA. *T:* Witchampton 422.

SHARP, Richard Lyall, CB 1977; Ceremonial Officer, Civil Service Department, since 1977; *b* 27 March 1915; *s* of late Alexander Sharp, Advocate, Aberdeen, and late Mrs Isabella Sharp, OBE; *m* 1950, Jean Helen, *er d* of late Sir James Crombie, KCB, KBE, CMG, and of Lady Crombie; two *s* two *d* (and one *d* decd). *Educ:* Fettes Coll.; Aberdeen Univ.; Clare Coll., Cambridge. MA with 1st Class Hons Classics, Aberdeen 1937; BA with 1st Class in Classical Tripos, Cambridge 1939. Served Royal Northumberland Fusiliers, 1939-46 (POW, Singapore and Siam, 1942-45). Principal, HM Treasury, 1946; Private Sec. to Chancellor of Exchequer, 1948-50 and to Minister of State for Economic Affairs, 1950; UK Treasury and Supply Delegn, Washington, 1952-56; Asst Sec., 1954; IDC, 1961; Under-Secretary: Nat. Bd for Prices and Incomes, 1966-68; HM Treasury, 1968-77. *Recreations:* playing the viola, gardening. *Address:* 15 Richmond Road, New Barnet, Herts. *T:* 01-449 6552. *Club:* Athenæum.
See also Baron Mackie of Benshie, A. G. Sharp.

SHARP, Robert Charles, CMG 1971; Director of Public Works, Tasmania, 1949-71; *b* 20 Sept. 1907; *s* of Robert George Sharp and Gertrude Coral (*née* Bellette); *m* 1935, Margaret Fairbrass Andrewartha; one *d. Educ:* Univ. of Tasmania. BE 1929. Bridge Engr, Public Works, 1935. Enlisted RAE (Major): comd 2/4 Aust. Field Sqdn RAE, 1942; 1 Aust. Port Mtce Co. RAE, 1943; HQ Docks Ops Gp, 1944. Chief Engr, Public Works, 1946; State Co-ordinator of Works, 1949-71. *Recreation:* golf. *Address:* 594 Sandy Bay Road, Hobart, Tasmania 7005, Australia. *T:* Hobart 25-1072. *Clubs:* Athenæum, Kingston Beach Golf, Royal Automobile of Tasmania (Hobart).

SHARP, Thomas, CBE 1951; MA, DLitt; FRIBA, FRTPI, PPILA; town and country planning consultant, architect, landscape architect, writer; *b* 12 April 1901; *s* of Francis Sharp and Margaret Beresford; *m* Rachel, *d* of Cameron Morrison. *Educ:* Council Schools. Worked in local govt offices, 1917-37; Lecturer then Reader, in Town and Country Planning, Univ. of Durham, 1937-45; Senior Research Officer, Ministry of Town and Country Planning, 1941-43; since 1945 in private practice; designer of plans for Durham, Exeter, Oxford, Salisbury, Chichester, King's Lynn, Taunton, St Andrews, Kensington, Todmorden, Minehead, Stockport, Rugby and other towns, new villages in Northumberland for Forestry Commission, new seaside village, Port-Eynon, S Wales; re-landscaping of St John's Backs, Cambridge; planning adviser, Vienna, 1955; Mellon Vis. Prof. Univ. of Illinois, 1965. President of Town Planning Institute, 1945-46; President of Institute of Landscape Architects, 1949-51; Mem. Council RIBA, 1958-60. Hon. Member: Austrian Inst. Planning, 1955; Mexican Soc. Architects, 1961; Hon. Fellow, Ancient Monuments Soc., 1969. *Publications:* Future Development of South-West Lancashire, 1930; Town and Countryside, 1932; A Derelict Area, 1935; English Panorama, 1937; Town Planning, 1940; Cathedral City, 1945; Anatomy of the Village, 1946; Exeter Phoenix, 1946; Oxford Replanned, 1948; Georgian City, 1949; Newer Sarum, 1949; Oxford Observed, 1952; Design in Town and Village (jointly), 1953; Northumberland, 1954; Dreaming Spires and Teeming Towers, 1963; Town and Townscape, 1968. *Address:* 1 Farndon Road, Oxford.

SHARP, Thomas; Department of Trade, since 1976; *b* 19 June 1931; *s* of William Douglas Sharp and Margaret Sharp (*née* Tout); *m* 1962, Margaret Lucy Hailstone; two *d*. *Educ:* Brown Sch., Toronto; Abbotsholme Sch., Derbs; Jesus Coll., Oxford. BoT and DTI (with short interval HM Treasury), 1954-73; Counsellor (Commercial), British Embassy, Washington, 1973-76. *Address:* 41 Hall Drive, SE26 6XL. *T:* 01-778 8776.

SHARP, William Johnstone; Controller, PSA Supplies, Department of the Environment, since 1976; *b* 30 May 1926; *s* of Frederick Matthew and Gladys Evelyn Sharp; *m* 1952, Joan Alice Clark, MBE, *d* of Arnold and Violet Clark. *Educ:* Queen Elizabeth Grammar Sch., Hexham; Emmanuel Coll., Cambridge (MA). Army Service, Reconnaissance Corps, Durham LI and Staff, 1944-48. Entered Min. of Transport, 1949; Private Sec. to Perm. Sec., 1951-53; Principal, Min. of Civil Aviation, 1953; Asst Sec., Min. of Transport, 1962; Under-Sec., DoE, 1970-76. *Recreations:* music, the Turf. *Address:* 23a Lee Terrace, Blackheath, SE3. *T:* 01-852 3222; Lintley View House, Slaggyford, Northumberland. *T:* Alston 352.

SHARPE, Brian Sidney; Executive Director, City Communications Centre; *b* 12 Feb. 1927; *s* of S. H. Sharpe and Norah Sharpe; *m* 1967, Susan Lillywhite; two *s*. *Educ:* Haberdashers' Aske's Sch., Hampstead; Guildhall Sch. of Music and Drama. Royal Fusiliers (att. Forces Broadcasting Service), 1945-48; BBC: Announcer, Midland Region, 1955; Television Presentation, 1956; Producer, African Service, External Services, 1957; Senior Producer: Overseas Talks and Features, 1965; The Financial World Tonight, Radio 4, 1974. *Publications:* How Money Works (with A. Wilson), 1975; several articles on corporate and other forms of communication. *Recreations:* offshore fishing, music. *Address:* 36 South Hill, Godalming, Surrey GU7 1JT. *T:* Godalming 21551.

SHARPE, Frank Victor, CMG 1972; OBE (mil.) 1943; ED 1942; Helicopter Consultant to Bell Helicopter Australia Pty Ltd, Brisbane International Airport; Avocado consultant and farm adviser since 1946; Director of several companies; *b* 21 Jan. 1903; *s* of Frederick Robert Sharpe, Avening, Glos, and Elizabeth Matilda Glassop, Sydney (third generation); *m* 1947, Millicent Adelaide Gardner; one *s* one *d*. *Educ:* Rudd's Clayfield Coll.; Queensland Univ. Became dir, family merchant tool business, 1923 (Chm. and Man. Dir and sole proprietor, 1946-). Commissioned Aust. Army, 1921 (Militia); served War of 1939-45, AIF, Australia and SW Pacific; Lt-Col, retd 1955. FAIM; Fellow, Australian Inst. Dirs. JP Brisbane 1947. *Recreations:* flying, farming, amateur radio. *Address:* 138 Adelaide Street, Clayfield, Brisbane, Qld 4011, Australia. *T:* 262.4842. *Clubs:* Athenæum (Melbourne); Queensland, Brisbane, United Service, Royal Queensland Yacht Squadron, Royal Queensland Aero, Queensland Turf, Tattersalls (Brisbane).

SHARPE, Hon. Sir Jack; see Sharpe, Hon. Sir John H.

SHARPE, Hon. Sir John Henry, (Hon. Sir Jack Sharpe), Kt 1977; CBE 1972; MHA; Prime Minister of Bermuda, 1975-77; *b* 8 Nov. 1921; *s* of Harry Sharpe; *m* 1948, Eileen Margaret, *d* of George Morrow, BC, Canada; one *s* one *d*. *Educ:* Warwick Acad., Warwick, Bermuda; Mount Allison, New Brunswick; Commercial Coll., Sackville, NB. Served War of 1939-45: Pilot Officer, with Bomber Comd, NW Europe, RAF. Became Vice-Pres. and Sec., Purvis Ltd (Importers), Bermuda. MHA for Warwick, Bermuda, 1963-; Minister of Finance, 1968-77; Dep. Leader of Govt, 1971-75. Formerly Member several Parliamentary Select Cttees, and of Bd of Educn, Bermuda; also Dep. Chm., Central Planning Authority and Defence Bd. Delegate to Constitutional Conf., London, 1966. Mem., War Veterans Assoc., Bermuda; Warden, Anglican Church. *Address:* Uplands, Harbour Road, Warwick West, Bermuda.

SHARPE, John Herbert S.; see Subak-Sharpe.

SHARPE, Sir Reginald (Taaffe), Kt 1947; QC; *b* 20 November 1898; *o s* of late Herbert Sharpe, Lindfield, Sussex; *m* 1st, 1922, Phyllis Maude (marr. diss. 1929), *d* of late Major Edward Whinney, Haywards Heath, Sussex; two *d*; 2nd, 1930, Eileen Kate (*d* 1946), *d* of Thomas Howarth Usherwood, Christ's Hospital, Sussex; 3rd, 1947, Vivien Travers (*d* 1971), *d* of late Rev. Herbert Seddon Rowley, Wretham, Norfolk; 4th, 1976, Mary Millicent, *d* of late Maj.-Gen. Patrick Barclay Sangster, CB, CMG, DSO, Roehampton. *Educ:* Westminster. Served European War: enlisted in Army, 1916; 2nd Lieut Grenadier Guards (SR), Jan. 1917; Lt, 1918; served with 2nd Bn in France (wounded). Called to Bar at Gray's Inn, Easter, 1920. Went South-Eastern Circuit and Sussex Sessions. Judge of High Court, Rangoon, 1937-48; Director of Supply, Burma (at Calcutta), 1942-44; Trustee of Rangoon University Endowment Fund, 1946-48; KC Feb. 1949; HM Comr of Assize: Western and Northern Circuits, 1949; Midland and Western Circuits, 1950; South-Eastern Circuit, 1952; North-Eastern Circuit, 1954; Birmingham October Assize, 1954; Midland Circuit, 1960. Special Comr for Divorce Causes, 1948-67. Chm., Nat. Health Service Tribunal for England and Wales, 1948-71. Deputy Chairman QS: E Sussex, 1949-69; W Kent, 1949-62; Kent, 1962-69; Mddx, 1963-65 (Asst Chm. 1951-63); Mddx area of Greater London, 1965-71; Asst Chm., W Sussex QS, 1950-70; Dep. Chm., Hailsham Petty Sessional Div., 1950-57 and 1959-70 (Chm., 1957-58). Mem. Standing Jt Cttee for E Sussex, 1958-65, for W Sussex, 1953-65. Mem., Nat. Arbitration Tribunal, 1951, and of Industrial Disputes Tribunal, 1951; Chairman, 1951-54, of Joint Council, and Independent Chairman, 1955-57, of Conciliation Board set up by Assoc. of Health and Pleasure Resorts and the Musicians' Union; Sole Commissioner to hold British Honduras Inquiry at Belize, March 1954; Chm., Departmental Cttee on Summary Trial of Minor Offences in Magistrates' Courts, 1954-55. Mem., Governing Body, Westminster Sch., 1955-. JP East Sussex. *Address:* Northfield India, Devonshire, Boreham Street, near Hailsham, East Sussex. *T:* Herstmonceux 2147. *Club:* East India, Devonshire, Sports and Public Schools.

SHARPE, William, OBE 1967; HM Diplomatic Service; HM Consul-General, Berlin, since 1975; *b* 9 Dec. 1923; *s* of late William Joseph Sharpe and of Phoebe Irene (*née* Standen); *m* 1959, Marie-Antoinette Rodesch; one *s*. *Educ:* High Sch., Chichester; London Univ. BA (Hons), MA, BSc Econ (Hons). Served RAF, 1943-47. Joined Foreign (subseq. Diplomatic) Service, 1947; Foreign Office 1947-52; Cologne and Bonn, 1952-54; Leopoldville, 1954-57; UK Mission to UN, New York, 1957-61; Foreign Office, 1961-66; Milan, 1966-70; FCO, 1971-72; Kuwait, 1972-75. *Recreations:* reading, music, golf. *Address:* c/o Foreign and Commonwealth Office, SW1. *Club:* Travellers'.

SHARPE, William James, CBE 1967 (OBE 1950); Director of Communications, Foreign and Commonwealth Office (formerly Foreign Office), 1965-69, retired; *b* 3 Jan. 1908; *s* of James Sharpe; *m* 1940, Doreen Winifred Cockell; three *s*. *Educ:* Aldershot Grammar School, 1927-39: Merchant Navy; Marconi International; Marine Communications Company. Commissioned Royal Corps of Signals, 1940; Served in France and South East Asia; Lt-Col 1945. Diplomatic Wireless Service, 1947; Deputy Director of Communications, 1959. *Address:* The Mount, Tingewick, Buckingham. *T:* Finmere 291.

SHARPLES, family name of Baroness Sharples.

SHARPLES, Baroness *cr* 1973 (Life Peer); Pamela Sharples; *b* 11 Feb. 1923; *o d* of late Lt-Comdr K. W. Newall and of Violet (who *m* 2nd, Lord Claud Hamilton, GCVO, CMG, DSO); *m* 1946, Major R. C. Sharples, MC, Welsh Guards (later Sir Richard Sharples, KCMG, OBE, MC, assassinated 1973); two *s* two *d*. *Educ:* Southover Manor, Lewes; Florence. WAAF, 1941-46. Occupation, farming. *Recreations:* sailing, riding, tennis, golf. *Address:* Southfield Farm, Chawton, Alton, Hants. *T:* Alton 83318; 01-589 6476.

SHARROCK, Prof. Roger Ian; Professor of English Language and Literature, University of London, King's College, since 1968; *b* Robin Hood's Bay, 23 Aug. 1919; *s* of Arthur and Iva France Sharrock; *m* 1940, Gertrude Elizabeth Adams, *d* of Edgar Leenie Adams, Bradford; one *s* two *d*. *Educ:* Queen Elizabeth's Sch., Wakefield; St John's Coll., Oxford (Open Exhibr). 1st cl. Hon. Sch. of Eng. Lang. and Lit., 1943; BLitt 1947. Served with King's Own Yorks LI, 1939-41; Nat. Buildings Record, 1942-44; Asst Master, Rugby Sch., 1944-46; Lectr, Univ. of Southampton, 1946; Reader, 1962; Prof. of English, Univ. of Durham, 1963. Editor, Durham Univ. Jl, 1964-68; Fulbright Vis. Prof., Univ. of Virginia, 1972; Warton Lectr of British Academy, 1972; Trustee, Dove Cottage Trust and Wordsworth Rydal Mount Trust; Chm., English Association. *Publications:* Songs and Comments, 1946; John Bunyan, 1954; (ed) Selected Poems of Wordsworth, 1958; (ed) Bunyan, The Pilgrim's Progress, 1960; (ed) Bunyan, Grace Abounding, 1962; (ed) Selected Poems of Dryden, 1963; (ed) Keats, Selected Poems and Letters, 1964; The Pilgrim's Progress, 1966; (ed) Oxford Standard Authors Bunyan, 1966; Solitude and Community in Wordsworth's Poetry, 1969; (ed) Pelican Book of English Prose, 1970; (ed) Casebook on Pilgrim's Progress, 1976; (ed) English Short Stories of Today, 1976; contrib. Encycl. Britannica, Essays in Criticism, Mod. Lang. Review, Review of English Studies, Tablet, etc. *Recreations:* walking, chess. *Address:* 12 Plough Lane, Purley, Surrey. *T:* 01-660 3248. *Club:* United Oxford & Cambridge University.

SHARWOOD-SMITH, Sir Bryan (Evers), KCMG 1955 (CMG 1950); KCVO 1956; KBE 1953; ED; Governor, Northern Nigeria, 1954-57 (Lieut-Governor, and President Northern House of Chiefs, 1952-54); retd 1957; *b* 5 Jan. 1899; *s* of late Edward Sharwood Smith; *m* 1st, 1926; one *d*; 2nd, 1939, Winifred Joan, *d* of late Thomas and Winifred Mitchell; two *s* one *d*. *Educ:* Newbury School; Aldenham School, Herts (Platt Schol.). Elected to Open Classical Schol., Emmanuel College, Cambridge, 1916, but entered army (RFC), 1917; served France, Rhine and North West Frontier India, 1917-20. Assistant Master St Cuthbert's Preparatory School, Malvern, 1920. Entered Colonial Administrative Service, 1920; served in British Cameroons, 1920-27, Nigeria, 1927-57. Military Service, 1940-42; Resident, 1942; Resident, Kano, Nigeria, 1950-52; and President of Northern Region House of Assembly, 1950-52. Acting Chief Commissioner, Northern Provinces, Sept.-Dec. 1950. *Publication:* But Always as Friends, 1969. *Address:* 47 Cooden Drive, Bexhill, East Sussex. *Club:* Royal Air Force.

SHATTOCK, Rear-Adm. Ernest Henry, CB 1955; OBE 1943; Consultant for Manufacturing Licences; Director, Filtration Specialists Ltd; *b* 22 October 1904; *s* of late Ernest Mark Shattock and late Evelyn Mabel (*née* Byrde); *m* 1958, Oz Armstrong; one *s* three *d* (of previous *m*). *Educ:* Osborne; Dartmouth. Entered Osborne, 1918; specialised in flying, 1927; Commander, 1938; Captain, 1943; Rear-Admiral, 1953. Served War of 1939-45; Chief of Staff to Flag Officer Naval Air Pacific, 1944-46; Director Naval Air Warfare Division, 1946-49; commanded HMS Glory, 1949-50. Directing Captain, Senior Officers' War College, 1951; Flag Officer, Malaya, Nov. 1953-April 1956; retired list, 1956. Naval ADC to the Queen, 1953. *Publication:* An Experiment in Mindfulness, 1958. *Recreations:* music, magic. *Address:* The Mill House, Newark, Ripley, Surrey. *T:* Ripley 3020.

SHATTOCK, John Swithun Harvey, CMG 1952; OBE 1946; HM Diplomatic Service, 1947-67; *b* 21 Nov. 1907; *s* of late Rev. E. A. Shattock, Kingston St Mary, Nr Taunton; unmarried. *Educ:* Westminster School; Christ Church, Oxford. Entered ICS, 1931; served in Bengal, 1931-36; Under Sec., Govt of India (Defence Dept), 1936-39; joined Indian Political Service, 1939; served in Kathiawar, Baroda, and Kashmir Residencies, 1939-44; Dep. Sec. to Crown Representative (Political Dept), New Delhi, 1944-46; Chief Minister, Chamba State, 1946-47; apptd HM Diplomatic Service, 1947; served in UK High Commission, New Delhi, 1947-49; Head of Far Eastern Dept, Foreign Office, London, 1950-51; Head of China and Korea Dept, FO 1951; FO Rep. at Imperial Defence Coll., London, 1952; Head of China and Korea Dept, FO, 1953; Counsellor, British Embassy, Belgrade, Dec. 1953-Nov. 1955; Political Representative, Middle East Forces, Cyprus, Jan. 1956-Nov. 1958. Deputy to UK Permanent Representative on North Atlantic Council, Paris, 1959-61; Minister, UK Delegation to Disarmament Conference, Geneva, 1961-63; FO, 1963-67. *Recreation:* travel. *Address:* St Mary's Cottage, Kingston St Mary, near Taunton, Somerset; Grindlay's Bank Ltd, 13 St James's Square, SW1. *Club:* Travellers'.

SHATWELL, Prof. Kenneth Owen; Emeritus Professor in the University of Sydney; *b* 16 Oct. 1909; *m* 1936, Betty, *d* of Thomas Rae Hogarth, Tasmania; one *s* one *d* (and one *d* decd). *Educ:* Lincoln College, Oxford. Served War of 1939-45: Lieut RANVR, on active service in Atlantic and Pacific. Prof. of Law and Dean of the Faculty of Law, Univ. of Tasmania, 1934-47; Challis Prof. of Law, Univ. of Sydney, 1947-74; Dean of the Faculty of Law, Univ. of Sydney, 1947-73; Dir, Inst. of Criminology, Sydney Univ., 1962-74. Vis. Prof., The Queen's Univ., Belfast, 1951; Australian Comr, S Pacific Commn, 1950-52; Sen. Research Fellow, Yale Univ., 1958-59, 1962; Visiting Professor: New York Univ. Law School Summer Workshop on Contracts, 1962; Temple Univ. Law School, 1968. Aust. Mem., Permanent Court of Arbitration under the Hague Convention, 1960-; Ministerial Cnsltnt to NSW Dept of Corrective Services, 1972-. FASSA. *Publications:* various articles in legal jls. *Recreation:* criminology. *Address:* 36 Chilton Parade, Turramurra, NSW 2074, Australia. *T:* Sydney 48-1189. *Clubs:* Athenæum; Tasmanian (Hobart).

SHAUGHNESSY, family name of **Baron Shaughnessy.**

SHAUGHNESSY, 3rd Baron, *cr* 1916, of Montreal; **William Graham Shaughnessy;** Vice-President, Secretary, since 1969, and Director, since 1955, Canada Northwest Land Ltd, Calgary; Director, Arbor Capital Resources Inc., Toronto, since 1972; *b* 28 March 1922; *s* of 2nd Baron and Marion (*d* 1936), *d* of late R. K. Graham, Montreal; *S* father, 1938; *m* 1944, Mary Whitley, *o d* of late John Whitley, Copthorne House, Letchworth; two *s* two *d*. *Educ:* Bishop's Univ., Lennoxville, Canada; BA 1941; MSc Columbia Univ., NY, 1947. Trustee, The Last Post Fund Inc., Canada. Major, Canadian Grenadier Guards, R of O. *Heir:* *s* Hon. Patrick John Shaughnessy, *b* 23 Oct. 1944. *Address:* Apt 1001, 1209 6th Street SW, Calgary, Alberta T2R 0Z5, Canada. *Clubs:* Ranchmen's (Calgary); University (Montreal).

SHAVE, Kenneth George, CEng, FIMechE; Member, London Transport Executive, 1967-73, retired; *b* 25 June 1908; *s* of George Shave and Frances Larkin; *m* 1935, Doris May Stone; one *s* one *d*. *Educ:* St Paul's School. Apprenticed London General Omnibus Company, 1925; Rolling Stock Engineer, East Surrey Traction Company, 1930; London Transport: Asst Divisional Engineer, 1935; Divisional Engineer, 1948; Rolling Stock Engineer, 1956; Chief Mechanical Engineer, 1965. CStJ 1971 (OStJ 1963). *Recreations:* golf, bridge, gardening. *Address:* 5 St Katherine's Road, Henley on Thames, Oxon RG9 7PJ. *T:* Turville Heath 327.

SHAW; *see* Byam Shaw.

SHAW, family name of **Baron Craigmyle** and **Baron Kilbrandon.**

SHAW, Alan Frederick, CBE 1977; JP; Chairman, Intervention Board for Agricultural Produce, since 1974; farmer since 1946; *b* 5 March 1910; *s* of Walter Frederick and Bessie Florence Shaw; *m* 1946, Angela Dearden (*née* Burges); one step *s*. *Educ:* Dulwich College. J. & J. Colman, Norwich, 1927-31; own business, gravel extraction, 1931-39. War Service: BEF, 1939-40; Middle East, 8th Army, 1941-43; 2nd Army, 1944-45; Lt-Col, RE. Vice-Pres. and Dep. Pres., NFU, 1968-70; Mem. Barker Cttee on Contract Farming, 1971-72; Mem. Intervention Bd, 1972-74; Dir, Nat. Seed Develt Organisation Ltd, 1971-; Mem., UK Seeds Exec., 1972-; Mem. Council, Nat. Inst. Agric. Botany, 1971-. JP Lincs, 1963. *Recreations:* golf; music (especially opera). *Address:* The Old Vicarage, Horbling, near Sleaford, Lincs. *T:* Billingborough 563. *Clubs:* Farmers', Royal Automobile; Spalding (Spalding).

SHAW, Anne Gillespie, (Mrs J. H. Pirie), CBE 1954; Chairman and Managing Director of: The Anne Shaw Organisation Ltd, 1945-74, Chairman, since 1974; Anne Shaw Data Processing Ltd since 1960; Office Reorganisation Ltd since 1960; Director, Wescot Ltd, since 1964; *b* Uddingston, Scotland, 28 May 1904; *d* of late Major David P. Shaw, Cameronians (killed in action, 1915), and late Mrs Helen B. Shaw; *m* 1937, John Henderson Pirie; one *s* two *d*. *Educ:* St Leonards School, St Andrews, Fife; Edinburgh University; Bryn Mawr College, Philadelphia, USA. MA (Edinburgh) 1927; Post-Graduate Diploma, Social Economy (Bryn Mawr), 1928. Metropolitan-Vickers Electrical Co. Ltd, 1930-45; Production Efficiency Board, advising Sir Stafford Cripps at MAP, 1942-45; Independent Member of Cotton Working Party, 1945-46. Member: National Advisory Council on Education for Industry and Commerce, 1948-60; Cttee of Enquiry on Training of Teachers for Technical Colleges; Milk Marketing Bd, 1964-73; NEDC for Post Office, 1963; Ct of Inquiry into Ford dispute, 1968; Robens Cttee on Safety and Health at Work, 1970-72. Chm. Management Consultants Assoc., 1967-68. Fellow, Inst. of Personnel Management (Pres. 1949-51); FBIM (Mem. Council, 1968-); CEng; FIProdE. Gilbreth Medal for contribution to scientific management (Soc. for Advancement of Management), 1948. *Publications:* Introduction to the Theory and Application of Motion Study, 1944; Purpose and Practice of Motion Study, 1952. *Recreations:* cine-photography, ski-ing, camping, gardening. *Address:* Coachman's Cottage, Macclesfield Road, Alderley Edge, Cheshire. *T:* Alderley Edge 583492. *Clubs:* University Women's; Royal Scottish Automobile (Glasgow).

SHAW, Arnold John; MP (Lab) Redbridge, Ilford South, since Feb. 1974 (Ilford South, 1966-70); *b* 12 July 1909; *s* of Solomon and Rachel Shaw; *m* 1935, Elizabeth Solomons; one *d. Educ:* Trafalgar Sq. (LCC) Primary Sch.; Coopers' Company's Sch.; Univ. of Southampton. BA (Hons) London, 1930. Entered teaching profession, 1932. Member: Stepney Borough Coun., 1934-48; Ilford Borough Coun., 1952-64 (Alderman, 1963-64); Redbridge, London Borough Coun., 1964-68, 1971-74. Contested (Lab) Ilford South, 1964. PPS to Minister for Housing and Construction, 1977-. *Recreation:* gardening. *Address:* 2a Claybury Broadway, Ilford, Essex.

SHAW, Rev. (Bernard) Arthur; Chairman of the Chester and Stoke on Trent District of the Methodist Church, since 1962; President of the Methodist Conference, June 1977-June 1978; *b* 12 Sept. 1914; *s* of John and Lillie Shaw; *m* 1944, Alma Kirk; two *s* one *d. Educ:* Queen Elizabeth Grammar Sch., Wakefield; Lancaster Royal Grammar Sch.; Richmond Coll. (Theological: London Univ.), Surrey. Filton, Bristol, 1941-43; RAF Chaplain, 1943-46; Stoke on Trent, 1946-51; Hinde Street Methodist Church, London Univ. Methodist Chaplaincy, 1951-57; Leeds Mission, 1957-62. DUniv Keele, 1977. *Recreations:* gardening, cricket. *Address:* 593 Crewe Road, Wistaston, Crewe, Cheshire CW2 6BX. *T:* Crewe 68720.

SHAW, Sir Bernard (Vidal), Kt 1957; *b* 28 April 1891; *s* of late Bernard Vidal Shaw; *m* 1929, Katharine Ceceley, *d* of Arthur Stanley Colls. *Educ:* St Paul's School. Indian Police, 1910-23; called to Bar, Gray's Inn, 1923; entered Colonial Service (Kenya), 1925; Resident Magistrate, 1928; Relieving President, District Court, Palestine, 1936; President, 1941; Chairman, Awqaf Commission, 1939-40; Puisne Judge, Supreme Court of Palestine, 1945-48. Chairman, North Midland District Valuation Board, 1950-55; Chm., Medical Appeal Tribunals, 1952-64; Sen. Puisne Judge, Cyprus, 1955-57. *Publications:* Kenya Law Reports, 1927-30 (Collator and Editor), and 1931-32 (Editor). *Recreation:* tennis. *Address:* 45 Rivermead Court, SW6 3RX. *T:* 01-736 1644. *Clubs:* Athenæum; Hurlingham.

SHAW, Charles Barry, CB 1974; QC 1964; Director of Public Prosecutions for Northern Ireland, since 1972; *b* 12 April 1923; *s* of late Ernest Hunter Shaw and Sarah Gertrude Shaw, Mayfield, Balmoral, Belfast; *m* 1964, Jane (*née* Phillips). *Educ:* Inchmarlo House, Belfast; Pannal Ash Coll., Harrogate; The Queen's Univ. of Belfast (LLB). Served War: commissioned RA, 97 A/Tk Regt RA, 15th (Scottish) Div., 1942-46. Called to Bar of Northern Ireland, 1948; called to Bar, Middle Temple, 1970. *Address:* Royal Courts of Justice (Ulster), Belfast, Northern Ireland BT1 3NX; Mayfield, 448 Lisburn Road, Belfast BT9 6GT. *Clubs:* Naval and Military; Ulster (Belfast).

SHAW, Prof. C(harles) Thurstan, CBE 1972; Professor of Archaeology, University of Ibadan, 1963-74; *b* 27 June 1914; 2nd *s* of late Rev. John Herbert Shaw and Grace Irene (*née* Woollatt); *m* Gilian Ione Maud, *e d* of late Edward John Penberthy Magor and Gilian Sarah (*née* Westmacott); two *s* three *d. Educ:* Blundell's Sch.; Sidney Sussex Coll., Cambridge; Univ. of London Inst. of Education. 1st cl. hons Arch. and Anthrop. Tripos 1936, MA, PhD Cantab; DipEd London. FRAI 1938; FSA 1947. Curator, Anthropology Museum, Achimota Coll., Gold Coast, 1937-45; Cambs Educn Cttee, 1945-51; Cambridge Inst. of Educn, 1951-63. Vis. Prof., Northwestern Univ., USA, 1969. Founder and Editor: W African Archaeological Newsletter, 1964-70; W African Jl of Archaeology, 1971-. Mem. Perm. Council, Internat. Union of Pre- and Proto-historic Sciences, 1965; Vice-Pres., Panafrican Congress on Prehistory and Study of Quaternary, 1966-77; Mem. Council, Univ. of Ibadan, 1969-71. Vis. Fellow, Clare Hall, Cambridge, 1973; Vis. Res. Prof. Ahmadu Bello Univ., 1975-78; Dir of Studies, Archaeology and Anthrop., Magdalene Coll., Cambridge, 1976. Amaury Talbot Prize, Royal Anthrop. Inst., 1970. Onunu-Ekwulu Ora of Igbo-Ukwu, 1972. *Publications:* Excavation at Dawu, 1961; Archaeology and Nigeria, 1964; (with J. Vanderburg) Bibliography of Nigerian Archaeology, 1969; (ed) Nigerian Prehistory and Archaeology, 1969; Igbo-Ukwu: an account of archaeological discoveries in eastern Nigeria, 2 vols, 1970; Discovering Nigeria's Past, 1975; Why 'Darkest' Africa?, 1975; Unearthing Igbo-Ukwu, 1976; numerous articles on African archaeology and prehistory in jls. *Recreations:* walking, music. *Address:* Silver Ley, 37 Hawthorne

Road, Stapleford, Cambridge CB2 5DU. *T:* Shelford 2283. *Club:* Athenæum.

SHAW, Colin Don; Director of Television, Independent Broadcasting Authority, since 1977; *b* 2 Nov. 1928; *s* of Rupert M. Shaw and late Enid F. Shaw (*née* Smith); *m* 1955, Elizabeth Ann, *d* of Paul Bowker; one *s* two *d. Educ:* Liverpool Coll.; St Peter's Hall, Oxford (MA). Called to the Bar, Inner Temple, 1960. Nat. Service, RAF, 1947-49. Joined BBC as Radio Drama Producer, North Region, 1953; Asst, BBC Secretariat, 1957-59; Asst Head of Programme Contracts Dept, 1959-60; Sen. Asst, BBC Secretariat, 1960-63; special duties in connection with recruitment for BBC2, 1963; Asst Head of Programmes, BBC North Region, 1963-66; various posts in TV Programme Planning, ending as Head of Group, 1966-69; Secretary to the BBC, 1969-72, Chief Secretary, 1972-76. Chm., Bd of Governors, Hampden House Sch., 1972-. *Publications:* several radio plays and a stage-play for children. *Recreations:* going to the theatre, reading. *Address:* Lesters, Little Ickford, Aylesbury, Bucks. *T:* Ickford 225.

SHAW, Dr Dennis Frederick, CBE 1974; Fellow of Keble College, since 1957; Keeper of Scientific Books, Bodleian Library, Oxford, since 1975; *b* 20 April 1924; 2nd *s* of Albert Shaw and Lily (*née* Hill), Teddington; *m* 1949, Joan Irene, *er d* of Sidney and Maud Chandler; one *s* three *d. Educ:* Harrow County Sch.; Christ Church, Oxford. BA 1945, MA 1950, DPhil 1950. Mem. Amer. Phys. Soc. 1957; FInstP 1971; FZS. Jun. Sci. Officer, MAP, 1944-46; Res. Officer in Physics, Clarendon Lab., Oxford, 1950-57, Sen. Res. Officer 1957-64; Univ. Lectr in Physics, Oxford, 1964-75. Vis. Scientist, CERN, Geneva, 1961-62; Vis. Prof. of Physics and Brown Foundn Fellow, Univ. of the South, Tennessee, 1974. Mem., Oxford City Council, 1963-67; Chm., Oxford City Civil Emergency Cttee, 1966-67; Mem., Home Office Sci. Adv. Council, 1966-; Chm., Oxford Univ. Delegacy for Educnl Studies, 1969-73; Chm., Home Office Police Equipment Cttee, 1969-70; Chm., Home Office Police Sci. Develt Cttee, 1971-74. *Publications:* An Introduction to Electronics, 1962, 2nd edn 1970; papers in sci. jls. *Recreations:* riding, gardening, enjoying music. *Address:* 29 Davenant Road, Oxford. *T:* Oxford 55521. *Club:* United Oxford & Cambridge University.

SHAW, Rev. Douglas William David; Dean of Faculty of Divinity, University of Edinburgh, and Principal of New College, since 1974; *b* 25 June 1928; *s* of William David Shaw and Nansie Smart. *Educ:* Edinburgh Acad.; Loretto; Ashbury Coll., Ottawa; Univs of Cambridge and Edinburgh. BA (Cantab), BD (Edin.), LLB (Edin.). WS. Practised law as Partner of Davidson and Syme, WS, Edinburgh, 1953-57. Ordained Minister of Church of Scotland, 1960; Asst Minister, St George's West Church, Edinburgh, 1960-63; Official Observer of World Alliance of Reformed Churches at Second Vatican Council, Rome, 1962; Lectr in Philosophy of Religion and Apologetics, Univ. of Edinburgh, 1963-. *Publications:* Who is God? 1968, 2nd edn 1970; trans. from German: F. Heyer: The Catholic Church from 1648 to 1870, 1969; various articles in theological jls. *Recreations:* squash (Scottish Amateur Champion, 1950-51-52), climbing. *Address:* 4/13 Succoth Court, Edinburgh EH12 6BZ. *T:* 031-337 2130. *Clubs:* New (Edinburgh); Royal Burgess Golfing Soc.; Luffness New; Edinburgh Sports.

SHAW, Frank Howard, MBE 1945; TD; MA; JP; Headmaster, King's College School, Wimbledon, 1960-75; *b* 13 June 1913; *s* of E. H. Shaw; *m* 1950, Harriette Alice, *d* of late His Honour Robert Peel; one *s* two *d. Educ:* Altrincham Grammar School; Hertford College, Oxford. Asst master: King's Coll. School, 1935-39; Marlborough College (and Housemaster), 1939-52; first Headmaster of Pakistan Air Force Public School, Murree Hills, 1952-58; Principal, Aden Coll., Aden, 1958-60. Chm., HMC, 1972. Served War of 1939-45 in Devonshire Regt; Jt Planning Staff, 1943-45. Lt-Col. JP, SW London, 1966-76. *Publications:* textbooks for teaching of English in Pakistan. *Recreation:* golf. *Address:* Medstead House, Medstead, near Alton, Hants. *T:* Alton 62195. *Clubs:* East India, Devonshire, Sports and Public Schools, MCC.

SHAW, Geoffrey Mackintosh; Convener, Strathclyde Regional Council, since 1974; *b* 9 April 1927; *s* of John James McIntosh Shaw, surgeon, and Mina Draper Shaw; *m* 1975, Sarah Dorothy Mason. *Educ:* Edinburgh Acad.; Edinburgh Univ. (MA, BD); Union Theol Seminary, NY. Boys' Leader, Church House, Bridgeton, Glasgow, 1955-57; Founder Mem., Gorbals Gp, 1957-75. Elected to Glasgow Corp., 1970, Leader, Labour Gp, 1973; elected to Strathclyde Regional Council, 1974. Mem., Royal Commn on Legal Services in Scotland, 1976-. *Address:* 14 Queen Mary Avenue, Glasgow G42 8DT. *T:* 041-424 3106.

SHAW, George Anthony Theodore, CBE 1965; Severn Trent Water Authority, since 1974; *b* 25 Oct. 1917; *s* of late G. E. Shaw, CMG, OBE, LLB; *m* 1st, Suzanne Alexandra Barber (marr. diss.), *d* of late H. C. Barber; one *s* one *d*; 2nd, Joan Margaret, *d* of late Rev. N. M. Livingstone, DCL, RN; two *d*. *Educ:* Marlborough Coll.; Clare Coll., Cambridge (MA). Intell. Corps, Army, 1941-46, Indian Civil Service, 1944-45; HM Overseas Civil Service, 1940-67: Malaya, Singapore, Sarawak, Brunei, Malaysia; State Sec., Sarawak, 1963-67; Milton Keynes Develt Corp., 1967-74. Order of Star of Sarawak (PNBS), 1966. *Recreations:* wide. *Address:* Coopers, Chestnut Square, Wellesbourne, Warwickshire. *Clubs:* East India, Devonshire, Sports and Public Schools; Royal Lymington Yacht.

SHAW, George N. B.; *see* Bowman-Shaw.

SHAW, Giles; *see* Shaw, J. G. D.

SHAW, Dr Ian James, OBE 1965; Assistant Chief Scientific Adviser (Studies), since 1974, and Director, Defence Operational Analysis Establishment, since 1977, Ministry of Defence; *b* 8 April 1919; *s* of Livingstone and Myrtle Shaw; *m* 1949, Audrey Jean Spalding; two *s*. *Educ:* Auckland UC, NZ (BSc); Cambridge Univ (BA, PhD). Joined Scientific Civil Service (Army Dept), 1950; transf. to MoD, 1958. *Recreations:* woodwork, gardening, baiting bureaucrats. *Address:* Woodilee, Mellersh Hill Road, Wonersh Park, Guildford, Surrey. *T:* Bramley 2436.

SHAW, Irwin; writer (US); *b* New York, 27 Feb. 1913; *s* of William Shaw and Rose (*née* Tompkins); *m* 1939, Marian Edwards (marr. diss.); one *s*. *Educ:* Brooklyn College (AB). Served War of 1939-45 in US Army. *Publications: plays:* Bury the Dead, 1936; The Gentle People, 1939; Quiet City, 1939; Retreat to Pleasure, 1941; Sons and Soldiers, 1943; The Assassin, 1945; Children From Their Games, 1963; *short stories:* Sailor Off the Bremen, 1940; Welcome to the City, 1942; Act of Faith, 1946; Mixed Company, 1952; Tip on a Dead Jockey, 1957; Love on a Dark Street, 1965; Whispers in Bedlam, 1972; God was Here, But He Left Early, 1973; *novels:* The Young Lions, 1948; The Troubled Air, 1951; Lucy Crown, 1956; Two Weeks in Another Town, 1960; Voices of a Summer Day, 1965; Rich Man, Poor Man, 1970; Evening in Byzantium, 1973; Nightwork, 1975; Beggarman, Thief, 1977; *travel:* In the Company of Dolphins, 1962; Paris! Paris!, 1976. *Address:* c/o Hope Leresche & Steele, 11 Jubilee Place, SW3 3TE.

SHAW, James John Sutherland, CB 1970; Chairman, Civil Service Appeal Board, 1973-77 (Deputy Chairman, 1972-73); *b* 5 Jan. 1912; *s* of Robert Shaw and Christina Macallum Sutherland; *m* 1947, Rosamond Chisholm Sharman; *no c. Educ:* Ardrossan Academy, Ayrshire; Glasgow and London Universities. Glasgow University: MA 1st Class Hons History, 1932, PhD 1935; Lecturer in History, 1936-40. Served War with RAF, 1940-45, Navigator, AC2 to Sqdn Leader (despatches). Senior Lecturer in History, Glasgow Univ., 1945-46; HM Treasury, 1946-68: Principal, Asst Sec., Under-Sec.; Under-Sec., 1968-69, Dep. Sec., 1969-72, CSD. OECD Consltnt on Greek CS, 1973; Chm., Internat. Commn on Reform, Sudan CS, 1973-74; consultant to Commn on Structure and Functions, Ghana CS, 1974, to States of Jersey on Jersey CS, 1975. *Recreations:* talking, walking and gardening. *Address:* North Field, Wootten Green, Stradbroke, Diss, Norfolk IP21 5JP. *T:* Stradbroke 535.

SHAW, John Dennis Bolton, MVO 1961; HM Diplomatic Service; Deputy High Commissioner, Kuala Lumpur, since 1976; *b* 5 July 1920; *er s* of William Bolton Shaw and Margaret Bolton Shaw, Manchester; *m* 1955, Isabel Lowe; two *s. Educ:* Manchester Grammar Sch.; Balliol Coll., Oxford (MA). Served War: in North Africa, Italy and India, Lieut RA and RWAFF, 1940-46. Colonial Office, 1948-55; District Comr and Dep. Financial Sec., Sierra Leone, 1955-57; Commonwealth Relations Office, 1957-58 and 1962-65; Karachi, 1958-61; Washington, 1961-62; apptd Counsellor, 1962; Nairobi, 1965-67; Counsellor for Trusteeship Affairs, UK Mission to the UN, 1967-71; Head of Gibraltar and General Dept, FCO, 1971-73; Ambassador to Somali Democratic Republic, 1973-76. *Recreations:* travel, archaeology, music. *Address:* c/o Foreign and Commonwealth Office, King Charles Street, SW1.

SHAW, (John) Giles (Dunkerley); MP (C) Pudsey since Feb. 1974; Marketing Director, Confectionery Division, Rowntree Mackintosh Ltd, 1970-74; *b* Nov. 1931, *y s* of Hugh D. Shaw; *m* Dione Patricia Crosthwaite Ellison; one *s* two *d. Educ:* Sedbergh Sch.; St. John's Coll., Cambridge (MA). President of the Union, Cambridge, 1954. Past Rural District Councillor; served on Flaxton RDC, 1957-64. Contested (C) Kingston upon Hull West, 1966. Mem. House of Commons Select Cttee on Nationalised Industries; Vice-Chm., Cons. Prices and Consumer Affairs Cttee; Joint-Sec., All Party Wool Textile Group; Treasurer Yorks Cons. Members' Group. *Recreations:* ornithology, fishing, tennis. *Address:* 20 Parkside, Horsforth, Leeds; House of Commons, SW1.

SHAW, Sir John J. K. B.; *see* Best-Shaw.

SHAW, John Michael, MC 1940; QC 1967; Barrister-at-Law; Regional Chairman of Industrial Tribunals, since 1972; *b* 14 Nov. 1914; *yr s* of late M. J. Shaw (killed in action, 1916); *m* 1940, Margaret L. *yr d* of Robert T. D. Stoneham, CBE; two *s* two *d. Educ:* Rugby; Worcester Coll., Oxford. Called to the Bar, Gray's Inn, 1937. Served War of 1939-45 (Major): commissioned Royal Fusiliers, 1940. *Recreations:* fishing, gardening. *Address:* South Knighton House, South Knighton, near Newton Abbot, Devon.

SHAW, Sir John Valentine Wistar, KCMG 1947 (CMG 1942); Kt 1946; *b* 1894; *m* 1926, Josephine Mary, *yr d* of Joseph Simpson, Horsehay, Shropshire; two *s. Educ:* Repton School. Served with Royal Engineers, 1914-19, in France and Palestine (despatches). Colonial Administrative Service, Gold Coast, 1921-35; Palestine, 1935-40; Colonial Sec. Cyprus, 1940-43 (despatches, CMG); Chief Sec. Palestine, 1943-46; Governor and C-in-C Trinidad and Tobago, 1947-50; retired, 1950. Attached War Office, 1950-54; Chairman, Commission of Inquiry into Industrial dispute and riots, Sierra Leone, 1955. *Address:* 2 White Close, Winchelsea, Sussex. *T:* Winchelsea 283.

SHAW, Max S.; *see* Stuart-Shaw.

SHAW, Michael Norman, JP; DL; MP (C) Scarborough, since 1974 (Scarborough and Whitby, 1966-74); Member, British Delegation to European Parliament, Strasbourg, since 1974; *b* 9 Oct. 1920; *e s* of late Norman Shaw; *m* 1951, Joan Mary Louise, *o d* of Sir Alfred L. Mowat, 2nd Bt; three *s. Educ:* Sedbergh. Chartered Accountant; Partner, Robson Rhodes; MP (L and C) Brighouse and Spenborough, March 1960-Oct. 1964; PPS: to Minister of Labour, 1962-63; to Sec. of State, Dept of Trade and Industry, 1970-72; to Chancellor of the Duchy of Lancaster, 1973. FCA. JP Dewsbury, 1953; DL W Yorks, 1977. *Address:* Duxbury Hall, Liversedge, W Yorkshire. *T:* Heckmondwike 402270. *Club:* Junior Carlton.

SHAW, Sir Robert, 7th Bt *cr* 1821; Design Engineer, T. Lamb, McManus & Associates Ltd, Calgary, Alberta; *b* Nairobi, Kenya, 31 Jan. 1925; *s* of Sir Robert de Vere Shaw, 6th Bt, MC, and Joan (*d* 1967), *d* of Thomas Cross; *S* father, 1969; *m* 1954, Jocelyn, *d* of late Andrew McGuffie, Swaziland; two *d. Educ:* Harrow; Univs of Oklahoma and Missouri, USA. RN, 1943-47 (Lieut RN retd). BS Civil Eng. Oklahoma, 1962; MS Civil Eng. Missouri, 1964; Professional Engineer, Alberta; Mem. Engineering Inst. of Canada. *Recreation:* sailing. *Heir: n* Charles de Vere Shaw, *b* 1 March 1957. *Address:* 234 40th Avenue SW, Calgary, Alberta T2S 0X3, Canada. *Club:* Alberta United Services Inst. (Calgary, Alberta).

SHAW, Robert; author and actor; *b* 9 Aug. 1927; *s* of a doctor; *m* 1st, 1952, Jennifer Bourke; four *d*; 2nd, 1963, Mary Ure (*d* 1975); two *s* two *d*; 3rd, 1976, Virginia Jansen. *Educ:* Truro Sch.; RADA. Shakespeare Memorial Theatre Co., 1949 and 1950; Rosenkrantz in Hamlet, 1951; Old Vic Co., 1951-52; Shakespeare Memorial Theatre Co., 1953. Subsequent West End plays: Tiger at the Gates; Caro William; Live Like Pigs; The Long and the Short and the Tall; One More River; A Lodging for the Bride; The Changeling; Broadway: The Caretaker; The Physicists; Old Times; Dance of Death. *Films:* The Dambusters; Hill in Korea; Sea Fury; The Valiant; Tomorrow at Ten; The Caretaker; From Russia with Love; The Luck of Ginger Coffey; The Battle of the Bulge; A Man for all Seasons; Custer of the West; The Birthday Party, 1968; Battle of Britain, 1968; Royal Hunt of the Sun, 1969; Figures in a Landscape, 1969; A Town Like Bastard, 1971; Reflections of Fear (previously called Labyrinth), 1971; Young Winston, 1972; The Hireling, 1973; The Sting, 1973; Jaws, 1974; The Judge and His Hangman, 1974; The Taking of Pelham 123, 1975; Diamonds, 1975; Black Sunday, 1976; The Swashbucklers, 1976; The Deep, 1976. *Television:* The Buccaneers (series); Luther, 1968; The Break, 1973; many television plays. *Plays:* Off the Mainland (perf. Arts Theatre, 1957); The Man in the Glass Booth (perf. St Martin's Theatre, 1967, Broadway, 1968). *Publications: novels:* The Hiding Place, 1959; The Sun Doctor, 1961 (Hawthornden Prize, 1962); The Flag, 1965; The Man in the Glass Booth, 1967; A Card from Morocco, 1969; *play:* Cato Street, 1970. *Recreations:* tennis, golf, squash. *Address:* c/o John French Artists' Agency Ltd, 26 Binney Street, WI. *Club:* Savage.

SHAW, Dr Robert Macdonald, CB 1968; Deputy Chief Medical Officer, Department of Health and Social Security (formerly Ministry of Health), 1965-77; b 16 Sept. 1912; s of late Peter Macdonald and Ellen Shaw; m 1941, Grace Helen Stringfellow; two s one d. Educ: Mill Hill School; Victoria Univ. of Manchester. Miscellaneous hospital appointments, etc, 1936-39. Emergency Commission, RAMC, 1939-45. Asst County MOH, Essex, 1945-48; Department of Health and Social Security (formerly Ministry of Health), 1948-77. QHP 1971-74. Address: 42 Chelmsford Road, Shenfield, Brentwood, Essex.

SHAW, Roy; Secretary General of the Arts Council of Great Britain since July 1975; b 8 July 1918; s of Frederick and Elsie Shaw; m 1946, Gwenyth Baron; five s two d. Educ: Firth Park Grammar School, Sheffield; Manchester Univ. BA(Hons). Newspaper printing department 'copy-holder', 1937; newspaper publicity, 1938; Library Asst, Sheffield City Library, 1939; Cataloguer, Manchester Univ. Library, 1945; Organizing Tutor, WEA, 1946; Adult Educn Lectr, Leeds Univ., 1947; Warden, Leeds Univ. Adult Educn Centre, Bradford, 1959; Professor and Dir of Adult Educn, Keele Univ., 1962. Vis. Prof., Centre for Arts, City Univ., London. Publications: contrib. chapters to: Trends in English Adult Education, 1959; The Committed Church, 1966; Your Sunday Paper, 1967; numerous articles on adult education, mass media and cultural policy. Recreations: reading, going to theatres, films, concerts and art galleries; watching the best of television—and sometimes the worst. Address: 48 Farrer Road, N8 8LB.

SHAW, Roy Edwin; Leader, Council, London Borough of Camden, since 1975; b 21 July 1925; s of Edwin Victor and Edith Lily Shaw. Hampstead Borough Council, 1956-62; St Pancras Borough, 1962-65; Camden Borough Council, 1964-. Formerly, Chairman of Planning and Finance Cttees, Chief Whip and Dep. Leader; Vice-Chm., and Dep. Leader, London Boroughs Assoc. Part-time Mem., London Electricity Bd; Mem., Transport Users Consultative Cttee for London. Recreations: listening to music; entertaining attractive women. Address: Town Hall, Euston Road, NW1 2RU. T: 01-278 4444. Club: Talacre Social (Kentish Town).

SHAW, Sir Run Run, Kt 1977; CBE 1974; President, Shaw Organisation, since 1963; b 14 Oct. 1907; m 1932, Lily Wong Mee Chun; two s two d. Left China for Singapore and began making films and operating cinemas, 1927; left Singapore for Hong Kong and built Shaw Movietown, making and distributing films, 1959. Pres., Hong Kong Red Cross Soc., 1972-. Chm., Hong Kong Arts Festival, 1974-; Vice-Chm. Bd of Governors, Hong Kong Arts Centre, 1974-. Mem. Council, Chinese Univ. of Hong Kong, 1977-. Recreations: shadow-boxing, golf. Address: 40 Island Road, Deepwater Bay, Hong Kong. T: 5-92596. Clubs: Hong Kong Country, Hong Kong, Royal Hong Kong Golf, Royal Hong Kong Jockey (Hong Kong).

SHAW, Rt. Hon. Sir Sebag, PC 1975; Kt 1968; Rt. Hon. Lord Justice Shaw; a Lord Justice of Appeal, since 1975; b 28 Dec. 1906; 2nd s of Henry and Marie Shaw; m 1928; one s. Called to Bar, Gray's Inn, 1931, Bencher 1967. QC 1962. Acting Deputy Chairman, County of London Sessions, 1949; Recorder of Ipswich, 1958-68; Prosecuting Counsel, Board of Trade, 1959-62; Judge of Queen's Bench Division, High Court of Justice, 1968-75. Member: Interdepartmental Cttee on Court of Criminal Appeal, 1964-65; Bar Council, 1964-68; Parole Bd, 1971-74, Vice-Chm., 1973-74. Fellow UCL, 1970-. Publication: Law of Meetings, 1947. Address: Royal Courts of Justice, Strand, WC2; 69 Wynnstay Gardens, W8. T: 01-937 4907.

SHAW, Sinclair, QC (Scotland) 1950; Sheriff Principal of Edinburgh, the Lothians and Peeblesshire and Sheriff of Chancery, 1966-73; b South Africa; m 1948, Denise Fanny (Mem. French Resistance, 1941-45, Médaille de la Résistance; Croix de Guerre avec Palme; Chevalier Légion d'Honneur), e d of Dr Charles Mantoux and Dr Dora Mantoux; no c. Called to Scots Bar, 1936. Chairman Scottish Council of Labour Party, 1947. Member New Towns Committee (Chm. Lord Reith) apptd by Govt to work out principles to be followed in building new towns, 1945-46. Contested (Lab): Moray and Nairn, 1945, S Aberdeen, 1951. Advocate-Depute, 1945-51; Sheriff Substitute of Fife, 1959-66. Address: 5 Randolph Cliff, Edinburgh EH3 7TZ. T: 031-225 4445; 28 Ecuble, France. T: Chartres 228702.

SHAW, Sydney Herbert, CMG 1963; OBE 1958; b 6 Nov. 1903; 2nd s of John Beaumont and Gertrude Shaw; m 1930, Mary Louise, e d of Ernest Lewin Chapman; one s one d. Educ: King's College School; Royal School of Mines, London University. BSc Hons 1st cl. Mining Engineering, 1925 and Mining Geology, 1926; MSc (Birm.) 1937; PhD (Lond.) 1949. Geophys. prospecting N and S Rhodesia, 1926-28; Imperial Geophys.

Experimental Survey, Aust., 1928-30; geophys. prospecting, Cyprus, 1930. Demonstrator, Geolog. Dept, Roy. Sch. of Mines, 1931; Lectr in Geology, Birmingham Univ., 1932-37; Govt Geologist, Palestine, 1937-48 (seconded as Dep. Controller Heavy Industries, Palestine, 1942-45); Colonial (later Overseas) Geological Surveys, London, 1949, Deputy Director, 1950, Dir, 1959-65; Head, Overseas Div., Inst. of Geological Sciences, 1965-68. Geological Adviser, Colonial Office (subseq. Dept of Tech. Co-op., then Min. of Overseas Develt), 1959-68. Retd, 1968. FIMM (Pres., 1968-69); FGS. Publications: scientific papers in various jls. Recreation: gardening. Address: Bisham Edge, Stoney Ware, Marlow, Bucks. T: Marlow 4951.

SHAW, Thomas Richard, CMG 1960; HM Diplomatic Service, retired; b 5 Sept. 1912; s of Colin R. and Ida L. Shaw, Bolton, Lancs; m 1939, Evelyn Frances Young; four s. Educ: Repton; Clare Coll., Cambridge. Appointed probationer vice-consul at Istanbul, Nov. 1934; transferred to Bushire, December 1937; acting Consul, Grade 2, Tientsin, 1938-39; transferred to Trieste, Jan. 1940, to Leopoldville, Oct. 1940, to Elisabethville, 1942; served at Casablanca, 1943; vice-consul, Rabat, Dec. 1943; appointed one of HM vice-consuls serving in Foreign Office, 1944; promoted to consul, 1945; transferred to Bremen as consul, 1949; Deputy Consul-General, New York, 1953; actg Consul-General, 1953; Consul-General, Izmir, 1955; Inspector of Foreign Service Establishments, 1957, Senior Inspector, 1961; Ambassador to the Republics of Niger, Upper Volta and the Ivory Coast, 1964-67 (also to the Republic of Dahomey, 1964-65); Minister, Tokyo, 1967-69; Ambassador to Morocco, 1969-71. Address: Upton, Harrow Road West, Dorking, Surrey.

SHAW, Thurstan; see Shaw, C. T.

SHAW, William Boyd Kennedy, OBE 1943 (MBE 1941); b 26 Oct. 1901; s of late Col. F. S. K. Shaw, CBE; m 1936, Eleanor, yr d of Maj. R. A. Dyott, Freeford, Lichfield; one s three d. Educ: Radley Coll.; University Coll., Oxford. Sudan Forest Service, 1924-29; later employed on archæological excavations in Near East; explorations in Libyan Desert, 1927, 1930, 1932, and 1935; awarded Gill Memorial of Royal Geographical Society, 1934; Department of Antiquities, Palestine Government, 1936-40; Land Agent, 1946-53. Military service, 1940-45 (despatches, MBE, OBE, Belgian Croix Militaire de 1ere Classe and Croix de Guerre 1940, avec palme); Officer Order of Orange Nassau, with swords. Publications: Long Range Desert Group, 1945; articles in periodicals on Libyan Desert. Address: The Guinea Garden, Elford, Tamworth, Staffs. T: Harlaston 279.

SHAW-STEWART, Sir Euan (Guy), 10th Bt cr 1667; independent; b 11 Oct. 1928; s of Sir (Walter) Guy Shaw-Stewart, 9th Bt, MC, and Diana (d 1931), d of late George Bulteel; S father, 1976; m 1st, 1953, Mary Louise Shaw (marr. diss. 1956); one d; 2nd, 1964, Victoria Ann Fryer (marr. diss. 1969); one d. Educ: St Peter's Court Prep. Sch.; Eton. Coldstream Guards, 1947-50; Fed. Malay Police, 1950-55; later attached War Office. Recreations: fishing, shooting, eating, sleeping. Heir: b Houston Mark Shaw-Stewart, MC, b 24 April 1931. Address: Forces Club, Sandell Street, SE1 8UJ. T: 01-928 6401. Club: Hokien and Mandarin (Taiping, Malaya).

SHAWCROSS, family name of Baron Shawcross.

SHAWCROSS, Baron, cr 1959 (Life Peer), of Friston; Hartley William Shawcross, PC 1946; GBE 1974; Kt 1945; QC 1939; Chairman: Panel on Take-overs and Mergers, since 1969; Press Council, since 1974; London and Continental Bankers, since 1974; International Chamber of Commerce Commission on Unethical Practices, since 1976; Upjohn & Co. Ltd (Director since 1967); Dominion Lincoln Assurance Co. Ltd; Chancellor, University of Sussex, since 1965; b 4 Feb. 1902; s of John Shawcross, MA, and Hilda Shawcross; m 1st, 1924, Rosita Alberta Shyvers (d 1943); 2nd, 1944, Joan Winifred Mather (d 1974); two s one d. Educ: Dulwich Coll.; abroad. Certificate of Honour for 1st place in Bar Final; called to Bar, Gray's Inn, 1925 (Bencher, 1939); practised on Northern Circuit. Sen. Law Lectr, Liverpool Univ., 1927-34. Chm., Enemy Aliens Tribunal, 1939-40; left practice at Bar for War Service, 1940; Chief Prosecutor for UK before Internat. Military Tribunal at Nuremberg. Asst Chm. of E Sussex QS, 1941; Recorder of Salford, 1941-45; Dep. Regional Comr, South-Eastern Region, 1941; Regional Comr, North-Western Region, 1942-45; Recorder of Kingston-upon-Thames, 1946-61; retired from practice at Bar, 1958. MP (Lab) St Helens, 1945-58; Attorney-General, 1945-51; Pres., BoT, April-Oct. 1951. A Principal Deleg. for UK to Assemblies of UN, 1945-49; a UK Mem., Permanent Court of Arbitration at The Hague, 1950-67. Independent Chm., Kent District Coal Mining Board, 1940; Chairman: Catering Wages Commn, 1943-45; Bar Council,

1952-57; Royal Commn on the Press, 1961-62; MRC, 1961-65; Internat. Law Section of British Inst. of Internat. and Comparative Law; Justice (British Br. of Internat. Commn of Jurists), 1956-72. President: Rainer Foundn (formerly London Police Court Mission), 1951-71; British Hotels and Restaurants Assoc., 1959-71. Member: Home Secretary's Adv. Council on Treatment of Offenders, 1944-45; Council, Internat. Law Assoc., 1958-; Exec. Cttee, Internat. Commn of Jurists, 1959. Hon. Member: Bar Council; Amer. and New York Bar Assoc.; Fellow, Amer. Bar Foundn. Director: Shell Transport and Trading Co., 1961-72; EMI Ltd, Rank-Hovis-McDougall Ltd, and Caffyns Motors Ltd, 1965-; Morgan et Cie International SA, 1966-; Morgan et Cie SA, 1967-; Times Newspapers Ltd, 1967-74; Hawker Siddeley Group Ltd, 1968-; Birmingham Small Arms Co. Ltd, 1968-73 (Chm., 1971-73); European Enterprises Development Co. SA, 1970- (Chm., 1973-); Chm., Thames Television Ltd, 1969-74; Special Adviser, Morgan Guaranty Trust Co. of New York (Chm., Internat. Adv. Council, 1967-74). Chm. Bd of Governors, Dulwich Coll.; Member: Court, London Univ., 1958-74; Council and Exec. Cttee, Sussex Univ., 1959- (Pro-Chancellor, 1960-65); Council, Eastbourne Coll. Hon. LLM Liverpool, 1932; Hon. LLD: Columbia, 1954; Liverpool, 1969; Hull 1970; Lehigh Univ.; Massachusetts; New Brunswick, Canada. JP Sussex, 1941-68. Chm., Soc. of Sussex Downsmen, 1962-75. Knight Grand Cross, Imperial Iranian Order of Homayoon, 1st Cl., 1974. *Recreations:* sailing, riding. *Address:* Friston Place, Sussex. *Clubs:* White's, Buck's; Travellers' (Paris); Royal Cornwall Yacht (Falmouth); Royal Yacht Squadron (Cowes); New York Yacht (US).

SHAWE-TAYLOR, Desmond (Christopher), CBE 1965; Music Critic, The Sunday Times, since 1958; *b* 29 May 1907; *s* of Frank Shawe-Taylor and Agnes Ussher. *Educ:* Shrewsbury Sch.; Oriel Coll., Oxford. Literary and occasional musical criticism, New Statesman, etc until 1939. Served War of 1939-45 with the Royal Artillery. Music Critic, New Statesman, 1945-58; Guest Music Critic, New Yorker, 1973-74. *Publications:* Covent Garden, 1948; (with Edward Sackville-West, later Lord Sackville), The Record Guide (with supplements and revisions, 1951-56). *Recreations:* travel, croquet, gramophone. *Address:* Long Crichel House, Wimborne, Dorset. *T:* Tarrant Hinton 250; 15 Furlong Road, N7. *T:* 01-607 4854. *Club:* Brooks's.

SHAWYER, Robert Cort, MA, PhD; Occasional Chairman, Civil Service Commission Interview Boards; *b* 9 Oct. 1913; *e s* of late Arthur Frederic Shawyer, sometime Gen. Manager, Martins Bank; *m* 1939, Isabel Jessie Rogers; two *d. Educ:* Charterhouse; Corpus Christi Coll., Oxford; Birkbeck Coll., Univ. of London. Bank of England, 1935-37. Commissioned RAEC, 1938 (Lt-Col 1945). Princ., Min. of Nat. Insce, 1948; Admty, 1951; Asst Sec., 1957; seconded to NATO, 1960; Nat. Def. Coll., Canada, 1961-62; Commonwealth Office, 1967; Consul-Gen., Buenos Aires, 1967-70; FCO, Cultural Relations Dept, 1970-72; retired. FRGS. *Publications:* articles in professional, etc, jls. *Recreations:* mediaeval and modern local government. *Address:* Keepers Corner, East Wretham, Norfolk; (winter) Apartamentos Damara, Calpe, Spain. *Clubs:* Royal Commonwealth Society, Royal Automobile.

SHEA, Patrick, CB 1972; OBE 1961; Chairman, Enterprise Ulster, since 1973; Director, Unico Finance Ltd, since 1976; *b* 1908; *s* of Patrick Shea and Mary Catherine Shea (*née* McLaughlin); *m* 1941, Eithne, *d* of Michael and Mary J. MacHugh, Balmoral, Belfast; two *s* one *d. Educ:* High Sch., Clones; Abbey Sch., Newry. Entered Northern Ireland Civil Service, 1926; Asst Sec., Min. of Finance, 1963; Perm. Sec., Min. of Education for N Ireland, 1969-73. Mem. Senate, QUB, 1973-. Hon. Mem., Royal Soc. of Ulster Architects, 1971. Trustee, Ulster Sports and Recreations Trust, 1975. FRSA 1977. *Publication:* (play) Waiting Night (prod. Abbey Theatre, Dublin), 1957. *Recreation:* occasional writer. *Address:* 6 Edenvale Park, The Green, Dunmurry, Belfast BT17 0EJ. *T:* Belfast 616293. *Club:* (Pres. 1961-62) Ulster Arts (Belfast).

SHEALS, Dr John Gordon; Keeper of Zoology, British Museum (Natural History), since 1971; *b* 19 Dec. 1923; *o s* of late John Joseph Sheals and Anne (*née* Ffoulkes); *m* 1945, Blodwen M. Davies (*d* 1972); two *s. Educ:* Caernarvon County Sch.; UC North Wales; Glasgow Univ. BSc, PhD, FIBiol. Asst Lectr, West of Scotland Agricultural Coll., Glasgow, 1948-56; Asst Advisory Entomologist, Min. of Agric., Fisheries and Food, 1956-58; Asst Keeper, 1958-68, and Dep. Keeper, 1968-71, Dept of Zoology, British Museum (Natural History). *Publications:* (with G. O. Evans and D. Macfarlane) The Terrestrial Acari of the British Isles: Introduction and Biology, 1961; papers on taxonomy and ecology of mites in scientific jls. *Recreation:* music. *Address:* 6 The Mount, Rickmansworth, Herts. *T:* Rickmansworth 77250.

SHEARER, Brigadier Eric James, CB 1942; CBE 1941; MC; Underwriting Member of Lloyd's; *b* 23 Nov. 1892; *s* of late Colonel Johnston Shearer, CB, DSO; *m* 1919; one *s*; *m* 1945, Mary, *d* of late Sir O. G. Holmden, KBE, JP, DL. *Educ:* Wellington; RMC, Sandhurst; Staff College. Indian Army, 1911; European War (MC, Brevet Major, despatches); Iraq Rebellion, 1919 (despatches); Malabar Rebellion, 1922; psc, 1922; General Staff, War Office, 1924-29; retired and joined Fortnum & Mason Ltd, Joint Managing Director, 1933-38; returned to Army on outbreak of war, 1939; DMI, MEF, 1940-42; retd; a Managing Director United Kingdom Commercial Corporation Ltd, 1942-45; Todd Shipyards Corporation, USA, 1945-50; Chm. Overseas Tankship (UK) Ltd, 1950-60; a Managing Director, Caltex Trading & Transport Co. Ltd, 1950-60; Director: London and Overseas Freighters Ltd, 1961-66. Member of Queen's Body Guard for Scotland (Royal Company of Archers); Livery Worshipful Company of Shipwrights, 1946; Freeman City of London, 1946. Coronation Medal, 1937; Special Constabulary Medal, 1938. *Address:* The New House, Wilton, near Marlborough, Wilts SN8 3SR. *T:* Great Bedwyn 653.

SHEARER, Rt. Hon. Hugh Lawson, PC 1969; Vice-President, Bustamante Industrial Trade Union, since 1960; *b* 18 May 1923. *Educ:* St Simons Coll., Jamaica. Journalist on weekly newspaper, Jamaica Worker, 1941-44, subseq. Editor. Apptd Asst Gen. Sec., Bustamante Industrial TU, 1947, Island Supervisor, 1953-67, Vice-Pres., 1960- (on leave of absence, 1967-72). Mem. Kingston and St Andrew Corp. Council, 1947; MHR for West Kingston, 1955-59; MLC (now Senator), 1962-67; Leader of Govt Business in Senate, 1962-67; Prime Minister of Jamaica, 1967-72; Minister of Defence and of External Affairs, 1967-72; Leader of the Opposition, 1972-74; Dep. Leader, Jamaica Labour Party, 1967-74. Hon. Dr of Laws, Howard Univ., Washington, DC, 1968. *Address:* Jamaica Labour Party, PO Box 536, Kingston 5, Jamaica.

SHEARER, Rt. Hon. Ian Hamilton; *see* Avonside, Rt Hon. Lord.

SHEARER, Janet Sutherland; *see* Avonside, Lady.

SHEARER, Moira, (Mrs L. Kennedy); Lecturer; Member, BBC General Advisory Council, since 1970; *b* Dunfermline, Fifeshire, 17 Jan. 1926; *d* of Harold King; *m* 1950, Ludovic Kennedy, *qv*; one *s* three *d. Educ:* Dunfermline High School; Ndola, N Rhodesia; Bearsden, Scotland. Professional training: Mayfair Sch.; Legat Sch.; Sadler's Wells School. Début with International Ballet, 1941; joined Sadler's Wells Ballet, 1942, during following ten years danced all major classic roles and full repertoire of revivals and new ballets; first ballerina rôle in Sleeping Beauty, 1946; created rôle of Cinderella, 1948; Titania in Old Vic production of A Midsummer Night's Dream (Edin. Festival, 1954, and tour of US and Canada); American tours with Sadler's Wells Ballet, 1949, 1950-51. Toured as Sally Bowles in I am a Camera, 1955; joined Bristol Old Vic, 1955; played in Man of Distinction, Edin. Fest., 1957; played Madame Ranevskaya in The Cherry Orchard, Royal Lyceum, Edin., 1977. Mem., Scottish Arts Council, 1971-73. Toured US, lecturing on history of ballet, March-April 1973; regular lecturing in England and Wales. Poetry and prose recitals, Edinburgh Festivals, 1974 and 1975. *Films:* Ballerina in The Red Shoes (première, 1948); Tales of Hoffmann, 1950; Story of Three Loves, 1952; The Man Who Loved Redheads, 1954; Peeping Tom, 1960; Black Tights, 1961. *Address:* Makerstoun, Roxburghshire.

SHEARER, Thomas Hamilton, CB 1974; Deputy Secretary, Department of the Environment, since 1972; Chairman, British Channel Tunnel Company, since 1975; *b* 7 Nov. 1923; *o s* of Thomas Appleby Shearer, OBE; *m* 1945, Sybil Mary Robinson, Stratford-on-Avon; one *s* one *d. Educ:* Haberdashers' Aske's, Hatcham; Emmanuel Coll., Cambridge (open exhibition in English). Served RAF, 1942-45 (despatches). Entered Air Ministry, as Asst Principal, 1948; Principal, 1951; Sec. to Grigg Cttee on Recruitment to Armed Forces, 1958; Asst Sec., 1959; transf. Min. of Public Building and Works, 1963; student, IDC, 1965; Under-Sec., 1967; Dir of Establishments, MPBW, 1967-70, DoE, 1970; Dir of Personnel Management, DoE, 1970-72; Dep. Chief Exec. II, PSA, DoE, 1972-73. Chm., Maplin Develt Authority, 1974-77. *Recreations:* opera, claret. *Address:* 9 Denny Crescent, SE11. *T:* 01-735 0921.

SHEARER, Rev. W(illiam) Russell; *b* 12 Oct. 1898; *s* of Henry S. and Jessie A. Shearer; *m* 1934, Phyllis Mary Wigfield. *Educ:* Harrogate Grammar School; Leeds University; Wesley House, Cambridge. Served European War, 1914-18, in Tank Corps. Since 1923 has been Methodist Minister at: Tunstall, Staffs; Manchester; Muswell Hill; Sutton, Surrey; Hanley. Chairman, Stoke-on-Trent Methodist District, 1943-50; Chairman,

Birmingham Methodist District, 1950-63. Pres. of Methodist Conference, 1954-55; Moderator, National Free Church Federal Council, 1959-60. Pres. UK Bd, Hope Union, 1960-74. *Address:* 32 Layton Lane, Shaftesbury, Dorset SP7 8PY. *T:* Shaftesbury 3431. *Club:* National Liberal.

SHEARMAN, Rt. Rev. Donald Norman; *see* Grafton, NSW, Bishop of.

SHEARMAN, Sir Harold (Charles), Kt 1965; MA; Chairman, Greater London Council, 1964-66; Member for Lewisham, 1964-67; Chairman: Inner London Education Cttee, 1964-65; Further and Higher Educn Sub-Cttee, 1964-67; *b* 14 March 1896; *e s* of late Rev. C. E. P. Shearman and late Mary Charlotte Shearman; *m* 1924, Frances Mary, *d* of late Henry Jameson, Hamsterley, Co. Durham; one *s*. *Educ:* Sulgrave National School; Magdalen College School, Brackley; Wolsingham Grammar School; St Edmund Hall, Oxford (1st Class, Modern History, 1922). Elementary Teacher, Durham, 1912-15. Served European War, 1914-18, Private RAMC, and Flying Officer (Observer) RAF, 1916-19. Contested (Lab) Isle of Wight, 1922. Tutor-organiser in Bedfordshire, WEA and Cambridge Extra Mural Board, 1927-35; Education Officer, WEA, 1935-45; Academic Adviser Tutorial Classes, Univ. of London, 1946-61. Member (Deptford) LCC 1946-65 (Chairman Education Cttee, 1955-61); Chairman: LCC, 1961-62; SE Gas Consultative Council, 1963-66; Member: UK delegation, UNESCO Conf., New Delhi, 1956; Committee on Higher Education (1961-63) and other Govt and Educational Cttees; Mem., Commonwealth Scholarships Commn, 1964-68; Pres. School Journey Assoc. of London, 1962-71. Chairman: Metropolitan Exam. Bd (Cert. of Sec. Educn), 1963-72; South Bank Polytechnic, 1970-75 (Hon. Fellow, 1976); Gov. Body, Kidbrooke Sch.; Southfields Sch.; Coombe Lodge Further Educn Coll., 1960-; Rachel Macmillan Coll. of Educn; Garnett College; Member: Court, Brunel Univ.; Univ. of London: Senate, 1966-70; King's College Delegacy; Sch. of Pharmacy, 1960-. DL Greater London, 1967-76. *Address:* 4 Selborne Road, New Malden, Surrey. *T:* 01-942 2581.

SHEARMAN, Prof. John Kinder Gowran, PhD, FBA 1976; Deputy Director, Courtauld Institute, since 1974; *b* 24 June 1931; *s* of Brig. C. E. G. Shearman; *m* 1957, Jane Dalrymple Smith; one *s* three *d*. *Educ:* St Edmund's, Hindhead; Felsted; Courtauld Inst., London Univ.; BA, PhD 1957. Lectr, Courtauld Inst., 1957-67; Research Fellow, Inst. for Advanced Study, Princeton, 1964; Reader, Courtauld Inst., 1967-74. *Publications:* Andrea del Sarto, 1965; Mannerism, 1967, 4th edn 1977; Raphael's Cartoons, 1972; contribs to British, French, German, American jls. *Recreations:* sailing, music. *Address:* Home Close, Long Lane, Rickmansworth, Herts WD3 5DQ. *Clubs:* Bembridge Sailing, Island Sailing (Cowes).

SHEEHAN, Harold Leeming, MD, DSc, FRCP, FRCOG; Professor of Pathology, University of Liverpool, 1946-65 (Professor Emeritus since 1965); *b* 4 Aug. 1900; *s* of Dr P. Sheehan, Carlisle; *m* 1934, E. S. G. Potter; no *c*. *Educ:* University of Manchester. Demonstrator and Lecturer in Pathology, University of Manchester, 1927-34; Rockefeller Medical Fellow in USA, 1934-35; Director of Research, Glasgow Royal Maternity Hosp., 1935-46; Hon. Lecturer in Pathology, Univ. of Glasgow, 1943-46. Served in RAMC, 1939-45; Colonel, Deputy Director of Pathology, AFHQ, Italy, 1945 (despatches, TD). Hon. Member: Fac. Med., Univ. of Chile; Fac. Med., Univ. of Concepcion; Hon. Fellow, Amer. Assoc. Obst. Gyn.; Hon. Member: Soc. Roy. Belge Gyn. Obst.; Soc. Chil. Obst. Gyn.; Soc. Argent. Neurol.; Soc. Med. Hop. Paris; Socs Endocrinology: Chile, Argentine, Roumania, Hungary. Foreign Corresp., Acad. Nat. Méd., France. *Publications:* papers on pathology, endocrinology and renal physiology in various med. jls. *Address:* 18 Knowsley Road, Liverpool L19 0PG. *T:* 051-427 2936.

SHEEN, Barry Cross, QC 1966; a Recorder of the Crown Court, since 1972; *b* 31 Aug. 1918; 2nd *s* of late Ronald Sheen, FCA, St John's Wood; *m* 1946, Diane, *d* of late C. L. Donne, MD; three *s*. *Educ:* Haileybury College, Hill School (USA); Trinity Hall, Cambridge (MA). Served in RNVR, 1939-46; Commanding Officer, HMS Kilkenzie, 1943-45. Called to Bar, Middle Temple, 1947, Master of the Bench, 1971; Member Bar Council, 1959-63; Junior Counsel to Admiralty, 1961-66. On Panel of Wreck Comrs (Eng.) under Merchant Shipping Acts, 1966-; Mem., Panel of Lloyd's Arbitrators in Salvage Cases, 1966-; Appeal Arbitrator, 1977; Arbiter under London Fisheries Convention, 1967. Life Governor, Haileybury. *Recreations:* swimming, golf. *Address:* 16 Parkside Gardens, Wimbledon Common, SW19. *T:* 01-946 8534. *Club:* Royal Wimbledon.

SHEEN, Most Rev. Fulton John, PhD, DD; Titular Archbishop of Newport, Gwent, since 1969; *b* 8 May 1895; *s* of Newton Morris and Delia Fulton Sheen. *Educ:* St Viator Coll.; St Paul Seminary; Catholic University of America; University of Louvain, Belgium; Sorbonne, Paris; Collegio Angelico, Rome. STB and JCB, Catholic Univ. of America, 1920; Univ. of Louvain: PhD 1923; Agrégé en Philosophie, 1925; Cardinal Mercier Internat. Prize for Philosophy, 1925; STD Rome, 1924. Ordained, 1919; Papal Chamberlain, 1934; Domestic Prelate, 1935; Auxiliary Bishop of New York (RC), 1951-66; National Director, Society for the Propagation of the Faith, 1950-66; Bishop of Rochester, NY (RC), 1966-69. Lectured in Westminster Cathedral, Cambridge Univ., and Santa Suzanna (Rome); Catholic Hour radio broadcasts for 25 years; started television series, Life Is Worth Living, 1952; taught in Cath. Univ. of Amer. for 25 years. Hon. LLD, LittD, LHD from various Universities and Colleges. *Publications:* about 60 books including: Freedom under God, 1940; Philosophies at War, 1943; Communism and Conscience of the West, 1948; Philosophy of Religion, 1948; Peace of Soul, 1949; Lift Up Your Heart, 1950; Three To Get Married, 1951; World's First Love, 1952; Way to Happiness, 1954; Thinking Life Through, 1955; Life is Worth Living, 1956; Life of Christ, 1958; This is the Mass (with D. Rops), 1958; This is Rome (with H. Morton), 1960; Go To Heaven, 1960; This Is The Holy Land, 1961; These Are the Sacraments, 1962; The Priest Is Not His Own, 1963; Missions and the World Crisis, 1964; The Power of Love, 1964; Walk with God, 1965; Christmas Inspirations, 1966; Footsteps in a Darkened Forest, 1967; The Quotable Fulton J. Sheen, 1967; Guide to Contentment, 1967; Children and Parents, 1970; Those Mysterious Priests, 1974; weekly column in secular press, 1949-. *Address:* 205 East 78th Street, New York, NY 10021, USA.

SHEFFIELD, 8th Baron; *see under* Stanley of Alderley, 8th Baron.

SHEFFIELD, Bishop of, since 1971; **Rt. Rev. William Gordon Fallows;** Clerk of the Closet to the Queen, since 1975; *b* 21 June 1913; *s* of William and Anne Joyce Fallows; *m* 1940, Edna Mary Blakeman; two *s* one *d*. *Educ:* Barrow Grammar School; St Edmund Hall, Oxford; Ripon Hall. BA 1935, MA 1939. Deacon, 1936; Priest, 1937; Curate of Holy Trinity, Leamington Spa, 1936-39; Vicar of Styvechale, Coventry, 1939-45; OCF 1941-44. Rural Dean of Preston, 1946-55; Proctor in Convocation, 1950-55; Archdeacon of Lancaster, 1955-59; Vicar of Preston, 1945-59; Principal of Ripon Hall, Oxford, 1959-68; Bishop Suffragan of Pontefract, 1968-71. Canon of Blackburn, 1952; Examining Chaplain to Bishop of Wakefield, 1968-71; Chaplain to the Queen, 1953-68. Select Preacher, Univ. of Oxford, 1961. *Publication:* Mandell Creighton and the English Church, 1964. *Recreation:* fell walking. *Address:* Bishopscroft, Snaithing Lane, Sheffield S10 3LG. *T:* Sheffield 302170. *Clubs:* Authors'; Sheffield.

SHEFFIELD, Provost of; *see* Curtis, Very Rev. W. F.

SHEFFIELD, Archdeacon of; *see* Johnson, Ven. Hayman.

SHEFFIELD, Maj.-Gen. John, CB 1967; CBE 1961; Commandant of the Star and Garter Home, Richmond, until 1977, a Governor, since 1977; *b* 28 April 1910; *s* of late Major W. G. F. Sheffield, DSO, and Mrs C. G. A. Sheffield (*née* Wing); *m* 1936, Mary Patience Vere (*née* Nicoll); one *s* one *d* (and one *s* decd). *Educ:* Winchester; RMA, Woolwich. Commd, 1930; served RA and RHA; transferred RAOC, 1939. Served War of 1939-45: BEF, 1939-40; MEF, 1944-48. Egypt, 1954-56; Cyprus, 1959-62; Comdr Base Organization, RAOC, 1964-67. Col Comdt, RAOC, 1970-74. *Recreations:* athletics (British Olympic Team, 1936), golf, sailing, numismatics. *Address:* 11 Pitt Street, W8. *T:* 01-937 3096. *Club:* Royal Automobile.

SHEFFIELD, John V.; Chairman: Norcros Ltd, since 1956; Portals Ltd, since 1968; Atlantic Assets Trust Ltd, since 1972; *b* 11 Nov. 1913; *y s* of Sir Berkeley Sheffield, 6th Bt; *m* 1st, 1936, Anne (*d* 1969), *d* of Sir Lionel Faudel-Phillips, 3rd Bt; one *s* three *d*; 2nd, 1971, Mrs France Crosthwaite, *d* of Brig.-Gen. Goland Clarke. *Educ:* Eton; Magdalene College, Cambridge (MA). Private Secretary to Minister of Works, 1943-44; High Sheriff of Lincolnshire, 1944-45. *Address:* Laverstoke House, Whitchurch, Hants. *T:* Overton 245. *Club:* White's.

SHEFFIELD, Sir Reginald (Adrian Berkeley), 8th Bt *cr* 1755; Director, M. B. P. Russell & Co. Ltd, Normanby Estate Co. Ltd, and other companies; Member of Lloyd's, since 1977; *b* 9 May 1946; *s* of Edmund Charles Reginald Sheffield, JP, DL (*d* 1977) and of Nancie Miriel Denise, *d* of Edward Roland Soames; *S* uncle, 1977; *m* 1969, Annabel Lucy Veronica (marr. diss.), *d* of T. A. Jones; two *d*; *m* 1977, Victoria, *d* of late R. C. Walker,

DFC. *Educ:* Eton. Member of Stock Exchange, 1973-75. *Heir:* uncle John V. Sheffield, *qv*. *Address:* Estate Office, Normanby, Scunthorpe, S Humberside. *T:* Scunthorpe 720618; The Old Rectory, West Tytherley, Salisbury, Wilts SP5 1NF. *T:* Lockerley 40345. *Club:* White's.

SHEHADIE, Sir Nicholas Michael, Kt 1976; OBE 1971; a managing director, in Australia; *b* 15 Nov. 1926; *s* of Michael and Hannah Shehadie; *m* 1957, Dr Marie Roslyn Bashir; one *s* two *d*. *Educ:* Sydney. Elected Alderman, City of Sydney, Dec. 1962; Dep. Lord Mayor, Sept. 1969-Sept. 1973; Lord Mayor of Sydney, Sept. 1973-Sept. 1975. *Recreations:* Rugby, golf, surfing, horse racing. *Address:* Town Hall, Sydney, Australia. *T:* 20263. *Clubs:* Australian Golf, Randwick Rugby, Royal Commonwealth Society, Tattersall's (all in Sydney).

SHELBOURNE, Philip; Chairman and Chief Executive, Samuel Montagu & Co., since 1974; Director, Midland Bank, since 1974; *b* 15 June 1924; *s* of late Leslie John Shelbourne. *Educ:* Radley Coll.; Corpus Christi Coll., Oxford (MA); Harvard Law School. Called to Bar, Inner Temple. Barrister specialising in taxation, 1951-62; Partner, N. M. Rothschild & Sons, 1962-70; Chief Exec., Drayton Corp., 1971-72; Chm., Drayton Gp and Drayton Corp., 1973-74. *Recreation:* music. *Address:* Theberton House, Theberton, Suffolk. *Clubs:* Brooks's, Beefsteak.

SHELBURNE, Earl of; Charles Maurice Petty-Fitzmaurice; *b* 21 Feb. 1941; *s* and *heir* of 8th Marquess of Lansdowne, *qv*; *m* 1965, Lady Frances Eliot, *o d* of 9th Earl of St Germans, *qv*; two *s* two *d*. *Educ:* Eton. Page of Honour to The Queen, 1956-57. Served with Kenya Regt, 1960-61; with Wiltshire Yeomanry (TA), amalgamated with Royal Yeomanry Regt, 1963-73; Pres., Wiltshire Playing Fields Assoc., 1965-74; Wiltshire County Councillor, 1970-; Vice-Chm., Finance Sub-Cttee, WCC, 1977-; Chm., Performance Review Panel, WCC, 1977-; Mem., South West Economic Planning Council, 1971-; Chairman: Working Committee Population & Settlement Patterns (SWEPC) 1972-; Calne and Chippenham RDC, 1972-73; North Wiltshire DC, 1973-76; President: Wiltshire Assocs Boys Clubs and Youth Clubs, 1976-; North-West Wiltshire District Scout Council 1977-. *Heir:* s Viscount Calne and Calstone, *qv*. *Address:* Bowood House, Calne, Wiltshire SN11 0LZ. *T:* Calne 813343; 3 Rutland Street, SW7. *T:* 01-584 1714. *Clubs:* Turf, White's.

SHELDON, Harold; County Councillor; Chairman, West Yorkshire County Council, May 1976-May 1977; *b* 22 June 1918; *s* of Charles Edwin Sheldon and Lily Sheldon (*née* Taylor); *m* 1941, Bessie Sheldon (*née* Barratt); two *s* one *d*. HM Forces, 1939-45 (Sgt; wounded D Day landings). Local Government: elected Batley Borough Council, 1953; W Yorkshire County Council, 1973-. *Recreation:* Sports Council. *Address:* 56 Healey Lane, Batley, West Yorkshire. *T:* Batley 473619. *Club:* Painthorpe Country (Wakefield).

SHELDON, John Gervase Kensington; His Honour Judge Sheldon; a Circuit Judge (formerly a County Court Judge), since 1968; *b* 4 Oct. 1913; *s* of John Henry Sheldon, MD, DPH, and Eleanor Gladys Sheldon, MB, BS; *m* 1st, 1940, Patricia Mary Mardon; one *s*; 2nd, 1960, Janet Marguerite Seager; two *s* one *d*. *Educ:* Winchester Coll.; Trinity Coll., Cambridge (MA; 1st Cl. Hons Law). Barrister-at-Law, called Lincoln's Inn, 1939 (Cert. of Honour, Cholmeley Schol.). Served RA (TA), 1939-45 (despatches twice): Egypt, N Africa, Italy; Major, RA, 1943. *Recreation:* family and home. *Address:* Hopton, Churt, Surrey GU10 2LD. *T:* Frensham 2035. *Club:* Hampshire (Winchester).

SHELDON, Rt. Hon. Robert (Edward), PC 1977; MP (Lab) Ashton-under-Lyne, since 1964; Financial Secretary to the Treasury, since June 1975; *b* 13 Sept. 1923; *m* 1st, 1945, Eileen Shamash (*d* 1969); one *s* one *d*; 2nd 1971, Mary Shield. *Educ:* Elementary and Grammar Schools; Engineering Apprenticeship; Technical Colleges in Stockport, Burnley and Salford. Engineering diplomas; external degree, London University. Contested Withington, Manchester, 1959; Chm., Labour Parly Economic Affairs and Finance Group, 1967-68; Opposition Front Bench Spokesman on Civil Service and Machinery of Govt, also on Treasury matters, 1970-74; Minister of State, CSD, March-Oct. 1974; Minister of State, HM Treasury, Oct. 1974-June 1975; Member: Public Accounts Cttee, 1965-70; Public Expenditure Cttee (Chm. Gen. Sub-Cttee), 1972-74; Mem. Civil Service Cttee, 1966-68. Chm., NW Gp of Labour MPs, 1970-74. Dir, Manchester Chamber of Commerce, 1964-74. *Recreations:* various arts and crafts. *Address:* 27 Darley Avenue, Manchester M20 8ZD; 2 Ryder Street, SW1.

SHELDON, Sir Wilfrid (Percy Henry), KCVO 1959 (CVO 1954); Physician-Pædiatrician to the Queen, 1952-71; Consulting Pædiatrician, King's College Hospital; Consulting Physician, Hospital for Sick Children, Great Ormond Street; Hon. Fellow of Royal Society of Medicine; *b* 23 Nov. 1901; *s* of John Joseph Sheldon, FLS; *m* 1927, Mabel Winifred Netherway; three *d*. *Educ:* King's College, London; King's College Hospital. MB, BS (Honours Anatomy and Medicine), 1921; MD London 1925. FRCP 1933; FAAP 1966; FRCOG 1972; MMSA, 1972. *Publications:* Acute Rheumatism following Tonsillitis, 1931; Amyoplasia Congenita, 1932; Congenital Pancreatic Lipase Deficiency, 1964; Text Book of Diseases of Infancy and Childhood, 8th edn, 1962. *Recreations:* golf, gardening. *Address:* Little Coombe, Warren Cutting, Kingston, Surrey. *T:* 01-942 0252.

SHELFORD, Cornelius William, DL; retired; *b* 6 July 1908; *s* of William Heard Shelford and Maud Ethel Shelford, Horncastle, Sharpthorne, Sussex, and Singapore; *m* 1934, Helen Beatrice Hilda Schuster; one *s* two *d*. *Educ:* private tutor and Trinity College, Cambridge. Chartered Accountant, 1934; Partner, Rowley Pemberton & Co., 1940 (retd 1960); Chm., Mills & Allen Ltd, 1964 (retd 1969); Chm., London County Freehold & Leasehold Properties Ltd, 1964 (retd 1970). East Sussex CC, 1952 (CA, 1957; Chm., 1964-67; Chm., Finance Cttee, 1970-74); High Sheriff of Sussex, 1954; DL Sussex, 1968-. *Recreations:* travelling, walking, gardening. *Address:* Chailey Place, near Lewes, E Sussex BN8 4DA. *T:* Newick 2881. *Club:* Carlton.

SHELLEY, Charles William Evans; Charity Commissioner, 1968-74; *b* 15 Aug. 1912; *s* of George Shelley and Frances Mary Anne Shelley (*née* Dain); *m* 1939, Patricia May Dolby; three *d* (and one *d* decd). *Educ:* Alleyn's Sch., Dulwich; Fitzwilliam House, Cambridge. Called to Bar, Inner Temple, 1937; practised at the Bar, to 1940. Served in Army: first in RAPC and later in Dept of Judge Advocate-General, rank Major, 1940-47. Joined Charity Commn as Legal Asst, 1947; Sen. Legal Asst, 1958; Dep. Comr, 1964. *Recreations:* English literature, listening to music, mountaineering. *Address:* Pen y Bryn, Llansilin, Oswestry, Salop. *T:* Llansilin 273. *Club:* Camping.

SHELLEY, Sir John (Richard), 11th Bt *cr* 1611; (professionally Dr J. R. Shelley); general medical practitioner; Partner, Drs Durstan-Smith, Shelley and Newth, Health Centre, South Molton, Devon, since 1974; *b* 18 Jan. 1943; *s* of John Shelley (*d* 1974), and of Dorothy, *d* of Arthur Irvine Ingram; *S* grandfather, 1976; *m* 1965, Clare, *d* of Claud Bicknell, *qv*; two *d*. *Educ:* King's Sch., Bruton; Trinity Coll., Cambridge (BA 1964, MA 1967); St Mary's Hosp., London Univ. MB, BChir 1967; DObstRCOG 1969. Partner in Drs Harris, Barkworth, Savile, Shelley and Gurney, Eastbourne, Sx, 1969-74. Member: Exeter Diocesan Synod for South Molton Deanery, 1976-79; BMA; CLA; Assoc. MRCGP. *Heir:* *b* Thomas Henry Shelley [*b* 3 Feb. 1945; *m* 1970, Katherine Mary Holton; two *d*]. *Address:* Molford House, 27 South Street, South Molton, Devon EX36 4AA. *T:* South Molton 2232.

SHELLEY, Ursula, MD, FRCP; retired 1971; Physician to Royal Free Hospital's Children's Department, 1940-71 (Assistant Physician, 1935-40), to Princess Louise (Kensington) Hospital for Children, 1944-71 (Assistant Physician, 1937-44), and to Queen Elizabeth Hospital for Children, 1946-71; *b* 11 Apr. 1906; *d* of Frederick Farey Shelley, FIC, and Rachel Hicks Shelley, MB, BS. *Educ:* St Paul's Girls' School; Royal Free Hospital School of Medicine. MB, BS Lond., Univ. Gold Medal, 1930; MD Lond., 1932; FRCP 1948. Member: Worshipful Society of Apothecaries; British Pædiatric Assoc., 1966; Liveryman, Soc. of Apothecaries; Freeman of City of London. *Publications:* numerous articles in medical journals. *Recreations:* gardening, lion dogs. *Address:* 15 Hyde Park Gate, SW7 5DG. *T:* 01-584 7941.

SHELTON, William Jeremy Masefield, MA Oxon; MP (C) Lambeth, Streatham, since 1974 (Clapham, 1970-74); Chairman, Fletcher Shelton Reynolds & Dorrell Ltd, since 1974; *b* 30 Oct. 1929; *s* of Lt-Col R. C. M. Shelton, MBE, St Saviour's, Guernsey, and Mrs R. E. P. Shelton (*née* Coode), London Place, Oxford; *m* 1960, Anne Patricia, *o d* of John Arthur Warder, *qv*; one *s* one *d*. *Educ:* Radley Coll.; Tabor Academy, Marion, Mass; Worcester Coll., Oxford; Univ. of Texas, Austin, Texas. Colman, Prentis & Varley Ltd, 1952-55; Corpa, Caracas, Venezuela, 1955-60; Managing Director: CPV (Colombiana) Ltd, Bogota, Colombia, 1960-64; CPV (International) Ltd, 1967-74 (Dir, 1964); Grosvenor Advertising Ltd, 1969-74 (Dir, 1964). Member for Wandsworth, GLC, 1967-70; Chief Whip, on ILEA, 1968-70. PPS to Minister of Posts and Telecommunications, 1972-74; PPS to Rt Hon. Margaret Thatcher, MP, 1975. *Recreations:* golf, reading, painting. *Address:* 94 Lupus Street, SW1. *T:* 01-834 6786; The Manor House, Long Crendon, Bucks. *T:* Long Crendon 208748. *Club:* Carlton.

SHENSTONE, Prof. Allen Goodrich, OBE 1943; MC 1918; FRS 1950; Professor-Emeritus of Physics, Princeton University, USA, Professor 1938; *b* 27 July 1893; British; *s* of Joseph Newton Shenstone and Eliza Hara; *m* 1st, 1923, Mildred Madeline Chadwick (*d* 1967); one *s* (and one *s* one *d* decd); 2nd, 1969, Locke Tiffin Harper. *Educ:* Princeton Univ.; Cambridge Univ. Instructor in Physics, Toronto University, 1922-25; Princeton Univ.: Asst Prof., 1925-28, Assoc. Prof., 1928-38, Actg Chm. Dept of Physics, 1949-50, Chm., 1950-60, Prof. Emeritus, 1962; leave of absence, 1940-45. Special Assistant to President of National Research Council of Canada for scientific liaison, 1940-45. Served European War, Royal Engineers (2nd Lt to Capt.), 1915-19 (despatches). Member: Physical Soc. USA; Optical Soc. of America (Meggers Prize, 1970); AAAS; FPhysS. Hon. DSc York Univ., Toronto, 1972. *Publications:* many papers on physics in various scientific journals, (mainly in spectroscopy). *Recreation:* sailing. *Address:* 111 Mercer St, Princeton, NJ 08540, USA. *T:* 609-924-2389. *Club:* Athenæum.

SHEPHARD, George Clifford; NCB Board Member for Industrial Relations since 1969; Director: Coal Products Division, NCB; Associated Heat Services Ltd; Compower Ltd; Chairman, Immingham Terminal; *b* 2 Aug. 1915; British; *m* 1942, Mollie Dorothy Mansfield; one *s* (one *d* decd). *Educ:* Chesterfield Grammar School. Bolsover Colliery Co. Ltd, Head Office, 1933-40. Served in Army, N Africa, various Comd HQs, 1940-45, commnd 1942. Official, National Union of Mineworkers, 1945-69. Member: CBI Cttees; ECSC. Hon. Sec., Coal Industry Social Welfare Organisation. Editor, various bulletins and tracts. FCIS, ACWA, MBIM. *Recreations:* golf, music. *Address:* Russett Lodge, 35 The Avenue, Hatch End, Pinner, Mddx HA5 4EL. *T:* 01-428 6444. *Club:* Grimsdyke Golf.

SHEPHARD, Air Cdre Harold Montague, CBE 1974 (OBE 1959); Provost Marshal (RAF) and Director of Security, 1971-74, retired; *b* 15 Aug. 1918; *s* of late Rev. Leonard B. Shephard and Lilian (*née* Robinson), Wanstead, Essex; *m* 1939, Margaret Isobel (*née* Girdlestone); one *s* one *d*. *Educ:* St John's, Leatherhead. Metropolitan Police (CID), 1937-41. Served War, RAF, 1941; commissioned for Provost duties, 1943. Seconded Public Safety Br., Control Commn, Germany, 1945; Wing Comdr, SIB, BAFO, 1947-50; OC, RAF Police Sch., 1951-52; then DAPM, Hong Kong; PMI, Air Ministry; Command Provost Marshal, Cyprus; OC, 4 RAF Police District; PM4, Air Ministry; Comdt, RAF Police Depot, Debden, 1963-64; CPM, FEAF, 1964-67; Comdt, Police Depot, 1967-69; Comd Provost and Security Officer, RAF Germany, 1969-71; Air Cdre, 1971. MBIM. *Recreations:* cricket, rugby, songwriting. *Address:* Le Moulin de Sourreau, Montcaret, 24 Vélines, Dordogne, France. *Clubs:* Royal Air Force, Kennel.

SHEPHEARD, Major-General Joseph Kenneth, CB 1962; DSO 1943, and Bar, 1945; OBE 1949; *b* 15 Nov. 1908; *s* of late J. D. Shepheard, Poole and Bournemouth; *m* 1939, Maureen, *d* of late Capt. R. McG. Bowen-Colthurst, Oak Grove, County Cork; three *d*. *Educ:* Monmouth School; RMA Woolwich; Christ's Coll., Cambridge (BA Hons). Commissioned RE, 1928; served in India with King George V's Own Bengal Sappers and Miners, 1933-38; served in France with BEF as Adjt 4 Div. RE, 1939-40; Staff College, Camberley, 1940; Bde Major 161 (Essex) Inf. Bde in UK, Sierra Leone and Western Desert, 1940-41; Bde Major 18 Indian Inf. Bde in Iraq, 1941; GSO1 4 Indian Div. in N Africa and Italy, 1942-44; Comd 6 Assault Regt RE, Normandy to Baltic, 1944-46; JSSC, Latimer, Bucks, 1947; GSO1, FarELF, 1948-49; Staff Officer to Dir of Operations, Malaya, 1950; Comd 27 Fd Enrg Regt and CRE 6 Armd Div., 1951-53; Defence Research Policy Staff, 1953-56; Imperial Defence Coll., 1957; CCRE 1 (Br.) Corps in Germany, 1958-60; Chief of Staff, Northern Comd, 1960-62; Chief Engineer, Northern Army Group and BAOR, 1962-64. Col Comdt, RE, 1967-72. Gen. Sec., The Officers' Assoc., 1966-74. *Address:* Comfrey Cottage, Fields Farm Lane, Layer-de-la-Haye, Colchester, Essex.

SHEPHEARD, Peter Faulkner, CBE 1972; PPRIBA, MRTPI, FILA; Architect, town planner and landscape architect in private practice since 1948 (Shepheard, Epstein & Hunter); Professor of Architecture and Environmental Design, and Dean of Graduate School of Fine Arts, University of Pennsylvania, since 1971; *b* 11 Nov. 1913; *s* of Thomas Faulkner Shepheard, FRIBA, Liverpool; *m* 1943, Mary Bailey; one *s* one *d*. *Educ:* Birkenhead Sch.; Liverpool Sch. of Architecture. BArch. (1st Cl. Hons) Liverpool, 1936; Univ. Grad. Scholar in Civic Design, 1936-37. Asst to Derek Bridgwater, 1937-40; Min. of Supply, Royal Ordnance Factories, 1940-43; Min. of Town and Country Planning: technical officer, first on Greater London Plan (Sir Patrick Abercrombie's staff), later on research and master plan for Stevenage New Town, 1943-47. Dep. Chief Architect and Planner, Stevenage Develt Corp., 1947-48. Vis. Prof., Landscape Architecture, Univ. of Pennsylvania, 1959 and 1962-71. Member: Nat. Parks Commn, 1966-68; Countryside Commn, 1968-71; Royal Fine Art Commn, 1968-71; Environmental Bd, 1977-. Artistic Advr, Commonwealth War Graves Commn, 1977-. Works include: housing and schools for GLC and other authorities; Landscape of part of Festival of Britain South Bank Exhibition, London, 1951; Master plan and buildings for University of Lancaster; work for the Universities of Keele, Liverpool, Oxford, and Ghana, and for Winchester College. Mem. Council of RIBA, 1950-75 (Pres., 1969-71); President: Architectural Association, 1954-55; Inst. of Landscape Architects, 1965-66. RIBA Distinction in Town Planning, 1956. Hon. FRAIC; Hon. FAIA. *Publications:* Modern Gardens, 1953; Gardens, 1969; various articles, lectures and broadcasts on architecture and landscape; drawings and illustrations of architecture and other things; illustr. A Book of Ducks, and Woodlands Birds (King Penguins). *Recreations:* music and poetry; drawing, gardening and the study of natural history. *Address:* 60 Kingly St, W1R 6EY. *T:* 01-734 8577. *Club:* Savile.

SHEPHEARD, Rex Beaumont, CBE 1949; Director of The Shipbuilding Conference, 1952-68, later Shipbuilders & Repairers National Association; *b* 9 Aug. 1902; *s* of Harold Beaumont Shepheard, MA, solicitor; *m* 1928, Helen H. Simmers; two *s* one *d*. *Educ:* Gresham's School; Glasgow University (BSc, Naval Architecture). Apprenticed with Fairfield Shipbuilding & Engineering Co. Ltd, and with J. Samuel White & Co. Ltd; Ship Surveyor, Lloyd's Register: London, 1928; Glasgow, 1930; Hamburg, 1935; Liverpool, 1939; USA, 1941. Seconded to Admiralty, and appointed Superintendent of Welding Development (Merchant Shipbuilding), 1942; Chief Ship Surveyor, Lloyd's Register of Shipping, 1944-52. Hon. Vice-Pres. Royal Inst. of Naval Architects; Hon. Fellow, NE Coast Instn of Engineers and Shipbuilders; Member: Inst. of Engineers and Shipbuilders in Scotland; Inst. of Marine Engineers. Past Prime Warden, Worshipful Company of Shipwrights. *Publications:* papers to professional institutions. *Address:* 7b South Cliff Tower, Eastbourne, East Sussex. *T:* Eastbourne 23430. *Club:* Devonshire (Eastbourne).

SHEPHEARD, Sir Victor (George), KCB 1954 (CB 1950); Director: William Denny & Brothers Ltd, Shipbuilders and Engineers, Dumbarton, 1959-63; Marinite Ltd, 1961-73; Director of Research, British Ship Research Association, 1959-63; *b* 21 March 1893; *e s* of late V. G. Shepheard, Shortlands, Kent; *m* 1924, Florence, *d* of late Capt. James Wood, Bridgwater. *Educ:* HM Dockyard School, Devonport; Royal Naval Coll., Greenwich. Royal Corps of Naval Constructors, 1915; Constructor Lieut, Grand Fleet, 1915-17; present at Battle of Jutland. Professor of Naval Architecture, RN College, Greenwich, 1934-39; Chief Constructor, 1939-42; Asst Director of Naval Construction, 1942-47; Deputy Director 1947-51; Director of Naval Construction, Admiralty, and Head of RCNC, 1951-58. Member Council Royal Inst. of Naval Architects, 1944-, Vice-Pres. 1952-, Hon. Vice-Pres., 1961, Treasurer, 1960-69; Hon. Vice-Pres., Soc. for Nautical Research; Member: Admty Adv. Cttee on Structural Steel; Cttee on application of Nuclear Power to Marine Purposes, 1961-63; HMS Victory Advisory Technical Cttee. Hon. Fell., NEC Inst.; Mem., Smeatonian Soc. of Civil Engineers, Pres., 1976; Liveryman of Worshipful Company of Shipwrights, Prime Warden, 1968; Board of Governors Cutty Sark Society; formerly Trustee, Nat. Maritime Museum. Froude Gold Medal for services to Naval Architecture and Shipbuilding, 1963. Chev. de la Légion d'Honneur, 1947. *Publications:* various papers to Professional Institutions. *Recreations:* gardening, music. *Address:* Manor Place, Manor Park, Chislehurst, Kent. *T:* 01-467 5455.

SHEPHERD, family name of **Baron Shepherd.**

SHEPHERD, 2nd Baron, *cr* 1946, of Spalding; **Malcolm Newton Shepherd,** PC 1965; Deputy Chairman, Sterling Group of Companies, since 1976; *b* 27 Sept. 1918; *s* of 1st Baron Shepherd, PC, and Ada Newton (*d* 1975); *S* father, 1954; *m* 1941, Allison Wilson Redmond; two *s*. *Educ:* Lower Sch. of John Lyon; Friends' Sch., Saffron Walden. War of 1939-45: commissioned RASC, 1941; served in Desert, N Africa, Sicily, Italy. Deputy Opposition Chief Whip, House of Lords, 1960. Member Parly Labour Party Exec., 1964; Deputy Speaker, House of Lords, subseq. Opposition Chief Whip, 1964; Captain of the Hon. Corps of Gentlemen-at-Arms and Government Chief Whip, House of Lords, 1964-67; Minister of State, FCO, 1967-70; Deputy Leader of the House of Lords, 1968-70; Opposition Dep. Leader, House of Lords, 1970-74; Lord Privy Seal and Leader, House of Lords, 1974-76, resigned. *Recreation:* golf. *Heir: s*

Hon. Graeme George Shepherd, *b* 6 January 1949. *Address:* 29 Kennington Palace Court, Sancroft Street, SE11. *T:* 01-735 0031. *Clubs:* Singapore, Tanglin, Royal Singapore Golf (Singapore).

SHEPHERD, Rear-Adm. Charles William Haimes, CB 1972; CBE 1968 (OBE 1958); *b* 10 Dec. 1917; *s* of William Henry Haimes Shepherd and Florence (*née* Hayter); *m* 1940, Myra Betty Joan Major; one *s. Educ:* Public Central Sch., Plymouth; HMS Fisgard and RNC Greenwich. Entered RN as Artificer Apprentice, 1933; specialised Engrg Officer, 1940; served War of 1939-45 in HMS: Repulse; Hero; Royal Sovereign; Gambia (RNZN); Staff of C-in-C Pacific (Sydney); R&D, Guided Weapons, 1946-49 and 1954-58 incl. Flotilla Eng Officer 3rd Trng Flotilla (HMS Crispin), 1949-51; Sen. Officers War Course, 1961-62; Tech. Dir, UK Polaris Weapon System, 1962-68; Dir Project Teams (Submarines), and Dep. Asst Controller (Polaris), MoD (Navy), 1968-71; Dep. Controller (Polaris), MoD, 1971-73. Sub-Lt 1940; Lieut 1941; Lt-Comdr 1949; Comdr 1952; Captain 1960; Rear-Adm. 1970; retired 1974. *Recreation:* Do-it-yourself. *Address:* 22 Thorkhill Gardens, Thames Ditton, Surrey.

SHEPHERD, Colin; MP (C) Hereford, since Oct. 1974; *b* 13 Jan. 1938; *s* of T. C. R. Shepherd; *m* 1966, Louise, *d* of Lt-Col E. A. M. Cleveland, MC. *Educ:* Oundle; Caius Coll., Cambridge; McGill Univ., Montreal. RCN, 1959-63. Marketing Dir, Haigh Engineering Co. Ltd, 1963-. Jt Sec., Cons. Parly Agr. Fish. and Food Cttee, 1975-; Sec., Cons. Parly Hort. Sub-Cttee, 1976-. *Address:* House of Commons, SW1A 0AA; Manor House, Ganarew, near Monmouth, Gwent. *T:* Symonds Yat 220. *Club:* Naval Officers.

SHEPHERD, David; *see* Shepherd, R. D.

SHEPHERD, Eric William, CB 1967; *b* London, 17 May 1913; *s* of late Charles Thomas Shepherd; *m* 1938, Marie Noele Carpenter; two *d. Educ:* Hackney Downs School; The Polytechnic, Regent Street. BSc 1st Class Hons (Maths and Physics) London 1932. Entered Post Office as Executive Officer, 1932. Served War of 1939-45, with Royal Engineers (Postal Section), 1940-46. Principal, Post Office, 1948; Treasury, 1949-52; Asst Accountant General, Post Office, 1952; Dep. Comptroller and Accountant General, 1953; Assistant Secretary, 1956; Director of Finance and Accounts, 1960; Senior Director, 1967-73. *Recreations:* music, especially choral singing, golf. *Address:* 2 Arkley View, Arkley, Barnet, Herts. *T:* 01-449 9316.

SHEPHERD, Geoffrey Thomas, BSc (Eng), FIMechE, FIEE; Chairman, Midlands Electricity Board, since 1972; part-time Member Central Electricity Generating Board, since 1977; *b* 1922; *s* of Thomas Henry and Louise Shepherd; *m* Irene Wilkes; one *d. Educ:* King Edward's Sch., Birmingham; Coll. of Technology, Birmingham. GEC Ltd, Witton; City of Birmingham Electricity Supply Dept; British Electricity Authority (several positions in Power Stations); Nuclear Ops Engr, CEGB, 1958-61; Asst Regional Dir (Western Div.), 1962-65; South of Scotland Electricity Bd, becoming Dir of Engineering, 1968; Dep. Chm., LEB, 1969-71. *Recreations:* sailing, railways. *Address:* Avon Reach, Church Street, Wyre Piddle, Pershore, Worcs. *T:* Pershore 3076.

SHEPHERD, His Honour Harold Richard Bowman A.; *see* Adie-Shepherd.

SHEPHERD, James Rodney; Under-Secretary, HM Treasury, since 1975; *b* 27 Nov. 1935; *s* of Richard James Shepherd and Winifred Mary Shepherd. *Educ:* Blundell's; Magdalen Coll., Oxford (PPE; Diploma in Statistics). National Inst. of Economic and Social Res., 1960-64; Consultant to OECD, 1964; HM Treasury, 1965-. *Publications:* articles in technical jls. *Address:* 32 Addison Grove, Bedford Park, W4. *T:* 01-994 8325.

SHEPHERD, John Dodson; Regional Administrator, Yorkshire Regional Health Authority, since 1977; *b* 24 Dec. 1920; *s* of Norman and Elizabeth Ellen Shepherd; *m* 1948, Marjorie Nettleton; one *s* two *d. Educ:* Barrow Grammar School. FCIS, FHA. RAF, 1940-46: N Africa, Italy, Middle East, 1943-46. Asst Sec., Oxford RHB, 1956-58; Dep. Sec., Newcastle upon Tyne HMC, 1958-62; Sec., East Cumberland HMC, 1962-67; Sec., Liverpool RHB, 1967-73; Reg. Administrator, Mersey RHA, 1973-77. Pres., Inst. of Health Service Administrators, 1974-75 (Mem. Council, 1969-). *Recreations:* golf, music. *Address:* c/o Yorkshire Regional Health Authority, Park Parade, Harrogate, N Yorks HG1 5AH. *T:* Harrogate 65061. *Club:* Caldy (Wirral) Golf.

SHEPHERD, Dame Margaret (Alice), DBE 1964 (CBE 1962); Chairman, Haigh Engineering Co. Ltd, Ross-on-Wye; *b* 1910; *d* of Percy S. Turner, Redcourt, Pyrford; *m* 1935, Thomas Cropper Ryley Shepherd (*d* 1975); three *s* one *d. Educ:* Wimbledon, Lausanne and London Univ. Chairman: Conservative and Unionist Women's National Advisory Cttee, 1960-63; National Union of Conservative and Unionist Assocs, 1963-64; Conservative Political Centre National Advisory Cttee, 1966-69; Pres., Nat. Union of Conservative and Unionist Assocs, 1971-72. *Recreations:* swimming, golf, gardening. *Address:* Moraston House, Bridstow, Ross-on-Wye, Herefordshire. *T:* Ross-on-Wye 2370.

SHEPHERD, Air Vice-Marshal Melvin Clifford Seymour, CB 1975; OBE 1963; Air Officer Administration, Strike Command, RAF, 1975-77; retired 1978; *b* 22 Oct. 1922; *s* of Clifford Charles Golding Shepherd and Isabella Davidson Shepherd (*née* Kemp); *m* 1949, Patricia Mary Large; one *s. Educ:* in South Africa. Commnd SAAF 1942; war service N Africa, Sicily, Burma, 1942-45; joined RAF, 1947 (Flt-Lt); comd No 73 (F) Sqdn Malta, 1950-53 (Sqdn Ldr); psa 1954; Chief Ops Officer, Western Sector UK, 1954-57; Comdr No 15 MU Wroughton, 1957-60 (Wing Comdr); Air Min. Air Plans, 1960-63; Dirg Staff, Jt Services Staff Coll., 1963-65; Chief Ops Officer, Far East Comd, 1966; ACOS (Intell.) 2ATAF, 1967-69; comd RAF Binbrook, 1969-72; SASO No 38 Gp, 1972-74; Dir of Ops (Air Defence and Overseas), 1974-75. *Recreations:* golf, gardening, shooting, fishing, reading. *Address:* 5 Barn Close, Toddington Lane, Wick, Sussex. *T:* Littlehampton 5904. *Clubs:* Royal Air Force, Royal Commonwealth Society.

SHEPHERD, Sir Peter (Malcolm), Kt 1976; CBE 1967; Chairman: Shepherd Building Group Ltd, since 1958; Construction Industry Training Board, 1973-76; *b* 18 Oct. 1916; *s* of Alderman Frederick Welton Shepherd and Mrs Martha Eleanor Shepherd; *m* 1940, Patricia Mary Welton; four *s. Educ:* Nunthorpe and Rossall Schs. Fellow Inst. of Building; British Inst. of Management, 1963. Chairman: Wool, Jute and Flax ITB, 1964-74; Jt Cttee, Textile ITBs, 1966-74. Inst. of Building: Pres., 1964-65; Mem., Nat. Council, 1956-; Vice-Chm., Professional Practice Bd, 1975- (Chm. 1963-75); Mem., Bd of Bldg Educn, 1967- (Chm. 1965-68); Chm., Site Management Study Gp; rep. on Nat. Consult. Council of Bldg and Civil Eng Industries, 1969-75; Standing Consult. Cttee on Bldg, 1969-71; Standing Consult. Cttee on EEC Liaison, 1973-75. British Inst. of Management: Mem., Nat. Council, 1965-71; Mem., Bd of Fellows, 1969-73; Founder Chm., Yorks and N Lincs Adv. Bd, 1969-71. Nat. Fedn of Building Trades Employers: Mem., President's Consult. Cttee, 1956-; former Mem., Management Trng Cttee and Cttee for Trng Gen. Foremen; Mem. Bd of Man., Bldg Adv. Service, 1959-73; Pres., York Assoc., 1952-53. Fedn of Civil Eng Contractors: Chm., Yorks Sect., 1953-54; former Mem., Nat. Council and Exec. Cttee. Chairman: Jt Cttee for Nat. Certificates and Diplomas in Bldg Industry, 1964-68; Council, Yorks Educnl Assoc. for Bldg Industry, 1956-67; Member: (founder) Technician Educn Council, 1973-; Yorks Adv. Cttee on Further Educn, 1958-65; Council and Res. Cttee, CIRIA, 1967-69; UK Adv. Council on Educn for Management, 1960-66. Member: Co. of Merchant Adventurers of City of York; York Rotary Club. Formerly: Sec., Chm., Area Chm., Hon. Pres. and Nat. Councillor, Round Table, York. Governor, St Peter's Sch., York. *Recreation:* sailing. *Address:* Galtres House, Rawcliffe Lane, York. *T:* York 24250. *Clubs:* Royal Yachting Association; Filey Sailing.

SHEPHERD, (Richard) David; artist; *b* 25 April 1931; *s* of Raymond Oxley Shepherd and Margaret Joyce Shepherd (*née* Williamson); *m* 1957, Avril Shirley Gaywood; four *d. Educ:* Stowe. Art trng under Robin Goodwin, 1950-53; started career as aviation artist (Founder Mem., Soc. of Aviation Artists). Frequent worldwide trips for aviation and paintings for Services. Exhibited, RA, 1956; began painting African wild life, 1960. First London one-man show, 1962; painted 15 ft reredos of Christ for army garrison church, Bordon, 1964; 2nd London exhibn, 1965; Johannesburg exhibns, 1966 and 1969; Collins Artist in Africa (publ.), 1967. Painted: HE Dr Kaunda, President of Zambia, 1967; HM the Queen Mother for King's Regt, 1969; HE Sheikh Zaid of Abu Dhabi, 1970; 3rd London exhibn, 1971. BBC made 50-minute colour life documentary, The Man Who Loves Giants, for worldwide TV, 1970; auctioned 5 wildlife paintings in USA and raised sufficient to purchase Bell Jet Ranger helicopter to combat game poaching in Zambia, 1971; painted Tiger Fire (raised £127,500 for Operation Tiger), 1973. Hon. DFA, Pratt Inst., New York, for services to wildlife conservation through his painting, 1971; Order of the Golden Ark, Netherlands, for services to wildlife conservation (Zambia, Operation Tiger, etc), 1973. *Publications:* Artist in Africa, 1967; (autobiog.) The Man who Loves Giants, 1975. *Recreations:*

conservation of wildlife (on Adv. Panel, Brit. Nat. Appeal World Wildlife Fund; preservation of steam locomotives, railways, etc (purchased two main line steam locomotives, full working order, Black Prince 92203 and Green Knight 75029, 1967; Chm., E Somerset Rlwy, Cranmore, Som., incl. Victorian station, track, 7 locomotives in working order, 6 coaches, etc; open to public, 1974-). *Address:* Winkworth Farm, Hascombe, Godalming, Surrey. *T:* Hascombe 220.

SHEPHERD, Prof. William Morgan, DSc (London); Professor of Theoretical Mechanics in Faculty of Engineering, University of Bristol, 1959-71, Emeritus, 1971; *b* 19 Dec. 1905; *s* of Charles Henry and Elizabeth Shepherd; *m* 1932, Brenda Coulson; two *d.* *Educ:* Wellington School; University College of the South West, Exeter; University College, London. Asst lecturer and lecturer in mathematics, University College of North Wales, Bangor, 1928-35; Lecturer in mathematics in Faculty of Engineering, University of Bristol, 1935-44; Reader in Elasticity, University of Bristol, 1944-59; Head of Department of Theoretical Mechanics, 1951-71. *Publications:* various publications, mainly on applied mathematics, in Proceedings of the Royal Society and other scientific journals. *Recreations:* gardening, cricket. *Address:* 2 Thorpe Lodge, Cotham Side, Bristol BS8 5TJ. *T:* Bristol 426284.

SHEPHERD, William Stanley; *b* 1918; *s* of W. D. Shepherd; *m* 1942, Betty, *d* of late T. F. Howard, MP for Islington South, 1931-35; two *s.* Served in Army, War of 1939-45. A managing director of businesses which he has established; MP (C) for Cheadle Division of Cheshire, 1950-66 (Bucklow Division of Cheshire, 1945-50); Member of the Select Committee on Estimates; Joint Hon. Sec. Conservative Parliamentary Committee in Trade and Industry, 1945-51. Director, Manchester Chamber of Commerce; Hon. Pres., Chair Frame Manufacturers Assoc.; Hon. Mem., Valuers Institution; Government Mem., Scientific Films Assoc. FREconS. *Address:* (office) 77 George Street, W1. *T:* 01-935 0753; (home) 33 Queens Grove, St John's Wood, NW8. *T:* 01-722 7526. *Club:* Carlton.

SHEPHERD-BARRON, Wilfrid Philip, MC, TD; LLD; FICE, FIMechE; *b* 2 May 1888; *s* of late James Barron, MInstCE, Aberdeen; *m* 1921, Dorothy Cunliffe (*d* 1953), *e d* of A. C. Shepherd; two *s.* *Educ:* Aberdeen Grammar School. Chief Engineer, Chittagong Port Commissioners; Chief Engineer, Karachi Port Trust. Served European War, 1914-18, France and Belgium, Royal Engineers, TF (despatches, MC); Past President, Institution of Civil Engineers; Colonel, Engineer and Railway Staff Corps, RE (TA); Chief Engineer, Port of London Authority, retired 1953. Hon. LLD Aberdeen, 1954. *Address:* 22 Ormonde Gate, Chelsea, SW3. *T:* 01-352 0170.

SHEPPARD, Rt. Rev. David Stuart; *see* Liverpool, Bishop of.

SHEPPARD, Leslie Alfred, MA; FSA; Deputy Keeper of Printed Books, British Museum, 1945-53; *b* 9 Jan. 1890; *o s* of late Alfred Sheppard, Keynsham; *m* 1918, Dorothy, *y d* of late Rev. H. Ewbank, St John's, Ryde; two *s.* *Educ:* Merrywood School, Bristol; St Catharine's College, Cambridge. Served with 1st British Red Cross Unit attached to Italian Army, 1915-19; entered British Museum, 1919; worked on Catalogue of books printed in XVth cent., now in BM, vols vi, viii-x; catalogued incunabula of Bodleian Library, Oxford, 1955-70. Member of Council of Bibliographical Society, 1936-46. *Publications:* A Fifteenth-Century Humanist, Francesco Filelfo, 1935; The Printers of the Coverdale Bible, 1935; Printing at Deventer in the XVth Century, 1943; A New Light on William Caxton and Colard Mansion, 1952; and other articles and reviews in Transactions of Bibliographical Society, Gutenberg Jahrbuch, and elsewhere. Translated Memoirs of Lorenzo da Ponte, 1929. *Address:* The Bishops House, 55 New Street, Henley-on-Thames, Oxon RG9 2BP. *T:* Henley 4658.

SHEPPARD, Tan Sri Dato Mervyn Cecil ffranck, PSM (Malaysia) 1969; DJPD (Malaysia), 1967; JMN (Malaysia), 1963; CMG 1957; MBE 1946; ED 1947; Vice-President and Editor, Malaysian Branch, Royal Asiatic Society; *b* 1905; *s* of late Canon J. W. ff. Sheppard; *m* 1940, Rosemary, *d* of late Major Edward Oakeley; one *d.* *Educ:* Marlborough; Magdalene Coll., Cambridge (MA). Cadet, Federated Malay States, 1928; Private Sec. to Chief Sec., 1929. Interned by Japanese, 1942-45. Director of Public Relations, 1946; District Officer, Klang, 1947-50; British Adviser, Negri Sembilan, 1952; Head of the Emergency Food Denial Organisation, Federation of Malaya, 1956. First Keeper of Public Records, 1957-62, and Director of Museums, 1958-63, Federation of Malaya. Hon. Curator, Nat. Museum, Kuala Lumpur. Panglima Setia Mahkota, 1969; Dato Jasa Purba Di-Raja, Negri Sembilan, 1967. *Publication:* Taman Indera, 1972. *Address:* Kenangan Road 9/3, Petaling Jaya, Malaysia. *Club:* United Oxford & Cambridge University.

SHEPPARD, Prof. Norman, FRS 1967; Professor of Chemical Sciences, University of East Anglia, Norwich, since 1964; *b* 16 May 1921; *s* of Walter Sheppard and Anne Clarges Sheppard (*née* Finding); *m* 1949, Kathleen Margery McLean; two *s* one *d* (and one *s* decd). *Educ:* Hymers Coll., Hull; St Catharine's Coll., Cambridge. BA Cantab 1st cl. hons 1943; PhD and MA Cantab 1947. Vis. Asst Prof., Pennsylvania State Univ., 1947-48; Ramsay Memorial Fellow, 1948-49; Senior 1851 Exhibn, 1949-51; Fellow of Trinity Coll., Cambridge and Asst Dir of Research in Spectroscopy, Cambridge Univ., 1957-64. *Publications:* scientific papers on spectroscopy in Proc. Roy. Soc., Trans. Faraday Soc., Jl Chem. Soc., Spectrochimica Acta, etc. *Recreations:* architecture, classical music, cricket. *Address:* 5 Hornor Close, Norwich NR2 2LY. *T:* Norwich 53052.

SHEPPARD, Prof. Percival Albert, (Peter), CBE 1969; FRS 1964; Professor of Meteorology, University of London (at Imperial College), 1952-74, now Emeritus; *b* 12 May 1907; *s* of Albert Edward Sheppard, Box, Wiltshire, and Flora Sheppard (*née* Archard); *m* 1933, Phyllis Blanche Foster (*d* 1976), Bath; two *s.* *Educ:* City of Bath Boys' School; University of Bristol. First Class Hons Physics, 1927; Demonstrator, H. H. Wills Physical Laboratory, University of Bristol, 1927-29; Resident Observer, Kew Observatory, 1929-32; British Polar Year Expedition, NWT, Canada, 1932-33; Meteorologist, Chemical Defence Research Establishment, Porton, 1934-39; Reader in Meteorology, Imperial Coll., Univ. of London, 1939-52. Served Meteorological Office, Air Min., 1939-45. Vis. Prof., Univ. of California, Los Angeles, 1963. Royal Meteorological Society: Editor and Hon. Sec., 1950-53; Pres., 1957-59; Symons Gold Medal, 1963; Hon. Mem., 1976. Chm., Meteorological Research Cttee, 1958-68; Mem. Science Res. Council, 1967-71 (Chm., Space Policy and Grants Cttee, 1965-71); Vice-Chm. of Council, ESRO, 1966-68 (Chm., Scientific and Technical Cttee, 1968-71); Mem. Council, Royal Soc., 1970-72. FInstP; Fellow, Amer. Meteorological Soc., 1967; Hon. ARCS. Hon. DSc: Leningrad, 1969; Bath, 1976. *Publications:* papers on atmospheric electricity and meteorology in various journals. *Recreation:* life. *Address:* Weathering, Longbottom, Seer Green, Bucks HP9 2UL. *T:* Beaconsfield 71297.

SHEPPARD, Richard, CBE 1964; RA 1972 (ARA 1966); FRIBA 1944 (ARIBA 1936); Architect in private practice (Richard Sheppard, Robson & Partners); work includes universities, schools and technical colleges, industrial and commercial buildings; *b* 2 July 1910; *e s* of William Sheppard and Hilda (*née* Kirby-Evans); *m* 1st, 1938, Jean Shufflebotham, ARIBA, MRTPI (*d* 1974); one *s* one *d*; 2nd, 1976, Marjorie Head. *Educ:* Bristol Grammar School; Architectural Association School of Architecture, Bedford Square. Hons Diploma, Architectural Assoc. 1935; foreign travel, 1935-37. Principal commissions include: City Univ., London; Brunel Univ., Uxbridge; Churchill College, Cambridge (competition), 1959; Collingwood College, Univ. of Durham; Campus West, Welwyn Garden City; Manchester Polytechnic; and other educnl and commercial bldgs. Vice-Pres. RIBA, 1969-70. Hon. DTech Brunel, 1972. *Publications:* Building for the People, 1945; Prefabrication and Building, 1946, etc; also technical articles. *Recreation:* looking at the work of others. *Address:* The Old Rectory, Little Berkhamsted, Herts. *T:* Cuffley 5066.

SHEPPARD, William Vincent, CBE 1963; Deputy Chairman, National Coal Board, 1971-75 (Member, since 1967); Chairman, PD/NCB (Consultants) Ltd, since 1975; *b* 15 Nov. 1909; *s* of late Dr H. P. Sheppard; *m* 1938, Nancy F. Watson; two *s* one *d.* *Educ:* Cheltenham College; Birmingham University (BSc (Hons) Min.). Mining Student with Bolsover Colliery Co. Ltd, 1931-35, Safety Officer to Co., 1935-37; Under Manager, Creswell Colliery, 1937; Manager, Rufford Colliery, 1938; Mining Devel. Engr, No 4 Area, East Midlands Div., NCB, 1947; Area Gen. Man., No 1 Area, East Midlands Div., NCB, 1948; Dir-Gen. of Reconstruction, NCB, 1957-60; Dir-Gen. of Production, NCB, 1960-67. Dir, Wide Range Engineering Services Ltd, 1976-. Past-Pres., Southern Counties Inst. of Instn of Mining Engineers; Hon. FIMinE. CStJ 1957. *Recreations:* gardening, model-making, Rugby football (County Cap, Glos). *Address:* Langshott Manor, Horley, Surrey. *T:* Horley 2282.

SHEPPARD FIDLER, Alwyn G.; *see* Fidler.

SHEPPERD, Alfred Joseph; Chairman and Chief Executive, The Wellcome Foundation Ltd, since 1977; *b* 19 June 1925; *s* of Alfred Charles Shepperd and Mary Ann Williams; *m* 1950, Gabrielle Marie Yvette Bouloux; two *d.* *Educ:* Archbishop Tenison's Sch.; University Coll., London (BSc Econ). Rank Organisation, 1949; Selincourt & Sons Ltd, 1963; Chamberlain Group, 1965; Managing Director, Keyser Ullmann Industries Ltd, 1967; Dir, Keyser Ullmann Ltd, 1967; Financial Dir,

Laporte Industries Ltd, 1971, Wellcome Foundation Ltd, 1972. *Address:* Court Mead, 6 Guildown Avenue, Guildford, Surrey GU2 5HB. *Clubs:* Athenæum, Naval, Oriental.

SHERBORNE, 7th Baron, *cr* 1784; **Charles Dutton;** *b* 13 May 1911; *e s* of 6th Baron, DSO and Ethel Mary (*d* 1969), *e d* of late William Baird; *S* father, 1949; *m* 1943, Joan Molesworth, *d* of Sir James Dunn, 1st Bt, and *widow* of John Anthony Jenkinson. *Educ:* Stowe. *Heir: b* Hon. George Edward Dutton [*b* 23 Sept. 1912; *m* 1959, Mrs Pauline Stewart Shephard, *d* of late Stewart Robinson]. *Address:* Lodge Park, Aldsworth, Cheltenham, Glos. *T:* Windrush 296. *Club:* White's.
See also Sir John Dutton Clerk .

SHERBORNE, Bishop Suffragan of, since 1976; **Rt. Rev. John Dudley Galtrey Kirkham;** Canon and Prebendary of Salisbury Cathedral, since 1977; *b* 20 Sept. 1935; *s* of Charles Dudley Kirkham and Doreen Betty Galtrey. *Educ:* Lancing Coll.; Trinity Coll., Cambridge (BA 1959, MA 1963). Commnd, Royal Hampshire Regt and seconded to 23 (K) Bn, King's African Rifles, 1954-56. Trinity Coll., Cambridge, 1956-59; Westcott House, 1960-62; Curate, St Mary-Le-Tower, Ipswich, 1962-65; Chaplain to Bishop of Norwich, 1965-69; Priest in Charge, Rockland St Mary w. Hellington, 1967-69; Chaplain to Bishop of New Guinea, 1969; Asst Priest, St Martin in the Fields and St Margaret's, Westminster, 1970-72; Domestic Chaplain to Archbishop of Canterbury, 1972-76; Canterbury Diocesan Director of Ordinands, 1972-76. Serving Brother Chaplain of the Order of St John of Jerusalem. Croix d'Argent de Saint-Rombaut, 1973. *Recreations:* skiing, walking, wood-work, reading. *Address:* Little Baillie, Sturminster Marshall, Wimborne, Dorset. *Clubs:* Army and Navy, Royal Commonwealth Society, Ski of Great Britain.

SHERBORNE, Archdeacon of; *see* Ward, Ven. E. J. G.

SHERBROOKE, Archbishop of, (RC), since 1968; **Most Rev. Jean-Marie Fortier;** *b* 1 July 1920. *Educ:* Laval University, Quebec. Bishop Auxiliary, La Pocatière, PQ, 1961-65; Bishop of Gaspé, PQ, 1965-68. Elected Pres., Canadian Catholic Conference, 1973-75. *Publication:* contrib. to Dictionnaire d'Histoire et de Géographie. *Address:* 130 rue de la Cathédrale, Sherbrooke, PQ, Canada. *T:* 569-6070.

SHERBROOKE-WALKER, Col Ronald Draycott, CBE 1961; TD 1945; TA (retired); Director of Securicor (Wales and South West) Ltd, 1965-72 (of Securicor Ltd, 1945-65); *b* 1 April 1897; *s* of Rev. George Sherbrooke Walker, sometime Rector of March, Cambs; *m* 1925, Ruth Bindley, *d* of William Allen Bindley, Edgbaston. *Educ:* Sherborne. Chartered Accountant, 1923. Served European War, 1914-19; Lieut Dorset Regt and RFC. Lieut to Major 8th Bn Middx Regt TA, 1925-31. Served War of 1939-45: Lieut-Col, Middx Regt and attached RAF Regt. Mem. Middx T&AFA, 1930-63 (Vice-Chm. 1951-56); Comdt Middx Army Cadet Force, 1948-54; Vice-Chm. Army Cadet Force Assoc., 1956-66 (Vice-Pres., 1966-); Mem. Amery Cttee, 1956-57; Mem. TA Advisory Cttee, 1956-64; Governor Cadet Training Centre, Frimley Park, 1959-. FCA. DL Middx, 1947-65; Vice-Lieutenant, Middx, 1963-65; DL Greater London, 1965-76. *Publications:* Khaki and Blue, 1952; contrib. to various jls. *Recreation:* gardening. *Address:* 22 Bathwick Hill, Bath BA2 6EW. *Club:* Naval and Military.

SHERFIELD, 1st Baron, *cr* 1964; **Roger Mellor Makins,** GCB 1960 (KCB 1953); GCMG 1955 (KCMG 1949; CMG 1944); Chancellor of Reading University, since 1970; Fellow, and Warden since 1974, Winchester College; Chairman: A. C. Cossor, since 1968; Raytheon Europe International Co., since 1970; Wells Fargo Ltd, since 1972; Lindemann Trust Fellowship Committee; Trustee, Kennedy Memorial Fund; President, Centre for International Briefing; Member of Council, Royal Albert Hall; *b* 3 Feb. 1904; *e s* of late Brigadier-General Sir Ernest Makins, KBE, CB, DSO; *m* 1934, Alice, *e d* of late Hon. Dwight F. Davis; two *s* four *d*. *Educ:* Winchester; Christ Church, Oxford. First Class Honours in History, 1925; Fellow of All Souls College, 1925-39 and 1957-; called to Bar, Inner Temple, 1927; Foreign Office, 1928; served Washington, 1931-34, Oslo, 1934; Foreign Office, 1934; Assistant Adviser on League of Nations Affairs, 1937; Sec. Intergovernmental Cttee on Refugees from Germany, 1938-39; Adviser on League of Nations Affairs, 1939; Acting First Secretary, 1939; Acting Counsellor, 1940; Adviser to British Delegation, International Labour Conference, New York, 1941; served on Staff of Resident Minister in West Africa, 1942; Counsellor, 1942; Asst to Resident Minister at Allied Force Headquarters, Mediterranean, 1943-44; Minister at British Embassy, Washington, 1945-47; UK rep. on United Nations Interim Commission for Food and Agriculture, 1945; Asst Under-Sec. of

State, FO, 1947-48, Dep. Under-Sec. of State, 1948-52; British Ambassador to the United States, 1953-56; Joint Permanent Secretary of the Treasury, 1956-59; Chairman: UKAEA, 1960-64; Hill, Samuel Group, 1966-70; Dir, Times Publishing Co. Ltd, 1964-67. Chairman: Finance for Industry Ltd, 1973-74; Finance Corp. for Industry Ltd, 1973-74; Industrial & Commercial Finance Corp., 1964-74; Estate Duties Investment Trust, 1966-73; Ship Mortgage Finance Co., 1966-74; Technical Develt Capital, 1966-74, and other companies. Pres., BSI, 1970-73. Pres., Parly and Scientific Cttee, 1969-73. Vice-Chm., The Ditchley Foundn, 1965-74 (Chm., 1962-65). Chm., Governing Body and Fellow of Imperial Coll. of Science and Technology, 1962-74. Chm., Marshall Aid Commemoration Commn, 1965-73. Trustee, The Times Trust, 1968-73. Hon. Student, Christ Church, Oxford, 1973; Hon. FICE 1964; Hon. DCL Oxford; Hon. LLD Reading; Hon. LLD: Sheffield; London; Hon. DL North Carolina; and other American universities and colleges. *Publication:* (ed) Economic and Social Consequences of Nuclear Energy, 1972. *Recreations:* shooting, gardening. *Heir: s* Hon. Christopher James Makins, *b* 23 July 1942. *Address:* 81 Onslow Square, SW7; Sherfield Court, near Basingstoke, Hants; Warden's Lodgings, Winchester College, Winchester, Hants. *Clubs:* Boodle's, Pratt's, MCC.
See also Baron Milford.

SHERGOLD, Harold Taplin, CMG 1963; OBE 1958 (MBE 1945); serving in Foreign and Commonwealth Office (formerly Foreign Office), since 1954; *b* 5 Dec. 1915; *s* of late Ernest Henry Shergold; *m* 1949, Bevis Anael, *d* of late William Bernard Reid; no *c. Educ:* Peter Symonds' School, Winchester; St Edmund Hall, Oxford; Corpus Christi Coll., Cambridge. Asst Master, Cheltenham Grammar Sch., 1937-40. Joined Hampshire Regt, 1940; transferred to Intelligence Corps, 1941; served in Middle East and Italy, 1941-46 (despatches). Joined Foreign Office, 1947; served in Germany, 1947-54. Mem., Royal Commonwealth Soc. *Address:* 1 Ancaster Court, Queens Road, Richmond, Surrey TW10 6JJ. *T:* 01-948 2048.

SHERIDAN, Cecil Majella, CMG 1961; *b* 9 Dec. 1911; *s* of late J. P. Sheridan, Liverpool, and Mrs Sheridan (*née* Myerscough), Preston, Lancs; *m* 1949, Monica, *d* of H. F. Ereaut, MBE, Jersey, CI; two *s* one *d. Educ:* Ampleforth College, York. Admitted Solicitor, England, 1934; called to Bar, Innner Temple, 1952. Practised as solicitor in Liverpool (Messrs Yates, Sheridan & Co.), 1934-40. Served in RAFVR, General Duties Pilot, 1940-46; resigned with hon. rank of Squadron Leader. Joined Colonial Legal Service, 1946; Crown Counsel and Dep. Public Prosecutor, Malayan Union, 1946-48; Legal Adviser, Malay States of Pahang, Kelantan, Trengganu and Selangor and Settlement of Penang, 1948-55; Legal Draftsman, Fedn of Malaya, 1955-57; Solicitor-General, Fedn of Malaya, 1957-59; Attorney-General, Fedn of Malaya, 1959-63; Attorney-General, Malaysia, retd. Mem. (Fedn of Malaya) Inter-Governmental Cttees for Borneo Territories and Singapore, 1962-63; Chm. Traffic Comrs, E Midland Traffic Area, 1965-; Pres., British Assoc. of Malaysia 1964-65. Chm., Malaysia Housing Soc., 1964-65. Hon. PMN (Malaysia), 1963. Associate Mem., Commonwealth Parly Assoc. (UK Branch). *Address:* 18 Private Road, Sherwood, Nottingham NG5 4DB. *Clubs:* East India, Devonshire, Sports and Public Schools; Nottinghamshire.

SHERIDAN, Sir Dermot (Joseph), Kt 1970; CMG 1965; Hon. Mr Justice Sheridan; Puisne Judge, High Court, Kenya, since 1972; *b* 3 Oct. 1914; *s* of late Sir Joseph Sheridan; *m* 1973, Mrs Marion Donnelly. *Educ:* Downside Sch.; Pembroke Coll., Cambridge (BA, 1st Cl. Hons Law Tripos); Harmsworth Scholar, Middle Temple. Called to Bar, 1936; practised at Bar, 1936-42; Colonial Legal Service, Resident Magistrate, Uganda, 1942-48; Crown Counsel, Uganda, 1948-51; Director of Public Prosecutions, Gold Coast, 1951-55; Puisne Judge, High Court, Uganda, 1955-70; Chief Justice, 1970-72; Acting Chief Justice, Jan.-June 1963, and 1968-70. *Recreations:* music, cricket, bridge, reading. *Address:* c/o The Standard Bank Ltd, 28 Northumberland Avenue, WC2. *Clubs:* MCC, East India, Sports and Public Schools; Muthaiga Country, Mombasa (Mombasa).

SHERIDAN, Peter, QC 1977; *b* 29 May 1927; *s* of Hugo and Marie Sheridan. *Educ:* eight schools; Lincoln Coll., Oxford Univ. BA Hons, 1950. Called to the Bar, Middle Temple, 1955. *Recreations:* motor cars, archery. *Address:* 17 Brompton Square, SW3. *T:* 01-584 7850; Pile Oak Lodge, Donhead St Andrew, Wilts. *T:* Donhead 484.

SHERLOCK, Sir Philip (Manderson), KBE 1967 (CBE 1953); Secretary-General, Association of Caribbean Universities & Research Institutes, since 1969; *b* Jamaica, 25 Feb. 1902; *s* of Rev. Terence Sherlock, Methodist Minister, and Adina

Sherlock; *m* 1942, Grace Marjorye Verity; two *s* one *d. Educ:* Calabar High Sch., Jamaica. Headmaster, Wolmer's Boys' Sch., Jamaica, 1933-38; Sec., Inst. of Jamaica, 1939-44; Educn Officer, Jamaica Welfare, 1944-47; Dir, Extra-Mural Dept, University Coll. of West Indies, 1947-60, also Vice-Principal, University Coll. of W Indies, 1952-62; Pro-Vice-Chancellor, Univ. of West Indies, 1962, Vice-Chancellor, 1963-69. Hon. LLD: Leeds, 1959; Carleton, 1967; St Andrews, 1968; Hon. DCL, New Brunswick, 1966; Hon. DLitt: Acadia, 1966; Miami, 1971; Univ. of WI, 1972. *Publications:* Anansi the Spider Man, 1956; (with John Parry) Short History of the West Indies, 1956; Caribbean Citizen, 1957; West Indian Story, 1960; Three Finger Jack, 1961; Jamaica, A Junior History, 1966; West Indian Folk Tales, 1966; West Indies, 1966; Land and People of the West Indies, 1967; Belize, a Junior History, 1969; The Iguana's Tail, 1969; West Indian Nations, 1973; Ears and Tails and Common Sense, 1974; Shout for Freedom, 1976; educational books and articles. *Recreations:* reading, writing, cooking. *Address:* Association of Caribbean Universities & Research Institutes, 18 Charlemont Avenue, Kingston 6, Jamaica, West Indies. *Clubs:* National Liberal, English-Speaking Union, Royal Commonwealth Society (West Indian).

SHERLOCK, Prof. Sheila Patricia Violet, MD; FRCP; FRCPEd; Professor of Medicine, University of London, at the Royal Free Hospital School of Medicine, since 1959; *b* 31 March 1918; *d* of Samuel Philip Sherlock and late Violet Mary Catherine Beckett; *m* 1951, David Geraint James; two *d. Educ:* Folkestone County Sch.; Edinburgh Univ. Ettles Scholar, 1941; Beit Memorial Research Fellow, 1942-47; Rockefeller Fellow, Yale University, USA, 1948. Physician and Lecturer in Medicine, Postgraduate Medical School of London, 1948-59; Bradshaw Lecturer, RCP, 1961; Rolleston Lecturer, RCP, 1968. RCP: Councillor, 1964-68; Censor, 1970-72; Senior Censor and Vice-Pres., 1976-77. Mem. Senate, Univ. of London, 1976-. Hon. Member: Gastro-enterological Societies of America, 1963, Australasia, 1965, Mexico, 1968, Czechoslovakia, 1968; Assoc. of Amer. Physicians, 1973; Assoc. of Alimentary Surgeons, 1973. Hon. FACP; Hon. FRCP (C). Hon. DSc, City Univ. of NY. William Cullen Prize, 1962 (shared). *Publications:* Diseases of the Liver and Biliary System, 5th edn, 1975; papers on liver structure and function in various medical journals, since 1943. *Recreations:* cricket, travel. *Address:* 41 York Terrace East, NW1 4PT. *T:* 01-486 4560.

SHERMAN, Sir Louis, (Sir Lou Sherman), Kt 1975; OBE 1967; JP; London cabby; Alderman, London Borough of Hackney; Chairman: London Boroughs Association; Housing Corporation, since 1977; Deputy Chairman: Harlow Development Corporation; Assoc. of Metropolitan Authorities, 1977-. Member: ILEA; English Tourist Bd, until 1977. Initiated Lea Valley Regional Park Authority. JP Inner London Area. *Recreations:* politics, reading, talking.

SHERRARD, Michael David, QC 1968; a Recorder of the Crown Court, since 1974; *b* 23 June 1928; *er s* of late Morris Sherrard and Ethel Sherrard; *m* 1952, Shirley (C. B. Piper, writer), *d* of late Maurice and Lucy Bagrit; two *s. Educ:* King's Coll., London. LLB 1949. Called to Bar, Middle Temple, 1949, Bencher 1977, Mem. Senate, 1977. Mem., SE Circuit, 1950. Mem., Winn Cttee on Personal Injury Litigation, 1966; Mem. Council and Exec. Cttee, Justice, British Section, Internat. Commn of Jurists, 1974-; Dept of Trade Inspector, London Capital Group, 1975-77; Chm., Normansfield Hosp. Inquiry, 1977-. Chm., St Michael's Hosp. Foundn for cardio-vascular diseases, 1973-77. *Recreations:* oil painting, listening to opera. *Address:* 2 Crown Office Row, Temple, EC4. *T:* 01-583 2681; 14 Burgess Hill, Hampstead, NW2. *T:* 01-435 7828.

SHERRILL, Rt. Rev. Henry Knox, DD; retired Bishop; Presiding Bishop of Protestant Episcopal Church in USA, 1947-58; a President, World Council of Churches, 1954-61; *b* Brooklyn, New York, 6 Nov. 1890; *s* of Henry Williams Sherrill, and Maria Knox Mills; *m* 1921, Barbara Harris, Brookline, Mass; three *s* one *d. Educ:* Hotchkiss School; Yale University; Episcopal Theological School, Cambridge, Mass. Deacon, 1914; Priest, 1915; Assistant Minister, Trinity Church, Boston, 1914-17; Rector, Church of Our Saviour, Brookline, 1919-23; Rector, Trinity Church, Boston, 1923-30; Bishop of Massachusetts, 1930-47; Red Cross and US Army Chaplain, AEF, France, July 1917-Jan. 1919; Pres. Nat. Council of Churches of Christ in USA, 1950-52; Board of Trustees: Massachusetts General Hospital, 1928-46 (Chairman of Board, 1934-46); Fellow Corporation of Yale University; Fellow American Academy of Arts and Sciences. Hon. DD Edinburgh, Oxford; numerous doctorates in Divinity, Law, Sacred Theology, Literature and Canon Law from American Universities and Colleges. *Publications:* William Lawrence: Later Years of a Happy Life,

1943; The Church's Ministry in Our Times (Lyman Beecher Lectures, Yale Univ.), 1949; Among Friends, 1962. *Address:* Boxford, Mass 01921, USA. *Clubs:* Graduates (New Haven); Union (Boston).

SHERRIN, Ned, (Edward George Sherrin); film, theatre and television producer, director and writer; *b* Low Ham, Som, 18 Feb. 1931; *s* of late T. A. Sherrin and D. F. Sherrin (*née* Drewett). *Educ:* Sexey's Sch., Bruton; Exeter Coll., Oxford; Gray's Inn. Producer: ATV, Birmingham, 1955-57; BBC TV, 1957-66 (prod. and dir. That Was The Week That Was). Produced films: The Virgin Soldiers (with Leslie Gilliat) 1968; Every Home Should Have One, 1969; (with Terry Glinwood) Up Pompeii, 1971; Up the Chastity Belt, 1971; Girl Stroke Boy, 1971; Rentadick, 1971; Up the Front, 1972; The National Health, 1972; TV plays (with Caryl Brahms) include: Little Beggars; Benbow was his Name; Take a Sapphire; The Great Inimitable Mr Dickens; Feydeau Farces; plays (with Caryl Brahms): No Bed for Bacon; Cindy-Ella or I Gotta Shoe, 1962-63; The Spoils, 1968; Nicholas Nickleby, 1969; Sing a Rude Song, 1970; Fish out of Water, 1971; Liberty Ranch, 1972; Nickleby and Me, 1975; directed: Come Spy with Me, Whitehall, 1967; (and appeared in) Side by Side by Sondheim, Mermaid, 1976, NY 1977. Guild of TV Producers and Directors' Awards; Ivor Novello Award, 1966. *Publications:* (with Caryl Brahms) Cindy-Ella or I Gotta Shoe, 1962; Rappell 1910, 1964; Benbow was his Name, 1967; Ooh la! la! (short stories), 1973; After You Mr Feydeau, 1975; many songs. *Address:* 234 New North Road, N1. *T:* 01-226 7782.

SHERRY, Mrs Vincent; *see* Robinson, Kathleen M.

SHERSBY, (Julian) Michael; MP (C) Hillingdon, Uxbridge, since 1974 (Uxbridge, Dec. 1972-1974); *b* Ickenham, 17 Feb. 1933; *s* of William Henry and Elinor Shersby; *m* 1958, Barbara Joan, *d* of John Henry Barrow; one *s* one *d. Educ:* John Lyon Sch., Harrow-on-the-Hill. Mem., Paddington Borough Council, 1959-64; Mem., Westminster City Council, 1964-71; Deputy Lord Mayor of Westminster, 1967-68. Chm., Uxbridge Div. Young Conservatives, 1951-52; Conservative and Unionist Party Organisation, 1952-58; Sec., Assoc. of Specialised Film Producers, 1958-62; Dir, British Industrial Film Assoc., 1962-66; Dir, British Sugar Bureau, 1966-77, Dir-Gen., 1977-. PPS to Minister of Aerospace and Shipping, DTI, 1974; Jt Sec., Conservative Party Parly Industry Cttee, 1972-74; Chm., Cons. Party Trade Cttee, 1974-76, Vice-Chm., 1977; Mem., Commonwealth Parly Assoc. Delegn to Caribbean, 1975; promoted Private Member's Bills: Town and Country Amenities Act, 1974; Parks Regulation (Amendment) Act, 1974; Stock Exchange (Completion of Bargains) Act, 1976. Jt Sec., Parly and Scientific Cttee, 1977. Mem. Court, Brunel Univ., 1975-; Pres., Abbeyfield Uxbridge Soc., 1975-. *Recreation:* sailing. *Address:* Anvil House, Park Road, Stoke Poges, Bucks. *T:* Farnham Common 4548. *Clubs:* Junior Carlton; Conservative (Uxbridge).

SHERSTON-BAKER, Sir Humphrey Dodington Benedict, 6th Bt, *cr* 1796; *b* 13 Oct. 1907; *s* of Lt-Col Sir Dodington Sherston-Baker, 5th Bt, and Irene Roper (*d* 1950), *yr d* of Sir Roper Parkington; *S* father, 1944; *m* 1938, Margaret Alice (Bobby) (marriage dissolved, 1953), *o d* of H. W. Binns, 9 Campden Street, W, and Blythburgh, Suffolk; one *s* three *d. Educ:* Downside; Christ's College, Cambridge. *Heir: s* Robert George Humphrey Sherston-Baker, *b* 3 April 1951. *Address:* 22 Frognal Court, NW3 5HP.

SHERWIN, Charles Edgar, CB 1969; Director of Warship Design, Ministry of Defence, 1966-69; *b* 1909; *s* of Charles William Sherwin; *m* 1935, Jennet Esther, *d* of F. Mason. *Educ:* Portsmouth; RNC, Greenwich. RCNC; FRINA. *Recreation:* golf. *Address:* 10 Dunsford Place, Bathwick Hill, Bath, Avon.

SHERWIN, Frederick George James, CB 1967; Chief Inspector, Board of HM Customs and Excise, 1963-69, retired; *b* 3 Sept. 1909; *s* of J. F. Sherwin and H. E. Sherwin, Woolston, Hants; *m* 1966, Margaret Dorothea Snow, *d* of Thomas L. H. Snow, Gidea Park, Essex; one *s. Educ:* Gosport Secondary Sch.; HM Dockyard Sch., Portsmouth. Civil Servant; entered Customs and Excise, 17 Feb. 1930. *Recreations:* gardening, walking. *Address:* 10 Maytree Avenue, Findon Valley, Worthing, West Sussex BN14 0HJ. *T:* Findon 3145.

SHERWIN-WHITE, Adrian Nicholas, MA; FBA 1956; Reader in Ancient History, University of Oxford, since 1966; Fellow and Tutor of St John's College, Oxford, since 1936; Keeper of the Groves, 1970; *b* 1911; *s* of H. N. Sherwin-White, Solicitors' Dept of LCC. *Educ:* Merchant Taylors' School; St John's College, Oxford (Derby Scholar, 1935; Arnold Historical Essay Prize, 1935; MA, 1937). War Service in RN and Admiralty,

1942-45. Conington Prize, 1947. Sarum Lecturer, Oxford Univ., 1960-61; Gray Lecturer, Cambridge Univ., 1965-66; Special Lectr, Open Univ., 1973-76. Pres., Soc. for Promotion of Roman Studies, 1974-77. Corresp. Fellow, Bayerische Akademie der Wissenschaften, 1977. *Publications:* Citizenship, 1939, enlarged edn 1973; Ancient Rome (Then and There Series), 1959; Roman Society and Roman Law in the New Testament, 1963; Historical Commentary on the Letters of Pliny the Younger, 1966; Racial Prejudice in Imperial Rome, 1967; ed Geographical Handbook Series, Admiralty; contrib. Jl Roman Studies. *Recreations:* watching horses and growing hardy plants. *Address:* St John's College, Oxford. *T:* Frilford Heath 496.

SHERWOOD, Bishop Suffragan of, since 1975; **Rt. Rev. Harold Richard Darby;** *b* 28 Feb. 1919; *s* of William and Miriam Darby; *m* 1949, Audrey Elizabeth Lesley Green; two *s* three *d*. *Educ:* Cathedral School, Shanghai; St John's Coll., Durham (BA). Military service, 1939-45; Durham Univ., 1946-50. Deacon 1950; priest 1951; Curate of Leyton, 1950-51; Curate of Harlow, 1951-53; Vicar of Shrub End, Colchester, 1953-59; Vicar of Waltham Abbey, 1959-70; Dean of Battle, 1970-75. *Recreation:* vintage cars. *Address:* Applegarth, Halam, Notts. *T:* Southwell 814041.

SHERWOOD, (Robert) Antony (Frank); Assistant Director-General, British Council, since 1977; *b* 29 May 1923; *s* of Frank Henry Sherwood and Mollie Sherwood (*née* Moore); *m* 1953, Margaret Elizabeth Simpson; two *s* two *d*. *Educ:* Christ's Hospital; St John's Coll., Oxford (BA 1949, MA 1953). War service, RAF, 1942-46. Apptd to British Council, 1949; Lectr, Turkey, 1949-50; Asst Dir, Ibadan, Nigeria, 1950-55; Lectr, Syria, 1955-56; Fellowships Dept, 1957; Asst Rep., Uganda, 1957-59; Representative: Somaliland Protectorate, 1959-60; Somali Republic, 1960-63; Dir, Commonwealth Dept, 1963-66; Dep. Controller, Home Div., 1966-69; Representative, Nigeria, 1969-72; Controller, Africa and Middle East Div., 1972-77. *Recreations:* reading, walking, current affairs, sport, theatre. *Address:* 18 Rivermount Gardens, Guildford, Surrey GU2 5DN. *T:* Guildford 38277. *Club:* Royal Commonwealth Society.

SHETH, Pranlal; Executive Director, Abbey Life Assurance Co. Ltd, since 1974; Legal Director, Hartford Europe Group of Companies, since 1977; Deputy Chairman, Commission for Racial Equality, since 1977; *b* 20 Dec. 1924; *s* of Purashotam Virji Sheth and Sakarben Sheth; *m* 1951, Indumati Sheth; one *s* one *d*. Called to the Bar, Lincoln's Inn, 1962. Journalist, Kenya, 1943-52; Chm., Nyanza Farmers' Cooperative Soc., 1954-60; Mem., Central Agriculture Bd, Kenya, 1963-66; Dep. Chm., Asian Hosp. Authority, 1964-66; Mem., Economic Planning and Develt Council, Kenya, 1964-66. Group Sec., Abbey Life Gp of Cos, 1971-; Chief Editor, Gujarat Samachar Weekly, 1972-73; Mem., N Metropolitan Conciliation Cttee, Race Relations Bd, 1973-77; Trustee, Project Fullemploy (Charitable Trust), 1977-. *Address:* (home) 70 Howberry Road, Edgware, Mddx. *T:* 01-952 2413; (business) Abbey Life House, 1/3 St Paul's Churchyard, EC4M 8AR. *T:* 01-248 9111.

SHEVILL, Rt. Rev. Ian (Wotton Allnutt), AO 1976; MA (Sydney); *b* 11 May 1917; *s* of Erson James Shevill; *m* 1st, 1959, Dr June (*d* 1970), *d* of Basil Stephenson, Worthing; two *s*; 2nd, 1974, Ann, *d* of A. Brabazon, Winton, Queensland. *Educ:* Scot's Coll., Sydney; Sydney Univ.; School of Oriental and African Studies, London Univ.; Moore Theological Coll., Sydney, BA, 1939, MA, 1945, Sydney; ThL, ThD, 1953, Moore Theol Coll. Deacon, 1940; Priest, 1941; Curate of St Paul, Burwood, 1940-45; Organising Secretary of the Australian Board of Missions, for Province of Queensland, 1946-47; Education Secretary, Society for the Propagation of Gospel, 1948-51; Bishop of North Queensland, 1953-70; Secretary, United Society for the Propagation of the Gospel, 1970-73; Asst Bishop, Diocese of London, 1971-73; Bishop of Newcastle, NSW, 1973-77. *Publications:* New Dawn in Papua, 1946; Pacific Conquest, 1948; God's World at Prayer, 1951; Orthodox and other Eastern Churches in Australia, 1964; Half Time, 1966; Going it with God, 1969. *Recreations:* travel, swimming. *Address:* c/o Bishopscourt, Newcastle, NSW 2300, Australia. *Clubs:* Athenæum, Australian (Sydney).

SHEWAN, Henry Alexander, CB 1974; OBE 1946; QC (Scotland) 1949; Commissioner of National Insurance, since 1955; *b* 7 November 1906; *s* of late James Smith Shewan, Advocate in Aberdeen; *m* 1937, Ann Fraser Thomson (*d* 1977), Aberdeen; two *s*. *Educ:* Robert Gordon's Coll., Aberdeen; Aberdeen Univ.; Emmanuel College, Cambridge. Advocate, 1933. Served War of 1939-45, RAF, 1940-45, Sqdn Leader. Standing Junior Counsel in Scotland: to Board of Trade, Customs and Excise, and Ministry of Labour, 1945-47; to Board of Inland Revenue, 1947-49. External Examiner in Law:

University of Aberdeen, 1946-49; University of Edinburgh, 1948-51. Member Scottish Medical Practices Cttee, 1948-55; Member Court of Session Rules Council, 1948-55; Dep. Chm. Panel of Arbiters and Referee under Coal Industry Nationalisation Act, 1949-55; Chm., Medical Appeal Tribunal National Insurance (Industrial Injuries) Act, 1950-55; Chairman General Nursing Council for Scot., 1960-62. *Address:* 7 Winton Loan, Edinburgh EH10 7AN. *T:* 031-445 3239. *Clubs:* New (Edinburgh); Honourable Company of Edinburgh Golfers (Muirfield).

SHEWELL-COOPER, Wilfred Edward, MBE 1946; NDH; Dip. Hort. (Wye); Director, International Horticultural Advisory Bureau, since 1960; Chairman of Council, The Good Gardeners' Association since 1964; *b* 15 September; *s* of Col E. Shewell-Cooper, RA, and Mabel Alice Read; *m* 1925, Irene Ramsay; two *s*. *Educ:* Diocesan College, Rondebosch, S Africa; Monkton Combe; Wye College, Univ. London. East Malling Research Station, 1922; Horticultural Adviser, Warwick CC, 1923; Head of Hort. Dept, Cheshire Agric. Coll., 1925; Hort. Supt, Swanley Hort. Coll., 1932, and Garden Editor, BBC (North Region); Director, Hort. Advisory Bureau, 1938; Command Hort. Officer, Eastern and S Eastern Commands, 1940-49; Lt-Col 1945; Adviser, BAOR, 1946-47; Principal, Thaxted Hort. Coll., 1950-60; Hon. Dir, Good Gardens Inst., 1961-78. Liveryman, Worshipful Company of Gardeners, 1956. Mem., Roy. Soc. of Teachers, 1923; FLS 1930; Fell. and Hon. Dr, Hort. Coll., Vienna, 1952; Chevalier du Mérite Agricole, France, 1952, Commandeur, 1964; Fell. Roy. Danish Hort. Soc., 1964. FRSL 1954; Hon. DLitt 1961. President: Internat. Mission to Miners; Farmers' Christian Postal Service; Mem. of the House of Laity, 1960-; International Clans' Chief, The Campaigners, 1966-76; Chm., British Assoc. of Consultants in Agric. and Hortic. 1966. Knight of the Order of Merit (Italy), 1966. *Publications:* over 80 books on horticulture beginning with The Garden, 1932, and including The Royal Gardeners, 22 Titles in the ABC series, The Complete Gardener, Mini-Work Gardening, The Complete Vegetable Gardener, Weekend Gardening, The Complete Greenhouse Gardener, Cut Flowers for the Home; New Basic Gardening Books series (12 titles), 1972; Compost Gardening, 1972; Flowers of the Desert, 1972; The Beginner's Book of Pot Plants, 1972; Tomatoes, Salads and Herbs, 1973; Compost Flower Growing, 1975; The Compost Fruit Grower, 1975; Compost Gardening, 1975; Grow Your Own Food, 1976; Soil, Humus and Health, 1976; The Basic Book of Fruit Growing, 1977; The Basic Book of Carnations and Pinks, 1977; and other standard works. *Recreations:* gardening, swimming. *Address:* Arkley Manor, Arkley, Herts. *T:* 01-449 3031/2177. *Club:* Army and Navy.

SHIACH, Sheriff Gordon Iain Wilson; Sheriff of Tayside, Central and Fife (formerly Fife and Kinross) at Dunfermline since 1972; *b* 15 Oct. 1935; *o s* of Dr John Crawford Shiach, FDS, QHDS, and Florence Bygott Wilson; *m* 1962, Margaret Grant Smith; two *d*. *Educ:* Gordonstoun Sch.; Edinburgh Univ. (MA, LLB). Admitted to Faculty of Advocates, 1960; practised as Advocate, 1960-72; Clerk to Rules Council of Court of Session, 1963-72. *Recreations:* reading, walking, music, the theatre. *Address:* 4 Craigleith Rise, Edinburgh EH4 3TR. *T:* 031-346 0874. *Club:* New (Edinburgh).

SHIELDS, John Sinclair; *b* 4 Feb. 1903; *s* of Rev. W. H. Shields and Margaret Louisa (*née* Sinclair); *m* 1st, 1924, Norah Fane Smith; three *d*; 2nd, 1963, Mrs Noreen Moultrie, widow of Comdr John Moultrie. *Educ:* Charterhouse; Lincoln Coll., Oxford (MA). Headmaster: Wem Grammar School, 1934-47; Queen Mary's School, Basingstoke, 1947-56; Headmaster, Peter Symonds' School, Winchester, 1957-63; Vice-Pres. Classical Assoc., 1958; Member: Broadcasting Cttee, 1960; Oxford Soc. (Sec. Hampshire Branch). *Recreation:* golf. *Address:* North End House, Hursley, Winchester, Hants.

SHIELDS, (Leslie) Stuart, QC 1970; a Recorder of the Crown Court, since 1972; *b* 15 May 1919; *m* 1941, Maureen Margaret McKinstry; two *s* two *d* (and one *s* decd). *Educ:* St Paul's School; Corpus Christi College, Oxford. Paid Local Serjeant, Oxford and Buckinghamshire Light Infantry, 1945-47. Called to the Bar, Middle Temple, 1948. *Recreation:* music. *Address:* Devereux Chambers, Devereux Court, Temple, WC2R 3JJ.

SHIELDS, Sir Neil (Stanley), Kt 1964; MC 1946; management consultant and company director; Director: Central and Sheerwood Ltd; Chesham Amalgamations and Investments Ltd; Newton Chambers & Co. Ltd; Sheerwood Corporate Services Ltd; The Sheerwood Trust Ltd; Trianco Group Ltd; Chairman: Holcombe Holdings Ltd; The Standard Catalogue Company Ltd; Neumo Ltd; *b* 7 September 1919; *o s* of late Archie Shields and Mrs Hannah Shields; *m* 1970, Gloria Dawn Wilson.

Member of Honourable Artillery Company 1939-. Served in Royal Artillery, 1939-46; commnd 1940; Major 1943. Prospective candidate (C) North St Pancras 1947 and contested by-election, 1949. Chairman: Camden Conservative Cttee, 1965-67; Hampstead Conservative Assoc., 1954-65 (Vice-Chm., 1951-54); Hon. Treas. 1965-67; National Union of Conservative and Unionist Assocs: Chm. of London Area, 1961-63 (Vice-Chm., 1959-61); Mem. of National Executive, 1955-59, 1961-67, 1968-69; Hampstead Borough Council: Mem. 1947-65; Deputy Leader, 1952-61; Chm. of Works Cttee, 1951-55; Chm. of Finance Cttee, 1955-59. Mem. Council, Aims for Freedom and Enterprise. *Recreations:* reading, music, walking, motoring, wining and dining. *Address:* 12 London House, Avenue Road, NW8 7PX. *T:* 01-586 4155. *Clubs:* Carlton, HAC.

SHIELDS, Maj.-Gen. Ronald Frederick, OBE 1943; BSc (Eng); CEng; FIEE; *b* 4 November 1912; *s* of late John Benjamin Frederic Shields, Chichester; *m* 1944, Lorna, *d* of late Frederick Murgatroyd, Manchester; one *s* one *d*. *Educ:* Portsmouth Grammar School. Lieut RAOC 1936. Served War of 1939-45 in Middle East and NW Europe; transferred to REME, 1942; Staff College Camberley, 1945; MELF, 1948-51; AQMG, HQ Northern Comd, 1952-55; War Office, 1956-59; REME Training Centre, 1959-62; DEME, HQ, BAOR, 1962-65; Comdt, Technical Group, REME, 1965-68; retd 1968. Col, 1955; Brig. 1962; Maj.-Gen. 1965. Col Comdt, REME, 1968-73. *Address:* 58 Petersfield Road, Midhurst, West Sussex.

SHIELDS, Ronald McGregor Pollock; Managing Director, Associated Newspapers Group Ltd, since Dec. 1970; *b* 30 July 1921; *s* of Thomas Shields and Beatrice Gordon; *m* 1948, Jacqueline (*née* Cowan); one *s* one *d*. *Educ:* Swanage Grammar Sch.; London Univ. (BSc (Econ)). Served War of 1939-45, Royal Artillery. Joined Associated Newspapers Gp; spent several years in various depts of the Co. and a year at Associated Rediffusion in charge of Audience Research. Set up the research co. National Opinion Polls, and was made Advertisement Dir of Associated Newspapers, 1963. Director: Associated Investments (Furniture) Ltd; Associated Investments Harmsworth Ltd; Associated Restaurants; Associated Special Publications Ltd; Consolidated Bathurst Ltd; Blackfriars Oil Co.; Blox Services Ltd; Bouverie Investments No 2 Ltd; Burton Reproductions Ltd; Copthall Developments Ltd; Crowvale Properties Ltd; Daily Mail Ltd; Evening News Ltd; E. & H. Grace Ltd; Greenwall Warehousing; Harmsworth Publishing Ltd; London Cab Co.; John M. Newton & Sons Ltd; NOP Market Research Ltd; Pizzaland Ltd; Purfleet Deep Wharf & Storage; G. T. Rackstraw Ltd; Retail Audits Ltd; Southern Television; Taylor Brothers; Frederick Tibbenham Ltd; Transport Group (Holdings) Ltd; Weekend Publications Ltd. FSS. *Recreations:* golf, the theatre. *Address:* New Carmelite House, Carmelite Street, EC4. *T:* 01-353 6000.

SHIELDS, Stuart; *see* Shields, L. S.

SHIELL, James Wyllie, BSc, FICE, FIWES; Consultant, R. H. Cuthbertson & Partners, Consulting Engineers, Edinburgh; *b* 20 Aug. 1912; *yr s* of late George Douglas Shiell, farmer, Rennieston, Jedburgh and Janet Gladstone Wyllie; *m* 1941, Maureen Cameron Macpherson Hunter, *d* of late Thomas Hunter, Leeds; two *s*. *Educ:* Jedburgh Grammar and Kelso High Schools; Edinburgh Univ. Municipal Engrg posts in Edinburgh, Southampton, Sunderland and Leeds, 1934-39; Sen. Engr on Staff of J. D. & D. M. Watson, Consulting Engrs, Westminster, 1939-43 and 1945-47; Civil Engr on wartime service with Admty, 1943-45; Sen. Engr, Min. of Agriculture, 1947-49; Engrg Inspector, Dept of Health for Scotland, 1949-62; Dep. Chief Engr, Scottish Development Dept, 1962-68; Chief Engr, Scottish Development Dept, 1968-75. Mem. Amenity Cttee set up by Sec. of State for Scotland under Hydro-Electric (Scotland) Devevlt Acts. Hon. FInstWPC. *Recreations:* walking, photography. *Address:* 25 Mortonhall Road, Edinburgh EH9 2HS. *T:* 031-667 8528. *Club:* Caledonian (Edinburgh).

SHIERLAW, Norman Craig; Senior Partner, N. C. Shierlaw & Associates (Stock and Sharebrokers), since 1968; *b* 17 Aug. 1921; *s* of Howard Alison Shierlaw and Margaret Bruce; *m* 1944, Patricia Yates; two *d*. *Educ:* Pulteney Grammar Sch., Adelaide; St Peter's Coll., Adelaide; Univ. of Adelaide (BE). Assoc. Mem. Australian Inst. Mining and Metallurgy; FSASM; Mining Manager's Certificate. War Service, AIF, 1941-45 (War Service medals). Mining Engr with North Broken Hill Ltd, 1949-58; Sharebroker's Clerk, 1959-60; Partner, F. W. Porter & Co. (Sharebrokers), 1960-68. Director: Australian Development Ltd, 1959-; Poseidon Ltd, 1968-; North Flinders Mines Ltd, 1969-; Nobelex NL, 1974-. FAIM 1971. *Recreations:* golf, tennis. *Address:* N. C. Shierlaw & Associates, 28 Grenfell Street, Adelaide, SA 5000, Australia. *T:* Adelaide 51-7468. *Clubs:*

Mining (Sydney); Naval, Military and Air Force, Stock Exchange, Kooyonga Golf (Adelaide); West Australian (Perth).

SHIFFNER, Sir Henry David, 8th Bt, *cr* 1818; Company Director; *b* 2 Feb. 1930; *s* of Major Sir Henry Shiffner, 7th Bt, and Margaret Mary, *er d* of late Sir Ernest Gowers, GCB, GBE, *S* father, 1941; *m* 1st, 1949, Dorothy Jackson (marr. diss. 1956); one *d* (and one *d* decd); 2nd, 1957, Beryl (marr. diss. 1970), *d* of George Milburn, Saltdean, Sussex; one *d*; 3rd, 1970, Joaquina Ramos Lopez. *Educ:* Rugby; Trinity Hall, Cambridge. Dir, Milupa, Spain. *Heir: cousin* George Frederick Shiffner [*b* 3 August 1936; *m* 1961, Dorothea Helena Cynthia, *d* of late T. H. McLean; one *s* one *d*]. *Address:* Apartado 14.791, Madrid 14, Spain. *Club:* Royal Automobile.

SHILLINGFORD, Prof. John Parsons, MD (Harvard and London), FRCP, FACC; Sir John McMichael Professor of Cardiovascular Medicine, Royal Postgraduate Medical School, London University, since 1976 (Director, Cardiovascular Research Unit, and Professor of Angiocardiology, 1966-76); *b* 15 April 1914; *s* of Victor Shillingford and Ethel Eugenie Parsons; *m* 1947, Doris Margaret Franklin; two *s* one *d*. *Educ:* Bishops Stortford; Harvard Univ.; London Hosp. Med. Sch. Rockefeller Student, Harvard Med. Sch., 1939-42; House agents, Presbyterian Hosp., New York, and London Hosp., 1943-45; Med. First Asst, London Hosp., 1945-52; Sen. Lectr Royal Postgrad. Med. Sch., 1958-62. Pres., Sect. Experimental Med., Royal Soc. Med., 1968; Sec., Brit. Cardiac Soc., 1963-70; Chm. Org. Cttee, Sixth World Congress Cardiology, 1970; Lumleian Lectr, RCP, 1972. Member: Assoc. Physicians Gt Brit.; Med. Res. Soc.; Med. Soc. London; Royal Soc. Med.; Comité Recherche Médicale, EEC; various cttees, Brit. Heart Foundn. Hon. Mem.: Hellenic Cardiac Soc.; Cardiac Soc. of Yugoslavia; Polish Cardiac Soc.; Cardiological Soc. of India; Corr. Mem., Australian Cardiac Soc.; Fellow, Amer. Coll. of Cardiology; Hon. FACP; Editor, Cardiovascular Research. Visiting Prof., Australian Heart Foundn, 1965; lectured extensively in Europe, USA, S America, Africa, Middle East. James Berry Prize, RCS. *Publications:* numerous scientific papers, mainly on heart disease and coronary thrombosis. *Recreation:* sailing. *Address:* 6 Hurlingham Court, Ranelagh Gardens, SW6 3SH. *T:* 01-736 6746; Forbes, Harbour Road, Old Bosham, West Sussex. *T:* Bosham 3060. *Clubs:* Hurlingham; Bosham Sailing.

SHILLINGTON, Courtenay Alexander Rives, CB 1953; CVO 1972; VRD 1941; DL; Commodore, RNVR, retired 1954; *b* 18 Mar. 1902; *s* of Thomas Courtenay Shillington, Glenmachan Tower, Belfast, and Bertha Wydown Hall, Charlottesville, Virginia, USA; one *d*. *Educ:* Bilston Grange; Rugby. Entered RNVR, Sub-Lt, 1924; ADC to: Duke of Abercorn, Northern Ireland, 1927-45; Earl Granville, Governor of Northern Ireland, 1945-52; Lord Wakehurst, Governor of Northern Ireland, 1952-64; Lord Erskine of Rerrick, Governor of NI, 1964-67; Lord Grey of Naunton, Governor of NI, 1967-73. Served War of 1939-45, in RN as Capt. RNVR, 1939-46; Comdr, Auxiliary Patrol, Scapa, 1939; Dep. Chief of Staff and Naval Liaison Officer to Field Marshal Lord Gort, Governor of Malta, 1942; Chief of Staff to Sen. Naval Officer, Persian Gulf, 1942; Naval Officer in Charge, Bahrain, 1943-45. DL County Down, 1956. *Recreation:* motor racing. *Address:* Glenganagh Farm Cottage, Groomsport, Bangor, County Down, Northern Ireland. *Clubs:* Royal Automobile; Ulster, Ulster Automobile (Belfast); Royal Ulster Yacht (Bangor).

SHILLINGTON, Sir (Robert Edward) Graham, Kt 1972; CBE 1970 (OBE 1959; MBE 1951); DL; Chief Constable, Royal Ulster Constabulary, 1970-73; *b* 2 April 1911; *s* of Major D. Graham Shillington, DL, MP, and Mrs Louisa Shillington (*née* Collen); *m* 1935, Mary E. R. Bulloch (*d* 1977), Holywood, Co. Down; two *s* one *d*. *Educ:* Sedbergh Sch., Yorks; Clare Coll., Cambridge. Royal Ulster Constabulary: Officer Cadet, 1933; 3rd Class District Inspector, 1934; 2nd Class District Inspector, 1936; 1st Class District Inspector, 1944; County Inspector, 1953; Commissioner, Belfast, 1961; Deputy Inspector General (Deputy Chief Constable), 1969-70. Chm., Belfast Voluntary Welfare Soc. DL Co. Down, 1975. King's Coronation Medal, 1937; Queen's Coronation Medal, 1953; Police Long Service and Good Conduct Medal, 1955. *Recreations:* golf, gardening. *Address:* Orchard Hill, Craigavad, Co. Down. *T:* Holywood 3471. *Clubs:* Royal Belfast Golf, Royal County Down Golf.

SHILLITO, Charles Henry; Under-Secretary, Ministry of Agriculture, Fisheries and Food, since 1974; *b* 8 Jan. 1922; *s* of Charles Cawthorne and Florence Shillito; *m* 1947, Elizabeth Jean (*née* Bull); two *d*. *Educ:* Hugh Bell Sch., Middlesbrough. Clerk, Min. of Agriculture and Fisheries, 1938; War Service, Lieut RNVR, 1941-46; Principal, MAFF, 1957; Asst Sec. 1966; Section Head, Nat. Econ. Develt Office, 1966-69 (on secondment). *Recreations:* gardening, nautical pursuits. *Address:* 62 Downs Road, Coulsdon, Surrey CR3 1AB. *T:* Downland 53392.

SHILLITO, Edward Alan, CB 1964; retired Civil Servant; a General Commissioner of Income Tax, since 1972; *b* 13 May 1910; *s* of late Rev. Edward and Mrs Annie Shillito, Buckhurst Hill, Essex; *m* 1934, Dorothy Jean, *d* of late Robert J. Davies, Buckhurst Hill, Essex; two *s* three *d. Educ:* Chigwell School; Oriel College, Oxford (Exhibitioner). Litt Hum 2nd Class, 1933. Customs and Excise, 1934-36; HM Treas., 1936-57; Under-Secretary, 1951; Admiralty, and MoD, 1957-69; Dir, Greenwich Hosp., 1969-71. Imperial Defence College course, 1953. *Recreations:* music, lacrosse (Oxford Univ., 1931-33, now spectator only). *Address:* 8 Baldwins Hill, Loughton, Essex. *T:* 01-508 1988.

SHIMELD, Kenneth Reeve; Permanent Secretary, Department of the Civil Service (NI), since 1976; *b* 5 Nov. 1921; *s* of Augustus John and Gertrude Shimeld; *m* 1949, Brenda, *d* of George and Millicent Barnard; two *d. Educ:* Coatham Sch.; Univ. of Durham (BA). Pres., Durham Univ. Union. Served Royal Signals, 1941-46. Asst Principal, Min. of Finance, NI Civil Service, 1949; Asst Sec. 1957; Sen. Asst Sec., Min. of Commerce, 1963; Head of Works Div., Min. of Finance, 1969, Second Secretary, 1971. *Recreations:* music, cricket, reading. *Address:* Flat 2, 9 Deramore Drive, Belfast, BT9 5JQ.

SHINDLER, George John, QC 1970; a Recorder of the Crown Court, since 1972; *b* 27 Oct. 1922; *yr s* of late Dr Bruno and Mrs Alma Schindler; *m* 1955, Eva Muller; three *s. Educ:* University Coll. Sch., Hampstead. Served in Royal Tank Regt, NW Europe, 1942-47. Called to Bar, Inner Temple, 1952. Standing Counsel to Inland Revenue at Central Criminal Court and all London sessions, 1965-70. *Recreations:* theatre, music, reading, watching soccer and cricket, travel. *Address:* Queen Elizabeth Building, Temple, EC4Y 9BS. *T:* 01-353 6453. *Clubs:* Reform, MCC; Glaziers.

SHINNIE, Prof. Peter Lewis; Professor of Archæology, in the University of Calgary, since 1970; *b* 1915; *s* of late Andrew James Shinnie, OBE; *m* 1st, 1940, Margaret Blanche Elizabeth Cloake; two *s* one *d*; 2nd, Ama Nantwi. *Educ:* Westminster Sch.; Christ Church, Oxford. Served War with RAF, 1939-45. Temp. Asst Keeper, Ashmolean Museum, 1945; Asst Commissioner for Archæology, Sudan Government, 1946; Commissioner for Archæology, Sudan Govt, 1948; Director of Antiquities, Uganda, 1956; Prof. of Archæology: Univ. of Ghana, 1958-66; Univ. of Khartoum, 1966-70. FSA. *Publications:* Excavation at Soba, 1955; Medieval Nubia, 1954; Ghazali: A Monastery in Northern Sudan, 1960; Meroe-Civilization of the Sudan, 1967; The African Iron Age, 1971; articles in Journal of Egyptian Archæology, Sudan Notes and Records, Kush. *Recreations:* reading, photography, travelling in Greece. *Address:* Department of Archæology, University of Calgary, Canada. *T:* 403-284-5227. *Club:* Athenæum.

SHINWELL, family name of **Baron Shinwell.**

SHINWELL, Baron *cr* 1970 (Life Peer), of Easington, Durham; **Emanuel Shinwell;** PC 1945; CH 1965; *b* London, 18 October 1884. MP (Lab) Linlithgow, 1922-24 and 1928-31, Seaham Div. of Durham, 1935-50, Easington Div. of Durham, 1950-70; Financial Secretary, War Office, 1929-30; Parliamentary Secretary to Department of Mines, 1924 and 1930-31; Minister of Fuel and Power, 1945-47; Secretary of State for War, 1947-50; Minister of Defence, 1950-51. Was Chairman and Member, National Executive Labour Party; Chairman, Parly Labour Party, 1964-67. Hon. DCL Durham, 1969. *Publications:* The Britain I Want, 1943; When the Men Come Home, 1944; Conflict without Malice, 1955; The Labour Story, 1963; I've Lived Through It All, 1973. *Address:* House of Lords, SW1.

SHIPWRIGHT, Sqdn Ldr Denis E. B. K., FRSA; psa; RAFRO (retired); Established Civil Servant (Telecomm. PO); Production and Administration, Gaumont British Picture Corporation, and Gainsborough Pictures; Director Cinephonic Music Co. Ltd; KStJ; *b* London, 20 May 1898; *y s* of late T. J. Shipwright and Adelina de Lara, OBE; *m* 1918, Kate (marriage dissolved, 1926; she *d* 1954), *o d* of late Sir Edward Hain, St Ives, Cornwall; one *s* two *d*; *m* 1947, Margaret *d* 1977), *o d* of late Robert Edgar Haynes, Woking, Surrey. *Educ:* France; University College, Oxford. Joined the Army as a private at the age of 16, 1914; despatch rider, 1915; wounded and crashed whilst flying in France in RFC; Flight Comdr, 1918; Capt. Royal 1st Devon Yeomanry, and North Devon Hussars; Capt. R of O RE, TA, to Apr. 1939; then Pilot Officer RAFVR; Flt Lt Nov. 1939; Sqdn Ldr 1940; passed out of RAF Staff College, 1940; served in

France, 1940 (despatches, 1939-43 Star); Special Mission to Gibraltar, 1942. Air ED 1944. Middle Temple, 1920; MP (C) Penryn and Falmouth, 1922-23; Representative on the Film Producers Group, Federation of British Industries; Adviser to the British Films Advancement Council; Member of the Kinematograph Advisory Committee; Life Member of the Commonwealth Parliamentary Association. Member: Surrey Special Constabulary, 1950; Company of Veteran Motorists, 1953; Order of Knights of Road, 1953; Civil Service Motoring Assoc.; Brooklands Soc.; British Unidentified Flying Object Research Assoc.; Chm. NE Surrey Gp, Contact UFO Research Investigation Assoc. Voluntary Driver, Surrey County Council Hospitals Car and Ambulance Service; Governor, Royal Hosp. and Home for Incurables. British Motor Racing Driver: Brooklands (winner 24th 100 mph Long Handicap); Speed Trials; Hill Climbs. Major, 11th (HG) Battalion, Queen's Royal Regt, 1953. Officer, Ministry of Agriculture and Food, Guildford, 1954. *Address:* Plym Lea, Triggs Lane, Woking, Surrey GU2 0EH. *T:* Woking 61736. *Clubs:* British Racing Drivers (Life Mem., and Life Mem., Silverstone Marshals Team), Royal Automobile; Oxford University Yacht (Oxford); Woking Conservative (Woking).

SHIRER, William Lawrence; broadcaster, journalist; author; *b* Chicago, 23 Feb. 1904; *s* of Seward Smith Shirer; *m* 1931, Theresa Stiberitz; two *d. Educ:* Coe College. Foreign Correspondent. DLitt (Hon.). Légion d'Honneur. *Publications:* Berlin Diary, 1941; End of a Berlin Diary, 1947; The Traitor, 1950; Mid-Century Journey, 1953; Stranger Come Home, 1954; The Challenge of Scandinavia, 1955; The Consul's Wife, 1956; The Rise and Fall of The Third Reich, 1960; The Rise and Fall of Adolf Hitler, 1961; The Sinking of the Bismarck, 1962; The Collapse of the Third Republic, 1970; Twentieth Century Journey: A Memoir of a Life and the Times, 1976. *Recreations:* walking, sailing. *Address:* Box 487, Lenox, Massachusetts 01240, USA. *Club:* Century (New York).

SHIRES, Sir Frank, Kt 1953; *b* 10 Aug. 1899; *s* of John Shires; *m* 1929, Mabel Tidds; one *s* one *d. Educ:* West Leeds High School. Joined H. J. Heinz Co. Ltd, 1925; Director of Manufacturing and Research, 1940; Director of Sales, 1950; Deputy Managing Director, 1950-55; Director: Marsh & Baxter Co. Ltd, 1958-64; C. & T. Harris (Calne) Ltd, 1958-64. Member of Exec. Cttee of Canners' (War Time) Assoc., 1942-49; Pres. Food Manufacturers' Federation, Inc., 1950-52; Member Council of British Food Manufacturing Industries Research Assoc., 1947-55; Chm. Governing Body of Nat. Coll. of Food Technology, 1950-66, Chm. Bd, 1970-; Member: Food Hygiene Advisory Council, 1955-73; Monopolies Commission, 1957-61; Council, Univ. of Reading, 1965-. Fellow, Inst. of Science Technology, 1965. *Recreations:* cricket, and golf; Rugby (Derbys, 1926-28, and Notts, Lincs and Derbys, 1926-28). *Address:* Redholt, Linksway, Northwood, Mddx. *T:* Northwood 22493.

SHIRLEY, family name of **Earl Ferrers.**

SHIRLEY, Evelyn Philip Sewallis, CMG 1952; OBE 1927; *b* 2 March 1900; *s* of late Ven. Archdeacon Shirley; *m* 1930, Marian Hamilton Bowen Powell; one *s. Educ:* Saint Columba's College, Dublin; Royal Military College, Sandhurst. Commissioned Royal Irish Fusiliers, 1918; served NW Persia and Iraq, 1920. Entered Somaliland Administrative Service, 1929; Chief Secretary and Commissioner for native affairs, Somaliland Protectorate, 1951-Nov. 1954; retd 1955. Military Service, 1940-45. *Address:* The Vicarage, Hempstead, Holt, Norfolk. *T:* Holt 3281.

SHIRLEY, Philip Hammond; retired; *b* 4 Oct. 1912; *s* of Frank Shillito Shirley and Annie Lucy (*née* Hammond); *m* 1st, 1936, Marie Edna Walsh (*d* 1972); one *s* one *d*; 2nd, 1973, Norma Jones. *Educ:* Sydney Church of England Grammar School (Shore). Qualified in Australia as Chartered Accountant, 1934; with Peat Marwick Mitchell & Co., Chartered Accountants, London, 1937-49; Personal Asst to Managing Director, J. Arthur Rank Organisation Ltd, 1949-51; with Unilever from 1951; Dep. Chief Accountant, 1951-52; Chief Accountant, 1952-58; Chm. Batchelors Foods Ltd 1958-61; Mem. BTC (Oct. 1961-Nov. 1962); Mem. BR Bd, 1962-67 (Vice-Chm. Bd, 1964-67); Dep. Chm., Cunard Steamship Co., 1968-71; Chief Commissioner, NSW, 1972-75. *Recreation:* golf. *Address:* Flat 5, 2a Telopea Street, Wollstonecraft, NSW 2065, Australia.

SHIRLEY, Air Vice-Marshal Sir Thomas (Ulric Curzon), KBE 1966 (CBE 1946); CB 1961; CEng; FIEE; FRAeS; DL; RAF (Retired); *b* 4 June 1908; *s* of late Captain T. Shirley, late 60 Rifles, and late Ellen Shirley; *m* 1935, Vera, *y d* of late George S. Overton, The Grange, Navenby, Lincolnshire; one *s* one *d. Educ:* Reading School. Royal Air Force Aircraft Apprentice,

1925-28; cadet RAF College, Cranwell, 1928-30; served in Army Co-operation Squadrons as pilot, 1930-36; in Far East and Middle East on Signals duties, 1936-41; Officer Commanding Signals Wings, 1941-45; RAF Staff College, 1945-46; Deputy Director of Signals, Air Ministry, 1946-47; Command Signals Officer, Transport Command, 1947-48; Joint Services Staff College, 1948-49; Deputy Director Technical Plans, Air Ministry, 1949-50; Director of Radio Engineering, 1950-53; Command Signals Officer, Fighter Command, 1953-55; Imperial Defence College, 1956; Air Officer Commanding and Commandant, Royal Air Force Technical College, Henlow, Beds 1957-59; Senior Technical Staff Officer, RAF Fighter Command, 1959-60; Deputy Controller of Electronics, Ministry of Aviation, 1960-64; Air Officer C-in-C Signals Command, 1964-66. ADC to King George VI, 1950-52, to the Queen, 1952-53. DL Leicester, 1967. *Address:* 210 Seagrave Road, Sileby, Loughborough, Leics. *T:* Sileby 2309. *Club:* Royal Air Force.

SHIRLEY-QUIRK, John Stanton, CBE 1975; bass-baritone singer; *b* 28 Aug. 1931; *s* of Joseph Stanley and Amelia Shirley-Quirk; *m* 1955, Patricia Hastie; one *s* one *d. Educ:* Holt School, Liverpool; Liverpool University. Violin Scholarship, 1945; read Chemistry, Liverpool Univ., 1948-53; BSc (Hons), 1952; Dipl. in Educn 1953; became professional singer, 1961. Officer in Education Br., RAF, 1953-57. Asst Lectr in Chemistry, Acton Technical Coll., 1957-61; Lay-clerk in St Paul's Cathedral, 1961-62. First Appearance Glyndebourne Opera in Elegy for Young Lovers, 1961; subseq. 1962, 1963. Sang in first performance of Curlew River, 1964, The Burning Fiery Furnace, 1966, The Prodigal Son, 1968, Owen Wingrave, 1970, Death in Venice, 1973, Confessions of a Justified Sinner, 1976, The Ice Break, 1977. Has sung in Europe, Israel, Australia, etc. First American tour, 1966; Australian tour, 1967; first appearance Metropolitan Opera, NY, 1974. Has made numerous recordings: operas, songs, cantatas, etc. Hon. RAM 1972; Hon. DMus Liverpool, 1976. Liverpool Univ. Chem. Soc. Medal, 1965; Sir Charles Santley Meml Gift, Worshipful Co. of Musicians, 1969. *Recreations:* trees, canals, clocks. *Address:* The White House, Flackwell Heath, Bucks. *T:* Bourne End 21325.

SHIRLEY-SMITH, Sir Hubert, Kt 1969; CBE 1965; Consulting Engineer with private practice, since 1967; Consultant to W. V. Zinn & Associates, since 1969; *b* 13 Oct. 1901; *s* of E. Shirley-Smith; *m* 1st, 1927, Joan Elizabeth Powell (*d* 1963); two *d* (and one *d* decd); 2nd, 1973, Marie Lynden-Lemon. *Educ:* City and Guilds Coll., London. BSc (Engrg) London, 1922; FICE (MICE 1936); FCGI 1965; FIC 1966; FIArb 1973. Assisted in design of Sydney Harbour Bridge, NSW, and Birchenough and Otto Beit Bridges, Rhodesia, 1923-36; worked on construction of Howrah Bridge, Calcutta, 1936-42. Dir, Cleveland Bridge & Engrg Co., 1951-60; Mem. Bd, of Cleveland Bridge, Dorman Long (Auckland) and ACD Bridge Co.; Agent i/c construction of Forth Road Bridge, 1960-65. Mem. Council, ICE, 1952- (Pres., 1967); Mem. Council, Fedn of Civil Engrg Contractors, 1958-65; Vice-Pres., Internat. Assoc. for Bridge and Structural Engrg, 1963-69. Member, Smeatonian Soc. of Civil Engrs. *Publications:* The World's Great Bridges, 1953 (revised, 1964); article on Bridges in Encyclopædia Britannica; papers in Proc. ICE, etc. *Recreations:* travel, writing. *Address:* 70 Broxbourne Road, Orpington, Kent. *T:* Orpington 32673. *Club:* Athenæum.

SHOCK, Maurice; Vice-Chancellor of Leicester University, since 1977; *b* 15 April 1926; *o s* of Alfred and Ellen Shock; *m* 1947, Dorothy Donald; one *s* three *d. Educ:* King Edward's Sch., Birmingham; Balliol Coll., Oxford (MA); St Antony's Coll., Oxford. Served Intell. Corps, 1945-48. Lectr in Politics, Christ Church and Trinity Coll., Oxford, 1955-56; Fellow and Praelector in Politics, University Coll., Oxford, 1956-77; Estates Bursar, 1959-74; Sen. Treasurer, Oxford Union Soc., 1954-72; Member: Franks Commn of Inquiry into the University of Oxford, 1964-66; Hebdomadal Council, Oxford Univ., 1969-75; Vis. Prof. of Govt, Pomona Coll., 1961-62, 1968-69. *Publications:* The Liberal Tradition, 1956; articles on politics and recent history. *Recreations:* gardening, theatre. *Address:* Knighton Hall, Leicester LE2 3WG. *T:* Leicester 706677.

SHOCKLEY, Dr William (Bradford); Medal of Merit (US) 1946; Alexander M. Poniatoff Professor of Engineering Science, Stanford University, 1963-75, Professor Emeritus 1975; Executive Consultant, Bell Telephone Laboratories, 1965-75; *b* 13 Feb. 1910; *s* of William Hillman Shockley and May (*née* Bradford); *m* 1933, Jean Alberta Bailey; two *s* one *d; m* 1955, Emmy I. Lanning. *Educ:* Calif. Inst. of Technology (BS); Mass Inst. Tech. (PhD). Teaching Fellow, Mass. Inst. Tech., 1932-36; Mem. Technical Staff, Bell Teleph. Laboratories, 1936-42 and 1945-54; Director Transistor Physics Department, 1954-55. Dir of Research, Anti-submarine Warfare Ops Research Gp, US Navy, 1942-44; Expert Consultant, Office of Secretary of War,

1944-45. Visiting Lectr, Princeton Univ., 1946; Scientific Advisor, Policy Council, Jt Research and Development Bd, 1947-49; Visiting Prof., Calif. Inst. Tech., 1954; Dep. Dir and Dir of Research, Weapons Systems Evaluation Gp, Dept of Defense, 1954-55; Dir, Shockley Semi-conductor Lab. of Beckman Instruments, Inc., 1955-58; Pres. Shockley Transistor Corp., 1958-60; Director, Shockley Transistor, Unit of Clevite Transistor, 1960-63; Consultant, 1963-65. Member: US Army Science Advisory Panel, 1951-63, 1964-; USAF Science Advisory Board, 1959-63; National Academy of Science, 1951-; Sigma Xi; Tau Beta Pi. Inducted into Inventors' Hall of Fame, 1974; more than 90 US Patents. Inventor of junction transistor; research on energy bands of solids, ferromagnetic domains, plastic properties of metals, theory of grain boundaries, order and disorder in alloys; semi-conductor theory and electromagnetic theory; mental tools for sci. thinking, ops res. on human quality statistics. Fellow AAAS. Hon. DSc: Pennsylvania, 1955; Rutgers 1956; Gustavus Adolphus Coll., 1963. Morris Liebmann Prize, IEEE, 1951; Air Force Citation of Honour, 1951; O. E. Buckley Prize (Amer. Physical Soc.), 1953; US Army Cert. of Appreciation, 1953; Comstock Prize (Nat. Acad. of Science), 1954; Wilhelm Exner Medal (Oesterreichischer Gewerberein), 1963; Holley Medal (Amer. Soc. Mech. Engrs), 1963. (Jt) Nobel Prize in Physics, 1956; Caltech Alumni Distinguished Service Award, 1966; NASA Certificate of Appreciation (Apollo 8), 1969; Public Service Group Achievement Award, NASA, 1969. *Publications:* Electrons and Holes in Semiconductors, 1950; Mechanics (with W. A. Gong), 1966; (ed) Imperfections of Nearly Perfect Crystals; over 100 articles in sci. and tech. jls. *Recreations:* mountain climbing, swimming, sailing. *Address:* 797 Esplanada Way, Stanford, Calif 94305, USA. *Clubs:* Cosmos, University (Washington, DC); Bohemian (San Francisco); Stanford Faculty; Palo Alto Yacht.

SHOENBERG, Prof. David, MBE 1944; FRS 1953; Professor of Physics, Cambridge University and Head of Low Temperature Physics Group, Cavendish Laboratory, since 1973; Fellow of Gonville and Caius College, 1947; *b* 4 Jan. 1911; *s* of Isaac and Esther Shoenberg; *m* 1940, Catherine Felicitée Fischmann; one *s* two *d. Educ:* Latymer Upper School, W6; Trinity College, Cambridge (Scholar). PhD 1935; Exhibition of 1851 Senior Student, 1936-39; Research in low temperature physics, 1932-, in charge of Royal Soc. Mond Laboratory, 1947-73; Univ. Lectr in Physics, 1944-52; Univ. Reader in Physics, 1952-73; UNESCO Adviser on Low Temperature Physics, NPL of India, 1953-54. Guthrie Lectr, 1961; Mellon Prof., Univ. of Pittsburgh, 1962; Gauss Prof., Univ. of Göttingen, 1964; Visiting Professor: Univ. of Maryland, 1968; Univ. of Toronto, 1974; Univ. of Waterloo, 1977. Dr (*hc*) Univ. of Lausanne, 1973. Fritz London Award for Low Temperature Physics, 1964. *Publications:* Superconductivity, 1938, revised edn, 1952; Magnetism, 1949; scientific papers on low temperature physics and magnetism. *Address:* Cavendish Laboratory, Madingley Road, Cambridge CB3 0HE. *T:* Cambridge 66477.

SHOLL, Hon. Sir Reginald (Richard), Kt 1962; MA, BCL, Oxon; MA Melbourne; Legal consultant and company director, Melbourne; *b* 8 Oct. 1902; *e s* of late Reginald Frank and Maud Sholl (*née* Mumby), Melbourne; *m* 1st, 1927, Hazel Ethel (*d* 1962), *yr d* of late Alfred L. and Fanny Bradshaw, Melbourne; two *s* two *d*; 2nd, 1964, Anna Campbell, *widow* of Alister Bruce McLean, Melbourne, and *e d* of late Campbell Colin and Edith Carpenter, Indiana, USA. *Educ:* Melbourne Church of England Grammar Sch.; Trinity Coll., Univ. of Melbourne; New Coll., Oxford. 1st Cl. Final Hons and exhibn, Sch. of Classical Philology, and Wyselaskie Schol. in Classical and Comparative Philology and Logic, Melbourne Univ., 1922; Rhodes Schol., Victoria, 1924; 1st Cl. Final Hons, School of Jurisprudence, Oxford, 1926, Bar Finals, London, 1926 and BCL, Oxford, 1927; Official Law Fellow, Brasenose Coll., Oxford, 1927. Called to Bar, Middle Temple, 1927; journalist, London, 1927; Tutor in Classics, Melbourne Univ., 1928-29; Lectr in law, 1928-38; Barrister, Melbourne, 1929-49; admitted to Bars of NSW and Tasmania, 1935. Served Aust. Army, 1940-44; Capt. retd. Chm. various Commonwealth Bds of Inquiry into Army contracts, 1941-42; KC Vic. and Tas., 1947, NSW 1948; Justice of the Supreme Court of Victoria, 1950-66; Australian Consul-Gen. in New York, 1966-69; Chm., Western Australian Parly Salaries Tribunal, 1971-75. Consultant to Russell, Kennedy & Cook, solicitors, Melbourne; Chairman, Aust. Superannuation Property Trust Management Ltd; Dir and Dep. Chm., Nat. Trustees Executors and Agency Co. of Australasia Ltd; Dir, Ecclesiastical Property Insurance Co. Pty Ltd. Trustee, Nat. Gall. of Vic., 1950-63, Dep. Chm. 1958; Pres. ESU (Vic. Br.) 1961-66; Fed. Chm., ESU in Aust., 1961-63, 1969-73; Member: Aust. Bd of Trustees, Northcote Children's Emigration Fund for Aust., 1950-; Bd US Educnl Foundn in Aust., 1961-64;

Archbishop-in-Council, Dio. Melbourne, 1958-66, 1969-; Advocate of Diocese of Melbourne, 1969-; Mem. Councils: Trinity Coll., Melbourne, 1939-66; C of E Grammar Sch., Melbourne, 1960-66; Peninsula Sch., Mt Eliza, 1960-63; Toorak Coll., 1969-71; C of E Girls' Grammar Sch., Melbourne, 1969-75. Pres. Somers Area, Boy Scouts Assoc. (Vic. Br.), 1955-64, 1972-76; Member: State Exec. Boy Scouts Assoc., 1958-66, (Vice-Pres., 1964-66); Nat. Council Australian Boy Scouts Assoc., 1959-69, 1975-; Cttee, Overseas Service Bureau (Australia), 1970-71; Foundn Dir, Winston Churchill Memorial Trust in Australia, 1965-66, Dep. Nat. Chm., 1972-75, Dep. Nat. Pres., 1975-; Chm., Nat. Fellowship Cttee, 1965-66, 1969-75; Mem., Victoria Cttee, Duke of Edinburgh's Award in Australia, 1964-66; Chairman, Vict. Supreme Court Rules Cttee, 1960-66; Chm., Royal Commn, Western Australia Inquiry into the airline system, 1974-75. Stawell Orator, 1970. *Publications:* contrib. to legal periodicals. *Recreations:* golf, lawn tennis, gardening; formerly football (Melbourne Univ. blue) and lacrosse (Oxford half-blue). *Address:* 257 Collins Street, Melbourne, Vic 3000, Australia. *Clubs:* Melbourne, Australian (Melbourne); Peninsula Country (Victoria).

SHOLOKHOV, Mikhail Aleksandrovich; Order of Lenin; novelist; Deputy to Supreme Soviet of USSR since 1946; Member: Communist Party of Soviet Union, 1932; CPSU Central Committee, 1961; Academy of Sciences, USSR, 1939; Praesidium, Union of Soviet Writers, 1954; Nobel Prize for Literature, 1965; Hon. LLD, St Andrews; *b* 24 May 1905; *m* Maria Petrovna Sholokhova. First published in 1923. *Publications:* The Don Stories, 1926 (including: Woman with Two Husbands; The Heart of Alyoshka; Dry Rot; The Mortal Enemy; The Family Man; The Colt; Harvest on the Don, etc); And Quiet Flows the Don (4 vols, 1928-40, State Prize, 1940); Virgin Soil Upturned (2 vols, 1932-59, Lenin Prize, 1960); They Fought for their Country, 1954; The Destiny of Man, 1957; Collected Works, Vols I-VIII, 1959-62, etc. *Address:* Stanitsa Veshenskaya, Rostov Region, USSR; Union of Soviet Writers, Ul. Vorovskogo 52, Moscow.

SHONE, Sir Robert Minshull, Kt 1955; CBE 1949; Visiting Professor, The City University, since 1967; Director: The Rank Organisation Ltd; M and G Group (Holdings) Ltd; *b* 27 May 1906; *s* of Robert Harold Shone. *Educ:* Sedbergh School; Liverpool University (MEng); Chicago Univ. (MA Economics). Commonwealth Fellow, USA, 1932-34; Lecturer, London School of Economics, 1935-36; British Iron and Steel Federation, 1936-39 and 1946-53, Director 1950-53; Iron and Steel Control, 1940-45, Gen. Dir, 1943-45; Executive Member, Iron and Steel Board, 1953-62; Joint Chairman, UK and ECSC Steel Committee, 1954-62; Dir-Gen., Nat. Economic Develt Council, 1962-66; Research Fellow, Nuffield Coll., Oxford, 1966-67; Special Prof., Nottingham Univ., 1971-73. Dir, A. P. V. Holdings Ltd, 1969-75. Hon. Fellow, LSE. Pres., Soc. of Business Economists, 1963-68. *Publications:* Price and Investment Relationships, 1975; contributions to: Some Modern Business Problems, 1937; The Industrial Future of Great Britain, 1948; Large Scale Organisation, 1950; Models for Decision, 1965; Britain and the Common Market, 1967; (ed) Problems of Investment, 1971; articles in journals. *Recreation:* golf. *Address:* 7 Windmill Hill, Hampstead, NW3. *T:* 01-435 1930. *Club:* Reform.

SHONFIELD, Andrew Akiba; Professor of Economics, European University Institute, Florence, since 1978; *b* 10 Aug. 1917; *s* of late Victor and Rachel Lea Schonfeld; *m* 1942, Zuzanna Maria Przeworska; one *s* one *d*. *Educ:* St Paul's; Magdalen Coll., Oxford. Hons BA (Oxon) Modern Greats, 1939. Served War of 1939-45, in RA, 1940-46; attached to AFHQ, Caserta, Italy, 1945 (despatches), Major. On Staff of Financial Times, 1947-57, Foreign Editor, 1950-57; Economic Editor, The Observer, 1958-61; Director of Studies, 1961-68, Research Fellow, 1969-71, Dir, 1972-77, RIIA; Chm., SSRC, 1969-71. Member: Royal Commn on Trade Unions, 1965-68; FCO Review Cttee on Overseas Representation, 1968-69; Reith Lectr, 1972. Fellow, Imperial Coll. of Science and Technology, 1970. Hon. DLitt Loughborough, 1972. *Publications:* British Economic Policy since the War, 1958; Attack on World Poverty, 1960; A Man Beside Himself, 1964; Modern Capitalism, 1965; (ed) North American and Western European Economic Policies, 1971; (ed) Social Indicators and Social Policy, 1972; Europe: journey to an unknown destination, 1973 (Cortina-Ulisse prize, 1974); (ed) International Economic Relations in the Western World, 1959-71, 1975. *Address:* 21 Paultons Square, SW3. *T:* 01-352 7364; c/o European University Institute, 50016 San Domenico di Fiesole, Italy. *Club:* Reform.

SHOOTER, Prof. Reginald Arthur; Professor of Medical Microbiology, London University, and Bacteriologist to St

Bartholomew's Hospital, since 1961; Dean, Medical College of St Bartholomew's Hospital, since 1972; *b* 1916; *s* of Rev. A. E. Shooter, TD and M. K. Shooter; *m* 1946, Jean Wallace, MB, ChB; one *s* three *d*. *Educ:* Mill Hill Sch.; Caius Coll., Cambridge; St Bartholomew's Hosp. BA 1937; MB, BChir 1940; MRCS, LRCP 1940; MA 1941; MD 1945; MRCP 1961; FRCP 1968; FRCS; FRCPath 1963 (Vice-Pres., 1971-74). After various Hosp. appts became Surgeon Lieut, RNVR. Appointments at St Bartholomew's Hospital from 1946; Rockefeller Travelling Fellow in Medicine, 1950-51; Reader in Bacteriology, University of London, 1953. Mem., City and E London AHA, 1974-. Mem., Public Health Laboratory Service Bd, 1970-; Chm., Dangerous Pathogens Adv. Gp, 1975-. *Publications:* books, and articles in medical journals. *Recreations:* squash, gardening, fishing. *Address:* 91 The Green, Ewell, Epsom, Surrey. *T:* 01-393 3530.

SHOPPEE, Prof. Charles William, FRS 1956; FAA 1958; Emeritus Professor of Chemistry, University of Sydney; *b* London, 24 Feb. 1904; *er s* of J. W. and Elizabeth Shoppee, Totteridge; *m* 1929, Eileen Alice West; one *d*. *Educ:* Stationers' Company's Sch.; Univs of London and Leeds. PhD, DSc (London); MA, DPhil (Basle). Sen. Student of Royal Commn for Exhibition of 1851, 1926-28; Asst Lecturer and Lecturer in Organic Chemistry, Univ. of Leeds, 1929-39; Rockefeller Research Fellow, Univ. of Basle, 1939-45; Reader in Chemistry, Univ. of London, at Royal Cancer Hosp., 1945-48; Prof. of Chemistry, Univ. of Wales, at University Coll., Swansea, 1948-56; Prof. of Organic Chemistry, Univ. of Sydney, 1956-70; Foundation Welch Prof. of Chemistry, Texas Tech. Univ., 1970-75. Visiting Professor of Chemistry: Duke Univ., N Carolina, USA, 1963; Univ. of Georgia, USA, 1966; Univ. of Mississippi, USA, 1968; Hon. Professorial Fellow in Chem., Macquarie Univ., 1976-. *Publications:* Scientific papers in Jl Chem. Soc. and Helvetica Chimica Acta. *Recreations:* bowls, music, bridge. *Address:* 41 Kenthurst Road, St Ives, Sydney, NSW 2075, Australia. *T:* 449 7603. *Club:* Royal Automobile.

SHORE, family name of **Baron Teignmouth.**

SHORE, Bernard Alexander Royle, CBE 1955; FRCM, FTCL, Hon. RAM, ARCM; retired as HM Inspector of Schools, Staff Inspector for Music (1948-59); viola player; Professor of the Viola at RCM; Music Advisor, Rural Music Schools Association; *b* 17 March 1896; *s* of Arthur Miers Shore and Ada Alice (*née* Clark); *m* 1922, Olive Livett Udale; two *d*. *Educ:* St Paul's School, Hammersmith; Royal College of Music (studied organ under Sir Walter Alcock). Served European War, 1914-18: enlisted in Artists Rifles, 1915, France; commissioned, 2nd Rifle Bde (wounded); seconded to RFC. Returned to RCM: studied viola under Arthur Bent and later with Lionel Tertis. Joined Queen's Hall Orchestra, 1922; first appearance as Soloist, Promenade Concert, 1925; Principal Viola, BBC Symphony Orchestra, 1930-40. War of 1939-45: RAF, 1940; Squadron Leader, 1942; demobilised, 1946. Adviser on Instrumental Music in Schools, Min. of Educn, 1946-47. *Publications:* The Orchestra Speaks, 1937; Sixteen Symphonies, 1947. *Recreations:* sketching, the viola. *Address:* Flat 6, 3 Palmeira Square, Hove, East Sussex.

SHORE, Dr Elizabeth Catherine; Deputy Chief Medical Officer, Department of Health and Social Security, since 1977; *b* 1927; *d* of Edward Murray Wrong and Rosalind Grace Smith; *m* 1948, Rt Hon. Peter David Shore, *qv*; one *s* two *d* (and one *s* decd). *Educ:* Newnham Coll., Cambridge; St Bartholomew's Hospital. MRCP, MRCS, FFCM, DRCOG. Medical Civil Service from 1962. *Recreations:* reading, cookery, swimming in rough seas. *Address:* c/o Department of Health and Social Security, Alexander Fleming House, Elephant and Castle, SE1.

SHORE, Rt. Hon. Peter (David), PC 1967; MP (Lab) Tower Hamlets, Stepney and Poplar, since 1974 (Stepney, 1964-74); Secretary of State for the Environment, since 1976; *b* 20 May 1924; *m* 1948, Elizabeth Catherine Wrong (*see* E. C. Shore); one *s* two *d* (and one *s* decd). *Educ:* Quarry Bank High Sch., Liverpool; King's Coll., Cambridge. Political economist. Joined Labour Party, 1948; Head of Research Dept, Labour Party, 1959-64. Member of Fabian Society. Contested (Lab) St Ives, Cornwall, 1950, Halifax, 1959. PPS to the Prime Minister, 1965-66; Jt Parly Sec.: Min. of Technology, 1966-67; Dept of Economic Affairs, 1967; Sec. of State for Economic Affairs, 1967-69; Minister without Portfolio, 1969-70; Dep. Leader of House of Commons, 1969-70; Opposition Spokesman on Europe, 1971-74; Sec. of State for Trade, 1974-76. *Publication:* Entitled to Know, 1966. *Recreation:* swimming. *Address:* House of Commons, SW1; 23 Dryburgh Road, SW15.

SHORROCK, James Godby; Barrister-at-Law; Recorder of Barrow-in-Furness, 1963-71; *b* 10 Dec. 1910; *s* of late William Gordon Shorrock, JP, Morland, Westmorland; *m* 1936, Mary Patricia, *d* of late George Herbert Lings, Burnage, Manchester; two *s* two *d*. *Educ:* Clifton; Hertford College, Oxford. Called to Bar, Inner Temple, 1934. Served War of 1939-45: Major RA (TA) and Judge Advocate General's Department. Dep. Chm., Westmorland QS, 1955-71. Legal Member, Mental Health Review Tribunal, 1960-63; Legal Chm., Manchester City Licensing Planning Cttee, 1964. *Recreations:* walking, fishing, gardening.

SHORT, family name of **Baron Glenamara.**

SHORT, Rt. Rev. Hedley Vicars Roycraft; *see* Saskatchewan, Bishop of.

SHORT, Rev. John, MA (Edinburgh); PhD (Edinburgh); Hon. DD (St Andrews); Minister of St George's United Church, Toronto, Canada, 1951-64; *b* Berwickshire, 27 March 1896; *m* 1st; one *s* one *d*; 2nd, 1939, Anneliese, 2nd *d* of Dr C. J. F. Bechler, Danzig; two *s*. *Educ:* Edinburgh University. Trained for a business career but attracted by religious convictions to the Christian ministry; began to study for same just before the war of 1914-18, joined army and served for 3 years and 6 months; commenced studies at Edinburgh; graduated MA. First class honours in Philosophy; awarded John Edward Baxter Scholarship in Philosophy for 3 years; received University Diploma in Education and Medal; trained for Teacher's Certificate; awarded Doctorate in Philosophy for a thesis on the Philosophic Character of English XIVth Century Mysticism; medallist in class of Moral Philosophy, and in Metaphysics; Prizeman in Psychology; trained in Scottish Congregational College for Ministry under Principal T. Hywel Hughes, DLitt, DD; called to Bathgate E. U. Congregational Church, 1924; Minister of Lyndhurst Road Congregational Church, Hampstead, 1930-37. Minister of Richmond Hill Congregational Church, Bournemouth, 1937-51; Chairman of the Congregational Union of England and Wales, 1949-50. Mason: 3° Home Lodge Amity, Poole, Dorset, 1938: Downend Chapter Rose Croix, Gloucester, 1953; affiliated Ashlar Lodge, 247 GRC, Toronto, 1952; 32° Moore Sovereign Consistory, Hamilton, Ont, 1964; 33° Supreme Council A&ASR, Dominion of Canada (Hon. Inspector Gen.), 1967. DD (hc): St Andrews Univ., 1950; McMaster Univ., Hamilton, Ontario, 1964. *Publications:* Can I Find Faith?, 1937; All Things are Yours (book of sermons), 1939; The Interpreter's Bible Exposition of I Corinthians; Triumphant Believing, 1952. *Recreations:* gardening, reading, and travel. *Address:* 162 Coldstream Avenue, Toronto M5N 1X9, Canada. *T:* 489-8614.

SHORT, Rt. Rev. Kenneth Herbert; an Assistant Bishop, Diocese of Sydney (Bishop in Wollongong), since 1975; also Archdeacon of Wollongong and Camden, since 1975; *b* 6 July 1927; *s* of Cecil Charles Short and Joyce Ellen Begbie; *m* 1950, Gloria Noelle Funnell; one *s* two *d*. *Educ:* Moore Theological Coll. (ThL and Moore Coll. Dipl.). Commissioned AIF, 1946; with BCOF, 1946-48; theological training, 1949-52; ordained Anglican Ministry, 1952; Minister in Charge, Provisional Parish of Pittwater, 1952-54; with CMS in Tanzania, E Africa, 1955-64; Chaplain, Tabora 1955, Mwanza 1955-62; first Principal, Msalato Bible School, 1961-64; Gen. Secretary, CMS NSW Branch, 1964-71, including Sec. for S America. Canon of St Andrew's Cathedral, Sydney, 1970-75; Exam. Chaplain to Archbishop of Sydney, 1971-; Rector of St Michael's, Vaucluse, 1971-75. *Publication:* Guidance, 1969. *Recreations:* fishing, reading, walking. *Address:* 20 Reserve Street, Wollongong, NSW 2500, Australia. *T:* 042 296927.

SHORT, Sir Noel (Edward Vivian), Kt 1977; MBE 1951; MC 1945; Speaker's Secretary, House of Commons, since 1970; *b* 19 Jan. 1916; *s* of late Vivian A. Short, CIE, Indian Police, and late Annie W. Short; *m* 1st, 1949, Diana Hester Morison (*d* 1951); one *s*; 2nd, 1957, Karin Margarete Anders; one *s* one *d*. *Educ:* Radley College; RMA Sandhurst. Commissioned Indian Army, 1936; joined 6th Gurkha Rifles, 1937. Active service: NW Frontier of India, 1937, 1940-41; Assam and Burma, 1942, 1944-45; New Guinea, 1943-44; Malaysia, 1950-51, 1952-53, 1956-57. Staff College, 1946-47; jssc, 1953; Comdr. 63 Gurkha Bde, Malaysia, 1960-61; Comdr, 51 Infty Bde, Tidworth, 1962-63. Principal, Home Office, 1964-70. *Publications:* contribs: Jl of RUSI; Army Quarterly. *Recreations:* ski-ing, photography. *Address:* Walters Green, Penshurst, Kent.

SHORT, Mrs Renee; MP (Lab) Wolverhampton North-East, since 1964; *m*; two *d*. *Educ:* Nottingham County Grammar Sch.; Manchester Univ. Freelance journalist. Member: Herts County Council, 1952-67; Watford RDC, 1952-64; West Herts Group Hosp. Management Cttee; former Chm. Shrodell's Hosp., Watford. Governor: Watford Coll. of Technology; Watford Grammar Sch. Contested (Lab) St Albans, 1955, Watford, 1959. TGWU sponsored Member of Parliament. Member: Delegation to Council of Europe, 1964-68; Expenditure Cttee, 1970- (Chm., Social Services and Employment Sub-Cttee); Vice-Chm., Parly East-West Trade Gp, 1968-; Chm., Anglo-GDR Parly Gp; Sec., Anglo-Soviet Parly Gp; Pres., British-Romanian Friendship Assoc. Mem., Nat. Exec. Cttee of Labour Party, 1970-. National President: Nursery Schools Assoc.; Campaign for Nursery Educn. Mem., Roundhouse Theatre Council; Chm., Theatres' Advisory Council, 1974-. *Address:* House of Commons, SW1A 0AA.

SHORT, Prof. Roger Valentine, FRS 1974; FRSE 1974; FRCVS 1976; Director, Medical Research Council Unit of Reproductive Biology, Edinburgh, since 1972; Honorary Professor, University of Edinburgh, since 1976; *b* 31 July 1930; *s* of F. A. and M. C. Short, Weybridge; *m* 1958, Dr Mary Bowen Wilson; one *s* three *d*. *Educ:* Sherborne Sch.; Univs of Bristol (BVSc, MRCVS), Wisconsin (MSc) and Cambridge (PhD, ScD). Mem., ARC Unit of Reproductive Physiology and Biochemistry, Cambridge, 1956-72; Fellow, Magdalene Coll., Cambridge, 1962-72; Lectr, then Reader, Dept of Veterinary Clinical Studies, Cambridge, 1961-72. *Publications:* (ed, with C. R. Austin) Reproduction in Mammals, vols 1-6, 1972; (ed, with D. T. Baird) Contraceptives of the Future, 1976; contrib. Jl Endocrinology, Jl Reproduction and Fertility, Jl Zoology. *Recreations:* gardening, wildlife. *Address:* Bonnyton House, Craigluscar Road, Dunfermline, Fife. *T:* Dunfermline 23687.

SHORTT, Maj.-Gen. Arthur Charles, CB 1951; OBE 1945; psc; *b* 2 April 1899; *s* of Charles William Shortt and Grace Evelyn Mary (*née* Skey; *m* 1st, 1927, Loraine (*née* Thomas), one *d*; 2nd, 1945, Nella (*née* Exelby). *Educ:* St Lawrence College; King's College, Cambridge; RMA Woolwich, 2nd Lt, RE, 1916. Served European War, 1914-18, in France and Belgium; 1st KGO Sappers and Miners, India, 1919-22; Staff College, Minley, 1939. War of 1939-45: Military Assistant to C-in-C, BEF 1940; Director of Technical Training, 1943; France and Germany, 1944-45. Military Attaché, Athens, 1947-49; Director of Military Intelligence, 1949-53; Chief Liaison Officer on UK Service Liaison Staff, Australia, 1953-56; Retired pay, 1956; Director of Public Relations, War Office, 1956-61; Col Comdt, Intelligence Corps, 1960-64. Mem. Governing Body, St Lawrence Coll. Officer, Legion of Honour (France), 1950. *Recreation:* numismatics. *Address:* Bolnore, Hayward's Heath, Sussex. *T:* 51386. *Club:* MCC.

SHORTT, Colonel Henry Edward, CIE 1941; FRS 1950; LLD 1952; Colonel IMS, retired; formerly Professor of Medical Protozoology, University of London, and Head of Department of Parasitology, London School of Hygiene and Tropical Medicine; *b* 15 April 1887; *m* 1921, Eleanor M. Hobson; one *s* one *d*. *Educ:* Univ. of Aberdeen. MB, ChB 1910; MD 1936; DSc 1938; KHP 1941-44; Inspector-Gen. of Civil Hospitals and Prisons, Assam, 1941-44; retired, 1944. President, Royal Society of Tropical Medicine and Hygiene, 1949-51; Technical Expert under Colombo Plan in E Pakistan, 1952-55. Straits Settlements Gold Medal, 1938; Kaisar-i-Hind Gold Medal, 1945; Laveran Prize, 1948; Mary Kingsley medal, 1949; Darling medal and prize, 1951; Stewart prize, 1954; Manson Medal, 1959; Gaspar Vianna Medal, 1962. *Publications:* over 130 scientific papers. *Recreations:* shooting and fishing. *Address:* Rivenhall, Lenten Street, Alton, Hants. *T:* Alton 83252.

SHOTTON, Prof. Edward; Professor of Pharmaceutics, University of London, 1956-Sept. 1977; *b* 5 July 1910; *s* of Ernest Richard and Maud Shotton; *m* 1943, Mary Constance Louise Marchant; one *d*. *Educ:* Smethwick (Junior) Technical School; Birkbeck College, University of London. Pharmaceutical Chemist (PhC), 1933; BSc (London), 1939; PhD (London), 1955; Hon. ACT (Birmingham), 1961. FRIC 1949. Pharmaceutical research and development work at Burroughs, Wellcome & Co., Dartford, 1939-48. Sen. Lecturer in Pharmaceutics, Univ. of London, 1948-56. Chairman, British Pharmaceutical Conference, 1966. *Publications:* (with K. Ridgway) Physical Pharmaceutics, 1974; research papers, mainly in Jl of Pharmacy and Pharmacology. *Recreations:* gardening, cricket, fly-fishing. *Address:* 10 Winston Gardens, Berkhamsted, Herts. *T:* 6402 Berkhamsted. *Club:* Athenæum.

SHOTTON, Prof. Frederick William, MBE 1946; FRS 1956; MA, ScD; FGS; CEng, FIMinE; MIWES; Professor of Geology, University of Birmingham, 1949-74, Emeritus Professor 1975 (Pro-Vice-Chancellor and Vice-Principal, 1965-71); *b* 8 Oct. 1906; *s* of F. J. and Ada Shotton, Coventry; *m* 1930, Alice L.

Linnett; two d. *Educ:* Bablake, Coventry; Sidney Sussex College, Cambridge. Wiltshire Prizeman and Harkness Scholar, Cambridge, 1926-27. Assistant Lecturer and Lecturer, University of Birmingham, 1928-36; Lecturer, Cambridge University, 1936-45. Served War of 1939-45, MEF and 21 Army Group, 1940-45. Prof. of Geology, Sheffield Univ., 1945-49. Mem., NERC, 1969-72. Pres., Geological Soc., 1964-66, Vice-Pres., 1966-68. Founder Fellow, Fellowship of Engineering, 1976. Hon. Mem., Royal Irish Acad., 1970. Prestwich Medal, Geological Soc. of London, 1954; Stopes Medal, Geologists' Assoc., 1967. *Publications:* numerous scientific. *Recreations:* archæology and natural history; gardening. *Address:* 111 Dorridge Road, Dorridge, West Midlands B93 8BP. *T:* Knowle 2820.

SHOVELTON, Prof. David Scott, FDSRCS; Professor of Conservative Dentistry, since 1964, and Director of the Dental School, since 1974, University of Birmingham; Consultant Dental Surgeon, Birmingham Area Health Authority (Teaching), since 1974; *b* 12 Sept. 1925; *s* of Leslie Shovelton, LDSRCS, and Marion de Winton (*née* Scott); *m* 1949, Pearl Holland; two *s*. *Educ:* The Downs Sch., Colwall; King's Sch., Worcester; Univ. of Birmingham (BSc, LDS, BDS). House Surg., Birmingham Dental Hosp., 1951; gen. dental practice, Evesham, Worcs, 1951; Dental Officer, RAF, 1951-53; Lectr in Operative Dental Surg., Univ. of Birmingham, 1953-60, Sen. Lectr, 1960-64. Vis. Asst Prof. of Clin. Dentistry, Univ. of Alabama, 1959-60. Cons. Dental Surg., United Birmingham Hosps, 1960-74, and Birmingham Reg. Hosp. Bd, 1962-74. Pres., British Soc. for Restorative Dentistry, 1970-71 (Vice-Pres., 1968-70 and 1971-72). Member: Gen. Dental Council, 1974-; Birmingham Area Health Authority (Teaching), 1974-. Ext. Examnr in dental subjects, univs and colls, 1968-. *Publications:* Inlays, Crowns and Bridges (jtly), 1963 (3rd edn 1977); articles in med. and dental jls, 1957-. *Recreations:* music, photography, gardening and caravanning. *Address:* 86 Broad Oaks Road, Solihull, West Midlands B91 1HZ. *T:* 021-705 3026. *Club:* Royal Air Force.

SHOVELTON, Walter Patrick, CB 1976; CMG 1972; Deputy Secretary (Civil Aviation and Shipping), Department of Trade, since 1976; *b* 18 Aug. 1919; *s* of late S. T. Shovelton, CBE, and M. C. Kelly, cousin of Patrick and Willie Pearse; *m* 1st, 1942, Marjorie Lucy Joan Manners (marr. diss. 1967); one *d*; 2nd, Helena Richards, 3rd *d* of D. G. Richards, *qv*. *Educ:* Charterhouse; Keble Coll., Oxford (scholar of both). Rep. Oxford Univ. at Eton Fives. Served in RA and RHA, 1940-46; DAAG, War Office, 1945-46. Entered Administrative Civil Service as Asst Principal, Min. of Transport, 1946; Principal 1947; Admin. Staff College, 1951; Private Sec. to Secretary of State for Co-ordination of Transport, Fuel and Power, 1951-53; Asst Sec., 1957; transferred to Min. of Aviation, 1959; IDC, 1962; Under Secretary, 1966; transferred to Min. of Technology, 1966, and to DTI, 1970; Mem., UK Negotiating Team for entry into EEC, 1970-72; Deputy Secretary: DTI, 1972-74; Dept of Prices and Consumer Protection, 1974-76. Leader, UK Negotiating Team for Bermuda 2, 1977. *Recreation:* golf. *Address:* Ashburton Cottage, 43 North Road, N6. *Clubs:* United Oxford & Cambridge University, MCC; Jesters; Hampstead Golf (Captain, 1975-76).

SHOWERING, Keith Stanley; Chairman and Chief Esxecutive, Allied Breweries Ltd, since 1975; Vice-Chairman, Guardian Royal Exchange Assurance Co., since 1974; *b* 6 Aug. 1930; *o* *s* of late Herbert and of Ada Showering; *m* 1954, Marie Sadie (*née* Golden); four *s* two *d*. *Educ:* Wells Cathedral School. Joined family business of Showerings Ltd, cider makers, 1947; Dir, 1951; Founder Dir, Showerings, Vine Products & Whiteways Ltd on merger of those companies, 1961; Dep. Chm., 1964; Chief Executive, 1971-75; Man. Dir, John Harvey & Sons Ltd and Harveys of Bristol Ltd, 1966-71, Chm., 1971; Allied Breweries Ltd: Dir, 1968; Vice-Chm., 1969-74; Dep. Chm., Jan.-Sept. 1975; also Director: Tooheys Ltd, Sydney, Australia, 1976-; other allied subsidiary cos. *Recreation:* shooting. *Address:* 156 St Johns Street, EC1P 1AR. *T:* 01-253 9911. *Clubs:* Bath, Arts, Buck's.

SHRAPNEL, Norman; Parliamentary Correspondent of the Guardian, 1958-75; *b* 5 Oct. 1912; *yr* *s* of Arthur Edward Scrope Shrapnel and Rosa Brosy; *m* 1940, Mary Lilian Myfanwy Edwards; two *s*. *Educ:* King's School, Grantham. Various weekly, evening and morning newspapers from 1930; Manchester Guardian (later the Guardian) from 1947, as reporter, theatre critic and reviewer; contributor to various journals. Political Writer of the Year Award (the Political Companion), 1969. *Publication:* A View of the Thames, 1977. *Recreations:* walking, music. *Address:* 27 Shooters Hill Road, Blackheath, SE3. *T:* 01-858 7123.

SHREWSBURY and WATERFORD, 21st Earl of, *cr* 1442 and 1446; **John George Charles Henry Alton Alexander Chetwynd Chetwynd-Talbot;** Baron of Dungarvan, 1446; Baron Talbot, 1733; Earl Talbot, Viscount Ingestre, 1784; Premier Earl of England, Hereditary Great Seneschal or Lord High Steward of Ireland; *b* 1 Dec. 1914; *s* of Viscount Ingestre, MVO (*d* 1915) and Lady Winifred Constance Hester Paget, *e* *d* of Lord Alexander (Victor) Paget (she *m* 1917, R. E. Pennoyer, and *d* 1965); *S* grandfather, 1921; *m* 1st, 1936, Nadine (marr. diss., 1963), *yr* *d* of late Brig.-Gen. C. R. Crofton, CBE; two *s* four *d*; 2nd, 1963, Aileen Mortlock. *Educ:* Eton. A godson of King George V and Queen Mary. Served War of 1939-45; Staff Officer to Duke of Gloucester, 1940-42; Middle Eastern and Italian Theatres of Operations, 1942-45. Pres., Staffs Agricultural Soc., 1935-60. Late CC and JP Staffs. *Heir:* *s* Viscount Ingestre, *qv*. *Address:* Au Marguery, Sentier de Priolaz 8, 1802 Corseaux, Vaud, Switzerland. *Club:* Royal Yacht Squadron.
See also G. R. F. Morris.

SHREWSBURY, Bishop Suffragan of, since 1970; **Rt. Rev. Francis William Cocks,** CB 1959; *b* 5 Nov. 1913; *o* *s* of late Canon W. Cocks, OBE, St John's Vicarage, Felixstowe; *m* 1940, Irene May (Barbara), 2nd *d* of H. Thompson, Bridlington; one *s* one *d*. *Educ:* Haileybury; St Catharine's Coll., Cambridge; Westcott House. Played Rugby Football for Cambridge Univ., Hampshire and Eastern Counties, 1935-38. Ordained, 1937. Chaplain RAFVR, 1939; Chaplain RAF, 1945; Asst Chaplain-in-Chief, 1950; Chaplain-in-Chief, and Archdeacon, Royal Air Force, 1959-65; Rector and Rural Dean of Wolverhampton, 1965-70. Mem. of Council, Haileybury and Imperial Service Coll., 1949-. Hon. Chaplain to HM the Queen, 1959-65. Prebendary of S Botolph in Lincoln Cathedral, 1959; Canon Emeritus, 1965-70; Prebendary of Lichfield Cathedral, 1968-70; Select Preacher, Univ. of Cambridge, 1960; Hon. Canon of Lichfield Cathedral, 1970-; Fellow, Woodard Schools, 1969-; Mem. Council: Denstone Sch., 1970-72; Shrewsbury Sch., 1971-; Ellesmere Coll., 1971-. Pres. Buccaneers CC, 1965-. *Recreations:* cricket, tennis, golf. *Address:* Athlone House, London Road, Shrewsbury SY2 6PG. *T:* Shrewsbury 56410. *Clubs:* MCC, Royal Air Force; Hawks (Cambridge).

SHREWSBURY, Bishop of, (RC), since 1962; **Rt. Rev. William Eric Grasar,** DCL, STL; *b* 18 May 1913. *Educ:* Brigg Grammar School; Panton; English College, Rome. Priest 1937; Vice-Rector, English College, Rome, 1942-46; Chancellor, Nottingham Diocese, 1948-52; Rector of St Hugh's College, Tollerton, 1952-56; Vicar-General, Nottingham Diocese, 1956-62. *Address:* The Council House, Shrewsbury SY1 2AY. *T:* Shrewsbury 3513.

SHREWSBURY, Auxiliary Bishop of, (RC); see Brewer, Rt. Rev. John.

SHRIMSLEY, Anthony; Assistant Editor, The Sun, and political adviser, News Group Newspapers, since 1976; *b* 12 June 1934; *s* of John Shrimsley and Alice Shrimsley, London; *m* 1961, Yvonne Ann, *d* of Harry and Gertrude Ross; one *s* one *d*. *Educ:* William Ellis Sch., Highgate, and elsewhere. Press Assoc., 1950; Edgware Post, 1951; RAF, 1952-54; Littlehampton Gazette; Reporter, Manchester Evening News, 1955, Polit. Corresp., 1959; Polit. Corresp., later Polit. Editor, Sunday Mirror, 1962-69; Polit. Editor, The Sun, 1969; Polit. Editor, Daily Mail, 1973, Asst Editor, 1975. Chm., Parly Lobby Journalists, 1975-76; Mem., BBC Consultative Gp on Business and Ind. Affairs, 1976-. *Publication:* The First Hundred Days of Harold Wilson, 1965. *Recreation:* sailing. *Address:* News Group Newspapers Ltd, 30 Bouverie Street, EC4Y 8EX. *T:* 01-353 3030. *Clubs:* Reform; Wembley Sailing.
See also Bernard Shrimsley.

SHRIMSLEY, Bernard; Editor, News of the World, since 1975; Director, News Group Newspapers Ltd, since 1975; *b* 13 Jan. 1931; *er* *s* of John and Alice Shrimsley, London; *m* 1952, Norma Jessie Alexandra, *d* of Albert and Maude Forster, Southport; one *d*. *Educ:* Kilburn Grammar School. Press Association, 1947; Southport Guardian, 1948; RAF, 1949-51; Daily Mirror, 1953; Dep. Northern Editor, Sunday Express, 1959; Northern Editor, Daily Mirror, 1963, subseq. Asst Editor, Asst Publicity Dir; Editor, Liverpool Daily Post, 1968; Dep. Editor, The Sun, 1969; Assoc. Editor, News of the World, 1972; Editor, The Sun, 1972-75. *Publication:* The Candidates, 1968. *Address:* 30 Bouverie Street, EC4Y 8EX. *T:* 01-353 3030.
See also A. Shrimsley.

SHRIVER, (Robert) Sargent; Lawyer; Senior Partner, Fried, Frank, Harris, Shriver & Jacobson, since 1971; *b* Westminster, Md, 9 Nov. 1915; *s* of Robert Sargent and Hilda Shriver; *m* 1953, Eunice Mary Kennedy; four *s* one *d*. *Educ:* parochial schools, Baltimore; Canterbury School, New Milford, Conn.; Yale College; Yale University. BA (*cum laude*) 1938; LLB 1941; LLD 1964. Apprentice Seaman, USNR, 1940; Ensign, 1941. Served War of 1941-45: Atlantic and Pacific Ocean Areas aboard battleships and submarines; Lt-Comdr, USNR. Admitted to: New York Bar, 1941; Illinois Bar, (retd) 1959; US Supreme Court, 1966; District of Columbia Bar, 1971. With legal firm of Winthrop, Stimson, Putnam & Roberts, NYC, 1940-41; Asst Editor, Newsweek, 1945-46; associated with Joseph P. Kennedy Enterprises, 1946-48; Asst Gen. Man., Merchandise Mart, 1948-61; President: Chicago Bd of Educn, 1955-60; Catholic Interracial Council of Chicago, 1954-59; Dir, Peace Corps, Washington, 1961-66; Dir, Office of Economic Opportunity and Special Asst to Pres. Johnson, 1964-68; US Ambassador to France, 1968-70. Vice-Presidential candidate (Democrat), Nov. 1972. Exec. Dir, Joseph P. Kennedy Jr Foundn. Democrat; Roman Catholic. *Address:* Timberlawn, Edson Lane, Rockville, Md, USA.

SHRUBSOLE, Alison Cheveley; Principal, Homerton College, Cambridge, since 1971; Fellow of Hughes Hall, Cambridge, since 1974; *b* 7 April 1925; *d* of Rev. Stanley and Mrs Margaret Shrubsole. *Educ:* Milton Mount Coll.; Royal Holloway Coll.; Inst. of Education. BA Hons London; MA Cantab; Postgraduate Cert. in Educn. FCP. Teaching in schools in South London, 1946-50; Lectr and Sen. Lectr, Stockwell Coll., 1950-57; Principal: Machakos Training Coll., Kenya, 1957-62; Philippa Fawcett Coll., London SW16, 1963-71. *Publications:* articles in TES, THES, Dialogue, Learning for Teaching. *Recreations:* music, architecture, travel, mountaineering, gardening, cooking. *Address:* Principal's House, Homerton College, Cambridge. *T:* Cambridge 45931. *Club:* English-Speaking Union.

SHUCKBURGH, Sir (Charles Arthur) Evelyn, GCMG 1967 (KCMG 1959; CMG 1949); CB 1954; HM Diplomatic Service, retired; Chairman: Executive Committee, since 1970, Council, since 1976, British Red Cross Society; Standing Commission, International Red Cross, since 1977 (Member, since 1974); *b* 26 May 1909; *e s* of late Sir John Shuckburgh, KCMG, CB; *m* 1937, Nancy Brett, 2nd *d* of 3rd Viscount Esher, GBE; two *s* one *d*. *Educ:* Winchester; King's College, Cambridge. Entered Diplomatic Service, 1933; served at HM Embassy, Cairo, 1937-39; seconded for service on staff of UK High Comr in Ottawa, 1940; transferred to Buenos Aires, 1942; Chargé d'Affaires there in 1944; First Secretary at HM Embassy, Prague, 1945-47. Head of South American Department, FO, 1947-48; Western Dept, 1949-50; Western Organizations Dept, 1950-51; Principal Private Secretary to Secretary of State for Foreign Affairs, 1951-54; Assistant Under-Secretary, Foreign Office, 1954-56; Senior Civilian Instructor, IDC, 1956-58; Asst Sec.-Gen. (Polit.) of NATO, Paris, 1958-60; Dep. Under-Sec., FO, 1960-62; Perm. Brit. Rep. to N Atlantic Council, in Paris, 1962-66; Ambassador to Italy, 1966-69. Dir, Commercial Union Assurance. Chm., N Home Counties Regional Cttee, National Trust, 1975-. *Address:* High Wood House, Watlington, Oxon. *Club:* Anglo-Belgian.

SHUCKBURGH, Sir Charles Gerald Stewkley, 12th Bt, *cr* 1660; TD; DL; JP; Major, late 11th (City of London Yeomanry) LAA; *b* 28 Feb. 1911; *s* of 11th Bt and Honour Zoë, OBE, *d* of Neville Thursby, of Harlestone, Northamptonshire; *S* father, 1939; *m* 1st, 1935, Remony (*d* 1936), *o d* of late F. N. Bell, Buenos Aires; 2nd, 1937, Nancy Diana Mary (OBE 1970), *o d* of late Capt. Rupert Lubbock, RN; one *s* two *d*. *Educ:* Harrow; Trinity College, Oxford. JP 1946, DL 1965, Warwickshire; High Sheriff, Warwickshire, 1965. *Heir: s* Rupert Charles Gerald Shuckburgh, *b* 12 Feb. 1949. *Address:* Shuckburgh, Daventry. *TA:* Daventry. *T:* Daventry 2523. *Club:* Bath.

SHUCKBURGH, Sir Evelyn; see Shuckburgh, Sir C. A. E.

SHUFFREY, Ralph Frederick Dendy; Assistant Under-Secretary of State, Home Office, since 1972; Registrar of the Baronetage; *b* 9 Dec. 1925; *s* of Frederick and late Mary Shuffrey; *m* 1953, Sheila, *d* of late Brig. John Lingham, CB, DSO, MC, and Juliet Judd; one *s* one *d*. *Educ:* Shrewsbury; Balliol Coll., Oxford. Served Army, 1944-47 (Captain). Entered Home Office, 1951; Private Sec. to Parly Under-Sec. of State, 1956-57; Private Sec. to Home Sec., 1965-66; Asst Sec., 1966-72. *Address:* 21 Claremont Road, Claygate, Surrey. *T:* Esher 65123.

SHULMAN, Drusilla Norman; see Beyfus, Drusilla N.

SHULMAN, Milton; writer, journalist, critic; *b* Toronto, 1 Sept. 1913; *s* of late Samuel Shulman, merchant, and of Ethel Shulman; *m* 1956, Drusilla Beyfus, *qv*; one *s* two *d*. *Educ:* Univ. of Toronto (BA); Osgoode Hall, Toronto. Barrister, Toronto, 1937-40. Armoured Corps and Intelligence, Canadian Army,

1940-46 (despatches, Normandy, 1945); Major. Film critic, Evening Standard and Sunday Express, 1948-58; book critic, Sunday Express, 1957-58; theatre critic, Evening Standard, 1953-; TV critic, Evening Standard, 1964-73; columnist, social and political affairs, Daily Express, 1973-75. Executive producer and producer, Granada TV, 1958-62; Asst Controller of Programmes, Rediffusion TV, 1962-64. IPC Award, Critic of the Year, 1966. *Publications:* Defeat in the West, 1948; How To Be a Celebrity, 1950; The Ravenous Eye, 1973; The Least Worst Television in the World, 1973; *children's books:* Preep, 1964; Preep in Paris, 1967; Preep and The Queen, 1970; *novel:* Kill Three, 1967; *novel and film story:* (with Herbert Kretzmer) Every Home Should Have One, 1970. *Recreations:* modern art, history, tennis. *Address:* 51 Eaton Square, SW1. *T:* 01-235 7162. *Club:* Hurlingham.

SHULTZ, George Pratt; President and Director, Bechtel Corporation, San Francisco, California, since 1975, Executive Vice President, 1974-75; *b* New York City, 13 Dec. 1920; *s* of Birl E. Shultz and Margaret Pratt; *m* 1946, Helena Maria O'Brien; two *s* three *d*. *Educ:* Princeton Univ., 1942 (BA Econ); Massachusetts Inst. of Technology, 1949 (PhD Industrial Econ). Served War, US Marine Corps, Pacific, 1942; Major, 1945. Faculty, MIT, 1948-57; Sen. staff economist, President's Council of Economic Advisers, 1955-56 (on leave, MIT); Univ. of Chicago, Graduate Sch. of Business: Prof. of Industrial Relations, 1957-62; Dean, 1962-69; Prof. of Management and Public Policy, Stanford Univ., Graduate Sch. of Business, 1974. Secretary of Labor, 1969-July 1, 1970; Dir, Office of Management and Budget, 1970-72; Secretary of the Treasury, 1972-74; Chm., Cost of Living Council, 1972-74; Asst to the President (Chm., Council on Econ. Policy and Council on Internat. Econ. Policy), 1972-74; US Governor, IMF, World Bank, Inter-American Bank, ADB, 1972-74; Chm., East-West Trade Policy Cttee, 1973-74; Mem., US Adv. Cttee on Reform of Internat. Monetary System, 1975-. Director: J. P. Morgan & Co.; Morgan Guaranty Trust Co.; Sears Roebuck and Co.; Trustee, Alfred P. Sloan Foundn. Hon. Dr of Laws: Notre Dame Univ., 1969; Loyola Univ., 1972; Pennsylvania, 1973; Rochester, 1973; Princeton, 1973; Carnegie-Mellon Univ., 1975. *Publications:* Pressures on Wage Decisions, 1951; The Dynamics of a Labor Market (with C. A. Myers), 1951; Management Organization and the Computer (with T. A. Whisler), 1960; Strategies for the Displaced Worker (with Arnold R. Weber), 1966; Guidelines, Informal Controls, and the Market Place (with Rober Z. Aliber), 1966; Workers and Wages in the Urban Labor Market (with Albert Rees), 1970. *Recreations:* golf, tennis. *Address:* (office) Bechtel Corporation, 50 Beale Street, San Francisco, Calif 94105, USA. *T:* (415) 768-7844; (home) Stanford, Calif, USA.

SHUTE, Prof. Charles Cameron Donald, MD; Professor of Histology, Cambridge University, since 1969; Fellow of Christ's College, Cambridge, since 1957; *b* 23 May 1917; *s* of late Cameron Deane Shute; *m* 1st, 1947, Patricia Cameron (*d* 1952), *d* of F. H. Doran; 2nd, 1954, Lydia May (Wendy) (*née* Harwood); one *s* three *d*. *Educ:* Eton; King's Coll., Cambridge; Middlesex Hosp., London. MA, MB, BChir Cambridge, 1945; MD Cambridge 1958. Resident posts at Middlesex Hosp., 1945-47; RAMC (otologist), 1947-49; Demonstrator and Lectr in Anatomy, London Hosp. Med. Coll., 1951; Univ. Demonstrator and Lectr, Cambridge, 1952-69; Univ. Reader in Neuroanatomy, Cambridge, 1969. *Publications:* papers in biological jls. *Recreations:* versifying, painting, seeing through gurus. *Address:* Milton House, Christ's Pieces, Cambridge. *T:* Cambridge 62035.

SHUTE, John Lawson, CMG 1970; OBE 1959; Member: Council of Egg Marketing Authorities of Australia, since 1970; Egg Marketing Board of New South Wales, since 1970; Director, Arthur Yates & Co. Pty Ltd, since 1970; *b* Mudgee, NSW, 31 Jan. 1901; *s* of J. Shute, Mudgee; *m* 1937, Constance W. M., *d* of J. Douglas; two *s*. *Educ:* Parramatta High Sch. Asst Sec., Primary Producers' Union, NSW, 1923-33; Gen.-Sec., 1933-43; Sec., Federated Co-operative Bacon Factories, 1927-43; Member: NSW Dairy Products Bd, 1934-46; Commonwealth Air Beef Panel, 1942; Dir, Commonwealth Dairy Produce Equalisation Cttee, 1941-46; 1st Sec. Aust. Dairy Farmers' Fedn, 1942; Mem. Exec. and Asst Sec., Empire Producers' Conf., 1938; Mem. Special Dairy Industry Cttee apptd by Commonwealth Govt, 1942; Dep. Controller, Meat Supplies, NSW, 1942-46. Chairman: Aust. Meat Bd, 1946-70; Aust. Cttee of Animal Production, 1947-70; Aust. Cattle and Beef Research Cttee, 1960-66; Belmont-Brian Pastures Res. Cttee, 1962-76; Aust. Meat Research Cttee, 1966-70; Aust. Frozen Cargo Shippers' Cttee, 1967-70; Member: Export Development Council, 1958-66; Overseas Trade Publicity Cttee, 1955-70; Australia Japan Business Co-operation Cttee, 1962-70; Industry

Co-operative Programme, FAO, 1975- (Chm., Working Gp on Integrated Meat Develt, 1976-); NSW Rural Reconstruction Bd, 1942-71. *Recreations:* Rugby Union (former Internat. rep.), cricket. *Address:* 5/2 Woonona Avenue, Wahroonga, NSW 2076, Australia. *Clubs:* Commercial Travellers' (NSW); Eastwood Rugby Union (NSW).

SHUTTLEWORTH, 5th Baron *cr* 1902, of Gawthorpe; **Charles Geoffrey Nicholas Kay-Shuttleworth; Bt** 1850; *b* 2 Aug. 1948; *s* of 4th Baron Shuttleworth, MC, and of Anne Elizabeth, *er d* of late Col Geoffrey Phillips, CBE, DSO; *S* father, 1975; *m* 1975, Mrs Ann Mary Barclay, *d* of James Whatman; one *s*. *Educ:* Eton. ARICS. *Heir: s* Hon. Thomas Edward Kay-Shuttleworth, *b* 29 Sept. 1976. *Address:* 14 Sloane Avenue, SW3 3JE; Leck Hall, Carnforth, Lancs. *Clubs:* Brooks's, MCC, City University.

SIBBALD, Maj.-Gen. Peter Frank Aubrey, OBE 1972; General Officer Commanding North West District, since 1977; *b* 24 March 1928; *s* of Major Francis Victor Sibbald, MBE, MM, BEM, and Mrs Alice Emma Hawking, The Hoe, Plymouth; *m* 1957, Margaret Maureen Entwistle; one *s* one *d*. *Educ:* ISC, Haileybury. Commnd, 1948; served with 1 KOYLI, 1948-53; Malayan Emergency, 1948-51 (mentioned in despatches); Korea, 1953-54; Kenya Emergency, 1954-55; Instr, Sch. of Inf., 1955-57; psc 1961; Aden, 1965-66; Bde Maj., 151 Inf. Bde, 1962-64; jssc 1964; GSO2 HQ FARELF, 1966-68; CO 2 LI, 1968-71; Col GS HQ BAOR, 1972; Comdr 51 Inf. Bde, 1972-74; Div. Brig., Light Div., 1975-77. MBIM 1973. *Recreations:* game shooting, fishing, squash, swimming. *Address:* Field House, 170 Sharoe Green Lane North, Fulwood, Preston, Lancs. *Club:* Army and Navy.

SIBERRY, John William Morgan; Under-Secretary, Welsh Office, 1964-73, retired; Secretary to Local Government Staff Commission for Wales, and NHS Staff Commission for Wales, 1973-75; *b* 26 Feb. 1913; *s* of late John William and Martha (*née* Morgan) Siberry; *m* 1949, Florence Jane Davies; one *s* one *d*. *Educ:* Porth County School, Rhondda; Univ. Coll. Cardiff. Entered Civil Service as Asst Principal, Unemployment Assistance Board (later Nat. Assistance Board), 1935; Principal, 1941; Asst Sec., 1947; transferred to Min. of Housing and Local Govt as Under-Sec., 1963; Welsh Secretary, Welsh Office and Office for Wales of the Ministry of Housing and Local Government, 1963-64. Chm., Working Party on Fourth Television Service in Wales, 1975. *Recreation:* golf. *Address:* Northgates, Pwllmelin Road, Llandaff, Cardiff CF5 2NG. *T:* Cardiff 564666. *Club:* Cardiff and County.

SIBLEY, Antoinette, CBE 1973; Prima Ballerina, The Royal Ballet, Covent Garden; *b* 27 Feb. 1939; *d* of Edward G. Sibley and Winifred M. Sibley (*née* Smith); *m* 1964, M. G. Somes, CBE (marr. diss. 1973); *m* 1974, Panton Corbett; one *d*. *Educ:* Arts Educational Sch. and Royal Ballet Sch. 1st performance on stage as Student with Royal Ballet at Covent Garden, a swan, Jan. 1956; joined company, July 1956. Leading role in: Swan Lake, Sleeping Beauty, Giselle, Coppelia, Cinderella, The Nutcracker, La Fille Mal Gardée, Romeo & Juliet, Harlequin in April, Les Rendezvous, Jabez & the Devil (created the role of Mary), La Fête Etrange, The Rakes Progress, Hamlet, Ballet Imperial, Two Pigeons, La Bayadère, Symphonic Variations, Scènes de Ballet, Lilac Garden, Daphnis & Chloe, The Dream (created Titania), Laurentia, Good Humoured Ladies, Aristocrat in Mam'zelle Angot, Façade, Song of the Earth, Monotones (created role), Jazz Calendar (created Friday's Child), Enigma Variations (created Dorabella), Thais (created pas de deux), Anastasia (created Kshessinska), Afternoon of a Faun, Triad (created the Girl), Pavanne, Manon (created title role). *Recreations:* doing nothing; opera and books. *Address:* Royal Opera House, WC2.

SICH, Sir Rupert (Leigh), Kt 1968; CB 1953; Registrar of Restrictive Trading Agreements, 1956-73; *b* 3 Aug. 1908; *s* of late A. E. Sich, Caterham, Surrey; *m* 1933, Elizabeth Mary, *d* of late R. W. Hutchison, Gerrards Cross; one *s* two *d*. *Educ:* Radley College; Merton College, Oxford. Called to Bar, Inner Temple, 1930. Board of Trade Solicitor's Dept, 1932-48; Treasury Solicitor's Dept, 1948-56. *Recreations:* J. S. Bach; gardening. *Address:* Norfolk House, The Mall, Chiswick, W4. *T:* 01-994 2133. *Clubs:* United Oxford & Cambridge University, MCC.

SICOT, Marcel Jean; Commandeur, Légion d'Honneur, 1954; Croix de Guerre, 1945; Médaille de la Résistance française, 1945; Médaille d'Honneur de la Police, etc.; Hon. Secretary General of ICPO (Interpol); *b* 19 Feb. 1898; *m* 1923, Agnès Demy; one *s*. *Educ:* in France (Brittany and Paris). Comr of French Sûreté, 1920; Divisional Comr, 1938; Sec. Gen. for Police, 1944; Under-Secretary, Police Judiciary, 1945; Director-

Inspector Gen., Nat. Sûreté, 1949; retired and appd Hon. Director-Inspector General, 1958; Sec. Gen. of Interpol, 1951; Hon. Sec. Gen., 1963. President of Honour of Assoc. Amicale des Cadres de la Sûreté Nationale; Mem. Council, Order of Civil Merit of Ministry of the Interior. Mem. jury of literary prize "Quai des Orfèvres". Comdr, Order of Vasa (Sweden); Comdr (Palm) Royal Order (Greece); Comdr, Order of Cedar (Lebanon); Comdr, Order of Dannebrog (Denmark). *Publications:* (jointly) Encyclopédie nationale de la police française, 1955; Servitude et grandeur policières-40 ans à la Sûreté, 1960; A la barre de l'Interpol, 1961; La Prostitution dans le Monde, 1964; Fausses et vraies identités, 1967. *Recreations:* fond of Association football and Breton folklore. *Address:* 4 rue Léon Delagrange, 75015 Paris, France. *T:* 250.91.95.

SIDDALL, Norman, CBE 1975; Member, National Coal Board, since 1971, Deputy Chairman since 1973 (Director General of Production, 1967-71); *b* 4 May 1918; *m* 1943; two *s* one *d*. *Educ:* King Edward VII School, Sheffield; Sheffield Univ. (BEng). National Coal Board: Production Manager, No 5 Area, East Midlands Div., 1951-56; General Manager, No 5 Area, East Midlands Div. 1956-57; General Manager, No 1 Area, East Midlands Div., 1957-66; Chief Mining Engineer, 1966-67. Chartered Engineer; FRSA; FIMinE; FBIM; 1st Vice-Chm., Organising Cttee, World Mining Congress, 1977; Member: Midland Counties Institution of Engineers (Silver Medal, 1951; Past President); Amer. Inst. Mining Engrs. National Association of Colliery Managers: Silver Medal, 1955; Bronze Medal, 1960; Coal Science Lecture Medal, 1972. Colliery Managers Certificate. *Publications:* articles in professional journals. *Address:* National Coal Board, Hobart House, Grosvenor Place, SW1. *T:* 01-235 2020; Brentwood, High Oakham Road, Mansfield, Notts. *T:* Mansfield 23479; 704 Hood House, Dolphin Square, SW1.

SIDDELEY, family name of **Baron Kenilworth.**

SIDDELEY, John (Tennant Davenport); Interior Designer; (3rd Baron Kenilworth, *cr* 1937, of Kenilworth); *b* 24 Jan. 1924; *o s* of 2nd Baron Kenilworth, CBE, TD, and Marjorie Tennant (*d* 1977), *d* of late Harry Firth; *S* father, 1971; *m* 1948, Jacqueline, *d* of late Robert Gelpi, Lyon, France; one *s* one *d*. *Educ:* Marlborough; Magdalene College, Cambridge (BA). Chairman: John Siddeley International Ltd; John Siddeley (Jewels) Ltd; Dir, Siddeley and Hammond, antiquarian booksellers. Consultant Designer to: Midleton Hotel Gp; Pedigree Toys; David Jones, Australia; Formica (Australia) Ltd. Contributing Editor, Vogue Living, Australia. Mem. of American Inst. of Interior Designers. Master, Coachmakers' and Coach Harness Makers' Company, 1969-70. FRSA. *Recreations:* opera, travel, good food. *Heir: s* Hon. John Randle Siddeley, *b* 16 June 1954. *Address:* 2 Lexham Walk, W8.

SIDDIQUI, Dr Salimuzzaman, MBE 1946; Tamgha-i-Pakistan 1958; Sitara-i-Imtiaz (Pakistan) 1962; FRS 1961; DPhil; Hon DMed; Director, Postgraduate Institute of Chemistry, University of Karachi, since 1966; *b* 19 Oct. 1897. *Educ:* Lucknow; MAO College, Aligarh, UP; University College, London; Univ. of Frankfurt-on-Main. Returned to India, 1928; planned and directed Research Inst. at Ayurvedic and Unani Tibbi Coll., Delhi, 1928-40. Joined Council of Scientific and Industrial Research (India): Organic Chemist, 1940; Actg Dir of Chemical Laboratories, 1944. Director of Scientific and Industrial Research, Pakistan, 1951; Director and Chairman of Pakistan Council of Scientific and Industrial Research, 1953-66; Chairman, Nat. Science Council, 1962-66; Pres., Pakistan Acad. of Sciences, 1968. A chemist, working on the chemistry of natural products; has led the promotion of scientific and industrial research in Pakistan; has rep. Pakistan at internat. scientific confs, etc. Gold Medal, Russian Acad.; President's Pride of Performance Medal (Pakistan), 1966. Elected Mem., Vatican Acad. of Sciences, 1964. Hon. DSc. *Address:* Postgraduate Institute of Chemistry, University of Karachi, Karachi, Pakistan. *T:* 413414.

SIDDONS, Arthur Harold Makins, MChir Cantab; FRCS; FRCP; Hon. Consulting Surgeon, St George's Hospital; *b* 17 Jan. 1911; *s* of late A. W. Siddons, Housemaster, Harrow School; *m* 1st, 1939, Joan Richardson Anderson (*née* McConnell) (*d* 1949); one *s* one *d*; 2nd, 1956, Eleanor Mary Oliver (*née* Hunter) (*d* 1970); 3rd, 1971, Margaret Christine Beardmore (*née* Smith). *Educ:* Harrow; Jesus College, Cambridge; St George's Hospital. MB, BCh Cantab 1935. Surgeon, St George's Hospital, 1941; Consultant General and Thoracic Surgeon, St George's Hosp. and others, 1948-76. Served RAF Medical Branch, 1942-46. Member of Court of Examiners, Royal College of Surgeons of England, 1958-63. *Publications:* Cardiac Pacemakers, 1967; sections on lung surgery in various textbooks. *Recreations:* travel, gardens. *Address:* Robin Hey, Tilford Road, Farnham, Surrey GU9 8HX. *T:* Farnham 5667.

SIDEBOTHAM, John Biddulph, CMG 1946; MA Cantab; retired as Assistant Secretary, Colonial Office (1941-54); *b* 23 Nov. 1891; *er s* of late Rev. Frederick William Gilbert Sidebotham, MA, Rector of Weeting, Norfolk; *m* 1st, 1917, Hilda, *d* of late F. Haviland; one *d*; 2nd, 1941, Mary, *d* of late A. Blascheck; 3rd, 1971, Audrey (*née* Sidebotham), *widow of* Major D. B. Williams. *Educ:* King's School, Canterbury; Gonville and Caius Coll., Cambridge (Stanhope Exhibitioner, Open Class Exhibitioner, Scholar). 1st cl. theolog. tripos, pt 1, 1914; BA 1914, MA 1920; 2nd Lieut Home Counties RE (TF), 1914; Lieut 1916; served in France, 1914-15 (wounded); Inland Revenue, Somerset House, 1920; transferred to Colonial Office as asst prin. under reconstruction scheme, Dec. 1922; sec. managing cttee, Bureau of Hygiene and Tropical Diseases, 1925; sec., East African guaranteed loan advisory cttee, 1927; pte sec. to Parliamentary Under-Sec. of State for Dominion Affairs, 1928; pte sec. Permt Under-Sec. for the Colonies, 1929, principal, 1930; accompanied Permt Under-Secretary of State for the Colonies (Sir J. Maffey) to W Indies, 1936. Visited St Helena, 1939 and 1955; also visited Ceylon, Borneo, Sarawak, Hong Kong, Fiji and Mauritius. Mem. managing cttee of Bureau of Hygiene and Tropical Diseases, 1941-73. *Address:* Nantwatcyn, Cwmystwyth, Aberystwyth, Dyfed SY23 4AG. *T:* Pontrhydygroes 217.

SIDEBOTTOM, Edward John; a Chief Inspector, Department of Education and Science, since 1973 (Divisional Inspector, 1969-73); *b* 1918; *s* of late Ernest Sidebottom, Wylam, Northumberland; *m* 1949, Brenda Millicent, *d* of late Alec H. Sadler, Wandsworth. *Educ:* Queen Elizabeth Grammar School, Hexham; Hatfield College, Durham (BSc). Entered Iraq Government education service, 1939; lecturer, Leavesden Green Emergency Training College, 1946; County Youth Organiser for Hampshire, 1947; HM Inspector of Schools, 1949-. Sec. to Albemarle Cttee on the Youth Service in England and Wales, 1958-59; seconded as Principal, Nat. Coll. for the Training of Youth Leaders, 1960-64; Member, Unesco Internat. Adv. Cttee for Out-of-School Educn, 1968-70. *Address:* 18 Nutborn House, Clifton Road, SW19.

SIDEY, Air Marshal Sir Ernest (Shaw), KBE 1972; CB 1965; MD, ChB, FFCM, DPH; Director-General, Chest, Heart and Stroke Association, since 1974; *b* 2 Jan. 1913; *s* of Thomas Sidey, Alyth, Perthshire; *m* 1946, Doreen Florence, *y d* of late Cecil Ronald Lurring, Dalkey, Ireland; one *d* (and one *d* decd). *Educ:* Morgan Acad., Dundee; St Andrews Univ. Commissioned in RAF, 1937. Served in Burma Campaign during War of 1939-45. Recent appts include: Chief, Med. Adv. Staff, Allied Air Forces Central Europe, 1957-59; PMO: Flying Trg Comd, 1961-63; Middle East Comd, 1963-65; Transport Command, 1965-66; DDGMS, RAF, 1966-68. PMO, Strike Command, 1968-70; DGMS, RAF, 1971-74. QHS 1966-74. Mem. Council, British Thoracic and Tuberculosis Assoc., 1977-. Governor, Star and Garter Home, 1974-. *Recreations:* racing, golf, bridge. *Address:* Callums, Tugwood Common, Cookham Dean, Berks. *T:* Marlow 3006. *Club:* Royal Air Force.

SIDEY, John MacNaughton, DSO 1945; Divisional Chief Executive, P&O Steam Navigation Co., since 1972 (Director, 1970-77); Chairman: P&O Energy Ltd, 1974-77; OMI Ltd London, since 1977; Director, Oil Mop Inc., Louisiana, USA, since 1977; *b* 11 July 1914; *e c* of John and Florence Sidey; *m* 1941, Eileen, *o d* of Sir George Wilkinson, 1st Bt, KCVO; one *s* (one *d* decd). *Educ:* Exeter School. Served War, 1939-45, with Royal Tank Regiment and Westminster Dragoons, finishing as Lt-Col commanding 22nd Dragoons. Mem., Southern Area Board, BTC, 1955-61 (Chm. Jan.-Dec. 1962); part-time Mem., British Railways Bd, 1962-68; Chm., Eastern Region Bd, British Railways, 1963-65. Chm., Transport Cttee of CBI, 1967-; Mem., Nat. Docks Labour Bd, 1977-. Pres., London Chapter, Nat. Defence Transportation Assoc. of America, 1961-62. *Recreations:* fishing, golf, gardening. *Address:* Acre Holt, Golf Club Road, Woking, Surrey GU22 0LS. *T:* Woking 4788.

SIDEY, Thomas Kay Stuart, CMG 1968; Managing Director, Wickliffe Press Ltd, since 1962; Barrister and Solicitor, NZ, since 1932; *b* 8 Oct. 1908; *s* of Sir Thomas Kay Sidey; *m* 1933, Beryl, *d* of Harvey Richardson Thomas, Wellington, NZ; one *s* one *d*. *Educ:* Otago Boys' High School; Univ. of Otago (LLM). Served War of 1939-45 (despatches): 2nd NZEF; 4 years, Middle East and Italy, rank of Major. Dunedin City Council, 1947-50, 1953-65; Dep. Mayor, 1956-59, 1968-; Mayor, 1959-65; Univ. of Otago Council, 1947-, Pro-Chancellor, 1959-70, Chancellor, 1970-76. Past President: Dunedin Chamber of Commerce;

Automobile Assoc., Otago; Otago Trustee Savings Bank; NZ Library Assoc.; Otago Old People's Welfare Council; Otago Boys' High Sch. Old Boys' Soc. *Recreations:* fishing, boating, ski-ing. *Address:* 16 Tolcarne Avenue, Dunedin, New Zealand. *T:* 60,068. *Club:* Dunedin (Dunedin, NZ).

SIDGWICK, Rear-Admiral John Benson, CB 1945; RN retd; late Deputy Engineer-in-Chief, Admiralty. Served European War, 1914-18; Engineer Captain, 1936; Engineer Rear-Admiral, 1942.

SIDMOUTH, 7th Viscount *cr* 1805; **John Tonge Anthony Pellew Addington;** *b* 3 Oct. 1914; *s* of 6th Viscount Sidmouth and of Gladys Mary Dever, *d* of late Thomas Francis Hughes; *S* father, 1976; *m* 1940, Barbara Mary, *d* of Bernard Rochford, OBE; two *s* five *d*. *Educ:* Downside School (Scholar); Brasenose Coll., Oxford (Scholar). Colonial Service, E Africa, 1938-54. Director, Joseph Rochford & Sons Ltd and other cos. Mem. Council and Chm. Glasshouse Cttee, Nat. Farmers Union, 1962-69; Member: Agricultural Research Council, 1964-74; Central Council for Agricultural Cooperation, 1970-73. Trustee, John Innes Charity, 1974. Knight of Malta, 1962. *Recreations:* sailing, gardening. *Heir: s* Christopher John Addington [*b* 10 April 1941; *m* 1963, Clio Mona, *o d* of John Peristiany]. *Address:* Stivers, Chalfont St Giles, Bucks. *T:* Little Chalfont 2192. *Clubs:* Institute of Directors; Royal Fowey Yacht; Nairobi (Kenya).

SIDNEY, family name of **Viscount De L'Isle.**

SIDNEY-WILMOT, Air Vice-Marshal Aubrey, CB 1977; OBE 1948; Director of Legal Services (Royal Air Force), since 1970; *b* 4 Jan. 1915; *s* of Alfred Robert Sidney-Wilmot and Harriet Sidney-Wilmot; *m* 1968, Ursula Hartmann; one *s* by former marriage. *Educ:* Framlingham College. Admitted Solicitor, 1938, practised, 1938-40. Commnd in Administrative Br., RAF, 1940; transf. to Office of JAG, 1942; DJAG (Army and RAF), Far East, 1948-50; transf. to Directorate of Legal Services (RAF), 1950; Dep. Dir of Legal Services (RAF), 1969. *Recreations:* travel, swimming, gardening. *Address:* Grove Cottage, Great Horkesley, Colchester, Essex CO6 4AG. *Club:* Royal Air Force.

SIDWELL, Martindale, FRAM; FRCO; Organist and Choirmaster, Hampstead Parish Church, since 1946; Organist and Director of Music, St Clement Danes (Church of the RAF), since 1957; Conductor, Hampstead Choral Society, since 1946; Conductor, Martindale Sidwell Choir, since 1956; Professor of Organ, Royal Academy of Music, since 1963; Director, Founder and Conductor, London Bach Orchestra, since 1967; *b* 23 Feb. 1916; *s* of John William Sidwell, Little Packington, Warwicks, and Mary Martindale, Liverpool; *m* 1944, Barbara Anne (*née* Hill) (pianist, harpsichordist and Prof. of Piano, Royal Coll. of Music, under the name Barbara Hill); two *s*. *Educ:* Wells Cathedral Sch., Somerset; Royal Academy of Music. Sub-Organist, Wells Cathedral, 1932. Served War of 1939-45, Royal Engineers. Organist, Holy Trinity Church, Leamington Spa, and Director of Music, Warwick School, 1943, also at same time Conductor of Royal Leamington Spa Bach Choir; Prof., RSCM, 1958-66. Mem. Council, Royal Coll. of Organists, 1966-. Harriet Cohen Bach Medal, 1967. Frequent broadcasts as Conductor and as Organ Recitalist, 1944-. *Address:* 1 Frognal Gardens, Hampstead, NW3. *T:* 01-435 9210. *Club:* Savage.

SIE, Sir Banja T.; *see* Tejan-Sie.

SIEFF, Joseph Edward; President, Marks & Spencer Ltd, since 1972 (Assistant Managing Director, 1946; Joint Managing Director, 1963-72; Vice-Chairman, 1963, Deputy Chairman, 1965, Chairman, 1967-72); *b* 28 Nov. 1905; *s* of Ephraim Sieff, Manchester; *m* 1929, Maisie, *d* of Dr Sidney Marsh; two *d*; *m* 1952, Lois, *d* of William Ross; one *s* one *d*. *Educ:* Manchester Grammar School; Manchester University. Joined Marks & Spencer Ltd, 1933. Chairman Joint Israel Appeal, 1961-65, President 1965-. Hon. President, Zionist Federation of Great Britain and Ireland, 1974- (Vice-Pres., 1965-74). Governor, Manchester Grammar School, 1974. *Address:* Michael House, Baker Street, W1A 1DN. *T:* 01-935 4422. *Club:* Savile.

SIEFF, Hon. Sir Marcus (Joseph), Kt 1971; OBE 1944; Chairman, Marks and Spencer Ltd, since 1972; Joint Managing Director, since 1967; *b* 2 July 1913; *yr s* of late Baron Sieff; *m* 1st, 1937, Rosalie Fromson (marr. diss., 1947); one *s*; 2nd, 1951, Elsa Florence Gosen (marr. diss., 1953); 3rd 1956, Brenda Mary Beith (marr. diss., 1962); one *d*; 4th, 1963, Mrs Pauline Lily Moretzki (*née* Spatz); one *d*. *Educ:* Manchester Grammar School; St Paul's; Corpus Christi College, Cambridge (BA), Hon. Fellow, 1975. Served War 1939-45, Royal Artillery. Joined Marks & Spencer Ltd, 1935; Dir, 1954; Asst Man. Dir, 1963, Vice-Chm., 1965; Dep. Chm., 1971. Mem., BNEC, 1965-71

(Chm., Export Cttee for Israel, 1965-68). Vice-Pres., Joint Israel Appeal. Vice Pres., PEP Exec., 1975-; Pres., Anglo-Israel Chamber of Commerce, 1975-. Patron, RCS, 1977. *Address:* Michael House, Baker Street, W1A 1DN.
See also Hon. M. D. Sieff.

SIEFF, Hon. Michael David, CBE 1975; Director, Marks & Spencer, since 1950 (Joint Managing Director, 1971-76; Joint Vice-Chairman, 1972-76); *b* 12 March 1911; *er s* of late Baron Sieff; *m* 1st, 1932, Daphne Madge Kerin Michael (marr. diss. 1975); one *s*; 2nd, 1975, Elizabeth Pitt. *Educ:* Manchester Grammar School. Served War of 1939-45, Col RAOC 1944; Hon. Col, TA, 1956. Joined Marks & Spencer Ltd, 1929; Asst Man. Dir, 1965-71. Member: European Trade Cttee, British Overseas Trade Bd, 1974-; British Overseas Trade Adv. Council, 1975-; Chm., British Overseas Trade Gp for Israel, 1972-; Vice-Chm., Anglo-Israel Chamber of Commerce, 1969-. Founder Fellow, Royal Post-Grad. Med. Sch. (Hammersmith Hosp.), 1972. *Address:* Michael House, Baker Street, W1A 1DN. *T:* 01-935 4422.
See also Hon. Sir M. J. Sieff.

SIEGBAHN, (Karl) Manne (Georg), DrSc; Professor Emeritus at the Royal Academy of Sciences, Director Nobel Institute for Physics, Stockholm; *b* Orebro, Sweden, 3 Dec. 1886; *m* 1914, Karin Hogbom (*d* 1972); two *s*. *Educ:* Hudiksvall, Stockholm. Studied mathematics, physics, chemistry, astronomy for the Master degree at the University of Lund; further work in physics for the DrSc (1911); Lecturer in Physics at Lund, 1911-20; Professor of Physics, Lund, 1920-23; Upsala, 1923-36; Member of the Royal Acad. of Science, Sweden 1922; For. Mem., Royal Society, London; Assoc. Mem., Acad. of Sciences, Paris; Member of the Academies in Moscow, Edinburgh, Copenhagen, Oslo, and Helsinki; Nobel Laureate, 1925; Hughes Medal of Royal Society, 1934; Rumford Medal of Royal Society, 1940; Duddel Medal of the Physical Society, London, 1948. Dr (hc) Univs in Paris, Oslo, Freiburg and Bucharest. *Publications:* The Spectroscopy of X-Rays, 1925; a number of scientific papers, especially on X-Rays. *Address:* Nobel Institute for Physics, 10405 Stockholm 50, Sweden.

SIEPMANN, Charles Arthur, MC; BA; Professor Emeritus, New York University, since 1967; Professor, Sarah Lawrence College, New York, 1968-71; *b* 10 Mar. 1899; *s* of Otto and Grace Florence Siepmann; *m* 1940, Charlotte Tyler; one *s* two *d*. *Educ:* Clifton Coll. (scholar); Keble Coll. Oxford (scholar). Served European War, 1917-18; Oxford, 1919-21; Brown Shipley and Co., 1922-24; housemaster and education officer, HM Borstal Instns, Feltham and Rochester, 1924-27; joined BBC, 1927; Dir of Talks, 1932-35, of Regional Relations, 1935-36, of Programme Planning, 1936-39; University Lecturer, Harvard University, 1939-42. Office of War Information, 1942-45, as Consultant, and, latterly, Deputy Director of its San Francisco Office; Professor of Education, New York Univ., 1946-67. Delivered television courses, Communication and Educn, and Communication and Society, 1967-68. *Publications:* Radio in Wartime; Radio's Second Chance; Radio, TV and Society; TV and our School Crisis; Educational TV in the United States. *Recreations:* walking, reading. *Address:* RFD Box 70, Newfane, Vermont 05345, USA; 21 Matlock Court, Kensington Park Road, W11.

SIERRA LEONE, Bishop of; *see under* West Africa, Archbishop of.

SIEVE, James Ezekiel Balfour, PhD, FCA; Finance Director, Metal Box Ltd, since 1970; *b* 31 July 1922; *s* of Isaac and Rachel Sieve; *m* 1953, Yvonne Manley; two *s*. *Educ:* London Sch. of Economics. BSc Econ, PhD. With Urwick Orr & Partners, 1950-54; Aquascutum & Associated Cos Ltd, 1954-68 (Finance Dir, 1957-68); Metal Box Ltd, 1968-. Governor, Home Farm Trust (Residential care of mentally handicapped), 1974-; Member: Tax Reform Cttee, 1975-; Nat. Freight Corp., 1977-. *Publication:* Income Redistribution and the Welfare State (with Adrian Webb), 1971. *Recreation:* relaxing with family. *Address:* 56 Hampstead Lane, NW3 7JP.

SIGNORET, Simone (pseudonym of **Simone Henriette Charlotte Montand**); actress; *b* Wiesbaden, 25 March 1921; *d* of Jean Kaminker and Louise (*née* Signoret); *m* 1947, Yves Allegret (marriage dissolved, 1950), motion picture director; one *d*; *m* 1950, Yves Montand, actor and singer. *Educ:* Cours Sicard, Paris. Worked as a teacher and typist before becoming actress. Films include: Dédée d'Anvers, La Ronde, Casque d'Or, Thérèse Raquin, La Mort en ce Jardin, Room at the Top (Oscar), Adua e le Compagne, Term of Trial, Ship of Fools, The Deadly Affair, Games, The Seagull, L'Aveu, Le Chat (Best Actress Award, Berlin Film Festival, 1971), La Veuve Couderc,

Les Granges brûlées, Rude journée pour la reine, La Chair de l'Orchidée. Has also appeared on the stage (including Lady Macbeth, Royal Ct, London 1966), and on television. Has won many awards in France, USA, England, etc, including Oscar of Acad. of Motion Picture Arts and Sciences for best actress, 1960. *Address:* 15 Place Dauphine, 75001 Paris, France.

SIGURDSSON, Niels P.; Ambassador of Iceland in Bonn, since 1976; *b* Reykjavik, 10 Feb. 1926; *s* of Sigurdur B. Sigurdsson and Karitas Einarsdóttir; *m* 1953, Olafia Rafnsdóttir; two *s* one *d*. *Educ:* Univ. of Iceland (Law). Joined Diplomatic Service 1952; First Sec., Paris Embassy, 1956-60; Dep. Permanent Rep. to NATO and OECD, 1957-60; Dir, Internat. Policy Div., Min. of Foreign Affairs, Reykjavik, 1961-67; Delegate to UN Gen. Assembly, 1965; Ambassador and Permanent Rep. of Iceland to N Atlantic Council, 1967-71. Ambassador: to Belgium and EEC, 1968-71; to UK, 1971-76. *Recreations:* swimming, riding. *Address:* Isländische Botschaft, Kronprinzenstrasse 6, 53 Bonn-Bad Godesberg, Germany.

SIKRI, Sarv Mittra; Chief Justice of India, 1971-73; *b* 26 April 1908; *s* of late Dr Nihal Chand; *m* 1937, Mrs Leila Sikri; one *s*. *Educ:* Trinity Hall, Cambridge (BA). Barrister-at-Law (Lincoln's Inn). Started practice in Lahore High Court, 1930; Asst Advocate Gen., Punjab, 1949; Advocate Gen., Punjab, 1951-64; Judge, Supreme Ct of India, 1964; alternate rep., UN Cttee on Codification and Develt of Internat. Law, 1947; Legal Adviser to Min. of Irrigation and Power, Govt of India, 1949; Mem. Internat. Law Assoc. Cttee on Internat. Rivers, 1955; Mem., Indian Law Commn, 1955-58. Delegate to: Law of the Sea Conf., Geneva, 1958; World Peace Through Law Conf., Tokyo, 1961, Athens, 1963; Accra Assembly, Accra, 1962. Pres., Indian Br. of Internat. Law Assoc., 1971-73; Member, Indian Commn of Jurists; Chairman, Sir Ganga Ram Hosp. Trust; Hon. Mem., Acad. of Political Sci., NY; Vice-Pres., Delhi Public School Soc. *Recreations:* golf, tennis, bridge. *Address:* B-18 Maharani Bagh, New Delhi, India. *T:* 630108. *Clubs:* Delhi Golf, Delhi Gymkhana (both in New Delhi).

SILBERSTON, (Zangwill) Aubrey; Official Fellow in Economics, since 1971, and Dean, since 1972, Nuffield College, Oxford; *b* 26 Jan. 1922; *s* of Louis and Polly Silberston; *m* 1945, Dorothy Marion, *d* of A. S. Nicholls; one *s* one *d*. *Educ:* Hackney Downs Sch., London; Jesus Coll., Cambridge. Econs Tripos Pt II, Cambridge, 1946. Courtaulds Ltd, 1946-50; Kenward Res. Fellow in Industrial Admin., St Catharine's Coll., Cambridge, 1950-53; University Lectr in Economics, Cambridge, 1953-71; Fellow, 1958-71, Dir of Studies in Econs, 1965-71, St John's Coll., Cambridge. Chm., Faculty Bd of Econs and Politics, 1966-70; Member: Monopolies Commn, 1965-68; Board of British Steel Corp., 1967-76; Departmental Cttee on Patent System, 1967-70; Economics Cttee, SSRC, 1969-73; Royal Commn on the Press, 1974-77; Management Cttee, SSRC, 1977-; Economic Adviser, CBI, 1972-74. Vis. Prof., Queensland Univ., 1977. *Publications:* Education and Training for Industrial Management, 1955; (with George Maxcy) The Motor Industry, 1959; (in collaboration with C. Pratten and R. M. Dean) Economies of Large-scale Production in British Industry, 1965; (in collaboration with K. H. Boehm) The Patent System, 1967; (with C. T. Taylor) The Economic Impact of the Patent System, 1973; (ed, with Francis Seton) Industrial Management: East and West, 1973; (with A. Cockerill) The Steel Industry, 1974; articles in Econ. Jl, Bulletin of Oxford Inst. of Statistics, Oxford Economic Papers, Jl of Royal Statistical Society. *Recreations:* music, ballet. *Address:* Nuffield College, Oxford OX1 1NF. *T:* 48014. *Club:* Royal Automobile.

SILK, Dennis Raoul Whitehall; Warden of Radley College, since 1968; *b* 8 Oct. 1931; 2nd *s* of late Rev. Dr Claude Whitehall Silk and of Mrs Louise Silk; *m* 1963, Diana Merilyn, 2nd *d* of W. F. Milton, Pitminster, Somerset; two *s* two *d*. *Educ:* Christ's Hosp.; Sidney Sussex Coll., Cambridge (Exhibr). BA (History) Cantab. Asst Master, Marlborough Coll., 1955-68 (Housemaster, 1957-68). *Publications:* Cricket for Schools, 1964; Attacking Cricket, 1965. *Recreations:* antiquarian, literary, sporting (Blues in cricket (Capt. Cambridge Univ. CC, 1955) and Rugby football). *Address:* The Warden's House, Radley College, Abingdon, Oxon. *T:* Abingdon 20585. *Clubs:* East India, Sports and Public Schools; Hawks (Cambridge).

SILK, Robert K.; *see* Kilroy-Silk.

SILKIN, 2nd Baron, *cr* 1950, of Dulwich [Disclaimed his peerage for life, 1972]; *see under* Silkin, Arthur.

SILKIN, Arthur; Lecturer in Public Administration, Civil Service College, Sunningdale, 1971-76, on secondment from Department of Employment; retired 1976; *b* 20 Oct. 1916; *e s* of

1st Baron Silkin, PC, CH; *S* father, 1972, as 2nd Baron Silkin, but disclaimed his peerage for life; *m* 1969, Audrey Bennett. *Educ:* Dulwich College; Peterhouse, Cambridge. BA 1938; Diploma in Govt Administration, 1959. Served 1940-45, Royal Air Force (A and SD Branch), Pilot Officer, 1941, subsequently Flying Officer. Entered Ministry of Labour and National Service, 1939; formerly 2nd Secretary, British Embassy, Paris. First Secretary: High Commissioner's Office, Calcutta, 1960-61; British Embassy. Dakar, May 1962-Mar. 1964; British Embassy, Kinshasa, 1964-66. *Publications:* contrib. to Public Administration, Political Qly. *Address:* Cuzco, 33 Woodnook Road, SW16. *T:* 01-677 8733.
See also Rt Hon. J. E. Silkin, Rt Hon. S. C. Silkin.

SILKIN, Rt. Hon. John Ernest, PC 1966; MP (Lab) Lewisham, Deptford, since 1974 (Deptford, July 1963-1974); Minister of Agriculture, Fisheries and Food, since 1976; *b* 18 March 1923; *y s* of 1st Baron Silkin, PC, CH; *m* 1950, Rosamund John (actress), *d* of Frederick Jones; one *s*. *Educ:* Dulwich College; University of Wales; Trinity Hall, Cambridge. BA 1944; LLB 1946; MA 1949. Joined Royal Navy, 1941, Lieutenant-Commander RNVR, served in HMS King George V and HMS Formidable. Admitted a Solicitor, 1950. Contested (Lab): St Marylebone, 1950; West Woolwich, 1951; South Nottingham, 1959. Government Pairing Whip, 1964-Jan. 1966; Lord Commissioner of the Treasury, Jan.-April 1966; Treasurer of the Household and Government Deputy Chief Whip, April-July 1966; Parly Sec. to the Treasury, and Govt Chief Whip, 1966-69; Dep. Leader, House of Commons, 1968-69; Minister of Public Building and Works, 1969-70; Minister for Planning and Local Govt, DoE, 1974-76. Dir, Pergamon Press, 1971-74. *Address:* 29 Tufton Street, SW1. *T:* 01-222 3341. *Clubs:* Garrick, Royal Automobile, Press, Farmers'.
See also Arthur Silkin, Rt Hon. S. C. Silkin.

SILKIN, Jon; poet; *b* 2 Dec. 1930; three *s* one *d* (and one *s* decd); *m* Lorna Tracy (American writer and co-editor of Stand). *Educ:* Wycliffe Coll.; Dulwich Coll.; Univ. of Leeds. BA Hons Eng. Lit. 1962. Journalist, 1947; Nat. Service, teaching in Educn Corps, Army; subseq. six years as manual labourer, London and two years teaching English to foreign students. Founded magazine Stand, 1952. Several poetry-reading tours, USA; Vis. Lectr, Denison Univ., Ohio; taught at Writers' Workshop, Univ. of Iowa, 1968-69; Vis. writer for Australian Council for the Arts, 1974. C. Day Lewis Fellowship, 1976-77. *Publications:* The Peaceable Kingdom, 1954, reprint 1976; The Two Freedoms, 1958; The Re-ordering of the Stones, 1961; Nature with Man, 1965 (Geoffrey Faber Meml Prize, 1966); (with Murphy and Tarn) Penguin Modern Poets 7, 1965; Poems New and Selected, 1966; Killhope Wheel, 1971; Amana Grass, 1971; Out of Battle: the poetry of the Great War, 1972; (with Nathan Zach) Translations of the Israeli Poet Amir Gilboa, 1972; (ed) Poetry of the Committed Individual, 1973; The Principle of Water, 1974; The Little Time-keeper, 1976. *Recreation:* travelling. *Address:* 19 Haldane Terrace, Newcastle upon Tyne NE2 3AN. *T:* Newcastle upon Tyne 812614.

SILKIN, Rt. Hon. Samuel Charles, PC 1974; QC 1963; MP (Lab) Southwark, Dulwich, since 1974 (Camberwell, Dulwich, Oct. 1964-1974); Attorney General, since 1974; *b* 6 March 1918; 2nd *s* of 1st Baron Silkin, PC, CH; *m* 1941, Elaine Violet (*née* Stamp); two *s* two *d*. *Educ:* Dulwich College (Schol.); Trinity Hall, Cambridge (schol.), BA (1st cl. hons Parts I and II of Law Tripos; Law Studentship, 1939). Called to Bar, Middle Temple, 1941 (Cert. of Honour 1940, Harmsworth Law Schol., 1946), Bencher 1969. Served War of 1939-45, Lt-Col RA (despatches). Member, Royal Commission on the Penal System for England and Wales, 1965-66. Chairman: Parly Labour Party's Group on Common Market and European Affairs, 1966-70; Select Cttee on Parly Privilege, 1967; Leader, UK Delegn to Assembly of Council of Europe, 1968-70; Chm. Council of Europe Legal Cttee, 1966-70; Opposition front-bench spokesman on Law Officer matters, 1970-74. Recorder of Bedford, 1966-71. Society of Labour Lawyers: Foundn Mem.; Chm., 1964-71; Vice Pres., 1971-. Governor, Royal Bethlem and Maudsley Hosps, 1970-74; Chm., British Inst. of Human Rights, 1972-74; Pres., Alcohol Educn Centre, 1973-. MacDermott Lectr, QUB, 1976. *Address:* House of Commons, SW1.
See also Arthur Silkin, Rt Hon. J. E. Silkin.

SILLARS, James; MP (SLP) South Ayrshire since March 1970; *b* Ayr, 4 Oct. 1937; *s* of Matthew Sillars; *m* 1957, Ann O'Farrell; one *s* one *d*. *Educ:* Newton Park Sch., Ayr; Ayr Academy. Former official, Fire Brigades Union; Past Member Ayr Town Council and Ayr County Council Educn Cttee; Mem., T&GWU. Head of Organization and Social Services Dept, Scottish TUC, 1968-70. Full-time Labour Party agent, 1964 and 1966 elections. Among the founders of the Scottish Labour

Party, Jan. 1976. Especially interested in education, social services, industrial relations, development policies. *Publications:* Labour Party pamphlet on Scottish Nationalism; Tribune Gp pamphlet on Democracy within the Labour Party. *Recreations:* reading, camping, tennis, swimming. *Address:* House of Commons, SW1.

SILLITOE, Alan; Writer since 1948; *b* 4 March 1928; *s* of Christopher Archibald Sillitoe and Sylvina (*née* Burton); *m* 1952, Ruth Esther Fainlight; one *s*. *Educ:* various elementary schools in Nottingham. Raleigh Bicycle Factory, 1942; wireless operator, RAF, 1946. Travelled in France, Italy, and Spain, 1952-58. Literary Adviser to W. H. Allen, 1970-. FRGS. *Publications:* Saturday Night and Sunday Morning (Authors' Club Award for best first novel of 1958; filmed, 1960, play, 1964); The Loneliness of the Long Distance Runner, 1959 (Hawthornden Prize; filmed, 1962); The General, 1960 (filmed 1967 as Counterpoint); The Rats and Other Poems, 1960; Key to the Door, 1961; The Ragman's Daughter, 1963 (filmed 1972); Road to Volgograd (travel), 1964; A Falling Out of Love (poems), 1964; The Death of William Posters (novel), 1965; A Tree on Fire (novel), 1967; The City Adventures of Marmalade Jim (children), 1967; Love in the Environs of Voronezh (poems), 1968; Guzman, Go Home (stories), 1968; (with Ruth Fainlight) All Citizens are Soldiers (play), 1969 (based on Lope de Vega, Fuente Ovejuna; first perf. Theatre Royal, Stratford, 1967); This Foreign Field (first perf. Roundhouse, 1970); A Start in Life (novel), 1970; Travels in Nihilon (novel), 1971; Raw Material (novel), 1972; Men, Women and Children (stories), 1973; The Flame of Life (novel), 1974; Storm and Other Poems, 1974; Barbarians and other poems, 1974; Mountains and Caverns (selected essays), 1975; The Widower's Son (novel), 1976; Pit Strike (TV play), 1977. *Recreation:* travel. *Address:* 21 The Street, Wittersham, Kent.

SILLS, Beverly, (Mrs P. B. Greenough); leading soprano, New York City Opera and Metropolitan Opera; *b* 25 May 1929; *d* of late Morris Silverman and of Sonia Bahn; *m* 1956, Peter B. Greenough; one *s* one *d*. *Educ:* Professional Children's Sch., NYC; privately. Vocal studies with Estelle Liebling, piano with Paulo Gallico. Operatic debut, Philadelphia Civic Opera, 1947; San Francisco Opera, 1953; New York City Opera, 1955; Vienna State Opera, 1967; Teatro Colon, Buenos Aires, 1968; La Scala, Milan, 1969; Teatro San Carlo, Naples, 1970; Royal Opera, Covent Garden, London, 1970; Deutsche Oper, W Berlin, 1971; NY Metropolitan Opera, 1975, etc. Repeated appearances as soloist with major US symphony orchestras; English orchestral debut with London Symphony Orch., London, 1971; Paris debut, orchestral concert, Salle Pleyel, 1971. Repertoire includes title roles of Norma, Manon, Lucia di Lammermoor, Maria Stuarda, Daughter of Regiment, Anna Bolena, Traviata, Lucrezia Borgia, Thais, Louise; Cleopatra in Giulio Cesare, Elizabeth in Roberto Devereux, Tales of Hoffmann, Elvira in Puritani, Rosina in Barber of Seville, Amina in La Sonnambula, etc. Subject of BBC-TV's Profile in Music (Nat. Acad. of TV Arts and Sciences Emmy Award, 1975). Hon. DMus: Temple Univ., 1972; New York Univ., 1973; New England Conservatory, 1973; Harvard Univ., 1974. *Recreations:* fishing, bridge. *Address:* c/o Edgar Vincent Associates, 156 East 52nd Street, New York, NY 10022, USA. *T:* (212) PL 2-3020.

SILONE, Ignazio; Writer and Politician; *b* Pescina dei Marsi, Abruzzi, Italy, 1 May 1900; *s* of Paolo and Annamaria Delli Quadri; *m* 1944, Darina Laracy, Dublin. *Educ:* various Catholic private and public schools. One of the leaders of the Italian Socialist Youth Movement, 1917-21; member Central Committee of Italian Communist Party and editor of various newspapers, 1921-29; in 1930 left Communist Party and has since been active mainly as an independent writer; with three warrants for arrest for underground political activity issued against him by the Fascist Special Tribunal, he was forced to go into exile in Switzerland, where he lived until the autumn of 1944; Member Executive Committee of Italian Socialist Party, 1941-47; Member of Italian Constituent Assembly, 1946-48; is now non-party independent Socialist. Pres. Italian Pen Club, 1945-59; Chm. Italian Cttee for Cultural Freedom; Co-Editor of Tempo Presente. Hon. DLitt; Yale; Warwick; Toulouse. Commandeur de la Légion d'Honneur. *Publications:* Fontamara, 1933; Fascism: its Origins and Growth, 1934; Mr Aristotle, 1935; Bread and Wine, 1937; The School for Dictators, 1938; Mazzini, 1939; The Seed beneath the Snow (novel), 1941; And He did Hide Himself (play), 1944; The God that failed (essay), 1950; A Handful of Blackberries (novel), 1953; The Secret of Luca (novel), 1959; The Fox and the Camellias (novel), 1961; Emergency Exit (essays), 1965; The Story of a Humble Christian (play), 1969. *Recreation:* watching football matches. *Address:* Via di Villa Ricotti 36, Rome, Italy.

SILSOE, 2nd Baron cr 1963; **David Malcolm Trustram Eve**, Bt 1943; QC 1972; Barrister, Inner Temple, since 1955; b 2 May 1930; er twin s of 1st Baron Silsoe, GBE, MC, TD, QC, and Marguerite (d 1945), d of late Sir Augustus Meredith Nanton, Winnipeg; S father, 1976; m 1963, Bridget Min, d of Sir Rupert Hart-Davis, qv; one s one d. Educ: Winchester; Christ Church, Oxford (MA); Columbia Univ., New York. 2nd Lt, Royal Welch Fusiliers, 1949-50; Lieut, Queen Victoria's Rifles (TA), 1950-53. Bar Auditor, Inner Temple, 1965-70; Bencher, 1970. Recreation: ski-ing. Heir: s Hon. Simon Rupert Trustram Eve, b 17 April 1966. Address: Neals Farm, Wyfold, Reading, Berks RG4 9JB. Club: Ski of Great Britain.

SILVER, Prof. **Peter H. S.**; see Spencer-Silver.

SILVER, Prof. **Robert Simpson**, CBE 1967; FRSE; FIMechE; FInstP; James Watt Professor of Mechanical Engineering, University of Glasgow, since 1967; b Montrose, Angus, 13 March 1913; s of Alexander Clark Silver and Isabella Simpson; m 1937, Jean McIntyre Bruce, er d of Alexander and Elizabeth Bruce (née Livingstone); two s. Educ: Montrose Academy; University of Glasgow. MA, 1932; BSc (1st Class Hons Nat. Phil) 1934; PhD 1938; DSc 1945. Research Physicist, ICI (Explosives), 1936-39; Head of Research, G. & J. Weir Ltd, 1939-46; Asst Director, Gas Research Board, 1947-48; Director of Research, Federated Founderies Ltd, 1948-54; Chief Designer, John Brown Land Boilers Ltd, 1954-56; Chief of Development and Research, G. & J. Weir Ltd, 1956-62 (Director 1958-); Prof. of Mech. Engrng, Heriot-Watt Coll. (now Univ.), 1962-66. FInstP 1942; MIMechE 1953; FRSE 1963. Unesco Prize for Science, 1968. Publications: An Introduction to Thermodynamics, 1971; papers on physics and engineering, with special emphasis on thermo-dynamics, desalination, combustion, phase-change, and heat transfer; also on philosophy of science and education; a few poems, as Robert Simpson. Recreations: fishing, music, theatre, Scottish history and affairs. Address: 14 Beech Avenue, Glasgow G41 5BX. T: 041-427 1322; Oakbank, Tobermory, Isle of Mull. T: Tobermory 2024. Clubs: Royal Over-Seas League; Royal Scottish Automobile (Glasgow).

SILVERLEAF, **Alexander**, CEng; FRINA; FICE; FCIT; Director, Transport and Road Research Laboratory, since 1971; b 29 Oct. 1920; m 1950, Helen Marion Scott; two d. Educ: Kilburn Grammar Sch., London; Glasgow Univ. (BSc 1941). Wm Denny and Bros Ltd, Shipbuilders, Dumbarton, 1937-51: Student apprentice, 1937-41; Head, Design Office, 1947-51; National Physical Laboratory, 1951-71: Superintendent, Ship Div., 1962-67; Dep. Dir, 1966-71. Hon. FIHE. Publications: papers in Trans. Royal Instn Naval Architects and other technical jls. Address: 64 Fairfax Road, Teddington, Mddx. T: 01-977 6261. Club: Athenæum.

SILVERMAN, **Herbert A.**; Industrial Consultant; b Leeds; m Margaret Pennington; two d. Educ: City of Leeds School; Univ. of Leeds (Senior City Scholar). Formerly Lecturer in Economics and Senior Tutor for Adult Education, University of Birmingham; Head of Department of Adult Education, University College, and Director of Vaughan College, Leicester; Director of Industrial Surveys, Nuffield College, Oxford. Publications: The Substance of Economics; The Economics of Social Problems; The Groundwork of Economics; Taxation: its Incidence and Effects; Economics of the Industrial System; Studies in Industrial Organisation (Nuffield College). Contributor to Adult Education in Practice, Consumer's Co-operation in Great Britain, Chambers's Encyclopædia, etc., and on industrial and financial subjects to various journals. Address: 15 Otterbourne Court, Budleigh Salterton, Devon EX9 6HB. T: Budleigh Salterton 3004.

SILVERMAN, **Julius**; MP (Lab) Birmingham, Erdington, 1945-55 and since 1974 (Birmingham, Aston, 1955-74); Barrister-at-law; b Leeds, 8 Dec. 1905; s of Nathan Silverman; m 1959, Eva Price. Educ: Central High School, Leeds (Matriculated). Entered Gray's Inn as student in 1928; called to Bar, 1931; joined Midland Circuit, 1933, practised in Birmingham since; Birmingham City Councillor, 1934-45; contested Moseley Division, 1935. Address: House of Commons, SW1.

SILVERWOOD-COPE, **Maclachlan Alan Carl**, CBE 1959; FCA 1960; HM Diplomatic Service, retired; Finance appointments with Aspro-Nicholas Ltd, Slough, since 1971; b 15 Dec. 1915; s of late Alan Lachlan Silverwood-Cope and late Elizabeth Masters; m 1st, 1940, Hilkka (née Halme) (marr. diss. 1970); one s one d; 2nd, 1971, Jane (née Monier-Williams); one s one d. Educ: Malvern College. ACA 1939. HM Forces, 1939-45 (Major, RA). Foreign (later Diplomatic) Service, 1939-: served as 3rd Sec., Stockholm, 1945-50; 1st Sec., Washington, 1951 and 1956-57; Tokyo, 1952-55; Copenhagen, 1960-64; Counsellor, Buenos Aires, 1966-68; FCO, 1968-71. Home Front Medal (Finland), 1940; Freedom Cross (Norway), 1945. Recreations: tennis, bridge, music. Address: Brock Hill Cottage, Winkfield Row, Berks RG12 6LS. T: Winkfield Row 2746.

SILVESTER, **Frederick John**; MP (C) Manchester, Withington, since Feb. 1974; Senior Associate Director, J. Walter Thompson; b 20 Sept. 1933; s of William Thomas Silvester and Kathleen Gertrude (née Jones); m 1971, Victoria Ann, d of James Harold and Mary Lloyd Davies; two d. Educ: Sir George Monoux Grammar Sch.; Sidney Sussex Coll., Cambridge. Called to the Bar, Gray's Inn, 1957. Teacher, Wolstanton Grammar School, 1955-57; Political Education Officer, Conservative Political Centre, 1957-60. Member, Walthamstow Borough Council, 1961-64; Chairman, Walthamstow West Conservative Association, 1961-64; MP (C) Walthamstow West, Sept. 1967-70; an Opposition Whip, 1974-76. Vice-Chm., Cons. Employment Cttee, 1976-. Address: House of Commons, SW1A 0AA.

SILVESTER, **Victor Marlborough**, OBE 1961; b 25 Feb. 1900; 2nd s of Rev. J. W. P. Silvester, sometime Vicar of Wembley, Middlesex; m 1922, Dorothy Francis Newton; one s. Educ: Ardingly College, Sussex; St John's, Leatherhead, Surrey; John Lyons, Harrow, Middlesex. Served European War, 1914-18, London Scottish and Argyll and Sutherland Highlanders, 1915-18. Started as a dancer, 1918; Winner of the World's Professional Ballroom Championship, 1922. Formed orchestra, 1935; has broadcast for the BBC, made records and televised ever since. Pres. Imperial Soc. of Teachers of Dancing Incorporated. Pres., Lord's Taverners, 1972. Italian Bronze Medal for Military Valour, 1917. Publications: Modern Ballroom Dancing, 1927 (57th edn, 1974); Theory and Technique of Ballroom Dancing, 1933; The Art of the Ballroom, 1936; Dancing is my Life, 1959. Recreation: physical culture. Address: 19 Boydell Court, St John's Wood Park, NW8. T: 01-586 1234.

SILYN ROBERTS, **Air Vice-Marshal** (retired) **Glynn**, CB 1959; CBE 1949; AFC 1939; b 2 April 1906; s of late R. Silyn Roberts, MA, and Mrs M. Silyn Roberts, MBE, BA. Educ: Bangor. Permanent Commission, RAF, 1930; No. 2 Squadron, 1930-32; Home Aircraft Depot 1932; Experimental Flying Dept, RAE, 1935; Aircraft Depot, Iraq, 1939; Chief Technical Officer, Empire Central Flying Sch., 1942; Dep. Dir Technical Development, MAP, 1943 (despatches); Director of Aircraft Research and Development, MAP, 1945; Commanding Officer, Experimental Flying Dept, RAE, 1947; Sen. Technical Staff Officer, No. 2 Group, Jan. 1949; Dep. Dir Military Aircraft Research and Development, Min. of Supply, Dec. 1949; Principal Dir of Aircraft Research and Development, Min. of Supply, 1955; Sen. Technical Staff Officer, Bomber Command, 1956; Dir-Gen. of Engineering, Air Min., 1958-61; retd, Nov. 1961. MSc, CEng, FRAeS. Recreations: fishing, shooting (Hon. Life Vice-Pres. RAF Small Arms Assoc.). Address: c/o Williams & Glyn's Bank Ltd, Kirkland House, 22 Whitehall, SW1. Clubs: Royal Air Force, Naval and Military.

SIM, Sir **Alexander**; see Sim, Sir G. A. S.

SIM, **David**, CMG 1946; retired; Deputy Minister of National Revenue for Customs and Excise, Canada, 1943-65; b Glasgow, Scotland, 4 May 1899; s of David Sim, and Cora Lilian Angus; m 1924, Ada Helen Inrig (d 1958); one s one d; m 1960, Winnifred Emily Blois. Educ: Haghill Public School, Glasgow; Kitchener-Waterloo Collegiate. Served European War, Canadian Army in Canada and Overseas with the 1st Canadian Infantry Battalion (wounded at Passchendaele). Bank of Nova Scotia, 1919-25; Waterloo Trust & Savings Co., 1926; Secretary to Minister of National Revenue, 1927-33; Commissioner of Excise, 1933-43; Administrator of Alcoholic Beverages, 1942-45; Administrator of Tobacco, 1942-46; Dir Commodity Prices Stabilization Corporation; Member of External Trade Advisory Cttee and Nat. Joint Council of the Public Service of Canada; Member, Board of Broadcast Governors, 1966-. Past President: Rotary Club; Canadian Club. Mem. Canadian delegation to: 1st Session of Preparatory Cttee for Internat. Conf. on Trade and Employment, London, 1946; 2nd Session of Preparatory Cttee for UN Conf. on Trade and Employment, Geneva, 1947. General Service, Victory, Jubilee and Coronation Medals. Recreations: golf, fishing, curling, reading. Address: 1833 Riverside Drive, Apt 616, Ottawa, Ontario, Canada. Clubs: Rideau, Canadian, Royal Ottawa Golf, Curling, Five Lakes Fishing (Ottawa).

SIM, Sir **(George) Alexander (Strachan)**, Kt 1956; b 18 Dec. 1905; s of late George Gall Sim, CSI, CIE and of Margaret Byers

Sim; *m* 1938, Florence May, *d* of late Jesse James Smith; one *d*. *Educ:* Winchester College. CA (Edinburgh), 1930. Director, Andrew Yule and Co. Ltd (Calcutta), 1939, Dep. Chm., 1948, Chm., 1953-56; Commissioner for the Port of Calcutta, 1950-55; Vice-Pres., Bengal Chamber of Commerce and Industry, 1954-55, Pres., 1955-56; Pres., Associated Chambers of Commerce of India, 1955-56; Director: Yule Catto & Co. Ltd, 1956-76; W. T. Henleys Telegraph Works Co. Ltd, 1957-59 (Chm., 1958-59); Peirce Leslie & Co. Ltd, 1964-68; Tote Investors Ltd, 1963-70; The Cementation Co. Ltd, 1961-70 (Dep. Chm., 1963-70). Chm., Horserace Totalisator Board, 1961-70. *Recreation:* golf. *Address:* East View, Iden, Rye, Sussex. *Clubs:* Oriental; Rye; Royal Calcutta Turf, Tollygunge (Calcutta).

SIM, John Mackay, MBE 1945; Deputy Chairman, Inchcape & Co. Ltd, since 1975 (Deputy Chairman/Managing Director, 1965-75); *b* 4 Oct. 1917; *s* of William Aberdeen Mackay Sim and Zoe Sim; *m* 1st, Dora Cecilia Plumridge Levita (*d* 1951); two *d*; 2nd, Mrs Muriel Harvard (Peggie) Norman. *Educ:* Glenalmond; Pembroke Coll., Cambridge (MA). Lieut RA, 1940, Captain 1942; served NW Europe (despatches). Smith Mackenzie & Co. Ltd (East Africa), 1946-62, Chm. 1960-62; Dir, subseq. Man. Dir, Inchcape & Co. Ltd, 1962. *Recreation:* gardening. *Address:* 6 Bryanston Mews West, W1H 7FR. *T:* 01-262 7673; Stone Lacey, Aston Sandford, near Aylesbury, Bucks. *T:* Haddenham (Bucks) 291217. *Clubs:* City of London, MCC.

SIM, Sir Wilfrid (Joseph), KBE 1951; MC 1918; QC (New Zealand), 1939; *b* 3 Nov. 1890; *s* of William Alexander Sim, a Judge of Supreme Court and Court of Appeal of New Zealand; *m* 1921, Hazel Dashwood Hill (*d* 1950), Christchurch, NZ; one *s* one *d*. *Educ:* Otago Boys' High School, Dunedin, NZ; Collegiate School, Wanganui, NZ; Victoria College University, NZ. Admitted to Bar, NZ, 1913. President NZ National Party, 1944-51. Served European War, 1914-18. NZ Expeditionary Force, Samoa, 1914; Argyll and Sutherland Highlanders, 1915-18 (Salonika), Médaille d'Honneur (France). Practised in Christchurch, NZ (Duncan, Cotterill and Co.), 1919-39, and, after taking silk, subsequently in Wellington. Member, Christchurch City Council, 1925-27, and Chairman, Citizens' Association, 1927-29. Trustee of Wanganui Collegiate School, 1939-70; NZ Cttee of Management for Doctor Barnardo's Homes. Director, Mount Cook Tourist Co. Member, Law Revision Cttee (now Law Revision Commission), 1936-69. *Publications:* Sim's Practice of Supreme Court and Court of Appeal, NZ, 11th edn 1972; Sim on Divorce, 8th edn 1970. *Recreations:* golf, gardening. *Address:* 74 Upland Road, Wellington, NZ. *Clubs:* Wellington (Wellington, NZ); Christchurch (Christchurch, NZ).

SIMCOCK, Rev. Canon James Alexander; Canon Residentiary and Treasurer of Truro Cathedral 1951-74; Canon Emeritus, since 1974; *b* 19 Dec. 1897; *m* 1923, Mary Dorothy, *d* of Rev. T. R. Pennington; one *s*. *Educ:* Egerton Hall, Manchester. Deacon, 1922; Priest, 1923; Curate of: St Luke, Weaste, 1922-24; Milnrow, 1924-27; Incumbent of St Mark, Chadderton, 1927-31; Rector of St Mark, Newton Heath, 1931-33; Organising Secretary, Church of England Children's Soc., for Dioceses of Bath and Wells, Exeter and Truro, and Curate of St Martin, Exminster, 1933-36; Rector of Calstock, 1936-43; Surrogate, 1939-; Vicar of St Gluvias with Penryn, 1943-51. Rural Dean of S Carnmath, 1946-49; Hon. Canon of St Germoe in Truro Cathedral, 1948-51. *Address:* 25 Kemp Close, Truro, Cornwall TR1 1EF. *T:* Truro 29277. *Club:* Royal Over-Seas League.

SIMCOX, Richard Alfred, CBE 1975 (MBE 1956); Member of the British Council; *b* 29 March 1915; *s* of Alfred William and Alice Simcox; *m* 1951, Patricia Elisabeth Gutteridge; one *s* two *d*. *Educ:* Gonville and Caius Coll., Cambridge. BA Class. Tripos. Served with N Staffs Regt, 1939-43; British Council from 1943: Rep. in Jordan, 1957-60; in Libya, 1960; in Jordan (again), 1960; Cultural Attaché, British Embassy, Cairo, 1968-71; British Council Representative, Iran, 1971-75. Governor, Gabbitas-Thring Educnl Trust. *Recreations:* gardening, philately. *Address:* Little Brockhurst, Lye Green Road, Chesham, Bucks. *T:* Chesham 3797.

SIME, William Arnold, MBE 1946; QC 1957; **His Honour Judge Sime;** a Circuit Judge, since 1972; *b* 8 Feb. 1909; *s* of William Sime, Wepener, OFS, South Africa, and Bedford, and Charlotte Edith Sime; *m* 1938, Rosemary Constance, *d* of Dr Cleaton Roberts, West Byfleet, Surrey; two *d*. *Educ:* Grahamstown, CP; Bedford School; Balliol College, Oxford. Called to the Bar, Inner Temple, 1932 (Master of the Bench, 1964); Recorder: Grantham, 1954-57, 1958-63; Great Grimsby, 1963-71; City of Birmingham, 1971; a Senior Puisne Judge, Cyprus, 1957-58; Senior Judge (non-resident) of the Sovereign Base Areas, Cyprus, 1960-. Served War of 1939-45 with RAF; Wing Comdr.

Recreations: golf, cricket (captained Bedfordshire CCC, 1931-33, captained Nottinghamshire CCC, 1947-50, Pres., 1975-77); Rugby (captained Bedford RUFC, 1932-37); racing. *Address:* Witsend, Wymeswold, Leicestershire; 6 King's Bench Walk, Temple, EC4. *Clubs:* MCC; Northampton and County.

SIMENON, Georges; Novelist; *b* Liège, Belgium, 13 February 1903; *s* of Désiré Simenon and Henriette Brull; *m* Denise Ouimet; three *s* one *d*. *Educ:* Collège St Servais, Liège, Belgium. His books are translated into 47 languages and have been published in 32 countries. *Publications:* 212 novels, including the 80 titles of the Maigret series; autobiographical works: When I Was Old, 1972; Letter to my Mother, 1976; Un Homme comme un autre, 1975; Des traces de pas, 1975; Les petits hommes, 1976; Vent du nord vent du sud, 1976; Un banc au soleil, 1977; De la cave au grenier, 1977. *Address:* Secretariat de Georges Simenon, avenue du Temple 19B, 1012 Lausanne, Switzerland. *T:* 33 39 79; 155 avenue de Cour, 1007 Lausanne.

SIMEON, Sir John Edmund Barrington, 7th Bt, *cr* 1815; Civil Servant in Department of Social Welfare, Provincial Government, British Columbia, retired 1975; lately in Real Estate business; *b* 1 March 1911; *s* of Sir John Walter Barrington Simeon, 6th Bt, and Adelaide Emily (*d* 1934), *e d* of late Col Hon. E. A. Holmes-à-Court; *S* father 1957; *m* 1937, Anne Robina Mary Dean; one *s* two *d*. *Educ:* Eton; Christ Church, Oxford. Motor business, 1931-39. Served with RAF, 1939-43; invalided, rank of Flight Lt, 1943. Civil Servant, Ministry of Agriculture, 1943-51. Took up residence in Vancouver, Canada, 1951. *Recreations:* sailing, painting. *Heir:* *s* Richard Edmund Barrington Simeon, PhD Yale; Associate Professor of Political Science, Queen's Univ., Kingston, Ont [*b* 2 March 1943; *m* 1966, Agnes Joan, *d* of George Frederick Weld; one *s* one *d*]. *Address:* c/o National Westminster Bank Ltd, Newport, Isle of Wight, 1704 Wolfe Street, North Vancouver, BC V7M 2Z1, Canada.

SIMEON, John Power Barrington; HM Diplomatic Service; Deputy High Commissioner and Head of Post, Ibadan, Nigeria, since 1975; *b* 15 Nov. 1929; *o s* of late Cornwall Barrington Simeon and Ellaline Margery Mary (*née* Le Poer Power, Clonmel, Co. Tipperary); *m* 1970, Carina Renate Elisabeth Schüller; one *s*. *Educ:* Beaumont Coll.; RMA, Sandhurst. Commnd 2nd Lieut Royal Corps of Signals, 1949; Lieut 1951; resigned, 1952; RARO, 1953-. Ferrous and non-ferrous metal broker, London and Europe, 1953-57; Rank Organisation: served in Germany, Thailand, Singapore, India, ME, N Africa, Hong Kong and London, 1957-65; HM Diplomatic Service, 1965-: First Sec. (Commercial): Colombo, 1967; Bonn, 1968-70; First Sec., and sometime Actg High Comr, Port of Spain, 1970-73; Republic of Ireland Dept, FCO, 1973-75. *Recreations:* travel, photography, shooting, riding. *Address:* c/o Foreign and Commonwealth Office, King Charles Street, SW1A 2AH. *Club:* Ibadan Polo.

SIMEONS, Charles Fitzmaurice Creighton, MA; Consultant: Environmental Control, Recovery, Disposal, Health and Safety at Work, Communications with Government; *b* 22 Sept. 1921; *s* of Charles Albert Simeons and Vera Hildegarde Simeons; *m* 1945, Rosemary (*née* Tabrum); one *s* one *d*. *Educ:* Oundle; Queens' Coll., Cambridge. Royal Artillery with 8th Indian Div., 1942-45. Man. Dir, supplier to photographic industry, 1957-70. MP (C) Luton, 1970-Feb. 1974. Chm., Luton Cons. Assoc., 1960-63. Pres., Luton, Dunstable and District Chamber of Commerce, 1967-68; District Gov., Rotary International, 1967-68; Chm. of cttees raising funds for disabled and cancer research. Chm., Adv. Cttee, Rotary Internat. Bd on Environmental Research and Resources, 1973-74; Vice Pres., Nat. Industrial Material Recovery Assoc.; Mem. Inst. of Environmental Sciences; Mem., Internat. Cttee, Water Pollution Control Federation, Washington, DC; Mem. Council, Smaller Business Assoc., 1974-76. Hon. Mem., Inst. of Water Pollution Control. Liveryman: Worshipful Co. of Feltmakers (and Asst to Court); Guild of Freemen of City of London. FIWM; FInstD. Pres., Old Oundelian Club, 1976-77. JP Luton, 1959-74. *Recreations:* watching football, cricket, gardening. *Address:* 21 Ludlow Avenue, Luton, Beds. *T:* Luton 30965. *Clubs:* City Livery, East India, Sports and Public Schools; Conservative (Luton).

SIMES, Charles Erskine Woollard, QC 1945; MA Oxon; *b* 1893; *s* of Frederick Albert Woollard Simes, Worcester; *m* 1923, Catherine Harriet (*d* 1964), *d* of W. M. Hayes, Vancouver, BC. *Educ:* Royal Grammar School, Worcester; St John's College, Oxford. Lieut 1/7th Batt. Worcestershire Regt, 1914-17; France, 1915; Hd Qr Staff W Midland Region, Ministry of National Service, 1917-18; Barrister-at-Law, Inner Temple, 1921; Bencher, 1961; Recorder of Banbury, 1938-51; Chm. Interdepartmental Cttee on Rating of Site Values, 1947-51; Dep. Chairman, Boundary Commission for England, 1950-56;

Member, Lands Tribunal, 1951-67; Chairman Harlow New Town Licensing Cttee; a Dep. Chm. Surrey QS, 1956-66; Mem. Boundary Commission for England, 1950-66. JP Surrey, 1953. Grand Registrar, United Grand Lodge of England, 1959-74. *Publications:* Joint Editor Lumley's Public Health (10th, 11th and 12th edns), Local Government Law and Administration. *Address:* Court House, Barnards Green, Malvern, Worcs WR14 3BU.

SIMKINS, Charles Anthony Goodall, CB 1968; CBE 1963; *b* 2 March 1912; *s* of Charles Wyckens Simkins; *m* 1938, Sylvia, *d* of Thomas Hartley, Silchester, Hants; two *s* one *d*. *Educ:* Marlborough; New Coll., Oxford (1st Class Hons Mod. Hist.). Barrister, Lincoln's Inn, 1936; served 1939-45 as Captain, Rifle Bde (POW); attached War Office (later MoD), 1945-71. *Address:* The Cottage, 94 Broad Street, near Guildford, Surrey. *T:* Guildford 72456. *Clubs:* Naval and Military, MCC.

SIMMONDS, Kenneth Willison, CMG 1956; FRSA; *b* Carmacoup, Douglas, Lanarkshire, 13 May 1912; *s* of late William Henry Simmonds, Civil Servant, and late Ida, *d* of John Willison, Acharn, Killin, Perthshire; *m* 1st, 1939, Ruth Constance Sargant (marr. diss. 1974); two *s*; 2nd, 1974, Mrs Catherine Clare Lewis, *y d* of late Col F. J. Brakenridge, CMG, Chew Magna. *Educ:* Bedford Sch.; Humberstone Sch.; St Catharine's Coll., Cambridge (MA). District Officer, Colonial Administrative Service, Kenya, 1935-48; Deputy Financial Secretary, Uganda, 1948-51; Financial Secretary, Nyasaland Protectorate, 1951-57; Chief Secretary, Aden, 1957-63. Exhibited paintings: Southern Arts Open Field, 1972-73; Royal Acad., 1973, 1974, 1977; Royal West of England Acad., 1976; group and collective exhbns. *Address:* North Close, Milverton, Taunton, Somerset TA4 1QZ. *T:* Milverton 235.

SIMMONDS, Sir Oliver Edwin, Kt 1944; CEng; FRAeS; President, E. F. G. Ltd, Nassau, Bahamas; *b* 1897; *e s* of Rev. F. T. Simmonds; *m* 1922, Gladys Evelyn Hewitt (*d* 1977); one *s* two *d*. *Educ:* Taunton; Magdalene College, Cambridge (Exhibnr; Mech. Sci. Tripos). Aerodynamic research, RAE (jt author first res. report on Supersonic flight); gave over 1000 lectures on future of civil aviation, 1922-35; joined Supermarine Aviation Works, 1924; responsible (jointly) for design Supermarines S4, S5, and S6 (Schneider Trophy Winners, 1926; from which Spitfire was subseq. developed); invented and patented interchangeable wings for aircraft (Simmonds Spartan biplane); formed Simmonds Aircraft Ltd, 1928 (produced Spartan landplane and seaplane), Simmonds Aerocessories Ltd, 1931, Simmonds Aerocessories, NY and Paris, 1936, Melbourne 1937, Montreal 1946. Chm., Air Transport Cttee, FBI. MP (U) Birmingham Duddeston, 1931-45. Founder-Pres. ARP Inst.; Chm., Parly ARP Cttee, 1938; led delegn to Berlin to study German ARP. Mem. Exec., 1922 Cttee, 1938-45; Chm. Govt Cttee on Brick Industry, 1941-42. Developed and patented electronic fuel gauge Pacitron. Moved to Bahamas, 1948; built Balmoral Club (now Balmoral Beach Hotel); Founder Pres., Friends of the Bahamas, 1954; Founder Pres., Bahamas Employers Confdn, 1966-68. Vice-Pres., RAeS, 1945-47. *Address:* PO Box 1480, Nassau, Bahamas. *Club:* Royal Thames Yacht.

SIMMONS, Fr Eric, CR; Superior of the Community of the Resurrection, Mirfield, Yorkshire, since May 1974; *b* 1930. *Educ:* Univ. of Leeds. BA (Phil) 1951. Coll. of the Resurrection, Mirfield, 1951; deacon, 1953, priest, 1954; Curate of St Luke, Chesterton, 1953-57; Chaplain, University Coll. of N Staffordshire, 1957-61; licensed to officiate: Dio. Wakefield, 1963-65 and 1967-; Dio. Ripon, 1965-67; Warden and Prior of Hostel of the Resurrection, Leeds, 1966-67; subseq. Novice Guardian, looking after young Community members; the Community is an Anglican foundation engaged in evangelism and teaching work, based in Yorkshire but with houses in Southern Africa. *Address:* House of the Resurrection, Mirfield, West Yorks. *T:* Mirfield 494318.

SIMMONS, Ernest Bernard, QC (Seychelles) 1949; *b* 7 Sept. 1913; *o s* of Bernard Simmons and Ethel (*née* Booth); *m* 1940, Edna Muriel Tomlinson; one *s* three *d*. Barrister-at-Law, Gray's Inn, 1936; Asst Attorney-Gen., Gibraltar, 1946; Attorney-Gen., Seychelles, 1949; Judge of the Supreme Court, Mauritius, 1952-58; Judge of the High Court, Tanganyika, 1958-61; retired. *Address:* The Gate House, 27 Middleton Road, Brentwood, Essex.

SIMMONS, Rev. F(rederic) P(earson) Copland, MA; *b* 7 July 1902; 7th *c* of Rev. Arthur Simmons, Kingskettle, Fife, Scotland; *m* 1933, Kathleen (*d* 1968), *d* of Rev. Henry Norwell, Helensburgh. *Educ:* Gateshead Secondary School; King's College, Newcastle; Westminster College, Cambridge. BA

Dunelm 1922, MA 1926. Ordained to Ministry, Ashington, Northumberland, 1925; Rutherford Church of Scotland, Glasgow, 1929; Egremont Presbyterian Church, Wallasey, 1938; St Andrew's Presbyterian Church Frognal, London, NW3, 1946; St Andrew's Presbyterian Church, Bournemouth, 1963-68; Chaplain at Scots Kirk, Nice, 1936-37. Moderator of the Free Church Federal Council of England and Wales, 1955-56; Moderator, Presbyterian Church of England, 1959-60; Minister, Monzie and Fowlis Wester Church, 1969-74. Visiting Preacher and Lectr in USA and Canada on nine occasions. *Recreations:* music, colour photography.

SIMMONS, Guy Lintorn, MVO 1961; HM Diplomatic Service; Commercial Counsellor, Copenhagen, since 1976; *b* 27 Feb. 1925; *s* of Captain Geoffrey Larpent Simmons, RN and late Frances Gladys Simmons (*née* Wright); *m* 1951, Sheila Jacob; three *d*. *Educ:* Bradfield Coll.; Oriel Coll., Oxford. RAF, 1943-46; CRO, 1949; 2nd Sec., British High Commn: Lahore, 1950; Dacca, 1952; CRO, 1954-58 and 1964-66; 1st Sec.: Bombay, 1958; New Delhi, 1961; Commercial Counsellor: New Delhi, 1966-68; Cairo, 1968-71; Head of Trade Policy Dept, FCO, 1971-73; Diplomatic Service Inspectorate, 1973-75. *Recreations:* fishing, riding, amateur dramatics. *Address: c/o* Foreign and Commonwealth Office, SW1. *Clubs:* Oriental, Royal Commonwealth Society.

SIMMONS, Jack; Professor of History, University of Leicester, 1947-75, now Professor Emeritus and Hon. Archivist; Pro-Vice-Chancellor, 1960-63; Public Orator, 1965-68; *b* 30 Aug. 1915; *o c* of Seymour Francis Simmons and Katharine Lillias, *d* of Thomas Finch, MB, Babbacombe, Devon. *Educ:* Westminster Sch.; Christ Church, Oxford. Beit Lectr in the History of the British Empire, Oxford Univ., 1943-47. FRSL; FRHistS; FSA. Mem., Adv. Council, Science Museum, 1970-; Vice-Chm., Nat. Railway Museum Cttee, York; Leicestershire Archæological and Historical Society: Hon. Editor, 1948-61; Pres. 1966-77. Chm., Leicester Local Broadcasting Council, 1967-70. Jt Editor, The Journal of Transport History, 1953-73. Editor: A Visual History of Modern Britain; Classical County Histories. *Publications:* African Discovery: An Anthology of Exploration (edited with Margery Perham), 1942; Southey, 1945; Edition of Southey's Letters from England, 1951; Journeys in England: an Anthology, 1951; Parish and Empire, 1952; Livingstone and Africa, 1955; New University, 1958; The Railways of Britain: an Historical Introduction, 1961; Transport, 1962; Britain and the World, 1965; St Pancras Station, 1968; Transport Museums, 1970; A Devon Anthology, 1971; (ed) Memoirs of a Station Master, 2 vols, 1973, 1977; Leicester Past and Present (2 vols), 1974; (ed) Rail 150: The Stockton and Darlington Railway and What Followed, 1975; The Railway in England and Wales, Vol. 1, 1978. *Address: c/o* Department of History, The University, Leicester LE1 7RH.

SIMMONS, Jean, (Mrs Richard Brooks); film actress; *b* London, 31 Jan. 1929; *m* 1950, Stewart Granger, *qv* (marriage dissolved, Arizona, 1960); one *d*; *m* 1960, at Salinas, Calif, Richard Brooks; one *d*. *Educ:* Orange Hill Sch.; Aida Foster School of Dancing. First film appearance in Give Us the Moon, 1942; minor parts in Cæsar and Cleopatra, The Way to the Stars, etc., 1942-44; since then has appeared in numerous British films, including: Great Expectations, Black Narcissus, Hungry Hill, Uncle Silas, Hamlet, So Long at the Fair, The Blue Lagoon, Trio, Adam and Evalyn, Clouded Yellow; The Grass is Greener, 1960; Life at the Top, 1965; Say Hello to Yesterday, 1971; began American film career, 1950; American films include: Androcles and the Lion, Ivanhoe, The Actress, Desirée, Footsteps in the Fog, Guys and Dolls, This Could Be the Night, Spartacus, Elmer Gantry, All the Way Home; Divorce, American Style, 1967; The Happy Ending, 1970. Musical: A Little Night Music, Adelphi, 1975. *Address: c/o* A. Morgan Maree, Jr & Assoc., Inc., 6363 Wilshire Boulevard, Los Angeles 48, California, USA.

SIMMONS, Robert, CMG 1954; CBE 1943; MRCVS; *b* 10 Dec. 1894; *m* 1923, Mary Dickinson Waugh; one *d*. *Educ:* Dunfermline High School; Royal Dick Veterinary College, Edinburgh. Served European War, 1914-19; Fife and Forfar Yeomanry, King's Own Scottish Borderers, Royal Scots. Entered Colonial Service, 1923; Director of Veterinary Services: Uganda, 1938; Nigeria, 1944. Adviser to Secretary of State, Colonial Office, 1948-55, retired. *Publications:* contributions to scientific journals. *Recreation:* golf. *Address:* Lindores, Summerfield, Dunbar, Scotland. *T:* Dunbar 63781.

SIMMONS, William Foster, CMG 1963; MB, ChM; FRACGP 1969; General Practitioner, 1919-66, retired; *b* 9 May 1888; *s* of William Alfred Simmons, JP, Vaucluse, NSW; *m* 1919, Edna Kathleen Millicent Goode; two *d* (and two *s* decd). *Educ:* Sydney Boys' High School; Sydney University. Served European

War, Australian Imperial Force, AAMC, 1914-19 (Major). Asst Hon. Physician, 1925, Hon. Consultant Physician, 1954, St George Hospital; Hon. Treasurer, Federal Council of BMA in Australia, 1946-62; Mem. Nat. Health and Medical Research Council, 1943-63. Chm. Medical Research Adv. Cttee, 1957-64; Dir Australasian Medical Publishing Co., 1946-74. Foundation Fellow, Aust. Coll. Gen. Practitioners, Oct. 1965. Awarded Gold Medal, BMA in Australia, 1961. *Recreations:* football and rowing (retired many years); gardening. *Address:* 78 Wentworth Road, Vaucluse, NSW 2030, Australia. *T:* 337-1770.

SIMMS, Most Rev. George Otto; *see* Armagh, Archbishop of, and Primate of All Ireland.

SIMON, family name of **Viscount Simon,** of **Baron Simon of Glaisdale** and of **Baron Simon of Wythenshawe.**

SIMON, 2nd Viscount, *cr* 1940, of Stackpole Elidor; **John Gilbert Simon,** CMG 1947; *b* 2 Sept. 1902; *o s* of 1st Viscount Simon, PC, GCSI, GCVO, and of Ethel Mary (*d* 1902), *d* of Gilbert Venables; *S* father, 1954; *m* 1930, James Christie, *d* of William Stanley Hunt; one *s* one *d. Educ:* Winchester; Balliol College, Oxford (Scholar). With Ministry of War Transport, 1940-47. Man. Dir, 1947-58, Dep. Chm., 1951-58, Peninsular and Oriental Steam Navigation Co. Chm., PLA, 1958-71; Mem., Nat. Ports Council, 1967-71. President: Chamber of Shipping of UK, 1957-58; Inst. of Marine Engineers, 1960-61; RINA, 1961-71; British Hydromechanics Res. Assoc. Officer Order of Orange Nassau, Netherlands. *Heir: s* Hon. Jan David Simon [*b* 20 July 1940; *m* 1969, Mary Elizabeth Burns, Sydney; one *d*]. *Address:* 51 The Strand, Topsham, Exeter EX3 0AS.

SIMON OF GLAISDALE, Baron *cr* 1971 (Life Peer), of Glaisdale, Yorks; **Jocelyn Edward Salis Simon,** PC 1961; Kt 1959; DL; a Lord of Appeal in Ordinary, 1971-77; *b* 15 Jan. 1911; *s* of Frank Cecil and Claire Evelyn Simon, 51 Belsize Pk, NW3; *m* 1st, 1934, Gwendolen Helen (*d* 1937), *d* of E. J. Evans; 2nd, 1948, Fay Elizabeth Leicester, JP, *d* of Brig. H. G. A. Pearson; three *s. Educ:* Gresham's School, Holt; Trinity Hall, Cambridge (Exhibitioner). Called to Bar, Middle Temple, 1934 (Blackstone Prizeman). Served War of 1939-45; commissioned RTR, 1939; comd Spec. Service Sqn, RAC, Madagascar, 1942; Burma Campaign, 1944; Lieut-Col. 1945. Resumed practice at Bar, 1946; QC 1951. MP (C) Middlesbrough West, 1951-62; Mem. of the Royal Commission on the Law relating to Mental Illness and Mental Deficiency, 1954-57. Jt Parly Under-Sec. of State, Home Office, 1957-58; Financial Sec. to the Treasury, 1958-59; Solicitor-General, 1959-62. President, Probate, Divorce and Admiralty Div. of the High Court of Justice, 1962-71. Elder Brother, Trinity House, 1975. Hon. Fellow, Trinity Hall, Cambridge, 1963. DL NR Yorks, 1973. *Publications:* Change is Our Ally, 1954 (part); Rule of Law, 1955 (part); The Church and the Law of Nullity, 1955 (part). *Address:* Midge Hall, Glaisdale Head, Whitby, North Yorks; Carpmael Building, Temple, EC4.

SIMON OF WYTHENSHAWE, 2nd Baron, *cr* 1947, of Didsbury; **Roger Simon;** *b* 16 Oct. 1913; *S* father, 1960 (but does not use the title and wishes to be known as Roger Simon); *m* 1951 (Anthea) Daphne May; one *s* one *d. Educ:* Gresham's School; Gonville and Caius College, Cambridge. *Heir: s* Hon. Matthew Simon, *b* 10 April 1955. *Address:* Oakhill, Chester Avenue, Richmond, Surrey.
See also B. Simon.

SIMON, Prof. Brian; Professor of Education, University of Leicester, since 1966; *b* 26 March 1915; *yr s* of 1st Baron Simon of Wythenshawe and Shena D. Potter; *m* 1941, Joan Home Peel; two *s. Educ:* Gresham's Sch., Holt; Schloss Schule, Salem; Trinity Coll., Cambridge; Inst. of Educn, Univ. of London. MA. Pres., Nat. Union of Students, 1939-40; Royal Corps of Signals, GHQ Liaison Regt (Phantom), 1940-45; teaching Manchester and Salford schs, 1945-50; Univ. of Leicester: Lectr in Educn, 1950-64; Reader, 1964-66; Dir, Sch. of Educn, 1968-70, 1974-77. Chm., History of Educn Soc., 1976; Pres., British Educn Res. Assoc., 1977-78. Editor, Forum (for discussion of new trends in educn), 1958-; Jt Editor, Students Library of Education, 1966-77. *Publications:* A Student's View of the Universities, 1943; Intelligence Testing and the Comprehensive School, 1953; The Common Secondary School, 1955; (ed) New Trends in English Education, 1957; (ed) Psychology in the Soviet Union, 1957; Studies in the History of Education 1780-1870, 1960; (ed, with Joan Simon) Educational Psychology in the USSR, 1963; (ed) The Challenge of Marxism, 1963; (ed) Non-streaming in the Junior School, 1964; Education and the Labour Movement 1870-1920, 1965; (ed) Education in Leicestershire 1540-1940, 1968; (with D. Rubinstein) The Evolution of the Comprehensive School 1926-66, 1969 (revised edn 1973); (with Caroline Benn)

Half-Way There: Report on the British Comprehensive School Reform, 1970 (revised edn 1972); Intelligence, Psychology and Education, 1971; (ed) The Radical Tradition in Education in Britain, 1972; The Politics of Educational Reform 1920-1940, 1974; (ed with Ian Bradley) The Victorian Public School, 1975. *Address:* School of Education, 21 University Road, Leicester LE1 7RF. *T:* 0533 24211.

SIMON, (Ernest Julius) Walter, CBE 1961; DrPhil, DLit; FBA 1956; Professor of Chinese, University of London, 1947-60, Emeritus Professor, 1960; Visiting Professor: University of Toronto, 1961-62; Australian National University, Canberra, 1962; Tokyo, Canberra and Melbourne, 1970; *b* Berlin, 10 June 1893; *m* 1921, Kate (*née* Jungmann); two *s. Educ:* Univ. of Berlin. Higher Library Service, Berlin Univ. Library, 1919-35; Exchange Librarian, Nat. Library of Peking, 1932-33; Lecturer in Chinese, Univ. of Berlin, 1926-32; Extraordinary Prof. of Chinese, Univ. of Berlin, 1932-34; Lecturer, School of Oriental Studies, 1936; Reader in Chinese, University of London, 1938. Editor, Asia Major, 1964-75. Hon. Fellow School of Oriental and African Studies, University of London; Toyo Bunko, Tokyo. Pres. Philological Soc., 1967-70, Vice-Pres., 1971-; Hon. Vice-Pres., Royal Asiatic Soc., 1976- (Gold Medal, 1977). *Publications:* Reconstruction of Archaic Chinese Final Consonants, 2 Parts, 1928-29 (in German); Tibetan Chinese Word Equations, 1930 (in German); Chinese Sentence Series, 3 volumes, 1942-44; New Official Chinese Latin Script, 1942; Chinese National Language (Gwoyeu) Reader, 1943 (2nd edn 1954, repr. 1972); 1200 Chinese Basic Characters, 1944 (4th repr. 1975); How to Study and Write Chinese Characters, 1944 (3rd repr. 1975); Structure Drill through Speech Patterns, I. Structure Drill in Chinese, 1945 (2nd edn 1959, repr. 1975); Beginners' Chinese-English Dictionary, 1947 (4th edn 1975); Introduction to: K. P. K. Whitaker's 1200 Basic Chinese Characters for Students of Cantonese, 1953 (3rd edn 1965); Y. C. Liu's Fifty Chinese Stories, 1960. Contribs to: Mitteilungen des Seminars für Orientalische Sprachen, Orientalistische Literaturzeitung, Bulletin of School of Oriental and African Studies, Harvard Journal of Oriental Studies, Asia Major, etc. *Address:* 13 Lisbon Avenue, Twickenham TW2 5HR. *T:* 01-894 3860.

SIMON, Neil; playwright; *b* NYC, 4 July 1927; *s* of Irving and Mamie Simon; *m* 1953, Joan Baim; two *d. Educ:* De Witt Clinton High Sch.; entered Army Air Force Reserve training programme as an engineering student at New York University; discharged with rank of corporal, 1946. Went to New York Offices of Warner Brothers Pictures to work in mail room. Wrote book for Little Me (produced 1962). *Screenplays include:* After The Fox (produced 1966); The Heartbreak Kid, 1973; The Prisoner on 2nd Avenue, 1975; The Sunshine Boys, 1976; Death by Murder, 1976. *Publications:* Come Blow Your Horn, 1963 (produced 1961); Barefoot in the Park, 1964 (produced 1963); The Odd Couple, 1965 (produced 1965); Sweet Charity, 1966 (with others) (produced 1966); The Star Spangled Girl, 1966 (produced 1966); Plaza Suite, 1969 (produced 1969); The Sunshine Boys, 1972 (produced 1972); The Good Doctor (produced 1974); The Gingerbread Lady, 1974; California Suite, 1976.

SIMON, Roger; *see* Simon of Wythenshawe barony.

SIMON, Walter; *see* Simon, (E. J.) W.

SIMON, William Edward; Secretary of the US Treasury, May 1974-Dec. 1976; *b* 27 Nov. 1927; *s* of Charles Simon and Eleanor Kearns; *m* 1950, Carol Girard; two *s* five *d. Educ:* Newark Academy, NJ; Lafayette Coll. (BA). Joined Union Securities, NYC 1952, Asst Vice-Pres. and Manager of firm's Municipal Trading Dept, 1955; Vice Pres., Weeden & Co., 1957-64; Sen. Partner, Salomon Brothers, NYC, 1964-72. Dep. Sec., US Treasury Dept, and Administrator, Federal Energy Office, 1973-74. Chairman: Economic Policy Bd, 1974-; Nat. Advisory Council on Internat. Monetary and Financial Policies; East-West Foreign Trade Bd, 1975-; Federal Financing Bank; Emergency Loan Guarantee Board; Council on Internat. Economic Policy; Council on Wage and Price Stability; past Chm., Oil Policy Cttee; Vice Chm., Nat. Commn on Supplies and Shortages; US Governor of: Internat. Monetary Fund; Internat. Bank for Reconstruction and Development; Inter-American Develt Bank; Asian Develt Bank. He has been very active in many public and private organizations. FORMER Trustee: Lafayette Coll.; Mannes Coll. of Music, NYC; Newark Academy. Hon. Dr of Laws: Lafayette Coll. 1973; Pepperdine Univ., 1975; Hon. DCL, Jacksonville Univ., 1976. *Address:* 1404 Langley Place, McLean, Virginia 22101, USA. *T:* 202-964-5300. *Clubs:* River (New York, NY); Maidstone (East Hampton, NY); Alfalfa (Washington DC); Burning Tree

(Maryland); Chevy Chase (Chevy Chase, Md); Balboa Bay (Calif); Morris County Golf (Convent Station, NJ).

SIMONET, Henri François; Foreign Minister, Belgium, and Secretary of State, Brussels Regional Economy, since 1977; *b* Brussels, 10 May 1931; *m* 1960, Marie-Louise Angenent; one *s* one *d*. *Educ:* Univ. Libre de Bruxelles (DenD, DèsSc); Columbia Univ., USA. Assistant, Univ. Libre de Bruxelles, 1956-58, now Prof.; Financial Adv., Inst. Nat. d'Etudes pour le Développement du Bas-Congo, 1958-59; Legal Adv., Commn of Brussels Stock Exchange, 1956-60; Dep. Dir, Office of Econ. Programming, 1961; Director of Cabinet: of Min. of Econ. Affairs and Power, 1961-65; of Dep. Prime Minister responsible for co-ordination of Econ. Policy, 1965. Mayor, Anderlecht, 1966-; Deputy from Brussels, 1968; Minister of Econ. Affairs, 1972; Vice-Pres., Commn of the European Communities, 1973-77. Officer, Order of Leopold II. *Publications:* various books and articles on economics, financial and political topics. *Address:* 1 Avenue des Crocus, 1070 Brussels, Belgium.

SIMONS, (Alfred) Murray; HM Diplomatic Service; Head of South East Asian Department, Foreign and Commonwealth Office, since 1975; *b* 9 Aug. 1927; *s* of late Louis Simons and of Fay Simons; *m* 1975, Patricia Jill, *d* of late David and May Barclay, Westbury on Trym, Bristol; one *s*. *Educ:* City of London Sch.; Magdalen Coll., Oxford (MA). FO, 1951; 3rd Sec., Moscow, 1952-55; FO, 1955-56; Columbia Univ., 1956; 2nd Sec., Bogota, 1957; 1st Sec., Office of Comr-Gen. for SE Asia, Singapore, 1958-61; FO, 1961-64; 1st Sec., British High Commn, New Delhi, 1964-68; FCO, 1968-71; Counsellor, 1969; British Embassy, Washington, 1971-75. *Recreations:* tennis, theatre. *Address:* 128 Longland Drive, N2O. *T:* 01-445 0896.

SIMPSON, Alan, MA, DPhil Oxon, LHD, LLD; President of Vassar College, Poughkeepsie, NY, since 1964; *b* Gateshead, Durham, England, 23 July 1912; *s* of George Hardwick Simpson and Isabella Simpson (*née* Graham); *m* 1938, Mary McQueen McEldowney, Chicago Heights, Ill; one *s* two *d*. *Educ:* Worcester Coll., Oxford (BA); Merton Coll., Oxford (MA, DPhil); Harvard Univ. (Commonwealth Fellow). Served War of 1939-45, RA, Major. Sen. Lectr in Modern British History and American History, Univ. of St Andrews, and Lectr in Constitutional Law, Law Sch., University Coll., Dundee, 1938-46; Asst Prof. of History, Univ. of Chicago, 1946-54; Associate Prof., 1954-59; Thomas E. Donnelley Prof. of History and Dean of the College, Univ. of Chicago, 1959-64. Member Board of Trustees: Colonial Williamsburg; Commn Independent Colls and Univs, State of NY; Amer. Hist. Assoc.; Conf. on British Studies; Amer. Antiquarian Soc.; Committee on the Second Regional Plan. Former Member: Council of the Inst. of Early Amer. History and Culture, Williamsburg, Va, 1957-60; Midwest Conf. of British Historians (Co-Founder, 1954; Sec., 1954-61); Commn on Academic Affairs and Bd of Dirs, Amer. Council on Educn; Commn on Liberal Learning, Assoc. of Amer. Colls; Hudson River Valley Commn. *Publications:* (Co-Editor) The People Shall Judge: Readings in the Formation of American Policy, 1949; Puritanism in Old and New England, 1955; The Wealth of the Gentry, 1540-1660: East Anglian Studies, 1961; (Co-Editor with Mary Simpson): Diary of King Philips War by Benjamin Church, 1975; I Too Am Here: a selection of letters of Jane Welsh Carlyle, 1976. *Address:* Vassar College, Poughkeepsie, New York, NY 12601, USA; Yellow Gate Farm, Little Compton, RI, USA. *Clubs:* Century (New York); Tavern (Chicago).

SIMPSON, Alan; author and scriptwriter since 1951 (in collaboration with Ray Galton, *qv*); *b* 27 Nov. 1929; *s* of Francis and Lilian Simpson; *m* 1958, Kathleen Phillips. *Educ:* Mitcham Grammar Sch. *Television:* Hancock's Half Hour, 1954-61; Comedy Playhouse, 1962-63; Steptoe and Son, 1962-, US TV Version, Sanford and Son, 1971-; Galton-Simpson Comedy, 1969; Clochemerle, 1971; Casanova, 1974; Dawson's Weekly, 1975; The Galton and Simpson Playhouse, 1976; *films:* The Rebel, 1960; The Bargee, 1963; The Wrong Arm of the Law, 1963; The Spy with a Cold Nose, 1966; Loot, 1969; Steptoe and Son, 1971; Steptoe and Son Ride Again, 1973; Den Siste Fleksnes (Norway), 1974; *theatre:* Way Out in Piccadilly, 1966; The Wind in the Sassafras Trees, 1968. Awards: Scriptwriters of the Year, 1959 (Guild of TV Producers and Directors); Best TV Comedy Series (Steptoe and Son, 1962/3/4/5 (Screenwriters Guild)); John Logie Baird Award (for outstanding contribution to Television), 1964; Best Comedy Series (Steptoe and Son, Dutch TV), 1966; Best Comedy Screenplay, Screenwriters Guild, 1972. *Publications:* (jointly with Ray Galton, *qv*): Hancock, 1961; Steptoe and Son, 1963; The Reunion and Other Plays, 1966; Hancock Scripts, 1974. *Recreations:* Hampton FC (Pres.), fishing. *Address:* c/o ALS Management Ltd, 67 Brook Street, W1. *T:* 01-629 9121.

SIMPSON, Alan; a Recorder of the Crown Court, since 1975; *b* 17 April 1937; *s* of William Henry Simpson and Gladys Simpson; *m* 1965, Maureen O'Shea; one *s* one *d*. *Educ:* Leeds Grammar Sch.; Corpus Christi Coll., Oxford (MA). Called to the Bar, Inner Temple, 1962. *Recreations:* music, books, sport (especially cricket and boxing). *Address:* The Keep, 41 Colton Road, Whitkirk, Leeds LS15 9AA. *T:* Leeds 605448. *Club:* St Anne's (Leeds).

SIMPSON, Alfred Henry; Hon. Mr Justice Simpson; Puisne Judge, High Court of Kenya, since 1967; *b* 29 Oct. 1914; *s* of John Robertson Simpson, Dundee; *m* 1941, Hilda Corson Rodgers; one *d*. *Educ:* Grove Academy; St Andrews University; Edinburgh University. MA St Andrews, 1935; LLB Edinburgh, 1938 and Solicitor. Served in RASC, 1940-46, Middle East and Italy; Military Mission to the Italian Army and Allied Commission, Austria. Legal Officer, BMA, Cyrenaica, 1946-48. Member of the Faculty of Advocates, 1952. Crown Counsel, Singapore, 1948-56; Legal Draftsman, Gold Coast, 1956; Solicitor-General, Ghana, 1957, then Puisne Judge, Supreme Court, 1957-61; Puisne Judge, Combined Judiciary of Sarawak, North Borneo and Brunei, 1962; Senior Puisne Judge, Fedn of Malaysia High Court in Borneo, 1964; Reader, Faculty of Law, ANU, Canberra, 1965; Barrister-at-Law, NSW, 1967. *Publication:* (with others) The Laws of Singapore, revised edn, 1955. *Recreation:* golf. *Address:* PO Box 30041, Nairobi, Kenya. *Clubs:* Royal Commonwealth Society; Royal Canberra Golf.

SIMPSON, Alfred Moxon, CMG 1959; Chairman: Simpson Pope Ltd; SA Telecasters Ltd; *b* 17 Nov. 1910; *s* of late A. A. Simpson, CMG, CBE; *m* 1938, Elizabeth Robson Cleland; one *s*. *Educ:* St Peter's College; University of Adelaide, (BSc). Associate (Commerce) of Univ. of Adelaide, 1940. Pres. Adelaide Chamber of Commerce, 1950-52; Sen. Vice-Pres. Associated Chambers of Commerce of Aust., 1953-55; Pres. SA Chamber of Manufrs, 1956-58; Pres. Associated Chambers of Manufrs of Aust., 1957-58. Director: Adelaide Steamship Co. Ltd; Bank of Adelaide; Elder Smith Goldsbrough Mort Ltd; QBE Insurance Group Ltd. Mem. Hulme Cttee on Rates of Depreciation, 1956. *Recreations:* carpentry, ski-ing. *Address:* 31 Heatherbank Terrace, Stonyfell, SA 5066, Australia. *T:* 31 12 85. *Clubs:* Adelaide, Mt Lofty Ski (Adelaide); Melbourne (Melbourne); Union (Sydney).

SIMPSON, Prof. (Cedric) Keith, CBE 1975; MA Oxon, MD London (Path.), FRCP; FRCPath; DMJ; Professor and Head of Department of Forensic Medicine to University of London, 1962-72, Professor Emeritus, since 1972 (Reader, 1946-62); Head of Department of Forensic Medicine, Guy's Hospital Medical School; *b* 20 July 1907; *s* of Dr George Herbert Simpson, Brighton, Sussex; *m* 1st, Mary McCartney Buchanan (*d* 1955); one *s* two *d*; 2nd, 1956, Jean Anderson Scott Dunn (*d* 1976). *Educ:* Brighton and Hove Grammar School, Sussex; University of London. Guy's Hospital Medical School: Gold Medallist (Golding-Bird) in Bacteriology, 1927; Beaney Prizeman, 1927; Gull Scholar and Astley Cooper Student, 1932; Lecturer in Pathology, 1932-37; Lecturer in Forensic Medicine, 1937-47; Lecturer in Forensic Med., Oxford Univ., 1961-73. Examiner in Forensic Medicine to Univs: London, 1945; St Andrews, 1948; Leeds, 1950; NUI, 1952-64; Wales, 1954; Oxford, 1957; Glasgow, 1964. Member, Home Office Scientific Advisory Council. Harvard Associate in Police Science, 1952; Medallist, Strasbourg University, 1954; President: Medico-Legal Society, 1961; British Assoc. in Forensic Medicine, 1966; British Council Lecturer, France 1954, Denmark 1961, India 1974. Corresponding Member: Société de Médicine Légale; Amer. Acad. of Forensic Sciences; Spanish and Italian Socs of Legal Medicine. Hon. MD, Ghent; Hon. LLD Edinburgh, 1976. *Publications:* Forensic Medicine, 1947 (7th edn, 1974; awarded RSA Swiney Prize, 1958); Modern Trends in Forensic Medicine, 1953 (2nd edn 1967); Doctor's Guide to Court, 1962 (2nd edn 1966); (ed) Taylor's Principles and Practice of Medical Jurisprudence, 12th edn, 1965; contrib. to medical and scientific journals. *Address:* Department of Forensic Medicine, Guy's Hospital, SE1. *T:* 01-407 0378; Dancers End Lodge, Tring, Herts. *Club:* Athenæum.

SIMPSON, Charles Valentine George; former Director: Wigham Poland Midlands Ltd; Walker, Moate, Simpson & Co. Ltd, Birmingham, since 1960; Wigham-Richardson and Bevingtons (Midlands) Ltd; *b* 14 Feb. 1900; 2nd *s* of Alexander Simpson, Ayrshire; *m*; two *s* one *d*; 2nd, Muriel Edwina, *e d* of Rev. Edwin Jones, Montgomeryshire; one *s*. *Educ:* Tindal Street Elementary Sch., Birmingham. RMLI, 1915-19; RNVR, 1939-45, rank of Lt-Comdr; served China, Med., Iceland, Germany. Councillor, Birmingham, 1935, Alderman, 1949-74; Chairman, Airports Cttee, 1950, Public Works Cttee, 1966-68; Lord Mayor, City of Birmingham, 1968-69. President: RN Assoc.,

City of Birmingham; Handsworth Wood Residents Assoc.; Birmingham Br., RNLI; County Pres., Birmingham Royal British Legion; Vice-Pres., Birmingham Bn, Boys' Brigade; Life Mem., Court of Governors, Birmingham Univ. Successfully inaugurated appeal, 1969, for a new lifeboat to be called City of Birmingham. *Recreations:* bowls, foreign travel (preferably by caravan). *Address:* 16 Knowle Wood Road, Dorridge, Warwickshire. *T:* Knowle 2427; (business) 021-236 7831. *Club:* Caravan.

SIMPSON, Commander Cortlandt James Woore, CBE 1956; DSC 1945; retired 1961; *b* 2 Sept. 1911; *s* of late Rear-Admiral C. H. Simpson, CBE, and, Edith Octavia (*née* Busby); *m* 1st, 1932, Lettice Mary Johnstone; 2nd, 1955, Ann Margaret Cubitt (*née* Tooth); 3rd, 1972, Joan Mary Watson; one *d*. *Educ:* St Ronans, Worthing; RN College, Dartmouth; London Univ. (BSc Engineering, Hons) Joined RN (Dartmouth), 1925; Lieut, 1934. Served War of 1939-45 in Home and Mediterranean Fleets; Commander, 1948. Summer expeditions to Greenland, 1950, 1951; Leader of British North Greenland Expedition, 1952-54. Polar Medal, 1954; Royal Geographical Society, Founder's Medal, 1955. *Recreations:* mountaineering, sailing, walking. *Publication:* North Ice, 1957. *Address:* Garden House, Bruisyard, Saxmundham, Suffolk. *Club:* Alpine.

SIMPSON, Sir Cyril; *see* Simpson, Sir J. C. F.

SIMPSON, Prof. David Rae Fisher; Director of The Fraser of Allander Institute, University of Strathclyde, since 1975; *b* 29 Nov. 1936; *s* of David Ebenezer Simpson and Roberta Muriel Wilson. *Educ:* Skerry's Coll.; Edinburgh and Harvard Univs. MA 1st cl. hons Econs Edinburgh; PhD Econs Harvard. Instr in Econs, Harvard Univ., 1963-64; Assoc. Statistician, UN Hdqtrs, NY, 1964-65; Res. Officer, Econ. Res. Inst., Dublin, 1965-67; Lectr in Polit. Economy, UCL, 1967-69; Sen. Lectr in Econs, Univ. of Stirling, 1969-74. Contested (SNP) Berwick and E Lothian Division, 1970 and Feb. 1974. *Publications:* Problems of Input-Output Tables and Analysis, 1966; General Equilibrium Analysis, 1975; articles in Econometrica, Rev. Econs and Statistics, Scientific American. *Recreations:* golf, tennis, walking. *Address:* 15 Ochlochy Park, Dunblane, Perthshire. *T:* Dunblane 822299.

SIMPSON, Dennis Charles; Industrial Director for Wales, Welsh Office, since 1975; *b* 24 Oct. 1931; *s* of late Arthur and Helen Simpson; *m* 1964, Margery Bruce Anderson; three *s* one *d*. *Educ:* Manchester Univ. (BA). FInstPS. 2nd Lieut Royal Signals, 1952-54; commercial appts, Philips Electrical Industries, 1956-63; Group Purchasing Manager: STC Ltd, 1963-66; Rank Organisation, 1966-69; Gen. Man., Cam Gears (S Wales) Ltd, 1969-72; Industrial Dir for Wales, Dept of Industry, 1972-75. *Recreations:* golf, bridge, reading war histories. *Address:* 9 Langland Bay Road, Langland, Swansea, West Glamorgan. *T:* Swansea 66648. *Club:* Langland Bay Golf.

SIMPSON, Edward Hugh, CB 1976; Deputy Secretary, Department of Education and Science, since 1973; *b* 10 Dec. 1922; *o s* of Hugh and Mary Simpson, of Brookfield, Ballymena, Co. Antrim; *m* 1947, Gladys Rebecca, *er d* of Samuel and Elizabeth Gibson, Ernevale, Kesh, Co. Fermanagh; one *s* one *d*. *Educ:* Coleraine Academical Institution; Queen's Univ., Belfast; Christ's Coll., Cambridge (Scholar). Dept of the Foreign Office, 1942-45; Min. of Education, 1947-50 and 1952-56; HM Treasury, 1950-52; Commonwealth Fund Fellow, USA, 1956-57; Private Sec. to Lord President of Council and Lord Privy Seal, 1957-60; Dep. Dir, Commonwealth Educn Liaison Unit, 1960-62; Sec., Commonwealth Educn Conf., New Delhi, 1962; Asst Sec., DES, 1962-68; Under-Sec., Civil Service Dept, 1968-71, DES, 1971-73. *Address:* 40 Frays Avenue, West Drayton, Mddx. *T:* West Drayton 43417.

SIMPSON, Esther Eleanor, MD, FRCP, FFCM, DPH, DCH; Senior Principal Medical Officer, Department of Education and Science, and Department of Health and Social Security; *b* 28 May 1919. *Educ:* Kendal High Sch.; London Univ. Medical Officer, London County Council, then to Province of Natal Centre, Inst. of Child Health; joined Medical Br., Min. of Education, 1961. *Recreations:* music, reading, walking. *Address:* 19 Belsize Lane, NW3 5AG. *T:* 01-794 4400.

SIMPSON, Ffreebairn Liddon, CMG 1967; General Manager, Central Water Authority, Mauritius, since 1976; *b* 11 July 1916; *s* of late James Liddon Simpson and of Dorothy (*née* Blyth); *m* 1947, Dorina Laura Magda, MBE (*née* Ilieva); one *s*. *Educ:* Westminster School; Trinity College, Cambridge. HM Diplomatic/Foreign Service, 1939-48; HM Treasury, 1948-50; Administrative Officer, Gold Coast, 1950-55; Dep. Colonial Sec., Mauritius, 1955; Perm. Secretary: Min. of Works and

Internal Communications, 1961; Premier's Office, 1966; Sec. to the Cabinet, Mauritius, 1967-76. *Recreations:* reading, philately. *Address:* Floreal, Mauritius. *Clubs:* United Oxford & Cambridge University; Stella Clavisque; Grand' Baie Yacht (Mauritius).

SIMPSON, General Sir Frank (Ernest Wallace), GBE 1953 (KBE 1947); KCB 1951 (CB 1944); DSO 1940; Chief Royal Engineer, 1961-67; Governor of Royal Hospital, Chelsea, 1961-69; *b* 21 March 1899; *s* of late Major Robert Wallace Simpson, MC; *m* 1934, Charlotte Dulcie Margaret Cooke; two *d*. *Educ:* Bedford School; Royal Military Academy, Woolwich; Trinity Hall, Cambridge. Commissioned in Royal Engineers, 1916; Lt-Col 1939; Col 1942; Maj.-Gen. 1944; Lt-Gen. 1946; Gen. 1950; served European War of 1914-18, France and Belgium (despatches, British War Medal, Victory Medal); Afghanistan and NW Frontier, 1919 (Medal with clasp); France, 1939-40 (DSO, 1939-45 Star, Defence Medal); Vice CIGS, 1946-48; GOC-in-C, Western Command, UK, 1948-51; Commandant, Imperial Defence College, 1952-54. ADC General to the King, 1951-52, to the Queen, 1952-54; retired pay, 1954; Mem. Eastern Electricity Board, 1954-63; Colonel Commandant: Royal Pioneer Corps, 1950-61; RE, 1954-67. Adviser to West Africa Cttee, 1956-66; Dir, United Services Trustee, 1961-69. JP Essex, 1955-61; DL Essex, 1956-65. Kt Gr Officer, Order of Orange-Nassau (with Swords), 1947. *Address:* 5 Northfields Close, Bath, Avon. *Clubs:* Naval and Military; MCC; Bath and County (Bath).

SIMPSON, Gerald Gordon, CMG 1967; HM Diplomatic Service, resigned; *b* 1 Sept. 1918; *s* of Major Gerald Gordon Simpson; *m* 1943, Peggy Ena Williams; one *d*. *Educ:* Royal Grammar Sch., Newcastle upon Tyne. Served in British and Indian Armies, 1938-46; (retd as Lt-Col). Ministry of Labour (seconded to Control Commission for Germany), 1947-48. Joined HM Foreign Service, 1948; served in: Ankara, 1950-52; Budapest, 1952-54; Foreign Office, 1954-58; Santiago de Chile, 1958-61; Washington, 1961-62; New York, 1962-65; Consul-Gen., Houston, 1965-68; seconded to Overseas Cttee of Unilever, 1969; Consul-Gen., Düsseldorf, 1970-74. *Recreations:* golf, gardening, painting; contemplating the folly of politicians. *Address:* Furnace Place, Haslemere, Surrey. *T:* Haslemere 51739.

SIMPSON, Gordon Russell, DSO 1944 and Bar 1945; TD; stockbroker; Partner, Bell, Cowan & Co. (now Bell, Lawrie, Macgregor & Co.), since 1938; *b* 2 Jan. 1917; *s* of A. Russell Simpson, WS; *m* 1943, Marion Elizabeth King (*d* 1976); two *s*. *Educ:* Rugby School. Served with 2nd Lothians and Border Horse, 1939-46 (comd 1944-46). Chm., Edinburgh Stock Exchange, 1961-63; Chm., Scottish Stock Exchange, 1965-66; Pres., Council of Associated Stock Exchanges, 1971-73; Dep. Chm., Stock Exchange, 1973-. Dir, General Accident Fire & Life Assurance Corp. Ltd, 1967; Chm., British Investment Trust Ltd, 1977. Member of Queen's Body Guard for Scotland (Royal Company of Archers). *Recreations:* music, ski-ing, archery. *Address:* Arntomie, Port of Menteith, Perthshire FK8 3RD. *Club:* New (Edinburgh).

SIMPSON, Maj.-Gen. Hamilton Wilkie, CB 1945; DSO 1940; late Royal Marines; *b* 1895. 2nd Lt Royal Marines, 1913; served European War, 1914-18; War of 1939-45 (DSO); retired list, 1946. *Address:* Briar Dene, Wellswood Avenue, Torquay, Devon TQ1 2QE.

SIMPSON, Henry George, OBE 1968; Controller of Housing to Greater London Council since 1974; *b* 27 April 1917; *s* of late William James and late Alice Simpson; *m* 1938, Gladys Lee; one *s*. *Educ:* Enfield Grammar School. FIH, FSVA. War Service 1940-46, Royal Fusiliers. Dir of Housing and Property Services, London Borough of Lambeth, 1962-72; Dir-Gen., Northern Ireland Housing Exec., 1972-74. *Recreations:* gardening, hi-fi. *Address:* c/o Greater London Council, County Hall, SE1 7PB.

SIMPSON, Ian; Principal, St Martin's School of Art, London, since 1972; *b* 12 Nov. 1933; *s* of Herbert William and Elsie Simpson; *m* 1958, Joan (*née* Charlton); two *s* one *d*. *Educ:* Bede Grammar Sch., Sunderland; Sunderland Coll. of Art; Royal Coll. of Art. ARCA 1958. Freelance artist and illustrator, 1958-63; Hornsey Coll. of Art: Lectr, 1963-66; Head, Dept of Visual Research, 1966-69; Head, Dept of Co-ordinated Studies, 1969-72. Exhibited various exhibns, Britain, USA, etc; one-man exhibn, Cambridge, 1975. *Publications:* Eyeline, 1968; Drawing: seeing and observation, 1973; Picture Making, 1973; *Television Programmes:* Eyeline (10 programmes), 1968, 1969; Picture Making (10 programmes), 1973, 1976; Reading the Signs (5 programmes), 1977-78. *Recreations:* reading, music. *Address:* 35 Slades Hill, Enfield, Mddx EN2 7DN. *T:* 01-363 8989.

SIMPSON, Sir James Dyer, Kt 1946; b 21 Aug. 1888; m Lucy Beavan; one s. Chief General Manager Royal Insurance Co. and The Liverpool & London & Globe Insurance Co.; retired 1949; Director General Administrative Services, Ministry of Supply, 1942. Past Chairman, British Insurance Assoc.; Insurance Institute of Liverpool. Chm., Liverpool Caledonian Assoc., 1976. JP (Liverpool) 1944-50. Publications: pamphlets on insurance. Address: Carlton Hotel, East Cliff, Bournemouth, Dorset. Club: Pilgrims.

SIMPSON, James Joseph Trevor, KBE (Hon.) 1965 (CBE 1957); (forename James added by deed poll, 1965); Chairman and Managing Director, James Simpson & Co. Ltd; retired as Chairman, Uganda Development Corporation, Ltd (1952-64); b 9 Jan. 1908; 2nd s of late Lieut-Colonel Herbert Simpson, OBE, MC, and of Mrs Henrietta Augusta Simpson; m 1940, Enid Florence (née Danzelman). Educ: Ardingly College, Sussex. Branch Manager, Vacuum Oil Co., Nakuru, Nairobi, Dar es Salaam, Mombasa, Kampala, 1932-46; General Manager, The Uganda Company Ltd, 1947-52; President, Uganda Chamber of Commerce, 1941, 1946-50. Member: Uganda Executive Council, 1952-55; Uganda Legislative Council, 1950-58 (Chm. Representative Members Organization 1951-58); E African Legislative Assembly, 1957-60, 1962-63; E African Railways and Harbours, Transport Advisory Council, 1948-61; E African Industrial Council, 1947-61; Uganda Electricity Bd, 1955-60; East African Airways Corporation, 1958-73; Minister of Economic Affairs, Uganda, 1962-63. Recreations: golf, bridge. Address: PO Box 48816, Nairobi, Kenya; c/o PO Box 4343, Kampala, Uganda. Clubs: East India, Sports and Public Schools; Muthaiga, Nairobi (Kenya).

SIMPSON, Sir (John) Cyril (Finucane), 3rd Bt, cr 1935; retired; b 10 Feb. 1899; s of Sir Frank Robert Simpson, 1st Bt, CB, and Alice Matilda (d 1950), d of late James Finucane Draper; S brother, 1968; m 1st, 1936, Betty (marr. diss. 1944), d of Frank J. Lambert; 2nd, 1945, Maria Teresa, d of Captain John Sutherland Harvey, Romerillo, Biarritz; no c. Educ: Rugby; Queen's Coll., Oxford. Stockbroker, 1922-63. Served European War, 1914-18, Pilot in RNAS; served abroad, 1917-18. Won Rackets Amateur Championship three years in succession and Open Championship two years, Doubles Championship four years; US Doubles Championship, 1928; Canadian Doubles Championship, 1924. Recreation: shooting. Heir: none. Address: Bradley Hall, Wylam, Northumberland. T: Wylam 2246. Clubs: Buck's; Northern Counties (Newcastle upon Tyne); Vincent's (Oxford).

SIMPSON, John Ferguson, FRCS; Consulting Surgeon to Ear, Nose and Throat Department, St Mary's Hospital, retired; formerly Civil Consultant, Ministry of Aviation; b 10 Oct. 1902; s of late Col P. J. Simpson, DSO, FRCVS, Maidenhead; m 1947, Winifred Beatrice Rood; one s one d. Educ: Reading Sch.; St Mary's Hosp. FRCS 1929; MRCS, LRCP 1926. Formerly: Lectr in Diseases of the Ear, Nose and Throat, Univ. of London; Specialist in Otorhino-laryngology, RAF; Hon. Surg. Royal Nat. Throat, Nose and Ear Hosp. FRSocMed (ex-President Section of Otology; Hon. Life Mem., Section of Laryngology). Publications: A Synopsis of Otorhinolaryngology (jointly), 1957. Chapters: Operative Surgery, 1957; ENT Diseases, 1965. Recreations: entomology; formerly Rugby football. Address: Long Barn, Waverley Abbey, Farnham, Surrey. T: Runfold 2555.

SIMPSON, John Liddle, CMG 1958; TD 1950; barrister; b 9 Oct. 1912; s of late James Simpson; m 1st, 1939, Nellie Lavender Mussett (d 1944); 2nd, 1959, Ursula Vaughan Washington (née Rigby). Educ: George Watson's Coll.; Edinburgh Univ. (MA, DLitt). Barrister, Middle Temple, 1937. Served War of 1939-45; GSO1, 1945. Principal, Control Office for Germany and Austria, 1946; Senior legal assistant, FO (German Section), 1948; transferred to Foreign (now Diplomatic) Service and promoted Counsellor, 1954; Legal Counsellor, FO, 1954-59 and 1961-68; Legal Adviser, United Kingdom Mission to the United Nations, New York, 1959-61; Dep. Legal Adviser, 1968-71; Second Legal Adviser, 1971-72, FCO; returned to practice, 1973. Freeman, City of London, 1976. Publications: Germany and the North Atlantic Community: A Legal Survey (with M. E. Bathurst), 1956; International Arbitration; Law and Practice (with Hazel Fox), 1959; articles and notes in legal journals. Address: 5 Paper Buildings, Temple, EC4Y 7HB. T: 01-353 8494; 137a Ashley Gardens, Thirleby Road, SW1P 1HN. T: 01-834 4814.

SIMPSON, Keith; see Simpson, Cedric K.

SIMPSON, Kenneth John, CMG 1961; HM Diplomatic Service, retired; b 5 Feb. 1914; s of Bernard and Ann Simpson,

Millhouses, Sheffield; m 1939, Harriet (Shan) Hughes; three s. Educ: Downing College, Cambridge. Entered HM Foreign (now Diplomatic) Service, 1937; lately Consul-Gen., Hanoi and Stuttgart, Inspector, Diplomatic Service and Counsellor, FCO. Address: 76 Wood Ride, Petts Wood, Kent. T: Orpington 24710.

SIMPSON, Oliver, CB 1977; MA, PhD, FInstP; Chief Scientist, Deputy Under-Secretary of State, Home Office, since 1974; b 28 Oct. 1924; y s of late Sir George C. Simpson, KCB, FRS, and Dorothy (née Stephen); m 1946, Joan, d of late Walter and Maud Morgan; one s (and one s decd). Educ: Highgate Sch.; Trinity Coll., Cambridge. War Service: Admiralty Research Laboratory, Teddington, on submarine detection, 1944-46. Research Scholar, 1946-49, Fellow of Trinity Coll., Cambridge, 1949-53; Asst Prof. of Physics, Univ. of Michigan, USA, 1949-52; Imperial Chemical Industries Fellow in Dept. of Theoretical Chemistry, Cambridge, 1952-53; joined Services Electronics Research Laboratory, Admty, 1953, Head of Solid State Physics, 1956-63; Supt, Basic Physics Div., Nat. Physical Laboratory, 1964-66; Dep. Dir, Nat. Physical Laboratory, 1966-69; Under-Sec., Cabinet Office, 1969-74. Publications: articles in scientific jls on infra-red detectors, semiconductors, fluorescence and standards of measurement. Address: 4 Highbury Road, Wimbledon, SW19. T: 01-946 3871. Club: Athenæum.

SIMPSON, Peter Miller, RDI 1974; FSIA; company director; Director, Bute Looms Ltd, since 1973; b 5 April 1921; s of David Simpson and Annie Simpson; m 1964, Orma Macallum; one s one d. Educ: Perth High Sch.; Dundee Coll. of Art (DA 1950). MSIA 1956, FSIA 1974. Study and work, USA, 1950-53. Mem. Scottish Cttee, Design Council. Recreations: gardening, pottery, walking. Address: 35 Lovers Lane, Scone, Perth. T: Perth 51573. Clubs: Caledonian; Arts (Edinburgh).

SIMPSON, Rayene Stewart, VC 1969; DCM 1964; with Australian Embassy, Tokyo, since 1972; b Sydney, Australia, 16 Feb. 1926; Australian parents (British stock); m 1952, Shoko Simpson (née Sakai); no c. Educ: Carlingford Public Sch., Sydney, Australia. Served War of 1939-45 (Pacific theatre): enlisted in AIF, 1944; discharged, 1947. Seasonal worker and merchant seaman, 1947-50; enlisted in Aust. Regular Army, 1951; served in Korea, 1951-54, with 3rd Bn, The Royal Australian Regt; served in Malaya, Oct. 1955-57, 2nd Bn, The Royal Australian Regt; 1st SAS, 1957-62; Aust. Army Trg Team, Vietnam (AATTV), July 1962-63; 1st SAS, July 1963-64; Aust. Army Trg Team, Vietnam (AATTV) July-Sept. 1964 (wounded in action, DCM, in hosp. 8 mths); 1st Bn City of Sydney Regt (Commando), 1965-66 (discharged 1966); re-enlisted Aust. Regular Army in Saigon, 1967, and served with AATTV (VC), in S Vietnam, 1970 (discharged from Army, 1970, after 21 years). Sales Representative, Caldbeck-Macgrigor & Co., Tokyo, 1970. Recreations: walking, reading (military history), watching boxing. Address: Australian Embassy, 1-14 Mita 2 Chome, Minato-Ku, Tokyo 108, Japan; No 5-30-1 Chome, Yayoicho, Nakano-ku, Tokyo 164, Japan. T: 373 1066. Clubs: Returned Services League (RSL), Paddington-Woollahra Sub-Branch (Sydney).

SIMPSON, Rev. Canon Rennie, MVO 1974; MA Lambeth 1970; Canon Residentiary, since 1974, Vice-Dean, since 1975, Chester Cathedral; b 13 Jan. 1920; o s of late Doctor Taylor Simpson and late May Simpson, Rishton; m 1949, Margaret, er d of late Herbert Hardy and Olive Hardy, South Kirkby; one s one d. Educ: Blackburn Tech. Coll.; Kelham Theol College. Curate of S Elmsall, Yorks, 1945-49; Succentor of Blackburn Cath., 1949-52; Sacrist and Minor Canon of St Paul's Cath., 1952-58, Hon. Minor Canon, 1958-, Jun. Cardinal, 1954-55, Sen. Cardinal, 1955-58; Vicar of John Keble Church, Mill Hill, 1958-63; Precentor, 1963-74, Acting Sacrist, 1973-74, Westminster Abbey. Chaplain, RNVR, 1953-55; Dep. Chaplain, Gt Ormond St Hosp., 1954-58; Asst Chaplain, 1956-64, Officiating Chaplain, 1964-, Sub-Prelate, 1973-, Order of St John of Jerusalem; Deputy Priest to the Queen, 1956-67; Priest-in-Ordinary to the Queen, 1967-74. Life Governor, Imperial Cancer Research Fund, 1963. Liveryman of Waxchandlers' Co. and Freeman of City of London, 1955. Jt Hon. Treas., Corp. Sons of the Clergy, 1967-74; Governor, King's School, Chester, 1974-. Recreations: football, cricket, theatre. Address: 13 Abbey Street, Chester CH1 2JF. T: Chester 20157.

SIMPSON, Rt. Hon. Dr Robert, PC (N Ireland) 1970; MP (U) Mid-Antrim, Parliament of Northern Ireland, 1953-72; b 3 July 1923; er s of Samuel and Agnes Simpson, Craigbilly, Ballymena; m 1954, Dorothy Isobel, 2nd d of Dr Robert Strawbridge, MA, DD, and Anne Strawbridge; two s one d. Educ: Ballymena Academy; Queen's University, Belfast. MB, BCh, BAO, 1946. House Surgeon, Belfast City Hosp., 1947; Resident Anaesthetist,

Royal Infirmary, Leicester, 1948; GP, Ballymena, Co. Antrim, 1949-; Medical Correspondent, Belfast Telegraph and Leicester Mercury; Medical Representative, NI, Europ Assistance; Medical Officer, Flexibox Ltd, Ballymena, Northern Dairies Ltd. Founder Chm., Ballymena Round Table, 1951. NI Deleg. to CPA Conf. in NZ and Australia, 1965. Minister of Community Relations, N Ireland, 1969-71. Director, John Atkinson & Co., etc. *Publications:* contribs to newspapers and magazines on medical, country and travel subjects. *Recreations:* the country, writing, music, France, food, travel. *Address:* Random Cottage, Craigbilly, Ballymena, Co. Antrim. *T:* Ballymena 3105. *Club:* Royal Over-Seas League.

SIMPSON, Robert Wilfred Levick, DMus; composer; BBC Music Producer, since 1951; *b* Leamington, Warwickshire, 2 March 1921; *s* of Robert Warren Simpson (British) and Helena Hendrika Govaars (Dutch); *m* 1946, Bessie Fraser. *Educ:* Westminster City Sch.; studied with Herbert Howells. DMus (Dunelm) 1952. Holder of: Carl Nielsen Gold Medal (Denmark), 1956; Medal of Honor of Bruckner Soc. of America, 1962. Mem., British Astronomical Assoc.; FRAS. *Compositions:* Symphonies: No 1, 1951 (recorded); No 2, 1956; No 3, 1962 (recorded); No 4, 1972; No 5, 1972; Nos 6 and 7, 1977; Piano Concerto, 1967; Violin Concerto, 1959; String Quartets: No 1, 1952 (recorded); No 2, 1953; No 3, 1954; No 4, 1973; No 5, 1974; No 6, 1975; No 7, 1977; Piano Sonata, 1946; Variations and Finale on a Theme of Haydn, for piano, 1948; Allegro Deciso, for string orchestra (from String Quartet No 3); Canzona for Brass, 1958 (recorded); Variations and Fugue for recorder and string quartet, 1959; Trio for clarinet, cello and piano, 1967; Quintet for clarinet, and strings, 1968 (recorded); Incidental Music to Ibsen's The Pretenders, 1965; Energy, Symphonic Study for brass band (test piece for 1971 World Championship); Quartet for horn, violin, cello and piano, 1976; *Media morte in vita sumus* (Motet for choir, brass, and timpani) 1975; Incidental Music to Milton's Samson Agonistes, 1974. *Publications:* Carl Nielsen, Symphonist, 1952; The Essence of Bruckner, 1966; numerous articles in various jls and three BBC booklets (Bruckner and the Symphony, Sibelius and Nielsen, and The Beethoven Symphonies); contrib. to: Encycl. Brit.; Musik in Geschichte und Gegenwart; (ed) The Symphony (Pelican), 1966. *Recreation:* astronomy. *Address:* Cedar Cottage, Chearsley, Aylesbury, Bucks HP18 0DA. *T:* Long Crendon 208436.

SIMPSON, Robin Muschamp Garry, QC 1971; a Recorder of the Crown Court, since 1976; *b* 19 June 1927; *s* of Ronald Maitland Simpson, actor and Lila Maravan Simpson (*née* Muschamp); *m* 1st, 1956, Avril Carolyn Harrisson; one *s* one *d*; 2nd, 1968, Mary Faith Laughton-Scott; one *s* one *d*. *Educ:* Charterhouse; Peterhouse, Cambridge (BA). Called to Bar, Middle Temple, 1951. Former Mem., Surrey and S London Sessions; Member: Central Criminal Court Bar Mess; SE Circuit. Appeal Steward, British Boxing Bd of Control. *Recreations:* riding, fox-hunting, sailing. *Address:* 9 Drayton Gardens, SW10. *T:* 01-373 3284.

SIMPSON, S(amuel) Leonard, MA, MD (Cambridge); FRCP; Chairman: S. Simpson, Ltd; Simpson (Piccadilly) Ltd; Daks-Simpson Ltd; President: Simpson Imports Ltd; Daks USA Inc., New York; Daks (Canada) Ltd, Montreal; Consultant in Industrial Psychology; Hon. Consulting Endocrinologist, St Mary's Hospital, London; *s* of late Simeon Simpson; *m* 1940, Heddy Monique, Baroness de Podmaniczky; one *d*. *Educ:* Westminster City School; Downing Coll., Cambridge. 1st Class Hons, Nat. Sci. Tripos, Pts I and II Physiology. Post-grad. research in America, Germany and Lister Institute, London. Member: Council, CBI (Past Mem., Grand Council of FBI); Council, Nat. Inst. of Industrial Psychology; British Nat. Council for Rehabilitation; Commonwealth Migration Council; Council, British Soc. of Endocrinology (Founder Mem.); Academic Cttee, Inst. of Social Psychiatry; Council, Inst. for Scientific Study of Delinquency; Hon. Mem. Endocrinological Socs of Argentine, Chile, France; Past Pres., Endocrine Section, RSocMed; Adv. Counsellor, English Speaking Union, 1976-. Humphrey Davy Rolleston Lectr, RCP, 1974. Life Mem., Brit. Horse Soc. Jt Founder, Walter Hagen Annual Award Trophy (in collab. with Golf Writers' Assoc. of USA), 1961, received Trophy, 1976. *Publications:* Major Endocrine Disorders, 1938, 3rd edn, 1959; contrib. Hutchison's Index of Therapeutics, Rolleston's Encyclopædia of Medical Practice, Endocrine Section of Price's Medicine, 1956, Endocrine Section of Medical Annual and Chambers's Encyclopædia; papers in Proc. Roy. Soc. Med., etc. *Recreations:* golf, painting, boxing (Capt. Cambridge Univ. 1922). *Address:* 28 Hyde Park Gate, SW7; Grouselands, Colgate, West Sussex. *Clubs:* Carlton, Simpson Services (Pres. and Founder), Machine Gun Corps Officers (Hon. Mem.); Sunningdale Golf (Sunningdale); Cowdray Park Polo; The Guards Polo.

SIMPSON, Prof. Scott, MA Cantab, Dr rer nat (Frankfurt-am-Main); Professor of Geology, University of Exeter, 1959-75, now Emeritus Professor; *b* 15 September 1915; *e s* of late Sir George C. Simpson, KCB, CBE, FRS; *m* 1940, Elisabeth, *er d* of late Dr Imre Szabo, Vienna; two *s* one *d*. *Educ:* Highgate School; Clare College, Cambridge. Research at University of Frankfurt-am-Main, 1937-39. Assistant Lecturer in Geology, 1939-46 (seconded to Department of Natural Philosophy, 1941-45) and Lecturer in Geology, 1946-49, University of Aberdeen; Lecturer, 1949-59, and Reader, 1959, in Geology, University of Bristol. Awarded E. J. Garwood Fund of Geological Society, 1956. *Publications:* various papers on Pleistocene geology and geomorphology, and Devonian stratigraphy and fossils; (jt Editor) Lexique Stratigraphique International, volumes for England, Scotland and Wales. *Address:* Restharrow, West Hill, Ottery-St-Mary, Devon.

SIMPSON, William James; Chairman, Health and Safety Commission, since 1974; *b* Falkirk, 20 May 1920; *s* of William Simpson and Margaret Nimmo; *m* 1942, Catherine McEwan Nicol; one *s*. *Educ:* Victoria Sch. and Falkirk Techn. Sch., Falkirk. Served War of 1939-45, Argyll and Sutherland Highlanders (Sgt). Apprenticed to moulding trade, 1935; returned to foundry, 1946. Mem. Nat. Exec. Council, Amalgamated Union of Foundry Workers, 1955-67; Gen. Sec., AUEW (Foundry Section), 1967-75. Mem. Nat. Exec. Cttee of Labour Party, 1962-; Chm. of Labour Party, 1972-73; Member: Race Relations Board; Ct of Inquiry into Flixborough explosion, 1974. *Publication:* Labour: The Unions and the Party, 1973. *Recreations:* golf, gardening. *Address:* 35 Fielding Road, Bedford Park, Chiswick, W4. *T:* 01-995 9677.

SIMPSON, William Wynn, OBE 1967; MA; FRSA; General Secretary, International Council of Christians and Jews; *b* 11 July 1907; *m* 1933, Winifred Marjorie Povey; one *s* one *d*. *Educ:* King Edward VI Grammar School, Camp Hill, Birmingham; Birmingham University; Wesley House and Fitzwilliam House, Cambridge. Asst Minister, Leysian Mission, London, 1929-32; Oxford Methodist Circuit, 1932-33; External Student, Jews' College, London and research into contemp. Jewish problems, 1933-35; Minister Amhurst Park Methodist Church, N London, 1935-38; General Secretary: Christian Council for Refugees, 1938-42; Council of Christians and Jews, 1942-74. Vice-Pres., Greater London Assoc. for the Disabled; Chm., Pestalozzi Children's Village Trust. Member: Soc. for Old Testament Study; London Soc. for Study of Religion. *Publications:* Readings in the Old Testament, 1932; Youth and Antisemitism, 1938; Christians and Jews Today (Beckly Social Service Lecture), 1942; (with A. I. Polack) Jesus in the Background of History, 1957; Jewish Prayer and Worship, 1965; Mini-Commentary on Pentateuch (Jerusalem Bible), 1969; Light and Rejoicing: a Christian's understanding of Jewish worship, 1976; pamphlets and articles on various aspects Jewish-Christian relations. *Recreation:* being alive. *Address:* 13 Woodside Road, Northwood, Mddx HA6 3QE. *Club:* Athenæum.

SIMPSON-JONES, Peter Trevor, CBE 1971; Président-Directeur Général, Société Française des Industries Lucas, since 1957; Partner, Ducellier & Co.; Director, Roto Diesel, Blois; *b* 20 March 1914; *s* of Frederick Henry Jones and Constance Agnès Simpson; *m* 1948, Marie-Lucy Sylvain; one *s* one *d*. *Educ:* Royal Navy School. British Chamber of Commerce, France: Vice-Pres., 1967-68 and 1970-72; Pres., 1968-70. Chevalier de la Légion d'Honneur, 1948, Officier 1973. *Recreation:* yachting. *Address:* 50 rue du Château, 92 Boulogne-sur-Seine, France. *T:* 825-01-20. *Clubs:* Special Forces; Polo, Racing (Paris).

SIMPSON-ORLEBAR, Michael Keith Orlebar; HM Diplomatic Service; Head of United Nations Department, Foreign and Commonwealth Office, since 1977; *b* 5 Feb. 1932; *s* of Aubrey Orlebar Simpson, Royal Artillery and Laura Violet, *d* of Captain Frederick Keith-Jones; *m* 1964, Rosita Duarte Triana; two *s* one *d*. *Educ:* Eton; Christ Church, Oxford (MA). Joined Foreign Service, 1954; 3rd Sec., Tehran, 1955-57; FO, 1957-62; Private Sec. to Parly Under-Sec. of State, 1960-62; 1st Sec. (Commercial) and Consul, Bogotá, 1962-65; seconded to Urwick, Orr and Partners Ltd, 1966; FO, 1966-68; 1st Sec., Paris, 1969-72; Counsellor (Commercial), Tehran, 1972-76. *Recreations:* gardening, fishing. *Address:* c/o Foreign and Commonwealth Office, SW1A 2AH; Orlingbury House, Forest Row, East Sussex RH18 5AA. *Club:* Travellers'.

SIMS, Prof. Geoffrey Donald, OBE 1971; Vice-Chancellor, University of Sheffield, since 1974; *b* 13 Dec. 1926; *s* of Albert Edward Hope Sims and Jessie Elizabeth Sims; *m* 1949, Pamela Audrey Richings; one *s* two *d*. *Educ:* Wembley County Grammar School; Imperial College of Science and Technology, London. Research physicist, GEC, 1948-54; Sen. Scientific

Officer, UKAEA, 1954-56; Lecturer/Senior Lecturer, University College, London, 1956-63; University of Southampton: Prof. and Head of Dept of Electronics, 1963-74; Dean, Faculty of Engrg, 1967-70; Dep. Vice-Chancellor, 1970-74. Consultant to various companies and to Department of Education and Science, 1957-; Consulting Editor, Chapman & Hall Ltd. Member: Council, British Association for the Advancement of Science, 1965-69 (Chm., Sheffield Area Council, 1974-); EDC for Electronics Industry, 1966-75; Adv. Cttee for Scientific and Technical Information, 1969-74; CNAA Electrical Engineering Bd, 1970-73; Planning Cttee for British Library, 1971-73 (Chm., British Library R&D Adv. Cttee, 1975-); Adv. Council, Science Museum, 1972-; British Nat. Cttee for Physics, 1972-; Royal Soc. Cttee on Sci. Information, 1972-; Electronics Res. Council, 1973-74; Annan Cttee on Future of Broadcasting, 1974-77; IUC Exec. Cttee, 1974-; Trent RHA, 1975-; Naval Educn Adv. Cttee, 1974-; Interim Action Cttee on British Film Industry, 1977-; Chm., British Council Engrg and Tech. Adv. Panel, 1976-. Chairman of Governors: Southampton College of Technology, 1967-69; Southampton Sch. of Navigation, 1972-74; Fellow, Midland Chapter, Woodard Schools, 1977-. FIEE 1963; FIERE 1966. Founder Mem., 1966, Reviews Editor, 1969-, Jl of Materials Science Bd. *Publications:* Microwave Tubes and Semiconductor Devices (with I. M. Stephenson), 1963; Variational Techniques in Electromagnetism (trans.), 1965; numerous papers on microwaves, electronics and education in learned jls. *Recreations:* golf, sailing, camping, music. *Address:* The Vice-Chancellor's Office, Sheffield University, Sheffield S10 2TN. *Clubs:* Athenæum; Sheffield (Sheffield).

SIMS, Monica Louie, OBE 1971; MA, LRAM, LGSM; Head of Children's Programmes, BBC Television, since 1967; *b* 27 Oct. 1925; *d* of late Albert Charles Sims and Eva Elizabeth Preen, both of Gloucester. *Educ:* Girls' High School, Gloucester; St Hugh's College, Oxford. Tutor in Literature and Drama, Dept of Adult Educn, Hull Univ., 1947-50; Educn Tutor, Nat. Fedn of Women's Institutes, 1950-53; BBC Sound Talks Producer, 1953-55; BBC Television Producer, 1955-64; Editor of Woman's Hour, BBC, 1964-67. *Recreations:* cinema and theatre. *Address:* 97 Gloucester Terrace, W2.

SIMS, Roger Edward, JP; MP (C) Chislehurst since Feb. 1974; *b* 27 Jan. 1930; *s* of Herbert William Sims and Annie Amy Savidge; *m* 1957, Angela Mathews; two *s* one *d*. *Educ:* City Boys' Grammar Sch., Leicester; St Olave's Grammar Sch., London. MInstM. National Service, 1948-50. Coutts & Co., 1950-51; Campbell Booker Carter Ltd, 1953-62; Dept Man., Dodwell & Co. Ltd, 1962-. Contested (C) Shoreditch and Finsbury, 1966 and 1970. Mem. Chislehurst and Sidcup UDC, 1956-62; JP Bromley, 1960-72 (Dep. Chm. 1970-72); Chm., Juvenile Panel, 1971-72. *Recreations:* swimming; music, especially singing (Mem. Royal Choral Soc. from 1950). *Address:* 68 Towncourt Crescent, Petts Wood, Orpington, Kent BR5 1PJ. *T:* Orpington 25676; House of Commons, SW1A 0AA.

SIMSON, Michael Ronald Fraser, OBE 1966; Secretary of the National Corporation for the Care of Old People, 1948-73; *b* 9 Oct. 1913; *er s* of Ronald Stuart Fraser Simson and Ethel Alice Henderson; *m* 1939, Elizabeth Joan Wilkinson; one *s*. *Educ:* Winchester Coll.; Christ Church, Oxford. OUAFC 1936 and 1937. Asst Master, West Downs Sch., 1938-40; RNVR, 1941-46; Asst Sec., Nat. Fedn of Housing Socs, 1946-48. Member: Min. of Labour Cttee on Employment of Older Men and Women, 1953-55; Cttee on Local Authority and Allied Personal Social Services (Seebohm Cttee), 1966-68; Supplementary Benefits Commn, 1967-76; Adv. Cttee on Rent Rebates and Rent Allowances, 1973-75, resigned 1975; Personal Social Services Council, 1973-. *Recreations:* gardening, interested in all forms of sport. *Address:* Summerhill, Kingsdon, Somerton, Somerset. *T:* Ilchester 858.

SINATRA, Francis Albert, (Frank); singer, actor, film producer, publisher; *b* Hoboken, New Jersey, USA, 12 Dec. 1915; *s* of late Natalie and Martin Sinatra; *m* 1st, 1939, Nancy Barbato (marr. diss.); one *s* two *d*; 2nd 1951, Ava Gardner (marr. diss.); 3rd, 1966, Mia Farrow (marr. diss.); 4th, 1976, Barbara Marx. *Educ:* Demarest High School, New Jersey. Started in radio, 1936; then became band singer with orchestras. First appearance in films, 1943. *Films include:* From Here to Eternity (Oscar for best supporting actor, 1953), Anchors Aweigh, On the Town, The Tender Trap, High Society, Guys and Dolls, The Man with the Golden Arm, Johnny Concho, The Joker is Wild, Kings Go Forth, Some Came Running, A Hole in the Head, Ocean's 11, The Devil at Four O'Clock, Sergeants Three, Manchurian Candidate, Come Blow Your Horn, Four for Texas, Robin and the Seven Hoods, None But the Brave, Marriage on the Rocks, Von Ryan's Express, Assault on a Queen, The Naked Runner,

Tony Rome, The Detective, Lady in Cement, Dirty Dingus Magee. Owner music publishing companies, etc. Jean Hersholt Humanitarian Award, 1971. *Publications:* composed numerous popular songs. *Address:* Sinatra Enterprises, Goldwyn Studios, 1041 N Formosa, Los Angeles, Calif 90046, USA.

SINCLAIR; *see* Alexander-Sinclair.

SINCLAIR, family name of **Earl of Caithness, Viscount Thurso, Baron Pentland,** and **Baron Sinclair of Cleeve.**

SINCLAIR, 17th Baron, *cr* 1449 (Scotland); **Charles Murray Kennedy St Clair,** MVO 1953; DL; Major, late Coldstream Guards; Extra Equerry to Queen Elizabeth the Queen Mother since 1953; Vice-Lord-Lieutenant, Dumfries and Galloway Region (District of Stewartry), since 1977; Member Queen's Body Guard for Scotland (Royal Company of Archers); *b* 21 June 1914; *o s* of 16th Baron Sinclair, MVO, and Violet (*d* 1953), *d* of Col J. Murray Kennedy, MVO; *S* father, 1957; *m* 1968, Anne Lettice, *yr d* of Sir Richard Cotterell, *qv*; one *s* two *d*. *Educ:* Eton; Magdalene Coll., Cambridge. Served War of 1939-45, Palestine, 1939 (wounded, despatches). Retired as Major Coldstream Guards, 1947. Portcullis Pursuivant of Arms, 1949-57; York Herald, 1957-68, retired. A Representative Peer for Scotland, 1959-63. DL Kirkcudbrightshire, 1969. *Heir: s* Master of Sinclair, *qv*. *Address:* Knocknalling, Dalry, Kirkcudbrightshire, Scotland. *T:* 221. *Club:* New (Edinburgh).

SINCLAIR, Master of; Matthew Murray Kennedy St Clair; *b* 9 Dec. 1968; *s* and *heir* of 17th Baron Sinclair, *qv*.

SINCLAIR OF CLEEVE, 1st Baron, *cr* 1957, of Cleeve, Co. Somerset; **Robert John Sinclair,** KCB 1946; KBE 1941 (MBE 1919); MA; United States Medal of Freedom with Gold Palm, 1947; *b* 1893; *s* of late R. H. Sinclair; *m* 1917, Mary Shearer Barclay; one *s* (and one killed in action, Middle East, 1942). *Educ:* Glasgow Acad.; Oriel College, Oxford (Hon. Fellow, 1959). Commnd Aug. 1914, 5th Bn KOSB; served Gallipoli (wounded, despatches), seconded to Ministry of Munitions, 1916, Deputy Director of Munitions Inspection, 1917-19; Member of Prime Minister's Advisory Panel of Industrialists, January 1939; Director-General of Army Requirements, War Office, 1939-42; Member: Supply Council, 1939-42; Army Council, 1940-42. Deputy for Minister of Production on Combined Production and Resources Board, Washington, 1942-43; Chief Executive, Ministry of Production, 1943, and subsequently with Board of Trade until Nov. 1945. Chairman, Committee to enquire into Financial Structure of Colonial Development Corporation, 1959; Member, UK Permanent Security Commission, 1965-77. Director: Imperial Tobacco Co. Ltd, 1933-67 (Chm., 1947-59, Pres., 1959-67); Bristol Waterworks Co., 1946-72 (Chm., 1960-71); Finance Corp. for Industry (Chm., 1960-64); Commonwealth Develt Finance Corp., 1953-67; General Accident Assurance Corp. Ltd, 1958-63; Debenture Corp. Ltd, 1961-73. Pro-Chancellor, Bristol Univ., 1946-71; Pres., Federation of British Industries, 1949-51; High Sheriff of Somerset, 1951-52. Hon. LLD (Bristol), 1959. *Recreations:* fishing, shooting, golf. *Heir: s* Lt-Col The Hon. John Robert Kilgour Sinclair, OBE 1963, Queen's Own Cameron Highlanders [*b* 3 Nov. 1919; *m* 1950, Patricia, *d* of Lawrence Hellyer, Lockerbie, Dumfriesshire; one *s* two *d*]. *Address:* Cleeve Court, Cleeve, Bristol BS19 4PE. *TA* and *T:* Yatton 832124. *Clubs:* United Oxford & Cambridge University, Army and Navy.

SINCLAIR, Alexander Riddell; HM Diplomatic Service, retired; *b* 28 Aug. 1917; *s* of Henry W. Sinclair and Mary Turner; *m* 1948, Alice Evelyn Nottingham; three *d*. *Educ:* Greenock High School. MIPR, DipCAM. Inland Revenue, 1935-37; Admty, 1938-47 (Comdr RNVR, 1945-46); 2nd Sec., HM Embassy, Moscow, 1947-48; Vice-Consul: Detroit, 1949; Mosul, 1950; FO, 1952; 1st Secretary, HM Embassy: Saigon, 1953-56; Amman, 1957-58; FO, 1959; 1st Sec. (Cultural), Budapest, 1962; FO, 1964; 1st Secretary (Information): Beirut, 1967-70; Rome, 1970-71; Consul-Gen., Genoa, 1972-76. Silver Jubilee Medal, 1977. *Publications:* literary articles in learned jls. *Recreations:* reading, book browsing, walking. *Address:* Ketton, 51 Clarence Road, Walton-on-Thames, Surrey. *Club:* Civil Service.

SINCLAIR, Allan Fergus Wilson; journalist and publicist; *b* Edinburgh, 1900; *o s* of Allan Wilson Sinclair; *m* 1st, one *s* one *d*; *m* 2nd; one *d*; 3rd, 1945, Naomi Sevilla, Cairo. *Educ:* George Heriot's, Edinburgh; Heriot-Watt (Hons English, Economics). Entered journalism, Edinburgh Evening Despatch, 1916; on staff, Daily Record, Glasgow, 1918; sent to London Office, 1919; went to The Times, 1921; Asst Editor, Sunday Chronicle, 1922; joined staff of The People, 1925, leaving as news editor, 1931; Editor Sunday Graphic until 1936; Editor Daily Sketch, 1936-

39; Assistant Director News Division, Ministry of Information, 1939-41; Press Relations Officer until 1943, then Director, British Information Services Middle East; Officer-in-Charge UN Photographic and Newsreel Pool, Cairo, Teheran, Fayoum, etc., Statesmen's Conferences, 1943 and 1945; Specialist Radio Photographic Adviser, India and Ceylon, 1945; Middle East Official Observer UN Assembly, London, 1946; joined Daily Herald, 1946; Scottish Editor, Daily Herald, 1950-53; rejoined London Staff, 1953, remaining when the paper became The Sun until May 1967; Production Editor, Club and Institute Journal, 1967-70; TV consultant on Middle East. *Recreations:* study of comparative religions, photography, painting in watercolour (exhibited London, Paris, New York, Switzerland; award winner, 1965). *Address:* 59 Westbourne Gardens, Hove, East Sussex.

SINCLAIR, Andrew Annandale; author; Managing Director, Lorrimer Publishing, Timon Films, since 1967; *b* 21 Jan. 1935; *m* 1960, Marianne, *d* of Mr and Mrs Arsène Alexandre; *m* 1972, Miranda, *o d* of Mr and Hon. Mrs George Seymour; two *s*. *Educ:* Eton Coll.; Trinity Coll., Cambridge (BA, PhD); Harvard. Harkness Fellow of the Commonwealth Fund, 1959-61; Dir of Historical Studies, Churchill Coll., Cambridge, 1961-63; Fellow of American Council of Learned Societies, 1963-64; Lectr in American History, University Coll., London, 1965-67. Dir/Writer Mem., ACTT. FRSL 1973; Fellow Soc. of American Historians, 1974. Somerset Maugham Literary Prize, 1966. *Films:* Directed: Under Milk Wood, 1971; Blue Blood, 1973; Produced: Malachi's Cove, 1973. *Publications:* The Breaking of Bumbo, 1958; My Friend Judas, 1959; The Project, 1960; Prohibition, 1962; The Hallelujah Bum, 1963; The Available Man: Warren E. Harding, 1964; The Better Half, 1964; The Raker, 1965; Concise History of the United States, 1966; Gog, 1967; The Greek Anthology, 1967; Adventures in the Skin Trade, 1968; The Last of the Best, 1969; Guevara, 1970; Magog, 1972; Dylan Thomas: poet of his people, 1975; The Surrey Cat, 1976; The Savage, 1977; Jack: the biography of Jack London, 1977. *Recreations:* old cities, old movies. *Address:* 47 Dean Street, W1. *T:* 01-734 1495/6/7.

SINCLAIR, Clive Marles; Chairman, Sinclair Radionics Ltd, since 1962; *b* 30 July 1940; *s* of George William Carter Sinclair and Thora Edith Ella (*née* Marles); *m* 1962, Ann (*née* Trevor Briscoe); two *s* one *d*. *Educ:* Boxgrove Prep. Sch., Guildford; Highgate; Reading; St George's Coll., Weybridge. Editor, Bernards Publishers Ltd, 1958-61. *Publications:* Practical Transistor Receivers, 1959; British Semiconductor Survey, 1963. *Recreations:* music, poetry, mathematics, science. *Address:* 18 Newton Road, Cambridge CB2 2AL. *T:* Cambridge 53726. *Club:* Carlton.

SINCLAIR, David Cecil; Director of Postgraduate Medical Education, Sir Charles Gairdner Hospital, Perth, Western Australia, since 1975; *b* 28 Aug. 1915; *s* of Norman James Sinclair and Annie Smart Sinclair; *m* 1945, Grace Elizabeth Simondson, Melbourne, Vic.; one *s* one *d*. *Educ:* Merchiston Castle Sch.; St Andrews University. MB, ChB (Commendation) St Andrews, 1937; MD (Hons and Rutherford Gold Medal) St Andrews, 1947; MA Oxon, 1948; DSc Western Australia, 1965. Served in RAMC, 1940-46: AMF, 1943-45; Head of Physiology Sect., Aust. Chem. Warfare Research and Experimental Stn, 1943-44; Dep. Chief Supt, Aust. Field Experimental Stn, 1944-45. Sen. Res. Off., Dept of Human Anatomy, Oxford, 1946-49; Univ. Demonstrator in Anatomy, Oxford, 1949-56; Lectr in Anatomy, Pembroke Coll., Oxford, 1950-56; Lectr in Anatomy, Ruskin Sch. of Fine Art, 1950-56; first Prof. of Anatomy, Univ. of W Australia, 1957-64; Dean of Med. Sch., 1964; Regius Prof. of Anatomy, Univ. of Aberdeen, 1965-75. FRCSE 1966. *Publications:* Medical Students and Medical Sciences, 1955; An Introduction to Functional Anatomy, 1957 (5th edn 1975); A Student's Guide to Anatomy, 1961; Cutaneous Sensation, 1967, Japanese edn 1969; Human Growth after Birth, 1969 (3rd edn 1978); Muscles and Fascia (section in Cunningham's Anatomy, 11th edn), 1972; Basic Medical Education, 1972; The Nerves of the Skin (section in Physiology and Pathophysiology of the Skin, ed Jarrett), 1973; Growth, section in Textbook of Human Anatomy (ed Hamilton), 1976; papers on chemical warfare, neurological anatomy, experimental psychology, and medical education; Editor, Jl of Anatomy, 1970-73. *Recreations:* reading, writing, photography, golf. *Address:* Sir Charles Gairdner Hospital, Nedlands, WA 6009, Australia.

SINCLAIR, Ernest Keith, CMG 1966; OBE 1946; DFC 1943; Commissioner, Australian Heritage Commission, since 1976; Associate Commissioner, Industries Assistance Commission, since 1974; Director: Australian Paper Manufacturers Ltd; *b* 13 November 1914; 2nd *s* of Ernest and Florence Sinclair, Victoria, Australia; *m* 1949, Jill, *d* of John and Muriel Nelder,

Pangbourne; one *s*. *Educ:* Melbourne High School, Australia. Literary staff, The Age, 1932-38; Served War of 1939-45, RAF, 1940-45 (despatches, 1944). Associate Editor, The Age, Melbourne, 1946-59, Editor, 1959-66. Consultant to Dept of Prime Minister and Cabinet, 1967-74 (to Prime Minister of Australia, 1967-72). Dep. Chm., Australian Tourist Commn, 1969-75 (Mem. 1966). Director: Australian Assoc. Press, 1959-66 (Chm., 1965-66); Gen. Television Corp. (Melbourne), 1959-66; Member: Australian Council, Internat. Press Inst., 1959-66; Schools Bd for the Humanities, Victoria Inst. of Colleges, 1969-72 (Chm.); Library Council of Victoria, 1966- (Dep. Pres., 1969-); Observer, Nat. Capital Planning Cttee, 1967-72; Dep. Chm., Building Trustees Library Council, Nat. Museum and Sci. Museum of Victoria, 1976-. *Recreation:* swimming. *Address:* 138 Toorak Road West, South Yarra, Victoria 3141, Australia. *T:* 26-4331. *Clubs:* Press (London); Melbourne (Melbourne); Commonwealth (Canberra).

SINCLAIR, Rear-Adm. Erroll Norman, CB 1963; DSC 1944; retired; *b* 6 Mar. 1909; *s* of late Col John Norman Sinclair, RHA; *m* 1940, Frances Elinor Knox-Gore; two *s*. *Educ:* RNC Dartmouth. Served HMS Cairo, 1936-38; HMS Gallant, 1938-40 (Dunkirk); in comd HMS Fortune, 1940, HMS Antelope, 1941-43, N African Landings; in comd HMS Eskimo, 10th Destroyer Flotilla, 1943-45 (DSC); First Lieut, RN Barracks, Chatham, 1946, Comdr 1946; Exec. Officer, RN Air Station, Eglinton, 1947; Staff Officer Ops to C-in-C, S Atlantic Station, Simonstown, and UK Liaison Officer to S Af. Naval Forces, until 1951. In comd HMS St Kitts, 5th Destroyer Sqdn, Home Fleet, 1951-53; Capt. 1952; Pres. Second Admiralty Interview Board, 1953-54; Naval Attaché at Ankara, Teheran and Tel Aviv, 1955; Capt. (D) 4th Destroyer Sqdn, HMS Agincourt, 1957-59; in comd HMS Sea Eagle and Sen. Naval Officer N Ireland, and Naval Director, Joint A/S School, Londonderry, 1959-61; Flag Officer, Gibraltar, and Admiral Superintendent, HM Dockyard, Gibraltar, also NATO Commander of Gibraltar sub areas, 1962-64; retd list, 1964; Naval Regional Officer (North), 1964-68. *Address:* Island Cottage, Wittersham, Kent. *T:* Wittersham 354.

SINCLAIR, Sir George (Evelyn), Kt 1960; CMG 1956; OBE 1950; MP (C) Dorking Division of Surrey, since October 1964; engaged in political work in United Kingdom and overseas, since 1960; *b* Cornwall, 6 November 1912; 2nd *s* of late F. Sinclair, Chynance, St Buryan, Cornwall; *m* 1st, 1941, Katharine Jane Burdekin (*d* 1971); one *s* three *d*; 2nd, 1972, Mary Violet, *widow* of George Lester Sawday, Saxmundham, Suffolk. *Educ:* Abingdon School; Pembroke College, Oxford. MA (Oxon). Entered Colonial Administrative Service, 1936; appointed to Gold Coast Administration; Asst District Comr, 1937. Military service, 1940-43. District Commissioner, Gold Coast, 1943; seconded to Colonial Office, 1943-45; Sec. to Commn on Higher Education in West Africa, 1943-45; returned to Gold Coast, 1945; Senior Assistant Colonial Secretary, 1947; Principal Assistant Secretary, 1950; Regional Officer, Trans-Volta Togoland Region, 1952; Deputy Governor, Cyprus, 1955-60; retired, 1961. Member, Parly Select Committees on: Procedure, 1965-66; Race Relations, 1969-70; Overseas Aid, 1969-70; Race Relations and Immigration, 1970-74; Members Interests, 1975; Abortion Act (Amendment) Bill; Joint Secretary: Cons. Parly Commonwealth Affairs Cttee, 1966-68; Cons. Parly Educn Cttee, 1974-, Vice-Chm., 1974; Member: Wimbledon Borough Council, 1962-65; Intermediate Technology Develt Gp (Vice-Pres., 1966-); Nat. Exec. Cttee, UNA (UK Branch), 1968-70; Council, Overseas Services Resettlement Bureau; Council of PDSA, 1964-70; Council, Christian Aid, 1973-. Trustee: Runnymede Trust, 1969-75; Human Rights Trust, 1971-74; Physically Handicapped and Able Bodied (Foundn Trustee), 1973-; Wyndham Place Trust. Chm., Bd of Governors, Abingdon School; Member: Assoc. of Governing Bodies of Independent Schools; Direct Grant Jt Cttee. *Recreations:* lawn tennis, golf, sailing, shooting. *Address:* Carlton Rookery, Saxmundham, Suffolk; 30 Ponsonby Terrace, SW1; South Minack, Porthcurno, Cornwall. *Clubs:* Athenæum, Royal Commonwealth Society.

SINCLAIR, Hugh Macdonald, DM, MA, BSc, FRCP, LMSSA; Director, International Institute of Human Nutrition, since 1972; Fellow, Magdalen College, Oxford, since 1937 (Vice-President, 1956-58); Visiting Professor in Food Science, University of Reading, since 1970; *b* Duddingston House, Edinburgh, 4 Feb. 1910; 2nd *s* of late Col H. M. Sinclair, CB, CMG, CBE, RE, and late Rosalie, *d* of Sir John Jackson, CVO, LLD; unmarried. *Educ:* Winchester (Senior Science Prize); Oriel College, Oxford. First Cl. Hons Animal Physiology, 1932; Gotch Prize, 1933; Senior Demy, Magdalen College, 1932-34; University Coll. Hosp. 1933-36 (Gold and Silver Medals for Clinical Medicine); Radcliffe Schol. in Pharmacology, 1934;

Radcliffe Travelling Fellow, 1937-38; Rolleston Prize, 1938. University Demonstrator and Lectr in Biochemistry, Oxford, 1937-47; Director, Oxford Nutrition Survey, 1942-47; Hon. Nutrition Consultant (with rank of Brig.), CCG, 1945-47; Lectr in Physiology and Biochemistry, Magdalen College, Oxford, 1937-76; Reader in Human Nutrition and Dir, Lab. of Human Nutrition, Oxford, 1951-58. Lectures: Cutter, Harvard, 1951; Schuman, Los Angeles, 1962; Golden Acres, Dallas, 1963. Member: Physiological Soc., Biochemical Soc.; Med. Research Soc.; Soc. for Experimental Biology; Soc. Philomathique; FChemSoc.; FInstBiol. Master, Apothecaries Co., 1967-68. Hon. DSc Baldwin-Wallace, USA, 1968. US Medal of Freedom with Silver Palm; Officer of Order of Orange Nassau, Holland. Editor-in-Chief, Internat. Encyclopedia of Food and Nutrition (24 vols), 1969-. *Publications:* papers on Human Nutrition and on Brain Metabolism in scientific and med. jls; Use of Vitamins in Medicine, in Whitla's Pharmacy, Materia Medica and Therapeutics (13th edn), 1939; Vitamins in Treatment, in Modern Therapeutics (Practitioner Handbooks), 1941; Nutrition, in Aspects of Modern Science, 1951; A Short History of Anatomical Teaching in Oxford (with A. H. T. Robb-Smith), 1950; (ed) The Work of Sir Robert McCarrison, 1953; (with McCarrison) Nutrition and Health, 1953 and 1961; (with Prof. Jelliffe) Nicholl's Tropical Nutrition, 1961; (with F. C. Rodger) Metabolic and Nutritional Eye Diseases, 1968; (with D. Hollingsworth) Hutchison's Food and Principles of Nutrition, 1969; articles on med. educn. *Recreations:* tennis, cricket, and gardening. *Address:* International Institute of Human Nutrition, High Street, Sutton Courtenay, Oxon OX14 4AW. *T:* Sutton Courtenay 246; Lady Place, Sutton Courtenay, Oxon. *Clubs:* Athenæum, MCC.

SINCLAIR, Ian David; Chairman and Chief Executive Officer, Director and Member of Executive Committee, Canadian Pacific Ltd; *b* Winnipeg, 27 Dec. 1913; *s* of late John David Sinclair and late Lillian Sinclair; *m* 1942, Ruth Beatrice, *d* of Robert Parsons Drennan, Montreal; two *s* two *d. Educ:* public schs, Winnipeg; Univ. of Manitoba (BA Econs 1937); Manitoba Law School (LLB 1941). Barrister, Guy Chappell & Co., Winnipeg, 1937-41; Lectr in Torts, Univ. of Manitoba, 1942-43; joined Canadian Pacific Law Dept as Asst Solicitor, Winnipeg, 1942; Solicitor, Montreal, 1946; Asst to General Counsel, 1951; General Solicitor, 1953; Vice-Pres. and Gen. Counsel, 1960; Vice-Pres., Law, 1960; Vice-Pres., Dir and Mem. Exec. Cttee, Canadian Pacific Rly Co., 1961; Pres., CPR Co., 1966; Chief Exec. Officer, CPR Co., 1969; Chm. and Chief Exec. Officer, Canadian Pacific Ltd, 1972. Hon. Dr of Laws, Manitoba, 1967. *Address:* Windsor Station, Montreal, Quebec H3C 3E4, Canada. *T:* (514) 861-6811. *Clubs:* Rideau (Ottawa); Mount Royal, Canadian Railway, Canadian, Canadian Chamber of Commerce-La Chambre de Commerce, Montreal Board of Trade (Montreal).

SINCLAIR, Rt. Hon. Ian (McCahon), PC 1977; MHR; Minister for Primary Industry, Australia, since 1975; Government Leader in House of Representatives, since 1975; Deputy Leader, National Country Party of Australia, since 1971; *b* 10 June 1929; *s* of George McCahon Sinclair and Gertrude Hazel Sinclair; *m* 1st, 1956, Margaret Tarrant (*d* 1967); one *s* two *d*; 2nd, 1970, Rosemary Fenton; one *s. Educ:* Knox Grammar Sch., Wahroonga, NSW; Sydney Univ. BA, LLB. Mem. Legislative Council, NSW, 1961-63; MHR for New England, 1963-; Minister for: Social Services, 1965-68; Shipping and Transport, 1968-71; Trade and Industry (Asst Minister), 1966-71; Primary Industry, 1971-72; Leader of House for Opposition, 1972-75; Country Party spokesman for Defence, Foreign Affairs, Law and Agriculture, 1973; Opposition spokesman on Agriculture, 1974-75; Minister for Agriculture and Minister for N Australia, Nov.-Dec. 1975. Govt, 1975. *Address:* Parliament House, Canberra, ACT 2600, Australia. *T:* (062) 726661. *Clubs:* Australian, American, Union (Sydney); Tamworth; Killara Golf.

SINCLAIR, Sir Ian (McTaggart), KCMG 1977 (CMG 1972); HM Diplomatic Service; Legal Adviser, Foreign and Commonwealth Office, since 1976; *b* 14 Jan. 1926; *s* of late John Sinclair, company director; *m* 1954, Barbara Elizabeth (*née* Lenton); two *s* one *d. Educ:* Merchiston Castle Sch. (Scholar); King's Coll., Cambridge; BA 1948, LLB 1949 (1st cl. hons). Served Intelligence Corps, 1944-47. Asst Legal Adviser, Foreign Office, 1950-56; Legal Adviser, HM Embassy, Bonn, 1957-60; Asst Legal Adviser, FO, 1960-64; Legal Adviser, UK Mission to the UN, New York, and HM Embassy, Washington, 1964-67; Legal Counsellor, FCO, 1967-71; Dep. Legal Advr, FCO, 1971-72; Second Legal Advr, FCO, 1973-75. Has been Legal Adviser to UK delegn at numerous internat. confs, incl. Geneva Conf. on Korea and Indo-China, 1954, and Brussels negotiations for UK entry into the EEC, 1961-63; Dep. Chm., UK delegn to Law of

Treaties Conf., Vienna, 1968-69; Legal Adviser to UK delegn on negotiations for UK entry into EEC, 1970-72. *Publications:* Vienna Convention on the Law of Treaties, 1973; articles in British Yearbook of International Law and International and Comparative Law Quarterly. *Recreations:* golf, fishing, watching sea-birds. *Address:* 24 Vineyard Hill Road, Wimbledon, SW19. *T:* 01-946 4269. *Club:* Athenæum.

SINCLAIR, Isabel Lillias, (Mrs J. G. MacDonald), QC (Scotland) 1964; Sheriff of Lothian and Borders (formerly Roxburgh, Berwick, and Selkirk), since 1968; *d* of William Sinclair, Glasgow, and Isabella (*née* Thomson), Glasgow; *m* 1938, J. Gordon MacDonald, BL, Solicitor, Glasgow. *Educ:* Shawlands Academy; Glasgow Univ.; Edinburgh Univ. MA 1932; BL 1946. Worked as a newspaper-woman from 1932. Admitted to Faculty of Advocates, Edinburgh, 1949. Sheriff-Substitute of Lanarkshire at Airdrie, 1966-68. *Address:* 6 St Vincent Street, Edinburgh EH3 6SH. *T:* 031-556 4806. *Club:* Ladies' Caledonian (Edinburgh).

SINCLAIR, John, MBE 1958; JP; DL; Lord Lieutenant of Caithness, 1965-73; *b* 24 March 1898; *s* of John Sinclair and Margaret Gray Sinclair; unmarried. *Educ:* Miller Academy, Thurso. Member of Thurso Town Council, 1929-63; Bailie (Magistrate), 1932-48; Provost, 1948-61; Free Burgess of the Burgh of Thurso, 1966. Hon. Sheriff Substitute, 1948; JP 1941, DL 1965, Caithness. Order of Founder of Salvation Army, 1968. *Recreations:* music, fishing. *Address:* 20 Millers Lane, Thurso. *T:* Thurso 2481.

SINCLAIR, Sir John (Rollo Norman Blair), 9th Bt, *cr* 1631; *b* 4 Nov. 1928; *s* of Sir Ronald Norman John Charles Udny Sinclair, 8th Bt, TD, and Reba Blair (Company Comdt, Auxiliary Territorial Service, 1938-41), *d* of Anthony Inglis, MS, Lismore, Ayrshire; *S* father 1952. *Educ:* Wellington College. Lt Intelligence Corps, 1948-49. Director: The Lucis Trust, 1957-61; The Human Development Trust, 1970-. *Publications:* The Mystical Ladder, 1968; The Other Universe, 1972. *Heir:* cousin Patrick Robert Richard Sinclair [*b* 21 May 1936; *m* 1974, Susan Catherine Beresford, *e d* of Geoffrey Clive Davies]. *Address:* (Seat) Barrock House, Wick, Caithness.
See also Baroness Masham of Ilton.

SINCLAIR, Air Vice-Marshal Sir Laurence (Frank), GC 1941; KCB 1957 (CB 1946); CBE 1943; DSO 1940 (and Bar, 1943); *b* 1908; *m* 1941, Valerie, *d* of Lt-Col Joseph Dalton White; one *s* one *d. Educ:* Imperial Service Coll.; RAF Coll. Cranwell. Comd No 110 Sqdn in 1940; Comd RAF Watton, 1941; Comd Tactical Light Bomber Force in North Africa and Italy, 1943-44; subsequently Sen. Air Staff Officer, Balkan Air Force; commanded No 2 Light Bomber Group (Germany), 1948-49; Assistant Commandant RAF Staff College, 1949-50; Commandant, Royal Air Force College Cranwell, 1950-52; Commandant, School of Land/Air Warfare, Old Sarum, Wiltshire, 1952-53; Asst Chief of the Air Staff (Operations), 1953-55; Comdr British Forces, Arabian Peninsula, 1955-57; Commandant Joint Services Staff College, 1958-60, retired from RAF. Controller of Ground Services, Min. of Aviation, 1960-61; Controller, Nat. Air Traffic Control Services, Min. of Avaiation, and MoD, 1962-66. Legion of Merit (American), 1943; Legion of Honour, 1944; Partisan Star (Yugoslavia), 1944. *Address:* Haines Land, Great Brickhill, Bletchley, Bucks.

SINCLAIR, Sir Leonard, Kt 1955; Company Chairman and Director; *b* 9 June 1895; *s* of John and Mary Sinclair, Broughton, Salford, Lancs; *m* 1926, Mary Levine; one *d. Educ:* Higher Grade School, Broughton, Salford, Lancs. Past Chm. Esso Petroleum Co. Ltd, 1951-58 (Dir, 1943-58). *Recreations:* golf, gardening. *Address:* Marlow, Deans Lane, Walton-on-the-Hill, Surrey. *T:* Tadworth 3844. *Clubs:* American, Royal Automobile.

SINCLAIR, Sir Ronald Ormiston, KBE 1963; Kt 1956; President, Court of Appeal: for the Bahamas and for Bermuda, 1965-70; for British Honduras, 1968-70; Chairman, Industrial Tribunals (England and Wales), 1966-69; *b* 2 May 1903; *yr s* of Rev. W. A. Sinclair, Auckland, NZ; *m* 1935, Ellen Isabel Entrican; two *s. Educ:* New Plymouth Boys' High School, NZ; Auckland University College, NZ; Balliol College, Oxford. Barrister and Solicitor of Supreme Court of New Zealand, 1924; LLM (NZ) 1925; Administrative Service, Nigeria, 1931; Magistrate, Nigeria, 1936; Resident Magistrate, Northern Rhodesia, 1938; Barrister-at-Law, Middle Temple, 1939; Puisne Judge, Tanganyika, 1946; Chief Justice, Nyasaland, 1953-55; Vice-President, East African Court of Appeal, 1956-57, Pres., 1962-64; Chief Justice of Kenya, 1957-62. *Address:* 158 Victoria Avenue, Remuera, Auckland, New Zealand.

SINCLAIR-LOCKHART, Sir Muir (Edward), 14th Bt *cr* 1636 (NS); retired sheep farmer; *b* 23 July 1906; 3rd *s* of Sir Robert Duncan Sinclair-Lockhart, 11th Bt and Flora Louisa Jane Beresford Nation (*d* 1937), *d* of Captain Edward Henry Power; *S* brother, 1970; *m* 1940, Olga Ann, *d* of Claude Victor White-Parsons; one *s* one *d*. *Recreation:* hunting (harrier). *Heir: s* Simon John Edward Francis Sinclair-Lockhart [*b* 22 July 1941; *m* 1973, Felicity Edith, *d* of late I. L. C. Stewart, NZ; twin *s*]. *Address:* Camnethan, RD 10, Feilding, New Zealand.

SINDEN, Donald Alfred; actor; *b* 9 Oct. 1923; *s* of Alfred Edward Sinden and Mabel Agnes (*née* Fuller), Sussex; *m* 1948, Diana Mahony; two *s*. *Educ:* Webber-Douglas Sch. of Dramatic Art. First appearance on stage, 1941, in Charles F. Smith's Co., Mobile Entertainments Southern Area; Leicester Repertory Co., 1945; Memorial Theatre Co., Stratford, 1946 and 1947; Old Vic and Bristol Old Vic, 1948; The Heiress, Haymarket, 1949-50; Bristol Old Vic, 1950; Red Letter Day, Garrick, 1951. Under contract to Rank Organisation, 1952-60, appearing in 23 films including Cruel Sea, Doctor in the House, etc. Returned to theatre, appearing in Odd Man In, St Martin's, 1957; Peter Pan, Scala, 1960; Guilty Party, St Martin's, 1961; Royal Shakespeare Co., 1963 and 1964 playing Richard Plantaganet in Henry VI (The Wars of the Roses), Price in Eh!, etc; British Council tour of S America, 1965; There's a Girl in my Soup, Globe, 1966; Assoc. Artist, RSC, 1967-; Lord Foppington in The Relapse, Aldwych, 1967; Not Now Darling, Strand, 1968; Royal Shakespeare Co., 1969 and 1970 playing Malvolio; Henry VIII; Sir Harcourt Courtly in London Assurance, revived at New Theatre, 1972, tour of the USA, 1974 (Drama Desk Award); In Praise of Love, Duchess, 1973; Stockmann in Enemy of the People, Chichester, 1975; Habeas Corpus, USA, 1975; Benedick in Much Ado About Nothing, King Lear, Stratford, 1976, Aldwych, 1977 (Variety Club of GB and Actor of the Year Awards, 1977); *recent films include:* The Day of the Jackal; The National Health; The Island at the Top of the World. Numerous TV appearances include: Our Man from St Marks series; Seven Days in the Life of Andrew Pelham; Two's Company; The Organisation. Member: Council, British Actors Equity Assoc., 1966-77; Adv. Council, V&A Museum, 1973-; Arts Council Drama Panel, 1973-77; Leicestershire Educn Arts Cttee, 1974-; BBC Archives Adv. Cttee, 1975-; London Acad. of Music and Dramatic Art Council, 1976-; RSA, 1972; Chairman: British Theatre Museum Assoc., 1971-77; Theatre Museum Adv. Council, 1973-; Pres., Fedn of Playgoers Socs, 1968-; Vice-Pres., London Appreciation Soc, 1960-. FRSA. *Recreations:* theatrical history, French history, architecture, ecclesiology, numismatology, genealogy, serendipity, London. *Address:* 60 Temple Fortune Lane, NW11; Rats Castle, Isle of Oxney, Kent. *Clubs:* Garrick, Beefsteak, MCC.

SINGER, Alfred Ernst; Chairman, Post Office Staff Superannuation Fund, since 1977; Director: Equity Capital for Industry, since 1976; Guinness Mahon & Co. Ltd, since 1977; *b* 15 Nov. 1924; *s* of late Dr Robert Singer and Mrs Charlotte Singer; *m* 1951, Gwendoline Doris Barnett; one *s* one *d*. *Educ:* Halesowen Grammar Sch. FCCA, FCIS, FBCS. Served War of 1939-45: Army, 1943-47. Subseq. professional and exec. posts with: Callingham, Brown & Co, Bunzl Pulp & Paper Ltd, David Brown Tractors Ltd; Rank Xerox Ltd, 1963-70 (Dir, 1967); Tesco Stores (Holdings) Ltd, 1970-73 (Finance and Dep. Managing Dir); Man. Dir (Giro), PO Corpn, 1973-76. Chm., Long Range Planning Soc., 1970-73; Mem. Council, Assoc. of Certified Accountants, 1972-. Member: Cttee for Industrial Technologies, DTI, 1972-76; National Economic Develt Corp.: Chm., Electronic Computers Sector Working Party; Member: Electronics EDC; Food and Drink Manufacturing Industry EDC, 1976-77. *Address:* 7 Bacon's Lane, South Grove, Highgate Village, N6 6BL. *T:* 01-340 0189. *Clubs:* Athenæum, MCC.

SINGER, Aubrey Edward; Controller, BBC 2, since 1974; *b* 21 Jan. 1927; *s* of Louis Henry Singer and Elizabeth (*née* Walton); *m* 1949, Cynthia Hilda Adams; one *s* three *d*. *Educ:* Giggleswick; Bradford Grammar School. Joined film industry, 1944; directed various films teaching armed forces to shoot; worked extensively in Africa, 1946-48; worked on children's films in Austria, 1948-49; joined BBC TV Outside Broadcasts, 1949; TV Producer Scotland, 1951; BBC New York Office, 1953; returned to London as Producer, 1956; produced many scientific programmes; Asst Head of Outside Broadcasts, 1959; Head of Science and Features, 1961; Head of Features Gp, BBC TV, 1967. Chm., Soc. of Film and Television Arts, 1971-73. *Recreations:* walking, talking, archery. *Address:* 11 Trevanion Road, W14. *T:* 01-603 7340.

SINGER, Very Rev. Samuel Stanfield; Dean of Diocese of Glasgow and Galloway, since 1974; Rector of Holy Trinity, Ayr, since 1975; *b* 1920. *Educ:* Trinity College, Dublin (BA 1942, MA 1961). Deacon 1943, priest, 1944, Dio. Down; Curate of Derriaghy, 1943-45; Minor Canon of Down Cathedral and Curate of Down, 1945-46; Curate of Wirksworth, 1946-49; Vicar of Middleton-by-Wirksworth, 1949-52; Rector: St George, Maryhill, Glasgow, 1952-62; All Saints, Jordanhill, Glasgow, 1962-75; Synod Clerk and Canon of Glasgow, 1966-74. *Address:* 12 Barns Terrace, Ayr, Ayrshire.

SINGH, Kanwar N.; *see* Natwar-Singh.

SINGH, Khushwant; Padma Bhushan, 1974; Editor, The Illustrated Weekly of India, Bombay 1; Barrister-at-Law; *b* Feb. 1915; *m* Kaval (*née* Malik); one *s* one *d*. *Educ:* Univ. of London (LLB); called to Bar. Practising Lawyer, High Court, Lahore, 1939-47; Min. of External Affairs, of India; PRO Ottawa and London, 1947-51; UNESCO, 1954-56. Visiting Lectr: Oxford (Spalding Trust), USA: Rochester, Princeton, Hawaii, Swarthmore; led Indian Delegn to Writers' Conf., Manila, Philippines, 1965; Guest Speaker at Montreal 'Expo 67'. Has written for many nat. dailies and foreign jls: New York Times; Observer and New Statesman (London); Harper's (USA); Evergreen Review (USA); London Magazine. Increased circulation of Illustrated Weekly of India from 80,000 to 300,000 in 4 yrs. *Broadcasting and Television:* All India Radio, BBC, CBC; LP recordings. Awards include: from Punjab Govt: 5,000 rupees and Robe of Honour, for contrib. to Sikh literature; Mohan Singh Award: 1,500 rupees for trans. of Sikh hymns, etc. *Publications: Sikh History and Religion:* The Sikhs, 1953; A History of the Sikhs: vol. i, 1469-1839, 1964; vol. ii, 1839-1964, 1967; Ranjit Singh, Maharajah of the Punjab, 1780-1839, 1963; Fall of the Kingdom of the Punjab; Sikhs Today; (ed) Sunset of the Sikh Empire, by Dr Sita Ram Kohli (posthumous); Hymns of Nanak The Guru. *Fiction:* The Mark of Vishnu and other stories, 1951; Train to Pakistan, 1956; I Shall Not Hear the Nightingales, 1961; *stories:* The Voice of God and other stories; Black Jasmine and other stories; A Bride for the Sahib and other stories. (*Co-author*): Sacred Writing of the Sikhs; (with Arun Joshi) Shri Ram: a biog., 1969; (with Satindra Singh) Ghadr Rebellion; (with Suneet Veer Singh) Homage to Guru Gobind Singh; *miscellaneous:* Love and Friendship (editor of anthology); Khushwant Singh's India—collection of articles (ed Rahul Singh); Shri Ram—a biography; *translations:* Umrao Jan Ada, Courtesan of Lucknow, by Mohammed Ruswa (with M. A. Husaini); The Skeleton (by Amrita Pritam); Land of the Five Rivers; I Take This Woman, by Rajinder Singh Bedi. *Recreation:* bird watching. *Address:* The Illustrated Weekly of India, Times of India Building, for D. Naoroji Road, Bombay 1, India. *T:* 268271. *Clubs:* Authors'; Imperial Gymkhana (New Delhi); Bombay Gymkhana (Bombay 1).

SINGH, Preetam, QC 1976; Member, Commission for Racial Equality, since 1977; *b* 1 Oct. 1914; *s* of Waryam Singh and late Balwant Kaur; *m* 1934, Rattan Kaur (*née* Bura); three *s* one *d*. *Educ:* A. V. High Sch., Mombasa, Kenya; King's Coll., London. LLD Punjab, 1977. Called to the Bar, Gray's Inn, 1951. Dep. Official Receiver, Kenya, 1960-64; Barrister, N Eastern Circuit, 1964-77. Contested (L) Hallam (Sheffield), 1970. *Recreations:* hunting, politics, religion, Indian classical music. *Address:* 129 Trinity Road, SW17 7HJ. *T:* 01-672 1762, (office) 01-242 9228. *Club:* Liberal.

SINGH, Sardar Swaran; President, Indian Council of World Affairs; *b* 19 Aug. 1907. *Educ:* Government College, Lahore; Lahore Law College. MSc (Physics) 1930; LLB 1932. Elected to Punjab Legislative Assembly, 1946; Punjab State Government: Minister for Development, Food and Civil Supplies, 1946-47; Member, Partition Committee, 1947; Minister: of Home, General Administration, Revenue, Irrigation and Electricity, 1947-49; of Capital Projects and Electricity, 1952; for Works, Housing and Supply, 1952-57, Govt of India; Member, Upper House of Indian Legislature, 1952-57; Member, Lower House of Indian Legislature, 1957; Minister: for Steel, Mines and Fuel, 1957-62; for Railways, 1962-63; for Food and Agriculture, 1963-64; for Industry and Supply, 1964; for External Affairs, 1964-66; Foreign Minister, 1970-74, Minister of Defence, 1966-70 and 1974-75. Has led many Indian delegations to the United Nations, its agencies, foreign countries and international conferences. *Address:* Sapru House, Bara Khamba Road, New Delhi, India.

SINGH BAHADUR, Maharawal Shri Sir Lakshman, GCIE 1947; KCSI 1935; *b* 7 March 1908; *S* father as Maharawal of Dungarpur, 1918; title no longer recognised by the Government of India, 1971; *m* grand-daughter of Raja Saheb of Bhinga, and *d* of Lieut-Col His late Highness Maharajadhiraj Sir Madan Singh Bahadur, KCSI, KCIE, of Kishengarh; three *s* four *d* (and one *s* decd). *Educ:* Mayo Coll., Ajmer. Visited England, Scotland,

Switzerland, France, and other European countries, 1927; invested with full ruling powers, 1928; Mem., Standing Cttee of Chamber of Princes, 1931-47; one of the select Princes chosen by his order to meet Cabinet Mission, 1946; elected Mem., Rajya Sabha, 1952-58; Leader, Rajasthan Assembly Swatantra Party and Leader of Opposition, 1962; Leader of Assembly Swatantra Party, Leader of SVD, and Leader of Opposition, 1967; President: Swatantra Party in Rajasthan, 1961-69; All-India Kshatriya Mahasabha, 1962-. Patron: Rajputana Cricket Assoc.; Cricket Club of India; Mem., MCC; captained Rajputana XI against MCC and Australian XI on four occasions. Is a keen naturalist and is interested in agriculture and study of wild life. *Address:* Udai Bilas Palace, Dungarpur, Rajasthan, India.
See also Dr K . Singhji Bahadur .

SINGHANIA, Sir Padampat, Kt 1943; President of the JK Organisation, India; *b* 1905; *s* of late Lala Kamlapat Singhania; *m* Srimati Anusiya Devi; four *s* one *d. Educ:* Home. A pioneer of Cotton, Rayon, Nylon, Jute, Woollen Textiles, Sugar, Aluminium, Steel and Engineering, Plastic, Strawboard, Paper, Chemicals, Oil Industries, Shipping, Cement, Electronics, Tyres and Tubes, Dry Cell Batteries, Banking, Insurance; Patron, large number of social, educational, political, and literary institutions. Founder of the Merchants' Chamber of UP: ex-Pres. of Federation of Indian Chambers of Commerce and Industry; ex-Pres., Employers' Assoc. of Northern India; Member 1st Indian Parliament, 1947-52, and many government and semi-govt bodies; formerly Chairman, Board of Governors, IIT Kanpur. Dr of Letters, Kanpur Univ., 1968. *Recreations:* riding, music, buildings, and studies. *Address:* Kamla Tower, Kanpur, India. *TA:* Laljuggi, Kanpur. *T:* 69854, 51147 and 62988. *Telex* KP215.

SINGHATEH, Alhaji Sir Farimang (Mohamadu), GCMG 1966; JP; Governor-General of The Gambia, 1965-70; *b* 30 Nov. 1912; *m* 1939; three *s* six *d* (and two *s* one *d* decd). *Educ:* Armitage Secondary School, Georgetown, The Gambia. Career as Druggist and Chemist. *Address:* 48 Grant Street, Banjul, The Gambia.

SINGHJI BAHADUR, Dr Karni; MP Indian Parliament; *b* 21 April 1924; *e s* of late Lt-Gen. HH Maharaja Sri Sadul Singhji Bahadur of Bikaner, GCSI, GCIE, CVO; *S* father as Maharaja of Bikaner, 1950; title no longer recognised by Government of India, 1971; *m* 1944, Princess Sushila Kumari, *d* of Maharawal Shri Sir Lakshman Singh Bahadur, *qv*; one *s* two *d . Educ:* St Stephen's Coll., Delhi; St Xavier's Coll., Bombay. BA (Hons) (History and Politics); PhD (thesis) Bombay Univ., 1964. Visited Middle East War Front in Nov. 1941 with his grandfather, Maharaja Sri Ganga Singhji Bahadur. Insignia Grand Commander: Order of Vikram Star (Bikaner), Order of Sadul Star (Bikaner), Order of Star of Honour (Bikaner); Africa Star; War Medal; India Service Medal; Arjun Award for Shooting, 1961. Has travelled extensively in Europe, Egypt, USA, Mexico, Honolulu and Far East, etc. Elected to House of People (Parliament of India) as an Independent, 1952; re-elected for 2nd and 3rd terms; elected 4th time, 1967, with largest margin (193816) in the country; elected 5th time, 1971; serving on various consultative cttees of different ministries. Mem., Asiatic Soc. of India; Mem., Bombay Natural History Soc. *Recreations:* tennis; shooting (National Champion in clay pigeon traps and skeet; rep. India, clay pigeon shooting, Olympic Games: Rome, 1960, Tokyo, 1964, Mexico, 1968; World Shooting Championships: Oslo, 1961; Cairo (Capt.), 1962 (2nd in world after tie for 1st place); Wiesbaden, 1966; Japan (1st Asian), 1967; Bologna, 1967; Mexico, 1968; San Sebastian, Spain, 1969; Seoul, 1971; Munich, 1972; golf; flying (qualified for private pilot's licence); cricket; mechanics; photography; painting; social service. *Address:* Lallgargh Palace, Bikaner, Rajasthan, India. *Clubs:* Willingdon Sports, Cricket Club of India, Bombay Flying, Bombay Presidency Golf, Western India Automobile Association, United Service (Bombay); Roshanara, Delhi Flying, Delhi Gymkhana, Delhi Golf (Delhi); Rajputana (Abu); Nat. Rifle Assoc. of India; Bikaner Thunderbolts Rifle.

SINGLETON, Sir Edward (Henry Sibbald), Kt 1975; solicitor; Member of Council, The Law Society, since 1961 (Vice-President of the Society, 1973, President, 1974); *b* 7 April 1921; *s* of W. P. Singleton, The Elms, Colwall, Malvern; *m* 1943, Margaret Vere Hutton; three *s* one *d. Educ:* Shrewsbury; BNC, Oxford. MA 1946. Served War, as Pilot, Fleet Air Arm, 1941-45. Solicitor, 1949; Partner in Macfarlanes, 1954, consultant 1977. Dir, Serck Ltd and other cos. *Recreations:* cricket (Oxford Univ. XI, 1940), boats, other odd jobs. *Address:* 57 Victoria Road, W8 5RH. *T:* 01-937 2277. *Clubs:* City of London; Vincent's (Oxford).

SINGLETON, Norman, CB 1966; Chairman, National Joint Council for Stable Staff; Deputy Chairman, Central Arbitration Committee; Deputy Chairman, Commission on Industrial Relations, 1973-74; (Secretary, 1969-72); *b* 21 March 1913; *s* of Charles and Alice Singleton, Bolton, Lancs; *m* 1936, Cicely Margaret Lucas, Claverdon, Warwick; one *s* two *d. Educ:* Bolton School; Emmanuel College, Cambridge. Min. of Labour, 1935; Under-Secretary: Civil Service Pay Research Unit, 1956-60; Min. of Labour (now Dept of Employment), 1960-69. *Publication:* Industrial Relations Procedures, 1976. *Address:* 34 Willoughby Road, Hampstead, NW3. *T:* 01-435 1504.

SINHA, 3rd Baron *cr* 1919, of Raipur; **Sudhindro Prosanno Sinha;** Chairman and Managing Director, MacNeill and Barry Ltd, Calcutta; *b* 29 Oct. 1920; *s* of Aroon Kumar, 2nd Baron Sinha (*s* of Satyendra Prasanna, 1st Baron Sinha, the first Indian to be created a peer) and Nirupama, *yr d* of Rai Bahadur Lalit Mohan Chatterjee; *S* father, 1967; *m* 1945, Madhabi, *d* of late Monoranjan Chatterjee, Calcutta; one *s* two *d* (and one *s* decd). *Educ:* Bryanston School, Blandford. *Heir: s* Hon. Sushanto Sinha, *b* 1953. *Address:* 7 Lord Sinha Road, Calcutta, India.

SINHA, Bhuvaneshwar Prasad; Chief Justice of India, 1959-64, retired; *b* 1 Feb. 1899; *s* of B. Kashi Nath Sinha and Sm. Sheila Devi; *m* 1914, Sm. Phulkesar Devi; three *s* three *d. Educ:* Arrah Zila School; Government College, Patna. BA (Patna) 1st Class Hons; 1st in History 1919 (Gold Medal); Post-Graduate Scholar, 1919-21; 1st in History, MA, 1921. Vakil, High Court, Patna, 1922; Advocate, High Court, Patna, 1927; Lecturer, Govt Law College, Patna, 1926-35; Govt Pleader, High Court, Patna, 1935-39; Asst Govt Advocate, High Court, Patna, 1940-43; Senior Advocate, Federal Court of India, 1942; Judge, High Court of Patna, 1943; Chief Justice, High Court, Nagpur, 1951-54; Judge, Supreme Court of India, Dec. 1954-Sept. 1959. *Recreations:* hiking and indoor games. *Address:* H-32, Green Park, New Delhi, India.

SINKER, Rt. Rev. George; *b* 5 May 1900; *s* of Rev. R. Sinker; *m* 1924, Eva Margaret Madden; two *s* two *d. Educ:* Rossall School; Brasenose College, Oxford. CMS Missionary, Kandy, Ceylon, 1921; ordained, 1924; Bannu, NWFP, India, 1924; Peshawar, 1932; Headmaster, Bishop Cotton School, Simla 1935; Canon of Lahore Cathedral, 1944; Gen. Sec. Bible Society, India and Ceylon, 1947; Bishop of Nagpur, 1949-54; Asst Bp of Derby, 1954-62; Vicar of Bakewell, 1955-62; Provost of Birmingham Cathedral and Asst Bishop of Birmingham, 1962-72. *Publications:* Jesus Loved Martha, 1949; What was Jesus doing on the Cross?, 1952; His Very Words, 1953. *Recreations:* reading, writing. *Address:* 7 The Close, Lichfield. *T:* Lichfield 53947.

SINKER, Rev. Canon Michael Roy; Rector of St Matthew, Ipswich, since 1967; Canon Emeritus of Lincoln Cathedral, since 1969; *b* 28 Sept. 1908; 3rd *s* of late Rev. Francis Sinker, sometime Vicar of Ilkley; *m* 1939, Edith Watt Applegate; one *s* two *d. Educ:* Haileybury; Clare College, Cambridge (MA); Cuddesdon College, Oxford. Curate of Dalston, Cumberland, 1932-34; Chaplain to South African Church Railway Mission, 1935-38; Curate of Bishop's Hatfield 1938-39; Vicar of Dalton-in-Furness, 1939-46; Vicar of Saffron Walden, 1946-63; Hon. Canon of Chelmsford Cathedral, 1955-63; Rural Dean of Saffron Walden, 1948-63; Archdeacon of Stow, 1963-67. *Address:* St Matthew's Rectory, Ipswich. *T:* Ipswich 51630.

SINNOTT, Ernest; Chairman, South Eastern Electricity Board, 1966-74; *b* 10 March 1909; *s* of John Sinnott and Emily (*née* Currie; *m* 1934, Simone Marie (*née* Petitjean); two *s. Educ:* Salford Grammar School. City Treasurer's Dept, Salford, 1924-31; City Accountant's Dept, Chester, 1931; Borough Treasurer's Dept, Warrington, 1931-32; Dep. Borough Treasurer, Middleton 1932-35, Worthing 1935-37; Borough Treasurer, Worthing, 1937-48; Chief Accountant, SE Electricity Bd, 1948-62, Dep. Chairman, 1962-66. Chartered Accountant (hons) 1935; FIMTA (Collins gold medal), 1932, now IPFA; Pres. 1956-57. *Publications:* (jointly) Brown's Municipal Bookkeeping and Accounts; contribs to learned journals on local government finance. *Recreations:* golf, music, reading and walking. *Address:* Little Court, West Parade, Worthing, West Sussex. *Club:* Worthing Golf.

SIRS, William, JP; General Secretary, Iron and Steel Trades Confederation, since 1975; *b* 6 Jan. 1920; *s* of Frederick Sirs and Margaret (*née* Powell); *m* 1941, Joan (*née* Clark); one *s* one *d . Educ:* Middleton St Johns, Hartlepool; WEA. Steel Industry, 1937-63; Iron and Steel Trades Confedn: Organiser, 1963; Divisional Officer, Manchester, 1970; Asst Gen. Sec., 1973. Member: Iron and Steel Industry Trng Bd, 1973; TUC Gen. Council, 1975-; Trade Union Steel Industry Cons. Cttee and Jt

Accident Prevention Adv. Cttee, 1973; Employment Appeal Tribunal, 1976-; Jt Sec., Jt Industrial Council for Slag Industry, 1973; Exec. Mem., Paul Finet Foundn, European Coal and Steel Community, 1974; Hon. Sec. (British Section), Internat. Metalworkers Fedn, 1975. Mem. RIIA, 1973. JP Hartlepool, Co. Durham, Knutsford, Cheshire, 1963. *Recreations:* sailing, squash, swimming, running. *Address:* Swinton House, 324 Gray's Inn Road, WC1X 8DD. *T:* 01-837 6691.

SISSON, Charles Hubert; writer; Joint Editor, PN Review; *b* 22 April 1914; *s* of late Richard Percy Sisson and Ellen Minnie Sisson (*née* Worlock); *m* 1937, Nora Gilbertson; two *d. Educ:* University of Bristol, and in France and Germany. Entered Ministry of Labour as Assistant Principal, 1936; HM Forces, in the ranks, mainly in India, 1942-45, Simon Senior Research Fellow, 1956-57; Dir of Establishments, Min. of Labour, 1962-68; Dir of Occupational Safety and Health, Dept of Employment, 1972. *Publications:* An Asiatic Romance, 1953; Versions and Perversions of Heine, 1955; The Spirit of British Administration, 1959; The London Zoo (poems), 1961; Numbers (poems); Christopher Homm, 1965; Art and Action, 1965; Catullus (translation), 1966; The Discarnation (poem), 1967; Essays, 1967; Metamorphoses (poems), 1968; English Poetry 1900-1950, 1971; The Case of Walter Bagehot, 1972; In the Trojan Ditch (poems), 1974; The Poetic Art, 1975; The Corridor (poem), 1975; The Poem on Nature (translation), 1976; (ed) The English Sermon, Vol. II 1650-1750, 1976; David Hume, 1976; Anchises (poems), 1976; (ed) Selected Poems of Jonathan Swift, 1977. *Address:* Moorfield Cottage, The Hill, Langport, Somerset. *T:* Langport 250845.

SISSON, Eric Roy, CEng, FRAeS; Chairman, Smiths Industries Ltd, since 1976; *b* 17 June 1914; *s* of Bernard Sisson and Violet (*née* Hagg); *m* 1943, Constance Mary Cutchey; two *s* two *d. Educ:* Regent Street Polytechnic. De Havilland Aircraft Co. Ltd, 1933-37; Flight Engineer and Station Engineer, BOAC, 1944-47; BOAC rep. at de Havilland Aircraft Co., 1948; Smiths Industries: joined, 1955; Divl Dir, 1964; Chief Exec., Aviation Div., 1966; Managing Dir, 1973; Chm. and Chief Exec., 1976. Pres., SBAC, 1973-74. FBIM. *Recreations:* sailing, tennis. *Address:* Gustard Wood House, Gustard Wood, near Wheathampstead, Herts. *Club:* Royal Dart Yacht.

SISSON, Marshall Arnott, CVO 1971; CBE 1959; RA 1963 (ARA 1956); FSA, FRIBA; Architect; *b* 14 Feb. 1897; *o s* of Arthur White Sisson, MIMechE, Hucclecote, Gloucestershire; *m* 1933, Marjorie (*d* 1972), *o d* of Harold Matthews, Portishead, Somerset. *Educ:* Bartlett School of Architecture, University of London. BA (Arch.) London 1923; Jarvis Rome Scholar in Architecture, 1924; Duveen Fellow, 1927. Architectural practice has included civic, collegiate, ecclesiastical, scholastic, dramatic, commercial and other buildings, and restoration of many historic buildings. Treasurer of the Royal Academy, 1965-70; Member: Ancient Monuments Board for England, 1959-76; Diocesan Adv. Cttees of Ely and Southwark; Architectural Panel of National Trust; Cathedrals Advisory Cttee; Architectural Adv. Panel for Westminster Abbey; Hon. Technical Adviser to the Georgian Group. Hon. D Fine Arts, Westminster Coll., Missouri, 1969. *Publications:* various papers in technical and archæological journals. *Address:* Farm Hall, Godmanchester, Huntingdon, Cambs. *T:* Huntingdon 53363. *Club:* Athenæum.

SITWELL, Rev. Francis Gerard, OSB, MA; Parish Priest of St Benedict's, Ampleforth, since 1969; *b* 22 Dec. 1906; *s* of late Major Francis Sitwell and Margaret Elizabeth, *d* of late Matthew Culley, Coupland Castle, Northumberland. *Educ:* Ampleforth; St Benet's Hall, Oxford. Received Benedictine Habit, 1924; Professed, 1925; Priest, 1933; Assistant Master at Ampleforth, 1933-39; Assistant Procurator at Ampleforth, 1939-47; Subprior of Ampleforth, 1946-47; Master of St Benet's Hall, Oxford, 1947-64; Priest of Our Lady and St Wilfrid, Warwick Bridge, Carlisle, 1966-69. *Publications:* Walter Hilton, Scale of Perfection, (trans. and ed); St Odo of Cluny; Medieval Spirituality; articles in Ampleforth Journal, Downside Review, Clergy Review, Month, etc. *Address:* Ampleforth Abbey, York YO6 4EN.

SITWELL, Sir Sacheverell, 6th Bt *cr* 1808; *b* Scarborough, 15 Nov. 1897; *s* of Sir George Sitwell, 4th Bt, and Lady Ida Emily Augusta Denison (*d* 1937), *d* of 1st Earl of Londesborough; *S* brother, 1969; *m* 1925, Georgia, *yr d* of Arthur Doble, Montreal; two *s. Educ:* Eton College. High Sheriff of Northamptonshire, 1948-49. *Publications:* Southern Baroque Art, 1924; All Summer in a Day, 1926; The Gothick North, 1929; Mozart, 1932; Life of Liszt, 1936; Dance of the Quick and the Dead, 1936; Conversation Pieces, 1936; La Vie Parisienne, 1937; Narrative Pictures, 1937; Roumanian

Journey, 1938; Old Fashioned Flowers, 1939; Mauretania, 1939; Poltergeists, 1940; Sacred and Profane Love, 1940; Valse des Fleurs, 1941; Primitive Scenes and Festivals, 1942; The Homing of the Winds, 1942; Splendours and Miseries, 1943; British Architects and Craftsmen, 1945; The Hunters and the Hunted, 1947; The Netherlands, 1948; Selected Poems, 1948; Morning, Noon, and Night in London, 1948; Spain, 1950, new edn 1975; Cupid and the Jacaranda, 1952; Truffle Hunt with Sacheverell Sitwell, 1953; Portugal and Madeira, 1954; Denmark, 1956; Arabesque and Honeycomb, 1957; Malta, 1958; Bridge of the Brocade Sash, 1959; Journey to the Ends of Time; Vol. I, Lost in the Dark Wood, 1959; Golden Wall and Mirador, 1961; The Red Chapels of Banteai Srei, 1962; Monks, Nuns and Monasteries, 1965; Forty-eight Poems (in Poetry Review), 1967; Southern Baroque Revisited, 1968; Gothic Europe, 1969; For Want of the Golden City, 1973; and 15 books of Poetry, 1918-36, with a further 40 small books of Poems, 1972-76. *Recreation:* 'Westerns'. *Heir: s* Sacheverell Reresby Sitwell [*b* 15 April 1927; *m* 1952, Penelope, *yr d* of late Col Hon. Donald Alexander Forbes, DSO, MVO; one *d*]. *Address:* Weston Hall, Towcester, Northants. *Club:* Beefsteak.

SIXSMITH, Maj.-Gen. Eric Keir Gilborne, CB 1951; CBE 1946; *b* 15 Oct. 1904; 2nd *s* of Charles Frederick Gilborne Sixsmith, Barry; *m* 1941, Rosemary Aileen, 4th *d* of Rev. Frederick Ernest Godden; two *s* one *d. Educ:* Harrow; RMC, Sandhurst. Commissioned The Cameronians (Scottish Rifles), 1924; Adjutant 1st Battalion, 1933-34; Staff College, Quetta, 1935-36. Served War of 1939-45; Bde Maj. 2 Inf. Bde, 1939-40; GSO1, 51st Highland Division, 1941-42; Commander 2nd Bn Royal Scots Fusiliers, Italy (wounded), 1944; commanded 2nd Bn Cameronians (Scottish Rifles), 1944; Deputy Director Staff Duties, War Office, 1945-46; Brigade Commander, India, 1946-47; Deputy Director Personnel Administration, War Office, 1947-50; idc 1951; Chief of Staff, Hong Kong, 1952; Chief of Staff, Far East Land Forces, 1952-54; Commanding 43 (Wessex) Infantry Division (TA) 1954-57; Assistant Chief of Staff (Organisation and Training) Supreme Headquarters, Allied Powers Europe, 1957-61, retired. *Publications:* British Generalship in the Twentieth Century, 1970; Eisenhower as Military Commander, 1973; Douglas Haig, 1976. *Recreations:* gardening, music. *Address:* Riversleigh, Langport, Somerset. *T:* Langport 250435. *Club:* Army and Navy.
See also *P. G. D. Sixsmith.*

SIXSMITH, (Philip) Guy (Dudley); Stipendiary Magistrate for Mid Glamorgan, 1966-75; *b* 5 Nov. 1902; *e s* of late C. F. G. Sixsmith, Barry, Glam; *m* 1933, Alice Mary (JP Glam), *d* of C. J. Birch; one *d* (one *s* decd). *Educ:* Barry County Sch.; Harrow; Lincoln Coll., Oxford (MA). Assistant master, Shanghai Cathedral School for Boys, 1929-35; called to the Bar, Inner Temple, 1936; Wales and Chester Circuit. Served War of 1939-45, gazetted 2nd Lt Cameronians (Scottish Rifles), 1940; Middle East and Paiforce, 1940-45. Deputy Judge Advocate (Major), 1942-45 and at War Crime Trials in Germany, 1946-48; Stipendiary Magistrate: Cardiff, 1948-66; Pontypridd, 1966-75; Dep. Chm., Glam QS, 1966-71. Chairman: Cardiff Rent Tribunal, 1947-48; Glam and Gwent Br., Oxford Soc.; Glamorgan Branch, Council for Protection of Rural Wales, 1967-69; Monmouth Diocesan Schools Cttee, 1968-70; Soc. of Stipendiary Magistrates of England and Wales; Pres., D. C. Jones Challenge Cup for Best Kept Village in Vale of Glamorgan, 1970-72 (Chm., 1967-69). Pres., Cardiff E District Scout Council. Vice-Pres., E Glam and Mon Br., Magistrates' Assoc. (Chm., 1954-66). Member: Council, Magistrates' Assoc., 1952-71; Monmouth Diocesan Board of Finance; Representative Body, Church in Wales; Court of Governors, University Coll. Cardiff; Court, University of Wales; Exec. Cttee, Council for Protection of Rural Wales, 1967-73. *Recreation:* procrastination. *Address:* St Julian's Cottage, Llanedeyrn, Cardiff CF3 9YJ. *T:* Cardiff 77846. *Club:* National Liberal.
See also *Maj.-Gen. E. K. G. Sixsmith.*

SKAE, Sheriff Victor Delvine Burnham; Sheriff of Lothian and Borders (formerly the Lothians) at Edinburgh, since 1968; *b* 25 Oct. 1914; *o s* of late Ernest Traill Skae, SSC and late Elsie Burnham; *m* 1939, Barbara Landale Melville; three *d. Educ:* Edinburgh Acad.; Bruges; Clifton Coll.; Peterhouse, Cambridge (BA); Edinburgh Univ. (LLB). RA, 1940-42, 652 (AOP) Sqdn; invalided out. Advocate, 1945; Advocate Depute, 1953-60; Sheriff Substitute: Falkirk, 1960-64; Linlithgow, 1964-68. *Recreations:* shooting, fishing. *Address:* 32 Garscube Terrace, Edinburgh EH12 6BN. *Club:* New (Edinburgh).

SKAN, Peter Henry O.; see Ogle-Skan.

SKEAPING, John (Rattenbury), RA 1959 (ARA 1950); sculptor; Professor of Sculpture, Royal College of Art, 1953-59; *b* 9 June

1901; *m* 1st, 1923, Barbara Hepworth (Dame Barbara Hepworth, DBE, *d* 1975) (marr. diss. 1933); one *s* (killed in action, RAF, 1953); 2nd, 1934, Morwenna Ward (marr. diss. 1969); three *s*; 3rd, 1969, Margery Scott. *Educ:* Royal Academy Schools. Rome Scholar, 1924. Exhibited: Royal Academy; Leicester Galls; Ackermann Galls. *Publications:* Animal Drawing, 1934; How to Draw Horses, 1938; The Big Tree of Mexico, 1952; Les Animaux dans l'Art, 1969 (Paris); Drawn from Life (autobiog.), 1977. *Recreations:* fishing and riding. *Address:* c/o A. Ackermann & Sons Ltd, 3 Old Bond Street, W1X 3TD; Moulin de la Taillade, Castries, Hérault, France.

SKEAT, Theodore Cressy, FBA 1963; BA; Keeper of Manuscripts and Egerton Librarian, British Museum, 1961-72; *b* 15 Feb. 1907; *s* of Walter William Skeat, MA; *m* 1942, Olive Martin; one *s*. *Educ:* Whitgift School, Croydon; Christ's College, Cambridge. Student at British School of Archaeology, Athens, 1929-31; Asst Keeper, Dept. of Manuscripts, British Musuem, 1931; Deputy Keeper, 1948. *Publications:* (with H. I. Bell) Fragments of an Unknown Gospel, 1935; (with H. J. M. Milne) Scribes and Correctors of the Codex Sinaiticus, 1938; The Reigns of the Ptolemies, 1954; Papyri from Panopolis, 1964; Catalogue of Greek Papyri in the British Museum, vol. VII, 1974; articles in papyrological journals. *Address:* 63 Ashbourne Road, W5 3DH. *T:* 01-998 1246.

SKEEN, Brig. Andrew, OBE 1945; psc; MP for Arundel (Rhodesian Parliament), 1965-74; *b* 1906; *s* of late Gen. Sir Andrew Skeen, KCB, KCIE, CMG; *m* 1939, Honor St Quintin Beasley; one *s* one *d*. *Educ:* Wellington College; Sandhurst. 2nd Lt R Berkshire Regt, 1926; Bde Maj., 1939; Lt-Col 1941; Brig., 1943. Served, 1939-45: France, N Africa, Middle East, India and Burma (despatches); retd 1947. Chairman, Industrial Boards; Member, Rhodesian Tourist Board. Life Vice-President, Manicaland Development and Publicity Assoc. Commissioner, Rhodesian Forestry Commission. Mem., Umtali-Odzi Road Council; Chm., Vumba Town Planning Authority. High Comr for Rhodesia in London, July-Nov. 1965. Independence Commemorative Decoration, Rhodesia, 1971. *Publication:* Prelude to Independence, 1966. *Address:* 19 Granta Road, Vainona, PO Borrowdale, Salisbury, Rhodesia. *T:* Salisbury 882097.

SKEET, Muriel Harvey; Chief Nursing Officer and Nursing Adviser, British Red Cross Society, since 1970; Chief Nursing Officer, St John of Jerusalem and BRCS Joint Committee, since 1970; *b* 12 July 1926; *y d* of late Col F. W. C. Harvey-Skeet, Suffolk. *Educ:* privately; Endsleigh House; Middlesex Hosp. SRN, MRSH. Gen. Nursing Trg at Middx Hosp., 1946-49; also London Sch. of Hygiene and Tropical Med. Ward Sister and Admin. Sister, Middx Hosp., 1949-60; Field Work Organiser, Opl Res. Unit, Nuffield Provincial Hosps Trust, 1961-64. Res. Org., Dan Mason Nursing Res. Cttee of Nat. Florence Nightingale Memorial Cttee of Gt Britain and N Ire., 1965-70; WHO Res. Consultant, SE Asia, 1970; European Deleg. and First Chm. of Bd of Commonwealth Nurses' Fed., 1971. Leverhulme Fellowship, 1974-75. Member: Hosp. and Med. Services Cttee, 1970; Ex-Services War Disabled Help Cttee, 1970; British Commonwealth Nurses War Memorial Fund Cttee and Council, 1970; Council of Management of Nat. Florence Nightingale Memorial Cttee, 1970; Council of Queen's Inst. of District Nursing, 1970; Royal Coll. of Nursing and Nat. Council of Nurses; Research Consultant, Internat. Hosp. Fedn. *Publications:* Waiting in Outpatient Departments (Nuffield Provincial Hospitals Trust), 1965; Marriage and Nursing (Dan Mason NRC), 1968; Home from Hospital (Dan Mason NRC), 1970; Home Nursing, 1975; Manual: Disaster Relief Work, 1977; various articles in professional jls. *Recreations:* music, opera, painting, reading. *Address:* 32 Onslow Square, SW7. *T:* 01-584 9066. *Clubs:* VAD, Anglo-Belgian, Royal Commonwealth Society.

SKEET, Trevor Herbert Harry; MP (C) Bedford since 1970; Barrister, Writer and Consultant; *b* 28 Jan. 1918; British; *m* 1958, Elizabeth Margaret Gilling (*d* 1973); two *s*. *Educ:* King's College, Auckland; University of New Zealand, Auckland (LLB). Served War of 1939-45, with NZ Engineers (sergeant); 2nd Lieut, NZ Anti-Aircraft (Heavy); Sub-Lieutenant, NZ Roy. Naval Volunteer Reserve; demobilised, 1945. Formerly Barrister and Solicitor of Supreme Court of New Zealand; Barrister, Inner Temple, 1947. Has considerable experience in public speaking. Contested (C): Stoke Newington and Hackney, North, Gen. Election, 1951; Llanelly Div. of Carmarthenshire, Gen. Election, 1955; MP (C) Willesden East, 1959-64. Formerly associated with Commonwealth and Empire Industires Assoc.; Mem. Council, Royal Commonwealth Soc., 1952-55, and 1956-69. Vice-Chm., Cons. Party Power Cttee, 1959-64; Energy Cttee, 1974-; Chairman: Oil Sub-Cttee, 1959-64; Cons. Party Trade

Cttee, 1971-74; Cons. Party Middle East Cttee (Foreign and Commonwealth Affairs), 1973-; Secretary: All-Party Cttee on Airships, 1971-; All-Party Gp on Minerals, 1971-; British-Japanese and British-Brazilian Gps. Mem., Econ. Cttee, Machine Tool Trades Association for several years; Member Technical Legislation Cttee, CBI. *Publications:* contrib. to numerous journals including New Commonwealth and Mining World, on oil, atomic energy, metals, commodities, finance, and Imperial and Commonwealth development. *Address:* (home) The Gables, Milton Ernest, Bedfordshire MK44 1RS. *T:* Oakley 2307; 1 Harcourt Buildings, Temple, EC4. *T:* 01-353 2214. *Clubs:* Junior Carlton, Royal Commonwealth Society.

SKEFFINGTON, family name of **Viscount Massereene and Ferrard.**

SKEFFINGTON-LODGE, Thomas Cecil; *b* 15 Jan. 1905; *s* of late Thomas Robert Lodge and late Winifred Marian Skeffington; unmarried. *Educ:* privately; Giggleswick and Westminster Schools. For some years engaged in Advertising and Publicity both in London and the North of England; later did Public Relations and administrative work in the Coal Trade as Northern Area Organiser for the Coal Utilisation Council, in which he served Cttees of Coal Trade in North-East, North-West and Yorkshire; on the outbreak of war, became a Mines Dept official; then volunteered for the Navy; from early 1941 a Naval Officer. Mem., Parly Delegn, Nüremberg Trials. Lecture tour in USA under auspices of Anglo-American Parly Gp, 1949. MP (Lab) Bedford, 1945-50; contested (Lab) York, 1951, Mid-Bedfordshire, 1955; Grantham, 1959; Brighton (Pavilion), March 1969; Personal Asst to Chm., Colonial Development Corp., 1950-52. Mem. of post-war Parly Delegns to Eire, Belgium, Luxembourg and USA; formerly Mem., Parly Ecclesiastical Cttee, and served on Parochial Church Council, St Margaret's, Westminster. Past-Pres. and Chm., Pudsey Divisional Labour Party; Pres., Brighton and Hove Fabian Soc.; Member: Labour Party many years; Exec. Cttee, Socialist Christian Movement; Parly Socialist Christian Group (past Chm.); Exec. Cttee, Brighton and Hove Br. UNA; German-British Christian Fellowship (past Chm.); Union of Shop, Distributive and Allied Workers; Wine and Food Society; CPRE (Chm., Brighton Dist Cttee, Sussex Branch); RSPB; Georgian Group; Friends of the Lake District; Amnesty Internat.; British-Soviet Friendship Soc.; Anglo-German Assoc.; Anglo-Belgian Assoc. *Recreations:* travel, politics and associating Christianity with them. *Address:* 5 Powis Grove, Brighton, East Sussex. *T:* Brighton 25472. *Clubs:* Savile; Royal Commonwealth Society (Hove).

SKELHORN, Sir Norman John, KBE 1966; QC 1954; a Recorder of the Crown Court, since 1977; Director of Public Prosecutions, 1964-77; *b* Glossop, Derbyshire, 10 Sept. 1909; *s* of late Rev. Samuel and late Bertha Skelhorn; *m* 1937, Rosamund, *d* of late Prof. James Swain, CB, CBE; no *c*. *Educ:* Shrewsbury School. Called to Bar, Middle Temple, 1931, Master of the Bench, 1962. Member of Western Circuit; employed in Trading with the Enemy Dept (Treasury and Board of Trade), 1940-42; in Admiralty, 1942-45, latterly as head of Naval Law Branch. Recorder, Bridgwater, 1945-54; Plymouth, 1954-62; Portsmouth, 1962-64. Chairman, Isle of Wight County Quarter Sessions, 1951-64. Member, Departmental Cttee on Probation Service, 1959-61; Appointed Member of Home Secretary's Advisory Council on Treatment of Offenders, 1962; Member Home Secretary's: Probation Advisory and Training Board, 1962-73; Criminal Law Revision Cttee, 1964. *Clubs:* Athenæum, Royal Automobile.

SKELMERSDALE, 7th Baron *cr* 1828; **Roger Bootle-Wilbraham;** Managing Director, Broadleigh Nurseries Ltd, since 1973; *b* 2 April 1945; *o s* of 6th Baron Skelmersdale, DSO, MC, and Ann (*d* 1974), *d* of late Percy Cuthbert Quilter; *S* father, 1973; *m* 1972, Christine Joan, *o d* of Roy Morgan; one *s* one *d*. *Educ:* Eton; Lord Wandsworth Coll., Basingstoke; Somerset Farm Institute; Hadlow Coll. VSO (Zambia), 1969-71; Proprietor, Broadleigh Gardens, 1972. *Recreations:* gardening, reading, bridge playing. *Heir:* *s* Hon. Andrew Bootle-Wilbraham, *b* 9 Aug. 1977. *Address:* Barr House, Bishops Hull, Taunton, Somerset. *T:* Taunton 86231.

SKELTON, Rt. Rev. Kenneth John Fraser; *see* Lichfield, Bishop of.

SKELTON, Rear-Adm. Peter, CB 1956; *b* 27 Dec. 1901; *s* of Peter John and Selina Frances Skelton; *m* 1928, Janice Brown Clark; two *d*. *Educ:* RN Colleges, Osborne and Dartmouth; Trinity Hall, Cambridge. Cadet, 1915; Midshipman, HMS Valiant, 1918; Commander, 1936; Capt. 1944; Rear-Adm., 1953. Served War of 1939-45, as Staff Officer in HMS Aurora, later at

Admiralty in Torpedo Division; Commander and Actg Capt. in HMS Royal Sovereign, 1942; Director of Trade Div., Admiralty, 1944; Supt of Torpedo Experimental Establishment, 1946; Sen. Naval Officer, Persian Gulf, 1949; Captain of Dockyard, Portsmouth, 1951; Admiral Superintendent, Rosyth, 1953-56; retired. Bucks CC, 1958. *Recreations:* golf, tennis, shooting. *Address:* Craigie Barns, Kippen, Stirlingshire.

SKELTON, Prof. Robin; author; Professor of English, since 1966, and Chairman of Department of Creative Writing, 1973-76, University of Victoria, British Columbia; *b* 12 Oct. 1925; *o s of* Cyril Frederick William and Eliza Skelton; *m* 1957, Sylvia Mary Jarrett; one *s* two *d. Educ:* Pocklington Grammar Sch., 1936-43; Christs Coll., Cambridge, 1943-44; Univ. of Leeds, 1947-51. BA 1950, MA 1951. Served RAF 1944-47. Asst Lectr in English, Univ. of Manchester, 1951; Lectr, 1954. Managing Dir, The Lotus Press, 1950-52; Examiner for NUJMB, 1954-58; Chm. of Examrs in English, 'O' Level, 1958-60; Co-founder and Chm., Peterloo Gp, Manchester, 1957-60; Founding Mem. and Hon. Sec., Manchester Inst. of Contemporary Arts, 1960-63; Centenary Lectr at Univ. of Massachusetts, 1962-63; Gen. Editor, OUP edn of Works of J. M. Synge, 1962-68; Associate Prof. of English, Univ. of Victoria, BC, 1963-66. Visiting Prof., Univ. of Michigan, Ann Arbor, 1967; Dir, Creative Writing Programme, Univ. of Victoria, 1967-73; Founder and co-Editor, Malahat Review, 1967-71, Editor 1972-. Mem. Bd of Dirs, Art Gall. of Greater Victoria, BC, 1968-69, 1970-73; Dir, Pharos Press, 1972-; Editor, Sono Nis Press, 1976-. FRSL 1966. *Publications:* poetry: Patmos and Other Poems, 1955; Third Day Lucky, 1958; Two Ballads of the Muse, 1960; Begging the Dialect, 1960; The Dark Window, 1962; A Valedictory Poem, 1963; An Irish Gathering, 1964; A Ballad of Billy Barker, 1965; Inscriptions, 1967; Because of This, 1968; The Hold of Our Hands, 1968; Selected Poems, 1947-67, 1968; An Irish Album, 1969; Georges Zuk, Selected Verse, 1969; Answers, 1969; The Hunting Dark, 1971; Two Hundred Poems from the Greek Anthology, 1971; A Different Mountain, 1971; A Private Speech, 1971; Remembering Synge, 1971; Three for Herself, 1972; Musebook, 1972; Country Songs, 1973; Timelight, 1974; Georges Zuk: The Underwear of the Unicorn, 1975; Callsigns, 1976; Because of Love, 1977; *prose:* John Ruskin: The Final Years, 1955; The Poetic Pattern, 1956; Cavalier Poets, 1960; Poetry (in Teach Yourself series), 1963; The Writings of J. M. Synge, 1971; J. M. Synge and His World, 1971; The Practice of Poetry, 1971; J. M. Synge (Irish Writers series), 1972; The Poet's Calling, 1975; Poetic Truth, 1978; Spellcraft, 1978; *edited texts:* J. M. Synge: Translations, 1961; J. M. Synge, Four Plays and the Aran Islands, 1962; J. M. Synge, Collected Poems, 1962; Edward Thomas, Selected Poems, 1962; Selected Poems of Byron, 1965; David Gascoyne, Collected Poems, 1965; J. M. Synge, Riders to the Sea, 1969; David Gascoyne, Collected Verse Translations (with Alan Clodd), 1970; J. M. Synge, Translations of Petrarch, 1971; Jack B. Yeats, Collected Plays, 1971; *anthologies:* Leeds University Poetry, 1949, 1950; Viewpoint, 1962; Six Irish Poets, 1962; Poetry of the Thirties, 1964; Five Poets of the Pacific Northwest, 1964; Poetry of the Forties, 1968; The Cavalier Poets, 1970; *symposia:* The World of W. B. Yeats (with Ann Saddlemyer), 1965; Irish Renaissance (with David R. Clark), 1965; Herbert Read: a memorial symposium, 1970. *Recreations:* book collecting, art collecting, making collages, stone carving, philately. *Address:* 1255 Victoria Avenue, Victoria, BC, Canada. *T:* (604) 592-7032.

SKEMP, Prof. Joseph Bright, MA Cantab, PhD Edinburgh; Emeritus Professor of Greek, in the University of Durham; *b* 10 May 1910; *s* of late Thomas William Widlake Skemp, solicitor and local government officer, and Caroline (*née* Southall); *m* 1941, Ruby James; no *c. Educ:* Wolverhampton Grammar School; Gonville and Caius College, Cambridge. Unofficial Drosier Fellow, Gonville and Caius College, Cambridge, 1936-47; Warden of Refugee Club and Asst Sec. to Refugee Cttee, Cambridge, 1940-46; Sec., Soc. for the Protection of Science and Learning, 1944-46; Lecturer in Greek and Latin, Univ. of Manchester, 1946-49; Reader in Greek, Univ. of Durham (Newcastle Div.), 1949-50; Prof. of Greek, Univ. of Durham, 1950-73; Vis. Prof., Univ. of Alexandria, 1977. Editor, Durham University Journal, 1953-57; Joint Editor, Phronesis, 1955-64. *Publications:* The Theory of Motion in Plato's Later Dialogues, 1942 (enlarged 1967); Plato's Statesman, 1952; The Greeks and the Gospel, 1964; Plato (supplementary vol. to periodical Greece and Rome), 1976. *Recreation:* walking. *Address:* 10 Highsett, Hills Road, Cambridge CB2 1NX. *T:* Cambridge 68292; 4 Heol y Dwr, Abergynolwyn, Tywyn, Gwynedd.

SKEMP, Terence Rowland Frazer, CB 1973; Joint Second Parliamentary Counsel, since Oct. 1973; Barrister-at-Law; *b* 14 Feb. 1915; *s* of Frank Whittingham Skemp and Dorothy Frazer; *m* 1939, Dorothy Norman Pringle; one *s* two *d. Educ:*

Charterhouse; Christ Church, Oxford. Called to Bar, Gray's Inn, 1938. Served War, Army, 1939-46. Entered Parliamentary Counsel Office, 1946; Parliamentary Counsel, 1964. *Address:* 997 Finchley Road, NW11. *Club:* Royal Commonwealth Society.

SKEMPTON, Prof. Alec Westley, DSc London 1949; FRS 1961; FICE; Professor of Civil Engineering in the University of London (Imperial College) since 1957; *b* 4 June 1914; *o c* of late A. W. Skempton, Northampton, and Beatrice Edridge Payne; *m* 1940, Mary, *d* of E. R. Wood, Brighouse, Yorks; two *d. Educ:* Northampton Grammar School; Imperial College, University of London (Goldsmiths' Bursar). Building Research Station, 1936-46; University Reader in Soil Mechanics, Imperial College, 1946-54; Professor of Soil Mechanics, Imperial College, 1955-57. Vice-Pres., 1974-76 (Member Council, 1949-54), Institute Civil Engineers; Pres., Internat. Soc. Soil Mechanics and Foundn Eng, 1957-61; Chm. Jt Cttee on Soils, Min. of Supply and Road Research Bd, 1954-59; Mem., Cathedrals Advisory Cttee, 1964-70; Mem., NERC, 1973-76; Lectures: Copenhagen, Paris, Harvard, Univ. of Illinois, Oslo, Stockholm, Madrid, Florence, Sydney, Quebec, Mexico City, Tokyo; Special Lectr, Architectural Assoc. 1948-57; Vis. Lectr Cambridge Univ. School of Architecture, 1962-66; Consultant to Binnie & Partners, John Mowlem & Co., etc. For. Associate, Nat. Acad. of Engineering, USA, 1976. Hon. DSc Durham, 1968. Ewing Medal, 1968; Lyell Medal, 1972; Dickinson Medal, 1974. Hon. Editor, Geotechnique, 1970-72. Silver Jubilee Medal, 1977. *Publications:* numerous papers on soil mechanics, engineering geology and history of construction; contributor to A History of Technology (ed Dr Charles Singer). *Recreations:* field and archive research on 18th cent. civil engineering and engineers, croquet. *Address:* Imperial College, SW7. *T:* 01-589 5111; 16 The Boltons, SW10. *T:* 01-370 3457. *Clubs:* Athenæum, Hurlingham.

SKERMAN, Ronald Sidney, CBE 1974; Chief Actuary, Prudential Assurance Co. Ltd, since 1968; *b* 1 June 1914; *s* of S. H. Skerman; *m* 1939, Gladys Mary Fosdike; no *c. Educ:* Hertford Grammar School. FIA. Actuarial Trainee with Prudential, 1932. Pres., Inst. Actuaries, 1970-72; Chm., Life Offices Assoc., 1973-74; Chm., British Insurers European Cttee, 1972-; Mem., Royal Commn on Civil Liability, 1973-. *Publications:* contrib. Jl Inst. Actuaries. *Recreations:* walking, travel, music. *Address:* 30 Springfields, Broxbourne, Herts EN10 7LX. *T:* Hoddesdon 63257.

SKILBECK, Dunstan, CBE 1957; MA Oxon; FIBiol; Principal, Wye College, University of London, 1945-68; Hon. Fellow, Wye College; *b* 13 June 1904; 2nd *s* of late Clement Oswald Skilbeck, FSA, and Elizabeth Bertha Skilbeck; *m* 1934, Elspeth Irene Jomini, *d* of late Edward Carruthers, MD, and Mary Carruthers; two *s* one *d. Educ:* University College School, London; St John's College, Oxford. Agricultural Economics Res. Inst., University of Oxford, 1927-30; Univ. Demonstrator in School of Rural Economy, University of Oxford; Director of St John's College Farm; Lecturer and Tutor in Rural Economy, St John's College, Oxford, 1930-40. Served with RAF Home and Middle East, Air Staff HQ, Middle East, 1940-45; as Wing Comdr, appointed Asst Director, Middle East Supply Centre (Food Production), 1942-45 (despatches). Vice-Chm. Imperial Coll. of Tropical Agric., 1958-60; Liaison Officer to Minister of Agriculture, for SE England, 1952-60; Mem., Ghana Commn on Univ. Educn., 1961; Chairman: Collegiate Council, Univ. of London, 1962-65 (Mem., Senate, 1959-68); Canterbury Diocesan Adv. Cttee, 1970-. Member Council: Voluntary Service Overseas, 1964-68; England and Wales Nature Conservancy, 1968-73; Vice-Chm., CPRE, 1974-. Trustee, Ernest Cook Trust, 1966-. Hon. Freeman Worshipful Co. of Fruiterers, 1960. *Publications:* contribs to scientific and agricultural jls. *Address:* Mount Bottom, Elham, near Canterbury, Kent. *T:* Elham 258.

SKILLICORN, Alice Havergal, CBE 1952; MSc; Principal of Homerton College, Cambridge, 1935-60, retired. *Educ:* privately; London Sch. of Economics. Teaching posts, London and St Hild's Coll., Durham, 1920-28; HM Inspector of Schools, 1929-35. *Recreations:* walking, foreign travel. *Clubs:* Women Graduates', English-Speaking Union (Cambridge).

SKILLINGTON, William Patrick Denny, CB 1964; a Deputy Secretary, Department of the Environment (formerly Ministry of Public Building and Works), 1966-73; Housing Commissioner, for Clay Cross UDC, 1973-74; *b* 13 Feb. 1913; *s* of late S. J. Skillington, Leicester; *m* 1941, Dorin Kahn, Sydney, Australia; two *d. Educ:* Malvern College; Exeter College, Oxford. BA 1935, MA 1939, Oxford. Articled to Clerk of Leicestershire CC, 1936-39. Commissioned in R Welch Fusiliers

(SR), 1933; served War of 1939-45 (despatches); regimental officer in France and Belgium, and on staff in Sicily, Italy and Greece; AA and QMG; Lt-Col. Entered Min. of Works as Principal, 1946; Asst Sec., 1952; Under-Sec. (Dir of Establishments), Min. of Public Building and Works, 1956-64; Asst Under-Sec. of State, Home Office, 1964-66. *Address:* 95a S Mark's Road, Henley-on-Thames, Oxon. *T:* Henley 3756. *Club:* United Oxford & Cambridge University.

SKINNARD, Frederick William; Retired as Registrar and External Director of Examinations, the Institute of Optical Science (1951-59); *b* 8 March 1902; *s* of late F. W. Skinnard, bookplate designer and engraver, Plymouth; *m* 1st, 1931, Muriel M. Lightfoot (*d* 1959); 2nd, 1960, Greta Cory Anthony. *Educ:* Devonport High School; Borough Road Training College, Isleworth. Taught under LCC Education Authority, 1922-24; from 1924 to 1945 served in Willesden schools where his pioneer work in citizenship training and local survey work attracted much attention. Lecturer to teachers' courses in England and abroad. Invited to tour the USA in 1937, and while there and in Canada made a special study of labour problems. Earliest political experience gained in the Union of Democratic Control under the late E. D. Morel. A member of the Labour Party since 1924; served on Harrow and Hendon Divisional Executives and as Vice-Pres.; MP (Lab) Harrow East, 1945-50; member of the Executive of Middlesex Federation of Labour Parties; Chairman Middlesex Labour Joint Consultative Committee. Visited Jamaica, 1946; Member Parliamentary Delegn to W Africa, 1947; Member Labour Party's Advisory Cttee on Imperial Affairs; Lecturer and writer on Colonial Problems; Mem. of Fabian Soc., NUT, Roy. Soc. of Teachers. Pres., Harrow Fifty Club. Hon. Fellow Inst. Optical Science, 1957. *Publications:* Willesden Memorandum, in The Extra School Year; Leaving Papers for Senior Schools (privately printed, 1934 and 1935); Co-editor of Education for Citizenship in the Elementary School, 1935; The Juvenile Delinquent and the Community (The World's Children), 1946; Training and Function of the Ophthalmic Optician, 1950; contrib. reviews on French literature and continental history to Books & Bookmen. *Recreations:* gardening and youth club work. *Address:* 4 Hawthorn Avenue, Bude, Cornwall EX23 8PT. *T:* Bude 3468.

SKINNER, Prof. Andrew Forrester, MA, BSc, PhD (St Andrews); MA (Columbia); FEIS; Professor of Education, Ontario College of Education, University of Toronto, 1954-70, now Emeritus Professor; *b* 21 May 1902; *s* of Alexander H. and Jessie F. Skinner, Kingskettle, Scotland; *m* 1932, Elizabeth Balmer Lockhart, Manchester. *Educ:* Bell-Baxter School, Cupar, Fife; University of St Andrews. MA, BSc, 1st Cl. Hons Maths and Phys Sci., 1925; Carnegie Research Fellow in Chemistry, PhD, 1928; Commonwealth Fund Fellow, Columbia, New York, 1929-31 (Educ. MA); Teacher in various schools, 1931-37; Asst Dir of Education, Co. of Aberdeen, 1937-39; Principal Lecturer in Methods, Dundee Trg Coll., 1939-41; Prof. of Education, Univ. of St Andrews, and Principal, Dundee Trg Coll., 1941-54. Vis. Prof. Ontario Coll. of Educ., Univ. of Toronto, 1950 and 1954; Visiting Professor: E. Tennessee State Coll., 1951, State Univ. of Iowa, 1951-52; Univ. of British Columbia, 1962; Univ. of Victoria, 1964; Queen's Univ., Kingston, 1971. Former Member: Scottish Council for Research in Education; Scottish Universities Entrance Bd; School Broadcasting Council for Scotland; Mem., Bd of Directors, Comparative Educn Soc. of USA; Mem. Exec., Comparative and Internat. Educn Soc. of Canada, Vice-Pres., 1968-69, Pres., 1969-70, now Hon. Mem. *Publications:* (Booklet) Scottish Education in Schools, 1942; (Booklet) Introductory Course on Education in Scotland, 1944; Citizenship in the Training of Teachers, 1948. Articles in Jl of Amer. Chem. Soc.; Trans. Chem. Soc.; Scottish Educnal Jl; The Year Book of Education; Educnal Forum: Educational Record of Quebec; The American People's Encyclopedia; Canadian and International Education; Canadian Education and Research Digest. *Recreations:* golf, gardening and walking. *Address:* 35 Clackmae Road, Edinburgh EH16 6NY. *T:* 031-664 7852.

SKINNER, Burrhus Frederic; Emeritus Professor, Harvard University, since 1975; *b* Susquehanna, 20 March 1904; *s* of William Arthur Skinner and Grace (*née* Burrhus); *m* 1936, Yvonne Blue; two *d*. *Educ:* Hamilton Coll.; Harvard Univ. AB Hamilton 1926; MA 1930, PhD 1931, Harvard. Res. Fellow NRC, Harvard, 1931-33; Jr Fellow, Harvard Soc. Fellows, 1933-36; Minnesota Univ.: Instr Psychol., 1936-37; Asst Prof., 1937-39; Assoc. Prof., 1939-45; conducted war research sponsored by Gen. Mills, Inc., 1942-43; Guggenheim Fellow, 1944-45; Prof. Psychol., Chm. Dept, Indiana Univ., 1945-48; Harvard Univ.: William James Lectr, 1947; Prof. Psychol., 1948-57; Edgar Pierce Prof., 1958-75. FRSA; Member: Brit. and Swedish Psychol Socs; Amer. Psychol Assoc.; AAAS; Nat. Acad. Sci.;

Amer. Acad. Arts and Scis; Amer. Phil Soc.; Phi Beta Kappa; Sigma Xi. Holds numerous hon. degrees; has won many awards. *Publications:* Behavior of Organisms, 1938; Walden Two, 1948; Science and Human Behavior, 1953; Verbal Behavior, 1957; (with C. B. Ferster) Schedules of Reinforcement, 1957; Cumulative Record, 1959, rev. 1961; (with J. G. Holland) The Analysis of Behavior, 1961; The Technology of Teaching, 1968; Contingencies of Reinforcement: A Theoretical Analysis, 1969; Beyond Freedom and Dignity, 1971; About Behaviorism, 1974; Particulars of My Life, 1975. *Address:* 11 Old Dee Road, Cambridge, Mass 02138, USA. *T:* 864-0848.

SKINNER, Cornelia Otis, (Mrs A. S. Blodget); actress, authoress, monologist; radio and motion picture actress; *d* of Otis Skinner and Maud Durbin; *m* 1928, Alden S. Blodget; one *s*. *Educ:* Baldwin School, Bryn Mawr, Pa; Bryn Mawr College; Sorbonne, Paris; Sociétaire of Comédie Française and School of Jacques Copeau. Appeared in: Blood and Sand; Will Shakespeare; Tweedles; In the Next Room; The Wild Westcotts; In His Arms; White Collars. Starred in: Candida; Theatre; The Searching Wind; Lady Windermere's Fan; Major Barbara; The Pleasure of His Company (which she wrote, with Samuel Taylor; it was filmed, 1961). Author and Producer of mono-dramas: The Wives of Henry VIII; The Empress Eugénie; The Loves of Charles II; Mansion on the Hudson; and original character sketches played in America and London; dramatized and produced mono-dramas of Margaret Ayer Barnes', Edna, His Wife, and full-length solo revue, Paris '90, with music by Kay Swift. Created and prepared scripts for radio series, William and Mary; also many other radio engagements including innumerable appearances on Information Please. Officier de l'Académie, 1953. *Publications:* Tiny Garments, 1931; Excuse It, Please, 1936; Dither and Jitters, 1937; Soap Behind the Ears (published in Eng. under title of Popcorn), 1941; Our Hearts Were Young and Gay (with Emily Kimbrough), 1942; Family Circle, 1948; omnibus publication of some of previous works, That's Me All Over, 1948; Nuts in May, 1950; Happy Family, 1950; Bottoms Up!, 1955; The Ape in Me, 1959; Elegant Wits and Grand Horizontals, 1962; Madame Sarah, 1967; Life With Lindsay & Crouse, 1976. *Recreation:* country. *Address:* 13 East 66th Street, New York City. *TA:* Courtesy. *T:* RH4-5894. *Clubs:* Colony, Cosmopolitan (NY).

SKINNER, Dennis Edward; MP (Lab) Bolsover since 1970; Miner at Glapwell Colliery; *b* 11 Feb. 1932; good working-class mining stock; *m* 1960; one *s* two *d*. *Educ:* Tupton Hall Grammar Sch.; Ruskin Coll., Oxford. Miner, 1949-70. Pres., Derbyshire Miners (NUM), 1966-70; Pres., NE Derbs Constituency Labour Party, 1968-71; Derbyshire CC, 1964-70; Clay Cross UDC, 1960-70. *Recreations:* tennis, cricket. *Address:* House of Commons, SW1; 86 Thanet Street, Clay Cross, Chesterfield, Derbyshire. *T:* Clay Cross 863429. *Clubs:* Miners' Welfares in Derbyshire; Bestwood Working Men's.

SKINNER, Ernest Harry Dudley, CBE 1957; Member, Colonial Development Corporation, 1958-60; *b* 1892; *m* 1921, Edith Lilian Stretton; one *s* one *d*. *Educ:* private school. Entered service of Bank of England, 1911; for several years acted as Private Secretary to Governor, Rt Hon. M. C. Norman, DSO (later Lord Norman); Deputy Secretary, 1932; Asst to Governors, 1935-45; General Manager to Finance Corporation for Industry from its formation in 1945 until 1948. Chm., Northern Div., NCB, 1948-50; Chairman, Durham Division, National Coal Board, 1950-57. Mem. of Council, OStJ for County Durham, 1951-57. Member, Newcastle Regional Hospital Board, 1958-59. Vice-Pres., NE Div., Northern Counties ABA, 1954-59. JP Durham County, 1957-59. *Address:* Danny House, Hurstpierpoint, Hassocks, West Sussex BN6 9BB. *T:* Hurstpierpoint 832220. *Club:* Reform.

SKINNER, Maj.-Gen. Frank Hollamby, CB 1947; CIE 1945; OBE 1942; Indian Army (retired); *b* 24 March 1897. *Address:* Herecombe Manor, Southview Road, Crowborough, Sussex. *T:* Crowborough 3476.

SKINNER, Henry Albert, QC 1965; **His Honour Judge Skinner;** a Circuit Judge, since 1975; *b* 20 May 1926; *s* of Albert and Emma Mary Skinner; *m* 1949, Joan Weston Cassin; two *d*. *Educ:* Wyggeston Grammar Sch., Leicester; St John's Coll., Oxford. Called to Bar, Lincoln's Inn, 1950, Bencher, 1973. Dep. Chm., Notts QS, 1966-69; a Recorder, 1966-75 (Recorder of Leicester, 1966-71); Chm., Lincolnshire (Lindsey) QS, 1968-71 (Dep. Chm., 1963-67). Mem. Parole Bd, 1970-73. Leader, Midland and Oxford Circuit, 1973-75. Treasurer, Univ. of Leicester, 1975-. *Recreations:* gardening, walking, listening to music. *Address:* 18 Pendene Road, Leicester LE2 3DQ. *T:* Leicester 704092.

SKINNER, James John, QC; Hon. Mr Justice Skinner; Chief Justice of Malaŵi, since 1970; *b* 24 July 1923; *o s* of late William Skinner, Solicitor, Clonmel, Ireland; *m* 1950, Regina Brigitte Reiss; three *s* two *d. Educ:* Clongowes Wood Coll.; Trinity Coll., Dublin; King's Inns, Dublin. Called to Irish Bar, 1946; joined Leinster Circuit; called to English Bar, Gray's Inn, 1950; called to Bar of Northern Rhodesia, 1951; QC (Northern Rhodesia) 1964; MP (UNIP) Lusaka East, 1964-68; Minister of Justice, 1964-65; Attorney-General, 1965-69 (in addition, Minister of Legal Affairs, 1967-68); Chief Justice of Zambia, March-Sept. 1969. Grand Comdr, Order of Menelik II of Ethiopia, 1965. *Recreation:* reading. *Address:* c/o The High Court, PO Box 30244, Chichiri, Blantyre 3, Malaŵi. *Club:* Irish.

SKINNER, Joyce Eva, CBE 1975; Director, Cambridge Institute of Education, since 1974; *b* 20 Sept. 1920; *d* of Matthew and Ruth Eva Skinner. *Educ:* Christ's Hosp.; Girls' High Sch., Lincoln; Somerville Coll., Oxford. BA 1941, MA 1945. Bridlington Girls' High Sch., 1942-45; Perse Girls' Sch., 1946-50; Keswick Sch., 1950-52; Homerton Coll., Cambridge, 1952-64; Vis. Prof., Queen's Coll., NY, 1955-56; Principal, Bishop Grosseteste Coll., Lincoln, 1964-74. Hon. Fellow, Coll. of Preceptors, 1971. *Recreations:* walking, reading, conversation. *Address:* 10 Natal Road, Cambridge CB1 3NS. *T:* Cambridge 40484.

SKINNER, Sir Keith; *see* Skinner, Sir T. K. H.

SKINNER, Martyn; *b* 1906; *s* of late Sir Sydney Skinner; *m* 1938, Pauline Giles; three *s* one *d* (and one *s* one *d* decd). *Educ:* two well-known Public Schools; Magdalen College, Oxford (no degree taken). Hawthornden prize, 1943; Heinemann Award, 1947; Runner-up, Barley Championship, Brewers' Exhibition, 1949. *Publications:* Sir Elfadore and Mabyna, 1935; Letters to Malaya I and II, 1941; III and IV, 1943; V, 1947; Two Colloquies, 1949; The Return of Arthur, 1966; Old Rectory (Prologue), 1970; Old Rectory (The Session), 1973; Old Rectory (Epilogue), 1977. *Address:* Fitzhead, Taunton, Somerset. *T:* Milverton 337.

SKINNER, Most Rev. Patrick James; *see* St John's (Newfoundland), Archbishop of (RC).

SKINNER, Sir Thomas (Edward), KBE 1976; JP; President, New Zealand Federation of Labour, since 1963; *b* 18 April 1909; *s* of Thomas Edward Skinner and Alice Skinner; *m* 1942, Mary Ethel Yardley; two *s* one *d. Educ:* Bayfield District Sch. Chm. of Dirs, NZ Shipping Line, 1973-; Dep. Chm., NZ Shipping Corp., 1973-; Dir, Container Terminals Ltd, 1975-. Chm., NZ Trade Union Trng Bd; Chm., St John Ambulance Trust Bd, Auckland, 1973-, KStJ 1970. JP New Zealand, 1943. *Recreations:* racing, boating, fishing. *Address:* 164 Kohimarama Road, St Heliers, Auckland 5, New Zealand. *T:* 587-571. *Clubs:* Avondale Jockey (New Zealand); Auckland Branch, International Lions.

SKINNER, Sir (Thomas) Keith (Hewitt), 4th Bt *cr* 1912; Director, International Publishing Corporation Ltd; Chairman and Chief Executive, IPC Business Press Ltd, since 1969, and other companies; *b* 6 Dec. 1927; *s* of Sir (Thomas) Gordon Skinner, 3rd Bt, and Mollie Barbara (*d* 1965), *d* of Herbert William Girling; *S* father, 1972; *m* 1959, Jill, *d* of Cedric Ivor Tuckett; two *s. Educ:* Charterhouse. Managing Director, Thomas Skinner & Co (Publishers) Ltd, 1952-60; also Director, Iliffe & Co Ltd, 1958-65; Director, Iliffe-NTP Ltd; Chm., Industrial Trade Fairs Holdings Ltd, 1977-. *Recreations:* publishing, shooting, fishing, gardening, golf. *Heir:* *s* Thomas James Hewitt Skinner, *b* 11 Sept. 1963. *Address:* Long Acre, West Clandon, Surrey; Laburnam Cottage, Southwold, Suffolk. *Clubs:* Royal Automobile; Aldeburgh Golf.

SKINNER, Thomas Monier, CMG 1958; MBE; MA Oxon; Company Chairman; *b* 2 Feb. 1913; *s* of Lt-Col and Mrs T. B. Skinner; *m* 1935, Margaret Adeline (*née* Pope) (*d* 1969); two *s. Educ:* Cheltenham Coll.; Lincoln Coll., Oxford. Asst District Officer (Cadet), Tanganyika, 1935; Asst District Officer, 1937; District Officer, 1947; Senior Asst Secretary, East Africa High Commission, 1952; Director of Establishments (Kenya), 1955-62, retired 1962. Member, Civil Service Commission, East Caribbean Territories, 1962-63; Chairman, Nyasaland Local Civil Service Commission, 1963; Salaries Commissioner, Basutoland, The Bechuanaland Protectorate and Swaziland, 1964. Reports on Localisation of Civil Service, Gilbert and Ellice Islands Colony and of British National Service, New Hebrides, 1968. *Recreation:* fishing. *Address:* Exeter Trust Ltd, Sanderson House, Blackboy Road, Exeter, Devon; Blackaton, Gidleigh, Chagford, near Newton Abbot, Devon.

SKIPWITH, Sir Patrick Alexander d'Estoteville, 12th Bt, *cr* 1622; Technical Editor, Bureau de Recherches Géologiques et Minières, Jeddah, since 1973; *b* 1 Sept. 1938; *o s* of Grey d'Estoteville Townsend Skipwith (killed in action, 1942), Flying Officer, RAFVR, and Sofka, *d* of late Prince Peter Dolgorouky; *S* grandfather, 1950; *m* 1st, 1964, Gillian Patricia (marr. diss. 1970), *d* of late Charles F. Harwood and Mrs Harwood; one *s* one *d* ; 2nd, 1972, Ashkhain, *d* of Bedros Atikian, Calgary, Alta. *Educ:* Harrow; Paris; Oxford; Dublin (MA); London (DIC, PhD). With Ocean Mining Inc., in Tasmania, 1966-67, Malaysia, 1967-69, W Africa, 1969-70; with Min. of Petroleum and Mineral Resources, Saudi Arabia, 1970-71 and 1972-73. *Heir:* *s* Alexander Sebastian Grey d'Estoteville Skipwith, *b* 9 April 1969. *Address:* c/o BRGM, PO Box 1492, Jiddah, Saudi Arabia. *Club:* Travellers'.

SKRIMSHIRE, Rt. Hon. Betty; *see* Harvie Anderson, Rt Hon. (Margaret) Betty.

SKUTSCH, Prof. Otto; Professor of Latin, University College London, 1951-72, now Emeritus Professor; *b* 6 Dec. 1906; *yr s* of Latinist Franz Skutsch and Selma Dorff; *m* 1938, Gillian Mary, *e d* of late Sir Findlater Stewart, GCB, GCIE, CSI; one *s* three *d. Educ:* Friedrichs-Gymnasium, Breslau; Univs of Breslau, Kiel, Berlin, Göttingen. DrPhil, Göttingen, 1934; Asst Thesaurus Linguae Latinae, 1932; Sen. Asst, Latin Dept, Queen's Univ., Belfast, 1938; Asst Lectr, Lectr, Sen. Lectr, Univ. of Manchester, 1939, 1946, 1949; Guest Lectr, Harvard Univ., 1958, Loeb Fellow, 1973; Vis. Andrew Mellon Prof. of Classics, Univ. of Pittsburgh, 1972-73; Guest Mem., Inst. for Advanced Study, Princeton, 1963, 1968, 1974; Vice-Pres., Soc. for Promotion of Roman Studies; For. Mem., Kungl. Vetenskaps-och Vitterhets- Samhället i Göteborg. *Publications:* Prosodische und metrische Gesetze der Iambenkürzung, 1934; Studia Enniana, 1968. Articles in classical journals, etc. *Address:* 3 Wild Hatch, NW11. *T:* 01-455 4876.

SKYRME, Stanley James Beresford, CBE 1975; Director: National Bus Company (Chief Executive, 1972-77); Lancashire United Transport Ltd; *b* 4 May 1912; *s* of late John Skyrme and late Kate Weeks; *m* 1938, Stephanie Mary Jay; one *s. Educ:* Norwich Sch. Served with cos in Tilling & BET Bus Gps, 1931-66; Exec. Dir, BET Group, 1966-68; Chm., SE Region, Nat. Bus Co., 1969-70; Dir of Manpower, Nat. Bus Co., 1971; Directorships of various Gp Cos, 1966-71; Pres., 1975-, and Mem. Council, Confedn of British Road Passenger Transport Operators; Chm., Nat. Bus Co. Consultancy Services, 1976-. FCIT. *Publications:* various papers for professional insts and assocs. *Recreations:* reading, gardening, walking. *Address:* Angles Cottage, Mulberry Lane, Ditchling, East Sussex. *T:* Hassocks 2170. *Club:* Royal Automobile.

SKYRME, Sir (William) Thomas (Charles), KCVO 1974; CB 1966; CBE 1953; TD 1949; JP; Secretary of Commissions, 1948-77, retired; President, Commonwealth Magistrates Association, since 1970; *b* 20 March 1913; *s* of Charles G. Skyrme, Hereford, and of Katherine (*née* Smith), Maryland, USA; *m* 1st, 1938, Hon. Barbara Suzanne Lyle (marr. diss. 1953), *yr d* of 1st Baron Lyle of Westbourne; one *s* two *d* ; 2nd, 1957, Mary, *d* of Dr R. C. Leaning. *Educ:* Rugby School; New College, Oxford (MA); Universities of Dresden and Paris. Called to the Bar, Inner Temple, 1935. Practised in London and on Western Circuit. Served War of 1939-45 in Royal Artillery in Middle East, North Africa and Italy (wounded twice). Lt-Col. Secretary to the Lord Chancellor, 1944. Governor and Member of Committee of Management of Queen Mary's Hosp., London, 1938-48. Chm., Interdepartmental Working Party on Legal Proceedings against Justices and Clerks, 1960; Mem., Interdepartmental Cttee on Magistrates Courts in London, 1961; Chm., Commonwealth Magistrates' Confs, London, 1970, Bermuda, 1972, Nairobi, 1973, Kuala Lumpur, 1975, Tonga, 1976; Vice-Chm., Adv. Cttee on Training of Magistrates, 1974-. Freeman of City of London, 1970; HM Lieut for City of London, 1977-; FRGS. JP (Oxfordshire), 1948, (London), 1952. *Recreations:* travel; rifle shooting (captained Oxford University, 1934). *Address:* Elm Barns, Blockley, Gloucestershire; Casa Larissa, Klosters, Switzerland. *Clubs:* Garrick; Royal Solent Yacht.
See also Sir T. G. Waterlow, Bt.

SLACK, Prof. Geoffrey Layton, CBE 1974 (OBE 1944); TD 1946; Professor of Community Dental Health, 1976-77 (formerly Professor of Dental Surgery, 1959-76), The London Hospital Medical College; *b* 27 March 1912; *er s* of late Charles Garrett Slack and Gertrude Wild, Southport; *m* Doreen Percival Ball, *d* of late Walter Knight Ball and Mary Percival, Birkdale; two *d. Educ:* Preparatory school, Croxton and Terra Nova; Leys School, Cambridge. LDS (with distinction) Univ. of Liverpool, 1934; DDS Northwestern Univ., Chicago, 1947; FDSRCS,

1948; Nuffield Fellow, 1949; Dipl. in Bacteriology, Manchester Univ. 1950. Private practice, 1934-39, 1945-46; House Surg., Liverpool Dental Hosp. 1934. TA, RASC, 1934-39; served in RASC, 1939-45; Major, DADST (T) Eastern Comd HQ, 1941-43; Lieut-Col ADST (T) HQ Second Army, 1943-44; Lieut-Col ADST (T) HQ 21 Army Gp, 1944-45; demobilized 1945. Lectr in Preventive Dentistry, Univ. of Liverpool, 1948-51; Sen. Lectr, 1951-59; Head of Dept of Preventive and Children's Dentistry, 1948-59; Consultant Dental Surgeon 1948-59, United Liverpool Hosps; Dean of Dental Studies, The London Hosp. Med. Coll. Dental Sch., 1965-69. Mem., Central Health Services Council, 1969-; Mem., 1956-, Chm., 1974-, Standing (Dental) Adv. Cttee to CHSS; Mem. General Dental Council, 1974-; Consultant Adviser, DHSS, 1974-77; Vice-Chm. Dental Health Cttee, British Dental Assoc., 1959. Hon. Dir, MRC Dental Epidemiology Unit, 1971-77, Hon. Consultant 1977-; Hon. Consultant in Dental Surgery to the Army, 1975-77; Civilian Consultant in Community Dentistry to the RAF, 1975-. Mem. Board of Faculty of Dental Surgery, RCS, 1961-77 (Vice-Dean, 1968-69, Dean, 1971-74); Governor: The London Hosp. Med. Coll., 1963-69; The London Hospital, 1963-69. WHO Consultant, 1963-. Fellow Am. College of Dentists, 1963; Guest Mem., Académie Dentaire, 1968-. RCS John Tomes Prize, 1960-62; RCS Charles Tomes Lectr, 1965. Hon. Dr of Odontology, Goteborg, 1974. Publications: (part-author) Dental Health, 1957; World Survey of Teaching Methods in Children's Dentistry, 1958; (with T. H. Melville) Bacteriology for Dental Students, 1960; (part-author) Demand and Need for Dental Care (Report to Nuffield Foundation), 1968; (part-author) Child Dental Health, 1969; (jt author) GSS Adult Dental Health in England and Wales in 1968, 1970; (ed) Dental Public Health, 1973; many contribs to medical and dental journals. Recreations: golf, sailing, the theatre; formerly hockey (played Lancashire 1933-39, 1945-52 (57 Caps), North of England, 1935-39, 1945-52, England XI 1938-39). Address: Flat 6, Donnington Lodge, 18 Westcliffe Road, Birkdale, Southport, Merseyside. Clubs: Savage, Royal Birkdale Golf.

SLACK, George Granville; His Honour Judge Granville Slack; a Circuit Judge (formerly a County Court Judge, since 1966); b 11 July 1906; s of George Edwin and Amy Beatrice Slack; m 1st, 1935, Ella Kathleen (d 1957), d of Henry Alexander Eason; one d; 2nd, 1958, Vera Gertrude, d of Reginald Ackland Spencer; one s one d. Educ: Accrington Grammar School; London University. BA (Hons History) 1926; LLB 1929; LLM 1932. Called to Bar, Gray's Inn, 1929. Served RAFVR, 1943-46. Contested (L): Twickenham, 1945; Dewsbury, 1950; Chairman: London Liberal Party, 1947-48, 1950-53; Liberal Party Organisation, 1956-57. Publications: Slack on War Damage, 1941; Liabilities (War Time Adjustment) Act, 1941; Liability for National Service, 1942. Address: 10 Baronsmede, Ealing, W5. T: 01-567 8164. Club: National Liberal.

SLACK, John Kenneth Edward, TD 1964; **His Honour Judge John Slack;** a Circuit Judge, since 1977; b 23 Dec. 1930; o s of late Ernest Edward Slack, formerly Chief Clerk Westminster County Court, and late Beatrice Mary Slack (née Shorten), Broadstairs; m 1959, Patricia Helen, MA Cantab, o d of late William Keith Metcalfe, Southport; two s. Educ: University College Sch., Hampstead; St John's Coll., Cambridge (MA). Captain, RAEC, 1950. Admitted Solicitor, 1957; Partner, Freeborough Slack & Co., 1958-76; Mem. No 1 (later No 14) Legal Aid Area, 1966-69; Deputy Registrar, County Courts, 1969-72; a Recorder of the Crown Court, 1972-77; Pres., Wireless Telegraphy Appeals Tribunal, 1974-77. Captain Club Cricket Conf., 1962-66; Captain Bucks County Cricket Club, 1967-69 (Minor County Champions 1969); Active Vice-Pres., Club Cricket Conf., 1969-. Mem. Council, University Coll. Sch., 1974-. Recreations: cricket (Cambridge Blue 1954); golf. Address: 33 Old Slade Lane, Iver, Bucks. T: Iver 653779. Clubs: MCC; Hawks (Cambridge); Beaconsfield Cricket, Beaconsfield Golf.

SLACK, Rev. Kenneth, MBE 1946; Director, Christian Aid Division, British Council of Churches, since 1975; b 20 July 1917; s of late Reginald Slack and late Nellie (née Bennett); m 1941, Barbara Millicent Blake; two s one d. Educ: Wallasey Grammar School; Liverpool Univ., BA Liverpool, 1937; Westminster College, Cambridge. Ordained to ministry of Presbyterian Church of England, 1941. Minister, St Nicholas', Shrewsbury, 1941-45. Chaplain, RAFVR, 1942-46, serving Air Command, South East Asia, 1943-46 (MBE). Minister, St James's, Edgware, 1946-55; General Secretary, 1955-65, British Council of Churches; Minister, St Andrew's Church, Cheam, 1965-67; Minister of the City Temple, London, 1967-75; Moderator, Gen. Assembly, United Reformed Church, 1973-74. Mem., Adv. Cttee, Conf. of European Churches, 1960-67. Vice-President, Toc H. Chm., Editorial Board, New Christian, 1965-

70. Select Preacher, Cambridge, 1961. Hon. LLD Southampton, 1971. Publications: The Christian Conflict, 1960; The British Churches Today, 1961, 2nd edn 1970; Despatch from New Delhi, 1962; Is Sacrifice Outmoded?, 1966; Uppsala Report, 1968; Martin Luther King, 1970; George Bell, 1971; Praying the Lord's Prayer Today, 1973; New Light on Old Songs, 1975; Nairobi Narrative, 1976. Recreations: reading, fell-walking. Address: 53 Cleaver Square, Kennington, SE11 4EA. T: 01-735 6891; 3 High Busk, Blue Hill Road, Ambleside. T: Ambleside 3670.

SLACK, Timothy Willatt, MA; Chairman of Sessions at Wilton Park and European Discussion Centre Conferences, Wiston House, Steyning, W Sussex; b 18 April 1928; yr s of Cecil Moorhouse Slack, MC, and late Dora Willatt, Beverley, Yorks; m 1957, Katharine, 2nd d of Walter Norman Hughes, MA, and Jean Sorsbie, Chepstow, Mon.; one s three d. Educ: Winchester Coll.; New Coll., Oxford. Hons. PPE, 1951. Asst, Lycée de Rennes, France, 1951; Asst master, the Salem School, Baden, Germany, 1952; Assistant master, Repton School, 1953-59; Headmaster of Kambawsa College, Taunggyi, Shan State, Burma, 1959-62; Headmaster, Bedales Sch., 1962-74. Chairman, Society of Headmasters of Independent Schools, 1968-70. Contested (L) Petersfield, Feb. and Oct. 1974. Address: Hamlet House, Hambledon, Portsmouth PO7 6RY.

SLACK, William Willatt, MA, MCh, BM, FRCS; Surgeon to the Queen, since 1975; Consultant Surgeon, Middlesex Hospital (and Senior Lecturer in Surgery, Middlesex Hospital Medical School), since 1962; also Surgeon: Hospital of St John and St Elizabeth, since 1970; King Edward VII Hospital for Officers, since 1975; b 22 Feb. 1925; s of Cecil Moorhouse Slack, MC, and Dora Slack (née Willatt); m 1951, Joan, 4th d of late Lt-Col Talbot H. Wheelwright, OBE; two s two d. Educ: Winchester Coll.; New Coll., Oxford; Middlesex Hosp. Med. Sch. Ho. Surg., Surgical Registrar and Sen. Surgical Registrar, Mddx Hosp., 1950-59; Jun. Registrar, St Bartholomew's Hosp., 1953; Fulbright Scholar, R. & E. Hosp., Univ. of Illinois, Chicago, 1959. Publications: various surgical articles in med. jls and textbooks. Recreations: skiing, gardening; Oxford blue for Association football, 1946. Address: 18 Upper Wimpole Street, W1M 7TB. T: 01-486 1191; 22 Platts Lane, NW3. T: 01-435 5887.
See also T. W. Slack.

SLADE, (Sir) Benjamin Julian Alfred, (7th Bt cr 1831, but does not use the title); b 22 May 1946; s of Sir Michael Slade, 6th Bt and Angela (d 1959), d of Captain Orlando Chichester; S father, 1962; m 1977, Pauline Carol, er d of Major Claude Myburgh. Educ: Millfield Sch. Recreations: hunting, shooting. Heir: kinsman Gerald Gordon Slade [b 27 Oct. 1899; m 1952, Netta Kathleen, d of Richard Edward Lloyd Maunsell, CBE]. Address: 164 Ashley Gardens, Emery Hill Street, SW1. T: 01-828 2809; Maunsel, North Newton, Bridgwater, Somerset.

SLADE, Col Cecil Townley M.; see Mitford-Slade.

SLADE, Hon. Sir Christopher John, Kt 1975; **Hon. Mr Justice Slade;** a Judge of the High Court of Justice, Chancery Division, since 1975; b 2 June 1927; s of late George Penkivil Slade, KC, and Mary Albinia Alice Slade; m 1958, Jane Gwenllian Armstrong Buckley; one s three d. Educ: Eton (Scholar); New Coll., Oxford (Scholar). Eldon Law Scholar, 1950. Called to Bar, Inner Temple, 1951; in practice at Chancery Bar, 1951-75; QC 1965; Bencher, Lincoln's Inn, 1973. Attorney General, Duchy of Lancaster and Attorney and Serjeant Within the County Palatine of Lancaster, 1972-75. Member: Gen. Council of the Bar, 1958-62, 1965-69; Senate of Four Inns of Court, 1966-69; Lord Chancellor's Legal Educn Cttee, 1969-71. Master, Ironmongers' Co., 1973. Address: 12 Harley Gardens, SW10. T: 01-373 7695. Clubs: Garrick, Beefsteak.

SLADE, Julian Penkivil; author and composer since 1951; b 28 May 1930; s of G. P. Slade, KC. Educ: Eton College; Trinity College, Cambridge (BA). Went to Bristol Old Vic Theatre School, 1951; wrote incidental music for Bristol Old Vic production of Two Gentlemen of Verona, 1952; joined Bristol Old Vic Co. as musical director, 1952. Wrote and composed Christmas in King St (with Dorothy Reynolds and James Cairncross) Bristol, 1952; composed music for Sheridan's The Duenna, Bristol, 1953; transferred to Westminster Theatre, London, 1954; wrote and composed The Merry Gentleman (with Dorothy Reynolds), Bristol, 1953; composed incidental music for The Merchant of Venice (1953 Stratford season). Wrote musical version of The Comedy of Errors for TV, 1954, and for Arts Theatre, London, 1956; wrote (with Dorothy Reynolds) Salad Days, Bristol, 1954, Vaudeville, London, 1954, Duke of York's, 1976; Free as Air, Savoy, London, 1957;

Hooray for Daisy!, Bristol, 1959, Lyric, Hammersmith, 1960; Follow that Girl, Vaudeville, London, 1960; Wildest Dreams, 1960; Vanity Fair (with Alan Pryce-Jones and Robin Miller), Queen's Theatre, London, 1962; Nutmeg and Ginger, Cheltenham, 1963; Sixty Thousand Nights (with George Rowell), Bristol, 1966; The Pursuit of Love, Bristol, 1967; composed music for songs in: As You Like It, Bristol, 1970; A Midsummer Night's Dream and Much Ado About Nothing, Regent's Park, 1970; adapted A. A. Milne's Winnie The Pooh, Phoenix Theatre, 1970, 1975; (music and lyrics) Trelawny, Bristol, then London West End, 1972; Out of Bounds (book, music and lyrics, based on Pinero's The Schoolmistress), 1973. *Publications:* Nibble the Squirrel (children's book), 1946; music of: The Duenna, 1954; Salad Days, 1954; Free as Air, 1957; Follow That Girl, 1967; Trelawny, 1974. *Recreations:* drawing, going to theatres and cinemas, listening to music. *Address:* 3 Priory Walk, SW10. *T:* 01-370 4859.

SLADE, Richard Gordon, OBE 1957; FRAeS; Chairman: Fairey Hydraulics Ltd, since 1975 (Gen. Manager, 1961-65; Managing Director, 1965-75); Fairey Hydraulics Inc., since 1973; *b* 10 Sept. 1912; *yr s* of late William Slade and late Helen Blanche Slade; *m* 1948, Eileen Frances, 2nd *d* of late Dr W. F. Cooper; two *s* two *d* (and one *s* decd). *Educ:* Dulwich College. Commissioned in RAF 1933. Served in Egypt and 30 Squadron, Iraq, 1933-37; with Aeroplane and Armament Experimental Establishment, Martlesham Heath, 1937-39; Boscombe Down, 1939-41. Commanded: 157 Sqdn, Fighter Command, 1942; Handling Sqdn Empire Central Flying School, 1943; 169 Sqdn and RAF Station, Swannington, Bomber Comd 1944-45; 148 and 138 Wings, British Air Forces of Occupation, 1945-46; Chief Test Pilot and Supt of Flying, Fairey Aviation Co., 1946-59. Director: Fairey Aviation Ltd, 1959-60; Fairey Air Surveys Ltd, 1959-72; Fairey Filtration Ltd, 1970-72. Member Council: SBAC, 1976-; CBI, 1976-. American Silver Star, 1946. Liveryman, Guild of Air Pilots and Air Navigators. *Recreations:* sailing, riding, ski-ing. *Address:* Mickledore, Maidenhead Thicket, Berks. *T:* Maidenhead 20052. *Clubs:* Royal Air Force, Naval and Military, Royal Aero.

SLANE, Viscount; Alexander Burton Conyngham; *b* 30 Jan. 1975; *s* and *heir* of Earl of Mount Charles, *qv*.

SLANEY, Prof. Geoffrey, FRCS; Barling Professor, Head of Department of Surgery, Queen Elizabeth Hospital, Birmingham, since 1971; Hon. Consultant Surgeon, United Birmingham Hospitals and Regional Hospital Board, since 1959; *b* 19 Sept. 1922; *er s* of Richard and Gladys Lois Slaney; *m* 1956, Josephine Mary Davy; one *s* two *d*. *Educ:* Brewood Grammar Sch.; Univs of Birmingham, London and Illinois, USA. MB, ChB (Birmingham) 1947, FRCS 1953, MS (Ill) 1956, ChM (Birmingham) 1961. Ho. Surg. and Surgical Registrar, Gen. Hosp. Birmingham, 1947-48. Captain RAMC, 1948-50. Surgical Registrar, Coventry, London and Hackney Hosps, 1950-53; Surgical Registrar, Lectr in Surgery and Surgical Research Fellow, Queen Elizabeth Hosp., Birmingham, 1953-59; Hunterian Prof., RCS, 1961-62; Prof. of Surgery, Univ. of Birmingham, 1966-. External Examr in Surgery to Univs of: Newcastle upon Tyne, London, Cambridge, Oxford, Liverpool, Lagos and Rhodesia. Visiting Professor: Durham, Cape Town, Witwatersrand, 1970; Richardson Meml Lectr, MGH, Boston, USA, 1975; Sir Logan Campbell and RACS Vis. Prof., NZ, 1977. Mem. Council, RCS, 1975-; Member: Moynihan Chirurgical Club; James IV Assoc. of Surgeons; Internat. Surgical Gp; Surgical Research Soc.; Internat. Soc. of Cardio-Vascular Surgeons; Vascular Surgical Soc., GB (Pres., 1974-75). Fellow: RSM; Assoc. of Surgeons GB and Ire. (Mem. Council, 1966-76, Treasurer, 1970-76). Jacksonian Prize and Medal, 1959. *Publications:* Metabolic Derangements in Gastrointestinal Surgery (with B. N. Brooke), 1967 (USA); numerous contribs to med. and surg. jls. *Recreations:* fishing and family. *Address:* 23 Aston Bury, Edgbaston, Birmingham B15 3QB. *T:* 021-454 0261.

SLANEY, George Wilson, (*Pseudonym:* **George Woden**); Novelist; *b* Wednesbury, Staffs, 1 Sept. 1884; *m* 1914, Edith Margaret Tomkinson, *g d* of John Tomkinson, Manchester; one *d*; *m* 1970, Dorothy Clare Sheppard. *Educ:* Queen Mary's Grammar School, Walsall; London University; France; Germany. Abandoned career as engineer; became a journalist, artist, musician; settled in Glasgow as a schoolmaster in 1909; retired. *Publications:* Sowing Clover, 1913; Paul Moorhouse, 1914; The New Dawn, 1915; Little Houses, 1919; The Money's The Thing (three-act play) Scottish National Theatre, Glasgow, 1921; The Wrenfield Mystery, 1923; Thistledown (three-act play) Play Actors, London, 1923; The Great Cornelius, 1926; The Gates of Delight, 1927; This Way to Fortune, 1929; The Parson and Clerk, 1930; Mungo, 1932; Love and Let Love, 1933;

Our Peter, 1934; Upside-Turvydown, 1934; Tannenbrae, 1935; Othersmith, 1936; Perhaps Young Man, 1936; The Bailie's Tale, 1937; The Cathkin Mystery, 1937; Happiness Has No Story, 1938; Holiday Adventure, 1939; Voyage Through Life, 1940; Dusk for Dreams, 1941; The Queer Folk Next Door, 1942; The Golden Lion, 1944; Ruffy & Sons, 1945; Messenger-at-Arms, 1946; The Lover's Tale, 1948; The Puzzled Policeman, 1949; Helen Enchanted, 1950; Mystery of the Amorous Music Master, 1951; Simonetta, 1952. *Recreation:* music. *Address:* 91 Marlborough Avenue, Glasgow G11 7BT. *Club:* Scottish PEN (President, 1944-47).

SLATCHER, William Kenneth, CVO 1975; HM Diplomatic Service; Consul-General, Osaka, since 1977; *b* 12 April 1926; *s* of John William and Ada Slatcher; *m* 1948, Erica Marjorie Konigs; one *s* one *d*. *Educ:* St John's Coll., Oxford (MA). Royal Artillery, 1950-57; HM Diplomatic Service, 1958: Peking, 1959-60; Tokyo, 1961-63; Paris, 1965-68; New Delhi, 1968-71; Tokyo, 1974-77. Order of Sacred Treasure (Japan), 1975. *Recreations:* travelling, oriental art and history, wild-fowling. *Address:* c/o Foreign and Commonwealth Office, SW1A 2AL. *T:* 265-5511. *Club:* Travellers'.

SLATER, Arthur Edward, CBE 1949; *b* 27 Nov. 1895; *s* of Harry Slater; *m* 1917, Kathleen Slater (*née* Spicer); one *s*. *Educ:* Beckenham County School; King's College, London. Served European War, 1914-18 (wounded), Devonshire Regt and Machine-Gun Corps; invalided, 1919. Appointed to Air Ministry as Asst Principal, 1919. Assistant Under-Secretary (Personnel), Air Ministry, 1951; Asst Under-Sec. (General), 1955; retired, 1956. *Recreation:* chess. *Address:* 3 The Homestead, Southwold, Suffolk. *T:* Southwold 3238.

SLATER, Duncan; UK Resident Representative to the International Atomic Energy Agency and UK Permanent Representative to the United Nations Industrial Development Organisation, Vienna, since 1975; *b* 15 July 1934; *m* 1972, Candida Coralie Anne Wheatley; one *s* one *d*. Joined FO, 1958; Asst Polit. Agent, Abu Dhabi, 1962-66; First Secretary: Islamabad, 1966; New Delhi, 1966-68; Head of Chancery, Aden, 1968-69; FO, 1969; Special Asst to Sir William Luce, 1970-71; First Sec., UK Representation to EEC, Brussels, 1973-75. *Recreations:* walking, sailing, studying Islamic art. *Address:* British Embassy, Reisnerstrasse 40, Vienna, Austria.

SLATER, Prof. Edward Charles, ScD; FRS 1975; Professor of Physiological Chemistry, University of Amsterdam, The Netherlands, since 1955; *b* 16 Jan. 1917; *s* of Edward Brunton Slater and Violet Podmore; *m* 1940, Marion Winifred Hutley; one *d*. *Educ:* Melbourne Univ. (BSc, MSc); Cambridge Univ. (PhD, ScD). Biochemist, Australian Inst. of Anatomy, Canberra, Aust., 1939-46; Research Fellow, Molteno Inst., Univ. of Cambridge, UK, 1946-55. Member: Royal Netherlands Acad. of Science and Letters, 1964; Hollandsche Maatschappij van Wetenschappen, 1970; Hon. Mem., Amer. Soc. of Biological Chemists, 1971; Foreign Corresp., Académie Royale de Méd., Belgium, 1973; Hon. Member: Academie Nacional de Ciencias Exactas, Fisicas y Naturales, Argentina, 1973; Japanese Biochemical Soc., 1973; For. Mem., Royal Swedish Acad. of Sciences, 1975. *Publications:* about 300 contrib. to learned jls. *Recreations:* yachting, skiing. *Address:* Elger 9, Monnickendam, The Netherlands. *T:* (house) 02995-1450, (work) 020-522 2150.

SLATER, Eliot Trevor Oakeshott, CBE 1966; MA, MD Cantab; FRCP; *b* 28 Aug. 1904; 2nd *s* of Gilbert Slater, MA, DSc; *m* 1935, Lydia (marriage dissolved), *d* of Leonid Pasternak; two *s* two *d*; *m* 2nd, 1946, Jeanie Fyfe Foster. *Educ:* Leighton Park; Cambridge University; St George's Hospital. Medical Officer, Maudsley Hospital, 1931-39; with Rockefeller Fellowship studied in Munich and Berlin, 1934-35; MRC Research grant, 1935-37; Clinical Director, Sutton Emergency Hosp., 1939-45; Physician in Psychological Medicine, National Hosp., Queen Sq., WC1, 1946-64; Dir, MRC Psychiatric Genetics Unit, 1959-69. Mem. Royal Commn on Capital Punishment, 1949. Hon. Fellow, Amer. Psychiatric Assoc.; Ehrenmitglied, Deutsche Gesellschaft für Psychiatrie. Hon. LLD Dundee, 1971. Hon. FRSocMed, 1976. Editor-in-chief, British Journal of Psychiatry, 1961-72. *Publications:* Introduction to Physical Methods of Treatment in Psychiatry (with W. Sargant), 1946; Patterns of Marriage (with M. Woodside), 1951; Psychotic and Neurotic Illness in Twins, 1953; Clinical Psychiatry (with W. Mayer-Gross and M. Roth), 1969; The Ebbless Sea (poems), 1968. Papers on genetical and psychiatric subjects. *Recreations:* Shakespeare studies, painting. *Address:* Institute of Psychiatry, SE5 8AF. *T:* 01-703 5411.

See also P. M. Oppenheimer.

SLATER, Gordon Archbold, OBE 1974; MusD (Dunelm); FRCO; JP; retired as Organist of Lincoln Cathedral (1930-66); Adjudicator at Music Festivals throughout UK since 1920; Organ Recitalist (including radio and TV, since 1920; *b* Harrogate, 1 Mar. 1896; *s* of late William Henry Slater, West Park, Harrogate; *m* 1920, Mary Hanson Thistlethwaite, *d* of late Samuel Newton, London; one *s* one *d. Educ:* privately; studied under Sir Edward C. Bairstow at York Minster, 1914-16. Served in HM Forces, 1916-19; Organist of Boston Parish Church, 1919-27; Conductor of Boston Choral Society, 1919-27; Billingborough Choral Society, 1924-27; Musical Director Holland Choirs' Triennial Festival, 1920-27; Gate Burton Players, 1925-27; Organist and Master of the Choir, Leicester Cathedral, 1927-30; Founder and Conductor Leicester Bach Choir, 1927-30; Melton Mowbray Choral Society, 1928-29; Lecturer in Singing, Leicester Univ. Coll. also in Music, Extra-Mural Dept, 1929-30; Conductor: Lincoln Musical Society, 1931-66; Symph. Orch., 1932-66; Lectr in Music, Extra Mural Dept, Nottingham Univ., 1932-59, Hull Univ., 1932-72, Sheffield Univ., 1972-74. Ferens Fine Art Lecturer, 1946-47; Adjudicated Canadian Musical Festivals, 1935, 1948. *Publications:* solo songs, choral songs, piano pieces, Church and Organ Music. *Recreation:* travelling. *Address:* 3 Pottergate, Lincoln LN2 1PH. *T:* Lincoln 26320.

SLATER, Gordon Charles Henry, CMG 1964; CBE 1956; Director, Branch Office in London of International Labour Office, 1964-70; Under-Secretary, Ministry of Labour, in the Overseas Department, 1960-64, retired; *b* 14 Dec. 1903; *s* of Matthew and Florence Slater; *m* 1928, Doris Primrose Hammond; one *s* one *d*. Entered Ministry of Labour, 1928, as Third Class Officer; Assistant Secretary, Organisation and Establishments, 1945, Disabled Persons Branch, 1949; Secretary of National Advisory Council on Employment of Disabled Persons, 1949-56; Sec. of Piercy Committee on Rehabilitation of Disabled, 1953-56; Under-Sec., Ministry of Labour, 1958. Member Governing Body, ILO, 1961-64; UK Govt delegate, IL Conf., 1961-64. Mem. Berkshire CC, 1970-, Vice-Chm., 1977-. *Address:* White House, Altwood Road, Maidenhead, Berks. *T:* Maidenhead 27463.

SLATER, James Derrick, FCA; *b* 13 March 1929; *o s* of Hubert and Jessica Slater; *m* 1965, Helen Wyndham Goodwyn; two *s* two *d. Educ:* Preston Manor County Sch. Accountant and then Gen. Man. to a gp of metal finishing cos, 1953-55; Sec., Park Royal Vehicles Ltd, 1955-58; Dep. Sales Dir, Leyland Motor Corp. Ltd, 1963; Chm., Slater Walker Securities Ltd, 1964-75; Dir, BLMC, 1969-75. FCA 1963 (ACA 1953). *Publication:* Return to Go, 1977. *Recreations:* chess, backgammon, golf, table tennis. *Address:* High Beeches, Blackhills, Esher, Surrey.

SLATER, John Fell, CMG 1972; Assistant Secretary, HM Treasury, since 1968; *b* 3 July 1924; *s* of J. Alan Slater, FRIBA, and Freide R. Slater (*née* Flight); *m* 1951, Susan Baron; two *s* two *d* (and one *d* decd). *Educ:* Abinger Hill Preparatory Sch.; Leighton Park Sch.; New Coll., Oxford (BA). *Recreations:* fly-fishing, sailing, parties, birdwatching, beer-making, squash. *Address:* 22 St Marks Crescent, Regents Park, NW1 7TU. *T:* 01-485 9446; Crow's Nest, Ferry Road, Walberswick, Suffolk. *Clubs:* Le Petit Club Français; Southwold Sailing.

SLATER, Kenneth Frederick, CEng, FIEE; Head of Military and Civil Systems Department and Deputy Director, Royal Signals and Radar Establishment, since 1977; *b* 31 July 1925; *s* of Charles Frederick and Emily Gertrude Slater; *m* 1965, Marjorie Gladys Beadsworth, Northampton. *Educ:* Hull Grammar Sch.; Manchester Univ. BSc Tech (Hons). Admiralty Signal Estab. Extension, 1943-46; RRE, 1949-63; UK Mem., NATO Air Defence Planning Team, 1964; Supt, Radar Div., RRE, 1965-68; Asst Dir of Electronics R&D, Min. of Technology, 1968-70, Dir, 1970-71; Head of Ground Radar Gp, 1971-75, of Electronics Gp, 1975, of Applied Physics Dept, and Dep. Dir, 1976, RRE. *Publications:* specialist contribs on Radar to Encyclopaedia Britannica and Encyclopaedic Dictionary of Physics; technical articles. *Recreations:* photography, music. *Address:* Wessenden, Blackheath Way, West Malvern WR14 4DR. *T:* Malvern 5576.

SLATER, Leonard, CBE 1976; JP; *b* 23 July 1908; *s* of S. M. Slater, Oldham, and Heysham, Lancs; *m* 1943, Olga Patricia George; two *s. Educ:* Hulme Grammar School, Oldham; St Catharine's College, Cambridge (MA). British Guiana Exped. 1929; Research at Cambridge, 1930-32; MA 1932. Lecturer in Geography, Univ. of Rangoon, 1932-37; Geography Master, Repton School, 1937. Served War, 1940-45; RE (Survey) in UK, India and SE Asia; Lieut-Col, 1944 and Hon. Lieut-Col, 1946. Durham Colleges, Univ. of Durham Geography Dept: Lectr, 1939; Reader, 1948; Pro-Vice-Chancellor, Durham Univ., 1969-73; Master, University Coll., Durham, 1953-73. Mem. Peterlee Develt Corp., 1956-63; JP, Durham, 1961; Chairman: Durham Hosp. Management Cttee, 1961-73; Durham AHA, 1973-77; Mem., Newcastle Regional Hosp. Bd, 1965-69 and 1971-74. *Publications:* articles in geographical periodicals. *Recreation:* travel. *Address:* 8 Farnley Ridge, Durham DH1 4HB. *T:* Durham 63319. *Club:* Pathfinders'.

SLATER, Richard Mercer Keene, CMG 1962; Adviser to Commercial Union Assurance Co.; *b* 27 May 1915; *s* of late Samuel Henry Slater, CMG, CIE; *m* 1939, Barbara Janet Murdoch; four *s. Educ:* Eton; Magdalene Coll., Cambridge. Indian Civil Service (Punjab Commission), 1939-47; joined HM Diplomatic Service, 1947; served in Karachi (on secondment to Commonwealth Relations Office), Lima, Moscow, Rangoon and Foreign Office; Ambassador to Cuba, 1966-70; High Comr in Uganda and Ambassador to Rwanda, 1970-72; Asst Under-Sec. of State, FCO, 1973. *Address:* Vicary's, Odiham, Hants.

SLATER, Admiral Sir Robin L. F. D.; *see* Durnford-Slater.

SLATTERY, Rear-Adm. Sir Matthew (Sausse), KBE 1960; Kt 1955; CB 1946; FRAeS 1946; *b* 12 May 1902; 3rd *s* of late H. F. Slattery, one-time Chairman of National Bank Ltd; *m* 1925, Mica Mary, *d* of Col G. D. Swain, CMG; two *s* one *d. Educ:* Stonyhurst Coll.; RN Colls, Osborne and Dartmouth. Joined RN, 1916; Director Air Material, Admiralty, 1939-41; commanded HMS Cleopatra, 1941-42; appointed Director-General of Naval Aircraft Development and Production, Ministry of Aircraft Production, 1941, and Chief Naval Representative, 1943; Vice-Controller (Air) and Chief of Naval Air Equipment at Admiralty, and Chief Naval Representative on Supply Council, Ministry of Supply, 1945-48; retd list, Royal Navy, 1946. Vice-Chm., Air Requirements Bd, 1960-74. Man. Dir, Short Brothers & Harland, Ltd, 1948-52, Chm. and Man. Dir, 1952-60; Chm.: (SB Realisations) Ltd, 1952-60; Bristol Aircraft Ltd, 1957-60; Dir Bristol Aeroplane Co. Ltd, 1957-60. Special Adviser to Prime Minister on Transport of Middle East Oil, 1957-59; Dir National Bank Ltd, 1959-60, 1963-69; Chairman: BOAC, 1960-63; BOAC-Cunard Ltd, 1962-63; R. & W. Hawthorn, Leslie & Co., 1966-73. Commander Legion of Merit (USA). DSc(*hc*) Queen's Univ., Belfast, 1954. *Recreations:* country pursuits. *Address:* Harvey's Farm, Warninglid, West Sussex.

SLATYER, Prof. Ralph Owen, FRS 1975; Professor, Department of Environmental Biology, Australian National University, Canberra, since 1967; *b* 16 April 1929; *s* of Thomas Henry and Jean Slatyer; *m* 1953, June Helen Wade; one *s* two *d. Educ:* Univ. of Western Australia. BSc (Agric.), MSc, DSc. CSIRO Res. Scientist, subseq. Chief Res. Scientist, 1951-67. Member: Australian Res. Grants Cttee, 1969-72; Nat. Capital Planning Cttee, 1973-; Australian Science and Technology Council, 1975-; Aust. Nat. Commn for Unesco, 1975- (Chm., 1976-); Pres., Ecol Soc. of Austr., 1969-71; Fellow, Austr. Acad. Sci., 1967. Edgeworth David Medal, 1960; Austr. Medal of Agric. Sci., 1968. For. Associate, US Nat. Acad. of Sciences, 1976. *Publications:* (with I. C. McIlroy) Practical Microclimatology, 1961 (Russian edn 1964); Plant-Water Relationships, 1967 (Russian edn 1970); (ed with R. A. Perry) Arid Lands of Australia, 1969; (ed jtly) Photosynthesis and Photorespiration, 1971; papers in learned jls. *Recreations:* ski-ing, bushwalking. *Address:* 10 Tennyson Crescent, Forrest, ACT 2603, Australia. *T:* (062)-73-2875.

SLAUGHTER, Frank Gill, MC; MD, FACS; novelist (self-employed); physician and surgeon (retd); *b* Washington, USA, 25 Feb. 1908; *s* of Stephen Lucius Slaughter and Sallie Nicholson Gill; *m* 1933, Jane Mundy; two *s. Educ:* Duke Univ. (AB); Johns Hopkins (MD). Served War, 1942-46 (MC): Major to Lt-Col, US Army Med. Corps. Intern, asst resident, and resident surgeon, Jefferson Hosp., Roanoke, Va, 1930-34; practice, specializing in surgery, Jacksonville, Fla, 1934-42; retired, 1946; Lectr, W. Colston Leigh, Inc., NY City, 1947-49. Res. Diplomate, Amer. Bd of Surgery. Mem., Sons of Amer. Revolution. Presbyterian (Elder). *Publications:* That None Should Die, 1941; Spencer Brade, MD, 1942; Air Surgeon, 1943; Battle Surgeon, 1944; A Touch of Glory, 1945; In a Dark Garden, 1946; The New Science of Surgery, 1946; The Golden Isle, 1947; Sangaree, 1948; Medicine for Moderns, 1948; Divine Mistress, 1949; The Stubborn Heart, 1950; Immortal Magyar, 1950; Fort Everglades, 1951; The Road to Bithynia, 1951; East Side General, 1952; The Galilieans, 1953; Storm Haven, 1953; The Song of Ruth, Apalachee Gold, 1954; The Healer, Flight from Natchez, 1955; The Scarlet Cord, 1956; The Warrior, 1956; Sword and Scalpel, 1957; The Mapmaker, 1957; Daybreak, 1958; The Thorn of Arimathea, 1958; The Crown and the Cross, 1959; Lorena, 1959; The Land and the Promise, 1960; Pilgrims in Paradise, 1960; Epidemic, 1961; The Curse of Jezebel, 1961;

David: Warrior and King, 1962; Tomorrow's Miracle, 1962; Devil's Harvest, 1963; Upon This Rock, 1963; A Savage Place, 1964; The Purple Quest, 1965; Constantine: The Miracle of the Flaming Cross, 1965; Surgeon, USA, 1966; God's Warrior, 1967; Doctor's Wives, 1967; The Sins of Herod, 1968; Surgeon's Choice, 1969; Countdown, 1970; Code Five, 1971; Convention, MD, 1972; Life blood, 1974; Stonewall Brigade, 1975; Cloque Ship, 1977; Devil's Gamble, 1978. *Recreations:* boating, hiking, reading. *Address:* 5051 Yacht Club Road, Jacksonville, Fla 32210, USA. *T:* 904-389-7677. *Club:* Timuquana Country (Jacksonville, Fla).

SLAUGHTER, James Cameron, CMG 1963; Executive Adviser, Brisbane City Council, since 1967 (Town Clerk and City Administrator, 1940-67); *b* 16 Aug. 1902; *s* of late Ernest E. Slaughter; *m* 1927, Ida M. Taylor; one *s* one *d*. *Educ:* Normal School, Brisbane. Trustee, City Debt Redemption Fund, 1940; Chm., Lang Park Trust, 1959; Town Clerk: Bundaberg City Coun., 1936-40; Coolangatta Town Coun., 1927-36; Shire Clerk: Gatton Shire Coun.; Inglewood Shire Coun.; Chief Clerk, Ithaca Town Council. AASA; FIMA. *Recreations:* bowls, fishing. *Clubs:* Johnsonian and Tattersalls; Rugby League, Booroodabin Bowling.

SLEEMAN, (Stuart) Colin; His Honour Judge Sleeman; a Circuit Judge, since 1976; *s* of Stuart Bertram Sleeman and Phyllis Grace (*née* Pitt); *m* 1944, Margaret Emily, *d* of late William Joseph Farmer; two *s* one *d*. *Educ:* Clifton Coll.; Merton Coll., Oxford (BA 1936, MA 1963). Called to the Bar, Gray's Inn, 1938; Bencher, 1974. World War II: Admin. Officer, Prize Dept, Min. of Economic Warfare, 1939-40; Lt-Col 16th-5th Lancers; Staff Captain: RAC Wing, Combined Trng Centre, 1941; 6th Armoured Div., 1942; Adjt, RAC Range, Minehead, 1942-44; Asst Judge Advocate Gen., HQ Allied Land Forces, SE Asia, 1945. London Corresp., Scottish Law Rev., 1949-54; a Recorder, 1975-76. *Publications:* The Trial of Gozawa Sadaichi and Nine Others, 1948; (with S. C. Silkin) The 'Double Tenth' Trial, 1950. *Recreations:* travel, genealogy. *Address:* Woodchurch, Knoll Road, Dorking, Surrey. *T:* Dorking 3616.

SLEIGH, Sir Hamilton (Morton Howard), Kt 1970; a non-executive Director, H. C. Sleigh Ltd, since 1975 (Chairman, 1947-75, and Managing Director, 1947-71); *b* 20 March 1896; *s* of Howard Crofton Sleigh and Marion Elizabeth Sleigh; *m* 1st, 1926, Doris Margherita Halbert (*d* 1968); two *s*; 2nd, 1973, Brenda, *widow* of J. W. Dodds. *Educ:* Sherborne Sch., Dorset. Kt Cross, Order of White Rose of Finland; Order of Lion of Finland. *Recreation:* gardening. *Address:* 42 Wallace Avenue, Toorak, Victoria 3142, Australia. *Clubs:* Australian (Melbourne and Sydney).

SLEIGHT, Sir John Frederick, 3rd Bt, *cr* 1920; *b* 13 April 1909; *s* of Major Sir Ernest Sleight, 2nd Bt and Margaret (*d* 1976), *d* of C. F. Carter, JP, The Limes, Grimsby; *S* father 1946; *m* 1942, Jacqueline Margaret Mundell, *widow* of Ronald Mundell and *o d* of late Major H. R. Carter of Brisbane, Queensland; one *s*. *Heir:* *s* Richard Sleight, *b* 27 May 1946. *Address:* The Garden House, 15 High Street, Thame, Oxon.

SLEIGHT, Prof. Peter, MD (Cantab), DM (Oxon), FRCP; Field-Marshal Alexander Professor of Cardiovascular Medicine in the University of Oxford, and Fellow of Exeter College, Oxford, since 1973; *b* 27 June 1929; *s* of William and Mary Sleight, Boston Spa, Yorks; *m* 1953, Gillian France; two *s*. *Educ:* Leeds Grammar Sch.; Gonville and Caius Coll., Cambridge; St Bartholomew's Hosp., London. Ho. Phys. and Ho. Surg., Med. and Surg. Professorial Units, Bart's, 1953; Sen. Registrar, St George's Hosp., London, 1959-64; Bissinger Fellow, Cardiovascular Research Unit, Univ. of California, San Francisco, 1961-63; MRC Scientific Officer, Depts of Physiology and Medicine, Univ. of Oxford, 1964-66; Consultant Physician, Radcliffe Infirmary, Oxford, 1966-73; Visiting Prof., Univ. of Sydney (Warren McDonald Sen. Overseas Fellow of Aust. Heart Foundn), 1972-73; Hon. Prof. of Medicine, Federal Univ. of Pernambuco, 1975. Young Investigators Award, Amer. Coll. of Cardiology, 1963. *Publications:* Modern Trends in Cardiology, 1976; contribs on nervous control of the circulation and hypertension in: Circulation Research; Jl Physiol. *Recreations:* golf, travel. *Address:* Wayside, 32 Crown Road, Wheatley, Oxon. *Club:* Royal Air Force.

SLEIGHTHOLME, Derek; Chairman of Tyne and Wear County Council, 1975-76; *b* 4 June 1935; *s* of George Henry Sleightholme and Evelyn Sleightholme; *m* 1957, Norma; one *s* one *d*. *Educ:* Washington Glebe. RAF, 1953-57; miner, 1957-75. *Recreations:* sport, agriculture. *Club:* Celtic (Washington).

SLEMON, Air Marshal Charles Roy, CB 1946; CBE 1943; retired from RCAF, 1964; Executive Vice-President, US Air Force Academy Foundation Inc., since 1964; *b* Winnipeg, Manitoba, Canada, 7 November 1904; *s* of Samuel Slemon and Mary Bonser; *m* 1935, Marion Pamela Slemon, Bowmanville, Ont; one *s* two *d*. *Educ:* University of Manitoba (BSc). Lieut COTC (Army), Canada, 1923; Cadet Royal Canadian Air Force, 1923; Royal Air Force Staff College Course, England, 1938; Senior Air Staff Officer at Western Air Command Headquarters, Canada, 1939-41; commanded Western Air Command, Canada, for 5 months in 1941; Director of Operations at RCAF HQ Ottawa, 1941-42; Senior Air Staff Officer, No. 6 (RCAF) Bomber Group, England, 1942-44; Air Vice-Marshal, 1945; Deputy AOC-in-C, RCAF Overseas, March 1945; Commanded Canadian Air Forces preparing for the Pacific, 1945; Air Council Member for Supply and Organization, 1946; Air Council Member for Operations and Training, 1947-48; AOC Trg Comd, RCAF, 1949-53; Chief of the Air Staff, Canada, 1953-57; Dep. C-in-C, N American Defence Comd (Canada-USA), 1957-64, retd. Hon. LLD (Univ. of Manitoba), 1953; Hon. DMSc (RMC), Kingston, Ont, 1965. USA Legion of Merit, 1946; French Legion of Honour and Croix de Guerre with Palm, 1947. *Recreations:* golf, swimming. *Address:* (business) Air Force Academy Foundation Inc., PO Box 1838, Colorado Springs, Colorado, USA; (home) 8 Thayer Road, Broadmoor Heights, Colorado Springs, Colorado 80906, USA.

SLESSER, Rt. Hon. Sir Henry, PC 1929; Kt 1924; JP Devon; a Lord Justice of Appeal, 1929-40; *b* London, 1883; *y s* of Ernest Slesser, Gerrards Cross, Bucks; *m* Margaret, *e d* of late Corrie Grant, KC. *Educ:* Oundle and St Paul's Schools; London Univ. Called to Bar, 1906, Bencher of the Inner Temple, 1924; KC, 1924; MP (Lab.) SE Leeds, 1924-29; HM Solicitor-General, 1924. Devon CC, 1946-68; Alderman, 1956; Chairman of Dartmoor Nat. Park Cttee, 1948-64. OSB (oblate); Hon. LLD Exeter, 1963. *Publications:* Trade Union Law, 1922 (3rd ed. 1928); Religio Laici, 1929; The Pastured Shire and Other Verses, 1935; Law (Heritage Series), 1936; Judgment Reserved, 1941; The Judicial Office and other matters, 1943; History of the Liberal Party, 1944; Order and Disorder, 1945; Administration of the Law, 1948; Middle Ages in the West, 1949 (2nd edn 1951); The Anglican Dilemma, 1952; The Art of Judgment and other legal studies, 1962. *Address:* Holcombe House, Moretonhampstead, Devon TQ13 8PW.

SLESSOR, Marshal of the Royal Air Force Sir John Cotesworth, GCB, *cr* 1948 (KCB 1943; CB 1942); DSO 1937; MC 1916; DL; *b* Rhanikhet, India, 3 June 1897; *s* of late Major Arthur Kerr Slessor, Sherwood Foresters; *m* 1st, 1923, Hermione Grace (*d* 1970), *d* of Gerald Seymour Guiness, and *widow* of Lt-Col Herbert Carter; one *s* one *d*; 2nd, 1971, Marcella Florence, *widow* of Brig. R. T. Priest. *Educ:* Dragon School; Haileybury. Served European War, RFC, 1915-18: London Air Defence, France, Egypt, and Sudan (despatches, wounded, MC); served RAF India, 1921-23; RAF Staff College, 1924-25; commanded No. 4 Squadron, 1925-28; Air Staff, Air Ministry, 1928-30; Instructor, Staff College, Camberley, 1931-34; India, 1935-37: commanded No. 3 Indian Wing, Quetta, 1935; Waziristan Operations, 1936-37 (despatches, DSO); Director of Plans, Air Ministry, 1937-41; ADC to the King, 1938; Air rep., Anglo-French Conversations, 1939 and Anglo-American (ABC) Staff Conversations, 1941; AOC 5 (Bomber) Group, 1941; ACAS, (Policy), 1942-43 (Casablanca Conf.); AOC-in-C Coastal Command, 1943; C-in-C, RAF, Mediterranean and Middle East, 1944-45; Member of Air Council for Personnel, 1945-47; Commandant Imperial Defence College, 1948-49; Principal Air ADC to the King, 1948-50; Air Commodore, 1939, Air Vice-Marshal, 1941; Air Marshal, 1943; Air Chief Marshal, 1946; Marshal of the RAF, 1950. Chief of the Air Staff, 1950-52; Rep. British Chief of Staffs, NATO Confs, Brussels, Rome, Lisbon, Paris, Washington; Mem. UK Delegations, Commonwealth Relations Confs, 1954, 1959. Order of Leopold, Belgium; Légion d'Honneur, France, Order of Phœnix, Greece; Order of St Olaf, Norway; Legion of Merit, USA; Order of the Sword, Sweden; Partisan Star, Jugoslavia. Pres. the Victory (ex-Services) Club; Chairman, Star and Garter Home, 1953-67; Vice-Pres., Inst. of Strategic Studies; Gov.: Haileybury, Sherborne, King's (Bruton). JP and CC Somerset, 1963-74; High Sheriff, Somerset, 1965; DL, Somerset, 1969. *Publications:* Air Power and Armies, 1936; Strategy for the West, 1954; The Central Blue, 1956; The Great Deterrent, 1959; What Price Co-existence, 1961; These Remain, 1969. RUSI gold medal, 1936; Chesney Memorial Award, 1965. *Address:* Rimpton Manor, Yeovil, Somerset. *T:* Marston Magna 223. *Clubs:* Royal Air Force, Naval and Military (Hon. Life).

SLEVIN, Brian Francis, CMG 1975; OBE 1973; QPM 1968; CPM 1965; Commissioner of Police, The Royal Hong Kong Police Force, since 1974; *b* 13 Aug. 1926; *s* of late Thomas and Helen Slevin; *m* 1972, Constance Gay, *e d* of Major Ronald Moody; one *s*. *Educ:* Blackrock Coll., Ireland. Palestine Police, 1946-48; Hong Kong Police, 1949-; Directing Staff, Overseas Police Courses, Metropolitan Police Coll., Hendon, London, 1955-57; Director, Special Branch, 1966-69; Sen. Asst Comr of Police, Comdg Kowloon Dist, 1969-70; Dir, Criminal Investigation Dept, 1971; Dep. Comr of Police, 1971, Hong Kong. *Recreations:* walking, golf, reading. *Address:* 50 Magazine Gap Road, The Peak, Hong Kong. *T:* 5-97112. *Clubs:* Royal Automobile; Hong Kong, Royal Hong Kong Golf, Royal Hong Kong Jockey (all three Hong Kong).

SLIGO, 10th Marquess of, *cr* 1800; **Denis Edward Browne; Baron** Mount Eagle, 1760; Viscount Westport, 1768; Earl of Altamont, 1771; Earl of Clanricarde, 1543 and 1800 (special remainder); Baron Monteagle (UK), 1806; *b* 13 Dec. 1908; *er s* of late Lt-Col Lord Alfred Eden Browne, DSO (5th *s* of 5th Marquess) and late Cicely, *d* of Edward Wormald, 15 Berkeley Square, W; *S* uncle, 1952; *m* 1930, José Gauche; one *s*. *Educ:* Eton. *Heir:* *s* Earl of Altamont, *qv*. *Address:* c/o Messrs Trower, Still and Keeling, 5 New Square, Lincoln's Inn, WC2.
See also Baron Brabourne.

SLIM, family name of Viscount Slim.

SLIM, 2nd Viscount *cr* 1960, of Yarralumla and Bishopston; **John Douglas Slim**, OBE 1973; Director: Boyden International Ltd; Frank O'Shanohun (Overseas) Ltd; *b* 20 July 1927; *s* of Field Marshal the 1st Viscount Slim, KG, GCB, GCMG, GCVO, GBE, DSO, MC, and of Aileen, *d* of Rev. J. A. Robertson, MA, Edinburgh; *S* father, 1970; *m* 1958, Elisabeth, *d* of Arthur Rawdon Spinney, CBE; two *s* one *d*. *Educ:* Prince of Wales Royal Indian Military College, Dehra Dun. Emergency Commn, Indian Army, 6 Gurkha Rifles, 1945-48; Lieut, Argyll and Sutherland Highlanders, 1948; Staff. Coll., Camberley, 1961; Brigade Major, HQ Infantry Bde (TA), 1962-64; JSSC 1964; GSO2, HQ Middle East Command, 1966-67; Lt-Col 1967; Comdr, 22 Special Air Service Regt, 1967-70; GSO1 (Special Forces) HQ UK Land Forces, 1970-72; retired 1972. President, Burma Star Association, 1971. *Heir:* *s* Hon. Mark William Rawdon Slim, *b* 13 Feb. 1960. *Address:* c/o Lloyds Bank Ltd, 6 Pall Mall, SW1. *Club:* Special Forces.

SLIMMINGS, Sir William Kenneth MacLeod, Kt 1966; CBE 1960; *b* 15 Dec. 1912; *s* of George and Robina Slimmings; *m* 1943, Lilian Ellen Willis; one *s* one *d*. *Educ:* Dunfermline High School. Chartered Accountant: Partner in Thomson McLintock & Co., Chartered Accountants, London, etc., 1946-. Member: Committee of Inquiry on the Cost of Housebuilding, 1947-53; Committee on Tax-paid Stocks, 1952-53; Committee on Cheque Endorsement, 1955-56; Performing Right Tribunal, 1963-; Chairman: Board of Trade Advisory Committee, 1957-66; Review Bd for Govt Contracts, 1971-; Accounting Standards Cttee, 1976-. Member: Council, Inst. Chartered Accountants of Scotland, 1962-66 (Pres., 1969-70); Scottish Tourist Bd, 1969-76; Review Body on Doctors' and Dentists' Pay, 1976-. Hon. DLitt, Heriot-Watt, 1970. *Recreation:* gardening. *Address:* (business) 70 Finsbury Pavement, EC2A 1SX. *T:* 01-638 6030; (home) 62 The Avenue, Worcester Park, Surrey. *T:* 01-337 2579. *Club:* Caledonian.

SLINGER, William; Deputy Secretary, Department of Education for Northern Ireland, since 1975; *b* 27 Oct. 1917; *yr s* of late William Slinger and Maud Slinger, Newcastle, Co. Down; *m* 1944, Muriel, *o d* of late R. J. Johnston, Belfast; three *d*. *Educ:* Methodist Coll., Belfast; Queen's Univ., Belfast (BComSc). Entered Northern Ireland Civil Service, 1937; Private Secretary: to Minister of Labour, 1942-43 and 1945-46; to Minister of Public Security, 1944; Sec. to Nat. Arbitration Tribunal (NI), 1946-48; Principal, Min. of Labour and Nat. Insurance, Industrial Relations Div., 1954-60; Asst Sec. and Head of Industrial Relations Div., 1961-69; Sec., Dept of Community Relations, 1969-75. *Recreations:* gardening, walking. *Address:* Cairnfield, Circular Road, Belfast BT4 2GD. *T:* Belfast 768240. *Clubs:* East India, Devonshire, Sports and Public Schools; Civil Service (N Ireland).

SLIVE, Prof. Seymour; Gleason Professor of Fine Arts at Harvard University since 1973; Director, Fogg Art Museum, since 1975; *b* Chicago, 15 Sept. 1920; *s* of Daniel Slive and Sonia (*née* Rapoport); *m* 1946, Zoya Gregorovna Sandomirsky; one *s* two *d*. *Educ:* Univ. of Chicago. BA 1943; PhD 1952. Served US Navy, Lieut, CO Small Craft, 1943-46. Instructor in Art History, Oberlin Coll., 1950-51; Asst Prof. and Chm. of Art Dept, Pomona Coll., 1952-54; Asst Prof. 1954-57, Assoc. Prof.

1957-61, Prof., 1961-73, Chm. of Dept 1968-71, Fine Arts, Harvard Univ.; Exchange Prof., Univ. of Leningrad, 1961. Ryerson Lectr, Yale, 1962. Slade Prof. of Fine Art, Univ. of Oxford, 1972-73. FAAAS 1964. For. Mem., Netherlands Soc. of Sciences, 1971. Hon. MA Harvard, 1958; Hon. MA Oxford, 1972. Officer, Order of Orange Nassau, 1962. *Publications:* Rembrandt and His Critics: 1630-1730, 1953; Drawings of Rembrandt, 1965; (with J. Rosenberg) Dutch Art and Architecture: 1600-1800, 1966; Frans Hals, 3 vols, 1970-74; contribs to learned jls. *Address:* 1 Walker Street Place, Cambridge, Mass 02138, USA.

SLOAN, Norman Alexander, QC (Scot.) 1953; Director, Swan Hunter Shipbuilders Ltd; *b* 27 Jan. 1914; *s* of George Scott Sloan and Margaret Hutcheson Smith; *m* 1944, Peggy Perry; two *s* one *d*. *Educ:* Glasgow Academy; Glasgow University (BL). Solicitor, 1935; Admitted to Faculty of Advocates, 1939; Served in RNVR 1940-46. Lecturer in Industrial Law, Edinburgh University, 1946-51; Standing Counsel to Department of Health for Scotland, 1946-51; Advocate-Depute, 1951-53. Director: The Shipbuilding Employers' Federation, 1955-68; Shipbuilders and Repairers Nat. Assoc., 1968-72; Swan Hunter Group Ltd, 1973-77. *Recreation:* golf. *Address:* Edenvale, 6 High Park, Morpeth, Northumberland NE61 2SS. *T:* Morpeth 55218; PO Box 1, Wallsend, Tyne and Wear NE28 6EQ. *T:* Newcastle upon Tyne 628921.

SLOANE, Maj.-Gen. John Bramley Malet, CB 1967; CBE 1962 (OBE 1951); DL; Director of Manning (Army), Ministry of Defence, 1964-67; retired; *b* 17 Sept. 1912; *m* 1939, Marjorie (*née* Crowley); three *s*. Late Argyll and Sutherland Highlanders. DL Beds, 1976. *Recreations:* golf, walking. *Address:* Jordans, Newton Blossomville, near Turvey, Beds. *T:* Turvey 392. *Club:* Army and Navy.

SLOCUM, Captain Frank Alexander, CMG 1953; OBE 1935; RN (retd); *b* 30 Sept. 1897; 2nd *s* of late Henry Slocum, Micheldever, Hampshire, and of Emily (*née* Clarke), *e d* of Capt. William Clarke, Roy. Fusiliers; *m* 1922, Vera, *e d* of late John Metherell Gard, Stoke, Devonport; two *d*. *Educ:* Royal Naval Establishments; Gonville and Caius College, Cambridge. Entered RN, 1914; served European War, 1914-18, in Grand Fleet; Lieut, 1918; 2nd Destroyer Flotilla, Home Fleet, 1920; qualified in (N) duties, 1921. Served in Persian Gulf, Mediterranean, and Home Fleets; psc RN Staff Coll., 1931; Mediterranean Fleet (Revenge and Resolution); staff of Tactical School, 1935; Actg Comdr, 1939; Actg Capt., 1940. Served War of 1939-45 as Dep. Dir Ops Div., Admiralty, and in charge of Auxiliary Patrol Flotillas; retd list, 1947, in war service rank of Captain. Temp. 1st Sec., British Embassy, Oslo, 1954-56. Trials Capt. for contract-built HM Ships, 1956. Croix de Guerre avec Palme (France), 1946; Comdr Legion of Merit (USA), 1946; King Haakon VII Liberty Cross (Norway), 1947; King Christian X's Freedom Medal (Denmark), 1947. *Publications:* naval and seafaring articles and short stories. *Recreations:* sailing, naval history, marine surveying. *Address:* Stone Cottage, 3a Camden Park, Tunbridge Wells, Kent. *T:* Tunbridge Wells 27395. *Clubs:* Naval and Military, Pratt's.

SLOMAN, Albert Edward, DPhil; Vice-Chancellor of University of Essex, since 1962; *b* Launceston, Cornwall, 14 Feb. 1921; *y s* of Albert Sloman; *m* 1948, Marie Bernadette, *d* of Leo Bergeron, Cognac, France; three *d*. *Educ:* Launceston Coll., Cornwall; Wadham Coll., Oxford (Pope Exhibitioner, 1939). Mediæval and Mod. Langs, 1941; MA (Oxon and Dublin); DPhil (Oxon). Served War of 1939-45 (despatches): night-fighter pilot with 219 and 68 squadrons; Flight-Lieut. Lecturer in Spanish, Univ. of California, Berkeley, USA, 1946-47; Reader in Spanish, in charge of Spanish studies, Univ. of Dublin, 1947-53; Fellow TCD, 1950-53; Gilmour Professor of Spanish, University of Liverpool, 1953-62; Dean, Faculty of Arts, 1961-62. Editor of Bulletin of Hispanic Studies, 1953-62. Reith Lecturer, 1963. Chairman, Dept of Education State Studentship Cttee (Humanities), 1965-; Pres., Conf. of European Rectors and Vice-Chancellors, 1969-74; Member: Council of Europe Cttee for Higher Educn and Research, 1963-72; Conf. of European Rectors and Vice-Chancellors, 1965-; Adm. Bd, Internat. Assoc., of Univs, 1965-75; Bd of Governors, Univ. of Guyana, 1966-; Internat. Assoc. of Universities, 1970- (Vice-Pres.); Economic and Social Cttee, EEC, 1973-. Hon. Doctorate, Nice, 1974. *Publications:* The Sources of Calderón's El Principe constante, 1950; The Dramatic Craftsmanship of Calderón, 1958; A University in the Making, 1964. Articles and reviews in Modern Language Review, Bulletin of Hispanic Studies, Hispanic Review, Romance Philology and other journals. *Recreation:* travel. *Address:* The University of Essex, Colchester. *Club:* Savile.

SLOMAN, Mrs (Margaret) Barbara; Principal, Civil Service College, since 1976 (Deputy Principal, 1975); *b* 29 June 1925; *d* of Charles and Margaret Pilkington-Rogers; *m* 1950, Peter Sloman, *qv*; one *s* one *d*. *Educ:* Cheltenham Ladies' Coll.; Girton Coll., Cambridge. BA Hons Classics. Asst Principal, Treasury, 1947, Principal 1954-65; Asst Sec., DES, 1965-69; Asst Sec., Civil Service Dept, 1970-75; Under-Sec., Civil Service Dept, 1975-. *Address:* 26 Glebe Road, SW13 0EA. *T:* 01-876 4429.

SLOMAN, Peter; Education Officer, Association of Metropolitan Authorities, since 1974; *b* Oct. 1919; *s* of H. N. P. Sloman and Mary Sloman (*née* Trinder); *m* 1950, Margaret Barbara (*see* M. B. Sloman); one *s* one *d*. *Educ:* Winchester Coll.; New Coll., Oxford. War Service (RA), 1939-46. Home Civil Service, 1946-74; Under-Secretary, 1968; Min. (later Dept) of Education; Treasury; Ministries of Defence, Land and Natural Resources, Housing and Local Govt. idc 1960. *Address:* 26 Glebe Road, SW13 0EA.

SLOSS; *see* Butler-Sloss.

SLOT, Peter Maurice Joseph; a Recorder of the Crown Court, since 1974; *b* 3 Dec. 1932; *s* of Joseph and Marie Slot; *m* 1962, Mary Eiluned Lewis; two *s* three *d*. *Educ:* Bradfield Coll.; St John's Coll., Oxford (MA). Called to Bar, Inner Temple, 1957. *Recreations:* golf, madrigals, argument. *Address:* The Red House, Betchworth, Surrey RH3 7DR. *T:* Betchworth 2010. *Club:* Walton Heath Golf.

SLYNN, Hon. Sir Gordon, Kt 1976; **Hon. Mr Justice Slynn;** a Judge of the High Court of Justice, Queen's Bench Division, since 1976; *b* 17 Feb. 1930; *er s* of late John Slynn and of Edith Slynn; *m* 1962, Odile Marie Henriette Boutin. *Educ:* Sandbach Sch.; Goldsmiths' Coll.; Trinity Coll., Cambridge (MA, LLB). Called to Bar, Gray's Inn, 1956; Master of Bench, Gray's Inn, 1970; QC 1974. Jun. Counsel, Min. of Labour, 1967-68; Jun. Counsel to the Treasury (Common Law), 1968-74; Leading Counsel to the Treasury, 1974-76. Recorder of Hereford, 1971; a Recorder, and Hon. Recorder of Hereford, 1972-76. Dep. Chief Steward of Hereford, 1977-. Hon. Vice-Pres., Union Internat. des Avocats, 1976- (Vice-Pres., 1973-76). Mem. Ct, Broderers Company. Chevalier du Tastevin. *Address:* Royal Courts of Justice, Strand, WC2. *Clubs:* Garrick, Beefsteak.

SLYTH, Arthur Roy, CB 1966; OBE 1957; *b* 30 May 1910; *s* of Thomas Slyth; *m* 1938, Anne Mary Muir Grieve (*d* 1973). *Educ:* Lincoln School. Entered Exchequer and Audit Department, 1929; Dep. Sec., 1963; Sec., 1963-73. *Recreation:* golf. *Address:* 28 Shepherd's Hill, N6. *T:* 01-340 0818.

SMAILES, Prof. Arthur Eltringham, MA, DLit London, FRGS; Emeritus Professor of Geography in the University of London; Professor of Geography at Queen Mary College, 1955-73; *b* Haltwhistle, Northumberland, 23 March 1911; *o s* of John Robert and Mary Elizabeth Smailes; *m* 1937, Dorothy Forster; one *d*. *Educ:* Grammar School of Queen Elizabeth, Hexham; University College, London. BA (London) with First Cl. Hons in Geography, 1930, MA 1933, DLit 1965. Lecturer, University College, London, from 1931 and Reader in Geography, 1950-53; Head of Department of Geography, Queen Mary College, University of London, 1953-73. Geographer Consultant, Middlesbrough Survey and Plan, 1944-45. Hon. Secretary, Inst. of British Geographers, 1951-62, Pres., 1970. Chm., Internat. Geog. Union Commn on Processes and Patterns of Urbanisation, 1972-76; Mem., UGC Social Studies Sub-Cttee, 1973-. Circuit Steward, West London Mission, Kingsway Hall, 1965-69. Research Medal, RSGS, 1964. *Publications:* The Geography of Towns, 1953; North England, 1960. Various articles in geographical and town planning journals. *Recreations:* gardening, travel. *Address:* 7 Lucerne Road, Milford-on-Sea, Hants.

SMALDON, Catherine Agnes, CBE 1964; Chairman, General Nursing Council for England and Wales, 1960-65; retired as Chief Nursing Officer and Principal, Queen Elizabeth School of Nursing, United Birmingham Hospitals (1955-63); *b* 23 April 1903; *d* of William Ernest Smaldon and Catherine Smaldon (*née* Fairley). *Educ:* The Old Palace School, Croydon; Charing Cross Hospital. Ward Sister, Princess Mary's Hosp., Margate, 1928-29; Charing Cross Hospital: Ward Sister, Theatre Sister, Out Patient Dept Sister, Night Supt, Asst Matron, 1930-36. Matron: Brompton Hosp., London, 1936-40; Queen Elizabeth Hosp., Birmingham, 1940-55. *Recreations:* gardening, walking. *Address:* Higher Longparks, Sydenham, Lewdown, Devon EX20 4PU.

SMALE, John Arthur, CBE 1953; AFC 1919; Technical consultant, Marconi's Wireless Telegraph Co. Ltd, 1957-62, retd; *b* 16 Feb. 1895; *s* of Charles Blackwell and Ann Smale; *m* 1920, Hilda Marguerita Watts; one *d* (one *s* killed on active service, RAF, 1941). *Educ:* Wycliffe Coll., Stonehouse; Bristol Univ. (BSc). Apprentice British Thompson Houston, Rugby, 1914; served European War, 1914-18, in RNAS; RAF, 1918-19. Engineer, Marconi's Wireless Telegraph Co. Ltd, 1919-29; Cable & Wireless Ltd, 1929-57, retired (Asst Engineer-in-Chief, 1935-48; Engineer-in-Chief, 1948-57). Chairman Cyprus Inland Telecommunications Authority, 1955-60, retired. FIEE 1941; Chairman, Radio Section of IEE, 1953; FIEEE 1958. *Recreations:* sport, music. *Address:* Cotswold, 21 Ilex Way, Goring-By-Sea, W Sussex BN12 4UZ.

SMALL, Sir (Andrew) Bruce, Kt 1974; JP; Member Legislative Assembly (for Surfers Paradise), Queensland, since 1972; Re-elected Mayor, City of Gold Coast, Queensland, 1976; *b* 11 Dec. 1895; *s* of William Andrew and Annie Elizabeth Small; *m* 1939, Lillian Ada Mitchell; one *s*. *Educ:* Govt schools, Melbourne, Vic. Cycle manufacturer, 1920-58 (Manager, Aust. teams: Cyclists Tour de France, 1928-31; Bol d'Or Record Breaker Teams: Eng. 1934, 1935, 1937; Sir Hubert Opperman); Radio and Refrigerator Retail Chain (115 stores, with factory warehouse in all 6 state capitals); Mayor, City of Gold Coast, 1967-73, Alderman, 1973-76. Retired to Gold Coast, Qld, 1959 and estab. land devel of satellite town on River Nerang, and canal waterways. JP Queensland, 1967. Hon. Col, Kentucky (USA); FAIM; KStJ 1974. *Recreation:* music (vocal, brass band). *Address:* Wanamara, Isle of Capri, Surfers Paradise, Gold Coast, Queensland, Australia. *T:* (business) 390777, (political) 390458, (residence) 390044.

SMALL, Prof. John Rankin; Professor and Head of Department of Accountancy and Finance, Heriot-Watt University, since 1967; Vice-Principal, Heriot-Watt University; *b* 28 Feb. 1933; *s* of David and Annie Small; *m* 1957, Catherine Wood; one *s* two *d*. *Educ:* Harris Academy, Dundee; Dundee Sch. of Econs. BScEcon London; FCCA, FCMA, JDipMA. Dunlop Rubber Co., 1956-60; Lectr, Univ. of Edinburgh, 1960-64; Sen. Lectr, Univ. of Glasgow, 1964-67; Dean of Faculty of Econ. and Social Studies, Heriot-Watt Univ., 1972-74. Dir, Edinburgh Instruments Ltd; Dir, Edinburgh Chamber of Commerce. Mem. Council, Assoc. of Certified Accountants, 1971-. *Publications:* (jtly) Introduction to Managerial Economics, 1966; (contrib.) Business and Accounting in Europe, 1973; articles in accounting and financial jls on accounting and financial management. *Recreation:* golf. *Address:* 39 Caiystane Terrace, Edinburgh EH10 6ST. *T:* 031-445 2638. *Club:* Caledonian.

SMALL, Very Rev. Robert Leonard, CBE 1975 (OBE 1958); DD; Minister of St Cuthbert's Parish Church, Edinburgh, 1956-75; Chaplain to the Queen in Scotland, 1967-75, Extra Chaplain since 1975; *b* N Berwick, 12 May 1905; *s* of Rev. Robert Small, MA, and Marion C. McEwen; *m* 1931, Jane May McGregor; three *s* one *d*. *Educ:* N Berwick High Sch.; Edinburgh Univ.; New Coll., Edinburgh. MA 1st cl. hons Classics; Sen. Cunningham Fellowship; studied in Rome, Berlin and Zurich; DD 1957. Ordained, 1931, to St John's, Bathgate; W High Church, Kilmarnock, 1935-44; Cramond Church, Edinburgh 1944-56. Convener: C of S Cttee on Huts and Canteens for HM Forces, 1946-58; Cttee on Temperance and Morals, 1958-63; Social and Moral Welfare Bd, 1963-64; Stewardship and Budget Ctee, 1964-69; Mem., Scottish Adv. Cttee on Treatment of Offenders; Regional Chaplain (Scotland), Air Trng Corps; Hon. Vice-Pres., Boys' Brigade. Warrack Lectr on Preaching, 1959. Guest Preacher: Knox Church, Dunedin, 1950; Fifth Ave., Presbyterian Church, NY, 1960; St Stephen's Presbyterian Church, Sydney, 1962, 1971, 1976; Scots Church, Melbourne, 1971, 1976. Moderator of the General Assembly of the Church of Scotland, 1966-67; First Chm., Scottish Parole Bd, 1967-73. TV Series, What I Believe, 1970. *Publications:* With Ardour and Accuracy (Warrack Lectures), 1959; No Uncertain Sound (Scholar as Preacher Series), 1964; No Other Name, 1966; contribs to The Expository Times. *Recreations:* boating, walking; formerly Association football (Edinburgh Univ. Blue, captained team, 1927-28; played as amateur for St Bernard's FC, 1928-29; capped *v* England (Amateur), 1929). *Address:* 5 Craighill Gardens, Edinburgh EH10 5PU. *T:* 031-447 4243. *Club:* Royal Over-Seas League.

SMALL, William Watson, JP; MP (Lab) Glasgow, Garscadden, since 1974 (Glasgow, Scotstoun, Oct. 1959-1974); *b* 19 Oct. 1909; *s* of Edward Small of Lochee, Dundee; *m* 1941, Isabella Scott, *d* of Matthew Murphy of Stevenston, Ayrshire; two *d*. *Educ:* Calder School, Motherwell. JP Ayrshire, 1948. PPS to: Min. of Power, 1964-65; Sec. of State for Colonies, 1965; Chancellor of Duchy of Lancaster, 1966-69. *Address:* Belle

Mara, 2 Diddup Drive, Stevenston, Ayrshire. *T:* Stevenston 63474.

SMALLEY, Beryl, FBA 1963; MA Oxon; PhD Manchester; History Tutor, 1943-69, Vice-Principal, 1957-69, Emeritus Fellow, St Hilda's College, Oxford; *b* 3 June 1905; *d* of Edgar Smalley. *Educ:* Cheltenham Ladies' College; St Hilda's College, Oxford. Assistant Lecturer, Royal Holloway College, 1931-35; Research Fellow, Girton College, 1935-40; Temporary Assistant in Dept of Western MSS, Bodleian Library, 1940-43. Ford's Lecturer, Oxford, 1966-67. Hon. DLitt Southampton, 1974. *Publications:* The Study of the Bible in the Middle Ages, 1952; English Friars and Antiquity, 1960; The Becket Conflict and the Schools, 1973; Historians in the Middle Ages, 1974; in Recherches de théologie ancienne et médiévale; Mediaeval and Renaissance Studies, etc. *Recreations:* walking, swimming, travel. *Address:* 5c Rawlinson Road, Oxford. *T:* Oxford 59525. *Club:* University Women's.

SMALLMAN, Barry Granger, CMG 1976; CVO 1972; HM Diplomatic Service; British High Commissioner to Bangladesh, since 1975; *b* 22 Feb. 1924; *s* of C. Stanley Smallman, CBE, ARCM, and Ruby Marian Granger; *m* 1952, Sheila Knight; two *s* one *d. Educ:* St Paul's School; Trinity College, Cambridge (Major Scholar, MA). Served War of 1939-45, Intelligence Corps, Australia 1944-46. Joined Colonial Office, 1947; Assistant Private Secretary to Secretary of State, 1951-52; Principal, 1953; attached to United Kingdom Delegation to United Nations, New York, 1956-57, 1958, 1961, 1962; seconded to Government of Western Nigeria, Senior Assistant Secretary, Governor's Office, Ibadan, 1959-60; transferred to CRO, 1961; British Deputy High Comr in Sierra Leone, 1963-64; Asst Sec., 1964; British Dep. High Comr in NZ, 1964-67; Imp. Defence Coll., 1968; FCO, 1969-71; Counsellor and Consul-Gen., British Embassy, Bangkok, 1971-74. *Recreations:* tennis, golf, making and listening to music, light verse. *Address:* c/o Foreign and Commonwealth Office, SW1; Golford House, Cranbrook, Kent. *T:* Sissinghurst 295.

SMALLPEICE, Sir Basil, KCVO 1961; Chartered Accountant; Chairman: Associated Container Transportation (Australia), since 1971; ACT (Australia)/Australian National Line Co-ordinating Board, since 1969; Administrative Adviser in HM Household since 1964; *b* 18 Sept. 1906; *s* of late Herbert Charles Smallpeice, Banker; *m* 1931, Kathleen Ivey Singleton Brame (*d* 1973), *d* of late Edwin Singleton Brame; *m* 1973, Rita Burns, *yr d* of late Major William Burns. *Educ:* Shrewsbury. Chartered Accountant, 1930. Accountant of Hoover Ltd, 1930-37; Chief Accountant and later Sec. of Doulton & Co. Ltd, 1937-48; Dir of Costs and Statistics, British Transport Commission, 1948-50; BOAC: Financial Comptroller, 1950-56; Member of Board, 1953-63; Deputy Chief Executive, 1954-56; Managing Director, 1956-63. Managing Director, BOAC-Cunard Ltd, from its inception in 1962 till end of 1963; Chairman: Cunard Steam-Ship Co. Ltd, 1965-71 (Dir, 1964; a Dep. Chm., 1965); Cunard Line Ltd, 1965-71; Cunard-Brocklebank, 1967-70; Cunard Cargo Shipping, 1970-71; a Dep. Chm., Lonrho Ltd, April 1972-May 1973; Director: Martins Bank Ltd, 1966-69; London Local Bd, Barclays Bank, 1969-74. Member Council: Inst. of Chartered Accountants, 1948-57; Inst. of Transport, 1958-61; Brit. Inst. of Management, 1959-64 and 1965- (Chm., 1970-72; a Vice-Pres., 1972-); Pres., Inst. of Freight Forwarders, 1977-. Mem., Cttee for Exports to the US, 1964-66. Chairman: Nat. Jt Council for Civil Air Transport, 1960-61; The English Speaking Union of the Commonwealth, 1965-68; Leatherhead New Theatre Trust, 1966-74; Air League, 1971-74. *Publications:* various articles in the 1940s on the development of industrial and management accounting. *Recreations:* gardening, golf. *Address:* 136 Fenchurch Street, EC3. *T:* 01-626 3233; Reed Thatch, 25 Clare Hill, Esher, Surrey. *T:* Esher 63020. *Clubs:* Athenæum, Boodle's; Melbourne (Melbourne, Vic); St George's Hill Golf (Weybridge, Surrey).

SMALLWOOD, Anne Hunter, CMG 1976; Commissioner, Board of Inland Revenue, since 1973; *b* 20 June 1922; *d* of Martin Wilkinson McNicol and Elizabeth Straiton Harper; *m* 1972, Peter Basil Smallwood (*d* 1977). *Educ:* High Sch. for Girls, Glasgow; Glasgow Univ. Entered Inland Revenue, 1943; Dep. Comptroller (Scotland), 1956-58; Min. of Land and Natural Resources, 1964-66; Min. of Housing and Local Govt, 1966; Under-Sec., Inland Revenue, 1971-73. *Address:* Bron, Long Grove, Seer Green, Beaconsfield, Bucks HP9 2QH. *Club:* United Oxford & Cambridge University.
See also G. P. McNicol.

SMALLWOOD, Air Chief Marshal Sir Denis (Graham), GBE 1975 (CBE 1961; MBE 1951); KCB 1969 (CB 1966); DSO 1944; DFC 1942; idc; jssc; psc; aws; Commander-in-Chief, UK Air Forces, 1975-76, and Commander-in-Chief, RAF Strike Command, 1974-76; *b* 13 Aug. 1918; *s* of Frederick William Smallwood, Moseley, Birmingham; *m* 1940, Frances Jeanne, *d* of Walter Needham; one *s* one *d. Educ:* King Edward VI School, Birmingham. Joined Royal Air Force, 1938. Served War of 1939-45, Fighter Command. Group Captain, 1957; commanded RAF Guided Missiles Station, Lincs, 1959-61; AOC and Commandant, RAF Coll. of Air Warfare, Manby, 1961-62; ACAS (Ops), 1962-65; AOC No 3 Gp, RAF Bomber Comd, 1965-67; SASO, Bomber Comd, 1967-68, Strike Comd, 1968-69; AOC-in-C, NEAF, Comdr, British Forces Near East, and Administrator, Sovereign Base Area, Cyprus, 1969-70; Vice-Chief of the Air Staff, 1970-74. Military Adviser to Chm. and Chief Exec., Aircraft Gp, BAe. ADC to the Queen, 1959-64. RAF Mem., Grand Military Race Cttee. Chm., Air League, 1978-. *Address:* The Flint House, Owlswick, Bucks. *Clubs:* Royal Air Force, Arts.

SMART, (Alexander Basil) Peter; HM Diplomatic Service; Counsellor and Head of Chancery, Canberra, since 1977; *b* 19 Feb. 1932; *s* of Henry Prescott Smart and Mary Gertrude Todd; *m* 1955, Joan Mary Cumming; three *s* (incl. twin *s*). *Educ:* Ryhope Grammar Sch., Co. Durham. Commnd RAEC, 1951; Supervising Officer, Educn, Gibraltar Comd, 1951-52; entered HM Foreign (later Diplomatic) Service, 1953; Vice Consul, Duala, 1955; Polit. Office, ME Forces, Cyprus, 1956; 2nd Sec. (Information), Seoul, 1959; News Dept, FO, 1964; Head of Chancery, Rangoon, 1968; FCO, 1971; Head of Communications Technical Services Dept, 1975. *Recreations:* wild nature, the arts; looking and listening. *Address:* c/o Foreign and Commonwealth Office, SW1A 2AL.

SMART, Andrew; Director, Royal Signals and Radar Establishment, Malvern, since 1978; *b* 12 Feb. 1924; *s* of late Mr and Mrs William S. Smart; *m* 1949, Pamela Kathleen Stephens; two *s* two *d. Educ:* Denny; High Sch. of Stirling; Glasgow Univ. MA 1944. TRE Malvern, 1943; Science 2 Air Min., 1950-53; Guided Weapons Gp, RRE, Malvern, 1953-70 (Head, 1968-70); Dep. Dir (Scientific B), DOAE, 1970; RAE, Farnborough: Head of Weapons Res. Gp, 1972; Head of Weapons Dept, 1973; Dep. Dir (W), 1974-77. *Recreations:* gardening, caravanning. *Address:* Hill Orchard, Shelsey Drive, Colwall, Malvern, Worcs. *T:* Colwall 40664.

SMART, Prof. Arthur David Gerald, FRTPI; Professor of Urban Planning in University of London, and Head of Bartlett School of Architecture and Planning, University College London, since 1975; *b* 19 March 1925; *s* of Dr A. H. J. Smart and A. O. M. Smart (*née* Evans); *m* 1955, Anne Patience Smart (*née* Baxter); two *d. Educ:* Rugby Sch.; King's Coll., Cambridge; Polytechnic of Central London. MA, DipTP; ARICS. Served in The Rifle Brigade, 1943-47 (Captain). Appts in local govt (planning), London, NE England, E Midlands, 1950-63; County Planning Officer, Hants CC, 1963-75; Member: Planning Adv. Gp, 1964-65, Cttee on Public Participation in Planning, 1968-69, Min. of Housing and Local Govt; Planning and Transportation Res. Adv. Council, DoE, 1975-. *Publications:* articles, conf. papers, in professional and other jls. *Recreations:* sailing, ornithology, music, walking. *Address:* University College London, Gower Street, WC1E 6BT. *T:* 01-387 7050; Lynch House, Bereweeke Road, Winchester, Hants SO22 6AP. *T:* Winchester 2818. *Club:* Athenæum.

SMART, Edwin; *see* Smart, L. E.

SMART, Professor George Algernon, MD, FRCP; Director, British Postgraduate Medical Federation, since 1971; *b* 16 Dec. 1913; *er s* of A. Smart, Alnwick, Northumb; *m* 1939, Monica Helen Carrick; two *s* one *d. Educ:* Uppingham; Durham Univ., BSc 1935, MB, BS 1937. MD 1939 (Durham); MRCP 1940, FRCP 1952. Commonwealth Fund Fellow, 1948-49. Lectr in Med., Univ. of Bristol, 1946-50; Reader in Medicine, Univ. of Durham, 1950-56; Prof. of Medicine, Univ. of Newcastle upon Tyne, 1968-71 (Post-graduate Sub-Dean, 1962-68, Dean of Medicine, 1968-71). Censor, 1965-67, Senior Censor and Senior Vice-Pres., 1972-73, RCP. *Publications:* contrib. to Price's Textbook of Medicine, and Progress in Clinical Medicine (Daley and Miller); (ed) Metabolic Disturbances in Clinical Medicine, 1958; (co-author) Fundamentals of Clinical Endocrinology, 1969, 2nd edn 1974. *Recreation:* photography. *Address:* British Postgraduate Medical Federation, 33 Millman Street, WC1N 3EJ; Chesters, Felden Drive, Hemel Hempstead, Herts. *Club:* Athenæum.

SMART, Henry Walter, CB 1966; formerly Director of Savings, GPO (1958-68); *b* 7 Sept. 1908; *m*; two *s. Educ:* Sir Thomas Rich's School, Gloucester. *Address:* Knapp Cottage, Sheepscombe, Stroud, Glos. *T:* Painswick 812091.

SMART, Jack, CBE 1976; JP; Leader, Wakefield Metropolitan District Council, since 1973; *b* 25 April 1920; *s* of James and Emily Smart; *m* 1941, Ethel King; one *d*. *Educ:* Altofts Colliery Sch. Miner, 1934-59; Branch Sec., Glasshoughton Colliery, NUM, 1949-59; Mem., Castleford Municipal Borough Council, 1949-74; Mayor of Castleford, 1962-63; Mem., Wakefield Metropolitan Dist. Council, 1973-; Chm., Assoc. of Metropolitan Authorities, 1977; Chm., Wakefield AHA, 1977; Mem., Layfield Cttee, 1974-76; Area Agent, NUM, Yorkshire Area, 1959. JP Castleford, 1960. *Recreations:* golf, music. *Address:* Churchside, Weetworth, Pontefract Road, Castleford, West Yorks. *T:* Castleford 554880.

SMART, (Louis) Edwin, Jr, JD; Chairman of Board and Chief Executive Officer, Trans World Airlines, Inc., since 1977; *b* 17 Nov. 1923; *s* of Louis Edwin Smart and Esther Guthery; *m* 1st, 1944, Virginia Alice Knouff; one *s* one *d*; 2nd, 1964, Jeanie Alberta Milone; one *s*. *Educ:* Harvard Coll. (AB *magna cum laude* 1947); Harvard Law Sch. (JD *magna cum laude* 1949). Admitted to NY Bar, 1950; Associate, Hughes, Hubbard & Ewing, NYC, 1949-56; Partner, Hughes, Hubbard & Reed, NYC, 1957-64; Pres., Bendix Internat. and Dir, Bendix Corp. and foreign subsids, 1964-67; Sen. Vice Pres., Trans World Airlines Inc., 1967-76, Vice Chm. 1976. Director: Southern Natural Resources, Inc.; ACF Industries, Incorp. *Address:* (office) 605 Third Avenue, New York, NY 10016, USA. *T:* (212) 557-5502; (home) 535 E 86th Street, New York, NY 10028; Coakley Bay, Christiansted, St Croix 00820, Virgin Islands. *Clubs:* Presidents, Sky (NYC).

SMART, Ninian; *see* Smart, R. N.

SMART, Peter; *see* Smart, A. B. P.

SMART, Maj.-Gen. Robert Arthur, CBE 1958; FRCP; Chief Medical Officer, Esso Petroleum Co., since 1975, Senior Medical Officer, 1972-75; *b* 29 April 1914; *s* of Arthur Francis Smart and Roberta Teresa Farquhar; *m* 1947, Josephine von Oepen; one *d*. *Educ:* Aberdeen Gram. Sch.; Aberdeen University. MB, ChB 1936; DPH (Eng.) 1948; MRCP 1965, FRCP 1977. Lt, RAMC, 1936; Capt. 1937; Maj. 1946; Lt-Col 1951; Col 1960; Brig. 1964; Maj.-Gen. 1967. Served in Palestine, Egypt, Western Desert, Eritrea, France and Germany, 1939-45; N Africa and E Africa, 1951-55; Asst Dir of Army Health, E Africa, 1952-55; Leader, Royal Society's Internat. Geophysical Year Expedn to Antarctica, 1956-57; Dep. Chief Med. Off., Supreme HQ Allied Powers Europe, 1960-62; Dep. Dir of Army Health, BAOR, 1962-64; Dir of Army Health, MoD, 1964-68; DMS, FARELF, 1968-70; DMS, BAOR, 1970-71; DDMS, HQ Army Strategic Comd, 1971-72, retired 1972. Polar Medal, 1958. QHS 1968-72. *Address:* 2 Tower Green, HM Tower of London, EC3. *Clubs:* Army and Navy, Caledonian.

SMART, Prof. (Roderick) Ninian; Professor of Religious Studies, University of Lancaster, since 1967, and concurrently Professor of Religious Studies, University of California, Santa Barbara, since 1976; *b* 6 May 1927; *s* of late Prof. W. M. Smart, FRSE, and Isabel (*née* Carswell); *m* 1954, Libushka Clementina Baruffaldi; one *s* two *d*. *Educ:* Glasgow Academy; The Queen's College, Oxford. Army service with Intelligence Corps, 1945-48, 2nd Lt, Captain, 1947; overseas service in Ceylon. Oxford: Mods (shortened), Class II, 1949; Lit. Hum. Class I, 1951; BPhil 1954; LHD Loyola. Asst Lecturer in Philosophy, Univ. Coll. of Wales, Aberystwyth, 1952-55, Lecturer, 1955; Vis. Lecturer in Philosophy, Yale Univ., 1955-56; Lecturer in History and Philosophy of Religion, Univ. of London, King's College, 1956-61; H. G. Wood Professor of Theology, University of Birmingham, 1961-66. Pro-Vice-Chancellor, Univ. of Lancaster, 1969-72. Visiting Lecturer, Banaras Hindu Univ., Summer, 1960; Teape Lectr, Univ. Delhi, 1964; Visiting Professor: Univ. Wisconsin, 1965; Princeton and Otago, 1971. First Gen. Sec., Inst. of Religion and Theology, 1973-. *Publications:* Reasons and Faiths, 1958; A Dialogue of Religions, 1960; Historical Selections in the Philosophy of Religion, 1962; Philosophers and Religious Truth, 1964; Doctrine and Argument in Indian Philosophy, 1964; The Teacher and Christian Belief, 1966; The Yogi and the Devotee, 1968; Secular Education and the Logic of Religion, 1968; The Religious Experience of Mankind, 1969; Philosophy of Religion, 1970; The Concept of Worship, 1972; The Phenomenon of Religion, 1973; The Science of Religion and the Sociology of Knowledge, 1973; Mao, 1974; A Companion to the Long Search, 1977; contrib. to Mind, Philosophy, Philosophical Quarterly, Review of Metaphysics, Religion, Religious Studies. *Recreations:* cricket, tennis, poetry. *Address:* Department of Religious Studies, University of Lancaster, Bailrigg, Lancaster LA1 4YG. *Club:* Athenæum.

SMART, William Norman H.; *see* Hunter Smart.

SMEALL, James Leathley, MA, JP; Principal, Saint Luke's College, Exeter, 1945-72; *b* 16 June 1907; *s* of late William Francis Smeall, MB, BCh (Edin.), and Ethel Mary Leathley; *m* 1936, Joan Rachel Harris; one *d*. *Educ:* Sorbonne; Queens' College, Cambridge (Scholar). Class I English Tripos, Class II Division 1 Anthropological and Archæological Tripos; Assistant Master, Merchiston, 1929-30; Staff, Royal Naval College, Dartmouth, 1930-34; Housemaster, Bradfield College, 1934-36; Head of the English Department, Epsom College, 1936-39; Headmaster, Chesterfield Grammar School, 1939-45; Commissioned RAFVR, 1941-44. Mayor of Exeter, 1965-66; Chm., Exeter Civic Soc., 1972-. Governor: Exeter Sch.; King's Coll., Taunton. *Publication:* English Satire, Parody and Burlesque, 1952. *Recreations:* gardening and travel. *Address:* Follett Orchard, Topsham, Exeter. *T:* Topsham 3892.

SMEDDLES, Thomas Henry; Chief General Manager, Royal Insurance Group, 1963-69; *b* 18 Dec. 1904; *s* of late T. H. Smeddles; *m* 1931, Dorothy Boardman; one *s*. Joined The Liverpool & London & Globe Insurance Co. Ltd, 1924. *Recreations:* gardening, sailing, golf. *Address:* Tinkers Revel, Burwood Park, Walton-on-Thames, Surrey. *T:* Walton-on-Thames 20706. *Club:* Junior Carlton.

SMEDLEY, (Frank) Brian, QC 1977; a Recorder of the Crown Court, since 1972; Barrister-at-Law; *b* 28 Nov. 1934. *Educ:* West Bridgford Grammar Sch.; London Univ. LLB Hons, 1957. Called to the Bar, Gray's Inn, 1960; Midland Circuit; Mem., Senate of the Inns of Court and the Bar, 1973-77. *Recreations:* travel, music. *Address:* The Barn, Wellingore, Lincolnshire. *T:* Lincoln 810386; 4 Hale Court, Lincoln's Inn, WC2. *T:* 01-242 4552. *Club:* Garrick.

SMEDLEY, George; *see* Smedley R. R. G. B.

SMEDLEY, Harold, CMG 1965; MBE 1946; British High Commissioner in New Zealand, and concurrently Governor of Pitcairn Island, since 1976; High Commissioner in Western Samoa, since 1977; *b* 19 June 1920; *s* of late Dr R. D. Smedley, MA, MD, DPH, Worthing; *m* 1950, Beryl Mary Harley Brown, Wellington, New Zealand; two *s* two *d*. *Educ:* Aldenham School; Pembroke College, Cambridge. Served War of 1939-45, Royal Marines. Entered Dominions Office (later Commonwealth Relations Office), 1946; Private Secretary to Permanent Under-Secretary of State, 1947-48; British High Commissioner's Office: Wellington, NZ, 1948-50; Salisbury, Southern Rhodesia, 1951-53; Principal Private Sec. to Sec. of State for Commonwealth Relations, 1954-57; Counsellor, British High Comr's Office: Calcutta, 1957; New Delhi, 1958-60; British High Comr in Ghana, 1964-67; Ambassador to Laos, 1967-70; Asst Under-Sec. of State, FCO, 1970-72; Sec. Gen., Commn on Rhodesian opinion, 1971-72; High Comr in Sri Lanka, and Ambassador to Republic of Maldives, 1972-75. *Address:* c/o Foreign and Commonwealth Office, SW1; Sherwood, Oak End Way, Woodham, Weybridge, Surrey. *Clubs:* Athenæum, United Oxford & Cambridge University; Wellington (New Zealand).

SMEDLEY, (Roscoe Relph) George (Boleyne); HM Diplomatic Service, Counsellor; Head of Nationality and Treaty Department, Foreign and Commonwealth Office, since 1977; *b* 3 Sept. 1919; *o s* of late Charles Boleyne Smedley and Aimie Blaine Smedley (*née* Relph); *m* 1947, Muriel Hallaway Murray (*d* 1975); one *s*. *Educ:* King's Sch., Ely; King's Coll., London (LLB). Called to Bar, Inner Temple. Artists Rifles TA; commnd S Lancs Regt, 1940; Indian Army, 1942-46 (Captain); Foreign Office, 1937 and 1946; Foreign Service (subseq. Diplomatic Service): Rangoon, 1947; Maymyo, 1950; Brussels, 1952; Baghdad, 1954; FO, 1958; Beirut, 1963; Kuwait, 1965; FCO, 1969; Consul-Gen., Lubumbashi, 1972-74; British Mil. Govt, Berlin, 1974-76; FCO 1976. *Address:* c/o Foreign and Commonwealth Office, SW1A 2AH. *Club:* Royal Automobile.

SMEDLEY, Susan M.; *see* Marsden-Smedley.

SMEETON, Vice-Adm. Sir Richard Michael, KCB 1964 (CB 1961); MBE 1942; FRAeS 1973; DL; Director and Chief Executive, Society of British Aerospace Companies, since 1966; *b* 24 Sept. 1912; *s* of Edward Leaf Smeeton and Charlotte Mildred Leighton; *m* 1940, Maria Elizabeth Hawkins; no *c*. *Educ:* RNC, Dartmouth. 800 Squadron i/c HMS Ark Royal, 1940-41; Assistant Naval Attaché (Air), Washington, DC, 1941-43; staff of Admiral Nimitz, USN 1943-44; Air Plans Officer, British Pacific Fleet, 1944-45; Captain (Air) Med., 1952-54; Imperial Defence College, 1955; Captain, HMS Albion, 1956-57; Director of Plans, Admiralty, 1958-59; Flag Officer Aircraft Carriers, 1960-62; NATO Deputy Supreme Allied Commander,

Atlantic, 1962-64; Flag Officer, Naval Air Command, 1964-65. Rear-Admiral, 1959; Vice-Admiral, 1962. Retired Nov. 1965, at own request. DL Surrey 1976. *Address:* St Mary's Cottage, Shamley Green, Surrey. *T:* Bramley 3478. *Club:* Army and Navy.

SMELLIE, Kingsley Bryce Speakman; Professor Emeritus of Political Science, London School of Economics, since 1965; Professor, 1949-65; *b* 22 Nov. 1897; *o s* of late John and Elizabeth Smellie; *m* 1931, Stephanie, *o d* of late A. E. Narlian. *Educ:* Mrs Bolwell, 15 Mall Road, Hammersmith; Latymer Upper School, Hammersmith; St John's College, Cambridge. Served European War, 1914-18, as private in London Scottish. Staff of London School of Economics, 1921-65. Laura Spelman Rockefeller Student in USA (Harvard Law School), 1925-26; Research Assistant, propaganda research unit of BBC, 1940; temp. principal: Ministry of Home Security, 1940-42, Board of Trade, 1942-45. *Publications:* The American Federal System, 1928; A Hundred Years of English Government, 1937; Civics, 1939; Reason in Politics, 1939; Our Two Democracies at Work, 1944; A History of Local Government, 1946; Why We Read History, 1948; British Way of Life, 1955; Great Britain since 1688, 1962. *Address:* 24 Parkside Gardens, SW19 5EU. *T:* 01-946 7869.

SMELLIE, Prof. R(obert) Martin S(tuart), PhD, DSc; FRSE 1964; FIBiol; Cathcart Professor of Biochemistry, since 1966 and Director of the Biochemical Laboratories, since 1972, University of Glasgow; *b* Rothesay, Bute, 1 April 1927; *s* of Rev. W. T. Smellie, OBE, MA and Jean (*née* Craig); *m* 1954, Florence Mary Devlin Adams, MB, ChB; two *s*. *Educ:* Dundee High Sch.; Glasgow Acad.; Univ. of St Andrews (BSc 1947); Univ. of Glasgow (PhD 1952, DSc 1963). FIBiol 1964. National Service, 1947-49: commnd Royal Scots Fusiliers; served with 2nd Bn Royal Scots and at CDEE, Porton. University of Glasgow: Asst Lectr in Biochemistry, 1949-52; Beit Memorial Res. Fellow, 1952-53; Lectr in Biochem., 1953-55 and 1956-59, Sen. Lectr, 1959-63; Reader in Molecular Biol., 1963-65. Res. Fellow, NY Univ. Coll. of Med., 1955-56. Biochemical Society: Mem. Cttee, 1967-71; Symposium Organiser, 1970-75. Member: European Molecular Biol. Org., 1964; MRC Physiol. Systems and Disorders Bd, 1977; Brit. Biophys. Soc., 1968; Brit. Assoc. for Cancer Res., 1961; Soc. for Endocrinology, 1968; Council, Trinity Coll., Glenalmond, 1976; Governor, Glasgow Academicals War Meml Trust, 1976-. Hon. Gen. Sec., RSE, 1976. *Publications:* A Matter of Life: DNA, 1969; The Biochemistry of the Nucleic Acids, 1976; (ed) Biochemical Society Symposia Nos 31-41; papers in scientific jls on nucleic acid biosynthesis and hormone control mechanisms. *Recreations:* fishing, walking, music, foreign travel,. *Address:* No 4 The University, Glasgow G12 8QQ. *T:* 041-339 5518; Corranbheag, Ochtertyre, Blair Drummond, Stirling FK9 7UN. *T:* Stirling 70524. *Clubs:* Royal Commonwealth Society; New (Edinburgh).

SMETHAM, Andrew James, MA; Headmaster, Wandsworth School, London, since 1974; *b* 22 Feb. 1937; *s* of Arthur James Smetham and Eunice (*née* Jones); *m* 1964, Sandra Mary (*née* Owen); two *s*. *Educ:* Vaynor and Penderyn Grammar Sch., Cefn Coed, Breconshire; King's Coll., Univ. of London (BA (Hons German) 1959, DipEd 1964, MA (Educn) 1968). Assistant Master: Wandsworth Sch., 1960-66; Sedgehill Sch., 1966-70; Dep. Headmaster, Holloway Sch., 1970-74. *Recreations:* music, walking. *Address:* 170 Court Lane, SE21 7ED. *T:* 01-693 3696.

SMETHURST, Stuart Wilson; Director, City of Birmingham Polytechnic, since 1970; *b* 22 Sept. 1923; *s* of Herbert Stuart Smethurst and Eliza (*née* Wilson); *m* 1954, Pamela Marguerite Soames; two *s* one *d*. *Educ:* Hull Grammar Sch.; University Coll., Hull. MSc; FIMA. Scientific Civil Service, 1944-45; posts in educn in Hull, Sunderland, Bradford and Leeds, 1946-70. Member: Educn Adv. Council, IBA, 1975-; Council, CNAA, 1973-. *Publications:* scientific papers in technical jls. *Address:* 106 Silhill Hall Road, Solihull, West Midlands. *T:* 021-705 1798.

SMETTEM, Colin William; Chairman, North Eastern Region, British Gas Corporation, 1973-76; *b* 1 June 1916; *s* of William Home Smettem and Agnes Grace; *m* 1945, Sylvia Elisabeth (*née* Alcock); two *s* two *d*. *Educ:* Scarborough High Sch. Solicitor (Hons). Asst Solicitor, Scarborough Corp., 1938. Served War, 1939-45: UK, India, Assam; GII at Tactical Trng Centre, India Command, 1944. Asst Town Clerk, Wallasey, 1948; Solicitor, North Western Gas Bd, 1950; Commercial Manager, North Western Gas Bd, 1961, and Mem. Bd, 1965-68; Dep. Chm., Eastern Gas Bd, 1968. *Recreation:* DIY. *Address:* Runlet End, Farnley Tyas, near Huddersfield HD4 6UP. *T:* Huddersfield 61276. *Club:* Naval and Military.

SMIETON, Dame Mary Guillan, DBE 1949; MA Oxon; Permanent Secretary, Ministry of Education, 1959-63, retired; *b* 5 Dec. 1902; *d* of John Guillan Smieton, late librarian and bursar Westminster Coll., Cambridge, and of Maria Judith Toop. *Educ:* Perse Sch., Cambridge; Wimbledon High Sch.; Bedford Coll., London (1 year) (Hon. Fellow, 1971); Lady Margaret Hall. Assistant Keeper, Public Record Office, 1925-28; Ministry of Labour and National Service, 1928-46; on loan to Home Office as General Secretary, Women's Voluntary Services, 1938-40, and to UN as Director of Personnel, 1946-48; Deputy Secretary, Ministry of Labour and National Service, 1955-59 (Under-Secretary, 1946-55). UK representative, Unesco Executive Board, 1962-68. Trustee, British Museum, 1963-73; Chm., Bedford Coll. Council, 1964-70. Member: Advisory Council on Public Records, 1965-73; Standing Commn on Museums and Galleries, 1970-73; Vice Pres., Museums Assoc., 1974-77. Hon. Fellow, Lady Margaret Hall, Oxford, 1959. *Address:* 14 St George's Road, St Margaret's on Thames, Middlesex. *T:* 01-892 9279. *Club:* United Oxford & Cambridge University.

SMIJTH-WINDHAM, Brig. William Russell, CBE 1946; DSO 1942; *b* 21 Oct. 1907; *s* of late Arthur Russell Smijth-Windham; *m* 1934, Helen Teresa, *d* of late Brig. H. Clementi Smith, DSO; one *s* three *d*. *Educ:* Wellington College; Royal Military Academy, Woolwich. Commissioned Royal Corps of Signals, 1927; Mount Everest Expedition, 1933 and 1936; Mohmand Ops, 1935; Army Revolver VIII, 1937-39; British Pistol VIII, 1939. Served War of 1939-45, Greece and Crete, 1941; Western Desert and Tunisia, 1942-43; France and Germany, 1944-45 (despatches); British Mil. Mission to Greece during Greek Civil War, 1948-49; Chief Signal Officer, Eastern Command, 1957-60, retd 1960; ADC to the Queen, 1957-60. FIEE. *Recreations:* shooting, sailing. *Address:* Icentown House, Pitney, Langport, Somerset. *T:* Langport 250525.

SMILEY, Sir Hugh Houston, 3rd Bt, *cr* 1903; late Grenadier Guards; JP; Vice-Lord-Lieutenant of Hampshire, since 1973; *b* 14 Nov. 1905; *s* of 2nd Bt and Valerie, *y d* of late Sir Claud Champion de Crespigny, 4th Bt; *S* father, 1930; *m* 1933, Nancy, *er d* of E. W. H. Beaton; one *s*. *Educ:* Eton; RMC, Sandhurst. Served with 1st Bn Grenadier Guards NW Europe, 1944-45. JP 1952, DL 1962, Hampshire; High Sheriff, 1959. Hon. Secretary Jane Austen Society, 1953-. *Heir: s* Major John Philip Smiley [*b* 24 Feb. 1934; *m* 1963, Davina Elizabeth, *e d* of late Denis Griffiths; two *s* one *d*. *Educ:* Eton; RMA, Sandhurst; Major Grenadier Guards]. *Address:* Ivalls, Bentworth, Alton, Hants GU34 5JU. *T:* Alton 63193. *Club:* Cavalry and Guards.

SMIRK, Sir (Frederick) Horace, KBE 1958; engaged in full-time research; Emeritus Research Professor of Medicine, University of Otago, Dunedin, New Zealand (Professor of Medicine, 1940-61); Director, Wellcome Research Institute, 1962; *b* 12 December 1902; *s* of Thomas Smirk and Betsy Ann (*née* Cunliffe); *m* 1931, Aileen Winifrede, *d* of Rev. Arthur Bamforth and Martha Bamforth; three *s* one *d*. *Educ:* Haslingden Gram. Sch.; Univ. of Manchester. Gaskill mathematical schol., 1919; MB, ChB 1st Cl. Hons 1925; MD Gold Medallist, 1927; FRCP 1940; FRACP (Hon.) 1940. Med. Registrar, Manchester Royal Infirmary, 1926-29; RMO 1929; Dickenson Travelling Scholar, University of Vienna, 1930; Beit Memorial Fell., successively Asst Depts of Pharmacology, and Medicine, Univ. Coll. London, 1930-34; Prof. of Pharmacology and Physician Postgrad. Dept, Egyptian Univ., 1935-39. Visiting Prof., Brit. Postgrad. Med. Sch., London, 1949; McIlraith Visiting Prof., Roy. Prince Alfred Hosp., Sydney, 1953; Holme Lectr Univ. Coll. Hosp. Med. Sch., 1949; Alexander Gibson Lectr, Edinburgh Coll. of Physicians, 1956; Dr N. D. Patel Inaugural lecture, Bombay, 1959; Member Board of Censors, later Senior Censor, 1940-58; Vice-President RACP, 1958-60; Chairman Clinical Reseach Committee, 1942-, Psychiatric Research Cttee, 1957-60; Mem. Council Med. Research Council of NZ, 1944-60; Mem. Expert Cttee on Hypertension and Ischaemic Heart Disease, of WHO; Life Member, New York Acad. of Science, 1961; formerly Councillor, International Society of Cardiology (Mem. Hypertension Research Sub-Cttee); Hon. overseas Mem. Assoc. of Physicians of GB, 1967. Hon. DSc: Hahneman Coll., Pa, 1961; Otago, 1975. Gairdner Foundn International Award for Research in Medicine, 1965. *Publications:* Hypotensive Drugs, 1956; Arterial Hypertension, 1957; jointly: Modern Trends in Geriatrics, 1956, Current Therapy, 1956, Annual Reviews of Medicine, 1955; Antihypertensive Agents, 1967; contrib. to med. jls, mainly on disorders of the heart. *Recreations:* reading, writing, travel. *Address:* 68 Cannington Road, Dunedin, New Zealand. *T:* 60.961. *Club:* Fernhill (Dunedin).

SMIRNOVSKY, Mikhail Nikolaevich; Soviet Ambassador to the Court of St James's, 1966-73; non-resident Ambassador to

Malta, 1967-73; *b* 1921; *m* Liudmila A.; one *s* two *d. Educ:* Moscow Aviation Institute. Mem. Soviet Foreign Service, 1948; Assistant, 1955, Deputy Head of American Div., Ministry for Foreign Affairs, 1957-58; Counsellor, 1958, Minister-Counsellor, Soviet Embassy in Washington, 1960-62; Head of US Div. and Mem. Collegium, Ministry for Foreign Affairs, 1962-66. Member: Central Auditing Commn of CPSU, 1966-; Soviet Delegations to several International Conferences. *Address:* Ministry of Foreign Affairs, 32-34 Smolenskaya Sennaya Ploshchad, Moscow, USSR.

SMITH; *see* Abel Smith and Abel-Smith.

SMITH; *see* Buchanan-Smith.

SMITH; *see* Delacourt-Smith.

SMITH; *see* Gordon-Smith.

SMITH; *see* Hamilton-Smith, family name of Baron Colwyn.

SMITH; *see* Hornsby-Smith.

SMITH; *see* Macdonald-Smith.

SMITH; *see* Nowell-Smith.

SMITH; *see* Spencer-Smith.

SMITH; *see* Stewart-Smith.

SMITH, family name of **Earl of Birkenhead, Viscount Hambleden, Barons Bicester** and **Kirkhill.**

SMITH, Alan; Head, Science and Technology Division, OECD, since 1977; *b* 19 Jan. 1930; *s* of John Smith and Alice (*née* Williams); *m* 1958, Adele Marguerite (*née* Buckle); two *s* two *d. Educ:* Rossall; St Catherine's Soc., Oxford. BSc Leeds 1957. MIMinE 1958. NCB, 1957-64; Principal Sci. Officer, Min. of Power, 1964; Sci. Counsellor, HM Embassy, Paris, 1965-70; Cabinet Secretariat, 1970-71; DTI, 1971-73; Dept of Industry, 1973-74; Sci. and Technol. Counsellor, HM Embassy, Washington, 1975-77. *Recreation:* engineering history. *Address:* Château de la Muette, Paris 16e, France.

SMITH, Alan Guy E.; *see* Elliot-Smith.

SMITH, Alastair Macleod M.; *see* Macleod-Smith.

SMITH, Sir Alex; *see* Smith, Sir Alexander M.

SMITH, Prof. Alexander Crampton (Alex. Crampton Smith); Nuffield Professor of Anaesthetics, Oxford University, since 1965; *b* 15 June 1917; *s* of William and Mary Elizabeth Crampton Smith; *m* 1953, Marjorie (*née* Mason); three *s* ; two *d* by a former marriage. *Educ:* Inverness Royal Acad.; Edinburgh University. Edinburgh Univ., 1935-41. Served War of 1939-45 (Croix de Guerre, despatches), RNVR, 1942-46. Consultant Anaesthetist, United Oxford Hospitals, 1951; Clinical Lectr in Anaesthetics, Oxford Univ., 1961. FFARCS 1953; MA Oxon 1961. Civilian Consultant Anaesthetist to Royal Navy, 1968. Mem. Bd, Faculty of Anaesthetists, 1965-. Mem. Trustees, Nuffield Medical Benefaction, 1973. *Publications:* Clinical Practice and Physiology of Artificial Respiration (with J. M. K. Spalding), 1963; contribs to anaesthetic, medical and physiological jls. *Recreations:* sailing, fishing. *Address:* 31 Croft Road, Thame, Oxfordshire. *T:* Thame 2338.

SMITH, Sir Alexander Mair, (Sir Alex), Kt 1975; Director of Manchester Polytechnic since 1969; *b* 15 Oct. 1922; *s* of late John S. and Anne M. Smith; *m* 1956, Doris Neil (*née* Patrick); three *d. Educ:* Univ. of Aberdeen. MA (Maths and Nat. Phil.), PhD, FInstP. Physicist, UKAEA, 1952-56; Head of Advanced Research, Rolls Royce Ltd, 1956-67; Dir and Chief Scientist, Rolls Royce & Associates Ltd, 1967-69. Chm., Cttee of Dirs of Polytechnics, 1974-76; Chm., Schools Council, 1975-. *Publications:* papers in learned jls. *Recreation:* golf. *Address:* 34 Fletsand Road, Wilmslow, Cheshire. *T:* Wilmslow 22011. *Club:* Athenæum.

SMITH, Sir (Alexander) Rowland, Kt 1944; formerly Chairman and Managing Director, Ford Motor Co. Ltd; formerly Director, National Provincial Bank Ltd; Ex-Member, UK Atomic Energy Authority and National Research Corp.; *b* Gillingham, Kent, 25 Jan. 1888; *s* of late Alexander James Frederick Smith, Gillingham, Kent; *m* 1913, Janet Lucretia (*d* 1972), *d* of late George Henry Baker, Gillingham, Kent; one *s* one *d. Educ:* Mathematical School, Rochester. Freeman, City of

London; Livery Cos: Glaziers (Past Master); Coachmakers and Coach Harness Makers; Member: Ministry of Aircraft Production Mission to USA, 1941; Ministry of Pensions Standing Advisory Cttee on Artificial Limbs, 1948; Cttee on Procedure for ordering Civil Aircraft, 1948. FIB; FRSA; CEng; FIMechE; Fell. Inst. of Bankers. *Recreation:* sailing. *Address:* The Manor House, Maresfield, W Sussex. *Clubs:* Athenæum; Royal Southern Yacht.

SMITH, Sir Allan Chalmers, Kt, *cr* 1953; MC 1918; *b* 22 Feb. 1893; *e s* of late Allan Frith Smith, Colonial Treasurer, Bermuda; *m* 1920, Elsie Joyce Martin; three *s* three *d. Educ:* Warwick Academy, Bermuda; Rossall School, Lancs, England; St John's College, Oxford. Rhodes Scholarship, Bermuda, 1912. Served European War, 1914-18 (despatches thrice), Temp. Capt. RFA. Called to Bar, Gray's Inn, 1920; law practice in Bermuda, 1920-34. Police Magistrate: Western District, 1928, Central District, 1931, Bermuda; Lagos, Nigeria, 1935. Puisne Judge: Trinidad, 1938, Gold Coast, 1944; Chief Justice, Sierra Leone, 1951-55; Assistant Justice, Bermuda, 1955-65. Judicial Comr of Plan for a British Caribbean Fedn, 1955. *Recreations:* golf, sailing. *Address:* Hilton, Paget, Bermuda.

SMITH, Andreas W.; *see* Whittam Smith.

SMITH, Dame Annis Calder; *see* Gillie, Dame A. C.

SMITH, Anthony (John Francis); writer, broadcaster; *b* 30 March 1926; 2nd *s* of Hubert Smith (formerly Chief Agent, National Trust) and Diana Watkin; *m* 1956, Barbara Dorothy Newman; one *s* two *d. Educ:* Dragon School, Oxford; Blundell's School, Devon; Balliol College, Oxford. MA Oxon., 1951. Served with RAF, 1944-48. Oxford University, 1948-51. Manchester Guardian, 1953 and 1956-57; Drum, Africa, 1954-55; Science Correspondent, Daily Telegraph, 1957-63. Scientific Fellow of Zoological Society. TV series include: Balloon Safari, Balloons over the Alps, Great Zoos of the World, Great Parks of the World, Wilderness. *Publications:* Blind White Fish in Persia, 1953; Sea Never Dry, 1958; High Street Africa, 1961; Throw Out Two Hands, 1963; The Body, 1968; The Seasons, 1970; The Dangerous Sort, 1970; Mato Grosso, 1971; Beside the Seaside, 1972; Good Beach Guide, 1973; The Human Pedigree, 1975; Animals on View, 1977; Wilderness, 1978. *Recreations:* travel, lighter-than-air flying. *Address:* 9 Steele's Road, NW3. *T:* 01-722 4928.

SMITH, Anthony Robert; Director of Statistics and Research, Department of Health and Social Security, since 1976; *b* 29 March 1926; *s* of late Ernest George Smith and Mildred Smith (*née* Murphy); *m* 1949, Helen Elizabeth Mary Morgan; two *d. Educ:* De La Salle Coll., Pendleton; Peterhouse, Cambridge; London Sch. of Economics (BScEcon). Royal Marines and Army, 1944-47. Admiralty (Asst Statistician), 1950; various Admty appts, 1950-64; Head of Naval Manpower Div. and Defence Manpower Studies Unit, 1964-68; Chief Statistician, Treasury, 1968; Civil Service Dept, 1968-76. Under-Sec., 1970; Chm., Manpower Planning Study Gp, 1967-70; Member: Council of Manpower Soc., 1970-75 (Hon. Vice-Pres., 1975-); Council of Inst. of Manpower Studies, 1968-; Nat. Cttee of Inst. of Personnel Management, 1972-; Consultant, Organisation for Economic Co-operation and Development, 1970-. FIPM 1975. *Publications:* Models of Manpower Systems (ed), 1970; Manpower and Management Science (with D. J. Bartholomew), 1971; (ed) Manpower Planning in the Civil Service, 1976; contributor to: books and jls concerned with statistics, operational research, personnel administration, management, psychology and public administration. *Recreation:* dabbling in plant and animal cultivation. *Address:* 16 Carlton Road, Redhill, Surrey. *T:* Redhill 62258.

SMITH, Anthony Thomas, QC 1977; a Recorder of the Crown Court, since 1977; *b* 21 June 1935; *s* of Sydney Ernest Smith and Winston Victoria Smith; *m* 1959, Letitia Ann Wheldon Griffith; one *s* two *d. Educ:* Northampton, Stafford, and Hinckley Grammar Schs; King's Coll., Cambridge (Exhibnr; MA). Called to the Bar, Inner Temple, 1958. Flying Officer, RAF, 1958-60. *Recreations:* music, reading, hunting, farming. *Address:* Skeffington House, Skeffington, Leics. *T:* Billesdon 445.

SMITH, Arnold Cantwell, CH 1975; Lester B. Pearson Professor of International Affairs, Carleton University, Ottawa, since 1975; *b* 18 Jan. 1915; *m* 1938, Evelyn Hardwick Stewart; two *s* one *d. Educ:* Upper Canada Coll., Toronto; Lycée Champoléon, Grenoble; Univ. of Toronto; Christ Church, Oxford (Rhodes Scholar for Ont) BA Toronto, 1935; BA (Jurisp) Oxon 1937 (MA 1968); BCL 1938. Editor, The Baltic Times, Tallinn, Estonia, and Assoc. Prof. of Polit. Econ., Univ. of Tartu, Estonia, 1939-40; Attaché, British Legation, Tallinn, 1940; Attaché, British

Embassy, Cairo, 1940-43; part-time Lectr in Polit. Sci. and Econs, Egyptian State Univ., Cairo, 1940-42; transf. to Canadian Diplomatic Service, 1943; Sec., Canadian Legation, Kuibyshev, USSR, 1943; Sec., Canadian Embassy, Moscow, 1943-45; Dept of External Affairs, Ottawa, 1946-47; Assoc. Dir, Nat. Def. Coll. of Canada, Kingston, Ont, 1947-49; Mem. Canadian Delegns to various UN Confs, 1947-51; Alternate Perm. Deleg. of Canada to UN Security Coun. and Atomic Energy Commn, 1949-50; Counsellor, Canadian Embassy, Brussels, and Head of Canadian Delegn to Inter-Allied Reparations Agency, 1950-53; Special Asst to Sec. of State for External Affairs, 1953-55; Internat. Truce Comr in Indochina, 1955-56; Canadian Minister to UK, 1956-58; Canadian Ambassador to UAR, 1958-61; Canadian Ambassador to USSR, 1961-63; Asst Under-Sec. of State for External Affairs, Ottawa, 1963-65; Secretary-General of the Commonwealth, 1965-75. Chairman: North-South Inst.; Hudson Inst. of Canada; Internat. Peace Acad., NY; Pres., Canadian Bureau of Internat. Educn; Trustee, Hudson Inst., Croton, NJ. Hon. Fellow, Lady Eaton Coll., Trent Univ. R. B. Bennett Commonwealth Prize, RSA, 1975. DCL, University of Michigan, 1966; Hon. LLD: Ricker Coll., 1964; Queen's Univ., Kingston, Ont, 1966; Univ. of New Brunswick, 1968; Univ. of BC, 1969; Univ. of Toronto, 1969; Leeds Univ., 1975; Hon. DCL Oxon, 1975. *Recreations:* fishing, reading, travelling, farming in France. *Address:* (office) The Norman Paterson School of International Affairs, Carleton University, Ottawa K1S 5B6, Canada; (home) 300 Queen Elizabeth Driveway, Townhouse Five, Ottawa, Canada. *Clubs:* Athenæum, Travellers'; Cercle Universitaire (Ottawa).

SMITH, Ven. Arthur Cyril, VRD 1955; MA; Archdeacon of Lincoln, 1960-76, now Archdeacon Emeritus; Rector of Algarkirk, 1960-76, now Canon Emeritus; *b* 26 Jan. 1909; *s* of late Arthur Smith and of Margaret Ryde, Manchester; *m* 1940, Patricia Marion Greenwood, *d* of late Lt-Col Ranolf Nelson Greenwood, MC, and Beatrice Marion, *d* of late Rev. Llewellyn L. Montford Bebb, DD; two *s* two *d*. *Educ:* St John's College, Winnipeg, Canada; Sheffield University; Westcott House, Cambridge. Curate of: Keighley, 1934-36; Bishop's Hatfield, 1936-40. Chaplain RNVR, 1940; HMS Hawkins, 1940-41; 13th Destroyer Flotilla Gibraltar, 1941-43; HMS Eaglet, 1943-44; Senior Chaplain, Liverpool 1945-46. Rector, South Ormsby Group of Parishes, 1946-60; Rural Dean, Hill North, 1955; Canon and Prebendary of Centum Solidorum, 1960. Member: Standing Cttee, House of Clergy, Church Assembly, 1966-76; Inspections Cttee, Adv. Council for Churches Ministry, 1967. Church Comr, 1968. Dir, Ecclesiastical Insurance Office Ltd. *Publications:* The South Ormsby Experiment, 1960; Deaneries: Dead or Alive, 1963; Team and Group Ministry, 1965; contributor: to Mission and Communication, 1963; to Theology; to The Caring Church, 1964. *Address:* Farthings, Church End, Great Rollright, Chipping Norton, Oxon OX7 5RX. *T:* Hook Norton 737769; 38 Pauls Lane, Overstrand, Cromer, Norfolk. *Club:* Army and Navy.

SMITH, Sir Arthur (Henry), Kt 1968; Chairman, United Africa Co. Ltd, 1955-69; Director of Unilever Ltd, 1948-69; retired; *b* 18 Jan. 1905; *s* of Frederick Smith; *m* 1930, Dorothy Percy; two *s*. *Educ:* Bolton School. Specialised in Company's interests in French and Belgian Africa, incl. several years' residence in those territories. Econ. Adviser to Brit. Govt's Econ. Mission to French W Africa, 1943. Officer, Legion of Honour, 1957 (Cross 1951); Commander, National Order of the Ivory Coast, 1969. *Recreations:* reading, theatre. *Address:* The Coach House, 31 Withdean Road, Brighton, East Sussex.

SMITH, Arthur Llewellyn, MBE 1945; MA Oxon; FSA 1964; FRIBA; Architect in private practice, 1937-70, as partner, Llewellyn Smith and Waters, now the Waters Jamieson Partnership; Consultant for historic buildings, since 1971; *b* 25 July 1903; *e s* of late Sir Hubert Llewellyn Smith, GCB, and of Edith (Maud Sophia) (*née* Weekley); unmarried. *Educ:* St Edmund's Sch., Hindhead; Winchester Coll. (Scholar); New Coll., Oxford (1st cl. Hon. Mods Oxon, 1924; 1st cl. Litt. Hum. Oxon, 1926); Bartlett Sch. of Architecture, London Univ. Asst in office of Troup & Steele, 1928-37. War service as Inspector in Passive Air Defence Div., Min. of Supply, 1939-45; seconded to Office of Chief Adviser, Factory ARP, Govt of India, 1941-45. Was mainly engaged on housing and domestic work, social and recreational buildings, churches and vicarages, and the restoration of historic buildings in Oxford and elsewhere. Jt Founder, Crown Club Hoxton (now Crown and Manor Boys' Club), 1926; Cons. Architect to Nat. Assoc. of Boys' Clubs, 1937-70; Hon. Sec., Crown and Manor (Boys') Club, Hoxton; Vice-Pres., Winchester Coll. Mission; Dep. Chm., Devas (Boys') Club, Battersea. Sec., Brit. Inst. of Industrial Art, 1927-33; Member, Art Workers Guild, 1946, Hon. Secretary, 1954-62, Master, 1964. Member Council RSA, 1966-72. Chm. of

Governors, Camberwell Sch. of Art and Crafts, 1969-. *Publications:* Buildings for Boys' Clubs, 1937; chapter in New Survey of London Life and Labour, Vol. VI, 1934; various articles and reviews in RIBA Jl, The Builder, RSA Jl, etc. *Recreation:* sketching. *Address:* 1 Ockley Road, Streatham, SW16 1UG. *T:* 01-769 2803. *Club:* United Oxford & Cambridge University.

SMITH, Arthur Norman E.; *see* Exton-Smith.

SMITH, Prof. Austin Geoffrey; Hives Professor of Thermodynamics, University of Nottingham, and Head of Department of Mechanical Engineering, since 1960; *b* 22 Aug. 1918; *s* of James Austin Smith and Olive Smith; *m* 1960, Vera Margaret Kennard; no *c*. *Educ:* Gillingham County School for Boys. Royal Scholar, Imperial College, London, 1937-40. Research engineer, Blackburn Aircraft Co., 1940-42; Engineer, Power Jets Ltd, 1942-46; Senior Scientific Officer and Principal Scientific Officer, National Gas Turbine Establishment, 1946-52; Reader in Gas Turbines, Imperial College, London, 1952-57; Professor of Aircraft Propulsion, The College of Aeronautics, 1957-60. *Publications:* many papers in the field of thermodynamics, heat transfer and aerodynamics. *Address:* The Manse, Church St, Bramcote, Nottingham NG9 3HD. *T:* Nottingham 258397.

SMITH, Basil Gerald P.; *see* Parsons-Smith.

SMITH, Basil Gerrard, TD 1950; Treasury Solicitor's Office, 1969-77; *b* 29 January 1911; *m* 1938, Marjorie Elizabeth Artz; one *s* two *d*. *Educ:* Epsom College, Surrey; Merton College, Oxford (MA). Solicitor (England), 1938. War Service, 1939-46; Hon. Lt-Col. District Judge, Pahang, 1946; joined Colonial Legal Service, 1946; District Judge: Selangor, 1947; Perak, 1948; President, Sessions Court: Ipoh, 1949; Georgetown, Penang, 1950; Barrister (Gray's Inn), 1950; Federal Counsel and Deputy Public Prosecutor, 1953; Asst Legal Draftsman, 1954; Actg Legal Draftsman, 1955; Judge, Supreme Court, Federation of Malaya, 1956-60; Attorney-General, Southern Cameroons, 1960-61; Legal Adviser to the UK Commissioner, Malta, 1962-64; Legal Asst, Solicitor's Dept, Post Office, 1964, Senior Legal Assistant, 1967-69. Adjudicator, Immigration Act; Law Revision Commissioner: Gilbert Islands; Tuvalu. *Address:* 17 Burdon Lane, Cheam, Surrey.

SMITH, Brian Percival, CEng, FIProdE, FIM; FBIM, FIMC; independent business consultant; Professor of Design Management, Royal College of Art, since 1977; *b* 3 Oct. 1919; *s* of Percival Smith and Hilda Judge; *m* 1943, Phoebe (Tina) Ginno; one *s*. *Educ:* Erith, Woolwich; London Univ. (BSc). MIMechE. Apprentice, 1936-41, Manager, 1941-46, Royal Ordnance Factories; Gen. Manager, Cumbrian Tool Co., 1946-49; PA Management Consultants: Consultant, 1949-59; Dir, R&D, 1959-66; Man. Dir, 1966-72; Chm. of Bd, 1972-76. Mem., Design Council, 1975-; Vice-Pres., Royal Soc. of Arts, 1976-; Member Council: BIM, 1972-74; Instn of Prod. Engrs, 1972-(Pres., 1973-74). *Publications:* Leadership in Management, 1968; Bureaucracy in Management, 1969; Management Style, 1973; Going into Europe, Why and How, 1975. *Recreations:* painting, writing, listening to music. *Address:* 4 Cliff Road, Eastbourne, East Sussex BN20 7RU. *T:* Eastbourne 31870.

SMITH, Bryan Crossley, CEng, FIGasE; Member for Marketing, British Gas Corporation, since 1977; *b* 28 Feb. 1925; *s* of Frank Riley Smith and Fanny Smith; *m* 1948, Patricia Mabbott; one *s* one *d*. *Educ:* Hipperholme Grammar Sch.; Bradford Technical Coll. CEng, FIGasE 1944. Articled pupil to John Corrigan, 1941; Operating Engr, Humphreys & Glasgow, 1944; Works Engr, Middlesbrough Corp. Gas Dept, 1948; N Eastern Gas Board: Asst Works Manager, Huddersfield, 1952; Engr and Man., Dewsbury, 1956; Group Sales Man., Wakefield, 1961; Conversion Man., 1966; Dep. Commercial Man., 1968; Chief Service Man., Gas Council, 1970; Service Dir, British Gas Corp., 1973. *Recreations:* golf, gardening. *Address:* Heron Path House, Wendover, Aylesbury, Bucks HP22 6NN. *T:* Wendover 622742.

SMITH, Sir Bryan Evers S.; *see* Sharwood Smith.

SMITH, Campbell (Sherston); *b* 24 April 1906; *s* of Herbert Smith and Carlotta Amelia Smith (*née* Newbury); *m* 1st, 1936, Leonora Florence Beeney (marr. diss., 1948); one *s*; 2nd, 1948, Gwenllian Elizabeth Anne Williams (marr. diss., 1963); one *s*; 3rd, 1964, Barbara Irene Winstone. *Educ:* City of London School. General Departmental Manager, Keith Prowse & Co. Ltd, 1932, Director and General Manager, 1936. Squadron Leader, RAF, 1939-45 (Defence Medal). Assistant Managing Director, Keith Prowse & Co. Ltd, 1945, Managing Director,

1951-54. Director, Performing Right Society, 1951-54; Managing Director, Mechanical Copyright Protection Society, 1945-57; Director of MEEC Productions Ltd, 1953-62; Administrator of the Arts Theatre Club, 1954-62. Man. Dir, Campbell Williams Ltd, 1960-75. *Recreation:* theatre. *Address:* 32 Wordsworth Road, Worthing, West Sussex. *Clubs:* Garrick, Arts Theatre.

SMITH, Sir Carl (Victor), Kt 1964; CBE 1946; Cadbury Fry Hudson (New Zealand): Managing Director, 1932-63; Chairman, 1939-63; retired 1964; Director, several NZ companies; *b* 19 April 1897; *s* of Dr James Smith, Edinburgh; *m* 1919, Catherine Elizabeth Gettings Johnston; two *s* one *d. Educ:* George Watson's College, Edinburgh. Served European War, 1914-18: 4th Royal Scots, Captain. Pres. NZ Manufrs Fedn, 1940-43; Member: Armed Services Appeal Board, 1940-45; Economic Stabilisation Commn, 1941; Coun. and Hon. Treas., Univ. of Otago, 1946-68; Roy. Commn on Parly Salaries, 1955, 1957, 1958; Roy. Commn on NZ Rlys, 1952; NZ Univ. Grants Cttee (3 years). Hon. LLD Otago. *Publication:* From N to Z, 1947. *Address:* Rowheath, Dudley Place, Dunedin, New Zealand. *T:* Dunedin 60076. *Club:* Dunedin.

SMITH, Catharine Mary S.; *see* Scott-Smith.

SMITH, Maj.-Gen. Sir Cecil (Miller), KBE 1951 (CBE 1944; OBE 1941); CB 1947; MC; CEng, MIMechE; psc; late RASC; *b* 17 June 1896; *s* of John Smith, Dromore, Co. Down; *m* 1930, Isabel Buswell; two *d. Educ:* Royal Belfast Academical Institution; Royal Military College, Sandhurst; Staff College, Camberley. Served European War, 1914-19, ASC and Royal Inniskilling Fusiliers. France and Belgium, 1916-18 (wounded, MC, two medals); War of 1939-45, Middle East, and NW Europe, 1940-44 (despatches, OBE, CBE). Lt-Col 1944; Col 1945; Maj.-Gen. 1944; Maj.-Gen. in charge of Administration, Northern Command, 1945-47; Chief of Staff, Northern Command, 1947-48; Director of Supplies and Transport, War Office, 1948-51; retired pay, 1951. Col Comdt, RASC, 1950-60. Chm. Ulster Society in London, 1964-73. Commander, Legion of Merit, US; Officier de la Légion d'Honneur (France). *Address:* Crosh, Southfield Place, Weybridge, Surrey. *T:* Weybridge 42199.

SMITH, Charles Edward Gordon, CB 1970; MD, FRCP, FRCPath; Dean, London School of Hygiene and Tropical Medicine, since 1971; *b* 12 May 1924; *s* of late John A. and Margaret Smith, Lundin Links, Fife; *m* 1948, Elsie, *d* of late S. S. McClellan, Lorton, Cumberland; one *s* two *d. Educ:* Forfar Academy; St Andrews University. MB, ChB (with commendation) 1947; MD (with hons and Singapore Gold Medal) 1956. House Surgeon and Physician, Cumberland Infirmary, Carlisle, 1947-48; HM Colonial Medical Service, 1948-57; Clinical appts Malacca, Kuala Lumpur, 1949-51; Virologist, Inst. for Med. Research, Kuala Lumpur, 1952-57; Sen. Lectr in Bacteriology, London Sch. of Hygiene and Trop. Med., 1957-61; Reader in Virology, London Sch. of Hygiene and Trop. Med., 1961-64; Director, Microbiological Research Estab., MoD, 1964-70. Chairman: Public Health Lab. Service Bd, 1972-; NERC Adv. Cttee to Unit of Invertebrate Virology, 1972-. A Wellcome Trustee, 1972-. Pres., Royal Soc. of Tropical Medicine and Hygiene, 1975-77. Chalmers Medal, Royal Soc. of Trop. Med. and Hygiene, 1961; Stewart Prize, BMA, 1973. Hon. DSc St Andrews, 1975. *Publications:* papers mainly on arthropod-borne animal viruses and leptospirosis. *Recreations:* gardening, golf. *Address:* London School of Hygiene and Tropical Medicine, Keppel Street, WC1E 7HT. *Club:* New Zealand Golf (West Byfleet).

SMITH, Charles H. G.; *see* Gibbs-Smith.

SMITH, Prof. C(harles) Holt, CBE 1955; MSc; FIEE; Professor of Instrument Technology, Royal Military College of Science, Shrivenham, 1949-68, now Emeritus; (seconded to the Indian Government for four years from 1st January, 1956, as Dean of the Institute of Armament Studies); *b* 27 Aug. 1903; *s* of Charles Smith and Emily (*née* Holt); *m* 1928, Gracie Alexandra Macdonald (*née* Livingstone); one *s* one *d. Educ:* Bolton Grammar School; Manchester University. Peel Connor Telephone Works, 1924-26; Royal Aircraft Establishment, Farnborough, 1926-30 and 1938-40. British Broadcasting Corporation, 1930-38. Telecommunications Research Establishment: Malvern, 1940-42; Defford, 1944-46; Malvern, 1946-49. Assistant Director of Directorate of Communications Development, Ministry of Supply, 1942-44. *Recreations:* bridge, fishing, shooting. *Address:* 37 Queens Park Avenue, Bournemouth, Dorset BH8 9LH. *T:* 57525.

SMITH, Charles Nugent C.; *see* Close-Smith.

SMITH, Prof. (Christopher) Colin; Professor of Spanish, University of Cambridge, since 1975; *b* 17 Sept. 1927; *s* of Alfred Edward Smith and Dorothy May Berry; *m* 1954, Ruth Margaret Barnes; three *d* (one *s* decd). *Educ:* Varndean Grammar Sch., Brighton; St Catharine's Coll., Cambridge (MA, PhD). BA 1st cl. hons 1950. Dept of Spanish, Univ. of Leeds: Asst Lectr 1953; Lectr 1956; Sen. Lectr 1964; Sub-Dean of Arts, etc, 1963-67; Cambridge Univ.: Univ. Lectr in Spanish, 1968; Fellow, St Catharine's Coll., 1968-, Professorial Fellow, 1975-, Tutor 1970; Chm. Faculty of Mod. and Med. Langs, 1973. General Editor, Modern Language Review, 1974-. *Publications:* Spanish Ballads, 1964; (ed) Poema de mio Cid, 1972, Spanish edn, 1976; Collins' Spanish-English, English-Spanish Dictionary, 1971, Spanish edn 1972; Estudios cidianos, 1977; contrib. Bull. Hispanic Studies, Mod. Lang. Rev., Bull. Hispanique, etc. *Recreations:* theatre, opera, squash, natural history (especially entomology), archaeology. *Address:* 56 Girton Road, Cambridge. *T:* Cambridge 76214.

SMITH, Christopher Patrick Crawford, MA; *b* Edinburgh, 9 May 1902; *s* of late George Smith; unmarried. *Educ:* Dulwich College; Trinity College, Oxford (Scholar, First in Classical Moderations, and First in Literae Humaniores). Assistant Master, Rugby School, 1926-38; Warden of Trinity College, Glenalmond, 1938-48; Headmaster of Haileybury, 1948-63. Chairman, Headmasters' Conference, 1961-62. *Address:* Windrush, St Andrews, Fife.

SMITH, Sir Christopher Sydney Winwood, 5th Bt, *cr* 1809; *b* 20 Sept. 1906; *s* of Sir William Sydney Winwood Smith, 4th Bt, and Caroline, *o d* of James Harris, County Cork; *S* father 1953; *m* 1932, Phyllis Berenice, *y d* of late Thomas Robert O'Grady, Grafton, New South Wales, and County Waterford, Ireland; three *s* two *d. Heir: s* Robert Sydney Winwood Smith, *b* 1939. *Address:* Junction Road, via Grafton, New South Wales 2460, Australia.

SMITH, Claude C.; *see* Croxton-Smith.

SMITH, Clifford Bertram Bruce H.; *see* Heathcote-Smith.

SMITH, Colin; *see* Smith, Christopher C.

SMITH, Colin; General Secretary, National Anti-Vivisection Society Ltd, since 1971; *b* 4 July 1941; *s* of Henry E. Smith and A. E. Smith. *Educ:* Upton House Sch., London. Asst Sec., National Anti-Vivisection Soc., 1962-71; Hon. Sec., Internat. Assoc. Against Painful Experiments on Animals, 1969-. Editor, Animals' Defender and Anti-Vivisection News, 1967-72. *Publications:* Progress without Pain, 1973; Animal Experiments: steps towards reform, 1975; numerous contribs to med. and scientific jls on the anti-vivisection case. *Recreations:* music, travel, gardening. *Address:* 51 Harley Street, W1N 1DD. *T:* 01-580 4034; (home) 40 Connaught Gardens, Palmers Green, N13. *T:* 01-886 1503.

SMITH, Cyril, MBE 1966; MP (L) Rochdale, since Oct. 1972; Liberal Chief Whip, 1975-76; Managing Director, Smith Springs (Rochdale) Ltd, since 1963; *b* 28 June 1928; unmarried. *Educ:* Rochdale Grammar Sch. for Boys. Civil Service, 1944-45; Wages Clerk, 1945-48; Liberal Party Agent, Stockport, 1948-50; Labour Party Agent, Ashton-under-Lyne, 1950-53, Heywood and Royton 1953-55; rejoined Liberal Party, 1967. Newsagent (own account), 1955-58; Production Controller, Spring Manufacturing, 1958-63; founded Smith Springs (Rochdale) Ltd, 1963. Councillor, 1952-66, Alderman, 1966-74, Mayor, 1966-67, Co. Borough of Rochdale (Chm., Education Cttee, 1966-72); Councillor, Rochdale Metropolitan DC, 1973-75. OStJ 1976. *Publication:* Big Cyril (autobiog.), 1977. *Recreations:* music (listener), reading, charitable work, local government. *Address:* 14 Emma Street, Rochdale, Lancs. *T:* Rochdale 48840.

SMITH, Cyril Robert, OBE 1945; consultant and lecturer; *b* 28 Dec. 1907; *s* of late Robert Smith and Rose Smith (*née* Sommerville); *m* 1933, Margaret Jane Kathleen Gwladys Hughes; two *s. Educ:* Whitgift; Queen Mary's Coll., Univ. of London. Served in Army, Europe, N Africa, 1939-45 (despatches, OBE; Col). Entered PO as Asst Traffic Supt Telephones, 1927; Asst Inspector, Telephone Traffic PO Headquarters, 1930; Asst Surveyor, Postal Services, 1935; Asst Principal, PO Headquarters, 1936; Asst Postal Controller, 1941; Instructor, PO Management Training Centre, 1954; Postal Controller, 1955; Asst Sec. i/c of Central Organisation and Methods Br., PO Headquarters, 1958; Director, Computer Development, 1965-67; Dir, National Data Processing, GPO, 1967-68. UN Advisor to Greek Govt on computers in public service, 1971-74. FBCS; FBIM. *Publications:* various papers on computer matters in Computer Jl, etc. *Address:* 64 Copse Avenue, West Wickham, Kent. *T:* 01-777 1100.

SMITH, Cyril Stanley, MSc, PhD; Secretary to Social Science Research Council, since 1975; *b* 21 July 1925; *s* of Walter and Beatrice May Smith; *m* 1968, Eileen Cameron; two *d* (by first marr.). *Educ:* Plaistow Municipal Secondary Sch.; London Sch. of Economics. HM Forces, Dorset Regt, 1943-47. Univ. of Birmingham, 1950-51; Univ. of Sheffield, 1951-52; Dulwich Coll. Mission, 1952-56; Nat. Coal Board, 1956-61; Univ. of Manchester, 1961-71; Civil Service Coll., 1971-75; Visiting Prof., Univ. of Virginia, 1965. Chm., British Sociological Assoc., 1972-74. *Publications:* Adolescence (sen. author), 1968; The Wincroft Youth Project, 1972; (ed jtly) Society and Leisure in Britain, 1973; numerous articles on youth, leisure and developments in social science. *Recreation:* walking. *Address:* Social Science Research Council, 1 Temple Avenue, EC4Y 0BD.

SMITH, Dan; *see* Smith, T. D.

SMITH, David Arthur George; JP; Headmaster of Bradford Grammar School, since 1974; *b* 17 Dec. 1934; *o s* of Stanley George and Winifred Smith, Bath, Somerset; *m* 1957, Jennifer, *e d* of John and Rhoda Anning, Launceston, Cornwall; one *s* two *d*. *Educ:* City of Bath Boys' Sch.; Balliol Coll., Oxford. MA, Dip. Ed (Oxon). Assistant Master, Manchester Grammar Sch., 1957-62; Head of History, Rossall School, 1963-70; Headmaster, The King's School, Peterborough, 1970-74. JP West Yorks, 1975. *Publications:* (with John Thorn and Roger Lockyer) A History of England, 1961; Left and Right in Twentieth Century Europe, 1970; Russia of the Tsars, 1971. *Recreations:* writing, tennis, cricket. *Address:* Bradford Grammar School, Bradford, West Yorks. *T:* Bradford 45461.

SMITH, David Buchanan; Sheriff of North Strathclyde at Kilmarnock, since 1975; *b* 31 Oct. 1936; *s* of William Adam Smith and Irene Mary Calderwood Hogarth; *m* 1961, Hazel Mary Sinclair; two *s* one *d*. *Educ:* Paisley Grammar Sch.; Glasgow Univ. (MA); Edinburgh Univ. (LLB). Advocate, 1961; Standing Junior Counsel to Scottish Educn Dept, 1968-75. *Publications:* articles in Scots Law Times, Juridical Rev. and newspapers. *Recreations:* Scottish legal history, curling, lapidary, music. *Address:* 72 South Beach, Troon, Ayrshire. *T:* Troon 312130; Sheriff's Chambers, Sheriff Court House, Kilmarnock.

SMITH, Prof. David Cecil, FRS 1975; Melville Wills Professor of Botany, since 1974, and Director of Biological Studies, since 1977, Bristol University; *b* 21 May 1930; *s* of William John Smith and Elva Emily Smith; *m* 1965, Lesley Margaret Mollison Mutch; two *s* one *d*. *Educ:* Colston's Sch., Bristol; St Paul's Sch., London; Queen's Coll., Oxford (Browne Schol., MA, DPhil). Christopher Welch Res. Schol., Oxford, 1951-54; Swedish Inst. Schol., Uppsala Univ., 1951-52; Browne Res. Fellow, Queen's Coll., Oxford, 1956-59; Harkness Fellow, Univ. Calif, Berkeley, 1959-60; Univ. Lectr, Dept Agric., Oxford Univ., 1960-74; Royal Soc. Res. Fellow, Wadham Coll., 1964-71; Tutorial Fellow and Tutor for Admissions, Wadham Coll., Oxford, 1971-74. Vis. Prof., Univ. Calif, Los Angeles, 1968. Editor and Trustee, New Phytologist, 1965-. Pres. British Lichen Soc., 1972-74. *Publications:* various articles on symbiosis, in New Phytol., Proc. Royal Soc., Biol. Rev., etc. *Address:* Hilbre, 1 Grove Road, Coombe Dingle, Bristol BS9 2RQ. *T:* Bristol 683828.

SMITH, David Douglas R.; *see* Rae Smith, D. D.

SMITH, David Dury H.; *see* Hindley-Smith.

SMITH, David Grahame G.; *see* Grahame-Smith.

SMITH, David Iser, CVO 1977; BA; Official Secretary to the Governor-General of Australia, since 1973; Secretary of the Order of Australia, since 1975; *b* 9 Aug. 1933; *s* of W. M. Smith; *m* 1955, June F., *d* of M. A. W. Forestier; three *s*. *Educ:* Scotch Coll., Melbourne; Melbourne Univ.; Australian National Univ., Canberra (BA). Entered Aust. Public Service, 1954; Dept of Customs and Excise, Melb., 1954-57; Trng Officer, Dept of the Interior, Canberra, 1957-58; Private Sec. to Minister for the Interior and Minister for Works, 1958-63; Exec. Asst to Sec., Dept of the Interior, 1963-66; Exec. Officer (Govt), Dept of the Interior, 1966-69; Sen. Adviser, Govt Br., Prime Minister's Dept, 1969-71; Sec., Federal Exec. Council, 1971-73; Asst Sec., Govt Br., Dept of the Prime Minister and Cabinet, 1972-73. Attached to The Queen's Household, Buckingham Palace, June-July 1975. Dist Comr, Capital Hill Dist, Scout Assoc. of Australia, 1971-74. CStJ 1974. *Recreations:* music, reading.

Address: Government House, Canberra, ACT 2600, Australia. *T:* 81.1211. *Club:* Commonwealth (Canberra).

SMITH, David MacLeish, FRS 1952; DSc; Consulting Mechanical Engineer; *b* 1900; *s* of David T. Smith, Elgin, Scotland; *m* 1941, Doris Kendrick; no *c. Educ:* Blairgowrie High School; Glasgow University. College Apprentice with Metropolitan Vickers Elect. Co. Ltd, Trafford Park, Manchester, 1920, and remained with that co. and its successor AEI Ltd, until 1966. DSc (Glasgow) 1932; Hon. LLD, Glasgow, 1967. MIMechE 1938; FRAeS 1949. *Publications:* Journal Bearings in Turbomachinery, 1969; various technical papers. *Address:* Flowermead, 4 Winton Road, Bowdon, Cheshire.

SMITH, Hon. Sir David (Stanley), Kt 1948; *b* 11 Feb. 1888; *s* of Rev. J. Gibson Smith; *m* 1st, 1915, Eva Jane (*d* 1917), *d* of late Duncan Cumming; one *d*; 2nd, 1923, Margaret Elizabeth (*d* 1954), *d* of Richard Wayne Gibbs; one *s. Educ:* Wellington Coll.; Victoria Univ. Coll., Wellington (LLM). Barrister, Solicitor and Notary Public; American non-national member of the Permanent Commission under the Treaty of Conciliation between the United States of America and Peru, 11 Feb. 1933; Chairman of Commission on Native Affairs, New Zealand, 1934; Member of Council of Victoria University College, 1939-45; Chairman of Royal Commission on Licensing of Alcoholic Liquors, 1945-46; Chancellor, Univ. of NZ, 1945-61; Judge of Supreme Court of NZ, 1928-48 (temp. Judge, 1949-50); retired 1948; Mem. Bd Dirs, US Educl Foundn in NZ, 1948-70. Chm. NZ Bd of Trade, 1950-59. Ex-Mem. Council of Internat. Bar Assoc. Hon. DCL Oxford, 1948; Hon. LLD Univ. of New Zealand, 1961. *Address:* 10 Sefton Street, Wellington 1, NZ. *Club:* Wellington (Wellington).

SMITH, Denis M.; *see* Mack Smith.

SMITH, Rt. Hon. Sir Derek Colclough W.; *see* Walker-Smith.

SMITH, Derek Cyril; Under-Secretary, Export Credits Guarantee Department, since 1974; *b* 29 Jan. 1927; *s* of Albert Cyril and Edith Mary Elizabeth Smith; *m* 1st, 1949, Ursula Kulich (marr. diss. 1967); two *d*; 2nd, 1967, Nina Munday; one *s . Educ:* Pinner Grammar Sch.; St Catherine's Soc., Oxford. BA Mod. History 1951. Asst Principal, Min. of Materials, 1952-55; BoT, 1955-57: Asst Private Sec., Minister of State; Private Sec., Parly Sec.; Principal, ECGD, 1958-67; Asst Sec., BoT and DTI, 1967-72: Sec. to Lord Cromer's Survey of Capital Projects Contracting Overseas; Asst Sec., ECGD, 1972-74. *Recreations:* walking, reading, model-building. *Address:* Minstead, Kiln Way, Grayshott, Hindhead, Surrey. *T:* Headley Down 2074.

SMITH, Derek Edward H.; *see* Hill-Smith.

SMITH, Maj.-Gen. Desmond; *see* Smith, Maj.-Gen. J. D. B.

SMITH, Dodie, (wrote under the name of C. L. Anthony up to 1935); Dramatist and Novelist; *b* 3 May 1896; *d* of Ernest Walter Smith and Ella Furber; *m* 1939, Alec Macbeth Beesley. *Educ:* St Paul's School for Girls. Studied at Royal Academy of Dramatic Art; on the stage for several years; gave up the stage and became a buyer at Heal and Son, Tottenham Court Road; wrote Autumn Crocus in 1930; produced Lyric Theatre, 1931; gave up business, 1931; wrote Service, 1932; produced Wyndham's Theatre, 1932; wrote Touch Wood, 1933; produced Theatre Royal, Haymarket, 1934; wrote Call It A Day, 1935; produced Globe Theatre, 1935; Bonnet Over the Windmill; produced New Theatre, 1937; wrote Dear Octopus, 1938; produced Queen's Theatre, 1938, revived Theatre Royal, Haymarket, 1967; wrote Lovers and Friends, 1942; prod. Plymouth Theatre, New York, 1943; Letter from Paris (adapted from novel, The Reverberator, by Henry James), Aldwych, 1952; wrote I Capture the Castle, 1952 (adapted from own novel of same name), prod. Aldwych Theatre, 1953; wrote These People-Those Books, 1957; prod. Leeds, 1958; wrote Amateur Means Lover, 1956; prod. Liverpool, 1961. *Publications: Plays by C. L. Anthony:* Autumn Crocus; Service; Touch Wood; *Plays by Dodie Smith:* Call It A Day; Bonnet Over the Windmill; Dear Octopus; Lovers and Friends; Letter from Paris; I Capture the Castle; *novels:* I Capture the Castle, 1949 (US 1948); The New Moon with the Old, 1963 (US 1963); The Town in Bloom, 1965 (US 1965); It Ends with Revelations, 1967 (US 1967); A Tale of Two Families, 1970 (US 1970); The Girl from the Candle-lit Bath, 1978; *children's books:* The Hundred and One Dalmatians, 1956 (US 1957); The Starlight Barking, 1967 (US 1968); The Midnight Kittens, 1978; *autobiography:* Look Back With Love, 1974; Look Back With Mixed Feelings, 1978. *Recreations:* reading, music, dogs, donkeys. *Address:* The Barretts, Finchingfield, Essex. *T:* Gt Bardfield 260.

SMITH, Donald Charles; a Master of the Supreme Court of Judicature (Chancery Division), 1969-73; *b* 23 Jan. 1910; *o s* of Charles Frederic Smith and Cecilia Anastasia Smith (*née* Toomey); *m* 1941, Joan Rowsell, twin *d* of Richard Norman Rowsell Blaker, MC. *Educ:* Stonyhurst College. Articled, Peacock & Goddard, Gray's Inn, 1927-31; admitted Solicitor, 1932; Solicitor with Thorold, Brodie & Bonham-Carter, Westminster, 1931-34; Legal Staff of Public Trustee Office, 1934-39; joined Chancery Registrars' Office, 1939; Chancery Registrar, 1952; Chief Registrar, 1963; first Chancery Registrar to be appointed a Master. Pres., Stonyhurst Assoc., 1969. Served in RNVR, Fleet Air Arm, 1943-46; Lieut, 1944-46. *Publications:* (Revising Editor) Atkin's Encyclopaedia of Court Forms, 1st edn, (Advisory Editor) 2nd edn; contribs to Law Jl. *Recreations:* cricket, walking, theatre, philately. *Address:* Reading Hall, Denham, Diss, Norfolk IP21 5DR. *T:* Eye (Suffolk) 500. *Club:* MCC.

SMITH, Ven. Donald John; Archdeacon of Suffolk, since 1975; Canon of St Edmundsbury and Ipswich; *b* 10 April 1926; *s* of late Dr John Arthur and Evelyn Peggy Smith; *m* 1948, Violet Olive Goss; two *s* one *d*. *Educ:* Clifton Theological Coll. Asst Curate: Edgware, 1953-56; St Margaret's, Ipswich, 1956-58; Vicar of St Mary, Hornsey Rise, Islington, 1958-62; Rector of Whitton, Ipswich, 1962-75. HCF 1964. *Recreations:* driving, foreign travel, chess, collecting Meerschaum and antiques, drama, reading, pastoral reorganisation, redundant churches. *Address:* Pond Hall, Botesdale, near Diss, Norfolk. *T:* Botesdale 685.

SMITH, Douglas Alexander; Commissioner of Inland Revenue, 1968-75; *b* 15 June 1915; *m* 1941, Mary Eileen Lyon; one *s* one *d*. *Educ:* Glasgow High Sch.; Glasgow Univ. MA, BSc 1937. Entered Inland Revenue, 1938; Asst Secretary: Inland Revenue, 1952-59; Office of Minister for Science, 1959-61; Under-Sec., Medical Research Council, 1964-67. *Recreations:* hockey, golf, bridge, gardening. *Address:* 66 Eastwick Drive, Great Bookham, Surrey. *T:* Bookham 54274. *Club:* Civil Service.

SMITH, Douglas Boucher; Under Secretary, Cabinet Office, since 1977; *b* 9 June 1932; *m* 1956, Mary Barbara Tarran. *Educ:* Leeds Modern Sch.; Leeds Univ. Entered Ministry of Labour, 1953; successively: Private Sec. to Minister of Labour, 1967-68; to First Sec. of State and Sec. of State for Employment and Productivity, 1968-70; to Sec. of State for Employment, 1970-71; Chief Conciliation Officer, 1971-74, Under Secretary, 1974-77, Dept. of Employment. *Address:* 17 Dundas Close, Bracknell, Berkshire. *T:* Bracknell 54573. *Club:* Athenæum.

SMITH, Dudley (Gordon); MP (C) Warwick and Leamington, since 1968 (Brentford and Chiswick, 1959-66); *b* 14 Nov. 1926; *o s* of late Hugh William and Florence Elizabeth Smith, Cambridge; *m* 1st, 1958, Anthea Higgins (marr. diss. 1975); one *s* two *d*; 2nd, 1976, Catherine Amos, *o d* of late Mr and Mrs Thomas Amos, Liverpool. *Educ:* Chichester High Sch., Sussex. Worked for various provincial and national newspapers, as journalist and senior executive, 1943-66; Asst News Editor, Sunday Express, 1953-59. Vice-Chm. Southgate Conservative Assoc., 1958-59; CC Middlesex, 1958-65. Chief Whip of Majority Group, 1961-63. A Divl Dir, Beecham Group, 1966-70; Dir, Sterling Health Services Ltd, 1974-76; Management Consultant. Contested (C) Camberwell-Peckham, General Election, 1955. PPS to Sec. for Tech. Co-operation, 1963-64; an Opposition Whip, 1965-66; an Opposition Spokesman on Industrial Affairs, 1969-70; Parliamentary Under-Secretary of State: Dept of Employment, 1970-74; (Army) MoD, 1974. Vice Chm., Parly Select Cttee on Race Relations and Immigration, 1974-. Promoted Town and Country Planning (Amendment) Act, 1977, as a private member. A Vice-Pres., District Councils' Assoc. Governor, Mill Hill and North London Collegiate Schs; Chm., United & Cecil Club, 1975-. *Publications:* Harold Wilson: A Critical Biography, 1964; etc. *Recreations:* books, travel, music, wild life preservation in South Africa. *Address:* Hunningham Hill, Hunningham, Warwicks. *T:* Marton 632515.

SMITH, Dr Edgar Charles B.; *see* Bate-Smith.

SMITH, Edgar Dennis; His Honour Judge Dennis Smith; a Circuit Judge (South-Eastern Circuit), since 1972; *b* 29 Jan. 1911; *yr s* of late George Henry Smith; *m* 1950, Mary, *yr d* of late Captain T. Drewery; two *s*. *Educ:* Queen Mary's School, Walsall; Birmingham University (LLM). Lord Justice Holker (Holt) Scholar, Gray's Inn, 1933. Called to Bar, Gray's Inn, 1935. Practised in London and on Oxford Circuit. Served War of 1939-45: Special Investigation Branch, Royal Military Police, 1940-46; Assistant Provost-Marshal, Special Investigation Branch, 1945. Headquarters Commissioner The Scout Association, 1947-58 (Silver Wolf, 1956); Mem. Council, The Scout Association, 1964- (Chm., Cttee of the Council, 1968-74). Dep. Chm., Agricultural Land Tribunal, S Eastern Region, 1959-63; Dep. Chm., Staffs QS, 1961-63; Metropolitan Stipendiary Magistrate, 1963-72; Chm., Inner London Juvenile Courts, 1968-72. *Publications:* (ed) The County Court Pleader; (Sen. Asst Ed.) Foa's Law of Landlord and Tenant (8th edn); various other legal works. *Recreations:* travel, music, theatre. *Address:* Chilham House, Rectory Lane, Pulborough, West Sussex RH20 2AE. *T:* Pulborough 2616. *Club:* Reform.

SMITH, Maj.-Gen. Sir Edmund Hakewill; *see* Hakewill Smith.

SMITH, Edward John Gregg; Under-Secretary, Ministry of Agriculture, Fisheries and Food, since 1971; *b* 1 Oct. 1930; *o s* of late Major J. W. Smith and Mrs V. H. E. Smith; *m* 1956, Jean Margaret Clayton; one *s* two *d*. *Educ:* Churcher's Coll., Petersfield; Queens' Coll., Cambridge (MA). FRGS. MAFF, 1953-68: Private Sec. to Minister, 1964-66; Head of Economic Policy Div., 1966-68; Principal Private Sec. to Lord President of Council and Leader of House of Commons, 1968-70; returned to MAFF: Head of Meat Div., 1970-71; Under-Sec. (External Relns), 1971-74; Under-Sec., Cabinet Office, 1974-76. *Address:* The Holme, Oakfield Road, Ashtead, Surrey. *T:* Ashtead 72311. *Club:* Reform.

SMITH, Sir (Edwin) Rodney; *see* Smith, Sir Rodney.

SMITH, Emma; Author; *b* 1923; *m* 1951, Richard Stewart-Jones (*d* 1957); one *s* one *d*. *Publications:* Maiden's Trip, 1948 (awarded John Llewellyn Rhys Memorial Prize, 1948); The Far Cry, 1949 (awarded James Tait Black Memorial Prize, 1949); Emily, 1959; Out of Hand, 1963; Emily's Voyage, 1966; No Way of Telling, 1972. *Address:* c/o Curtis Brown, 1 Craven Hill, W2.

SMITH, Dame Enid Mary R. R.; *see* Russell-Smith.

SMITH, Sir Eric; *see* Smith, Sir J. E.

SMITH, Eric John R.; *see* Radley-Smith.

SMITH, Eric Norman, CMG 1976; HM Diplomatic Service; Counsellor, British High Commission, Singapore, since 1975; *b* 28 Jan. 1922; *s* of Arthur Sidney David Smith; *m* 1955, Mary Gillian Horrocks. *Educ:* Colfe's Sch., London. Served War, Royal Corps of Signals, 1941-46. Foreign Office, 1947-53; HM Embassy, Cairo, 1953-55; UK Delegn to the UN, New York, 1955-57; FO, 1957-60; HM Embassy, Tehran, 1960-64; FO, 1964-68; British Information Services, New York, 1968-71; FCO, 1971-75. *Recreations:* music, photography. *Address:* c/o British High Commission, Tanglin Circus, Singapore 10.

SMITH, E(rnest) Lester, DSc; FRS 1957; formerly Consultant, Glaxo Laboratories, Greenford; *b* 7 August 1904; *s* of Lester and Rose Smith; *m* 1931, Winifred R. Fitch; *n c*. *Educ:* Wood Green County School; Chelsea Polytechnic. Joined Glaxo Laboratories, 1926, as first post after graduation. Various posts in development, Fine Chemical Production (Head), then Biochemical Research. Shared responsibility for production of penicillin during War of 1939-45; isolation of vitamin B_{12} accomplished, 1948. *Publications:* Vitamin B_{12} (in series of Biochemical Monographs), 1960, 3rd edn 1965. Numerous research papers in various scientific journals, 1927-. *Recreation:* horticulture. *Address:* Quarry Wood, 23 Grange Road, Hastings, East Sussex TN34 2RL.

SMITH, Sir Ewart; *see* Smith, Sir Frank Ewart.

SMITH, Maj.-Gen. Francis Brian W.; *see* Wyldbore-Smith.

SMITH, Francis Edward Viney, CMG 1942; BSc; *b* 1902; *m* 1st, 1926, Winifred Nellie Nicholson (*d* 1951), Salisbury, Wilts; three *s* one *d*; 2nd, 1956, Annie McLaren, London. *Educ:* Colston's School, Bristol; Bristol University, Department of Scientific and Industrial Research, 1921; Senior Assistant Mycologist, Ministry of Agriculture and Fisheries, 1924; Government Microbiologist, Jamaica, 1927; Comr of Commerce and Industry, Jamaica, to 1944; Devel. Sec. in charge of postwar planning and reconstruction, Nigerian Govt Secretariat, 1944-46; Commissioner on Special Duty, Nigeria, 1947-53; Chm. Cameroons Development Corp., 1947-52. Services made available, by HM Govt, to Ghana, to establish National Research Council, 1958-61. *Address:* Milbourne Cottage, Malmesbury, Wilts. *T:* Malmesbury 2306.

SMITH, Prof. Francis Graham, FRS 1970; Director, Royal Greenwich Observatory, since 1976 (Director-Designate, 1974-76); *b* 25 April 1923; *s* of Claud Henry and Cicely Winifred Smith; *m* 1945, Dorothy Elizabeth (*née* Palmer); three *s* one *d*.

Educ: Epsom Coll.; Rossall Sch.; Downing Coll., Cambridge. Nat. Sci. Tripos, Downing Coll., 1941-43 and 1946-47; PhD Cantab 1952. Telecommunications Research Estab., Malvern, 1943-46; Cavendish Lab., 1947-64; 1851 Exhibr 1951-52; Warren Research Fellow of Royal Soc., 1959-64; Fellow of Downing Coll., 1953-64, Hon. Fellow 1970; Prof. of Radio Astronomy, Univ. of Manchester, 1964-74. Vis. Prof. of Astronomy, Univ. of Sussex, 1975. Sec., Royal Astronomical Soc., 1964-71, Pres., 1975-77. *Publications:* Radio Astronomy, 1960; (with J. H. Thomson) Optics, 1971; Pulsars, 1977; papers in Monthly Notices of RAS, Nature and other scientific jls. *Recreations:* sailing, walking. *Address:* Royal Greenwich Observatory, Herstmonceux Castle, near Hailsham, East Sussex BN27 1RP; Rock's Farm, Herstmonceux, Hailsham, East Sussex.

SMITH, (Francis) Raymond (Stanley); retired as Librarian and Curator, Corporation of London (1943-56); *b* Fenny Stratford, Bucks, 12 Dec. 1890; *o s* of Rev. H. S. Smith, Baptist Minister, and Lina F. Smith. *Educ:* privately; Mercers' School. Junior Clerk, Guildhall Library, 1908. Served European War, 1916-19, Lt RAPC. Librarian and Curator, Guildhall Library and Museum, 1943; Director, Guildhall Art Gallery, 1945; Member Council of Library Assoc., 1951. Chm. Reference and Special Libraries Section, 1951-54; Chm. Exec. Cttee, Roman and Mediaeval London Excavation Council, 1952-56. Liveryman of Clockmakers Company; Hon. Librarian, Clockmakers and Gardeners Companies, 1943-56; Guild Master, Civic Guild of Old Mercers, 1952-53. Member: Soc. of Archivists; London Topographical Soc.; Cons. Librarian and Archivist, French Protestant Church of London, 1965. FLA, 1929; FSA 1944. *Publications:* Classification of London literature, 1926; The City of London: a Select Book List, 1951; (with P. E. Jones) Guide to the Records at Guildhall, London, 1951; ed Guildhall Miscellany, 1952-56; The pictorial history of the City of London, 1953; The Living City, a new view of the City of London, 1957, 2nd edn 1966; The Worshipful Company of Masons, 1960; Sea Coal for London, 1961; Ceremonials of the Corporation of London, 1962; The Irish Society 1613-1963, 1966; The Archives of the French Protestant Church of London, a handlist, 1972; The Royal Bounty and other records in the Huguenot Library, University College, a handlist, 1974; contrib. to professional journals and books on libraries, archives, etc. *Recreations:* book-hunting, gardening, music. *Address:* 61 Sutton Road, Seaford, East Sussex.

SMITH, Sir (Frank) Ewart, Kt 1946; FRS 1957; MA; CEng; Hon. FIMechE; FIChemE; a past Deputy Chairman, Imperial Chemical Industries, Ltd; *b* 31 May 1897; *s* of late Richard Sidney Smith; *m* 1924, Kathleen Winifred, *d* of late H. Rudd Dawes; one *d* (one *s* decd). *Educ:* Christ's Hospital; Sidney Sussex College, Cambridge (Scholar, 1st Class Mech. Science Tripos, John Winbolt Prizeman). War service, 1916-19, RA; ICI Ltd, Billingham Works in various engineering and managerial posts, 1923-42; chief engineer, 1932-42; Chief Engineer and Supt of Armament Design, Ministry of Supply, 1942-45; Formerly Member: Advisory Council on Scientific Policy; Scientific Advisory Council of Ministry of Works and Ministry of Fuel and Power; British Productivity Council, Cttee on Scientific Manpower; Chairman, National Health Service Advisory Council for Management Efficiency (England and Wales), etc. Hon. Fellow Sidney Sussex College; Hon. Member, City and Guilds of London Institute; Hon. FWSOM; Hon. Associate, Univ. of Aston. James Clayton Prize, IMechE. American Medal of Freedom with Palm, 1946. *Publications:* various technical papers. *Recreations:* cabinet making, gardening. *Address:* Manesty, Weydown Road, Haslemere, Surrey. *T:* Haslemere 2167. *Club:* Athenæum.

SMITH, Frank William G.; see Glaves-Smith.

SMITH, Frederick Llewellyn, CBE 1964; MSc, DPhil, CEng, FIMechE; *b* 25 July 1909; *s* of late James Brooksbank Smith; *m* 1943, Alice Mary McMurdo; one *s* two *d*. *Educ:* Rochdale High Sch.; Univ. of Manchester; Balliol Coll., Oxford. Joined Rolls-Royce Ltd, 1933; Dir, 1947; Group Man. Dir, Automotive and subsidiary cos, 1970; Chm., Rolls-Royce Motors Ltd, 1971; retired 1972. Pres. Soc. of Motor Manufacturers & Traders Ltd, 1955-56. Mem. Nat. Research Development Corp., 1959-73. Pres., Motor Industry Research Assoc., 1963-65. *Address:* 4 Raglan Close, Reigate, Surrey RH2 0EU.

SMITH, Prof. Frederick Viggers; Professor of Psychology, University of Durham, 1950-77; *b* Hamilton, New South Wales, 24 Jan. 1912; *s* of Frederick Thomas Smith and Agnes (*née* Viggers); unmarried. *Educ:* Newcastle (NSW) High School; Sydney and London Universities. BA 1938, MA 1941, Lithgow Schol., Sydney; PhD London 1948. FBPsS, 1950. Pres., British

Psychological Society, 1959-60. Research Office, Dept of Educ., NSW, 1936; Lecturer in Psychology, The Teachers' Coll., Sydney, 1938; Lectr, Birkbeck Coll., Univ. of London, 1946; Lectr, Univ. of Aberdeen, 1948. Visiting Prof., Cornell Univ., USA, 1957, Christchurch and Wellington Univs, NZ, 1960. Consultant, Council of Europe Sub-Cttee on Crime Problems, 1973; Unesco Consultant, Univ. of Riyadh, 1973. *Publications:* The Child's Point of View (Sydney), 1946 (under pseudonym Victor Southward); Explanation of Human Behaviour (London), 1951, 1960; Attachment of the Young: Imprinting and Other Developments, 1969; Purpose in Animal Behaviour, 1971; papers to psychol and philosophical journals. *Recreations:* mountain walking, ski-ing, photography, music, golf. *Address:* Winslea, Deyncourt, Lowes' Barns, Durham. *T:* Durham 64971.

SMITH, Frederick William, CMG 1947; MC 1917; retired as Chief Contracts Officer to the Central Electricity Authority (1950-56); and as Contracts Adviser to Central Electricity Authority (1957-Dec. 1959); *b* 7 March 1896; *m* 1921, Emma Sarah Sharman (*d* 1971); one *s*. *Educ:* Haberdashers' Aske's Hampstead School. European War, 1914-18, army service, concluded as DAAG 51st Highland Division 1914-19; Croix de Chevalier de l'Ordre de Leopold, 1917; Belgian Croix de Guerre, 1917. Civil Service: Inland Revenue Dept, Air Ministry, Ministry of Aircraft Production, Viceroy of India, Ministry of Works, Cabinet Office, Treasury, Ministry of Fuel and Power, 1920-50; Deputy Secretary, Ministry of Fuel and Power, 1948-50. *Address:* Beechwood, Tower Road, Faygate, Horsham, West Sussex.

SMITH, Sir Gengoult; see Smith, Sir Harold G.

SMITH, Geoffrey Ellrington Fane, CMG 1955; Senior Provincial Commissioner, Northern Rhodesia, 1951-55, retired; Colonial Office, 1956-61, Department of Technical Co-operation (later Ministry of Overseas Development), 1961-66; *b* 1903; *m* 1933, Olga Smith. *Educ:* King Edward VI Grammar School, Louth; Lincoln College, Oxford. Cadet, Northern Rhodesia, 1926-29; District Officer, 1929; Provincial Commissioner, Northern Rhodesia, 1947-51. *Address:* 26 Vincent Road, Stoke D'Abernon, Cobham, Surrey.

SMITH, Geoffrey J.; see Johnson Smith.

SMITH, Vice-Adm. Sir Geoffrey T.; see Thistleton-Smith.

SMITH, Prof. George, MBE 1945; Regius Professor of Surgery, University of Aberdeen, since 1962, and Director, Institute of Environmental and Offshore Medicine, since 1975; *b* 4 June 1919; *s* of John Shand Smith and Lilimina Myles Mathers Smith; *m* 1951, Vivienne Marie Tuck, BA, Wooster, Ohio, USA; two *s* one *d*. *Educ:* Grove Academy; Queen's College, Univ. of St Andrews. MB, ChB (St Andrews) 1942; MD (Hons) 1957, ChM (Hons) 1959; DSc (Glasgow) 1964; FRFP&S (Glasgow) 1949; FRCS (Edinburgh) 1949; FACS 1958; FACCP 1963; FInstBiol 1963. Commonwealth Fund Fellow, 1949-51 (Johns Hopkins and Western Reserve Medical Schools). Formerly Reader in Cardiovascular Surgery, Univ. of Glasgow. Dean of Medicine, Aberdeen Univ., 1974-76. Chm., NE Region Med. Postgrad. Cttee; Civil Consultant in surgery to RN; Governor: Robert Gordon's Coll.; Amer. Coll. of Chest Physicians. *Publications:* sections in books and various papers, mainly on cardio-vascular and respiratory topics. *Recreations:* sailing, gardening, golf. *Address:* Cairn-Cot, 21 Cairn Road, Bieldside, Aberdeenshire AB1 9AL. *T:* Aberdeen 47556. *Clubs:* Naval; RNVR (Glasgow).

SMITH, George; formerly Director-General of Ordnance Factories (Finance), 1972-76; *b* 13 Dec. 1914; *s* of George Smith and Catherine Annie Smith (*née* Ashby); *m* 1939, Alice May Smith; two *s*. *Educ:* Alderman Newton's Sch., Leicester. FCCA. Various posts in industry, 1929-40; joined Min. of Supply, 1940, various posts in Royal Ordnance factories, 1940-52; Asst Dir of Ordnance Factories (Accounts), 1952; Civil Asst, ROF Woolwich, 1958; Dir of Ordnance Factories (Accounts), 1962. *Recreations:* gardening, walking, bowls. *Address:* 14 Blenheim Gardens, Sanderstead, Surrey. *T:* 01-657 5826.

SMITH, George Fenwick, CBE 1969; General Secretary, Union of Construction, Allied Trades and Technicians (formerly Amalgamated Society of Woodworkers and Painters), since 1959; Operatives Secretary, National Joint Council for Building Industry; *b* 24 June 1914; *s* of James Guthrie Smith and Agnes Pearson Fenwick; *m* 1937, Doris Ferguson Drever; two *s* one *d*. *Educ:* Inverbrothock and Downfield Schs. Amalgamated Society of Woodworkers: National Organizer, 1945-48; Asst Gen. Sec., 1949-59. Member: TUC Gen. Council, 1959 (Chm. TUC, 1972); Commonwealth Development Corp., 1967-; Council, Advisory, Conciliation and Arbitration Service, 1974-.

Recreations: photography, handcrafts. *Address:* 72 Maryland Road, Thornton Heath, Surrey. *T:* 01-764 1149.

SMITH, George William Q.; *see* Quick Smith.

SMITH, Gerard Gustave L.; *see* Lind-Smith.

SMITH, Gerard Thomas Corley, CMG 1952; HM Diplomatic Service, retired; Secretary General, Charles Darwin Foundation for the Galapagos Islands; *b* 30 July 1909; *s* of late Thomas and Nina Smith; *m* 1937, Joan Haggard; one *s* three *d. Educ:* Bolton Sch.; Emmanuel Coll., Cambridge. Gen. Consular Service, 1931; has served in Paris, Oran, Detroit, La Paz, Milan, St Louis, New York, Brussels, and at various times in the Foreign Office. Became 1st Sec. and Consul, on appt as Labour Attaché to Embassy in Brussels 1945; Counsellor UK Deleg. to UNO at New York and UK Alternate Rep. on UN Economic and Social Council, 1949-52; Press Counsellor, Brit. Embassy, Paris, 1952-54; Labour Counsellor, Brit. Embassy, Madrid, 1954-59; British Ambassador: to Haiti, 1960-62; to Ecuador, 1962-67. *Recreations:* music, mountains, birds. *Address:* Greensted Hall, Chipping Ongar, Essex. *Club:* Travellers'.

SMITH, Sir Gilbert; *see* Smith, Sir T. G.

SMITH, Sir Gordon; *see* Smith, Sir W. G.

SMITH, Gordon E.; *see* Etherington-Smith.

SMITH, Sir Guy Bracewell-; *see* Bracewell-Smith.

SMITH, Colonel Sir (Harold) Gengoult, Kt 1934; VD; JP; FRCPE, LRCP and SE, LRFP and SG; Chairman of Royal Visit (1949) Committee of Melbourne; *b* 25 July 1890; *s* of Hon. Louis Laurence Smith and Marion Higgins; *m* 1933, Cynthia Mary (decd), *d* of Sir Norman E. Brookes; one *s* one *d. Educ:* Melbourne Church of England Gram. Sch.; Melbourne and Edinburgh Univs; Royal College of Surgeons, Edinburgh. Australian Military Forces, 1907-47; Lt-Col Brighton Rifles (seconded), 2nd Dragoon Guard (Res. Regt), 1915, 2nd Lt; Served France, 1915-16; Qualified Royal College of Surgeons, 1917; House Surgeon, Royal Edinburgh Infirmary, 1917; Medical Clinical Asst, 1923-24; Comd Balcombe Casualty Clearing Station, 1941; CO 111th Australian General Hospital, 1944; elected Melbourne City Council, 1921; Lord Mayor, 1931-32, 1932-33 and 1933-34; Chairman Victorian and Melbourne Centenary Celebrations Council, 1934-35; President Children's Cinema Council; Patron, Partially Blinded Soldiers' Assoc.; Chm. Exhibition Trustees; Zoological Board of Victoria; Board of Eye and Ear Hospital; Board of Infectious Diseases Hospital; Council of Old Colonists' Homes; Chairman of Public Works Cttee. *Recreations:* fox-hunting (Oaklands Hounds), golf, fishing, shooting, travelling. *Address:* 720 Orrong Road, Toorak, Victoria 3142, Australia. *Clubs:* Athenæum, Peninsula Country (Melbourne); Victoria Racing.

SMITH, Admiral Harold Page; Legion of Merit (twice); US Navy; Commander-in-Chief, Atlantic and US Atlantic Fleet and Supreme Allied Commander, Atlantic, 1963-65; *b* Mobile, Alabama, 17 Feb. 1904; *s* of Harvey Samuel and Elizabeth Warren Smith; *m* Helen Dee Rogers, Oklahoma, USA; no *c. Educ:* University Military School, Mobile; US Naval Academy. Instructor: Naval Acad.; Naval Gun Factory, Washington, DC. Served War (Navy Cross, 1942; Netherlands Order of the Bronze Lion, 1942; campaign and service medals); CO, USS Stewart, 1940; on Staff of C-in-C, US Fleet (War Plans Section); commanded Destroyer Division 7, later Destroyer Squadron Four, 1943-45. Chief of Staff, Commander Destroyer Force, Atlantic Fleet, 1949-50; Deputy Chief of Information, Navy Dept, 1950-51; Director, Office of Foreign Military Affairs, Office of the Secretary of Defense, 1951; Chief of Staff to Supreme Allied Commander, Atlantic, 1956-58; Chief of Navy Personnel, 1958-60; C-in-C, US Naval Forces, Europe, 1960-63. Capt. 1943; Rear-Adm. 1952; Vice-Adm. 1956; Adm. 1960.

SMITH, Lt-Col Harry Cyril, CBE 1945 (OBE 1919); MC 1917; Russian Order of St Anne (2nd Class) 1920; *b* 1888; *s* of late Arthur B. Smith, Birmingham; *m* 1st, 1920, Catherine Koulikoff, Petrograd (marr. diss.), *d* of late Baroness v. Breugel-Douglas, The Hague; one *s* ; *m* 2nd, Ida Eleanor, widow of Capt. Lawder B. S. Smith, MC, and *e d* of late William Raymond FitzMaurice Clark, Kilballyskea, Shinrone, Offaly, Eire. *Educ:* Royal Grammar School, Worcester and Birmingham. Joined RE (TA), 1908; Engineering, S America, 1909-14; served European War, 1914-18, RE (despatches twice); CRE 28th Division, 1919; Assistant Railway Adviser, British Military Mission with Denekin, S Russia, 1919-20; Asst Director of Railways, GHQ Constantinople and simultaneously Mil.

Director, Anatolian and Baghdad Rly and Pres. Inter-Allied Rly Commission in Turkey, 1920-23; Manager and Dir Anatolian Rly Co., rep. interests of Anglo-Turkish Trust Co., and Dir Port of Haidar Pasha and Mersina, Tarsus, Adana Rly Co. 1923-27; reported on transport conditions in Italy, 1928; organised Indian Roads and Transport Devel. Assoc., 1929-39; Member, Bombay Leg. Council and Indian Central Leg. Assembly (Delhi and Simla); served on various Govt Transport cttees and confs; served with Transportation Directorate, GHQ Middle East, Cairo, 1940-41. Dir-Gen., Iraqi State Railways, Baghdad, 1941-50; temp. Amir Al Liwa' (Maj.-Gen.) Iraq Army. Silver Jubilee Medal, 1935; Coronation Medal, 1937. *Address:* 5 Hickman's Close, Lindfield, Sussex.

SMITH, Hedworth Cunningham, CBE 1972; Chairman, Medical Appeal Tribunals and Pensions Appeals Tribunals, England; Judge of the Supreme Court of the Bahama Islands 1965-72, retired; *b* 12 May 1912; *s* of James Smith and Elizabeth (née Brown); unmarried. *Educ:* George Watson's Coll., Edinburgh; Edinburgh University. MA 1933; LLB 1936. Solicitor, Scotland, 1937-40; Barrister-at-Law, Gray's Inn, London, 1950. Served War of 1939-45: commnd 1940; Staff Officer, GHQ India Command, 1943-46 (Major). District Magistrate, 1946, Senior District Magistrate, 1950, Gold Coast; Judge of Supreme Court of Ghana, 1957; retd from Ghana Govt service, 1961; Legal Adviser, Unilever Ltd Gp of Cos in Ghana, 1962-64. *Recreation:* golf. *Address:* c/o 40 Thorne Road, Doncaster, Yorks. *T:* Doncaster 62819. *Club:* East India, Devonshire, Sports and Public Schools.

SMITH, Sir Henry Martin, Kt 1971; CBE 1952 (OBE 1943; MBE 1941); retired as HM Chief Inspector of Fire Services (1948-72); *b* 10 Feb. 1907; *s* of William and Helen Smith; *m* 1937, Anita Marie Sullivan; no *c. Educ:* Roan School, Greenwich, London. Chief Regional Fire Officer, Southern Region, National Fire Service, 1941-46; Acting Chief of Fire Staff and Inspector-in-Chief, 1947-48. *Address:* 203 Upper Woodcote Road, Caversham, Reading, Berks. *T:* Reading 473932.

SMITH, Major Henry Owen H.; *see* Hugh Smith.

SMITH, Prof. Henry Sidney; Edwards Professor of Egyptology, University College London, since 1970; *b* 14 June 1928; *s* of Sidney Smith, *qv* ; *m* 1961, Hazel Flory Leeper. *Educ:* Merchant Taylors' Sch., Northwood; Christ's Coll., Cambridge (MA). Lectr in Egyptology, Univ. of Cambridge, 1954-63; Budge Fellow in Egyptology, Christ's Coll., Cambridge, 1955-63; Reader in Egyptian Archaeology, University Coll. London, 1963-70. Field Dir for Egypt Exploration Soc. in Nubia, 1961, 1964-65, and at Saqqara, Egypt, 1970-76. *Publications:* Preliminary Reports of the Egypt Exploration Society's Nubian Survey, 1962; A Visit to Ancient Egypt, 1974; The Fortress of Buhen: the inscriptions, 1976; articles in Kush, Jl of Egyptian Arch., Orientalia, Rev. d'Egyptologie, etc. *Address:* Ailwyn House, Upwood, Huntingdon, Cambs.

SMITH, Sir Henry (Thompson), KBE 1962; CB 1957; *b* 25 Feb. 1905; *y s* of late Ralph Smith, Gateshead; *m* 1929, Jane Harrison, *y d* of late Robert Wilson, Seahouses; three *d. Educ:* Sunderland Road School, Gateshead; London School of Economics. Post Office: Boy messenger, 1918; Sorting-clerk and telegraphist, 1922; Customs and Excise: Clerical officer, 1928; Officer, 1932; Asst Principal, 1934; Air Ministry: Principal, 1940; Asst Secretary, 1944; Assistant Under-Secretary of State, 1953-58; Deputy Under-Secretary of State, 1958-64; Dep. Under-Sec. of State (Air Force Dept), Min. of Defence, 1964-65, retd. *Recreations:* woodwork, gardening. *Address:* 130 Wantage Road, Wallingford, Oxfordshire. *T:* Wallingford 36330.

SMITH, Sir Henry Wilson; *see* Wilson Smith.

SMITH, Herbert Cecil, CBE 1945; BSc; MBOU; *b* Tunbridge Wells, Kent, 27 Jan. 1893; *m* 1925, Jane Bell Blair; one *s* one *d. Educ:* Eastbourne College; Edinburgh University. Joined Indian Forest Service in Burma, 1915; Served with 1/70th Burma Rifles in India, Egypt and Palestine, 1917-19. Continued as a Forest Officer in Burma until May 1942; on Reconstruction with Govt of Burma in Simla till June 1945; returned to Burma as Chief Forest Officer in the Civil Affairs Service (Burma); retired from Indian Forest Service, 1946. *Address:* Hazel Cottage, Maypole, Rockfield, Gwent.

SMITH, Sir Howard (Frank Trayton), KCMG 1976 (CMG 1966); HM Diplomatic Service; British Ambassador in Moscow, since 1976; *b* 15 Oct. 1919; *m* 1943, Winifred Mary Cropper; one *d. Educ:* Sidney Sussex Coll., Cambridge. Employed in FO, 1939; apptd Foreign Service, 1946. Served Oslo; transf.

Washington, 2nd Sec. (Inf.) 1950; 1st Sec., Dec. 1950; 1st Sec. and Consul, Caracas, 1953; FO, 1956; Counsellor: Moscow, 1961-63; Foreign Office, 1964-68; Ambassador to Czechoslovakia, 1968-71; UK Rep. in NI, 1971-72; Dep. Sec., Cabinet Office, on secondment, 1972-75. *Address:* c/o Foreign and Commonwealth Office, SW1. *Club:* Travellers'.

SMITH, Sir Hubert S.; *see* Shirley-Smith.

SMITH, Hon. Hugh Adeane Vivian, MBE; Chairman, Charter Consolidated Ltd, 1969-71 (Dep. Chm. 1966); Executive Director, British South Africa Co., 1962-66; Director, Anglo American Corp. of South Africa, 1947-70 (Managing Dir, 1948-52); *b* 25 April 1910; *s* of 1st Baron Bicester and Lady Sybil McDonnell; *m* 1933, Lady Helen Primrose, *d* of 6th Earl of Rosebery, KT, PC, DSO, MC, and his 1st wife, Lady Dorothy Grosvenor (*d* 1966); one *s* one *d.* Partner, Messrs Rowe & Pitman (stockbrokers), 1935-46. Served War of 1939-45 (despatches): in Hertfordshire Regt, then Irish Guards. *Recreation:* golf. *Address:* Souldern Manor, Bicester, Oxon OX6 9JP. *T:* Fritwell 374. *Clubs:* Brooks's, Pratt's, White's.

SMITH, Captain Hugh D.; *see* Dalrymple-Smith.

SMITH, Captain Humphry Gilbert B.; *see* Boys-Smith.

SMITH, Iain-Mór L.; *see* Lindsay-Smith.

SMITH, Ian Douglas; Prime Minister of Rhodesia, April 1964-11 Nov. 1965, and Leader of the Rhodesia Front regime, since 11 Nov. 1965; *b* Selukwe, S Rhodesia, 8 April 1919; *m* Janet Watt; two *s* one *d. Educ:* Selukwe Sch.; Chaplin Sch., Gwelo, S Rhodesia; Rhodes Univ., Grahamstown, S Africa (B Com.). Served War of 1939-45: 130 Sqdn RAF, and 237 (Rhodesia) Sqdn Western Desert and Europe, 1941-45 (Flight-Lieut). Farmer. MLA (Rhodesia Party), Southern Rhodesia, 1948; Mem. Federal Parliament (United Federal Party) 1953; Chief Govt Whip, 1958; resigned from United Federal Party, 1961; Foundn Mem., Rhodesian Front, President, 1965-; MLA (Rhodesian Front), and appointed Minister of the Treasury, S Rhodesia, Dec. 1962; Minister of Defence, April 1964-May 1965; Minister of External Affairs, April-Aug. 1964. Independence Decoration, Rhodesia, 1970. *Address:* 8 Chancellor Avenue, Salisbury, Rhodesia; Gwenoro Farm, Selukwe, Rhodesia. *Clubs:* Salisbury, Salisbury Sports (Rhodesia).

SMITH, Ida Phyllis B.; *see* Barclay-Smith.

SMITH, Ivor Otterbein, CMG 1963; OBE 1952; retired as Chairman of Public Service and Police Service Commissions and Member of Judicial Service Commission, British Guiana (1961-66); *b* Georgetown, British Guiana, 13 Dec. 1907; *s* of Bryce Otterbein Smith and late Florette Maud Smith (*née* Chapman); *m* 1936, Leila Muriel Fowler; one *s* two *d. Educ:* Queen's Coll., British Guiana; Pitman's Commercial Coll., London. Joined Brit. Guiana CS, as Clerical Asst, Treas., 1925; Sec. Commissioners of Currency, 1933; Asst Dist. Comr, 1941; Private Sec. to Gov., 1943; Dist Comr, 1945; Comr, Cayman Is, 1946-52; Dep. Comr of Local Govt, Brit. Guiana, 1953; Governor's Sec., and Clerk Exec. Coun., 1956; Dep. Chief Sec., 1960; Acted as Chief Sec. on several occasions and was Officer Administering the Govt, Sept.-Oct. 1960. Served with S Caribbean Force, 1941-43; Major, Staff Officer, Brit. Guiana Garrison. Hon. Col, British Guiana Volunteer Force, 1962-66. Chm., Nat. Sports Coun, 1962-66. *Recreations:* tennis; interested in sports of all kinds; rep. Brit. Guiana at Association and Rugby football, cricket, hockey. *Address:* Suite No 54, 2020 Comox Street, Vancouver, BC, Canada.

SMITH, Jack, ARCA 1952; artist; *b* 18 June 1928; *s* of John Edward and Laura Smith; *m* 1956, Susan Craigie Halkett. *Educ:* Sheffield College of Art; St Martin's School of Art; Royal College of Art. Exhibitions: Whitechapel Art Gallery, 1959, 1971; Beaux Arts Gallery, 1952-58; Matthiesen Gallery, 1960, 1963; Catherine Viviano Gallery, New York, 1958, 1961; Pittsburgh International, 1955, 1957, 1964; Grosvenor Gallery, 1965; Marlborough Gallery, 1968; Konsthallen, Gothenburg, Sweden, 1968; Hull Univ., 1969; Bear Lane Gallery, Oxford, 1970; Whitechapel Gall., 1970; Redfern Gall., 1973 and 1976. Guggenheim Award (Nat.), 1960. Work in permanent collections: Tate Gallery; Arts Council of Great Britain; Contemporary Art Society; British Council. *Address:* 29 Seafield Road, Hove, Sussex. *T:* Brighton 738312.

SMITH, Jack Stanley, CMG 1970; Professor, and Chairman, Graduate School of Business Administration, University of Melbourne, 1973-77, retired; *b* 13 July 1916; *s* of C. P. T. Smith,

Avoca, Victoria; *m* 1940, Nancy, *d* of J. C. Beckley, Melbourne; one *s* two *d. Educ:* Ballarat Grammar Sch.; Melbourne Univ. Construction Engineer, Australasian Petroleum Co., 1938-41. Served in Australian Imperial Forces, 1942-45, Lieut. Project Engineer, Melbourne & Metropolitan Bd of Works, 1946-48. P.A. Management Consultants, UK and Australia, 1949-72, Managing Dir, 1964-72. *Recreations:* golf, tennis. *Address:* 15 Glyndebourne Avenue, Toorak, Victoria 3142, Australia. *T:* 20 4581. *Clubs:* Melbourne (Melbourne); Lawn Tennis Association of Victoria, Metropolitan Golf (Vic.).

SMITH, James Aikman, TD; Sheriff of Lothian and Borders (formerly the Lothians and Peebles) at Edinburgh, 1968-76; Hon. Sheriff, 1976; *b* 13 June 1914; *s* of Rev. W. J. Smith, DD; *m* 1947, Ann, *d* of Norman A. Millar, FRICS, Glasgow; three *d. Educ:* Glasgow Academy; The Queen's Coll., Oxford; Edinburgh Univ. BA (Oxford) 1936; LLB (Edinburgh) 1939; Mem. of Faculty of Advocates, 1939. Served War of 1939-45 (despatches): Royal Artillery, 1939-46; Lt-Col 1944. Sheriff-Substitute of Renfrew and Argyll, 1948-52; of Roxburgh, Berwick and Selkirk, 1952-57; of Aberdeen, Kincardine and Banff, 1957-68. Pres., Sheriffs-Substitute Assoc., 1969; Pres., Sheriffs' Assoc., 1971-72. Member Departmental Cttee on Probation Service, 1959-62. Chm., Edinburgh and E of Scotland Br., English-Speaking Union, 1971. Bronze Star (US), 1945. *Publications:* occasional articles in legal journals. *Address:* East Carrine, Southend, Campbeltown, Argyll PA28 6RN; 6 Murrayfield Avenue, Edinburgh EH12 6AX. *Club:* New (Edinburgh).

SMITH, James Alfred, CBE 1964; TD; **Hon. Mr Justice Smith;** Senior Justice, Supreme Court of the Bahamas since 1975; *b* Llandyssul, Cardiganshire, May 1913; *s* of late Charles Silas and Elizabeth Smith (*née* Williams), Timberdine, Lampeter, Cardiganshire. *Educ:* Christ Coll., Brecon. Solicitor of the Supreme Court, 1937; called to the Bar, Lincoln's Inn, 1949. Served War of 1939-45: various Army Staff appointments; on staff of Supreme Allied Commander, South-East Asia, with rank of Major, 1944-45. Appointed to Colonial Legal Service, as Resident Magistrate, Nigeria, 1946; Chief Magistrate, 1951; Chief Registrar of the Supreme Court, Nigeria, 1953; Puisne Judge, Nigeria, 1955; Judge, High Court, Northern Nigeria, 1955; Senior Puisne Judge, High Court, N Nigeria, 1960-65; Puisne Judge, Supreme Court, Bahamas, 1965-75. *Address:* Supreme Court of the Bahamas, Nassau, Bahamas. *Clubs:* Naval and Military, Royal Commonwealth Society; Lyford Cay (Nassau).

SMITH, James Andrew Buchan, CBE 1959; DSc; retired as Director of the Hannah Dairy Research Institute, Ayr, Scotland, 1951-70 (Acting Director, 1948-51); *b* 26 May 1906; *yr s* of late Dr James Fleming Smith, JP, MB, CM, Whithorn, Wigtownshire; *m* 1933, Elizabeth Marion, *d* of James Kerr, Wallasey, Cheshire; four *d. Educ:* Leamington College, Warwicks; Univ. of Birmingham. PhD (Birmingham) 1929; DSc (London) 1940. Graduate Research Asst: at UCL, 1929-30; at Imperial College, London, 1930-32; Lectr in Biochemistry, Univ. of Liverpool, 1932-36; Biochemist, Hannah Dairy Research Inst., 1936-46; Lectr in Biochemistry, Univ. of Glasgow, 1946-47. President: Society of Dairy Technology, 1951-52; Nutrition Society, 1968-71; Treasurer, Internat. Union of Nutritional Sciences, 1969-75. FRIC; FRSE. Hon. LLD Glasgow, 1972. *Publications:* scientific papers in Biochemical Jl, Jl of Dairy Research, Proc. Nutrition Soc., etc. *Recreation:* gardening. *Address:* Hazelwood, 9 St Leonard's Road, Ayr. *T:* Ayr 64865. *Club:* Farmers'.

SMITH, James Archibald Bruce; Controller, Personnel and Staff Recruitment Division, British Council, since 1977; *b* 12 Sept. 1929; *s* of James Thom Smith and Anna Tyrie; *m* 1957, Anne Elizabeth Whittle; three *d. Educ:* Forfar Acad.; Edinburgh Univ. (MA 1952); Sch. of Econs, Dundee (BScEcon 1953); Jesus Coll., Cambridge. RAF, 1953-55. HMOCS, Dist Officer, Kenya, 1956-62; British Council, 1962-: Asst, Edinburgh, 1962-65; Asst Rep., Tanzania, 1965-66; Reg. Dir, Kumasi, Ghana, 1966-69; Rep., Sierra Leone, 1969-72; seconded to ODM, 1973-75; Dir, Personnel Dept, 1975-77. *Recreations:* Angusiana, reading, walking, collecting. *Address:* 38 Poplar Walk, SE24 0BU. *T:* 01-274 8945; Corodale, Hillside Road, Forfar, Angus. *T:* Forfar 4140.

SMITH, James Cadzow, CEng; FIMechE, FIEE, FIMarE; Chairman, East Midlands Electricity Board, since 1977; *b* 28 Nov. 1927; *s* of James Smith and Margaret Ann Cadzow; *m* 1954, Moira Barrie Hogg; one *s* one *d. Educ:* Bellvue Secondary Sch.; Heriot-Watt Coll.; Strathclyde Univ. Diploma of Royal Coll. of Science and Technology, Glasgow. Engineer Officer, Mercantile Marine, 1948-53; various positions in Fossil and

Nuclear Power Generation, 1953-73; Director of Engineering, N Ireland Electricity Service, 1973-74; Deputy Chairman and Chief Executive, 1974-77. *Recreations:* music and drama, mountaineering. *Address:* 398 Coppice Road, Arnold, Nottingham NG5 7HX. *T:* Nottingham 269711.

SMITH, Maj.-Gen. (James) Desmond (Blaise), CBE 1944; DSO 1944; CD 1948; Chairman and Chief Executive, Pillar Engineering Ltd; Chairman: Blaise Investments Ltd; Desmond Smith Investments Ltd; Director, RTZ Industries Ltd and numerous other companies; Vice-President, Engineering Industries Association; *b* 7 Oct. 1911; *s* of William George Smith, Ottawa, Canada; *m* 1937, Miriam Irene Blackburn (*d* 1969); two *s*. *Educ:* Ottawa University, Canada; Royal Military College, Canada. Joined Canadian Army, Royal Canadian Dragoons, 1933; National Defence HQ, Ottawa, as Assistant Field Officer in Bde Waiting to Governor-General of Canada, 1939. Served War of 1939-45, in England, Italy and N W Europe holding following commands and appts: CO Royal Canadian Dragoons; Comdr: 4th Cdn Armoured Bde; 5th Cdn Armoured Bde; 1st Cdn Inf. Bde: 5th Cdn Armoured Div.; 1st Cdn Inf. Div.; Chief of Staff, 1st Cdn Corps. Comdt Canadian Army Staff Coll., 1946; Imp. Defence Coll., 1947; Sec. Chiefs of Staff Cttee, 1948-50; Military Sec. Cdn Cabinet Defence Cttee, 1948-50; QMG, Canadian Army, 1951; Chairman, Canadian Joint Staff, London, 1951-54; Commandant, National Defence College of Canada, 1954-58; Adjutant-General of the Canadian Army, 1958-62. Colonel, HM Regt of Canadian Guards, 1961-66. Croix de Guerre, 1944, Chevalier, Legion of Honour, 1944 (France); Comdr Military Order of Italy, 1944; Officer Legion of Merit (USA), 1944; Order of Valour (Greece), 1945. KStJ 1961 (CStJ 1952). *Recreations:* shooting, tennis, ski-ing, painting. *Address:* 20 Eaton Place, Belgravia, SW1. *Clubs:* Carlton, Mark's; Queen's Tennis.

SMITH, Sir (James) Eric, Kt 1977; CBE 1972; FRS 1958; ScD; Secretary, Marine Biological Association of the UK, and Director Plymouth Laboratory, 1965-74; *b* 23 Feb. 1909; *er s* of Walter Smith and Elsie Kate Smith (*née* Pickett); *m* 1934, Thelma Audrey Cornish; one *s* one *d*. *Educ:* Hull Grammar School; King's College, London. Student Probat., Plymouth Marine Biol Lab., 1930-32; Asst Lecturer: Univ. of Manchester, 1932-35; Univ. of Sheffield, 1935-38; Univ. of Cambridge, 1938-50; Prof. of Zoology, Queen Mary Coll., Univ. of London, 1950-65 (Vice-Principal, 1963-65). Trustee, British Museum (Natural History), 1963-74; Chm. Trustees, 1969-74. Formerly Vice-President, Zoological Society; Member: Senate, Univ. of London, 1963-65; Scientific Advisory Committee, British Council; Science Research Council, 1965-67; Nature Conservancy, 1969-71; Royal Commn, Barrier Reef, 1970; Adv. Bd for the Research Councils, 1974-. FKC 1964; Fellow, Queen Mary College, 1967. Hon. Prof., Madurai Univ., India, 1969. Hon. DSc Exeter, 1968. *Publications:* various on marine biology, embryology, nervous anatomy and behaviour. *Recreations:* walking, gardening. *Address:* Wellesley House, 7 Coombe Road, Saltash, Cornwall PL12 4ZR. *Club:* Royal Western Yacht.

SMITH, James Ian, CB 1974; Secretary, Department of Agriculture and Fisheries for Scotland, since 1972; *b* 22 April 1924; *s* of James Smith, Ballater, Aberdeenshire, and Agnes Michie; *m* 1947, Pearl Myra Fraser; one *s*. *Educ:* Alderman Newton's Sch., Leicester; St Andrews Univ. Served War of 1939-45: India and Burma; RA (attached Indian Mountain Artillery), Lieut, 1943-46. Entered Dept of Agriculture for Scotland, 1949; Private Sec. to Parly Under-Sec. of State, Scottish Office, 1953; Dept of Agriculture for Scotland: Principal, 1953; Asst Sec., 1959; Asst Sec., Scottish Development Dept, 1965-67; Under-Sec., Dept of Agriculture and Fisheries for Scotland, 1967-72. Mem. ARC, 1967-72. *Recreation:* golf. *Address:* 31 Hillpark Way, Edinburgh EH4 7ST. *T:* 031-336 4652. *Club:* Royal Commonwealth Society.

SMITH, James Stewart, CMG 1955; Nigerian Administrative Service, retired; *b* 15 Aug. 1900; 4th *s* of late Charles Stewart Smith, HM Consul-General at Odessa; *m* 1955, Rosemary Stella Middlemore, *er d* of late Dr and Mrs P. T. Hughes, Bromsgrove, Worcs. *Educ:* Marlborough; King's College, Cambridge. Entered Nigerian Administrative Service, 1924; Senior District Officer 1943; Resident 1945; Senior Resident 1951; retired 1955. Papal Order of Knight Commander of Order of St Gregory the Great, 1953. *Recreations:* gardening, fly-fishing, watching cricket, chess. *Address:* Wyre House, Wyre Piddle, Pershore, Worcs. *T:* Pershore 2516. *Club:* United Oxford & Cambridge University.

SMITH, Janet (B.) A.; *see* Adam Smith.

SMITH, Dr John, OBE 1945; TD 1950; Deputy Chief Medical Officer, Scottish Home and Health Department, 1963-75, retired; *b* 13 July 1913; *e s* of late John Smith, DL, JP, Glasgow and Symington, and Agnes Smith; *m* 1942, Elizabeth Fleming, twin *d* of late A. F. Wylie, Giffnock; three *s* one *d* (and one *s* decd). *Educ:* High Sch., Glasgow; Sedbergh Sch.; Christ's Coll., Cambridge; Glasgow Univ. BA 1935; MA 1943; MB, BChir Cantab 1938; MB, ChB Glasgow 1938; MRCPG 1965; FRCPG 1967; FRCPE 1969; FFCM 1972. TA (RA) from 1935 (RAMC from 1940); War Service, 1939-46; ADMS Second Army, DDMS (Ops and Plans) 21 Army Group (despatches); OC 155 (Lowland) Fd Amb., 1950-53; ADMS 52 (Lowland) Div., 1953-56; Hon. Col 52 Div. Medical Service, 1961-67. House appts Glasgow Victoria and Western Infirmaries; joined Dept of Health for Scotland, 1947; Medical Supt, Glasgow Victoria Hosp., 1955-58; rejoined Dept of Health for Scotland, 1958; specialised in hospital planning. QHP 1971-74. Officier, Ordre de Leopold I (Belgium), 1947. *Publications:* articles on medical administration and hospital services in various medical jls. *Recreations:* rifle shooting (shot in Scottish and TA representative teams); hill walking, gardening. *Address:* Murrayfield, Biggar, Lanarkshire. *T:* Biggar 20036. *Clubs:* Naval and Military; Western (Glasgow), New (Edinburgh).

SMITH, John; MP (Lab) Lanarkshire North, since 1970; Minister of State, Privy Council Office, since 1976; *b* 13 Sept. 1938; *s* of Archibald Leitch Smith and Sarah Cameron Smith; *m* 1967, Elizabeth Margaret Bennett; three *d*. *Educ:* Dunoon Grammar Sch.; Glasgow Univ. (MA, LLB). Solicitor in Glasgow, 1963-66; admitted to Faculty of Advocates, 1967. Contested East Fife, 1961 by-election and 1964. PPS to Sec. of State for Scotland, Feb.-Oct. 1974; Parly Under-Sec. of State, 1974-75, Minister of State, 1975-76, Dept of Energy. Winner, Observer Mace, Nat. Debating Tournament, 1962. *Recreations:* tennis, sailing. *Address:* 44 Craiglea Drive, Edinburgh EH10 5PF. *T:* 031-447 3667.

SMITH, Professor John Cyril, FBA 1973; Professor of Law in the University of Nottingham since 1958, and Head of Department of Law 1956-74, and since 1977; *b* 15 Jan. 1922; 2nd *s* of Bernard and Madeline Smith; *m* 1957, Shirley Ann Walters; two *s* one *d*. *Educ:* St Mary's Grammar Sch., Darlington; Downing Coll., Cambridge (Hon. Fellow, 1977). Served Royal Artillery, 1942-47 (Captain). BA 1949, LLB 1950, MA 1954, LLD 1975 Cantab. Called to Bar, Lincoln's Inn, 1950; Hon. Bencher, 1977. Assistant Lecturer in Law, Nottingham University, 1950-52. Commonwealth Fund Fellow, Harvard Law School, 1952-53. Lecturer, 1952-56, Reader, 1956-57, Pro-Vice-Chancellor, 1973-77, Nottingham University. *Publications:* (with Professor J. A. C. Thomas) A Casebook on Contract, 1957; (with Brian Hogan) Criminal Law, 1965; Law of Theft, 1968; Criminal Law, Cases and Materials, 1975; articles in legal periodicals. *Recreations:* walking, gardening. *Address:* 445 Derby Road, Lenton, Nottingham NG7 2EB. *T:* Nottingham 782323.

SMITH, John Derek, MA, PhD; FRS 1976; Member of Scientific Staff, Medical Research Council, Laboratory of Molecular Biology, Cambridge, since 1962; *b* 8 Dec. 1924; *s* of Richard Ernest Smith and Winifred Strickland Smith (*née* Davis); *m* 1955, Ruth Irwin Aney (marr. diss. 1968). *Educ:* King James' Grammar Sch., Knaresborough; Clare Coll., Cambridge. Mem., Scientific Staff, Agricl Research Council Virus Research Unit, Cambridge, 1945-59; Research Fellow, Clare Coll., 1949-52; with Institut Pasteur, Paris, 1952-53; Rockefeller Foundn Fellow, Univ. of California, Berkeley, 1955-57; California Institute of Technology: Sen. Research Fellow, 1959-62; Sherman Fairchild Scholar, 1974-75. *Publications:* numerous papers in scientific jls on biochemistry and molecular biology. *Recreation:* travel. *Address:* MRC Laboratory of Molecular Biology, Hills Road, Cambridge CB2 2QH. *T:* Cambridge 48011; 12 Stansgate Avenue, Cambridge. *T:* Cambridge 47841.

SMITH, Rear-Adm. John Edward D.; *see* Dyer-Smith.

SMITH, (John) Edward (McKenzie) L.; *see* Lucie-Smith.

SMITH, John Gerald, CB 1966; *b* 2 Jan. 1907; *s* of Frederick and Mary Smith; *m* 1934, Christine Mary Till; no *c*. Joined Min. of Transport, 1935, after experience and training with Consulting Engineers and local authority. Commissioned RE, 1939; served in France, Middle East and Italy (despatches) attained rank of Major. Returned to Min. of Transport, Senior Engineer, 1948; Asst Chief Engineer at HQ of Min. of Transport, 1957; Deputy Chief Engineer, 1958; Chief Highway Engineer, 1964; retired 1966. CEng, FICE. *Address:* 5 Regent's Close, Belgrave Road, Seaford, East Sussex BN25 2EB.

SMITH, John Herbert, CBE 1977; FCA, IPFA, CIGasE, FBCS; Deputy Chairman, British Gas Corporation, since 1976; *b* 30 April 1918; *s* of Thomas Arthur Smith and Pattie Lord; *m* 1945, Phyllis Mary Baxter; two *s* three *d*. *Educ:* Salt High Sch., Shipley, Yorks. Articled Clerk, Bradford and Otley, 1934-39. Served War: RAMC, 1940-46. Dep. Clerk and Chief Financial Officer, Littleborough, Lancs, 1946-49; West Midlands Gas Bd, 1949-61 (various posts, finishing as Asst Chief Accountant); Chief Accountant, Southern Gas Bd, 1961-65; Director of Finance and Administration, East Midlands Gas Bd, 1965-68; Mem. (full-time), East Midlands Gas Bd, 1968 (Dep. Chm., 1968-72); Mem. for Finance, Gas Council, June-Dec. 1972; Mem., British Gas Corp., 1973-. Member, Management Committee: Pension Funds Property Unit Trust, 1975; Lazard American Exempt Fund, 1976; Chm., Moracrest Investments Ltd, 1977. *Recreations:* music, piano playing, choral activities. *Address:* 64A Beaconsfield Road, Blackheath, SE3 7LG.

SMITH, John Hilary, CBE 1970 (OBE 1964); Governor of Gilbert and Ellice Islands, 1973-76, of Gilbert Islands since 1976; *b* 20 March 1928; 2nd *s* of late P. R. Smith, OBE and Edith Prince; *m* 1964, Mary Sylvester Head; two *s* one *d*. *Educ:* Cardinal Vaughan Sch., London; University Coll. London; University Coll., Oxford. BA Hons London 1948. Mil. service, 1948-50, commnd Queen's Own Royal W Kent Regt. Cadet, Northern Nigerian Administration, 1951; Supervisor, Admin. Service Trng, 1960; Dep. Sec. to Premier, 1963; Dir Staff, Develt Centre, 1964; Perm. Sec., Min. of Finance, Benue Plateau State, 1968; Vis. Lectr, Duke Univ., 1970; Financial Sec., British Solomon Is, 1970. *Publications:* How to Write Letters that get Results, 1965; Colonial Cadet in Nigeria, 1968; articles in S Atlantic Quarterly, Administration, Jl of Overseas Administration, Nigeria. *Recreations:* walking, writing, music. *Address:* Government House, Tarawa, Gilbert Islands; 26 Edinburgh Gardens, Windsor, Berks. *T:* Windsor 65203. *Clubs:* East India, Devonshire, Sports and Public Schools, Royal Commonwealth Society.

SMITH, Sir John Kenneth N.; *see* Newson-Smith.

SMITH, John M.; *see* Maynard Smith, J.

SMITH, John (Lindsay Eric), CBE 1975; Lord-Lieutenant of Berkshire; *b* 3 April 1923; *s* of Captain E. C. E. Smith, MC, LLD; *m* 1952, Christina, *d* of late Col U. E. C. Carnegy of Lour, DSO, MC; two *s* three *d*. *Educ:* Eton; New Coll., Oxford (MA). Served Fleet Air Arm 1942-46 (Lieut RNVR). Chm., National Trust General Purposes Cttee, 1960-64. MP (C) Cities of London and Westminster, Nov. 1965-1970; Mem., Public Accounts Cttee, 1968-69. Member: Standing Commission on Museums and Galleries, 1958-66; Inland Waterways Redevelopment Cttee, 1959-62; Historic Buildings Cttee, National Trust, 1952-61; Council and Exec. Cttee, National Trust, 1961-; Historic Buildings Council, 1971-; Redundant Churches Fund, 1972-74. Director: Coutts & Co., 1950-; Financial Times Ltd, 1959-68; Rolls Royce Ltd, 1955-75; Dep. Governor, Royal Exchange Assurance, 1961-66. Founder, Manifold and Landmark Charitable Trusts. High Steward of Maidenhead, 1966-75. Fellow of Eton College, 1974-. FSA; Hon. FRIBA, 1973. JP Berks, 1964. *Address:* Shottesbrooke Park, Maidenhead, Berks; 1 Smith Square, SW1. *Clubs:* Pratt's, Beefsteak, Brooks's; Leander.

SMITH, John Roger B.; *see* Bickford Smith.

SMITH, Rev. John Sandwith B.; *see* Boys Smith.

SMITH, Hon. Kenneth George, OJ 1973; Hon. Mr Justice Smith; Chief Justice of Jamaica since 1973; *b* 25 July 1920; *s* of Franklin C. Smith; *m* 1942, Hyacinth Whitfield Connell; two *d*. *Educ:* Primary schs; Cornwall Coll., Jamaica; Inns of Court Sch. of Law, London. Barrister-at-Law, Lincoln's Inn. Asst Clerk of Courts, 1940-48; Dep. Clerk of Courts, 1948-53; Clerk of Courts, 1953-56; Crown Counsel, 1956-62; Asst Attorney-Gen., 1962-65; Supreme Court Judge, 1965-70; Judge of Appeal, Jamaica, 1970-73. *Recreations:* swimming, gardening. *Address:* 16 Farringdon Drive, Kingston 6, Jamaica; Supreme Court, Kingston, Jamaica, W1. *T:* (office) 922-2933. *Clubs:* Royal Over-Seas League, Royal Commonwealth Society.

SMITH, Kenneth Graeme Stewart, CMG 1958; JP; retired as Civil Secretary, The Gambia, West Africa, 1962; *b* 26 July 1918; 3rd *s* of late Prof. H. A. Smith, DCL; unmarried. *Educ:* Bradfield; Magdalen College, Oxford. Cadet, Colonial Administrative Service, Tanganyika, 1940; appointments in Colonial Service, 1945-62. JP Dorset, 1967. *Address:* The Old House, Newland, Sherborne, Dorset DT9 3AQ. *T:* Sherborne 2754.

SMITH, Kenneth Manley, CBE 1956; FRS 1938; DSc, PhD; formerly Director Virus Research Unit, Agricultural Research Council, Cambridge; Hon. Fellow, Downing College, Cambridge; *b* Helensburgh, Scotland; *m* 1923, Germaine Marie Noël (French); one *s*. *Educ:* Dulwich College; Royal College of Science. Served European War; Senior Lecturer and Adviser in Agricultural Entomology, University of Manchester. Vis. Prof., Dept of Botany, Univ. of Texas, Austin, 1964-69. *Publications:* A Textbook of Agricultural Entomology; Recent Advances in the Study of Plant Viruses; Plant Viruses, 6th edn 1977; A Textbook of Plant Virus Diseases, 3rd edn, 1972; The Virus; Life's Enemy; Beyond the Microscope; Virus-Insect Relationships, 1976; contributions to scientific journals. *Recreation:* gardening. *Address:* Hedingham House, 3 Sedley-Taylor Road, Cambridge CB2 2PW. *T:* Cambridge 47238.

SMITH, Kenneth Shirley, MD, BSc London, FRCP; Lieutenant-Colonel RAMC 1942; Hon. Physician and Cardiologist, Charing Cross Hospital and to the London Chest Hospital; Chief Medical Officer Marine and General Mutual Life Assurance Society; formerly Consulting Physician, Samaritan Free Hospital for Women; Staff Examiner in Medicine, University of London; Examiner in Medicine, Conjoint Board; *b* 23 Jan. 1900; *s* of E. Shirley Smith; *m* 1929, Alice Mary Hoogewerf; one *s* two *d*. *Educ:* London University; Middlesex Hospital (Senior Scholar). BSc, 1st Class Hons in Physiology, London, 1923; formerly House Physician, Casualty Medical Officer and Medical Registrar Middlesex Hospital; also Resident Medical Officer, Nat. Hosp. for Diseases of the Heart, 1927; Pres., British Cardiac Soc. Member, Assoc. of Physicians of Great Britain. Editor, British Heart Journal. Organizing Secretary, First European Congress of Cardiology, London, 1952. Served with 1st Army in N Africa, later with CMF in Italy, Greece and Austria. Gold Staff Officer, Coronation of King George VI. *Publications:* Contributor to British Encyclopaedia of Medical Practice, 1937; Papers on cardiological and pulmonary subjects in British Heart Journal, American Heart Journal, Quarterly Journal of Medicine, Lancet, British Medical Journal, Practitioner, etc. *Recreation:* sketching. *Address:* 5 Asmun's Hill, Hampstead Garden Suburb, NW11. *T:* 01-455 2706.

SMITH, Sir Laurence Barton G.; *see* Grafftey-Smith.

SMITH, Lawrence Delpré; Senior Puisne Judge of the Supreme Court of Sarawak, North Borneo and Brunei, 1951-64, retired; *b* 29 October 1905; *m*; one *s* three *d*. *Educ:* Christ's Hospital; Hertford College, Oxford; Gray's Inn. Colonial Administrative Service, 1929; Colonial Legal Service, 1934; Tanganyika, 1929; Palestine, 1946; Gambia, 1948. *Address:* 34 The Avenue, Muswell Hill, N10 2QL. *T:* 01-883 7198.

SMITH, Leslie Charles, OBE 1968; Managing Director, Lesney Products, since 1973 (Founder and Joint Managing Director, since 1947); Director, Eastway Zinc Alloy Co. Ltd, since 1965; *b* 6 March 1918; *s* of Edward A. Smith and Elizabeth Smith; *m* 1948, Nancy Smith; two *s* one *d*. *Educ:* Enfield Central School. Export Buyer, 1938-40; Lieut, RNVR, 1940-46. FInstM; FBIM 1976. *Recreations:* ski-ing, sailing, golf. *Address:* White Timbers, 9a Broad Walk, N21. *T:* 01-886 1656. *Clubs:* Naval; RNVR Sailing, Royal Ocean Racing, Royal Motor Yacht, Parkstone Yacht, Poole Harbour Yacht; North Middlesex Golf, South Hertfordshire Golf.

SMITH, Sir Leslie (Edward George), Kt 1977; Chairman, BOC International Ltd (formerly The British Oxygen Co. Ltd), since 1972; *b* 15 April 1919; *m* 1st, 1943, Lorna Bell Pickworth; two *d*; 2nd, 1964, Cynthia Barbara Holmes; one *s* one *d*. *Educ:* Christ's Hospital, Horsham, Sussex. Served War, Army (Royal Artillery, Royal Fusiliers), 1940-46. Variety of activities, 1946-55. Joined British Oxygen as Accountant, holding successive appts (until succ. as Chm.), 1956-72. FCA. *Recreations:* unremarkable. *Address:* Cookley House, Cookley Green, Swyncombe, near Henley-on-Thames, Oxon RG9 6EN.

SMITH, Maggie, (Mrs Margaret Natalie Cross), CBE 1970; Actress; *b* 28 Dec. 1934; *d* of Nathaniel Smith and Margaret Little (*née* Hutton); *m* 1st, 1967, Robert Stephens, *qv* (marr. diss. 1975); two *s*; 2nd, 1975, Beverley Cross, *qv*. *Educ:* Oxford High School for Girls. Studied at Oxford Playhouse School under Isabel van Beers. Hon. DLitt St Andrews, 1971. First appearance, June 1952, as Viola in OUDS Twelfth Night; 1st New York appearance, Ethel Barrymore Theatre, June 1956, as comedienne in New Faces. Played in Share My Lettuce, Lyric, Hammersmith, 1957; Veredane in The Stepmother, St Martin's, 1958. Old Vic Co., 1959-60 season: Lady Plyant in The Double Dealer; Celia in As You Like It; Queen in Richard II; Mistress Ford in The Merry Wives of Windsor; Maggie Wylie in What

Every Woman Knows; Daisy in Rhinoceros, Strand, 1960; Kathy in Strip the Willow, Cambridge, 1960; Lucille in The Rehearsal, Globe, 1961; The Private Ear and The Public Eye (Evening Standard Drama Award, best actress of 1962), Globe, 1962; Mary, Mary, Queen's, 1963 (Variety Club of Gt Britain, best actress of the year); The Country Wife, Chichester, 1969; Design for Living, LA, 1971; Private Lives, Queen's, 1972, Globe, 1973, NY, 1975 (Variety Club of GB Stage Actress Award, 1972); Peter in Peter Pan, Coliseum, 1973; Snap, Vaudeville, 1974; *at National Theatre:* 1963: Silvia in The Recruiting Officer; 1964: Desdemona in Othello, Hilda Wangel in The Master Builder, Myra Arundel in Hay Fever; 1965: Beatrice in Much Ado About Nothing, Miss Julie in Miss Julie; A Bond Honoured, 1966; The Beaux' Stratagem, 1970 (also USA); Hedda in Hedda Gabler, 1970 (Evening Standard Best Actress award); *at Stratford, Ontario:* 1976: Antony and Cleopatra, The Way of the World, Measure for Measure, The Three Sisters; 1977: Midsummer Night's Dream, Richard III, The Guardsman, As You Like It, Hay Fever. *Films:* The VIP's, 1963; The Pumpkin Eater, 1964; Young Cassidy, 1965; Othello, 1966; The Honey Pot, 1967; Hot Millions, 1968 (Variety Club of GB Award); The Prime of Miss Jean Brodie, 1968 (Oscar; SFTA award); Oh! What a Lovely War, 1968; Love and Pain (and the Whole Damned Thing), 1973; Travels with my Aunt, 1973; Murder by Death, 1976. *Recreation:* reading. *Address:* c/o Fraser and Dunlop, 91 Regent Street, W1R 8RU. *T:* 01-734 7311.

SMITH, Dame Margôt, DBE 1974; *b* 5 Sept. 1918; *d* of Leonard Graham Brown, MC, FRCS, and Margaret Jane Menzies; *m* 1947, Roy Smith; two *s* one *d*. *Educ:* Westonbirt. Chm., Nat. Conservative Women's Adv. Cttee, 1969-72; Chm., Nat. Union of Conservative and Unionist Assocs, 1973-74. Mem., NSPCC Central Exec. Cttee. *Recreations:* foxhunting, riding, tapestry, gardening. *Address:* Badger Bank, Norton Conyers, near Ripon, North Yorkshire HG4 5LT. *T:* Melmerby 252.

SMITH, Mark Barnet; His Honour Judge Mark Smith; a Circuit Judge since 1972; *b* 11 Feb. 1917; *s* of David Smith and Sophie Smith (*née* Abrahams); *m* 1943, Edith Winifred Harrison; two *d*. *Educ:* Freehold Council Sch., Oldham; Manchester Grammar Sch.; Sidney Sussex Coll., Cambridge. MA (Hons) (Natural Sci.). Asst Examr in HM Patent Office, 1939 (and promoted Examr in 1944, while on war service). Served War, RA (Staff Sergt), 1940-46. Returned to Patent Office, 1946. Called to Bar, Middle Temple, 1948. Left Patent Office, end of 1948; pupil at the Bar, 1949. Temp. Recorder of Folkestone, 1971; a Recorder of the Crown Court, Jan.-Apr. 1972. *Address:* 28 Avenue Elmers, Surbiton, Surrey KT6 4SL. *T:* 01-399 0634.

SMITH, Maurice George; retired; Under-Secretary, Ministry of Overseas Development, 1968-76; *b* 4 Sept. 1915; *s* of Alfred Graham and Laura Maria Smith; *m* 1940, Eva Margaret Vanstone; two *s*. *Educ:* Sir Walter St John's School, Battersea. Examiner, Estate Duty Office, 1939. Flt Lieut RAF, 1942-46. Asst Principal, Min. of Civil Aviation, 1947; Principal, 1948; transferred to Colonial Office, 1950; seconded Commonwealth Office, 1954-55; Asst Secretary, Colonial Office, 1959; transferred to Dept of Technical Co-operation, 1961; Min. of Overseas Development, 1964; Under-Sec. and Principal Finance Officer, ODM, 1968. Chairman, Knights' Assoc. of Christian Youth Clubs, Lambeth, 1970- (Hon. Sec., 1950-70). *Recreations:* voluntary work in youth service, travel. *Address:* 52 Woodfield Avenue, SW16. *T:* 01-769 5356.

SMITH, Prof. Michael G.; Special Adviser to the Prime Minister of Jamaica, since 1975; *b* 18 Aug. 1921; *m*; three *s*. *Educ:* University College London. BA 1948, PhD 1951. Research Fellow, Inst. of Social and Economic Research, University Coll. of the West Indies, 1952-56, Sen. Research Fellow, there, 1956-58; Sen. Research Fellow, Nigerian Inst. of Social and Economic Research, Ibadan, 1958-60; Sen. Lectr (Sociology), Univ. Coll. of the WI, 1960-61; Prof. of Anthropology: Univ. of California, Los Angeles, 1961-69; University Coll. London, 1969-75. Hon. LLD McGill 1976. Order of Merit (Jamaica), 1973. *Publications:* The Economy of Hausa Communities of Zaria, 1955; Labour Supply in Rural Jamaica, 1956; (with G. J. Kruijer) A Sociological Manual for Caribbean Extension Workers; Government in Zazzau, 1800-1950, 1960; Kinship and Community in Carriacou, 1962; West Indian Family Structure, 1962; Dark Puritan, 1963; The Plural Society in the British West Indies, 1965; Stratification in Grenada, 1965; (ed, with Leo Kuper) Pluralism in Africa, 1969; Corporations and Society, 1974. *Address:* 96 Woodwarde Road, SE22 8UT.

SMITH, Michael J. B.; see Babington Smith.

SMITH, Michael K.; see Kinchin Smith.

SMITH, Murray S.; see Stuart-Smith.

SMITH, (Newlands) Guy B.; see Bassett Smith.

SMITH, Patrick Wykeham M.; see Montague-Smith.

SMITH, Peter Claudius G.; see Gautier-Smith.

SMITH, Philip; Deputy Director Warship Design (Electrical), Ministry of Defence (Navy), 1969-73, retired; *b* 19 May 1913; *m* 1940, Joan Mary Harker; one *s* one *d*. *Educ:* Bishop Wordsworth's Sch., Salisbury; Bristol Univ. BSc (First Cl. Hons). Graduate Trainee Apprentice, BTH Co., 1934-37; Outside Construction Engrg, BTH Co., 1937-38; Central Electricity Bd, 1938-39; Admty (Electrical Engrg Dept) (now MoD Navy), 1939-: past service at Chatham Dockyard and Dockyard Dept, HQ; Electrical Engrg Design Divs; Head of Electrical Dept, Admty Engrg Laboratory, West Drayton. CEng, FIEE, FIMechE. *Recreations:* horticulture, golf. *Address:* Myrfield, Summer Lane, Combe Down, Bath. *T:* Combe Down 833408. *Club:* Bath Golf.

SMITH, Philip George, CBE 1973; Chairman, Metal Market & Exchange Co. Ltd, since 1967 (Director since 1954); Director, Bassett Smith & Co. Ltd, since 1946. *Educ:* St Lawrence Coll., Ramsgate; Royal School of Mines, London. ARSM, BSc (Eng). Mem. Inst. Exports; Mem. Metals Soc.; Mem. Cttee, London Metal Exchange, 1949-64 (Chm. 1954-64). Adviser to Dept of Trade and Industry; part-time Mem. Sugar Bd, 1967-76. *Address:* 1 Metal Exchange Buildings, Whittington Avenue, EC3V 1LB. *T:* 01-626 0111.

SMITH, Phyllis B.; see Barclay-Smith.

SMITH, Ralph E. K. T.; see Taylor-Smith.

SMITH, Raymond; see Smith, (Francis) Raymond (Stanley).

SMITH, (Raymond) Gordon (Antony); see Etherington-Smith.

SMITH, Sir Raymond (Horace), KBE 1967 (CBE 1960); Chairman of Hawker Siddeley Brush and other British cos in Venezuela; Representative, Rolls-Royce and British Aircraft Corporation; Economist; *b* 1917; *s* of Horace P. Smith and Mabelle (*née* Osborne-Couzens); *m* 1943, Dorothy, *d* of Robert Cheney Hart. *Educ:* Salesian College, London; Barcelona University. Served War of 1939-45, with British Security Co-ordination, NY, and with Intelligence Corps, in France, India, Burma, Malaya and Indonesia. Civil Attaché British Embassy, Caracas, 1941-43; Negotiator, sale of British Railway Cos to Venezuelan Govt, 1946-50; Pres. British Commonwealth Assoc. of Venezuela, 1955-57; Companion of Royal Aeronautical Society. Venezuelan Air Force Cross. *Recreations:* tennis, water ski-ing, winter sports (Cresta Run and ski-ing). *Address:* Edificio las Américas, Calle Real de Sabana Grande, Caracas, Venezuela. *Club:* Caracas Country (Venezuela).

SMITH, Reginald Arthur; Journalist and author; writer on education, religion, politics and social relations; *b* 23 July 1904; *e* surv. *s* of late Arthur and late Clara Smith, Burton-on-Trent; *m* 1931, Doris Fletcher Lean; one *s* one *d*. *Educ:* Victoria Road and Guild Street elementary schools, Burton-on-Trent. Junior Asst, Burton-on-Trent public library, 1918-21; reporter, Burton Daily Mail, Burton-on-Trent, 1921-30; sub-editor, Sheffield Mail, 1930-31; editor Westmorland Gazette, Kendal, 1931-34; reporter and special corresst Manchester Guardian, 1934-43; editor: Manchester Guardian Weekly, 1943-47; British Weekly, 1947-50; managing editor, Liberal Party publications, 1951-60; Hon. Sec., Friends' Temperance and Moral Welfare Union, 1975- (Sec., 1960-); Personal Asst to Ernest Bader, Scott-Bader Commonwealth, 1960-62; Sec., Soc. for Democratic Integration in Industry, 1961-63; Chm. of the Religious Weekly Press Group, 1950-51. Mem. of Soc. of Friends. *Publications:* Can Conscience be Measured?, 1940; Towards a Living Encyclopaedia, 1942; King of Little Everywhere, 1942; A Liberal Window on the World, 1946; Industrial Implications of Christian Equality, 1949; (joint editor with A. R. J. Wise) Voices on the Green, 1945. *Address:* Walnut, Albury Heath, Guildford, Surrey. *Club:* National Liberal.

SMITH, Mrs Reginald Donald; see Manning, Olivia.

SMITH, Reginald John, CVO 1954; *b* 21 Aug. 1895; *o s* of late John Smith, Hardwicke, Gloucestershire; *m* 1921, Irene Victoria Hauser; two *d*. *Educ:* Sir Thomas Rich's School, Gloucester. Joined Metropolitan Police, 1915; served Royal Artillery,

France and Flanders, 1917-19; rejoined Met. Police, 1919; Sergt, 1920; Inspector, 1932; Supt 1940; Assistant Chief, British Police Mission to Greece, 1945-46; Deputy Commander, 1946; Commander, 1947-58. King's Police Medal, 1945 for distinguished service during Flying Bomb attack. Chevalier, The Order of Dannebrog, 1951; OStJ. *Recreations:* cricket, bowls. *Address:* Foxwold, East Dean, Eastbourne, East Sussex. *T:* East Dean 3229.

SMITH, Sir Reginald Verdon; see Verdon-Smith.

SMITH, Prof. Richard Edwin; Professor of Ancient History, University of Manchester, 1953-74, Pro-Vice-Chancellor, 1971-74; *b* Moscow, 15 June 1910; *s* of James Ford Smith and Katherine Louise Smith (*née* Lunn); unmarried. *Educ:* Market Bosworth and Emmanuel Coll., Cambridge. Charles Oldham Classical Scholar, University of Cambridge, 1934. Assistant Lecturer in Classics, University College, Nottingham, 1935-38; Lecturer in Ancient History, Trinity College, University of Toronto, 1938-41, Assistant Professor, 1941. Served War of 1939-45, with RCAF, 1941-45. Classical Tutor, Queens' Coll., Cambridge, 1945-46; Professor of Latin, University of Sydney, 1946-53. *Publications:* The Failure of the Roman Republic, 1955; Service in the post-Marian Roman Army, 1959; Cicero the Statesman, 1966; articles in Classical Quarterly, Classical Philology, Historia, Greece and Rome. *Address:* 113 Marlborough Park Central, Belfast, Northern Ireland BT9 6HP. *T:* Belfast 666677.

SMITH, Richard H. S.; see Sandford Smith.

SMITH, Richard Maybury H.; see Hastie-Smith.

SMITH, Sir Richard P.; see Prince-Smith, Sir (William) Richard.

SMITH, Sir Richard R. V.; see Vassar-Smith.

SMITH, Prof. R(ichard) Selby, MA (Oxon), MA (Harvard); Professor of Education and Dean of Faculty of Education, University of Tasmania, since 1973; *b* 1914; *s* of Selby Smith, Hall Place, Barming, Maidstone, Kent, and Annie Rachel Smith (*née* Rawlins); *m* 1940, Rachel Hebe Philippa Pease, Rounton, Northallerton, Yorks; two *s*. *Educ:* Rugby Sch.; Magdalen Coll., Oxford; Harvard Univ. Asst Master, Milton Acad., Milton, Mass, USA, 1938-39; House Tutor and Sixth Form Master, Sedbergh Sch., 1939-40; War of 1939-45: Royal Navy, 1940-46; final rank of Lt-Comdr, RNVR. Administrative Asst, Kent Education Cttee, 1946-48; Asst Education Officer, Kent, 1948-50; Dep. Chief Education Officer, Warwickshire, 1950-53; Principal, Scotch Coll., Melbourne, 1953-64; Foundation Prof. of Educn, Monash Univ., 1964, Dean of Faculty of Educn, 1965-71; Principal, Tasmanian Coll. of Advanced Education, 1971-73. Chairman: Victorian Univs and Schools Examinations Bd, 1967-71; State Planning and Finance Cttee, Australian Schools Commn; Mem. Council and Executive, Australian Council for Educnl Research. *Recreations:* fishing, shooting and ornithology. *Address:* 297 Nelson Road, Mount Nelson, Tasmania 7007, Australia. *Clubs:* Naval; Melbourne (Melbourne).

SMITH, Prof. Robert Allan, CBE 1960; PhD; FRS 1962; PRSE 1977 (FRSE 1969); Principal Emeritus and Hon. Professor, Heriot-Watt University; PRSE 1977 (FRSE 1969); *b* Kelso, Scotland, 14 May 1909; *s* of G. J. T. Smith; *m* 1934, Doris M. L. Ward; one *s* two *d*. *Educ:* Edinburgh Univ.; Cambridge University. Carnegie Research Fellow, St Andrews Univ., 1935-38; Lecturer, Reading Univ., 1939; Royal Radar Establishment, 1939-61 (Head of Physics Dept, 1947-61); Professor of Physics, Sheffield Univ., 1961-62; Professor of Physics, and First Director of Center of Materials, Science and Engineering, Mass Inst. of Technology, 1962-68; Principal and Vice-Chancellor, Heriot-Watt Univ., 1968-74. Hon. DSc Heriot-Watt, 1975. *Publications:* Radio Aids to Navigation, 1947; Aerials for Meter and Decimeter Wave-lengths, 1949; The Physical Principles of Thermodynamics, 1952; The Detection and Measurement of Infra-Red Radiation, 1957; Semiconductors, 1959; The Wave Mechanics of Crystalline Solids, 1961. *Address:* 2/18 Succoth Court, Edinburgh EH12 6BZ. *Clubs:* Caledonian; New (Edinburgh).

SMITH, Robert Courtney, MA, CA, JP; Partner, Arthur Young McClelland Moores & Co., Chartered Accountants, since 1957; Chairman, Scottish United Investors Ltd; Director: Finance for Industry Ltd; Standard Life Assurance Company; Sidlaw Industries Ltd; *b* 10 Sept. 1927; 4th *s* of late John Smith, DL, JP, and Agnes Smith, Glasgow and Symington; *m* 1954, Moira Rose, *d* of late Wilfred H. Macdougall, CA, Glasgow; one *s* two *d* (and one *s* decd). *Educ:* Kelvinside Academy, Glasgow;

Sedbergh Sch.; Trinity Coll., Cambridge. BA 1950, MA 1957. Served, Royal Marines, 1945-47, and RMFVR, 1951-57. Member: Scottish Industrial Develt Adv. Bd, 1972-; Council, Inst. of Chartered Accountants of Scotland, 1974-; Horserace Betting Levy Bd, 1977-. Deacon Convener, Trades House of Glasgow, 1976-78; Pres., Business Archives Council of Scotland; Dir, Nat. Register of Archives (Scotland). OStJ. *Recreations:* formerly: Rugby football and athletics; now: tennis, racing, gardening. *Address:* North Lodge, Dunkeld, Perthshire. *T:* Dunkeld 574; (professional) 151 West George Street, Glasgow G2 2JF. *Clubs:* East India, Devonshire, Sports and Public Schools, Caledonian; Western (Glasgow); Royal (Perth); Hawks (Cambridge).

SMITH, Roderick Philip, QC 1966; **His Honour Judge Smith;** a Circuit Judge, since 1972; *b* 29 April 1926; *s* of John Philip Smith and Hettie Smith (*née* Mayall); *m* 1957, Jean Rodham Hudspith; two *s* two *d*. *Educ:* Newcastle upon Tyne Royal Grammar Sch.; Merton Coll., Oxford. BA 1950. Served Royal Navy, 1945-47. Called to the Bar, Middle Temple, 1951. Recorder of Sunderland, 1967-70; of Newcastle upon Tyne, 1970-71; Dep.-Chm., Durham QS, 1967-71. *Recreations:* cricket, gardening. *Address:* Oaklands Manor, Riding Mill, Northumberland. *Club:* MCC.

SMITH, Sir Rodney, KBE 1975; MS, FRCS; Surgeon, St George's Hospital, London; Hon. Consulting Surgeon: Royal Prince Alfred Hospital, Sydney, NSW; Wimbledon Hospital; Examiner in Surgery, University of London; External Examiner in Surgery, Universities of Cambridge, Birmingham and Hong Kong; former Advisor in Surgery to Department of Health and Social Security; Hon. Consultant in Surgery to the Army, since 1972; *b* 10 May 1914; *o s* of Dr Edwin Smith and Edith Catherine (*née* Dyer); *m* 1st, 1938, Mary Rodwell (marr. diss. 1971); three *s* one *d*; 2nd, 1971, Susan Fry. *Educ:* Westminster Sch.; London Univ. (St Thomas's Hospital). MB, BS London, MRCS, LRCP 1937; FRCS 1939; MS London 1941. Surgical Registrar, Middlesex Hospital, 1939-41; Surgeon RAMC, 1941-45; appointed Surgeon, St George's Hospital 1946. Royal College of Surgeons: Hunterian Professor, 1947 and 1952; Arris and Gale Lecturer, 1959; Jacksonian Prizewinner, 1951; Penrose May Tutor in Surgery, 1957-63; Dean, Inst. of Basic Medical Sciences, 1966-71; Mem., Ct of Examiners, 1963-69, Chm. Feb.-July 1969; Mem. Council, 1965-; Pres., 1973-77; Hunterian Orator, 1975. Vis. Lectr to S Africa Assoc. of Surgeons, 1957; McIlrath Guest Professor in Surgery, Royal Prince Alfred Hospital, Sydney, NSW, 1966; Lectures: First Datuk Abdul Majid Ismail Oration and Gold Medal, Malaysian Assoc. of Surgeons, 1972; Robert Whitmarsh Oration, Providence, 1972; Cheselden, St Thomas's Hosp., 1975; Philip Mitchiner, 1976; Balfour, Toronto, 1976; Colles, RCSI, 1976; Faltin (and Medal), Helsinki, 1976; Sir Ernest Finch Meml, Sheffield, 1978; Telford Meml, Manchester, 1978; Annual Oration Med. Soc. of London, 1978; Sir William MacEwen Meml, Glasgow, 1978. Hon. Member: Soc. of Grad. Surgeons of LA County Hosp., 1965; Finnish Surgical Soc., 1976; Surgical Res. Soc., 1976; Surgical Soc. of Phoenix, Arizona. Hon. FRACS 1957; Hon. FRCSEd 1975; Hon. FACS 1975; Hon. FRCSCan 1976; Hon. FRCSI 1976; Hon. FRCS S Africa 1976. Hon. DSc: Exeter, 1974; Leeds, 1976. Biennial Prize, Internat. Soc. of Surgery, 1975. *Publications:* Acute Intestinal Obstruction, 1947; Surgery of Pancreatic Neoplasms, 1951; Progress in Clinical Surgery, 1953, 1961, 1969; Operative Surgery (8 Vols) 1956-57 (14 Vols) 1968-69; Surgery of the Gallbladder and Bile Ducts, 1965; Clinical Surgery (Vols 1-14), 1965-67; papers in learned journals on pancreatic surgery, general abdominal surgery, intestinal obstruction. *Recreations:* music, cricket, golf, bridge. *Address:* 149 Harley Street, W1. *T:* 01-935 4444. *Clubs:* MCC; Temple Golf.

SMITH, Prof. Roland; Professor of Marketing, University of Manchester Institute of Science and Technology, since 1966; *b* 1 Oct. 1928; *s* of late Joshua Smith and of Mrs Hannah Smith; *m* 1954, Joan (*née* Shaw); no *c*. *Educ:* Univs of Birmingham and Manchester. BA, MSc, PhD (Econ). Flying Officer, RAF, 1953. Asst Dir, Footwear Manufacturers' Fedn, 1955; Lectr in Econs, Univ. of Liverpool, 1960; Dir, Univ. of Liverpool Business Sch., 1963; Non-Executive Chairman: Senior Engineering Ltd, 1973; Barrow Hepburn Group, 1974; Tremletts Ltd, 1975; Dir-Consultant to a number of public companies. *Recreation:* walking. *Address:* Branksome, Enville Road, Bowdon, Cheshire. *T:* 061-928 1119.

SMITH, Ron, CBE 1973; Member, British Steel Corporation, 1967-77; (Managing Director (Personnel and Social Policy) 1967-72); *b* 15 July 1915; *s* of Henry Sidney Smith and Bertha Clara (*née* Barnwell); *m* 1940, Daisy Hope (*d* 1974), *d* of Herbert Leggatt Nicholson; one *d*. *Educ:* Workers' Education

Association. Post Office Messenger, 1929; Postman, 1934; Postal and Telegraph Officer, 1951; Treasurer, Union of Post Office Workers, 1953; Gen. Sec., Union of Post Office Workers, 1957-66. General Council, TUC, 1957-66; Civil Service National Whitley Council, 1957-66; Exec. Cttee, Postal, Telegraph and Telephone International, 1957-66; Vice-Chairman, Post Office Dept, Whitley Council, 1959-66. Member: Cttee on Grants to Students, 1958-60; Development Areas, Treasury Advisory Cttee, 1959-60; Cttee on Company Law, 1960-62; National Economic Development Council, 1962-66; Court of Enquiry into Ford Motor Co. Dispute, 1963; Cttee of Enquiry into Pay, etc, of London Transport Bus Staff, 1963-64; Organising Cttee for Nat. Steel Corp., 1966; President, Postal, Telegraph and Telephone Internat., 1966. Director, BOAC, 1964-70. *Recreations:* photography, golf. *Address:* 33 Grosvenor Place, SW1. *T:* 01-235 1212. *Club:* Royal Automobile.

SMITH, Ronald A. D.; *see* Dingwall-Smith.

SMITH, Sir Rowland; *see* Smith, Sir Alexander R.

SMITH, Air Vice-Marshal Roy David A.; *see* Austen-Smith.

SMITH, Rupert Alexander A.; *see* Alec-Smith.

SMITH, Rupert R. R.; *see* Rawden-Smith.

SMITH, Sidney, LittD, FBA 1941; Professor Emeritus, University of London; *b* Aug. 1889; *m* Mary, *d* of H. W. Parker; one *s* one *d*. *Educ:* City of London Sch.; Queens' Coll., Cambridge (Scholar, Hon. Fellow, 1935). Director of Antiquities, Iraq, 1929-30; Hon. Fellow, School of Oriental and African Studies, University of London. Foreign Member Royal Flemish Acad. of Belgium. *Address:* Cawthorne, Barcombe, Lewes, East Sussex.
  See also H.S.Smith.

SMITH, Sidney William; Regional Administrator, East Anglian Regional Health Authority, since 1975; *b* 17 May 1920; *s* of Sidney John and Harriet May Smith; *m* 1943, Doreen Kelly; one *s* one *d*. *Educ:* Wirral Grammar Sch., Cheshire. FHA, ACIS. Dep. Group Sec.: Mansfield Hosp. Management Cttee, 1948-61; Wolverhampton Hosp. Management Cttee, 1961-63; Group Sec., Wakefield Hosp. Management Cttee, 1963-73; Area Administrator, Wakefield Area Health Authority, 1973-75. Mem. Management Side, Ancillary Staff, Whitley Council, 1969-; Chm., Assoc. of Chief Administrators of Health Authorities, 1974-76. *Recreations:* gardening, walking. *Address:* 77 Gough Way, Cambridge CB3 9LN. *T:* Cambridge 62307; Dalar Wen, Denbigh, Clwyd, North Wales LL16 3HT.

SMITH, Prof. Stanley Desmond, FRS 1976; FRSE 1972; Professor of Physics and Head of Department of Physics, Heriot-Watt University, Edinburgh, since 1970; *b* 3 March 1931; *s* of Henry George Stanley Smith and Sarah Emily Ruth Smith; *m* 1956, Gillian Anne Parish; one *s* one *d*. *Educ:* Cotham Grammar Sch., Bristol; Bristol Univ. (BSc, DSc); Reading Univ. (PhD). SSO, RAE, Farnborough, 1956-58; Research Asst, Dept of Meteorology, Imperial Coll., London, 1958-59; Lectr, then Reader, Univ. of Reading, 1960-70. Chm., Edinburgh Instruments Ltd, 1971-. C. V. Boys Prizeman, Inst. of Physics, 1976. *Publications:* Infra-red Physics, 1966; numerous papers on semi-conductor and laser physics and satellite meteorology. *Recreations:* tennis, skiing, mountaineering. *Address:* 4 Cherry Tree View, Balerno, Edinburgh EH14 5AP. *T:* 031-449 4520.

SMITH, Stanley Frank, MA; CEng, FIMechE, AFRAeS; Chief Mechanical Engineer, London Transport, since 1972; *b* 15 Dec. 1924; *s* of Frederick and Edith Maria Smith; *m* 1960, Margaret (*née* Garrett); two *s* three *d*. *Educ:* Purley Sch.; Hertford Coll., Oxford (MA). Served War, RAF Pilot, 1943-46. Oxford Univ., 1946-49. Rolls-Royce Ltd, 1949-65 (Chief Research Engineer, 1963); British Railways, 1965-71 (Dir of Engineering Research, 1965; Dir of Research, 1966); joined London Transport 1971; Dir-Gen. of Research and Develt, 1971-72. *Recreations:* tennis, sailing. *Address:* Bridge House, Cromford, Derbyshire. *T:* Matlock 3210.

SMITH, Stanley G.; *see* Graham Smith.

SMITH, Stewart Ranson; Controller, Overseas B, British Council, since 1976; *b* 16 Feb. 1931; *s* of John Smith and Elizabeth Smith; *m* 1960, Lee Tjam Mui. *Educ:* Bedlington Grammar Sch., Northumberland; Nottingham Univ. (BA, MA); Yale Univ., USA (MA). British Council: Asst Rep., Singapore, 1957-59; Reg. Officer, Overseas A, 1959-61; Dir, Curitiba, Brazil, 1961-65; Asst Rep., Sri Lanka, 1965-69; Planning Officer, London, 1969-70; seconded Min. of Overseas Develt,

1970-73; Rep., Kenya, 1973-76. *Recreations:* music, cricket, football, writing. *Address:* 53 Sutherland Avenue, Petts Wood, Kent BR5 1QY.

SMITH, Stuart Hayne Granville; *see* Granville-Smith.

SMITH, Sydney, CBE 1957; *b* 2 Nov. 1900; *s* of John Ickringill Smith and Annie Shields Smith (*née* Hutton); *m* 1st, 1926, Claudia Jane Warburton (*d* 1947); two *s*; 2nd, 1948, Sheina Baird Wright. *Educ:* Belle Vue Sch., Bradford, Yorkshire; Bradford Technical Coll. Dep. Engineer and Manager, Gas Dept, Dunfermline, Fife, 1928-35; Chief Asst Engineer and Works Manager, Bristol Gas Co., 1935-39; Engineer and Manager, Gas Dept, Paisley, Renfrewshire, 1939-45; General Manager and Chief Engineer, Romford Gas Co., Essex, 1945-49; Dep. Chairman, East Midlands Gas Board, 1949-52; Chairman: East Midlands Gas Board, 1952-56; The Scottish Gas Board, 1956-65. Member, Scottish Tourist Board, 1965-69. *Publications:* contrib. to technical journals. *Recreations:* motoring, photography, golf, fishing. *Address:* Eastfield, Erskine Road, Gullane, East Lothian EH31 2DR. *T:* Gullane 842287.

SMITH, Alderman Sydney Herbert, MA; *s* of late Charles Edward and Emma Hedges, of London, Woodbridge, Suffolk, and Aylesbury, Bucks. *Educ:* Ruskin Coll.; St Catherine's, Oxford Univ. (Hons graduate). Member Hull City Council, 1923-70; Hon. Alderman; Lord Mayor, 1940-41; Hon. Freeman of Hull, 1968. MP (Lab) Hull, South-West, 1945-50. Life Mem., Court of Hull University. Former Chairman, Hull Education Cttee and Hull Housing and Town Planning Cttee. Hon. LLD Hull, 1967. Queen Marie of Roumania's Cross for Services, 1917. *Address:* 16 Southfield, Hessle, North Humberside. *T:* 648979.

SMITH, Prof. Thomas Broun, QC Scotland 1956; DCL Oxon, 1956; LLD Edinburgh, 1963; FRSE 1977; FBA 1958; Member of Scottish Law Commission, since 1972; Hon. Professor of Edinburgh University, since 1972; *b* 3 Dec. 1915; 2nd *s* of late J. Smith, DL, JP, and Agnes Smith, Symington, Lanarkshire; *m* 1940, Ann Dorothea, *d* of late Christian Tindall, CIE, ICS, Exmouth, Devon; one *d* (one *s* one *d* decd). *Educ:* High Sch. of Glasgow; Sedbergh Sch.; Christ Church, Oxford (MA). Boulter Exhibitioner, 1st Class Hons School of Jurisprudence, 1937; Eldon Scholar, 1937; Edinburgh Univ.; 1st Class and Certificate of Honour English Bar Final, Called to English Bar by Grays Inn, 1938. Served TA from 1937; War Service, 1939-46; BEF, Home Forces, Middle East and Central Mediterranean; London Scottish (Gordon Highlanders) and RA (Fd.); variously employed on regimental and intelligence duties and at School of Infantry; Lieut-Colonel (despatches); Lieut-Colonel (TA) Gordon Highlanders, 1950; OC Aberdeen University Contingent, Officers Training Corps, 1950-55; Hon. Colonel, 1964-73. Attached to Foreign Office, 1946-47. Examined by and admitted to Faculty of Advocates in Scotland, 1947. Professor of Scots Law, University of Aberdeen, 1949-58; Dean of Faculty of Law, 1950-53 and 1956-58; Prof. of Civil Law, University of Edinburgh, 1958-68, of Scots Law, 1968-72. Hon. Sheriff of Aberdeen, 1950 and of Lothians and Peebles, 1964; Member Scottish Law Reform Cttee, 1954. Director Scottish Universities Law Inst., 1960; Hon. Member Council Louisiana State Law Inst., 1960; Mem., Academic Advisory Cttee, Universities of St Andrews and Dundee, 1964-; Ford Visiting Professor, Tulane Univ. (Louisiana), 1957-58; Visiting Lecturer, Cape Town and Witwatersrand Universities, 1958; Visiting Prof., Harvard Law Sch., 1962-63. Hon. Foreign Mem., Amer. Acad. of Arts and Sciences, 1969. Hon. LLD: Cape Town, 1959; Aberdeen, 1969. *Publications:* Doctrines of Judicial Precedent in Scots Law, 1952; Scotland: The Development of its Laws and Constitution, 1955; British Justice: The Scottish Contribution, 1961; Studies Critical and Comparative, 1962; A Short Commentary on the Law of Scotland, 1962; contribs to legal publications on Scottish, historical and comparative law. *Recreations:* gardening, foreign travel. *Address:* 11 India Street, Edinburgh EH3 6HA. *T:* 031-225 8030; Kirkton of Morham, Morham, Haddington, East Lothian EH41 4LQ. *Clubs:* Naval and Military; New (Edinburgh).

SMITH, T(homas) Dan; Development Officer (Northern), Howard League for Penal Reform, since 1977; *b* 11 May 1915; *m* 1939; one *s* two *d*. Company Director. City Councillor, Newcastle upon Tyne, 1950-65 (Chairman, Finance Cttee); Member: Nat. Sports Council, 1965-69; Royal Commission on Local Government, 1966-69; Shakespeare Theatre Trust, 1968-. Chairman: Northern Economic Planning Council, 1965-70; Peterlee and Aycliffe Develt Corp., 1968-70. Hon. DCL Newcastle University, 1966. *Publications:* Essays in Local Government, 1965; contrib. to Which Way, 1970; Education,

Science and Technology (paper to British Assoc. for Advancement of Science), 1970; An Autobiography, 1971. *Recreations:* painting, music, swimming, sport. *Address:* Leazes Edge, 13 Bell Grove Terrace, Spital Tongues, Newcastle upon Tyne NE2 4LL.

SMITH, Rt. Rev. Thomas Geoffrey Stuart; *b* 28 Feb. 1901; *s* of late Rev. Albert James Smith and late Amy Florence Smith; *m* 1930, Barbara Agnes Read; two *s* one *d. Educ:* Felsted Sch.; Jesus Coll., Cambridge; Ridley Hall, Cambridge. BA 1924; Carus Prize, 1924; MA 1927. Deacon 1925, Priest 1926, Southwark; Curate of St Mary Magdalene, Bermondsey, 1925-28; Chaplain of Ridley Hall, Cambridge, 1928-30; Examining Chaplain to Bishop of Chelmsford, 1929-30 and 1960-62. Vice-Principal, Diocesan Theological Instn, and Missionary, Kottayam, S India, 1930-39; Archdeacon of Mavelikkara, 1939-47; consecrated Bishop of North Kerala (Church of S India), 1947; resigned, 1953. Vicar of Burwell, 1954-60; Rector of Danbury, 1960-66; Assistant Bishop of Chelmsford, 1961-66; Hon. Canon of Chelmsford, 1961-66; Rector of Swithland, 1966-73; Asst Bishop of Leicester, 1966-73; Hon. Canon of Leicester, 1966-72; Canon Emeritus, 1977. Select Preacher, University of Cambridge, 1957. *Publication:* (in Malayalam) The Prison Epistles of St Paul, A Commentary, 1938. *Address:* 3 Ulverscroft Road, Loughborough, Leics. *T:* Loughborough 67882.

SMITH, Sir (Thomas) Gilbert, 4th Bt, *cr* 1897; Area Manager; *b* 2 July 1937; *er s* of Sir Thomas Turner Smith, 3rd Bt, and Agnes, *o d* of Bernard Page, Wellington, New Zealand; *S* father, 1961; *m* 1962, Patricia Christine Cooper; two *s* one *d. Educ:* Huntley Sch.; Nelson Coll. *Recreation:* skiing. *Heir: s* Andrew Thomas Smith, *b* 17 Oct. 1965. *Address:* PO Box 654, 50 Titoki Street, Masterton, New Zealand.

SMITH, Thomas I.; *see* Irvine Smith.

SMITH, Ven. Timothy D.; *see* Dudley-Smith.

SMITH, Timothy John; MP (C) Ashfield, since April 1977; *b* 5 Oct. 1947; *s* of late Captain Norman Wesley Smith, CBE and of Nancy Phyllis Smith. *Educ:* Harrow Sch.; St Peter's Coll., Oxford (MA). ACA. Articled with Gibson, Harris & Turnbull, 1969; Audit Sen., Peat, Marwick, Mitchell & Co., 1971; Co. Sec., Coubro & Scrutton (Holdings) Ltd, 1973. Pres., Oxford Univ. Conservative Assoc., 1968; Chm., Coningsby Club, 1977. *Recreations:* athletics, cricket. *Address:* 6 Morley Street, Sutton-in-Ashfield, Notts. *Clubs:* Sutton-in-Ashfield Conservative; Hucknall Conservative.

SMITH, Adm. Sir Victor (Alfred Trumper), AC 1975; KBE 1969 (CBE 1963); CB 1968; DSC 1941; Chairman, Australian Chiefs of Staff Committee, 1970-75; Military Adviser to SEATO, 1970-74; *b* 9 May 1913; *s* of George Smith; *m* 1944, Nanette Suzanne Harrison; three *s. Educ:* Royal Australian Naval College. Sub-Lieut, 1935; Lieut, 1936; Lieut-Commander, 1944; Commander, 1947; Captain, 1953; Rear-Admiral, 1963; Vice-Admiral, 1968; Chief of Naval Staff and First Naval Member, Austr. Commonwealth Naval Bd, 1968-70; Admiral, 1970. *Recreation:* walking. *Address:* Fishburn Street, Red Hill, ACT 2603, Australia. *T:* Canberra 958942.

SMITH, Walter Campbell, CBE 1949; MC; TD; MA, ScD; *b* 30 Nov. 1887; 2nd *s* of late George Hamilton Smith, Solihull, Warwickshire; *m* 1936, Susan, *y d* of late John Finnegan, Belfast; one *s* one *d. Educ:* Solihull; Corpus Christi, Cambridge. Wiltshire Prize, Cambridge Univ., 1909; Assistant, Dept of Minerals, British Museum, 1910; Deputy Keeper, 1931-37; Deputy Chief Scientific Officer, British Museum (Natural History), 1948-52; also Keeper of Minerals, 1937-52; Non-resident Fellow Corpus Christi, Cambridge, 1921-24; Honorary Secretary, Geological Society of London, 1921-33 (Murchison Medallist, 1945), President, 1955-56; General Secretary, Mineralogical Society, 1927-38, President, 1945-48; President, geological section, British Assoc., 1950; Governor, Royal Holloway Coll., 1922-43, representing Cambridge University; served in the Artists' Rifles, 1910-35 and 1939-42; European War, France, 1914-18 (MC, despatches twice, 1914 Star); Acting Lieut-Colonel, 1918; Brevet Lieut-Colonel, 1935; Second-in-Command, 163 OCTU (The Artists' Rifles), 1939-41. *Publications:* numerous papers on minerals, rocks and meteorites. *Address:* Flat 2, Burley Lodge, Rockdale Road, Sevenoaks, Kent.

SMITH, Walter Purvis, OBE 1960 (MBE 1945); Director General, Ordnance Survey, since 1977; *b* 8 March 1920; *s* of John William Smith and Margaret Jane (*née* Purvis); *m* 1946, Bettie Cox; one *s* one *d. Educ:* Wellfield Grammar Sch., Co.

Durham; St Edmund Hall, Oxford (MA). FRICS 1951. Commnd RE (Survey), 1940; served War, UK and Europe, 1940-46; CO 135 Survey Engr Regt (TA), 1957-60. Directorate of Colonial (later Overseas) Surveys: served in Ghana, Tanzania, Malawi, 1946-50; Gen. Man., Air Survey Co. of Rhodesia Ltd, 1950-54; Fairey Surveys Ltd, 1954-75 (Man. Dir, 1969-75); Adviser, Surveying and Mapping, UN, NY, 1975-77. Mem., Field Mission, Argentine-Chile Frontier Case, 1965. 15th British Commonwealth Lectr, RAeS, 1968. Pres., Photogrammetric Soc., 1972-73; Mem., Gen. Council, RICS, 1967-70 (Chm., Land Survey Cttee, 1963-64). *Publications:* papers and technical jls. *Recreations:* music, walking, golf. *Address:* Northcroft, Winchester Hill, Romsey, Hants. *T:* Romsey 512391; (office) Southampton 775555. *Club:* Oriental.

SMITH, Walter Riddell, CB 1973; FRAgSs 1971; FIBiol; Welsh Secretary, Ministry of Agriculture, Fisheries and Food, since 1975; *b* 18 Sept. 1914; *s* of John Riddell Smith and Ethel Smith (*née* Liddell); *m* 1942, Janet Henderson Mitchell; one *s* one *d. Educ:* Lamesley C. of E. Sch., Co. Durham; Johnston Techn. Sch., Durham City. NDA 1936; BSc(Agric.) 1936. Record Keeper: Cockle Park, Northumberland, 1936-37; School of Agriculture, Durham, 1937-39; Asst Agricultural Organiser, Northumberland CC, 1939-42; Animal Husbandry Officer, Northumberland War Agric. Exec. Cttee, 1942-47; Nat. Agric. Adv. Service, 1948-; Livestock Adviser: WR, 1948-52; Eastern Region, 1952-55; Wales, 1955-61; Dep. Regional Director, Yorks and Lancs, 1961-64; Regional Director, Northern Region, 1964-66; Dir, Nat. Agricultural Adv. Service, 1967-71; Dep. Dir-Gen., Agricultural Develt and Adv. Service, 1971-75. President: Univ. of Newcastle upon Tyne Agricultural Soc., 1969; British Grassland Soc., 1971-72; NPK Club, 1971. *Publications:* contributions to press, popular agric. and technical journals. *Recreations:* gardening, sport, theatre. *Address:* 36 Cwm Aur, Llanilar, Aberystwyth. *T:* Llanilar 326. *Club:* Farmers'.

SMITH, William Frederick Bottrill, CBE 1964; Accountant and Comptroller General of Inland Revenue, 1958-68; Principal, Uganda Resettlement Board, 1972-74; *b* 29 Oct. 1903; *s* of late Arthur and Harriet Frances Smith; *m* 1926, Edyth Kilbourne (*d* 1970); *m* 1971, M. Jane Smith, Washington DC; three step *c. Educ:* Newton's, Leicester. Entered the Inland Revenue Dept, Civil Service, 1934. President, Inland Revenue Staff Federation, 1945-47. Vice-Pres., CS Fedn Drama Socs; Chm., Pett Level Naturalists' Soc. Churchwarden, Pett Parish Church. *Address:* Boulder House, Pett Level, Hastings, East Sussex.

SMITH, Sir (William) Gordon, 2nd Bt *cr* 1945; VRD; Lieut-Commander, RNR, retired; *b* 30 Jan. 1916; *s* of Sir Robert Workman Smith, 1st Bt, and Jessie Hill, *yr d* of late William Workman, Belfast; *S* father, 1957; *m* 1st, 1941, Diana Gundreda, *d* of late Major C. H. Malden, Aberdeenshire; 2nd, 1958, Diana Goodchild; two *s. Educ:* Westminster; Trinity Coll., Cambridge (BA). Called to Bar, Inner Temple, 1939. Served War of 1939-45 as Lieut, RNVR (despatches). *Recreation:* yachting (Winner, International Dragon Gold Cup, 1961). *Heir: s* Robert Hill Smith, *b* 15 April 1958. *Address:* 15 Cadogan Court, Draycott Avenue, SW3 3BX; (Seat) Crowmallie, Pitcaple, Aberdeenshire. *Clubs:* Royal Yacht Squadron; New (Edinburgh).

SMITH, William Jeffrey, CB 1976; Under-Secretary, Northern Ireland Office, 1972-76; *b* 14 Oct. 1916; 2nd *s* of Frederick Smith, Sheffield, and Ellen Hickinson, Nottingham, Derbyshire; *m* 1942, Marie Hughes; one *s* one *d. Educ:* King Edward VII Sch., Sheffield; University Coll., Oxford (Schol.) (MA). Employed by Calico Printers' Assoc., Manchester, 1938-40 and in 1946. Served War, Army: enlisted Sept. 1939, embodied, 1940; RA and York and Lancaster Regt (Captain), 1940-46. Dominions Office (subseq. CRO), 1946; Principal, 1948; Office of UK High Commissioner in South Africa, 1953-56; Asst Sec., 1959; sundry internat. confs; Dept of Technical Co-operation, 1961-64; Min. of Overseas Development, 1964-70; Overseas Develt Admin., 1970-72; UK Rep. to UNESCO, 1969-72. Sec. to Widgery Tribunal on loss of life in Londonderry, 1972; Northern Ireland Office, 1972. *Recreations:* theatre, scrambling up mountains, walking, ski-ing. *Address:* Salmons, 121 Salmons Lane, Whyteleafe, Surrey CR3 0HB. *T:* 01-660 5493.

SMITH, William McGregor, OBE 1970; HM Inspector of Constabulary for Scotland, 1970-75, retired; *b* 14 April 1910; *s* of John Smith, Milngavie and Agnes Smith (*née* Haldane); *m* 1939, Alice Mary Ewen, Montrose; one *s* one *d. Educ:* Bearsden Academy and Glasgow University (MA 1930). Joined City of Glasgow Police, 1933; Deputy Commandant, Scottish Police College, 1951; Chief Constable of Aberdeen, 1963. *Recreations:* golf, bridge. *Address:* Sherwood, 2 Cherry Tree Park, Balerno, Midlothian. *Clubs:* Luffness Golf, Baberton Golf.

SMITH, Sir William Reardon Reardon-, 3rd Bt, *cr* 1920; Major, RA (TA); *b* 12 March 1911; *e s* of Sir Willie Reardon-Smith, 2nd Bt, and Elizabeth Ann, *d* of John and Mary Wakely; *S* father, 1950; *m* 1st, 1935, Nesta (marr. diss., 1954; she *d* 1959), *d* of late Frederick J. Phillips; three *s* one *d*; 2nd, 1954, Beryl, *d* of William H. Powell; one *s* three *d. Educ:* Blundell's Sch., Tiverton. Served War of 1939-45. *Heir: s* William Antony John Reardon-Smith [*b* 20 June 1937; *m* 1962, Susan, *d* of H. W. Gibson, Cardiff; two *s* one *d. Educ:* Wycliffe Coll., Glos]. *Address:* Rhode Farm, Romansleigh, S Molton, Devon. *T:* Bishops Nympton 371. *Club:* Cardiff and County (Cardiff).

SMITH, Sir William Reginald Verdon; *see* Verdon-Smith.

SMITH, William W.; *see* Wenban-Smith.

SMITH-DODSWORTH, Sir John (Christopher), 8th Bt, *cr* 1784; *b* 4 March 1935; *s* of Sir Claude Smith-Dodsworth, 7th Bt, and Cyrilla Marie Louise von Sobbe, 3rd *d* of William Ernest Taylor, Linnet Lane, Liverpool; *S* father, 1940; *m* 1961, Margaret Anne (*née* Jones); one *s* one *d. Educ:* Ampleforth Coll., Yorks. *Heir: s* David John Smith-Dodsworth, *b* 23 Oct. 1963. *Address:* Thornton Watlass Hall, Ripon, North Yorkshire.

SMITH-GORDON, Sir (Lionel) Eldred (Peter), 5th Bt *cr* 1838; *b* 7 May 1935; *s* of Sir Lionel Eldred Pottinger Smith-Gordon, 4th Bt, and of Eileen Laura, *d* of late Captain H. G. Adams-Connor, CVO; *S* father, 1976; *m* 1962, Sandra Rosamund Ann, *d* of late Wing Commander Walter Farley, DFC and of Mrs Dennis Poore; one *s* one *d. Educ:* Eton College; Trinity College, Oxford. *Heir: s* Lionel George Eldred Smith-Gordon, *b* 1 July 1964. *Address:* 76 Brondesbury Park, NW2 5JU. *T:* 01-459 6113.

SMITH-MARRIOTT, Sir Ralph George Cavendish, 10th Bt, *cr* 1774; retired Bank Official; *b* 16 Dec. 1900; *s* of late George Rudolph Wyldbore Smith-Marriott and of Dorothy Magdalene, *d* of Rev. John Parry; *S* uncle, 1944; *m* 1st, Phyllis Elizabeth (*d* 1932), *d* of Richard Kemp (late Governor HM Prison, Bristol); two *s* one *d*; 2nd, 1933, Doris Mary (*d* 1951), *d* of R. L. C. Morrison, Tenby, Pembs; 3rd, 1966, Mrs Barbara Mary Cantlay. *Educ:* Cranleigh Sch., Surrey. Bristol Univ. OTC, 1918. *Recreations:* tennis, golf, cricket. *Heir: s* Hugh Cavendish Smith-Marriott [*b* 22 March 1925; *m* 1953, Pauline Anne, *d* of F. F. Holt, Bristol; one *d*]. *Address:* 28a Westover Road, Westbury-on-Trym, Bristol. *T:* Bristol 628827.

SMITH-ROSE, Reginald Leslie, CBE 1952; DSc, PhD, FCGI, FIEE, FIRE; FIC; Director of Radio Research, Department of Scientific and Industrial Research, 1948-Sept. 1960; *b* 2 April 1894; *m* 1919, Elsie Masters; two *d. Educ:* Latymer Upper Sch., Hammersmith; Imperial College of Science, London Univ. Board of Education, Royal Schol. (1st Place) 1912; Imperial College, Governor's Prize in Physics (1st Place) 1914; London Univ.: BSc, Hons Physics, Cl. 1, 1914; PhD, Science, 1923; DSc, Science, 1926. Assistant Engineer, Siemens Bros Ltd, Woolwich, 1915-19. National Physical Laboratory: Scientific Officer, Electricity Div., 1919-33; Principal Scientific Officer, Radio Div., 1933-39; Supt Radio Div., 1939-47; acting Director, 1950 and 1956. Institution of Electrical Engineers: Chairman, Radio Section, 1942-43; Member Council, 1953-56, 1960-61; Vice-President, 1961-64; Fellow, Institute of Electrical and Electronics Engineers (USA) (Vice-President, 1948); FIEEE. Member, various scientific and technical committees of Government Departments and other Institutions; delegate to various international scientific radio conferences in various countries; President, Internat. Scientific Radio Union, 1960-63; Chairman, Study Group V, Internat. Radio Consultative Cttee, 1951-70; Secretary-General, Inter-Union Cttee on Frequency Allocations for Radio Astronomy and Space Research, 1961-73. Chairman, PMG's Frequency Advisory Cttee, 1960-; Member PMG's Cttee on Broadcasting, 1960. Coronation Medals, 1937, 1953; US Medal of Freedom with Silver Palm, 1947. *Publications:* many original papers published in Proc. of Royal and Phys. Societies, Instn Elect. Engrs, and elsewhere. *Address:* 21 Tumblewood Road, Banstead, Surrey. *Club:* Athenæum.

SMITH-RYLAND, Charles Mortimer Tollemache; Lord-Lieutenant of Warwickshire since 1968; *b* 24 May 1927; *s* of Charles Ivor Phipson Smith-Ryland and Leila Mary Tollemache; *m* 1952, Hon. Jeryl Marcia Sarah Gurdon, *d* of Hon. Robin Gurdon; two *s* three *d. Educ:* Eton. Lt, Coldstream Guards, 1945-48; Reserve, Warwickshire Yeomanry. Warwickshire: CC, 1949; DL, 1955; Alderman, 1958; Vice-Chm. CC, 1963; Chm. CC, 1964-67; Vice-Chm. Police Authority, 1966-68; Chm., Warwickshire and Coventry Police Authority, 1969-74; High Sheriff, 1967-68. Chm. Council, RASE, 1976-. KStJ 1968. *Recreations:* hunting, shooting, golf.

Address: Sherbourne Park, Warwick. *T:* Barford 255. *Clubs:* Turf, White's; Leamington Tennis.
See also Baron Cranworth.

SMITHERMAN, Frank, MBE 1951; HM Diplomatic Service, retired; *b* 13 Oct. 1913; *s* of Lt-Col H. C. Smitherman and Mildred E. Holten; *m* 1937, Frances Ellen Rivers Calvert; one *s* one *d. Educ:* Sir Joseph Williamson's Mathematical Sch., Rochester. Indian Police, Burma, 1933; served in: Yenangyaung; Rangoon; Myitkyina; Sagaing; Thayetmyo; Thaton. Served War of 1939-45 (despatches, 1945), Burma Army Reserve of Officers; Maj. 1945. Joined Civil Affairs Service; Foreign Office, 1949; subseq. service in: Amoy; Cairo; Rome; Khartoum; Miami; Consul-General, Bordeaux, 1967-69; Counsellor, Moscow, 1969-70; Ambassador to Togo and Dahomey, 1970-73. *Recreations:* fishing, gardening. *Address:* Pickwick Cottage, New Buckenham, Norfolk. *T:* New Buckenham 388.
See also Sir T. F. V. Buxton, Bt.

SMITHERS, Prof. Sir David (Waldron), Kt 1969; MD, FRCP, FRCS, FRCR; Professor of Radiotherapy in the University of London, 1943-73, now Emeritus; Director of the Radiotherapy Department at the Royal Marsden Hospital, 1943-73; *b* 17 Jan. 1908; *s* of late Sir Waldron Smithers, MP; *m* 1933, Gwladys Margaret (Marjorie), *d* of Harry Reeve Angel, Officer (1st class) Order of White Rose of Finland; one *s* one *d. Educ:* Boxgrove School, Guildford; Charterhouse; Clare College, Cambridge; St Thomas's Hospital. MRCS, LRCP 1933; MB, BChir (Cantab) 1934; MD (Cantab) 1937; DMR (London) 1937; MRCP 1946; FRCP 1952; FFR 1953, now FRCR; FRCS 1963. Pres. British Inst. of Radiology, 1946-47; President, Faculty of Radiologists, 1959-61; Kt Comdr, Order of St John of Jerusalem, Kts of Malta, 1973. *Publications:* papers on cancer and radiotherapy. *Recreation:* growing roses. *Address:* Ringfield, Knockholt, Kent. *T:* Knockholt 2122.

SMITHERS, Donald William, CB 1967; retired; *b* 21 Aug. 1905; *s* of William John and Mary Smithers, Portsmouth, Hants; *m* 1929, Kathleen Margery Gibbons; three *s* one *d. Educ:* Portsmouth; Royal Naval Coll., Greenwich. Asst Constructor until 1937, then Constructor, Chatham; Principal Ship Overseer, 1939-44; Constructor Captain to C-in-C Mediterranean, 1944-47; Chief Constructor: Admiralty, 1947-52; Portsmouth, 1952-54; Singapore, 1954-56; Asst Dir of Dockyards, 1956-58; Manager HM Dockyard, Chatham, 1958-61; Director of Dockyards, 1961-67; retd 1967. CEng; FRINA; RCNC. *Address:* Chevithorne, Greenway Lane, Bath. *T:* Bath 311093.

SMITHERS, Professor Geoffrey Victor; Professor of English Language, University of Durham, 1960-74, now Emeritus; *b* 5 May 1909; *s* of William Henry and Agnes Madeline Smithers; *m* 1953, Jean Buglass Hay McDonald; three *s* one *d. Educ:* Durban High School; Natal University College; Hertford College, Oxford. Rhodes Schol. for Natal, 1930; 1st Cl. in Final Hon. School of English, Oxford, 1933. Asst Lecturer: King's Coll., London, 1936; University Coll., London, 1938; Lectr in English Language, 1940, Senior Lecturer in English Language, 1950, Reader in Medieval English, 1954, Univ. of Oxford, and professorial Fellow of Merton Coll., 1954. *Publications:* 2nd edn of C. Brown's Religious Lyrics of the Fourteenth Century, 1952; Kyng Alisaunder, Vol. I 1952, Vol. II 1957; (with J. A. W. Bennett and N. Davis) Early Middle English Verse and Prose, 1966 (2nd edn 1968); papers in Med. Æv., English and Germanic Studies, Archivum Linguisticum, Rev. Eng. Studies. *Recreation:* music. *Address:* 20 The Peth, Durham. *T:* 3940.

SMITHERS, Sir Peter (Henry Berry Otway), Kt 1970; VRD with clasp; DPhil Oxon; Lt-Comdr RNR, retired; *b* 9 Dec. 1913; *o s* of late Lt-Col H. O. Smithers, JP, Hants, and Ethel Berry; *m* 1943, Dojean, *d* of late T. M. Sayman, St Louis, Mo; two *d. Educ:* Hawtrey's; Harrow Sch.; Magdalen Coll., Oxford. Demyship in History, 1931; 1st cl. Hons Modern History, 1934. Called to Bar, Inner Temple, 1936; joined Lincoln's Inn, 1937. Commn, London Div. RNVR, 1939; British Staff, Paris, 1940; Naval Intelligence Div., Admiralty; Asst Naval Attaché, British Embassy, Washington; Actg Naval Attaché, Mexico, Central Amer. Republics and Panama. RD Councillor, Winchester, 1946-49. MP (C) Winchester Div. of Hampshire, 1950-64; PPS to Minister of State for Colonies, 1952-56 and to Sec. of State for Colonies, 1956-59; Deleg., Consultative Assembly of Council of Europe, 1952-56 and 1960; UK Deleg. to UN Gen. Assembly, 1960-62; Parly Under-Sec. of State, FO, 1962-64; Sec.-Gen., Council of Europe, 1964-69; Senior Research Fellow, UN Inst. for Trng and Research, 1969-72; General Rapporteur, European Conf. of Parliamentarians and Scientists, 1970-. Chairman: British-Mexican Soc., 1952-55; Conservative Overseas Bureau, 1956-59; Vice-Chm., Conservative Parly Foreign Affairs Cttee, 1958-62; Vice-Pres., European Assembly of Local Authorities,

1959-62. Master, Turners' Co., 1955; Liveryman, Goldsmiths' Co. Dr of Law *hc* Zürich, 1969. Chevalier de la Légion d'Honneur. Orden Mexicana del Aguila Azteca. Alexander von Humboldt Gold Medal, 1969. *Publication:* Life of Joseph Addison, 1954, 2nd edn, 1966. *Recreations:* observational astronomy, gardening. *Address:* CH-6911 Vico Morcote, Switzerland. *Clubs:* Carlton; Metropolitan (New York); The Everglades.

SMITHIES, Kenneth Charles Lester; His Honour Judge Smithies; a Circuit Judge, since 1975; *b* 15 Aug. 1927; *s* of late Harold King Smithies and Kathleen Margaret (*née* Walsh); *m* 1950, Joan Winifred (*née* Ellis); one *s* two *d*. *Educ:* City of London Sch. (Corporation Scholar); University College London (LLB). Volunteered 60th Rifles, 1945, later commnd in Royal Artillery, in India; demobilised, 1948. Called to Bar, Gray's Inn, 1955. *Recreations:* music, gardening, bridge. *Address:* 1 Russell Place, Southampton SO2 1NU. *Club:* Hampshire (Winchester).

SMITHSON, Peter Denham; architect in private practice since 1950; *b* 18 Sept. 1923; *s* of William Blenkiron Smithson and Elizabeth Smithson; *m* 1949, Alison Margaret (*née* Gill); one *s* two *d*. *Educ:* The Grammar School, Stockton-on-Tees; King's College, Univ. of Durham. Served War of 1939-45: Queen Victoria's Own Madras Sappers and Miners, India and Burma, 1942-45. Asst in Schools Div. LCC, 1949-50; subseq. in private practice with wife. *Buildings:* Hunstanton School, 1950-54; Economist Building, St James's, 1959-64; Robin Hood Gardens, Tower Hamlets, 1963-72; Garden Bldg, St Hilda's Coll., Oxford, 1968-70. *Publications:* (all with A. Smithson) Uppercase 3, 1960; The Heroic Period of Modern Architecture, 1965; Urban Structuring Studies of Alison and Peter Smithson, 1967; Team 10 Primer, 1968; The Euston Arch, 1968; Ordinariness and Light, 1970; Without Rhetoric, 1973; theoretical work on town structuring in Architectural Review, Architectural Design and most foreign periodicals (most with A. Smithson). *Relevant publication:* synopsis of professional life in Arch. Assoc.'s Arena, Feb. 1966. *Address:* 24 Gilston Road, SW10. *T:* 01-373 7423.

SMOLKA, H. P.; *see* Smollett, H. P.

SMOLLETT, Harry Peter, OBE 1944; author and journalist; *b* Vienna, 17 Sept. 1912; *s* of Albert V. Smolka and Vilma Wottitz; naturalised British subject since 1938; changed name to Smollett by deed poll in 1938, but continues to use Smolka as writer's name; *m* 1933, Lotte Jaeckl; two *s*. *Educ:* Vienna Gymnasium; University of Vienna; London School of Economics. London Correspondent Central European Newspapers and Central European Adviser to Exchange Telegraph Co. Ltd, 1934-38; Head of Foreign Dept, Exchange Telegraph Co., 1938-39; War Service, Min. of Information, 1939-45; Vienna Correspondent of The Times, 1947-49. Chairman and Managing Director: Vienna Metal Goods Manufacturing Co.; Vienna Metal Goods Trading Co.; Jt Man. Dir Tyrolia Metal and Sporting Goods Trading Co., Munich, Germany. Commercial Advisor to Pres. of Austria, 1973. Travels: all European countries, USA, Mexico, USSR, Israel. *Publication:* 40,000 Against the Arctic. *Recreation:* chess. *Address:* Lindauergasse 9, A.1238 Vienna, Austria.

SMOUT, Professor Charles Frederick Victor; Professor of Anatomy, University of Birmingham, 1948-61, retired; *b* 23 Oct. 1895; *s* of Thomas and Mary Elizabeth Smout; *m* 1923, Ethel May Butterworth; no *c*. *Educ:* King Edward's School, Birmingham, MB, ChB 1923; MRCS, LRCP 1923. MD (Birmingham) 1943. *Publications:* Anatomy for Students of Physiotherapy, 1943 (rev. 5th edn, Gynaecological and Obstetrical Anatomy, Descriptive and Applied, 1968); Basic Anatomy and Physiology, 1961; An Introduction to Midwifery, 1962; The Story of the Progress of Medicine, 1964; A Layman looks at life in general and at the Bible in particular, 1966. *Address:* 111 Touchwood Hall Close, off Lode Lane, Solihull, West Midlands B91 2UE. *T:* 021-704 4637. *Club:* University Staff (Birmingham).

SMOUT, David Arthur Lister, QC 1975; a Recorder of the Crown Court, since 1972; *b* 17 Dec. 1923; *s* of Sir Arthur Smout and Hilda Smout (*née* Fellows); *m* 1957, Kathleen Sally, *d* of Dr J. L. Potts, Salisbury; two *s* two *d*. *Educ:* Leys Sch.; Clare Coll., Cambridge (MA, LLB); Birmingham Univ. (LLM). Served War, F/O, RAFVR, 1943-45. Cecil Peace Prize, 1948. Admitted solicitor, 1949; called to Ontario Bar, 1949. Lectr, Osgoode Hall, Toronto, 1949-53, Vis. Prof., 1977. Called to English Bar, Gray's Inn, 1953; Midland and Oxford Circuits. Dir, Murex Ltd and associated cos, 1954-67. Bar Council, 1958-62; prosecuting counsel, DTI, 1967-75; Dep.-Chm., Lincs QS (parts of Holland), 1968-71. *Publications:* Chalmers, Bills of Exchange (13th edn),

1964; (with B. E. Basden) Department of Trade Investigations: Bernard Russell Ltd, 1975; Blanes Ltd, 1975. *Recreations:* fishing, Canadiana. *Address:* Long Swan Cottage, Haddenham, Bucks; 1 King's Bench Walk, Temple, EC4Y 7DB.

SMYLY, Col Dennis Douglas Pilkington, DSO 1945; JP; *b* 1913; *s* of late Major R. J. Smyly, OBE, Sweethay Court, Trull, Somerset; *m* 1939, Hon. Dorothy Margaret Berry, 3rd *d* of 1st and last Baron Buckland; three *s* one *d*. *Educ:* Sherborne; RMC Sandhurst. 2 Lt 16/5 Lancers, 1933; served War of 1939-45, North Africa, 1942-43; Italy (despatches), 1944-45; commanded 16/5 Lancers, 1944-47. Colonel 16/5 Queens Royal Lancers, 1959-69. JP Northants, 1955-67; High Sheriff Northants, 1961; DL Northants, 1965-68; JP Glos, 1969. *Address:* 120 Marsham Court, Marsham Street, SW1. *T:* 01-834 5276. *Club:* Cavalry and Guards.

SMYTH, Rev. Canon Charles Hugh Egerton, MA, FRHistS; Fellow of Corpus Christi College, Cambridge, 1925-32 and since 1937; *b* Ningpo, China, 31 March 1903; *s* of Richard Smyth, MD; *m* 1934, Violet, *e d* of Rev. Canon Alexander Copland, Forfar. *Educ:* Repton; Corpus Christi College, Cambridge (Scholar); Wells Theological Coll. 1st class, Historical Tripos, Part 1, 1923, and Part 2, 1924; Thirlwall Medal and Gladstone Prize, 1925. Tutor and Lectr in History, Harvard Univ., USA, 1926-27; Deacon, 1929; Priest, 1930; University Lecturer in History, Cambridge, 1929-32 and 1944-46; Curate of St Clement's, Barnsbury, Islington, 1933-34; of St Saviour's, Upper Chelsea, 1934-36; of St Giles', Cambridge, 1936-37. Birkbeck Lecturer in Ecclesiastical History, Trinity College, Cambridge, 1937-38; Dean of Chapel, Corpus Christi College, 1937-46; Hon. Canon of Derby and Chaplain to Bishop of Derby at the University of Cambridge, 1938-46; Select Preacher, Oxford, 1941-43 and 1965; Canon of Westminster and Rector of St Margaret's, Westminster, 1946-56; Hon. Canon and Prebendary of Nassington in Lincoln Cathedral, 1965-; Canon Emeritus of Derby Cathedral, 1977-. Editor of the Cambridge Review, 1925 and 1940-41. *Publications:* Cranmer and the Reformation under Edward VI, 1926; The Art of Preaching (747-1939), 1940; Simeon and Church Order (Birkbeck Lectures), 1940; Religion and Politics, 1943; The Friendship of Christ, 1945; Dean Milman, 1949; Church and Parish (Bishop Paddock Lectures), 1955; Good Friday at St Margaret's, 1957; Cyril Forster Garbett, Archbishop of York, 1959; The Two Families, 1962; The Church and the Nation, 1962. *Address:* 12 Manor Court, Grange Road, Cambridge CB3 9BE. *T:* Cambridge 56390; Corpus Christi College, Cambridge.

SMYTH, Prof. David Henry, FRS 1967; Professor of Physiology, Sheffield University, 1946-73, now Emeritus; Pro-Vice-Chancellor, 1962-66; *b* 9 Feb. 1908; *s* of late Joseph Smyth, Lisburn, Co. Antrim; *m* 1942, Edith Mary Hoyle; no *c*. *Educ:* Royal Belfast Academical Institution; Queen's Univ., Belfast. QUB: BSc 1929; MB, BCh 1932; MSc 1934; MD 1935; PhD London, 1940. RMO Royal Victoria Hospital, Belfast, 1932; Demonstrator in Physiology, Belfast, 1933; Musgrave Student in Physiology at Göttingen, Germany, 1936; Lectr in Physiology, University Coll., London, 1937. Mem. Editorial Bd, Journal of Physiology, 1961-68 (Chm., 1966-68). Chm., British Nat. Cttee for Physiology, 1974-; Foreign Sec., Physiological Soc., 1972-. Leverhulme Emeritus Fellow, 1973-75. Robert Campbell Memorial Orator, Ulster Med. Soc., 1968. Hon. DSc Belfast, 1976. *Publications:* papers in Journal of Physiology, Quarterly Journal of Experimental Physiology, Biochemical Journal, British Medical Journal, 1934-73. *Recreations:* pedigree dogs, music. *Address:* The Swevic, Foolow, Derbyshire. *T:* Tideswell 871330. *Club:* Kennel.

SMYTH, Brig. Rt. Hon. Sir John (George), 1st Bt *cr* 1955; VC 1915; PC 1962; MC 1920; *b* 24 Oct. 1893; *e s* of W. J. Smyth, Indian Civil Service; *m* 1920, Margaret, *d* of late Charles Dundas, ICS, Sialkot; one *s* one *d* (and two *s* decd, of whom *e s* killed in action 1944); *m* 1940, Frances Read, *d* of late Lieut-Colonel R. A. Chambers, OBE, IMS. *Educ:* Repton; Sandhurst. Entered army, 1912; served European War, 1914-15 (despatches, VC, Russian Order of St George); Senussi Campaign, Western Egypt, 1915-16; Mohmand Expedition, India, 1916; Afghan War, 1919; Waziristan Frontier Expedition, 1919-20 (despatches, MC); Mesopotamia Insurrection, 1920-21 (despatches); Operations on NW Frontier, 1930 (despatches); Mohmand Operations, 1935 (despatches); Brevet-Major, 1928; Brevet Lieut-Colonel, 1933; Colonel, 1936; Instructor, Staff College, Camberley, 1931-34; Comdt 45th Rattrays Sikhs, 1936-39; GSO1, 2nd London Division, 1939-40; Commander 127 Inf. Bde in operations with BEF in France and Belgium (despatches); Acting Maj.-Gen. 1941; raised 19th Division in India; Comd 17th Division in Burma at time of Japanese invasion; retired, Nov. 1942; Hon. Brig. 1943. Military

Correspondent: Kemsley newspapers, 1943-44; Daily Sketch and Sunday Times, 1945-46; Lawn Tennis Correspondent: Sunday Times, 1946-51; News of the World, 1956-57. Author, Wimbledon Programme articles, 1947-73. Comptroller Royal Alexandra and Albert School, 1948-63; Governor: Gypsy Road and West Norwood Secondary Schs, 1947-49; Strand and West Norwood Secondary Schools, 1949-51; St Martin's High School for Girls, 1950-52; Dragon School, Oxford, 1953-66; Queen Mary's Hosp., Roehampton, 1956-62. Exec., Returned Brit. POW Assoc., 1946-51. First Chm. Victoria Cross Assoc., 1956-71 (Centenary of the Victoria Cross), Life Pres. 1966; Vice-Pres. Not Forgotten Assoc., 1956; Pres. S London Branch Burma Star Assoc., 1957-; Vice-Pres. Distinguished Conduct Medal League, 1957, Pres. 1958-70; Director Creative Journals Ltd, 1957-63. Govt Apptd Trustee, Far East POW and Internee Fund, 1959-61; Hon. Vice-Pres. Far Eastern POW Federation, 1960; President Old Reptonian Society, 1960 and 1961; Vice-President: Dunkirk Veterans Assoc., 1963-; Internat. Lawn Tennis Club of GB, 1966. Contested (C) Wandsworth Central, 1945. MP (C) Norwood Div. of Lambeth, 1950-66; Parly Sec., Min. of Pensions, 1951-53; Jt Parly Sec., Min. of Pensions and Nat. Insce, 1953-55. Freeman of City of London in Worshipful Co. of Farriers, 1951; Master of Farriers' Co., 1961-62. *Publications:* Defence Is Our Business, 1945; The Western Defences (ed and introd), 1951; Lawn Tennis, 1953; The Game's the Same, 1956; Before the Dawn (story of two historic retreats), 1957; Paradise Island (children's adventure story), 1958; The Only Enemy (autobiography), 1959; Trouble in Paradise, 1959; Ann Goes Hunting (children's book), 1960; Sandhurst (A History of the Military Cadet Colleges), 1961; The Story of the Victoria Cross, 1962; Beloved Cats, 1963; Blue Magnolia, 1964; (with Col Macauley) Behind the Scenes at Wimbledon, 1965; Ming (the story of a cat family), 1966; The Rebellious Rani (a story of the Indian Mutiny), 1966; Bolo Whistler (biography), 1967; The Story of the George Cross, 1968; In This Sign Conquer (The Story of the Army Chaplains), 1968; The Valiant, 1969; Will to Live: the story of Dame Margot Turner, 1970; Percival and the Tragedy of Singapore, 1971; Jean Borotra: the Bounding Basque, 1974; Leadership in War, 1939-1945, 1974; Leadership in Battle, 1914-1918, 1975; Great Stories of the Victoria Cross, 1977; *plays:* Burma Road (with Ian Hay), 1945; Until the Morning (with Ian Hay), 1950. *Heir: g s* Timothy John Smyth, *b* 16 April 1953. *Address:* 807 Nelson House, Dolphin Square, SW1A 3PA. *Clubs:* Queen's, All England Lawn Tennis, Carlton; International Lawn Tennis Clubs of Britain, USA and France.

SMYTH, Margaret Jane, CBE 1959 (OBE 1955); *b* 23 Sept. 1897; *d* of late Colonel John Smyth, IMS. *Educ:* Uplands School (Church Education Corporation); Clifton High School. Trained at Univ. Settlement, Bristol; Health Visitors Certificate. Roy. Sanitary Inst., 1918; Central Midwives Board, SCM, 1920; Maternity and Child Welfare Certificate, RSI, 1921; SRN, 1925, trained in Nightingale Trng School, St Thomas Hosp.; Sister, St Thomas Hosp., 1926-34; Matron, St Thomas Babies' Hostel, 1934-37; Warden, St Christopher's Nursery Trng College, 1937-39; Dep. Matron, St Thomas Hosp., 1939-45, Supt, Nightingale Trng School and Matron, St Thomas Hospital, 1945-55; Chairman of the General Nursing Council for England and Wales, 1955-60; President Royal College of Nursing, 1960-62; Chairman, South West Metropolitan Area, Nurse Training Cttee, 1952-64, Mem., 1964-66; Vice-Chm., Long Grove Hospital Management Cttee, 1964-67; Mem., Kingston and Long Grove Hosp. Management Cttee, 1967-69. *Address:* 9 Stockbridge Gardens, Chichester, West Sussex. *Club:* Naval and Military.

SMYTH, Captain Sir Philip Weyland Bowyer-, 14th Bt, *cr* 1661; RN retired; *b* 4 Feb. 1894; *s* of late Clement Weyland Bowyer-Smijth, *b* of 13th Bt, and Maud, *d* of W. Gray, Sydney, NSW; *S* uncle, 1927; *m* 1922, Margaret Joan, OBE 1952, TD (marr. diss. 1951), *o d* of late S. McCall-McCowan, Sydney; no *c*; *m* 1951, Veronica Mary, 2nd *d* of Capt. C. W. Bower, DSC, RN retd, Fordwich, Kent; one *s* one *d.* Naval Attaché at Rome, 1939-40; ADC to the King, 1946; retired list, 1946. *Heir: s* Thomas Weyland Bowyer-Smyth, *b* 25 June 1960. *Address:* La Provençale, 06870 Plascassier, France. *Club:* Royal Yacht Squadron.

SMYTHE, Clifford Anthony, (Tony); Director, Mind (National Association for Mental Health), since 1973; *b* 2 Aug. 1938; *s* of Clifford John and Florence May Smythe; *m*; four *d. Educ:* University College School. Conscientious Objector, 1958; General Secretary, War Resisters' International, 1959-64; Council Member, Internat. Confederation for Disarmament and Peace, 1963-71; Gen. Sec., Nat. Council for Civil Liberties, 1966-72; Field Dir, American Civil Liberties Union, 1973. Member: Bd, Internat. League for the Rights of Man, 1973; Nat.

Adv. Council on Employment of Disabled People, 1975. *Publications:* Conscription: a World Survey, 1968; (with D. Madgwick) The Invasion of Privacy, 1974. *Address:* 136 Stapleton Hall Road, N4.

SMYTHE, Captain George Quentin Murray, VC 1942; Officer Instructor, Department of Defence, South Africa, since 1970; *b* 6 Aug. 1916; *s* of Edric Murray Smythe and *g s* of 1st Administrator of Natal (Hon. Charles Smythe, Methven Castle, Perthshire, Scotland); *m* 1945, Dale Griffiths (marr. diss. 1970), Capetown; three *s* one *d; m* 1970, Margaret Joan Shatwell. *Educ:* Estcourt High Sch. Went through Abyssinian Campaign with Regt, Natal Carabineers; Sgt at Alem Hanza, Egypt (VC). *Recreations:* cricket, tennis, fishing. *Address:* Private Bag, SACC S Bn, Eersterivier, 7100 Cape Province, South Africa.

SMYTHE, Henry James Drew-, MC, TD; MS, MD (London); FRCS; MMSA; FRCOG; late Hon. Consulting Gynæcologist United Bristol Hospitals and Southmead General Hospital; late Gynæcologist, Weston-super-Mare and Burnham Hospitals; Colonel RAMCT; *b* 1 June 1891; *s* of Frank Thompson Smythe and Ada Josephine Drew; *m* 1914, Enid Audrey Cloutman (*d* 1971); two *s. Educ:* Taunton School; Bristol Medical School; London Hospital. Qualified 1913; House Surgeon and House Physician Bristol Children's Hospital, 1913-14; House Surgeon Bristol General Hospital, 1914; served European War, 1914-19; also served War of 1939-45; House Surgeon Royal Infirmary, 1919; Demonstrator of Anatomy, Royal Free Hospital for Women, 1921; Post-Graduate Course London Hospital, 1921-22; Surgical Registrar, Bristol General Hospital, 1923; Asst Gynæcologist, 1925; Professor of Obstetrics, University of Bristol, 1934-51. Liveryman Society of Apothecaries; Freeman of City of London. *Publications:* various in Practitioner, Bristol Med. Chir. Jl, Jl of Obst. of British Empire, etc; Operative Obstetrics (Butterworth's Modern Trends), 1949. *Recreations:* Rugby football, hockey, tennis. *Address:* 2 Chariton Close, Charlton Kings, Cheltenham, Glos. *T:* Cheltenham 25117.

SMYTHE, Patricia Rosemary; *see* Koechlin, P. R.

SMYTHE, Sir Reginald Harry, KBE 1971; JP; Managing Director, New Zealand Forest Products Ltd, since 1963; *b* 2 May 1905; *s* of Reginald Harry Smythe; *m* 1930, Colleen Valmar, *d* of George Mobberley; one *s. Educ:* Auckland Grammar Sch.; FCIS. Accountant to: Morris Duncan & Gylls, 1922-24; Smith Wylie Co. Ltd, 1924-30; Asst Sec., 1930-32, Sec., 1932-35, NZ Perpetual Forests; NZ Forest Products Ltd: Sec., 1935-60; Dir, 1954-; Gen. Manager, 1960-63; Chairman: D. Henry & Co. Ltd; Carter Kumeu Ltd; Fibre Products NZ Ltd; Dir, NZ Paper Mills Ltd. JP 1948-. *Recreation:* gardening. *Address:* NZ Forest Products Ltd, O'Rorke Road, Penrose, Auckland; 178 Remuera Road, Auckland 5, New Zealand.

SMYTHE, Tony; *see* Smythe, C. A.

SNAGGE, John Derrick Mordaunt, OBE 1944; *b* 1904; 2nd *s* of late Judge Sir Mordaunt Snagge; *m* 1936, Eileen Mary, *e d* of H. P. Joscelyne, Alvechurch, Worcestershire. *Educ:* Winchester College; Pembroke College, Oxford. Assistant Station Director BBC, Stoke-on-Trent, 1924; Announcer London (Savoy Hill), 1928; Assistant Outside Broadcast Department 1933; Commentator Oxford and Cambridge Boat Race, 1931-; Assistant Director Outside Broadcasts, 1939; Presentation Director BBC, 1939-45; Head of Presentation (Home Service), 1945-57; Head of Presentation (Sound) BBC, 1957-63; Special Duties, BBC, 1963-65. Retired from BBC 1965. Chairman of the Lord's Taverners, 1956, 1960, 1961; President, 1952, 1964; Secretary, 1965-67; Trustee, 1970-76. *Publications:* (with Michael Barsley) Those Vintage Years of Radio, 1972. *Recreation:* fishing. *Address:* Willow Tree Cottage, West End Lane, Stoke Poges, Bucks. *T:* Farnham Common 4400. *Clubs:* MCC, Leander, Lord's Taverners, Sportsman's.

SNAGGE, Dame Nancy (Marion), DBE 1955 (OBE 1945); *b* 2 May 1906; *d* of late Henry Thomas Salmon; *m* 1962, Thomas Geoffrey Mordaunt Snagge, DSC, *e s* of late His Hon. Sir Mordaunt Snagge. *Educ:* Notting Hill, High Sch. Joined the WAAF on its inception, March 1939; served as a commnd officer in the WAAF and WRAF from Sept. 1939. ADC to King George VI, 1950-52; ADC to the Queen, 1952-56; Director Women's Royal Air Force, 1950-56, retired as Air Commandant. *Address:* Test Lodge, Longstock, Stockbridge, Hampshire. *T:* Stockbridge 558.

SNAITH, George Robert, FRINA; Director of Research, British Ship Research Association, since 1976; *b* 9 July 1930; *s* of late Robert and Clara Snaith; *m* 1953, Verna Patricia (*née* Codling); one *s* one *d. Educ:* University of Durham. BSc Applied Science

(Naval Architecture), 1952. A. Kari & Co., Consulting Naval Architects, Newcastle, 1952-57; Northern Aluminium Co. Ltd, Bambury, 1957-59; Burness, Corlett & Partners, Consulting Naval Architects, Basingstoke, 1959-64; British Ship Research Association, 1964-. Member of Council, Royal Instn of Naval Architects. *Recreations:* reading, literature and discussion. *Address:* 10 Fieldhouse Close, Hepscott, Morpeth, Northumberland. *T:* Morpeth 55319. *Club:* Athenæum.

SNAITH, Group Captain Leonard Somerville, CB 1952; AFC 1933; retired; *b* 30 June 1902; *s* of David Somerville Snaith; *m* 1931, Joyce Edith Taylor; two *s. Educ:* Carlisle Cathedral Sch. Commnd, 1927; Comd 83 Sqdn, 1937-40; service in: Iraq, 1934-36; USA (Test flying), 1940-41; Egypt, Italy, Palestine, Aden, 1945-47. Schneider Trophy Team, 1931; Commandant Empire Test Pilot School, 1948-50; Comdg Officer, Experimental Flying, Royal Aircraft Establishment, Farnborough, 1950-52; retired from RAF, 1952. DL Beds, 1961-69. *Address:* 27 Montrose Drive, Pietermaritzburg, Natal, S Africa. *Clubs:* Royal Air Force; Victoria (Natal).

SNAITH, Rev. Norman Henry, DD; *b* 21 April 1898; *s* of John Allen Snaith and Mary Ann (*née* Bunn); *m* 1925, Winifred Howson Graham; one *s* two *d. Educ:* Paston Sch., North Walsham; Duke's Sch., Alnwick; Manchester Grammar Sch.; Corpus Christi and Mansfield Colls, Oxford. Open Mathematical Schol., Corpus Christi, Oxon, 1917; BA Hons Maths 1920, MA 1924, DD 1948, Oxford. Junior Kennicott Hebrew Schol., 1924, Senior Kennicott Hebrew Schol., 1925. Entered Methodist Ministry, 1921. Tutor in Hebrew and Old Testament subjects, Wesley College, Headingley, Leeds, 1936-61; Principal, 1954-61. Pres., Soc. for Old Testament Study, 1957; Vis. Prof. United Theol. Coll., Bangalore, 1957. Pres., Methodist Conf., 1958-59. Speaker's Lectr in Biblical Studies, Oxford, 1961-65. Hon. DD Glasgow, 1952; Hon. LittD Leeds, 1961. *Publications:* Studies in the Psalter, 1934; Have Faith in God, 1935; The Distinctive Ideas of the Old Testament, 1944; Study Notes on Bible Books, 1945-54; The Jewish New Year Festival, 1948; The Jews from Cyrus to Herod, 1949; I believe in..., 1949; Hymns of the Temple, 1951; New Men in Christ Jesus, 1952; Mercy and Sacrifice, 1953; Commentary on Amos, Hosea and Micah, 1956; Editor: Hebrew Bible (for British and Foreign Bible Society), 1958; Leviticus and Numbers, New Century Bible, 1966; The Book of Job, 1968; The God that never was, 1971. *Address:* Greenacres, Castle Lane, Thetford, Norfolk. *T:* Thetford 2848.

SNAITH, Stanley, FLA; author and librarian; Borough Librarian, Bethnal Green Public Libraries, 1950-65; *b* Kendal, 16 Dec. 1903; *e s* of J. W. Snaith, JP, and Margaret Tebay. Held senior posts in the Kendal, Kingston-upon-Thames and Islington public libraries. Local Secretary, Ministry of Information, 1940-42; HM Forces (Heavy Anti-Aircraft Batteries), 1942-46. *Publications:* April Morning, 1926; A Flying Scroll, 1928; The Silver Scythe, 1933; North, 1934; Fieldfaring, 1935; London Pageant, 1935; Men Against Peril, 1936; Green Legacy, 1937; Modern Poetry (A Bibliography), 1937; At Grips with Everest, 1937; Alpine Adventure, 1944; Stormy Harvest, 1944 (chosen as an Ambassador Book to the USA); The Inn of Night, 1946; The Flowering Thorn, 1946; (with George F. Vale) Bygone Bethnal Green, 1948; The Naked Mountain, 1949; The Common Festival, 1950; The Mountain Challenge, 1952; The Siege of the Matterhorn, 1956; The Books in My Life, 1957; The Special Shelf, 1958; The Lost Road, 1968; *poems:* Nanga Parbat, awarded Shirley Carter Greenwood Prize, 1949; Homage to Rilke and The Hawthorn in the Bombed Church, awarded 1st Prize, Nat. Shakespearian Sonnets Competition, 1964; scripts for BBC, and numerous papers and pamphlets on antiquarian matters; texts for two pageants; contributor to Oxford Junior Encyclopædia, Encyclopædia Britannica, and to many anthologies and periodicals. *Recreations:* reading, music. *Address:* 17 Newton Rise, Swanage, Dorset.

SNAPE, Peter Charles; MP (Lab) West Bromwich East since Feb. 1974; an Assistant Government Whip, since Nov. 1975; *b* 12 Feb. 1942; *s* of Thomas and Kathleen Snape; *m* 1963, Winifred Grimshaw; two *d. Educ:* St Joseph's RC Sch., Stockport; St Winifred's Sch., Stockport. Railway signalman, 1957-61; regular soldier, RE & RCT, 1961-67; goods guard, 1967-70; clerical officer BR, 1970-74. Mem., Council of Europe and WEU, May-Nov. 1975. Mem., Bredbury and Romiley UDC, 1971-74 (Chm., Finance Cttee). *Address:* 29 Bailey Crescent, Congleton, Cheshire. *T:* Congleton 3934.

SNEDDEN, Rt. Hon. Billy Mackie, PC 1972; QC (Australia); Federal Member of Parliament for Bruce (Victoria), Commonwealth of Australia, since 1955; Speaker, House of Representatives, since 1976; *b* 31 Dec. 1926; *s* of A. Snedden, Scotland; *m* 1950, Joy; two *s* two *d. Educ:* Univ. of Western Australia (LLB). Barrister, admitted Supreme Ct of Western Australia, 1951; admitted Victorian Bar, 1955. Australian Govt: Attorney-General, 1963-66; Minister for Immigration, 1966-69; Leader of the House, 1966-71; Minister for Labour and Nat. Service, 1969-71; Treasurer, 1971-72; Leader of the Opposition, 1972-75; Leader, Parliamentary Liberal Party, 1972-75 (Dep. Leader, 1971-72). *Recreations:* squash, tennis. *Address:* 22 Pine Crescent, Ringwood, Victoria 3134, Australia. *Clubs:* Melbourne, Melbourne Scots, Naval and Military (Melbourne).

SNEDDON, Prof. Ian Naismith, OBE 1969; MA Cantab, DSc Glasgow; FRSE; FIMA; Member of the Polish Academy of Sciences; Simson Professor of Mathematics in the University of Glasgow since 1956; *b* 8 Dec. 1919; *o s* of Naismith Sneddon and Mary Ann Cameron; *m* 1943, Mary Campbell Macgregor; two *s* one *d. Educ:* Hyndland School, Glasgow; The University of Glasgow; Trinity College, Cambridge (Senior Scholar, 1941). Scientific Officer, Ministry of Supply, 1942-45; Research Worker, H. H. Wills Physical Lab., Univ. of Bristol, 1945-46; Lecturer in Natural Philosophy, Univ. of Glasgow, 1946-50; Professor of Mathematics in University Coll. of N Staffordshire, 1950-56 (Senior Tutor of the College, 1954-56); Dean of Faculty of Science, Univ. of Glasgow, 1970-72, Senate Assessor on Univ. Court, 1973-; Visiting Prof.: Duke Univ., North Carolina, 1959 and 1960; Michigan State Univ., 1967; Adjunct Prof., North Carolina State Univ., 1965-72; Visiting Lecturer: Univ. of Palermo, 1953; Serbian Acad. of Sciences, 1958; Univ. of Warsaw, 1959, 1973, 1975; Canadian Mathematical Congress, 1961; Polish Acad. of Sciences, 1962; US Midwest Mechanics Research Seminar, 1963; Univ. of Zagreb, 1964; Univ. of Calgary, 1968; Indiana Univ., 1970, 1971, 1972; Kuwait Univ., 1972; CISM, Udine, 1972, 1974; NSF Distinguished Vis. Scientist, State Univ., New York, 1969. Member: various govt scientific cttees, 1950-; Adv. Council on Scientific Research and Tech. Development, Min. of Supply, 1953-56, Min. of Defence, 1965-68; Univs Science and Technology Bd (SRC), 1965-69; Adv. Council of Scottish Opera, 1972-; Bd of Scottish Nat. Orch., 1976-; Bd of Citizens Theatre, Glasgow, 1975-; Vice-Pres., RSE, 1966-69. Kelvin Medal, Univ. of Glasgow, 1948; Makdougall-Brisbane Prize, RSE, 1956-58. FRSA. Mem., Order of Long-Leaf Pine, USA, 1964; Hon. Fellow, Soc. of Engng Sci., USA; Hon. DSc Warsaw, 1973. Comdr's Cross, Order of Polonia Restituta, 1969. *Publications:* (with N. F. Mott) Wave Mechanics and Its Applications, 1948; Fourier Transforms, 1951; Special Functions of Mathematical Physics and Chemistry, 1956; The Elements of Partial Differential Equations, 1956; Introduction to the Mathematics of Biology and Medicine (with J. G. Defares), 1960; Fourier Series, 1961; Zagadnienie Szczelin w Teorii Sprezystasci, 1962; Mixed Boundary Value Problems in Potential Theory, 1966; Crack Problems in the Mathematical Theory of Elasticity (with M. Lowengrub), 1969; An Introduction to the Use of Integral Transforms, 1972; Metoda Transformacji Calkowych w Mieszanych Zogadnieniach Brzegowych, 1974; The Linear Theory of Thermoelasticity, 1974; (ed) Encyclopedic Dictionary of Mathematics for Engineers, 1976; (with G. Eason, W. Nowacki and Z. Olesiak) Integral Transform Methods in Elasticity, 1977; articles in Handbuch der Physik, 1956-58; scientific papers on quantum theory of nuclei, theory of elasticity, and boundary value problems in jls. *Recreations:* music, painting and photography. *Address:* 15 Victoria Park Gardens South, Glasgow G11 7BX. *T:* 041-339 4114. *Club:* Authors'.

SNEDDON, Robert, CMG 1976; MBE 1945; HM Diplomatic Service; Counsellor, Foreign and Commonwealth Office, since 1971; *b* 8 June 1920; *m* 1945, Kathleen Margaret Smith; two *d. Educ:* Dalziel High Sch., Motherwell; Kettering Grammar Sch.; University Coll., Nottingham. HM Forces, 1940-46: 8th Army, ME and Italy, 1942-45; 30 Corps, Germany (Major), 1945-46. Joined Foreign (subseq. Diplomatic) Service, 1946; 3rd Sec., Warsaw, 1946; 2nd Sec., Stockholm, 1950; FO, 1954; 1st Sec., Oslo, 1956; 1st Sec., Berlin, 1961; FO, 1963; Counsellor, Bonn, 1969. *Recreations:* tennis, squash, ski-ing, music. *Address:* Windrose, Church Road, Horsell, Woking, Surrey. *T:* Woking 4335.

SNELGROVE, Ven. Donald George, TD 1972; Archdeacon of the East Riding since 1970, and Rector of Cherry Burton; *b* 21 April 1925; *s* of William Henry Snelgrove and Beatrice Snelgrove (*née* Upshell); *m* 1949, Sylvia May Lowe; one *s* one *d. Educ:* Queens' Coll. and Ridley Hall, Cambridge (MA). Served War, commn (Exec. Br.) RNVR, 1943-46. Cambridge, 1946-50; ordained, 1950; Curate: St Thomas, Oakwood, 1950-53; St Anselm's, Hatch End, 1953-56; Vicar of: Dronfield with Unstone, Dio. Derby, 1956-62; Hessle, Dio. York, 1963-70.

Rural Dean of Hull, 1966-70; Canon of York, 1969. Chaplain T&AVR, 1960-73. *Recreation:* travel. *Address:* Cherry Burton Rectory, Beverley, North Humberside. *T:* Leconfield 50293.

SNELL, Ven. Basil Clark; Archdeacon of St Albans, 1962-73, now Archdeacon Emeritus; *b* 2 Feb. 1907; *s* of Charles Clark Snell, Vicar of Littlehampton; *m* 1933, Isobel Eills Nedeham Browne (*d* 1975); two *d. Educ:* King's School, Canterbury; Queens' College, Cambridge. Curate of Crosthwaite, Keswick, 1933-35; Chaplain of Aldenham School, 1935-40; Chaplain, Loretto Sch. and Army Chaplain, 1940-47; Rector of Tattingstone, Suffolk, 1947-55; Residentiary Canon of St Edmundsbury, 1955-58; Dir of Religious Education: Dio. of St Edmundsbury and Ipswich, 1947-58; Dio. of St Albans, 1958-68. Archdeacon of Bedford, 1958-62. *Recreations:* golf, gardening. *Address:* Glebe House, Melbourn, Royston, Herts.

SNELL, Frederick Rowlandson, MA, BSc; *b* 18 Sept. 1903; *s* of Rev. C. D. Snell; *m* 1928, Margaret Lucy Sidebottom; one *s* three *d. Educ:* Winchester College (Scholar); Oriel College, Oxford (Scholar). BA, 1925; BSc, 1927; Lecturer in Chemistry, St John's College, Agra, UP, India, 1927-32; Senior Science Master, Eastbourne College, 1932-38; Rector of Michaelhouse, Natal, SA, 1939-52; Founder and first Rector of Peterhouse, Rhodesia, 1953-67; Treasurer, Anglican Church in Central Africa, 1968-76. *Recreations:* walking and music. *Address:* 54 1st Street, Marandellas, Rhodesia. *Club:* Royal Commonwealth Society.

SNELL, Rt. Rev. Geoffrey Stuart; see Croydon, Bishop Suffragan of.

SNELL, Rt. Rev. George Boyd, DD, PhD; *b* Toronto, Ontario, 17 June 1907; *s* of John George Snell and Minnie Alice Boyd; *m* 1934, Esther Mary. *Educ:* Trinity College, Toronto. BA 1929, MA 1930, PhD 1937, DD 1948. Deacon, Toronto, 1931; Priest, Niagara (for Tor.), 1932; Curate of St Michael and All Angels, Tor., 1931-39; Rector, 1940-48; Private Chaplain to Bp of Tor., 1945-48; Rector of Pro-Cathedral, Calgary, and Dean of Calgary, 1948-51; Exam. Chaplain to Bp of Calgary, 1948-51; Rector of St Clem. Eglinton, Tor., 1951-56; Archdeacon of Toronto, 1953-56; Exam. Chaplain to Bp of Toronto, 1953-55. Consecrated Bp Suffragan of Toronto, 1956; elected Bp-Coadjutor of Toronto, 1959; Bishop of Toronto, 1966-72. Hon. DD: Wycliffe Coll., Toronto, 1959; Huron Coll., Ontario, 1968. *Address:* 1210 Glen Road, Mississauga, Ont., Canada. *Club:* National (Toronto).

SNELL, William Edward, MD; FRCP; Consultant Physician Superintendent, Colindale Chest Hospital, 1938-67; Demonstrator in Tuberculosis, St Bartholomew's Hospital Medical College, 1948-67; Consultant Chest Physician, Napsbury and Shenley Hospitals, 1963-67; *b* 16 Aug. 1902; *er s* of late S. H. Snell, MD; *m* 1934, Yvonne Creagh Brown; two *s* one *d. Educ:* Stubbington House; Bradfield College; Corpus Christi College, Cambridge (Exhibitioner and Prizeman); University College Hospital. MA Cambridge; BSc Hons London; MD; FRCP; DPH. Tuberculosis Scholarship Tour, Canada and USA, 1930. Formerly: Pres. Brit. Tuberculosis Assoc., 1955-57; Chairman: NW Metropolitan Thoracic Soc.; Metropolitan Branch, Soc. of Med. Supts; Editorial Cttee TB Index; Member: Management Cttees, Hendon and Chelsea Groups of Hosps; Brit. Tuberculosis Research Cttee; Examiner to Gen. Nursing Council. Mem. Council (twice Vice-Pres.), History of Medicine Section, RSM. *Publications:* articles in medical press relating to tuberculosis and chest disease, accidents to patients and history of medicine. *Recreations:* gardening, sailing, collecting ship models and prints; late part owner 15 ton ketch Craignair. *Address:* Yewden Manor, Hambleden, Henley-on-Thames, Oxon. *T:* Hambleden 351. *Clubs:* Keyhaven Yacht, Cambridge University Cruising, etc.

SNELLGROVE, David Llewellyn, LittD, PhD; FBA 1969; Professor of Tibetan in the University of London, since 1974 (Reader, 1960-74, Lecturer, 1950-60); Director of Institute of Tibetan Studies, Tring, since its foundation in 1966; *b* Portsmouth, 29 June 1920; *s* of Lt-Comdr Clifford Snellgrove, RN, and Eleanor Maud Snellgrove. *Educ:* Christ's Hospital, Horsham; Southampton Univ.; Queens' Coll., Cambridge. Served War of 1939-45: commissioned in Infantry, 1942; Intell. Officer in India until 1946. Then started seriously on oriental studies at Cambridge, 1946, cont. Rome, 1950-54. BA Cantab 1949, MA Cantab 1953; PhD London 1954; LittD Cantab 1969. Made expedns to India and the Himalayas, 1953-54, 1956, 1960, 1964 and 1967; founded with Mr Hugh E. Richardson an Inst. of Tibetan Studies, 1966. Apptd Consultant to Vatican in new Secretariat for non-Christian Religions, 1967. *Publications:* Buddhist Himalaya, 1957; The Hevajra Tantra, 1959;

Himalayan Pilgrimage, 1961; Four Lamas of Dolpo, 1967; The Nine Ways of Bon, 1967; A Cultural History of Tibet (with H. E. Richardson), 1968; articles in Arts Asiatiques (Paris), Bulletin of the Secretariat for non-Christian Religions (Rome), etc. *Recreations:* travel: involving photography, filming, recording (esp. in India and the Himalayas), personal and professional visits to W Europe (fluent in several languages). *Address:* c/o Institute of Tibetan Studies, Tring, Herts; Rest-harrow, 113 Cross Oak Road, Berkhamsted, Herts. *T:* Berkhamsted 4782.

SNELLGROVE, John Anthony; HM Diplomatic Service, retired; Secretary, British Brush Manufacturers' Association, since 1977; *b* 29 Jan. 1922; *s* of late John Snellgrove and of Anne Mary Priscilla (*née* Brown); *m* 1956, Rose Jeanne Marie Suzanne (*née* Paris); two *d. Educ:* Wimbledon Coll.; Stonyhurst Coll.; Peterhouse, Cambridge (1940-41 and 1945-48; BA and MA). Served War, Royal Navy, latterly as temp. actg Lieut, RNVR, 1941-45. Asst Principal, Colonial Office, 1948-49; joined Foreign Service, Oct. 1949; 2nd Sec., Prague, 1950-51; FO (Econ. Relations Dept), 1951-53; HM Vice-Consul, Tamsui (Formosa), 1953-56; 1st Sec., 1954; FO (SE Asia Dept and UN (E&S) Dept), 1956-59; 1st Sec., Bangkok, 1959-62; 1st Sec. and Consul, Mogadishu (Somali Republic), 1962-63; FO (Arabian and European Econ. Org. Depts), 1963-66; 1st Sec., Holy See, 1967-71; Counsellor, 1971; Dep. Sec.-Gen. (Economic), CENTO, 1971-73; Counsellor and Head of Chancery, Carácas, 1973-75, retired, 1976. *Recreations:* golf, music, bridge. *Address:* 13 Chantry Hurst, Woodcote, Epsom, Surrey KT18 7BN. *Club:* Challoner.

SNELLING, Sir Arthur (Wendell), KCMG 1960 (CMG 1954); KCVO 1962; HM Diplomatic Service, retired; *b* 7 May 1914; *s* of Arthur and Ellen Snelling; *m* 1939, Frieda, *d* of late Lt-Col F. C. Barnes; one *s. Educ:* Ackworth Sch., Yorks; University Coll., London (BSc Econ.). Study Gp Sec., Royal Inst. of Internat. Affairs, 1934-36; Dominions Office, 1936; Private Sec. to Parl. Under-Sec., 1939; Joint Sec. to UK Delegn to Internat. Monetary Conference, Bretton Woods, USA, 1944; accompanied Lord Keynes on missions to USA and Canada, 1943 and 1944; Dep. High Comr for UK in New Zealand, 1947-50, in S Africa, 1953-55; Assistant Under-Secretary of State, Commonwealth Relations Office, 1956-59; British High Comr in Ghana, 1959-61; Dep. Under-Sec. of State, FCO (formerly CRO), 1961-69; Ambassador to South Africa, 1970-72. Dir, Gordon and Gotch Holdings Ltd, 1973-. Fellow, UCL, 1970; Mem., College Cttee, UCL, 1976. Vice-Pres., UK-S Africa Trade Assoc. *Address:* 19 Albany Park Road, Kingston-upon-Thames, Surrey KT2 5SW. *T:* 01-549 4160. *Club:* Reform.

SNELSON, Sir Edward Alec Abbott, KBE 1954 (OBE 1946); Justice, Supreme Restitution Court, Herford, German Federal Republic, since 1962; Judge, Arbitral Tribunal for Agreement on German External Debts and Mixed Commission, Koblenz, 1969-77; *b* 31 Oct. 1904; *er s* of Thomas Edward and Alice Martha Snelson; *m* 1956, Prof. Jean Johnston Mackay, MA, 3rd *d* of Donald and Isabella Mackay; two *s. Educ:* St Olave's; Gonville and Caius Coll., Cambridge. Called to Bar, Gray's Inn, 1929; entered ICS 1929; served in Central Provinces, District and Sessions Judge, 1936; Registrar, High Court, 1941; Legal Secretary, 1946; Joint Secretary, Govt of India, 1947; retired, 1947; Official Draftsman, Govt of Pakistan, 1948; Sec. Min. of Law, 1951-61, also of Parliamentary Affairs, 1952-58. Mem. Exec. Cttee, Arts Council of Pakistan, 1953-61. *Publication:* Father Damien, 1938. *Recreations:* sailing, music, theatre. *Address:* c/o Barclays Bank, Piccadilly Circus, W1A 3BJ; c/o Supreme Restitution Court, Herford, BFPO 15. *Clubs:* United Oxford & Cambridge University; Challoner.

SNELUS, Alan Roe, CMG 1960; retired as Deputy Chief Secretary, Sarawak (1955-64); *b* 19 May 1911; *s* of John Ernest Snelus, late of Ennerdale Hall, Cumberland; *m* 1947, Margaret Bird Deacon-Elliott; one *s* one *d. Educ:* Haileybury Coll.; St Catharine's Coll., Cambridge. Barrister, Gray's Inn, 1934. Joined Sarawak Civil Service as an Administrative Officer, 1934; Actg Chief Sec., 1958-59; Officer Administering the Government of Sarawak, March-April 1959. *Recreations:* gardening and contemplation. *Address:* Cleaveside, Morcombelake, Bridport, Dorset.

SNODGRASS, Prof. Anthony McElrea; Laurence Professor of Classical Archaeology, University of Cambridge, since 1976; Fellow of Clare College, Cambridge, since 1977; *b* 7 July 1934; *s* of William McElrea Snodgrass, MC (Major, RAMC), and Kathleen Mabel (*née* Owen); *m* 1959, Ann Elizabeth Vaughan (now separated); four *d. Educ:* Marlborough Coll.; Worcester Coll., Oxford (BA 1959, MA, DPhil 1963). Served with RAF in Iraq, 1953-55 (National Service). Student of the British School,

Athens, 1959-60; University of Edinburgh: Lectr in Classical Archaeology, 1961; Reader, 1969; Prof., 1975. Corresp. Mem., German Archaeol. Inst., 1977-. *Publications:* Early Greek Armour and Weapons, 1964; Arms and Armour of the Greeks, 1967; The Dark Age of Greece, 1971; contrib. Jl of Hellenic Studies, Proc. of Prehistoric Soc., Gnomon, etc. *Recreations:* mountaineering, skiing. *Address:* Museum of Classical Archaeology, Little St Mary's Lane, Cambridge CB2 1RR. *T:* Cambridge 65621 (ext. 204).
See also J. M. O. Snodgrass.

SNODGRASS, John Michael Owen; HM Diplomatic Service; Head of Pacific Dependent Territories Department, Foreign and Commonwealth Office, since 1977; *b* 12 Aug. 1928; *e s* of Major W. M. Snodgrass, MC, RAMC; *m* 1957, Jennifer James; three *s.* *Educ:* Marlborough Coll.; Trinity Hall, Cambridge (MA, Maths and Moral Scis). Diplomatic Service: 3rd Sec., Rome, 1953-56; FO, 1956-60; 1st Sec., Beirut, 1960-63; S Africa, 1964-67; FCO, 1967-70; Consul-Gen., Jerusalem, 1970-74; Counsellor, South Africa, 1974-77. CStJ 1975. *Recreations:* ski-ing, tennis, travel. *Address:* c/o Foreign and Commonwealth Office, SW1; The Old School, Eastbury, Berks. *Clubs:* Hurlingham, Royal Commonwealth Society, Ski Club of Great Britain.
See also A. McE. Snodgrass.

SNOW, family name of **Baron Burntwood** and **Baron Snow.**

SNOW, Baron *cr* 1964 (Life Peer); **Charles Percy Snow,** Kt 1957; CBE 1943; writer; *b* 15 Oct. 1905; *m* 1950, Pamela Hansford Johnson, *qv*; one *s.* *Educ:* Alderman Newton's Sch., Leicester; Univ. Coll., Leicester; Christ's Coll., Cambridge. Parly Sec., Min. of Technology, 1964-66. Fellow, Churchill Coll., Cambridge; Hon. Fellow, Christ's Coll., Cambridge. Foreign Mem., American Academy-Institute; hon. doctorates, and other awards, from American, Canadian, English, Scottish and Soviet universities, colleges and academies, inc. NY Univ. and Louisville, 1976, Pace, 1977. *Publications:* Death Under Sail, 1932; New Lives for Old, 1933; The Search, 1934 (revised and republished, 1958); occupied, 1935-70, with novel-sequence of eleven volumes (general title, Strangers and Brothers): George Passant, 1940; The Light and the Dark, 1947; Time of Hope, 1949; The Masters, 1951; The New Men, 1954 (James Tait Black Memorial Prize, awarded in conjunction with The Masters); Homecomings, 1956; The Conscience of the Rich, 1958; The Affair, 1960; Corridors of Power, 1964; The Sleep of Reason, 1968; Last Things, 1970; The Two Cultures and the Scientific Revolution (Rede Lecture), 1959; Science and Government (Godkin Lectures), 1961; Appendix to Science and Government, 1962; The Two Cultures and a Second Look, 1964; Variety of Men, 1967; Public Affairs, 1971; *novels:* The Malcontents, 1972; In Their Wisdom, 1974; *critical biography:* Trollope, 1975; *plays:* View over the Park, produced Lyric, Hammersmith, 1950; The Affair (adapted by Ronald Millar), Strand, 1961-62; The New Men (adapted by Ronald Millar), Strand, 1962; The Masters (adapted by Ronald Millar), Savoy, Piccadilly, 1963-64; Time of Hope (adapted by Arthur and Violet Ketels), Philadelphia, 1963; The Case in Question (adapted from In Their Wisdom by Ronald Millar), Haymarket, 1975. *Address:* 85 Eaton Terrace, SW1. *Clubs:* Garrick, MCC; Century (NY).

SNOW, Rt. Hon. Lady; see Johnson, Pamela Hansford.

SNOW, Rt. Rev. George D'Oyly; *b* 2 Nov. 1903; *s* of Lt-Gen. Sir Thomas D'Oyly Snow, KCB, KCMG, and Charlotte Geraldine Coke; *m* 1942, Joan Monica, *y d* of late Maj. Henry J. Way, VD; three *s.* *Educ:* Winchester College; Oriel College, Oxford. Assistant Master at Eton College, 1925-36; ordained, 1933; Chaplain at Charterhouse, 1936-46; Headmaster of Ardingly College, Sussex, 1946-61; Prebend of Chichester Cathedral, 1959-61; Suffragan Bishop of Whitby, 1961-71; Rural Dean, Purbeck, 1973-76. Chairman National Society, 1963-73. Chaplain to retired clergy and widows in Dorset Archdeaconry, 1976-. *Publications:* A Guide to Prayer, 1932; A Guide to Belief, 1935; A School Service Book, 1936; A Guide to Confirmation, 1936; Our Father, 1938; Letters to a Confirmand, 1946; Into His Presence, 1946; The Public School in the New Age, 1959; Forth in His Name, 1964. *Recreations:* gardening, D-I-Y, caravan camping, music. *Address:* Meadow Cottage, Corfe Castle, Wareham, Dorset. *T:* Corfe Castle 589.

SNOW, Thomas; Secretary to Oxford University Appointments Committee, since 1970; Fellow, New College, Oxford, since 1973; *b* 16 June 1929; *e s* of Thomas Maitland Snow, *qv*; *m* 1961, Elena Tidmarsh; two *s* one *d.* *Educ:* Winchester Coll.; New Coll., Oxford. Joined Crittall Manufacturing Co. Ltd as Management Trainee, 1952; Dir 1966; Director: Crittall Hope Ltd, Darlington Simpson Rolling Mills, Minex Metals Ltd, 1968. Held various positions in local govt; Marriage Councillor,

1964-70; Chm., Oxford Marriage Guidance Council, 1974-. JP 1964-69. *Address:* 157 Woodstock Road, Oxford.

SNOW, Thomas Maitland, CMG 1934; *b* 21 May 1890; *s* of Thomas Snow, Cleve, Exeter, and Edith Banbury; *m* 1st, 1927, Phyllis Annette Malcolmson; three *s*; 2nd, 1949, Sylvia, *d* of W. Delmar, Buda-Pest. *Educ:* Winchester; New Coll., Oxford. 1st Secretary, HM Diplomatic Service, 1923; Counsellor, 1930; Minister: to Cuba, 1935-37; to Finland, 1937-40; to Colombia, 1941-44 (Ambassador, 1944-45); to Switzerland, 1946-49. Retired, 1950. *Recreation:* fishing. *Address:* La Combe, Tartegnin, Switzerland.
See also Thomas Snow.

SNOWDEN, Rt. Rev. John Samuel Philip; see Cariboo, Bishop of.

SNOWDEN, Joseph Stanley; *b* 16 Oct. 1901; *e s* of late Joseph Snowden, JP, and late Fanny Ruth Snowden, Morecambe and Heysham; *m* 1938, Agnes Enid Mitchell; no *c.* *Educ:* Sedbergh; St John's Coll., Cambridge. Law Tripos (Cantab) 1923 (BA, LLB); called to the Bar, Inner Temple, 1925; joined North-Eastern Circuit, 1925; Dep. Chm., W Riding of Yorks QS, 1960-71. Contested (L) Bradford East Div., 1945 and 1950, Dewsbury Div., 1951 and 1955, Pudsey Div., 1959. Recorder of Scarborough, 1951-71; a Recorder, and hon. Recorder of Scarborough, 1972-73. Chairman, Yorkshire and Lancashire Agricultural Land Tribunal, 1963-71. *Recreation:* politics. *Address:* Oakburn, 20 St James Road, Ilkley, West Yorkshire LS29 9PY. *T:* Ilkley 609401.

SNOWDON, 1st Earl of, *cr* 1961; **Antony Charles Robert Armstrong-Jones,** GCVO 1969; Viscount Linley, 1961; an Artistic Adviser to the Sunday Times and Sunday Times Publications Ltd, since 1962; Constable of Caernarvon Castle since 1963; *b* 7 March 1930; *s* of Ronald Owen Lloyd Armstrong-Jones, MBE, QC, DL (*d* 1966), and of the Countess of Rosse; *m* 1960, HRH The Princess Margaret; one *s* one *d.* *Educ:* Eton; Jesus Coll., Cambridge. Joined Staff of Council of Industrial Design, 1961, continuing on a consultative basis, 1962, also an Editorial Adviser of Design Magazine. Designed: Snowdon Aviary, London Zoo, 1965; Chairmobile, 1972. Mem. Council, National Fund for Research for the Crippled Child. Hon. Fellow: Institute of British Photographers; Royal Photographic Soc.; Soc. of Industrial Artists and Designers; Manchester College of Art and Design; Hon. Member: North Wales Society of Architects; South Wales Institute of Architects; Royal Welsh Yacht Club; Patron: Welsh Nat. Rowing Club; National Youth Theatre; Metropolitan Union of YMCAs; British Water Ski Federation. President: Contemp. Art Society for Wales; Civic Trust for Wales; British Theatre Museum; Welsh Theatre Company. FRSA. *Television films:* Don't Count the Candles, 1968 (2 Hollywood Emmy Awards; St George Prize, Venice; awards at Prague and Barcelona film festivals); Love of a Kind, 1969; Born to be Small, 1971 (Chicago Hugo Award); Happy being Happy, 1973; Mary Kingsley, 1975; Burke and Wills, 1975. *Exhibitions:* Photocall, London, 1958; Assignments, Cologne, London, Brussels, USA, 1972, Japan, 1975. *Publications:* London, 1958; Malta (in collaboration), 1958; Private View (in collaboration), 1965; Venice, 1972; Assignments, 1972. *Heir:* s Viscount Linley, *qv.* *Address:* 22 Launceston Place, W8 5RL. *Clubs:* Leander (Henley-on-Thames); Hawks (Cambridge).
See also under Royal Family, and Earl of Rosse.

SNOY ET d'OPPUERS, Baron Jean-Charles, Hon. KBE 1975 (OBE 1948); Grand Officier de l'Ordre de Léopold, Belgium; Grand Officier de l'Ordre de la Couronne, Belgium; Member of Belgian Parliament, 1968-71; Minister of Finance, Belgium, 1968-72; *b* 2 July 1907; *s* of 9th Baron and of Claire de Beughem de Houtem; *m* 1935, Nathalie, Countess d'Alcantara; two *s* five *d.* *Educ:* Collège Saint-Pierre, Uccle; University of Louvain; Harvard Univ. Secretary Société Belge de Banque, 1932; Attaché Cabinet Minister of Economic Affairs, 1934; Directeur Ministry Econ. Aff., 1936; Secrétaire Général, Ministère des Affaires Economiques, 1939-60; Président du Conseil de l'Union Benelux, 1945-60. War Service: Services de Renseignements et d'Action, 1940-44. Chairman, Four Party Supply Cttee, Belgium, 1945; Président du Conseil, Organisation Européenne de Coopération Economique, 1948-50 (OEEC in English); Chm., Steering Board for Trade, OEEC, 1952-61; Chef de la délégation Belge pour la négociation des Traités de Rome, 1957; Président, Comité Intérimaire du Marché Commun et de l'Euratom, 1957-58; Representant Permanant de la Belgique, Communauté Economique Européenne, 1958-59; Administrateur-Délégué de la Compagnie Lambert pour l'Industrie et la Finance, Brussels, 1960-68. Holds several foreign decorations. *Publications:* La Commission des Douanes,

1932; L'Aristocratie de Demain, 1936; La Profession et l'Organisation de la Production, 1942; Revue Générale Belge. *Recreations:* shooting, tennis. *Heir: s* Bernard, Baron Snoy, *b* 27 March 1945. *Address:* Château de Bois-Seigneur-Isaac, 1421 Ophain, Belgium. *T:* Nivelles 22.22.27. *Club:* Club de la Fondation Universitaire (Brussels).

SNYDER, John Wesley; Director, The Overland Corporation, 500 Security Building, Toledo, Ohio, since 1953 (Chairman Finance Committee and President, 1953-66); *b* 21 June 1895; *s* of Jerre Hartwell Snyder and Ellen Hatcher; *m* 1920, Evlyn Cook (*d* 1956); one *d. Educ:* Jonesboro Grade and High Sch.; Vanderbilt Univ. Various offices in Arkansas and Missouri banks, 1920-30; national bank receiver, office of Comptroller of the Currency, Washington, DC, 1930-37; in 1937 selected to head St Louis Loan Agency of RFC; and Exec. VP and Director of Defense Plant Corp., a subsidiary; early in 1943 resigned all Federal posts to become Exec. VP First National Bank of St Louis; Federal Loan Administrator, Washington, 30 April 1945; Dir of Office War Mobilization and Reconversion, July 1945-June 1946; Secretary of the Treasury, United States, 1946-53; US Governor of International Monetary Fund and International Bank for Reconstruction and Development, 1946-53; Advr, US Treasury, 1955-69. Delegate International Financial Conferences: Mexico City, 1945-52; Rio de Janeiro, 1957; London, 1947; Paris, 1950-52; Ottawa, 1951; Rome, 1951; Lisbon, 1952. Served as Captain, Field Artillery, 57th Bde, during War, 1917-18; retired Colonel US Army. 1955. Member: Omicron Delta Kappa; American Legion; Reserve Officers' Association. Trustee, Harry S. Truman Memorial Library. Episcopalian. *Address:* 8109 Kerry Lane, Chevy Chase, Maryland 20015, USA. *Clubs:* Missouri Athletic (St Louis); Chevy Chase, Alfalfa, National Press (Washington); Toledo (Toledo, Ohio).

SOAME, Sir Charles Burnett Buckworth-Herne-, 11th Bt *cr* 1697; late King's Shropshire Light Infantry; *b* 26 Sept. 1894; *s* of 10th Bt and Mary, *d* of John Edge and *widow* of P. B. Pring; *S* father, 1931; *m* 1924, Elsie May (*d* 1972), *d* of Walter Alfred Lloyd, Coalbrookdale, Salop; one *s* one *d.* Served European War, 1914-16 (wounded). *Heir: s* Charles John Buckworth-Herne-Soame [*b* 28 May 1932; *m* 1958, Eileen Margaret Mary, *d* of Leonard Minton; one *s*]. *Address:* Sheen Cottage, Coalbrookdale, Salop.

SOAMES, Rt. Hon. Sir (Arthur) Christopher (John), PC 1958; GCMG 1972; GCVO 1972; CBE 1955; Director, N. M. Rothschild & Sons, since 1977; *b* 12 Oct. 1920; *m* 1947, Mary, *d* of late Rt Hon. Sir Winston Churchill, KG, PC, OM, CH, FRS, and of Baroness Spencer-Churchill, *qv*; three *s* two *d. Educ:* Eton; Royal Military Coll., Sandhurst. 2nd Lieut, Coldstream Guards, 1939; Captain, 1942; served Middle East, Italy and France. Assistant Military Attaché British Embassy, Paris, 1946-47, MP (C) Bedford Division of Bedfordshire, 1950-66. Parliamentary Private Secretary to the Prime Minister, 1952-55; Parliamentary Under-Secretary of State, Air Ministry, Dec. 1955-Jan. 1957; Parliamentary and Financial Secretary, Admiralty, 1957-58; Secretary of State for War, Jan. 1958-July 1960; Minister of Agriculture, Fisheries and Food, 1960-64. Director: Decca Ltd, 1964-68; James Hole & Co. Ltd, 1964-68. Ambassador to France, 1968-72. A Vice-Pres., Commn of the European Communities, 1973-Jan. 1977. Pres., RASE, 1973. Hon. LLD St Andrews, 1974. Croix de Guerre (France), 1942; Grand Officier de la Légion d'honneur, 1972; Grand Cross of St Olav (Norway), 1974. Medal of the City of Paris, 1972. *Clubs:* White's, Portland.

SOAMES, Rt. Hon. Sir Christopher; *see* Soames, Rt Hon. Sir A. C. J.

SOBELL, Sir Michael, Kt 1972; Chairman: GEC (Radio & Television) Ltd; Radio & Allied (Holdings) Ltd; President, National Society for Cancer Relief; *b* 1 Nov. 1892; *s* of Lewis and Esther Sobell; *m* 1917, Anne Rakusen; two *d. Educ:* Central London Foundation Sch. Freeman and Liveryman, Carmen Co. Hon. Fellow: Bar Ilan Univ.; Jews' Coll. *Recreations:* racing, charitable work. *Address:* Bakeham House, Englefield Green, Surrey. *T:* Egham 4111. *Clubs:* Royal Automobile, City Livery; Jockey (Newmarket).

SOBERS, Sir Garfield (St Aubrun), Kt 1975; cricketer; *b* Bridgetown, Barbados, 18 July 1936; *m* 1970, Prudence; one *s. Educ:* Bay Street Sch., Barbados. First major match, 1953, for Barbados; played in 86 Test Matches for West Indies, 39 as Captain, 1953-74 (made world record Test Match score, Kingston, 1958); captained West Indies and Barbados teams, 1965-74; Captain of Nottinghamshire CCC, 1968-74. On retirement from Test cricket held the following world records in

Test Matches: 365 not out; 26 centuries; 235 wickets; 110 catches. *Publications:* Cricket Advance, 1965; Cricket Crusader, 1966; King Cricket, 1967; (with J. S. Barker) Cricket in the Sun, 1967; Bonaventure and the Flashing Blade, 1967; *relevant publication:* Sir Gary: a biography by Trevor Bailey, 1976.

SOBHA SINGH, Hon. Sardar Bahadur Sir Sardar, Kt, *cr* 1944; OBE 1938; landlord, millowner and contractor; Member of the Council of State, Delhi; Chairman, Nerbudda Valley Refrigeration Products Co. Ltd, Bhopal; Director: Machinery Manufacturers Corp. Ltd, Bombay, and several other leading Indian firms; *b* 1890; *m* Shrimati Wariam Kaur; four *s* one *d.* Member Indian Overseas League. *Address:* Baikunth, New Delhi 11, India. *Clubs:* Delhi Gymkhana, Chelmsford (New Delhi); Cricket Club of India (Bombay).

SOBHI, Mohamed Ibrahim; Order of Merit, 1st Class, Egypt, 1974; Director General, International Bureau of Universal Postal Union, since 1975; *b* Alexandria, 28 March 1925; *s* of Gen. Ibrahim Sobhi and Mrs Zenab Afifi; *m* 1950, Laila Ahmed Sobhi; two *s* one *d. Educ:* Cairo Univ. (BE 1949). Construction of roads and airports, Engr Corps, 1950; Technical Sec., Communications Commn, Permanent Council for Develt and National Prodn, 1954; Fellow, Vanderbilt Univ., Nashville, Tenn (studying transport and communications services in USA), 1955-56; Tech. Dir, Office of Minister of Communications for Posts, Railways and Coordination between means of transp. and communications, 1956-61; Dir-Gen., Sea Transp. Authority (remaining Mem. Tech. Cttees, Postal Org.), 1961-64; Under Sec. of State for Communications and Mem. Bd, Postal Org., 1964-68; Chm. Bd, Postal Org., and Sec.-Gen., African Postal Union, 1968-74. Universal Postal Union: attended Congress, Ottawa, 1957; attended Cons. Council for Postal Studies session, Brussels, 1958; Head of Egyptian Delegn, Tokyo and Lausanne Congresses, and sessions of CCPS (set up by Tokyo Congress), 1969-74. Dir, Exec. Bureau i/c Egyptian projs in Africa, incl. construction of Hôtel de l'Amitié, Bamako, Mali, and roads, 1963-74. *Recreations:* croquet, philately, music. *Address:* Bureau international de l'Union postale universelle, Weltpoststrasse 4, CH-3000 Berne 15, Switzerland. *T:* Berne 43 22 11.

SODDY, Dr Kenneth; Consulting Physician, University College Hospital, London, 1976 (Physician in charge, Children's and Adolescents' Psychiatric Department and Lecturer in Child Psychiatry, 1948-76); Hon. Lecturer in Child Development, University College, London, 1951-76; Hon. Consultant in Child Psychiatry, Royal Free Hospital, 1973-76; *b* 27 July 1911; *s* of Rev. T. E. Soddy, BA; *m* 1936, Emmeline (*d* 1972), *d* of H. E. Johnson; one *s* two *d*; *m* 1972, Mary, *d* of Canon N. S. Kidson, MC, MA. *Educ:* Taunton Sch.; University College, London; University College Hospital Medical School. MB, BS 1934; DPM 1937; MD 1938; FRCPsych (Foundn Fellow). Commonwealth Fund Fellowship in Child Guidance, 1938; Psychiatrist, London Child Guidance Clinic, 1939. Temp. Commn, RAMC, 1940; Specialist Psychiatrist (Major), 1941; Advisor in Psychiatry (Lieut-Colonel), AG's Dept, India Comd, 1943; Dep. Director, Selection of Personnel, India Comd, (Colonel), 1944; Hon. Lieut-Colonel, RAMC, 1946. Medical Director, National Assoc. for Mental Health, 1946; Psychiatrist, Tavistock Clinic, 1947; Psychiatrist, 1948, Med. Dir, 1953-58, Child Guidance Training Centre. Scientific Adviser, World Federation for Mental Health, 1961-64 (Hon. Secretary, 1948; Assistant Director, 1949; Scientific Director, 1958); Member, Expert Panel on Mental Health, World Health Organisation, 1949-; Mem., St Lawrence's Hosp., Caterham, Management Cttee, 1962-74; Consultant: to WHO, 1950 and 1957; to UKAEA, 1964-74; to Nat. Spastics Soc., 1965-; Pres., Inst. of Religion and Medicine, 1975-76 (Chm., 1964-71; Pro-Chm., 1971-74). Member various Study Groups, etc; Hon. Mem. American Psychiatric Assoc., 1953. *Publications:* Clinical Child Psychiatry, 1960; (with R. F. Tredgold) Mental Retardation, 11th edn, 1970; (with Mary C. Kidson) Men in Middle Life, 1967; Editor: Mental Health and Infant Development, 2 vols, 1955; Identity; Mental Health and Value Systems, 1961; (with R. H. Ahrenfeldt) Mental Health in a Changing World, 1965; Mental Health and Contemporary Thought, 1967; Mental Health in the Service of the Community, 1967; many articles in British, American and internat. medical and sociological jls. *Recreations:* organ playing, chamber music, moor and mountain walking. *Address:* The Manor Cottage, Doccombe, Moretonhampstead, Newton Abbot, Devon TQ13 8SS. *T:* Moretonhampstead 378.

SODOR AND MAN, Bishop of, since 1974; **Rt. Rev. Vernon Sampson Nicholls,** JP; *b* 3 Sept. 1917; *s* of Ernest C. Nicholls, Truro, Cornwall; *m* 1943, Phyllis, *d* of Edwin Potter, Stratford-on-Avon; one *s* one *d. Educ:* Truro Sch.; Univ. of Durham and

Clifton Theological Coll., Bristol. Curate: St Oswald, Bedminster Down, Bristol, 1941-42; Liskeard, Cornwall, 1942-43. CF, 1944-46 (Hon. CF 1946). Vicar of Meopham, 1946-56; Rural Dean of Cobham, 1953-56; Vicar and Rural Dean of Walsall, and Chaplain to Walsall Gen. Hosp., 1956-67; Preb of Curborough, Lichfield Cath., 1964-67; Archdeacon of Birmingham, 1967-74; Diocesan Planning Officer and Co-ordinating Officer for Christian Stewardship, 1967-74. Dean of St German's Cathedral, Peel, 1974-. MLC, Tynwald, IoM; Member: IoM Bd of Educn; IoM Bd of Social Security. JP, IoM. *Recreations:* meeting people, gardening, motoring. *Address:* The Bishop's House, Quarterbridge Road, Douglas, Isle of Man. *T:* Douglas 22108.

SOLDATOV, Aleksandr Alekseyevich; Rector, Moscow State Institute of International Relations, since 1970; *b* 27 Aug. 1915; *m* Rufina B.; *two d. Educ:* Moscow Teachers' Training Inst. (grad. Hist. Sciences, 1939). Member Soviet Foreign Service, 1941; Senior Counsellor of Soviet Delegation to the UN and Representative on Trusteeship Council, 1948-53; Head of UN Div., 1953-54, of American Div., 1954-60, Soviet Foreign Ministry; Soviet Ambassador to the Court of St James's, 1960-66; Deputy Foreign Minister, 1966-68; Ambassador in Cuba, 1968-70. Member Soviet Delegation to Geneva Conferences: on Germany, 1959; on Laos, 1961. Mem., CPSU Central Auditing Commn, 1966-71. *Address:* Moscow State Institute of International Relations, Ul. Metrostroerskaya 53, Moscow, USSR.

SOLER, Antonio R.; *see* Ruiz Soler, A.

SOLESBY, Tessa Audrey Hilda; HM Diplomatic Service; on secondment to NATO International Staff, Brussels, since 1975; *b* 1932; *d* of Charles Solesby and Hilda Solesby (*née* Willis). *Educ:* Clifton High School; St Hugh's College, Oxford. MA. Min. of Labour and Nat. Service, 1954-55; joined Diplomatic Service, 1956; FO, 1956; Manila, 1957-59; Lisbon, 1959-62; FO, 1962-64; First Sec., UK Mission to UN, Geneva, 1964-68; FO, 1968-70; First Sec., UK Mission to UN, NY, 1970-72; FCO, 1972-75, Counsellor, 1975. *Recreations:* hill-walking, music. *Address:* c/o Foreign and Commonwealth Office, SW1A 2AH.

SOLLBERGER, Edmond, FBA 1973; Keeper of Western Asiatic Antiquities, The British Museum, since 1974 (Deputy Keeper, 1970-74); *b* 12 Oct. 1920; *s* of W. Sollberger and M.-A. Calavassy; *m* 1949, Ariane Zender; *two d. Educ:* Univ. of Geneva, LicLitt 1945; DLitt 1952. Asst Keeper of Archæology, Musée d'art et d'histoire, Geneva, 1949; Keeper, 1952; Principal Keeper, 1958; Actg-Dir, 1959; Privat-Docent for Sumerian and Akkadian, Faculty of Letters, Univ. of Geneva, 1956-61; Asst Keeper of Western Asiatic Antiquities, The British Museum, 1961. Member: Council and Exec. Ctte, British Sch. of Archaeology in Iraq, 1961; Council of Management, British Inst. of Archæology at Ankara, 1961-70; Council, British Sch. of Archæology, Jerusalem, 1974; Governing Body, SOAS, 1975. Corresp. Mem., German Archæological Inst., 1961. *Publications:* Le Système verbal dans les inscriptions royales présargoniques de Lagash, 1952 (Geneva); Corpus des inscriptions royales présargoniques de Lagash, 1956 (Geneva); Ur Excavations Texts VIII: Royal Inscriptions, 1965 (London); The Business and Administrative Correspondence under the Kings of Ur, 1966 (New York); (with J. R. Kupper) Inscriptions royales sumériennes et akkadiennes, 1971 (Paris); Pre-Sargonic and Sargonic Economic Texts, 1972 (London); numerous articles on Cuneiform and related studies in learned jls; jt editor: Littératures anciennes du Proche Orient, 1963- (Paris); Texts from Cuneiform Sources, 1965- (New York); Cambridge Ancient History, vols I-IV (rev. edn), 1969-. *Address:* 26 Kingfisher Drive, Ham, Richmond, Surrey. *T:* 01-940 4465.

SOLOMON, CBE 1946; pianist; *b* London, 9 Aug. 1902; *m* 1970, Gwendoline Byrne. First public appearance at Queen's Hall at age of eight, June 1910; frequent appearances till 1916 then studied in London and Paris; reappeared in London at Wigmore Hall, Oct. 1921, and has since toured in the British Isles, America, France, Germany, Holland, Italy, Australia, and New Zealand. Hon. LLD St Andrews; Hon. MusD Cantab. *Recreations:* golf, bridge, motoring. *Address:* 16 Blenheim Road, NW8.

SOLOMON, (Alan) Peter; His Honour Judge Solomon; a Circuit Judge, since 1973; *b* 6 July 1923; *s* of late Jacob Ovid Solomon, Manchester; *m* 1st, 1954, Deirdre Anne Punter (marr. diss. 1969); *one d*; 2nd, 1973, Gloria Sophia, *d* of Samuel Turower; *one d. Educ:* Mill Hill Sch.; Lincoln College, Oxford; MA. Served War 1942-46, Fleet Air Arm, Petty Officer Airman. Called to Bar, Inner Temple, 1949; practised South-Eastern circuit. *Publications:* poetry: The Lunatic, Balance, in Keats

Prize Poems, 1973. *Recreations:* the turf, travel, poetry, burgundy. *Address:* The Crown Court, Middlesex Guildhall, Parliament Square, Westminster, SW1. *Club:* Garrick.

SOLOMON, Sir David (Arnold), Kt 1973; MBE 1944; *b* 13 Nov. 1907; *s* of Richard Solomon and Sarah Annie Solomon (*née* Simpson); *m* 1935, Marjorie Miles; *two s one d. Educ:* Leys Sch., Cambridge; Liverpool Univ. Qualified a Solicitor, 1933; became Mem. Liverpool Stock Exchange, 1935. Served War of 1939-45, RAF (MBE). Practised as a Stockbroker until retirement, March 1969. Chairman: Liverpool RHB, 1968-73; Community Health Council, SE Cumbria, 1973-76. *Recreation:* music. *Address:* Short Nab, Storrs Park, Windermere, Cumbria LA23 3JG. *T:* Windermere 3434. *Club:* Athenæum (Liverpool).

SOLOMON, Edwin, CBE 1972; QPM 1967; DL; Chief Constable, West Midlands Constabulary, 1967-74; *b* 20 Sept. 1914; *s* of Richard and Jane Solomon, Co. Durham; *m* 1942, Susan Clarke; *two s. Educ:* The Grammar Sch., Chester-le-Street. Joined Metropolitan Police as Constable, 1934; served through ranks to Supt; Dep. Chief Constable, Newcastle upon Tyne, 1956; Chief Constable, Walsall County Borough, 1964. DL Staffs, 1969. *Recreations:* walking, fishing, gardening. *Address:* Catalan Cottage, Gibralter Lane, Dunsley Road, Kinver, near Stourbridge, West Midlands. *T:* Kinver 2047.

SOLOMON, Dr Patrick Vincent Joseph; High Commissioner for Trinidad and Tobago in London, 1971-76, concurrently Ambassador for Trinidad and Tobago to Switzerland, France, Germany, Austria, Luxembourg, Denmark, Norway, Sweden, Italy, Netherlands and Finland; President of Assembly, IMCO, 1976-77; *b* 12 April 1910; *s* of late Charles William Solomon and late Euphemia Alexia (*née* Payne); *m*; *two s*; *m* 1974, Mrs Leslie Richardson, *widow* of late William A. Richardson, Trinidad and Tobago. *Educ:* Tranquility Boys' Sch.; St Mary's Coll., Trinidad; Island Science Scholar, 1928; studied Medicine at Belfast and Edinburgh Univs, graduating in 1934. Practised medicine in Scotland, Ireland and Wales, to 1939; Leeward Island Medical Service, 1939-42; practised medicine in Trinidad, 1943-. Entered Politics, 1944. Elected: MLC, 1946-50 and 1956; MP (MHR) 1961; Minister of: Education, 1956-60; Home Affairs, 1960-64; External Affairs, 1964-66; Dep. Prime Minister, 1962-66; Dep. Political Leader of People's Nat. Movement, 1956-66; Permanent Rep. of Trinidad and Tobago to the United Nations, NY, 1966-71; Vice-Pres., UN General Assembly, 21st Session, 1966; Chm., UN Fourth Cttee, 23rd Session, 1968; Trinidad and Tobago Rep., Special Cttee on Apartheid, 1966-71, and Special Cttee of 24 on question of Decolonization; Mem. Preparatory Cttees concerning: celebration of Tenth Anniversary of Declaration on granting of Independence to Colonial Countries and Peoples (Resolution 1514, xv), 1968 and 1969; Commemoration of 25th Anniversary of United Nations. Is a Roman Catholic. *Recreations:* bridge, fishing. *Address:* c/o Ministry of External Affairs, Knowsley, Queen's Park West, Port of Spain, Trinidad.

SOLOMON, Peter; *see* Solomon, A. P.

SOLOMONS, Prof. David; Professor of Accounting in the University of Pennsylvania (Wharton School), USA, since 1959, Chairman of Accounting Department, 1969-75, designated Arthur Young Professor, 1974; *b* London, 11 Oct. 1912; *e s* of Louis Solomons and Hannah Solomons (*née* Isaacs); *m* 1945, Kate Miriam (*née* Goldschmidt); *one s one d. Educ:* Hackney Downs Sch., London, E8; London School of Economics. BCom (London) 1932; DSc (Econ.) (London), 1966. Chartered accountant, 1936; engaged in professional accountancy until Sept. 1939. Enlisted in ranks on outbreak of war; 2nd Lieut, RASC, 1941; Temp. Captain, 1942; Petrol Supply Officer, HQ 88 Area (Tobruk), 1942; prisoner-of-war in Italy and Germany, 1942-45. Lectr in Accounting, LSE, 1946; Reader in Accounting, Univ. of London, 1949-55; Prof. of Accounting, University of Bristol, 1955-59. Visiting Assoc. Prof., University of California, 1954; Prof. at Institut pour l'Etude des Méthodes de Direction de l'Enterprise (IMEDE), Lausanne, 1963-64; Director of Research, Amer. Accounting Assoc., 1968-70, Pres., 1977; Vis. Erskine Fellow, Univ. of Canterbury, NZ, 1976. Mem., AICPA Study on Establishment of Accounting Principles, 1971-72; directed (UK) Adv. Bd of Accountancy Educn Long-range Enquiry into Educn and Trg for Accountancy Profession, 1972-74. AICPA Award for Notable Contribution to Accounting Literature, 1969. *Publications:* Divisional Performance: Measurement and Control, 1965; ed and contrib. to Studies in Cost Analysis, 1968; Prospectus for a Profession, 1974; articles in Economic Jl, Economica, Jl of Business, Accounting Review, Accountancy, etc. *Address:* 205 Elm Avenue, Swarthmore, Pa 19081, USA. *T:* 215-KI 4-8193.

SOLOVEYTCHIK, George M. de, MA (Oxon); author, journalist, and lecturer; *b* St Petersburg, Russia; *s* of late Michael A. de Soloveytchik, Chairman and Managing Director of the Siberian Bank of Commerce, and *g s* of Founder thereof; Resident in Great Britain since 1919 and naturalised British subject, 1934; unmarried. *Educ:* St Catharine's and The Reformation Schools, Petrograd; Queen's Coll., Oxford; Paris and Berlin Universities. Has travelled extensively all over Europe since tender age of one. Escaped from Soviet Russia to England, 1918; began to write and lecture while still at Oxford; frequent free-lance contributor to leading British and overseas newspapers and periodicals chiefly on international affairs, history and biography, Editor, *Economic Review*, 1926-27; Foreign Editor, *Financial Times*, 1938-39; business in City of London, 1925-36; Director of Publicity, Internat. Colonial Exhibition, Paris, 1931; Special adviser to exiled Belgian Govt in London, 1941-45; official lectr to HM Forces, 1940-45; delivered addresses to American Academy of Political and Social Science, and at Princeton, Yale, etc, 1944; numerous lecture tours in USA, Canada and Europe since 1946; special mission to Scandinavian countries on behalf of UNESCO, 1947; Visiting Lecturer, Graduate Inst. of International Studies, Geneva Univ., 1948-56, also at School of Economics, St Gallen. FJI; Member: RIIA, 1934-74; American Academy of Political and Social Science, 1944-74; Hon. Member International Mark Twain Society, USA. Officier, Légion d'Honneur; Kt Comdr 1st cl. with Star, Lion of Finland; Comdr Leopold II; Comdr, White Lion; 1st cl. Kt of the Vasa; 1st cl. Kt of St Olav; 1st cl. Kt of the Dannebrog; Officier Ordre de la Couronne, Order of Orange-Nassau, Officier, White Rose of Finland, Danish Liberation Medal, etc. *Publications:* The Naked Year (Editor), New York, 1928; Ivar Kreuger-Financier, 1933; Potemkin-A Picture of Catherine's Russia, 1938; Ships of the Allies, 1942; Peace or Chaos, 1944; Russia in Perspective, 1946; Great Britain since the War (in Swedish), 1947; Switzerland in Perspective, 1954; Leu and Co.: Two Centuries of History in the Life of a Swiss Bank, 1955; Benelux, 1957; chapter on How Switzerland is really governed, in Swiss Panorama, 1963 (new edn 1974); chapters on Russia in Universal Encyclopædia. *Recreations:* travel, theatre, music, Russian ballet, art; also studying human eccentricities and foibles. *Address:* 26a North Audley Street, W1. *T:* 01-629 6208. *Club:* Savage.

SOLTI, Sir Georg, KBE 1971 (CBE (Hon.) 1968); Music Director, Chicago Symphony Orchestra, since 1970; *b* Budapest, 21 Oct. 1912; adopted British nationality, 1972; *m* 1st, 1946, Hedwig Oeschli; 2nd, 1967, Ann Valerie Pitts; two *d*. *Educ:* High School of Music, Budapest. Studied with Kodály, Bartók, and Donhnányi. Conductor and pianist, State Opera, Budapest, 1930-39; first prize, as pianist, Concours Internationale, Geneva, 1942; Musical Director, Munich State Opera, 1946-52; Musical Director, Frankfurt Opera, and Permanent Conductor, Museums Concerts, Frankfurt, 1952-61; Musical Director: Covent Garden Opera Co., 1961-71; Orchestre de Paris, 1971-75. Guest Conductor: Berlin, Salzburg, Paris, London (first conducted London Philharmonic Orchestra, 1947; Covent Garden début, 1959), Glyndebourne Festival, Edinburgh Festival, San Francisco, New York, Los Angeles, Chicago, etc. Has made numerous recordings (many of which have received international awards or prizes, incl. Grand Prix Mondiale du Disque (8 times)). Hon. DMus: Leeds, 1971; Oxon, 1972; Yale Univ., 1974. *Address:* Chalet Haut Près, Villars s. Ollon, Switzerland. *Club:* Athenæum.

SOLZHENITSYN, Alexander Isayevitch; author; Hon. Fellow, Hoover Institution on War, Revolution and Peace, 1975; *b* 11 Dec. 1918; *m* ; three *s*. *Educ:* Univ. of Rostov (degree in maths and physics); Moscow Inst. of History, Philosophy and Literature (correspondence course). Joined Army, 1941; grad. from Artillery School, 1942; in comd artillery battery and served at front until 1945 (twice decorated); sentenced to eight years' imprisonment, 1945, released, 1953; exile in Siberia, 1953-56; officially rehabilitated, 1957; taught and wrote in Ryazan and Moscow; expelled from Soviet Union, 1974. Member Union of Soviet writers, 1962, expelled 1969; Member Amer. Acad. of Arts and Sciences, 1969. Awarded Nobel Prize for Literature, 1970. *Publications:* One Day in the Life of Ivan Denisovich, 1962, new edn 1970, filmed 1971; An Incident at Krechetovka Station, and Matryona's House (publ. US as We Never Make Mistakes, 1969), 1963; For the Good of the Cause, 1964; The First Circle, 1968; Cancer Ward, part 1, 1968, part 2, 1969 (Prix du Meilleur Livre Etranger, Paris); The Love Girl and the Innocent, 1969; Stories and Prose Poems, 1970; August 1914, 1972; One Word of Truth: the Nobel speech on literature, 1972; The Gulag Archipelago: an experiment in literary investigation, vol. 1, 1973, vol. 2, 1974, vol. 3, 1976; A Calf Banged its Head against an Oak (autobiog.), 1975; Lenin in Zurich, 1975; Prussian Nights (poem), 1977. *Address:* c/o Harper & Row Inc., 10 East 53rd Street, New York, NY 10022, USA.

SOMARE, Rt. Hon. Michael Thomas, PC 1977; first Prime Minister of Papua New Guinea, since Sept. 1975; *b* 9 April 1936; *m* 1965, Veronica Somare; three *s* two *d*. *Educ:* Sogeri Secondary Sch.; Admin. Coll. Teaching, 1956-62; Asst Area Educn Officer, Madang, 1962-63; Broadcasts Officer, Dept of Information and Extension Services, Wewack, 1963-66; Journalism, 1966-68. Member for E Sepik Region (Nat. Parl.) House of Assembly, 1968-; Parly Leader, Pangu Pati, 1968-; First Chief Minister, 1972-75; Dep. Chm., Exec. Council, 1972-73, Chm., 1973-. Mem., Second Select Cttee on Constitutional Develt, 1968-72; Mem. Adv. Cttee, Australian Broadcasting Commission. *Address:* Office of the Prime Minister, PO Box 2501, Konedobu, Papua New Guinea. *T:* 44501; (home) Karan, Murik Lakes, East Sepik, Papua New Guinea.

SOMERFIELD, Stafford William; editorial consultant, since 1970; *b* 9 Jan. 1911; *m* 1st, 1933, Gertrude Camfield (marr. diss. 1951); two *d*; 2nd, 1951, Elizabeth Montgomery (*d* 1977). *Educ:* Ashleigh Road School, Barnstaple. Exeter Express and Echo, Bristol Evening World, Daily Telegraph, 1934-39; News Chronicle, 1939, until outbreak of War. Rifleman, Queen's Westminsters, 1939-40; Major, Gloucestershire Regt. 1945. News of the World: Features Editor, Asst Editor, Northern Editor, Dep. Editor; Editor, 1960-70. *Publication:* John George Haigh, 1950. *Recreation:* pedigree dogs. *Address:* Woodlands, Swain Road, St Michaels, Tenterden, Kent. *T:* Tenterden 2544. *Clubs:* Kennel, Press.

SOMERLEYTON, 3rd Baron *cr* 1916; **Savile William Francis Crossley;** Bt 1863; DL; farmer; *b* 17 Sept. 1928; *er s* of 2nd Baron Somerleyton, MC; *S* father, 1959; *m* 1963, Belinda Maris Loyd, *d* of late Vivian Loyd and of Mrs Gerald Critchley; one *s* four *d*. *Educ:* Eton Coll. Captain Coldstream Guards, 1948; retired, 1956. Royal Agricultural Coll., Cirencester, 1958-59; farming, 1959-. DL Suffolk, 1964. *Heir: s* Hon. Hugh Francis Savile Crossley, *b* 27 Sept. 1971. *Address:* Somerleyton Hall, Lowestoft, Suffolk. *T:* Lowestoft 730308. *Club:* Turf.

SOMERS, 8th Baron *cr* 1784; **John Patrick Somers Cocks;** Bt 1772; *b* 30 April 1907; *o s* of 7th Baron and Mary Benita (*d* 1950), *d* of late Major Luther M. Sabin, United States Army; *S* father, 1953; *m* 1st, 1935, Barbara Marianne (*d* 1959), *d* of Charles Henry Southall, Norwich; 2nd, 1961, Dora Helen, *d* of late John Mountfort. *Educ:* privately; Royal College of Music, London. 2nd Music Master, Westonbirt School, 1935-38; Director of Music, Epsom Coll., 1949-53; Prof. of Composition and Theory, RCM, 1967-77. BMus, ARCM. *Publications:* Three Sketches for Oboe and Piano; (song) New Year's Eve; The Song of the Redeemed (for chorus and orchestra); Sonatina for Oboe and Piano, Four Psalms for two-part Choir; Organ Sonata. *Heir: cousin* Philip Sebastian Somers-Cocks, *b* 4 Jan. 1948. *Address:* 35 Links Road, Epsom, Surrey. *Club:* Royal Commonwealth Society.

SOMERS, Finola, Lady, CBE 1950; *b* 1896; *d* of late Captain Bertram Meeking, 10th Hussars, and late Mrs Herbert Johnson; *m* 1921, 6th Baron Somers, KCMG, DSO, MC (*d* 1944); one *d*. *Educ:* home. Chief Commissioner, Girl Guides' Association, 1943-49. *Address:* Garden Cottage, Eastnor, Herefordshire. *T:* Ledbury 2305.

SOMERSCALES, Thomas Lawrence, CBE 1970; General Secretary, Joint Committee of the Order of St John of Jerusalem and the British Red Cross Society, since 1960; *b* 1 July 1913; *s* of Wilfred Somerscales; *m* 1941, Ann Teresa, *d* of Robert Victor Kearney; three *s* one *d*. *Educ:* Riley High Sch., Hull. FCA 1939. Finance Sec., Jt Cttee, OStJ and BRCS, 1953-60. Mem., Adv. Council, ITA, 1964-67. *Address:* 17 Hamilton Way, Finchley, N3.

SOMERSET, family name of **Duke of Beaufort** and of **Baron Raglan.**

SOMERSET, 18th Duke of *cr* 1546; **Percy Hamilton Seymour;** Bt 1611; DL; Major, Wilts Regt, retired; *b* 27 Sept. 1910; *e surv. s* of 17th Duke of Somerset, DSO, OBE, and Edith Mary (*d* 1962), *d* of W. Parker, JP, Whittington Hall, Derbyshire; *S* father, 1954; *m* 1951, Gwendoline Collette (Jane), 2nd *d* of late Major J. C. C. Thomas and Mrs Thomas; two *s* one *d*. *Educ:* Blundell's Sch., Tiverton; Clare Coll., Cambridge. BA 1933. DL Wiltshire, 1960. *Heir: s* Lord Seymour, *qv*. *Address:* Maiden Bradley, Warminster, Wilts. *Clubs:* MCC, Surrey CC, British Automobile Racing.

SOMERSET, Sir Henry Beaufort, Kt 1966; CBE 1961; *b* 21 May 1906; *s* of Henry St John Somerset; *m* 1930, Patricia Agnes Strickland; two *d*. *Educ:* St Peter's Coll., Adelaide; Trinity Coll., University of Melbourne; MSc 1928. Chairman: Humes Ltd;

Australian Titan Products Pty Ltd; Goliath Portland Cement Co. Ltd; Perpetual Exors Trustees Ltd; Director: Associated Pulp & Paper Mills Ltd (Man. Dir, 1948-70); Electrolytic Zinc Co. of Australasia Ltd. Chancellor, University of Tasmania, 1964-72; Member: Australasian Inst. of Mining and Metallurgy (President, 1958 and 1966); Exec., CSIRO, 1965-74; Council, Nat. Museum of Victoria, 1968-; Pres., Australian Mineral Foundn, 1972-. Hon. DSc Tasmania, 1973. FRACI. *Address:* 193 Domain Road, South Yarra, Victoria 3141, Australia. *Clubs:* Melbourne, Australian (Melbourne); Tasmanian (Hobart).

SOMERSET, Brigadier Hon. Nigel FitzRoy, CBE 1945; DSO; MC; *b* Cefntilla Court, Usk, Monmouthshire, 27 July 1893; 3rd *s* of 3rd Baron Raglan, GBE, CB; *m* 1922, Phyllis Marion Offley Irwin, Western Australia; one *s* one *d. Educ:* King William's Coll., IOM; RMC Sandhurst. Served France with 1st Bn Gloucestershire Regt, 12 Aug. 1914 till wounded at the Battle of the Aisne, 15 Sept. 1914; 3 Dec. 1914, till wounded at Cuinchy, 12 May 1915; Mesopotamia, Oct. 1916-May 1919, comdg 14th Light Armoured Motor Battery (despatches thrice, DSO, MC); Bt Majority on promotion to Subst. Captain, 1918; Afghan War, 1919, with Armoured Motor Brigade (Medal and Clasp); ADC to Governor of South Australia, 1920-22; Assistant Military Secretary, Headquarters, Southern Command, India, 1926-30; Major 1933; Lieut-Colonel Comdg 2nd Bn The Gloucestershire Regt, 1938; served War of 1939-45 comdg 145 Inf. Bde (PoW 1940-45; despatches; CBE); Comdg Kent Sub District, 1946-47; Brig. Special Appt Germany, 1947-48; retired pay, 1949. *Address:* 18 St Anne's Crescent, Lewes, Sussex.

SOMERVILLE, David, CB 1971; Under-Secretary, Department of Health and Social Security, 1968-77; *b* 27 Feb. 1917; *e s* of late Rev. David Somerville and of Euphemia Somerville; *m* 1950, Patricia Amy Johnston; two *s* two *d. Educ:* George Watson's Coll.; Fettes Coll.; Edinburgh Univ.; Christ Church, Oxford. Served with Army, 1940-45; Major, Royal Artillery. Entered Civil Service as Asst Principal, Ministry of Health, 1946; Cabinet Office, 1953-55; Ministry of Health, 1956; Under-Secretary, Min. of Health, 1963-67. *Recreations:* golf, gardening. *Address:* Conifers, Grange Road, Leatherhead, Surrey. *T:* Ashtead 75642. *Club:* Effingham Golf.
See also R. M. Somerville.

SOMERVILLE, Jane, MD; FRCP; Consultant Physician, National Heart Hospital, since 1974; Hon. Consultant Physician, Hospital for Sick Children, Great Ormond Street, since 1968; *b* 24 Jan. 1933; *d* of Joseph Bertram Platnauer and Pearl Ashton; *m* 1957, Dr Walter Somerville, *qv*; three *s* one *d. Educ:* Queen's Coll., London; Guy's Hosp., London Univ. MB, BS (Treasurer's Gold Medal for Clin. Surg.) 1955; MD 1966. MRCS 1955; FRCP 1973 (LRCP 1955, MRCP 1957). FACC 1972. Guy's Hospital: Ho. Phys., Dept of Med., 1955; Ho. Surg. under Lord Brock, 1956; Med. Registrar, 1956-58; Registrar, Nat. Heart Hosp., 1958-59; First Asst to Dr Paul Wood, 1959-63, Sen. Lectr 1964-74, Inst. of Cardiol.; Hon. Cons. Phys., Nat. Heart Hosp., 1967-74. 6 months' sabbat. leave, Neonatal Unit, UCH, 1973; Lectr in Cardiovascular Disease, Turin Univ., 1973. Vis. Prof. and Guest Lectr, Europe, ME, USA, Mexico, S America, 1968-. Mem. Council, and Scientific Sec., Assoc. Europ. Pæd. Cardiol., 1975-; Member: British Cardiac Soc.; Assoc. Europ. Pæd. Cardiol.; Jt Cttee on Higher Med. Trng (Council Mem. and Org. Sec., 12th Annual Meeting, London, 1974); British Ped. Soc.; Anglo-Argentine Soc.; Hon. Mem., Argentine Pæd. Soc. Mem. RSocMed. Governor, Queen's Coll., London. Woman of the Year, 1968. *Publications:* numerous contribs to med. lit. on heart disease in children, congenital heart disease and results of cardiac surgery; chapters in Paul Wood's Diseases of Heart and Circulation (3rd edn). *Recreations:* collecting stone eggs, pictures, porcelain soldiers; chess, roof gardening. *Address:* 30 York House, Upper Montagu Street, W1H 1FR. *T:* 01-262 2144.

SOMERVILLE, John Arthur Fownes, CB 1977; CBE 1964; an Under-Secretary, Government Communications Headquarters, since 1969; *b* 5 Dec. 1917; *s* of late Admiral of the Fleet Sir James Fownes Somerville, GCB, GBE, DSO; *m* 1945, Julia Elizabeth Payne; one *s* two *d. Educ:* RNC Dartmouth. Midshipman 1936; Sub-Lieut 1938; Lieut 1940; Lieut-Comdr 1945; retd 1950. Govt Communications Headquarters, 1950-. *Recreation:* walking. *Address:* Hoefield House, The Leigh, Gloucester. *T:* Coombe Hill 281. *Club:* Army and Navy.

SOMERVILLE, Mrs (Katherine) Lilian, CMG 1971; OBE 1958; FMA 1962; Director, Fine Arts Department, British Council, 1948-70; *b* 7 Oct. 1905; *d* of Captain Arthur George Tillard and Emily Katherine Close-Brooks; *m* 1928, Horace Somerville (*d* 1959); one *d. Educ:* Abbot's Hill; Slade School of Art, London.

Painted until war. Joined British Council, 1941. Fellow, UCL, 1973. Hon. Dr, RCA, 1972. *Address:* The Studio, 16a Hill Road, NW8 9QG. *T:* 01-286 1087. *Club:* Institute of Contemporary Arts.

SOMERVILLE, Sir Robert, KCVO 1961 (CVO 1953); MA; FSA; FRHistS; Clerk of the Council of the Duchy of Lancaster, 1952-70; *b* 5 June 1906; *s* of late Robert Somerville, FRSE, Dunfermline; *m* 1932, Marie-Louise Cornelia Bergené (*d* 1976); one *d. Educ:* Fettes; St John's Coll., Cambridge (1st cl. Class. Tripos, 1929); Edinburgh Univ. Entered Duchy of Lancaster Office, 1930; Ministry of Shipping, 1940; Chief Clerk, Duchy of Lancaster, 1945; Hon. Research Asst, History of Medicine, UCL, 1935-38; Chairman: Council, British Records Assoc., 1957-67 (Hon. Secretary, 1947-56); London Record Soc.; Member: Advisory Council on Public Records, 1959-64; Royal Commn on Historical MSS, 1966-; Corr. Member, Indian Historical Records Commn. Alexander Medallist, Royal Historical Society, 1940. *Publications:* History of the Duchy of Lancaster, 2 vols, 1953, 1970; The Savoy, 1960; Handlist of Record Publications, 1951; Duchy of Lancaster Office-Holders from 1603, 1972; (joint editor) John of Gaunt's Register, 1937; contribs to Chambers's Encyclopædia, historical journals, etc. *Address:* 15 Foxes Dale, Blackheath, SE3.

SOMERVILLE, Maj.-Gen. Ronald Macaulay, CB 1974; OBE 1963; General Manager, Scottish Special Housing Association, since 1975; *b* 2 July 1919; 2nd *s* of late Rev. David Somerville and of Euphemia Somerville; *m* 1947, Jean McEwen Balderston; no *c. Educ:* George Watson's Coll., Edinburgh. Joined TA, 1939; commnd RA, 1940; regtl and Staff War Service in UK, NW Europe and Far East, 1939-45 (MBE, despatches, 1945); psc 1944; jssc 1956; comd Maiwand Battery, Cyprus Emergency, 1957-59 (despatches, 1958); CO 4th Light Regt RA, 1963-65; Borneo Emergency, 1965; CRA 51st (H) Div., 1965-66; idc 1967; DQMG, BAOR, 1968-70; GOC Yorks District, 1970-72; Vice-QMG, MoD, 1972-74; Chm., Logistic Reorganisation Cttee, 1974-75; retd 1975. Hon. Col, 3rd Bn Yorkshire Volunteers, 1972-77; Col Comdt, RA, 1974-. Comr, Royal Hospital Chelsea, 1972-74; Chm., RA Council for Scotland, 1975-. MBIM 1974. Kt Officer, Order of Orange Nassau, with Swords, 1946. *Recreations:* golf, gardening, fishing. *Address:* 6 Magdala Mews, Edinburgh EH12 5BX. *T:* 031-346 0371; Bynack Mhor, Boat of Garten, Inverness-shire. *T:* Boat of Garten 245. *Club:* New (Edinburgh).
See also David Somerville.

SOMERVILLE, Most Rev. Thomas David; *see* New Westminster, Archbishop of.

SOMERVILLE, Walter, MD, FRCP; Physician to Department of Cardiology, Middlesex Hospital, since 1954; to Cardiac Surgical Unit, Harefield Hospital, since 1952; Lecturer in Cardiology, Middlesex Hospital Medical School, since 1954; Consultant in Cardiology to the Army, since 1963; Hon. Civil Consultant in Cardiology to Royal Air Force, Civil Aviation Authority, and Royal Hospital, Chelsea, since 1963, to Association of Naval Officers, since 1960; to King Edward VII Convalescent Home for Officers, Osborne, since 1970; *b* 2 Oct. 1913; *s* of late Patrick and Catherine Somerville, Dublin; *m* 1957, Jane Platnauer (*see* Jane Somerville); three *s* one *d. Educ:* Belvedere Coll., Dublin; University College, Dublin. House appts, Mater Hosp., Dublin, 1937; out-patients Assistant, Brompton Hosp. and Chelsea Chest Clinic, 1938-39; served in War 1939-45, Lt-Col RAMC 1944. Fellow in Med., Mass General Hosp., Boston, 1946; Registrar, British Postgraduate Med. School, Hammersmith, 1947; studied in Paris, Stockholm and Univ. of Michigan, 1948; Fellow in Medicine, Peter Bent Brigham Hosp. and Boston and Harvard Med. Sch., 1949; Med. Registrar, Nat. Heart Hosp. and Inst. of Cardiology, 1951; Sen. Med. Registrar, Middlesex Hosp., 1951-54. Editor, British Heart Journal, 1973-; Editl Bd, Postgrad. Medical Journal, 1960-; Pres., British Cardiac Soc., 1976-; former Pres., British Acad. of Forensic Sciences; Mem., Assoc. of Physicians of Great Britain and Ireland and other socs; Corr. Member: Colombian Soc. of Cardiology; Chilean Soc. of Cardiology; Fellow, Amer. Coll. of Cardiology. Officer, Legion of Merit, USA, 1945. *Publications:* (ed) Paul Wood's Diseases of the Heart and Circulation (3rd edn), 1968; various articles on cardiovascular subjects in British and American journals. *Address:* 149 Harley Street, W1. *T:* 01-935 4444; 30 York House, Upper Montagu Street, W1H 1FR. *T:* 01-262 2144.

SOMES, Michael (George), CBE 1959; Principal Repetiteur, Royal Ballet, Covent Garden; *b* 28 Sept. 1917; British; *m* 1956, Deirdre Annette Dixon (*d* 1959). *Educ:* Huish's Grammar Sch., Taunton, Somerset. Started dancing at Sadler's Wells, 1934; first important rôle in Horoscope, 1938; Leading Male Dancer,

Royal Ballet, Covent Garden, 1951-68; Asst Director, 1963-70. *Recreation:* music.

SOMMER, André D.; *see* Dupont-Sommer.

SONDES, 5th Earl *cr* 1880; **Henry George Herbert Milles-Lade;** Baron Sondes, 1760; Viscount Throwley, 1880; *b* 1 May 1940; *o s* of 4th Earl Sondes, and Pamela (*d* 1967), *d* of Col H. McDougall; *S* father, 1970; *m* 1968, Primrose Creswell (marr. diss. 1969), *d* of late Lawrence Stopford Llewellyn Cotter; *m* 1976, Sissy Fürstin zu Salm-Reifferscheidt-Raitz. *Recreations:* shooting, skiing. *Address:* Stringman's Farm, Faversham, Kent. *T:* Chilham 336.

SONDHEIM, Stephen Joshua; domposer-lyricist; *b* 22 March 1930; *s* of Herbert Sondheim and Janet (*née* Fox). *Educ:* Willisms Coll. (BA 1950). Lyrics: West Side Story, 1957; Gypsy, 1959; Do I Hear a Waltz?, 1965. Music and Lyrics: A Funny Thing Happened on the Way to the Forum, 1962; Anyone Can Whistle, 1964; Company, 1970; Follies, 1971; A Little Night Music, 1973; Pacific Overtures, 1976. Pres., Dramatists Guild, 1973-. Hon. Doctorate, Willisms Coll., 1971. *Publications:* (book and vocal score): West Side Story, 1958; Gypsy, 1960; A Funny Thing Happened on the Way to the Forum, 1963; Anyone Can Whistle, 1965; Do I Hear a Waltz?, 1966; Company, 1971; Follies, 1972; A Little Night Music, 1974; Pacific Overtures, 1977. *Address:* 246 East 49th Street, New York, NY 10017, USA.

SONDHEIMER, Professor Ernst Helmut, MA, ScD; Professor of Mathematics, Westfield College, University of London, since 1960; *b* 8 Sept. 1923; *er s* of Max and Ida Sondheimer; *m* 1950, Janet Harrington Matthews, PhD; one *s* one *d. Educ:* University College School; Trinity Coll., Cambridge. Smith's Prize, 1947; Fellow of Trinity Coll., 1948-52; Research Fellow, H. H. Wills Physical Lab., University of Bristol, 1948-49; Research Associate, Massachusetts Inst. of Technology, 1949-50; Lecturer in Mathematics, Imperial College of Science and Technology, 1951-54; Reader in Applied Mathematics, Queen Mary Coll., Univ. of London, 1954-60. Vis. Research Asst Prof. of Physics, Univ. of Illinois, USA, 1958-59; Vis. Prof. of Theoretical Physics, University of Cologne, 1967. Member of Council, Queen Elizabeth Coll., London. *Publications:* Green's Functions for Solid State Physicists (with S. Doniach), 1974; papers on the electron theory of metals. *Recreation:* mountaineering. *Address:* 51 Cholmeley Crescent, Highgate, N6. *T:* 01-340 6607. *Club:* Alpine.
See also Prof. Franz Sondheimer.

SONDHEIMER, Prof. Franz, FRS 1967; PhD (London), DIC; Royal Society Research Professor, University College, London, since 1967; *b* 17 May 1926; *yr s* of Max and Ida Sondheimer; *m* 1958, Betty Jane Moss; one step *d* (decd). *Educ:* Highgate School; Imperial College of Science, London. Research Fellow, Harvard University, 1949-52; Associate Director of Research, Syntex SA, Mexico City, 1952-56; Vice-President, Research, 1961-63; Head of Organic Chemistry Department, Weizmann Institute of Science, Rehovoth, Israel, 1956-64; Rebecca and Israel Sieff Professor of Organic Chemistry, 1960-64; Royal Soc. Research Prof., Univ. of Cambridge, 1964-67; Fellow of Churchill Coll., Cambridge, 1964-67; Vis. Prof., Ohio State Univ., 1958, Rockefeller Univ., NY, 1972; Lectures: Andrews, Univ. of New South Wales, 1962; Edward Clark Lee, Univ. of Chicago, 1962; Tilden, Chem. Soc., 1965; Pacific Coast, 1969. Israel Prize in the Exact Sciences, 1960; Corday-Morgan Medal and Prize, Chem. Soc., 1961; Adolf-von-Bayer Medal, German Chem. Soc., 1965; Synthetic Organic Chemistry Award, Chem. Soc., 1973; Award for creative work in synthetic organic chemistry, Amer. Chem. Soc., 1976. For. Mem., German Acad. of Sciences, Leopoldina, 1966. *Publications:* scientific papers in chemical jls. *Recreations:* classical music, travel. *Address:* Chemistry Dept, University College, 20 Gordon Street, WC1H 0AJ. *T:* 01-387 7050; 43 Green Street, W1Y 3FJ. *T:* 01-629 2816.
See also Prof. E. H. Sondheimer.

SONNEBORN, Prof. Tracy Morton; Distinguished Professor of Zoology, Indiana University, Bloomington, Indiana, 1953-76, now Emeritus; *b* 19 Oct. 1905; *s* of Lee and Daisy (Bamberger) Sonneborn; *m* 1929, Ruth Meyers; two *s. Educ:* Johns Hopkins Univ., Baltimore. Johns Hopkins University: Fellow, Nat. Research Coun., USA, 1928-30; Research Asst, 1930-31; Research Associate, 1931-33; Associate in Zoology, 1933-39; Indiana University: Associate Prof. in Zoology, 1939-43; Prof. of Zoology, 1943-53; Actg Chm., Div. of Biological Sciences, 1963-64. Foreign Mem., Royal Soc., London, 1964. Hon. Member: French Soc. of Protozoology, 1965; Genetics Soc. of Japan, 1976. Hon. DSc: Johns Hopkins Univ., 1957; Northwestern Univ., 1975; Univ. of Geneva, 1975. Newcomb-Cleveland

Research Prize, Amer. Assoc. for Advancement of Science, 1946; Kimber Genetics Award, Nat. Acad. of Sciences, USA, 1959; Mendel Medal, Czechoslovak Acad. of Sciences, 1965. *Publications:* The Control of Human Heredity and Evolution, 1965; numerous chapters in books and articles in scientific jls on genetics, cell biology, micro-organisms. *Address:* 1305 Maxwell Lane, Bloomington, Indiana 47401, USA. *T:* Area 812-336-5796.

SOOTHILL, Ronald Gray; Chairman, Turner and Newall Ltd, 1959-67, Hon. President, 1967-73; *b* 19 Aug. 1898; *o s* of late Rev. Alfred Soothill, BA, Headmaster of Ashville College, Harrogate, and late H. E. Soothill (*née* Gray); *m* 1926, Thelma, *e d* of late Edwin James Bird. *Educ:* Ashville College, Harrogate; Mill Hill; Jesus Coll., Cambridge (MA). Officer in Royal Artillery, 1917-18. Cadbury Bros Ltd, 1922-28; Turner and Newall Ltd since 1928: Dir, 1942-69; Jt Man. Dir, 1949; Dep. Chm., 1958. Director: District Bank Ltd, 1959-69; Royal Insurance Co. Ltd, 1960-71; Liverpool & London & Globe Insurance Co. Ltd, 1960-71; London & Lancashire Insurance Co. Ltd, 1962-71; Tube Investments Ltd, 1963-68; William Mallinson and Sons Ltd, 1957-70. Mem., Cttee of Inquiry into Shipping, 1967-70; Mem. Ct, Manchester Univ., 1959-72; Chm. of Governors, Ashville Coll., Harrogate, 1957-75; Vice-Pres., Nat. Assoc. for Care and Resettlement of Offenders. *Address:* Manor Beeches, Maids Moreton, Buckingham. *T:* Buckingham 2014. *Club:* Bath.

SOPER, family name of **Baron Soper.**

SOPER, Baron, *cr* 1965 (Life Peer); **Rev. Donald Oliver Soper,** MA Cantab; PhD (London); Methodist Minister; President of the Methodist Conference, 1953, Superintendent West London Mission, Kingsway Hall, since 1936; *b* 31 Jan. 1903; *s* of late Ernest and Caroline Soper; *m* 1929, Marie Dean, *e* of late Arthur Dean, Norbury; four *d. Educ:* Aske's School, Hatcham; St Catharine's College, Cambridge University; Wesley House, Cambridge; London School of Economics, London University. Hon. Fellow, St Catharine's Coll., Cambridge, 1966. Minister, South London Mission, 1926-29; Central London Mission, 1929-36. Chm., Shelter, 1974-. President, League against Cruel Sports. *Publications:* Christianity and its Critics; Popular Fallacies about the Christian Faith; Will Christianity Work?; Practical Christianity To-day; Questions and Answers in Ceylon; All His Grace (Methodist Lent Book for 1957); It is hard to work for God; The Advocacy of the Gospel; Tower Hill 12.30; Aflame with Faith; Christian Politics. *Recreations:* music and most games. *Address:* Kingsway Hall, WC2B 6TA.

SOPER, Dr Frederick George, CBE 1950; FRSNZ 1949; FRIC 1936; Hon. FNZIC 1965; PhD 1924; DSc (Wales) 1928; Vice-Chancellor, University of Otago, Dunedin, NZ, 1953-63, retired; Emeritus Professor since 1964; Professor of Chemistry, University of Otago, 1936-53; *b* 5 April 1898; *m* 1st, 1921, Frances Mary Gwendolen Richardson; one *s* one *d* ; 2nd, 1938, Eileen Louise Service. *Educ:* St Asaph Grammar Sch.; University College of North Wales, 1920; Lecturer, 1921-36. Director NZ Woollen Mills Research Assoc., 1937-50; Pres. NZ Institute of Chemistry, 1947; Member of Council of Univ. of Otago, 1944-51, 1953-63; Dean of Faculty of Science, 1948-50; Member of Senate, Univ. of NZ, 1946-61. Served RA, 1916-19, and TA. Dep. Dir of Scientific Development (Chemical), DSIR (NZ), 1942-45; Member: Defence Science Advisory Cttee (NZ), 1942-53; NZ Science Deleg. to Roy. Soc. Empire Science Conf., London, 1946; Leader NZ Deleg. to Unesco Conf., Paris, 1951. Mem. NZ Med. Research Council, 1960-65; Vice-Pres., Roy. Soc. of NZ, 1962-63; Chm., NZ Nuffield Advisory Cttee, 1960-72; Pres. Dunedin Public Art Gallery Coun., 1963-66; Mem. Exec., NZ Wool Research Organisation, 1964-71 (Vice-Chm., 1966-71); Mem. Exec., Wool Industries Research Inst., 1957-68; Mem. UGC Research Cttee, 1964-74. Hon. DSc Otago, 1967. *Publications:* a number of papers in Journal of Chemical Society, mainly on mechanism of chemical reactions. *Recreations:* walking and gardening. *Address:* 6 Howard Street, Macandrew Bay, Dunedin, NZ. *T:* 75.461. *Club:* Fernhill (Dunedin).

SOPER, Dr J. Dewey; naturalist, explorer; Canadian Wildlife Service, Department of Indian Affairs and Northern Development, Ottawa, retired Nov. 1952; *b* Guelph, Ont, 5 May 1893; *m* 1927, C. K. Freeman, Wetaskiwin, Alberta; one *s* one *d. Educ:* Alberta Coll. and Univ. of Alberta, Edmonton. Studied music 6 yrs; then took up science, specialising in ornithology and mammalogy, especially the latter; naturalist to the Canadian Arctic Expedition of 1923, visiting Greenland, Ellesmere, North Devon and Baffin Islands; engaged in biological research and exploration on Baffin Island for the Canadian Government, 1924-26; engaged in biological research, exploration and mapping of Foxe Land, Baffin Island, for Dept of the Interior,

Canada, 1928-29, resulting among other things in the discovery of the mysterious breeding grounds of the Blue Goose, and for Dept of Interior, Lake Harbour region, Baffin Island, 1930-31, and Wood Buffalo Park, Alta, and NWT 1932-34, then transferred as Chief Federal Migratory Bird Officer for the Prairie Provinces. Hon. LLD Univ. Alberta, 1960. *Publications:* The Weasels of Canada; Bird Life in the Alberta Wilds; Mammalian and Avian Fauna of Islay, Alberta; Mammals of Wellington and Waterloo Counties, Ontario; Birds of Wellington and Waterloo Counties, Ontario; Mammals of the Ridout Region, Northern Ontario; A Biological Reconnaissance of Nipissing and Timiskaming Districts, Northern Ontario; A Faunal Investigation of Southern Baffin Island; Discovery of the Breeding Grounds of the Blue Goose; The Blue Goose; Solitudes of the Arctic; Intimate Glimpses of Eskimo Life in Baffin Island; The Lake Harbour Region, Baffin Island; Notes on the Beavers of Wood Buffalo Park; Local Distribution of Eastern Canadian Arctic Birds; History, Range and Home Life of the Northern Bison; Mammals of Wood Buffalo Park; Birds of Wood Buffalo Park and Vicinity; Life History of the Blue Goose; The Mammals of Southern Baffin Island, NWT; Ornithological Results of the Baffin Island Expeditions of 1928-29 and 1930-31, together with more Recent Records; Mammals of the Northern Great Plains along the International Boundary in Canada; Observations on Mammals and Birds in the Rocky Mountains of Alberta; Field Data on the Mammals of Southern Saskatchewan; The Mammals of Manitoba; The Mammals of Alberta; The Mammals of Jasper National Park, Alberta; The Conquest of Pangnirtung Pass; The Mammals of Waterton Lakes National Park, Alberta; Kingnait Pass; Baffin Island; The mysterious West Coast. *Recreations:* water-colour painting, reading and writing. *Address:* 7115 81st Street, Edmonton, Alberta T6C 2T3, Canada.

SOPWITH, Sir Charles (Ronald), Kt 1966; Second Counsel to Chairman of Committees, House of Lords, since 1974; *b* 12 Nov. 1905; *s* of Alfred Sopwith, S Shields, Co. Durham; *m* 1946, Ivy Violet (*d* 1968), *d* of Frederick Leonard Yeates, Gidea Park, Essex. *Educ:* S Shields High School. Chartered Accountant, 1928; Solicitor, 1938. Assistant Director, Press Censorship, 1943-45; Assistant Solicitor, 1952-56, Principal Asst Solicitor, 1956-61, Solicitor, 1963-70, Board of Inland Revenue; Public Trustee, 1961-63; Deputy Sec., Cabinet Office, 1970-72. *Recreations:* music, reading history, golf. *Address:* House of Lords, SW1. *Club:* Reform.

SOPWITH, Sir Thomas Octave Murdoch, Kt 1953; CBE 1918; President Hawker Siddeley Group Ltd (Chairman, 1935-63); *s* of Thomas Sopwith, MICE; *b* 1888; *m* 1st, 1914, Hon. Beatrix Mary Leslie Hore-Ruthven (*d* 1930), *d* of 8th Baron Ruthven; no *c*; 2nd, 1932, Phyllis Brodie, 2nd *d* of late F. P. A. Gordon; one *s.* Founded the Sopwith Aviation Co. Ltd, Kingston-on-Thames, 1912; Chairman, 1925-27, Society of British Aircraft Constructors. *Recreations:* yachting, shooting, fishing. *Address:* Compton Manor, Kings Somborne, Hampshire. *Clubs:* Carlton; Royal Yacht Squadron.

SOREF, Harold Benjamin; Chairman, since 1976, and Managing Director, since 1959, Soref Bros Ltd; *b* 18 Dec. 1916; *o s* of late Paul Soref and Zelma Soref (*née* Goodman), Hampstead. *Educ:* Hall Sch., Hampstead; St Paul's Sch.; Queen's Coll., Oxford. Served with Royal Scots and Intell. Corps, 1940-45. Contested (C): Dudley, 1951; Rugby, 1955. MP (C) Lancashire, Ormskirk, 1970-Feb. 1974. Delegate, first all-British Africa Conf. held Bulawayo, 1938, to form Africa Defence Fedn; formerly Vice-Chm., Monday Club; Chm., Africa Cttee, Monday Club; Mem. Council: Anglo-Jewish Assoc.; Anglo-Rhodesian Soc.; Anglo-Zanzibar Soc.; Founder Mem., Conservative Commonwealth Council. *Publications:* (jtly) The War of 1939, 1940; (with Ian Greig) The Puppeteers, 1965; numerous articles in press and periodicals. *Recreations:* research, reading, writing. *Address:* 125 Beaufort Mansions, Chelsea, SW3. *T:* 01-352 6461; 69-85 Old Street, EC1. *T:* 01-253 9311. *Clubs:* Carlton, PEN, 1900; Royal Scots (Edinburgh).

SOREL CAMERON, Brig. John, CBE 1957; DSO 1943; DL; retired as Chief of Staff, Headquarters Scottish Command (Oct. 1958-60); ADC to the Queen, 1957-60; *b* 19 July 1907; *er s* of late Lt-Col G. C. M. Sorel Cameron, CBE and Mrs Sorel Cameron, Gorthleck, Inverness-shire; *m* 1937, Catherine Nancy, *yr d* of late Frank Lee, JP, Halifax, Yorks; one *d.* *Educ:* Wellington; RMC Sandhurst. Gazetted 2nd Lieut Queen's Own Cameron Highlanders, 1927; regimental service, 1927-40; served War of 1939-45 in Middle East, Sicily, NW Europe (wounded thrice, despatches twice); Staff Coll., 1940; Staff, 1940-42; comd: 5/7th Gordons, 1942; 5th Camerons, 1943; Staff, 1944-50; comd: 1st Camerons, 1951-53; 154 Highland Bde, 1953-55; Chief of Staff, British Commonwealth Forces in Korea, 1955-56;

BGS, HQ Scottish Comd, 1957. DL Inverness, 1971-. *Recreations:* field sports, history. *Address:* 47 Drummond Road, Inverness, Scotland. *T:* Inverness 30029.

SORINJ, Dr L. T.; *see* Tončić-Sorinj.

SORN, Hon. Lord; James Gordon McIntyre, MC; Senator of College of Justice in Scotland, 1944-63, retired; *b* 21 July 1896; *s* of late T. W. McIntyre, of Sorn; *m* 1923, Madeline (*d* 1954), *d* of late Robert Scott Moncrieff, Downhill; one *s* one *d.* *Educ:* Winchester; Balliol Coll., Oxford (BA); Glasgow Univ. (LLB). Served European War, 1914-18, Ayrshire Yeomanry, Captain 1917 (MC and bar, French Croix de Guerre); called Scottish Bar, 1922; KC 1936; Dean of the Faculty of Advocates, 1939-44. Hon. LLD Glasgow University. *Recreation:* fishing. *Address:* Sorn Castle, Ayrshire. *Club:* New (Edinburgh).

SOROKOS, Lt-Gen. John A., Greek Gold Medal for Gallantry (3 times); Greek Military Cross (twice); Medal for Distinguished Services (3 times); Silver and Gold Cross (with swords) of Order of George I; Comdr, Order of George I and Order of Phoenix; Military Medal of Merit (1st Class); Ambassador of Greece to the United States of America, 1972-74; *b* 1917; *s* of A. and P. Sorokos; *m* 1954, Pia Madaros; one *s.* *Educ:* Mil. Acad. of Greece; Staff and Nat. Defence Colls, Greece; British Staff Coll., Camberley; US Mil. Schools. Company Comdr: in Second World War in Greece, 1940-41; in El Alamein Campaign, N Africa, 1942-43; Div. Staff Officer and Bn Comdr, 1947-49; served as Staff Officer: in Mil. Units in Army HQ and Armed Forces HQ, 1952-63; in NATO Allied Forces Southern Europe, 1957-59; Instructor, Nat. Defence Coll., Greece, 1963-64; Regt Comdr, 1965; Mil. Attaché to Greek Embassies in Washington and Ottawa, 1966-68; Div. Comdr, 1968-69; Dep. Comdr, Greek Armed Forces, 1969; Ambassador to UK, 1969-72. Officer, Legion of Merit (US). *Recreations:* horses, boating, fishing. *Address:* Mimnermou 2, Athens 138, Greece.

SORRELL, Alec Albert; Assistant Director, Central Statistical Office, Cabinet Office, since 1972; *b* 20 July 1925; *s* of Albert Edward Sorrell and Jessie (*née* Morris); *m* 1962, Eileen Joan Orchard; one *s.* *Educ:* George Gascoigne Sch., Walthamstow; SW Essex Technical College. BSc (Econ). Statistical Officer, MAP, 1945; Board of Trade: Asst Statistician, 1950; Statistician, 1954; Chief Statistician, 1966; Chief Statistician: Min. of Technology, 1969; Dept of Trade and Industry, 1970; Central Statistical Office, 1971. *Publications:* various articles in trade, professional and learned jls. *Recreations:* walking, reading, beachcombing. *Address:* 8 Ravensmere, Epping, Essex. *T:* Epping 73961; River Cottage, West Putford, Devon.

SORSBIE, Sir Malin, Kt 1965; CBE 1956 (OBE 1942); Chairman, The Munitalp Foundation; *b* 25 May 1906; *s* of late Rev. William Frances Sorsbie and late Blanche Georgina Sorsbie; *m* 1955, Constantine Eugenie, *d* of late Albert Wheeler Johnston, Greenwich, Connecticut, USA; one step *d.* *Educ:* Brighton College; Manitoba University. Royal Canadian Mounted Police, 1926-29; RAF, 1930-35; Imperial Airways, 1936-39; BOAC, 1940-47; East African Airways (Gen. Manager), 1947-56. Life Fellow, RGS. KStJ. *Publications:* Dragonfly, 1971; Brandy for Breakfast, 1972. *Address:* PO Box 45337, Nairobi, Kenya. *T:* 65331 and 65343. *Clubs:* Bath, Royal Air Force; RAF Yacht; Muthaiga Country, Nairobi (Nairobi).

SORSBY, Arnold, CBE 1966; MD, FRCS; Consultant Adviser, Ministry of Health, 1966-71; Editor, Journal of Medical Genetics, 1964-69; Research Professor in Ophthalmology, Royal College of Surgeons and Royal Eye Hospital, 1943-66; Emeritus Professor, 1966; Hon. Director, Wernher Research Unit on Ophthalmological Genetics, Medical Research Council, 1953-66; Vice-President, Internat. Organization against Trachoma, 1951-68; Member, Expert Advisory Panel on Trachoma, WHO, 1953-68; *b* 10 June 1900. *Educ:* Leeds Univ. Consultant, WHO, 1969-70. Sir Arthur Keith Medal (RCS), 1966; Grimshaw Award (Nat. Fedn of the Blind), 1968. *Publications:* (ed) Tenements of Clay, 1974; Diseases of the Funus Oculi, 1976; books and papers on ophthalmology, genetics and on medical history. *Address:* 19 Parham Court, Grand Avenue, Worthing, West Sussex. *T:* Worthing 40607.

SOSKICE, family name of **Baron Stow Hill.**

SOTERIADES, Antis Georghios; Ambassador of Cyprus to Egypt, since 1966, concurrently accredited to Syrian Arab Republic and Lebanon, since 1967; *b* 10 Sept. 1924; *m* 1962, Mona, *yr d* of Petros Petrides, Nicosia; one *s* one *d.* *Educ:* London Univ.; Inns of Court, London. Practising lawyer until 1956; joined patriotic Organization EOKA and fought British Colonialism in Cyprus, 1956-59; President of the first political party formed in Cyprus after independence, 1959; High Commissioner for Cyprus in the UK, 1960-66. Kt Order of St Gregory the Great (Vatican), 1963. *Address:* 16 Cleopatra Road, Heliopolis, Cairo, Egypt.

SOTHERS, Donald Bevan, CIE 1944; Chief Conservator Forests, Bombay (retired); *b* 11 March 1889; *s* of George Henry Sothers; *m* 1922, Dorothy, *d* of A. G. Edie, CIE; one *s* one *d. Educ:* Reading School; St John's College, Oxford. Joined Indian Forest Service, 1911; War Service, 1915-18, IARO attached 114th Mahrattas, Mesopotamia; Conservator Forests, 1932; Chief Conservator, 1942; re-employed as Land Development Officer, Bombay, 1944-46. *Recreations:* shooting, golf. *Address:* Leyfield, The Chase, Reigate.

SOUKOP, Wilhelm Josef, RA 1969 (ARA 1963); RBA 1950; FRBS 1956; Master of Sculpture, Royal Academy Schools, since 1969; freelance sculptor; *b* 5 Jan. 1907; *s* of Karl Soukop and Anna Soukop (*née* Vogel); *m* 1945, Simone (*née* Moser), Paris; one *s* one *d. Educ:* Vienna State School; apprenticed to an engraver; Academy of Fine Art, Vienna. Arrived in England, Dartington Hall, 1934; taught at Dartington Hall, Bryanston and Blundell's Schools, 1935-45; moved to London, 1945, and taught at Bromley Sch. of Art, 1945-46, Guildford Sch. of Art, 1945-47; sculpture teacher, Chelsea Sch. of Art, 1947-72. Examr for Scotland, 1959-62. Sculptures for new schools in Herts, Leics, Derbs, Staffs, LCC. Work for housing estates. Sculptures in museums: USA; Cordova Mus., Boston; Chantry Bequest; Tate Gallery; Cheltenham Mus. and Gall.; Collection of LCC Educn Cttee. Work in many private collections England, America, Canada, Europe. Archibald McIndoe Award, 1964. *Recreation:* gardening. *Address:* 26 Greville Road, NW6. *T:* 01-624 5987.

SOULBURY, 2nd Viscount *cr* 1954, of Soulbury; **James Herwald Ramsbotham;** Baron 1941; *b* 21 March 1915; *s* of 1st Viscount Soulbury, PC, GCMG, GCVO, OBE, MC, and Doris Violet (*d* 1954), *d* of late S. de Stein; *S* father, 1971; *m* 1949, Anthea Margaret (*d* 1950), *d* of late David Wilton. *Educ:* Eton; Magdalen College, Oxford. *Heir: b* Hon. Sir Peter Edward Ramsbotham, *qv.*

SOUROZH, Metropolitan of; *see* Anthony, Archbishop.

SOUSTELLE, Jacques; Officier, Légion d'Honneur, 1955; Member, Lyon Municipal Council, 1954-62 and 1971-77; *b* 3 Feb. 1912. *Educ:* Ecole Normale supérieure, Paris; Univ. of Lyon. Agrégé de l'Université 1932, PhD 1937. Asst Dir, Musée de l'Homme, 1937; Nat. Comr for Information in London, 1942; Head of French special services, Algiers, 1943-44; Governor of Bordeaux, 1945; Minister of Information and Colonies, 1945-46. Prof. of Sociology, Ecole des Hautes Etudes, 1951. Mem. Nat. Assembly, 1945-46, 1951-59, 1973-. Gov.-Gen. of Algeria, 1955-56; Minister of Information, 1958; Minister delegate to the Prime Minister, France, 1959-60. FRAI. Order of Polonia Restituta, 1944; US Medal of Freedom, 1945; Hon. CBE, Great Britain, 1946. *Publications:* Mexique, terre indienne, 1935; Envers et contre tout, 1947; La Vie quotidienne des Aztèques, 1955 (Daily Life of the Aztecs, 1962); Aimée et souffrante Algérie, 1956; L'espérance trahie, 1962; Sur une route nouvelle, 1964; L'Art du Mexique ancien, 1966 (Arts of Ancient Mexico, 1967); Archæologia Mundi: Mexique, 1967 (Archæologia Mundi: Mexico, 1967, repr. as The Ancient Civilizations of Mexico, 1969); Les quatre soleils, 1967 (The Four Suns, 1971); La longue marche d'Israël, 1968 (The Long March of Israel, 1969); Vingt-huit ans de Gaullisme, 1968; Les Aztèques, 1970; Lettre ouverte aux victimes de la décolonisation, 1973; papers and memoirs on anthropology and ethnology, in learned jls. *Address:* 85 avenue Henri-Martin, 75016 Paris, France.

SOUTAR, Air Vice-Marshal Charles John Williamson, MBE 1958; QHS 1974; Principal Medical Officer, Strike Command, RAF, since Oct. 1975; *b* 12 June 1920; *s* of Charles Alexander Soutar and Mary Helen (*née* Watson); *m* 1944, Joy Dorée Upton; one *s* two *d. Educ:* Brentwood Sch.; London Hosp. MB, BS, LMSSA, MFCM, DPH, DIH. Commissioned RAF, 1946. Various appts, then, PMO, Middle East Command, 1967-68; Dep. Dir, Med. Organisation, RAF, 1968-70; OC, PMRAF Hosp., Halton, 1970-73; Comdt, RAF Inst. of Aviation Medicine, 1973-75. CStJ 1972. *Recreations:* sport, gardening, ornithology, music. *Address:* (private) Oak Cottage, High Street, Aldeburgh, Suffolk IP15 5DT. *T:* Aldenburgh 2201; (office hours) *T:* High Wycombe 26200, ext. 2652. *Club:* Royal Air Force.

SOUTER, family name of **Baron Audley.**

SOUTH, Sir Arthur, Kt 1974; JP; Managing Director, Arthur South Furs (Wholesale) Ltd, since 1962; Senior Partner, Norwich Fur Company, since 1947; *b* 29 Oct. 1914; *s* of Arthur and Violet South, Norwich; *m* 1937, May Adamson (marr. diss. 1976); two *s*; *m* 1976, Mary June, *widow* of Robert Edward Carter, JP, DL. *Educ:* City of Norwich Sch. RAF and MAP, 1941-46. Mem., Norwich, Lowestoft, Gt Yarmouth Hosp. Management Cttee, 1948-74 (Vice-Chm., 1954-66, Chm., 1966-74); Chm., Norfolk Area Health Authority, 1974-; Mem., E Anglia Regional Hosp. Bd, 1969-74. Member: Assoc. of Educn Cttees, 1963-74; Assoc. of Municipal Corporations, 1965-74; E Anglia Econ. Planning Council, 1966-; E Anglia Rent Assessment Panel, 1967-74; E Anglia Adv. Cttee to BBC, 1970-74; Univ. of E Anglia Council, 1964- (Life Mem., Court, 1964). Norwich: City Councillor, 1935-41 and 1946-61; Alderman, 1961-74; Sheriff, 1953-54; Lord Mayor, 1956-57, Dep. Lord Mayor, 1959-60; JP 1949; Dep. Leader, Norwich City Council, 1959-60; Chm., Labour Party Gp and Leader Norwich City Council, 1960-. Norwich City Football Club: Vice-Pres., 1957-66; Dir, 1966-73; Chm., 1973-. *Recreations:* football, bowls, cricket. *Address:* The Lowlands, Drayton, Norfolk NR8 6HA. *T:* Norwich 867625. *Clubs:* City, Mitre Bowls, Rotary, Labour (Norwich); Norfolk Cricket, Norwich City Football.

SOUTHALL, Kenneth Charles; Under-Secretary, Inland Revenue, since 1975; *b* 3 Aug. 1922; *s* of Arthur and Margarette Jane Southall; *m* 1947, Audrey Kathleen Skeels; one *s. Educ:* Queen Elizabeth's Grammar Sch., Hartlebury, Worcs. Inland Revenue, 1939; RAF, 1942-46; Administrative Staff College, 1962. *Address:* Tewin Vale, New Road, Digswell, Welwyn, Herts AL6 0AH. *T:* Welwyn 4014.

SOUTHAM, Alexander William, CBE 1948; *b* 6 Jan. 1898. *Educ:* Oundle; Christ's College, Cambridge (MA 1925). Served European War, 1915-19 (despatches, foreign orders). British Petroleum Co. Ltd, 1922-34; managed oil shale cos in Baltic States owned by Gold Fields of S Africa Ltd, 1934-40; various war work from 1939 in Europe and Middle East; joined British Element of Allied Commn for Austria, 1945; Dir, Economic Gp, and British Chm., Economic Directorate, 1946-48; Dir, Investigation and Research Div., Internat. Authority for Ruhr, 1949-52. Man. Dir, 1953-64, and Pres., 1958-64, British Newfoundland Corp. Ltd, Canada. *Address:* c/o Potchett Investment Ltd, 39th Floor, 1155 Dorchester Boulevard West, Montreal, Quebec, Canada H3B 3V2. *Clubs:* University, Royal Montreal Golf (Montreal); Rideau (Ottawa).

SOUTHAM, Gordon Ronald, BSc; AInstP; Headmaster, Ashville College, 1958-77; *b* 20 March 1918; *s* of G. H. Southam, Brackley; *m* 1948, Joan, *d* of W. Thompson; one *d. Educ:* Magdalen College School, Brackley; Westminster College, and King's College, London. BSc (Gen. Hons) 1938, BSc (Special Physics) 1st Class Hons 1939. Teacher's diploma, 1947, AInstP 1947. Served Royal Air Force, 1940-46: Bomber Comd, 1940-43; Staff Officer in HQ, ACSEA, 1943-46 (Sqdn Ldr). Senior Physics Master, Culford School, 1947-49; Lecturer, Royal Military Academy, Sandhurst, 1950-52; Head of Department of Science, Royal Military Academy, Sandhurst, 1953-57. *Recreations:* motoring, electronics; formerly Rugby football, athletics. *Address:* Greycott, Hartley, Kirkby Stephen, Cumbria. *T:* Kirkby Stephen 70652.

SOUTHAMPTON, Barony of (*cr* 1780); title disclaimed by 5th Baron; *see under* FitzRoy, Charles.

SOUTHAMPTON, Bishop Suffragan of, since 1972; **Rt. Rev. John Kingsmill Cavell;** *b* 4 Nov. 1916; *o s* of late William H. G. Cavell and Edith May (*née* Warner), Deal, Kent; *m* 1942, Mary Grossett (*née* Penman), Devizes, Wilts; one *d. Educ:* Sir Roger Manwood's Sch., Sandwich; Queens' Coll., Cambridge; MA; Wycliffe Hall, Oxford. Ryle Reading Prize. Ordained May 1940; Curate: Christ Church, Folkestone, 1940; Addington Parish Church, Croydon, 1940-44; CMS Area Secretary, dio. Oxford and Peterborough, and CMS Training Officer, 1944-52; Vicar: Christ Church, Cheltenham, 1952-62; St Andrew's, Plymouth, 1962-72; Rural Dean of Plymouth, 1967-72; Prebendary of Exeter Cathedral, 1967-72. Hon. Canon, Winchester Cathedral, 1972-; Bishop to Prisons and Borstals, 1975-. Proctor in Convocation; Member of General Synod; Surrogate. Chm., Home Cttee, CMS London. Chaplain, Greenbank and Freedom Fields Hosps, Plymouth; Member: Plymouth City Educn Cttee, 1967-72; City Youth Cttee; Plymouth Exec. Council, NHS, 1968-72. Fellow, Pilgrim Soc., Massachusetts, 1974. Governor: Cheltenham Colls of Educn; King Alfred's College of Educn, 1973-; Chairman: St Mary's Coll. Building Cttee, 1957-62; Talbot Heath Sch., Bournemouth, 1975-. *Recreations:* historical research, philately, cricket. *Address:* Shepherds, Shepherds Lane, Compton, Winchester, Hants. *T:* Twyford 713285.

SOUTHBOROUGH, 3rd Baron *cr* 1917; **Francis John Hopwood;** Kt 1953; retired as Managing Director "Shell" Transport & Trading Co., 1951-70 (Director, 1946-70); *b* 7 March 1897; *s* of 1st Baron Southborough, PC, GCB, GCMG, GCVO, KCSI and his 2nd wife, Florence Emily, *d* of late Lieut-Gen. Samuel Black; *S* half-brother (2nd Baron), 1960; *m* 1918, Audrey Evelyn Dorothy, *d* of late Edgar George Money; one *s* one *d. Educ:* Westminster School. Served European War, 1914-18, Sub-Lieut, RNVR, Admiralty and Foreign Office; seconded, 1917, to staff of Irish Convention in Dublin and later was Sec. to War Trade Advisory Cttee. Joined Royal Dutch Shell Group of Companies, 1919; Pres. Asiatic Petroleum Corporation, USA, (also represented Petroleum Board), 1942-46; Managing Director The Shell Petroleum Co., and Bataafse Petroleum Maatschappij NV, 1946-57, retired. Mem., Oil Supply Adv. Cttee. Commander of the Order of Orange-Nassau. *Heir:* s Hon. Francis Michael Hopwood, late Lieut The Rifle Brigade [*b* 3 May 1922; *m* 1945, Moyna Kemp, *d* of Robert J. K. Chattey]. *Address:* Bingham's Melcombe, near Dorchester, Dorset. *T:* Milton Abbas 202. *Club:* Brooks's.
See also J. M. Rank.

SOUTHBY, Sir (Archibald) Richard (Charles), 2nd Bt *cr* 1937; OBE 1945; Lt-Col (retd), Rifle Brigade; *b* 18 June 1910; *s* of Sir Archibald Richard James Southby, 1st Bt, and Phyllis Mary (*d* 1974), *er d* of late Charles Henry Garton, Banstead Wood, Surrey; *S* father, 1969; *m* 1st, 1935, Joan Alice (marr. diss. 1947), *o d* of Reginald Balston; 2nd, 1947, Olive Marion (marr. diss. 1964), *d* of late Sir Thomas Bilbe-Robinson; one *s*; 3rd, 1964, Hon. Ethel Peggy, *d* of 1st Baron Cunliffe and *widow* of Brig. Bernard Lorenzo de Robeck, MC, RA. *Educ:* Eton; Magdalen Coll., Oxford (MA). Medal of Freedom (US). *Heir:* s John Richard Bilbe Southby [*b* 2 April 1948; *m* 1971, Victoria, *d* of William James Sturrock; one *s* one *d*]. *Address:* 24 Broadway Avenue, Newlands, Cape, South Africa.

SOUTHEND, Archdeacon of; *see* Moses, Ven. J. H.

SOUTHERN, Michael William; Regional Administrator, South West Thames Regional Health Authority, since 1973; *b* 22 June 1918; *s* of William Southern and Ida Frances Southern; *m* 1945, Nancy Russell Golsworthy; three *d. Educ:* Tiffin Boys' Sch., Kingston-upon-Thames; London Univ. (DPA); Open Univ. (BA Humanities). FHA. Surrey CC Public Health Dept, 1934-39 and 1945-48; served with RAMC (NCO), 1939-45: Technician in No 1 Malaria Field Lab., 1940-41; POW Germany, 1941-44 (captured in Crete); Planning Officer and later Sec. of SW Metropolitan Regional Hosp. Bd, 1948-73. *Publications:* various articles in Hospital and Health Services Review, Health and Social Service Jl. *Recreations:* music, travel, philately. *Address:* 14 Poole Road, West Ewell, Epsom, Surrey KT19 9RY. *T:* 01-393 5096, (office) 01-262 8011, ext. 362.

SOUTHERN, Richard; Theatre Consultant (private) since 1947; *b* 5 Oct. 1903; *o s* of Harry Southern and Edith (*née* Hockney); *m* 1933, Grace Kathleen Loosemore; two *d. Educ:* St Dunstan's College; Goldsmiths' Art School; Royal Academy of Art. Designed scenery, 1928-, for over fifty shows (Everyman Theatre, Cambridge Festival Theatre and various London theatres); also acted and stage-managed; specialized in study of stage technique and theatre architecture. Technical Lectr, Goldsmiths' College, 1932, London Theatre Studio, 1937, Royal Academy of Dramatic Art, 1945, Old Vic Theatre Centre, 1947; Theatre planning adviser to Arts Council, 1947; Director, Nuffield Theatre, Univ. of Southampton, 1964-66; Lectr, Drama Dept, Bristol Univ., 1959-60, and Special Lectr in Theatre Architecture, 1961-69, retired. Has planned various modern theatres and stages includ. Bristol Univ., 1951, Royal College of Art, 1952, Glasgow, 1953, Reading University, 1957, Nottingham, 1961, Southampton University, 1961, University Coll., London, 1967, also various reconstructions of historical theatres, Richmond, Yorkshire, 1950, King's Lynn, 1951, Williamsburg, Virginia, 1953. Hon. DLitt (Bristol), 1956. *Publications:* Stage Setting, 1937; Proscenium and Sightlines, 1939; The Georgian Playhouse, 1948; The Essentials of Stage Planning (with Stanley Bell and Norman Marshall), 1949; Changeable Scenery, 1952; The Open Stage, 1953; The Medieval Theatre in the Round, 1957; The Seven Ages of the Theatre, 1961; The Victorian Theatre, 1970; The Staging of Plays before Shakespeare, 1973; contrib. to specialist journals and encyclopædias. *Recreation:* figure drawing. *Address:* 37 Langham Road, Teddington TW11 9HF. *T:* 01-977 6686.

SOUTHERN, Sir Richard (William), Kt 1974; FBA 1960; President of St John's College, Oxford, since 1969; *b* 8 Feb. 1912; 2nd *s* of Matthew Henry Southern, Newcastle upon Tyne; *m* 1944, Sheila (*née* Cobley), *widow* of Sqdn Ldr C. Crichton-Miller; two *s. Educ:* Royal Grammar Sch., Newcastle upon Tyne; Balliol College, Oxford (Domus Exhibr). 1st Class Hons Modern History, 1932. Junior Research Fellow, Exeter College, Oxford, 1933-37; studied in Paris, 1933-34 and Munich, 1935; Fellow and Tutor, Balliol Coll., Oxford, 1937-61 (Hon. Fellow 1966). Served Oxford and Bucks LI, 1940; 2nd Lt Durham LI 1941; 155th Regt RAC, 1942; Captain 1943; Major 1944; Political Intelligence Dept, Foreign Office, 1943-45. Junior Proctor, Oxford Univ., 1948-49; Birkbeck Lectr in Ecclesiastical History, Trinity College, Cambridge, 1959-60; Chichele Prof. of Modern History, Oxford, 1961-69; President: Royal Historical Soc., 1968-72; Selden Soc., 1973-76. Lectures: Raleigh, British Academy, 1962; David Murray, Glasgow Univ., 1963; Gifford, Glasgow Univ., 1970-72. Corr. Fellow, Medieval Academy of America, 1965; For. Hon. Mem., Amer. Acad. of Arts and Scis, 1972. Hon. Fellow, Sidney Sussex Coll., Cambridge, 1971; Hon. DLitt: Glasgow, 1964; Durham, 1969; Cantab, 1971; Bristol, 1974; Newcastle, 1977; Hon. LLD Harvard, 1977. *Publications:* The Making of the Middle Ages, 1953 (numerous foreign translations); (ed) Eadmer's Vita Anselmi, 1963; St Anselm and his Biographer, 1963; Western Views of Islam in the Middle Ages, 1962; (ed with F. S. Schmitt) Memorials of St Anselm, 1969; Medieval Humanism and other studies, 1970 (RSL award 1970); Western Society and the Church in the Middle Ages, 1970; articles in English Historical Review, Medieval and Renaissance Studies, etc. *Address:* President's Lodgings, St John's College, Oxford. *T:* Oxford 44419.

SOUTHERN, Sir Robert, Kt 1970; CBE 1953; General Secretary, Co-operative Union Ltd, 1948-72; *b* 17 March 1907; *s* of Job Southern and Margaret (*née* Tonge); *m* 1933, Lena Chapman; one *s* one *d. Educ:* Stand Grammar Sch.; Co-operative Coll.; Manchester University. Co-operative Wholesale Soc., Bank Dept, 1925-29; Co-operative Union Ltd, 1929. *Publication:* Handbook to the Industrial and Provident Societies' Act, 1938. *Recreations:* photography, gardening. *Address:* 22 Glebelands Road, Prestwich, Manchester M25 5NE. *T:* 061-773 2699.

SOUTHERTON, Thomas Henry, BSc (Eng); CEng, MIEE; Senior Director Data Processing, Post Office, since 1975; *b* 1 July 1917; *s* of C. H. Southerton, Birmingham; *m* 1945, Marjorie Elizabeth Sheen; one *s. Educ:* Bemrose Sch., Derby; Northampton Coll., London (BSc(Eng)). PO Apprentice, Derby, 1933-36; Engineering Workman, Derby and Nottingham, 1936-40; Inspector, Engineer-in-Chief's Office, 1940-45; Engineer, 1945-50; Sen. Exec. Engr, 1950-53; Factory Manager, PO Provinces, 1953-56; Dep. Controller, Factories Dept, 1956-64; Controller, Factories Dept, 1964-67; Dir, Telecommunications Management Services, 1967-73; Sen. Dir Telecommunications Personnel, 1973-75. *Recreations:* art, architecture. *Address:* 92 Greenways, Hinchley Wood, Esher, Surrey. *T:* 01-398 1985.

SOUTHESK, 11th Earl of *cr* 1633; **Charles Alexander Carnegie,** KCVO, *cr* 1926; DL; Major late Scots Guards; Baron Carnegie, 1616; Baron Balinhard (UK), 1869; Bt of Nova Scotia, 1663; *b* 23 Sept. 1893; *e s* of 10th Earl of Southesk and Ethel (*d* 1947), *o c* of Sir Alexander Bannerman, 9th Bt of Elsick; *S* father, 1941; *m* 1st, 1923, HH Princess Maud (*d* 1945), 2nd *d* of HRH Princess Louise, Princess Royal and late Duke of Fife; one *s*; 2nd, 1952, Evelyn, *e d* of Lieut-Colonel A. P. Williams-Freeman, and *widow* of Major Ion E. F. Campbell, DCLI. *Educ:* Eton; Sandhurst. DL Angus. *Heir:* s Duke of Fife, *qv. Address:* Kinnaird Castle, Brechin, Angus. *T:* Bridge of Dun 209.
See also Vice-Admiral Sir E. M. C. Abel Smith.

SOUTHEY, Air Commodore Harold Frederic George, CB 1954; HM Diplomatic Service, retired; *b* 18 Feb. 1906; *s* of Rev. William George Southey and Edith Mary Roffey; *m* 1929, Joan Mary Gordon Davies; no *c. Educ:* Downside; RAF Coll., Cranwell. Served War of 1939-45 (despatches twice); AOC No 247 Group, and Senior British Officer, Azores, 1945; Air Attaché, Brussels, 1947; West Union Defence Organisation, 1951; SASO Transport Command, 1952; AOC, RAF Maritime HQ, Chatham, 1954; retired 1957; Queen's Messenger, 1959-71. *Recreations:* fishing, shooting, and sailing. *Address:* 17 Knightsbridge Court, SW1. *T:* 01-235 6927. *Clubs:* Royal Air Force, Royal Thames Yacht.

SOUTHEY, Sir Robert (John), Kt 1976; CMG 1970; Chairman, Wm Haughton & Co. Ltd, since 1968; Federal President, Liberal Party of Australia, 1970-75; *b* 20 March 1922; *s* of Allen Hope Southey and Ethel Thorpe McComas, MBE; *m* 1946, Valerie Janet Cotton, *y d* of late Hon. Sir Francis Grenville Clarke, KBE, MLC; five *s. Educ:* Geelong Grammar Sch.; Magdalen Coll., Oxford (MA). Coldstream Guards, 1941-46 (Captain 1944). BA, 1st cl. PPE Oxon, 1948. Wm Haughton & Co. Ltd: Dir 1953; Man. Dir, 1959-75; Chm. 1968; Director: British

Petroleum Co. of Australia Ltd; Port Phillip Mills Pty Ltd; Buckley & Nunn Ltd; Kinnears Ltd; Vericast Australia Ltd; Timbersales Ltd; Mem. Australian Adv. Council, General Accident Assurance Corp. Ltd. Victorian State Pres., Liberal Party, 1966-70; Chm. of Council, Geelong Grammar Sch., 1966-72; Chm. Australian Adv. Cttee, Nuffield Foundn, 1970-; Mem., Rhodes Scholarship Selection Cttee, Victoria, 1973-76. *Recreations:* fishing, golf. *Address:* Denistoun Avenue, Mount Eliza, Victoria 3930, Australia. *T:* 7871701. *Clubs:* Cavalry and Guards, MCC; Melbourne, Australian (Melbourne); Union (Sydney); Leander.

SOUTHGATE, Air Vice-Marshal Harry Charles, CB 1976; CBE 1973 (MBE 1950); Director General of Engineering and Supply Policy and Planning, Ministry of Defence (Air), 1973-76, retired; *b* 30 Oct. 1921; *s* of George Harry Southgate and Lily Maud (*née* Clarke); *m* 1945, Violet Louise Davies; one *s*. *Educ:* St Saviour's Sch., Walthamstow. Entered RAF, 1941; India, 1942-45; HQ 90 Gp, 1946-50; RAF Stafford, 1950-52; Air Min., 1952-53; transf. to Equipment Br., 1953; RAF Tangmere, 1953-55; Singapore, 1955-57; psc 1957; Air Min., 1958-60; jssc 1961; Dirg Staff, RAF Staff Coll., Bracknell, 1961-64; CO 35 MU RAF Heywood, 1965-66; SESO, RAF Germany, 1967-68; idc 1969; Dir Supply Management, MoD Air, 1970-73. *Recreations:* travel, golf, painting, bird-watching. *Address:* The Rushings, Winksley, near Ripon, North Yorkshire HG4 3NR. *T:* Kirkby Malzeard 582. *Club:* Royal Air Force.

SOUTHGATE, Ven. John Eliot; Archdeacon of Cleveland since 1974; *b* 2 Sept. 1926; *m* 1958, Patricia Mary Plumb; two *s* one *d*. *Educ:* City of Norwich Sch.; Durham Univ. BA 1953, DipTh 1955. Ordained 1955; Vicar of Plumstead, 1962; Rector of Old Charlton, 1966; Dean of Greenwich, 1968; York Diocesan Sec. for Mission and Evangelism and Vicar of Harome, 1972-77. *Recreations:* music, sailing, Egyptology. *Address:* 79 Middleton Road, Pickering, N Yorks YO18 8NQ. *T:* Pickering 73605.

SOUTHWARD, Dr Nigel Ralph; Apothecary to the Queen, Apothecary to the Household and to the Households of Princess Alice Duchess of Gloucester and the Duke and Duchess of Gloucester, since 1975; *b* 8 Feb. 1941; *s* of Sir Ralph Southward, *qv*; *m* 1965, Annette, *d* of J. H. Hoffmann; one *s* two *d*. *Educ:* Rugby Sch.; Trinity Hall, Cambridge; Middlesex Hosp. Med. Sch. MA, MB, BChir, 1965; MRCP 1969. Ho. Surg., Mddx Hosp., 1965; Ho. Phys., Royal Berkshire Hosp., Reading, 1966; Ho. Phys., Central Mddx Hosp., 1966; Casualty MO, Mddx Hosp., 1967; Vis. MO, King Edward VII Hosp. for Officers, 1972-. *Recreations:* sailing, golf, ski-ing. *Address:* 9 Devonshire Place, W1N 1PB. *T:* 01-935 8425; 56 Primrose Gardens, NW3 4TP.

SOUTHWARD, Sir Ralph, KCVO 1975; Apothecary to the Household of Queen Elizabeth the Queen Mother, since 1966 (Apothecary to Household of HRH the Duke of Gloucester, 1966-75, to HM Household, 1964-74, to HM the Queen, 1972-74); *b* 12 Jan. 1908; *s* of Henry Stalker Southward; *m* 1935, Evelyn, *d* of J. G. Tassell; four *s*. *Educ:* High School of Glasgow; Glasgow Univ. MB, ChB (Glasgow) 1930; MRCP 1939; FRCP 1970. Western Infirmary, and Royal Hospital for Sick Children, Glasgow; Postgraduate Medical School, Hammersmith, London. Served War of 1939-45: Medical Officer, 215 Field Ambulance, North Africa, 1940-41; Medical Specialist, Egypt, India and Ceylon, and Lieut-Colonel in charge Medical Division, 1942-43; Colonel Comdg Combined General Hospital, 1944-45. *Recreations:* trout and salmon fishing. *Address:* 9 Devonshire Place, W1. *T:* 01-935 7969; Amerden Priory, Taplow, Bucks. *T:* Maidenhead 23525.
See also N . R . Southward.

SOUTHWARK, Archbishop and Metropolitan of, (RC), since 1977; **Most Rev. Michael George Bowen**; *b* 23 April 1930; *s* of late Major C. L. J. Bowen and of Lady Makins (who *m* 1945, Sir Paul Makins, Bt, *qv*). *Educ:* Downside; Trinity Coll., Cambridge; Gregorian Univ., Rome. Army, 1948-49, 2nd Lieut Irish Guards; Wine Trade, 1951-52; English Coll., Rome, 1952-59; ordained 1958; Curate at Earlsfield and at Walworth, South London, 1959-63; taught theology, Beda Coll., Rome, 1963-66; Chancellor of Diocese of Arundel and Brighton, 1966-70; Coadjutor Bishop with right of succession to See of Arundel and Brighton, 1970-71; Bishop of Arundel and Brighton, 1971-77. *Recreations:* golf, tennis. *Address:* Archbishop's House, St George's Road, Southwark, SE1 6HX. *T:* 01-928 2495/5592.

SOUTHWARK, Bishop of, since 1959; **Rt. Rev. Arthur Mervyn Stockwood**, DD; *b* 27 May 1913; *s* of late Arthur Stockwood, solicitor, and Beatrice Ethel Stockwood; unmarried. *Educ:* Kelly Coll., Tavistock; Christ's Coll., Cambridge (MA). Curate of St Matthew, Moorfields, Bristol, 1936-41; Blundell's Sch.,

Missioner, 1936-41; Vicar, St Matthew, Moorfields, Bristol, 1941-55; Hon. Canon of Bristol, 1952-55; Vicar of the University Church, Cambridge, 1955-59. Freeman of City of London, 1976. DD Lambeth, 1959; DLitt Sussex, 1963. *Publications:* There is a Tide, 1946; Whom They Pierced, 1948; Christianity and Marxism, 1949; I Went to Moscow, 1955; The Faith To-day, 1959; Cambridge Sermons, 1959; Bishop's Journal, 1965. *Recreation:* fishing. *Address:* Bishop's House, 38 Tooting Bec Gardens, SW16 1QZ.

SOUTHWARK, Auxiliary Bishop in, (RC); *see* Henderson, Rt Rev. C. J.

SOUTHWARK, Provost of; *see* Frankham, Very Rev. H. E.

SOUTHWARK, Archdeacon of; *see* Whinney, Ven. M. H. D.

SOUTHWELL, family name of **Viscount Southwell.**

SOUTHWELL, 7th Viscount, *cr* 1776; **Pyers Anthony Joseph Southwell;** Bt 1662; Baron Southwell, 1717; International Management and Marketing Consultant; *b* 14 Sept. 1930; *s* of Hon. Francis Joseph Southwell (2nd *s* of 5th Viscount) and Agnes Mary Annette Southwell (*née* Clifford); *S* uncle, 1960; *m* 1955, Barbara Jacqueline Raynes; two *s*. *Educ:* Beaumont Coll., Old Windsor, Berks; Royal Military Academy, Sandhurst. Commissioned into 8th King's Royal Irish Hussars, 1951; resigned commission, 1955. *Recreation:* golf. *Heir: s* Hon. Richard Andrew Pyers Southwell, *b* 15 June 1956. *Address:* 4 Rosebery Avenue, Harpenden, Herts. *T:* Harpenden 5831. *Clubs:* Army and Navy, MCC.

SOUTHWELL, Bishop of, since 1970; **Rt. Rev. John Denis Wakeling,** MC 1945; *b* 12 Dec. 1918; *s* of Rev. John Lucas Wakeling and Mary Louise (*née* Glover); *m* 1941, Josephine Margaret, *d* of Dr Benjamin Charles Broomhall and Marion (*née* Aldwinckle); two *s*. *Educ:* Dean Close Sch., Cheltenham; St Catharine's Coll., Cambridge. MA Cantab 1944. Commnd Officer in Royal Marines, 1939-45 (Actg Maj.). Ridley Hall, Cambridge, 1946-47. Deacon, 1947; Priest, 1948. Asst Curate, Barwell, Leics, 1947; Chaplain of Clare Coll., Cambridge, and Chaplain to the Cambridge Pastorate, 1950-52; Vicar of Emmanuel, Plymouth, 1952-59; Prebendary of Exeter Cathedral, 1957, Prebendary Emeritus, 1959; Vicar of Barking, Essex, 1959-65; Archdeacon of West Ham, 1965-70. Entered House of Lords, June 1974. Chairman: Archbishops' Council on Evangelism, 1976; Lee Abbey Council, 1976. *Recreations:* cricket; formerly hockey (Cambridge Univ. Hockey Club, 1938, 1939, 1945, 1946, English Trials Caps, 1939, 1946, 1947, 1948, 1949). *Address:* Bishop's Manor, Southwell, Notts. *Clubs:* Army and Navy, National; Hawks (Cambridge).

SOUTHWELL, Provost of; *see* Pratt, Very Rev. J. F.

SOUTHWELL, Sir (Charles Archibald) Philip, Kt 1958; CBE 1953; MC 1918; Director, Kuwait Oil Co. Ltd, since 1946 (Managing Director, 1946-59); *s* of late Dr Charles Edward Southwell, Stoke-on-Trent; *m* 1926, Mary Burnett, *d* of Thomas Scarratt, Belmont Hall, Ipstones, Staffs; two *s*. *Educ:* Birmingham Univ. (BSc (Pet.)). President: Inst. of Petroleum, 1951-52; Oil Industries Club, 1953. Petroleum Technologist to Government of Trinidad, 1922-28. Served European War, 1914-18, with RA (MC); War of 1939-45; temp. Lt-Col. Govt Cttee Business Training, 1945. Royal Society of Arts: Silver Medal, 1953; Council, 1958. Cadman Memorial Medal, Inst. of Petroleum, 1954; Hon. Fellow, 1959. Chairman: Brown and Root (UK) Ltd; Highland Fabricators; Dir, Halliburton Gp of Cos. Liveryman, Company of Shipwrights. Bailiff Grand Cross OStJ; late Dir-Gen. St John Ambulance, 1968. Comdr, Order of Cedar of Lebanon, 1958. *Publications:* on petroleum technology. *Recreation:* gardening. *Address:* Manor House, Tendring, Essex. *T:* Weeley 286. *Clubs:* Garrick, Royal Thames Yacht.

SOUTHWELL, Ven. Roy; Archdeacon of Northolt, since 1970; *b* 3 Dec. 1914; *s* of William Thomas and Lilian Southwell; *m* 1948, Nancy Elizabeth Lindsay Sharp; two *d*. *Educ:* Sudbury Grammar Sch.; King's Coll., London (AKC 1942). Curate: St Michael's, Wigan, 1942-44; St John the Divine, Kennington, 1944-48; Vicar of Ixworth, 1948-51; Vicar of St John's, Bury St Edmunds, 1951-56; Rector of Bucklesham with Brightwell and Foxhall, 1956-59; Asst Director of Religious Education, Diocese of St Edmundsbury and Ipswich, 1956-58, Director, 1959-67. Hon. Canon of St Edmundsbury, 1959-68; Vicar of Hendon, 1968-71. *Recreations:* reading, singing and watching TV. *Address:* Gayton Lodge, 71 Gayton Road, Harrow, Middlesex HA1 2LY. *T:* 01-863 1530.

SOUTHWOOD, Captain Horace Gerald, CBE 1966; DSC 1941; Royal Navy; Managing Director, Silley, Cox & Co. Ltd, Falmouth Docks, since 1974; Chairman, Falmouth Group, since 1976; *b* 19 April 1912; *s* of late Horace George Southwood; *m* 1936, Ruby Edith Hayes; two *s* one *d. Educ:* HMS Fisgard, RN Coll., Greenwich. Joined RN, 1927; HMS Resolution, Medit. Stn, 1932-34; HMS Barham, 1934-35; RN Coll., Greenwich, 1935-36; HMS Royal Oak, Home Fleet, 1936-38; specialised in Submarines, 1938; HMS Lucia, 1938-39. HM Submarine, Regent, 1939-41; HMS Medway, China and Medit., 1941-42 (despatches, DSC); HM Submarine, Amphion (first of Class), 1943-45. HMS Dolphin, 1946-48; HMS Vengeance, 1948-49; Comdr, 1948; HMS Glory, 1949-51; HMS Forth, 1951-52; Admty, Whitehall, 1952-54; HM Dockyard, Portsmouth (Dep. Man.), 1954-58; jssc, 1958-59; Capt., 1958. Chief Engr, Singapore, 1959-62; Sen. Officers' War Course, 1962; Manager, Engrg Dept, HM Dockyard, Portsmouth, 1963-67; Gen. Manager, HM Dockyard, Devonport, 1967-72, retd. Management Consultant, Productivity and Management Services Ltd, 1972-74. CEng, FIMechE, MBIM. *Recreations:* sailing, fishing, golf, caravanning. *Address:* Dolphin Cottage, Riverside, Newton Ferrers, Devon. *T:* Newton Ferrers 649. *Clubs:* Naval; Royal Naval and Royal Albert Yacht (Portsmouth); Royal Western Yacht (Plymouth); Yealm Yacht (Newton Ferrers).

SOUTHWOOD, Prof. Thomas Richard Edmund, FRS 1977; Professor of Zoology and Applied Entomology, University of London; Head of Department of Zoology and Applied Entomology and Director of Field Station, Imperial College, since 1967; *b* 20 June 1931; *s* of Edmund W. Southwood and late A. Mary, *d* of Archdeacon T. R. Regg; *m* 1955, Alison Langley, *d* of A. L. Harden, Harpenden, Herts; two *s. Educ:* Gravesend Grammar Sch.; Imperial Coll., London. BSc, ARCS 1952; PhD London, 1955; DSc London, 1963. ARC Research Schol., Rothamsted Experimental Station, 1952-55; Res. Asst and Lecturer, Zoology Dept, Imperial Coll., London, 1955-64; Vis. Prof., Dept. of Entomology, University of California, Berkeley, 1964-65; Reader in Insect Ecology, University of London, 1964-67. Dean, Royal Coll. of Science, 1971-72. Chm., Division of Life Sciences, Imperial Coll., 1974-77. Member: ARC Adv. Cttee on Plants and Soils, 1970-72; ARC Res. Grants Bd, 1972-; JCO Arable and Forage Crops Bd, 1972-; NERC Terrestrial Life Sciences (formerly Nature Conservancy) Grants Cttee, 1971-76 (Chm., 1972-76); Royal Commn on Environmental Pollution, 1974-; Council, St George's House, Windsor, 1974-; Adv. Bd, Research Councils, 1977-; Pres., British Ecological Soc., 1976-78 (Hon. Treas., 1960-64 and 1967-68). Governor, Glasshouse Crops Research Inst., 1969-; Trustee, British Museum (Natural History), 1974-; Plenary speaker, 15th Internat. Congress on Entomology, Washington, 1976; Spencer Lectr, Univ. of British Columbia, 1978. Scientific Medal, Zool. Soc., London, 1969. *Publications:* (with D. Leston) Land and Water Bugs of the British Isles, 1959; Life of the Wayside and Woodland, 1963; Ecological Methods, 1966; many papers in entomological and ecological jls. *Recreations:* natural history, gardening. *Address:* 8 Silwood Close, Ascot, Berks. *T:* Ascot 21676. *Club:* Athenæum.

SOUTHWOOD, William Frederick Walter, MD; MChir; FRCS; Consultant Surgeon, Bath Health District, since 1966; *b* 8 June 1925; *s* of Stuart W. Southwood, MC, and Mildred M. Southwood; *m* 1965, Margaret Carleton Holderness, *d* of late Sir Ernest Holderness, Bt, CBE, and Lady Holderness; two *s. Educ:* Charterhouse; Trinity Coll., Cambridge (MA 1951, MD 1964, MChir 1956); Guy's Hosp. FRCS 1954. Surg. Registrar, West London Hosp. and St Mark's Hosp. for Diseases of the Rectum, 1954-60; Sen. Surg. Registrar, Royal Infirmary, Bristol, 1960-66. Hunterian Prof., RCS, 1961. Member: Court of Assts, Worshipful Soc. of Apothecaries of London, 1975-; Temp. Registration Assessment Bd, GMC, 1976-. Esamr in Anatomy and Surgery to GNC, 1957-72. *Publications:* articles in surgical jls. *Recreations:* fishing, snooker. *Address:* Upton House, Bathwick Hill, Bath, Avon. *T:* Bath 5152. *Club:* Bath and County (Bath).

SOUTHWORTH, Sir Frederick, Kt 1965; QC; Chief Justice, Malawi, 1964-70; *b* Blackburn, Lancashire, 9 May 1910; *m* 1942, Margaret, *d* of James Rice, Monaghan, Iceland; three *d. Educ:* Queen Elizabeth's Grammar Sch., Blackburn; Exeter Coll., Oxford. Called to the Bar, Gray's Inn, 1936. War of 1939-45; commissioned 1939; Department of the Judge Advocate General in India, 1943; Hon. Colonel, Crown Counsel, Palestine, 1946; Crown Counsel, Tanganyika, 1947; Attorney General of the Bahamas, 1951-55; QC Bahamas, 1952; Acting Governor, July-Aug. 1952; Acting Chief Justice, July-Oct. 1954; Puisne Judge, Nyasaland, 1955; Acting Governor-General, Malawi, at various times, 1964-66. *Address:* c/o Barclays Bank, Halkett Place, St Helier, Jersey.

SOUTHWORTH, Jean May, QC 1973; a Recorder of the Crown Court, since 1972; *b* 20 April 1926; *o c* of late Edgar and Jane Southworth, Clitheroe. *Educ:* Queen Ethelburga's Sch., Harrogate; St Anne's Coll., Oxford (MA). Served in WRNS, 1944-45. Called to Bar, Gray's Inn, 1954. Standing Counsel to Dept of Trade and Industry for Central Criminal Court and Inner London Sessions, 1969-73. Fellow, Woodard Corporation (Northern Div.), 1974. *Recreations:* music, watching cricket. *Address:* 21 Caroline Place, W2 4AN; Queen Elizabeth Building, Temple, EC4Y 9BS.

SOUYAVE, Hon. Sir (Louis) Georges, Kt 1971; Hon. Mr Justice Souyave; Resident Judge of the High Court of the New Hebrides and British Judge of the Joint Court of the New Hebrides, since 1976; *b* 29 May 1926; *m* 1953, Mona de Chermont; two *s* four *d. Educ:* St Louis Coll., Seychelles; Gray's Inn, London. Barrister-at-Law, Gray's Inn, 1949. In private practice, Seychelles, 1949-56; Asst Attorney-Gen., Seychelles, 1956-62; Supreme Court, Seychelles: Additional Judge, 1962-64; Puisne Judge, 1964-70; Chief Justice, 1970-76. *Recreations:* fishing, sailing. *Address:* British Judge's Chambers, Joint Court, Port Vila, New Hebrides, Western Pacific.

SOUZAY, Gérard (*né* Gérard Marcel Tisserand), Chevalier, Légion d'Honneur; Chevalier de l'Ordre des Arts et Lettres; French baritone; *b* 8 Dec. 1921. *Educ:* Paris Conservatoire Musique. World Première, Stravinsky's Canticum Sacrum, Venice Festival, 1956; Bach B Minor Mass at Salzburg Festival; Pelléas et Mélisande, Rome Opera, Opera Comique, 1962, Scala, Milan, 1973; Don Giovanni, Paris Opera, 1963; second tour of Australia and New Zealand, 1964. Also tours in US, South America, Japan, Africa, Europe. Annual Lieder recitals, Salzburg Festival. Has made recordings; Grand Prix du Disque, for Ravel Recital, etc. *Recreations:* tennis, painting. *Address:* 26 rue Freycinet, 75116 Paris, France.

SOWMAN, Air Cdre John Edward Rudkin, CB 1959; CBE 1957; DL; RAF, retired; *b* West Clandon, Surrey, 8 May 1902; *s* of Alfred William Rudkin Sowman and Ellen Sowman (*née* Bone); *m* 1928, Olive Rosa Trimmer; two *s* one *d. Educ:* Bedford Sch. Engineer Training, 1919-24; Pilot Officer, RAF, Oct. 1926; Flying Officer No 70 Sqdn, Iraq, 1929-30; Flt Lieut, No 33 Sqdn, Bicester, 1930-34, No 47 Sqdn, Khartoum, 1934-36; RAF Staff Coll., 1937; Air Ministry, Sqdn Leader, Wing Comdr, Group Captain, 1938-43 (responsible for provision of radio equipment); on HQ Staff, MAAF, Algiers, 1943-45; Comdr No 351 MU Algiers, 1945-46 (clearance of N Africa); Staff appts at HQ No 40 Group and Flying Training Comd, 1946-51; Air Cdre and SESO, MEAF, 1951-53; SASO, HQ No 40 Group, 1953-56; Director of Mechanical Transport and Marine Craft, Air Ministry, Sept. 1956-Nov. 1959. DL Beds 1973. *Recreation:* rifle shooting (RAF Team, 7 times, once as Captain), won Alexandra Cup at Bisley, 1949. *Address:* 58 St Michaels Road, Bedford MK40 2LU. *T:* Bedford 66415. *Club:* Royal Air Force.

SOWREY, Air Marshal Frederick Beresford, CB 1968; CBE 1965; AFC 1954; UK Representative, Permanent Military Deputies Group, Central Treaty Organisation, since 1977; *b* 14 Sept. 1922; *s* of late Group Captain Frederick Sowrey, DSO, MC, AFC; *m* 1946, Anne Margaret, *d* of late Captain C. T. A. Bunbury, OBE, RN; one *s* one *d. Educ:* Charterhouse. Joined RAF 1940; flying training in Canada, 1941; Fighter-reconnaissance Squadron, European theatre, 1942-44; Flying Instructors Sch., 1944; Airborne Forces, 1945; No 615 (Co. of Surrey) Squadron, RAuxAF, 1946-48; Fighter Gunnery Sch., 1949-50, comdg 615 Sqdn, 1951-54; RAF Staff Coll., Bracknell, 1954; Chiefs of Staff Secretariat, 1955-58; comdg No 46 Sqdn, 1958-60; Personal Staff Officer to CAS, 1960-62; comdg RAF Abingdon, 1962-64; IDC 1965; SASO, Middle East Comd (Aden), 1966-67; Dir Defence Policy, MoD, 1968-70; SASO, RAF Trng Comd, 1970-72; Comdt, Nat. Defence Coll., 1972-75; Dir-Gen. RAF Training, 1975-77. *Publications:* contribs and book reviews for defence jls. *Recreations:* motoring sport (internat. records 1956), veteran aircraft and cars, mechanical devices of any kind, fishing. *Address:* c/o British Embassy, Sehit Ersan Caddesi, 46A, Cankaya, Ankara, Turkey. *Club:* Royal Air Force.

SOYSA, Sir Warusahennedige Abraham Bastian, Kt 1954; CBE 1953 (MBE 1950); JP; formerly Mayor of Kandy, Sri Lanka; Proprietor of W. B. Soysa & Co., Sri Lanka. *Address:* W. B. Soysa & Co., 184 Colombo Street, Kandy, Sri Lanka.

SPAAK, Fernand Paul Jules, Dr en droit; Head of Delegation to USA, Commission of the European Communities, since 1976; *b* 8 Aug. 1923; *s* of Paul-Henri Spaak and Marguerite Malevez; *m* 1953, Anne-Marie Farina; three *d. Educ:* Université Libre de Bruxelles (Dr en droit); Univ. of Cambridge (BA Econs).

National Bank of Belgium, 1950-52; High Authority, European Coal and Steel Community, Luxembourg: Exec. Asst to Pres., Jean Monnet and to Pres. René Mayer, 1953-58; Dir, Cartels and Concentrations Div., 1958-60; Dir Gen., Supply Agency, Euratom, Brussels, 1960-67; Dir Gen. of Energy, Commn of European Communities, Brussels, 1967-75. *Address:* 2534 Belmont Road NW, Washington, DC 20008, USA. *T:* (202) 483-0254.

SPAFFORD, Very Rev. Christopher Garnett Howsin; Provost and Vicar of Newcastle, since 1976; *b* 10 Sept. 1924; *s* of Rev. Canon Douglas Norman Spafford and Frances Alison Spafford; *m* 1953, Stephanie Peel; three *s. Educ:* Marlborough Coll.; St John's Coll., Oxford (MA 2nd Cl. Hons Modern History); Wells Theological Coll. Curate of Brighouse, 1950; Curate of Huddersfield Parish Church, 1953; Vicar of Hebden Bridge, 1955; Rector of Thornhill, Dewsbury, 1961; Vicar of St Chad's, Shrewsbury, 1969. *Recreations:* reading, gardening, walking. *Address:* The Cathedral Vicarage, 23 Montague Avenue, Gosforth, Newcastle upon Tyne NE3 4HY. *T:* Newcastle upon Tyne 853472.

SPAFFORD, George Christopher Howsin; a Recorder of the Crown Court, since 1975; Chancellor, Manchester Diocese, since 1976; *b* 1 Sept. 1921; *s* of Christopher Howsin Spafford and Clara Margaret Spafford; *m* 1959, Iola Margaret, 3rd *d* of Bertrand Leslie Hallward, *qv*; one *s* one *d. Educ:* Rugby; Univ. of Oxford (MA, BCL Hons). Served RA, 1939-46 (Captain). Called to Bar, Middle Temple, 1948. *Recreation:* painting pictures. *Address:* 460 The Royal Exchange, Cross Street, Manchester M2 7EW.

SPAGHT, Monroe E., MA, PhD; Director, Royal Dutch Petroleum Co., since 1970 (Managing Director, 1965-70); Director, Shell Oil Co., USA, since 1970 (Executive Vice-President, 1953-60, President, 1961-65, Chairman, 1965-70); *b* Eureka, California, 9 Dec. 1909; *s* of Fred E. and Alpha L. Spaght; *m*; two *s* one *d. Educ:* Stanford Univ.; University of Leipzig. AB 1929, MA 1930, PhD 1933, Stanford Univ. (Chemistry). Research Scientist Shell Oil Co., 1933-45; Vice-President, Shell Development Co., 1945-48, President, 1949-52; Exec. Vice-President, Shell Oil Co., 1953-60, President, 1961-65; Man. Dir, Royal Dutch/Shell Group, 1965-70; Director: Stanford Research Inst., 1953-70; Inst. of International Education, 1953- (Chm., 1971-74); American Petroleum Inst., 1953-; The Boston Co., 1971-; American Standard, 1972-. Chm., Internat. Adv. Bd of Chemical Bank, 1977-; Mem., Internat. Adv. Cttee, Wells Fargo Bank, 1977-. Trustee, Stanford Univ., 1955-65. President, Economic Club of New York, 1964-65. Hon. DSc: Rensselaer Polytechnic Inst., 1958; Drexel Inst. of Technology, 1962; Hon. LLD: Manchester, 1964; California State Colleges, 1965; Millikin Univ., Illinois, 1967; Wesleyan Univ., Middletown, Conn, 1968; Hon. DEng, Colorado Sch. of Mines, 1971. Order of Francisco de Miranda, Venezuela, 1968; Cmdr, Order of Oranje Nassau, 1970. *Publications:* contribs to scientific journals. *Address:* Shell Centre, London SE1. *T:* 01-934 1234. *Clubs:* Athenæum; Blind Brook Country, Links (New York).

SPAIN, Stephen William; Under Secretary, Department of Energy, since 1974; *b* 18 Oct. 1924; 2nd *s* of Peter Valentine and Ellen Gammon; *m* 1950, Jean Margaret Evitt; three *s* one *d. Educ:* Hendon Grammar Sch.; LSE. Lieut (A) RNVR, 1942-46. Asst Principal, Min. of Labour, 1949; Commonwealth Dept of Labour, Melbourne, 1957-59; UK Delegn to Council of Europe, Western European Union, ILO, 1959-61; Hon. Sec., First Division Assoc., 1961-64; Min. of Technology: Asst Sec., 1965-69; Under-Sec., 1969-; Dir, Central Computer Agency, CSD, 1971-73. *Recreations:* natural history, walking, gardening. *Address:* 9 Sherland Court, Radlett, Herts. *T:* Radlett 4273. *Club:* Athenæum.

SPALDING, Prof. Dudley Brian, MA, ScD; FIMechE, FInstF; Professor of Heat Transfer in the University of London at the Imperial College of Science and Technology, since 1958; *b* New Malden, Surrey, 9 Jan. 1923; *s* of H. A. Spalding; *m* 1947, Eda Ilse-Lotte (*née* Goericke); two *s* two *d. Educ:* King's College Sch., Wimbledon; The Queen's Coll., Oxford; Pembroke Coll., Cambridge. BA (Oxon) 1944; MA (Cantab) 1948, PhD (Cantab) 1951. Bataafsche Petroleum Matschapij, 1944-45; Ministry of Supply, 1945-47; National Physical Laboratory, 1947-48; ICI Research Fellow at Cambridge Univ., 1948-50; Cambridge University Demonstrator in Engineering, 1950-54; Reader in Applied Heat, Imperial College of Science and Technology, 1954-58. Managing Director: Combustion, Heat and Mass Transfer Ltd, 1970-. Concentration, Heat and Momentum Ltd, 1975-. *Publications:* Some Fundamentals of Combustion, 1955; (with E. H. Cole) Engineering Thermodynamics, 1958;

Convective Mass Transfer, 1963; (with S. V. Patankar) Heat and Mass Transfer in Boundary Layers, 1967, rev. edn 1970; (co-author) Heat and Mass Transfer in Recirculating Flows, 1969; (with B. E. Launder) Mathematical Models of Turbulence, 1972; numerous scientific papers. *Recreations:* squash, poetry. *Address:* (home) 2 Vineyard Hill Road, SW19. *T:* 01-946 2514; (business) Imperial College, Exhibition Road, SW7. *T:* 01-589 5111.

SPALDING, Rear-Adm. Ian Jaffery L.; *see* Lees-Spalding.

SPANSWICK, (Ernest) Albert (George), JP; General Secretary, Confederation of Health Service Employees, since 1974; Member, TUC General Council, since 1977; *b* 2 Oct. 1919; *m* Joyce Redmore; one *s* two *d.* SRN, RMN. Regional Sec., Northern Region, Confedn of Health Service Employees, 1959; apptd National Officer, 1962; elected Asst General Secretary, 1969; elected General Secretary, 1973, and took up duties in July 1974. JP Co. Surrey, 1970. *Recreations:* swimming, walking, fishing. *Address:* Confederation of Health Service Employees, Glen House, High Street, Banstead, Surrey. *T:* Burgh Heath 53322.

SPARK, Mrs Muriel Sarah, OBE 1967; writer; *b* Edinburgh; *d* of Bernard Camberg and Sarah Elizabeth Maud (*née* Uezzell); *m* 1937 (marr. diss.); one *s. Educ:* James Gillespie's School for Girls, Edinburgh. General Secretary, The Poetry Society, Editor, The Poetry Review, 1947-49. FRSL 1963. Hon. DLitt Strathclyde, 1971. *Publications:* critical and biographical: (ed jtly) Tribute to Wordsworth, 1950; (ed) Selected Poems of Emily Brontë, 1952; Child of Light: a Reassessment of Mary Shelley, 1951; (ed jtly) My Best Mary: the letters of Mary Shelley, 1953; John Masefield, 1953; (joint) Emily Brontë: her Life and Work, 1953; (ed) The Brontë Letters, 1954; (ed jointly) Letters of John Henry Newman, 1957; *poems:* The Fanfarlo and Other Verse, 1952; *fiction:* The Comforters, 1957; Robinson, 1958; The Go-Away Bird, 1958; Memento Mori, 1959 (adapted for stage, 1964); The Ballad of Peckham Rye, 1960 (Italia prize, for dramatic radio, 1962); The Bachelors, 1960; Voices at Play, 1961; The Prime of Miss Jean Brodie, 1961 (adapted for stage, 1966, filmed 1969); Doctors of Philosophy (play), 1963; The Girls of Slender Means, 1963, adapted for radio, 1964, and BBC TV, 1975; The Mandelbaum Gate, 1965 (James Tait Black Memorial Prize); Collected Stories I, 1967; Collected Poems I, 1967; The Public Image, 1968; The Very Fine Clock (for children), 1969; The Driver's Seat, 1970 (filmed 1974); Not to Disturb, 1971; The Hot House by the East River, 1973; The Abbess of Crewe, 1974 (filmed 1977); The Takeover, 1976. *Recreations:* poetry, friends, cats, racing. *Address:* c/o Macmillan & Co. Ltd, Little Essex Street, WC2.

SPARKMAN, John J.; US Senator from Alabama since Nov. 1946; Chairman, Senate Committee on Foreign Relations, since 1975; *b* 20 Dec. 1899; *s* of Whitten J. Sparkman and Julia Mitchell (*née* Kent); *m* 1923, Ivo Hall; one *d. Educ:* University of Alabama. AB 1921, LLB 1923, AM 1924; Phi Beta Kappa. Admitted to Alabama Bar, 1925; practised as Attorney, Huntsville, Ala, 1925-36; US Commissioner, 1930-31; Member of US House of Representatives, 1937-46; Democratic Nomination for Vice-Presidency, 1952. Chm., Senate Banking Cttee, 1967. Hon. degrees: Alabama; Spring Hill Coll., Ala; Athens Coll., Ala; Huntingdon Coll., Ala; Auburn; Seoul, Korea. Methodist. *Address:* Huntsville, Alabama 35801, USA; Senate Office Building, Washington, DC 20510, USA. *Clubs:* Army-Navy Country, 1925 F Street (both Washington); Huntsville Country (Alabama).

SPARKS, Arthur Charles, BSc (Econ); Under-Secretary, Ministry of Agriculture, Fisheries and Food, 1959-74; *b* 1914; *s* of late Charles Herbert and Kate Dorothy Sparks; *m* 1939, Betty Joan, *d* of late Harry Oswald and Lilian Mary Simmons; three *d. Educ:* Selhurst Grammar Sch.; London School of Economics. Clerk, Ministry of Agriculture and Fisheries, 1931; Administrative Grade, 1936; National Fire Service, 1942-44; Principal Private Secretary to Minister of Agriculture and Fisheries, 1946-47; Asst Secretary, Ministry of Agriculture and Fisheries, 1947-49 and 1951-59; Asst Secretary, Treasury, 1949-51. Chm., Internat. Wheat Council, 1968-69. *Recreations:* reading, walking. *Address:* 7 Cottenham Place, West Wimbledon, SW20. *T:* 01-947 1908.

SPARKS, Rev. Hedley Frederick Davis, DD Oxon, 1949; FBA 1959; Oriel Professor of the Interpretation of Holy Scripture, University of Oxford, 1952-76; *b* 14 Nov. 1908; *s* of late Rev. Frederick Sparks and late Blanche Barnes Sparks (formerly Jackson); *m* 1953, Margaret Joan, *d* of C. H. Davy; two *s* one *d. Educ:* St Edmund's Sch., Canterbury; BNC, Oxford; Ripon Hall, Oxford. Hon. DD (St Andrews), 1963. *Publications:* The

Old Testament in the Christian Church, 1944; The Formation of the New Testament, 1952; A Synopsis of the Gospels, part I: The Synoptic Gospels with the Johannine Parallels, 1964, 2nd edn 1970; part II: The Gospel according to St John with the Synoptic Parallels, 1974, combined volume edn, 1977; *Joint Editor:* Novum Testamentum Domini Nostri Iesu Christi Latine secundum editionem Sancti Hieronymi, Part ii, fasc. 5, 1937, fasc. 6, 1939, fasc. 7, 1941, Part iii, fasc. 2, 1949, fasc. 3, 1953; Biblia Sacra iuxta Vulgatam versionem, 1969, 2nd edn 1975; *Contributor:* The Bible in its Ancient and English Versions, 1940, 2nd edn 1954; Studies in the Gospels, 1955; The Cambridge History of the Bible, vol. 1, 1970, 2nd edn, 1975. *Recreations:* music and railways. *Address:* 48 London Road, Canterbury, Kent.

SPARKS, Joseph Alfred; Mayor of the Borough of Acton, 1957-58; *b* 30 Sept. 1901; *s* of late Samuel and Edith Sparks; *m* 1928, Dora Brent; two *s. Educ:* Uffculm School and Central Labour College. Alderman of Borough of Acton and County of Middlesex, 1958-61; retired. Clerk Western Region, British Railways; President, London District Council NUR, 1934-45; Parliamentary Labour Candidate, Taunton, 1929, Chelmsford, 1931, and Buckingham, 1935. MP (Lab) Acton, 1945-Sept. 1959. Freeman of the Borough of Acton. *Publications:* A Short History of Dunteswell Abbey, 1969; A History of Sheldon, Devon, 1975. *Address:* 10 Emanuel Avenue, W3. *T:* 01-992 2069.

SPARROW, (Albert) Charles, QC 1966; barrister; *b* Kasauli, India, 16 Sept. 1925; *e s* of late Captain Charles Thomas Sparrow, sometime Essex Regt, and Antonia Sparrow; *m* 1949, Edith Rosalie Taylor; two *s* one *d. Educ:* Royal Grammar Sch., Colchester. Served Civil Defence, 1939-43; joined Army, 1943; posted as cadet to India, commnd into Royal Signals and served in Far East, 1944-47; OC, GHQ Signals, Simla, 1947. Admitted to Gray's Inn, 1947 (Holker Senior Scholar, Atkin Scholar, Lee Prizeman and Richards Prizeman); called to Bar, 1950, Master of the Bench, 1976; LLB London Univ., 1951; admitted to Lincoln's Inn, 1967; in practice in Chancery and before Parliament, 1950-. Member: Chancery Procedure Cttee, 1968-; General Council of the Bar, 1969-73; Senate of the Four Inns of Court, 1970-73. Hon. Legal Adviser to Council for British Archæology (concerned notably with legal protection of antiquities and reform of treasure trove; produced two draft Antiquities Bills), 1966-. Chm., independent Panel of Inquiry for affairs of RSPCA, 1973-74. FSA 1972. Pres., Essex Archaeological Soc., 1975-78. Chm., Stock Branch, British Legion, 1970-75. Freeman, City of London. *Recreation:* Romano-British archæology. *Address:* 13 Old Square, Lincoln's Inn WC2A 3UA. *T:* 01-242 6105; Croyde Lodge, Stock, Essex.

SPARROW, John Hanbury Angus, OBE 1946; Warden of All Souls College, Oxford, 1952-77; *b* New Oxley, near Wolverhampton, 13 Nov. 1906; *e s* of I. S. Sparrow and Margaret Macgregor; unmarried. *Educ:* Winchester (Scholar); New Coll., Oxford (Scholar). 1st Class, Hon. Mods, 1927; 1st Class, Lit Hum, 1929; Fellow of All Souls Coll., 1929 (re-elected 1937, 1946); Chancellor's Prize for Latin Verse, 1929; Eldon Scholar, 1929; called to Bar, Middle Temple, 1931; practised in Chancery Division, 1931-39; enlisted in Oxford and Bucks LI, 1939; Commnd Coldstream Guards, 1940; Military Asst to Lt-Gen. Sir H. C. B. Wemyss in War Office and on Military Mission in Washington, Feb.-Dec. 1941; rejoined regt in England, 1942; DAAG and AAG, War Office, 1942-45; resumed practice at Bar, 1946; ceased to practise on appointment as Warden of All Souls Coll., 1952; Hon. Bencher, Middle Temple, 1952; Fellow of Winchester Coll., 1951; Hon. Fellow, New Coll., 1956. Hon. DLitt, Univ. of Warwick, 1967. *Publications:* various; mostly reviews and essays in periodicals, some of which were collected in Independent Essays, 1963, and Controversial Essays, 1966; Sense and Poetry: essays on the place of meaning in contemporary verse; Mark Pattison and the Idea of a University (Clark Lectures), 1967; After the Assassination, 1968; Visible Words (Sandars Lectures), 1969. *Address:* Beechwood House, Iffley, Oxford. *Clubs:* Garrick, Reform, Beefsteak.

SPAUL, Eric A., DSc, PhD (London); FZS; FIBiol; Professor of Zoology, The University, Leeds, 1933-60; Professor Emeritus, 1960; *b* 27 Aug. 1895. *Educ:* Owen's School, London; Birkbeck Coll., Univ. of London. War Service, 1915-19, Commissioned Rank, London Regt and RE; Gen. Reserve, 1942-46. Graduated BSc (London), 1921, PhD 1924, DSc, 1930; Assistant Lecturer, 1921; Lecturer, 1924; Reader in Zoology, University of London, 1930-33. *Publications:* contributed to: The Natural History of the Scarborough District, Vols I & II, 1956; Van Nostrand's Scientific Encyclopedia, 3rd edn, 1958; and to Journal of Experimental Biology, Proceedings of the Zoological Soc., etc.

Recreations: sports, travel. *Address:* 6 Churchdown Road, Poolbrook, Malvern, Worcs.

SPEAKMAN-PITT, William, VC 1951; *b* 21 Sept. 1927; *m* 1st, 1956, Rachel Snitch; one *s*; 2nd, Jill; one *d. Educ:* Wellington Road Senior Boys' Sch., Altrincham. Entered Army as Private. Served Korean War, 1950-53 (VC), King's Own Scottish Borderers. *Recreations:* swimming, and ski-ing.

SPEAR, Harold Cumming, CBE 1976; Member, Central Arbitration Committee, since 1976; *b* 26 Oct. 1909; *yr s* of late Rev. Edwin A. and Elizabeth Spear; *m* 1935, Gwendolen (*née* Richards); one *s* one *d. Educ:* Kingswood Sch., Bath. Asst to Employment Manager, Gramophone Co. Ltd, 1928-33; Labour and Welfare Supervisor, Mitcham Works Ltd, 1933-35; Employment Supervisor, Hoover Ltd, 1935-38; Personnel Manager, Sperry Gyroscope Co. Ltd, 1938-40; appts with British Overseas Airways Corp., finally as Chief Personnel Officer, 1941-59; Dir of Personnel Management, Central Electricity Generating Bd, 1959-72; Mem., Electricity Council, 1972-76. Pres., Inst. of Personnel Management, 1969-71; CIPM. *Recreation:* golf. *Address:* Gayhurst, Bank,near Lyndhurst, Hants SO4 7FD. *T:* Lyndhurst 3377. *Club:* Roehampton.

SPEAR, Ruskin, RA 1954 (ARA 1944); artist; *b* 30 June 1911; *s* of Augustus and Jane Spear; *m* 1935, Mary Hill; one *s. Educ:* Brook Green School; Hammersmith School of Art; Royal College of Art, Kensington, under Sir William Rothenstein. Diploma, 1934; first exhibited Royal Academy, 1932; elected London Group, 1942; President London Group, 1949-50; Visiting teacher, Royal College of Art, 1952-77. Pictures purchased by Chantrey Bequest, Contemporary Art Society, Arts Council of Great Britain, and British Council. Exhibited work in Pushkin Museum, Moscow, 1957; has also exhibited in Paris, USA, Belgium, S Africa, Australia, NZ. Commissions include: Altar Piece for RAF Memorial Church, St Clement Danes, 1959; four mural panels for P&O Liner Canberra. Recent portraits include: Lord Adrian; Herbert Butterfield; Sir Stewart Duke-Elder; Sir Laurence Olivier as Macbeth (Stratford Memorial Theatre); Lord Chandos; Sir Ian Jacob; Sir Robin Darwin; Miss Ruth Cohen; Sir Eric Ashby; S. S. Eriks, KBE; Dr Ramsey, Archbishop of Canterbury; Sir Aubrey Lewis; Arthur Armitage; Harold Wilson; 5th Duke of Westminster; Sir Hugh Greene; Lord Goodman; Dr Charles Bosanquet; Sir James Tait; Sir John Mellor; Sir Alan Herbert; Sir Geoffrey Taylor; G. F. Taylor; Sir Peter Allen; Sir Maurice Bridgeman. Visiting teacher, RCA, until 1976. *Address:* 20 Fielding Road, Chiswick, W4. *T:* 01-995 9736; (Studio) 60 British Grove, Hammersmith, W6.

SPEARING, George David; Under Secretary, Department of Transport, since 1976, and Director, Highways Planning and Management, since 1974; *b* 16 Dec. 1927; *s* of George Thomas and Edith Lydia Anna Spearing; *m* 1951, Josephine Mary Newbould; two *s* one *d. Educ:* Rotherham Grammar Sch.; Sheffield Univ. BEng; MICE, FIHE. RAF, Airfield Construction Br., 1948. Asst Divl Surveyor, Somerset CC, 1951; Asst Civil Engr, W Riding of Yorks CC, 1953; Asst Engr, MoT, 1957; Supt. Engr, Midland Road Construction Unit, 1967; Asst Chief Engr, MoT, 1969; Regional Controller (Roads and Transportation), West Midlands, 1972; Dep. Chief Engr, DoE, 1973; Under Sec., DoE, 1974-76. *Publications:* papers in Proc. Instn CE and Jl Instn HE. *Address:* Wysswood, Dayseys Hill, Outwood, Surrey RH1 5QY. *T:* Smallfield 2715.

SPEARING, Nigel John; MP (Lab) Newham South, since May 1974; *b* 8 Oct. 1930; *s* of Austen and May Spearing; *m* 1956, Wendy, *d* of Percy and Molly Newman, Newport, Mon; one *s* two *d. Educ:* Latymer Upper School, Hammersmith. Ranks and commission, Royal Signals, 1950-52; St Catharine's Coll., Cambridge, 1953-56. Tutor and later Sen. Geography Master, Wandsworth School, 1956-68; Director, Thameside Research and Development Group, Inst. of Community Studies, 1968-69; Housemaster, Elliott School, Putney, 1969-70. Chairman: Barons Court Labour Party, 1961-63; Hammersmith Local Govt Cttee of the Labour Party, 1966-68. Contested (Lab) Warwick and Leamington, 1964. MP (Lab) Acton, 1970-74; Secretary: Parly Lab. Party Educn Gp, 1971-74; Parly Inland Waterways Gp, 1970-74; Member Select Cttee: Overseas Develt, 1973-74; Members' Interests, 1974-75; Procedure, 1975-. Vice-Pres., River Thames Soc; Pres., Socialist Envt and Resources Assoc., 1977-. Co-opted Mem. GLC Cttees, 1966-73. *Publication:* The Thames Barrier-Barrage Controversy (Inst. of Community Studies), 1969. *Recreations:* rowing, reading. *Address:* House of Commons, SW1. *T:* 01-219 3000.

SPEARMAN, Sir Alexander Cadwallader Mainwaring, Kt 1956; *b* 1901; *s* of late Commander A. C. M. Spearman, Royal Navy;

m 1928, Diana (marriage dissolved, 1951), *d* of Colonel Sir Arthur Doyle, 4th Bt; *m* 1951, Diana Josephine, *d* of Colonel Sir Lambert Ward, 1st Bt, CVO, DSO, TD; four *s* one *d. Educ:* Repton; Hertford College, Oxford. Contested Mansfield Div., Gen. Election, 1935, Gorton Div. of Manchester, By-Election, 1937; MP (C) Scarborough and Whitby, 1941-66, retd. PPS to President of the Board of Trade, 1951-52. *Address:* The Old Rectory, Sarratt, Herts. *T:* King's Langley 64733; 14 Cadogan Square, SW1. *T:* 01-235 1529. *Club:* Beefsteak.

SPEARMAN, Sir Alexander Young Richard Mainwaring, 5th Bt *cr* 1840; *b* 3 Feb. 1969; *s* of Sir Alexander Bowyer Spearman, 4th Bt, and Martha, *d* of John Green, Naauwpoort, S Africa; *S* father, 1977. *Heir:* uncle Dr Richard Ian Campbell Spearman, FLS, FZS, *b* 14 Aug. 1926. *Address:* Windwards, Klein Constantia Road, Constantia, Cape Town, 7800, S Africa.

SPEARMAN, Clement; HM Diplomatic Service; Ambassador to the Dominican Republic, since 1975; *b* 10 Sept. 1919; *y s* of late Edward and Clara Spearman; *m* 1950, Olwen Regina Morgan; one *s* two *d. Educ:* Cardiff High School. RNVR, 1942-46. Entered Foreign (subseq. Diplomatic) Service, 1948; 3rd Sec., Brussels, 1948-49; 2nd Sec., FO, 1949-51; HM Consul, Skoplje, 1951-53; FO, 1953-56; 1st Sec., Buenos Aires, 1956-60; FO, 1960-62; Dep. Sec.-Gen., CENTO, Ankara, 1962-65; Reykjavik, 1965-69; FCO, 1969-71; Manila, 1971-74; Toronto, 1974-75. *Recreations:* tennis, swimming. *Address:* c/o Foreign and Commonwealth Office, SW1A 2AH. *Clubs:* Travellers', Naval, Roehampton.

SPECTOR, Prof. Roy Geoffrey, MD, PhD; FRCP, FRCPath; Professor of Applied Pharmacology, Guy's Hospital Medical School, since 1972; *b* 27 Aug. 1931; *s* of Paul Spector and Esther Cohen; *m* 1960, Evie Joan Freeman; two *s* one *d. Educ:* Roundhay Sch., Leeds; Sch. of Medicine, Leeds Univ. (MB, ChB, MD); PhD Lond 1964, Dip. in Biochem. 1966. FRCP 1971; FRCPath 1976; FRSM. Lectr in Paediatric Res. Unit, Guy's Hosp., 1961-67; Guy's Hosp. Medical School: Reader in Pharmacology, 1968-71; Sub Dean for Admissions, 1975-. Vice Chm., British Univs' Film Council, 1976-. *Publications:* The Nerve Cell, 1964; Clinical Pharmacology in Dentistry, 1975; Mechanisms in Pharmacology and Therapeutics, 1976; contribs to jls on pathology, gen. science, and applied pharmacology. *Recreations:* music, pottery, walking. *Address:* Department of Pharmacology, Guy's Hospital Medical School, SE1 9RT. *T:* 01-407 7600, ext. 3384.

SPECTOR, Prof. Walter Graham; Professor of Pathology in the University of London at St Bartholomew's Hospital Medical College, since 1962; Consultant Pathologist, St Bartholomew's Hospital; Secretary, Beit Memorial Fellowships Advisory Board; *b* 20 Dec. 1924; *o s* of H. Spector, London; *m* 1957, June, *o d* of Col W. F. Routley, OBE, Melbourne, Australia; two *s. Educ:* City of London School; Queens' Coll., Cambridge; UCH Med. School (Graham Schol.). MB 1947, MA 1949, Cambridge; MRCP 1948; FRCP 1966; FRCPath 1972. Beit Memorial Fellow in Medical Research, 1951; Lecturer in Pathology, University College Hospital Med. School, 1953; Rockefeller Trav. Fell., 1956; Litchfield Lectr, Univ. of Oxford, 1957; Sen. Lectr in Pathology, Univ. Coll. Hosp. Med. School, 1960. Mem. Council, Imperial Cancer Res. Fund. Treas., Path. Soc. GB and Ireland. Editor-in-chief, Jl Path. *Publications:* An Introduction to General Pathology, 1977; numerous scientific papers and review articles in Pathology. *Recreation:* amateur sociology. *Address:* Department of Pathology, St Bartholomew's Hospital, West Smithfield, EC1A 7BE. *T:* 01-600 9000; 14 Islington Park Street, N1 1PU. *T:* 01-607 8903.

SPEED, (Herbert) Keith, RD 1967; MP (C) Ashford since Oct. 1974; Consultant, Rank Hovis McDougall Ltd; *b* 11 March 1934; *s* of late Herbert Victor Speed and of Dorothy Barbara (*née* Mumford); *m* 1961, Peggy Voss Clarke; two *s* one *d* (and one *s* decd). *Educ:* Greenhill Sch., Evesham; Bedford Modern Sch.; RNC, Dartmouth and Greenwich. Officer, RN, 1947-56; now Lt-Comdr RNR. Sales Man., Amos (Electronics) Ltd, 1957-60; Marketing Man., Plysu Products Ltd, 1960-65; Officer, Conservative Res. Dept, 1965-68. MP (C) Meriden, March 1968-Feb. 1974; An Asst Govt Whip, 1970-71; a Lord Comr of HM Treasury, 1971-72; Parly Under-Sec. of State, DoE, 1972-74; Opposition spokesman on local govt, 1976-. *Publications:* Blue Print for Britain, 1965; contribs to various political jls. *Recreations:* classical music, motor cycling, reading. *Address:* Strood House, Rolvenden, Cranbrook, Kent. *Clubs:* St Stephen's; Elwick (Ashford); Tenterden.

SPEED, Marjorie Jane, OBE 1959; Matron, The Middlesex Hospital, London, W1, 1946-65; *d* of F. C. Marriott, Kingston-on-Thames, Surrey; *m* 1972, James Grant Speed. Guy's

Hospital: Nursing Training, 1928-32; Asst Matron, 1939-40; Matron, County Hosp., Orpington, 1940-46. Vice-President: The Royal Coll. of Nursing; National Florence Nightingale Memorial Cttee. *Recreations:* music, painting. *Address:* Braemore Lodge, Dunbeath, Caithness.

SPEED, Sir Robert (William Arney), Kt 1954; CB 1946; QC 1963; Counsel to the Speaker since 1960; *b* 1905; *s* of late Sir Edwin Arney Speed; *m* 1929, Phyllis, *d* of Rev. P. Armitage; one *s* one *d. Educ:* Rugby; Trinity College, Cambridge. Called to Bar, Inner Temple, 1928; Bencher, 1961; Principal Assistant Solicitor, Office of HM Procurator-General and Treasury Solicitor, 1945-48; Solicitor to the Board of Trade, 1948-60. *Address:* Upper Culham, Wargrave, Berks. *T:* Henley-on-Thames 4271. *Club:* United Oxford & Cambridge University.

SPEELMAN, Sir Cornelis Jacob, 8th Bt *cr* 1686; BA; *b* 17 March 1917; *s* of Sir Cornelis Jacob Speelman, 7th Bt and Maria Catharina Helena, Castendijk; *S* father, 1949; *m* 1972, Julia Mona Le Besque. Education Dept, Royal Dutch Army, 1947-49; with The Shell Company (Marketing Service Dept), 1950. Student, Univ. of Western Australia, 1952; formerly Master of Modern Languages at Clifton Coll., Geelong Grammar Sch. and Exeter Tutorial Coll. *Address:* The Nab House, Flat 5, Beach House Road, Bembridge, IoW.

SPEIDEL, General Hans, Dr phil; Knight, Württemberg Order of Merit (1914-18); Kt, Iron Cross, 1943; President, Foundation of Science and Politics, since 1964; Hon. Professor, 1971; *b* Metzingen/Württemberg, 28 Oct. 1897; *m* 1925, Ruth Stahl; one *s* two *d. Educ:* Eberhard-Ludwig-Gymnasium of the Humanities, Stuttgart; Univs of Berlin and Tübingen, Technische Hochschule, Stuttgart. Ensign, Grenadier Regt, König Karl (5. Württ.) Nr 123, 1914; Regimental Adjutant, Western Front, 1915-18; entered Reichswehr (3 years at Military Academy); during War of 1939-45 was successively Chief of Staff of Army Corps and Army (8) (Eastern Front), and of Field Marshal Rommel's Army Group (Western Front); arrested on Himmler's orders, 1944; released from Gestapo imprisonment at end of the War. Lecturer, Tübingen Univ. and Leibniz University Coll.; Military Adviser, Federal Govt, 1951; Military Delegate-in-Chief to EDC (European Defence Community) and NATO negotiations, 1951-55; Commander-in-Chief of Combined German Forces, 1955-57; Commander Allied Land Forces, Central Europe, 1957-63; Special Counsellor to Federal Government, W Germany, 1963-64. Commander, US Legion of Merit, 1961; Grosses Verdienstkreuz BRD mit Stern und Schulterband; Ehrenbürger, Stadt Metzingen, 1972. *Publications:* Invasion 1944 (a contribution to the fate of Rommel and the Reich), 1949; Zeitbetrachtungen, 1969; Editor and commentator on Vol. of Essays by Gen. Ludwig Beck, 1955; essays on Ernst Jünger, Theodor Heuss, Eugen Bircher, Gneisenau and Beck, etc. *Recreation:* study of history and literature. *Address:* Am Spitzenbach 21, Bad Honnef, Germany.

SPEIGHT, Johnny; writer; *b* 2 June 1920; *s* of John and Johanna Speight; *m* 1956, Constance Beatrice Barrett; two *s* one *d. Educ:* St Helen's RC School. Has written for: Arthur Haynes Show; Morecambe and Wise Show; Peter Sellers; Till Death Us Do Part (Screenwriters Guild Award, 1966, 1967, 1968). *Plays:* Compartment (Screenwriters Guild Award, 1962); Playmates; Salesman; Knackers Yard; If There Weren't any Blacks You Would Have to Invent Them (Prague Festival Award, 1969). *Publications:* It Stands to Reason, 1974; The Thoughts of Chairman Alf, 1974; various scripts. *Recreation:* golf. *Address:* 9 Orme Court, W2. *Clubs:* Eccentric; White Elephant; Stage Golf, Variety Golf, Pinner Hill Golf.

SPEIR, Wing Comdr Robert Cecil Talbot, OBE 1945; Vice-Lieutenant of Nairn since 1970; *b* 8 Oct. 1904; *e s* of late Lt-Col Guy Thomas Speir, North Berwick; *m* 1st, 1932, Elizabeth Findlay (*d* 1958), *d* of Sir John R. Findlay, 1st Bt, KBE; two *s* two *d*; 2nd, 1961, Dolce Maria, *d* of late Henry Hanselman. *Educ:* Eton; RMC Sandhurst. Served War, 1939-45: Bomber Comd, Gps 1, 2 and 4 (despatches thrice), and War Cabinet Office; Wing Comdr 1943; RAFVR(T), 1947-51. Mem., Royal Company of Archers (Queen's Body Guard for Scotland). DL Nairn, 1951-70. *Recreation:* shooting. *Address:* Linkside, Nairn. *T:* Nairn 53357.

SPEIR, Sir Rupert (Malise), Kt 1964; Chairman: Crossley Building Products Ltd; Matthew Hall & Co. Ltd; Common Brothers Ltd; Director of other companies; *b* 10 Sept. 1910; *y s* of late Guy Thomas Speir and late Mary Lucy Fletcher, of Saltoun. *Educ:* Eton Coll.; Pembroke Coll., Cambridge (BA). Admitted Solicitor, 1936. Special Mem., Hops Marketing Board, 1958. Served in Army throughout War of 1939-45;

commissioned in Intelligence Corps, Sept. 1939; retired with rank of Lt-Col, 1945. Contested (C) Linlithgow, 1945, Leek, 1950; MP (C) Hexham Div. of Northumberland, 1951-66, retired. Sponsor of: Litter Act, 1958; Noise Abatement Act, 1960; Local Government (Financial Provisions) Act, 1963; Parliamentary Private Secretary: to Minister of State for Foreign Affairs and to Parly Sec., CRO, 1956-59; to Parly and Fin. Sec., Admty and to Civil Lord of Admty, 1952-56. Hon. Fellow, Inst. of Public Cleansing; Vice-Pres., Keep Britain Tidy Group. *Recreations:* golf, shooting, fishing. *Address:* 120 Cheapside, EC2. *T:* 01-588 4000; 240 Cranmer Court, Sloane Avenue, SW3. *T:* 01-589 2057; Birtley Hall, Hexham, Northumberland. *T:* Wark 30275.

SPEIRS, Graham Hamilton; Secretary, Convention of Scottish Local Authorities, since 1975; *b* 9 Jan. 1927; *s* of Graham Mushet Speirs and Jane (*née* McChesney); *m* 1954, Myra Reid (*née* Mills); one *s* one *d*. *Educ:* High Sch. of Glasgow; Glasgow Univ. (MA 1950, LLB 1952). Anderson, Young and Dickson, Writers, Glasgow, 1950-52; Legal Asst, Dunbarton CC, 1952-54; Sen. Legal Asst, Stirling CC, 1954-59; Depute Sec., then Sec., Assoc. of County Councils in Scotland, 1959-75. *Recreation:* golf. *Address:* (home) 3 Dirleton Avenue, North Berwick EH39 4AX. *T:* North Berwick 2801; (office) 3 Forres Street, Edinburgh EH3 6BL. *T:* 031-225 1626. *Clubs:* Royal Scottish Automobile (Glasgow); North Berwick Golf (North Berwick).

SPELLER, Maj.-Gen. Norman Henry, CB 1976; Government Relations Adviser, ICL International Division, since 1976; *b* 5 March 1921; *s* of late Col Norman Speller and Emily Florence Speller (*née* Lambert); *m* 1950, Barbara Eleanor (*née* Earle); two *s*. *Educ:* Wallingford Grammar School. Commnd RA, 1940; War Service N Africa; transf. to RAOC, 1945; psc 1952; DAA&QMG 39 Inf. Bde, 1953-55; Dirg Staff, Staff Coll., 1955-58; OC 20 Ordnance Field Park, 1958-60; Admin. Staff Coll., 1961; AA&QMG N Ireland, 1961-63; D/SPO COD Donnington, 1964-65; Col AQ 54 (EA) Div./District, 1965-66; AAG AG9, MoD, 1967; DDOS 1 British Corps, 1968-69; idc 1970; Dir of Systems Coordination, MoD, 1971-73; Dir of Ordnance Services, MoD, 1973-76, retired. *Recreations:* sailing, golf. *Address:* 1 Steeple Close, SW6. *Clubs:* Army and Navy; Royal Southampton Yacht.

SPENALE, Georges; Officer de la Légion d'Honneur; Palmes Académiques; First Vice-President of the European Parliament, since 1977 (President, 1975-77); Deputy from Tarn, French National Assembly, since 1962; *b* Carcassonne, 29 Nov. 1913; *m* 1935, Carmen Delcayré; one *s* one *d*. *Educ:* Licencié en Droit; Diplômé de l'Ecole Nationale de la France d'outre-Mer. Economic Bureau, French Guinea, 1938-39; served War, with the colours, 1939-40 and 1943-45; Chief of District, Upper Volta, 1941-42; Inspector of Labour, Ivory Coast, 1942-43; Director of Cabinet for Fedn of Equatorial Africa, 1946-48; Chief of Information Service, Ivory Coast, 1949-50; Director of Cabinet, Fr. Cameroons, 1951-53, Sec.-Gen. 1953-54, acting High Comr 1954-55; Ministry of France d'outre-Mer: Adj. Dir, 1955-56; Governor, 1956; Director, Cabinet of M Gaston Defferre (took part in framing Fundamental Law), 1956-57; High Comr in Togo (until Independence), 1957-60. European Parliament: Mem., 1964-; Pres., Commn of Finances, 1967-75; Pres., Socialist Group, 1974-75. Mayor of Saint-Sulpice, Tarn, 1965; Vice-Pres., Regional Council, Midi-Pyrénées, 1975. Mem. Directing Cttee, Fr. Socialist Party, 1968-71. Holds decorations from African countries. *Address:* Faubourg Saint-Jean, 81370 Saint-Sulpice, France. *T:* 578003 (63).

SPENCE, Allan William, MA, MD Cantab; FRCP; Hon. Consultant Physician: St Bartholomew's Hospital, since 1965; Luton and Dunstable Hospital, since 1965; King George Hospital, Ilford, since 1967; Governor, St Bartholomew's Hospital Medical College, since 1965; *b* 4 Aug. 1900; *s* of late William Ritchie Spence and Emma (*née* Allan), Bath; *m* 1930, Martha Lena, *d* of late Hugh Hamilton Hutchison, JP, Girvan, Ayrshire; two *s*. *Educ:* King Edward's VI School, Bath; Gonville and Caius College, Cambridge; St Bartholomew's Hospital, London. Brackenbury Schol. in Medicine, 1926, Lawrence Research Schol. and Gold Medal, 1929-30, Cattlin Research Fell., 1938, St Bartholomew's Hosp.; Rockefeller Travelling Fellow, USA, 1931-32. House Phys., 1927, Demonstrator of Physiology, 1928-30, of Pathology, 1930-31, First Asst, 1933-36, Asst Dir of Med. Unit, 1936-37, St Bartholomew's Hospital; Physician St Bartholomew's Hosp., London, 1937-65; King George Hospital, Ilford, 1938-67; Luton and Dunstable Hospital, 1946-65; Hon. Consultant in Endocrinology to Army at Home, 1954-65; Med. Referee to Civil Service Commn, 1952-70; Physician on Med. Appeal Tribunal, DHSS, 1965-72; Member Medical Research Coun. Adv. Cttee: on Iodine Deficiency and Thyroid Disease, 1933-39; and on Hormones,

1937-41. Hon. Lt-Col, RAMC; service in North Africa and Greece as OC Med. Div., 97th Gen. Hosp., 1943-45. Mem. Assoc. of Physicians of Gt Brit.; Foundation Mem. Soc. for Endocrinology, to 1965; Fellow RSM, 1926-72 (Vice-Pres., Section of Med., 1949, Pres. Section of Endocrinology, 1951-52, Councillor, 1958-61); Foundn Mem. Internat. Soc. of Internal Medicine; Fellow Medical Soc. of London, 1937-72 (Councillor, 1957-60); Foundn Mem., London Thyroid Club; Mem., Physiological Soc., 1935-52; Emeritus Mem., Endocrine Society, USA, 1966. Examr in Medicine: Univ. of Cambridge, 1946-50; to Society of Apothecaries of London, 1947-52; in Therapeutics to University of London, 1953-57; to the Conjoint Examining Bd in England, 1955-59; to Fellowship of Faculty of Anæsthetists, RCS, 1964-66. Mem. of Editorial Bd, Jl of Endocrinology, 1956-63. Freeman of City of London; Member of Livery, Society of Apothecaries of London. *Publications:* Clinical Endocrinology, 1953 (translated into Spanish); articles to medical and scientific journals on endocrinological and general medical subjects. *Recreations:* reading, gardening; formerly rowing (Pres. Caius Boat Club, 1922-23). *Address:* Oak Spinney, Liphook Road, Lindford, Bordon, Hants GU35 0PN. *T:* Bordon 2450. *Club:* Hawks (Cambridge).

SPENCE, Gabriel John; Under-Secretary, and Head of Arts and Libraries Branch, Department of Education and Science, since 1973; *b* 5 April 1924; *s* of G. S. and D. A. Spence, Hope, Flints; *m* 1950, Averil Kingston (*née* Beresford); one *s* decd. *Educ:* Arnold House; King's Sch., Chester (King's Schol., Head of School); Wadham Coll., Oxon (Schol.). MA 1949; Stanhope Prize and Proxime, Gibbs Schol., Oxon, 1947; Haldane Essay Prize, Inst. Public Admin, 1959. Civil Service from 1949 (Min. of Works, Science Office, Min, of Housing and Local Govt, DES); Jt Sec., Adv. Council on Scientific Policy, 1959-62; Sec., Council for Scientific Policy, 1964-67. Admin. Staff Coll., Henley, 1957. *Recreations:* natural history, photography. *Address:* Old Heath, Hillbrow Road, Liss, Hants. *T:* Liss 3235. *Clubs:* Athenæum, MCC.

SPENCE, Henry Reginald, OBE; *b* 22 June 1897; *s* of James Henry Easton Spence and Gertrude Mary Hawke; *m* 1939, Eileen Beryl Walter; one *s* one *d*. Commissioned RFC 1915; with No. 16 Sqdn, 1916-17 and 12 Wing RAF, 1918 (under Ginger Mitchell). British Cross Country Ski Champion, Mürren, 1929. Was Area Commandant of ATC for North-East Scotland. MP (C) Central Division, County of Aberdeen and Kincardine, 1945-50, West Aberdeenshire, 1950-59. *Recreations:* ski-ing, sailing, golf, shooting. *Address:* 11 Wynnstay Gardens, Allen Street, W8 6UP.

SPENCE, John Deane; MP (C) Thirsk and Malton, since 1974 (Sheffield, Heeley, 1970-74); civil engineering and building contractor; director of various companies connected with construction industry; *b* 7 Dec. 1920; *s* of George Spence, Belfast; *m* 1944, Hester Nicholson; one *s* one *d*. *Educ:* Queen's Univ. of Belfast. Mem., Public Relations and Organization Cttee, Building Industry, 1967; Nat. Pres., UK Commercial Travellers' Assoc., 1965-66. Mem., Speaker's Panel of Cttee Chairmen. Hon. Secretary: Yorks Cons. Members Gp, 1970-; Cons. Back-benchers' Industry Cttee, 1971-72; Jt Hon. Sec., Cons. Back-benchers' Agriculture, Fisheries and Food Cttee, 1974-; Mem., Select Cttee, Nationalised Industries, 1974-. PPS to Minister of Local Govt and Develt, 1971-74. Member: NFU; Country Landowners' Assoc.; Yorkshire Derwent Trust; Anglo-Israel Friendship Soc. *Recreations:* golf, walking, travel. *Address:* House of Commons, SW1A OAA; Greystones, Maltongate, Thornton Dale, North Yorkshire. *Clubs:* Constitutional, Junior Carlton, Royal Automobile.

SPENCER, family name of **Viscount Churchill** and of **Earl Spencer.**

SPENCER, 8th Earl *cr* 1765; **Edward John Spencer,** MVO 1954; DL; JP; Baron and Viscount Spencer, 1761; Viscount Althorp, 1765; Viscount Althorp (UK), 1905; President, Northamptonshire Association of Boys' Clubs; Chairman National Association of Boys' Clubs; *b* 24 Jan. 1924; *o s* of 7th Earl Spencer, TD, and Lady Cynthia Elinor Beatrix Hamilton, DCVO, OBE (*d* 1972), *d* of 3rd Duke of Abercorn; *S* father, 1975; *m* 1st, 1954, Hon. Frances Ruth Burke Roche (marr. diss. 1969), *yr d* of 4th Baron Fermoy; one *s* three *d* (and one *s* decd); 2nd, 1976, Raine (*see* Countess Spencer). *Educ:* Eton; RMC Sandhurst and RAC, Cirencester. ADC to Gov. of South Australia, 1947-50; Equerry to the Queen, 1952-54 (to King George VI, 1950-52). Formerly Capt RS Greys. Hon. Col The Northamptonshire Regt (Territorials), T&AVR, 1967-71; a Dep. Hon. Col, The Royal Anglian Regt, 1971-. Trustee: King George's Jubilee Trust; Queen's Silver Jubilee Appeal; Mem. UK Council European Architectural Heritage Year, 1975. CC

Northants; High Sheriff of Northants, 1959; DL Northants, 1961; JP Norfolk, 1970. *Heir: s* Viscount Althorp, *qv. Address:* Althorp, Northampton NN7 4HG. *Clubs:* Turf, Brooks's, MCC, Royal Over-Seas League.

SPENCER, Countess; Raine Spencer; *b* 9 Sept. 1929; *d* of late Alexander George McCorquodale and of Barbara Cartland, *qv*; *m* 1st, 1948, Earl of Dartmouth (marr. diss. 1976), *qv*; three *s* one *d*; 2nd, 1976, Earl Spencer, *qv*. Westminster City Councillor, 1954-65 (served on various cttees); Member: for Lewisham West, LCC, 1958-65 (served on Town Planning, Parks, Staff Appeals Cttees); for Richmond upon Thames, GLC, 1967-73; GLC Gen. Purposes Cttee, 1971-73; Chm., GLC Historic Buildings Bd, 1968-71; Mem., Environmental Planning Cttee, 1967-71; Chm., Covent Garden Develt Cttee, 1971-72; Chm., Govt working party on Human Habitat in connection with UN Conf. on Environment, Stockholm (June 1972), 1971-72 (report: How Do You Want to Live?); Member: English Tourist Bd, 1971-75; BTA Infrastructure Cttee, 1972-; Chm., UK Exec., European Architectural Heritage Year, 1975. Patron, West Lewisham Con. Assoc.; Pres., Barnes Day Club for Old People; Patron, 29th Westminster Scouts The Countess of Dartmouth's Own. Formerly LCC Voluntary Care Cttee Worker, Wandsworth and Vauxhall. Hon. Dr Laws, Dartmouth Coll., USA. *Publication:* What Is Our Heritage?, 1975. *Address:* 48 Grosvenor Square, W1. *T:* 01-629 6255.

SPENCER, Alan Douglas, FBIM; Chairman and Managing Director, Boots The Chemists Ltd, since 1977; *b* 22 Aug. 1920; *s* of Thomas Spencer and late Laura Spencer; *m* 1944, Dorothy Joan Harper; two *d*. *Educ:* Prince Henry's Grammar Sch., Evesham. FBIM 1975. Commnd Gloucester Regt, 1940; served War with Green Howards, 1940-45; Instr, Sch. of Infantry, 1945-47. Joined Boots Co., 1938; rejoined 1947; Man. Dir, 1975. *Recreation:* shooting. *Address:* Oakwood, Grange Road, Edwalton, Nottingham. *T:* Nottingham 231722. *Club:* Naval and Military.

SPENCER, Brian; HM Diplomatic Service; Counsellor (Administration) and Consul General, Moscow, since 1975; *b* 20 March 1922; *s* of Alphaeus and Ethel Audrey Palmer Spencer; *m* 1950, Jean Edmunds; one *s*. *Educ:* Holgate Grammar Sch., Barnsley. Entered Civil Service in Mines Dept, BoT, 1939. Army, 1940-46: commnd, S Staffs Regt, 1942, with subseq. service in E Surrey Regt, N Africa, Sicily, Italy, Austria and Greece (Captain, despatches). Joined FO, 1950; Second Sec., Bagdad, 1952, Jakarta, 1955; FO, 1956; First Sec., Singapore, 1959; FO, 1962; First Secretary (Information): Helsinki, 1964; Canberra, 1967; Sydney, 1968; First Sec., Ottawa, 1969; Consul, Chicago, 1971; FCO, 1972. *Recreations:* tennis, cricket, football, ballet, music. *Address:* c/o Foreign and Commonwealth Office, SW1A 2AH; 68 Old Shoreham Road, Hove, Sussex. *Club:* Royal Over-Seas League.

SPENCER, Cyril Charles, CMG 1951; First Deputy Executive Director, International Coffee Organisation, London, 1964-68; *b* 1 Feb. 1912; *s* of Albert Edward Spencer, CBE, and late Elsie Maud Spencer; *m* 1st, 1938; one *d*; 2nd, 1949, Catherine Dewar Robertson. *Educ:* Royal Grammar Sch., Worcester; St John's Coll., Cambridge (BA 1934). Uganda: Asst Treas., 1935; Asst District Officer, 1937; Asst Financial Sec., 1946; Economic Sec., E Africa High Commission, 1948; Financial Sec., 1948; Acting Chief Sec. at various dates; Acting Governor, July 1951; Chairman: Uganda Lint Marketing Bd; Uganda Coffee Marketing Board; Member: Uganda Electricity Board; Uganda Development Corp.; Comr on Special Duty, Uganda, 1953-61; Sec.-Gen., Inter-African Coffee Organisation, Paris, 1961-64. *Recreations:* golf, fishing. *Address:* Shandon, Coreway, Sidford, Sidmouth, Devon. *Club:* MCC.

SPENCER, Gilbert, RA 1959 (ARA 1950); RWS 1949 (ARWS 1943); Hon. ARCA; Member: NEAC; Society of Mural Painters; Faculty of Prix de Rome; *b* 1893; *s* of late William and Anna Spencer; *m* 1930, Margaret Ursula Bradshaw (*d* 1959); one *d*. *Educ:* privately and Slade School. Served War of 1914-18, RAMC and East Surrey Regt. Professor of Painting, Royal Coll. of Art, 1932-48; Head of Department of Painting and Drawing, Glasgow School of Art, 1948-50; Head of Dept of Painting and Drawing, Camberwell Sch. of Arts and Crafts, 1950-57. Exhibitions: Goupil Gall., 1922, 1926 (with Mark Gertler and John Nash, RA), 1928, 1931; Leicester Galls, 1933, 1937, 1943, 1946, 1948; work rep. in many public galleries, including: Tate Gallery, Victoria and Albert Museum, Imperial War Museum, Aberdeen, Belfast, Capetown and Durban Art Galls. Commissioned by Imperial War Museum, 1919, and War Artists' Advisory Council, 1940 and 1943. Murals, Foundation Legend of Balliol Coll.; The Scholar Gipsy Students Union, Univ. of London; An Artist's Progress, Royal Academy.

Publications: Stanley Spencer, 1961; Memoirs of a Painter, 1974. *Address:* Church Rise Cottage, Walsham-le-Willows, Bury St Edmunds, Suffolk. *T:* Walsham-le-Willows 509.

SPENCER, Air Vice-Marshal Ian James, CB 1963; DFC 1941 (Bar 1943); Senior Partner, I. J. Spencer and Partners; Chairman, Spencer Partners SA (Geneva and The Hague); *b* 6 June 1916; *s* of late Percival James Spencer; *m* 1940, Kathleen Jeune Follis, *d* of late Canon Charles Follis; two *s*. Commissioned 1937. War of 1939-45: bomber sqdns of No 2 Gp (despatches). RAF Staff College, 1948; Air Attaché, Berne, 1950-53; CO, Univ of London Air Sqdn, 1954-56; Director of Plans Second Allied TAF, 1956-59; commanded RAF Benson, 1959-61; AOA, Transport Command, 1961-64; Dir of Personnel, MoD, 1964-65; AOA, Far East Air Force, 1965-67; retired 1968. Member: CPRE; Franco-British Soc.; Anglo-Swiss Soc.; Internat. Inst. for Strategic Studies; BIM. Governor, Sherborne Sch. Freeman, Guild of Air Pilots and Air Navigators. Croix de Guerre, 1944; Légion d'Honneur 1945. Interests: internat. affairs, the countryside and country pursuits. *Address:* Rossals, Rotherfield, Sussex TN6 3LU. *T:* Rotherfield 2219. *Clubs:* Royal Air Force, MCC; Sussex CCC.

SPENCER, Mrs Joanna Miriam, CB 1971; CBE 1961; CompIGasE; *b* 26 July 1910; *d* of late Rev. R. S. Franks; *m* 1954, Frank Woolley Sim Spencer (*d* 1975). *Educ:* Redland High School for Girls, Bristol; Girton College, Cambridge (MA). Asst, Lancs County Library, 1934-35; Asst Librarian: Hull Univ. Coll., 1936-37; Regent Street Polytechnic, 1938; Librarian, Selly Oak Colls, 1938-42. Temp. Civil Servant, Min. of Aircraft Production, 1942-45. Principal, Min. of Supply, 1946; Assistant Secretary, Min. of Supply, 1949-55, Board of Trade, 1955-56, Min. of Power, 1957-64; Under-Secretary: Min. of Power, 1964-69; Min. of Technology, 1969-70; DTI, 1970-72. *Address:* 4 Rostrevor Road, SW19 7AP. *T:* 01-946 4969.

SPENCER, John Loraine, TD; Headmaster, Berkhamsted School, since 1972; *b* 19 Jan. 1923; *s* of Arthur Loraine Spencer, OBE, and Emily Maude Spencer, OBE, Woodford Green; *m* 1954, Brenda Elizabeth (*née* Loft); two *s* one *d*. *Educ:* Bancroft's Sch.; Gonville and Caius Coll., Cambridge (MA). 1st cl. hons Class. Tripos Pts I and II. War Service in Essex Regt, 1942-45 (Captain, despatches). Asst Master, Housemaster and Sixth Form Classics Master, Haileybury Coll., 1947-61; Headmaster, Lancaster Royal Grammar Sch., 1961-72. Mem. Council, Lancaster Univ., 1968-72. *Address:* Wilson House, Berkhamsted School, Berkhamsted, Herts. *T:* Berkhamsted 4827.

SPENCER, Sir Kelvin (Tallent), Kt 1959; CBE 1950; MC 1918; Chief Scientist, Ministry of Power, 1954-59, retired; *b* 7 July 1898; *s* of Charles Tallent and Edith Ælfrida Spencer; *m* 1927, Phœbe Mary Wills; one *s*. *Educ:* University College School, Hampstead; City and Guilds Engineering Coll., London Univ. Mem. Council, Exeter Univ. Founder Mem., Scientific and Medical Network. FCGI 1959. Formerly MICE, FRAeS. *Address:* Wootans, Branscombe, Seaton, Devon EX12 3DN. *T:* Branscombe 242. *Club:* Farmers'.

SPENCER, Noël, ARCA (London); retired as Principal, Norwich School of Art (1946-64); *b* 29 Dec. 1900; *s* of late John William Spencer; *m* 1929, Vera K. Wheeler; no *c*. *Educ:* Ashton-under-Lyne School of Art; Manchester School of Art; Royal College of Art. Art Teacher, Central School of Arts and Crafts, Birmingham, 1926-32; Headmaster, Moseley School of Art, Birmingham, 1929-32; Second Master, Sheffield College of Arts and Crafts, 1932-34; Headmaster, Huddersfield Art School, 1934-46. *Exhibitions:* Royal Academy, New English Art Club, Royal Birmingham Society of Artists, Sheffield Society of Artists, Liverpool, Bradford, Wakefield and Doncaster Art Galleries, Norwich Art Circle and Twenty Group, Chicago Art Institute and Los Angeles Art Museum, USA, etc. *Publications:* A Scrap Book of Huddersfield, Book I, 1944, Book II, 1948; (with Arnold Kent) The Old Churches of Norwich, 1970; Sculptured Monuments in Norfolk Churches, 1977. *Recreations:* drawing and painting. *Address:* 18 Upton Close, Norwich, Norfolk. *T:* Norwich 51683.

SPENCER, Oscar Alan, CMG 1957; Economic Adviser to Government of Seychelles, since 1976; *b* Eastleigh, Hants, 12 Dec. 1913; *m* 1952, Diana Mary, *d* of late Edmund Walker, Henley-on-Thames; two *s* one *d*. *Educ:* Mayfield Coll., Sussex; London Sch. of Economics. BCom (Hons) 1936. Premchand Prize in Banking and Currency, 1936; John Coleman Postgraduate Scholar, 1936-37. Served War of 1939-45, Lt-Col (despatches twice). Economic Adviser and Development Comr, British Guiana, 1945; also Comr, Interior, 1949; Economic Sec., Malaya, 1950; Member, 1951, Minister, 1955, for Economic Affairs, Economic Adviser, and Head of Economic Secretariat,

Fedn of Malaya, 1956-60. UN Tech. Assistance Service, 1960-76: Econ. Adviser to Govt of Sudan, 1960-64; Sen. Regl Adviser on Public Finance and Head of Fiscal Sect., UN Econ. Commn for Africa, 1964-66; Financial Adviser to Govt of Ethiopia, 1966-76. Chm., Central Electricity Board, Malaya, 1952-55, 1956-60; British Guiana Delegate, Caribbean Commn, 1948; Malayan Adviser to Sec. of State. Commonwealth Finance Ministers' Conf., 1951; Leader of Malayan Reps, Internat. Rubber Study Gp, London, 1952, Copenhagen, 1953; Malayan Deleg., Internat. Tin Conf., Geneva, 1953; Adviser to Malayan Delegation, London Constitutional and Financial Confs, 1956 and 1957. Comdr, Order of St Agatha, San Marino, 1944; Knight of the Order of Defenders of the Realm (PMN), Malaya, 1958. *Publications:* The Finances of British Guiana, 1920-45, 1946; The Development Plan of British Guiana, 1947. *Recreation:* tennis. *Address:* Gatehurst, Pett, near Hastings, East Sussex. *T:* Pett 2197; Department of Cabinet Affairs, President's Office, Mahé, Seychelles. *T:* 2041. *Club:* East India, Devonshire, Sports and Public Schools.

SPENCER, Terence John Bew; Professor of English Language and Literature, Birmingham University, since 1958; Director of the Shakespeare Institute, since 1961; Member Board, Young Vic, since 1974; *b* 21 May 1915; *s* of Frederick John and Dorothy Emmie Spencer, Harrow; *m* 1948, Katharine Margaret, *d* of Francis William Walpole, Limpsfield, Surrey; three *d. Educ:* Lower School of John Lyon, Harrow; University of London (King's Coll. and University Coll.); British School at Rome. Assistant, English Department, King's Coll., London, 1938-40; Brit. Council Lectr, Brit. Inst., Rome, and Inst. of English Studies, Athens, 1939-41. Served War, 1941-46 (despatches); Cyprus Regt and Royal Pioneer Corps; commissioned 1941; Maj. 1943; actg Lt-Col 1945. Asst Lectr and Lectr in English, 1946-55, UCL; Prof. of English, QUB, 1955-58; Public Orator, Birmingham Univ., 1966-73. Turnbull Prof. of Poetry, Johns Hopkins Univ., 1968; Berg Prof. of English, NY Univ., 1974. Hon. Sec., The Shakespeare Association, 1950-; Gov., Royal Shakespeare Theatre, 1968-; Chm. Adv. Cttee, Young Vic, 1970-74; Mem. Bd, Nat. Theatre, 1968-76. Hon. Life Mem., Modern Humanities Res. Assoc., 1975. General Editor: New Penguin Shakespeare; Penguin Shakespeare Library; English Editor, Modern Language Review, 1956-75 (General Editor, 1959-71); Editor, Year Book of English Studies, 1971-75. *Publications:* Fair Greece, Sad Relic: Literary Philhellenism from Shakespeare to Byron, 1954; (ed with James Sutherland) On Modern Literature by W. P. Ker, 1955; From Gibbon to Darwin, 1959; The Tyranny of Shakespeare, 1959; Byron and the Greek Tradition, 1960; Shakespeare: The Roman Plays, 1963; ed, Shakespeare's Plutarch, 1964; ed, Shakespeare: A Celebration, 1964; ed, Romeo and Juliet, 1967; ed, A Book of Masques, 1967; Elizabethan Love Stories, 1968; contribs to other books, and to journals. *Address:* The Shakespeare Institute, The University, Birmingham B15 2RX.

SPENCER-CHURCHILL, family name of **Duke of Marlborough** and of **Baroness Spencer-Churchill.**

SPENCER-CHURCHILL, Baroness *cr* 1965 (Life Peer), of Chartwell; **Clementine Ogilvy Spencer-Churchill,** GBE 1946 (CBE 1918); *b* 1885; *d* of late Sir Henry Hozier and late Lady Blanche Hozier, *d* of 9th Earl of Airlie; *m* 1908, Rt Hon. Sir Winston Churchill, KG, PC, OM, CH, FRS (*d* 1965); two *d* (one *s* and two *d* decd). *Educ:* at home; Berkhamsted Girls' Sch.; Sorbonne, Paris. Organised Canteens for munition workers on behalf of YMCA in NE Metropolitan Area, 1914-18; Chairman of the Red Cross Aid to Russia Fund, 1939-46; President of YWCA War Time Appeal; Chairman of Fulmer Chase Maternity Hospital for Wives of Junior Officers, 1940-46; Chairman of National Hostels Committee of YWCA, 1948-51. Freedom of Wanstead and Woodford, 1945. Hon. LLD: Glasgow University, 1946; Bristol Univ., 1976; Hon. DCL Oxford University, 1946. CStJ. *Address:* 7 Princes Gate, SW7. *See also W. S. Churchill, Baron Duncan-Sandys, Rt. Hon. Sir. A. C. J. Soames.*

SPENCER CHURCHILL, John George; *see* Churchill, J. G. S.

SPENCER-NAIRN, Sir Robert (Arnold), 3rd Bt *cr* 1933; *b* 11 Oct. 1933; *s* of Sir Douglas Spencer-Nairn, 2nd Bt, TD, and Elizabeth Livingston, *d* of late Arnold J. Henderson; *S* father, 1970; *m* 1963, Joanna Elizabeth, *d* of late Lt-Comdr G. S. Salt, RN; two *s* one *d. Educ:* Eton College; Trinity Hall, Cambridge (MA). *Heir: s* James Robert Spencer-Nairn, *b* 7 Dec. 1966. *Address:* Barham, Cupar, Fife KY15 5RG. *Clubs:* New (Edinburgh); Royal and Ancient Golf (St Andrews).

SPENCER PATERSON, Arthur; *see* Paterson, A. S.

SPENCER-SILVER, Prof. Peter Hele; S. A. Courtauld Professor of Anatomy in the University of London, at the Middlesex Hospital Medical School, since 1974, Sub-Dean, since 1976; *b* 29 Oct. 1922; 2nd *s* of late Lt-Col J. H. Spencer Silver; *m* 1948, Patricia Anne, *e d* of late Col J. A. F. Cuffe, CMG, DSO, Wyke Mark, Winchester; two *s* one *d. Educ:* Harrow School; Middlesex Hosp. Med. School, Univ. of London. MRCS, LRCP; MB, BS London 1945; PhD London 1952. Res., Middlesex Hosp., 1945-46. RAF, 1946-48. Demonstrator in Anatomy, Middlesex Hosp. Med. Sch., 1948-57; Mem. 2nd Internat. Team in Embryology, Hübrecht Laboratory, Utrecht, Netherlands Govt Fellowship, 1956; Reader in Anatomy, Univ. of London, 1957; US Nat. Inst. of Health Post-doctoral Travelling Fellowship, 1961; Carnegie Inst. of Washington, Dept of Embryology, Baltimore, 1961-62; Prof. of Embryology, Mddx Hosp. Medical Sch., 1964-74. FRSM. *Publications:* contribs to Jl Embryology and Experimental Morphology, Jl Physiol., Jl Anat., Lancet, etc. *Recreation:* music. *Address:* 7 More's Garden, 90 Cheyne Walk, SW3 5BB. *T:* 01-352 2990.

SPENCER-SMITH, Maj.-Gen. Jeremy Michael, CB 1971; OBE 1959; MC 1945; Director of Manning (Army), Ministry of Defence, 1970-72; retired; *b* 28 July 1917; *s* of Michael Spencer-Smith, DSO, MC, and Penelope, *née* Delmé-Radcliffe (she *m* 2nd, 1934, Elliot Francis Montagu Butler, and *d* 1974). *Educ:* Eton; New Coll., Oxford. Welsh Guards, 1940; Adjutant, 1st Bn, 1944-46; Staff, 1st Guards Brigade, MELF, 1950-51; comd 3 KAR, Kenya, 1959-60; Staff, HQ BAOR, 1960-63; comd 148 Infantry Bde (TA), 1964-67; Dep. Dir of Manning, Ministry of Defence (Army), 1967-68; GOC Wales, 1968-70. *Recreations:* shooting, racing, travel. *Address:* The White Cottages, Cheveley, Newmarket, Suffolk.

SPENCER-SMITH, Sir John Hamilton-, 7th Bt, *cr* 1804; contract gardener; *b* 18 March 1947; *s* of Sir Thomas Cospatric Hamilton-Spencer-Smith, 6th Bt, and Lucy Ashton, *o d* of late Thomas Ashton Ingram, Hopes, Norton-sub-Hamdon, Somerset; *S* father, 1959. *Educ:* Milton Abbey; Lackham College of Agriculture, Wilts. *Recreations:* watching polo and local football. *Heir: cousin* Peter Compton Hamilton-Spencer-Smith [*b* 12 Nov. 1912; *m* 1950, Philippa Mary, *yr d* of late Captain Richard Ford; two *s*]. *Address:* Iping Mill, Iping, Midhurst, West Sussex GU29 0PE.

SPENCER WILLS, Sir John; *see* Wills.

SPENDER, Hon. Sir Percy Claude, KCVO 1957; KBE 1952; QC (NSW), 1935; BA; LLB; President of the International Court of Justice at The Hague, 1964-67 (Judge, 1958-64); Australian lawyer; *b* Sydney, 5 Oct. 1897; *s* of late Frank Henry Spender, Sydney, and Mary Hanson (*née* Murray); *m* 1925, Jean Maude (*d* 1970), *d* of Samuel B. Henderson; two *s. Educ:* Fort Street High Sch., Sydney; Sydney Univ. BA 1918 (distinction in economics); LLB 1922, with 1st class Honours and University Medal; George and Matilda Harris Scholar, 1920; Special Wigram Allen Prize for proficiency in Roman and Constitutional Law, 1918; Morven K. Nolan Memorial Prize for Political Science, 1920; Member of Sydney Univ. Senate, 1939-44; called to NSW Bar, 1923. Member of Menzies Ministry, 1939-41; Vice-President, Fed. Exec. Council, 1940 (Member 1939); Minister without portfolio assisting Treas., and Ministerial Secretary to Cabinet, 1939; Acting Treas. 1939, Treas. 1940; Member of Economic Cabinet, 1939-40; Chairman Australian Loan Council, 1939-40; Chairman of Nat. Debt Commn, 1940; Minister for the Army, Chairman of Mil. Board, and Member War Cabinet, 1940-41; Government, then Opposition Member of Advisory War Council, 1940-45; Minister for External Affairs and of External Territories, Australia, 1949-51; MHR for Warringah, 1937-51; Australian Ambassador to the United States, 1951-58. Chairman: Australian Delegn at Conference of British Commonwealth Foreign Ministers, Colombo, 1950 (at which he put forward a plan for economic aid to S and SE Asia, subseq. known as the Colombo Plan); Conf. of British Commonwealth Consultative Cttee on Economic Aid to S and SE Asia, Sydney, 1950; Australian delegate at British Commonwealth Consultative Cttee Meeting, London, 1950; Vice-Pres., 5th General Assembly, UN, 1950-51, and Chm. and Vice-Chm., Australian Delegn UN General Assembly, 1952-56; Australian Representative at negotiation Canberra and subsequently at signing Regional Security Treaty between USA, NZ, and Australia, San Francisco, 1951; Vice-President Jap. Peace Treaty Conf., San Francisco, 1951 (Chm., Australian Delegn); Australian Governor of Internat. Monetary Fund and Internat. Bank, 1951-53; alternate Governor, Internat. Monetary Fund, 1954; Chm. Australian Delegn to UN Commemorative Session,

San Francisco, 1955; Special Envoy on goodwill mission to South and Central America, July-Aug. 1955; Chairman, Australian Delegation Internat. Sugar Conf., May-June 1956 and Conf. to establish Atomic Energy Internat. Agency, Sept.-Oct. 1956; Chairman, Australian Delegation to 2nd Suez Conf., London, Sept. 1956, and to Commonwealth Finance Ministers' meeting, Washington, Oct. 1956. Mem. Gen. Council, Assicurazioni Generali (Italy), 1969-. European War, 1914-18, enlisted AIF, 1918; War of 1939-45, Lieut-Colonel on Active List AMF part-time special duties, 1942-45; now on retired list with hon. rank of Lieut-Colonel. Member: Board of Directors of USA Educational Foundation in Australia, 1950-51; US Cttee of Study and Training in Australia, 1950-51; Member of Council (1949-51) and Life Member Convocation Australian Nat. Univ.; Vice-President, Royal Commonwealth Society (President, NSW Br., 1949-51); President: Sydney Club, 1967-; NSW Br. of Overseas League, 1967-72. Chm., Aust. Museum Bd of Trustees for compilation of National Photographic Index of Australian Birds, 1969-. Hon. LLD: Univ. of British Columbia; Hamilton Coll., NY, 1952; Univ. of Colorado, 1953; Trinity Coll., Hartford, Conn, 1955; Yale, 1957; California, 1965; University of the East (Philippines), 1966; Sydney, 1973; Hon. DCL and Hon. Chancellor, Union Univ., Schenectady, 1955; Hon. LittD Springfield Coll., Mass, 1955. Coronation Medal, 1937 and 1953. KStJ 1958. Grande Ufficiale del' Ordine al Merito della Repubblica Italiana, 1976. C of E. *Publications:* Company Law and Practice, 1939; Australia's Foreign Policy, the Next Phase, 1944; Exercises in Diplomacy, 1969; Politics and a Man, 1972. *Recreations:* reading, surfing, golf. *Address:* Headingley House, Wellington Street, Woollahra, NSW 2025, Australia. *Clubs:* Elanora Country, Australasian Pioneers (Sydney); Athenæum (Melbourne).

SPENDER, Stephen (Harold), CBE 1962; poet and critic; Professor of English, University College, London University, 1970; *b* 28 Feb. 1909; *s* of Edward Harold Spender and Violet Hilda Schuster; *m* 1st, 1936, Agnes Marie (Inez), *o d* of late William Henry Pearn; 2nd, 1941, Natasha Litvin; one *s* one *d*. *Educ:* University College Sch.; University College, Oxford (Hon. Fellow, 1973). Co-editor Horizon Magazine, 1939-41; Counsellor, Section of Letters, Unesco, 1947; Co-Editor, Encounter, 1953-67. Fireman in NFS, 1941-44. Hon. Mem. Phi Beta Kappa (Harvard Univ.); Elliston Chair of Poetry, Univ. of Cincinnati, 1953; Beckman Prof., Univ. of California, 1959; Visiting Lecturer, Northwestern Univ., Illinois, 1963; Consultant in Poetry in English, Library of Congress, Washington, 1965; Clark Lectures (Cambridge), 1966; Mellon Lectures, Washington, DC, 1968; Northcliffe Lectures (London Univ.), 1969. Pres., English Centre, PEN Internat., 1975-. Fellow, Inst. of Advanced Studies, Wesleyan Univ., 1967. Vis. Prof., Univ. of Connecticut, 1969. Hon. Mem. Amer. Acad. of Arts and Letters and Nat. Inst. of Arts and Letters, 1969. Queen's Gold Medal for Poetry for 1971. Hon. DLitt: Montpellier Univ.; Loyola Univ. *Publications:* 20 Poems; Poems, the Destructive Element, 1934; Vienna, 1934; The Burning Cactus, 1936; Forward from Liberalism, 1937; Trial of a Judge, 1937; Poems for Spain, 1939; The Still Centre, 1939; Ruins and Visions, 1941; Life and the Poet, 1942; Citizens in War and After, 1945; Poems of Dedication, 1946; European Witness, 1946; The Edge of Being, 1949; essay, in The God that Failed, 1949; World Within World (autobiog.), 1951; Learning Laughter (travels in Israel), 1952; The Creative Element, 1953; Collected Poems, 1954; The Making of a Poem, 1955; Engaged in Writing (stories), 1958; Schiller's Mary Stuart (trans.), 1958; The Struggle of the Modern, 1963; Selected Poems, 1965; The Year of the Young Rebels, 1969; The Generous Days (poems), 1971; (ed) A Choice of Shelley's Verse, 1971; (ed) D. H. Lawrence: novelist, poet, prophet, 1973; Love-Hate Relations, 1974; T. S. Eliot, 1975; (ed) W. H. Auden: a tribute, 1975. *Address:* 15 Loudoun Road, NW8.

SPENS, family name of **Baron Spens.**

SPENS, 2nd Baron *cr* 1959; **William George Michael Spens;** *b* 18 Sept. 1914; *s* of 1st Baron Spens, PC, KBE, QC, and Hilda Mary (*d* 1962), *e d* of Lt-Col Wentworth Grenville Bowyer; *S* father, 1973; *m* 1941, Joan Elizabeth, *d* of late Reginald Goodall; two *s* one *d*. *Educ:* Rugby; New Coll., Oxford (MA). Barrister, Inner Temple, 1945. Served War of 1939-45 with RA; British Control Commission (later High Commission), Germany, 1945-55. *Heir:* *s* Hon. Patrick Michael Rex Spens, ACA [*b* 22 July 1942; *m* 1966, Barbara Janet Lindsay, *d* of Rear-Adm. Ralph Lindsay Fisher; one *s* one *d*].

SPENS, Colin Hope, CB 1962; FICE, FIWES, FInstWPC; Deputy Chairman, Sutton and District Water Co. since 1971; Chairman, Public Works and Municipal Services Congress Council, since 1970; *b* 22 May 1906; *er s* of late Archibald Hope

Spens, Lathallan, Fifeshire and Hilda Constance Hooper; *m* 1941, Josephine, *d* of late Septimus Simond; two *s* one *d*. *Educ:* Lancing Coll.; Imperial College of Science and Technology. Consulting engineering experience, 1928-39. Served War of 1939-45 with Royal Signals, 1939-41; PA to Director of Works in Ministry of Works, 1941-44; Engineering Inspectorate of Min. of Health, 1944-51, Min. of Housing and Local Govt, 1951-60; Chief Engineer, Min. of Housing and Local Govt, 1960-67. Senior Consultant, Rofe, Kennard and Lapworth, 1967-76. Pres., IWES, 1974-75. Hon. FInstPHE. *Address:* 10 Ashbourne Court, Burlington Place, Eastbourne BN21 4AX. *T:* Eastbourne 638742.

SPENSER-WILKINSON, Sir Thomas Crowe, Kt 1959; *b* 28 Sept. 1899; *o surv. s* of late Henry Spenser Wilkinson and Victoria Amy Eveline Crowe; *m* 1930, Betty Margaret, *o d* of late David Aitken Horner; one *s* one *d*. *Educ:* RN Colleges Osborne and Dartmouth; Balliol Coll., Oxford. Served as Midshipman and Sub-Lieut in Grand Fleet, 1915-18; in Destroyers in Baltic, 1918-19; Lieut 1920. Barrister-at-Law, Gray's Inn, 1925; Advocate and Solicitor, Singapore, 1928; practising in Singapore, 1928-38; President, District Court, Nicosia, Cyprus, 1938, and Famagusta, 1940; Lt-Comdr 1940; Naval Control Service in Cyprus and Port Said, 1940-42; on staff of C-in-C, S Atlantic, Capetown, 1942-44; Malaya Planning Unit in London, 1945; Chief Legal Adviser, Civil Affairs, British Mil. Administration, Malaya, Sept. 1945-April 1946; Judge, Supreme Court, Malaya, 1946; Chief Justice, Nyasaland, 1956-62; Chm., Medical Appeals Tribunal, Liverpool, 1962-72. *Publication:* Merchant Shipping Law of the Straits Settlements, 1946. *Recreation:* gardening. *Address:* Whitecroft, Pentre Close, Ashton, Chester. *T:* Kelsall 51531. *Clubs:* Royal Commonwealth Society, English-Speaking Union.
See also L. J. H. Horner.

SPENSLEY, Philip Calvert, DPhil, FRIC; Director, Tropical Products Institute, Ministry of Overseas Development, since 1966; *b* 7 May 1920; *s* of late Kent and Mary Spensley, Ealing; *m* 1957, Sheila Ross Fraser, *d* of Alexander and late Annie Fraser, Forres, Scotland; one *s* three *d*. *Educ:* St Paul's Sch., London; Keble Coll., Oxford (MA, BSc). Technical Officer, Royal Ordnance Factories, Ministry of Supply, 1940-45; Research Chemist, Nat. Inst. for Medical Research, MRC, 1950-54; Scientific Secretary, Colonial Products Council, Colonial Office, 1954-58; Asst Director, Tropical Products Inst., DSIR, 1958-61, Dep. Director, 1961-66, Director, 1966. Chairman, Cttee of Visitors, Royal Institution, 1959. Member: FAO/WHO/Unicef Protein Adv. Gp, 1968-71; Cttee on Technical Assistance to Developing Countries, Internat. Union of Food Science and Technology, 1970-; Food Science and Technol. Bd, MAFF/ARC/Dept of Agric. and Fisheries for Scotland Jt Consultative Organisation, 1973-; UK Rep., CENTO Council for Scientific Educn and Research, 1970-. Received MRC/NRDC Inventors Awards, 1963 and 1971. *Publications:* Tropical Products Institute Crop and Product Digests, vol. 1, 1971; various research and review papers, particularly in the fields of chemotherapeutic substances, plant sources of drugs, aflatoxin, and work of Tropical Products Inst.; patents on extraction of hecogenin from sisal. *Recreations:* gardening, lawn tennis, boating. *Address:* 96 Laurel Way, Totteridge, N20. *T:* 01-445 7895. *Clubs:* Athenæum, Royal Automobile; Island Cruising.

SPERRY, Rt. Rev. John Reginald; *see* Arctic, Bishop of The.

SPICER, Clive Colquhoun; Director, Medical Research Council Computer Unit, since 1967; *b* 5 Nov. 1917; *s* of John Bishop Spicer and Marion Isobel Spicer; *m* 1941, Faith Haughton James, MB; one *s* two *d*. *Educ:* Charterhouse Sch.; Guy's Hospital. Operational research on war casualties, 1941-46; Hon. Sqdn Leader, RAF; Staff, Imperial Cancer Research Fund, 1946-49; Dept of Biometry, University Coll., London, 1946-47; Public Health Laboratory Service, 1949-59; WHO Fellow, Univ. of Wisconsin, 1952-53; Vis. Scientist, US Nat. Insts of Health, 1959-60; Statistician, Imperial Cancer Research Fund, 1960-62; Chief Medical Statistician, General Register Office, 1962-66. Main interest has been in application of mathematical methods to medical problems. *Publications:* papers in scientific journals on epidemiology and medical statistics. *Recreations:* sailing, reading. *Address:* 10 Fortior Court, Hornsey Lane, N6.

SPICER, James Wilton; MP (C) Dorset West since Feb. 1974; company director and farmer; *b* 4 Oct. 1925; *s* of James and Florence Clara Spicer; *m* 1954, Winifred Douglas Shanks; two *d*. *Educ:* Latymer. Regular army, 1943-57, retd (Major); commnd Royal Fusiliers, 1944; served with King's African Rifles; Para. Regt, 1951-57. Mem., European Parlt, 1975-; Chm., Cons. Group for Europe, 1975-. *Recreations:* swimming, tennis, squash. *Address:* Whatley, Beaminster, Dorset. *T:* Beaminster 337. *Clubs:* Naval and Military, St Stephen's.

SPICER, Hon. Sir John Armstrong, Kt 1963; Chief Judge, Australian Industrial Court, 1956; President, Copyright Tribunal, since 1968; *b* Armadale, Victoria, 5 March 1899; *m* 1924, Lavinia M., *d* of Robert S. Webster; one *s*. *Educ:* Torquay (England); Hawksburn (Victoria); University of Melbourne. Admitted as Barrister and Solicitor, 1921; KC 1948; Attorney-General, Commonwealth of Australia, 1949-56. Senator in Commonwealth Parliament, 1940-44 and 1949-56. Chairman, Senate Cttee on Regulations and Ordinances, 1940-43. *Address:* 153 Glen Iris Road, Glen Iris, Victoria 3146, Australia. *T:* 25.2882. *Clubs:* Australian, Constitutional (Melbourne).

SPICER, Lancelot Dykes, DSO, MC; *b* 22 March 1893; *y s* of Rt Hon. Sir Albert Spicer, 1st Bt; *m* 1920, Iris Cox (who obtained a divorce, 1935); (one *s* killed in action, 31 May 1944); *m* 1951, Dorothy Beverley, *d* of late Frank Edwin Gwyther, CIE. *Educ:* Rugby Sch.; Trinity Coll., Cambridge. Granted temp. Commn in Army, Sept. 1914; T/Capt., July 1916; Bde-Major, April 1918; served European War (MC Oct. 1917; bar to MC May 1918; DSO Sept. 1918). Chairman, Spicers Ltd, 1950-59. *Address:* Salisbury Place, Shipton under Wychwood, Oxford OX7 6BP. *Club:* Hurlingham.
See also P. J. Spicer.

SPICER, Michael; *see* Spicer, W. M. H.

SPICER, (Sir) Peter James, 4th Bt *cr* 1906 (but does not use the title); Senior Editor, Religious Books, Oxford University Press; *b* 20 May 1921; *s* of Captain Sir Stewart Dykes Spicer, 3rd Bt, RN, and Margaret Grace (*née* Gillespie) (*d* 1967); *S* father, 1968; *m* 1949, Margaret, *e d* of Sir Steuart Wilson (*d* 1966), and Ann Mary Grace, now Lady Boult; one *s* three *d* (and one *d* decd). *Educ:* Winchester Coll. (Schol.); Trinity Coll., Cambridge (Exhibr); Christ Church, Oxford (MA). Served War of 1939-45 (despatches, 1944); Royal Sussex Regt, then RN (Temp. Lieut, RNVR). Trinity Coll., Cambridge, 1939-40; Christ Church, Oxford, 1945-47. Joined Staff of Oxford University Press, 1947. Co-opted Member, Educn Cttee of Oxfordshire CC, 1959-74 (Chairman, Libraries Sub-Cttee, 1961-74). Congregational Rep., British Council of Churches, 1963-72; Chm., Educational Publishers' Council, 1976-. *Recreations:* gardening, walking, sailing, music, large family gatherings. *Heir: s* Nicholas Adrian Albert Spicer *b* 28 Oct. 1953. *Address:* 8 Swan Street, Osney Town, Oxford OX2 0BJ. *T:* Oxford 722858. *Club:* United Oxford & Cambridge University.
See also L. D. Spicer.

SPICER, (William) Michael (Hardy); MP (C) South Worcestershire since Feb. 1974; Managing Director, Economic Models Ltd, since 1970; *b* 22 Jan. 1943; *s* of Brig. L. H. Spicer; *m* 1967, Patricia Ann Hunter; one *s* two *d*. *Educ:* Wellington Coll.; Emmanuel Coll., Cambridge (MA Econs). Asst to Editor, The Statist, 1964-66; Conservative Research Dept, 1966-68; Dir, Conservative Systems Research Centre, 1968-70. *Publications:* contrib. Jl Royal Inst. Public Admin. *Recreations:* painting, tennis, writing, travelling. *Address:* House of Commons, SW1. *T:* 01-219 3000.

SPICKERNELL, Rear-Adm. Derek Garland, CB 1974; CEng, FIMechE, FIProdE, MIPM, MBIM, MIMarE; Technical Director, British Standards Institution, since 1976; *b* 1 June 1921; *s* of late Comdr Sidney Garland Spickernell, RN, and Florence Elizabeth (*née* March); *m* 1946, Ursula Rosemary Sheila Money; two *s* one *d*. *Educ:* RNEC, Keyham. Served War, HM Ships Abdiel, Wayland, and Engr Officer HM Submarine Statesman, 1943-45. Engr Officer HM Submarines Telemachus, Tudor and Alcide, 1945-50; Submarine Trials Officer, 1950-51; Engrg Dept, HM Dockyard, Portsmouth, 1951-53; SEO: Portsmouth Frigate Sqdn, 1954-55; 2nd Submarine Sqdn, 1956-57; Supt, ULE, Bournemouth, 1958-59; Dep. Captain Supt, AUWE, Portland, 1959-62; Dep. Manager, Engrg Dept, HM Dockyard, Portsmouth, 1962-64; in command, HMS Fisgard, 1965-66; Dep. Dir, Naval Ship Production, 1967-70; Dep. Chief Exec., Defence Quality Assurance Bd, 1970-71; Dir-Gen., Quality Assurance, MoD (PE), 1972-75; Chm., Nat. Council for Quality and Reliability, 1973-75; A Vice-Pres., Inst. of Quality Assurance, 1974-(Hon. FIQA); Member: Internat. Acad. of Quality Assurance, 1977-; Govt Adv. Council for Calibration and Measurement; Council, British Approvals Service for Electrical Equipment in Flammable Atmospheres; Res. Bd, British Non-Ferrous Metal Technol. Centre. Member: Exec. Cttee, RoSPA; Ct, Cranfield Inst. of Technol. *Publications:* papers on Quality Assurance. *Recreation:* golf. *Address:* Ridgefield, Shawford, Hants. *T:* Twyford 712157. *Clubs:* English-Speaking Union, Anglo-Belgian; Royal Fowey Yacht.

SPIERS, Prof. Frederick William, CBE 1962; Part-time Director, Bone Dosimetry Research, University of Leeds, 1972-78; Professor of Medical Physics, University of Leeds, 1950-72; *b* 29 July 1907; *er s* of Charles Edward and Annie Spiers; *m* 1936, Kathleen M. Brown; one *d*. *Educ:* Prince Henry's Grammar Sch., Evesham; University of Birmingham. 1st Class Hons Physics, 1929; PhD 1932; DSc 1952. Anglo-German Exchange Scholar, Univ. of Munich, 1930. Demonstrator in Physics, University of Leeds, 1931; Senior Physicist, General Infirmary, Leeds, 1935; Vis. Lecturer, Washington Univ., St Louis, USA, 1950. Hon. Director: MRC Environmental Radiation Unit, 1959-72; MRC Regional Radiological Protection Service, Leeds, 1963-70; Chief Regional Scientific Adviser for Civil Defence, NE Region, 1952-77; President, British Inst. of Radiology, 1955-56; Chairman: Hospital Physicists Assoc., 1944-45; British Cttee on Radiation Units and Measurements, 1967-77; Home Defence Scientific Adv. Standing Conference, 1972-77; Hon. Mem., Royal Coll. of Radiologists; Member: MRC Protection Cttee; Radio-active Substances Adv. Cttee, 1960-70; Internat. Commn on Radiation Units and Measurements, 1969-73; Statutory Adv. Cttee to National Radiological Protection Bd; Adv. Council on Calibration and Measurement, 1973-77. Silvanus Thompson Meml Lectr, British Inst. Radiology, 1973. Routgen Prize, 1950; Barclay Medal, 1970; Sulver Jubilee Medal, 1977. FInstP 1970. *Publications:* Radioisotopes in the Human Body, 1968; articles on radiation physics and radiobiology in scientific journals; contribs in: British Practice in Radiotherapy, 1955; Radiation Dosimetry, 1956, 1969; Encyclopedia of Medical Radiology, 1968; Manual on Radiation Haematology, 1971. *Recreations:* photography, music, gardening. *Address:* Lanesfield House, Old Lane, Bramhope, near Leeds LS16 9AZ. *T:* Arthington 842680.

SPIERS, Ronald Ian; Minister, United States Embassy in London, since 1974; *b* 9 July 1925; *s* of Tomas H. and Blanca De P. Spiers; *m* 1949, Patience Baker; one *s* three *d*. *Educ:* Dartmouth Coll., New Hampshire (BA); Princeton Univ. (Master in Public Affairs, PhD). Mem., US Delegn to UN, 1956-60; US Department of State: Dir, Office of Disarmament and Arms Control, 1960-62; Dir, Office of NATO Affairs, 1962-66; Political Counsellor, London, 1966-69; Asst Sec. of State, Politico-Military Affairs, 1969-73; Ambassador to the Bahamas, 1973-74. *Recreations:* swimming, music, theatre-going, gardening. *Address:* 1 Cottesmore Gardens, W8 5PR. *T:* 01-937 4120.

SPINELLI, Altiero; a Deputy (Independent), Parliament of Italy, since 1976; *b* 31 Aug. 1907; *s* of Carlo Spinelli and Maria Ricci; *m* 1944, Ursula Hirschmann; three *d*. *Educ:* Univ. of Rome. Political prisoner in Italy, 1927-43; partisan in Italian Resistance, 1943-45; Leader of European Federalist Movement, 1945-61. Visiting Prof., Johns Hopkins Univ. Center for Advanced Internat. Studies, in Bologna, 1961-64. Founder and Director, Istituto Affari Internationali, Rome, 1965-70; Mem., Commn of the European Communities, 1970-76. *Publications:* Degli Stati Sovrani agli Stati Uniti d'Europa, 1952; L'Europa non cade dal cielo, 1960; Tedeschi al bivio, 1960; The Eurocrats, 1966; The European Adventure, 1973; Il lungo monologo, 1970. *Address:* Camera dei Deputati, Rome, Italy; Cliro Rutario 5, 00152 Roma, Italy.

SPINK, Prof. John Stephenson; Professor of French Language and Literature in the University of London (Bedford College), 1952-73; *b* 22 Aug. 1909; *s* of William Spink and Rosetta Spink (*née* Williamson); *m* 1940, Dorothy Knowles, MA, DèsL, LRAM. *Educ:* Pickering Grammar Sch.; Universities of Leeds and Paris. BA (Leeds), 1930; MA (Leeds), 1932; Docteur de l'Université de Paris, 1934; Lauréat de l'Académie Française, 1935. Assistant at Lycée Henri IV, Paris, 1930-33; Lecteur at the Sorbonne, 1931; Asst Lectr in Univ. of Leeds, 1933-36; Lectr in Univ. of London, King's Coll., 1937-50; Prof. of French at University College, Southampton, 1950-52. Officier de l'ordre nat. du mérite, 1973. *Publications:* J.-J. Rousseau et Genève, 1934 (Paris); critical edition of J.-J. Rousseau, Les Rêveries du Promeneur solitaire, 1948; Literature and the sciences in the age of Molière, 1953; French Free-Thought from Gassendi to Voltaire, 1960; critical edn of Rousseau's educational writings in Pléiade œuvres complètes, t. IV, 1969; (ed jointly) Diderot, Œuvres complètes, I, II, 1975; articles in Annales J.-J. Rousseau, Mercure de France, Revue d'Histoire littéraire, Modern Language Review, French Studies, Bulletin des Historiens du théâtre, Horizon, Europe, Revue de Littérature Comparée, Problèmes des Genres Littéraires, Cahiers de l'Association Internat. des Études Françaises, Dix-huitième siècle; trans. of Krimov, The Tanker Derbent, 1944 (Penguin). *Address:* 48 Woodside Park Road, N12.

SPINKS, Dr Alfred, FRS 1977; CChem, FRIC; FIBiol; Research Director, Imperial Chemical Industries Ltd, since 1970; *b* 25 Feb. 1917; *s* of Alfred Robert Spinks and Ruth (*née* Harley); *m* 1946, Patricia Kilner; two *d*. *Educ:* Soham Grammar Sch.; University Coll., Nottingham (BSc); Imperial Coll., London (PhD, DIC); Worcester Coll., Oxford (MA). CChem 1975; FRIC 1971; FIBiol 1976. Joined ICI Dyestuffs Div., 1941; Res. Chemist, Imperial Coll., 1941-42; research with ICI Dyestuffs Div., 1942-50; Oxford Univ., 1950-52; Res. Pharmacologist, ICI, 1952-61; Pharmaceuticals Division, ICI: Biochem. Res. Manager, 1961-65; Res. Dir, March-June 1966; Dep. Chm., 1966-70. Dep. Chm., AECI Ltd, S Africa, 1975-. Member: Council, RIC, 1974-77; Council, Chem. Soc., (Pres. elect, 1978). Member: Adv. Council, Applied R&D, 1976-; Adv. Bd for Res. Councils, 1977-. Fellow, Imperial Coll., London, 1975. *Publications:* Evaluation of Drug Toxicity, 1958; papers in scientific jls. *Recreations:* photography, travel, theatre. *Address:* Woodcote, Torkington Road, Wilmslow, Cheshire SK9 2AE. *T:* Wilmslow 22316. *Clubs:* Athenæum, United Oxford & Cambridge University.

SPINKS, Rev. Dr G(eorge) Stephens; Vicar, St Paul's, Scouthead, Oldham, 1966-69; Examining Chaplain to Bishop of Manchester, 1967-70; *b* Cambridge, 1903; *m* 1968, Mrs Annie Nightingale. *Educ:* Cathedral Choir Sch., Rochester; Manchester College and St Catherine's Society, Oxford; University College and King's Coll., London. MA (London), PhD (London); Hibbert Research Student, 1944-45; Upton Lecturer, Manchester Coll., Oxford, 1947-48 and 1949-50. Minister of All Souls' Church, Golders Green, London, 1937-47. Editor of the Hibbert Journal, 1948-51. Rector of Great Lever, Bolton, 1952-55; Rector of Clovelly, 1955-59; Priest-in-Charge, St Swithun's, Littleham by Bideford, 1962-64. Ext. Lectr, Exeter, 1956-66. Frequent broadcast talks on BBC European Service. Exeter University Extension Lecturer; Joyce Lecturer, Dio. Exeter, 1961; Tele-Lecture (from England to W Virginia, USA), 1968. *Publications:* (with E. L. Allen and James Parkes) Religion in Britain since 1900, 1952; The Fundamentals of Religious Belief, 1961; Psychology and Religion, 1963 (also published US, Holland, Japan); Origins of Religious Experience, chapter in Encyclopedia of Psychology, vol. III, 1972; articles in periodicals in Holland, India, Japan, UK, USA. *Address:* 35 Greenmount Drive, Greenmount, Tottington, near Bury, Lancs. *T:* Tottington 2677.

SPIRO, Sidney, MC 1945; *b* 27 July 1914; *Educ:* Cape Town Univ. (Law degree). RA in Middle East, Italy, 1939-45. Joined Anglo American Corp., 1953, Exec. Dir 1961-77; Man. Dir and Dep. Chm., Charter Consolidated, 1969, Chm. 1971-76; Director: Rio Tinto-Zinc Corp. Ltd; Barclays Bank International Ltd; De Beers Consolidated Mines Ltd. Mem., Internat Adv. Council, Canadian Imperial Bank of Commerce; Chm., Société Minière de Tenke-Fungurume. *Recreations:* shooting, golf, tennis, music. *Address:* 43 Lowndes Square, SW1. *Clubs:* White's, MCC; Rand (Johannesburg); Sunningdale Golf.

SPITZ, Mrs Heinz; *see* Gales, Kathleen Emily.

SPITZER, Prof. Lyman (Jr), BA; PhD; Professor of Astronomy (Charles A. Young Professor since 1952), Chairman of Astrophysical Sciences Department, and Director of Observatory, Princeton University, since 1947; Chairman, Research Board, 1967-72; *b* 26 June 1914; *s* of Lyman Spitzer and Blanche B. (*née* Brumback); *m* 1940, Doreen D. Canaday; one *s* three *d*. *Educ:* Phillips Academy, Andover; Yale Univ. (BA); Cambridge Univ., England; Princeton Univ. (PhD). Instructor in Physics and Astronomy, Yale Univ., 1939-42; Scientist, Special Studies Group, Columbia Univ. Div. of War Research, 1942-44; Dir, Sonar Analysis Group, Columbia Univ. Div. of War Research, 1944-46; Assoc. Prof. of Astrophysics, Yale Univ., 1946-47. Dir Project Matterhorn, Princeton Univ., 1953-61; Chm. Exec. Cttee, Plasma Physics Lab., Princeton Univ., 1961-66; Principal Investigator, Princeton telescope on Copernicus satellite. Member: Nat. Acad. of Sciences; American Academy of Arts and Sciences; American Philosophical Society; Internat. Acad. of Astronautics; Corr. Member, Société Royale des Sciences, Liège; Foreign Associate, Royal Astronomical Soc.; Pres., American Astronomical Soc., 1959-61. Hon. Dr of Science: Yale Univ., 1958; Case Inst. of Technology, 1961; Harvard, 1975; Hon. Dr of Laws, Toledo Univ., 1963. Rittenhouse Medal, 1957; NASA Medal, 1972; Bruce Medal, 1973; Draper Medal, 1974; Maxwell Prize, 1975; Dist. Public Service Medal, NASA, 1976. *Publications:* (ed) Physics of Sound in the Sea, 1946; Physics of Fully Ionized Gases, 1956 (2nd edn 1962); Diffuse Matter in Space, 1968; papers in Astrophysical Jl, Monthly Notices of Royal Astronomical Soc., Physical Review, Physics of Fluids, on interstellar matter, stellar dynamics, plasma physics, etc. *Recreations:* ski-ing, mountain climbing. *Address:* 659 Lake Drive, Princeton, NJ 08540, USA. *T:* 609-924 3007. *Club:* American Alpine.

SPOCK, Dr Benjamin McLane; Professor of Child Development, Western Reserve University, USA, 1955-67, now writing and working for peace; *b* New Haven, Connecticut, 2 May 1903; *s* of Benjamin Ives Spock and Mildred Louise (*née* Stoughton); *m* 1st, 1927, Jane Davenport Cheney (marr. diss.); two *s*; 2nd, 1976, Mrs Mary Councille. *Educ:* Yale Univ. (BA); Yale Medical Sch.; Coll. Physicians and Surgeons, Columbia Univ. (MD). In practice (Pediatrics) from 1933; Cornell Med. Coll.; NY Hospital; NYC Health Dept. Served, 1944-46 in US Navy. Subseq. on Staff of: Rochester (Minn) Child Health Inst., Mayo Clinic, University of Minnesota; Prof. of Child Development, University of Pittsburgh, 1951-55. *Publications:* Common Sense Book of Baby and Child Care, 1946 (repr. as Pocket Book, 1946); (with John Reinhart and Wayne Miller) A Baby's First Year, 1955; (with Miriam E. Lowenberg) Feeding Your Baby and Child, 1955; Dr Spock Talks with Mothers, 1961; Problems of Parents, 1962; (with Marion Lerrigo) Caring for Your Disabled Child, 1964; (with Mitchell Zimmerman) Dr Spock on Vietnam, 1968; Decent and Indecent: our personal and political behaviour, 1970; A Young Person's Guide to Life and Love, 1971; Raising Children in a Difficult Time, 1974 (UK as Bringing Up Children in a Difficult Time, 1974). *Relevant publications:* The Trial of Doctor Spock, by Jessica Mitford, 1969; Dr Spock: biography of a conservative radical, by Lynn Z. Bloom, 1972. *Address:* Box N, Rogers, Arkansas 72756, USA.

SPOFFORD, Charles Merville, CBE (Hon.) 1945; DSM and Purple Heart (US), 1945; Lawyer (US); Trustee: Carnegie Corporation of New York; Juillard Musical Foundation; Director Emeritus: Council on Foreign Relations; Metropolitan Opera Association (Chairman Exec. Cttee, 1956-71, Member since 1971, President, 1946-50); Vice-Chairman and Director Emeritus, Lincoln Center for the Performing Arts, Inc.; Member Exec. Cttee, American Branch, International Law Association; former Member Exec. Council, American Society International Law, etc.; Trustee, The Mutual Life Insurance Co. of New York; *b* 17 Nov. 1902; *s* of Charles W. and Beulah Merville Spofford; *m* 1st, 1930, Margaret Mercer Walker (marr. diss. 1959); two *s* two *d*; 2nd, 1960, Carolyn Storrs Andre (*d* 1970); 3rd, 1970, Sydney Brewster Luddy. *Educ:* Northwest Univ.; University of Grenoble; Yale Univ. (AB 1924; Hon. MA 1956); Harvard Law Sch. JD 1928. Instructor, European History, Yale Univ., 1924-25, and sometime Alumni Fellow; practised Law, Chicago, 1929-30, New York (Davis Polk & Wardwell), 1930-40; member of firm, 1940-50 and 1952-. Lieut-Colonel 1942, AFHQ Algiers; adv. on econ. and supply, French N Africa and French W Africa, 1942-43; Chief of Planning Staff (for AMG Sicily and Italy); Dep. Chief Civil Affairs Officer for Sicily and S Italy, 1943-44; AFHQ, Asst Chief of Staff, (G-5) Med. Theatre, 1944-45; War Dept as Military Adv. to State Dept, 1945; Colonel, 1943; Brig-General, 1944. Asst to President and Special Counsel to American National Red Cross, 1946-50; also other former civic activities. Deputy US Representative, North Atlantic Council, and Chairman, North Atlantic Council Deputies, 1950-52; Member European Co-ordinating Cttee (US); resigned 1952, to rejoin law firm. Formerly Director: American Univ. in Beirut, 1957-63; Nat. Council, English-Speaking Union, 1955-64; The Distillers Co. Ltd, 1952-76; subsid. CIBA Corp., 1957-71; Inst. for Defense Analyses, 1960-70. Carnegie Lectr, Hague Acad. of Internat. Law, 1964. Hon. LLD Northwestern Univ., 1959. Comdr, Order of Nishan Iftikhar, Tunisia, 1943; Croix de Guerre with palm, France, 1945; Commander, Order of SS Maurice and Lazarus, Italy, 1945; Commander, Legion of Honour, France, 1952; Commander with Star, Order of the Falcon, Iceland, 1953; Grand Officer, Order of the Crown, Belgium. *Recreation:* golf. *Publications:* articles in journals. *Address:* (business) 1 Chase Manhattan Plaza, New York, NY 10005, USA; (residence) Windmill Lane, East Hampton, New York, NY 11937. *Clubs:* Century Association, Links (New York); Maidstone (East Hampton).

SPOKES, John Arthur Clayton, QC 1973; a Recorder of the Crown Court, since 1972; *b* 6 Feb. 1931; 2nd *s* of late Peter Spencer Spokes and of Lilla Jane Spokes (*née* Clayton), Oxford; *m* 1961, Jean, *yr d* of late Dr Robert McLean, Carluke, and Jean Symington McLean (*née* Barr); one *s* one *d*. *Educ:* Westminster Sch.; Brasenose Coll., Oxford. BA 1954; MA 1959. Nat. Service, Royal Artillery, 1949-51 (commnd 1950). Called to Bar, Gray's Inn, 1955. *Recreations:* gardening, walking. *Address:* 3 Pump Court, Temple, EC4Y 7AJ. *T:* 01-353 0711. *Club:* Leander (Henley-on-Thames).

SPOONER, Edward Tenney Casswell, CMG 1966; MD, MA, MRCS, LRCP; FRCP; *b* 22 May 1904; *s* of William Casswell Spooner, MB, and Edith Maud Spooner, Blandford, Dorset; *m* 1948, Colin Mary Stewart. *Educ:* Epsom Coll.; Clare Coll., Cambridge; St Bartholomew's Hospital. Foundation Scholar of Clare Coll., 1923; House Physician, St Bartholomew's Hospital, 1927-28; Commonwealth Fellow, Harvard Medical Sch., 1929-31; Fellow of Clare Coll., 1929-47; Tutor of Clare Coll., 1939-47; University Demonstrator and Lecturer, Dept of Pathology, University of Cambridge, 1931-46; Professor of Bacteriology and Immunology, London School of Hygiene and Tropical Medicine, 1947-60, Dean, 1960-70. Temporary Major, RAMC, in No 1 Medical Research Section, 1942-43; Director, Emergency Public Health Laboratory, Cambridge, 1943-44; Editor, Journal of Hygiene, 1949-55; Member Medical Research Council, 1953-57; Member Council Epsom Coll., 1955-65; Chm., Public Health Lab. Service Bd, 1963-72. *Publications:* papers on tetanus, certain virus diseases and wound infection. *Address:* Wolverley, Burnhams Road, Little Bookham, Surrey. *Club:* Athenæum.

SPOONER, Edwin George, CIE 1946; Director and General Manager, Whitehead Iron & Steel Co. Ltd, Newport, Mon, 1954-63; *b* 1898; *s* of George Henry Spooner, Birmingham; *m* Thelma Marie, *d* of Eric Albert Bibra, Melbourne, Australia. *Educ:* Secondary Sch., Birmingham. Served in France with Coldstream Guards, European War, 1914-19. Iron and Steel Controller, Dept of Supply, India, 1944-47. *Address:* Flat 8, Hartshill Court, 104 Golf Links Road, Ferndown, Dorset BH22 8DA. *T:* Ferndown 873568.

SPOONER, Prof. Frank Clyffurde, MA, PhD; Professor of Economic History, University of Durham, since 1966; *b* 5 March 1924; *s* of Harry Gordon Morrison Spooner. *Educ:* Bromley Grammar Sch.; Christ's Coll., Cambridge. Hist. Tripos, 1st cl., Pt I 1947 and Pt II 1948; MA 1949; PhD 1953. War Service, Sub-Lt (S) RNVR, 1943-46; Bachelor Research Scholar, 1948; Chargé de Recherches, CNRS, Paris, 1949-50; Allen Scholar, 1951; Fellow, Christ's Coll., Cambridge, 1951-57; Commonwealth Fund Fellow, 1955-57 at Chicago, Columbia, New York, and Harvard Univs; Ecole Pratique des Hautes Etudes, VI Section, Sorbonne, 1957-61; Lectr, Univ. of Oxford, 1958-59; Vis. Lectr in Econs, Harvard Univ., 1961-62; Irving Fisher Research Prof. of Econs, Yale Univ., 1962-63; Univ. of Durham: Lectr, 1963; Reader, 1964; Resident Tutor-in-charge, Lumley Castle, 1965-70; Dir, Inst. of European Studies, 1969-76; Leverhulme Fellow, 1976-78. Prix Limantour de l'Académie des Sciences Morales et Politiques, 1957. FRHS 1970. *Publications:* L'économie mondiale et les frappes monétaires en France, 1493-1680, 1956, revised edn The International Economy and Monetary Movements in France, 1493-1725, 1972; contrib. Congrès et Colloques, 1965; Mediterraneo e Oceano Indiano, 1970; Annales (ESC); Annales de Normandie; Cambridge Hist. Jl; Revised Cambridge Modern History; Cambridge Econ. History of Europe; essays in honour of Armando Sapori, Amintore Fanfani and Fernand Braudel. *Recreations:* music, photography, walking. *Address:* 145 Gilesgate, Durham DH1 1QQ. *Club:* United Oxford & Cambridge University.

SPORBORG, Henry Nathan, CMG 1945; Chairman: SKF (UK) until 1975; Stirling-Astaldi; Gomme Holdings; Bishopsgate Property and General Investments; Berkeley Hambro Property Co. until 1975; Vice-Chairman, Sun Alliance & London Insurance Ltd, since 1969; Deputy Chairman, Thorn Electrical Industries, since 1973; Director of other companies; Commissioner to Earl Fitzwilliam; *b* 17 Sept. 1905; *e c* of late H. N. and M. A. Sporborg; *m* 1935, Mary Rowlands; one *s* three *d*. *Educ:* Rugby Sch.; Emmanuel Coll., Cambridge. Admitted Solicitor, 1930; partner in firm of Slaughter & May, 1935; joined Ministry of Economic Warfare, 1939; Director and later Vice-Chief, Special Operations Executive, 1940-46. A Director, Hambros, until 1977. Mem., Port of London Authority, until 1975. Chairman, Board of Governors, St Mary's Hospital, 1964-74. JP Herts, 1957. Chevalier, Legion of Honour, Croix de Guerre, Order of St Olav (Norway), etc. *Recreation:* foxhunting. *Address:* Culver, Much Hadham, Herts. *T:* Much Hadham 2506. *Clubs:* Boodle's, Carlton.

SPOTSWOOD, Marshal of the Royal Air Force Sir Denis (Frank), GCB 1971 (KCB 1966; CB 1961); CBE 1946; DSO 1943; DFC 1942; Vice-Chairman, Rolls Royce Ltd, since 1974; *b* 26 Sept. 1916; *s* of late F. H. Spotswood and M. C. Spotswood; *m* 1942, Ann (*née* Child); one *s*. Commissioned in RAF, 1936; UK Service in Squadrons, 1937-41; No 209 Squadron, 1939-41. Served War of 1939-45 (despatches twice, DSO). Chief Instructor, Operation Training Unit, 1941-42; Officer Commanding No 500 (County of Kent) Squadron, RAuxAF,

1942-43; Director of Plans, HQ Supreme Allied Commander, South-East Asia, 1944-46; Directing Staff, RAF Staff Coll., 1946-48; Officer Commanding RAF (Fighter) Stations, Horsham St Faith and Coltishall, 1948-50; Directing Staff, Imperial Defence Coll., 1950-52; Exchange Duties, HQUSAF in USA, 1952-54; Officer Commanding RAF (Fighter) Station, Linton-on-Ouse, 1954-56; Deputy Director of Plans, Air Ministry, 1956-58; AOC and Commandant, RAF Coll., Cranwell, 1958-61; Assistant Chief of Staff (Air Defence), SHAPE, 1961-63; AOC No 3 Group, RAF Bomber Command, 1964-65; C-in-C RAF Germany, 1965-68; Commander, 2nd Allied Tactical Air Force, 1966-68; AOC-in-C, RAF Strike Command, 1968-71; Comdr, UK Air Defence Region, 1968-71; Chief of the Air Staff, 1971-74. Group Captain, 1954; Air Commodore, 1958; Air Vice-Marshal, 1961; Air Marshal, 1965; Air Chief Marshal, 1968; Marshal of the RAF, 1974. ADC to the Queen, 1957-61, Air ADC to the Queen, 1970-74. Director: RR/Turbomeca Ltd; Turbo Union Ltd. Vice-Pres., SBAC. Governor, Star and Garter Home; Chm. of Trustees, RAF Museum. FRAeS. Officer of the Legion of Merit (USA). *Recreations:* golf, sailing, shooting, bridge. *Address:* c/o Williams and Glyn's Bank Ltd, Whitehall, SW1. *Club:* Royal Air Force.

SPRAGG, Cyril Douglas, CBE 1949; Hon. FRIBA 1971 (Hon. ARIBA 1959); Secretary, Royal Institute of British Architects, 1945-59; *b* 22 July 1894; *y s* of late Charles and Emily Spragg; unmarried. *Educ:* Christ's Hospital. Served European War, Queen's Westminster Rifles, 1914-19. Asst Secretary, RIBA, 1926-44. Governor of Christ's Hospital; Thames Conservancy, 1966-70; Hon. Member American Institute of Architects, 1955; Hon. Corresp. Member, Royal Architectural Inst. of Canada, 1956; Hon. Associate Royal Australian Inst. of Architects, 1957; Hon. Fellow, New Zealand Institute of Architects, 1957; Hon. Member Inst. South African Architects; Hon. Member Ghana Society of Architects, 1959; Hon. Fellow Royal Incorporation of Architects in Scotland, 1960; Hon. Member Ceylon Inst. of Architects, 1960; Hon. Member Fedn of Malaya Society Architects, 1961. Hon. MA Durham Univ., 1958. Member: Middlesex CC, 1961; Surrey CC, 1965, Alderman, 1967-70. *Address:* Tower Cottage, Vicarage Road, Egham, Surrey TW20 9JN. *T:* Egham 4224.

SPRECKLEY, John Nicholas Teague; HM Diplomatic Service; Counsellor and Head of Chancery, Tokyo, since 1976; *b* 6 Dec. 1934; *s* of late Air Marshal Sir Herbert Spreckley, KBE, CB, and Winifred Emery Teague; *m* 1958, Margaret Paula Jane, *er d* of Prof. W. McC. Stewart, *qv*; one *s* one *d*. *Educ:* Winchester Coll.; Magdalene Coll., Cambridge (BA). Tokyo, 1957-62; American Dept, FO, 1962-64; Asst Private Sec. to Lord Carrington and Mr Padley, 1964; Defence Dept, FO, 1964-66; Head of Chancery, Dakar, 1966-70; Paris, 1970-75; Head of Referendum Unit, FCO, 1975. *Address:* c/o Foreign and Commonwealth Office, SW1A 2AL. *Clubs:* Army and Navy; International House (Tokyo).

SPREULL, Professor James (Spreull Andrew); William Dick Professor of Veterinary Surgery, at the University of Edinburgh, 1959-78; *b* 2 May 1908; *s* of late Lt-Col Andrew Spreull, DSO, TD, MRCVS, and Effie Andrew Spreull; *m* 1951, Kirsten Brummerstedt-Hansen; three *s*. *Educ:* Dundee High Sch.; Edinburgh Univ. (PhD); Royal Dick Veterinary Coll. (MRCVS). Royal Dick Veterinary College: Demonstrator of Anatomy, 1930-34, Lecturer in Applied Anatomy, 1931-34. Engaged in general practice in Dundee, 1934-59. FRSE 1965. *Publications:* various contributions to Veterinary Journals. *Recreations:* agriculture, fishing, badminton, antiques. *Address:* Spencerfield House, Hillend, Fife KY11 5LA. *T:* Inverkeithing 4255. *Club:* University (Edinburgh).

SPRIGGS, Leslie, JP; MP (Lab) St Helens since June 1958; *b* 22 April 1910; British; *m* 1931, Elfrida Mary Brindle Parkinson. *Educ:* Council Sch.; Trade Union Adult Schools. TU Scholarship to Belgium, 1951. Merchant Service, then Railway man until 1958. President, NW (NUR) District Council, Political Section, 1954; Vice-President, Industrial Section, 1955. Served as Auditor to Lancs and Cheshire Region of the Labour Party. Formerly Lecturer, National Council of Labour Colleges on Industrial Law, Economics, English, Foreign Affairs, Local Government, Trade Union History. JP N Fylde, 1955. *Recreations:* Rugby league, athletics, water polo. *Address:* House of Commons, SW1; 38 Knowle Avenue, Cleveleys, near Blackpool, Lancs. *T:* Cleveleys 2746. *Clubs:* Windle Labour (St Helens); Wortley Hall (Yorks) (Vice-Pres.).

SPRING, Frank Stuart, FRS 1952; DSc (Manchester), PhD (Liverpool), FRIC; Director, Laporte Industries Ltd, London, W1, 1959-71; retired; *b* 5 Sept. 1907; 3rd *s* of Captain John

Spring and Isabella Spring, Crosby, Liverpool; *m* 1932, Mary, 2nd *d* of Rev. John Mackintosh, MA, Heswall; one *s* one *d*. *Educ:* Waterloo Grammar Sch.; University of Liverpool. United Alkali Research Scholar, University of Liverpool, 1928-29; University Fellow, Liverpool, 1929-30. Assistant Lecturer, Lecturer and Senior Lecturer in Chemistry, University of Manchester, 1930-46; Freeland Professor of Chemistry, The Royal College of Science and Technology, Glasgow, 1946-59. Chemical Society, Tilden Lecturer, 1950. Hon. DSc, University of Salford, 1967. *Publications:* papers in chemical journals. *Address:* Flat 26, 1 Hyde Park Square, W2. *T:* 01-262 8174.

SPRING RICE, family name of **Baron Monteagle of Brandon.**

SPRINGALL, Harold Douglas; Professor of Chemistry, University of Keele, 1950-75, now Emeritus (Head of Department, 1950-74); *b* 24 June 1910; *o s* of Harold Springall and Margaret Springall (*née* Wright); *m* 1940, Jean Helen McArthur Gordon, *d* of L. McArthur Gordon and H. Violet Gordon (*née* Holbeche); two *s* one *d*. *Educ:* Colfe's Grammar School, London; Lincoln College, Oxford (Scholar). BA (1st cl.) 1934; BSc 1934; Magdalen College, Oxford (Senior Demy), 1934-36; DPhil 1936; MA Oxon 1938. Commonwealth Fund Fellowship, Calif Tech., Pasadena, Calif, Cornell Univ., 1936-38; Rockefeller Research Grant, Oxford, 1938-39. Min. of Supply: Sci. Officer (Armament Res. Dept) 1939-44; Sen. Sci. Officer, 1944-45. Univ. of Manchester: Lectr in Chemistry, 1945-48, Sen. Lectr, 1948-50; Asst Tutor to Faculty of Science, 1949-50; Tutor in Chemistry, Dalton Hall, 1945-50; Univ. Coll. of North Staffs: Dir of Studies, 1951-52; Vice-Principal, 1957-59; Actg Vice-Principal, 1960-61. Mem. Council Chem. Soc., 1954-57; Mem. Publication Cttee, Faraday Soc., 1957-71. CChem; FRIC 1948; FRSA 1971. DSc Keele, 1972. *Publications:* The Structural Chemistry of Proteins, 1954; Sidgwick's Organic Chemistry of Nitrogen, 1966; A Shorter Sidgwick's Organic Chemistry of Nitrogen, 1969; articles in Jl Chem. Soc., Jl Amer. Chem. Soc., Trans. Faraday Soc., Nature, etc. *Recreations:* music; hill and mountain walking and climbing. *Address:* 21 Springpool, The University, Keele, Staffordshire. *T:* Newcastle (Staffs) 627395. *Club:* Climbers'.

SPRINGER, Sir Hugh (Worrell), KCMG 1971; CBE 1961 (OBE 1954); Secretary-General, Association of Commonwealth Universities, since 1970; Barrister-at-Law; *b* 1913; 2nd *s* of late Charles W. Springer, Barbados, and late Florence Springer; *m* 1942, Dorothy Drinan, 3rd *d* of late Lionel Gittens, Barbados, and Cora Gittens; three *s* one *d*. *Educ:* Harrison Coll., Barbados; Hertford Coll., Oxford (Hon. Fellow 1974). BA 1936, MA 1944. Called to Bar, Inner Temple, 1938. Practice at the Bar, Barbados, 1938-47; MCP, 1940-47, MEC 1944-47, Barbados; Gen.-Sec., Barbados Lab. Party, 1940-47; Organiser and first Gen.-Sec., Workers' Union, 1940-47; Mem., West Indies Cttee of the Asquith Commn on Higher Educn, 1944; Mem., Provisional Council, University Coll. of the West Indies, 1947; first Registrar, Univ. Coll. of WI, 1947-63; John Simon Guggenheim Fellow and Fellow of Harvard Center for Internat. Affairs, 1961-62; first Dir, Univ. of WI Inst. of Educn, 1963-66; Commonwealth Asst Sec.-Gen., 1966-70. Past Mem., Public Service and other Commns and Cttees; Sen. Vis. Fellow of All Souls Coll., Oxford, 1962-63; Actg Governor of Barbados, 1964; Mem., Bermuda Civil Disorder Commn, 1968. Chm., Commonwealth Caribbean Med. Res. Council (formerly Brit. Caribbean Med. Research Cttee), 1965-; Vice-Pres., British Caribbean Assoc., 1974-; Trustee, Bernard Van Leer Foundn, 1967-; Barbados Trustee, Commonwealth Foundn, 1967-, and Chm., 1974-77; Member, Court of Governors: LSE, 1970-; Exeter Univ., 1970-; Hull Univ., 1970-; London Sch. of Hygiene and Tropical Medicine, 1974-; Inst. of Commonwealth Studies, 1974-. Jt Sec., UK Commonwealth Scholarships Commn, 1970-; Exec. Sec., Marshall Scholarships Commn, 1970-; Sec., Kennedy Memorial Trust, 1970-; Chm., Commonwealth Human Ecology Council, 1971-; Member: Council, USPG, 1972-; Adv. Cttee, Sci. Policy Foundn, 1977-; Pres., Educn Section, British Assoc., 1974-75. Hon. DSc Soc Laval, 1958; Hon. LLD: Victoria, BC, 1972; Univ. of WI, 1973; Hon. DLitt: Warwick, 1974; Ulster, 1974; Heriot-Watt, 1976; Hong Kong, 1977; St Andrews, 1977. *Publications:* Reflections on the Failure of the First West Indian Federation, 1962 (USA); articles and lectures on West Indian and Commonwealth Educn and Development, in: The Round Table, Commonwealth, RSA Jl, Caribbean Quarterly, Internat. Organisation, Jl of Negro History, etc. *Recreations:* walking, talking. *Address:* (home) 22 Kensington Court Gardens, W8. *T:* 01-937 4626; (office) 36 Gordon Square, WC1H 0PF. *T:* 01-387 8572. *Clubs:* Athenæum, Royal Commonwealth Society; Kingston Cricket (Jamaica).

SPRINGER, Tobias; a Metropolitan Stipendiary Magistrate, since 1963; Barrister-at-law; *b* 3 April 1907; *o c* of late Samuel Springer, MBE; *m* 1937, Stella Rauchwerger. *Educ:* Mill Hill Sch.; Caius Coll., Cambridge. Law Tripos 1928; called to Bar, Gray's Inn, 1929. Practised London and SE Circuit. Served War of 1939-45: 60th Rifles, 1940-45; Lt-Col GSO1, GHQ, H Forces, 1944. Returned to practise at Bar, 1945. Actg Dep. Chm., Co. London Sessions, periods 1962, 1963. Life Governor: Mill Hill School; Metropolitan Hosp. *Recreations:* travel, golf, reading. *Address:* 82 Cholmley Gardens, NW6 1UN. *T:* 01-435 0817. *Clubs:* Royal Automobile; Porters Park Golf.

SPRINGETT, Jack Allan, MA(Cantab); County Education Officer, Essex, since 1973; *b* 1 Feb. 1916; *s* of Arthur John and Agnes Springett; *m* 1950, Patricia Winifred Singleton; three *s* one *d*. *Educ:* Windsor Grammar Sch.; Fitzwilliam House, Cambridge. Asst Master, Christ's Hospital, Horsham, 1938-47. Served War, Royal Signals and Gen. Staff, 1940-46. Administrative Asst, North Riding, 1947-52; Asst Educn Officer, Birmingham, 1952-62; Dep. Educn Officer, Essex, 1962-73. Mem., Technician Educn Council; Hon. Sec., County Educn Officers' Soc. *Recreations:* music, mountain walking. *Address:* 3 Roxwell Road, Chelmsford, Essex CM1 2LY. *T:* Chelmsford 58669.

SPRINGFORD, John Frederick Charles, OBE 1970; Counsellor, Cultural Affairs, British High Commission, Ottawa, and British Council Representative in Canada, since 1974; *b* 6 June 1919; *s* of Frederick Charles Springford and Bertha Agnes Springford (*née* Trenery); *m* 1945, Phyllis Wharton; one *s* two *d*. *Educ:* Latymer Upper Sch.; Christ's College, Cambridge (MA). Served War 1940-46, RAC; seconded Indian Armoured Corps, 1942; Asst Political Agent II in Mekran, 1945. British Council Service, Baghdad and Mosul, Iraq, 1947-51, Isfahan, Iran, 1951-52; British Council Representative: Tanzania, 1952-57; Sudan, 1957-62; Dir, Overseas Students Dept, 1962-66; Representative: Jordan, 1966-69; Iraq, 1969-74. *Recreations:* archaeology, organ music. *Address:* Precinct, Crowhurst, Battle, East Sussex TN33 9AA. *T:* Crowhurst 200.

SPROAT, Iain Mac Donald; MP (C) Aberdeen (South) since 1970; *b* Dollar, Clackmannanshire, 8 Nov. 1938; *s* of late William Sproat and of Lydia B. Sproat. *Educ:* Melrose; Winchester; Oxford. *Recreations:* collecting books, cricket. *Address:* Dhualt House, near Banchory, Grampian.

SPROTT, Rt. Rev. John Chappell, MA; DD St Andrews 1965; *b* 16 Oct. 1903; *s* of Thomas Sprott, Master Mariner, and Catherine Chappell; *m* 1932, Winifred Helen Cameron, *d* of late Sir David W. Bone, CBE, LLD; three *s* one *d*. *Educ:* Castle Hill Sch., Ealing; Glasgow Univ.; Edinburgh Theological Coll. Deacon, 1927; Priest, 1928; Chaplain and Succentor, St Mary's Cathedral, Edinburgh, 1927-29; Lecturer in Music, Edinburgh Theological College, 1928-29; Curate, All Saints, Glasgow, 1929-33; St George the Martyr, Holborn, 1933-37; Rector, West Hackney, 1937-40; Provost of St Paul's Cathedral, Dundee, 1940-59; Bishop of Brechin, 1959-75. *Recreation:* music. *Address:* 5 Sandilands, Bentinck Drive, Troon, Ayrshire.

SPRY, Brig. Sir Charles Chambers Fowell, Kt 1964; CBE 1956; DSO 1943; retired as Director-General, Australian Security Intelligence Organization, 1950-70; *b* 26 June 1910; *s* of A. F. Spry, Brisbane; *m* 1939, Kathleen Edith Hull, *d* of Rev. Godfrey Smith; one *s* two *d*. *Educ:* Brisbane Grammar School. Graduated Royal Military College, Duntroon. Served War of 1939-45 as Col, Australian Imperial Force in SW Pacific (DSO) and Middle East. Director of Military Intelligence, 1946-50. *Recreation:* golf. *Address:* 18 Balmoral Crescent, Mont Albert, Victoria 3127, Australia. *Clubs:* Melbourne; Royal Melbourne Golf.

SPRY, Maj.-Gen. Daniel Charles, CBE 1945; DSO 1944; CD; *b* Winnipeg, Man, 4 Feb. 1913; *s* of Major-General Daniel William Bigelow Spry and Ethelyn Alma (*née* Rich); *m* 1939, Elisabeth, *d* of Roy Fletcher Forbes, Halifax, NS; one *s* one *d*. *Educ:* Public Schools, Calgary and Halifax; Ashford School, England; Dalhousie University. Served with Canadian Militia; 2nd Lt, Princess Louise Fusiliers, 1932; Royal Canadian Regt (permanent force), 1934. Served War, 1939-46 (CBE, DSO, CD, despatches twice); Captain 1939, Major 1940, Lt-Col 1943, Brig. 1943, Maj.-Gen. 1944; GOC 3rd Canadian Infantry Div., 1944-45; retired as Vice-Chief of Gen. Staff, 1946. Col, The Royal Canadian Regt, 1965. Chief Exec. Comr, The Boy Scouts' Assoc. of Canada, 1946-51; Dep. Dir, Boy Scouts World Bureau, 1951-53, Dir, 1953-65. Commander, Order of the Crown of Belgium, 1945; Croix de Guerre, Belgium, 1945. *Recreations:* sailing, gardening, fishing. *Address:* 4 Rock Avenue, Ottawa, Ontario K1M 1A6, Canada. *Club:* Rideau (Ottawa).
See also Graham Spry.

SPRY, Graham, CC 1971; Agent General for Saskatchewan in the United Kingdom and Europe, 1947-67, retired 1968; *b* St Thomas, Ontario, 20 Feb. 1900; *e s* of Maj.-Gen. D. W. B. Spry, OBE, ED, and Ethelyn Alma Rich; *m* 1938, Professor Irene Mary Biss; one *s* one *d* (and one *s* decd). *Educ:* public schools, Toronto, Montreal and Winnipeg; University of Manitoba (BA, Rhodes Scholar); University College, Oxford (MA); Sorbonne, Paris. Served Canadian Army, Gunner, 1918. Editorial Staff, Winnipeg Free Press, 1919-22 (while at University); Internat. Labour Office, Geneva, 1925-26; Nat. Sec., Assoc. of Canadian Clubs, 1926-32. Organized and chm. of Canadian Radio League (voluntary group which advocated and secured, by unanimous vote of House of Commons, establishment of public service broadcasting), 1929-33; Canadian Politics, 1933-37. California Standard Oil Co. Ltd, London, Eng., 1938-39, Dir, and Manager, 1940-46; Director: Associated Ethyl Co., Ceylon Petroleum Co., 1940-47; British Ethyl Corp., 1944-47; Personal Asst to Rt Hon. Sir Stafford Cripps, Lord Privy Seal and Minister of Aircraft Production, 1942-45, Member of Mission to India, 1942; duties in USA for Sir Stafford Cripps, 1942, and for Rt Hon. R. K. Law, 1943. Member Inter-deptl Cttee on Internat. Civil Aviation, War Corresp., Canadian Army, Italy, Aug.-Sept., 1944, and Germany, April-May, 1945. XXth Century Fund Survey of Turkey, 1947; FRAI. Hon. LLD: Brock, 1968; Saskatchewan, 1968; York, 1976. *Publications:* (joint) Social Planning for Canada, 1934; Canada 1941; Canada, 1946; (joint) Turkey: An Economic Appraisal, 1949. *Recreations:* books, history, ski-ing, and Tuscany. *Address:* 446 Cloverdale Road, Ottawa, Ontario K1M 0Y6, Canada; Shield's Edge, Kingsmere, Quebec. *Clubs:* Brooks's; Travellers'; Leander (Hon. Mem.); Rideau (Ottawa).
See also D. C. Spry.

SPRY, Hon. Sir John (Farley), Kt 1975; Chief Justice of Gibraltar, since 1976; *b* 11 March 1910; *s* of Joseph Farley Spry and Fanny Seagrave Treloar Spry; *m* 1st (marr. diss. 1940); one *s* one *d*; 2nd, Stella Marie (*née* Fichat). *Educ:* Perse School and Peterhouse, Cambridge (MA). Solicitor, 1935; Asst Registrar of Titles and Conveyancer, Uganda, 1936-44; Chief Inspector of Land Registration, Palestine, 1944; Asst Director of Land Registration, Palestine, 1944-48; Registrar-General, Tanganyika 1948-50, Kenya 1950-52; Tanganyika: Registrar-Gen., 1952-56; Legal Draftsman, 1956-60; Principal Sec., Public Service Commn, 1960-61; Puisne Judge, 1961-64; Justice of Appeal, Court of Appeal for Eastern Africa, 1964-70; Vice-President, 1970-75; Chm., Pensions Appeal Tribunals, 1975-76. *Publications:* Sea Shells of Dar es Salaam, Part I, 1961 (3rd edn 1968), Part II, 1964; Civil Procedure in East Africa, 1969. *Recreation:* conchology. *Address:* The Supreme Court, Gibraltar.

SPURGEON, Maj.-Gen. Peter Lester; Commander, Training Group, Royal Marines, since 1977; *b* 27 Aug. 1927; *s* of Harold Sidney Spurgeon and Emily Anne (*née* Bolton); *m* 1959, Susan Ann (*née* Aylward); one *s* one *d*. *Educ:* Merchant Taylors' Sch., Northwood. Commnd, 1946; 1949-66: HMS Glory; Depot, RM Deal; 40 Commando RM; ADC to Maj.-Gen. Plymouth Gp RM; DS Officers' Sch., RM; RAF Staff Coll., Bracknell; Staff of Comdt Gen. RM; 40 Commando RM; Jt Warfare Estab.; GS02 HQ: ME Comd, Aden, 1967; Army Strategic Comd, 1968-69; Second-in-Comd, 41 Commando RM, 1969-71; DS National Defence Coll., Latimer, 1971-73; CO RM Poole, 1973-75; Dir of Drafting and Records, RM, 1975-76. *Recreations:* golf, dinghy sailing, tennis. *Address:* Eastney House, Southsea, Hants PO4 9PP. *T:* Portsmouth 22351, ext. 6149. *Club:* Army and Navy.

SPURLING, Antony Cuthbert, QC (Sierra Leone); *b* 12 Oct. 1906; 3rd *s* of late Cuthbert Spurling; *m* 1935, Elizabeth Frances, *d* of late J. C. Stobart; two *s* one *d*. *Educ:* Berkhamsted; St Paul's; Hertford College, Oxford. Called to Bar, Inner Temple, 1931; Temp. Legal Asst, Ministry of Health, 1934; Resident Magistrate, Kenya, 1935; Crown Counsel, Kenya, 1939; Solicitor-General, Trinidad, 1946; Attorney-General, Gambia, 1951. Attorney-General, Sierra Leone, 1955-61. Retired, 1961. *Publication:* Digest and Guide to the Criminal Law of Kenya, 1946. *Recreation:* gardening. *Address:* Wheelwright Cottage, Bodle Street Green, Nr Herstmonceux, Sussex. *T:* Herstmonceux 2308.

SPURLING, Hon. Sir (Arthur) Dudley, Kt 1975; CBE 1963; JP; Barrister and Attorney; Senior Partner, Appleby, Spurling & Kempe; Speaker of the House of Assembly, Bermuda, 1972-76; *b* 9 Nov. 1913; *m* 1941, Marian Taylor, *d* of Frank Gurr, St George's, Bermuda; three *s* one *d*. *Educ:* St George's Grammar Sch.; Saltus Grammar Sch.; Rossall Sch., Lancs; Trinity Coll., Oxford (Rhodes Scholar); Lincoln's Inn. Called to Bar: Lincoln's Inn, 1937; Bermuda 1938. Served War, 1939-45, Bermuda Volunteer Rifle Corps. MHA, 1943-; MEC, 1957-69; former Chairman: Educn Bd; Bd of Public Works; Bd of Immigration; Bd of Trade. JP Bermuda. *Recreations:* golf, boating, swimming. *Address:* Three Chimneys, St George's, Bermuda. *Clubs:* Royal Bermuda Yacht, Royal Hamilton Amateur Dinghy, Mid Ocean, St George's Dinghy and Sports (all in Bermuda).

SPURLING, Maj.-Gen. John Michael Kane, CB 1957; CBE 1953; DSO 1944; *b* 9 May 1906; *s* of late Dr Clement and Mrs Spurling, Oundle, Northants; *m* 1930, Penelope, *d* of Rt Rev. Neville Lovett, CBE, DD, sometime Bishop of Portsmouth and subsequently of Salisbury; one *s* one *d* (and one *s* decd). *Educ:* Oundle. Commissioned Roy. Leics Regt, 1927; served India, UK and Palestine, 1927-38; Staff College, Camberley, 1938-39; served UK and Burma, 1940-43; North-West Europe, 1944-45, including command of 131 Bde, 7th Armoured Division, War Office, and command of a Parachute Bde, 1945-50; Commandant, Senior Officers' School, 1950-53; Chief of Staff, West Africa, 1953-55; Chief of Staff, HQ Northern Command, 1955-58, retired. Col, 4th (Leics) Battn, The Royal Anglian Regt, 1965-68; Dep. Col, The Royal Anglian Regiment (Leicestershire and Rutland), 1968-70. Governor, Milton Abbey Public School, 1961. *Recreation:* shooting. *Address:* The Manor, Fifehead Neville, Dorset. *T:* Hazelbury Bryan 458.

SPURRIER, Mabel Annie, HRI; Freelance Artist; Royal Birmingham Society of Artists, 1930; *b* Moseley, Birmingham; *y d* of late William James and Caroline Spurrier, Moseley, Birmingham; unmarried. *Educ:* The Woodroughs, Moseley; College of Arts and Crafts, Birmingham, and London. *Address:* 30 Spencer House, 11 Belsize Park Gardens, NW3. *T:* 01-722 9984.

SQUIBB, George Drewry, QC 1956; JP; President Transport Tribunal, since 1962; Chief Commons Commissioner, since 1971; Norfolk Herald Extraordinary since 1959; Earl Marshal's Lieutenant, Assessor and Surrogate in the Court of Chivalry, since 1976; *b* 1 Dec. 1906; *o s* of Reginald Augustus Hodder Squibb, Chester; *m* 1st, 1936, Bessie (*d* 1954), *d* of George Whittaker, Burley, Hants; one *d*; 2nd, 1955, Evelyn May, *d* of Frederick Richard Higgins, of Overleigh Manor, Chester. *Educ:* King's School, Chester; Queen's College, Oxford (BCL, MA). Barrister-at-Law, Inner Temple, 1930; Bencher, 1951; Reader, 1975; Treasurer, 1976. Army Officers' Emergency Reserve, 1938. Deputy Chairman Dorset Quarter Sessions, 1950-53, Chairman, 1953-71; Junior Counsel to the Crown in Peerage and Baronetcy Cases, 1954-56; Hon. Historical Adviser in Peerage Cases to the Attorney-General, 1965-. Member: Cttee on Rating of Charities, 1958-59; Adv. Council on Public Records, 1964-; Council, Selden Soc., 1961- (Vice-Pres., 1969-72). FSA, 1946; FSG 1973. JP Dorset, 1943-. *Publications:* The Law of Arms in England, 1953; Wiltshire Visitation Pedigrees, 1623, 1955; Reports of Heraldic Cases in the Court of Chivalry, 1956; The High Court of Chivalry, 1959; Visitation Pedigrees and the Genealogist, 1964; Founders' Kin, 1972; Doctors' Commons, 1977; papers in legal and antiquarian journals. *Recreation:* genealogical and heraldic research. *Address:* 5 Paper Buildings, Temple, EC4Y 7HB. *T:* 01-353 3436; The Old House, Cerne Abbas, Dorset DT2 7JQ. *T:* Cerne Abbas 272. *Clubs:* Athenæum, United Oxford & Cambridge University.

SQUIRE, Clifford William, MVO 1972; Counsellor, Washington, since 1976; *b* 7 Oct. 1928; *s* of Clifford John Squire and Eleanor Eliza Harpley; *m* 1st, 1959, Marie José Carlier (*d* 1973); one *s* two *d* (and one *s* decd); 2nd, 1976, Sara Laetitia Hutchison; one *s*. *Educ:* Royal Masonic Sch., Bushey; St John's Coll., Oxford; Coll. of Europe, Bruges. British Army, 1947-49. Nigerian Admin. Service, 1953-59; FO, 1959-60; British Legation, Bucharest, 1961-63; FO, 1963-65; UK Mission to UN, New York, 1965-69; Head of Chancery, Bangkok, 1969-72; Head of SE Asian Dept, FCO, 1972-75; Extramural Fellow, Sch. of Oriental and African Studies, London Univ., 1975-76. *Address:* c/o Foreign and Commonwealth Office, SW1; 5226 Loughborough Road NW, Washington, DC 20016, USA. *T:* 966-1122. *Clubs:* Travellers'; Cosmos (Washington, DC).

SQUIRE, Peter John; Headmaster, Bedford Modern School, since 1977; *b* 15 Feb. 1937; *s* of Leslie Ernest Squire and Doris Eileen Squire; *m* 1965, Susan Elizabeth (*née* Edwards); one *s* one *d*. *Educ:* King Edward's Sch., Birmingham; Jesus Coll., Oxford (BA 1960, MA 1964); Pembroke Coll. and Dept of Educn, Cambridge (Cert. in Educn 1961). Asst Master, Monkton Combe Sch., Bath, 1961-65; Haberdashers' Aske's Sch., Elstree, 1965-77; Sen. Boarding Housemaster, 1968-77; Sen. History Master, 1970-77. *Recreations:* Rugby, squash, gardening, antique collecting. *Address:* Bedford Modern School, Manton Lane, Bedford MK41 7NT. *T:* Bedford 64331.

SQUIRE, Raglan, FRIBA, MSIA; Senior Partner Raglan Squire & Partners, Consultants in Architecture, Engineering, Town Planning, etc; *b* 30 Jan. 1912; *e s* of late Sir John Squire, Kt; *m* 1st, 1938, Rachel, (*d* 1968), *d* of James Atkey, Oxshott, Surrey; two *s*; 2nd, 1968, Bridget Lawless. *Educ:* Blundell's; St John's Coll., Cambridge. Private practice in London, 1935-. War service with Royal Engineers, 1942-45. Founded firm of Raglan Squire & Partners, 1948. Principal projects: housing, educational and industrial work, 1935-41; pre-fabricated bldgs and industrial design, 1945-48; Eaton Sq. Conversion Scheme, 1945-56; Rangoon Univ. Engineering Coll., 1953-56; Associated Architect, Transport Pavilion, Festival of Britain Exhib., 1951; Town Planning Scheme for Mosul, Iraq, 1955; Bagdad airport report, 1955; factories at Weybridge, Huddersfield, etc; office buildings London, Eastbourne, Bournemouth, etc; gen. practice at home and over-seas incl. major hotels at Teheran, Tunis, Nicosia, Malta and Singapore, Gibraltar, Caribbean and Middle East, 1955-74. Sec. RIBA Reconstruction Cttee, 1941-42; Council of Architectural Assoc., 1951-52; Guest Editor Architects' Journal, 1947. *Publications:* articles in technical press on organisation of Building Industry, Architectural Education, etc. *Recreations:* ocean racing and designing small yachts. *Address:* 73 Elizabeth Street, SW1. *T:* 01-730 7225. *Clubs:* Royal Thames Yacht, Royal Ocean Racing; Royal Southern Yacht (Hamble).

SQUIRES, James Duane; Professor of History, Colby College, New Hampshire, USA, since 1933; Historical Consultant to NH War Records Committee, since 1944; *b* Grand Forks, North Dakota, 9 Nov. 1904; *s* of Vernon Purinton Squires and Ethel Claire Wood; *m* 1928, Catherine Emily Tuttle, Grand Forks, North Dakota; two *s*. *Educ:* Public Schools, Grand Forks, North Dakota. BA University of North Dakota, 1925; MA, University of Minnesota, 1927; PhD, Harvard Univ., 1933; Professor of History, State College, Mayville, North Dakota, 1927-31; Graduate Student, Harvard University, 1931-33; Lecturer and writer; Official Delegate to the Harvard Tercentenary, 1936; Member: US Constitution Sesquicentennial Commission for New Hampshire, 1938; NH State Council of Defense, 1942-45; Special Consultant to USAAF, War Dept, 1943; Chm. of USO in NH, 1944. President: NH Council of Religious Educn, 1944-45; NH Library Trustees Assoc., 1957; Old Number Four Associates, 1957; Amer. Baptist Historical Soc., 1969-. Member: NH Historical Soc. (Hon. Mem. 1975); Cttee of 1000 for World Congress of Religion in 1948; Lincoln Soc.; Peabody Award Cttee for Radio; Citizens Cttee for UN Reform; Hoover Cttee for Govtl Reorganization in US, 1949; Citizens' Adv. Cttee for US Commn on Govt Security, 1957; Nat. Archives Adv. Council for New England; NH Library Adv. Cttee; Cttee for a New England Bibliography; Chairman UN Day Cttee in NH, 1949-57; Pres. NH Sons of the American Revolution, 1949; Chm. NH American Revolution Bicentennial Cttee, 1970-; Deleg.-at-large to Nat. Republican Convention, Chicago, 1952; San Francisco, 1956, 1964 (Mem. Platform Cttee of Convention, 1964); Official Deleg. Second Assembly of World Council of Churches, Evanston, Ill, 1954; Chm., Bicentennial Council of the Original Thirteen States, 1973-74. Director of NH Victory Speakers' Bureau, 1943; Newcomen Soc. in N America; Trustee: NH Baptist Convention; NH YMCA; NH Christian Civic League, etc; Mem., NH Commn on Historical Sites, 1950; Chm. NH Centennial Commn on the Civil War, 1958-; Mem. Bd of Governors, Amer. Revolution Bicentennial Admin., 1974- Vice-Chm., 1975-). Judge, New London District Court, 1969-. George Washington Honor Medal of Freedoms' Foundation, 1954. LLD Univ. of N Dakota, 1958. Granite State Award, Univ. of New Hampshire, 1970; NH Boy Scout Honor Medal, 1975; Charles Pettee Honor Medal, Univ. of NH, 1976; Bicentennial Award, Amer. Baptist Churches, 1976. *Publications:* A History of the University of North Dakota, 1931; British Propaganda at Home and in the United States, 1914-17, 1935; Ballooning in the American Civil War, 1937; editor, The Centennial of Colby Junior College, 1937; editor, The Sesquicentennial of the Baptist Church of New London, New Hampshire, 1939; co-author, Western Civilization, 2 vols, 1942; The Founding of the Northern RR, 1948; Abraham Lincoln and the Civil War, 1949; A History of New London, New Hampshire since 1900, 1952; Experiment in Cooperation, 1953; Community Witness, 1954; A History of New Hampshire since 1623, 1956; The Story of New Hampshire, 1964. Contributor to: Journal of Modern History, American Historical Review, Christian Century, Dictionary of American Biography and Dictionary of American History, Encyclopedia Britannica. *Recreations:* fishing, numismatics. *Address:* New London, New Hampshire 03257, USA. *T:* 526-4561. *Clubs:* Forum (New London); Boys.

SQUIRRELL, Leonard Russell, RE 1919 (ARE 1917); RWS 1941 (ARWS 1935); artist (painter and etcher); *b* 30 Oct. 1893; *s*

of Frank Squirrell and Henrietta Clements (both British); *m* 1923, Hilda Victoria Bird (*d* 1972); one *d* (one *s* decd). *Educ:* British School, Ipswich; Ipswich School of Art; Slade School, London. Gold and Silver Medals, Nat. Competitions of Schools of Art, 1911-15; British Institution Scholarship in Engraving, 1915; Internat. Print-Makers' Exhibs at Los Angeles: silver medal, 1923; Gold medals, 1925 and 1930. Exhibitor Roy. Acad., 1912-59; official purchases by Toronto, British Museum, Victoria and Albert Museum, Fitzwilliam Museum, Cambridge, Brighton, Derby, Rochdale, etc. and Permanent Collection, Ipswich. *Publications:* Landscape Painting in Pastel, 1938; Practice in Water-Colour, 1950. *Address:* Merrydown, Witnesham, Suffolk. *T:* Witnesham 354.

SRAFFA, Piero, FBA 1954; MA; Fellow of Trinity College, Cambridge, since 1939; Emeritus Reader in Economics, University of Cambridge; *b* Turin, Italy, 1898. *Educ:* Univ. of Turin. *Publications:* (ed) The Works and Correspondence of David Ricardo, 11 vols, 1951-73; Production of Commodities by Means of Commodities, 1960. *Address:* Trinity College, Cambridge.

SRIVASTAVA, Chandrika Prasad, Padma Bhushan 1972; Secretary-General, Inter-Governmental Maritime Consultative Organization, since 1974; *b* 8 July 1920; *s* of B. B. Srivastava; *m* 1947, Nirmala Salve; two *d. Educ:* Lucknow, India. 1st cl. BA 1940, 1st cl. BA Hons 1941, 1st cl. MA 1942, 1st cl. LLB 1944; gold medals for proficiency in Eng. Lit. and Polit. Science. Under-Sec., Min. of Commerce, India, 1948-49; City Magistrate, Lucknow, 1950; Addtl Dist. Magistrate, Meerut, 1951-52; Directorate-Gen. of Shipping, 1953; Dep. Dir-Gen. of Shipping, 1954-57; Dep. Sec., Min. of Transport, and Pvte Sec. to Minister of Transport and Communications, 1957-58; Sen. Dep. Dir-Gen. of Shipping, 1959-60; Man. Dir, Shipping Corp. of India, 1961-64; Jt Sec. to Prime Minister, 1964-66; Chm. and Man. Dir, Shipping Corp. of India, 1966-73; Director: Central Inland Water Transport Corp., 1967; Central Bd, Reserve Bank of India, 1972-73; Chm., Mogul Line Ltd, 1967-73. President: Indian Nat. Shipowners' Assoc., 1971-73; Inst. Mar. Technologists, India; UN Conf. on Code of Conduct for Liner Confs; Chm., Cttee of Invisibles, 3rd UN Conf. on Trade and Develt, 1972; Member: Nat. Shipping Bd, 1959-73; Merchant Navy Trng Bd, 1959-73; Nat. Welfare Bd for Seafarers, 1966-73; Amer. Bureau of Shipping, 1969; Governing Body, Indian Inst. of Foreign Trade, 1970; State Bd of Tourism, 1970; Nat. Harbour Bd, 1970-73; Gen. Cttee, Bombay Chamber of Commerce and Ind., 1971; Governing Body Indian Inst. of Management, 1972-73. Vice-Pres., Sea Cadet Council. *Publications:* articles on shipping in newspapers and jls. *Recreation:* music. *Address:* 56 Ashley Gardens, SW1. *Clubs:* Anglo-Belgian, Curzon House; Willingdon (Bombay); Delhi Symphony Society.

STABB, William Walter, QC 1968; **His Honour Judge Stabb;** a Circuit Judge (formerly Official Referee, Supreme Court of Judicature), since 1969; *b* 6 Oct. 1913; 2nd *s* of late Sir Newton Stabb, OBE and late Lady E. M. Stabb; *m* 1940, Dorothy Margaret Leckie; four *d. Educ:* Rugby; University Coll., Oxford. Called to the Bar, 1936; Master of the Bench, Inner Temple, 1964. Served with RAF, 1940-46, attaining rank of Sqdn Ldr. Junior Counsel to Ministry of Labour, 1960; Prosecuting Counsel to BoT, 1962-68. Chm. 1961-69, Dep. Chm. 1969-71, Bedfordshire QS. *Recreations:* fishing, golf. *Address:* The Pale Farm, Chipperfield, Kings Langley, Herts. *T:* Kings Langley 63124; 1 King's Bench Walk, Temple, EC4. *T:* 01-353 8436.

STABLE, Maj.-Gen. Hugh Huntington, CB 1947; CIE 1938; Major-General, IA (retired) *b* 1896; *s* of late Alfred Henry Stable, MA and Ada Huntington; *m* 1923, Cyrille Helen Dorothy, *d* of late Rev. M. A. Bayfield, MA. *Educ:* Malvern. First Commission 2/4th Dorset Regt 1914; served Palestine, 1917-18 (despatches); Central India Horse, 1919; Bt Lt-Col 1935; Staff Coll., Camberley, 1929-30; Army Headquarters, India, Staff Officer to Major-General Cavalry, 1932; Assistant Military Secretary (Personal) to Commander-in-Chief, 1933-36; Military Secretary to the Viceroy of India, 1936-38; Comdt, 8th KGO Cavalry, 1939-40; Bde Comdr, 1941-43; DQMG, GHQ, India, 1943-44; Comdr Lucknow Sub Area, 1945-46; Comdr Bihar and Orissa Area, 1947; QMG India, Dec. 1947; retd 1950. A Governor, Malvern Coll.; Emeritus Comr, Boy Scouts of South Africa. *Address:* 810 Rapallo, Sea Point, Cape Town, SA. *Clubs:* Army and Navy; City and Civil Service (Cape Town).

STABLE, (Rondle) Owen (Charles), QC 1963; a Recorder of the Crown Court, since 1972; *b* 1923; *yr s* of Rt Hon. Sir Wintringham Norton Stable, *qv*; *m* 1949, Yvonne Brook, *y d* of late Maj. L. B. Holliday, OBE; two *d. Educ:* Winchester. Served with Rifle Bde, 1940-46 (Capt.). Barrister, Middle Temple, 1948;

Bencher, 1969. Dep. Chm., QS, Herts, 1963-71; Board of Trade Inspector: Cadco Group of Cos, 1963-64; H. S. Whiteside & Co Ltd, 1965-67; International Learning Systems Corp. Ltd, 1969-71; Pergamon Press, 1969-73. Sec. National Reference Tribunal for the Coal Mining Industry, 1953-64; Chancellor of Diocese of Bangor, 1959-; Member, Governing Body of the Church in Wales, 1960-; Licensed Parochial Lay Reader, Diocese of St Albans, 1961-; Member: General Council of the Bar, 1962-66; Senate of 4 Inns of Court, 1971-74; Senate of the Inns of Court and the Bar, 1974-75. Chm., Horserace Betting Levy Appeal Tribunal, 1969-74. JP Hertfordshire, 1963-71. *Publication:* (with R. M. Stuttard) A Review of Coursing, 1971. *Recreations:* shooting, listening to music. *Address:* Buckler's Hall, Much Hadham, Hertfordshire. *T:* Much Hadham 2604. *Club:* Boodle's.
See also P. L. W. Owen.

STABLE, Rt. Hon. Sir Wintringham (Norton), PC 1965; Kt 1938; MC; a Judge of the High Court of Justice, Queen's Bench Division, 1938-68; *b* 19 March 1888; *s* of Daniel Wintringham Stable and Gertrude Mary Law; *m* 1916, Lucie Haden (*d* 1976), *widow* of Richard Bayly Murphy and *d* of late F. F. Freeman, Tavistock; two *s. Educ:* Winchester; Christ Church, Oxford (MA). 2nd Class Honours School History; Bar, Middle Temple, 1913; served with the Montgomeryshire Yeomanry and 25th Battalion Royal Welch Fusiliers, 1914-18, Egypt, Palestine and France (MC, despatches); QC 1935; Chairman of Quarter Sessions for the Counties of Shropshire, 1947-67, and Merioneth, 1944-; Chancellor of Diocese of Portsmouth, 1937-38. Hon. Student of Christ Church, Oxford, 1960. *Recreation:* country life. *Address:* Plas Llwyn Owen, Llanbrynmair, Powys.
See also P. L. W. Owen, R. O. C. Stable.

STABLEFORTH, Dr Arthur Wallace, CB 1962; retired as Project Manager, UN Special Fund Sheep Diseases Research Laboratories, Pendik, Turkey, 1964-70; *b* 15 March 1902; *s* of W. Parkinson and Florence Kate Stableforth; *m* 1926, Hilda Dorothy Allen; one *s* one *d. Educ:* Allhallows School; Royal Veterinary College; London University. Demonstrator, Asst, Research Institute of Animal Pathology, 1926-33; in charge of Preventive Medicine, Royal Veterinary College, 1933-39. Veterinary Laboratory, Ministry of Agriculture and Fisheries: Senior Research Officer, 1939-49, Deputy Director, 1949-50. Director of Veterinary Laboratories and Investigation Service, 1951-63; Animal Health Officer, Food and Agriculture Organisation of the UN, 1963. Hon. FRCVS, 1968. John Henry Steele Medal, 1956; Thomas Baxter Prize, 1957. Doctor Medicinae Veterinarie (*hc*), Copenhagen, 1974. *Publications:* contributions to scientific jls and books in this and other countries; Co-editor, Infectious Diseases of Animals. *Recreations:* gardening and music. *Address:* 11 The Paddock, Merrow, Guildford, Surrey. *Clubs:* Royal Society of Medicine, Royal Over-Seas League.

STABLER, Arthur Fletcher; District Councillor, Newcastle upon Tyne; Member, Supplementary Benefits Commission, since 1976; *b* 1919; *s* of Edward and Maggie Stabler; *m* 1948, Margaret Stabler; two *s. Educ:* Cruddas Park Sch. Engineer apprenticeship, Vickers Armstrong, 1935-39. Served War, Royal Northumberland Fusiliers, 1939-46. With Vickers Armstrong, 1946-76. Newcastle upon Tyne: City Councillor, 1963-74; District Councillor, 1973-; Chairman: Housing Renewals, 1975-76; Arts and Recreation, 1976-77; Case Work Sub-Cttee, 1974-77; Tenancy Relations Sub-Cttee, 1975-77; Community Develt Sub-Cttee, 1975-76; Town Moor Sub-Cttee, 1976-77; Vice-Chairman: Social Services Cttee, 1974-76; Housing Management Cttee, 1975-76. Mem., numerous Tenants' Assocs. Pres., No 6 Br., AUEW. Chm., Westerhope Golf Club Jt Sub-Cttee, 1976-77. *Recreations:* social work, local history. *Address:* 10 Whitebeam Place, Elswick, Newcastle upon Tyne NE4 7EJ. *T:* Newcastle upon Tyne 32362. *Clubs:* Pineapple CIU, Polish White Eagle (Newcastle upon Tyne).

STACEY, Air Vice-Marshal John Nichol, CBE 1971; DSO 1945; DFC 1942; Director, Stonham Housing Assoc., since 1976; *b* 14 Sept. 1920; *s* of Captain Herbert Chambers Stacey and Mrs May Stacey; *m* 1950, Veronica Satterley; two *d. Educ:* Whitgift Middle Sch., Croydon. Merchant Marine Apprentice, 1937-38; joined RAF, 1938; flying throughout War of 1939-45; comd No 160 Sqdn, 1944-45; Asst Air Attaché, Washington, 1947-48; psc 1949; on staff at Staff Coll., 1958-60; Chief of Air Staff, Royal Malayan Air Force, 1960-63 (JMN); comd RAF Laarbruch, Germany, 1963-66; AOC, Air Cadets, 1968-71; Dir, Orgn and Admin. Planning (RAF), MoD, 1971-74; AOA, Support Comd, 1974-75, retired. *Recreations:* sailing, golf. *Address:* Riseden Cottage, Riseden, Goudhurst, Cranbrook, Kent. *T:* Goudhurst 239. *Clubs:* Royal Air Force; Dale Hill Golf.

STACEY, Prof. Maurice, CBE 1966; FRS 1950; Mason Professor of Chemistry, 1956-74, now Emeritus, and Head of Department, 1956-74, University of Birmingham; Dean of Faculty of Science, 1963-66; Hon. Senior Research Fellow, 1974-76; *b* 8 April 1907; *s* of J. H. Stacey, Bromstead, Newport, Shropshire; *m* 1937, Constance Mary, *d* of Wm Pugh, Birmingham; two *s* two *d. Educ:* Adam's School, Newport, Shropshire; Universities of Birmingham, London and Columbia (New York). BSc (Hons) Birmingham Univ., 1929; Demonstrator, Chemistry, Birmingham Univ., 1929-32; PhD 1932; Meldola Medal, 1933; Beit Memorial Fellow for Medical Research, School of Tropical Medicine, London Univ., 1933-37 (DSc 1939); Travelling Fellow, Columbia Univ., New York, 1937; Lecturer in Chemistry, Univ. of Birmingham, 1937-44, Reader in Biological Chemistry, 1944-46, Prof. of Chemistry, 1946-56. Tilden Lecturer of Chemical Society, 1946; P. F. Frankland Lectr, Roy. Inst. of Chemistry, 1955; Ivan Levinstein Lectr, Soc. Chem. Industry, 1956; Vice-Pres. Chemical Society, 1950-53, 1955-58, 1960-63, 1968-71; Associate Editor, Advances in Carbohydrate Chem., 1950-; Editor, Advances in Fluorine Chem., 1960-73; Editor-in-Chief, European Polymer Jl. Chief Scientific Adviser for Civil Defence, Midland Region, 1957-; Governor, National Vegetable Research Institute, 1961-73. Former Member, Court of Governors: Univ. of Keele; Univ. of Warwick; Univ. of Loughborough; Gov., Adam's Sch., 1956-74; Mem. Council, Edgbaston High Sch. for Girls, 1963-; Mem., Home Office Science Council, 1966-. Sugar Research Prize of National Academy of Science, New York, 1950; John Scott Medal and Award, 1969; Haworth Meml Medal, 1970. Captain, 2nd in Command Birmingham Home Guard, Chemical Warfare School, 1942-44. Defence Medal, 1945. Visiting Lecturer, Universities of Oslo, Stockholm, Uppsala and Lund, 1949, Helsinki, 1955. Has foreign Hon. doctorate and medals. John Scott Medal and Award, 1969; Haworth Meml Medal, 1970. Hon. DSc Keele, 1977. *Publications:* (with S. A. Barker) Polysaccharides of Micro-organisms, 1961, and Carbohydrates of Living Tissues; about 400 scientific contribs to Jl of Chem. Soc., Proc. Royal Soc., etc., on organic and biological chemistry subjects. *Recreations:* foreign travel, athletics (Hon. Life Mem. AAA), horticulture, science antiques. *Address:* 12 Bryony Road, Weoley Hill, Birmingham B29 4BU. *T:* 021-475 2065; The University, Birmingham. *T:* 021-472 1301. *Club:* Athenæum.

STACEY, Rear-Adm. Michael Lawrence; Flag Officer, Gibraltar, since 1976; *b* 6 July 1924; *s* of Maurice Stacey and Dorice Evelyn (*née* Bulling); *m* 1955, Penelope Leana (*née* Riddoch); two *s. Educ:* Epsom Coll. Entered RN as Cadet, 1942; Normandy landings, HMS Hawkins, 1944; served on HM Ships Rotherham, Cambrian, Shoreham, Hornet, Vernon, Euryalus, Bermuda, Vigilant; Comdr 1958; staff of RN Staff Coll.; in comd HMS Blackpool, 1960-62; JSSC; Captain 1966; Chief Staff Officer to Admiral Commanding Reserves, 1966-68; in comd HMS Andromeda and Captain (F) Sixth Frigate Sqdn, 1968-70; Dep. Dir of Naval Warfare, 1970-73; in comd HMS Tiger, 1973-75; Asst Chief of Naval Staff (Policy), 1975-76. ADC to the Queen, 1975. *Recreations:* golf, gardening. *Address:* Little Hintock, 40 Lynch Road, Farnham, Surrey. *T:* Farnham 3032. *Club:* Army and Navy.

STACEY, Rev. Nicolas David; Director of Social Services for Kent County Council, since 1974; *b* 27 Nov. 1927; *s* of David and Gwen Stacey; *m* 1955, Hon. Anne Bridgeman, *er d* of 2nd Viscount Bridgeman, *qv*; one *s* two *d. Educ:* RNC, Dartmouth; St Edmund Hall, Oxford (hons degree Mod. Hist.); Cuddesdon Theol Coll., Oxford. Midshipman, HMS Anson, 1945-46; Sub-Lt, 1946-48. Asst Curate, St Mark's, Portsea, 1953-58; Domestic Chap. to Bp of Birmingham, 1958-60; Rector of Woolwich, 1960-68; Dean of London Borough of Greenwich, 1965-68; Dep. Dir of Oxfam, 1968-70; Dir of Social Services, London Borough of Ealing, 1971-74. Sporting career: internat. sprinter, 1948-52, incl. British Empire Games, 1949, and Olympic Games, 1952 (semi-finalist 200 metres and finalist 4×400 metres relay); Pres., OUAC, 1951; winner, Oxf. v Cambridge 220 yds, 1948-51; Captain, Combined Oxf. and Camb. Athletic Team, 1951. *Publication:* Who Cares (autobiog.), 1971. *Recreations:* reading, golf, gardening. *Address:* The Old Vicarage, Selling, Faversham, Kent ME13 9RD. *T:* Selling 833. *Clubs:* Beefsteak; Royal St George's Golf (Sandwich, Kent).

STACEY, Air Marshal Sir William John, KCB 1977; CBE 1972; MRAeS; C-in-C RAF Germany and Commander Second Allied Tactical Air Force, since 1977; *b* 1 Dec. 1923; *s* of Edward William John Stacey; *m* 1952, Frances Jean, *d* of Prof. L. W. Fawcett, USA; one *s* two *d*. Commnd 1944; served S Africa, Far East and UK; flying instructor, Central Flying Sch., 1951-52; BJSM Washington, 1952-55; comdg 54 Sqdn, 1955; Chief of Atomic Ops Br., 2nd Allied Tactical Air Force, 1959-62;

Bomber Comd, 1963-65; Dep. Dir Bomber Ops, MoD, 1965-68; Comdr Fighter Station Coltishall, 1968-69; Comdr RAF Akrotiri, 1969-72; RCDS 1972; COS 46 Gp, Strike Comd, 1972-74; ACAS (Policy), MoD, 1974-76; Dep. C-in-C RAF Strike Command, 1976-77. *Address:* HQ RAF Germany, BFPO 40. *Club:* Royal Air Force.

STACK, (Ann) Prunella, (Mrs Brian St Quentin Power); Director of The Women's League of Health and Beauty; *b* 28 July 1914; *d* of Capt. Hugh Bagot Stack, 8th Ghurka Rifles, and Mary Meta Bagot Stack, Founder of The Women's League of Health and Beauty; *m* 1st, 1938, Lord David Douglas-Hamilton (*d* 1944); two *s*; 2nd, 1950, Alfred G. Albers, FRCS (*d* 1951), Cape Town, S Africa; 3rd, 1964, Brian St Quentin Power. *Educ:* The Abbey, Malvern Wells. Mem. of the National Fitness Council, 1937-39. *Publications:* The Way to Health and Beauty, 1938; Movement is Life, 1973. *Recreations:* poetry, music, travel. *Address:* Buckham Hill House, Uckfield, East Sussex; 14 Gertrude Street, SW10.

STACK, Air Chief Marshal Sir (Thomas) Neville, KCB 1972 (CB 1969); CVO 1963; CBE 1965; AFC 1957; Air Secretary, since 1976; *b* 19 Oct. 1919; *s* of late T. Neville Stack, AFC, and Edythe Neville Stack; *m* 1955, Diana Virginia, *d* of late Oliver Stuart Todd, MBE; one *s* one *d*. *Educ:* St Edmund's College, Ware; RAF College, Cranwell. Served on flying boats, 1939-45; Coastal Command, 1945-52; Transport Support flying in Far East and UK, 1954-59; Dep. Captain of The Queen's Flight, 1960-62; Transport Support in Far East, 1963-64; Comdt, RAF Coll., Cranwell, 1967-70; UK Perm. Mil. Deputy, CENTO, Ankara, 1970-72; AOC-in-C, RAF Trng Commnd, 1973-75. Air ADC to the Queen, 1976-. FRMetS; MBIM. *Recreations:* various outdoor sports; undergardening. *Address:* 182 Rivermead Court, Hurlingham, SW6; The Grange, Wellingore, Lincoln. *Clubs:* Royal Air Force, Boodle's.

STACPOOLE, John Wentworth; Under-Secretary, Children's Division, Department of Health and Social Security, since 1973; *b* 16 June 1926; *s* of G. W. Stacpoole and Mrs M. G. Butt; *m* 1954, Charmian, *d* of late J. P. Bishop and Mrs E. M. Bishop; one *s* one *d*. *Educ:* Sedbergh; Magdalen Coll., Oxford (Demy; MA). Army, 1944-47 (Lieut, Assam Regt). Asst Principal, Colonial Office, 1951; Asst Private Sec. to Sec. of State, 1954-56; seconded to Sierra Leone Govt, 1958-60; jt sec. to Uganda Relationships Commn, 1960-61; Principal Private Sec. to Sec. of State, 1964-65; Asst Sec., 1965; transf. to Min. of Social Security, 1968. *Recreations:* reading, walking, sketching. *Address:* Fairseat Lodge, Fairseat, near Sevenoaks, Kent. *T:* Fairseat 822201.

STACY, Reginald Joseph William, CB 1955; *b* 1 Jan. 1904; *e s* of late Frank Dixon Stacy and Alice Summers; *m* 1932, Nina Grace Holder; one *s* one *d*. *Educ:* Wirtemburg (now Stonhouse) Street Elementary School; Sir Walter St John's School, London; Trinity College, Cambridge (Sen. Schol.). BA 1925 (Double First, Mod. Lang. Tripos). Entered Board of Trade, Commercial Relations and Treaties Department, 1927; Ottawa Imperial Conference, 1932; Commercial Mission to Colombia, 1938; led UK Trade Delegation to Warsaw, 1948-49; accompanied Minister of State, Board of Trade to South America, 1954; Insurance and Companies Department, 1956; Internat. Conferences on Insurance; Under-Sec., Bd of Trade, 1949-64, retd; French and Latin Master, Parkside Preparatory School, 1967-69. *Address:* 2 Beech Court, Easington Place, Guildford, Surrey. *T:* Guildford 60761.

STAFFORD, 14th Baron *cr* 1640, *confirmed* 1825; **Basil Francis Nicholas Fitzherbert;** *b* 7 April 1926; *s* of late Capt. Hon. Thomas Charles Fitzherbert, AM 1917, and Beryl (*d* 1959), 2nd *d* of John Waters and *widow* of Major Henry Brougham, RA; *S* uncle, 1941; *m* 1952, Morag Nada, *yr d* of late Lt-Col Alastair Campbell, Altries, Milltimber, Aberdeenshire; three *s* three *d*. *Educ:* Ampleforth College, York. Lieut Scots Guards, 1945-48. Local Director, Barclays Bank Ltd (Birmingham); President: Stafford Rugby FC; Staffs Assoc. of Boys' Clubs; Staffs Playing Fields Assoc.; North Staffs Br. Inst. of Marketing, 1955-76; Patron, City of Stoke on Trent Amateur Operatic Soc.; Pres., Staffs CLA; Show Dir, Staffs Agric. Soc.; President: Old Amplefordian Cricket Club; North Staffs Sporting Club; Nat. Assoc. of Young Cricketers; Dep. Pres., Staffs Gentleman CC. FInstM. *Recreations:* cricket, shooting, yachting, fishing, tennis. *Heir: s* Hon. Francis Melfort William Fitzherbert, *b* 13 March 1954. *Address:* Swynnerton Park, Stone, Staffordshire. *TA* and *T:* Swynnerton 228; Salt Winds, West Wittering, Chichester, West Sussex. *T:* West Wittering 2181. *Clubs:* Army and Navy; IZ; Free Foresters; MCC; Lord's Taverners.

STAFFORD, Bishop Suffragan of, since 1975; **Rt. Rev. John Waine;** *b* 20 June 1930; *s* of William and Ellen Waine; *m* 1957, Patricia Zena Haikney; three *s*. *Educ:* Prescot Grammar Sch.; Manchester Univ. (BA); Ridley Hall, Cambridge. Deacon 1955, Priest 1956; Curate of St Mary, West Derby, 1955-58; Curate in Charge of All Saints, Sutton, 1958-60; Vicar of Ditton, 1960-64; Vicar of Holy Trinity, Southport, 1964-69; Rector of Kirkby, 1969-75. *Recreation:* caravanning. *Address:* St Thomas Lodge, Radford Rise, Stafford ST17 4PS. *T:* Stafford 52366.

STAFFORD, Archdeacon of; *see* Ninis, Ven. R. B.

STAFFORD, Frank Edmund, CMG 1951; CBE 1946 (OBE 1931); Malayan CS, retired 1951; *b* 24 Aug. 1895; *s* of late Frank Stafford and Marie Stafford; *m* 1943, Ida Wadham (marr. diss., 1950), *d* of late Conway Burton-Durham; one *s*; *m* 1953, Catherine Rolfe. *Educ:* Royal Gram. School, Guildford. Served European War, 1914-18, "Queen's" Regt. Joined staff of Civil Commissioner, Iraq, 1919; appointed to High Commission, Iraq, 1921; Financial Secretary, 1924; Financial Adviser, British Embassy, Baghdad, 1931; Colonial Service, Nigeria, 1936 (Asst Treasurer, Principal Asst Sec., Actg Financial Sec.). War of 1939-45, commissioned in Army (Lt-Col) for service with Occupied Enemy Territory Administration, 1941; Financial Adviser, Ethiopian Govt, 1942; attached LHQ Australia, 1944; Col, Military Administration, British Borneo, 1945; demobilized, 1946 (Brig.); seconded to Foreign Office, 1946; Member UK Delegn Italian Peace Conference and Council of Foreign Ministers; Head UK Delegn Four Power Commission, 1947; Member UK Delegn to UN, 1948, 1949, 1950, 1952; Foreign Office Adviser (Minister) to Chief Administrator, Eritrea, 1951-53; Adviser to Ethiopian Govt, 1953-60. FRAS, FRGS. Order Star of Ethiopia, 1944; Grand Officer, Star of Honour, 1955. *Publications:* contributions to Encyc. Britannica and to International Affairs. *Recreations:* astronomy, horticulture, walking. *Address:* 3 Holbrook Park, Horsham, West Sussex RH12 4PW. *T:* Horsham 2497. *Clubs:* Travellers', National Liberal.

STAFFORD, Godfrey Harry, CBE 1976; PhD; FInstP; Director, Rutherford Laboratory, Chilton, Didcot, Oxon, since 1969; *b* 15 April 1920; *s* of Henry and Sarah Stafford; *m* 1950, Helen Goldthorp (*née* Clark); one *s* twin *d*. *Educ:* Rondebosch Boys High Sch., S Africa; Univ. of Cape Town; Gonville and Caius Coll., Cambridge. MSc Cape Town, 1941; South African Naval Forces, 1941-46; Ebden Scholar, PhD Cantab 1950; Harwell, 1949-51; Head of Biophysics Subdiv., CSIR, Pretoria, 1951-54; Cyclotron Gp, AERE, 1954-57; Rutherford Laboratory: Head of Proton Linear Accelerator Gp, 1957; Head of High Energy Physics Div., 1963; Dep. Dir, 1966. Visiting Fellow, St Cross Coll., Oxford, MA, 1971. CERN appointments: UK deleg. to Council, 1973; Vice-Pres., Council, 1973; Scientific Policy Cttee, 1973, Vice-Chm., 1976. Vice-Pres. for meetings, Inst. of Physics, 1976. *Publications:* papers and articles in learned jls on: biophysics, nuclear physics, high energy physics. *Address:* Ferry Cottage, North Hinksey Village, Oxford OX2 0NA. *T:* (home) Oxford 47621, (office) Abingdon 21900.

STAFFORD, Jack, CB 1953; Chief Statistician, Price Commission, since 1973; *b* 1909; *s* of late John William and Ruth Stafford; *m* 1932, Miriam Claire Holt; two *s*. *Educ:* Baines' Grammar School; Manchester Univ. Asst Lecturer in Economics, Manchester Univ., 1930; Lecturer in Economics, Manchester Univ., 1934; Rockefeller Fellow, 1938; Statistician, Central Statistical Office, 1941, Acting Director, 1946; Dir of Statistics, DTI (formerly BoT), 1948-72. *Publications:* Essays on Monetary Management, 1933; articles and papers in Jl of Royal Statistical Soc., Trans Manchester Statistical Soc., Economic Jl, Manchester School. *Recreation:* gardening. *Address:* 8 Normandy Gardens, Horsham, West Sussex. *T:* Horsham 67045.

STAFFORD, John, OBE 1977; Diplomatic Service; First Secretary (Commercial); New Delhi, since 1974; *b* 15 June 1920; *s* of late Frank and Gertrude Stafford, Sheffield; *m* 1949, Mary Jocelyn Goodwin, *d* of late Capt. J. G. Budge, RN. *Educ:* High Storrs Grammar Sch. Exchequer and Audit Dept, 1939. Joined RAF, 1940; Reconnaissance Pilot, Western Desert; invalided out as Warrant Officer/Pilot, 1945. Board of Trade, 1946; Assistant Trade Commissioner, Delhi, 1946-49; Karachi, 1950-54; Bulawayo, 1954-56; Trade Commissioner, Karachi, 1956; Lahore, 1957; Bombay, 1958-60; Lahore, 1963-65; Dep. High Comr in Lahore, 1965-69; Consul, Houston, Texas, 1969-71; on secondment to DTI, 1972-74. *Recreations:* cricket, tennis, amateur dramatics, music. *Address:* c/o Foreign and Commonwealth Office, SW1. *Clubs:* East India, Devonshire, Sports and Public Schools; Punjab (Lahore); and various in India and Pakistan.

STAFFORD-CLARK, David, MD; DPM; FRCP; FRCPsych; Consultant Emeritus, Guy's Hospital; formerly Physician in Charge, Department of Psychological Medicine, and Director of The York Clinic, Guy's Hospital, 1954-73; Chairman, Psychiatric Division, Guy's Group, 1973-74; Consultant Physician, Bethlem Royal and Maudsley Hospitals and the Institute of Psychiatry, 1954-73; retired; *b* 17 March 1916; *s* of Francis and Cordelia Susan Stafford Clark; *m* 1941, Dorothy Stewart (*née* Oldfield); three *s* one *d. Educ:* Felsted; University of London. Guy's Hospital. MRCS, LRCP, 1939; MB, BS, 1939. Served War of 1939-45, RAFVR; trained as Medical Parachutist (despatches twice); demobilised 1945. Guy's Hosp., MRCP, Nuffield Med. Fellow, 1946; 3 years postgrad. trg appts, Inst. of Psychiatry, Maudsley Hosp.; MD London, 1947, DPM London, 1948; Registrar, Nat. Hosp., Queen Sq., 1948. Resident Massachusetts Gen. Hosp., Dept of Psychiatry, and Teaching Clinical Fellow, Harvard Med. School, 1949; First Asst, Professorial Unit, Maudsley Hosp., 1950; Mem. Assoc. for Research in Mental and Nervous Disorders, NY, 1950-53; Consultant Staff, Guy's Hosp., 1950; Lectureship, Psychology (Faculty of Letters), Reading Univ., 1950-54. Member: Archbishop of Canterbury's Commn on Divine Healing; Council, Royal Medico-Psychological Assoc.; Council, Medico-Legal Soc.; Examr, RCP London and Cambridge MD; Editorial Bds, Guy's Hosp. Reports, and Mod. Med. of Gt Britain. Acted as adviser to various motion picture companies (Universal International etc) on medical aspects of their productions; has also acted as adviser and director on a large number of medical programmes on sound radio, and both BBC and Independent Television, including the "Lifeline" series of programmes for the BBC, and documentary programmes for ITV on the emotional and intellectual growth of normal children, and the life and work of Freud; Author of Brain and Behaviour Series in Adult Education Television Programmes on BBC Channel 2; Mind and Motive Series, 1966. FRCP, 1958; Mem., NY Acad. of Sciences; FRSA (Silver Medal), 1959; Hon. RCM, 1966; Foundn Fellow, RCPsych, 1972, Hon. Fellow, 1976. *Publications:* poetry: Autumn Shadow, 1941; Sound in the Sky, 1944; Psychiatry Today (Pelican), 1951; Psychiatry for Students, 1964, rev. edn, 1973; What Freud Really Said, 1965; Five Questions in Search of an Answer, 1970, repr. 1972; chapters in: Emergencies in Medical Practice, 1st, 2nd and 3rd edns, 1948, 1950, 1952; Compendium of Emergencies, 1st and 2nd edns; Case Histories in Psychosomatic Medicine, 1952; Taylor's Medical Jurisprudence, 12th edn, 1965; Schizophrenia: Somatic Aspects, 1st edn, 1957; Frontiers in General Hospital Psychiatry, 1961; A Short Textbook of Medicine, 1963; The Pathology and Treatment of Sexual Deviation, 1964; Modern Trends in Psychological Medicine, 1970; Psychiatric Treatment, Concepts of, in Encyclopædia Britannica, 200th anniv. edn, 1973; contributions to various medical textbooks and to medical and scientific jls. *Recreations:* travel, reading, writing, making and watching films, theatre.

STAFFORD-KING-HARMAN, Sir Cecil William Francis, 2nd Bt, *cr* 1913; *b* 6 Jan. 1895; *s* of late Rt Hon. Sir Thomas Stafford, Bt, CB, and Frances Agnes King-Harman; *S* father, 1935; assumed additional surname of King-Harman, 1932; *m* 1917, Sarah Beatrice, *y d* of late Col A. D. Acland, CBE, and Hon. Mrs Acland, Feniton Court, Honiton, Devon; (one *s* killed in action) two *d. Educ:* RN Colleges, Osborne and Dartmouth; RMC Sandhurst; Christ Church, Oxford. Formerly Midshipman, Royal Navy, retired, 1912; commissioned 2nd Lt, The King's Royal Rifle Corps, 1914; Captain, 1917; served throughout European War in France and Italy (despatches); after war went to Christ Church, Oxford, MA (Hons) Agriculture; Steward, Irish Turf Club, 1938-40, 1943-46, 1948-51, 1952-55, 1959-62; Mem. of Racing Board, 1945-50. Appointed Member, Council of State for Ireland, 1956. War substantive Captain, 1940; Temporary Major, 1941; Temporary Lt-Col 1942. *Recreations:* shooting, racing, fishing. *Address:* St Catherines Park, Leixlip, Co. Kildare, Ireland. *T:* 280421. *Clubs:* Kildare Street and University, Irish Turf (Dublin).

STAGG, Prof. Geoffrey Leonard, MBE 1945; Professor, and Chairman, Department of Hispanic Studies, University of Toronto, since 1973; *b* 10 May 1913; *s* of Henry Percy Stagg and Maude Emily Bradbury; *m* 1948, Amy Southwell, Wellesley Hills, Mass, USA; two *s* one *d. Educ:* King Edward's School, Birmingham (Scholar); Trinity Hall, Cambridge (Scholar). BA 1st cl. Hons Modern and Medieval Languages Tripos, 1934; MA 1946; Joseph Hodges Choate Mem. Fellow, Harvard Univ., 1934-36; AM (Harvard), 1935; Modern Languages Master, King Edward's School, Birmingham, 1938-40, 1946-47; served in Intelligence Corps, 1940-46; Lecturer in Spanish and Italian, Nottingham Univ., 1947-53, and Head of Dept of Spanish, 1954-56; Dept of Italian and Hispanic Studies, Toronto Univ.: Prof., 1956-73; Chm., 1956-66, 1969-73. Vice-Pres., Assoc. of Teachers

of Spanish and Portuguese of GB and Ireland, 1948-; Pres., Canadian Assoc. of Hispanists, 1964-66, 1972-74. Fellow, New Coll., Univ. of Toronto, 1962; Senior Fellow, Massey Coll., Univ. of Toronto, 1965-70; Canada Council Senior Fellowship, 1967-68. *Publications:* articles on Spanish literature in learned jls. *Address:* Department of Hispanic Studies, University of Toronto, Toronto M5S 1A1, Canada.

STAGG, Air Commodore (retired) Walter Allan, CB 1958; CBE 1953 (OBE 1950); *b* 2 April 1903; *s* of late Frederick Edward and late Emma Jane Stagg; *m* 1943, Olive Georgina Legg; no *c. Educ:* privately. Commnd in RAF, 1926; served India, 1928-33 (India General Service Medal, NW Frontier Clasp, 1930-31). Air Ministry (Directorate of Equipment), 1935-37. Joined HMS Glorious in Mediterranean, 1937-39. On staff of HQ Training, Flying Training and Maintenance Comds, 1940-43; Dep. Director of Equipment (2) in Air Ministry, 1943-45; Senior Equipment Staff Officer, No 214 Group, Italy, 1945; Comd No 25 Maintenance Unit, 1945-46. In Ministry of Civil Aviation, 1946-47; on staffs of HQ Maintenance Comd, 40 Group and Flying Training Comd, 1947-51; Dep. Asst Chief of Staff (Logistics) at SHAPE, 1951-53; Director of Equipment (A) Air Ministry, 1954-55; Director of Movements, Air Ministry, 1955-58; Director, Supply Services Division, NATO. Maintenance Supply Services Agency, 1958-60, retired. *Address:* 3 Ingleside Court, Budleigh Salterton, Devon. *T:* Budleigh Salterton 5282. *Club:* Royal Air Force.

STAHL, Professor Ernest Ludwig; Taylor Professor of the German Language and Literature and Fellow of The Queen's College, Oxford, 1959-69, Supernumerary Fellow, since 1969; *b* Senekal, OFS, S Africa, 10 Dec. 1902; *s* of Philip and Theresa Stahl; *m* 1942, Kathleen Mary Hudson; no *c. Educ:* Capetown, Oxford, Heidelberg and Berne Universities. MA Capetown, 1925; First Class Hons, Oxford, 1927; PhD Berne *magna cum laude* 1931. Assistant Lecturer in German, Birmingham, 1932; Lecturer in German, Oxford, 1935; Reader in German Literature, Oxford, 1945; Student of Christ Church, Oxford, 1945, Student Emeritus, 1960. Vis. Professor: Cornell, 1956; Princeton, 1958; Yale, 1964; Kansas, 1968; Calif (Davis), 1969-70. Gold Medal, Goethe Gesellschaft, 1966. *Publications:* Die religiöse und die philosophische Bildungsidee und die Entstehung des Bildungsromans, 1934; Hölderlin's Symbolism, 1944; The Dramas of Heinrich von Kleist, 1948 (revised edn, 1961); Schiller's Drama: Theory and Practice, 1954; Goethe's Iphigenie auf Tauris, 1962. Editions of Goethe's Werther, 1942 (new edn, 1972), Lessing's Emilia Galotti, 1946, Goethe's Torquato Tasso, 1962, and R. M. Rilke's Duino Elegies, 1965; revised edn, Oxford Book of German Verse, 1967; (with W. E. Yuill) Introduction to German Literature, vol. III, 1970; The Faust Translation in Time Was Away: the world of Louis MacNeice, 1975; articles in Modern Language Review, Germanic Review, German Life and Letters, Journal of English and Germanic Philology, Oxford German Studies, Yearbook of Comparative Criticism; contrib. to Festschrift for Ralph Farrell. *Address:* 43 Plantation Road, Oxford.

STAINFORTH, Maj.-Gen. Charles Herbert, CB 1969; OBE 1955; Editor, Army Quarterly and Defence Journal, since 1974; *b* 12 Dec. 1914; *s* of Lt-Col Stainforth, CMG, 4th Cavalry, IA, and Georgina Helen, *d* of Maj.-Gen. H. Pipon, CB; *m* Elizabeth, *d* of late John Tait Easdale; one *s* one *d. Educ:* Wellington Coll.; RMC, Sandhurst. Commnd into 2nd Royal Lancers, IA; transferred British Army, 1947; Chief of Staff, Southern Comd, 1965-66; GOC Aldershot District and SE Dist, 1966-69; Head of UK Future Command Structure, MoD, 1969-72. Col Comdt, RCT, 1970-72. Chm. Combined Cadet Forces, 1970-72. Consultant to Nat. Tourist Bds, 1973-. *Address:* Powderham House, Dippenhall, near Farnham, Surrey. *Clubs:* Army and Navy, MCC.
See also G. H. Stainforth.

STAINFORTH, Graham Henry; *b* 3 Oct. 1906; *s* of Lt-Col H. G. Stainforth, CMG, Indian Cavalry, and Georgina Helen, *d* of Maj.-Gen. H. Pipon, CB; *m* 1943, Ruth Ellen Douglas-Cooper; one *s* two *d. Educ:* Wellington Coll., Berks; Emmanuel Coll., Cambridge. Assistant Master at Merchant Taylors' Sch., 1928-35, and Assistant Housemaster, 1933-35; Assistant Master and Tutor at Wellington Coll., and Head of the English Department, 1935-45; Hon. Secretary of Wellington College Clubs at Walworth, 1935-45; Headmaster of Oundle and Laxton Grammar Schools, 1945-56; Master of Wellington, 1956-66. Mem., Berks Educn Cttee, 1961-74; Fellow of Woodard Corp., 1966-; Governor: Ardingly College, 1966-; Portsmouth Grammar School, 1966-77; Wallingford Comprehensive School, 1976. Hon. Liveryman, Grocers' Co., 1975. *Address:* The Cottage, Winterbrook, Wallingford, Oxon OX10 9EF. *T:* Wallingford 36414.
See also C. H. Stainforth.

STAINTON, Sir Anthony (Nathaniel), KCB 1974 (CB 1967); QC 1975; First Parliamentary Counsel to HM Treasury, 1972-76 (Parliamentary Counsel, 1956-72); *b* 8 Jan. 1913; *s* of Evelyn Stainton, Barham Court, Canterbury; *m* 1st, 1947, Barbara Russell; three *d* ; 2nd, 1966, Rachel Frances, *d* of late Col C. E. Coghill, CMG. *Educ:* Eton; Christ Church, Oxford. Called to the Bar, Lincoln's Inn, 1937.

STAINTON, John Ross, CBE 1971; Member, British Airways Board, since 1971, Deputy Chairman (Commercial Operations), since 1977; *b* 27 May 1914; *s* of late George Stainton and Helen Ross; *m* 1939, Doreen Werner; three *d*. *Educ:* Glengorse, Eastbourne; Malvern Coll., Worcestershire. Joined Imperial Airways as Trainee, 1933; served in Italy, Egypt, Sudan. Served with RAF in England and West Indies, 1940-42. BOAC in USA, 1942; Man. N America, 1949-53; General Sales Man. BOAC, and other Head Office posts, 1954-64; Commercial Director, 1964; Dep. Man. Dir, 1968-71; Man. Dir, 1971-72; Mem., BOAC (AC), 1961-72; Mem., BOAC Bd, 1968, Chm. and Chief Exec., 1972, until merged into British Airways, 1974. FCIT (Pres., 1970-71). FBIM. *Address:* Tees Green, Prior Road, Camberley, Surrey. *Clubs:* Royal Air Force; Sunningdale Golf.

STAINTON, Keith; MP (C) Sudbury and Woodbridge since Dec. 1963; *b* 8 Nov. 1921; *m* 1946, Vanessa Ann Heald; three *s* three *d*. *Educ:* Kendal Sch.; Manchester Univ. (BA (Com.) Dist. in Economics). Insurance clerk, 1936-39. Served War of 1939-45: Lieut, RNVR, Submarines, 1940-46. Manchester Univ., 1946-49; Leader Writer, Financial Times, 1949-52; Industrial Consultant, 1952-57; joined Burton, Son & Sanders, Ltd, 1957, Man. Dir 1961-69, Chm. 1962-69; Chm. Scotia Investments Ltd, 1969-72. Croix de Guerre avec Palmes, Ordre de l'Armée, 1943. *Address:* Little Bealings House, Woodbridge, Suffolk. *T:* Kesgrave 4205.

STAIR, 13th Earl of, *cr* 1703; **John Aymer Dalrymple,** CVO 1964; MBE 1941; Bt 1664 and (Scot.) 1688; Viscount Stair, Lord Glenluce and Stranraer, 1690; Viscount Dalrymple, Lord Newliston, 1703; Baron Oxenfoord (UK) 1841; Colonel (retired) Scots Guards; Lord-Lieutenant of Wigtown, since 1961; Captain General of the Queen's Body Guard for Scotland, Royal Company of Archers, since 1973; *b* 9 Oct. 1906; *e s* of 11th Earl of Stair, KT, DSO, and Violet Evelyn (*née* Harford) (*d* 1968); *S* father, 1961; *m* 1960, Davina, *d* of late Hon. Sir David Bowes-Lyon, KCVO; three *s*. *Educ:* Eton; Sandhurst. Bde Major, 3rd (London) Infantry Bde and Regimental Adjt Scots Guards, 1935-38; served Middle East, 1941; Bde Major, 16th Inf. Bde (despatches, MBE); Lieut-Colonel 1942; commanded 1st Scots Guards, 1942-43; AMS Headquarters AAI, 1944; Comd Trg Bn Scots Guards, 1945; Comd 2nd Scots Guards, 1946-49; Comd Scots Guards, Temp. Colonel, 1949-52; retired, 1953; retired as Hon. Colonel Scots Guards, 1953. *Heir: s* Viscount Dalrymple, *qv. Address:* Lochinch Castle, Stranraer, Wigtownshire. *Club:* Cavalry and Guards.
See also Lady Marion Philipps , Lady Jean Rankin .

STALKER, Prof. Alexander Logie, TD; DL; Regius Professor of Pathology, University of Aberdeen, since 1972; Consultant Pathologist, North East Regional Hospital Board, since 1955; *b* 15 Feb. 1920; *s* of late J. S. Stalker and Jean Logie; *m* 1945, Mary E. C. MacLean, MB, ChB; one *s* three *d*. *Educ:* Morrison's Academy, Crieff; Univ. of Aberdeen. MB, ChB 1942; MD 1961; FRCPath 1970. RAMC War Service, 1942-47 and TA Service, 1948-64; ADMS 51 (H) Div., 1958-64; QHS, 1963-65. Univ. of Aberdeen: Sen. Lectr in Pathology, 1948-65; Reader in Pathology, 1965-69; Personal Prof. of Pathology, 1969-72. County Comr Scouts, City of Aberdeen, 1965-68. Pres., British Microcirculation Soc., 1968-73; Pres., European Soc. for Microcirculation, 1970-72; Mem., Pathological Soc. of Gt Britain and Ireland. DL Aberdeen, 1967. *Publications:* scientific papers in medical jls, esp. in field of microcirculation. *Recreations:* fishing, hill walking, Norwegian studies. *Address:* Coach End, Banchory, Kincardineshire AB3 3HS. *T:* Banchory 2460.

STALLARD, Albert William; MP (Lab) Camden, St Pancras North, since 1974 (St Pancras North, 1970-74); an Assistant Government Whip, since 1976; *b* 5 Nov. 1921; *m* 1944; one *s* one *d*. *Educ:* Low Waters Public School; Hamilton Academy, Scotland. Engineer, 1937-65; Technical Training Officer, 1965-70. Councillor, St Pancras, 1953-59, Alderman, 1962-65; Councillor, Camden, 1965-70, Alderman, 1971-. PPS to: Minister of State, Agriculture, Fisheries and Food, 1974; Minister of State for Housing and Construction, 1974-76. Chairman: Camden Town Disablement Cttee (Mem., 1951-); Camden Assoc. for Mental Health. Mem., Inst. of Training Officers, 1971. AEU Order of Merit, 1968. *Address:* House of Commons, SW1A 0AA. *T:* 01-219 4214.

STALLARD, Sir Peter (Hyla Gawne), KCMG 1961 (CMG 1960); CVO 1956; MBE 1945; Lieutenant Governor of the Isle of Man, 1966-74; *b* 6 March 1915; *y c* of Rev. L. B. Stallard and Eleanor, *e d* of Colonel J. M. Gawne; *m* 1941, Mary Elizabeth Kirke, CStJ; one *s* one *d*. *Educ:* Bromsgrove Sch.; Corpus Christi Coll., Oxford (MA). Cadet, Colonial Administrative Service, Northern Nigeria, 1937. Military Service; Nigeria, Gold Coast, Burma, 1939-45. Secretary to the Prime Minister of the Federation of Nigeria, 1958-61; Governor and Commander-in-Chief of British Honduras, 1961-66. Mem., Bath and Wells Diocesan Synod, 1974. Governor, Bromsgrove Sch., 1975. Pres., Devon and Cornwall Rent Assessment Panel, 1976-. KStJ 1961; Chapter-Gen., Order of St John, 1976-. *Recreation:* golf. *Address:* 18 Henley Road, Taunton, Somerset. *T:* Taunton 81505. *Club:* Athenæum.
See also R. D. Wilson.

STALLIBRASS, Geoffrey Ward, CB 1972; OBE 1952; FRAeS; Controller, National Air Traffic Services (Civil Aviation Authority/Ministry of Defence), 1969-74 (Joint Field Commander, 1966-69); *b* 17 Dec. 1911; *s* of Thomas and Ivy Stallibrass, Midhurst; *m* 1940, Alison, *e d* of late James and Rita Scott, Norwich; two *s* three *d*. *Educ:* Wellingborough Sch. Air Service Training, Hamble (Commercial Pilot/Instrument Rating Course), 1948. Dep. Director, Civil Aviation Ops, Ministry of Civil Aviation, 1946; attached to BOAC, 1949; Dep. Director of Control and Navigation (Development), 1950; Director of Aerodromes (Tech.), Ministry of Transport and Civil Aviation, 1953; Director of Flight Safety, Min. of Aviation, 1961. *Publications:* articles on aviation subjects. *Recreations:* walking, birdwatching, photography, music. *Address:* Turkey Island Corner, East Harting, Petersfield, Hants. *T:* Harting 220.

STALLWOOD, Frank, CMG 1967; OBE 1955; *b* 5 Sept. 1910; *s* of late Henry Robert Stallwood and late Ethel (*née* Cheeseman); *m* 1935, Cora Cécile Frances (*née* Brady); one *s* one *d*. *Educ:* Owen's Sch.; St Luke's Coll., Exeter. BA Hons London. Schoolmaster, 1932-40. Army, Captain, Intelligence Corps, Service in ME, 1940-46. Diplomatic Service, 1946-68, retired. *Recreations:* fly-fishing, conversation. *Address:* 5 Macklin Close, Hungerford, Berks. *T:* Hungerford 3584.

STALLWORTHY, Sir John (Arthur), Kt 1972; Nuffield Professor of Obstetrics and Gynæcology, University of Oxford, 1967-73, now Emeritus; Fellow Emeritus, Oriel College, Oxford, 1973, Hon. Fellow, 1974; *b* 26 July 1906; *s* of Arthur John Stallworthy; *m* 1934, Margaret Wright Howie; one *s* twin *d*. *Educ:* Auckland Grammar Sch.; Universities of Auckland and Otago, NZ. Distinction and gold medal in surgery, gynæcology and obstetrics, 1930; travelling med. schol., 1931; obstetrical travelling schol., 1932; postgrad. experience in Melbourne, London and Vienna. MRCOG 1935; FRCS 1936; FRCOG 1951. Joseph Price Orator, US, 1950; McIlrath Guest Prof., Sydney, 1952; Sommer Mem. Lecturer, US, 1958; Hunterian Prof., RCS, 1963; Sims Black Prof. S Africa, 1964. Sometime Examiner in Obstetrics and Gynæcology for RCOG, RCS of S Africa, Universities of Oxford, Birmingham, Leeds, E Africa and Singapore. Hon. Cons., Royal Prince Alfred Hospital, Sydney, 1952; Assoc. Obstetrician, National Maternity Hospital, Dublin, 1959. Vice-Pres., RCOG, 1969; President: RSM, 1974-75 (Hon. Fellow, 1976); Medical Protection Soc.; BMA, 1975. Hon. Fellow, Surgical, Obstetrical and Gynæcological Societies in US, Wales, Canada, S Africa, Spain and Turkey; Hon. FACS 1954; Hon. FCOG (SA) 1964; Hon. FACOG 1974; Hon. FRCSI 1976. Hon. DSc: Otago, 1975; Leeds, 1975. Victor Bonney Prize, RCS, 1970. Member, Honourable Order of Kentucky Colonels, 1968. *Publications:* (jointly) Problems of Fertility in General Practice, 1948; (jointly) Recent Advances in Obstetrics and Gynæcology, 1966; (jointly) Bonney's Gynaecological Surgery, 8th edn; joint contrib. to British Obstetric Practice and British Gynæcological Practice, 1959, and 1963. *Recreations:* formerly Rugby football, tennis, swimming, driving fast cars; now gardening. *Address:* Shotover Edge, Headington, Oxford. *T:* Oxford 62481. *Club:* Athenæum.
See also J . H . Stallworthy .

STALLWORTHY, Jon Howie; James Wendell Anderson Professor of English Literature, Cornell University, since 1977; *b* 18 Jan. 1935; *s* of Sir John (Arthur) Stallworthy, *qv* ; *m* 1960, Gillian Meredith (*née* Waldock); two *s* one *d* . *Educ:* The Dragon Sch., Oxford; Rugby Sch.; Magdalen Coll., Oxford (MA, BLitt). Served RWAFF (pre-Oxford). At Oxford won Newdigate Prize, 1958 (runner-up, 1957). Joined Oxford Univ. Press, 1959, Dep. Head, Academic Div., 1975-77. Gave Chatterton Lecture on an English Poet to British Academy, 1970; during a sabbatical year, 1971-72, was a Visiting Fellow at All Souls Coll., Oxford. FRSL, 1971. *Publications:* poems: (6 collections) The Astronomy of Love, 1961; Out of Bounds, 1963;

Root and Branch, 1969; Positives, 1969; The Apple Barrel: selected poems, 1955-63, 1974; Hand in Hand, 1974; *criticism*: Between the Lines, W. B. Yeats's Poetry in the Making, 1963; Vision and Revision in Yeats's Last Poems, 1969; *biography*: Wilfred Owen, 1974 (winner of Duff Cooper Meml Prize, W. H. Smith Literary Award and E. M. Forster Award); *translations*: (with Peter France) Alexander Blok: The Twelve and other poems, 1970; (with Jerzy Peterkiewicz) poems for 2nd edn of Five Centuries of Polish Poetry, 1970; ed, The Penguin Book of Love Poetry, 1973. *Address*: Department of English, Cornell University, Ithaca, NY 14853, USA; (Christmas and summer) Long Farm, Elsfield Road, Old Marston, Oxford. *Club*: Vincent's (Oxford).

STAMER, Sir (Lovelace) Anthony, 5th Bt, *cr* 1809; MA; AMIMI; *b* 28 Feb. 1917; *s* of Sir Lovelace Stamer, 4th Bt, and Eva Mary (*d* 1974), *e d* of R. C. Otter; *S* father, 1941; *m* 1st, 1948, Stella Huguette (marr. diss., 1953), *d* of Paul Burnell Binnie, Brussels; one *s* one *d*; 2nd, 1955, Margaret Lucy (marr. diss., 1959), *d* of late Major Belben and Mrs Stewart, Marandellas, S Rhodesia; 3rd, 1960, Marjorie June (marr. diss. 1968), *d* of T. C. Noakes, St James, Cape. *Educ*: Harrow; Trinity Coll., Cambridge; Royal Agricultural Coll., Cirencester. BA 1947; MA 1963; AMIMI 1963. Served RAF 1939-41; Officer in ATA 1941-45. Executive Director: Bentley Drivers Club Ltd, 1969-72; Bugatti & Ferrari Owners Club, 1972-74. *Heir*: *s* Peter Tomlinson Stamer, Flying Officer, RAF, *b* 19 Nov. 1951. *Address*: Summer Cottage, Turville Heath, near Henley-on-Thames, Oxon.

STAMLER, Samuel Aaron, QC 1971; a Recorder of the Crown Court, since 1974; *b* 3 Dec. 1925; *s* of late Herman Stamler and Bronia Stamler; *m* 1953, Honor, *d* of A. G. Brotman; two *s* one *d*. *Educ*: Berkhamsted; King's College, Cambridge. Called to Bar, Middle Temple, 1949. *Recreations*: tennis, children. *Address*: 1 Essex Court, Temple, EC4. *T*: 01-353 5362. *Club*: Athenæum.

STAMM, Temple Theodore, FRCS; Orthopædic Surgeon Emeritus, Guy's Hospital; *b* 22 Dec. 1905; *s* of Dr Louis Edward Stamm, Streatham, and Louisa Ethel (*née* Perry), Caterham, Surrey; *m* 1945, Pamela, *d* of Charles Russell, Chislehurst, Kent. *Educ*: Rose Hill Sch., Surrey; Haileybury Coll.; Guy's Hospital Medical School. MB, BS (London), 1930, MRCS, LRCP 1928, FRCS 1934. Fellow Royal Society of Medicine; Fellow British Orthopædic Assoc.; Member British Med. Assoc. Formerly: Orthopædic Surgeon, Bromley Hospital, 1941-66; Asst Orthopædic Surgeon and Orthopædic Registrar, Royal Nat. Orthopædic Hospital; Asst Orthopædic Surgeon, Orthopædic Registrar, Asst Anæsthetist and Demonstrator of Anatomy, Guy's Hospital. Major RAMC. *Publications*: Foot Troubles, 1957; Guide to Orthopædics, 1958; Surgery of the Foot, British Surgical Practice, Vol. 4. Contributions to Blackburn and Lawrie's Textbook of Surgery, 1958. Articles in: Lancet, Guy's Hospital Reports, Journal of Bone and Joint Surgery, Medical Press, etc. *Recreations*: farming, sailing, music. *Address*: Bosloggas, St Mawes, Cornwall.
See also Air Vice-Marshal W. P. Stamm.

STAMM, Air Vice-Marshal William Percivale, CBE 1960; Senior RAF Consultant in Pathology and Tropical Medicine and Officer Commanding RAF Institute of Pathology and Tropical Medicine, 1951-69, retired; *b* 27 Aug. 1909; *s* of Dr L. E. Stamm and L. E. (*née* Perry); *m* 1939, Mary Magdalene Van Zeller; two *s* one *d*; *m* 1974, Mrs J. M. Turner (*née* Erleigh). Educ: Haileybury Coll.; Guy's Hospital. MRCS, LRCP, 1932; MB, BS (London) 1933; DCP (London) 1946; DTM&H 1947; MRCP 1951; FRCP 1956; FRCPath 1964. House appointments, anatomy demonstrator, Guy's Hospital. Commissioned RAF, 1934; specialised in pathology and tropical medicine, 1938; comd RAF Hospital, Takoradi, 1942-43; Member Council: Royal Society Trop. Med. and Hygiene, 1951-57, 1959-69, 1971-72 (Vice-President, 1957-59, and 1969-71); Assoc. of Clinical Pathologists, 1958-61 (President, 1966-67); United Services Sect., Royal Society Med., 1952-62 and 1966-69. Pres., British Div., Internat. Acad. Pathology, 1966; Hon. lectr, tropical pathology, Royal Free Med. Sch.; Cons., King's Coll. Hospital. QHS 1959-69. *Publications*: contrib. to Symposium, The Pathology of Parasitic Diseases; papers in Lancet, BMJ, Journal Clin. Pathology, Trans. Royal Society Tropical Med. and Hygiene, and Proc. Royal Society of Medicine. *Recreations*: building and decorating, opera and theatre. *Address*: 17 Ennismore Gardens, SW7. *T*: 01-589 5351. *Club*: Royal Air Force.
See also T. T. Stamm.

STAMMERS, Professor Francis Alan Roland, CBE 1945; TD (with clasp) 1949; Emeritus Professor of Surgery, University of Birmingham (Professor, 1946-63); Hon. Cons. Surgeon, United Birmingham Hospitals; Cons.-Adviser in Surgery to Birmingham Regional Hospital Board, 1963-68, Hon. Cons.-Adviser, 1968-71; *b* 31 Jan. 1898; *s* of Charles Roland Stammers and Eliza Nellie Pettitt; *m* 1933, Lois Mildred Marris; one *s* two *d*. *Educ*: Dudley Grammar School; Birmingham Univ.; London Hospital; Mayo Clinic, USA. Served European War, 1914-18, 2nd Lieut, Lieut RGA, 1916-18; BSc (Birmingham) 1920; MB, ChB (Birmingham), MRCS, LRCP 1923; FRCS 1925; ChM (Birmingham), 1936. Late Surgeon: General, Children's and Queen Elizabeth Hospitals, 1929; Rockefeller Fellowship Mayo Clinic, USA, 1928; served War of 1939-45: surgical specialist and OC Surgical Division, RAMC, 1939-42; Cons. Surgeon, Brigadier AMS, W Command and forward areas of and Italy, 1942-45 (despatches); Hon. Colonel, AMS; Late Member Council (late Member Court of Examiners), Royal College of Surgeons, 1957-65; late External Examiner: University of London; University of Durham. Visiting Surgeon to Harvard University Medical School, Boston, Mass, USA, 1950; President, Surgical Section of Royal Society of Med. (now Hon. Member), 1952-53; British Council and BMA Lecturer in Cyprus, Baghdad and Khartoum, 1952; Australasian Postgrad. Federation in Medicine Lecturer, 1958. President: Assoc. of Surgeons of Great Britain and Ireland, 1960-61; Midland Med. Society, 1960-61; Moynihan Chirurgical Club, 1962-63; W Midlands Surgical Soc., 1955; Mem. Council and Cases Cttee, Medical Protection Society. *Publications*: Partial Gastrectomy Complications with Metabolic Consequences (with J. Alexander Williams), 1963; numerous articles in medical and surgical journals and textbooks. *Recreations*: gardening, bowls, reading. *Address*: 56 Middle Park Road, Weoley Hill, Birmingham B29 4BJ. *T*: 021-475 1022. *Club*: University Staff (Birmingham).

STAMP, family name of Baron Stamp.

STAMP, 3rd Baron, *cr* 1938, of Shortlands; **Trevor Charles Stamp**, MA, MD, FRCPath; Emeritus Professor of Bacteriology, Royal Postgraduate Medical School, University of London (Reader, 1937-48, Professor, 1948-70); *b* 13 Feb. 1907; *s* of 1st Baron Stamp, GCB, GBE; *S* brother, 1941; *m* 1932, Frances Dawes, *d* of late Charles Henry Bosworth, Evanston, Illinois, USA; two *s*. *Educ*: Leys Sch., Cambridge; Gonville and Caius Coll., Cambridge; St Bartholomew's Hospital. MRCS, LRCP, BCh Cambridge, MA Cambridge, 1931; MB Cambridge, 1937. MD 1966. Demonstrator in Bacteriology, 1932-34, Lecturer in Bacteriology, 1934-37, London School of Hygiene and Tropical Medicine; attached to the Ministry of Supply, 1941-45; Governor of Imperial College of Science and Technology; Governor of Leys School; Chm. of Governors, Queenswood School. Mem., Parly Delegn to Egypt, 1973, to Tokyo, 1974. Founder Fellow, College of Pathologists, 1963 (now RCPath); Fellow, Royal Postgrad. Med. Sch., 1972. US Medal of Freedom with Silver Palm, 1947. Hon. Freedom, Barbers' Company, 1958. *Publications*: Various papers on bacteriological subjects. *Recreation*: gardening. *Heir*: *s* Dr the Hon. Trevor Charles Bosworth Stamp, MD, BCh, MRCP [*b* 18 Sept. 1935; *m* 1st, 1963, Anne Carolynn Churchill (marr. diss. 1971); two *d*; 2nd, 1975, Carol Anne, *d* of Keith Russell, Lower Bourne, Farnham, Surrey; one *d*]. *Address*: Middle House, 7 Hyde Park Street, W2. *T*: 01-723 8363; Pennyroyal, Hedgerley, Bucks. *T*: Farnham Common 2737. *Club*: Athenæum.

STAMP, Hon. Arthur Maxwell; Member, Civil Aviation Authority, since 1976; Director: Hill Samuel & Co. Ltd, 1958-76; The De La Rue Co. Ltd, 1960; Triplex Holdings Ltd, 1963-75; Economics International Inc.; Chairman: Maxwell Stamp Associates Ltd; Maxwell Stamp (Africa) Ltd; Maxeast Ltd; *b* 20 Sept. 1915; 3rd *s* of 1st Baron Stamp, GCB, GBE; *m* 1944, Alice Mary Richards; one *s* two *d*. *Educ*: Leys Sch., Cambridge; Clare Coll., Cambridge. Called to the Bar, Inner Temple, 1939; War of 1939-45, 2nd Lieut Intelligence Corps, 1940; Major 1943; Lieut-Colonel 1944. Financial Adviser, John Lewis Partnership Ltd, 1947-49; Acting Adviser, Bank of England, 1950-53. Alternate Executive Director for the UK, International Monetary Fund, Washington, DC, USA, 1951-53; Director, European Department, International Monetary Fund, 1953-54. Adviser to the Governors, the Bank of England, 1954-57. Member: Council of Foreign Bondholders, 1950-53, 1955-57; Council, Internat. Chamber of Commerce, 1961-75; Exec. Cttee, Nat. Inst. of Economic and Social Research, 1962; Exec. Cttee, European League for Economic Co-operation, 1962; Council, Trade Policy Research Centre; Economic Cttee, CBI, 1968-; Chm., Home Office Cttee on London Taxi-Cab Trade, 1967. Mem., Panel of Conciliators, Internat. Centre for Settlement of Investment Disputes, Washington, 1968. Chm., The Rehearsal Orchestra. Governor, LSE, 1968. *Recreations*: music, photography. *Address*: Mulberry Green Farmhouse, Copford, Essex. *T*: Colchester 210231; 19 Clarence Gate Gardens, Glentworth Street, NW1. *T*: 01-723 9538. *Club*: Athenæum.

STAMP, Prof. Edward, MA (Cantab), CA; J. Arthur Rank Research Professor in Accountancy since 1975 (Professor of Accounting Theory, 1971-75), Director of International Centre for Research in Accounting, since 1971, University of Lancaster; *b* 11 Nov. 1928; *s* of William Stamp and Anne Wilson; *m* 1953, Margaret Douglas Higgins, *d* of Douglas Gordon Higgins, MC, Toronto, Canada; one *s* three *d*. *Educ:* Quarry Bank, Liverpool; Cambridge Univ. Open Exhibnr, Foundation Scholar, Prizeman, First cl. Hons Natural Sciences. Lieut, RCNR. With Arthur Young, Clarkson, Gordon & Co., Chartered Accountants and Management Consultants, Toronto and Montreal, 1951-62 (Manager, 1957; Partner, 1961); Sen. Lectr in Accountancy, Victoria Univ. of Wellington, NZ, 1962-65; Prof. of Accountancy, 1965-67; Prof. and Head of Dept of Accounting and Finance, Univ. of Edinburgh, 1967-71. Hon. Treas., NZ Inst. of Internat. Affairs, 1963-65; Member: Govt Cttee on Taxation, NZ, 1967; Bd of Research and Pubn, NZ Soc. of Accountants, 1964-67; Jt Standing Cttee on Degree Studies and Accounting Profession (UK), 1967-72 (Exec. Cttee, 1969-72); UK Adv. Bd of Accountancy Educn, 1969-72. Advr, HM Treasury, 1971-76 (resigned); Consultant, Price Commission, 1974-. Editorial Bd, Abacus (Australia), 1969-, Jl of Business Finance, 1969-, Internat. Register of Research in Accounting and Finance, 1971-, The Accounting Review (USA), 1972-, Accountancy, 1974-, Management Internat. Review (Germany), 1974-. Chm., Brit. Accounting and Finance Assoc., 1968-71 (Life Vice-Pres., 1971-); Member: Steering Cttee, Long-Range Enquiry into Accounting Educn, 1971-; ASSC Working Party on scope and aims of Financial Accounts, 1974-75. Visiting Prof.: Univ. of Sydney, 1966; Univ. of NSW, 1967; European Inst. of Business Admin. (INSEAD), Fontainebleau, 1969 and 1970; Univ. of Nairobi, 1969 and 1972; AAA Distinguished Internat. Vis. Lectr, USA, 1977. *Publications:* The Elements of Consolidation Accounting, 1965; Looking at Balance Sheets, 1967; Accounting Principles and the City Code: the case for reform, 1970; Corporate Financial Reporting, 1972; (jtly) The Corporate Report, 1975; articles and papers in professional and academic jls in several countries, also papers to World Congresses of Accountants. *Recreation:* tormenting dinosaurs. *Address:* Roxburghe House, Haverbreaks, Lancaster. *T:* Lancaster 2056; International Centre for Research in Accounting, Gillow House, Bailrigg, Lancaster. *T:* Lancaster 65201. *Clubs:* Reform; Lancaster Golf and Country (Lancaster).

STAMP, Rt. Hon. Sir (Edward) Blanshard, PC 1971; Kt 1964; **Rt. Hon. Lord Justice Stamp;** a Lord Justice of Appeal, since 1971; *b* 21 March 1905; *s* of late Alfred Edward Stamp, CB, and Edith Florence Guthrie; *m* 1st, 1934, Mildred Evelyn (*d* 1971), *d* of John Marcus Poer O'Shee; no *c*; 2nd, 1973, Mrs Pamela Joan Peters. *Educ:* Gresham's Sch., Holt; Trinity Coll., Cambridge. Called to Bar, Inner Temple, 1929; Bencher of Lincoln's Inn, 1956. Served War of 1939-45 as civilian attached General Staff, War Office. Junior Counsel to Commissioners of Inland Revenue (Chancery), 1954; Junior Counsel to Treasury (Chancery), 1960-64; a Judge of the High Court of Justice, Chancery Div., 1964-71. Mem., Restrictive Practices Court, 1970-71. *Recreations:* walking, travelling. *Address:* 30 Hanover House, St John's Wood, NW8. *Clubs:* United Oxford & Cambridge University, Garrick.

STAMPER, John Trevor, MA, CEng, FRAeS; Technical Director, British Aerospace, since 1977; *b* 12 Oct. 1926; *s* of late Col Horace John Stamper and Clara Jane (*née* Collin); *m* 1950, Cynthia Joan Parsons; two *s* one *d*. *Educ:* Loughborough Grammar Sch.; Jesus Coll., Cambridge (MA 1951). FRAeS 1965; CEng 1966; Fellow, Fellowship of Engrg, 1977. Blackburn Aircraft Ltd: Post-grad. apprenticeship, 1947; Dep. Head of Aerodynamics, 1955; Head of Structures, 1956; Flight Test Manager, 1960; Chief Designer (Buccaneer), 1961; Dir and Chief Designer, 1963; Hawker Siddeley Aviation Ltd (following merger): Exec. Dir Design (Military), 1966; Exec. Dir and Dep. Chief Engr (Civil), 1968; Tech. Dir, 1968. Member: Council RAeS, 1971-77; Tech. Bd, SBAC, 1966- (Chm., 1972-74); Council, Aircraft Res. Assoc., 1966- (Chm., 1976-); Aeronautical Res. Council, 1971-74; Air Warfare Adv. Bd, Defence Scientific Adv. Council, 1973-; Noise Adv. Council, 1975-; Comité Technique et Industriel, Assoc. Européenne des Constructeurs de Matériel Aerospatial, 1971- (Chm., 1974-); Airworthiness Requirements Bd, CAA, 1976-. Hodgeson Prize, RAeS, 1975; British Gold Medal for Aeronautics, RAeS, 1976. *Publications:* (contrib.) The Future of Aeronautics, 1970; papers in Jl RAeS. *Recreations:* sailing, photography. *Address:* 8 Brendon Drive, Esher, Surrey KT10 9EQ. *T:* Esher 66009.

STAMPER, Thomas Henry Gilborn, CIE 1938; MC; FRICS 1906; Formerly Consulting Surveyor to the Government of Bombay; *b* 27 Oct. 1884; *m* 1923, Edith, *d* of late Rev. Stephen Edward Gladstone; two *s* one *d*. Served European War, 1914-18

(despatches, MC, with two Bars, French Croix de Guerre). *Address:* Wath Cottage, Damerham, Fordingbridge, Hants. *T:* Rockbourne 250.

STANBRIDGE, Air Vice-Marshal Brian Gerald Tivy, CBE 1974; MVO 1958; AFC 1952; Defence Services Secretary, Ministry of Defence, since 1975; *b* 6 July 1924; *s* of late Gerald Edward Stanbridge and of Violet Georgina Stanbridge; *m* 1949, Kathleen Diana Hayes, Cheltenham; two *d*. *Educ:* Thurlestone Coll., Dartmouth. Served War: RAFVR, 1942; commnd, 1944; No 31 Sqdn (SE Asia), 1944-46; No 47 Sqdn, 1947-49; 2FTS/CFS, 1950-52; British Services Mission to Burma, 1952-54; The Queen's Flight (personal pilot and flying instructor to Duke of Edinburgh), 1954-58; Naval Staff Coll., 1958; PSO to AOC-in-C Coastal Comd, 1958-59; W/Cdr, Flying, RAF St Mawgan, 1960-62; jssc, 1962; RAFDS, Army Staff Coll., Camberley, 1962-63; Gp Captain on staff of NATO Standing Gp, Washington, DC, 1963-66; RAF Dir, Jt Anti-Submarine Sch., Londonderry, and Sen. RAF Officer, NI, 1966-68; Gp Captain Ops, HQ Coastal Comd, 1968-70; IDC, 1970; Air Cdre, 1970; Sec., Chiefs of Staff Cttee, MoD, 1971-73; Dep. Comdt, RAF Staff Coll., Bracknell, 1973-75; ADC to the Queen, 1973-75; Air Vice-Marshal, 1975. Chm., RAF Gliding and Soaring Assoc. *Recreations:* travel, walking, gardening, woodwork, gliding. *Address:* 9 Paines Lane, Pinner, Middx HA5 3DF. *T:* 01-866 6643. *Club:* Royal Air Force.

STANBRIDGE, Ven. Leslie Cyril; Archdeacon of York since 1972; *b* 19 May 1920. *Educ:* Bromley County Grammar Sch., Kent; St John's Coll., Durham Univ. (MA, DipTheol). Asst Curate of Erith Parish Church, Kent, 1949-51; Tutor and Chaplain, St John's Coll., Durham, 1951-55; Vicar of St Martin's, Hull, 1955-64; Examining Chaplain to the Archbishop of York, 1962-; Rector of Cottingham, Yorks, 1964-72; Canon of York, 1968-; Rural Dean of Kingston-upon-Hull, 1970-72. *Recreations:* fell walking, cycling. *Address:* 14 St George's Place, York YO2 2DR. *T:* York 23775.

STANBRIDGE, Air Vice-Marshal (retired) Reginald Horace, CB 1956; OBE 1944; MRCS, LRCP, DPM, DIH; *b* 24 Nov. 1897; *s* of Horace John Stanbridge; *m* 1945, Inez Valerie, *d* of Arthur Holland; one *s*. *Educ:* Eastbourne; St Mary Coll., London Univ.; London Hospital Medical College. Served War, 1915-18, Lieut RGA, and RFC. Principal Medical Officer in following RAF Commands: Aden, 1938-41; Transport, 1948-49; Bomber, 1950-53; KHP, 1952, QHP, 1952-56; Principal Medical Officer, Middle East Air Force, 1953-56; retired, 1956. BoT later CAA Med. Dept, 1966-. Liveryman, Soc. of Apothecaries; Freeman, City of London. CStJ. *Publications:* various articles in The Lancet, RAF Quarterly, Wine and Food. *Recreations:* sailing, tennis. *Address:* The Dial House, Birdshill Road, Oxshott, Surrey. *T:* Oxshott 2175. *Club:* Royal Air Force.

STANBROOK, Ivor Robert; MP (C) Bromley, Orpington, since 1974 (Orpington, 1970-74); Barrister-at-Law; *b* 13 Jan. 1924; *y s* of Arthur William and Lilian Stanbrook; *m* 1946, Joan (*née* Clement); two *s*. *Educ:* State Schools and London and Oxford Universities. Colonial Administrative Service, Nigeria, 1950-60. Called to the Bar, Inner Temple, 1960; practising barrister, 1960-. *Address:* 6 Sevenoaks Road, Orpington, Kent. *T:* Orpington 20347.

STANBURY, Richard Vivian Macaulay; HM Diplomatic Service, retired; *b* 5 Feb. 1916; *s* of late Gilbert Vivian Stanbury and Doris Marguerite (*née* Smythe); *m* 1953, Geraldine Anne, *d* of late R. F. W. Grant and of Winifred Helen Grant; one *s* one *d*. *Educ:* Shrewsbury Sch.; Magdalene Coll., Cambridge. Sudan Political Service, 1937-50 (District Comr in 12 districts, and Magistrate); HM Foreign Service, 1951-71. *Recreations:* tennis, golf, and, once upon a time, cricket (played for Somerset) and polo; trying to avoid playing bridge; growing peaches and orchids. *Address:* Quinta da Boa Esperanca, Quinta da Larga Vista, S. B. Messines, Algarve, Portugal. *Clubs:* Bath; Hawks (Cambridge); Hurlingham (Buenos Aires).

STANBURY, Prof. Sydney William, MD, FRCP; Professor of Medicine, University of Manchester, since 1965; *b* 21 April 1919; *s* of F. A. W. Stanbury and A. B. Stanbury (*née* Rowe); *m* 1943, Helen, *d* of Harry and Patty Jackson; one *s* four *d*. *Educ:* Hulme Grammar Sch., Oldham; Manchester Univ. MB, ChB (1st Cl. Hons) 1942; MD (Gold Medal) 1948; MRCP 1947, FRCP 1958. Served RAMC, Burma and India, 1944-47. Beit Meml Res. Fellow, 1948-51; Rockefeller Travelling Fellow, 1951-52; Registrar, Lectr and Reader, Dept of Medicine, Manchester Royal Infirmary, 1947-65; Consultant Phys., United Manchester Hosps, 1959-; Dir, Metabolic Ward, Manch. Royal Inf., 1963-. Member: Assoc. of Physicians; Medical Res. Soc.; Bone and Tooth Soc. John Howard Means Vis. Prof.,

Massachusetts Gen. Hosp., Boston, 1958; Henry M. Winans Vis. Prof., Univ. of Texas, Dallas, 1958; Weild Lectr, RCP and S, Glasgow, 1958; Vis. Lectr: Univ. of Washington, Mayo Clinic, etc. *Publications:* contrib. European and American med. books and jls on: renal function, electrolyte metabolism, metabolic bone disease and vitamin D metabolism. *Recreation:* gardening. *Address:* Department of Medicine, Royal Infirmary, Manchester M13 9WL; Hey Tor, Leicester Road, Hale, Cheshire. *T:* 061-928 5247.

STANCLIFFE, Very Rev. Michael Staffurth, MA; Dean of Winchester, since 1969; *b* 8 April 1916; *s* of late Rev. Canon Harold Emmet Stancliffe, Lincoln; *m* 1940, Barbara Elizabeth, *yr d* of late Rev. Canon Tissington Tatlow; two *s* one *d. Educ:* Haileybury; Trinity Coll., Oxford. Curate of St James, Southbroom, Devizes, 1940-43; priest-in-charge, Ramsbury, 1943-44; curate of Cirencester and priest-in-charge of Holy Trinity, Watermoor, 1944-49; Chaplain and Master, Westminster School, 1949-57; Canon of Westminster and Rector of St Margaret's, Westminster, 1957-69; Speaker's Chaplain, 1961-69; Preacher to Lincoln's Inn, 1954-57. Mem., General Synod, 1970-; Chm., Council for Places of Worship, 1972-75. Fellow, Winchester Coll., 1973. *Publication:* contrib. to A House of Kings, 1966. *Address:* The Deanery, Winchester, Hants.

STANDING, John; see Leon, Sir J. R.

STANDING, Michael Frederick Cecil, CBE 1959; retired as Controller of Programme Organisation (sound), BBC, 1957-70; *b* 28 Feb. 1910; *s* of late Sir Guy Standing, KBE, and of late Lady Standing; *m* 1947, Helen Jean Dawson, *widow* of Flying Officer Michael Hope Lumley and *d* of late Lt-Comdr Dawson Miller, CBE, RN, retired; one *s* two *d* (one *s* decd). *Educ:* Charterhouse. Baring Brothers & Co. Ltd, 1927-35; BBC, 1935; Director of Outside Broadcasting, 1940-45; Head of Variety, 1945-52; Controller of Sound Entertainment, BBC, 1952-57. *Recreations:* painting, gardening, cricket. *Address:* Trottiscliffe House, near West Malling, Kent. *T:* Fairseat 822293.

STANFIELD, Hon. Robert Lorne, PC (Canada) 1967; QC; MP (Progressive C) Halifax, NS, since 1968 (Colchester-Hants, NS, 1967); Leader of Opposition and National Leader of Progressive Conservative Party of Canada, 1967-76; *b* Truro, NS, 11 April 1914; *s* of late Frank Stanfield, sometime MLA and Lieutenant-Governor of NS, and Sarah (*née* Thomas); *m* 1st, 1940, N. Joyce (*d* 1954), *d* of C. V. Frazee, Vancouver; one *s* three *d* ; 2nd, 1957, Mary Margaret (*d* 1977), *d* of late Hon. W. L. Hall, Judge of Supreme Court and formerly Attorney-Gen. of NS. *Educ:* Colchester County Academy, Truro; Ashbury Coll., Ottawa; Dalhousie Univ.; Harvard Law Sch. Southam Cup, Ashbury Coll.; BA Political Science and Economics 1936, Governor-General's Gold Medal, Dalhousie Univ.; LLB Harvard, 1939. War of 1939-45: attached Halifax Office of Wartime Prices and Trade Bd as Regional Rentals Officer, later as Enforcement Counsel. Admitted Bar of NS, 1940. Practised law, McInnes and Stanfield, Halifax, 1945-56; KC 1950. President, Nova Scotia Progressive Cons. Assoc., 1947-; Leader, Nova Scotia Progressive Cons. Party, 1948-67; elected to Legislature of NS, 1949, Mem. for Colchester Co.; re-elected Mem., 1953, 1960, 1963, 1967; Premier and Minister of Education, NS, 1956; resigned as Premier of NS, 1967. Hon. LLD: University of New Brunswick, 1958; St Dunstan's Univ., PEI, 1964; McGill Univ., PQ, 1967; St Mary's Univ., NS, 1969. Anglican. *Address:* The House of Commons, Ottawa, Canada; 136 Acacia Avenue, Rockcliffe Park, Ottawa, Ontario K1M 0R1.

STANFORD, William Bedell, MA, LittD; Regius Professor of Greek in University of Dublin, since 1940, Pro-Chancellor, since 1977; Fellow of Trinity College, Dublin, since 1934 (Senior Fellow since 1962); Tutor, 1938-54; Public Orator, 1970-71 (Deputy Public Orator, 1958-60); Senior Master, Non-regent, 1960-62; *b* 1910; *s* of Rev. Bedell Stanford, then Rector of Trinity Church, Belfast, and Susan Stanford; *m* 1935, Dorothy Isobel Wright; two *s* two *d. Educ:* Bishop Foy Sch., Waterford; Trinity Coll., Dublin (Scholar). Formerly External Examiner in Greek for National Univ., Queen's Univ., University of Wales, University of Leeds and Royal Colleges of Physicians and Surgeons, Ireland. MRIA. Sather Professor of Classical Literature, University of California, Berkeley, 1966; Visiting Prof., McGill Univ., Montreal, 1968, Wayne State Univ., 1971, Princeton Univ., 1974. Has lectured on over 40 other campuses in North America. Editor of Hermathena, 1942-62. Rep. of Dublin Univ. in the Irish Senate, 1948-69. Irish Rep., Council of Europe, Strasbourg, 1951, European Parliamentary Conf., Vienna, 1956 and Inter-parliamentary Conf., Warsaw, 1959. Member Irish Radio Advisory Council until 1952. Governor, Erasmus Smith's Sch.; Mem., General Synod and Dublin

Diocesan Synod of Church of Ireland and of Episcopal Electoral Coll. for Southern Province; Sec., Appointments Cttee, TCD, 1936-37, Hon. Sec., TCD Assoc., 1950-55. Mem. Council, Hellenic Soc., 1965-68; Pres., Birmingham Branch, Classical Assoc., 1968; Vice-Pres. RIA, 1969; Chairman: Irish Nat. Cttee for Greek and Latin Studies, 1968-72; Council of Dublin Inst. for Advanced Studies. *Publications:* Greek Metaphor, 1936; Ambiguity in Greek Literature, 1939; Livy XXIV edited for schools, 1942; Aeschylus in His Style, 1942; Homer's Odyssey, edited, 1947-48 (2nd edn, 1961-62); The Ulysses Theme, 1954 (2nd edn, 1963); Aristophanes' Frogs, edited, 1957 (2nd edn, 1963); Sophocles' Ajax, edited, 1963; The Sound of Greek, 1967; (with R. B. McDowell) Mahaffy, 1971; (with J. V. Luce) The Quest for Ulysses, 1975; (with Robert Fagles) Aeschylus: The Oresteia, 1976; Ireland and the Classical Tradition, 1976; various shorter publications on literary, linguistic, ecclesiastical and historical subjects. *Address:* 40 Trinity College, Dublin; 2 Mount Salus, Dalkey, Co. Dublin. *T:* Dublin 803329. *Club:* Royal Irish Yacht (Dun Laoghaire).

STANFORD-TUCK, Wing Commander Robert Roland, DSO 1940; DFC (2 bars); *b* 1 July 1916; *s* of Stanley Lewis Tuck and Ethel Constance Tuck; *m* 1945; two *s. Educ:* St Dunstan's Preparatory School and College, Reading. Left school, 1932, and went to sea as a cadet with Lamport and Holt; joined Royal Air Force, Sept. 1935; posted to No 65 Fighter Sqdn, Aug. 1936, and served with them until outbreak of war; posted to 92 (F) Sqdn, and went through air fighting at Dunkirk, shooting down 8 enemy aircraft (DFC); posted to Comd No 257 Burma Fighter Sqdn, Sept. 1940, till July 1941, when given command of Wing; comd Duxford and Biggin Hill Wings; prisoner 1942, escaped 1945. Record to end July 1941: 27 confirmed victories, 8 probably destroyed, 6 damaged; wounded twice, baled out 4 times. Retired list, 1948. *Relevant publication:* Fly For Your Life (by L. Forrester). *Recreations:* fencing, riding, shooting. *Address:* Mallards, North Road, Sandwich Bay, Sandwich, Kent CT13 9PJ.

STANHOPE, family name of **Earl of Harrington.**

STANIER, Brigadier Sir Alexander Beville Gibbons, 2nd Bt, *cr* 1917; DSO 1940 (and Bar, 1945); MC; DL, JP; CStJ; *b* 31 Jan. 1899; *s* of 1st Bart, and Constance (*d* 1948), *d* of late Rev. B. Gibbons; *S* father, 1921; *m* 1927, Dorothy Gladys (*d* 1973), *e d* of late Brig.-Gen. Alfred Douglas Miller, CBE, DSO; one *s* one *d. Educ:* Eton; RMC, Sandhurst. Served European War in France, 1918 (MC); served War of 1939-45, in France 1940 and 1944 (despatches, DSO and Bar, American Silver Star, Comdr Order of Leopold of Belgium with palm, Belgian Croix de Guerre with palm). Adjutant 1st Bn Welsh Guards, 1923-26; Military Secretary, Gibraltar, 1927-30; commanded 2nd Battalion Welsh Guards, 1939-40; temp. Brigadier, 1940-45; Lieut-Colonel Commanding Welsh Guards, 1945-48. CC Salop, 1950-58. High Sheriff of Shropshire, 1951. County President of the St John Ambulance Bde, 1950-60. *Heir:* *s* Beville Douglas Stanier [*b* 20 April 1934; *m* 1963, Shelagh, *er d* of late Major and Mrs J. S. Sinnott, Tetbury, Glos; one *s* two *d*]. *Address:* East Farndon Manor, Market Harborough, Leics. *T:* 2104; Park Cottage, Ludford, Ludlow. *T:* Ludlow 2675.

STANIER, Maj.-Gen. John Wilfred, MBE 1961; Commandant, Staff College, Camberley, 1975-78; *b* 6 Oct. 1925; *s* of late Harold Allan Stanier and Penelope Rose Stanier (*née* Price); *m* 1955, Cicely Constance Lambert; four *d. Educ:* Marlborough Coll.; Merton Coll., Oxford. MBIM, FRGS. Commd in 7th Queen's Own Hussars, 1946; served in N Italy, Germany and Hong Kong; comd Royal Scots Greys, 1966-68; comd 20th Armd Bde, 1969-70; GOC 1st Div., 1973-75. *Recreations:* hunting, fishing, sailing, talking. *Address:* Whitewater House, Dipley, Hartley Wintney, Hants. *Club:* Cavalry and Guards.

STANIER, Robert Spenser; Master of Magdalen College School, Oxford, 1944-67; *b* 9 Aug. 1907; *s* of C. E. Stanier, Civil Engineer to the Underground Railways; *m* 1935, Maida Euphemia Kerr Burnett; two *s. Educ:* Berkhamsted School; Wadham Coll., Oxford. Assistant Master at King's School, Canterbury, 1929-35; Usher at Magdalen College School, Oxford, 1935-44. *Publications:* Selections from the Greek Lyric Poets, 1935; Magdalen School, 1940 (republished by Oxford Historical Society, 1941; augmented edition, 1958); Oxford Heraldry for the Man in the Street, 1974; articles in 'Journal of Hellenic Society' and 'Greece and Rome'. *Address:* 211 Morrell Avenue, Oxford. *T:* Oxford 40269.

STANIFORTH, John Arthur Reginald, CBE 1969; Director: John Brown & Co., Ltd; Constructors John Brown Ltd (Chief Executive and Managing Director, 1958-77); John Brown Engineering (Clydebank) Ltd (Chairman, 1970-77); *b* 19 Sept.

1912; *o s* of Captain Staniforth, MC, Anston House, Anston, Yorks; *m* 1936, Penelope Cecile, *y d* of Maj.-Gen. Sir Henry Freeland; one *s* one *d. Educ:* Marlborough Coll. Joined John Brown Group 1929-. Mem., Export Guarantees Adv. Council, 1971-76, Dep. Chm., 1975-76. Founder Chm., British Chemical Engrg Contractors Assoc., 1965-68. Governor: Cranborne Chase Sch.; Bryanston Sch. *Recreations:* golf, fishing, sailing. *Address:* Spindlewood, Old Bosham, West Sussex. *T:* Bosham 572401. *Clubs:* Flyfishers', MCC; Goodwood Golf.

STANISTREET, Rt. Rev. Henry Arthur, DD (*jure dig*), Dublin University, 1958; *b* 19 March 1901; *s* of late Rev. Precentor A. H. Stanistreet; *m* 1938, Ethel Mary Liversidge; one *d. Educ:* Trent Coll., Derbyshire; St Columba's Coll., Rathfarnham; Trinity Coll., Dublin (MA). Ordained 1924. Curate, Clonmel with Innislonagh, 1924-27; Curate in charge, Corbally and Chaplain, Roscrea Hospital, 1927-30; Rector: Templeharry with Borrisnafarney, 1930-31; Roscrea, 1931-43; Surrogate, 1931; Rural Dean, Ely O'Carroll, 1933-43; Canon, Killaloe, 1940-43; Dean of Killaloe Cathedral, 1943-57; Prebendary, Killaloe, Rural Dean, O'Mullod, Rector, St Flannan with O'Gonnilloe and Castletownarra, 1943-57; Rural Dean, Traderry, 1949-57; Prebendary, St Patrick's Cathedral, Dublin, 1955-57; Bishop of Killaloe, Kilfenora, Clonfert and Kilmacduagh, 1957-72. *Address:* Woodville, Dunmore East, Co. Waterford, Ireland.

STANLEY, family name of **Earl of Derby** and **Baron Stanley of Alderley**.

STANLEY OF ALDERLEY, 8th Baron (UK) *cr* 1839; **Thomas Henry Oliver Stanley;** Bt 1660; Baron Sheffield (Ire), 1783; Baron Eddisbury, 1848; Captain (retired), Coldstream Guards; Tenant Farmer of New College, Oxford, since 1954; *b* 28 Sept. 1927; *s* of Lt-Col The Hon. Oliver Hugh Stanley, DSO, JP (3rd *s* of 4th Baron) (*d* 1952), and Lady Kathleen Stanley (*d* 1977), *e d* of 5th Marquess of Bath; *S* cousin (known as Baron Sheffield), 1971; *m* 1955, Jane Barrett, *d* of Ernest George Hartley; three *s* one *d. Educ:* Wellington College, Berks. Coldstream Guards, 1945-52; Guards Parachute Battalion and Independent Company, 1947-50; Northamptonshire Institute of Agriculture, 1952-53. *Recreations:* sailing, skiing, fishing. *Heir: e s* Hon. Richard Oliver Stanley, *b* 24 April 1956. *Address:* Rectory Farm, Stanton St John, Oxford. *T:* Stanton St John 214; Trysglwyn Fawr, Amlwch, Anglesey. *T:* Amlwch 830364. *Club:* Farmers'.

STANLEY, Brian Taylor, MA; In-Service Training Adviser, St Mary's College of Education, Newcastle upon Tyne, since 1972; *b* 1907; *s* of T. T. and Ada A. Stanley, Birmingham; *m* 1938, Audrey, *d* of H. and E. C. Topsfield, Sunbury on Thames; one *s* one *d. Educ:* King Edward's Sch., Birmingham; Christ Church, Oxford; London Day Trng Coll., Columbia Univ., New York; Pädagogische Akademie, Hanover. Teacher under the Warwickshire County Council and Resident Tutor, Fircroft Working Men's College, 1931; Lecturer in Education, Manchester University, 1932; Professor of Education, King's College, Newcastle upon Tyne, 1936-48; Director Institute of Education: Univ. of Durham, 1948-63, Univ. of Newcastle upon Tyne, 1963-72. Order of St Olav, Norway, 1972. *Publications:* The Education of Junior Citizens, 1945; contributions to various educational jls, at home and abroad. *Address:* 5 Corchester Avenue, Corbridge, Northumberland. *T:* Corbridge 2075.

STANLEY, Charles Orr, CBE 1945 (OBE 1943); Chairman, Sunbeam Wolsey Ltd; Director: Arts Theatre Trust; Stanley Foundation Ltd; Orr Investments Ltd; *b* 15 April 1899; *s* of John and Louisa A. Stanley; *m* 1st, 1924, Elsie Florence Gibbs; one *s*; 2nd, 1934, Velma Dardis Price (*d* 1970); 3rd, 1971, Lorna Katherine Sheppard (*d* 1977). *Educ:* Bishop Foy School, Waterford; City and Guilds, Finsbury. Served European War, RFC, 1917-18; Civil Engineer, 1922. Chm., Radio Industry Council, 1962-65; Pres., British Radio Equipment Manufrs Assoc., 1962-64. Hon. Pres., Pye of Cambridge Ltd. Hon. LLD Trinity College, Dublin, 1960. FCGI 1961. *Address:* Sainsfoins, Little Shelford, Cambs; Lisselan, Clonakilty, County Cork, Ireland. *T:* Bandon 43249. *Clubs:* Royal Thames Yacht; Royal Cork Yacht.

STANLEY, Prof. Eric Gerald, MA (Oxford and Yale); PhD (Birmingham); Rawlinson and Bosworth Professor of Anglo-Saxon in the University of Oxford, since Jan. 1977; *b* 19 Oct. 1923; *m* 1959, Mary Bateman, MD, FRCP; one *d. Educ:* Queen Elizabeth's Grammar Sch., Blackburn; University Coll., Oxford. Lectr in Eng. Lang. and Lit., Birmingham Univ., 1951-62; Reader in Eng. Lang. and Lit., 1962-64, Prof. of English, 1964-75, Univ. of London at QMC; Prof. of English, Yale Univ., 1975-76. Co-Editor, Notes and Queries, 1963-. Member: Mediaeval Acad. of America, 1975-; Connecticut Acad. of Arts

and Scis, 1976-. *Publications:* academic articles and books. *Recreation:* photography. *Address:* Pembroke College, Oxford.

STANLEY, Henry Sydney Herbert Cloete, CMG 1968; HM Diplomatic Service; British High Commissioner to Trinidad and Tobago and (non-resident) to Grenada, since 1977; *b* 5 March 1920; *er s* of late Sir Herbert Stanley, GCMG and Reniera (*née* Cloete), DBE; *m* 1941, Margaret, *d* of late Professor H. B. Dixon, CBE, FRS; three *s. Educ:* Eton; Balliol College, Oxford. Served with King's Royal Rifle Corps, 1940-46 (Capt.); N-W Europe, 1944-46, also HQ, CCG. Appointed to Commonwealth Relations Office, 1947. Served in Pakistan, 1950-52; Swaziland and South Africa, 1954-57; USA, 1959-61; Tanganyika, 1961-63; Kenya, 1963-65; Inspector, HM Diplomatic Service, 1966-68, Chief Inspector, 1968-70; High Comr, Ghana, 1970-75; Asst Under Sec. of State, FCO, 1975-77; High Comr for the New Hebrides (non-resident), 1976-77. *Address:* c/o Foreign and Commonwealth Office, SW1; 10 More's Garden, Cheyne Walk, SW3. *Club:* Travellers'.

STANLEY, Dr Herbert Muggleton, FRS 1966; *b* Stratford-upon-Avon, 20 July 1903; *m* 1930, Marjorie Mary (*née* Johnson); two *s* two *d. Educ:* King Edward VI Grammar School, Stratford-on-Avon; Birmingham University (1919-29). BSc 1923; MSc 1925; PhD 1930, FRIC; Mem. Council, Royal Soc., 1968. *Publications:* articles in numerous journals, including Jl Chem. Soc., Soc. Chem. Ind. *Recreations:* archæology, gardening. *Address:* West Halse, Bow, Crediton, Devon. *T:* Bow 262.

STANLEY, John Paul; MP (C) Tonbridge and Malling since Feb. 1974; *b* 19 Jan. 1942; *s* of H. Stanley; *m* 1968, Susan Elizabeth Giles; one *s* one *d. Educ:* Repton Sch.; Lincoln Coll., Oxford (MA). Conservative Research Dept with responsibility for Housing, 1967-68; Research Associate, Internat. Inst. for Strategic Studies, 1968-69; Rio Tinto-Zinc Corp. Ltd, 1969-74. Mem. Parly Select Cttee on Nationalised Industries, 1974; PPS to Rt Hon. Mrs Margaret Thatcher, 1976-. *Publications:* (jtly) The International Trade in Arms, 1972. *Recreations:* music and the arts, sailing. *Address:* House of Commons, SW1A 0AA. *Club:* Leander (Henley-on-Thames).

STANLEY, Michael Charles, MBE 1945; Director of The Proprietors of Hay's Wharf Ltd, and various subsidiary companies; *b* 11 Aug. 1921; *s* of late Col Rt Hon. O. F. G. Stanley, PC, MC, MP, and Lady Maureen Stanley (*née* Vane-Tempest-Stewart); *m* 1951, Ailleen Fortune Hugh Smith, *d* of Owen Hugh Smith, Old Hall, Langham, Rutland; two *s. Educ:* Eton; Trinity College, Cambridge. Served 1939-46 with Royal Signals (Capt. 1943); N Africa, Sicily and Italy with 78th Infantry Div. Trinity, 1946-49 (Nat. Science and Engineering, MA). Served Engineering Apprenticeship with Metropolitan Vickers Electrical Co. Ltd, 1949-52. CEng 1966; MIEE 1966 (AMIEE 1952). High Sheriff for Westmorland, 1959; Westmorland County Councillor, 1961-74; Vice-Lieutenant of Westmorland, 1965-74; DL Westmorland, 1964-74, Cumbria, 1974; High Sheriff, Cumbria, 1975. *Recreations:* idleness, walking, wine. *Address:* Halecat, Witherslack, Grange-over-Sands, Cumbria LA11 6RU. *T:* Witherslack 229. *Clubs:* Turf, White's, Beefsteak, Brooks's; St James's (Manchester); Puffins (Edinburgh).
See also K. E. H. Dugdale.

STANLEY, Hon. Pamela Margaret; *b* 6 Sept. 1909; *d* of 5th Lord Stanley of Alderley and Margaret Evans Gordon; *m* 1941, Sir David Cunynghame, *qv* ; three *s. Educ:* Switzerland; France. Studied at Webber-Douglas School of Acting and Singing; first appearance Lyric, Hammersmith, 1932, in Derby Day; six months at Oxford Repertory, 1933; with Martin Harvey in The Bells, Savoy, 1933; Sydney Carroll's Open Air Theatre, 1934; Wendy in Peter Pan, 1934; Queen Victoria in Victoria Regina, Gate Theatre, 1935; went to USA with Leslie Howard in Hamlet, 1936; Queen Victoria in Victoria Regina, Lyric, 1937-38; Open Air Theatre, 1938; Queen Victoria in The Queen's Highland Servant, Savoy, 1968. *Address:* 15 Madeline Road, SE20. *T:* 01-778 7740.

STANLEY, Captain Hon. Richard Oliver; Grenadier Guards; *b* 29 Jan. 1920; 2nd *s* of Colonel Rt Hon. Lord Stanley, PC, MC (*d* 1938), and Sibyl Louise Beatrix Cadogan (*d* 1969), *e d* of Henry Arthur, late Viscount Chelsea, and Lady Meux; *g s* of 17th Earl of Derby, KG, PC, GCB, GCVO; *b* and *heir-pres* to 18th Earl of Derby, *qv*; *m* 1965, Susan (*d* 1976) *o d* of Sir John Aubrey-Fletcher, *qv. Educ:* Eton. Served War of 1939-45; 2nd Lieutenant, Grenadier Guards, 1940, later Captain. Joined staff of Conservative Central Office after the war. Parliamentary Private Secretary to First Lord of the Admiralty, 1951-55. MP (C) N Fylde Div. of Lancashire, 1950-66, retired. Joint Treasurer, Conservative Party, 1962-66. Mem., Gaming Bd,

1968-. *Address:* 26a North Audley Street, W1. *T:* 01-493 0813; New England House, Newmarket, Suffolk. *T:* Cambridge 811394.

STANLEY, Sir Robert (Christopher Stafford), KBE 1954 (OBE 1942); CMG 1944; *b* 12 May 1899; *o s* of Frederic Arthur and Mary Stanley; *m* 1927, Ursula Cracknell; one *d. Educ:* Westminster; RMA, Woolwich. RGA, 1918-21; war service in Palestine; Reuter's editorial staff, 1923-24; entered Nigerian Administrative Service, 1925; transferred Cyprus, 1935; Commissioner, Larnaca, 1936-37; Chief Assistant Secretary to Govt of Cyprus, 1938-41; Colonial Secretary, Barbados, 1942; Colonial Secretary, Gibraltar, 1945; Chief Secretary, Northern Rhodesia, 1947-52; High Commissioner for Western Pacific, 1952-56, retd. Speaker of Mauritius Legislative Council, 1957-59. *Publication:* King George's Keys, 1975. *Address:* Tragariff, Bantry, Co. Cork, Ireland. *T:* Bantry 74. *Club:* Royal Commonwealth Society.
See also Sir C. D. P. T. Haskard.

STANLEY-CLARKE, Brig. Arthur Christopher Lancelot, CBE 1940; DSO 1918; *b* 1886; *s* of late Ronald Stanley Clarke and late Mabel Octavia Shadwell; *m* 1931, Olive, 3rd *d* of late Thomas Carroll-Leahy of Woodfort, Mallow, Co. Cork; no *c. Educ:* Winchester; Oxford. Capt. OUAFC, 1908-9; gazetted The Cameronians (Scottish Rifles), 1909; commanded 1st Royal Scots Fusiliers, 1931-34; Assist Comdt and Chief Instructor, Netheravon Wing, Small Arms School, 1934-37, Comdr 154th (Argyll and Sutherland) Infantry Brigade TA, 1937; Commander Lothian and Border District, 1941-44; retired pay, 1944. Served European War, 1914-18 (despatches, DSO, and bar, Legion of Honour, Croix de Guerre); War of 1939-45 (CBE). *Address:* Shiel, Baily, Co. Dublin, Ireland.

STANLEY PRICE, Peter, QC 1956; *His Honour Judge Stanley Price*; a Circuit Judge (formerly a Judge of the Central Criminal Court), since 1969; President, National Reference Tribunal, Conciliation Scheme for Deputies employed in Coal-Mining Industry, since 1967; Judge of the Chancery Court of York, since 1967; *b* 27 Nov. 1911; *s* of late Herbert Stanley Price and late Gertrude Rangeley S. P. (*née* Wightman); *m* 1st, 1946, Harriett Ella Theresa (*d* 1948), *o d* of late Rev. R. E. Pownall; two *s*; 2nd, 1950, Margaret Jane, *o d* of late Samuel Milkins (she *m* 1937, William Hebditch, RAF; he *d* 1941); one *d* one step *s. Educ:* Cheltenham; Exeter College, Oxford (1st cl. Final Hons Sch. of Jurisprudence, 1933). Barrister, Inner Temple, 1936, Master of the Bench, 1963. Served War of 1939-45, Lieut (S) RNVR. Recorder of Pontefract, 1954, of York, 1955, of Kingston-upon-Hull, 1958, of Sheffield, 1965-69. Dep. Chm., N Riding QS, 1955-58, 1970-71, Chm., 1958-70; Judge of Appeal, Jersey and Guernsey, 1964-69; Solicitor-General, County Palatine of Durham, 1965-69. *Recreations:* birds and trees; gardening, shooting. *Address:* Church Hill, Great Ouseburn, York. *T:* Green Hammerton 30252. *Clubs:* Brooks's, Bath; Yorkshire (York).

STANNARD, Rt. Rev. Robert William, MA; *b* 20 Oct. 1895; *s* of late Robert John and Fanny Rebecca Stannard; *m* 1922, Muriel Rose Sylvia Knight; one *s* (elder son killed in action April 1945). *Educ:* Westminster; Christ Ch., Oxford; Cuddesdon Theological College. Served army, 1915-19, Lieut Middlesex Regiment. Oxford: Distinction in Lit. Hum., First in Theology, Liddon Student; Ordained, 1922; Curate Bermondsey Parish Church, 1922-24; Curate-in-Charge S Mary's, Putney, 1924-27; Vicar of St James, Barrow-in-Furness, 1927-34; Rural Dean of Dalton, 1934; Rector of Bishopwearmouth (Sunderland), 1934-41; Rural Dean of Sunderland, 1937-41; Archdeacon of Doncaster, 1941-47; Chaplain to the King, 1944-47; Bishop Suffragan of Woolwich, 1947-59; Dean of Rochester, 1959-66. Grand Chaplain, United Grand Lodge of England, 1948-50. Master, Worshipful Co. of Gardeners, 1972-73. *Recreations:* gardening and music. *Address:* Dendron, Reading Road North, Fleet, Hants. *T:* Fleet 4059.

STANNER, Prof. William Edward Hanley, CMG 1972; PhD; FASSA; Emeritus Professor; Consultant, Commonwealth Department of Aboriginal Affairs; *b* 24 Nov. 1905; *s* of late Andrew Edwin Stanner and Mary Catherine Stanner (*née* Hanley), Sydney; *m* 1962, Patricia Ann Williams; two *s. Educ:* Univ. of Sydney (MA, cl. I Hons, 1934); London Sch. of Economics (PhD 1938). Served War: 2nd AIF, 1942-46, Lt-Col (Personal Staff of Minister for the Army, 1941-42). Field research in North and Central Australia (Aust. Nat. Res. Council), 1932, 1934-35; Kenya (Oxf. Soc. St. Res. Cttee), 1938-39; Papua-New Guinea, Fiji, W Samoa (Inst. Pacific Relns), 1946-47; Northern Territory (ANU), 1952-62. Foundn Dir, East African Inst. Soc. Res. (Makerere, Uganda), 1947-49. Australian National Univ.: Reader, 1949-64; Prof. of

Anthropology and Sociology, 1964-70; Emer. Prof. and Hon. Fellow, 1971. Chm., Governing Body, 1954, Bursar, 1954-55, and Hon. Mem., 1960-, Univ. House, ANU; Vis. Fellow, Dept of Prehistory and Anthropology, Sch. of Gen. Studies, ANU, 1975-77. Personal staff of NSW Premier, 1933-34, Commonwealth Treasurer, Imperial Conf., 1937; Australian Comr, S Pacific Commn, 1953-55; Convenor and Chm., Commonwealth Conf. on Aboriginal Studies, 1961; First Exec. Officer, Aust. Inst. of Aboriginal Studies, 1961-62. Mem., Commonwealth Council for Aboriginal Affairs, 1967-76; Technical Adviser, House of Reps Standing Cttee on Aboriginal Affairs, Commonwealth Parlt, 1974-75. Boyer Lectr, 1968. Mueller Medallist, ANZAAS, 1971; Cilento Medal, 1972. Hon. DLitt, ANU, 1972. *Publications:* The South Seas in Transition, 1953; On Aboriginal Religion, 1964; After the Dreaming, 1968; numerous articles in learned jls. *Recreations:* fishing, reading. *Address:* 75 Empire Circuit, Forrest, Canberra, ACT 2603, Australia. *T:* 731305. *Club:* Commonwealth (Canberra).

STANSFIELD, James Warden; *His Honour Judge Stansfield*; a Circuit Judge (formerly County Court Judge), since 1963; *b* 7 April 1906; *s* of James Hampson Stansfield, Sunny Lea, Wilmslow, Cheshire; *m* 1937, Florence Evelyn, *d* of Arthur Harry Holdcroft, Congleton, Cheshire; two *s* one *d. Educ:* King's School, Macclesfield; Sidney Sussex College, University of Cambridge. BA 1927; LLB 1928; MA 1935. Called to the Bar, Inner Temple, 1929; practised Northern Circuit. Contested (C) Platting Division of Manchester, 1935. Served War of 1939-45: Royal Air Force, Middle East, and Staff of Judge Advocate-General; formerly RAFVR (Squadron Leader). Chairman: Manchester Licensing Planning Cttee, 1955-63; Manchester Mental Health Review Tribunal, 1962; Warrington Licensed Premises Cttee, 1970. *Recreations:* golf, walking. *Address:* Oak Lea, Victoria Road, Wilmslow, Cheshire. *T:* Wilmslow 23915.

STANSFIELD, Walter, CBE 1974; MC 1945; QPM 1969; Chief Constable of Derbyshire, since 1967; *b* 15 Feb. 1917; *er s* of Frederick and Annie Georgina Stansfield; *m* 1939, Jennie Margery Biggs; one *d. Educ:* Chartres, Eure et Loire, France; Heath Grammar Sch., Halifax. West Riding Constabulary, 1939-42, 1950-56, 1959-64 (Asst Chief Constable, 1962-64). Served War, 1942-46: commnd in RA (Field), 1943; Special Ops Exec., 1943-45. Control Commission (Germany), 1945-46; seconded to: Special Police Corps, Germany, 1946-50; Cyprus Police Force, 1956-59. Chief Constable of Denbighshire, 1964-67. Colonial Police Medal, 1959; OStJ 1974. Croix de Guerre (France), 1947. *Recreations:* music, photography, gardening. *Address:* Butterley Hall, Ripley, Derby DE5 3RS. *T:* Ripley 3551. *Clubs:* Special Forces; County (Derby).

STANSGATE, Viscountcy of (*cr* 1942, of Stansgate); title disclaimed by 2nd Viscount.

STANTON, Maj.-Gen. Anthony Francis, OBE 1955; *b* 6 Aug. 1915; *s* of Brig.-Gen. F. H. G. Stanton and Hilda Margaret (*née* Parkin); *m* 1943, Elizabeth Mary, *d* of John Reginald Blackett-Ord, Whitfield Hall, Hexham; one *s* two *d. Educ:* Eton Coll.; RMA Woolwich. Commissioned RA, 1936. Served in: India, 1936-41; ME, 1941-43; NW Europe, 1944-45; subseq. in Germany, Far East and UK; Imp. Def. Coll., 1962; COS, HQ Northern Comd, 1967-70, retired 1970. Col Comdt, RA, 1972-77. *Recreation:* country sporting pursuits. *Address:* Wooperton Hall, Alnwick, Northumberland. *T:* Wooperton 241. *Club:* Army and Navy.

STANTON, Blair R. H.; *see* Hughes-Stanton.

STANTON, Rev. John Maurice, MA; Rector of Chesham Bois, since 1973; *b* 29 Aug. 1918; *s* of Frederick William Stanton, MInstCE and Maude Lozel (*née* Cole); *m* 1947, Helen Winifred (*née* Bowden); one *s* two *d. Educ:* King's School, Rochester (King's Scholar); University College, Oxford (Gunsley Scholar in Science). 2nd Class Hons, Final Hon. Sch. of Nat. Science, 1947; MA 1947. Fellow of Chemical Society, 1947. Commissioned Royal Artillery, 1940, 92nd Field Regt, RA, 1940-43. ISLD, CMF, 1943-46. Assistant Master, Tonbridge School, 1947-59; Headmaster, Blundell's School, Tiverton, Devon, 1959-71; Curate, St Matthew's, Exeter, 1972. Ordained Deacon, 1952; Priest, 1953. *Recreations:* water colour painting (Mem. Royal Water Colour Soc.'s Art Club), gardening. *Address:* The Rectory, Chesham Bois, Amersham, Bucks HP6 5NA.

STANTON, Walter Kendall, MA, DMus Oxon; Hon. RCM; Emeritus Professor of Music, University of Bristol, 1958; *b* 29 Sept. 1891; *s* of W. B. Stanton; *m* 1931, Edith Monica Leslie Wood (*d* 1956). *Educ:* Choristers' Sch., Salisbury; Lancing Coll. Organ Scholar, Merton Coll., Oxford, 1909-13. Director of

Music, St Edward's Sch., Oxford, 1915-24, Wellington Coll., Berks, 1924-37; Reading Univ., 1927-37; Music Dir, Midland Region, BBC, 1937-45; Prof. of Music, Univ. of Bristol, 1947-58. President: Incorporated Society of Musicians, 1953 (Treasurer, 1959-71); Union of Graduates in Music, 1953-57. Private organist to Duke of Marlborough, 1912-14, 1918-20; City Organist, Bristol, 1956-58; Conductor, Bristol Choral Soc., 1958-60. Examiner in Music at Oxford, Durham and Edinburgh Universities and the University of Wales. Mem., Management Board, Bournemouth Symph. Orch., 1967 (Chm., 1967-68). Editor-in-Chief, BBC Hymn Book. Vice-President: Wilts Music Festival, 1974 (Chm., 1960-73); Wilts Rural Music Sch.; President: N Wilts Orchestra, 1966-; Childrens' Concerts, Salisbury, 1968-; Vice-Pres., Western Orchestral Soc., 1973-. *Address:* Hays, Sedgehill, Shaftesbury, Dorset. *T:* East Knoyle 543.

STANWAY, Rt. Rev. Alfred; President, Trinity Episcopal School for Ministry, Pittsburgh, since 1975; *b* 9 Sept. 1908; *s* of Alfred Stanway, Millicent, S Australia, and Rosa Dawson; *m* 1939, Marjory Dixon Harrison. *Educ:* Melbourne High Sch.; Ridley Coll., Melbourne; Australian Coll. of Theology (ThL (Hons), 1934); Melbourne Teachers Coll. MA (Lamb), 1951. Diocese of Melbourne: Curate of St Albans, 1935-36; Mission of St James and St John, 1936-37; Diocese of Mombasa: Missionary, Giriama District, 1937-44; Principal Kaloleni Sch., 1938-44; Acting Gen. Sec., Victorian Branch, Church Missionary Soc., 1941; Hon. CF, 1942-46; Missionary, Maseno District, 1944-45; Rural Dean of Nyanza, 1945-47; Examining Chaplain to Bishop of Mombasa, 1945-51; Sec. African Council and African Education Board, Diocese of Mombasa, 1948-50; Commissary to Bishop of Mombasa, 1949-51; Archdeacon and Canon of Diocese of Mombasa, 1949-51; Bishop of Central Tanganyika, 1951-71; Dep. Principal, Ridley Coll., Melbourne Univ., 1971-75. *Recreation:* chess. *Address:* 341 Henry Avenue, Sewickley, Pa 15143, USA. *T:* (412) 741-5252.

STANYER, Maj.-Gen. John Turner, CBE 1971 (OBE 1967); Director General of Supply Co-ordination, Ministry of Defence, since 1975; *b* 28 July 1920; *s* of late Charles T. Stanyer and late Mrs R. H. Stanyer; *m* 1942, Mary Patricia Pattie; three *s* four *d.* *Educ:* Latymer Upper Sch., Hammersmith. Served War, 2/Lieut The Middlesex Regt, 1941; Lieut to Captain, The Middlesex Regt, 1941-47: Iceland, France, Germany, Palestine. Captain, Royal Army Ordnance Corps, 1947; Student, Staff Coll., Camberley, 1951; AA&QMG, UN Force in Cyprus, 1966; Dir of Ordnance Services, BAOR, 1968-71; Commandant, Central Ordnance Depot, Bicester, 1971-73; Comdr, Base Orgn, RAOC, 1973-75, retired. Col Comdt, RAOC, 1977-. *Recreation:* sailing. *Address:* 36 Jack Straws Lane, Headington, Oxford. *T:* Oxford 68757. *Club:* Army and Navy.

STAPLES, Rev. Canon Edward Eric, CBE 1977 (OBE 1973); Chaplain to the Queen since 1973; Chaplain to the Anglican congregations in Helsinki and throughout Finland, in Moscow, Leningrad and elsewhere in the Soviet Union, and in Outer Mongolia, since 1964; Hon. Chaplain, British Embassy: Helsinki since 1967, Moscow since 1968, Ulan Bator since 1970; Hon. Lecturer, English History, University of Helsinki, since 1972; Hon. Canon of Gibraltar Cathedral, since 1974; *b* 15 Nov. 1910; *yr s* of Christopher Walter Staples and Esther Jane Staples; *m* 1962, Kate Ethel Thusberg (*née* Rönngren); two step *d.* *Educ:* Chichester Theol Coll. (earlier opportunities so misused that it is unwise to name the establishments concerned!). MA, PhD. Niger Company, 1932. Served with RNVR, 1939-46. Ordained 1948. Kt, Order of the Lion (Finland), 1976. *Recreations:* climbing, cricket (no longer actively), fishing, gardening, historical research. *Address:* Aarnivalkeantie 10 E, 00210 Espoo 10, Finland. *T:* Helsinki 467530; Suvisaari, Ruokavesi, Heinävesi, Finland. *Clubs:* MCC; Helsinki Cricket (Founder Mem.); Moscow Cricket (Founder Mem.).

STAPLES, Hubert Anthony Justin; HM Diplomatic Service; Counsellor and Consul-General, Bangkok, since 1974; *b* 14 Nov. 1929; *s* of Francis Hammond Staples, formerly ICS, and Catherine Margaret Mary Pownall; *m* 1962, Susan Angela Collingwood Carter; one *s* one *d.* *Educ:* Downside; Oriel Coll., Oxford. Served in RAF 1952-54 (Pilot Officer). Entered Foreign (later Diplomatic) Service, 1954; 3rd Sec., Bangkok, 1955; Foreign Office, 1959; 1st Sec., Berlin (Dep. Political Adviser), 1962; Vientiane, 1965 (acted as Chargé d'Affaires in 1966 and 1967); transf. to FO and seconded to Cabinet Office, 1968; Counsellor, UK Delegn to NATO, Brussels, 1971; acting Chargé d'affaires, Bangkok, 1975 and 1977. *Address:* c/o Foreign and Commonwealth Office, SW1. *Clubs:* Travellers'; Royal Bangkok Sports.

STAPLES, Sir John (Richard), 14th Bt *cr* 1628; *b* 5 April 1906; *s* of John Molesworth Staples (*d* 1948) and of Helen Lucy Johnstone, *yr d* of late Richard Williams Barrington; *S* kinsman, Sir Robert George Alexander Staples, 13th Bt, 1970; *m* 1933, Sybella, *d* of late Dr Charles Henry Wade; two *d.* Heir: *cousin* Thomas Staples [*b* 9 Feb. 1905; *m* 1952, Frances Ann Irvine]. *Address:* Butter Hill House, Dorking, Surrey.

STAPLETON, Sir Alfred; *see* Stapleton, Sir H. A.

STAPLETON, Air Vice-Marshal Deryck Cameron, CB 1960; CBE 1948; DFC; AFC; psa; British Aircraft Corporation Representative, CENTO Area, Teheran, since 1970; *b* 1918; *s* of John Rouse Stapleton, OBE, Sarnia, Natal; *m* 1942, Ethleen Joan Clifford, *d* of late Sir Cuthbert William Whiteside. *Educ:* King Edward VI Sch., Totnes. Joined RAF, 1936; served Transjordan and Palestine (AFC), 1937-39; War of 1939-45 (DFC). Middle East, N Africa, Italy. Asst Sec. (Air), War Cabinet Offices, 1945-46; Secretary, Chiefs of Staff Cttee, Ministry of Defence, 1947-49; OC RAF, Odiham, 1949-51; subsequently, Plans, Fighter Comd HQ; OC, RAF, Oldenburg (Germany); Plans, Bomber Comd HQ, 1957-60; Air Ministry, 1960-62; Dir, Defence Plans, Min. of Defence, 1963-64; AOC No 1 Group, RAF Bomber Command, 1964-66; Comdt, RAF Staff Coll., Bracknell, 1966-68. BAC Area Manager, Libya, 1969-70. Assoc. Fellow, British Interplanetary Soc., 1960. *Recreations:* most sports. *Address:* c/o National Westminster Bank, Haymarket, SW1. *Clubs:* Royal Air Force, White's.

STAPLETON, Sir (Henry) Alfred, 10th Bt *cr* 1679; *b* 2 May 1913; *s* of Brig. Francis Harry Stapleton, CMG (*d* 1956) (*g s* of 7th Bt), and Maud Ellen (*d* 1958), *d* of late Major Alfred Edward Wrottesley; *S* kinsman, 1977; *m* 1961, Rosslyne Murray, *d* of late Captain H. S. Warren, RN. *Educ:* Marlborough; Christ Church, Oxford. Served War of 1939-45, Oxfordshire and Bucks Light Infantry. *Recreations:* cricket umpiring, campanology. Heir: none. *Address:* Mereworth, Mill Lane, Donhead St Andrew, Shaftesbury, Dorset. *Clubs:* Garrick, MCC.

STAPLETON-COTTON, family name of **Viscount Combermere.**

STAREWICZ, Artur, 2 Orders of Banner of Labour (1st cl.); Polonia Restituta; and other orders; Ambassador of Poland to the Court of St James's, since 1971; *b* Warsaw, 20 March 1917; *m* 1947, Maria Rutkiewicz; two *s* two *d.* *Educ:* Warsaw Univ.; Institut Chimique de Rouen; Lvov Technical Univ., Charkov Chem. Inst., 1940-43. Chemical engr. Mem., revolutionary youth orgns incl. Communist Union of Polish Youth; arrested 1935 and 1936; studied in France, 1937-38; Soviet electrochemical ind., 1943-44; Mem., Polish Workers Party (PPR), 1944-48; worked in PPR Voivoidship Cttees: Rzeszow; Cracow; Warsaw; First Sec., Wroclaw, 1947-48; Polish United Workers Party (PZPR): Mem., 1948-; Head of Propaganda, Central Cttee, 1948-53; Sec., Central Council of Trade Unions, 1954-56; Alternate Mem., Central Cttee, 1954-59, Mem., 1959-71; Head of Press Office, 1957-63; Sec., Central Cttee, 1963-71. Dep. Editor-in-Chief, daily newspaper Trybuna Ludu, 1956. Mem., Seym, 1957-72; Chm., Polish Gp, Interparty Union. *Recreation:* acquatic sport. *Address:* Polish Embassy, 47 Portland Place, W1; Stepinska 49a 10, Warsaw, Poland.

STARK, Sir Andrew (Alexander Steel), KCMG 1975 (CMG 1964); CVO 1965; Deputy Under-Secretary of State, Foreign and Commonwealth Office, since 1976; *b* 30 Dec. 1916; *yr s* of late Thomas Bow Stark and of late Barbara Black Stark (*née* Steel), Fauldhouse, West Lothian; *m* 1944, Helen Rosemary, *er d* of Lt-Col J. Oxley Parker, *qv*; two *s* (and one *s* decd). *Educ:* Bathgate Acad.; Edinburgh Univ. MA (Hons), Eng. Lit, Edinburgh, 1938. Served War of 1939-45, 2nd Lieut Green Howards, 1940; Capt. 1942; Major 1945. Entered Foreign Service, 1948, and served in Foreign Office until 1950; 1st Secretary, Vienna, 1951-53; Asst Private Sec. to Foreign Secretary, 1953-55; Head of Chancery: Belgrade, 1956-58; Rome, 1958-60; Counsellor: FO, 1960-64; Bonn, 1964-68; attached to Mission to UN with rank of Ambassador, Jan. 1968; British Mem., Seven Nation Cttee on Reorganisation of UN Secretariat; seconded to UN, NY, as Under-Secretary-General, Oct. 1968-1971; HM Ambassador to Denmark, 1971-76. Grosses Verdienstkreuz, German Federal Republic, 1965; Grand Cross, Order of the Dannebrog, Denmark, 1974. *Recreations:* ski-ing, tennis. *Address:* 41 Eaton Place, SW1. *T:* 01-235 7624; Fambridge Hall, White Notley, Essex. *T:* Braintree 83117. *Clubs:* Travellers', MCC; Royal Danish Yacht.

STARK, Dame Freya (Madeline), DBE 1972 (CBE 1953); *d* of late Robert Stark, sculptor, Ford Park, Chagford, Devon; *m* 1947, Stewart Perowne, *qv.* *Educ:* privately in Italy; Bedford

College, London University; School of Oriental Studies, London. Engaged on Govt service in Middle East and elsewhere, 1939-45. Awarded Back Grant, 1933, for travel in Luristan; Triennial Burton Memorial Medal from Royal Asiatic Society, 1934; Mungo Park Medal from Royal Scottish Geographical Society, 1936; Founder's Medal from Royal Geographical Society, 1942; Percy Sykes Memorial Medal from R Central Asian Soc., 1951. Sister of the Order of St John of Jerusalem, 1949. LLD Glasgow Univ., 1951; DLitt Durham, 1971. *Publications:* Bagdad Sketches, 1933, enlarged edition, 1937; The Valleys of the Assassins, 1934; The Southern Gates of Arabia, 1936; Seen in the Hadhramaut, 1938; A Winter in Arabia, 1940; Letters from Syria, 1942; East is West, 1945; Perseus in the Wind, 1948; Traveller's Prelude, 1950; Beyond Euphrates, 1951; The Coast of Incense, 1953; Ionia: a Quest, 1954; The Lycian Shore, 1956; Alexander's Path, 1958; Riding to the Tigris, 1959; Dust in the Lion's Paw, 1961; The Journey's Echo, 1963; Rome on the Euphrates, 1966; The Zodiac Arch, 1968; Space, Time and Movement in Landscape, 1969; The Minaret of Djam, 1970; Turkey: a sketch of Turkish History, 1971; Letters (ed Lucy Moorehead): vol. 1, The Furnace and the Cup, 1914-1930, 1974; vol. 2, The Open Road 1930-35, 1975; vol. 3, The Growth of Danger, 1976; Vol. 4, The Bridge of the Levant 1940-1943, 1977; A Peak in Darien, 1976. *Recreations:* travel, mountaineering and embroidery. *Address:* Via Canova, Asolo (Treviso), Italy; c/o John Murray, 50 Albemarle Street, W1.

STARKE, Hon. Sir John Erskine, Kt 1976; **Hon. Mr Justice Starke;** Judge of Supreme Court of Victoria, Australia, since 1964. Admitted to Victorian Bar, 1939; QC 1955; Judge, 1946. *Address:* Supreme Court, Melbourne, Victoria 3000, Australia; Mount Eliza, Victoria, Australia.

STARKE, Leslie Gordon Knowles, CBE 1953; *b* 23 May 1898; *s* of William and Martha Starke; *m* 1929, Joan Mary Davidson; no *c. Educ:* Andover Grammar School; University College, Southampton; Queen's College, Oxford. Served European War, 1914-18, RE (Signal Service), 1918. Entered Government Actuary's Dept, 1919; Ministry of Food, 1939-46 (Director of Statistics and Intelligence, 1943-46); Principal Actuary and Establishment Officer, Government Actuary's Dept, 1946-58; Deputy Government Actuary, 1958-63. *Recreations:* gardening, walking. *Address:* Brack Mound House, Castle Precincts, Lewes, East Sussex. *T:* Lewes 4139.

STARKER, Janos; concert cellist, recording artist; Distinguished Professor of Music, Indiana University, since 1958; *b* 5 July 1924; *s* of F. Sandor and M. Margit; *m* 1944, Eva Uranyi; one *d*; *m* 1960, Rae D. Busch; one *d. Educ:* Franz Liszt Academy of Music, Budapest; Zrinyi Gymnasium, Budapest. Solo cellist: Budapest Opera and Philh., 1945-46; Dallas Symphony, 1948-49; Metropolitan Opera, 1949-53; Chicago Symphony, 1953-58; numerous recordings. Grand Prix du Disque, 1948; George Washington Award. Holds an Hon. Doctorate of Music, 1961. *Publications:* Cello Method: an organised method of string playing, 1963; Bach Suites, 1971; Cadenzas, 1976; many articles in various magazines. *Recreations:* writing, swimming, ping-pong. *Address:* Indiana University Music Department, Bloomington, Ind 47401, USA.

STARKEY, Sir John (Philip), 3rd Bt *cr* 1935; *b* 8 May 1938; *s* of Sir William Randle Starkey, 2nd Bt, and Irene Myrtle Starkey (*née* Francklin) (*d* 1965); *S* father, 1977; *m* 1966, Victoria Henrietta Fleetwood, *y d* of Lt-Col Christopher Fuller, TD; one *s* three *d. Educ:* Eton College; Christ Church, Oxford. Sloan Fellow, London Business School. *Recreation:* cricket. *Heir: s* Henry John Starkey, *b* 13 Oct. 1973. *Address:* Norwood Park, Southwell, Notts. *T:* Southwell 812762. *Club:* MCC.

STARLEY, Hubert Granville, CBE 1946; FIMI; Chairman: Starley Marine, Shepperton, Middlesex, since 1974; Starleys Estates Ltd; *b* Skipton, 16 April 1909; *s* of late Hubert Ernest and Fanny Starley, Coventry; great nephew of J. K. Starley, founder of Rover Co.; *g g s* of James Starley of Coventry, inventor of the bicycle and differential gear; *m* 1933, Lilian Amy Heron, Bournemouth; one *s* one *d. Educ:* Ermysteds; Skipton, Yorks. Man. Dir, 1963-72, Vice-Chm., 1972-73, Champion Sparking Plug Co. Ltd; Assistant to Lord Beaverbrook, Minister of Supply, 1941; Advisor to War Office and Air Ministry on Stores Packaging, 1943; Hon. Chairman Anglo-American Packaging Exhibition Committee, 1944; Member Barlow Mission to the USA, 1944; Hon. Chm., Motor Industry Jubilee Committee, 1946; Society of Motor Manufacturers and Traders, Ltd: Chm., Accessory and Component Manufrs' Cttee, 1945-46, 1953-55, 1961-62; Mem. Council Management Cttees, 1953-73; Mem., General Purposes Cttee, 1968-72; Vice-Pres., 1972-73. Chm., Fellowship of the Motor Industry, 1969-70; Pres., Cycle

and Motor Cycle Assoc., 1970 (Mem., 1950-75); Trustee, Nat. Motor Mus., Beaulieu, 1973-77; Hon. Chm. Inter-Services Packaging Cttee, MoD, 1958-65; Founder, Mem. Council and Dir, Aims of Industry, Ltd, 1942-71, Vice-Pres., 1972-77. Vice-Pres., Inst. of Motor Industry, 1973-75; Mem. Council, CBI, 1970-75; Councillor, Aeronautical Educn Trust, 1970-77. Hon. Chm., Home Office Mobile Crime Prevention Cttee, 1968-69. Past Pres. and Patron, Twickenham Conservative Assoc. Master, Livery Company of Coachmakers and Coach Harness Makers, 1966-67; Pres., Pickwick Bicycle Club, 1954. Hon. Pageant Master and Organiser, History of British Motoring Cavalcade, Lord Mayor's Show, 1964; Hon. Organiser, 6 day Cycle Race, Earl's Court, 1967. *Address:* Rothesay House, London Road, Twickenham TW1 1ES. *T:* 01-892 5187. *Clubs:* Carlton, Royal Automobile, Royal Thames Yacht; Royal Motor Yacht (Sandbanks, Poole).

STARLING, Brigadier John Sieveking, CBE 1945; retired; *b* 18 Jan. 1898; *o s* of late Prof. Ernest H. Starling, CMG, MD, FRS, and Florence, *d* of late Sir Edward Sieveking; *m* 1st, 1934, Vivian Barbara, *d* of late Henry J. Wagg, OBE (marriage dissolved 1948); one *s*; 2nd, 1948, Marion, *d* of late A. G. Pool, and *widow* of C. A. Morell-Miller. *Educ:* University College School; Royal Military Academy; Trinity College, Cambridge. Commissioned 2nd Lt RA, 1916; served European War, France and Flanders, 1916-18 (wounded twice); normal career of a Regimental Officer in UK, Egypt and India. Attached French Army, 1939; served France and Flanders, Middle East and Italy, 1939-46 (despatches, wounded, CBE); retired from Regular Army as Hon. Brig., 1948. *Recreations:* fishing, shooting, sailing. *Address:* Le Hurel, Trinity, Jersey, CI. *T:* 61066. *Club:* Army and Navy.

STASSEN, Harold Edward; lawyer, politician, educator, United States; Partner in law firm Stassen, Kostos and Mason; Chairman, International Law Committee of Philadelphia Bar Association, 1973; *b* W St Paul, Minn, 13 April 1907; *s* of William Andrew Stassen and Elsie Emma Mueller; *m* 1929, Esther G. Glewwe; one *s* one *d. Educ:* Univ. of Minnesota Coll. (BA 1927; LLB 1929); Law School. Has several hon. degrees. Admitted to Minnesota Bar, 1929; practised South St Paul; County Attorney, Dakota County, 1930-38; thrice elected Governor of Minnesota, 1939-43; resigned for service with Navy; Lt Comdr, USN; Comdr on staff of Admiral Halsey in South Pacific, 1943-44; Asst Chief of Staff, 1944; Capt., USN; released to inactive duty, 1945. One of US delegates to San Francisco Conference, drafting and signing UN Charter, 1945. Pres., Minnesota Young Republicans; Delegate to Republican Convention, 1936; Temporary Chairman and Keynoter of Republican National Convention and floor manager for Wendell Wilkie, 1940; twice elected National Chairman National Governors' Conference, and of Council of State Governments, 1940-41. President, University of Pennsylvania, 1948-53. President International Council of Religious Education, 1942, 1950; Vice-Pres. and a Founder, Nat. Council of Churches, 1951-52; President, Div. of Christian Educ. of Nat. Council of Churches, 1953-. Director Foreign Operations Admin., 1953-55; Special Assistant to the President for Disarmament, 1955-58; Dep. US Rep. on Disarmament Commn, UN, 1955-58. Chief Consultant to ME Tech. Univ., Ankara, 1958; Mem., Nat. Security Council, 1953-58. Delivered Godkind Lectures on Human Rights, Harvard Univ., 1946; candidate for Republican nomination for President of US, 1948 and 1952. Chm., World Law Day, Geneva, 1968. Bronze Star, 1944; Legion of Merit, Six Battle Stars (Western Pacific campaign), 1945. Baptist. Mason. *Publications:* Where I Stand, 1947; Man was meant to be Free, 1951. *Address:* (office) 2300 Two Girard Plaza, Philadelphia, Pennsylvania 19102, USA.

STATHAM, Sir Norman, KCMG 1977 (CMG 1967); CVO 1968; HM Diplomatic Service; Ambassador to Brazil, since 1977; *b* Stretford, Lancs, 15 Aug. 1922; *s* of Frederick William and Maud Statham; *m* 1948, Hedwig Gerlich; two *s* one *d. Educ:* Seymour Park Council School, Stretford; Manchester Grammar School; Gonville and Caius College, Cambridge (MA). Intelligence Corps, 1943-47; Manchester Oil Refinery Ltd and Petrochemicals Ltd, 1948-50; Foreign Service, 1951: Foreign Office, 1951; Consul (Commercial), New York, 1954-58; First Secretary (Commercial), Bonn, 1958-63; Administrative Staff College, Henley, 1963; Foreign Office, 1964; Counsellor, Head of European Economic Integration Dept, 1965-68, 1970-71; Consul-General, São Paulo, 1968-70; Minister (Economic), Bonn, 1971-75; Asst Under Sec. of State, FCO, 1975; Dep. Under Sec. of State, FCO, 1975-77. *Recreations:* gardening, hill-walking, reading. *Address:* c/o Foreign and Commonwealth Office, SW1; Underhill House, Underhill Park Road, Reigate, Surrey. *Clubs:* Travellers'; Lancashire County Cricket.

STATON, Air Vice-Marshal William Ernest, CB 1947; DSO and Bar, 1940; MC 1918; DFC and Bar, 1918; *b* 1898; *m* 1st, 1919, Norah Carina Workman (*d* 1969); two *s*; 2nd, 1973, Jean Patricia Primrose (*née* Richardson). Served European War, 1914-19 (despatches); War of 1939-45 (despatches); Wing Comdr, 1939; Group Capt., 1940; Actg Air Commodore, 1941; Air Vice-Marshal, 1950; SASO Singapore, 1942; prisoner of war, Japan, 1942-45 (despatches); ADC to the King, 1940-46; AOC No. 46 Group, 1945-47; Commandant Central Bomber Establishment, 1947-49; Air Officer-in-Charge of Administration, Technical Training Command, 1949-52; retired 1952. Helper, RAF Benevolent Fund, 1952-. Chm. RAF Small Arms Assoc., 1947-52; Capt. British Shooting Teams, Olympic Games, 1948 and 1952. Ex-Mem. of Councils; Internat. Shooting Union, Stockholm; Nat. Rifle Assoc.; Nat. Small Bore Rifle Assoc.; Brit. Olympic Assoc. (1952-57). *Address:* Wildhern, Creek End, Emsworth, Hants. *Club:* Emsworth Sailing (Flag Officer, 1968; Commodore, 1972-).

STAUGHTON, Christopher Stephen Thomas Jonathan Thayer, QC 1970; a Recorder of the Crown Court, since 1972; *b* 24 May 1933; *yr s* of late Simon Thomas Samuel Staughton and Edith Madeline Jones; *m* 1960, Joanna Susan Elizabeth, *er d* of late George Frederick Arthur Burgess; two *d. Educ:* Eton Coll. (Scholar); Magdalene Coll., Cambridge (Scholar). 2nd Lieut, 11th Hussars PAO, 1952-53; Lieut, Derbyshire Yeomanry TA, 1954-56. George Long Prize for Roman Law, Cambridge, 1955; BA 1956; MA 1961. Called to Bar, Inner Temple, 1957. Mem., Senate of the Inns of Court and the Bar, 1974-. Chm., St Peter's Eaton Square Church of England Sch., 1974-. *Publication:* (Jt Editor) The Law of General Average (British Shipping Laws vol. 7), 1964, new edn, 1975. *Recreations:* bridge, growing dahlias. *Address:* 11 Wilton Street, SW1. *T:* 01-235 5791; Sarratt Hall, Sarratt, Herts. *T:* King's Langley 62698. *Club:* Brooks's.

STAVELEY, Martin Samuel, CMG 1966; CVO 1966; CBE 1962 (MBE 1955); *b* 3 Oct. 1921; fourth *s* of late Herbert Samuel Staveley and Edith Ellen Staveley (*née* Shepherd); *m* 1942, Edith Eileen Baker; one *s* two *d. Educ:* Stamford School; Trinity College, Oxford. Appointed Cadet, Colonial Administrative Service, Nigeria, 1942; Secretary, Development and Welfare Organisation in the West Indies, 1946-57; Secretary to Governor-General, Federation of the West Indies, 1958-62; Administrator, British Virgin Islands, 1962-67; HM Diplomatic Service, 1967-74; Home Civil Service, 1974-. *Recreations:* golf, music. *Address:* The Cottage Farm House, Great Bentley, Essex.

STAVELEY, Rear-Adm. William Doveton Minet; Flag Officer Carriers and Amphibious Ships, and NATO Commander, Carrier Striking Group Two, since 1977; *b* 10 Nov. 1928; *s* of late Adm. Cecil Minet Staveley, CB, CMG, and Margaret Adela (*née* Sturdee); *m* 1954, Bettina Kirstine Shuter; one *s* one *d. Educ:* West Downs, Winchester; RN Colls, Dartmouth and Greenwich. Entered Royal Navy as Cadet, 1942; Midshipman, HMS Ajax, Mediterranean, 1946-47; Sub-Lieut/Lieut, HM Ships Nigeria and Bermuda, S Atlantic, 1949-51; Flag Lieut to Adm. Sir George Creasy, C-in-C Home Fleet, HM Ships Indomitable and Vanguard, 1952-54; Staff, Britannia, RNC, Dartmouth, 1954-56; HM Yacht Britannia, 1957; First Lieut, HMS Cavalier, Far East, 1958-59; Lt-Comdr, 1958; RN Staff Coll., 1959; Staff, C-in-C Nore and Flag Officer Medway, 1959-61; Comdr 1961; Sen. Officer, 104th and 6th Minesweeping Sqdn, HMS Houghton, Far East, 1962-63; Comdr, Sea Trng, Staff of Flag Officer, Sea Trng, Portland, 1964-66; comd HMS Zulu, ME and Home Station, 1967; Captain 1967; Asst Dir, Naval Plans, Naval Staff, 1967-70; Command: HM Ships Intrepid, Far and ME, 1970-72; Albion, Home Station, 1972; RCDS, 1973; Dir of Naval Plans, Naval Staff, 1974-76; Flag Officer, Second Flotilla, 1976-77. Member: Royal Naval Sailing Assoc.; Royal Yachting Assoc.; Royal Nat. Rose Soc. A Younger Brother of Trinity House, 1973. *Recreations:* gardening, shooting, tennis, sailing. *Address:* Old Graingers, Plaxtol, Sevenoaks, Kent TN15 0QB. *Club:* Royal Naval and Royal Albert Yacht (Portsmouth).

STAWELL, Maj.-Gen. William Arthur Macdonald, CB 1945; CBE 1944; MC 1917; *b* 22 Jan. 1895; *s* of G. C. Stawell, ICS; *m* 1926, Amy, *d* of C. W. Bowring, New York; one *s. Educ:* Clifton College; RMA, Woolwich. Served European War, 1914-21, France, Greek Macedonia, Serbia, Bulgaria, Turkey (wounded, MC); 2nd Lieut 1914; Temp. Captain, 1916-17; Acting Major, Mar.-April 1917 and 1918-19; Captain, 1917; Major 1929; Lieut-Col 1937; Col 1940; Brig. 1940. GSO3 War Office, 1931-32; Brigade Maj., Aldershot, 1932-35; DAAG India, 1935-37; CRE 1937-40; AA and QMG Feb.-July 1940; GSO1 July-Nov. 1940; DDMI War Office, 1940-42; Brig., Comdr Home Forces, Feb.-Nov. 1942; Brig. General Staff, Home Forces, 1942-43; MEF

and CMF, 1943-45 (CBE, CB); Temp. Maj.-Gen. 1943-45; Deputy Chief of Operations UNRRA, Nov. 1945-Aug. 1946; Deputy Chief Intelligence Division, CCG, 1947-48; retired. *Recreations:* yachting, golf. *Address:* Park Hill, Oulton, near Lowestoft, Suffolk. *T:* Lowestoft 730322. *Clubs:* Army and Navy; Royal Norfolk and Suffolk Yacht.

STAYNER, Brig. Gerrard Francis Hood, CB 1945; CBE 1943 (OBE 1941); psc; retired; late Inf.; *b* 29 July 1900; 2nd *s* of Hewlett James Stayner and Mabel Palmer, Llanstephan, Teignmouth, Devon; *m* 1927, Leslie Edna, 2nd *d* of Horace and Diana Imber; no *c. Educ:* Cheltenham College; RMC Sandhurst. 2nd Lieut Leicestershire Regiment, 1919; served with Sudan Defence Force, 1925-35; Eritrean Campaign (OBE); Malta 1942-43 (CBE); Italy 1944-45 (CB, Legion of Merit Degree of Officer, USA); seconded to UNRRA Oct. 1945; Dep. Chief of Mission for Supply and Distrib., UNRRA Greece, 1945-46. OC Troops and Brigadier i/c Administration, Fortress HQ Gibraltar, 1950-53; retd 1953. Controller, Airborne Forces Security Fund, 1962-66. *Address:* 6 Lansdowne House, Lansdowne Road, W11 3LP. *T:* 01-727 4829.

STEAD, Christina Ellen; Fellow in Creative Arts, Australian National University, Canberra, since 1969; *b* 17 July 1902; *d* of Ellen Butters and David George Stead; *m* William J. Blake (*d* 1968). *Educ:* Sydney Univ., NSW. In business: London, 1928-29, Paris, 1930-35. Cinema: Senior Writer, MGM, Hollywood, Calif, 1943. Instructor, Workshop in the Novel, New York Univ., 1943-44. *Publications:* Short Story Collection: Salzburg Tales, London, 1934, NY, 1935, Melbourne, 1966. Novels: Seven Poor Men of Sydney, London and NY, 1935, Sydney and London, 1966 (new edn, 1970); The Beauties and Furies, London and NY, 1936; House of All Nations, London and NY, 1938, NY 1972; The Man who Loved Children, London, 1941, NY, 1940, new edn 1965, London 1966; For Love Alone, NY, 1944, London, 1945, new edn, New York, 1965, new edn, London, 1966, Sydney, 1969; Letty Fox, Her Luck, NY, 1946, London, 1947; A Little Tea, A Little Chat, NY, 1948; The People with the Dogs, Boston, 1951; Dark Places of the Heart, New York, 1966; The Little Hotel, 1974; Miss Herbert, the Suburban Wife, NY, 1976; The Puzzleheaded Girl, novellas, 1967; short stories: in Southerly, 1963; in Kenyon Review, Saturday Evening Post, 1965; in Meanjin, 1968, 1970; in Hemisphere, 1970; in New Yorker, 1970; in Commentary, 1971; in Partisan Review, 1971; in Overland, 1972. *Address:* c/o Laurence Pollinger, Ltd, 18 Maddox Street, W1.

STEAD, Rev. Canon George Christopher; Ely Professor of Divinity, Cambridge University, since 1971; Professorial Fellow, King's College, Cambridge, since 1971; Canon Residentiary of Ely Cathedral, since 1971; *b* 9 April 1913; *s* of Francis Bernard Stead, CBE, and Rachel Elizabeth, *d* of Rev. Canon G. C. Bell; *m* 1958, Doris Elizabeth Odom; two *s* one *d. Educ:* Marlborough Coll.; King's Coll., Cambridge (scholar). 1st cl. Classical Tripos Pt I, 1933; Pitt Scholar, 1934; 1st cl. Moral Science Tripos Pt II, 1935; BA 1935, MA Cantab 1938; New Coll., Oxford (BA 1935); Cuddesdon Coll., Oxford, 1938. Ordained, 1938; Curate, St John's, Newcastle upon Tyne, 1939; Fellow and Lectr in Divinity, King's Coll., Cambridge, 1938-48; Asst Master, Eton Coll., 1940-44; Fellow and Chaplain, Keble Coll., Oxford, 1949-71 (MA Oxon 1949). *Publications:* contributor to: Faith and Logic, 1957; New Testament Apocrypha, 1965; Divine Substance, 1977; articles and reviews in Jl of Theological Studies, Vigiliae Christianae. *Recreations:* walking, sailing, music. *Address:* The Black Hostelry, Ely, Cambs.

STEAD, Gilbert; Professor Emeritus of Physics in the University of London since 1953; Consultant Physicist Emeritus to Guy's Hospital since 1953; *b* 3 Feb. 1888; *s* of late Richard Stead, Folkestone; *m* 1916, Margaret (*d* 1976), *d* of late Thomas Gallimore, Leamington; one *s* two *d. Educ:* Bradford Grammar School; Clare College, Cambridge (Scholar). 1st Class Nat. Sci. Tripos, Pt I, 1908, Pt II, 1909; BA 1909; MA 1913; DSc (London), 1940; Assistant Demonstrator, Cavendish Laboratory, 1910; attached to HM Signal School, Portsmouth, 1915-19; Reader in Physics, Guy's Hospital Medical School, University of London, 1923-38, Professor of Physics, 1939-53; Honorary Consulting Physicist to Guy's Hospital, 1948-53; Governor of Guy's Hospital Medical School, 1948-53; University Lecturer in Physics as applied to Medical Radiology, Cambridge, 1925-38; Sec. for Cambridge Diploma in Medical Radiology, 1927-42; FInstP; FRSA; Hon. Member of Indian Radiological Assoc.; Member British Institute of Radiology, Pres., 1947-48. Hon. Mem., RCR; Fellow of Cambridge Philosophical Society; Member Hospital Physicists' Association (President, 1951-52; Hon. Member 1960). *Publications:* Elementary Physics, 1924; Notes on Practical Physics, 1939; various original papers in Proc. Roy. Soc., Philosophical

Magazine, Journ. Institution of Electrical Engineers, Proc. Cambridge Philosophical Soc. *Address:* Flat 8, Coombe Court, Station Approach, Tadworth, Surrey KT20 5AL. *T:* Tadworth 2466.

STEAD, Ralph Edmund, FCA, FCMA; Chairman, Eastern Region, British Gas Corporation, since 1977; *b* 7 Jan. 1917; *s* of Albert Stead and Mabel Stead; *m* 1946, Evelyn Annie Ness; two *s* two *d*. *Educ:* Manchester Grammar Sch.; Ilford County High Sch. FCA 1949; FCMA 1952. Served War, RASC, 1940-46. Asst Divl Accountant, Cambridge Div., Eastern Gas Bd, 1949-50; N Eastern Gas Board: Asst Chief Accountant, 1950-53; Group Accountant, Bradford Gp, 1953-57; N Western Gas Board: Gp Accountant, Manchester Gp, 1957-61; Gen. Man., West Lancs Gp, 1961-65; Head of Management Services, 1966-71; Dir of Finance, 1971-73; Dep. Chm., Eastern Reg., British Gas Corp., 1973-77. *Recreations:* golf, gardening, reading. *Address:* 1 Cashio Lane, Letchworth, Herts. *T:* Letchworth 71218.

STEAD, Robert, CBE 1965; retired as Controller, BBC North Region, 1958-69; *b* 10 Aug. 1909; *s* of Charles Fearnley Stead and Mary Ellen Taylor; *m* 1932, Constance Ann Sharpley; two *s*. *Educ:* Morley Gram. Sch. In Journalism, 1926-40; served in RN, 1940-45. Talks Producer, BBC North Region, 1946-48; Head of North Region Programmes, 1948-53; BBC Australian Representative, 1953-57. *Recreations:* golf, gardening, theatre. *Address:* Orchard Close, Wilmslow, Cheshire. *T:* Wilmslow 25536.

STEADMAN, Ralph Idris; freelance cartoonist; illustrator; *b* 15 May 1936; *s* of Lionel Raphael Steadman (English), and Gwendoline (Welsh); *m* 1st, 1959, Sheila Thwaite (marr. diss. 1971); two *s* two *d*; 2nd, 1972, Anna Deverson; one *d*. *Educ:* Abergele Grammar Sch.; London Coll. of Printing and Graphic Arts. Apprentice, de Havilland Aircraft Co., 1952; Cartoonist, Kemsley (Thomson) Newspapers, 1956-59; freelance for Punch, Private Eye, Telegraph, during 1960s. Retrospective exhibition, Nat. Theatre, 1977. D and AD Gold Award (for outstanding contribution to illustration), 1977, and Silver Award (for outstanding editorial illustration), 1977. *Publications:* (with Frank Dickens) Fly Away Peter, 1961; (with Mischa Damjan): The Big Squirrel and the Little Rhinoceros, 1962; The False Flamingoes, 1963; The Little Prince and the Tiger Cat, 1964; (with Richard Ingrams) The Tale of Driver Grope, 1964; (with Fiona Saint) The Yellow Flowers, 1965; (with Mischa Damjan) Two Cats in America, 1968; (with Tariq Ali) The Thoughts of Chairman Harold, 1968; Jelly Book, 1968; Still Life with Raspberry; collected drawings, 1969; The Little Red Computer, 1970; Dogs Bodies, 1971; Bumper to Bumper Book, 1973; Two Donkeys and the Bridge, 1974; Flowers for the Moon, 1974; The Watchdog and the Lazy Dog, 1974; America: drawings, 1975; America: collected drawings, 1977; Cherrywood Cannon, 1978; designed and printed, Steam Press Broadsheets; *illustrated:* Love and Marriage, 1964; Where Love Lies Deepest, 1964; Alice in Wonderland, 1967; Midnight, 1967; Fear and Loathing in Las Vegas, 1972; Contemporary Poets set to Music series, 1972; Through the Looking Glass, 1972; Night Edge: poems, 1973; The Poor Mouth, 1973; John Letts Limericks, 1974; The Hunting of the Snark, 1975. *Recreations:* gardening, collecting, writing, fishing. *Clubs:* Chelsea Arts; City Golf.

STEARN, Dr William Thomas; botanical consultant; retired as Senior Principal Scientific Officer, Department of Botany, British Museum (Natural History), 1976; Hon. Botanical Curator, Linnean Society, since 1959; Editor, Annales Musei Coulandris, since 1976; *b* 16 April 1911; *e s* of late Thomas Stearn, Cambridge; *m* 1940, Eldwyth Ruth Alford, *d* of late Roger R. Alford, Tavistock; one *s* two *d*. *Educ:* Cambridge High Sch. for Boys; part-time research at Botany Sch., Cambridge; apprentice antiquarian bookseller, Bowes & Bowes, Cambridge, 1929-32. Librarian, Royal Horticultural Soc., 1933-41, 1946-52. Served RAF, in Britain, India and Burma, 1941-46. Botanist, British Museum (Natural History), 1952-76. Hon. Sec., Internat. Cttee for Nomenclature of Cultivated Plants, 1950-53; former Council Member: Botanical Soc. of British Isles (Vice-Pres., 1973-77); British Soc. for History of Science (Vice-Pres., 1969-72); British Soc. for History of Medicine; Field Studies Council; Garden History Soc. (Founder Mem., 1965; Pres., 1977-); Linnean Soc. (Vice-Pres., 1961-62); Ray Soc. (Vice-Pres., 1964-67, 1970-73, Pres., 1974-77); Richmond Scientific Soc. (Pres., 1969-71); Soc. for Bibliography of Natural History (Founder Mem., 1936, Hon. Mem., 1976); Systematics Assoc. Masters Meml Lectr, 1964; Sandars Reader in Bibliography, Cambridge, 1965; Vis. Prof., Dept of Botany and Agricl Botany, Univ. of Reading, 1977-. Has lectured in Australia, Austria, Germany, Greece, Holland, Jamaica, Papua New Guinea, Sweden, USA; botanical collections made in

Europe, Jamaica, USA, Australia. Royal Horticultural Society: Hon. Fellow, 1946; Veitch Meml Medal, 1964; Victoria Medal of Honour, 1965. FLS 1934; FIBiol 1967 (MIBiol 1965); Hon. Member: Kungl. Vetenskaps-Societeten i Uppsala, 1967; Svenska Linné-Sällskapet, 1971. Hon. Fellow, Sidney Sussex Coll., Cambridge, 1968. DSc *hc* Leiden, 1960; Hon. ScD Cantab, 1967; FilDr *hc* Uppsala, 1972. Boerhaave Commem. Medal, Leiden, 1969; Linnaeus Medal, Royal Swedish Acad. of Sciences, 1972; Linnaean Gold Medal, Linnean Soc., 1976. *Publications:* (with H. B. D. Woodcock) Lilies of the World, 1950; (with E. Blatter and W. S. Millard) Some Beautiful Indian Trees, 1955; Introduction to the *Species Plantarum* of Carl Linnaeus, 1957; Early Leyden Botany, 1961; Botanical Latin, 1966, 2nd edn 1973; Three Prefaces on Linnaeus and Robert Brown, 1967; Humboldt, Bonpland, Kunth and Tropical American Botany, 1968; (with C. N. Goulimis and N. Goulandris) Wild Flowers of Greece, 1968; (with A. W. Smith) Gardener's Dictionary of Plant Names, 1972; (with W. Blunt) Captain Cook's Florilegium, 1973; (with M. Page) Culinary Herbs, 1974; (with W. Blunt) Australian Flower Paintings of Ferdinand Bauer, 1976; numerous bibliographical, biographical, botanical and horticultural contribs to learned jls (listed in Biological Jl of Linnean Soc. vol. 8, 1976), RHS Dictionary of Gardening, Chambers Encyclopaedia, Dictionary of Scientific Biography, Flora Europaea, etc. *Recreations:* gardening, talking. *Address:* 17 High Park Road, Kew Gardens, Richmond, Surrey.

STEDMAN, family name of **Baroness Stedman.**

STEDMAN, Baroness *cr* 1974 (Life Peer), of Longthorpe, Peterborough; **Phyllis Stedman,** OBE 1965; a Baroness-in-Waiting (a Government Whip), since 1975; *b* 14 July 1916; *o d* of Percy and Emmie Adams; *m* 1941, Henry William Stedman. *Educ:* County Grammar Sch., Peterborough. Branch Librarian, Peterborough City Council, 1934-41; Group Officer, National Fire Service, 1942-45. County Councillor: Soke of Peterborough, 1946-65; Huntingdon and Peterborough, 1965-74; Cambridgeshire, 1974-76; Vice-Chm., Cambridgeshire County Council, 1974-76. Board Member, Peterborough Development Corp., 1972-76. *Address:* Green Pastures, Grove Lane, Longthorpe, Peterborough PE3 6ND.

STEDMAN, Sir George (Foster), KBE 1957; CB 1948; MC 1919; Civil Service, retired; *b* 1895; *s* of James Mathew and Marguerite Adele Stedman, Leytonstone, Essex; *m* 1925, Olive May Scrivener; one *d* (one *s* decd). *Educ:* Mercers' School, London; Trinity Coll., Camb. Served European War, 1914-18, with York and Lancaster Regt, France and Macedonia (MC, despatches twice). Entered Civil Service, Ministry of Transport, 1920; Private Secretary to Minister, 1926-30; Under-Sec., 1946. Deputy Secretary, Ministry of Transport and Civil Aviation, 1954-57. *Address:* Fosters, Main Street, Oxton, Southwell, Notts.

STEEDMAN, Air Chief Marshal Sir Alexander McKay Sinclair, (Sir Alasdair Steedman), KCB 1976 (CB 1973); CBE 1965; DFC 1944; UK Military Representative to NATO, since 1977; *b* 29 Jan. 1922; *s* of late James Steedman, Hampton-on-Thames, Mddx, and late Anna McKay Steedman (*née* Sinclair), Fulford, York; *m* 1945, Dorothy Isobel, *d* of Col Walter Todd, Knockbrex, Kirkcudbright; one *s* two *d*. *Educ:* Hampton Grammar School. Entered RAF, 1941; Flt Comdr, 241 Sqdn, 1942-44, 2 Sqdn, 1945; Air Min., 1945-48; comd 39 Sqdn, Khartoum, 1948-49; comd 8 Sqdn, Aden, 1949-50; CFS Course, 1951; Trng Sqdn Comdr, 201 AFS, 1951-53; Syndicate Ldr, Aircrew Selection Centre, Hornchurch, 1953-54; psa 1955; Chief Instructor, CFS (B), 1955-57; Comdr Royal Ceylon Air Force, Katanyake, 1957-59; jssc 1959-60; Directing Staff, Jt Services Staff Coll., 1960-62; Comdr RAF Lyneham, 1962-65; Gp Capt. (Ops), HQ Transport Comd, 1965; CAS, Royal Malaysian Air Force, 1965-67; Dir of Defence Plans (Air), MoD, 1967-68. Dir, Defence Ops Staff, MoD, 1968-69; ACAS (Policy), MoD, 1969-71; SASO, Strike Comd, 1971-72; Comdt, RAF Staff Coll., 1972-75; Air Member for Supply and Organisation, 1976-77. ARAeS 1960; FBIM 1976. Johan Mangku Negara (Malaysia), 1967. *Recreations:* golf, tennis, squash, motoring. *Address:* c/o Barclays Bank Ltd, 7 High Street, Hampton-on-Thames, Middlesex; Villa du Lac, 243 Chaussée de la Hulpe, 1170 Bruxelles. *Clubs:* Royal Air Force; Royal Selangor (Kuala Lumpur).

STEEDMAN, Maj.-Gen. John Francis Dawes, CMG 1963; CBE 1945; MC 1918; *b* 30 Nov. 1897; *s* of John Francis Steedman, FRCS, Streatham; *m* 1931, Olive Ursula (Kaisar-i-Hind Medal, Silver Jubilee Medal, 1935), *d* of Earl Oliver Besant, Reading; one *d*. *Educ:* Bradfield; RMA, Woolwich. 2nd Lt, RE, 1916; Served European War, 1914-18, Salonika (MC, despatches twice); Afghanistan, 1919; Waziristan (MBE, despatches), 1920-21; Khajuri (despatches), 1930-31; Malaya, as CRE 11 Ind. Div. (Despatches), 1941-42; Comdt QVO Madras Sappers and Miners, 1942-43; Burma, as CE 33 Ind. Corps and XII Army (CBE, despatches), 1944-46; Chief Engineer, Southern Command, India, 1946; Engineer-in-Chief, Dominion of India, 1947; Chief Engineer, Southern Command, UK, 1948-51; ADC to HM King George VI, 1949-51; retired as Hon. Maj.-Gen., 1951; Director of Works, Commonwealth War Graves Commission, 1951-63. *Address:* Valley Farm House, East Knoyle, Salisbury, Wiltshire. *T:* East Knoyle 329.

STEEDMAN, Martha, (Mrs R. R. Steedman); *see* Hamilton, M.

STEEGMULLER, Francis; writer; *b* New Haven, Conn, 3 July 1906; *s* of Joseph Francis Steegmuller and Bertha Tierney; *m* 1st, 1935, Beatrice Stein (decd); 2nd, 1963, Shirley Hazzard. *Educ:* Columbia University, New York. Member, Nat. Inst. of Arts and Letters, 1966. Chevalier de la Légion d'Honneur, 1957. *Publications:* O Rare Ben Jonson (under pseudonym Byron Steel), 1928; Flaubert and Madame Bovary, 1939, reprinted 1947, 1958, 1968; States of Grace, 1947; Maupassant, 1950, repr. 1973; Blue Harpsichord (under pseudonym David Keith), 1950; The Two Lives of James Jackson Jarves, 1953; (trans. and ed) The Selected Letters of Gustave Flaubert, 1954; La Grande Mademoiselle, 1955; The Christening Party, 1961; Le Hibou et la Poussiquette, 1961; Apollinaire, 1963, repr. 1973; Papillot, Clignot et Dodo (with Norbert Guterman), 1965; (trans.) Gustave Flaubert, Intimate Notebook, 1967; Cocteau, 1970 (Nat. Book Award 1971); Stories and True Stories, 1972 (trans. and ed) Flaubert in Egypt, 1972; (ed) Your Isadora, 1975; works published abroad include a translation of Madame Bovary (1957) and many short stories and articles in The New Yorker. *Address:* 200 East 66th Street, New York, NY 10021, USA. *Clubs:* Athenæum; Century; Coffee House (New York).

STEEL, Byron; *see* Steegmuller, Francis.

STEEL, Brig. Charles Deane, CMG 1957; OBE 1941; *b* 29 May 1901; *s* of Dr Gerard Steel, JP, Leominster, Herefs; *m* 1932, Elizabeth Chenevix-Trench (*d* 1973); two *s*. *Educ:* Bedford; Royal Military Academy, Woolwich. Prize Cadetship, Woolwich, 1919. Armstrong Memorial Prize, 1921. Commissioned 2nd Lieut RE, 1921; served in India (Bengal Sappers and Miners), 1924-29; Staff College, Camberley, 1936-37; War of 1939-45; E Africa and Abyssinia, 1941; Western Desert, 1942; POW, 1942; Switzerland, 1943; Dep. Head, British Mil. Mission to Greece, 1945-49; Dep. Mil Sec., 1949-52; retd Feb. 1952; Head of Conference and Supply Dept, Foreign Office, 1952-64; Head of Accommodation Department Diplomatic Service, 1965-67. *Recreations:* golf, and gardening. *Address:* Little Hill, Nettlebed, Oxfordshire. *T:* Nettlebed 287. *Clubs:* Naval and Military, Shikar.

STEEL, Very Rev. David; Minister of St Michael's, Linlithgow, 1959-76, now Minister Emeritus; Moderator of the General Assembly of the Church of Scotland, 1974-75; *b* 5 Oct. 1910; *s* of John S. G. Steel and Jane Scott, Hamilton; *m* 1937, Sheila Martin, Aberdeen; three *s* two *d*. *Educ:* Peterhead Academy; Robert Gordon's Coll., Aberdeen; Aberdeen Univ. MA 1932, BD 1935. Minister of Church of Scotland: Denbeath, Fife, 1936-41; Bridgend, Dumbarton, 1941-46; Home Organisation Foreign Mission Secretary, 1946-49; Minister of Parish of East Africa and of St Andrew's, Nairobi, 1949-57; Associate Minister, St Cuthbert's, Edinburgh, 1957-59. Chm. of Governors Callendar Park Coll. of Educn. Vice-Pres., Boys' Brigade. Hon. DD Aberdeen 1964; Hon. LLD Dundee, 1977. *Publications:* History of St Michael's, Linlithgow; contrib. theological and church jls. *Recreation:* trout fishing. *Address:* 13A Chamberlain Road, Edinburgh. *T:* 031-447 2180. *Clubs:* Scottish Liberal (Edinburgh); Edinburgh Amateur Angling
See also Rt Hon . D . M . Steel.

STEEL, Sir David (Edward Charles), Kt 1977; DSO 1940; MC 1945; TD; Chairman: British Petroleum Company, since 1975; *b* 29 Nov. 1916; *s* of late Gerald Arthur Steel, CB; *m* 1956, Ann Wynne, *d* of Maj.-Gen. C. B. Price, CB, DSO, DCM, VD, CD; one *s* two *d*. *Educ:* Rugby School; University Coll., Oxford, BA. Inns of Court Regt, 1938; Commissioned 9 QR Lancers, 1940; served 1940-45 France, Middle East, North Africa, Italy (DSO, MC, despatches thrice). Admitted a Solicitor, June 1948; Linklaters and Paines, 1948-50; Legal Dept of The British Petroleum Co. Ltd, 1950-56; Pres. BP (N Amer.) Ltd, 1959-61; Man. Dir, Kuwait Oil Co. Ltd, 1962-65; Man. Dir, 1965-75 and a Dep. Chm., 1972-75, BP. Governor, Rugby Sch. Order of TAJ III, 1974. *Address:* 18 Princes Gate, SW7; Queen Wood Farm, Christmas Common, near Watlington, Oxon. *Clubs:* Cavalry and Guards; Links (New York).

STEEL, Rt. Hon. David (Martin Scott), PC 1977; MP (L) Roxburgh, Selkirk and Peebles since 1965; Leader of the Liberal Party, since 1976; journalist and broadcaster; *b* 31 March 1938; *s* of Very Rev. Dr David Steel, *qv*; *m* 1962, Judith Mary, *d* of W. D. MacGregor, CBE, Dunblane; two *s* one *d*. *Educ:* Prince of Wales School, Nairobi, Kenya; George Watson's College and Edinburgh University. MA 1960; LLB 1962. President: Edinburgh University Liberals, 1959; Students' Representative Council, 1960. Visited Soviet Union, 1961. Asst Secretary, Scottish Liberal Party, 1962-64; Youngest Member of 1964-66 Parliament; Liberal Chief Whip, 1970-75; Mem. Parly Delegn to UN Gen. Assembly, 1967; Sponsor, Private Member's Bill to reform law on abortion, 1966-67; Pres., Anti-Apartheid Movement of GB, 1966-69; Chm., Shelter, Scotland, 1969-73. Member: Acton Trust, 1970-; British Council of Churches, 1971-75; Council of Management, Centre for Studies in Social Policy, 1971-76; Adv. Council, European Discussion Centre, 1971-. BBC television interviewer in Scotland, 1964-65; Presenter of STV weekly religious programme, 1966-67, and for Granada, 1969, and BBC 1971-. *Publications:* Boost for the Borders, 1964; Out of Control, 1968; No Entry, 1969; The Liberal Way Forward, 1975; A New Political Agenda, 1976; contrib. to The Times, The Guardian, other newspapers and political weeklies. *Recreations:* angling, riding, motoring, gardening. *Address:* House of Commons, SW1A 0AA; Cherry Dene, Ettrick Bridge, Selkirkshire. *T:* Ettrick Bridge 253. *Club:* Scottish Liberal (Edinburgh).

STEEL, Major Sir (Fiennes) William Strang, 2nd Bt, *cr* 1938; DL; JP; Major (retired), 17/21st Lancers; Forestry Commissioner, 1958-73; *b* 24 July 1912; *e s* of Sir Samuel Steel, 1st Bt and of Hon. Vere Mabel (*d* 1964), *d* of 1st Baron Cornwallis; *S* father, 1961; *m* 1941, Joan, *d* of late Brig.-Gen. Sir Brodie Haldane Henderson, KCMG, CB, Braughing, Ware; two *s* (one *d* decd). *Educ:* Eton; RMC, Sandhurst; joined 17/21st Lancers, 1933; Major, 1941; retired, 1947. Convener, Selkirk CC, 1967-75. DL Selkirkshire, 1955, JP 1965. *Heir: s* Major Fiennes Michael Strang Steel, 17/21 Lancers [*b* 22 Feb. 1943; *m* 1977, Sarah Russell]. *Address:* Philiphaugh, Selkirk. *T:* Selkirk 21216. *Club:* Cavalry and Guards.

STEEL, Henry, CMG 1976; OBE 1965; HM Diplomatic Service; Legal Counsellor, Foreign and Commonwealth Office, since 1976; *b* 13 Jan. 1926; *yr s* of late Raphael Steel; *m* 1960, Jennifer Isobel Margaret, *d* of late Brig. M. M. Simpson, MBE; two *s* two *d*. *Educ:* Christ's Coll., Finchley; New Coll., Oxford. BA Oxon 1950. Called to Bar, Lincoln's Inn, 1951; Legal Asst, Colonial Office, 1955; Senior Legal Asst, CO, 1960; Asst Legal Adviser, CRO, 1965; Legal Counsellor, FCO, 1967-73; Legal Adviser, UK Mission to UN, NY, 1973-76. Military Service, RASC and Intelligence Corps, 1944-47. *Address:* c/o Foreign and Commonwealth Office, SW1; Wentways, Priestwood, Meopham, Kent. *T:* Meopham 812183.

STEEL, Sir James, Kt 1967; CBE 1964; Lord-Lieutenant of Tyne and Wear, since 1974; President, Northern Group, Royal Institute of Public Administration; Chairman, Furness Withy & Co. Ltd; Director: Acrow Ltd; Dunlop Industrial Group; Northern Shipbuilding & Industrial Holdings Ltd; Hall Russell & Co. Ltd; Rea Brothers Ltd (Deputy Chairman); Stag Line Ltd; North of England Building Society; Newcastle upon Tyne Local Board, Barclays Bank; Aeronautical and General Instruments Ltd; Shipping Investment Trust Ltd; *b* 19 May 1909; *s* of Alfred Steel and Katharine (née Meikle); *m* 1935, Margaret Jean MacLauchlan; two *s* two *d*. *Educ:* Trent College. Steel & Co. Ltd: Apprentice, 1927; Employee, 1931; Director, 1935; Dep. Man. Dir, 1942; Chm. and Man. Dir, 1956. Mem., Commn on the Constitution, 1969-73. Trustee, Sir John Priestman Charity Trust; Mem. Council, Durham University. Chairman: British Productivity Council, 1966-67; Textile Council, 1968-72; Pres., YMCA, Sunderland; Vice-President: Young Enterprise Nat. Council; NE Div., Nat. Council of YMCAs; Jt Pres., Council of the Order of St John for Northumbria. Liveryman, Worshipful Co. of Founders. FBIM. JP Sunderland, 1964; Durham: DL 1969; Sheriff 1972-73. KStJ 1975. *Recreations:* ornithology, photography. *Address:* Fawnlees Hall, Wolsingham, County Durham DL13 3LW. *T:* 307. *Club:* Junior Carlton.

STEEL, Sir (Joseph) Lincoln (Spedding), Kt 1965; JP; formerly Director Charterhouse Investment Trust; Chairman, Triplex Holdings Ltd, 1961-66 (Deputy Chairman, 1960-61); *b* 24 March 1900; *s* of late Comdr Joseph Steel, RD, RNR, and Esther Alice (née Spedding); *m* 1st, 1928, Cynthia Smith (*d* 1929); one *s* ; 2nd, 1938, Barbara I. T., *y d* of late Colonel S. G. Goldschmidt; one *s*. *Educ:* Christ's Hospital; St John's College, Oxford (Open Scholar, MA). Served RE, 1918-19. Joined Brunner Mond & Co. Ltd, 1922; Delegate Dir, ICI (Alkali) Ltd,

1932; Man. Dir, Alkali Div. of ICI Ltd, 1942; Chm. Alkali Div. of ICI Ltd, 1943; Dir, Imperial Chemical Industries Ltd, 1945-60, retd. Chm. British Nat. Cttee of International Chamber of Commerce, 1951-63; Pres. Internat. Chamber of Commerce, 1963-65; Vice-Pres. 1951-63; Hon. Pres. 1965-; Chairman Overseas Cttee of FBI, 1950-65; Member: Council of CBI, 1965-68; EFTA Consultative Cttee, 1960-69. Leader, UK Industrial Mission to W Indies, 1952. Member Cheshire County Council, 1937-45; JP Cheshire, 1939; JP Bucks, 1960; Gen. Comr for Income Tax, Burnham District, 1968-75. FRSA 1963. *Recreations:* gardening, walking, travel. *Address:* The Warren, 87 Bois Lane, Chesham Bois, Amersham, Bucks. *T:* Amersham 6406. *Clubs:* Carlton, Beefsteak.

STEEL, Robert; Secretary-General, Royal Institution of Chartered Surveyors, since 1968; *b* 7 April 1920; *e s* of late John Thomas Steel, Wooler, Northumberland; *m* 1943, Averal Frances, *d* of Arthur Pettitt; one *s* one *d. Educ:* Duke's Sch., Alnwick, Northumb.; Univ. of London (BSc 1945); Gray's Inn (Barrister, 1956). Surveyor, 1937-46; Asst Sec., Under Sec., Royal Instn of Surveyors, 1946-61; Dir of Town Development, Basingstoke, 1962-67. Sec.-Gen., Internat. Fedn of Surveyors, 1967-69, Vice-Pres., 1970-72; Sec., Commonwealth Assoc. of Surveying and Land Economy, 1969-; Sec., Aubrey Barker Trust, 1970-; Member: South East Economic Planning Council, 1974-76; Council, British Consultants Bureau, 1977-. Chm., Geometers Liaison Cttee, EEC, 1972-. Hon. Editor, Commonwealth Surveying and Land Economy. FRICS; FRGS. *Publications:* on Property Law; contrib. professional jls. *Recreations:* mountain walking, travel, music. *Address:* 2 Oaklands Close, Romsey Road, Winchester, Hants. *T:* Winchester 68050. *Clubs:* Athenæum, Royal Commonwealth Society.

STEEL, Prof. Robert Walter, BSc, MA Oxon; Principal, University College of Swansea, since 1974; *b* 31 July 1915; *er s* of late Frederick Grabham and Winifred Barry Steel; *m* 1940, Eileen Margaret, *er d* of late Arthur Ernest and Evelyn Beatrice Page, Bournemouth; one *s* two *d. Educ:* Great Yarmouth Grammar Sch.; Cambridge and County High School for Boys; Jesus College, Oxford (Open Exhibitioner in Geography). RGS Essay Prize, 1936. Drapers' Co. Research Scholarship for Geography, 1937-39, for work in Sierra Leone; Departmental Lectr in Geography, Univ. of Oxford, 1939-47; Naval Intelligence Div., Admiralty, 1940-45; attached to Sociological Dept of W African Inst. of Arts, Industry and Social Science as geographer to Ashanti Social Survey, Gold Coast, 1945-46; University of Oxford: Univ. Lectr in Colonial Geography, 1947-56; Lectr in Geography, St Peter's Hall, 1951-56; Official Fellow and Tutor in Geography, Jesus Coll., 1954-56; Univ. of Liverpool: John Rankin Prof. of Geography, 1957-74; Dean, Faculty of Arts, 1965-68, Pro-Vice-Chancellor, 1971-73. Murchison Grant (RGS), 1948; Council RGS, 1949-53, 1968-71; Inst. of Brit. Geographers: Council, 1947-60; Actg Sec., 1948, Asst Sec., 1949-50; Hon. Editor of Publications, 1950-60; Vice-Pres., 1966-67, Pres. 1968, Hon. Mem. 1974; President: Section E (Geography), British Association for the Adv. of Science, 1966; African Studies Assoc. of the UK, 1970-71 (Vice-Pres., 1969-70); Geographical Assoc., 1973. Dir, Commonwealth Geographical Bureau, 1972-; Mem., Inter-Univ. Council for Higher Educn Overseas, 1974-; Chm., Universities Council for Adult Educn, 1976-; Vice-Pres., Royal African Soc., 1977-; Council, Nat. Inst. of Adult Educn, 1977-. Vis. Prof., Univ. of Ghana, 1964; Canadian Commonwealth Vis. Fellow, Carleton Univ., 1970; Supernumerary Fellow, Jesus Coll., Oxford, 1974-75. Hon. Prof., UCW, 1974. Hon. DSc Salford, 1977. *Publications:* ed (with A. F. Martin), and contrib. to, The Oxford Region: a Scientific and Historical Survey, 1954; ed (with C. A. Fisher), and contrib. to Geographical Essays on British Tropical Lands, 1956; ed (with R. M. Prothero), and contrib. to Geographers and the Tropics: Liverpool Essays, 1964; ed (with R. Lawton), and contrib. to Liverpool Essays on Geography: a Jubilee Collection, 1967; (with Eileen M. Steel) Africa, 1974; ed, Human Ecology and Hong Kong: report for the Commonwealth Human Ecology Council, 1975; articles, mainly on tropical Africa, in Geographical Jl and other geog. jls. *Address:* Danver House, 236 Gower Road, Swansea SA2 9JJ. *T:* Swansea 22329. *Club:* Royal Commonwealth Society.

STEEL, Major Sir William Strang; see Steel, Major Sir F. W. S.

STEELE, Prof. Alan John; Professor of French, University of Edinburgh, since 1972; *b* Bellshill, Lanark, 11 April 1916; *s* of John Steele, MA, BD, and Anne (*née* Lawson); *m* 1947, Claire Alice Louise Belet; one *s* one *d. Educ:* Royal Grammar School, Newcastle upon Tyne; Blyth Secondary School, Northumberland; Universities of Edinburgh, Grenoble and Paris. MA 1st Cl. Hons in French Language and Literature,

Vans Dunlop Schol., Univ. of Edinburgh, 1938. Served War of 1939-45, at sea with 4th Maritime AA Regt, RA, 1941-42; commissioned, 1942, with 64th LAA Regt RA in Algeria, Italy and Greece. Lecturer in French, University of Edinburgh, 1946, Prof. of French Literature, 1961-72. Chairman: Scottish Central Cttee for Modern Languages; Assoc. of Univs. Profs of French, 1974-75. Editor, Modern Language Review (French Section). Chevalier, Légion d'Honneur, 1973. *Publications:* (with R. A. Leigh) Contemporary French Translation Passages, 1956; Three Centuries of French Verse, 1956, new edn, 1961; contrib. to Cahiers de l'Assoc. Internat. des Etudes françaises, Modern Language Review. *Recreation:* golf. *Address:* 17 Polwarth Grove, Edinburgh EH11 1LY. *T:* 031-337 5092.

STEELE, (Francis) Howard, FCGI, BSc(Eng), CEng, FIEE, FIERE; Managing Director, Sony Broadcasting, since 1978; *b* Gt Bookham, Surrey, 23 Sept. 1929; *s* of Arnold Francis Steele, MBE, and Florence Anne Winifred Steele; *m* 1953, Elaine Barnes Steele (*née* Mason); two *s. Educ:* Mill Hill School; Imperial College of Science and Technology. Engineer, Marconi Company, Chelmsford, 1952-57; Asst Engineer in Charge, Alpha Television Services, Birmingham, 1957-58; Head of Planning and Installation Dept, 1958-61, Chief Engineer, 1961-66, ABC Television Ltd; Chief Engineer, ITA, 1966-69; Dir of Engineering, ITA, later IBA, 1969-77. Hon. Fellow, British Kinematograph, Sound and Television Soc., 1974. *Recreations:* motoring and sailing. *Address:* Little Thatch, Crawley, near Winchester, Hants.

STEELE, Frank Fenwick, OBE 1969; HM Diplomatic Service, retired; joined Kleinwort, Benson as Adviser, 1975; *b* 11 Feb. 1923; *s* of Frank Robert and Mary Fenwick Steele; *m* ; one *s* one *d. Educ:* St Peter's Sch., York; Emmanuel Coll., Cambridge (MA). Army, 1943-47. Joined HM Diplomatic Service, 1951; FO, 1951; Vice-Consul, Basra, 1951; Third, later Second Sec., Tripoli, 1953; Foreign Office, 1956; Second Sec., Beirut, 1958; FO, 1961; First Sec.: Amman, 1965; Nairobi, 1968; Counsellor and Dep. UK Rep., Belfast, 1971; FCO, 1973; retd 1975. *Recreation:* travel. *Address:* 9 Ashley Gardens, SW1. *T:* 01-834 7596. *Club:* Travellers'.

STEELE, Commander Gordon Charles, VC, RN, retired; Hon. Captain, RNR, 1949; Captain Superintendent of Thames Nautical Training College, HMS Worcester, off Greenhithe, 1929-57; Fellow of Institute of Navigation, 1951; *b* Exeter, 1892; *s* of late Captain H. W. Steele, RN, and S. M., *d* of Major-General J. C. Symonds, RMLI. *Educ:* Vale College, Ramsgate; HMS Worcester. Midshipman, Royal Navy Reserve; joined P & OSN Co. as cadet and served in RNR and P & O till outbreak of war; served in HM Submarines D8 and E22 and in Q ships; transferred to Royal Navy as Sub-Lieutenant for distinguished service in action, Aug. 1915; served in HMS Royal Oak as Lieut RN in Jutland, and in Iron Duke; commanded HM ships P63 and Cornflower, 1917-18; served in coastal motor boat raid on Kronstadt Harbour, Aug. 1919 (VC); specialised in anti-submarine duties; Naval Interpreter in Russian; retired list, 1931; served in HMS Osprey as Anti-Submarine Commander, and Inspector of Anti-Submarine Equipment, in War, 1939-45; a Younger Brother of Trinity House; Member Worshipful Company of Shipwrights; Freeman City of London; a Lay-Reader. Silver Jubilee Medal, 1977. *Publications:* Electrical Knowledge for Ships' Officers, 1950; The Story of the Worcester, 1962; To Me, God is Real, 1973; About My Father's Business, 1975; In My Father's House, 1976. *Address:* Winkleigh Court, Winkleigh, Devon. *Club:* East India, Sports and Public Schools.

STEELE, Lt-Col Harwood (Robert Elmes), MC; FRGS; Author and Journalist; at present engaged on History of Royal Canadian Mounted Police; *b* Fort Macleod, Alberta, Canada, 5 May 1897; *o s* of late Maj.-Gen. Sir S. B. Steele, KCMG, and Lady Steele (*née* de Lotbiniere Harwood), *d* of co-seigneur of Vaudreuil, Quebec. *Educ:* England, Canada and South Africa. Served European War, 1914-18 (Capt., MC, despatches); Capt. Winnipeg Grenadiers, 1915-26; Capt. 17th DYRC Hussars 1926; Major, 1929; Lieut-Colonel and OC 1938. Historian, Canadian Govt Arctic Expedition. CGS Arctic, 1925, to Far North; Asst Press Representative, CPR, 1925-27; lectured, with Govt endorsement, on RCM Police through Canada and Eastern US, 1928-30. Served War of 1939-45 in England, Northern Ireland, NW Frontier, India, 14th Army, East of Brahmaputra and GHQ, India Command; War Subst. Major 17/21 Lancers, 1939; Temp. Lt-Col 1944 (despatches). Lectured in England and Canada on India, Canada and RCMP, 1945-63. Hon. Chief, E Kootenay Indians (Canada), and other similar honours. *Publications:* Cleared for Action (Naval Poems), 1914;

The Canadians in France, 1915-18, 1920; Spirit of Iron, novel, 1923; I Shall Arise, novel, 1926; The Ninth Circle, novel, 1927; Policing the Arctic, history of RCMP in Far North, 1936; India: Friend or Foe? a political study, 1947; To Effect An Arrest, short stories of RCMP, 1947; Ghosts Returning (novel), 1950; The Marching Call, early life of Sir S. B. Steele, 1955; The Red Serge, short stories of RCMP, 1961; Royal Canadian Mounted Police: a short history, 1968; poems, short stories, broadcasts, articles. *Address:* Warenne Lodge, Pulborough, West Sussex. *Club:* Savage.

STEELE, Howard; *see* Steele, F. H.

STEELE, John Roderic; Deputy Secretary, Department of Trade, since 1976; *b* 22 Feb. 1929; *s* of late Harold Graham Steele and Doris Steele (*née* Hall); *m* 1956; two *s* two *d. Educ:* Queen Elizabeth Grammar Sch., Wakefield; Queen's Coll., Oxford (MA). Asst Principal, Min. Civil Aviation, 1951; Private Sec. to Parly Sec., MTCA, 1954; Principal, Road Trans. Div., 1957; Sea Transport, 1960; Shipping Policy, 1962; Asst Sec., Shipping Policy, BoT, 1964; Counsellor (Shipping), British Embassy, Washington, 1967; Asst Sec., Civil Aviation Div., DTI, 1971, Under-Sec., Space Div., 1973, Shipping Policy Div., 1974, Gen. Div., 1975, Dept of Trade. *Recreations:* normal. *Address:* 7 Kemerton Road, Beckenham, Kent. *Club:* Philippics.

STEELE, Kenneth Walter Lawrence, OBE 1967; KPM 1936; Chief Constable, Avon and Somerset Constabulary, since 1974; *b* 28 July 1914; *s* of Walter and Susan Steele, Godalming, Surrey; *m* 1940, Ursula, *d* of late Major J. N. Biggs-Davison, RA. *Educ:* Wellington Sch., Wellington, Somerset. Served War: with Somerset LI and Royal Northumberland Fusiliers, 1942-45. Asst Chief Constable, Buckinghamshire, 1953-55; Chief Constable: Somerset, 1955-66; Somerset and Bath, 1966-74. *Recreations:* golf, badminton, tennis. *Address:* Chief Constable's Office, Bristol BS99 7BH. *T:* Bristol 290721.

STEELE, Thomas; Member, Scottish Board, British Rail; *b* 15 Nov. 1905; *s* of late James Steele, miner; *m* 1939, Helen Thomson; two *s*. Stationmaster to 1945; MP (Lab) Lanark Division of Lanarkshire, 1945-50, West Dunbartonshire, 1950-70; Parliamentary Secretary, Ministry of National Insurance, 1946-50. Member GMC, 1965-75. *Address:* Windyridge, Lesmahagow, Lanark.

STEELE, Tommy, (Thomas Hicks); Actor; *b* Bermondsey London, 17 Dec. 1936; *s* of Thomas Walter Hicks and Elizabeth Ellen (*née* Bennett); *m* 1960, Ann Donoghue; one *d. Educ:* Bacon's Sch. for Boys, Bermondsey. First appearance on stage in variety, Empire Theatre, Sunderland, Nov. 1956; first London appearance, variety, Dominion Theatre, 1957; Buttons in Rodgers and Hammerstein's Cinderella, Coliseum, 1958; Tony Lumpkin in She Stoops to Conquer, Old Vic, 1960; Arthur Kipps in Half a Sixpence, Cambridge Theatre, London, 1963-64 and Broadhurst Theatre (first NY appearance), 1965; Truffaldino in The Servant of Two Masters, Queen's, 1969; Dick Whittington, London Palladium, 1969; Meet Me In London, Adelphi, 1971; London Palladium: The Tommy Steele Show, 1973; Hans Andersen, 1974 and 1977. Entered films in Kill Me Tomorrow, 1956; subseq. films include: The Tommy Steele Story; The Duke Wore Jeans; Tommy the Toreador; Touch It Light; It's All Happening; The Happiest Millionaire; Half a Sixpence; Finian's Rainbow; Where's Jack?. Composed and recorded, My Life, My Song, 1974. *Recreations:* football, painting. *Address:* c/o Talent Artists Ltd, 13 Bruton Street, W1X 8JY. *T:* 01-493 0343.

STEELE-PERKINS, Surgeon Vice-Admiral Sir Derek (Duncombe), KCB 1966 (CB 1963); KCVO 1964 (CVO 1954); FRCS; FRACS; *b* 19 June 1908; *s* of late Dr Duncombe Steele-Perkins, Honiton, Devon, and Sybil Mary Hill-Jones, Edinburgh; *m* 1937, Joan Boddan, Birkdale, Lancashire; three *d. Educ:* Allhallows School, Rousdon; Edinburgh University and College of Surgeons (Edin.). Entered RN, 1932; RN Hosp., Haslar, 1932; HMS Mantis, China, 1934-36; HMS Ganges, Shotley, 1936-38; HMS Vindictive, 1938-39; RN Hospitals: Haslar, 1939-40; Chatham, 1940-44; Sydney, Australia, 1944-46; Malta, 1946-50; RY Gothic, 1951-52; Chatham, 1952-59; Senior Surgical Specialist, RN Hosp., Bighi, Malta, Oct. 1959-61; Medical Officer-in-Charge, Royal Naval Hospital, Haslar, 1961; Command MO to C-in-C, Portsmouth, 1962-63; Medical Director of the Navy, 1963-66. FRSocMed Royal Commonwealth Tours, 1953-54, 1959. QHS 1961. CStJ. *Recreations:* sailing, fly-fishing, shooting. *Address:* c/o National Westminster Bank, Haven Road, Canford Cliffs, Dorset. *Club:* Army and Navy.

STEEN, Anthony David; MP (C) Liverpool Wavertree, since Feb. 1974; first Director of Neo Government Urban Renewal and Community Development Foundation, YVFF, 1968-June 1974, retd; *b* 22 July 1939; *s* of Stephen Nicholas Steen, *qv*; *m* 1965, Carolyn Padfield, educational psychologist; one *s* one *d. Educ:* Westminster Sch.; occasional student University Coll., London. Called to Bar, Gray's Inn, 1962; Practising Barrister, 1962-74, Defence Counsel, MoD. Founded Task Force to help London's old and lonely, with Govt support, 1964. Advisor to Federal and Provincial Govts of Canada on unemployment, student problems, youth and community work, 1972-73. Involved with detached youth work, Settlements, and a variety of community action projects in many parts of Britain, and has raised about £1 million for charity projects since 1964. Vice Pres., Liverpool Regional Fire Liaison Panel; Member: Council, VSO Management; Community Transport; Exec. Council, NPFA; Vice-Chm., Task Force. *Recreations:* piano, hill climbing, tennis, swimming, cycling. *Address:* 15 Sutherland Street, SW1. *T:* 01-828 3979; 15 Ullet Road, Liverpool L17 3BL. *T:* 051-733 2184. *Clubs:* Athenæum (Liverpool), Old Swan Conservatives; Wavertree Cricket, Kensington Close Swimming.

STEEN, Robert Elsworth, MD, Past President RCPI; FRCP Glasgow (Hon.); Hon. Consulting Pædiatrician: National Children's Hospital, Dublin; Monkstown Hospital, Dublin; Sunshine Home, Foxnock; Stewart's Hospital, Palmerstown; formerly Consulting Pædiatrician, St Kevin's Hospital, Dublin; sometime Professor of Pædiatrics, Dublin University; *b* 11 April 1902; *s* of David Miller Steen and Jane Elsworth (*née* Orr); *m* 1939, Elizabeth Margaret Cochrane; one *s* one *d. Educ:* St Andrew's College and Trinity College, Dublin. Graduated 1924; held following posts: Demonstrator in Biochemistry and Pathology, Dublin University; House Surgeon and House Physician, Monkstown Hospital, Dublin, and French Hospital, London; House Physician, Hospital for Sick Children, Great Ormond Street, London; Assistant Physician, Royal City of Dublin Hospital and Meath Hospital, Dublin; Physician, Dr Steeven's Hospital, Dublin, and Meath Hospital, Dublin; Medical Director, St Patrick's Infant Hosp. and Nursery Training Coll., Temple Hill, Blackrock; formerly Lecturer in Hygiene, Metropolitan School of Nursing, Dublin, and Pædiatrician to the Rotunda Hospital, Dublin and Royal Victoria Eye and Ear Hosp., Dublin. Fellow and late President Section of Pædiatrics, Royal Academy of Medicine in Ireland; late President: Irish Cardiac Soc.; Irish Pædiatric Assoc.; Dublin University Biological Assoc.; British Pædiatric Assoc.; Hon. Member, Assoc. of European Pædiatric Cardiologists; Sen. Member, Assoc. of Physicians of GB and Ireland; Extraordinary Member, British Cardiac Soc. Past Master, Knights of the Campanile, TCD. *Publications:* Infants in Health and Sickness; numerous publications in medical journals. *Recreations:* hunting, music, croquet, bridge. *Address:* Department of Pædiatrics, University of Dublin, National Children's Hospital, Harcourt Street, Dublin 2. *T:* Dublin 752355; Mountsandel, Carrickmines, Co. Dublin. *T:* 893184. *Clubs:* Kildare Street and University, Friendly Brother House (Dublin); Royal Irish Yacht; Dublin University Boat (Pres.).

STEEN, Stephen Nicholas; President, Smith & Nephew Associated Companies Ltd, since 1976 (Chairman, 1968-76); Chairman, British Tissues Limited, 1971-77; Director, Gala Cosmetics Group Ltd, since 1971; *b* 19 July 1907; *m* 1934; one *s* one *d.* Arthur Berton & Co. Ltd, 1943; Director, Smith & Nephew Associated Companies Ltd, 1958, Dep. Chm. 1962. Underwriting Member, Matthews Wrightson Pulbrook Ltd; called to the Bar, Gray's Inn, 1949. Mem., Ct of Patrons, RCS, 1973-. *Recreation:* golf. *Address:* (office) 2 Temple Place, WC2R 3BP. *T:* 01-836 7922. *Club:* Carlton.
See also A. D. Steen.

STEER, Francis William; Maltravers Herald Extraordinary since 1972; Archivist and Librarian to the Duke of Norfolk since 1956; Archivist to New College, Oxford, since 1965 and to College of Arms, 1969-77; Librarian of Chichester Cathedral; *b* Ashingdon, 10 Aug. 1912; *s* of William Francis Steer and Edith Caroline (*née* Todd); *m* 1934, Mabel Alice Holdstock; no *c. Educ:* Ashingdon; Southend-on-Sea High Sch.; privately. MA, FSA, FSA (Scot.), FRHistS. Asst Archivist, Essex Record Office, 1946-53; County Archivist: E and W Sussex, 1953-59; W Sussex, 1959-69; Archivist to Bp and Dean and Chapter of Chichester, 1953-69; Hon. Sec., Essex Archaeological Soc., 1953; Mem. Council, Sussex Arch. Soc., 1954-, President, 1973-77, Vice-Pres., 1977-; Editor, Sussex Archaeological Collections, 1959-73; Jt Literary Dir, Sussex Record Soc., 1958- (Mem. Council, 1954-); Hon. Sec., Marc Fitch Fund, 1956-; Mem. Exec. Cttee, Sussex Historic Churches Trust; served as mem. various cttees concerned with archives, local history, museums, etc. Citizen and Scrivener of London; Parish Clerk of St Benet,

Paul's Wharf, London; Mem., Parish Clerks' Co. Hon. MA Oxon, 1974; Hon. DLitt Sussex, 1974. OStJ 1967. *Publications:* Farm and Cottage Inventories of Mid-Essex, 1635-1749, 1950 (2nd edn 1969); History of the Dunmow Flitch Ceremony, 1951; (ed, with L. J. Redstone) Local Records, their nature and care, 1953; (with A. S. Duncan-Jones) The Story of Chichester Cathedral, 1955; John Philipot's Roll of the Constables of Dover Castle, 1956; Catalogue of the Ashburnham Archives, 1958; I am, my dear Sir, 1959; Records of the Corporation of Seaford, 1959; Catalogue of the Shiffner Archives, 1959; Catalogue of the Crookshank Collection, 1960; Samuel Tufnell of Langleys, 1960; Bibliotheca Norfolciana, 1961; Catalogue of the Mitford Archives, vol. 1, 1962, vol. 2, 1970; A Catalogue of Sussex Estate and Tithe Award Maps, vol. 1, 1962, vol. 2, 1968; The Hawkins Papers: a catalogue, 1962; Minute Book of the Common Council of Chichester, 1783-1826, 1963; The Maxse Papers: a catalogue, 1964; The Cobden Papers: a catalogue, 1964; Catalogue of the Lavington Archives, 1964; A Catalogue of the Earl Marshal's Papers at Arundel Castle, 1965; The Letters of John Hawkins and Samuel and Daniel Lysons, 1812-1830, 1966; The Wilberforce Archives: a catalogue, 1966; (with I. M. Kirby) Records of the Diocese of Chichester, vol. 1, 1966, vol. 2, 1967; Scriveners' Company Common Paper, 1357-1678, 1968; Arundel Castle Archives: a catalogue, vol. 1, 1968, vol. 2, 1973, vol. 3, 1976; (with N. H. Osborne) The Petworth House Archives, 1968; (with J. E. A. Venables) The Goodwood Estate Archives, vol. 1, 1970, vol. 2, 1972; The Life of St Philip Howard, 1971 (revised edn); Centenary of Arundel Cathedral: a monograph, 1973; History of the Worshipful Company of Scriveners, 1973; The Archives of New College, Oxford: a catalogue, 1974; An 18th Century Survey of Arundel Castle, 1976; numerous articles, reviews, monographs. *Recreations:* looking at flowers, reading, working, talking to friends. *Address:* 63 Orchard Street, Chichester, West Sussex. *T:* Chichester 83490. *Clubs:* Athenæum, City Livery.

STEER, Kenneth Arthur, MA, PhD, FRSE, FSA, FSAScot; Secretary, Royal Commission on the Ancient and Historical Monuments of Scotland, since 1957; *b* 12 Nov. 1913; *o s* of Harold Steer and Emily Florence Thompson; *m* 1941, Rona Mary Mitchell; one *d. Educ:* Wath Grammar School; Durham University. Research Fellowship, 1936-38. Joined staff of Royal Commission on Ancient and Historical Monuments of Scotland, 1938. Intelligence Officer in Army, 1941-45 (despatches twice). Monuments, Fine Arts and Archives Officer, North Rhine Region, 1945-46. Corresponding Member, German Archæological Inst.; Horsley Memorial Lecturer, Durham University, 1963; Rhind Lectr, 1968. Mem., Ancient Monuments Board for Scotland. Pres., Soc. of Antiquaries of Scotland, 1972-75. *Publications:* Late Medieval Monumental Sculpture in the West Highlands (with J. W. M. Bannerman), 1976; numerous articles in archæological journals. *Address:* 18 Esslemont Road, Edinburgh. *T:* 031-667 5167. *Club:* New (Edinburgh).

STEER, Rt. Rev. Stanley Charles; Bishop of Saskatoon, 1950-70; *s* of S. E. and E. G. Steer; *m* 1936, Marjorie Slater. *Educ:* Guildford Gram. Sch.; Univ. of Saskatchewan (B), Oxford Univ. (MA). Hon. DD: Wycliffe Coll., Toronto, 1947, Emmanuel Coll., Saskatoon, 1952; St Chad's Coll., Regina, 1964. Missionary at Vanderhoof, BC, 1929; Chaplain, St Mark's Church, Alexandria, 1931; Chaplain, University Coll., Oxford, 1932-33; St John's Hall, Univ. of London: Tutor, 1933; Vice-Principal, 1936. Chaplain, The Mercers' Company, City of London, 1937; Principal, Emmanuel Coll., Saskatoon, 1941; Hon. Canon of St John's Cathedral, Saskatoon, and CF (R of O), 1943. *Recreation:* tennis. *Address:* 2383 Lincoln Road, Victoria, BC, Canada. *T:* 592 9888.

STEER, Wilfred Reed, QC 1972; *b* 23 Aug. 1926; *s* of George William and Dorothy Steer; *m* 1953, Jill Park; one *s* one *d*, and two step *s. Educ:* Bede Collegiate Sch., Sunderland, Co. Durham; London Sch. of Economics. LLB (Lond.) 1949. Called to the Bar, Gray's Inn, 1950. *Address:* 51 Westgate Road, Newcastle upon Tyne. *T:* Newcastle upon Tyne 20541.

STEER, William Reed Hornby, DL, MA, LLB, Barrister-at-Law; Recorder of South Molton, 1936-51; Deputy Chairman, London County Council, 1948-49; Lt-Col in the Army (released); *b* 5 April 1899; *s* of late Rev. W. H. Hornby Steer, TD MA, JP; unmarried. *Educ:* Eton; Trinity College, Cambridge. Commissioned in Royal Field Artillery; served European War, France and Belgium; called to Bar, Inner Temple, 1922; joined Western Circuit; Standing Counsel to Commons, Open Spaces, and Footpaths Preservation Society; to Council for Preservation of Rural England; to National Smoke Abatement Society and to Pure Rivers Society; an Examiner in Law to Chartered Institute of Secretaries; Legal Member of Town Planning Inst.; Fellow of Royal Soc. of Health; Associate of Royal Institution of Chartered Surveyors; a representative for Hampstead on London County Council, 1931-52; a representative of London County Council on International Union of Local Authorities; Master of Worshipful Company of Turners, 1949-50; a Governor of Haberdashers' Aske's Schools and of Royal Free Hospital; a Governor and an Almoner of Christ's Hospital, Dep. Chm. Council of Almoners, 1970-; Chairman Children's Hospital, Hampstead; Vice-Chairman London Old Age Pensions Committee; Treasurer, London Soc.; Kt of Justice, Order of St John; Joint Hon. Secretary of League of Mercy; Gold Staff Officer at Coronation of King George VI; Inspector of Metropolitan Special Constabulary; Army Officers Emergency Reserve, 1938; Extra Regimentally Employed, Military Dept, Judge Advocate-General's Office, 1939; Deputy Judge Advocate-General, Malta, 1941-43; graded Assistant Adjutant-General, War Office, 1944; Staff Officer (I), Control Commission for Germany, 1945; Captain, 1939; Major, 1941; Lt-Col 1943; Member of Territorial Army and Air Force Association of the County of London. *Publications:* articles on the law relating to Highways; Assistant Editor of Glen's Public Health Act, 1936; Steer's Law of Smoke Nuisances, 1938, 2nd edn 1948; contributions to Lord Macmillan's Local Government Law and Administration. *Recreation:* sailing. *Address:* 71A Whitehall Court, SW1A 2EL. *T:* 01-930 3160. *Clubs:* United Oxford & Cambridge University, Carlton, Pratt's, MCC; Royal Corinthian Yacht (Burnham-on-Crouch).

STEERS, James Alfred, CBE 1973; MA; Professor Emeritus of Geography and Emeritus Fellow of St Catharine's College, Cambridge; Chairman, National Committee of Geography, 1967-72; Coastal Consultant to Conservation Committee of Council of Europe, 1968; Chairman: Coastal Conferences, 1966-67; *b* 8 Aug. 1899; *s* of J. A. Steers, Bedford; *m* 1942, Harriet, *d* of J. A. Wanklyn, Cambridge; one *s* one *d. Educ:* Elstow (Private) School, Bedford; St Catharine's Coll., Cambridge. Senior Geography Master, Framlingham Coll., 1921-22; elected Fellow of St Catharine's, 1925, subsequently Dean, Tutor and President, Univ. Demonstrator, 1926-27; Univ. Lecturer, 1927-49; Prof. of Geography, 1949-66; Member of the British Expedition to the Great Barrier Reefs, 1928; Leader of Geographical Expedition to the Reefs, 1936; Expedition to the Jamaica Cays, 1939; War Service, 1917-18; Vice-Pres., Royal Geographical Soc., 1959-63, 1967-72, Hon. Vice-Pres., 1972-, Hon. Mem., 1977-; Pres. Norfolk and Norwich Naturalists Soc., 1940-41; Pres., Section E British Association (Oxford), 1954; President, Inst. Brit. Geographers (Reading), 1956; President: Geographical Assoc., 1959; Estuarine and Brackish Water Science Assoc., 1977. Corresp. Mem., Royal Dutch Geographical Soc.; Hon. Mem., Ges. für Erdkunde Berlin; Member: Council of Senate, Cambridge, 1941-48; Wild Life Conservation Cttee; Nature Conservancy, 1949-54, 1957-66; Scientific Policy Cttee, 1949-66; Cttee for England, 1949-68, 1970-73; Nat. Parks Commn, 1966-66; Properties Cttee, Nat. Trust, until 1976; Hon. Adviser on Coastal Preservation to Ministry of Town and Country Planning and to Department of Health, Scotland; Departmental Cttee on Coastal Flooding, 1953; Advisory Committee... to improve Sea Defences, 1954-; Hydraulics Research Board, DSIR, 1957-61; Visiting Prof., Berkeley, Calif, 1959; Visiting Fellow, Aust. Nat. Univ., 1967. Hon LLD Aberdeen, 1971. Victoria Medal, RGS, 1960; Scottish Geographical Medal, 1969. *Publications:* Introduction to the Study of Map Projections, 1927, 15th edn 1970; The Unstable Earth, 1932 (new edn 1950); Editor and contrib. to Scolt Head Island, 1934, 2nd rev. edn, 1960; The Coastline of England and Wales, 1946 (2nd edn 1969); A Picture Book of the Whole Coast of England and Wales, 1948; The Sea Coast, 1953, 4th edn 1969; The Coast of England and Wales in Pictures, 1960; The English Coast and the Coast of Wales, 1966; Coasts and Beaches, 1969; Introduction to Coastline and Development, 1970; The Coastline of Scotland, 1973; Editor: new edns of P. Lake's Physical Geography, 1958; Vol. on Field Studies in the British Isles, Internat. Geog. Union. London meeting, 1964; Brit. Assoc. Advancement of Science, The Cambridge Region, 1965; Engl. edn of V. P. Zenkovitch, Processes of Coastal Development, 1967; papers on Coastal Physiography, Coral Islands, etc., in various scientific publications. *Recreations:* walking, philately, travel. *Address:* 47 Gretton Court, Girton, Cambridge CB3 0QN. *T:* Cambridge 76007. *Clubs:* Travellers', Geographical.

STEIL, John Wellesley, CMG 1951; MBE 1937; *b* 15 Aug. 1899; *s* of late Lt W. J. Steil, RN; *m* Annetta Elise (*d* 1961), 2nd *d* of late S. Fichat, Nairobi, Kenya; one *s* one *d. Educ:* Christ's Hospital, Horsham; Portsmouth Grammar School; Cadet Ship HMS Conway. Served European War, 1917-19, Harwich Force, HMTB 85, HMS Dragon, Malayan American Rubber Co., Malaya and Sumatra, 1920-24; Colonial Administrative Service,

Cadet, Uganda, 1925; Asst District Officer, 1927; District Officer, 1936; Provincial Comr, 1947, Senior Provincial Commissioner, 1949; Secretary for African Affairs, Uganda, MEC and MLC, 1950-51. Farming in WA, 1957-62. *Address:* The Weld Club, GPO Box B54, Perth, WA 6001, Australia. *Clubs:* Royal Commonwealth Society; Weld (Perth, WA).

STEIN, John, CBE 1970; Manager, Celtic Football Club, since 1965; *b* 5 Oct. 1922; *s* of George Stein and Jane Armstrong; *m* 1946, Jean McAuley; one *s* one *d*. *Educ:* Greenfield Public Sch., Lanarkshire. Miner, 1937-50; Professional Footballer, 1950-57; Coach, 1957-60; Manager: Dunfermline, 1960-64; Hibernians, 1964-65; Celtic, 1965-. Under his management, Celtic won: Scottish League Cup, 1965-66, 1966-67, 1967-68, 1968-69, 1969-70, 1974-75; Scottish Cup, 1964-65, 1966-67, 1968-69, 1970-71, 1971-72, 1973-74, 1974-75, 1976-77; European Cup, 1966-67; Scottish League Championship, 1965-74 inclusive, 1976-77. *Recreations:* golf, bowling. *Address:* 9 Southwood Drive, Glasgow G44 5SH.

STEIN, John Alan, CIE 1943; *b* 31 Oct. 1888; *s* of late Hamilton Stein; *m* 1st, 1920, Phyllis (*d* 1949), *d* of Lindsay Horne, Aberdeen; one *d*; 2nd, Vera Craig, *d* of T. H. Patterson, Sunderland. *Educ:* Bedford School; City and Guilds College, London Univ. Joined Indian Service of Engineers, 1912, apptd to Bengal; served with Indian Sappers and Miners in Mesopotamia, Palestine, and Syria, 1916-19 (wounded); Executive Engineer, 1919; Under Secretary, Govt of Bengal, 1926; Superintending Engineer, 1931-41; Chief Engineer, Communications and Works Dept, Bengal, 1941-43; Chief Engineer, Civil Supplies Dept, Bengal, 1945-47. Handicapper, Royal Calcutta Turf Club, 1947-52. *Address:* 99 Peterborough Road, SW6 3BU. *Clubs:* East India, Devonshire, Sports and Public Schools; Royal Calcutta Turf.

STEIN, Prof. Peter Gonville, FBA 1974; JP; Regius Professor of Civil Law in the University of Cambridge, and Fellow of Queens' College, since 1968; *b* 29 May 1926; *o s* of late Walter Stein, MA, Solicitor, and Effie Stein (*née* Walker); *m* 1953, Janet Mary, PhD, *yr d* of late Clifford Chamberlain, Desborough, Northants; three *d*. *Educ:* Liverpool Coll.; Gonville and Caius Coll., Camb. (Classical Exhibitioner); University of Pavia. Served in RN, Sub-lieut (Sp) RNVR, 1944-47. Admitted a Solicitor, 1951; Italian Govt Scholar, 1951-52; Asst Lecturer in Law, Nottingham Univ., 1952-53; Lecturer in Jurisprudence, 1953-56, Prof. of Jurisprudence, 1956-68, Dean of Faculty of Law, 1961-64, Aberdeen Univ.; Chm., Faculty Bd of Law, Cambridge, 1973-76; Vice Pres., Queens' Coll., 1974-. Visiting Prof. of Law: Univ. of Virginia, 1965-66; Colorado, 1966; Witwatersrand, 1970; Louisiana State Univ., 1974; Fellow, Winchester Coll., 1976-. Member: Council, Max Planck Inst. for European Legal History, Frankfurt, 1966-; Council, Internat. Assoc. of Legal History, 1970-; Sec. of State for Scotland's Working Party on Hospital Endowments, 1966-69; Bd of Management, Royal Cornhill and Assoc. (Mental) Hospitals, Aberdeen, 1963-68 (Chm. 1967-68); UGC, 1971-75. JP Cambridge, 1970-. *Publications:* Fault in the formation of Contract in Roman Law and Scots Law, 1958; editor, Buckland's Textbook of Roman Law, 3rd edn, 1963; Regulae Iuris: from juristic rules to legal maxims, 1966; Roman Law in Scotland in Ius Romanum Medii Aevi, 1968; Roman Law and English Jurisprudence, 1969; (with J. Shand) Legal Values in Western Society, 1974; (ed jtly) Adam Smith's Lectures on Jurisprudence, 1977; articles in legal periodicals mainly on Roman Law and legal history. *Recreation:* hill walking. *Address:* Queens' College, Cambridge. *T:* Cambridge 65511.

STEIN, Prof. William Howard; Professor of Biochemistry, Rockefeller University, New York, since 1955; *b* NYC, 25 June 1911; *s* of Fred M. and Beatrice B. Stein; *m* 1936, Phoebe Hockstader; three *s*. *Educ:* Lincoln Sch. of Teachers Coll., Columbia; Phillips Exeter Acad.; Univs of Harvard and Columbia. BS Harvard, 1933; PhD Columbia, 1938. Rockefeller Inst. for Medical Research: Asst, 1939-43; Associate, 1943-49; Associate Mem., 1949-52; Mem., 1952. Member: Nat. Acad. of Sciences; Amer. Acad. of Arts and Sciences; Amer. Soc. of Biological Chemists; Biochem. Soc., London; Amer. Chem. Soc.; Amer. Assoc. for Advancement of Science; Harvey Soc. of NY; Past Member: Editorial Cttee, Jl of Biological Chemistry (Chm. 1958-61); Editorial Bd, Jl of Biological Chemistry, 1962-64 (Assoc. Editor, 1964-68; Editor, 1968-71); Council, Inst. of Neurological Diseases and Blindness of NIH, 1961-66; Chm., US Nat. Cttee for Biochemistry, 1968-69. Harvey Lectr, 1956; Phillips Lectr, Haverford Coll., 1962; Philip Schaffer Lectr, Washington Univ., 1965. Vis. Prof., Univ. of Chicago, 1961; Vis. Prof., Harvard Univ., 1964. Mem. Med. Adv. Bd, Hebrew Univ.-Hadassah Med. Sch., 1957-70; Trustee, Montefiore Hosp., 1948-74. Amer. Chem. Soc. Award in Chromatography and

Electrophoresis (jtly), 1964; Richards Medal, Amer. Chem. Soc. (jtly), 1972; Kaj Linderstrøm-Lang Award (jtly), 1972; Nobel Prize in Chemistry (jtly), 1972; Columbia Univ. Graduate Faculty and Alumni Assoc. Award of Excellence, 1973. Hon. DSc: Columbia, 1973; Albert Einstein Coll. of Medicine, Yeshiva Univ., 1973. *Publications:* numerous papers in Jl Biological Chemistry, Biochemistry, Jl Amer. Chem. Soc., Analytical Chemistry, etc. *Address:* 530 East 72nd Street, New York, NY 10021, USA. *T:* 535-7022.

STEINBERG, Jack; Chairman, Steinberg Group, since 1966; *b* 23 May 1913; *s* of Alexander and Sophie Steinberg; *m* 1938, Hannah Anne, *d* of late Solomon Wolfson, JP; two *d*. *Educ:* privately, London. Underwriting Member of Lloyd's. Chairman: Horrockses Fashions Ltd; Butte-Knit (London) Ltd; Member, NEDC; Vice-President: British Mantle Manufacturers' Assoc.; Clothing Export Council (Chm., 1970-74). Member of Plumbers' Livery Co.; Freeman, City of London. *Recreation:* farming. *Address:* 74 Portland Place, W1. *T:* 01-580 5908; Chartners Farm, Hartfield, Sussex. *T:* Hartfield 248. *Clubs:* Brooks's, Portland, Carlton.

STEINBERG, William; Conductor and Musical Director of the Pittsburgh Symphony Orchestra, Pennsylvania, USA, 1952-76, simultaneously, Music Director of the Boston Symphony Orchestra, 1969-72; *b* Cologne, 1 Aug. 1899; *s* of Julius Steinberg and Bertha Matzdorf; *m* 1934, Lotti Stern; one *s* one *d*. *Educ:* School of Higher Musical Studies, Cologne University. Studied piano with Uzielli, composition with Boelsche and conducting with Abendroth. Conductor Cologne Opera House, 1920; Opera Director, German Theatre, Prague, 1925-29; subseq. General Music Director, Frankfort Opera House, Guest Conductor, Berlin State Opera House, Conductor, Ceska Philharmonie, Prague, Museum Gesellschaft, Frankfort, and Palestine Orchestra. Went to USA, 1938; Guest Conductor with orchestras of many US cities; Conductor, San Francisco Opera, 1944-58; Musical Director: Buffalo Philharmonic Orch., 1945-52; London Philharmonic Orch., 1958-60. Has made many gramophone records. *Address:* 44 James Avenue, Atherton, Calif. 94025, USA; (Manager) Ronald A. Wilford, Columbia Artists, 165 West 57th Street, New York, NY 10019, USA.

STEINER, Prof. George, MA, DPhil; Extraordinary Fellow, Churchill College, Cambridge, since 1969; Professor of English and Comparative Literature, University of Geneva, since 1974; *b* 23 April 1929; *s* of Dr F. G. and Mrs E. Steiner; *m* 1955, Zara Steiner (*née* Shakow); one *s* one *d*. *Educ:* Paris (BèsL); Univ. of Chicago (BA); Harvard (MA); Oxford (DPhil). Member, staff of the Economist, in London, 1952-56; Inst. for Advanced Study, Princeton, 1956-58; Gauss Lectr, Princeton Univ., 1959-60; Massey Lectr, 1974; Fellow of Churchill Coll., 1961-. Fulbright Professorship, 1958-69; O. Henry Short Story Award, 1958; Guggenheim Fellowship, 1971-72; Zabel Award of Nat. Inst. of Arts and Letters of the US, 1970. Pres., English Assoc., 1975. FRSL 1964. Hon. DLitt East Anglia, 1976. *Publications:* Tolstoy or Dostoevsky, 1958; The Death of Tragedy, 1960; Anno Domini, 1964; Language and Silence, 1967; Extraterritorial, 1971; In Bluebeard's Castle, 1971; The Sporting Scene: White Knights in Reykjavik, 1973; After Babel, 1975 (adapted for TV as The Tongues of Men, 1977). *Recreations:* music, chess, mountain walking. *Address:* 32 Barrow Road, Cambridge. *T:* Cambridge 61200. *Clubs:* Athenæum, Savile; Harvard (New York).

STEINER, Rear-Adm. Ottokar Harold Mojmir St John, CB 1967; Asst Chief of Defence Staff, 1966-68, retired; *b* 8 July 1916; *e s* of late O. F. Steiner; *m* 1st, 1940, Evelyn Mary Young (marr. diss. 1975); one *s* one *d*; 2nd, 1975, Eleanor, *widow* of Sqdn Leader W. J. H. Powell, RAF. *Educ:* St Paul's School. Special entry cadet, RN, 1935. Served War of 1939-45 (despatches twice), HMS Ilex, Havelock, Frobisher, Superb. Naval Staff Course, 1947; Staff of C-in-C, Far East Fleet, 1948-50; Comdr 1950; jssc 1953; HMS Ceylon, 1953-54; NATO Defence Coll., 1955; HMS Daedalus, 1955-56; Capt. 1956; Admiralty, 1956-58; in comd HMS Saintes and Capt. (D) 3rd Destroyer Sqdn, 1958-60; Naval Adviser to UK High Commission, Canada, 1960-62; Senior Offrs War Course, 1962; In Comd HMS Centaur, 1963-65; Rear-Adm., 1966. Chm. Council, Shipwrecked Fishermen and Mariners Royal Benevolent Soc. Freeman, City of London; Liveryman, Coachmakers and Coach Harness Makers. *Recreations:* sailing, golf. *Address:* The Cottage, Mouns Hill, Totland, IoW. *T:* Freshwater 3404. *Clubs:* Royal Cruising; Royal Yacht Squadron; Royal Naval and Royal Albert Yacht (Portsmouth); Royal Solent; Union (Malta).

STEINER, Prof. Robert Emil; Professor of Diagnostic Radiology, University of London, Royal Postgraduate Medical

School, since 1961; *b* 1 Feb. 1918; *s* of Rudolf Steiner and Clary (*née* Nordlinger); *m* 1945, Gertrude Margaret Konirsch; two *d*. *Educ:* University of Vienna; University College, Dublin. Dep. Director, Dept of Radiology, Hammersmith Hosp.; Lecturer Diagnostic Radiology, Postgraduate Med. School of London, 1950, Sen. Lecturer, 1955, Director, 1955-. Consultant Adviser in Radiology to DHSS; Civil Consultant in Radiology to Med. Dir.-Gen., Navy. Warden of Fellowship, Faculty of Radiologists. Past Pres., British Inst. Radiology; Pres., RCR, 1977. Hon. Fellow: Amer. Coll. of Radiology; Australian Coll. of Radiology; Faculty of Radiologists, RCSI. Barclay Medal British Inst. of Radiology. Former Editor, British Jl of Radiology. *Publications:* Clinical Disorders of the Pulmonary Circulation, 1960; Recent Advances of Radiology, 1974; contrib. to British Journal of Radiology, Clinical Radiology, British Heart Jl, Lancet, BMJ, etc. *Address:* 12 Stonehill Road, East Sheen, SW14. *T:* 01-876 4038.

STEMBRIDGE, David Harry; a Recorder of the Crown Court, since 1977; *b* 23 Dec. 1932; *s* of Percy G. Stembridge and Emily W. Stembridge; *m* 1956, Therese C. Furer; three *s* one *d*. *Educ:* St Chad's Cathedral Choir Sch., Lichfield; Bromsgrove Sch.; Birmingham Univ. (LLB Hons). Called to the Bar, Gray's Inn, 1955; practising barrister, 1956-. *Recreations:* flute and organ playing, sailing. *Address:* Heath Lodge, Ullenhall, Warwickshire. *Clubs:* Bar Yacht, Royal Dart Yacht.

STENHOUSE, Sir Nicol, Kt 1962; *b* 14 Feb. 1911; 2nd *s* of late John Stenhouse, Shanghai, China, and Tring, Hertfordshire; *m* 1951, Barbara Heath Wilson; two *s* one *d*. *Educ:* Repton. Joined Andrew Yule & Co. Ltd, Calcutta, India, 1937; Managing Director, 1953-59; Chairman and Senior Managing Director, 1959-62; President: Bengal Chamber of Commerce and Industry, Calcutta, 1961-62; Associated Chambers of Commerce of India, Calcutta, 1961-62. *Recreation:* gardening. *Address:* Church Farm Cottage, Sixpenny Handley, near Salisbury, Wilts SP5 5NP. *Clubs:* Bengal, Tollygunge (Calcutta).

STENING, Sir George (Grafton Lees), Kt 1968; ED; Hon. Consultant Gynæcological Surgeon, Royal Prince Alfred Hosp., Sydney; Chancellor, Order of St John, in Australia; *b* 16 Feb. 1904; *s* of George Smith Stening and Muriel Grafton Lees; *m* 1935, Kathleen Mary Packer; one *s* one *d*. *Educ:* Sydney High Sch.; Univ. of Sydney. MB, BS (Syd.) 1927 (Hons Cl. II); FRCS (Ed.) 1931; FRACS 1935; FRCOG 1947; Carnegie Trav. Fellow, 1948. Served War of 1939-45: Middle East, New Guinea, Australia; OC, 3rd Aust. Surgical Team, Libyan Desert, 1941; CO, 2/11 Aust. Gen. Hosp., 1941-44; CO, 113 Aust. Gen. Hosp., 1945. Hon. Col, RAAMC; GCStJ 1971. Pres., Sen. Golfers' Soc. of Aust. *Publication:* A Text Book of Gynæcology (co-author), 1948. *Recreations:* golf, yachting. *Address:* 6/22 Wolseley Road, Point Piper, NSW 2027, Australia. *Clubs:* Australian, Royal Sydney Golf (Sydney).

STEPHEN, Sir Alastair (Edward), Kt 1973; solicitor; director of public companies; *b* 27 May 1901; *o s* of late Sir Colin Campbell Stephen, Sydney, solicitor and Dorothy, *d* of late Edward William Knox, Sydney; *m* 1st, 1942, Diana Heni (*d* 1943), *d* of late Richard Allen, Christchurch, NZ; one *d*; 2nd, 1946, Winifred Grace, *d* of late James Atkinson Bonnin; one *s* two *d*. *Educ:* Tudor House Sch.; Geelong C of E Grammar Sch.; St Paul's Coll., Univ. of Sydney. BA Sydney 1923. Solicitor, Supreme Court of NSW, 1926; partner, Stephen Jaques & Stephen, Sydney, 1926-75. Dir, Royal Prince Alfred Hosp., Sydney, 1944-73 (Vice-Chm. 1953-62, Chm. 1962-73); Pres., Australian Hosp. Assoc., 1969-71. *Recreations:* ski-ing, sailing, fishing, racing. *Address:* 60 Fairfax Road, Bellevue Hill, Sydney, NSW, Australia. *T:* 36-6402. *Clubs:* Union, Australian, Royal Sydney Golf, Australian Jockey (Sydney).

STEPHEN, Sir Andrew, Kt 1972; Chairman of the Football Association; *b* 20 May 1906; *s* of Alexander Stephen and Margaret Martin Stephen; *m* 1934, Frances Barker; three *s*. *Educ:* Peterhead Academy, Aberdeenshire; Aberdeen Univ. (MB, ChB). Various hosp. appts in Aberdeen and London, as resident MO, 1928-30; Gen. Practitioner, Sheffield, 1930-66. Pres., Sheffield Div. of BMA; Pres., Sheffield Medico-Chirurgical Soc. Served on: Exec. Council, Local Medical Cttee, and Hospital Management Cttee, in Sheffield. *Recreations:* shooting activities, including game shooting. *Address:* Wisewood House, Wisewood Road, Sheffield S6 4WB. *T:* Sheffield 343177.

STEPHEN, Derek Ronald James, CB 1975; Deputy Under-Secretary of State (Navy), Ministry of Defence, since 1973; *b* 22 June 1922; *s* of Ronald James Stephen; *m* 1948, Gwendolen Margaret, *d* of late William James Heasman, CBE; two *s* one *d*

(and one *s* decd). *Educ:* Bec Sch.; Christ's Coll., Cambridge (Scholar). 1st cl. Class. Tripos, Pt I, 1941; 1st cl. Class. Tripos, Pt II, 1946. Served War, 1941-45; Royal Armoured Corps (Captain), N Africa, Italy, NW Europe. Asst Principal, War Office, 1946; Asst Private Sec. to Sec. of State for War, 1949-50; Principal, 1951; Private Sec. to Sec. of Cabinet, 1958-60; Asst Sec., WO (later Ministry of Defence), 1960; IDC 1966; HM Treasury, 1968; Civil Service Dept (on its formation), 1968; Under-Sec., 1971; Asst Under-Sec. of State, MoD, 1972-73. *Recreations:* tennis, travel, music. *Address:* 30 Oaken Lane, Claygate, Surrey. *T:* Esher 63383.

STEPHEN, Harbourne Mackay, DSO 1941; DFC and bar 1940; Managing Director, Daily Telegraph and Sunday Telegraph, since 1963; *b* 18 April 1916; *s* of Thomas Milne Stephen, JP, and Kathleen Vincent Park; *m* 1947, Sybil Erica Palmer; two *d*. *Educ:* Shrewsbury. Staff of Allied Newspapers, London, 1931; Evening Standard, 1936-39. RAFVR, 1937; served RAF, 1939-45 (destroyed numerous enemy aircraft): 605 and 74 Sqdns, 1939-40; at MAP, 1941, then formed 130 Sqdn and comd 234 Sqdn; served Far East, 1942-45; Wing Comdr (Flying) Dum Dum; RAF Jessore, Bengal; comd 166 Fighter Wing; then to Fighter Ops, 224 Gp Arakan; Ops "A" Air Comd SEA. Was OC 602 City of Glasgow (F) Sqdn RAuxAF, 1950-52. Returned to Beaverbrook Newspapers, Oct. 1945; worked on Scottish Daily Express, Scottish Sunday Express, and Evening Citizen in Glasgow, 1945-55. General Manager, Sunday Express, 1958; General Manager, Sunday Graphic, 1960, and thereafter General Manager, Thomson Papers, London. Dir, Internat. Newspaper Colour Assoc., Darmstadt, 1964-69. Council Mem., RSPB, 1972-73. *Recreations:* normal, occasionally. *Address:* Donnington Holt, Newbury, Berks. *T:* Newbury 40105. *Clubs:* Bath, Royal Automobile, Royal Air Force.

STEPHEN, Henrietta Hamilton, (Rita Stephen), MBE 1973; Executive Secretary, Association of Professional, Executive, Clerical and Computer Staff, since 1965; *b* 9 Dec. 1925; *d* of late James Pithie Stephen, engine driver, Montrose and late Mary Hamilton Morton, South Queensferry. *Educ:* Wolseley Street and King's Park Elem. Schs, Glasgow; Queen's Park Sen. Secondary, Glasgow; Glasgow Univ. (extra-mural); LSE (TUC Schol.). Imperial Relations Trust Schol., McGill Univ. and Canada/US Travel, 1958-59; Duke of Edinburgh's Commonwealth Study Conf., 1968. Law office junior, 1941; Clerk, Labour Exchange (Mem. MLSA), 1941-42; Post Office Telephonist, 1942-60; Mem. Union of Post Office Workers, Glasgow Br., 1942-60 (Br. Cttee Mem., Vice-Chm., Chm., Sec., Deleg. to Trades Council, UPW District Council, Scottish Council, Annual Conf., etc); Mem. UPW Parly Panel, 1957; Glasgow City Labour Party Deleg., 1955; Educn Officer, Cathcart Ward Labour Party, 1955-58; Election Agent (Municipal); London and Home Counties Area Organiser, CAWU, 1960-65; Asst Sec., CAWU, 1965 (Union renamed APEX and post renamed Exec. Sec., 1972). Negotiator in public and private sectors of industry, 1960-; Editor, The Clerk, 1965-71; Union Educn Officer, 1965-; Delegate: TUC; Labour Party Annual Confs; Member: EDC for Distributive Trades, 1966-; WEA Nat. Cttee, 1968-; Food Standards Cttee, 1968-; Industrial Soc. Council and Exec., 1968-; Mary Macarthur Educnl Trust, 1965 (Hon. Sec. 1972-); Distributive Industry Trng Bd, 1968-73; Monopolies and Mergers Commn, 1973-; British Wool Marketing Bd, 1973-; Governor: Ruskin Coll., 1966-; Duke of Edinburgh's 1974 Commonwealth Study Conf., 1973; LSE, 1976-. *Publications:* (jtly) Training Shop Stewards, 1968; (with Roy Moore) Statistics for Negotiators, 1973; contrib. Clerk, Industrial Soc. Jl, Target, etc. *Recreations:* food, walking, conversation, theatre, reading. *Address:* 3 Pond Road, SE3. *T:* 01-852 7797, 01-947 3131.

STEPHEN, Sir James Alexander, 4th Bt, *cr* 1891; *b* 25 Feb. 1908; *o c* of 3rd Bt and Barbara, *y d* of late W. Shore-Nightingale of Embley, Hants and Lea Hurst, Derbyshire; *S* father, 1945. *Educ:* Eton; Trinity College, Cambridge. Law Student, Inner Temple; embraced Roman Catholic faith, 1936; Resident, Toynbee Hall, 1936-39; Air Raid Warden, 1940; served RA (AA), 1940-41, discharged unfit; worked on the land as a volunteer, 1941-45; certified insane, 1945; name restored to vote, 1960; discharged from hospital, 1972. *Heir:* none. *Recreation:* contract bridge. *Address:* 44 Princess Road, Branksome, Poole, Dorset BH12 1BH. *T:* Bournemouth 764481.

STEPHEN, John Low, ChM (Aberdeen), FRCSE, FRCS; Surgeon St Mary's Hospital, W2 since 1958; Senior Surgeon, St Mary's Hospital, W9, since 1948; *b* 13 May 1912; 2nd *s* of late Dr J. H. Stephen, Aberdeen; *m* 1938, Mary Milne, MA, BSc; one *s* one *d*. *Educ:* Aberdeen Grammar School; Aberdeen and Edinburgh Universities. MA 1931, MB 1935, Aberd.; FRCSEd, 1937; ChM Aberd., 1945; FRCS (ad eundem), 1968. Various university and hospital appointments in Scotland and England. Associate Teacher in Surgery, St Mary's Hosp. Med. School, 1950-. FRSocMed. *Publications:* chapters in Operative Surgery (Smith and Rob); various articles on abdominal surgery in Brit. Jl of Surgery. *Recreations:* golf, motoring. *Address:* Luibeg, Groombridge, East Sussex.

STEPHEN, Lessel Bruce; His Honour Judge Stephen, a Circuit Judge, since 1972; *b* 15 Feb. 1920; *s* of L. P. Stephen, FRCS(E); *m* 1949, Brenda (*née* Tinkler). *Educ:* Marlborough; Sydney Sussex Coll., Cambridge (BA). Called to the Bar, Inner Temple, 1948; subsequently practised NE Circuit; Recorder, 1972. *Recreations:* golf, wine. *Address:* 2 Harcourt Buildings, Temple, EC4Y 9DB. *T:* 01-353 2548.

STEPHEN, Hon. Sir Ninian Martin, KBE 1972; QC; Justice of the High Court of Australia since 1972; *b* 15 June 1923; *o s* of late Frederick Stephen and Barbara Stephen (*née* Cruickshank); *m* 1949, Valery Mary, *d* of late A. Q. Sinclair and of Mrs G. M. Sinclair; five *d. Educ:* Edinburgh Acad.; St Paul's Sch., London; Scotch Coll., Melbourne; Melbourne Univ. (LLB). Served War, HM Forces (Australian Army), 1941-46. Admitted as Barrister and Solicitor, in State of Victoria, 1949; signed Roll of Victorian Bar, 1951; QC 1966. Appointed Judge of Supreme Court of Victoria, 1970. *Recreations:* sailing, reading. *Address:* 631 Burke Road, Hawthorn, Victoria 3122, Australia. *T:* Melbourne 82-2131.

STEPHEN, Rita; *see* Stephen, H. H.

STEPHEN, Maj.-Gen. Robert Alexander, CB 1965; CBE 1958 (OBE 1954); MD, ChM; FRCS; QHS 1960-67; Director of Army Surgery and Consulting Surgeon to the Army, Royal Army Medical College, 1959-67; Consultant in Surgery, Royal Hospital, Chelsea; *b* 20 June 1907; *s* of late James Alexander Stephen, MB, ChB, DPH; *m* 1st, 1935, Audrey Vivien (*d* 1972), *d* of late George William Royce, Cambridge; one *d* ; 2nd, 1977, Mrs Patricia O'Reilly (*née* Wrixon-Harris). *Educ:* Aberdeen Grammar School; Aberdeen University. MD 1933, ChM 1960, Aberdeen. FRCS 1947. MS Malaya, 1959. Lieut, RAMC, 1934. Served War of 1939-45, in France, Egypt, Libya, Greece, Crete, Belgium, Holland and Germany; Lt-Col 1941. Formerly Asst Prof. of Military Surgery, Royal Army Medical College, London; Consulting Surgeon, FARELF, 1956-59; Hon. Consulting Surgeon, General Hospital, Singapore, 1956; Brigadier, 1958; Major-General, 1961. Hunterian Prof., RCS, 1958. Fellow: Royal Society of Medicine; Assoc. of Surgeons of Great Britain and Ireland. OStJ. *Recreations:* golf and gardening. *Address:* Pinnocks, 44a Shortheath Road, Farnham, Surrey GU9 8SL. *T:* Farnham 23848.

STEPHENS, Air Commandant Dame Anne, DBE 1961 (MBE 1946); Hon. ADC to the Queen, 1960-63; Director, Women's Royal Air Force, 1960-63; *b* 4 Nov. 1912; *d* of late General Sir Reginald Byng Stephens, KCB, CMG and late Lady Stephens. *Educ:* privately. Joined WAAF, 1939; served in UK, Belgium and Germany, 1939-45. Command WRAF Depot, Hawkinge, 1950-52; promoted Group Officer, 1951; Inspector WRAF, 1952-54; Deputy Director, 1954-57; Staff Officer, HQ 2nd TAF, 1957-59; promoted Air Commandant, 1960. *Address:* The Forge, Sibford Ferris, Banbury, Oxfordshire. *T:* Swalcliffe 452.

STEPHENS, Anthony William, CMG 1976; Under Secretary, Northern Ireland Office, since 1976; *b* 9 Jan. 1930; *s* of late Donald Martyn Stephens and Norah Stephens (*née* Smith-Cleburne); *m* 1954, Mytyl Joy, *d* of late William Gay Burdett; four *d. Educ:* Bradfield Coll.; Bristol Univ. (LLB); Corpus Christi Coll., Cambridge. RM, 1948-50. Colonial Administrative Service, 1953; District Officer, Kenya, 1954-63; Home Civil Service, 1964; Principal, MoD, 1964-70; Asst Private Sec. to successive Secretaries of State for Defence, 1970-71; Asst Sec., 1971; Chief Officer, Sovereign Base Areas, Cyprus, 1974-76. *Recreations:* travel and the outdoor life, music, theatre. *Address:* c/o Northern Ireland Office, Stormont Castle, Belfast BT4 3ST. *Club:* Royal Commonwealth Society.

STEPHENS, Prof. Arthur Veryan, MA Cantab; CEng; FRAeS; Professor of Aeronautical Engineering, The Queen's University, Belfast, 1956-73, now Emeritus Professor; *b* 9 July 1908; *s* of Arthur John Stephens and Mildred, *d* of Robert Fowler Sturge; *m* 1938, Jane Dows, *d* of F. W. Lester; three *s* one *d. Educ:* Clifton College; St John's College, Cambridge (Mechanical Sciences Tripos, John Bernard Seely Prize). Scientific Officer, Royal Aircraft Establishment, 1930-34; Fellow of St John's College, Cambridge, 1934-39; Lawrence Hargrave Professor of Aeronautics, 1939-56, Dean of the Faculty of Engineering, 1947-56, University of Sydney, NSW. Edward Busk Memorial Prize of RAeS, 1934; Member: Australian Flying Personnel Research

Cttee, 1940-45; Australian Council for Aeronautics, 1941-46; Chairman, Aeronautical Research Consultative Cttee, 1947-54; Chairman, Australian Aeronautical Research Committee, 1954-56; Member Australian Defence Research and Development Policy Committee, 1953-56; Chairman, Australian Division of Royal Aeronautical Society, 1947-56. Dean of Faculty of Applied Science and Technology, 1961-64; Vice-President (Buildings), 1964-67. *Publications:* numerous papers on applied aerodynamics published by Aeronautical Research Council, Australian Dept of Supply and in Jl of RAeS. *Recreations:* golf, gliding. *Address:* The Forge, Hallow Lane, Wilton, near Marlborough, Wilts. *Club:* Athenæum.

STEPHENS, Cedric John; barrister-at-law; consultant; retired; *b* 13 Feb. 1921; *s* of late Col J. E. Stephens, Truro, Cornwall. *Educ:* London University (BSc (Eng.) Hons). Entered Scientific Civil Service, 1951; Dir, Space Activities, Min. of Aviation, 1961; Mem. Coun., European Launcher Development Organisation, Paris, 1962; Chm. Technical Cttee, European Coun. on Satellite Communications, 1964; Imperial Defence Coll., 1965; Director, Signals Research and Develt Estabt, Min. of Technology, 1966-67; Chief Scientific Adviser, Home Office, 1968; Dir-Gen. of Research and Chief Scientist, Home Office, 1969-73; Chm. Selection Bds, Civil Service Commn, 1974-75. Called to Bar, Gray's Inn, 1971. Mem., Electronics Div. Bd, IEE, 1972. *Publications:* papers on forensic evidence. *Recreations:* classical philology, especially Arabic; growing orchids. *Address:* 7 Exeter Court, Wharncliffe Road, Christchurch, Dorset. *Clubs:* Athenæum, MCC.

STEPHENS, Christopher Wilson T.; *see* Stephens, Wilson T.

STEPHENS, Sir David, KCB 1964; CVO 1960; Clerk of the Parliaments, House of Lords, 1963-74; *b* 25 April 1910; *s* of late Berkeley John Byng Stephens, CIE, and Gwendolen Elizabeth (*née* Cripps), Cirencester; *m* 1st, 1941, Mary Clemency, JP (*d* 1966), *er d* of late Colonel Sir Eric Gore Browne, DSO, OBE, TD; three *s* one *d* ; 2nd, 1967, Charlotte Evelyn, widow of Henry Manisty, *d* of late Rev. A. M. Baird-Smith; three step *s. Educ:* Winchester College; Christ Church. Oxford (2nd cl. Lit. Hum.). Laming Travelling Fellow, the Queen's College, Oxford, 1932-34; Clerk in the Parliament Office, House of Lords, 1935-38; Member Runciman Mission to Czechoslovakia, 1938; Transf. HM Treasury, 1938; Political Warfare Executive, 1941-43; Prin. Priv. Sec. to the Lord Pres. of the Council (Mr Herbert Morrison), 1947-49; Asst Sec., HM Treasury, 1949; Secretary for Appointments to two Prime Ministers (Sir Anthony Eden and Mr Harold Macmillan), 1955-61; Reading Clerk and Clerk of the Journals, House of Lords, 1961-63. Chm., Redundant Churches Fund, 1976-. Chm. of Governors, Maidwell Hall Sch., 1964-70. Mem., Cotswold DC, 1976-. Pres., Friends of Cirencester Parish Church, 1976-. *Recreations:* gardening, tennis and country life; preserving the Cotswolds. *Address:* The Old Rectory, Coates, near Cirencester, Glos. GL7 6NS. *T:* Kemble 258. *Clubs:* Brooks's, MCC.

STEPHENS, Frederick James; retired 1971; Managing Director, The "Shell" Transport and Trading Co. Ltd, 1957-71 (Director since 1951; Chairman, 1961-67); Chairman, The Shell Petroleum Co. Ltd, 1961-71 (Managing Director, 1951-61); Managing Director, Shell International Petroleum Co. Ltd, 1959-61; Director, Bataafse Petroleum Maatschappij NV (Principal Director, 1956-61, Delegate Member of Board from 1951); *b* 30 July 1903; *er s* of late Canon John Frederick Douglas Stephens and Frances Mary (*née* Mirrlees); *m* 1948, Sara Clark (*d* 1954), Dallas, Texas; no *c. Educ:* Marlborough Coll.; Grenoble Univ., France; Pembroke Coll., Cambridge. BA 1926, MA 1956, Cambridge. Joined Royal Dutch Shell Group of Companies, 1926, and served in Venezuela, London and US; Director and Exec. Vice-Pres. of Asiatic Petroleum Corp., New York, 1946; returned to London, 1948. Hon. Fellow, University Coll., London, 1958; Visiting Fellow Nuffield Coll., Oxford, 1961; Member of Court, University of Reading, 1962. Comdr, Order of Orange-Nassau, 1968. *Recreations:* gardening, walking. *Address:* Noel House, Les Ruisseaux, St Brelade, Jersey, CI. *Clubs:* Junior Carlton; New Zealand Golf (Byfleet); Victoria; Royal Channel Islands Yacht (Jersey).

STEPHENS, Mrs George Arbour; *see* Williams, Mary.

STEPHENS, Engineer Rear-Admiral George Leslie, CB 1946; CBE 1943; Royal Canadian Navy, retired; *b* 2 Jan. 1889; *s* of George Selleck and Ernestine Stephens; *m* 1913, Edna Louise Woodill; one *s* two *d. Educ:* Plympton Public School, Plympton; Stoke Public School, Devonport. Naval Engineer training, HM Dockyard, Devonport, England, 1903-10; joined Royal Canadian Navy as Engine-room Artificer, 1910. Warrant Rank, 1912; Engineer Lieut 1915; Engineer Comdr 1929; Engineer

Capt. 1940; Engineer-in-Chief, Naval Service HQ, Ottawa, 1941; Engineer Rear-Adm. 1943. *Recreations:* curling and golf. *Address:* Apt. 301 The Croydon, 201 McLeod Street, Ottawa K2P 0Z9, Ontario, Canada.

STEPHENS, Ian Melville, CIE 1935; MA Cantab; *b* 1903; *e s* of J. A. Melville Stephens, Fleet, Hants; unmarried; hon. adopted son, Dr Arthur Kwok Cheung Li. *Educ:* Winchester; King's Coll., Cambridge (foundn scholar, R. J. Smith research student); 1st class hons, Natural Sciences Tripos, Pt I, 1924, and Historical Tripos, Pt II, 1925. Business appts, 1927-30; Deputy Dir, Bureau of Public Information, Govt of India, 1930-32; wrote the M & MP Reports for 1929-30 and 1930-31; was Indian corresp., The Round Table; Publicity Officer, Indian Franchise (Lothian) Cttee, 1932; Dir, Bureau of Public Information, 1932-37; Asst Editor, The Statesman newspaper, Calcutta and Delhi, 1937; also on the Board, 1939; Editor, 1942-51 (also aeronautical corresp., and a staff photographer). War Corresp., SEAC and SHAEF, 1943-45. Member: Standing Cttee, All-India Newspaper Editors' Conf., 1942-51; Indian Delegn to Commonwealth Press Conf., Canada, 1950; Brit. Group, Inst. of Pacific Relations Conf., Lucknow, 1950. Retired from India, 1951. Fellow, King's Coll., Cambridge, 1952-58; also Mem. Council, and Hon. Treasurer Appeals Cttee, New Hall, Cambridge. Chm., Mount Vernon (Ceylon) Tea Co., 1953-57. Historian, Pakistan Govt, GHQ, Rawalpindi, 1957-60. Has travelled in South Asia, Australia, NZ, Canada, USA. *Publications:* Horned Moon, illus. with own photographs, 1953 (3rd edn 1966); Pakistan, 1963 (paperback edn 1964, 3rd edn 1967); Monsoon Morning, 1966; (ed) Sir R. Reid's Years of Change, 1966; The Pakistanis, 1968; A Curiosity, 1970; Unmade Journey, 1977; contribs to Chambers's Encyclopaedia (1966 edn); articles, lectures, broadcasts, reviews. *Address:* c/o Lloyds Bank, 3 Sidney Street, Cambridge.

STEPHENS, Maj.-Gen. Keith Fielding, CB 1970; OBE 1957; Medical Officer, Department of Health and Social Security, since 1970; *b* Taplow, Bucks, 28 July 1910; *s* of late Edgar Percy and Mary Louise Stephens; *m* 1937, Margaret Ann, *d* of late Alexander MacGregor; two *s. Educ:* Eastbourne College; St Bartholomew's Hospital. MB, BS London 1934; FFARCS 1953; DA 1945. Commissioned into RAMC, 1937; served in India, 1937-43; France and Germany, 1944-46; Cyprus, 1954-56; Adviser in Anæsthetics to the Army, 1949-53 and 1957-66; Commandant and Director of Studies, Royal Army Medical College, 1966-68; DDMS, Southern Command, 1968-70, retired. FRSocMed (Pres., Sect. of Anæsthetics, 1970-71); Hon. Member, Assoc. of Anæsthetists of Gt Brit. and Ireland. Fellow, Med. Soc. of London. Hon. FFARCS (Ireland), 1970; QHS, 1964-70. Hon. Col, 221 (Surrey) Field Ambulance RAMC(V), 1972-76. Mitchiner Medal, 1962. CStJ 1967. *Publications:* numerous articles in medical journals. *Address:* 3 Carnegie Place, Parkside, Wimbledon, SW19. *T:* 01-946 0911. *Club:* Naval and Military.

STEPHENS, Peter Norman Stuart; Associate Editor, The Sun, since 1975; *b* 19 Dec. 1927; *s* of J. G. Stephens; *m* 1950, Constance Mary Ratheram; two *s* one *d. Educ:* Mundella Secondary Sch., Nottingham. Newark Advertiser, 1945-48; Northern Echo, 1948-50; Daily Dispatch, 1950-55; Daily Mirror, Manchester, 1955-57; Asst Editor, Newcastle Journal, 1957-60; Asst Editor, Evening Chronicle, Newcastle, 1960-62; Editor 1962-66; Editor, Newcastle Journal, 1966-70; Asst Editor, The Sun, 1970-72, Dep. Editor 1972; Associate Editor, News of the World, 1973, Editor, 1974-75. *Recreation:* supporting Derby County Football Club. *Address:* 30 Bouverie Street, EC4Y 8DE. *T:* 01-353 3030.

STEPHENS, Peter Scott, CMG 1962; *b* 25 Nov. 1910; *s* of Major John August Stephens, TD, and Elsie Evelyn Stephens (*née* Watson). *Educ:* Sherborne School; Oriel Coll., Oxford. HM Consular Service, 1933; served New York and Manila; transferred to Foreign Office, 1941; Leopoldville and Elizabethville, Belgian Congo, 1942-45; in charge of Consular Section, British Embassy, Brussels, 1945-47; transf. to Foreign Office, 1947; First Secretary, Washington, 1949; First Secretary and First Secretary (Commercial), British Embassy, Havana, 1951-54; acted as Chargé d'Affaires, there, in 1951, 1952, 1953 and 1954; Counsellor (Commercial) British Embassy, Caracas, April 1955-Nov. 1958; acted as Chargé d'Affaires, there, in 1955, 1956, 1957 and 1958; Commercial Counsellor, Madrid, 1959-62; HM Consul-General, Milan, 1962-68. *Address:* The Garden House, Thornhill, Stalbridge, Dorset. *T:* Stalbridge 62366. *Club:* Travellers'.

STEPHENS, Major Robert, CVO 1964; ERD; Northern Ireland Civil Servant, since 1964; Administrative Officer, Hillsborough Castle (formerly Government House), since 1973; *b* 1909; *s* of

late John Samuel Stephens; *m* 1939, Kathleen, *d* of late R. I. Trelford, Helen's Bay, Belfast. *Educ:* Campbell Coll., Belfast. Ulster Bank, 1929-39. Served War of 1939-45: RA, Middle East, 1941-45. Commercial Manager, Newforge Ltd, 1946-55; Private Secretary to the Governor of Northern Ireland, 1955-73; Comptroller to: Lord Wakehurst, 1955-64; Lord Erskine of Rerrick, 1964-68; Lord Grey of Naunton, 1968-73. *Recreation:* golf. *Address:* Hillsborough Castle, Hillsborough, Co. Down, Northern Ireland. *T:* Hillsborough 682244.

STEPHENS, Robert; actor; *b* 14 July 1931; *s* of Rueben Stephens and Gladys (*née* Deverell); *m* 1st, Tarn Bassett; one *d*; 2nd, 1967, Maggie Smith, *qv* (marr. diss. 1975); two *s. Educ:* Bradford Civic Theatre School. Started with Caryl Jenner Mobile Theatre Co.; Mem. English Stage Co., Royal Court, 1956, played in The Crucible, Don Juan, The Death of Satan, Cards of Identity, The Good Woman of Setzuan and The Country Wife (also at Adelphi, 1957); The Apollo de Bellac, Yes-and After, The Making of Moo, How Can We Save Father?, The Waters of Babylon, Royal Court, 1957; The Entertainer, Palace, 1957; Epitaph for George Dillon, Royal Court, Comedy, Golden (NY), 1958 and Henry Miller, 1959; Look After Lulu (also at New) and The Kitchen (also 1961), Royal Court, 1959; The Wrong Side of the Park, Cambridge, 1960; The Sponge Room, Squat Betty, Royal Court, 1962; Chichester and Edinburgh Festival, 1963; joined National Theatre Company, 1963: played in Hamlet, St Joan, The Recruiting Officer, 1963; Andorra, Play, The Royal Hunt of the Sun (also Chichester Fest.), Hay Fever, 1964; Much Ado About Nothing, Armstrong's Last Goodnight, Trelawny of the Wells (also Chichester Fest.), 1965; A Bond Honoured, Black Comedy, 1966; The Dance of Death, The Three Sisters (at Los Angeles, 1968), As You Like It, Tartuffe, 1967; Most Unwarrantable Intrusion (also dir.), Home and Beauty, 1968; Macrune's Guevara (also co-dir), 1969; The Beaux' Stratagem (also Los Angeles), Hedda Gabler, 1970; Design for Living (Los Angeles), 1971; Private Lives, Queen's, 1972; The Seagull, Chichester, 1973; Apropos The Falling Sleet (dir.), Open Space, 1973; Ghosts, The Seagull, Hamlet, Greenwich, 1974; Sherlock Holmes, NY and Canada, 1975; Murderer, Garrick, 1975; Zoo Story, 1975, Othello, 1976, Open Air, Regent's Park. *Films:* A Taste of Honey; Cleopatra; The Small World of Sammy Lee; The Prime of Miss Jean Brodie; The Private Life of Sherlock Holmes; Travels with my Aunt; The Asphyx; Luther; QBVIII, etc. TV performances include: Vienna 1900 (6 part series), 1973; Tribute to J. B. Priestley, 1974. Variety Club Award for stage actor, 1965. *Recreations:* cooking, gymnastics, swimming. *Address:* c/o Film Rights Ltd, 113-117 Wardour Street, W1. *T:* 01-437 7151.

STEPHENS, William Henry, CB 1961; DSc, MSc, CEng, FRAeS; Executive Director, General Technology Systems Ltd, since 1974; *b* Kilkenny, Ireland, 18 March 1913; *s* of William Henry Stephens, MBE, and Helena Read Stephens (*née* Cantley); *m* 1938, Elizabeth Margaret Brown, BSc; one *s* one *d. Educ:* Methodist College and Queen's University, Belfast. Air Ministry, Royal Aircraft Establishment (Aerodynamic Research), 1935-38; War Office, Woolwich (Rocket Research), 1938-39; Ministry of Aircraft Prod., London (Air Defence Research), 1939-44; Asst Scientific Attaché and Asst Director, UK Scientific Mission, British Commonwealth Scientific Office, Washington, USA, 1944-47; Min. of Supply, RAE, Head of Guided Weapons Dept and later Dep. Director, 1947-58; Dir-Gen. Ballistic Missiles, Ministry of Aviation, 1959-62; Technical Dir, European Space Launcher Develt Organisation, Paris, 1962-69; Minister, Defence R&D, British Embassy, Washington, 1969-72; Special Advr (Internat. Affairs), Controllerate of Res., MoD, 1972-73. Mem., Internat. Acad. of Astronautics; Fellow, British Interplanetary Soc. *Publications:* contrib. to Jl Royal Aeronautical Soc.; Proc. Brit. Assoc.; Proc. Internat. Congress of Aeronautical Sciences. *Recreations:* travel, music, art, theatre. *Address:* Rosebrook House, Oriel Hill, Camberley, Surrey. *Club:* Athenæum.

STEPHENS, Wilson (Treeve); Editor of The Field, 1950-77; *b* 2 June 1912; *s* of Rev. Arthur Treeve Stephens, Shepton Beauchamp, Somerset, and Margaret Wilson; *m* 1st, 1934, Nina, *d* of Arthur Frederick Curzon, Derby; two *d*; 2nd, 1960, Marygold Anne, *o d* of Major-General G. O. Crawford, *qv*; two *d. Educ:* Christ's Hosp. Formerly on editorial staffs of several provincial newspapers, and of The Daily Express. Served War of 1939-45, Royal Artillery. *Publications:* is a contributor to numerous journals. *Recreation:* fly-fishing. *Address:* c/o 8 Stratton Street, W1. *T:* 01-499 7881. *Club:* Kennel.

STEPHENS SPINKS, Rev. Dr G.; *see* Spinks.

STEPHENSON, Donald, CBE 1957 (OBE 1943); Controller, Overseas and Foreign Relations, BBC, 1966-71; *b* 18 May 1909; *yr s* of late J. V. G. Stephenson; *m* 1940, Alison (*d* 1965), *yr d* of late Wynn ap H. Thomas, OBE, LLB; one *s* three *d. Educ:* Denstone College (Scholar); Paris; Baghdad. Banking business, 1925-31; permanent commission, RAF, 1932; Flt Lt, 1936; served France and Middle East, 1935-37; language specialist (interpreter, French and Arabic); Special Duty List, 1938; Arabic Editor, BBC, 1939; Director, BBC, New Delhi, 1944-45; Director, Eastern Services, 1946-47; Asst Controller in Overseas Div., 1948; Controller, North Region, 1948-56; Controller, Overseas Relations, BBC, 1956-58; Chief Executive, Anglia Television Ltd, 1959; Head of Overseas and Foreign Relations, BBC, Dec. 1960. A Governor of Manchester Univ., 1950-58. A delegate to 5th Commonwealth Broadcasting Conf., Canada, 1963, to 7th Conf., NZ, 1968, and 8th Conf., Jamaica, 1970. *Recreation:* family life. *Address:* Essington Corner, Pains Hill, Oxted, Surrey. *T:* Limpsfield Chart 3151. *Club:* Athenæum.

STEPHENSON, Ven. Edgar, MM 1918; TD 1950; Archdeacon Emeritus of Rochdale, since 1962, Archdeacon, 1951-62; Director of Religious Education in Diocese of Manchester, 1955-62; *b* 24 Sept. 1894; *y s* of late T. J. Stephenson, Tamworth, Staffs; *m* 1926, Kathleen, *d* of late William Taws, Macclesfield, Cheshire; no *c. Educ:* Manchester University. BA 1922; BD 1925; MA 1929. CF(TA), 1933-50. Vicar of St Mary's, Oldham, 1947-55. *Recreations:* reading, walking, gardening. *Address:* Gwelfryn, 15A Francis Avenue, Colwyn Bay, Clwyd LL28 4DW. *T:* Colwyn Bay 48793.

STEPHENSON, Colonel Eric Lechmere, DSO 1940; MC and two bars; *b* 18 April 1892; *s* of late Dr O. T. and Jane Marriott Stephenson; *m* 1934, Helen Joyce Marples; one *s. Educ:* King Alfred's School, Wantage. Regular Commission in Army, 1912; retired pay, 1946. *Recreations:* cricket and polo. *Address:* 2 Comptons Lea, Comptons Lane, Horsham, West Sussex. *Club:* Army and Navy.

STEPHENSON, Lieut-Col Sir Francis; *see* Stephenson, Lt-Col Sir (Henry) F. (B).

STEPHENSON, Prof. Gordon, CBE 1967; FRIBA, FRTPI, LFRAIA, LFRAPI, FILA, DisTP; Professor Emeritus of Architecture, University of Western Australia; Member, National Capital Planning Committee, Canberra, 1967-73; *b* 6 June 1908; *s* of Francis E. and Eva E. Stephenson, Liverpool; *m* 1938, Flora Bartlett Crockett, Boston, USA; three *d. Educ:* Liverpool Institute; University of Liverpool; University of Paris; Massachusetts Institute of Technology. Elmes Scholar, Univ. of Liverpool, 1925-30; Holt Scholar, 1928; First Cl. Hons in Architecture, 1930; Chadwick Scholar at Brit. Inst. in Paris and Univ. of Paris, 1930-32; BArch; MCP(MIT). Lecturer and Studio Instructor in Architecture, University of Liverpool, 1932-36; Commonwealth Fellow and Medallist, Massachusetts Inst. of Technology, 1936-38; Studio Master, Architectural Assoc., School of Architecture, 1939-40; Lever Professor of Civic Design, School of Architecture, University of Liverpool, 1948-53; Professor of Town and Regional Planning in the University of Toronto, Canada, 1955-60; Prof. of Architecture, Univ. of WA, 1960-72. Architectural and Planning practice: asst to Corbett, Harrison and McMurray, NY City, 1929; asst to Le Corbusier and Pierre Jeanneret, Paris, 1930-32; Div. Architect, with W. G. Holford, on Royal Ordnance Factory work, 1940-42; Research Officer, Sen. Research Officer, and Chief Planning Officer, Min. of Works and Planning, and Min. of Town and Country Planning, 1942-47; seconded to assist Sir Patrick Abercrombie on Greater London Plan, 1943-44; Cnslt Architect, Univ. of WA, 1960-69; in partnership with R. J. Ferguson, as architects and planners for Murdoch Univ., WA, 1972-76; in private practice, houses, militia camp, university bldgs, community centre, housing schemes, town and regional planning studies. Editor, Town Planning Review, 1949-54. Hon. MCIP 1960. Hon. LLD Univ. of WA. *Publications:* (with Flora Stephenson) Community Centres, 1941; (with F. R. S. Yorke) Planning for Reconstruction, 1944; (with J. A. Hepburn) Plan for the Metropolitan Region of Perth and Fremantle, 1955; a Redevelopment Study of Halifax, Nova Scotia, 1957; (with G. G. Muirhead) A Planning Study of Kingston, Ontario, 1959; The Design of Central Perth, 1975; articles and papers in British, Australian, Canadian Technical Professional Jls. *Recreations:* architectural practice, drawing and travel. *Address:* 22 Princess Road, Claremont, WA 6010, Australia. *T:* 311923. *Club:* Weld (Perth).

STEPHENSON, Lt-Col Sir (Henry) Francis (Blake), 2nd Bt, *cr* 1936; OBE 1941; TD; DL; *b* 3 Dec. 1895; *e s* of late Lieut-Colonel Sir Henry Kenyon Stephenson, DSO, and Frances, *e d* of late Major W. G. Blake, DL, JP, *S* father, 1947; *m* 1925, Joan, *d* of Maj. John Herbert Upton (formerly Upton Cottrell-Dormer), JP; one *s. Educ:* Eton. Lt Col (QO) Yorks Dragoons; served European War, 1914-18, BEF, 1915-18 (1914-15 Star, two medals); War of 1939-45; Middle East, 1939-42 (OBE). JP City of Sheffield; DL Derbyshire, 1948; High Sheriff of Derbyshire, 1948-49. Hon. LLD, Sheffield, 1955. *Heir: s* Henry Upton Stephenson, High Sheriff of Derbyshire, 1975 [*b* 26 Nov. 1926; *m* 1962, Susan, *o d* of Major J. E. Clowes, Ashbourne, Derbyshire, and of Mrs Nuttall; four *d*]. *Address:* Hassop Green, Bakewell, Derbyshire. *T:* Great Longstone 233.

STEPHENSON, Henry Shepherd, CEng, FIMinE; Chairman, Mining Qualifications Board, 1970-75; *b* 1 Oct. 1905; *m* 1934, Faith Estelle, 3rd *d* of Tom Edward Arnold, Bolton Old Hall, Bradford; two *d. Educ:* Whitehaven Grammar School; Armstrong College, Durham University (BSc). Articled apprentice Mining Engineer, Whitehaven Colliery Co., 1924-28; official posts, Whitehaven Colliery Co., 1928-35; HM Junior Inspector of Mines Northern Div., 1935-39;· Mining Agent, Cumberland Coal Co., 1939-41; HM Junior Inspector of Mines and Quarries (Yorkshire), 1941-44; Senior Inspector (Scotland), 1944-47; Senior Dist Inspector (Durham), 1948-52; Senior Dist Inspector (West Midland), 1952-58; Divisional Inspector (East Midland), 1958-62; Deputy Chief Inspector, Jan. 1962; Chief Inspector, 1962-70. Hon. DSc Newcastle upon Tyne, 1971. *Recreations:* gardening, golf. *Address:* Flat 13, The Redlands, Manor Road, Sidmouth, Devon.

STEPHENSON, Hugh; Editor, The Times Business News, since 1972; *b* 18 July 1938; *s* of late Sir Hugh Stephenson, GBE, KCMG, CIE, CVO, and of Lady Stephenson; *m* 1962, Auriol Stevens; two *s* one *d. Educ:* Winchester Coll.; New Coll., Oxford (BA); Univ. of Calif, Berkeley. Pres., Oxford Union, 1962. HM Diplomatic Service, 1964-68; joined The Times, 1968. Councillor, London Bor. of Wandsworth, 1971-78. *Publication:* The Coming Clash, 1972. *Address:* 28 Gwendolen Avenue, SW15. *T:* 01-788 5047.

STEPHENSON, (James) Ian (Love), ARA 1975; painter; Director, Postgraduate Painting, Chelsea School of Art, since 1970; *b* 11 Jan. 1934; *o s* of James Stephenson and Mary (*née* Emery); *m* 1959, Kate, *o d* of James Brown; one *s* one *d . Educ:* King Edward VII School of Art; King's Coll., Univ. of Durham, Newcastle upon Tyne (3 prizes; Hatton Schol.; BA Dunelm 1956, 1st Class Hons in Fine Art). Tutorial Student, 1956-57, Studio Demonstrator, 1957-58, King's Coll., Newcastle upon Tyne; Boise Schol. (Italy), Univ. of London, 1958-59; Vis. Lectr, Polytechnic Sch. of Art, London, 1959-62; Vis. Painter, Chelsea Sch. of Art, 1959-66; Dir, Foundn Studies, Dept of Fine Art, Univ. of Newcastle, 1966-70. Member: Visual Arts Panel, Northern Arts Assoc., Newcastle, 1967-70; Fine Art Panel, NCDAD, 1972-74; Perm. Cttee, New Contemp. Assoc., 1973-75; Fine Art Board, CNAA, 1974-75; Adv. Cttee, Nat. Exhibn of Children's Art, Manchester, 1975-; Selection Cttee, Arts Council Awards, 1977-78. *Exhibitions include:* British Painting in the Sixties, London, 1963; 5e Biennale, Paris, 1967; Junge Generation Grossbritannien, Berlin, 1968; Retrospective, Newcastle, 1970; La Peinture Anglaise Aujourd'hui, Paris, 1973; Elf Englische Zeichner, Baden Baden and Bremen, 1973; Recente Britse Tekenkunst, Antwerp, 1973; 13a Bienal, São Paulo, 1975; Arte Ingelese Oggi, Milan, 1976; Retrospective, London, 1977; Englische Kunst der Gegenwart, Bregenz, 1977; British Painting 1952-77, London, 1977; *illustrations include:* Cubism and After (BBC film), 1962; Contemporary British Art, 1965; Private View, 1965; Blow Up (film), 1966; Art of Our Time, 1967; Recent British Painting, 1968; Adventure in Art, 1969; In Vogue, 1975; Painting in Britain 1525—1975, 1976; Contemporary Artists, 1977; *work in collections:* Arts Council, British Council, BP Co., Contemp. Art Soc., DoE, Gulbenkian Foundn, Northern Arts Assoc., Nuffield Foundn, Stuyvesant Foundn, Tate Gall., Victoria Art Gall., Whitworth Art Gall., Bristol City Art Gall. *Prizes include:* Junior Section, Moores Exhibn, Liverpool, 1957; European Selection, Premio Marzotto, Valdagno, 1964; First, Northern Painters' Exhibn, 1966. *Address:* 49 Elm Park Gardens, Chelsea, SW10 9PA. *T:* 01-352 1310.

STEPHENSON, Jim; a Recorder of the Crown Court, since 1974; barrister-at-law; *b* 17 July 1932; *s* of late Alex Stephenson, Heworth, Co. Durham, and of Mrs Stephenson; *m* 1964, Jill Christine, *d* of Dr Lindeck, Fairwarp, Sussex; three *s . Educ:* Royal Grammar Sch. and Dame Allan's Sch., Newcastle; Exeter Coll., Oxford (Exhibnr, BA). Pres., Oxford Univ. Law Society, Michaelmas, 1955. Called to Bar, Gray's Inn, 1957. Mem., General Council of the Bar, 1961-64; Junior, NE Circuit, 1961. *Recreations:* reading, fell-walking. *Address:* 51 Westgate Road, Newcastle upon Tyne NE1 1SS. *T:* Newcastle upon Tyne 20541.

STEPHENSON, Rt. Hon. Sir John (Frederick Eustace), PC 1971; Kt 1962; **Rt. Hon. Lord Justice Stephenson;** a Lord Justice of Appeal, since 1971; *b* 28 March 1910; 2nd *s* of late Sir Guy Stephenson, CB, and of late Gwendolen, *d* of Rt Hon. J. G. Talbot; *m* 1951, Frances Rose, *yr d* of late Lord Asquith of Bishopstone, PC; two *s* two *d. Educ:* Winchester College (Schol.); New Coll., Oxford (Schol.). 1st Cl. Hon. Mods. 1930, 1st Cl. Litt Hum. 1932, BA 1932, MA 1956. Called to Bar, Inner Temple (Entrance Scholarship), 1934; Bencher, 1962. Sapper RE (TA), 1938; War Office, 1940; Intelligence Corps, Captain 1943, Major 1944 and Lieut-Col 1946; Middle East and NW Europe; Regional Intelligence Officer, Hamburg, 1946; Recorder of Bridgwater, 1954-59; Recorder of Winchester, 1959-62; Chancellor of the Diocese: of Peterborough, 1956-62; of Winchester, 1958-62; QC 1960; Dep. Chm., Dorset QS, 1962-71; Judge of Queen's Bench Div., High Court of Justice, 1962-71. *Publication:* A Royal Correspondence, 1938. *Address:* Royal Courts of Justice, Strand, WC2; 30 Drayton Gardens, SW10. *T:* 01-373 8289. *Clubs:* Hurlingham; MCC.

STEPHENSON, Air Vice-Marshal John Noel Tracy, CB 1956; CBE 1954; Retired; Member Directing Staff, Administrative Staff College, 1960, Director of Studies, 1968-69, retired 1970; *b* Nov. 1907; *m* 1959, Jill Sheila Fitzgerald, *d* of William Fitzgerald Hervey. *Educ:* Whitgift; RAF College. Served War of 1939-45: in UK, in Burma and on loan to Australian Defence Ministry. Berlin Airlift, 1948. Comdt, RAF Staff Coll., 1949-52; Dir of Organisation (Air Ministry), 1952-54; Sen. Air Staff Officer, Middle East Air Forces, 1954-57; Suez Operations, 1957 (despatches); Asst Chief of Air Staff, 1957-59. Officer, American Legion of Merit. *Address:* Hill Grove, Dymock, Glos. *Club:* Royal Air Force.

STEPHENSON, Margaret Maud; see Tyzack, M. M.

STEPHENSON, Prof. Patrick Hay, MA, CEng, FIMechE; Head of Research Requirements Branch 2, Department of Industry, since 1972; Professor of Mechanical Engineering, University of Strathclyde, since 1967; *b* 31 March 1916; *e s* of late Stanley George Stephenson; *m* 1947, Pauline Coupland; two *s* one *d. Educ:* Wyggeston Sch., Leicester; Cambridge Univ. (MA). Apprenticeship and Research Engr, Brit. United Shoe Machinery Co., 1932-39. War Service as Ordnance Mechanical Engr and REME, India and Far East, 1939-45. Chief Mechanical Engr, Pye Ltd, 1949-67; Dir, Inst. of Advanced Machine Tool and Control Technology, Min. of Technology, 1967-70; Dir, Birniehill Inst. and Manufacturing Systems Group, DTI, 1970-72. Mem. Council, IMechE, 1960-68; Member: Bd, UKAC, 1964-73; Engrg Bd, SRC, 1973-. *Publications:* papers and articles in technical press. *Recreations:* music, vintage motoring. *Address:* Toft Lane, Great Wilbraham, Cambridge. *T:* Cambridge 880854. *Clubs:* Army and Navy; Vintage Sports Car.

STEPHENSON, Sir Percy, Kt 1971; company director; *b* 10 April 1909; *s* of James and Elizabeth Stephenson; *m* 1934, Kathleen, *d* of James Percy Bilbie; one *s* one *d. Educ:* Aylwin College. Articled to Accountancy, 1926; entered motor industry, 1930. Served on Lancashire County Council, 1956-57; Chm., Ormskirk Constituency Conservative Assoc., 1960-65; Conservative North Western Provincial Area: Dep. Treasurer, 1964; Vice-Chm., 1965; Chm., 1966-71. Lancaster University: Chm., Buildings Cttee, 1968-; Mem. Council, 1968-; Mem. Court, 1968-; Mem., Finance Cttee; Chm., Safety Cttee, 1974-. *Recreations:* fell-walking, gardening. *Address:* Plaisance, Alderney, Channel Islands. *T:* Alderney 2466. *Club:* Junior Carlton.

STEPHENSON, Philip Robert, CMG 1962; OBE 1951; *b* 29 May 1914; *s* of late Robert Barnard Stephenson and Lilian Stephenson (*née* Sharp); *m* 1947, Marianne Hurst Wraith; two *s. Educ:* Berkhamsted School; Imperial College, London; Downing College, Cambridge; Imperial College of Tropical Agriculture, Trinidad. Colonial Agricultural Service, Entomologist, Uganda, 1938. Military Service, 1940-43. East African Anti-Locust Directorate, 1943-47, Director, Desert Locust Survey, 1948-62, HM Overseas Service. Member, British Advisory Mission on Tropical Agriculture in Bolivia, Dept of Technical Co-operation, 1963-64. *Address:* c/o Lloyds Bank, Berkhamsted, Herts. *Club:* MCC.

STEPHENSON, Sir William Samuel, Kt 1945; MC; DFC; *b* 11 Jan. 1896; *s* of Victor Stephenson, Canada; *m* 1924, Mary French, *d* of William Simmons, of Tennessee. *Educ:* Canada. Served European War, Capt. RFC, 1914-18. Formerly: Personal Representative of Winston Churchill, and Director of British Security Co-ordination in the Western Hemisphere, 1940-46; Chairman Caribbean Development Corporation. Croix de Guerre avec Palmes, 1918; French Légion d'Honneur; US Medal for Merit. *Relevant publications:* (biography by H. M. Hyde) The Quiet Canadian, 1962 (as Room 3603, in USA); Heroes of the Sunlit Sky, by Arch Whitehouse, USA, 1968; Canadians at War, vol. II, 1969; The Two Bills, by Col C. H. Ellis, 1972; A Man called Intrepid, by William Stevenson, 1973. *Address:* Camden House, Camden North, Paget, Bermuda. *TA:* Inter, Bermuda. *Clubs:* Junior Carlton; Royal Yacht (Bermuda).

STEPNEY, Suffragan Bishop of, 1968-78; **Rt. Rev. Trevor Huddleston,** DD; designate Bishop of Mauritius, from May 1978; *b* 15 June 1913; *s* of late Capt. Sir Ernest Huddleston, CIE, CBE; unmarried. *Educ:* Lancing; Christ Church, Oxford; Wells Theological College. 2nd class Hon. Mod. Hist., Oxford, 1934 (BA), MA 1937. Deacon, 1936; Priest, 1937. Joined Community of the Resurrection; Professed, 1941. Apptd Priest-in-charge Sophiatown and Orlando Anglican Missions, diocese Johannesburg, Nov. 1943; Provincial in S Africa, CR, 1949-55; Guardian of Novices, CR, Mirfield, 1956-58; Prior of the London House, Community of the Resurrection, 1958-60; Bishop of Masasi, 1960-68. A Vice-Pres., Anti-Apartheid Movement, 1969-. Trustee, Runnymede Trust, 1972-. Hon. DD (Aberdeen Univ.), 1956; Hon. DLitt Lancaster, 1972. *Publications:* Naught for Your Comfort, 1956; The True and Living God, 1964; God's World, 1966. *Recreations:* walking and listening to music. *Address:* 400 Commercial Road, E1. *T:* 01-790 4382; (from May 1978) Phoenix, Mauritius.

STERLING, Jeffrey Maurice, CBE 1977; Chairman: Sterling Guarantee Trust Ltd, since 1969; Town & City Properties Ltd, since 1974; *b* 27 Dec. 1934; *s* of Alice and Harry Sterling. *Educ:* Reigate Grammar Sch.; Preston Manor County Sch.; Guildhall School of Music. Paul Schweder & Co. (Stock Exchange), 1955-57; Dir, Eberstadt & Co. (Investment Bankers), 1957-63; Fin. Dir, General Guarantee Corp., 1963-64; Man. Dir, Gula Investments Ltd, 1964-69. Mem. Exec., 1966-, Chm. Organisation Cttee, 1969-73, World ORT Union; Chm., ORT Technical Services, 1974-. Dep. Chm. and Hon. Treasurer, London Celebrations Cttee, Queen's Silver Jubilee, 1975-. Chm., Young Vic Co., 1975-; Governor, Royal Ballet Sch., 1976-. *Recreations:* music, chess, swimming, skin-diving, tennis. *Address:* 17 Brompton Square, SW3; Quennells, Plaistow, Sussex. *Clubs:* Carlton, Hurlingham.

STERN, family name of **Baron Michelham.**

STERN, Isaac; violinist; *b* Kreminiecz, Russia, 21 July 1920; *s* of Solomon and Clara Stern; *m* 1948, Nora Kaye; *m* 1951, Vera Lindenblit; three *c.* Studied San Francisco Conservatory, 1930-37. First public concert as guest artist San Francisco Symphony Orchestra, 1934; played with Los Angeles Philharmonic Orchestra and in concerts in Pacific Coast cities; New York début, 1937. Has since played in concerts throughout USA, in Europe, Israel, Australia, South America, Japan, India, The Philippines, Soviet Union and Iceland; has played with major American and European orchestras. Took part in Prades Festivals, 1950-52; Edinburgh and other major festivals in Europe and US. President, Carnegie Hall, NY. *Address:* c/o ICM Artists Ltd, 40 West 57th Street, New York, NY 10019, USA.

STERN, Vivien Helen; Director, National Association for the Care and Resettlement of Offenders (NACRO), since 1977; *b* 25 Sept. 1941; *d* of Frederick Stern and Renate Mills. *Educ:* Kent Coll., Pembury, Kent; Bristol Univ. (BA, MLitt, CertEd). Lectr in Further Educn until 1970; Community Relations Commn, 1970-77. *Address:* National Association for the Care and Resettlement of Offenders, 125 Kennington Park Road, SE11.

STERNBERG, family name of **Baron Plurenden.**

STERNBERG, Sir Sigmund, Kt 1976; FCommA; JP; Founder, Mounststar Metal Corporation; Chairman, Commodities Research Unit Ltd; Director, Forex Research Ltd; Lloyds Underwriter; *b* Budapest, 2 June 1921; *s* of Abraham and Elizabeth Sternberg; *m* 1970, Hazel (*née* Everett Jones); two *s* two *d.* Served War of 1939-45, Civil Defence Corps. Pres., British Secondary Metals Assoc., 1965-66. Treasurer, 1972 Industry Gp. Co-Chm., Arbitration Cttee, Bureau International de la Récupération, 1966-; Mem., Waste Management Adv. Council. Chm., Inst. for Archaeo-Metallurgical Studies. Vice-Pres., Coll. of Speech Therapists; Chm., Nat. Speech Therapy Develt Trust. Treasurer, Council of Christians and Jews. Instituted Res. Gp for Labour Shadow Cabinet, 1973-74; Chm., Appeals Cttee, Fabian Soc., 1975-77; Mem., Economic and Industry Cttee, Fabian Soc., 1976-. Mem. Ct, Essex Univ. Chairman: St Charles Gp HMC, 1974; NW Metrop. RHB, 1974; Member: Camden and Islington AHA; Middlesex Probation

(Case) Cttee, 1973. Mem. Finance and Gen. Purposes Cttee, NAMH, 1972. Former Ring-Dealing Mem., London Stock Exchange. Mem., Rotary Club, London. Mem., Company of Horners. Freeman, City of London. JP Middlesex, 1965. *Recreations:* golf, swimming. *Address:* 55 Gower Street, WC1E 6HJ. *T:* 01-637 2886. *Telex* 26408. *Clubs:* Reform, City Livery.

STERNE, Laurence Henry Gordon, MA, CEng, FIMechE, FIMA; *b* 2 July 1916; *o s* of late Henry Herbert Sterne and late Hilda Davey; *m* 1944, Katharine Clover; two *d*. *Educ:* Culford Sch.; Jesus Coll. (Open Exhibnr and Hon. Schol.), Oxford (MA). Royal Aircraft Establishment: Structures and Mechanical Engrg Depts, 1940; Aerodynamics Dept, 1949; Head of Naval Air Dept, 1954; Chief Supt at Bedford, 1955. Prof. and Dir, von Karman Inst., Rhode Saint Genèse, Belgium, 1958-62; Aviation Mem., Research Policy Staff, MoD, 1962-64; Dir, Royal Naval Aircraft and Helicopters, 1964-68; Dep. Dir, Nat. Engineering Lab., E Kilbride, 1968-76. Vis. Prof., Strathclyde Univ., 1971-76. *Publications:* reports and memoranda of Aeronautical Research Council; ed jtly, early vols of Progress in Aeronautical Sciences. *Recreation:* gardening. *Address:* 10 Trinity Street, Bungay, Suffolk NR35 1EH.

STEVAS, Norman Antony Francis St J.; *see* St John-Stevas.

STEVEN, Guy Savile, MBE 1945; Chairman of Allied Ironfounders Ltd, 1960-70, retired; *b* 24 Nov. 1906; *s* of John Hugh Steven and Ernestine May Shepherd; *m* 1937, Marion Grace Mackenzie-Kennedy; one *s*. *Educ:* Preparatory School; Marlborough College. Joined McDowall, Steven & Co., Ltd, Ironfounders, Falkirk, April 1925; this company became a member of Allied Ironfounders Ltd on the Group's formation, 1929. Director, Allied Ironfounders, 1947; Dep. Man. Dir, 1954; Man. Dir, 1956-67. Served War of 1939-45 (despatches): RASC in Middle East, Italy and North West Europe (Lieut-Col). *Recreations:* shooting and tennis. *Address:* Pickhurst, Chiddingfold, Surrey. *T:* Wormley 2919. *Club:* Hurlingham.

STEVENS, Air Marshal Sir Alick (Charles), KBE, *cr* 1952; CB 1944; retired; *b* 31 July 1898; *s* of late Charles Edward Russell Stevens, Jersey; *m* 1927, Beryl, *d* of B. J. Gates, Wing, Bucks; one *s*. *Educ:* Victoria College, Jersey. Joined RNAS 1916; transferred to RAF on formation, 1918; Wing Comdr, 1937; Air Commodore, 1942. Dep. Director, 1940-42, and then Director of Operations (Naval Co-operation) at Air Ministry, 1942-43; SASO, No 18 Group, 1943-44 (despatches); AOC, RAF, Gibraltar, 1944-45; AOC No 47 Group, 1945; AOC No 4 Group, Transport Command, 1946; Air Vice-Marshal, 1947; AOC No 22 Group, Technical Training Comd, 1946-48; AOC British Forces, Aden, 1948-50; SASO, Coastal Comd, 1950-51; AOC-in-C, Coastal Comd, 1951-53; Air C-in-C, Eastern Atlantic Area, Atlantic Comd, 1952-53; Allied Maritime Air C-in-C Channel and Southern North Sea, Channel Comd, 1952-53; retd Dec. 1953; Vice-Chairman, Gloucestershire T&AFA, 1955-63. *Address:* Cherry Tree Cottage, Cadmore End, near High Wycombe, Bucks. *T:* High Wycombe 881569. *Club:* Royal Air Force.

STEVENS, Anthony John; Deputy Chief Veterinary Officer, Ministry of Agriculture, Fisheries and Food, since 1973; *b* 29 July 1926; *s* of John Walker Stevens and Hilda Stevens; *m* 1954, Patricia Frances, *d* of Robert Gill, Ponteland; one *s* two *d*. *Educ:* Liverpool and Manchester Univs; Magdalene Coll., Cambridge. MA, BVSc, MRCVS, DipBact. Veterinary Investigation Officer, Cambridge, 1956-65; Animal Health Expert for UNO, 1959-63; Suptg Veterinary Investigation Officer, Leeds, 1965-68; Dep. Dir, Central Vet. Lab., 1968-71; Asst Chief Vet. Officer, 1971-73. External Examr, Dublin, Liverpool and Edinburgh Univs., 1964-70. Past Pres., Veterinary Research Club. FRSA. *Publications:* UN/FAO Manual of Diagnostic Techniques; regular contributor to Veterinary Record, etc. *Recreations:* canals, sailing and anything near water. *Address:* Chalkdene, 13 Great Quarry, Guildford, Surrey. *T:* Guildford 65375.

STEVENS, Prof. Denis William; President and Artistic Director, Accademia Monteverdiana, since 1961; *b* 2 March 1922; *s* of William J. Stevens and Edith Driver; *m* 1st, 1949, Sheila Elizabeth Holloway; two *s* one *d*; 2nd, 1975, Leocadia Elzbieta Kwasny. *Educ:* Jesus College, Oxford. Served War of 1939-45, RAF Intelligence, India and Burma, 1942-46. Producer, BBC Music Div., 1949-54; Assoc. Founder and Conductor, Ambrosian Singers, 1952; Vis. Professor of Musicology, Cornell Univ., 1955, Columbia Univ., 1956; Secretary, Plainsong and Mediaeval Music Soc., 1958-63; Editor, Grove's Dictionary of Music and Musicians, 1959-63. Professor, Royal Acad. of Music, 1960. Vis. Prof. Univ. of California (Berkeley), 1962; Dist. Vis. Prof., Pennsylvania State Univ., 1962-63; Prof. of Musicology, Columbia Univ., 1964-76; Vis. Prof. Univ. of

California (Santa Barbara), 1974-75; Brechemin Dist. Vis. Prof., Univ. of Washington, Seattle, 1976; Vis. Prof., Univ. of Michigan, Ann Arbor, 1977. Lectures on music, especially British, in England, France, Germany, Italy, USA; concerts, conducting own and ancillary ensembles at internat. festivals in GB, Europe and USA; TV and radio programmes in Europe and N America; cons. for films. FSA; Member Worshipful Company of Musicians. Hon. RAM, 1960. Hon.D, Humane Letters, Fairfield Univ., Connecticut, 1967. *Publications:* The Mulliner Book, 1952; Thomas Tomkins, 1957, rev. edn 1966; A History of Song, 1960, rev. edn, 1971; Tudor Church Music, 1966; A Treasury of English Church Music (I), 1965; (ed) First and Second Penguin Book of English Madrigals, 1967, 1971; Early Tudor Organ Music (II), 1969; Music in Honour of St Thomas of Canterbury, 1970; Monteverdi: sacred, secular and occasional music, 1977; Gen. Editor, The Penn State Music Series; many edns of early music, including Monteverdi Vespers and Orfeo; articles in English and foreign journals; also many stereo recordings ranging from plainsong to Beethoven. *Recreations:* travel, photography. *Address:* 2203 Las Tunas Road, Santa Barbara, Calif 93103, USA. *Club:* Garrick.

STEVENS, Frank Leonard; formerly Editor, FBI Review and Publicity Officer, Federation of British Industries; *b* Mexborough, 8 Jan. 1898; *s* of late Frederick Thomas Stevens; *m* 1925, Winifred, 2nd *d* of Alexander Bruce, JP; two *s*. *Educ:* Mexborough Grammar School; University College, London. After a year as teacher, three years in the Army (1916-19), entered journalism, South Yorkshire Times, Allied Newspapers, Manchester; Manchester Evening News; assistant editor, John O' London's Weekly; Daily News sub-editorial staff; associate editor, Everyman; joint editor, monthly Clarion. *Publications:* Through Merrie England, 1926; On Going to Press, 1928; Under London, 1939. *Recreations:* reading and sketching. *Address:* Barn Cottage, Singleton, Chichester, West Sussex. *T:* Singleton 653.

STEVENS, Geoffrey Paul; Chartered Accountant, 1926; *b* 10 Nov. 1902; *yr s* of late Alfred Stevens and Maria Ennriquetta Stevens, both of London. *Educ:* Westminster School. Partner with Pannell Fitzpatrick & Co., 1930-70. Contested (C) Park Division of Sheffield, general election, 1945; MP (C) Portsmouth, Langstone, 1950-64. *Recreation:* gardening. *Address:* Littlewick Place, Littlewick Green, near Maidenhead, Berks. *T:* Littlewick Green 2813. *Club:* United and Cecil.

STEVENS, Herbert Lawrence, CBE 1952 (OBE 1936); Consulting Engineer with Messrs Sandberg, 40 Grosvenor Gardens, SW1, since 1954; *b* 26 April 1892; *s* of Thomas Waghorn Stevens and Louisa Cecillia (*née* Davis); *m* 1st, 1917, Beryl Marjorie Gentry (*d* 1949); one *s* two *d* (and one *s* killed in action); 2nd, 1950, Amelia Beatrice Paice. *Educ:* Bradfield College, Berks; Downing College, Cambridge. Schriner Schol., Downing Coll., 1911; 2nd Cl. hons, Part I Maths Trip., 1912; 2nd Cl. hons, Mech. Sci. Trip., 1914; BA Cantab. 1914. Joined Royal Aircraft Establt, Farnborough, 1914 (became head of full-scale flying sect.); Chief Tech. Officer, Aeroplane and Armament Exper. Estab., RAF Martlesham Heath, 1927; Head of Structures Dept, RAE, 1931; Supt of Scientific Research. RAE, 1937; Dep. Dir, Brit. Air Commn, Washington, 1940; Dep. Dir, RAE, 1941; Prin. Dir Equipment Research and Develt (Air), Min. of Supply, 1950; retd from Govt service, 1953. Fellow Roy. Aeronautical Soc.; MIMechE. *Publications:* various papers to Aeronautical Research Council. *Recreations:* photography and gardening. *Address:* Kariba, Copse Avenue, Weybourne, Farnham, Surrey.

STEVENS, Jocelyn Edward Greville; Deputy Chairman and Managing Director, Beaverbrook Newspapers, since 1974, Director, since 1971; *b* 14 Feb. 1932; *s* of Major C. G. B. Stewart-Stevens and of Mrs Greville Stevens; *m* 1956, Jane Armyne Sheffield; two *s* two *d*. *Educ:* Eton; Cambridge. Military service in Rifle Bde, 1950-52; Journalist, Hulton Press Ltd, 1955-56; Chairman and Managing Dir, Stevens Press Ltd, and Editor of Queen Magazine, 1957-68; Personal Asst to Chairman of Beaverbrook Newspapers, May-Dec. 1968; Managing Director: Evening Standard Co. Ltd, 1969-72; Daily Express, 1972-74. *Recreation:* shooting. *Address:* 48 Chelsea Park Gardens, SW3. *T:* 01-352 6276; Testbourne, Longparish, near Andover, Hants. *T:* Longparish 232. *Clubs:* Buck's, Beefsteak, White's.

STEVENS, John Edgar, PhD; FBA 1975; Fellow of Magdalene College, Cambridge, since 1950; Reader in English and Musical History, University of Cambridge, 1974-78; Professor of Medieval and Renaissance English, University of Cambridge, from Oct. 1978; *b* 8 Oct. 1921; *s* of William Charles James and Fanny Stevens; *m* 1946, Charlotte Ethel Mary (*née* Somner);

two s two d. Educ: Christ's Hospital, Horsham; Magdalene College, Cambridge (Schol.; MA, PhD). Served Royal Navy; Temp. Lieut RNVR. Cambridge University: Bye-Fellow 1948, Research Fellow 1950, Fellow 1953 and Tutor 1958-74, Magdalene Coll.; Univ. Lectr in English, 1954-74. Publications: Medieval Carols (Musica Britannica vol. 4), 1952, 2nd edn 1958; Music and Poetry in the Early Tudor Court, 1961; Music at the Court of Henry VIII (Musica Britannica vol. 18), 1962, 2nd edn 1969; (with Richard Axton) Medieval French Plays, 1971; Medieval Romance, 1973; Early Tudor Songs & Carols (Musica Britannica vol. 36), 1975. Recreations: viol-playing, sailing, bricklaying. Address: Highfield Farm, Apthorpe Street, Fulbourn, Cambridge. T: Cambridge 880601.

STEVENS, Vice-Adm. Sir John (Felgate), KBE 1955 (CBE 1945); CB 1951; b 1 June 1900; o surv. s of late Henry Marshall Stevens, Droveway Corner, Hove; m 1928, Mary, o d of J. Harry Gilkes, JP, Wychcote, Patcham, Sussex; one s two d. Midshipman, 1918; King's Coll., Cambridge, 1922, specialised in Navigation, 1924; Staff College, 1930; Commander, 1933; Captain, 1940. Served War of 1939-45 (despatches, CBE); Director of Plans, Admiralty, 1946-47; commanded HMS Implacable, 1948-49; Rear-Admiral, 1949; Director of Naval Training, 1949-50; Chief of Staff to Head of British Joint Services Mission. Washington, 1950-52; Flag Officer, Home Fleet Training Squadron, 1952-53; Commander-in-Chief, America and West Indies Station, and Deputy Supreme Allied Commander, Atlantic, 1953-55; retired list, 1956. Address: Withy Springs, Petworth Road, Haslemere, Surrey. T: Haslemere 2970. Club: Naval and Military.

STEVENS, Hon. John Paul; Associate Justice, Supreme Court of the United States, since 1975; b 20 April 1920; s of Ernest James Stevens and Elizabeth Stevens (née Street); m 1942, Elizabeth Jane Sheeren; one s three d. Educ: Univ. of Chicago (AB 1941); Northwestern Univ. (JD 1947). Served War, USNR, 1942-45 (Bronze Star). Law Clerk to US Supreme Ct Justice Wiley Rutledge, 1947-48; Associate, Poppenhusen, Johnston, Thompson & Raymond, 1948-50; Associate Counsel, sub-cttee on Study Monopoly Power, Cttee on Judiciary, US House of Reps, 1951; Partner, Rothschild, Hart, Stevens & Barry, 1952-70; US Circuit Judge, 1970-75. Lectr, anti-trust law, Northwestern Univ. Sch. of Law, 1953; Univ. of Chicago Law Sch., 1954-55; Mem., Attorney-Gen.'s Nat. Cttee to study Anti-Trust Laws, 1953-55. Mem., Chicago Bar Assoc. (2nd Vice-Pres. 1970). Order of Coif, Phi Beta Kappa, Psi Upsilon, Phi Delta Phi. Publications: chap. in book, Mr Justice (ed Dunham and Kurland); contrib. to Antitrust Developments: a supp. to Report of Attorney-Gen.'s Nat. Cttee to Study the Anti-trust Laws, 1955-68; various articles etc, in Ill. Law Rev., Proc. confs, and reports. Recreations: flying, tennis, bridge, reading, travel. Address: Supreme Court of the United States, Washington, DC 20543, USA.

STEVENS, Kenneth Henry; Chief Executive Commissioner, The Scout Association, since 1970; b 8 Oct. 1922; s of late Horace J. Stevens, CBE, sometime Senior Principal Inspector of Taxes, and Nora Stevens (née Kauntze); m 1947, Yvonne Grace Ruth (née Mitchell); one s one d. Educ: Brighton Coll.; Brighton Technical Coll. South Coast Civil Defence, 1941-44. Alliance Assurance Co., 1944-47; Asst Dir of Adult Leader Training, Internat. Scout Training Centre, Gilwell Park, Chingford, 1947-56; Organising Comr, World Scout Jamboree, Indaba and Rover Moot, Sutton Coldfield, 1956-58; Dep. Dir of Adult Leader Training, Internat. Scout Training Centre, 1958-61; Asst Chief Exec. Comr, The Scout Assoc., 1961-63; Dep. Chief Exec. Comr, 1963-70. MBIM. Publication: Ceremonies of The Scout Movement, 1958. Recreations: motoring, gardening. Address: 69 Ashley Road, Epsom, Surrey. T: Epsom 25031. Club: MCC.

STEVENS, Prof. Kenneth William Harry; Professor of Theoretical Physics, University of Nottingham since 1958; b 17 Sept. 1922; s of Harry and Rose Stevens; m 1949, Audrey A. Gawthrop; one s one d. Educ: Magdalen College School, Oxford; Jesus and Merton Colleges, Oxford. MA 1947, DPhil 1949. Pressed Steel Company Ltd Research Fellow, Oxford University, 1949-53; Research Fellow, Harvard University, 1953-54; Reader in Theoretical Physics, University of Nottingham 1953-58. (Jointly) Maxwell Medal and Prize, 1968. Publications: contrib. to learned journals. Recreations: music, tennis, squash. Address: The University, Nottingham.

STEVENS, Philip Theodore; Professor of Greek in the University of London (Bedford College), 1950-74, now Emeritus; b 11 Nov. 1906; s of late Rev. Herbert Stevens, Vicar of Milwich; m 1939, Evelyn Grace, 2nd d of late G. L. Crickmay, FRIBA, Oatlands Park, Weybridge, Surrey; one s. Educ: Wolverhampton Grammar School; New Coll., Oxford (Scholar). 1st Cl. Hon.

Mods, 1927; 2nd Cl. Lit. Hum., 1929; Asst Master, Liverpool Institute, 1929-30; Tutor at Univ. Corresp. Coll., Cambridge, 1930-32; Asst Lecturer in Greek, Univ. of Aberdeen, 1933-38; PhD Aberdeen 1939. Lectr in Classics, Univ. of Cape Town, 1938-41. War Service, S African Mil. Intelligence, 1941-45. Lecturer in Latin and Greek, University of Liverpool, 1945-50. Publications: Euripides, Andromache, 1971; Colloquial Expressions in Euripides, 1976; contribs to English and foreign classical periodicals. Recreation: music. Address: Baywell Cottage, Charlbury, Oxon. Club: Reform.

STEVENS, Sir Roger Bentham, GCMG 1964 (KCMG 1954; CMG 1947); Director, British Bank of the Middle East, 1964-77; Member, United Nations Administrative Tribunal, since 1972; b 8 June 1906; s of F. Bentham Stevens, JP, and Cordelia Wheeler; m 1st, 1931, Constance Hallam Hipwell (d 1976); one s; 2nd, 1977, Jane Chandler (née Irvine); two step s. Educ: Wellington; Queen's Coll., Oxford; Hon. Fellow 1966. Entered Consular Service, 1928; served in Buenos Aires, New York, Antwerp, Denver and FO; Secretary of British Civil Secretariat, Washington, 1944-46; Foreign Office, 1946-48; Assistant Under-Secretary of State, Foreign Office, 1948-51; British Ambassador to Sweden, 1951-54; British Ambassador to Persia, 1954-58. Adviser to First Secretary of State on Central Africa, 1962; Deputy Under-Secretary of State, Foreign Office, 1958-63; Vice-Chancellor, Leeds Univ., 1963-70; Chm., Yorks and Humberside Economic Planning Council, 1965-70; Mem., Panel of Inquiry into Greater London Develt Plan, 1970-72; Chm., Cttee on Mineral Planning Control, 1972-74. Publication: The Land of the Great Sophy, 1962, new edn 1971. Address: Hill Farm, Thursley, Surrey; Parsons Close, Giggleswick, Yorks. Club: Travellers'.

STEVENS, HE Dr Siaka (Probyn); First Prime Minister and First Executive President, Republic of Sierra Leone, since April 1971; b 24 Aug. 1905; m 1940, Rebecca Stevens; seven s five d. Educ: Albert Academy, Freetown; Ruskin Coll., Oxford. Joined Sierra Leone Police Force, 1923, and became 1st Cl. Sergt and Musketry Instr; worked for Sierra Leone Development Co., and became first Gen. Sec. of United Mine Workers Union (co-founder), 1931-46. Member: Moyamba Dist Council; Freetown City Council (rep. Protectorate Assembly); several Govt Cttees, 1946-48; Sec., Sierra Leone TUC, 1948-50; MLC (elec. by Assembly), 1951, and became first Minister of Lands, Mines and Labour; Dep. Leader of (the now dissolved) Peoples' National Party, 1958-60; formed Election before Independence Movement (which later became the All Peoples' Congress), 1960; became Leader of the Opposition, All Peoples' Congress, 1962; apptd Mayor of Freetown, 1964; sworn in as Prime Minister of Sierra Leone in 1967, re-appointed 1968. Hon. DCL Univ. of Sierra Leone, 1969. Recreation: walking. Address: State House, Freetown, Sierra Leone.

STEVENS, Prof. Thomas Stevens, FRS 1963; FRSE 1964; Emeritus Professor of Chemistry, University of Sheffield; b 8 Oct. 1900; o c of John Stevens and Jane E. Stevens (née Irving); m 1949, Janet Wilson Forsyth; no c. Educ: Paisley Grammar School; Glasgow Academy; Universities of Glasgow and Oxford. DPhil 1925. Assistant in Chemistry, Univ. of Glasgow, 1921-23, Lecturer, 1925-47; Ramsay Memorial Fellow, Oxford, 1923-25; Sen. Lectr in Organic Chemistry, Univ. of Sheffield, 1947-49, Reader, 1949-63, Prof., 1963-66; Visiting Prof. of Chemistry, Univ. of Strathclyde, Oct. 1966-Sept. 1967. Publications: (with W. E. Watts) Selected Molecular Rearrangements, 1973; contrib. to Elsevier-Rodd, Chemistry of Carbon Compounds, 1957-60. Papers in scientific jls. Recreation: unsophisticated bridge. Address: 313 Albert Drive, Glasgow G41 5RP.

STEVENS, Thomas Terry Hoar; see Terry-Thomas.

STEVENS, Thomas Wilson, CBE 1962; RD 1942; Commodore, Royal Mail Line Fleet, 1961-63, retired; b 16 Oct. 1901; s of John Wilson Stevens and Susan Eliza Smith; m 1939, Mary Doreen Whitington; one s one d. Educ: Sir Walter St John's, Battersea. Joined Royal Mail Steam Packet Co. as a Cadet, 1917; joined Royal Naval Reserve as Sub-Lieut 1927. Active service, Royal Navy, 1939-47. Younger Brother of Trinity House, 1944. Captain Royal Mail Lines, 1947; Captain Royal Naval Reserve, 1950. Recreation: golf. Address: 79 Offington Lane, Worthing, West Sussex. T: Worthing 61100.

STEVENS, Timothy John; Director, Merseyside County Council Art Galleries, since 1974; b 17 Jan. 1940; s of Seymour Stevens; m 1969, Caroline Sankey; twin s. Educ: King's Sch., Canterbury; Hertford Coll., Oxford (MA); Courtauld Inst., Univ. of London (Academic Diploma, History of Art). Walker Art Gallery: Asst Keeper of British Art, 1964-65; Keeper of Foreign Art, 1965-67;

Dep. Dir, 1967-70; Dir, 1971-74. *Recreation:* gardening. *Address:* Walker Art Gallery, William Brown Street, Liverpool L3 8EL. *T:* 051-227 5234.

STEVENSON, Dr Alan Carruth; engaged in research in drug-induced cell damage, Royal Northern Infirmary, Inverness; *b* 27 Jan. 1909; *s* of Allan Stevenson, CBE, and Christina Kennedy Lawson; *m* 1937, Annie Gordon Sheila Steven; two *s* one *d. Educ:* Glasgow Academy; Glasgow University. BSc 1930, MB, ChB 1933, MD 1946, Glasgow; MRCP 1935; FRCP 1955. Appointments: Royal Infirmary, Glasgow; Highgate Hospital, London; London Hospital. Served RAMC 1939-45 (despatches); retired with hon. rank of Lieutenant-Colonel, 1946-48. Professor of Social and Preventive Medicine, The Queen's University, Belfast, 1948-58; Reader in Public Health, London University; Dir, MRC Population Genetics Unit, Oxford, and Lectr in Human Genetics, Oxford Univ, 1958-74. *Publications:* Recent Advances in Social Medicine, 1948; Build your own Enlarger, 1943; Genetic Counselling, 1971; articles on Tropical and Preventive Medicine and human genetics in appropriate scientific journals. *Recreation:* fishing. *Address:* Old Laboratories, Royal Northern Infirmary, Inverness and Dunera, Dores Road, Inverness.

STEVENSON, Alan Leslie; Metropolitan Magistrate, 1951-73; *b* 1 Apr. 1901; *yr s* of late James Stevenson, London and Calcutta. *Educ:* Bradfield College; Christ Church, Oxford (BA). Called to the Bar, Inner Temple, 1926; South Eastern Circuit, Kent and London Sessions. Part time Ministry of Food, London Divisional Food Office, Licensing (Revocations) Officer, 1942-49; Chairman Milk Marketing Board Disciplinary Committee, 1950-51. *Recreations:* golf and tennis. *Address:* 48 Lincoln House, Basil Street, SW3. *T:* 01-589 9026. *Clubs:* Bath; Royal St George's Golf (Sandwich); Royal Cinque Ports Golf (Deal).

STEVENSON, Rt. Hon. Sir (Aubrey) Melford (Steed), PC 1973; Kt 1957; **Rt. Hon. Mr Justice Melford Stevenson;** Justice of the High Court since 1957 (Queen's Bench Division since 1961; Probate, Divorce and Admiralty Division, 1957-61); *b* 17 October 1902; *o s* of late Rev. J. G. Stevenson; one *d* (by 1st marriage); *m* 2nd, Rosalind Monica, *d* of late Orlando H. Wagner; one *s* one *d. Educ:* Dulwich Coll. LLB (London). Called to Bar, Inner Temple, 1925, Treasurer, 1972; Major and Dep. Judge Advocate, 1940-45; KC 1943; Bencher, 1950. Recorder of Rye, 1944-51, of City of Cambridge, 1952-57; Dep. Chairman, West Kent Quarter Sessions, 1949-55; Presiding Judge, South-Eastern Circuit, 1970-75. Mem. Inter-Departmental Committee on Human Artificial Insemination, 1958-60. *Recreation:* golf. *Address:* Royal Courts of Justice, WC2A 2LL; Truncheons, Winchelsea, East Sussex. *T:* Winchelsea 223. *Club:* Garrick.

STEVENSON, Sir David; *see* Stevenson, Sir H. D.

STEVENSON, Dennis; *see* Stevenson, H. D.

STEVENSON, Dr Derek Paul, CBE 1972; MRCS, LRCP; Member, Health Services Board, since 1977 (Member, Scottish Committee); *b* 11 July 1911; *s* of late Frederick Stevenson and Maud Coucher; *m* 1941, Pamela Mary, *d* of late Col C. N. Jervelund, OBE; two *s* one *d. Educ:* Epsom College; Guy's Hospital. Lieut RAMC, 1935 (Montefiore Prize, Royal Army Med. Coll., 1935); Capt. RAMC 1936; Maj. 1942; Lt-Col 1943; service in China and Malaya. Asst Director-General Army Medical Service, War Office, 1942-46; Sec. Army Medical Advisory Bd 1943-46. War Office rep. on Central Med., War Cttee, 1943-46. British Medical Association: Asst Sec., 1946-48; Dep. Sec., 1948-58; Sec., 1958-76. Sec. Jt Consultants Cttee, 1958-76. Vice-Pres. British Medical Students Assoc.; Hon. Sec./Treas., British Commonwealth Med. Conf.; Delegate, Gen. Assembly World Medical Association: Sydney, 1968, Paris, 1969, Oslo, 1970, Ottawa, 1971, Amsterdam, 1972, Munich, 1973, Stockholm, 1974, Chm. Council, 1969, 1970-71 (Mem. Council, 1967-). Medical Sec. to Nat. Ophthalmic Treatment Board Assoc.; Mem. Council of London Hospital Service Plan; Mem. Cttee of Management: Medical Insurance Agency; Medical and Dental Retirement Adv. Service. Adviser: Sterling Winthrop, Mediscope Jl; Mem. Adv. Bd, Allied Investments; Gen. Comr, Inland Revenue. Hon. Sec. and Treas., British Commonwealth Medical Assoc., 1964; Sec. Gen., Permanent Cttee of Doctors, EEC, 1973-76; Hon. Sec., British Life Assurance Trust. Liaison Officer, MoD, 1964. Mem. Bd of Governors, Epsom College; Pres., Old Epsomian Club, 1974-75. Fellow, Royal Commonwealth Soc., 1968; Fellow, BMA, 1976 (Gold Medal, 1976). Hon. LLD, Manchester, 1964. *Publications:* contrib. Irish Medical Jl; BMA Lecture delivered to Irish Medical Assoc.; contrib. Canadian Med. Assoc. Jl, and address at Centennial meeting, Montreal; NHS Reorganisation

(in RSH Jl), address to RSH Congress 1973; regular contribs to Medical Interface. *Recreations:* golf, sailing, gardening. *Address:* Bodrigy, Holycombe, Liphook, Hants. *T:* Liphook 724205. *Clubs:* Athenæum, Garrick, Royal Commonwealth Society; Hindhead Golf.

STEVENSON, Henry Dennistoun, (Dennis Stevenson); Partner, Specialist Research Unit, since 1972; Chairman, Newton Aycliffe and Peterlee New Town Development Corporation, since 1971; *b* 19 July 1945; *s* of Alexander James Stevenson and Sylvia Florence Stevenson (*née* Ingleby); *m* 1972, Charlotte Susan, *d* of Hon. Peter Vanneck, *qv*; one *s. Educ:* Edinburgh Academy; Trinity Coll., Glenalmond; King's Coll., Cambridge (MA). Subseq. involved in commercial market research and self-financed research into social problems, esp. recent studies of unemployment among young West Indians, Old Age Pensioners, etc. Apptd Chm. of indep. govt working party on role of voluntary movements and youth in the environment, 1971, which produced the report '50 Million Volunteers' (HMSO). Chairman: Indep. Advisory Cttee on Pop Festivals, 1972-76, which produced report 'Pop Festivals, Report and Code of Practice' (HMSO); Nat. Assoc. of Youth Clubs, 1973-. Dir, Nat. Building Agency, 1977-. *Recreations:* watching most sports, cooking, reading, writing, talking. *Address:* 42 Waveney Road, Peterlee, Co. Durham. *T:* Peterlee 862219; 20 Surrey Square, SE17 2JX. *T:* 01-703 8316. *Club:* MCC.

STEVENSON, Dame Hilda (Mabel), DBE 1967 (CBE 1963; OBE 1960); Vice-President, Royal Children's Hospital, Melbourne, Victoria, Australia, 1938-72; *b* 1895; *d* of H. V. McKay, CBE, Sunshine, Vic; *m* 1st, Cleveland Kidd (*d* 1925); one *d*; 2nd, Col G. I. Stevenson (*d* 1958), CMG, DSO, VD. *Educ:* Presbyterian Ladies' College. Hon. LLD Melbourne, 1973. *Address:* 17 St George's Road, Toorak, Victoria 3142, Australia. *T:* 24-4628. *Clubs:* International Sportsmen's; Sunningdale Golf; Alexandra (Melbourne).

STEVENSON, Vice-Adm. Sir (Hugh) David, KBE 1977 (CBE 1970); AC 1975; Royal Australian Navy, retired; *b* 24 Aug. 1918; *s* of late Rt Rev. William Henry Webster Stevenson, Bishop of Grafton, NSW, and Mrs Katherine Saumarez Stevenson; *m* 1944, Myra Joyce Clarke; one *s* one *d. Educ:* Southport Sch., Qld; RAN Coll. psc RN 1956; idc 1966. Commnd, 1938; served War: Mediterranean, East Indies, Pacific; minesweeping post, SW Pacific; specialised in navigation, 1944 (HM Navigation Sch.); Commands: HMAS Tobruk and 10th Destroyer Sqdn, 1959-60; HMNZS Royalist, 1960-61; HMAS Sydney, 1964; HMAS Melbourne, 1965-66; Dir of Plans, 1962-63; Naval Officer i/c W Australian area, 1967; Dep. Chief of Naval Staff, 1968-69; Comdr Aust. Fleet, 1970-71; Chief of: Naval Personnel, 1972-73; Naval Staff, 1973-76; retd 1976. Comdr 1952; Captain 1958; Cdre 1967; Rear-Adm. 1968; Vice-Adm. 1973. Chm. for Territories, Queen Elizabeth Jubilee Fund for Young Australians, 1977. *Publication:* (contrib.) The Use of Radar at Sea, 1952. *Recreations:* golf, fishing, gardening. *Address:* 4 Charlotte Street, Red Hill, ACT 2603, Australia. *T:* Canberra 95-6172. *Clubs:* Royal Commonwealth Society; Canberra Yacht, Federal Golf (Canberra).

STEVENSON, Air Vice-Marshal Leigh Forbes, CB 1944; *b* 24 May 1895; *s* of John Henry Stevenson and Mary Ann Irving; *m* 1926, Lillian Myrtle Comber; two *d. Educ:* Richibucto Grammar School, Richibucto, NB, Canada. Canadian Expeditionary Force, 1914-17; Commissioned, 1916; RFC 1917-18; RAF 1918-19; RCAF 1920-45. Air Vice-Marshal, 1942; Graduate Royal Naval Staff College, Greenwich, 1930; AOC, RCAF Overseas, 1940-41; retired, Oct. 1945. MLA of BC, 1946-53. US Commander of Legion of Merit, 1945. *Recreations:* shooting, fishing. *Address:* 1163 Balfour Avenue, Vancouver, BC, Canada. *Club:* Vancouver (BC).

STEVENSON, Sir Matthew, KCB 1966 (CB 1961); CMG 1953; Deputy Chairman, Mersey Docks and Harbour Board, 1970-71; Member, British Steel Corporation, 1971-76; *b* 1910; *s* of James Stevenson; *m* 1937, Mary Sturrock Campbell White. Under-Sec., HM Treasury, Oct. 1955-61; Permanent Sec., Ministry of Power, 1965-66 (Deputy Sec., 1961-65); Permanent Sec., Min. of Housing and Local Govt, 1966-70. *Address:* Arden, Towncourt Crescent, Petts Wood, Kent. *T:* Orpington 22626. *Club:* Travellers'.

STEVENSON, Rt. Hon. Sir Melford; *see* Stevenson, Rt Hon. Sir A. M. S.

STEVENSON, Prof. Olive; Professor of Social Policy and Social Work, University of Keele, since 1976; *b* 13 Dec. 1930; *d* of John and Evelyn Stevenson. *Educ:* Purley County Grammar Sch. for Girls; Lady Margaret Hall, Oxford (BA EngLitt, MA 1955);

London Sch. of Economics (Dip. in Social Studies, Dip. in Child Care). Tavistock Clinic; Child Care Officer, Devon CC, 1954-58; Lecturer in Applied Social Studies: Univ. of Bristol, 1959-61; Univ. of Oxford, 1961-68; Social Work Adviser, Supplementary Benefits Commn, 1968-70; Reader in Applied Social Studies, Univ. of Oxford, and Professorial Fellow, St Anne's Coll., Oxford, 1970-76. Mem., Royal Commn on Civil Liability, 1973-. *Publications:* Someone Else's Child, 1965, rev. edn 1977; Claimant or Client?, 1970; contrib. Brit. Jl Social Work. *Recreations:* music, cookery, conversation. *Address:* 223 Church Plantation, University of Keele, Staffs.

STEVENSON, Robert, MA; Writer and Motion Picture Director, Walt Disney Productions Inc., California; *b* 1905; *s* of late Hugh Hunter Stevenson, Buxton; *m* Ursula Henderson, MB, BS (London), FAPA (USA). *Educ:* Shrewsbury School; St John's College, Cambridge (Scholar), 1st Class Mechanical Sciences Tripos and John Bernard Seely Prize for Aeronautics, 1926; Editor of Granta 1927; President of Cambridge Union Society, and research in psychology, 1928. Entered motion picture industry 1929. Motion Picture Producer for US War Dept, 1942, Capt, 1943-46; Maj. US Army Res., 1946-53. Films directed include Tudor Rose (in America, Nine Days a Queen), King Solomon's Mines, Owd Bob (in America, To the Victor), The Ware Case, Young Man's Fancy, Tom Brown's Schooldays, Back Street, Joan of Paris, Jane Eyre, To the Ends of the Earth, Walk Softly Stranger, The Las Vegas Story, Old Yeller, Darby O'Gill and the Little People, Kidnapped, The Absent-minded Professor, The Castaways, Son of Flubber, Mary Poppins, That Darn Cat, The Gnome-Mobile, Blackbeard's Ghost, The Love Bug, Bedknobs and Broomsticks, Herbie Rides Again, Island on Top of the World, One of Our Dinosaurs is Missing, The Shaggy D. A. Has also written and directed very many television films. Film stories which he has written include Tudor Rose and Young Man's Fancy. *Publication:* Darkness in the Land, 1938. *Address:* c/o Walt Disney Productions, 500 South Buena Vista Street, Burbank, Calif 91521, USA.

STEVENSON, Robert Barron Kerr, CBE 1976; MA; FSA; FMA; Keeper, National Museum of Antiquities of Scotland, since 1946, Trustee, since 1975; *b* 16 July 1913; *s* of late Professor William B. Stevenson; *m* 1950, Elizabeth M. Begg; twin *s.* Member: Ancient Monuments Board for Scotland, 1961-; Cttees of Inquiry: Field Monuments, 1966-68; Provincial Museums, 1972-73. Pres., Soc. of Antiquaries of Scotland, 1975-. Fellow, UCL, 1977. *Address:* 8 Cobden Crescent, Edinburgh EH9 2BG. *T:* 031-667 3164.

STEVENSON, Sir Simpson, Kt 1976; Chairman: Greater Glasgow Health Board, since 1973; Scottish Health Services Common Service Agency, 1973-77; *b* 18 Aug. 1921; *s* of T. H. Stevenson, Greenock; *m* 1945, Jean Holmes Henry, JP, Port Glasgow. *Educ:* Greenock High Sch. Member: Greenock Town Council, 1949-67 and 1971-; Inverclyde DC, 1974-; Provost of Greenock, 1962-65; Vice-Chm., Clyde Port Authority, 1966-69. Member: Western Regional Hosp. Bd (Scotland), 1959-; Scottish Hosp. Administrative Staffs Cttee, 1965-74 (Chm., 1972-74); Chm., W Regional Hosp. Bd (Scotland), Glasgow, 1967-74; Member: Scottish Hosp. Endowments Commn, 1969-70; Scottish Health Services Planning Council; Royal Commn on the NHS, 1976-. Chm., Consortium of Local Authorities Special Programme (CLASP), 1974. *Recreations:* football, reading, choral singing. *Address:* Greater Glasgow Health Board, 351 Sauchiehall Street, Glasgow, G2 3HT. *T:* 041-332 2977; 64A Reservoir Road, Gourok, Renfrewshire.

STEVENSON, Sir William Alfred, KBE 1965 (OBE 1954); JP (NZ); civil engineering contractor; Managing Director: W. Stevenson and Sons Ltd; The Roose Shipping Co. Ltd; Director, Dillingham Corporation of NZ Ltd; Formerly Mayor of Howick for 9 years. Manager and Coach, rowing section, Empire Games team, Vancouver, BC, 1954; Manager, NZ Olympic team, Tokyo, 1964. KStJ 1968. *Recreation:* NZ Champion: single sculls, 1923, 1924, 1926. 1927; double sculls, 1925, 1926. *Address:* W. Stevenson and Sons Ltd, Otahuhu, Auckland, New Zealand; Cockle Bay Road, Howick, Auckland.

STEWARD, Prof. Frederick Campion, FRS 1957; Charles A. Alexander Professor of Biological Sciences and Director of Laboratory for Cell Physiology and Growth, Cornell University, Ithaca, NY, 1965-72, now Professor Emeritus (Professor of Botany in the University, 1950-65); *b* 16 June 1904; *s* of Fredk Walter and Mary Daglish Steward; *m* 1929, Anne Temple Gordon, Richmond, Va, USA; one *s. Educ:* Heckmondwike Gram. Sch., Yorks; Leeds Univ. Demonstrator in Botany, Leeds Univ., 1926; Rockefeller Fellow: Cornell Univ., 1927, Univ. of California, 1928; Asst Lecturer, Univ. of Leeds (Botany), 1929; Rockefeller Foundation Fellow, 1933-34; Reader in Botany,

Univ. of London (Birkbeck Coll.), 1934; War Service with MAP (Dir of Aircraft Equipment), 1940-45; Prof. of Botany and Chm. of Dept, Univ. of Rochester, Rochester, NY, 1946-50. John Simon Guggenheim Fell., 1963-64; Sir C. V. Raman Vis. Prof., Madras Univ., 1974. Fellow American Academy of Arts and Sciences, 1956. Merit Award, Botanical Society of America, 1961. Hon. DSc Dehli, 1974. *Publications:* Plants at Work, 1964; Growth and Organisation in Plants, 1968; Plants, Chemicals and Growth, 1971; (ed) Treatise on Plant Physiology (6 vols and 11 tomes), 1959-72; papers in scientific journals and proceedings of learned societies. *Recreations:* gardening, swimming. *Address:* 1612 Inglewood Drive, Charlottesville, Va 22901, USA.

STEWARD, George Coton, MA, ScD, DSc; Professor of Mathematics, The University, Hull, 1930-61, Emeritus Professor, since 1961; *b* 6 April 1896; *o c* of Joseph Steward and Minnie, *d* of William Coton, Wolverhampton; unmarried. *Educ:* The Grammar School, Wolverhampton; Gonville and Caius College, Cambridge (Senior Scholar). Wrangler, with distinction, Mathematical Tripos, 1920; ScD, 1937; First Class Honours in Mathematics in BSc (Honours), Univ. of London, 1917; MSc, 1919; DSc, 1926; Smith's Prize, Univ. of Cambridge, 1922, for contributions on Geometrical and Physical Optics; Member of Scientific Staff of Optics Department of National Physical Laboratory, 1918; Assistant Lecturer in Applied Mathematics, University of Leeds, 1920; Fellow of Gonville and Caius College, Cambridge, 1922; Fellow and Mathematical Lecturer, Emmanuel College, Cambridge, 1923. *Publications:* The Symmetrical Optical System, Cambridge Mathematical and Physical Tracts, No 25, 1928, 1958; papers on Geometrical and Physical Optics, and Plane Kinematics, in Transactions of Royal Society, of Cambridge Philosophical Society, etc. *Address:* 42 South Street, Cottingham, North Humberside. *T:* Hull 847654.

STEWARD, Nigel Oliver Willoughby, OBE 1946; MA Oxon, BA Cantab; Consul-General, Haifa, 1955-59, retired; *b* 16 October 1899; *s* of Arthur Bennett Steward, ICS, and Alice Willoughby; *m* 1933, Raquel Wyneken, of Viña del Mar, Chile; three *d. Educ:* Winchester (Scholar); Trinity College, Oxford. Entered Consular Service, 1924. Vice-Consul at San Francisco, Valparaiso, Guatemala (Second Secretary), and Paris; Consul and First Secretary at Montevideo; Minister (local rank) to Paraguay; First Secretary, Bucharest, 1946; Deputy Consul-Gen., New York, 1946-48; Minister to Nicaragua, 1948-52; Consul-General, Nice and Monaco, 1952-55. *Address:* Middle Park Farmhouse, Beckley, Oxford OX3 9SX. *Club:* United Oxford & Cambridge University.

STEWARD, Stanley Feargus, CBE 1947; CEng; FIProdE; Chairman: William Steward (Holdings) Ltd; William Steward & Co. Ltd; George Thurlow and Sons Ltd; Thurlow Nunn & Sons Ltd; Thurlow Wright Ltd; Thurlow Nunn International Ltd; *b* 9 July 1904; *s* of late Arthur Robert and late Minnie Elizabeth Steward, Mundesley, Norfolk; *m* 1929, Phyllis Winifred, *d* of late J. Thurlow, Stowmarket, Suffolk; one *s* one *d. Educ:* The Paston Sch., North Walsham, Norfolk. Was apprenticed to East Anglian Engineering Co. (subseq. Bull Motors Ltd) and subseq. held positions of Chief Designer, Sales Manager and Dir. Min. of Supply Electrical Adviser to Machine Tool Control, 1940; Director of Industrial Electrical Equipment, 1941-44; Dir Gen. of Machine Tools, 1944-45; Chm. Machine Tool Advisory Council, 1946-47; Chm. Gauge & Tool Advisory Council, 1946-47. Director: E. R. & F. Turner, Ltd, Ipswich, 1944-48. Chm., South Western Electricity Board, 1948-55. Member: British Electricity Authority, 1952-53; Elect. Engineering EDC, 1962-71; Machine Tool EDC, 1971; Chm., British Electrical Development Assoc., 1954; Dir, Electrical Res. Assoc. Ltd; President: Ipswich and District Electrical Assoc., 1964-67, 1972-; Electrical Industries Club, 1966-67; Assoc. of Supervisory and Exec. Engineers, 1970-74; Electrical and Electronic Industries Benevolent Assoc., 1971-72. Managing Director: Lancashire Dynamo Holdings Ltd, 1956-59 (Chm. 1957-58); BEAMA, 1959-71. Formerly Chairman: Lancashire Dynamo and Crypto Ltd; Lancashire Dynamo Electronic Products Ltd; Lancashire Dynamo Group Sales; Pres., Exec. Cttee, Organisme de Liaison des Industries Metalliques Europeénes, 1963-67. Freeman of City of London; Master, Worshipful Company of Glaziers and Painters of Glass, 1964. *Publications:* Twenty Five Years of South Western Electricity, 1973; regular 'Personal View' contribs to Electrical Review and other jls. *Recreations:* books, music. *Address:* 41 Fairacres, Roehampton Lane, SW15 5LX. *T:* 01-876 2457. *Club:* Athenæum.

STEWARD, Sir William Arthur, Kt 1955; Director of food manufacturing companies; gentleman farmer; *b* 20 Apr. 1901; *s* of late W. A. Steward and of Mrs C. E. Steward, Norwich; *m* 1939. *Educ:* Norwich Model Sch., and privately. Freeman of

City of London; Master, Worshipful Co. of Distillers, 1964-65; Liveryman, Worshipful Co. of Fruiterers. Served RAF, 1938-45; Sen. Catering Officer at Air Min., 1943-45; retired with rank of Squadron Leader. MP (C) Woolwich West, 1950-59; Chm. Kitchen Cttee, House of Commons, Nov. 1951-Sept. 1959. Mem. of London County Council for Woolwich West, 1949-52. Chm., London Conservative Union, 1953-55. *Address:* Hethersett Hall, near Norwich, Norfolk.

STEWART, family name of **Earl of Galloway** and **Baroness Stewart of Alvechurch.**

STEWART; *see* Vane-Tempest-Stewart, family name of Marquess of Londonderry.

STEWART, Hon. Lord; Ewan George Francis Stewart, MC 1945; a Senator of the College of Justice in Scotland, since 1975; *b* 9 May 1923; *s* of late George Duncan Stewart, CA, Edinburgh, and late Catherine Wilson Stewart; *m* 1953, Sheila Margaret, *er d* of late Major K. G. Richman, East Lancs Regt; one *s* one *d*. *Educ:* George Watson's Coll., Edinburgh; Edinburgh Univ. Served War of 1939-45 with 7/9 (Highlanders) Bn, The Royal Scots, in 52 (L) Division. Mem. of Faculty of Advocates, 1949; QC (Scotland) 1960; standing junior counsel to Min. of Civil Aviation in Scotland, 1955-60; Hon. Sheriff-Substitute of the Lothians and Peebles, 1961-64; practised at New Zealand Bar, 1962-64; resumed practice at Scottish Bar, 1964; Home Advocate-Depute, 1965-67; Solicitor-General for Scotland, 1967-70; Scottish Law Commissioner, 1971-75. Mem., Cttee on Preparation of Legislation, 1973-75; Chm., Cttee on Alternatives to Prosecution, 1977-. Governor, St Denis School, Edinburgh, 1967-76; Chm., Court, Univ. of Stirling, 1976-. *Address:* 5 Munro Drive, Edinburgh EH13 0EG; Canty Bay, East Lothian. *Club:* Caledonian.

STEWART OF ALVECHURCH, Baroness *cr* 1974 (Life Peer), of Fulham; **Mary Elizabeth Henderson Stewart,** JP; *d* of Herbert and Isabel Birkinshaw; *m* 1941, Rt Hon. Michael Stewart, *qv*. *Educ:* King Edward VI High Sch., Birmingham; Bedford Coll., London Univ. (BA Hons Philosophy). Served War with WRAF, 1941-45. Tutor, WEA, 1945-64. Mem., Fabian Soc. Executive, 1950- (Chm. 1963); Chairman: Governors, Charing Cross Hosp., 1966-74; Fulham-Gilliatt Comprehensive School, 1974-. JP Co. London, 1949; Chm. Juvenile Court, 1956-66. *Publications:* Fabian Society pamphlets. *Recreations:* walking, music. *Address:* 11 Felden Street, SW6. *T:* 01-736 5194.

STEWART, Dr Alan, CBE 1972; Vice-Chancellor of Massey University since 1964; *b* 8 Dec. 1917; *s* of Kenneth and Vera Mary Stewart; *m* 1950, Joan Cecily Sisam; one *s* three *d*. *Educ:* Massey Agricultural College; University College, Oxford. Sen. Lectr, Massey Agric. Coll., 1950-54; Chief Consulting Officer, Milk Marketing Board, England and Wales, 1954-58; Principal, Massey Agric. Coll., 1959-63. *Address:* Massey University, Palmerston North, New Zealand.

STEWART, Alastair Lindsay; Sheriff of South Strathclyde, Dumfries and Galloway, at Airdrie since 1973; *b* 28 Nov. 1938; *s* of Alexander Lindsay Stewart and Anna Stewart; *m* 1968, Annabel Claire Stewart, *yr d* of Prof. W. McC. Stewart, *qv*; two *s*. *Educ:* Edinburgh Academy; St Edmund Hall, Oxford (BA); Univ. of Edinburgh (LLB). Admitted to Faculty of Advocates, 1963; Tutor, Faculty of Law, Univ. of Edinburgh, 1963-73; Standing Junior Counsel to Registrar of Restrictive Trading Agreements, 1968-70; Advocate Depute, 1970-73. *Publications:* various articles in legal jls. *Recreations:* reading, gardening, listening to music. *Address:* 45 Victoria Road, Lenzie, Kirkintilloch, Glasgow G66 5AP. *T:* 041-776 3333.

STEWART, Alexander Boyd, CBE 1962; Director of Macaulay Institute for Soil Research, Aberdeen, 1958-68, retired; *b* 3 Nov. 1904; *s* of late Donald Stewart, Farmer, Tarland, Aberdeenshire; *m* 1939, Alice F., 3rd *d* of late Robert Bowman, Aberdeen; one *s*. *Educ:* Aberdeen University; Zürich Polytechnic. Aberdeen: MA 1925; BSc (1st Cl. Hons) 1928; PhD 1932. Macaulay Inst. for Soil Research, Craigiebuckler, Aberdeen: Head of Dept of Soil Fertility, 1932; Asst Dir, 1943; Dep. Dir, 1945; seconded as Agronomist to Ind. Council of Agric. Research, 1945-46; part-time mem., Develt Commn team to survey agric., forestry and fishery products in UK, 1949-51; Strathcona-Fordyce Professor of Agriculture, University of Aberdeen, 1954-58. Mem. various tech. cttees of Dept of Agric. for Scotland, Agric. Res. Council, Colonial Office and Forestry Commn. Has visited most West European Countries, India, USA, and Canada. Hon. LLD Aberdeen, 1971. *Publications:* papers on soils and agriculture in agric. jls. *Recreations:* bowls, golf. *Address:* 3 Woodburn Place, Aberdeen AB1 8JS. *T:* Aberdeen 34348. *Club:* Farmers'.

STEWART, Prof. Andrew; *b* 17 Jan. 1904; *s* of Andrew Stewart, Edinburgh, Scotland, and Marcia Sabina (*née* Sprot); *m* 1931, Jessie Christobel Borland; four *s* two *d*. *Educ:* Daniel Stewart's College, Edinburgh, Scotland; East of Scotland College of Agriculture (CDA); University of Manitoba. BSA 1931, MA 1932 (Univ. of Manitoba). Lecturer in Agricultural Economics, Univ. of Manitoba, 1932-33; Lecturer, 1935, Prof. 1946, of Political Economy, Dean of Business Affairs, 1949, President, 1950-59, Univ. of Alberta; Chm. Bd of Broadcast Governors, Ottawa, 1958-68; Chm. Alberta Univs Commn, 1968-70; Prof. of Education, Univ. of Ibadan, Nigeria, 1970-72. Member of Royal Commissions: Province of Alberta (Natural Gas), 1948; Canada (Economic Prospects), 1955-57; Canada (Price Spreads of Food Products) (Chairman), 1958-59; Pres. Nat. Conf. of Canadian Univs, 1958; Chm. Assoc. of Univs of British Commonwealth, 1958. Hon. LLD Manitoba, New Brunswick, Melbourne, Alberta; Hon. DEcon Laval; FRSC; Fellow, Agricultural Inst. of Canada. *Address:* 10435 Allbay Road, Sidney, BC, Canada.

STEWART, Andrew, CBE 1954; *b* 23 June 1907; *s* of James Stewart; *m* 1937, Agnes Isabella Burnet, *d* of James McKechnie, JP. *Educ:* Glasgow University (MA). Hon LLD Glasgow, 1970. Joined BBC at Glasgow, 1926; Glasgow Representative, 1931-35; Scottish Programme Director, 1935-48; Controller (N Ire.), 1948-52; Controller (Home Service), 1953-57; Controller, Scotland, 1957-68. Min. of Information, 1939-41. Director, Scottish Television, 1968-77. Chm., Scottish Music Archive, 1972-; Chm., Films of Scotland Committee. Governor, National Film School, 1971-76. *Recreations:* reading, the theatre, mountaineering. *Address:* 36 Sherbrooke Avenue, Glasgow G41 4EP.

STEWART, Andrew Charles, CMG 1955; OBE 1942; DL; Ambassador to Libya, 1962-63; *b* 22 April 1907; *s* of Frederick Naylor F. Stewart; *m* 1935, Emily Caroline Martin; two *s* one *d*. *Educ:* Scarborough Coll.; RMC Sandhurst. Commissioned Indian Army, 1927; transferred to Indian Political Service, 1933; appointed to Foreign Service, 1947; British Minister to Korea, 1954-56; Consul-General at Jerusalem, 1957-59; Ambassador and Consul-General, Iceland, 1959-61. DL Ross and Cromarty, 1976. *Recreation:* golf. *Address:* The Cottage, Dunvegan, Skye. *T:* Dunvegan 213. *Club:* East India, Devonshire, Sports and Public Schools.

STEWART, (Bernard Harold) Ian (Halley), RD 1972; MP (C) Hitchin since Feb. 1974; Director: Brown, Shipley & Co. Ltd, Merchant Bankers, since 1971; Victory Insurance Co. Ltd, since 1976; *b* 10 Aug. 1935; *s* of Prof. H. C. Stewart, *qv*; *m* 1966, Deborah Charlotte, *d* of Hon. William Buchan and late Barbara Howard Ensor, JP; one *s* two *d*. *Educ:* Haileybury; Jesus Coll., Cambridge (MA). 1st cl. hons Class. Tripos Cantab. Nat. Service, RNVR, 1954-56; subseq. Lt-Cmdr RNR. Seccombe, Marshall & Campion Ltd, bill brokers, 1959-60; joined Brown, Shipley & Co. Ltd, 1960, Asst Man. 1963, Man. 1966, Dir 1971. Jt Sec., Cons. Parly Finance Cttee, 1975-76. Mem. British Academy Cttee for Sylloge of Coins of British Isles, 1967-; Hon. Treas., Westminster Cttee for Protection of Children, 1960-70, Vice-Chm., 1975-. FSA (Mem. Council 1974-76); FSA Scot; Dir, British Numismatic Soc., 1965-75 (Sanford Saltus Gold Medal 1971); FRNS (Parkes Weber Prize). Vice-Pres., Hertfordshire Soc., 1974-; Mem. Council, British Museum Soc., 1975-76. Life Governor, Haileybury, 1977. Esquire, Order of St John, 1974. *Publications:* The Scottish Coinage, 1955 (2nd edn 1967); Scottish Mints, 1971; many papers in Proc. Soc. Antiquaries of Scotland, Numismatic Chronical, British Numismatic Jl, etc. *Recreations:* history; tennis (Captain CU Tennis Club, 1958-59; 1st string v Oxford, 1958 and 1959; winner Coupe de Bordeaux 1959; led 1st Oxford and Cambridge Tennis and Rackets team to USA, 1958; played squash for Herts); Homer. *Address:* 121 St George's Road, SE1 6HY. *Clubs:* MCC; Hawks, Pitt (Cambridge).

STEWART, Brian Thomas Webster, CMG 1969; HM Diplomatic Service; Counsellor, Foreign and Commonwealth Office, since 1974; *b* 27 Apr. 1922; *s* of Redvers Buller Stewart and Mabel Banks Sparks, Broich, Crieff; *m* 1946, Millicent Peggy Pollock (marr. diss. 1970); two *d*; *m* 1972, Sally Nugent; one *s* one *d*. *Educ:* Trinity Coll., Glenalmond; Worcester Coll., Oxford (MA). Commnd The Black Watch (RHR), 1942; served Europe and Far East (Capt.). Joined Malayan Civil Service, 1946; studying Chinese Macau, 1947; Asst Sec., Chinese Affairs, Singapore, 1949; Devonshire Course, Oxford, 1950; Asst Comr for Labour, Kuala Lumpur, 1951; Sec. for Chinese Affairs, Supt of Chinese Schs, Malacca and Penang, 1952-57; joined HM Diplomatic Service, 1957; served Rangoon, Peking, Shanghai, Manila, Kuala Lumpur, Hanoi; Asst Sec., Cabinet Office, 1968-72; Counsellor, Hong Kong, 1972-74. *Publication:* All Men's

Wisdom (anthology of Chinese Proverbs), 1957. *Recreations:* climbing, sailing, ski-ing, chamber music, orientalia particularly chinoiserie. *Address:* c/o Foreign and Commonwealth Office, SW1; Broich, Crieff, Perthshire. *T:* Crieff 2544. *Clubs:* Athenæum, Royal Commonwealth Society.

STEWART, Sir Bruce Fraser, 2nd Bt *cr* 1920; Chairman, Pigeon Bay Road Board; ex-Flying Officer, New Zealand Air Force; *b* Sept. 1904; *s* of 1st Bt; *S* father, 1924; *m* 1925, Constance, *d* of W. S. Gray, Cambridge; two *d. Educ:* Eton; Cambridge. Past-President, Canterbury Aero Club. *Recreations:* polo, flying, boating, and golf. *Address:* Strathmore, Pigeon Bay, Banks Peninsula, Canterbury, NZ.

STEWART, Charles Cosmo Bruce, CMG 1962; Head of Cultural Relations Department, Foreign and Commonwealth Office (formerly Foreign Office), 1967-72; *b* 29 July 1912; *o s* of late Brig.-Gen. Cosmo Gordon Stewart, CB, CMG, DSO, and Mrs Gladys Berry Stewart (*née* Brand). *Educ:* Eton; King's Coll., Cambridge. Barrister-at-law, Middle Temple, 1938. Served War, 1939-46. Foreign Service Officer, 1946; First Sec., Rome, 1949; First Secretary (Commercial), Cologne, 1951; transf. to Foreign Office, 1954; Head of Information Policy Dept, 1955-58; Counsellor and Consul-General, Saigon, Vietnam, 1958-61; Counsellor and Head of Chancery, Copenhagen, 1961-63; Consul-General at Luanda, 1963-68. *Club:* Travellers'.

STEWART, Colin MacDonald, FIA, FSS; Directing Actuary, Government Actuary's Department, London, since 1974; *b* 26 Dec. 1922; *s* of John Stewart and Lillias Cecilia MacDonald Fraser; *m* 1948, Gladys Edith Thwaites; three *d. Educ:* Queen's Park Secondary Sch., Glasgow. Clerical Officer, Rosyth Dockyard, 1939-42. Served War: Fleet Air Arm (Lieut (A) RNVR), 1942-46. Govt Actuary's Dept, London, 1946-. FIA 1953. *Publications:* numerous articles on actuarial and demographic subjects in British and internat. jls. *Recreations:* golf, genealogical research, reading about (and where possible visiting) other countries, participation in affairs of Inst. of Actuaries. *Address:* 8 The Chase, Coulsdon, Surrey CR3 2EG. *T:* 01-660 3966.

STEWART, Air Vice-Marshal Colin Murray, CB 1962; CBE 1952 (OBE 1945); RAF, retired; *b* 17 June 1910; *s* of Archie Stewart, Sherborne, Dorset; *m* 1940, Anthea, *d* of Maynard Loveless, Stockbridge, Hants; four *s. Educ:* Wycliffe College, Stonehouse, Glos. Joined RAF, 1932; served in 5 Sqdn, NWF, India, and 16 Sqdn at home; specialised in Signals, 1937. Served War of 1939-45 (despatches, OBE): CSO various formations at home and in Europe. Chairman: British Joint Communications Board, 1952-55; Communications Electronics Cttee of Standing Group, Washington, 1955-57; AOC, No 27 Gp, 1957-58; Comd Electronics Officer, Fighter Comd, 1958-61; Dir-Gen. of Signals, Air Ministry, 1961-64; STSO, Fighter Comd, 1964-67; SASO, Technical Training Comd, 1967-68, retired. Controller, Computing Services, Univ. of London, 1968-73. *Recreations:* fishing, gardening, etc. *Address:* Byelanes, Moult Road, Salcombe, S Devon. *T:* Salcombe 2042.

STEWART, Sir David (Brodribb), 2nd Bt *cr* 1960, TD 1948; Managing Director, Francis Price (Fabrics) Ltd, Manchester, since 1960; *b* 20 Dec. 1913; *s* of Sir Kenneth Dugald Stewart, 1st Bt, GBE, and Noel (*d* 1946), *y d* of Kenric Brodribb, Melbourne; *S* father, 1972; *m* 1963, Barbara Dykes, *widow* of Donald Ian Stewart and *d* of late Harry Dykes Lloyd. *Educ:* Marlborough College; Manchester College of Technology (BSc (Tech), Textile Technology). Joined Stewart Thomson & Co. Ltd, Textile Merchant Converters, 1935; continuously employed in this company, except for six years war service, until absorbed into the Haighton & Dewhurst Group, 1958; Francis Price (Fabrics) Ltd is a subsidiary of this Group. Commissioned 8th Bn Lancashire Fusiliers (TA), 1934; war service, 1939-45; joined Duke of Lancaster's Own Yeomanry (TA) on re-formation of TA, 1947; in comd, 1952-56; retd with rank of Bt Col. *Recreation:* gardening. *Heir: b* Robin Alastair Stewart [*b* 26 Sept. 1925; *m* 1953, Patricia Helen, *d* of late J. A. Merrett; one *s* three *d*]. *Address:* Delamere, Heyes Lane, Alderley Edge, Cheshire SK9 7JY. *T:* Alderley Edge 2312.

STEWART, Sir David James H.; *see* Henderson-Stewart.

STEWART, Desmond Stirling; *b* 20 April 1924; *e s* of late R. M. Stewart, MD, FRCP and of Agnes Maud Stewart (*née* Stirling of Muiravonside); unmarried. *Educ:* Haileybury College (classical scholar); Trinity College, Oxford (classical scholar). MA Hons; BLitt. Asst Prof. of English, Baghdad Univ., 1948-56; Inspector of English in Islamic Maqâsid Schs of Beirut, 1956-58; thereafter chiefly resident in Egypt, writing fiction and non-fiction with a

Middle Eastern background. FRSL 1973. *Publications:* Fiction: Leopard in the Grass, 1951; Memoirs of Alcibiades, 1952; The Unsuitable Englishman, 1955; A Woman Besieged, 1959; The Men of Friday, 1961; The Sequence of Roles, a trilogy (The Round Mosaic, 1965; The Pyramid Inch, 1966; The Mamelukes, 1968); The Vampire of Mons, 1976; Non-fiction: (with J. Haylock) New Babylon: a portrait of Iraq, 1956; Young Egypt, 1958; Turmoil in Beirut: a personal account, 1958; The Arab World (with Editors of 'Life'), 1962; Turkey (with Editors of 'Life'), 1965; Early Islam (with Editors of 'Life'), 1967; Orphan with a Hoop, 1967; Great Cairo, Mother of the World, 1968; The Middle East: Temple of Janus, 1972; Theodor Herzl: artist and politician, 1974; T. E. Lawrence, 1977; Translations: A. R. Sharkawi, Egyptian Earth, 1962; F. Ghanem, The Man Who Lost His Shadow, 1966. *Recreations:* swimming, walking. *Address:* Ilex House, Wells-next-the-Sea, Norfolk; 8 Sharia Yusif el-Gindi, Bab el-Louk, Cairo, Egypt.

STEWART, Rt. Hon. Donald James, PC 1977; MP (SNP) Western Isles, since 1970; *b* 17 Oct. 1920; *m* 1955, Christina Macaulay. *Educ:* Nicolson Institute, Stornoway. Provost of Stornoway, 1958-64 and 1968-70; Hon. Sheriff, 1960. Leader, Parly SNP, 1974-. *Recreations:* fishing, photography, gardening. *Address:* 20 Holm Road, Stornoway, Isle of Lewis. *T:* Stornoway 2672.

STEWART of Appin, Sir Dugald Leslie Lorn, KCVO 1972; CMG 1969; HM Diplomatic Service, retired; British Ambassador to Yugoslavia, 1971-77; *b* 10 Sept. 1921; *m* 1947, Sibyl Anne Sturrock, MBE; three *s.* one *d. Educ:* Eton; Magdalen College, Oxford. Foreign Office, 1942. Served in Belgrade, Berlin, Iraq, Cairo; Counsellor (Commercial), Moscow, 1962; IDC, 1965; Inspector Diplomatic Service, 1966; Counsellor, Cairo, 1968. *Recreations:* shooting, fishing, golf. *Address:* Salachail, Glen Creran, Appin, Argyll.

STEWART, Sir Euan Guy S.; *see* Shaw-Stewart.

STEWART, Ewan George Francis; *see* Stewart, Hon. Lord.

STEWART, Ewen; Sheriff at Wick since 1962; *b* 22 April 1926; *o s* of late Duncan Stewart and Kate Blunt, and *gs* of late Ewen Stewart, Kinlocheil; *m* 1959, Norma Porteous Hollands, *d* of late William Charteris Hollands, Earlston; one *d. Educ:* Edinburgh University. BSc (Agric.) 1946; MA (Econ.) 1950; LLB 1952. Asst Agricultural Economist, East of Scotland Coll. of Agriculture, 1946-49; practised at Scottish Bar, 1952-62; lectr on Agricultural Law, Univ. of Edinburgh, 1957-62; former standing junior counsel, Min. of Fuel and Power; Parly Cand. (Lab.) Banffshire, 1962; Chm., Caithness Gen. Comrs for Inland Revenue; Chm., Scrabster Harbour Trust. *Address:* Strath of Bylbster, Watten, Wick, Caithness KW1 5UQ. *T:* Watten 210.

STEWART, Prof. Sir Frederick (Henry), Kt 1974; FRS 1964; PhD Cantab; FRSE; FGS; Regius Professor of Geology, since 1956, Dean of Science Faculty, 1966-68, and Member, University Court, 1969-70, Edinburgh University; *b* 16 Jan. 1916; *o s* of Frederick Robert Stewart and Hester Alexander, Aberdeen; *m* 1945, Mary Florence Elinor Rainbow (*see* Mary Stewart); no *c. Educ:* Fettes Coll.; Univ. of Aberdeen (BSc); Emmanuel Coll., Cambridge. Mineralogist in Research Dept of ICI Ltd (Billingham Div.), 1941-43; Lectr in Geology, Durham Colls in the Univ. of Durham, 1943-56. Vice-Pres., Geological Soc. of London, 1965-66; Member: Council for Scientific Policy, 1967-71; Adv. Council for Applied R&D, 1976-; Chairman: NERC, 1971-73 (Mem., Geol. Geophysics Cttee, 1967-70); Adv. Bd for Res. Councils, 1973- (Mem., 1972-73); Mem. Council, Royal Soc., 1969-70. Lyell Fund Award, 1951, J. B. Tyrrell Fund, 1952, Geological Soc. of London; Mineralogical Soc. of America Award, 1952; Lyell Medal, 1970; Clough Medal, Edinburgh Geol. Soc., 1971; Sorby Medal, Yorks Geol. Soc., 1975. Hon. DSc: Aberdeen, 1975; Leicester, 1977. *Publications:* papers in Mineralogical Magazine, Jl of Geol. Soc. of London, etc., dealing with igneous and metamorphic petrology and salt deposits. *Recreation:* fishing. *Address:* King's Buildings, West Mains Road, Edinburgh EH9 3JW. *T:* 031-667 1011. *Club:* Athenæum.

STEWART, George Girdwood, MC 1945, TD 1954; Commissioner for Forest and Estate Management, Forestry Commission, since 1969; *b* 12 Dec. 1919; *o s* of late Herbert A. Stewart, BSc, and of Janetta Dunlop Girdwood; *m* 1950, Shelagh Jean Morven Murray; one *s* one *d. Educ:* Kelvinside Academy, Glasgow; Glasgow Univ.; Edinburgh Univ. (BSc). Dist. Officer, Forestry Commn, 1949; Asst Conservator, 1961; Conservator, West Scotland, 1966. Served RA 1940-46 (MC, despatches); Comdg Officer, 278 (Lowland) Field Regt RA (TA), 1957-60. FRSA; FIFor. Pres., Scottish Ski Club, 1971-75;

Vice-Pres., Nat. Ski Fedn of GB; Chm., Alpine Racing Cttee, 1975. *Recreations:* ski-ing, gardening. *Address:* Ferryhills, North Queensferry, Inverkeithing, Fife. *T:* Inverkeithing 3507. *Club:* Ski Club of Great Britain.

STEWART, Prof. Gordon Thallon, MD; Mechan Professor of Public Health, University of Glasgow, since 1972; Hon. Consultant in Epidemiology and Preventive Medicine, Glasgow Area Health Board; *b* 5 Feb. 1919; *s* of John Stewart and Mary L. Thallon; *m* 1946, Joan Kego; two *s* two *d*; *m* 1975, Neena Walker. *Educ:* Paisley Grammar Sch.; Univs of Glasgow and Liverpool. BSc 1939; MB, ChB 1942; DTM&H 1947; MD (High Commendation) 1949; FRCPath 1964; FFCM 1972; MRCPGlas 1972; FRCPGlas 1975. House Phys. and House Surg., 1942-43; Surg. Lieut RNVR, 1943-46; Res. Fellow (MRC), Univ. of Liverpool, 1946-48; Sen. Registrar and Tutor, Wright-Fleming Inst., St Mary's Hosp., London, 1948-52; Cons. Pathologist, SW Metrop. Regional Hosp. Bd, 1954-63; Res. Worker at MRC Labs Carshalton, 1955-63; Prof. of Epidem. and Path., Univ. of N Carolina, 1964-68; Watkins Prof. of Epidem., Tulane Univ. Med. Center, New Orleans, 1968-72. Vis. Prof., Dow Med. Coll., Karachi, 1952-53 and Cornell Univ. Med. Coll., 1970-71; Cons. to WHO, 1953-54, and to NYC Dept of Health, 1970-72; Vis. Lectr and Examr, various univs in UK and overseas. Sen. Fellow, Nat. Science Foundn, Washington, 1964; Delta omega, 1969. *Publications:* (ed) Trends in Epidemiology, 1972; (ed jtly) Penicillin Allergy, 1970; Penicillin Group of Drugs, 1965; papers on chemotherapy of infectious diseases, drug allergy and epidemiology in various med. and sci. jls. *Recreations:* sailing, drawing, music. *Address:* 23 Hamilton Drive, Glasgow G12. *T:* 041-946 7120. *Clubs:* Naval; Royal Northern Yacht.

STEWART, Gordon William, CVO 1964; Chairman and General Manager, Scottish Region, British Railways, 1967-71; Chairman and Managing Director, British Transport Ship Management (Scotland) Ltd, 1967-71; Director, British Transport Hotels Ltd, 1968-71, retired; *b* 13 April 1906; *s* of James E. Stewart and Margaret Stewart; *m* 1935, Dorothy Swan Taylor. *Educ:* Daniel Stewart's Coll.; George Heriot Sch., Edinburgh. L&NER: Traffic Apprentice, 1929; appts in London, Lincoln and Manchester, 1942-52; Prin. Asst to Gen. Man., Eastern Region, 1952; Asst Gen. Man., Scottish Region, 1956. Member: Stirling CC, 1972-75; Bridge of Allan Town Council, 1972-75. *Recreations:* golf, shooting. *Address:* Creag Mor, Blairforkie Drive, Bridge of Allan, Stirlingshire. *T:* Bridge of Allan 832266.

STEWART, Prof. Harold Charles, CBE 1975; FRCP; FRSE; DL; Head of Pharmacology Department, St Mary's Hospital Medical School, 1950-74; Professor of Pharmacology in the University of London 1965-74, now Emeritus Professor (Reader, 1949-64); Consultant in Pharmacology to: St Mary's Hospital, 1946; Ministry of Defence (Army), since 1961; *b* 23 Nov. 1906; *s* of Bernard Halley Stewart, MA, MD, FRSE, FKC, Pres. of Sir Halley Stewart Trust, and Mabel Florence Wyatt; *m* 1st, 1929, Dorothy Irene Lowen (*d* 1969); one *s* one *d*; 2nd, 1970, Audrey Patricia Nicolle. *Educ:* Mill Hill Sch.; University Coll. London; Jesus Coll., Cambridge; University Coll. Hospital. Cambridge Univ.: BA 1928, MA 1934; MB, BCh 1931, MD 1935. London Univ.: PhD 1941, MRCP 1949. Gen. practice, Barnet, Herts, 1932-36. Sub-Dean, St Mary's Hospital Med. Sch., 1950-52; Gresham Prof. in Physic, City Univ., 1968-70. Examr now or formerly, Univs of London, Cambridge, Birmingham, Bristol and Wales, RCS, Soc. of Apothecaries. Research work, mainly on fat absorption and transport in the human subject, and on problems of pain and analgesia. Cons. in Pharmacology to Army; Med. Adviser and Mem. Commonwealth Council, Brit. Commonwealth Ex-Services League; Trustee Sir Halley Stewart Trust for Research and Buttle Trust for Children; Mem. Asthma Research Council; Dir-Gen., St John Ambulance Assoc., 1976- (Dep Dir-Gen., 1973-76; Dist Surg. for London, SJAB, 1950-64); Mem. Chapter-Gen., Order of St John (KStJ); Mem. Council, Stewart Soc.; Vice-Chairman: Med. Council of Alcoholism; St Christopher's Hospice for terminal cases; Liveryman, Soc. of Apothecaries of London; Freeman, City of London: Mem. Physiolog., Brit. Pharmacolog., Nutrition and Genealog. Socs. FFA, RCS, 1969. FRSE 1974. RAMC, T, 1935; Mem. LDV, later Major and Med. Adviser, HG; comd and reformed Med. Unit, Univ. of London STC as Major RAMC, 1942-46. Defence Medal; Gen. Serv. Medal, 1939-46; Coronation Medal, 1953; Guthrie Meml Medal, 1974. DL Greater London, 1967. *Publications:* Drugs in Anæsthetic Practice (with F. G. Wood-Smith), 1962; (with W. H. Hughes) Concise Antibiotic Treatment, 2nd edn 1973; contribs to jls. *Recreations:* voluntary service; sport (lacrosse: Cambridge Half-Blue 1928; lawn tennis); genealogy and heraldry. *Address:* 41 The Glen, Green Lane, Northwood, Mddx. *T:* Northwood 24893. *Club:* Athenæum.
See also B. H. I. H. Stewart.

STEWART, Sir Hector (Hamilton), KBE 1976; MD; FRCS, FRACS; *b* 4 Nov. 1901; *s* of Hector Joseph Stewart and Maggie Russell Robertson; *m* 1935, Viotti Winifred Wheatley; three *s* one *d*. *Educ:* Modern Sch., Perth; Univ. of WA (MB, BS 1926); Univ. of Vic. (MD). FRCS 1930; FRACS 1933. AMF, 1939-45 (Lt-Col). WA Branch, BMA: Mem. Council, 1933-48; Pres., 1948; Mem. Council, Aust. Coll. of Surgeons, 1958-69; Fellow, Aust. Med. Assoc., 1965. Univ. of WA: Mem. Senate, 1962-74; Pro Chancellor, 1970-74. *Recreations:* sailing, golf, bowls. *Address:* 20 Mounts Bay Road, Crawley, WA 6009, Australia. *T:* 862676. *Club:* Weld (Perth).

STEWART, Sir Herbert (Ray), Kt 1946; CIE 1939; FRCScI, DIC, NDA, MSc; *b* 10 July 1890; *s* of Hugh Stewart, Ballyward, Co. Down; *m* 1917, Eva (*d* 1955), *d* of William Rea, JP, Ballygawley, Co. Tyrone; one *d*; *m* 1957, Elsie, *d* of Walter J. Pyne, London. *Educ:* Excelsior Academy, Banbridge; Royal College of Science, Dublin; Imperial College of Science and Technology, London. Military Service, 1915-19; entered the Indian Agricultural Service as Deputy Director of Agriculture, 1920; Professor of Agriculture, Punjab, 1921-27; Assistant Director of Agriculture, 1928-32; Agricultural Expert, Imperial Council of Agricultural Research, Government of India, 1938; Director of Agriculture, Punjab, 1932-43; Member of the Punjab Legislative Council from time to time, 1927-36; Fellow of the University of the Punjab, 1929-43; Dean of the Faculty of Agriculture, 1933-43; Agriculture Commissioner with Government of India, 1943-46; Vice-Chairman, Imperial Council of Agricultural Research, 1944-46; Agricultural Adviser to British Middle East Office, Cairo, 1946-51; Principal Consultant, Agriculture, to UN Economic Survey Mission for Middle East, 1949; Agricultural Adviser to UN Relief and Works Agency for Palestine Refugees, 1950-51; Chief, Agricultural Mission to Colombia of Internat. Bank for Reconstruction and Development, 1955-56; Agricultural Consultant to Bank Missions to Pakistan, 1956, 1958, Italy, 1957, Yugoslavia and Uganda, 1960 and Kenya, 1961-62. *Publications:* various pamphlets and reports on agriculture and farm accounts in India, and on agriculture in Middle East. *Address:* 29 Alyth Road, Bournemouth, Dorset BH3 7DG. *T:* Bournemouth 764782.

STEWART, Sir Hugh Charlie Godfray, 6th Bt, *cr* 1803, of Athenree; Major; DL; High Sheriff, Co. Tyrone, 1955; *b* 13 April 1897; *s* of Colonel Sir George Powell Stewart, 5th Bt, and Florence Maria Georgina, *d* of Sir James Godfray; *S* father, 1945; *m* 1st, 1929 (marr. diss. 1942); one *s* one *d*; 2nd, 1948, Diana Margaret, *d* of late Capt. J. E. Hibbert, MC, DFC, and late Mrs R. B. Bannon, Jersey; one *s* one *d*. *Educ:* Bradfield Coll., Berkshire; RMC, Sandhurst. Served European War, Royal Inniskilling Fusiliers, 1916; Arras, 1917 (wounded); France, 1939-40. Foreign Service has included India, Iraq, China, Malaya, South Africa and Syria; retired. DL Co. Tyrone, 1971. *Heir:* *s* David John Christopher Stewart [*b* 19 June 1935; *m* 1959, Bridget Anne, *er d* of late Patrick W. Sim and of Mrs Leslie Parkhouse]. *Address:* Lough Macrory Lodge, Co. Tyrone, N Ireland. *Club:* Tyrone County.

STEWART, Sir Iain (Maxwell), Kt 1968; BSc, FIMechE, FRINA, FIMarE; Chairman, Higher Productivity (Organisation and Bargaining) Ltd; Deputy Chairman, British Caledonian Airways; Director: Beaverbrook Newspapers Ltd; Dorchester Hotel Ltd; Dunbar & Co. Ltd; Eagle Star Insurance Co. Ltd; Heatherset Management and Advisory Services Ltd; Lyle Shipping Co. Ltd; Royal Bank of Scotland Ltd; Scottish Television Ltd; Industrial Communications Ltd; APV Holdings Ltd; *b* 16 June 1916; *s* of William Maxwell Stewart and Jessie Naismith Brown; *m* 1941, Margaret Jean Walker (marr. diss. 1967); two *s* two *d*. *Educ:* Loretto Sch.; Glasgow Univ. (BSc Mech. Eng.). Apprenticeship at Thermotank Ltd, 1935-39. Served War of 1939-45, Technical Adjutant, Fife and Forfar Yeomanry, 1939-41. Dir. Thermotank Ltd, 1941, Man. Dir, 1946, Chairman, 1950-65; Chm., Fairfields (Glasgow) Ltd, 1966-68; Dep. Chm., Upper Clyde Shipbuilders Ltd, 1967-68. Mem. Bd, BEA, 1966-73. Pres., Inst. of Engineers & Shipbuilders in Scotland, 1961-63; Prime Warden, Worshipful Co. of Shipwrights; Mem. Chamber of Commerce, Glasgow. President's Medal, IPR, 1970. Hon. LLD Strathclyde, 1975. *Recreation:* golf. *Address:* Lochbrae House, Bearsden, Glasgow. *T:* 041-942 0202. *Clubs:* Carlton, Garrick, Caledonian; Western (Glasgow).

STEWART, Ian; *see* Stewart, B. H. I. H.

STEWART, Jackie; *see* Stewart, John Young.

STEWART, James Cecil Campbell, CBE 1960; Deputy Chairman, Nuclear Power Co. Ltd, since 1975; Chairman,

British Nuclear Forum, since 1974; *b* 1916; *s* of late James Stewart and Mary Campbell Stewart; *m* 1946, Pamela Rouselle, *d* of William King-Smith; one *d. Educ:* Armstrong College and King's College, Durham University (BSc Physics). Telecommunications Research Establishment, 1939-46; Atomic Energy Research Establishment, Harwell, 1946-49; Industrial Group, UKAEA, 1949-63; Dep. Chm., British Nuclear Design and Construction, 1969-75; Member: UKAEA, 1963-69; Central Electricity Generating Bd, 1965-69. *Recreation:* gardening. *Address:* Whitethorns, Higher Whitley, Cheshire. *T:* Norcott Brook 377. *Club:* East India, Devonshire, Sports and Public Schools.

STEWART, Prof. James Douglas; Principal, Lincoln University College of Agriculture, since 1974; *b* 11 Aug. 1925; *s* of Charles Edward Stewart and Edith May Stewart (*née* Caldwell); *m* 1953, Nancy Elizabeth Dunbar; one *s* three *d. Educ:* Lincoln UC (Dip. Valuation and Farm Management); Canterbury Univ. (MA); Reading Univ. (DPhil). Lectr in Farm Management, Lincoln Coll., NZ, 1951-59; Research Fellow, Reading Univ., 1959-61; Sen. Lectr, Lincoln Coll., 1962-64; Prof. of Farm Management, Lincoln Coll., 1964-74. Chm., Govt Adv. Cttee on External Aid and Develt, 1975-. Queen's Jubilee Medal, 1977. *Publications:* contrib. Jl Agric. Econs, Jl Farm Econs, Econ. Record, etc. *Recreations:* Provincial Rugby Union Coach, squash raquets, fishing. *Address:* PO Box 16, Lincoln College, Canterbury, NZ. *T:* Lincoln 796.

STEWART, James Gill, CB 1958; CBE 1952; Hon. FITO; *b* 13 March 1907; *s* of John Stewart (builder) and Isabella Stewart, late of Edinburgh; *m* 1936, Jessie Dodd; one *s* one *d. Educ:* George Watson's College, Edinburgh; Edinburgh University. Passed Home Civil Service Administrative Class Competition, 1929; entered Min. of Labour, Asst Principal, 1930; Private Sec. to Permanent Sec., 1934; Principal, 1936; Asst Sec., 1941; on loan to Min. of Works, 1941-43; on loan to UN (Bureau of Personnel), 1946-47; on loan to Cabinet Office, 1947-49; Industrial Relations Dept, 1950-53; Under-Sec., Employment Dept, 1953; Training Dept, 1960, retired, 1967. Trustee, Industrial Training Foundn, 1967. *Recreations:* choral singing, hill walking. *Address:* 104 Highgate West Hill, N6. *T:* 01-340 2014.

STEWART, James Lablache; *see* Granger, Stewart.

STEWART, James (Maitland), DFC with 2 oak leaf clusters (US); Air Medal with 3 oak leaf clusters; DSM (US); actor, stage and film; *b* Indiana, Pa, 20 May 1908; *s* of Alexander Maitland Stewart and Elizabeth Ruth (*née* Jackson); *m* 1949, Gloria McLean; two *s* twin *d. Educ:* Mercersburg Academy, Pa; Princeton University (BS Arch.). War Service, 1942-45: Lt-Col Air Corps; Europe, 1943-45 (Air Medal, DFC); Colonel, 1945. USAF Reserve; Brig.-Gen. 1959. Dir, Air Force Assoc. First New York appearance, Carry Nation, 1932; subseq. played in Goodbye Again, Spring in Autumn, All Good Americans, Yellow Jack, Divided by Three, Page Miss Glory, A Journey by Night. Entered films, 1935; *films include:* Murder Man, Next Time We Love, Seventh Heaven, You Can't Take It With You, Made for Each Other, Vivacious Lady, The Shopworn Angel, Mr Smith Goes to Washington, Destry Rides Again, No Time for Comedy, Philadelphia Story, The Shop around the Corner, Pot o' Gold, Ziegfeld Girl, Come Live with Me, It's a Wonderful Life, Magic Town, On Our Merry Way, You Gotta Stay Happy, Call Northside 777, Rope, The Stratton Story, Malaya, The Jackpot, Harvey, Winchester '73, Broken Arrow, No Highway in the Sky, Bend of the River, Carbine Williams, The Greatest Show on Earth, Thunder Bay, Naked Spur, The Glen Miller Story, Rear Window, The Man from Laramie, The Far Country, Strategic Air Command, The Man Who Knew Too Much, Night Passage, Spirit of St Louis, Midnight Story, Vertigo, Bell, Book and Candle, Anatomy of a Murder, The FBI Story, The Mountain Road, The Man Who Shot Liberty Valance, Mr Hobbs Takes a Vacation, Take her, She's Mine, Cheyenne Autumn, Shenandoah, The Rare Breed, Firecreek, Bandalero, The Cheyenne Social Club, Fool's Parade, Dynamite Man from Glory Jail, The Shootist, Airport 77. *Play* Harvey (Broadway), 1970, (Prince of Wales), 1975. Holds many awards including: five Academy Award nominations; Oscar award as best actor of the year; two NY Film Critics best actor awards; Venice Film Festival best actor award; France's Victoire Trophy for best actor; Screen Actors Guild award. Hon. degrees include: DLitt, Pennsylvania; MA, Princeton. *Address:* PO Box 550, Beverly Hills, Calif., USA.

STEWART, James Robertson, CBE 1971 (OBE 1964); Clerk of the University Court, University of London, since 1950 (Deputy Clerk, 1946-49); *b* 1917; *s* of James and Isabella Stewart; *m* 1941, Grace Margaret Kirsop; two *s* one *d. Educ:* Perth Acad.;

Whitley and Monkseaton High Sch.; Armstrong Coll. (later King's Coll.), Newcastle, Univ. of Durham. BA Dunelm (1st cl. hons Mod. History) 1937; DThPT (1st cl.) 1938; research in Canada (Canada Co.), 1938-39; awarded Holland Rose Studentship, Cambridge, and William Black Noble Fellowship, Durham, 1939; MA Dunelm 1941. Served Army, 1939-46: Royal Artillery (BEF); Combined Ops HQ; Directorate of Combined Ops, India; Major (Actg Lt-Col); Certif. of Good Service. *Recreations:* golf, stamp collecting, gardening, watching (now) soccer and cricket. *Address:* 84 Fir Tree Road, Banstead, Surrey. *T:* Burgh Heath 54370. *Clubs:* Athenæum; Cuddington (Banstead) Golf.

STEWART, Very Rev. James Stuart, MA, Hon. DD; Professor Emeritus of New Testament Language, Literature and Theology, University of Edinburgh, New College (retired 1966); Extra Chaplain to the Queen in Scotland (Chaplain, 1952-66); *b* 21 July 1896; *s* of William Stewart, Dundee, and Katharine Jane Stuart Duke; *m* 1931, Rosamund Anne Barron, Berkeley Lodge, Blandford, Dorset; two *s. Educ:* High School, Dundee; St Andrews University (MA, BD); New College, Edinburgh; University of Bonn, Germany. Minister of following Church of Scotland Congregations: St Andrews, Auchterarder, 1924-28; Beechgrove, Aberdeen, 1928-35; North Morningside, Edinburgh, 1935-46. Hon. DD, St Andrews Univ., 1945. Held following special lectureships: Cunningham Lectures, New Coll., Edinburgh, 1934; Warrack Lectures, Edinburgh and St Andrews Univs, 1944; Hoyt Lectures, Union Seminary, New York, 1949; Lyman Beecher Lectures, Yale University, USA, 1952; Duff Missionary Lectures, 1953; Turnbull Trust Preacher, Scots Church, Melbourne, 1959; Stone Lectures, Princeton, 1962; Earl Lectures, Berkeley, California, 1967; Moderator of General Assembly of Church of Scotland, May 1963-64. *Publications:* The Life and Teaching of Jesus Christ, 1932; A Man in Christ: St Paul's Theology, 1935; The Gates of New Life, 1937; The Strong Name, 1941; Heralds of God, 1945; A Faith To Proclaim, 1953; Thine Is The Kingdom, 1956; The Wind of the Spirit, 1968; River of Life, 1972; King for Ever, 1975; Joint Editor, English Trans. of Schleiermacher, The Christian Faith, 1928. *Address:* 6 Crawfurd Road, Edinburgh EH16 5PQ. *T:* 031-667 1810.

STEWART, Sir James (Watson), 4th Bt, *cr* 1920; *b* 8 Nov. 1922; *s* of Sir James Watson Stewart, 3rd Bt and Janie Steuart Stewart (*née* Sim) (she *m* 2nd, 1961, Neil Charteris Riddell); *S* father 1955; *m* 1946, Anne Elizabeth Glaister; no *c. Educ:* Uppingham; Aberdeen University. Served 1940-47: Royal Artillery; 1st Special Air Service: Parachute Regiment. *Heir: brother* John Keith Watson Stewart [*b* 25 Feb. 1929; *m* 1954, Mary Elizabeth, *d* of John Francis Moxon; two *s* one *d*]. *Address:* Wellwood, Highfield, Fairlie, Ayrshire, Scotland. *T:* Fairlie 567.

STEWART, Sir Jocelyn Harry, 12th Bt, *cr* 1623; *b* 24 Jan. 1903; *s* of Sir Harry Jocelyn Urquhart Stewart, 11th Bt, and Isabel Mary (*d* 1956), 2nd *d* of Col Mansfield, DL, Castle Wray, Co. Donegal; *S* father, 1945; *m* 1st, Constance Shillaber (*d* 1940); one *s*; 2nd, 1946, Katherine Christina Sweeney, Tamney, Co. Donegal; two *s* two *d. Heir: s* Alan D'Arcy Stewart [*b* 29 Nov. 1932; *m* 1952, Patricia, *d* of Lawrence Turner, Ramelton, Co. Donegal; two *s* two *d*].

STEWART of Ardvorlich, John Alexander MacLaren, TD; Vice-Lord-Lieutenant, Perth and Kinross (formerly Perthshire), since 1974; *b* 25 March 1904; *s* of late Major William Stewart of Ardvorlich and of Lily, *d* of late Dr A. C. MacLaren, Harley Street, London; *m* 1930, Violet Hermione, *er d* of late Col Sir Donald Walter Cameron of Lochiel, KT, CMG; one *s* one *d. Educ:* Wellington Coll., Berks. Landowner and farmer. Served War, 1939-45: 6th Bn, The Black Watch (France, 1940; Tunisia, 1943; Italy, 1944). *Publications:* The Stewarts, 1954, 2nd edn 1963; The Grahams, 1958, 2nd edn 1970; The Camerons- A History of Clan Cameron, 1974. *Recreations:* normal country pursuits in Highlands. *Address:* Ardvorlich, Lochearnhead, Perthshire. *T:* Lochearnhead 218. *Clubs:* Farmers'; Royal Perth Golfing, County and City (Perth).

STEWART, John Anthony Benedict, OBE 1973; HM Diplomatic Service; Counsellor, and Head of Hong Kong Department, Foreign and Commonwealth Office, since 1976; *b* 24 May 1927; *e s* of late Edward Vincent Stewart and Emily Veronica (*née* Jones); *m* 1960, Geraldine Margaret, *o d* of late Captain G. C. Clifton; one *s* one *d* (and one *s* decd). *Educ:* St Illtyd's Coll.; Univ. of Wales (BSc, MA); Cambridge Univ.; Imperial Coll. of Science and Technology, London Univ. (Dip. in Geochem.); Cox Gold medal for Geology, 1950. RNVR Ordinary Seaman, later Midshipman, 1944-47. Colonial Geol. Survey Service, Somaliland Protectorate, 1952-56; Dist Officer, 1956-57; seconded to Anglo-Ethiopian Liaison Service, 1957-60 (Sen.

Liaison Officer, 1960); transf. N Rhodesia as Dist Officer, 1960, Dist Comr, 1962-64; Resident Local Govt Officer, Barotseland, 1964-67. Entered HM Diplomatic Service, 1968; served FCO, Barbados, Uganda; RCDS, 1974; Ambassador to Democratic Republic of Vietnam, 1975-76. *Publications:* The Geology of the Mait Area, 1955; papers in geological jls. *Recreations:* shooting, fishing, flying light aeroplanes. *Address:* c/o Foreign and Commonwealth Office, SW1; Kingfishers, Abbotswood, Guildford. *T:* Guildford 64362. *Clubs:* Travellers'; Three Counties Aero (Blackbushe).

STEWART, Captain John Christie, CBE 1947; DL; JP; Lord Lieutenant of Lanarkshire, 1959-63; Chairman Red Cross Council for Scotland, 1956-59; *b* 1 Aug. 1888; *o surv s* of late Sir Robert King Stewart, KBE; *m* 1928, Agnes Violet Averil, JP Lanarks (*d* 1975), *d* of Brig.-Gen. Douglas Campbell Douglas, CB, and Hon. Mrs Douglas. *Educ:* Eton; University Coll., Oxford. MA Oxon, 1912. Served 1914-19 with HLI, and on general staff as Captain. Member of Royal Company of Archers (Queen's Body Guard for Scotland). Chairman Red Cross Exec. Cttee for Scotland, 1942-56. Grand Master Mason of Scotland, 1942-46. JP 1926, DL 1933, VL, 1957-59, Lanarkshire. *Recreations:* shooting and travelling. *Address:* Murdostoun Castle, Newmains, Lanarkshire. *T:* Wishaw 4757. *Clubs:* United Oxford & Cambridge University; New (Edinburgh).

STEWART, John Innes Mackintosh; Reader in English Literature, Oxford University, 1969-73; Student of Christ Church, Oxford, 1949-73, now Emeritus; *b* 30 Sept. 1906; *s* of late John Stewart, Director of Education in the City of Edinburgh, and Eliza Jane, *d* of James Clark, Golford, Nairn; *m* 1932, Margaret Hardwick; three *s* two *d*. *Educ:* Edinburgh Academy; Oriel College, Oxford. Bishop Fraser's Scholar, 1930; 1st class Eng. Lang. and Lit. 1928; Matthew Arnold Memorial Prize, 1929; Lectr in English in Univ. of Leeds, 1930-35; Jury Professor of English in Univ. of Adelaide, 1935-45; Lectr in Queen's Univ., Belfast, 1946-48; Walker-Ames Prof., Univ. of Washington, 1961. Hon. DLitt New Brunswick, 1962. *Publications:* Montaigne's Essays: John Florio's Translation, 1931; Character and Motive in Shakespeare, 1949; Eight Modern Writers, 1963; Rudyard Kipling, 1966; Joseph Conrad, 1968; Thomas Hardy, 1971; Shakespeare's Lofty Scene (Shakespeare Lectr, British Acad.), 1971. Detective novels and broadcast scripts (under pseudonym of Michael Innes) Death at the President's Lodging, 1936; Hamlet Revenge!, 1937; Lament for a Maker, 1938; Stop Press, 1939; There Came Both Mist and Snow, 1940; The Secret Vanguard, 1940; Appleby on Ararat, 1941; The Daffodil Affair, 1942; The Weight of the Evidence, 1944; Appleby's End, 1945; From London Far, 1946; What Happened at Hazelwood, 1947; A Night of Errors, 1948; The Hawk and the Handsaw, 1948; The Journeying Boy, 1949; Operation Pax, 1951; A Private View, 1952; Christmas at Candleshoe, 1953; Appleby Talking, 1954; The Man From the Sea, 1955; Old Hall, New Hall, 1956; Appleby Talks Again, 1956; Appleby Plays Chicken, 1956; The Long Farewell, 1958; Hare Sitting Up, 1959; The New Sonia Wayward, 1960; Silence Observed, 1961; A Connoisseur's Case, 1962; Money from Holme, 1964; The Bloody Wood, 1966; A Change of Heir, 1966; Appleby at Allington, 1968; A Family Affair, 1969; Death at the Chase, 1970; An Awkward Lie, 1971; The Open House, 1972; Appleby's Answer, 1973; Appleby's Other Story, 1974; The Mysterious Commission, 1974; The Appleby File, 1975; The Gay Phoenix, 1976; Honeybath's Haven, 1977; (*novels* as J. I. M. Stewart) Mark Lambert's Supper, 1954; The Guardians, 1955; A Use of Riches, 1957; The Man Who Wrote Detective Stories, 1959; The Man Who Won the Pools, 1961; The Last Tresilians, 1963; An Acre of Grass, 1965; The Aylwins, 1966; Vanderlyn's Kingdom, 1967; Cucumber Sandwiches, 1969; Avery's Mission, 1971; A Palace of Art, 1972; Mungo's Dream, 1973; quintet, A Staircase in Surrey, 1974-78 (The Gaudy, 1974; Young Pattullo, 1975; A Memorial Service, 1976; The Madonna of the Astrolabe, 1977; Full Term, 1978). *Recreation:* walking. *Address:* Fawler Copse, Fawler, Wantage, Oxon.
See also M. J. Stewart.

STEWART, John Philip, MD, FRCSE, FSA Scotland; Consulting Surgeon, Deaconess Hospital; Hon. Consulting Surgeon, Royal Infirmary, Edinburgh; former Hon. Senior Lecturer and Head of Department of Otorhinolaryngology, member, Faculty of Medicine and Senatus Academicus, University of Edinburgh; *b* 1 Feb. 1900; *s* of late George Stewart, SSC, JP, and Flora Philip, MA; *m* 1928, Elizabeth Josephine Forbes Wedderburn. *Educ:* Daniel Stewart's College and University, Edinburgh; Paris and Vienna. 2nd Lieut RFA 1918; MB, ChB Edinburgh Univ. 1923; MD 1925; FRCSE 1926; Lt-Col RAMC, Adviser in Oto-Rhino-Laryngology, BLA; served France, 1940; Egypt and Persia, 1942-43; North-West Europe, 1944-45 (despatches). *Publication:* Turner's Diseases of Ear,

Nose and Throat. *Recreation:* golf. *Address:* Gleven, 20 Gallow Hill, Peebles EH45 9BG. *T:* Peebles 20447.

STEWART, John Young, (Jackie Stewart), OBE 1972; racing driver, retired 1973; *b* 11 June 1939; *s* of late Robert Paul Stewart and of Jean Clark Young; *m* 1962, Helen McGregor; two *s*. *Educ:* Dumbarton Academy. First raced, 1961; competed in 4 meetings, 1961-62, driving for Barry Filer, Glasgow; drove for Ecurie Ecosse and Barry Filer, winning 14 out of 23 starts, 1963; 28 wins out of 53 starts, 1964; drove Formula 1 for BRM, 1965-67 and for Ken Tyrrell, 1968-73; has won Australian, New Zealand, Swedish, Mediterranean, Japanese and many other non-championship, major internat. Motor Races; set up new world record by winning his 26th World Championship Grand Prix (Zandvoort), July 1973, and 27th (Nurburgring), Aug. 1973; 3rd in World Championship, 1965; 2nd in 1968 and 1972; World Champion, 1969, 1971, 1973. BARC Gold Medal 1971. Daily Express Sportsman of the Year, 1971, 1973; BBC Sports Personality of the Year, 1973; Scottish Sportsman of the Year, 1973; US Sportsman of the Year, 1973; Segrave Trophy, 1973. *Film:* Weekend of a Champion, 1972. *Publication:* Faster!, 1972 (with Peter Manse). *Recreations:* golf, fishing; shooting (Mem. British Team for Clay Pigeon shooting; former Scottish, English, Irish, Welsh and British Champion; won Coupe des Nations, 1959 and 1960; reserve for two-man team, 1960 Olympics). *Address:* Clayton House, 1268 Begnins, Vaud, Switzerland. *T:* Geneva 61.01.52. *Clubs:* (Hon.) Royal Automobile, British Racing Drivers' (Vice-Pres.); (Hon.) Royal Scottish Automobile; (Pres.) Scottish Motor Racing (Duns).

STEWART, Kenneth Hope, PhD; Director of Research, Meteorological Office, since 1976; *b* 29 March 1922; *s* of Harry Sinclair Stewart and Nora Hassan Parry; *m* 1950, Hilary Guest; four *s* four *d*. *Educ:* Trinity Coll., Cambridge (MA, PhD). Entered Meteorol Office, 1949; Dep. Dir, Physical Res., 1974. *Publications:* Ferromagnetic Domains, 1951; contrib. physical and meteorol jls. *Address:* 33 Ravenswood Avenue, Crowthorne, Berks.

STEWART, Mary (Florence Elinor), (Lady Stewart); *b* 17 Sept. 1916; *d* of Rev. Frederick A. Rainbow, Durham Diocese, and Mary Edith (*née* Matthews), NZ; *m* 1945, Sir Frederick Henry Stewart, *qv*; no *c*. *Educ:* Eden Hall, Penrith, Cumberland; Skellfield School, Ripon, Yorks; St Hild's Coll., Durham Univ. BA 1941. MA 1941. Asst Lectr in English, Durham Univ., 1941-45; Part-time Lectr in English, St Hild's Training Coll., Durham, and Durham Univ., 1948-56. FRSA 1968. *Publications:* novels: Madam, Will You Talk?, 1954; Wildfire at Midnight, 1956; Thunder on the Right, 1957; Nine Coaches Waiting, 1958; My Brother Michael, 1959; The Ivy Tree, 1961; The Moonspinners, 1962; This Rough Magic, 1964; Airs Above the Ground, 1965; The Gabriel Hounds, 1967; The Wind Off The Small Isles, 1968; The Crystal Cave, 1970; The Little Broomstick, 1971; The Hollow Hills, 1973; Ludo and the Star Horse, 1974; Touch Not the Cat, 1976; also articles, poems, radio plays. *Recreations:* gardening, music, painting. *Address:* 79 Morningside Park, Edinburgh EH10 5EZ. *T:* 031-447 2620.

STEWART, Rt. Hon. Michael, PC 1964; CH 1969; MP (Lab) Hammersmith, Fulham, since 1974 (Fulham East, 1945-55; Fulham, 1955-74); *b* 6 Nov. 1906; *s* of Robert Wallace Stewart, DSc and Eva Stewart; *m* 1941, Mary Elizabeth (*see* Baroness Stewart of Alvechurch); no *c*. *Educ:* Christ's Hosp.; St John's Coll., Oxford. Pres. Oxford Union, 1929; Asst Master, Merchant Taylors' Sch., 1930-31; Asst Master, Coopers' Company's School, and Lectr for Workers' Educational Assoc., 1931-42. Joined Army Intelligence Corps, 1942. Trans. to Army Educational Corps, 1943; commissioned and promoted to Capt., 1944. Contested (Lab) West Lewisham, 1931 and 1935; Vice-Chamberlain of HM Household, 1946-47; Comptroller of HM Household, 1946-47; Under-Sec. of State for War, 1947-51; Parly Sec., Min. of Supply, May-Oct. 1951; Sec. of State for Education and Science, Oct. 1964-Jan. 1965; Sec. of State for Foreign Affairs, Jan. 1965-Aug. 1966; First Sec. of State, 1966-68; Sec. of State for Economic Affairs, 1966-67; Secretary of State for Foreign and Commonwealth Affairs, 1968-70. Mem., European Parlt, 1975-76. Freeman of Hammersmith, 1967. Hon. Fellow, St John's Coll. Oxford, 1965; Hon. LLD Leeds, 1966; Hon. DSc Benin, 1972. *Publications:* The Forty Hour Week (Fabian Soc.), 1936; Bias and Education for Democracy, 1937; The British Approach to Politics, 1938; Modern Forms of Government, 1959. *Recreations:* chess, painting. *Address:* 11 Felden Street, SW6. *T:* 01-736 5194. *Club:* Reform.

STEWART, Michael James; Reader in Political Economy, University College, London University, since 1969; *b* 6 Feb. 1933; *s* of John Innes Mackintosh Stewart, *qv*; *m* 1962, Hon. Frances Kaldor, *d* of Baron Kaldor, *qv*; one *s* three *d*. *Educ:*

Campbell Coll., Belfast, St Edward's Sch., Oxford; Magdalen Coll., Oxford. 1st cl. PPE (Oxon), 1955. Asst Res. Off., Oxford Univ. Inst. of Statistics, 1955-56; Barnett Fellow, Cornell Univ., 1956-57; Econ. Asst, HM Treasury, 1957-60; Sec. to Council on Prices, Productivity and Incomes, 1960-61; Econ. Adviser, HM Treasury, 1961-62, Cabinet Office, 1964-67 (Senior Econ. Advr, 1967), Kenya Treasury, 1967-69; Special Adviser to Sec. of State for Trade, Apr.-Oct. 1974; Economic Adviser to Malta Labour Party, 1970-73; Special Econ. Advr to Foreign Sec., 1977-. Contested (Lab): Folkestone and Hythe, 1964; Croydon North-West, 1966. Asst Editor, Nat. Inst. Econ. Review, 1962-64. Consultant to various UN agencies, 1971-. *Publications:* Keynes and After, 1967; The Jekyll and Hyde Years: politics and economic policy since 1964, 1977. *Recreation:* walking. *Address:* 79 South Hill Park, NW3 2SS. *T:* 01-435 3686.

STEWART, Sir Michael (Norman Francis), KCMG 1966 (CMG 1957); OBE 1948; HM Diplomatic Service, retired; Director, Sotheby's, since 1977; *b* 18 Jan. 1911; *s* of late Sir Francis Stewart, CIE, and of Lady Stewart; *m* 1951, Katharine Damaris Houssemayne du Boulay; one *s* two *d. Educ:* Shrewsbury; Trinity College, Cambridge. Assistant Keeper, Victoria and Albert Museum, 1935-39; Ministry of Information, 1939-41; Press Attaché: HM Embassy, Lisbon, 1941-44; HM Embassy, Rome, 1944-48; employed in Foreign Office, 1948-51; Counsellor, Office of Comr-Gen. for UK in SE Asia, 1951-54; Counsellor, HM Embassy, Ankara, 1954-59; HM Chargé d'Affaires, Peking, 1959-62; Senior Civilian Instructor, IDC, 1962-64; HM Minister, British Embassy, Washington, 1964-67; Ambassador to Greece, 1967-71. Dir, Ditchley Foundn, 1971-75. *Recreation:* country life. *Address:* Lower Farm, Combe, near Newbury, Berks.

STEWART, Dame Muriel (Acadia), DBE 1968; Headmistress, Northumberland LEA, since 1940; *b* 22 Oct. 1905; *d* of late James Edmund Stewart. *Educ:* Gateshead Grammar Sch.; Durham Univ. BA Hons 1926; MA 1929. Teacher: Newcastle upon Tyne, 1927-29; Northumberland, 1929-; Shiremoor Middle School, 1969-70. Nat. Pres., Nat. Union of Teachers, 1964-65; Chm., Schools Council, 1969-72. Vice-Chm., Bullock Cttee. Hon. MEd, Newcastle Univ., 1965. *Recreation:* music. *Address:* 44 Caldwell Road, Gosforth, Newcastle upon Tyne NE3 2AX. *T:* Newcastle upon Tyne 853400.

STEWART, Potter; Associate Justice of the Supreme Court of the United States, since 1958; *b* 23 Jan. 1915; *s* of James Garfield Stewart and Harriet Loomis Stewart (*née* Potter); *m* 1943, Mary Ann Bertles; two *s* one *d. Educ:* Hotchkiss School, Lakeville, Connecticut; Yale College; Yale Law School. One-year fellowship, Cambridge, Eng. General practice of law as associate with Debevoise, Stevenson, Plimpton and Page, New York City, 1941-42, 1945-47; associate with Dinsmore, Shohl, Sawyer and Dinsmore, Cincinnati, O, 1947; partner of that firm, 1951-54; Judge, US Court of Appeals for 6th Circuit, 1954-58. Member, Cincinnati City Council, 1950-53 (Vice-Mayor, 1952-53). Hon. LLD: Yale Univ., 1959; Kenyon Coll., 1960; Wilmington Coll., 1962; Univ. of Cincinnati, 1963; Ohio Univ., 1964; Univ. of Michigan, 1966; Miami Univ., 1974. *Address:* Supreme Court Building, Washington, DC 20543, USA. *Clubs:* Camargo (Cincinnati, Ohio); Chevy Chase (Chevy Chase, Md).

STEWART, Richard, CBE 1976; JP; Leader of Administration, Strathclyde Regional Council, since 1974; *b* 27 May 1920; *s* of Richard Stewart and Agnes (*née* Cunningham); *m* 1942, Elizabeth Peat; one *d. Educ:* Harthill Sch., Harthill. Mem., Lanark CC for 15 years (Chm. several cttees, finally Chm., Social Work Cttee). Full-time Sec./Organiser, Labour Party; Agent for: Rt Hon. Miss Margaret Herbison for 20 years; Mr John Smith, MP, 1970-. Past Chairman: Scottish Council of Labour Party; Nat. Union of Labour Organisers. JP Lanark County Council 1964. *Recreations:* music, chess. *Address:* 28 Hawthorn Drive, Harthill, Shotts ML7 5SG. *T:* Harthill 303.

STEWART, Lt-Col Robert Christie, TD 1962; Lord Lieutenant of Kinross-shire, 1966-74; *b* 3 Aug. 1926; *m* 1953, Ann Grizel Cochrane; three *s* two *d. Educ:* Eton; University College, Oxford. Lt Scots Guards, 1945-49. Oxford Univ., 1949-51 (BA Agric.). TA, 7 Argyll and Sutherland Highlanders, 1948-66; Lt-Col Comdg 7 A & SH, 1963-66. Hon. Col, 1/51 Highland Volunteers, 1972. DL Kinross 1956, VL 1958; Chairman Kinross County Council, 1963-73. *Address:* Arndean, By Dollar, Kinross-shire. *T:* Dollar 2527. *Club:* New (Edinburgh).

STEWART, Rt. Hon. Robert Maitland Michael; *see* Stewart, Rt Hon. Michael.

STEWART, Dr Robert William, FRS 1970; FRSC 1967; Director-General, Ocean and Aquatic Sciences, Pacific Region,

Fisheries and Marine Service, Department of Environment, Canada, since 1974; Hon. Professor of Physics and Oceanography, University of British Columbia; *b* 21 Aug. 1923; *m* 1st, 1948, V. Brande (marr. diss. 1972); two *s* one *d*; 2nd, 1973, Anne-Marie Robert, one *s. Educ:* Queen's Univ., Ontario. BSc 1945, MSc 1947, Queen's; PhD Cantab 1952. Canadian Defence Research Bd, 1950-61; Prof. of Physics and Oceanography, Univ. of British Columbia, 1961-70; Dir, Marine Scis Br., Pacific Reg., Environment Canada, 1970-74. Vis. Professor: Dalhousie Univ., 1960-61; Harvard Univ., 1964; Pennsylvania State Univ., 1964; Commonwealth Vis. Prof., Cambridge Univ., 1967-68. Vice-Chm., Jt Organizing Cttee, Global Atmospheric Res. Program, 1968-72. *Publications:* numerous, on turbulence, oceanography and meteorology. *Address:* Ocean and Aquatic Sciences, Pacific Region, Department of Environment, 1230 Government Street, 5th Floor, Victoria, BC, Canada. *Club:* University of British Columbia Faculty (Vancouver).

STEWART, Sir Ronald (Compton), 2nd Bt, *cr* 1937; DL; Chairman, London Brick Co. Ltd; *b* 14 Aug. 1903; *s* of Sir (Percy) Malcolm Stewart, 1st Bt, OBE, and Cordelia (*d* 1906,) *d* of late Rt Hon. Sir Joseph Compton Rickett, DL, MP; *S* father, 1951; *m* 1936, Cynthia, OBE, JP, *d* of Harold Farmiloe. *Educ:* Rugby; Jesus College, Cambridge. High Sheriff of Bedfordshire, 1954, DL 1974. *Heir: half-b* Malcolm Stewart [*b* 20 Dec. 1909; *m* 1935 Mary Stephanie (marr. diss. 1957), *d* of Frederick Ramon de Bertodano, 8th Marquis del Moral (Spain)]. *Address:* Maulden Grange, Maulden, Bedfordshire.

STEWART, Stanley Toft; Company Director; *b* 13 June 1910; *s* of Charles Campbell Stewart and Jeanette Matilda Doral; *m* 1935, Therese Zelie de Souza; seven *d. Educ:* St Xavier's Instn, Penang; Raffles Coll., Singapore. Straits Settlements CS, 1934-46; Overseas Civil Service, 1946-. District Officer, Butterworth, Province Wellesley, 1947-52; Dep. Chm., Rural Board, Singapore, 1952-54; Chm., Rural Board, Singapore, 1954; Dep. Sec., Ministry of Local Government, Lands and Housing, Singapore, 1955, Actg Permanent Sec., 1955; Actg Chief Sec., Singapore, Oct. 1957-Jan. 1958; Permanent Secretary: Home Affairs, 1959-63; to Prime Minister, 1961-66; Singapore High Comr in Australia, 1966-69; Permanent Sec., Min. of Foreign Affairs, Singapore, 1969-72; Exec. Sec., Nat. Stadium Corp., 1973. *Recreations:* cricket, tennis, gardening. *Address:* 103 Holland Road, Singapore 10. *Clubs:* Singapore Recreation; Club 200.

STEWART, Mrs Suzanne Freda; *see* Norwood, S. F.

STEWART, Brigadier Thomas G.; *see* Grainger-Stewart.

STEWART, Dr William, CB 1977; DSc; Deputy Controller of Aircraft A, Ministry of Defence (Procurement Executive), since 1973; *b* Hamilton, 29 Aug. 1921. *Educ:* St John's Grammar Sch.; Hamilton Acad.; Glasgow Univ. BSc Hons (engin.); DSc 1958. RAE, Farnborough, 1942-53; British Jt Services Mission, Washington, 1953-56; Dep. Head of Naval Air Dept, RAE, Bedford, 1956-63; Imperial Defence College, 1964; Asst Dir, Project Time and Cost Analysis, 1965-66; Dir, Anglo-French Combat Trainer Aircraft Projects, 1966-70; Dir-Gen., Multi-Role combat Aircraft, 1970-73. *Address:* 25 Brickhill Drive, Bedford; MoD(PE), Main Building, Horse Guards Avenue, SW1.

STEWART, Prof. William Alexander Campbell, MA, PhD; DL; Vice-Chancellor, University of Keele, since 1967; *b* Glasgow, 17 Dec. 1915; *s* of late Thomas Stewart, Glasgow, and Helen Fraser, Elgin, Morayshire; *m* 1947, Ella Elizabeth Burnett, of Edinburgh; one *s* one *d. Educ:* Colfe's Grammar Sch., London; University Coll., and Inst. of Education, Univ. of London. Exhibitioner, University Coll., London., 1934-37; BA 1937; MA 1941; PhD 1947; Diploma in Education, 1938; Fellow, UCL, 1975. Sen. English Master: (and Housemaster), Friends' School, Saffron Walden, Essex, 1938-43; Abbotsholme School, Derbyshire, 1943-44 (Member of Governing Body, 1960-; Chm., Council, 1974); Asst Lectr and Lectr in Education, University Coll., Nottingham, 1944-47; Lectr in Education, Univ. of Wales (Cardiff), 1947-50; Prof. of Education, Univ. of Keele, 1950-67. Vis. Prof., McGill Univ., 1957, Univ. of Calif., Los Angeles 1959; Simon Vis. Prof., Univ. of Manchester, 1962-63; Prestige Fellow, NZ Univs, 1969. Chairman: YMCA Educn Cttee, 1962-67; Nat. Adv. Council for Child Care, 1968-71; Univs Council for Adult Educn, 1969-73; Member: Inter-Univ. Council for Higher Education Overseas; Commonwealth Univ. Interchange Council; Council of Fourah Bay Coll., Univ. of Sierra Leone, 1968-72; Adv. Council, Supply and Training of Teachers, 1974-. Fellow, Internat. Inst. of Art and Letters. DL Stafford, 1973. Hon. DLitt Ulster, 1973. *Publications:* Quakers and Education,

1953; (ed with J. Eros) Systematic Sociology of Karl Mannheim, 1957; (with K. Mannheim) An Introduction to the Sociology of Education, 1962; contrib. to The American College (ed Sanford), 1962; The Educational Innovators (Vol. 1, with W. P. McCann), 1967; The Educational Innovators (Vol. 2), 1968; Progressives and Radicals in English Education 1750-1970, 1972. *Recreations:* formerly most games; travelling, talking, theatre, music. *Address:* The Clock House, The University, Keele, Staffs. *T:* Keele Park 394. *Clubs:* Athenæum, Oriental; Federation House (Stoke on Trent).

STEWART, Prof. William Duncan Paterson, PhD, DSc; FRS 1977; FRSE; Boyd-Baxter Professor of Biology and Head of Department of Biological Sciences, University of Dundee, since 1968; *b* 7 June 1935; *s* of John Stewart and Margaret (*née* Paterson); *m* 1958, Catherine MacLeod; one *s*. *Educ:* Bowmore Junior Secondary Sch., Isle-of-Islay; Dunoon Grammar Sch.; Glasgow Univ. (BSc, PhD, DSc). FRSE 1973. Asst Lectr, Univ. of Nottingham, 1961-63; Lectr, Westfield Coll., Univ. of London, 1963-68. Vis. Res. Worker, Univ. of Wisconsin, 1966 and 1968. *Publications:* Nitrogen Fixation in Plants, 1966; (jtly) The Blue-Green Algae, 1973; Algal Physiology and Biochemistry, 1974; (ed) Nitrogen Fixation by Free-living Organisms, 1975; papers in learned jls of repute. *Recreations:* soccer, playing the bagpipes. *Address:* Department of Biological Sciences, University of Dundee, Dundee DD1 4HN. *T:* Dundee 23181, ext. 324; 45 Fairfield Road, West Ferry, Dundee. *T:* Dundee 76702.

STEWART, William Ian; *see* Allanbridge, Hon. Lord.

STEWART, William McCausland; Professor of French, University of Bristol, 1945-66; Emeritus, 1966; *b* 17 Sept. 1900; *yr s* of late Abraham McCausland Stewart, Londonderry, and Alexandrina Catherine Margaret Elsner, Dublin; *m* 1933, Ann Cecilia Selo (*d* 1969); two *d*. *Educ:* Foyle Coll., Londonderry; Trinity Coll., Dublin (Sizar, Schol. and Sen. Moderator in Mod. Literature-French and German; Prizeman in Old and Middle English; Vice-Chancellor's Prizeman in English Verse). BA 1922; MA 1926; Lecteur d'Anglais, Univ. of Montpellier, 1922-23 (Certificat de Licence en Phonétique, 1923). Resident Lecteur d'Anglais at Ecole Normale Supérieure, Paris, 1923-26; also studied Sorbonne (Diplôme d'Etudes Supérieures de Lettres: Langues Classiques, 1925) and Ecole des Hautes Etudes, Paris, and taught Collège Sainte-Barbe, Paris; Lectr in French, Univ. of Sheffield, 1927 and 1928; Lectr in French and Joint Head of French Dept, Univ. of St Andrews and University College, Dundee, from 1928 onwards. Seconded for War Service in Foreign Research and Press Service (Chatham House), Balliol College, Oxford, Sept. 1939; Head of French Section of same, 1940-43; Head of French Section, Research Dept of Foreign Office, 1943-45. Chairman, University of Bristol Art Lectures Committee, 1946-66; Dean of Faculty of Arts, 1960-62; Visiting Professor, Univ. of Auckland, 1967. Member Council, RWA; Pres., Clifton Arts Club; Governor, Bath Academy of Art, Corsham Court; Chairman, Bristol-Bordeaux Assoc., 1953-76; Corr. Mem. Acad. des Sciences, Belles Lettres et Arts de Bordeaux and of Acad. Montesquieu. Chevalier de la Légion d'Honneur, 1950. Officier des Palmes Académiques, 1957, Commandeur, 1966. DLitt (*hc*), Nat. Univ. of Ireland, 1963. *Publications:* Les Etudes Françaises en Grand Bretagne, Paris, 1929 (with G. T. Clapton); translation of Paul Valéry's Eupalinos, with Preface, Oxford, 1932, and of his Dialogues, Bollingen Series XLV, New York, 1956 and London, 1958; Les Chœurs d'Athalie (record), 1958; Aspects of the French Classical Ideal, 1967; Tokens in Time (poems), 1968; Alcaics for our Age, 1976; Bristol-Bordeaux: The First Thirty Years, 1977; contribs to literary reviews and learned periodicals, mainly on Classical and Modern France (incl. Descartes, Racine, Montesquieu, Valéry). *Address:* 5 Cotham Park, Bristol BS6 6BZ. *T:* Bristol 48156. *Club:* Europe House.
  See also J. N. T. Spreckley, A. L. Stewart.

STEWART-CLARK, Sir John, 3rd Bt *cr* 1918; Managing Director, Pye of Cambridge Ltd, since 1975; *b* 17 Sept. 1929; *e s* of Sir Stewart Stewart-Clark, 2nd Bt, and of Jane Pamela, *d* of late Major Arundell Clarke; *S* father, 1971; *m* 1958, Lydia Frederike, *d* of J. W. Loudon, Holland; one *s* four *d*. *Educ:* Eton; Balliol College, Oxford; Harvard Business School. Commissioned with HM Coldstream Guards, 1948-49. Oxford, 1949-52. With J. & P. Coats Ltd, 1952-69; Managing Director: J. & P. Coats, Pakistan, Ltd, 1961-67; J. A. Carp's Garenfabrieken, Holland, 1967-69; Philips Electrical Ltd, London, 1971-75. Member Royal Company of Archers, Queen's Body Guard for Scotland. Contested (U) North Aberdeen, Gen. Election, 1959. *Recreations:* golf, tennis, shooting, photography, vintage cars. *Heir: s* Alexander Dudley Stewart-Clark, *b* 21 Nov. 1960. *Address:* Holmsley House, near Cowden, Kent. *T:* Cowden 541.

Clubs: White's; Hon. Company of Edinburgh Golfers, Royal Ashdown Golf.

STEWART-JONES, Mrs Richard; *see* Smith, Emma.

STEWART-MOORE, Alexander Wyndham Hume; Chairman, Gallaher Ltd, since 1975 (Managing Director, 1966-75); Director, American Brands Inc., since 1975; *b* 14 Feb. 1915; 2nd *s* of late James Stewart-Moore, DL, Ballydivity, Dervock, Co. Antrim, and of Katherine Marion (*née* Jackson); *m* 1948, Magdalene Clare, *y d* of Sir David Richard Llewellyn, 1st Bt, LLD, JP; three *s* one *d*. *Educ:* Shrewsbury. Joined Gallaher Ltd, Nov. 1934. Served War, Royal Artillery (Middle East and Italy), 1939-46. *Recreations:* farming, fishing, gardening. *Address:* 1 Stavordale Lodge, Melbury Road, W14. *T:* 01-602 3661; Seaport, Portballintrae, Bushmills, Co. Antrim, NI. *T:* Bushmills 31361. *Club:* Ulster.

STEWART-RICHARDSON, Sir Simon (Alaisdair), 17th Bt *cr* 1630; *b* 9 June 1947; *er s* of Sir Ian Rorie Hay Stewart-Richardson, 16th Bt, and of Audrey Meryl (who *m* 1975, P. A. P. Robertson, *qv*), *e d* of Claude Odlum; *S* father, 1969. *Educ:* Trinity College, Glenalmond. *Heir: b* Ninian Rorie Stewart-Richardson, *b* 20 Jan. 1949. *Address:* Lynedale House, Longcross, near Chertsey, Surrey KT16 0DP. *T:* Ottershaw 2329.

STEWART-SMITH, Rev. Canon David Cree, MA; Home Secretary of Jerusalem and Middle East Church Association, since 1976; *b* 22 May 1913; 3rd *s* of late Thomas Stewart Stewart-Smith, JP, Heathlands, Kinver, Staffs, and Mabel (*née* McDougall); *m* 1943, Kathleen Georgiana Maule Ffinch, *d* of Rev. K. M. Ffinch, Ifield, Kent. *Educ:* Marlborough; King's Coll., Cambridge; Cuddesdon Theol. College. BA 1939, MA 1943. Vicar-Choral and Sacrist, York Minster, 1944-49; Vicar of Shadwell, Leeds, 1949-52; Warden, Brasted Place Coll., 1952-63; Dean of St George's Cath., Jerusalem, and Administrator of St George's Coll., 1964-67; Commissary for Archbishop in Jerusalem, 1968-; Archdeacon of Bromley and Hon. Canon of Rochester, 1968-69; Archdeacon of Rochester and Canon Residentiary of Rochester Cathedral, 1969-76; Hon. Canon of Rochester, 1976-; Director of Ordinands, dio. Rochester, 1968-74; Mem., C of E Pensions Bd, 1970-; a Church Commissioner, 1973-; Fellow of Woodard Corp.: Northern Div., 1949-52; Southern Div., 1959-64. *Recreations:* architecture, music, travel, collecting. *Address:* Flat 3, 7 Fortfield Terrace, Sidmouth, Devon EX10 8NT. *T:* Sidmouth 4440. *Club:* United Oxford & Cambridge University.

STEWART-SMITH, (Dudley) Geoffrey; Director, Foreign Affairs Research Institute, since 1976; *b* 28 Dec. 1933; *s* of Dudley Cautley Stewart-Smith; *m* 1956, Kay Mary; three *s*. *Educ:* Winchester; RMA Sandhurst. Regular Officer, The Black Watch, 1952-60. Director, Foreign Affairs Circle; Editor, East-West Digest; Dir, Foreign Affairs Publishing Co.; Financial Times, 1968. MP (C) Derbyshire, Belper, 1970-Feb 1974. *Publications:* The Defeat of Communism, 1964; No Vision Here: Non-Military Warfare in Britain, 1966; (ed) Brandt and the Destruction of NATO, 1973; contribs to various foreign, defence and communist affairs jls at home and overseas. *Recreations:* walking, swimming, shooting and stalking. *Address:* Church House, Petersham, Surrey. *T:* 01-940 2885.

STEWART-WILSON, Lt-Col Blair Aubyn; Deputy Master of the Household and Equerry to Her Majesty, since 1976; *b* 17 July 1929; *s* of late Aubyn Wilson and Muriel Stewart; *m* 1962, Helen Mary Fox; three *d*. *Educ:* Eton; Sandhurst. Commnd Scots Guards, 1949; served with Regt and on Staff several times in Germany and Far East; ADC to Viscount Cobham, Governor General and C-in-C, New Zealand, 1957-59; Equerry to late Duke of Gloucester, 1960-62; GSO1, Foreign Liaison Sect. (Army), MoD, 1970-73; Defence, Military and Air Attaché, British Embassy, Vienna, 1975-76. *Address:* 3 Browning Close, W9 1BW. *T:* 01-286 9891; Thorn Falcon House, Taunton, Somerset. *T:* Henlade 442248. *Clubs:* Turf, Pratt's.

STEWARTSON, Prof. Keith, FRS 1965; Goldsmid Professor of Mathematics, University College, London, since 1964; *b* 20 Sept. 1925; *s* of late G. C. Stewartson and M. Stewartson (*née* Hyde); *m* 1953, Elizabeth Jean Forrester; two *s* one *d*. *Educ:* Stockton Secondary Sch.; St Catharine's Coll., Cambridge. Lectr in Applied Mathematics at Bristol Univ., 1949-53; Research Fellow in Aeronautics, California Inst. of Technology, 1953-54; Reader in Applied Mathematics at Bristol Univ., 1954-58; Prof. of Applied Mathematics, Durham Univ. (late Durham Colls), 1958-64. FIMA, 1964. *Publications:* Laminar Compressible Boundary Layers, 1964; papers in Mathematical and Aeronautical Journals. *Address:* 51 Dunstan Road, NW11. *T:* 01-455 1702.

STIBBE, Philip Godfrey, MA; Head Master of Norwich School, since 1975; *b* 20 July 1921; *m* 1956, Mary Joy, *d* of late Canon C. G. Thornton; two *s* one *d*. *Educ:* Mill Hill Sch.; Merton Coll., Oxford (MA). Served War of 1939-45; joined Royal Sussex Regt, 1941; seconded King's (Liverpool) Regt, 1942; 1st Wingate Expedn into Burma (wounded, despatches), 1943; POW, 1943-45. Asst Master, 1948-75, Housemaster, 1954-74, Bradfield Coll. *Publication:* Return via Rangoon, 1947. *Recreations:* people, places, books. *Address:* 16 The Close, Norwich NR1 4DZ. *T:* Norwich 25425. *Club:* East India, Devonshire, Sports and Public Schools.

STIBBS, Prof. Douglas Walter Noble, MSc Sydney, DPhil Oxon; FRAS, FRSE; Napier Professor of Astronomy and Director of the University Observatory, University of St Andrews, since 1959; *b* 17 Feb. 1919; 2nd *s* of Edward John Stibbs, Sydney, NSW; *m* 1949, Margaret Lilian Calvert, BSc, DipEd (Sydney), AID, *er d* of Rev. John Calvert, Sydney, NSW; two *d*. *Educ:* Sydney High Sch.; Univ. of Sydney; New College, Oxford. Deas Thomson Scholar, Sch. of Physics, Univ. of Sydney, 1940; BSc (Sydney), 1st Class Hons, Univ. Medal in Physics, 1942; MSc (Sydney), 1943; DPhil (Oxon), 1954. Johnson Memorial Prize and Gold Medal for Advancement of Astronomy and Meteorology, Oxford Univ., 1956. Res. Asst, Solar Observatory, Canberra, ACT, 1940-42; Asst Lectr, Dept of Mathematics and Physics, New England University Coll., Armidale, NSW (now the Univ. of New England), 1942-45; Scientific Officer and Sen. Scientific Officer, Commonwealth Observatory, Canberra, ACT, 1945-51; Radcliffe Travelling Fellow in Astronomy, Radcliffe Observatory, Pretoria, S Africa, and Univ. Observatory, Oxford, 1951-54; PSO, UKAEA, 1955-59; Vis. Prof. of Astrophysics, Yale Univ. Observatory, 1966-67; British Council Vis. Prof., Univ. of Utrecht, 1968; Prof., Collège de France, 1975-76. Member: Internat. Astronomical Union, 1951- (Chm. Finance Cttee, 1964-67, 1973-76, 1976-); Amer. Astronomical Soc., 1956-73; Adv. Cttee on Meteorology for Scotland, 1960-69, 1972-75; Board of Visitors, Royal Greenwich Observatory, 1963-65; Council RAS, 1964-67, 1970-73 (Vice-Pres., 1972-73), Editorial Board, 1970-73; Council, RSE, 1970-72; National Cttee for Astronomy, 1964-76; SRC Cttees for Royal Greenwich Observatory, 1966-70, and Royal Observatory, Edinburgh, 1966-76, Chm., 1970-76; SRC Astronomy, Space and Radio Bd, 1970-76; SRC, 1972-76; S African Astron. Obs. Adv. Cttee, 1972-76; Chairman: Astronomy Policy and Grants Cttee, 1972-74; Astronomy II Cttee, 1974-75; Centre National de la Recherche Scientifique Cttee, Obs. de Haute Provence, 1973-78. Mem. New Coll. Soc., 1953-. *Publications:* The Outer Layers of a Star (with Sir Richard Woolley), 1953; contrib. Theoretical Astrophysics and Astronomy in Monthly Notices of RAS and other jls. *Recreations:* music, photography. *Address:* University Observatory, Buchanan Gardens, St Andrews, Fife KY16 9LZ. *T:* St Andrews 2643. *Club:* Royal and Ancient (St Andrews).

STIFF, Rt. Rev. Hugh Vernon; Rector of St James Cathedral and Dean of Toronto, since 1974; Assistant Bishop, Diocese of Toronto, since 1977; *b* 15 Sept. 1916; unmarried. *Educ:* Univ. of Toronto (BA); Trinity Coll., Toronto (LTh). BD General Synod; Hon. DD, Trinity Coll., Toronto. Bishop of Keewatin, 1969-74. *Address:* 65 Church Street, Toronto, Ontario, Canada.

STIGLITZ, Prof. Joseph Eugene, PhD; Drummond Professor of Political Economy, Oxford University, since 1976; *b* 9 Feb. 1943; *m*; one *s* one *d*. *Educ:* Amherst Coll. (BA 1964); MIT (PhD 1966); Cambridge Univ. (MA 1970). Professor of Economics: Yale Univ. 1970-74; Stanford Univ., 1974-76. Fellowships: Nat. Sci. Foundn, 1964-65; Fulbright, 1965-66; SSRC Faculty, 1969-70; Guggenheim, 1969-70. Consultant: Nat. Sci. Foundn, 1972-75; Ford Foundn Energy Policy Study, 1973; Dept of Labor (Pensions and Labor Turnover), 1974; Dept of Interior (Offshore Oil Leasing Programs), 1975; Federal Energy Admin (Intertemporal Biases in Market Allocation of Natural Resources), 1975-; World Bank (Cost Benefit Analysis; Urban Rural Migration; Natural Resources), 1975-; Electric Power Res. Inst., 1976-. Gen. Editor, Econometric Soc. Reprint Series; Associate Editor: Jl of Economic Theory, 1968-73; American Economic Rev., 1972-75; Co-editor, Jl of Public Economics, 1968-; American Editor, Rev. of Economic Studies, 1968-. Fellow, Econometric Soc., 1972 (Sec./Treasurer, 1972-75). Hon. MA Yale, 1970; Hon. DHL Amherst, 1974. *Publications:* (ed) Collected Scientific Papers of P. A. Samuelson, 1965; (ed with H. Uzawa) Readings in Modern Theory of Economic Growth, 1969; contribs on economics of growth, development, natural resources, information, uncertainty, imperfect competition, corporate finance and public finance in Amer. Econ. Rev., Qly Jl of Econs, Jl of Pol. Econ., Econometrica, Internat. Econ. Rev., Econ. Jl, Rev. of Econ. Studies, Jl of Public Econs, Jl of Econ. Theory, Oxford Econ. Papers. *Address:* 28 Parktown, Oxford.

STIKKER, Dirk Uipko, Hon. GCVO 1958; Hon. GBE 1951; Grand Cross, Order of Orange Nassau; Knight, Order of Netherlands Lion; former Director: Friesch-Groningsche Hypotheekbank; Wm H. Müller & Co.; Deli-Maatschappij, and other companies; *b* 5 Feb. 1897; *s* of Uipko Obbo Stikker and Ida Meursing; *m* 1922, Catherina Paulina van der Scheer; two *s*. *Educ:* Latin-grammar school; University of Groningen (Doctor of Law, 1922). Manager, Lissense Bank Vereniging, Lisse, 1931; Man. Dir, Heinekens Bierbrouwerijen, 1935; Bd of Directors, Nederlandse Bank en Nederlandse Handel Maatschappij; Organiser and Pres., Netherlands Labour Foundation, 1945; Organiser and Chm., Party of Freedom, later known as People's Party for Freedom and Democracy (liberal), 1946. Member Netherlands Govt Delegation to Round Table Conf. on political status of Netherlands West-Indies, 1946; Round Table Conf. with reps of Indonesia and preparation for Independence of Indonesia, 1948; Netherlands Minister of Foreign Affairs, 1948-52; Member Political Purging Council, 1945; Netherlands rep., Council, OEEC, 1950; Chairman OEEC, 1950-52; Netherlands Envoy Extraordinary and Minister Plenipotentiary to Icelandic Republic, 1954-56; Netherlands Ambassador at the Court of St James's, 1952-58; Netherlands Ambassador to the Icelandic Republic, 1956-58. Chairman Netherlands Delegation to Economic and Social Council, UN, 1955-56. Netherlands Permanent Representative on the North Atlantic Council and to the Council of OEEC in Paris, 1958-61; Secretary-General of NATO, 1961-64; Consultant to Unctad, 1966. Holds Grand Cross of several orders in Europe, South America, etc. *Publications:* Men of Responsibility, 1966; (for UNCTAD) The role of private enterprise in investment and promotion of exports in developing countries, 1967; many articles. *Recreation:* golf. *Address:* Stoeplaan 11, Wassenaar, Netherlands.

STILES, Walter Stanley, OBE 1946; FRS 1957; PhD, DSc; formerly Deputy Chief Scientific Officer, The National Physical Laboratory, Teddington, retired 1961; *b* 15 June 1901; *s* of Walter Stiles and Elizabeth Catherine (*née* Smith); *m* 1928, Pauline Frida Octavia, *d* of Judge Henrik Brendstrup, Hillerød, Denmark; no *c*. *Educ:* University College, London; St John's College, Cambridge. Andrews Scholar, University Coll., London, 1918. Demonstrator in Physics, 1920-22; PhD London 1929, DSc London 1939; Carpenter Medallist, London Univ., 1944. Technical Officer, RN Signal School, 1923-25; Scientific Officer, Nat. Physical Lab., 1925-61. Gen. Sec. Internat. Commn on Illumination, 1928-31; Vice-President Physical Soc., 1948-49; President, Illuminating Engineering Soc., 1960, Gold Medallist, 1967; Chm. Colour Group of Physical Soc., 1949-51, Newton Lectr, 1967; Thomas Young Orator (Physical Soc.), 1955; Regents' Lectr (UCLA), 1964; Tillyer Medallist (Optical Society of America), 1965; Finsen Medallist (Congr. Internat. de Photobiologie), 1968. *Publications:* Thermionic Emission, 1932; Color Science (with G. Wyszecki), 1967; many papers on illuminating engineering and physiological optics in Proc. Royal Soc., Trans Illum. Eng Soc., etc. *Recreation:* painting. *Address:* 89 Richmond Hill Court, Richmond, Surrey. *T:* 01-940 4334.

STINSON, David John; His Honour Judge David Stinson; a Circuit Judge (formerly County Court Judge), since 1969; Chancellor, Diocese of Carlisle, since 1971; *b* 22 Feb. 1921; *s* of late Henry John Edwin Stinson, MC, MA, LLB, Beckenham, Kent (sometime Chief Commoner of City of London, solicitor), and late Margaret Stinson (*née* Little); *m* 1950, Eleanor Judith (*née* Chance); two *s* two *d* (and one *s* decd). *Educ:* Eastbourne Coll.; Emmanuel Coll., Cambridge. MA 1946; Jesters Club, 1949 (Rugby Fives). Served War of 1939-45: Essex Yeomanry, Captain, RA, and Air OP, 1941-46 (despatches). Called to Bar, Middle Temple, 1947; Dep. Chm., Herts QS, 1965-71; Suffolk and Essex County Court Circuit, 1973-. Liveryman, Worshipful Co. of Needlemakers. *Recreations:* bird-watching, sailing. *Address:* The Maltings, Waldringfield, Woodbridge, Suffolk IP12 4QZ. *T:* Waldringfield 280. *Club:* Army and Navy.

STIRLING, Alexander John Dickson, CMG 1976; HM Diplomatic Service; Ambassador to Iraq, since 1977; *b* 20 Oct. 1926; *e s* of late Brig. A. Dickson Stirling, DSO, MB, ChB, DPH, and of Isobel Stirling, MA, DipEd, DipPsych, *d* of late Rev. J. C. Matthew (former senior Presidency Chaplain, Bombay); *m* 1955, Alison Mary, *y d* of Gp Capt. A. P. Campbell, CBE; two *s* two *d*. *Educ:* Edinburgh Academy; Lincoln Coll., Oxford (MA). RAFVR, 1945-48 (Egypt, 1945-47). Entered Foreign Office, 1951; Lebanon, 1952; British Embassy, Cairo, 1952-56 (Oriental Sec., 1955-56); FO, 1956-59; First Sec., British Embassy, Baghdad, 1959-62; First Sec. and Consul, Amman, 1962-64; First Sec., British Embassy, Santiago, 1965-67; FO, 1967-69; British Political Agent, Bahrain, 1969-71, Ambassador, 1971-72; Counsellor, Beirut, 1972-75; RCDS 1976. *Address:* c/o Williams & Glyn's Bank Ltd, Kirkland House, Whitehall, SW1.

STIRLING, Alfred, CBE 1953 (OBE 1941); *b* Melbourne, Victoria, Australia, 8 Sept. 1902; *s* of Robert Andrew and Isabel Stirling. *Educ:* Scotch College, Melbourne; Melbourne Univ.; University Coll., Oxford (MA, LLB). Victorian Bar, 1927-33. Private Secretary to Attorney-General of Commonwealth (Rt Hon. R. G. Menzies), 1934-35; Assistant External Affairs Officer, London, 1936; head of Political Section, Dept of External Affairs, Canberra, 1936-37; External Affairs Officer, London, 1937-45; Counsellor, Australian Legation to Netherlands, 1942-45; High Commissioner for Australia in Canada, 1945-46; Australian Minister in Washington, 1946-48; Australian High Comr in S Africa, 1948-50; Australian Ambassador: to the Netherlands, 1950-55; to France, 1955-59; to the Philippines, 1959-62; to Greece, 1964-65; to Italy, 1962-67. Grand Cross of St Gregory; Grand Cordon of Royal George (Greece). *Publications:* Victorian (jtly), 1934; Joseph Bosisto, 1970; The Italian Diplomat, and Italy and Scotland, 1971; Gang Forward, 1972; On the Fringe of Diplomacy, 1973; Lord Bruce: the London Years, 1974; A Distant View of the Vatican, 1975. *Address:* Flat 30, St Ives, 166 Toorak Road West, South Yarra, Victoria 3141, Australia. *Clubs:* Caledonian (London); Melbourne (Melbourne).

STIRLING, (Archibald) David, DSO 1942; OBE 1946; Chairman, Television International Enterprises Ltd; *b* 15 Nov. 1915; *s* of late Brigadier-General Archibald Stirling of Keir, and Hon. Mrs Margaret Stirling, OBE, 4th *d* of 13th Baron Lovat. *Educ:* Ampleforth College, Yorks; (for a brief period) Cambridge University. In Sept. 1939 was Mem. SRO, Scots Guards and served with that Regt for first six months of War when he was transferred to No 3 Commando (Brigade of Guards) and went out with this unit to Middle East; subseq. served with First SAS Regt (POW, 1943-45). President, Capricorn Africa Society, 1947-59, living at that time in Africa based on Salisbury and Nairobi. Officer, Légion d'Honneur; Officer, Orange Nassau. *Address:* 22 South Audley Street, W1. *T:* 01-499 9252. *Clubs:* White's, Turf, Pratt's.

STIRLING, Sir Charles (Norman), KCMG 1955 (CMG 1941); KCVO 1957; *b* 19 Nov. 1901; *er s* of late F. H. Stirling, Victoria, British Columbia; *m* 1950, Ann, *o d* of J. H. Moore; one *s* two *d*. *Educ:* Wellington College; Corpus Christi College, Oxford. Third Secretary, Diplomatic Service, 1925; Second Secretary, 1930; First Secretary, 1937; Head of a Department in Ministry of Economic Warfare, 1939-42; Acting Counsellor in the Foreign Office, 1942; Counsellor, British Embassy, Lisbon, 1946; Consul-General, Tangier, 1949-51; Ambassador to Chile, 1951-54; Ambassador to Portugal, 1955-60. *Recreation:* fishing. *Address:* 17 Park Row, Farnham, Surrey. *Club:* Travellers'.

STIRLING, David; *see* Stirling, Archibald D.

STIRLING, Duncan Alexander; Director: London Life Association, since 1935 (President, 1951-65); Baring Foundation; *b* 6 Oct. 1899; 4th *s* of late Major William Stirling, JP, DL, of Fairburn, Ross-shire, and Charlotte Eva, *d* of late Æneas Mackintosh, Daviot, Inverness-shire; *m* 1926, Lady Marjorie Murray, *e d* of 8th Earl of Dunmore, VC, DSO, MVO; two *s*. *Educ:* Harrow; New College, Oxford. Coldstream Guards, 1918 and again 1940-43. Partner, H. S. Lefevre & Co., Merchant Bankers, 1929-49; Director: Westminster Bank, 1935-69 (Chm. 1962-69); Westminster Foreign Bank, 1935-74 (Chm. 1962-69); National Westminster Bank, 1968-74 (Chm., 1968-69). Pres., Inst. of Bankers, 1964-66; Chm., Cttee of London Clearing Bankers and Pres., British Bankers', Assoc., 1966-68. Prime Warden Fishmongers Co., 1954-55. *Address:* 28 St James's Place, SW1; Lake House, Avington, Winchester, Hants. *Club:* Brooks's.

STIRLING, James Frazer, ARIBA 1950; Architect; *b* 1926; *s* of Joseph Stirling and Louisa Frazer; *m* 1966, Mary, *d* of Morton Shand and Sybil Sissons; one *s* two *d*. *Educ:* Quarry Bank High Sch., Liverpool; Liverpool Sch. of Art, 1942. Served War of 1939-45: Lieut, Black Watch and Paratroops (D-Day Landing). Sch. of Architecture, Liverpool Univ., 1945-50. With Assoc. of Town Planning and Regional Research, London, 1950-52; worked for Lyons, Israel and Ellis, London, 1953-56; entered a series of architectural competitions, and Mem. ICA Indep. Gp, 1952-56. Private practice, 1956- (Partners: James Gowan until 1963 and Michael Wilford, 1971-). Projects include: Flats at Ham Common, 1955-58; Churchill Coll. Comp., 1958 (finalist); Selwyn Coll., Cambridge, 1959; Leicester Univ. Engrg Bldg, 1959-63 (USA Reynolds Award); History Faculty, Cambridge Univ., 1964-67; Andrew Melville Hall, St Andrews Univ., 1964-68; Dorman Long Steel Co. HQ, 1965; Runcorn New Town Housing, 1968-; Florey Bldg at Queen's Coll., Oxford, 1967-71; Olivetti Trng Sch., Surrey, 1969-. Visiting teacher at: Architectural Assoc., London, 1955; Regent Street Polytechnic,

London, 1956-57; Cambridge Univ. Sch. of Architecture, 1958; RIBA Lecture (An Architect's Approach to Architecture), 1965; lectures in Europe and USA, 1960-; Charles Davenport Visiting Prof., Yale Univ. Sch. of Architecture, USA, 1970. Redevelopment plan of West Mid-Town Manhatten, for New York City Planning Commn, USA, 1968-69; invited UK Architect, in internat. limited competitions for Govt/United Nations low cost housing for Peru, 1969, and Siemens AG Computer Centre Munich, 1970. Hon. Mem., Akademie der Kunst, Berlin, 1969; Hon. FAIA, 1976. Exhibitions: "James Stirling—Three Buildings", at Museum of Modern Art, NY, USA, 1969; (drawings) RIBA Heinz Gall., 1974 (associated pubn, James Stirling, 1974). BBC/Arts Council film, James Stirling's Architecture, 1973. *Relevant publication:* James Stirling: Buildings and Projects, 1950-74, 1975. *Address:* 75 Gloucester Place, W1H 3PF.

STIRLING, John Bertram, OC 1970; Hon. Chairman of Board E. G. M. Cape & Co. Ltd since 1965 (Chairman, 1960-65); Chancellor, Queen's University, Kingston, Ontario, 1960-73; *b* 29 Nov. 1888; *s* of Dr James A. Stirling and Jessie Bertram, Picton, Ont; *m* 1928, Emily P., *d* of Col and Mrs E. T. Sturdee, Saint John, NB; one *d*. *Educ:* Queen's University, Kingston, Canada. BA 1909, BSc 1911, Queen's Univ., Kingston. Resident Engineer, Chipman and Power, Cons. Engineers, Toronto, 1911-15; with E. G. M. Cape and Co. Ltd from 1915; Field Engineer, 1915; Supt 1924; Gen. Supt, 1930; Vice-Pres., 1940. President: Canadian Construction Assoc., 1942; Montreal Board of Trade, 1950; Engineering Inst. of Canada, 1952. Hon. LLD: Queen's, Kingston, 1951; Toronto, 1961; Hon. DSc: Royal Mil. Coll., Canada, 1962; McGill, 1963. Hon. Col 3rd Field Regt Royal Can. Engrs. Sir John Kennedy Medal of Eng. Inst. of Canada, 1954; Montreal Medal, Queen's Univ. Alumni Assoc., 1955; Julian Smith Medal, Eng. Inst. of Canada, 1963. *Recreations:* sailing, country life, music. *Address:* 10 Richelieu Place, Montreal 109, Canada. *Clubs:* Saint James's, Forest and Stream (Montreal).

STIRLING, Rear-Adm. Michael Grote; Agent-General for British Columbia in the United Kingdom and Europe, 1968-75; *b* 29 June 1915; *s* of late Hon. Grote Stirling and late Mabel Katherine (*née* Brigstocke), Kelowna, British Columbia; *m* 1942, Sheelagh Kathleen Russell; two *s* one *d*. *Educ:* Shawnigan Lake School, BC; RNC Greenwich. Cadet, RCN, 1933; HMS Frobisher for training till 1934, then as Midshipman and Sub-Lt in RN, returning Canada Jan. 1938; Ships of RCN until 1941; specialized in Signals at HM Signal School, Portsmouth, then Home Fleet; Deputy Director, Signal Div., Naval Service HQ, Ottawa, 1942-43; SSO to C-in-C, Canadian North-West Atlantic, 1943-44; Commanded destroyers, 1944-46; Director Naval Communications, rank of Commander, 1949-51; promoted Captain and staff of Supreme Allied Commander Atlantic, Norfolk, Va, 1953-55; Commanded HMCS Cornwallis, 1955-57; 2nd Cdn Escort Sqdn, 1957-58; Naval Member of Directing Staff, Nat. Defence College as Commodore, 1958-61; Senior Canadian Officer Afloat, 1961-62; Chief of Naval Personnel and Rear-Admiral, 1962-64; Flag Officer Pacific Coast and Maritime Commander, Pacific, 1964-66; Director, Univ. of Victoria Foundation, 1967-68. *Recreations:* golf, ski-ing. *Address:* 1662 St Francis Wood, Victoria, BC V8S 1X6, Canada. *Clubs:* Union Club of British Columbia, Victoria Golf (Victoria, BC).

STIRLING, Viola Henrietta Christian, CBE 1947; TD 1951; DL; *b* 3 June 1907; *d* of late Charles Stirling of Gargunnock, *Educ:* Queen Ethelburga's Sch., Harrogate; Lady Margaret Hall, Oxford (BA). Joined Auxiliary Territorial Service, 1939; Deputy Director ATS Scottish Command, 1945; released with Hon. Rank of Controller, 1949. Member: Finance Committee, ATS Benevolent Fund, 1948-64; of Stirling and Clackmannan Hospitals Board of Management, 1948-64; selected military member TA & AFA, County of Stirling, 1948-68; Hon. Colonel 317 (Sc. Comd) Bn WRAC/TA, 1959-62. Member of Stirling County Council, 1958-67; DL Co. of Stirling, 1965. *Address:* Gargunnock, Stirlingshire. *T:* Gargunnock 202. *Club:* Ladies' Caledonian (Edinburgh).

STIRLING-HAMILTON, Sir Robert William; *see* Hamilton.

STOBART, Patrick Desmond, CBE 1976 (MBE 1950); HM Diplomatic Service; on secondment to Commercial Relations and Exports Division, Department of Trade; *b* 14 Feb. 1920; *s* of late Reginald and Eva Stobart; *m* 1951, Sheila (marr. diss. 1973), *d* of late A. W. Brown, Belfast; three *s* one *d*. *Educ:* Cathedral and Cleveland House Schools, Salisbury; St Edmund Hall, Oxford. Served Royal Artillery and Wilts Regiment, 1940-46. Tübingen University, 1946; Political Officer, Trucial Oman, 1947; Chancery, Bonn, 1951-53; FO, 1953-54; Consul, Benghazi,

1954-58; FO, 1958-60; Commercial Counsellor, British Embassy, Helsinki, 1960-64, Copenhagen, 1964-66; Consul-General, Gothenburg, 1966-68; seconded to Aero-Engine Div., Rolls-Royce Ltd, 1968-69; Gwilym Gibbon Research Fellow, Nuffield College, Oxford, 1969-70; Head of Export Promotion Dept, FCO, 1970-71; Consul-Gen. Zürich, 1971-75. *Recreations:* history, sailing, fishing. *Address:* 44B Manor View, Finchley, N3. *T:* 01-346 7322. *Club:* Travellers'.

STOBY, Sir Kenneth Sievewright, Kt 1961; Chairman, Guyana Match Co. Ltd; Director, Shawinigan Engineering (Guyana) Co. Ltd; *b* 19 Oct. 1903; *s* of late Mr and Mrs W. S. Stoby; *m* 1935, Eunice Badley; one *s* one *d*. *Educ:* Christ Church Sch., Georgetown; Queen's Coll., Georgetown. Called to Bar, Lincoln's Inn, 1930; private practice until 1940; seconded Dep. Controller of Prices, 1944; seconded again, 1947, Controller Supplies and Prices; acted Legal Draftsman; Chairman several Boards and Committees; Magistrate Nigeria, 1948; Registrar of Deeds and Supreme Court, British Guiana, 1950; Puisne Judge, 1953; Chief Justice, Barbados, 1959-65; Chancellor of the Judiciary, Guyana, 1966-68. Pro-Chancellor, Univ. of Guyana, 1966-. *Address:* 7A New Providence, East Bank, Demerara, Guyana.

STOCK, Allen Lievesley; Chairman, The Morgan Crucible Co. Ltd, 1959-69; *b* 24 September 1906; 2nd *s* of late Cyril Lievesley and Irene Mary Stock; *m* 1933, Rosemary Nancy Hopps; two *s* one *d*. *Educ:* Charterhouse; Faraday House; Christ's College, Cambridge. Belliss & Morcom, 1926-27; The British Thomson-Houston Co. Ltd, Rugby, 1928-32; The Morgan Crucible Company Ltd, 1932-69. Chairman, London Chamber of Commerce, 1958-62, Vice-Pres., 1962-; Member: Post Office Users' Council, 1966-69; Commn of Inquiry into Industrial Representation, 1971-72. Hon. Treasurer, The Sail Training Assoc., 1969-71. *Recreations:* boats, gardening, bird-watching. *Address:* Furzefield Cottage, Bosham Hoe, W Sussex. *T:* Bosham 573231. *Club:* Hawks (Cambridge).

STOCK, Prof. Francis Edgar, CBE 1977 (OBE 1961); FRCS, FACS; Principal and Vice-Chancellor of the University of Natal, South Africa, 1970-77; retired; *b* 5 July 1914; *o s* of late Edgar Stephen and Olive Blanche Stock; *m* 1939, Gwendoline Mary Thomas; two *s* one *d*. *Educ:* Colfe's Grammar Sch., Lewisham; (Sambrooke schol.) King's Coll., London; King's Coll. Hosp., London (Jelf medal, Todd medal and prize in clin. med.; Hygiene and Psychological med. prizes); Univ. of Edinburgh. AKC, MB, BS (Lond), FRCS, FACS, DTMH (Edin.). Ho. Surg., Cancer Research Registrar, Radium Registrar, King's Coll. Hosp., 1938-39; MO, Colonial Med. Service, Nigeria, 1940-45; Lectr and Asst to Prof. of Surg., Univ. of Liverpool, 1946-48; Prof. of Surgery, Univ. of Hong Kong, 1948-63; Cons. in Surg. to Hong Kong Govt, Brit. Mil. Hosps in Hong Kong, and Ruttonjee Sanatorium, 1948-63; Cons. Surg., RN, 1949-70; Dean, Fac. of Med., Univ. of Hong Kong, 1957-62; Med. Coun., Hong Kong, 1957-60; Pro-Vice-Chancellor, Univ. of Hong Kong, 1959-63; McIlrath Guest Prof., Royal Prince Alfred Hosp., Sydney, NSW, 1960 (Hon. Cons. Surg., 1960-); Prof. of Surg., Univ. of Liverpool, 1964-70; Cons. Surg., Liverpool Royal Infirmary and Liverpool Regional Hosp. Bd, 1964-70; Dean, Fac. of Med., Univ. of Liverpool, 1969-70. Visiting Prof. or Lectr: Univs of Alberta, Edinburgh, Qld, Singapore, W Australia, QUB, State Univ. of NY. Brit. Council Lectr: in Thailand, Burma, Fiji, Mauritius; Hunterian Prof., RCS London, 1948 and 1951. Member: BMA (Council 1964-69); Bd of Governors, United Liverpool Hosps, 1967-70; Med. Adv. Council and Chm. Techn. Adv. Cttee on Surg., Liverpool Reg. Hosp. Bd, 1964-70; Gen. Med. Council, 1969-70; Med. Appeals Tribunals, Liverpool and N Wales, 1966-70; Council, Edgewood Coll. of Education, 1976-77; Univs Adv. Council, 1976-; Cttee of Univ. Principals, 1970-77 (Chm., 1976-77). Examr in Surgery: to Univs of Edinburgh, Glasgow, Liverpool, Hong Kong, Malaya, Singapore and NUI, at various times, 1949-70; to Soc. of Apothecaries, 1958-60; Mem. Ct of Examrs, RCS, 1965-69. Sen. Fellow, Assoc. of Surgeons of Gt Brit. and Ire.; Sen. Mem. Pan Pacific Surg. Assoc. (past Mem. Coun. and Bd of Trustees). Mem., Board of Control, Nat. Inst. of Metallurgy, 1975-77. Hon. FACCP. *Publications:* Surgical Principles (with J. Moroney), 1968; chapters in: Surgery of Liver and Bile Ducts (ed Smith and Sherlock); Clinical Surgery (ed Rob and Smith); Scientific Foundations of Surgery (ed Wells and Kyle); Abdominal Operations (ed Maingot), and others; numerous articles in scientific jls. *Recreations:* swimming (Univ. of London colours, 1934, Kent Co. colours, 1935), sailing, gardening, photography; Pres., Hong Kong Yacht Racing Assoc., 1961-63, Vice-Pres., Far East Yacht Racing Fedn, 1961-62. *Address:* Hebe Haven, 7 Old Forge Lane, Fauvic, Jersey, CI. *T:* Central 53269. *Clubs:* Royal Over-Seas League; Royal Hong Kong Yacht (Hong Kong); Royal Channel Islands Yacht (Jersey); Durban, Durban Country, Royal Natal Yacht (Durban).

STOCK, Keith L(ievesley), CB 1957; Under Secretary, Department of Economic Affairs, 1965-68, retired; *b* 24 Oct. 1911; *s* of late Cyril Lievesley Stock and Irene Mary Stock (née Tomkins); *m* 1937, Joan Katherine Stock (née Milne); two *s* one *d*. *Educ:* Charterhouse; New College, Oxford. Petroleum Department, Board of Trade, 1935; Ministry of Fuel and Power, 1942; Imperial Defence College, 1951; Cabinet Office, 1954; Ministry of Fuel and Power, 1955; Min. of Technology, 1964. *Address:* c/o Barclays Bank, Millbank, SW1.

STOCK, Raymond, QC 1964; His Honour Judge Stock; a Circuit Judge (formerly Judge of County Courts), since 1971; *b* 1913; *s* of late A. E. and M. E. Stock; *m* 1969, E. Dorothy Thorpe, JP. *Educ:* West Monmouth School; Balliol College, Oxford. Barrister-at-law, Gray's Inn, 1936, Bencher, 1969. Royal Artillery, 1939-45. Recorder: Penzance, 1962-64; Exeter, 1964-66; Southampton, 1966-71; Dep. Chm., Dorset QS, 1964-71. *Address:* Shellwood Manor, Leigh, Surrey; 2 King's Bench Walk, Temple, EC4. *Club:* Hampshire.

STOCKDALE, Sir Edmund (Villiers Minshull), 1st Bt *cr* 1960; Kt 1955; JP; *b* 16 April 1903; 2nd *s* of late Major H. M. Stockdale, JP, and Mrs Stockdale, Mears Ashby Hall, Northants; *m* 1937, Hon. Louise Fermor-Hesketh, *er d* of 1st Lord Hesketh; two *s* one *d*. *Educ:* Wellington College. Entered Bank of England, 1921; Assistant to Governors, Reserve Bank of India, 1935; Asst Principal, Bank of England, 1937, Dep. Principal, 1941; pensioned, 1945. Elected Court of Common Council, City of London, 1946, Alderman, Ward of Cornhill, 1948; one of HM Lieuts, City of London, Comr of Assize, 1948-63; Sheriff, City of London 1953; Lord Mayor of London, 1959-60; Chm., Lord Mayor's Appeal Fund, King George's Jubilee Trust, 1960; Mem., Adv. Bd, etc., Holloway Prison, 1948-60. Chairman 1951-53; Member, Holloway Discharged Prisoners Aid Society Cttee, 1964; Vice-President, The Griffins (formerly Holloway DPAS), 1965; Member, Boards: Bridewell, Christ's, Royal Bethlem and Maudsley Hosps, 1948-63; Mem., Emerg. Bed Service Cttee, King Edward Hosp. Fund, 1963-69; Vice-Pres. King Edward's School, Witley, 1960-63; Governor, United Westminster Schools, 1948-54; Wellington College, 1955-74. Director, Embankment Trust Ltd, 1948-74, and other Cos. A Church Comr for England, 1962; Mem. Winchester Dioc. Bd of Finance (Exec. Cttee), 1963. Junior Grand Warden (Acting), Grand Lodge of England, 1960-61. Partner, Read Hurst-Brown and Co.; Member: London Stock Exchange, 1946-60; Court of Assistants, Carpenters' Co. (Master, 1970), Glaziers' Co. (Master 1973). JP London (Inner London Sessions), 1968. Grand Officer, Legion of Honour; Grand Cross, Order of Merit, Peru; Grand Official, Order of Mayo, Argentina; Knight Comdr, Order of Crown, Thailand; Order of Triple Power, Nepal; Comdr, Royal Order of North Star, Sweden; KStJ. Gold Medal, Madrid. *Publication:* The Bank of England, 1934. *Recreations:* shooting, drawing. *Heir: er s* Thomas Minshull Stockdale [*b* 7 Jan. 1940; *m* 1965, Jacqueline Ha-Van-Vuong; one *s* one *d*]. *Address:* Hoddington House, Upton Grey, Basingstoke. *T:* Long Sutton 437; Delnadamph, Strathdon, Aberdeenshire. *T:* Corgarff 253. *Clubs:* Buck's, MCC.

STOCKDALE, Eric; His Honour Judge Eric Stockdale; a Circuit Judge since 1972; *b* 8 Feb. 1929; *m* 1952, Joan (née Berry); two *s*. *Educ:* Collyers Sch., Horsham; London Sch. of Economics. LLB, BSc(Econ.), LLM, PhD. 2nd Lieut, RA, 1947-49. Called to the Bar, Middle Temple, 1950. Mem. Council: Inst. for the Study and Treatment of Delinquency (ISTD), 1966-; Nat. Assoc. for the Care and Resettlement of Offenders (NACRO), 1970-; Pres., Barnet Marriage Guidance Council, 1972-. *Publications:* The Court and the Offender, 1967; A Study of Bedford Prison 1660-1877, 1977. *Address:* 20 Lyonsdown Road, New Barnet, Herts. *T:* 01-449 7181.

STOCKDALE, Frank Alleyne, MA; His Honour Judge Stockdale; a Circuit Judge (County Court Judge, since 1964, Ilford and Westminster Courts); *b* 16 Oct. 1910; *er s* of late Sir Frank Stockdale, GCMG, CBE, MA, FLS; *m* 1942, Frances Jean, *er d* of late Sir FitzRoy Anstruther-Gough-Calthorpe, Bt; one *s* two *d*. *Educ:* Repton; Magdalene College, Cambridge. Called to Bar, Gray's Inn, 1934; Bencher, 1964. Served War of 1939-45: 5th Royal Inniskilling Dragoon Guards, BEF, 1939-40; North Africa, 1942-43 (despatches); psc; Lt-Col. Dep. Chm., Hampshire QS, 1954-66; Dep. Chm., Greater London QS, 1966-71. Mem., Inter. Deptl Cttee on Adoption Law, 1969-, Chm. 1971-72; *Address:* 4 Verulam Buildings, Gray's Inn, WC1. *T:* 01-242 3916. *Club:* Garrick.

STOCKDALE, Maj.-Gen. Reginald Booth, CB 1963; CMG 1975; OBE 1945; BSc (Eng); CEng; FIMechE; retired; *b* 12 Jan. 1908; *s* of late Reginald Hind Stockdale, Preston, Lancs; *m* 1940, Betty Celia, *d* of late William Alexander Tucker, Bromley, Kent; two *s* one *d. Educ:* Bedford Modern School. psc. Lieut, RAOC, 1931. Served War of 1939-45: BEF, 1939-40; UK, 1940-42; transferred to REME as Major, 1942; MEF, 1942-43; CMF, 1943-45. MELF, 1945-46; East Africa, 1946-48; Lt-Col, 1948; BAOR, 1948-50; Colonel, 1951; BAOR, 1952-53; DDME, Southern Command, 1953-56; DEME, BAOR, 1956-59; Commandant, Technical Group, REME, 1960-63. Brigadier, 1958; Major-General, 1960. Col Comdt, REME, 1963-68. An internat. official with WEU, Paris, 1963-74. *Address:* 9 St Ann Street, Salisbury, Wilts SP1 2DP. *T:* Salisbury 28168. *Club:* Army and Navy.

STOCKER, Prof. Bruce Arnold Dunbar, FRS 1966; MD; Professor of Medical Microbiology in Stanford University, since 1966; *b* 26 May 1917. *Educ:* King's College, London; Westminster Hospital, MB, BS, 1940; MRCS, LRCP, 1940; MD 1947. Guinness Prof. of Microbiology, Univ. of London, and Dir of Guinness-Lister Microbiological Research Unit, Lister Inst. of Preventive Med., until Dec. 1965. *Publications:* articles in scientific jls. *Address:* Department of Medical Microbiology, Stanford University, Stanford, Calif 94305, USA.

STOCKER, Hon. Sir John (Dexter), Kt 1973; MC, TD; **Hon. Mr Justice Stocker;** a Judge of the High Court, Queen's Bench Division, since 1973; Presiding Judge, South-Eastern Circuit, since 1976; *b* 7 Oct. 1918; *s* of late John Augustus Stocker and Emma Eyre Stocker (*née* Kettle), Hampstead; *m* 1956, Margaret Mary Hegarty; no *c. Educ:* Westminster Sch.; London University. 2nd Lt, QO Royal West Kent Regt, 1939; France, 1940; Middle East, 1942-43; Italy, 1943-46; Maj. 1943; Lt-Col 1945. LLB London 1947. Called to Bar, Middle Temple, 1948, Master of the Bench, 1971. QC 1965; a Recorder, 1972-73. *Recreations:* golf, cricket. *Address:* 24 Wallgrave Road, SW5. *T:* 01-373 1295. *Clubs:* Bath, MCC, Royal Wimbledon Golf.

STOCKHAUSEN, Karlheinz; composer and conductor; *b* 22 Aug. 1928; *s* of late Simon and Gertrud Stockhausen; *m* 1st, 1951, Doris Andreae; four *c*; 2nd, 1967, Mary Bauermeister; two *c. Educ:* Hochschule für Musik, and Univ., Cologne, 1947-51; studied with: Messaien, 1952-53; Prof. Werner Meyer-Eppler, Bonn Univ., 1954-56. With Westdeutscher Rundfunk Electronic Music Studio, 1953-, Artistic Dir, 1963-. Lectr, Internat. Summer Sch. for New Music, Darmstadt, 1953-; Dir, Interpretation Group for live electronic music, 1964-; Founder, and Artistic Dir, Kölner Kurse für Neue Musik, 1963-68; Visiting Professor: Univ. of Pa, 1965; Univ. of Calif., 1966-67; Cologne State Conservatory, 1971-. Co-Editor, Die Reihe, 1954-59. First annual tour of 30 concert-lectures, 1958, USA and Canada, since then throughout world. Has made over 70 records of his own works. *Publications:* Texte, 4 vols, 1963-77; *compositions:* Chöre für Doris, Drei Lieder, Chöre 1950-51; Sonatine, Kreuzspiel, Formel, 1951; Schlagtrio Spiel für Orchester, Etude, 1952; Punkte, 1952, rev. 1962, Klavierstücke I-XI, 1952-56, 1961; Kontra-Punkte, 1953; Elektronische Studien I and II, 1953-54; Zeitmasze, Gesang der Jünglinge, 1956; Gruppen, 1957; Zyklus, Refrain, 1959; Carré, Kontakte, 1960; Originale (musical play), 1961; Plus Minus, 1963; Momente, 1962-64; Mixtur (new arr. 1967), Mikrophonie I, 1964; Mikrophonie II, Stop (new arr. 1969), 1965; Telemusik, Solo, Adieu, 1966; Hymnen, Prozession, Ensemble, 1967; Kurzwellen, Stimmung, Aus den sieben Tagen, Spiral, Musik für ein Haus, 1968; Hymnen mit Orchester, Fresco, Dr K-Sextett, 1969; Pole, Expo, Mantra, Für Kommende Zeiten, 1970; Sternklang, Trans, 1971; Alphabet, Am Himmel Wandre ich, (Indianerlieder), Ylem, 1972; Vortrag über Hu, Inori, 1973-74; Herbstmusik, Atmen gibt das Leben..., 1974; Musik im Bauch, Tierkreis, Harlekin, 1975; Sirius, 1975-76; Amour, 1976; Jubiläum, In Freundschaft, 1977. *Address:* Studio für Elektronische Musik, Westdeutscher Rundfunk, Wallrafplatz, Cologne, Germany.

STOCKIL, Sir Raymond (Osborne), KBE 1964 (OBE 1958); Farmer and Director of Companies; *b* 15 April 1907; *s* of Francis Robert Stockil and Ruth (*née* Coventry); *m* 1929, Virginia Fortner (*d* 1972); one *s* three *d* (and one *s* decd); *m* 1973, Margot Susan Lovett Hodgson. *Educ:* Heldeberg College, Cape Province; Washington University, USA (BA). Took up Civil Aviation and Manufacturing in USA, 1929-33 (5 USA Patents); returned to Natal, 1934; commenced farming in Fort Victoria, 1936. Served War of 1939-45 with SR Signal Corps. MP for Victoria, 1946-62; Leader of Opposition, 1948-53 and 1956-59; resigned from Parliament, 1962. Chairman, Hippo Valley Estates Ltd, 1956. *Recreation:* owner and trainer of racehorses. *Address:* 7 Addington Lane, Borrowdale, Salisbury, Rhodesia. *T:* 882501. *Club:* Salisbury (Salisbury, Rhodesia).

STOCKLEY, David Dudgeon, BSc (Engineering, London 1st Class Hons 1921); Principal, Aston Technical College, 1936-60; *b* 2 July 1900; *s* of Charles Rennie Stockley and L. Dudgeon; *m* 1928, Elizabeth Nina Baty; no *c. Educ:* Sunderland Technical College. Industrial posts, 1921-25; Lecturer Huddersfield Technical College, 1925-27; Sunderland Technical College, 1927-30; Head of Engineering Department, School of Engineering and Navigation, Poplar, 1930-32; Head of Dept of Engineering and Building, Borough Polytechnic, SE1, 1932-36. *Publications:* Papers on technical and educational subjects. *Recreation:* fishing. *Address:* 15 South Grange Road, Ripon, Yorks HG4 2NH.

STOCKLEY, Gerald Ernest, CBE 1957; *b* Simla, India, 15 Dec. 1900; *s* of late Brig.-Gen. E. N. Stockley, DSO, late RE, and Elsie Shewell Cooper; *m* 1st, Phillipina Mary Prendergast (marr. diss.); two *d*; 2nd, Katharine Noel Parker. *Educ:* Wellington Coll.; Christ's Coll., Cambridge, BA Hons, English and Mod. Langs. China Consular Service, 1925, and served at numerous posts in China: Consul (Grade II) 1935, Consul, Foochow, 1936-38, and Tengyüeh, 1938-40; Consul (Grade I) 1939, Acting Consul-Gen., Kunming, 1939; served with British Military Mission in China, 1941-43; Acting Consul-General, Kweilin, 1943-44; Consul, Seattle (USA), 1944-45; Consul-Gen., Hankow, 1946-48; Counsellor, FO, 1948-49; Minister to Republic of Honduras, 1950-54; Consul-General, Naples, 1954-59; retired, Dec. 1959; Consul and Consul-General (personal rank), Nice, 1960-66. *Address:* 6 Harrogate House, 29 Sloane Square, SW1.

STOCKMAN, Henry Watson, CBE 1949; *b* London, 20 April 1894; *s* of late Henry Stockman; *m* 1921, Margaret Reid Robertson; one *s* one *d. Educ:* Battersea Polytechnic. National Health Insurance Commn (England), 1912-19; Ministry of Health, 1919-44; Ministry of National Insurance (later Min. of Pensions and Nat. Insurance), 1945-55; Asst Secretary, 1945-50; Chief Insurance Officer, 1950-53; Under-Secretary, 1953-55; International Labour Office, Geneva, Social Security Division, 1957-59; Technical Adviser, International Social Security Association, Geneva, 1959-64. *Publications:* History and Development of Social Security in Great Britain, 1957; Development and Trends in Social Security in Great Britain, 1962. *Recreation:* gardening. *Address:* Christmas Cottage, 22 Grove Road, Beaconsfield, Bucks HP9 1UP. *T:* Beaconsfield 3722.

See also Sir Hermann Bondi.

STOCKPORT, Suffragan Bishop of, since 1965; **Rt. Rev. Rupert Gordon Strutt,** BD; *b* 15 Jan. 1912; *s* of Rupert Henry and Maude Mortlock Strutt; *m* 1st, 1936, Eva Gertrude Rabbitts; one *s* one *d*; 2nd, 1949, Constance Mary Fergusson Foden; one *s* two *d. Educ:* University of London; London College of Divinity; Wycliffe Hall, Oxford. Deacon, 1942; Priest, 1943. Curate of Carlton-in-the-Willows, 1942-43; Chaplain to the Forces (Emergency Commission), 1943-45; Rector of Normanton-on-Soar, 1945-48; Vicar of Holy Trinity, Leicester, 1948-52; Curate-in-Charge, St John the Divine, Leicester, 1949-52; Vicar of Addiscombe, Diocese of Canterbury, 1952-59. Chaplain to HM Prison, Leicester, 1948-52. Commissary to the Bishop of Saskatoon, 1958-. Archdeacon of Maidstone and Canon Residentiary of Canterbury Cathedral; also Prior of St John's Hospital, Canterbury, 1959-65. *Address:* Bishop's Lodge, Macclesfield Road, Alderley Edge, Cheshire. *T:* Alderley Edge 582074.

STOCKS, Alfred James; Chief Executive, Liverpool City Council, since 1973; *b* 24 March 1926; *s* of James and Mary Stocks; *m* 1958, Jillian Margery Gedye; one *s* one *d. Educ:* Bootham Sch., York; Clare Coll., Cambridge (MA). Admitted solicitor, 1949. Appointed Dep. Town Clerk, Liverpool, 1968. *Address:* 38 Glendyke Road, Liverpool L18 6JR. *T:* 051-724 2448. *Club:* Athenæum (Liverpool).

STOCKWELL, Air Cdre Edmund Arthur, CB 1967; MA; Command Education Officer, Training Command, 1968-72 (Flying Training Command, 1964-68); retired 1972; *b* 15 Dec. 1911; *s* of Arthur Davenport Stockwell, Dewsbury; *m* 1937, Pearl Arber; one *s* two *d*; *m* 1955, Lillian Gertrude Moore (*d* 1965), OBE, MRCP; two *s*; *m* 1970, Mrs Kathleen (Betty) Clarke, Chesham. *Educ:* Wheelwright Grammar School; Balliol Coll., Oxford. Entered RAF Educational Service, Cranwell, 1935; RAF Educn in India, 1936; Punjab and NW Frontier, 1936-38; RAFVR (Admin and Special Duties), 1939; Lahore, Simla, Delhi, 1939-44; Group Educn Officer, No 6 (RCAF) Group, 1944; Air Min., 1944-48; OC, RAF Sch. of Educn, 1948-51; Comd Educn Officer, Coastal Comd, 1951-53; Comd Educn Officer, Far East Air Force, 1953-55; Principal Educn Officer, Halton, 1956-59; Comd Educn Officer, Maintenance Comd,

1959-62; Dep. Dir of Educational Services, Air Min., 1962-64. Group Captain, 1954; Air Commodore, 1964. *Recreations:* golf, gardening. *Address:* Saroman, Faringdon Road, Abingdon, Oxon. *T:* Abingdon 20816.

STOCKWELL, Gen. Sir Hugh Charles, GCB 1959 (KCB 1954; CB 1946); KBE 1949 (CBE 1945); DSO 1940 and Bar 1957; late Infantry; Chairman: Inland Waterways Amenity Advisory Council, 1971-74; Kennet and Avon Canal Trust, 1966-75; Member: British Waterways Board, 1971-74; Water Space Amenity Commission, 1973-74; *b* 16 June 1903; *s* of late Lt-Col H. C. Stockwell, OBE, late Highland Light Infantry, Chief Constable of Colchester, and Gertrude Forrest; *m* 1931, Joan Rickman Garrard, *d* of Charles and Marion Garrard, Kingston Lisle, Berkshire; two *d. Educ:* Cothill House, Abingdon; Marlborough; Royal Military Coll., Sandhurst. Joined 2/Royal Welch Fusiliers, 1923; served West Africa, 1929-35; Instructor, Small Arms School, Netheravon, 1935-38; Brigade-Major, Royal Welch Brigade, 1938-40; served in Norway (DSO); 30 East African Bde, 1942-43; 29th Independent Bde, 1943-45; Burma (CB); Commander 82 (WA) Division, Jan. 1945-June 1946; Commander, Home Counties District, UK, July 1946-47; Commander Sixth Airborne Division, Palestine, 1947-48; Commandant, RMA, Sandhurst, 1948-50; Comdr, 3rd Inf. Div., and Comdr, East Anglian Dist, 1951-52; General Officer Commanding: Malaya, 1952-54; 1 Corps, BAOR, 1954-56; Ground Forces, Suez Operation, 1956; Military Secretary to the Secretary of State for War, 1957-59; Adjutant-General to the Forces, 1959-60; Deputy Supreme Allied Commander, Europe, 1960-64, retired. Gen., 1957. Col, The Royal Welch Fusiliers, 1952-65; Col, The Royal Malay Regt 1954-59; Col Commandant, Army Air Corps, 1957-63; Col Commandant, Royal Army Educational Corps October 1959-64. ADC General to the Queen, 1959-62. Governor, Felsted School, 1954-65. Grand Officier, Légion d'Honneur (France), 1958. *Recreations:* conservation, painting, travel. *Address:* Horton, near Devizes, Wilts. *T:* Cannings 617; The Clydesdale Bank, 31 St James's Street, SW1. *Clubs:* MCC, Army and Navy.

STOCKWOOD, Rt. Rev. Arthur Mervyn; *see* Southwark, Bishop of.

STODART, Rt. Hon. (James) Anthony, PC 1974; *b* 6 June 1916; *yr s* of late Col Thomas Stodart, CIE, IMS, and of Mary Alice Coullie; *m* 1940, Hazel Jean Usher. *Educ:* Wellington. Farming at Kingston, North Berwick, 1934-58, and now at Leaston, Humbie, East Lothian. Hon. Pres., Edinburgh Univ. Agricultural Soc., 1952; Pres. East Lothian Boy Scouts' Assoc., 1960-63. Contested: (L) Berwick and East Lothian, 1950; (C) Midlothian and Peebles, 1951; Midlothian, 1955; MP (C) Edinburgh West, 1959-Oct. 1974; Jt Parly Under-Sec. of State, Scottish Office, Sept. 1963-Oct. 1964; An Opposition spokesman on Agriculture and on Scottish Affairs, 1966-69; Parly Sec., MAFF, 1970-72; Minister of State, MAFF, 1972-74; Vice-Chm., Conservative Agric. Cttee, House of Commons, 1962-63, 1964-65, 1966-70. Led Parly Delegn to Canada, 1974. Chm., Agricultural Credit Corp. Ltd, 1975-. *Publications:* (jt author) Land of Abundance, a study of Scottish Agriculture in the 20th Century, 1962; contrib. on farming topics to agricultural journals and newspapers. *Recreations:* music, playing golf and preserving a sense of humour. *Address:* Lorimers, North Berwick, East Lothian. *T:* North Berwick 2457. *Clubs:* Caledonian; New (Edinburgh); Hon. Company of Edinburgh Golfers.

STODDART, David Leonard; MP (Lab) Swindon, since 1970; a Lord Commissioner, HM Treasury, since 1976; *b* 4 May 1926; *s* of Arthur Leonard Stoddart, coal miner, and Queenie Victoria Stoddart (*née* Price); *m* 1961, Jennifer Percival-Alwyn; two *s* one *d. Educ:* elementary; St Clement Danes and Henley Grammar Schools. Youth in training, PO Telephones, 1942-44; business on own account, 1944-46; Railway Clerk, 1947-49; Hospital Clerk, 1949-51; Power Station Clerical Worker, 1951-70. Joined Labour Party, 1947; Member Reading County Borough Council, 1954-72; served at various times as Chairman of Housing, Transport and Finance Cttees; Leader of the Reading Labour Group of Councillors, 1962-70. Contested (Lab) Newbury, 1959 and 1964, Swindon, 1969. PPS to Minister for Housing and Construction, 1974-75; an Asst Govt Whip, 1975. *Recreations:* gardening, music. *Address:* Sintra, 37A Bath Road, Reading, Berks. *T:* Reading 56726.

STOESSEL, Walter J., Jr; US Ambassador to the Federal Republic of Germany, since 1976; *b* 24 Jan. 1920; *s* of Walter John Stoessel and Katherine Stoessel (*née* Haston); *m* 1946, Mary Ann (*née* Ferrandou); three *d. Educ:* Lausanne Univ.; Stanford Univ. (BA); Russian Inst., Columbia Univ.; Center for Internat. Affairs, Harvard Univ. US Foreign Service, 1942;

Polit. Officer, Caracas, 1942-46; Dept of State, 1946-47; Moscow, 1947-49; Bad-Nauheim, 1950-52; Officer i/c Soviet Affairs, Dept of State, 1952-56; White House, 1956; Paris, 1956-59; Dir, Exec. Secretariat, Dept of State, 1960-61; Polit. Adviser to SHAPE, Paris, 1961-63; Moscow, 1963-65; Dep. Asst Sec. for European Affairs, Dept of State, 1965-68; US Ambassador to Poland, 1968-72; Asst Sec. for European Affairs, Dept of State, 1972-74; US Ambassador to USSR, 1974-76. *Recreations:* tennis, ski-ing, swimming, painting. *Address:* American Embassy, Bonn, Federal Republic of Germany.

STOGDON, Norman Francis; a Recorder of the Crown Court, since 1972; *b* 14 June 1909; *s* of late F. R. Stogdon and late L. Stogdon (*née* Reynolds); *m* 1959, Yvonne (*née* Jaques). *Educ:* Harrow; Brasenose Coll., Oxford (BA, BCL). Called to Bar, Middle Temple, 1932. War Service, Army, 1939-45: served with Royal Fusiliers, King's African Rifles, 1941-45; Staff Officer; sc Middle East 1944. *Publications:* contrib. 2nd and 3rd edns Halsbury's Laws of England. *Recreations:* golf, ski-ing. *Address:* 2 Harcourt Buildings, Temple, EC4Y 9DB. *T:* 01-353 2548. *Club:* Moor Park Golf.

STOICHEFF, Prof. Boris Peter, FRS 1975; FRSC 1965; Centennial Medal of Canada, 1967; Professor of Physics, since 1974 and University Professor, since 1977, University of Toronto; *b* 1 June 1924; *s* of Peter and Vasilka Stoicheff; *m* 1954, Lillian Joan Ambridge; one *s* one *d. Educ:* Univ. of Toronto, Faculty of Applied Science and Engineering (BASc), Dept of Physics (MA, PhD). McKee-Gilchrist Fellowship, Univ. of Toronto, 1950-51; Nat. Research Council Fellowship, Ottawa, 1952-53; Res. Officer in Div. of Pure Physics, Nat. Res. Council of Canada, 1953-64; Visiting Scientist, Mass Inst. of Technology, 1963-64. Chm., Engrg Science, Univ. of Toronto, 1972-77. Izaak Walton Killam Meml Scholarship, 1977. Fellow, Optical Soc. of America, 1965 (Pres. 1976); Fellow, Amer. Phys. Soc., 1969; Hon. Fellow, Indian Acad. of Scis, 1971; Gold Medal for Achievement in Physics of Canadian Assoc. of Physicists, 1974. *Publications:* numerous scientific contribs to phys. and chem. jls. *Address:* Department of Physics, University of Toronto, Toronto, Ontario M5S 1A7, Canada. *T:* (416) 978-2948.

STOKE-UPON-TRENT, Archdeacon of; *see* Borrett, Ven. C. W.

STOKER, Prof. Michael George Parke, CBE 1974; FRS 1968, FRSE 1960; Director, Imperial Cancer Research Fund Laboratories, London, since 1968; *b* 4 July 1918; *e s* of Dr S. P. Stoker, Maypole, Monmouth; *m* 1942, Veronica Mary English; three *s* two *d. Educ:* Oakham Sch.; Sidney Sussex Coll., Cambridge; St Thomas' Hosp., London, MRCS, LRCP 1942; MB, BChir 1943; MD 1947. RAMC, 1942-47; Demonstrator in Pathology, Cambridge Univ., 1947-48; Univ. Lecturer in Pathology, 1948-50; Huddersfield Lecturer in Special Pathology, 1950-58; Fellow of Clare Coll., 1948-58; Asst Tutor and Dir of Medical Studies, Clare Coll., 1949-58; Prof. of Virology, Glasgow Univ., and Hon. Dir, MRC Experimental Virus Research Unit, 1959-68. WHO Travel Fellow, 1951; Vis. Prof., UCL, 1968-74. Leeuwenhoek Lecture, Royal Soc., 1971. Member: European Molecular Biology Organisation; Council for Scientific Policy, DES, 1970-73. For. Hon. Mem., Amer. Acad. of Arts and Scis, 1973. Hon. Fellow, Clare Coll., Cambridge, 1976. *Publications:* various articles on cell biology and virology. *Address:* Oxley House, Lenham, Kent. *Club:* Athenæum.

STOKES, family name of **Baron Stokes.**

STOKES, Baron *cr* 1969 (Life Peer), of Leyland; **Donald Gresham Stokes,** Kt 1965; TD; DL; CEng, FIMechE; MSAE; FIMI; FCIT; President, British Leyland Ltd, since 1975; Chairman and Managing Director, 1968-75, Chief Executive, 1973-75, British Leyland Motor Corporation Ltd; *b* 22 March 1914; *o s* of Harry Potts Stokes; *m* 1939, Laura Elizabeth Courteney Lamb; one *s. Educ:* Blundell's School; Harris Institute of Technology, Preston. Started Student Apprenticeship, Leyland Motors Ltd, 1930. Served War of 1939-45: REME, 1939-46 (Lt-Col). Re-joined Leyland as Exports Manager, 1946; General Sales and Service Manager, 1950; Director, 1954; Managing Director, and Deputy Chairman, Leyland Motor Corp., 1963, Chm. 1967; Chm. and Man. Dir, British Leyland UK, 1973. Director: National Westminster Bank, 1969; London Weekend Television Ltd, 1967-71; Vice-President, Empresa Nacional de Autocamiones SA, Spain, 1959-73. Chm., British Arabian Adv. Co. Ltd, 1977-. President: SMMT, 1961-62; Motor Industry Res. Assoc., 1965-66; Manchester Univ. Inst. of Science and Technology, 1972-76 (Vice-Pres., 1968-71); Vice-Pres., IMechE, 1971, Pres., 1972; Chm., EDC for Electronics Industry, 1966-67; Member: NW Economic Planning Council, 1965-70; IRC, 1966-71 (Dep.

Chm. 1969); EDC for the Motor Manufacturing Industry, 1967-; Council, Public Transport Assoc.; Cttee of Common Market Constructors, 1972-; Worshipful Co. of Carmen. DL Lancs 1968. Hon. Fellow, Keble Coll., Oxford, 1968. Hon. LLD Lancaster, 1967; Hon. DTech Loughborough, 1968; Hon. DSc: Southampton, 1969; Salford, 1971. Officier de l'Ordre de la Couronne (Belgium), 1964; Commandeur de l'ordre de Leopold II (Belgium), 1972. *Recreation:* boating. *Address:* Nuffield House, 41-46 Piccadilly, W1V 0BD. *Clubs:* Royal Western Yacht, Royal Motor Yacht.

STOKES, Prof. Eric Thomas, MA, PhD; Smuts Professor of the History of the British Commonwealth, Cambridge, since 1970; *b* 10 July 1924; *s* of Walter John Stokes; *m* 1949, Florence Mary Lee; four *d. Educ:* Holloway Sch.; Christ's Coll., Cambridge. MA 1949; PhD 1953. War Service, 1943-46: Lieut, RA; Royal Indian Mountain Artillery. Lecturer in: History, Univ. of Malaya, Singapore, 1950-55; Colonial History and Administration, Univ. of Bristol, 1955-56; Prof. of History, Univ. Coll. of Rhodesia and Nyasaland, 1956-63; Lecturer in History (Colonial Studies), Univ. of Cambridge, and Fellow and Tutor, St Catharine's Coll., 1963-70; Reader in Commonwealth History, 1970. Member: Inter-Univ. Council for Higher Educn Overseas, 1972-; India Cttee, British Council, 1972-; Indian Hist. Records Commn, 1976-. Hon. DLitt Mysore, 1977. *Publications:* The English Utilitarians and India, 1959; The Political Ideas of English Imperialism, an inaugural lecture, 1960; The Peasant and the Raj, 1978; (ed with Richard Brown) The Zambesian Past, 1966; contributed to: Historians of India, Pakistan and Ceylon (ed C. H. Philips), 1961; Elites in South Asia (ed E. R. Leach and S. N. Mukherjee), 1970; Rudyard Kipling (ed John Gross), 1972; Historical Perspectives: studies in English thought and society in honour of J. H. Plumb (ed N. McKendrick), 1974; Indian Society and the Beginnings of Modernization circa 1830-50 (ed C. H. Philips and M. D. Wainwright), 1976; Land Tenure and Peasant in South Asia (ed R. E. Frykenberg, 1977); articles in Historical Jl, Past and Present, etc. *Address:* St Catharine's College, Cambridge. *T:* Cambridge 59445. *Club:* Royal Commonwealth Society.

STOKES, John Fisher, MA, MD, FRCP; Physician, University College Hospital, since 1947; *b* 19 Sept. 1912; *e s* of late Dr Kenneth Stokes and Mary (*née* Fisher); *m* 1940, Elizabeth Joan, *d* of Thomas Rooke and Elizabeth Frances (*née* Pearce); one *s* one *d. Educ:* Haileybury (exhibitioner); Gonville and Caius Coll., Cambridge (exhibitioner); University Coll. Hosp. (Fellowes Silver Medal for clinical medicine). MB BChir (Cambridge) 1937; MRCP 1939; MD (Cambridge) 1947 (proxime accessit, Horton Smith prize); FRCP 1947; FRCPE 1975; Thruston Medal, Gonville and Caius Coll., 1948. Appointments on junior staff University Coll. Hosp. and Victoria Hosp. for Children, Tite St, 1937-42; RAMC 1942-46; served in Far East, 1943-46, Lt-Col (despatches). Examiner in Medicine, various Univs, 1949-70. Member of Council, Royal Soc. of Med., 1951-54, 1967-69. Vice-Pres., RCP, 1968-69. Amateur Squash Rackets Champion of Surrey, 1935, of East of England, 1936, Runner-up of British Isles, 1937; English International, 1938; Technical Adviser to Squash Rackets Assoc., 1948-52; Chm. Jesters Club, 1953-59. *Publications:* Examinations in Medicine (jtly), 1976; contrib. on liver disease and general medicine in medical journals. *Recreations:* music, tennis, painting. *Address:* Ossicles, Newnham Hill, near Henley-on-Thames, Oxon RG9 5TL. *Clubs:* Athenæum, Savile.
See also Prof. W. D. M. Paton.

STOKES, John Heydon Romaine; MP (C) Halesowen and Stourbridge, since 1974 (Oldbury and Halesowen, 1970-74); *b* 23 July 1917; *o* surv. *s* of late Victor Romaine Stokes, Hitchin; *m* 1939, Barbara Esmée, *y d* of late R. E. Yorke, Wellingborough; one *s* two *d. Educ:* Temple Grove; Haileybury Coll.; Queen's Coll., Oxford. BA 1938; MA 1946. Hon. Agent and Treas., Oxford Univ. Conservative Assoc., 1937; Pres., Monarchist Soc., 1937; Pres., Mermaid Club, 1937. Asst Master, Prep. Sch., 1938-39. Served War, 1939-46: Dakar Expedn, 1940; wounded in N Africa, 1943; Mil. Asst to HM Minister Beirut and Damascus, 1944-46; Major, Royal Fusiliers. Contested (C): Gloucester, 1964; Hitchin, 1966. Personnel Officer, Imperial Chemical Industries, 1946-51; Personnel Manager, British Celanese, 1951-59; Dep. Personnel Manager, Courtaulds, 1957-59; Partner, Clive & Stokes, Personnel Consultants, 1959-. Mem. Exec. Cttee, Oxford Soc.; Chm., Gen. Purposes Cttee, Primrose League; Vice-Chm., Royal Soc. of St George. Order of Merit (Syria), 1946. *Publications:* articles on political and personnel subjects. *Recreations:* gardening, tennis, travel, English history. *Address:* Jasmine Cottage, Aston Rowant, Oxford OX9 5ST. *T:* Kingston Blount 51506. *Club:* Carlton.

STOKES, (Hon.) Brig. Ralph Shelton Griffin, CBE 1942 (OBE 1919); DSO 1917; MC 1916; *b* 31 July 1882; *s* of Francis Griffin Stokes, BA Oxon; *m* 1921, Lora Mary Bradford; four *d. Educ:* St Mark's, Windsor and privately. Served Anglo-Boer War, Paget's Horse, 1901-02, with Methuen's Columns in W Transvaal; European War, 1914-18 (DSO, MC, despatches thrice); Field Company, RE; Tunnelling Companies; Lieut-Col, Controller of Mines, First Army; Colonel, Chief Engineer, Allied Forces, Archangel, North Russia, 1918-19 (OBE, despatches twice); War of 1939-45: with RE; France, 1939-40; Narvik 1940 (despatches); CE Xth Corps, 1940; Brig. CE Airfields, Middle East, 1941-43 (CBE; despatches twice); War Office, 1943-44; has record of active service in the three wars of the century. Field Engineer, International Nickel Co., New York, 1912-14; Superintendent of Mines, De Beers Consolidated, Kimberley, 1920-28; Consulting Engineer, and Manager, Central Mining & Investment Corporation, 1928-44, Director, 1944-59. Chairman of Trinidad Leaseholds Ltd, 1944-47. Past President: Geological Soc. of S Africa; SA Inst. of Mining and Metallurgy; Instn of Mining and Metallurgy, London; Past Vice-Pres., Royal African Soc. *Publication:* Mines and Minerals of the British Empire, 1908. *Address:* Highfield, Leweston, Sherborne, Dorset DT9 6EL. *T:* Holnest 425. *Clubs:* Army and Navy; Rand (Johannesburg).

STOKES, William Henry, CBE 1950; JP 1950; Personnel Manager, Armstrong Siddeley Motors Ltd, Coventry, 1954-59; Member, Coventry Pre-Retirement Committee, since 1968; *b* 18 Nov. 1894; *s* of William Henry Stokes, Coventry, and Annie Maria (*née* Jenkins); *m* 1918, Frances Emily Beckett; no *c. Educ:* Coventry. Chm. Midland Regional Bd for Industry, 1945-50; Vice-Chm. Midland Regional Production Bd, 1940-45; Member: Nat. Production Advisory Council, 1940-50; Local Employment Cttee; BBC Advisory Cttee, Midland Region; Divisional Organiser, Amalgamated Engineering Union (Coventry area), 1937-50; Iron and Steel Corporation of Great Britain, 1950-53; (part-time), East Midlands Electricity Board, 1959-65; former Chm., Coventry Pre-Retirement Cttee; Mem., Coventry Probus. *Recreations:* interest in Rugby football (a Vice-Pres. Coventry RFC); golf, pottery, sculpture. *Address:* 57 Rochester Road, Coventry CV5 6AF. *T:* Coventry 72860.

STONE, family name of **Baron Stone.**

STONE, Baron *cr* 1976 (Life Peer), of Hendon; **Joseph Ellis Stone,** Kt 1970; Medical Practitioner; *b* 27 May 1903; 2nd *s* of late Henry Silverstone and Rebecca Jane Silverstone (*née* Ellis); *m* 1932, Beryl, *y d* of late Alexander and Jane Bernstein; one *s* one *d. Educ:* Llanelli County Intermediate Sch.; Cardiff Univ.; Westminster Hosp., SW1. MB, BS London 1927; MRCS, LRCP 1925. Casualty Officer and Ho. Surg., Westminster Hosp., 1925-26; Sen. Ho. Surg., N Staffs Royal Infirmary, 1926-28; MO, St George in the East Hosp., 1928-32; gen. med. practice, 1932-. Served RAMC, 1940-45, Captain; graded med. specialist. Personal Physician to PM, 1964-70 and 1974-76. Mem. Med. Soc. of London; Mem. Hampstead Med. Soc. Yeoman of Worshipful Soc. of Apothecaries. *Recreation:* golf. *Address:* 615 Finchley Road, Hampstead, NW3. *T:* 01-435 7333.

STONE, Alan Reynolds; *see* Stone, Reynolds.

STONE, Bertram Gilchrist, OBE 1955; *b* 3 June 1903; *s* of late Reverend William Arthur Stone, Warden of St Thomas' Coll., Colombo, and of Clare Frances Stone; *m* 1933, Dorothy Kneale, *y d* of late D. E. McCracken, OBE, Liverpool; two *s. Educ:* Bromsgrove School; Sidney Sussex College, Cambridge (Scholar), Classical Tripos, BA 1925, MA 1929. District Officer, Colonial Administrative Service, Nigeria, 1925-36; Administrative Officer, Nat. Council of Social Service, 1937-43; Midland Regional Officer, 1944-47; Colonial Office, 1947; official visits to Nigeria, 1955 and 1959, Aden and Somaliland, 1957; Head of Students Branch, Colonial Office and Ministry of Overseas Development, 1956-65. Foundn Fellow, Univ. of Surrey. *Publications:* contrib. to educational journals. *Recreations:* gardening, reading. *Address:* Manor Barn, Kingston, Lewes, East Sussex. *T:* Lewes 4569. *Club:* Royal Commonwealth Society.

STONE, Prof. Francis Gordon Albert, FRS 1976; Head of Department of Inorganic Chemistry, and Professor since 1963, Bristol University; *b* 19 May 1925; *s* of Sidney Charles and Florence Stone; *m* 1956, Judith M. Hislop, Sydney, Australia; three *s. Educ:* Exeter Sch.; Christ's Coll., Cambridge. BA 1948, MA and PhD 1952, ScD 1963, Cambridge. Fulbright Schol., Univ. of Southern Calif., 1952-54; Instructor and Asst Prof., Harvard Univ., 1954-62; Reader, Queen Mary Coll., London, 1962-63. Vis. Professor: Monash Univ., 1966; Princeton Univ., 1967; Univ. of Arizona, 1970; Carnegie-Mellon Univ., 1972;

Guggenheim Fellow, 1961; Sen. Vis. Fellow, Australian Acad. of Sciences, 1966; A. R. Gordon Distinguished Lectr, Univ. of Toronto, 1977. Lectures: Boomer, Univ. of Alberta, 1965; Firestone, Univ. of Wisconsin, 1970; Tilden, Chem. Soc., 1971. Member: Council, Chem. Soc., 1968-70; Dalton Council, 1971-74 (Vice-Pres. 1973); SRC Chemistry Cttee, 1971-74. Organometallic Chemistry Medal, Chem. Soc., 1972. *Publications:* (Editor) Inorganic Polymers, 1962; Hydrogen Compounds of the Group IV Elements, 1962; (Editor) Advances in Organometallic Chemistry, vols 1-16, 1964-74; numerous papers in Jl Chem. Soc., Jl Amer. Chem. Soc., etc. *Recreation:* world travel. *Address:* 6 Rylestone Grove, Bristol BS9 3UT. *T:* Bristol 627408.

STONE, Frederick Alistair; solicitor; Clerk and Chief Executive, Surrey County Council, since 1973; *b* 13 Sept. 1927; *s* of Cyril Jackson and Elsie May Stone; *m* 1963, Anne Teresa Connor; one *s* one *d*. *Educ:* William Hulme's Grammar Sch.; Dulwich Coll.; Brasenose Coll., Oxford (BCL, MA). Asst Solicitor: Norwich City Council, 1954-58; Hampshire CC, 1958-60; Sen. Solicitor, CC of Lincoln (Parts of Lindsey), 1960-63; Asst Clerk, Hampshire CC, 1963-65; Dep. Clerk, Cheshire CC, 1965-73. *Recreations:* music, walking, gardening. *Address:* (office) County Hall, Kingston upon Thames, Surrey. *T:* 01-546 1050; (home) North Lodge, Brockham Green, Betchworth RH3 7JS. *T:* Betchworth 2178.

STONE, Gilbert Seymour, FCA; private practice as chartered accountant; *b* 4 Feb. 1915; *s* of J. Stone; *m* 1941, Josephine Tolhurst; one *s*. *Educ:* Clifton College. War service as Air Gunner with RAF, 1939-45 (Sqdn-Ldr); with Industrial & Commercial Finance Corp. Ltd, 1945-59, latterly Asst Gen. Manager; Dir, Gresham Trust Ltd, 1959-61; practised on own account, 1961-72; Dir, Industrial Develt Unit, DTI, 1972-74. Director: Babcock & Wilcox Ltd; Industrial and Commercial Finance Corp. Ltd; London Amer. Finance Corp. Ltd (non-exec. Dep. Chm., 1975-); Export Credit and Marketing Corp.; New Shakespeare Co. Ltd; Hamilton Leasing Ltd (Chm.); Manganese Bronze Holdings Ltd; Antofagasta (Chile) and Bolivia Railway Co. Ltd; Queensway Discount Warehouses Ltd. *Recreations:* golf, travel. *Address:* Deepcut Place, Deepcut, Surrey. *Clubs:* Garrick; Sunningdale Golf.

STONE, Sir (John) Leonard, Kt 1943; OBE 1943; QC 1948; *b* 6 Nov. 1896; *s* of late John Morris Stone, Blackheath and Lincoln's Inn, and late Edith Emily Stone, *d* of Alderman Edward Hart; *m* 1923, Madeleine Marie, *d* of late Frederick Scheffler, New York; one *s*. *Educ:* Malvern College. Served European War, 1914-22, commissioned Worcester Regt, Oct. 1914, Gallipoli, Army of the Black Sea, Control Officer Eskishehir, 1919-20; Inter-Allied Commission of Inquiry Turco-Greek War, 1921 (despatches, thrice). Called to Bar, Gray's Inn, 1923; joined Lincoln's Inn, 1931; Bencher, Gray's Inn, 1942, Treas., 1956. Pres., Commission of Inquiry, Bombay Explosions, 1944; Chief Justice High Court, Bombay, 1943-47; Vice-Chancellor, County Palatine of Lancaster, 1948-63. Chairman of Departmental Committee on Hallmarking, 1956-58. Mem. Council, Imp. Soc. of Knights Bachelor. *Address:* 2 Gray's Inn Square, WC1. *Clubs:* MCC; Cheltenham Croquet.
See also R. F. Stone.

STONE, (John) Richard (Nicholas), CBE 1946; MA; P. D. Leake Professor of Finance and Accounting, University of Cambridge, since 1955; Fellow of King's College, Cambridge, since 1945; *b* 30 Aug. 1913; *o c* of late Sir Gilbert Stone; *m* 1941, Feodora Leontinoff (*d* 1956); one *d*; *m* 1960, Mrs Giovanna Croft-Murray, *d* of Count Aurelio Saffi. *Educ:* Westminster School; Gonville and Caius College, Cambridge (Hon. Fellow, 1976). With C. E. Heath and Co., Lloyd's Brokers, 1936-39; Ministry of Economic Warfare, 1939-40; Offices of the War Cabinet, Central Statistical Office, 1940-45; Dir Dept of Applied Economics, Cambridge, 1945-55. Mem., Internat. Statistical Inst. Pres., Econometric Soc., 1955; Hon. Member: Soc. of Incorp. Accountants, 1954; Amer. Economic Assoc., 1976; For. Hon. Mem., Amer. Acad. of Arts and Sciences, 1968. FBA 1956. ScD 1957. Hon. doctorates, Univs of Oslo and Brussels, 1965, Geneva, 1971, Warwick, 1975. *Publications:* The Role of Measurement in Economics, 1951; (with others) The Measurement of Consumers' Expenditure and Behaviour in the United Kingdom 1920-1938, vol. 1 1954, vol. 2 1966; Quantity and Price Indexes in National Accounts, 1956; Input-Output and National Accounts, 1961; (with G. Stone) National Income and Expenditure, 10th edn, 1977; Mathematics in the Social Sciences, and Other Essays, 1966; Mathematical Models of the Economy, and other Essays, 1970; Demographic Accounting and Model Building, 1971; gen. editor and pt author series A Programme for Growth, 1962-74; numerous articles in learned journals, particularly on social accounting and econometrics,

1936-. *Recreation:* staying at home. *Address:* 13 Millington Road, Cambridge.

STONE, Prof. Julius, OBE 1973; Professor of Law, University of New South Wales, since 1973; Distinguished Professor of International Law and Jurisprudence, Hastings College of Law, California University, since 1973; Emeritus Professor, University of Sydney; Member of New Zealand and Victorian Bars; Solicitor, Supreme Court, England; *b* 7 July 1907; *s* of Israel and Ellen Stone, Leeds, Yorkshire; *m* 1934, Reca Lieberman, BSc, LDS; two *s* one *d*. *Educ:* Univs of Oxford, Leeds, Harvard. BA, BCL, DCL (Oxford); LLM (Leeds); SJD (Harvard). Asst Lectr, University Coll., Hull, 1928-30; Rockefeller Fellow in Social Sciences, 1931; Asst Prof. of Law, Harvard Univ., 1933-36; Prof. of Internat. Law and Organisation, Fletcher Sch. of Law and Diplomacy, USA, 1933-36; Lectr in Law, Univ. of Leeds, 1936-38; Prof. and Dean Faculty of Law, Auckland University Coll., NZ, 1938-42; Challis Prof. of Internat. Law and Jurisprudence, Univ. of Sydney, 1942-72. Vis. Prof., New York Univ. and Fletcher Sch. of Law and Diplomacy, 1949; Acting Dean, Sydney Faculty of Law, 1954-55, 1958-59; Visiting Professor: Columbia Univ., 1956; Harvard Univ., 1956-57; Hague Academy of Internat. Law, 1956; Charles Inglis Thomson Guest Prof., Univ. of Colorado, 1956; Award of Amer. Soc. of Internat. Law, 1956; Prize of Legatum Visserianum, Leyden Univ., 1956; Roscoe Pound Lectr, Univ. of Nebraska, 1957; John Field Sims Memorial Lectr, Univ. of New Mexico, 1959; first Pres., Internat. Law Assoc., Aust., Br., 1959; Council, Internat. Commn of Jurists, Aust. Section, 1959; Vis. Prof., Indian Sch. of Internat. Affairs, Delhi, 1960; Vis. Prof. and Wilfred Fullagar Lectr, Monash Univ., 1972; Fellow, Woodrow Wilson Internat. Center for Scholars, 1973. Mem. Titulaire, Inst. of Internat. Law; Associate, Internat. Acad. of Comparative Law. Chm., NSW Research Group, Aust. Inst. of Internat. Affairs, 1942-45; Vice-Chm., Prime Minister's Cttee on National Morale, and with Directorate of Research, LHQ, War of 1939-45 (Lt-Col). Founding and Exec. Mem., Aust. SSRC; Fellow, Aust. Acad. of Social Sciences; Chm. Aust. Unesco Cttee for Social Sciences; Aust. Deleg., 6th Unesco Gen. Conf., Paris, 1951; Aust. rep., Second Corning Conf. on The Individual in the Modern World, 1961; Official Observer of Internat. Commn of Jurists, Eichmann Trial, 1961; General Editor, Sydney Law Review, 1953-60; cont. on Editorial Cttee; Hon. Life Member: Amer. Soc. Internat. Law, 1962; Indian Soc. Internat. Law, 1964. Joint Swiney Prize, RSA, 1964; Fellow: Centre for Study of the Behavioral Sciences, 1964; World Acad. of Arts and Sciences, 1964. Patron, Amnesty International, 1963. Mem., Advisory Cttee, Internat. League for Rights of Man, 1964; Regular Broadcaster on Internat. Affairs (Australian Broadcasting Commn), 1945-. Hon. LLD Leeds, 1973. *Publications:* International Guarantees of Minority Rights, 1932; Regional Guarantees of Minority Rights, 1933; The Atlantic Charter—New Worlds for Old, 1943; Stand Up and Be Counted, 1944; The Province and Function of Law, Law as Logic, Justice and Social Control (Aust., Eng. and Amer. edns), 1946, 1947, 1950, 1961, 1968; (with the late S. P. Simpson) Law and Society (3 vols), 1949-50; Legal Controls of International Conflict, A Treatise on the Dynamics of Disputes- and War- Law, 1954 (Aust., Eng. and Amer. Edns; revised impression, 1958); Sociological Inquiries concerning International Law, 1956; Aggression and World Order, 1958 (Aust., Eng. and Amer. edns); Legal Education and Public Responsibility, 1959; Quest for Survival, 1961 (German, Portuguese and Arabic trans); The International Court and World Crisis, 1962; Legal System and Lawyers' Reasonings, 1964; Human Law and Human Justice, 1965; Social Dimensions of Law and Justice, 1966, 1971; Law and the Social Sciences in the 2nd Half-Century, 1966; The Middle East Under Cease-Fire, 1967; No Peace—No War in The Middle East, 1969; Approaches to International Justice, 1970; (with R. K. Woetzel) Towards a Feasible International Criminal Court, 1970; Of Law and Nations, 1974; numerous articles in Anglo-American legal journals. *Recreations:* swimming, gardening, landscape gardening. *Address:* 24 Blake Street, Rose Bay, NSW 2029, Australia. *T:* 36.6927.

STONE, Prof. Lawrence, MA Oxon; Dodge Professor of History, since 1963, and Director, Shelby Cullom Davis Center for Historical Studies, since 1968, Princeton University; *b* 4 Dec. 1919; *s* of Lawrence Frederick Stone and Mabel Julia Annie Stone; *m* 1943, Jeanne Caecilia, *d* of Prof. Robert Fawtier, Membre de l'Institut, Paris; one *s* one *d*. *Educ:* Charterhouse School, 1933-38; Sorbonne, Paris, 1938; Christ Church, Oxford, 1938-40, 1945-46. Lieut RNVR 1940-45. Bryce Research Student, Oxford Univ., 1946-47; Lectr, University Coll. Oxford, 1947-50; Fellow, Wadham Coll., Oxford, 1950-63; Mem. Inst. for Advanced Study, Princeton, 1960-61; Chm., Dept of History, 1967-70. Mem., Amer. Philosophical Soc., 1970.

Fellow, Amer. Acad. of Arts and Sciences, 1968. *Publications:* Sculpture in Britain: The Middle Ages, 1955; An Elizabethan: Sir Horatio Palavicino, 1956; The Crisis of the Aristocracy, 1558-1641, 1965; The Causes of the English Revolution, 1529-1642, 1972; Family and Fortune: Studies in Aristocratic Finance in the 16th and 17th Centuries, 1973; (ed) The University in Society, 1975; (ed) Schooling and Society, 1977; Family, Sex and Marriage in England 1500-1800, 1977; numerous articles in History, Economic History Review, Past and Present, Archæological Jl, English Historical Review, Bulletin of the Inst. for Historical Research, Malone Soc., Comparative Studies in Society and History, History Today, etc. *Address:* 266 Moore Street, Princeton, NJ 08540, USA. *T:* Princeton 921.2717; 231 Woodstock Road, Oxford. *T:* Oxford 59174.

STONE, Sir Leonard; see Stone, Sir J. L.

STONE, Marcus; Sheriff of Glasgow and Strathkelvin, since 1976; Advocate; *b* 22 March 1921; *s* of Morris and Reva Stone; *m* 1956, Jacqueline Barnoin; three *s* two *d. Educ:* High Sch. of Glasgow; Univ. of Glasgow (MA 1940, LLB 1948). Served War of 1939-45, RASC: overseas service, West Africa, att. RWAFF. Admitted Solicitor, 1949; Post Grad. Dip., Psychology, Univ. of Glasgow, 1953; admitted Faculty of Advocates, 1965; apptd Hon. Sheriff Substitute, 1967, Sheriff, 1971-76, of Stirling, Dunbarton and Clackmannan, later N Strathclyde at Dumbarton. *Recreations:* swimming, golf. *Address:* Sheriff's Chambers, Sheriff Court, County Buildings, Ingram Street, Glasgow. *T:* 041-552 3434.

STONE, Reynolds, CBE 1953; RDI 1956; FRSA 1964; Designer and Engraver; *b* 13 March 1909; *s* of Edward Wellington and Laura Neville Stone; *m* 1938, Janet Woods; two *s* two *d. Educ:* Eton; Magdalene College, Cambridge. Studied printing at the University Press, Cambridge, after taking degree in History Tripos, 1930. Worked in a printing house, Barnicott & Pearce of Taunton, for two years, then as a free-lance designer and engraver. Served in RAF (photo interpretation), 1941-45. Designs for printers and publishers chiefly, and has decorated a number of books and produced many devices and book labels with an emphasis on lettering. Also designs and executes memorial tablets and engraves glass. Designed 3d Victory Stamp 1946, seal and device for The Arts Council, book-labels for National Trust and The British Council and an engraving of the Royal Arms for HM Stationery Office, 1956, Five Pound and Ten Pound Notes. Designed and executed the Winston Churchill Memorial for Westminster Abbey, 1965. One-man exhibn of water colours, New Grafton Gall., London, 1972; Prints in Ashmolean Museum, Oxford. *Publications:* Among the books decorated are: A Shakespeare Anthology, 1935; Rousseau's Confessions, 1938; Old English Wines and Cordials, 1938; The Praise and Happiness of the Countrie Life, Guevara, 1938; Apostate, Forrest Reid, 1946; The Open Air, Adrian Bell, 1949; Omoo, 1967; St Thomas Aquinas, 1969. *Recreations:* hunting in second-hand bookshops; interest in trees and 19th century wood-engraving. *Address:* Litton Cheney Old Rectory, Dorchester, Dorset. *T:* Long Bredy 383.

STONE, Richard; see Stone, J. R. N.

STONE, Richard Evelyn, CMG 1962; HM Overseas Civil Service, retired; Administrator, Agricultural Economics Institute, Oxford University, since 1967; *b* 20 Dec. 1914; 2nd *s* of late R. G. and late A. L. Stone, Yetminster, Dorset; *m* 1948, Mavis, 2nd *d* of late E. D. Tongue, OBE, and late E. E. Tongue. *Educ:* Blundell's School; Wadham College, Oxford. MA (Hons jurisprudence). Served War of 1939-45 (despatches): Adjt 34th Bn KAR; Staff Captain, 21st (EA) Inf. Bde; qualified Staff Coll., Quetta, 1945. Dist Comr, Uganda, 1948-55; Permanent Sec. of various Mins; Dep. Resident, Buganda, 1959, Resident, 1960-62. Retd 1963, on Independence of Uganda. Farmed in Devon, 1963-67. Sen. Treasurer, Oxford Univ. Cricket Club. *Recreations:* fishing, cricket. *Address:* Brackenhurst, Boars Hill, Oxford. *Clubs:* MCC; Vincent's (Oxford).

STONE, Richard Frederick, QC 1968; *b* 11 March 1928; *s* of Sir Leonard Stone, *qv*; *m* 1st, 1957, Georgina Maxwell Morris (decd); two *d*; 2nd, 1964, Susan van Heel; two *d. Educ:* Lakefield College Sch., Canada; Rugby; Trinity Hall, Cambridge (MA). Lt, Worcs Regt, 1946-48. Called to Bar, Gray's Inn, 1952, Bencher, 1974; Mem., Bar Council, 1957-61; Member: Panel of Lloyd's Arbitrators in Salvage Cases; Panel of Wreck Comrs. *Recreation:* sailing. *Address:* 5 Raymond Buildings, Gray's Inn, WC1. *T:* 01-242 2697; Orchard Gap, Wittering Road, Hayling Island, Hants.

STONE, Riversdale Garland, CMG 1956; OBE 1946; HM Consul-General, Los Angeles, 1957-59; *b* 19 Jan. 1903; *m* 1927,

Cassie Gaisford; no *c.* Information Officer, Rio de Janeiro, Brazil, 1946; transf. to Singapore, 1948; First Secretary (Economic), Staff of Commissioner-General for the UK in SE Asia, 1948; Transf. to Batavia, 1949; Counsellor (Commercial), Mexico City, 1952; Counsellor, HM Diplomatic Service, retired. *Address:* c/o National Westminster Bank Ltd, Piccadilly Circus Branch, Glasshouse Street, W1.

STONEFROST, Maurice Frank; Comptroller of Financial Services, Greater London Council, since 1973; *b* 1 Sept. 1927; *s* of Arthur and Anne Stonefrost, Bristol; *m* 1953, Audrey Jean Fishlock; one *s* one *d. Educ:* Merrywood Grammar Sch., Bristol (DPA). IPFA, FBCS, FRSS, MBIM. Nat. Service, RAF, 1948-51; local govt finance: Bristol County Borough, 1951-54; Slough Borough, 1954-56; Coventry County Borough, 1956-61; W Sussex CC, 1961-64; Sec., Inst. of Municipal Treasurers and Accountants, 1964-73. *Recreation:* gardening. *Address:* 33 Birdham Road, Chichester, Sussex. *T:* Chichester 83304. *Club:* Reform.

STONEHOUSE, John Thomson; *b* 28 July 1925; *m* 1948, Barbara Joan Smith; one *s* two *d. Educ:* Elementary Sch. and Tauntons Sch., Southampton; Univ. of London (London Sch. of Econs and Political Science). Asst to Senior Probation Officer, Southampton, 1941-44. Served in RAF as pilot and education officer, 1944-47. Studied at LSE, 1947-51 (Chm., Labour Soc., 1950-51); BSc (Econ.) Hons, 1951. Man. for African Co-op. Socs in Uganda, 1952-54; Sec., Kampala Mutual Co-op Soc. Ltd (Uganda), 1953-54; Dir of London Co-operative Soc. Ltd, 1956-62 (Pres., 1962-64); Mem. until 1962 of Development Cttee of the Co-operative Union; Dir of Society Footwear Ltd until 1963. Contested Norwood, London CC Election, 1949; contested (Lab): Twickenham, General Election, 1950; Burton, General Election, 1951; MP (Lab Co-op): Wednesbury, Feb. 1957-74; Walsall N, 1974-76, (English Nat. Party, April-Aug. 1976); Parly Sec., Min. of Aviation, 1964-66; Parly Under-Sec. of State for the Colonies, 1966-67; Minister of Aviation, 1967; Minister of State, Technology, 1967-68; Postmaster-General, 1968-69; Minister of Posts and Telecommunications, 1969-70. Chm., Parly Cttee of ASTMS, 1974-75; Mem. Exec. Cttee, UK Br. IPU. UK Deleg. to Council of Europe and WEU, 1962-64; Leader, UK Govt Delegns, Independence Ceremonies in Botswana and Lesotho, 1966; attended Independence Ceremonies in Uganda, 1962, Kenya, 1963, Zambia, 1964, and Mauritius, 1968, as special guest of Independence Governments. Granted citizenship of Bangladesh, 1972. Councillor, Islington Borough Council, 1956-59. Member, RIIA, 1955-65. *Publications:* Prohibited Immigrant, 1960; (part author) Gangrene, 1959; Death of an Idealist, 1975. *Recreations:* music, learning to ski, desmology. *Club:* Royal Automobile.

STONES, Prof. Edward Lionel Gregory, MA, PhD; Professor of Mediæval History, University of Glasgow, 1956-Sept. 1978; *b* Croydon, 4 March 1914; *s* of Edward Edison Stones, Elland, Yorks, and Eleanor Gregory; *m* 1947, Jeanne Marie Beatrice, *d* of A. J. Fradin and Florence B. Timbury; one *s* one *d. Educ:* Glasgow High Sch.; Glasgow Univ.; Balliol Coll., Oxford. 1st Cl. English Lang. and Lit. (Glasgow), 1936; 1st Class Modern History (Oxford), 1939; PhD (Glasgow), 1950; FRHistS, 1950; FSA, 1962. Asst Lectr in History, Glasgow Univ., 1939. War of 1939-45: joined Royal Signals, 1940; Major 1943; GSO2, GHQ, New Delhi (Signals Directorate), 1943-45. Lectr in History, Glasgow, from 1945. Lay Mem., Provincial Synod, Episcopal Church of Scotland, 1963-66. Pres., Glasgow Archaeological Soc., 1969-72; Member: Ancient Monuments Board for Scotland, 1964- (Chm. 1968-73); Council, Royal Hist. Soc., 1968-72; Council, Soc. Antiquaries, London, 1972-74. *Publications:* Anglo-Scottish Relations, 1174-1328, 1965; (ed) Maitland's Letters to Neilson, 1976; (with G. G. Simpson) Edward I and the Throne of Scotland, 1978; and articles in various historical journals. *Recreations:* books, music, photography. *Address:* 70 Oakfield Avenue, Glasgow G12 8LS. *T:* 041-339 3333.

STONES, (Elsie) Margaret, MBE 1977; botanical artist; Artist in Residence, Louisiana State University, Baton Rouge, since 1977; *b* 28 Aug. 1920; *d* of Frederick Stones and Agnes Kirkwood (née Fleming). *Educ:* Swinburne Technical Coll., Melbourne; Melbourne National Gall. Art Sch. Came to England, 1951; working independently as botanical artist, 1951-: at Royal Botanic Gardens, Kew; Nat. Hist. Museum; Royal Horticultural Soc., and at other botanical instns; Principal Contrib. Artist to Curtis's Botanical Magazine, 1957-. Drawings (water-colour): 20, Aust. plants, National Library, Canberra, 1962-63; 250, Tasmanian endemic plants, 1962-77; Basalt Plains flora, Melbourne Univ., 1975-76; to spend 3-4 months annually for 10 years at Louisiana State Univ. doing 200 water-colour drawings of Louisiana flora, 1977-. Exhibitions: Colnaghi's,

London, 1967, 1971, 1973 and 1975; Retrospective Exhibn, Melbourne Univ., 1976. *Publications:* The Endemic Flora of Tasmania (text by W. M. Curtis): Pt 1, 1967; Pt 2, 1969; Pt 3, 1971; Pt 4, 1973; Pt 5, 1975; Pt 6, 1978; illus. various books. *Recreations:* gardening, reading. *Address:* 1 Bushwood Road, Kew, Richmond, Surrey. *T:* 01-940 6183.

STONEY, Brigadier Ralph Francis Ewart, CBE 1952 (OBE, 1943); Director-General, The Royal Society for the Prevention of Accidents, 1959-68; *b* 28 June 1903; *o s* of late Col R. D. S. Stoney, The Downs, Delgany, Co. Wicklow and of Mrs E. M. M. Stoney; *m* 1939, Kathleen Nina (*née* Kirkland) (*d* 1973); one *d. Educ:* Royal Naval Colleges, Osborne and Dartmouth; Royal Military Academy, Woolwich. Commissioned Royal Engineers, 1923; Staff College, Camberley, 1937-38. Served War of 1939-45 as GSO, 1939-43 (OBE) and as CRE, 82 Div., 1943-46, in Burma (despatches twice). CRE 5th Div. and 2nd Div., 1947-48; Col GS (Intelligence), War Office, 1949-51; Brig. GS (Intelligence), Middle East, 1952-54. Retired, 1954. *Recreations:* sailing; workshop practice. *Address:* Chota Ghur, Crakell Road, Reigate, Surrey. *T:* Reigate 42521.

STONHOUSE, Sir Philip (Allan), 18th Bt, *cr* 1628, and 14th Bt *cr* 1670; Assessor and Land Appraiser, Government of Alberta; *b* 24 Oct. 1916; *s* of Sir Arthur Allan Stonhouse, 17th Bt, and Beatrice C. Féron; *S* father, 1967; *m* 1946, Winnifred Emily Shield; two *s. Educ:* Western Canada Coll.; Queen's Univ., Kingston, Ontario. Gold Mining, 1936-40; General Construction, 1940-42; Ranching, 1942-54; Assessing, 1954-68. Is a Freemason. *Recreations:* water-fowl and upland game hunting, tennis, ski-ing. *Heir: s* Rev. Michael Philip Stonhouse, BA, LTh [*b* 4 Sept. 1948. *Educ:* Wycliffe Coll., Toronto]. *Address:* 521-12 Street SW, Medicine Hat, Alberta, Canada. *T:* 526-5832. *Club:* Medicine Hat Ski.

[*But his name does not, at the time of going to press, appear on the Official Roll of Baronets.*]

STONHOUSE-GOSTLING, Maj.-Gen. Philip Le Marchant Stonhouse, CB 1955; CBE 1953; retired; *b* 28 August 1899; *s* of Colonel Charles Henry Stonhouse-Gostling and Alice Seton (*née* Fraser-Tytler); *m* 1946, Helen Rimington Myra (*née* Pereira), Ottawa, Ontario, Canada. *Educ:* Cheltenham College; RMA Woolwich. Entered RA, 1919; served India with RA, 1920-26; Mil. Coll. of Science, 1927-29; i/c Technical Intelligence, WO, 1930; Woolwich Arsenal: Asst Inspector Guns and Carriages, 1931-38; Supt Carriage Design, 1939; Technical Adviser to Canadian Govt and British Purchasing Commn for Armaments, 1939-40; Dep. Dir of Supply, British Supply Mission, Washington, 1941-44; Director of Supply (Armaments), 1944-46; Dep. Dir Technical Services, British Jt Staff Mission, 1942-46; Director, 1946-50; Dep. Chief Engineer, Armaments Design Establishment in UK, 1951; President, Ordnance Board, Feb. 1954-Feb. 1955; Retired from Army, March 1955. Exec. Engineer, Beemer Engineering Co., Philadelphia, 1955-64. Legion of Merit (Officer), USA 1944. *Recreations:* sailing, photography. *Address:* Island House West, Tequesta, Florida 33458, USA; c/o Lloyds Bank, Cox's and King's Branch, 6 Pall Mall, SW1.

STONIER, George Walter, MA; author; critic; journalist; *b* Sydney, Australia, 1903; *m* 1951, Patricia, *d* of James Nelson Dover. *Educ:* Westminster School; Christ Church, Oxford. Assistant Literary Editor of the New Statesman and Nation, 1928-45. Has written plays for BBC: Robert Tasker Deceased, Squeaky Shoes, Chap in a Bowler Hat, etc. *Publications:* Gog Magog, 1933; The Shadow Across the Page, 1937; Shaving Through the Blitz, 1943; My Dear Bunny, 1946; The Memoirs of a Ghost, 1947; Round London with the Unicorn, 1951; Pictures on the Pavement, 1954; English Countryside in Colour, 1956; Off the Rails, 1967; Rhodesian Spring, 1968; (ed) International Film Annual, vols 2 and 3. Contributions to Observer, New Statesman and Nation, Punch, Sunday Telegraph, Sight and Sound. *Address:* 1 Riebeeck, Acton Road, Rondebosch, Cape Town, South Africa.

STONOR, family name of **Baron Camoys.**

STOODLEY, Peter Ernest William; County Treasurer of Kent, since 1972; *b* 27 July 1925; *s* of Ernest and Esther Stoodley; *m* 1970, June (*née* Bennett). *Educ:* Weymouth Grammar Sch.; Administrative Staff Coll.; Inst. of Public Finance Accountants. Accountant with County Council of: Dorset, 1947-56; Staffordshire, 1956-61; Kent, 1961-65; Asst Co. Treasurer of Kent, 1965-69; Dep. Co. Treasurer of Kent, 1969-72. MBCS, MBIM. *Recreations:* ornithology, cricket. *Address:* Cranby, Horseshoe Lane, Leeds, Maidstone, Kent. *T:* Maidstone 861287.

STOOKE, Sir George Beresford-, KCMG 1948 (CMG 1943); Gentleman Usher of the Blue Rod in the Order of St Michael and St George, 1959-71; *b* 3 Jan. 1897; *m* 1931, Creenagh, *y d* of late Sir Henry Richards; one *s* one *d.* Royal Navy, 1914-19; Colonial Service, 1920-48; Governor and C-in-C, Sierra Leone, 1948-53; Second Crown Agent for Oversea Governments and Administrations, 1953-55. Member, Kenya Camps Inquiry, 1959. Overseas Comr, Boy Scouts Assoc., 1954-61. Vice-Chm., Internat. African Inst., 1954-74. President, Anglo-Sierra Leone Society, 1962-72. 2nd Class Order of Brilliant Star of Zanzibar, 1942. KStJ, 1951. *Address:* Little Rydon, Hillfarrance, Taunton, Somerset.
See also W. F. Page.

STOPFORD, family name of **Earl of Courtown.**

STOPFORD, Edward Kennedy, CB 1955; Assistant Under-Secretary of State, Ministry of Defence, 1964-71, retired; *b* 10 Oct. 1911; *yr s* of late Major Heneage Frank Stopford, Royal Field Artillery, and Margaret, *d* of late Edward Briggs Kennedy; *m* 1952, Patricia Iona Mary, *widow* of Duncan Stewart, CMG, and *d* of late Howard Carrick; one *s. Educ:* Winchester; New College, Oxford. 1st Class, Lit Hum, 1933. Entered War Office, 1936; Under-Secretary, 1954-64. *Address:* The Folly, Fifield, Oxford. *T:* Shipton-under-Wychwood 830484.

STOPFORD, Rear-Admiral Frederick Victor, CBE 1952; retired; *b* 6 July 1900; *yr s* of late Rear-Admiral Hon. W. G. Stopford; *m* 1924, Mary Guise, *d* of late Captain F. C. U. Vernon-Wentworth; three *s* one *d. Educ:* Osborne; Dartmouth. Served European War, 1916-18; Commander, 1933; War of 1939-45; Captain, 1943; Rear-Admiral, 1950. ADC, 1948-50. *Address:* Ash Farm House, Grenofen, Tavistock, S Devon.

STOPFORD, Robert Jemmett, CMG 1946; Commander of the Order of Orange Nassau; US Medal of Freedom; Vice-Chairman, Imperial War Museum, 1954-68; *b* 19 May 1895; *s* of late Jemmett J. Stopford, Dublin; unmarried. *Educ:* St Paul's Sch.; Magdalene Coll., Cambridge. Served European War, 1914-18; Banking, 1921-38. Private Sec. to Chm., Indian Statutory Commission, 1928-30; Member of Runciman Mission to Czechoslovakia, 1938; Liaison Officer for Refugees with the Czechoslovak Govt, 1938-39; Financial Counsellor, British Embassy, Washington, 1940-43; War Office, 1943-45. Formerly Chairman National Film Finance Corporation. *Address:* Oyles Mill Cottage, Iwerne Minster, Blandford, Dorset. *Club:* Athenæum.

STOPPARD, Tom, FRSL; playwright and novelist; *b* 3 July 1937; *yr s* of late Eugene Straussler and of Mrs Martha Stoppard; *m* 1st, 1965, Jose (marr. diss. 1972), *yr d* of John and Alice Ingle; two *s*; 2nd, 1972, Dr Miriam Moore-Robinson; two *s. Educ:* abroad; Dolphin Sch., Notts; Pocklington, Yorks. Journalist: Western Daily Press, Bristol, 1954-58; Bristol Evening World, 1958-60; freelance, 1960-63. Hon. MLitt Bristol, 1976. *Plays:* Enter a Free Man, London, 1968 (TV play, A Walk on the Water, 1963); Rosencrantz and Guildenstern are Dead, Nat. Theatre, 1967, subseq. NY, etc (Tony Award, NY, 1968; NY Drama Critics Circle Award, 1968); The Real Inspector Hound, London, 1968; After Magritte, Ambiance Theatre, 1970; Dogg's Our Pet, Ambiance Theatre, 1972; Jumpers, National Theatre, 1972 (Evening Standard Award); Travesties, Aldwych, 1974 (Evening Standard Award; Tony Award, NY, 1976); Dirty Linen, Newfoundland, Ambiance Theatre, 1976; Every Good Boy Deserves Favour (music-theatre), 1977; *radio:* The Dissolution of Dominic Boot, 1964; M is for Moon Among Other Things, 1964; If You're Glad I'll Be Frank, 1965; Albert's Bridge, 1967 (Prix Italia); Where Are They Now?, 1970; Artist Descending a Staircase, 1972; *television:* A Separate Peace, 1966; Teeth, 1967; Another Moon Called Earth, 1967; Neutral Ground, 1968; (with Clive Exton) Boundaries, 1975; (adapted) Three Men in a Boat, 1976; Professional Foul, 1977; *film script:* (with T. Wiseman) The Romantic Englishwoman, 1975. John Whiting Award, Arts Council, 1967; Evening Standard Award for Most Promising Playwright, 1968. *Publications:* (short stories) Introduction 2, 1964; (novel) Lord Malquist and Mr Moon, 1965; *plays:* Rosencrantz and Guildenstern are Dead, 1967; The Real Inspector Hound, 1968; Albert's Bridge, 1968; Enter a Free Man, 1968; After Magritte, 1971; Jumpers, 1972; Artists Descending a Staircase, and, Where Are They Now?, 1973; Travesties, 1975; Dirty Linen, and New-Found-Land, 1976. *Address:* Fernleigh, Wood Lane, Iver Heath, Bucks.

STORAR, Leonore Elizabeth Therese; Director, Colombo Plan Bureau, Colombo, Sri Lanka, 1976; *b* 3 May 1920. Served HM Forces, 1942-46. Min. of Labour, 1941; Min. of Works, 1947; joined CRO, 1948; First Sec., Delhi and Calcutta, 1951-53; Salisbury, 1956-58; Colombo, 1960-62; Counsellor, 1963; Head of General and Migration Dept, CRO, 1962; Dep. Consul-Gen., NY, 1967; Consul-Gen., Boston, 1969; Head of Commonwealth Co-ordination Dept, FCO, 1971-75. *Address:* c/o 16 Grosvenor Court, Grosvenor Hill, Wimbledon, SW19.

STORER, Prof. Roy; Professor of Prosthodontics since 1968 and Dean of Dentistry since 1977 (Clinical Sub-Dean, 1970-77) The Dental School, University of Newcastle upon Tyne; *b* 21 Feb. 1928; *s* of Harry and Jessie Storer; *m* 1953, Kathleen Mary Frances Pitman; one *s* two *d. Educ:* Wallasey Grammar Sch.; Univ. of Liverpool. LDS (Liverpool) 1950; FDSRCS 1954; MSc (Liverpool) 1960. House Surg., 1950, and Registrar, 1952-54, United Liverpool Hosps; Lieut (later Captain) Royal Army Dental Corps, 1950-52; Lectr in Dental Prosthetics, Univ. of Liverpool, 1954-61; Visiting Associate Prof., Northwestern Univ., Chicago, 1961-62; Sen. Lectr in Dental Prosthetics, Univ. of Liverpool, 1962-67; Hon. Cons. Dental Surgeon: United Liverpool Hosps, 1962-67; United Newcastle Hosps (now Newcastle Area Health Authority (T)), 1968-. Mem. Council and Sec., British Soc. for the Study of Prosthetic Dentistry, 1960-69 (Pres., 1968-69). Pres., Med. Rugby Football Club (Newcastle), 1968-; Mem., Northern Sports Council, 1973-; Chm., Div. of Dentistry, Newcastle Univ. Hosps, 1972-75. External Examiner in Dental Subjects: Univs of Belfast, Birmingham, Bristol, Dublin, Dundee, Leeds, London, Newcastle upon Tyne, and Royal Coll. of Surgeons of England. *Publications:* A Laboratory Course in Dental Materials for Dental Hygienists (with D. C. Smith), 1963; Immediate and Replacement Dentures (with J. N. Anderson), 2nd edn, 1973; papers on sci. and clin. subjects in dental and med. jls. *Recreations:* Rugby football, cricket, squash, gardening. *Address:* Department of Prosthodontics, The Dental School, Northumberland Road, Newcastle upon Tyne NE1 8TA; 164 Eastern Way, Darras Hall, Ponteland, Newcastle upon Tyne NE20 9RH. *T:* Ponteland 24399. *Clubs:* MCC; East India, Sports and Public Schools; Northumberland County Rugby and Cricket.

STOREY, family name of Baron Buckton.

STOREY, Christopher, MA, PhD; Headmaster, Culford School, Bury St Edmunds, 1951-71; *b* 23 July 1908; *s* of William Storey and Margaret T. B. Cowan, Newcastle upon Tyne; *m* 1937, Gertrude Appleby, Scarborough; four *s. Educ:* Rutherford Coll., Newcastle upon Tyne; King's Coll., Univ. of Durham (BA Hons French, cl. I); Univ. of Strasbourg (PhD). Modern Languages Master, Mundella Sch., Nottingham, 1931-34; French Master: Scarborough High Sch. for Boys, 1934-36; City of London Sch., 1936-42. Headmaster, Johnston Grammar Sch., Durham, 1942-51. Officier d'Académie, 1947. *Publications:* Etude critique de la Vie de St Alexis, 1934; Apprenons le mot juste!, 1939; La Vie de St Alexis, 1946; Sprechen und Schreiben (with C. E. Bond), 1950; articles in Modern Language Review, French Studies, and Medium Aevum. *Address:* 36 Lakeside, Oxford OX2 8JH. *T:* Oxford 52328.

STOREY, David Malcolm; writer and dramatist; *b* 13 July 1933; *s* of Frank Richmond Storey and Lily (*née* Cartwright); *m* 1956, Barbara Rudd Hamilton; two *s* two *d. Educ:* Queen Elizabeth Grammar Sch., Wakefield, Yorks; Slade School of Fine Art, London; Fellow, UCL, 1974. *Plays:* The Restoration of Arnold Middleton, 1967 (Evening Standard Award); In Celebration, 1969 (Los Angeles Critics' Award); The Contractor, 1969 (Writer of the Year Award, Variety Club of GB, NY Critics' Award); Home, 1970 (Evening Standard Award, Critics' Award, NY); The Changing Room, 1971 (Critics' Award, NY); Cromwell, 1973; The Farm, 1973; Life Class, 1974; Mother's Day, 1976. *Publications:* This Sporting Life, 1960 (Macmillan Fiction Award, US); Flight into Camden, 1960 (John Llewellyn Meml Prize, Somerset Maugham award); Radcliffe, 1963; Pasmore, 1972 (Geoffrey Faber Meml Prize, 1973); A Temporary Life, 1973; Edward, 1973; Saville, 1976 (Booker Prize, 1976). *Address:* c/o Jonathan Cape Ltd, 30 Bedford Square, WC1B 3EL.

STOREY, (M.) Gladys, OBE 1919; authoress; *b* Hampstead; *d* of Prof. G. A. Storey, RA, and Emily Hayward, London. *Educ:* Allen-Olney Sch., Hampstead. On stage, ingénue parts with Sir George Alexander, gave up stage for war-work; pioneer of Women's Services; commenced recruiting on own initiative, gaining approval of Lord Roberts; became only female recruiter at HQ Recruiting Depot, Whitehall, 1914; ran fund (under own name) for providing Bovril to soldiers in trenches in every theatre of war, 1914-18; donations, King George V; grant from the Army Council; supplied British Military Mission in N and S Russia (by special request of GOC), 1919-20; transferred from Recruiting HQ to supervise staff at HQ National Registration, London, 1915-17; Sept. 1939, re-inauguration of Great War

Fund (under own name) providing Bovril for HM Forces in all war and other areas; continuation of supplies after European War by request of Field-Marshal Montgomery to British Army of the Rhine, 1945-47, and British Troops, Jerusalem, 1946-47. Fund supported by King George VI and War Office. *Publications:* Humorous Stories of Famous People, 1916; All Sorts of People, 1929; Dickens and Daughter (at her request), 1939; made drawing (1925) of Mrs Perugini (Kate Dickens) bound in at beginning of vol. containing Charles Dickens' letters to his wife, Br. Museum, 1934.

STOREY, Maude; Registrar, General Nursing Council for England and Wales, since 1977; *b* 24 March 1930; *d* of late Henry Storey and of Sarah Farrimond Storey. *Educ:* Wigan and District Mining and Techn. Coll.; St Mary's Hosp., Manchester; Lancaster Royal Infirmary; Paddington Gen. Hosp.; Royal Coll. of Nursing, Edinburgh; Queen Elizabeth Coll., London. SRN 1952; SCM 1953; RCI (Edin.) 1962; RNT 1965. Domiciliary Midwife, Wigan County Borough, 1953-56; Midwifery Sister, St Mary's Hosp., Manchester, 1956-57; Charge Nurse, Intensive Therapy, Mayo Clinic, USA, 1957-59; Theatre Sister, Clinical Instructor, 1959-63, subseq. Nurse Tutor, 1965-68, Royal Albert Edward Infirmary, Wigan; Lectr in Community Nursing, Manchester Univ., 1968-71; Asst. subseq. Principal Regional Nursing Officer, Liverpool Regional Hosp. Bd, 1971-73; Regional Nursing Officer, Mersey RHA, 1973-77. *Recreations:* travel, painting. *Address:* 14 Conifer Drive, Long Lane, Tilehurst, Berks.

STORIE-PUGH, Dr Peter David, MBE 1945; MC 1940; TD 1945 and 3 clasps; DL; President, Federation of Veterinarians of the EEC, since 1975 (UK delegate, Liaison Committee, since 1962, President, 1973-75); Lecturer, University of Cambridge, since 1953; Fellow of Wolfson College, Cambridge, since 1967; *b* 1 Nov. 1919; *s* of Prof. Leslie Pugh, *qv*; *m* 1st, 1946, Alison (marr. diss. 1971), *d* of late Sir Oliver Lyle, OBE; one *s* two *d*; 2nd, 1971, Leslie Helen, *d* of Earl Striegel; two *s. Educ:* Malvern; Queens' Coll., Cambridge (Hon. Foundn Scholar); Royal Veterinary Coll., Univ. of London. MA, PhD, FRCVS, CChem, MRIC. Served War of 1939-45, Queen's Own Royal W Kent Regt; comd 1st Bn, Cambs Regt, comd 1st Bn Suffolk and Cambs Regt; Col, Dep. Comdr, 161 Inf. Bde, ACF County Comdt. Mem. Council, RCVS, 1956- (Chm. Parly Cttee, 1962-67; Jun. Vice-Pres., 1976-77, Pres., 1977-); President: Cambridge Soc. for Study of Comparative Medicine, 1966-67; Internat. Pig Vet. Soc., 1967-69 (Life Pres., 1969); British Veterinary Assoc., 1968-69 and 1970-71; Mem. Exec. Cttee, Cambridgeshire Farmers Union, 1960-65; Chm., Eurovet, 1971-; Mem. Jt RCVS/BVA Cttee on European Vet. Affairs, 1971-; Observer, European Liaison Gp for Agric., 1972-; Jt Pres., 1st European Vet. Congress, Wiesbaden, 1972; Permanent Mem. EEC Adv. Vet. Cttee, 1976-; Mem. Council, Secrétariat Européen des Professions Libérales, Intellectuelles et Sociales, 1976-; Mem. Permanent Cttee, World Vet. Assoc. Member: Parly and Sci. Cttee, 1962-67; Home Sec.'s Adv. Cttee (Cruelty to Animals Act, 1876), 1963-; Nat. Agric. Centre Adv. Bd, 1966-69; Production Cttee, Meat and Livestock Commn, 1967-70; Min. of Agriculture's Farm Animal Adv. Cttee, 1970-73. Chm., Nat. Sheep Breeders' Assoc., 1964-68; Vice-Pres., Agric. Section, British Assocn, 1970-71. Robert von Ostertag Medal, German Vet. Assoc., 1972. DL Cambs, 1963. *Publications:* (and ed jtly) Eurovet: an anatomy of Veterinary Europe, 1972; Eurovet-2, 1975. *Address:* Tyrells Hall, Shepreth, Royston, Herts SG8 6QS. *T:* Royston 60430. *Clubs:* United Oxford & Cambridge University, Europe House.

STORK, Herbert Cecil, CIE 1945; *b* 28 June 1890; *s* of Herbert William and Florence Stork; *m* 1919, Marjorie (*née* Cosens); two *d. Educ:* Merchant Taylors' School; Queen's College, Oxford (BA). Appointed to ICS, Dec. 1913; served Bengal and Assam, various posts, concluding with Legal Remembrancer and Secretary to Government of Assam; retired from ICS, 1947. Served European War, 1914-18; GSO III, 9th (Secunderabad) Division, and Staff Captain, Dunsterforce, MEF. *Recreations:* cricket, tennis. *Address:* 127 Cumnor Hill, Oxford. *T:* Cumnor 2692. *Club:* Oxford Union Society.

STORK, Joseph Whiteley, CB 1959; CBE 1949; retired as Director of Studies, Britannia Royal Naval College, Dartmouth (1955-59) (Headmaster, 1942-55); *b* Huddersfield, 9 Aug. 1902; *s* of John Arthur Stork, Huddersfield; *m* 1927, Kathleen, *d* of Alderman J. H. Waddington, JP, Halifax; one *s* three *d. Educ:* Uppingham; Downing Coll., Cambridge (scholar). 1st Class Nat. Sci. Tripos Pt 1, 2nd Class Nat. Sci. Tripos Pt II (Zoology); Senior Biology Master, Cambridge and County School, 1926; Head of Biological Dept, Charterhouse School, 1926-36; Headmaster, Portsmouth Grammar School, 1936-42. *Publications:* Joint Author of: Fundamentals of Biology, 1932,

Junior Biology, 1933, Plant and Animal Ecology, 1933. *Address:* Peverell Old School, Peverell Terrace, Portleven, Helston, Cornwall TR13 9DH.

STORMONT, Viscount; Alexander David Mungo Murray; *b* 17 Oct. 1956; *s* and *heir* of 8th Earl of Mansfield and Mansfield, *qv*. *Address:* Scone Palace, Perthshire.

STORMONTH DARLING, James Carlisle, CBE 1972; MC 1945; TD; Director, The National Trust for Scotland, since 1971 (Secretary, as Chief Executive, 1949-71); *b* 18 July 1918; *s* of late Robert Stormonth Darling, Writer to the Signet, Rosebank, Kelso, Roxburghshire, and late Beryl Madeleine Sayer, Battle, Sussex; *m* 1948, Mary Finella, BEM 1945, *d* of late Lt.-Gen. Sir James Gammell, KCB, DSO, MC; one *s* two *d*. *Educ:* Winchester Coll.; Christ Church, Oxford; BA 1939, MA 1972; Edinburgh Univ.; LLB 1949. 2nd Lt KOSB (TA), 1938; War Service, 1939-46, in KOSB and 52nd (L) Reconnaissance Regt, RAC, of which Lt-Col comdg in 1945 (TD). Admitted Writer to the Signet, 1949. Member, Queen's Body Guard for Scotland (Royal Company of Archers), 1958-. *Address:* Chapel Hill House, Dirleton, East Lothian. *T:* Dirleton 296; National Trust for Scotland, 5 Charlotte Square, Edinburgh EH2 4DU. *Club:* New (Edinburgh).

STORR, (Charles) Anthony, FRCP, FRCPsych; writer and psychiatrist; Clinical Lecturer in Psychiatry, Faculty of Medicine, University of Oxford, since 1974; *b* 18 May 1920; *y s* of Vernon Faithfull Storr, Subdean of Westminster and Katherine Cecilia Storr; *m* 1st, 1942, Catherine Cole; three *d*; 2nd, 1970, Catherine Barton (*née* Peters). *Educ:* Winchester Coll.; Christ's Coll., Cambridge; Westminster Hosp. Medical School. MB, BChir Cantab; Qual. in medicine, 1944; postgrad. trng in psychiatry, Maudsley Hosp., 1947-50; held various positions as psychiatrist in different hospitals; Consltnt Psychotherapist, Oxford AHA, 1974-. *Publications:* The Integrity of the Personality, 1960; Sexual Deviation, 1964; Human Aggression, 1968; Human Destructiveness, 1972; The Dynamics of Creation, 1972; Jung, 1973; contrib. several books and jls. *Recreations:* music, broadcasting, journalism. *Address:* 7 St Margaret's Road, Oxford OX2 6RU. *T:* Oxford 53348. *Club:* Savile.

STORR, Norman, OBE 1947; with Charity Commission, 1967-73; *b* 9 Dec. 1907; *s* of Herbert Storr and Beatrice Emily Storr, Barnsley; *m* 1937, Kathleen Mary Ward; two *s* one *d*. *Educ:* Holgate's Grammar School, Barnsley; Keble College, Oxford. Open schol. in Mod. History, Keble Coll., Oxford, 1926; BA Hons Mod. History, 1929. Entered Indian Civil Service, 1930; Session Judge, 1935; Registrar, Allahabad High Court, 1939; Registrar, Federal Court of India, 1943-47. Principal, Home Office, 1947; Principal, 1952, Establishment Officer, 1958, Comr and Sec., 1962, Prison Commission; Asst Sec., Estab. Div. Home Office, 1966-67, retired. *Recreation:* painting. *Address:* Moorlands, Amberley, near Stroud, Glos. *Club:* Royal Over-Seas League.

STORRAR, Sir John, Kt, *cr* 1953; CBE 1949; MC 1917; Town Clerk of Edinburgh, 1941-56; *b* 8 Dec. 1891; *s* of late Rev. Wm Storrar, Hardgate, Dalbeattie, Kirkcudbrightshire; *m* Agnes Drennan, *d* of late James Cameron, Hollos, Lenzie; one *d*. *Educ:* Castle Douglas Academy; Edinburgh Univ. Solicitor, 1914. Served European War, Royal Scots, 1914-19 (despatches, MC). Local Government service, 1923; Depute Town Clerk, Edinburgh, 1934. Member of various government committees. Hon. LLD Edinburgh, 1957. *Address:* 13 Cadogan Road, Edinburgh EH16 6LY. *T:* 031-664 3503.

STORRAR, Air Vice-Marshal Ronald Charles, CB 1957; OBE 1945; retired as Senior Air Staff Officer, RAF Maintenance Command; *b* 4 Sept. 1904; *m* 1932, Vera Winifred Butler; one *s*; psa; Royal Air Force; serving in the Equipment Branch. Air Commodore, 1954; Air Vice-Marshal, 1959; retired, 1963. *Address:* Apartado 45, Fuengirola, near Malaga, Spain. *Club:* Royal Air Force.

STOTESBURY, Herbert Wentworth; Assistant Under-Secretary of State, Home Office, 1966-75; Probation and Aftercare Department, 1969-75; *b* 22 Jan. 1916; *s* of Charles and Ada Stotesbury; *m* 1944, Berenice Mary Simpson; one *s* two *d*. *Educ:* Christ's Hospital; Emmanuel College, Cambridge. Home Office, 1939; Army, 1940-45. Lecturer, Military Coll. of Science, 1941-45. Home Office, 1945-75; Asst Secretary, 1953. Chm., Working Party on Marriage Guidance, 1976-. *Recreations:* music, camping. *Address:* 65 Woodside, Wimbledon, SW19. *T:* 01-946 9523.

STOTT, Rt. Hon. Lord; George Gordon Stott, PC 1964; QC (Scotland) 1950; Senator of College of Justice in Scotland since 1967; *b* 22 Dec. 1909; *s* of Rev. Dr G. Gordon Stott; *m* 1947, Nancy, *d* of A. D. Braggins; one *s* one *d*. *Educ:* Cramond Sch.; Edinburgh Acad.; Edinburgh Univ. Advocate 1936; Advocate-Depute, 1947-51; Editor, Edinburgh Clarion, 1939-44; Member, Monopolies Commission, 1949-56; Sheriff of Roxburgh, Berwick and Selkirk, 1961-64; Lord Advocate, 1964-67. *Address:* 12 Midmar Gardens, Edinburgh. *T:* 031-447 4251.

STOTT, Rt. Hon. George Gordon; *see* Stott, Rt Hon. Lord.

STOTT, Rev. John Robert Walmsley, MA Cantab; Rector of All Souls Church, Langham Place, W1, 1950-75, now Rector Emeritus; Hon. Chaplain to the Queen, since 1959; *b* 27 April 1921; *s* of late Sir Arnold W. Stott, KBE, physician, and late Emily Caroline Holland. *Educ:* Rugby Sch.; Trinity Coll., Cambridge; Ridley Hall, Cambridge. Curate of All Souls, Langham Place, 1945; Rector of All Souls, 1950, with St Peter's, Vere Street, 1952. Chm., C of E Evangelical Council, 1967. Hon. DD, Trinity Evangelical Divinity Sch., Deerfield, USA, 1971. *Publications:* Men with a Message, 1954; What Christ Thinks of the Church, 1958; Basic Christianity, 1958; Your Confirmation, 1958; Fundamentalism and Evangelism, 1959; The Preacher's Portrait, 1961; Confess Your Sins, 1964; The Epistles of John, 1964; Canticles and Selected Psalms, 1966; Men Made New, 1966; Our Guilty Silence, 1967; The Message of Galatians, 1968; One People, 1969; Christ The Controversialist, 1970; Understanding the Bible, 1972; Guard the Gospel, 1973; Balanced Christianity, 1975; Christian Mission in the Modern World, 1975; Baptism and Fullness, 1975; Christian Counter-Culture, 1978. *Recreations:* bird watching and photography. *Address:* 13 Bridford Mews, Devonshire Street, W1.

STOTT, Peter Frank, MA, FICE, FIHE, FIEAust, FCIT; Director-General, National Water Council, since 1973; *b* 8 Aug. 1927; *s* of Clarence Stott and Mabel Sutcliffe; *m* 1953, Vera Watkins; two *s*. *Educ:* Bradford Grammar Sch.; Clare Coll., Cambridge. Partner, G. Maunsell & Partners, Consulting Engineers, 1955-63; Deputy Chief Engineer (Roads) and later Chief Engineer, London County Council, 1963-65; Dir of Highways and Transportation, GLC, 1964-67; Traffic Comr and Dir of Transportation, GLC, 1967-69; Controller of Planning and Transportation, GLC, 1969-73. President: Reinforced Concrete Assoc., 1964; Concrete Soc., 1967; Instn of Highway Engineers, 1971-72; Mem. Council, ICE, 1966-71, 1972-75 and 1976-. *Address:* 7 Frank Dixon Way, SE21. *T:* 01-693 5121. *Club:* Athenæum.

STOTT, Sir Philip Sidney, 3rd Bt *cr* 1920; ARIBA, AIAA; Senior Architect in private practice; *b* 23 Dec. 1914; *e s* of Sir George Edward Stott, 2nd Bt, and Kate (*d* 1955), *o d* of late George Swailes, Oldham; *S* father 1957; *m* 1947, Cicely Florence, widow of V. C. W. Trowbridge and *o d* of Bertram Ellingham; two *s*. *Educ:* Rossall; Trinity Hall, Cambridge. Registered Chartered and Incorporate Architect; ARIBA 1947; AIAA 1950. *Recreations:* astronomy, chess, music and tennis. *Heir: s* Adrian George Ellingham Stott, *b* 7 Oct. 1948.

STOTT, Roger; MP (Lab) Westhoughton, since May 1973; *b* 7 Aug. 1943; *s* of Richard and Edith Stott; *m* 1969, Irene Mills; two *s*. *Educ:* Rochdale Tech. Coll. Served in Merchant Navy, 1959-64. Post Office Telephone Engineer, 1964-73. PPS to Sec. of State for Industry, 1975-76; PPS to the Prime Minister, 1976-. *Recreations:* football, cricket, gardening. *Address:* House of Commons, SW1A 0AA; 10 Firs Park Crescent, Aspull, Wigan. *T:* Wigan 57732.

STOUGHTON, Raymond Henry, ARCS; DSc (London); LLD (Toronto); retired as Principal, University College of Ghana, 1957-61; *b* 8 Jan. 1903; *yr s* of Arnold Stoughton-Harris and Mary Townsend Jefferis; *m* 1925, Audrey Milne Rennie (*d* 1950); three *s*. *Educ:* St Peter's Sch., York; Imperial Coll. of Science and Technology, ARCS, 1923; BSc London 1924; DSc London 1932; Mycologist, Rubber Research scheme, Ceylon 1924-26; Assistant Mycologist, Rothamsted Experimental Station, 1926-33. Professor of Horticulture, University of Reading, 1933-57. Victoria Medal of Honour, RHS, 1955, Vice-Pres., RHS, 1976. *Publications:* various on plant pathology and bacterial cytology in Proceedings of the Royal Society, Annals of Applied Biology, etc., and on physiology and horticulture in various journals. *Recreations:* philately and art history. *Address:* Lane's Corner, North Warnborough, Basingstoke, Hants. *T:* Odiham 2783.

STOURTON, family name of **Baron Mowbray, Segrave and Stourton.**

STOURTON, Sir Ivo (Herbert Evelyn Joseph), Kt 1961; CMG 1951; OBE 1939; KPM 1949; Inspector General of Colonial Police 1957-66; b 18 July 1901; s of late Major H. M. Stourton, OBE, and late Hon. Mrs H. Stourton; m 1st, 1926, Lilian (d 1942), d of late G. Dickson; two s one d; 2nd, 1945, Virginia, d of Sir Horace Seymour, qv; one d. Educ: Stonyhurst College, Lancs. Joined Colonial Police Service, 1921; Asst Supt of Police; served Mauritius, 1921-33; Commissioner of Police: Bermuda, 1933-39; Zanzibar, 1939-40; Aden, 1940-45; Uganda, 1945-50; Nigeria, 1950; Inspector-Gen. of Police, Nigeria, 1951, retd 1953. Re-appointed as Deputy Inspector General of Colonial Police, 1953-57. Kt of Malta. Address: The Old Bakery, Kimpton, Andover, Hants. T: Weyhill 2446.

STOURTON, Hon. John Joseph, TD; b 5 March 1899; yr s of 24th Lord Mowbray; m 1st, 1923, Kathleen Alice (marr. diss. 1933), d of late Robert Louis George Gunther, of 8 Princes Gardens and Park Wood, Englefield Green, Surrey; two s two d; 2nd, 1934, Gladys Leila (marr. diss. 1947), d of late Col Sir W. J. Waldron. Educ: Downside School. MP (C) South Salford, 1931-45. Served N Russian Relief Force at Archangel, 1919; and in European War, 1939-43; late Lt 10th Royal Hussars; Major The Royal Norfolk Regiment.
See also Earl of Gainsborough, H. L. C. Greig.

STOUT, Alan Ker, MA, FAHA; FASSA; Professor of Philosophy, University of Sydney, 1939-65, now Emeritus Professor; s of late Professor G. F. Stout and Ella Ker; m Evelyn Roberts, BA; one s one d. Educ: Fettes College, Edinburgh; Oriel College, Oxford. First Class Hon. Mods Oxford; Second Class Lit Hum Oxford; Bishop Fraser Research Scholar, Oriel Coll., 1922; Lecturer in Philosophy, Univ. College of North Wales, Bangor, 1924-34, Univ. of Edinburgh, 1934-39. Visiting Prof., Univ. of Wisconsin, 1966. Pres., Council for Civil Liberties, 1964-67; Member: Aust. National Film Board, 1945-47; Aust. Nat. Adv. Cttee for UNESCO, 1949-74; Bd of Dirs, Tasmanian Theatre Co.; Governor, Aust. Film Inst., 1960-75. Mem. Council, Aust. Consumers' Assoc. Fellow, Univ. Senate, Univ. of Sydney, 1954-69. Editor, Australasian Jl of Philosophy, 1950-67. Publications: Articles and Reviews (especially on the Philosophy of Descartes and on Moral Theory) in Mind, Proceedings of Aristotelian Soc., Philosophy, Australasian Journal of Philosophy, Australian Quarterly, etc., from 1926; Editor God and Nature (posthumously published Gifford lectures of G. F. Stout), 1952. Recreation: the theatre. Address: 12 Lambert Avenue, Sandy Bay, Hobart, Tasmania 7005, Australia.

STOUT, Sir Duncan; see Stout, Sir T. D. M.

STOUT, Samuel Coredon; HM Diplomatic Service, retired; b 17 Feb. 1913; m 1st, Mary Finn (d 1965); two s one d; 2nd, 1966, Jill Emery. Ministry of National Insurance, 1937-40; Admiralty, 1940-46; Board of Trade, 1946-65 (Trade Commissioner, Singapore, Bombay and Melbourne); Counsellor (Commercial), Canberra, 1966-68; Dep. High Comr and Minister (Commercial), Karachi, 1968-70; Consul-Gen., St Louis, USA, 1970-72. Address: Richmond House, Alverston Avenue, Woodhall Spa, Lincs.

STOUT, Sir (Thomas) Duncan (Macgregor), Kt 1962; CBE 1943 (OBE 1919); DSO 1917; ED; MB, MS London; FRCS; FRACS; FACS; Hon. Cons. Surgeon, Wellington Hospital; Past Member Council and past Chancellor, Victoria University of Wellington; Past Member: Senate, University of New Zealand; Council, Massey Agricultural College; Trustee, NZ Cancer Societies; Past President, Wellington Branch (NZ) British Empire Cancer Campaign; b 25 July 1885; s of late Rt Hon. Sir R. Stout, KCMG; m 1919, Agnes I. Pearce; three s one d. Educ: Wellington College, NZ; Guy's College and Hospital. Consultant Surgeon, Wellington Hospital (NZ); served European War, 1914-18, Samoan Force (OBE, DSO); attached to No 1 NZ Stationary Hospital at Port Said, Salonica, and France; Divisional Surgeon at Brockenhurst (NZ Hospital in England); War of 1939-45 (England, Middle East and Italy); Consultant Surgeon 2nd NZEF (CBE). Editor NZ Medical War History, 1939-45; President, NZ Branch BMA, 1937-38. Hon. LLD: Victoria Univ. of Wellington; Univ. of NZ. Recreations: golf and bowls. Address: 1 Katherine Avenue, Wellington N1, New Zealand. T: 737-425. Club: Wellington (Wellington, NZ).

STOUT, William Ferguson, CB 1964; Security Adviser to Government of Northern Ireland, 1971-72, retired; b Holywood, Co. Down, 22 Feb. 1907; s of late Robert and Amelia Stout; m 1938, Muriel Kilner; one s one d. Educ: Sullivan Upper Sch., Holywood; Queen's Univ., Belfast. Ministry of Home Affairs: Principal, 1943; Asst Sec., 1954; Senior Asst Sec., 1959; Permanent Sec., 1961-64; Permanent Secretary: Min. of Health

and Local Govt, 1964; Min. of Development, 1965-71. Recreation: golf.

STOW, Archdeacon of; see Scott, Ven. David.

STOW, Sir Edmond Cecil P.; see Philipson-Stow.

STOW, Sir John Montague, GCMG 1966 (KCMG 1959; CMG 1950); KCVO 1966; Governor-General of Barbados, 1966-67; retired, 1967; since employed as consultant by Stewart Wrightson Ltd; Director, Tradewinds Airways; b 3 Oct. 1911; s of late Sir Alexander Stow, KCIE; m 1939, Beatrice Tryhorne; two s. Educ: Harrow School; Pembroke College, Cambridge. Administrative Officer, Nigeria, 1934; Secretariat, Gambia, 1938; Chief Sec., Windward Islands, 1944; Administrator, St Lucia, BWI, 1947; Dir of Establishments, Kenya, 1952-55; Chief Sec., Jamaica, 1955-59; Governor and C-in-C Barbados, 1959-66. Vice-Chm., Commonwealth Soc. for Deaf. KStJ 1959. Recreations: cricket, tennis. Address: 26a Tregunter Road, SW10. T: 01-370 1921. Clubs: Caledonian, MCC.

STOW, (Julian) Randolph; writer; b Geraldton, W Australia, 28 Nov. 1935; s of Cedric Ernest Stow and Mary Stow (née Sewell). Educ: Guildford Grammar Sch., W Australia; Univ. of Western Australia. Lecturer in English Literature: Univ. of Leeds, 1962; Univ. of Western Australia, 1963-64; Harkness Fellow, United States, 1964-66; Lectr in English and Commonwealth Lit., Univ. of Leeds, 1968-69. Miles Franklin Award, 1958; Britannica Australia Award, 1966. Publications: poems: Outrider, 1962; A Counterfeit Silence, 1969; novels: To The Islands, 1958; Tourmaline, 1963; The Merry-go-round in the Sea, 1965; music theatre (with Peter Maxwell Davies): Eight Songs for a Mad King, 1969; Miss Donnithorne's Maggot, 1974; for children: Midnite, 1967. Address: c/o Richard Scott Simon Ltd, 32 College Cross, N1 1PR.

STOW, Ralph Conyers, FCIS, FBS; Managing Director, Cheltenham & Gloucester Building Society, since 1973; b 19 Dec. 1916; s of Albert Conyers Stow and Mabel Louise Bourlet; m 1943, Eleanor Joyce Appleby; one s one d. Educ: Woodhouse Sch., Finchley. FCIS 1959; FBS 1952. Supt of Branches, Temperance Permanent Bldg Soc., 1950, Asst Manager 1958; Gen. Man. and Sec., Cheltenham & Gloucester Bldg Soc., 1962, Dir 1967. Pres., Bldg Socs Inst., 1971-72; Chm., Midland Assoc. of Bldg Socs, 1973-74; Chm., Bldg Socs Assoc., 1977. Mem., Glos AHA. Mem. Council, Cheltenham Coll.; Governor, Bournside Sch., Cheltenham. Recreations: beekeeping, photography, oil painting. Address: Cheltenham & Gloucester Building Society, Clarence Street, Cheltenham, Glos GL50 3JR. T: Cheltenham 36161. Clubs: Royal Automobile; Rotary (Cheltenham).

STOW, Randolph; see Stow, J. R.

STOW HILL, Baron cr 1966 (Life Peer), of Newport; Frank Soskice, PC 1948; Kt, cr 1945; QC 1945; b 23 July 1902; m 1940, Susan Isabella Cloudesley Hunter; two s. Educ: St Paul's School; Balliol College, Oxford. Called to Bar, Inner Temple, 1926; Bencher, 1945. MP (Lab) for Birkenhead East, 1945-50, for Neepsend Div. of Sheffield, (April) 1950-55, for Newport (Monmouthshire), (July) 1956-66; Solicitor-General, 1945-51; Attorney-General, April-Oct. 1951; Home Secretary, 1964-65; Lord Privy Seal, 1965-66. UK Delegate to UN General Assembly, 1950. Treasurer, Inner Temple, 1968. Address: House of Lords, SW1.

STOWE, Kenneth Ronald, CB 1977; Principal Private Secretary to the Prime Minister, since 1975; b 17 July 1927; er s of Arthur and Emily Stowe; m 1949, Joan Frances Cullen; two s one d. Educ: County High Sch., Dagenham; Exeter Coll., Oxford (MA). Asst Principal, Nat. Assistance Board, 1951; Principal, 1956; seconded UN Secretariat, New York, 1958; Asst Sec., 1964; Asst Under-Sec. of State, DHSS, 1970-73; Under Sec., Cabinet Office, 1973-75; Dep. Sec., 1976. Recreations: opera, theatre, hill walking. Address: 6 Church Road, Newton, Suffolk.

STOWERS, Arthur, BSc (Eng), London; ACGI, FIMechE, MICE, FMA; retired; b 24 Jan. 1897; yr s of James H. Stowers, MD; m 1929, Freda, d of Richard Hall, FRIBA; two s. Educ: Haileybury; City and Guilds (Engineering) College, South Kensington. Contracts Engr, after 3 yrs pupilage, at W. H. Allen, Sons & Co., Bedford, 1923; Asst Keeper, Science Museum, South Kensington, 1930. Min. of Aircraft Production, 1940; Keeper, Science Museum, Department of Mechanical and Civil Engineering, 1950-62. Jt Hon. Sec. Newcomen Soc., 1933-48, Pres., 1955-57; Dickinson Memorial Medal, 1962. Address: 27 Woodgavil, The Drive, Banstead, Surrey SM7 1AA.

STOY, Prof. Philip Joseph; Professor of Dentistry, Queen's University of Belfast, 1948-73, now Professor Emeritus; *b* 19 Jan. 1906; *m* 1945, Isabella Mary Beatrice Crispin; two *s*. *Educ:* Wolverhampton School. Queen's Scholar, Birmingham Univ., 1929; LDS, RCS, 1931; BDS (Hons), Birmingham 1932; FDS, RCS, 1947; Fellow of the Faculty of Dentistry, RCSI, 1963 (FFDRCSI). Lectr in Dental Mechanics, Univ. of Bristol, 1934; Lectr in Dental Surgery, Univ. of Bristol, 1940. *Publications:* articles in British Dental Journal, Dental Record. *Recreations:* reading, walking, painting, dental history, chess. *Address:* Westward Ho!, 57 Imperial Road, Exmouth, Devon EX8 1DQ. *T:* Exmouth 5113.

STOYLE, Roger John B.; *see* Blin-Stoyle.

STRABANE, Viscount; James Harold Charles Hamilton; *b* 19 Aug. 1969; *s* and *heir* of Marquess of Hamilton, *qv*.

STRABOLGI, 11th Baron of England, *cr* 1318; **David Montague de Burgh Kenworthy;** Captain of the Yeomen of the Guard (Deputy Government Chief Whip), since 1974; *b* 1 Nov. 1914; *e s* of 10th Baron Strabolgi and Doris, *o c* of late Sir Frederick Whitley-Thomson, MP; *S* father, 1953; *m* 1961, Doreen Margaret, *e d* of late Alexander Morgan, Ashton-under-Lyne. *Educ:* Gresham's School, Holt; Chelsea Sch. of Art. Served with HM Forces, BEF, 1939-40; MEF, 1940-45, as Lt-Col RAOC. Mem. Parly Delegations to USSR, 1954, SHAPE, 1955. PPS to Minister of State, Home Office, 1968-69; PPS to Leader of the House of Lords and Lord Privy Seal, 1969-70; Asst Opposition Whip, and spokesman on the Arts, House of Lords, 1970-74; Member: Franco-British Parly Relations Cttee; House of Lords' Offices Cttee. Dir, Bolton Building Soc., 1958-74; Member: Labour Party; Council, Franco-British Soc.; Jt Vice-Chm., Labour Parly Films Gp, 1968-70. *Heir-pres: b* Rev. Hon. Jonathan Malcolm Atholl Kenworthy, MA, Rector of Yelvertoft, Northants; Chaplain HM's Forces [*b* 16 Sept. 1916; *m* 1st, 1943, Joan Gaster (*d* 1963); two *d*; 2nd, 1963, Victoria Hewitt; two *s* one *d*]. *Address:* House of Lords, SW1.
See also Sir Harold Hood, Bt.

STRACEY, Sir John (Simon), 9th Bt *cr* 1818; *b* 30 Nov. 1938; *s* of Captain Algernon Augustus Henry Stracey (2nd *s* of 6th Bt) (*d* 1940) and Olive Beryl (*d* 1972), *d* of late Major Charles Robert Eustace Radclyffe; *S* cousin, 1971; *m* 1968, Martha Maria, *d* of late Johann Egger; two *d*. *Heir: cousin* Henry Mounteney Stracey [*b* 24 April 1920; *m* 1st, 1943, Susanna, *d* of Adair Tracey; one *d*; 2nd, 1950, Lysbeth, *o d* of Charles Ashford, NZ; one *s* one *d*; 3rd, 1961, Jeltje, *y d* of Scholte de Boer]. *Address:* 652 Belmont Avenue, Westmount, Quebec H3Y 2W2, Canada. *T:* (514) 489-8904. *Club:* Royal St Lawrence Yacht (Montreal).

STRACHAN, Hon. Lord; James Frederick Strachan; Senator, College of Justice in Scotland, 1948-67; *b* 11 October 1894; *s* of James K. Strachan, Glasgow; *m* 1926, Irene Louise, *d* of Timothy Warren, LLD, Glasgow; two *s* one *d*. *Educ:* Glasgow Academy; Glasgow Univ. MA, LLB; admitted Faculty of Advocates, 1921; Advocate Depute, 1936-38; KC 1938; Vice-Dean Faculty of Advocates, 1941-48; Procurator Church of Scotland, 1938-48. Sheriff of Argyll, 1942-45; Sheriff of Perth and Angus, 1945-48. Hon. LLD Glasgow, 1961. *Address:* Woodville, Canaan Lane, Edinburgh EH10 4SG. *Club:* New (Edinburgh).

STRACHAN, Alexander William Bruce, OBE 1971; HM Diplomatic Service, retired; *b* 2 July 1917; *s* of William Fyfe and Winifred Orchar Strachan; *m* 1940, Rebecca Prince MacFarlane; one *s* one *d*. *Educ:* Daniel Stewart's Coll., Edinburgh; Allen Glen's High Sch., Glasgow. Doctorate of Commonsense (self awarded). Joined GPO, 1935; service with Army, 1939-46; Asst Postal Controller, 1953-64; Postal Adviser to Iraq Govt, 1964-66; FCO, 1967-68; 1st Sec. (Development), Jordan, 1968-72; 1st Sec. (Commercial) and Consul, Addis Ababa, 1972-73; Consul General, Lahore, 1973-74; Counsellor (Economic and Commercial) and Consul General, British Embassy, Islamabad, 1975-77. Order of Istiqlal, Hashemite Kingdom of Jordan, 1971. *Recreations:* bridge, golf. *Address:* c/o Barclays Bank Ltd, 12 Station Parade, Sanderstead, Surrey CR2 0PH. *Club:* Punjab (Lahore).

STRACHAN, Major Benjamin Leckie; HM Diplomatic Service; Ambassador to Yemen Arab Republic, since 1977; *b* 4 Jan. 1924; *e s* of late Dr C. G. Strachan, MC, FRCPE and Annie Primrose (*née* Leckie); *m* 1958, Lize Lund; three *s* and one step *s* one step *d*. *Educ:* Rossall Sch. (Scholar); RMCS. Royal Dragoons, 1944; France and Germany Campaign, 1944-45 (despatches); 4th QO Hussars, Malayan Campaign, 1948-51; Middle East Centre for Arab Studies, 1952-53; GSO2, HQ British Troops Egypt, 1954-

55; Technical Staff Course, RMCS, 1956-58; 10th Royal Hussars, 1959-61; GSO2, WO, 1961; retd from Army and joined Foreign (subseq. Diplomatic) Service, 1961; 1st Sec., FO, 1961-62; Information Adviser to Governor of Aden, 1962-63; FO, 1964-66; Commercial Sec., Kuwait, 1966-69; Counsellor, Amman, 1969-71; Trade Comr, Toronto, 1971-74; Consul General, Vancouver, 1974-76. *Recreations:* golf, tennis, squash, fishing. *Address:* c/o Foreign and Commonwealth Office, SW1; Mill of Strachan, Strachan, Kincardineshire; 17 Pembroke Crescent, Hove, East Sussex.

STRACHAN, Lt-Col Henry, VC 1917; MC 1917; Fort Garry Horse; retired; Hon. ADC to Governor General of Canada from 1935; Field Representative, The Canadian Bank of Commerce, from 1928; *b* Bo'ness, Scotland, 7 Nov. 1884; *m*; one *d*. *Educ:* Royal High School, Edinburgh; Edinburgh University. Ranches in Alberta, Canada; joined FGH, 1914; Commission July 1916; served European War, 1914-18 (MC, wounded, VC); War of 1939-45, Lt-Col Cmdg 1st Bn Edmonton Fusiliers. *Recreations:* badminton, golf. *Address:* 3008 West 31st Avenue, Vancouver 8, British Columbia, Canada. *Clubs:* Alberta Golf, Country (Calgary).

STRACHAN, James Frederick; *see* Strachan, Hon. Lord.

STRACHAN, Michael Francis, MBE 1945; Chairman, Ben Line Steamers Ltd and Ben Line Containers Ltd, since 1970; Director, Bank of Scotland; *b* 23 Oct. 1919; *s* of Francis William Strachan and Violet Blackwell (*née* Palmer); *m* 1948, Iris Hemingway; two *s* two *d*. *Educ:* Rugby Sch. (Scholar); Corpus Christi Coll., Cambridge (Exhibnr, MA). Served in Army, 1939-46; Bde Major 26th Armd Bde, Italy, 1944-45 (MBE, despatches); demobilised 1946 (Lt-Col); subseq. served with Lothians and Border Horse, TA. Joined Wm Thomson & Co., Edinburgh, Managers of Ben Line, 1946; Partner, 1950-64; Jt Man. Dir, Ben Line Steamers Ltd, 1964. Chm., Associated Container Transportation Ltd, 1971-75. Trustee, Nat. Galleries of Scotland, 1972-74; Chm. Bd of Trustees, Nat. Library of Scotland, 1974-. Member of Queen's Body Guard for Scotland. *Publications:* The Life and Adventures of Thomas Coryate, 1962; (ed jtly) The East India Company Journals of Captain William Keeling and Master Thomas Bonner, 1615-1617, 1971; articles in Blackwood's, Hakluyt Society's Hakluyt Handbook, History Today, Jl Soc. for Nautical Research. *Recreations:* country pursuits, silviculture. *Address:* 33 St Mary's Street, Edinburgh EH1 1TN. *Clubs:* Naval and Military; New (Edinburgh).

STRACHAN, Robert Martin; Agent-General for British Columbia in the United Kingdom and Europe, 1975-77; *b* 1 Dec. 1913; *s* of Alexander Strachan and Sarah Martin; *m* 1937, Anne Elsie Paget; two *s* one *d*. *Educ:* schools in Glasgow, Scotland. Mem., British Columbia Legislature, 1952-75; Leader of Opposition, 1956-69; Minister: of Highways, 1972-73; of Transport and Communications, 1973-75; resigned seat Oct. 1975, to accept appointment as Agent-General. *Recreations:* swimming, fishing, painting. *Address:* RR2, Cedar Road, Nanaimo, Vancouver Island, British Columbia. *Club:* Royal Over-Seas League.

STRACHAN, Walter, CBE 1967; CEng, FRAeS; Consulting Engineer since 1971; *b* 14 Oct. 1910; *s* of William John Strachan, Rothes, Morayshire, and Eva Hitchins, Bristol; *m* 1937, Elizabeth Dora Bradshaw, Aldershot; two *s*. *Educ:* Newfoundland Road Sch., Bristol; Merchant Venturers Technical Coll., Bristol. Bristol Aeroplane Co.: Apprentice, 1925; Aircraft Ground Engr, 1932; RAE, Farnborough, 1934; Inspector: Bristol Aeroplane Co., 1937. BAC Service Engr, RAF Martlesham Heath, 1938; BAC: Asst Service Manager, 1940; Asst Works Manager, 1942; Manager, Banwell, building Beaufort and Tempest aircraft, 1943; Gen.-Manager, Banwell and Weston Factories, manufrg Aluminium Houses, 1945; Gen. Manager, Banwell and Weston Factories, building helicopters and aircraft components, 1951; Managing Dir, Bristol Aerojet, Banwell, Rocket Motor Develt and Prod., 1958. *Recreations:* golf, music, ornithology. *Address:* 38 Clarence Road South, Weston-Super-Mare, Somerset. *T:* Weston-Super-Mare 23878. *Clubs:* Naval and Military; Royal Automobile.

STRACHEY, family name of **Baron O'Hagan.**

STRACHEY, Charles, (6th Bt *cr* 1801, but does not use the title); *b* 20 June 1934; *s* of Rt Hon. Evelyn John St Loe Strachey (*d* 1963) and of Celia, 3rd *d* of late Rev. Arthur Hume Simpson; *S* to baronetcy of cousin, 2nd Baron Strachie, 1973; *m* 1973, Janet Megan, *d* of Alexander Miller; one *d*. *Heir: kinsman* John Ralph Severs Strachey [*b* 22 Oct. 1905; *m* 1st, 1933, Isobel Bertha (marr. diss. 1942), *d* of Ronald Leslie; one *d*; 2nd, 1945,

Rosemary, *d* of Douglas Mavor; one *s*]. *Address:* 30 Gibson Square, N1 0RD. *T:* 01-226 8216.

STRADBROKE, 4th Earl of, *cr* 1821; **John Anthony Alexander Rous;** Bt 1660; Baron Rous, 1796; Viscount Dunwich, 1821; Lord-Lieutenant and Custos Rotulorum for the County of Suffolk since 1948; Commander Royal Navy, retired list; *b* 1 April 1903 (to whom Queen Alexandra stood sponsor); *e s* of 3rd Earl of Stradbroke, KCMG, CB, CVO, CBE, and Helena Violet Alice, DBE, *cr* 1927, Lady of Grace of St John (*d* 1949), *d* of Gen. Keith Fraser; *S* father, 1947; *m* 1929, Barbara (*d* 1977), *yr d* of late Lord Arthur Grosvenor; two *d. Educ:* RN Colleges, Osborne and Dartmouth; Christ Church (Hon. MA), Oxford. Member E Suffolk CC 1931-45, Alderman 1953-64. Private Sec. to Governor of Victoria and Acting Governor General, Australia, 1946-47. Estate Owner, Agriculturist and Forester. National Vice-Pres. (Pres. Eastern Area), Royal British Legion; Vice-Pres., Assoc. of (Land) Drainage Authorities. Dir, Daejan Holdings Ltd. Served Royal Navy, 1917-28, and on Naval Staff, Admiralty 1939-46. Lately Hon. Colonel 660 HAA Regiment (TA); Vice-Pres., TA&VRA for E Anglia. FRSA. Grand Master, Grand Lodge of Mark Master Masons; Provincial Grand Master, Freemasons, Province of Suffolk. KStJ. *Heir: b* Hon. (William) Keith Rous [*b* 10 Mar. 1907; *m* 1st, 1935, Pamela Catherine Mabell (marr. diss. 1941), *d* of late Capt. Hon. Edward James Kay.-Shuttleworth; two *s*; 2nd, 1943, April Mary, *d* of late Brig.-General Hon. Arthur Melland Asquith, DSO; one *s* three *d*]. *Address:* Henham, Wangford, Beccles, Suffolk. *T:* Wangford 212 and 214. *Clubs:* Travellers'; Jockey Club Rooms; Royal Norfolk and Suffolk Yacht.

STRADLING, Rt. Rev. Leslie Edward, MA; *b* 11 Feb. 1908; *er s* of late Rev. W. H. Stradling; unmarried. *Educ:* King Edward VII Sch., Sheffield; The Queen's Coll., Oxford; Westcott House, Cambridge. Curate of St Paul's, Lorrimore Square, 1933-38; Vicar of St Luke's Camberwell, 1938-43; of St Anne's, Wandsworth, 1943-45; Bishop of Masasi, 1945-52; Bishop of South West Tanganyika, 1952-61; Bishop of Johannesburg, 1961-74. Hon. DCL Bishops' Univ., Lennoxville, Canada, 1968. *Publications:* A Bishop on Safari, 1960; The Acts through Modern Eyes, 1963; An Open Door, 1966; A Bishop at Prayer, 1971; Praying Now, 1976; Praying the Psalms, 1977. *Address:* 197 Main Road, Kalk Bay, South Africa 7975. *Clubs:* United Oxford & Cambridge University; City and Civil Service (Cape Town).

STRADLING THOMAS, John; MP (C) Monmouth, since 1970; farmer; *b* 10 June 1925; *s* of Thomas Roger Thomas and Catherine Thomas (*née* Delahay); *m* 1957, Freda Rhys Evans; one *s* two *d. Educ:* Rugby School. Contested (C) Aberavon, 1964; Cardigan, 1966. Asst Govt Whip, 1971-73; a Lord Comr, HM Treasury, 1973-74; an Opposition Whip, 1974-; Mem., Select Cttee on the Civil List, 1971. Member Council, NFU, 1963-70. *Address:* House of Commons, SW1A 0AA.

STRAFFORD, 7th Earl of, *cr* 1847; **Robert Cecil Byng;** Baron Strafford (UK), 1935; Viscount Enfield, 1847; *b* 29 July 1904; *o* surv. *s* of late Hon. Ivo Francis Byng (4th *s* of 5th Earl) and late Agnes Constance, *d* of S. Smith Travers, Hobart, Tasmania; *S* uncle 1951; *m* 1st, 1934, Maria Magdalena Elizabeth (marr. diss. 1947), *d* of late Henry Cloete, CMG, Alphen, S Africa; two *s*; 2nd, 1948, Clara Evelyn, *d* of late Sir Ness Nowrosjee Wadia, KBE, CIE. *Heir: s* Viscount Enfield, *qv. Address:* 98 Cheyne Walk, SW10 0DQ.

STRAIGHT, Whitney Willard, CBE 1944; MC; DFC; Legion of Merit (USA); Norwegian War Cross; Deputy Chairman, Post Office Corporation, 1969-74; Chairman: Arran Trust Ltd; Rolls-Royce Realizations Ltd, since 1976; Director, Midland Bank Ltd; Hon. Companion, Royal Aeronautical Society; *b* 6 Nov. 1912; *e s* of late Maj. W. D. Straight and Mrs Dorothy Whitney Elmhirst; *m* 1935, Lady Daphne Finch-Hatton, *d* of 14th Earl of Winchilsea and Nottingham; two *d. Educ:* Lincoln Sch., USA; Dartington Hall; Trinity Coll., Cambridge. Became professional motor car driver and won many International races and held speed records. Gave up motor racing in 1934 to enter Civil Aviation. Started a number of Companies and was appointed to Govt and other National Cttees. Served War of 1939-45, in RAF; Fighter Comd, Transport Comd, Air Cdre 1942 (despatches, MC, DFC, CBE, Norwegian War Cross, American Legion of Merit). Air ADC 1944. Chm., Straight Corp. and subsidiary cos, 1935-39; Dep. Chm. BEA, 1946-47; Man. Dir (Chief Exec.), BOAC, 1947-49, Dep. Chm., 1949-55; Exec. Vice-Chm., 1956-57, Dep. Chm., 1957-71, Chm., 1971-76, Rolls-Royce Ltd. Member: Aerodrome Owners Assoc., 1936; Air Registration Bd, 1939-42, 1947-54; Council, RCA, 1955-58; Council, Business Aircraft Users Assoc., 1962; CoID, 1957-66; Council, UK S African Trade Assoc., 1969; Nat. Adv. Council

on Art Educn, 1959-65; Cttee, RGS; former Chm., Contemporary Art Soc.; Vice-Pres., British Light Aircraft Centre; Chm., 1946-51, Vice-Pres., 1951-68, Royal Aero Club; Pres., PO Art Club of GB, 1969; Vice-Pres., Geoffrey de Havilland Flying Foundn, 1966; Chairman: Govt Adv. Cttee on Private Flying, 1947; Exec. Cttee, Alexandra Day, 1957. Royal Air Forces Assoc.: Pres., Ealing Br., 1965. Member: Inst. Transport; Inst. of Navigation; British Air Line Pilots Assoc.; Fellow: Royal Soc. for Protection of Birds; Brit. Inst. of Management; FRSA; FRGS (Vice-Pres., 1974); FZS. Liveryman: Guild of Air Pilots and Navigators; Worshipful Co. of Goldsmiths; Worshipful Co. of Coachmakers and Coachharnessmakers. *Publications:* numerous articles on aviation subjects. *Recreations:* ski-ing, music, art, industrial design. *Address:* The Aviary, Windmill Lane, Southall, Middlesex UB2 4NG. *T:* 01-574 2711. *Clubs:* Buck's; Royal Yacht Squadron, Cruising Association; International des Anciens Pilotes de Grand Prix FI (Lausanne); Corviglia Ski (St Moritz).

STRAKER, Rear-Adm. Bryan John, OBE 1966; Assistant Chief of Naval Staff (Policy), since 1976; *b* 26 May 1929; *s* of late George Straker and Marjorie Straker; *m* 1954, Elizabeth Rosemary, *d* of Maj.-Gen. C. W. Greenway, CB, CBE, and Mrs C. W. Greenway; two *d. Educ:* St Albans Sch. MBIM 1976. Cadet, RNC Dartmouth, 1946; Flag Lieut to Flag Officer, Malayan Area, 1952-53; qual. in communications, 1955; Flag Lieut and Staff Ops Officer to Sen. Naval Officer, WI, 1960-62; CO: HMS Malcolm, 1962-63; HMS Defender, 1966-67; Asst Dir, Naval Operational Requirements, MoD, 1968-70; CO HMS Fearless, 1970-72; Dir of Naval Plans, MoD, 1972-74; Sen. Naval Officer, WI, and Island Comdr, Bermuda, 1974-76. Freeman, City of London. *Recreations:* tennis, cricket, gardening. *Address:* The Cottage, Durford Court, Petersfield, Hants. *T:* Liss 3497. *Clubs:* Farmers', Forty, West India.

STRAKER, Michael Ian Bowstead, CBE 1973; JP; farmer, since 1951; *b* 10 March 1928; *s* of late Edward Charles Straker and of Margaret Alice Bridget Straker. *Educ:* Eton. Served in Coldstream Guards, 1946-50. Director, Newcastle and Gateshead Water Co., 1975; Chairman, Newcastle upon Tyne Area Health Authority (Teaching), 1973-; Chm., Newcastle Univ. HMC, 1971; Mem. Newcastle Univ. Court and Council, 1972-; Chm., Northern Area Conservative Assoc., 1969-72. High Sheriff of Northumberland, 1977; JP Northumberland, 1962. *Address:* High Warden, Hexham, Northumberland. *T:* Hexham 2083. *Clubs:* Brooks's; Northern Counties (Newcastle upon Tyne).

STRAND, Prof. Kenneth T.; Professor, Department of Economics and Commerce, Simon Fraser University, since 1968; *b* Yakima, Wash, 30 June 1931; US citizen; *m* 1960, Elna K. Tomaske; no *c. Educ:* Washington State Coll. (BA); Univ. of Wisconsin (PhD, MS). Woodrow Wilson Fellow, 1955-56; Ford Foundn Fellow, 1957-58; Herfurth Award, Univ. of Wisconsin, 1961 (for PhD thesis). Asst Exec. Sec., Hanford Contractors Negotiation Cttee, Richland, Wash, 1953-55; Asst Prof., Washington State Univ., 1959-60; Asst Prof., Oberlin Coll., 1960-65 (on leave, 1963-65); Economist, Manpower and Social Affairs Div., OECD, Paris, 1964-66; Assoc. Prof., Dept of Econs and Commerce, Simon Fraser Univ., 1966-68; Pres., Simon Fraser Univ., 1969-74 (Acting Pres., 1968-69). Member: Industrial Relations Research Assoc.; American Econ. Assoc.; Internat. Industrial Relations Assoc.; Canadian Econs Assoc. FRSA 1972. *Publications:* Jurisdictional Disputes in Construction: The Causes, The Joint Board and the NLRB, 1961; contribs to Review of Econs and Statistics, Amer. Econ. Review, Industrial Relations, Sociaal Mannblad Arbeid. *Recreations:* sailing, ski-ing. *Address:* RR1, Group Box 9C, Bedwell Bay Road, Port Moody, BC V3J 5H6, Canada.

STRANG, family name of **Baron Strang.**

STRANG, 1st Baron, *cr* 1954, of Stonesfield; **William Strang,** GCB 1953 (KCB 1948; CB 1939); GCMG 1950 (KCMG 1943; CMG 1932); MBE 1918; Chairman, National Parks Commission, 1954-66; Member Nature Conservancy, 1954-66; Chairman Food Hygiene Advisory Council, 1955-71; Chairman, Royal Institute of International Affairs, 1958-65; a Deputy Speaker and Deputy Chairman of Committees, House of Lords, 1962; *b* 1893; *e s* of late James Strang, Englefield, Berks; *m* 1920, Elsie Wynne (*d* 1974), *y d* of late J. E. Jones; one *s* one *d. Educ:* Palmer's School; University Coll., London; Sorbonne. BA (London), 1912; Quain Essay, 1913; served European War with 4th Bn Worcestershire Regt, and HQ, 29th Div. (MBE); entered Foreign Office, 1919; 3rd Sec., Belgrade, 1919; 2nd Sec., 1920; Foreign Office, 1923; 1st Sec., 1925; acting Counsellor of Embassy at Moscow, 1930; Counsellor, 1932; Asst Under-Sec. of

State in Foreign Office, 1939-43; UK Representative on European Advisory Commission, with rank of Ambassador, 1943-45; Political Adviser to C-in-C, British Forces of Occupation in Germany, 1945-47; Permanent Under-Sec., FO (German Section), 1947-49; Permanent Under-Sec. of State, Foreign Office, 1949-53; retired 1953. Fellow University College, London, 1946; Chairman College Committee, 1963-71. Hon. LLD (London), 1954. *Publications:* The Foreign Office, 1955; Home and Abroad, 1956; Britain in World Affairs, 1961; The Diplomatic Career, 1962. *Heir: s* Hon. Colin Strang [*b* 12 June 1922; *m* 1955, Barbara Mary Hope (*see* Prof. Barbara Strang); one *d*]. *Address:* 14 Graham Park Road, Gosforth, Newcastle upon Tyne NE3 4BH. *Club:* Travellers'.

STRANG, Prof. Barbara Mary Hope; Professor of English Language and General Linguistics, University of Newcastle upon Tyne, since 1964; *b* 20 April 1925; *d* of Frederick A. and Amy M. Carr; *m* 1955, Hon. Colin Strang, *s* of Baron Strang, *qv*; one *d* . *Educ:* Coloma Convent of the Ladies of Mary, Croydon; Univ. of London (King's Coll.). BA 1945, MA 1947. Asst Lectr, Westfield Coll., Univ. of London, 1947-50; Lectr, Armstrong Coll., Newcastle, 1950-63. Mem., Univ. Grants Cttee, 1975-. *Publications:* Modern English Structure, 1962, 2nd edn 1968; A History of English, 1970, paperback, 1974; contribs to Trans Philological Soc.; Durham Univ. Jl; English Studies Today; Lingua; Notes and Queries; various Proc. and Festschriften, etc. *Recreation:* horsemanship. *Address:* School of English, The University, Newcastle upon Tyne NE1 7RU. *T:* Newcastle upon Tyne 28511.

STRANG, Gavin Steel; MP (Lab) Edinburgh East since 1970; Parliamentary Secretary, Ministry of Agriculture, Fisheries and Food, since Oct. 1974; *b* 10 July 1943; *s* of James Steel Strang and Marie Strang (*née* Finkle); *m* . *Educ:* Univs of Edinburgh and Cambridge. BSc Hons Edinburgh, 1964; DipAgricSci Cambridge, 1965; PhD Edinburgh, 1968. Mem., Tayside Econ. Planning Consultative Group, 1966-68; Scientist with ARC, 1968-70. Parly Under-Sec. of State, Dept of Energy, March-Oct. 1974. *Publications:* articles in Animal Production. *Recreations:* golf, swimming, films. *Address:* 80 Argyle Crescent, Edinburgh EH15 2QD. *T:* 031-669 5999. *Club:* New Craighall Miners' Welfare (Edinburgh).

STRANG, William John, CBE 1973; PhD; FRS 1977, CEng, FRAeS; Technical Director, British Aircraft Corporation Ltd, Commercial Aircraft Division, since 1971; *b* 29 June 1921; *s* of John F. Strang and late Violet Strang (*née* Terrell); *m* 1946, Margaret Nicholas Howells; three *s* one *d* . *Educ:* Torquay Grammar Sch.; King's Coll., London Univ. (BSc). Bristol Aeroplane Co., Ltd, Stress Office, 1939-46; King's Coll., London Univ., 1946-48; Aeronautical Research Lab., Melbourne, Aust., 1948-51; Bristol Aeroplane Co. Ltd: Dep. Head, Guided Weapons Dept, 1951-52; Head of Aerodynamics and Flight Research, 1952-55; Chief Designer, 1955-60; British Aircraft Corp. Ltd (Filton Div.): Director and Chief Engr, 1960-67; Technical Dir, 1967-71. Fellow, Fellowship of Engineering, 1977. *Recreation:* sailing. *Address:* Homefield, Barrow Gurney, Avon BS19 3RU. *T:* Flax Bourton 2115. *Clubs:* Royal Yachting Association; Island Cruising (Salcombe), Salcombe Yacht.

STRANG STEEL, Major Sir F. W.; *see* Steel, Major Sir F. W. S.

STRANGE, 15th Baron *cr* 1628 (title abeyant, 1957-65); **John Drummond;** *b* 6 May 1900; *s* of late Capt. Malcolm Drummond of Megginch, Grenadier Guards, and late Geraldine Margaret, *d* of 1st Baron Amherst of Hackney; *m* Violet Margaret (*d* 1975), *d* of Sir R. B. Jardine, 2nd Bt of Castlemilk; three *d* (co-heiresses to Barony). *Educ:* Eton. *Publications:* The Bride Wore Black, 1942; Pocket Show Book, 1943; Charter for the Soil, 1944; Playing to the Gods, 1944; Inheritance of Dreams, 1945; A Candle in England, 1946; Behind Dark Shutters, 1948; Gold over the Hill, 1950; The Naughty Mrs Thornton, 1952; Proof Positive, 1956. *Address:* Tholt-E-Will, Sulby Glen, Isle of Man. *Club:* Bath.
See also Sir Peter Agnew, Bt.

STRANGER-JONES, Leonard Ivan; Registrar of the Principal Registry of the Family Division of the High Court of Justice, since 1967; *b* 8 May 1913; *s* of Walter Stranger-Jones; *m* 1st, 1935, Elizabeth Evelyn Williams (marr. diss., 1942); 2nd, 1943, Iris Christine Truscott; one *s* one *d* . *Educ:* Lancing; Oriel Coll., Oxford (MA). Called to the Bar, 1938. Served War of 1939-45: RAF, Sept. 1939; Pilot, 1942. Returned to the Bar, Sept. 1945; Bencher, Middle Temple, Nov. 1967. *Publication:* Eversley on Domestic Relations, 1951. *Recreations:* photography, history. *Address:* 18 Chelmsford Square, Brondesbury Park, NW10 3AR. *T:* 01-459 3757.

STRANGWAYS; *see* Fox-Strangways, family name of Earl of Ilchester.

STRANKS, Ven. Charles James; Archdeacon of Auckland, 1958-73, now Emeritus; 10th Canon of Durham, 1958-73; *b* 10 May 1901; *s* of Joseph and Elizabeth Stranks; *m* 1930, Elsie Lilian, *d* of John and Anne Buckley; two *s*. *Educ:* St Chad's Coll., Durham; St Boniface Coll., Warminster. BA, 1925; MA and Diploma in Theology, 1928; MLitt, 1937. Curate of All Saints, Leeds, 1926-28; Missionary, Dio. Kobe, Japan, 1928-40; Examining Chaplain to Bishop in Kobe, 1938-40; SPG Organizing Sec., 1940-41; Vicar of St Barnabas, Morecambe, 1941-47; Warden of Whalley Abbey, Canon of Blackburn, and Dir of Relig. Educ., 1947-54; Proctor in Convocation for Archdeaconry of Blackburn, 1949-54; Sixth Canon of Durham Cathedral, 1954. Chm., Lord Crewe's Trustees, 1963-74. *Publications:* The Apostle of the Indies, 1933; Japan in the World Crisis, 1941; The Approach to Belief, 1947; Our Task Today, 1950; The Life and Writings of Jeremy Taylor, 1952; Dean Hook, 1954; Anglican Devotion, 1961; Country Boy: The Autobiography of Richard Hillyer, 1966; (ed) The Path of Glory: The Autobiography of John Shipp, 1969; This Sumptuous Church: the story of Durham Cathedral, 1973; contrib. Encyclopædia Britannica. *Recreations:* walking, gardening. *Address:* 1 The Corner House, Shincliffe Village, Durham. *T:* Durham 2719. *Club:* Royal Commonwealth Society.

STRASSER, Sir Paul, Kt 1973; Chairman, Bridge Oil Ltd; *b* 22 Sept. 1911; *s* of Eugene Strasser and Elizabeth Klein de Ney; *m* 1935, Veronica Gero; one *s*. *Educ:* Univ. of Budapest. Dr of Law, 1933; practised in Hungary for 10 yrs; emigrated to Australia, 1948. Career in fields of construction, mining and oil exploration, hotel and motel chains, meat processing and exporting, merchant banking. Associated with and promoter of several charitable foundns, etc, incl. Jewish Residential Coll. at Univ. of NSW and Children's Surgical Research Fund. *Recreations:* playing bridge, swimming, reading. *Address:* 8 Carrington Avenue, Bellevue Hill, Sydney, NSW 2023, Australia. *T:* 36-6407. *Clubs:* American, Sydney Turf (Sydney).

STRATFORD, Neil Martin; Keeper of Medieval and Later Antiquities, British Museum, since 1975; *b* 26 April 1938; *s* of Dr Martin Gould Stratford and Dr Mavis Stratford (*née* Beddall); *m* 1966, Anita Jennifer Lewis; two *d* . *Educ:* Marlborough Coll.; Magdalene Coll., Cambridge (BA Hons English 1961, MA); Courtauld Inst., London Univ. (BA Hons History of Art 1966). 2nd Lieut Coldstream Guards, 1956-58; Trainee Kleinwort, Benson, Lonsdale Ltd, 1961-63; Lecturer Westfield Coll., London Univ., 1969-75. Liveryman, Haberdashers' Company 1959-. Hon. Mem., Académie de Dijon, 1975. *Publications:* articles in French and English periodicals. *Recreations:* opera, food and wine, cricket and football. *Address:* 17 Church Row, NW3. *T:* 01-794 5688. *Clubs:* MCC, I Zingari; University Pitt, Hawks (Cambridge).

STRATHALLAN, Viscount; John Eric Drummond; *b* 7 July 1935; *e s* of 17th Earl of Perth, *qv*; *m* 1963, Margaret Ann (marr. diss.), *o d* of Robin Gordon; two *s*. *Heir: s* Hon. James David Drummond, *b* 24 Oct. 1965. *Address:* Stobhall, by Perth.

STRATHALMOND, 3rd Baron *cr* 1955; **William Roberton Fraser;** *b* 22 July 1947; *s* of 2nd Baron Strathalmond, CMG, OBE, TD, and of Letitia, *d* of late Walter Krementz, New Jersey, USA; *S* father, 1976; *m* 1973, Amanda Rose, *yr d* of Rev. Gordon Clifford Taylor; one *s*. *Educ:* Loretto. *Heir: s* Hon. William Gordon Fraser, *b* 24 Sept. 1976. *Address:* 36 Pyrmont Road, W4 3NR.

STRATHCARRON, 2nd Baron, *cr* 1936, of Banchor; **David William Anthony Blyth Macpherson;** Bt, *cr* 1933; Partner, Strathcarron & Co.; Director: Kirchhoff (East Africa) Ltd; Kirchhoff (London) Ltd; Seabourne Shipping Co.; Dorada Holdings Ltd; Forster and Hales Ltd; *b* 23 Jan. 1924; *s* of 1st Baron and Jill (*d* 1956), *o d* of Sir George Rhodes, 1st Bt; *S* father, 1937; *m* 1st, 1947, Valerie Cole (marr. annulled on his petition, 1947); 2nd, 1948, Mrs Diana Hawtrey Curle (*d* 1973), *o d* of Comdr R. H. Deane; two *s*; 3rd 1974, Mrs Eve Samuel, *o d* of late J. C. Higgins, CIE. *Educ:* Eton; Jesus College, Cambridge. Served War of 1939-45, RAFVR, 1942-47. Motoring Correspondent of The Field. Member, British Parly Delegn to Austria, 1964. President: Guild of Motoring Writers; Inst. of Freight Forwarders, 1974-75. *Publication:* Motoring for Pleasure, 1963. *Recreations:* motor-racing, flying, golf. *Heir: s* Hon. Ian David Patrick Macpherson, *b* 31 March 1949. *Address:* 55 Cumberland Terrace, Regent's Park, NW1. *T:* 01-935 5913; Otterwood, Beaulieu, Hants. *T:* Beaulieu 612334. *Clubs:* Boodle's, Royal Air Force.

STRATHCLYDE, 1st Baron, *cr* 1955, of Barskimming; **Thomas Dunlop Galbraith,** PC 1953; Commander, Royal Navy, retired; *b* 20 March 1891; 2nd *s* of William Brodie Galbraith, JP, CA, Glasgow, and Annie Dunlop; *m* 1915, Ida, *e d* of Thomas Galloway, Auchendrane, Ayrshire; four *s* (and one killed in action, 1940), two *d. Educ:* Glasgow Academy; RN Colleges, Osborne and Dartmouth. Entered Royal Navy, 1903; served throughout European War, 1914-18, in HMS Audacious and HMS Queen Elizabeth; RN Staff College, Greenwich, 1920-22; retired 1922; War of 1939-45, on Staff of C-in-C Coast of Scotland, 1939-40; Deputy British Admiralty Supply Representative in USA, 1940-42. MP (Nat. C) for Pollok Div. of Glasgow, 1940-April 1955; Jt Parly Under-Sec. of State for Scotland, 1945 and 1951-55; Minister of State, Scottish Office, 1955-58, resigned; Chm., North of Scotland Hydro-Electric Board, 1959-67; Mem., South of Scotland Electricity Board, 1965-67. Chartered Accountant, 1925; Partner Galbraith, Dunlop & Co., CA, Glasgow, 1925-70; Member of Corporation of Glasgow, 1933-40; Magistrate, 1938-40. President, Electrical Research Association, 1965-66. Hon. FRCPE; Hon. FRCPSGlas; a Governor of Wellington College, 1948-61; Hon. Governor, Glasgow Academy. Freedom of Dingwall, 1965; Freedom of Aberdeen, 1966. *Heir: s* Hon. Thomas Galloway Dunlop Galbraith, *qv. Address:* Barskimming, Mauchline, Ayrshire. *Clubs:* Carlton, Naval and Military; New (Edinburgh); Western (Glasgow).

STRATHCONA and MOUNT ROYAL, 4th Baron, *cr* 1900; **Donald Euan Palmer Howard;** Joint Deputy Leader of the Opposition, House of Lords, since 1976; *b* 26 Nov. 1923; *s* of 3rd Baron Strathcona and Mount Royal and Diana Evelyn, twin *d* of 1st Baron Wakehurst; *S* father 1959; *m* 1954, Lady Jane Mary Waldegrave (marr. diss. 1977), 2nd *d* of Earl Waldegrave, *qv*; two *s* four *d. Educ:* King's Mead, Seaford; Eton; Trinity Coll., Cambridge; McGill University, Montreal (1947-50). Served War of 1939-45: RN, 1942-47: Midshipman, RNVR, 1943; Lieutenant, 1945. With Urwick, Orr and Partners (Industrial Consultants), 1950-56. Lord in Waiting (Govt Whip), 1973-74; Parly Under-Sec. of State for Defence (RAF), MoD, 1974. Chairman, Bath Festival Society, 1966-70. Dep. Chm., SS Great Britain Project, 1970-73. *Recreations:* gardening, sailing. *Heir: s* Hon. Donald Alexander Smith Howard, *b* 24 June 1961. *Address:* 89 Barkston Gardens, SW5 0EU. *T:* 01-370 5180; Kiloran, Isle of Colonsay, Scotland. *T:* Colonsay 301. *Club:* Brooks's.

STRATHEDEN, 4th Baron, *cr* 1836, **and CAMPBELL,** 4th Baron, *cr* 1841; **Alastair Campbell,** CBE 1964; *b* 21 Nov. 1899; *s* of late Hon. John Beresford Campbell and Hon. Alice Susan Hamilton (*d* 1949), *d* of 1st Baron Hamilton of Dalzell; *S* grandfather, 1918; *m* 1st, 1923, Jean, CBE 1954 (*d* 1956), *o d* of late Col W. Anstruther-Gray; three *d*; 2nd, 1964, Mrs Noël Vincent. *Educ:* Eton; Sandhurst. Joined Coldstream Guards, 1919; Regimental Adjutant, 1931-34; Staff Officer Local Forces, Kenya and Uganda, 1936-39; Lt-Col, 1941; served War of 1939-45 (wounded, despatches); Regtl Lt-Col, 1945-46; Brig., 1946; Comd 32nd Guards Bde, 1946, 4th Inf. Bde, 1947-49; Deputy Director Personal Services, War Office, 1949; retired 1950. Captain, Royal Company of Archers, Queen's Body Guard for Scotland. Chm. Roxburgh, Berwick and Selkirk-shires T&AFA, 1958-63; Chm. Edinburgh and E of Scotland Coll. of Agriculture, 1956-70; Chm. Hill Farming Research Organisation, 1958-69; Convener Roxburgh County Council, 1960-68; Pres., Assoc. of County Councils in Scotland, 1966-68. Chm., Historic Buildings Council for Scotland, 1969-76. DL Roxburgh, 1946, Vice-Lieutenant, 1962-75. Hon. LLD Edinburgh Univ. *Heir: b* Major Hon. Gavin Campbell, late KRRC [*b* 28 Aug. 1901; *m* 1933, Evelyn, *d* of late Col H. A. Smith, CIE; one *s*]. *Address:* Hunthill, Jedburgh, Scotland. *T:* Jedburgh 2413. *Clubs:* Cavalry and Guards; New (Edinburgh). *See also Hon. Nicholas Ridley.*

STRATHMORE and KINGHORNE, 17th Earl of, *cr* 1677; Earl (UK), *cr* 1937; **Fergus Michael Claude Bowes Lyon;** DL; Baron Glamis (Scot.), 1445; Earl of Kinghorne, Lord Lyon, Baron Glamis, 1606; Viscount Lyon, Lord Glamis, Tannadyce, Sydlaw, and Strathdichtie, 1677; Baron Bowes (UK), 1887; *b* 31 Dec. 1928; *e s* of Hon. Michael Claude Hamilton Bowes Lyon (5th *s* of 14th Earl) (*d* 1953), and Elizabeth Margaret (*d* 1959), *d* of late John Cator; *S* cousin, 1972; *m* 1956, Mary Pamela, *d* of Brig. Norman Duncan McCorquodale, MC; one *s* two *d. Educ:* Eton; RMA, Sandhurst. Commissioned Scots Guards, 1949; Captain 1953; transferred to RARO, 1961. Member of Edinburgh Stock Exchange, 1963. Member of Royal Company of Archers, Queen's Body Guard for Scotland. DL Angus, 1973. *Recreations:* shooting, fishing. *Heir: s* Lord Glamis, *qv. Address:* Glamis Castle, Forfar, Angus. *T:* Glamis 244. *Clubs:* White's, Pratt's; New (Edinburgh).

STRATHNAVER, Lord; Alistair Charles St Clair Sutherland; Master of Sutherland; *b* 7 Jan. 1947; *e s* of Charles Noel Janson, DL, and the Countess of Sutherland, *qv*; *heir* to mother's titles; *m* 1968, Eileen Elizabeth, *o d* of Richard Wheeler Baker, Jr, Princeton, NJ; two *d. Educ:* Eton; Christ Church, Oxford. BA. Metropolitan Police, 1969-74.

STRATHSPEY, 5th Baron, *cr* 1884; **Donald Patrick Trevor Grant of Grant,** 17th Bt, of Nova Scotia, *cr* 1625; 32nd Chief of Grant; Lieutenant-Colonel retired; *b* 18 March 1912; *s* of 4th Baron and Alice Louisa (*d* 1945), *d* of T. M. Hardy-Johnston, MICE London, of Christchurch, NZ; *S* father, 1948; *m* 1st, 1938, Alice (marr. diss. 1951), *o c* of late Francis Bowe, Timaru, NZ; one *s* two *d*; 2nd, 1951, Olive, *d* of W. H. Grant, Norwich; one *s* one *d. Educ:* Stowe Sch.; South Eastern Agricultural Coll. War Dept Land Agent and Valuer, Portsmouth, 1944-48; Command Land Agent, HQ Scottish Command, 1948-60; Asst Chief Land Agent and Valuer, War Office, 1960-63; Command Land Agent, HQ Cyprus District, 1963-64; Asst Director of Lands, NW Europe, 1964-66; Asst Chief Land Agent, MoD HQ, 1966-72. Associate, Land Agents' Soc. Fellow, Royal Institution of Chartered Surveyors, retd 1972. Member: Standing Council of Scottish Chiefs; Highland Soc. of London; West Wittering Horticultural Soc.; Hon. Member: Los Angeles Saint Andrew's Soc.; Mark Twain Soc., Missouri; Patron, American Scottish Foundn. Defence Medal; Coronation medal. *Recreations:* yachting, gardening. *Heir: s* Hon. James Patrick Grant of Grant, *b* 9 Sept. 1943. *Address:* Elms Cottage, Elms Ride, West Wittering, West Sussex. *Clubs:* Lancia Motor, House of Lords Motor, Civil Service Motoring Association, West Wittering Sailing.

STRATTEN, Thomas Price; President, Union Corporation Limited, since 1972 (Managing Director, 1954-67; Chairman, 1962-72); *b* Kimberley, Cape Province, S Africa, 4 June 1904; *m* 1930, Mary A. Morris, New York, USA; two *s* one *d. Educ:* University of Cape Town; Balliol College, Oxford (Rhodes Scholar). Dir of War Supplies, S Africa, 1940-45. Director: Charter Consolidated Ltd, 1972; South African Reserve Bank, 1966-72; Comr, Electricity Supply Commission, 1954-69. Past President, Associated Scientific and Technical Societies of South Africa; Past President and Hon. Member, S African Inst. of Electrical Engrs. Hon. LLD, Univ. of Witwatersrand, 1966. *Recreation:* golf. *Address:* (home) 16 Pallinghurst Road, Westcliff, Johannesburg, South Africa; (office) 74-78 Marshall Street, Johannesburg. *Clubs:* Rand, Johannesburg Country, Royal Johannesburg Golf (Johannesburg).

STRATTON, Andrew, MSc, FInstP, CEng, FIEE, FInstNav, FIMA; Under Secretary, Ministry of Defence, on secondment as Consultant to Imperial Chemical Industries Ltd, since 1977; *b* 5 Sept. 1918; *m* 1949, Ruth Deutsch; one *s* one *d. Educ:* Skinners' Company Sch., Tunbridge Wells; University Coll. of the South West, Exeter; Univ. of London (BSc 1st cl. Hons Physics). RAE Farnborough: Air Defence and Armament Depts, 1939-54; Supt, Instruments and Inertial Navigation Div., 1954-62; Head of Weapon Research and Assessment Group, 1962-66; Prof. and Head of Maths Dept, Coll. of Aeronautics, Cranfield, 1966-68; Dir, Defence Operational Analysis Estabt, 1968-76. Faraday Lecture, IEE, 1972-73. Former Chm. and Mem. of Cttees, Aeronautical and Electronics Research Councils; Mem., Home Office Scientific Adv. Council. Pres., Inst. of Navigation, 1967-70; Chm. of Convocation, Univ. of Exeter. Hon. DSc Exeter, 1972. Hodgson Prize, RAeS, 1969; Bronze Medal, 1971 and 1975, Gold Medal, 1973, Royal Inst of Navigation. US Medal of Freedom with Bronze Palm, 1947. *Publications:* contrib. to Unless Peace Comes, 1968; to The Future of Aeronautics, 1970; papers on aircraft instruments, navigation, air traffic, operational analysis in Jl IEE, Jl IMechE, Jl RAeS, Jl Inst. Navigation. *Recreations:* painting, rambling. *Address:* Chartley, 39 Salisbury Road, Farnborough, Hants. *T:* Farnborough 42514.

STRATTON, Ven. Basil; Archdeacon of Stafford and Canon Residentiary of Lichfield Cathedral, 1959-April 1974; Archdeacon Emeritus, since 1974; Chaplain to the Queen, 1965-76; *b* 1906; *s* of Reverend Samuel Henry Stratton and Kate Mabel Stratton; *m* 1934, Euphemia Frances Stuart; one *s* three *d. Educ:* Lincoln School; Hatfield College, Durham University. Deacon 1930; Priest 1931; Curate, St Stephen's, Grimsby, 1930-32; SPG Missionary, India, 1932-34; Indian Ecclesiastical Establishment, 1935-47. Chaplain to the Forces on service in Iraq, India, Burma and Malaya, 1941-46 (despatches); officiated as Chaplain-General in India, 1946. Vicar of Figheldean with Milston, Wilts, 1948-53; Vicar of Market Drayton, Shropshire, 1953-59. *Address:* Woodlands Cottage, Mere, Wilts. *T:* Mere 235. *Club:* Army and Navy.

STRATTON, Julius Adams, ScD; President Emeritus, Massachusetts Institute of Technology; *b* Seattle, 18 May 1901; *s* of Julius A. Stratton and Laura (*née* Adams); *m* 1935, Catherine N. Coffman; three *d. Educ:* Univ. of Washington; Mass Inst. of Technology (SB, SM); Eidgenössische Technische Hochschule, Zurich (ScD). Expert Consultant, Sec. of War, 1942-46. MIT: Res. Assoc. in Communications, 1924-26; Asst Prof., Electrical Engrg, 1928-31; Asst Prof., Physics, 1931-35; Assoc. Prof., Physics, 1935-41; Prof., Physics, 1941-51; Mem. Staff, Radiation Lab., 1940-45; Dir, Res. Lab. of Electronics, 1945-49; Provost, 1949-56; Vice-Pres., 1951-56; Chancellor, 1956-59; Actg Pres., 1957-59; Pres., 1959-66; Pres. Emer., 1966-. Chm. of Board, Ford Foundn, 1966-71. Chm., Commn on Marine Science, Engrg and Resources, 1967-69. Life Mem. Corp., MIT; Trustee, Boston Museum of Science. Hon. FIEEE; Fellow: Amer. Acad. of Arts and Scis; Amer. Phys. Soc.; Member: Amer. Philos. Soc.; Council on For. Relations, Nat. Acad. of Engrg; Nat. Acad. of Scis; Sigma Xi; Tau Beta Pi; Zeta Psi; Eminent Mem., Eta Kappa Nu. Hon. Fellow, Coll. of Science and Technology, Manchester, England, 1963; Hon. Mem. Senate, Technical Univ. of Berlin, 1966. Holds numerous hon. doctorates of Engrg, Humane Letters, Laws and Science incl. DSc: Leeds, 1967; Heriot-Watt, 1971; ScD Cantab 1972. Medal for Merit, 1946; Certif. of Award, US Navy, 1957; Medal of Honor, Inst. Radio Engrs, 1957; Faraday Medal, IEE (England), 1961; Boston Medal for Distinguished Achievement, 1966. Officer, Legion of Honour, France, 1961; Orden de Boyacá, Colombia, 1964; Kt Comdr, Order of Merit, Germany, 1966. *Publications:* Electromagnetic Theory, 1941; Science and the Educated Man, 1966; numerous papers in scientific and professional jls. *Address:* (home) 100 Memorial Drive, Cambridge, Mass 02142, USA; (office) Massachusetts Institute of Technology, Cambridge, Mass 02139. *Clubs:* Century Association, University (New York); St Botolph (Boston).

STRATTON, Richard James, CMG 1974; HM Diplomatic Service; Assistant Under-Secretary of State, Foreign and Commonwealth Office, since 1977; *b* 16 July 1924; *s* of William Henry and Cicely Muriel Stratton. *Educ:* The King's Sch., Rochester; Merton Coll., Oxford. Served in Coldstream Guards, 1943-46. Joined Foreign Service, Oct. 1947; British Embassy, Rio de Janeiro, 1948-50; FO, 1951-53; British Embassy, Tokyo, March-Aug. 1953; British Legation, Seoul, 1953-55; Private Sec. to Parly Under-Sec. of State, FO, Nov. 1955-Feb. 1958; NATO Defence Coll., Paris, Feb.-Aug. 1958; British Embassy, Bonn, Sept. 1958-July 1960; British Embassy, Abidjan, Ivory Coast, Aug.-1960-Feb. 1962; Private Sec. to Lord Carrington, as Minister without Portfolio, FO, 1963-64; to Minister of State for Foreign Affairs, 1964-66; Counsellor, British High Commn, Rawalpindi, 1966-69; IDC, 1970; FCO, 1971-72; Political Adviser to Govt of Hong Kong, 1972-74; HM Ambassador: to Republic of Zaire and People's Republic of the Congo, 1974-77; to Republic of Burundi, 1975-77; to Rwandan Republic, 1977. *Recreations:* tennis, bridge. *Address:* c/o Foreign and Commonwealth Office, SW1. *Club:* Travellers'.

STRATTON, Mrs Roy Olin; see Dickens, Monica Enid.

STRATTON, Air Vice-Marshal William Hector, CB 1970; CBE 1963; DFC 1939 and Bar 1944; company director; Chief of the Air Staff, RNZAF, 1969-71, retired 1971; *b* 22 July 1916; *s* of V. J. Stratton; *m* 1954, Dorothy M., *d* of J. D. Whyte; one *s* two *d. Educ:* Hawera Tech. High School, and privately. RAF, 1937-44. Appointments include: in comd RNZAF, Ohakea; Air Member for Personnel; assistant chief of Air Staff; Head NZ Defence Staff, Canberra; Head NZ Defence Staff, London. *Address:* 62 Paramatta Road, Doubleview, Perth, WA 6018, Australia.

STRATTON, Lt-Gen. Sir William (Henry), KCB 1957 (CB 1948); CVO 1944; CBE 1943; DSO 1945; *b* 1903; *o s* of late Lt-Col H. W. Stratton, OBE; *m* 1930, Noreen Mabel Brabazon, *d* of late Dr and Mrs F. H. B. Noble, Sittingbourne, Kent; no *c. Educ:* Dulwich Coll.; RMA, Woolwich. 2nd Lieut RE 1924; psc; Lt-Col (temp.), 1940; Brig. (temp.), 1941; Col 1945; ide 1946; Maj.-Gen. 1947; Chief of Staff, BAOR, 1947-49; Comdt Joint Services Staff Coll., 1949-52; Commander British Army Staff, and Military Member British Joint Services Mission, Washington, 1952-53; Comdr 42 (Lancs) Inf. Div. (TA), 1953-55; Lt-Gen. 1955; Commander, British Forces, Hong Kong, 1955-57; Vice-Chief of the Imperial General Staff, 1957-60, retired. Col Comdt RE, 1960-68; Inspector-General of Civil Defence, Home Office, 1960-62. Chairman: Edwin Danks (Oldbury) Ltd, 1961-71; Penman & Co. Ltd, 1961-71; Babcock-Moxey Ltd, 1965-71.

STRAUSS, Claude L.; see Levi-Strauss.

STRAUSS, Franz Josef; Grand Cross, Order of Merit, Federal Republic of Germany; Member of Bundestag, Federal Republic of Germany, since 1949; President, Christian Social Union (CSU), since 1961; *b* Munich, 6 Sept. 1915; *s* of Franz Josef Strauss and Walburga (*née* Schiessl); *m* 1957, Marianne (*née* Zwicknagl); two *s* one *d. Educ:* Gymnasium, Munich; Munich Univ. Served in War of 1939-45, Lieut. In Bavarian State Govt, 1946-49; Pres., Govt Cttee on Youth in Bavaria, 1946-49; Minister for Special Tasks, 1953-55; Minister for Atomic Questions, 1955-56; Minister of Defence, 1956-62; Minister of Finance, 1966-69. President: Landrat (County Commissioner) of Schongau, 1946-49; Committee on Questions of European Security. Dr *hc*: Detroit University, USA, 1956; Kalamazoo College, 1962; Case Institute of Technology, Cleveland (Ohio), 1962; De Paul University, Chicago, 1964. Holds decorations from other European countries. *Publications:* The Grand Design, 1965; Herausforderung und Antwort, 1968; Challenge and Response: A programme for Europe, 1969; Finanzpolitik: Theorie und Wirklichkeit, 1969; many articles on political affairs in newspapers and periodicals. *Address:* Lazarettstrasse 33, Munich, Germany. *T:* 123-215.

STRAUSS, Rt. Hon. George Russell, PC 1947; MP (Lab) for Vauxhall Division of Lambeth since 1950 (North Lambeth, 1929-31 and 1934-50); *b* 18 July 1901; *s* of Arthur Strauss, formerly MP (C) Camborne Div. of Cornwall and N Paddington; *m* 1932, Patricia O'Flynn (*see* P. F. Strauss); two *s* one *d. Educ:* Rugby. PPS to Minister of Transport, 1929-31, to Lord Privy Seal, and later Minister of Aircraft Production, 1942-45; Parly Sec., Min. of Transport, 1945-47; Minister of Supply, 1947-51 (introd. Iron and Steel Nationalisation Bill, 1949). CC Representative: N Lambeth, 1925-31; SE Southwark, 1932-46; LCC Chm. Highways Cttee, 1934-37; Vice-Chm. Finance Cttee, 1934-37; Chm. Supplies Cttee, 1937-39; Mem. London and Home Counties Traffic Advisory Cttee, 1934-39. Introduced Theatres Bill for the abolition of stage censorship, 1968. Father of the House of Commons, 1974. *Recreations:* painting and chess. *Address:* 1 Palace Green, W8. *T:* 01-937 1630; Naylands, Slaugham, West Sussex. *T:* Handcross 270.

STRAUSS, Hon. Jacobus Gideon Nel, QC (South Africa) 1944; Leader of the South African United Party, 1950-56; MP for Germiston District 1932-57; *b* Calvinia CP, 17 Dec. 1900; *s* of late H. J. Strauss; *m* 1928, Joy Carpenter; two *s* two *d* (and one *s* decd). *Educ:* Calvinia High Sch.; Univ. of Cape Town; Univ. of South Africa. Private Sec. to the Prime Minister (General J. C. Smuts), 1923-24; practice at Johannesburg Bar, 1926-53; Minister of Agriculture and Forestry in Smuts Cabinet, 1944; succeeded Field Marshal J. C. Smuts as Leader of the Opposition, 1950. *Recreations:* riding, mountaineering and golf. *Address:* PO Box 67398, Bryanston, Transvaal 2021, South Africa. *Clubs:* Rand, Royal Johannesburg Golf (Johannesburg); Bryanston Country; City (Cape Town).

STRAUSS, Patricia Frances, (Mrs G. R. Strauss); Governor: the Old Vic since 1951; Sadler's Wells Theatre since 1951; St Martin's School of Art, since 1952; the Royal Ballet since 1957; Whitechapel Art Gallery since 1957; Ballet Rambert, since 1958; London Opera Centre, since 1965; Sadler's Wells Opera (Coliseum), since 1968; Goldsmith School of Art, since 1969; *b* 21 Oct. 1909; *m* 1932, Rt Hon. George Russell Strauss, *qv*; two *s* one *d.* Member of London County Council, 1946-58; Chairman: Parks Cttee (LCC), 1947-49; Supplies Cttee (LCC), 1949-52. Contested (Lab) South Kensington, Parliamentary General Election, 1945. Governor, Royal Ballet Sch., 1951-72. *Publications:* Bevin and Co., 1941; Cripps, Advocate and Rebel, 1942. *Recreations:* painting, chess, foreign travel. *Address:* 1 Palace Green, W8. *T:* 01-937 1630; Naylands, Slaugham, Sussex. *T:* Handcross 270.

STRAW, Jack, (John Whitaker Straw); Barrister-at-law; *b* 3 Aug. 1946; *s* of Walter Arthur Whitaker Straw and of Joan Sylvia Straw; *m* 1968, Anthea Lilian Weston; one *d* (decd). *Educ:* Brentwood Sch., Essex; Univ. of Leeds. LLB 1967. Called to Bar, Inner Temple, 1972. Political Advr to Sec. of State for Social Services, 1974-76; Special Advr to Sec. of State for Environment, 976-77. Pres., Leeds Univ. Union, 1967-68; Pres., Nat. Union of Students, 1969-71; Mem., Islington Borough Council, 1971-; Dep. Leader, Inner London Educn Authority, 1973-74; Mem., Labour Party's Nat. Exec. Sub-Cttee on Educn and Science, 1970-; Mem., Social Morality Council Enquiry into Future of Broadcasting, 1973; Chm., Jt Adv. Cttee on Polytechnics of N London, 1973-75. Contested (Lab) Tonbridge and Malling, Feb. 1974; Prospective Parly Cand. (Lab), Blackburn, 1977-. *Publications:* Granada Guildhall Lecture, 1969; contrib. pamphlets, articles. *Recreations:* cycling, walking, tennis. *Address:* 31 Battledean Road, N5 1UX; Francis Taylor Building, Temple, EC4.

STRAWSON, Maj.-Gen. John Michael, CB 1975; OBE 1964; idc, jssc, psc; Head of Cairo office, Westland Aircraft Ltd, since 1976; *b* 1 Jan. 1921; *s* of late Cyril Walter and Nellie Dora Strawson; *m* 1960, Baroness Wilfried von Schellersheim; two *d*. *Educ:* Christ's Coll., Finchley. Joined Army, 1940; commnd, 1942; served with 4th QO Hussars in Middle East, Italy, Germany, Malaya, 1942-50, 1953-54, 1956-58; Staff Coll., Camberley, 1950; Bde Major, 1951-53; Instructor, Staff Coll. and Master of Drag Hounds, 1958-60; GSO1 and Col GS in WO and MoD, 1961-62 and 1965-66; comd QR Irish Hussars, Malaysia and BAOR, 1963-65; comd 39 Inf. Bde, 1967-68; idc 1969; COS, Live Oak, SHAPE, 1970-72; COS, HQ UKLF, 1972-76. Col, Queen's Royal Irish Hussars, 1975-. US Bronze Star, 1945. *Publications:* The Battle for North Africa, 1969; Hitler as Military Commander, 1971; The Battle for the Ardennes, 1972; The Battle for Berlin, 1974; contribs to The Times, Blackwood's Magazine, Army Quarterly, RUSI Jl. *Recreations:* equitation, golf, reading. *Address:* The Old Rectory, Boyton, Warminster, Wilts BA12 0SS. *Club:* Cavalry and Guards.
   See also Sir P . F . Strawson .

STRAWSON, Sir Peter (Frederick), Kt 1977; FBA 1960; Fellow of University College, Oxford, 1948-Aug. 1968, subsequently Fellow of Magdalen College; Waynflete Professor of Metaphysical Philosophy in the University of Oxford, since Aug. 1968 (Reader 1966-68); *b* 23 November 1919; *s* of late Cyril Walter and Nellie Dora Strawson; *m* 1945, Grace Hall Martin; two *s* two *d*. *Educ:* Christ's College, Finchley; St John's College, Oxford (scholar; Hon. Fellow, 1973). Served War of 1939-45, RA, REME, Capt. Asst Lecturer in Philosophy, University Coll. of N. Wales, 1946; John Locke Schol., Univ. of Oxford, 1946; Lecturer in Philosophy, 1947, Fellow and Praelector, 1948, University Coll., Oxford. Vis. Prof., Duke Univ., N Carolina, 1955-56; Fellow of Humanities Council and Vis. Associate Prof., Princeton Univ., 1960-61, Vis. Prof., 1972. For. Hon. Mem., Amer. Acad. Arts and Scis, 1971. *Publications:* Introduction to Logical Theory, 1952; Individuals, 1959; The Bounds of Sense, 1966; (ed) Philosophical Logic, 1967; (ed) Studies in the Philosophy of Thought and Action, 1968; Logico-Linguistic Papers, 1971; Freedom and Resentment, 1974; Subject and Predicate in Logic and Grammar, 1974; contrib. to Mind, Philosophy, Proc. Aristotelian Soc., Philosophical Review, etc. *Address:* 25 Farndon Road, Oxford. *T:* Oxford 55026.
   See also J. M. Strawson.

STREAT, Sir (Edward) Raymond, KBE 1957 (CBE 1930); Kt 1942; Member, Court of Governors, Manchester University (Member Council, 1943-72, Chairman, 1957-65, Treasurer, 1951-57); Hon. Fellow, Nuffield College, Oxford (Visiting Fellow, 1944-59); Vice-President, Lancashire and Merseyside Industrial Development Association, 1946-75; Trustee, John Rylands Library, 1960-75; *b* 7 Feb. 1897; *s* of late Edward Streat, Prestwich; *m* Doris (*d* 1976), *d* of late Amos Davies, JP; two *s* (and one *s* died of wounds, 1944). *Educ:* Manchester Grammar School. Lt 10th Manchester Regiment (TA), 1915-18; Assistant Secretary, Manchester Chamber of Commerce, 1919; Director and Secretary, 1920-40; Hon. Director, Lancashire Industrial Development Council, 1931-40; Chairman, The Cotton Board, Manchester, 1940-57; President, Manchester Statistical Soc., 1936-38; President, Association of Technical Institutions, 1944-45; Secretary, Export Council, Board of Trade, Jan.-June 1940; Member, Advisory Council, DSIR, 1942-47; President, Manchester Luncheon Club, 1946-47; Pres., the Textile Institute, 1946-48; Chairman: Manchester Joint Research Council, 1948-51; N-Western Electricity Consultative Council, 1960-68; Member, Gen. Advisory Council, BBC, 1947-52. Hon. LLD, Manchester University, 1963. Commander of Order of Orange Nassau (Netherlands). *Address:* 4 Mill Street, Eynsham, Oxford. *T:* Oxford 881562.

STREATFEILD, Sir Geoffrey Hugh Benbow, Kt 1947; MC; Judge of the High Court of Justice, Queen's Bench Division, 1947-66; *b* 28 July 1897; *yr s* of late Maj. H. S. Streatfeild, Ryhope, Co. Durham, and Barlay, Balmaclellan, Kirkcudbrightshire; *m* 1918, Marjorie, *yr d* of late Charles Booth, Sunderland; three *d*. *Educ:* Rugby School. Served with 4th Batt. Durham Light Infantry and Royal Flying Corps and RAF, 1914-19, Capt. 1917 (MC); called to Bar, Inner Temple, 1921; KC 1938. Joined North Eastern Circuit, 1922; Recorder of Rotherham, 1932-34; Huddersfield, 1934-43; Kingston-upon-Hull, 1943-47; Solicitor-General and Attorney General of the County Palatine of Durham, 1939-47; Bencher of the Inner Temple, 1945; Major (Deputy Judge Advocate), 1940; Lt-Col Asst Judge Advocate-General, 1942-43; Comr of Assize, Western Circuit, 1946. Chairman, Inter-Departmental Cttee on the Business of the Criminal Courts, 1958-60; Deputy

Chairman, Somerset Quarter Sessions. Hon. DCL Durham Univ., 1957. *Address:* Cheddon Corner, Cheddon Fitzpaine, Taunton, Somerset. *T:* Kingston St Mary 277.

STREATFEILD, Noel; Novelist; *d* of late William Champion Streatfeild, Bishop of Lewes and late Janet Mary Venn; *b* 24 Dec. 1895. unmarried. *Educ:* Laleham; Eastbourne. *Publications:* Whicharts, 1931; Parson's Nine, 1932; Tops and Bottoms, 1933; Children's Matinee, 1934; Shepherdess of Sheep, 1934; Ballet Shoes, 1936; It Pays to be Good, 1936; Wisdom Teeth: a play, 1936; Tennis Shoes, 1937; Caroline England, 1937; Circus is Coming (Carnegie Gold Medal), 1938; Luke, 1940; Secret of the Lodge, 1940; House in Cornwall, 1940; Children of Primrose Lane, 1941; Winter is Past, 1942; I Ordered a Table for Six, 1942; Myra Carrol, 1944; Curtain Up, 1944; Saplings, 1945; Party Frock, 1946; Grass in Piccadilly, 1947; Painted Garden, 1949; Mothering Sunday, 1950; (ed) Years of Grace, 1950; White Boots, 1951; Aunt Clara, 1952; (ed) By Special Request, 1953; The Fearless Treasure, 1953, new edn, 1963; The First Book of Ballet, 1953 (US), rev. edn, 1963 (UK); The Bell Family, 1954; (ed) Growing Up Gracefully, 1955; The Grey Family, 1956; Judith, 1956; (ed) The Day Before Yesterday, 1956; Wintles Wonders, 1957; Magic and the Magician, 1958; Bertram, 1959; The Royal Ballet School, 1959; The Ballet Annual, 1960; Christmas with the Crystals, 1960; Look at the Circus, 1960; New Town, 1960; Queen Victoria, 1961; The Silent Speaker, 1961; Apple Bough, 1962; Lisa Goes to Russia, 1963; A Vicarage Family (autobiog.), 1963; The Children on the Top Floor, 1964; Away from the Vicarage (autobiog.), 1965; Let's Go Coaching, 1965; Enjoying Opera, 1966; The Growing Summer, 1966; Old Chairs to Mend, 1966; The Thames, 1966; Before Confirmation, 1967; Caldicott Place, 1967; The Barrow Lane Gang, 1968; (ed) Nicholas, 1968; Red Riding Hood, 1970; Thursday's Child, 1970; Beyond the Vicarage (autobiog.), 1971; The First Book of Shoes, 1971; Ballet Shoes for Anna, 1972; The Boy Pharaoh, Tutankhamen, 1972; When the Siren Wailed, 1974; Gran-Nannie, 1976; Far To Go, 1976. *Recreation:* wild flowers. *Address:* 51 Elizabeth Street, Eaton Square, SW1W 9PP. *T:* 01-730 5673.

STREATFEILD, Maj.-Gen. Timothy Stuart Champion, MBE 1960; Chief of Staff, Logistic Executive, Ministry of Defence, since 1976; *b* 9 Sept. 1926; *s* of Henry Grey Champion and Edythe Streatfeild; *m* 1951, Annette Catherine, *d* of Sir John Clague, CMG, CIE, and Lady Clague; two *s* one *d*. *Educ:* Eton; Christ Church, Oxford. MBIM. Commnd into RA, 1946; Instructor, Staff Coll., Camberley, 1963-65; Chief Instructor, Sudan Armed Forces Staff Coll., 1965-67; Commander, 7th Parachute Regt, RHA, 1967-69; Col Adjt and QMG, 4 Div., 1969-70; Commander, RA 2 Div., 1971-72; Royal Coll. of Defence Studies, 1973; Brigadier Adjt and QMG, 1st Corps, 1974-75. *Recreations:* fishing, sporting, the countryside, music. *Address:* Warley, Links Road, Winchester, Hants. *T:* Winchester 2962. *Clubs:* Army and Navy, Flyfishers', MCC.

STREDDER, James Cecil; Headmaster, Wellington School, Somerset, 1957-73; *b* 22 Sept. 1912; 4th *s* of late Rev. J. Clifton Stredder and late Mrs Stredder; *m* 1938, Catherine Jane, *er d* of late Rev. A. R. Price, RN (Retd), Paignton, Devon; one *d*. *Educ:* King Edward VI School, Stratford-on-Avon; Jesus College, Oxford. Senior Chemistry Master at: Victoria College, Alexandria, Egypt, 1935; St Lawrence Coll., Ramsgate, 1936; Fettes Coll., Edinburgh, 1940; Tonbridge School, 1942-57. BA (Hons) Natural Science (Chemistry) Oxon 1935, MA 1943. *Recreations:* rowing and walking. *Address:* Fair View, Lawrenny Road, Cresselly, Kilgetty, Dyfed.

STREET, Prof. Harry, LLM, PhD; FBA 1968; Professor of English Law, Manchester University, since 1960; Member, Monopolies and Mergers Commission, since 1973; *b* 17 June 1919; *s* of Alfred and Lilian Street; *m* 1947, Muriel Hélène Swain; two *s* one *d*. *Educ:* Farnworth Grammar School; Manchester Univ. LLB 1938, LLM 1948; PhD 1951. Qualified as Solicitor, 1940. Flt-Lt, RAF, 1942-46. Lectr in Law, Manchester Univ., 1946-47; Commonwealth Fund Fellow at Columbia Univ., USA, 1947-48; Lectr in Law, 1948-51, Senior Lectr in Law, 1951-52, Manchester Univ.; Prof. of Law, Nottingham Univ., 1952-56; Prof. of Public Law and Common Law, Manchester Univ., 1956-60. Visiting Prof. of Law, Harvard Univ., USA, 1957-58. Chairman: Cttee on Racial Discrimination, 1967; Royal Commn on Fiji electoral system, 1975-76; Mem., Commn on the Constitution, 1969-73. Hon. LLD Southampton, 1974. *Publications:* Principles of Administrative Law (with J. A. G. Griffith), 1952, 5th edn 1973; A Comparative Study of Governmental Liability, 1953; Law of Torts, 1955, 6th edn 1976; Law of Damages, 1961; Freedom, the Individual and the Law, 1963, 4th edn 1977; Law relating to Nuclear Energy (with F. R. Frame), 1966; Road Accidents (with

D. W. Elliott), 1968; Justice in the Welfare State (Hamlyn Lectures), 1968. Articles in numerous English, Canadian and American Jls of law and public administration. *Recreation:* mountain walking. *Address:* Faculty of Law, Manchester University, Manchester M13 9PL; 1 Queen's Gate, Bramhall, Cheshire SK7 1JT. *T:* 061-439 4922.

STREET, John Edmund Dudley, CMG 1966; Assistant Under-Secretary of State, Ministry of Defence, since 1976; *b* 21 April 1918; *er s* of late Philip Edmund Wells Street and of Elinor Gladys Whittington-Ince; *m* 1940, Noreen Mary, *o d* of Edward John Griffin Comerford and Mary Elizabeth Winstone; three *s* one *d. Educ:* Tonbridge School; Exeter College, Oxford. Served War of 1939-45, HM Forces, 1940-46. Entered Foreign Service, 1947; First Secretary: British Embassy, Oslo, 1950; British Embassy, Lisbon, 1952; Foreign Office, 1954; First Secretary and Head of Chancery, British Legation, Budapest, 1957-60; HM Ambassador to Malagasy Republic, 1961-62, also Consul-General for the Island of Réunion and the Comoro Islands, 1961-62; Asst Sec., MoD, 1967-76. *Recreations:* reading, golf, bridge. *Address:* 162 Oatlands Drive, Weybridge, Surrey. *T:* Weybridge 46205.

STREET, John Hugh, CB 1965; Lecturer, Department of Town and Regional Planning, Sheffield University, since 1976; *b* 24 Aug. 1914; *s* of Hugh W. Street and Augusta Street; *m* 1938, Alicia, *d* of Oscar Kumpula, Wakefield, Mich., USA; two *d. Educ:* Aldenham School; Pembroke College, Cambridge. Home Office, 1937-46; Ministry of Town and Country Planning, 1946-47; Central Land Board, 1947-53; Treasury, 1953-54; Ministry of Housing and Local Government, 1955-70 (Under-Sec., 1956); Dept of the Environment, 1970-74. *Recreations:* looking at pictures, gardening, travel. *Address:* 43 Teignmouth Road, NW2. *T:* 01-452 5337.

STREET, Hon. Sir Laurence (Whistler), KCMG 1976; **Hon. Mr Justice Street;** Lieutenant-Governor of New South Wales since 1974; Chief Justice of New South Wales since 1974; *b* Sydney, 3 July 1926; *s* of Hon. Sir Kenneth Street, KCMG; *m* 1952, Susan Gai, *d* of E. A. S. Watt; two *s* two *d. Educ:* Cranbrook Sch.; Univ. of Sydney (LLB Hons). Ord. Seaman, RANR, 1943-44; Midshipman, RANVR, 1944-45; Sub-Lt 1945-47; Comdr, Sen. Officer RANR Legal Br., 1964-65. Admitted to NSW Bar, 1951; QC 1963; Judge, Supreme Court of NSW, 1965; Judge of Appeal, 1972-74; Chief Judge in Equity, 1972-74. Lectr in Procedure, Univ. of Sydney, 1962-63, Lectr in Bankruptcy, 1964-65; Mem., Public Accountants Regn Bd, 1962-65; Mem., Companies Auditors Bd, 1962-65; Pres., Courts-Martial Appeal Tribunal, 1971-74; Pres., Cranbrook Sch. Council, 1966-74. KStJ 1976. Grand Officer of Merit, Order of Malta, 1977. *Address:* 20 Wallaroy Road, Double Bay, NSW, Australia. *T:* 2308218. *Clubs:* Union (Sydney); Royal Sydney Golf.

STREETEN, Paul Patrick; Warden of Queen Elizabeth House, Director, Institute of Commonwealth Studies, and Fellow of Balliol College, Oxford, since Oct. 1968; Senior Economic Adviser, World Bank, 1976-Sept. 1978; *b* 18 July 1917; *e s* of Wilhelm Hornig, Vienna; changed name to Streeten under Army Council Instruction, 1943; *m* 1951, Ann Hilary Palmer, *d* of Edgar Higgins, Woodstock, Vermont; two *d* (and one step *s*). *Educ:* Vienna; Aberdeen Univ.; Balliol Coll., Oxford (Hon. Schol.); 1st cl. PPE, 1947; Student, Nuffield Coll., Oxford, 1947-48. Mil. service in Commandos, 1941-43; wounded in Sicily, 1943. Fellow, Balliol Coll., Oxford, 1948-66; Associate, Oxford Univ. Inst. of Econs and Statistics, 1960-64; Dep. Dir-Gen., Econ. Planning Staff, Min. of Overseas Develt, 1964-66; Prof. of Econs, Fellow and Dep. Dir of Inst. of Develt Studies, Sussex Univ., 1966-68. Rockefeller Fellow, USA, 1950-51; Fellow, Johns Hopkins Univ., Baltimore, 1955-56; Fellow, Center for Advanced Studies, Wesleyan Univ., Conn.; Sec., Oxford Econ. Papers, until 1961, Mem. Edit. Bd, 1971-; Editor, Bulletin of Oxford Univ. Inst. of Econs and Statistics, 1961-64; Chm., Edit. Bd, World Development; Member: UK Nat. Commn of Unesco, 1966; Provisional Council of Univ. of Mauritius, 1966-72; Commonwealth Develt Corp., 1967-72; Statutory Commn, Royal Univ. of Malta, 1972-; Royal Commn on Environmental Pollution, 1974-76. Mem., Internat. Adv. Panel, Canadian Univ. Service Overseas. Vice-Chm., Social Sciences Adv. Cttee, 1971; Member, Governing Body: Queen Elizabeth House, Oxford, 1966-68; Inst. of Develt Studies, Univ. of Sussex, 1968- (Vice-Chm.); Dominion Students' Hall Trust, London House; Council, Overseas Develt Institute. Pres., UK Chapter, Soc. for Internat. Develt until 1976. *Publications:* (ed) Value in Social Theory, 1958; Economic Integration, 1961; contrib. to Economic Growth in Britain, 1966; The Teaching of Development Economics, 1967; (ed with M. Lipton) Crisis in Indian Planning, 1968; (contrib. to) Gunnar Myrdal, Asian Drama, 1968; (ed) Unfashionable Economics, 1970; (ed, with

Hugh Corbet) Commonwealth Policy in a Global Context, 1971; Frontiers of Development Studies, 1972; (ed) Trade Strategies for Development, 1973; The Limits of Development Research, 1975; (with S. Lall) Foreign Investment, Transnationals and Developing Countries, 1977; contribs to learned journals. *Address:* (until Sept. 1978) Room D446, International Bank for Reconstruction and Development, 1818 H Street NW, Washington, DC 20433, USA. *T:* (202) 477.4545; Queen Elizabeth House, 20 St Giles, Oxford OX1 3LA. *T:* Oxford 52952 (office); Oxford 59000 (home). *Club:* United Oxford & Cambridge University.

STREETER, John Stuart; His Honour Judge Streeter; a Circuit Judge (formerly Deputy Chairman 1967-71, Chairman 1971, Kent Quarter Sessions); *b* 20 May 1920; *yr s* of late Wilfrid A. Streeter, osteopath, and of Mrs R. L. Streeter; *m* 1956, Margaret Nancy Richardson; one *s* two *d. Educ:* Sherborne. Served War of 1939-45 (despatches): Captain, Royal Scots Fusiliers, 1940-46. Called to Bar, Gray's Inn, Nov. 1947. Post Office Counsel SE Circuit, 1957; Treasury Counsel, London Sessions, 1959; Part-time Dep. Chm., Kent Quarter Sessions, 1963. *Recreation:* gardening. *Address:* Triscombe, 10 Burntwood Road, Sevenoaks, Kent. *T:* Sevenoaks 52000.

STREETON, Terence George, MBE 1969; HM Diplomatic Service; Counsellor and Head of Joint Administration Office, Brussels, since 1975; *b* 12 Jan. 1930; *er s* of Alfred Victor Streeton and Edith Streeton (*née* Deiton); *m* 1962, Molly Horsburgh; two *s* two *d. Educ:* Wellingborough Grammar School. Inland Revenue, 1946; Prison Commission, 1947; Government Communications Headquarters, 1952; Foreign Office (Diplomatic Wireless Service), 1953; Diplomatic Service, 1965-: First Secretary, Bonn, 1966; FCO, 1970; First Secretary and Head of Chancery, Bombay, 1972. *Recreations:* private flying, golf. *Address:* c/o Foreign and Commonwealth Office, SW1A 2AH; The Langtons, Olney, Bucks MK46 5AE. *T:* Bedford 711761. *Club:* Royal Aero of Belgium (Brussels).

STREIT, Clarence Kirshman; President, International Movement for Atlantic Union, since 1958, and Federal Union, Inc., USA, since 1939; author; lecturer since 1939; Editor, Freedom & Union, since 1946; *b* 21 Jan. 1896; *s* of Louis L. Streit and Emma Kirshman, California, Mo, USA; *m* 1921, Jeanne Defrance, of Paris, France; one *s* two *d. Educ:* Missouri and Montana public schs; State Univ. of Montana; Sorbonne; University Coll., Oxford (Rhodes Schol.), Hon. LLD, LittD, DHL. US public land surveyor in Montana and Alaska, 1912-16; served as volunteer in American Expeditionary Force, France, 1917-19, first as private, 18th Engineers Railway, then as sergeant in Intelligence Service, attached to American Delegation, Paris Peace Conference; then Rhodes Scholar, Oxford; correspondent Philadelphia Public Ledger, 1920-24, Greco-Turk War, Rome, Istanbul, Paris; correspondent, New York Times, 1925-39, Carthage excavations, Riff war, Vienna, New York, Latin America, Geneva, 1929-38, Washington, DC, 1938-39. First Recipient, Estes Kefauver Union of the Free Award, 1968. *Publications:* Where Iron is, There is the Fatherland, 1920; Hafiz: The Tongue of the Hidden (rubaiyat), 1928; Report on How to Combat False News, League of Nations, 1932; Union Now, 1939; Union Now with Britain, 1941; Chapter on Briand in Dictators and Democrats, 1941; (joint) The New Federalist, 1950; Freedom Against Itself, 1954; Freedom's Frontier-Atlantic Union Now, 1960. *Address:* (home) 2853 Ontario Road NW, Washington, DC 20009, USA; (office) 1875 Connecticut Avenue NW, Washington DC 20009, USA.

STRELCYN, Stefan, FBA 1976; Reader in Semitic Languages, University of Manchester, since 1973 (Lecturer, 1970-73); *b* 28 June 1918; *s* of Szaja Strelcyn and Cywia (*née* Frank); *m* 1940, Maria Kirzner; two *s. Educ:* Gimnazjum Ascola and Tech. Engrg Sch., Warsaw; Université Libre de Bruxelles; Université de Montpellier; Sorbonne (LèsL); Ecole Nationale des Langues Orientales Vivantes (Dipl.); Ecole des Langues Orientales Anciennes (Dipl.); Ecole Pratique des Hautes Etudes, IVe Section (Dipl.). Served War of 1939-45; in Polish Forces in France, 1940 and French Résistance, 1941-44; deported to Germany, Eutritzsch near Leipzig, 1944-45. Croix de Guerre. Attaché de Recherches, CNRS, Paris, 1949-50; University of Warsaw: Assoc. Prof. 1950-54, then Prof. of Semitic Studies, 1954-69; Head of Dept of Semitic Studies, 1950-69; Dir, Inst. of Oriental Studies, 1961-65; Dir, Centre of African Studies, 1962-69; Vis. Lectr in Semitic Studies, SOAS, Univ. of London, 1969-70. Dep. Dir, Inst. of Oriental Studies, Polish Acad. of Scis, 1953-62; Vice-Pres., Cttee of Oriental Studies, Polish Acad. of Scis, 1954-66. Research journeys to Ethiopia, 1957-58, 1966. Unesco missions: Somalia, 1966; Ethiopia, 1974. Haile Sellassie Award for Ethiopian Studies, 1967. FRAS 1977. Editor: Catalogue des manuscrits orientaux des collections polonaises,

1957-67; Africana Bulletin, 1964-69; Jt editor: Rocznik Orientalistyczny, 1954-68; Prace Orientalistyczne, 1954-68; Jl of Semitic Studies, 1976-. *Publications:* Catalogue des manuscrits éthiopiens (Collection Griaule), tome IV, 1954; Prières magiques éthiopiennes pour délier les charmes, 1955; Kebra Nagast czyli Chwała Królów Abisynii, 1956; Mission scientifique en Ethiopie, 1959; Inscriptions palmyréniennes in: K. Michałowski, Palmyre: fouilles polonaises, 1959-60, 1960, 1961, 1962 (resp. 1961, 1962, 1963, 1964); Médecine et plantes d'Ethiopie: (vol. I) Les traités médicaux éthiopiens, 1968; (vol. II) Enquête sur les noms et l'emploi des plantes en Ethiopie, 1973; Catalogue of Ethiopic Manuscripts in the John Rylands University Library of Manchester, 1974; Catalogue des manuscrits éthiopiens de l'Accademia Nazionale dei Lincei: Fonds Conti Rossini et Fonds Caetani 209, 375-378, 1976; articles and reviews in jls of learned socs. *Address:* Department of Near Eastern Studies, University of Manchester, Manchester M13 9PL.

STRETTON, Eric Hugh Alexander, CB 1972; Deputy Chief Executive in Property Services Agency, Department of the Environment, 1972-76, Deputy Chairman, 1973-76; *b* 22 June 1916; *y s* of Major S. G. Stretton, Wigston, Leicester; *m* 1946, Sheila Woodroffe Anderson, MB, BS, *d* of Dr A. W. Anderson, Cardiff (formerly of Ogmore Vale); one *s* one *d. Educ:* Wyggeston Sch; Pembroke Coll., Oxford. BA 1939, MA 1942. Leics Regt and 2/4 PWO Gurkha Rifles (Major), 1939-46. Asst Sec., Birmingham Univ. Appointments Board, 1946. Entered Ministry of Works, 1947; Prin. Private Sec. to Minister of Works, 1952-54; Asst Sec., 1954; Under-Secretary: MPBW, 1962-70; DoE, 1970-72; Dep. Sec., 1972. *Address:* Dacre Castle, Penrith, Cumbria. *T:* Pooley Bridge 375. *Club:* United Oxford & Cambridge University.

STRICKLAND, Maj.-Gen. Eugene Vincent Michael, CMG 1960; DSO 1944; OBE 1955; MM 1940; Chief of Joint Services Liaison Organization, British Forces, Germany, 1966-69, retired; *b* 25 Aug. 1913; *s* of Capt. V. N. Strickland (*d* of wounds, 1917) and of Mary Erina Strickland (*née* O'Sullivan); *m* 1939, Barbara Mary Farquharson Meares Lamb; four *s* one *d. Educ:* Mayfield College; RMC Sandhurst. Commissioned, 1934; served in India, 1935; War of 1939-45, in France and Belgium, 1940; N Africa, 1942-43; Italy, 1943-45; Greece, 1945-46; Egypt, 1948; WO, (MI), 1948-50; Min. of Defence, 1952-54; Arab Legion, 1955-56; Sen. British Officer, Jordan, 1956-57; Min. of Defence, on staff of Chief of Defence Staff, 1957-58; Mil. Adviser to King Hussein of Jordan, 1958-59; Director of Plans, War Office, 1960-63; psc 1947; jssc 1952; idc 1960; NATO Defence College, 1963; DAQMG 1st Corps, 1963-66. Star of Jordan, 1959. CStJ 1960. *Recreations:* shooting, cricket, etc. *Address:* 46 Olivers Battery Road, Winchester, Hants.

STRICKLAND, Hon. Mabel Edeline, OBE 1944; Leader of the Progressive Constitutional Party in Malta, since 1953; *b* Malta, 8 Jan. 1899; 3rd *d* of 1st and last Baron Strickland, of Sizergh Castle, Kendal (and 6th Count della Catena in the Island of Malta) and of late Lady Edeline Sackville. *Educ:* privately in Australia. Attached Naval HQ, Malta, 1917-18; War Correspondent, attached 21st Army Group, BAOR, Aug. 1945. Asst Sec., Constitutional Party, 1921-45; Editor: Times of Malta, 1935-50; Sunday Times of Malta, 1935-56; Member: Malta Legislative Assembly, 1950, 1951-53, 1962-66; Malta Chamber of Commerce; Man. Dir, Allied Malta Newspapers Ltd, 1940-55; Chairman: Xara Palace Hotel Co. Ltd, 1949-61, 1966-; Allied Malta Newspapers Ltd, 1950-55, 1966-; Director, Progress Press Co. Ltd, 1957-61, 1966-. Life Member: Commonwealth Parliamentary Assoc.; Air League; RSA; Mem. Royal Horticultural Soc.; Hon. Corresp. Sec. (Malta), Royal Commonwealth Soc. Astor Award, CPU, 1971. CStJ 1969. Coronation medal, 1953. *Publications:* A Collection of Essays on Malta, 1923-54; Maltese Constitutional and Economic Issue, 1955-59. *Recreations:* swimming, gardening. *Address:* Villa Parisio, Lija, Malta. *T:* 41286. *Clubs:* Lansdowne; Malta Sports.

STRICKLAND-CONSTABLE, Sir Robert (Frederick), 11th Bt *cr* 1641; *b* 22 Oct. 1903; 2nd *s* of Lt-Col Frederick Charles Strickland-Constable (*d* 1917) (*g g s* of 7th Bt) and Margaret Elizabeth (*d* 1961), *d* of late Rear-Adm. Hon. Thomas Alexander Pakenham; *S* brother, 1975; *m* 1936, Lettice, *y d* of late Major Frederick Strickland; two *s* two *d. Educ:* Magdalen Coll., Oxford (BA 1925, MA 1936, DPhil 1940). Served War of 1939-45, Lieut Comdr RNVR. Teaching Staff, Chem. Engineering Dept, Imperial Coll., Univ. of London, 1948-71, Readership 1963-71. Mem. Faraday Soc. *Publications:* Kinetics and Mechanism of Crystallization, 1968; contribs to jls. *Recreations:* music, mountains, bird-watching. *Heir:* *s* Frederick Strickland-Constable, *b* 21 Oct. 1944. *Address:* Combe Wood, Brasted, Westerham, Kent.

STRINGER, Donald Arthur, OBE 1975; Port Director, Port of Southampton, since 1970; Member: British Transport Docks Board, since 1969; National Dock Labour Board, since 1976; *b* 15 June 1922; *s* of late Harry William Stringer and Helen Stringer; *m* 1945, Hazel Handley; one *s* one *d. Educ:* Dorking High Sch.; Borden Grammar Sch. FCIT. Joined Southern Railway Co., 1938; service with RAF, 1941-46; Docks Manager: Fleetwood, 1957-58; East Coast Scottish Ports, 1958-62; Chief Docks Man., Southampton, 1963-67; Dep. Man. Dir, British Transport Docks Bd, 1967-71; Chairman: Southampton Bd, BTDB, 1972-; Southampton Cargo Handling Co. Ltd, 1968-; Southampton Port Employers Assoc., 1970-; Mem. Exec. Cttee. Nat. Assoc. of Port Employers, 1964-; Dir, Southampton Chamber of Commerce, 1970-. Col, E and RS Corps, T&AVR. *Recreations:* gardening, sailing. *Address:* Hillcrest, Pinehurst Road, Bassett, Southampton. *T:* Southampton 768887. *Clubs:* Army and Navy; (Hon.) Royal Yacht Squadron, (Hon.) Royal Southern Yacht, Royal Southampton Yacht.

STRINGER, Pamela Mary; Headmistress, Clifton High School for Girls, since 1965; *b* 30 Aug. 1928; *e d* of late E. Allen Stringer. *Educ:* Worcester Grammar Sch. for Girls; St Hugh's Coll., Oxford. MA (Hons Lit Hum). Asst Classics Mistress, Sherborne Sch. for Girls, 1950-59; Head of Classics Dept, Pate's Grammar Sch. for Girls, Cheltenham, 1959-64 (Dep. Head, 1963-64). Member: Exec. Cttee, Assoc. of Headmistresses, 1975-; Exec. Cttee, Girls Schools Assoc., 1975 (Hon. Treas., 1976-). *Recreations:* travel in Tuscany and Umbria, reading, theatre, cooking. *Address:* Glendower House, Clifton Park, Clifton, Bristol BS8 3JX.

STRONACH, Ancell, ARSA 1934; DA (Edin); *b* Dundee, 6 Dec. 1901; *s* of Alexander Stronach and Margaret Ancell; *m* 1941, Joan Cunningham. *Educ:* Hutcheson's Grammar School; privately. GSA (diploma), 1920; Guthrie Award bronze and silver medallist; travelling scholarship; Terrance Memorial Prize given by G. A. Lauder Prize GAC. Exhibited at Paris Salon, RA, WAG, RSA, Canada, New Zealand and America; official purchasers, Ross and Thorburn and Modern Arts Association permanent collections. Professor of Mural Painting, Glasgow School of Art, to 1939. *Recreations:* walking, menagerie and collection of British and foreign fish and reptiles. *Address:* Alma House, 25 Gillingham Road, Gillingham, Kent. *T:* Medway 54077.

STRONACH, David Brian, OBE 1975; FSA; Director, British Institute of Persian Studies, since 1961; *b* 10 June 1931; *s* of Ian David Stronach, MB, FRCSE, and Marjorie Jessie Duncan (*née* Minto); *m* 1966, Ruth Vaadia; two *d. Educ:* Gordonstoun; St John's Coll., Cambridge (MA). Pres., Cambridge Univ. Archaeological Field Club, 1954. British Inst. of Archaeology at Ankara: Scholar, 1955-56; Fellow, 1957-58; Fellow, British Sch. of Archaeology in Iraq, 1957-60; Brit. Acad. Archaeological Attaché in Iran, 1960-61. Asst on excavations at: Istanbul, 1954; Tell Rifa'at, 1956; Beycesultan, 1956-57; Hacilar, 1957-59; Nimrud, 1957-60; Charsada, 1958. Dir, excavations at: Ras al'Amiya, 1960; Yarim Tepe, 1960-62; Pasargadae, 1961-63; Tepe Nush-i Jan, 1967-; Co-dir, excavs at Shahr-i Qumis, 1967-. Mem., Internat. Cttee of Internat. Congresses of Iranian Art and Archaeology, 1968-. Hagop Kevorkian Visiting Lectr in Iranian Art and Archaeology, Univ. of Pennsylvania, 1967; Rhind Lectr, Edin., 1973; Vis. Prof., Jerusalem, 1977. Mem., German Archaeological Inst., 1973 (Corr. Mem., 1966). *Publications:* Pasargadae, a Report on the Excavations conducted by the British Institute of Persian Studies, 1977; archaeological articles in: Jl of Near Eastern Studies; Iran; Iraq; Anatolian Studies, etc. *Recreations:* fly fishing, mediaeval architecture, tribal carpets; repr. Cambridge in athletics, 1953. *Address:* British Institute of Persian Studies, PO Box 2617, Tehran, Iran. *Clubs:* Achilles; Hawks (Cambridge).

STRONG, Sir Charles Love, KCVO 1974 (MVO 1962); chartered physiotherapist in private practice in London, since 1938; *b* 16 April 1908; *o s* of late Alfred Strong; *m* 1st, 1933, Ivy Maud (*d* 1976), *yr d* of late Arthur Stockley; one *d* ; 2nd, 1977, Ruth Hermon-Smith. *Educ:* privately (Bailey Sch., Durham). Miner and merchant seaman, 1924-26; RN (Sick Berth Br.), qualified MCSP; Physiotherapist, RN Hosps, Haslar and Malta. Devised new apparatus and technique for treatment of injury to humans by faradism; developed manipulative techniques, 1926-38; running parallel with human practice designed special apparatus and technique for treatment of injuries to horses by faradism with outstanding success; under observation of leading equine veterinarian treated 100 cases of lameness in horses which had failed to respond to previous treatment, curing 88 per cent; some hundreds of races have now been won by horses cured of lameness by this method and which had failed to respond to other treatments. Formed firm of 'Transeva' for development, manufacture and marketing of horse apparatus, which is now supplied to many parts of the world. Served War, RAF Marine Section, 1st cl. Coxwain, 1940-44 (invalided). *Publications:* Common-Sense Therapy for Horses' Injuries, 1956; Horses' Injuries, 1967. *Recreation:* racing. *Address:* 73 Portland Place, W1N 3AL. *T:* 01-935 4523.

STRONG, Air Cdre David Malcolm, CB 1964; AFC 1941; *b* 30 Sept. 1913; *s* of Theo Strong; *m* 1941, Daphne Irene Warren-Brown; two *s* one *d. Educ:* Cardiff High School. Pilot, under trng, 1936; Bomber Sqdn, 1937-41; POW, 1941-45. Station Commander, RAF Jurby, RAF Driffield, 1946-48; Staff Coll. (psa), 1949; Staff Officer, Rhodesian Air Trng Grp, 1949-51; Directing Staff, Staff Coll., 1952-55; Air Warfare Coll. (pfc), 1956; Station Comdr, RAF Coningsby, 1957-59; Dir of Personnel, Air Min., 1959-61; Senior Air Staff Officer, RAF Germany, 1962-63; Officer Commanding, RAF Halton, 1964-66. Retired, 1966. Chairman: RAF Rugby Union, 1954-56; RAF Golf Soc., 1964-66. *Recreation:* golf. *Address:* Clematis Cottage, Great Kimble, Bucks. *T:* Princes Risborough 3985. *Clubs:* Royal Air Force; Ashridge Golf.

STRONG, Julia Trevelyan; *see* Oman, J. T.

STRONG, Maj.-Gen. Sir Kenneth William Dobson, KBE 1966 (OBE 1942); Kt 1952; CB 1945; Director: Philip Hill Investment Trust, 1966-77; Eagle Star Insurance Co., 1966-77; *o s* of late Prof. John Strong, CBE, LLD, and of late Mrs Strong, Eastbourne; unmarried. *Educ:* Montrose Academy; Glenalmond; RMC, Sandhurst. 2nd Lt 1st Bn Royal Scots Fusiliers, 1920. Military career, 1920-47 (which included command of 4/5 Bn Royal Scots Fusiliers, Camberley Staff College Course); Mem. of Saar force, 1935; Defence Security Officer, Malta and Gibraltar; staff appts at WO (2 years as Hd of German Section); a tour of duty as Military Attaché, Berlin, and residence in Germany, France, Italy and Spain prior to qualifying as an interpreter in the languages of these countries; Head of Intelligence Home Forces, 1942; Head of General Eisenhower's Intelligence Staff, 1943, remaining with the Supreme Commander during his campaigns in Africa, Sicily, Italy, France and Germany, leaving him at the dissolution of Supreme HQ in July 1945 (despatches). Member, delegns for conducting Armistice negotiations with Italy, in Lisbon and Sicily, 1943; and with Germany in Rheims and Berlin, 1945. Director General of Political Intelligence Dept of Foreign Office, 1945-47; retired pay, 1947. First Director of Joint Intelligence Bureau, Ministry of Defence, 1948-64; first Director-General of Intelligence, Min. of Defence, 1964-66. Distinguished Service Medal (USA), Legion of Merit (USA). Chevalier and Officer of Legion of Honour, Croix de Guerre with Palms (France); Order of the Red Banner (Russia). *Publications:* Intelligence at the Top, 1968; Men of Intelligence, 1970; various newspaper articles on business organisation and export problems. *Recreation:* golf. *Address:* 25 Kepplestone, Eastbourne, East Sussex. *Club:* Army and Navy.

STRONG, Maurice F.; Chairman, Petro-Canada, since 1976; *b* 29 April 1929; *s* of Frederick Milton Strong and late Mary Fyfe Strong; *m* 1950; two *s* two *d. Educ:* Public and High Sch., Oak Lake, Manitoba, Canada. Served in UN Secretariat, 1947; Pres. or Dir, various Canadian and internat. corporations, 1954-66; Dir-Gen., External Aid Office (later Canadian Internat. Develt Agency), Canadian Govt, 1966-71; Under-Sec.-Gen. with responsibility for environmental affairs, and Sec.-Gen. of 1972 Conf. on the Human Environment, Stockholm, 1971-72; Exec. Dir, UN Environmental Programme, 1972-75. Chairman: Canadian Internat. Develt Bd; Centre for Internat. Management Studies, Geneva, Switzerland, 1971-; Alt. Governor, IBRD, ADB, Caribbean Develt Bank. Trustee: Rockefeller Foundn, 1971-; Aspen Inst., 1971-. Holds numerous hon. degrees from univs and colls in Canada, USA and UK. *Publications:* articles in Foreign Affairs Magazine and Natural History Magazine. *Recreations:* swimming, skin-diving, reading. *Address:* Petro-Canada, PO Box 2844, Calgary, Canada. *T:* Calgary 403-264 7015. *Clubs:* Mount Royal (Montreal); Canadian, Yale, Century (New York); Rideau (Ottawa); Ranchmen's (Calgary).

STRONG, Most Rev. Philip Nigel Warrington, KBE 1970; CMG 1958; MA Cantab; ThD ACT; DD Lambeth, 1968; *b* Sutton-on-the-Hill, Etwall, 11 July 1899; *s* of late Rev. John Warrington Strong, Oxford, formerly Vicar of Dodford with Brockhall, and late Rosamond Maria, *d* of late John Digby Wingfield Digby, Sherborne Castle, Dorset. *Educ:* King's School, Worcester; Selwyn Coll., Cambridge; Bishops' College, Cheshunt. Served European War with RE (Signal Service), 1918-19; BA Cambridge, 1921; MA 1924; Deacon, 1922; Priest, 1923; Curate of St Mary's, Tyne Dock, 1922-26; Vicar of Christ Church, Leeds, 1926-31; Vicar of St Ignatius the Martyr, Sunderland,

1931-36; Proctor of Convocation of York and Member of Church Assembly for Archdeaconry of Durham, 1936; Bishop of New Guinea, 1936-62; MLC, Territory of Papua and New Guinea, 1955-63; Archbishop of Brisbane and Metropolitan of Queensland, 1962-70; Primate of Australia, 1966-70. Senior CF (Australian Army), 1943-45. Hon. Fellow, Selwyn College, Cambridge, 1966. Sub-Prelate, Order of St John of Jerusalem, 1967. *Publication:* Out of Great Tribulation, 1947. *Address:* 11 Cathedral Close, Wangaratta, Victoria 3677, Australia. *T:* Wangaratta 21-5603. *Clubs:* University (Sydney); Melbourne.

STRONG, Roy Colin, PhD, FSA; Director, Victoria and Albert Museum, since 1974; *b* 23 Aug. 1935; *s* of G. E. C. Strong; *m* 1971, Julia Trevelyan Oman, *qv. Educ:* Edmonton Co. Grammar Sch.; Queen Mary Coll., London; Warburg Inst., London. Asst Keeper, 1959, Director, Keeper and Secretary 1967-73, Nat. Portrait Gallery. Ferens Prof. of Fine Art, 1971. Walls Lectures, Pierpont Morgan Library, 1974. Lecturer, critic, contributor to radio and TV and organiser of exhibitions. *Publications:* Portraits of Queen Elizabeth I, 1963; (with J. A. van Dorsten) Leicester's Triumph, 1964; Holbein and Henry VIII, 1967; Tudor and Jacobean Portraits, 1969; The English Icon: Elizabethan and Jacobean Portraiture, 1969; (with Julia Trevelyan Oman) Elizabeth R, 1971; Van Dyck: Charles I on Horseback, 1972; (with Julia Trevelyan Oman) Mary Queen of Scots, 1972; (with Stephen Orgel) Inigo Jones: the theatre of the Stuart court, 1973; contrib. Burke's Guide to the Royal Family, 1973; Splendour at Court: Renaissance Spectacle and Illusion, 1973; (with Colin Ford) An Early Victorian Album: the Hill-Adamson collection, 1973; Nicholas Hilliard, 1975; contrib. Spirit of the Age, 1975; The Cult of Elizabeth: Elizabethan Portraiture and Pageantry, 1977; contributor to learned jls. *Recreations:* gardening, cooking, country life. *Address:* 2E Morpeth Terrace, SW1P 1EW. *Clubs:* Beefsteak, Garrick, Grillions.

STRONGE, Captain Rt. Hon. Sir (Charles) Norman (Lockhart), 8th Bt *cr* 1803; PC N Ireland, 1946; MC; HM Lieutenant for Co. Armagh, since 1939; President, Royal British Legion, Northern Ireland Area, since 1946; *b* 23 July 1894; *s* of Sir Charles Edmond Sinclair Stronge, 7th Bt, and Marian (*d* 1948), *d* of Samuel Bostock, The Hermitage, Epsom; *S* father 1939; *m* 1921, Gladys Olive Hall, OBE 1943, OStJ, of Knockbrack, Athenry, Co. Galway, *o d* of Major H. T. Hall, late 18th Hussars; one *s* two *d* (and one *d* decd). *Educ:* Eton. Served European War, 1914-19, R Inniskilling Fusiliers and R Irish Rifles (MC, despatches twice, Belgian Croix-de-Guerre). MP Mid-Armagh, N Ireland Parlt, 1938-69; Asst Parliamentary Sec., Ministry of Finance, Northern Ireland, 1941-42; Parliamentary Sec., Ministry of Finance (Chief Whip), 1942-44; Speaker, Northern Ireland House of Commons, 1945-69. JP Co, Londonderry; JP Co. Armagh; High Sheriff Co. Londonderry, 1934; Chm., Armagh County Council, 1944-55. Dir, Commercial Insurance Co. of Ireland Ltd. North Irish Horse (Royal Armoured Corps), invalided. Hon. Col 5th Bn Royal Irish Fusiliers (TA), 1949-63. KStJ; Comdr of the Order of Leopold (Belgium), 1946. *Recreations:* shooting, fishing. *Heir: s* James Matthew Stronge [*b* 21 June 1932. *Educ:* Eton; Christ Church, Oxford (MA). Captain, Grenadier Guards, RARO. MP (N Ireland), Mid-Armagh, 1969-73; Member (U) NI Assembly, for Armagh, 1973-76. JP Co. Armagh]. *Address:* Tynan Abbey, Tynan, Co. Armagh, Northern Ireland. *TA:* Tynan. *T:* Middletown 205. *Club:* Ulster (Belfast).

STRONGE, Rt. Hon. Sir Norman; *see* Stronge, Rt Hon. Sir C. N. L.

STROUD, Prof. (Charles) Eric, FRCP; Professor of Child Health, King's College Hospital Medical School, and Director, Department of Child Health, since 1968; *b* 15 May 1924; *s* of Frank Edmund and Lavinia May Stroud; *m* 1950, June, *d* of Harold Neep; one *s* two *d. Educ:* Cardiff High Sch. for Boys; Welsh National Sch. of Medicine. BSc 1945, MB, BCh 1948 (Wales); MRCP 1955, DCH 1955, FRCP 1968 (London). Sqdn Ldr, RAF, 1950-52. Med. Qual., 1948; Paediatric Registrar, Welsh Nat. Sch. of Med.; Sen. Registrar, Great Ormond Street Children's Hosp., 1957-61; Paediatrician, Uganda Govt, 1958-60; Asst to Dir, Dept of Child Health, Guy's Hosp., 1961-62; Cons. Paediatrician, King's Coll. Hosp., 1962-68. *Publications:* chapters in Textbook of Obstetrics, 1958; Childhealth in the Tropics, 1961; various articles in med. jls. *Recreations:* bad golf, good fishing, cheap antiques. *Address:* 84 Copse Hill, Wimbledon, SW20. *T:* 01-947 1336.

STROUD, Dorothy Nancy, MBE 1968; Assistant Curator, Sir John Soane's Museum, since 1945; *b* London, 11 Jan. 1910. *Educ:* Claremont, Eastbourne; Edgbaston High Sch. On staff of: Country Life, 1930-41; National Monuments Record, 1941-45;

Sir John Soane's Museum, 1945-. Mem., Historic Buildings Council, 1974-; FSA 1951; Hon. RIBA, 1975. *Publications:* Capability Brown, 1950, new edn 1975; The Thurloe Estate, 1959; The Architecture of Sir John Soane, 1961; Humphry Repton, 1962; Henry Holland, 1966; George Dance, 1971; The South Kensington Estate of Henry Smith's Charity, 1975. *Address:* 24 Onslow Square, SW7 3NS.

STROWGER, Gaston Jack, CBE 1976; Managing Director, Thorn Electrical Industries, since 1970; *b* 8 Feb. 1916; *s* of Alfred Henry Strowger, Lowestoft boat-owner, and Lily Ellen Tripp; *m* 1939, Katherine Ellen Gilbert; two *s* one *d. Educ:* Lowestoft Grammar School. Joined London Electrical Supply Co., 1934; HM Forces, 1939-43. Joined TEI, as an Accountant, 1943; Group Chief Accountant, 1952; joined Tricity Finance Corp. as Dir, 1959; Exec. Dir, TEI, 1961; full Dir 1966; Financial Dir 1967; Dep. Chm., Tricity Finance Corp., 1968. FBIM 1971. *Recreations:* gardening, bowling. *Address:* Kesslee, 29 Beech Hill Avenue, Hadley Wood, Barnet, Herts EN4 0IN. *T:* 01-449 6289.

STROYAN, Ronald Angus Ropner, QC 1972; **His Honour Judge Stroyan**; a Circuit Judge, since 1975; *b* 27 Nov. 1924; *e s* of Ronald S. Stroyan of Boreland, Killin; *m* 1st, 1952, Elizabeth Anna Grant (marr. diss. 1965), *y d* of Col J. P. Grant of Rothiemurchus; one *s* two *d* ; 2nd, 1967, Jill Annette Johnston, *d* of late Sir Douglas Marshall; one *s. Educ:* Harrow School; Trinity College, Cambridge; BA(Hons). Served 1943-45 with The Black Watch (NW Europe); attd Argyll and Sutherland Highlanders, Palestine, 1945-47 (despatches); Captain; later with Black Watch TA. Barrister-at-Law, 1950, Inner Temple. Dep. Chm., North Riding QS, 1962-70, Chm., 1970-71; a Recorder of the Crown Court, 1972-75. Mem. Gen. Council of the Bar, 1963-67, 1969-73 and 1975. *Recreations:* shooting, stalking, fishing. *Address:* Chapel Cottage, Whashton, near Richmond, Yorks; Duncroisk, Killin, Perthshire. *T:* Killin 309. *Clubs:* Caledonian; Yorkshire (York).

STRUDWICK, Air Cdre Arthur Sidney Ronald, CB 1976; DFC 1945; Defence Liaison Officer, The Singer Co., Link-Miles Division, since 1976; *b* 16 April 1921; *s* of Percival and Mary Strudwick; *m* 1941, Cissily (*née* Stedman); two *s* one *d . Educ:* Guildford Tech. Coll.; RAF Colls. Joined RAF 1940; War Service as Fighter Pilot, 941-43; POW Germany, 1944; Test Flying, Canada, 1948-50; CO No 98 Sqdn, 1951-53; Staff Coll., Camberley, 1954; Commanded Jt Services Trials Unit, Woomera, 1956-59; JSSC, 1959-60; MoD Planning Staff, 1960-62; Dir of Plans, Far East, 1962-64; Commanded RAF Leuchars, 1965-67; Air Cdre Plans, Strategic Comd, 1967-69; IDC 1969; Dir of Flying (R&D), MoD PE, 1970-73; AOC Central Tactics and Trials Orgn, 1973-76, retired 1976. *Recreations:* golf and gardening. *Address:* c/o Williams & Glyn's Bank Ltd, Whitehall, SW1. *Club:* Royal Air Force.

STRUDWICK, John Philip, CBE 1970; CVO 1973; Assistant Secretary, Board of Inland Revenue, 1950-74, retired; *b* 30 May 1914; *s* of Philip Strudwick, FRICS and Marjorie Strudwick (*née* Clements); *m* 1942, Elizabeth Marion Stemson; two *s* three *d* (and one *d* decd). *Educ:* Eltham Coll.; St John's Coll., Cambridge. BA 1936, MA 1973. Asst Principal, Bd of Inland Revenue, 1937; Principal 1942. Sec., Millard Tucker Cttee on Taxation Treatment of Provisions for Retirement, 1951-53. *Recreations:* music, gardening, voluntary social work (Chm., Univ. of Sussex Catholic Chaplaincy Assoc., 1972-76). *Address:* The Moat, Cowden, Edenbridge, Kent TN8 7DP. *T:* Cowden 441.

STRUTT, family name of **Barons Belper** and **Rayleigh**.

STRUTT, Sir Austin; *see* Strutt, Sir Henry Austin.

STRUTT, Hon. Charles Richard; *b* 25 May 1910; *s* of 4th Baron Rayleigh and Lady Mary Hilda Strutt, *d* of 4th Earl of Leitrim;*b* and *heir-pres* of 5th Baron Rayleigh, *qv* ; *m* 1952, Jean Elizabeth, *d* of 1st Viscount Davidson, PC, GCVO, CH, CB; one *s* two *d. Educ:* Eton; Trinity College, Cambridge. Governor of Felsted School, 1936-74. Member, Church Army Bd, 1950 (Vice-Pres. 1963). Hon. Treas., Soc. for Psychical Research, 1954. Director of various companies including Australian Estates Co. Ltd (1949-75) and Lord Rayleigh's Farms Inc. (Chairman), 1957. King Christian IX Liberation Order (Denmark). *Recreation:* gardening. *Address:* Berwick Place, Hatfield Peverel, Chelmsford, Essex. *T:* Chelmsford 380321. *Club:* Brooks's.

STRUTT, Sir (Henry) Austin, KCVO 1953 (CVO 1943; MVO 1937); CB 1949; MA; JP; Extra Gentleman Usher to the Queen since 1961; Chairman: Council of Voluntary Welfare Work,

1962; Church of England Pensions Board, 1965-74; *b* 23 Jan. 1903; *er s* of late Henry Strutt and Elizabeth Maher, Rathkeale, Co. Limerick; *m* 1927, Gladys May (*d* 1974), *o d* of late Arthur Salter Holt; two *d. Educ:* Roan School; Magdalen College, Oxford. 1st Class Modern History, 1924; Senior Demy, 1925-26; Home Office, 1925-61; Principal Private Secretary to Mr Herbert Morrison, 1940-43; Assistant Under-Secretary of State, Home Office, 1943-57; Principal Establishment and Organisation Officer, Home Office, 1945-57; subseq. Dep. Under-Sec. of State, Home Office. Registrar of the Baronetage, 1945-61; Director, John Lewis Partnership Ltd, 1962-67. JP Bucks. KStJ. Jubilee Medals, 1935, 1977; Coronation Medals, 1937, 1953. *Address:* 51 Sussex Place, Slough, Berks. *T:* Slough 21008.

STRUTT, Sir Nigel (Edward), Kt 1972; TD; DL; FRAgS; Chairman and Managing Director, Strutt & Parker (Farms) Ltd; Managing Director, Lord Rayleigh's Farms Inc.; *b* 18 Jan. 1916; *yr s* of late Edward Jolliffe Strutt. *Educ:* Winchester; Wye Agricultural College (Fellow, 1970). Essex Yeomanry (Major), 1937-56. Member: Eastern Electricity Bd, 1964-76; Agricultural Advisory Council, 1963- (Chm. 1969-73; Chm., Adv. Council for Agriculture and Horticulture, 1973-); NEDC for Agriculture, 1967-. President: Country Landowners' Association, 1967-69; British Friesian Cattle Soc., 1974-75. Master, Farmers' Co., 1976-77. DL Essex 1954; High Sheriff of Essex, 1966. Massey Ferguson Award, 1976. Von Thünen Gold Medal, Kiel Univ., 1974. *Recreations:* shooting, ski-ing. *Address:* Sparrows, Terling, Essex. *T:* Terling 213. *Clubs:* Brooks's, Farmers'.

STRUTT, Rt. Rev. Rupert Gordon; *see* Stockport, Suffragan Bishop of.

STUART, family name of **Earl Castle Stewart, Earl of Moray** and **Viscount Stuart of Findhorn**.

STUART; *see* Crichton-Stuart, family name of Marquess of Bute.

STUART OF FINDHORN, 2nd Viscount *cr* 1959; **David Randolph Moray Stuart**; *b* 20 June 1924; *s* of 1st Viscount Stuart of Findhorn, PC, CH, MVO, MC, and Lady Rachel Cavendish OBE (*d* 1977), 4th *d* of 9th Duke of Devonshire; *S* father, 1971; *m* 1st, 1945, Grizel Mary Wilfreda (*d* 1948), *d* of D. T. Fyfe and *widow* of Michael Gillilan; one *s* ; 2nd, 1951, Marian Emelia, *d* of Gerald H. Wilson; one *s* three *d. Educ:* Eton; Cirencester Agricultural College. FRICS. Partner, Bernard Thorpe & Partners. *Heir: s* Hon. James Dominic Stuart, *b* 25 March 1948. *Address:* Flat 6, 6 Collingham Gardens, SW5 0HW. *T:* 01-373 8810. *Clubs:* White's, Bath, Buck's.

STUART, Viscount; Andrew Richard Charles Stuart; *b* 7 Oct. 1953; *s* and *heir* of 8th Earl Castle Stewart, *qv* ; *m* 1973, Annie Le Poulain, St Malo, France; one *d . Educ:* Wynstones, Glos; Millfield, Som. *Address:* Truance Cottage, Honiton, Devon.

STUART, Prof. Alan; Professor Emeritus, University of Exeter, 1959 (Professor, and Head Department of Geology, 1957-59); *b* 25 April 1894; *s* of James Anderson Stuart and Elizabeth (*née* Gladwell); *m* 1921, Ruth May Hugill; one *s* two *d. Educ:* Gateshead Secondary Sch.; Armstrong Coll. (now University of Newcastle upon Tyne). BSc Hons Geology, 1921; MSc 1923. Dip. RMS, 1973. Asst Lectr, Lectr and First Lectr, Dept of Geology, University Coll. of Swansea, 1921-47; Indep. Head of Dept of Geology, University Coll., Exeter, 1947-57. War Service: RAMC Dardanelles and Egypt, 1915-16; India, 1916-18; Indian Army, (TC), 2/27 Punjabis (Adjutant), Afghan War, 1919. Civil Defence, 1939-45; at University Coll., Swansea, during War, worked on crystallography of explosives for Ministry of Supply. *Publications:* (with N. H. Hartshorne): Crystals and the Polarising Microscope, 4th edn, 1970; Practical Optical Crystallography, 2nd edn 1969. Contribs to jls mainly concerned with sedimentary petrology and applications of microscopy to chemical problems. *Recreations:* photography, study of landscape, microscopy, problems of water supply. *Address:* Bridge House, Neopardy, Crediton, Devon. *T:* Crediton 2992.

STUART, Alexander John Mackenzie; *see* Mackenzie Stuart, Hon. Lord.

STUART, Andrew Christopher, CPM 1961; HM Diplomatic Service; Counsellor, Jakarta, since 1975; *b* 30 Nov. 1928; *s* of Rt Rev. Cyril Edgar Stuart, *qv* ; *m* 1959, Patricia Kelly; two *s* one *d. Educ:* Bryanston; Clare Coll., Cambridge (MA). Royal Navy, 1947-49. Colonial Admin. Service, Uganda, 1953; retd from HMOCS as Judicial Adviser, 1965. Called to Bar, Middle Temple, 1965. Entered HM Diplomatic Service, 1965; 1st Sec.

and Head of Chancery, Helsinki, 1968; Asst, S Asian Dept, FCO, 1971; Head of Hong Kong and Indian Ocean Dept, FCO, 1972-75. *Recreations:* sailing, gliding, squash, mountaineering. *Address:* c/o Foreign and Commonwealth Office, SW1A 2AH; 13 The Waldrons, Oxted, Surrey. *T:* Oxted 2752. *Clubs:* United Oxford & Cambridge University, Alpine; Jesters.

STUART, Rt. Rev. Cyril Edgar; *s* of Canon E. A. Stuart, Canterbury, and Emily Ada Guy; *m* 1924, Mary Summerhayes; two *s. Educ:* Repton; St John's College, Cambridge; MA. Public School Brigade, 1914; 3rd N Staffs, 1915; Salonica, 1916-19; ordained as Curate of St Mary's, Hornsey Rise, 1920; Chaplain and Lecturer, Ridley Hall, Cambridge, 1921-24; Chaplain and Librarian Achimota College, Gold Coast, 1925-30; CMS Missionary, Uganda, 1931; Asst Bishop of Uganda, 1932-34; Bishop of Uganda, 1934-53; Assistant Bishop of Worcester and Rector of St Andrew's and All Saints with St Helen's, St Alban's and St Michael's, Worcester, 1953-56; Residentiary Canon of Worcester Cathedral, 1956-65. *Address:* 4 Eddystone Court, Churt, Farnham, Surrey.
See also A. C. Stuart.

STUART, Francis; *b* Queensland, Australia, 1902; *s* of Henry and Elizabeth Stuart, Co. Antrim, Ireland; *m* 1st, 1920, Iseult Gonne; one *s* one *d*; 2nd, 1954, Gertrude Meiszner. *Educ:* Rugby. First book, poems, which received an American prize and also award of the Royal Irish Academy, published at age of twenty-one; first novel published in 1931 at age of 29; contributor to various newspapers and periodicals. *Publications:* novels: Women and God, 1930; Pigeon Irish, 1932; The Coloured Dome, 1933; Try the Sky, 1933; Glory, 1934; The Pillar of Cloud, 1948; Redemption, 1949; The Flowering Cross, 1950; Good Friday's Daughter, 1951; The Chariot, 1953; The Pilgrimage, 1955; Victors and Vanquished, 1958; Angels of Providence, 1959; Black List, Section H, 1971; Memorial, 1973; A Hole in the Head, 1977; *poetry:* We Have Kept the Faith; *autobiography:* Things to Live For, 1936. *Recreations:* horse-racing, golf. *Address:* 2 Highfield Park, Dublin 14, Ireland.

STUART, James Keith; Managing Director, British Transport Docks Board, since 1977; *b* 4 March 1940; *s* of James and Marjorie Stuart; *m* 1966, Kathleen Anne Pinder (*née* Woodman); three *s* one *d*. *Educ:* King George V School, Southport; Gonville and Caius College, Cambridge (MA). FCIT, FBIM. District Manager, South Western Electricity Bd, 1970-72; Secretary, British Transport Docks Bd, 1972-75, Gen. Manager, 1976-77. *Recreation:* music. *Address:* 8 Thamesfield Gardens, Mill Road, Marlow on Thames, Bucks SL7 1PZ. *T:* Marlow 73107. *Club:* United Oxford & Cambridge University.

STUART, Prof. John Trevor, FRS 1974; Professor of Theoretical Fluid Mechanics since 1966 and Head of Mathematics Department since 1974, Imperial College of Science and Technology, University of London; *b* 28 Jan. 1929; *s* of Horace Stuart and Phyllis Emily Stuart (*née* Potter); *m* 1957, Christine Mary (*née* Tracy); two *s* one *d*. *Educ:* Gateway Sch., Leicester; Imperial Coll., London. BSc 1949, PhD 1951. Aerodynamics Div., Nat. Physical Lab., Teddington, 1951-66; Sen. Principal Scientific Officer (Special Merit), 1961. Vis. Lectr, Dept of Maths, MIT, 1956-57; Vis. Prof. of Maths, MIT, 1965-66. *Publications:* (contrib.) Laminar Boundary Layers, ed L. Rosenhead, 1963; articles in Proc. Royal Soc., Phil. Trans Royal Soc., Jl Fluid Mech., Proc. 10th Int. Cong. Appl. Mech., Jl Lub. Tech. (ASME). *Recreations:* gardening, reading, do-it-yourself, ornithology. *Address:* Mathematics Department, Imperial College, SW7 2AZ. *T:* 01-589 5111; 3 Steeple Close, Wimbledon, SW19 5AD. *T:* 01-946 7019.

STUART, Prof. Sir Kenneth (Lamonte), Kt 1977; MD, FRCP, FRCPE, FACP, DTM&H; Medical Adviser, Commonwealth Secretariat, since 1976; *b* 16 June 1920; *s* of Egbert and Louise Stuart; *m* 1958, Barbara Cecille Ashby; one *s* two *d*. *Educ:* Harrison Coll., Barbados; Queen's Univ., Belfast (MB, BCh, BAO 1948). Consultant Physician, University Coll. Hospital of the West Indies, 1954-76; University of the West Indies: Prof. of Medicine, 1966-76; Dean, Medical Faculty, 1969-71; Head, Dept of Medicine, 1972-76; Mem. Council, 1971-76. Rockefeller Foundation Fellow in Cardiology, Massachusetts Gen. Hosp., Boston, 1956-57; Wellcome Foundation Research Fellow, Harvard Univ., Boston, 1960-61; Consultant to WHO on Cardiovascular Disorders, 1969-. *Publications:* articles on hepatic and cardiovascular disorders in medical journals. *Recreations:* tennis, music. *Address:* Commonwealth Secretariat, Marlborough House, Pall Mall, SW1Y 5HX. *T:* 01-839 3411.

STUART, Malcolm Moncrieff, CIE 1947; OBE 1944; ICS retired; Recorder to Council of Lord High Commissioners to the

General Assembly of the Church of Scotland; *b* 21 May 1903; *s* of George Malcolm Stuart and Mary Elizabeth Scott Moncrieff; *m* 1928, Grizel Graham Balfour Paul; one *s* one *d*. *Educ:* Sedbergh; St John's College, Cambridge; Queen's Coll., Oxford. Entered ICS 1927; served as Dist Magistrate of various districts and was on special duty for Govt Estates, 1938; during War of 1939-45 was mostly Dist Magistrate of Chittagong and also Comr there. Served in Pakistan until 1950, as additional Member, Board of Revenue. *Publications:* Bob Potts at Murshedabad (Bengal Past and Present), 1933; Handbook to Bengal Records, 1948; and other stories. *Recreations:* golf, shooting, bridge. *Address:* Old Manse, Pilmuir, Haddington, East Lothian. *Clubs:* New (Edinburgh); Muirfield Golf.

STUART, Michael Francis Harvey; Treasury Adviser, UK Mission to the United Nations, since 1974; *b* 3 Oct. *s* of late Willoughby Stuart and Ethel Stuart; *m* 1961, Ruth Tennyson-d'Eyncourt; one *s* one *d*. *Educ:* Harrow; Magdalen Coll., Oxford. Air Min., 1950-65; DEA, 1965-69; HM Treasury, 1969-74. Mem., UN Adv. Cttee on Administrative and Budgetary Questions, 1975. *Recreations:* music, tennis, golf. *Address:* 147 White Plains Road, Bronxville, New York, NY 10708, USA. *T:* (914) 793 3872.

STUART, Sir Phillip (Luttrell), 9th Bt *cr* 1660; late F/O RCAF; President, Agassiz Industries Ltd; *b* 7 September 1937; *s* of late Luttrell Hamilton Stuart and late Irene Ethel Jackman; *S* uncle, Sir Houlton John Stuart, 8th Bt, 1959; *m* 1st, 1962, Marlene Rose Muth (marr. diss. 1968); two *d*; 2nd, 1969, Beverley Clare Pieri; one *s* one *d*. *Educ:* Vancouver. Enlisted RCAF, Nov. 1955; commnd FO (1957-62). *Heir:* *s* Geoffrey Phillip Stuart, *b* 5 July 1973. *Address:* 3 Windermere Bay, Winnipeg, Manitoba R3T 1B1, Canada.
[*But his name does not, at the time of going to press, appear on the official Roll of Baronets.*]

STUART-FORBES, Sir Charles Edward; *see* Forbes.

STUART-HARRIS, Sir Charles (Herbert), Kt 1970; CBE 1961; MD; FRCP; Postgraduate Dean of Medicine, University of Sheffield, 1972-77, Professor of Medicine, 1946-72; Physician United Sheffield Hospitals, 1946-74; *b* 12 July 1909; *s* of late Dr and Mrs Herbert Harris, Birmingham; *m* 1937, Marjorie, *y d* of late Mr and Mrs F. Robinson, Dulwich; two *s* one *d*. *Educ:* King Edward's School, Birmingham; St Bartholomew's Hospital Medical School. MB, BS London 1931 (Gold Medal); MD 1933 (Gold Medal); FRCP 1944. House-Physician and Demonstrator in Pathology, St Bartholomew's Hosp.; First Asst, Dept of Medicine, Brit. Postgrad. Medical Sch., 1935; Sir Henry Royce Research Fellow. Univ. of London, 1935; Foulerton Research Fellow, Royal Society, 1938. War Service, 1939-46; Specialist Pathologist Comdg Mobile Bacteriological, Command and Field Laboratories; Colonel RAMC, 1945. Goulstonian Lectr, Royal College of Physicians, 1945; Visiting Prof. of Medicine, Albany Medical Coll., New York, 1953; Sir Arthur Sims Commonwealth Travelling Prof., 1962. Vis. Professor of Medicine: Vanderbilt Univ., Tennessee, 1961; Univ. of Southern California, Los Angeles, 1962; Croonian Lectr, Royal Coll. of Physicians, 1962; Henry Cohen Lectr, Hebrew Univ. of Jerusalem, 1966; Waring Prof., Univ. of Colorado and Stanford Univ., Calif., 1967; Harveian Orator, RCP, 1974. Member: MRC, 1957-61; Public Health Lab. Service Bd, 1954-66; UGC 1968-77; Chm., Med. Sub-Cttee, UGC, 1973-77. Pres., Assoc. of Physicians of GB and Ireland, 1971. Hon. Member: Assoc. of Amer. Physicians; Infectious Diseases Soc. of Amer. Hon. DSc Hull, 1973. *Publications:* (co-author) Chronic bronchitis emphysema and cor pulmonale, 1957; (co-author) Virus and Rickettsial Diseases, 1967; (co-author) Influenza—the Viruses and the Disease, 1976; papers in med. and scientific jls on influenza, typhus and bronchitis. *Recreation:* music. *Address:* 28 Whitworth Road, Sheffield S10 3HD. *T:* Sheffield 301200.

STUART-MENTETH, Sir James; *see* Menteth.

STUART-SHAW, Max, CBE 1963; Executive Director, Olympic Airways, 1969-71; *b* 20 Dec. 1912; *e s* of Herman and Anne Louise Stuart-Shaw; *m* 1967, Janna Job, *d* of C. W. Howard. *Educ:* Belmont School, Sussex; St Paul's, London. Imperial Airways/BOAC, 1931-46; Aer Lingus Irish Airlines; Traffic Manager, Commercial Manager, Asst Gen. Manager, 1947-57; Chief Exec. and Gen. Manager Central African Airways, Salisbury, Rhodesia, 1958-65; Man. Dir, BUA, 1966-67; Vice-Chairman, British United Airways, 1967-68. FCIT. *Recreation:* air transport. *Address:* c/o Barclays Bank, 160 Piccadilly, W1A 2AB. *Club:* Salisbury (Rhodesia).

STUART-SMITH, Murray, QC 1970; a Recorder of the Crown Court, since 1972; *b* 18 Nov. 1927; *s* of Edward Stuart-Smith and Doris Mary Laughland; *m* 1953, Joan Elizabeth Mary Motion, BA, JP; three *s* three *d*. *Educ:* Radley; Corpus Christi Coll., Cambridge (MA, LLB). Called to the Bar, Gray's Inn, 1952; Bencher 1977. *Recreations:* playing 'cello, shooting. *Address:* Serge Hill, Abbots Langley, Herts. *T:* Kings Langley 62116. *Club:* Bath.

STUART TAYLOR, Sir Richard (Laurence), 3rd Bt *cr* 1917; *b* 27 Sept. 1925; *s* of Sir Eric Stuart Taylor, 2nd Bt, OBE, MD, and Evelyn Thérèse (*d* 1946), *er d* of late James Calvert, CBE, MD, FRCP; *S* father, 1977; *m* 1950, Iris Mary, *d* of Rev. Edwin John Gargery; one *s* one *d*. *Educ:* Winchester; King's College, Cambridge (BA 1949, MA 1959). Served War of 1939-45 with RAC and Royal Gloucestershire Hussars. *Heir: s* Nicholas Richard Stuart Taylor, *b* 14 Jan. 1952. *Address:* White Lodge, Hambrook, Chichester, West Sussex.

STUART-WHITE, Christopher Stuart; a Recorder of the Crown Court, since 1974; barrister-at-law; *b* 18 Dec. 1933; *s* of Reginald Stuart-White and Catherine Mary Wigmore Stuart-White (*née* Higginson); *m* 1957, Pamela (*née* Grant); one *s* two *d*. *Educ:* Winchester; Trinity Coll., Oxford (BA). Called to Bar, Inner Temple, 1957. Practising Barrister on the Midland and Oxford Circuit, 1958-. *Recreations:* gardening, hill walking. *Address:* The Moat House, Cutnall Green, near Droitwich, Worcs WR9 0PH. *T:* Cutnall Green 238.

STUBBLEFIELD, Sir (Cyril) James, Kt 1965; FRS 1944; FGS; FZS; DSc (London); ARCS; formerly Director, Geological Survey of Great Britain and Museum of Practical Geology, 1960-66; Director, Geological Survey in Northern Ireland, 1960-66; *b* 6 Sept. 1901; *s* of late James Stubblefield; *m* 1932, Muriel Elizabeth, *d* of late L. R. Yakchee; two *s*. *Educ:* The Perse Sch.; Chelsea Polytechnic; Royal College of Science, London (Royal Scholar); London Univ. Geology Scholar, 1921. Demonstrator in Geology, Imperial College of Science and Technology, 1923-28; Warden of first Imperial Coll. Hostel, 1926-28. Apptd Geological Survey as Geologist, 1928; Chief Palæontologist, 1947-53; Asst Director, 1953-60. Mem., Anglo-French Commn of Surveillance, Channel Tunnel, 1964-67. Pres. Geological Soc. of London, 1958-60; Bigsby Medallist, 1941; Murchison Medallist, 1955. Sec. of Palæontographical Soc., 1934-48; Pres., 1966-71, Hon. Mem., 1974. Member Council Brit. Assoc. for Advancement of Science, 1946-52, 1958-63; Pres. Section C (Geology), Oxford, 1954. Pres. Internat. Congress Carboniferous Stratigraphy and Geology, 6th Session, Sheffield, 1967. Vice-Pres. International Paleontological Union, 1948-56. Corresp. Paleont. Soc. (USA), 1950-; Corresp. Mem. Geol Soc. Stockholm, 1952-; Senckenbergische Naturforschende Gesellschaft, 1957-. Mem. Council, Royal Soc., 1960-62. Hon. Fellow Pal. Soc. India, 1961-. Fellow Imperial Coll. of Science and Technology, 1962-; Hon. Member: Geologists' Assoc., 1973-; Liverpool Geol Soc., 1960-; For. Corr., Geol Soc., France, 1963-, For. Vice-Pres., 1966. Hon. DSc Southampton, 1965. *Publications:* papers on Palæozoic fossils and rocks and contributions to: Geological Survey Memoirs; Trilobita, Zoological Record, 1938-51, 1965-. Joint Editor of the Handbook of the Geology of Great Britain, 1929; Review, Introduction to Palæontology (A. Morley Davies), 3rd edn, 1961. *Address:* 35 Kent Avenue, Ealing, W13 8BE. *T:* 01-997 5051.

STUBBS, John F. A. H.; see Heath-Stubbs.

STUBBS, William Frederick, CMG 1955; CBE 1952 (OBE 1941); HMOCS, retired; *b* 19 June 1902; *e s* of late Lawrence Morley Stubbs, CSI, CIE, ICS (retd); *m* 1929, Eileen Mary (*d* 1963), *y d* of late Sir W. E. Stanford, KBE, CB, CMG, Rondebosch, S Africa; one *d*. *Educ:* Winchester. Joined British S Africa Police, S Rhodesia, 1921; N Rhodesia Police on transfer, 1924; Colonial Administrative Service, Northern Rhodesia, 1926; District Officer, 1928; District Comr of various districts; seconded to Labour Department, 1940; Labour Comr, 1944-48; Provincial Comr, 1949; acted as Secretary for Native Affairs, 1951 and 1953; Secretary for Native Affairs, 1954-57; *Ex-officio* member of Executive and Legislative Councils (Speaker, Legislative Council, and Chm. Public Service Commn Somaliland Protectorate, 1960, until Union with Somalia). Associate Commonwealth Parliamentary Association. *Recreations:* shooting and fishing. *Address:* Nash Court Farm House, Marnhull, Dorset. *Club:* Royal Commonwealth Society.

STUCHBERY, Arthur Leslie, CBE 1971 (OBE 1968); Chairman, Remploy, 1969-72; *b* 14 Feb. 1903; *s* of Harry and Martha Stuchbery; *m* 1930, Dorothy Blanche Willmott; one *s* one *d*. *Educ:* Hackney Techn. Coll.; Borough Polytechnic. CEng, FIMechE, FIProdE, FRSA. Metal Box Co.: Plant Manager,

1929; Chief Engr, 1939; Dir of R&D, 1961. Founder Councillor, PERA (Chm. 1962-67); Founder Mem., IProdE, 1924, President 1969-72; Chm., Brunel Univ., 1965-73. Clayton Lectr, 1966. Hon. DTech Brunel, 1970. *Publications:* numerous technical papers. *Recreations:* hand crafts, motoring. *Address:* Dyke End House, Littlestone, Kent. *T:* New Romney 2076. *Clubs:* City Livery, St Stephen's.

STUCLEY, Major Sir Dennis Frederic Bankes, 5th Bt, *cr* 1859; DL; JP; *b* 29 Oct. 1907; *s* of Sir Hugh Nicholas Granville Stucley, 4th Bt, and Gladys (*d* 1950), *d* of W. A. Bankes, Wolfeton House, Dorchester; *S* father, 1956; *m* 1932, Hon. Sheila Bampfylde, *o d* of 4th Baron Poltimore; one *s* four *d* (and one *s* decd). *Educ:* Harrow; RMC Sandhurst. 2nd Lt Grenadier Guards, 1927; retired, 1932. Devon CC, 1934, CA, 1955. Capt. Royal Devon Yeomanry, 1937, Major, 1944. JP Devon, 1936; Deputy Lieutenant, Devon, 1955; Mayor of Bideford, 1954-56; High Sheriff of Devon, 1956, County Alderman, Devon, 1956. Joint Master, Dulverton Foxhounds, 1952-54. Chairman: Regional Adv. Cttee, Forestry Commn, SW, 1958-75; Timber Growers Organization, 1966-69; Exmoor Nat. Park (Devon) Cttee, 1968-74. *Recreations:* hunting, shooting and fishing. *Heir: s* Lieut Hugh George Coplestone Bampfylde Stucley, Royal Horse Guards [*b* 8 Jan. 1945; *m* 1969, Angela Caroline, *er d* of Richard Toller, Theale, Berks; two *s* one *d*]. *Address:* Hartland Abbey, Bideford, Devon. *T:* Hartland 234; Court Hall, North Molton, South Molton, Devon. *T:* North Molton 224. *Club:* Cavalry and Guards.
See also Viscount Boyne, Baron Cobbold, Sir C. H. M. Peto, Bt, J. H. A. Stucley.

STUCLEY, John Humphrey Albert, DSC 1945; **His Honour Judge Stucley;** a Circuit Judge, since 1974; *b* 12 July 1916; 2nd *s* of Sir Hugh Stucley, 4th Bt, Affeton Castle, Devon; *m* 1941, Natalia, *d* of Don Alberto Jiménez, CBE and Natalia Cossio de Jiménez; no *c*. *Educ:* RN Colls, Dartmouth and Greenwich. Cadet, RN, 1930; served China, Mediterranean and Home stns and throughout War of 1939-45; Lt-Comdr 1945. Called to Bar, Middle Temple, 1957. A Recorder of the Crown Court, 1972-74. Dep. Chm., SE England Agricultural Land Tribunal, 1971. *Recreation:* shooting. *Address:* 14 Chester Row, SW1W 9JH. *T:* 01-730 6742.
See also Major Sir D. F. B. Stucley, Bt.

STUDD, Sir Edward (Fairfax), 4th Bt *cr* 1929; Director, Inchcape & Co. Ltd and other Inchcape Group Companies, since 1974; *b* 3 May 1929; *s* of Sir Eric Studd, 2nd Bt, OBE, and Stephana (*d* 1976), *o d* of L. J. Langmead; *S* brother, 1977; *m* 1960, Prudence Janet, *o d* of Alastair Douglas Fyfe, OBE, Riding Mill, Northumberland; two *s* one *d*. *Educ:* Winchester College. Lieutenant Coldstream Guards, London and Malaya, 1947-49; Macneill & Barry Ltd, Calcutta, 1951-62; Inchcape & Co. Ltd, London, 1962-. Under Renter Warden, Merchant Taylors' Company, 1977. *Recreations:* walking, shooting, fishing. *Heir: s* Philip Alastair Fairfax Studd, *b* 27 Oct. 1961. *Address:* Danceys, Clavering, near Saffron Walden, Essex. *T:* Clavering 444. *Clubs:* City of London; Royal Calcutta Turf (Calcutta).

STUDD, Sir Peter Malden, GBE 1971; Kt 1969; Director: Thomas De La Rue & Co. Ltd; Beaver Housing Society; Lloyds & Scottish Ltd; W. & F. C. Bonham & Sons Ltd; City of London (Arizona) Corporation; *b* 15 Sept. 1916; *s* of late Brig. Malden Augustus Studd, DSO, MC; *m* 1943, Angela Mary Hamilton (*née* Garnier); two *s*. *Educ:* Harrow; Clare Coll., Cambridge (MA). Served War of 1939-45, ME and European campaigns. Alderman, City of London, 1960-76; Sheriff, 1967-68; Lord Mayor of London, 1970-71; Hon. DSc City Univ., 1970. Mem., Canada Permanent Mortgage Corp. (London Adv. Bd). Pres., Florence Nightingale Aid in Sickness Trust; Vice-Chm., Admin. Council, King George's Jubilee Trust, 1972; Chm., the Queen's Silver Jubilee Appeal Council, 1976-; Vice-Chm., Admin. Council, the Queen's Silver Jubilee Trust, 1977. Governor: Lady Eleanor Holles Sch., Hampton; Cripplegate Foundation; Harrow Sch.; Trustee, St Paul's Cathedral Trust. Master, Merchant Taylors' Co., 1973-74 (Asst, 1959-); Hon. Liveryman, Worshipful Cos of Fruiterers and Plaisterers. Surrey County Pres., St John Ambulance. KStJ. *Recreations:* gardening, fishing, shooting, 'lighting up the Thames'. *Address:* Arbourne, Copsem Lane, Esher, Surrey. *T:* Esher 65252. *Clubs:* City Livery, MCC.

STUDHOLME, Sir Henry (Gray), 1st Bt, *cr* 1956; CVO 1953; DL; *b* 13 June 1899; *s* of late William Paul Studholme, Perridge House, Exeter; *m* 1929, Judith, *d* of Henry William Whitbread, Norton Bavant Manor, Warminster; two *s* one *d*. *Educ:* Eton; Magdalen Coll., Oxford (MA). Served European War with Scots Guards, 1917-19; Member LCC, 1931-45; rejoined Scots

Guards, 1940; Staff appointments, 1941-44. MP (C) Tavistock Division, 1942-66. PPS to late Comdr R. Brabner, Under-Sec. of State for Air, Nov. 1944-March 1945; Conservative Whip, 1945-56; Joint Treas. of the Conservative Party, 1956-62. Vice-Chamberlain of King George VI's Household, 1951-52, of the Queen's Household, 1952-56. DL Devon, 1969. *Heir: s* Paul Henry William Studholme, late Capt. Coldstream Guards [*b* 16 Jan. 1930; *m* 1957, Virginia Katherine, *yr d* of late Sir Richmond Palmer, KCMG; two *s* one *d*]. *Address:* Wembury House, Wembury, Plymouth. *T:* Plymouth 862210.

STURDEE, Rear-Adm. Arthur Rodney Barry, CB 1971; DSC 1945; RN retired; Flag-Officer, Gibraltar, 1969-72; *b* 6 Dec. 1919, *s* of Comdr Barry V. Sturdee, RN, and Barbara (*née* Sturdee); *m* 1953, Marie-Claire Amstoutz, Mulhouse, France; one *s* one *d*. *Educ:* Canford Sch. Entered Royal Navy as Special Entry Cadet, 1937. Served War of 1939-45: Midshipman in HMS Exeter at Battle of the River Plate, 1939; Lieut, 1941; specialised in Navigation, 1944; minesweeping in Mediterranean, 1944-45 (DSC). Lt-Comdr, 1949; RN Staff Coll., 1950-51; Staff of Navigation Sch., 1951-52; Comdr, 1952; JSSC, 1953; BJSM, Washington, 1953-55; Fleet Navigating Officer, Medit., 1955-57; Exec. Officer, RNAS, Culdrose, 1958-59; Captain 1960; NATO Defence Coll., 1960-63; Queen's Harbour-Master, Singapore, 1963-65; Staff of Chief of Defence Staff, 1965-67; Chief of Staff to C-in-C, Portsmouth (as Cdre), 1967-69; Rear-Adm. 1969. ADC to the Queen, 1969. *Address:* 9 Avenue Road, Malvern, Worcestershire. *T:* Malvern 5402.

STURDY, Henry William, OBE 1975 (MBE 1968); HM Diplomatic Service; Deputy Consul General and Counsellor Commercial, Chicago, since 1976; *b* 17 Feb. 1919; *s* of Henry William Dawson Sturdy and late Jemima Aixill; *m* 1945, Anne Jamieson Marr; one *s* one *d*. *Educ:* Woolwich Polytechnic (Mechanical Engineering). Served War in Middle East, 1939-45; Allied Control Commission, Germany, 1946. Executive Branch of Civil Service and Board of Trade, 1951; tour in Trade Commission Service, 1953; appointments: Pakistan, Bangladesh, Sri Lanka, Canada. First Secretary, Diplomatic Service, 1965; Counsellor, Korea, 1976. Defence Medal; 1939-45 Medal; General Service Medal, 1939, with Palestine Clasp, 1945. *Recreations:* squash, bridge, reading, argument, international cuisine. *Address:* Apt 16D, 3240 Lakeshore Drive, Chicago, Ill. 60602, USA. *T:* 312-871-1210; 5 Partridge Drive, Orpington, Kent. *Clubs:* Royal Commonwealth Society; Cliffdwellers, Rotary One (Chicago).

STURGE, Arthur Collwyn, MC 1945; President, A. L. Sturge (Holdings) Ltd, since 1977; *b* 27 Sept. 1912; *yr s* of Arthur Lloyd Sturge and Jessie Katherine Howard; *m* 1938, Beryl Gwenllian, *yr d* of Thomas Arthur, Hong Kong; two *s* two *d*. *Educ:* Harrow; Brasenose Coll., Oxford (BA). Underwriting Member of Lloyd's, 1933; Mem., Cttee of Lloyd's, 1967-75 (Dep. Chm., 1969, 1970); Mem. Gen. Cttee, Lloyd's Register of Shipping, 1969-77. Partner, R. W. Sturge & Co.; Chairman: Lloyd's of London Press Ltd; Officers' Families Fund. Commissioned 64 Field Regt RA (TA), 1937; served War of 1939-45, Middle East, Italy. High Sheriff, East Sussex, 1977. *Recreations:* golf, shooting. *Address:* 15 Arundel Court, Jubilee Place, SW3; Faircrouch, Wadhurst, Sussex. *T:* Wadhurst 2281. *Clubs:* City of London; Rye Golf.
See also R. W. Sturge.

STURGE, Harold Francis Ralph; Metropolitan Magistrate, 1947-68; *b* 15 May 1902; *y s* of Ernest Harold Sturge; *m* 1936, Doreen, *e d* of Sir Percy Greenaway, 1st Bt; two *s* (and one *s* decd). *Educ:* Highgate Sch.; Oriel Coll., Oxford, BA (Lit. Hum.). Called to Bar, Inner Temple, 1925; Midland Circuit. War of 1939-45, served on staff of Judge Advocate-General. Member Departmental Cttee on the Probation Service, 1959; President, Old Cholmelian Society, 1962-63. *Publications:* The Road Haulage Wages Act, 1938; (jointly with T. D. Corpe, OBE) Road Haulage Law and Compensation, 1947. *Recreation:* painting. *Address:* 10 Tilney Court, Catherine Road, Surbiton, Surrey KT6 4HA.

STURGE, Maj.-Gen. Henry Arthur John; Assistant Chief of Defence Staff (Signals), since 1977; *b* 27 April 1925; *s* of Henry George Arthur Sturge and Lilian Beatrice Sturge; *m* 1953, Jean Ailsa Mountain; two *s* one *d*. *Educ:* Wilson's Sch., (formerly) Camberwell; London; Queen Mary Coll., London. Commissioned, Royal Signals, 1946; UK, 1946-50; Egypt, 1950-53; UK, incl. psc, 1953-59; Far East, 1959-62; jssc, 1962; BAOR, 1963-64; RMA, Sandhurst, 1965-66; BAOR, incl. Command, 1966-69; Min. of Defence, 1970-75; Chief Signal Officer, BAOR, 1975-77. *Recreations:* sailing, (formerly) Rugby. *Address:* Border Hill, Dippenhall, Farnham, Surrey. *Club:* Army and Navy.

STURGE, Raymond Wilson; Chairman of Lloyd's, 1964, 1965 and 1966; *b* 10 June 1904; *er s* of late Arthur Lloyd Sturge and late Jessie Katharine (*née* Howard); *m* 1929, Margaret, *y d* of late Walter J. Keep, Sydney, NSW; one *s* four *d*. *Educ:* Harrow; Brasenose Coll., Oxford (BA). Mem. of Lloyd's, 1926; first elected to Committee, 1953; Dep. Chm., 1963. Served War of 1939-45, Royal Scots Fusiliers, Staff Duties. Pres., Insurance Institute of London, 1967-68 (Dep. Pres., 1966-67). *Address:* Ashmore, near Salisbury, Wilts. *T:* Fontmell Magna 261. *Club:* City of London.
See also Hon. J. D. Eccles, A. C. Sturge.

STUTTAFORD, Dr (Irving) Thomas; medical practitioner; *b* 4 May 1931; 2nd *s* of late Dr W. J. E. Stuttaford, MC, Horning, Norfolk; *m* 1957, Pamela, *d* of late Col Richard Ropner, TD, DL, Tain; three *s*. *Educ:* Gresham's Sch.; Brasenose Coll., Oxford; West London Hosp. 2nd Lieut, 10th Royal Hussars (PWO), 1953-55; Lieut, Scottish Horse (TA), 1955-59. Qualif. MRCS, LRCP, 1959; junior hosp. appts, 1959 and 1960. Gen. Med. practice, 1960-70. Mem. Blofield and Flegg RDC, 1964-66; Mem., Norwich City Council, 1969-71. MP (C) Norwich S, 1970-Feb. 1974; Mem. Select Cttee Science and Technology, 1970-74. Contested (C) Isle of Ely, Oct. 1974. Vis. Physician, BUPA Medical Centre; Clinical Assistant to: The London Hosp.; Queen Mary's Hosp. for East End; Moorfields Eye Hosp. Member: Council, Research Defence Soc., 1970-; Birth Control Campaign Cttee, 1971-; British Cancer Council, 1971-. *Recreation:* country life. *Address:* Snowre Hall, Hilgay, Downham Market, Norfolk. *Clubs:* Athenæum, Reform, Cavalry and Guards; Norfolk (Norwich).

STYLE, Lt-Comdr Sir Godfrey (William), Kt 1973; CBE 1961; DSC 1941; RN; Governor, Queen Elizabeth's Foundation; Member of Council, Sir Oswald Stoll Foundation; also Member of a number of allied advisory bodies and panels; a Member of Lloyd's, since 1945; *b* 3 April 1915; *er s* of Brig.-Gen. R. C. Style (*y s* of Sir William Henry Marsham Style, 9th Bt), and Hélène Pauline, *d* of Herman Greverus Kleinwort; *m* 1st, 1942, Jill Elizabeth Caruth (marr. diss. 1951); one *s* two *d*; 2nd, 1951, Sigrid Elisabeth Julin (*née* Carlberg); one *s*. *Educ:* Eton. Joined Royal Navy as a Regular Officer, 1933; served in Royal Yacht Victoria and Albert, 1938. Served War, Flag-Lieut to C-in-C, Home Fleet, 1939-41 (despatches, DSC, 1941; wounded, 1942, in Mediterranean); despatches, 1943; invalided from Royal Navy, due to war wounds and injuries, 1945. Dep. Underwriter at Lloyds, 1945-55; thereafter concentrated increasingly on work of, and concerned with, the National Advisory Council on Employment of Disabled People (Chm., 1963-74). *Recreations:* the field sports, horticulture (esp. orchid growing), lapidary work. *Address:* Rocklands, Norton-sub-Hamdon, Somerset TA14 6SR. *T:* Chiselborough 279. *Clubs:* Naval and Military; Union (Malta).

STYLE, Sir William Montague, 12th Bt, *cr* 1627; *b* 21 July 1916; *s* of Sir William Frederick Style, 11th Bt, and Florence (*d* 1918), *d* of J. Timm; *S* father, 1943; *m* 1941, La Verne, *d* of T. M. Comstock; two *s*. *Heir: s* William Frederick Style, *b* 13 May 1945.

STYLES, Fredrick William, BEM 1943; Member for Greenwich, Greater London Council; Chairman, Royal Arsenal Co-operative Society, since 1975 (Director, since 1968); *b* 18 Dec. 1914; *s* of Henry Albert Styles and Mabel Louise (*née* Sherwood); *m* 1942, Mary Gwendoline Harrison; one *s* three *d*. *Educ:* LCC elementary sch.; London Univ. (Dipl. economics); NCLC (Dipls Local and Central Govt). Salesman, Co-op, 1929-39. RAFVR Air Sea Rescue Service, 1939-46. Royal Humane Soc. Silver Medal, 1939; BEM for gallantry, 1943. Trade union official, NUPE (London divisional officer), 1946-52; social worker, hospital, 1952-58; social worker, LCC and GLC, 1958-68. Vice-Chm., 1974-75, Chm., 1975-76, ILEA. Chm. Staff and General Cttee, ILEA, 1977-. *Recreations:* problems, people, politics. *Address:* 49 Court Farm Road, Mottingham, SE9 4JN. *T:* 01-857 1508.

STYLES, Lt-Col Stephen George, GC 1972; retired; company director, since 1974; *b* 16 March 1928; *s* of Stephen Styles and Grace Lily Styles (*née* Preston); *m* 1952, Mary Rose Styles (*née* Woolgar); one *s* two *d*. *Educ:* Collyers Sch., Horsham; Royal Military Coll. of Science. Ammunition Technical Officer, commissioned RAOC, Nov. 1947; seconded to 1 Bn KOYLI, 1949-51 (despatches, 1952); RMCS, 1952-56; HQ Ammunition Organisation, 1956-58; OC 28 Commonwealth Bde, Ordnance Field Park, Malaya, 1958-61; 2i/c 16 Bn RAOC, Bicester, 1961-64; OC Eastern Command Ammunition Inspectorate, 1964-67; Sen. Ammo Tech. Officer, 3 BAPD, BAOR, 1967-68; OC 1(BR) Corps Vehicle Company, 1968-69; Sen. Ammo Tech. Officer, Northern Ireland, 1969-72; Chief Ammo Tech. Officer (EOD),

HQ DOS (CILSA), 1972-74. Member: Royal Soc. of St George, NRA, NSRA. *Publications:* Bombs Have No Pity, 1975; contrib. Proc. ICE, Jl of Forensic Science Soc. *Recreation:* rifle and game shooting, cartridge collector. *Address:* c/o Barclays Bank Ltd, Wantage. *Club:* Institute of Directors.

SUÁREZ, Dr Eduardo; Mexican Ambassador to Great Britain, 1965-70; *b* Texcoco, Mexico, 3 Jan. 1895; *s* of Eduardo Suárez and Antonia Aránsolo de Suárez; *m* 1935, Maria de la Luz Dávila; four *s* one *d.* (and one *s* decd). *Educ:* Col. Municipal, Texcoco; Col. Inglés, Tacubaya; Nat. Univ. of Mexico. Supt Under Sec., State of Hidalgo; Pres., Central Conciliation and Arbitration Bd of City of Mexico; Prof. of Jurisprudence, Nat. Univ. of Mexico, at different times, 1916-48. Counsel for Mexico, in Claims between: Mexico and the US, June 1926-Aug. 1927; Mexico and Gt Britain, Aug.-Dec. 1928; Member, Arbitration Tribunal between Mexico and France. Head of Legal Dept, Min. of For. Affairs, 1929-31, 1931-34, Jan.-June 1935; Minister of Finance and Public Credit, 1935-46. Dr (*hc*) Nat. Univ. of Mexico; holds foreign decorations. *Publications:* pamphlets, articles. *Address:* Paseo de la Reforma 645, Lomas, Mexico 10, DF, Mexico. *Clubs:* White's, Clermont; Club de Banqueros (Mexico).

SUAREZ, Juan L.; see Lechin-Suarez.

SUBAK-SHARPE, Prof. John Herbert, FRSE 1970; Professor of Virology, University of Glasgow, since 1968; Hon. Director, Medical Research Council Virology Unit, since 1968; *b* 14 Feb. 1924; *s* of late Robert Subak and late Nelly (*née* Bruell), Vienna, Austria; *m* 1953, Barbara Naomi Morris; two *s* one *d.* *Educ:* Humanistic Gymnasium, Vienna; Univ. of Birmingham. BSc (Genetics) (1st Cl. Hons) 1952; PhD 1956. Refugee from Nazi oppression, 1939; farm pupil, 1939-44; HM Forces (Parachute Regt), 1944-47. Asst Lectr in Genetics, Glasgow Univ., 1954-56; Mem. scientific staff, ARC Animal Virus Research Inst., Pirbright, 1956-60; Nat. Foundn Fellow, California Inst. of Technology, 1961; Mem. Scientific staff of MRC, in Experimental Virus Research Unit, Glasgow, 1961-68. Vis. Prof., US Nat. Insts of Health, Bethesda, Md, 1967; Sec., Genetical Soc., 1966-72, Vice-Pres. 1972-75, Trustee 1971-. Member: European Molecular Biology Orgn, 1969- (Chm., Course and Workshops Cttee, 1976-); Genetic Manipulation Adv. Gp, 1976-; British Nat. Cttee of Biophysics, 1970-76; Governing Body, W of Scotland Oncological Orgn, 1974-. *Publications:* articles in scientific jls on genetic studies with viruses and cells. *Recreations:* mountain walking and bridge. *Address:* 17 Kingsborough Gardens, Glasgow G12 9NH. *T:* 041-334 1863. *Club:* Athenæum.

SUBONO, Adm. Richardus; Ambassador of Indonesia to the Court of St James's, since 1974; *b* 27 June 1927; *s* of R. S. Suryosumarno and Sukimah Suryosumarno; *m* 1959, Veronica Maria Umboh; one *s* three *d.* *Educ:* naval sch. and coll.; courses in Indonesia and abroad (Holland and UK). Various appts in fleet and Naval HQ, 1950-61; Dep. C-in-C Theatre Comd for liberation of West Irian, 1962; Dir-Gen. Planning, Naval HQ, 1963; Dep. Governor, Nat. Defence Coll., 1964; Dep. Chief of Staff of Navy, 1966; Chief of Gen. Staff, Armed Forces HQ, 1969; Chief of Staff of Navy, 1973. Awarded 22 medals, 1950-74. *Recreation:* golf. *Address:* Indonesian Embassy, Grosvenor Square, W1X 9AD. *T:* 01-499 7661. *Club:* Highgate Golf.

SUBRAMANIAM, Chidambaram; Minister of Finance, Government of India, 1974-77; *b* 30 Jan. 1910; *s* of Chidambara Gounder and Valliammal; *m* 1945, Sakuntala; one *s* two *d.* *Educ:* Madras (BA, LLB). Set up legal practice, Coimbatore, 1936; took active part in freedom movt, imprisoned 1932, 1941 and again 1942; Pres., District Congress Committee, Coimbatore; Mem. Working Cttee of State Congress Cttee; Mem. Constituent Assembly; Minister of Finance, Educn and Law, Govt of Madras, 1952; MP 1962; Minister of Steel, 1962-63; Minister of Steel, Mines and Heavy Engrg, 1963-64; Minister of Food and Agric., 1964-66; Minister of Food and Agriculture, CD and Coopn, 1966-67; Chm. Cttee on Aeronautics Industry, 1967-69; Interim Pres., Indian Nat. Congress, July-Dec. 1969; Chm. Nat. Commn on Agric., 1970; Minister of Planning and Dep. Chm., Planning Commn, 1971; also i/c Dept of Science and Technology; Minister of Industrial Develt and Science and Technology, 1972 (also Agric., temp., 1974). Hon. DLitt: Wattair; Sri Venkateswara; Madurai; Hon. LLD Andhra. *Publications:* Nan Sendra Sila Nadugal (Travelogues); War on Poverty; Ulagam Sutrinen (in Tamil); India of My Dreams (in English); Strategy Statement for Fighting Protein Hunger in Developing Countries. *Recreation:* yoga. *Address:* 26 Tughlak Crescent, New Delhi 110011, India. *T:* 375838. *Clubs:* Cosmopolitan, Gymkhana (Madras); Cosmopolitan (Coimbatore).

SUCKSDORFF, Mrs Åke; see Jonzen, Mrs Karin.

SUCKSMITH, W., FRS 1940; DSc Leeds; Professor of Physics, Sheffield University, 1940-63, Emeritus since 1963. Formerly Reader in Magnetism, Bristol University. Hon. DSc Sheffield, 1972. *Address:* 27 Endcliffe Grove Avenue, Sheffield S10 3EJ.

SUCRE-TRIAS, Dr Juan Manuel; Ambassador of Venezuela to the Court of St James's, since 1977; *b* 25 Oct. 1940; *m* 2nd, 1977, Tatiana Perez; three *s* of former marriage. Economist. Economist, Corporación Venezolana de Guayana; as Economist, Ministry of Public Works, Caracas: Head of Studies Unit; Asst Director of Programming and Budgeting. Member of Congress, Venezuela; President, Finance Commission of Congress of the Republic. Holds several military decorations (Venezuelan). *Recreations:* swimming, tennis, golf. *Address:* Venezuelan Embassy, 3 Hans Crescent, SW1. *T:* 01-584 5375. *Clubs:* Les Ambassadeurs, Belfry, Annabel's.

SUDBURY, Archdeacon of; see Child, Ven. Kenneth.

SUDBURY, Col Frederick Arthur, OBE 1942; ERD 1951; JP; *b* 14 Sept. 1904. *Educ:* Colfe Grammar School, Lewisham; London School of Economics. Tate & Lyle, 1922-69. Served War of 1939-45, Army Officers Emergency Reserve; Col, Dir of Inland Water Transport, Iraq, 1941-43; Col, Movements and Transportation, 14th Army, 1944-45; Lt-Col Supplementary Reserve, 1947-51; Col, Army Emergency Reserve, 1951-62; Hon. Col., RE (AER), 1951-66. Mem. Thames Conservancy, 1958-65 (Vice-Chm., 1960-65). Underwriting Mem. of Lloyd's. Liveryman and Mem. Court Shipwrights' Co.; Freeman and Mem. Court, Co. of Watermen and Lightermen (Master, 1960-61-62). JP Inner London, 1962-. *Recreation:* yachting. *Address:* 1 Abbotsbury Close, W14. *T:* 01-603 2880. *Club:* Royal Thames Yacht.

SUDDABY, Arthur, PhD, MSc; CChem, MRIC; CEng, MIChemE; Provost, City of London Polytechnic, since 1970; *b* 26 Feb. 1919; *e s* of George Suddaby, Kingston-upon-Hull, Yorks; *m* 1944, Elizabeth Bullin Vyse (decd), *d* of Charles Vyse; two *s.* *Educ:* Riley High Sch., Kingston-upon-Hull; Hull Technical Coll.; Chelsea Polytechnic; Queen Mary Coll. London. Chemist and Chemical Engr, in industry, 1937-47; Lectr in Physical Chemistry, and later Sen. Lectr in Chem. Engrg, West Ham Coll. of Technology, 1947-50; Sir John Cass Coll.: Sen. Lectr in Physics, 1950-61; Head of Dept of Physics, 1961-66; Principal, 1966-70. Chm., Cttee of Directors of Polytechnics, 1976-; Member: Chem. Engrg Cttee, 1948-51; London and Home Counties Regional Adv. Council, 1971-; Bd of Examrs and Educn Cttee, Inst. of Chem. Engrs, 1948-51; CNAA: Chem. Engrg Bd, 1969-75; Nautical Studies Bd, 1972-75; Court of the City University, 1967-; Chm., Assoc. of Navigation Schs, 1972. Scientific consultant on physical and chemical problems of carriage of goods by sea, 1955-. *Publications:* various original research papers in theoretical physics, in scientific jls; review articles. *Recreation:* hunting. *Address:* Flat 3, 16 Elm Park Gardens, Chelsea, SW10. *T:* 01-352 9164; Bothkerran House, Dengie, Essex. *T:* Tillingham 340.

SUDDARDS, (Henry) Gaunt; His Honour Judge Suddards; a Circuit Judge (formerly Judge of County Courts), since 1963; *b* 30 July 1910; *s* of Fred Suddards and Agnes Suddards (*née* Gaunt); unmarried. *Educ:* Cheltenham College; Trinity College, Cambridge (MA). Barrister, Inner Temple, 1932; joined NE Circuit, 1933. Served War of 1939-45, RAFVR, 1940-46. Recorder of Pontefract, 1960-61; Recorder of Middlesbrough, 1961-63; Dep. Chm., West Riding QS, 1961-71; Chairman, Agricultural Land Tribunal, Northern Area, 1961-63, Dep. Chairman 1960. *Recreations:* fishing, shooting, sailing. *Address:* Rockville, Frizinghall, Shipley, West Yorkshire. *Club:* Union (Bradford).

SUDELEY, 7th Baron *cr* 1838; **Merlin Charles Sainthill Hanbury-Tracy;** *b* 17 June 1939; *o c* of late Captain Michael David Charles Hanbury-Tracy, Scots Guards, and Colline Ammabel, *d* of late Lt-Col C. G. H. St Hill and *widow* of Lt-Col Frank King, DSO, OBE; *S* cousin, 1941. *Educ:* at Eton and in the ranks of the Scots Guards. Vice-Pres., Prayer Book Soc.; Member: Cttee of Human Rights Soc.; Exec., Monday Club. Patron, St Peter's, Petersham, Richmond, Surrey. *Publications:* contribs to Quarterly Review, Contemporary Review, Trans of Bristol and Gloucestershire Archaeol. Soc., Montgomeryshire Collections, Die Waage (Zeitschrift der Chemie Grünenthal). *Recreations:* ancestor worship; cultivating his sensibility. *Heir:* kinsman Claud Edward Frederick Hanbury-Tracy-Domvile, TD [*b* 11 Jan. 1904; assumed by deed poll, 1961, additional surname of Domvile; *m* 1st, 1927, Veronica May (marr. diss. 1948), *d* of late Cyril Grant Cunard; two *s* one *d*; 2nd, 1954,

Marcella Elizabeth Willis, er d of late Rev. Canon John Willis Price]. *Address:* c/o Williams & Glyn's Bank Ltd, 21 Grosvenor Gardens, SW1. *Clubs:* Brooks's, (as Member of Parliament) House of Lords.

SUDLEY, Viscount; Arthur Desmond Colquhoun Gore; b 14 July 1938; er s of 8th Earl of Arran, qv; m 1974, Eleanor, er d of Bernard van Cutsem and Lady Margaret Fortescue; two d. *Educ:* Eton; Balliol College, Oxford. 2nd Lieutenant, 1st Bn Grenadier Guards (National Service). Asst Manager, Daily Mail, 1972-73; Man. Dir, Clark Nelson, 1973-74; Asst Gen. Manager Daily and Sunday Express, June-Nov. 1974. Co-Vice-Chm., Children's Country Holidays Fund. *Recreations:* tennis, shooting, gardening. *Address:* 28 Pembroke Road, Kensington, W8. *T:* 01-602 4228. *Club:* Turf.

SUENENS, His Eminence Cardinal Leo Joseph, DTheol, DPhil; Cardinal since 1962; Archbishop of Malines-Brussels and Primate of Belgium, since 1961; b Ixelles (Brussels), 16 July 1904. *Educ:* primary sch., Inst. of Marist Brothers, Brussels; secondary sch., St Mary's High Sch., Brussels; Gregorian Univ., Rome (BCL, DPhil, DrTheol). Priest, 1927; Teacher, St Mary's High Sch., Brussels, 1929; Prof. of Philosophy, Diocesan Seminary, Malines, 1930; Vice-Rector, Cath. Univ. of Louvain, 1940; Vicar-Gen., Archdio. of Malines, 1945; Auxiliary Bp to Archbp of Malines, 1945. Moderator of Second Vatican Council, 1962-65; Pres., Belgian Bishops' Conf. Templeton Prize for Religion, 1976. *Publications:* Theology of the Apostolate of the Legion of Mary, 1951 (Cork); Edel Quinn, 1952 (Dublin); (ed) The Right View on Moral Rearmament, 1953 (London); (ed) The Gospel to Every Creature, 1955 (London); (ed) Mary the Mother of God, 1957 (New York); (ed) Love and Control, 1959 (London); (ed) Christian Life Day by Day, 1961 (London); (ed) The Nun in the World, 1962 (London); (ed) Co-responsibility in the Church, 1968 (New York), 1969 (London); (ed, with Archbp Ramsey) The Future of the Christian Church, 1971 (New York); A New Pentecost?, 1975 (New York). *Address:* Wollemarkt 15, 2800 Mechelen, Belgium. *T:* 015/21.65.01.

SUENSON-TAYLOR, family name of **Baron Grantchester.**

SUFFIELD, 11th Baron cr 1786; **Anthony Philip Harbord-Hamond,** Bt, cr 1745; MC 1950; Major, retired, 1961; b 19 June 1922; o s of 10th Baron and Nina Annette Mary Crawfuird (d 1955), e d of John Hutchison of Laurieston and Edingham, Stewartry of Kirkcudbright; S father 1951; m 1952, Elizabeth Eve, er d of late Judge Edgedale; three s one d. *Educ:* Eton. Commission, Coldstream Guards, 1942; served War of 1939-45, in North African and Italian campaigns, 1942-45; Malaya, 1948-50. One of HM Hon. Corps of Gentlemen-at-Arms, 1973-. Officer of the Order of Orange Nassau, 1950. *Recreations:* normal. *Heir:* s Hon. Charles Anthony Assheton Harbord-Hamond [b 3 Dec. 1953; commissioned Coldstream Guards, 1972]. *Address:* Langham Lodge, Holt, Norfolk. *T:* Binham 373. *Clubs:* Army and Navy, Pratt's.

SUFFIELD, Sir (Henry John) Lester, Kt 1973; Head of Defence Sales, Ministry of Defence, 1969-76; b 28 April 1911; m 1940, Elizabeth Mary White; one s one d. *Educ:* Camberwell Central, LCC. Served with RASC, 1939-45 (Major). LNER, 1926-35; Morris Motors, 1935-38 and 1945-52; Pres., British Motor Corp., Canada and USA, 1952-64; Dep. Man. and Dir, British Motor Corp., Birmingham, 1964-68; Sales Dir, British Leyland Motor Corp., 1968-69. *Recreation:* golf. *Address:* 1 Somerset Square, W14. *T:* 01-602 4737. *Clubs:* Royal Automobile; Royal Wimbledon Golf.

SUFFOLK and BERKSHIRE, 21st Earl of, cr 1603; **Michael John James George Robert Howard;** Viscount Andover and Baron Howard, 1622; Earl of Berkshire, 1626; b 27 March 1935; s of 20th Earl (killed by enemy action, 1941) and Mimi (d 1966), yr d of late A. G. Forde Pigott; S father 1941; m 1st, 1960, Mme Simone Paulmier (marr. diss. 1967), d of late Georges Litman, Paris; (one d decd); 2nd, 1973, Anita, d of R. R. Fuglesang, Haywards Heath, Sussex; one s one d. Owns 5,000 acres. *Heir:* s Viscount Andover, qv. *Address:* Charlton Park, Malmesbury, Wilts.

See also Hon. G. R. Howard.

SUFFOLK, Archdeacon of; see Smith, Ven. Donald John.

SUGDEN, family name of **Baron St Leonards.**

SUGDEN, Arthur; Chief Executive Officer, Co-operative Wholesale Society Ltd, since 1974; b 12 Sept. 1918; s of late Arthur and Elizabeth Ann Sugden; m 1946, Agnes Grayston; two s. *Educ:* Thomas Street, Manchester. Certified Accountant, Chartered Secretary. FIB. Served War of 1939-45, Royal

Artillery; CPO 6th Super Heavy Battery; Adjt 12th Medium Regt; Staff Captain 16th Army Group. CWS Ltd: Accountancy Asst, 1946; Office Man., 1950; Factory Man., 1954; Group Man., Edible Oils and Fats Factories, 1964; Controller, Food Div., 1967; Dep. Chief Exec. Officer, 1971. Director: Co-operative Bank Ltd; Co-operative Commercial Bank Ltd; Co-operative City Investments Ltd; Co-operative Pension Funds Unit Trust Managers' Ltd; Co-operative Bank (Insurance Services) Ltd; Associated Co-operative Creameries Ltd; FC Finance Ltd; CWS Svineslagterier A/S Denmark; CWS (Overseas) Ltd; CWS (Longburn) Ltd; CWS (New Zealand Holdings) Ltd; Spillers French Holdings Ltd; J. W. French (Milling & Baking Holdings) Ltd; Chancelot Mill Ltd; Centenary Finance (Glasgow) Ltd; Shaw's Smokers' Products Ltd; North Eastern Co-operative Soc. Ltd; Inst. of Grocery Distribution Ltd; Manchester Chamber of Commerce. *Recreations:* music, reading, walking. *Address:* 56 Old Wool Lane, Cheadle Hulme, Cheadle, Cheshire. *T:* 061-485 1019.

SUGDEN, John Goldthorp, MA; ARCM; Headmaster, Wellingborough School, 1965-73; b 22 July 1921; s of A. G. Sugden, Brighouse, Yorkshire; m 1954, Jane Machin; two s. *Educ:* Radley; Magdalene College, Cambridge. War Service, Royal Signals, 1941-46. Asst Master, Bilton Grange Prep. School, 1948-52; Asst Master, The King's School, Canterbury, 1952-59; Headmaster, Foster's School, Sherborne, 1959-64. *Recreations:* music, golf, tennis. *Address:* Woodlands, 2 Linksview Avenue, Parkstone, Poole, Dorset BH14 9QT. *T:* Parkstone 707497.

SUGDEN, Theodore Morris, CBE 1975; MA, ScD; FRS 1963; Master of Trinity Hall, Cambridge, since 1976; b 31 Dec. 1919; s of Frederick Morris Sugden and Florence Sugden (née Chadwick); m 1945, Marian Florence Cotton; one s. *Educ:* Sowerby Bridge Grammar School; Jesus College, Cambridge (Hon. Fellow 1977). Stokes Student, Pembroke Coll., Cambridge, 1945-46; H. O. Jones Lecturer in Physical Chemistry, Univ. of Cambridge, 1950-60; Reader in Physical Chemistry, Univ. of Cambridge, 1960-63; Fellow, Queens' Coll., Cambridge, 1957-63 (Hon. Fellow, 1976). Dir, Thornton Research Centre, Chester, 1967-75; Chief Executive, Shell Research Ltd, 1974-75. Associate Prof., Molecular Sciences, Univ. of Warwick, 1965-74; Vis. Prof. Chemical Technology, Imp. Coll., 1974-75. Hon. DTech Bradford, 1967; Hon. DSc: York, Ont, 1973; Liverpool, 1977. Medallist of the Combustion Inst., 1960, 1976; Davy Medal, Royal Soc., 1975. *Publications:* (with C. N. Kenney) Microwave Spectroscopy of Gases, 1965; articles in Proc. Royal Soc., Transactions of Faraday Soc., Nature, etc. *Recreations:* pianoforte, travel. *Address:* The Master's Lodge, Trinity Hall, Cambridge CB2 1TJ.

SUGG, Aldhelm St John, CMG 1963; retired as Provincial Commissioner, Southern Provinces of Northern Rhodesia, August 1963; b 21 Oct. 1909; s of H. G. St J. Sugg; m 1935, Jessie May Parker; one s one d. *Educ:* Colchester Royal Grammar School. Palestine Police, 1930-31; Northern Rhodesia Police, 1932-43; Colonial Administrative Service, in N Rhodesia, 1943-63. Retired to England, 1963. *Recreations:* sailing, field sports. *Address:* Bushbury, Blackboys, Uckfield, East Sussex. *T:* Framfield 282. *Club:* Royal Commonwealth.

SUIRDALE, Viscount; Richard Michael John Hely-Hutchinson; b 8 Aug. 1927; er s of 7th Earl of Donoughmore, qv; m 1951, Sheila, o c of late Frank Frederick Parsons, and of Mrs Roy Smith-Woodward; four s. *Educ:* Winchester; New College, Oxford (MA; BM, ChB). *Heir:* s Hon. John Michael James Hely-Hutchinson, b 7 Aug. 1952. *Address:* Manoir de Buzenval, 58 bis rue du 19 Janvier, 92 Garches, France. *Clubs:* Kildare Street and University (Dublin); Jockey (Paris).

SULEIMAN, Mohammed Ahmed, Order of Two Niles, 1971; Ambassador of the Democratic Republic of the Sudan to Nigeria, since 1975; b 14 Jan. 1924; m 1955, N. B. al Rayah; three d. *Educ:* Cairo Univ. Licencé en Droit. Minister of Agriculture, Forestry and Rural Waters, 1964; Ambassador to USSR, 1969; Minister: of Nat. Economy and Foreign Trade, 1969-70; of Industry, 1970-71; of Justice, 1971-73; Ambassador to London, 1973-75. *Address:* Sudan Embassy, 40 Awolowo Road, Ikoyi, PO Box 2428, Lagos, Nigeria.

SULLIVAN, Albert Patrick Loisol, CBE 1944 (MBE 1941); MM; MIFireE; b 19 October 1898; s of late William Sullivan, Cobh, Eire; m 1st, 1920, Margaret Elizabeth Mary Andrews (d 1951); one s; 2nd, 1964, Rose Mabel, d of late Richard John Dance. Served European War (France), 1915-19. London Fire Brigade 1919-41; Chief Supt LFB 1940-41; Deputy Chief of Fire Staff, National Fire Service, 1941-47; Chief of Fire Staff and Inspector in Chief, NFS, Mar.-Nov. 1947; Chief Fire Officer to the Ministry of Civil Aviation, 1948-50. President Institution of Fire Engineers, 1946-47; OStJ; King's Police and Fire Services Medal, 1948. *Address:* 28 Park Rise, Harpenden, Herts AL5 3AL. *T:* Harpenden 2147. *Club:* Royal Over-Seas League.

SULLIVAN, David Douglas Hooper, QC 1975; barrister-at-law; *b* 10 April 1926; *s* of Michael and Maude Sullivan; *m* 1951, Sheila, *d* of Henry and Georgina Bathurst; three *d*. *Educ:* Haileybury (schol.); Christ Church, Oxford (schol.). MA 1949, BCL 1951. Served War, with RNVR (Sub-Lieut), 1944-46. Called to Bar, Inner Temple, 1951. *Recreations:* painting, walking, geology. *Address:* Wyldes, North End, NW3 7HS. *T:* 01-455 1571.

SULLIVAN, Prof. (Donovan) Michael; Professor of Oriental Art since 1966, Christensen Professor since 1975, Stanford University, California; *b* 29 Oct. 1916; *s* of Alan Sullivan and Elisabeth Hees; *m* 1943, Khoan, *d* of Ngo Eng-lim, Kulangsu, Amoy, China; no *c*. *Educ:* Rugby School; Corpus Christi College, Cambridge (MA); Univ. of London (BA Hons); Harvard Univ. (PhD); LittD Cambridge, 1966; MA, DLitt Oxon, 1973. Chinese Govt Scholarship, Univ. of London, 1947-50; Rockefeller Foundn Travelling Fellowship in USA, 1950-51; Bollingen Foundn Research Fellowship, 1952-54; Curator of Art Museum and Lectr in the History of Art, Univ. of Malaya (now Univ. of Singapore), Singapore, 1954-60; Lectr in Asian Art, Sch. of Oriental and African Studies, Univ. of London, 1960-66. Vis. Prof. of Far Eastern Art, Univ. of Michigan (Spring Semester), 1964; Slade Prof. of Fine Art, Oxford Univ., 1973-74; Guggenheim Foundn Fellowship, 1974; Vis. Fellow, St Antony's Coll., Oxford, 1976-77. FRSA; Fellow, Amer. Acad. of Arts and Sciences, 1977. *Publications:* Chinese Art in the Twentieth Century, 1959; An Introduction to Chinese Art, 1961; The Birth of Landscape Painting in China, 1962; Chinese Ceramics, Bronzes and Jades in the Collection of Sir Alan and Lady Barlow, 1963; Chinese and Japanese Art, 1965; A Short History of Chinese Art, 1967; The Cave Temples of Maichishan, 1969; The Meeting of Eastern and Western Art, 1973; Chinese Art: recent discoveries, 1973; The Arts of China, 1973; The Three Perfections, 1975; contrib. to learned journals, Encyclopedia Britannica, Chambers's Encyclopædia, etc. *Address:* Department of Art, Stanford University, Stanford, Calif 94305, USA. *Club:* Athenæum.

SULLIVAN, Very Rev. Martin Gloster; Dean of St Paul's, 1967-77, Dean Emeritus since 1977; Dean of the Order of the British Empire, 1967-77, of the Order of St Michael and St George, 1968-77; *b* Auckland, 30 March 1910; *s* of Denis Sullivan; *m* 1st, 1934, Doris (*d* 1972), *d* of Canon C. H. Grant Cowen; 2nd, 1973, Elizabeth Roberton. *Educ:* Auckland Grammar School; St John's (Theological) College, Auckland University College. MA (NZ). Deacon 1932; Priest 1934; Asst Curate, St Matthew's, Auckland, 1932; Vicar, St Columba, Grey Lynn, 1934; Te Awamutu, 1936-46; Exam. Chap. to Bp of Waikato, 1937-46; on staff, St Martin-in-the-Fields, London, 1945-46; Chaplain to SCM Wellington, 1946-49; CF, 1941-46; Principal, College House, Christchurch, 1950-58; Dean of Christchurch, 1951-62; Vicar-General, 1952-62; Commissary to Bp of Christchurch, 1962; Archdeacon of London and Canon Residentiary of St Paul's, 1963-67. Council of Univ. of Canterbury, 1953-62; Senate of Univ. of NZ, 1961-62; Court of Directors, Royal Humane Soc. of NZ, 1956-62; Rep. of Vice-Chancellor of Univ. of Canterbury on Assoc. of Univs of Brit. Commonwealth, 1962. Member Central Council, Royal Over-Seas League; Mem., Guild of Freemen of City of London. Governor: St Paul's Sch., 1967-; Haileybury, 1971-75. Freeman: London, 1965; Merchant Taylors' Co., 1967. Chaplain and Sub-Prelate, Order of St John, 1968. Hon. LittD Auckland, 1976. *Publications:* Children Listen, 1955; Listen Again, 1956; A Word for Everyman, 1956; Draw Near with Faith, 1956; On Calvary's Tree, 1957; Approach With Joy, 1961; A Dean Speaks to New Zealand, 1962; A Funny Thing Happened to me on the way to St Paul's, 1968; Watch How You Go, 1975. *Recreations:* reading, theatre. *Address:* (temp.) c/o 45 Speight Road, Kohimarama, Auckland 5, New Zealand. *Club:* Athenæum.

SULLIVAN, Prof. Michael; see Sullivan, D. M.

SULLIVAN, Richard Arthur, (9th Bt *cr* 1804, but does not use the title); Vice-President, McClelland Engineers, since 1973; *b* 9 Aug. 1931; *s* of Sir Richard Benjamin Magniac Sullivan, 8th Bt, and Muriel Mary Paget, *d* of late Francis Charles Trayler Pineo; *S* father, 1977; *m* 1962, Elenor Mary, *e d* of K. M. Thorpe; one *s* three *d*. *Educ:* Univ. of Cape Town (BSc); Massachusetts Inst. of Technology (SM). Chartered Engineer, UK; Professional Engineer, Texas and Louisiana. *Publications:* technical papers to international conferences and geotechnical journals. *Recreation:* tennis. *Heir:* *s* Charles Merson Sullivan, *b* 15 Dec. 1962.

Address: 25 Davenham Avenue, Northwood, Middlesex HA6 3HW. *T:* Northwood 23112.

SULLIVAN, Tod; National Secretary, Association of Clerical, Technical and Supervisory Staffs, since 1974; *b* 3 Jan. 1934; *s* of Timothy William and Elizabeth Sullivan; *m* 1963, Patricia Norma Roughsedge; one *s* three *d*. *Educ:* Fanshawe Crescent Sch., Dagenham. Merchant Navy, 1950-52; RAF, 1952-55; Electrician, 1955-60; Children's Journalist, 1960-68; Industrial Relations Officer: ATV, 1968-71; CIR, 1971-72; Gen. Sec., Union of Kodak Workers, 1973-74 (until transfer of engagements to TGWU). *Recreations:* reading, music, golf. *Address:* 267 Luton Road, Harpenden, Herts. *T:* Harpenden 5034.

SULLY, Leonard Thomas George, CBE 1963; Covent Garden Market Authority, since 1967; Member, Industrial Tribunals Panel, since 1976; *b* 25 June 1909; British; *m* 1935, Phyllis Emily Phipps, Bristol; one *d*. *Educ:* elementary schs; Fairfield Grammar Sch., Bristol. Public Health Dept, Bristol Corp., 1927; Assistance Officer, Unemployment Assistance Board, Bristol District, 1934; subseq. served in Bath, Weston-super-Mare, etc.; Staff Officer, Air Ministry, London, 1943; Principal, and allocated to Air Ministry, 1949; Asst Sec., 1954, Dir of Contracts, 1960; Dir of Contracts (Air) MoD, 1964. *Recreation:* gardening. *Address:* Coppins, 20 Brackendale Close, Camberley, Surrey. *T:* Camberley 63604.

SULTAN, Syed Abdus; *b* 1 Feb. 1917; Bengali Muslim; lawyer; Supreme Court of Bangladesh, Dacca, since 1976; *m* 1938, Begum Kulsum Sultan; two *s* two *d*. *Educ:* Calcutta and Dacca Univs. Grad. Calcutta 1936, LLB Dacca 1949. Joined Dacca High Court Bar, 1949; Mem. Nat. Assembly of Pakistan, 1962; Delegate Inter-Parly Union Conf., Belgrade, 1963; toured Europe and Middle East; Mem. Pakistan Bar Council, 1967; Mem. Pakistan Nat. Assembly, 1970 with Sheikh Mujibur Rahman (Mem. Constitution Drafting Cttee); joined Bangladesh liberation movt, 1971; visited India, UK, USA and Canada to project cause of Bangladesh; Mem. Unofficial Delegn of Govt of Bangladesh to UN; Ambassador, later High Comr, for Bangladesh in UK, 1972-75. Member: Bangladesh Inst. of Law and Internat. Affairs; Bangla Academy. *Publications:* (in Bengali): Biography of M. A. Jinnah, 1948; Pancha Nadir Palimati, 1953; Ibne Sina, 1955; Man Over the Ages (history), 1969; Manirag (Belles Lettres), 1969; translations of short stories. *Recreations:* tennis, cricket, literature, literary and cultural activities. *Address:* Supreme Court Bar Association, Dacca, Bangladesh.

SULZBERGER, Arthur Ochs; President and Publisher of The New York Times since 1963; *b* 5 Feb. 1926; *s* of late Arthur Hays Sulzberger; *m* 1st, 1948, Barbara Grant (marr. diss. 1956); one *s* one *d*; 2nd, 1956, Carol Fox Fuhrman; one *d* (and one adopted *d*). *Educ:* Browning School, New York City; Loomis School, Windsor, Conn; Columbia University, NYC. Reporter, Milwaukee Journal, 1953-54; Foreign Correspondent, New York Times, 1954-55; Asst to the Publisher, New York Times, 1956-57; Asst Treasurer, New York Times, 1957-63. Hon. LLD: Dartmouth, 1964; Bard, 1967; Hon LHD Montclair State Coll. *Recreation:* golf. *Address:* 229 West 43rd Street, New York, NY 10036, USA. *T:* 556-1771. *Clubs:* Overseas Press, Century Country, Explorers (New York); Metropolitan, Federal City (Washington, DC).

SUMMERFIELD, Prof. Arthur, BSc Tech; BSc; FBPsS; Professor of Psychology, University of London, and Head of the Department of Psychology at Birkbeck College since 1961; *b* 31 March 1923; *s* of late Arthur and Dora Gertrude Summerfield; *m* 1st, 1946, Aline Whalley; one *s* one *d*; 2nd, 1974, Angela Barbara, MA Cantab, PhD London, *d* of late George Frederick Steer and of Estelle Steer. *Educ:* Manchester Grammar Sch.; Manchester Univ.; University Coll. London (1st cl. hons Psychology). Served War of 1939-45, Electrical Officer, RNVR, 1943-46. Asst Lectr in Psychology, University Coll. London, 1949-51, Lectr, 1951-61, Hon. Research Associate, 1961-70; Hon. Research Fellow, 1970-; first Dean, Fac. of Econs, Birkbeck Coll., 1971-72; Hon. Lectr in Psychology, Westminster Med. Sch., 1974-76. Mem. Council, British Psychological Soc., 1953-65, 1967-75, 1977- (Hon. Gen. Sec., 1954-59; Pres., 1963-64; Vice-Pres., 1964-65; first Chm., Scientific Affairs Bd, 1974-75); Mem. Cttee on Internat. Relations in Psychology, Amer. Psychological Assoc., 1977-; Pres., International Union of Psychological Science, 1976- (Mem., Exec. Cttee, 1963-, Assembly, 1957-; Vice-Pres., 1972-76); Pres., Section J (Psychology) BAAS, 1976-77; Mem., Prog. Cttee, Internat. Soc. Sci. Council, 1973-; Chm., Dept of Education and Science Working Party on Psychologists in Educn Services, 1965-68. Vis. Prof., Univ. of California (at Dept of Psychobiology, Irvine

Campus), 1968. Governor, Enfield Coll. of Technology, 1968-72. Asst Editor, Brit. Jl Psychology (Statistical Section), 1950-54; Editor, British Journal of Psychology, 1964-67; Scientific Editor, British Med. Bulletin issues on Experimental Psychology, 1964, Cognitive Psychology, 1971. *Publications:* articles on perception, memory, statistical methods and psychopharmacology in scientific periodicals. *Address:* Birkbeck College, Malet Street, WC1E 7HX.

SUMMERFIELD, Hon. Sir John (Crampton), Kt 1973; CBE 1966 (OBE 1961); **Hon. Mr Justice Summerfield;** Chief Justice of Bermuda, since 1972; Judge of the Grand Court and Chief Justice of the Cayman Islands, since 1977; *b* 20 Sept. 1920; *s* of late Arthur Fred Summerfield and late Lilian Winifred Summerfield (*née* Staas); *m* 1945, Patricia Sandra Musgrave; two *s* two *d. Educ:* Lucton Sch., Herefordshire. Called to Bar, Gray's Inn, 1949. Served War, 1939-46: East Africa, Abyssinia, Somaliland, Madagascar; Captain, Royal Signals. Crown Counsel, Tanganyika (now Tanzania), 1949; Legal Draftsman, 1953; Dep. Legal Sec., EA High Commission, 1958. Attorney-Gen., Bermuda, 1962; QC (Bermuda) 1963; MEC, 1962-68, and MLC, 1962-68 (Bermuda). *Publications:* Preparation of Revised Laws of Bermuda, 1963 and 1971 edns. *Recreations:* photography, chess, sailing. *Address:* Supreme Court, Bermuda. *T:* 21350. *Clubs:* Naval and Military; Royal Bermuda Yacht, Royal Hamilton Amateur Dinghy (Bermuda).

SUMMERHAYES, Sir Christopher (Henry), KBE 1955 (MBE 1929); CMG 1949; *b* 8 March 1896; *s* of late Rev. H. Summerhayes; *m* 1921, Anna (Johnson) (*d* 1972); two *s* two *d.* Served HM Forces, 1914-19 and 1940-45, Gloucestershire Regt (despatches). HM Foreign Service; Consul-General at Alexandria, 1946-51; Ambassador to Nepal, 1951-55. *Address:* Limpsfield, Surrey.
See also D. M. Summerhayes.

SUMMERHAYES, David Michael, CMG 1975; HM Diplomatic Service; Minister, British Embassy, Pretoria/Cape Town, South Africa, since 1974; *b* 29 Sept. 1922; *s* of Sir Christopher Summerhayes, *qv*; *m* 1959, Jean van der Hardt Aberson; two *s* one *d. Educ:* Marlborough; Emmanuel Coll., Cambridge. Served War of 1939-45 in Royal Artillery (Capt.) N Africa and Italy. 3rd Sec., FO, 1948; Baghdad, 1949; Brussels, 1950-53; 2nd Sec., FO, 1953-56; 1st Sec. (Commercial), The Hague, 1956-59; 1st Sec. and Consul, Reykjavik, 1959-61; FO, 1961-65; Consul-General and Counsellor, Buenos Aires, 1965-70; Head of Arms Control and Disarmament Dept, FCO, 1970-74. Hon. Officer, Order of Orange Nassau. *Recreations:* sailing, tennis, wildlife. *Address:* c/o Foreign and Commonwealth Office, SW1; 6 Kingsmere Road, Wimbledon, SW19. *Clubs:* United Oxford & Cambridge University; Hurlingham; Itchenor Sailing; Pretoria Country.

SUMMERS, (Sir) Felix Roland Brattan, 2nd Bt *cr* 1952; does not use the title and his name is not on the Official Roll of Baronets.

SUMMERS, Henry Forbes, CB 1961; Under-Secretary, Department of the Environment (formerly Ministry of Housing and Local Government), 1955-71; *b* 18 August 1911; *s* of late Rev. H. H. Summers, Harrogate, Yorks; *m* 1937, Rosemary, *d* of late Robert L. Roberts, CBE; two *s* one *d. Educ:* Fettes Coll., Edinburgh; Trinity College, Oxford. *Address:* Folly Fields, Tunbridge Wells, Kent. *T:* 27671.

SUMMERS, Janet Margaret, (Mrs L. J. Summers); see Bateley, J. M.

SUMMERSCALE, David Michael, MA; Master of Haileybury, since 1976; *b* 22 April 1937; *s* of Noel Tynwald Summerscale and Beatrice (*née* Wilson); *m* 1975, Pauline,*d* of Prof. Michel Fleury, Président de la IVème Section de l'Ecole des Hautes Etudes, Paris. *Educ:* Northaw; Sherborne Sch.; Trinity Hall, Cambridge. Lectr in English Literature and Tutor, St Stephen's Coll., Univ. of Delhi, 1959-63; Charterhouse, 1963-75 (Head of English, Housemaster). Oxford and Cambridge Schs Examination Bd Awarder in English. Member: Managing Cttee of Cambridge Mission to Delhi; C. F. Andrews Centenary Appeal Cttee. *Publications:* articles on English and Indian literature; dramatisations of novels and verse. *Recreations:* music, play production, reading, mountaineering, games (squash (Mem. SRA), cricket, tennis, rackets (Mem. Tennis and Rackets Assoc.), golf, football, cross-country, hockey). *Address:* The Master's Lodge, Haileybury, Hertford SG13 7NU. *T:* Hoddesdon 62352. *Clubs:* Athenæum, Royal Commonwealth Society; I Zingari, Free Foresters, Jesters.

SUMMERSCALE, Sir John (Percival), KBE 1960 (CBE 1951); Retired 1960, as Minister (Commercial), British Embassy, Rio

de Janeiro; Editor, Penguin Books, 1961; *b* 23 Nov. 1901; *s* of Annie and Percy Summerscale; *m* 1931, Nelle Blossom Stogsdall (*d* 1977); two *s* two *d. Educ:* Latymers' School, Edmonton; Cambridge University. Levant Consular Service, 1926; served in Beirut, Hamadan, Shiraz, Tehran, Bagdad. Commercial Secretary (Grade II), Washington, 1938; Counsellor (Commercial) there, 1945; transferred to Board of Trade, 1946, and to Warsaw, 1948 as Commercial Counsellor; Consul-Gen., Munich, 1951; Minister (Commercial), Rio de Janeiro, 1954-60. *Recreation:* tennis. *Address:* Crossways, Tarrant Hinton, Blandford, Dorset.

SUMMERSKILL, Baroness (Life Peer), *cr* 1961, of Ken Wood, **(Edith),** PC 1949; CH 1966; Member, Political Honours Scrutiny Committee, 1967-76; *b* Doughty St, London, 1901; *d* of William and Edith Summerskill; *m* 1925, Dr E. Jeffrey Samuel; one *s* one *d. Educ:* King's Coll., London; Charing Cross Hosp. Qualified as a doctor, 1924. Member of Middlesex County Council for Green Lanes division of Tottenham, 1934-41. Contested Parly by-election in Putney, 1934, and Bury div. General Election, 1935; MP (Lab) for West Fulham, 1938-55, for Warrington, 1955-61. Parly Sec., Min. of Food, 1945-50; Minister of National Insurance, 1950-51. Chm. of Labour Party, 1954-55. Hon. LLD Newfoundland, 1968. *Publications:* Babies without Tears, 1941; The Ignoble Art, 1956; Letters to my Daughter, 1957; A Woman's World, 1967. *Address:* Pond House, Millfield Lane, Highgate, N6.
See also Dr the Hon. S. C. W. Summerskill.

SUMMERSKILL, Dr the Hon. Shirley Catherine Wynne; MP (Lab) Halifax since 1964; Parliamentary Under-Secretary of State, Home Office, since 1974; Medical Practitioner since 1960; *b* London, 9 Sept. 1931; *d* of Dr E. J. Samuel and of Baroness Summerskill, *qv*; *m* 1957, John Ryman (marr. diss. 1971). *Educ:* St Paul's Girls' Sch.; Somerville Coll., Oxford; St Thomas' Hospital. MA, BM, BCh., 1958. Treas., Oxford Univ. Labour Club, 1952. Resident House Surgeon, later House Physician, St Helier Hosp., Carshalton, 1959. Contested (Lab) Blackpool North by-election, 1962. UK delegate, UN Status of Women Commn, 1968 and 1969; Mem. British delegn, Council of Europe and WEU, 1968, 1969. Vice-Chm., Parly Labour Party Health Group, 1964-69, Chm., 1969-70. Opposition spokesman on health, 1970-74. *Publication:* A Surgical Affair (novel), 1963. *Address:* House of Commons, SW1.

SUMMERSON, Sir John (Newenham), Kt 1958; CBE 1952; FBA 1954; BA(Arch); FSA; ARIBA; Curator of Sir John Soane's Museum since 1945; *b* 25 Nov. 1904; *o s* of late Samuel James Summerson of Darlington and Dorothea Worth Newenham; *m* 1938, Elizabeth Alison, *d* of H. R. Hepworth, CBE, Leeds; three *s. Educ:* Harrow; University College, London. From 1926 worked in architects' offices, including those of late W. D. Caröe and Sir Giles Gilbert Scott, OM. Instructor in Sch. of Architecture, Edinburgh Coll. of Art, 1929-30. Asst Editor, Architect and Building News, 1934-41; Dep. Dir, National Buildings Record, 1941-45. Lectr in History of Architecture: Architectural Assoc., 1949-62; Birkbeck Coll., 1950-67; Slade Prof. of Fine Art, Oxford, 1958-59; Ferens Prof. of Fine Art, Hull, 1960-61 and 1970-71; Slade Prof. of Fine Art, Cambridge, 1966-67; Bampton Lectr, Columbia Univ., 1968; Page-Barbour Lectr, Virginia Univ., 1972. Silver Medallist (Essay), RIBA, 1937. Member: Royal Fine Art Commn, 1947-54; Royal Commn on Historical Monuments (England), 1953-74; Historic Buildings Council, 1953-78; Arts Council Art Panel, 1953-56; Historical Manuscripts Commn, 1959-; Listed Buildings Cttee Min. of Housing and Local Govt, 1944-66 (Chm., 1960-62); Adv. Council on Public Records, 1968-74; Council, Architectural Assoc., 1940-45; Trustee, National Portrait Gallery, 1966-73. Hon. Fellow, Trinity Hall, Cambridge, 1968; Fellow, UCL. Foreign Hon. Mem., Amer. Acad. of Arts and Sciences, 1967; Chairman, National Council for Diplomas in Art and Design, 1961-70. Hon. DLitt: Leicester, 1959; Oxford, 1963; Hull, 1971; Newcastle, 1973; Hon. DSc Edinburgh, 1968; Hon. Dr, RCA, 1975. RIBA Royal Gold Medal for Architecture, 1976. *Publications:* Architecture Here and Now (with C. Williams-Ellis), 1934; John Nash, Architect to George IV, 1935; The Bombed Buildings of Britain (with J. M. Richards), 1942 and 1945; Georgian London, 1946, rev. edn 1970; The Architectural Association (Centenary History), 1947; Ben Nicholson (Penguin Modern Painters), 1948; Heavenly Mansions (essays), 1949; Sir John Soane, 1952; Sir Christopher Wren, 1953; Architecture in Britain, 1530-1830 (Pelican History of Art), 1953, 5th edn 1969; New Description of Sir J. Soane's Museum, 1955; The Classical Language of Architecture, 1964; The Book of John Thorpe (Walpole Soc., vol. 40), 1966; Inigo Jones, 1966; Victorian Architecture (four studies in evaluation), 1969; (ed) Concerning Architecture, 1969; The London Building World of the Eighteen-Sixties, 1974; (with H. M. Colvin and D.

R. Ransome) The History of the King's Works, vol. 3, 1976. *Recreation:* music. *Address:* 1 Eton Villas, NW3. *T:* 01-722 6247. *Clubs:* Athenæum, Beefsteak.

SUMMERSON, Thomas Hawksley, OBE 1971; JP; *b* 22 April 1903; *s* of late Robert Bradley Summerson, Coatham Mundeville, Co. Durham; *m* 1943, Joan, *d* of late Walter Rogers, Ashington, Sussex; three *s* one *d. Educ:* Harrow. Dir for Steel Castings, Iron and Steel Control, Ministry of Supply, 1940-43; Chairman and Joint Man. Dir, Summerson Holdings Ltd, 1944-65; Chairman: British Steel Founders' Association, 1951-54; NE Industrial and Development Association, 1952-55; Home Affairs and Transport Division, Assoc. of British Chambers of Commerce, 1952-59 (Vice-President, 1954, Deputy President, 1960-62, President, 1962-64); Darlington and N Yorks Local Employment Cttee, 1953-74; Design Panel, British Transport Commn, 1956-63; St Paul's Jarrow Development Trust, 1971-75; Civic Trust for NE, 1970-76; Trustee, Civic Trust, 1970-76; Dep. Chairman, Peterlee Development Corp., 1954-55. Chairman, North Eastern Area Board, British Transport Commission, 1955, and Part-time Member of the Commission, until 1962; Part-time Member, British Railways Board, Jan. 1963-Oct. 1963, and Chm. North Eastern Railway Bd, Jan.-Oct. 1963. Member: Aycliffe New Town Development Corp., 1947-61; Development Areas Treasury Advisory Cttee, 1951-55; President: Tees-side and S-W Durham Chamber of Commerce, 1948-50; Tees-side Industrial Development Board, 1954-57; Member, Independent Television Authority, 1957-60; Mem., North East Development Council, 1965-73. Mem Darlington RDC, 1937-74 (Chm. 1949-52); Chm., Sedgefield Div. Conservative and Unionist Assoc., 1965-71. JP Co. Durham, 1946; Chm. Darlington County Bench, 1951-53 and 1955-61; High Sheriff, County Durham, 1953-54; DL County Durham, 1958-76. Chm. South Durham Hunt, 1955-73. *Recreations:* shooting, fishing. *Address:* The Old Manse, Errogie, Inverness. *T:* Gorthleck 649; 3 Terrett's Place, Upper Street, Islington, N1. *Club:* Brooks's.

SUMMERVILLE, Sir (William) Alan (Thompson), Kt 1968; DSc, FAIAS; Agent-General for Queensland in London, 1964-70; Chairman, Queensland Sugar Board, 1970-73; Queensland Government representative on international sugar affairs; *b* 6 Feb. 1904; *s* of W. H. Summerville, Ipswich, Queensland; *m* 1930, Ethel, *d* of T. F. Barker; two *d. Educ:* Ipswich Grammar School; University of Queensland. Entomological Investigations, 1930-36; Plant Physiology Research, 1937-45. Studied Agricultural Research Methods in Ceylon, Egypt, Palestine, GB, USA, Canada, Hawaii and NZ, 1936-37 and 1955. Dir, Div. of Plant Industry, Dept of Agric. and Stock, Qld, 1955-58; Dir-Gen. and Under-Sec., Dept of Agric. and Stock, Qld, 1958-64. Vice-President: Australia-Britain Soc.; Exec. Cttee, Inst. Internat. Affairs (Qld). Hon. LLD (Qld), 1963. *Publications:* various, on entomological and physiological subjects. *Recreations:* bowls, gardening. *Address:* 25 Munro Street, Indooroopilly, Queensland 4068, Australia. *Club:* Johnsonian (Brisbane).

SUMNER, Donald; see Sumner, W. D. M.

SUMNER, (William) Donald (Massey), OBE 1945; QC 1960; His Honour Judge Sumner; a Circuit Judge (formerly Judge of County Courts), since 1961; *b* 13 Aug. 1913; *s* of Harold Sumner, OBE, Standish, Lancs. *Educ:* Charterhouse; Sidney Sussex Coll., Cambridge. Called to the Bar, Lincoln's Inn, 1937. Served War of 1939-45 with Royal Artillery; Lt-Col and Asst Adjutant-General, 21st Army Group. Mem. Orpington UDC, 1950-53. Acted as Asst Recorder of Plymouth frequently, 1954-61. MP (C) Orpington Div. of Kent, Jan. 1955-Oct. 1961; PPS to Solicitor-General, Nov. 1959-Oct. 1961. Officier, Ordre de la Couronne and Croix de Guerre (Belgian); Bronze Star Medal (American). *Address:* 2 Harcourt Buildings, Temple, EC4; East Brabourne House, near Ashford, Kent.

SUMSION, Herbert Whitton, CBE 1961; DMus, Cantuar; MusBac, Dunelm; FRCM, Hon. RAM, FRCO, FRSCM; Organist of Gloucester Cathedral, 1928-67; Director of Music, Ladies' Coll., Cheltenham, 1935-68; *b* Gloucester, 19 Jan. 1899; *m* 1927, Alice Hartley Garlichs, BA; three *s.* Organist and Choirmaster at Christ Church, Lancaster Gate; Director of Music, Bishop's Stortford College; Asst Instructor in Music at Morley Coll., London; Teacher of Harmony and Counterpoint, Curtis Institute, Philadelphia, 1926-28; Conductor Three Choirs Fest., 1928, 1931, 1934, 1937, 1947, 1950, 1953, 1956, 1959, 1962, 1965. *Publications:* Introduction and Theme for Organ, 1935; Morning and Evening Service in G, 1935; Two pieces for Cello and Piano, 1939 (No. 1 arranged for String Orchestra); Magnificat and Nunc Dimittis in G for Boys' Voices, 1953, for Men's Voices, 1953, for Boys' Voices in D, 1973; Cradle Song for

Organ, 1953; Benedicite in B flat, 1955; Four Carol Preludes for Organ, 1956; Festival Benedicite in D, 1971. *Address:* Hartley, Private Road, Rodborough Common, Stroud, Glos GL5 5BT. *T:* Amberley 3528.

SUNDARAVADIVELU, Neyyadupakkam Duraiswamy; Vice-Chancellor, University of Madras, 1969-75; *b* 15 Oct. 1912. *Educ:* Univ. of Madras (MA, Licentiate in Teaching). Asst Panchayat Officer (organising and directing village panchayats), 1935-40; Madras Educnl Subordinate Service, inspection of primary schs, 1940-42; Madras Educnl Service, inspection of secondary schs and gen. direction of primary schs, 1942-54; Dir of Public Instruction, and Comr for Public Examns, Tamil Nadu, 1954-65; Dir of Higher Educn, Tamil Nadu, 1965-66; Dir of Public Libraries, Tamil Nadu, 1954-69; Jt Educnl Adviser to Govt of India, Min. of Educn, New Delhi, 1966-68; Chief Educnl Adviser and Additional Sec. to Govt of Tamil Nadu, Educn Dept, 1968-69; Dir of Collegiate Educn, Tamil Nadu, 1968-69. Visited: UK, 1951, 1962, 1973; USSR, 1961, 1967, 1971, 1973; USA, 1964, 1970; France, 1951, 1968, 1970, 1971, 1973; Malaysia, 1966, 1975; Philippines, 1971, 1972; Ghana, 1971; Canada, 1970; Singapore, 1966, 1975; Hong Kong, 1970, 1975; German Dem. Republic, 1973; participated in various confs, meetings, etc. Mem., Nat. Council of Educnl Research and Trng, New Delhi; Past Mem., Nat. Commn on UNESCO; Mem., Nat. Council for Rural Higher Educn; Pres., Madras Cttee of World Univ. Service (Vice-Pres., Indian Nat. Cttee); Mem., Nat. Bd of Adult Educn; Chm., Southern Languages Book Trust; Mem., Standing Cttee of Inter-Univ. Bd of India and Ceylon, New Delhi; Vice-Pres., Indian Adult Educn Assoc.; Mem., Central Cttee of Tamil Nadu Tuberculosis Assoc.; Chm., Kendriya Vidyalaya, Gill Nagar, Madras. Originator of schemes, Free Mid-day Meals, School Improvement, and Free Supply of Uniforms to School Children, recommended to all Asian countries for adoption (personally commended by Pres. of India, 1960). Padma Shri (presidential award), 1961. *Publications:* 30 books in Tamil, incl. 13 for children. *Address:* 90C Shenoynagar, Madras 600030, India. *T:* Madras 612516.

SUNDERLAND, (George Frederick) Irvon; DL; His Honour Judge Sunderland; a Circuit Judge (formerly Judge of County Courts), since 1963; *b* 8 May 1905; *o s* of Frederick and Mary Jane Sunderland; *m* 1929, Mary Katharine, *d* of Arthur John Bowen; three *s* (and one *s* decd). *Educ:* privately. Called to Bar, Gray's Inn, 1932 (H. C. Richards Prizeman); joined Midland Circuit; Assistant Recorder: Birmingham Quarter Sessions, 1960-63; Coventry Quarter Sessions, 1962-63; County Court Judge, Derbyshire, 1964-66; Chairman, Warwick County QS, 1967-71. Deputy Chairman: East Midlands Agricultural Land Tribunal, 1959-63; Birmingham Mental Health Review Tribunal, 1959-63; Chm., Birmingham Local Bar Cttee, 1959-63. DL Warwicks, 1967. *Recreations:* gardening, the theatre. *Address:* 70 Woodbourne, Augustus Road, Edgbaston, Birmingham B15 3PJ. *T:* 021-454 7236.

SUNDERLAND, Prof. Sir Sydney, Kt 1971; CMG 1961; FAA 1954; Professor of Experimental Neurology, 1961-75, now Emeritus Professor, and Dean of the Faculty of Medicine 1953-71, University of Melbourne; *b* Brisbane, Aust., 31 Dec. 1910; *s* of Harry and Anne Sunderland; *m* 1939, Nina Gwendoline Johnston, LLB; one *s. Educ:* University of Melbourne. BM, BS 1935, DSc 1945, DMed 1946, Melbourne. FRACP 1941; FRACS 1952. Sen. Lectr in Anatomy, Univ. of Melbourne, 1936-37; Demonstrator in Human Anatomy, Oxford, 1938-39; Prof. of Anatomy, Univ. of Melbourne, 1940-61. Visiting Specialist (Hon. Major) 115 Aust. Gen. Mil. Hosp., 1941-45. Mem. Zool. Bd of Vict., 1944-65 (Chm. Scientific Cttee, 1958-62); Dep. Chm., Adv. Cttee to Mental Hygiene Dept, Vict., 1952-63; Mem. Nat. Health and MRC, 1953-69; Chm., Med. Research Adv. Cttee of Nat. Health and MRC, 1964-69. Visiting Prof. of Anatomy, Johns Hopkins Univ., 1953-54; Sec., Div. of Biol Sciences, Aust. Acad. Sci., 1955-58; Member: Nat. Radiation Adv. Cttee, 1957-64 (Chm. 1958-64); Defence Research and Development Policy Cttee, 1957-75; Med. Services Cttee, Dept of Defence, 1957-; Council, AMA, Victorian Branch, 1960-68; Safety Review Cttee, Aust. Atomic Energy Commn, 1961-74 (Chm.); Aust. Univs Commn, 1962-76; Cttee of Management, Royal Melbourne Hosp., 1963-71; Protective Chemistry Research Adv. Cttee, Dept of Supply, 1964-73 (Chm.); Victorian Med. Adv. Cttee, 1962-71; Board of Walter and Eliza Hall Inst. of Med. Research, 1968-75. Governor, Ian Potter Foundn, 1964-. Trustee: National Museum, 1954-; Van Cleef Foundn, 1971-. Fogarty Scholar in residence, Nat. Inst. of Health, Bethesda, USA, 1972-73. Foundn Fellow, Aust. Acad. of Science, 1954, and rep. on Pacific Science Council, 1957-69. Hon. MD: Tasmania, 1970; Queensland, 1975; Hon. LLD Melbourne, 1975. *Publications:* Nerves and Nerve Injuries, 1968; about 100 articles in scientific jls in Gt Britain, Europe, US and Australia. *Address:* 11 Scotsburn Grove, Toorak, Victoria 3142, Australia. *T:* 203431. *Club:* Melbourne.

SUNG CHIH-KUANG; Ambassador of the People's Republic of China to the Court of St James's, since 1972; *b* April 1916; *m* 1945, Chang Ju; two *s* one *d. Educ:* University, China. Counsellor, Chinese Embassy, German Democratic Republic; Dep. Dir, Dept of West European Affairs, Min. of Foreign Affairs, China; Counsellor, Chinese Embassy, Paris; Ambassador to German Democratic Republic. *Address:* 31 Portland Place, W1N 3AG. *T:* 01-636 5726.

SUNLIGHT, Joseph; Architect; *b* 2 Jan. 1889; *s* of Israel and Minnie Sunlight. *Educ:* Private School, Kingston-on-Thames. MP (L) Shrewsbury, 1923-24. *Address:* 14 Victoria Square, SW1. *T:* 01-834 4734; Hallside, Knutsford, Cheshire. *T:* Knutsford 3339; Sunlight House, Manchester. *T:* 061-834 7113.

SUPHAMONGKHON, Dr Konthi, Kt Grand Cordon of the White Elephant, Kt Grand Cordon, Order of the Crown of Thailand; Kt Grand Commander, Order of Chula Chom Klao; Hon. GCVO 1972; Ambassador of Thailand to the Court of St James's, 1970-76; *b* 3 Aug. 1916; *m* 1951, Dootsdi Atthakravi; two *s* one *d. Educ:* Univ. of Moral and Political Sciences, Bangkok (LLB); Univ. of Paris (Dr-en-Droit). Joined Min. of Foreign Affairs, 1940; Second Sec., Tokyo, 1942-44; Chief of Polit. Div., 1944-48; Dir-Gen., Western Affairs Dept, 1948-50; UN Affairs Dept, 1950-52; Minister to Australia, 1952-56, Ambassador, June 1956-59, and to New Zealand, Oct. 1956-59; Dir-Gen. of Internat. Organizations, 1959-63; Adviser on Foreign Affairs to the Prime Minister, 1962-64; Sec.-Gen., SEATO, 1964-65; Ambassador to Federal Republic of Germany, 1965-70, and to Finland, 1967-70. Frequent Lecturer, 1944-; notably at Thammasat Univ., 1944-52, at National Defence Coll., 1960-62, and at Army War Coll., Bangkok, 1960-63. Holds foreign decorations. *Publication:* Thailand and her relations with France, 1940 (in French). *Recreations:* tennis, golf, swimming. *Address:* c/o Ministry of Foreign Affairs, Bangkok, Thailand. *Clubs:* Travellers', Hurlingham; Royal Wimbledon Golf, Cuddington Golf.

SURREY, Archdeacon of; *see* Evans, Ven. J. M.

SURRIDGE, Brewster Joseph, CMG 1950; OBE 1941; Adviser on Co-operatives to Minister of Overseas Development, 1964-67 (to Secretary of State for Colonies, 1947-64); retired 1967; *b* 12 Feb. 1894; *e s* of E. E. Surridge; *m* 1922, Winifred Bywater-Ward (*née* Lawford). *Educ:* Felsted School; Downing College, Cambridge. Served European War, Army, 1914-17. Colonial Administrative Service, Cyprus, 1918-33; Registrar of Co-operative Societies, Cyprus, 1934-43; Financial Secretary, Gold Coast, 1943-45; retired, 1946. Adviser on Co-operation to the Government of Iraq, 1946-47. *Publications:* A Survey of Rural Life, Cyprus, 1931; A Manual of Co-operative Law and Practice, 1948. *Address:* 2 Furze Croft, Hove, Sussex BN3 1PB. *T:* Brighton 70027.

SURRIDGE, Sir (Ernest) Rex (Edward), Kt, *cr* 1951; CMG 1946; retired; *b* 21 Feb. 1899; *s* of late E. E. Surridge, Coggeshall, Essex; *m* Roy, *d* of late Major F. E. Bradstock, DSO, MC; two *s. Educ:* Felsted; St John's College, Oxford. European War, 1917-20, Lieut 7th Bn DCLI; St John's College, Oxford, 1920-22, Mod. Hist. (Hons) Colonial Admin. Service, 1924, Tanganyika; Assistant Chief Secretary, Tanganyika, 1936; Deputy Chief Secretary, Kenya, 1940; Chief Secretary to Govt of Tanganyika, 1946-51; Salaries Comr, Cyprus, 1953-54; Financial Comr, Seychelles, 1957-58; Salaries Comr, High Commn Territories (South Africa), 1958-59; Salaries Comr, Gibraltar, 1959-60. *Address:* Flat 4, Wytham Abbey, Oxford. *T:* Oxford 44733.

SURTEES, John, MBE 1961; motor racing since 1961; also controlling companies involved in automobile construction and development, and property; *b* 11 Feb. 1934; *s* of late John Norman and Dorothy Surtees; *m* 1962, Patricia Phyllis Burke; no *c. Educ:* Ashburton School, Croydon. 5 year engineering apprenticeship, Vincent Engrs, Stevenage, Herts. Motorcycle racing, 1952-60; British Champion, 1954, 1955; World 500 cc Motorcycle Champion, 1956; World 350 and 500 cc Motorcycle Champion, 1958, 1959, 1960. At end of 1960 he retd from motorcycling and subseq. began motor racing. With Ferrari Co., won World Motor Racing title, 1964; 5th in World Championship, 1965 (following accident in Canada due to suspension failure); in 1966 left Ferrari in mid-season and joined Cooper, finishing 2nd in World Championship; in 1967 with Honda Motor Co. as first driver and develt engr (1967-68); 3rd in World Championship; with BRM as No 1 driver, 1969; designed and built own Formula 1 car, 1970. *Publications:*

Motorcycle Racing and Preparation, 1958; John Surtees Book of Motorcycling, 1960; Speed, 1963; Six Days in August, 1968. *Recreations:* music, architecture; interested in most sports. *Address:* c/o Surtees Racing Organisation, Station Road, Edenbridge, Kent. *T:* Edenbridge 3773.

SUSMAN, Maurice Philip, MB, ChM Sydney; FRCS; FRACS; AAMC; Hon. Consulting Surgeon, Sydney Hospital, 1958; Hon. Consulting Thoracic Surgeon, Royal North Shore Hospital, Sydney, 1958; *b* 4 Aug. 1898; *s* of Philip Tasman Susman and Gertrude Lehane; *m* 1934, Ina May Shanahan; one *d. Educ:* Sydney Church of England Grammar School; University of Sydney. *Publications:* various papers on surgical subjects. *Recreations:* chess, being idle, flying. *Address:* 22 Bathurst Street, Woollahra, NSW 2025, Australia. *T:* 389 6053. *Club:* Royal Aero (NSW).

SUSSKIND, (Jan) Walter; conductor, composer and concert pianist; *b* 1 May 1913; of Czech parents; one *s* by former marr. *Educ:* Prague State Conservatorium. Conductor Prague Opera, 1934-37; Principal Conductor Royal Carl Rosa Opera Co., 1943-45; Principal Conductor Sadler's Wells Opera Co., 1946; Conductor of the Scottish National Orchestra, 1946-52; Principal Conductor Glyndebourne Opera Co. (at 1st Edinburgh Festival), 1947; Resident Conductor, Victorian Symphony Orch., Melbourne (8 mths each yr), 1954-56; Principal Conductor, Toronto Symphony Orch., 1956-65; Music Dir and Principal Conductor, St Louis Symphony Orch., 1968-75. Records for numerous companies (over two hundred records so far). Regular Guest Conductor, NYC Opera, 1961-; Guest Conductor of most leading orchestras in Europe, 1952-; many world tours as guest conductor of the world's leading orchestras; has conducted in over thirty countries on all five continents. Music Director of: Mendelssohn Choir, 1958-64; National Youth Orchestra of Canada, 1960-; Music Festival, Aspen, Colorado, 1961-68; Mississippi River Festival (St Louis Symphony's summer festival), 1968-75. Conductor and Mem. Adv. Cttee, Internat. Festival of Youth Orchestras, St Moritz, Switzerland, later at Lausanne. Dir, Amer. Inst. of Orchestral Conducting. Orchestrator of many piano works. Hon. Dr of Humanities, Univ. of Southern Illinois, 1969; Hon. Dr of Fine Arts, Washington Univ., 1975. *Address:* c/o Ingpen & Williams, 14 Kensington Court, W8.

SUTCLIFF, Rosemary, OBE 1975; writer of historical novels for adults and children; *b* 14 Dec. 1920; *d* of George Ernest Sutcliff and Elizabeth Sutcliff (*née* Lawton). *Educ:* privately. *Publications:* Chronicles of Robin Hood, 1950; The Queen Elizabeth Story, 1950; The Armourer's House, 1951; Brother Dusty-feet, 1952; Simon, 1953; The Eagle of the Ninth, 1954; Outcast, 1955; Lady in Waiting, 1956; The Shield Ring, 1956; The Silver Branch, 1957; Warrior Scarlet, 1958; Rider of the White Horse, 1959; Lantern Bearers, 1959; Houses and History, 1960; Knights Fee, 1960; Rudyard Kipling, 1960; Beowulf, 1961; Dawn Wind, 1961; Sword at Sunset, 1963; The Hound of Ulster, 1963; The Mark of the Horse Lord, 1965; Heroes and History, 1965; The Chief's Daughter, 1967; The High Deeds of Finn McCool, 1967; A Circlet of Oak Leaves, 1968; The Flowers of Adonis, 1969; The Witches' Brat, 1970; Tristan and Iseult, 1971; The Capricorn Bracelet, 1973; The Changeling, 1974; Blood Feud, 1977; Sun House, Moon House, 1977; Shifting Sands, 1977. *Recreations:* painting, needlework, dogs, travel. *Address:* Swallowshaw, Walberton, Arundel, West Sussex. *T:* Yapton 551316.

SUTCLIFFE, Edward Davis, QC 1959; **His Honour Judge Sutcliffe;** a Circuit Judge and Additional Judge of the Central Criminal Court, since 1969; *b* 25 Aug. 1917; 3rd *s* of late Richard Joseph and Anne Sutcliffe; *m* 1939, Elsie Eileen Brooks; two *d. Educ:* University College School, Hampstead; Wadham College, Oxford (MA). Served Royal Artillery, 1939-46 (despatches). Called to Bar, Inner Temple, 1946; Bencher, 1966. Recorder of Canterbury, 1968-69, and Hon. Recorder, 1974-. Mem., Criminal Injuries Compensation Board, 1964-69; Legal Assessor, GMC and GDC, 1967-69. Governor: Bedford Coll., London, 1968-76; St Michael's Sch., Otford. Liveryman, Needleworkers' Co. *Address:* Central Criminal Court, Old Bailey, EC4.

SUTCLIFFE, Prof. Frank Edmund; Professor of Classical French Literature, University of Manchester, since 1966; *b* 8 Aug. 1918; *er s* of Charles Edmund Taylor Sutcliffe and of Ellen Sutcliffe; *m* 1966, Jane Ceridwen Bevan. *Educ:* Huddersfield College; University of Manchester. BA 1940, MA 1948, PhD 1958. Served War of 1939-45, with Royal Artillery and Hong Kong and Singapore Royal Artillery, 1940-46. Asst lectr in French, 1946-49. Lecturer in French, 1949-55, Senior Lecturer in French, 1955-61. Professor of Modern French Literature, 1961-

66, Univ. of Manchester, Dean of Faculty of Arts, 1972-74. Visiting Professor: Univ. of Kiel, 1968; Université Laval, Québec, 1968-69. Chevalier de l'Ordre National du Mérite, 1965. *Publications:* La Pensée de Paul Valéry, 1955; Guez de Balzac et son temps; littérature et politique, 1960; Le réalisme de Charles Sorel: problèmes humains du XVIIe siècle, 1965; (ed) Discours politiques et militaires by Fr de la Noue, 1967; (trans.) Descartes, Discours de la Méthode, 1968; Politique et culture 1560-1660, 1973; book reviews; contrib. to French Studies, Le Bayou (Houston, Texas), Jahrbuch (Univ. of Hamburg), Bulletin of the John Rylands Library. *Address:* 61 Daisy Bank Road, Victoria Park, Manchester M14 5QL. *T:* 061-224 1864.

SUTCLIFFE, Geoffrey Scott, OBE 1944; TD 1952; *b* 12 June 1912; *o s* of late John Walton Sutcliffe and late Alice Mary Sutcliffe (*née* Scott); *m* 1946, Mary Sylvia, *d* of late George Herbert Kay; two *s* one *d. Educ:* Repton. TA 2nd Lieut, 1939; Lt-Col, 1943; GSO1, AFHQ, N Africa and Italy; served France and Belgium, 1940; N Africa and Italy, 1943-45 (despatches, OBE). Ferodo Ltd, 1932: Works Dir, 1947; Home Sales Dir, 1952; Man. Dir, 1955; Chm., 1956-67; Turner & Newall Ltd: Dir, 1957-75; Jt Man. Dir, 1963-74; Dep. Chm., 1967-74. *Recreations:* gardening, swimming. *Address:* Brierwood House, Disley, Cheshire. *T:* Disley 2292.

SUTCLIFFE, John Harold Vick; Barrister-at-Law; *b* 30 April 1931; *o s* of late Sir Harold Sutcliffe and Emily Theodora Cochrane; *m* 1959, Cecilia Mary, *e d* of Ralph Meredyth Turton; three *s* one *d. Educ:* Winchester Coll.; New Coll., Oxford (Scholar; MA). 2nd Lieut RA, 1950-51. Called to Bar, Inner Temple, 1956; practised until 1960, Midland Circuit. Company Director. Contested (C): Oldham West, 1959; Chorley, Lancs, 1964; Middlesbrough West, 1966. MP (C) Middlesbrough W, 1970-Feb. 1974. Contested (C) Teesside Thornaby, Oct. 1974. *Recreations:* gardening, travel, reading. *Address:* Chapelgarth, Great Broughton, Middlesbrough, Cleveland. *T:* Wainstones 228.

SUTCLIFFE, Joseph Richard, ED, BSc; Member the Stock Exchange of Melbourne, 1950-74; *b* 25 Jan. 1897; *s* of late A. H. Sutcliffe and Kate Elizabeth Haybittle; *m* 1923, Aileen, *d* of Henry H. Batchelor, NZ; one *s* one *d. Educ:* Palmerston North Boys' High School; Victoria University College, New Zealand. War Service, 1916-19, with NZ Machine Gun Corps and Royal Air Force; Major retd; Headmaster Scots College, Wellington, NZ, 1930-38; Melbourne Church of England Grammar School, 1938-49. *Publication:* Why be a Headmaster?, 1977. *Address:* 35 York Avenue, Ivanhoe, Melbourne, Victoria 3079, Australia. *Club:* Melbourne (Melbourne).

SUTCLIFFE, Kenneth Edward; Headmaster, Latymer Upper School, Hammersmith, W6, 1958-71; *b* 24 March 1911; *s* of late Rev. James Sutcliffe; *m* 1937, Nora, *d* of late Charles Herbert Burcham; two *d. Educ:* Manchester Grammar School; King's College, Cambridge (Scholar). BA Modern and Medieval Languages Tripos 1932; MA 1936. Assistant Master, Stockport Grammar School, 1933-38; Assistant Master, Liverpool Institute High School, 1938-46; Headmaster, Cockburn High School, Leeds, 1946-57. Served with Royal Armoured Corps and Intelligence Corps, 1940-46, Captain (General Staff). Lay Reader, Wedmore Parish Ch, dio. Bath and Wells, 1972-. *Publications:* German Translation and Composition, 1948; French Translation and Composition, 1951; Fahrt ins Blaue (a German course for schools), 1960. *Address:* Hatherlow, Springfield Drive, Wedmore, Somerset.

SUTCLIFFE, Prof. Reginald Cockcroft, CB 1961; OBE 1942; FRS 1957; BSc, PhD Leeds; Professor of Meteorology, Reading University, 1965-70, now Emeritus Professor; *b* 16 Nov. 1904; 2nd *s* of late O. G. Sutcliffe and late Jessie Sutcliffe (*née* Cockcroft), Cleckheaton, Yorkshire; *m* 1929, Evelyn, *d* of late Rev. William Williams, Halkyn; two *d. Educ:* Whitcliffe Mount Grammar Sch., Cleckheaton; Leeds Univ.; University Coll., Bangor. Professional Asst, Meteorological Office, 1927; Meteorological Office appointments: Malta, 1928-32; Felixstowe, 1932-35; Air Ministry, 1935-37; Thorney Island, 1937-39. Squadron Leader RAFVR, France, 1939-40; Sen. Meteorological Officer, No. 3 Bomber Group RAF, 1941-44; Group Capt., Chief Meteorological Officer AEAF, later BAFO, Germany, 1944-46. Research in Meteorological Office, 1946-; Director of Research, 1957-65. President, Commission for Aerology of World Meteorological Organization, 1957-61; Mem. Adv. Cttee, World Meteorological Organization, 1964-68; Mem. Council, Royal Soc., 1968-70; Pres., Internat. Assoc. of Meteorology, 1967-71; Pres. Royal Meteorological Soc., 1955-57; Hon. Mem., Amer. Meteorological Soc., 1975-; Editor, Quarterly Jl, 1970-73 (Buchan Prize, 1950, Symons Gold Medal, 1955); Charles Chree Medal, Physical Soc., 1959; Internat.

Meteorological Organization Prize, 1963. *Publications:* Meteorology for Aviators, 1938; Weather and Climate, 1966; meteorological papers in jls. *Address:* Green Side, Winslow Road, Nash, Milton Keynes, Bucks MK17 0EJ. *T:* Whaddon 343.

SUTCLIFFE, Air Cdre Walter Philip, CB 1958; DFC 1940; *b* 15 Aug. 1910; *s* of late W. Sutcliffe, Brampton, Cumberland; *m* 1947, Margery Anne Taylor, *d* of W. L. Taylor, Tulse Hill, SW2; one *s. Educ:* Durham School; Royal Air Force Coll., Cranwell. Fleet Air Arm, 1933-35 and 1937-39; Central Flying Sch., 1936. War of 1939-45: Bomber Command, 1939-42, India and Burma, 1942-45 (despatches). RAF Staff College, 1946; Director of Operational Training, Air Ministry, 1948-50; Standing Group, NATO, 1950-51; RAF Station, Wittering, 1953-55; SHAPE, 1955-56; Atomic Weapon Trials, Australia, 1957; Director of Intelligence, Air Ministry, 1958-61; retd April 1961; Officers' Association, 1961-75. Officer, Legion of Merit (USA), 1945. *Address:* The Pond House, Pluckley, Kent. *T:* Pluckley 209.

SUTHERLAND, family name of Countess of Sutherland.

SUTHERLAND, 6th Duke of, *cr* 1833; **John Sutherland Egerton,** TD; DL; Bt 1620; Baron Gower, 1703; Earl Gower, Viscount Trentham, 1746; Marquis of Stafford (county), 1786; Viscount Brackley and Earl of Ellesmere, 1846; *b* 10 May 1915; *o s* of 4th Earl of Ellesmere and Violet (*d* 1976) *e d* of 4th Earl of Durham; *S* father, 1944; *S* kinsman as Duke of Sutherland, 1963; *m* 1939, Lady Diana Percy, *yr d* of 8th Duke of Northumberland. Served War of 1939-45 (prisoner). DL Berwickshire, 1955. *Heir: c* Cyril Reginald Egerton [*b* 7 Sept. 1905; *m* 1st, 1934, Mary (*d* 1949), *d* of late Rt Hon. Sir Ronald Hugh Campbell, PC, GCMG; one *s* three *d* ; 2nd, 1954, Mary, *d* of late Sir Sydney Lea, Dunley Hall, Worcestershire]. *Address:* Mertoun, St Boswell's, Roxburghshire; Lingay Cottage, Hall Farm, Newmarket. *Clubs:* White's, Turf; Jockey (Newmarket).
See also J. M. E. Askew, Lady M. Colville, Baron Home of the Hirsel , Viscount Rochdale .

SUTHERLAND, Countess of (24th in line) *cr (c)* 1235; **Elizabeth Millicent Sutherland;** Lady Strathnaver (*c*) 1235; Chief of Clan Sutherland; *b* 30 March 1921; *o c* of Lord Alastair St Clair Sutherland-Leveson-Gower, MC (*d* 1921; 2nd *s* of 4th Duke), and Baroness Osten Driesen (*d* 1931); *niece* of 5th Duke of Sutherland, KT, PC; *S* (to uncle's Earldom of Sutherland and Lordship of Strathnaver), 1963; *m* 1946, Charles Noel Janson, DL, late Welsh Guards; two *s* one *d* (and one *s* decd). *Educ:* Queen's College, Harley Street, W1, and abroad. Land Army, 1939-41; Laboratory Technician: Raigmore Hospital, Inverness, 1941-43; St Thomas' Hospital, SE1, 1943-45. Chairman: Trentham Gardens Ltd; The Northern Times Ltd. *Recreations:* reading, swimming. *Heir: e s* Lord Strathnaver, qv. *Address:* Dunrobin Castle, Sutherland; House of Tongue, by Lairg, Sutherland; 39 Edwardes Square, W8. *T:* 01-603 0659.

SUTHERLAND, Anthony (Frederic Arthur); Under-Secretary, Department of Employment, retired; *b* 19 Oct. 1916; *e s* of Bertram and Grace Sutherland; *m* 1940, Betty Josephine Glass; one *s* two *d. Educ:* Christ's Hosp.; Gonville and Caius Coll., Cambridge (Classical Schol.). 1st cl. hons Classics, 1938; MA 1944. HM Forces, 1940-45 (Major, Mddx Regt). Asst Prin., Min. of Labour, 1938; Prin., 1943; Prin. Private Sec. to Ministers of Labour, 1948-53; Counsellor (Labour), British Embassy, Rome, 1953-55; Asst Sec., 1955; Imp. Def. Coll., 1960; Under-Sec., 1967. Coronation Medal, 1953; Silver Jubilee Medal, 1977. *Recreation:* philately (Mem., Royal Philatelic Soc. of London). *Address:* 53 Wieland Road, Northwood, Mddx. *T:* Northwood 22078. *Clubs:* Army and Navy, Civil Service.

SUTHERLAND, Sir (Benjamin) Ivan, 2nd Bt, *cr* 1921; *b* 16 May 1901; *er surv. s* of Sir Arthur Munro Sutherland, 1st Bt, KBE, and Fanny Linda (*d* 1937), 2nd *d* of Robert Hood Haggie; *S* father 1953; *m* 1st, 1927, Marjorie Constance Daniel (marriage dissolved, 1944), *yr d* of late Frederic William Brewer, OBE, MA, Newcastle upon Tyne; two *s* ; 2nd, 1944, Margaret, *d* of Albert Owen, Chalfont St Giles, Bucks; three *s. Heir: s* John Brewer Sutherland [*b* 19 Oct. 1931; *m* 1958, Alice Muireall, *d* of late W. Stanford Henderson, Kelso; three *s* one *d*]. *Address:* Dunstan Steads, Embleton, Northumberland.

SUTHERLAND, Carol Humphrey Vivian, CBE 1970; FBA 1970; Keeper of the Heberden Coin Room, Ashmolean Museum, Oxford, 1957-75; Student of Christ Church, Oxford, 1945-75, Emeritus Student since 1975; *b* 5 May 1908; *s* of late George Humphreys Vivian and Elsie Sutherland; *m* 1933, Monica La Fontaine Porter (*see* Monica La F. Sutherland); no *c. Educ:* Westminster Sch.; Christ Church, Oxford. Barclay Head Prize for Ancient Numismatics, 1934; Asst Keeper of Coins,

Ashmolean Museum, Oxford, 1932-52; Deputy Keeper, 1952-57; University Lecturer in Numismatics, 1939-75; DLitt, 1945. Curator of Pictures, Christ Church, 1947-55, 1970-75; President, Royal Numismatic Society, 1948-53; Winslow Lectr, Hamilton Coll., Clinton, NY, 1949 and 1957; Huntington Medallist of the American Numismatic Soc., 1950; Royal Numismatic Soc. Medallist, 1954; Silver Medallist, Royal Soc. of Arts, 1955; ed Numismatic Chronicle, 1953-66; Pres., Commn Internationale de Numismatique, 1960-73; Pres., Centro Internazionale di Studi Numismatici, Naples, 1966-73; Visiting Mem. Inst. for Advanced Study, Princeton, 1962-63, 1968, 1973; Leverhulme Emeritus Fellow, 1977-79; Mem. Royal Mint Advisory Cttee, 1963-; Hon. Member: Société française de numismatique; Société royale de numismatique de Belgique; Commission Internationale de Numismatique; Corresp. Mem., German Archaeol Inst. Governor, Wallingford Sch. Officier, Palmes Académiques (France), 1965. Publications: Coinage and Currency in Roman Britain, 1937; (with H. Mattingly, E. A. Sydenham and R. A. G. Carson) The Roman Imperial Coinage, 1939-; The Romans in Spain, 1939; Anglo-Saxon Gold Coinage in the Light of the Crondall Hoard, 1948; (with J. G. Milne and J. D. A. Thompson) Coin Collecting, 1950; Coinage in Roman Imperial Policy, 1951; Art in Coinage, 1955; Gold, 1959; The Cistophori of Augustus, 1970; English Coinage, 600-1900, 1973; Roman Coins, 1974; (with C. M. Kraay) Catalogue of the Coins of the Roman Empire in the Ashmolean Museum, 1976; The Emperor and the Coinage, 1976; articles in Numismatic Chronicle, Jl Roman Studies, etc. Recreations: music, gardening. Address: Westfield House, Cumnor, Oxford. T: Cumnor 2178.

SUTHERLAND, Sir (Frederick) Neil, Kt 1969; CBE 1955; MA; Chairman, The Marconi Co. (formerly Marconi's Wireless Telegraph Co. Ltd), and of Marconi Instruments, 1965-69, retired; Director, English Electric Co. Ltd, 1965; b 4 March 1900; s of late Neil Hugh Sutherland; m 1st, 1931, Naruna d'Amorim Jordan (d 1970); one s; 2nd, 1973, Gladys Jackman. Educ: St Catharine's College, Cambridge. MA 1922. Served apprenticeship with English Electric Co. Ltd; Gen. Manager, English Electric Co. in Brazil, 1928; Man. Dir, English Electric (South Africa) Ltd, 1937; Gen. Manager, Marconi's Wireless Telegraph Co. Ltd, 1948; Man. Dir, Marconi Co. Ltd, 1958-65, Chm., 1962-65. Recreation: golf. Address: 44 Springfield Green, Chelmsford, Essex. T: Chelmsford 53980.

SUTHERLAND, Sir Gordon (Brims Black McIvor), Kt 1960; FRS 1949; Hon. LLD St Andrews, 1958; Hon. DSc, Strathclyde, 1966; Master of Emmanuel College, Cambridge, 1964-77; b Watten, Caithness, 8 April 1907; y s of late Peter Sutherland and late Eliza Hope Sutherland, Dundee, Scotland; m 1936, Gunborg Elisabeth, er d of Konstnar Filip and Anna Wahlström, Gothenburg, Sweden; three d. Educ: Morgan Academy, Dundee; St Andrews Univ. (MA, BSc); Cambridge Univ. (PhD, ScD). Commonwealth Fund Fellow, 1931-33; Stokes Studentship, Pembroke Coll., 1934-35; Fellow and Lectr, Pembroke Coll., Cambridge, 1935-49. Leverhulme Fellow 1939, for study in US; Asst to Director of Scientific Research, Min. of Supply, 1940-41; Head of group carrying out extra-mural research in Cambridge Univ. for Min. of Aircraft Prodn, Min. of Supply and Admiralty, 1941-45; Asst Dir of Research in Dept of Colloid Science, Cambridge, 1944-47; Foster Lecturer, Univ. of Buffalo, 1948; Univ. Proctor, Cambridge, 1943-44; Member of Council of Senate 1946-49; Reader in Spectroscopy, Cambridge, 1947-49; Prof. of Physics in the Univ. of Michigan, 1949-56; Dir, National Physical Laboratory, 1956-64; Reilly Lectr, Univ. of Notre Dame, 1954-55; Guggenheim Fellow, 1956; Governor: Coll. of Aeronautics, Cranfield, 1957-63; London Sch. of Economics, 1957-65; Northampton Coll. of Advanced Technology, 1960-65. Hon. Fellow: Pembroke Coll., Cambridge, 1959; Wolfson Coll., Cambridge, 1977. Vice-Pres., Royal Soc., 1961-63; Internat. Organisation for Pure and Applied Biophysics, 1961-64; Internat. Cttee on Data for Science and Technology, 1968-72; Pres., Triple Commn for Spectroscopy, 1962-63; Vice-Pres., Internat. Union of Pure and Applied Physics, 1963-69; President: Inst. of Physics and the Physical Soc., 1964-66 (Glazebrook Medal and Prize, 1972); Section X, British Assoc., 1968; Mem., Council for Scientific Policy, 1965-68. A Trustee of the National Gallery, 1971-. Fellow, Center for Advanced Study in Behavioral Scis, Stanford, 1972; For. Mem., Amer. Philosophical Soc.; For. Hon. Member: Amer. Acad. of Arts and Sciences, 1968; Société Royale des Sciences de Liège, 1960. Publications: Infra-Red and Raman Spectra, 1935. Scientific papers and articles on Infra-red Spectroscopy, Molecular Structure and Science Policy. Recreation: golf. Address: 38 Courtyards, Little Shelford, Cambridge CB2 5ER.

SUTHERLAND, Graham (Vivian), OM 1960; Painter; Designer; b London, 24 Aug. 1903; e s of late G. H. V. Sutherland, Civil

Servant, and E. Sutherland; m 1928, Kathleen Frances Barry; one s (died in infancy). Educ: Epsom Coll.; Goldsmiths' College School of Art, Univ. of London. Retrospective Exhibitions: XXVI Biennale Venice, 1952; Musée Nationale d'Art Moderne, Paris, 1952; Stedelijk Museum, Amsterdam, 1953; Kunsthaus, Zürich, 1953; Tate Gallery, London, 1953; New London Gallery, 1962; Galleria d'Arte Moderna, Turin, 1965; Basel, Munich, The Hague and Cologne, 1966-68; Marlborough Fine Art Gallery, 1968, 1973, 1977; Milan, 1973; first exhibn of portraiture, Nat. Portrait Gall., 1977. Rep. permanent collection: Tate Gallery; British Museum; Victoria and Albert Museum; Museum of Modern Art, New York; Musée de l'Art Moderne, Paris; Musée des Beaux-Arts, Brussels; The Albertina, Vienna; Museum des 20 Jahrhunderts Künstmuseum, Basel; New Pinaleotok, Munich. Trustee of Tate Gallery, 1948-54. Graham Sutherland Gallery, Pembrokeshire, established under the Picton Castle Trust, 1976. Designed tapestry, "Christ in Majesty", hung in Coventry Cathedral, 1962. Hon. Member: Inst. of Arts and Letters; Acad. of Arts and Letters, USA. Hon. DLitt: Oxford, 1962; Leicester, 1965. Museum of Modern Art, São Paulo, Prize; Foreign Secretary's Prize, Tokyo; Shakespeare Prize, Hamburg, 1974. Citoyen d'honneur, Ville de Menton. Commandeur des Arts et Lettres, France. Relevant publications: The Work of Graham Sutherland, by Douglas Cooper, 1961; Sutherland by Francesco Arcangeli, 1976. Address: La Villa Blanche, Route de Castellar, 06 Menton, France. Clubs: Athenæum, Curzon.

SUTHERLAND, Iain Johnstone Macbeth, CMG 1974; HM Diplomatic Service; Assistant Under-Secretary of State, Foreign and Commonwealth Office, since 1976; b Edinburgh, 15 June 1925; s of late Dr D. M. Sutherland, MC, RSA, and of Dorothy Johnstone, ARSA; m 1955, Jeanne Edith Nutt; one s two d. Educ: Aberdeen Grammar School; Aberdeen Univ.; Balliol College, Oxford. Served in HM Forces (Lieut, RA), 1944-47. Entered Foreign (now Diplomatic) Service, 1950; Third Secretary, Moscow, 1951; Foreign Office, 1953; First Secretary, Belgrade, 1956; Head of Chancery, Havana, 1959; transf. Washington, 1962; Asst, Northern Dept, FO, 1965; Counsellor and Consul-Gen., Djakarta, 1967-69; Head of South Asian Dept, FCO, 1969-73; Fellow, Centre for Internat. Affairs, Harvard Univ., 1973-74; Minister, Moscow, 1974-76. Address: c/o Foreign and Commonwealth Office, SW1; 24 Cholmeley Park, Highgate, N6. Club: Travellers'.

SUTHERLAND, Ian, MA; Director of Education and Training to Health Education Council, since 1971; b 7 July 1926; m 1951, Virginia Scovil Bliss; one s one d. Educ: Wyggeston Grammar School, Leicester; Sidney Sussex College, Cambridge. Assistant Professor of Classics, Univ. of New Brunswick, NB, Canada, 1949-50; Asst Master: Christ's Hospital, 1951-52; Harrow School, 1952-60; Head Master, St John's School, Leatherhead, 1960-70; Dir of Educn, Health Educn Council, 1970-71. FRSA 1969. Publication: From Pericles to Cleophon, 1954. Recreations: painting, cricket. Address: 57 Burntwood Grange Road, Wandsworth Common, SW18 3JY. Clubs: MCC, Free Foresters'.

SUTHERLAND, Dr Ian Boyd; Regional Medical Officer, South Western Regional Health Authority, since 1973; b 19 Oct. 1926; s of William Sutherland and Grace Alexandra Campbell; m 1950, Charlotte Winifred Cordin; two d. Educ: Bradford Grammar Sch.; Edinburgh Univ. MB, ChB; FFCM, DPH. Medical Officer, RAF, 1950-52; Asst MOH, Counties of Roxburgh and Selkirk, 1953-55; Dep. MOH, County and Borough of Inverness, 1955-59; Dep. County MOH, Oxfordshire CC, 1959-60; Asst Sen. MO, Leeds Regional Hosp. Bd, 1960-63. South Western Regional Hosp. Bd: Dep. Sen. Admin. MO, 1963-70; Sen. Admin. MO, 1970-73. Recreations: golf, reading, archaeology. Address: The Penthouse, Telford House, North Road, Leigh Woods, Bristol BS8 3PP.

SUTHERLAND, Sir Ivan; see Sutherland, Sir Benjamin Ivan.

SUTHERLAND, James, CBE 1974; Partner, McClure Naismith Brodie & Co., Solicitors, Glasgow and East Kilbride, since 1951; b 15 Feb. 1920; s of James Sutherland, JP and Agnes Walker; m 1948, Elizabeth Kelly Barr; two s. Educ: Queens Park Secondary Sch., Glasgow; Glasgow Univ. MA 1940, LLB 1948. Served Royal Signals, 1940-46. Examr in Scots Law, 1951-55 and Mercantile Law and Industrial Law, 1968-69, Glasgow Univ.; Chm., Glasgow South Nat. Insce Tribunal, 1964-66; Member: Bd of Management, Glasgow Maternity and Women's Hosps, 1964-74 (Chm. 1966-74); Council, Law Soc. of Scotland, 1959-77 (Vice-Pres. 1969-70; Pres. 1972-74); Council, Internat. Bar Assoc., 1972-; GDC, 1975-; Vice-Chm., Glasgow Eastern Health Council, 1975-77; Deacon, Incorporation of Barbers, Glasgow, 1962-63; Sec., Local Dental Cttee, City of Glasgow,

1955-65; Dean, Royal Faculty of Procurators in Glasgow, 1977-. *Recreation:* golf. *Address:* Biggarford, Newlands Road, Glasgow G43 2JD. *T:* 041-649 1961. *Clubs:* Caledonian; Western (Glasgow).

SUTHERLAND, Prof. James Runcieman, FBA 1953; MA, BLitt; Emeritus Professor of Modern English Literature, University College, London (Lord Northcliffe Professor, 1951-67); *b* Aberdeen, 26 April 1900; *s* of Henry Edward Sutherland, Stockbroker; *m* 1st, 1931, Helen (*d* 1975) *d* of Will H. Dircks; 2nd, 1977, Eve Betts, *widow* of Ernest Betts. *Educ:* Aberdeen Grammar Sch.; Univ. of Aberdeen; Oxford Univ. Lecturer in English, Univ. of Saskatchewan, 1921-23; Merton Coll., Oxford, 1923-25; Chancellor's English Essay Prize, Oxford, 1925; Lecturer in English, University College, Southampton, 1925; BLitt, Oxford, 1927; Lecturer in English, University of Glasgow, 1925-30; Senior Lecturer in English, University College, London, 1930-36; Professor of English Literature, Birkbeck College, London, 1936-44; Prof. of English Language and Literature, Queen Mary College, London, 1944-51; Warton lecturer on English Poetry to the British Academy, 1944; editor of The Review of English Studies, 1940-47. Visiting Professor: Harvard Univ., 1947; Indiana Univ., 1950-51; Univ. California, Los Angeles, 1967-68; Mellon Prof., Univ. of Pittsburgh, 1965; Berg Prof., NY Univ., 1969-70. Sir Walter Scott Lectures, Edinburgh University, 1952; Clark Lectures, Cambridge University, 1956; Alexander Lectures, Toronto University, 1956; Public Orator, University of London, 1957-62; W. P. Ker Memorial Lecture, Glasgow Univ., 1962; Clark Library Fellow, Univ. of California, Los Angeles, 1962-63. Hon. Mem. Modern Language Assoc. of America, 1960. Hon. LLD Aberdeen, 1955; Hon. DLitt Edinburgh, 1968; Hon. Doctor, Liège, 1974. *Publications:* Leucocholy (Poems), 1926; Jasper Weeple, 1930; The Medium of Poetry, 1934; Defoe, 1937; Background for Queen Anne, 1939; The Dunciad, 1943; English in the Universities, 1945; A Preface to Eighteenth Century Poetry, 1948; The English Critic, 1952; The Oxford Book of English Talk, 1953; On English Prose, 1957; English Satire, 1958; English Literature of the late Seventeenth Century, 1969; Daniel Defoe: a critical study, 1971; editions of plays by Nicholas Rowe, Thomas Dekker, John Dryden, William Shakespeare, and of Lucy Hutchinson's Memoirs of the Life of Colonel Hutchinson, 1973; (ed) The Oxford Book of Literary Anecdotes, 1975; contributions to various literary journals. *Recreations:* fishing, second-hand book catalogues. *Address:* Courtenay Pitts, All Saints Lane, Sutton Courtenay OX14 4AG. *T:* Sutton Courtenay 237.

SUTHERLAND, Joan, AC 1975; CBE 1961; Prima Donna, Royal Opera House, Covent Garden, since 1952; *b* 7 Nov. 1926; *d* of McDonald Sutherland, Sydney, NSW; *m* 1954, Richard Bonynge, *qv*; one *s*. *Educ:* St Catherine's, Waverley, Sydney. Début as Dido in Purcell's Dido and Aeneas, Sydney, 1947; subsequently concerts, oratorios and broadcasts throughout Australia. Came to London, 1951; joined Covent Garden, 1952; début as First Lady in The Magic Flute. Rôles at Covent Garden include: Countess, in Figaro; Agathe, in Der Freischütz; Olympia, Antonia and Giulietta, in The Tales of Hoffman; Pamina, in The Magic Flute; Gilda, in Rigoletto; Desdemona, in Otello; Lucia, in Lucia di Lammermoor; Violetta, in La Traviata; Amina, in La Sonnambula, by Bellini (opening Covent Garden season, 1960-61); Queen of the Night in The Magic Flute; Marie in La Fille du Regiment; Elvira in I Puritani; Norma (title role). Countess, in Figaro, in bicentenary celebration of Mozart's birth, Glyndebourne. Donna Anna, in Don Giovanni, Sept. 1959, Desdemona and Donna Anna, Dec. 1959, Vienna State Opera; Italian début, Feb. 1960 (Alcina); French début April 1960 (Lucia); US début, Nov. 1960, followed by tour, 1961; appeared at the Metropolitan Opera, New York, in season 1961-62; début, La Scala, Milan, April 1961 (Lucia); then sang Bellini's Beatrice di Tenda there (first time in over 100 years); re-engaged for La Scala, 1962 and 1963; opened 1961-62 Season, San Francisco; opened 1961-62 Season, Chicago. Has made many recordings in GB and France. *Recreations:* collecting autographed opera scores, 19th century operatic lithographs and 19th century books on singers of that period. *Address:* c/o Royal Opera House, Covent Garden, WC2.

SUTHERLAND, Dame Lucy Stuart, DBE 1969 (CBE 1947); DLitt Oxon 1955; Principal, Lady Margaret Hall, Oxford, 1945-71, Hon. Fellow, 1971; Pro-Vice-Chancellor, Univ. of Oxford, 1960-69; *b* 21 June 1903; *d* of Alexander Charles Sutherland, MA, MCE, and Margaret Mabel Goddard. *Educ:* Roedean School, South Africa; University of the Witwatersrand, S Africa (Herbert Ainsworth Scholar, MA (Distinction), 1925); Somerville College, Oxford (BA (Hons) Modern History Cl. I, 1927; MA 1931). Fellow and Tutor of Somerville College, Oxford, 1928-45; first Temp. Principal, then Temp. Assistant

Secretary, Board of Trade, 1941-45; Chm. Lace Working Party, 1946; Pres. GPDST; Member: Cttee of Enquiry into Distribution and Exhibition of Cinematograph Films, 1949; Royal Commission on Taxation of Profits and Income, 1951; Committee of Enquiry into Grants for Students, 1958; Hebdomadal Council, Oxford Univ., 1953-71; Sponsoring Body, Univ. of Kent, Canterbury; UGC, 1964-69; Editorial Bd, The History of Parliament Trust. Governor, Administrative Staff Coll., Henley, 1964-69. FRSA 1950; FBA 1954. Hon. LittD: Cantab, 1963; Kent, 1967; Hon. LLD Smith College, Northampton, Mass, 1964; Hon. DLitt: Glasgow, 1966; Keele, 1968; Hon. DLit Belfast, 1970; Hon. DCL Oxon, 1972. Foreign Hon. Member, Amer. Acad. of Arts and Sciences, 1965. *Publications:* A London Merchant (1695-1774), 1933; edited (with M. McKisack) Mediaeval Representation and Consent, by M. V. Clarke, 1936, and Fourteenth Century Studies, by M. V. Clarke, 1937; edited (with H. Cam and M. Coate) Studies in Manorial History, by A. E. Levett, 1938; (joint) Report of the Lace Working Party, 1947; The East India Company in Eighteenth Century Politics, 1952; edited The Correspondence of Edmund Burke, Vol. II, 1960; The University of Oxford in the Eighteenth Century, 1973; contributions to English Historical Review, Economic History Review, Economic History, Transactions of the Royal Historical Society, etc. *Address:* 59 Park Town, Oxford. *T:* Oxford 56159.

SUTHERLAND, Sir Maurice, Kt 1976; Leader of Opposition, Cleveland County Council, since 1977; Chairman, Northern Economic Planning Council, since 1977; *b* 12 July 1915; *s* of Thomas Daniel and Ada Sutherland; *m* 1st, 1941, Beatrice (*née* Skinner); one *s*; *m* 2nd, 1960, Jane Ellen (*née* Bell); one step-*d*. *Educ:* Stockton Secondary Sch. War service with Green Howards and RCS, N Africa and NW Europe. Solicitor, 1937-. Mem. Stockton Borough Council, 1957-67; Chm., Teesside Steering Cttee, 1966-67; Leader of Labour Party, Teesside County Borough Council, 1967-74; Mayor of Teesside, 1973-74; Leader of Cleveland CC, 1973-77. *Recreations:* cricket, walking, chess, politics. *Address:* 15 Valley Drive, Leven Road, Yarm, Cleveland. *T:* Eaglescliffe 782799.

SUTHERLAND, Monica La Fontaine; author; *d* of C. M. McAnally, Hon. Canon of Norwich, and Mabel Adelaide McAnally (*née* La Fontaine); *m* 1st, R. W. Porter, Hon. Canon of Chelmsford, Vicar of East Ham; two *d* (one *s* killed in action); 2nd, C. H. V. Sutherland, *qv*; no *c*. *Educ:* Eastbourne; Paris. Formerly: served in National Fire Service and Red Cross Prisoner-of-War Books Section, 1941-45. Formerly Vice-Chm., Oxford Diocesan Council for Social Work. *Publications:* La Fontaine, 1953; Louis XIV and Marie Mancini, 1956; The San Francisco Disaster, 1959; various newspaper and magazine articles. *Recreations:* travel, languages. *Address:* Westfield House, Cumnor, Oxford. *T:* Cumnor 2178.

SUTHERLAND, Sir Neil; *see* Sutherland, Sir F. N.

SUTHERLAND, Prof. Norman Stuart, MA, DPhil; Professor of Experimental Psychology, University of Sussex, since 1965; *b* 26 March 1927; *s* of Norman McLeod Sutherland; *m* 1966, Jose Louise Fogden; two *d*. *Educ:* Magdalen Coll., Oxford. BA Hons Lit. Hum. 1949 and PPP 1953; John Locke Scholar 1953. Fellow; Magdalen Coll., 1954-58; Merton Coll., 1962-64; Oxford Univ. Lectr in Exper. Psychol., 1960-64. Vis. Prof., MIT, 1961-62, 1964-65. Director: William Schlackman Ltd, 1968-; Bond Street Antiques. *Publications:* Shape Discrimination by Animals, 1959; (ed jtly) Animal Discrimination Learning, 1969; (with N. J. Mackintosh) Mechanisms of Animal Discrimination Learning, 1971; Breakdown: a personal crisis and a medical dilemma, 1976; scientific papers mainly on perception and learning. *Address:* Centre for Research on Perception and Cognition, Sussex University, Brighton BN1 9QG. *T:* Brighton 66755.

SUTHERLAND, Ranald Iain, QC (Scot) 1969; *b* 23 Jan. 1932; *s* of J. W. and A. K. Sutherland, Edinburgh; *m* 1964, Janice Mary, *d* of W. S. Miller, Edinburgh; two *s*. *Educ:* Edinburgh Academy; Edinburgh University. MA 1951, LLB 1953. Admitted to Faculty of Advocates, 1956; Advocate Depute, 1962-64, 1971-77; Standing Junior Counsel to Min. of Defence (Army Dept), 1964-69. Mem., Criminal Injuries Compensation Bd, 1977. *Recreations:* sailing, shooting. *Address:* 38 Lauder Road, Edinburgh. *T:* 031-667 5280. *Clubs:* New (Edinburgh); Royal Forth Yacht.

SUTHERLAND, Scott, RSA 1970; Head of Sculpture Department, Duncan of Jordanstone College of Art, Dundee, 1947-75, retired; *b* 15 May 1910; *s* of Major David Sutherland, MC, TD; *m* 1942; one *s* two *d*. *Educ:* Wick Academy; Wick High Sch.; Edinburgh Coll. of Art; Ecole des Beaux Arts, Paris.

Works include: Commando Memorial, Spean Bridge, 1952; Black Watch Memorial, 1959; Hercules Linton 'Cutty Sark' Meml, Inverbervie, 1969; Leaping Salmon fountain gp for Norie-Miller Walk, Perth, 1971; The Beacon Lighter, silver statuette presented to HM the Queen by ROC, 1977. *Address:* 17 Norwood, Newport-on-Tay, Fife. *T:* Newport-on-Tay 3336.

SUTHERLAND-HARRIS, Sir Jack (Alexander), KCVO 1968; CB 1959; Second Crown Estate Commissioner, 1960-68; *b* 8 May 1908; *s* of late Lieut-Colonel A. S. Sutherland-Harris, DL, JP, Burwash, Sussex; *m* 1934, Rachel Owen Jones, *yr d* of late Capt. Owen Jones, CBE, Worplesdon, Surrey; two *s* two *d*. *Educ:* Winchester Coll.; New Coll., Oxford. Entered Min. of Agriculture and Fisheries as Asst Principal, 1932; Principal Private Secretary to Minister of Agriculture and Fisheries, 1941-43; Asst Sec., 1943-50; Under-Sec., 1950-60. *Address:* Old Well Cottage, Bury, Pulborough, West Sussex. *T:* Bury 465. *Club:* Royal Commonwealth Society.

SUTTIE, Sir (George) Philip Grant-, 8th Bt, *cr* 1702; *b* 20 Dec. 1938; *o s* of late Maj. George Donald Grant-Suttie and Marjorie Neville, *d* of Capt. C. E. Carter, RN, of Newfoundland; *S* cousin, 1947; *m* 1962, Elspeth Mary (marr. diss. 1969), *e d* of Maj.-Gen. R. E. Urquhart, *qv*; one *s*. *Educ:* Sussex Composite High School, Wilts, Canada; Macdonald College, McGill University, Montreal. *Heir: s* James Edward Grant-Suttie, *b* 29 May 1965. *Address:* (seat) Balgone, North Berwick; Sheriff Hall, North Berwick, East Lothian. *T:* 2569. *Club:* New (Edin.).

SUTTILL, Dr Margaret Joan, (Mrs G. A. Rink); Chief Medical Adviser, British Council, since 1976; *d* of Ernest Montrose and Caroline Hyde; *m* 1st, 1935, F. A. Suttill, DSO, LLB (*d* 1945); two *s*; 2nd, 1949, G. A. Rink, QC, *qv*. *Educ:* Royal Free Hospital Medical School. MB BS 1935; MRCP (London) 1972. British Council: Dep. Director, Medical Dept, 1945; Director, 1948-76. *Recreations:* music (especially opera), reading, walking, bird watching, consumer problems. *Address:* 173 Oakwood Court, W14. *T:* 01-602 2143.

SUTTON, Alan John; Industrial Director, Welsh Office, since 1976; *b* 16 March 1936; *s* of William Clifford Sutton and Emily Sutton (*née* Batten); *m* 1957, Glenis (*née* Henry); one *s* one *d*. *Educ:* Bristol Univ. BSc (Hons) Elec. Engrg; MIEE. Design, Production and Trials Evaluation of Guided Missiles, English Electric Aviation Ltd, 1957-63; Design, Production, Sales and General Management of Scientific Digital, Analogue and Hybrid Computers, Solartron Electronic Group Ltd, 1963-69; International Sales Manager, Sales Director, of A. B. Electronic Components Ltd, 1969-73; Managing Director, A. B. Connectors, 1973-76. *Recreations:* squash, golf. *Address:* 56 Heol-y-Delyn, Lisvane, Cardiff CF4 5SR. *T:* (office) Cardiff 62131, ext. 468, (home) Cardiff 753194.

SUTTON, Denys; Editor of Apollo since 1962; Art critic to Financial Times; *b* 10 Aug. 1917; *s* of Edmund Sutton and Dulcie Laura Wheeler; *m* 1940, Sonja Kilbansky (marr. diss.); 1952, Gertrud Kœbke-Knudson (marr. diss.); 1960, Cynthia Sassoon; one *s* one *d*. *Educ:* Uppingham School; Exeter Coll., Oxford (BA, BLitt). Foreign Office Research Dept, 1940-46; Sec., Internat. Commn for Restitution of Cultural Material, 1946; Fine Arts Specialist at UNESCO 1948; Visiting lectr at Yale Univ., 1949. Organiser: Bonnard Exhibition, RA, 1966; France in the 18th Century, RA, 1968; British Art, Columbus, Ohio, 1971; Venice Rediscovered, Wildenstein, London, 1972; Irish Art, Columbus, Ohio, 1974. Formerly: Art Critic to Country Life; Saleroom Correspondent of Daily Telegraph. Corresp. Membre de l'Institut. Chevalier, Légion d'Honneur. *Publications:* Watteau's Les Charmes de la Vie, 1946; Matisse, 1946; Picasso, Blue and Pink Periods, 1948; French Drawings of the 18th Century, 1949; American Painting, 1949; Flemish Painting, 1950; Bonnard, 1957; Christie's since the War, 1959; André Derain, 1959; Nicholas de Staël, 1960; Gaspard Dughet, 1962; Toulouse-Lautrec, 1962; Titian, 1963; Nocturne; The Art of Whistler, 1964; Sergio de Castro, 1965; Triumphant Satyr, 1966; Whistler: Paintings, Drawings, Etchings and Water-colours, 1966; Vélazquez, 1967; An Italian Sketchbook by Richard Wilson RA, 1968; (ed and introd) Letters of Roger Fry, 1973; Walter Sickert: a biography, 1976; *introductions:* Vlaminck, Dangerous Corner, 1961; R. A. M. Stevenson, Velasquez, 1962; *jointly:* Artists in 17th Century Rome (with Denis Mahon), 1955; Catalogue of French, Spanish and German schools in Fitzwilliam Museum, Cambridge (with J. W. Goodison), 1960; Painting in Florence and Siena (with St John Gore), 1965; Richard Ford in Spain (with Brinsley Ford), 1974; contribs to magazines, etc. *Recreation:* theatre. *Address:* 22 Chelsea Park Gardens, SW3. *T:* 01-352 5141; Westwood Manor, Bradford-on-Avon, Wilts. *Club:* Travellers'.

SUTTON, Sir Frederick (Walter), Kt 1974; OBE 1971; Founder and Chairman of Directors of the Sutton Group of Companies; *b* 1 Feb. 1915; *s* of late William W. Sutton and Daisy Sutton; *m* 1934, Adriene Marie Gardener; three *s*. *Educ:* Sydney Technical College. Motor Engineer, founder and Chief Executive of the Sutton group of Companies; Mem. Bd of Directors, and life Governor, Royal New South Wales Inst. for Deaf and Blind Children. *Recreations:* flying, going fishing, boating. *Address:* 114 Bourke Street, East Sydney, NSW, Australia. *T:* Sydney 357-1777. *Clubs:* Royal Aero of NSW (Life Member); Royal Automobile of Australia; Royal Automobile of Victoria; American (Sydney).

SUTTON, Prof. John, FRS 1966; FGS; DSc, PhD; ARCS; Professor of Geology, Imperial College of Science and Technology, London, since 1958; Dean, Royal School of Mines, 1965-68 and since 1974; *b* 8 July 1919; *s* of Gerald John Sutton; *m* 1949, Janet Vida, *d* of Professor D. M. S. Watson, FRS. *Educ:* King's School, Worcester; Royal College of Science, London. Service with RAOC and REME, 1941-46. Imperial College: Research, 1946-48; Lecturer in Geology, 1948; Reader in Geology, 1956; Head of Geol. Dept, 1964-74. A Trustee, BM (Nat. Hist.), 1976-. Mem., NERC, 1976-. President, Geologists' Association, 1966-68. A Vice-Pres., Royal Society, 1976-. Bigsby Medal, Geological Society of London, 1965 (jointly with Mrs Sutton); Murchison Medal, 1975. *Publications:* papers dealing with the Geology of the Scottish Highlands. *Recreation:* gardening. *Address:* Imperial College of Science and Technology, SW7; Hartfield, Sandy Drive, Cobham, Surrey. *T:* Oxshott 3129.

SUTTON, Rev. Keith Norman; Principal of Ridley Hall, Cambridge, since 1973; *b* 23 June 1934; *s* of Norman and Irene Sutton; *m* 1963, Edith Mary Jean Geldard; three *s* one *d*. *Educ:* Jesus College, Cambridge (MA 1959). Curate, St Andrew's, Plymouth, 1959-62; Chaplain, St John's Coll., Cambridge, 1962-67; Tutor and Chaplain, Bishop Tucker Coll., Mukono, Uganda, 1968-73. *Recreations:* walking, music. *Address:* Principal's Lodge, Ridley Hall, Cambridge. *T:* Cambridge 58665.

SUTTON, Leslie Ernest, FRS 1950; MA, DPhil Oxon; Fellow and Lecturer in Chemistry, Magdalen College, Oxford, 1936-73, Fellow Emeritus, 1973; Reader in Physical Chemistry, 1962-73 (University Demonstrator and Lecturer in Chemistry, 1945-62); *b* 22 June 1906; *o c* of Edgar William Sutton; *m* 1st, 1932, Catharine Virginia Stock (*d* 1962), *er d* of Wallace Teall Stock, Maplewood, NY, USA; two *s* one *d*; 2nd, 1963, Rachel Ann Long, *er d* of Lt-Col J. F. Batten, Swyncombe, Henley-on-Thames; two *s*. *Educ:* Watford Gram. Sch.; Lincoln Coll., Oxford (Scholar). 1st Class Hon. School Chemistry, 1928; research at Leipzig Univ., 1928-29, and at Oxford University; Meldola Medal (R Inst. of Chemistry), 1932; Fellow by Examination, Magdalen College, 1932-36; Rockefeller Fellow, California Inst. of Technology, 1933-34; Harrison Prize (Chemical Soc.), 1935; Tilden Lecturer (Chemical Soc.), 1940. Vice-Pres., Magdalen College, 1947-48. Hon. Sec. Chemical Society, 1951-57; a Vice-Pres., 1957-60. Visiting Prof., Heidelberg Univ., 1960, 1964, 1967. Hon. DSc Salford, 1973. *Publications:* papers in scientific jls; (as scientific Editor) Tables of Interatomic Distances and Configuration in Molecules and Ions, 1958, 1964; Chemische Bindung und Molekülstruktur, 1961. *Address:* 62 Osler Road, Headington, Oxford OX3 9BN. *T:* Oxford 66456.

SUTTON, Rt. Rev. Peter (Eves); *see* Nelson, NZ, Bishop of.

SUTTON, Peter John; Principal Assistant Solicitor (Under Secretary, Legal), Customs and Excise, since 1976; *b* 31 May 1917; *s* of William Bertram and May Ethel Sutton; *m* 1949, Yvonne Joyce Swain. *Educ:* Gladstone's, Cliveden Place, London; Westminster School. Served War of 1939-45: Royal Gloucester Hussars, 1939; commnd Grenadier Guards, 1940; served N Africa, Italy, 1943-44. Articled Hempsons, Solicitors, 1936; admitted Solicitor, 1947. Legal Asst, Customs and Excise, 1948; Sen. Legal Asst, 1952; seconded as Legal Consultant, Cyprus Sovereign Base Areas, 1960-61; Asst Solicitor, 1969. Member, Law Society. *Recreations:* tennis, golf, motoring, boating, railways, space travel. *Address:* Heywood Close, Boldre, Lymington, Hants. *T:* Brockenhurst 2183. *Club:* Roehampton.

SUTTON, Philip John, ARA 1977; *b* 20 Oct. 1928; *m* 1954; one *s* three *d*. *Educ:* Slade Sch. of Fine Art, UCL. One-man exhibitions: Roland Browse and Delbanco Gallery, London, annually 1953-56, biennially 1958-; Geffrye Museum, London, 1959; Leeds City Art Gallery, 1960; Newcastle-on-Tyne, 1962; Bradford, 1962; Edinburgh, 1962; Sydney, 1963, 1966, 1970, 1973; Perth, 1963; Battersea, 1963, 1972; Detroit, 1967; Bristol,

1970; Folkestone, 1970, 1974; Cape Town, 1976; Johannesburg, 1976. *Recreations:* swimming, running. *Address:* 10 Soudan Road, Battersea, SW11 4HH. *T:* 01-622 2647.

SUTTON, Richard Lewis; Regional Director, Northern Region, Department of Industry, since 1974; *b* 3 Feb. 1923; *s* of William Richard Sutton and Marina Susan Sutton (*née* Chudleigh); *m* 1944, Jean Muriel (*née* Turner). *Educ:* Ealing County Grammar Sch. Board of Trade, 1939. Served War: HM Forces (Lieut RA), 1942-47. Asst Trade Comr, Port of Spain, 1950-52; BoT, 1953-62; Trade Comr, Kuala Lumpur, 1962-66; Monopolies Commn, 1966; BoT, 1967-68; Dir, British Industrial Develt Office, New York, 1968-71; Regional Dir, West Midland Region, Dept of Trade and Industry, 1971-74. *Recreations:* music, walking, bridge. *Address:* Littleburn, St James Close, Riding Mill, Northumberland NE44 6BS. *T:* Riding Mill 555.

SUTTON, Sir Robert Lexington, 8th Bt, *cr* 1772; *b* 18 Jan. 1897; *s* of Sir Arthur Sutton, 7th Bt, and Cecil (Blanche) (*d* 1948), *d* of W. D. Dumbleton, Cape Colony; *S* father, 1948; *m* 1936, Gwladys, *d* of Maj. A. C. Gover, MC; two *s. Educ:* Wellington; RMC, Sandhurst. Served European War, 1915-19. *Heir: s* Richard Lexington Sutton [*b* 27 April 1937; *m* 1959, Fiamma Ferrari; one *s* one *d*]. *Address:* Clinger Farm, Cucklington, Wincanton, Somerset BA9 9QQ. *T:* Wincanton 33209.

SUTTON, Robert William, CB 1962; OBE 1946; retired as Superintendent and Chief Scientific Officer, Services Electronics Research Laboratories, Baldock, Herts, 1946-70; *b* 13 Nov. 1905; *s* of late William Sutton; *m* 1951, Elizabeth Mary, *d* of George Maurice Wright, CBE, Chelmsford; one *s* two *d. Educ:* Brighton College; Royal College of Science, London University. Formerly with Ferranti Ltd, and then with E. K. Cole Ltd until 1938. Admiralty from 1939. *Address:* 33 Hitchin Street, Baldock, Herts. *T:* Baldock 3373.

SUTTON, Shaun Alfred Graham; Head of Drama Group, BBC Television Service, since 1969; *b* 14 Oct. 1919; *s* of late Graham Sutton and Beryl Astley-Marsden; *m* 1948, Barbara Leslie; one *s* three *d. Educ:* Latymer Upper Sch.; Embassy Sch. of Acting, London. Actor and Stage Manager, Q, Embassy, Aldwych, Adelphi, Arts, Criterion Theatres, 1938-40. Royal Navy, 1940-46, Lieut RNVR. Stage Dir, Embassy and provincial theatres, 1946-48; Producer, Embassy, Buxton, Croydon Theatres, 1948-50; toured S Africa as Producer, 1950; Producer, Embassy, Ipswich, Buxton, 1951-52; entered BBC TV Service, 1952; produced and wrote many children's TV plays and serials; directed many series incl. Z Cars, Softly Softly, Sherlock Holmes, Kipling, etc; Head of BBC Drama Serials Dept, 1966-69; dramatised Rogue Herries and Judith Paris for BBC Radio, 1971. *Publications:* A Christmas Carol (stage adaptation), 1949; Queen's Champion (children's novel), 1961. *Recreations:* gardening, walking. *Address:* The Firs, Marsh Lane, Mill Hill, NW7. *T:* 01-959 2613; Meadow Cottage, Brewery Road, Trunch, Norfolk. *Club:* Lord's Taverners.

SUTTON, Sir Stafford William Powell F.; *see* Foster-Sutton.

SUTTON, Thomas Francis; Director, J. Walter Thompson Co. Ltd, since 1960 (Managing Director, 1960-66); Director and Executive Vice-President, J. Walter Thompson Co., New York, since 1966; *b* 9 Feb. 1923; *m* 1950, Anne Fleming; one *s* two *d. Educ:* King's School, Worcester; St Peter's College, Oxford. Research Officer, British Market Research Bureau Ltd, 1949-51; Advertising Manager, Pasolds Ltd, 1951-52; Managing Director, J. Walter Thompson GmbH, Frankfurt, Germany, 1952-59. FIPA; FIS; Fellow, Royal Statistical Soc. Mem. Adv. Bd, Sch. of Internat. Business, Rutgers Univ. Internat. Advertising Man of the Year Award, 1970. *Recreations:* chess, skiing, tennis, riding. *Address:* Coldharbour, Warninglid, Sussex; 45 E 89th Street, New York, NY 10028, USA.

SUTTON, William Godfrey; Principal and Vice-Chancellor, University of the Witwatersrand, Johannesburg, 1954-62; *b* 28 March 1894; *s* of late William Godfrey Sutton, and late Mary Sutton (*née* Bennett); *m* 1st, 1954, Aletta McMenamin (*née* Wilson) (*d* 1967); 2nd, 1970, Olive Henwood (*née* Hiles) (*d* 1973). *Educ:* King Edward VII School, Johannesburg; University of Cape Town. Served European War, 1916-18, in German East African Campaign; Asst Engineer, Union Irrigation Dept, 1918-26; attached to US Reclamation Service, 1921-22; Professor of Civil Engineering, Univ. of the Witwatersrand, Johannesburg, 1926-54; War of 1939-45 Gen. Manager Central Organisation for Tech. Trg, Dept of Defence, 1941-44; Chief Technical Advisor, Dept of Commerce and Industries, 1944-45. President: South African Institute of Engineers, 1936; SA Instn of Civil Engrs, 1945; Associated Scientific and Tech. Socs of SA, 1951. Member: Smuts Meml

Cttee; US-S Africa Leader Exchange Program; Trustee, S Africa Foundn. Hon. LLD Rand, 1963. KStJ 1972. *Recreation:* bowls. *Address:* 48 Eastwood Road, Dunkeld, Johannesburg, South Africa. *T:* 42-1680. *Clubs:* Rand, Country (Johannesburg).

SUTTON CURTIS, John, CBE 1974; Chairman: Thames Board Mills Ltd, 1969-76; Workington Saw Mills Ltd, since 1966; *b* 2 July 1913; *s* of Harold Ernest Curtis; *m* 1936, Muriel Rose Hastwell; one *s. Educ:* Watford Grammar School. Served War of 1939-45, Royal Artillery. Thames Board Mills Ltd: Director, 1958; Vice-Chm., 1965; Dep. Chm. and Man. Dir, 1966-69. Chm., Assoc. of Board Makers, 1965-70; Pres., British Paper and Board Makers' Assoc., 1971-73 (Dep. Pres., 1973-75); Pres., Confederation of European Pulp, Paper and Board Industries (CEPAC), 1974-75 (Vice-Pres., 1973). Paper Industry Gold Medal, 1973. *Recreations:* golf, motoring. *Address:* Covertside, 115a Langley Road, Watford, Herts WD1 3RP. *T:* Watford 26375. *Club:* West Herts Golf.

SUVA, Archbishop of, (RC), since 1976; **Most Rev. Petero Mataca;** *b* 28 April 1933; *s* of Gaberiele Daunivucu and Akeneta Nai. *Educ:* Holy Name Seminary, Dunedin, NZ; Propaganda Fidei, Rome. Priest, Rome, 1959; Vicar-Gen. of Archdiocese of Suva, 1966; Rector of Pacific Regional Seminary, 1973; Auxiliary Bishop of Suva, 1974. Pres., Fiji Council of Churches. *Address:* Archbishop's House, Box 393, Suva, Fiji. *T:* 22851.

SUYIN; *see* Han Suyin.

SUZMAN, Mrs Helen; MP (Progressive Reform Party (earlier Progressive Party)), Houghton, Republic of South Africa, since 1961 (United Party, 1953-61); *b* 7 Nov. 1917; *d* of late Samuel Gavronsky; *m* Dr M. M. Suzman, FRCP; two *d. Educ:* Parktown Convent, Johannesburg; Univ. of Witwatersrand (BCom). Lectr in Economic History, Univ. of Witwatersrand, 1944-52. Hon. Fellow: St Hugh's Coll., Oxford, 1973; London Sch. of Economics, 1975. Hon. DCL Oxford, 1973; Hon. LLD: Harvard, 1976; Witwatersrand, 1976; Columbia, 1977; Smith Coll., 1977. *Recreations:* golf, swimming, fishing, bridge. *Address:* 49 Melville Road, Hyde Park, Sandton, 2146 Transvaal, South Africa. *T:* 42-1493. *Clubs:* Lansdowne; River, Wanderers, Wanderers Golf, Houghton Golf, Glendower (Johannesburg).

SUZMAN, Janet; actress; *b* 9 Feb. 1939; *d* of Saul Suzman; *m* 1969, Trevor Nunn, *qv. Educ:* Kingsmead Coll., Johannesburg; Univ. of the Witwatersrand (BA); London Acad. of Music and Dramatic Art. Roles played for Royal Shakespeare Co. incl.: Joan La Pucelle and Lady Anne in The Wars of the Roses, 1963-64; Lulu in The Birthday Party, Rosaline, Portia, 1965; Ophelia, 1965-66; Katharina, Celia, and Berinthia in The Relapse, 1967; Beatrice, Rosalind, 1968-69; Cleopatra and Lavinia, 1972-73. Kate Hardcastle, and Carmen in The Balcony, Oxford Playhouse, 1966; Hester in Hello and Goodbye, King's Head Theatre, 1973; Masha in Three Sisters, Cambridge, 1976; Good Woman of Setzuan, Newcastle, 1976, Royal Court, 1977; Hedda Gabler, Duke of York's, 1977. *Films:* A Day in the Death of Joe Egg, 1970; Nicholas and Alexandra, 1971; The Black Windmill, 1973; The Voyage, 1976. Plays for BBC and ITV incl.: St Joan, 1968; The Three Sisters, 1969; Macbeth, 1970; Hedda Gabler, 1972; Twelfth Night, 1973; Antony and Cleopatra, 1974; Clayhanger, serial, 1975-76. Evening Standard Drama Awards, Best Actress, 1973, 1976; Plays and Players Award, Best Actress, 1976. Mem., Theatres Trust, 1977-. *Recreation:* reading. *Address:* William Morris (UK) Ltd, 147/149 Wardour Street, W1V 3TB. *T:* 01-734 9361.

SVENNINGSEN, Nils Thomas; Grand Cross, Order of Dannebrog, Denmark; *b* 28 March 1894; *s* of Anders Svenningsen (Norwegian), Average Adjuster, and Anna Svenningsen (*née* Bennet, Swede); *m* 1922, Eva (*née* Larsen) (*d* 1960); one *d. Educ:* University of Copenhagen. Candidatus juris, 1917; practised as Assistant to a Danish Advocate in Copenhagen; entered Min. of Justice, Copenhagen, 1918. Joined Danish Foreign Service, 1920; Secretary to Danish Legation in Berlin, 1924-30; then different posts in Danish Foreign Ministry. Permanent Under-Secretary of State for Foreign Affairs, 1941-45; and 1951-61; Danish Ambassador to: Stockholm, 1945-50; Paris, 1950-51; the Court of St James's, 1961-64; retd. Chm., Swedish-Norwegian Commn on reindeer grazing, 1964. Hon. GBE 1957. *Recreation:* riding. *Address:* Overgaden oven Vandet 50, Copenhagen K, Denmark. *T:* 571566.

SVENSON, Mrs Sven G.; *see* Grey, Beryl.

SVOBODA, Prof. Josef; Chief Scenographer, National Theatre, Prague, CSSR, since 1948; Professor at Academy of Applied Arts, since 1968; *b* Cáslav, 10 May 1920; *m* 1948, Libuše

Svobodová; one d. *Educ:* Gymnasium; special sch. for interior architecture; Academy of Applied Arts (architecture). EXPO 58, Brussels: success with Laterna Magica; EXPO 67, Montreal: polyvision, polydiaekran. He co-operates with many theatres all over the world (Metropolitan Opera, New York; Covent Garden; Geneva; Bayreuth; Frankfurt, etc.); Chief of Laterna Magica, experimental scene of National Theatre, Prague, 1973-. Laureate of State Prize, 1954; merited Artist of CSSR, 1966; National Artist of CSSR, 1968; Hon. RA, London, 1969. *Publications:* relevant monographs: Josef Svoboda (by Theatre Inst.) 1967 (Prague); Josef Svoboda (by Denis Bablet) 1970 (France); The Scenography of J. Svoboda (by Jarka Burian) 1971, 1974 (USA); Teatr Josefa Svobody (by V. Berjozkin) 1973 (USSR). *Recreations:* theatre, photography, creative arts, music, literature. *Address:* Filmařská 780, 150 00 Prague 5, CSSR.

SWAFFIELD, Sir James (Chesebrough), Kt 1976; CBE 1971; RD 1967; Director-General and Clerk to the Greater London Council, since 1972; Clerk of Lieutenancy for Greater London; solicitor; *b* 16 Feb. 1924; *s* of Frederick and Kate Elizabeth Swaffield, Cheltenham; *m* 1950, Elizabeth Margaret Ellen, 2nd *d* of A. V. and K. E. Maunder, Belfast; two *s* two *d. Educ:* Cheltenham Grammar Sch.; Haberdashers' Aske's Hampstead Sch.; London Univ. (LLB); MA Oxon 1974. RNVR, 1942-46. Articled Town Clerk, Lincoln, 1946-49; Asst Solicitor: Norwich Corp., 1949-52; Cheltenham Corp., 1952-53; Southend-on-Sea Corp., 1953-56; Dep. Town Clerk, subseq. Town Clerk and Clerk of Peace, Blackpool, 1956-62; Sec., Assoc. of Municipal Corpns, 1962-72. Vice-Pres., Royal Inst. of Public Admin. (Chm., Exec. Council, 1969-71); Member: Council, Law Soc.; Exec. Council, Soc. of Local Authority Chief Executives; Internat. City Management Assoc.; UK delegn to CLRAE (Council of Europe); Foundn Sec., Local Govt Training Bd. Vis. Fellow, Nuffield Coll., Oxford. Hon. Fellow, Inst. Local Govt Studies, Birmingham Univ. Member: Ct of Governors, Admin. Staff Coll. Governing Body, Centre for Environmental Studies; Bd of Governors, Nat. Inst. for Social Work. *Address:* 10 Kelsey Way, Beckenham, Kent. *Clubs:* Reform, Naval.

SWAIN, Air Commodore (Francis) Ronald Downs, CB 1954; CBE 1946 (OBE 1941); AFC 1937; psa; retired; *b* 31 Aug. 1903; *s* of late Major Charles Sanchez de Pina Swain, TD, Southsea, Hants; *m* 1938, Sarah Mitchell, *d* of Charles H. Le Fèvre, Washington, DC; three *d. Educ:* Stonyhurst Coll. Joined Royal Air Force, 1922; Wing Comdr, 1939; Air Commodore, 1949. Commanded Cairo-Rhodesia Flight, 1933; gained World High Altitude Record, 1936 (AFC); served War of 1939-45 (despatches, OBE, CBE); Air Officer Commanding No 28 Group, RAF, 1949-50; Senior Air Staff Officer and Deputy Head of Air Force Staff, British Joint Services Mission, Washington, 1950-54, retired 1954. *Address:* c/o National Westminster Bank Ltd, 133 Westbourne Grove, W2; St Martins, Emsworth, Hants.

SWAIN, Freda Mary, FRCM; composer and pianist; *b* Portsmouth, Hants; *d* of Thomas Swain and Gertrude Mary Allen; *m* Arthur Alexander (pianist, composer, Prof. at RCM) (*d* 1969). *Educ:* St John's Southsea (private sch.); Matthay Pianoforte Sch. (under Dora Matthay); RCM. Won Associated Board Exhibition for piano, Ada Lewis Scholarship for piano (RAM) and Portsmouth-Whitcombe Scholarship for Composition (RCM), all at an early age; chose latter and studied under Sir Charles Villiers Stanford at RCM and (during last year) under Arthur Alexander (piano); Sullivan Prize for composition and Ellen Shaw Williams Prize for piano; Prof. of piano, RCM, for 14 years; founded British Music Movement, later NEMO concerts, with which former is now incorporated; founded NEMO Music Teaching Centre (Oxon & Bucks), Matthay Method, 1971. Extensive tours of S Africa and Australia (lecturing and piano), mainly on behalf of British music. FRCM 1963. *Works in manuscript* include: orchestral; concertos (two piano, one clarinet); chamber music (two string quartets, one pianoforte quartet, violin and piano sonata, poems for violin and piano, sonata for violin solo, Summer Rhapsody for viola and piano, Rhapsody No. 2 for viola and piano, Sonata for right hand (piano), Three Movements for violin and piano); anthems and wedding anthems; hymns, various; a one-act opera; Perceptions (for two pianos); Flourish (for two pianos); over 100 songs; arrangements of works for two pianos, various folk songs, pieces for recorder. *Repro works:* Carol of the Seasons, Te Deum, Jubilate, Cantata in Memoriam, Bird of the Wilderness (Song Cycle); Hymns; Ballet-Scherzo for three pianos; Setting of Psalms 150 and 121; Two Sonatas, Prelude and Toccata; Unseen Heralds (choral); Sing to Heaven (negro spiritual style). Fanfare and Anthem for 70th anniv. Tormead Sch., 1976, Guildford Cath.; A Queen's Prayer, to words by Elizabeth I, Fanfare for a Queen, and Royal Fanfare, first performance Royal Jubilee Concert, Guildford Cath., 1977; wedding anthems; anthems;

various and numerous songs. *Publications* include: *Piano:* Humoresque; Mountain Ash; An English Idyll; Two S African Impressions; Autumn Landscape; Wayward Waltz; Marionette on Holiday; Croon of the Sea; Musical Box; Windmill; *Clarinet:* The Willow Tree; Two Contrasts; Waving Grass; Laburnum Tree; Three Whimsies (solo); Rhapsody (with piano); *Oboe and Piano:* Paspy; Fantasy-Suite; *Violin or Flute:* Tambourin Gai (with piano); *Organ:* English Pastoral; *Hymn:* Breathe on me; *Songs:* Winter Field; Experience; Blessing; Country Love; The Lark on Portsdown Hill; The Green Lad from Donegal; Song for Scouts and Guides; *Choral:* A Chinnor Carol; Sweet Content; Two Christmas Carols; A Gaelic Prayer. *Recreations:* reading, the English countryside. *Address:* High Woods, Chinnor Hill, Chinnor, Oxfordshire. *T:* Kingston Blount 51285.

SWAIN, Henry Thornhill, CBE 1971; RIBA; County Architect, Nottinghamshire County Council, since 1964; *b* 14 Feb. 1924; *s* of Thornhill Madge Swain and Bessie Marion Swain; *m*; two *d. Educ:* Bryanston Sch.; Architectural Assoc. (Hons Dipl.). Served with RN, 1943-46. Herts County Architect's Dept, 1949; worked in primary school group; Notts CC, 1955; Group Leader i/c initial develt of CLASP construction; Dep. County Architect, 1958. *Publications:* many articles in architectural jls. *Recreation:* sailing. *Address:* 50 Loughborough Road, West Bridgford, Nottingham. *T:* Nottingham 864970.

SWAIN, Thomas Henry; MP (Lab) Derbyshire North-East since Oct. 1959; *b* 29 Oct. 1911; *s* of late Thomas Henry Swain, Burton-on-Trent; *m* 1931, Ruth Hannah (*d* 1969), *d* of Frank Wootton, Staveley, Derbyshire; six *s* four *d* ; *m* 1969, Rosemary Fischer. *Educ:* Broadway School, Burton-on-Trent. Miner. Member: Staveley UDC, 1944-56; Derbyshire CC, 1946-49. Vice-Pres., Derbyshire Area Exec., and Branch Sec., National Union of Mineworkers. *Address:* House of Commons, SW1; Rosemarie, 165 Clowne Road, Stanfree, Chesterfield, Derbyshire S44 6AR.

SWAINE, Edward Thomas William, CMG 1968; MBE 1952; Director, Exhibitions Division, Central Office of Information, 1961-71, retired; *b* 17 July 1907; *s* of Edward James Swaine; *m* 1942, Ruby Louise (*née* Ticehurst) (*d* 1974). Entered Govt Service, Min. of Information, 1940; Festival of Britain, 1948-52; Dir of Exhibns, British Pavilion, Montreal World Exhibn, 1967; UK Dep. Comr-Gen. and Dir of Exhbns, Japan World Exhbn, 1970. *Recreation:* photography. *Address:* 6/12 Northwood Hall, Highgate, N6. *T:* 01-340 4392.

SWALLOW, John Crossley, PhD; FRS 1968; physical oceanographer, Institute of Oceanographic Sciences (formerly National Institute of Oceanography), since 1954; *b* 11 Oct. 1923; *s* of Alfred Swallow and Elizabeth (*née* Crossley); *m* 1958, Mary Morgan (*née* McKenzie); one *step d. Educ:* Holme Valley Gram. Sch.; St John's Coll., Cambridge. Admty Signal Estabt, 1943-47; research in marine geophysics, at Cambridge and in HMS Challenger, 1948-54; work on ocean circulation, in RRS Discovery II, and in RRS Discovery, and other vessels, 1954-. Rossby Fellow, Woods Hole Oceanographic Inst., 1973-74. Murchison Grant of RGS, 1965. Foreign Hon. Mem., Amer. Acad. of Arts and Sciences, 1975. Holds American awards in oceanography. *Publications:* papers on physical oceanography. *Address:* Crossways, Witley, Surrey. *T:* Wormley 2819.

SWALLOW, Sydney; Chief Procurement Officer, Post Office, since 1977; *b* 29 June 1919; *s* of William and Charlotte Lucy Swallow; *m* 1950, Monica Williams; one *s. Educ:* Woking County Sch.; St Catharine's Coll., Cambridge (MA). Mines Dept, Board of Trade, 1940-42. Served War: Royal Engineers (Survey), 1942-46. Nat. Coal Bd, 1946-59; Central Electricity Generating Bd, 1959-65; Associated Electrical Industries Ltd, 1965-68; General Electric Co. Ltd, 1968; Dir of Supplies, GLC, 1968-77. Chm., Educn Cttee, Inst. of Purchasing and Supply, 1967-77; Visiting Prof., Univ. of Bradford Management Centre, 1972-75; Vis. Fellow, ASC, 1976-. FInstPS. *Publications:* various articles on purchasing and supply in professional jls. *Recreations:* narrowboats, cricket. *Address:* 101 Muswell Hill Road, N10. *T:* 01-444 8775.

SWALLOW, Sir William, Kt 1967; FIMechE; *b* 2 Jan. 1905; *s* of William Turner Swallow, Gomersal, Yorks; *m* 1929, Kathleen Lucy Smith; no *c. Educ:* Batley and Huddersfield Technical Colleges. Draughtsman, Karrier Motors Ltd, 1923; senior draughtsman, chief body designer, Short Bros, 1926; Gilford Motors Ltd, 1930; development engineer, Pressed Steel Co., 1932; chief production engineer, Short Bros, 1943; development engineer, General Motors Overseas Operations, New York, 1947; i/c manufacturing staff, General Motors Ltd, 1948; gen. man., A. C. Sphinx Spark Plug Div. of Gen. Motors Ltd, 1950; Managing Director, General Motors Ltd, 1953, Chairman,

1958; Chm., Vauxhall Motors Ltd, Luton, Beds, 1961-66 (Man. Dir, 1961-65). Mem., Advisory Council on Technology, 1968-70; Chairman: NPL Adv. Bd, 1969-; Shipbuilding and Shiprepairing Council, 1967-71; EDC for Hotel and Catering Industry, 1966-72; Shipbuilding Industry Bd, 1966-71. Governor, Ashridge Coll., 1965-72. ARAeS; MSAE. President: SMMT, 1964-65 (Dep. Pres. 1966-67); Inst. Road Tspt Engrs, 1966-68. *Address:* Alderton Lodge, Ashridge Park, Berkhamsted, Herts. *T:* Little Gaddesden 2284.

SWAMINATHAN, Dr Monkombu Sambasivan, FRS 1973; Director-General, Indian Council of Agricultural Research and Secretary to the Government of India, since 1972; *b* 7 Aug. 1925; *m* Mina Swaminathan; three *d. Educ:* Univs of Kerala, Madras and Cambridge. BSc Kerala, 1944; BSc (Agric.) Madras, 1947; Assoc. IARI 1949; PhD Cantab, 1952. Responsible for developing Nat. Demonstration Project, 1964, and for evolving Seed Village concept; actively involved in devel't of High Yielding Varieties, Dryland Farming and Multiple Cropping Programmes. Vice-Pres., Internat. Congress of Genetics, The Hague, 1963; Gen. Pres., Indian Science Congress, 1976. First Zakir Hussain Meml Lectr, 1970; UGC Nat. Lectr, 1971; lectures at many internat. scientific symposia. Foreign Associate, US Nat. Acad. of Scis; Hon. Mem., Swedish Seed Assoc.; Hon. Fellow, Indian Nat. Acad. of Sciences. FNA. Shanti Swarup Bhatnagar Award for contribs in Biological Scis, 1961; Mendel Centenary Award, Czechoslovak Acad. of Scis, 1965; Birbal Sahni Award, Indian Bot. Soc., 1965; Ramon Magsaysay Award for Community Leadership, 1971; Silver Jubilee Award, Indian Nat. Science Acad., 1973. Padma Shri, 1967; Padma Bhushan, 1972. Hon. DSc from ten universities. *Publications:* numerous scientific papers. *Address:* Indian Council of Agricultural Research, Krishi Bhavan, Dr Rajendra Prasad Road, New Delhi 110001, India.

SWAN, Conrad Marshall John Fisher, PhD; York Herald of Arms, since 1968; Genealogist: Order of the Bath, since 1972; of Grand Priory, OStJ, since 1976; *b* 13 May 1924; *yr s* of late Dr Henry Peter Swan, Major RAMC and RCAMC, of BC, Canada and Colchester, Essex, and of Edna Hanson Magdalen (*née* Green); *m* 1957, Lady Hilda Susan Mary Northcote, *yr d* of 3rd Earl of Iddesleigh; one *s* four *d. Educ:* St George's Coll., Weybridge; Sch. of Oriental and African Studies, Univ. of London; Univ. of Western Ontario; Peterhouse, Cambridge. BA 1949, MA 1951, Univ. of W Ont; PhD 1955, Cambridge. Served Europe and India (Capt. Madras Regt, IA), 1942-47. Assumption Univ. of Windsor, Ont.: Lectr in History, 1955-57; Asst Prof. of Hist., 1957-60; Univ. Beadle, 1957-60. Rouge Dragon Pursuivant of Arms, 1962-68. On Earl Marshal's staff for State Funeral of Sir Winston Churchill and Investiture of HRH Prince of Wales, 1969. In attendance: upon HM The Queen at Installation of HRH Prince of Wales as Great Master of Order of the Bath, 1975; during Silver Jubilee Thanksgiving Service, 1977; on Australasian Tour, 1977. Woodward Lectr, Yale, 1964; Centennial Lectr, St Thomas More Coll., Univ. of Saskatchewan, 1967; Inaugural Sir William Scott Meml Lectr, Ulster-Scot Hist. Foundn, 1968; first Herald to execute duties in Tabard across Atlantic (Bermuda, 1969) and in S Hemisphere (Brisbane, Qld, 1977); to visit Australia, 1970, S America, 1972, Thailand, Japan, 1973, NZ, 1976. World lecture tours, 1970, 1973, 1976. Adviser to PM of Canada on establishment of Nat. Flag of Canada and Order of Canada, 1964-67. Hon. Citizen, State of Texas; Freemanships in USA; Freeman: St George's, Bermuda, 1969; City of London, 1974. Fellow, 1976-, Hon. Vice-Pres. and a Founder, Heraldry Soc. of Canada; Fellow, Geneal. Soc. of Victoria (Australia), 1970; FSA 1971. Liveryman and Freeman, Gunmakers' Co., 1974. KStJ 1976. Kt of Grace and Devotion, SMO of Malta, 1964 (Genealogist Br. Assoc., 1974-). *Publications:* Heraldry: Ulster and North American Connections, 1972; Canada: Symbols of Sovereignty, 1977; many articles in learned jls on heraldic, sigillographic and related subjects. *Recreations:* hunting, driving (horse drawn vehicles), rearing ornamental pheasants and waterfowl, marine biology. *Address:* College of Arms, Queen Victoria Street, EC4V 4BT. *T:* 01-248 1850; Boxford House, Boxford, near Colchester. *T:* Boxford (Suffolk) 210208.

SWAN, Maj.-Gen. Dennis Charles Tarrant, CB 1953; CBE 1948; *b* 2 Sept. 1900; *s* of late Lt-Col C. T. Swan, IA; *m* 1930, Patricia Ethel Mary Thorne (*d* 1960); one *s* one *d. Educ:* Wellington Coll., Berks; Royal Military Academy, Woolwich. Commissioned as 2nd Lt RE, 1919; served War of 1939-45 (despatches twice): with BEF France, Feb.-May 1940; CRE 1 Burma Div., 1941; Comdt No 6 Mech. Eqpt Group, IE, 1944; Chief Engineer, 15 Ind. Corps, 1945; District Chief Engineer, BAOR, 1946, Chief Engineer, 1948; Director of Fortification and Works, War Office, 1952-55, retired. Captain 1930; Adjutant, 36 (Mx) AA Bn, 1935; Major, 1938; Lt-Col, 1945;

Colonel 1947; Brig. 1948; Maj.-Gen., 1952. Pres., Instn of Royal Engineers, 1961-65. *Address:* 15 Lancastrian Grange, Tower Street, Chichester, West Sussex. *T:* Chichester 86899.

SWAN, Dermot Joseph, MVO 1972; HM Diplomatic Service; HM Consul-General, Marseilles, 1971-77; *b* 24 Oct. 1917; *s* of Dr William Swan and Anne Cosgrave; *m* 1947, Jeanne Labat; one *d. Educ:* St George's, Weybridge; University Coll., London Univ. BA (Hons) French and German. Served War, HM Forces, 1939-46. HM Foreign (later Diplomatic) Service: Vice-Consul, Marseilles, 1947; Saigon, 1949; Foreign Office, 1951; Brazzaville, 1951; Budapest, 1953; FO 1955; First Sec., 1958; Head of Chancery, Phnom Penh, 1959, and Budapest, 1961; UK Mission, New York, 1963; FO (later FCO), 1967; Counsellor, Special Asst to Sec.-Gen. of CENTO, Ankara, 1969. *Recreations:* concerts and opera; tennis, ice-skating, swimming. *Address:* 35 Lennox Gardens, SW1. *Club:* Roehampton.

SWAN, Sheriton Clements; Director, Henry Hall (Gateshead) Ltd; *b* 15 Jan. 1909; *s* of late Sir Charles Sheriton Swan, Stocksfield-on-Tyne; *m* 1936, Rosalind Maitland, *d* of late D. S. Waterlow; two *s* one *d. Educ:* Cambridge Univ. Went to Architectural Assoc. in London to complete architectural training; joined firm of Swan, Hunter and Wigham Richardson, Ltd, in 1935. *Address:* Milestone Cottage, Wall, Hexham, Northumberland. *T:* Humshaugh 319.

SWAN, Thomas, MA, LLB; Partner in Warren Murton & Co., Solicitors, 1927-67; Chairman of Smith's Group of cos, 1963-67, and a director of other public cos; *b* 11 Aug. 1899; *s* of Thomas David Swan; *m* 1922, Iola Blanche Winfield Roll (*d* 1973); two *s* two *d. Educ:* Royal Grammar School, Newcastle upon Tyne; Emmanuel College, Cambridge. Served European War, 1914-18: Lt, The Black Watch, 1918-19; served War of 1939-45: Major, RA, 1940-45. Emmanuel College, 1919-21. Admitted Solicitor, 1923. Member of Worshipful Company of Fan Makers (Master, 1956-57). *Recreations:* golf and bridge. *Address:* 5A Old Palace Lane, Richmond, Surrey TW9 1PG. *T:* 01-940 4338. *Club:* Naval and Military.

SWAN, Lt-Col William Bertram, CBE 1968; TD 1955; JP; farmer since 1933; Lord-Lieutenant of Berwickshire since 1969; *b* 19 Sept. 1914; *er s* of late N. A. Swan, Duns, Berwickshire; *m* 1948, Ann Gilroy, *d* of late G. G. Hogarth, Ayton, Berwickshire; four *s. Educ:* St Mary's Sch., Melrose; Edinburgh Academy. Served 1939-42 with 4 Bn KOSB (UK and France) and 1942-45 with IA. Pres., Nat. Farmers Union of Scotland, 1961-62; Pres., Scottish Agric. Organisation Society Ltd, 1966-68; Mem., Development Commn, 1964-76. Pres., Scottish Cricket Union, 1972-73. JP 1964. *Recreation:* sport. *Address:* Blackhouse, Reston, Eyemouth, Berwickshire. *T:* Cumleage 242.

SWANN, Sir Anthony (Charles Christopher), 3rd Bt *cr* 1906; CMG 1958; OBE 1950; Minister for Defence and Internal Security, Kenya, 1959-63; *b* 29 June 1913; *s* of Sir (Charles) Duncan Swann, 2nd Bt; *m* 1940, Jean Margaret Niblock-Stuart; one *s. Educ:* Eton College; New College, Oxford. Joined Colonial Service, Kenya, 1936. Served, 1940-43, with King's African Rifles (Major). District Commissioner, Kenya, 1946-54; Provincial Commissioner, Kenya, 1955-59. Chairman East African Land Forces Organisation, 1959-60. *Recreations:* music, reading, fishing, shooting. *Heir:* s Michael Christopher Swann [*b* 23 Sept. 1941; *m* 1965, Hon. Lydia Mary Hewitt, *e d* of Viscount Lifford, *qv*; two *s* one *d*]. *Address:* 23 Montpelier Square, SW7. *Clubs:* Carlton, Pratt's.

SWANN, Benjamin Colin Lewis; Controller, Finance, British Council, since 1975; *b* 9 May 1922; *s* of Henry Basil Swann and Olivia Ophelia Lewis; *m* 1946, Phyllis Julia Sybil Lewis; three *s* one *d. Educ:* Bridgend County School. CA. RAFVR, 1941; Transatlantic Ferry, 1942; Flt Lieut, Transport Command, 1944; Flt Supervisor, BOAC, 1946. Apprentice Chartered Accountant, 1950; Audit Asst, George A. Touche & Co., 1953; Treasury Acct, Malaya, 1954; Financial Adviser, Petaling Jaya, 1956; Partner, Milligan Swann & Co., Chartered Accountants, Exeter, 1957; British Council, 1960; Regional Acct, SE Asia, 1961; Dep. Dir Audit, 1965; Asst Representative, Delhi, 1970; Director, Budget, 1972; Dep. Controller, Finance, 1972. *Recreations:* cuisine, lepidoptery. *Address:* 10 Probyn Road, SW2. *T:* 01-671 2179; Les Malardeaux, St Sernin de Duras 47120, France.

SWANN, Donald Ibrahim, MA; composer and performer, free-lance since 1948; *b* 30 Sept. 1923; *s* of late Dr Herbert William Swann, Richmond, Surrey and Naguimé Sultan; *m* 1955, Janet Mary (*née* Oxborrow), Ipswich, Suffolk; two *d. Educ:* Westminster School; Christ Church, Oxford. Hons Degree Mod. Lang. (Russian and Mod. Greek). Contributed music to London revues, including Airs on a Shoestring, 1953-54, as joint leader writer with Michael Flanders; Wild Thyme, musical play, with Philip Guard, 1955; in At the Drop of a Hat, 1957, appeared for first time (with Michael Flanders) as singer and accompanist of own songs (this show ran over 2 yrs in London, was part of Edinburgh Festival, 1959; Broadway, 1959-60; American and Canadian tour, 1960-61; tour of Great Britain and Ireland, 1962-63); At the Drop of Another Hat (with Michael Flanders), Haymarket, 1963-64, Globe, 1965; Aust. and NZ tour, 1964; US Tour, 1966-67. Arranged concerts of own settings: Set by Swann, An Evening in Crete; Soundings by Swann; Between the Bars: an autobiography in music; A Crack in Time, a concert in search of peace. Works in song-writers' trio with Jeremy Taylor and Sydney Carter. Founded Albert House Press for special publications, 1974. Compositions and Publications include: satirical music to Third Programme series by Henry Reed, ghosting for Hilda Tablet. London Sketches with Sebastian Shaw, 1958; Festival Matins, 1962; Perelandra, music drama with David Marsh based on the novel of C. S. Lewis, 1961-62; Settings of John Betjeman Poems, 1964; Sing Round the Year (Book of New Carols for Children), 1965; (with Arthur Scholey) The Song of Caedmon, 1971; The Road Goes Ever On, book of songs with J. R. R. Tolkien, 1968; The Space Between the Bars: a book of reflections, 1968; Requiem for the Living, to words of C. Day Lewis, 1969; The Rope of Love: around the earth in song, 1973; Swann's Way Out: a posthumous adventure, 1974; (with Albert Friedlander) The Five Scrolls, 1975; Omnibus Flanders and Swann Songbook, 1977. Recreation: going to the launderette. Address: 13 Albert Bridge Road, SW11 4PX. T: 01-622 4281.

SWANN, Frederick Ralph Holland, CBE 1974 (OBE 1944); Chairman, Royal National Lifeboat Institution, 1972-75; b 4 Oct. 1904; s of F. Holland Swann, JP, Steeple, Dorset; m 1940, Philippa Jocelyn Braithwaite (d 1968); no c. Educ: Eton; Trinity Coll., Cambridge (MA). Mem. London Stock Exchange, 1932-64. Joined RNVSR, 1937; served in HMS Northern Gift, 1939-40 (despatches); comd HMS Sapphire, 1940-41; Senior fighter Direction Officer, HMS Formidable, 1941-43; Comdr RNVR 1944; Exec. Officer, HMS Biter, 1944 and HMS Hunter, 1944-45 (in comd, 1945). Mem. Cttee of Management, RNLI, 1953, Dep. Chm. 1964-72. A Vice-Pres., Royal Humane Soc., 1973; Hon. Life Mem., Norwegian Soc. for Sea Rescue, 1975. A Comr of Income Tax, City of London, 1964-76. Recreations: sailing, fishing, gardening. Address: Stratford Mill, Stratford-sub-Castle, Salisbury, Wilts. T: Salisbury 6563. Clubs: United Oxford & Cambridge University, Royal Cruising (Cdre 1966-72); Royal Corinthian Yacht.

SWANN, Julian Dana Nimmo H.; see Hartland-Swann.

SWANN, Sir Michael (Meredith), Kt 1972; MA, PhD; FRS 1962; FRSE 1952; Chairman of the BBC, since 1973; b 1 March 1920; er s of late M. B. R. Swann, MD, Fellow of Gonville and Caius Coll., Cambridge, and of Marjorie (she m 2nd, Sir Sydney Roberts, he d 1966); m 1942, Tess, ARCM, ARCO, d of late Prof. R. M. Y. Gleadowe, CVO, Winchester; two s two d. Educ: Winchester; Gonville and Caius College, Cambridge. Served War, 1940-46, in various capacities, mainly scientific (despatches, 1944). Fellow of Gonville and Caius College, Cambridge, 1946-52; University Demonstrator in Zoology, Cambridge, 1946-52; Professor of Natural History, University of Edinburgh, 1952-65; Dean, Faculty of Science, 1963-65, Principal and Vice-Chancellor, 1965-73, Univ. of Edinburgh. Member: Adv. Council on Educn in Scotland, 1957-61; Fisheries Adv. Cttee, Develt Commn, 1957-65. Council St George's School for Girls, 1959-75; Edinburgh Univ. Court, 1959-62; MRC, 1962-65; Cttee on Manpower Resources, 1963-68; Council for Scientific Policy, 1965-69; SRC, 1969-73; Adv. Council, Civil Service Coll., 1970-76; Chairman: Nuffield Foundation Biology Project, 1962-65; Jt Cttee on Use of Antibiotics in Animal Husbandry and Veterinary Medicine, 1967-68; Scottish Health Services Scientific Council, 1971-72; Jt Cttee of Inquiry into the Veterinary Profession, 1971-75; Council for Science and Society, 1973-. Author of Swann reports on Scientific Manpower, 300 GEV Accelerator, Antibiotics, Veterinary Profession. Director: Inveresk Res. Internat., Midlothian, 1969-72; New Court Natural Resources Ltd, 1973-. Mem. Bd of Trustees, Wellcome Trust, 1973-. FIBiol; Hon. FRCSE 1967; Hon. FRCPE 1972; Hon. ARCVS 1976. Hon. LLD Aberdeen, 1967; DUniv York, 1968; Hon. DSc Leicester, 1968; Hon. DLitt Heriot Watt, 1971. Publications: papers in scientific journals. Recreations: gardening, sailing. Address: Ormsacre, 41 Barnton Avenue, Edinburgh EH4 6JJ. T: 031-336 1325; Broadcasting House, W1. T: 01-580 4468. Clubs: Athenæum; New (Edinburgh).
See also Bishop of Truro.

SWANN, Robert Swinney, MBE 1947; HM Diplomatic Service, retired; Escort Officer, Government Hospitality Fund, since 1975; b 17 Nov. 1915; s of R. N. and F. Swann. Educ: George Watson's Boys' College, Edinburgh; Edinburgh University. Indian Civil Service, 1938-47; joined Diplomatic Service, 1947; Counsellor Addis Ababa, 1965-69; Diplomatic Service Inspector, 1969-72; Counsellor, Bonn, 1972-74. Now engaged in legal-historical research. Recreations: music, theatre. Address: 6 Collingham Gardens, SW5. T: 01-373 0445.

SWANSEA, 4th Baron cr 1893; John Hussey Hamilton Vivian, Bt 1882; DL; b 1 Jan. 1925; s of 3rd Baron and Hon. Winifred Hamilton (d 1944) (d of 1st Baron Holm Patrick; S father, 1934; m 1956, Miriam Antoinette (marr. diss. 1973; she d 1975), 2nd d of A. W. F. Caccia-Birch, MC, of Guernsey Lodge, Marton, NZ; one s two d. Educ: Eton; Trinity Coll., Cambridge. DL Powys (formerly Brecknock), 1962. Recreations: shooting, fishing, rifle shooting. Heir: s Hon. Richard Anthony Hussey Vivian, b 24 Jan. 1957. Address: Glanyrafon, Erwood, Powys. T: Erwood 662. Clubs: Junior Carlton; Cardiff and County (Cardiff).

SWANSEA and BRECON, Bishop of, since 1976; Rt. Rev. Benjamin Noel Young Vaughan; b 25 Dec. 1917; s of Alderman and Mrs J. O. Vaughan, Newport, Pembs; m 1945, Nesta Lewis. Educ: St David's Coll., Lampeter (BA); St Edmund Hall, Oxford (MA); Westcott House, Cambridge. Deacon, 1943; Priest, 1944. Curate of: Llannon, 1943-45; St David's, Carmarthen, 1945-48; Tutor, Codrington Coll., Barbados, 1948-52; Lecturer in Theology, St David's Coll., Lampeter, and Public Preacher, Diocese of St David's, 1952-55; Rector, Holy Trinity Cathedral, Port of Spain, and Dean of Trinidad, 1955-61; Bishop Suffragan of Mandeville, 1961-67; Bishop of British Honduras, 1967-71; Assistant Bishop and Dean of Bangor, 1971-76. Examining Chaplain to Bishop of Barbados, 1951-52, to Bishop of Trinidad, 1955-61; Commissary for Barbados, 1952-55. Formerly Chairman: Nat. Council for Educn in British Honduras; Govt Junior Secondary Sch.; Provincial Commn on Theological Educn in WI; Provincial Cttee on Reunion of Churches, Christian Social Council of British Honduras; Ecumenical Commn of British Honduras; Agric. Commn of Churches of British Honduras. Chairman: Provincial Cttee on Missions, Church in Wales; Church and Society Dept, Council of Churches for Wales; Adv. Cttee on Church and Society, Church in Wales, 1977; Judge of Provincial Court, Church in Wales. Member: Council, St David's Univ. Coll., Lampeter, 1976; Council and Ct, Swansea Univ. Coll., 1976. Sub-Prelate, OStJ, 1977; Order of Druids, Gorsedd y Beirdd. Publications: Structures for Renewal, 1967; Wealth, Peace and Godliness, 1968; The Expectation of the Poor, 1972. Address: Ely Tower, Brecon, Powys.

SWANSON, Gloria, (Gloria May Josephine Swanson); American film actress; b Chicago, 27 March 1899; d of Joseph and Adelaide Swanson; m 1st, Wallace Beery (marr. diss.); 2nd, Herbert K. Somborn (marr. diss.); one d; 3rd, Marquis de la Falaise de la Coudraye (marr. diss.); 4th, Michael Farmer (marr. diss.); one d; 5th, William N. Davey (marr. diss.); 6th, William Dufty. Began career at Essanay in Chicago, then Keystone Comedies, Hollywood; starred in Triangle Films, for Cecil B. DeMille (six consec. films) and 20 for Famous Players-Lasky in Hollywood and NY; later formed Gloria Swanson Productions; and became owner-member of United Artists which released Sonya (which opened NY Roxy Theatre), Sadie Thompson, Queen Kelly (unreleased), The Trespasser, and the first all-talking picture, What a Widow, and Perfect Understanding (with Laurence Olivier, made in England); among many other films starred in Music in the Air, Father Takes a Wife, Sunset Boulevard, 1950, and Airport, 1975. Has also appeared in various theatrical rôles: 20th Century, with José Ferrer, Broadway, 1951; The Inkwell, 1962-63, and Reprise, 1967; Butterflies are Free, toured and on Broadway, 1970-72. Own television show, The Gloria Swanson Hour, 1948. Palms and Officer, Académie des Beaux Arts; Cross of Honour and Merit, SMO Malta; OStJ 1963; Award from City of Paris and, among others, Foreign Critics Award; Neiman-Marcus Award for style; Hon. Comr of Youth and Fitness of NY, 1976. Recreations: sculpture, painting. Address: Swanson/Dufty Enterprises Ltd, 920 5th Avenue, New York, NY 10021, USA.

SWANSTON, Commander David, DSO 1945; DSC 1941, and Bar, 1942; RN; Deputy Serjeant at Arms, House of Commons, since 1976; b 13 Feb. 1919; s of late Capt. D. S. Swanston, OBE RN; m 1st, 1942, Sheila Ann Lang (marr. diss.); one s (and one s decd); 2nd, 1953, Joan Margaret Nest Stockwood, d of late I. H. Stockwood and Mrs Stockwood; one s one d. Educ: Royal Naval College, Dartmouth. Joined Royal Navy, 1932; served in submarines at Home, Mediterranean, and East Indies Stations, from 1939. Comd Shakespeare, 1944-45; Alaric, 1948; Tudor, 1949; Naval Liaison Officer, RMA Sandhurst, 1951-53; passed RN Staff course, 1953; Commander, 1953; invalided from Royal Navy, 1955. Asst Serjeant at Arms, House of Commons, 1957-76. Industrial employment, 1955-56. *Recreations:* golf, rifle shooting. *Address:* Speaker's Court, House of Commons, SW1A 0AA. *T:* 01-219 5611; High Meadow, Linchmere, Haslemere, Surrey GU27 3NF.

SWANTON, Ernest William, OBE 1965; formerly Cricket and Rugby football Correspondent to the Daily Telegraph, retired 1975; BBC Commentator, since 1934; *b* 11 Feb. 1907; *s* of late William Swanton; *m* 1958, Ann, *d* of late R. H. de Montmorency and *widow* of G. H. Carbutt. *Educ:* Cranleigh. Evening Standard, 1927-39. Played Cricket for Middlesex, 1937-38. Served 1939-46; captured at Singapore, 1942; POW Siam, 1942-45; Actg Maj. Bedfordshire Yeomanry (RA). Joined Daily Telegraph staff, 1946. Covered 20 Test tours to Australia, W Indies, S Africa, New Zealand and India; managed own XI to West Indies, 1956 and 1961 and to Malaya and Far East, 1964. Editorial Director, The Cricketer. Cttee, MCC and Kent CC. *Publications:* (with H. S. Altham) A History of Cricket, editions 1938, 1946, 1948, 1962 (in 2 vols); Denis Compton, A Cricket Sketch, 1948; Elusive Victory (with F. R. Brown's Team in Australia), 1951; Cricket and The Clock, 1952; Best Cricket Stories (An Anthology), 1953; The Test Matches of 1953, 1953; West Indian Adventure, 1954; Victory in Australia, 1954/5, 1955; The Test Matches of 1956, 1956; Report from South Africa (with P. B. H. May's MCC Team, 1956-1957), 1957; West Indies Revisited, 1960; The Ashes in Suspense, 1963. General Editor of The World of Cricket, 1966; Cricket from all Angles, 1968; Sort of a Cricket Person (memoirs), 1972; Swanton in Australia, 1975; Follow On, 1977. *Recreations:* cricket, golf. *Address:* Delf House, Sandwich, Kent. *Clubs:* MCC, Bath; Royal and Ancient.

SWANWICK, Betty, ARA 1972; RWS 1976; artist; book illustrator and mural painter; now painting in watercolours; *b* 22 May 1915; *d* of Henry Gerrad Swanwick. *Educ:* Lewisham Prendergast Sch.; Goldsmiths' Coll. Sch. of Art; Royal Coll. of Art. Has designed posters and press advertisements for LPTB, Shell-Mex, etc; murals for various organizations. *Publications:* The Cross Purposes, 1945; Hoodwinked, 1957; Beauty and the Burglar, 1958. *Recreation:* gardening. *Address:* Caxton Cottage, Frog Lane, Tunbridge Wells, Kent.

SWANWICK, Hon. Sir Graham Russell, Kt 1966; MBE 1944; **Hon. Mr Justice Swanwick;** Judge of the High Court of Justice (Queen's Bench Division), since 1966; Presiding Judge, Midland and Oxford Circuit, since 1975; *b* 24 August 1906; *s* of Eric Drayton Swanwick and Margery Eleanor (*née* Norton), Whittington House, Chesterfield; *m* 1st, 1933, Helen Barbara Reid (marr. diss., 1945; she *d* 1970); two *s*; 2nd, 1952, Audrey Celia Parkinson. *Educ:* Winchester Coll.; University Coll., Oxford (BA). Called to Bar, Inner Temple, 1930, Master of the Bench, 1962; QC 1956; Leader Midland Circuit, 1961-65. Wing Comdr RAFVR, 1940-45 (MBE). Recorder: City of Lincoln, 1957-59; City of Leicester, 1959-66; Judge of Appeal, Channel Islands, 1964-66; Derbyshire QS: Chm., 1963-66; Dep. Chm., 1966-71. *Recreations:* tennis, shooting. *Address:* 4 Holland Park Road, W14 8LZ. *T:* 01-602 2652; Burnett's Ashurst, Steyning, West Sussex. *T:* Partridge Green 710241.

SWARBRICK, James, PhD, DSc; FRIC; Dean, School of Pharmacy, University of London, since 1976; *b* 8 May 1934; *s* of George Winston Swarbrick and Edith M. C. Cooper; *m* 1960, Pamela Margaret Oliver. *Educ:* Sloane Grammar Sch.; Chelsea Coll., Univ. of London (BPharm Hons 1960; PhD 1964; DSc 1972). MPS 1961; FRIC 1970. Asst Lectr, 1962, Lectr, 1964, Chelsea Coll.; Vis. Asst Prof., Purdue Univ., 1964; Associate Prof., 1966, Prof. and Chm. of Dept of Pharmaceutics, 1969, Asst Dean, 1970, Univ. of Conn; Dir of Product Develt, Sterling-Winthrop Res. Inst., NY, 1972; first Prof. of Pharmaceutics, Univ. of Sydney, 1975-76. Vis. Scientist, Astra Labs, Sweden, 1971; Indust. Cons., 1965-72, 1975-; Cons., Aust. Dept. of Health, 1975-76; Mem., Cttee on Specifications, National Formulary, 1970-75; Chm., Jt US Pharmacopoeia-Nat. Formulary Panel on Disintegration and Dissolution Testing, 1971-75. Member: Cttee on Grad. Programs, Amer. Assoc. of Colls of Pharmacy, 1969-71; Practice Trng Cttee, Pharm. Soc. of NSW, 1975-76; Academic Bd, Univ. of Sydney, 1975-76; Collegiate Council, 1976; Educn Cttee, Pharmaceutical Soc. of GB, 1976. FAAAS 1966; Fellow, Acad. of Pharm. Sciences, 1973. Mem. Editorial Board: Jl of Biopharmaceutics and Pharmacokinetics, 1973; Drug Development Communications, 1974; series Editor, Current Concepts in the Pharmaceutical Sciences, and, Drugs and the Pharmaceutical Sciences. *Publications:* (with A. N. Martin and A. Cammarata) Physical

Pharmacy, 1960 (2nd edn 1969); contributed: American Pharmacy, 6th edn 1966 and 7th edn 1974; Remington's Pharmaceutical Sciences, 14th edn 1970 and 15th edn 1975; contrib. Current Concepts in the Pharmaceutical Sciences: Biopharmaceutics, 1970; res. contribs to internat. sci. jls. *Recreation:* chasing golf and tennis balls. *Address:* The School of Pharmacy, University of London, 29/39 Brunswick Square, WC1N 1AX. *T:* 01-837 7651.

SWART, Hon. Charles Robberts, DMS 1972; BA, LLB; State President, Republic of South Africa, May 1961-May 1967, retired; *b* 5 Dec. 1894; *m* 1924, Nellie de Klerk; one *s* one *d.* *Educ:* University Coll. of OFS, South Africa (BA, LLB); Columbia University, New York. Practised as Advocate, Supreme Court, S Africa, 1919-48; MP (Nat) for Ladybrand, OFS, 1923-38 and for Winburg, OFS, 1941-59; Minister of Justice, 1948-59; also Minister of Education Arts and Science, 1949-50; Deputy Prime Minister and Leader of the House, 1954-59; Acting Prime Minister, 1958; Governor-General of the Union of South Africa, 1960-61. Hon. Col, Regt, Oos-Vrystaat, 1953-; Hon. Col Regt Univ. Oranje-Vrystaat, 1963-. Chancellor, Univ. of OFS, 1951-. Hon. LLD, Univ. of OFS, 1955, Rhodes Univ., 1962, and Potchefstroom Univ., 1963; Hon. Fellow, Coll. of Physicians, Surgeons and Gynaecologists of SA, 1963-; Hon. Mem. SA Acad. of Science and Art; Life Mem. Federn of Afrikaans Cultural Socs; Hon. Pres., Automobile Assoc. (SA); Hon. Fellow, SA Inst. of Architects; Life Patron-in-Chief, SA Voortrekker Youth Movement. Hon. Freeman: Johannesburg; Durban; Bloemfontein; Kimberley, etc. *Publications:* (both in Afrikaans Language) Kinders van Suid-Africa, 1933; Die Agterryer, 1939. *Address:* De Aap, Brandfort, OFS, Republic of South Africa.

SWARTZ, Rt. Rev. George Alfred; a Bishop Suffragan of Cape Town, since 1972; Canon of St George's Cathedral, Cape Town, since 1969; *b* 8 Sept. 1928; *s* of Philip and Julia Swartz; *m* 1957, Sylvia Agatha (*née* George); one *s* one *d .* *Educ:* Umbilo Road High Sch., Durban; Univ. of the Witwatersrand, Johannesburg; Coll. of the Resurrection, Mirfield, Yorks; St Augustine's Coll., Canterbury. BA, Primary Lower Teacher's Cert., Central Coll. Dip. (Canterbury). Asst Teacher, Sydenham Primary Sch., 1951-52; Deacon, 1954; Priest, 1955; Asst Curate, St Paul's Church, Cape Town, 1955-56; Priest in Charge, Parochial Dist of St Helena Bay, Cape, 1957-60; St Augustine's Coll., Canterbury, 1960-61; Dir, Cape Town Dio. Mission to Muslims, 1962-63; Dir, Mission to Muslims and Rector St Philip's Church, Cape Town, 1963-70; Regional Dean of Woodstock Deanery, 1966-70; Priest in Charge, Church of the Resurrection, Bonteheuwel, Cape, 1971-72. *Recreations:* cinema, music (traditional jazz; instruments played are guitar and saxophone). *Address:* Bishopsholme, 18 Rue Ursula, Glenhaven, Bellville 7530, Republic of South Africa. *T:* 94 1518.

SWARTZ, Col Hon. Sir Reginald (William Colin), KBE 1972 (MBE 1948); ED; JP; MBIM; company director; *b* 14 April 1911; *s* of late J. Swartz, Toowoomba, Qld; *m* 1936, Hilda, *d* of late G. C. Robinson; two *s* one *d.* *Educ:* Toowoomba and Brisbane Grammar Schs. Commonwealth Military Forces, 1928-40, Lieut, 1934. Served War of 1939-45: Captain 2-26 Bn, 8 Div., AIF, 1940; Malaya (PoW): Singapore, Malaya, Thailand (Burma-Thailand Rly); CMF, in Darling Downs Regt, Lt-Col, AQMG, CMF, N Comd, Col (RL), 1961. Hon. Col Australian Army Aviation Corps, 1969-75. MHR (L) Darling Downs, Qld, 1949-72; Parly Under-Sec. for Commerce and Agric., 1952-56; Parly Sec. for Trade, 1956-61; Minister: (of State) for Repatriation, Dec. 1961-Dec. 1964; for Health, 1964-66; for Social Services, 1965; for Civil Aviation, 1966-69; for Nat. Develt, 1969-72; Leader, House of Representatives, Canberra, 1971-72. Leader of many delegns overseas incl. Aust. Delegn to India, 1967, and Trade Mission to SE Asia, 1958; Parly Delegn to S and SE Asia, 1966. Patron and/or Vice-Pres. or Mem. of numerous public organizations. Member, RSL. JP Queensland 1947. *Recreations:* bowls, boating. *Address:* 31 Furlong Street, Rio Vista, Surfers Paradise, Qld 4217, Australia. *Clubs:* Number 10; United Service, Anzac (Brisbane); Royal Auto (Toowoomba); Royal Automobile Club of Victoria; Australian (Melbourne); Twin Towns Services (Tweed Head); Surfers Paradise Bowls; Darling Downs Aero; Southport Yacht (Queensland).

SWASH, Stanley Victor, MC 1917 and Bar 1918; *b* 29 February 1896; British; *s* of A. W. Swash, JP and Sylvia Swash; *m* 1924; *m* 1955, Jane Henderson. *Educ:* Llandovery College; St John's College, Oxford; Lincoln's Inn. Served European War, 1915-19, RFA. MA (Mathematics); short period in Ministry of Pensions; served Royal Navy as Lieut Inst., 1921-24; worked in Woolworth Company, 1924-55; Director, 1939, Chairman, 1951-55; retired 1955. Called to Bar, Lincoln's Inn, 1938. OC 57

County of London Home Guard Battalion, Lieut-Colonel, 1940-45. Chairman, Horticultural Marketing Advisory Council, 1958; Member Milk Marketing Board, 1957-63; Chm. BOAC/MEA Cttee of Enquiry, 1963-64. *Recreations:* golf, bridge. *Address:* Park Avenue, St Andrews, Malta. *Club:* United Oxford & Cambridge University.

SWAYNE, Ronald Oliver Carless, MC 1945; Chairman, Overseas Containers Ltd, since 1973; Director: Ocean Transport & Trading Ltd; National Freight Corporation, since 1973; *b* 11 May 1918; *s* of Col. O. R. Swayne, DSO, and Brenda (*née* Butler); *m* 1941, Charmian, *d* of Major W. E. P. Cairnes, Bollingham, Herefordshire; one *s* one *d*. *Educ:* Bromsgrove Sch., Worcester; University Coll., Oxford, 1936-39 and 1945-46 (MA). Served with Herefordshire Regt, 1939-40, No 1 Commando, 1940-45 (MC). Joined Ocean Steam Ship Co., 1946; became partner of Alfred Holt & Co. and Man. Dir of Ocean Steam Ship Co., 1955. Dir, 1965, Dep. Chm., 1969, Overseas Containers Ltd. Vice-Chm., British Shipping Fedn, 1967; Pres., Cttee des Assocs d'Armateurs of EEC, 1974-75; Vice-Pres., Gen. Council of British Shipping, 1977-78. Industrial Adviser, Churchill Coll., Cambridge, 1974; Member: Design Council, 1975; Careers Res. Adv. Council, 1975; New Philharmonia Trust, 1968. *Recreations:* fishing, shooting, music, bull terriers. *Address:* Puddle House, Chicksgrove, Tisbury, Salisbury SP3 6NA. *T:* Teffont 454. *Clubs:* Travellers'; Houghton (Stockbridge).

SWAYTHLING, 3rd Baron, *cr* 1907; **Stuart Albert Samuel Montagu,** Bt, *cr* 1894; OBE 1947; late Grenadier Guards; formerly director, Messrs Samuel Montagu and Co. Ltd; *b* 19 Dec. 1898; *e s* of 2nd Baron and Gladys Helen Rachel, OBE, (*d* 1965), *d* of late Col A. E. Goldsmid; *S* father, 1927; *m* 1925, Mary Violet (from whom he obtained a divorce, 1942), *e d* of late Major Levy, DSO, and late Hon. Mrs Ionides; two *s* one *d*; *m* 1945, Mrs Jean Knox, Director ATS (*see* Lady Swaythling). *Educ:* Clifton; Westminster; Trinity College, Cambridge. JP: Co. Southampton, 1928-48; Surrey, 1948-. Pres., English Guernsey Cattle Society, 1950-51, 1971-72; Dep. Pres., Royal Assoc. of British Dairy Farmers, 1970-72, 1973-74 (Pres., 1972-73). Master of The Company of Farmers, 1962-63. *Heir: s* Hon. David Charles Samuel Montagu, *qv*. *Address:* Crastock Manor, Crastock, Woking, Surrey GU22 0RJ. *T:* Worplesdon 2265. *Club:* Bath.
See also Hon. E. E. S. Montagu, Ivor Montagu.

SWAYTHLING, Lady, (Jean M.), CBE 1943; Chief Controller and Director, Auxilliary Territorial Service, 1941-43 (as Mrs Jean Knox); *b* 14 Aug. 1908; *m* Squadron Leader G. R. M. Knox; one *d*; *m* 1945, 3rd Baron Swaythling, *qv*. *Address:* Crastock Manor, Crastock, Woking, Surrey. *T:* Worplesdon 2265.

SWEANEY, William Douglas, CMG 1965; retired 1972, as Establishment Officer, Overseas Development Administration, Foreign and Commonwealth Office; *b* 12 Nov. 1912; *s* of late Lt-Comdr William Sweaney, MBE, RN, and late Elizabeth Bridson; *m* 1939, Dorothy Beatrice Parsons; one *s*. *Educ:* Gillingham Gram. Sch.; London Sch. of Economics. Clerical Officer, Inland Revenue (Special Comrs of Income Tax), 1929; Officer of Customs and Excise, 1932; seconded to Colonial Office, 1943 (promoted Surveyor of Customs and Excise *in absentia*); transferred to Colonial Office, 1948; Principal, 1948; Private Sec. to Minister of State for Colonial Affairs, 1953; Asst Sec., 1955; Dept of Technical Co-operation, 1961; ODM, later ODA, FCO, 1964-72, Establishment Officer, 1965. *Recreations:* walking, ornithology. *Address:* Crowlink, Borde Hill Lane, Haywards Heath, West Sussex. *T:* Haywards Heath 50341.

SWEENEY, Very Rev. Canon Garrett Daniel; *b* 30 Sept. 1912; *s* of Daniel Sweeney and Margaret Helen Sweeney (*née* Payne). *Educ:* Derby Sch.; Cotton Coll.; Ven. English Coll., Rome; Christ's Coll. and St Edmund's House, Cambridge. Priest (RC) 1937; BA (London) 1940; MA (Cantab) 1952. Asst Priest, Leicester, 1937-41; Parish Priest, Shirebrook, Derbys, 1941-46; Asst Master, 1948-56, and Headmaster, 1956-64, St Hugh's Coll., Tollerton, Nottingham; Master, St Edmund's House, Cambridge, 1964-76, Hon. Fellow, 1976. *Address:* The Priest's House, 203 Park Road, Loughborough LE11 2HE. *T:* Loughborough 212534.

SWEENEY, Maj.-Gen. Joseph A.; *b* Burton Port, 13 June 1897; *s* of John and Margaret Sweeney Burton Port; two *s* one *d*. MP (SF) West Donegal, 1918-22; Member, of Dail for County Donegal, 1922-23; GOC Donegal Command, 1923-24; GOC Curragh Command, 1924-26; GOC Athlone Command, 1926-28; Adjutant General, 1928-30; Quartermaster-General, 1930-31; Chief of Staff, General Headquarters, Dublin, 1930-31; GOC

Curragh Command, 1931-38; GOC Athlone Command, 1938-40; retired, 1940. Area Officer, Irish Red Cross Society, 1950-54; Dep. Sec. Gen., 1954-56; Gen. Sec., 1956-62. Retd Dec. 1962. Mem. Board of Governors, Michael Collins Memorial Foundation, 1965. *Address:* 26 Orchardstown Park, Dublin 14.

SWEET, Prof. Peter Alan, MA, PhD; Regius Professor of Astronomy in the University of Glasgow, since Oct. 1959; *b* 15 May 1921; *s* of David Frank Sweet; *m* 1947, Myrtle Vera Parnell; two *s*. *Educ:* Kingsbury County Grammar School, London; Sidney Sussex College, Cambridge. Open Maj. Schol. in Maths, Sidney Sussex Coll., 1940-42, Wrangler, 1942, BA Cantab 1943. Junior Scientific Officer, Min. of Aircraft Prod., 1942-45; BA Scholar, at Sidney Sussex Coll., 1945-47; MA Cantab 1946; Mayhew Prizeman, 1946, PhD Cantab 1950. Lectr in Astronomy, Univ. of Glasgow, 1947-52; Lectr in Astronomy and Asst Director of the Observatory, Univ. of London, 1952-59. Visiting Asst Professor of Astronomy, Univ. of California, Berkeley, 1957-58; Vis. Res. Fellow, NASA Inst. for Space Studies, NY, 1965-66. *Publications:* papers on Stellar Evolution, Cosmic Magnetism, and Solar Flares in Monthly Notices of Royal Astronomical Soc., etc. *Recreations:* music, gardening. *Address:* 17 Westbourne Crescent, Glasgow G61 4HB. *T:* 041-942 4425.

SWEETING, William Hart, CMG 1969; CBE 1961; Chairman, Board of Directors, Bank of London and Montreal, since 1970; *b* 18 Dec. 1909; *s* of late Charles Cecil Sweeting, Nassau, Bahamas; *m* 1950, Isabel Jean (*née* Woodall). *Educ:* Queen's Coll., Nassau; London Univ. Entered Bahamas Public Service as Cadet, 1927; served in Colonial Secretary's Office, 1927-37; acted as Asst Colonial Sec. for short periods in 1928 and 1936; transferred to Treasury, 1937; Cashier, Public Treasury, 1941; Asst Treasurer and Receiver of Crown Dues, 1946; seconded as Financial Sec., Dominica, 1950-52; Receiver-Gen. and Treasurer, Bahamas, 1955; MLC, Bahamas, 1960-64; Chm., Bahamas Currency Comrs, 1955-63; Chm., Bahamas Broadcasting and Television Commn, 1957-62. Acted as Governor various periods 1959, 1964, 1965, 1966, 1968, 1969; acted as Colonial Secretary various periods, 1962-63; Chief Secretary, Bahamas 1964; Dep. Governor, Bahamas, 1969, retired 1970. Mem., Bahamas Music Soc.; Elder, St Andrew's Presbyterian Church; Chairman: Trinity Coll. of Music Local Exams Cttee; Bahamas Br., Bible Soc. in WI; Hon. Treasurer, United Word Coll. of the Atlantic Local Cttee. *Recreations:* tennis, swimming, painting, music, bird watching. *Address:* PO Box N 573, Nassau, Bahamas. *T:* 3-1518. *Clubs:* Corona; Bankers (Nassau).

SWEETMAN, Mrs Ronald Andrew; *see* Dickson, Jennifer J.

SWEETMAN, Seamus George, MBE 1945; Vice-Chairman, Unilever Ltd, since 1974; a Deputy Chairman, Price Commission, ince 1977; *b* 7 Nov. 1914; *s* of late James Michael Sweetman, KC and Agnes (*née* Fottrell); *m* 1939, Mary Alberta Giblett; one *s*. *Educ:* Beaumont Coll.; St John's Coll., Cambridge (BA). Pte Suffolk Regt, 1939; commnd The Buffs, 1940; Italian campaign (despatches); Lt-Col, GSO1, Sec. to Supreme Allied Comdr, Mediterranean, 1944-45. Various Unilever subsids, 1936-39; D. & W. Gibbs, 1950-55; Unilever NV, Rotterdam, 1955-57; Margarine Union, Germany, 1957-61; Director: Unilever Ltd and Unilever NV, 1961-; Commonwealth Development Finance Co., 1975. Trustee, Leverhulme Trust. FBIM. Officer, US Legion of Merit. *Recreations:* history, gardening, mountain walking. *Address:* Greenloaning, West Common Close, Harpenden, Herts. *T:* Harpenden 3221.

SWEETT, Cyril, CEng, AIStructE, FRICS, FIArb; Senior Partner, Cyril Sweett & Partners, Chartered Quantity Surveyors; *b* 7 April 1903; *s* of William Thomas Sweett; *m* 1931, Barbara Mary, *d* of late Henry Thomas Loft, Canterbury and London; one *d*. *Educ:* Whitgift Sch.; Coll. of Estate Management. Artists Rifles, TA, 1923-27. Army Service: RE, 1939-43, France, N Africa and Italy; demob. as Lt-Col. Mem. Council, RICS (Founder Chm., Cost Research Panel, 1956-60); Chm., Nat. Jt Consultative Cttee of Architects, Quantity Surveyors and Builders, 1962-63. Mem. Cttee, London Library. Master, Worshipful Co. of Painter Stainers, 1964-65, 1966-67; Sheriff of City of London, 1965-66. Jordanian Star, 1966; Silver Star of Honour, Austria, 1966. *Address:* 22 Raynham, Norfolk Crescent, W2 2PG. *T:* 01-262 8600; 26 Warnham Court, Grand Avenue, Hove, Sussex BN3 2NJ. *T:* Brighton 777292. *Clubs:* Garrick; Royal Thames Yacht, Royal Ocean Racing, Royal Burnham Yacht (Cdre, 1963-65).

SWIFT, Margaret; *see* Drabble, Margaret.

SWIFT, Reginald Stanley, CB 1969; Under-Secretary, Department of Health and Social Security, 1968-76, retired; *b* 2 Nov. 1914; *e s* of Stanley John and Annie Swift; *m* 1940, Mildred Joan Easter; no *c. Educ:* Watford Grammar School; Christ's College, Cambridge. BA Cantab (1st Cl. Hons in Classics) 1936; MA Cantab 1940; BSc (Econ.) London 1944. Entered Civil Service as Asst Comr, National Savings Cttee, 1938; transferred to Min. of National Insurance as Principal, 1947; Principal Private Secretary to Minister, 1953-54; Assistant Secretary, 1954; Under-Secretary, 1962. *Recreations:* gardening, golf. *Address:* Woodpeckers, The Chase, Kingswood, Tadworth, Surrey. *T:* Mogador 2951. *Club:* Kingswood Golf.

SWINBURN, Maj.-Gen. Henry Robinson, CB 1947; OBE 1945; MC 1922; *b* 8 May 1897; *e s* of late Henry Swinburn; *m* 1932, Naomi Barbara, *yr d* of late Major-General Sir C. P. Amyatt Hull, KCB; two *s.* Entered Indian Army, 1918; Royal Ludhiana Sikhs: served European War, 1914-18, Operations, NWF India, 1919, Iraq, 1920, Kurdistan, 1922-23 (wounded, MC); BEF France, 1940 (despatches, OBE). Staff College, Quetta, 1929-30; psc†; GSO II, GHQ India, 1932-36; Instructor Staff Coll., Camberley, 1937-38; Instructor Senior Staff College, Minley, 1939; Chief Instructor School of Military Intelligence, 1939-40; GSO I, 51 Highland Div., 1940; Director of Morale, India, 1945; Deputy Mil. Sec., GHQ India, 1946; Military Secretary, GHQ India, 1946-47; retired, 1948. Bt Major, 1934; Bt Lt-Col, 1939; Temp. Maj.-Gen., 1946; Subs Col, 1947; Counsellor, UK High Commn in India, 1948-49. Schools Liaison Officer, 1952-60. *Recreation:* fishing. *Address:* Stoney Close, Nunton, Salisbury, Wilts. *T:* Salisbury 29741. *Club:* Naval and Military.
See also Field Marshal Sir R. A. Hull.

SWINBURNE, Ivan Archie, CMG 1973; Member of Legislative Council of Victoria, Australia, since 1946; *b* 6 March 1908; *s* of George Arthur and Hilda Maud Swinburne; *m* 1950, Isabella Mary, *d* of James Alexander Moore; one *d. Educ:* Hurdle Creek West and Milawa State Schs; Wangaratta and Essendon High Schs. MLC, for NE Prov., 1946; Dep. Leader of Country Party, 1954-69; Leader of Country Party in Legislative Council, 1969-; Minister of Housing and Materials, 1950-52; Mem., Subordinate Legislation Cttee, 1961-67 and 1973. Councillor, Shire of Bright, 1940-47 (Pres., 1943-44). Mem., Bush Nursing Council of Victoria, 1948-; Chm. Cttee of Management, Mount Buffalo National Park, 1963-. *Recreation:* football administration. *Address:* PO Box 341, Myrtle Street, Myrtleford, Victoria 3737, Australia. *T:* Myrtleford 521167. *Clubs:* RACV, CTA Victoria (Melbourne); Wangaratta (Wangaratta).

SWINBURNE, Nora; actress; *b* Bath, 24 July 1902; *d* of H. Swinburne Johnson; *m* 1st, Francis Lister (marr. diss.); one *s*; 2nd, Edward Ashley-Cooper (marr. diss.); 3rd, 1946, Esmond Knight, *qv. Educ:* Rossholme College, Weston-super-Mare; Royal Academy of Dramatic Art. First West End appearance, 1916; went to America, 1923; returned to London stage, 1924; New York, again, 1930; continuous successes in London, from 1931; went into management, 1938, in addition to acting. Played as Diana Wentworth in The Years Between (which ran for more than a year), Wyndhams, 1945; Red Letter Day, Garrick; A Woman of No Importance, Savoy, 1953; The Lost Generation, Garrick, 1955; Fool's Paradise, Apollo, 1959; Music at Midnight, Westminster, 1962. *Films include:* Jassy, Good Time Girl, The Blind Goddess, Fanny by Gaslight, They Knew Mr Knight, Quartet, Christopher Columbus, My Daughter Joy, The River (made in India), Quo Vadis, also Helen of Troy (made in Italy), Third Man on the Mountain, Conspiracy of Hearts, Music at Midnight, Interlude, Anne of the Thousand Days. Has appeared on television (incl. Forsyte Saga, Post Mortem, Kate serial, Fall of Eagles). *Address:* 35 Bywater Street, Chelsea, SW3.

SWINDLEHURST, Rt. Rev. Owen Francis; Bishop Auxiliary of Hexham and Newcastle, (RC), since 1977; Titular Bishop of Chester-le-Street; *b* 10 May 1928; *s* of Francis and Ellen Swindlehurst. *Educ:* Ushaw College, Durham; English College, Rome. PhL, STL, LCL (Gregorian Univ., Rome). Assistant Priest: St Matthew's, Ponteland, 1959-67; St Bede's, Denton Burn, Newcastle, 1967-72; Parish Priest at Holy Name, Jesmond, Newcastle, 1967-77. *Recreations:* walking, gardening, reading. *Address:* c/o Bishop's House, 800 West Road, Newcastle upon Tyne 5.

SWINDON, Archdeacon of; *see* Maples, Ven. J. S.

SWINFEN, 3rd Baron *cr* 1919; **Roger Mynors Swinfen Eady;** *b* 14 Dec. 1938; *s* of 2nd Baron Swinfen and of Mary Aline, *d* of late Col H. Mynors Farmar, CMG, DSO; *S* father, 1977; *m* 1962, Patricia Anne, *o d* of late F. D. Blackmore, Dundrum, Dublin; one *s* three *d. Educ:* Westminster; RMA, Sandhurst.

ARICS 1970. With Jackson-Stops and Staff, Curzon Street, W1. *Heir: s* Hon. Charles Roger Peregrine Swinfen Eady, *b* 8 March 1971. *Address:* Dene House, Wingham, Canterbury.

SWINGLAND, Owen Merlin Webb, QC 1974; Barrister-at-Law; *b* 26 Sept. 1919; *er s* of Charles and Maggie Eveline Swingland; *m* 1941, Kathleen Joan Eason (*née* Parry), Newport, Mon; one *s* two *d. Educ:* Haberdashers' Aske's Hatcham Sch.; King's Coll., London. LLB 1941, AKC. Called to Bar, Gray's Inn, 1946; practice at Chancery Bar, 1948-; Barrister of Lincoln's Inn, 1977. Assistant Comr, Boundary Commn for England. Liveryman, Haberdashers' Co.; Freeman of the City of London. Foundation Governor, Haberdashers' Aske's Hatcham Schools. *Publications:* contribs to books, and articles in periodicals on estate duty and trusts. *Recreations:* music, theatre, fishing, sailing, reading; interested in most competitive sports. *Address:* Ightham Warren, Kent. *T:* Borough Green 884157. *Club:* Old Askean.

SWINGLER, Bryan Edwin; Minister; Education Adviser, British High Commission, New Delhi, and Head of British Council Division, India, since 1977; *b* 2 Sept. 1924; *s* of late George Edwin Swingler, Birmingham, and Mary Eliza Frayne; *m* 1954, Herta, *er d* of late Edwin Jaeger, Schoenlinde; one *d. Educ:* King Edward's Sch., Birmingham; Peterhouse, Cambridge (Sen. Schol.); Charles Univ., Prague. BA 1948, MA 1953. Served War, Royal Navy (Leading Signalman), 1943-46. Apptd to British Council, 1949; Vienna, 1949-52; Lahore, 1952-55; Karachi, 1955-56; Oslo, 1956-59; Berlin, 1959-61; Cologne, 1961-63; Dir, Scholarships, 1963-67; Dep. Controller, Commonwealth Div., 1967-68; Rep. Indonesia, Djakarta, 1968-71; Controller Finance, 1972-73; Controller, Home, 1973-75; Asst Dir-Gen., 1975-77. Vice-Chm., British Council Staff Assoc., 1965-67; Member: British-Austrian Mixed Commn, 1973-77; British-French Mixed Commn, 1976-77. *Recreations:* music, painting, oriental ceramics, sailing in warm waters. *Address:* c/o Foreign and Commonwealth Office, SW1; 2 South End Road, New Delhi 110011. *T:* 374956; 10 Meadow Bank, Blackheath, SE3 9XD. *T:* 01-852 1666; Beverley, Porthpean, St Austell, Cornwall. *T:* St Austell 3347.

SWINGLER, Raymond John Peter; journalist; *b* 8 Oct. 1933; *s* of Raymond Joseph and Mary Swingler; *m* 1960, Shirley, *e d* of Frederick and Dorothy Wilkinson, Plymouth; two *d. Educ:* St Bede's Coll., Christchurch, NZ; Canterbury Univ. Journalist, The Press, Christchurch, NZ, 1956-57; Marlborough Express, 1957-59; Nelson Mail, 1959-61; freelance Middle East, 1961-62; Cambridge Evening News, 1962-. Member: Press Council, 1975-, Press Council Complaints Cttee, 1976-; Nat. Exec. Council, Nat. Union of Journalists, 1973-75; Provincial Newspapers Industrial Council, 1976-; Chm., General Purposes Cttee (when journalists' Code of Professional Conduct (revised) introduced), 1974-75. *Recreations:* horses, and horsewomen. *Address:* Wicken Hall, Wicken, Cambs CB7 5XT. *T:* Ely 720745.

SWINLEY, Captain Casper Silas Balfour, DSO 1941; DSC 1940; Royal Navy; *b* 28 Oct. 1898; *y s* of late Gordon Herbert Swinley, Assam, India, and Margaret Eliza, *d* of late Prof. J. H. Balfour, Edin.; *m* 1928, Sylvia Jocosa, 4th *d* of late Canon W. H. Carnegie, Rector of St Margaret's, Westminster, and Sub-Dean of Westminster Abbey; two *s* twin *d. Educ:* Epsom College. Entered Royal Navy with Special Entry Cadetship, 1916; served European War, 1916-18, as Midshipman and Sub-Lieut in HMS New Zealand; HMS Ceres, evacuation of Odessa, 1919-20; Queens' Coll., Cambridge, 1920; ADC and Private Sec. to Sir Charles O'Brien, Governor of Barbados, 1921-22; HMS Curacoa, evacuation of Smyrna, 1922-23; HMS Calcutta, Flagship West Indies Station, 1924-26; HMS Ganges, Boys' Training Establishment, Shotley, 1926-28; Flag-Lieut to Adm. Sir E. Alexander-Sinclair, C-in-C the Nore, 1928-30; HMS Repulse, 1930-32; HMS Carlisle, Africa Station, under Adm. Sir Edward Evans, 1932-34; Comdr 1934; commanded HMS Express, 5th Destroyer Flotilla, Abyssinian crisis, Spanish War, Jubilee Review, 1935-37; NID, Admiralty Naval Staff, 1937-39; commanded HMS Impregnable, Boys' Training Establishment, Devonport, 1939; commanded HMS Codrington and Dover Patrol Destroyers, taking King George VI to France and back; also Mr Winston Churchill to Boulogne, 1939-40; French Destroyer Brestois for Liaison duties; evacuation of Namsos, Norway; commanded demolition party at Calais (DSC), 1940; commanded HMS Isis, North Sea, Genoa, Greece, Crete (DSO); Syrian campaign, 1940-41; commanded HMS Miranda and Minesweepers, Great Yarmouth; Capt. 1942; Chief Staff Officer to Vice-Adm. Sir Ralph Leatham, Malta, 1942; Director of Service Conditions, Admiralty, 1943-45; Commanded HMS Arethusa, 1945; Chief Staff Officer to Vice-Adm. Sir F. Dalrymple Hamilton, Malta, 1946; commanded HMS Flamingo and Senior Officer Reserve Fleet, Devonport, 1946-47; Chief of Naval Information, Admiralty, 1947-48; Captain in Charge, Captain Superintendent and King's Harbour Master, Portland, 1949-51. Naval ADC to King George VI, 1951; Commodore and Chief of Staff, Royal Pakistan Navy, 1953-54. Senior Whale Fishery Inspector, South Georgia, 1959-60. Appeals Organiser, BRCS, Gloucestershire, 1963-67. *Recreation:* scrap-book collecting. *Address:* Broughtons, near Newnham, Glos. *T:* Westbury-on-Severn 328.

SWINNERTON, Frank Arthur; novelist and critic; President, Royal Literary Fund, 1962-66; *b* Wood Green, 12 Aug. 1884; *y s* of Charles Swinnerton and Rose Cottam; *m* 1924, Mary Dorothy Bennett; one *d. Publications:* The Merry Heart, 1909; The Young Idea, 1910; The Casement, 1911; The Happy Family, 1912; George Gissing: a Critical Study, 1912; On the Staircase, 1914; R. L. Stevenson: a Critical Study, 1914; The Chaste Wife, 1916; Nocturne, 1917; Shops and Houses, 1918; September, 1919; Coquette, 1921; The Three Lovers, 1922; Young Felix, 1923; The Elder Sister, 1925; Summer Storm, 1926; Tokefield Papers, 1927; A London Bookman, 1928; A Brood of Ducklings, 1928; Sketch of a Sinner, 1929; Authors and the Book Trade, 1932; The Georgian House, 1932; Elizabeth, 1934; The Georgian Literary Scene, 1935; Swinnerton: an Autobiography, 1937; Harvest Comedy, 1937; The Two Wives, 1939; The Reviewing and Criticism of Books, 1939; The Fortunate Lady, 1941; Thankless Child, 1942; A Woman in Sunshine, 1944; English Maiden, 1946; The Cats and Rosemary, (US) 1948, (England) 1950; Faithful Company, 1948; The Doctor's Wife Comes to Stay, 1949; A Flower for Catherine, 1950; The Bookman's London, 1951; Master Jim Probity, 1952; Londoner's Post, 1952; A Month in Gordon Square, 1953; The Sumner Intrigue, 1955; Authors I Never Met, 1956; Background with Chorus, 1956; The Woman from Sicily, 1957; A Tigress in Prothero, 1959; The Grace Divorce, 1960; Death of a Highbrow, 1961; Figures in the Foreground, 1963; Quadrille, 1965; A Galaxy of Fathers, 1966; Sanctuary, 1966; The Bright Lights, 1968; Reflections from a Village, 1969; On the Shady Side, 1970; Nor all thy Tears, 1972; Rosalind Passes, 1973; Some Achieve Greatness, 1976; Arnold Bennett: the last word, 1978. *Address:* Old Tokefield, Cranleigh, Surrey. *Club:* Reform (Hon. Life Mem.).

SWINNERTON-DYER, Prof. Sir (Henry) Peter (Francis), 16th Bt *cr* 1678; FRS 1967; Professor of Mathematics, University of Cambridge, since 1971 (Lecturer 1960-71); Master of St Catharine's College, Cambridge, since 1973; *b* 2 Aug. 1927; *s* of Sir Leonard Schroeder Swinnerton Dyer, 15th Bt, and of Barbara, *d* of Hereward Brackenbury, CBE; *S* father, 1975. *Educ:* Eton; Trinity College, Cambridge. Trinity College, Cambridge: Research Fellow, 1950-54; Fellow, 1955-73; Dean, 1963-73; Univ. Lectr, Mathematical Laboratory, Cambridge, 1960-67. Commonwealth Fund Fellow, Univ. of Chicago, 1954-55. Vis. Prof., Harvard Univ., 1971. *Publications:* numerous papers in mathematical journals. *Recreation:* tennis. *Heir:* kinsman Richard Stewart Dyer-Bennet [*b* 6 Oct. 1886; *m* 1912, Miriam Wolcott (*d* 1973), *d* of late Prof. Edward B. Clapp; four *s* one *d*]. *Address:* St Catharine's College, Cambridge.

SWINTON, 2nd Earl of, *cr* 1955; **David Yarburgh Cunliffe-Lister,** JP; Viscount Swinton, 1935; Baron Masham, 1955; *b* 21 March 1937; *s* of Major Hon. John Yarburgh Cunliffe-Lister (*d* of wounds received in action, 1943) and Anne Irvine (*d* 1961), *yr d* of late Rev. Canon R. S. Medlicott (she *m* 2nd, 1944, Donald Chapple-Gill); *S* grandfather, 1972; *m* 1959, Susan Lilian Primrose Sinclair (*see* Baroness Masham of Ilton); one *s* one *d* (both adopted). *Educ:* Winchester; Royal Agricultural College. Member: N Riding Yorks CC, 1961-74; N Yorks CC, 1973-77. JP North (formerly NR) Yorks, 1971. *Heir: b* Hon. Nicholas John Cunliffe-Lister [*b* 4 Sept. 1939; *m* 1966, Elizabeth Susan, *e d* of Rt Hon. William Whitelaw, *qv*; one *s* one *d*]. *Address:* Dykes Hill House, Masham, N Yorks. *T:* Masham 241; c/o Midland Bank Ltd, 1 Sydney Place, Onslow Square, SW7.

SWINTON, Countess of; *see* Masham of Ilton, Baroness.

SWINTON, Maj.-Gen. John, OBE 1969; General Officer Commanding London District and Major-General Commanding Household Division, since 1976; Brigadier, Queen's Body Guard for Scotland (Royal Company of Archers); *b* 21 April 1925; *s* of late Brig. A. H. C. Swinton, MC, Scots Guards; *m* 1954, Judith, *d* of late Harold Killen, Merribee, NSW; three *s* one *d. Educ:* Harrow. Enlisted, Scots Guards, 1943, commissioned, 1944; served NW Europe, 1945 (twice wounded); Malaya, 1948-51 (despatches); ADC to Field Marshal Sir William Slim, Governor-General of Australia, 1953-54; Staff College, 1957; DAA&QMG 1st Guards Brigade, 1958-59; Regimental Adjutant Scots Guards, 1960-62; Adjutant,

RMA Sandhurst, 1962-64; comd 2nd Bn Scots Guards, 1966-68; AAG PS12 MoD, 1968-70; Lt Col Comdg Scots Guards, 1970-71; Comdr, 4th Guards Armoured Brigade, BAOR, 1972-73; RCDS 1974; Brigadier Lowlands and Comdr Edinburgh and Glasgow Garrisons, 1975-76. *Address:* HQ London District, Horse Guards, SW1; Kimmerghame, Duns, Berwickshire.

SWIRE, John Anthony, CBE 1977; Chairman, John Swire & Sons Ltd, since 1966; Director: British Bank of the Middle East, since 1975; Royal Insurance Co. Ltd, since 1975; Ocean Transport & Trading Ltd, since 1977; *b* 28 Feb. 1927; *s* of John Kidston Swire, *qv*; *m* 1961, Moira Cecilia Ducharne; two *s* one *d. Educ:* Eton; University Coll., Oxford (MA). Served Irish Guards, UK and Palestine, 1945-48. Joined Butterfield & Swire, Hong Kong, 1950; Dir, John Swire & Sons Ltd, 1955. Chm., Hong Kong Assoc., 1975. *Address:* Luton House, Selling, near Faversham, Kent ME13 9RQ. *T:* Selling 234. *Clubs:* Brooks's, City, Flyfishers'; Union (Sydney).

SWIRE, John Kidston; Director, John Swire & Sons, Ltd, 1920-68 (Chairman, 1946-66); Hon. President, Cathay Pacific Airways Ltd; Member, General Committee, Lloyd's Register of Shipping, 1940-68; *b* 19 Feb. 1893; *er s* of late John Swire, Hillingdon House, Harlow, Essex; *m* 1923, Juliet Richenda, *d* of Theodore Barclay, Fanshaws, Hertford; two *s* two *d. Educ:* Eton Coll.; University Coll., Oxford. Major Essex Yeomanry, with whom he served in European War 1914-19. DL Essex, 1928-68; High Sheriff, Essex, 1941-42. Min. of Shipping Rep. at Min. of Economic Warfare and on the Contraband Cttee, 1939-40; Chm. Port Employers in London and Port Labour Exec. Cttee, 1941-45. Chm. China Association, 1951-55. *Address:* Hubbards Hall, Harlow, Essex. *TA* and *T:* Harlow 29470. *Clubs:* Turf, Cavalry and Guards, City of London.

SWISS, Sir Rodney (Geoffrey), Kt 1975; OBE 1964; JP; LDSRCS; President, General Dental Council, since 1974 (Member since 1957); *b* 4 Aug. 1904; *e s* of Henry H. Swiss, Devonport, Devon, and Emma Jane Swiss (*née* Williams); *m* 1928, Muriel Alberta Gledhill. *Educ:* Plymouth Coll.; Dean Close Sch., Cheltenham; Guy's Hosp. LDSRCS 1926. General dental practice, Harrow, Mddx, 1930-69 (Hon. dental surgeon, Harrow Hosp., 1935-67). NHS Mddx Exec. Council, 1947-74 (Chm., 1970-71); Chm., Visiting Cttee and Bd of Visitors, Wormwood Scrubs Prison, 1958-63; Mem., Central Health Services Council, 1964-74; Chairman: Standing Dental Advisory Cttee, 1964-74; Hendon Juvenile Court, 1959-64; Gore Petty Sessional Div., 1965-67 and 1970-74; Management Cttee, Sch. for Dental Auxiliaries, 1972-74. JP Mddx area, 1949. *Publications:* contribs to dental press. *Recreation:* philately. *Address:* Shrublands, 23 West Way, Pinner, Mddx HA5 3NX. *Club:* Savage.

SWORD, John Howe; Special Assistant to the President, University of Toronto, since 1974; *b* Saskatoon, Saskatchewan, 22 Jan. 1915; *m* 1947, Constance A. Offen; one *s* one *d. Educ:* public and high schs, Winnipeg; Univ. of Manitoba (BA); Univ. of Toronto (MA). Served War, RCAF, Aircrew navigation trg and instr in Western Canada. Taught for six years, before War, in Roland, Teulon and Winnipeg, Manitoba. Secretary, Manitoba Royal Commn on Adult Educn, 1945-46. Univ. of Toronto: Asst Sec. and Sec., Sch. of Grad. Studies, 1947-60; Exec. Asst to the President, 1960-65; Vice-Provost, 1965-67; Actg Pres., 1967-68; Exec. Vice-Pres. (Academic), and Provost, 1968-71; Actg Pres., 1971-72; Vice-Pres., Institutional Relations and Planning, 1972-74. Hon. LLD, Univ. of Manitoba, 1970. *Recreations:* tennis, swimming. *Address:* 8 Wychwood Park, Toronto, Ontario M6G 2V5, Canada. *T:* 6565876. *Clubs:* Faculty (Univ. of Toronto); Arts and Letters, Queen's (Lambton).

SWYER, Dr Gerald Isaac Macdonald, FRCP; Consultant Endocrinologist, Department of Obstetrics and Gynæcology, University College Hospital, London, WC1, since 1951; *b* 17 Nov. 1917; *s* of Nathan Swyer; *m* 1945, Lynda Irene (*née* Nash); one *s* one *d. Educ:* St Paul's School; Magdalen College and St John's College, Oxford; University of California; Middlesex Hospital Medical School. Foundation Schol. and Leaving Exhib., St Paul's School, 1931-36; Open Exhib. and Casberd Schol., St John's Coll., Oxford, 1936-39; Welsh Memorial Prize, 1937; Theodore Williams Schol. in Anatomy, 1938; 1st Cl. Final Honour School of Animal Physiology, 1939; Senior Demy, Magdalen Coll., 1940; Rockefeller Medical Student, Univ. of Calif, 1941. MA, DPhil, BM Oxon 1943; MD Calif, 1943; DM Oxon 1948; MRCP 1945; FRCP 1964; Hon FRCOG 1975. Mem. of Scientific Staff, Nat. Inst. for Med. Res., 1946-47; Endocrinologist, UCH Med. Sch., 1947. 1st Sec., formerly Chm., Soc. for the Study of Fertility; formerly Mem. Council, Soc. for Endocrinology; formerly Pres., Sect. of Endocrinology,

Roy. Soc. Med.; formerly Sec.-Gen., Internat. Fedn of Fertility Societies and Mem. Exec. Sub-Cttee Internat. Endocrine Soc.; Mem. Council, British Soc. for Population Studies. *Publications:* Reproduction and Sex, 1954; papers in medical and scientific journals. *Recreations:* music, sailing. *Address:* 2 Prince Arthur Road, NW3 6AU. *T:* 01-435 4723.

SWYNNERTON, Sir Roger (John Massy), Kt 1976; CMG 1959; OBE 1951; MC 1941; consultant in tropical agriculture and development, including part-time to Booker Agriculture International Ltd, since 1976; *b* S Rhodesia, 16 Jan. 1911; *s* of late C. F. M. Swynnerton, CMG, formerly Dir Tsetse Research, Tanganyika, and Mrs N. A. G. Swynnerton (*née* Watt Smyth); *m* Grizel Beryl Miller, *d* of late R. W. R. Miller, CMG, formerly Member for Agriculture and Natural Resources, Tanganyika; two *s*. *Educ:* Lancing Coll.; Gonville and Caius Coll., Cambridge (BA Hons 1932; DipAgric 1933); Imperial Coll. of Tropical Agriculture, Trinidad. AICIA 1934. O/c CUOTC Artillery Bty, 1932-33; TARO, 1933-60. Entered Colonial Agricultural Service as Agric. Officer and Sen. Agric. Officer, 1934-50, in Tanganyika Territory. Served War, 1939-42, with 1/6 Bn KAR (Temp. Capt.), Abyssinian Campaign. Seconded to Malta on Agric. duty, 1942-43. Transferred to Kenya on promotion, Asst Director of Agric., 1951, Dep. Dir, 1954, Director, 1956. Nominated Member of Kenya Legislative Council, 1956-60; Permanent Sec., Min. of Agriculture, 1960-62; Temp. Minister for Agriculture, Animal Husbandry and Water Resources, 1961, retd 1963; Mem. Advisory Cttee on Development of Economic Resources of S Rhodesia, 1961-62; Agric. Adviser and Mem. Exec. Management Bd, Commonwealth Develt Corp., 1962-76. *Publications:* All About KNCU Coffee, 1948; A Plan to Intensify the Development of African Agriculture in Kenya, 1954; various agricultural and scientific papers. *Address:* 35 Lower Road, Fetcham, Leatherhead, Surrey KT22 9EL. *Clubs:* Royal Commonwealth Society, Royal Over-Seas League; Nairobi (Kenya).

SYCAMORE, Thomas Andrew Harding, CBE 1949; retired; a Managing Director, Liebig's Extract of Meat Co. Ltd, 1963-66; Chairman, Chipmunk Ltd, 1962-66; Director: Beefex Products Ltd, 1954-66; Bellamy's Wharf & Dock Ltd, 1958-66; Oxo Ltd, 1954-66 (Managing Director 1954-63); Oxo (Canada) Ltd, 1954-66; Oxo (Ireland) Ltd, 1954-66; Oxo (USA) Ltd, 1954-66; Thames Side Properties Ltd, 1955-66; Produits Liebig SA, Basle, 1965-66; Euro-Liebig SC, Antwerp, 1964-66; Compagnie Française des Produits Liebig SA, Paris, 1963-66; Compagnie Liebig SA, Antwerp, 1963-66; Compagnia Italiana Liebig SpA, Milan, 1963-66; Nederlandse Oxo Maatschappij NV, Rotterdam, 1963-66; Liebig GmbH, Cologne, 1963-66; Beefco Corp., New York, 1963-66 (Chairman, 1964-66); London Philharmonic Society Ltd, 1960-66; *b* 31 Aug. 1907; *s* of late Henry Andrew and Caroline Helen Sycamore; *m* 1932, Winifred Clara Pellett; one *s* two *d*. *Educ:* privately. At Oxford Univ. Press, 1924-35; Manufacturing Confectioners' Alliance, 1936-40 (Asst Sec. 1940); Food Manufacturers' Federation Inc., 1936-54; Asst Sec., 1940; Sec., 1945; Director and Gen. Sec., 1947. Secretary, Bacon Marketing Bd, and many other food manufacturers' associations, etc; Mem., Food Research Adv. Cttee, 1960-66; Vice-Pres., Assoc. Internat. de l'Industrie des Bouillons et Potages (Paris), 1963-65. Member Council: British Food Manufacturing Industries Research Association (formerly Sec.); Food Manufacturers' Federation, Inc.; Grocers' Institute (a Vice-Pres. 1958-66, Hon. Treas. 1961-66); English Stage Soc.; Mem. Grand Council, FBI (member many committees); Deputy Leader and Sec. of two productivity teams which went to the US; helped to create Food Industries Council (Sec. for many years); helped in formation of National College of Food Technology, and to establish British Food Fair at Olympia (Sec. for many years). Served on Councils or Committees of various other bodies; a Governor of several schools. President of Appeal, Royal Commercial Travellers' Schools, 1960-61; Life Hon. Vice-President, Huddersfield Branch, United Commercial Travellers' Assoc., 1962; Chm., Nat. Music Council of Gt Brit., 1963-64. Freeman, City of London. Liveryman, Worshipful Company of Loriners; Life Mem., Guild of Freemen of City of London; FREconS; Hon. Fellow, Grocers' Institute; Officier de l'Ordre de la Couronne (Belgium), 1965. *Recreations:* music, theatre, reading, tennis, cricket. *Address:* Gainsborough, 38 Warren Lane, Friston, near Eastbourne, East Sussex. *T:* East Dean 2127.

SYDNEY, Archbishop of, since 1966; (Metropolitan of the Province of New South Wales); **Most Rev. Marcus Lawrence Loane,** KBE 1976; DD; *b* 14 Oct. 1911; *s* of K. O. A. Loane; *m* 1937, Patricia Evelyn Jane Simpson Knox; two *s* two *d*. *Educ:* The King's School, Parramatta, NSW; Sydney University (MA). Moore Theological College, 1932-33; Australian College of Theology (ThL, 1st Class, 1933; Fellow, 1955). Ordained Deacon, 1935, Priest, 1936; Resident Tutor and Chaplain,

Moore Theological College, 1935-38; Vice-Principal, 1939-53; Principal, 1954-59. Chaplain AIF, 1942-44. Canon, St Andrew's Cathedral, 1949-58; Bishop-Coadjutor, diocese of Sydney, 1958-66. Hon. DD Wycliffe College, Toronto, 1958. *Publications:* Oxford and the Evangelical Succession, 1950; Cambridge and the Evangelical Succession, 1952; Masters of the English Reformation, 1955; Life of Archbishop Mowll, 1960; Makers of Religious Freedom, 1961; Pioneers of the Reformation in England, 1964; Makers of Our Heritage, 1966; The Hope of Glory, 1968; This Surpassing Excellence, 1969; They Were Pilgrims, 1970; They Overcame, 1971; By Faith We Stand, 1971; The King is Here, 1973. *Address:* PO Box Q190, Queen Victoria Building, York Street, Sydney, NSW 2000, Australia. *TA:* Anglican.

SYDNEY, Archbishop of, (RC), since 1971; **His Eminence Sir James Darcy Cardinal Freeman,** KBE 1977; Knight of the Holy Sepulchre; *b* 19 Nov. 1907; *s* of Robert Freeman and Margaret Smith. *Educ:* Christian Brothers' High School, St Mary's Cathedral, Sydney; St Columba's Coll., Springwood, NSW; St Patrick's Coll., Manly, NSW. Priest, 1930; Private Secretary to HE Cardinal Gilroy, Archbishop of Sydney, 1940-46; Auxiliary Bishop to HE Cardinal Gilroy, 1957; Bishop of Armidale, 1968. Cardinal, 1973. Hon. DD 1957. *Address:* St Mary's Cathedral, Sydney, NSW 2000, Australia. *T:* 232-3788.

SYDNEY, Assistant Bishops of; *see* Cameron, Rt Rev. E. D., Dain, Rt Rev. A. J., Reid, Rt Rev. J. R., Robinson, Rt Rev. D. W. B., Short, Rt Rev. K. H.

SYER, William George, CVO 1961; CBE 1957; Joint Secretary, West Africa Committee, since 1970; *b* 22 June 1913; *s* of late William Robert Syer and late Beatrice Alice Theresa Syer, Alton, Hants; *m* 1948, Marjorie Leila, *d* of late S. G. Pike, Essex; no *c*. *Educ:* Kent College, Canterbury. Joined Colonial Police Service, 1933; Gibraltar, 1933-35; Jamaica, 1935-40; Nigeria, 1940-51; Comr of Police, Sierra Leone, 1951; retired, 1962; Comr of Police, Swaziland, 1964-68. Formerly Comr St John Ambulance Brigade, Sierra Leone. CStJ 1969. *Recreations:* gardening, birdwatching, walking. *Address:* South Grays, Highercombe Road, Haslemere, Surrey.

SYERS, Sir Cecil George Lewis, KCMG 1949 (CMG 1947); CVO 1941; JP; *b* 29 March 1903; *s* of late G. W. Syers; *m* Yvonne, *d* of late Inglis Allen; one *s*. *Educ:* St Paul's; Balliol Coll., Oxford (Scholar). 1st Class Honour Mods 1922, and Lit. Hum. 1925; MA 1929. Entered Dominions Office, 1925; Asst Private Sec. to Sec. of State for Dominion Affairs, 1930-34; Private Sec. to Prime Minister, 1937-40; Asst Sec., Treasury, 1940; Dep. UK High Comnr in the Union of South Africa, 1942-46; an Asst Under-Sec. of State, CRO, 1946-48, Dep. Under-Sec. of State, 1948-51; High Comnr for the UK in Ceylon, 1951-57; Doyen of Diplomatic Corps, Ceylon, 1953-57. Sec., UGC, 1958-63. Pres., Ceylon Branch, Oxford Soc., 1954-57; Pres., Classical Assoc. of Ceylon, 1956, 1957. Mem. Governing Body, SOAS, Univ. of London, 1963-73; Dir, Foundation Fund Appeal, Univ. of Kent at Canterbury 1964-66. JP Hove, 1967. *Address:* 25 One Grand Avenue, Hove, Sussex BN3 2LA. *T:* Brighton 732545.

SYKES, (Arthur) Frank (Seton), CVO 1962; DL; Agricultural Adviser to the Queen at Windsor, 1950-71; *b* 4 July 1903; *e s* of late Sir Percy Sykes, KCIE, CB, CMG; *m* Barbara Godolphin, *e d* of W. H. Yeatman Biggs; one *s*. *Educ:* Rugby. Chm., Frank Sykes Ltd. Mem. Royal Commission on East Africa, 1953. Vice-Pres., RASE, 1970. Alderman, Wilts CC, 1952; High Sheriff of Wilts, 1964; DL Wilts, 1968. Gold Medal, RASE, 1974. Chevalier de la Légion d'Honneur. *Publications:* This Farming Business, 1944; Living from the Land, 1957. *Recreations:* travel, hunting, fishing. *Address:* Stockton, Warminster, Wilts.

SYKES, Lt-Col Arthur Patrick, MBE 1945; JP; DL; *b* 1 Sept. 1906; *e s* of late Herbert R. Sykes, JP; *m* 1936, Prudence Margaret, *d* of late Maj.-Gen. D. E. Robertson, CB, DSO, Indian Army; one *s* one *d*. *Educ:* Eton; Magdalene College, Cambridge. 2nd Lt 60th Rifles, 1929; served India, Burma, Palestine; ADC to Governor of Bengal, 1933-35; War of 1939-45, Middle East (wounded); Lt-Col 1944. JP 1950, DL 1951, High Sheriff, 1961, Salop. *Address:* Lydham Manor, Bishops Castle, Salop. *T:* Bishops Castle 486.

SYKES, Bonar Hugh Charles; farmer; formerly Counsellor in HM Diplomatic Service; *b* 20 Dec. 1922; *s* of late Sir Frederick Sykes and of Isabel, *d* of Andrew Bonar Law; *m* 1949, Mary, *d* of late Sir Eric Phipps and of Frances Phipps; four *s*. *Educ:* Eton; The Queen's Coll., Oxford. War service in Navy (Lieut RNVR), 1942-46. Trainee with Ford Motor Co. (Tractor Div.), 1948-49. Joined Foreign Service, 1949: served in Prague, Bonn, Tehran, Ottawa, FCO; retired 1970. Pres., Wiltshire Archaeological and

Natural History Soc., 1975-. *Address:* Conock Manor, Devizes, Wiltshire. *T:* Chirton 227.

SYKES, Sir Charles, Kt 1964; CBE 1956; FRS 1943; FInstP; DSc, PhD; DMet; Director, Thos Firth and John Brown Ltd, Sheffield, 1944-73 (Managing Director, 1951-67; Deputy Chairman, 1962-64); Chairman, Firth Brown Ltd, 1962-67; *b* 27 Feb. 1905; *m* 1930, Norah Staton. *Educ:* Staveley; Netherthorpe Grammar School; Sheffield Univ. Superintendent, Metallurgy Dept, National Physical Laboratory, 1940-44; Superintendent Terminal Ballistics Branch, Armament Research Dept, 1943-44; Director of Research, Brown-Firth Research Laboratories, 1944-51. Pres., Inst. of Physics, 1952-54; Member, Council for Scientific and Industrial Research, 1962-65; Chairman, Adv. Councils on Research and Development, Min. of Power, later Dept of Trade and Industry: Fuel and Power, 1965-70; Iron and Steel, 1967-72. Pro-Chancellor, Sheffield University, 1967-71. Iron and Steel Inst. Bessemer Gold Medal, 1956; Glazebrook Medal and Prize (IPPS), 1967. *Address:* Upholme, Blackamoor Crescent, Dore, Sheffield. *T:* Sheffield 360339.

SYKES, Christopher Hugh, FRSL; author; Member, London Library Committee, 1965-74; *b* 17 Nov. 1907; 2nd *s* of late Sir Mark Sykes, Bt, Sledmere; *m* 1936, Camilla Georgiana, *d* of El Lewa Sir Thomas Russell Pasha, CMG; one *s*. *Educ:* Downside; Christ Church, Oxford. Hon. Attaché to HM Embassy, Berlin, 1928-29, and to HM Legation, Tehran, 1930-31. Served War of 1939-45: 7 Battalion The Green Howards; GHQ, Cairo; HM Legation, Tehran; SAS Bde (despatches, Croix de Guerre). Special correspondent of the Daily Mail for the Persian Azerbaijan Campaign, 1946; Deputy Controller, Third Programme, BBC, 1948; Features Dept, BBC, 1949-68. *Publications:* Wassmuss, 1936; (with late R. Byron), Innocence and Design, 1936; Stranger Wonders, 1937; High Minded Murder, 1943; Four Studies in Loyalty, 1946; The Answer to Question 33, 1948; Character and Situation, 1949; Two Studies in Virtue, 1953; A Song of A Shirt, 1953; Dates and Parties, 1955; Orde Wingate, 1959; Cross Roads to Israel, 1965; Troubled Loyalty: a Biography of Adam von Trott, 1968; Nancy, the life of Lady Astor, 1972; Evelyn Waugh, 1975. *Recreation:* music. *Address:* Swyre House, Swyre, Dorchester, Dorset.

SYKES, Dr Donald Armstrong; Principal of Mansfield College, Oxford, since 1977; *b* 13 Feb. 1930; *s* of Rev. Leonard Sykes and Edith Mary Sykes (*née* Armstrong); *m* 1962, Marta Sproul Whitehouse; two *s*. *Educ:* The High Sch. of Dundee; Univ. of St Andrews (MA 2nd cl. Classics 1952; Guthrie Scholar); Mansfield Coll., Oxford (BA 1st cl. Theol. 1958; MA 1961; DPhil 1967); Univ. of Glasgow (DipEd). Fellow in Theology, 1959-77, and Senior Tutor, 1970-77, Mansfield Coll., Oxford. Vis. Prof. in Religion, St Olaf Coll., Northfield, Minn, 1969-70. *Publications:* articles and reviews in Jl Theological Studies, Studia Patristica. *Recreations:* gramophone records, gardening, walking. *Address:* The Principal's Lodgings, Mansfield College, Oxford OX1 3TF. *T:* Oxford 42340 and 43507.

SYKES, Edwin Leonard, CMG 1966; Secretary, Office of the Parliamentary Commissioner for Administration, 1967-74; *b* 1 May 1914; *m* 1st, 1946, Margaret Elizabeth McCulloch (*d* 1973); 2nd, 1976, Dorothy Soderberg. *Educ:* Leys School, Cambridge (Schol.); Trinity Coll., Cambridge (Senior Schol.). Entered Dominions Office, 1937; Asst Priv. Sec. to Secretary of State, 1939. Served War, 1939-45 (despatches). Served in British High Commissions, Canada, 1945-47, India, 1952-54; idc 1955; Dep. UK High Commissioner in Federation of Rhodesia and Nyasaland, 1956-59; Asst Under-Sec. of State, CRO, 1964-65; Dep. UK High Commissioner in Pakistan, 1965-66. *Address:* Sandway, Upper Rose Hill, Dorking, Surrey.

SYKES, Sir Francis (Godfrey), 9th Bt, *cr* 1781, of Basildon; *b* 27 Aug. 1907; *s* of Francis William Sykes (*d* 1945) (*g g s* of 2nd Bt) and Beatrice Agnes Sykes (*née* Webb) (*d* 1953); *S* cousin, Rev. Sir Frederic John Sykes, 8th Bt, 1956; *m* 1st, 1934, Eira Betty (*d* 1970), *d* of G. W. Badcock; one *s* one *d*; 2nd, 1972, Nesta Mabel, *d* of late Col and Mrs Harold Platt Sykes. *Educ:* Blundell's School, Devon; Nelson College, New Zealand. Tea planting, 1930; Air Ministry, 1939; fruit farming and estate management, 1945-57; Regional Sec., Country Landowners' Assoc., 1957-72. FCIS. *Heir:* *s* Francis John Badcock Sykes [*b* 7 June 1942; *m* 1966, Susan Alexandra, *er d* of Adm. of the Fleet Sir E. B. Ashmore, *qv*; three *s*]. *Address:* White Lodge, Bishops Castle, Salop. *T:* Bishops Castle 487. *Club:* Salop (Shrewsbury).

SYKES, Frank; *see* Sykes, A. F. S.

SYKES, Dr John Bradbury; Deputy Chief Editor, The Oxford English Dictionaries, since 1971; Editor, Concise and Pocket Oxford Dictionaries; *b* Folkestone, Kent, 26 Jan. 1929; *s* of Stanley William Sykes and Eleanor Sykes Sykes (*née* Bradbury); *m* 1955, Avril Barbara Hart; one *s*. *Educ:* Wallasey Grammar Sch.; Rochdale High Sch.; St Lawrence Coll.; Wadham Coll., Oxford (BA Maths 1950); Balliol Coll., Oxford (Skynner Sen. Student); Merton Coll., Oxford (Harmsworth Sen. Schol., MA and DPhil Astrophysics 1953). AERE, Harwell, 1953-71 (Head of Translations Office 1958, Principal Scientific Officer 1960); Member, Internat. Astronomical Union, 1958 (Pres., Commn for Documentation, 1967-73). Fellow, Inst. of Linguists, 1960; Mem. Council, 1977. *Publications:* (with B Davison) Neutron Transport Theory, 1957; (ed) Technical Translator's Manual, 1971; (ed) Concise Oxford Dictionary (6th edn), 1976; translations of many Russian textbooks in physics and astronomy; contribs to Incorporated Linguist. *Recreation:* crossword-solving (National Champion 1958, 1972-75 and 1977). *Address:* 20 Milton Lane, Steventon, Abingdon, Oxon OX13 6SA. *T:* Abingdon 831291.

SYKES, Sir John (Charles Anthony le Gallais), 3rd Bt *cr* 1921; *b* 19 April 1928; *s* of Stanley Edgar Sykes (*d* 1963) (2nd *s* of 1st Bt) and Florence Anaise le Gallais (*d* 1955); *S* uncle, 1974; *m* (marr. diss.). *Educ:* Churchers College. In textile trade. Member: British Epicure Soc.; International Wine & Food Soc. *Recreations:* golf, wine, food, travel. *Heir:* *b* Michael le Gallais Sykes [*b* 4 Jan. 1932; *m* 1976, Jacqueline Susan, *o d* of Captain C. Melia; two *s* by previous marriage]. *Address:* 120 Hartscroft, Linton Glade, Croydon, Surrey CR0 9LE. *T:* 01-651 2279.

SYKES, Joseph Walter, CMG 1962; CVO 1953; Chairman, Fiji Public Service Commission, since 1971; *b* 10 July 1915; *s* of Samuel Sykes and Lucy M. Womack; *m* 1940, Elima Petrie, *d* of late Sir Hugh Hall Ragg; three *s* two *d*. *Educ:* De La Salle Coll., Sheffield; Rotherham Gram. Sch.; Jesus Coll., Oxford. Colonial Administrative Service, Fiji; Cadet, 1938; Dist Officer, 1940; District Commissioner, 1950; Deputy Secretary for Fijian Affairs, 1952; Assistant Colonial Secretary, 1953; transferred to Cyprus as Dep. Colonial Sec., Nov. 1954; Admin. Sec., Cyprus. 1955-56; Colonial Sec., Bermuda, 1956-68; Chief Sec., Bermuda, 1968-71; retired. *Publication:* The Royal Visit to Fiji 1953, 1954. *Recreations:* photography, tennis. *Address:* c/o Public Service Commission, PO Box 2211, Suva, Fiji. *Club:* United Oxford & Cambridge University.

SYKES, Prof. Keble Watson; Head of Chemistry Department, since 1959, Professor of Physical Chemistry, since 1956, Queen Mary College, University of London; *b* 7 Jan. 1921; *s* of Watson and Victoria May Sykes; *m* 1950, Elizabeth Margaret Ewing Forsyth; three *d* (and one *s* decd). *Educ:* Seascale Preparatory Sch.; St Bees Sch.; The Queen's Coll., Oxford, MA, BSc, DPhil (Oxon.). ICI Research Fellow, Physical Chemistry Lab., Oxford, 1945-48; Lecturer, 1948-51, and Senior Lecturer in Chemistry, 1951-56, University Coll. of Swansea, Univ. of Wales; Dean, Fac. of Science, QMC, London, 1970-73. Hon. Sec. Chemical Soc. of London, 1960-66, Vice-Pres., 1966-69, Mem. Council, 1977-. Member Council, Westfield College, University of London. *Publications:* scientific papers in journals of Royal Society, Faraday Soc. and Chem. Soc. *Address:* 58 Wood Vale, Muswell Hill, N10 3DN. *T:* 01-883 1502.

SYKES, Sir (Mark Tatton) Richard T.; *see* Tatton-Sykes.

SYKES, Sir Richard (Adam), KCMG 1977 (CMG 1965); MC 1945; HM Diplomatic Service; Ambassador to the Netherlands, since 1977; *b* 8 May 1920; *s* of late Brig. A. C. Sykes, CBE, DSO; *m* 1953, Ann Georgina, *d* of late Brig. A. F. Fisher, CBE, DSO; two *s* one *d*. *Educ:* Wellington Coll.; Christ Church, Oxford. Served Army, 1940-46; Major, Royal Signals. Joined HM Foreign Service, 1947; served: Foreign Office, 1947-48; Nanking, 1948-50; Peking, 1950-52; Foreign Office, 1952-56; Brussels, 1956-59; Santiago, 1959-62; Athens, 1963-66; Foreign and Commonwealth Office, 1967-69; Ambassador to Cuba, 1970-72; Minister, Washington, 1972-75; Dep. Under-Sec., FCO, 1975-77. Croix de Guerre (France), 1945. *Address:* c/o National Westminster Bank Ltd, Warminster, Wilts. *Club:* Army and Navy.

SYKES, Rev. Prof. Stephen Whitefield, MA; Van Mildert Canon Professor of Divinity, Durham University, since 1974; *b* 1939; *m* 1962; one *s* two *d*. *Educ:* St John's Coll., Cambridge. BA (Cantab) 1961 (1st cl. Theol), Pt iii Theol Tripos 1962 (1st cl. with dist.); MA (Cantab) 1964. Univ. Asst Lectr in Divinity, Cambridge Univ., 1964-68, Lectr, 1968-74; Fellow and Dean, St John's Coll., Cambridge, 1964-74. Mem., Archbishop's Cttee on Religious Educn, 1967. Examining Chaplain to Bishop of Chelmsford, 1970-. *Publications:* Friedrich Schleiermacher, 1971; Christian Theology Today, 1971; (ed) Christ, Faith and History, 1972. *Address:* 14 The College, Durham.

SYKES, Air Vice-Marshal William, OBE; CEng, FRAeS; MBIM; RAF retired, 1975; General Manager, British Airport Corporation Ltd (Oman); *b* 14 March 1920; *s* of Edmund and Margaret Sykes, Appleby, Westmorland; *m* 1946, Jean Begg, *d* of Alexander and Wilemena Harrold, Watten, Caithness; one *s* one *d. Educ:* Raley Sch. and Technical Coll., Barnsley, Yorks. HNC Mech. and Aero Eng. 1942; CEng, AFRAeS 1968, FRAeS 1974, MBIM 1975. Joined RAF as Aircraft Apprentice, 1936. Served War: No 51 (Bomber) Sqdn, 1939-41; various engrg specialist courses; commissioned, 1942; Coastal Command: Invergordon, Pembroke Dock, Gibraltar, Hamworthy, Reykjavik (Iceland) and Tain. After 1945: appts at Marine Aircraft Exptl Estabt, Felixstowe; HQ No 23 Gp; Central Servicing Develt Estabt (CSDE); RAE; 2nd TAF, Germany; Dept of ACAS(OR); Electrical Specialist Course, 1948; Staff Coll., 1953-54; jssc 1959-60. During period 1960-72: served a further tour with CSDE as OC Projects Wing; was OC Engrg Wing, Wyton; Station Comdr, No 8 of TT, Weeton; Comd Engrg Officer, FEAF; Dir of Mechanical Engrg (RAF), MoD (AFD); Air Officer Engrg, NEAF; Vice-Pres., Ordnance Board, 1972-74, Pres., 1974-75. Attended IDC, 1967. *Recreations:* travel, motor sports. *Address:* PO Box 3074, Seeb Airport, Muscat, Sultanate of Oman; 5 Clifton Court, Clifton Drive South, St Anne's-on-Sea, Lancs. *T:* St Anne's 727689. *Club:* Royal Air Force.

SYLVESTER, Albert James, CBE 1920; JP; *b* Harlaston, Staffs, 24 Nov. 1889; *s* of late Albert and Edith Sylvester; *m* Evelyn (*d* 1962), *d* of late Rev. W. Welman, Reading; one *d. Educ:* Guild Street School, Burton-on-Trent; privately. Private Secretary to Sec. of Cttee of Imperial Defence, 1914-21; Private Sec. to Sec. of War Cabinet and of Cabinet, 1916-21; Private Secretary to Secretary, Imperial War Cabinet, 1917; Private Secretary to British Secretary, Peace Conference, 1919; Private Secretary to successive Prime Ministers, 1921-23; Principal Secretary to Earl Lloyd George of Dwyfor, 1923-45. Film, The Very Private Secretary, BBC TV, 1974. JP Wilts, 1953. Commander of the Order of the Crown of Italy, and Sacred Treasure of Japan. Supreme Award (with Honours), Ballroom and Latin American Dancing, Imperial Soc. of Teachers of Dancing, 1977. *Publications:* The Real Lloyd George, 1947; Life with Lloyd George (diaries, ed Colin Cross), 1975. *Recreations:* riding and golf. *Address:* Rudloe Cottage, Corsham, Wilts. *T:* Hawthorn 810375. *Club:* National Liberal.
See also A. Sylvester-Evans.

SYLVESTER, George Harold, CBE 1967; retired 1967 as Chief Education Officer for Bristol; *b* 26 May 1907; *s* of late George Henry and Martha Sylvester; *m* 1936, Elsie Emmett; one *s. Educ:* Stretford Grammar School; Manchester University. BA Manchester 1928; MA Bristol 1944. Teaching, Manchester, 1929-32; Administrative posts (Education) in Wolverhampton and Bradford, 1932-39; Assistant Education Officer, Bristol, 1939-42; Chief Education Officer, Bristol, 1942-67. Hon. MEd Bristol, 1967. *Recreations:* golf, music. *Address:* 43 Hill View, Henleaze, Bristol BS9 4QE. *T:* Bristol 62-8144.

SYLVESTER-BRADLEY, Prof. Peter Colley; Professor of Geology, University of Leicester, since 1959; *b* 21 May 1913; 2nd *s* of Lt-Col C. R. Sylvester-Bradley; *m* 1945, Joan Eveleen Mary Campbell; three *s* one *d. Educ:* Haileybury College; University of Reading. Lecturer, Seale Hayne Agricultural College, 1937-39. Served War of 1939-45, Royal Navy. Assistant Lecturer, Lecturer, and Senior Lecturer, University of Sheffield, 1946-59; Rose Morgan Professor, University of Kansas, 1955-56; Internat. Commissioner of Zoological Nomenclature, 1953-58. Vice-Pres., Palæontographical Soc. *Publications:* (ed) The Species Concept in Paleontology, 1956; (ed) The Geology of the East Midlands, 1968; papers on palæontology, stratigraphy, taxonomy, evolution and the origin of life. *Recreations:* natural history, travel, landscape gardening, photography, the gramophone, country wines. *Address:* Department of Geology, University of Leicester, LE1 7RH. *T:* Leicester 50000; Noon's Close, Stoughton, Leicester. *T:* Leicester 713764.

SYLVESTER-EVANS, Alun, CB 1975; Deputy Chief Executive, Property Services Agency, Department of the Environment, since 1973; *b* 21 April 1918; *o c* of Daniel Elias Evans and Esther Evans, Rhymney, Mon.; *m* 1945, Joan Maureen, *o c* of A. J. Sylvester, *qv*; two *s. Educ:* Lewis' School, Pengam; University of Wales, Aberystwyth. Armed services, 1940-46. Asst Research Officer, Min. of Town and Country Planning, 1946-47; Asst Principal, 1947-48; Principal Private Sec. to Minister of Housing and Local Govt, 1954-57; Asst Secretary, 1957-66, Under-Sec., 1966-73, Min. of Housing and Local Govt, later DoE. *Recreation:* golf. *Address:* 2 Enmore Road, Putney, SW15. *T:* 01-788 3043. *Club:* Hurlingham.

SYME, Sir Colin (York), AK 1977; Kt 1963; LLB; company director; Chairman, Broken Hill Pty Co. Ltd, 1952-71 (Director, since 1937); *b* 22 April 1903; *s* of Francis Mark Syme; *m* 1933, Patricia Baird; three *s* one *d. Educ:* Scotch College, Claremont, WA; Universities of Perth and Melbourne, Australia. Partner, Hedderwick, Fookes & Alston, Solicitors, 1928-66. Pres., The Walter & Eliza Hall Inst. of Medical Research; Chairman: Cttee of Inquiry into Victorian (Aust.) Health Services, 1973-75; Victorian Health Planning Cttee, 1975-; Hon. Mem., Aust. Inst. of Mining and Metallurgy. Hon. DSc Univ. of NSW, 1960. Storey Medal, Aust. Inst. Management, 1971. *Recreation:* fishing. *Address:* 22 Stonnington Place, Toorak, Victoria 3142, Australia. *Clubs:* Melbourne, Australian (Melbourne); Adelaide (Adelaide); Newcastle (Newcastle); Links (New York).

SYME, Sir Ronald, OM 1976; Kt 1959; FBA 1944; retired as Camden Professor of Ancient History, Oxford, 1949-70; *b* 11 March 1903; *e s* of David and Florence Syme, Eltham, New Zealand. *Educ:* NZ; Oriel College, Oxford (Classical Prizes and First Class Hons, Lit Hum, 1927). Fellow of Trinity College, 1929-49; Conington Prize, 1939. Press Attaché with rank of First Secretary, HM Legation, Belgrade, 1940-41; HM Embassy, Ankara, 1941-42; Professor of Classical Philology, University of Istanbul, 1942-45; President, Society for the Promotion of Roman Studies, 1948-52; President, International Federation of Classical Societies, 1951-54; Secretary-General, Internat. Council for Philosophy and Humanistic Studies, 1952-71, Pres., 1971-75; Vice-President: Prize Cttee of Balzan Foundation, 1963; Assoc. Internat. pour l'Etude du Sud-Est Européen, 1967. Hon. Fellow: Oriel College, Oxford, 1958; Trinity College, Oxford, 1972; Emeritus Fellow, Brasenose College, 1970; Fellow, Wolfson Coll., 1970. Hon. LittD NZ, 1949; Hon. DLitt: Durham, 1952; Liège, 1952; Belfast, 1961; Graz, 1963; Emory, US, 1963; D ès L: Paris, 1963; Lyon, 1967; Ohio, 1970; Boston Coll., 1974; Tel-Aviv, 1975; Louvain, 1976. Membre Associé de l'Institut de France (Académie des Inscriptions et Belles-Lettres), 1967; Corresp. Member, German Archæological Institute, 1931, Member, 1953; Member, Royal Danish Acad. of Letters and Sciences, 1951; For. Mem. Lund Society of Letters, 1948. Corresponding Member Bavarian Academy, 1955; For. Member: American Philosophical Soc., 1959; Amer. Acad. of Arts and Sciences, 1959; Massachusetts Historical Society, 1960; Istituto di Studi Romani, 1960; Amer. Historical Soc., 1963; Real Academia de la Historia, 1963; Istituto Lombardo, 1964; Acc. Torino, 1972; Corresponding Member Austrian Academy, 1960. Kenyon Medal, British Acad., 1975. Commandeur de la Légion d'Honneur, 1975; Member, Orden Pour le Mérite für Wissenschaften und Künste, 1975. *Publications:* The Roman Revolution, 1939; Tacitus (2 vols), 1958; Colonial Elites, 1958; Sallust, 1964; Ammianus and the Historia Augusta, 1968; Ten Studies in Tacitus, 1970; Emperors and Biography, 1971; The Historia Augusta: a call for clarity, 1971; Danubian Papers, 1971; chaps in Cambridge Ancient History. *Address:* Wolfson College, Oxford. *Club:* Odd Volumes (Boston).

SYMES, Maj.-Gen. George William, CB 1946; MC; *b* 12 Jan. 1896; *o s* of late George and Eliza Symes; *m* 1st, 1939, Katherine Bellairs Lucas (*d* 1961); 2nd, 1967, Kathleen Champion de Crespigny. *Educ:* Bridport Gram. Sch. Commissioned 1915, York and Lancaster Regt; served with MG Corps, 1915-19 (MC and bar); Staff College, Camberley, 1930-31; Bt Major, 1932; Major, 1938; Bt Lt-Col, 1939; Col, 1942; Acting Maj.-Gen. 1942; Temp. 1943; Subst. Maj.-Gen., 1944. Comd 8th Inf. Bde, 1940-41; Brig.-Gen. Staff, Eastern Comd, 1941-42; Comd 70th Division, 1942-43; Deputy Commander Special Force, India, 1943-44; Deputy Commander L of C 21st Army Group, May-Nov. 1944 (despatches); Comd L of C Comd, SEAC, 1944-45; Comd South Burma District, June-Dec. 1945 (despatches); Commander South-Western District, Taunton, Som., 1946-48, and 43rd (Wessex) Division TA, 1947-48; retired April 1949. Colonel, York and Lancaster Regt, 1946-48; Hon. Col, 10th Bn Adelaide Rifles, 1958-60. Founded Nat. Trust of S Australia, 1954, Vice-Pres. 1965-. *Publications:* contribs. to Australian Dictionary of Biography. *Recreations:* historical research, golf. *Address:* 81 Esplanade, Tennyson, SA 5022, Australia. *T:* 356-8568. *Club:* Adelaide (Adelaide).

SYMES, (Lilian) Mary; Clerk to Justices, 6 Divisions in Suffolk, 1943-74; Chairman, Norfolk and Suffolk Rent Tribunal, since 1974; *b* 18 Oct. 1912; *d* of Walter Ernest and Lilian May Hollowell; *m* 1953, Thomas Alban Symes; one *s. Educ:* St Mary's Convent, Lowestoft; Great Yarmouth High School. Articled in Solicitor's Office; qualified as Solicitor, 1936. Became first woman Clerk to Justices (Stowmarket), 1942; first woman Deputy Coroner, 1945; Clerk to the Justices, Woodbridge, 1946, Bosmere and Claydon, 1951; first woman Coroner, 1951; Deputy Coroner, Northern District, Suffolk, 1956-. *Recreations:* Worcester porcelain, gardening. *Address:* Little Orchard, Westerfield, Ipswich, Suffolk. *T:* Ipswich 54634.

SYMINGTON, David, CSI 1947; CIE 1943; *b* 4 July 1904; 2nd *s* of James Halliday Symington, merchant, Bombay, India, and Maud McGrigor (*née* Aitken); *m* 1929, Anne Ellen Harker; one *s* one *d. Educ:* Cheltenham College; Oriel College, Oxford (Scholar). Entered Indian Civil Service, 1926; held various appointments including Backward Classes Officer, Bombay Province, 1934-37; Municipal Commissioner, City of Bombay, 1938; ARP Controller, Bombay, 1941; Secretary to Government of Bombay, Home Dept, 1942, Secretary to Governor, 1943-47; retired from ICS, 1948; Member, John Lewis Partnership, 1948-52; Director, N Rhodesia Chamber of Mines, 1953-60; Chairman Copperbelt Technical Foundation, 1955-60. Councillor, Royal Borough of Kensington, 1950. Member of Council, Cheltenham College, 1961-76. *Publications:* Report on Aboriginal Tribes of the Bombay Province, 1938; (as James Halliday): I Speak of Africa, 1965; A Special India, 1968; also short stories; (TV play) The Brahmin Widow, 1968. *Recreations:* writing, bridge. *Address:* 5 Paragon Terrace, Cheltenham, Glos.

SYMINGTON, Stuart; United States Senator from Missouri, 1952-76; *b* Amherst, Massachusetts, 26 June 1901; *s* of William Stuart and Emily Haxall Symington; *m* 1924, Evelyn Wadsworth (decd); two *s. Educ:* Yale University; International Correspondence School. Joined Symington Companies, Rochester, New York, 1923; President Colonial Radio Co., Rochester, 1930-35; President, Rustless Iron & Steel Co., Baltimore, 1935-37; President and Chairman, Emerson Electric Manufacturing Co., St Louis, 1938-45; Surplus Property Administrator, Washington, 1945-46; Assistant Secretary of War for Air, 1946-47; Secretary of Air Force, National Defense, 1947-50; Chairman, National Security Resources Board, 1950-51; Administrator, Reconstruction Finance Corporation, 1951-52. Is a Democrat. *Address:* Apt 704-N Watergate East, 2510 Virginia Avenue, NW, Washington, DC 20037, USA.

SYMINGTON, Prof. Thomas, MD; FRSE; Director, since 1970, and Professor of Pathology, since 1971, Institute of Cancer Research, Royal Cancer Hospital; *b* 1 April 1915; *m* 1943, Esther Margaret Forsyth, MB, ChB; two *s* one *d. Educ:* Cumnock Academy. BSc 1936; MB ChB, 1941; MD 1950. St Mungo (Notman) Prof. of Pathology, Univ. of Glasgow, 1954-70. Visiting Prof. of Pathology, Stanford Univ., Calif., 1965-66. Member, Medical Research Council, 1968-72. FRSE, 1956; FRIC, 1958 (ARIC, 1951); FRCP(G), 1963; FRFPS (G), 1958; FRCPath, 1964; FIBiol, 1970. Hon. MD Szeged Univ., 1971. *Publications:* Functional Pathology of the Human Adrenal Gland, 1969; numerous papers on problems of adrenal glands in Journals of Endocrinology and Pathology. *Recreation:* golf. *Address:* 130 Northey Avenue, Cheam, Surrey. *T:* 01-642 7628. *Club:* Athenæum.

SYMMERS, Prof. William St Clair; Professor of Histopathology (formerly Morbid Anatomy), in the University of London, Charing Cross Hospital Medical School, and Hon. Consultant Pathologist and Lecturer in Morbid Anatomy and Histology, Charing Cross Hospital Group, since 1953; *b* 16 Aug. 1917; *s* of William St Clair Symmers (Professor of Pathology and Bacteriology, QUB) and Marion Latimer (*née* Macredie); *m* 1941, Jean Noble Wright; one *s. Educ:* Royal Belfast Academical Institution; Queen's University of Belfast; Guy's Hospital Medical School. MB, BCh, BAO (QUB), 1939; MD (QUB), 1946; PhD (Birmingham), 1953; MRCP (Lond.), 1946; FRCP (Lond.), 1959; MRCP (Edin.), 1965; MRCP (Ireland), 1976; FRCPA (MCPA 1967); FRCPath, 1963-75. Extern Surgeon, Royal Victoria Hospital, Belfast, 1940. Served War of 1939-45, Surgeon Lieutenant, RNVR, 1940-46. Demonstrator in Pathology and pupil of Prof. G. Payling Wright, Guy's Hosp. Med. Sch., 1946-47; Registrar in Clinical Pathology, Guy's Hospital, 1946-47; Deptl Demonstrator of Pathology, University of Oxford, 1947; Senior Assistant Pathologist, Radcliffe Infirmary, Oxford, 1947-48; Senior Lecturer in Pathology, Univ. of Birmingham, 1948-53; Hon. Cons Pathologist: United Birmingham Hosps, 1948-53; Birmingham Regional Hosp. Bd, 1949-53. Visiting Prof. of Pathology: Univ. of Heidelberg, 1962; Univ. of Cincinnati, 1962; New York Univ., 1963; Vargas Hosp. School of Medicine, Univ. of Caracas, Venezuela, 1963; Univ. of Otago, 1966; Univ. of São Paulo, 1969, 1972; Med. Univ. of S Carolina, 1969, 1972; Univ. of Kentucky, 1972; Univ. of Bahia, Salvador, Brazil, 1972; Baghdad Univ., 1974. Univ. of Buenos Aires, 1977. Visiting Scholar, Louisiana State Univ., 1962; Guest Speaker, Mayo Clinic, 1962. Visiting Lecturer, 1961 onwards, in Universities of Europe, Asia, Africa, North and South America and Australasia, inc. Ehrlich, Frankfurt, 1962; Dr Dhayagude Meml, Seth GS Med. Sch., Univ. of Bombay, 1967; Pasteur, Dakar, 1969; Koch, Berlin, 1970; Examiner, Universities of: Birmingham, 1948-53; London, 1953-61, 1966-; Cambridge,

1956-67, 1970-75; the West Indies, 1963, 1965; Cairo, 1966; East Africa, 1966; Ceylon, 1966; Malaya, 1967-69, 1975-76; Lagos, 1967-70; Bristol, 1967-69; Nat. Univ. of Ireland, 1970-74, 1978-; Malta, 1970; Zambia, 1970-72, 1974-75; Riyadh, 1975-76; Oxford, 1976; Examining Bd in England, 1962-66; RCP, 1966-72; RCS, 1968-75; Conjoint Bd Ireland, 1974-77; Inst. of Medical Laboratory Technology, 1949-55. Pres., Section of Pathology, RSM, 1969-70. Fellow, Ulster Med. Soc. Yamagiwa Medal, Univ. of Tokyo, 1969; Scott-Heron Medal, Royal Victoria Hosp., Belfast, 1975. *Publications:* contrib. Brit. and foreign medical works; jt ed., Systemic Pathology (1st edn, with late Prof. G. Payling Wright), 1966, 2nd edn, 5 Vols, 1976-78; Curiosa, 1974. *Address:* Whitefriars, 30 Sandy Lodge Way, Northwood, Middlesex HA6 2AS. *T:* Northwood 25688; Department of Histopathology, Charing Cross Hospital Medical School, Fulham Palace Road, W6 8RF. *T:* 01-748 2040 (ext. 2726), 01-748 3749.

SYMON, Mrs David; *see* Moore, Miss Jocelyn A. M.

SYMONDS, Sir Charles (Putnam), KBE 1946; CB 1944; MA, DM Oxon; FRCP, Hon. FRCPEd; Air Vice-Marshal RAFVR; Consulting Physician Emeritus for Nervous Diseases, Guy's Hospital; Consulting Physician Emeritus, The National Hospital, Queen Square; Hon. Consulting Neurologist, RAF; *b* 1890; *s* of Sir Charters Symonds; *m* 1st, 1915, Janet Palmer Poulton (*d* 1919); 2nd, 1920, Edythe Dorton; four *s. Educ:* Rugby; New Coll., Oxford; Guy's Hospital; Entrance Scholarships Rugby and Guy's Hospital. Served European War, 1914-18 (Médaille Militaire). Held appts at Guy's Hosp., at Throat Nose and Ear Hosp., and at Nat. Hosp., Queen Square, from 1919 until retirement. Radcliffe Travelling Fellow, Oxford University, 1920; FRSM (Ex-Pres. Sections of Psychiatry and Neurology); Ex-Pres., Assoc. of British Neurologists, 1956. Hon. Visiting Neurologist, Johns Hopkins Hosp.; Sims Commonwealth Travelling Professor for 1953; Harveian Orator, RCP, 1954. Hon. Member, Amer. Neurological Assoc.; Membre Correspondant de la Société de Neurologie de Paris; Hon. Member, New York Neurological Soc. Hon. Fellow RSM 1964. *Publications:* Studies in Neurology, 1970; Section on Nervous Diseases in Taylor's Textbook of Medicine; papers on neurological subjects in scientific journals. *Recreations:* photography, bird-watching, fly-fishing. *Address:* 180 Chiltern Court, Baker Street, NW1. *Club:* Royal Air Force.
. *See also* R . C . Symonds .

SYMONDS, Jane Ursula; *see* Kellock, J. U.

SYMONDS, Joseph Bede, OBE 1957; *b* 17 Jan. 1900; *m* 1921; four *s* six *d* (three *s* decd). *Educ:* St Bede's Secondary School, Jarrow. Councillor, Jarrow, 1929; Alderman 1935; Mayor 1945; County Councillor, Durham, 1946; Freeman, Borough of Jarrow, 1955. Past Chairman National Housing Town Planning Council, 1948-50 (Exec. Member, 1938-); Chairman Jarrow Housing Cttee, 1935-. MP (Lab) Whitehaven, June 1959-70. *Recreations:* cricket; welfare work (old people); Air Training Corps. *Address:* 11 Hedworth View, Jarrow, Tyne and Wear NE32 4EW. *T:* Jarrow 897246.

SYMONDS, Ronald Charters, CB 1975; a Special Adviser to the Royal Commission on Gambling, since 1976; *b* 25 June 1916; *e s* of Sir Charles Symonds, *qv*; *m* 1939, Pamela Painton; two *s* one *d. Educ:* Rugby Sch.; New Coll., Oxford. British Council, 1938-39 and 1946-51. Military Service, 1939-45. War Office, later MoD, 1951-76, retired. United States Bronze Star, 1948. *Recreations:* walking, ornithology. *Address:* 10 Bisham Gardens, N6 6DD.

SYMONETTE, Hon. Sir Roland Theodore, Kt 1959; Premier of the Bahamas, 1964-67; Member of HM Executive Council, Bahamas, since 1949; Leader of Government in the House of Assembly, 1955-67; MHA since 1925; shipyard owner, Bahamas; Contractor for the Construction of roads, wharfs, and harbours; *b* 16 Dec. 1898; *m* 1945, Margaret Frances Thurlew; four *s* one *d* (and one *d* decd). *Educ:* day school at Current Eleuthera, Bahama Islands. *Recreation:* yachting. *Address:* 601 Bay Street, Nassau, Bahamas. *Clubs:* Nassau Yacht (Bahamas); North American Yacht Racing Association (New York).

SYMONS, Ernest Vize, CB 1975; Director General, Board of Inland Revenue, 1975-77; *b* 19 June 1913; *s* of Ernest William Symons and Edith Florence Elphick; *m* 1938, Elizabeth Megan Jenkins; one *s* two *d. Educ:* Stationers' Company's Sch.; University Coll., London. Asst Inspector, 1934; Admin. Staff Coll., Henley, 1956; Principal Inspector of Taxes, 1957; Sen. Principal Inspector of Taxes, 1961; Dep. Chief Inspector of Taxes, 1964-73; Chief Inspector of Taxes, 1973-75. Mem. College Cttee, UCL, 1975. *Recreations:* chess, bridge. *Address:* Awelon, Links Drive, Totteridge, N20. *T:* 01-445 3015.

SYMONS, Julian Gustave, FRSL; author; *b* 30 May 1912; *y s* of M. A. Symons; *m* 1941, Kathleen Clark; one *s* (one *d* decd). Editor, Twentieth Century Verse, 1937-39. Chairman: Crime Writers Association, 1958-59; Cttee of Management, Soc. of Authors, 1970-71; Sunday Times Reviewer, 1958-. Pres., Detection Club, 1976-. Mem. Council, Westfield Coll., Univ. of London, 1972-75. FRSL 1975. *Publications:* Confusions About X, 1938; (ed) Anthology of War Poetry, 1942; The Second Man, 1944; The Immaterial Murder Case, 1945; A Man Called Jones, 1947; Bland Beginning, 1949; The Thirty First of February, 1950; A. J. A. Symons, 1950; Charles Dickens, 1951; Thomas Carlyle, 1952; The Broken Penny, 1952; The Narrowing Circle, 1954; Horatio Bottomley, 1955; The Paper Chase, 1956; The General Strike, 1957; The Colour of Murder, 1957 (CWA Critics' Award); The Gigantic Shadow, 1958; The Progress of a Crime, 1960 (MWA Edgar Allan Poe Award); A Reasonable Doubt, 1960; The Thirties, 1960; The Killing of Francie Lake, 1962; The Detective Story in Britain, 1962; Buller's Campaign, 1963; The End of Solomon Grundy, 1964; The Belting Inheritance, 1965; England's Pride, 1965; Critical Occasions, 1966; A Picture History of Crime and Detection, 1966; The Man Who Killed Himself, 1967; The Man Whose Dreams Came True, 1968; (ed) Essays and Biographies by A. J. A. Symons, 1969; The Man Who Lost His Wife, 1970; Bloody Murder: from the detective story to the crime novel, a history, 1972 (MWA Edgar Allan Poe Award); Notes from Another Country, 1972; The Players and the Game, 1972; Between the Wars, 1972; The Plot Against Roger Rider, 1973; A Three Pipe Problem, 1975; The Hungry Thirties, 1976; several plays for television. *Recreations:* watching cricket and Association football, wandering in cities. *Address:* 147 Ramsden Road, SW12 8RF. *T:* 01-673 3671.

SYMONS, Noel Victor Housman, CIE 1941; MC 1916; JP; Major, Army in India Reserve of Officers, 1934; *b* 27 Nov. 1894; *s* of late Edward William Symons, MA (Oxon.), Headmaster King Edward VI's School, Bath, and Katharine Elizabeth, *sister* of A. E. and Laurence Housman; *m* 1924, Cicely Dorothea Richards; no *c. Educ:* King Edward VI's School, Bath. British Army, 1914-19, Lt Worcestershire Regt; Indian Civil Service, 1920; District work till 1931; Secretary, Board of Revenue, 1931-34; Private Secretary to Governor of Bengal, 1934-35; Revenue Secretary, Govt of Bengal, 1938-40; Commissioner, Presidency Division, and ARP Controller, Bengal, 1940; Commissioner, Rajshahi Division, and Additional Secretary, Civil Defence, Bengal, 1941; Joint Secretary, Civil Defence Dept, Govt of India, 1942; Director-General, Civil Defence, and Additional Secretary, Defence Dept, Govt of India, 1943; retired from ICS Aug. 1946. JP Hampshire, 1951. Appointed to Appeal Cttee, Quarter Sessions, 1959; Dep. Chm., Lymington Petty Sessions and Mem. Council, Magistrates' Assoc., 1964; Chm., Lymington Petty Sessions, 1966; supplemental list, 1969. *Publication:* The Story of Government House (Calcutta), 1935. *Recreations:* yachting, beagling, fell walking. *Address:* Bucklands, Lymington, Hants. *T:* Lymington 72719. *Club:* Royal Lymington Yacht.

SYMS, John Grenville St George, QC 1962; Barrister-at-Law; a Recorder of the Crown Court, since 1972; *b* 6 Jan. 1913; *s* of late Harold St George Syms and Margaret (*née* Wordley); *m* 1951, Yvonne Yolande (*née* Rigby) (marr. diss. 1971); one *s. Educ:* Harrow; Magdalen College, Oxford (BA). Called to the Bar, 1936. Dep. Chm., Huntingdon and Peterborough QS, 1965-71. Chm., SE Agricultural Law Tribunal, 1972. Served in RAFVR, 1940-45 (despatches); Wing Commander, 1944. *Recreations:* hunting, shooting and fishing. *Address:* Willinghurst, Shamley Green, Surrey. *T:* Cranleigh 2828. *Club:* Flyfishers'.

SYNGE, Henry Millington; Chairman, Union International Co. Ltd, since 1969 (Director since 1955); Partner in Tilney & Co. (Stockbrokers), Liverpool and Shrewsbury; *b* 3 April 1921; *s* of Richard Millington Synge, MC, Liverpool and Eileen Hall; *m* 1947, Joyce Helen, *d* of Alexander Ross Topping and Mrs Topping (*née* Stileman); two *s* one *d. Educ:* Shrewsbury School. Mercantile Marine: Radio Officer, 1941; Purser, Bibby Line, 1943; demobilised, 1946. Partner, Sing White & Co. (Stockbrokers), 1947. Manager, Liverpool Trustee Savings Bank, 1957, Chm. 1968-69; Manager, Trustee Savings Bank of Wales and Border Counties, 1970. *Recreations:* private flying, fishing, amateur radio. *Address:* Wilcot House, Nesscliffe, Shrewsbury, Salop SY4 1BJ. *T:* Nesscliffe 392. *Club:* Salop (Shrewsbury).

SYNGE, John Lighton, FRS 1943; MA, ScD Dublin; MRIA, FRSC (Tory Medal, 1943); Senior Professor, School of Theoretical Physics, Dublin Institute for Advanced Studies, 1948-72, now Emeritus; *b* Dublin, 1897; *y s* of Edward Synge; *m* 1918, Elizabeth Allen; three *d. Educ:* St Andrew's Coll., Dublin;

Trinity Coll., Dublin. Senior Moderator and Gold Medallist in Mathematics and Experimental Science, 1919; Lecturer in Mathematics, Trinity College, Dublin, 1920; Assistant Professor of Mathematics, University of Toronto, 1920-25; Secretary to the International Mathematical Congress, Toronto, 1924; Fellow of Trinity College, Dublin, and University Professor of Natural Philosophy, 1925-30; Treas., Royal Irish Academy, 1929-30. Sec., 1949-52. Pres., 1961-64; Professor of Applied Mathematics, Univ. of Toronto, 1930-43; Professor of Mathematics and Chm. of Dept, Ohio State Univ., 1943-46; Prof. of Mathematics and Head of Dept, Carnegie Inst. of Technology, 1946-48; Visiting Lecturer, Princeton Univ., 1939; Vis. Prof.: Brown Univ., 1941-42; Inst. for Fluid Dynamics and Applied Maths, University of Maryland, 1951. Ballistics Mathematician, United States Army Air Force, 1944-45. Hon. FTCD. Hon. LLD St Andrews, 1966; Hon. ScD: QUB, 1969; NUI, 1970. Boyle Medal, RDS, 1972. *Publications:* Geometrical Optics, 1937; (with B. A. Griffith) Principles of Mechanics, 1942; (with A. E. Schild) Tensor Calculus, 1949; Science: Sense and Nonsense, 1951; Geometrical Mechanics and de Broglie Waves, 1954; Relativity: the Special Theory, 1956; The Hypercircle in Mathematical Physics, 1957; The Relativistic Gas, 1957; Kandelman's Krim, 1957; Relativity: the General Theory, 1960; Talking about Relativity, 1970; papers on geometry and applied mathematics; Ed. Sir W. R. Hamilton's Mathematical Papers, Vol. I. *Address:* Torfan, Stillorgan Park, Blackrock, Co. Dublin. *T:* 881251.

SYNGE, Richard Laurence Millington, FRS 1950; Hon. Professor, School of Biological Sciences, University of East Anglia, since 1968; *b* 28 Oct. 1914; *s* of late Laurence M. Synge and Katharine C. Synge (*née* Swan), Great Barrow, Chester; *m* 1943, Ann, *d* of late Adrian L. Stephen and Karin Stephen (*née* Costelloe), both of London; three *s* four *d. Educ:* Winchester College; Trinity College, Cambridge (Hon. Fellow, 1972). International Wool Secretariat Research Student, University of Cambridge, 1938; Biochemist: Wool Industries Research Assoc., Leeds, 1941; Lister Institute of Preventive Medicine, London, 1943; Rowett Research Inst., Bucksburn, Aberdeen, 1948; Food Research Inst., Norwich, 1967-76. Editorial Board, Biochemical Journal, 1949-55. Hon. MRIA 1972; Hon. DSc, Univ. of East Anglia, 1977. (Jtly) Nobel Prize for Chemistry, 1952. *Publications:* papers in biochemical and chemical journals, etc, 1937-. *Address:* ARC Food Research Institute, Colney Lane, Norwich NR4 7UA; 19 Meadow Rise Road, Norwich NR2 3QE. *T:* Norwich 53503.

SYNGE, Sir Robert Carson, 8th Bt, *cr* 1801; Manager and Owner, Rob's Furniture; *b* 4 May 1922; *s* of late Neale Hutchinson Synge (2nd *s* of 6th Bt) and Edith Elizabeth Thurlow (*d* 1933), Great Parndon, Essex; *m* 1944, Dorothy Jean Johnson, *d* of T. Johnson, Cloverdale; two *d. S* uncle, 1942. *Heir: cousin* Neale Francis Synge [*b* 28 Feb. 1917; *m* 1939, Kathleen Caroline Bowes; one *s* one *d*]. *Address:* 19364 Fraser Highway, RR4, Langley, British Columbia, Canada.

SYNNOTT, Pierce Nicholas Netterville, CB 1952; Deputy Under-Secretary of State, Ministry of Defence, 1964-65; *b* 6 Sept. 1904; *e s* of Nicholas J. Synnott, JP, Furness, Naas, and Barbara (*née* Netterville); *m* 1939, Ann (from whom he obtained a divorce, 1948), *d* of Sir Abe Bailey, 1st Bt, KCMG; one *s. Educ:* Oratory School; Balliol College, Oxford. 1st Class Mods and 1st Class Litterae Humaniores, Oxford. Asst Principal, Admiralty, 1928; Principal, 1936. Served War of 1939-45 in Army (6oth Rifles), in African and Italian campaigns. Returned to Admiralty, 1945; Under-Secretary, 1947; Deputy Secretary, 1958. Chancellor, Irish Assocs, Order of Malta, 1971-. JP County of London, 1961. Order of St Olav, Norway (1st Class), 1947. *Address:* Furness, Naas, Co. Kildare. *T:* Naas 97203.

SYSONBY, 3rd Baron, *cr* 1935, of Wonersh; **John Frederick Ponsonby;** *b* 5 Aug. 1945; *s* of 2nd Baron Sysonby, DSO and Sallie Monkland, *d* of Dr Leonard Sanford, New York; *S* father 1956. *Address:* Newby Hall, Ripon, North Yorks.

SYTHES, Percy Arthur; Comptroller and Auditor General for Northern Ireland, since Dec. 1974; *b* 21 Dec. 1915; *s* of William Sythes and Alice Maud Grice; *m* 1941, Doreen Smyth Fitzsimmons; three *d. Educ:* Campbell Coll., Belfast; Trinity Coll., Dublin. Exhibr, Scholar; BA (Mod. Lit.), 1st cl. hons Gold Medal 1938; Vice-Chancellor's Prizeman 1939. Asst Master: Royal Sch., Dungannon, 1939; Portadown Coll., 1940. Royal Artillery, 1940-46 (Major); GSO2, 1946. Asst Principal, NI Civil Service, 1946; Private Sec. to Dame Dehra Parker, 1950; Principal 1958; Asst Sec. 1963; Sen. Asst Sec., NI Min. of Develt, 1970, Dep. Sec. 1971; Dep. Sec., NI Executive, 1974. Mem. Bd of Governors, Strathearn Sch., 1966. *Recreations:* gardens, family. *Address:* Malory, 37 Tweskard Park, Belfast BT4 2JZ. *T:* Belfast 63310.

SZEMERÉNYI, Prof. Oswald John Louis, DrPhil (Budapest); Professor of Indo-European and General Linguistics, University of Freiburg-im-Breisgau, since 1965; *b* London, 7 Sept. 1913; *m* 1940, Elizabeth Kövér; one *s. Educ:* Madách Imre Gimnazium; University of Budapest. Classics Master in Beregszász and Mátyásföld, 1939-41; Lecturer in Greek, 1942-45, Reader, 1946, Professor of Comparative Indo-European Philology in University of Budapest, 1947-48. Came to England, Oct. 1948; employed in industry, 1949-52; Research Fellow, Bedford Coll., London, 1952-53; Asst Lecturer, 1953-54, Lecturer, 1954-58, Reader, 1958-60, in Greek at Bedford College; Professor of Comparative Philology, University College, London, 1960-65. Collitz Prof., Linguistic Inst., USA, 1963; Vis. Prof., Seattle, 1964. *Publications:* The Indo-European liquid sonants in Latin, 1941; Studies in the Indo-European System of Numerals, 1960; Syncope in Greek and Indo-European, 1964; Einführung in die vergleichende Sprachwissenschaft, 1970; Richtungen der modernen Sprachwissenschaft, part I, 1971; contrib. Comparative Linguistics in Current Trends in Linguistics 9, 1972; The Kinship Terminology of the Indo-European Languages, 1977; contrib. to British and foreign learned journals. *Recreations:* motoring, chess. *Address:* Albert-Ludwigs-Universität, Freiburg-im-Breisgau, W Germany.

SZENT-GYORGYI, Albert, MD, PhD Cantab, Dhc; Scientific Director, National Foundation for Cancer Research, Massachusetts, USA, since 1975; *b* Budapest, 16 Sept. 1893; *s* of Nicholas Szent-Györgyi and Josephine, *d* of Joseph Lenhossék, Professor of Anatomy; *m* 1st, 1941; one *d*; 2nd, Marcia Houston. *Educ:* Budapest University; Cambridge University. Matriculated Medical Faculty, Budapest, 1911; war service, 1914-18 (wounded); Assistant, University Pozsony, 1918; working at Prague and Berlin, 1919; in Hamburg in scientific research, 1919-20; Assistant at Univ. Leiden, Holland, 1920-22; privaat dozent at Groningen, 1922-26; working at Cambridge, England, with the interrruption of one year spent in USA, 1926-30; Prof. of Medical Chemistry, Szeged Univ., 1931-45; Professor of Biochemistry Univ. of Budapest, Hungary, 1945-47; Dir of Research, Inst. of Muscle Research, Mass, 1947-75. Formerly: Pres. Acad. of Sciences, Budapest; Vice-Pres. Nat. Acad., Budapest. Prix Nobel of Medicine, 1937; Visiting Prof., Harvard Univ., 1936; Franchi Prof., Univ. of Liége, Belgium, 1938. Cameron Prize (Edinburgh), 1946. Lasker Award, 1954. Hon. ScD Cantab, 1963. Hon. Fellow, Fitzwilliam Coll., Cambridge, 1967. *Publications:* Oxidation, Fermentation, Vitamins, Health and Disease, 1939; Muscular Contraction, 1947; The Nature of Life, 1947; Contraction in Body and Heart Muscle, 1953; Bioenergetics, 1957; Submolecular Biology, 1960; Science, Ethics and Politics, 1962; Bioelectronics, 1968; The Living State, 1972; Electronic Biology and Cancer, 1976; many scientific papers. *Recreations:* sport of all kinds, chiefly sailing, swimming and fishing. *Address:* Marine Biological Laboratory, Woods Hole, Mass 02543, USA; Penzance, Woods Hole, Mass, USA.

SZERYNG, Henryk; Hon. Professor, Faculty of Music, Mexican National University, Mexico City; Concert Violinist; *b* Warsaw, 22 Sept. 1921; Mexican Citizen since 1946. *Educ:* Warsaw, Berlin, Paris. Graduated violin class of Carl Flesch, Berlin, 1933; 1st Prize special mention, Paris Conservatoire, 1937; Composition study with Nadia Boulanger, 1934-39. War of 1939-45: played over 300 concerts for Allied Armed Forces, Red Cross and other welfare institutions in Scotland, England, Canada, USA, Caribbean area, Middle East, North Africa, Brazil and Mexico. Has covered the five continents in recitals, also soloist with major orchestras, 1953-. Mexican Cultural Ambassador, 1960-; Cultural Adviser to Mexican delegn, UNESCO, Paris, and to Mexican Foreign Ministry, 1970-. Numerous recordings; Grand Prix du Disque, 1955, 1957, 1960, 1961, 1967, 1969. Hon. Mem., RAM, 1969. Hon. Pres., Musical Youth of Mexico, 1974. Officer of Cultural Merit, Roumania, 1935; Kt Comdr, Order of Polonia Restituta (Poland), 1956; Silver Medal of City of Paris, 1963; Officer, Order of Arts and Letters (France), 1964; Comdr, Order of the Lion (Finland), 1966; Chevalier, Légion d'Honneur, 1972; Mozart Medal, Salzburg, 1972; Comdr Al Merito (Italy), 1974; Comdr, Order of Flag with Golden Star (Yugoslavia), 1976. 1974; Comdr, Order of Flag with Golden Star (Yugoslavia), 1976. *Publications:* several chamber music works, also for piano and violin. Revised violin concertos by Nardini, Vivaldi and others; re-discovered Paganini Concerto No 3 (World Première, London, 1971). *Recreations:* climbing, golf, motoring, reading. *Address:* c/o London Artists, 124 Wigmore Street, W1H 0AX.

SZWARC, Michael M., FRS 1966; Distinguished Professor of Chemistry of the State University of New York; *b* 9 June 1909; Polish; *m* 1933, Marja Frenkel; one *s* two *d. Educ:* Warsaw Inst. of Technology (Chem. Eng. 1933); Hebrew Univ., Jerusalem

(PhD 1942). University of Manchester (Lecturer), 1945-52; PhD (Phys. Chem.) 1947; DSc 1949; State University Coll. of Environmental Scis at Syracuse, NY, 1952-: Prof. of Physical and Polymer Chemistry; Research Prof.; Distinguished Prof. of Chemistry; Dir, Polymer Research Inst. Baker Lectr, Cornell Univ., 1972. Nobel Guest Prof., Univ. of Uppsala, 1969; Vis. Prof., Univ. of Leuven, 1974. Hon. Dr: Leuven, Belgium, 1974, Uppsala, Sweden, 1975. Amer. Chem. Soc. Award for Outstanding Achievements in Polymer Chemistry, 1969; Gold Medal, Soc. of Plastic Engrs, 1972. *Publications:* Carbanions, Living Polymers and Electron Transfer Processes, 1968; Ions and Ion-pairs in Organic Chemistry, Vol. I, 1972, Vol. II, 1974; numerous contribs to Jl Chem. Soc., Trans Faraday Soc., Proc. Royal Soc., Jl Am. Chem. Soc., Jl Chem. Phys., Jl Phys. Chem., Jl Polymer Sci., Nature, Chem. Rev., Quarterly Reviews, etc. *Address:* 406 Hillsboro Parkway, Syracuse, New York 13214, USA. *T:* 446-2448.

T

TABOR, Prof. David, FRS 1963; PhD, ScD; Professor of Physics in the University of Cambridge, since 1973 (Reader, 1964-73), and Head of Physics and Chemistry of Solids, Cavendish Laboratory; Fellow of Gonville and Caius College, Cambridge, since 1957; *b* 23 Oct. 1913; *s* of Charles Tabor and Rebecca Weinstein; *m* 1943, Hannalene Stillschweig; two *s. Educ:* Regent St Polytechnic; Universities of London and Cambridge. BSc London 1934; PhD Cambridge 1939; ScD Cambridge 1956. Inaugural Gold Medal of Tribology, Inst. of Engrs, 1972; Guthrie Medal, Inst. Physics, 1975. *Publications:* The Hardness of Metals, 1951; Gases, Liquids and Solids, 1969; (with F. P. Bowden) Friction and Lubrication of Solids, Part I, 1950 (rev. edn, 1954); Part II, 1964; contributions to learned jls on friction, adhesion, lubrication and hardness. *Recreation:* Judaica. *Address:* Cavendish Laboratory, Madingley Road, Cambridge CB3 0HE; Gonville and Caius College, Cambridge; 8 Rutherford Road, Cambridge. *T:* Trumpington 3336.

TABOR, Maj.-Gen. David John St Maur, CB 1977; MC 1944; late Royal Horse Guards; GOC Eastern District, 1975-77; *b* 5 Oct. 1922; *y s* of late Harry Tabor, Hitchin, Herts; *m* 1955, Hon. Pamela Roxane, 2nd *d* of 2nd Baron Glendyne; two *s. Educ:* Eton; RMA, Sandhurst. Served War: 2nd Lieut, RHG, 1942; NW Europe, 1944-45 (wounded, 1944); Major, 1946. Lt-Col Comdg RHG, 1960; Lt-Col Comdg Household Cavalry, and Silver Stick in Waiting, 1964; Col, 1964; Brig., 1966; Comdr Berlin Infty Bde, 1966; Comdr, British Army Staff and Mil. Attaché, Washington, 1968; RCDS, 1971; Maj.-Gen., 1972; Defence Attaché, Paris, 1972-74. *Recreations:* shooting, fishing, sailing, golf, gardening. *Address:* Upton Manor, Andover, Hants. *T:* Hurstbourne Tarrant 250. *Clubs:* Turf, Royal Automobile, MCC; Royal Yacht Squadron.

TABOUIS, Geneviève; Officier de la Légion d'Honneur, 1959; Commandeur de l'Ordre National du Mérite; Rédacteur Diplomatique quotidien à Paris Jour, à Radio-Luxembourg, La Dépêche du Midi, Juvénal; *d* du peintre Le Quesne; nièce de l'Ambassadeur Jules Cambon et du Général Tabouis; *m* 1916, Robert Tabouis (*d* 1973), Président-Directeur Général de la Cie Générale de Télégraphie sans Fil; one *s* one *d. Educ:* Couvent de l'Assomption; Faculté des lettres, Paris, Ecole archéologique du Louvre. Journaliste diplomatique; débuta en 1924 à la SDN comme correspondante de La Petite Gironde, du Petit Marseillais; chargée de 1924 à 1932 de toutes les grandes enquêtes diplomatiques, de tous les grands reportages politiques et de nombreuses conférences diplomatiques; diplomatic Leader à La Petite Gironde et Le Petit Marseillais, 1932-37, à L'Œuvre 1932-40; fonda et dirigea l'hebdomadaire français, Pour La Victoire, New York, 1939-45; retour à Paris, 1946-56; diplomatic leader à La France Libre, L'Information, L'Espoir. Correspondant diplomatique du Sunday Dispatch de Londres, de La Critica de Buenos-Ayres; collaboratrice à de nombreux journaux et revues; déploié une grande activité dans les meetings politiques et les conférences politiques et diplomatiques; nombreuses hautes décorations étrangères. Hon. Vice-Présidente de l'Association de la Presse Diplomatique française. *Publications:* 4 livres historiques couronnés par l'Académie Française: Tout Ank Amon, Nabuchodonosor, Salomon, Sybaris; une biographie: Jules Cambon par l'un des siens (couronné par l'Académie Française): un livre de politique: Le Chantage à la Guerre; Albion Perfide ou Loyale; tous ces ouvrages ont paru également en Angleterre; Ils l'ont appelée

Cassandre (New York); Grandeurs et Servitudes américaines (Paris); Quand Paris Résiste; 20 Ans de Suspense Diplomatique. *Recreations:* Aucune récréation; travaille tout le temps, même le dimanche, ne connait pas le week-end; comme seule distraction aime recevoir diplomates, hommes politiques et amis; sa table est célèbre par ses surtouts extraordinaires; objets d'art, ou céramiques commandées à L. E. Chevallier, et décors originaux adaptés aux événements diplomatiques d'actualité. *Address:* 3 square Claude-Debussy, 75017 Paris, France. *Club:* Soroptimist Interallié.

TACON, Air Cdre Ernest William, CBE 1958; DSO 1944; MVO 1950; DFC 1940 (Bar 1944); AFC 1942 (Bar 1953); *b* 6 Dec. 1917; *s* of Ernest Richard Tacon, Hastings, New Zealand; *m* 1st, 1949, Clare Keating (*d* 1956), *d* of late Michael Keating, Greymouth, NZ; one *s* two *d*; 2nd, 1960, Bernardine, *d* of Cecil Leamy, Wellington, NZ; three *s. Educ:* St Patrick's College, Silverstream, New Zealand. Joined RNZAF, 1938. Served with RAF, 1939-46. Transferred to RAF, 1946. CO, King's Flight, Benson, 1946-49. Overseas Services since War: Canal Zone, 1951-53; Cyprus, 1956-58; Persian Gulf, 1961-63; Commandant, Central Fighter Establishment, 1963-65; Air Cdre, Tactics, HQ Fighter Comd, 1966-67; AOC Military Air Traffic Ops, 1968-71, retired. *Address:* 69 McLean Road, Bucklands Beach, Auckland, NZ. *Club:* United Services Officers (Wellington).

TAFT, Charles Phelps; Attorney at Law; Mayor of Cincinnati, USA, 1955-57; Hon. Chairman, US Advisory Committee on Voluntary Foreign Aid (Agency for International Development) (formerly Chairman); General Counsel, Committee for a National Trade Policy; *b* 20 Sept. 1897; *s* of William H. Taft (27th President of the US and Chief Justice) and Helen Herron; *m* 1917, Eleanor Kellogg (*d* 1961), *d* of Irving H. Chase of Ingersoll-Waterbury Co.; two *s* three *d* (and two *d* decd). *Educ:* The Taft School, Watertown, Connecticut; Yale University. BA 1918, LLB 1921; Hon. LLD (Yale), 1952, etc.; Doctor of Hebrew Letters, Hebrew Union College, 1948. Enlisted 12 FA 2nd Div., AEF, 1917 (Fr., Jan.-Dec. 1918), discharged as 1st Lt 1919. Prosecuting Attorney Hamilton County, 1927-28; Partner Taft: Stettinius & Hollister, 1924-37; Headley, Sibbald & Taft, 1946-59; Taft & Lavercombe, 1959-66; Taft & Luken, 1967-74; Chm. Fed. Steel Mediation Bd, 1937; Dir, Community War Services, Fed. Security Agency, 1941-43; Dir, Wartime Economic Affairs. Department of State, 1944-45; City Councilman of Cincinnati, 1938-42, 1948-51, 1955-77. Trustee, Twentieth Century Fund, Carnegie Institution of Washington, Committee for Economic Development; Senior Warden, Christ Episcopal Church, Cincinnati; Pres. Fed. Council of Churches of Christ in America, 1947-48. Medal for Merit, 1946. *Publications:* City Management: The Cincinnati Experiment, 1933; You and I-and Roosevelt, 1936; Why I am for the Church, 1947; Democracy in Politics and Economics, 1950. *Recreations:* fishing, local politics, topical daily broadcasting. *Address:* (office) 1071 Celestial Street, Cincinnati, Ohio 45202, USA; (home) Highland Towers, Cincinnati, Ohio 45202, USA.

TAGGART, John S.; *see* Scott-Taggart.

TAHOURDIN, John Gabriel, CMG 1961; HM Diplomatic Service, retired; *b* 15 Nov. 1913; *s* of late John St Clair Tahourdin; *m* 1957, Margaret Michie; one *s* one *d. Educ:* Merchant Taylors' School; St John's College, Oxford. Served HM Embassy, Peking, 1936-37; Private Secretary to HM Ambassador at Shanghai, 1937-40; BoT, 1940-41; Vice-Consul, Baltimore, 1941; Foreign Office, 1942; Private Secretary to Parliamentary Under-Secretary of State, 1943, and to Minister of State, 1945; Athens, 1946; returned to Foreign Office, 1949; Counsellor, British Embassy, The Hague, 1955; Foreign Office, 1957; Minister, UK Delegn to 18 Nation Disarmament Conf., Geneva, 1963-66; HM Ambassador to: Senegal, 1966-71, and concurrently to Mauritania, 1968-71, to Mali, 1969-71, and to Guinea, 1970-71; Bolivia, 1971-73. Mem., Internat. Inst. for Strategic Studies. Price Commission, 1975-. *Recreations:* music cinematography, foreign languages, travel. *Address:* Swafield Hall, North Walsham, Norfolk. *Clubs:* Athenæum, Travellers', Norfolk.
See also P. A. I. Tahourdin.

TAHOURDIN, Dr Peter Anthony Ivan, CBE 1970 (OBE 1956); Deputy Director General, British Council, since 1977; *b* 12 Oct. 1920; *yr s* of John St Clair Tahourdin and Suzanne Perscheid; *m* 1945, Betty Yeo, Court Colman, Glam; one *s* two *d. Educ:* Merchant Taylors' Sch.; University Coll., Oxford (Open Scholar, Edmund Spenser Exhibr, MA, BSc, DPhil). Research scientist, UK Atomic Energy Project, 1942-46; joined British Council, 1946: Science Officer, Italy, 1946-54; Asst Rep., Yugoslavia, 1954-58; Rep., Israel, 1958-61; Asst Controller, Books, Arts and Science Div., 1961-67; Rep., Yugoslavia, 1967-

69; Dep. Controller, Books, Arts and Science Div., 1969-70; Controller, Educn and Science Div., 1970-73; Asst Dir-Gen., 1973-77. *Publications:* contrib. professional jls on sci. subjects and the cinema. *Recreations:* talking, the cinema, industrial archaeology, photography. *Address:* 2 Twyford Avenue, W3 9QA. *T:* 01-992 5758.
See also J. G. Tahourdin.

TAILYOUR, General Sir Norman (Hastings), KCB 1966 (CB 1964); DSO 1945, and Bar to DSO 1956; Captain of Deal Castle, since 1972; *b* 12 Dec. 1914; *s* of late Lt-Col G. H. F. Tailyour and Mrs Tailyour (*née* Hutcheson); *m* 1st, 1941, Priscilla June Southby (*d* 1971); one *s* one *d*; 2nd, 1973, Juliet, *d* of late Col. K. N. Colvile and of Mrs K. N. Colvile, and *widow* of J. A. Greig; two step *s* one step *d. Educ:* Nautical College, Pangbourne. 2nd Lieutenant, RM 1933; seconded to Royal West African Frontier Force (Nigeria Regiment), Captain RM, 1939; 5th Battalion RM, RM Div., 1941; Staff College, Camberley, 1943; G2, HQs RM Div., 1943; OCRM, HMS Robertson, then Exec. Officer, HMS St Mathew (Landing Craft Base), 1943-44; CO 27th Bn RM, NW Europe, 1945 (despatches, DSO); OC Training Cadre, Inf. Sch., RM, 1946; Sen. Course, US Marine Corps, Quantico, USA, Major RM, 1947; Chief Instr Amphibious Sch., RM, 1948; GI Plans and Ops RN Rhine Flotilla, 1949; JSSC, Latimer, 1951; GI Amphibious Warfare HQ, London, 1952; Lieut-Col Comdg Officer 45 Commando, RM, Cyprus (Bar to DSO), Port Said (wounded, despatches), 1954; NATO Defence Coll., Paris, 1957; CO RM Barracks, Plymouth, 1957; Chief of Amphibious Warfare's Rep., BJSM, Washington, 1958; Asst Naval Mem., Mil. Staff Cttee, UN, Col RM; Comdr 3rd Commando Bde, RM, Brig. RM, 1960; Comdr Plymouth Gp, RM, Maj.-Gen., 1962; Lt-Gen. 1965; General 1967. Comdt-Gen., Royal Marines, 1965-68. Adm. in Texas Navy, 1972. Patron: Goodwin Sands and Downs RNLI; Deal Soc.; Council Member: Officers' Pension Soc.; Stoll Foundn. MBIM. *Recreation:* sailing. *Address:* West Brae, Johnshaven, by Montrose, Angus. *T:* Benholm 372. *Clubs:* Savile, Army and Navy; Royal Yacht Squadron; (Life Vice-Cdre) Royal Marines Sailing; Royal Naval Sailing Association (Rear Commodore, 1961-65).
See also Col Sir O. W. Williams-Wynn, Bt.

TAIT, Prof. Alan Anderson; Chief, Fiscal Analysis Division, International Monetary Fund, Washington, since 1976; *b* 1 July 1934; *s* of Stanley Tait and Margaret Ruth (*née* Anderson); *m* 1963, Susan Valerie Somers; one *s. Educ:* Heriot's Sch., Edinburgh; Univ. of Edinburgh (MA); Trinity Coll., Dublin (PhD). Lectr, Trinity Coll., Dublin, 1959-71 (Fellow, 1968, Sen. Tutor, 1970); Visiting Prof., Univ. of Illinois, 1965-66. Economic adviser to Irish Govt on industrial develt and taxation and chief economic adviser to Confedn of Irish Industry, 1967-71; International Monetary Fund: Visiting Scholar, 1972; Consultant, 1973 and 1974. Prof. of Money and Finance, Univ. of Strathclyde, 1971-77. *Publications:* The Taxation of Personal Wealth, 1967; (with J. Bristow) Economic Policy in Ireland, 1968; (with J. Bristow) Ireland: some problems of a developing economy, 1971; The Value Added Tax, 1972; articles on public finance in Rev. of Economic Studies, Finanzarchiv, Public Finance, etc. *Recreations:* sailing, painting. *Address:* 4284 Vacation Lane, Arlington, Va 22207, USA. *T:* 477-4416. *Club:* Royal Northern Yacht (Rhu); Royal Irish Yacht (Dun Laoghaire).

TAIT, Vice-Adm. Sir (Alan) Gordon, KCB 1977; DSC 1943; Chief of Naval Personnel and Second Sea Lord, since 1977; *b* 30 Oct. 1921; *s* of Allan G. Tait and Ann Gordon, Timaru, NZ; *m* 1952, Philippa, *d* of Sir Bryan Todd, *qv*; two *s* two *d. Educ:* Timaru Boys' High Sch.; RNC Dartmouth. Commanded HM Submarines: Teredo, 1947; Solent, 1948; ADC to Governor-General of New Zealand, 1949-51; commanded HM Submarines: Ambush, 1951; Aurochs, 1951-53; Tally Ho, 1955; Sanguine, 1955-56; commanded HM Ships: Caprice, 1960-62; Ajax, 1965-66; Maidstone, 1967; commanded: 2nd Destroyer Squadron (Far East), 1965-66; 3rd Submarine Sqdn, 1967-69; Britannia RNC, 1970-72; Naval Adviser, UK High Commn, Canada, 1965-66; Naval Secretary, 1972-74; Flag Officer, Plymouth, Port Admiral, Devonport, Comdr Central Sub Area, Eastern Atlantic, and Comdr Plymouth Sub Area, Channel, 1975-77. Naval ADC to the Queen, 1977. *Address:* 29 Chelsea Park Gardens, SW3. *Club:* Royal Yacht Squadron.

TAIT, Sir James (Blair), Kt 1963; QC (Australia); Barrister; *b* 15 October 1890; *s* of John Tait; *m* 1st, 1922, Annie Frances (*d* 1962), *d* of Dr George Howard; one *s* one *d*; 2nd, 1964, Sophie, *widow* of Dr J. Thomson-Tait. *Educ:* Geelong College; Melbourne University. War, 1914-18: Lt Aust. Flying Corps; Pilot Officer in France. Called to Bar in Victoria, 1919; KC 1945. Hon. Treas., Victorian Bar Council; Past Pres., Graduate

Union, Melbourne Univ.; Chairman: Equity Trustees Co, Ltd; Barristers' Chambers Ltd; Millbank Investment Fund (Aust.) Inc. Chairman, Cttee of Inquiry into Stevedoring Industry in Australia, 1955-57. *Recreations:* golf and bowls. *Address:* Owen Dixon Chambers, 205 William Street, Melbourne, Victoria 3000, Australia. *T:* Melbourne 60.0791. *Clubs:* Australian (Melbourne); Metropolitan Golf.

TAIT, Prof. James Francis, PhD; FRS 1959; Joel Professor of Physics as Applied to Medicine, University of London, since 1970; *b* 1 December 1925; *s* of Herbert Tait and Constance Levinia Brotherton; *m* 1956, Sylvia Agnes Simpson (*née* Wardropper) (*see* S. A. Tait). *Educ:* Darlington Grammar Sch.; Leeds Univ. Lectr in Medical Physics, Middlesex Hospital Medical School, 1948-55; External Scientific Staff, Medical Research Council, Middlesex Hospital Medical School, 1955-58; Senior Scientist, Worcester Foundation for Experimental Biology, USA, 1958-70. *Publications:* papers on medical physics, biophysics and endocrinology. *Recreations:* squash rackets, boating, gardening. *Address:* Department of Physics as Applied to Medicine, Middlesex Hospital Medical School, Cleveland Street, W1P 6DB. *T:* 01-636 8333 (ext. 642).

TAIT, Sir James (Sharp), Kt 1969; DSc, LLD, PhD, BSc(Eng), CEng, FIEE, FIMechE; Vice-Chancellor and Principal, The City University, 1966-74, retired (formerly Northampton College of Advanced Technology, London, of which he was Principal, 1957-66); *b* 13 June 1912; *s* of William Blyth Tait and Helen Sharp; *m* 1939, Mary C. Linton; two *s* one *d. Educ:* Royal Technical College, Glasgow; Glasgow Univ. (BSc (Eng.), PhD). Lecturer, Royal Technical Coll., Glasgow, 1935-46; Head of Electrical Engineering Department: Portsmouth Municipal Coll., 1946-47; Northampton Polytechnic, EC1, 1947-51; Principal, Woolwich Polytechnic, SE18, 1951-56. Member: Adv. Council on Scientific Policy, 1959-62; National Electronics Council, 1964-76, Hon. Mem., 1976. Pres., Inst. of Information Scientists, 1970-72. Hon. Fellow: Inst. of Measurement and Control, 1970; Inst. of Inf. Scientists, 1973. Hon. LLD Strathclyde, 1967; Hon. DSc City, 1974. *Recreation:* open-air pursuits. *Address:* 23 Trowlock Avenue, Teddington, Mddx. *T:* 01-977 6541.

TAIT, Sir Peter, KBE 1975 (OBE 1967); JP; Sharebroker, New Zealand; Director: Rothman's Industries Ltd; Peros Ltd, NZ; Municipal Insurance Co. Ltd; *b* Wellington, NZ, 5 Sept. 1915; *s* of John Oliver Tait and Barbara Ann Isbister; *m* 1946, Lilian Jean Dunn; one *s* one *d. Educ:* Wellington Coll., NZ. MP, New Zealand National Party, 1951-54; Mayor, City of Napier, 1956-74; Pres., NZ Municipal Assoc., 1968-69. Chairman: Napier Fire Bd, 1956-75; Hawke's Bay Airport Authority, 1962-74; Napier Marineland Trust Bd, 1963-; Princess Alexandra Hosp. Bd, 1972-. Exec., Hawke's Bay Med. Res. Foundn; Patron, Napier Develt Assoc.; Freeman, City of Napier. JP 1956-. *Recreations:* bowls, gardening. *Address:* 13 Simla Terrace, Napier, New Zealand. *T:* (private) 53894, (business) 55555. *Clubs:* Royal Over-Seas League; Lions, (Hon.) Cosmopolitan (both Napier).

TAIT, Mrs Sylvia Agnes Sophia, (Mrs James F. Tait), FRS 1959; biochemist; distinguished for her work on the hormones controlling the distribution of salts in the body; *m* 1956, James Francis Tait, *qv. Address:* Department of Physics as Applied to Medicine, Middlesex Hospital Medical School, W1P 6DB.

TAIT, Air Vice-Marshal Sir Victor Hubert, KBE 1944 (OBE 1938); CB 1943; *b* 8 July 1892; *s* of Samuel Tait, Winnipeg; *m* 1st, 1917; one *d* ; 2nd, 1929; one *s* ; 3rd, 1957, Nancy Margaret, *d* of late Andrew Muecke, Adelaide, Australia. *Educ:* University of Manitoba (BSc). Canadian Army, 1914-17; RFC and RAF, 1917-45. Director of Radar and Director-General of Signals, Air Ministry, 1942-45; Operations Director, BOAC, 1945-56. Chairman: International Aeradio Ltd, 1946-63; Lindley Thompson Transformer Co., 1959-66; Ultra Electronics (Holdings) Ltd, 1963-67 (Dir, 1955-72); Dir, Ultra Electronics Ltd, 1956-72. Air Transport Electronic Council, UK, 1958. Governor, Flight Safety Foundn of America, 1959-69. President, British Ice Hockey Assoc., 1958-71. Mem. Council, RGS, 1965-70. Order of the Nile (Egypt), 1936; Order of Merit (USA), 1945. *Address:* 81 Swan Court, SW3. *T:* 01-352 6864. *Clubs:* Hurlingham, Royal Air Force.

TALBOT, family name of **Baron Talbot of Malahide.**

TALBOT OF MALAHIDE, 9th Baron *cr* 1831 (Ire.); **Joseph Hubert George Talbot;** Baron Malahide of Malahide (Ire.), 1831; Hereditary Lord Admiral of Malahide and adjacent seas (15 Edward IV); retired; *b* 22 April 1899; *s* of John Reginald Charles Talbot (*d* 1909) and Maria Josephine (*d* 1939), *d* of 3rd Duc de Stacpoole; *S* brother, 1975; *m* 1st, 1924, Hélène (*d* 1961), *o d* of M. Gouley; 2nd, 1962, Beatrice Bros (marr. diss. 1970). *Educ:* Beaumont College. *Heir: cousin* Reginald John Richard Arundell [*b* 9 Jan. 1931; *m* 1955, Laura Duff, *yr d* of late Group Captain Edward John Tennant, DSO, MC; one *s* four *d*]. *Address:* 2 Fern Cottage, West Hoathly, Sussex.

TALBOT, Vice-Adm. Sir (Arthur Allison) FitzRoy, KBE 1964; CB 1961; DSO 1940 and Bar 1942; DL; Commander-in-Chief, Plymouth, 1965-67; retired; *b* 22 October 1909; *s* of late Henry FitzRoy George Talbot, Captain Royal Navy, and of Susan Blair Athol Allison; *m* 1940, Joyce Gertrude Linley; two *d. Educ:* RN College, Dartmouth. Served War of 1939-45: Comd 10th A/S Striking Force, North Sea, 1939, and 3rd MGB Flotilla, Channel, 1940-41 (DSO); Comd HMS Whitshed, East Coast, 1942 (Bar to DSO); Comd HMS Teazer, Mediterranean, 1943-44. Comdr 1945; Chief Staff Officer, Commodore Western Isles, 1945; Staff Officer Ops to C-in-C Brit. Pacific Fleet and Far East Station, 1947-48; Comd HMS Alert, 1949. Capt. 1950; Naval Attaché, Moscow and Helsinki, 1951-53. Imperial Defence College, 1954. Capt. (D) 3rd Destroyer Squadron, 1955-57; Commodore RN Barracks Portsmouth, 1957-59; Rear-Adm. 1960; Flag Officer: Arabian Seas and Persian Gulf, 1960-61; Middle East, 1961-62; Vice-Adm. 1962; Commander-in-Chief, S Atlantic and S America, 1963-65. DL Somerset, 1973. *Recreations:* riding, shooting. *Address:* Thickthorn Manor, Ilminster, Somerset. *T:* Ilminster 2738. *Club:* Naval and Military.

TALBOT, Maj.-Gen. Dennis Edmund Blacquière, CB 1960; CBE 1955; DSO 1945; MC 1944; DL; *b* 23 Sept. 1908; *s* of late Walter Blacquière Talbot, St John, Jersey and The White House, Hadlow, Kent; *m* 1939, Barbara Anne, *o d* of late Rev. R. B. Pyper, Rector of Pluckley, Kent; three *s* two *d. Educ:* Tonbridge; RMC Sandhurst. 2nd Lieut Roy. West Kent Regt, 1928. Served War of 1939-45 (despatches, DSO, MC); Brigade Major, 30th Infantry, Bde, BEF; GSO 2, HQ 1st Corps; GSO 2 and 1, Combined Ops; 2nd i/c 5th Bn Dorset Regt; in command, 7th Bn Hampshire Regt, NW Europe, 1944-45. I/c 2nd Bn Royal W Kent Regt, 1945-46; GSO 1, HQ, Far ELF, 1947-48; Senior UK Army Liaison Officer, NZ, 1948-51; Lt-Col 1949; Col 1952; i/c 18th Inf. Bde and 99th Gurkha Inf. Bde, Malaya, 1953-55; Brig. 1956; BGS, HQ, BAOR, 1957-58; Maj.-Gen. 1958; GOC, E Anglian Dist and 54th Inf. Div. (TA), 1958-61; Dep. Comdr, BAOR, and Comdr British Army Group Troops, 1961-63; Chief of Staff, BAOR, and GOC Rhine Army Troops, 1963-64, retired; Civil Service, 1964-73. Graduate of: Staff Coll., Camberley; RN Staff Coll., Greenwich; Joint Services Staff Coll., Latimer; Imperial Defence College, London; Civil Defence Staff Coll., Sunningdale. Col, The Queen's Own Royal West Kent Regt, 1959-61; Dep. Colonel, The Queen's Own Buffs, The Royal Kent Regt, 1961-65; Hon. Col, 8 Queen's Cadre (formerly 8 Bn The Queen's Regt (West Kent)), 1968-71. DL Kent, 1964. Knight Commander 1962, Grand Cross 1965, Order of the Dannebrog (Denmark). *Recreation:* gardening. *Address:* Oast Court, Barham, near Canterbury, Kent.

TALBOT, Vice-Adm. Sir FitzRoy, *see* Talbot, Vice-Adm. Sir A. A. F.

TALBOT, Frank Heyworth, QC 1949; LLB (London) 1929; Barrister; *b* 4 June 1895; *s* of Edward John Talbot and Susan (*née* Heyworth); *m* 1st, 1922, Mabel (*d* 1956), *d* of John Williams, Brecon; two *s* ; 2nd, 1969, Heather, *d* of J. F. Williams, Great Missenden, Bucks. *Educ:* Tottenham Grammar School; London Univ. Civil Service, 1912-31. Inns of Court Regt, 1918. Called to the Bar, Middle Temple, 1931; practice at the Bar, 1931-. Bencher, Middle Temple, 1958. *Recreation:* music. *Address:* Flat no 11, 24 Old Buildings, Lincoln's Inn, WC2; *T:* 01-242 0494; 11 New Square, Lincoln's Inn, WC2. *T:* 01-242 4017.

TALBOT, Godfrey Walker, MVO 1960; OBE 1946; author, broadcaster, lecturer, journalist; Senior News Reporter and Commentator on staff of British Broadcasting Corporation, 1946-69; official BBC observer accredited to Buckingham Palace, 1948-69; *b* 8 Oct. 1908; *s* of Frank Talbot and Kate Bertha Talbot (*née* Walker); *m* 1933, Bess, *d* of Robert and Clara Owen, Bradford House, Wigan; one *s* (and one *s* decd). *Educ:* Leeds Grammar School. Joined editorial staff on The Yorkshire Post, 1928; Editor of The Manchester City News, 1932-34; Editorial Staff, Daily Dispatch, 1934-37. Joined BBC, 1937; War of 1939-45: BBC war correspondent overseas, 1941-45 (despatches, OBE); organised BBC Home Reporting Unit, as Chief Reporter, after the war. BBC Commentator, Royal Commonwealth Tour, 1953-54, and other overseas visits by HM the Queen. *Publications:* Speaking from the Desert, 1944; Ten Seconds from Now, 1973; Queen Elizabeth the Queen Mother,

1973; Permission to Speak, 1976; Royal Heritage, 1977; Royalty Annual, 1952, 1953, 1954, 1955, 1956. *Recreations:* keeping quiet and walking. *Address:* Holmwell, Hook Hill, Sanderstead, Surrey. *T:* 01-657 3476.

TALBOT, Hon. Sir Hilary Gwynne, Kt 1968; **Hon. Mr Justice Talbot;** a Judge of the High Court of Justice, Queen's Bench Division, since 1968; *b* 22 Jan. 1912; *s* of late Rev. Prebendary A. T. S. Talbot, RD, and Mrs Talbot; *m* 1963, Jean Whitworth, *o d* of late Mr and Mrs Kenneth Fisher. *Educ:* Haileybury Coll.; Worcester Coll., Oxford. MA Oxon. Served War of 1939-45; Captain, RA. Called to Bar by Middle Temple Jan. 1935. Dep. Chm., Northants QS, 1948-62; Chm., Derbyshire QS, 1958-63; Dep. Chm. Hants QS, 1964-71; Judge of County Courts, 1962-68; a Presiding Judge, Wales and Chester Circuit, 1970-74. Formerly Dep. Chm., Agricultural Land Tribunals. *Recreations:* fishing, walking, bird-watching. *Address:* Royal Courts of Justice, WC2. *Club:* Athenæum.

TALBOT, Commandant Mary (Irene), CB; Director, Women's Royal Naval Service, 1973-76; *b* 17 Feb. 1922. *Educ:* Bristol Univ. BA Hons, Philosophy and Economics. Joined WRNS as a Naval recruiting asst, Nov. 1943; Officer training course, 1944, and apptd to HMS Eaglet, in Liverpool, as an Educn and Resettlement Officer; served on staffs of C-in-Cs: Mediterranean; the Nore; Portsmouth, 1945-61; First Officer, and apptd to staff of Dir Naval Educn Service, 1952; subseq. served HMS Condor, Dauntless and Raleigh; Chief Officer, and apptd Sen. WRNS Officer, the Nore, 1960; on staff of Dir Naval Manning, 1963-66, and then became Asst Dir, WRNS; Superintendent, and served on staff of C-in-C Naval Home Command, 1969; Supt in charge, WRNS training estabt, HMS Dauntless, near Reading, 1972-73. Hon. ADC, 1973-76. Dir, Norland Nursing Training Coll. *Recreations:* usual spinster ones: bridge, gardening, racing. *Address:* Sonning Cottage, Pound Lane, Sonning-on-Thames. *T:* Sonning 3323; Flat 2, 35 Buckingham Gate, SW1. *T:* 01-834 2579.

TALBOT, Very Rev. Maurice John; Dean Emeritus of Limerick; *b* 29 March 1912; 2nd *s* of late Very Rev. Joseph Talbot, sometime Dean of Cashel; *m* 1942, Elisabeth Enid Westropp; four *s*. *Educ:* St Columba's College; Trinity College, Dublin (MA). Curate of Nantenan, 1935; Rector of Rathkeale, 1942; Rector of Killarney, 1952; Dean of Limerick, 1954-71; Prebendary of Taney, St Patrick's Nat. Cathedral, Dublin; Bishop's Curate, Kilmallock Union of Parishes, 1971-73. *Publications:* Pictorial Guide to St Mary's Cathedral, Limerick, 1969; contrib. to North Munster Studies, 1967; The Monuments of St Mary's Cathedral, 1976. *Recreations:* tennis, shooting, fishing. *Address:* 4 Meadow Close, Caherdavin, Limerick, Ireland.

TALBOT, Lt-Gen. Sir Norman (Graham Guy), KBE 1969 (OBE 1945); TD 1950; Medical Director, Margaret Pyke Centre; Director-General, Army Medical Services, 1969-73; *b* Hastings, 16 Feb. 1914; *s* of late Rev. Richard Talbot, MA, and late Ethel Maude Talbot (*née* Stuart); *m* 1939, Laura Winifred, *d* of late William Kilby, Donington, Lincs; two *s* one *d*. *Educ:* Reigate Grammar Sch.; King's Coll., London; King's Coll. Hosp. MRCS, LRCP 1937; MB, BS London 1938; DA England 1939; MRCOG 1951; MD London 1953; FRCOG 1960; FRCP 1973. Commission into RAMC from RAMC (TA), Aug. 1939. Served War of 1939-45 (despatches, twice, OBE): in BEF, 1939-40; Egypt, Palestine and Syria, 1941-43; Sicily and Italy, 1943-46. Consultant Adviser in Obstetrics and Gynæcology to Army, 1951-58 and 1963-66. Served in Malta, 1958-61, and in Germany, 1961-63; DDMS, 1 (Br.) Corps, 1967-68; Comdt and Dir of Studies, Roy. Army Med. Coll., 1968-69. Brig. 1967; Maj.-Gen. 1968; Lt-Gen. 1969. Comr, Royal Hosp. Chelsea, 1969-73; Mem. Control Bd, Army Benevolent Fund, 1972-; Vice-Pres., Finsbury Rifles OCA. FRSM; Mem. Council, Section of Obstetrics of RSM, 1968-71; Vice-Pres., United Services Section, RSM, 1969-73; Examiner: RCOG; Central Midwives Board. Fellow, 1968-77, and Counsellor, 1973-74, Med. Soc. London; Member: Anglo-German Med. Soc.; Soc. of Apothecaries of London. QHS 1968-73. CStJ 1970 (OStJ 1966). *Publications:* contribs to various medical jls. *Recreations:* gardening, travel. *Address:* The Beeches, 76 Church Road, Fleet, Hants GU13 8LB. *T:* Fleet 7727.

TALBOT, Richard Michael Arthur Chetwynd; His Honour Judge Chetwynd-Talbot; a Circuit Judge, since 1972; *b* 28 Sept. 1911; 3rd *s* of late Reverend Prebendary A. H. Talbot and late Mrs E. M. Talbot; unmarried. *Educ:* Harrow; Magdalene College, Cambridge (MA). Called to Bar by Middle Temple, 1936, Bencher, 1962. Mem. Bar Council, 1957-61. Dep. Chm., 1950-67, Chm., 1967-71, Shropshire QS; Recorder of Banbury, 1955-71, Hon. Recorder, 1972-. Served War of 1939-45, in

Army. Major, King's Shropshire Light Infantry. *Address:* 7 St Leonard's Close, Bridgnorth, Salop WV16 4EJ. *T:* Bridgnorth 3619.

TALBOT, Thomas George, CB 1960; QC 1954; Assistant Counsel to the Chairman of Committees, House of Lords, since 1977; *b* 21 Dec. 1904; *s* of late Rt Hon. Sir George John Talbot and late Gertrude Harriet, *d* of late Albemarle Cator, Woodbastwick Hall, Norfolk; *m* 1933, Hon. Cynthia Edith Guest; one *s* three *d*. *Educ:* Winchester; New Coll., Oxford. Called to Bar, Inner Temple, 1929; Bencher, 1960. RE (TA), 1938; Scots Guards, 1940-44 (Hon. Captain). Assistant, subsequently Deputy, Parliamentary Counsel to Treasury, 1944-53; Counsel to Chm. of Cttees, H of L, 1953-77. *Address:* Falconhurst, Edenbridge, Kent. *T:* Cowden 641; House of Lords, SW1. *Club:* Brooks's.

TALBOYS, Rt. Hon. Brian Edward, PC 1977; MP for Wallace, New Zealand, since 1957; Deputy Leader, National Party, since 1974; Deputy Prime Minister, since 1974; Minister of Foreign Affairs and Overseas Trade, since 1975; *b* Wanganui, 1921; *m*; two *s*. *Educ:* Wanganui Collegiate Sch.; Univ. of Manitoba; Victoria Univ., Wellington (BA). Served war of 1939-45, RNZAF. Parly Under-Sec. to Minister of Trade and Industry, 1960; Minister of Agriculture, 1962-69; Minister of Science, 1964-72; Minister of Education, 1969-72; Minister of Overseas Trade and Trade and Industry, 1972; Minister of Nat. Develt, 1975-77. Leader of a member of NZ delegns to overseas confs. Owns 500 acre sheep farm, Heddon Bush. *Address:* Parliament House, Wellington, New Zealand.

TALINTYRE, Douglas George; Head of Policy and Planning, Manpower Services Commission, since 1977; *b* 26 July 1932; *o s* of late Henry Matthew Talintyre and of Gladys Talintyre; *m* 1956, Maureen Diana Lyons; one *s* one *d*. *Educ:* Harrow County Grammar School; London School of Economics. BSc (Econ.) 1956. Joined National Coal Board, 1956: Administrative Assistant, 1956-59; Marketing Officer, Durham Div., 1959-61; Head of Manpower Planning and Intelligence, HQ, 1961-62; Dep. Head of Manpower, HQ, 1962-64; Head of Wages and Control, NW Div., 1964-66. Entered Civil Service, 1966; Principal, Naval Personnel (Pay) Div., MoD, 1966-69; Senior Industrial Relations Officer, CIR, 1969-71; Director of Industrial Relations, CIR, 1971-74; Asst Secretary, Training Services Agency, 1974-75; Counsellor (Labour), Washington DC, 1975-77. *Recreations:* squash, chess, gardening. *Address:* Woodwards, School Lane, Cookham Dean, Berks SL6 9PQ.

TALLACK, Sir Hugh M.; *see* Mackay-Tallack.

TALLBOYS, Richard Gilbert, OBE 1974; FCA; FCIS; HM Diplomatic Service; Counsellor Commercial, Seoul, since 1976; *b* 25 April 1931; *s* of late Harry Tallboys; *m* 1954, Margaret Evelyn, *d* of Brig. H. W. Strutt, DSO, ED, Hobart; two *s* two *d*. *Educ:* Palmer's School. LLB (London), BCom (Tasmania). Lt-Comdr RANR. Accounting profession in Australia, 1955-62; Alderman, Hobart City Council, 1958-62; Director, National Heart Foundation of Australia, 1958-62; Australian Govt Trade Commissioner, Johannesburg, Singapore, Jakarta, 1962-68. HM Diplomatic Service, 1968; First Secretary i/c Brasilia, 1969; First Secretary and Head of Chancery, Phnom Penh, 1972; FO, 1973. *Address:* c/o Bank of New South Wales, Sackville Street, W1. *Clubs:* Travellers'; Tasmanian, Naval, Military and Air Force (Hobart).

TALLERMAN, Dr Kenneth H., MC; MA, MD, FRCP; retired; Consulting Physician, Paediatric Department, The London Hospital; Consulting Paediatrician, St Margaret's Hospital, Epping; Hon. Lieutenant-Colonel RAMC; *b* London, 1894; *s* of late P. Tallerman and late Mrs C. G. L. Wolf; *m* 1st, 1929, Alice Campbell (*d* 1960), *yr d* of late D. C. Rose, Otago, NZ; 2nd, 1961, Florence M., *widow* of Frank Keeble and *d* of late Canon Small. *Educ:* Charterhouse School; Caius College, Cambridge University. Served in the Royal Field Artillery during European War, 1914-1919, and in the RAMC during War of 1939-45; graduated Medicine from St Thomas's Hosp., and obtained the degree MD (Cantab.); FRCP (London); late Cons. Pædiatrician, North-East Metropolitan Regional Board and Dr Barnardo's Home, and Physician to The Infants, and Paddington Green Children's Hospitals, Asst to the Medical Unit St Thomas's Hospital, Fellow and Instructor in Pediatrics, Washington University School of Medicine, USA, etc. Hon. Member (Past Pres.) Brit. Pædiatric Assoc.; Past Pres. Pædiatric Section, RSM. *Publications:* The Principles of Infant Nutrition (with C. K. Hamilton), 1928; numerous scientific and medical papers, 1920-58. *Recreation:* gardening. *Address:* Brantham Lodge, Brantham, near Manningtree, Essex. *T:* Holbrook 385. *Club:* Savile.

TALLIS, Gillian Helen; see Mackay, G. H.

TALLIS, Mrs Walter; see Mackay, G. H.

TAMBLIN, Air Cdre Pamela Joy; Director, Women's Royal Air Force, since 1976; *b* 11 Jan. 1926; *d* of late Albert Laing and of Olga Victoria Laing; *m* 1970, Douglas Victor Tamblin; one step *s* one step *d*. *Educ:* James Gillespie's High Sch., Edinburgh; Heaton High Sch., Newcastle upon Tyne; Durham Univ. (BA Hons). ATS, 1943-45. Essex County Council Planning Officer, 1949-51. Joined Royal Air Force, 1951; served Education Branch, 1951-55: RAF Locking; RAF Stanmore Park; RAF Wahn, Germany; Secretarial (now Administrative) Branch, 1955-76; Schools Liaison Recruiting, 1955-59; Accountant Officer, RAF St Mawgan and RAF Steamer Point, Aden, 1959-61; Staff College, 1962-63; MoD, Air Secretary's Dept, 1963-66; Sen. Trng Officer, RAF Spitalgate, 1966-68; Admin. Plans Officer, HQ Maintenance Comd, 1968-69; Command WRAF Admin. Officer, HQ Strike Comd, 1969-71; Station Comdr, RAF Spitalgate, 1971-74; Command Accountant, HQ Strike Comd, 1974-76. Chm., Cttee on Women in Nato Forces, 1977-. *Recreations:* fell-walking, gardening, cookery, tapestry, woodworking. *Address:* 2 Carlton Court, Eastbury Road, Watford, Herts. *Club:* Royal Air Force.

TAME, William Charles, CB 1963; Deputy Secretary, Ministry of Agriculture, Fisheries and Food, 1967-71; *b* 25 June 1909; *s* of late Charles Henry Tame, Wimbledon, Surrey; *m* 1935, Alice Margaret, *o d* of late G. B. Forrest, Witherslack, Westmorland; one *s* one *d*. *Educ:* King's College School, Wimbledon; Hertford College, Oxford. Entered Ministry of Agriculture as Assistant Principal, 1933. Chairman: International Whaling Commission, 1966-68; Fisheries R&D Bd, 1972-. Member: Council, Royal Veterinary Coll., Univ. of London, 1972- (Vice-Chm., 1973-); Governing Body, Animal Virus Res. Inst., 1972-76. *Recreation:* music. *Address:* Windrush, Walton Lane, Bosham, Chichester. *T:* Bosham 573217.

TAMMADGE, Alan Richard; Headmaster, Sevenoaks School, since 1971; *b* 9 July 1921; *m* 1950, Rosemary Anne Broadribb; two *s* one *d*. *Educ:* Bromley County Sch.; Dulwich Coll.; Emmanuel Coll., Cambridge. BA (Maths) 1950; MA 1957. Royal Navy Special Entry, 1940; resigned, 1947 (Lt); Cambridge, 1947-50; Lectr, RMA Sandhurst, 1950-55; Asst Master, Dulwich College, 1956-58; Head of Mathematics Dept, Abingdon School, 1958-67; Master, Magdalen College School, Oxford, 1967-71. FIMA 1965. *Publications:* Complex Numbers, 1965; (jtly) School Mathematics Project Books 1-5, 1965-69; (jtly) General Education, 1969; Parents' Guide to School Mathematics, 1976; articles in Mathemat. Gazette, Mathematics Teacher (USA), Aspects of Education (Hull Univ.). *Recreations:* music, gardens. *Address:* Sevenoaks School, Sevenoaks, Kent. *T:* Sevenoaks 55133.

TAMUNO, Prof. Tekena Nitonye, PhD; Vice-Chancellor, University of Ibadan, Nigeria, since 1975; *b* 28 Jan. 1932; *s* of Chief Mark Tamuno Igbiri and late Mrs Ransoline I. Tamuno; *m* 1963, Olu Grace Tamuno (*née* Esho); two *s* two *d*. *Educ:* University Coll., Ibadan; Birkbeck Coll., Univ. of London; Columbia Univ., New York City. BA (Hons) History, PhD History (London). Univ. of Ibadan: Professor of History, 1971; Head, Dept of History, 1972-75; Dean of Arts, 1973-75; Chairman, Cttee of Deans, 1974-75. Principal, University Coll., Ilorin, Oct.-Nov. 1975. Nat. Vice-Pres., Historical Soc. of Nigeria, 1974-. JP Ibadan, 1976. *Publications:* Nigeria and Elective Representation, 1923-1947, 1966; The Police in Modern Nigeria, 1961-1965, 1970; The Evolution of the Nigerian State: The Southern Phase, 1898-1914, 1972; (ed, with Prof. J. F. A. Ajayi) The University of Ibadan, 1948-1973: A History of the First Twenty-Five Years, 1973; History and History-makers in Modern Nigeria, 1973. *Recreations:* music, photography, swimming, horse-riding. *Address:* University of Ibadan, Ibadan, Nigeria. *T:* (office) 23248, (home) 21165. *Club:* (Hon.) Senior Staff (University of Ibadan).

TAMWORTH, Viscount; Robert William Saswalo Shirley; *b* 29 Dec. 1952; *s* and *heir* of 13th Earl Ferrers, *qv. Educ:* Ampleforth. Teaching in Kenya, under Youth Service Abroad Scheme, 1971-72. Articled to Whinney Murray & Co, CA, 1972-76; admitted to Inst. of Chartered Accountants of England and Wales, 1976. *Address:* Hedenham Hall, Bungay, Suffolk.

TANBURN, Jennifer Jephcott; Head of Research and Consumer Affairs, since 1975, a Director, since 1976, Booker McConnell UK food distribution division; Member, Marketing Policy Committee of Central Council for Agricultural and Horticultural Co-operation; *b* 6 Oct. 1929; *d* of late Harold Jephcott Tanburn and of Elise Noel Tanburn (*née* Armour).

Educ: St Joseph's Priory, Dorking; Settrington Sch., Hampstead; University Coll. of the South West, Exeter (BSc(Econ)). Market Research Dept, Unilever Ltd, 1951-52; Research and Information, Lintas Ltd, 1952-66; Head of Div., 1962-66; Head of Special Projects, 1966-74. Member: Market Research Soc.; Marketing Gp of GB; BA Bd, 1974-76. *Publications:* Food, Women and Shops, 1968; People, Shops and the '70s, 1970; Superstores in the '70s, 1972; Retailing and the Competitive Challenge: a study of retail trends in the Common Market, Sweden and the USA, 1974; articles on retailing and marketing subjects. *Recreations:* travel, golf, gardening, dressmaking, television viewing, reading. *Address:* 8 Ellwood Rise, Vache Lane, Chalfont St Giles, Bucks HP8 4SU. *T:* Chalfont St Giles 5205. *Club:* Beaconsfield Golf.

TANCRED, Sir H. L.; see Lawson-Tancred.

TANDY, Jessica; actress, stage and screen; *b* London, 7 June 1909; *d* of Harry Tandy and Jessie Helen (*née* Horspool); *m* 1st, 1932, Jack Hawkins (marr. diss.); one *d*; 2nd, 1942, Hume Cronyn (Young); one *s* one *d*. *Educ:* Dame Owen's Girls' Sch.; Ben Greet Acad. of Acting. Birmingham Repertory Theatre, 1928; first London appearance, 1929; first New York appearance, 1930; subsequently alternated between London and New York. *New York plays include:* The Matriarch, 1930; The Last Enemy, 1930; Time and the Conways, 1937; The White Steed, 1939; Geneva, 1940; Jupiter Laughs, 1940; Anne of England, 1941; Yesterday's Magic, 1942; A Streetcar Named Desire, 1947-49 (Antoinette Perry Award, 1948); Hilda Crane, 1950; The Fourposter, 1951-53 (Comœdia Matinee Club Bronze Medallion, 1952); Madame Will You Walk?, 1953; Face to Face, 1954; the Honeys, 1955; A Day by the Sea, 1955; The Man in the Dog Suit, 1957-58; Triple Play, 1959; Five Finger Exercise, 1959 (New York League's Delia Austria Medal, 1960); The Physicists, 1964; A Delicate Balance, 1966-67; Camino Real, 1970; Home, 1971; All Over, 1971; Promenade All (tour), 1972; Happy Days, Not I (Samuel Beckett Festival), 1972 (Drama Desk Award, 1973); Tours: Not I, 1973; Many Faces of Love, 1974, 1975 and 1976; Noel Coward in Two Keys, 1974, 1975. *London plays include:* The Rumour, 1929; Autumn Crocus, Lyric, 1931; Children in Uniform, Duchess, 1932; Hamlet, New, 1934; French without Tears, Criterion, 1936; Anthony and Anna, Whitehall, 1935. Open-Air Theatre, London, 1933 and 1939; Old Vic, 1937 and 1940, leading Shakespearian rôles, etc. Toured Canada, 1939; tour of US with husband, (poetry and prose readings), 1954; they also toured Summer Theatres (in plays), 1957. Opening Season of the Tyrone Guthrie Theatre Minneapolis, USA: 1963: Hamlet; Three Sisters; Death of A Salesman; 1965: The Way of the World, The Cherry Orchard and The Caucasian Chalk Circle. The Miser, Los Angeles, 1968; Heartbreak House, Shaw Festival, Niagara-on-the-Lake, Ontario, 1968; Tchin-Tchin, Chicago, 1969; Eve, The Way of the World and A Midsummer Night's Dream, Stratford, Ontario Festival, 1976; Long Day's Journey Into Night, London, Ontario, 1977; The Gin Game, Long Wharf Theatre, New Haven, Conn, 1977. *Films include:* The Indiscretions of Eve, The Seventh Cross, The Valley of Decision, Dragonwyck, The Green Years, A Woman's Vengeance, Forever Amber, September Affair, Rommel-Desert Fox, A Light in the Forest, Adventures of a Young Man, The Birds, Butley. *Television:* all major American dramatic programs. Obie Award, 1972-73. Hon. LLD, Univ. of Western Ontario, 1974. *Address:* Pound Ridge, New York 10576, USA.

TANG, Sir Shiu-kin, Kt 1964; CBE 1957 (OBE 1949; MBE 1934); JP; Chairman and Managing Director of Kowloon Motor Bus Co. (1933) Ltd since its inception; *b* 21 Mar. 1901; *s* of late Tang Chi-Ngong, JP; *m* May Fung. *Educ:* Queen's Coll., Hong Kong; St Stephen's Coll., Hong Kong. Dir, Tung Wah Hosp., 1924 (Chm. Bd of Dirs, 1928); Life Mem., Court of Univ. of Hong Kong; Member: Urban Coun., 1938-41; St John Coun. for Hong Kong, St John Ambulance Assoc. and Bde; Grantham Scholarships Fund Cttee; Cttee of Aberdeen Tech. Sch.; Chinese Temples Cttee, 1934-64; Bd of Chinese Perm. Cemetery; Tung Wah Gp of Hosps Adv. Bd; Po Leung Kuk Perm. Bd of Dirs (Chm. 1932); Exec. Cttee, Nethersole, Alice and Ho Miu Ling Hosp.; Trustee, Street Sleepers' Shelter Soc.; Vice-Pres. and Trustee of Hong Kong Br., Brit. Red Cross Soc.; Vice-President: The Boy Scouts' Assoc.; S China Athletic Assoc.; Adviser: Hongkong Juvenile Care Centre; Chinese Chamber of Commerce. Hon. LLD, Hong Kong, 1961. JP Hong Kong, 1929. Certificate of Honour Class I, and Life Mem., British Red Cross Soc., 1967. KStJ 1962. *Address:* 5 Broom Road, Hong Kong.

TANGE, Sir Arthur (Harold), AC 1977; Kt 1959; CBE 1955 (OBE 1953); Secretary, Department of Defence, since 1970; *b* 18 August 1914; 2nd *s* of late Charles L. Tange, Solicitor, Gosford,

New South Wales; *m* 1940, Marjorie Florence, 2nd *d* of late Professor Edward O. G. Shann; one *s* one *d*. *Educ:* Gosford High School; Western Australia University (BA; 1st Cl. Hons Economics). Joined Bank of NSW, 1931; Economist, Bank of NSW, 1938; Economic Research in Commonwealth Depts, Canberra, 1942-46. Entered Australian Diplomatic Service, 1946; First Secretary, Australian Mission to United Nations, 1946-48; Counsellor, United Nations Division, Canberra, 1948-50; Assistant Secretary, Department of External Affairs, Canberra, 1950-53; Minister at Australian Embassy, Washington, 1953-54; Secretary of Dept of External Affairs, Canberra, 1954-65; High Comr in India and Ambassador to Nepal, 1965-70. Represented Australia at many international economic and trade conferences, 1944-63. *Publication:* (jointly) Australia Foots the Bill, 1942. *Recreation:* fishing. *Address:* 12 La Perouse Street, Canberra, ACT 2603, Australia. *Club:* Commonwealth (Canberra).

TANGNEY, Dame Dorothy Margaret, DBE 1968; Senator for West Australia, 1943-68; *b* 13 March 1911; *d* of E. Tangney, Claremont, West Australia. *Educ:* St Joseph's Convent, Fremantle, University of West Australia. Teaching staff, Education Department, West Australia. First woman to be elected to Commonwealth Senate. Mem., Standing Cttee, Convocation, University of West Australia. *Recreations:* tennis, motoring, badminton, reading. *Address:* 12 Mary Street, Claremont, WA 6010, Australia. *T:* 31 2631.

TANKERVILLE, 9th Earl of, *cr* 1714; **Charles Augustus Grey Bennet;** Baron Ossulston, 1682; Flight Lieutenant RAFVR; *b* 28 July 1921; *er s* of 8th Earl of Tankerville, and of Roberta, *d* of late Percy Mitchell; *S* father, 1971; *m* 1943, Virginia Diether (from whom he obtained a divorce, 1950), Vancouver; one *d*; 1954, Georgiana Lilian Maude, *d* of late Gilbert Wilson, DD, of Vancouver, Canada; one *s* two *d* (of whom one *s* one *d* are twins). Joined RAF 1941; Flight Lieut 1943. *Heir: s* Lord Ossulston, *qv. Address:* 139 Olympia Way, San Francisco, Calif, USA.

TANLAW, Baron *cr* 1971 (Life Peer), of Tanlawhill, Dumfries; **Simon Brooke Mackay;** Chairman and Managing Director: Chronolog Systems Ltd, since 1973; Fandstan Ltd, since 1973; *b* 30 March 1934; *s* of 2nd Earl of Inchcape; *m* 1st, 1959, Joanna Susan, *d* of Major J. S. Hirsch; one *s* two *d* (and one *s* decd); 2nd, 1976, Rina Siew Yong Tan, *d* of late Tiong Cha Tan and Mrs Tan. *Educ:* Eton College; Trinity College, Cambridge (MA 1966). Served as 2nd Lt XII Royal Lancers, Malaya. Trinity Coll., Cambridge, 1954-57. Inchcape Group of Companies, India and Far East, 1960-66; Managing Director, Inchcape & Co., 1967-71; Chairman, Thwaites & Reed Ltd, 1970-74. Chm., Building Cttee, UC at Buckingham, 1973-. Contested (L) Galloway, by-election and gen. election, 1959, and gen. election, 1964. Joint Treasurer, 1971-72, Dep. Chm., 1972, Scottish Liberal Party; Pres., Kensington Lib. Assoc. Pres., Sarawak Assoc., 1973-75. Inventor, Chronolog system of time measurement. *Recreations:* normal. *Address:* Tanlawhill, Eskdalemuir, By Langholm, Dumfriesshire. *T:* Eskdalemuir 273; 14/16 Cockspur Street, SW1. *T:* 01-839 1414. *Clubs:* White's, Buck's, National Liberal.

TANN, Florence Mary, CBE 1952; MA Cantab; *b* 12 Aug. 1892; *d* of William Robert Baldwin Tann, organist and choirmaster. *Educ:* Norwich High School; Girton Coll., Cambridge. Teaching in schools in S Africa, 1915-18; English Lecturer, University of Witwatersrand, Johannesburg, 1918-19; Organiser, National Union of Societies for Equal Citizenship, 1920-21; HM Inspector of Schools, 1921; Divisional Inspector, Board of Education, 1940-45; Chief Inspector, Primary Schools, Ministry of Education, 1945-52. Member National Book League. *Recreations:* gardening and needlework. *Address:* 17 Cedar Way, Henfield, West Sussex. *T:* Henfield 2488. *Club:* University Women's.

TANNER, Dr Bernice Alture; General Practitioner in London W11 area; Member, Supplementary Benefits Commission, since 1976; *b* 23 Sept. 1917; *m* 1942, Prof. James M. Tanner, MD, FRCP, FRCPsych; one *s* one *d*. *Educ:* Cornell Univ., USA; New York Univ.; McGill Univ., Canada; Medical Coll. of Pennsylvania, USA. BA 1939; MD 1943 (Med. Coll., Pa); MRCGP 1962. Convenor, Educational Cttee, London NW Faculty RCGP; Course organizer, St Charles Hosp. Vocational Trng Scheme for Gen. Practice; Mem., AHA Cttee paediatric care, London NW Area. *Publication:* (ed) Language and Communication in General Practice, 1976. *Recreations:* music, postgraduate medical education. *Address:* 21 Holland Villas Road, W14 8DH. *T:* 01-603 7881.

TANNER, Sir Edgar (Stephen), Kt 1968; CBE 1957; ED; Member for Ripponlea, then for Caulfield, Victoria, in Victorian Legislative Assembly (Chairman of Committees), since 1955; Chairman (formerly Hon. Secretary and Treasurer), Australian Olympic Federation; *b* 1914; *s* of late Edgar Tanner; *m* 1938, Edna, *d* of late Miles de H. Ponsonby; one *s* one *d*. *Educ:* All Saints' Gram. Sch., Melbourne; Melbourne Univ. Served War of 1939-45 as Captain AIF (prisoner). Victorian Legislative Assembly: Member: Industries and Labour Cttee; Constitution Cttee; State Develt Cttee; Liberal Party Jt Policy Cttee. Hon. Sec. Organising Cttee, Olympic Games, Melbourne, 1956; Hon. Gen. Manager Australian Teams: Olympic Games, London, 1948; Commonwealth Games, Perth, 1962; Member Australian Delegn: Olympic Games, Helsinki 1952, Rome 1960, Tokyo 1964, Mexico City 1968, Munich 1972, Montreal 1976; Commonwealth Games, Auckland 1950, Edinburgh 1970, Christchurch 1973. President: Olympians International; Australian Amateur Boxing Union; Victorian AAA; Aust. Sen. Execs Soc. Life Member: Royal Children's Hosp.; Aust. Olympic Fedn; Aust. Commonwealth Games Assoc.; Victorian Olympic Council; Victorian Amateur Boxing Assoc.; Victorian Amateur Wrestling Assoc.; Commonwealth Parly Assoc.; Caulfield Historical Soc. *Address:* 190 Hawthorn Road, Caulfield, Vic. 3161, Australia. *Clubs:* Naval and Military, Amateur Sports, Melbourne Cricket (Melbourne); Elwood Serviceman's.

TANNER, Dr John Ian; Director, Royal Air Force Museum, since 1963; *b* London, 2 Jan. 1927; *o s* of R. A. and I. D. M. Tanner; *m* 1953, April Rothery; one *d*. *Educ:* City of London Library Sch.; Universities of London and Nottingham. MA, PhD Nottingham. Reading Public Library, 1950; Archivist-Librarian, Kensington Library, 1950-51; Leighton House Art Gall. and Museum, 1951-53; Curator, Librarian and Tutor, RAF Coll., 1953-63; Hon. Sec., Old Cranwellian Assoc., 1956-64; Extra-mural Lectr in History of Art, Univ. of Nottingham, 1959-63. Chm., Internat. Air Museum Cttee; Vice-Pres., Guild of Aviation Artists. FLA, FMA, FRHistS, FRAeS, FSA. Freeman, City of London, 1966; Liveryman, Worshipful Co. of Gold and Silver Wyre Drawers, 1966. Hon. Mem. Collegio Araldico of Rome, 1963; CStJ 1975. *Publications:* (ed) List of Cranwell Graduates, 2nd edn, 1963; (jtly) Encyclopedic Dictionary of Heraldry, 1968; How to trace your Ancestors, 1971; Man in Flight (limited edn), 1973; The Royal Air Force Museum: one hundred years of aircraft history, 1973; (with W. E. May and W. Y. Carman) Badges and Insignia of the British Armed Services, 1974; Charles I, 1974; Who's Famous in Your Family: a Reader's Digest guide to genealogy, 1975; Wings of the Eagle (exhibition catalogue), 1976; Editor, RAF Museum Air Publication series, 5 vols; General Editor: Museums and Libraries (Internat. Series); Studies in Air History; reviews and articles in professional and other jls. *Recreations:* cricket, opera, reading. *Address:* Flat One, 57 Drayton Gardens, SW10 9RU. *Clubs:* Athenæum, Buck's, Reform, MCC, Royal Air Force.

TANNER, John W., FRIBA, FRTPI; Director, United Nations Relief and Works Agency for Palestine Refugees, Jordan, since 1971; *b* 15 Nov. 1923; *s* of Walter George Tanner and Elizabeth Wilkes Tanner (*née* Humphreys); *m* 1948, Hazel Harford Harford-Jones; one *s* two *d*. *Educ:* Clifton Coll.; Liverpool Univ. Sch. of Architecture and Dept of Civic Design. MCD, BArch (Hons). Sen. Planning Officer, Nairobi, 1951; Architect i/c African Housing, 1953; Hon. Sec., Kenya Chapter of Architects, 1954; UN Relief and Works Agency: Architect and Planning Officer, Beirut, 1955; Chief Techn. Div., 1957; Actg Chef de Cabinet, 1970. Past Mem. Cttee, Fedn of Internat. Civil Servants Assoc., 1968-70. *Buildings:* vocational and teacher training centres, schools; low cost housing and health centres; E African Rugby Union HQ, Nairobi; training centres: Damascus Vocational, Syria; Siblin, Lebanon; Ramallah Women's; Wadi Seer; Amman, Jordan. *Publications:* The Colour Problem in Liverpool: accommodation or assimilation, 1951; Building for the UNRWA/UNESCO Education and Training Programme, 1968. *Recreations:* formerly: Rugby football (Waterloo, Lancs, 1950; Kenya Harlequins (Captain 1955), Kenya and E Africa); skiing. *Address:* UNRWA, Jordan; 10 Yeomans Drive, Aston, Hants. *Clubs:* Ski Club of GB; Kandahar Ski; Delhamyeh Country (Lebanon); City, Royal Jordanian Automobile (Jordan).

TANNER, Lawrence Edward, CVO 1953 (MVO 1932, 5th cl. 1932, 4th cl. 1948); MA, FSA; Emeritus Librarian, Westminster Abbey (Librarian, 1956-72; Keeper of the Muniments, 1926-66); Secretary HM's Royal Almonry, 1921-64; *b* 12 Feb. 1890; *y s* of Ralph Tanner, Senior Assistant Master, Westminster School, and Lucy L. le G., *d* of G. L. Phipps Eyre; *m* 1945, Joan Doreen (*d* 1971), *e d* of Hon. Assheton N. Curzon. *Educ:* Westminster; Pembroke College, Cambridge. Hist. Tripos Pts I and II;

Winchester Reading Prize, Cambridge University, 1912; BA, 1912; MA, 1919; Lieutenant (Gen. List), European War; Master, History Form, Westminster School, 1919-32; Clerk to Worshipful Company of Weavers, 1919-60 (Member Court, 1960); Upper Bailiff, Weavers Company, 1963-64. FSA 1926 (Vice-President, 1951-55); FRHistS, 1929 (Council, 1936-39); Vice-President, Society of Genealogists, 1939; Hon. Vice-Pres., R Arch. Inst. 1952. President, Brit. Archæological Association, 1951-56. OStJ, 1931. Gold Staff Officer, Coronations 1937 and 1953. Hon. DLitt Southampton, 1967. *Publications:* Westminster School, its Buildings and their Associations, 1923; Story of Westminster Abbey, 1932; Westminster School: A History, 1934 (2nd ed 1951); Recent Investigations regarding the fate of the Princes in the Tower, 1935; Unknown Westminster Abbey (King Penguin), 1948; The History of the Coronation, 1952; The History and Treasures of Westminster Abbey, 1953; Recollections of a Westminster Antiquary, 1969; articles and lectures on Westminster Abbey, etc. *Recreation:* fishing. *Address:* 32 Westminster Mansions, Great Smith Street, SW1P 3BP. *T:* 01-222 5753. *Club:* Athenæum.

TANNER, Norman Cecil, FRCS; Hon. Consulting Surgeon: Charing Cross Hospital; St James's Hospital, London; *b* 13 June 1906; *s* of late Henry John Tanner and of Mrs Annie Tanner, Bristol; *m* 1940, Dr Evelyn Winifred Glennie, Aberdeen; two *s* one *d. Educ:* Merchant Venturers School, Bristol; Bristol University. MB, ChB 1929, MD 1954, Bristol; MRCS, LRCP 1929; FRCS 1931. Resident hosp. appts, many Bristol and London hosps. Inaugurated gastro-enterological dept at St James's Hosp., 1939; Jacksonian Prize, 1948; Lectures: First Simpson-Smith Memorial, 1949; Macarthur, Edinburgh, 1951; Lettsomian, London, 1954; Price, Univ. of Utah, 1966; Gallie, Univ. of Toronto, 1968; Moynihan, Leeds, 1969; Visiting Prof. of Surgery: Ein Shams Univ., Cairo, 1954; Royal North Shore Hosp., Sydney, Australia, 1960; Canadian Univs, 1965; Univ. of Los Angeles, 1968; Univ. of Quebec, 1971; Univ. of Singapore, 1971; Hunterian Prof., RCS, 1960 (Past Mem. Council, RCS). Mem., Editorial Bd, Indian Jl of Cancer; formerly: Vice-Chm., British Journal of Surgery; Asst Editor, Gut. Visitor for King Edward VII Hosp. Fund for London. Former Examr in Surgery to Univs of Cambridge and London. President: Clinical Sect, RSM, 1961-63; Sect of Surgery, 1965-66; British Soc. Gastro-enterology, 1967-68; W London Med. Chirurgical Soc., 1968-69. Hon. Lectr in Surgery, St Thomas' Hosp. Liveryman, Soc. of Apothecaries, 1971; Freeman, City of London, 1969. Hon. FACS 1966; Hon. FRCSI, 1969; Hon. FRSM 1976; Hon. Member: Bristol Medico-Chirurgical Soc.; Wessex Surgeons Club; Hellenic Soc. of Surgery, 1973; Hon. Fellow, Assoc. of Surgeons of E Africa. Grand Cross, Patriarchal Order, St Mark, Alexandria; Grand Band of Star of Africa (Liberia). *Publications:* (ed) Tumours of the Oesophagus, 1961; chapters in: Techniques in British Surgery, 1950; Recent Advances in Surgery, 1959; Modern Operative Surgery, 1956; Operative Surgery, 1956; Management for Abdominal Operations, 1953, 1957; Abdominal Operations, 1952; Modern Trends in Gastroenterology, 1958; Demonstrations of Operative Surgery for Nurses; Cancer, Vol. 4 1958; many publications in The Medical Annual, Brit. Jl of Surg., Lancet, BMJ, etc. *Recreations:* golf, ski-ing, music. *Address:* 89 Rivermead Court, SW6 3SA. *T:* 01-736 2312. 5 Beaufort Road, Clifton, Bristol BS8 2JT. *Clubs:* Athenæum, Hurlingham, Coombe Wood Golf.

TANSLEY, Sir Eric (Crawford), Kt 1953; CMG 1946; Chairman, Pacol, 1962-72; formerly Director: Bank of West Africa; Standard Bank Ltd; Standard & Chartered Banking Group Ltd; *b* 25 May 1901; *o s* of William and Margaret Tansley; *m* 1931, Iris, *yr d* of Thomas Richards; one *s* one *d. Educ:* Mercers' Sch. Formerly: Mem., Colonial, now Commonwealth, Development Corporation, 1948-51, 1961-68; Chairman: London Cocoa Terminal Market Assoc., 1932; Cocoa Assoc. of London, 1936-37; Marketing Director, West African Produce Control Board (Colonial Office), 1940-47. Retired, 1961 as Managing Director, Ghana Cocoa Marketing Co. and Adviser, Nigerian Produce Marketing Co. *Address:* 11 Cadogan Square, SW1. *T:* 01-235 2752.

TANZANIA, Archbishop of, since 1970; **Most Rev. John Sepeku;** Bishop of Dar-es-Salaam since 1965. *Educ:* Hegongo Theological College. Deacon, 1938; priest, 1940; Curate, Diocese of Zanzibar, 1938-55; Priest-in-charge, 1955-60; Canon of Zanzibar, 1957-60; Archdeacon of Magila, 1960-63; Vicar-General of Zanzibar, 1963-65; Assistant Bishop of Zanzibar, 1963-65. *Address:* PO Box 25016, Ilala, Dar-es-Salaam, Tanzania, E Africa.

TAPLIN, Walter; author and journalist; *b* Southampton, 4 Aug. 1910; *m*; three *s* two *d. Educ:* University College, Southampton (Foundation Scholar); The Queen's Coll., Oxford (Southampton

Exhibitioner). Tutor-Organiser for Adult Education, W Hants and E Dorset, 1936-38; Editorial Staff of The Economist, 1938-40; Ministry of Food, 1940-42; Offices of the War Cabinet (Central Statistical Office), 1942-45; joined the Spectator as Asst Editor, 1946; Editor, 1953-54; Senior Economist, Iron and Steel Board, 1955-56; Research Fellow in Advertising and Promotional Activity, London School of Economics and Political Science, 1957-61. Editor: Accountancy, 1961-71; Accounting and Business Research, 1971-75. *Publications:* Advertising: A New Approach, 1960; Origin of Television Advertising, 1961; History of the British Steel Industry (with J. C. Carr), 1962. *Recreation:* reading. *Address:* Parson's Field, Long Bredy, Dorchester, Dorset. *T:* Long Bredy 360. *Club:* Reform.

TAPP, Maj.-Gen. Sir Nigel (Prior Hanson), KBE 1960 (CBE 1954); CB 1956; DSO 1945; DL; *b* 11 June 1904; *y s* of late Lt-Col J. Hanson Tapp, DSO, and of late Mrs Hanson Tapp (*née* Molesworth), Duns, Berwickshire; *m* 1948, Dorothy, *y d* of late Alexander Harvey. *Educ:* Cheltenham College; Royal Military Academy, Woolwich. 2nd Lieutenant RA, 1924; Sudan Defence Force, 1932-38; ADC to Governor-General, Sudan, 1935-36; Staff College, Camberley, 1939; GSO 3, 1 Corps BEF, 1940; GSO 2, War Office, 1940-41; GSO 1 Staff College, Camberley, 1941-42; CO, 7 Field Regt, RA, UK, Normandy, Belgium, and Holland, 1942-45; Comd RA 25 Div., SEAC, 1945; District Commander, Eritrea, 1946-47; Dep. Dir Land/Air Warfare, 1948; Dep. Dir RA, 1949; idc, 1950; Commander 1 Corps Royal Artillery, BAOR, 1951-53; General Officer Commanding 2 AA Group, 1954; Director of Military Training, War Office, 1955-57; GOC East Africa Command, 1957-60; retd 1961; Lieut-Governor and Sec., Royal Hosp., Chelsea, 1967-73. Pres., Assoc. of Service Newspapers, 1974-. Col Comdt, Royal Regt of Artillery, 1963-68. DL Greater London, 1973. *Recreations:* riding and fishing. *Address:* 9 Cadogan Square, SW1. *Club:* Army and Navy.

TAPPER-JONES, Sydney, LLB (London); Town Clerk and Clerk of the Peace, Cardiff, 1942-70; *b* 12 March 1904; *s* of David and Frances Caroline Mary Jones; *m* 1947, Florence Mary (Joan) Hellyer; one *d. Educ:* Pentre (Rhondda) Secondary School. Articled Cousins, Botsford & Co., Solicitors, Cardiff. LLB Lond. (External) (Hons), 1924. Solicitors' Final Exam. (Hons), 1925; Admitted Solicitor, 1925. Managing Clerk with Allen Pratt & Geldard (with whom were amalgamated Vachell & Co.), Solicitors, Cardiff, 1925-27; Cardiff Corporation: Conveyancing Solicitor, 1927-29, Prosecuting Solicitor, 1929-33; Deputy Town Clerk and Deputy Clerk of the Peace, 1933-42; Commissioner for Oaths. Member of Convocation, 1925. Member, Order of St John, 1966. *Address:* Maes-y-Coed, 59 Heath Park Avenue, Cardiff. *T:* Cardiff 751306.

TAPPS-GERVIS-MEYRICK, Lt-Col Sir George David Eliott; see Meyrick.

TAPSELL, Peter Hannay Bailey; MP (C) Horncastle (Lincs) since 1966 (Nottingham West, 1959-64); Junior Conservative Spokesman on Foreign and Commonwealth Affairs, since 1976; *b* 1 Feb. 1930; *s* of late Eustace Tapsell; *m* 1st, 1963, Hon. Cecilia Hawke (marr. diss. 1971), 3rd *d* of 9th Baron Hawke; one *s*; 2nd, 1974, Mlle Gabrielle Jocelyne Mahieu, *e d* of late Jean Mahieu, Normandy, France. *Educ:* Tonbridge; Merton Coll., Oxford (MA). Nat. Service Commn, Royal Sussex Regt, 1948-50 (Middle East). 1st Cl. Hons Mod. Hist., 1953; Hon. Postmaster of Merton Coll., 1953; Librarian of Oxford Union, 1953; Rep. Oxford Union on debating tour of United States, 1954. Personal Asst to Prime Minister (Anthony Eden) during 1955 General Election Campaign. Conservative Research Department, 1954-57 (Social Services and Agriculture). Contested (C) Wednesbury, bye-election, 1957. Member of London Stock Exchange; Member, James Capel & Co. (Stockbrokers); Chairman, Coningsby Club, 1957-58; Jt Chm., British-Caribbean Assoc., 1963-64. Court Mem., Univs of Nottingham and Hull. Vice Pres., Tennyson Soc. Hon. Mem., Brunei Govt Investment Adv. Bd, 1976-. Mem. Organising Cttee, Zaire River Expedn, 1974-75. Hon. Life Mem., 6th Sqdn RAF, 1971. Brunei Dato, 1971. *Recreations:* overseas travel, walking over Lincolnshire wolds, reading. *Address:* Albany, Piccadilly, W1. *T:* 01-734 6641; Roughton Hall, near Woodhall Spa, Lincolnshire. *T:* Horncastle 2572. *Clubs:* Carlton, Hurlingham.

TARBAT, Viscount; John Ruaridh Blunt Grant MacKenzie; *b* 12 June 1948; *s* and *heir* of 4th Earl of Cromartie, *qv*; *m* 1973, Helen, *d* of John Murray. *Educ:* Rannoch School, Perthshire; Strathclyde University. *Recreations:* mountaineering, art, astronomy, geology. *Address:* Castle Leod, Strathpeffer, Ross-shire. *Clubs:* Army and Navy; Scottish Mountaineering.

TARN, Prof. John Nelson; Roscoe Professor of Architecture, University of Liverpool, since 1974; *b* 23 Nov. 1934; *s* of Percival Nelson Tarn and Mary I. Tarn (*née* Purvis); unmarried. *Educ:* Royal Grammar Sch., Newcastle upon Tyne; Univ. of Durham (BArch); Univ. of Cambridge (PhD). 1st cl. hons Dunelm; FRIBA, FRSA, FRHistS. Lectr in Architecture, Univ. of Sheffield, 1963-70; Prof. of Architecture, Univ. of Nottingham, 1970-73. *Publications:* Working Class Housing in Nineteenth Century Britain, 1971; The Peak District National Park: its architecture, 1971; Five Per Cent Philanthropy, 1974. *Recreation:* music. *Address:* 2 Ashmore Close, Barton Hey Drive, Caldy, Wirral, Merseyside L48 2JX. *T:* 051-625 9557.

TARVER, Major-General Charles Herbert, CB 1961; CBE 1958; DSO 1945; DL; jssc; psc; late Infantry; retired Feb. 1964; *b* 6 Oct. 1908; *s* of Major-General A. L. Tarver, CB, CIE, DSO; *m* 1932, Margaret Poad; three *s. Educ:* King's School, Bruton; RMC, Sandhurst. Deputy Director of Military Intelligence, War Office, 1956-58; Assistant Chief of Staff (Intelligence) at Supreme Headquarters, Allied Powers Europe, 1958-61; Chief of Staff to C-in-C Allied Forces Northern Europe, 1961-64. Colonel 1953; Brigadier, 1957; Major-General, 1958. Dep. Col, The Queen's Regt, 1967-71; Hon. Col., 7th Bn, The Queen's Regt (E Kent), 1970-71. DL, Kent, 1968. *Recreations:* golf, fishing. *Address:* Flat 2, 23 Clifton Crescent, Folkestone, Kent.

TASKER, Antony Greaves, CBE 1966 (OBE 1945; MBE 1943); Assistant Secretary-General and Managing Director Commonwealth Fund for Technical Co-operation, Commonwealth Secretariat, 1974-78; *b* 27 March 1916; *o s* of late Captain R. G. Tasker, Worcestershire Regt, and of Vera, *d* of Rev. T. M. Everett (she *m* 2nd, Harold Raymond, OBE, MC, who *d* 1975); *m* 1940, Elizabeth Gilmor, JP, *e d* of late Maj. Harold Carter, TD. *Educ:* Bradfield Coll.; Christ Church, Oxford. Served War of 1939-45 (despatches twice); Western Desert, Sicily, Italy, NW Europe, SE Asia; Col GS(I). Org. Dir, Internat. Tea Market Expansion Bd, 1948-52; Dir Public Rel., Booker Gp of Cos in Guyana, 1954-62 (Chm., 1962-67); Dir, Overseas Develt Inst., 1968-74. Member, Br. Guiana Senate, 1961-64 (MLC, 1957-61); Governor: Inst. of Develt Studies, Sussex, 1968-78; Oversea Service Coll., 1968-78; Mem. Council, Overseas Develt Inst., 1975-78. Member: Econ. and Social Cttee, EEC, 1973-74; Exec. Cttee, British Council, 1970-74; Voluntary Cttee on Overseas Aid and Develt, 1968-74; British Volunteer Programme, 1968-74. US Bronze Star, 1944; Officer, US Legion of Merit, 1945.

TASKER, Rev. Canon Derek Morris Phipps; Canon Residentiary and Treasurer of Southwark Cathedral since 1962; Director of Post-ordination Training for Diocese of Southwark, since 1965; Director of Ordinands, since 1968; *b* 15 Nov. 1916; *er s* of late Morris Bennet and Geraldine Emily Tasker. *Educ:* Sherborne Sch.; Exeter Coll., Oxford (BA, DipTheol); Westcott House, Cambridge. Curate, St Mary Redcliffe, Bristol, 1939-47; Vicar, St Stephen, Southmead, Bristol, 1947-55; King George VI Training Officer, Church of England Youth Council, 1955-62. *Publications:* The Parish and Young People, 1957; Letters to an Apprentice, 1958; Vocation and Work, 1960; Training the Youth Group, 1960. *Recreations:* English literature, contemporary theatre, cricket. *Address:* 2 Sandover House, Ormond Road, Richmond, Surrey. *T:* 01-948 0463.

TASKER, Sir Theodore James, Kt 1937; CIE 1932; OBE 1919; Indian Civil Service; retired; County Councillor, Dorset (Swanage-East), 1946; County Alderman, 1955-70; *b* 20 Jan. 1884; *s* of late Rev. John Greenwood Tasker, DD; *m* 1915, Jessie Helen Mellis-Smith (Kaisar-i-Hind Gold Medal) (*d* 1974); three *s* one *d. Educ:* King Edward's School, Birmingham; Trinity Coll., Cambridge (Major Scholar in Classics, First Class Honours Classical Tripos). Entered ICS 1908; Under-Secretary to Madras Govt, 1913-15; District Magistrate, Civil and Military Station, Bangalore, 1917-22; Commissioner of Coorg, 1923-26; services lent to Government of Nizam of Hyderabad as Director-General of Revenue and Revenue Secretary, 1927-35, and Member of Council, 1935-42; Supervisor, ICS. Probationers' Training, Dehra Dun, 1942-44; retired, 1944. *Address:* Southover, Swanage, Dorset BH19 2JF. *T:* Swanage 2033.

TASMANIA, Bishop of, since 1963; **Rt. Rev. Robert Edward Davies,** MA, ThD; *b* Birkenhead, England, 30 July 1913; *s* of late R. A. Davies, Canberra; *m* 1953, Helen M., *d* of H. M. Boucher; two *d. Educ:* Cessnock High School; Queensland University; St John's Theological College, Morpeth, NSW. Assistant Priest, Christ Church Cathedral, Newcastle, NSW, 1937-41. War of 1939-45: Toc H Army Chaplain, 1941-42; Chaplain, Royal Australian Air Force, Middle East and Mediterranean, 1942-46. Vice-Warden, St John's College,

University of Queensland, Brisbane, 1946-48; Archdeacon of Canberra and Rector of Canberra, 1949-53; Archdeacon of Wagga Wagga, NSW, 1953-60; Assistant Bishop of Newcastle and Warden of St John's Theological College, Morpeth, NSW, 1960-63. *Recreations:* golf, tennis. *Address:* Bishopscourt, 26 Fitzroy Place, Sandy Bay, Tasmania 7005, Australia. *Clubs:* Tasmanian, Naval Military and Air Force of Tas. (Tas.).

TATA, Dr Jamshed Rustom, FRS 1973; Head, Laboratory of Developmental Biochemistry, National Institute for Medical Research, since 1973; *b* 13 April 1930; *s* of Rustom and Gool Tata; *m* 1954, Renée Suzanne Zanetto; two *s* one *d. Educ:* Univ. of Bombay (BSc); Univ. of Paris, Sorbonne (D-ès-Sc). Postdoctoral Fellow, Sloan-Kettering Inst., New York, 1954-56; Beit Memorial Fellow, Nat. Inst. for Med. Research, 1956-60; Vis. Scientist, Wenner-Gren Inst., Stockholm, 1960-62; Mem., Scientific Staff, MRC, Nat. Inst. for Med. Research, 1962-. Visiting Prof.: King's Coll., London, 1968-69, and 1970-77; Univ. of California, Berkeley, 1969-70; Vis. Senior Scientist, Nat. Institutes of Health, USA. Van Meter Award, 1954; Colworth Medal, 1966; Medal of Soc. for Endocrinology, 1973. *Publications:* (jtly): The Thyroid Hormones, 1959; The Chemistry of Thyroid Diseases, 1960; papers in jls of: Biochemistry; Developmental Biology. *Address:* 15 Bittacy Park Avenue, Mill Hill, NW7 2HA. *T:* 01-346 6291.

TATE, Ellalice; *see* Hibbert, Eleanor.

TATE, Francis Herbert; Vice-Chairman, Tate & Lyle Ltd, since 1962; *b* 3 April 1913; 2nd *s* of late Alfred Herbert Tate and late Elsie Tate (*née* Jelf Petit); *g g s* of Sir Henry Tate, Bt, founder of Henry Tate & Sons (now Tate & Lyle, Ltd) and donor of the Tate Gallery; *m* 1937, Esther, *d* of late Sir John Bromhead-Matthews, KC, JP, and late Lady Matthews, JP; one *s* two *d. Educ:* Private Tutor; Christ Church Oxford (BA 1934, MA 1963). Called to the Bar, Inner Temple, 1937. War Service, 1940-46, Royal Corps of Military Police (Lt-Col). Joined Tate & Lyle Ltd, 1946; Man. Dir, 1949. Chairman: British Sugar Bureau, 1966-; Council, London Chamber of Commerce, 1962-64 (Vice-Pres., 1964-); Federation of Commonwealth Chambers of Commerce, 1964-69. Chm. Central Council, Royal Commonwealth Society, 1969-72; Mem. Council, Australia Soc., 1974. Governor, Commonwealth Inst., 1975-. Dir, Lloyds Bank Ltd, Southern Region, 1977-. Master of Mercers' Company, 1967-68. *Recreations:* golf (played for Oxford, 1934-35); motoring. *Address:* High Housen, Hook Heath, Woking, Surrey. *T:* Woking 60532. *Club:* Carlton.

TATE, Lt-Col Sir Henry, 4th Bt, *cr* 1898; TD; DL; late Royal Welch Fusiliers TA; *b* 29 June 1902; *s* of Sir Ernest Tate, 3rd Bt and Mildred Mary, 2nd *d* of F. H. Gossage of Camp Hill, Woolton, Liverpool; *S* father, 1939; *m* 1927, Nairne, *d* of late Saxon Gregson-Ellis, JP; two *s.* Sometime Lt Grenadier Guards. Joint Master Cottesmore Hounds, 1946-58. Councillor Rutland CC, 1958-69, 1970-74; High Sheriff of Rutland, 1949-50. Commanding 1st Bn Rutland Home Guard, 1954-57. DL, Co. of Rutland, 1964. *Heir: s* Henry Saxon Tate [*b* 28 Nov. 1931; *m* 1st, 1953, Sheila Ann (marr. diss. 1975), *e d* of Duncan Robertson; four *s*, including twin *s*; 2nd, 1975, Virginia Sturm]. *Address:* Preston Lodge, Withcote, Oakham, Rutland, Leics LE15 8PP; Galltfaenan, Trefnant, Clwyd. *Club:* Buck's.

TATE, Phyllis (Margaret Duncan), (Mrs Alan Frank); composer (free-lance); *b* 6 April 1911; *d* of Duncan Tate, FRIBA, and Annie S. Holl; *m* 1935, Alan Frank; one *s* one *d. Educ:* Royal Academy of Music, London. FRAM 1964. *Works:* (some commissioned by the BBC, and for festivals, etc, and several commercially recorded): Saxophone Concerto, 1944; Nocturne for four voices, 1945; Sonata for clarinet and cello, 1947; String Quartet, 1952; Choral Scene from The Bacchae, 1953; The Lady of Shalott, for tenor and instruments, 1956; Air and Variations for violin, clarinet and piano, 1958; London Fields, 1958; Witches and Spells, choral suite, 1959; Opera: The Lodger, 1960; Television Opera: Dark Pilgrimage, 1963; A Victorian Garland, for two voices and instruments, 1965; Gravestones, for Cleo Laine, 1966; Seven Lincolnshire Folk Songs, for chorus and instruments, 1966; A Secular Requiem, for chorus and orchestra, 1967; Christmas Ale, for soloist, chorus and orchestra, 1967; Apparitions, for tenor and instruments, 1968; Coastal Ballads, for baritone and instruments, 1969; Illustrations, for brass band, 1969; To Words by Joseph Beaumont, for women's chorus, 1970; Variegations, for solo viola, 1970; Serenade to Christmas, for mezzo-soprano, chorus and orchestra, 1972; Lyric Suite, for piano duet, Explorations around a Troubadour Song, for piano solo, 1973; The Rainbow and the Cuckoo, for oboe, violin, viola and cello, 1974; Sonatina Pastorale for harmonica and harpsichord, 1974; Songs of Sundrie Kindes, for tenor and lute, 1975; St Martha and the

Dragon, for narrator, soloists, chorus and orchestra, 1976; A Seasonal Sequence, for viola and piano, 1977; Panorama, for strings, 1977; All the World's a Stage, for chorus and orchestra, 1977; and many small choral pieces, songs and works for young people, including: Street Sounds, The Story of Lieutenant Cockatoo, Twice in a Blue Moon; A Pride of Lions; Invasion. *Address:* 12 Heath Hurst Road, NW3. *T:* 01-435 0607.

TATHAM, Francis Hugh Currer; Editor of Whitaker's Almanack since 1950; Director, Sporting Handbooks Ltd; *b* 29 May 1916; *s* of late Harold Lewis Tatham, Gravesend, Kent, and late Frances Eva (*née* Crook); *m* 1945, Nancy Margaret, *d* of John Robins, Newton Abbot; two *s*. *Educ:* Charterhouse; Christ Church, Oxford. Missioner, Shrewsbury School Mission, Liverpool, 1939-42; Sub-Warden, Mary Ward Settlement, 1942-45; Army Cadet Force, 1943-45; Editor, Church of England Newspaper, 1945-47. Vice-Pres., Harrow RFC. *Recreations:* cricket, walking. *Address:* Two Trees, Fee Farm Road, Claygate, Surrey. *T:* Esher 62493. *Clubs:* Lansdowne, MCC.

TATI, Jacques, (Jacques Tatischeff); French film actor and Director; *b* Pecq, Seine et Oise, 9 Oct. 1908. Stage début as Music Hall artist; subsequently, 1933-, Actor, Director and Script-writer, Gérant de Cady Films. *Films* (many of which have received international awards or prizes) include: Gai Dimanche, 1935; Soigne ton gauche, 1936; L'Ecole des Facteurs, 1947; Jour de Fête, 1947; Les Vacances de Monsieur Hulot, 1951; Mon Oncle, 1958; Play Time, 1968; Trafic (originally titled Yes Monsieur Hulot), 1971; Parade, 1974. Has won several awards for films. *Address:* 12 rue du Château, 92 La Garenne-Colombes, France.

TATISCHEFF, Jacques; see Tati, Jacques.

TATLOW, John Colin, PhD, DSc (Birmingham); CChem; FRIC; Professor of Organic Chemistry since 1959, and Head of Department of Chemistry since 1974, University of Birmingham; *b* 19 Jan. 1923; *s* of Thomas George and Florence Annie Tatlow, Cannock, Staffs; *m* 1946, Clarice Evelyn Mabel, *d* of Eric Millward and Mabel Evelyn Joiner, Sutton Coldfield; two *d*. *Educ:* Rugeley Grammar School, Staffs; University of Birmingham. Scientific Officer, Min. of Supply, 1946-48; University of Birmingham: Lectr in Chemistry, 1948-56; Sen. Lectr, 1956-57; Reader in Organic Chemistry, 1957-59. Council of Chemical Society, 1957-60. Examiner, Royal Inst. of Chemistry, 1963-67. *Publications:* scientific papers mainly in Jl of Chem. Soc., Tetrahedron, Nature, and Jl of Fluorine Chem.; Editor: Advances in Fluorine Chemistry; Jl of Fluorine Chemistry. *Address:* 30 Grassmoor Road, King's Norton, Birmingham B38 8BP. *T:* 021-458 1260.

TATTON BROWN, William Eden, CB 1965; ARIBA; architect; *b* 13 Oct. 1910; *m* 1936, Aileen Hope Johnston Sparrow; two *s* one *d* (and one *d* decd). *Educ:* Wellington Coll.; King's Coll., Cambridge (MA); Architectural Association School, London; School of Planning, London. Special Final Examination of Town Planning Institute. Chief Design Asst, Messrs Tecton, Architects, 1934-38; private practice, 1938-40; Finsbury Borough Council, 1940-41. Served in HM Forces, Major, Royal Engineers, 1941-46. Asst Regional Planning Officer, Min. of Town and Country Planning, 1946-48; Dep. County Architect, Herts CC, 1948-59; Chief Architect, Min. of Health, later Dept of Health and Social Security, 1959-71. Steuben-Corning Research Fellowship, Travelling Scholarship to USA, 1957. Guest Lectr, Internat. Hosp. Confs: Finland, 1966; Holland, 1967; Australia, 1967; Düsseldorf, 1969; Tunisia, 1969; Sweden, 1970; Canada, 1970; S Africa, 1971; WHO Commn to Madrid, 1968. Lecturer and broadcaster. *Publications:* contributor to technical and national press. *Recreations:* building, water-skiing. *Address:* 47 Lansdowne Road, W11. *T:* 01-727 4676.

TATTON-SYKES, Sir (Mark Tatton) Richard, 7th Bt, *cr* 1783; JP; DL; Chairman, Driffield Magistrates, 1969-75; *b* 24 Aug. 1905; *s* of Sir Mark Sykes, 6th Bt, MP, and late Edith Violet, 3rd *d* of Rt. Hon. Sir J. E. Gorst; *S* father, 1919; changed name by deed poll to Tatton-Sykes, 1977; *m* 1942, Virginia (*d* 1970), *o d* of John Gilliat and Lillian (*widow* of 5th Marquess of Anglesey and *d* of Sir George Chetwynd, 4th Bt); four *s* two *d*. *Educ:* Downside; Trinity Coll., Cambridge. Member East Riding County Council, 1931-70, Alderman 1946-70; President: Bridlington Div. Conservative Assoc., 1948-77; East Riding Georgian Soc., 1962-75; E Yorkshire Local History Soc. 1968-71; Northern Counties Concert Soc. Lieutenant 5th Bn The Green Howards, 1925-27; Lt 7th Bn The Green Howards, 1939; served France, 1940; Captain, 1940. Lt-Col 1958. Jt Master, E Middleton Foxhounds, 1931-39; Member, Jockey Club, 1947-; JP E Yorks and N Humberside, 1945-. High Sheriff, Yorks, 1948-49; DL Yorks, 1953, N Humberside, 1974. *Recreations:*

horse breeding, coursing, organist. *Heir:* s Tatton Christopher Mark Sykes, *b* 24 Dec. 1943. *Address:* Sledmere, Driffield, North Humberside. *Club:* White's.

TAUNTON, Suffragan Bishop of, since 1977; **Rt. Rev. Peter John Nott;** *b* 30 Dec. 1933; *s* of Cecil Frederick Wilder Nott and Rosina Mabel Bailey; *m* 1961, Elizabeth May Maingot; one *s* three *d*. *Educ:* Bristol Grammar School; Dulwich Coll.; RMA Sandhurst; Fitzwilliam House, Cambridge; Westcott House, Cambridge (MA). Curate of Harpenden, 1961-64; Chaplain of Fitzwilliam Coll., Cambridge, 1964-69; Fellow of Fitzwilliam Coll., 1967-69; Chaplain of New Hall, Cambridge, 1966-69; Rector of Beaconsfield, 1969-77. *Recreations:* music, sketching, gardening, sport. *Address:* Sherford Farm House, Sherford, Taunton, Somerset TA1 3RS. *T:* Taunton 88759.

TAUNTON, Archdeacon of; see Olyott, Ven. L. E.

TAUNTON, Doidge Estcourt, CB 1951; DSO and bar 1945; DL; Secretary, Northamptonshire TA and AFA, 1952-68; *b* 9 Nov. 1902; *s* of late J. G. C. Taunton, Launceston, Cornwall; *m* 1930, Rhona Caroline Wetherall (*d* 1951); one *s* (and one *s* decd). *Educ:* Cheltenham College; RMC Sandhurst; 2nd Lt Northamptonshire Regt, 1923; Lt 1925; Capt. 1935, and Adjt TA, 1932-36; Major 1940; Lt-Col 1941; Col 1948; Temp. Brig. 1945-47 and 1948-52. Served NWF India, 1936-38 (Medal and 2 clasps); War of 1939-45, India and Burma, 1936-45; French Indo-China and Netherlands East Indies, 1945-46 (Medal and clasp); Comd Somaliland Area, 1948-50; Comd 2nd Inf. Brigade, 1950-51; retired pay, 1951. DL Northants, 1969. *Address:* Great Hayne, Duston, Northampton.

TAUSKY, Vilem; FGSM 1968; Director of Opera, Guildhall School of Music, since 1966; Artistic Director, Phoenix Opera Co., since 1967; BBC Conductor since 1950; *b* 20 July 1910; *s* of Emil Tausky, MD, Prerov, Czechoslovakia, and Josefine Ascher, opera singer; *m* 1948, Margaret Helen Powell. *Educ:* Univ. of Brno; Janáček Conservatoire, Brno; Meisterschule, Prague. Military Service in France and England, 1939-45. National Opera House, Brno, Czechoslovakia, 1929-39; Musical Director, Carl Rosa Opera, 1945-49. Guest Conductor: Royal Opera House, Covent Garden, 1951-; Sadler's Wells Opera, 1953-. Czechoslovak Military Cross, 1944; Czechoslovak Order of Merit, 1945. *Publications:* Czechoslovak Christmas Carols, 1942; Oboe Concerto, 1957; Concertino for harmonica and orchestra, 1963; Divertimento for strings, 1966; Soho: Scherzo for orchestra, 1966; Concert Overture for Brass Band, 1969; Cakes and Ale: Overture for Brass Band, 1971; Ballad for Cello and Piano; From Our Village: orchestral suite, 1972; Sonata for Cello and Piano, 1976. *Recreation:* country life. *Address:* 44 Haven Green Court, W5. *T:* 01-997 6512; Rose Cottage, Towersey, near Thame, Oxon. *T:* Thame 2192.

TAVARÉ, Andrew Kenneth; Special Commissioner of Income Tax, since 1976; *b* 10 Jan. 1918; *s* of late L. A. Tavaré, Bromley, Kent; *m* 1950, June Elinor Attwood, Beckenham, Kent; three *s*. *Educ:* Chatham House School, Ramsgate; King's College, London University. LLB (London). Solicitor of the Supreme Court. Served War with 79th HAA Regt (Hertfordshire Yeomanry), RA, 1940-45; N Africa and Italy, rank of Captain. Admitted Solicitor, 1948; Solicitor's Office, Inland Revenue, 1953-; Assistant Solicitor, 1965-75. Consultant Editor of Sergeant on Stamp Duties, 4th edition 1963, to 7th edition 1977. *Publications:* (contrib.) Simon's Taxes, 2nd edn, 1965, and 3rd edn, 1970. *Address:* 32 Marlborough Crescent, Sevenoaks, Kent. *T:* Sevenoaks 51789.

TAVENER, John; composer; Professor of Music at Trinity College of Music since 1969; *b* 28 Jan. 1944; *m* Victoria Marangopoulou. *Educ:* Highgate Sch.; Royal Academy of Music (LRAM). Hon. ARAM, Hon. FTCL. *Publications:* compositions: Piano Concerto; Three Holy Sonnets (Donne); Cain and Abel (1st Prize, Monaco); Little Concerto for Orchestra; The Cappe-makers; Three Songs of T. S. Eliot; Grandma's Footsteps; In Memoriam Igor Stravinsky; Responsorium in memory of Annon Lee; The Whale; Introit for March 27th; Three Surrealist Songs; In Alium; Celtic Requiem; Ultimos Ritos; Thérèse (opera); The Gentle Spirit (opera); Kyklike Kinesis (chamber orch. and tape); Palintropos (solo piano); Canticle of the Mother of God; Last Prayer of Mary Queen of Scots. *Address:* c/o J. & W. Chester Ltd, 7 Eagle 3ourt, EC1.

TAVERNE, Dick, QC 1965; The Director, Institute for Fiscal Studies, since 1970; *b* 18 Oct. 1928; *s* of Dr N. J. M. and Mrs L. V. Taverne; *m* 1955, Janice Hennessey; two *d*. *Educ:* Charterhouse School; Balliol College, Oxford (First in Greats). Oxford Union Debating tour of USA, 1951. Called to Bar, 1954.

MP (Lab) Lincoln, March 1962-Oct. 1972, resigned; MP (Democratic Lab) Lincoln, March 1973-Sept. 1974; Parliamentary Under-Secretary of State, Home Office, 1966-68; Minister of State, Treasury, 1968-69; Financial Secretary to the Treasury, 1969-70. Chm., Public Expenditure (General) Sub-Cttee, 1971-72. Director: Equity and Law Life Assurance Co. Ltd; BOC International. *Publication:* The Future of the Left: Lincoln and after, 1973. *Recreations:* squash, sailing. *Address:* 60 Cambridge Street, SW1V 4QQ.

TAVISTOCK, Marquess of; Henry Robin Ian Russell; a Director, Trafalgar House, since 1977; *b* 21 Jan. 1940; *s* and *heir* of 13th Duke of Bedford, *qv*; *m* 1961, Henrietta Joan, *d* of Henry F. Tiarks, *qv*; three *s. Educ:* Le Rosey, Switzerland; Harvard University. Chm., Cedar Investment Trust, 1977-; Dir, Touche, Remnant and Co., 1977-. *Heir:* s Lord Howland, *qv*. *Address:* Woburn Abbey, Woburn, Bedfordshire. *T:* Woburn 666; 3 Clarendon Place, W2. *T:* 01-262 5588. *Clubs:* White's, Buck's; Jockey Club Rooms; The Brook (New York).

TAYLER, Harold Clive; a Recorder of the Crown Court, since 1974; *b* 4 Nov. 1932; *m* 1959, Catherine Jane (*née* Thomas); two *s* one *d. Educ:* Solihull Sch.; Balliol Coll., Oxford. BCL and BA (Jurisprudence). Called to the Bar, Inner Temple, 1956; in practice, Birmingham, from 1958; Midland and Oxford Circuit. *Recreations:* gardening, swimming, caravanning. *Address:* Drayton House, Drayton Bassett, Tamworth, Staffs B78 3TP. *T:* Tamworth 62709.

TAYLOR; *see* Suenson-Taylor, family name of Baron Grantchester.

TAYLOR, family name of **Barons Taylor, Taylor of Gryfe** and **Taylor of Mansfield.**

TAYLOR, Baron *cr* 1958 (Life Peer), of Harlow; **Stephen James Lake Taylor,** MD, BSc, FRCP; FRCGP; Visiting Professor of Medicine, Memorial University of Newfoundland, since 1973; *b* 30 Dec. 1910; *s* of John Reginald Taylor, MInstCE, and Beatrice Violet Lake Taylor; *m* 1939, Dr May Doris Charity Clifford (*see* Lady Taylor); two *s* one *d. Educ:* Stowe Sch.; St Thomas's Hosp. Med. Sch., Univ. of London. BSc 1st cl. Hons; MB, BS (Hons Hygiene and Forensic Medicine); MD. FRCP 1960. Served War of 1939-45: Surg. Lt-Comdr (Neuro-psychiatric Specialist), RNVR; Dir of Home Intelligence and Wartime Social Survey, MOI, 1941-45. Formerly: Casualty Officer and HP, St Thomas' Hosp.; Grocers' Co. Research Scholar, Med. Unit, St Thomas' Hosp.; Sen. Resident Med. Officer, Royal Free Hosp.; HP, Bethlem Royal Hosp.; Asst Med. Officer, Maudsley Hosp. MP (Lab) Barnet Div. of Herts, 1945-50; PPS to Dep. Prime Minister and Lord President of Council, 1947-50; Under-Sec. of State for Commonwealth Relations and Colonies, 1964-65. Consultant in Occupational Health, Richard Costain Ltd, 1951-64 and 1966-67; Med. Dir, Harlow Industrial Health Service, 1955-64 and 1965-67; Pres. and Vice-Chancellor, Meml Univ. of Newfoundland, 1967-73. Visiting Research Fellow, Nuffield Provincial Hospitals Trust, 1953-55; Chadwick Lectr, RSH, 1963. Mem., Harlow New Town Develt Corp., 1950-64 and 1966-67. Chm., Labour Party Study Group on Higher Educn; Vice-Chm., British Film Inst.; Member: N-W Metropolitan Regional Hosp. Bd; Health Adv. Cttee of Labour Party; Cohen Cttee on Gen. Practice, Beveridge Cttee on BBC; Bd of Governors, UCH. Clarke Lectr, Univ. of Surrey, 1975. Hon. LLD St Thomas Univ., NB, 1972. *Publications:* Scurvy and Carditis, 1937; The Suburban Neurosis, 1938; Mental Illness as a Clue to Normality, 1940; The Psychopathic Tenth, 1941; The Study of Public Opinion, 1943; Battle for Health, 1944; The Psychopath in our Midst, 1949; Shadows in the Sun, 1949; Good General Practice, 1954; The Health Centres of Harlow, 1955; The Survey of Sickness, 1958; First Aid in the Factory, 1960; Mental Health and Environment, 1964; articles in Lancet, etc. *Address:* Plas y Garth, Glyn Ceiriog, near Llangollen, Clwyd. *T:* Glyn Ceiriog 216.

TAYLOR, Lady, (Charity), MB, BS, MRCS, LRCP; retired as Assistant Director and Inspector of Prisons (Women), (1959-66); Member, BBC General Advisory Council, 1964-67; President, Newfoundland and Labrador Social Welfare Council, 1968-71; *b* Sept. 1914; *d* of W. George and Emma Clifford; *m* 1939, Stephen J. L. Taylor (*see* Lord Taylor); two *s* one *d. Educ:* The Grammar School, Huntingdon; London (Royal Free Hospital) School of Medicine for Women. HS Royal Free Hospital; HS Elizabeth Garrett Anderson Hospital; Assistant Medical Officer HM Prison, Holloway; Medical Officer, HM Prison Holloway; Governor, HM Prison Holloway, 1945-59. *Recreations:* reading, conversation. *Address:* Plas y Garth, Glyn Ceiriog, near Llangollen, Clwyd.

TAYLOR OF GRYFE, Baron *cr* 1968 (Life Peer), of Bridge of Weir; **Thomas Johnston Taylor;** DL; FRSE; Chairman: Economic Forestry Group, since 1976; Morgan Grenfell (Scotland) Ltd, since 1973; *b* 27 April 1912; *m* 1943, Isobel Wands; two *d. Educ:* Bellahouston Acad., Glasgow. Member: British Railways Bd, 1968- (Chm., Scottish Railways Board, 1971-); Board of Scottish Television Ltd, 1968-; Forestry Commn, 1963-76 (Chm., 1970-76). President, Scottish CWS, 1965-70; Mem., Scottish Economic Council, 1971-74. Director: Scottish Civic Trust; Whiteaway Laidlaw & Co. Ltd (Bankers), 1971-; Friends' Provident and Century Gp, 1972-; Scottish Metropolitan Property Co. Ltd, 1972-; BR Property Ltd; Mem., Adv. Bd, Morgan Grenfell. DL Renfrewshire, 1970. Hon. LLD Strathclyde, 1974. *Recreations:* theatre, golf, walking. *Address:* The Cottage, Auchenames, Kilbarchan, Renfrewshire PA10 2PM. *T:* Kilbarchan 2648. *Clubs:* Caledonian; New (Edinburgh).

TAYLOR OF MANSFIELD, Baron *cr* 1966 (Life Peer), of Mansfield; **Harry Bernard Taylor,** CBE 1966; *b* 18 Sept. 1895; *s* of Henry Taylor, Mansfield Woodhouse; *m* 1921, Clara, *d* of John Ashley; one *s. Educ:* Council Schools. A Coal Miner. MP (Lab.) Mansfield Div. of Nottinghamshire, 1941-66; Parliamentary Private Secretary to Parliamentary Secretary, Ministry of Aircraft Production, 1942; to Minister of National Insurance, 1945; Parliamentary Secretary, Ministry of National Insurance, 1950-51. *Publication:* Uphill all the Way (autobiog.), 1973. *Address:* 47 Shakespeare Avenue, Mansfield Woodhouse, Nottinghamshire.

TAYLOR, Alan John Percivale, FBA 1956; historian and journalist; Hon. Fellow of Magdalen College, Oxford, 1976; *b* Birkdale, Lancs, 25 March 1906; *o s* of Percy Lees and Constance Sumner Taylor; four *s* two *d. Educ:* Bootham School, York; Oriel Coll., Oxford. Formerly Lectr in Modern History, University of Manchester. Lecturer in International History, Oxford University, 1953-63; Tutor in Modern History, Magdalen College, 1938-63, Fellow, 1938-76. Lectures: Ford's, in English History, Oxford Univ., 1955-56; Leslie Stephen, Cambridge Univ., 1960-61; Creighton, London Univ., 1973; Andrew Lang, St Andrews Univ., 1974; Benjamin Meaker Vis. Prof. of History, Bristol Univ., 1976-78. Pres., City Music Soc. (London). Hon. DCL, New Brunswick, 1961; DUniv York, 1970. *Publications:* (many of them translated into other languages): The Italian Problem in European Diplomacy 1847-49, 1934; Germany's First Bid for Colonies 1884-85, 1938; The Habsburg Monarchy 1815-1918, 1941, rewritten 1948; The Course of German History, 1945; From Napoleon to Stalin, 1950; Rumours of Wars, 1952; The Struggle for Mastery in Europe, 1848-1918, 1954; Bismarck, 1955; Englishmen and Others, 1956; The Trouble Makers: Dissent over Foreign Policy, 1792-1939, 1957; The Russian Revolution of 1917, 1958 (script of first lectures ever given on television); The Origins of the Second World War, 1961; The First World War: an Illustrated History, 1963; Politics in Wartime and Other Essays, 1964; English History, 1914-1945, 1965; From Sarajevo to Potsdam, 1966; Europe: Grandeur and Decline, 1967; War by Timetable, 1969; Beaverbrook, 1972; The Second World War: an illustrated history, 1975; Essays in English History, 1976; The Last of Old Europe, 1976; (ed) Lloyd George: twelve essays, 1971; (ed) Lloyd George, a Diary by Frances Stevenson, 1971; (ed) Off the Record: political interviews 1933-43 by W. P. Crozier, 1973; (ed) My Darling Pussy: the letters of Lloyd George and Frances Stevenson, 1975. *Address:* c/o National Westminster Bank, 1 St James's Square, SW1.

TAYLOR, Prof. (Alfred) Maurice, PhD, MA; FInstP; Professor of Physics, University of Southampton, 1945-68, now Emeritus Professor; *b* 6 Feb. 1903; *o s* of Alfred Ernest Taylor, MA, Clerk in Holy Orders, and Helen Caroline Georgiana (*née* Adams); *m* 1938, Sarah Margaret Alston, *yr d* of Edward Judge; one *s* one *d. Educ:* Reigate Grammar School; Trinity College, Cambridge. Sen. Schol., Alhusen and Coutts-Trotter Research Student, etc, Trinity Coll., Cambridge, 1921-27; PhD Cambridge 1927, MA 1928. Madden Prizeman, TCD, 1928; Ramsay Memorial Fellow, 1927-29. Asst Prof. of Physical Optics, Univ. of Rochester, NY, USA, 1929-34; Lectr in Natural Philosophy, Univ. of St Andrews, Scotland, 1934-45 (seconded to Southampton in 1941); Dep. Prof. of Physics, University Coll., Southampton, 1941-45; Vis. Lectr on the Tallman Foundation, Bowdoin Coll., Brunswick, Maine, USA, 1964-65; Vis. Professor: Hollins Coll., Virginia, USA, 1965-66; Bowdoin Coll., Brunswick, Maine, USA, 1968-69, 1969-70. *Publications:* (with F. I. G. Rawlins) Infra-red Analysis of Molecular Structure, 1929. Imagination and the Growth of Science (Tallman Lectures, 1964-65, given at Bowdoin College, USA), 1966. Papers in Proceedings Royal Society, Philosophical Magazine, Trans Faraday Soc., Proc. Physical Soc., Jl of Scientific

Instruments, Jl of Optical Soc. of Amer., etc. *Recreations:* gardening, caravanning. *Address:* Randal's, Chilworth, Southampton SO1 7WS. *T:* Southampton 68114.

TAYLOR, Lt.-Gen. Sir Allan (Macnab), KBE 1972; MC 1944; Deputy Commander-in-Chief, United Kingdom Land Forces, 1973-76, retired; *b* 26 March 1919; *s* of Alexander Lawrence Taylor and Winifred Ethel (*née* Nisbet); *m* 1945, Madeleine Turpin (marr. diss. 1963); two *d. Educ:* Fyling Hall School, Robin Hood's Bay. Joined TA, 1938; Troop Leader, 10th R Tank Regt, 1940; Squadron Leader, 7th R Tank Regt, 1942; 6th R Tank Regt, 1946; Staff College, 1948; GSO 2, 56 London Armoured Div., 1949; Bde Major 20 Armoured Bde, 1952; Instructor, Staff College, 1954; Squadron Leader, 1st R Tank Regt, 1957; Second in Comd 5th RTR, 1959; Comdg Officer: 5th RTR, 1960 and 3rd, 1961; AA & QMG, 1st Div., 1962; Commandant, RAC Gunnery School, 1963; Comd Berlin Brigade, 1964; Imperial Defence College, 1967; Comdr, 1st Div., 1968; Commandant, Staff College, Camberley, 1969-72; GOC South East District, April-Dec. 1972. Chm., Cttee on Regular Officer Training, 1972-. Col Comdt, RTR, 1973-. *Recreation:* golf. *Address:* 4 Mill Close, Middle Assendon, Henley-on-Thames, Oxon.

TAYLOR, Sir Alvin B.; *see* Burton-Taylor.

TAYLOR, Andrew James, CBE 1965; Chairman, British Manufacturing and Research Co., Grantham, Lincs, 1968-73; *b* 1902; *s* of late Alfred George Ralph Meston Taylor, Broughty Ferry, Dundee; *m* 1925, Mary Ann Symmers, *d* of George Cowie, Aberdeen; three *s* one *d. Educ:* Robert Gordon's Coll., Aberdeen. Dir of Manufacture and Exec. Dir, Ford Motor Co. Ltd, 1962-65; Deputy Managing Director, 1965-67. *Recreations:* photography, fishing. *Address:* Flat 107, Queen's Court, Queen's Promenade, Ramsey, Isle of Man. *Club:* Royal Automobile.

TAYLOR, Mrs Ann; *see* Taylor, Mrs W. A.

TAYLOR, Arnold Joseph, CBE 1971; DLitt, MA; FBA 1972; FSA; President, Society of Antiquaries, since 1975 (Vice-President, 1963-64; Secretary, 1964-70; Director, 1970-75); *b* 24 July 1911; *y s* of late John George Taylor, Headmaster of Sir Walter St John's School, Battersea; *m* 1940, Patricia Katharine, *d* of late S. A. Guilbride, Victoria, BC; one *s* one *d. Educ:* Merchant Taylors' School; St John's College, Oxford (MA). Assistant master, Chard School, Somerset, 1934; Assistant Inspector of Ancient Monuments, HM Office of Works, 1935. Served War of 1939-45, Intelligence Officer, RAF, 1942-46. Inspector of Ancient Monuments for Wales, Min. of Works, 1946-54, Asst Chief Inspector, 1954-61; Chief Inspector of Ancient Monuments and Historic Buildings, MPBW, later DoE, 1961-72. Commissioner: Royal Commissions on Ancient and Historical Monuments (Wales and Monmouthshire), 1956-; Historical Monuments (England), 1963-; Mem., Ancient Monuments Board: for England, 1973-; for Scotland, 1974-; for Wales, 1974-. Member: Cathedrals Advisory Cttee, 1964; Adv. Bd for Redundant Churches, 1973 (Chm., 1975-77); Vice-Pres., Royal Archaeol. Inst., 1968; President: Cambrian Archaeolog. Assoc., 1969; London and Mddx Archaeolog. Soc., 1971-74; Soc. for Medieval Archaeology, 1972-75. Mem., Sir Walter St John's Schools Trust, 1970. Hon. DLitt Wales, 1970. *Publications:* Records of the Barony and Honour of the Rape of Lewes, 1940; official guides to various historical monuments in care Ministry of Works (now DoE), 1939-56; chapter on Military Architecture, in vol. Medieval England, 1958; (part author) History of the King's Works, 1963; contribs on medieval architectural history in Eng. Hist. Rev., Antiquaries Jl, Archaeologia Cambrensis, etc. *Address:* Rose Cottage, Lincoln's Hill, Chiddingfold, Surrey. *T:* Wormley 2069. *Club:* Athenæum.

TAYLOR, Prof. Arthur John; Professor of Modern History, Leeds University, since 1961; *b* 29 Aug. 1919; *s* of Victor Henry and Mary Lydia Taylor, Manchester; *m* 1955, Elizabeth Ann Jeffries; one *s* two *d. Educ:* Manchester Grammar School; Manchester University. Assistant Lecturer in History, University Coll., London, 1948; Lecturer, 1950. Pro-Vice Chancellor, Leeds Univ., 1971-73. Chm., Jt Matriculation Bd, 1970-73. *Publications:* Laissez-faire and State Intervention in Nineteenth Century Britain, 1973; The Standard of Living in Britain in the Industrial Revolution, 1975; (with P. H. J. H. Gosden) Studies in the History of a University: Leeds 1874-1974, 1975; contrib. to books and learned journals. *Address:* Redgarth, Leeds Road, Collingham, Wetherby, West Yorks. *T:* Collingham Bridge 2930.

TAYLOR, Arthur John Ernest, OBE 1968; Chairman, Skelmersdale Development Corporation, since 1975; *b* 25 May 1913; *s* of Henry and Margaret Jane Taylor; *m* 1939, Lillian Joyce Mitchell; one *s* two *d. Educ:* Bootle Grammar Sch.; Liverpool Univ. (LLM). Solicitor. Royal Navy, 1941-45. Deputy Town Clerk, Bootle, 1947-63; Town Clerk and Chief Executive, Bootle, 1963-74; Chief Executive, Sefton Metropolitan District Council, 1974. SBStJ 1972. *Recreations:* gardening, travel. *Address:* Meresden, 14 St Andrews Road, Blundellsands, Liverpool L23 7UR. *T:* 051-924 2150.

TAYLOR, Arthur Robert; President, CBS Inc., since 1972; *s* of Arthur Earl Taylor and Marian Hilda Scott; *m* 1959, Marion McFarland Taylor; three *d. Educ:* Brown Univ., USA (AB, MA). Exec. Vice-Pres./Director, Internat. Paper Co., May 1970-July 1972; Vice-Pres./Dir, The First Boston Co., Jan. 1961-May 1970. Asst Dir, Admissions, Brown Univ., June 1957-Dec. 1960. Hon. degrees: Dr Humane Letters: Simmons Coll., 1975; Rensselaer Polytechnic Inst., 1975; Dr of Humanities, Bucknell Univ., 1975. *Publication:* contrib. chapter to The Other Side of Profit, 1975. *Recreations:* sailing, tennis. *Address:* CBS, 51 West 52 Street, New York, NY 10019, USA. *T:* (212) 975-5152. *Clubs:* The Brook, Century, Larchmont Yacht, Links Golf (all NY); California (Los Angeles); Lyford Cay (Nassau, The Bahamas).

TAYLOR, Arthur Wood, CB 1953; *b* 23 June 1909; *s* of late Richard Wood and Ann Taylor; *m* 1936, Mary Beatrice Forster; one *d. Educ:* Royal School, Wolverhampton; Wolverhampton Grammar School; Sidney Sussex College, Cambridge. Wrangler (Tyson Medal), 1930; joined HM Customs and Excise, 1931; Principal, 1936; Asst Secretary, 1943. Comr of Customs and Excise, 1949; Under-Secretary, HM Treasury, 1957-63; Comr of Customs and Excise, 1964-65, Dep. Chm., 1965-70. Chm., Horserace Totalisator Bd, 1970-72 (Dep. Chm., 1972-73). *Publications:* Amusements with Prizes: social implications, 1974 (report for Churches Council on Gambling); History of Beaconsfield, 1976. *Address:* 72 Wattleton Road, Beaconsfield, Bucks. *T:* 2285. *Club:* Reform.

TAYLOR, Dr Charity; *see* Taylor, Lady.

TAYLOR, Prof. Charles Margrave, DPhil; Chichele Professor of Social and Political Theory, and Fellow of All Souls College, University of Oxford, since 1976; *b* 5 Nov. 1931; *s* of Walter Margrave Taylor and Simone Beaubien; *m* 1956, Alba Romer; five *d. Educ:* McGill Univ. (BA History); Oxford Univ. (BA PPE, MA, DPhil). Fellow, All Souls Coll., Oxford, 1956-61; McGill University: Asst Prof., later Associate Prof., later Prof. of Polit. Science, Dept of Polit. Science, 1961-76; Prof. of Philosophy, Dept. of Philos., 1973-76; Prof. asst, later Prof. agrégé, later Prof. titulaire, Ecole Normale Supérieure, 1962-64, Dept de Philos., 1963-71, Univ. de Montréal. Vis. Prof. in Philos., Princeton Univ., 1965; Mills Vis. Prof. in Philos., Univ. of Calif, Berkeley, 1974. *Publications:* The Explanation of Behavior, 1964; Patterns of Politics, 1970; Hegel, 1975; Erklarung und Interpretation in den Wissenschaften vom Menschen, 1975. *Recreations:* skiing, swimming. *Address:* All Souls College, Oxford OX1 4AL.

TAYLOR, Sir Charles (Stuart), Kt 1954; TD; MA Cantab; DL; *b* 10 April 1910; *s* of Alfred George and Mary Taylor; *m* 1936, Constance Ada Shotter; three *s* one *d. Educ:* Epsom College; Trinity College, Cambridge (BA 1932); Hons Degree Law Tripos. Chm., Onyx Country Estates Co. Ltd, and other cos; formerly: Man. Dir, Unigate & Cow & Gate Ltd; Dir, Trust House Ltd; Chm., later Pres., Grosvenor House (Park Lane) Ltd. President, Residential Hotels Association of Great Britain, until 1948 and Vice-Chairman of Council of British Hotels and Restaurants Association until 1951; Mem. of Honour, Internat. Hotels Assoc.; Vice-President Building Societies Association. MP (C) Eastbourne, March 1935-Feb. 1974; Leader of Parly Delegns to Germany, Ethiopia, Mauritius; Mem., Parly Delegn to Romania. Joined TA 1937 (Royal Artillery), Capt., August 1939; DAAG and Temp. Major, Jan. 1941; attended Staff College, June 1941 (war course), graduated sc. Hon. Colonel. DL Sussex, 1948. Serving Brother, Order of St John. Under Warden, Worshipful Co. of Bakers. Hon. Freeman, Co. Borough of Eastbourne, 1971. Paduka Seri Laila Jasa (Dato), Brunei, 1971. *Recreations:* yachting (rep. Gt Britain *v* USA and Old World *v* New World in six-metre yacht races, 1955), shooting, fishing. *Address:* 4 Reeves House, Reeves Mews, W1. *T:* 01-499 3730. *Clubs:* 1900, Buck's, MCC; Royal Thames Yacht; Ski Club of Great Britain (Hon. Life Mem.).

TAYLOR, Christopher Albert, CB 1976; Inspector General of the Insolvency Service, Department of Trade, 1971-76, retd; *b* 25 Nov. 1915; *s* of Christopher Charles Albert Taylor and Violet Alma Taylor; *m* 1940, Ethel Kathleen Boon; one *s* two *d. Educ:* Woolwich Central Sch.; Woolwich Commercial Inst. (Silver

Medal for Commercial Subjects). FCIS. Clerk: Linotype and Machinery Ltd, 1932; London County Freehold and Leasehold Properties Ltd, 1936; Asst Examiner, Companies Winding-up Dept, Board of Trade, 1939. RAF, 1940-46: Wireless Mechanic (Sgt), 1940-43; Signals Officer (Flt-Lt), Udine, Italy, 1946. Asst Official Receiver, London Suburban Bankruptcy Office, 1950; Official Receiver: Sheffield, 1951-52; Northampton and Cambridge, 1952-62; Companies Winding-Up Dept, 1962-67, Sen. Official Receiver, 1967-70; Dep. Inspector General, Insolvency Service, 1970-71. Mem., Insolvency Law Review Cttee. *Recreations:* photography, amateur radio (G3AEH). *Address:* Bruerne House, Stoke Bruerne, Towcester, Northants NN12 7SB. *T:* Roade 862353. *Club:* Civil Service.

TAYLOR, Dr Daniel Brumhall Cochrane; Vice-Chancellor, Victoria University of Wellington, New Zealand, since 1968; *b* 13 May 1921; *s* of Daniel Brumhall Taylor, Coleraine, NI and Anna Martha Taylor (*née* Rice); *m* 1955, Elizabeth Page, Christchurch, NZ; one *s* one *d. Educ:* Coleraine Academical Instn, NI; Queen's Univ., Belfast. BSc (Mech. Engrg) 1942, BSc (Elec. Engrg) 1943, MSc 1946, PhD 1948, QUB; MA Cantab 1956; FIMechE 1968. Lecturer in Engineering: Liverpool Univ., 1948-50; Nottingham Univ., 1950-53; ICI Fellow, Cambridge Univ., 1953-56; Lectr in Mechanical Sciences, Cambridge Univ., 1956-68; Fellow of Peterhouse, 1958-68, Fellow Emeritus, 1968; Tutor of Peterhouse, 1958-65, Senior Tutor, 1965-68. Member: NZ/USA Educnl Foundn, 1970-; Council, Assoc. of Commonwealth Univs, 1974-77 (Chm., 1975-76); Chm., NZ Vice-Chancellors' Cttee, 1975-77. *Publications:* numerous engrg and metallurgical papers. *Recreations:* golf; formerly rowing (Ireland VIII, Olympic Games, 1948). *Address:* Victoria University of Wellington, Private Bag, Wellington, New Zealand. *T:* Wellington 721-166. *Clubs:* Leander (Henley-on-Thames); Wellington (NZ).

TAYLOR, Desmond Maxwell; Chief Assistant to the Director-General (Regions), BBC, since 1977; *b* 1 June 1928; *s* of Alexander Taylor and Jane Bell; *m* 1958, Rosemary Anne Overfield. *Educ:* Ballymena Academy; Royal Belfast Academical Instn; Queen's Univ., Belfast. Northern Whig, 1951-53; Belfast Telegraph, 1953-54; BBC, 1954-; Editor, News and Current Affairs, BBC, 1971-77. *Address:* BBC, Broadcasting House, W1A 1AA. *T:* 01-580 4468.

TAYLOR, Desmond S.; see Shawe-Taylor.

TAYLOR, Dorothy Mary, CBE 1960; MD, DPH; late Senior Medical Officer, for Maternity and Child Welfare, Ministry of Health; *b* 17 August 1902; *d* of late Thomas Taylor, Highfield, Dreghorn Loan, Colinton, Edinburgh 13; unmarried. *Educ:* George Watson's Ladies' Coll., Edinburgh; Edinburgh Univ. House Surgeon Female VD Department, Edinburgh Royal Infirmary, 1925-26; Clinical Assistant, Maternity and Child Welfare Department, Edinburgh, Apr.-Oct. 1926; House Physician, Royal Hospital for Sick Children, Edinburgh, 1926-27; Resident Medical Officer, Sick Children's Hospital, Newcastle on Tyne, 1927-28; Senior Clinical Assistant, Female VD Department, Royal Infirmary, Edinburgh, 1928-30; Medical Officer, Maternity and Child Welfare Department, Edinburgh, 1930-31; Assistant MOH, Maternity and Child Welfare Department, Sunderland, 1932-35. *Address:* 4 Clerk's Acre, Keymer, Hassocks, West Sussex BN6 8QY. *T:* Hassocks 2143. *Club:* University Women's.

TAYLOR, Ven. Edward; Archdeacon of Warwick, since 1974; *b* 1921; *s* of Albert and Emily Taylor; *m* 1945, Mary Jane Thomson, *e d* of John and Margaret Bell; two *d. Educ:* King's Coll., London (AKC 1948); St Boniface Coll., Warminster. British Army, 1940-42; commnd, 14th Punjab Regt, 1942-46; Hon. Captain, DWR, 1946. Deacon 1949, priest 1950, diocese of Norwich; Curate of Diss, 1949-51; Vicar: St Paul, Stockingford, 1951-57; St Nicholas, Radford, Coventry, 1957-64; Rector of Spernall, Morton Bagot and Oldberrow, 1965-74; Priest-in-charge of Coughton with Sambourne, 1965-70, Vicar 1970-74; Vicar of Sherbourne, 1975-77; Hon. Canon of Coventry, 1969. Proctor in Convocation, 1960. *Recreations:* not playing bridge and golf with great fervour and enthusiasm. *Address:* The Archdeacon's House, Sherbourne, Warwick CV35 8AB. *T:* Barford 624344. *Club:* National Liberal.

TAYLOR, Edward Macmillan; MP (C) Cathcart Division of Glasgow since 1964; journalist and author; *b* 18 April 1937; *s* of late Edward Taylor and of Minnie Hamilton Taylor; *m* 1970, Sheila Duncan; two *s. Educ:* Glasgow High School and University (MA (Hons) Econ. and Politics). Commercial Editorial Staff of Glasgow Herald, 1958-59; Industrial Relations Officer on Staff of Clyde Shipbuilders' Assoc., 1959-64. Parly Under-Sec. of State, Scottish Office, 1970-71, resigned; Parly

Under-Sec. of State, Scottish Office, 1974. *Publications:* (novel) Hearts of Stone, 1968; contributions to the press. *Address:* 77 Newlands Road, Glasgow G43 2JP.

TAYLOR, Edward Plunket, CMG 1946; President: Lyford Cay Co. Ltd; Windfields Farm Ltd; Chairman: New Providence Development Co., Nassau; International Housing Ltd, Bermuda; Director: Royal Bank of Canada International Ltd, Nassau; Trust Corp. of Bahamas Ltd, Nassau; RoyWest Banking Corp. Ltd, Nassau; and other companies; *b* Ottawa, Ontario, 29 January 1901; *s* of late Lieut-Colonel Plunket Bourchier Taylor and Florence Gertrude Magee; *m* 1927, Winifred Thornton, *d* of late Charles F. M. Duguid, Ottawa, Ontario; one *s* two *d. Educ:* Ashbury College; Ottawa Collegiate Institute, Ottawa; McGill University, Montreal (BSc in Mechanical Engineering, 1922). Director Brading Breweries Limited, 1923, also entered the investment house of McLeod, Young, Weir & Co., Limited, Ottawa, 1923, a Director 1929, resigned to become Pres. Canadian Breweries Ltd, 1930 (Chm. of Board, 1944). Mem. Bd of Governors: Trinity Coll. Sch.; Ashbury College. Wartime appointments held: Member, Executive Committee, Dept of Munitions and Supply, Ottawa, April 1940; Joint Director-General of Munitions Production, Nov. 1940; Executive Assistant to the Minister of Munitions and Supply, Feb. 1941; President War Supplies Limited, Washington, DC, April 1941; by Prime Minister Churchill appointed President and Vice-Chairman, British Supply Council in North America, Sept. 1941; Director-General British Ministry of Supply Mission, Feb. 1942; Canadian Deputy Member on the Combined Production and Resources Board, Nov. 1942; also Canadian Chairman, Joint War Aid Committee, US-Canada, Sept. 1943. Chm. and Chief Steward, Jockey Club of Canada; Hon. Chm., Ontario Jockey Club; Mem., Jockey Club, NY. Member, Delta Upsilon Fraternity. Anglican. *Recreation:* riding. *Address:* Lyford Cay, New Providence, Bahamas. *Clubs:* Buck's, Turf; Royal Yacht Squadron (Cowes); Toronto, York (Toronto); Rideau (Ottawa); Metropolitan (New York); Lyford Cay (Nassau).

TAYLOR, Edward Wilfred, CBE 1946; FRS 1952; Hon. DSc Leeds, 1957; FRMS; *b* 29 April 1891; *s* of Harold Dennis Taylor and Charlotte Fernandes Barff; *m* 1921, Winifred Mary, *d* of Edward George Hunter, Hastings; one *s. Educ:* Oundle School. Joined Messrs Cooke Troughton & Simms, 1908; served European War, 1914-19, Lieut RNVR Admiralty War Staff; Optical Manager, 1923; Technical Manager, 1932; Joint Managing Director, 1937-56; Director, 1956-61. Govt sponsored missions, US, 1943; Jena, 1945; Delegate, Commission Internationale d'Optique, 1948, 1950, 1953, 1956 and 1959. President Yorkshire Naturalists' Trust, 1952-70. DUniv York, 1977. *Publications:* Design and Construction of Surveying Instruments, 1938; contributions to technical and scientific journals, including Proceedings of the Royal Society, on microscopy and surveying. *Recreations:* fishing and ornithology. *Address:* 7 St Peter's Grove, York YO3 6AQ. *T:* York 22621.

TAYLOR, Elizabeth; film actress; *b* London, 27 Feb. 1932; *d* of Francis Taylor and Sara (*née* Sothern); *m* 1st, 1950, Conrad Nicholas Hilton, Jr (marr. diss.; he *d* 1969); 2nd, 1952, Michael Wilding, *qv* (marr. diss.); two *s*; 3rd, 1957, Mike Todd (*d* 1958); one *d*; 4th, 1959, Eddie Fisher (marr. diss.); 5th, 1964, Richard Burton, *qv* (marr. diss.; remarried 1975; marr. diss. 1976); 7th, 1976, John Warner. *Educ:* Byron House, Hampstead; Hawthorne School, Beverly Hills; Metro-Goldwyn-Mayer School; University High School, Hollywood. *Films include:* Lassie Come Home, 1942; National Velvet, 1944; Courage of Lassie, 1946; Little Women, 1948; The Conspirator, 1949; Father of the Bride, 1950; A Place in the Sun, 1950; Ivanhoe, 1951; Beau Brummel, 1954; Giant, 1956; Raintree County, 1957; Suddenly Last Summer, 1959; Butterfield 8 (Academy Award for Best Actress), 1960; Cleopatra, 1963; the VIPs, 1963; The Sandpiper, 1965; Who's Afraid of Virginia Woolf?, 1966; The Taming of the Shrew, 1967; Boom, 1968; The Comedians, 1968; Reflections in a Golden Eye, 1968; Secret Ceremony, 1968; The Only Game in Town, 1970; Under Milk Wood, 1972; Zee and Co., 1972; Hammersmith is Out, 1972; Night Watch, 1973; Blue Bird, 1975; A Little Night Music, 1976. *Publication:* Elizabeth Taylor, 1966. *Address:* c/o Major D. Neville-Willing, 85 Kinnerton Street, Belgravia, SW1. *T:* 01-235 4640.

TAYLOR, Eric Scollick, PhD; Clerk of Committee Records, House of Commons, since 1975; *b* 16 April 1918; *s* of late Percy Scollick Taylor and Jessie Devlin. *Educ:* Durham Univ. (MA); Edinburgh Univ. (PhD 1942). Asst Clerk, House of Commons, 1942; Dep. Principal Clerk, 1962; Principal Clerk, 1972. Clerk to: Cttee of Privileges, 1949-57; Estimates Cttee, 1957-64; Cttee of Public Accounts, 1964-68; Clerk of the Journals, 1972-75. *Publications:* The House of Commons at Work (Penguin), 1951,

8th edn 1971; The Liberal Catholic Church-what is it?, 1966 (also foreign trans); The Houses of Parliament, 1976; contribs to Times Lit. Supp., etc. *Recreations:* walking, listening to music, preaching to the converted, worship. *Address:* 113 Beaufort Street, SW3 6BA. *T:* 01-351 1765; 71 Woodbine Road, Gosforth, Newcastle upon Tyne NE3 1DE. *T:* Newcastle upon Tyne 857040.

TAYLOR, Eric W., RE 1948 (ARE 1935); ARCA 1934; ASIA (Ed) 1965; printmaker, painter and sculptor; *b* 6 Aug. 1909; *s* of Thomas John and Ethel Annie Taylor; *m* 1939, Alfreda Marjorie Hurren; one *s* one *d*. *Educ:* William Ellis School, Hampstead; Royal College of Art, South Kensington. Worked for 3 years in London Studio; then as a free-lance illustrator; won British Inst. Scholarship, 1932; runner-up in Prix de Rome, 1934, while at Royal College of Art. Exhibited: Royal Academy; Royal Scottish Academy; Doncaster Art Gallery; New York; Brooklyn; Chicago; London Group; New English Art Club. Pictures in permanent Collections of Stockholm Art Gallery, Art Inst. of Chicago, Washington Art Gallery, War Museum, London. Logan Prize for best Etching in International Exhibition of Etching and Engraving at Art Institute of Chicago, 1937. Selected by British Council to exhibit in Scandinavian Exhibition, 1940, S America, 1942-44, Spain and Portugal, 1942-44, Turkey, 1943-45, Iceland, 1943, Mexico, 1943-45, China, 1945, Czechoslovakia, 1948, and Rotterdam, 1948. Associate Chicago Society of Etchers, 1937. War pictures bought by National Gallery Advisory Committee for Imperial War Museum, 1945. Volunteered for RA, Nov. 1939. Instructor at Northern Command Camouflage School, 1941-43; Royal Engineers, France and Germany, 1943-45; instructing for Educational Corps Germany, 1946; Art Instructor Camberwell School of Art, 1936-39; Willesden School of Art, 1936-49; Central School of Art, 1948-49; Examiner: Bristol Univ., 1948-51; Durham Univ., 1971-72; Min. of Education NDD Pictorial Subjects, 1957-59. Designer and Supervisor of Lubeck School of Art for the Services, 1946. Head of the Design School, Leeds Coll. of Art, 1949-56, Principal, 1956-69; Hd of Faculty of Art and Design, Leeds Polytechnic, 1969-71. Leverhulme Research Awards, 1958-59, visiting Colleges of Art in Austria, Germany, Holland, Denmark and Italy. Study of Mosaics, Italy, 1965. Representative Exhibitions: Wakefield Art Gall., 1960; Goosewell Gall., Menston, 1972, 1973, 1976; Middlesbrough Art Gall., 1972; Northern Artists Gall., Harrogate, 1977. British Representative Speaker, International Design Conference, Karachi, 1962. Print selected by Royal Soc. of Painter Etchers for Presentation to Print Collections Club, 1947. Mem. of Senefelder Club, 1947. Picture purchased by British Council, 1948. *Publications:* Etching Published in Fine Prints of the Year, 1935, 1936, 1937, and in 1939 and 1940 issues of Print Collectors Quarterly. *Address:* Gordale, 13 Tredgold Avenue, Bramhope, near Leeds, W Yorks.

TAYLOR, Ernest Richard; Headmaster of Wolverhampton Grammar School, 1956-April 1973; *b* Oldham, 9 Aug. 1910; *e s* of late Louis Whitfield and Annie Taylor; *m* 1936, Muriel Hardill; twin *s*. *Educ:* Hulme Grammar School, Oldham; Trinity College, Cambridge. Hist. Tripos, Class I, 1931; Sen. Schol. and Earl of Derby Research Student (Trinity), 1931-32; Thirlwall and Gladstone Prizes, 1933; MA 1935. Asst Master, Culford School, 1932-36; Moseley Gram. Sch., Birmingham, 1936-39; Manchester Gram. Sch., 1939-47. War Service in RA and AEC, 1940-46. Headmaster of Quarry Bank High School, Liverpool, 1947-56; Member, Schools Council for Curriculum and Examinations (formerly Secondary Schools Examinations Council), 1962-. Walter Hines Page Scholar, HMC, 1964. Pres. Incorporated Assoc. of Head Masters, 1965; Chm. Central Exec., Jt Four Secondary Assocs, 1970-72. Mem., President's Council of Methodist Church, 1976-. *Publications:* Methodism and Politics, (1791-1851), 1935; Padre Brown of Gibraltar, 1955; Religious Education of pupils from 16 to 19 years, 1962. *Recreation:* golf. *Address:* Highcliff, Whitcliffe, Ludlow, Salop. *T:* Ludlow 2093.

TAYLOR, Sir Francis, (Sir Frank Taylor), Kt 1974; Founder, Taylor Woodrow Group; Director: Taylor Woodrow of Canada Ltd since 1953; Monarch Investments Ltd, Canada, since 1954; Taylor Woodrow Blitman Inc., since 1962; *b* 7 Jan. 1905; *s* of late Francis Taylor and late Sarah Ann Earnshaw; *m* 1st, 1929 (marr. diss.); two *d*; 2nd, 1956, Christine Enid Hughes; one *d*. Founded, 1921, Taylor Woodrow, Building, Civil & Mechanical Engineering Contractors, which became Public Company, in 1935. Member of Advisory Council to Minister of State, 1954-55; Chm. Export Group for Constructional Industries, 1954-55; President Provident Institution of Builders' Foremen and Clerks of Works, 1950; Dir, Freedom Federal Savings and Loan Assoc., Worcester, Mass, 1972-. Dir, BOAC, 1958-60. Governor: Queenswood School for Girls, 1948-; London Grad. Sch. of

Business Studies. Hon. DSc Salford, 1973. Fellow Inst. of Builders. *Recreations:* tennis, swimming, riding. *Address:* (office) 10 Park Street, W1Y 4DD; (home) Long Common, Wanborough, near Guildford, Surrey GU3 2JL. *Clubs:* Royal Automobile, Queen's, Hurlingham, All England.

TAYLOR, Sir Frank; *see* Taylor, Sir Francis.

TAYLOR, Frank, CBE 1969; QFSM 1965; Chief Fire Officer, Merseyside County Fire Brigade, 1974-76 (Liverpool Fire Brigade, 1962-74); *b* 6 April 1915; *s* of Percy and Beatrice Taylor; *m* 1940, Nancy (*née* Hefford); two *s* two *d*; *m* 1976, Florence Mary Latham. *Educ:* Council Sch., Sheffield. Fireman, Sheffield Fire Bde, 1935-41; Instr, NFS West Riding, 1941-42; Company Officer up to Station Officer (ops), NFS in Yorkshire, 1942-49; Chief Officer, Western Fire Authority, N Ire., 1949-51; Divl Officer N Ire. Fire Authority, 1951-57; Belfast: Dep. Chief Officer, 1958-60; Chief Officer, 1960-62. *Recreations:* football, gardening. *Address:* Onchan, Hall Lane, Wrightington, near Wigan, Lancs.

TAYLOR, Dr Frank; Deputy Director and Principal Keeper, The John Rylands University Library of Manchester, since 1972; Hon. Lecturer in Manuscript Studies, University of Manchester, since 1967. *Educ:* Univ. of Manchester (MA, PhD). FSA. Served with RN, 1942-46: Lieut, RNVR, 1943-46. Research for Cttee on History of Parlt, 1934-35; Keeper of Western Manuscripts, 1935-49, Keeper of Manuscripts, 1949-72, Librarian, 1970-72, John Rylands Library. Jt. Hon. Sec., Lancs Parish Record Soc., 1937-57, Hon. Sec., 1957-. Editor, Bulletin of the John Rylands Univ. Lib. of Manchester. *Publications:* various Calendars of Western Manuscripts and Charter Room collections in the Rylands Library, 1937-; The Chronicle of John Strecche for the Reign of Henry 5, 1932; An Early Seventeenth Century Calendar of Records Preserved in Westminster Palace Treasury, 1939; The Parish Registers of Aughton, 1541-1764, 1942; contrib. to Some Twentieth Century Interpretations of Boswell's Life of Johnson (ed J. L. Clifford), 1970; The Oriental Manuscript Collections in the John Rylands Library, 1972; (ed with J. S. Roskell) Gesta Henrici Quinti, 1975; (with G. A. Matheson) Hand-List of Personal Papers from the Muniments of the Earl of Crawford and Balcarres, 1976; articles in Bulletin of John Rylands Library, Indian Archives. *Recreations:* cricket, walking. *Address:* The John Rylands University Library of Manchester, Deansgate, Manchester M3 3EH. *T:* 061-834 5343.

TAYLOR, Frank Henry; Consultant to two firms of Chartered Accountants: Frank H. Taylor & Co., City of London; W. T. Flower & Co. Wimbledon; *b* 10 Oct. 1907; 2nd *s* of George Henry Taylor, Cambridgeshire; *m* 1936, Margaret Dora Mackay (*d* 1944), Invernesshire; one *d*; *m* 1948, Mabel Hills, Hertfordshire; two *s*. *Educ:* Rutlish School, Merton, Surrey, FCIS 1929; FCA 1930. Commenced in practice as Chartered Accountant, 1930; Ministry of Food Finance Director of Tea, Coffee and Cocoa, 1942; Min. of War Transport Finance Rep. overseas, 1944; visited over 30 countries on financial missions. Lt-Colonel comdg 1st Caernarvonshire Bn Home Guard, 1943. Contested (C) Newcastle under Lyme, 1959; MP (C) Manchester, Moss Side, Nov. 1961-Feb. 1974. Governor of Rutlish School, 1946-. Liveryman, City of London. Member: Court of Worshipful Co. of Bakers, 1947; Guild of Air Pilots. *Recreations:* numerous including Rugby (for Surrey County), Sculling (Thames Championship), punting (several Thames championships), golf (Captain RAC 1962). *Address:* 2A Barrie House, Lancaster Gate, W2. *T:* 01-723 3289; Tinker Taylor, Sennen Cove, Cornwall. *T:* Sennen 220. *Clubs:* City Livery, Royal Automobile, British Sportsman's.

TAYLOR, Prof. Frederick William, MA Cantab, LLM Wales; Professor of Law, University of Hull, 1956-74, now Emeritus (Dean of Faculty of Arts, 1954-57); *b* 8 March 1909; *o s* of late James Edward Taylor, Solicitor, and of Emily Price; *m* 1938, Muriel Vera Markreed, *d* of Onek Vosguerchian; two *d*. *Educ:* Twynyrodyn Elementary and Cyfarthfa Secondary Schools, Merthyr Tydfil; University College of Wales, Aberystwyth; St John's College, Cambridge. Solicitor, 1931; LLB Wales, Sir Samuel Evans Prize 1933, BA Cantab, Scholar of St John's Coll., 1935; Asst Lectr in Law, University Coll., Hull, 1935; Acting Head, Dept of Law: University Coll., Southampton, 1940; Hull, 1941; called to Bar, Cert. of Honour, Middle Temple Prize, 1943; Head of Dept of Law, University Coll., Hull, 1949; LLM Wales 1954. Formerly Mem. of Bd of Studies in Laws of Univ. of London. Equity draftsman and conveyancer, 1944-, formerly at Leeds and later at Hull. *Publications:* articles in Law Journal, The Conveyancer, Jl of Soc. of Public Teachers of Law, Solicitors' Journal, The Solicitor, Secretaries Chronicle. *Recreations:* natural history, etc. *Address:* Imperial Chambers, Bowlalley Lane, Hull. *T:* Hull 23264; 1 Hurn View, Beverley, North Humberside. *T:* 883561.

TAYLOR, Sir George, Kt 1962; DSc; FRS 1968, FRSE, FLS; Director, Stanley Smith Horticultural Trust, since 1970; Visiting Professor, Reading University, since 1969; *b* 15 February 1904; *o s* of George William Taylor and Jane Sloan; *m* 1st, 1929, Alice Helen Pendrich (*d* 1977); two *s*; 2nd, Norah English (*d* 1967); 3rd, Beryl, Lady Colwyn. *Educ:* George Heriot's Sch., Edinburgh; Edinburgh Univ. BSc (1st class hons Botany), 1926; Vans Dunlop Scholar. Member of Botanical Expedition to South Africa and Rhodesia, 1927-28; Joint Leader of British Museum Expedition to Ruwenzori and mountains of East Africa, 1934-35; Expedition to SE Tibet and Bhutan, 1938. Principal in Air Ministry, 1940-45. Deputy Keeper of Botany, British Museum (Natural History), 1945-50; Keeper of Botany, 1950-56; Dir, Royal Botanic Gardens, Kew, 1956-71. Botanical Sec. Linnean Soc., 1950-56; Vice-Pres. 1956. Percy Sladen Trustee, 1951-. Royal Horticultural Soc.: Mem. Council, 1951-73, Vice-Pres., and Prof. of Botany, 1974-; Council Member: National Trust (Chm. Gardens Cttee), 1961-72; RGS 1957-61 (Vice-Pres. 1964); Mem. Min. of Transport Adv. Cttee on Landscaping Treatment of Trunk Roads, 1956- (Chm. 1969-). Editor, Curtis's Botanical Magazine, 1962-71. Gen. Sec., Brit. Assoc. for the Advancement of Science, 1951-58. Hon. Botanical Adviser, Commonwealth War Graves Commn, 1956-. President: Botanical Society of British Isles, 1955; Division of Botany, Internat. Union Biol Sci., 1964-69; Internat. Assoc. for Plant Taxonomy, 1969-72. Member Royal Society Science, Uppsala, 1956; Corr. Member Royal Botanical Soc. Netherlands; Hon. Mem., Botanical Soc. of S Africa; Hon. Mem., American Orchid Soc. Hon. FRHS 1948. Hon. Freeman, Worshipful Co. of Gardeners, 1967. Hon. LLD Dundee, 1972. VMH 1956; Veitch Gold Medal, Royal Horticultural Soc., 1963; Bradford Washburn Award, Museum of Science, Boston, USA, 1969. Hon. DrPhil Gothenburg, 1958. *Publications:* An Account of the Genus Meconopsis, 1934; contributions on flowering plants to various periodicals. *Recreations:* angling, gardening, music. *Address:* Belhaven House, Dunbar, East Lothian EH42 1NS. *T:* Dunbar 62392, 63546; 26 Harley Place, W1. *T:* 01-580 1736. *Clubs:* Athenæum; New (Edinburgh).

TAYLOR, George Francis, CBE 1943; Chairman, Bank of London and South America, 1970-71 (Deputy Chairman, 1966-70; Director, 1950); *b* 13 Jan. 1903; *s* of George Arthur Taylor and Anna Maria (*née* Ryan); *m* 1937, Vivian Judith Elizabeth, *d* of late Lt-Comdr Vivian Rose Price, RN; one *s* two *d. Educ:* Xavier Coll., Melbourne; Melbourne Univ. (MA, LLB). Served 1939-45 with Special Ops, (SOE), Middle East, Greece, Yugoslavia, India, SE Asia and SW Pacific; Chief of Staff, HQ, 1940-42; Colonel. TARO, 1945-53. FRSA 1967. *Recreations:* fishing, sailing, riding, tennis. *Address:* 20 Keane Street, Peppermint Grove, WA 6011, Australia. *Club:* Boodle's.

TAYLOR, Prof. Gerard William, MS, FRCS; Professor of Surgery, University of London, since 1960; Surgeon and Director Surgical Professorial Unit, St Bartholomew's Hospital, London; Honorary Consultant in Vascular Surgery to the Army since 1962; *b* 23 September 1920; *s* of William Ivan Taylor; *m* 1951, Olivia Gay; one *s* one *d. Educ:* Bemrose School, Derby; St Bartholomew's Hospital Medical College. Served War of 1939-45, Capt. RAMC, 1944-47. Fellow in Surgery, Asst Resident, Fulbright Schol., Stanford Univ. Hosp., San Francisco, Calif., 1950-51; Surgeon, St Bartholomew's Hosp., London, Reader in Surgery, Univ. of London, 1955; Hunterian Prof., RCS, 1962; Vis. Prof. of Surgery: Univ. of Calif., Los Angeles, 1965; Univ. of Melbourne, 1969; Sir James Wattie Prof., NZ, 1972. Examiner in Surgery: Univ. of London, 1960; NUI, 1966; Univ. of Cambridge, 1966; Trinity Coll., Dublin, 1969; Univ. of Liverpool, 1974. Governor, St Bartholomew's Hosp., 1971; Mem. Council, Epsom Coll., 1972. President: Vascular Surgical Soc. of GB and Ireland, 1975; Surgical Res. Soc., 1976. *Publications:* articles on general and arterial surgery in scientific journals. *Recreation:* motoring. *Address:* Maple Farm, Shantock Lane, Bovingdon, Herts. *T:* Hemel Hempstead 833170.

TAYLOR, Gordon Rattray; author, specialising in understanding social change; *b* Eastbourne, 11 Jan. 1911; *o s* of Frederick Robert Taylor and Adèle Baker; *m* 1st, 1945, Lysbeth Morley Sheaf (marr. diss.); two *d*; 2nd, 1962, Olga Treherne Anthonisz. *Educ:* Radley Coll.; Trinity Coll., Cambridge. Morning Post, 1933-36; freelance, 1936-38; Daily Express (leader and feature writer), 1938-40; Monitoring Service and European News Broadcasts, BBC, 1940-44; Psychological Warfare Div., SHAEF, 1944-45; freelance writer, broadcaster and author, 1945-50; Dir, social research organisation, 1950-54; writing and devising science television programmes for BBC, 1958-66 (Chief Science Advisor, 1963-66); wrote Eye on Research series (Ondas award, 1961); Challenge series; Science Internat. series (first science programmes to attract over 10 million viewers) incl. Machines like Men (Brussels award, 1961); Editor, Horizon,

1964-66; full-time author, 1966-. Editorial consultant: Discovery, 1963-65; Science Jl, 1965-68. Other activities included devising British pavilion display for Turin Fair, 1961; Advisor, Triumphs of British Genius Exhbn, and ed, catalogue/book, 1977; lecture tours in US. Founder and Past Pres., Internat. Science Writers Assoc., etc. *Publications:* Economics for the Exasperated, 1947; Conditions of Happiness, 1949; Are Workers Human?, 1950; Sex in History, 1953; The Angel Makers: a study in the psychological origins of historical change 1750-1850, 1958; (abridgement, with an introductory essay) of The Mothers (by Robert Briffault), 1959; Eye on Research, 1960; The Science of Life: a picture history of biology, 1963; Growth (with Dr James Tanner), 1965; The Biological Time Bomb, 1968; The Doomsday Book (Yorkshire Post book-of-the-year award), 1970; Rethink: a paraprimitive solution, 1972; How to Avoid the Future, 1975; A Salute to British Genius, 1977; contrib. Focus feature to Science Jl, from inception; ed numerous research reports for Acton Soc. Trust; contributor to: Encounter, The Observer, Futures, etc. *Recreations:* wine, gardening, baroque music, thought. *Address:* c/o Coutts and Co., 10 Mount Street, W1. *Club:* Savile.

TAYLOR, Greville Laughton; company director; *b* 23 Oct. 1902; *s* of Rowland Henry and Edith Louise Taylor; *m* 1947, Mary Eileen Reece Mahon; one *s* one *d. Educ:* Lodge School, Barbados; St John's College, Oxford. Called to the Bar, Lincoln's Inn, 1927. Clerk to the House of Assembly, Barbados, 1930-36. Police Magistrate, Barbados, 1936-44; Army 1940-44 (UK, N Africa, Italy); Registrar, Barbados, 1944-46; Judge of the Assistant Court of Appeal, Barbados, 1947-57; Puisne Judge, Windward Islands and Leeward Islands, 1957-64. *Recreations:* reading, shooting, fishing. *Address:* Cole's House, Cole's, St Philip, Barbados, West Indies. *T:* 207. *Clubs:* Royal Barbados Yacht; Bridgetown (Bridgetown).

TAYLOR, Harold George K.; *see* Kirwan-Taylor.

TAYLOR, Harold Joseph, CBE 1966; Chief Director, Prison Department, Home Office, 1965-68, retired; *b* 7 May 1904; *s* of Herbert Taylor and Gertrude Mary Taylor; *m* 1940, Olive Alice Slade, *d* of Harry Slade, Honor Oak Park, SE; one *s* (adopted). *Educ:* Blandford Sec. Gram. Sch.; Southampton University. Teacher, Brighton Education Authority, 1924-28; Asst Housemaster, Prison Commission, HM Borstal, Portland, 1928; Housemaster, Portland Borstal, 1930; Superintendent, Borstal Training School, Thayetmyo, Burma, 1933-37; Governor, HM Borstal: Feltham, Middx, 1938-41; Lowdham Grange, 1941-46; Governor, HM Prison: Camp Hill, IoW, 1946-49; Sudbury, Derby, 1949-51; Asst Comr, HM Prison Commission, 1951-57; Comr and Director of Borstal Administration, 1958-65. *Recreations:* fishing, country lore, tinkering. *Address:* 45 Church Way, Pagham, Bognor Regis, West Sussex. *T:* Pagham 3750.

TAYLOR, Harold McCarter, CBE 1955; TD 1945; retired, 1967; *b* Dunedin, New Zealand, 13 May 1907; *s* of late James Taylor, and late Louisa Urquhart Taylor; *m* 1st, 1933, Joan (*d* 1965), *d* of late George Reginald Sills, Lincoln; two *s* two *d*; 2nd, 1966, Dorothy Judith, *d* of late Charles Samuel, Liverpool. *Educ:* Otago Boys' High School and Univ. of Otago, NZ; Clare Coll., Cambridge. MSc New Zealand, 1928; MA, PhD Cambridge, 1933. Allen Scholar and Smith's Prizeman, 1932. Fellow of Clare College, Cambridge, 1933-61; Hon. Fellow, 1961-; Lecturer in Mathematics, University of Cambridge, 1934-45; Treasurer of the University, 1945-53; Secretary General of the Faculties, 1953-61; Vice-Chancellor, University of Keele, 1961-67 (Principal, University College of North Staffordshire, 1961-62); Rede Lecturer, Cambridge University, 1966. Mem., Royal Commn on Historical Monuments (England), 1972-. Pres., Royal Archaeol Inst., 1972-75; Vice-Pres., Soc. of Antiquaries of London, 1974-77. Hon. LLD Cambridge, 1967; Hon. DLitt Keele, 1968. Commissioned in TA, NZ, 1925; served War of 1939-45 as Major and Lieut-Col RA; Instructor and Senior Instructor in Gunnery at School of Artillery, Larkhill. *Publications:* (with Joan Taylor) Anglo-Saxon Architecture, 1965; many articles in nat. and county archaeological jls. *Recreations:* mountaineering and ski-ing; Anglo-Saxon art and architecture; photography. *Address:* 192 Huntingdon Road, Cambridge CB3 0LB. *T:* 76324.

TAYLOR, Henry Archibald; CBE 1952; journalist; *s* of George Taylor and Ellen E. Collins; *m* Mollie Little (Capt., WRAC, Retd); two *s*. After provincial experience, joined staff of Daily Chronicle; served European War, Western Front; Royal Fusiliers and Staff. Chm. Newspaper Features, Ltd, 1923-64; Editor, Empire Review, 1943-44; special political contributor, Evening Standard, 1945-46, Yorkshire Post, 1949-60; leader writer, Country Life 1956-; President Institute of Journalists,

1938; Member: Court of Bristol Univ., 1936-68; Lord Chancellor's Cttee on Law of Defamation, 1939-48. Chairman Restoration Cttee St Bride's Church, Fleet Street, 1951-57. Parliamentary Candidate (C) Doncaster, 1939-45, NE Leicester, 1949, contesting that division at General Election and subsequent by-election, 1950. *Publications:* Goodbye to the Battlefields, 1930; Smith of Birkenhead, 1931; The Strange Case of Andrew Bonar Law, 1932; Robert Donald, 1934; Jix, Viscount Brentford, 1935; Will You Be Left? (in collaboration), 1945; The British Press: a Critical Survey, 1961; (with Sir Linton Andrews), Lords and Labourers of the Press, 1970. *Address:* Oldwell House, Dummer, Basingstoke, Hants. *T:* Dummer 227. *Clubs:* Press, Whitefriars.

TAYLOR, Henry George, DSc(Eng); Director of Electrical Research Association, 1957-69; *b* 4 Nov. 1904; *m* 1931, Gwendolyn Hilda Adams; one *s* two *d. Educ:* Taunton School; Battersea Polytechnic Inst., City and Guilds Engineering College. Metropolitan Vickers, 1929-30; Electrical Research Assoc., 1930-38; Copper Development Assoc., 1938-42; Philips Lamps Ltd, 1942-47; British Welding Research Assoc., 1947-57. *Publications:* contribs to: Instn of Electrical Engineers Jl, Jl of Inst. of Physics, etc. *Recreation:* walking. *Address:* 9 La Valette Court, Qawra Point, St Paul's Bay, Malta GC.

TAYLOR, Hermon, MA, MD, MChir, FRCS; Consulting Surgeon: London Hospital, E1; King George Hospital, Ilford; *b* 11 May 1905; *s* of Enoch Oliver Taylor and L. M. Taylor (née Harrison); *m* 1932, Méarie Amélie Pearson; three *s* two *d. Educ:* Latymer School, Edmonton; St John's Coll., Cambridge (scholar); St Bartholomew's Hospital (Entrance Scholar). BA 1926; MRCS, LRCP 1929; MB, ChB Cantab. 1930; FRCS Eng. 1930. House Surgeon, Demonstr of Pathology, St Bart's Hosp.; Res. Surgical Officer: Hertford Co. Hosp., Lincoln Co. Hosp.; Surgical Registrar, Prince of Wales' Hosp., Tottenham. MChir Cantab 1932; MD Cantab 1934; Horton Smith Prize, Univ. Cantab; Luther Holden Research Scholar, St Bartholomew's Hospital; BMA Research Scholar, Surgical First Assistant London Hospital. Moynihan Fellow, Assoc. of Surgeons of GB and Ireland; Hunterian Professor, RCS. Past President, British Society of Gastro-enterology; Hon. Member Amer. Gastro-enterological Assoc. *Publications:* Carcinoma of the Stomach, in Modern Trends in Gastro-Enterology, 1952; contrib. to BMJ, Lancet, etc, 1942-. *Address:* 9 Cambridge Gate, Regent's Park, NW1. *T:* 01-935 5212. *Club:* Athenæum.

TAYLOR, Prof. Ian Galbraith; Ellis Llwyd Jones Professor of Audiology and Education of the Deaf, University of Manchester, since 1964; *b* 24 Apr. 1924; *s* of David Oswald Taylor, MD, and Margaret Ballantine Taylor; *m* 1954, Audrey Wolstenholme; two *d. Educ:* Manchester Grammar Sch.; Univ. of Manchester. MB, ChB, DPH Manchester; MD (Gold Medal) Manchester 1963; MRCP 1973; FRCP 1978. Ho. Surg., Manchester Royal Infirm., 1948; DAD, Army Health of N Regional Canal Zone, and OC Army Sch. of Hygiene, ME, 1949-51; Asst MO, City of Manchester, 1951-54. Univ. of Manchester: Hon. Special Lectr and Ewing Foundn Fellow, Dept of Education of the Deaf, 1956-60; Lectr in Clinical Audiology, 1963-64. Consultant in Audiology, United Manchester Hosps, 1968. FCST (Hon.) 1966. *Publication:* Neurological Mechanisms of Hearing and Speech in Children, 1964. *Recreations:* gardening, fishing. *Address:* 7 Hall Moss Lane, Bramhall, Cheshire SK7 1RB. *T:* 061-428 6894.

TAYLOR, Ivor Ralph, QC 1973; **His Honour Judge Taylor;** a Circuit Judge, since 1976; *b* 26 Oct. 1927; *s* of Abraham Taylor and late Ruth Taylor; *m* 1st, 1954, Ruth Cassel (marr. diss. 1974); one *s* one *d* (and one *d* decd); 2nd, 1974, Jane Elizabeth Ann Gibson; two step *d. Educ:* Stand Grammar Sch., Whitefield; Manchester Univ. Served War of 1939-45, AC2 in RAF, 1945. Called to Bar, Gray's Inn, 1951. Standing Counsel to Inland Revenue, N Circuit, 1969-73; a Recorder of the Crown Court, 1972-76. Pres., Manchester and District Medico Legal Soc., 1974, 1975. *Recreations:* walking, indifferent golfing. *Address:* 7 Moorside House, Oakleigh Court, Stockport Road, Timperley, Cheshire WA15 6UG. *T:* 061-969 7046. *Club:* Dunham Forest Golf and Country.

TAYLOR, Sir James, Kt 1966; MBE 1945; DSc, FRIC, Hon. FInstP, Hon. MIMinE; Deputy Chairman: Royal Ordnance Factories Board, 1959-72 (Member, 1952-72); Chairman: Chloride Silent Power Ltd, since 1974; Fulmer Research Institute Ltd, since 1976; *b* 16 Aug. 1902; *s* of James and Alice Taylor; *m* 1929, Margaret Lennox Stewart; two *s* one *d. Educ:* Bede College, Sunderland; Rutherford College, Newcastle upon Tyne; Universities of Durham, Sorbonne, Utrecht, Cambridge. BSc (1st cl. Hons Physics) 1923; PhD 1925; Dr of Physics and Maths (*cum laude*) Utrecht, 1927; DSc Dunelm, 1931. ICI Ltd:

joined Nobel Div. 1928; Research Dir, 1946; Jt Man. Dir, 1951; Director, 1952-64. Chairman: Yorkshire Imperial Metals Ltd, 1958-64; Imperial Aluminium Co. Ltd, 1959-64; Imperial Metal Industries Ltd, 1962-64. Director: Nuclear Developments Ltd, 1961-64; European Plumbing Materials Ltd, 1962-64; BDH Group Ltd, 1965-67; Oldham & Son Ltd, 1965-69; Oldham (International) Ltd., 1969-72. Member: Adv. Coun. on Scientific Research and Tech. Develt, MoD, 1965-68; NPL Steering Committee, 1966; Adv. Coun. on Calibration and Measurement, 1966; Chm., Glazebrook Cttee, NPL, 1966. Member: Court, Brunel Univ., 1967; Council, British Non-Ferrous Metals Research Assoc., 1954-67 (Vice-Chm. 1961-67); Council, City and Guilds of London, 1969-71; Court, RCA, 1969-71; Pres. Section B British Assoc. 1960, Council 1965; Pres. Inst. of Physics and Physical Society, 1966-68 (Hon. Treas. 1957-66); FRIC 1945; MIMinE 1947 (Hon. Member, 1960); FInstP 1948 (Hon. FInstP 1972); FRSA 1962 (Member Council 1964-, Vice-Pres., 1969, Chm., 1969-71; Silver Medal, 1969); Hon. Pres., Research and Development Soc., 1970; Hon. Mem., Newcomen Soc. in N America, 1970. Mem., Inst. of Dirs, 1964. Hon. DSc Bradford, 1968; Hon. DCL Newcastle, 1969. Medal, Society Chemical Industry, 1965; Silver Medal, Chem. Soc., 1972. *Publications:* On the Sparking Potentials of Electric Discharge Tubes, 1927; Detonation in Condensed Explosives, 1952; British Coal Mining Explosives, 1958; Solid Propellent and Exothermic Compositions, 1959; The Modern Chemical Industry in Great Britain (Cantor Lectures, Jl of Roy. Soc. Arts), 1961; Restrictive Practices (Soc. of Chem. Ind. Lecture), 1965; Monopolies and Restrictive Practices (RSA), 1967; The Scientist and The Technologist in Britain today (Pres. Address, IPPS), 1967; Britain's Technological Future (IOP Jubilee Address), 1968; Arts, Crafts and Technology (RSA), 1969; Cobalt, Madder and Computers (RSA), 1969; The Seventies and the Society (RSA), 1970; The American Dream and the RSA, 1971; New Horizons in Research and Development (RSA), 1971; The Scientific Community, 1973; numerous contribs to Proc. Roy. Soc., Phil. Mag., Trans Inst. Min. Eng., Advancement of Science, ICI Magazine. *Recreations:* gardening and writing. *Address:* Culvers, Seale, near Farnham, Surrey GU10 1JN. *T:* Runfold 2210. *Clubs:* Number Ten; RNVR Carrick (Hon.) (Glasgow).

TAYLOR, Air Vice-Marshal James Clarke, CB 1970; OBE 1953; Deputy Director General, RAF Medical Services, 1968-70, retired; *b* 6 July 1910; *s* of William and Agnes Taylor; *m* 1961, Moira Jane, *d* of late Sir Hector Macneal, KBE; no *c. Educ:* Glasgow Acad.; Glasgow Univ. Commissioned RAF, 1937; various appts; PMO, Arabian Peninsula, 1957-59; PMO, Near East Air Force, 1961-64; Officer Commanding Central Medical Estab., RAF, London, 1965-66; PMO, Bomber Command, 1967-68, Strike Command, 1968-69. QHP 1967-70. *Recreation:* golf. *Address:* Dormer Cottage, Aston Clinton, Bucks. *T:* Aylesbury 630217. *Clubs:* Royal Air Force; Royal and Ancient (St Andrews).

TAYLOR, Sir John (Aked), Kt 1972; OBE 1960; TD 1951; JP; Chairman and Managing Director, Timothy Taylor & Co. Ltd; Vice Lord-Lieutenant of West Yorkshire, since 1976; *b* 15 Aug. 1917; *s* of Percy Taylor, Knowle Spring House, Keighley, and Gladys Broster (who *m* 2nd, 1953, Sir (John) Donald Horsfall, 2nd Bt); *m* 1949, Barbara Mary, *d* of Percy Wright Stirk, Keighley; two *d. Educ:* Shrewsbury Sch. Served War of 1939-45: Duke of Wellington's Regt and Royal Signals, Major; Norway, Middle East, Sicily, NW Europe and Far East. Mem., Keighley Town Council, 1946-67 (Mayor, 1956; Chm., Educn Cttee, 1949-61; Chm. Finance Cttee, 1961-67); Mem. Council, Magistrates' Assoc., 1957- (Vice-Chm., Exec. Cttee, 1975-76; Chm., Licensing Cttee, 1969-76; Past Pres. and Chm., WR Br.); Chm., Keighley Conservative Assoc., 1952-56 and 1957-67 (Jt Hon. Treas.), 1947-52, and Chm., Young Conservatives, 1946-47); Chm., Yorkshire Area, Nat. Union of Conservative and Unionist Assocs, 1966-71 (Vice-Chm., 1965-66); Chm., Exec. Cttee of Nat. Union of Conservative and Unionist Assocs, 1971-76 (Mem., 1964-). Hon. Treasurer, Magistrates' Assoc., 1976-. Gen. Comr of Income Tax, 1965. JP Borough of Keighley 1949; DL West (formerly WR) Yorks, 1971. *Recreation:* cricket. *Address:* Fieldhead, Keighley, West Yorkshire. *T:* Keighley 603895. *Club:* Carlton.

TAYLOR, Brigadier John Alexander Chisholm, DSO 1918; MC, TD; DL; FRIBA; late RA; Chartered Architect; *s* of late Tom Taylor; *m* 1927, Jean Bell, *d* of late Dr Johnstone. *Educ:* Sedbergh Sch. Served European War, 1914-18 (despatches, DSO, MC with bar). War of 1939-45. DL Lancs 1946. *Address:* Torbeckhill, Waterbeck, Dumfriesshire.

TAYLOR, John Barrington, MBE 1945; TD 1957; JP; **His Honour Judge John Taylor;** a Circuit Judge, since 1977; *b* 3 Aug. 1914; *y s* of Robert Edward Taylor, Bath; *m* 1941,

Constance Aleen, *y d* of J. Barkly Macadam, Edinburgh and Suffolk; two *s* three *d* (and one *s* decd). *Educ:* King Edward's Sch., Bath. LLB (London). Admitted a Solicitor, 1936, and practised at Bath until 1960. Served War, enlisting, Somerset LI, 1939; overseas service 1942-46: DAAG, HQ 5 Corps, 1943; AAG, Allied Commn for Austria, 1945; AAG, No 1 Dist. (Milan), 1946. HM Coroner, City of Bath, 1958-72; Registrar, Bath Gp of County Courts, 1960-77; a Recorder of the Crown Court, 1972-77. One of examnrs apptd for Dio. Bath and Wells under Ecclesiastical Jurisdiction Measure, 1963. JP Somerset, 1962. *Recreation:* gardening. *Address:* Turleigh Combe, Bradford-on-Avon, Wilts. *T:* Limpley Stoke 2235.

TAYLOR, Ven. John Bernard; Archdeacon of West Ham, since 1975; *b* 6 May 1929; *s* of George Ernest and Gwendoline Irene Taylor; *m* 1956, Linda Courtenay Barnes; one *s* two *d*. *Educ:* Watford Grammar Sch.; Christ's Coll., Cambridge; Jesus Coll., Cambridge. MA Cantab. Vicar of Henham and Elsenham, Essex, 1959-64; Vice-Principal, Oak Hill Theological Coll., 1964-72; Vicar of All Saints', Woodford Wells, 1972-75. Examining Chaplain to Bishop of Chelmsford, 1962-. *Publications:* A Christian's Guide to the Old Testament, 1966; Evangelism among Children and Young People, 1967; Tyndale Commentary on Ezekiel, 1969. *Address:* 4 Russell Road, Buckhurst Hill, Essex IG9 5QJ. *T:* 01-504 5218.

TAYLOR, Dr John Bryan, FRS 1970; Head of Theoretical Physics Division, Culham Laboratory, since 1963; *b* 26 Dec. 1928; *s* of Frank and Ada Taylor, Birmingham; *m* 1951, Joan M. Hargest; one *s* one *d*. *Educ:* Oldbury Grammar Sch.; Birmingham Univ., 1947-50 and 1952-55. RAF, 1950-52. Atomic Weapons Research Establishment, Aldermaston, 1955-59 and 1960-62; Harkness Fellow, Commonwealth Fund, Univ. of California (Berkeley), 1959-60; Culham Laboratory (UKAEA), 1962-69 and 1970-; Inst. for Advanced Study, Princeton, 1969. FInstP 1969. Maxwell Medal, IPPS, 1971. *Publications:* contribs to scientific learned jls. *Recreation:* gliding. *Address:* Culham Laboratory, Abingdon, Oxon. *T:* Abingdon 21840.

TAYLOR, John Clayton, PhD; Reader in Theoretical Physics, Oxford University, since 1964; *b* 4 Aug. 1930; *s* of Leonard Taylor and Edith (*née* Tytherleigh); *m* 1959, Gillian Mary (*née* Schofield); two *s*. *Educ:* Selhurst Grammar Sch., Croydon; Cambridge Univ. (MA). Lectr, Imperial Coll., London, 1956-60; Lectr, Cambridge Univ., and Fellow of Peterhouse, 1960-64; Reader, Oxford Univ., and Supernumerary Fellow of University Coll., Oxford, 1964-. *Publication:* Gauge Theories of Weak Interactions, 1976. *Recreation:* pottering about. *Address:* 75 Mill Street, Kidlington, Oxford OX5 2EE.

TAYLOR, Rt. Hon. John David, PC (N Ire.) 1970; Member (UU), for North Down, Northern Ireland Constitutional Convention, 1975-76; *b* 24 Dec. 1937; *er s* of George D. Taylor and Georgina Baird; *m* 1970, Mary Frances Todd; one *s* three *d*. *Educ:* Royal Sch., Armagh; Queen's Univ. of Belfast (BSc, CEng). AMInstHE, AMICEI. MP (UU) S Tyrone, NI Parlt, 1965-73; Mem. (UU), Fermanagh and S Tyrone, NI Assembly, 1973-75; Parly Sec. to Min. of Home Affairs, 1969-70; Minister of State, Min. of Home Affairs, 1970-72. Partner, G. D. Taylor and Associates, Architects and Civil Engineers, 1966-74; Director: Bramley Apple Restaurant Ltd, 1974-; West Ulster Estates Ltd, 1968-; West Ulster Hotels Co. Ltd, 1976-; Gosford Housing Assoc. Ltd, 1977-. *Address:* Windy Ridge, Portadown Road, Armagh, Northern Ireland. *T:* Armagh 522409. *Club:* Armagh County (Armagh).

TAYLOR, John D.; *see* Debenham Taylor.

TAYLOR, John Grigor; HM Diplomatic Service; Counsellor, UK Delegation to Conference of Committee on Disarmament, Geneva, since 1974; *b* 25 Nov. 1921; *m* 1954 (marr. diss. 1965); one *s* one *d*. *Educ:* Cheltenham Coll.; Christ's Coll., Cambridge (Econs Tripos). Indian Army, 1941-45; joined HM Foreign (subseq. Diplomatic) Service, 1947; served in: Delhi (twice); The Hague, Rangoon; NATO Delegn in Paris; UK Delegn to UN, New York; FCO (twice); Washington. *Recreation:* walking. *Address:* c/o Foreign and Commonwealth Office, SW1A 2AH. *Club:* Royal Commonwealth Society.

TAYLOR, John Hugh; Assistant Under Secretary of State, Ministry of Defence, 1972-76; *b* 1 Dec. 1916; *yr s* of late Arthur and Etna Taylor, Steeton, Yorks; *m* 1954, Romayne F. E. Good, *d* of late I. E. Good, Fulmer; two *s*. *Educ:* Boys' Grammar Sch., Keighley; Peterhouse, Cambridge (Scholar). 1st Cl. Historical Tripos Part I, 1938, 1st Cl. Part II, 1939. Administrative Class, Civil Service, 1939, Asst Principal, Admiralty; Private Secretary to Civil Lord 1941-1942; Private Secretary to Civil Lord and

also to Parliamentary Secretary, 1942-43; Principal Private Secretary to First Lord, 1950-51; Assistant Secretary, 1951-61; Under-Secretary, Admiralty, 1961-64; Asst Under-Sec. of State, MoD, 1964-69; Under-Sec., Civil Service Dept, 1969-70; Dep. Principal, Civil Service Coll., 1970-72. Coronation Medal, 1953. *Recreations:* ornithology and photography. *Address:* 14 Duke's Wood Drive, Gerrards Cross, Bucks. *T:* Gerrards Cross 84241. *Club:* United Oxford & Cambridge University.

TAYLOR, John Lang, CMG 1974; HM Diplomatic Service; Ambassador to Venezuela, since 1975; *b* 3 Aug. 1924; *y s* of Sir John William Taylor, KBE, CMG; *m* 1952, Molly, *o d* of James Rushworth; five *s* three *d*. *Educ:* Prague; Vienna; Imperial Services Coll., Windsor; Baltimore Polytechnic Inst., Md; Cornell Univ.; Trinity Coll., Cambridge. RAFVR, 1944-47 (Flt-Lt 1946). Joined HM Foreign (now Diplomatic) Service, 1949; served in: FO, 1949-50 and 1957-60; Saigon, 1950-52; Hanoi, 1951; Beirut, 1952-55; Prague, 1955-57; Montevideo, 1960-64; Bonn, 1964-69; Minister (Commercial), Buenos Aires, 1969-71; RCDS, 1972; Head of Industry, Science and Energy Dept, FCO, 1972-73; Asst Under-Sec. of State, FCO, 1973-74; Under-Sec., Dept of Energy, 1974-75. *Address:* c/o Foreign and Commonwealth Office, SW1. *Club:* Travellers'.

TAYLOR, John Mark; Leader of West Midlands Metropolitan County Council, since 1977; *b* 19 Aug. 1941; *s* of Wilfred and Eileen Martha Taylor. *Educ:* Eversfield Prep. School; Bromsgrove School and College of Law. Admitted Solicitor, 1966; Partner in Reynolds & Co., 1968. Member: Solihull County Borough Council, 1971; W Midlands Metropolitan County Council, 1973-; Opposition (Conservative) Leader, 1975-77. Contested (C) Dudley East, Feb. and Oct. 1974. *Recreations:* fellowship, cricket, reading. *Address:* 19 Emscote Green, Solihull, West Midlands B91 1TB. *T:* 021-704 9212. *Clubs:* Carlton, MCC; Birmingham (Birmingham).

TAYLOR, John Ralph Carlisle, CIE 1943; Past Director, Davy-Ashmore International Co. Ltd; *b* Sydney, NSW, Australia, 18 Aug. 1902; *o s* of Charles Carlisle Taylor and Jean Sawers; *m* 1933, Nancy (Ann) Marguerite Sorel-Cameron (*d* 1972); one *s* decd. *Educ:* Winchester. Shaw Wallace & Co., London, Calcutta, Karachi, 1921-28; Burmah-Shell, 1928-39 and 1945-54; General Manager in India, 1951-54. Service in RIASC (Lt-Col) 1941-42, GHQ India (Lt-Col) 1942; Petroleum Officer; *ex-officio* Dep. Sec., Defence Dept, Govt of India, 1942-45. Chairman, Shell Group of Companies in Australia, 1955-60; retired from Shell, 1960. *Recreations:* walking, reading, racing. *Address:* 166 Oakwood Court, W14. *Clubs:* Hurlingham, Oriental.

TAYLOR, John Russell; Professor, Department of Cinema, University of Southern California, since 1972; *b* 19 June 1935; *s* of Arthur Russell and Kathleen Mary Taylor (*née* Picker). *Educ:* Dover Grammar Sch.; Jesus Coll., Cambridge (MA); Courtauld Inst. of Art, London. Sub-Editor, Times Educational Supplement, 1959; Editorial Asst, Times Literary Supplement, 1960; Film Critic, The Times, 1962-73. Lectr on Film, Tufts Univ., in London, 1970-71. *Publications:* Anger and After, 1962; Anatomy of a Television Play, 1962; Cinema Eye, Cinema Ear, 1964; Penguin Dictionary of the Theatre, 1966; The Art Nouveau Book in Britain, 1966; The Rise and Fall of the Well-Made Play, 1967; The Art Dealers, 1969; Harold Pinter, 1969; The Hollywood Musical, 1971; The Second Wave, 1971; David Storey, 1974; Directors and Directions, 1975; Peter Shaffer, 1975; Hitchcock, 1977; Cukor's Hollywood, 1978. *Address:* Division of Cinema-Performing Arts, University of Southern California, University Park, Los Angeles, Calif 90007, USA.

TAYLOR, Rt. Rev. John Vernon; *see* Winchester, Bishop of.

TAYLOR, John William Ransom; Editor and Compiler, Jane's All the World's Aircraft, since 1959; *b* 8 June 1922; *s* of late Victor Charles Taylor and late Florence Hilda Taylor (*née* Ransom); *m* 1946, Doris Alice Haddrick; one *s* one *d*. *Educ:* Ely Cathedral Choir Sch., Soham Grammar Sch., Cambs. FRHistS, MRAeS, FSLAET. Design Dept, Hawker Aircraft Ltd, 1941-47; Editorial Publicity Officer, Fairey Aviation Gp, 1947-55; Author/Editor, 1955-; Air Corresp., Meccano Magazine, 1943-72; Editor, Air BP Magazine, British Petroleum, 1956-72; Jt Editor, Guinness Book of Air Facts and Feats, 1974-; Contributing Editor, Air Force Magazine (USA), 1971-. Vice-President: Horse Rangers Assoc.; Guild of Aviation Artists. C. P. Robertson Memorial Trophy, 1959. *Publications:* Spitfire, 1946; Aircraft Annual, 1949-75; Civil Aircraft Markings, 1950-; Wings for Tomorrow, 1951; Military Aircraft Recognition, 1952-; Civil Airliner Recognition, 1953-; Picture History of Flight, 1955; Science in the Atomic Age, 1956; Rockets and Space Travel, 1956; Best Flying Stories, 1956; Jane's All the

World's Aircraft, 1956-; Helicopters Work Like This, 1957; Royal Air Force, 1957; Fleet Air Arm, 1957; Jet Planes Work Like This, 1957; Russian Aircraft, 1957; Rockets and Missiles, 1958; CFS, Birthplace of Air Power, 1958; Rockets and Spacecraft Work Like This; British Airports, 1959; US Military Aircraft, 1959; Warplanes of the World, 1959, rev. as Military Aircraft of the World; BP Book of Flight Today, 1960; Combat Aircraft of the World, 1969; Westland 50, 1965; Pictorial History of the Royal Air Force, 3 vols 1968-71; Aircraft Aircraft, 1967, 4th edn 1974; Encyclopaedia of World Aircraft, 1966; The Lore of Flight, 1971; Rockets and Missiles, 1971; Light Plane Recognition, 1970-; Civil Aircraft of the World, 1970-; British Civil Aircraft Register, 1971; (with M. J. H. Taylor) Missiles of the World, 1972-; (with D. Mondey) Spies in the Sky, 1972; (with K. Munson) History of Aviation, 1973, 2nd edn, 1977; History of Aerial Warfare, 1974; (with S. H. H. Young) Passenger Aircraft and Airlines, 1975; Jets, 1976; (with M. J. H. Taylor) Helicopters of the World, 1976. *Recreations:* historical studies, travel, ski-ing. *Address:* 36 Alexandra Drive, Surbiton, Surrey KT5 9AF. *T:* 01-399 5435. *Clubs:* Royal Aero, Royal Air Force (Hon.); Fenland Motor.

TAYLOR, Kenneth, CB 1975; Secretary, Export Credits Guarantee Department, since 1975; *b* 10 Oct. 1923; *s* of William and May Taylor; *m* 1952, Mary Matilda Jacobs; one *s* one *d.* *Educ:* Merchant Taylors' Sch., Crosby; University Coll., Oxford (MA). Commnd RAF, 1943; Flt-Lt 212 Sqdn, 1944-45. Entered Min. of Civil Aviation as Asst Principal, 1947; BoT, later DTI, 1948-56, 1959-74; Treasury, 1957-59; Asst Sec. 1963; idc 1967; Under-Sec., 1969-73; Dep. Sec., 1973; Secretary, Price Commn, 1973-74. Mem., BOTB, 1975-. *Recreations:* squash, tennis, chess. *Address:* High Trees, West Hill Way, Totteridge, N20. *T:* 01-445 7173. *Club:* Overseas Bankers.

TAYLOR, Kenneth John; His Honour Judge Kenneth Taylor; a Circuit Judge, ince 1977; *b* 29 March 1929; *s* of Hereford Phillips Taylor and Florence Gertrude Taylor; *m* 1953, Joan Cattermole; one *s* one *d.* *Educ:* William Hulme's Grammar Sch., Manchester; Manchester Univ. (LLB). Called to Bar, Middle Temple, 1951. A Recorder of the Crown Court, 1972-77. *Recreations:* photography, reading, watching cricket. *Address:* 25 Mill Lane, off The Bank, Scholar Green, Stoke-on-Trent. *T:* Stoke-on-Trent 512102.

TAYLOR, Kenneth Roy Eldin, CVO 1955; *b* 27 Sept. 1902; *s* of late Thomas Taylor, Welbourn, Lincoln; *m* 1926, Katharine Mary, *er d* of late Frederick Ernest Taylor, FRCS, LRCP, Brancaster, Norfolk; three *s.* *Educ:* Lincoln School; Selwyn College, Cambridge (BA, LLM, Exhibitioner and Univ. Squire Law Schol.). Called to the Bar, Lincoln's Inn, 1970. Chm., Industrial Appeals Tribunals, 1967-74; Sec., Diocesan Conf., 1966-68; Solicitor for Affairs of HM Duchy of Lancaster, 1942-67; former Member of Council, British Records Association; Chm., Portsmouth Diocesan Parsonages Bd. *Recreations:* literature, rowing. *Address:* 22 Lingfield Court, Pembroke Park, Old Portsmouth, Hants. *T:* 26293. *Clubs:* Leander; Royal Naval and Royal Albert Yacht (Portsmouth).

TAYLOR, Len Clive; Head of Educational Programme Services, Independent Broadcasting Authority, since 1977; *b* 4 Aug. 1922; *s* of late S. R. Taylor, Calcutta, India; *m* 1951, Suzanne Dufault, Spencer, Massachusetts, USA; one *s* two *d.* *Educ:* Sevenoaks School; New College, Oxford; Chicago University. New College, Oxford; 1st Cl. Hons Mod. Hist.; Commonwealth Fund Fellowship. Assistant Master, St Paul's School, Darjeeling, India, 1940-42 and 1945-46; Indian Army Intelligence Corps, 1942-45; New College, Oxford, 1946-49; Chicago University, 1949-50; Senior History Master, Repton School, 1950-54; Headmaster, Sevenoaks School, 1954-68; Dir, Mediterranean Educnl Innovation Project, OECD, Paris, 1972-77. Dir, Nuffield Foundn 'Resources for Learning' Project, 1966-72. *Publications:* Experiments in Education at Sevenoaks, 1965; Resources for Learning, 1971. *Address:* 43 The Drive, Sevenoaks, Kent. *T:* Sevenoaks 51448.

TAYLOR, Leon Eric Manners; Research Analyst, University of Sussex, since 1973; *b* 28 Oct. 1917; *s* of late Leon Eric Taylor and Veronica Dalmahoy (*née* Rogers); *m* 1963, Margaret Betty Thompson; no *c.* *Educ:* Fettes Coll., Edinburgh; Oriel Coll., Oxford. Captain RA (Service, 1939-46). Asst Principal, 1945, Principal, 1948, in Bd of Trade until 1963. First Sec., UK Delegn to the European Communities, 1963-66; Econ. Counsellor, British High Commn, Kuala Lumpur, 1966-70. Called to Bar, Inner Temple, 1951. Attended Joint Services Staff College, 1952. Hon. Visiting Fellow, Centre for Contemporary European Studies, University of Sussex, 1970-71; Counsellor (Commercial), The Hague, 1971-72. *Recreations:* walking, amateur theatre, golf. *Address:* Sam's Hill Cottage, 47 North

Street, Middle Barton, Oxford OX5 4BH. *T:* Steeple Aston 47256.

TAYLOR, Leonard Whitworth, OBE 1947; MA Oxon; retired; *b* 29 March 1880; *s* of Thomas Taylor, JP, CA; *m* 1904, Madeline Hills; no *c.* *Educ:* Warwick School; New College, Oxford. Assistant Master Stratford-on-Avon; Second Master, Bournemouth School; Headmaster Darlington Grammar School, 1913-33; Captain OTC and 5th Battalion DLI; served European War in France, 1916-18 (wounded, prisoner); Pres. IAHM, 1931; Secretary IAHM and HMC, 1934-55. *Address:* 8 Inman's Lane, Sheet, Petersfield, Hants. *Club:* National Liberal.

TAYLOR, Martin; lawyer; *b* Hereford, England, 15 Dec. 1885; *s* of James Durham and Mary Taylor (*née* Preece); *m* 1915, Caroline Strong Reboul (decd); one *d.* *Educ:* Trinity Coll.; Columbia Univ., USA. Admitted New York Bar, 1913. Practice, New York; Former Counsel: New York State Tax Commission; Reed, Hoyt Taylor & Washburn. Rep. numerous British interests in USA; Mem., Internat. Law Assoc.; Chm. Cttee on Constitutional Law, New York Bar Assoc.; Mem. Assoc. of The Bar of City of New York. Formerly: Director of Consolidated RR of Cuba, The Cuba Company, Relief for Americans in the Philippines; Common Law Foundation; Library of Sei-Kiu-Do Common Law Inst., Tokyo; National Jail Assoc.; New York Post Graduate Med. Sch. and Hospital. Founder, Village of Nissequogue; Co-Founder, Tilney-Taylor Prize. Episcopalian. *Publications:* Reorganization of the Federal Judiciary (Supreme Court Controversy), 1937; The Common Law Foundation, 1963; A Footnote to History, 1970. *Recreations:* book collecting, bridge and tennis. *Address:* (residence) 163 E 81st Street, New York, NY 10028, USA. *Clubs:* Beefsteak, Portland; Union, University (NYC).

TAYLOR, Maurice; see Taylor, A. M.

TAYLOR, General Maxwell Davenport, DSC (US) 1944; DSM (US) 1945 (3 Oak Leaf Clusters, 1954, 1959, 1964); Silver Star 1943 (Oak Leaf Cluster, 1944); Legion of Merit; Bronze Star; Purple Heart; Consultant to President of US; President, Institute of Defense Analyses; Member, Foreign Intelligence Advisory Board, since 1965; *b* 26 Aug. 1901; *s* of John Earle Maxwell Taylor and Pearle Davenport; *m* 1925, Lydia Gardner (*née* Happer); two *s.* *Educ:* US Milit. Academy (BS). Became artillery commander of 82nd Airborne Division by Dec. 1942; served in Sicilian and Italian Campaigns; in 1944 became Commanding Gen. of 101st Airborne Div., which he led in the airborne invasion of Normandy, the airborne invasion of Holland, and in the Ardennes and Central Europe Campaigns; supt US Mil. Acad., 1945; Chief of Staff, European Comd HQ, Heidelberg, Jan. 1949; first US Comdr, Berlin, Sept. 1949; Asst Chief of Staff for Ops, G3, Dept of Army, Feb. 1951; Dep. Chief of Staff for Ops and Admin. of Army, Aug. 1951; Comdg Gen., 8th US Army in Korea, 1953; Comdr of all ground forces in Japan, Okinawa and Korea, at Camp Zama, Japan, Nov. 1954; C-in-C of Far East Comd and UN Comd, 1955; Chief of Staff, US Army, 1955-59; Mil. Representative of the President of the USA, 1961-62; Chairman, Joint Chiefs of Staff, US, Oct. 1962-June 1964; American Ambassador to South Vietnam, 1964-65; Special Consultant to President, 1965-69. Formerly Director of companies (including Chairman Board, Mexican Light & Power Co.); was also President, Lincoln Center for the Performing Arts. Holds fifteen Honorary doctorates. Many foreign decorations. *Publications:* The Uncertain Trumpet, 1960; Responsibility and Response, 1967; Swords and Plowshares, 1972. *Recreations:* tennis, handball and squash. *Address:* 2500 Massachusetts Avenue NW, Washington, DC 20008, USA. *Clubs:* University (NYC); Army and Navy, International, Chevy Chase, Alibi (Washington).

TAYLOR, Neville; Director of Information, Department of the Environment, since 1974; *b* 17 Nov. 1930; *y s* of late Frederick Taylor and of Lottie Taylor; *m* 1954, Margaret Ann, *y d* of late Thomas Bainbridge Vickers and Gladys Vickers; two *s.* *Educ:* Sir Joseph Williamson's Mathematical Sch., Rochester; Coll. of Commerce, Gillingham, Kent. Junior Reporter, Chatham News Group, 1947; Royal Signals, 1948-50; Journalism, 1950-58; Asst Information Officer, Admiralty, 1958; Information Officer (Press), Admiralty, 1960; Fleet Information Officer, Singapore, 1963; Chief Press Officer, MoD, 1966; Information Adviser to Nat. Economic Develt Office, 1968; Dep. Dir, Public Relns (Royal Navy), 1970; Head of Information, Min. of Agriculture, Fisheries and Food, 1971; Dep. Dir of Information, DoE, 1973-74. *Recreation:* fishing. *Address:* 227 Bredhurst Road, Wigmore, Kent ME8 0QX. *T:* Medway 34502.

TAYLOR, Nicholas George Frederick, CMG 1970; FIPR 1973; Development Director, East Caribbean; Higgs & Hill (UK) Ltd, since 1973; Higgs & Hill (St Kitts) Ltd (Chairman), since 1973; Director: Cariblue Hotels Ltd, St Lucia, since 1968; St Lucia (Co-operative) Bank Ltd, since 1973; Local Adviser, Barclays Bank International, St Lucia, since 1974; *b* 14 Feb. 1917; 3rd *s* of Louis Joseph Taylor and Philipsie (*née* Phillip); *m* 1952, Morella Agnes, *e d* of George Duncan Pitcairn and Florence (*née* La Guerre); two *s* two *d*. *Educ:* St Mary's Coll., St Lucia; LSE, London; Gonville and Caius Coll., Cambridge. Clerk, various Depts, St Lucia, 1937-46; Asst Social Welfare Officer, 1948-49; Public Relations and Social Welfare Officer, 1949-54; District Officer, and Authorised Officer, Ordnance Area, St Lucia, 1954-57; Dep. Dir St Lucia Br., Red Cross Soc., 1956-57; Perm. Sec., Min. of Trade and Production, 1957-58 (acted Harbour Master in conjunction with substantive duties); Commn for W Indies in UK: Administrative Asst, 1959; Asst Sec.-Chief Community Development Officer, Migrants Services Div., 1961; Commn in UK for Eastern Caribbean Govts: Officer-in-Charge, 1962-63; Actg Comr, 1964-66; Comr for E Caribbean Govts in UK, 1967-73. Mem., Civil Service Appeals Bd, 1973-77. Vice-Chm. Commonwealth Assoc., Bexley, Crayford and Erith, 1965-67; a Patron, British-Caribbean Assoc., 1962-73. Member: West India Committee Executive, 1968-; Bd of Governors, Commonwealth Inst., 1968-73. Assoc. Mem. 1951, Mem. 1962, Fellow, 1973, (British) Inst. of Public Relations. Chairman: Central Library Bd, St Lucia, 1973-; Central Housing Authority, 1975-77. Founder Life Mem., Cambridge Soc., 1976. JP 1948. Coronation Medal, 1953; British Red Cross Medal, 1949-59. *Recreations:* cricket, lawn tennis, reading. *Address:* PO Box 428, Castries, St Lucia, West Indies. *T:* 8513. *Clubs:* Royal Commonwealth Society (West Indian), Travellers'.

TAYLOR, Peter Murray, QC 1967; a Recorder of the Crown Court, since 1972; *b* 1 May 1930; *s* of Herman Louis Taylor, medical practitioner and Raie Helena Taylor (*née* Shockett); *m* 1956, Irene Shirley, *d* of Lionel and Mary Harris; one *s* three *d*. *Educ:* Newcastle upon Tyne Royal Gram. Sch.; Pembroke Coll., Cambridge (Exhibr). Called to Bar, Inner Temple, 1954, Bencher, 1975. Recorder of: Huddersfield, 1969-70; Teesside, 1970-71; Dep. Chm., Northumberland QS, 1970-71. Leader of NE Circuit, 1975-. *Recreation:* music. *Address:* 21 Graham Park Road, Gosforth, Northumberland. *T:* Gosforth 854506; 11 King's Bench Walk, EC4. *T:* 01-353 3337.

TAYLOR, Philippe Arthur; Chief Executive, Scottish Tourist Board, since 1975; *b* 9 Feb. 1937; *s* of Arthur Peach Taylor and Simone Vacquin; *m* 1973, Margaret Nancy Wilkins; two *s*. *Educ:* Trinity College, Glenalmond; St Andrews University. Procter & Gamble (Graduate Trainee), 1963; Masius International (International Co-ordinator), 1967; British Tourist Authority, 1970; Scottish Tourist Board, 1975. *Publications:* Captain Crossjack and the Lost Penguin, 1970; various papers and articles on tourism. *Recreations:* sailing, making things, tourism, reading. *Address:* 16 Belgrave Crescent, Edinburgh EH4 3AJ. *Clubs:* Royal Yachting Association; Royal Northumberland Yacht (Blyth); Royal Forth Yacht (Edinburgh).

TAYLOR, Raymond Charles; Managing Director, Renmark Development Co. Pty Ltd, since 1976; Chairman, Waninga Pty Ltd; Director: Allumba Development Pty Ltd; South Australian Industries Assistance Corp.; Consul for the Netherlands in South Australia, since 1975; *b* 7 Nov. 1926; *s* of Frank Reeves Taylor and Doris Mills, Perth, WA; *m* 1959, Hilary Thérèse, *d* of A. J. Flanagan, Perth, WA; two *s* two *d*. *Educ:* James Street High Sch., Perth, WA. Asst to Gen. Manager, Western Australia Farmers Co-operative Ltd, 1948-54; Ampol Petroleum Ltd, 1954-71: Sales Manager, South Australia, 1961, Victoria, 1965; Branch Manager, South Australia, 1967-71; Agent-General and Trade Comr for S Australia in London, 1971-74; Chm., Monarto Develt Commn, 1974-76. Pres., SA Soccer Fedn Inc. *Recreation:* golf. *Address:* Renmark Development Co. Pty Ltd, 56 Carrington Street, Adelaide, S Australia 5000; 508 Greenhill Road, Hazelwood Park, S Australia 5066. *Club:* East India, Devonshire, Sports and Public Schools.

TAYLOR, Sir Richard Laurence S.; see Stuart Taylor.

TAYLOR, Robert Carruthers; a Recorder of the Crown Court, since 1976; *b* 6 Jan. 1939; *o s* of John Houston Taylor, CBE, TD, MA, DL and Barbara Mary Taylor, JP (*née* Carruthers); *m* 1968, Jacqueline Marjorie, *er d* of Nigel and Marjorie Chambers; one *s* one *d*. *Educ:* Moorlands School, Leeds; Wycliffe Coll., Stonehouse; St John's College, Oxford (Exhibitioner). MA 1967. Called to the Bar, Middle Temple, 1961; Member, North Eastern Circuit, 1962- (Circuit Junior, 1964). *Recreations:* reading, music, gardening, domestic life. *Address:* 37 Park Square, Leeds LS1 2PB. *T:* Leeds 452702; 2 Harcourt Buildings, Temple, EC47 7BE. *T:* 01-353 2548. *Club:* Leeds (Leeds).

TAYLOR, Robert George; MP (C) Croydon North West since 1970; *b* 7 Dec. 1932; 2nd *s* of late Frederick Taylor and of Grace Taylor, Eastbourne; *m* 1964, Rosemary (*née* Box); one *s* one *d*. *Educ:* Cranleigh School. Exec. Dir, G. & S. Allgood Ltd; Chm., (South African subsidiary) G. & S. Allgood (Pty) Ltd; Dir, Syncronol Industries Ltd. Mem. Council, Building Materials Export Gp. Contested (C) North Battersea, 1959 and 1964. Mem., Select Cttee of Public Accounts, 1975-. TA parachutist. *Recreations:* bridge; formerly Rugby football (played for Sussex). *Address:* Hinterland House, Effingham Common, Surrey. *T:* Bookham 52691. *Clubs:* Junior Carlton, East India, Devonshire, Sports and Public Schools.

TAYLOR, Sir Robert (Mackinlay), Kt 1963; CBE 1956; Chairman, Thomas Tilling Ltd, since 1976; Deputy Chairman: Standard Chartered Bank Ltd, since 1973; Standard Bank, since 1973; Chartered Bank, since 1973; Director: Standard Bank Investment Corporation, Johannesburg; Standard Bank of South Africa; *b* 29 Sept. 1912; *s* of late Commander R. M. Taylor, DSC, Royal Navy, and late Mrs Taylor; *m* 1944, Alda Cecilia Ignesti; one *d*. *Educ:* Plymouth College; Hele's School, Exeter; University Coll. of the SW, Exeter (MSc(Econ.) London). Entered Home CS, 1937; transf. Colonial Service, 1948. Dep. Comr, Nat. Savings Cttee, 1939. War Service, 1939-46; Commnd 2 Lieut, RA, 1940; Occupied Enemy Territory Admin., Eritrea, 1941-43, Finance Officer (Major); Dep. Controller Finance and Accounts (Lt-Col), Brit. Somaliland, Reserved Areas of Ethiopia, Italian Somaliland, 1943-45; Controller, Finance and Accounts (Col) E Africa Comd, 1945, Middle East Comd, 1945-46. Economic Adviser, Govt of Fiji, 1947; Fin. Sec., Fiji, 1948-52; Fin. Sec., N Rhodesia, 1952-58; seconded to Govt of Fedn of Rhodesia and Nyasaland, 1953; Sec. for Transport until end 1954; thereafter Sec. to Federal Treasury; retd from HMOCS, Dec. 1958. Chm., Richard Costain Ltd, 1969-73. Mem. Adv. Commn on Review of Constitution of Rhodesia and Nyasaland (Monckton Commn), 1960. *Publication:* A Social Survey of Plymouth, 1937. *Recreation:* golf. *Address:* Flat 8, 24 Park Road, NW1. *Clubs:* Athenæum, Naval and Military; MCC; Salisbury (Rhodesia).

TAYLOR, Robert Martin, OBE 1976; Editorial Director, The Croydon Advertiser Ltd, 1967-76; *b* 25 Nov. 1914; *s* of Ernest H. and Charlotte Taylor; *m* 1947, Ray Turney; one *s* one *d*. *Educ:* Simon Langton, Canterbury. Croydon Advertiser: Editor, 1950-58; Managing Editor, 1958-74; Dir, 1967-76. Mem., Nat. Council for the Training of Journalists, 1967-71; Pres., Guild of British Newspaper Editors, 1971-72, Hon. Life Pres., 1976; Mem., Press Council, 1974-76. *Publication:* Editor and co-author, Essential Law for Journalists, 1954, 6th edn 1975. *Address:* Glengarry, Milton, Drumnadrochit, Inverness-shire. *T:* Drumnadrochit 291.

TAYLOR, Robert Richardson, QC (Scotland) 1959; MA, LLB, PhD; Sheriff-Principal of Tayside Central and Fife, since 1975; *b* 16 Sept. 1919; *m* 1949, Märtha Birgitta Björkling; two *s* one *d*. *Educ:* Glasgow High School; Glasgow University. Called to Bar, Scotland, 1944; called to Bar, Middle Temple, 1948. Lectr in Internat. Private Law, Edinburgh Univ., 1947-69; Sheriff-Principal, Stirling, Dunbarton and Clackmannan, 1971-75. Contested (U and NL): Dundee East, 1955; Dundee West, 1959 and Nov. 1963. Chm., Central and Southern Region, Scottish Cons. Assoc., 1969-71. *Recreations:* fishing, ski-ing. *Address:* 51 Northumberland Street, Edinburgh. *T:* 031-556 1722.

TAYLOR, (Robert) Ronald, CBE 1971; Chairman, Glenrothes Development Corporation, since 1964; Chairman: Forth Alloys Ltd; Tayforth Foundry Ltd; *b* 25 Aug. 1916; *e s* of late Robert Taylor, ironfounder, Larbert; *m* 1941, Margaret, *d* of late William Purdie, Coatbridge; two *s* two *d*. *Educ:* High Sch., Stirling. *Recreations:* fishing, shooting, golf. *Address:* Beoraid, Caledonian Crescent, Gleneagles, Perthshire. *Clubs:* Army and Navy; New (Edinburgh).

TAYLOR, Most Rev. Robert Selby; *b* 1 March 1909; *s* of late Robert Taylor, Eden Bank, Wetheral, Cumberland; unmarried. *Educ:* Harrow; St Catharine's Coll., Cambridge; Cuddesdon Coll. Ordained deacon, 1932; priest, 1933; served as a curate at St Olave's, York; went out to Diocese of Northern Rhodesia in 1935 as a Mission priest; Principal of Diocesan Theological Coll., 1939; Bishop of Northern Rhodesia, 1941-51; Bishop of Pretoria, 1951-59; Bishop of Grahamstown, 1959-64; Archbishop of Cape Town, 1964-74. Hon. Fellow, St Catharine's Coll., Cambridge, 1964. DD (Hon.) Rhodes Univ., 1966. *Address:* Seaspray, Main Road, Kalk Bay, CP, South Africa. *T:* 8-5588. *Clubs:* Royal Commonwealth Society; Civil Service (Cape Town).

TAYLOR, Ronald; see Taylor, R. R.

TAYLOR, Rupert Sutton, OBE 1945; TD (three bars) 1943; FDS, RCS; MRCS, LRCP; Hon. Consulting Dental Surgeon, Westminster Hospital Teaching Group and Seamen's Hospital Group, 1970; Consultant Dental Surgeon, Westminster Hospital, 1937-70, Seamen's Hospital, 1930-70; Recognised Teacher, University of London, since 1948; b 18 July 1905; s of G. W. and M. F. Taylor; m 1951, Mary Angela Tebbs. Educ: Newtown School, Waterford; Middlesex Hospital; Royal Dental Hospital. LDS 1928; commissioned RAMC, TA (Hygiene Coys), 1928; Dental Ho. Surg., Middlesex Hosp., 1928; Clin. Asst, Dental Dept, Westminster Hosp., 1929-31; Sen. Clin. Asst. to Dental Surgeon, Nose, Ear, and Throat Hosp., Golden Square, 1931-32; Hon. Dental Surgeon, Nat. Hosp., Queen's Square, 1933-37. External Examr Dental Surgery and Materia Medica, Queen's Univ., Belfast, 1938-39 and 1945-48. Dental Member, London Exec. Council (National Health Service), 1948-62; Chm. London Executive Council, 1953 and 1954-Mar. 1956 (Vice-Chm., 1951-53); FDS, RCS (by election), 1948. Served with RAMC War of 1939-45; Major, 1938-42, Lt-Col, 1942-45; commanded 127 Light Field Amb. and 146 Field Amb.; 161 Field Ambulance, TA, 1957-58; Hon. Col Medical Units 54 (EA) Infantry division, 1959-66. OStJ 1959; CStJ 1961. Publications: various articles on oral surgery. Recreations: sailing, fishing. Address: Thie-ny-Chibbyr, Lezayre Road, Ramsey, Isle of Man. T: Ramsey, IoM 812585. Club: Savage.

TAYLOR, Selwyn Francis, DM, FRCS; Dean of the Royal Postgraduate Medical School, London, 1965-74; Senior Lecturer in Surgery, and Surgeon, Hammersmith Hospital; Examiner in Surgery, Universities of Oxford, London, Manchester, Leeds, National University of Ireland, West Indies, Makerere and Society of Apothecaries; b Sale, Cheshire, 16 Sept. 1913; s of late Alfred Petre Taylor and Emily Taylor, Salcombe, Devon; m 1939, Ruth Margaret, 2nd d of late Sir Alfred Howitt, CVO; one s one d. Educ: Peter Symonds, Winchester; Keble College, Oxford; King's College Hospital. BA (Hons) Oxford, 1936; Burney Yeo Schol., King's Coll. Hosp., 1936; MA Oxon; MRCS, LRCP, 1939; FRCS 1940; MCh, 1946; DM 1959. Surgical Registrar, King's Coll. Hosp., 1946-47; Oxford Univ. George Herbert Hunt Travelling Schol., Stockholm, 1947; Rockefeller Travelling Fellow in Surgery, 1948-49; Research Fellow, Harvard Univ., and Fellow in Clin. Surgery, Massachusetts Gen. Hosp., Boston, Mass, USA, 1948-49. RNVR, 1940-46; Surgeon Lt-Comdr; Surgeon Specialist, Kintyre, East Indies, Australia; Surgeon: Belgrave Hosp. for Children, 1946-65; King's Coll. Hospital, 1951-65. Consultant Surgeon to RN. Bradshaw Lectr, RCS, 1977. Pres., Harveian Soc., 1969; Member: Council, RCS, 1966- (Senior Vice-Pres., 1976-77; GMC, 1974-; Surgical Research Soc.; Internat. Soc. for Surgery; Fellow Assoc. Surgeons of GB; FRSM; Hon. FRSEd 1976; Corresp. Fellow Amer. Thyroid Assoc.; Pres., London Thyroid Club and Sec., Fourth Internat. Goitre Conference. Mem., Senate of London Univ., 1970-75. Chm., Heinemann Medical Books. Joll Prize, 1976. Publications: books and papers on surgical subjects and thyroid physiology. Recreations: sailing, tennis, wine. Address: 5 Addisland Court, W14. T: 01-603 5533; Trippets, Bosham, West Sussex. T: Bosham 573387. Clubs: Garrick, Hurlingham.

TAYLOR, Stanley Grisewood, CIE 1946; Indian Police (retired); b 19 May 1893; s of Edmund Judkin Taylor, Solicitor, Bristol; m 1919, Coralie May, d of Robert Elphinstone Bradley, Indian Police; one d (one s decd). Educ: Clifton Coll. Appointed to Indian Police, 1913; seconded to Indian Army, 1916-19, serving in Mesopotamia, 1917-18; Principal, Police Training College, Bengal and Assam, 1936-39; Dep. Inspector-General of Police, Bengal, 1939; Inspector-General of Police, Bengal, 1945; retired 1947. Intelligence Officer, Ministry of Food, Tunbridge Wells, 1948; Deputy Chief Constable, Ministry of Civil Aviation Police, London, 1949; Commandant, Police College, Federation of Malaya, 1951-53. King's Police Medal, 1934; Indian Police Medal, 1944. Address: 1 Apsley Court, Ticehurst, Wadhurst, Sussex TN5 7BJ. T: Ticehurst 200264.

TAYLOR, Thomas Whiting, MA, PhD Cantab; BD London; Headmaster, Haberdashers' Aske's School, Elstree, Hertfordshire, 1946-73; b 29 Nov. 1907; m 1937, Margaret, y d of late Prof. H. H. Swinnerton, CBE; one s five d. Educ: Liverpool Collegiate School; Christ's College, Cambridge, 1926-30 (Classical Scholar, Classical Tripos Pt I 1st class honours, Pt II 2nd class honours, Burney Prize); Frankfurt-am-Main University, 1931-32; Christ's College, Cambridge, 1932-34. Senior Classical Master at Worksop College, Notts, 1930-31; Assistant Tutor in Classics at Handsworth College, Birmingham, 1934-36; Sixth Form Classical Master at Bradford Grammar School, Yorks, 1936-39; Headmaster, City of Bath School, 1940-46. Chm., Exec. Cttee, Nat. Youth Orchestra; Chm., ESU Brit.-Amer. Schoolboy Scholarships Cttee; Schools Adviser, Central Bureau for Educnl Visits and Exchanges; Member: Council, Royal Holloway College, Univ. of London; Council, Sch. of Slavonic Studies, Univ. of London; Educnl Interchange Council. Governor: North London Collegiate Sch.; Camden Sch.; Henrietta Barnett Sch. Hon. Freeman and Liveryman, Worshipful Company of Haberdashers. Hon. ARAM; Hon. ARCM. Recreations: drama, music, foreign travel. Address: 42 The Dell, Sandpit Lane, St Albans, Herts AL1 4HF. T: St Albans 67949.

TAYLOR, Walter R.; see Ross Taylor.

TAYLOR, Dr William; Director, University of London Institute of Education, since 1973; b 31 May 1930; s of Herbert and Maud E. Taylor, Crayford, Kent; m 1954, Rita, d of Ronald and Marjorie Hague, Sheffield; one s two d. Educ: Erith Grammar Sch.; London Sch. of Economics; Westminster Coll.; Univ. of London Inst. of Educn. BSc Econ 1952, PhD 1960. Teaching in Kent, 1953-56; Deputy Head, Slade Green Secondary Sch., 1956-59; Sen. Lectr, St Luke's Coll., Exeter, 1959-61; Head of Educn Dept, Bede Coll., Durham, 1961-64; Tutor and Lectr in Educn, Univ. of Oxford, 1964-66; Prof. of Educn and Dir of Sch. of Educn, Univ. of Bristol, 1966-73. Research Consultant, Dept of Educn and Science (part-time), 1968-73; Chm., European Cttee for Educnl Research, 1969-71. UK Rep., Permanent Educn Steering Cttee, Council of Europe, 1971-73; Chairman: UK Nat. Commn for UNESCO, 1975- (Mem., 1973-); Educnl Adv. Council, IBA, 1974-; UCET, 1976-. Member: UGC Educn Cttee, 1971-; British Library Res. and Develt Cttee, 1975-; Open Univ. Academic Adv. Cttee, 1975-; SSRC Educnl Research Board, 1976-; Adv. Cttee on Supply and Training of Teachers, 1976-; Teacher Educn Adv. Cttee, 1977-; Working Gp on Management of Higher Educn, 1977-; Steering Cttee on Future of Examinations at 16+, 1977-. Mem. Senate, Univ. of London, 1977-. Commonwealth Vis. Fellow, Australian States, 1975; NZ UGC Prestige Fellowship, 1977. Hon. DSc Aston (Birmingham), 1977. Publications: The Secondary Modern School, 1963; Society and the Education of Teachers, 1969; (ed with G. Baron) Educational Administration and the Social Sciences, 1969; Heading for Change, 1969; Planning and Policy in Post Secondary Education, 1972; Theory into Practice, 1972; Research Perspectives in Education, 1973; (ed with R. Farquar and R. Thomas) Educational Administration in Australia and Abroad, 1975; Research and Reform in Teacher Education, 1978. Recreations: writing, walking. Address: Institute of Education, Bedford Way, WC1H 0AL. T: 01-636 1500.

TAYLOR, Lt-Comdr William Horace, GC 1941; MBE 1973; Commissioner of the Scout Association, since 1946; b 23 Oct. 1908; s of William Arthur Taylor; m 1946, Joan Isabel Skaife d'Ingerthorpe; one s three d. Educ: Manchester Grammar Sch. Junior Partner, 1929; Managing Dir, 1937. Served War: Dept of Torpedoes and Mines, Admiralty, 1940 (despatches, 1941); Founder Mem., Naval Clearance Divers, HMS Vernon (D), 1944. Travelling Commissioner for Sea Scouts of UK, 1946; Field Commissioner for SW England, Scout Association, 1952-74, Estate Manager, 1975-. Recreations: scouting, boating, music. Address: The Bungalow, Carbeth, Blanefield, near Glasgow. T: Blanefield 70847. Clubs: Naval; Manchester Cruising Association.

TAYLOR, William Leonard, JP; DL; solicitor in private practice; b 21 Dec. 1916; s of Joseph and May Taylor; m 1943, Gladys Carling; one s. Educ: Whitehill School; Glasgow Univ. (BL). Chairman: Livingston Develt Corp., 1965-72; Scottish Water Adv. Cttee, 1969-72; Mem., Scottish Adv. Cttee on Civil Aviation, 1965-72; Chm., Panel of Assessors, River Clyde Planning Study, 1972-74. Chairman: Planning Exchange, 1972-; Scottish Adv. Council on Social Work, 1974-; Vice-Chm., Commn for Local Authority Accounts in Scotland, 1974-; Mem., Housing Corp., 1974-; Dep. Chm. Scottish Special Housing Assoc., 1976; Member: Scottish Economic Council, 1975-; Extra-Parly Panel under Private Legislation Procedure (Scotland) Act 1936, 1971-. Councillor, City of Glasgow, 1952-69; Magistrate, City of Glasgow, 1956-60; Sen. Magistrate, 1960-61; Leader, Labour Gp in Glasgow Corp., 1962-69; Leader of Council, 1962-68; Convener of Cttees: Planning, Glasgow Airport, Sports Centre, Parly Bills. Governor, Centre for Environmental Studies, 1966-; Trustee, Scottish Civic Trust, 1967-; Chm., Glasgow Citizens' Theatre Ltd, 1970-; Mem., Nat. Executive (and Chm. Scottish Exec.), Town & Country Planning Assoc. Hon. FRTPI. JP 1953; DL Glasgow, 1971. Knight, Order of Polonia Restituta (Poland), 1969. Recreations: fishing, golf, reading. Address: Cruachan, 18 Bruce Road, Glasgow G41 5EF. T: 041-429 1776. Club: Arts (Glasgow).

TAYLOR, Mrs (Winifred) Ann; MP (Lab) Bolton West, since Oct. 1974; an Assistant Government Whip since 1977; *b* Motherwell, 2 July 1947. *Educ:* Bolton Sch.; Bradford Univ.; Sheffield Univ. Formerly teaching. Past part-time Tutor, Open Univ. (Univ. of the Air); interested in economic affairs, regional policy, and education. Mem., Association of Univ. Teachers; (formerly) Union of Shop, Distributive and Allied Workers. Is a Parish Councillor; Holmfirth Urban District Council, 1972-74. Contested (Lab) Bolton West, Feb. 1974. PPS to Sec. of State for Educn and Science, 1975-76; PPS to Sec. of State for Defence, 1976-. *Address:* 7 Bellgreave Avenue, New Mill, Huddersfield; c/o House of Commons, SW1. *Club:* Labour (Bolton).

TAYLOR-SMITH, Dr Ralph Emeric Kasope; High Commissioner in London for Sierra Leone, since 1974; Ambassador to Norway, Sweden and Denmark, since 1974; *b* 24 Sept. 1924; *m* 1953, Sarian Dorothea; five *s*. *Educ:* CMS Grammar Sch., Sierra Leone; Univ. of London (BSc (2nd Cl. Hons Upper Div.); PhD (Org. Chem.)). FRIC. Analytical chemist, 1954; Demonstrator, Woolwich Polytechnic, 1956-59; Lectr, Fourah Bay Coll., Sierra Leone, 1959-62 and 1963; postdoctoral Fellow, Weizmann Inst. of Sci., 1962-63; Research Associate, Princeton Univ., 1965-69; Fourah Bay College: Sen. Lectr, 1965; Dean, Faculty of Pure and Applied Sci., 1967; Associate Prof., 1968 and 1969; Visiting Prof., Kalamazoo Coll., Mich, 1969. Ambassador of Sierra Leone to Peking, 1971-74. Service in academic and public cttees, including: Mem. Council, Fourah Bay Coll., 1963-65 and 1967-69; Member: Senate, 1967-69, Court, 1967-69, Univ. of Sierra Leone; Mem., Student Welfare Cttee, 1967-69; Univ. Rep., Sierra Leone Govt Schol. Cttee, 1965-68; Mem., Bd of Educn, 1970. Pres., Teaching Staff Assoc., Fourah Bay Coll., 1971. Chm., Sierra Leone Petroleum Refining Co., 1970. Delegate or observer to academic confs, 1958-69, incl. those of W African Science Assoc., and Commonwealth Univ. Conf., Sydney, Aust., 1968. Fellow, Thames Polytechnic, 1975. *Publications:* papers to learned jls, especially on Investigations on Plants of West Africa. *Recreations:* tennis, swimming. *Address:* Sierra Leone High Commission, 33 Portland Place, W1; Sans Souci, South View Road, Pinner Hill, Mddx. *T:* 01-866 7645.

TAYLOR THOMPSON, John Derek; Commissioner of Inland Revenue, since 1973; *b* 6 Aug. 1927; *o s* of John Taylor Thompson and Marjorie (*née* Westcott); *m* 1954, Helen Laurie Walker; one *d*. *Educ:* St Peter's Sch., York; Balliol Coll., Oxford. 1st cl. Mods, 2nd cl. Lit. Hum., MA. Asst Principal, Inland Revenue, 1951; Private Sec. to Chm., 1954; Principal, Inland Revenue, 1956; Private Sec. to Minister without Portfolio, 1962; Asst Sec., Inland Revenue, 1965. *Address:* Jessops, Nutley, Sussex. *Club:* United Oxford & Cambridge University.

TAYLOUR, family name of **Marquess of Headfort.**

TEAGUE, Colonel John, CMG 1958; CBE 1946 (OBE 1925); MC 1916; Retired; *b* 16 Nov. 1896; *y s* of William and Helen Teague; *m* 1st, 1926, Heather Fairley (*d* 1966), *d* of late Captain James William Fairley, Tunbridge Wells; two *s* one *d*; 2nd, 1973, Mrs Nora Ballard. *Educ:* Portsmouth Grammar School. Studied music under Dr A. K. Blackall, FRAM, and was his Assistant Organist at St Mary's, Warwick, 1913. Commissioned Royal Warwickshire Regt, 1914; served in France, 1915-17 (wounded twice, despatches, MC). Transf. Indian Army (Baluch Regt). With Sykes' Mission in South Persia and Staff Capt., Shiraz Brigade, 1918. Attached Indian Political Service as Vice-Consul Shiraz, 1919. Iraq Insurrection (despatches) 1920. General Staff (intelligence), GHQ Baghdad, 1920, later with RAF, Iraq, Kurdistan Operations (severely wounded), 1922. NW Frontier, India, 1930. Language student in Persia (Interpreter), 1933. Liaison Officer, RAF Palestine during Arab Revolt, 1936-39. GHQ, Middle East, 1942. Transferred to Foreign Office, 1945. Director, Passport Control, 1953-58. Polonia Restituta, 1946; Legion of Merit (USA), 1946; White Lion (Czechoslovakia), 1947. *Publications:* occasional articles for press about Middle East. *Recreations:* music, reading and walking. *Address:* 5 Hungershall Park, Tunbridge Wells, Kent. *T:* Tunbridge Wells 26959. *Club:* Royal Air Force.

TEAKLE, Prof. Laurence John Hartley, CMG 1970; Deputy Vice-Chancellor, University of Queensland, 1963-70, retired; *b* 2 Aug. 1901; *s* of David John and Bertha Teakle; *m* 1927, Beatrice Elizabeth Inch; three *s* one *d*. *Educ:* Perth Modern Sch., WA; Univ. of Western Australia; Univ. of California (Berkeley). Dept of Agriculture, WA: Agricultural Adviser, 1923; Research Officer, 1928-46; Comr for Soil Conservation, 1946-47; Univ. of Queensland: Prof. of Agriculture, 1947-62; Dep. Vice-Chancellor, 1963-70; Acting Vice-Chancellor, 1968-70. Hon. LLD Queensland, 1969. *Publication:* Fertilizers for the Farm and Garden (Teakle and Boyle), 1958. *Address:* 51 Goldieslie

Road, Indooroopilly, Queensland 4068, Australia. *T:* 378.1502. *Clubs:* Rotary of Brisbane, University of Queensland Staff (Brisbane).

TEALE, Rear-Adm. Godfrey Benjamin, CB 1962; CBE 1953; retired as Chief Staff Officer (Administration) on staff of C-in-C, Portsmouth (1960-63); *b* 27 Oct. 1908; *s* of Captain G. C. Teale; *m* 1933, Frances Evelyn Turreff; one *s* one *d*. *Educ:* Radley. Entered Royal Navy, 1926; Sec. to Admiral of the Fleet Sir Rhoderick McGrigor, GCB, DSO, 1938-55; Director of Manning, Admiralty, 1957-60. *Recreations:* cricket, tennis. *Address:* Apartado 92, Marbella, Malaga, Spain. *Club:* Royal Naval and Royal Albert Yacht (Portsmouth).

TEAR, Robert; FRSA; concert and operatic tenor; *b* 8 March 1939; *s* of Thomas Arthur and Edith Tear; *m* 1961, Hilary Thomas; two *d*. *Educ:* Barry Grammar Sch.; King's Coll., Cambridge (MA). Mem., King's Coll. Choir, 1957-60; subseq. St Paul's Cathedral and solo career; joined English Opera Group, 1964. By 1968 worked with world's leading conductors, notably Karajan, Giulini, Bernstein and Solti; during this period created many rôles in operas by Benjamin Britten. Has appeared in all major festivals; close association with Sir Michael Tippett, 1970-; Covent Garden: début, The Knot Garden, 1970, closely followed by Lensky in Eugène Onégin; Fledermaus, Rake's Progress, 1977. appears regularly with Royal Opera. Started relationship with Scottish Opera (singing in La Traviata, Alceste, Don Giovanni, Peter Grimes, etc), 1974; Paris Opera; début, 1976; Lulu 1977. Has worked with every major recording co. and made numerous recordings (incl. solo recital discs). *Recreations:* any sport, TV absorption, digging; interested in 18th and 19th century English water colours. *Address:* 101D Clarendon Road, W11. *T:* 01-727 5680. *Club:* Garrick.

TEARE, Dr (Hugo) Douglas, CVO 1973; Physician Superintendent, King Edward VII Hospital, Midhurst, Sussex, 1971-77; *b* 20 April 1917; *s* of A. H. Teare, JP, and Margaret Green; *m* 1945, Evelyn Bertha Hider; three *s*. *Educ:* King William's Coll., Isle of Man; Gonville and Caius Coll., Cambridge; St George's Hospital, London. BA 1938; MRCS, LRCP 1941; MB, BChir 1942. House Physician and Casualty Officer, St George's Hospital, 1941; Resident Surgical Officer and Med. Registrar, Brompton Hospital, 1943; Dep. Med. Superintendent, King Edward VII Hospital (Sanatorium), Midhurst, 1946-70. OStJ. *Recreation:* golf. *Address:* Keeill-ny-Magher, Bride, Isle of Man. *T:* Kirk Andreas 455.
See also R . D . Teare.

TEARE, R(obert) Donald, MD, FRCP, FRCPath; Professor Emeritus in Forensic Medicine, University of London (Reader, 1963-67, Professor, 1967-75); Hon. Lecturer in Forensic Medicine, Charing Cross Hospital Medical School, 1976; *b* 1 July 1911; *s* of late A. H. Teare, JP, and Margaret Green; *m* 1937, Kathleen Agnes Gracey, JP; three *s* one *d*. *Educ:* King William's College, Isle of Man; Gonville and Caius College, Cambridge; St George's Hospital. BA 1933; MRCS 1936; MB, BCh 1937; MRCP 1937; MA, MD 1948; FRCP 1962; DMJ, FRCPath 1963. Past Consultant Pathologist, St George's Hosp.; Past Lectr in Forensic Medicine, St Bartholomew's Hosp. Med. Coll. and Metropolitan Police Coll. Examr in Forensic Medicine at various times in Univs of Oxford, London, Bristol, Nat. Univ. of Ireland, Riyadh, Soc. of Apothecaries, and in Pathology in Univ. of Cambridge. Past Pres., Med. Defence Union; Past Pres., Medico-Legal Soc.; Past Treasurer, RCPath; Past Sec. and Pres., Brit. Assoc. in Forensic Medicine; Brit. Council Lectr, Denmark, 1964. Master, Soc. of Apothecaries of London, 1976. Hon. LLD Sheffield, 1977. *Publications:* scientific papers in Lancet, BMJ, Jl of Bone and Joint Surgery, Thorax, and many forensic jls. *Recreations:* golf, gardening. *Address:* 8 Highdown Road, Putney, SW15. *T:* 01-788 6663; St George's Hospital, SW1. *T:* 01-235 6303; Ripple Cottage, Castletown, Isle of Man. *T:* Castletown 3353. *Clubs:* MCC; Royal Wimbledon Golf.
See also H . D . Teare.

TE ATAIRANGIKAAHU, Arikinui, DBE 1970; Arikinui and Head of Maori Kingship, since 1966; *b* 23 July 1931; *o d* of King Koroki V; *m* 1952, Whatumoana; two *s* five *d*. *Educ:* Waikato Diocesan School, Hamilton, NZ. Elected by the Maori people as Head of the Maori Kingship on the death of King Koroki, the fifth Maori King, with title of Arikinui (Queen), in 1966. *Recreation:* the fostering of all aspects of Maori culture and traditions. *Heir:* s Tuheitia, *b* 21 April, 1955. *Address:* Turongo House, Turangawaewae Marae, Ngaruawahia, New Zealand.

TEBALDI, Renata; Italian Soprano; *b* Pesaro, Italy, 1 Feb. 1922; *o c* of Teobaldo and Giuseppina (Barbieri) Tebaldi. Studied at Arrigo Boito Conservatory, Parma; Gioacchino Rossini Conservatory, Pesaro; subsequently a pupil of Carmen Melis and later of Giuseppe Pais. Made professional début as Elena in Mefistofele, Rovigo, 1944. First sang at La Scala, Milan, at post-war reopening concert (conductor Toscanini), 1946. Has sung at Covent Garden and in opera houses of Naples, Rome, Venice, Pompeii, Turin, Cesana, Modena, Bologna and Florence; toured England, France, Spain and South America. American début in title rôle Aïda, San Francisco, 1950; Metropolitan Opera House Season, New York, 1955. Recordings of complete operas include: Otello; Adriana Lecouvreur; Il Trittico; Don Carlo; La Gioconda; Un Ballo in Maschera; Madame Butterfly; Mefistofele; La Fanciulla Del West; La Forza Del Destino; Andrea Chenier; Manon Lescaut; La Tosca; Il Trovatore; Aida, La Bohème. *Address:* c/o S. A. Gorlinsky Ltd, 35 Dover Street, W1; 1 Piazza della Guastella, Milan, Italy.

TEBBIT, Sir Donald (Claude), KCMG 1975 (CMG 1965); HM Diplomatic Service; British High Commissioner in Australia, since 1976; *b* 4 May 1920; *m* 1947, Barbara Margaret Olson Matheson; one *s* three *d. Educ:* Perse School; Trinity Hall, Cambridge (MA). Served War of 1939-45, RNVR. Joined Foreign (now Diplomatic) Service, 1946; Second Secretary, Washington, 1948; transferred to Foreign Office, 1951; First Secretary, 1952; transferred to Bonn, 1954; Private Secretary to Minister of State, Foreign Office, 1958; Counsellor, 1962; transferred to Copenhagen, 1964; Commonwealth Office, 1967; Asst Under-Sec. of State, FCO, 1968-70; Minister, British Embassy, Washington, 1970-72; Chief Clerk, FCO, 1972-76. *Address:* c/o Foreign and Commonwealth Office, SW1; Westminster House, 76 Empire Circuit, Canberra, ACT 2600, Australia.

TEBBIT, Norman (Beresford); MP (C) Waltham Forest, Chingford, since 1974 (Epping, 1970-74); journalist; *b* 29 March 1931; 2nd *s* of Leonard and Edith Tebbit, Enfield; *m* 1956, Margaret Elizabeth Daines; two *s* one *d. Educ:* Edmonton County Grammar Sch. Embarked on career in journalism, 1947. Served RAF: commissioned GD Branch; qualif. Pilot, 1949-51; Reserve service RAuxAF, No 604 City of Mddx Sqdn, 1952-55. Entered and left publishing and advertising, 1951-53. Civil Airline Pilot, 1953-70 (Mem. BALPA; former holder various offices in that Assoc.). Active mem. and former holder various offices, Conservative Party, 1946-. PPS to Minister of State, Dept of Employment, 1972-73; Chm., Cons. Members Aviation Cttee; former Vice-Chm. and Sec., Cons. Members Housing and Construction Cttee; Sec. House of Commons New Town Members Cttee. *Recreations:* formerly politics, now aviation. *Address:* House of Commons, SW1.

TEBBLE, Norman, DSc; FRSE; FIBiol; Director, Royal Scottish Museum, since 1971; *b* 17 Aug. 1924; 3rd *s* of late Robert Soulsby Tebble and Jane Anne (*née* Graham); *m* 2 March 1954, Mary Olivia Archer, *o d* of H. B. and J. I. Archer, Kenilworth; two *s* one *d. Educ:* Bedlington Grammar School; St Andrews Univ.; BSc 1950, DSc 1968; MA, Merton Coll., Oxford, 1971; FIBiol 1971, FRSE 1976. St Andrews Univ. Air Squadron, 1942-43; Pilot, RAFVR, Canada, India and Burma, 1943-46. Scientific Officer, British Museum (Natural History), 1950, Curator of Annelida; John Murray Travelling Student in Oceanography, Royal Soc., 1958; Vis. Curator, Univ. of California, Scripps Inst. of Oceanography, 1959; Curator of Molluscs, British Museum, 1961; Univ. Lecturer in Zoology and Curator, zoological collection, Univ. of Oxford, 1968; Curator, Oxford Univ. Museum, 1969. Member Council: Marine Biological Assoc., UK, 1963-66; Scottish Marine Biological Assoc., 1973-78; Museums Assoc., 1972- (Vice-Pres., 1976-77; Pres., 1977-78). *Publications:* (ed jtly) Speciation in the Sea, 1963; British Bivalve Seashells, 1966, 2nd edn 1976; (ed jtly) Bibliography British Fauna and Flora, 1967; scientific papers in Systematics of Annelida and Distribution in the World Oceans. *Recreations:* reading, walking seashores with the family, hill-walking. *Address:* 4 Bright's Crescent, Edinburgh EH9 2DB. *T:* 031-667 5260.

TEBBUTT, Dame Grace, DBE 1966 (CBE 1960); JP; Member of Sheffield City Council, 1929-67, Alderman, 1934-67; *b* 5 January 1893; *d* of Alfred and Ann Elizabeth Mellar; *m* 1913, Frank Tebbutt; two *d. Educ:* Coleridge Road School, Sheffield 9. Chairman: Parks Cttee, Sheffield, 1934-47 and 1950-55; Health Cttee, 1947-49; Children's Committee, 1956-67. Formerly: Vice-Chm., Nat. Bureau for Co-operation in Child Care; Mem., Home Office Central Adv. Council in Child Care and Central Training Council in Child Care. Lord Mayor of Sheffield, 1949-50; JP 1950; Hon. Freeman of Sheffield, 1959. Hon. LLD Sheffield Univ., 1965. *Address:* Edgelow, 501 Lowedges Crescent, Sheffield S8 7LN. *T:* Sheffield 746783.

TEDDER, family name of **Baron Tedder.**

TEDDER, 2nd Baron, *cr* 1946, of Glenguin; **John Michael Tedder,** MA, ScD, PhD, DSc; Purdie Professor of Chemistry, St Salvator's College, University of St Andrews, since 1969; *b* 4 July 1926; 2nd and *er* surv. *s* of 1st Baron Tedder, GCB, and Rosalinde (*née* Maclardy); *S* father, 1967; *m* 1952, Peggy Eileen Growcott; two *s* one *d. Educ:* Dauntsey's School, Wilts; Magdalene College, Cambridge (MA 1951; ScD 1965); University of Birmingham (PhD 1951; DSc 1961). Roscoe Professor of Chemistry, University of Dundee, 1964-69. Mem., Ct of Univ. of St Andrews, 1971-76. FRSE; FRIC. *Publications:* Valence Theory, 1966; Basic Organic Chemistry, 1966; papers in Jl of Chemical Society, Trans of Faraday Society, and other scientific jls. *Heir: s* Hon. Robin John Tedder, *b* 6 April 1955. *Address:* Little Rathmore, Kennedy Gardens, St Andrews, Fife. *T:* St Andrews 3546; Department of Chemistry, St Salvator's College, St Andrews, Fife, Scotland. *T:* St Andrews 5771.

TEELOCK, Sir Leckraz, Kt 1972; CBE 1968; MB, ChB, DTM, LM; High Commissioner for Mauritius in UK since 1968 (Commissioner, 1964-68); Ambassador Extraordinary and Plenipotentiary to the Holy See, The Netherlands, Luxembourg, Norway, Finland, Sweden and Denmark; *b* 1909; *m* Vinaya Kumari Prasad, BA, Barrister-at-Law, Middle Temple; one *s* one *d. Educ:* Royal College, Curepipe; Edinburgh University; Liverpool University, and Dublin. Medical practitioner, 1939-64. Member Legislative Assembly, 1959-63. Chairman, Mauritius Family Planning Association, 1959-62; Director, Mauritius Free Press Service Ltd, 1940-63. Ambassador Extraordinary and Plenipotentiary to Belgium and EEC, 1971-76. *Address:* (office) 32-33 Elvaston Place, SW7; (home) Flat 1, Chelsea House, Lowndes Street, SW1. *T:* 01-235 6299.

TEESDALE, Edmund Brinsley, CMG 1964; MC 1945; *b* 30 Sept. 1915; *s* of late John Herman Teesdale and late Winifred Mary (*née* Gull); *m* 1947, Joyce, *d* of late Walter Mills and of Mrs J. T. Murray; three *d. Educ:* Lancing; Trinity College, Oxford. Entered Colonial Administrative Service, Hong Kong, 1938. Active Service in Hong Kong, China, India, 1941-45. Subsequently various administrative posts in Hong Kong; Colonial Secretary, Hong Kong, 1963-65. Dir, Assoc. of British Pharmaceutical Industry, 1965-76. *Recreations:* gardening, swimming, reading. *Address:* The Hogge House, Buxted, Sussex.

TEI ABAL, Sir, Kt 1976; CBE 1974; MHA, PNG; Leader of the Opposition, United Party, Papua New Guinea; *b* 1932; *m* ; six *c*. Became a tea-planter and trader in Papua New Guinea; a Leader of the Engi Clan in Western Highlands. Member for Wabag, open electorate, PNG; Former Member (Ministerial) in 1st, 2nd and 3rd Houses of Assembly. *Address:* c/o PO Box 3534, Port Moresby, Papua New Guinea; Wabag, Papua New Guinea.

TEIGNMOUTH, 7th Baron, *cr* 1797; **Frederick Maxwell Aglionby Shore;** Bt 1792; DSC and Bar 1944; *b* 2 Dec. 1920; *yr s* of 6th Baron and Anna Adelaide Caroline (*d* 1976), *d* of Col Marsh; *S* father, 1964; *m* 1947, Daphne Beryl (marriage annulled, 1952), *o d* of W. H. Freke-Evans, Hove. *Educ:* Wellington College. Served War of 1939-45: Lieut, RNVR (despatches twice, DSC and Bar). *Recreations:* fishing, shooting, painting. *Heir:* none. *Address:* Brownsbarn, Thomastown, Co. Kilkenny, Eire.

TEJAN-SIE, Sir Banja, GCMG 1970 (CMG 1967); Governor-General of Sierra Leone, 1970-71 (Acting Governor-General, 1968-70); *b* 7 Aug. 1917; *s* of late Alpha Ahmed Tejan-Sie; *m* 1946, Admira Stapleton; three *s* one *d. Educ:* Bo Sch., Freetown; Prince of Wales Sch., Freetown; LSE, London University. Called to Bar, Lincoln's Inn, 1951. Station Clerk, Sierra Leone Railway,1938-39; Nurse, Medical Dept, 1940-46; Ed., West African Students' Union, 1948-51; Nat. Vice-Pres., Sierra Leone People's Party, 1953-56; Police Magistrate: Eastern Province, 1955; Northern Province, 1958; Sen. Police Magistrate Provinces, 1961; Speaker, Sierra Leone House of Representatives, 1962-67; Chief Justice of Sierra Leone, 1967-70. Mem. Keith Lucas Commn on Electoral Reform, 1954. Hon. Sec. Sierra Leone Bar Assoc., 1957-58. Chm. Bd of Management, Cheshire Foundn, Sierra Leone, 1966. Has led delegations and paid official visits to many countries throughout the world. Pres., Freetown Golf Club, 1970-. Grand Cross (Nigeria), 1970; Grand Band, Order of Star of Africa (Liberia), 1969; Special Grand Cordon, Order of propitious clouds (Taiwan), 1970; Grand Cordon, Order of Knighthood of Pioneers (Liberia), 1970; Order of Cedar (Lebanon), 1970. *Recreations:* music, reading. *Address:* 3 Tracy Avenue, NW2. *T:* 01-452 2324. *Club:* Royal Commonwealth Society.

TE KANAWA, Kiri, OBE 1973; opera singer; *m* 1967, Desmond Stephen Park. *Educ:* St Mary's Coll., Auckland, NZ; London

Opera Centre. Major rôles at Royal Opera House, Covent Garden, include: the Countess, in Marriage of Figaro; Elvira, in Don Giovanni; Mimi, in La Bohème; Desdemona, in Otello; Marguerite, in Faust; Amelia, in Simon Boccanegra; Fiordiligi, in Cosi Fan Tutti; Tatiana, in Eugene Onegin; title rôle in Arabella. Has sung leading rôles at Metropolitan Opera, New York, notably, Desdemona, Elvira, and Countess; also at the Paris Opera as Elvira, Fiordiligi and Pamina in Magic Flute; at San Francisco Opera, Amelia and Pamina; at Sydney Opera House, Mimi nd Amelia. *Recreations:* golf, swimming. *Address:* c/o Artists' International Management, AG Ltd, 5 Regent's Park Road, NW1.

TELFER, Rev. Andrew Cecil, MA; FRAS; *b* 1893; 2nd *s* of Rev. A. Telfer, Faversham, Kent; *m* 1928, Dorothy, *y d* of C. J. Britton, Ford End, Essex; two *d. Educ:* King's School, Canterbury; Selwyn College, Cambridge. Deacon, 1943; Priest, 1944; served European War, 1914-19 (wounded); Captain CUH and H, 1913-20; President CUAC, 1919-20; Assistant Master Felsted School, 1920-27; Headmaster Ludlow Grammar School, 1927-33; Housemaster, Felsted School, 1933-46; retired, 1960. Co-Founder Achilles Club. *Address:* Felsted, Essex.

TELFORD, Robert, CBE 1967; CEng, FIEE, FIProdE, FBIM, FRSA; Managing Director: The Marconi Co. Ltd, since 1965; GEC-Marconi Electronics Ltd, since Dec. 1968; Director, General Electric Co., since 1973; *b* 1 Oct. 1915; *s* of Robert and Sarah Annie Telford; *m* 1st, 1941 (marr. diss. 1950); one *s*; 2nd, 1958, Elizabeth Mary (*née* Shelley); three *d. Educ:* Quarry Bank Sch., Liverpool; Queen Elizabeth's Grammar Sch., Tamworth; Christ's Coll., Cambridge (MA). Works Manager, Hackbridge Works, Marconi's W. T. Co. Ltd, 1940-46; Man. Dir, Companhia Marconi Brasileira, 1946-50; Personal Asst to Gen. Manager, Marconi's W. T. Co. Ltd, 1950-53; Gen. Works Manager, Marconi's W. T. Co. Ltd, 1953-61; Gen. Manager, The Marconi Co. Ltd, 1961-65. *Address:* Rettendon House, Rettendon, Chelmsford, Essex. *T:* Wickford 3131. *Club:* Royal Air Force.

TELLER, Prof. Edward; University Professor, University of California, Berkeley, 1971-75, now Emeritus (Professor of Physics, 1960-71); Chairman, Department of Applied Science, University of California, 1963-66; Associate Director, Lawrence Radiation Laboratory, University of California, 1954-75, now Emeritus; *b* Budapest, Hungary, 15 January 1908; *s* of a lawyer; became US citizen, 1941; *m* 1934, Augusta Harkanyi; one *s* one *d. Educ:* Karlsruhe Technical Inst., Germany; Univ. of Munich; Leipzig (PhD). Research Associate, Leipzig, 1929-31; Research Associate, Göttingen, 1931-33; Rockefeller Fellow, Copenhagen, 1934; Lectr, Univ. of London, 1934-35; Prof. of Physics, George Washington Univ., Washington, DC, 1935-41; Prof. of Physics, Columbia Univ., 1941-42; Physicist, Manhattan, Engineer District, 1942-46, Univ. of Chicago, 1942-43; Los Alamos Scientific Laboratory, 1943-46; Prof. of Physics, Univ. of Chicago, 1946-52; Asst Dir, Los Alamos (on leave, Chicago), 1949-52; Consultant, Livermore Br., Univ. of Calif, Radiation Laboratory, 1952-53; Prof. of Physics, Univ. of Calif, 1953-60; Dir, Livermore Br., Lawrence Livermore Lab., Univ. of Calif, 1958-60. Mem. Nat. Acad. of Sciences, etc. Holds several hon. degrees, 1954-. Has gained awards, 1957-, incl. Harvey Prize, Israel, 1975. *Publications:* The Structure of Matter, 1949; Our Nuclear Future, 1958; The Legacy of Hiroshima, 1962; The Reluctant Revolutionary, 1964; The Constructive Uses of Nuclear Explosives, 1968; Great Men of Physics, 1969; Nuclear Energy in a Developing World, 1977. *Address:* Stanford, Ca 94305, USA.

TELLO, Manuel, CMG (Hon.) 1975; Ambassador of Mexico to the Court of St James's, since 1977; *b* 15 March 1935; *s* of late Manuel Tello and Guadalupe M. de Tello; *m* 1959, Sonia D. de Tello. *Educ:* schools in Mexico City; Georgetown Univ.; Sch. for Foreign Service, Washington, DC; Escuela Libre de Derecho; Institut de Hautes Etudes Internationales, Geneva. Equivalent of BA in Foreign Service Studies and post-grad. studies in Internat. Law. Joined Mexican Foreign Service, 1957; Asst Dir Gen. for Internat. Organizations, 1967-70, Dir Gen., 1970-72; Dir for Multilateral Affairs, 1972-74; Dir for Political Affairs, 1974-76. Alternate Rep. of Mexico to: OAS, 1959-63; Internat. Orgs, Geneva, 1963-64; Conf. of Cttee on Disarmament, Geneva, 1964-67. Rep. of Mexico to: Org. for Proscription of Nuclear Weapons in Latin America, 1967-70; 3rd UN Conf. on Law of the Sea, 1971-76. Has attended seven Sessions of UN Gen. Assembly. Holds decorations from Chile, France, Italy, Jordan, Panama, Venezuela, Yugoslavia. *Publications:* contribs to learned jls in the field of international relations. *Recreations:* theatre, music. *Address:* 48 Belgrave Square, SW1X 8QY. *T:* 01-235 2522; Jardín 15, San Angel Inn, México 20, DF. *T:* 548 45 22. *Clubs:* Travellers', Les Ambassadeurs, Annabel's, Tramps.

TEMIN, Prof. Howard M(artin), PhD; Professor of Oncology, since 1969, Wisconsin Alumni Research Foundation Professor of Cancer Research, since 1971 and American Cancer Society Professor of Viral Oncology and Cell Biology, since 1974, University of Wisconsin-Madison; *b* 10 Dec. 1934; *s* of Henry Temin and Annette Lehman Temin; *m* 1962, Rayla Greenberg; two *d. Educ:* Swarthmore Coll., Swarthmore, Pa (BA 1955); Calif Inst. of Technol., Pasadena (PhD 1959). Postdoctoral Fellow, Calif Inst. of Technol., Pasadena, 1959-60; Asst Prof. of Oncology, Univ. of Wis-Madison, 1960-64, Associate Prof. of Oncol., 1964-69. US Public Health Service Res. Career Develt Award, National Cancer Inst., 1964-74; (jtly) Nobel Prize for Physiology or Medicine, 1975. Hon. DSc: Swarthmore Coll., 1972; NY Med. Coll., 1972; Univ. of Pa, 1976; Hahnemann Med. Coll., 1976; Lawrence Univ., 1976. *Publications:* articles on viruses and cancer and on RNA-directed DNA synthesis. *Address:* McArdle Laboratory, University of Wisconsin-Madison, Madison, Wis 53706, USA. *T:* 608-252-1209.

TEMPEST, Margaret (Mary), (Lady Mears; Author and Illustrator; *d* of Charles Ernest Tempest, JP, Ipswich; *m* 1951, Sir Grimwood Mears, KCIE (*d* 1963). *Educ:* Westminster Sch. of Art; Royal Drawing Soc.; Chelsea Illustrators. *Publications:* author and illustrator of: The Lord's Prayer for Children, 1943; A Thanksgiving, 1944; A Belief, 1945; The Christchild, 1947; A Sunday Book, 1954; The Little Lamb of Bethlehem, 1956; also of The Pinkie Mouse and Curly Cobbler series, 1944. Has illustrated many books including (1929-) The Grey Rabbit series. *Recreations:* yachting; yacht-racing. *Address:* 3 St Edmund's Road, Ipswich, Suffolk. *T:* 54261. *Club:* Royal Harwich Yacht.

TEMPEST, Prof. Norton Robert; William Roscoe Professor of Education, Liverpool University, 1954-72, now Emeritus; *b* 29 Dec. 1904; *s* of James Henry and Veronica Tempest (*née* Fletcher); *m* 1st, 1932, Mary MacDermott (*d* 1962), Danvers, Mass, USA; one *s*; 2nd, 1970, Maureen Kennedy, Litherland, Liverpool. *Educ:* Liverpool Univ.; Harvard Univ. William Noble Fellow, Liverpool Univ., 1927-28; Commonwealth Fund Fellow, 1930-32. Taught in Grammar Schools; asst lecturer, later lecturer, Manchester and Sheffield Univs, 1932-45; senior lecturer in Education, Liverpool Univ., 1945-49; Director, Sheffield Univ. Inst. of Education, 1949-54. *Publications:* The Rhythm of English Prose, 1930; Teaching Clever Children 7-11, 1974; articles and reviews in various journals. *Address:* 5 Parson's Walk, Pembridge, Leominster, Herefordshire HR6 9EP.

TEMPLE OF STOWE, 7th Earl, *cr* 1822; **Ronald Stephen Brydges Temple-Gore-Langton;** *b* 5 November 1910; *s* of Captain Hon. Chandos Graham Temple-Gore-Langton (*d* 1921); granted rank, title and precedence as an Earl's son, which would have been his had his father survived to succeed to the title; nephew of 5th Earl; *S* brother, 966. Company representative. *Recreations:* sailing, swimming, bird watching, conservation. Resident in Victoria, Australia.

TEMPLE, Ernest Sanderson, MBE; MA; QC 1969; **His Honour Judge Temple;** a Circuit Judge, since 1977; *b* 23 May 1921; *o s* of Ernest Temple, Oxenholme House, Kendal *m* 1946, June Debonnaire, *o d* of W. M. Saunders, JP, Wennington Hall, Lancaster; one *s* two *d. Educ:* Kendal School; Queen's Coll., Oxford. Served in Border Regt in India and Burma, attaining temp. rank of Lt-Col (despatches, 1945). Barrister-at-Law, 1943. Joined Northern Circuit, 1946; Chm., Westmorland QS, 1969-71; a Recorder of the Crown Court, and Hon. Recorder of Kendal, 1972-77. *Recreations:* farming and horses. *Address:* Yealand Hall, Yealand Redmayne, near Carnforth, Lancs. *T:* Burton (Cumbria) 781200. *Club:* St James's (Manchester).

TEMPLE, Frances Gertrude Acland, (Mrs William Temple); *b* 23 Dec. 1890; *yr d* of late Frederick Henry Anson, 72 St George's Square, SW1; *m* 1916, William Temple, later Archbishop of Canterbury (*d* 1944). *Educ:* Francis Holland School for Girls, SW1; Queen's College, Harley Street, W1. JP for City of Manchester, 1926-29. Member of Care of Children Cttee (The Curtis Cttee), 1945-47. Church Commissioner, 1948-59; Mem. of Board of Visitors of Rochester Borstal Institution, 1943-60. A Vice-Pres., YHA. MA (*hc*) Manchester Univ., 1954. *Address:* Brackenlea, Shawford, Winchester, Hants.

TEMPLE, Rt. Rev. Frederick Stephen; *see* Malmesbury, Bishop Suffragan of.

TEMPLE, George, CBE 1955; FRS 1943; PhD, DSc, MA; Sedleian Professor of Natural Philosophy, University of Oxford, 1953-68, now Professor Emeritus; Honorary Fellow of Queen's College, Oxford; *b* 2 Sept. 1901; *o s* of late James Temple,

London; *m* 1930, Dorothy Lydia, *e d* of late Thomas Ellis Carson, Liverpool. *Educ:* Ealing County School; Birkbeck College, University of London; Trinity College, Cambridge. Research Assistant and Demonstrator, Physics Dept, Birkbeck College, 1922-24; Assistant Lecturer, Maths Dept, City and Guilds (Eng.) College, 1924-28; Keddey Fletcher Warr Studentship, 1928; 1851 Exhibition Research Student, 1928-30; Assistant Professor in Maths Dept, Royal College of Science, 1930-32; Professor of Mathematics, University of London, King's College, 1932-53. Seconded to Royal Aircraft Establishment, Farnborough, 1939-45. Chairman, Aeronautical Research Council, 1961-64. Leverhulme Emeritus Fellowship, 1971-73. Hon. DSc: Dublin, 1961; Louvain, 1966; Hon. LLD W Ontario, 1969. Sylvester Medal (Royal Soc.), 1970. *Publications:* An Introduction to Quantum Theory, 1931; Rayleigh's Principle, 1933; General Principles of Quantum Theory, 1934; An Introduction to Fluid Dynamics, 1958; Cartesian Tensors, 1960; The Structure of Lebesque Integration Theory, 1971; papers on Mathematical Physics, Relativity, Quantum Theory, Aerodynamics, Distribution Theory, History of Mathematics. *Address:* 341 Woodstock Road, Oxford; The Queen's College, Oxford. *Club:* Athenæum.

TEMPLE, John Meredith, JP; DL; *b* 1910; *m* 1942, Nancy Violet, *d* of late Brig.-Gen. Robert Wm Hare, CMG, DSO, DL, Cobh, Eire, and Norwich; one *s* one *d. Educ:* Charterhouse; Clare College, Cambridge (BA). Served War of 1939-45 (despatches). ADC to Governor of S Australia, 1941. MP (C) City of Chester, Nov. 1956-Feb. 1974. Vice-Pres., Chester Conservative Club; Vice-Pres., Army Benevolent Fund (Chester Branch); Vice-Chm., British Group, IPU, 1973-74; Vice-Pres., Salmon and Trout Assoc.; Mem. Council, RASE; Chairman: Anglo-Colombian Society; British Latin-American Parly Gp, 1970-74; Vice-Chm., Cons. Finance Cttee, 1966-68. Mem., NW Region Bd, Abbey Nat. Building Soc. JP Cheshire 1949, DL Cheshire 1975. Great Officer: Order of San Carlos, Colombia, 1973; Order of Boyacà, Colombia, 1974; Order of the Liberator, Venezuela, 1974. *Address:* Picton Gorse, near Chester CH2 4JU. *T:* Mickle Trafford 300239. *Clubs:* Carlton, Army and Navy; Racquet (Liverpool); City (Chester).

TEMPLE, Rawden John Afamado, CBE 1964; QC 1951; Barrister; Chief National Insurance Commissioner, since 1975 (a National Insurance Commissioner, 1969); a Referee under Child Benefit Act, 1975, since 1976; *b* 1908; *m* 1936, Margaret Jessie Wiseman, *d* of late Sir James Gunson, CMG, CBE; two *s. Educ:* King Edward's School, Birmingham; The Queen's College, Oxford. BA 1930; BCL, 1931; called to Bar, 1931; Master of the Bench, Inner Temple, 1960; Vice-Chairman, General Council of the Bar, 1960-64. War Service, 1941-45. Liveryman Worshipful Company of Pattenmakers, 1948. *Recreations:* fishing; collecting portraits and oriental rugs. *Address:* 3 King's Bench Walk North, Temple, EC4.

TEMPLE, Reginald Robert; HM Diplomatic Service; Counsellor, Foreign and Commonwealth Office, since 1975; *b* 12 Feb. 1922; *s* of Lt-Gen. R. C. Temple, CB, OBE, RM, and Z. E. Temple (*née* Hunt); *m* 1952, Julia Jasmine Anthony; one *s* one *d. Educ:* Wellington College; Peterhouse, Cambridge. HM Forces, 1940-46, RE and Para Regt; Stockbroking, 1947-51; entered Foreign Service, 1951; Office of HM Comr Gen. for SE Asia, 1952-56; 2nd Sec., Beirut, 1958-62; 1st Sec., Algiers, 1964-66, Paris, 1967-69; FCO, 1969-; Counsellor 1975. American Silver Star, 1944. *Recreations:* sailing. *Address:* c/o Foreign and Commonwealth Office, SW1A 2AH; 16 Quarrendon Street, SW6. *T:* 01-736 2795. *Clubs:* Army and Navy; Royal Cruising, Royal Ocean Racing, Hurlingham.

TEMPLE, Sir Richard Anthony Purbeck, 4th Bt, *cr* 1876; MC 1941; *b* 19 Jan. 1913; *s* of Sir Richard Durand Temple, 3rd Bt, DSO; *S* father, 1962; *m* 1st, 1936, Lucy Geils (marr. diss., 1946), 2nd *d* of late Alain Joly de Lotbinière, Montreal; two *s*; 2nd, 1950, Jean, *d* of late James T. Finnie, and *widow* of Oliver P. Croom-Johnson; one *d. Educ:* Stowe; Trinity Hall, Cambridge; Lausanne University. Served War of 1939-45 (wounded, MC). Sometime Major, KRRC. *Recreation:* sailing. *Heir:* s Richard Temple [*b* 17 Aug. 1937; *m* 1964, Emma Rose, 2nd *d* of late Maj.-Gen. Sir Robert Laycock, KCMG, CB, DSO; three *d*]. *Address:* Idbury Manor, Idbury, Oxon.

TEMPLE, Mrs William; *see* Temple, F. G. A.

TEMPLE-BLACKWOOD; *see* Blackwood, Hamilton-Temple-.

TEMPLE-GORE-LANGTON, family name of **Earl Temple of Stowe.**

TEMPLE-MORRIS, His Honour Sir Owen, Kt 1967; QC 1937; Judge of Cardiff County Court Circuit No 27, 1968-69; Monmouthshire Quarter Sessions, 1950-69; Chancellor of Diocese of Llandaff since 1935; *s* of late Dr Frederick Temple Morris, Cardiff, and Florence, *e d* of Col Charles Lanyon Owen, CB, Portsmouth; *m* 1927, Vera, *er d* of D. Hamilton Thompson; one *s*. Solicitor for five years in practice; Deputy Magistrate's Clerk, Dinas Powis Div., Glamorgan; called to Bar, Gray's Inn, 1925; Wales and Chester Circuits; Judge of County Court Circuit No 24, Cardiff, etc, 1955-68 (Circuit No 31, 1942-48; No 30, 1948-55). Comr of Assize, Oxford Autumn Assize, 1946; Comr of Assize, Welsh Circuit Summer Assize, 1960, 1961, Autumn Assize, 1963, Winter Assize and Summer Assize, 1965, 1966, 1967, 1968, 1969. Mem. Royal Commn on the Police, 1960-62. Prosecuting Counsel to the Post Office, South Wales Circuit, 1931-37; Recorder of Merthyr Tydfil, 1936-42; Acting Recorder of Swansea, 1940-42; Dep. Recorder of Cardiff, 1969-71; Chm. of Quarter Sessions: Town and Co. Haverfordwest, 1942-48; Co. Carmarthenshire, 1942-50; Brecknockshire, 1948-55; Dep.-Chm. of Quarter Sessions: Glamorgan, 1938-48; Pembrokeshire, 1942-48; formerly Chm., County Court Rule Cttee. MP (Nat C) Cardiff East, 1931-42; contested Caerphilly Division of Glamorgan, General Election, 1929; Vice-Pres. Wales and Mon Conservative and Unionist Association, 1931-42; Chm. Wales and Mon Conservative Education Cttee, 1938-42; Mem. Governing Body, Association of Conservative Clubs, 1929-42; Chm. Wales and Mon Conservative Clubs Advisory Cttee, 1929-42; Mem. of Governing Body and Vice-Chm., Representative Body of the Church in Wales; President, Provincial Court of Church in Wales; Chm. of Legal Cttee and Pensions Cttee of Representative Body, 1945-55; Hon. Lay Sec. Llandaff Diocesan Conf., 1927-35; Mem. of Cymmrodorion Soc.; Chief Comdt Cardiff Volunteer Special Constabulary, 1938-45; Chm. and Sec. Commandants of Special Constabularies Conf., No 8 Region, 1942-45. CStJ. *Address:* 8 Raglan House, Westgate Street, Cardiff. *Club:* Cardiff and County (Cardiff).

See also P . Temple -Morris .

TEMPLE-MORRIS, Peter; MP (C) Leominster since Feb. 1974; *b* 12 Feb. 1938; *o s* of His Honour Sir Owen Temple-Morris, *qv*; *m* 1964, Tahéré, *e d* of HE Senator Khozeimé Alam, Teheran; two *s* two *d. Educ:* Hillstone Sch., Malvern; Malvern Coll.; St Catharine's Coll., Cambridge (MA). Chm., Cambridge Univ. Conservative Assoc., 1961; Mem. Cambridge Afro-Asian Expedn, 1961. Called to Bar, Inner Temple, 1962. Judge's Marshal, Midland Circuit, 1958; Mem., Young Barristers' Cttee, Bar Council, 1962-63; in practice on Wales and Chester Circuit, 1963-66; London and SE Circuit, 1966-76; 2nd Prosecuting Counsel to Inland Revenue, SE Circuit, 1971-74. Contested (C): Newport (Mon), 1964 and 1966; Norwood (Lambeth), 1970. Mem. Exec. Cttee, Soc. of Conservative Lawyers, 1968-71; Chm., Hampstead Conservative Political Centre, 1971-73; Mem. Council, Iran Soc., 1968-; Secretary: Anglo-Iranian Parly Gp; Anglo-Lebanese Parly Gp; Treas., Anglo-Lebanese Parly Gp; Mem. Royal Inst. Internat. Affairs; Chm., Bow Group Standing Cttee on Home Affairs, 1975-; Vice-Chm., Soc. of Cons. Lawyers' Standing Cttee on Criminal Law, 1976-; Sec., Conservative Parly Transport Cttee, 1976-; Mem. Exec. British Branch, IPU; British delegate, IPU fact-finding mission on Namibia, 1977-. Freeman, City of London; Liveryman, Basketmakers' Co. Governor, Malvern Coll., 1975-. *Recreations:* shooting; wine and food; family relaxation. *Address:* 7 Redington Road, NW3 7QX. *T:* 01-435 4255; Huntington Court, Huntington, Hereford HR4 7RA. *T:* Hereford 2684. *Club:* Carlton.

TEMPLEMAN, Geoffrey, MA London; PhD Birmingham; FSA; Vice-Chancellor, University of Kent at Canterbury, since 1963; *b* 15 February 1914; *s* of R. C. Templeman; *m* 1939, Dorothy May Heathcote; two *s* one *d. Educ:* Handsworth Grammar School; Universities of Birmingham, London and Paris. University of Birmingham: teaching history from 1938, Registrar, 1955-62. Chairman: Northern Univs Jt Matric. Bd, 1961-64; Universities Central Council on Admissions, 1964-75; Schs Cttee, Bd of Educn, General Synod of C of E, 1971-76 (Mem., 1971-); Univ. Authorities Panel, 1972-. Mem., SE Metropolitan Reg. Hosp. Bd, 1972-74; Mem., SE Thames RHA, 1974-. Mem. Review Body on Doctors' and Dentists' Remuneration, 1965-70. Hon. DTech Brunel, 1974. *Publications:* Dugdale Soc. Pubs vol. XI together with articles in learned jls, incl. Trans Royal Hist. Soc. and Cambridge Hist. Jl. *Address:* The University, Canterbury, Kent. *Club:* Athenæum.

TEMPLEMAN, Hon. Sir Sydney (William), Kt 1972; MBE 1946; **Hon. Mr Justice Templeman;** Judge of the High Court of Justice, Chancery Division, since 1972; *b* 3 March 1920; *s* of late Herbert William and Lilian Templeman; *m* 1946, Margaret Joan (*née* Rowles); two *s. Educ:* Southall Grammar School; St John's

College, Cambridge (schol.). MA 1940. Served War of 1939-45: commnd 4/1st Gurkha Rifles, 1941; NW Frontier, 1942; Arakan, 1943; Imphal, 1944; Burma with 7 Ind. and 17 Ind. Divisions, 1945 (despatches; Hon. Major). Called to the Bar, 1947; Harmsworth and MacMahon schols; Mem., Middle Temple and Lincoln's Inn; Mem., Bar Council, 1961-65, 1970-72; QC 1964; Bencher, Middle Temple, 1969. Attorney Gen. of the Duchy of Lancaster, 1970-72. Member: Tribunal to inquire into matters relating to the Vehicle and General Insurance Co., 1971; Adv. Cttee on Legal Education, 1972-74; Royal Commn on Legal Services, 1976-. Treasurer, Senate of the Four Inns, 1972-74; Pres., Senate of the Inns of Court and the Bar, 1974-76. Hon. Member: Canadian Bar Assoc., 1976; Amer. Bar Assoc., 1976. *Address:* Manor Heath, Knowl Hill, Woking, Surrey. *T:* Woking 61930.

TEMPLER, Field-Marshal Sir Gerald (Walter Robert), KG 1963; GCB 1955; GCMG 1953; KBE 1949; DSO 1936; *b* 11 Sept. 1898; *o s* of late Lt-Col Walter Francis Templer, CBE, DL; *m* 1926, Ethel Margery, *o d* of Charles Davie, JP, Bishops Tawton, Barnstaple; one *s* one *d*. *Educ:* Wellington Coll.; RMC, Sandhurst. Joined Royal Irish Fus, 1916; Capt. Loyals 1928; Bt Maj. 1935; Capt. Royal Irish Fus 1937; Bt Lt-Col 1938; commanded between 1942 and 1944 2 Corps, 47th (London) Div., 1st Div., 56th (London) Div. and 6th Armd Div.; Dir of Milit. Govt 21 Army Group, 1945-46; Director of Military Intelligence, War Office, 1946-48; Vice-CIGS, 1948-50; GOC-in-C, Eastern Command, 1950-52; High Commissioner, and Director of Operations, Federation of Malaya, 1952-54; Chief of the Imperial General Staff, 1955-58. Colonel: The Royal Irish Fusiliers, 1946-60; Fedn Regiment of Malaya, 1954-59; 7th Gurkha Rifles, 1956-64; Royal Horse Guards (The Blues) 1963-69, The Blues and The Royals, 1969-; Gold Stick to the Queen 1963-. Served European War, 1914-18; operations in North-West Persia and Mesopotamia, 1919-21 (medal and two bars); operations in Palestine, 1936 (despatches, DSO); War of 1939-45 (wounded, OBE, CB). ADC General: to King George VI, 1951-52; to Queen Elizabeth II, 1952-54. Constable, HM Tower of London, 1965-70. HM Lieutenant of Greater London, 1967-73. Trustee: Nat. Portrait Gallery, 1958-72; Imperial War Museum, 1959-66; Historic Churches Preservation Trust, 1963-. Member: Council, Outward Bound Trust, 1954-74; Exec. and Finance Cttees, National Trust, 1959-74; Exec. Cttee and Council, Voluntary Service Overseas, 1961-; Council, Scout Assoc., 1968-; Chm. Exec. Cttee and Mem. Council, Nat. Army Museum, 1960-; President: Soc. of Army Historical Research, 1965-; British Horse Soc., 1968-70. Comr, Royal Hospital Chelsea, 1969-. Commander, Legion of Merit (USA); Commander, Order of Crown, with Palm (Belgium); Croix de Guerre (Belgium); Kt Grand Cross, Order of Orange Nassau with Swords (Netherlands); Kt Grand Cross, Most Distinguished Order of Defender of Realm (Malaya). Hon. Freeman, Armourers' and Brasiers' Co., 1965. Hon. DCL Oxon; Hon. LLD St Andrews, 1974. *Address:* Flat 7, 31 Sloane Court West, SW3 4TE. *Clubs:* Boodle's, Buck's.

TEMPLETON, Darwin Herbert, CBE 1975; Senior Partner, Price Waterhouse & Co., Northern Ireland (formerly Ashworth Rowan Craig Gardner & Co.), since 1967; *b* 14 July 1922; *s* of Malcolm and Mary Templeton; *m* 1950, Hazel Gregg; two *s* one *d*. *Educ:* Rocavan Sch.; Ballymena Academy. FICAI. Qualified as Chartered Accountant, 1945. Partner, Ashworth Rowan, 1947. Chm., Ulster Soc. of Chartered Accountants, 1961-62; Pres., ICAI, 1970-71. Chm., Industries Develt Cttee for Northern Ireland, 1968-; Mem., Royal Commn on Legal Services, 1976-. Chairman: William W. Cleland Holdings Ltd; W. W. Cleland Ltd; Cleland (Belfast) Ltd; Oullingtree Trust Ltd; Director: Ulsterbus Ltd; Citybus Ltd; Shaftesbury Estates of Lough Neagh Ltd; Byturn Developments Ltd; Nationwide Building Soc.; NI Post Office and Telecommunications Bd. *Recreations:* music, golf, motor racing. *Address:* Braes, 169 Malone Road, Belfast, Northern Ireland BT9 6TA. *T:* (home) Belfast 660033; (office) 44001. *Clubs:* Number 10; Belfast (Ulster).

TEMPLETON, Mrs Edith; author, since 1950; *b* 7 April 1916; *m* Edmund Ronald, MD; one *s*. *Educ:* Prague and Paris; Prague Medical University. During War of 1939-45 worked in American War Office, in office of Surgeon General. Conference (1945-46) and Law Court Interpreter for British Forces in Germany, rank of Capt. *Publications:* Summer in the Country, 1950 (USA 1951); Living on Yesterday, 1951; The Island of Desire, 1952; The Surprise of Cremona, 1954 (USA 1957); This Charming Pastime, 1955; Three (USA 1971). Contributor to The New Yorker, Holiday, Atlantic Monthly, Vogue, Harper's Magazine. *Recreation:* travel, with the greatest comfort possible. *Address:* 55 Compayne Gardens, NW6 3DG.

TEMPLETON-COTILL, Rear-Adm. John Atril, CB 1972; RN retired; Director: Sotheby Parke-Bernet (France), since 1974; Sotheby Parke-Bernet (Monaco), since 1975; *b* 4 June 1920; *s* of late Captain Jack Lionel Cottle, Tank Corps. *Educ:* Canford Sch.; New Coll., Oxford. Joined RNVR, 1939; served war 1939-45; HMS Crocus, 1940-41; British Naval Liason Officer, French warship Chevreuil, 1941-42; staff, GOC New Caledonia (US), 1942; US Embassy, London, 1943; Flag Lieutenant to Vice-Adm., Malta, 1943-44; 1st Lieut, MTB 421, 1944-45; ADC to Governor of Victoria, 1945-46; served in HMS London, Loch Quoich, Whirlwind, Jutland, Barrosa and Sparrow, 1946-55; Comdr 1955; comd HMS Sefton and 108th Minesweeping Sqdn, 1955-56; jssc 1956; Comdr-in-Charge, RN School of Work Study, 1957-59; HMS Tiger, 1959-61; Captain 1961; British Naval Attaché, Moscow, 1962-64; comd HMS Rhyl and Captain (D), 23rd Escort Sqdn, 1964-66; Senior Naval Mem., Defence Operational Analysis Estabt, 1966-68; comd HMS Bulwark, 1968-69; Rear-Adm. Jan. 1970; Chief of Staff to Comdr Far East Fleet, 1970-71; Flag Officer, Malta, and NATO Comdr, SE Area Mediterranean, 1971-73; Comdr, British Forces Malta, 1972-73. *Recreations:* riding, shooting, skiing, walking, travel. *Address:* 85 rue du Faubourg St Honoré, 75008 Paris, France; Château de Roaix, 84110 Vaison-la-Romaine, France. *Club:* Automobile Club de France (Paris).

TEMPLETOWN, 5th Viscount, Ireland, *cr* 1806; **Henry Augustus George Mountjoy Heneage Upton;** *cr* Baron 1776; late Lieut Royal East Kent Mounted Rifles; *b* 12 Aug. 1894; *o surv. s* of 4th Viscount and Lady Evelyn Georgina Finch-Hatton (*d* 1932), *d* of 9th Earl of Winchilsea and Nottingham; *S* father, 1939; *m* 1st, 1916, Alleyne (*d* 1974), *d* of late Henry Lewes Conran, RN; one *d* (one *s* decd); 2nd, 1975, Margaret Violet Louisa, *widow* of Sir Lionel George Archer Cust, CBE. *Educ:* Eton; Magdalen College, Oxford. *Recreations:* shooting, fishing, ski-ing. *Heir:* none. *Address:* The Holme, Balmaclellan, Castle Douglas, Kirkcudbrightshire. *T:* New Galloway 243.

TENBY, 2nd Viscount, *cr* 1957, of Bulford; **David Lloyd George;** *b* 4 Nov. 1922; *s* of 1st Viscount Tenby and Edna, Viscountess Tenby (*d* 1971); *S* father, 1967. *Educ:* Eastbourne Coll.; Jesus Coll. (Scholar), Cambridge (MA). Served War 1942-47: as Captain, Royal Artillery, NW Europe, 1944-45. Called to the Bar, Inner Temple, 1953. *Heir:* b Hon. William Lloyd George [*b* 7 Nov. 1927; *m* 1955, Ursula Diana Ethel Medlicott; one *s* two *d*]. *Address:* Flat 2, 40 Preston Park Avenue, Brighton, East Sussex. *Club:* Reform.

TENCH, William Henry; Chief Inspector of Accidents, Department of Trade, since 1974; *b* 2 Aug. 1921; *s* of Henry George Tench and Emma Rose Tench (*née* Osborn); *m* 1944, Margaret Ireland; one *d*. *Educ:* Portsmouth Grammar School. CEng, MRAeS. Learned to fly in Fleet Air Arm, 1940; pilot with oil co. in S America, 1947 and 1948; joined KLM Royal Dutch Airlines, W Indies Div., 1948; transf. to Holland, 1951, flying N and S Atlantic, S African, ME and European routes; joined Min. of Transport and Civil Aviation as Inspector of Accidents, 1955. *Recreations:* music, sailing. *Address:* 1 Latchmoor Avenue, Gerrards Cross, Bucks. *T:* Gerrards Cross 84447. *Clubs:* Civil Service; Royal Air Force Yacht.

TENISON; see Hanbury-Tenison.

TENISON; see King-Tenison.

TENISON, Lt-Col William Percival Cosnahan, DSO 1917; late Royal Artillery; *b* 25 June 1884; *e s* of Col William Tenison, DL, JP, of Loughbawn, Ballybay, Ireland; *m* 1915, Olive Leonora, *d* of late C. L. Mackenzie and Baroness Wesselenyi of Hadad, Hungary; two *d*. *Educ:* Marlborough; RMA, Woolwich. First commn, 1903; served European War, 1914-17 (DSO); retired pay, 1922. Guildford Borough Council, 1925-31; Hon. Associate British Museum (Natural History); FLS, FZS (Mem. Council, 1943-47), MBOU; Compiler Zoological Record (Aves, 1944-63); zoological artist; Field Studies Council; Worshipful Company of Farriers; Mem., Old Contemptibles Association; a Governor of Archbishop Tenison's Grammar School. Raised and commanded 54th Surrey (Wimbledon) Bn Home Guard, 1940-45. *Address:* 2 Wool Road, SW20 0HW.

TENNANT, family name of Baron Glenconner.

TENNANT, Hon. Colin (Christopher Paget); Governing Director, Tennants Estate Ltd, since 1967; Chairman, Mustique Co. Ltd, since 1969; *b* 1 Dec. 1926; *s* and *heir* of 2nd Baron Glenconner, *qv*; *m* 1956, Lady Anne Coke, *e d* of 5th Earl of Leicester, MVO; three *s* twin *d*. *Educ:* Eton; New College, Oxford. Director, C. Tennant Sons & Co. Ltd, 1953; Deputy Chairman, 1960-67, resigned 1967. *Recreations:* shopping, talking. *Address:* 27 Eldon Road, W8. *T:* 01-937 6963. *Club:* Bath.

TENNANT, Harry; Commissioner of Customs and Excise, since 1975; *b* 10 Dec. 1917; *s* of late Robert and Mary Tennant; *m* 1944, Bernice Baker; one *s*. *Educ:* Oldham High School. Appointed Officer of Customs and Excise, 1938; Inspector, 1960; Principal Inspector, 1970; Asst Sec., 1971; Dep. Chief Inspector, 1973. *Publications:* Moses My Servant, 1966, repr. 1975; The Man David, 1968, repr. 1973. *Recreations:* walking, travel. *Address:* Strathtay, Alexandra Road, Watford, Herts WD1 3QY. *T:* Watford 22079.

TENNANT, Captain Iain Mark, JP; Lord-Lieutenant of Morayshire, since 1964; Crown Estate Commissioner, since 1970; *b* 11 March 1919; *e s* of late Col Edward Tennant, Innes, Elgin and Mrs Georgina Tennant; *m* 1946, Lady Margaret Helen Isla Marion Ogilvy, 2nd *d* of 12th Earl of Airlie, Kt, GCVO, MC; two *s* one *d*. *Educ:* Eton College; Magdalene College, Cambridge. Scots Guards, 1939-46. Caledonian Cinemas, 1947; Chm., Grampian Television Ltd, 1968-; Director: Times Publishing Co. Ltd, 1962-66; Clydesdale Bank Ltd, 1968-; Chm., The Glenlivet Distillers Ltd, 1964-. Chm. Bd of Governors, Gordonstoun School, 1954-71. FRSA 1971. DL Moray, 1954; JP Moray, 1961. *Recreations:* shooting, fishing; formerly rowing (rowed for Eton, 1937). *Address:* (home) Lochnabo, Lhanbryde, Moray. *T:* Lhanbryde 228; (office) Innes House, Elgin, Moray. *T:* Lhanbryde 410.

TENNANT, Sir Mark (Dalcour), KCMG 1964 (CMG 1951); CB 1961; Deputy Secretary, Department of the Environment, 1970-71; *b* 26 Dec. 1911; *o surv. s* of late N. R. D. Tennant, Haileybury, Hertford; *m* 1936, Clare Elisabeth Ross, *o d* of late Sir Ross Barker, KCIE, CB. *Educ:* Marlborough; New College, Oxford (Open Classical Schol.). Entered Min. of Labour as Asst Principal, 1935; Private Secretary to Parliamentary Secretary, Ministry of Labour, 1938-39; and to Parliamentary Secretary, Ministry of Food, 1939-40. Served War of 1939-45, Royal Artillery, 1942-44. Assistant Secretary, 1945; Member of UK Delegation to International Labour Conference, 1949-53; Student Imperial Defence College, 1956; Under-Secretary, 1957; Secretary-General Monckton Commission on the Review of the Constitution of the Federation of Rhodesia and Nyasaland, 1960; Dir Organisation and Establishments, Min. of Labour, 1960; Secretary, Central African Office, 1962-64. Third Secretary, HM Treasury, 1964-65; Dep. Sec., Min. of Public Building and Works, 1965-70. *Address:* c/o Barclays Bank Ltd, 1 Pall Mall East, SW1. *Club:* Travellers'.

TENNANT, Sir Peter (Frank Dalrymple), Kt 1972; CMG 1958; OBE 1945; Director-General, British National Export Council, 1965-71; Industrial Adviser, Barclays Bank International Ltd, since 1972; Director: Prudential Assurance Company Ltd, since 1973; C. Tennant Sons & Company Ltd, since 1972; Anglo-Rumanian Bank, since 1973; *b* 29 Nov. 1910; *s* of G. F. D. Tennant and Barbara Tennant (*née* Beck); *m* 1st, 1934 (marr. diss., 1952), Hellis, *d* of Professor Fellenius, Stockholm; one *s* two *d*; 2nd, 1953, Galina Bosley, *d* of K. Grunberg, Helsinki; one *step s*. *Educ:* Marlborough; Trinity College, Cambridge. Sen. Mod. Languages Scholar, Trinity College, Cambridge, 1929; Cholmondely Studentship, Lincoln's Inn; 1st Cl. Hons Mod. Langs Tripos, 1931; BA 1931, MA 1935, Cambridge. Cambridge Scandinavian Studentship, Oslo, Copenhagen, Stockholm, 1932-33; Fellow Queens' College, Cambridge, and University Lecturer, Scandinavian Languages, 1933; Press Attaché, British Legation, Stockholm, 1939-45; Information Counsellor, British Embassy, Paris, 1945-50; Deputy Commandant, British Sector, Berlin, 1950-52; resigned Foreign Service to become Overseas Director, FBI, 1952-63. Deputy Director-General, FBI, 1963-65. Special Advr, CBI, 1964-65. Former Mem., Council of Industrial Design; Member: Wilton Park Academic Council; Bd, Centre for Internat. Briefing, Farnham Castle; Chairman: Gabbitas Thring Educational Trust; London Chamber of Commerce and Industry, 1976-. *Publications:* Ibsen's Dramatic Technique, 1947; The Scandinavian Book, 1952. *Recreations:* writing, talking, painting, travel, languages, sailing, country life. *Address:* Blue Anchor House, Linchmere Road, Haslemere, Surrey GU27 3QF. *T:* Haslemere 3124. *Clubs:* Travellers', Special Forces.

TENNEKOON, Victor; Chief Justice of the Republic of Sri Lanka, since 1974; *b* 9 Sept. 1914; *s* of Loku Banda Tennekoon and Nandu Menike Tennekoon (*née* Rambukwella); *m* 1946, Semitha Muriel Wijeyewardene; one *s* two *d*. *Educ:* St Anthony's Coll., Kandy; University Coll., Colombo. BA London Univ. (External) 1935. Called to Sri Lanka Bar, 1942. QC 1965. Practised at Kegalle, 1943-46; Crown Counsel, 1946; Solicitor-General, 1964; Attorney-General, 1970; Judge of

Court of Appeal, Sri Lanka, 1973. *Recreations:* tennis, billiards, bridge, chess. *Address:* (office) Chief Justice's House, 129 Wijerama Mawatha, Colombo 7, Sri Lanka. *T:* 95364; (home) No 9, 25th Lane, Green Path, Colombo 3, Sri Lanka. *T:* 20853. *Clubs:* Orient, Sinhalese Sports (Colombo).

TENNYSON, family name of **Baron Tennyson.**

TENNYSON, 4th Baron *cr* 1884; **Harold Christopher Tennyson;** *b* 25 March 1919; *e s* of 3rd Baron and Hon. Clarissa Tennant (*d* 1960), *o d* of 1st Baron Glenconner; *S* father 1951. *Educ:* Eton; Trinity Coll., Cambridge. BA 1940. Employed War Office, 1939-46. Hon. Freeman, City of Lincoln, 1964. *Heir:* *b* Hon. Mark Aubrey Tennyson, DSC 1943; RN ret. [*b* 28 March 1920; *m* 1964, Deline Celeste Budler. *Educ:* RN College, Dartmouth. Served War of 1939-45 (despatches, DSC); Comdr RN, 1954]. *Address:* 18 Rue Galilée, 75016 Paris, France. *Clubs:* White's, Royal Automobile; Royal and Ancient.

TENNYSON-d'EYNCOURT, Sir (John) Jeremy (Eustace), 3rd Bt *cr* 1930; *b* 8 July 1927; *s* of Sir Eustace Gervais Tennyson-d'Eyncourt, 2nd Bt, and Pamela (*d* 1962), *d* of late W. B. Gladstone; *S* father, 1971; *m* 1st, 1964, Mrs Sally Fyfe-Jamieson (marr. diss.), *e d* of Robin Stratford, QC; 2nd, 1972, Brenda Mary Veronica (marr. diss. 1976), *d* of Dr Austin Stafford. *Educ:* Eton; Glasgow University. Former Mem., Inst. of Management Consultants. Liveryman and Freeman, Fishmongers' Co.; Freeman, City of London. Served as Sub Lieut, RNVR, 1945-48. *Recreations:* shooting, fishing and wild-life; cooking and gardening. *Heir:* *b* Giles Gervais Tennyson-d'Eyncourt [*b* 16 April 1935; *m* 1966, Juanita, *d* of Fortunato Borromeo; one *s*]. *Address:* 106 Delarey Road, Rivonia, Johannesburg, South Africa. *Clubs:* Rand (Johannesburg); Inanda (Transvaal).

TENZING NORGAY, GM 1953; Sherpa Climber; Director of Field Training, Himalayan Mountaineering Institute, Darjeeling (established by Indian Government, 1954); *b* Tami, Nepal, 1914; *m* Anglahmu; two *d*; *m* 1962, Dawa Phuti; one *s*. Migrated to Bengal, 1932. High altitude Sherpa in British mountaineering expeditions, 1935, 1936 and 1938; took part in expeditions to Karakoram, 1950, and Nanda Devi, 1951, climbing to east peak; Sirdar and full Member to 2 Swiss expedns (climbing record 28,215 ft), 1952; Sirdar and Full Member to Sir John Hunt's expedition, 1953; with Sir Edmund Hilary reached summit of Mount Everest, May 1953. President of Sherpa Buddhist and Climber's association. Coronation Medal, 1953; Hon. Citizen of Chamonix, 1954. Star of Nepal, 1953. Holds numerous foreign medals and awards. *Publication:* After Everest (autobiog.), 1977; *relevant publication:* Man of Everest by James Ramsay Ullman, 1955 (Amer. edn Tiger of the Snows). *Address:* Himalayan Mountaineering Institute, Birch Hill, Darjeeling, W Bengal; 1 Tonga Road, Ghang-La, Darjeeling, W Bengal.

TERESHKOVA, Valentina N.; *see* Nikolayeva-Tereshkova.

TERRAINE, John Alfred; author; *b* 15 Jan. 1921; *s* of Charles William Terraine and Eveline Holmes; *m* 1945, Joyce Eileen Waite; one *d*. *Educ:* Stamford Sch.; Keble Coll., Oxford. Joined BBC, 1944; Pacific and S African Programme Organiser, 1953-63; resigned from BBC, 1964. Associate producer and chief scriptwriter of The Great War, BBC TV, 1963-64; part-scriptwriter The Lost Peace, BBC TV, 1965; scriptwriter, The Life and Times of Lord Mountbatten, Rediffusion/Thames TV, 1966-68; scriptwriter, The Mighty Continent, BBC TV, 1974-75. *Publications:* Mons: The Retreat to Victory, 1960; Douglas Haig: The Educated Soldier, 1963; The Western Front, 1964; General Jack's Diary, 1964; The Great War: An Illustrated History, 1965 (NY); The Life and Times of Lord Mountbatten, 1968; Impacts of War 1914 and 1918, 1970; The Mighty Continent, 1974; Trafalgar, 1976. *Recreation:* convivial and congenial conversation. *Address:* 74 Kensington Park Road, W11. *T:* 01-229 8152; Vittoria, Church Street, Amberley, Arundel, West Sussex. *T:* Bury 638.

TERRELL, Edward, OBE 1953; QC 1955; Chairman, Chevrons Club for Non-commissioned Officers of Royal Navy, Army, Royal Air Force and Commonwealth, to 1975; Honorary Recorder of Newbury, since 1972; *b* 12 June 1902; *s* of Thomas Terrell, KC; *m* 1928, Winifred Packard Shyvers; one *s*. *Educ:* Berkhamsted School; London University. Called to Bar, Gray's Inn, 1924; Member of Middle Temple. Recorder of Newbury, 1935-71; a Recorder of the Crown Court, 1972-74. War Service: joined RNVR as Temp. Lieut 1940; Lieut-Comdr (acting), 1941; Comdr (acting), 1942; Capt. (acting), 1944; apptd to personal staff of First Sea Lord (Adm. of the Fleet Sir Dudley Pound) for duties on U-Boat Warfare, 1941-45; inventor of Plastic Armour (July 1940) which was fitted to 10,000 Allied War and Merchant

Ships, 1940-44 (award from Royal Commission on Awards to Inventors, 1949); inventor of first Allied Rocket Bomb for attacks on U-Boat shelters. *Publications:* The Law of Running Down Cases, Edns, 1931, 1936, 1965; Admiralty Brief (an autobiography of the War), 1958. Hon. Recorder, Newbury, 1972-74. *Recreations:* tennis, yachting, inventing. *Address:* 14 Keats Grove, Hampstead, NW3. *T:* 01-435 2402; 4 Brick Court, Temple, EC4. *TA:* 77 Temple. *T:* 01-353 2725.

TERRELL, Captain Sir Reginald, Kt 1959; *b* 1889; *y s* of late George Terrell; *m* 1923, Marjorie Ethel, 2nd *d* of late Mr O'Connor; two *d. Educ:* Harrow. Served his apprenticeship in sailing ships. Joined the London and North-Western Works at Crewe. Entered the Grenadier Guards, 1915; served European War, 1915-19; MP (C) Henley Division of Oxfordshire, December 1918-October 1924. *Address:* Cliff Lodge, Cliff Road, The Leas, Folkestone, Kent. *T:* Folkestone 51806. *Clubs:* Hon. Life Member: Carlton, Royal Thames Yacht.

TERRELL, Colonel Stephen, OBE 1952; TD; QC 1965; DL. Called to the Bar, Gray's Inn, 1946; Bencher, Gray's Inn, 1970. South Eastern Circuit. Pres., Liberal Party, 1972-. Contested (L) Eastbourne, Feb. 1974. DL Middlesex, 1961. *Address:* 10 South Square, Gray's Inn, WC1. *T:* 01-242 2902.

TERRINGTON, 4th Baron, *cr* 1918, of Huddersfield; **James Allen David Woodhouse;** Member, Stock Exchange; Partner in Sheppards and Chase; Deputy Chairman: Wider Share Ownership Council; London Group, Oxford Committee for Famine Relief; *b* 30 December 1915; *er s* of 3rd Baron Terrington and Valerie (*née* Phillips) (*d* 1958), Leyden's House, Edenbridge, Kent; *S* father, 1961; *m* 1942, Suzanne, *y d* of Colonel T. S. Irwin, DL, JP, late Royal Dragoons, Justicetown, Carlisle, and Mill House, Holton, Suffolk; three *d. Educ:* Winchester; Royal Military College, Sandhurst. Joined Royal Norfolk Regiment, 1937. Served War of 1939-45 in India, North Africa and Middle East (wounded); ADC to GOC Madras, 1940; psc 1944; GSOII, Allied Force HQ Algiers, Ninth Army, Middle East, and War Office, Military Operations; retired as Major, 1948; joined Queen's Westminster Rifles (KRRC), TA. Joined Messrs Chase Henderson and Tennant, 1949 (now Sheppards and Chase). Deputy Chairman of Cttees, House of Lords, 1961-63. *Recreations:* shooting, racing. *Heir: b* Hon. Christopher Montague Woodhouse, *qv. Address:* Alward House, Alderbury, Salisbury, Wilts; 23 Sloane Gardens, SW1. *Clubs:* Boodle's, Pratt's.

TERRY, Major Sir Edward Henry Bouhier I.; *see* Imbert-Terry.

TERRY, George Walter Roberts, CBE 1976; QPM 1967; Chief Constable of Sussex, since 1973; *b* 29 May 1921; *s* of late Walter George Tygh Terry and of Constance Elizabeth Terry; *m* 1942, Charlotte Elizabeth Kresina; one *s. Educ:* Peterborough, Northants. Served War, Northamptonshire Regt, in Italy, 1942-46 (Staff Captain). Chief Constable: Pembrokeshire, 1958-65; East Sussex, 1965-67; Dep. Chief Constable, Sussex, 1968-69; Chief Constable, Lincolnshire, 1970-73. Mem. Council, Inst. of Advanced Motorists, 1974. OStJ. *Recreations:* horticulture, motoring. *Address:* Police Headquarters, Malling House, Lewes, Sussex BN7 2DZ. *T:* Lewes 5432.

TERRY, Sir John Elliott, Kt 1976; Managing Director, National Film Finance Corporation, since 1958; *b* 11 June 1913; *s* of Ernest Fairchild Terry, OBE, FRICS, and Zabelle Terry (*née* Costikyan), Pulborough, Sussex; *m* 1940, Joan Christine, *d* of Frank Alfred Ernest Howard Fell and Ethel Christine Fell (*née* Nilson), Stoke D'Abernon, Surrey; one *s* one *d. Educ:* Mill Hill School; Univ. of London (LLB). Articled with Denton Hall & Burgin, London; admitted solicitor, 1938. London Fire Service, 1939-40; Friends' Ambulance Unit, 1941-44; Nat. Council of Social Service, 1944-46; Film Producers' Guild, 1946-47; The Rank Organisation's Legal Dept, 1947-49; joined Nat. Film Finance Corp. as Solicitor, 1949, becoming Secretary also, 1956. *Address:* Still Point, Fairmile Lane, Cobham, Surrey.

TERRY, Michael, FRGS; FRGS(A); explorer and author; *b* Newcastle upon Tyne, 3 May 1899; *s* of late Major A. M. and late Catherine Terry; *m* 1940, Ursula (marr. diss. 1945), *yr d* of Captain Noel Livingstone-Learmonth. *Educ:* Preston House School; King Edward School, Birmingham; Durham University. Served in Russia; invalided out; went to Australia upon discharge; took first motor across Northern Australia from Winton, Queensland, to Broome on the North-West Coast, in 1923; Cuthbert-Peek Grant in support of expedition undertaken, 1925, from Darwin to Broome; authorised to name Dummer Range and Mount Rosamund; third expedition started Port Hedland, 1928; proceeded Broome, Halls Creek, Tanami, Alice Springs, Melbourne. Made gold and potassium nitrate

discoveries. Explored extensively in N Territory, also in S and W Australia, 1929-33; found Hidden Basin, a 40x20 mile subsided area, covered 1200 miles on camels and collected data for Waite Research Inst., Met. Bureau, and Lands Dept; Sept.-Nov. 1933, Tennants Creek Goldfield; 1934-36, prospecting NE of Laverton, WA; farming, Terrigal, NSW, 1946-63. Received by Prince of Wales, 1926; presented to King George, 1940. Has completed 14 Australian inland expeditions. Life Member: Aust. Soc. Authors; War I Aero Historians Soc. of NSW; Life Associate, Path Finders Assoc. of NSW. *Publications:* Across Unknown Australia, 1925; Through a Land of Promise, 1927; Untold Miles, 1928; Hidden Wealth and Hiding People, 1931; Sand and Sun, 1937; Bulldozer, 1945; War of the Warramullas, 1974; (autobiog.) Thanks, Kind Fate, 1978, etc; and in numerous journals. *Recreations:* surfing, riding. *Address:* c/o GPO Box 5089, Sydney, NSW 2001, Australia.

TERRY, Air Marshal Peter David George, CB 1975; AFC 1968; Vice-Chief of the Air Staff, since 1977; *b* 18 Oct. 1926; *s* of James George Terry and Laura Chilton Terry (*née* Powell); *m* 1946, Betty Martha Louisa Thompson; two *s* one *d. Educ:* Chatham House Sch., Ramsgate. Joined RAF, 1945; commnd in RAF Regt, 1946; Pilot, 1953. Staff Coll., 1962; OC, No 51 Sqdn, 1966-68; OC, RAF El Adem, 1968-70; Dir, Air Staff Briefing, MoD, 1970-71; Air Cdre and Dir of Forward Policy for RAF, 1971-74; Air Vice-Marshal, 1974; ACOS (Policy and Plans), SHAPE, 1975-77; Air Marshal, 1977. *Recreation:* golf. *Address:* VCAS, Ministry of Defence, Main Building, Whitehall, SW1A 2HB. *Club:* Royal Air Force.

TERRY, Walter Frederick; Member of Political Staff, The Sun, since 1976; *b* 18 Aug. 1924; *s* of Frederick George Terry and Helen MacKenzie Bruce; *m* 1950, Mavis Landen; one *s* one *d* (and one *s* decd). *Educ:* at school and later by experience. Entered journalism, Glossop Chronicle, 1943; Derby Evening Telegraph, 1947; Nottingham Journal, 1943; Daily Mail, Manchester, 1949; Daily Mail: Parliamentary Staff, 1955; Political Correspondent, 1959; Political Editor, 1965; Washington Correspondent, 1969; Dep.-Editor, 1970-71; Political Editor, 1971-73; Political Editor, Daily Express, 1973-75. Journalist of the Year (first awards), 1963. *Address:* St Germans House, Eliot Place, SE3 0QL. *T:* 01-852 2526; 8 Fort Rise, Newhaven Harbour, Sussex BN9 9DW. *T:* Newhaven 4347. *Clubs:* Reform; Newhaven and Seaford Sailing.

TERRY-THOMAS, (Thomas Terry Hoar Stevens); Actor; *b* 14 July 1911; *s* of Ernest Frederick Stevens and Ellen Elizabeth (*née* Hoar); *m* 1938, Ida Patlanskey; *m* 1963, Belinda Cunningham; two *s. Educ:* Ardingly Coll., Sussex. Served War of 1939-45: in army, Royal Corps of Signals, 1941-46. Piccadilly Hayride, Prince of Wales Theatre, 1946-47; Radio Series: To Town With Terry, 1948-49; Top Of The Town, 1951-52; TV Series: How Do You View, 1951-52. *Films:* Private's Progress, Green Man, 1956; Brothers-in-Law, Blue Murder at St Trinians, Lucky Jim, Naked Truth, 1957; Tom Thumb, Happy is the Bride, 1958; Carlton Browne of the FO, I'm All Right Jack, Too Many Crooks, 1959; Make Mine Mink, School for Scoundrels, His and Hers, 1960; A Matter of Who, Bachelor Flat, Operation Snatch, The Wonderful World of the Brothers Grimm, 1961; Kill or Cure, Its a Mad, Mad, Mad, Mad World, 1962; Wild Affair, 1963; How to Murder Your Wife, 1964; Those Magnificent Men in their Flying Machines, 1965; Jules Verne's Rocket to the Moon, 1967; Don't Look Now, 1968; Where Were You When the Lights Went Out?, 1968; Monte Carlo or Bust!, 1969; Thirteen, 1970; Seven Times Seven, 1970; Arthur, Arthur, 1970; Atlantic Wall, 1970; Dr Phibes, 1970; Lei, Lu., Loro, la Legge, 1971; Dr Phibes rises again, 1972; The Heros, 1972; Tom Jones, 1975; Side by Side, 1975; Spanish Fly, 1975; The Last Remake of Beau Geste, 1976. *Publication:* (as Terry-Thomas) Filling the Gap, 1959. *Recreations:* horse-riding and water ski-ing. *Address:* Suite Eleven, 15 Berkeley Street, W1. *T:* 01-499 3034. *Club:* Savage.

TESH, Robert Mathieson, CMG 1968; HM Diplomatic Service; Ambassador to the Socialist Republic of Vietnam, since 1976; *b* 15 Sept. 1922; *s* of late E. Tesh, Hurst Green; *m* 1950, Jean Bowker; two *s* one *d. Educ:* Queen Elizabeth's, Wakefield; Queen's College, Oxford (MA). Oxford, 1940-42 and 1945-47; Rifle Brigade, 1942-45; HM Foreign Service, 1947: New Delhi, 1948-50; FO, 1950-53 and 1957-60; Delegation to NATO, Paris, 1953-55; Beirut, 1955-57; Bangkok, 1960-64; Dep. High Comr, Ghana, 1965-66; Lusaka, 1966; Consul-General British Interests Section, Canadian Embassy, Cairo, 1966-67; Counsellor, British Embassy, Cairo, 1968; IDC, 1969; Head of Defence Dept, FCO, 1970-72; Ambassador to Bahrain, 1972-75; Ambassador to the Democratic Republic of Vietnam, 1976. *Recreations:* riding, sea fishing, water ski-ing. *Address:* c/o National Westminster Bank, Tothill Street, SW1. *Club:* Travellers'.

TESLER, Brian; Managing Director, London Weekend Television Ltd, since 1976; *b* 19 Feb. 1929; *s* of late David Tesler and of Stella Tesler; *m* 1959, Audrey Mary Maclean; one *s*. *Educ:* Chiswick County School for Boys; Exeter Coll., Oxford (State Schol.; MA). Theatre Editor, The Isis, 1950-51; Pres., Oxford Univ. Experimental Theatre Club, 1951-52. British Forces Broadcasting Service, 1947-49; Producer/Director: BBC Television, 1952; ATV, 1957; ABC Television: Head of Features and Light Entertainment, 1960; Programme Controller, 1961; Dir of Programmes, 1962; Dir of Programmes, Thames Television, 1968; Dep. Chief Exec., London Weekend Television, 1974. Daily Mail Nat. Television Award, 1954; Guild of Television Producers and Directors Award, 1957. *Recreations:* books, theatre, cinema, music, walking dogs. *Address:* London Weekend Television Ltd, South Bank Television Centre, Kent House, Upper Ground, SE1 9LT. *T:* 01-261 3434.

TESTAFERRATA, Marquis; *see* St Vincent Ferreri, Marquis of.

TETLEY, Sir Herbert, KBE 1965; CB 1958; Government Actuary, 1958-73; *b* 23 April 1908; *s* of Albert Tetley, Leeds; *m* 1941, Agnes Maclean Macfarlane Macphee; one *s*. *Educ:* Leeds Grammar School; The Queen's College, Oxford. Hastings Scholar, Queen's College, 1927-30; 1st Cl. Hons Mods (Mathematics), 1928; 1st Cl. Final Hons School of Mathematics, 1930. Fellow of Institute of Actuaries, 1934; Fellow of Royal Statistical Society; served with London Life Assoc., 1930-36; Scottish Provident Instn, 1936-38; National Provident Instn, 1938-51 (Joint Actuary). Joined Government Actuary's Dept as Principal Actuary, 1951; Deputy Government Actuary, 1953; Chairman: Civil Service Insurance Soc., 1961-73; Cttee on Economics Road Research Board, 1962-65; Cttee on Road Traffic Research, 1966-73. Pres., Inst. of Actuaries, 1964-66. *Publications:* Actuarial Statistics, Vol. I, 1946; (jointly) Statistics, An Intermediate Text Book, Vol. I, 1949, Vol. II, 1950. *Recreations:* gardening, music, fell-walking. *Address:* 8-b Langley Avenue, Surbiton, Surrey KT6 6QL. *T:* 01-399 3001.

TETLEY, Kenneth James; a Recorder of the Crown Court, since 1972; *b* Ashton-under-Lyne, Lancs, 17 Oct. 1921; *o s* of William Tetley, Dukinfield, Cheshire, and Annie Lees, Oldham; *m* 1945, Edna Rita, *e d* of Peter Charles Spurrin Gray and Annie Gray, Audenshaw, Manchester; one *s* three *d*. *Educ:* Ashton-under-Lyne Grammar Sch.; Manchester Univ. Served War of 1939-45: joined RN, 1941; Lieut RNVR (attached Combined Ops); discharged, 1945. Admitted Solicitor, 1947; Councillor, Ashton-under-Lyne Borough Council, 1955; Alderman, 1967. *Recreations:* Rugby Union football, golf, photography. *Address:* Green Meadows, Ley Hey Park, Marple, Cheshire. *T:* 061-427 3755. *Clubs:* Rugby, Golf (Ashton-under-Lyne); Romiley Golf; Lancashire County RFU.

TETT, Sir Hugh (Charles), Kt 1966; ARCS, BSc, DIC; Director, Pirelli General Cable Works Ltd, since 1970; Chairman, Bristol Composite Materials Ltd, since 1974 (Director, since 1972); *b* Exeter, Devon, 28 Oct. 1906; *e s* of late James Charles Tett and late Florence Tett (*née* Lihou); *m* 1st, 1931, Katie Sargent (*d* 1948); one *d*; 2nd, 1949, Joyce Lilian (*née* Mansell); one *d*. *Educ:* Hele's School, Exeter; University College, Exeter; Royal College of Science (Kitchener's Scholar). Joined Esso Petroleum Co. Ltd, 1928; Technical Advisory Committee, Petroleum Board, 1940-45; Lieut-Colonel, Combined Intelligence Objectives Sub-Cttee, 1944-45; Chairman of Council, Institute of Petroleum, 1947-48; Managing Director, Esso Research Ltd, 1947-49; Director, Esso Petroleum Co. Ltd, 1951, Chairman, 1959-67. Member: Council for Scientific and Industrial Research, 1961-64; Advisory Council, Ministry of Technology, 1964-67. Chairman, Economic Development Cttee for Motor Manufacturing Industry, 1967-69. Pro-Chancellor, Univ. of Southampton, 1967-. Fellow, Imperial Coll. of Science and Technology, 1964. Hon. DSc: Southampton, 1965; Exeter, 1970. *Recreation:* golf. *Address:* Ladymead Cottage, West Strand, West Wittering, West Sussex. *Clubs:* Athenæum; Ham Manor Golf (Sussex).

TEUSNER, Hon. Berthold Herbert, CMG 1972; JP; Solicitor since 1931; Speaker, South Australian Parliament, 1956-62; *b* 16 May 1907; *s* of Carl Theodor Teusner and Agnes Sophie Elisabeth Teusner (*née* Christian); *m* 1934, Viola Hilda Kleeman; two *s*. *Educ:* Immanuel Coll., Adelaide; Univ. of Adelaide (LLB). Legal Practice at Tanunda, SA, 1932-. MP for Angas, S Australian Parlt, 1944-70; Govt Whip, 1954-55; Dep. Speaker and Chm. of Cttees: 1955-56, 1962-65 and 1968-70. Councillor, Dist. Council of Tanunda, 1936-56 (Chm. for 17 years); JP, 1939-. Member: Bd of Governors, Adelaide Botanical Gdns, 1956-70; SA Nat. Fitness Council, 1953-70; Royal Adelaide Hosp. and Queen Elizabeth Hosp. Advisory Cttees

(Chm., 1959-62); Immanuel Coll. Council, 1933-71; Hon. Assoc. Life Mem., SA Br. of Commonwealth Parly Assoc.; Mem., Transport Control Bd of SA, 1971-74. *Recreation:* bowls. *Address:* 18 Elizabeth Street, Tanunda, South Australia. *T:* 32422.

TEVIOT, 2nd Baron, *cr* 1940, of Burghclere; **Charles John Kerr;** *b* 16 Dec. 1934; *s* of 1st Baron Teviot, DSO, MC, and Florence Angela, *d* of late Lt-Col Charles Walter Villiers, CBE, DSO; *S* father, 1968; *m* 1965, Patricia Mary Harris; one *s* one *d*. *Educ:* Eton. Sales Representative; Bus Conductor and Driver; Salesman; genealogical and historical record agent. Mem., Adv. Council on Public Records, 1974-. Fellow, Soc. of Genealogists, 1975. *Recreations:* reading, walking. *Heir:* *s* Hon. Charles Robert Kerr, *b* 19 Sept. 1971. *Address:* 12 Grand Avenue, Hassocks, West Sussex. *T:* Hassocks 4471.

TEW, Prof. John Hedley Brian, PhD; Midland Bank Professor of Money and Banking, University of Nottingham, since 1967; *b* 1 Feb. 1917; *s* of Herbert and Catherine Mary Tew; *m* 1944, Marjorie Hoey Craigie; one *s* one *d*. *Educ:* Mill Hill School, Leicester; University College, Leicester; Peterhouse, Cambridge. BSc (Econ.) London; PhD Cantab. Iron and Steel Control, 1940-42; Ministry of Aircraft Production, 1942-45; Industrial and Commercial Finance Corp., 1946; Professor of Economics, Univ. of Adelaide (Australia), 1947-49; Professor of Economics, University of Nottingham, 1950-67; Part-time Member: Iron and Steel Board, 1964-67; East Midlands Electricity Board, 1965-76; Tubes Div., BSC, 1969-73; Mem., Cttee of Enquiry on Small Firms, Dept of Trade and Industry, 1969-71. *Publications:* Wealth and Income, 1950; International Monetary Co-operation 1952; (jt editor) Studies in Company Finance, 1959; Monetary Theory, 1969; The Evolution of the International Monetary System, 1977. *Address:* 121 Bramcote Lane, Wollaton, Notts.

TEWKESBURY, Bishop Suffragan of, since 1973; **Rt. Rev. Thomas Carlyle Joseph Robert Hamish Deakin;** *b* 16 Feb. 1917; *s* of Rev. Thomas Carlyle Deakin (Rector of Uley, Glos, 1943-57), and Harriet Herries Deakin; *m* 1942, Marion, *d* of E. J. and Mrs E. Anson Dyer, Stratford Abbey, Stroud; one *s* (and one *s* decd). *Educ:* Wadham Coll., Oxford (MA); Wells Theological Coll. Deacon 1940, priest 1941, Diocese of Gloucester. Curate of St Lawrence, Stroud, 1940-44; Vicar of Holy Trinity, Forest of Dean, 1944-49; Vicar of Charlton Kings, 1949-73; Rural Dean of Cheltenham, 1963-73; Hon. Canon of Gloucester, 1966-73. *Address:* Green Acre, 166 Hempsted Lane, Gloucester GL2 6LG. *T:* Gloucester 21824.

TEWSON, Sir (Harold) Vincent, Kt 1950; CBE 1942; MC; *b* 4 Feb. 1898; *s* of late Edward Tewson, Bradford, Yorks; *m* 1929, Florence Elizabeth Moss; two *s*. *Educ:* Bradford. Secretary Organisation Dept, TUC, 1925-31; Asst Gen. Sec., 1931-46; Gen. Sec. 1946-60, retired. Member of the Economic Planning Board, 1947-60; Pres., Internat. Confedn of Free Trade Unions, 1953-55; Part-time Mem. London Electricity Board, 1960-68. Mem., ITA, 1964-69. *Address:* 7 Campana Court, Blenheim Road, Barnet, Herts. *T:* 01-449 0386.

TEYNHAM, 20th Baron *cr* 1616; **John Christopher Ingham Roper-Curzon;** *b* 25 Dec. 1928; *s* of 19th Baron Teynham, DSO, DSC, and Elspeth Grace (who *m* 2nd, 1958, 6th Marquess of Northampton, DSO, and *d* 1976), *e d* of late William Ingham Whitaker; *S* father, 1972; *m* 1964, Elizabeth, *yr d* of Lt-Col the Hon. David Scrymgeour-Wedderburn, DSO (killed on active service 1944), and of the Countess of Dundee; two *s* four *d* (of whom one *s* one *d* are twins). *Educ:* Eton. A Land Agent. Late Captain, The Buffs (TA), formerly Coldstream Guards; active service in Palestine, 1948. ADC to Governor of Bermuda, 1953 and 1955; ADC to Governor of Leeward Islands, 1955; Private Secretary and ADC, 1956; ADC to Governor of Jamaica, 1962. Pres., Inst. of Commerce, 1972-. Member of Council, Sail Training Association, 1964-. OStJ. *Recreations:* shooting and fishing. *Heir:* *s* Hon. David John Henry Ingham Roper-Curzon, *b* 5 Oct. 1965. *Address:* The Severalls, Hatherop, Cirencester, Gloucestershire. *T:* Coln St Aldwyns 364. *Clubs:* Turf; House of Lords Yacht; Puffins (Edinburgh).

THACKER, Charles, CBE 1961; Director, Ford Motor Co. Ltd, 1953-64, retired; *b* 13 Feb. 1897; *m* 1927, Edith May Genese (*d* 1976); one *d*. Joined Ford Motor Co. Ltd, 1924: General Manager (Germany), 1945; Belgium, 1946-48); Managing Director, England, 1957-62, retired. Served in Army, European War, 1914-19. *Address:* 11 Luard Road, Cambridge.

THACKER, Prof. Thomas William, MA Oxon; Director of School of Oriental Studies, and Professor of Semitic Philology, University of Durham, 1951-77; *b* 6 Nov. 1911; *s* of late Thomas William and of Edith Maud Thacker; *m* 1939, Katharine E.

Hawthorn; one *s. Educ:* City of Oxford School; St Catherine's, Oxford; Berlin University. Clothworkers' Exhibitioner, 1931-33; BA 1933; Goldsmiths' Research Scholar, 1933-35; University Senior Student, Oxford, 1935-37; Mark Quested Exhibitioner, Oxford, 1937-39; studied in Berlin, 1933-36. Member of Egypt Exploration Society's expedition to Tell-el-Amarna, 1935; Asst Lecturer in Semitic Languages, University Coll. of N Wales, Bangor, 1937; Reader in Hebrew, Univ. of Durham, 1938-45; Prof. of Hebrew and Oriental Languages, Univ. of Durham, 1945-51; Foreign Office, 1940-45. Examiner at Univs of Wales (Hebrew and Old Testament), Manchester, Liverpool and Leeds (Semitic Languages), Oxford (Egyptology and Hebrew). Foreign Mem., Royal Flemish Acad. *Publications:* The Relationship of the Semitic and Egyptian Verbal Systems, 1954; articles and reviews in various periodicals. *Address:* 28 Church Street, Durham. *T:* Durham 64385.

THALBEN-BALL, George Thomas, CBE 1967; DMus Cantuar 1935; ARCM; FRCM 1951; FRCO; FRSCM 1956 (diploma 1963); FRSA; Bard Ylewyth Mur; Freeman of City of London; Civic and University Organist, Birmingham, 1949; Organist, the Temple Church; Curator-Organist, The Royal Albert Hall, London; Professor and Examiner, the Royal College of Music; Examiner to the Associated Board of the Royal Academy of Music and the Royal College of Music; Member of the Council and Examiner of Royal College of Organists; Examiner on behalf of the Cape University, 1925; Adviser and Consultant to BBC, 1941; *b* Sydney, NSW; *s* of George Charles Thalben-Ball and Mary Hannah Spear, Newquay, Cornwall; *m* Evelyn (*d* 1961), *d* of Francis Chapman, NZ; one *s* one *d. Educ:* private tuition. Exhbnr and Grove Scholar, RCM, Chappell and Hopkinson Gold Medallist; Lafontaine Prize, RCO; Organist: Whitefield's Tabernacle; Holy Trinity Church, Castlenau; Paddington Parish Church; acting Organist, the Hon. Socs of Temple, 1919, Organist, 1923-; studied pianoforte with Fritz Hartvigson, Franklin Taylor, and Fanny Davies; harmony and composition with Sir Frederick Bridge, Sir Charles Stanford, and Dr Charles Wood; musical history with Sir Hubert Parry; organ with Sir Walter Parratt and F. A. Sewell. President: London Soc. of Organists, 1936; RCO, 1948; Incorporated Assoc. of Organists, 1944-46; Mem. Bd of Governors, Royal Normal Coll. of the Blind. FRSA 1971. Hon. RAM 1973. Hon. Bencher, Inner Temple, 1959. Guest Organist, Les Amis de l'Orgue, Paris, 1937; Toured Australia as guest organist in connection with Jubilee of the formation of the Commonwealth, 1951, toured: South Africa, 1954, New Zealand, 1971; Guest of honour, Amer. Guild of Organists Convention, NY, 1956; Guest, Philadelphia, 1973; toured USA and Canada, 1975 (opening organ recital, Carnegie Hall, NY). Mem. Jury, Concours international d'orgue, Grand Prix de Chartres, 1973. EMI Gold Disc, 1963. Has played the organ on the Continent and in America and was a regular broadcaster and performer at the Sir Henry Wood Promenade Concerts. Composer of Organ and Choral music including Sursum Corda for chorus, orchestra and trumpet fanfares (commissioned by BBC). Hon. DMus and Gold Medal, Birmingham, 1972. *Recreations:* golf and riding. *Address:* 3 Paper Buildings, Inner Temple, EC4. *Club:* Athenæum.

THALMANN, Dr Ernesto; Swiss Ambassador to the Court of St James's, since 1976; *b* 14 Jan. 1914; *s* of Friedrich Thalmann and Clara (*née* Good); *m* 1943, Paula Degen; two *s* one *d. Educ:* Gymnasien, Berne and Zürich; Univ. of Zürich (LLD). Entered Federal Dept of Public Economy, 1941; Federal Political Dept (Swiss Foreign Office), 1945; Minister/Counsellor and Dep. Head of Mission, Swiss Embassy, Washington, 1957-61; Permanent Observer to UN, New York (Ambassador Extraordinary and Plenipotentiary), 1961-66; Head of Internat. Organizations Div., Fed. Political Dept, Berne, 1966-71; Special Mission in Jerusalem, after 6-day war, as Personal Rep. of UN Secretary-General, U Thant, 1967; Secretary-General, Fed. Political Dept and Director of Political Affairs, 1971-75. *Address:* 16-18 Montagu Place, W1H 2BQ. *T:* 01-723 0701; (residence) 21 Bryanston Square, W1H 7FG.

THAPAR, Prem Nath, CIE 1944; lately Vice-Chancellor, Punjab Agricultural University, Lydhiana, 1962-68; Indian Civil Service; *b* 13 April 1903; *s* of Diwan Bahadur Kunj Behari Thapar, CBE; *m* 1932, Leela Dutta; one *s* two *d. Educ:* Govt Coll., Lahore; New Coll., Oxford. Joined ICS 1926. Dep. Commissioner, Kangra, Attock; Deputy Commissioner and Colonisation Officer, Montgomery, 1934-37; Settlement Officer, Jhelum, 1937-41; Joint Secretary, Information and Broadcasting Department, Government of India, 1941-46; Secretary, Food and Civil Supplies Department, Punjab, 1946-47; Commissioner, Lahore Division, 1947; Financial Commissioner, East Punjab, 1947-53; Chief Administrator, Chandigarh Capital Project, 1950-53; Adviser, Planning Commission, Government

of India, 1953-54; Sec., Min. of Food and Agric, Govt of India, 1954-58; Member, Atomic Energy Commission and *ex officio* Secretary to Government of India, Dept of Atomic Energy, Bombay, 1958-62. Mem. Punjab Admin. Reforms Commn, 1964-65; Consultant, Review Team, FAO, UN, Rome, 1966-67. Trustee, Internat. Rice Research Inst., Manila, Philippines. *Publications:* Settlement Report, Jhelum District, 1945; Customary Law, Jhelum District, 1946. *Address:* Ashok Farm, PO Maidan Garhi, New Delhi-30, India. *T:* 72382.

THATCHER, Arthur Roger, CB 1974; Deputy Secretary and Director of Statistics, Department of Employment, since 1972; *b* 22 Oct. 1926; *s* of Arthur Thatcher; *m* 1950, Mary Audrey Betty (*née* Street); two *d. Educ:* The Leys Sch.; St John's Coll., Cambridge (MA). Royal Navy, 1947-49. North Western Gas Board, 1949-52; Admiralty, 1952-61; Cabinet Office, 1961-63; Ministry of Labour, 1963-68; Director of Statistics, Dept of Employment, 1968-72. *Publications:* official publications; articles in statistical jls. *Address:* Department of Employment, 8 St James' Square, SW1Y 4JB. *T:* 01-214 6124. *Club:* Army and Navy.

THATCHER, Rt. Hon. Mrs Margaret (Hilda), PC 1970; MP (C) Barnet, Finchley, since 1974 (Finchley, 1959-74); Leader of the Opposition, since 1975; *b* 13 Oct. 1925; *d* of late Alfred Roberts, Grantham, Lincs; *m* 1951, Denis Thatcher; one *s* one *d* (twins). *Educ:* Kesteven and Grantham Girls' School; Somerville College, Oxford (MA, BSc). Research Chemist 1947-51; called to the Bar, Lincoln's Inn, 1953, Hon. Bencher, 1975. Joint Parly Sec., Min. of Pensions and National Insurance, Oct. 1961-64; Sec. of State for Educn and Sci., 1970-74. Co-Chm., Women's Nat. Commn, 1970-74. Hon. Fellow, Somerville Coll., Oxford, 1970. *Recreations:* music, reading. *Address:* House of Commons, SW1. *Club:* Carlton.

THAW, Mrs John; *see* Hancock, Sheila.

THAYRE, Albert Jesse, MBE 1945; Chief General Manager and Director, Halifax Building Society, since 1974; *b* 30 May 1917; *s* of Alfred and Louisa Thayre; *m* 1940, Margaret Elizabeth Wheeler; one *d. Educ:* Bromley County Sch. for Boys; City of London Coll. BCom (London) 1948. Stockbrokers' Clerk, 1933-39. Served War: Rifleman/NCO with 2/London Irish Rifles, 1939-41; Lieut to Captain 51 (H) Bn Reconnaissance Corps, 1941-42; Captain, then Major and Lt-Col 14 Highland LI, 1942-46 (incl. appts as DAQMG and AA&QMG). Investment Analyst, 1946-50; Halifax Building Soc.: Clerk, then Inspector and Br. Manager, 1951-55; Staff Manager, 1955-56; Asst Gen. Man., 1956-60; Gen. Man., 1960; Dir, 1968; Asst Chief Gen. Man., 1970. Bradford Univ.: Mem. Council and Chm. Finance Cttee, 1966; Pro-Chancellor, 1969. Mem., Univs Authorities Panel, 1970; Dir and Dep. Chm., Univs Superannuation Scheme Ltd, 1974. FSS, FBS. *Recreation:* public speaking. *Address:* Stonedale, 42 Northowram Green, Halifax, West Yorkshire HX3 7SL. *T:* Halifax 202581.

THELLUSSON, family name of **Baron Rendlesham.**

THELWELL, Norman; freelance artist-cartoonist since 1957; *b* Birkenhead, 3 May 1923; *s* of Christopher Thelwell and Emily (*née* Vick); *m* 1949, Rhona Evelyn Ladbury; one *s* one *d. Educ:* Rock Ferry High Sch., Birkenhead; Liverpool Coll. of Art. Nat. Diploma of Art; ATD. Teacher of Art, Wolverhampton Coll. of Art, 1950-57. Regular contributor to Punch, 1952-; cartoonist for: News Chronicle, 1956-60; Sunday Dispatch, 1960-61; Sunday Express, 1962-. Drawings for general publications, advertising, book jackets, illustrations, etc. *Publications:* Angels on Horseback, 1957; Thelwell Country, 1959; A Place of Your Own, 1960; Thelwell in Orbit, 1961; A Leg at Each Corner, 1962; The Penguin Thelwell, 1963; Top Dog, 1964; Thelwell's Riding Academy, 1965; Drawing Ponies, 1966; Up the Garden Path, 1967; Thelwell's Compleat Tangler, 1967; Thelwell's Book of Leisure, 1968; This Desirable Plot, 1970; The Effluent Society, 1971; Penelope, 1972; Three Sheets in the Wind, 1973; Belt Up, 1974; Thelwell Goes West, 1975; Thelwell's Brat Race, 1977; A Plank Bridge by a Pool, 1978. *Recreations:* trout and salmon angling, painting. *Address:* Herons Mead, Timsbury, Romsey, Hants SO5 0NE. *T:* Braishfield 68238. *Club:* Savage.

THEORELL, (Axel) Hugo (Teodor), MD; Director of Nobel Medical Institute, Department of Biochemistry, Stockholm, 1937-70; *b* Linköping, Sweden, 6 July 1903; *s* of Ture and Armida (Bill) Theorell; *m* 1931, Margit Alenius; three *s. Educ:* Linköpings Högre Allm. Läroverk; Pasteur Institute, Paris; Royal Caroline Medico-Surgical Institute, Stockholm. MD Stockholm, 1930. Asst Professor of Biochemistry, Uppsala University, 1932; with Prof. Otto Warburg Kaiser Wilhelm Institut für Zellphysiologie, Berlin-Dahlem, 1933-35; engaged upon research into enzyme structure; awarded Nobel Prize in Physiology and Medicine, 1955, for discoveries concerning nature and effects of oxidation enzymes. Secretary, Swedish Society of Physicians and Surgeons, 1940-46 (Chm., 1946-47 and 1957-58, Hon. Mem., 1956); Chairman: Wenner-Gren Society; Wenner-Gren Center Foundation; Swedish Chemists' Assoc., 1947-49; Stockholm Symphony Soc., 1951-73. Pres., Internat. Union of Biochemistry, 1967-73; Member: Swedish Academy of Science (President, 1967-69); Swedish Academy of Engineering Science; Swedish Acad. of Music; Royal Danish Acad. Scis and Letters; Norwegian Acad. Sci. and Letters; Royal Norwegian Soc. Arts and Scis; Amer. Acad. Arts and Scis; Nat. Acad. Scis, Washington; Amer. Philos. Soc., Philadelphia; NY Acad. of Sci.: l'Accademia Nazionale del XL of Rome; Polish Acad. Naukoznawcze; Indian Acad. Sci. For. Mem., Roy. Soc. Hon. Dr: Univ. Sorbonne, Paris; Univ. Pennsylvania USA; Univ. Louvain; Univ. Libre, Brussels, Belgium; Univ. Brasil, Rio de Janeiro; Univ. Kentucky, USA; Univ. Michigan, USA. 1st Cl. Comdr Royal Order of the Northern Star; 1st Cl. Comdr, Order of Finnish Lion; Comdr Royal Norwegian Order of St Olav; Comdr, Légion d'Honneur (France); Officer, Order of Southern Cross (Brazil). Trafvenfelt Medal, 1945; Scheele Medal, 1956; Caroline Inst. 150 years Jubilee Medal, 1960; Emanuel e Paterno Medal, 1962; Paul Karrer Medal, 1965; Ciba Medal, 1971; Semmelweiss Medal, 1971. *Recreation:* music. *Address:* Karolinska Institutet, Medicinska Nobelinstitutet, Biokemiska advelningen, Laboratorium för Enzymforskning, Solnavägen 1, 10401 Stockholm 60, Sweden; Sveavägen 166H, 11346 Stockholm, Sweden.

THEROUX, Paul Edward; writer; *b* 10 April 1941; *s* of Albert Eugene Theroux and Anne Dittami Theroux; *m* 1967, Anne Castle; two *s*. *Educ:* Univ. of Massachusetts (BA). Lecturer: Univ. of Urbino, 1963; Soche Hill Coll., Malawi, 1963-65; Makerere Univ., Kampala, Uganda, 1965-68; Univ. of Singapore, 1968-71; Writer-in-Residence, Univ. of Virginia, 1972. *Publications: novels:* Waldo, 1967; Fong and the Indians, 1968; Girls at Play, 1969; Murder in Mount Holly, 1969; Jungle Lovers, 1971; Sinning with Annie, 1972; Saint Jack, 1973; The Black House, 1974; The Family Arsenal, 1976; The Consul's File, 1977; Picture Palace, 1978; *criticism:* V. S. Naipaul, 1972; *travel:* The Great Railway Bazaar, 1975; reviews in The Times, New York Times, New Statesman, etc. *Recreation:* snooker. *Address:* 35 Elsynge Road, SW18 2HR.

THESIGER, family name of **Viscount Chelmsford.**

THESIGER, Hon. Sir Gerald (Alfred), Kt 1958; MBE 1946; **Hon. Mr Justice Thesiger;** Judge of the High Court of Justice, Queen's Bench Division, since 1958; *b* 25 Dec. 1902; *s* of late Maj.-Gen. George Thesiger, CB, CMG; *m* 1932, Marjorie Guille (*d* 1972), d of late Raymond Guille, Long Island, NY; three *d*. *Educ:* Greshams School, Holt; Magdalen College, Oxford (MA). Demy, 1921; BA, 1924; called to Bar, Inner Temple, 1926, Bencher, 1956; South Eastern Circuit; QC 1948; Member General Council of the Bar, 1936-41, 1958; Recorder of Rye, 1937-42; Recorder of Hastings, 1943-57; Recorder of Southend, 1957-58; Chairman, West Kent Quarter Sessions, 1947-58; Member Borough Council, Fulham, 1934-37, Chelsea, 1937-58; Alderman, 1945; Chief Warden, Chelsea, 1939-41; Major, Deputy Judge Advocate Staff, 1941-45; Mayor of Chelsea, 1944-46, Hon. Freeman, 1963; Chairman, Departmental Cttee on Licensing of Road Passenger Services, 1953-54; Chairman Governors, United Westminster Schools, 1947-58; Dep. Chm., Boundary Commn (England), 1962-74. Pres. British Acad. of Forensic Sciences, 1973-74. *Address:* Royal Courts of Justice, Strand, WC2. *Club:* Hurlingham.

THESIGER, Roderic Miles Doughty; Director, P. & D. Colnaghi and Co. Ltd, 1955-71; *b* 8 Nov. 1915; *y s* of late Hon. Wilfred Thesiger, DSO, and Mrs Reginald Astley, CBE; *m* 1st, 1940, Mary Rose (marr. diss. 1946; she *d* 1962), d of Hon. Guy Charteris; 2nd, 1946, Ursula, d of A. W. Whitworth, Woollas Hall, Pershore; one *s* one *d*. *Educ:* Eton; Christ Church, Oxford; Courtauld Institute. Served War of 1939-45, Welsh Guards, 1939-41; 1st Parachute Bde, 1941-44 (twice wounded, POW). Assistant, Tate Gallery, 1945-46; afterwards worked with Messrs Sotheby and privately until 1954. *Recreations:* visiting Italy and France. *Address:* The Paddocks, Lucton, Leominster, Herefordshire. *T:* Yarpole 327. *Club:* Brooks's.
See also W. P. Thesiger.

THESIGER, Wilfred Patrick, CBE 1968; DSO 1941; MA Oxon; *b* 3 June 1910; *e s* of late Hon. Wilfred Thesiger, DSO, and Mrs Reginald Astley, CBE. *Educ:* Eton; Magdalen College, Oxford (MA). Repres. Oxford at boxing, 1930-33; Captain Oxford Boxing Team, 1933; Hon. Attaché Duke of Gloucester's Mission to Abyssinia, 1930; served Middle East, 1941 (DSO); explored

Danakil country of Abyssinia and the Aussa Sultanate, 1933-34 (awarded Back Grant by RGS, 1935); Sudan Political Service, Darfur-Upper Nile, 1935-40; served in Ethiopian, Syrian and Western Desert campaigns with SDF and SAS regiment with rank of Major; explored in Southern Arabia, 1945-49; twice crossed the Empty Quarter. Founder's Medal, RGS, 1948; Lawrence of Arabia Medal, RCAS, 1955; Livingstone Medal, RSGS, 1962; W. H. Heinemann Award (for 1964), RSL, 1965; Burton Memorial Medal, Roy. Asiatic Soc., 1966. FRSL; Hon. DLitt Leicester. 3rd Class Star of Ethiopia. *Publications:* Arabian Sands, 1959; The Marsh Arabs, 1964. *Recreations:* travelling, photography. *Address:* 15 Shelley Court, Tite Street, SW3. *T:* 01-352 7213. *Clubs:* Brooks's, Pratt's, Travellers'.
See also R. M. D. Thesiger.

THETFORD, Bishop Suffragan of, since 1977; **Rt. Rev. Hugh Charles Blackburne;** *b* 4 June 1912; *s* of late Very Rev. Harry William Blackburne; *m* 1944, Doris Freda, *widow* of Pilot Officer H. L. N. Davis; two *s* one *d*. *Educ:* Marlborough; Clare Coll., Cambridge (MA); Westcott House, Cambridge. Deacon 1937; Priest, 1938; Curate of Almondbury, Yorks, 1937-39. Chaplain to the Forces, 1939-47; served with 1st Guards Bde, 11th Armoured Div., HQ Anti-Aircraft Comd, and as Chaplain, RMC, Sandhurst. Rector, Milton, Hants, 1947-53; Vicar, St Mary's, Harrow, 1953-61. Rector of the Hilborough Group, 1961-72; Vicar of Ramworth and Chaplain for the Norfolk Broads, 1972-77; Hon. Canon of Norwich, 1965-77; Chaplain to the Queen, 1962-77. *Recreations:* sailing, bird-watching. *Address:* Caistor St Edmund Rectory, Norwich NR14 8QS. *T:* Framlingham Earl 2490.
See also Sir Kenneth Blackburne.

THEUNISSEN, Most Rev. John Baptist Hubert, DD; Titular Archbishop of Skálholt, since 1968; *b* Schimmert, Holland, 3 Oct. 1905; *Educ:* Schimmert and Oirschot, Holland; Rome University. DD 1929. Professor, Major Seminary, Oirschot, Holland, 1930; Professor, Major Seminary, Portugal, 1935; Superior Regional of the Missions in Portuguese East Africa, 1937; Superior Provincial of Dutch Province of Montfort Fathers, 1947; consecrated Bishop of Blantyre, 1950; Archbishop of Blantyre, Malawi, 1959; Apostolic Administrator of Iceland, 1967; retd, 1968. Knight, Order of the Lion (Netherlands), 1960. *Recreation:* music. *Address:* Bishop's House, Langstraat 84, Schimmert (L.), The Netherlands.

THIESS, Sir Leslie Charles, Kt 1971; CBE 1968; Chairman, Thiess Group of Companies, since 1968; *b* 8 April 1909; *m* 1929, Christina Mary (*née* Erbacher); two *s* three *d*. *Educ:* Drayton, Queensland. Founded Thiess Bros as a private company, 1933; Managing Dir, Thiess Holdings Ltd when it was formed in 1950; also when firm became a public company, 1958. FCIT (London), 1971. Order of the Sacred Treasure (third class), Japan, 1972. *Recreations:* deep sea fishing. *Address:* 121 King Arthur Terrace, Tennyson, Qld 4105, Australia. *T:* 48 1147. *Clubs:* Brisbane, Tattersalls, Royal Queensland Yacht, Royal Queensland Aero (all of Brisbane); Huntington, NSW Sports (NSW).

THIMANN, Prof. Kenneth Vivian; Professor of Biology, since 1965, and Provost of Crown College, 1966-72, Emeritus Professor, recalled to duty, 1972, University of California, Santa Cruz, Calif, USA; *b* 5 Aug. 1904; *s* of Phoebus Thimann and Muriel Kate Thimann (*née* Harding); *m* 1931, Ann Mary Bateman, Sutton Bridge, Lincs; three *d*. *Educ:* Caterham Sch., Surrey; Imperial Coll., London. BSc, ARCS 1924; DIC 1925; PhD 1928. Beit Memorial Res. Fellow, 1927-29; Demonstr in Bacteriology, King's Coll. for Women, 1926-28; Instr in Biochem., Calif Inst. of Techn., 1930-35; Harvard University: Lectr on Botany, 1935; (Biology): Asst Prof., 1936, Associate Prof., 1939, Prof., 1946, and Higgins Prof., 1962-65, now Prof. Emeritus. Vis. Professor: Sorbonne, 1954; Univ. of Massachusetts, 1974. Scientific Consultant, US Navy, 1942-45. Dir, Amer. Assoc. for Adv. of Science, 1968-71. Pres., XIth Internat. Botanical Congress, Seattle, USA, 1969; 2nd Nat. Biol Congress, Miami, 1971. Hon. AM Harvard, 1940; PhD (Hon.) Univ. of Basle, 1959; Doctor (Hon.) Univ. of Clermont-Ferrand, 1961. Fellow: Nat. Acad. of Scis (Councillor, 1967-71); Amer. Acad. of Arts and Scis; Amer. Philosophical Soc. (Councillor, 1973-76); and professional biological socs in USA and England; Foreign Member: Royal Society (London); Accademia Nazionale dei Lincei (Rome); Leopoldina Akademie (Halle); Roumanian Academy (Bucharest); Botanical Societies of Japan and Netherlands. *Publications:* (in USA) Phytohormones (with F. W. Went), 1937; The Action of Hormones in Plants and Invertebrates, 1948; The Life of Bacteria, 1955, 2nd edn 1963 (German edn 1964); The Natural Plant Hormones, 1972; Hormones in the Whole Life of Plants, 1977; about 250 papers in biological and biochemical jls. *Recreations:* music (piano), gardening. *Address:* 36 Pasatiempo Drive, Santa Cruz, California 95060, USA. *T:* 423-0437. *Clubs:* Harvard Faculty (Cambridge, Mass); Harvard (San Francisco).

THIMONT, Bernard Maurice; Controller of Her Majesty's Stationery Office and Queen's Printer of Acts of Parliament, since 1977; *b* 1 July 1920; *s* of Georges André Thimont; *m* 1949, Joy Rowe; one *s* one *d. Educ:* St Ignatius Coll., London. Served War of 1939-45, in Army (Major), 1939-48. Foreign Office, 1948-50; HM Treasury, 1950-65; IDC, 1966; Cabinet Office, 1967; HM Treasury, 1967-68; Civil Service Dept, 1968-77. *Recreations:* music, building. *Address:* 2 Worple Avenue, Wimbledon, SW19 4JQ. *T:* 01-946 0918.

THIRD, Rt. Rev. Richard Henry McPhail; *see* Maidstone, Bishop Suffragan of.

THIRKELL, Lancelot George, (Lance Thirkell); Controller, Administration, External Broadcasting, BBC, since 1975; *b* 9 Jan. 1921; *s* of George Lancelot Thirkell, engineer, and Angela Margaret Mackail (Angela Thirkell, novelist); *m* 1946, Katherine Mary Lowinsky, *d* of Thomas Esmond Lowinsky, artist, and Ruth Jeanette Hirsch; two *s* two *d. Educ:* Saint Paul's School (Schol.); Magdalen Coll. Oxford (Demy). HM Forces, 1942-46; active service D-day to the Rhine with Essex Yeo. and in SE Asia with RA. HM Foreign Service, 1946-50; granted Civil Service Certificate, 1946; Third Sec., Western Dept, 1946; Third Sec., Budapest, 1947; Second Sec., Eastern Dept, 1948. Joined BBC as Report Writer, Monitoring Service, 1950; Assistant, Appointments Dept, 1953; Assistant Staff Administration, 1956; Head of Secretariat, 1961; Controller, Staff Trng and Appointments, 1964; Chief Asst to Man. Dir, External Broadcasting, 1972-75. Dir, Caribbean Relay Co., 1976. Governor, Thomson Foundn Television Coll., 1964-72. Councillor, Royal Borough of Kensington, 1959-62; Chm. Notting Hill Adventure Playground, 1964-76; Appeals Sec., Portobello Project for unattached youth; Mem., European Adv. Council, Salzburg Seminar in American Studies. *Publications:* A Garden Full of Weeds, 1962; (with Ruth Lowinsky) Russian Food for Pleasure, 1953. *Recreations:* ski-ing, sailing. *Address:* 31 Lansdowne Road, W11. *T:* 01-727 6046; Oxbow, Harkstead, Suffolk. *Clubs:* Leander (Henley-on-Thames); Royal Harwich Yacht.

THIRKETTLE, William Ellis, CBE 1959; Principal, London College of Printing, 1939-67; *b* 26 July 1904; *s* of William Edward Thirkettle; *m* 1930, Alva, *d* of Thomas Tough Watson; two *s. Educ:* Tiffin School. Principal, Stow College of Printing, Glasgow, 1936-39. *Address:* The Brae, Seend Cleeve, Wilts.

THIRLWALL, Air Vice-Marshal George Edwin, CB 1976; Air Officer Engineering, Strike Command, since 1976; *b* 24 Dec. 1924; *s* of Albert and Clarice Editha Thirlwall; *m* 1949, Daphne Patricia Wynn Giles (*d* 1975). *Educ:* Sheffield Univ.; Cranfield Inst. of Technology. BEng, MSc, CEng, FRAeS, MBIM. Joined RAF, 1950; OC RAF Sealand, 1969; Dir Air Guided Weapons, MoD, 1972; AO Ground Trng, RAF Trng Comd, 1974-76. *Recreation:* gardening. *Address:* Oaks Cottage, Oaks Close, Hitchin, Herts. *T:* Hitchin 50123. *Club:* Royal Air Force.

THIRSK, Dr (Irene) Joan, FBA 1974; Reader in Economic History in the University of Oxford, since 1965; Fellow of St Hilda's College, Oxford, since 1965; *b* 19 June 1922; *d* of William Henry Watkins and Daisy (*née* Frayer); *m* 1945, James Wood Thirsk; one *s* one *d. Educ:* Camden School for Girls, NW5; Westfield Coll., Univ. of London. BA, PhD London; MA Oxford. Subaltern, ATS, Intelligence Corps, 1942-45. Asst Lectr in Sociology, LSE, 1950-51; Sen. Res. Fellow in Agrarian History, Dept of English Local History, Leicester Univ., 1951-65. Ford Lectr in English History, Oxford, 1975. Mem., Royal Commn on Historical Monuments (England), 1977-. Editor, Agricultural History Review, 1964-72; Gen. Editor, The Agrarian History of England and Wales, 1974- (Dep. Gen. Ed., 1966-74). Mem. Exec. Cttee, British Agricultural History Soc., 1953-, Chm. Cttee 1974-77; Mem. Council, Economic History Soc., 1955-; Mem. Editorial Bd, Past and Present, 1956-. *Publications:* English Peasant Farming, 1957; Suffolk Farming in the Nineteenth Century, 1958; Tudor Enclosures, 1959; The Agrarian History of England and Wales vol. IV, 1500-1640, 1967; (with J. P. Cooper) Seventeenth-Century Economic Documents, 1972; The Restoration, 1976; articles in Economic History Rev., Agric. History Rev., Past and Present, History, Jl Modern History, etc. *Recreations:* gardening, sewing. *Address:* The Kilns, Lewis Close, Headington, Oxford.

THISTLETHWAITE, Frank; Vice-Chancellor, University of East Anglia, Norwich, since 1961; *b* 24 July 1915; *s* of late Lee Thistlethwaite and of Florence Nightingale Thistlethwaite; *m*

1940, Jane, *d* of H. Lindley Hosford, Lyme, Connecticut, USA; one *s* three *d* (and one *s* decd). *Educ:* Bootham School; St John's College, Cambridge (Exhibitioner and Scholar). Pt I, Historical Tripos, Class 1, Pt I, English Tripos, Class 1 BA 1938, MA 1941. Editor, The Cambridge Review, 1937. Commonwealth Fund Fellow, University of Minnesota, 1938-40; British Press Service, New York, 1940-41. Served in RAF, 1941-45; seconded to Office of War Cabinet, 1942-45. Fellow, St John's College, Cambridge, 1945-61; at various times, Tutor, Praelector, Steward; University Lecturer in Faculty of Economics and Politics, 1949-61; Visiting Prof. of American Civilization, Univ. of Pennsylvania, 1956; Vis. Fellow, Henry E. Huntington Library, Calif, 1973. Member: Inst. for Advanced Study, Princeton, 1954; Academic Adv. Committee: Chelsea Coll. of Science and Technology, 1964-66; Open Univ., 1969-74; Provisional Council, Univ. of Zambia, 1965-69; Univ. of Malawi, 1971-75; Univ. of Mauritius, 1974-; Marshall Aid Commemoration Commn, 1964-; US-UK Educnl Commn, 1964-; European Adv. Council, Salzburg Seminar in Amer. Studies, 1969-74; Inter-Univ. Council for Higher Educn Overseas, 1962- (Vice-Chm., 1974-77, Chm., 1977); Bd, British Council, 1971-; British Cttee of Award, Harkness Fellowships, 1974-; Chairman: British Assoc. for American Studies, 1955-59; Cttee of Management, Inst. of US Studies, Univ. of London; Adviser to Nat. Council of Higher Educn Ceylon, 1967. Governor, Sedbergh Sch., 1958-73. Hon. Fellow, St John's Coll., Cambridge, 1974. Hon. LHD Colorado, 1972. FRHistS. *Publications:* The Great Experiment: An Introduction to the History of the American People, 1955; The Anglo-American Connection in the Early Nineteenth Century, 1958; Report on the Establishment of the University of Colombo, 1967; contrib. New Cambridge Modern History and others' historical works and journals; New Universities in the Modern World (ed. M. G. Ross). *Recreation:* music. *Address:* University of East Anglia, Norwich NR4 7TJ. *Club:* Athenæum.

THISTLETON-SMITH, Vice-Admiral Sir Geoffrey, KBE 1959; CB 1956; GM 1941; DL; *b* 10 May 1905; *m* 1931, Mary Katherine Harvey (*d* 1976); one *s* one *d. Captain,* 1944; HMS Pembroke, Royal Naval Barracks, Chatham (in Command), 1952; Chief of Staff to C-in-C Home Fleet and Eastern Atlantic, Dec. 1953; Rear-Admiral, 1954; Admiral Commanding Reserves, 1956-58; Vice-Admiral, 1957; Adm'ral, British Joint Services Mission, Washington, 1958-60, retd. CC West Sussex, 1964-77. DL Sussex, 1972. *Address:* Down Place, Harting, Petersfield, Hants.

THODAY, Prof. John Marion, FRS 1965; BSc Wales, PhD, ScD Cantab; Arthur Balfour Professor of Genetics, Cambridge University, since 1959; Fellow of Emmanuel College, 1959; *b* 30 Aug. 1916; *s* of Professor D. Thoday, FRS; *m* 1950, Doris Joan Rich, PhD (Fellow, Lucy Cavendish College); one *s* one *d. Educ:* Bootham School, York; University Coll. of N Wales, Bangor; Trinity College, Cambridge. Photographic Intelligence, Royal Air Force, 1941-46; Cytologist, Mount Vernon Hospital, 1946-47; Asst Lectr, then Lectr for Cytogenetics. Departments of Botany and Zoology, University of Sheffield, 1947-54; Head of Department of Genetics, Sheffield, 1954-59. Director, OECD Project for reform of secondary school Biology teaching 1962, 1963. Pres., Genetical Soc., 1975. *Publications:* articles on radiation cytology, experimental evolution, the genetics of continuous variables, biological progress and on genetics and society. *Address:* 7 Clarkson Road, Cambridge.

THODE, Dr Henry George, CC (Canada) 1967; MBE 1946; FRS 1954; FRSC 1943; FCIC 1948; Professor of Chemistry, McMaster University, Canada, since 1944; *b* 10 September 1910; Canadian; *m* 1935, Sadie Alicia Patrick; three *s. Educ:* University of Saskatchewan (BSc 1930, MSc 1932); University of Chicago (PhD 1934). Research Asst, Columbia Univ., 1936-38; Research Chemist, US Rubber Co., 1938; McMaster University: Asst Prof. of Chem., 1939-42; Assoc. Prof. of Chem., 1942-44; Head, Department of Chemistry, 1948-52; Dir of Res., 1947-61; Principal of Hamilton Coll., 1949-64; Vice-Pres., 1957-61; Pres. and Vice-Chancellor, 1961-72. California Inst. of Technology, Pasadena, Calif: Nat. Science Foundn Sen. Foreign Res. Fellow, 1970; Sherman Fairchild Distinguished Scholar, 1977. National Research Council, War Research-Atomic Energy, 1943-45. Member: Nat. Research Council, 1955-61; Defence Research Bd, 1955-61; Commn on Atomic Weights, IUPAC; Canadian Nat. Cttee, IUPAC; Board of Governors, Ontario Research Foundation; Director: Atomic Energy of Canada Ltd; Steel Co. of Canada Ltd. Hon. Fellow, Chemical Inst. of Canada, 1972; Shell Canada Merit Fellowship, 1974. Hon. DSc: Universities: Toronto, 1955; EC, Acadia, 1960; Laval, 1963; RMC, 1964; McGill, 1966; Queen's, 1967; York, 1972; McMaster, 1973. Hon. LLD Sask. 1958. Medal of Chemical Inst. of Canada, 1957; Tory Medal, Royal Society of

Canada, 1959. *Publications:* 134 publications on nuclear chemistry, isotope chemistry, isotope abundances in terrestrial and extraterrestrial material, separation of isotopes, magnetic susceptibilities, electrical discharges in gases, sulphur concentrations and isotope ratios in lunar materials. *Recreations:* swimming, farming. *Address:* Department of Chemistry, Nuclear Research Building, McMaster University, 1280 Main Street West, Hamilton, Ontario L8S 4K1, Canada. *T:* (416) 525-9140. *Club:* Rotary (Hamilton, Ont.).

THODY, Prof. Philip Malcolm Waller; Professor of French Literature, University of Leeds, since 1965; *b* Lincoln, 21 March 1928; *s* of Thomas Edwin Thody and Florence Ethel (*née* Hart); *m* 1954, Joyce Elizabeth Woodin; two *s* two *d. Educ:* Lincoln Sch.; King's Coll., Univ. of London. Temp. Asst Lectr, Univ. of Birmingham, 1954-55; Asst Lectr, subseq. Lectr, QUB, 1956-65; Chairman: Dept of French, Univ. of Leeds, 1968-72, 1975-; Bd of Faculties of Arts, Social Studies and Law, Univ. of Leeds, 1972-74. Vis. Professor: Univ. of Western Ontario, Canada, 1963-64; Berkeley Summer Sch., 1964; Harvard Summer Sch., 1968; Centenary Vis. Prof., Adelaide Univ., 1974; Canterbury Vis. Fellow, Univ. of Canterbury, NZ, 1977. *Publications:* Albert Camus, a study of his work, 1957; Jean-Paul Sartre, a literary and political study, 1960; Albert Camus, 1913-1960, 1961; Jean Genet, a study of his novels and plays, 1968; Jean Anouilh, 1968; Choderlos de Laclos, 1970; Jean-Paul Sartre, a biographical introduction, 1971; Aldous Huxley, a biographical introduction, 1973; Roland Barthes: a conservative estimate, 1977; A True Life Reader for Children and Parents, 1977; contribs to French Studies, Times Literary Supplement, Times Higher Educational Supplement, Modern Languages Review, London Magazine, Twentieth Century, Encounter. *Recreations:* talking; Wodehouse inter-war first editions. *Address:* 6 The Nook, Primley Park, Alwoodley, Leeds LS17 7JU. *T:* Leeds 687350.

THOM, Alexander; Professor of Engineering Science, Oxford University, 1945-61; *b* 26 March 1894; Scottish parents; *m* 1917, Jeanie Boyd Kirkwood (*d* 1975); one *s* one *d* (one *s* killed 1945). *Educ:* Glasgow University. BSc 1915, PhD 1926, DSc 1929, Glasgow; MA (Oxford) 1945; Emeritus Fellow, Brasenose College, 1961. Employed by various engineering and aeronautical firms, 1913-21; Lectr, Glasgow University, 1922-39; Royal Aircraft Establishment, Farnborough, on aeronautical research, 1939-45. Hon. LLD Glasgow, 1960; Hon. DSc Strathclyde, 1976. *Publications:* Standard Tables and Formulae for Setting out Road Spirals, 1935; (with C. J. Apelt) Field Computations in Engineering and Physics, 1960; Megalithic Sites in Britain, 1967; Megalithic Lunar Observatories, 1971; papers to various scientific institutions. *Recreation:* sailing. *Address:* The Hill, Dunlop, Ayrshire.

THOM, James Robert; Forestry Consultant, Food and Agriculture Organisation, Rome, since 1973; *b* 22 July 1910; *er s* of late Wm and Caroline Thom; *m* 1937, Constance Daphne, *d* of late Dr A. C. L. La Frenais, British Guiana; two *s. Educ:* George Watson's Coll., Edinburgh; Edinburgh University. BSc (Forestry) Edinburgh Univ., 1932. District Officer, Forestry Commission, 1933; Divisional Officer, 1940; Conservator, 1946; Director of Forestry for Wales, 1958-63, for England, 1963-65; Dir of Research, 1965-68, Forestry Commn; Project Manager: UN Forest Industries Devlt Survey, Guyana, 1968-70; UN Devlt Prog., Sarajevo, Yugoslavia, 1970-73. *Recreations:* Rugby football (represented Scotland, 1933), gardening. *Address:* 11 Abbotsford Crescent, Edinburgh EH10 5DY. *T:* 031-447 1005. *Club:* Caledonian.

THOM, Kenneth Cadwallader; HM Diplomatic Service; Head of Accommodation and Services Department, Foreign and Commonwealth Office, since 1974; *b* 4 Dec. 1922; *m* 1948, Patience Myra (*née* Collingridge); three *s* one *d. Educ:* University College School, London; St Andrews Univ.; MA(Hons). Army Service, 1942-47; Assistant District Officer, then District Officer, Northern Nigerian Administration, 1950-59; 1st Secretary: FO, 1959; UK Mission to UN, NY, 1960-63; FO, 1963-66; Budapest, 1966-68; FCO, 1968-72; Counsellor, Dublin, 1972-74. *Address:* c/o Foreign and Commonwealth Office, SW1. *Club:* Royal Commonwealth Society.

THOMAS, family name of **Baron Thomas.**

THOMAS, Baron *cr* 1971 (Life Peer), of Remenham, Berks; **William Miles Webster Thomas,** Kt 1943; DFC; CEng; FIMechE; MSAE; FRAeS; President, National Savings Committee, 1965-72 (also Chairman, 1965-70); Chairman: Britannia Airways Ltd; Chesham Amalgamations and Investments Ltd; Director: Sun Insurance Office, Ltd; Dowty Group Ltd; Thomson Organisation (Sunday Times, etc);

Thomson Travel Ltd; *b* 2 March 1897; *s* of late William Henry Thomas and Mary Elizabeth Webster; *m* 1924, Hylda Nora Church, Kidlington, Oxford; one *s* one *d. Educ:* Bromsgrove School. Served as Engineering Premium Pupil at Bellis and Morcom Ltd, Birmingham; joined Armoured Car Squadron as private; served in German East African campaign as Armoured Car Driver; Commissioned to RFC in Egypt; Stunt Flying and Aerial Fighting Instructor at Heliopolis; afterwards served with RAF in Mesopotamia, Persia and Southern Russia (DFC); Demobilised, 1919; became editor on technical journals; joined Lord Nuffield (then Mr W. R. Morris) as adviser on Sales Promotion, 1924; founded Morris-Oxford Press in 1926; Director and General Sales Manager of Morris Motors Ltd, 1927; Director and General Manager of Morris Commercial Cars Ltd, Birmingham, 1934; of Wolseley Motors Ltd, Birmingham, 1935; Managing Director of Wolseley Motors Ltd in 1937; Vice-Chairman and Managing Director of Morris Motors Ltd and Subsidiary Companies, 1940-47. Chairman: Cruiser Tank Production Group and member of Advisory Panel on Tank Production, 1941; British Tank Engine Mission to US, 1942; Govt of Southern Rhodesia Development Co-ordinating Commission, 1947; Oxfordshire Council, Order of St John, 1947. President, Soc. of Motor Manufacturers, 1947-48; Director, Colonial Development Corporation, 1948-51; Chairman of BOAC, 1949-56; Dep. Chm., P. Leiner & Sons Ltd, 1961-71; President: Advertising Assoc., 1949-53; International Air Transport Assoc., 1951-52; Carbon Electric Holdings Ltd, 1971-72 (Chm. 1964-70); Neumo Ltd. Member: BBC General Advisory Council, 1952-56; Brit. Productivity Council, 1957-62 (Chm., 1959); Chairman: Monsanto Chemicals Ltd, 1956-63; Welsh Adv. Cttee for Civil Aviation, 1961-66; Development Corp. for Wales, 1958-67; Vice-Chm., Welsh Econ. Council, 1965-66. Comdr of Cedar of the Lebanon, Lebanon. *Publications:* Treatise on the development and use of multi-wheel vehicles for cross-country and military purposes, 1924; numerous articles, broadcast talks and television "Brains Trust" and "Get Ahead", 1934-64. (Autobiography) Out on a Wing, 1964. *Recreations:* modest motoring and simple gardening. *Address:* Remenham Court, Henley-on-Thames, Oxon. *T:* Henley 5400. *Clubs:* Athenæum, Royal Automobile, Royal Air Force; The Links (New York).

THOMAS, Rt. Rev. Albert; *see* Bathurst (NSW), Bishop of, (RC).

THOMAS, Ambler Reginald, CMG 1951; Under-Secretary, Ministry of Overseas Development, retired 1975; *b* 12 Feb. 1913; *s* of late John Frederick Ivor Thomas, OBE, MICE, MIME and of Elizabeth Thomas; *m* 1943, Diana Beresford Gresham; two *s* three *d. Educ:* Gresham's School, Holt; Corpus Christi College, Cambridge. Entered Home Civil Service as Asst Principal and apptd to Ministry of Agriculture and Fisheries, 1935; transferred to Colonial Office, 1936. Asst Private Sec. to Sec. of State for Colonies, 1938-39; Principal, Colonial Office, 1939; Asst Sec., 1946; Chief Sec. to Govt of Aden, 1947-49; Establishment and Organization Officer, Colonial Office, 1950-52; Assistant Under-Sec. of State, Colonial Office, 1952-64; Under-Sec., Min. of Overseas Develt, and Overseas Develt Administration, 1964-73. Member, Exec. Cttee, British Council, 1965-68. Chm., Commn of Inquiry into Gilbert Is Develt Authority, 1976. *Address:* Champlands, North Chideock, Bridport, Dorset. *Club:* United Oxford & Cambridge University.

THOMAS, Prof. (Antony) Charles, FSA; Professor of Cornish Studies, University of Exeter, and Director, Institute of Cornish Studies, since 1971; *b* 24 April 1928; *s* of Donald Woodroffe Thomas and Viva Warrington Thomas; *m* 1959, Jessica Dorothea Esther Mann; two *s* two *d. Educ:* Winchester; Corpus Christi Coll., Oxon (BA Hons Jurisp.); Univ. of London (Dipl. Prehist. Archaeol.). Lectr in Archaeology, Univ. of Edinburgh, 1957-67; Prof. of Archaeology, Univ. of Leicester, 1967-71. Leverhulme Fellowship, 1965-67; Lectures: Hunter Marshall, Univ. of Glasgow, 1968; O'Donnell, Univ. of Edinburgh, 1970; Jarrow, 1973; Willans, UC, Aberystwyth, 1975. President: Council for British Archaeology, 1970-73; Royal Instn of Cornwall, 1970-72; Chairman: BBC SW Reg. Adv. Council, 1975-; DoE Area Archaeol Cttee, Cornwall and Devon, 1975-; Hon. Archaeol Consultant, National Trust, 1970-. Hon. Mem., Royal Irish Acad., 1973; Hon. Fellow, RSAI, 1975. *Publications:* Christian Antiquities of Camborne, 1967; The Early Christian Archaeology of North Britain, 1971; Britain and Ireland in Early Christian Times, 1971; (with A. Small and D. Wilson) St Ninian's Isle and its Treasure, 1973; (with D. Ivall) Military Insignia of Cornwall, 1974. *Recreations:* military history, archaeological fieldwork. *Address:* Lambessow, St Clement, Truro, Cornwall; Pencobben, Gwithian, Cornwall.

THOMAS, Brig. Arthur Frank Friend, CIE 1942; *b* 8 Aug. 1897; *s* of Arthur Ernest Thomas, Parkhurst, South Norwood; *m* 1928, Elizabeth Stephenson Walker, MB, BCh, DPH, *d* of Rev. S. Walker, MA, Donaghadee, Co. Down; one *s* one *d*. *Educ:* Melbourne College. ADC, EEF, 1920-21; DADOS Waziristan District, 1928-31; Staff Capt. AHQ 1931-33; DADOS, AHQ, 1933-36; AD of C, AHQ, 1936-39; DD of C 1939-40; D of C 1940; CCPM 1940-41; Deputy Controller-General of Inspection, GHQ, India, 1941-45; Director of Civil Personnel, 1945-47; retired, 1947. Served European War, 1914-21, Egypt, 1914-16, France, 1916-17, EEF 1918 (wounded, despatches); NW Frontier, India, 1930; War of 1939-45. *Recreations:* gardening, cine-photography. *Address:* Drayton House, Loxley Road, Stratford-on-Avon, Warwicks.

THOMAS, Brian (Dick Lauder), OBE 1961; Mural Painter and Stained Glass Designer; *b* 19 Sept. 1912; *s* of Frank Leslie Thomas, MB, BS, and Margaret Mary (*née* Lauder). *Educ:* Bradfield College. Rome Scholarship in Mural Painting, 1934; Camouflage Directorate, Min. of Home Security, 1939-45; Principal, Byam Shaw Sch. of Art, 1946-54; Master, Art Workers Guild, 1957, Editor, Artifex, 1968-71; Fellow, Brit. Soc. of Master Glass Painters, 1958; Chm. of Governors, Hurstpierpoint Coll., 1958-67; Mem. Council, Artists' Gen. Benevolent Instn, 1964; Chm. Council, Fedn of British Craft Socs, 1971-73; Mem., Crafts Adv. Cttee, 1971-73. Vice-Pres., SPCK, 1976. Master, Glaziers Co., 1976. *Principal works:* St Paul's Cathedral (stained glass in American and OBE Chapels); Westminster Abbey (stained glass); Winchester Cathedral (shrine of St Swithun); Wellington Cathedral, NZ (War Memorial windows); St George's Chapel, Windsor (panels in altar rails); St George's Church, Stevenage New Town (stained glass); Livery Co. Windows: London Guildhall, Pewterers' Hall; memorials to Dame Nellie Melba, John Ireland, Russell Colman, Sir Harold Graham-Hodgson, Lord Webb-Johnson and others; painted ceiling at Templewood, Norfolk; murals and mosaics in many religious and secular buildings of London and the provinces. *Publications:* Vision and Technique in European Painting, 1952; Geometry in Pictorial Composition, 1971; (ed) Directory of Master Glass-Painters, 1972. *Address:* The Studio, 3 Hill Road, NW8. *T:* 01-286 0804. *Clubs:* Arts, Athenæum.

THOMAS, Brinley, CBE 1971 (OBE 1955); MA, PhD; FBA 1973; Professor of Economics, University College, Cardiff, 1946-73; Ford Visiting Research Professor, University of California, Berkeley, 1976-77; *b* 6 Jan. 1906; *e s* of late Thomas Thomas and Anne Walters; *m* 1943, Cynthia, *d* of late Dr Charles T. Loram, New Haven, Connecticut; one *d*. *Educ:* Port Talbot County School; University College of Wales, Aberystwyth; London School of Economics. MA (Wales) (with distinction), 1928; Fellow of the University of Wales, 1929-31; Social Science Research Training Scholar, 1929-31; PhD (London), 1931; Hutchinson Silver Medal, London School of Economics, 1931; Acland Travelling Scholar in Germany and Sweden, 1932-34; Lecturer in Economics, London School of Economics, 1931-39; War Trade Department, British Embassy, Washington, 1941-42; Dir, Northern Section, Political Intelligence Dept of Foreign Office, 1942-45; Member: National Assistance Bd, 1948-53; Anderson Cttee on Grants to Students, 1958-60; Dept of Employment Retail Prices Index Advisory Cttee; Prince of Wales Cttee, 1969-76. Chairman: Welsh Advisory Cttee of British Council, 1966-74; Welsh Council, 1968-71; Assoc. of Univ. Teachers of Econs, 1965-68; Member, Exec. Committee: British Council, 1966-74; Atlantic Economic Soc. Nat. Science Foundn Fellow, 1971. Governor, Centre for Environmental Studies, 1972-74. *Publications:* Monetary Policy and Crises, A Study of Swedish Experience, 1936; Migration and Economic Growth, A Study of Great Britain and the Atlantic Economy, 1954, 2nd edn 1973; International Migration and Economic Development: A Trend Report and Bibliography, 1961; Migration and Urban Development, 1972; (ed) Economics of International Migration, 1958; (ed) The Welsh Economy: studies in expansion, 1962; articles in various journals. *Address:* 44a Church Road, Whitchurch, Cardiff. *T:* Cardiff 62835. *Club:* Reform.

THOMAS, Charles; *see* Thomas, A. C.

THOMAS, Dr Claudius Cornelius; Commissioner for the Eastern Caribbean Governments in the United Kingdom, since 1975; *b* 1 Oct. 1928; *s* of Charles Malin Thomas and Ada Thomas (*née* Dyer). *Educ:* Castries Intermed. Sch., St Lucia; London Univ. (LLB); Univ. de Strasbourg (Dr en droit). Called to Bar, Gray's Inn, 1957. Cadet Officer, Commn for the West Indies in UK, 1961; Translator, EEC, Brussels, 1962; Attaché, L'Institut Internat. des Sciences Administratives, Brussels, 1962-63; Free University of (West) Berlin: Wissenschaftlicher Asst, 1963-72, Asst Prof., 1972. *Publications:* contrib. to and assisted in, Multjtudo Legum Ius Unum, 1973; contrib. Deutches Jahrbuch des Offentlichen Rechts, 1966, and other legal ls. *Recreations:* cricket, table tennis, sailing. *Address:* Paddock Cottage, Hampton Court Road, Hampton Court, Surrey. *T:* 01-977 5686.

THOMAS, Colin Agnew; chartered accountant; Secretary-General of Lloyd's, since 1976; *b* 14 Feb. 1921; *s* of Harold Alfred Thomas and Nora (*née* Williams); *m* 1947, Jane Jardine Barnish, *d* of Leonard Barnish, FRIBA; one *s* one *d*. *Educ:* Oundle School. Lieut, RNVR, 1941-46. Finance Comptroller, Lloyd's, 1964-75. *Recreations:* golf, sailing, gardening. *Address:* 33 Cobham Road, Leatherhead, Surrey KT22 9AY. *T:* Leatherhead 74335; 15 Ravenspoint, Trearddur Bay, Anglesey. *Clubs:* Effingham Golf, Holyhead Golf, Trearddur Bay Sailing.

THOMAS, Dafydd Elis; MP (Plaid Cymru) Merioneth, since Feb. 1974; *b* 18 Oct. 1946; *m* 1970, Elen M. Williams; one *s*. *Educ:* Ysgol Dyffryn Conwy; UC North Wales. Research worker, Bd of Celtic Studies, 1970; Tutor in Welsh Studies, Coleg Harlech, 1970; Lectr, Dept of English, UC North Wales, 1974. Part-time freelance broadcaster, BBC Wales, HTV, 1970-73. *Recreations:* hill walking, camping. *Address:* 7 Fron Wnion, Dolgellau, Gwynedd LL40 1SL. *T:* (home) Dolgellau 422303; (constituency office) Dolgellau 422661; (London) 01-219 4172/5021. *Club:* Sport and Social (Trawsfynydd).

THOMAS, David Bowen, PhD; Keeper, Department of Museum Services, Science Museum, since 1973; *b* 28 Dec. 1931; *s* of Evan Thomas and Florence Annie Bowen. *Educ:* Tredegar Grammar Sch.; Manchester Univ. (BSc). Research Fellow, Wayne Univ., Detroit, USA, 1955-57; Research Scientist, Min. of Agriculture, Fisheries and Food, Aberdeen, 1957-61; Asst Keeper, Science Museum, Dept of Chemistry, 1961-73. *Publications:* The First Negatives, 1964; The Science Museum Photography Collection, 1969; The First Colour Motion Pictures, 1969. *Recreation:* country walking. *Address:* 6 Malcolm Lodge, Darlaston Road, Wimbledon SW19 4LQ. *T:* 01-947 3705.

THOMAS, David Churchill; Assistant Secretary, Cabinet Office, since 1973; *b* 21 Oct. 1933; *o s* of David Bernard Thomas and Violet Churchill Thomas (*née* Quicke); *m* 1958, Susan Petronella Arrow; one *s* two *d*. *Educ:* Eton Coll.; New Coll., Oxford (Exhibnr). Mod. Hist. 1st Cl., 1957. Army, 2nd Lieut, Rifle Brigade, 1952-54. Foreign Office, 1958; 3rd Sec., Moscow, 1959-61; 2nd Sec., Lisbon, 1961-64; FCO, 1964-68; 1st Sec. (Commercial), Lima, 1968-70; FCO, 1970-73; Head of South West European Dept, 1974. *Recreations:* photography, listening to music. *Address:* 1 Lion Gate Gardens, Richmond, Surrey TW9 2DF. *T:* 01-940 3074. *Club:* London Welsh RFC.

THOMAS, David Hamilton Pryce, CBE 1977; solicitor; President, Rent Assessment Panel for Wales, since 1971; *b* 3 July 1922; *s* of Trevor John Thomas and Eleanor Maud Thomas; *m* 1948, Eluned Mair Morgan; two *s* one *d*. *Educ:* Barry County Sch.; University College, Cardiff. Served War of 1939-45; British and Indian Armies, terminal rank T/Captain (GSO III), 1941-46. Qualified as Solicitor, 1948, with hons; Partner in J. A. Hughes & Co., Solicitors, Barry, 1950-75; Notary Public, 1953. Director 1962, Vice-Chm. 1967, Chm. 1971, Barry Mutual Building Society. Member: Rent Assessment Panel for Wales, 1966; Adv. Cttee on Fair Rents, 1973; Chm., E Glam. Rent Tribunal, 1967-71; Dep. Chm., Land Authority for Wales, 1975. District Comr of Scouts, Barry and District 1963-70; Chm., Barry District Scout Assoc. 1971; Vice-Chm., S Glam. Scout Council, 1975. *Recreations:* books, music. *Address:* 27 Romilly Park, Barry, South Glamorgan. *T:* Barry 732229.

THOMAS, David Monro; Insurance Consultant, YWCA of Great Britain; Legal & General Assurance Soc ety Ltd, 1951-75; *b* 31 July 1915; *s* of late Henry Monro and Winifred Thomas, East Hagbourne, Berks; *m* 1948, Ursula Mary, *d* of late H. W. Liversidge; two *s* one *d*. *Educ:* St Edward's School, Oxford; St Edmund Hall, Oxford. Oxford House, 1937; Army, 1939, Major, Royal Welch Fusiliers; Head of Oxford House, 1946-48; Secretary of Greek House, 1948-51. *Address:* Watcombe Corner, Watlington, Oxon. *T:* Watlington 2403.

THOMAS, David Owen, QC 1972; a Recorder of the Crown Court, since 1972; *b* 22 Aug. 1926; *s* of Emrys Aeron Thomas and Dorothy May Thomas; *m* 1967, Mary Susan Atkinson; four *d*. *Educ:* Queen Elizabeth's, Barnet; John Bright Sch., Llandudno; Queen's Univ., Belfast. Served War, HM Forces, 1943-45 and to 1948. Called to the Bar, Middle Temple, 1952; Dep. Chairman, Devon QS, 1971. *Recreations:* acting, cricket, Rugby football. *Address:* 2 King's Bench Walk, Temple, EC4Y 7DE. *T:* 01-353 1746; 8 Chesil Street, Winchester, Hants. *T:* Winchester 65142. *Clubs:* MCC; Hampshire (Winchester).

THOMAS, Derek Morison David, CMG 1977; HM Diplomatic Service; Assistant Under Secretary of State, Foreign and Commonwealth Office, since 1976; *b* 31 Oct. 1929; *s* of K. P. D. Thomas and Mali McL. Thomas; *m* 1956, Carolina Jacoba van der Mast; one *s* one *d. Educ:* Radley Coll., Abingdon; Trinity Hall, Cambridge (MA). Mod. Langs Tripos. Articled apprentice, Dolphin Industrial Developments Ltd, 1947. Entered HM Foreign Service, 1953; Midshipman 1953, Sub-Lt 1955, RNVR; FO, 1955; 3rd, later 2nd, Sec., Moscow, 1956-59; 2nd Sec., Manila, 1959-61; UK Delegn to Brussels Conf., 1961-62; 1st Sec., FO, 1962; Sofia, 1964-67; Ottawa, 1967-69; seconded to Treasury, 1969-70; Financial Counsellor, Paris, 1971-75; Head of N American Dept, FCO, 1975-76. *Recreations:* listening to people and music; being by, in or on water. *Address: c/o* Foreign and Commonwealth Office, SW1; William the Conqueror, Widdington, Saffron Walden, Essex. *T:* Saffron Walden 40524. *Club:* United Oxford & Cambridge University.

THOMAS, Dewi Alun, MBE; **His Honour Judge Thomas;** a Circuit Judge since 1972; *b* 3 Dec. 1917; *e s* of late Joshua and Martha Ann Thomas; *m* 1952, Doris Maureen Smith, Barrister; one *s* one *d. Educ:* Christ Coll., Brecon; Jesus Coll., Oxford (MA). Served War of 1939-45 (MBE, despatches): mobilised with TA (RA), 1939; served Sicily, Italy, the Balkans; Major, 2nd in Comd, No 2 Commando; demobilised 1946. Called to Bar, Inner Temple, 1951, Bencher 1969. *Recreations:* golf, watching Rugby football. *Address:* 16 Westhall Park, Warlingham, Surrey. *T:* Upper Warlingham 4127. *Club:* Cardiff and County.

THOMAS, Prof. Dewi-Prys, BArch, DipCD; FRIBA, MRTPI; (first) Professor of Architecture, since 1964, and Head of Welsh School of Architecture, since 1960, University of Wales Institute of Science and Technology, Cardiff; *b* Liverpool, 5 Aug. 1916; *o s* of A. Dan Thomas, Martin's Bank, and Elysabeth Watkin Thomas; *m* 1965, Joyce Ffoulkes Davies, *e d* of Rev. Robert Ff. Parry, Ballarat and Geelong, Australia; two step *s* two step *d. Educ:* Liverpool Inst.; Univ. of Liverpool Sch. of Architecture. Ravenhead Schol. and John Lewis Partnership Prizeman, 1935; John Rankin Prizeman, 1935 and 1936; Holland, Hannen and Cubitts Prizeman and Holt Travelling Schol., 1936; RIBA Archibald Dawnay Schol., 1936-38; Honan Trav. Schol., 1938-39; BArch (1st Cl. Hons) 1938; DipCD (Distinction) Liverpool, 1942. Architect in office of T. Alwyn Lloyd, FRIBA, PPTPI, Cardiff (S Wales Outline Plan), 1942-47; Lectr and Sen. Lectr, Univ. of Liverpool, 1947-60. Dean of Environmental Design, UWIST, 1967-69 and 1971-73; Vice-Principal, UWIST, 1969-71. Comr, Royal Commn on Ancient Monuments in Wales, 1970-; Member Board: Civic Trust for Wales,1964-; Univ. of Wales Press, 1969-75; Member: Court of Governors, Nat. Theatre for Wales, 1967-; Court, Univ. of Wales, 1972-; Founder Mem., Cardiff 2000 (Cardiff Civic Soc.), 1964- (Chm., 1973-75). Frequent lectr and broadcaster (Welsh and English) radio and TV, 1942-; Sir Sydney Jones Meml Lectures (The British Underground), Univ. of Liverpool, 1975; BBC Wales TV Heritage Year Lecture (Arthur Lives!), 1975. *Publications:* Treftadaeth: the heritage, 1975; (memoir in) Artists in Wales, 3, 1976; contrib. to jls. *Recreations:* Celtic affairs, Welsh poetry and history, art. *Address:* The Welsh School of Architecture, UWIST, Cardiff CF1 3NU. *T:* Cardiff 42522; Taldir, Dolgellau. *T:* Dolgellau 422201.

THOMAS, Donald Martin; *see* Thomas, Martin.

THOMAS, Ebenezer Rhys, OBE 1941; DCL, MA, MSc; retired Part-time Lecturer, Physics Department, University of Newcastle upon Tyne; *s* of late D. Thomas, Aberystwyth; *m* Mary Foster (*d* 1956), *d* of Hugh Richardson, MA, Stocksfield, Northumberland; three *s. Educ:* Aberystwyth School and University College; Emmanuel College, Cambridge. Late Headmaster Royal Grammar School, Newcastle upon Tyne; formerly Head of Science Dept, Rugby School; did work on high explosives during the European War; later DAQMG, GHQ, BEF, France (despatches). *Publications:* papers in Journal of Chemical Society and other scientific journals; articles in Listener; School Science Review; New Scientist; Editor of Classics of Scientific Method; joint author of Newton and the Origin of Colours. *Recreations:* research on singing sands, chamber music. *Address:* Clova, 2 Clothersholme Road, Ripon, North Yorkshire.

THOMAS, Prof. Edgar, CBE 1958; BSc Wales; BLitt Oxon; Professor of Agricultural Economics, University of Reading, 1945-65, Emeritus Professor since 1965 (Dean of the Faculty of Agriculture and Horticulture, 1955-59); *b* 24 July 1900; *y s* of Henry Jones Thomas, JP, Penrhos, Llanfynydd, Carmarthenshire, and Elizabeth Lewis; *m* 1927, Eurwen Parry-

Williams (*d* 1951); two *d. Educ:* Llandeilo County Scho.; University Coll. of Wales, Aberystwyth; Wadham College, Oxford; Royal Agricultural Coll., Copenhagen. Research Assistant, Agricultural Economics Research Institute, Oxford, 1926-27; Chief Advisory Officer and Lecturer in Agricultural Economics, Reading Univ., 1927-45. First Pres., Thames Valley Rent Assessment Panel, 1966-72. Vice-President, Internat. Conference of Agricultural Economists, 1952-64; Hon. Sec., Agricultural Economics Society, 1930-52, President, 1953-54; Chairman of Curators of Museum of English Rural Life, 1954-65; Corresponding Member: Accad. Economico-Agraria dei Georgofili, Florence, 1958; Scientific Agricultural Society of Finland, 1961; a Vice-President of Hon. Society of Cymmrodorion. *Publications:* The Economics of Smallholdings, 1927; An Introduction to Agricultural Economics, 1946. Contributions to Journal of Agricultural Economics, Proceedings International Conference of Agricultural Economists and to other economic journals and Reviews. *Address:* 81 Elm Road, Earley, Reading, Berks. *T:* 81474.

THOMAS, Emyr, LLB, LMRTPI; General Manager, Telford New Town Development Corporation, since 1969; *b* 25 April 1920; *s* of late Brinley Thomas, MA, Aldershot; *m* 1947, Barbara J. May; one *d. Educ:* Aldershot County High School. Served War of 1939-45, RASC. Admitted Solicitor, 1947. Asst Solicitor, Exeter City Council, 1947-50; Sen. Asst Solicitor, Reading County Borough Council, 1950-53; Dep. Town Clerk, West Bromwich County Borough Council, 1953-64; Sec. and Solicitor, Dawley (later Telford) Development Corp., 1964-69. *Recreation:* gardening. *Address:* 8 Kynnersley Lane, Leighton, near Shrewsbury, Salop. *T:* (business) Telford 613131.

THOMAS, Rt. Rev. Eryl Stephen; *b* 20 Oct. 1910; *s* of Edward Stephen and Margaret Susannah Thomas; *m* 1939, Jean Mary Alice Wilson; three *s* one *d . Educ:* Rossall Sch.; St John's Coll., Oxford; Wells Theological Coll. BA 2nd Class Hon. Theology, Oxford, 1932; MA 1935. Curate of Colwyn Bay, 1933-38, of Hawarden, 1938-43; Vicar of Risca, Mon, 1943-48; Warden of St Michael's Theological Coll., Llandaff, 1948-54; Dean of Llandaff, 1954-68; Bishop of Monmouth, 1968-71, of Llandaff, 1971-75. Chaplain and Sub-Prelate, Order of St John of Jerusalem, 1969. *Address:* 17 Orchard Close, Gilwern, Abergavenny, Gwent NP7 0EN. *T:* Gilwern 831050.

THOMAS, Frank; *see* Thomas, J. F. P.

THOMAS, Frederick Maginley, CMG 1962; retired Civil Servant; *b* 1 July 1908; 3rd *s* of Rev. Canon F. Thomas; *m* 1941, Dorothea Mary (*d* 1969), *o d* of Edward North; two *d. Educ:* Truro Cathedral School; Exeter College, Oxford. Cadet, Colonial Administrative Service, 1931; District Officer, Northern Rhodesia, 1933; Asst Secretary, 1949; Provincial Commissioner, 1954; Minister of Native Affairs, Northern Rhodesia Government, 1960-63; Deputy Governor, Northern Rhodesia, 1964-65. Served 1940-47; 3rd Battalion KAR; 3 Bn NRR; GSO1 Civil Affairs, Lt-Col. *Publication:* Historical Notes on the Bisa, 1953. *Recreations:* most outdoor pursuits and water colours. *Address:* Rock House, Halse, Taunton, Somerset. *T:* Bishops Lydeard 432293.

THOMAS, Sir Frederick William, Kt 1959; Councillor, City of Melbourne, 1953-65 (Lord Mayor, 1957-59); *b* 27 June 1906; *s* of F. J. Thomas; *m* 1908, Dorothy Alexa Gordon; three *s* by former marr. *Educ:* Melbourne Grammar School. Served War of 1939-45, RAAF (Air Efficiency Award, two bars); Group Captain. Comdr Order of Orange Nassau with swords (Holland), 1943. *Recreation:* golf. *Address:* 35 Hitchcock Avenue, Barwon Heads, Victoria 3227, Australia. *Clubs:* Naval and Military, Australian (Melbourne); Barwon Heads Golf.

THOMAS, Air Vice-Marshal Geoffrey Percy Sansom, CB 1970; OBE 1945; retired; *b* 24 April 1915; *s* of Reginald Ernest Sansom Thomas, New Malden; *m* 1940, Sally, *d* of Horace Biddle, Gainsborough; one *s* one *d. Educ:* King's College School, Wimbledon. Commissioned RAF, 1939; served India and Ceylon, 1942-45; lent to Turkish Air Force, 1950-52; Group Captain, 1958; served with RAAF, 1960-62; Air Commodore, 1965; Director of Movements, 1965; Air Vice-Marshal, 1969; SASO, Maintanance Comd, 1969-71. *Address:* Elms Wood House, Elms Vale, Dover, Kent. *T:* Dover 206375.

THOMAS, Rt. Hon. George; *see* Thomas, Rt Hon. T. G.

THOMAS, Maj.-Gen. George Arthur, CB 1960; CBE 1957; retired; *b* 2 May 1906; *s* of Colonel F. H. S. Thomas, CB, and Diana Thomas; *m* 1936, Diana Zaidee Browne; one *s* one *d. Educ:* Cheltenham College; Royal Military Academy, Woolwich. Commissioned, Royal Artillery, 1926; served in UK and Egypt; Staff College, 1940; CO 17 Field Regt, 1st Army, 1942-43; GSO1, 4 Division, 1943-44; BGS 8th Army, 1944-45; CRA 16 Airborne Div., 1947-48; Imperial Defence Coll., 1952; BGS, MELF, 1955-57; Chief of Staff, HQ Northern Command, 1958-60; Chief of Staff, GHQ Far ELF, 1960-62. Retired, 1962. *Recreations:* games and sports of all kinds. *Address:* Cherrywell, Salisbury Road, Andover, Hants. *T:* Andover 2120. *Club:* Army and Navy.

THOMAS, Gilbert Oliver; author and journalist; *b* 1891; *s* of late J. Oliver Thomas, Leicester; *m* 1928, Dorothy Kathleen, *y d* of late Robert Dann, Hythe, Kent; one *s* one *d. Educ:* Wyggeston School, Leicester; Leys, Cambridge. Editorial Staff, Chapman & Hall, 1910-14; Editor, The Venturer, 1919-21. *Publications:* Birds of Passage (Poems), 1912; The Wayside Altar (Poems), 1913; The Voice of Peace, and other Poems, 1914; The Grapes and the Thorns: Thoughts in War Time, 1915; The Further Goal and other Poems, 1915; Towards the Dawn, and other Poems, 1918; Things Big and Little (Essays), 1919; Poems: 1912-1919, 1920; Sparks from the Fire (Essays), 1923; Mary of Huntingdon and other Poems, 1928; Calm Weather (Essays), 1930; John Masefield (Modern Writers Series), 1932; The Master Light; Letters to David, 1932; William Cowper and the Eighteenth Century, 1935, revised edition, 1949; The Inner Shrine: anthology of the author's devotional poems, 1943; Builders and Makers (literary essays), 1944; Times May Change (essays), 1946. Autobiography: 1891-1941, 1946; Paddington to Seagood: The Story of a Model Railway, 1947; Selected Poems Old and New, 1951; Window in the West (Essays), 1954; Later Poems, 1960; Double Headed: Two Generations of Railway Enthusiasm (in collaboration with David St John Thomas), 1963; One Man Speaks (Text of broadcast poem), 1967; Collected Poems, 1969; contributor, Observer, Sunday Times, Spectator, and many others. For some years wrote regular weekly book feature for Birmingham Post. *Recreations:* music, model railways. *Address:* Queenswood, Cliffgrove, Chilwell, Nottingham. *T:* Nottingham 255328.

THOMAS, Sir (Godfrey) Michael (David), 11th Bt, *cr* 1694; Member of Stock Exchange, London, since 1959; *b* 10 Oct. 1925; *o s* of Rt Hon. Sir Godfrey Thomas, PC, GCVO, KCB, CSI, 10th Bt, and Diana, *d* of late Ven. B. G. Hoskyns; *S* father 1968; *m* 1956, Margaret Greta Cleland, *yr d* of John Cleland, Stormont Court, Godden Green, Kent; one *s* two *d,* of whom one *s* one *d* are twins. *Educ:* Harrow. The Rifle Brigade, 1944-56. *Heir: s* David John Godfrey Thomas, *b* 11 June 1961. *Address:* 2 Napier Avenue, SW6. *T:* 01-736 6896. *Clubs:* MCC, Hurlingham.

THOMAS, Gwyn; author; *b* 6 July 1913; *s* of Walter and Ziphorah Thomas; *m* 1938, Eiluned Thomas. *Educ:* Porth Grammar Sch.; St Edmund Hall, Oxford Univ.; Madrid Univ. BA Hons Oxon, 1934. Univ. Extension Lectr, 1934-40; Schoolmaster (Mod. Langs), 1940-62. Television appearances, 1962-. *Publications: novels:* The Dark Philosophers, 1946; Where Did I Put My Pity, 1946; The Alone To The Alone, 1947; All Things Betray Thee, 1949; The World Cannot Hear You, 1951; Now Lead Us Home, 1952; A Frost On My Frolic, 1953; The Stranger At My Side, 1954; Point Of Order, 1956; Gazooka, 1957; The Love Man, 1958; Ring Delirium 123, 1959; A Welsh Eye, 1964; A Hatful of Humours, 1965; Leaves In The Wind, 1968; The Sky of Our Lives, 1972; *plays:* The Keep, 1961; Loud Organs, 1962; Jackie the Jumper, 1962; The Loot, 1965; SAP, 1974; The Breakers, 1976; *autobiog:* A Few Selected Exits, 1968. *Recreations:* opera, staring. *Address:* Cherry Trees, Wyndham Park, Peterston-super-Ely, Cardiff. *T:* Peterston-super-Ely 435. *Club:* Pontcanna Studio (Cardiff).

THOMAS, Gwyn Edward Ward; *see* Ward Thomas.

THOMAS, Prof. Horatio Oritsejolomi, CBE 1963; CON 1965; FRCS; Vice-Chancellor, University of Ibadan, 1972-75; *b* 31 Aug. 1917; *s* of James Awadagin and Alero Ogiedi Thomas; *m* 1940, Dorothy Irene (*née* Williams); one *s* two *d. Educ:* Univ. of Birmingham. MB, ChB 1942; MRCS 1942, LRCP, FRCS 1949. University Coll., Ibadan (now Univ. of Ibadan): Lectr in Surgery, 1949-52; Sen. Lectr in Surgery, 1952-62; Univ. of Lagos: Prof. and Head of Dept of Surgery, Coll. of Medicine of the Univ., 1962-72; Dean and Provost, Coll. of Medicine, 1962-69; Chm.; Bd of Management, Lagos Univ. Teaching Hosp., 1962-66. Hon. DSc, Univ. of Ife, 1967; Hon. FRCSI, 1970. *Publications:* contribs (chap.) to Diseases of Children in the Subtropics and Tropics (ed Trowell and Jelliffe), 1970; also to: Lancet; Brit. Jl of Surgery; Jl of Med. Educn; W African Med. Jl. *Recreations:* gardening, water-skiing, books (reading, designing and publishing). *Address:* St Thomas's Clinic, PO Box 1, Sapele, Nigeria. *Clubs:* Metropolitan, 400, Lagos Motor Boat (all in Lagos).

THOMAS, Howard, CBE 1967; Chairman: Thames Television Ltd and Thames Television International Ltd, since 1974 (Managing Director of ABC Television, 1955-68, of Thames Television, 1968-74); Independent Television News, 1974-76 (Director, since 1956); *b* 5 March 1909; *s* of W. G. Thomas and A. M. Thomas; *m* 1934, Hilda, *d* of Harrison Fogg; two *d.* Trained in advertising, journalism and broadcasting. Started Commercial Radio Department, London Press Exchange Ltd, 1938. Writer and Producer for BBC Sound Radio and during 3 years directed and produced 500 programmes. Entered film industry as Producer-in-Chief, Associated British Pathé Ltd, 1944. Divnl Dir, EMI Ltd; Director: EMI Film and Theatre Corp. Ltd; EMI Film Distributors Ltd; Euston Films Ltd; Independent Television Companies Association; Literators Ltd; Argus Press Ltd; BAFTA Management Ltd 1975-; Thames Valley Broadcasting Ltd, 1975-. Member: Advertising Standards Authority, 1962-73; Govt Adv. Cttee on Appt of Advertising Agents. Vice-Chm., Advertising Assoc., 1973-. A Vice-Pres., Gtr London Arts Assoc.; Dir, Internat. Council, Nat. Acad. of TV Arts & Scis (USA), 1971-. A Governor, BFI, 1974-; Mem., 'London Looks Forward' Silver Jubilee 1977 Conf. Hon. Fellow, British Kinematograph Sound & Television Soc., 1967; FRSA 1975; Vice-Pres., Royal Television Soc., 1976-; Mem., Internat. Inst. of Communications. Radio Programmes: Showmen of England, Beauty Queen, The Brains Trust, Shipmates Ashore, etc. Films: Elizabeth is Queen (Coronation) and many documentaries. *Publications:* The Brighter Blackout Book, 1939; How to Write for Broadcasting, 1940; Britain's Brains Trust, 1944; The Truth About Television, 1962; With an Independent Air, 1977. *Address:* Thames Television House, Euston Road, NW1. *T:* 01-387 9494; 6 Lowndes Square, SW1X 9HR; Beechwood, Lambridge Lane, Henley-on-Thames, Oxon. *Clubs:* Lord's Taverners, Pilgrims, Variety; Phyllis Court.

THOMAS, Hugh Swynnerton; Historian; Professor of History, 1966-76, and Chairman, Graduate School of Contemporary European Studies, 1973-76, University of Reading; *b* 21 Oct. 1931; *s* of Hugh Whitelegge Thomas, CMG, Colonial Service, Gold Coast (Ghana) and Margery Swynnerton; *m* 1962, Vanessa Jebb, *d* of 1st Baron Gladwyn, *qv*; two *s* one *d. Educ:* Sherborne; Queens' Coll., Cambridge (Scholar); Sorbonne, Paris. Pres. Cambridge Union, 1953. Foreign Office, 1954-57; Sec. to UK delegn to UN Disarmament Sub-Cttee, 1955-56; Lectr at RMA Sandhurst, 1957; prospective parly candidate (Lab) Ruislip-Northwood, 1957-58; worked for UNA, 1960-61, as Dir of its Disarmament Campaign; Chm., Writers for Europe, 1975. Governor, Univ. of the Negev, 1976. Somerset Maugham Prize, 1962. *Publications:* Disarmament: the way ahead (Fabian pamphlet), 1957; The World's Game, 1957; The Oxygen Age, 1958; (ed) The Establishment, 1959; (with Gen. Sir Ronald Adam and Charles Judd) Assault at Arms, 1960; Death of a Conference (UNA pamphlet), 1960; The Spanish Civil War, 1961, rev. edn 1977; The Story of Sandhurst, 1961; The Suez Affair, 1967; (ed) Crisis in the Civil Service, 1968; Cuba, or the Pursuit of Freedom, 1971; (ed) The selected writings of José Antonio Primo de Rivera, 1972; Goya and The Third of May 1808, 1972; Europe, the Radical Challenge, 1973; John Strachey, 1973; The Cuban Revolution, 1977; contributor to: Conviction, 1958; A Century of Conflict, 1966; The Politics of Conformity in Latin America, 1967; European Fascism, 1968; Troubled Neighbours, 1971; The International Regulation of Civil Wars, 1972; The World of Malraux, 1976; The Distant Drum, 1976. *Recreation:* travelling in Italy. *Address:* 29 Ladbroke Grove, W11. *T:* 01-727 2288. *Club:* Beefsteak.

THOMAS, Ivor B.; *see* Bulmer-Thomas.

THOMAS, Ivor Owen; Retired; *b* 5 Dec. 1898; *s* of late Benjamin L. and Margaret Thomas, Briton Ferry, Glamorgan; *m* 1929, Beatrice, *d* of late Councillor William Davis, Battersea; one *d. Educ:* Vernon Place Council Sch., Briton Ferry; London Labour College, 1923-25. Gwalia Tinplate Works, Briton Ferry, 1912-19; Engine Cleaner GWR, Pontypool Rd, 1919-23; NUR Head Office Staff, 1925-45. Member Battersea Borough Council, 1928-45; Chm. Housing Cttee, 1934-38. MF (Lab) the Wrekin Division of Shropshire, 1945-55. Resumed NUR Head Office Staff, 1955-58. Waterloo CCE Dept British Rlys, Southern Region, 1960-64; Westminster City Council, Land Use Survey, 1965-66. *Address:* Marobea, 26 Sumburgh Road, SW12. *T:* 01-228 2874.

THOMAS, Jeffrey, QC 1974; MP (Lab) Abertillery since 1970; a Recorder of the Crown Court, since 1975; *b* 12 Nov. 1933; *s* of John James Thomas and Phyllis Thomas (*née* Hile); *m* 1960, Margaret Jenkins, BSc(Econ). *Educ:* Abertillery Grammar Sch.; King's Coll. London; Gray's Inn. Called to the Bar, Gray's Inn, 1957. Pres., Univ. of London Union, 1955-56. Served Army (National Service): commnd in Royal Corps of Transport, 1959

(Senior Under Officer); later served in Directorate of Army Legal Services: Major, Dep. Asst Dir, HQ BAOR, 1961. Contested (Lab) Barry, 1966. Chm., Brit. Caribbean Assoc.; Mem. Council, Justice; Mem. Exec. Cttee, British Gp, IPU. Member Court of Governors: University Coll. of Wales, Aberystwyth; Nat. Museum of Wales (ex officio); Nat. Library of Wales; Vice Pres., North Monmouthshire Youth Rugby Union. *Recreations:* watching Rugby football, travelling. *Address:* (home) 60 Lamont Road, SW10. *T:* 01-351 1303; (chambers) 3 Temple Gardens, Temple, EC4. *T:* 01-583 8333. *Clubs:* Reform; Abertillery Rugby Football.

THOMAS, Jeremy Cashel; HM Diplomatic Service; Head of Permanent Under-Secretary's Department, Foreign and Commonwealth Office, since 1977; *b* 1 June 1931; *s* of Rev. H. C. Thomas and Margaret Betty (*née* Humby); *m* 1957, Diana Mary Summerhayes; three *s. Educ:* Eton; Merton Coll., Oxford. HM Forces, 1949-51; entered FO, 1954; served Singapore, Rome and Belgrade; Dep. Head, Personnel Ops Dept, FCO, 1970-74; Counsellor and Head of Chancery, UK Mission to UN, NY, 1974-76. *Recreations:* sailing, fishing. *Address:* Moffat, Pains Hill, Limpsfield, Surrey. *T:* Limpsfield Chart 3176. *Clubs:* Leander, Oxford and Cambridge Sailing Society, Itchenor Sailing.

THOMAS, (John) Frank (Phillips); Director, Network Planning Department, Post Office, since 1972; *b* 11 April 1920; *s* of late John and of Catherine Myfanwy Phillips Thomas; *m* 1942, Edith V. Milne; one *s* one *d. Educ:* Christ's Coll., Finchley; Univ. of London (BSc). CEng, MIEE. Joined Post Office Research Dept, 1937; trans-oceanic telephone cable system develt, 1947-63; planning UK inland telephone network, 1963-69; Dep. Dir London Telephone Region, 1969-71; Dep. Dir Engrg, Network Planning Dept, 1971. *Publications:* contrib. scientific and technical jls on telecommunications subjects. *Recreation:* tennis (Vice-Captain, Rickmansworth Tennis Club). *Address:* 24 Shepherds Way, Rickmansworth, Herts. *T:* Rickmansworth 72992.

THOMAS, Rt. Rev. John James Absalom, DD Lambeth 1958; *b* 17 May 1908; *s* of William David and Martha Thomas; *m* 1941, Elizabeth Louise, *d* of Very Rev. H. L. James, DD, former Dean of Bangor; one *s. Educ:* University College of Wales, Aberystwyth; Keble College, Oxford. Curate of Llanguicke, 1931-34; Curate of Sketty, 1934-36; Bishop's Messenger and Examining Chaplain, 1936-40; Warden of Church Hostel, Bangor, and Lecturer in University Coll. of N Wales, 1940-44; Vicar of Swansea, 1945-58, also Chaplain to Bishop of Swansea and Brecon; Canon of Brecon Cathedral, 1946; Precentor, 1952; Rural Dean of Swansea, 1952-54; Archdeacon of Gower, 1954-58; Bishop of Swansea and Brecon, 1958-76. Chm. of Governors, Christ Coll., Brecon, 1961-. Chaplain and Sub-Prelate, Order of St John of Jerusalem, 1965. *Address:* Woodbine Cottage, St Mary Street, Tenby, Dyfed.

THOMAS, (John) Maldwyn; Chairman, Rank Xerox Ltd, since 1972; *b* 17 June 1918. *Educ:* Porth Rhondda Grammar Sch. FCIS. Called to Bar, Gray's Inn, 1953; Solicitor, 1965. Admin. posts, Porthcawl, 1937-39; Lewis & Tylor Ltd, Cardiff, 1940-56: Asst Sec. 1944; Sec. 1947; Dir 1954; Signode Ltd, Swansea, 1956-59; Commercial Agreements Man., UKAEA, 1959-63; Rank Xerox Ltd: Sec. 1964-70; Man. Dir 1970-72. Vice-Pres., London Welsh Rugby Football Club. Contested (L) Aberavon, 1950. *Address:* Rank Xerox House, 338 Euston Road, NW1 3BH.

THOMAS, Prof. John Meurig, PhD, DSc; FRS 1977; Professor and Head of Department of Chemistry, University College of Wales, Aberystwyth, since 1969; *b* Llanelli, Wales, 15 Dec. 1932; *s* of David John and Edyth Thomas; *m* 1959, Margaret, *d* of William Hubert and Catherine Ann Edwards; two *d. Educ:* Gwendraeth Grammar Sch.; University College of Swansea; Queen Mary Coll., London. Scientific Officer, UKAEA, 1957-58; Asst Lectr 1958-59, Lectr 1959-65, Reader 1965-69, in Chemistry, UCNW, Bangor. Visiting appointments: Holland, 1962; USA, 1963, 1975; Germany, 1966; Israel, 1969; Italy, 1972; Egypt, 1973. Corday Morgan Silver Medal, Chem. Soc., 1967; first Pettinos Prize, American Carbon Soc., 1969; Tilden Medal and Lectr, Chem. Soc., 1973. *Publications:* (with W. J. Thomas) Introduction to the Principles of Heterogeneous Catalysis, 1967; numerous articles on solid state and surface chemistry, and influence of crystalline imperfections, in Proc. Royal Soc., Jl Chem. Soc., etc. *Recreations:* ancient civilizations, bird watching, hill walking, Welsh literature. *Address:* Edward Davies Chemical Laboratories, University College of Wales, Aberystwyth SY23 1NE. *T:* Aberystwyth 7645.

THOMAS, Gen. Sir (John) Noel, KCB 1969 (CB 1967); DSO 1945; MC 1945; BEng; Member, since 1971, Vice-Chairman, since 1974, Commonwealth War Graves Commission; *b* 28 Feb. 1915; *s* of John Ernest Thomas; *m* 1946, Jill, *d* of Edward Gordon Cuthbert Quilter; two *s. Educ:* Royal Grammar School, Newcastle upon Tyne; Liverpool University. 2nd Lieut, Royal Engineers, 1936. Served War of 1939-45 (MC, DSO). Imperial Defence College, 1963; General Officer Commanding 42 (Lancashire and Cheshire) Div. (TA), North West District, 1963-65; Director, Combat Development (Army), MoD, 1965-68; Dep. Chief of Defence Staff (Operational Requirements), MoD, 1968-70; Master-Gen. of the Ordnance, 1971-74. Lt-Gen. 1968; Gen. 1971. Hon. Col, Liverpool Univ. Contingent, OTC, 1965-. Colonel Commandant: Royal Pioneer Corps, 1968-75; Royal Engineers, 1968-73. FRSA 1971. Hon. DEng Liverpool, 1972. *Address:* Chandlers House, The Trippet, Old Bosham, Sussex. *Club:* Royal Ocean Racing.

THOMAS, Rev. John Roland Lloyd; Principal of St David's College, Lampeter, 1953-75; Canon of St David's, 1956-75, Chancellor, 1963-75; *b* 22 Feb. 1908; 2nd *s* of late John Thomas, ME, and Mrs Ann Thomas; *m* 1949, Mrs Elizabeth Swaffield (*née* Rees); three *d. Educ:* King's Coll., Taunton; St David's Coll., Lampeter; Jesus College, Oxford. Welsh Church Scholar, St David's College, Lampeter, BA (1st Class Hons History), 1930, Senior Scholar, 1929-30; Meyricke Graduate Scholar, 1930-32, Jesus Coll., Oxford, BA (2nd Class Th. Hons), 1932; MA 1936. Deacon, 1932; priest, 1933; Curate of St John Baptist, Cardiff, 1932-40. CF (EC) 1940-44. Rector of Canton, Cardiff, 1944-49; Vicar of St Mark's, Newport, 1949-52; Dean of Monmouth and Vicar of St Woolos Parish, Newport, 1952-53. CF(TA), 1949-52; SCF (TA), 1950-52; Hon. CF 1952. Hon. LLD Wales, 1976. *Address:* 1 Rock House, St Julian Street, Tenby, Dyfed. *T:* Tenby 2679.

THOMAS, John S.; *see* Stradling Thomas.

THOMAS, Prof. Joseph Anthony Charles; Professor of Roman Law in the University of London, since 1965; *b* 24 Feb. 1923; *e c* of Joseph and Merle Thomas, Bridgend, Glam; *m* 1949, Margaret (marr. diss. 1970), *d* of John and Jean Hookham, Cambridge; three *s* one *d. Educ:* County Grammar School, Bridgend; Trinity College, Cambridge. MA, LLB Cantab 1949; Barrister, Gray's Inn, 1950. Lecturer in Law, Nottingham Univ., 1949-54; Sen. Lecturer, Univ. of Glasgow, 1954-57; Douglas Professor of Civil Law, University of Glasgow, 1957-64. Served with Intelligence Corps, Psychological Warfare Branch, and Allied Commission, Austria, 1942-46. Crabtree Orator, 1969. Medaglia d'oro dei benemeriti della cultura della Repubblica italiana, 1974. *Publications:* Private International Law, 1955, repr. 1975; (with J. C. Smith) A Casebook on Contract, 1957 (6th edn 1977); The Institutes of Justinian, 1975; Textbook of Roman Law, 1976; articles in legal periodicals. *Recreations:* walking, reading, watching cricket. *Address:* University College, Gower Street, WC1. *T:* 01-387 7050; 1 Hornton Street, W8. *T:* 01-937 1688. *Club:* MCC.

THOMAS, Keith Henry Westcott, OBE 1962; CEng, FRINA, RCNC; General Manager, HM Dockyard, Devonport, since 1977; *b* 20 May 1923; *s* of Henry and Norah Thomas; *m* 1946, Brenda Jeanette Crofton; two *s. Educ:* Portsmouth Southern Secondary Sch.; HM Dockyard Sch., Portsmouth; RNC, Greenwich. Asst Constructor, Admiralty Experiment Works, Haslar, 1947-49; Constructor, London, 1949-56; Large Carrier Design Section, Admty, Bath, 1956-60; Submarines and New Construction, HM Dockyard, Portsmouth, 1960-63; Project Leader, Special Refit HMS Hermes, Devonport, 1963-66; Dep. Planning Manager, HM Dockyard, Devonport, 1966-68; Project Man., Ikara Leanders, MoD(N), 1968-70; Dir-Gen. of Naval Design, Dept of Navy, Canberra, Aust. (on secondment), 1970-73; Planning Man., 1973-75; Gen. Man., 1975-77, HM Dockyard, Rosyth. MBIM. *Recreations:* music, fencing, lapidary. *Address:* Carrickmore, Westella Road, Yelverton, Devon.

THOMAS, Kenneth Rowland; General Secretary, Civil and Public Services Association, since 1976; *b* 7 Feb. 1927; *s* of William Rowland Thomas and Annie Thomas; *m* 1955, Nora (*née* Hughes); four *s. Educ:* St Joseph's Elementary Sch., Penarth; Penarth Grammar Sch. Trainee Reporter, South Wales Echo and Western Mail, 1943-44; Civil Servant, 1944-54; Asst Sec., Civil and Public Services Assoc., 1955, Dep. Gen. Sec., 1967. Mem., TUC Gen. Council, 1977-. *Recreations:* sailing, building harpsichords, music. *Address:* 66 Canonbie Road, SE23 3AG. *T:* 01-699 9762.

THOMAS, Maj.-Gen. Lechmere Cay, CB 1948; CBE 1945 (OBE 1939); DSO 1940 and Bar 1942; MC and Bar 1917; Major-

General, retired; late Royal Northumberland Fusiliers; *b* 20 Oct. 1897; *s* of late Kempson Thomas, Farnham, Surrey; *m* 1st, 1929, Kathleen Primrose (*d* 1929), 2nd *d* of late Albert White, JP, Birney Hill, Ponteland, Northumberland; 2nd, 1951, Sylvia E., *widow* of Eric Smith, Colonial Service, and *d* of late Newman Hall, Forest Hill, Jersey, CI. *Educ:* Cranleigh School, Surrey. Served European War, 1914-18, in France and Belgium (wounded, MC and Bar, two medals); Iraq, 1920 (wounded); commanded 2nd Battalion King's African Rifles, 1934-39; served War of 1939-45, in France, Malaya and Burma (despatches, DSO, and Bar, CBE); Commander: 9th Bn R Northumberland Fusiliers, 1940-42; 1st Bn, Wilts Regt, 1942; 88th Indian Inf. Bde, 1942-43; 36th Indian Inf. Bde, 1943-45; Inspector General, (Indigenous) Burma Army, 1945-47; GOC (Indigenous) Burma Army, 1947-48. *Address:* Forest Hill, Beaumont, Jersey, CI. *Club:* Army and Navy.

THOMAS, Leslie John; author; *b* 22 March 1931; *s* of late David James Thomas and late Dorothy Hilda Court Thomas, Newport (Mon); *m* 1st, 1956, Maureen Crane (marr. diss.); two *s* one *d*; 2nd, 1970, Diana Miles; one *s*. *Educ:* Dr Barnardo's, Kingston-upon-Thames; Kingston Technical Sch.; SW Essex Technical Coll., Walthamstow. Local Newspapers, London area, 1948-49 and 1951-53; Army, 1949-51 (rose to Lance-Corporal); Exchange Telegraph News Agency, 1953-55; Special Writer, London Evening News, 1955-66; subseq. author. *Publications: autobiography:* This Time Next Week, 1964; *novels:* The Virgin Soldiers, 1966; Orange Wednesday, 1967; The Love Beach, 1968; Come to the War, 1969; His Lordship, 1970; Onward Virgin Soldiers, 1971; Arthur McCann and All His Women, 1972; The Man with Power, 1973; Tropic of Ruislip, 1974; Stand up Virgin Soldiers, 1975; Dangerous Davies, 1976; Bare Noll, 1977; *non-fiction:* Some Lovely Islands, 1968; TV Plays and Documentaries, etc. *Recreations:* golf, islands, antiques, cricket. *Address:* Vennards, North Gorley, Hants. *Clubs:* Wig and Pen; Variety.

THOMAS, (Lewis John) Wynford V.; *see* Vaughan-Thomas.

THOMAS, Lowell; Author, Producer, Radio Commentator; *b* 6 April 1892; *s* of Colonel Harry G. Thomas, MD, and Harriet Wagner; *m* 1st, 1917, Frances Ryan; one *s*; 2nd, 1977, Marianna Munn. *Educ:* University of Northern Indiana (BSc); Univ. of Denver (BA, MA); Princeton Univ. (MA). Reporter Chicago Journal until 1914; Professor of Oratory, Chicago Kent College of Law, 1912-14; Instructor Dept of English, Princeton, 1914-16; Chief of Civilian Mission for historical record of First World War (Palestine Campaign and Arabian revolution). Associate-Editor, Asia Magazine, 1919-23. Studied international aviation (25,000 mile flight over 21 countries), 1926-27. Made many war broadcasts from European and Far Eastern war points; Tibetan Expedition, 1949. Brought out Cinerama for the first time 1952; producer of This Is Cinerama, The Seven Wonders of The World, and Search for Paradise. In 1957, 1958, 1959; organised many TV expedns and prod. TV programmes in remote parts of the World. FAGS, FRGS. Member English-Speaking Union (hon. life), Life member, American Museum of Natural History. Fraternities: Kappa Sigma; Tau Kappa Alpha; Phi Delta Phi; Sigma Delta Chi; Alpha Epsilon. Mason. *Publications:* With Lawrence in Arabia, 1924; The First World Flight, 1925; Beyond Khyber Pass, 1925; Count Luckner, The Sea Devil, 1927; European Skyways, 1927; The Boy's Life of Colonel Lawrence, 1927; Raiders of the Deep, 1928; Adventures in Afghanistan for Boys, 1928; Woodfill of the Regulars, 1929; The Sea Devil's Fo'c's'le, 1929; The Hero of Vincennes, 1929; India, Land of the Black Pagoda, 1930; Wreck of the Dumaru, 1930; Lauterback of the China Sea, 1930; Rolling Stone, 1931; Tall Stories, 1931; Kabluk of the Eskimo, 1932; This Side of Hell, 1932; Old Gimlet Eye, 1933; The Untold Story of Exploration, 1935; Fan Mail, 1935; A Trip to New York with Bobby and Betty, 1936; Men of Danger, 1936; Kipling Stories, and a Life of Kipling, 1936; Seeing Canada with Lowell Thomas, 1936; Seeing India with Lowell Thomas, 1936; Seeing Japan with Lowell Thomas, 1937; Seeing Mexico with Lowell Thomas, 1937; Adventures among Immortals, 1937; Hungry Waters, 1937; Wings Over Asia, 1937; Magic Dials, 1939; In New Brunswick We'll Find It, 1939; Soft Ball! So What? 1940; How to Keep Mentally Fit, 1940; Stand Fast for Freedom, 1940; Pageant of Adventure, 1940; Pageant of Life, 1941; Pageant of Romance, 1943; These Men Shall Never Die, 1943; Back to Mandalay, 1951; Great True Adventures, 1955; The Story of the New York Thruway, 1955; The Seven Wonders of the World, 1957; History as You Heard It, 1958; The Vital Spark, 1959; Sir Hubert Wilkins: His World of Adventure, 1961; More Great True Adventures, 1963; Book of the High Mountains, 1964; Story of the St Lawrence Seaway, 1971; Famous First Flights that Changed History, 1968; Burma Jack, 1971; Good Evening Everybody (autobiog.), 1976; Doolittle, a biography, 1976.

Recreations: ski-ing, riding, golf. *Address:* Hammersley Hill, Pawling, NY 12564, USA; (office) 24E 51st Street, New York City, NY 10022, USA. *Clubs:* Royal and Ancient (St Andrews); Princeton, Explorers, Dutch Treat, Overseas Press (New York); Bohemian (San Francisco); Pine Valley Golf (New Jersey); Assoc. of Radio and TV News Analysts; Marco Polo.

THOMAS, Maldwyn; *see* Thomas, J. M.

THOMAS, Margaret, RBA 1947; FRSA 1951; NEAC 1950; Women's International Art Club, 1940; Contemporary Portrait Society, 1970; Royal West of England Academy, 1971; Practising Artist (Painter); *b* 26 Sept. 1916; *d* of late Francis Stewart Thomas and of Grace Wetherly. *Educ:* privately; Slade Sch.; RA Schools. Slade Scholar, 1936. Hon. Sec. Artists International Assoc., 1944-45; Group exhibitions, Wildensteins, 1946, 1949 and 1962; First one-man show at Leicester Galls, 1949, and subsequently at same gallery, 1950; one-man shows in Edinburgh (Aitken Dotts), 1952, 1955, 1966 and at Outlook Tower, Edinburgh, during Internat. Fest., 1961; RBA Galleries, London, 1953; at Canaletto Gall. (a barge, at Little Venice), 1961; Exhibition of Women Artists, Wakefield Art Gall., 1961; Howard Roberts Gallery Cardiff, 1963, The Minories, Colchester, 1964, QUB, 1967, Mall Galls, London, 1972; Octagon Gall., Belfast, 1973; Court Lodge Gallery, Kent, 1974; Gallery Paton, Edinburgh, 1977; Regular exhibitor Royal Academy and Royal Scottish Academy. Official purchases: Prince Philip, Duke of Edinburgh; Chantrey Bequest; Arts Council; Exeter College, Oxford; Min. of Education; Min. of Works; Wakefield, Hull, Paisley and Carlisle Art Galleries; Edinburgh City Corporation; Nuffield Foundation Trust; Steel Co. of Wales; Financial Times; Mitsukoshi Ltd, Tokyo. GLC and county education authorities in Yorks, Bucks, Monmouth, Derbyshire, Hampshire and Wales. Coronation painting purchased by Min. of Works for British Embassy in Santiago. *Publications:* work reproduced in: Daily Telegraph, News Chronicle, Listener, Studio, Scottish Field, Music and Musicians, The Lady, Arts Review, Western Mail. *Recreations:* antique collecting, gardening, vintage cars. *Address:* Halfway Cottage, 11a North Road, Highgate Village, N6 4BD. *T:* 01-340 2527; 8 North Bank Street, Edinburgh EH1 2LP. *T:* 031-225 3343.

THOMAS, Martin; a Recorder of the Crown Court, since 1976; *b* 13 March 1937; *s* of Hywel and Olwen Thomas; *m* 1961, Nan Thomas (*née* Kerr); three *s* one *d*. *Educ:* Grove Park Grammar Sch., Wrexham; Peterhouse, Cambridge. MA, LLB (Cantab). Solicitor at Wrexham, 1961-66; Lectr in Law, 1966-68; called to the Bar, Gray's Inn, 1967; Barrister, Wales and Chester Circuit, 1968-; Dep. Circuit Judge, 1974-76. Contested (L): W Flints, 1964, 1966, 1970; Wrexham, Feb. and Oct. 1974; Vice Chm., Welsh Liberal Party, 1967-69, Chm. 1969-74; Pres., Wrexham Liberal Assoc., 1975-. *Recreations:* Rugby football, golf, music-making, amateur theatre. *Address:* Glasfryn, Cresford, Wrexham, Clwyd. *T:* Gresford 2205. *Clubs:* Reform; Wrexham Rugby Football, Wrexham Golf.

THOMAS, Rt. Rev. Maxwell McNee; *see* Wangaratta, Bishop of.

THOMAS, Melbourne, QPM 1953; Chief Constable, South Wales Constabulary, 1969-71; *b* 1 May 1906; *s* of David and Charlotte Frances Thomas; *m* 1930, Marjorie Elizabeth Phillips; one *d*. *Educ:* Newport (St Julian's) High School. Metropolitan Police, 1928-29; Newport Borough Police, 1929-45 (Dep. Chief Constable, 1941-45); Chief Constable: Merthyr Borough Police, 1945-63; Glamorgan Constabulary, 1963-69. Chm., Bd of Governors, Coleg-y-Fro, 1971; Dir of Ceremonies, St John Priory, Wales, 1973-. KStJ 1974. *Recreations:* Rugby, cricket, athletics. *Address:* The Old Malthouse, Llantwit Major, South Glam. *T:* Llantwit Major 153.

THOMAS, Air Vice-Marshal Meredith, CSI 1946; CBE 1941; DFC 1922; AFC; Royal Air Force, retired; *b* 6 July 1892. Served European War, 1914-19; Flying Officer, RFC, 1917; Group Captain, 1938; SASO, No 5 Grp, 1938; Dir of Techn. Trg, Air Min., 1940; Air Cdre, 1943; AOC, India, 1944-46; retired, 1946. *Address:* c/o Ministry of Defence (Air), Whitehall, SW1.

THOMAS, Sir Michael, 3rd Bt; *see* Thomas, Sir W. M. M.

THOMAS, Sir Michael, 11th Bt; *see* Thomas, Sir G. M. D.

THOMAS, Michael David, QC 1973; *b* 8 Sept. 1933; *s* of D. Cardigan Thomas and late Kathleen Thomas; *m* 1958, Jane Lena Mary, *e d* of Francis Neate; two *s* two *d*. *Educ:* Chigwell Sch., Essex; London Sch. of Economics. LLB 1954. Called to Bar, Middle Temple, 1955 (Blackstone Entrance Schol., 1952; Harmsworth Schol., 1957). Nat. Service with RN, Sub-Lt

RNVR, 1955-57. In practice at Bar from 1958. Junior Counsel to Minister of Defence (RN) and to Treasury in Admty matters, 1966-73. Wreck Commissioner under Merchant Shipping Act 1970; one of Lloyd's salvage arbitrators. Governor, Chigwell Sch., 1971-. *Publications:* (ed jtly) Temperley: Merchant Shipping Acts, 6th edn 1963 and 7th edn 1974. *Recreations:* music, travel. *Address:* 3 The Little Green, Richmond, Surrey. *T:* 01-940 4819; 2 Essex Court, Temple, EC4Y 9AP. *T:* 01-353 4559. *Club:* Garrick.

THOMAS, Michael Stuart, (Mike Thomas); MP (Lab and Co-op), Newcastle upon Tyne East, since Oct. 1974; Parliamentary Private Secretary to Rt Hon. Roy Hattersley, MP, since 1975; Member, Select Committee on Nationalised Industries, since 1975; *b* 24 May 1944; *s* of Arthur Edward Thomas. *Educ:* Latymer Upper Sch.; King's Sch., Macclesfield; Liverpool Univ. (BA). Pres., Liverpool Univ. Guild of Undergraduates, 1965-66; Past Mem. Nat. Exec., NUS. Head of Research Dept, Co-operative Party, 1966-68; Sen. Res. Officer, Political and Economic Planning, 1968-73; Dir, Volunteer Centre, 1973-74. Mem., USDAW; founder of parly jl The House Magazine. *Publications:* Participation and the Redcliffe Maud Report, 1970; various PEP pamphlets, contribs, etc, 1971-; various articles, reviews, etc. *Recreations:* theatre, music, cooking, collecting political and historical objects (particularly pottery). *Address:* House of Commons, SW1A 1AA. *T:* 01-219 3000. *Clubs:* Walker Social, Walkergate Social (Newcastle upon Tyne).

THOMAS, Neville; *see* Thomas, R. N.

THOMAS, Sir Noel; *see* Thomas, Sir J. N.

THOMAS, Norman; HM Chief Inspector of Schools since 1973; *b* 1 June 1921; *s* of Bowen Thomas and Ada Thomas (*née* Redding); *m* 1942, Rose Henshaw; one *s* one *d. Educ:* Latymer's Sch., Edmonton; Camden Coll. Qual. Teacher. Commerce and Industry, then primary schs in London and Herts, 1948-56; Head, Longmeadow Sch., Stevenage, 1956-61; HM Inspector of Schools, Lincs and SE England, 1962-68; HMI, Staff Inspector for Primary (Junior and Middle) Schs, 1969-73. *Recreations:* photography, reading. *Address:* Department of Education and Science, Elizabeth House, York Road, SE1 7PH. *T:* 01-928 9222.

THOMAS, Sir Patrick (Muirhead), Kt 1974; DSO 1945; TD 1945; Chairman, Scottish Transport Group, 1968-77; *b* 31 Jan. 1914; *s* of Herbert James Thomas, Barrister-at-Law and Charis Thomas (*née* Muirhead); *m* 1939, Ethel Mary Lawrence; one *s* three *d. Educ:* Clifton Coll.; Corpus Christi Coll., Cambridge (MA). FInstT. Served War of 1939-45, France, N Africa, Italy, Greece, Middle East, Austria; Lt-Col comdg 71st Field Regt RA, 1944-45. Steel Industry, United Steel Cos and Arthur Balfour & Co. Ltd, Sheffield, 1935-39; Wm Beardmore & Co. Ltd, Parkhead Steelworks, Glasgow, 1946: Man. Dir, 1954; Dir, 1967-76. Hon. Vice-Pres., Iron and Steel Inst., 1968. Col Comdt, City of Glasgow Army Cadet Force, 1956 (Hon. Col 1963-70, 1977-). Pres., FBI Scottish Council, 1961-62; Pres., Scottish Engrg Employers' Assoc., 1967-68; Part-time Mem., Scottish Gas Board, 1966-72; Director: Brightside Engrg Holdings Ltd, 1967-71; Midland Caledonian Investment Trust Ltd, 1972-75. Chm., Scottish Opera, 1976- (Dir, 1965-); Member: Court, Univ. of Strathclyde, 1970- (Chm., 1970-75); Lloyd's Register of Shipping Scottish Cttee, 1967-; Panel Mem., Industrial Tribunals, 1967-; Mem. Exec. Cttee, Officers Assoc. (Scotland), 1964-75; Deacon Convener, Trades of Glasgow, 1970-71; Mem. Exec. Cttee, Officers Assoc. (Scotland), 1964-75; Chm., Lady Haig's Poppy Factory, 1967-72; Mem. Exec. Cttee, Earl Haig Fund (Scotland), 1964-75. Hon. LLD Strathclyde, 1973. US Bronze Star, 1945. OStJ 1970. *Recreations:* golf, gardening. *Address:* Bemersyde, Kilmacolm, Renfrewshire PA13 4EA. *T:* Kilmacolm 2710.

THOMAS, Rt. Hon. Peter John Mitchell, PC 1964; QC 1965; MP (C) Barnet, Hendon South, since 1974 (Hendon South, 1970-74); a Recorder of the Crown Court, since 1974; *b* 31 July 1920; *o s* of late David Thomas, Solicitor, Llanrwst, Denbighshire, and Anne Gwendoline Mitchell; *m* 1947, Frances Elizabeth Tessa, *o d* of Basil Dean, CBE and Lady Mercy Greville; two *s* two *d. Educ:* Epworth College, Rhyl; Jesus College, Oxford (MA). Served War of 1939-45, in RAF; Prisoner of War (Germany), 1941-45. Called to Bar, 1947, Middle Temple, Bencher, 1971, Member of Wales and Chester Circuit. MP (C) Conway Div. of Caernarvonshire, 1951-66; PPS to the Solicitor-General, 1954-59; Parly Secretary, Min. of Labour, 1959-61; Parly Under-Sec. of State, Foreign Office, 1961-63; Minister of State for Foreign Affairs, 1963-64; Opp. Front Bench Spokesman on Foreign Affairs and Law, 1964-66; Sec. of State for Wales, 1970-74. Chm., Cons. Party

Organisation, 1970-72. Pres., Nat. Union of Conservative and Unionist Assocs, 1974 and 1975. Dep. Chairman: Cheshire QS, 1966-70; Denbighshire QS, 1968-70. Member, Historic Buildings Council for Wales, 1965-67. *Address:* 145 Kennington Road, SE11. *T:* 01-735 6047; Millicent Cottage, Elstead, Surrey. *Clubs:* Carlton; Cardiff and County (Cardiff).

THOMAS, Ralph Philip, MC 1942; Film Director; *b* Hull, Yorks, 10 Aug.; *m* 1944, Joy Spanjer; one *s* one *d. Educ:* Tellisford School, Clifton. Entered film industry, 1932, and worked in all production depts, particularly editing, until 1939. Served War of 1939-45, as Regimental Officer 9th Lancers until 1944; thereafter Instructor Royal Military College. Returned to Film Industry, in Rank Organisation Trailer Dept, 1946; Joined Gainsborough Pictures, 1948, and directed Once Upon a Dream, Traveller's Joy. Films directed at Pinewood Studios: The Clouded Yellow, Appointment with Venus, The Venetian Bird, A Day to Remember, Doctor in the House, Mad About Men, Above Us The Waves, Doctor at Sea, The Iron Petticoat, Checkpoint, Doctor at Large, Campbell's Kingdom, A Tale of Two Cities, The Wind Cannot Read, The 39 Steps, Upstairs and Downstairs, Conspiracy of Hearts, Doctor in Love, No My Darling Daughter, No Love for Johnnie, The Wild and the Willing, Doctor in Distress, Hot enough for June, The High Bright Sun, Doctor in Clover, Deadlier than the Male, Nobody Runs Forever, Some Girls Do, Doctor in Trouble, Quest, Percy, It's a 2 foot 6 inch Above the Ground World, Percy's Progress. *Address:* Boundary House, Beaconsfield, Bucks. *Clubs:* Cavalry and Guards, Royal Automobile.

THOMAS, Lt-Col Reginald Silvers W.; *see* Williams-Thomas.

THOMAS, Robert Antony C.; *see* Clinton-Thomas.

THOMAS, Sir Robert (Evan), Kt 1967; DL, JP; Leader, Greater Manchester Metropolitan County Council, 1973-77; Deputy Chairman, Manchester Ship Canal, 1971-74; *b* 8 Oct. 1901; *s* of Jesse and Anne Thomas; *m* 1924, Edna Isherwood; one *s* one *d. Educ:* St Peter's, Leigh, Lancs. Miner, 1914; served Army, 1919-21; Bus Driver, 1924-37; Trade Union Official, 1937-66; Member, Manchester City Council, 1944-74; Lord Mayor of Manchester, 1962-63. Chairman: Assoc. of Municipal Corps, 1973-74; Assoc. of Metropolitan Authorities, 1974-77; British Sector, Internat. Union of Local Authorities, 1974-. JP Manchester, 1948; DL: County Palatine of Lancaster, 1967-73; County Palatine of Greater Manchester, 1974. Hon. MA Manchester, 1974. *Recreations:* dancing, gardening, photography. *Address:* 29 Milwain Road, Manchester M19 2PX. *T:* 061-224 5778.

THOMAS, (Robert) Neville, QC 1975; barrister-at-law; a Recorder of the Crown Court, since 1975; *b* 31 March 1936; *s* of Robert Derfel Thomas and Enid Anne Thomas; *m* 1970, Jennifer Anne Brownrigg; one *s* one *d. Educ:* Ruthin Sch.; University Coll., Oxford (MA, BCL). Called to Bar, Inner Temple, 1962. *Recreations:* fishing, walking, reading. *Address:* Eithinog Hall, Cyfronydd, Welshpool, Powys SY21 9ED.

THOMAS, Roger Lloyd; Assistant Secretary, Department of the Environment, since 1974; *b* 7 Feb. 1919; *er s* of Trevor John Thomas and Eleanor Maud (*née* Jones), Abercarn, Mon; *m* 1945, Stella Mary, *d* of Reginald Ernest Willmett, Newport, Mon; three *s* one *d. Educ:* Barry County Sch.; Magdalen Coll., Oxford (Doncaster Schol.; Heath Harrison Trav. Schol.). BA 2nd Mod. Langs, 1939; MA 1946. Served 1939-46, RA and Gen. Staff (Major GSO2) in India, Middle East, N Africa, Italy and Germany. Civil Servant, 1948-70: Min. of Fuel and Power, Home Office, Treasury, Welsh Office and Min. of Housing and Local Govt; Private Sec. to Perm. Under-Sec. of State, Home Office, 1950 and to successive Parly Under-Secs of State, 1951-53; Sec., Interdeptl Cttee on powers of Subpoena, 1960; Asst Sec., 1963; Sec., Aberfan Inquiry Tribunal, 1966-67; Chm., Working Party on Building by Direct Labour Organisations, 1968-69. Gen. Manager, The Housing Corporation, 1970-73. *Publications:* sundry reports. *Recreation:* growing flowers. *Address:* 5 Park Avenue, Caterham, Surrey. *T:* Caterham 42080. *Club:* Union (Oxford).

THOMAS, Ronald Richard; MP (Lab) Bristol North-West, since Oct. 1974; *b* March 1929. *Educ:* Ruskin Coll. and Balliol Coll., Oxford (MA). Sen. Lectr, Econ. and Indust. Studies, Univ. of Bristol. Contested (Lab) Bristol North-West, Feb. 1974. Member: Bristol DC; ASTMS. *Address:* House of Commons, SW1A 0AA; 64 Morris Road, Lockleaze, Bristol BS7 9TA.

THOMAS, Rev. Ronald Stuart; poet; Vicar of St Hywyn, Aberdaron, with St Mary, Bodferin, since 1967; Rector of Rhiw with Llanfaelrhys, since 1973; *b* 1915; *m* Mildred E. Eldridge;

one *s*. *Educ:* University of Wales (BA); St Michael's College, Llandaff. Ordained deacon, 1936; priest, 1937. Curate of Chirk, 1936-40; Curate of Hanmer, in charge of Talarn Green, 1940-42; Rector of Manafon, 1942-54; Vicar of Eglwysfach, 1954-67. First record, reading his own poems, 1977. Queen's Gold Medal for Poetry, 1964. *Publications:* poems: Stones of the Field (privately printed), 1947; Song at the Year's Turning, 1955 (Heinemann Award of the Royal Society of Literature, 1956); Poetry for Supper, 1958; Tares, 1961; Bread of Truth, 1963; Pieta, 1966; Not That He Brought Flowers, 1968; H'm, 1972; Selected Poems 1946-1968, 1974; Laboratories of the Spirit, 1976; edited: A Book of Country Verse, 1961; George Herbert, A Choice of Verse, 1967; A Choice of Wordsworth's Verse, 1971. *Address:* Aberdaron Vicarage, Pwllheli, Gwynedd.

THOMAS, Ryland Lowell Degwel, CB 1974; Deputy Director of Public Prosecutions, 1971-74; *b* 24 April 1914; *er s* of Rev. William Degwel Thomas and Sarah Maud Thomas (*née* Richards), Neath, Glam; *m* 1942, Mair Eluned, *d* of Rev. J. L. Williams, Swansea, Glam; one *s* one *d*. *Educ:* University Coll. of Wales, Aberystwyth (LLB); Trinity Hall, Cambridge (MA). Barrister-at-Law, Inner Temple. Ministry of Supply, 1941; Dept of Dir of Public Prosecutions, 1942; Asst Dir, 1965. *Recreations:* walking, motoring, travel. *Address:* 58 Strathearn Avenue, Whitton, Twickenham, Mddx. *Club:* London Welsh RFC (Vice-Pres.).

THOMAS, Swinton Barclay, QC 1975; a Recorder of the Crown Court, since 1975; *b* 12 Jan. 1931; *s* of Brig. William Bain Thomas, CBE, DSO, and Mary Georgina Thomas; *m* 1967, Angela, Lady Cope; one *s* one *d*. *Educ:* Ampleforth Coll.; Lincoln Coll., Oxford (Scholar) (MA). Called to Bar, Inner Temple, 1955. *Recreations:* reading, travel. *Address:* 36 Sheffield Terrace, W8. *T:* 01-727 2923. *Club:* Garrick.

THOMAS, Terry; *see* Terry-Thomas.

THOMAS, Terry, MA, LLB Cantab, BSc London and Wales, PhD London; Headmaster, Leeds Grammar School, 1923-53; *b* 19 Oct. 1888; *e s* of late David Terry Thomas, Cardiff; *m* 1915, Mair, *e d* of late Major Henry Davies, OBE, CC, Cardiff; two *d*. *Educ:* Howard Gardens; University College, Cardiff (Isaac Roberts' Science Scholar); St John's Coll., Cambridge (Foundation Scholar). First Class Honours in Physics, BSc Wales; Second Class Honours in Physics BSc, London; 1st Cl. Natural Sci. Tripos, Part II, Physics; Second Class Mathematical Tripos, Part I; Third Class Law Tripos, Part II. Chief Science Master, Inverurie Academy, 1909-11; Head of Military and Engineering Side, Haileybury Coll., 1914-22; former Mem. of Headmasters' Conference Committee; Captain OTC; Chm., Leeds XIII Discussion Club, 1929-; Pres. of the Incorporated Association of Headmasters, 1936, Hon. Treas., 1938-46; former Member Secondary School Examination Council; Member of Norwood Committee; formerly Mem. Court, Univ. of Leeds; JP, Leeds, 1937-; Chm. Visiting Magistrates, Leeds Prison, 1948-63; Chm., Leeds Medical and Legal Gp on Psychiatry and the Law, 1948-53; Dep. Chairman Leeds Group B Hospital Management Committee, 1948-54; Chm. Leeds Bench, 1950-63; Pres. W Riding Branch Magistrates' Association, 1956, 1957, and 1958; President Leeds Lit. and Philosophical Society, 1952 and 1953. Mem. Nat. Assistance Bd Tribunal; Education Adviser, RAF Benevolent Fund. Hon. LLD Leeds, 1948. *Publications:* Mathematical and Science Papers for Army Candidates; Revision Arithmetic and Mensuration; Notes on Dynamics; Outlines of the Calculus; The Leeds Intelligence Test; The Science of Marking. *Recreations:* fly-fishing, golf, painting. *Address:* Fairmount, 25 Shire Oak Road, Leeds LS6 2DD. *T:* Leeds 751895.

THOMAS, Rt. Hon. (Thomas) George, PC 1968; MP Cardiff West; Speaker of the House of Commons, since 1976. *Educ:* University Coll., Southampton. PPS, Min. of Civil Aviation, 1951. Chm., Welsh Parly Labour Party, 1950-51. Member, Chairman's Panel, House of Commons, 1951-64; Pres., National Brotherhood Movement, 1955. Schoolmaster. Vice-Pres. the Methodist Conference, 1960-61. MP (Lab): Cardiff Central, 1945-50; Cardiff W, 1950-76 (when elected Speaker); First Chm. of the Welsh Parliamentary Grand Committee; Jt Parly Under-Sec. of State, Home Office, 1964-66; Minister of State: Welsh Office, 1966-67; Commonwealth Office, 1967-68; Secretary of State for Wales, 1968-70; Dep. Speaker and Chm. of Ways and Means, House of Commons, 1974-76. Hon. Fellow, UC Cardiff, 1972; Hon. LLD: Asbury Coll., Kentucky, 1976; Univ. of Southampton, 1977; Univ. of Wales, 1977. Freeman: Borough of Rhondda, 1970; City of Cardiff, 1975. Dato Setia Negara, Brunei, 1971. *Publication:* The Christian Heritage in Politics. *Address:* Tilbury, 173 King George V Drive East, Cardiff. *T:* Cardiff 757460.

THOMAS, Trevor, BA; artist, author; retired; *b* 8 June 1907; 2nd *s* of William Thomas and Mary Richards; *m* 1947; two *s*. *Educ:* Sir Alfred Jones Scholar, University Coll. of Wales, Aberystwyth. Demonstrator, Dept of Geography and Anthropology, University Coll. of Wales, Aberystwyth, 1929-30; Secretary and Lecturer-Assistant, Department of Geography, Victoria University, Manchester, 1930-31; Cartographer to Geographical Association, Manchester, 1930-31; Keeper, Departments of Ethnology and Shipping, Liverpool Public Museums, 1931-40; Rockefeller Foundation Museums Fellow, USA, 1938-39; Director, Museum and Art Gallery, Leicester, 1940-46; Surveyor, Regional Guide to Works of Art, Arts Council of Great Britain, 1946-48; Designer of Exhibitions for the British Institute of Adult Education, 1946-48; Director, Crafts Centre of Great Britain, 1947-48; Programme Specialist for Education through the Arts, UNESCO, Paris, 1949-56; Visiting Prof. of Art Education, Teachers' Coll., Columbia Univ., NY, USA, 1956; Prof. of Art, State Univ. of New York, College for Teachers, Buffalo, 1957-58; Prof. of Art Hist., University of Buffalo, and Art Critic, Buffalo Evening News, 1959-60; Art Editor, Gordon Fraser Gall. Ltd, 1960-72. Mem. Exec. Cttee, Campaign for Homosexual Equality, 1976-78. *Publications:* Penny Plain Twopence Coloured: the Aesthetics of Museum Display (Museums Jl, April 1939); Education and Art: a Symposium (jt Editor with Edwin Ziegfeld), Unesco, 1953; Creating with Paper: basic forms and variations (Foreword and associate writer with Pauline Johnson), 1958; contribs to: Museums Journal, Dec. 1933, April 1935, April 1939, Oct. 1941; Parnassus, Jan. and April 1940; Unesco Eduen Abstracts, Feb. 1953. *Recreations:* art, music, theatre, lecturing. Research: Art. *Address:* 36 Pembroke Street, Bedford. *T:* 53879.

THOMAS, Trevor Cawdor, MA, LLB Cantab, LLB Wales; Vice-Chancellor, University of Liverpool, 1970-76; Emeritus Professor, 1976; *b* 19 April 1914; *o s* of James Elwyn Thomas and Charlotte Thomas (*née* Ivatt); *m* 1943, Mrs Marjory Molony, widow of John Bernard Molony, and *y d* of Samuel Harry Guteridge Higgs and Fanny Higgs, Reading. *Educ:* University College of Wales, Aberystwyth; Trinity Hall, Cambridge. LLB Wales 1936 (first class (at Aberystwyth) and Sir Samuel Evans prizeman); Foundn Schol., Trinity Hall, 1937; Trinity Hall Law Studentship, 1938; Joseph Hodges Choate Memorial Fellowship, 1938; LLB Cantab 1938 (first class, Pt II Law Tripos, 1937; first class with dist. in LLB). Entrance Schol., Gray's Inn, 1936; Bar Final Examinations, 1940 (first class with certif. of honour); called to Bar, Gray's Inn, 1941, Hon. Bencher, 1975. Lecturer in Law, Univ. of Leeds, 1939-41. RAF, Intell. Br., 1941-45. Fellow of Trinity Hall, Cambridge, 1945-60, Hon. Fellow, 1970; Univ. Lectr in Law, Univ. of Cambridge, 1945-60; Fellow and Sen. Bursar, St John's Coll., Cambridge, 1960-69; Hon. Fellow, Darwin Coll., Cambridge, 1972. Mem. Statutory Commn for Royal Univ. of Malta, 1960-69. JP, City of Cambridge, 1966-69. Hon. LLD Liverpool, 1972. *Publications:* co-editor, Jenks' Digest of English Civil Law, 4th edn 1947; articles in Cambridge Law Jl. *Recreations:* gardening, travel, fishing. *Address:* Dolphins, Roncombe Lane, Sidbury, near Sidmouth, Devon EX10 0QL. *Club:* Farmers'.

THOMAS, Maj.-Gen. Vivian Davenport, CB 1949; CBE 1946 (OBE 1942); Royal Marines, retired; *b* 31 Oct. 1897; *s* of Arnold Frederick Davenport Thomas, London; *m* 1929, Theresa, *d* of Colonel E. J. Previte, VD, TD, Burstow, Surrey; one *s*. *Educ:* St Paul's. Served European War, 1914-18: with Royal Marines, 1914-19; HMS Princess Royal, 1st Battle Cruiser Squadron, 1915-18. War of 1939-45, North Africa; Lieutenant-Colonel, 1942; acting Colonel Commandant (temp. Brig.) 1943; Comdr 1st RM AA Bde, India, 1943; COS to Chief of Combined Ops, 1944-46; Maj.-Gen. 1946; COS to Comdt Gen., RM, 1946-50; Chief of Amphibious Warfare, 1950-54; retired, 1954. Cdre, 1951-55, Life Vice-Cdre, 1974, Royal Naval Sailing Assoc. Hon. Col Comdt, Plymouth Group Royal Marines, 1957-61. Master, Armourers' and Brasiers' Company, 1962-63. *Address:* Glebe House, Framfield, Uckfield, East Sussex. *Clubs:* Caledonian; Royal Yacht Squadron.

THOMAS, Maj.-Gen. Walter Babington, CB 1971; DSO 1943; MC and Bar, 1942; Commander, HQ Far East Land Forces, Nov. 1970-Nov. 1971 (Chief of Staff, April-Oct. 1970); retired Jan. 1972; *b* Nelson, NZ, 29 June 1919; *s* of Walter Harington Thomas, Farmer; *m* 1947, Iredale Edith Lauchlan (*née* Trent); three *d*. *Educ:* Motueka Dist High Sch., Nelson, NZ. Clerk, Bank of New Zealand, 1936-39. Served War of 1939-45 (despatches, MC and Bar, DSO): 2nd NZEF, 1940-46, in Greece, Crete, Western Desert, Tunis and Italy; Comd 23 (NZ) Bn, 1944-45; Comd 22 (NZ) Bn, in Japan, 1946; transf. to Brit. Army, Royal Hampshire Regt, 1947; Bde Major, 39 Inf. Bde Gp, 1953-55 (despatches); GSO2, UK JSLS, Aust., 1958-60; AA&QMG, HQ 1 Div. BAOR, 1962-64; Comd 12 Inf. Bde Gp,

1964-66; IDC, 1967; GOC 5th Div., 1968-70. Silver Star, Medal, 1945 (USA). *Publications:* Dare to be Free, 1951; Touch of Pitch, 1956. *Recreation:* riding. *Address:* PO Box 2161, Darwin, NT 5794, Australia.

THOMAS, William Herbert Evans, CBE 1941; retired; *b* 28 Dec. 1886; *s* of late John Owen Thomas and Mary Elizabeth Evans, Llantwit Major, Glamorgan; *m* ; two *s* one *d. Educ:* Privately; London University. Joined Chartered Bank of India, Australia and China, 1907; Manager at Peking, Tientsin and Hong Kong Branches; Inspector of Branches, 1939; British Member Stabilization Board of China, 1943. Financial Counsellor, HBM Embassy, Chungking, 1944, 1945-46. *Publication:* Vanished China. *Address:* c/o Chartered Bank, 38 Bishopsgate, EC2.

THOMAS, Sir William James Cooper, 2nd Bt, *cr* 1919; TD; JP; DL; Captain RA; *b* 7 May 1919; *er s* of Sir William James Thomas, 1st Bt, and Maud Mary Cooper, Bexhill-on-Sea; *S* father 1945; *m* 1947, Freida Dunbar, *yr d* of late F. A. Whyte; two *s* one *d. Educ:* Harrow; Downing Coll., Cambridge. Barrister, Inner Temple, 1948. Member TA, 1938. Served War of 1939-45. Monmouthshire: JP 1958; DL 1973; High Sheriff, 1973. *Heir: s* William Michael Thomas, *b* 5 Dec. 1948. *Address:* Rockfield Park, Monmouth, Gwent. *T:* Monmouth 2757. *Club:* Army and Navy.

THOMAS, Sir (William) Michael (Marsh), 3rd Bt *cr* 1918; Managing Director of Goss Nurseries Ltd, 1955; *b* 4 Dec. 1930; *s* of Sir William Eustace Rhyddlad Thomas, 2nd Bt, and Enid Helena Marsh; *S* father 1957; *m* 1953, Geraldine Mary, *d* of Robert Drysdale, Anglesey; three *d. Educ:* Oundle School, Northants. *Heir: u* Robert Freeman Thomas [*b* 8 Jan. 1911; *m* 1947, Marcia, *d* of Walter Lucas]. *Address:* Belan, Rhosneigr, Gwynedd.

THOMAS, William R.; *see* Rees-Thomas.

THOMAS, Wyndham; General Manager, Peterborough New Town Development Corporation, since 1968; *b* 1 Feb. 1924; *s* of Robert John Thomas and Hannah Mary; *m* 1947, Elizabeth Terry Hopkin; one *s* three *d. Educ:* Maesteg Grammar School. Served Army (Lieut, Royal Welch Fusiliers), 1943-47. Schoolmaster, 1950-53; Director, Town and Country Planning Association, 1955-67; Member, Land Commission, 1967-68; Member, Commission for the New Towns, 1964-68. Mayor of Hemel Hempstead, 1958-59. *Publications:* many articles on town planning, housing, etc, in learned jls. *Recreations:* collecting old furniture, work, golf. *Address:* 20 High Street, Castor, Peterborough. *T:* Castor 409.

THOMAS, Wynford V.; *see* Vaughan-Thomas.

THOMASON, Prof. George Frederick; Montague Burton Professor of Industrial Relations, University College, Cardiff, since 1969; *b* 27 Nov. 1927; *s* of George Frederick Thomason and Eva Elizabeth (*née* Walker); *m* 1953, Jean Elizabeth Horsley; one *s* one *d. Educ:* Kelsick Grammar Sch.; Univ. of Sheffield (BA); Univ. of Toronto (MA); PhD (Wales). CIPM,MBIM. University College, Cardiff: Research Asst, 1953; Asst Lectr, 1954; Research Associate, 1956; Lectr, 1959; Asst Man. Dir, Flex Fasteners Ltd, Rhondda, 1960; University College, Cardiff: Lectr, 1962; Sen. Lectr, 1963; Reader, 1969; Dean, Faculty of Economics, 1971-73; Dep. Principal (Humanities), 1974-77. *Publications:* Welsh Society in Transition, 1963; Personnel Manager's Guide to Job Evaluation, 1968; Professional Approach to Community Work, 1969; The Management of Research and Development, 1970; Improving the Quality of Organization, 1973; Textbook of Personnel Management, 1975, 2nd edn 1976. *Recreation:* gardening. *Address:* The Red House, 12 Mill Road, Llanishen, Cardiff CF4 5XB. *T:* Cardiff 754236. *Clubs:* Athenæum, Royal Commonwealth Society; Cardiff and County (Cardiff).

THOMPSON, Alan; Deputy Secretary, Department of Education and Science, since 1975; *b* 16 July 1920; *s* of Herbert and Esther Thompson; *m* 1944, Joyce Nora Banks; two *s* one *d . Educ:* Carlisle Grammar Sch.; Queen's Coll., Oxford. Joined Min. of Education, 1946; Private Sec. to Minister of Education, 1954-56; Asst Sec., Further Education Br., 1956-64; Under Sec., UGC, 1964-71; Under Sec., Science Br., DES, 1971-75. *Address:* 1 Drax Avenue, Wimbledon, SW20. *T:* 01-946 1837.

THOMPSON, Prof. Alan Eric; Professor of the Economics of Government, Heriot-Watt University, since 1972; Scottish Governor, BBC, since 1976; *b* 16 Sept. 1924; *o c* of late Eric Joseph Thompson and of Florence Thompson; *m* 1960, Mary Heather Long; three *s* one *d. Educ:* University of Edinburgh. MA 1949, MA (Hons Class I, Economic Science), 1951, PhD

1953, Carnegie Research Scholar, 1951-52; Asst in Political Economy, 1952-53, Lectr in Economics (formerly Political Economy), 1953-59, and 1964-71, Univ. of Edinburgh. Parly Adviser to Scottish Television, 1966-67. Visiting Professor, Graduate School of Business, Stanford Univ., USA, 1966, 1968. MP (Lab) Dunfermline, 1959-64. Chm., Adv. Bd on Economics Educn (Esmée Fairbairn Research Project), 1970-76; Member: Scottish Cttee, Public Schools Commn, 1969-70; Cttee enquiring into conditions of service life for young servicemen, 1969; Royal Fine Art Commn for Scotland, 1975-; Chm., Northern Offshore (Maritime) Resources Study, 1974-. Hon. Vice-Pres., Assoc. of Nazi War Camp Survivors, 1960-; Pres., Edinburgh Amenity and Transport Assoc., 1970-75. Has broadcast and appeared on TV (economic and political talks and discussions) in Britain and USA. FRSA 1972. *Publications:* contribs to learned journals. *Recreation:* writing children's stories and plays. *Address:* 11 Upper Gray Street, Edinburgh EH9 1SN. *T:* 031-667 2140. *Clubs:* New, Edinburgh University Staff (Edinburgh); Loch Earn Sailing.

THOMPSON, Aubrey Denzil Forsyth, CMG 1944; CVO 1947; CBE 1941; *b* 3 Oct. 1897; *s* of Ernest Alfred Thompson; *m* 1924, Kathleen Esther Murray; one *s* one *d. Educ:* Weenen County College, Natal; New College, Oxford. Served European War, France, RFA, Lieut 1917-19; Oxford, 1919-20 (BA); Administrative Officer, Uganda, 1921-37; Asst Resident Commissioner and Govt Secretary, Bechuanaland Protectorate, 1937-42; Resident Commissioner, 1942-46; Resident Commissioner, Basutoland, 1946-51; retired, 1951. *Recreation:* gardening. *Address:* 269 West Street, Pietermaritzburg, Natal, S Africa.

THOMPSON, Aubrey Gordon D.; *see* Denton-Thompson.

THOMPSON, Brenda, (Mrs Gordon Thompson); writer on education; Head Teacher, Northwold I (Primary) School, since 1971; *b* 27 Jan. 1935; *d* of Thomas Barnes Houghton and Marjorie Houghton; *m* 1956, Gordon Thompson; one *s. Educ:* Leeds Univ. BSc Hons in Biochemistry. Food chemist with J. Lyons & Co, 1957; Hosp. Biochemist, Chelsea Women's Hosp., 1958-60. Entered primary school teaching, 1964. Mem., Press Council, 1973-76. Indep. Councillor for London Borough of Islington, 1968-71. *Publications:* Learning to Read, 1970; Learning to Teach, 1973; The Pre-School Book, 1976; Editor various children's books; Contributor to: Teachers' World; Child Education. *Address:* 101 Barnsbury Street, Islington, N1. *T:* 01-607 5307.

THOMPSON, Charles Allister; HM Diplomatic Service, retired; *b* 21 July 1922; *yr s* of late Herbert Ivie and Margaret (*née* Browne-Webber) Thompson, Managua, Nicaragua; *m* 1950, Jean Margaret, *er d* of late Alexander Bruce Dickson; two *s* two *d. Educ:* Haileybury; Hertford Coll., Oxford (MA, BLitt). War Service, 1942-46, 1st King's Dragoon Guards. Joined Foreign Service (now Diplomatic Service), 1947, and served in FO until 1949; 3rd Sec., Prague, 1949-50; 2nd Sec. (Commercial), Mexico City, 1950-53; FO 1953-56; 1st Sec., Karachi, 1956-59; Head of Chancery, Luxembourg, 1959-62; FO, 1962-65; Counsellor, 1965; Dep. Consul-Gen., New York, 1965-67; Dep. High Comr, Port of Spain, 1967-70; HM Consul-Gen., Philadelphia, 1970-74; Vis. Fellow, Centre for Internat. Studies, LSE, 1974-75; Head of Training Dept, FCO, and Dir, Diplomatic Service Language Centre, 1975-76. *Recreations:* sailing, fishing, photography. *Address:* c/o Williams and Glyn's Bank Ltd, Holts Branch, Whitehall, SW1.

THOMPSON, Charles Norman, FInstPet; CChem; FRIC; Director (Research Administration), Shell Research Ltd, London, since 1961; *b* 23 Oct. 1922; *s* of Robert Norman Thompson and Evelyn Tivendale Thompson (*née* Wood); *m* 1946, Pamela Margaret Wicks; one *d. Educ:* Birkenhead Institute; Liverpool Univ. (BSc). Research Chemist, Thornton Research Centre (Shell Refining & Marketing Co. Ltd), 1943; Lectr, Petroleum Chemistry and Technology, Liverpool Coll. of Technology, 1947-51; Personnel Supt and Dep. Associate Manager, Thornton Research Centre, Shell Research Ltd, 1959-61. Mem. Council, Inst. of Petroleum, 1976- (Chm., Res. Adv. Cttee, 1973-). Pres., RIC, 1976-78. *Publications:* Reviews of Petroleum Technology, vol. 13: insulating and hydraulic oils, 1953; numerous papers in Jl Inst. Petroleum, Chem. and Ind., Chem. in Brit., on hydrocarbon dielectrics, insulating oils, diffusion as rate-limiting factor in oxidation, antioxidants in the oil industry, mechanism of copper catalysis in insulating oil oxidation, scientific manpower, etc. *Recreation:* golf. *Address:* Delamere, Horsell Park, Woking, Surrey GU21 4LW. *T:* Woking 4939.

THOMPSON, Charles Paxton, CMG 1961; OBE 1956; Bursar, University of Birmingham, 1961-73; *b* 31 May 1911; *s* of W. P. Thompson; *m* 1938, Gweneth Barbara Toby; one *s* one *d*. *Educ:* Merchant Taylors' School, London; University College, London; Trinity Hall, Cambridge. Cadet, Colonial Administrative Service (Nigeria), 1933; Economic Secretary to Prime Minister of Federation of Nigeria, 1958; Permanent Secretary, Ministry of Economic Development, Lagos, 1960. *Recreations:* reading omnivorously; gardening. *Address:* Cock and Dog Cottage, Stoke Prior, Bromsgrove, Worcs. *T:* Bromsgrove 31751. *Club:* Oriental.

THOMPSON, Colin Edward; Director, National Galleries of Scotland, since 1977; *b* 2 Nov. 1919; *s* of late Edward Vincent Thompson, CB, and Jessie Forbes Cameron; *m* 1950, Jean Agnes Jardine O'Connell; one *s* one *d*. *Educ:* Sedbergh Sch.; King's College, Cambridge; Chelsea Polytechnic Sch. of Art. MA (Cantab). FS Wing CMP, 1940-41; Foreign Office, 1941-45. Lectr, Bath Acad. of Art, Corsham, 1948-54; Asst Keeper, 1954, Keeper, 1967, National Gall. of Scotland. Sen. Adviser, Res. Centre in Art Educn, Bath Acad. of Art, 1962-65; Mem., Scottish Arts Council, 1976-. *Publications:* (with Lorne Campbell) Hugo van der Goes and the Trinity Panels in Edinburgh, 1974; guide books, catalogues and a history of the National Gallery of Scotland; articles in Burlington Magazine, Museums Jl, etc. *Address:* Edenkerry, Lasswade, Midlothian. *T:* 031-663 7927. *Club:* New (Edinburgh).

THOMPSON, Daniel Varney; author and columnist; Registered Professional Engineer (Massachusetts); *b* 29 Dec. 1902; *s* of Daniel Varney and Grace Randall Thompson; *m* 1927, Cécile de Luze Simonds (*d* 1972); one *d* (one *s* decd). *Educ:* Harvard. AB *cum laude* Harvard 1922; AM 1926; Instr and tutor, Harvard Univ., 1923-24, 1925-26 (Sheldon Fellow, 1922-23, 1924-25); Technical Adviser, Fogg Art Museum China Expedition 1924-25; Instructor and Assistant Professor of the History of Art in Yale University, 1926-33 (Sterling Fellow, 1931-32); Research Fellow of American Council of Learned Societies, 1933-34; Research and Technical Adviser Courtauld Institute of Art, 1934-36; Head of its Scientific Department, 1936-38; Professor of the History of the Technology of Art in University of London, 1938-46. Man. Dir, Daniel Varney Ltd, 1943-47. Technical Consultant, Head of Research and Development, E-Z Mills, Inc., 1948-50. Sen. Staff Consulting Engr, AVCO Corp. Res. and Advanced Develt, Missile Systems Div., Advanced Electronics Gp, 1956-68, retd. Member Royal Institution (Board of Visitors, 1946-48); Technical Consultant, Sylvania Electric Products, Electronics Division, 1951; Comstock & Wescott, Inc., 1952 and 1955-67; Chief Engineer, Jarrell-Ash Co., 1953-55; Vice-Pres. Swett & Sibley Co. 1955-57. Food and Garden Editor, North Shore Magazine, 1966-. Hon. Mem. Soc. of Painters in Tempera (London). *Publications:* Il Libro dell' Arte 1932; The Craftsman's Handbook, 1933 (rev. 1936); De Arte Illuminandi: The Technique of Manuscript Illumination, 1933; The Practice of Tempera Painting, 1936 (1962); The Materials of Medieval Painting, 1936 (repr. as The Materials and Techniques of Medieval Painting, 1957); (introd) C. E. Francatelli's The Modern Cook, 1846, 1973; contrib. various learned and tech. jls, magazines and newspapers. *Address:* Box 1569, Manchester, Mass 01944, USA. *Club:* Athenæum.

THOMPSON, David Richard, CB 1974; Master of the Crown Office and Queen's Coroner and Attorney, Registrar of Criminal Appeals and of the Courts Martial Appeal Court since 1965; *b* 11 Feb. 1916; *s* of William George Thompson; *m* 1952, Sally Jennifer Rowntree Thompson (*née* Stockton); two *s* four *d*. *Educ:* Alleyn's Sch., Dulwich; Jesus Coll., Oxford. BA Physics 1938. Royal Corps of Signals, 1939-46 (despatches). Called to Bar, Lincoln's Inn, 1946; Office of Director of Public Prosecutions, 1948-54; Dep. Asst Registrar, then Asst Registrar, Court of Criminal Appeal, 1954-65. *Publication:* (with H. W. Wollaston) Court of Appeal Criminal Division, 1969. *Recreation:* rough gardening. *Address:* 54 Highbury Grove, N5. *T:* 01-226 6514.

THOMPSON, Dennis Cameron; Consultant to UN; Director, Restrictive Practices and Dominant Positions, Commission of the European Communities, 1973-76; *b* 25 Oct. 1914; *s* of late Edward Vincent Thompson, CB, and late Jessie Forbes; *m* 1959, Maria von Skramlik; one *d*. *Educ:* Oundle; King's Coll., Cambridge. Nat. Sci. Tripos Pt I, Law Pt II; MA 1949. RAF, 1940-45: Sqdn-Ldr, personnel staff, Desert Air Force, and Germany. Called to Bar, Inner Temple, 1939; practised London and Midland Circuit, 1946-63; Asst Dir (European Law), British Inst. of Internat. and Comparative Law, 1963-66; Legal Adviser, Secretariat of EFTA, Geneva, 1967-73; participated in negotiations for European Patent Convention, 1969-73. Trustee, Federal Trust, 1962. *Publications:* (ed) Kennedy, CIF

Contracts, 3rd edn 1959; (with Alan Campbell) Common Market Law, 1962; The Proposal for a European Company, 1969; articles in Internat. and Compar. Law Quarterly; (ed jtly) Common Market Law Review, 1963-67; founder and Editor, Jl of World Trade Law, 1967. *Recreations:* walking, ski-ing, sailing. *Address:* 8 rue des Belles Filles. 1299 Crans, Switzerland. *T:* (22) 76 16 87. *Club:* United Oxford & Cambridge University.

THOMPSON, Donald Henry, MA Oxon; JP; Headmaster, Chigwell School, Essex, 1947-71; *b* 29 Aug. 1911; *s* of H. R. Thompson, solicitor, Swansea; *m* 1942, Helen Mary Wray; four *s*. *Educ:* Shrewsbury School; Merton College, Oxford. Postmaster in Classics, Merton Coll., Oxford, 1930; 1st Class Hon. Mod., 1932; 1st Class Literae Humaniores, 1934; Asst Master Haileybury Coll., Hertford, 1934-46. Served War of 1939-45, RA, 1940-45. JP Essex, 1955. *Recreations:* cricket, bird-watching, walking. *Address:* The Haylands, Maldon Road, Mundon, near Maldon, Essex. *T:* Maldon 740254.

THOMPSON, Rev. Douglas Weddell; President of the Methodist Conference, 1966-67; *b* 4 July 1903; *s* of Nathan Ellis and Florence Thompson; *m* 1929, Gladys Wentworth (*d* 1972); one *d*; *m* 1973, Margret Forrest. *Educ:* Gateshead Grammar Sch.; Handsworth Coll., Birmingham. Missionary, Hunan, China, 1925-27; Chaplain, Bengal, India, 1927-28; Hunan, China, 1929-39. Served War, 1939-45 (despatches): Chaplain, HMF, W Africa, Western Desert; POW Chaplain, Italy, Germany. Methodist Home Missions, London and Portsmouth, 1945-58. Eastbourne Central Church, 1968; Lewes and villages, 1971. WEA Lectr on Eastern Affairs. Gen. Sec. and Chm. of Officers, Methodist Overseas Mission Dept, 1958-68. *Publications:* Wisdom of the Way, 1945; About to Marry, 1945; Into Red Starlight, 1950; Captives to Freedom, 1951; The Mystery of the White Stone, 1961; The World He Loves, 1963; Donald Soper: a biography, 1971; numerous articles in Ecumenical and Missionary jls. *Recreation:* mountain and fell-walking. *Address:* 3 Ashmore House, 12 High Street, East Hoathly, East Sussex BN8 6DP. *Club:* Royal Commonwealth Society.

THOMPSON, Prof. Edward Arthur, FBA 1964; Professor of Classics, University of Nottingham, since 1948 *b* 22 May 1914; *s* of late Robert J. Thompson and late Margaret Thompson, Rathmines, Dublin. *Educ:* Trinity Coll., Dublin. Lecturer in Classics: Dublin, 1939-41; Swansea, 1942-45; King's College, London, 1945-48. Vis. Bentley Prof. of History, Univ. of Michigan, 1969-71. *Publications:* The Historical Work of Ammianus Marcellinus, 1947; A History of Attila and The Huns, 1948; A Roman Reformer and Inventor, 1952; The Early Germans, 1965; The Visigoths in the Time of Ulfila, 1966; The Goths in Spain, 1969. *Address:* The University, Nottingham.

THOMPSON, Sir Edward (Hugh Dudley), Kt 1967; MBE 1945; TD; Director: Allied Breweries Ltd; P-E Consulting Group Ltd (Chm., 1971-73); *b* 12 May 1907; *s* of Neale Dudley Thompson and Mary Gwendoline Scutt; *m* 1st, 1931, Ruth Mencia, 3rd *d* of Charles Henry Wainwright, JP; two *s*; 2nd, 1947, Doreen Maud, *d* of George Tibbitt; one *s* one *d*. *Educ:* Uppingham; Lincoln Coll., Oxford. Served War of 1939-45 (despatches twice, MBE); 1st Derbyshire Yeomanry, 1939-43, in N Africa; General Staff, 1943-45, in Italy and Germany. Solicitor, 1931-36. Asst Man. Dir, Ind Coope & Allsopp Ltd, 1936-39, Managing Director, 1939; Chairman: Ind Coope Ltd, Burton on Trent, 1955-62; Allied Breweries Ltd (formerly Ind Coope Tetley Ansell Ltd), 1961-68. Director: Sun Insurance Ltd, 1946-59; Sun Alliance & London Insurance Ltd, 1959-77. Chm. Brewers' Soc., 1959-61; Founder Member of World Security Trust; Trustee, Civic Trust; Mem., Northumberland Foot and Mouth Cttee. Mem. Council, Nottingham Univ., 1969-. Mem. Council, RASE, 1972-. High Sheriff of Derbyshire, 1964. *Recreations:* farming, sailing, ski-ing. *Address:* Culland Hall, Brailsford, Derby. *T:* Brailsford 247. *Club:* Boodle's.

THOMPSON, Sir Edward (Walter), Kt 1957; JP; Chairman John Thompson Ltd, Wolverhampton, 1947-67, now Hon. President; Director, Barclays Bank, 1958-73; Local Director, Barclays Bank (Birmingham), 1952-73; *b* 11 June 1902; *s* of late Albert E. Thompson and late Mary Thompson; *m* 1930, Ann E., *d* of Rev. George L. Amphlett, Four Ashes Hall, Stourbridge, Worcs; one *s* three *d*. *Educ:* Oundle; Trinity Hall, Cambridge. MA (Engineering) Cambridge. Joined family firm of John Thompson's, 1924; Dir John Thompson Watertube Boilers, 1930; Joint Man. Dir John Thompson Ltd, 1936-62. Chm. Watertube Boilermakers Assoc., 1951-54; Pres. Brit. Engineers Assoc., 1957-59 (Vice-Pres. 1956). Mem. Midland Chapter Woodard Schools. Chairman: Birmingham Regional Hosp. Bd, 1957-61; Redditch Development Corp., 1964-74; Leader SE Asia Trade Delegation, 1961. JP Co. Salop, 1953; Dep. Chm.

Bridgnorth Bench, 1956-66; High Sheriff, Staffordshire, 1955-56. *Recreations:* shooting, fishing, gardening. *Address:* Gatacre Park, Bridgnorth, Salop. *T:* Bobbington 211. *Club:* Brooks's. *See also Viscount Bledisloe.*

THOMPSON, Estelle Merle O'Brien; see Oberon, Merle.

THOMPSON, Prof. Francis Michael Longstreth; Director, Institute of Historical Research, and Professor of History in the University of London, since 1977; *b* 13 Aug. 1925; *s* of late Francis Longstreth-Thompson, OBE; *m* 1951, Anne Challoner; two *s* one *d. Educ:* Bootham Sch., York; Queen's Coll., Oxford (Hastings Schol.; MA, DPhil). ARICS 1968. War service, with Indian Artillery, 1943-47; James Bryce Sen. Schol., Oxford, 1949-50; Harmsworth Sen. Schol., Merton Coll., Oxford, 1949-51; Lectr in History, UCL, 1951-63; Reader in Economic History, UCL, 1963-68; Prof. of Modern Hist., Univ. of London and Head of Dept of Hist., Bedford Coll., London, 1968-77. Joint Editor, Economic History Review, 1968-; Mem. Senate and Academic Council, Univ. of London, 1970-. *Publications:* English Landed Society in the Nineteenth Century, 1963; Chartered Surveyors: the growth of a profession, 1968; Victorian England: the horse-drawn society, 1970; Countrysides, in The Nineteenth Century, ed Asa Briggs, 1970; Hampstead: building a borough, 1650-1964, 1974; introd. to General Report on Gosford Estates in County Armagh 1821, by William Greig, 1976; numerous articles in Economic History Review, History, English Historical Review, etc. *Recreations:* gardening, walking, carpentry, tennis, pony-watching. *Address:* Holly Cottage, Sheepcote Lane, Wheathampstead, Herts. *T:* Wheathampstead 3129.

THOMPSON, Air Commodore Frederick William, CBE 1957; DSO 1944; DFC 1942; AFC 1944; Executive Director, Air Weapons, Hawker Siddeley Dynamics Co. Ltd, since 1972; *b* 9 July 1914; *s* of William Edward Thompson, Winster, Poulton-le-Fylde, Lancs; *m* 1941, Marian, *d* of Wm Bootyman, Hessle, E Yorks; two *d. Educ:* Baines's Grammar School; Liverpool University. BSc 2nd Cl. Hons Maths; Advanced Diploma in General Hygiene (Hons). Joined RAF, 1935, invalided 1936. S Rhodesian Education Dept, 1936-39. Served War of 1939-45 (despatches, DFC, AFC, DSO): S Rhodesian Air Force, 1940, Pilot Officer; seconded to RAFVR, 4 Gp Bomber Command, 1940; Flight Comdr 10 Sqdn Bombers, 1941; 1658 HCU, 1942; CO 44 Bomber Sqdn, 1944; Bomber Command Instructor's School, 1944; Station Commander, RAF Heany, 1945; HQ Mid Med., 1946-47; Min. of Defence, 1947-50; HQ CC, 1950-53; OC Aswdu, 1953; Group Capt., CO Luqa, 1954; Deputy Director Operational Requirements (1), Air Ministry, 1957-60. Air Cdre Imperial Defence Coll., 1960; Director of Guided Weapons (Trials), Ministry of Aviation, 1961. Retired from RAF at own request to join de Havilland Aircraft Co. Ltd as Representative of the Company on the West Coast of America; Engrg Manager, Hawker Siddeley Dynamics Co. Ltd, 1964. idc, jssc, psc, cfs. *Recreations:* tennis, swimming. *Address:* Westwick, Lye Green Road, Chesham, Bucks. *T:* Chesham 5413. *Club:* Royal Air Force.

THOMPSON, Rt. Rev. Geoffrey Hewlett; see Willesden, Bishop Suffragan of.

THOMPSON, Lt-Gen. Sir Geoffrey (Stuart), KBE 1960 (MBE 1941); CB 1954; DSO 1944; late Royal Artillery; *b* 6 Jan. 1905; 3rd *s* of late Brig.-Gen. W. A. M. Thompson, CB, CMG; *m* 1934, Agnes Mary Colville (*d* 1974), *e d* of late Captain H. D. Wakeman-Colville, RN retd; one *d. Educ:* Sherborne Sch.; RN Colls, Osborne and Dartmouth. Commissioned, 1925; served War of 1939-45 (North Africa and Italy); Commander 1st Field Regiment RA, Italy, 1944-45; Commander No. 2 Army Group, Royal Artillery, Egypt, 1950-52; Director Land/Air Warfare and Dir for NATO Standardisation, War Office, 1952-54; Senior Army Instructor, Imperial Defence College, 1955-57; Director of Staff Duties, War Office, 1957-59; Military Secretary to the Secretary of State for War, 1959-61. Col Comdt, RA, 1961-69. Asst Man. Dir, Arthur Guinness Son & Co., Dublin, 1961-70. Officer of Legion of Merit, USA, 1945; Commander of Order of Leopold, Belgium, 1950; Croix de Guerre, Belgium, 1950. *Recreations:* fishing, hunting. *Address:* Swainstown, Dunsany, Co. Meath. *T:* (046) 25312. *Club:* Army and Navy.

THOMPSON, George H.; MP (SNP) Galloway, since Oct. 1974; *b* Sept. 1928. *Educ:* Dalry Sch.; Kirkcudbright Acad.; Edinburgh Univ. Teacher, modern languages, Kirkcudbright Academy. Contested (SNP) Galloway, Feb. 1974. Former SNP Asst Nat. Sec.; SNP Spokesman: on health, Oct. 1974-; on forestry, 1975. *Address:* House of Commons, SW1A 0AA.

THOMPSON, Gerald Francis Michael Perronet; Chairman, Kleinwort Benson Ltd, 1971-75, retired (Director 1961, Vice-Chairman 1970); Member, Accepting Houses Committee, 1971-75; *b* 10 Oct. 1910; *s* of late Sir John Perronet Thompson, KCSI, KCIE, and Ada Lucia Tyrrell; *m* 1944, Margaret Mary Bodenham Smith; two *s* one *d. Educ:* Repton; King's Coll., Cambridge (Scholar, MA); London Sch. of Economics (post graduate). Kleinwort Sons & Co., 1933. Served War, RAFVR, 1939-46 (despatches): in France, UK, and Middle East, Wing Comdr. Director: Kleinwort Sons & Co., 1960; Kleinwort Benson Lonsdale Ltd, 1970-. *Recreations:* travel, skiing. *Address:* Whitewebs, Margaretting, Essex. *T:* Ingatestone 2002. *Clubs:* United Oxford & Cambridge University, City University. *See also Rear-Adm. J. Y. Thompson, L. P. Thompson-McCausland.*

THOMPSON, Gertrude C.; see Caton-Thompson.

THOMPSON, Godfrey; see Thompson, W. G.

THOMPSON, Mrs Gordon; see Thompson, B.

THOMPSON, Sir Harold (Warris), Kt 1968; CBE 1959; FRS 1946; MA, DSc (Oxon); PhilD (Berlin); Professor of Chemistry, Oxford University, 1964-75, now Emeritus; *b* 15 Feb. 1908; *m* 1938, Grace Penelope Stradling; one *s* one *d. Educ:* King Edward VII Sch., Sheffield; Trinity College, Oxford (Open Millard Scholar); Berlin University. 1st Class Hons Chemistry, Oxford, 1929; Junior Research Fellow, St John's College, Oxford; Official Fellow and Tutor, St John's College, 1930-64, Professorial Fellow, 1964-75, Hon. Fellow, 1975; University Reader in Infra red spectroscopy, 1954-64; Leverhulme Research Fellow (Pasadena), 1937; Tilden Lecturer, 1943; Gnehm Lecturer, Zürich, 1948; Reilly Lecturer, 1961; Cherwell Memorial Fellow, 1961. Chemical Research for Ministry of Supply and Ministry of Aircraft Production, 1939-45; Member, Chemical Research Board, DSIR, 1949-54 and Committees of Scientific Advisory Council and MRC, 1947-55; Scientific Adviser, Home Office Civil Defence, Southern Region, 1952-63; Member General Board, Oxford University, 1949-55; Hebdomadal Council, 1957-61; President: Internat. Council of Scientific Unions, 1963-66; Inst. Information Scientists, 1967-70; Aslib, 1973-74; Chm., Commn on Molecular Spectroscopy of Internat. Union of Pure and Applied Chem., 1955-61, and of IUPAC Publications Cttee, 1957-; Pres., IUPAC, 1973-75 (Mem. Bureau, 1963-71; Exec Cttee, 1967-71, Vice-Pres., 1971-73); Member: UK Unesco Commn, 1966-; Exec. Cttee, British Council, 1966-; Chm., GB/China Cttee, 1972-74; Chm., China Centre, 1974-; Mem. Council, Royal Soc., 1959-64, Vice-Pres., 1963-64, 1965-71, For. Sec., 1965-71; Vice-Pres., Chem. Soc., 1970-73. Hon. Corresp. Mem., Inst. Nat. Sci., Ecuador, 1971; Hon. Member: Leopoldina Acad.; Japan Chemical Soc. Ciamician Medal, Bologna, 1959; Davy Medal of Royal Society, 1965; John Torrance Tate Gold Medal (Am. Inst. Physics), 1966. Hon. Treasurer OUAFC, 1931-; Founder and Chairman of Pegasus FC, Secretary, 1948-54; Member, FA Coun., 1941-, Vice-Chm., 1967-76, Chm., 1976-; Life Vice-Pres., AFA (Pres. 1969-71); Mem., Exec. Cttee UEFA, 1974-. Editor, Spectrochimica Acta, 1957-. Hon. Counsellor, Spanish SRC, 1971-. Hon. DSc: Newcastle upon Tyne, 1970; Strasbourg, 1972; Hon. ScD Cambridge, 1974. Order of Aztec Eagle, Mexico, 1970; Chevalier, Légion d'Honneur, 1971; Grand Service Cross, German Federal Republic, 1971. *Publications:* A Course in Chemical Spectroscopy, 1938; (ed) Advances in Spectroscopy, Vol. I 1959, II 1961; Papers in Proc. of scientific socs and journals. *Recreation:* Association football (Oxford *v* Cambridge, 1928-29). *Address:* 33 Linton Road, Oxford. *T:* Oxford 58925.

THOMPSON, Sir Herbert; see Thompson, Sir (Joseph) Herbert.

THOMPSON, Sir (Humphrey) Simon M.; see Meysey-Thompson.

THOMPSON, James Craig; Managing Director, South Eastern Newspapers Ltd, since 1975 (Director since 1973); *b* 27 Oct. 1933; *s* of Alfred Thompson and Eleanor (*née* Craig); *m* 1957, Catherine (*née* Warburton); one *s* one *d. Educ:* Heaton Grammar Sch., Newcastle upon Tyne; Rutherford Coll., Newcastle upon Tyne. Mem. Inst. of Marketing. Sales Executive: Chivers & Sons Ltd, 1955-58; Revlon Internat. Corp., 1958-60; Internat. Latex Corp., 1960-63; Advertising Executive: Thomson Organisation Ltd; Newcastle Chronicle & Journal, 1963-64; The Scotsman, 1964-65; Classified Advertisement Manager, Liverpool Daily Post and Echo, 1965-67; Advertising Manager, Kent Messenger Gp, 1967-70, Marketing Controller, 1970-71, Director, 1972-, Dep. Man. Dir, 1974-. Director: Ad Builder Ltd, 1971-; Bilabel Ltd, 1973-; Moadford Ltd, 1973-; Union Motors Kent Ltd, 1973-; SE Magazines Ltd, 1973-;

Larkfield Web Offset Ltd, 1973-; Messenger Print Ltd, 1974-; Seacoast Newspapers Ltd, 1976-; Kentish Express (Igglesdon & Co.) Ltd, 1977-; Chatham, Rochester & Gillingham Evening Post Ltd, 1977-; Commercial Union Assurance Co. Ltd, 1977-; Man. Dir, Adverkit Internat. Ltd, 1973-. Mem. Bd of Governors, St Simon Stock Sch., 1972-. Life Governor, Kent County Agricl Soc., 1976. Pres., Maidstone Circle, Catenian Assoc., 1974-75; Chm., Membership Cttee, Weekly Newspaper Advtsg Bureau, 1972-74; Mem. Management Cttee, Southern Football League, 1975-77 (Chm., 1977-); Pres., Eastern Professional Floodlight League, 1976-; Chm., Maidstone United FC, 1970-. Mem., Internat. Advertising Assoc.; MInstD. Distinguished Service Award, Internat. Classified Advertising Assoc., Baltimore, 1968. *Publications:* numerous articles on commercial aspects of newspaper publishing. *Recreations:* squash, Northumbrian history. *Address:* Prescott House, Otham, Kent ME15 8RL. *T:* Maidstone 861606. *Clubs:* Eccentric, Fleet Street Column, Press; Elwick (Ashford); Maidstone (Maidstone); Fairchild Wine Society (Oklahoma); Kent CCC.

THOMPSON, Hon. Sir John, Kt 1961; Hon. **Mr Justice Thompson;** Judge of the High Court of Justice, Queen's Bench Division since 1961; *b* Glasgow, 16 Dec. 1907; *e s* of Donald Cameron Thompson and Jeanie Dunn Thompson (*née* Nisbet); *m* 1934, Agnes Baird, *o d* of John and Jeanie Drummond, Glasgow; two *s*. *Educ:* Bellahouston Academy; Glasgow University; Oriel College, Oxford. Glasgow University: MA and Arthur Jones Memorial Prize, 1928; Ewing Gold Medal, 1929; Oxford University: BA, 1930; MA 1943. Barrister-at-Law, Powell Prize, Middle Temple, 1933. QC 1954; Bencher, Middle Temple, 1961; Lent Reader, 1977; Dep. Treasurer, 1977. Vice-Chm., Gen. Council of the Bar, 1960-61 (Mem. 1958-61). Commissioner of Assize (Birmingham) 1961. *Publications:* (edited with H. R. Rogers) Redgrave's Factories, Truck and Shops Acts. *Recreation:* golf. *Address:* 73 Sevenoaks Road, Orpington, Kent. *T:* Orpington 22339.

THOMPSON, John Alan, CMG 1974; HM Diplomatic Service, retired; *b* 21 June 1926; *m* 1956, Maureen Sayers. *Educ:* Bromsgrove Sch.; Brasenose Coll., Oxford. Control Commission for Germany, 1952; Vice-Consul, Hanoi, 1954; Second Sec., Saigon, 1956; Warsaw, 1959; Foreign Office, 1961; First Sec. (Commercial), Havana, 1964; First Sec., FO (later FCO), 1966-75; Counsellor, 1973. *Recreations:* music, mountains. *Address:* Flat 3, 15 Dawson Place, W2. *T:* 01-229 7919. *Club:* United Oxford & Cambridge University.

THOMPSON, John Brian; Director of Radio, Independent Broadcasting Authority, since 1973; *b* 8 June 1928; *y s* of John and Lilian Thompson; *m* 1957, Sylvia, *d* of late Thomas Waterhouse, CBE, and of Doris Waterhouse (*née* Gough); two *s* one *d*. *Educ:* St Paul's; Pembroke College, Oxford (BA; MA). Eileen Power Studentship, LSE, 1950; Glaxo Laboratories Ltd, 1950-54; Masius & Fergusson Ltd, 1955; Asst Editor, Truth, 1956-57; Daily Express, 1957-59 (New York Correspondent; Drama Critic); ITN, 1959-60 (Newscaster/Reporter); Editor, Time and Tide, 1960-62; News Editor, The Observer, 1962-66; Editor, Observer Colour Magazine, 1966-70; Publisher and Editorial Dir, BPC Publishing Ltd, 1971. Sen. Advr on Radio to Minister of Posts and Telecommunications, 1972. *Address:* 4 Edith Grove, SW10. *T:* 01-352 5414.

THOMPSON, John Crighton, CB 1965; CBE 1958; retired as Director of Electrical Engineering, Navy Department, Ministry of Defence; *b* 14 July 1902; *s* of William Thompson and Margaret Thompson (*née* Turner); *m* 1928, Jessie Walker, *née* Ashton; three *s* one *d* (and one *d* decd). *Educ:* King Edward VI School, Norwich; Faraday House Elec. Engineering Coll., London. BSc (Eng) London 1922. Pupil, Brush Elec. Engineering Co., Loughborough, 1922-23; Asst Engineer, Callenders Cable and Construction Co., 1923-26; Asst Elec. Engineer, Admiralty, 1927; after service at home and abroad, apptd Director of Electrical Engineering and Head of RNES, 1960; retd, 1964. FIEE. *Recreations:* motoring, gardening, fishing. *Address:* 135 Bradford Road, Combe Down, Bath. *T:* Combe Down 832228.

THOMPSON, John Derek T.; *see* Taylor Thompson.

THOMPSON, Prof. John Griggs, PhD; Rouse Ball Professor of Mathematics, University of Cambridge, since 1971; Fellow of Churchill College, since 1968; *b* Kansas, 13 Oct. 1932; *s* of John and Eleanor Thompson; *m* 1960, Diane Oenning; one *d*. *Educ:* Yale (BA 1955); Chicago (PhD 1959); MA Cantab 1972. Prof. of Mathematics, Chicago Univ., 1962-68; Vis. Prof. of Mathematics, Cambridge Univ., 1968-70. Cole Prize, 1966; Field Medal, 1970. *Address:* Churchill College, Cambridge.

THOMPSON, John Kenneth, CMG 1963; Director of the Commonwealth Institute, 1969-77; *b* Halstead, Essex, 12 May 1913; *e s* of late W. Stanton Thompson, MBE. *m* 1937, Jenny More; two *s*. *Educ:* Dover County School; King's College, London; Lausanne Univ. BA, AKC, DipEd Mod. Lang. Master, Queen's Royal Coll., Trinidad, 1935-39; Censor, Trinidad, 1939-41; Chief Censor, 1941-42; Asst Sec., Postal and Tel. Censorship, London, 1943-45; Principal, Colonial Office, 1945-49; Colonial Attaché, Brit. Embassy, Washington, 1950-53; Asst Sec., Colonial Office, 1953-59; Director, Colombo Plan Bureau, SE Asia, 1959-62; Asst Sec., Dept of Technical Co-operation, 1962-64; Dir of Overseas Appointments, ODM, 1964-69. Governor: Hartwell House, Aylesbury; Centre for Internat. Briefing, Farnham Castle. Trustee, Central Bureau for Educnl Visits and Exchanges. Chm. Exec. Cttee, Royal Commonwealth Soc. for the Blind. *Address:* 9 Grove Way, Esher, Surrey. *T:* 01-398 4461. *Club:* Royal Commonwealth Society.

THOMPSON, John Leonard C.; *see* Cloudsley-Thompson.

THOMPSON, Air Commodore John Marlow, CBE 1954; DSO 1943; DFC 1940 (and Bar 1942); AFC 1952; RAF retired; Director, Monte Carlo Golf Club, Monaco, since 1973; *b* 16 Aug. 1914; *s* of late John Thompson and Florence Thompson (*née* Marlow); *m* 1938, Margaret Sylvia Rowlands; one *s* one *d* (and one *s* decd). *Educ:* Bristol Grammar School. Joined RAF 1934; comd 111 Sqdn, Battle of Britain; Spitfire Wing, Malta, 1942-43; SASO 11 Group, 1952-54; comd RAF Leeming, 1956-57; Dir of Air Defence, Air Ministry, 1958-60; AOC, Military Air Traffic Ops, 1962-65; Gen. Manager, Airwork Services, Saudi Arabia, 1966-68. Graduate Imperial Defence College, 1961. Belgian MC 1st Class, 1942; Danish Order of Dannebrog, 1951. *Recreation:* golf. *Address:* Le Bahia, Avenue Princesse Grace, Monte-Carlo, Principauté de Monaco. *T:* Monte-Carlo (93) 304137. *Clubs:* Royal Air Force; RAF Reserves; Monte-Carlo.

THOMPSON, John William McWean; Editor, Sunday Telegraph, since 1976; *b* 12 June 1920; *s* of Charles and Charlotte Thompson; *m* 1947, Cynthia Ledsham; one *s* one *d*. *Educ:* Roundhay Sch., Leeds. Previously on staffs of Yorkshire Evening News, Evening Standard, London, and The Spectator (Dep. Editor); joined Sunday Telegraph, 1970; Asst Editor, 1975. *Publication:* (as Peter Quince) Country Life, 1975. *Address:* St Andrew's Cottage, Much Hadham, Herts SG10 6DH. *T:* Much Hadham 2309. *Club:* Travellers'.

THOMPSON, Rear-Adm. John Yelverton, CB 1960; DL; retired 1961; *b* 25 May 1909; *s* of late Sir John Perronet Thompson, KCSI, KCIE, and Ada Lucia, Lady Thompson (*née* Tyrrell); *m* 1934, Barbara Helen Mary Aston Key; two *s*. *Educ:* Mourne Grange, Kilkeel, Co. Down; RN College, Dartmouth. Midshipman: HMS Repulse and Berwick, 1926-29; Sub-Lieutenant: HMS Warspite, 1931; Lieutenant: HMS Queen Elizabeth, 1931-32, Restless 1933, Excellent 1933-34, Queen Elizabeth 1935, Glasgow 1936-39; Lieut-Commander: HMS Excellent 1939-41, Anson 1941-43; Commander: Admiralty, Naval Ordnance Dept, 1943-45; US Fifth Fleet, 1946; HMS Liverpool, 1947; HMS Newcastle, 1948; Captain: Ordnance Board, 1948-50; HMS Unicorn, 1951-52; Director, Gunnery Division, Naval Staff, 1952-54; Imperial Defence College, 1955; Commodore: Royal Naval Barracks, Portsmouth, 1956-57; Rear-Admiral: Admiralty Interview Boards, 1958; Adm. Superintendent, HM Dockyard, Chatham, 1958-61. ADC to the Queen, 1957. Governor, Aldenham Sch., 1967-73. DL: Hertfordshire, 1966-73; Cornwall, 1973. American Legion of Merit, 1953. *Address:* Flushing Meadow, Manaccan, near Helston, Cornwall.
See also G. F. M. P. Thompson, L. P. Thompson-McCausland.

THOMPSON, Sir (Joseph) Herbert, Kt 1947; CIE 1945; *b* 9 March 1898; *o s* of J. Arnold Thompson, JP, and Ellen Stewart Fraser, Wilmslow, Cheshire; *m* 1925, Kathleen (Kaiser-i-Hind Silver medal, 1948), *d* of J. H. Rodier; three *d*. *Educ:* Manchester Grammar School; Brasenose College, Oxford (MA). Royal Naval Air Service (Sub-Lt) 1916, RAF (Capt.) 1918 and served principally as a fighter pilot (despatches). Assistant Master, Oundle School, 1921-22; ICS 1922; served in Madras Presidency; appointed to Foreign and Political Department, Govt of India (later Indian Political Service), 1926; Served NWF Province, Hyderabad and Rajputana, 1926-41; Dep. Sec., Political Department, 1941-43; Revenue and Divisional Commissioner NWF Province, 1943; Resident for Kolhapur and Deccan States, 1944-45; Resident for the Punjab States, 1945-47; on special duty in connection with lapse of Paramountcy, 1947, retd 1949. General Secretary, London Council of Social Service, 1949-50; Diocesan Secretary, Worcester, 1951-53; Rowing Corresp., Sunday Times, 1954-68; BBC (Appointments Dept),

1956-59. Member: Bd of Governors, St Thomas' Hosp., 1950-70; SW Metropolitan Regional Hospitals Board, 1959-63. *Recreations:* walking, gardening and rowing. *Address:* Fair Acre, Haddenham, Bucks HP17 8HB. *T:* Haddenham 291212. *Clubs:* Leander; Vincent's (Oxford).

THOMPSON, Sir Kenneth (Pugh), 1st Bt *cr* 1963; Chairman, Merseyside County Council, since 1977, Leader, Conservative Group, since 1974; *b* 24 Dec. 1909; *s* of Ernest S. and Annie Thompson; *m* 1936, Nanne Broome, Walton; one *s* one *d. Educ:* Bootle Grammar School. Formerly newspaper reporter, and subsequently entered commercial life; lectured for the Economic League. Worked for Ministry of Information as Regional Officer during War of 1939-45. Member of Liverpool City Council, 1938-58. Director of several Liverpool companies. MP (C) Walton Div. Liverpool, 1950-64; Chairman Conservative Nat. Advisory Cttee on Local Govt, 1956-57; Assistant Postmaster-General, 1957-Oct. 1959; Parliamentary Secretary, Ministry of Education, October 1959-July 1962. *Publications:* Member's Lobby, 1966; Pattern of Conquest, 1967. *Heir: s* Paul Anthony Thompson [*b* 6 Oct. 1939; *m* 1971, Pauline Dorothy Spencer, *d* of Robert Spencer, Bolton, Lancs]. *Address:* Atherton Cottage, Formby, Merseyside.

THOMPSON, Sir Lionel; *see* Thompson, Sir L. L. H. *and* Thompson, Sir T. L. T., Bt.

THOMPSON, Major Lloyd H.; *see* Hall-Thompson, Major R. L.

THOMPSON, Sir (Louis) Lionel (Harry), Kt 1953; CBE 1946; Deputy Master and Comptroller of the Royal Mint and *ex-officio* Engraver of HM's Seals, 1950-57; retired 1957; *b* 10 March 1893; *o s* of William Thompson, Eaton, Retford; *m* Mary, *d* of William White, MD, Hadfield, Derbyshire; two *s. Educ:* King Edward VI School, Retford; Sheffield Univ.; Exeter Coll., Oxford (scholar). First Cl. Classical Mods, 1913. Served European War, 1914-18, Cheshire Regt (Territorial), Temp. Major. Asst Principal Treasury, 1919; Asst Secretary to Commissioner for Special Areas, 1937-39; Under-Secretary, Treasury, 1947-50. *Recreations:* walking, gardening. *Address:* 61 Woodbury Avenue, Petersfield, Hants. *T:* 3277. *Club:* United Oxford & Cambridge University.

THOMPSON, Norman Sinclair; Chairman, Mass Transit Railway Corporation, Hong Kong, since 1975; *b* 7 July 1920; *s* of Norman Whitfield Thompson and Jane Thompson (*née* Robinson); *m* 1945, Peggy Sivil; two *s* (one *d* decd). *Educ:* Middlesbrough High Sch. Qual. Chartered Accountant, 1947 (FCA); Cost and Management Accountant (ACMA). Served War, Merchant Seaman, 1940-45. Asst Sec., Paton's and Baldwin's Ltd, 1947; Commercial Manager, Cowan's Sheldon & Co. Ltd, 1955; Group Secretary, Richardson's Westgarth & Co. Ltd, 1957; Financial Dir, David Brown & Sons (Huddersfield) Ltd, 1961; Gen. Manager, Malta Drydocks, Swan Hunter Group Ltd, 1963; apptd Swan Hunter Bd, 1964; Overseas Dir, 1967; Dep. Managing Dir, 1969. The Cunard Steam-Ship Co. Ltd: Man. Dir, Cargo Shipping, 1970; Man. Dir, 1971-74. *Recreations:* sailing, music. *Address:* Shadrach House, Burton Bradstock, Dorset. *T:* Burton Bradstock 670; 9 Strawberry Hill, The Peak, Hong Kong. *Clubs:* Oriental; Hong Kong; Royal Hong Kong Yacht.

THOMPSON, Oliver Frederic, OBE 1945; Pro-Chancellor of The City University, 1966-72; *b* 26 Jan. 1905; 3rd *s* of late W. Graham Thompson and late Oliveria C. Prescott; *m* 1939, Frances Phyllida, *d* of late F. H. Bryant; one *s* three *d. Educ:* Tonbridge. Mem. Shell Gp of Cos, 1924-64: managerial posts in USA, Caribbean, London. Head of Oil Sect., Min. of Econ. Warfare, and Mem. War Cabinet Sub-Cttee on Oil, 1942-46; rep. UK, Suez Canal Users Assoc.; rep. UK on various UN and OECD Cttees; Mem. Parly and Sci. Cttee, 1955-65. Past Master and Mem. Ct, Worshipful Co. of Skinners. Chm. Governing Body, Northampton Coll. of Advanced Technology, 1956-66 (now City University); Governor, Tonbridge Sch. and Kingston Polytechnic. FInstP (Past Mem. Council); Chm. Qualifications Cttee, British Computer Society, 1968 (Hon. Fellow, 1972). County Councillor, Surrey, 1965- (Majority Leader, 1970-73). Hon. DSc, City Univ., 1967. *Publications:* various papers on economics of energy and petroleum. *Recreation:* country pursuits. *Address:* 32 Park Road, Aldeburgh, Suffolk IP15 5EU.

THOMPSON, Sir Peile, 5th Bt *cr* 1890; OBE 1959 (MBE 1950); Lieutenant-Colonel (retired), The Manchester Regiment and King's African Rifles; *b* 11 Feb. 1911; *s* of Sir Peile Beaumont Thompson, 4th Bt, and Stella Mary (*d* 1972), *d* of late Arthur Harris; *S* father, 1972; *m* 1937, Barbara Johnson, *d* of late H. J. Rampling, Old Manor House, Harston; one *s* one *d. Educ:* Canford School; St Catharine's College, Cambridge (BA 1933,

MA 1950). 2nd Lieutenant, Manchester Regt, 1932; served War of 1939-45; commanded 26 Bn, KAR, Kenya Emergency, 1954-56 (despatches). *Recreation:* gardening. *Heir: s* Christopher Peile Thompson [*b* 21 Dec. 1944; *m* 1969, Anna, *d* of Major Arthur Callander; one *s* one *d*]. *Address:* Old Farm, Augres, Trinity, Jersey, CI. *T:* Jersey Central 62289.

THOMPSON, Peter Anthony, FCIT; Chief Executive, National Freight Corporation, since 1977; *b* 14 April 1928; *s* of late Herbert Thompson and of Sarah Jane Thompson; *m* 1958, Patricia Anne Norcott; one *s* two *d . Educ:* Royal Drapers Sch.; Bradford Grammar Sch.; Leeds Univ. BA. Unilever, 1952-62; GKN, 1962-64; Transport Controller, Rank Organisation, 1964-66; Head of Transport, BSC, 1968-72; Group Co-ordinator, BRS Ltd, 1972-75; Exec. Vice-Chm. (Operations), NFC, 1976-77. *Recreations:* golf, tennis, squash, Rugby (at one time). *Address:* 37 Newlands Avenue, Radlett, Herts. *T:* Radlett 5996; (office) National Freight Corporation, Argosy House, 215 Great Portland Street, W1. *T:* 01-636 8688.

THOMPSON, Reginald Aubrey, CMG 1964; *b* 22 Nov. 1905; *s* of John Thompson, Mansfield; *m* 1932, Gwendoline Marian Jackson; one *s. Educ:* Brunts Sch., Mansfield; University Coll., Nottingham. BSc London (1st Cl. Hons Chemistry), 1927. Research, Organic Chemistry, 1927-29; Science Master, various grammar schools, 1929-41; Scientific Civil Service, Min. of Supply, 1941-46; transf. to Admin. Class (Principal), 1946; Asst Sec., 1953; Assistant Secretary, Department of Education and Science (formerly Office of Minister of Science), 1956-64; Ministry of Technology, 1964; retd, 1966. Led UK Delegn at Confs on: liability of operators of nuclear ships, Brussels Convention, 1962; liability for nuclear damage, Vienna Convention, 1963. *Recreations:* golf, gardening, music. *Address:* Qualicum, Bentsbrook Park, North Holmwood, Dorking, Surrey. *T:* Dorking 2289.

THOMPSON, Reginald Stanley; Headmaster of Bloxham School, 1952-65, retired; *b* 23 Sept. 1899; *s* of late Reverend Canon C. H. Thompson, formerly Vicar of Eastleigh, Hants, and of Newport, Isle of Wight; *m* 1938, Phyllis Barbara, *y d* of Henry White, Solicitor, Winchester, Hants; one *s* two *d. Educ:* Hereford Cathedral School; Lancing College; Oriel College, Oxford. Assistant Master at Sherborne School, 1922-52 (Housemaster, 1936-52). *Recreations:* music, gardening, books, cricket. *Address:* Westcott Close, Clifton-upon-Teme, Worcestershire. *T:* Shelsley Beauchamp 234.

THOMPSON, Sir Richard (Hilton Marler), 1st Bt *cr* 1963; *b* Calcutta, India, 5 Oct. 1912; *m* 1939, Anne Christabel de Vere, *d* of late Philip de Vere Annesley, MA, and of Mrs Annesley, BEM; one *s. Educ:* Malvern College. In business in India, Burma and Ceylon, 1930-40; travelled in Tibet, Persia, Iraq, Turkey, etc. Served in RNVR, 1940-46, volunteering as ordinary seaman; commissioned, 1941 (despatches, 1942); Lieut-Comdr 1944. MP (C) Croydon West, 1950-55; Assistant-Government Whip, 1952; Lord Commissioner of the Treasury, 1954; MP (C) Croydon South, 1955-66 and 1970-Feb. 1974; Vice-Chamberlain of HM Household, 1956; Parly Sec., Ministry of Health, 1957-59; Under-Secretary of State, CRO, 1959-60; Parly Sec., Ministry of Works, Oct. 1960-July 1962. Mem., Public Accounts Cttee, 1973-74. A Cottonian family Trustee of the British Museum, 1951-63; re-apptd as a Prime Minister's Trustee, 1963, 1971, 1976. Chm., Overseas Migration Bd, 1959; led UK delegation to ECAFE in Bangkok, 1960; signed Indus Waters Agreement with India, Pakistan and World Bank for UK, Sept. 1960; led UK Parly Delegn to Tanganyika, to present Speaker's chair, Jan. 1963. Chm., Capital and Counties Property Co., 1971-77, retired; Pres., British Property Fedn, 1976-77; Director: Rediffusion Television Ltd; Rediffusion Holdings Ltd. Chm., British Museum Society, 1970-74. *Recreations:* gardening, collecting, study of history. *Heir: s* Nicholas Annesley Marler Thompson, *b* 19 March 1947. *Address:* Rhodes House, Sellindge, Kent. *Club:* Carlton.

THOMPSON, Sir Robert Grainger Ker, KBE 1965; CMG 1961; DSO 1945; MC 1943; *b* 12 April 1916; *s* of late Canon W. G. Thompson; *m* 1950, Merryn Newboult; one *s* one *d. Educ:* Marlborough; Sidney Sussex College, Cambridge (MA). Cadet, Malayan Civil Service, 1938. Served War of 1939-45 (MC, DSO), RAF, 1941-46. Asst Commissioner of Labour, Perak, 1946; jssc 1948-49; Staff Officer (Civil) to Director of Operations, 1950; Co-ordinating Officer, Security, 1955; Dep. Sec. for Def., Fedn of Malaya, 1957; Perm. Sec. for Def., 1959-61; Head, British Advisory Mission to Vietnam, 1961-65. Consultant to Govts, including the White House. Johan Mangku Negara (JMN), Malaya, 1958. *Publications:* Defeating Communist Insurgency, 1966; The Royal Flying Corps, 1968; No Exit from Vietnam, 1969; Revolutionary War in World

Strategy, 1945-1969, 1970; Peace Is Not At Hand, 1974. *Recreations:* all country pursuits. *Address:* Pitcott House, Winsford, Minehead, Som. *Club:* Special Forces.

THOMPSON, Robert Henry Stewart, CBE 1973; MA, DSc, DM, BCh; FRS 1974; FRCP; FRCPath; Courtauld Professor of Biochemistry, Middlesex Hospital Medical School, University of London, 1965-76; now Emeritus Professor; Trustee, Wellcome Trust, 1963; *b* 2 Feb. 1912; *s* of Dr Joseph Henry Thompson and Mary Eleanor Rutherford; *m* 1938, Inge Vilma Anita Gebert; one *s* two *d. Educ:* Epsom College; Trinity College, Oxford; Guy's Hospital Medical School. Millard Scholar, Trinity College, Oxford, 1930; Theodore Williams Scholar in Physiology, Oxford, 1932; 1st Class Animal Physiology, Oxford, 1933; Senior Demy, Magdalen College, Oxford, 1933; Univ. Scholar, Guy's Hosp. Med. School, 1933; Adrian Stokes Travelling Fellowship to Hosp. of Rockefeller Inst., New York, 1937-38; Gillson Research Scholar in Pathology, Soc. of Apothecaries of London, 1938; Fellow of University Coll., Oxford, 1938-47; Demonstrator in Biochemistry, Oxford, 1938-47; Dean of Medical School, Oxford, 1946-47; Prof. of Chemical Pathology, Guy's Hosp. Medical School, Univ. of London, 1947-65; Secretary-General International Union of Biochemistry, 1955-64; Hon. Sec. Royal Society of Medicine, 1958-64; Mem. of Medical Research Council, 1958-62; Mem., Bd of Governors, Middlesex Hosp., 1972-74. Radcliffe Prize for Medical Research, Oxford, 1943. Served War of 1939-45, Major, RAMC, 1944-46. *Publications:* (with C. W. Carter) Biochemistry in relation to Medicine, 1949; Joint Editor (with E. J. King) Biochemical Disorders in Human Disease, 1957; numerous papers on biochemical and pathological subjects in various scientific journals. *Recreation:* gardening. *Address:* 1 Church Way, Hurst Green, Oxted, Surrey RH8 9EA. *T:* Oxted 3526; Orchard's Almshouses, Launcells, N Cornwall. *T:* Bude 3817. *Club:* Athenæum.

THOMPSON, Major Robert Lloyd H.; *see* Hall-Thompson.

THOMPSON, Sir (Thomas) Lionel Tennyson, 5th Bt, *cr* 1806; Barrister-at-Law; *b* 19 June 1921; *s* of Lt-Col Sir Thomas Thompson, 4th Bt, MC, and of Milicent Ellen Jean, *d* of late Edmund Charles Tennyson-d'Eyncourt, Bayons Manor, Lincolnshire; *S* father, 1964; *m* 1955, Mrs Margaret van Beers (marr. diss. 1962), *d* of late Walter Herbert Browne; one *s* one *d. Educ:* Eton. Served War of 1939-45: Royal Air Force Volunteer Reserve, 1940; Flying Officer, 1942 (invalided, 1944); Able Seaman, Royal Fleet Auxiliary, 1944-46. Awarded 1939-45 Star, Aircrew (Europe) Star, Defence and Victory Medals. Called to the Bar, Lincoln's Inn, 1952. *Recreations:* shooting, sailing, flying and photography. *Heir: s* Thomas d'Eyncourt John Thompson, *b* 22 Dec. 1956. *Address:* Queen Elizabeth Building, Temple, EC4Y 9BS. *T:* 01-353 6453, 01-353 7855; 16 Old Buildings, Lincoln's Inn, WC2. *T:* 01-405 7929. *Club:* Naval and Military.

THOMPSON, Maj.-Gen. (Hon. Lt-Gen.) Sir Treffry Owen, KCSI 1947; CB 1946; CBE 1942; KHP 1944; County Patron BRCS, Devon Branch; *b* 9 Aug. 1888; *s* of late Rev. W. F. Thompson (Chaplain, India), Fyfield, Abingdon, Berks; *gs* of Sir Charles Bell, Anatomist and Surgeon; *m* 1916, Mary Emily (*d* 1958), *d* of late Rev. Canon Medd, North Cerney, Gloucester; two *s* two *d* ; *m* 1959, Vera Elaine, *d* of late E. J. F. A. Ward and Mrs Ward. *Educ:* Dragon Sch., Oxford; Priory, Repton; St John's Coll., Oxford; St George's Hosp., London. House appointments Radcliffe, Oxford; RAMC, 1914; served European War, 1914-19, with RAMC; Lt, 1914; Capt., 1915; Major, 1926; DAD Hygiene, India, 1926-29; Lt-Col, 1935; AD Hygiene and Path., India, 1933-37; AD of Hygiene, War Office, 1938-39; DD Hygiene, and Pathology, India, 1939; Col, 1941; DDMS L of C Iraq Forces; Brig., 1942; DDMS Burma, Jan.-May 1942; Acting Maj.-Gen. 1942; DDMS Cen. Command, India; DDMS Eastern Army, 1943-44; Maj.-Gen. 1944; Medical Adviser SACSEA; DMS ALFSEA, 1944-45; DMS SACSEA, 1945; DMS in India, 1946-47; Lt-Gen. (local) 1947; retd, 1948; Col Comdt RAMC, 1950-53. Br. Red Cross Comr for relief work in India and Pakistan, 1947-49; Editor, RAMC Journal, 1950; writer for Official Medical History, Campaigns of World War, 1939-45. County Dir British Red Cross Soc. Devonshire Br., 1951-65. CStJ 1945; Special Service Cross, BRCS 1960. Italian Croce di Guerra, 1917. *Publications:* scientific (Hygiene) articles. *Recreations:* hockey (Oxford Occasionals, Oxford County, 1910-14), cricket, Rugby football, tennis, squash, fishing, bee-keeping. *Address:* Savourys, Chulmleigh, N Devon EX18 7ES. *T:* Chulmleigh 314.

See also M. E. D. Poore.

THOMPSON, Vernon Cecil, MB, BS London; FRCS; retired 1970 as Surgeon to Department of Thoracic Surgery, The London Hospital; Surgeon, London Chest Hospital; Hon. Consulting Thoracic Surgeon to: West London Hospital, Hammersmith; King Edward VII Hospital, Windsor; Harefield Hospital, Middlesex; Broomfield and Black Notley Hospitals, Essex; *b* 17 Sept. 1905; 2nd *s* of Dr C. C. B. Thompson, Tidenham, Glos; *m* 1942, Jean, *d* of late H. J. Hilary; one *s* one *d. Educ:* Monmouth School; St Bartholomew's Hospital. Resident House appointments followed by First Assistant to a Surgical Unit, St Bartholomew's Hospital, 929-37. Dorothy Temple Cross Travelling Fellowship, Vienna, and University Hosp., Ann Arbor, Michigan, USA, 1937. President, Soc. of Thoracic Surgeons of Great Britain and Ireland, 1966; Hon. Mem. Amer. Soc. for Thoracic Surgery, 1967. *Publications:* contrib. on surgical diseases of the chest to j s and text books. *Recreations:* fishing, shooting, gardening. *Address:* Vicarage House, Llowes, Hereford. *T:* Glasbury 323.

THOMPSON, William Bell, MA, PhD; Professor of Physics, University of California, since 1965; Chairman, Department of Physics, University of California at San Diego, 1969-72; *b* N Ireland, 27 Feb. 1922; *m* 1953, Gertrud Helene Goldschmidt, PhD (marr. diss. 1972); one *s* one *d* ; *m* 1972 Johanna Elzelina Ladestein Korevaar. *Educ:* Universities of British Columbia and Toronto, Canada. BA 1945, MA 1947, Univ. of BC; PhD Toronto, 1950. AERE Harwell: Senior Research Fellow, 1950; Deputy Chief Scientist, 1959. Visiting Prof., Univ. of California, 1961; Head, Theoretical Physics Division, Culham Laboratory, UKAEA, 1961-63; Prof. of Theoretical Plasma Physics, Oxford Univ., 1963-65. *Publications:* Introduction to Plasma Physics, 1962; numerous papers in learned journals, on controlled thermonuclear research, plasma physics, kinetic theory, etc. *Recreations:* music, literature, and gardening (alas!). *Address:* Physics Department, University of California at San Diego, La Jolla, California 92037, USA.

THOMPSON, William David James C.; *see* Cargill Thompson.

THOMPSON, (William) Godfrey; Guildhall Librarian and Director of Art Gallery, City of London, since 1966; *b* 28 June 1921; *s* of late A. and E. M. Thompson, Coventry; *m* 1946, Doreen Mary Cattell; one *s. Educ:* King Henry VIII Sch., Coventry. Served with Royal Signals, 1941-45. Entered Library Service, Coventry, 1937; Dep. Borough Librarian, Chatham, 1946; Dep. City Librarian: Kingston-upon-Hull, 1952; Manchester, 1958; City Librarian, Leeds, 1953. Hon. Librarian to Clockmakers' Co. and Gardeners' Co., 1956. Pres., Assoc. of Assistant Librarians, 1962. Member: Council, Library Assoc., 1968- (Hon. Treasurer, 1974-); Council, Aslib, 1968-; Hon. Sec. Internat. Assoc. Metropolitan Libraries, 1968-70; Adv. Bd, New Library World. Governor, St Bride Foundn. FLA 1947. MA Loughborough, 1977. *Publications:* London's Statues, 1971; Planning and Design of Libraries, 1972, 2nd edn 1977; (ed) London for Everyman, 1969; (ed) Encyclopædia of London, 1969. *Address:* Guildhall Library, EC2. *T:* 01-606 3030. *Club:* Press.

THOMPSON, Willoughby Harry, CMG 1974; CBE 1968 (MBE 1954); *b* 3 Dec. 1919; *s* of late Willoughby Thompson and of Dorothy Thompson (*née* Lowe); *m* 1963, Sheelah O'Grady; no *c. Educ:* varied, and privately. Territorial Army, 1937. Served War: RA, and E African Artillery, 1939-47. Kenya Govt Service, 1947-48; Colonial Administrative Service (Dist. Officer, Dist. Comr), Kenya, 1948-63; Colonial Sec., Falkland Islands, 1963-69 (Actg Governor, 1964 and 1967); Actg Judge, Falkland Islands and Dependencies Supreme Court, 1965-69; Actg Administrator, British Virgin Islands, May-July 1969; HM Commissioner in Anguilla, July 1969-71; Governor of Montserrat, 1971-74. *Recreations:* gardening, painting. *Address:* 38 Holland Park, Clacton on Sea, Essex. *Club:* Royal Commonwealth Society.

THOMPSON HANCOCK, P(ercy) E(llis); *see* Hancock.

THOMPSON-McCAUSLAND, Lucius Perronet, CMG 1966; *b* 12 Dec. 1904; *e s* of late Sir John Perronet Thompson, KCSI, KCIE and Ada Lucia Tyrrell; *m* Helen Laura, *d* of late Rt Hon. M. M. McCausland, sometime Lieut of Co. Londonderry; two *s* three *d* (and one *s* decd). *Educ:* Repton; King's Coll., Cambridge (Scholar). Helbert Wagg & Co., 1928; Financial News, 1929-34; Moody's Economist Service, 1929-39; Bank of England, 1939-65, Adviser to Governor, 1949-65 (accompanied Lord Keynes to pre-Bretton Woods Conf., 1943, Havana Conf., 1948); Consultant to HM Treasury on internat. monetary problems, 1965-68. Director: Dun & Bradstreet Ltd, 1965-75; Tricentrol Ltd, 1967-76 (Chm., 1970-76); Moodies Services Ltd, 1968-75 (Chm., 1970-75). Governor of Repton, 1952-77 (Chm., 1959-71); Chm., Corp. of Working Men's Coll. 1964-69, Principal, 1969-. High Sheriff of Hertfordshire, 1965-66. *Recreations:*

garden, travel. *Address:* Epcombs, Hertingfordbury, Hertford. *T:* Hertford 52580. *Clubs:* Athenæum; Leander (Henley).
See also G. F. M. P. *Thomson, Rear-Adm. J. Y. Thomson.*

THOMSON, family name of **Barons Thomson of Fleet** and **Thomson of Monifieth.**

THOMSON, Hon. Lord; Alexander Thomson; a Senator of the College of Justice, Scotland, since 1965; *b* 9 Nov. 1914; *s* of James Stuart Thomson, Dunfermline, Fife; *m* 1957, Marie Wilson, *o d* of late David G. Cowan, Milngavie. *Educ:* Dunfermline High School; Edinburgh University (MA, LLB). Served War of 1939-45, Capt., RA. Mem. Faculty of Advocates, Edinburgh, 1946 (Dean, 1964-65); QC (Scotland) 1955; Sheriff of Renfrew and Argyll, 1962-64; a Judge of Nat. Industrial Relations Court, 1971-74. *Address:* 9 Moray Place, Edinburgh EH3 6DT.

THOMSON OF FLEET, 2nd Baron *cr* 1964; **Kenneth Roy Thomson;** newspaper proprietor; Chairman, Thomson Organisation, since 1976 (Joint Chairman, 1971-76); Co-President, Times Newspapers Ltd, since 1971 (Chairman, 1968-70, Deputy Chairman, 1966-67); Chairman of the Board, President and Director, Thomson Newspapers Limited (owners of 65 newspapers in Canada); President and Director, Thomson Newspapers Inc. (owners of 47 newspapers in the United States); Director: Toronto Dominion Bank; Scottish and York Ltd; Abitibi Paper Co. Ltd; President, Vice-President or Director of numerous newspapers and other communications companies in Canada and the US; *b* Toronto, Ont., 1 Sept. 1923; *s* of 1st Baron Thomson of Fleet, GBE, and Edna Alice (*d* 1951) *d* of John Irvine, Drayton, Ont.; *S* father, 1976; *m* 1956, Nora Marilyn, *d* of A. V. Lavis; two *s* one *d*. *Educ:* Upper Canada Coll.; Univ. of Cambridge, England (MA). Served War of 1939-45 with RCAF. Began in editorial dept of Timmins Daily Press., Timmins, Ont., 1947; Advertising Dept, Galt Reporter, Galt, 1948-50, General Manager, 1950-53; returned to Toronto Head Office of Thomson Newspapers to take over direction of Company's Canadian and American operations. Member, Baptist Church. *Recreation:* collecting antiques. *Heir: s* Hon. David Kenneth Roy Thomson, *b* 12 June 1957. *Address:* (home) 8 Kensington Palace Gardens, W8; 8 Castle Frank Road, Toronto, Ont.; (office) Times Newspapers Limited, New Printing House Square, Grays Inn Road, WC1X 8EZ; Thomson Newspapers Ltd, 65 Queen Street West, Toronto, Ont. *Clubs:* National, Toronto, Granite, York, Toronto Hunt (Toronto).

THOMSON OF MONIFIETH, Baron *cr* 1977 (Life Peer), of Monifieth, Dundee; **George Morgan Thomson,** PC 1966; Chairman: Advertising Standards Authority, since 1977; European Movement in Britain, since 1977; First Crown Estate Commissioner, since 1977; Chancellor, Heriot-Watt University, since 1977; *b* 16 Jan. 1921; *s* of late James Thomson, Monifieth; *m* 1948, Grace Jenkins; two *d*. *Educ:* Grove Academy, Dundee. Served War of 1939-45, in Royal Air Force, 1940-45. Assistant Editor, Forward, 1946, Editor, 1948-53. Contested (Lab) Glasgow, Hillhead, 1950; MP (Lab) Dundee East, July 1952-72. Member: Fabian Commonwealth Bureau; Exec. Council, CPA; Joint Chm., Council for Education in the Commonwealth, 1959-64; Adviser to Educational Institute of Scotland, 1960-64. Minister of State, Foreign Office, 1964-66; Chancellor of the Duchy of Lancaster, 1966-67; Joint Minister of State, Foreign Office, 1967; Secretary of State for Commonwealth Affairs, Aug. 1967-Oct. 1968; Minister Without Portfolio, 1968-69; Chancellor of the Duchy of Lancaster, 1969-70; Shadow Defence Minister, 1970-72. Chm., Labour Cttee for Europe, 1972-73; Commissioner, EEC, 1973-Jan. 1977. Chm., David Davies Inst. of Internat. Studies, 1971-. Hon. LLD Dundee, 1967; Hon. DLitt Heriot-Watt, 1973; Hon. DSc Aston, 1976. *Address:* 102 Rochester Row, SW1. *Club:* Brooks's.

THOMSON, Adam, CBE 1976; Chairman, Caledonian Airways Group, since 1970 (formerly Airways Interests (Thomson) Ltd, Chairman and Managing Director, 1964-70); Chairman and Chief Executive, British Caledonian Airways; *b* 7 July 1926; *s* of Frank Thomson and Jemina Rodgers; *m* 1948, Dawn Elizabeth Burt; two *s*. *Educ:* Rutherglen Acad.; Coatbridge Coll.; Royal Technical Coll., Glasgow. Pilot; Fleet Air Arm, 1944-47; Flying Instructor 1947-50; BEA, West African Airways, Britavia, 1951-59. Chairman: Blue Sky Holidays Ltd; Associated & Internat. Hldg Co. Establishment; Consultores Hoteleros del Mediterraneo SA. Mem., Airworthiness Requirements Bd. Mem. Council, Inst. of Dirs. FRAeS; FCIT; FBIM. Businessman of the Year, Hambro Award, 1970; first Scottish Free Enterprise Award, Aims for Freedom and Enterprise, 1976. *Recreations:* squash, sailing, skin-diving. *Address:* 154 Buckswood Drive, Crawley, West Sussex. *Clubs:* Caledonian, Institute of Directors.

THOMSON, Alexander; *see* Thomson, Hon. Lord.

THOMSON, Alfred Reginald, RA 1945 (ARA 1939); RP 1944; RBA 1973; *b* Bangalore, India; father, Civil Service, India; *m*; one *s* one *d*. Farm training in Kent and Buckingham. *Murals:* Hotel, Duncannon Street; The Science Museum, London; private houses near Cannes, France; The Queen Mary; County Hall of Essex, Chelmsford; The Dental Hospital, Birmingham, etc.; official artist to Royal Air Force (portraits of the Queen and members of Royal Family for RAF Commem. Dinner). *Portraits:* King George of Greece; Cardinal Godfrey; Bishop of London, 1961; Bishop of Southwark, 1961; Lord Mayors of Liverpool, Duke of Marlborough, Lord Vansittart, Lord Trenchard, etc; other principal works: White Collar Dinner of the Pytchley Hunt at Althorp, The Houses of Parliament in Session, The Greater London Council, The Royal Yacht Squadron, Court of Grocers' Company, 40th Anniversary of RAF, mural for children's library, Darlington, 1974; book illustrations. The XIV Olympiad Gold Medallist for painting of sports, London, 1948. FSA 1948. *Recreation:* talking nonsense. *Address:* Milton House, 2 Fernshaw Road, SW10. *Clubs:* Chelsea Arts, London Sketch.

THOMSON, Bryden; Orchestral Conductor; Artistic Director and Principal Conductor, Ulster Orchestra, since 1977; *b* Ayr, Scotland. *Educ:* Ayr Academy; Royal Scottish Academy of Music; Staatliche Hochschule für Musik, Hamburg. BMus. Dunelm; DipMusEd (Hons) RSAM; LRAM; ARCM. Asst Conductor, BBC Scottish Orchestra, 1958; Conductor: Royal Ballet, 1962; Den Norske Opera, Oslo, 1964; Stora Teatern, Göteborg, Sweden, 1965; Royal Opera, Stockholm, 1966; Associate Conductor, Scottish National Orch., 1966; Principal Conductor, BBC Northern Symphony Orch., 1968-73. Guest Conducting: Norway; Sweden; Denmark; Canada; Germany; S Africa. *Recreations:* golf, learning about music. *Address:* c/o Music International, 13 Ardilaun Road, Highbury, N5.

THOMSON, Sir David; *see* Thomson, Sir F. D. D.

THOMSON, David Kinnear, CBE 1972 (MBE 1945); JP; Chairman, Peter Thomson (Perth) Ltd, whisky blenders and exporters; Chairman, Tayside Health Board, 1973-77; *b* Perth, 26 March 1910; *s* of Peter Thomson, whisky blender, and Jessie Kinnear; unmarried. *Educ:* Perth Academy; Strathallan School. Mem., Perth Local Authority, 1949-72; Chm. Bd of Management, Perth Technical Coll., 1972-75; Mem., ITA (Scottish Br.), 1968-73; Mem., Scottish Economic Council, 1968-75; Director: Scottish Transport Gp, 1972-76; Scottish Opera, 1973-; Chm., Perth Festival of the Arts, 1973-. Lord Provost of Perth, 1966-72, and Hon. Sheriff of Perth; DL 1966-72, JP 1955, Perth. OStJ. *Recreations:* golf, walking, listening to music. *Address:* Fairhill, Oakbank Road, Perth. *T:* Perth 26593. *Club:* Royal Perth Golfing Society.

THOMSON, Hon. David Spence, MC 1942; ED; MP (National) for Stratford, New Zealand since 1963; Minister of Justice, New Zealand, since 1975; *b* Stratford, 14 Nov. 1915; *s* of Percy Thomson, MBE; *m* 1942, June Grace Adams; one *s* three *d*. *Educ:* Stratford Primary and High Sch. Territorial Army, 1931-59; served Middle East, 1939-42; Prisoner of War, 1942-45; Brigadier (Reserve of Officers); Chairman Federated Farmers Sub-provincial Exec., 1959-63; Minister of Defence, 1966-71, holding in addition from time to time portfolios of Tourism, Publicity, War Pensions, Rehabilitation, and Minister Assistant to Prime Minister; Minister of Labour and Immigration, 1971-72. *Recreations:* golf, gardening, classical music. *Address:* Parliament Buildings, Wellington, New Zealand.

THOMSON, Sir Evan (Rees Whitaker), Kt 1977; FRCS, FRACS, FACS; Hon. Consultant Surgeon, Princess Alexandra Hospital, Brisbane; *b* 14 July 1919; *s* of Frederick Thorpe Thomson and Ann Margaret Thomson (*née* Evans); *m* 1955, Mary Kennedy. *Educ:* Brisbane Boys' Coll.; Univ. of Queensland (MB BS). Full time staff, Brisbane General Hospital, 1942-48; RAAF Reserve, 1942-45; Visiting Surgeon: Brisbane General Hospital, 1950-56; Princess Alexandra Hospital, 1956-71; Clinical Lectr in Surgery, Univ. of Queensland, 1951-71. Qld Branch, Australian Medical Association: Councillor, 1966-; Pres., 1967-68; Chm. of Council; Chm. of Ethics Cttee. Pres., 4th Aust. Med. Congress, 1971. Member: Med. Bd of Queensland; North Brisbane Hospitals Bd; Wesley Hospital Bd, etc. Silver Jubilee Medal, 1977. *Publications:* papers in medical and allied jls. *Recreations:* golf, swimming. *Address:* Alexandra, 201 Wickham Terrace, Brisbane, Queensland 4000, Australia. *T:* 221 4688. *Clubs:* Queensland; Headland Golf; Mooloolaba Yacht.

THOMSON, Ewen Cameron, CMG 1964; nutrition consultant; *b* 12 April 1915; *s* of Francis Murphy Thomson, Woodhill, Forfar, Angus; *m* 1948, Betty, *d* of Lt-Col J. H. Preston, MBE, Far Horizons, Trearddur Bay, Anglesey; one *s* three *d*. *Educ:* Forfar Academy; St Andrews University. Cadet, Northern Rhodesia Provincial Admin., 1938. War Service, 1st Bn Northern Rhodesia Regt, 1939-46. District Commissioner, 1946; Dep. Prov. Comr, 1956; Prov. Comr, 1957; Senior Provincial Commissioner, 1961; Permanent Sec. for Native Affairs, 1962; Minister for Native Affairs, 1962; Permanent Secretary, Ministry of Transport and Works, Zambia, 1964; Director of Communications, Contingency Planning Organisation, Zambia, 1966; Exec. Sec., Nat. Food and Nutrition Commn, Zambia, 1967; Temp. Project Manager, UNDP/FAO, Nat. Food and Nutrition Programme, Zambia, 1970. Consultant: SIDA Nat. Food and Nutrition Programme Tanzania, 1972; World Bank, 1974-77; Nat. Food and Nutrition Projects, Indonesia and Brazil, 1974-76; Urban Projects, Kenya and Botswana; Leader FFHC UK Reconnaissance Mission, Malaŵi, 1972; Co-Dir, Preparatory Team, Tanzania Food and Nutrition Centre, 1973. Leader, Planning Team, Nat. Food and Nutrition Programme, Malaŵi, 1973. Gave keynote address, Rockefeller Conf. on Nutrition and Govt Policy in Developing Countries, 1975. *Recreations:* golf, cooking. *Address:* Acorns, Roundhill, Woking, Surrey. *T:* Woking 73223. *Club:* Royal Commonwealth Society.

THOMSON, Rt. Rev. Francis; *see* Motherwell, Bishop of, (RC).

THOMSON, Francis Paul, OBE 1975; CEng, MIERE; Consultant on Post Office and Bank Giro Systems, since 1968; *b* Corstorphine, Edinburgh, 17 Dec. 1914; *y s* of late William George and Elizabeth Hannah Thomson, Goring-by-Sea; *m* 1954, E. Sylvia, *e d* of late Lokförare J. Erik Nilsson, Bollnäs, Sweden. *Educ:* Friends' Sch., Sibford Ferris; Sch. of Engrg, Polytechnic, London; in Denmark and Sweden. TV and radar research, 1935-42; Special Ops Exec., 1942-44; Sen. Planning Engr, Postwar research and reconstruction, communications industry; founded British Post Giro Campaign, 1946 and conducted Campaign to victory in Parlt, 1965; Lectr, Stockholm Univ. Extension, 1947-49; Founder, and Man. Editor, English Illustrated, 1950-61; techn. exports promotion with various firms, esp. electronic equipment, 1950-60; pioneered electronic language laboratory equipment and methods, 1930, subseq. joined consultancy-production groups; Bank Computerisation Consultant, 1967-. Governor, Watford Coll. of Technology, 1965-70 (Engrg Dept Adv. Cttee, 1972-); Mem., Communication of Technical Information Adv. Cttee, CGLI; Advr to PO Users' Nat. Council's Giro Sub Cttee, 1975; Founder and first Hon. Sec., SW Herts Post Office Adv. Cttee, 1976; Cttee Mem., Writers Guild of GB, 1974-; First British Cttee Mem., Internat. Centre for Ancient and Modern Tapestry (CITAM), Lausanne, 1974-. Founder and Hon. Sec., St Andrews Residents' Assoc. (Watford). AMBIM. Hon. Fellow, Inst. of Scientific and Technical Communicators, 1975. Life Member; Corstorphine Trust; Anglo-Swedish Soc. *Publications:* Giro Credit Transfer Systems, 1964; Money in the Computer Age, 1968; (ed jtly) Banking Automation, 1971; (ed with E. S. Thomson) rev. repr. of A History of Tapestry (2nd edn), by W. G. Thomson, 1973; (with S. J. L. Blumlein) A. D. Blumlein (1903-42): engineer extraordinary, 1977; numerous papers in European and other learned jls. *Recreations:* gardening, archaeology. *Address:* The Cottage, 39 Church Road, Watford, Herts WD1 3PY. *T:* Watford 36673. *Club:* Special Forces.

THOMSON, Sir (Frederick Douglas) David, 3rd Bt *cr* 1929; Managing Director, Ben Line Steamers Ltd, since 1964; Chairman, Ben Line Ship Management, since 1972; *b* 14 Feb. 1940; *s* of Sir James Douglas Wishart Thomson, 2nd Bt, and of Evelyn Margaret Isabel, (Bettina), *d* of Lt-Comdr D. W. S. Douglas, RN; *S* father, 1972; *m* 1967, Caroline Anne, *d* of Major Timothy Stuart Lewis; two *s* one *d*. *Educ:* Eton; University College, Oxford (BA Agric). Joined family business, Ben Line, 1961; Partner, Wm Thomson & Co., 1963-64. Member: Queen's Body Guard for Scotland, Royal Company of Archers. *Recreations:* farming, shooting. *Heir: s* Simon Douglas Charles Thomson, *b* 16 June 1969. *Address:* Glenbrook House, Balerno, Midlothian. *T:* 031-449 4116. *Club:* New (Edinburgh).

THOMSON, Garry; Scientific Adviser to the Trustees and Head of the Scientific Department, National Gallery, London, since 1960; *b* 13 Sept. 1925; *s* of Robert Thomson and Mona Spence; *m* 1954, M. R. Saisvasdi Svasti; four *s*. *Educ:* Charterhouse; Magdalene College, Cambridge (MA). Editorial Staff of A History of Technology, 1951; Research Chemist, National Gallery, 1955; Hon. Editor, Studies in Conservation (jl of Internat. Inst. for Conservation of Historic and Artistic Works), 1959-67. *Publications:* Recent Advances in Conservation (Ed.),

1963; Museum Climatology (Ed.), 1967; reviews and articles in Nature, Museums Journal, Studies in Conservation, etc. *Recreation:* underwater swimming. *Address:* Squire's Hill, Tilford, Surrey. *T:* Runfold 2206. *Club:* Athenæum.

THOMSON, Prof. George Derwent; Professor of Greek, University of Birmingham, 1937-70; *b* 19 Aug. 1903; *s* of William Henry and Minnie Thomson; *m* 1934, Katharine Fraser Stewart; two *d*. *Educ:* Dulwich College; King's College, Cambridge. Craven Student, University of Cambridge, 1926-27; Fellow of King's College, Cambridge, 1927-35 and 1934-36. Member, Czechoslovak Academy of Sciences, 1960-. *Publications:* Greek Lyric Metre, 1929 (new edn, 1960); Aeschylus, Prometheus Bound, 1932; M. O'Sullivan, Twenty Years A-Growing (trans. from the Irish), 1933 (World's Classics edition, 1953); Aeschylus, Oresteia, 2 vols, 1938 (new edn, 1966); Aeschylus and Athens, 1941 (new edn 1973); Marxism and Poetry, 1946 (new edn, 1954); Studies in Ancient Greek Society, Vol. I, The Prehistoric Aegean, 1949 (new edn 1973); Vol. II, The First Philosophers, 1955 (new edn, 1973); The Greek Language, 1960 (new edn, 1966); Geras: Studies Presented to G. T. on his Sixtieth Birthday, 1963; A Manual of Modern Greek, 1966; Palamas, Twelve Lays of the Gipsy, 1969; From Marx to Mao Tse-tung, 1971; Capitalism and After, 1973; The Human Essence, 1975; books in Irish and Greek and articles in learned and other journals; foreign editions of his books in 21 languages. *Address:* 58 Billesley Lane, Birmingham B13 9QS. *T:* 021-449 2656.

THOMSON, George Ewart; Director, C. E. Heath & Co. Ltd, 1941-69 (Chairman, 1959-66); *b* 7 May 1897; *s* of John and Alice Susanna Thomson; *m* 1930, Wilhelmina Marjory (née Morrison); three *s* one *d*. *Educ:* Caterham Sch., Surrey; Rastrick Grammar Sch., Yorks. Joined C. E. Heath & Co. Ltd, 1914. Served European War, 1914-18, Infantry, 1916-19. Member of Lloyd's, 1933; Director, C. E. Heath & Co. Ltd, 1941; Member Cttee of Lloyd's, 1945-63; Dep. Chairman of Lloyd's, 1956, Chairman of Lloyd's, 1961. Export Credits Guarantee Advisory Council, 1959-67. *Recreation:* golf. *Address:* Red Hatch, Ridgeway, Hutton, Brentwood, Essex. *T:* Brentwood 220070.

THOMSON, Rev. George Ian Falconer; Director of the Bible Reading Fellowship, 1968-77; *b* 2 Sept. 1912; *s* of Rev. G. D. Thomson, DD; *m* 1st, 1938, Hon. Bridget de Courcy (marr. diss. 1951), *e d* of 34th Baron Kingsale, DSO; one *d*; 2nd, 1952, Mary Josephine Lambart Dixon, OBE, *d* of Archdeacon H. T. Dixon, DD, Hereford; one *s*. *Educ:* Shrewsbury Sch.; Balliol Coll., Oxford (MA); Westcott House, Cambridge. Ellerton Theol Essay Prize, Oxford, 1936. Pilot, RAFO, 1932-37; Chaplain, RAFVR, 1942-46. Curate, St Luke's, Chelsea, 1936-37; Chaplain, Hertford Coll., Oxford, 1937-46, Junior Dean and Dean of Degrees, 1939-42; Rector of Hilgay, Norfolk, 1946-51; Sec. of Gen. Ordination Examn, 1946-52; Master, Maidstone Grammar Sch., 1951-62; Chaplain and Sen. Lectr, St Paul's Coll., Cheltenham, 1962-66; Exam. Chaplain to Bp of Gloucester, 1964-76; Vis. Lectr, McMaster Univ., Ont, 1964; Dir, research project, Conf. of British Missionary Socs, 1966-68; re-visited China during Cultural Revolution, 1967. Rowing Corresp., The Observer, 1938-65. Freeman, City of London. *Publications:* History of the Oxford Pastorate, 1946; Experiment in Worship, 1951; The Rise of Modern Asia, 1957; Changing Patterns in South Asia, 1961; Two Hundred School Assemblies, 1966; Mowbray's Mini-Commentary No 4, 1970. *Recreations:* rowing (Oxford Blue, 1934), travel, writing. *Address:* Jackson's Farm, Yarnton, Oxford. *Clubs:* Royal Air Force; Leander.

THOMSON, George Malcolm; Author and Journalist; *b* Leith, Scotland, 2 Aug. 1899; *e s* of Charles Thomson, journalist, and Mary Arthur, *d* of John Eason; *m* 1926, Else (d 1957), *d* of Harald Ellefsen, Tønsberg, Norway; one *s* one *d*; *m* 1963, Diana Van Cortland Robertson. *Educ:* Daniel Stewart's College, Edinburgh; Edinburgh University. Journalist. *Publications:* Caledonia, or the Future of the Scots, 1927; A Short History of Scotland, 1930; Crisis in Zanat, 1942; The Twelve Days, 1964; The Robbers Passing By, 1966; The Crime of Mary Stuart, 1967; Vote of Censure, 1968; A Kind of Justice, 1970; Sir Francis Drake, 1972; Lord Castlerosse, 1973; The North-West Passage, 1975; Warrior Prince: Prince Rupert of the Rhine, 1976. *Address:* 5 The Mount Square, NW3. *T:* 01-435 8775. *Clubs:* Garrick, Beefsteak.

THOMSON, Very Rev. Ian; *see* White-Thomson.

THOMSON, Sir Ivo Wilfrid Home, 2nd Bt, *cr* 1925; *b* 14 Oct. 1902; *s* of Sir Wilfrid Thomson, 1st Bt, and Ethel Henrietta, 2nd *d* of late Hon. Reginald Parker; *S* father 1939; *m* 1st, 1933, Sybil Marguerite (from whom he obt. a divorce), *yr d* of C. W. Thompson, The Red House, Escrick; one *s* and one *d* decd);

2nd, 1954, Viola Mabel (who *m* 1937, Keith Home Thomson, from whom she obt. a divorce), *d* of Roland Dudley, Linkenholt Manor, Andover. *Educ:* Eton. *Heir:* s Mark Wilfrid Home Thomson [*b* 29 Dec. 1939; *m* 1976, Lady Jacqueline Rufus Isaacs, *d* of 3rd Marquess of Reading, *qv*]. *Address:* Frilsham Manor, Hermitage, Newbury, Berks. *T:* Hermitage 201291.

THOMSON, Tun Sir James (Beveridge), KBE 1966; Kt 1959; *b* 24 March 1902, *e* s of late Rev. William Archibald Thomson, Dalmellington, Ayrshire; *m* 1931, Dr Florence Adam; one *s*. *Educ:* Dalmellington Village School; George Watson's College, Edinburgh; Edinburgh University. MA, 1st Cl. Hons History, Edin. Called to English Bar, Middle Temple, 1929; admitted Advocate in Scotland, 1955. District Officer, 1926 and Resident Magistrate, 1932, N Rhodesia; Judge, Fiji, Chief Justice of Tonga and a Judicial Commissioner for Western Pacific, 1945-48; Judge, Federation of Malaya, 1948; Chief Justice 1956; (first) Lord President of the Federal Court of Malaysia, 1963-66; (last) President of the High Court of S Arabia, 1967; Chm., Delimitation Commn, Republic of Botswana, 1968. Hon. Sheriff, Inverness, 1972. Meritorious Service Medal (Perak), 1957; Panglima Mangku Negara (Federation of Malaya), 1958; Seri Maharajah Mangku Negara (Malaysia), 1966. *Publications:* The Laws of the British Solomon Islands, 1948; The Law of Tonga, 1951. *Address:* Craig Gowan, Carr Bridge, Inverness-shire. *T:* Carr Bridge 257.
See also *W. A. R. Thomson*.

THOMSON, James Frederick Gordon; *see* Migdale, Hon. Lord.

THOMSON, Prof. James Leonard, CBE 1955; Professor Emeritus in Civil Engineering, Royal Military College of Science, Shrivenham, since 1970; *b* 9 Aug. 1905; *s* of James Thomson, Liverpool. *Educ:* University of Manchester; St John's College, Cambridge. Mather & Platt, Ltd, Manchester, 1923-26; Univ. of Manchester, 1926-30 (BSc (Tech.) 1st Cl. Hons and Stoney Prizeman); Lecturer, Technical College, Horwich, 1930-32; Whitworth Senior Scholar, 1931; St John's Coll., Cambridge, 1932-34 (BA 1934, MA 1938); Research Engineer, ICI, Billingham-on-Tees, 1934-38; Lecturer, Dept of Civil and Mechanical Engineering, Univ. of London, King's College, 1938. Seconded for War-time Service: Managing Engineer, HM Royal Ordnance Factory, Pembrey, Carms, 1940-42; Principal Technical Officer, School of Tank Technology, 1942-46. Royal Military College of Science, Shrivenham: Prof. of Mechanical Engrg and Head of Dept of Civil and Mechanical Engrg, 1946-61; Prof. of Civil Engrg and Head of Dept of Civil Engrg, 1965-70; seconded to ME Technical Univ., Ankara, Turkey, 1961-65: Consultant Dean and Mechanical Engrg Specialist; later Chief Technical Adviser for UNESCO project in Turkey. *Publications:* various scientific papers dealing with High Pressure Techniques. *Recreations:* mountaineering, sailing. *Address:* Astral House, Netherbury, Bridport, Dorset DT6 5LU.

THOMSON, Maj.-Gen. James Noel, CB 1946; DSO 1917; MC; *b* 25 Dec. 1888; *s* of James Thomson and Margaret Stuart; *m* 1929, Lorna Carmen, *d* of late Sir Edward Buck, CBE; no *c*. *Educ:* Fettes; RMA Woolwich. Senior Under Officer RMA Woolwich, 1909; Commissioned in Royal Field Artillery, 1909; European War France and Germany, 1914-19 (DSO, MC, despatches thrice, French Croix de Guerre); Adjutant Royal Military Academy, 1919-21; Staff College, Camberley, 1921; War Office, 1922-23; Brigade Major 1st Rhine Brigade, 1923-24; General Staff Rhine Army (Operations and Intelligence) 1924-25; Staff Officer to Major-General Royal Artillery, India, 1927-30; Lieut Colonel, 1929; idc 1932; Asst Master Gen. of the Ordnance in India, 1934-37; Col, 1935; Brig. RA, N Command, India, 1938-41; Comdr 6 Ind. Div., 1941; Temp. Maj.-Gen., 1942; Dep. Master Gen. of Ord. GHQ, India, 1943. ADC to the King, 1939; retired pay, 1946, with hon. rank of Maj.-Gen. *Recreations:* horses, racing. *Address:* c/o Meerut Race Club, Meerut, UP, India.

THOMSON, Sir John, KBE 1972; TD 1944; MA; Lord-Lieutenant of Oxfordshire since 1963; Director: Barclays Bank Ltd (Chairman, 1962-73); Union Discount Company of London Ltd, 1960-74; *b* 1908; *s* of late Guy Thomson, JP, Woodperry, Oxford; *m* 1935, Elizabeth, JP (*d* 1977), *d* of late Stanley Brotherton, JP, Thornhaugh Hall, Peterborough; no *c*. *Educ:* Winchester; Magdalen College, Oxford. Commanded Oxfordshire Yeomanry Regt, RATA, 1942-44 and 1947-50. Deputy High Steward of Oxford University; a Curator of Oxford University Chest, 1949-74; Chairman: Nuffield Medical Trustees; Nuffield Orthopædic Centre Trust. President, British Bankers' Association, 1964-66 (Vice-President, 1963-64); FIB. Mem. Royal Commn on Trade Unions and Employers' Assocs, 1965-68; Mem. BNEC, 1968-71. Hon. Fellow St Catherine's Coll., Oxford. Hon. Colonel: 299 Fd Regt RA (TA), 1964-67; Oxfordshire Territorials, 1967-75; Bt Col, 1950. DL Oxfordshire, 1947-57; High Sheriff of Oxfordshire, 1957; Vice-Lieut, 1957-63. A Steward, Jockey Club, 1974-. Hon. DCL Oxford, 1957. KStJ 1973. *Address:* Manor Farm House, Spelsbury, Oxford. *T:* Charlbury 266; Achnaba, Lochgilphead, Argyll. *T:* Lochgilphead 2537. *Club:* Cavalry and Guards.

THOMSON, John Adam, CMG 1972; HM Diplomatic Service; High Commissioner to India, since 1976; *b* 27 April 1927; *m* 1953, Elizabeth Anne McClure; three *s* one *d*. Foreign Office, 1950; Third Secretary, Jedda, 1951; Damascus, 1954; Foreign Office, 1955; Private Secretary to Permanent Under-Secretary, 1958-60; First Secretary, Washington, 1960-64; Foreign Office, 1964; Acting Head of Planning Staff, 1966; Counsellor, 1967; Head of Planning Staff, Foreign Office, 1967; seconded to Cabinet Office as Chief of Assessments Staff, 1968-71; Minister and Dep. Permanent Rep. to N Atlantic Council, 1972-73; Head of UK Delegn to MBFR Exploratory Talks, Vienna, 1973; Asst Under-Sec. of State, FCO, 1973-76. *Recreation:* castles. *Address:* c/o Foreign and Commonwealth Office, SW1; Lochpatrick Mill, Kirkpatrick Durham, Castle Douglas, Kirkcudbrightshire. *Club:* Athenæum.

THOMSON, John (Ian) Sutherland, CMG 1968; MBE 1944; Independent Chairman, Fiji Sugar Industry, since 1971, and Chairman, Fiji Coconut Board, since 1973; *b* 8 Jan. 1920; *s* of late William Sutherland Thomson and of Jessie McCaig Malloch; *m* 1945, Nancy Marguerite Kearsley, Suva, Fiji; seven *s* one *d*. *Educ:* High Sch. of Glasgow; Univ. of Glasgow (MA Hons). Served War of 1939-45: Black Watch, 1940; Fiji Military Forces, 1941-45 (Captain). Appointed Cadet, Colonial Administrative Service, Fiji and Western Pacific, 1941; District Administration and Secretariat, Fiji, 1946-54; Seconded to Colonial Office, 1954-56; Dep. Comr, Native Lands and Fisheries, Fiji, 1957-58; Comr of Native Reserves and Chairman, Native Lands and Fisheries Commission, Fiji, 1958-62; Divisional Commissioner, Fiji, 1963-66; Administrator, British Virgin Islands, 1967-71. *Recreations:* golf, tennis. *Address:* Honson Building, Thomson Street, GPO Box 644, Suva, Fiji.

THOMSON, Nigel Ernest Drummond; Sheriff of Lothian and Borders, at Edinburgh, since 1976; *b* 19 June 1926; *y* s of late Rev. James Kyd Thomson, and late Joan Drummond; *m* 1964, Snjólaug Magnússon, *yr d* of Consul-General Sigursteinn Magnússon; one *s* one *d*. *Educ:* George Watson's College, Edinburgh; Univs of St Andrews and Edinburgh. Served with Scots Guards and Indian Grenadiers, 1944-47. MA (St Andrews) 1950; LLB (Edin.) 1953. Called to Scottish Bar, 1953. Standing Counsel to Scottish Educn Dept, 1961-66; Sheriff of Lanarkshire, later S Strathclyde, Dumfries and Galloway, at Hamilton, 1966-76. Pres., Speculative Soc., Edinburgh, 1960. Chm., Strathaven Arts Guild. *Recreations:* music, woodwork, golf. *Address:* 5 Abinger Gardens, Edinburgh. *T:* 031-337 2066.

THOMSON, Peter; Sheriff of South Strathclyde, Dumfries and Galloway (formerly Lanarkshire) at Hamilton, 1962-77; *b* 1914; *s* of John Thomson, SSC, and Martha Lindsay Miller; *m* 1939, Jean Laird Nicoll; two *s* one *d*. *Educ:* Royal High School, Edinburgh; Edinburgh University. Gordon Highlanders, 1941-46; Capt. 1944. Called to Scottish Bar, 1946. Founded Scottish Plebiscite Society, 1947. Sheriff Substitute of Caithness, Sutherland, Orkney and Zetland, 1955. Chairman, Thistle Prize, 1964. *Recreations:* walking, golf. *Address:* Haughhead Farm House, Uddingston, Lanarkshire. *Club:* University (Aberdeen).

THOMSON, Robert Howard Garry; *see* Thomson, Garry.

THOMSON, Robert John Stewart, CMG 1969; MBE 1955; Ministry of Defence, since 1970; *b* 5 May 1922; *s* of late John Stewart Thomson, FRIBA, and Nellie Thomson (*née* Morris). *Educ:* Bromsgrove Sch.; Worcester Coll., Oxford. Service with Sudan Defence Force, 1943-45. Sudan Political Service, 1943-54 (District Commissioner, 1950-54). Attached Ministry of Defence, 1955-56; First Sec., British High Commission, Accra, 1956-60, 1962-64, Counsellor, 1966-69. *Recreations:* gardening, singing. *Address:* 75 Hill Rise, Rickmansworth, Herts WD3 2NT. *Clubs:* Royal Over-Seas League; Polo (Accra).

THOMSON, Air Vice-Marshal Ronald Bain, CB 1959; DSO 1943; DFC 1942; *b* 15 April 1912; *s* of George Thomson, Aberdeen, and Christina Ann (*née* Reid); *m* 1940, Elizabeth Napier (*née* Ayling); two *d*. *Educ:* Robert Gordon's College, Aberdeen. Joined Royal Auxiliary Air Force (612 County of Aberdeen Squadron), 1937. Senior Lecturer Physical Educ. and Hygiene, Pretoria Technical College, S Africa, 1939. War of 1939-45, Coastal Command. AOC, RAF, Gibraltar, 1958-60;

AOC, RAF, Scotland and Northern Ireland, 1960-63; AOA, Flying Training Command, 1963-66; retired. Member of the Queen's Body Guard for Scotland, The Royal Company of Archers. Commander Order of St Olav, 1963. *Recreations:* shooting, golf. *Club:* Royal Air Force.

THOMSON, Sir Ronald (Jordan), Kt 1950; Lord Lieutenant of Peeblesshire, 1956-68; *b* 13 March 1895; *s* of William Thomson, shipowner; *m* 1919, Patricia Martha Burrell Guild (*d* 1955); one *s* (one *d* decd). Commissioned Border Regiment, 1914; served European War, 1914-18; resigned commission on account of wounds, 1917. Elected Peeblesshire County Council, 1922; Convener of Peeblesshire, 1932-58; President, Association of County Councils in Scotland, 1948-50; Civil Defence Controller, Eastern Scotland, 1954-60; Chairman, Scottish Special Housing Association, 1952-62. JP 1922-69; DL 1930, VL 1945, Peeblesshire. *Address:* Kaimes, West Linton, Peeblesshire. *T:* West Linton 413.

THOMSON, Thomas Davidson, CMG 1962; OBE 1959; *b* 1 April 1911; *s* of J. A. Thomson, FFA, FRSE, and Barbara M. Davidson, Edinburgh; *m* 1947, Marjorie Constance, *d* of T. R. Aldred, Limbe, Nyasaland; one *s*. *Educ:* George Watson's Coll., Edinburgh; Edinburgh Univ. (MA, LLB); Magdalene Coll., Cambridge. Editor, The Student, 1932; Travel Secretary, Scottish National Union of Students, 1932; Cadet, Nyasaland Administration, 1934; Civil Demobilisation Officer, 1945; Assistant Secretary, Nyasaland, 1947; Officer in charge, Domasi Community Development Scheme, 1949; Officer in charge, School of Local Government, 1955, Social Development, 1958; retired as Commissioner for Social Development, Nyasaland, 1963. Carried out survey of Adult Education in Nyasaland, 1956-57; organised Nyasaland Council of Social Service, 1959. Served War of 1939-45, E Africa (Major). Sec., Eastern Border Development Assoc., 1962-67. Chairman: Scottish Community Development Cttee, 1968-75; Berwicks Council of Social Service, 1971-75; Hon. Vice-Pres., Scottish Council of Social Service, 1976-. Pres., Berwickshire Naturalists' Club, 1969-70. Vice-Pres., Soc. of Antiquaries of Scotland, 1971-74. Brain of Britain, BBC Radio, 1969. *Publications:* A Practical Approach to Chinyanja, 1947; Coldingham Priory, 1973; sundry reports and papers on Nyasaland affairs; papers in Hist. Berwickshire Naturalists' Club; sundry papers in philatelic jls. *Recreations:* gardening, philately, contemplative archaeology, Scouting (Chief Commissioner, Nyasaland, 1958; County Commissioner, Berwickshire, 1966-75). *Address:* The Hill, Coldingham, Berwickshire. *T:* Coldingham 209. *Club:* Caledonian (Edinburgh).

THOMSON, William Archibald Robson, MD; FRCPEd; Editor of The Practitioner, 1944-73; Medical Correspondent, The Times, 1956-71; Medical Consultant, The Daily Telegraph; Chairman: The Leprosy Study Centre; Council, Sesame; Deputy Chairman, Executive Council, British Academy of Forensic Sciences; *b* 6 Nov. 1906; 2nd *s* of late Rev. W. A. Thomson; *m* 1934, Marion Lucy Nannette, *d* of late Sir Leonard Hill, FRS; two *s*. *Educ:* Dalmellington HGP Sch.; Wigan Grammar Sch.; University of Edinburgh. MB, ChB 1929, MD (Hons), 1933, University of Edinburgh; FRCPEd 1976. Clin. Asst, Ho. Phys. and Clin. Tutor, Royal Infirmary, Edinburgh; Asst, Dept of Medicine, also Davidson Research Fellow in Applied Bacteriology, Univ. of Edinburgh; Surg. Lieut, RN, seconded for res. work on deep diving; Paterson Research Scholar and Chief Asst, Cardiac Dept, London Hospital; First Assistant, Medical Unit, St Thomas' Hospital. FRSocMed; FRIPHH; Founder Member, The British Academy of Forensic Sciences. Bengué Meml Award Lectr, RIPH&H; Cavendish Lectr, W London Medico-Chirurgical Soc., 1975. Abercrombie Award, RCGP, 1973. *Publications:* Black's Medical Dictionary, 31st edn 1976; Thomson's Concise Medical Dictionary, 1973; The Searching Mind in Medicine, 1960; (ed) The Practitioner's Handbook, 1960; (ed) Practical Dietetics, 1960; (ed) Calling the Laboratory, 3rd edn, 1971; (ed) The Doctor's Surgery, 1964; (ed) Sex and Its Problems, 1968; Herbs That Heal, 1976; A Dictionary of Medical Ethics and Practice, 1977; contribs to: Gradwohl's Legal Medicine, 3rd edn 1976; Encyclopaedia Britannica, 14th and 15th edns; various articles on medical and cardiological subjects in Quarterly Journal of Medicine, British Heart Jl, Lancet, etc. *Address:* 4 Rutland Court, Queens Drive, W3 0HL. *T:* 01-992 8685. *Club:* Athenæum.
See also Tun Sir James Thomson.

THOMSON, William Oliver, MD, DPH, DIH; Chief Administrative Medical Officer, Lanarkshire Health Board, since 1973; *b* 23 March 1925; *s* of William Crosbie Thomson and Mary Jolie Johnston; *m* 1956, Isobel Lauder Glendinning Brady; two *s*. *Educ:* Allan Glen's Sch., Glasgow; Univ. of Glasgow (MB ChB, MD). DPA; FFCM. Captain, RAMC, 1948-50.

Hospital appointments, 1951-53; appointments in Public Health, Glasgow, 1953-60; Admin. MO, Western Regional Hospital Bd, 1960-70; Group Medical Superintendent, Glasgow Maternity and Women's Hospitals, 1970-73. *Publications:* articles on clinical medicine, community medicine, general practice, occupational health and health education, in various medical jls. *Recreations:* walking, talking, writing. *Address:* 14 Stewarton Drive, Cambuslang, Glasgow G72 8DF. *T:* 041-641 2300.

THONEMANN, Peter Clive, MSc, DPhil; Professor and Head of Department of Physics, University College, Swansea, since 1968; *b* 3 June 1917. *Educ:* Melbourne Grammar Sch., Melbourne; Sydney and Oxford Univs. BSc Melbourne, 1940; MSc Sydney, 1945; DPhil Oxford, 1949. Munition Supply Laboratories, Victoria, Australia, 1940; Amalgamated Wireless, Australia, 1942; University of Sydney, Commonwealth Research Fellow, 1944; Clarendon Laboratory, Oxford, ICI Research Fellow, 1946; United Kingdom Atomic Energy Authority, 1949; Dep. Dir, Culham Laboratory, 1967-68. *Address:* Department of Physics, University College, Swansea, Singleton Park, Swansea, Wales; 33 Cumnor Hill, Oxford.

THORLEY, Charles Graham; Specialist Adviser, House of Lords, since 1975; *b* 4 Jan. 1914; *s* of Charles Lord Thorley; *m* 1958, Peggy Percival Ellis (*née* Boor); one step *s* one step *d*. *Educ:* Manchester Grammar Sch.; King's Coll., Cambridge (Mod. Lang. Scholar). Served War of 1939-45, Eritrea and Cyrenaica (Lt-Col). Entered Civil Service as Economist, Bd of Trade, 1936; attached to British Embassy, China, 1936-38; Mem. British Economic Mission to Belgian Congo, 1940-41; HM Treasury, 1940-57; served on UK financial delegns and missions in Japan, US, Egypt, France, Switzerland, W Germany, etc; Min. of Power, 1957; Under-Secretary and Head of Coal Div., 1965-69; Acct-Gen. and Dir of Finance, 1969. Chm., NATO Petroleum Planning Cttee, 1962-65; Under-Sec., Min. of Technology and DTI, 1969-74. *Recreation:* travel. *Address:* Preston House, Corton Denham, Sherborne, Dorset DT9 4LS. *T:* Corton Denham 269. *Club:* United Oxford & Cambridge University.

THORLEY, Sir Gerald (Bowers), Kt 1973; TD; Chairman: Allied Breweries Ltd, 1970-75; British Sugar Corporation Ltd since 1968; MEPC Ltd, since 1976; Vice-Chairman, Rockware Group Ltd, since 1976; Director, British-American Tobacco Industries Ltd; *b* 26 Aug. 1913; *s* of Clement Thorley and Ethel May Davy; *m* 1947, Beryl Preston, *d* of G. Preston Rhodes; one *s* one *d*. *Educ:* Ratcliffe College. FRICS. FRSA. Served War of 1939-45, RA; BEF, 1939-40; Malaya, 1941; POW, 1942-45. Ind Coope & Allsopp Ltd, 1936. Underwriting Member of Lloyd's, 1952. *Recreations:* gardening, golf. *Address:* Church House, Bale, Fakenham, Norfolk. *T:* Thursford 314. *Club:* Naval and Military.

THORN, John Leonard, MA; Headmaster of Winchester College since 1968; *b* 28 April 1925; *s* of late Stanley L. Thorn and of Winifred M. Thorn (*née* King); *m* 1955, Veronica Laura, *d* of late Sir Robert Maconochie, OBE, QC; one *s* one *d*. *Educ:* St Paul's School; Corpus Christi College, Cambridge. Served War of 1939-45, Sub-Lieutenant, RNVR, 1943-46. 1st Class Historical Tripos, Parts I and II, 1948-49; Assistant Master, Clifton College, 1949-61 (Head of History Dept, 1951-58, Housemaster, 1958-61); Headmaster, Repton School, 1961-68. Dir, Royal Opera House, Covent Garden, 1971-76. *Publication:* (joint) A History of England, 1961. *Address:* Headmaster's House, Winchester College, Winchester. *T:* 4328. *Club:* Garrick.

THORN, Sir Jules, Kt 1964; President of Thorn Electrical Industries Limited, since 1976 (Chairman 1937-76, Managing Director, 1937-69); other companies are included in the Thorn Group. Chairman, Radio Industry Council, 1966. Hon. Master of the Bench, Middle Temple, 1969. President: British Radio Equipment Manufacturers' Assoc., 1964-68; Conf. of Electronics Industry, 1971; Mem., Sch. Council, UCH Med. Sch. FRSA; CIEE; Hon. FIES. *Recreations:* travelling, reading, music. *Address:* Thorn Electrical Industries Limited, Thorn House, Upper St Martins Lane, WC2H 9ED. *T:* 01-836 2444.

THORNE, Rear-Adm. Edward Courtney, CB 1975; CBE 1971; Chief of Naval Staff, New Zealand, 1972-75, retired; *b* 29 Oct. 1923; *s* of Ernest Alexander Thorne and Ethel Violet Thorne; *m* 1949, Fay Bradburn (*née* Kerr); three *s*. *Educ:* Nelson Coll., NZ. Joined RNZN, 1941. Mem. Nat. Council, Duke of Edinburgh Award Scheme. Mem. Nat. Council, United World Colls. *Recreations:* golf, gardening. *Address:* 75 Hatton Street, Karori, Wellington 5, New Zealand. *Club:* Wellington (New Zealand).

THORNE, Rt. Rev. Frank Oswald, CBE 1957; DD; *b* 21 May 1892; *s* of Leonard Temple Thorne and Ada Theodosia Franklin; unmarried. *Educ:* St Paul's School; Christ Church, Oxford (Scholar). 2nd Class Hon. Mods, 1913; BA (War Degree), 1918; 2nd Class Theology, 1921; MA 1935; Served European War, 13th (S) Bn The Manchester Regt, Captain and Adjutant, 1915-17; Brigade Major, No 1 Section Tyne Garrison, 1918-19 (wounded, MC); Ordained, 1922; Curate All Souls' Clapton Park, 1922-25; joined Universities Mission to Central Africa, 1925; First Warden of S Cyprian's Theological Coll., Tunduru, Diocese of Masasi, Tanganyika Territory, 1930-34; Bishop of Nyasaland, 1936-61; Dean of Prov. of Central Africa, 1955-61. MLC Nyasaland, 1937-43, 1946-49. DD Lambeth, 1958. *Address:* College of St Barnabas, Blackberry Lane, Lingfield, Surrey.

THORNE, Peter Francis, CBE 1966; Serjeant at Arms, House of Commons, since 1976; *b* 1914; *y s* of late Gen. Sir Andrew Thorne, KCB, CMG, DSO; *m* 1959, Lady Anne Pery, MA, DPhil, Senior Lecturer, Imperial College of Science and Technology, *d* of 5th Earl of Limerick, GBE, CH, KCB, DSO, TD; one *s* three *d. Educ:* Eton; Trinity Coll., Oxford. Served War of 1939-45: with 3rd Bn Grenadier Guards (wounded), 1939-41; HQ 2nd Div., 1941-42; Staff College, Quetta, 1942; on staff of India Command and HQ, SACSEA, 1943-45; demobilised with rank of Hon. Lieut-Col, 1946. With Imperial Chemical Industries Ltd, 1946-48. Assistant Serjeant at Arms, House of Commons, 1948-57, Dep. Serjeant at Arms, 1957-76. *Address:* Speaker's Green, House of Commons, SW1. *T:* 01-219 4774. *Clubs:* Cavalry and Guards; Royal Yacht Squadron.
See also Dowager Countess of Limerick.

THORNE, Robin Horton John, CMG 1966; OBE 1963; HM Overseas Service, retired; with Vice-Chancellors' Committee, 1967-77; *b* 13 July 1917; *s* of late Sir John Anderson Thorne; *m* 1946, Joan Helen Wadman; one *s. Educ:* Dragon Sch., Oxford; Rugby (open scholar); Exeter College, Oxford (open scholar). War Service, Devonshire Regiment and King's African Rifles, 1939-46. Colonial Administrative Service (now HM Overseas Civil Service), 1946-67; Tanganyika Administration, 1946-58; Aden, 1958-67; Asst Chief Sec. (Colony), MLC and Mem. of Governor's Exec. Coun., 1959-63; Ministerial Sec. to Chief Minister, 1963-65; Assistant High Commissioner, 1966-67. Trustee of Aden Port Trust, 1959-66. *Recreations:* various. *Address:* The Old Vicarage, Old Heathfield, East Sussex. *T:* Heathfield 3160. *Club:* Royal Commonwealth Society.

THORNE, Stanley George; MP (Lab) Preston South since Feb. 1974; *b* 22 July 1918; *s* of postman and dressmaker; *m* Catherine Mary Rand; two *s* three *d. Educ:* Ruskin Coll., Oxford; Univ. of Liverpool. Dip. Social Studies Oxon 1968; BA Hons Liverpool 1970. 30 yrs in industry and commerce: coal-miner, semi-skilled fitter, chartered accountant's clerk, rly signalman, office manager, auditor, commercial manager, etc; lectr in govt and industrial sociology. *Recreations:* chess, bridge, golf. *Address:* 17A Chislehurst Avenue, Liverpool L25 2SG. *T:* (office) 01-219 4183.

THORNELY, Gervase Michael Cobham; Headmaster of Sedbergh School, 1954-75; *b* 21 Oct. 1918; *er s* of Major J. E. B. Thornely, OBE, and Hon. Mrs M. H. Thornely; *m* 1954, Jennifer Margery, *d* of Sir Hilary Scott, *qv*, Knowle House, Addington, Surrey; two *s* two *d. Educ:* Rugby Sch.; Trinity Hall, Cambridge. Organ Scholar; 2nd Cl. Hons, Modern and Mediæval Languages Tripos; BA, 1940; MA, 1944. FRSA 1968. Assistant Master, Sedbergh School, 1940. *Recreations:* music, fly-fishing. *Address:* High Stangerthwaite, Killington, Cumbria. *T:* Sedbergh 20444. *Club:* East India, Devonshire, Sports and Public Schools.

THORNEYCROFT, family name of **Baron Thorneycroft.**

THORNEYCROFT, Baron *cr* 1967 (Life Peer), of Dunston; **(George Edward) Peter Thorneycroft,** PC 1951; Barrister-at-law; late RA; Chairman of the Conservative Party, since 1975; Chairman: Pye Holdings; Pye of Cambridge Ltd; Pirelli General Ltd; Pirelli Ltd; Trust Houses Forte Ltd; Director, Securicor; *b* 26 July 1909; *s* of late Major George Edward Mervyn Thorneycroft, DSO, and Dorothy Hope, *d* of Sir W. Franklyn, KCB; *m* 1st, 1938, Sheila Wells Page (who obtained a divorce, 1949); one *s* ; 2nd, 1949, Countess Carla Roberti; one *d. Educ:* Eton; Roy. Mil. Acad., Woolwich. Commissioned in Royal Artillery, 1930; resigned Commission, 1933; called to Bar, Inner Temple, 1935; practised Birmingham (Oxford Circuit); MP (C) Stafford, 1938-45, Monmouth, 1945-66. Parliamentary Secretary, Ministry of War Transport, 1945. President of the Board of Trade, October 1951-January 1957; Chancellor of the Exchequer, Jan. 1957-Jan. 1958, resigned; Minister of Aviation,

July 1960-July 1962; Minister of Defence, 1962-64; Secretary of State for Defence, Apr.-Oct. 1964. Chairman: SITPRO, 1968-75; BOTB, 1972-75. Exhibitions of paintings, Trafford Gallery, 1961, 1970. Associate, Royal Soc. of British Artists, 1977. *Address:* House of Lords, SW1. *T:* 01-219 4093. *Club:* Army and Navy.

THORNHILL, Lt-Col Edmund Basil, MC 1918; Vice-Lieutenant of Cambridgeshire and Isle of Ely, 1965-75; *b* 27 Feb. 1898; *e s* of late E. H. Thornhill, Manor House, Boxworth, Cambridge; *m* 1934, Diana Pearl Day, *d* of late Hubert G. D. Beales, Hambleden and Cambridge; two *s* one *d. Educ:* St Bees School; Royal Military Academy. 2nd Lieut Royal Artillery, 1916; served European War, 1914-18, France and Belgium (wounded, MC); served War of 1939-45, France, Western Desert (Eighth Army) and Italy (despatches); psc 1934; Lt-Col 1945; retd 1948. Chm., Cambs and I of Ely TA & AFA, 1957-62. DL Cambs and Isle of Ely, 1956. *Address:* Manor House, Boxworth, Cambridge. *T:* Elsworth 209. *Club:* Army and Navy.

THORNLEY, Sir Colin (Hardwick), KCMG 1957 (CMG 1953); CVO 1954; *b* 1907; *s* of late Dr and Mrs J. H. Thornley; *m* 1940, Muriel Betty Hobson; one *s* two *d. Educ:* Bramcote School, Scarborough; Uppingham; Brasenose College, Oxford. MA (hons jurisp.). Colonial Administrative Service, The Tanganyika Territory, 1930-39, seconded to Colonial Office, 1939-45; Principal Private Secretary to Secretary of State for the Colonies, 1941-45; Admin. Secretary, Kenya, 1945-47; Dep. Chief Secretary, Kenya, 1947-52; Chief Secretary, Govt of Protectorate of Uganda, 1952-55; Governor and Commander-in-Chief, British Honduras, 1955-61; retired, 1962. Dir-Gen., Save the Children Fund, 1965-74 (Dep. Dir, 1963-65). Mem., Regional Boundaries Commn, Kenya, 1962; Trustee, Imp. War Museum, 1968-77. *Recreations:* lawn tennis, golf, cricket. *Address:* Spinaway Cottage, Church Lane, Slindon, near Arundel, West Sussex. *T:* Slindon 308. *Clubs:* East India, Devonshire, Sports and Public Schools, Royal Commonwealth Society.

THORNTON, Dr (Clara) Grace, CBE 1964 (OBE 1959); MVO 1957; Secretary, Women's National Commission, Cabinet Office, since 1973; *b* 27 June 1913; *d* of late Arthur Augustus Thornton and Clara Maud Hines; unmarried. *Educ:* Kettering High School; Newnham Coll., Cambridge (MA, PhD). Research: Iceland, Cambridge, 1935-39. Min. of Information, 1940-45. Press Attaché, Copenhagen, 1945-48; Vice-Consul, Reykjavik, 1948-51 (Chargé d'Affaires during 1949 and 1950); Foreign Office, 1951-54; 1st Sec. and Consul, Copenhagen, 1954-60; 1st Sec. and Information Officer, Brussels, 1960-62; 1st Sec. and Consul, Djakarta, 1962-64 (Consul-General, 1963-64); Consul-General, Lisbon, 1965-70; Head of Consular Dept, FCO, 1970-73. Associate Fellow, Newnham Coll., Cambridge, 1972-. President: London Assoc. of University Women, 1974-; Associates of Newnham Coll., 1975-. FRSA 1969. Danish Freedom Medal, 1945; Order of Dannebrog, 1957. *Publications:* (trans. and ed) A Visit to Portugal, by Hans Christian Andersen, 1972; (trans. and ed) A Visit to Spain, by Hans Christian Andersen, 1975. *Recreations:* music, embroidery, Scandinavica, cats. *Address:* 17 Onslow Court, Drayton Gardens, SW10. *T:* 01-373 2965. *Club:* University Women's (Chm. 1976-).

THORNTON, Ernest, MBE 1951; JP; DL; *b* Burnley, Lancs, 18 May 1905; *s* of Charles Thornton and Margaret (*née* Whittaker); *m* 1930, Evelyn, *d* of Fred Ingham, Blacko, Nelson; one *s* (and one *s* decd). *Educ:* Walverden Council Sch., Nelson, Lancs. Cotton weaver, 1918-26; costing clerk, 1926-29. Rochdale Weavers and Winders' Assoc.; Asst Secretary, 1929-40, Secretary, 1940-70. President, Amalgamated Weavers' Assoc., 1960-65. Secretary, United Textile Factory Workers' Assoc., 1943-53. Member: Lord President's Advisory Council for Scientific and Industrial Research, 1943-48; Council of British Cotton Industry Research Assoc., 1948-53. MP (Lab) Farnworth, 1952-70; Joint Parliamentary Secretary, Min. of Labour, 1964-66. Member: UK Trade Mission to China, 1946; Anglo-American Cotton Textile Mission to Japan, 1950; Cotton Board's Mission to India, 1950. Mayor of County Borough of Rochdale, 1942-43. Comp. TI 1966. JP 1944. DL Manchester Metropolitan County (formerly Lancaster), 1970. *Address:* 31 Lynnwood Drive, Rochdale, Lancs. *T:* Rochdale 31954.

THORNTON, George Edwin, CMG 1948; MBE 1932; *b* 1899; *m* 1926, Charlotte, *d* of Edward Brian Coulson. Served European War 1914-18, in E Africa, 1916-17; Colonial Service, Northern Rhodesia, 1918; Financial Secretary, Northern Rhodesia, 1945-51. *Address:* 79 Kew Drive, Highlands, Salisbury, Rhodesia.

THORNTON, Dr Grace; *see* Thornton, Dr C. G.

THORNTON, Jack Edward Clive, OBE 1964 (MBE 1945); Chief Education Adviser and Under-Secretary, Ministry of Overseas Development (formerly Overseas Development Administration in the Foreign and Commonwealth Office), since 1970; *b* 22 Nov. 1915; *s* of late Stanley Henry Thornton and Elizabeth Daisy (*née* Baxter). *Educ:* Solihull Sch.; Christ's Coll., Cambridge (Open Exhibnr 1936). Cert. Educn 1939; MA 1942. Served in RASC, 1939-46 (despatches, 1946); Lt-Col 1944. Teaching in UK, 1946-47; Asst, then Dep. Educn Officer, City of York, 1947-51; Asst Educn Officer, WR Yorks, 1951-54; Dep. Dir of Educn, Cumberland, 1954-62; Sec., Bureau for External Aid for Educn, Fed. Govt of Nigeria, 1962-64; Educn Consultant, IBRD, 1964-65; Adviser on Educn in W Africa and Controller Appts Div., British Council, 1965-68; Dep. Educn Adviser, Min. of Overseas Develt, 1968-70. Governor: Imperial Coll. of Science and Technology; SOAS; Member: Commonwealth Scholarship Commn; Inter-Univ. Council for Higher Educn Overseas; Bd, Technical Educn and Training Orgn for Overseas Countries. *Recreations:* books, mountains, music, travel. *Address:* 131 Dalling Road, W6 0ET. *T:* 01-748 7692.

THORNTON, Lt.-Gen. Sir Leonard (Whitmore), KCB 1967 (CB 1962); CBE 1957 (OBE 1944); Chairman, Alcoholic Liquor Advisory Council; *b* Christchurch, 15 Oct. 1916; *s* of late Cuthbert John Thornton and Frances Caverhill Thornton; *m* 1942, Gladys Janet Sloman, Wellington; three *s*; *m* 1971, Ruth Leicester, Wellington. *Educ:* Christchurch Boys' High Sch.; Royal Military Coll., Duntroon, Australia. Commissioned in New Zealand Army, 1937. Served War of 1939-45 (despatches twice, OBE), Middle East and Italy in 2nd New Zealand Expeditionary Force; Commander, Royal Artillery, 2 New Zealand Division. Commander, Tokyo Sub-area, 1946; Deputy Chief of General Staff, 1948; idc 1952; Head, New Zealand Joint Service Liaison Staff, 1953 and 1954; QMG, New Zealand, 1955; AG, 1956-58; Chief, SEATO Planning Office, Thailand, 1958-59; Chief of General Staff, NZ, 1960-65; Chief of Defence Staff, NZ, 1965-71; Ambassador for New Zealand in S Vietnam and Khmer Republic, 1972-74. *Recreation:* fishing. *Address:* 67 Bedford Street, Wellington 5, New Zealand. *Clubs:* Wellington, United Services Officers (Wellington).

THORNTON, Michael James, MC 1942; Chief of Economic Intelligence Department, Bank of England, 1967-78; *b* 6 Dec. 1919; *s* of late Arthur Bruce Thornton and Dorothy Kidston Thornton (*née* Allsop); *m* 1949, Pauline Elizabeth Heppell; one *s* two *d*. *Educ:* Christ's Hospital; London Sch. of Economics (BSc(Econ)). Entered Bank of England, 1938; Deputy Chief Cashier, 1962-67. *Recreation:* sailing. *Address:* Vaughans, Church Square, Shere, Guildford, Surrey GU5 9HG.

THORNTON, Sir Peter (Eustace), KCB 1974 (CB 1971); Director: Hill Samuel Group, Courtaulds, Rolls Royce, since 1977; Permanent Secretary, Department of Trade, 1974-77; *b* 28 Aug. 1917; *s* of Douglas Oscar Thornton and Dorothy (*née* Shepherd); *m* 1946, Rosamond Hobart Myers, US Medal of Freedom, Sewanee, Tennessee; two *s* one *d*. *Educ:* Charterhouse; Gonville and Caius Coll., Cambridge. Served with RA, mainly in Middle East and Italy, 1940-46. Joined Board of Trade, 1946. Secretary, Company Law Cttee (Jenkins Cttee), 1959-62; Assistant Under-Secretary of State, Department of Economic Affairs, 1964-67; Under-Sec., 1967-70, Dep. Sec., 1970-72, Cabinet Office, with central co-ordinating role during British negotiations for membership of EEC; Dep. Sec., DTI, March-July 1972; Sec. (Aerospace and Shipping), DTI, 1972-74; Second Permanent Sec., Dept of Trade, 1974. *Recreations:* sailing, walking. *Address:* 22 East Street, Alresford, Hants SO24 9EE. *T:* Alresford 3010. *Club:* United Oxford & Cambridge University.

THORNTON, Peter Kai, FSA 1976; Keeper Department of Furniture and Woodwork, Victoria and Albert Museum, London, since 1966; *b* 8 April 1925; *s* of Sir Gerard Thornton, FRS, and of Gerda, *d* of Kai Nørregaard, Copenhagen; *m* 1950, Mary Ann Rosamund, *d* of E. A. P. Helps, Cregane, Rosscarbery, Co. Cork; three *d*. *Educ:* Bryanston Sch.; De Havilland Aeronautical Technical Sch.; Trinity Hall, Cambridge. Served with Army, Intelligence Corps, Austria, 1945-48; Cambridge, 1948-50; Voluntary Asset Keeper, Fitzwilliam Museum, Cambridge, 1950-52; Joint Secretary, National Art-Collections Fund, London, 1952-54; entered Victoria and Albert Museum as Asst Keeper, Dept of Textiles, 1954; transf. to Dept of Woodwork, 1962. *Publications:* Baroque and Rococo Silks, 1965; contribs to several joint works including World Furniture, 1965; articles on textiles and furniture in Burlington Magazine, Gazette des Beaux Arts and other journals. *Address:* 15 Cheniston Gardens, W8. *T:* 01-937 8868; Carrigillihy, Union Hall, Co. Cork; Phillips Farm Cottage, Eaton Hastings, Faringdon, Oxon.

THORNTON, Robert John; Assistant Under Secretary of State and Director General of Supplies and Transport (Naval), Ministry of Defence, since 1977; *b* 23 Dec. 1919; *s* of Herbert John Thornton and Ethel Mary Thornton (*née* Dunning); *m* 1944, Joan Elizabeth Roberts; three *s*. *Educ:* Queen Elizabeth Grammar School, Atherstone. MBIM 1970. Joined Naval Store Dept, Admiralty, as Asst Naval Store Officer, 1938; Singapore, 1941; Dep. Naval Store Officer, Colombo, 1942; Support Ship Hong Siang, 1943; Naval Store Officer, Admiralty, 1945; Gibraltar, 1951; Asst Dir of Stores, 1955; Superintending Naval Store Officer, Portsmouth, 1960; Dep. Dir of Stores, 1964; Dir of Victualling, 1971; Dir of Supplies and Transport (General Stores and Victualling), 1971. *Recreations:* squash, fly fishing, gardening. *Address:* 6 Peppercorn Orchard, Great Hinton, near Trowbridge, Wilts.

THORNTON, Robert Ribblesdale, CBE 1973; DL; solicitor; Member, Local Government Boundary Commission for England, since 1976; *b* 2 April 1913; *s* of Thomas Thornton and Florence Thornton (*née* Gatenby); *m* 1940, Ruth Eleonore Tuckson; one *s* one *d*. *Educ:* Leeds Grammar Sch.; St John's Coll., Cambridge (MA, LLB). Asst Solicitor, Leeds, 1938-40 and 1946-47. Served War, 1940-46. Asst Solicitor, Bristol, 1947-53; Dep. Town Clerk, Southampton, 1953-54; Town Clerk: Salford, 1954-66; Leicester, 1966-73; Chief Exec., Leicester CC, 1973-76. Pres., Soc. of Town Clerks, 1971. DL Leicestershire 1974. French Croix de Guerre, 1946. *Recreations:* music, sport. *Address:* Brackenfell, 6 Mill Road, Woodhouse Eaves, Leics LE12 8RD. *T:* Woodhouse Eaves 890646. *Club:* National Liberal.

THORNTON, Sir Ronald (George), Kt 1965; a Director, Bank of England, 1966-70; *b* 21 July 1901; *s* of late Henry George Thornton; *m* 1927, Agnes Margaret (*née* Masson); one *s* one *d*. *Educ:* St Dunstan's Coll., Catford. Director, Barclays Bank Ltd, 1961 (General Manager, 1946; Vice-Chairman, 1962-66); formerly Director: Friends' Provident & Century Life Office; The Century Insurance Co. Ltd; Century Insurance Trust Ltd; United Dominions Trust Ltd, 1962-71; Member: Cttee of Inquiry on Decimal Currency, 1961-62; Export Council for Europe, 1960-64; Chairman: Exec. Cttee, Banking Inf. Service, 1962-66; Bank Education Service, 1965-66. FRSA 1971. Fellow, Inst. of Bankers. *Address:* South Bank, Rectory Lane, Brasted, Westerham, Kent TN16 1JU.

THORNTON, Colonel Thomas Anson, CVO 1939; Order of Sword of Sweden, 1935; *b* 1887; *s* of late T. W. Thornton, JP, Brockhall, Northampton; *m* 1916, Constance Maude Stuart (*d* 1964); *d* of late Sir S. Fraser, KCSI, CIE; two *d* (*er s* killed in action, 1944; *yr s* decd 1951). *Educ:* Harrow; RMC, Sandhurst. Joined 7th Hussars, 1906; served European War, 1914-19 with 7th Hussars and in Afghanistan on Staff, 1919; Lt-Col Commanding 7th Hussars, 1927-31; re-employed, 1940-44. Equerry to Prince Arthur of Connaught, 1932-38; High Sheriff of Northamptonshire for 1946-47; DL Northamptonshire, 1947; Colonel of 7th Hussars, 1948-52. *Address:* Brockhall, Northampton. *T:* Weedon 40445. *Club:* Cavalry and Guards.

THORNTON-DUESBERY, Rev. Canon Julian Percy, MA; Canon-Theologian at Liverpool Cathedral, since 1968; *b* 7 Sept. 1902; *s* of late Rt Rev. Charles Leonard Thornton-Duesbery (formerly Bishop of Sodor and Man) and late Ethel Nixon Baumgartner. *Educ:* Forest Sch., Snaresbrook; Rossall Sch.; Balliol Coll., Oxford (Domus Exhbn); Wycliffe Hall, Oxford. Goldsmiths' Exhibition, 1922; *prox acc* Craven Scholarship, 1922; 1st Class Hon. Moderations (Classics), 1923; 1st Class Lit Hum 1925; 1st Class Theology, 1926; Junior Canon Hall Greek Testament Prize, 1926; Senior Denyer and Johnson Scholarship, 1928; Deacon, 1926; Priest, 1927; Chaplain of Wycliffe Hall, Oxford, 1926-27; Vice-Principal, 1927-33; Chaplain, Fellow, and Librarian of Corpus Christi Coll., Oxford, 1928-33; Headmaster of St George's Sch., Jerusalem, 1933-40; Master of St Peter's Hall, 1940-45; Rector of St Peter-le-Bailey, Oxford, 1940-45, 1955-61; Acting Principal, Wycliffe Hall, 1943-44; Principal of Wycliffe Hall, Oxford, 1944-55; Master, St Peter's Coll. (formerly St Peter's Hall), Oxford, 1955-68, Hon. Fellow, 1968. Commissary to Bishop in Jerusalem, 1943-63; Member of Council: St Lawrence Coll., Ramsgate, 1941-; Headington Sch., 1943-74; Forest Sch., Snaresbrook, 1958-68; St Stephen's Coll., Broadstairs, 1970-77. Examining Chaplain to: Bishop of Blackburn, 1927-33; Bishop in Jerusalem, 1933-40; Bishop of Worcester, 1941-70; Bishop of Oxford, 1955-68; Bishop of Sodor and Man, 1967-. Select Preacher, University of Oxford, 1943-45. *Publication:* The Open Secret of MRA, 1964. *Recreation:* walking. *Address:* 26 Beech Court, Allerton Road, Liverpool L18 3JZ. *T:* 051-724 4958; Hillside Cottage, Corony Hill, Maughold, Isle of Man. *T:* Ramsey, IoM 3020.

THORNYCROFT, John Ward, CBE 1957; CEng; FIMechE; beef farmer; Hon. President, John I. Thornycroft & Co. Ltd, since 1966 (Chairman, 1960-66; Managing Director, 1942-66); Director, Southampton, Isle of Wight and South of England Royal Mail Steam Packet Co. Ltd, since Jan. 1961; *b* 14 Oct. 1899; *s* of late Sir John E. Thornycroft; *m* 1930, Esther Katherine, *d* of J. E. Pritchard; one *s* one *d. Educ:* Royal Naval Colleges, Osborne, Dartmouth and Keyham; Trinity Coll., Cambridge. Served War, 1914-18, HMS Canada, HMS Opal, HM Submarine G10, HMS Spenser (1914-15 War Service Star). Hon. Vice-Pres., RINA; FRSA. *Recreations:* golf, sailing and gardening. *Address:* Steyne, Bembridge, Isle of Wight. *T:* Bembridge 2502. *Clubs:* Naval and Military; Bembridge Sailing (IOW).
See also Baron Inverforth .

THOROGOOD, Kenneth Alfred Charles; Executive Chairman, Tozer Kemsley & Millbourn (Holdings) Ltd, international finance and investment group, since 1972; *b* 1924; *s* of Albert Jesse and Alice Lucy Thorogood; *m* 1947, José Patricia Smith; two *d. Educ:* Highbury County Grammar School. Flt Lt RAF, 1942-46. Pres., BMW Concessionaires (GB) Ltd; Director: Alexanders Discount Co. Ltd; Royal Insurance Co. Ltd; Liverpool, London & Globe Insurance Co. Ltd; London & Lancashire Insurance Co. Ltd. Chairman, Brit. Export Houses Assoc., 1968-70, Vice-Pres., 1973-76; Mem., Cttee of Invisibles, 1968-70. *Recreations:* aviation, music. *Address:* 71 Chester Square, SW1W 9DU. *Clubs:* Travellers', City of London; Wanderers (Johannesburg).

THOROLD, Captain Sir Anthony (Henry), 15th Bt, *cr* 1642; OBE 1942; DSC 1942, and Bar 1945; DL; JP; RN Retired; *b* 7 Sept. 1903; *s* of Sir James (Ernest) Thorold, 14th Bt; *S* father, 1965; *m* 1939, Jocelyn Elaine Laura, *er d* of late Sir Clifford Heathcote-Smith, KBE, CMG; one *s* two *d. Educ:* Royal Naval Colleges Osborne and Dartmouth. Entered RN 1917; qualified as Navigating Officer, 1928; psc 1935; Commander, 1940; served in Mediterranean and Home Fleets, 1939-40; Staff Officer Operations to Flag Officer Commanding Force 'H', 1941-43; in command of Escort Groups in Western Approaches Comd, 1944-45; Captain, 1946; Naval Assistant Secretary in Cabinet Office and Ministry of Defence, 1945-48; Sen. Officer, Fishery Protection Flotilla, 1949-50; Captain of HMS Dryad (Navigation and Direction Sch.), 1951-52; Commodore in Charge, Hong Kong, 1953-55; ADC to the Queen, 1955-56; retired, 1956. DL Lincs, 1959; JP Lincolnshire (Parts of Kesteven), 1961; High Sheriff of Lincolnshire, 1968. Chairman: Grantham Hospital Management Cttee, 1963-74; Lincoln Diocesan Trust and Board of Finance, 1966-71; CC Kesteven, 1958-74; Mem., Lincs County Council, 1973-. *Recreation:* shooting. *Heir: s* (Anthony) Oliver Thorold [*b* 15 April 1945; *m* 1977, Genevra M., *y d* of John Richardson, Midlothian]. *Address:* Syston Old Hall, Grantham, Lincs. *T:* Honington 270. *Club:* Army and Navy.

THORPE, Bernard; Senior Partner, Bernard Thorpe & Partners, since 1922; Land Agent, Surveyor, Farmer; *b* 27 June 1895; *m* 1916, Hilda Mary (*d* 1971), *d* of Edwin Wilkinson, Coventry; one *s* one *d* (and one *s* killed as Pilot Officer Royal Air Force). *Educ:* private tutor; Nottingham Univ. Member Godstone (Surrey) RDC and of its Board of Guardians, 1926-36; Past President, (1939) and Past Chairman, Surrey and Sussex Br. Incorp. Society of Auctioneers and Landed Property Agents; sometime Member Council, Home Grown Timber Marketing Assoc.; Director (Tile Section), Redland Holdings Ltd; Chairman, Park Investments Ltd, 1958-63; Chairman, Assoc. of Land and Property Owners, 1962-64. Past Master, Worshipful Company of Gold and Silver Wyre Drawers, 1966 (Member 1938, and Past Warden); Member Court of Assistants, Worshipful Company of Paviors 1938 (past Warden; Master, 1975); Freeman, City of London. Freemason. *Recreations:* hunting and shooting; formerly Rugby football. *Address:* Malin House, The Close, Aldwick Bay, Bognor Regis, Sussex. *T:* Pagham 4694. *Club:* City Livery.

THORPE, Rt. Hon. (John) Jeremy, PC 1967; MP (L) North Devon since Oct. 1959; Leader of the Liberal Party, 1967-76; Chairman, United Nations Association, since 1976; *b* 29 April 1929; *s* of late J. H. Thorpe, OBE, KC, MP (C) Rusholme, and Ursula, *d* of late Sir John Norton-Griffiths, Bt, KCB, DSO, sometime MP (C); *m* 1st, 1968, Caroline (*d* 1970), *d* of Warwick Allpass, Kingswood, Surrey; one *s* ; 2nd, 1973, Marion, *d* of late Erwin Stein. *Educ:* Rectory Sch., Connecticut, USA; Eton Coll.; Trinity Coll., Oxford, Hon. Fellow, 1972. President, Oxford Union Society, Hilary, 1951; Barrister, Inner Temple, 1954. Member Devon Sessions. Contested (L) N Devon, 1955. Hon. Treasurer, Liberal Party Organisation, 1965-67. A Vice-Pres., Anti-Apartheid Movement, 1969-. FRSA. Hon. LLD Exeter,

1974. *Publications:* (jtly) To all who are interested in Democracy, 1951; (jtly) Europe: the case for going in, 1971; contrib. to newspapers and periodicals. *Recreations:* music; collecting Chinese ceramics. *Address:* House of Commons, SW1. *Club:* National Liberal.

THORPE, Ronald Laurence G.; *see* Gardner-Thorpe.

THORPE, Prof. William Homan, FRS 1951; MA, ScD (Cantab); Fellow since 1932, President, 1969-72, Jesus College, Cambridge; Professor of Animal Ethology, Cambridge University, 1966-69, now Emeritus; Joint Editor of "Behaviour: an International Journal of Comparative Ethology"; Chairman: Arthur Stanley Eddington Memorial Trust, 1946-75; International Council for Bird Preservation (British Section), since 1965; *b* 1 April 1902; *o s* of Francis Homan and Mary Amelia Thorpe (*née* Slade), Hastings and Weston-super-Mare; *m* 1936, Winifred Mary, *o d* of Preb. G. H. Vincent; one *d. Educ:* Mill Hill Sch.; Jesus Coll., Cambridge. Research Fellow of International Education Board (Rockefeller Foundation) at University of California, 1927-29; Research Entomologist at Farnham Royal Parasite Laboratory of Imperial Bureau of Entomology, 1929-32; Tutor Jesus Coll., Cambridge, 1932-45; Lecturer in Entomology in the University, 1932-59; Leverhulme Research Fellow in East Africa, 1939; Senior Tutor, Jesus Coll., Cambridge, 1945-47. President, Association for Study of Animal Behaviour, 1948-52; President, Society British Entomology, 1951-53; Prather Lecturer in Biology, Harvard Univ., 1951-52; President of British Ornithologists Union, 1955-60; President Sect. D (Zoology) British Association (Sheffield), 1956; Visiting Prof., University of California, 1958; Eddington Lecturer, 1960; Riddell Lecturer, Durham Univ., 1961; Fremantle Lecturer, Balliol Coll., Oxford, 1962-63; Gifford Lectr, St Andrews Univ., 1969-71. Leverhulme Emeritus Fellowship, 1971-72. Godman-Salvin Gold Medal, British Ornithologists' Union, 1968. *Publications:* Learning and Instinct in Animals, 1956; (ed with O. L. Zangwill) Current Problems in Animal Behaviour, 1961; Bird Song: The Biology of Vocal Communication and Expression in Birds, 1961; Biology and the Nature of Man, 1962; Science, Man and Morals, 1965; Quakers and Humanists, 1968; (ed with A. M. Pantin) The Relations Between the Sciences, by late C. F. A. Pantin, 1968; Duetting and Antiphonal Song in Birds, 1972; Animal Nature and Human Nature, 1974; Purpose in a World of Chance, 1978; The Origins and Rise of Ethology, 1978; articles in Encyclopædia Britannica, 15th edn, 1974; numerous papers on Entomology, Ornithology, Comparative Physiology and Animal Behaviour (Ethology): in Journal Society Exp. Biology, Biol. Reviews, Ibis, Behaviour, etc. *Recreations:* music, swimming. *Address:* Jesus College, Cambridge; 9 Wilberforce Road, Cambridge. *T:* 50943.

THORPE DAVIE, Cedric; *see* Davie, C. T.

THORSON, Hon. Joseph T., PC Canada, 1941; President of Exchequer Court, Canada, from 1942, retired; Barrister-at-law, Winnipeg; *b* Winnipeg, 15 March 1889; *s* of Stephen Thorson who came from Iceland, 1887; *m* 1916, Alleen B. Scarth; one *s* two *d. Educ:* Manitoba Coll., Winnipeg; New Coll., Oxford. BA University of Manitoba, 1910; First Class Honours and Silver Medal in Classics. Rhodes Scholar for Manitoba, 1910; BA in Jurisprudence, University of Oxford, 1912; LLB University of Manitoba, 1921; Juris Doctor (Hon.), University of Iceland, 1930; Hon. LLD University of Manitoba, 1958; called to Bar, Middle Temple, 1913; Manitoba, 1913; enlisted CEF, 1916; served in France, rank Captain; Dean of Manitoba Law School, 1921-26; MP (L) Winnipeg South Centre, 1926-30; MP (L) Selkirk, 1935-42, Canadian House of Commons; Minister National War Services, Canada, 1941-42; KC 1930; appointed one of delegates of Canada to assembly of League of Nations, Sept. 1938; Chairman, War Expenditures Cttee, House of Commons, 1941; President, International Congress of Jurists, Berlin, 1952, Athens, 1955. Awarded the Grand Cross of the Order of the Falcon, Iceland. Religion: Anglican. *Recreations:* gardening, golf. *Address:* 20 Crescent Road, Rockcliffe, Ottawa, Canada. *Club:* Canadian (Ottawa).

THOULESS, Robert Henry; Reader Emeritus in the University of Cambridge since 1961; Fellow of Corpus Christi College, Cambridge, since 1945; *b* 15 July 1894; *s* of Henry James Thouless; *m* 1924, Priscilla Gorton; one *s* one *d. Educ:* City of Norwich Sch.; Corpus Christi Coll., Cambridge. BA (Nat. Sci.), 1915. Served European War, 2nd Lieut, RE, British Salonika Force, 1917. PhD (Cambridge) 1922; Lecturer in Psychology, Manchester Univ., 1921, Glasgow Univ., 1926, Cambridge Univ., 1938; Reader in Educational Psychology, 1945-61; Consultant NFER, 1964. President, Section J British Association, 1937; Riddell Memorial Lecturer, 1940; President, Society for Psychical Research, 1942; President, British

Psycholog. Society, 1949 (Hon. Fellow 1962); Hulsean Lecturer, 1951. Lecturing in Australia, 1962, 1966; Eddington Memorial Lecturer, 1963, T. B. Davie Memorial Lecturer (Cape Town), 1964. ScD (Cambridge), 1953. *Publications:* An Introduction to the Psychology of Religion, 1923 (rev. edn 1971); The Lady Julian, 1924; Social Psychology, 1925; The Control of the Mind, 1927; Straight and Crooked Thinking, 1930, rev. edn, 1974; General and Social Psychology, 1937, 1951 and 1957; Straight Thinking in War Time, 1942; Authority and Freedom, 1954; Experimental Psychical Research, 1963; Map of Educational Research, 1969; Missing the Message, 1971; From Anecdote to Experiment in Psychical Research, 1972; Articles in British Journal of Psychology, Proc. of Society of Psychical Research, Journal of Parapsychology, etc. *Recreations:* camping and painting. *Address:* 2 Leys Road, Cambridge.

THOURON, Sir John (Rupert Hunt), KBE 1976 (CBE 1967); *b* 10 May 1908; *m* 1st, 1930, Lorna Ellett (marr. diss. 1939); one *s*; 2nd, 1953, Esther duPont. *Educ:* Sherborne School, Dorset. Served War of 1939-45; Major, Black Watch. With Lady Thouron, Founder of the Thouron University of Pennsylvania Fund for British-American Student Exchange, 1960. *Recreations:* shooting, fishing, golf, gardening. *Address:* Glencoe Farm, Unionville, Chester County, Pa 19375, USA. *T:* (215) 384-5542. *Clubs:* White's; Sunningdale Golf; Royal St George Golf; Wilmington, Wilmington Country, Biderman Golf (all Delaware); Pine Valley, British Officers Club of Philadelphia (Pennsylvania); Ristigouche Salmon (Canada); Seminole Golf (Florida).

THOYTS, Robert Francis Newman; Principal Assistant Solicitor, Department of Health and Social Security, 1971-78; *b* 13 March 1913; *o s* of late Lt-Comdr Robert Elmhirst Thoyts, RN, and late Kathleen Olive Thoyts (*née* Hobbs); *m* 1938, Joyce Eliza Gillingham, *er d* of late Rev. William Samuel Probert and late Evangeline Eliza Probert; one *s* four *d. Educ:* Bradfield Coll. Admitted Solicitor, 1936. Entered Solicitor's Dept, Min. of Labour, 1936. Served War, RAF, 1941-45; Flt Lieut. Transf. to Min. of Nat. Insurance, 1945; Asst Solicitor, Min. of Pensions and Nat. Insurance, 1962. Mem. Gen. Purposes Cttee, Civil Service Legal Soc., 1945-75, Gen. Sec. 1945-50, Vice-Chm. 1963-65, Chm. 1965-67. Mem. Salaried Solicitors' Cttee of Law Soc., 1948-. *Recreations:* sailing (Civil Service Rep. Sailing Badge, 1966); amenity interests. *Address:* 37 Queen's Drive, Thames Ditton, Surrey KT7 0TJ. *T:* 01-398 0469. *Clubs:* Law Society; Civil Service Sailing Assoc. (Hon. Life Mem., Chm., 1959-74; Rear-Cdre, 1977-); River Thames Soc. (Vice-Chm. 1971); Littleton Sailing (Vice-Cdre, 1959-61, Cdre, 1961-65; Hon. Life Mem.); Frostbite Yacht Club of America (Hon. Cdre); Island Sailing, etc.

THRELFALL, Richard Ian, QC 1965; *b* 14 Jan. 1920; *s* of William Bernhard and Evelyn Alice Threlfall; *m* 1948, Annette, *d* of George C. H. Matthey; two *s* three *d* (and one *s* decd). *Educ:* Oundle; Gonville and Caius Coll., Cambridge. War service, 1940-45 (despatches twice); Indian Armoured Corps (Probyn's Horse) and Staff appointments. Barrister, Lincoln's Inn, 1947, Bencher 1973. FSA, 1949. Member: Court of Assistants, Worshipful Co. of Goldsmiths; British Hallmarking Council. *Address:* Gray's Inn Chambers, Gray's Inn, WC1. *T:* 01-405 7211; Pebble Hill House, Limpsfield, Surrey. *T:* Oxted 2452.

THRING, Rear-Adm. George Arthur, CB 1958; DSO 1942 and Bar 1952; DL; *b* 13 Sept. 1903; *s* of late Sir Arthur Thring, KCB; *m* 1929, Betty Mary, *er d* of Colonel Stewart William Ward Blacker, DSO; two *s* two *d. Educ:* Royal Naval Colleges, Osborne and Dartmouth. Commander, 1941; Captain, 1946; Rear-Admiral, 1956; retired, 1958. Commanded: HMS Deptford, 1940-41; 42nd and 20th Escort Groups, Atlantic, 1943-45; HMS Ceylon, 1951-52; Flag Officer, Malayan Area, 1956-58. Officer, Legion of Merit (USA), 1945. DL Somerset, 1968. *Recreations:* golf, shooting and fishing. *Address:* Alford House, Castle Cary, Somerset. *T:* Wheathill 329.

THRING, Prof. Meredith Wooldridge; Professor of Mechanical Engineering, Queen Mary College, London University, since 1964; *b* 17 Dec. 1915; *s* of Captain W. H. C. S. Thring, CBE, RN, and Dorothy (*née* Wooldridge); *m* 1940, Alice Margaret Hooley; two *s* one *d. Educ:* Malvern Coll., Worcs; Trinity Coll., Cambridge (Senior Scholar, 1937). Hons Degree Maths and Physics, 1937; ScD, 1964. Student's Medal, Inst. of Fuel, for work on producer gas mains, 1938; British Coal Utilisation Research Assoc.: Asst Scientific Officer, 1937; Senior Scientific Officer and Head of Combustion Research Laboratory, 1944; British Iron and Steel Research Assoc.: Head of Physics Dept, 1946; Superintendent, 1950; Assistant Director, 1953; Prof. of Fuel Technology and Chemical Engineering, Sheffield Univ., 1953-64. Sir Robert Hadfield medal of Iron and Steel Inst. for

studies on open hearth furnaces, 1949; Parsons Memorial Lecture on Magnetohydrodynamics, 1961; General Superintendent International Flame Radiation Research Foundn, 1951-. Visitor: Production Engineering Research Assoc., 1967; Machine Tool Industry Research Assoc., 1967. Member Clean Air Council, 1957-62; Fuel Research Board, 1957-58; Fire Research Board, 1961-64; BISRA Council, 1958-60; President, Inst. of Fuel, 1962-63 (Vice-President, 1959-62); Member: Adv. Council on Research and Development, Ministry of Power, 1960-66; Acad. Adv. Council, University of Strathclyde, 1962-67; Education Cttee, RAF, 1968-76. FInstP 1944; FInstF 1951; FIChemE 1972 (MIChemE 1956); FIMechE 1968 (MIMechE 1964); FIEE 1968 (MIEE 1964); Fellow, Fellowship of Engineering, 1976; FRSA 1964; MRI 1965; FRAeS 1969. Elected Mem., Royal Norwegian Scientific Soc., 1974. *Publications:* The Science of Flames and Furnaces, 1952, 2nd edn, 1960; (with J. H. Chesters) The Influence of Port Design on Open Hearth Furnace Flames (Iron and Steel Institute Special Report 37), 1946; (with R. Edgeworth Johnstone) Pilot Plants, Models and Scale-up Methods in Chemical Engineering, 1957; (ed.) Air Pollution, 1957; Nuclear Propulsion, 1961; Man, Machines and Tomorrow, 1973; Machines—Masters or Slaves of Man?, 1973; (ed with R. J. Crookes) Energy and Humanity, 1974; (with E. R. Laithwaite) How to Invent, 1977. *Recreations:* carpentry, wood-carving. *Address:* 27 Greenhill, High Road, Buckhurst Hill, Essex. *Club:* Athenæum.

THROCKMORTON, Sir Robert George Maxwell, 11th Bt, *cr* 1642; *b* 15 Feb. 1908; *s* of Lt-Col Courtenay Throckmorton (killed in action, 1916), and Lilian (*d* 1955), *o d* of Colonel Langford Brooke, Mere Hall, Cheshire; *S* grandfather, 1927; *m* 1st, 1942, Jean (marr. diss. 1948), (former wife of Arthur Smith-Bingham, *d* of late Charles Garland; she *m* 1959, 3rd Baron Ashcombe, and *d* 1973); 2nd, 1953, Lady Isabel Guinness, *d* of 9th Duke of Rutland. *Educ:* Downside; RMC, Sandhurst. 2nd Lieut, Grenadier Guards, 1928-30; Lieut (A) RNVR, 1940-44. *Heir:* cousin Nicholas Joseph Anthony Throckmorton [*b* 24 Nov. 1913; *m* 1955, Rosemary Anne, *o c* of Major Edward Rowland Miles Alston, MBE]. *Address:* Coughton Court, Alcester, Warwickshire; Molland Bottreaux, South Molton, N Devon. *Clubs:* Army and Navy, White's.

THROWER, Percy John; with garden centre and nursery business (Murrells of Shrewsbury, Portland Nurseries, Shrewsbury); Parks Superintendent, Shrewsbury, 1946-74; *b* 30 Jan. 1913; British; *m* 1939, Constance Margaret (*née* Cook); three *d. Educ:* Church of England Sch., Little Horwood. NDH 1945. Improver, Horwood House Gdns, Winslow, 1927-31; Journeyman Gardener, Royal Gdns, Windsor, 1931-35; Journeyman Gardener, City of Leeds Parks Dept, 1935-37; Asst Parks Supt, Borough of Derby Parks Dept, 1937-46. Frequent broadcaster, radio and TV, 1947-. RHS: Associate of Honour, 1963; VMH 1974. *Publications:* In Your Garden Week by Week, 1959, rev. edn 1973; Encyclopædia of Gardening, 1962; In Your Greenhouse, 1963, rev. edn 1972; Colour in Your Garden, 1966, rev. 1976; Everyday Gardening, 1969; Vegetables and Fruit, 1977; My Lifetime of Gardening, 1977; contrib. Amateur Gardening, Daily Mail. *Recreation:* shooting. *Address:* The Magnolias, Bomere Heath, Shrewsbury, Salop SY4 3QJ. *T:* Bomere Heath 225.

THRUSH, Dr Brian Arthur, FRS 1976; Reader in Physical Chemistry, University of Cambridge, since 1969; Fellow of Emmanuel College, Cambridge, since 1960; *b* Hampstead Garden Suburb, 23 July 1928; *s* of late Arthur Albert Thrush and of Dorothy Charlotte Thrush (*née* Money); *m* 1958, Rosemary Catherine Terry; one *s* one *d. Educ:* Haberdashers' Aske's Sch.; Emmanuel Coll., Cambridge (Schol. 1946-50). BA 1949, MA, PhD 1953, ScD 1965. University of Cambridge: Demonstrator in Physical Chemistry, 1953; Asst Dir of Research, 1959; Dir of Studies in Chemistry, 1963-; Lectr in Physical Chemistry, 1964; Tutor, Emmanuel Coll., 1963-67. Consultant Physicist, US Nat. Bureau of Standards, Washington, 1957-58; Sen. Vis. Scientist, Nat. Res. Council, Ottawa, 1961, 1971. Tilden Lectr, Chem. Soc., 1965; Member: Faraday Council, Chem. Soc., 1976-; US Nat. Acad. of Scis Panel on Atmospheric Chemistry, 1975-. *Publications:* papers on gas kinetics and spectroscopy in Proc. Royal Soc., Trans Faraday Soc., etc. *Recreations:* wine, fell-walking, collecting. *Address:* Brook Cottage, Pemberton Terrace, Cambridge CB2 1JA. *T:* Cambridge 57637.

THUILLIER, Lt-Col Henry Shakespear, DSO 1940; late Royal Artillery (Regular); *b* 10 Sept. 1895; *s* of late Maj.-Gen. Sir Henry Thuillier, KCB, CMG; *m* Beatrice Winifred, *d* of late Captain F. H. Walter, RN; two *s. Educ:* Dragon Sch.; Dover Coll.; RMA, Woolwich. Commissioned RA, 1915; Captain,

1917; Major, 1935; Acting Lt-Col, 1940; Lt-Col, 1942; served Gallipoli and Mesopotamia, 1915-20; BEF, France, 1939-40 (DSO); North African Campaign, 1942-43; Italian Campaign, 1944-45 (despatches twice); retired, 1946; Commissioned RCA, 1950, appointed Lt-Col (SR); retired, 1955. *Address:* 2424 Beach Drive, Victoria, BC, Canada.

THUILLIER, Maj.-Gen. Leslie de Malapert, CB 1958; CVO 1966; OBE 1944; Consultant, Airwork Services Ltd, since 1969; *b* 26 Sept. 1905; *s* of late Lt-Col L. C. Thuillier, Indian Army; *m* 1936, Barbara Leonard Rawlins; one *s* two *d. Educ:* Berkhamsted Sch.; Royal Military Academy, Woolwich. Commissioned as 2nd Lieut, Royal Corps of Signals, 1926; Lieut, 1929; Captain, 1937; Staff Coll., Camberley, 1939; Temp. Major, 1940; Temp. Lt-Col, 1941; Temp. Colonel, 1945; Colonel, 1949, Brigadier, 1951; Maj.-Gen., 1955. War Office, 1940-41; Middle East and Italy, 1941-45; Chief Signal Officer, Northern Ireland District, 1945-46; British Troops in Egypt, 1951-53; Northern Command, 1954-55; Director of Telecommunications, War Office, 1955-58; Asst Sec., Cabinet Office, 1958-67. CEng; MIEE 1968 (AMIEE 1958). *Recreation:* gardening. *Address:* The Bear House, Sandy Lane, Chippenham, Wilts. *T:* Bromham 281. *Club:* Naval and Military.

THURBURN, Gwynneth Loveday, OBE 1956; Hon. FCST; Principal, Central School of Speech and Drama, 1942-67; *b* 17 July 1899; *d* of Robert Augustus Thurburn and Bertha Loveday. *Educ:* Birklands, St Albans; Central School of Speech and Drama. Vice-Pres., Central Sch. of Speech and Drama. *Publication:* Voice and Speech. *Address:* Church Cottage, Darsham, Saxmundham, Suffolk.

THURBURN, Brigadier Roy Gilbert, CB 1950; CBE 1945 (OBE 1941); Secretary, Army Museums Ogilby Trust, 1957-72; *b* 6 July 1901; *y s* of late Reginald Phibbs Thurburn; *m* 1936, Rhona Moneen Hignett; one *s. Educ:* St Paul's Sch.; Royal Military Coll., Sandhurst. Commissioned in the Cameronians (Scottish Rifles), 1921; took part in operations in Southern Kurdistan, 1923; attended Staff Coll., Camberley, 1933-34. Served War of 1939-45, in Middle East, North Africa and Italy (despatches twice). ADC to the Queen, 1952-53; retired, 1953. Gold Medallist, United Services Institution of India, 1932. Legion of Merit (USA), 1947. *Publications:* various in journals. *Recreations:* many. *Address:* 2 Eversleigh, Buckingham Close, Guildford, Surrey.

THURLOW, 8th Baron *cr* 1792; **Francis Edward Hovell-Thurlow-Cumming-Bruce,** KCMG 1961 (CMG 1957); Governor and C-in-C of the Bahamas, 1968-72; *b* 9 March 1912; *s* of 6th Baron Thurlow and Grace Catherine, *d* of Rev. Henry Trotter; *S* brother, 1971; *m* 1949, Yvonne Diana Aubyn Wilson, CStJ 1969; two *s* two *d. Educ:* Shrewsbury Sch.; Trinity Coll., Cambridge. Asst Principal, Dept of Agriculture for Scotland, 1935; transferred to Dominions Office, 1937; Asst Private Sec. to Sec. of State, 1939; Asst Sec., Office of UK High Comr in NZ, 1939; Asst Sec., Office of UK High Comr in Canada, 1944; Secretariat, Meeting of Commonwealth Prime Ministers in London, 1946; served with UK Delegn at Paris Peace Conf., 1946, and at UN Gen. Assemblies, 1946 and 1948; Principal Private Sec. to Sec. of State, 1946; Asst Sec., CRO, 1948; Head of Political Div., Office of UK High Comr in New Delhi, 1949; Establishment Officer, CRO, 1952; Head of Commodities Dept, CRO, 1954; Adviser on External Affairs to Governor of Gold Coast, 1955; Deputy High Comr for the UK in Ghana, 1957; Asst Under-Sec. of State, CRO, April 1958; Deputy High Comr for the UK in Canada, 1958; High Comr for UK: in New Zealand, 1959-63; in Nigeria, 1964-67. KStJ 1969. *Recreations:* fishing, golf. *Heir: s* Hon. Roualeyn Robert Hovell-Thurlow-Cumming-Bruce, *b* 13 April 1952. *Address:* 16 Warwick Avenue, W2. *Club:* Travellers'.
See also Hon. Sir J. R. H.-T.-Cumming-Bruce.

THURLOW, Very Rev. Alfred Gilbert Goddard, MA; Dean of Gloucester, since 1972; *b* 6 April 1911; *s* of Rev. A. R. Thurlow; *m* 1955, Thelda Mary Hook; two *s. Educ:* Selwyn Coll., Cambridge; Cuddesdon Coll., Oxford. MA Cantab, 1936. Curate, All Saints, Wokingham, 1934-39; Precentor of Norwich Cathedral, 1939-55; Rector of St Clement, St George Colegate and St Edmund Norwich, 1943-52; Vicar of: St Andrew and St Michael at Plea, Norwich, 1952-55; St Nicholas, Great Yarmouth, 1955-64; Canon Residentiary of Norwich, 1964-72, Vice-Dean, 1969-72. FSA 1948; FRHistS 1962. *Publications:* Church Bells and Ringers of Norwich, 1947; St George Colegate Norwich, a Redundant Church, 1950; The Mediæval Painted Panels of Norwich Cathedral, 1959; Norwich Cathedral, 1962; Great Yarmouth Priory and Parish Church, 1963; Cathedrals at Work, 1966; City of Norwich, 1970; Cathedrals in Colour, 1971;

Norwich Cathedral, 1972; Biblical Myths and Mysteries, 1974; Gloucester and Berkeley: Edward II, Martyr King, 1976. *Recreations:* change ringing, travel, interpreting historic buildings. *Address:* The Deanery, Gloucester GL1 2BP. *T:* Gloucester 24167. *Clubs:* Cambridge Union; Rotary.

THURSO, 2nd Viscount *cr* 1952, of Ulbster; **Robin Macdonald Sinclair;** Bt 1786; JP; Lord-Lieutenant of Caithness, since 1973; Chairman, Lochdhu Hotels Ltd; Director: Caithness Glass Ltd; Stephens (Plastics) Ltd; Thurso Fisheries Ltd; Morgan Grenfell (Scotland) Ltd; *b* 24 Dec. 1922; *s* of 1st Viscount Thurso, KT, PC, CMG, and Marigold (*d* 1975), *d* of late Col J. S. Forbes, DSO; *S* father, 1970; *m* 1952, Margaret Beaumont Brokensha, *widow* of Lieut G. W. Brokensha, DSC, RN, and *d* of Col J. J. Robertson, DSO, DL, TD; two *s* one *d. Educ:* Eton; New College, Oxford; Edinburgh Univ. Served RAF, 1941-46; Flight Lieut 684 Sqdn, 540 Sqdn, commanded Edinburgh Univ. Air Sqdn, 1946; Captain of Boats, Edinburgh Univ. Boat Club, 1946-47, Green 1946, Blue, 1947. Caithness CC, 1949, 1952, 1955, 1958; Thurso Town Council, 1957, 1960, resigned 1961, re-elected 1965, 1968, 1971, Dean of Guild 1968, Baillie 1960, 1969, Police Judge 1971. Pres. North Country Cheviot Sheep Soc., 1951-54; Chm. Caithness and Sutherland Youth Employment Cttee, 1957-75; Mem., Red Deer Commn, 1965-74. DL 1952, JP 1959, Vice-Lieutenant, 1964-73, Caithness. *Recreations:* fishing, shooting, amateur drama. *Heir: s* Hon. John Archibald Sinclair [*b* 10 Sept. 1953; *m* 1976, Marion Ticknor, *d* of Louis D. Sage, Connecticut, USA, and of Mrs A. R. Ward]. *Address:* Thurso East Mains, Thurso, Caithness, Scotland. *T:* Thurso 2600. *Clubs:* Royal Air Force; Naval (Edinburgh).

THURSTAN, Violetta, MM, FRGS; *o d* of Edward Paget Thurstan, MD. *Educ:* Ladies' Coll., Guernsey; Germany; LLA St Andrews. Honours in Aesthetics and Fine Art. Sent to Brussels in Aug. 1914 by the Order of St John of Jerusalem; and served throughout the War in Belgium and Russia (Military Medal, 1914 Star, etc); Officer WRNS, 1939-44. Late Director of Bedouin Industries Frontier Districts Administration, Egypt. Officer in Allied Commission, Austria, 1946-48. Fellow Society of Designer-Craftsmen, 1975. *Publications:* Field Hospital and Flying Column; The People Who Run, Tragedy of the Refugees in Russia; Desert Songs; The Use of Vegetable Dyes; Decorative Textiles and Tapestries, 1934; Weaving Patterns of Yesterday and To-day; History of Ancient Fabrics (republished 1954); Weaving without Tears, 1956; Stormy Petrel, 1964; The Foolish Virgin, 1966; The Lucky Mary, 1973; The Hounds of War Unleashed, 1977. *Recreations:* travelling, gardening, weaving. *Address:* Old Mill House, The Square, Penryn, Cornwall. *T:* Penryn 2339.

THURSTON, Gavin, CBE 1966; FRCP, FRCGP; HM Coroner, Inner West London, since 1965 (Western District, County of London, 1956-65); Deputy Coroner to the Royal Household since 1964; *b* 26 March 1911; 4th *s* of John Bourdas Thurston, London; *m* 1st, 1935, Ione Witham (*d* 1967), *d* of J. T. Barber, JP; one *s* one *d*; 2nd, 1969, Janet Hazell, MB, ChB, LRAM. *Educ:* Dulwich Coll.; Guy's Hosp. Med. School. MRCS, LRCP 1933; MRCP, 1937; DCH, 1937; FRCP 1969; FRCGP 1969. Barrister, Inner Temple, 1952. Treasurer's Cert. in Clinical Surgery, Guy's, 1933; Res. MO, Pembury Hosp. and Belgrave Hosp., 1933-35. Served War of 1939-45, RAMC, India and NW Europe; Specialist in Medicine, Lt-Col. Asst Dep. Coroner: South Essex, 1946-56; City of London, 1950-56; Dep. Coroner: Metropolitan Essex, 1949-56; North London, 1952-56; West Ham, 1950-56; Hon. Treasurer, Coroners' Soc., 1950-56. Hon. Treasurer, Coroners' Soc., 1958-60; Lecturer in Forensic Medicine, W London Hosp. Med. Sch., 1956-60; Sen. Lectr in Forensic Medicine, Charing Cross Hosp. Med. Sch., 1969-71; Hon. Editor, Medico-Legal Journal, 1958-; Founder Member, British Acad. of Forensic Sciences, 1959; Vice-Pres., Medical Defence Union, 1960-; Hon. Sec., Coroners' Soc. of England and Wales, 1960-71, Pres. 1971-72; President: Medico-Legal Soc., 1969-71; Chelsea Clinical Soc., 1976-77; Examiner for DMJ, 1963-72; Examiner for Milburn Prize, 1961-. Chm., Authors' Club, 1967-69. DMJ (hc) 1963. *Publications:* Coroner's Practice, 1958; contrib. to Atkin's Court Forms, 1961, and 1974; contrib. to Encyclopædia of General Practice, 1963; The Great Thames Disaster, 1965; The Clerkenwell Riot, 1967; Coroners, in Halsbury's Laws of England, 4th edn, 1974; Coronership, 1977; articles on medico-legal subjects. *Recreations:* reading and writing. *Address:* Coroner's Court, 65 Horseferry Road, SW1P 2ED. *T:* 01-834 6515; Ripe, Lewes, East Sussex BN8 6AS. *Clubs:* Authors', Savage.

THWAITE, Anthony Simon; poet; co-editor of Encounter since 1973; *b* 23 June 1930; *s* of Hartley Thwaite, *qv; m* 1955, Ann Barbara Harrop; four *d. Educ:* Kingswood Sch.; Christ Church,

Oxford (MA). Vis. Lectr in English, Tokyo Univ., 1955-57; Producer, BBC, 1957-62; Literary Editor, The Listener, 1962-65; Asst Prof. of English, Univ. of Libya, 1965-67; Literary Editor, New Statesman, 1968-72; Henfield Writing Fellow, Univ. of East Anglia, 1972; Vis. Prof., Kuwait Univ., 1974. *Publications: poetry:* Home Truths, 1957; The Owl in the Tree, 1963; The Stones of Emptiness, 1967 (Richard Hillary Memorial Prize, 1968); Inscriptions, 1973; New Confessions, 1974; A Portion for Foxes, 1977; *criticism:* Contemporary English Poetry, 1959; Poetry Today, 1973; Twentieth Century English Poetry, 1977; *travel:* (with Roloff Beny) Japan, 1968; The Deserts of Hesperides, 1969; (with Roloff Beny and Peter Porter) In Italy, 1974; *editor:* (with Geoffrey Bownas) Penguin Book of Japanese Verse, 1964; (with Peter Porter) The English Poets, 1974; *for children:* Beyond the Inhabited World, 1976. *Recreations:* archaeology, travel. *Address:* The Mill House, Tharston, Norfolk NR15 2YN. *T:* Fundenhall 569.

THWAITE, Hartley, JP; Yorkshire District Manager, Lloyds Bank Ltd, retired (Yorkshire Regional Director, 1963-70); *b* Kalutara, Ceylon, 5 Aug. 1903; *e s* of late Rev. Simon and Susannah Thwaite; *m* 1928, Alice Evelyn Mallinson; one *s*. *Educ:* Kingswood, Bath; Leeds Univ. (research). MPhil 1972; FSA 1957; FIB 1949; FSG 1973. Entered service of Lloyds Bank, 1920. Mem. Council, Inst. of Bankers, 1950-53, Chm. Huddersfield Centre, 1950-53, Pres. Leeds Centre, 1959-60; Chm., Leeds Coll. of Commerce, Banking Adv. Sub-Cttee, 1959-60; British Bankers' Assoc. rep., BSI Cttee on documentary reproduction, 1948-49. Mem., Nat. Register of Archives, WR (North) Cttee, 1952-75. Pres., Huddersfield Union Discussion Soc., 1958-59; Chm., Scarcroft Conservative Assoc., 1964-68. Yorkshire Archaeological Soc.: Sen. Vice-Pres.; Mem. Council, 1954-; Hon. Treas., 1955-59; 11 yrs Chm., Parish Register Section; Chm., Family Studies Section, 1973-76. Member: Leeds Library Cttee; Leeds Watch Cttee, 1966-68; Chm., Leeds Parole Cttees, 1971 and 1972; Chm., Leeds Prison Bd, 1973 and 1974 (Dep. Chm., 1970-72). Dir, Northern and Scottish Bd, Legal & General Assce Soc. Ltd, 1963-73. Dir, Kirkstall Lodge Ltd (ex-prisoners' hostel), 1970-77. Pres., Kingswood Old Boys' Assoc., 1969-70. JP Leeds City, 1962 (Court Chm.; Chm. Betting and Gaming Licensing Cttee). Frequent lectr on genealogy, parish registers, the history of probate and admin, etc. *Publications:* Parish Register of Wensley, Yorks, 1701-1837, 1967; Abstracts of Abbotside Wills, 1552-1688, 1968; contrib. Genealogists' Magazine. *Recreations:* genealogy, archaeology, local history. *Address:* Rose Cottage, Manor Park, Scarcroft, Leeds LS14 3BW. *T* Leeds 892367. *Clubs:* East India, Devonshire, Sports and Public Schools; Leeds (Leeds); Huddersfield and Borough (Huddersfield).
See also A. S. Thwaite.

THWAITES, Brian St George, CMG 1958; *b* 22 April 1912; *s* of late Henry Thwaites and Ada B. Thwaites (*née* Macnutt); *m* 1938, Madeleine Elizabeth Abell; one *s* two *d*. *Educ:* Canford School; Clare Coll., Cambridge. Entered Colonial Service (now HM Overseas Civil Service), 1935; served as Administrative Officer in Eastern Nigeria, 1935-47 and 1948-57; Palestine, 1947-48; retired, 1957. *Address:* Cox Hill, Marnhull, Sturminster Newton, Dorset DT10 1NZ. *T:* Marnhull 286.

THWAITES, Dr Bryan, MA, PhD; FIMA; Principal of Westfield College since 1966; *b* London, 6 December 1923; *e s* of late Ernest James and Dorothy Marguerite Thwaites; *m* 1948, Katharine Mary, 4th *c* of late H. R. Harries and late Mrs L. Harries, Longhope, Glos; four *s* two *d*. *Educ:* Dulwich College; Winchester College; Clare College, Cambridge. Scientific Officer, National Physical Laboratory, 1944-47; Lecturer, Imperial College, London, 1947-51; Assistant Master, Winchester College, 1951-59; Professor of Theoretical Mechanics, Southampton Univ., 1959-66. Chm. of Collegiate Council, London Univ., 1973-76. Chm. and Mem. ARC Cttees, 1948-69. Special Lecturer, Imperial College, 1951-58. Director of the School Mathematics Project, 1961-75, Chm. of Trustees, 1967-; Member: United States Educational Commn, 1966-76; Ct of London Univ., 1975-; Chm. of Delegacy, Goldsmiths' Coll., 1975-; Mem. Acad. Advisory Committee: Univ. of Bath, 1963-72; Open Univ., 1969-75; Chairman: Council of C of E Colleges of Education, 1969-71; Church of England Higher Educn Cttee, 1974-76; Northwick Park Hosp. Management Cttee, 1970-74; Brent and Harrow AHA, 1973-; King's Fund Enquiry into Sen. Management Trng in NHS, 1975-76. Gresham Prof. in Geometry, City Univ., 1969-72; Mercier Lectr, Whitelands Coll., 1973. Shadow Vice-Chancellor, Independent Univ., July-Nov. 1971; Hon. Sec. and Treasurer, Dulwich College Mission, 1946-57; Member of Approved School Committee, Hampshire CC, 1954-58, 1961-66; JP, Winchester City Bench, 1963-66; Governor of various schools. Pres. Institute of Mathematics and its Applications, 1966-67. *Publications:* (ed) Incompressible

Aerodynamics, 1960; (ed) On Teaching Mathematics, 1961; The SMP: the first ten years, 1973; numerous contributions to Proc. Royal Soc., Reports and Memoranda of Aeronautical Research Council, Quart. Jl of Applied Mech., Jl of Royal Aeronautical Soc., etc. *Recreations:* music, sailing. *Address:* Milnthorpe, Winchester, Hants. *T:* Winchester 2394; The Old House, Westfield College, NW3. *T:* 01-794 2090. *Clubs:* Athenæum; Hollington (SE5).

THWAITES, Jacqueline Ann, JP; Principal of Inchbald Schools of Design and Fine Arts since 1960; *b* 16 Dec. 1931; *d* of Mrs Donald Whitaker; *m* 1st, 1955, Michael Inchbald, FSIA (marr. diss. 1964); one *s* one *d*; 2nd, 1974, Brig. Peter Trevenen Thwaites, *qv*. *Educ:* Convent of the Sacred Heart, Brighton; House of Citizenship, London. Founded: Inchbald Sch. of Design, 1960; Inchbald Sch. of Fine Arts, 1970; Inchbald Sch. of Garden Design, 1972. Member: Monopolies Commn, 1972-75; Whitford Cttee on Copyright and Design, 1974-76; London Electricity Cons. Council, 1973-76; Westminster City Council (Warwick Ward). JP South Westminster, 1976. *Publications:* Directory of Interior Designers, 1966; Bedrooms, 1968; Design and Decoration, 1971. *Recreations:* fishing, travel. *Address:* 47 Sussex Street, SW1. *T:* 01-828 1587; The Manor, Ayot St Lawrence, Herts; (office) 7 Eaton Gate, SW1W 9BA.

THWAITES, Brig. Peter Trevenen, Chairman, Joint Staff, Sultan of Oman's Armed Forces, since 1977; *b* 30 July 1926; *yr* surv. *s* of late Lt-Col Norman Graham Thwaites, CBE, MVO, MC, and Eleanor Lucia Thwaites, Barley End, Tring, Herts; *m* 1st, 1950, Ellen Theresa King (marr. diss.; she *d* 1976); one *s* two *d* (and one *s* decd); 2nd, 1974, Jacqueline Ann Inchbald (*see* Jacqueline Ann Thwaites). *Educ:* Rugby. Commnd Grenadier Guards, 1944; served 1st, 2nd and 4th Bns in Germany, Egypt, British Cameroons, British Guiana; Mem., Sir William Penney's Scientific Party to UK Atomic Trials in S Australia, 1956; Staff Coll., Malaya, JSSC, MoD, 1958-67; Aden, 1967; comd Muscat Regt, Sultan of Muscat's Armed Forces, 1967-70; AQMG London Dist, 1970-71; Comdr, British Army Staff, Singapore (Col), and Governor, Singapore Internat. Sch., 1971-73; Dep. Dir, Defence Operational Plans (Army), 1973-74; Brig. 1975; Head of MoD Logistics Survey Team to Saudi Arabia, 1976, retired 1977. Sultan's Commendation, 1967; Sultan's Dist. Service Medal, 1969; Sultan's Bravery Medal, 1970. *Publications: plays:* (with Charles Ross) Love or Money, 1958; (with Charles Ross) Master of None, 1960; Roger's Last Stand, 1976; *revue:* (with Myles Rudge and Ted Dicks) Caught in the Act, 1976. *Recreations:* polo, shooting. *Address:* 47 Sussex Street, SW1V 4RJ; The Manor House, Ayot St Lawrence, Herts. *Club:* Cavalry and Guards.

THYNE, William, OBE 1969; President, William Thyne (Holdings) Ltd, since 1973 (Chairman, 1948-73); Director, Clydesdale Bank Ltd, since 1948 (Chairman, 1969-75); *b* 23 March 1901; *e s* of late William Thyne and late Christian Seton Watt; *m* 1931, Virginia Neeb Williams (*d* 1968); two *s* two *d*. *Educ:* George Watson's Coll., Edinburgh; CIT, Pittsburg. Director: Clydesdale Bank Finance Corp. Ltd (Chm., 1969-75); Clydesdale Bank Insurance Services Ltd (Chm., 1969-75); Midland Bank Ltd, 1970-75; Henry Ballantyne & Sons Ltd; Man. Dir, A. & R. Scott Ltd, 1941-54. Pres., Edinburgh Chamber of Commerce and Mfrs, 1950-52; Chm., Council of Scottish Chambers of Commerce, 1964-66; Pres., Grocers' Inst., 1957-60; Past Convener of Commerce Advisory Cttee, Edinburgh Univ., and Past Mem., Industrial Liaison Cttee, Edinburgh Univ.; Mem., Scottish Nat. Cttee, English-Speaking Union; Mem., Scottish Tourist Board, 1965-69. *Recreations:* fishing, shooting. *Address:* The Yair, by Galashiels, Selkirkshire. *T:* Clovenfords 212.

THYNN, Alexander; *see* Weymouth, Viscount.

THYNNE, family name of **Marquess of Bath.**

THYNNE, John Corelli James, PhD, DSc; Counsellor (Scientific), British Embassy, Moscow, since 1974; *b* 27 Nov. 1931; *s* of Corelli James Thynne and Isabel Anne (*née* Griffiths). *Educ:* Milford Haven Grammar Sch.; Nottingham Univ. (BSc, PhD); Edinburgh Univ. (DSc). Res. Chemist, English Electric Co. (Guided Missile Div.), 1956-58; Fellow: Nat. Res. Council, Ottawa, 1958-59; UCLA, 1959-60; Univ. of Leeds, 1960-63; Lectr in Chemistry and Dir of Studies, Univ. of Edinburgh, 1963-70; Principal, DTI, 1970-73. *Publications:* contribs on physical chemistry to scientific journals. *Recreations:* skiing, sailing, cricket. *Address:* c/o Foreign and Commonwealth Office, SW1; 5 Eldon Grove, NW3. *T:* 01-794 7439. *Club:* Athenæum.

TIARKS, Rt. Rev. Geoffrey Lewis, MA Cantab; Rural Dean of Lyme Bay and Chaplain to Retired Clergy and Widows in the Archdeaconry of Sherborne, since 1976; *b* 8 Oct 1909; *s* of Lewis Herman Tiarks, Clerk in Holy Orders, and Edith Margaret Tiarks; *m* 1934, Betty Lyne, *d* of Henry Stock; one *s* (one *d* decd). *Educ:* Marlborough; S John's College, Cambridge. Ordained at Southwark, 1932; Curate of St Saviour's with St Peter, Southwark, 1932-33; Chaplain, RN, 1934-47; Chaplain, Diocesan College, Rondebosch, CP, 1948-50; Rector of S Paul's, Rondebosch, 1950-54; Vicar of Lyme Regis, Dorset, 1954-61; Archdeacon of the Isle of Wight, 1961-65; Archdeacon of Portsmouth, 1965-69; Bishop Suffragan of Maidstone, 1969-76; Senior Chaplain to Archbishop of Canterbury, 1969-74. *Address:* Primrose Cottage, Netherbury, Bridport, Dorset. *T:* Netherbury 277.

TIARKS, Henry Frederic, FRAS; *b* 8 Sept. 1900; *e s* of late Frank Cyril Tiarks, OBE; *m* 1st, 1930, Lady Millicent Olivia Taylour (marr. diss. 1936), *d* of 4th Marquess of Headfort; (one *s* decd); 2nd, 1936, Joan, *d* of Francis Marshman-Bell, one *d* (one *s* decd). *Educ:* Eton College. Served European War 1914-19. Midshipman RNVR 1918; Sqdn Ldr AAF, 1940; Wing Commander, 1942-43, Retd (invalided). Former directorships: J. Henry Schroder & Co., Partner 1926-57, J. Henry Schroder & Co. Ltd, 1957-62, J. Henry Schroder Wagg & Co. Ltd, 1962 (May to Sept.), Schroders Ltd, 1962-65; J. Henry Schroder Banking Corpn, NY, 1945-62; Antofagasta (Chili) and Bolivia Railway Co. Ltd, 1926-67 (Chairman 1966-67); Securicor Ltd (founder) 1939-68; Pressed Steel Co. Ltd, 1936-66; Joseph Lucas Ltd, 1946-68; Bank of London & South America Ltd, 1958-68; Bank of London & Montreal Ltd, Nassau, 1959-69; Anglo-Scottish Amalgamated Corpn Ltd, 1935-68. Member: Dollar Exports Council, 1952-60; Western Hemisphere Exports Council, 1960-64; European League for Economic Co-operation (European Central Council); Internat. EFTA Action Cttee, 1967-75; Vice-Pres., European-Atlantic Gp. Mem., The Wildfowl Trust; Trustee, World Wildlife Fund (International), Morges, Switzerland, 1966-76. Mem. Cttee of Managers, RI, 1960-62. Gran Oficial, Order of Merit, Chile. *Recreations:* golf, shooting, astronomy, photography. *Address:* Casa Ina, Marbella Club, Marbella, (Malaga) Spain; 120 Cheapside, EC2. *Clubs:* Overseas Member: White's, Royal Thames Yacht; Royal and Ancient Golf (St Andrews), Swinley Forest Golf (Ascot), Royal St George's Golf (Sandwich), Berkshire Golf (Bagshot), The Brook (New York), Lyford Cay (Nassau, Bahamas).
See also Marquess of Tavistock.

TIBBER, Anthony Harris; His Honour Judge Tibber; a Circuit Judge, since 1977; *b* 23 June 1926; *s* of Maurice and Priscilla Tibber; *m* 1954, Rhona Ann Salter; three *s*. *Educ:* University College School, London; Magdelen College School, Brackley. Served in Royal Signals, 1945-48; called to the Bar, Gray's Inn, 1950; a Recorder of the Crown Court, 1976. *Recreations:* boating, idling, pottering. *Address:* 48 Bancroft Avenue, N2 0AS. *T:* 01-348 3605.

TIBBITS, Captain Sir David (Stanley), Kt 1976; DSC 1942; MNI; RN retired; Deputy Master and Chairman of Board, Trinity House, 1972-76; *b* 11 April 1911; *s* of late Hubert Tibbits, MB, BCh, Warwick, and Edith Lucy (*née* Harman) Tibbits; *m* 1938, Mary Florence Butterfield, Hamilton, Bermuda; two *d*. *Educ:* Wells House Sch., Malvern Wells; RNC, Dartmouth. RN Cadet 1925; served War, 1939-45: Navigating Officer; started RN Radar/Plotting Sch. and Action Information Trng Centre, 1943-44; Navigating Officer, HMS Anson, Far East (present at re-occupation of Hong Kong); Comdr 1946; Captain 1953; Dir, Radio Equipment Dept, Admty, 1953-56; in comd, HM Ships Manxman, Dryad and Hermes, 1956-61; retd. Trinity House: Elder Brother, 1961; Warden, 1969. Hon. Sec., King George's Fund for Sailors; Lay Vice-Pres., Missions to Seamen. Mem., Court Worshipful Co. of Shipwrights, 1976. Trustee, National Maritime Museum, 1974-77. Governor, Pangbourne Coll., 1973-. Founder Mem., Nautical Inst., 1972. *Recreations:* sailing, colour photography, classical music. *Address:* Harting Hill, Point Shares, Pembroke, Bermuda; c/o Trinity House, Tower Hill, EC3N 4DH. *Clubs:* Army and Navy; Royal Yacht Squadron (Naval Mem.); Royal Bermuda Yacht (Bermuda).

TIBBS, Craigie John; Under Secretary (Director of Land Economy), Departments of the Environment and Transport, since 1976; *b* 17 Feb. 1935; *s* of Arthur and Gladys Tibbs; *m* 1959, Carol Ann (*née* Linsell); two *d*. *Educ:* King George V School, Southport; Heaton Grammar School, Newcastle upon Tyne; RMA Sandhurst; London University. BSc; FRICS. Trainee Estates Officer, London Transport, 1959-62; Valuer and Senior Valuer, Luton Corp., 1962-67; Chief Valuer and Surveyor, London Borough of Newham, 1967-71; Development

Officer, City of Birmingham, 1971-73; County Estates Officer, Hants County Council, 1973-76. *Recreations:* music, reading, writing, walking, swimming, golf, the Well Game. *Address:* c/o Department of the Environment, 2 Marsham Street, SW1. *T:* 01-212 3530.

TICKELL, Crispin Charles Cervantes, MVO 1958; HM Diplomatic Service; Chef de Cabinet to Rt Hon. Roy Jenkins, President of the Commission of the European Communities, since 1977; *b* 25 Aug. 1930; *s* of late Jerrard Tickell and Renée (*née* Haynes); *m* 1st, 1954, Chloë (marr. diss. 1976), *d* of late Sir James Gunn, RA, PRP; two *s* one *d*; 2nd, 1977, Penelope Thorne Thorne. *Educ:* Westminster (King's Schol.); Christ Church, Oxford (Hinchliffe and Hon. Schol.). 1st Cl. Hons Mod. Hist. 1952. Served with Coldstream Guards, 1952-54; entered HM Diplomatic Service, 1954. Served at: Foreign Office, 1954-55; The Hague, 1955-58; Mexico, 1958-61; FO (Planning Staff), 1961-64; Paris, 1964-70; Private Sec. to successive Chancellors of the Duchy of Lancaster (Rt Hon. George Thomson, MP; Rt Hon. Anthony Barber, MP; Rt Hon. Geoffrey Rippon, QC, MP), 1970-72; Head of Western Organisations Dept, FCO, 1972-75; Fellow, Center for Internat. Affairs, Harvard Univ., 1975-76. Officer, Order of Orange Nassau (Holland), 1958. *Publications:* (contrib.) The Evacuees, 1968; (contrib.) Life After Death, 1976; Climatic Change and World Affairs, 1977. *Recreations:* anthropology, pre-Columbiana, walking. *Address:* 1 avenue des Gaulois, 1040 Bruxelles, Belgium. *Club:* Brooks's.

TICKELL, Maj.-Gen. Marston Eustace, CBE 1973 (MBE 1955); MC 1945; CEng, FICE; Commandant Royal Military College of Science, since 1975; *b* 18 Nov. 1923; *er s* of late Maj.-Gen. Sir Eustace Tickell, KBE, CB, MC; *m* 1961, Pamela Vere, *d* of Vice-Adm. A. D. Read, CB; no *c*. *Educ:* Wellington Coll.; Peterhouse, Cambridge (MA). Commnd in RE, 1944; NW Europe Campaign and Middle East, 1944-45; psc 1954; Mil. Ops, MoD, 1955-57; served in Libya, Cyprus and Jordan, 1958-59; US Armed Forces Staff Coll. and Instructor RMCS and Staff Coll., 1959-62; Defence Planning Staff, MoD, 1962-64; CRE 4th Div., 1964-66; comd 12 Engr Bde, 1967-69; Indian Nat. Defence Coll., 1970; COS Northern Ireland, 1971-72; E-in-C, MoD, 1972-75. FICE 1974. *Recreation:* sailing. *Address:* Royal Military College of Science, Shrivenham, Oxon; Shaw Top House, Chipstead, Sevenoaks, Kent. *Clubs:* Army and Navy; Royal Ocean Racing.

TICKLE, Brian Percival; Registrar, Principal Registry of the Family Division, High Court of Justice, since 1970; *b* 31 Oct. 1921; *m* 1945, Margaret Alice Pendrey; one *s* one *d*. *Educ:* The Judd Sch., Tonbridge. Entered Civil Service, 1938. Served War, Royal Signals, 1939-45. Civil Service, 1946-70. *Publications:* Rees Divorce Handbook, 1963; Atkins Court Forms and Precedents (Probate), 1974. *Recreation:* golf. *Address:* 23 Coniston Avenue, Tunbridge Wells, Kent.

TICKLE, Rt. Rev. Gerard William; Titular Bishop of Bela and Bishop-in-Ordinary to HM Forces (RC), since Nov. 1963; *b* 2 Nov. 1909; 2nd *s* of William Joseph Tickle and Rosanna Kelly. *Educ:* Douai School; Venerable English College, Rome. Priest, 1934. Curate at St Joseph's Church, Sale, 1935-41; Army Chaplain, 1941-46; Vice-Rector, 1946, Rector, 1952, Venerable English College, Rome. Privy Chamberlain to Pope Pius XII, 1949; Domestic Prelate to Pope Pius XII, 1953. *Address:* 54 Ennismore Gardens, SW7 1AJ. *T:* 01-589 1273.

TIERNEY, Dom Francis Alphonsus, OSB, MA; Prior of Douai Abbey, since 1973; *b* 7 March 1910; *s* of James Francis Tierney and Alice Mary Claypoole. *Educ:* Douai; St Benet's Hall, Oxford. Headmaster of: Douai Junior School, Ditcham Park, 1948-52; Douai Sch., 1952-73. *Address:* Douai Abbey, Woolhampton, Berkshire. *T:* Woolhampton 3163.

TIERNEY, Sydney; JP; MP (Lab) Birmingham, Yardley, since Feb. 1974; President, Union of Shop, Distributive and Allied Workers, since 1977; *b* Sept. 1923. *Educ:* Secondary Modern Sch., Dearne; Plater Coll., Oxford. Formerly: Mem., Co-operative Party; an Official and Member, Union of Shop, Distributive and Allied Workers. Vice-Chm., W Midlands Labour Gp of MPs. PPS to Min. of State for Agriculture. JP Leicester, 1966. *Address:* 64 Northdene Road, Leicester LE2 6FH; House of Commons, SW1A 0AA.

TIGHE, Maj.-Gen. Patrick Anthony Macartan, CB 1977; MBE 1958; MBIM; *b* 26 Feb. 1923; *s* of late Macartan H. Tighe, BA, RUI, Barrister-at-Law, Dublin and Dorothy Isabel (*née* Vine); *m* 1st, 1950, Elizabeth Frazer Stewart (*d* 1971); two *s*; 2nd, 1972, Princine Merendino Calitri, authoress, W Virginia, USA. *Educ:* Christ's Hospital. Served RAF, 1940-41; commnd Royal

Signals, 1943; served NW Europe, 1944-45, Palestine, 1945-47; psc 1955; DAAQMG Gurkha Bde Malaya, 1956 (MBE); Mil. Asst Comd British Forces Hong Kong, 1963; Force Signals Officer Borneo, 1964-66 (despatches); Asst Mil. Sec., 1966; Col Asst Adjt Gen., 1968; Brig. Comd Trng Bde Royal Signals, 1970; Inspector of Intell. Corps, 1973; Signal Officer-in-Chief (Army), 1974-77. Col Comdt, Royal Signals, 1977. *Publications:* radio plays (BBC), film and book reviews for press and radio in Far East. *Recreations:* cinema (Mem. British Film Inst. 1947), golf. *Address:* c/o Lloyds Bank, 6 Pall Mall, SW1Y 5NH. *Club:* Army and Navy.

TILBE, Douglas Sidney, OBE 1973; JP; *b* 27 May 1931; *s* of late Norrie Ethelbert Sidney George Tilbe and of Ethel Tilbe (*née* Scott); *m* 1957, Janet Ann Ainger; three *s* one *d. Educ:* LSE; Avery Hill Coll. of Educn; Univ. of Essex (MA Soc. Service Planning). Gen. Sec., Soc. of Friends Race Relations Cttee, 1965-71; Dir, British Council of Churches Community and Race Relations Unit, 1971-73; Chm., Priority Area Children, 1971-73; Mem., Uganda Resettlement Bd, 1972-74; Chm., Co-ordinating Cttee for Welfare of Evacuees from Uganda, 1972-73; Dir, Shelter, 1974-77. Chm., Welwyn Garden City UDC, 1972-73. Contested (Lab) Rye, 1959 and 1964. Member: NW Metrop. Mental Health Review Tribunal, 1971-; Oxford Region Mental Health Review Tribunal, 1974-. Chm. Governors, Heronswood Sch. JP Herts 1967. Hon. MA Open. *Publications:* East African Asians, 1968; The Ugandan Asian Crisis, 1972. *Recreations:* soccer referee; watching football, cricket, golf and tennis. *Address:* 15 Beehive Green, Welwyn Garden City, Herts. *T:* Welwyn Garden 27373.

TILEY, Arthur, CBE 1972; JP; Insurance Broker and Marine Underwriter; Chairman: Clarkson Tiley & Hargreaves Ltd, Incorporated Insurance Brokers, Bradford and Halifax; Northern Capital Ltd; Bradford & Northern Housing Assoc. Ltd; *b* 17 January 1910; *m* 1936, Mary, *d* of late Craven and Mary Tankard, Great Horton; one *s* one *d. Educ:* Grange High School, Bradford. Treasurer, Young Women's Christian Association, Bradford, 1934-50. Contested (C and Nat. L) Bradford Central, 1951. MP (C and Nat. L) Bradford West, 1955-66. Served War of 1939-45 as Senior Company Officer, National Fire Service. Mem. Council, Churchill Memorial Trust, 1965-76. JP Bradford, 1967. *Address:* 10 Petersgarth, Moorhead Lane, Shipley, West Yorks.

TILL, Barry Dorn; Principal of Morley College, London, since 1965; *b* 1 June 1923; *s* of John Johnson and Hilda Lucy Till; *m* 1st, 1954, Shirley Philipson (marr. diss. 1965); two *s*; 2nd, 1966, Antonia, *d* of Sir Michael Clapham, *qv*; two *d. Educ:* Harrow; Jesus College and Westcott House, Cambridge. Lightfoot Scholar, University of Cambridge, 1949. Deacon, 1950; Priest, 1951; Asst Curate, Bury Parish Church, Lancs, 1950-53; Fellow of Jesus Coll., Cambridge, 1953-60, Chaplain, 1953-56, Dean, 1956-60, Tutor, 1957-60; Univ. Preacher, Cambridge, 1955; Examining Chaplain to Bishop of Lichfield, 1957-60; Dean of Hong Kong, 1960-64. Chm., Asia Christian Colleges Assoc., 1968-76, Vice-Pres., 1976-. Governor, British Inst. of Recorded Sound, 1967-72; Mem. Board, Youth and Music, 1965-; Adviser to Baring Foundn, 1973-; Mem., Adv. Council, V&A Museum, 1977-. Governor, St Olaf's Grammar Sch., 1973-; Mem., Cultural Cttee, European Culture Foundn, 1976-. *Publications:* contrib. to The Historic Episcopate, 1954; Change and Exchange, 1964; Changing Frontiers in the Mission of the Church, 1965; contrib. to A Holy Week Manual, 1967; The Churches Search for Unity, 1972. *Recreations:* travel, gardening, opera. *Address:* 44 Canonbury Square, N1 2AW. *T:* 01-359 0708.

TILLARD, Maj.-Gen. Philip Blencowe, CBE 1973; Assistant Director (Outdoor Activities), Borough of Brighton, since 1977; *b* 2 Jan. 1923; *s* of late Brig. John Arthur Stuart Tillard, OBE, MC and of Margaret Penelope (*née* Blencowe); *m* 1953, Patricia Susan (*née* Robertson); three *s* one *d. Educ:* Winchester College. Commnd into 60th Rifles, 1942; served Syria, Italy and Greece, 1943-46; transf. to 13th/18th Royal Hussars (QMO), 1947; served in Libya, Malaya and Germany, comd Regt, 1964-66; psc 1956; jssc 1962; Comdr RAC 3rd Div., 1967-69; BGS (Army Trng), MoD, 1970-73; ADC to the Queen, 1970-73; COS, BAOR, 1973-76. *Recreations:* normal family pursuits; shooting. *Address:* Church House, Chailey Green, Lewes, East Sussex. *T:* Newick 2759. *Clubs:* Farmers'; Sussex.

TILLETT, Mrs Emmie Muriel; Managing Director, Ibbs & Tillett, since 1948; *b* 7 December 1896; *d* of Arthur and Florence Bass; *m* 1941, John Hudson Tillett; no *c. Educ:* privately. With Chappell & Co. Ltd (Music Publishers), 1916-22; joined the firm of Ibbs & Tillett, 1922. *Recreations:* water colour painting, reading. *Address:* 11 Elm Tree Road, St John's Wood, NW8. *T:*

01-286 6161; Three Ash House, Bungay, Suffolk. *T:* Bungay 2485.

TILLING, George Henry Garfield; Chairman, Scottish Postal Board, since 1977; *b* 24 Jan. 1924; *s* of Thomas and Anne Tilling, Old Colwyn; *m* 1956, Margaret Meriel, *d* of late Rear-Adm. Sir Alexander McGlashan, KBE, CB, DSO; two *s* two *d. Educ:* Hardye's Sch., Dorchester; University Coll., Oxford (Open Exhibnr, Kitchener Schol., Farquharson Prizeman, MA). Served War of 1939-45, NW Europe: Captain, Dorset Regt, 1943-46. Post Office: Asst Principal, 1948; Principal, 1953; Private Sec. to Postmaster General, 1964; Dep. Dir of Finance, 1965; Dir, Eastern Postal Region, 1967; Sec. of the Post Office, 1973-75; Dir of Postal Ops, 1975-77. Mem. Council, Order of St John for London, 1975-77. *Recreations:* orders and medals, heraldry, uniforms. *Address:* Scottish Postal Board, 102 West Port, Edinburgh EH3 9HS. *T:* 031-228 5200. *Club:* United Oxford & Cambridge University.

TILLINGHAST, Charles Carpenter, Jr; Vice-Chairman, White, Weld & Co. Incorporated, since 1977; Director, Trans World Airlines, Inc. (Chairman and Chief Executive, 1969-76); *b* 30 Jan. 1911; *s* of Charles Carpenter Tillinghast and Adelaide Barrows Shaw; *m* 1935, Elizabeth (Lisette) Judd Micoleau; one *s* three *d. Educ:* Horace Mann Sch.; Brown Univ. (PhB); Columbia Univ. (JD). Associate, Hughes, Schurman & Dwight, 1935-37; Dep. Asst Dist Attorney, NY County, 1938-40; Associate, Hughes, Richards, Hubbard & Ewing, 1940-42; Partner, Hughes, Hubbard and Ewing (and successor firm, Hughes, Hubbard, Blair & Reed), 1942-57; Vice-Pres. and Dir, The Bendix Corp., 1957-61; Pres., Chief Exec. Officer, Dir, Trans World Airlines Inc.; Director: Amstar Corp., 1964-; Merck & Co., 1962-; Trustee: Mutual Life Ins. Co. of NY, 1966; Brown Univ., 1954-61, 1965- (Chancellor, 1968-); Mem. IATA Executive Cttee, 1969-. Hon. Degrees: LHD, South Dakota Sch. of Mines and Tech., 1959; LLD: Franklin Coll., 1963; Univ. of Redlands, 1964; Brown Univ., 1967; Drury Coll., 1967; William Jewell Coll., 1973. *Recreations:* golf, shooting, gardening, woodworking, reading, Philharmonic and opera. *Address:* (business) One Liberty Plaza, New York, NY 10006, USA. *T:* (212) 285-7944; (home) 56 Oakledge Road, Bronxville, NY 10708, USA. *T:* (914) 337-6941. *Clubs:* Blind Brook, Brown Univ. (New York); Economic (NY); Hope (RI); Sky; Sakonnet Golf; Siwanoy Country (all in USA).

TILLOTSON, Prof. Kathleen Mary, FBA 1965; MA, BLitt; Hildred Carlile Professor of English in the University of London, at Bedford College, 1958-71, now Emeritus; *b* 3 April 1906; *e d* of late Eric A. Constable, BLitt (Durham), journalist, and Catherine H. Constable, Berwick-on-Tweed and Birmingham; *m* 1933, Geoffrey Tillotson, FBA (*d* 1969); two adopted *s. Educ:* Ackworth School; Mount School, York; Somerville College, Oxford (Exhibitioner and Shaw Lefevre Scholar). Charles Oldham Shakespeare Scholarship, 1926; BA 1927; temporary tutor, Somerville College, 1928-29; BLitt 1929; teaching at Somerville and St Hilda's Colleges, 1929-39; part-time Assistant, later Junior Lecturer, 1929, Lecturer, 1939, Fellow, 1971, Bedford College; Reader in the University of London at Bedford College, 1947-58. Vice-Pres., Dickens Fellowship; Trustee: Dove Cottage; Martindale Trust. Warton Lecture, British Academy, 1956; Annual Tennyson Lecture, 1974. James Bryce Memorial Lecturer, Somerville College, Oxford, 1963, Hon. Fellow, 1965. Hon. DLit Belfast, 1972. Rose Mary Crawshay prize, British Academy, 1943. *Publications:* (with J. W. Hebel and B. H. Newdigate) Works of Michael Drayton, Vol. V, 1941; Novels of the Eighteen-Forties, 1954; Matthew Arnold and Carlyle (Warton Lecture), 1957; (with John Butt) Dickens at Work, 1957; Introductions to Trollope's Barsetshire novels, 1958-75; The Tale and the Teller (inaug. lect.), 1959; Vanity Fair (ed with G. Tillotson), 1963; Mid-Victorian Studies (with G. Tillotson), 1965; Letters of Charles Dickens, vol. 1, 1965, vol. 2, 1969, vol. 3, 1974 (Associate Editor); vol. 4, 1977 (Editor); Oliver Twist, 1966; (ed with A. Trodd) The Woman in White, 1969; Dickens Memorial Lecture, 1970; General editor, Clarendon Dickens; contributions to periodicals. *Address:* 23 Tanza Road, NW3. *T:* 01-435 5639. *Club:* University Women's.

TILMAN, Harold William, CBE 1973; DSO 1945; MC; FRGS (Founder's Medal); LLD; late RA; *b* 14 Feb. 1898; *s* of late John Hinkes Tilman. *Educ:* Berkhamsted School; Royal Military Academy, Woolwich. Commissioned Royal Artillery, July 1915; served on Western Front with RFA and RHA until end of War (MC and bar); resigned, 1919; Reserve of Officers; Farming in Kenya, 1919-33; expeditions to Mts Kenya, Kilimanjaro, and Ruwenzori; various expeditions to Himalaya; Mt Everest Reconnaissance, 1935; Nanda Devi, 1934-36; Leader Mt Everest, 1938; two journeys to Sinkiang, 1947, 1948; two journeys to Nepal, 1949-50; annual voyages to sub-antarctic, antarctic and arctic islands, 1955-76. Served with Royal Artillery in France (despatches), Syria, Irak, Western Desert, Tunisia, 1939-43; with Albanian partisans, 1943-44, and with Italian partisans, 1944-45 (DSO, Freeman of City of Belluno, N Italy). Hon. LLD University of St Andrews, 1954. Blue Water Medal of Cruising Club of America, 1956. *Publications:* Ascent of Nanda Devi, 1937; Snow on the Equator, 1938; When Men and Mountains Meet, 1947; Mount Everest, 1938, 1948; Two Mountains and a River, 1949; China to Chitral, 1951; Nepal Himalaya, 1952; Mischief in Patagonia, 1957; Mischief Among the Penguins, 1961; Mischief in Greenland, 1964; Mostly Mischief, 1966; Mischief goes South, 1968; In Mischief's Wake, 1972; Ice with Everything, 1974; Triumph and Tribulation, 1976. *Address:* Bodowen, near Barmouth, Gwynedd. *T:* Barmouth 630. *Clubs:* Alpine, Naval and Military, Ocean Cruising, Royal Cruising.

TILMOUTH, Prof. Michael; first Tovey Professor of Music, University of Edinburgh, since 1971; *b* 30 Nov. 1930; *s* of Herbert George Tilmouth and Amy Tilmouth (*née* Hall); *m* 1966, Mary Jelliman; two *s* one *d*. *Educ:* Wintringham Grammar Sch., Grimsby; Christ's Coll., Cambridge (MA, PhD). Lectr, Glasgow Univ., 1959-71; Dean, Faculty of Music, Edinburgh Univ., 1973-76. Dir, Scottish Opera, 1975-. Mem., BBC Archives Adv. Cttee, 1975-. Mem. Council, Royal Musical Assoc., 1970-76 (Editor, Research Chronicle, 1968-77); Member, Editorial Committee: Musica Britannica, 1972-; Purcell Soc., 1976-. *Publications:* (ed) Matthew Locke: Chamber Music (Musica Britannica, vols xxxi and xxxii), 1971 and 1972; (ed) Purcell: Collected Works, vol. v, 1976; contribs to: Galpin Soc. Jl, Music & Letters, Proc. of Royal Musical Assoc., Musical Times, Musical Quarterly, Royal Mus. Assoc. Res. Chronicle, Encyc. de la Pléiade, Die Musik in Geschichte und Gegenwart, Grove's Dictionary, Monthly Mus. Record, The Consort, Brio, Early Music. *Recreations:* skiing, squash, hill walking. *Address:* 62 Northumberland Street, Edinburgh EH3 6JE. *T:* 031-556 3293.

TILNEY, Charles Edward, CMG 1956; Minister for Finance and Economics, Tanganyika, 1957-60; *b* 13 April 1909; *yr s* of late Lt-Col N. E. Tilney, CBE, DSO, and late Mrs Tilney; *m* 1952, Rosalind Hull, *e d* of late Lt-Col E. C. de Renzy-Martin, CMG, DSO, MC, and Mrs de Renzy-Martin; two *s*. *Educ:* Rugby School; Oriel College, Oxford. Ceylon Civil Service, 1932; Tanganyika: Asst Chief Secretary (Finance), 1948; Dep. Financial Secretary, 1948; Secretary for Finance, 1950; Member for Finance and Economics, 1953. Retd from E Africa, 1960. *Address:* 8 Butts Close, Biddestone, Chippenham, Wilts. *T:* Corsham 714770.

TILNEY, Guinevere, (Lady Tilney); UK Representative on United Nations Commission on Status of Women, 1970-73; *b* 8 Sept. 1916; *y d* of late Sir Hamilton Grant, 12th Bt, KCSI, KCIE, and late Lady Grant; *m* 1st, 1944, Captain Lionel Hunter (*d* 1947), Princess Louise Dragoon Guards; one *s*; 2nd, 1954, Sir John Tilney, *qv*. *Educ:* Westonbirt. WRNS, 1941-45; Private Sec. to Earl of Selborne, 1949-54; Vice-Chm., SE Lancs Br., British Empire Cancer Campaign, 1957-64; Founder Mem., 1st Chm., 1st Pres., Merseyside Conservative Ladies Luncheon Club, 1957-75, now 1st Hon. Life Mem.; Nat. Council of Women of Great Britain: Vice-Pres., 1958-61, Pres., 1961-68, Liverpool and Birkenhead Br.; Sen. Nat. Vice-Pres., 1966-68; Nat. Pres., 1968-70; Co-Chm., Women's Nat. Commn, 1969-71; Mem., North Thames Gas Consultative Council, 1967-69; Mem., BBC Gen. Adv. Council, 1967-76. Co-Chm., Women Caring Trust, 1972-75. DL: Co. Palatine of Lancaster, 1971-74; Co. Merseyside, 1974-76. *Recreations:* reading, music, theatre. *Address:* 3 Victoria Square, SW1. *T:* 01-828 8674.

TILNEY, Sir John (Dudley Robert Tarleton), Kt 1973; TD; JP; *b* 19 Dec. 1907; *yr s* of late Col R. H. Tilney, DSO; *m* 1954, Guinevere Tilney, *qv*; one step *s*. *Educ:* Eton; Magdalen College, Oxford. Member, Stock Exchange. Served during War of 1939-45 (despatches), with 59th (4th West Lancs) Medium Regt, RA, and 11th Medium Regt, RA; commanded 47/49 359 (4th West Lancs), Medium Regt RATA; Hon. Col 470 (3 W Lancs), LAA Regt, 1957-61. Governor, Liverpool Coll.; Trustee Bluecoat Sch.; Mem. of Cathedral Cttee, The Liverpool Merchants' Guild; Chairman, Liverpool Luncheon Club, 1948-49; Chm. of Liverpool Branch of Royal Commonwealth Soc., 1955-60, Pres., 1965. MP (C) Wavertree, Liverpool, 1950-Feb. 1974; Parliamentary Private Sec. to: Sec. of State for War, 1951-55; Postmaster-General, 1957-59; Chm. Inter-Parly Union, Brit. Gp, 1959-62; Chm. Conservative Commonwealth Council W Africa Cttee, 1954-62; PPS to Minister of Transport, 1959-62; Parly Under-Sec. of State for Commonwealth Relations, 1962-64 and for the Colonies, 1963-64; Member: Select Cttee on

Expenditure; Exec. Cttee, Nat. Union of Conservative and Unionist Assocs, 1965-73; Chm. Merseyside Conservative MPs, 1964-74 (Vice-Chm., NW Area Cttee); Treasurer, UK Branch, Commonwealth Parly Assoc., 1968-70; Mem., Exec. Cttee, Cons. Political Centre, 1972-. Chm., Winston Churchill Meml Statue Cttee. Mem., Exec. Cttee, Westminster Soc., 1975-; Chm., Victoria Square Assoc., 1959-. JP Liverpool, 1946. Croix de Guerre with Gilt Star, 1945; Legion of Honour, 1960. *Recreations:* gardening, travel. *Address:* 3 Victoria Square, SW1W 0QZ. *T:* 01-828 8674. *Clubs:* Pratt's, MCC, Carlton; Jesters; Liverpool Cricket, Liverpool Racquet.

TILNEY, Brig. Robert Adolphus George, CBE 1962; DSO 1945; TD; *b* 2 November 1903; *s* of late Colonel William Arthur Tilney and late Hylda Paget, Sutton Bonington, Notts; *m* 1933, Frances Moore, *d* of late Robert Cochrane Barclay, Virginia, USA; three *d* (one *s* decd). *Educ:* Eton; Cambridge University. Joined Leics Yeo., 1924; Major 1935; Lt-Col Comdg Leics Yeo., 1940-43; Brig. Comdg 234 Bde 1943; Comdg Fortress Leros, 1943 (despatches). Retired as Chm., Sale Tilney & Co. Ltd, Byward Street, EC3, 1965. High Sheriff, Leics, 1953. *Address:* Bucks Lane, Sutton Bonington, Loughborough, Leics.
See also Baron Elton, T. J. King.

TILSTON, Col Frederick Albert, VC 1945; CD; *b* Toronto, Ontario, 11 June 1906; *s* of late Fred Tilston, English birth, and late Agnes Estelle Le May, Cdn birth; *m* 1946; one *s*. *Educ:* De La Salle Collegiate, Toronto; Ontario College of Pharmacy (graduated 1929). Salesman for Sterling Products Ltd, Windsor, Ont., manufacturers of nationally advertised drug products, 1930-36; Canadian Sales Manager for Sterling Products Ltd, 1937-40; Vice-Pres. in charge of sales, Sterling Products Ltd, Windsor, Ontario, 1946-57; Pres., Sterling Drug Ltd, 1957-70; retired 1971. Canadian Army, 1941-46. Hon. Col, Essex and Kent Scottish Regt. CStJ. Hon. Dr Laws Windsor, 1977. *Recreations:* swimming, ice hockey, golf; amateur pianist. *Address:* Wellington Street West, Aurora, Ont, Canada. *T:* Aurora Area 416, 727-4617. *Clubs:* New Windsor, Press, Essex County Golf and Country (Windsor, Ont); Royal Canadian Military Institute (Toronto); Summitt Golf and Country (Oak Ridges).

TILTMAN, Brig. John Hessell, CMG 1954; CBE 1944 (OBE 1930); MC; late King's Own Scottish Borderers; *b* 25 May 1894; *s* of late A. Hessell Tiltman, FRIBA; *m* 1926, Tempe Monica Robinson; one *d*. *Educ:* Charterhouse. *Address:* 4740 Connecticut Avenue NW, Washington, DC 20008, USA. *Club:* Army and Navy.

TIMBERLAKE, Herman Leslie Patterson; Chief General Manager, since 1971, Director, since 1972 and Deputy Chairman, since 1976, Abbey National Building Society; *b* 3 Feb. 1914; *s* of William Walter and Mabel Timberlake; *m* 1940, Betty (*née* Curtis); two *s*. *Educ:* Watford Grammar Sch. FCIS; FBS; FBIM. Served War of 1939-45. Joined Abbey Road Building Soc., 1930; Asst Branch Manager, Watford, 1936; became Abbey National Building Soc., 1944; Branch Manager appts, 1946-59; Manager: Branches Admin. Dept, 1959; Investments Admin. Dept, 1964; Branches and Agencies, 1966; Jt General Manager, 1968. Mem. Council, Building Societies Assoc.; Pres., Building Societies Institute, 1977-78. *Address:* 1 Rochester Drive, Pinner, Mddx HA5 1DA. *T:* 01-866 1554.

TIMMS, Dr Cecil, DEng, CEng, FIMechE, FIProdE; Engineering Consultant, Department of Trade and Industry, later Department of Industry, since 1974; *b* 13 Dec. 1911; *m*; no *c*. *Educ:* Liverpool Univ. Head of Metrology, Mechanisms and Noise Control Div., 1950-61, Supt of Machinery Group, 1961-65, National Engrg Laboratory; Head of Machine Tools Branch, Min. of Technology, later DTI, 1965-73. *Publications:* contribs to Proc. IMechE, Metalworking Prod. and Prod. Engr. *Address:* Broom House, Ballsdown, Chiddingfold, Surrey. *T:* Wormley 2014.

TIMMS, Ven. George Boorne; Archdeacon of Hackney since 1971; Vicar of St Andrew, Holborn, since 1965; *b* 4 Oct. 1910; *s* of late George Timms and Annie Elizabeth Timms (*née* Boorne); unmarried. *Educ:* Derby Sch.; St Edmund Hall, Oxford; Coll. of the Resurrection, Mirfield. MA Oxon. Deacon, 1935; Priest, 1936; Curate: St Mary Magdalen, Coventry, 1935-38; St Bartholomew, Reading, 1938-49; Oxford Diocesan Inspector of Schools, 1944-49; Sacrist of Southwark Cath., 1949-52; Vicar of St Mary, Primrose Hill, NW3, 1952-65; Rural Dean of Hampstead, 1959-65; Prebendary of St Paul's Cathedral, 1964-71. Proctor in Conv., 1955-59, 1965-70, 1974-; Member: Standing Cttee Church Assembly, 1968-70; Anglican-Methodist Unity Commn, 1965-69. Dir of Ordination Trg, and Exam. Chap. to Bp of London, 1965-; Chm., Alcuin Club, 1968-. Papal

Medallion for services to Christian Unity, 1976. *Publications:* Dixit Cranmer, 1946; The Liturgical Seasons, 1965; contributor to A Manual for Holy Week, 1967; (ed) English Praise, 1975. *Address:* St Andrew's Vicarage, St Andrew Street, EC4A 3AB. *T:* 01-353 3544. *Club:* United Oxford & Cambridge University.

TINBERGEN, Dr Jan; Officer, Order of The Lion; Commander, Order of Orange Nassau; Professor, Netherlands School of Economics, since 1933; *b* 12 April 1903; *s* of Dirk Cornelis Tinbergen and Jeannette Van Eek; *m* 1929, Tine Johanna De Wit; three *d* (and one *d* decd). *Educ:* Leiden University. On Staff, Central Bureau of Statistics, 1929-45; Staff, League of Nations, 1936-38; Director, Central Planning Bureau (Dutch Government), 1945-55; Advisor to various governments and international organisations, 1955-; Chm., UN Develt Planning Cttee, 1965-72. Hon. Degrees from 20 Universities, 1954-. (Jointly) Prize in Economics to the memory of Alfred Nobel, 1969. *Publications:* Economic Policy, Principles and Design, 1956; Selected Papers, 1959; Shaping the World Economy, 1962; Income Distribution, 1975; articles. *Recreations:* languages, drawing. *Address:* Haviklaan 31, The Hague, Netherlands. *T:* 070-394884.
See also N. Tinbergen.

TINBERGEN, Prof. Nikolaas, DPhil, MA; FRS 1962; Professor in Animal Behaviour, Oxford University, 1966-74, Emeritus Professor, 1977 (Lecturer, 1949-60, Reader, 1960-66); Fellow of Wolfson College, 1966-74, now Emeritus; *b* 15 April 1907; *s* of Dirk C. Tinbergen and Jeannette Van Eek; *m* 1932, Elisabeth A. Rutten; two *s* three *d*. *Educ:* Leiden; Vienna; Yale. Lecturer, 1936, Prof. of Experimental Zoology, 1947, Leiden University; Fellow, Merton Coll., Oxford Univ., 1950-66. Hon. DSc: Edinburgh, 1973; Leicester, 1974. Godman-Salvin Medal, British Ornithol. Union, 1969. Italia Prize (documentaries), 1969; Swammerdam Medal, 1973; Nobel Prize for Physiology or Medicine (jt), 1973. *Publications:* Eskimoland, 1935; The Study of Instinct, 1951; The Herring Gull's World, 1953; Social Behaviour in Animals, 1953; Curious Naturalists, 1959; Animal Behaviour, 1965; Signals for Survival, 1970; The Animal in its World, vol. 1, 1972, vol. 2, 1973; contribs to German, Dutch, British and American journals. *Address:* 88 Lonsdale Road, Oxford. *T:* Oxford 58662.
See also Dr J. Tinbergen.

TINDAL-CARILL-WORSLEY, Air Commodore Geoffrey Nicolas Ernest, CB 1954; CBE 1943; Royal Air Force, retired; *b* 8 June 1908; *s* of late Philip Tindal-Carill-Worsley; *m* 1st, 1937, Berys Elizabeth Gilmour (marr. diss., 1951; she *d* 1962); one *s*; 2nd, 1951, Dorothy Mabel Murray Stanley-Turner. *Educ:* Eton; RAF Coll., Cranwell. Commanding Officer, RAF Station, Halton, Bucks, 1954-56; Sen. Technical Staff Officer, Far East Air Force, 1956-59; Director of Technical Training, Air Ministry, 1959; retired 1960. *Recreations:* fishing, shooting. *Club:* Army and Navy.

TINDALE, Lawrence Victor Dolman, CBE 1971; Deputy Chairman: Finance For Industry, Industrial & Commercial Finance Corporation, Finance Corporation For Industry, Finance For Shipping, Technical Development Capital, all since 1974; Chairman, Edbro (Holdings), since 1974; Member, National Research & Development Corporation, since 1974; *b* 24 April 1921; *s* of late John Stephen and Alice Lilian Tindale; *m* 1946, Beatrice Mabel (Betty) Barton; one *s* one *d*. *Educ:* Upper Latymer Sch., Hammersmith; Inst. of Chartered Accountants of Scotland. Apprenticed McClelland Ker, 1938. Served War, Army, in E Africa and Burma, 1941-45. Returned to McClelland Ker, and qualified, 1946; Partner, 1951. Invited to join ICFC Ltd as Asst Gen. Manager, 1959; Dir and Gen. Manager, 1966-72. On secondment, DTI, as Dir of Industrial Development, 1972-74. Member, DTI Cttee of Inquiry on Small Firms, 1969-71; Chm., EDC for Mechanical Engrg Industry, 1968-72. Director: Commodore Shipping Co. Ltd, 1969-; Guernsey Gas Light Co. Ltd, 1970-; Investment Trust of Guernsey Ltd, 1970-; Reyrolle Parsons, 1974-; General Funds Investment Trust, 1974-; Estates House Investment Trust, 1975-; London American Finance Corp. Ltd, 1975-; Trind Ltd (Chm.), 1975-; Flextech Oil Pipe (Holdings) Ltd, 1975-. Mem. Council: Consumer Assoc., 1970-; BIM, 1974-; Soc. for Preservation of Ancient Buildings (Hon. Treasurer), 1974-. CA; FBIM. *Recreation:* opera. *Address:* 3 Amyand Park Gardens, Twickenham, TW1 3HS. *T:* 01-892 9457; Le Bouillon House, St George's Esplanade, St Peter Port, Guernsey. *T:* Guernsey 21688. *Clubs:* Reform; St James's (Manchester).

TINDALE, Patricia Randall; Director, Housing Development Directorate, Department of the Environment, since 1974; *b* 11 March 1926; *d* of Thomas John Tindale and May Tindale (*née* Uttin). *Educ:* Blatchington Court, Seaford, Sussex;

Architectural Assoc. Sch. of Architecture (AADip.). ARIBA. Architect, Welsh Dept, Min. of Educn, 1949-50; Min. of Educn Develt Gp, 1951-60; Min. of Housing and Local Govt R&D Gp, 1960-70; DoE Housing Develt Gp, 1970-72; Head, Building Regulations Professional Div., DoE, 1972-74. Mem., AA Council, 1965-68. *Publication:* Housebuilding in the USA, 1966. *Recreations:* weaving, travel. *Address:* 34 Crescent Grove, SW4 7AH.

TINDALL, Rev. Canon Frederick Cryer, BD 1923; AKC 1922; Principal Emeritus of Salisbury Theological College since 1965; Canon and Prebendary of Salisbury Cathedral since 1950; *b* 2 July 1900; *s* of late Frederick and Frances Tindall, Hove, Sussex; *m* 1942, Rosemary Phyllis, *d* of late Frank and Katharine Alice Newman, Woking; one *s* (one *d* decd). *Educ:* Brighton Grammar Sch.; King's Coll., London (Fellow, 1951-); Ely Theological College. Curate of S Cyprian, S Marylebone, 1924-28; Lecturer and Bursar, Chichester Theological College, 1928-30, Vice-Principal, 1930-36; Warden of Connaught Hall and Lecturer in Theology, University College, Southampton, 1936-39; Vicar of St Augustine, Brighton, 1939-50; Principal, Salisbury Theological Coll., 1950-65 (Sabbatical Year 1965-66). Proctor in Convocation for Diocese of Chichester, 1936-45, 1949-50; Examining Chaplain to Bishop of Chichester, 1941-50, Canon and Prebendary of Chichester Cathedral, 1948-50; Proctor in Convocation for Diocese of Salisbury, 1950-75; Vice-Pres. and Chm. House of Clergy, Salisbury Diocesan Synod, 1970-76; Chm., Salisbury Diocesan Liturgical Cttee, 1973-; Member: Commn for Revision of the Catechism, 1958; Church Assembly Standing Orders Cttee, 1963; Archbishop's Commn on London and SE England, 1965; Greater London Area Liaison Cttee, 1968; Pastoral Measure Appeal Tribunal, 1969-75; General Synod Standing Orders Cttee, 1970-75. Clerical Judge, Court of Arches, Canterbury, 1969-. Pro-Prolocutor, Lower House of Convocation of Canterbury, 1959-75. *Publications:* England Expects, 1946; a History of S Augustine's Brighton, 1946; Christian Initiation, Anglican Principles and Practice, 1951; contributor to: History of Christian Thought, 1937; Encyclopædia Britannica Year Book, 1939; Baptism To-Day, 1949; Theology, Church Quarterly Review, Guardian, etc. *Recreations:* music, travelling, golf, gardening. *Address:* Bemerton House, 71 Lower Road, Salisbury, Wilts SP2 9NH. *T:* Salisbury 22373. *Clubs:* Athenæum, Royal Commonwealth Society, Ski Club of Great Britain.

TINDALL, Gillian Elizabeth; *b* 4 May 1938; *d* of D. H. Tindall and U. M. D. Orange; *m* 1963, Richard G. Lansdown; one *s*. *Educ:* Univ. of Oxford (BA 1st cl.). Freelance journalism: for Observer; subseq. Guardian and New Statesman, 1960-; for Evening Standard, 1973. *Publications:* novels: No Name in the Street, 1959; The Water and the Sound, 1961; The Edge of the Paper, 1963; The Youngest, 1967; Someone Else, 1969, 2nd edn 1975; Fly Away Home, 1971 (Somerset Maugham Award, 1972); Dances of Death, 1973; The Traveller and His Child, 1975, etc; *biography:* The Born Exile (George Gissing), 1974; *other non -fiction:* A Handbook on Witchcraft, 1965; The Fields Beneath, 1977; contribs to: Encounter, Punch. *Recreations:* keeping house, foreign travel. *Address:* c/o Curtis Brown Ltd, 1 Craven Hill, W2.

TINDEMANS, Leo; Prime Minister, Belgium, since 1974; President, European People's Party; Vice-President, European Union of Christian Democrats; Visiting Professor in the Faculty of Social Sciences, Catholic University, Louvain; *b* Zwijndrecht, 16 April 1922; *m* 1960, Rosa Naesens; two *s* two *d*. *Educ:* State Univ., Ghent; Catholic Univ., Louvain. Mem., Chamber of Deputies (Christian Social Party), 1961; Mayor of Edegem, 1965-76; Minister of: Community Affairs, 1968-71; Agriculture and Middle Class Affairs, 1972-73; Dep. Prime Minister and Minister for the Budget and Institutional Problems, 1973-74. Awarded Charlemagne Prize, 1976. Hon. DLitt, City Univ., 1976. *Publications:* Ontwikkeling van de Benelux, 1958; L'autonomie culturelle, 1971; Regionalized Belgium, Transition from the Nation State to the Multinational State, 1972; Een handvest voor woelig België, 1972; Dagboek van de werkgroep Eyskens, 1973; European Union, 1975; Europe, Ideal of our Generation, 1976. *Recreations:* reading, writing, walking. *Address:* Prime Minister's Office, Wetstraat 16, B-1000 Brussels, Belgium. *T:* 02/513-80-20; (home) Jan Verbertlei 24, B-2520 Edegem, Belgium.

TINDLE, David, ARA 1973; painter; *b* 29 April 1932; *m* 1969, Janet Trollope; one *s* two *d*. *Educ:* Coventry Sch. of Art. Worked as scene painter and commercial artist, 1946-51; subseq. taught at Hornsey Coll. of Art; Vis. Tutor, Royal Coll. of Art, 1972-. First showed work, Archer Gall., 1952 and 1953; regular one-man exhibns, Piccadilly Gall., from 1954; one-man exhibns at many public and private galleries in Gt Britain; Galerie du

Tours, San Francisco and Los Angeles, 1964; Gallerie Vinciana, Milan, 1968; Galleria Carbonesi, Bologna, 1968; Gallery XX, Hamburg, 1974, 1977; rep. in exhibns at: Piccadilly Gall., 1954-; Royal Acad.; Internat. Biennale of Realist Art, Bruges, 1958 and Bologna, 1967; British Exhibn Art, Basel, 1958; John Moores, 1959 and 1961; Arts Council Shows: British Self-Portraits; Painters in East Anglia; Thames in Art; Salon de la Jeune Peinture, Paris, 1967; Mostra Mercato d'Arte Contemporanea, Florence, 1967; British Painting 1974, Hayward Gall.; British Painting 1952-77, RA. Work rep. in numerous public and private collections; Chantrey Bequest purchases, 1974 and 1975. Critic Prize, 1962; Europe Prize for Painting, 1969; Critics' Choice, Tooths, 1974; Waddington Prize, Chichester Nat. Art Exhibn, 1975. *Address:* Old Chapel, East Haddon, Northants.

TING, Prof. Samuel Chao Chung; Thomas D. Cabot Institute Professor, Massachusetts Institute of Technology, since 1977; *b* 27 Jan. 1936; *s* of K. H. Ting and late T. S. Wang; *m* 1960, Kay Louise Kuhne; two *d*. *Educ:* Univ. of Michigan (PhD). Ford Fellow, CERN, Geneva, 1963; Asst Prof. of Physics, Columbia Univ., 1965; Prof. of Physics, MIT, 1969. Nobel Prize for Physics (jt), 1976. *Publications:* articles in Physical Review and Physical Review Letters. *Address:* 15 Moon Hill Road, Lexington, Mass 02173, USA.

TINKER, Brian; TD; JP; *b* 4 Apr. 1892; *s* of Charles Shaw Tinker, JP, CC, Meal Hill, Hepworth, Yorks; *m* Helen Violet Brameld, *d* of Frank Johnson, Scarborough; no *c. Educ:* Repton; Magdalene College, Cambridge. Studied Mining Engineering with H. St John Durnford at Doncaster; entered Tinker Bros Ltd, 1913; joined QO Yorks Dragoons, 1912; served with them during European War; retired with rank of Major, 1930; commanded the Huddersfield and Wakefield Squadron. JP WR Yorks, 1928. *Recreations:* hunting, Master, Rockwood Harriers, 1927-31, Master, Badsworth Hounds, 1931-34; Master, Grove Hounds, 1937-39. *Address:* Meal Hill, New Mill, Huddersfield, West Yorks. *TA:* New Mill. *T:* Holmfirth 3170.

TINKER, Prof. Hugh Russell; Professor of Politics, University of Lancaster, since 1977; *b* 20 July 1921; *s* of late Clement Hugh Tinker and of Gertrude Marian Tinker; *m* 1947, Elisabeth McKenzie (*née* Willis); three *s. Educ:* Taunton Sch.; Sidney Sussex Coll., Cambridge (BA Scholar). Indian Army, 1941-45; Indian civil admin, 1945-46. Lectr, Reader and Prof., SOAS, 1948-69; Dir, Inst. of Race Relations, 1970-72; Sen. Fellow, Inst. of Commonwealth Studies, Univ. of London, 1972-77. Prof., Univ. of Rangoon, 1954-55; Prof., Cornell Univ., USA, 1959. Mem. Council, Minority Rights Gp; Trustee, Noel Buxton Trust. Contested (L) Barnet, gen. elecs 1964 and 1966. *Publications:* The Foundations of Local Self-Government in India, Pakistan and Burma, 1954; The Union of Burma, a Study of the First Years of Independence, 1957 (4th edn 1967); India and Pakistan, a Political Analysis, 1962; Ballot Box and Bayonet, People and Government in Emergent Asian Countries, 1964; Reorientations, Studies on Asia in Transition, 1965; South Asia, a Short History, 1966; Experiment with Freedom, India and Pakistan 1947, 1967; (ed and wrote introduction) Henry Yule: Narrative of the Mission to the Court of Ava in 1855, 1969; A New System of Slavery: the export of Indian labour overseas 1830-1920, 1974; Separate and Unequal: India and the Indians in the British Commonwealth 1920-1950, 1976; The Banyan Tree: overseas emigrants from India, Pakistan and Bangladesh, 1977; Race, Conflict and the International Order: from Empire to United Nations, 1977. *Recreations:* writing, walking. *Address:* Montbegon, Hornby, near Lancaster; Aspen Lea, Little Hampden, Bucks.

TINN, James; MP (Lab) Teesside, Redcar, since 1974 (Cleveland, 1964-74); an Assistant Government Whip, since 1976; *b* 23 Aug. 1922; *s* of James Tinn and Nora (*née* Davie). *Educ:* Consett Elementary School; Ruskin College; Jesus College, Oxford. Cokeworker until 1953; Branch official, Nat. Union of Blastfurnacemen. Full-time study for BA (PPE Oxon). Teacher, secondary modern school, 1958-64. PPS to Sec. of State for Commonwealth (formerly for Commonwealth Relations), 1965-66, to Minister for Overseas Development, 1966-67. *Address:* 1 Norfolk Road, Moorside, Consett, Co. Durham. *T:* Consett 509313; 8 Woodlands Gate, Putney, SW15. *T:* 01-870 1800. *Club:* United Oxford & Cambridge University.

TINNISWOOD, Maurice Owen; *b* 26 March 1919; *y s* of late Robert Tinniswood, OBE; *m* 1946, Anne Katharine, *yr d* of late Rev. J. Trevor Matchett; one *s* one *d. Educ:* Merchant Taylors' School. Served with Royal Hampshire Regt, 1939-46 (Major). Joined PO, 1938 as Executive Officer, Principal, 1949; Asst Secretary, 1958; Imperial Defence College, 1963; Director of Establishments and Organisation, 1965; Director of Reorganization, 1966; Secretary to the Post Office, 1969-70; Dir

of Personnel, BBC, 1970-77. FBIM 1974. *Address:* Little Croft, Weston Green Road, Thames Ditton, Surrey. *T:* 01-398 4561. *Club:* Royal Automobile.

TINSLEY, Charles Henry, FRICS; Deputy Chief Valuer, Inland Revenue Valuation Office, since 1974; *b* 3 March 1914; *s* of Arthur William and Teresa Tinsley; *m* 1938, Solway Lees; two *s* one *d. Educ:* Ratcliffe Coll., Leicester. Served War: joined TA, 1939; commn in Royal Artillery, 1941; with Lanarkshire Yeomanry, RA, in ME, Sicily and Italy; GSOII, in ME Supply Centre, Tehran, 1945-46. Nottinghamshire and W Riding of Yorkshire County Valuation Depts, 1929-39; Co. Valuer, N Riding of Yorkshire, 1948. Re-joined TA, 1948, and retd as Lt-Col, 1955. Joined Valuation Office, 1949; Suptg Valuer (Rating) Northern Region, 1949-68; Asst Chief Valuer, 1968. *Recreations:* violin making, fishing. *Address:* 44 Belgrave Manor, Brooklyn Road, Woking, Surrey GU22 7TW. *T:* Woking 67444.

TINSLEY, Rt. Rev. Ernest John; *see* Bristol, Bishop of.

TIPPETT, Sir Michael (Kemp), Kt 1966; CBE 1959; Composer; *b* 2 Jan. 1905; *s* of Henry William Tippett and Isabel Kemp. *Educ:* Stamford Grammar Sch.; Royal College of Music (Foley Scholar). Ran Choral and Orchestral Society, Oxted, Surrey, and taught French at Hazelwood School, till 1931. Entered Adult Education work in music (LCC and Royal Arsenal Co-operative Soc. Educn Depts), 1932. Director of Music at Morley College, London, 1940-51. Sent to prison for 3 months as a conscientious objector, June 1943. A Child of Our Time first performed March 1944, broadcast Jan. 1945. 1st Symphony performed Nov. 1945 by Liverpool Philharmonic Society. Artistic Dir, Bath Festival, 1969-74. Hon. Mem., AAAL, 1973. Cobbett Medal for Chamber Music, 1948; Gold Medal, Royal Philharmonic Society, 1976. Hon. MusD: Cambridge, 1964; Trinity Coll., Dublin, 1964; Leeds, 1965; Oxford, 1967; DUniv York, 1966; Hon. DLitt Warwick, 1974. *Works include:* String Quartet No 1, 1935; Piano Sonata, 1937; Concerto for Double String Orchestra, 1939; A Child of Our Time, Oratorio, 1941; Fantasia on a theme of Handel for Piano and Orchestra, 1942; String Quartet, No 2, 1943; Symphony No 1, 1945; String Quartet No 3, 1946; Little Music for Strings, 1946; Suite in D, 1948; Song Cycle, The Heart's Assurance, 1951; Opera, The Midsummer Marriage, 1952 (first performed 1955); Ritual Dances, excerpts from the Opera for Orchestra, 1952; Fantasia Concertante on a Theme of Corelli for String Orchestra, 1953 (commnd for Edinburgh Festival); Divertimento, 1955; Concerto for piano and orchestra, 1956 (commnd by City of Birmingham Symphony Orch.); Symphony No 2, 1957 (commnd by BBC); Crown of the Year (commnd by Badminton School), 1958; Opera, King Priam (commnd by Koussevitsky Foundation of America), 1961; Magnificat and Nunc Dimittis (commnd by St John's Coll., Cambridge), 1961; Piano Sonata No 2, 1962; Incidental music to The Tempest, 1962; Praeludium for Brass etc (commnd by BBC), 1962; Cantata, The Vision of St Augustine, 1966; The Shires Suite, 1970; Opera, The Knot Garden, 1970; Songs for Dov, 1970; Symphony No 3, 1972; Piano Sonata no 3, 1973; Opera, The Ice Break, 1977; Symphony No 4, 1977 (commnd by Chicago SO). *Publication:* Moving into Aquarius, 1959, rev. edn 1974. *Recreation:* croquet. *Address:* c/o Schott & Co., 48 Great Marlborough Street, W1. *TA:* Shotanco, London. *T:* 01-437 1246.

TIPPETTS, Rutherford Berriman; *b* 8 Feb. 1913; *s* of late Percy William Berriman Tippetts and Katherine Brown Rutherford; *m* 1948, Audrey Helen Wilson Cameron; one *s* one *d. Educ:* Rugby; Trinity Coll., Oxford (MA). Asst Principal, BoT, 1936; Principal Private Sec. to Ministers of Supply and Presidents of BoT, 1941-45; idc 1954; Chief Exec., Dollar Exports Council, 1959-61; served in Commercial Relations and Exports, Industry and Tourism Divs of BoT; Under-Sec., Export Services Div., DTI, 1970-73. Master, Worshipful Co. of Armourers and Brasiers, 1975-76. *Recreation:* gardening. *Address:* 23 Clareville Grove, SW7. *T:* 01-373 2759. *Clubs:* Junior Carlton, Roehampton.

TITCHENER, John Lanham Bradbury, CMG 1955; OBE 1947; Director: International Insurance Services, Iran, since 1974; Hamworthy Engineering (Iran), since 1973; Hagen International A/S, since 1977; *b* 28 Nov. 1912; *s* of late Alfred Titchener and late Alicia Marion Leonora Bradbury; *m* 1937, Catherine Law Clark (marr. diss. 1958); no *c; m* 1958, Rikke Marian Lehmann (*née* Bendixsen), *e d* of late Frederik Carl Bendixsen and Kammerherreinde Nina Grandjean of Vennerslund, Falster, Denmark; two step *s. Educ:* City of London Sch.; Royal College of Music. Nat. Council of Education of Canada, 1934; BBC 1938-43; War of 1939-45: served HM Forces, Jan.-Aug. 1943; Psychological Warfare

Branch, Allied Force HQ, Algiers, 1943; 15th Army Group HQ, Italy, 1944-45; Asst Dep. Director, Political Warfare Div., SACSEA, 1945; Political Warfare Adviser to C-in-C, Netherlands East Indies, 1945-46; First Secretary, HM Foreign Service, 1947; served in FO until 1950, when transferred to HM Embassy, Moscow; then at HM Embassy, Ankara, 1953-54; Economic Counsellor, HM Embassy, Tehran, 1954-56, Chargé d'Affaires, 1955. Resigned HM Foreign Service, 1957. *Recreations:* music, gardening, fishing. *Address:* PO Box 1627, Tehran, Iran; 3 Impasse du Château, 06190 Roquebrune Village, France. *T:* (93) 350785. *Club:* Travellers'.

TITE, Dr Michael Stanley, FSA; Keeper, British Museum Research Laboratory, since 1975; *b* 9 Nov. 1938; *s* of Arthur Robert Tite and late Evelyn Frances Violet Tite (*née* Endersby); *m* 1967, Virginia Byng Noel; two *d* . *Educ:* Trinity Sch. of John Whitgift, Croydon; Christ Church, Oxford (MA, DPhil). FSA 1977. Research Fellow in Ceramics, Univ. of Leeds, 1964-67; Lectr in Physics, Univ. of Essex, 1967-75. *Publications:* Methods of Physical Examination in Archaeology, 1972; papers on scientific methods applied to archaeology in various jls. *Recreation:* travelling with "The Buildings of England". *Address:* Crossing Cottage, Boley Road, White Colne, Colchester, Essex. *T:* Earls Colne 2161.

TITFORD, Rear-Adm. Donald George, CEng, FRAeS; Deputy Controller of Aircraft, Ministry of Defence, since 1976; *b* 15 June 1925; *s* of late Percy Maurice Titford and Emily Hannah Titford (*née* McLaren). *Educ:* Highgate Sch.; Royal Naval Engineering Coll.; Coll. of Aeronautics, Cranfield. MSc. MIMechE. Entered RN as Cadet, 1943; Comdr 1959; Air Engr Officer, HMS Victorious, 1965; Captain 1967; comd, RN Air Station, Lee-on-Solent, 1972-74; Comd Engr Officer, Naval Air Comd, 1974-76. *Recreations:* modern pentathlon, old English watercolours. *Address:* Merry Hill, North Road, Bath BA2 6HD. *T:* Bath 62132. *Club:* Army and Navy.

TITHERIDGE, Roger Noel, QC 1973; a Recorder of the Crown Court since 1972; Barrister-at-Law; *b* 21 Dec. 1928; *s* of Jack George Ralph Titheridge and Mabel Titheridge (*née* Steains); *m* 1963, Annabel Maureen (*née* Scott-Fisher); two *d*. *Educ:* Midhurst Grammar Sch.; Merton Coll., Oxford (Exhibnr). MA (History and Jurisprudence). Called to the Bar, Gray's Inn, 1954; Holker Sen. Scholar, Gray's Inn, 1954. *Recreations:* tennis, sailing. *Address:* 1 Paper Buildings, Temple, EC4. *T:* 01-353 3728; 13 The Moat, Traps Lane, New Malden, Surrey. *T:* 01-942 2747.

TITMAN, Sir George (Alfred), Kt 1954; CBE 1948 (OBE 1937); MVO (4 cl.) 1942; Secretary, Lord Chamberlain's Office, 1939-54, retired; *b* 12 July 1889; *o s* of late George Titman, Lewisham; *m* 1914, Eva Ellen, *e d* of late Charles Comfort, Cheltenham; one *s* one *d* (twins). Clerk, Duchess of Albany's Household, 1910-16; served in The King's (Liverpool) Regt, 1916; Clerk in Queen Mary's Household, 1916-19; Central Chancery of Orders of Knighthood, 1919-22; entered Lord Chamberlain's Office, 1922; First Clerk, 1932; Asst Secretary, 1936; a Sergeant-at-Arms to King George VI, 1946-52, to the Queen, 1952-54. Order of St John; Officer Legion of Honour; Chev. Order of Dannebrog (Denmark); Officer House of Orange (Netherlands); Chevalier (Cl. IV), Order of Vasa (Sweden); Cav. Crown of Italy; Order of Menelik II (Cl. IV); Star of Ethiopia (3). *Publication:* Dress and Insignia Worn at Court, 1937. *Address:* 42 Chadacre Road, Stoneleigh, Epsom, Surrey. *T:* 01-393 1683.

TITO, President (Josip Broz); Marshal of Yugoslavia since 1943; Prime Minister and Minister of National Defence, Yugoslavia, since 1945; President of Yugoslavia, since 1953, Life President, since 1974; President of the League of Communists of Yugoslavia; Supreme Commander of the Yugoslav Army; *b* 7 May 1892; *s* of Franjo and Marija Broz; a Croatian; *m* 1st, 1918 (wife decd); one *s* ; 2nd, 1939 (marr. diss.); one *s* ; 3rd, 1952, Jovanka Budisavljevic. Served in Austro-Hungarian Army, 1913-15; war prisoner, Russia, 1915-17; fought with Red Army, 1917-20; returned to Yugoslavia, worked as machinist and mechanic, and became Croatian Labour leader working with Metal Workers' Union; was imprisoned for five years for conspiracy after taking part in illegal Communist activities, 1928; left the country, on release, and recruited Yugoslavs for the International Brigades in Spanish Civil War, 1936-37; became Member of Central Committee, 1934; Secretary General of the Yugoslav Communist Party, 1937; returned to Yugoslavia before War of 1939-45, during which, at head of Yugoslav Communist Party, led general people's uprising and revolution in occupied Yugoslavia; Supreme Commander of Yugoslav National Liberation Army. Elected Marshal of Yugoslavia and President Nat. Liberation Cttee, 1943. Elected President of the Yugoslav Government, 1945; elected President of the Republic,

1953, re-elected 1954, 1958, 1963, 1967 and 1971. Decorations: Grand Star of Yugoslavia; Order of Liberty; 3 orders of National Hero; Hero of Socialist Work; National Liberation; War Flag; Great Cordon of Yugoslav Flag; Partisan Star with Golden Wreath; Merit for the People with Golden Star; Fraternity and Unity with Golden Wreath; Outstanding Courage; Order of the October Revolution; Hon. GCB 1972; in all about 70 high foreign decorations. *Publications:* twenty-three volumes of articles, speeches and other documents covering the period 1941-68. *Address:* Užička 15, Belgrade, Yugoslavia.

TITTERTON, Prof. Sir Ernest (William), Kt 1970; CMG 1957; FRSA; FAA; Professor of Nuclear Physics, Australian National University, since 1950; Dean of the Research School of Physical Sciences, Australian National University, 1966-68, Director of Research School of Physical Sciences, 1968-73; *b* 4 March 1916; *e s* of W. A. Titterton, Tamworth, Staffs; *m* 1942, Peggy Eileen, *o d* of Captain A. Johnson, Hagley, Worcs; one *s* two *d*. *Educ:* Queen Elizabeth's Grammar Sch., Tamworth; University of Birmingham (BSc, MSc, PhD). Research Officer, Admiralty, 1939-43; Member British Scientific Mission to USA on Atomic Bomb development, 1943-47; Sen. Member of Timing Group at 1st Atomic Bomb Test, Alamagordo, 1945; Adviser on Instrumentation, Bikini Atomic Weapon Tests, 1946; Head of Electronics Div., Los Alamos Lab., USA, 1946-47; Group Leader in charge of Research team at AERE, Harwell, 1947-50. Member Australian Atomic Energy Commn Scientific Advisory Cttee, 1955-64; Dep. Chairman Australian Atomic Weapons Safety Cttee, 1954-56; Chm., Atomic Weapons Safety Cttee, 1957-73 (in this capacity attended all British Atom Bomb tests in Australia, 1952-57); Member, Defence Research and Development Policy Cttee, 1958-75; Member National Radiation Advisory Cttee, 1957-73. Vice-Pres., Aust. Inst. of Nuclear Science and Engineering, 1968-72, Pres., 1973-75. *Publications:* Facing the Atomic Future (London, New York, Melbourne), 1956; some 212 papers mainly on nuclear physics, atomic energy and electronics in technical journals. *Recreations:* music and tennis. *Address:* 8 Somers Crescent, Forrest, Canberra, ACT 2603, Australia. *T:* Canberra 7-32280.

TIVERTON, Viscount; Adam Edward Giffard; *b* 3 June 1934; *o s* of 3rd Earl of Halsbury, *qv* ; *m* 1963, Ellen, *d* of late Brynjolf Hovde. *Educ:* Stowe; Jesus Coll., Cambridge.

TIZARD, Prof. Jack, CBE 1973; Professor of Child Development, University of London, Institute of Education, 1964-71, Research Professor since 1971; Director, Thomas Coram Research Unit; *b* 25 Feb. 1919; *s* of John Marsh Tizard; *m* 1947, Barbara Patricia Parker; two *s* one *d* (and one *d* adopted). *Educ:* Timaru Boys' High Sch.; Canterbury University Coll., NZ; Universities of Oxford and London. MA NZ 1940; BLitt Oxford 1948; PhD London 1951. Army Service, 2 NZEF, MEF, and CMF, 1940-45. Lecturer in Psychology, St Andrews, 1947-48; Sci. Staff, MRC, Social Psychiatry Research Unit, 1948-64. Bartholomew Lecturer, University of Keele, 1966; Emanuel Miller Lecture, Assoc. for Child Psychology and Psychiatry, 1973; Dorothy Gardner Lecture, 1975. Kennedy International Scientific Award, 1968. Member, Social Science Research Council and Chm. of its Educational Research Board, 1969-71; Consultant Adv. in Mental Subnormality, Dept of Health and Social Security, 1965-75; Consultant to Home Office Res. Unit, 1975-; Chairman: Spastics Soc. Educational Adv. Cttee, 1966-; Sec. of State's Adv. Cttee on Handicapped Children, 1970-73; Assoc. of Child Psychology and Psychiatry, 1964-65; Member: Chief Scientist's Res. Cttee, DHSS, 1973-77; Child Health Services Cttee. Pres., British Psychological Soc., 1975-76. Consultant on Mental Subnormality, WHO. Hon. Mem., British Paediatric Assoc. FBPsS, FRSM. Res. Award, Amer. Assoc. on Mental Deficiency, 1973. *Publications:* The Social Problem of Mental Deficiency (with N. O'Connor), 1956; The Mentally Handicapped and their Families (with J. C. Grad), 1961; Community Services for the Mentally Handicapped, 1964; Education, Health and Behaviour (with M. L. Rutter and T. K. Whitmore), 1970; Patterns of Residential Care (with R. D. King and N. V. Raynes), 1971; (with R. Clarke and I. Sinclair) Varieties of Residential Experience, 1975; (with P. Moss and J. Perry) All Our Children, 1976; articles on mental retardation and child development. *Address:* 4 The Gables, Vale of Health, NW3. *T:* 01-435 4475.

TIZARD, John Peter Mills; Professor of Pædiatrics, University of Oxford, since May 1972; Hon. Consultant Children's Physician, United Oxford Hospitals, since 1972; Fellow, Jesus College, Oxford, since 1972; *b* London, 1 April 1916; *e s* of late Sir Henry Thomas Tizard, GCB, AFC, FRS, and late Lady (Kathleen Eleanor) Tizard; *m* 1945, Elisabeth Joy, *yr d* of late Clifford John Taylor, FRCSE; two *s* one *d*. *Educ:* Rugby Sch.; Oriel Coll., Oxford; Middlesex Hospital. BA Oxon 1938 (3rd cl.

Hons Honour Sch. of Natural Science); Oxford and Cambridge School. (Biochemistry and Physiology), Middlesex Hospital, 1938; MA, BM, BCh Oxon 1941; MRCP 1944; FRCP 1958; DCH England 1947. Served War of 1939-45 with RAMC, 1942-46 (Temp. Major). Med. Registrar and Pathologist, Hospital for Sick Children, Great Ormond Street, 1947; Asst Director, Pædiatric Unit, St Mary's Hospital Medical Sch., 1949; Physician, Paddington Green Children's Hospital, 1949; Nuffield Foundation Medical Fellow, 1951; Research Fellow in Pediatrics, Harvard Univ., 1951; Reader in Child Health, 1954-64, Prof. of Pædiatrics, Inst. of Child Health, Royal Postgraduate Med. Sch., Univ. of London, 1964-72; Hon. Cons. Children's Physician, Hammersmith Hosp., 1954-72; Chm., Med. Cttee, Hammersmith Hosp., 1970-71. Lectures: Blackfan Meml, Harvard Univ., 1963; Samuel Gee, RCP, 1972; Carl Fridericksen, Danish Paediatric Soc., 1972; Perlstein, Louisville Univ., 1973; Clausen Meml, Rochester Univ., NY, 1975; Choremis Meml, Hellenic Paediatric Soc., 1975; Orator, Reading Pathological Soc., 1973. Mem. Ct of Assistants, Soc. of Apothecaries of London, 1971-. Member: British Pædiatric Assoc., 1953; European Pædiatric Research Soc., 1959 (Pres., 1970-71); Neonatal Society, 1959- (Hon. Sec. 1964-66; Pres., 1975-); Assoc. Physicians of Great Britain and Ireland, 1965; Assoc. British Neurologists, 1969; German Acad. of Scientists, Leopoldina, 1972; Harveian Soc., 1974- (Pres., 1977); Corresp. Member: Société française de Pédiatrie, 1969; Pædiatric Soc. of Chile, 1968; Austrian Paediatric Soc., 1972; Swiss Paediatric Soc., 1973; Hon. Member: Pædiatric Soc. of Concepcion, 1968; Czechoslovak Med. Assoc. J. E. Purkynĕi, 1971; Dutch Pædiatric Soc., 1971; Amer. Pediatric Soc., 1976. *Publications:* Medical Care of Newborn Babies (jtly), 1972; papers in scientific and medical journals. *Address:* Ickenham Manor, Ickenham, Uxbridge, Mddx UB10 8QT. *T:* Ruislip 32262; Jesus College, Oxford OX1 3DW. *Club:* Athenæum.

TIZARD, Hon. Robert James; MP for Otahuhu (Pakuranga), New Zealand; *b* 7 June 1924; *s* of Henry James and Jessie May Tizard; *m* 1951, Catherine Anne Maclean; one *s* three *d*. *Educ:* Auckland Grammar Sch.; Auckland Univ. MA, Hons Hist., 1949. Served War: RNZAF, 1943-46, incl. service in Canada and Britain; (commnd as a Navigator, 1944). Pres., Students' Assoc., Auckland Univ., 1948; Lectr in History, Auckland Univ., 1949-53; teaching, 1954-57 and 1961-62. MP 1957-60 and 1963-; Minister of Health and State Services, 1972-74; Dep. Prime Minister and Minister of Finance, 1974-75; Dep. Leader of the Opposition, 1975-. *Recreations:* golf, squash. *Address:* 84A Beresford Street, Auckland 1, New Zealand.

TOBIAS, Prof. Stephen Albert, DSc, PhD Edinburgh, MA Cantab, DiplEng Budapest; FIMechE; FIProdE; Chance Professor of Mechanical Engineering and Head of Department, University of Birmingham, since 1959; *b* Vienna, 10 July 1920; *s* of Bela and Zelma; *m* 1945, Stephanie Paula Garzo; two *s*. *Educ:* Josef Eotvos Gymnasium, Budapest; Technological Univ., Budapest; Edinburgh Univ. DiplEng Technological Univ., Budapest, 1943. MASME. Machine Tool Design Engineer, 1943-47; British Council Scholarship, 1947; ICI Research Fellow, 1951-54; Assistant Director of Research, Department of Engineering, Cambridge Univ., 1956. Visiting Professor: Univ. of Cairo, 1963; Univ. of Denver, 1969; Univ. of California, 1969; Nat. Univ. of Mexico, 1970. UNESCO Consultant to Brazil, 1971. Dir, Engineering DRD Ltd. Member: Engineering Industry Trng Bd, ASME, 1967- (Chm. Technologist Trng Panel); SRC Manufacturing Technology Cttee, 1972-75; CIRP. T. Bernard Hall Prize, 1957, and Whitworth Prize, 1959, of Instn of Mechanical Engineers; Blackall Machine Tool Award, 1958, of American Society of Mech. Engineers. Co-editor in chief, Procs Internat. Conf. for Machine Tool Design and Res., 1963-; Editor in Chief, Internat. Jl for Machine Tool Design and Res., 1977- (co-editor in chief, 1959-76). *Publications:* Schwingungen an Werkzeugmaschinen, 1961; Machine-Tool Vibration, 1965 (Japanese edn, 1969, Spanish edn, 1971); over 120 contributions to engineering journals and proceedings of learned societies dealing with linear and non-linear vibrations, dynamic stability of metal cutting process, high energy rate forming, design and impact noise. *Recreations:* colour photography, music, cultivation of cactus plants, petroforging. *Address:* Department of Mechanical Engineering, PO Box 363, University of Birmingham, Birmingham B15 2TT. *T:* 021-472 1301. *Club:* Athenæum.

TOD, Sir John Hunter H.; *see* Hunter-Tod.

TODD, family name of **Baron Todd.**

TODD, Baron, *cr* 1962, of Trumpington (Life Peer); **Alexander Robertus Todd,** OM 1977; Kt 1954; FRS 1942; DSc Glasgow; Dr Phil nat Frankfurt; DPhil Oxon; MA Cantab; FRIC; Master

of Christ's College, Cambridge, since 1963 (Fellow, 1944); Professor of Organic Chemistry, University of Cambridge, 1944-71; (first) Chancellor, University of Strathclyde, Glasgow; President of the Royal Society, since 1975; Director, Fisons Ltd; *b* Glasgow, 2 Oct. 1907; *e s* of Alexander Todd, JP, Glasgow; *m* 1937, Alison Sarah, *e d* of Sir H. H. Dale, OM, GBE, FRS; one *s* two *d*. *Educ:* Allan Glen's Sch.; University of Glasgow. Carnegie Research Scholar, University of Glasgow, 1928-29; Univ. of Frankfurt a M, 1929-31; 1851 Exhibition Senior Student, Univ. of Oxford, 1931-34; Assistant in Medical Chemistry, 1934-35, and Beit Memorial Research Fellow, 1935-36, University of Edinburgh; Member of Staff, Lister Institute of Preventive Medicine, London, 1936-38; Reader in Biochemistry, University of London, 1937-38; Visiting Lecturer, California Institute of Technology, USA, 1938; Sir Samuel Hall Professor of Chemistry and Director of Chemical Laboratories, University of Manchester, 1938-44. Chairman, Advisory Council on Scientific Policy, 1952-64. Visiting Professor: University of Chicago, 1948; University of Sydney, 1950; Mass. Inst. Tech., 1954. Chemical Society, Tilden Lecturer, 1941, Pedler Lecturer, 1946; Meldola Medal, 1936; Leverhulme Lecturer, Society of Chemical Industry, 1948; President: Chemical Soc., 1960-62; Internat. Union of Pure and Applied Chemistry, 1963-65; British Assoc. Advancement of Science, 1969-70. Chairman: Royal Commn on Medical Education, 1965-68; Board of Governors, United Cambridge Hospitals, 1969-74. Member Council, Royal Society, 1967-70; Mem., NRDC, 1968-76. Hon. Member French, German, Spanish, Belgian, Swiss Chemical Societies; Foreign Member: Nat. Acad. Sciences, USA; American Acad. of Arts and Sciences; Akad. Naturf. Halle; American Phil. Soc.; Australian, Austrian, Indian, New York and Polish Academies of Science. Hon. Fellow: Australian Chem. Institute; Manchester College Technology; Royal Society Edinburgh. Chairman, Managing Trustees, Nuffield Foundation, 1973- (Trustee, 1950-); Lavoisier Medallist, French Chemical Society, 1948; Davy Medal of Royal Society, 1949; Bakerian Lecturer, 1954; Royal Medal of Royal Society, 1955; Nobel Prize for Chemistry, 1957; Cannizzaro Medal, Italian Chemical Society, 1958. Paul Karrer Medal, Univ. Zürich, 1962; Stas Medal, Belgian Chemical Society, 1962; Longstaff Medal, Chemical Society, 1963; Copley Medal, Royal Society, 1970. Hon. FRCP 1975. Hon. Fellow: Oriel Coll., Oxford, 1955; Churchill Coll., Cambridge, 1971. Hon. LLD: Glasgow, Melbourne, Edinburgh, Manchester, California; Hon. Dr rer nat Kiel; Hon. DSc: London, Madrid, Exeter, Leicester, Aligarh, Sheffield, Wales, Yale, Strasbourg, Harvard, Liverpool, Adelaide, Strathclyde, Oxford, ANU, Paris, Warwick, Durham, Michigan; Hon. DLitt Sydney. Pour le Mérite, German Federal Republic, 1966. Master, Salters' Company, 1961. *Publications:* numerous scientific papers in chemical and biochemical journals. *Recreations:* fishing, golf. *Address:* Master's Lodge, Christ's College, Cambridge. *T:* Cambridge 56688. *Club:* Athenæum.

TODD, Rev. Alastair, CMG 1971; Priest-in-charge, St Augustine's, Brighton, since 1977; *b* 21 Dec. 1920; *s* of late Prof. James Eadie Todd, MA, FRHistS (formerly Prof. of History, Queen's University, Belfast) and Margaret Simpson Johnstone Maybin; *m* 1952, Nancy Hazel Buyers; two *s* two *d*. *Educ:* Royal Belfast Academical Institution; Fettes Coll., Edinburgh; Corpus Christi Coll., Oxford; London Univ. (External); Salisbury and Wells Theological Coll. BA (Oxon), DipTheol (London). Served War, Army, 1940-46, Capt. RHA. Apptd Colonial Administrative Service, Hong Kong, 1946; Joint Services Staff Coll., 1950; Defence Sec., Hong Kong, 1957-60; Dep. Colonial Sec., Hong Kong, 1963-64; Dir of Social Welfare, also MLC, 1966-68; and, again, Defence Sec., 1968-71, retd. Ordained Deacon by Bishop of Chichester, 1973 and Priest, 1974; Asst Curate, Willingdon, 1973-77. *Recreations:* reading, walking, embroidery, gardening. *Address:* St Augustine's Vicarage, 32 Florence Road, Brighton. *T:* Brighton 561755.

TODD, (Alfred) Norman, FCA; CompIEE; Chairman, National Bus Company, 1969-71; retired; *b* 18 Oct. 1904; *s* of late Alfred and Rachel Todd; *m* 1935, Mary Watson; one *s* one *d*. *Educ:* Bishops Stortford College. With Deloitte Plender Griffiths & Co., 1929-48; Assistant, then Deputy Chief Accountant, Merseyside and North Wales Electricity Board, 1948-51; Assistant Chief Accountant, British Electricity Authority, 1951-54; Chief Accountant, London Electricity Board, 1954-56; Dep. Chairman, London Electricity Board, 1956-61; Chairman, East Midlands Electricity Board, 1962-64. Member, Central Electricity Generating Board, 1965-68. Hon. Treasurer, IEE, 1972-75. *Recreation:* golf. *Address:* Allendale, 139 Cooden Drive, Bexhill-on-Sea, East Sussex. *T:* Cooden 4147.

TODD, Ann; Actress; *m* 1933, Victor Malcolm; one *s*; *m* 1939, Nigel Tangye; one *d*; *m* 1949, David Lean, *qv* (marr. diss.). Stage plays and films include: *Plays:* Peter, in Peter Pan, Winter

Garden, 1942-43; Lottie, in Lottie Dundass, Vaudeville, 1943; Madeleine Smith, in The Rest is Silence, Prince of Wales, 1944; Francesca Cunningham in The Seventh Veil, Princes, 1951; Foreign Field, 1953; Old Vic Season, 1954-55; Macbeth; Love's Labour's Lost; Taming of the Shrew; Henry IV, Parts I and II; Jennifer Dubedat in The Doctor's Dilemma, Saville, 1956; Four Winds, New York, 1957; Duel of Angels, London, 1958. *Films:* The Seventh Veil, 1945; Daybreak, 1948; The Paradine Case, 1948; So Evil My Love, 1948; The Passionate Friends, 1949; Madeleine, 1950; The Sound Barrier, 1952; The Green Scarf, 1954; Time Without Pity, 1956; Taste of Fear, 1960; Son of Captain Blood, 1961; 90 Degrees in the Shade, 1964; The Vortex, 1965; Beware my Brethren, 1970; The Fiend, 1971; produced, wrote and appeared in Diary Documentaries, 1964-74: Thunder in Heaven (Kathmandu); Thunder of the Gods (Delphi); Thunder of the Kings (Egypt); Persian Fairy Tale; Free in the Sun (Australia); Thunder of Silence (Jordan); Thunder of Light (Scotland). Appears frequently on radio and television both in US and Great Britain, incl. The Last Target, BBC, 1972. *Address:* 57 Melbury Road, Kensington, W14; Sea Green Cottage, Walberswick, Suffolk.

TODD, Arthur James Stewart; retired; *b* 12 Feb. 1895; *s* of George Todd, ISO, and Emily Mary Ellerman; *m* 1927, Marjorie Elizabeth Moughton; one *d*. *Educ:* St Paul's Sch.; University of Lausanne. Served at home and abroad during the European War in the Army from the outbreak to end 1916 and the Naval Auxiliary Services during 1918 (Mons medal, Army medal, Allied medal, Naval medal). Home Guard, 1940-44; Staff Captain, 1943-44. Joined family shipping co. (nephew of Sir John Ellerman, 1st Bt, CH) after World War I; Dir, Westcott & Laurance Line, Ellerman's Wilson Line and other subsidiary cos; Dir, 1929, Alliance Assce Co., later Sun Alliance & London Insce Gp; retired after 40 years. *Recreations:* rugby commentator, philately. *Address:* Flat 42, 4 Grand Avenue, Hove, East Sussex. *Clubs:* Sussex County Cricket, St James' Cricket, Brighton Rugby.

TODD, Sir Bryan (James), Kt 1976; Chairman: Todd Petroleum Mining Co. Ltd, since 1955; Viking Mining Co. Ltd, since 1970; Director: Todd Motors Ltd, since 1924; Shell, BP & Todd Oil Services Ltd, since 1955; *b* 8 Sept. 1902; *s* of Charles Todd and Mary (*née* Hegarty); *m* 1928, Helen Ann Buddo; three *d*. *Educ:* Christian Bros, Dunedin, NZ; Riverview Coll., Sydney, NSW, Australia. Automotive industry, 1922-; prominent in petroleum industry of NZ, 1930-; Founder and formerly Managing Director: Europa Oil (NZ) Ltd (marketing and refining); Todd Petroleum Mining Co. Ltd (exploration and production of oil and gas in NZ); Viking Mining Co. Ltd (ironsand prodn, refining and export). Chairman: Ruapehu Alpine Lifts Ltd, 1953-; Todd Foundn, 1972-. *Recreations:* skiing, sailing, golf, shooting. *Address:* 38 Wesley Road, Wellington, New Zealand. *T:* (home) 727 040, (office) 722 970. *Clubs:* Wellington, Wellesley (Wellington, NZ); Wellington Golf (Heretaunga, NZ); Ruapehu Ski (NZ).

See also Adm . Sir Gordon Tait .

TODD, Hon. Garfield; see Todd, Hon. R. S. G.

TODD, Sir Geoffrey Sydney, KCVO 1951 (CVO 1947); OBE 1946; DL; MB, ChM, FRCP; FRACP; Medical Superintendent, King Edward VII Hospital, Midhurst, 1934-70; *b* 2 Nov. 1900; *s* of late George William Todd, and Amy Louisa Webb; *m* 1955, Margaret Alan Sheen, *o d* of late F. A. Sheen, MC, and of Mrs Sheen, Tudor Cottage, Midhurst. *Educ:* King's Sch., Parramatta, Australia; Sydney Univ., Australia. Resident MO, 1925-26, Medical Superintendent, 1926-27, Wagga District Hospital; House Physician 1929, House Surgeon 1930, Resident MO 1930-34, Brompton Hospital for Chest Diseases, London. DL Sussex, 1968, West Sussex, 1974. Guthrie Meml Medal, 1971. CStJ. *Publications:* various, in medical journals, 1936-56. *Recreations:* sailing, golf, photography. *Address:* Friars Gate, 1 Priory Road, Chichester, West Sussex. *T:* Chichester 82798. *Club:* Naval and Military.

TODD, Sir Herbert John, Kt 1947; CIE 1944; retired as Chief Representative, Iraq Petroleum Company and Associate Companies, Baghdad (1952-59); *b* 15 Oct. 1893; *m* 1919, Nancy, 2nd *d* of Colonel A. F. Pullen, RA; two *d*. Imperial Police, Burma, 1913; 11th Bengal Lancers (Probyns Horse), 1917; Civil Administration, Mesopotamia, 1919; Indian Political Service, 1921; Asst Political Agent, Sibi, 1921; Kalat, 1922; Political Agent, Gilgit, 1927; Quetta-Pishin, 1932; Political Agent, E Rajputana States, 1935; Prime Minister and Vice-President, Council of State, Jaipur, 1939; Political Agent, Mewar, 1940; Secretary, Baluchistan, 1941; Resident for the Madras States, 1943; Resident for the Eastern States, 1944-47. *Address:* Grey Gables, Sandy Lane, Old Oxted, Surrey RH8 9LU. *T:* Oxted 3926.

TODD, James Maclean, MA; Secretary to the Oxford University Delegacy for the Inspection and Examination of Schools and Oxford Secretary to the Oxford and Cambridge Schools Examination Board, 1964-74; Founder Fellow of St Cross College, Oxford; *b* 1907; *s* of late John Todd, Oxford, and Mary, *d* of late Robert Spottiswoode, Gattonside; *m* 1944, Janet, *d* of late Andrew Holmes, Glasgow; one *s* one *d*. *Educ:* City of Oxford School; The Queen's Coll., Oxford (Open Mathematical Scholar). First Class Mathematical Mods, 1928; 2nd Class Lit. Hum., 1930; 2nd Class Hon. School of Theology, 1931. Awarded Holwell Studentship in Theology. Assistant Master, Radley, Bryanston, Bromsgrove and Stowe. Headmaster, The High School, Newcastle, Staffs, 1948-63. *Publications:* The Ancient World, 1938; Hymns and Psalms for use in Newcastle High School (New Edn), 1951; Voices from the Past: a Classical Anthology (with Janet Maclean Todd), 1955 (Grey Arrow edn, 1960); Peoples of the Past (with Janet Maclean Todd), 1963. *Address:* The White House, Headington Quarry, Oxford. *T:* Oxford 63624.

TODD, John Arthur, FRS 1948; PhD; Emeritus Reader in Geometry in the University of Cambridge; Fellow of Downing College, 1958-73, Hon. Fellow 1973; *b* 23 Aug. 1908; *s* of John Arthur and Agnes Todd. *Educ:* Liverpool Collegiate School; Trinity Coll., Cambridge. Assistant Lecturer in Mathematics, University of Manchester, 1931-37; Lecturer in Mathematics in the University of Cambridge, 1937-60, Reader in Geometry 1960-73. *Publications:* Projective and Analytical Geometry, 1947; various mathematical papers. *Address:* 30 Glebe Hyrst, Sanderstead, South Croydon, Surrey CR2 9JE. *T:* 01-657 4994.

TODD, John Francis James, PhD, CChem, FRIC; Master of Rutherford College, University of Kent at Canterbury, since 1975; Senior Lecturer in Chemistry, Faculty of Natural Sciences, University of Kent at Canterbury, since 1973; *b* 20 May 1937; *o s* of late Eric Todd and Annie Lewin Todd (*née* Tinkler); *m* 1963, Mavis Georgina Lee; three *s* . *Educ:* Leeds Grammar Sch.; Leeds Univ. (BSc, Cl. I Hons Chem.). Research Fellow: Leeds Univ., 1962-63; Yale Univ., USA, 1963-65; Univ. of Kent at Canterbury: Asst Lectr in Chemistry, 1965-66; Lectr in Chemistry, 1966-73. 'J. B. Cohen Prizeman, Leeds Univ., 1963; Fulbright Research Scholar, 1963-65. Chm., Kent Section of Chem. Soc., 1975. Mem., Amer. Soc. of Sigma Xi, Yale Chapter. *Publications:* (jt ed) Dynamic Mass Spectrometry, Vol. 4, 1975; reviews and papers, mainly on mass spectrometry, in Jl of Chem. Soc. and Jl of Physics, etc. *Recreations:* music, travel. *Address:* Rutherford College, University of Kent at Canterbury. *T:* Canterbury 66822 (ext. 470); West Bank, 122 Whitstable Road, Canterbury, Kent. *T:* Canterbury 69552.

TODD, Mary Williamson Spottiswoode, MA; Headmistress of Harrogate College, 1952-73; *b* 11 June 1909; *d* of John and Mary Todd, Oxford. *Educ:* Oxford High School; Lady Margaret Hall, Oxford. MA Hons Oxon. Final Hon. Sch.: Mathematics, 1932, Nat. Science, 1933; London Diploma in Theology, 1941. Various teaching posts: St Felix School, Southwold, 1933-37; Clifton High School, Bristol, 1937-39; Westonbirt School, Glos, 1939-46; Headmistress of Durham, 1946-52. *Address:* 93 Oakdale, Harrogate, North Yorks. *T:* Harrogate 66411.

TODD, Norman; see Todd, A. N.

TODD, Hon. R(eginald) S(tephen) Garfield; *b* 13 July 1908; *s* of late Thomas and Edith C. Todd; *m* 1932, Jean Grace Wilson; three *d*. *Educ:* Otago Univ.; Glen Leith Coll.; University of Witwatersrand. Minister Oamaru Church of Christ, NZ, 1932-34; Superintendent Dadaya Mission, 1934-53, Chm. Governing Bd 1963-. Man. Dir, Hokonui Ranching Co. MP for Shabani, 1946-58; elected leader, United Rhodesia Party and Prime Minister of S Rhodesia, 1953-58; Federal President, Central Africa Party, 1959-60; President, New Africa Party, 1961. First Vice-President World Convention of Churches of Christ (Disciples), 1955-60; awarded Citation for Christian Leadership in Politics and Race Relations; Member Executive: United Coll. of Educn, Bulawayo, 1965-; Rhodesian Christian Council, 1967-. Has lectured widely, USA, Canada, UK, Australia, NZ, S Africa. Holds hon. doctorates. Arrested by Smith regime in 1965 and confined to ranch for one year; arrested by Smith regime in 1972 and imprisoned without charge or trial for five weeks, then detained at home on Hokonui Ranch, the area being gazetted as a 'protected area' and closed to public under police guard; detention order lifted June 1976; a Political Adviser to Mr Joshua Nkomo at Geneva Conf. on Future of Rhodesia, 1976. *Address:* PO Dadaya, Rhodesia. *Club:* Bulawayo.
See also Baron Acton.

TODD, Richard, (Richard Andrew Palethorpe-Todd); actor; *b* 11 June 1919; *s* of Major A. W. Palethorpe-Todd, Castlederg, Co.

Tyrone, and Marvil Agar-Daly, Ballymalis Castle, Kerry; *m* 1st, 1949, Catherine Stewart Crawford Grant-Bogle (marr. diss. 1970); one *s* one *d*; 2nd, 1970, Virginia Anne Rollo Mailer; two *s*. *Educ:* Shrewsbury; privately. Entered the theatre in 1937. Served in King's Own Yorkshire Light Infantry and The Parachute Regt, 1940-46. Films since War of 1939-45 include: The Hasty Heart, 1949; Stage Fright, 1950; Robin Hood, 1952; Rob Roy, 1953; A Man Called Peter, 1954; The Dambusters, 1954; The Virgin Queen, 1955; Yangtse Incident, 1957; Chase a Crooked Shadow, 1957; The Long and the Short and the Tall, 1960; The Hellions, 1961; The Longest Day, 1962; Operation Crossbow, 1964; Coast of Skeletons, 1964; The Love-Ins (USA), 1967; Subterfuge, 1968; Dorian Grey, 1969; Asylum, 1972; Secret Agent 008, 1976. Stage appearances include: An Ideal Husband, Strand, 1965-66; Dear Octopus, Haymarket, 1967; USA tour, The Marquise, 1972; Australia tour, Sleuth, 1973; led RSC N American tour, 1974; Equus, Australian Nat. Theatre Co., 1975; On Approval (S Africa), 1976; nat. tour of Quadrille, and The Heat of the Moment, 1977. Formed Triumph Theatre Productions, 1970. *Recreations:* shooting and farming. *Address:* Chinham Farm, Faringdon, Oxon; Little Ponton House, near Grantham, Lincs. *Club:* Army and Navy.

TODD, Ronald Ruskin; Colonial Administrative Service, retired; *b* 23 March 1902; *er s* of late A. E. Todd, Histon, Cambridge; *m* 1947, Madge, *yr d* of late Captain H. Griffiths, Wallasey; one *s*. *Educ:* Cambridge and County High School; Emmanuel Coll., Cambridge (Scholar). Colonial Administrative Service, Hong Kong, 1924; various administrative posts, 1927-41; Acting Financial Secretary, 1941; interned by Japanese, 1942-45; Secretary for Chinese Affairs, Hong Kong, 1946-55, and Member of Executive and Legislative Councils. Acting Colonial Secretary various occasions, 1946-53. *Recreation:* tennis. *Address:* Manston, Kippington Road, Sevenoaks, Kent. *T:* Sevenoaks 51582. *Club:* Royal Commonwealth Society.

TODD-JONES, Sir (George) Basil, Kt 1957; *s* of Edgar William Todd-Jones and Theodora, *d* of Captain David Anderson; *m* 1st, 1928, Margaret Helen (*d* 1950), *d* of Sir Alexander Mackenzie, KCSI; no *c*; 2nd, 1954, Anne Elizabeth, *d* of William Scott Adie. *Educ:* Sherborne; University College, Oxford. Served European War, 1914-18; RFA, 1916-19, France 1917 and 1918. Called to Bar, 1922, Midland Circuit. Office of Solicitor of Inland Revenue, 1928-36; Special Commissioner of Income Tax, 1945-63; Presiding Commissioner, 1953-63. Retired, 1963. *Address:* 93 Rivermead Court, Ranelagh Gardens, SW6. *T:* 01-736 1654. *Club:* Hurlingham.

TOH CHIN CHYE, BSc, PhD, DipSc; Member of Parliament, Singapore, since 1959; Minister for Health, since 1975; *b* 10 Dec. 1921; *m*. *Educ:* Raffles Coll., Singapore; University College, London; Nat. Inst. for Medical Research, London. Reader in Physiology, 1958-64, Research Associate 1964, Vice-Chancellor, 1968-75, Univ. of Singapore. Dep. Prime Minister of Singapore, 1959-68; Chm., People's Action Party, 1954- (a Founder Mem.); Minister for Science and Technology, 1968-75. Chm. Board of Governors: Singapore Polytechnic, 1959-75; Regional Inst. of Higher Educn and Develt, 1970-74; Mem. Admin. Bd, Assoc. of SE Asian Insts of Higher Learning, 1968-75. DLitt (*hc*) Singapore, 1976. *Publications:* papers in Jl of Physiology and other relevant jls. *Address:* 23 Greenview Crescent, Singapore 11.

TOKATY, Prof. Grigori Alexsandrovich; Chief Scientific Adviser, Walmica Technical Services Institute, since 1976; *b* North Caucasus, Russia, 13 Oct. 1910; naturalized British. *Educ:* Moscow Higher Technical Coll.; Zhukovsky (Military Air Force) Academy of Aeronautics, Moscow. DEng, PhD, DAeSc, CEng, CanTechSc. Zhukovsky Academy: Aeronautical Research Engineer, 1937-38; Head of Aerodynamics Laboratory, 1938-41; Lectr in Aerodynamics and Aircraft Design, 1941-45; Acting Prof. of Aviation, Moscow Engrg Inst, 1939-45; Rocket scientist, Berlin, 1945-47. Varied work for HM Govt, London, 1948-52; Imperial Coll., and Coll. of Aeronautics, Cranfield, 1953-56; work on theoretical rocket dynamics and orbital flight mechanics associated with Apollo programme, 1956-68; Reader in Aeronautics and Astronautics, Northampton Coll. of Advanced Technology, 1958-59; Prof. of Astronautics, and Flight Mechanics Advr, USA, 1959-60; Head of Dept of Aeronautics and Space Technology, Northampton Coll. of Advanced Technology, 1960-67; Prof. and Head of Dept of Aeronautics, City Univ., 1967-75, now Emeritus. Vis. Prof.-Advr, Nigeria Univ., 1973, Academic Rep. of Vice-Chancellor in UK, 1974-76; Leverhulme Emeritus Fellow, 1976-78. FRAeS, FAIAA, FIMA. *Publications:* numerous, including seven books: Rocketdynamics, 1961; The History of Rocket Technology (jt), 1964; A History and Philosophy of Fluid Mechanics, 1971; Cosmonautics-Astronautics, 1976; articles and booklets (alone or jointly) in the fields of fluid mechanics, gasdynamics, rocketdynamics, theory and philosophy of educn, and non-scientific subjects. *Recreations:* writing, broadcasting, travelling. *Address:* Department of Aeronautics, The City University, St John Street, EC1V 4PB. *T:* 01-253 4399 (Ext. 264); Imperial House, 15-19 Kingsway, WC2B 6UU. *T:* 01-240 5361.

TOLER; *see* Graham-Toler, family name of Earl of Norbury.

TOLER, Maj.-Gen. David Arthur Hodges, OBE 1963; MC 1945; Emergency Planning Officer, Lincolnshire County Council, since 1974; *b* 13 Sept. 1920; *s* of Major Thomas Clayton Toler, DL, JP, Swettenham Hall, Congleton; *m* 1951, Judith Mary, *d* of James William Garden, DSO, Aberdeen; one *s* one *d*. *Educ:* Stowe; Christ Church, Oxford (MA). 2nd Lieut Coldstream Guards, 1940; served War of 1939-45, N Africa and Italy; Regimental Adjt, Coldstream Guards, 1952-54; Bde Major, 4th Gds Bde, 1956-57; Adjt, RMA Sandhurst, 1958-60; Bt Lt-Col 1959; comd 2nd Bn Coldstream Guards, 1962-64; comd Coldstream Guards, 1964-65; comd 4th Guards Bde, 1965-68; Dep. Comdt, Staff Coll., Camberley, 1968-69; Dep. Comdr, Army, N Ireland, 1969-70; GOC E Midland Dist, 1970-73; retired 1973. *Recreations:* shooting, fishing, gardening. *Address:* Grove House, Fulbeck, Lincs. *Club:* Army and Navy.

TOLLEMACHE, family name of **Baron Tollemache.**

TOLLEMACHE, 5th Baron *cr* 1876; **Timothy John Edward Tollemache;** Director: Tollemache & Cobbold Breweries Ltd, since 1973; NRG London Re-insurance Co. Ltd; *b* 13 Dec. 1939; *s* of 4th Baron Tollemache, MC, DL, and of Dinah Susan, *d* of late Sir Archibald Auldjo Jamieson, KBE, MC; *S* father, 1975; *m* 1970, Alexandra Dorothy Jean, *d* of late Col Hugo Meynell, MC; one *s* one *d*. *Educ:* Eton. Commissioned into Coldstream Guards, 1959; served Kenya and Persian Gulf, 1960-62; Course of Estate Management at Sandringham, Norfolk, 1962-64; Trainee, Barings Bank Ltd, 1964-65; joined Tollemache & Cobbold Breweries Ltd, 1965. *Recreations:* shooting, fishing, natural history. *Heir: s* Hon. Edward John Hugo Tollemache, *b* 12 May 1976. *Address:* Helmingham Hall, Stowmarket, Suffolk IP14 6EF. *T:* Helmingham 217. *Clubs:* White's, Pratt's, Boodle's.

TOLLEMACHE, Maj.-Gen. Sir Humphry (Thomas), 6th Bt *cr* 1793; CB 1952; CBE 1950; DL; *b* 10 Aug. 1897; *s* of Sir Lyonel Tollemache, 4th Bt (*d* 1952), and Hersilia Henrietta Diana (*d* 1953), *d* of late H. R. Oliphant; *S* brother, 1969; *m* 1926, Nora Priscilla, *d* of John Taylor, Broomhill, Eastbourne; two *s* two *d*. *Educ:* Eastbourne Coll. 2nd Lieut, Royal Marines, 1915; served European War, 1914-19; War of 1939-45 in Middle East and Far East; Bt Major, 1934; Bt Lt-Col, 1942; Actg Colonel Comdt, temp. Brigadier, 1943; Colonel, 1946; Maj.-Gen., 1949; commanded Portsmouth Group, Royal Marines, 1949-52 and Hon. Colonel Comdt, 1958-60; Colonel Comdt, Royal Marines, 1961-62; Rep. Colonel Comdt, 1961. Member Hampshire CC, 1957; Alderman, 1969-74. Chm., C of E Soldiers, Sailors and Airmen Clubs, 1955-65, Pres., 1974. DL, Hampshire, 1965. *Heir: s* Lyonel Humphry John Tollemache [*b* 10 July 1931; *m* 1960, Mary Joscelyne, *e d* of William Henry Whitbread, *qv*; two *s* two *d*]. *Address:* Sheet House, Petersfield, Hants.

TOLLERFIELD, Albert Edward, CB 1963; Assistant Comptroller, Patent Office, 1959-66; retired from Civil Service; *b* 8 Dec. 1906; *s* of late Frank Tollerfield; *m* 1st, 1930, Lilian May (*d* 1972); three *d*; 2nd, 1974, Adelaide Mary. *Educ:* Royal Dockyard School, Portsmouth. Fitter Apprentice, 1922-27; Design Draughtsman, 1929; Examiner, Patent Office, 1930; Intelligence Department, Min. of Shipping, 1939-43; Superintending Examiner and Hearing Officer, Patent Office, 1955-59. Chairman, Patents Appointments Boards, Civil Service Commn, 1966-69. *Recreation:* do-it-yourself. *Address:* 12 Wenham Drive, Westcliff-on-Sea, Essex. *T:* Southend 40992.

TOLLEY, Major Cyril James Hastings, MC; Councillor (Conservative), County Borough of Eastbourne, 1958-62; *b* London, 14 Sept. 1895; *yr* and *o surv. s* of late James T. Tolley and late Christiana Mary Pascall. *Educ:* University College, Oxford. Served European War, Royal Tank Corps, 1915-19 (MC); Prisoner of War, 1917-18; Royal Sussex Regt, 1940-45. Liberal Candidate South Hendon, Feb. 1950; Hon. Treasurer London Liberal Party, 1950-51. Pres., Eastbourne Downs Golf Club; former Pres., Eastbourne Society of Artists; Vice-President Eastbourne Downs Artisans' Golf Club. British Amateur Golf Champion, 1920 and 1929; French Open Golf Champion, 1924 and 1928; Welsh Open Amateur Golf Champion, 1921 and 1923; Captain Royal and Ancient, St Andrews, 1948; Captain, Oxford and Cambridge Golfing Society, 1946-48. London Stock Exchange, 1921-29, and 1933-

39. Publication: The Modern Golfer, 1924. *Recreations:* golf, bowls, croquet; apiarist; philately. *Address:* Pommern Lodge, Eastbourne, East Sussex. *Clubs:* Royal Automobile; Vincent's, Bullingdon (Oxford); Royal and Ancient (St Andrews); Oxford and Cambridge Golfing Society; Royal Eastbourne Golf; Woking; Pine Valley Golf (Pa, USA), etc; Eastbourne (Saffrons) Bowling, Preston (Brighton) Bowling, Compton Croquet.

TOLLEY, Rev. Canon George; Principal, Sheffield City Polytechnic (formerly Sheffield Polytechnic), since 1969; Curate, St Andrew's, Sharrow; Hon. Canon of Sheffield Cathedral, since 1976; *b* 24 May 1925; *s* of George and Elsie Tolley, Old Hill, Staffordshire; *m* 1947, Joan Amelia Grosvenor; two *s* one *d. Educ:* Halesowen Grammar Sch.; Birmingham Central Tech. Coll. (part-time); Princeton Univ., USA. BSc, MSc, PhD (London); FRIC; FBIM. Rotary Foundation Fellow, Princeton Univ., 1949-50. Head, Department of Chemistry, College of Advanced Technology, Birmingham, 1954-58; Head of Research and Experimental Dept, Allied Ironfounders Ltd, 1958-61; Principal, Worcester Tech. College, 1961-65; Senior Director of Studies, Royal Air Force Coll., Cranwell, 1965-66; Principal, Sheffield Coll. of Technology, 1966-69. Chairman: Council, Plastics Inst., 1959-61; Further Educn Adv. Cttee, Food, Drink and Tobacco Ind. Trng Bd; Hon. Sec., Assoc. of Colleges of Further and Higher Educn; Member: CNAA (Chm. Management Studies Bd); British Council; Nat. Adv. Council on Educn for Industry and Commerce; Local Govt Trng Bd; Univ. and Polytechnics Industry Cttee; Editorial Bd, Univs Qly. *Publications:* Meaning and Purpose in Higher Education, 1976; many papers relating to plastics and education in British and foreign journals. *Recreations:* music, hill walking, bird watching. *Address:* 74 Furniss Avenue, Dore, Sheffield S17 3QP. *Club:* Royal Commonwealth Society.

TOLLEY, Leslie John, CBE 1973; Chairman: Renold Ltd, since 1972; Fodens Ltd, since 1975-77; *b* Oxford, 11 Nov. 1913; *s* of late Henry Edward Charles and Gertrude Eleanor Tolley; *m* 1939, Margaret Butterfield, *d* of late Walter Bishop and Nellie May Butterfield; one *s* one *d. Educ:* Oxford Sch. of Technology. CEng; FIProdE; FBIM. Gen. Manager, Nuffield Metal Products, 1941-52; Gen. Works Manager, 1952, Works Dir, 1954, Renold Chains Ltd; Gp Man. Dir, Renold Ltd, 1962; Dir, NW Regional Bd, Lloyds Bank Ltd, 1975—. Member: NW Industrial Develt Bd, 1972-; NW Postal Bd, 1973-77. A Vice-Chm., BIM, 1973-; Chm., Bd of Directors, BIM Foundn. *Recreation:* golf. *Address:* Silver Birches, Dale Brow, Prestbury, Macclesfield SK10 4BN. *T:* Prestbury 49073. *Club:* Royal Automobile.

TOLLINTON, Richard Bartram Boyd, CBE 1955 (OBE 1947); *b* London, 28 Aug. 1903; *o s* of Rev. Canon Tollinton, DD, DLitt, and Minnie Tollinton (*née* Boyd Carpenter); *m* 1931, Mary Judith Paulina (*d* 1977), *d* of late Judge Harold Chaloner Dowdall. *Educ:* Rugby; Balliol Coll., Oxford. Levant Consular Service, 1926; Acting Vice-Consul, Tehran, 1928; Bushire, 1929; Vice-Consul, Rotterdam, 1931; Consul (local rank) and Commercial Secretary (local rank), Sofia, 1934; Vice-Consul, Casablanca, 1938; seconded to British Council, London, 1939-40; Vice-Consul and Second Secretary (local rank), Washington, 1940; Acting Consul, Boston, 1941, Consul 1944; First Secretary and Consul, Sofia, 1944; Acting Political Rep., Rome, 1946-47; Consul, Oporto, 1947; Consul-General, 1948; Consul-General, Leopoldville, 1952; HM Ambassador to Nepal, 1955-57; HM Foreign Service, Levant Dept, Foreign Office, 1957-60, HM Ambassador to Honduras, 1960-63, retired. *Publications:* Economic Conditions in Bulgaria, 1935 and 1937. *Recreations:* hill scrambling, tennis, amateur theatricals. *Clubs:* Royal Automobile; Oxford Union; Himalayan.

TOLSTOY, Alexandra; Farmer, Speaker, Writer; President, Tolstoy Foundation Inc. (for Russian Welfare and Culture), New York, since 1939; *b* Yasnaia Poliana, Russia, 1 July 1884; *d* of Leo and Sophia Tolstoy. *Educ:* Moscow; Home. Secretary to Tolstoy, 1901-10; in 1911, fulfilled Tolstoy's will, edited his posthumous works; bought land of father's estate with money secured and distributed it among Yasnaia Poliana Peasants (1800 acres); 1914 went to war first as a nurse, then as representative for refugees at the Western front; worked as a chief of a sanitary detachment at the Western Front; in 1918 organised a society in Moscow to study and work on a complete edition of Tolstoy's works (91 volumes); organised Museums, several schools in Yasnaia Poliana, kindergartens, a hospital; worked in Russia till 1929; compelled to leave because the Soviets instilled anti-religious propaganda in Tolstoy's museums and schools; in 1929 went to Japan, lectured there; entered USA 1931; lectured all over America, now lives on a farm (Resettlement Center of Tolstoy Foundn; Chm. Nursing Home and Homes for the Aged, etc, of the Tolstoy Foundation Inc. of which she is President); in 1941 became an American citizen. Hon. DHL, Hobart and William Smith Colleges, USA, 1962. *Publications:* Tragedy of Tolstoy (numerous trans.); I Worked for the Soviet, 1934; Tolstoy-a Life of My Father, 1953 (numerous trans.); The Real Tolstoy, 1968; contrib. magazines. *Address:* Tolstoy Foundation Inc., 250 West 57th Street (Room 1101), New York, NY 10019, USA; (home) Valley Cottage, Tolstoy Foundation Resettlement Center, New York 10989, USA.

TOLSTOY, Dimitry, (Dimitry Tolstoy-Miloslavsky), QC 1959; Barrister-at-Law; *b* 8 Nov. 1912; *s* of late Michael Tolstoy-Miloslavsky and Eileen May Hamshaw; *m* 1st, 1934, Frieda Mary Wicksteed (marr. diss.); one *s* one *d* ; 2nd, 1943, Natalie Deytrikh; one *s* one *d. Educ:* Wellington; Trinity Coll., Cambridge. President of Cambridge Union, 1935. Called to Bar, Gray's Inn, 1937. Lecturer in Divorce to Inns of Court, 1952-68. *Publications:* Tolstoy on Divorce (7th edn), 1971; articles in legal periodicals. *Address:* San Spyridon, Javea CM. 216 (Alicante), Spain.

TOMBS, Francis Leonard; Chairman, Electricity Council, since 1977; *b* 17 May 1924; *s* of Joseph and Jane Tombs; *m* 1949, Marjorie Evans; three *d. Educ:* Elmore Green Sch., Walsall; Birmingham Coll. of Technology. BSc (Econ), CEng, FIMechE, FIEE; FBIM. Hon. LLD Strathclyde, 1976. *Recreations:* music, golf, sailing. *Address:* 15 Highgate Close, N6 4SD. *Club:* Athenæum.

TOMKINS, Sir Edward Emile, GCMG 1975 (KCMG 1969; CMG 1960); CVO 1957; HM Diplomatic Service, retired; HM Ambassador to France, 1972-75; *b* 16 Nov. 1915; *s* of late Lt-Col E. L. Tomkins; *m* 1955, Gillian Benson; one *s* two *d. Educ:* Ampleforth Coll.; Trinity Coll., Cambridge. Foreign Office, 1939. Military service, 1940-43. HM Embassy, Moscow, 1944-46; Foreign Office, 1946-51; HM Embassy, Washington, 1951-54; HM Embassy, Paris, 1954-59; Foreign Office, 1959-63; HM Embassy, Bonn, 1963-67; HM Embassy, Washington, 1967-69; Ambassador to the Netherlands, 1970-72. Mem., Bucks CC, 1977-. Chm., Friends of UC at Buckingham, 1977. *Address:* Winslow Hall, Winslow, Bucks. *T:* Winslow 2323; 17 Thurloe Place Mews, SW7. *T:* 01-589 9623. *Clubs:* Beefsteak, Garrick, Turf.

TOMKINS, Rt. Rev. Oliver Stratford, MA, DD, LLD; *b* 9 June 1908; *s* of Rev. Leopold Charles Fellows Tomkins and Mary Katie (*née* Stratford); *m* 1939, Ursula Mary Dunn; one *s* three *d. Educ:* Trent Coll; Christ's Coll, Cambridge; Westcott House, Cambridge. Asst Gen. Sec., Student Christian Movement, 1933-40, and Editor, Student Movement Magazine, 1937-40. Deacon, 1935; Priest, 1936; Vicar of Holy Trinity, Millhouses, Sheffield, 1940-45; an Associate Gen. Sec. World Council of Churches and Sec. of its Commission on Faith and Order, 1945-52; Warden of Lincoln Theological College (Scholae Cancellarii) and Canon and Prebend, Lincoln Cathedral, 1953-59; Bishop of Bristol, 1959-75. Mem. Central Cttee, World Council of Churches, 1968-75. DD (*hon. causa*) Edinburgh University, 1953; Hon LLD Bristol, 1975. *Publications:* The Wholeness of the Church, 1949; The Church in the Purpose of God, 1950. Editor and contributor The Universal Church in God's Design, 1948; Intercommunion, 1951; (ed) Faith and Order (Lund Conference Report), 1953; Life of E. S. Woods, Bishop of Lichfield, 1957; A Time for Unity, 1964; Guarded by Faith, 1971. *Recreation:* walking. *Address:* 14 St George's Square, Worcester WR1 1XH. *T:* Worcester 25330.

See also Ven . T . W . I . Cleasby .

TOMKINSON, John Stanley, FRCS; Obstetric Surgeon, Queen Charlotte's Maternity Hospital, since 1953; Obstetric and Gynæcological Surgeon, Guy's Hospital, since 1953; Gynæcological Surgeon, Chelsea Hospital for Women, since 1971; Consultant Adviser in Obstetrics and Gynæcology to Department of Health and Social Security (formerly Ministry of Health), since 1966; *b* 8 March 1916; *o s* of Harry Stanley and Katie Mills Tomkinson, Stafford; *m* 1954, Barbara Marie Pilkington; two *s* one *d. Educ:* Rydal Sch.; Birmingham University Medical Sch.; St Thomas' Hospital. MRCS, LRCP 1941; MB, ChB Birmingham 1941; FRCS 1949; MRCOG 1952; FRCOG 1967. Medal in Surgery and Priestley-Smith Prize, Birmingham. Demonstrator of Anatomy, Birmingham Medical School, 1946; appointments in General Surgery, Obst. and Gynæcol., at Birmingham and Midland Hosp. for Women, Birmingham Maternity Hospital, and Queen Elizabeth Hospital, Birmingham, 1941-42 and 1947-52; Registrar, Professorial Unit in General Surgery and Professorial Unit in Obst. and Gynæcol., Birmingham; Chief Asst, Chelsea Hospital for Women, 1952-53; Resident Obstetrician and Tutor in Obstetrics (Postgrad. Inst. of Obst. and Gynæcol. of University of London), Queen

Charlotte's Maternity Hospital, 1952-53. Travelling Fellow (Guy's Hospital), USA and Canada, 1954. Vis. Prof., Spanish Hospital, Mexico City, 1972. William Hawksworth Meml Lectr, 1969; Sir Winston Churchill Meml Lectr, Canterbury, 1970; Foundn Lectr, Amer. Assoc. of Gynaecol. and Obstetrics, 1978. Examiner for Central Midwives Board, Univ. of London, RCOG, QUB, Univ. of Oxford, Univ. of Cambridge, Univ. of East Africa, Univ. of Haile Sellassie I, Ethiopia, Conjoint Examng Bd, Univ. of Birmingham. FRSM. Member: Gynæcological Club of Great Britain; Birmingham and Midland Obst. and Gynæcol. Society; Central Midwives Board (Dep. Chm.); Member Council: RCOG; RCS; section of Obstetrics and Gynæcology, RSM; Sec. Gen., Internat. Fedn of Obstetrics and Gynaecology (Mem. Exec. Council and Cttee on Maternal Mortality); Chm., Jt Study Working Gp of Internat. Confedn of Midwives and Internat. Fedn of Gynaecology and Obstetrics. Jt Editor, Report on Confidential Enquiries into Maternal Deaths in England and Wales, 1964-66, 1967-69, 1970-72. Foreign Member, Continental Gynæcol. Society (of America). Surgeon Lieut, RNVR, 1942-46. *Publications:* (ed) Queen Charlotte's Textbook of Midwifery; papers of general surgical, obstetric and gynæcological interest. *Recreations:* fishing, fly-fishing, painting, and the arts generally. *Address:* 109 Harley Street, W1. *T:* 01-935 5855; 140 Priory Lane, SW15. *T:* 01-876 2006. *Clubs:* Athenæum; MCC.

TOMKYS, William Roger; HM Diplomatic Service; Head of Near East and North Africa Department, Foreign and Commonwealth Office, since 1977; *b* 15 March 1937; *s* of William Arthur and Edith Tomkys; *m* 1963, Margaret Jean Abbey; one *s* one *d. Educ:* Bradford Grammar Sch.; Balliol Coll., Oxford (Domus Scholar; 1st cl. Hons Lit. Hum.). Entered Foreign Service, 1960; MECAS, 1960; 3rd Sec., Amman, 1962; 2nd Sec., FCO, 1964; 1st Sec., Head of Chancery, Benghazi, 1967; Planning Staff, FCO, 1969; Head of Chancery, Athens, 1972; Counsellor, seconded to Cabinet Office, 1975. *Address:* c/o Foreign and Commonwealth Office, SW1A 2AH; 7 Grotes Place, Blackheath, SE3. *T:* 01-852 4629. *Club:* Travellers'.

TOMLIN, Eric Walter Frederick, CBE 1965 (OBE 1959); FRSL; author; *b* 30 Jan. 1913; *s* of Edgar Herbert Tomlin and Mary (*née* Dexter); *m* 1st, 1945, Margaret Stuart (marr. diss. 1952); one *s*; 2nd, 1974, Judith, *yr d* of Lt-Gen. Sir Euan Miller, *qv. Educ:* Whitgift; Brasenose Coll., Oxford. Asst Master: Sloane Sch., Chelsea, 1936-38; Marlborough, 1939; Resident Tutor, Wilts, Bristol Univ. Bd of Extra-Mural Studies, 1939-40; joined Local Defence Volunteers, 1940; British Council Lecturer, Staff Coll. Baghdad and RMC, 1940-41; worked in Information Dept, British Embassy, Baghdad, 1941; British Council: Ankara, 1941-42; Regional Dir, S Turkey, 1942-45; Headquarters London, 1945-47 and 1952-56; Paris, 1947-51; Rep. in Turkey and Cultural Attaché British Embassy, Ankara, 1956-61; Rep. in Japan and Cultural Counsellor British Embassy, Tokyo, 1961-67; Leverhulme Foundn Fellow, 1967-69; British Council Rep. in France, and Cultural Attaché, British Embassy, Paris, 1969-71. Bollingen Foundn Fellow and Vis. Prof., Univ. of Southern California, 1961; Vis. Fellow, Univ. Coll., Cambridge, 1971-72; Vis. Prof., Nice, 1972-74. Fellow: Royal Asiatic Soc.; Inst. of Cultural Research; Life Mem., Royal Inst. of Cornwall; Associate Mem., Magic Circle; Pres., Royal Soc. of St George, Tokyo, 1965. *Publications:* The Modern Miracle, 1939; Life in Modern Turkey, 1946; The Approach to Metaphysics, 1947; The Western Philosophers, 1950; The Eastern Philosophers, 1952; Simone Weil, 1954; R. G. Collingwood, 1954; Wyndham Lewis, 1955; Living and Knowing, 1955; La Vie et l'Oeuvre de Bertrand Russell, 1963; (ed) T. S. Eliot: a Tribute from Japan, 1965; Tokyo Essays, 1967; Wyndham Lewis: an Anthology of his Prose, 1969; (ed) Charles Dickens, a Centenary Volume, 1969; Japan, 1973; Man, Time and the New Science, 1973; The Last Country, 1974; contribs to Criterion, Scrutiny, Times Literary Supplement, Economist, and many foreign reviews, etc. *Recreations:* travel, reading, music. *Address:* Tall Trees, Morwenstow, Cornwall. *T:* Morwenstow 206; 31 Redan Street, W14. *T:* 01-602 6414. *Clubs:* Athenæum; Union Society (Oxford).

TOMLINSON, (Alfred) Charles, FRSL; Reader in English Poetry, University of Bristol, since 1968; *b* 8 Jan. 1927; *s* of Alfred Tomlinson and May Lucas; *m* 1948, Brenda Raybould; two *d. Educ:* Longton High School; Queens' Coll., Cambridge (MA); Royal Holloway and Bedford Colls, Univ. of London (MA). Lecturer, Bristol Univ., 1957-68. Visiting Prof., Univ. of New Mexico, 1962-63; O'Connor Prof., Colgate Univ., NY, 1967-68. Arts Council Poetry Panel, 1964-66; Witter Bynner Lectr, Univ. of New Mexico, 1976. Exhibition of Graphics: Ely House, OUP, London, 1972; Clare Coll., Cambridge, 1975. Hon. Fellow, Queens' Coll., Cambridge, 1975. FRSL 1975. *Publications: poetry:* Relations and Contraries, 1951; The

Necklace, 1955, repr. 1966; Seeing is Believing, 1960 (US 1958); A Peopled Landscape, 1963; Poems, 1964; American Scenes, 1966; The Poem as Initiation, (US) 1968; The Way of a World, 1969; Poems, in Penguin Modern Poets, 1969; Renga, (France) 1970, (US) 1972; Written on Water, 1972; The Way In, 1974; Selected Poems, 1978; The Shaft, 1978; *graphics:* Words and Images, 1972; In Black and White, 1975; *translations:* Versions from Fyodor Tyutchev, 1960; Castilian Ilexes: Versions from Antonio Machado, 1963; Ten Versions from Trilce by Cesar Vallejo, (US) 1970; *edited:* Marianne Moore: A Collection of Critical Essays, (US) 1969; William Carlos Williams: A Collection of Critical Essays, 1972; William Carlos Williams: Selected Poems, 1976; contribs to: Essays in Criticism, Hudson Review, Poetry (Chicago), Sewanee Review, Times Lit. Supp. *Recreations:* music, walking. *Address:* c/o English Department, University of Bristol, Bristol BS8 1TH.

TOMLINSON, David (Cecil MacAlister); Actor; *b* 7 May 1917; *s* of C. S. Tomlinson, Solicitor, Folkestone, Kent, and F. E. Tomlinson (*née* Sinclair-Thomson); *m* Audrey Freeman, actress; four *s. Educ:* Tonbridge Sch. Served War of 1939-45: Flight Lieut, Pilot, RAF; demobilised, 1946. Chief roles include: Henry, in The Little Hut, Lyric, Aug. 1950-Sept. 1953; Clive, in All for Mary, Duke of York's, June 1954-May 1955; David, in Dear Delinquent, Westminster and Aldwych, June 1957-July 1958; Tom, in The Ring of Truth, Savoy, July 1959; Robert in Boeing Boeing, Apollo, 1962; acted and directed: Mother's Boy (Nero), Globe, 1964; A Friend Indeed, Cambridge, 1966; The Impossible Years, Cambridge, 1966; On the Rocks (Prime Minister), Dublin Festival, 1969; A Friend Indeed, and A Song at Twilight, South Africa, 1973-74; The Turning Point, Duke of York's, 1974. First appeared in films, 1939; since then has appeared, in leading roles, in over 50 films. *Recreation:* antique collecting. *Address:* Brook Cottage, Mursley, Bucks. *T:* Mursley 213. *Club:* Travellers'.

TOMLINSON, Sir (Frank) Stanley, KCMG 1966 (CMG 1954); HM Diplomatic Service, retired; Member, Governing Body of School of Oriental and African Studies, London University, since 1972; Chairman, Council of International Social Service, since 1973; Member, panel of Chairmen, Civil Service Selection Board, since 1973; Chairman, Royal Society for Asian Affairs, since 1974; *b* 21 March 1912; *m* 1959, Nancy, *d* of late E. Gleeson-White and Mrs Gleeson-White, Sydney, Australia. *Educ:* High Pavement Sch., Nottingham; University College, Nottingham. Served in various consular posts in Japan, 1935-41; Saigon, 1941-42; United States, 1943; Washington, 1945; Acting Consul-General, Manila, 1945; Chargé d'Affaires, 1946; Foreign Office, 1947; Washington, 1951; Imperial Defence Coll., 1954; Counsellor and Head, SE Asia Dept, 1955; Dep. Commandant, Berlin, 1958; Minister, UK Permanent Delegation to NATO, 1961-64; Consul General, New York, 1964-66; British High Comr, Ceylon, 1966-69; Dep. Under-Sec. of State, FCO, 1969-72. Hon. LLD Nottingham, 1970. *Recreations:* trout fishing, oenophily, reading about the remoter human past. *Address:* 6/24 Buckland Crescent, NW3; 32 Long Street, Devizes, Wilts. *Club:* Brooks's.

TOMLINSON, Rt. Rev. Mgr George Arthur; Prelate of Honour to HH Pope Paul VI; Canon of the Chapter of Westminster; *b* Hampstead, NW, 21 May 1906; *s* of late George Henry and Frances Tomlinson. *Educ:* Hastings Grammar Sch.; Keble Coll., Oxford. BA 1929; MA 1942. Ordained in Church of England, 1930; Curate of South Kirby, Yorkshire, 1930-32; received into Catholic Church, 1932; Pontifical Beda Coll., Rome, 1933-37; Priest, 1937; Chaplain to the Oratory Sch., 1937-41; Curate at Kentish Town, 1941; Brentford, 1942; Headmaster, The Oratory Sch., South Oxon, 1943-53; re-established Oratory Preparatory Sch., Branksome Park, Dorset, 1946; Senior Catholic Chaplain to University of London, 1953-64; Administrator Westminster Cathedral, 1964-67; Rector, St James's, Spanish Place, 1967-77. Member: Westminster Diocesan Ecumenical Commn; Council, Royal Sch. of Church Music. Painter of Frescoes in chapel of Our Lady and the English Martyrs, Little Crosby, Lancs, and various smaller works. *Publications:* regular contributor to theological reviews. *Recreations:* music, painting, swimming. *Address:* Spetchley Park, Worcester.

TOMLINSON, John Edward; MP (Lab) Meriden, since Feb. 1974; Parliamentary Under-Secretary of State: Foreign and Commonwealth Office, since 1976; Ministry of Overseas Development, since 1977; *b* 1 Aug. 1939; *s* of Frederick Edwin Tomlinson, headmaster, and Doris Mary Tomlinson; *m* 1963, Marianne Solveig Sommar, Stockholm; three *s. Educ:* Westminster City Sch.; Co-operative Coll., Loughborough; Nottingham Univ. (Dip. Polit. Econ. Social Studies). Sec., Sheffield Co-operative Party, 1961-68; Head of Research Dept, AUEW, 1968-70; Lectr in Industrial Relations, 1970-74. PPS to

Prime Minister, 1975-76. *Address:* 19 Ash Grove, Wheathampstead, Herts. *T:* Wheathampstead 3615. *Clubs:* Kingshurst Labour, Arley Working Men's, Atherstone Miners Welfare.

TOMLINSON, Reginald R., OBE 1959; RBA (Hon. Mem., 1971); ARCA; Senior Inspector of Art to the LCC, 1925-51; *b* Overton, Hants, 10 Oct. 1885; *s* of F. C. Tomlinson; *m* 1914, Emily E., *d* of A. E. Mullins; two *s* one *d*. *Educ:* Farnham Grammar Sch. Apprentice Designer to Minton, Hollins & Co.; Pottery Painter and Designer for Bernard Moore, 1906-09; Royal College of Art; Art Director to the Crown Staffordshire China Co. Ltd, 1913-19; Principal of Cheltenham Coll. of Arts and Crafts, 1922-25; Acting Principal, Central School of Arts and Crafts, London, 1935-36 and 1939-46; President English Speaking Nations International Art Congress, Brussels, 1935; Chairman British Cttee for International Art Congress, Paris, 1937; awarded two international Gold Medals for Design and Craftsmanship, in collaboration with Bernard Moore, at Ghent and Turin; exhibited at Principal Exhibitions and Art Galleries. Chm., Bd of Examiners for ATD, Univ. of London. Hon. Fellow, Institute of British Decorators; Hon. Fellow, College of Handicrafts. Liveryman of Company of Goldsmiths; Freeman of City of London; Past President Royal Drawing Society; President Artists Annuity and Benevolent Fund; Master Art Workers' Guild, 1955. *Works purchased:* Pottery in Museums in this country and abroad; *Portraits:* Lady Arkell, Sir Aylmer Firebrace, J. J. Mallon, CH, Sir Arthur Middleton, Sir William Houghton, Lord Alexander, etc. *Publications:* Lettering for Arts and Crafts; Memory and Imaginative Drawing; Picture Making by Children, 1934; contributed Encyclopædia Britannica, Art in General Education; Crafts for Children, 1935; Children as Artists (King Penguin), 1945; Picture and Pattern Making by Children, 1950; (with J. F. Mills) Growth of Child Art, 1966. *Recreation:* gardening. *Address:* Chestnut Cottage, The Drive, Chichester, West Sussex. *T:* Chichester 527551.

TOMLINSON, Sir Stanley; *see* Tomlinson, Sir F. S.

TOMNEY, Frank; MP (Lab) Hammersmith North since 1950; sales and marketing analyst; *b* 24 May 1908; *s* of Arthur Tomney, Bolton, Lancs; *m* 1936, Gladys Winifred, *d* of Andrew Isham, Watford; one *s* one *d*. Branch Secretary, General and Municipal Workers Union, 1940-50. Mem., House of Commons Select Cttees, 1954-60; Deleg., Council of Europe and WEU, 1963-64, 1971-73, 1974-; Leader, UK Delegn to UN, 1968; Mem., European Parlt, 1976-. Member: Watford Town Council, 1946-50; Herts CC, 1950-54. *Recreation:* collecting English and continental water colours. *Address:* 27 Shepherds Way, Rickmansworth, Herts.

TOMONAGA, Dr Sin-itiro; Professor Emeritus, since 1969, Tokyo Kyoiku University (Tokyo University of Education); *b* 31 March 1906; *s* of Sanjuro and Hide Tomonaga; *m* 1940, Ryoko Sekiguchi; two *s* one *d*. *Educ:* Kyoto Imperial University. Research Student, Institute of Physical and Chemical Research, 1932-39; studied at University of Leipzig, Germany, 1937-39; Asst, Inst. of Physical and Chemical Research, 1939-40; Lecturer, Tokyo Bunrika Univ. (absorbed into Tokyo University of Education, 1949), 1940; Prof. of Physics, Tokyo Bunrika Univ., 1941; studied at Inst. for Advanced Study, Princeton, USA, 1949-50; Prof. of Physics, Tokyo Univ. of Educn, 1949-69 (President, 1956-62); Director, Inst. for Optical Research, 1963-69; Pres., Science Council of Japan, 1963-69. Japan Academy Prize, 1948; Order of Culture, Japan, 1952; Lomonosov Medal, USSR, 1964; Nobel Prize for Physics (jointly), 1965. *Publications:* Quantum Mechanics, Vol. I, 1962, Vol. II, 1966. *Recreation:* rakugo. *Address:* 3-17-12 Kyonan-cho, Musashinoshi, Tokyo, Japan.

TOMPKINS, Prof. Frederick Clifford, FRS 1955; Professor in Physical Chemistry, Imperial College of Science and Technology, SW7, 1959-77, now Emeritus; Editor and Secretary of Faraday Division of The Chemical Society (formerly The Faraday Society), 1950-77, President, 1978; *b* 29 Aug. 1910; *m* 1936, Catherine Livingstone Macdougal; one *d*. *Educ:* Yeovil Sch.; Bristol Univ. Asst Lectr, King's Coll., Strand, 1934-37; Lectr and Senior Lectr, Natal Univ., Natal, S Africa, 1937-46; ICI Fellow, King's College, Strand, 1946-47; Reader in Physical Chemistry, Imperial College of Science and Technology, 1947; Hon. ARCS 1964. Hon. DSc Bradford, 1975. *Publications:* contributions to Proc. Royal Society, Journal Chem. Soc., Trans Faraday Soc., Jl Chem. Physics, Zeitung Elektrochem. *Address:* 9 St Helens Close, Southsea, Portsmouth, Hants. *T:* Portsmouth 731901.

TOMPKINS, (Granville) Richard (Francis); Founder, Chairman and Managing Director: Green Shield Trading Stamp Co. Ltd, since 1958; Argos Distributors Ltd, since 1973; *b* 15 May 1918; *s* of Richard and Ethel May Tompkins; *m* 1970, Elizabeth Nancy Duke; one *d*. *Educ:* Pakeman St LCC Sch., London, N7. Laundry delivery man and filling station attendant, 1932; van salesman, 1934; engineering draughtsman, 1938. Founded several companies in printing and advertising, 1945; also Green Shield Trading Stamp Co., 1958. *Recreations:* travel, theatre, golf. *Address:* 7 Belgrave Square, SW1.

TOMS, Carl, OBE 1969; First Head of Design, and Associate Director, for the Young Vic at the National Theatre, since 1970; *b* 29 May 1927. *Educ:* High Oakham Sch., Mansfield, Notts; Mansfield College of Art; Royal Coll. of Art; Old Vic Sch. Designing for theatre, films, opera, ballet, etc, on the London stage, 1957-; also for productions at Glyndebourne, Edinburgh Festival, Chichester Festival, and Aldeburgh (world première of Midsummer Night's Dream, 1960). Theatre designs include: Vivat! Vivat Regina!, Chichester and London, 1970, NY 1972; Sherlock Holmes, London, 1974, NY 1974 (Drama Desk Award for Theatre Design); Travesties, London, 1974, NY 1975, Vienna Burgtheater, 1976; Long Day's Journey into Night, LA 1977; Man and Superman, Malvern Festival and London, 1977. Designs for the Royal Opera House, Covent Garden, include: Gala perf. for State Visit of King and Queen of Nepal, 1960; Iphigénie en Tauride, 1961; Ballet Imperial, 1963; Die Frau ohne Schatten (costumes), 1967; Fanfare for Europe, 1973; Queen's Silver Jubilee Gala, 1977; for Sadler's Wells: Cenerentola, 1959; The Barber of Seville, 1960; Our Man in Havana, 1963; for Nat. Theatre: Edward II, 1968; Cyrano de Bergerac, 1970; for NY City Opera: Die Meistersinger von Nürnberg, 1975; The Marriage of Figaro, 1977; The Voice of Ariadne, 1977; for San Diego Opera Co.: Norma, 1976; La Traviata, 1976; The Merry Widow, 1977; for San Francisco Opera: Thais, 1976. Other companies and theatres designed for include Royal Shakespeare Company, Old Vic, Young Vic, Welsh Nat. Opera, NY State Opera. Completed re-designing of Theatre Royal, Windsor, 1965; design consultant for Investiture of Prince of Wales, Caernarvon Castle, 1969. Has designed sets and costumes for numerous films; work has incl. dec. of restaurants, hotels, houses, etc; has also designed exhibns, programmes, cards, etc. *Publications:* Winter's Tale (designs for stage prod.), 1975; Scapino (designs for stage prod.), 1975. *Recreations:* gardening, travel, parrots. *Address:* The White House, Beaumont, near Wormley, Broxbourne, Herts EN10 7QJ. *T:* Hoddesdon 63961.

TOMS, Edward Ernest; Counsellor, British Embassies Bonn and Vienna, since 1977; *b* 10 Dec. 1920; *s* of Alfred William and Julia Harrington Toms; *m* 1946, Veronica Rose, Dovercourt, Essex; three *s* one *d*. *Educ:* St Boniface's Coll. and HM Dockyard Sch., Devonport; Staff Coll., Camberley (psc), Nat. Defence Coll. (jssc). War service 1939-45; Captain Seaforth Highlanders; Special Forces, W Desert, Italy, Balkans, NW Europe; Regular Army, 1946, Seaforth Highlanders and QO Highlanders; Brigade Major, Berlin, 1959-61; Col GS, 1967-69. Principal, Home Civil Service, 1969; Asst Sec., Dept of Employment, 1973; seconded as Diplomatic Service Counsellor, 1977. *Publications:* infrequent contribs to Punch and Pick of Punch. *Recreations:* hill-walking (founder Mem., Aberdeen Mountain Rescue Assoc., 1964), squash. *Address:* British Embassy, Bonn, BFPO 19. *Clubs:* Army and Navy, Civil Service.

TOMSETT, Alan Jeffrey, OBE 1974; Finance Director and Member British Transport Docks Board, since 1974; chartered accountant; *b* 3 May 1922; *s* of Maurice Jeffrey Tomsett and Edith Sarah (née Mackelworth); *m* 1948, Joyce May Hill; one *s* one *d*. *Educ:* Trinity School of John Whitgift, Croydon; Univ. of London (BCom). JDipMA. Joined Hodgson Harris & Co., Chartered Accountants, London, 1938. Served War with RAF, 1941-46 (Middle East, 1942-45). With Smallfield Rawlins & Co., Chartered Accountants, London, 1951; Accountant and Asst Sec. (later Sec.), Northern Mercantile & Investment Corp. Ltd, 1955; William Baird & Co. Ltd, 1962-63. British Transport Docks Board: Dep. Chief Accountant, 1963; Chief Accountant, 1964; Financial Controller, 1970. Director: BTDB (Pension Trustees) Ltd; Kenny (Stevedores) Ltd, 1975. FCA, FCMA, IPFA, FCIS, FCIT. *Address:* 102 Ballards Way, Croydon, Surrey CR0 5RG. *T:* 01-657 5069.

TONBRIDGE, Bishop Suffragan of, since 1973; **Rt. Rev. Philip Harold Ernest Goodrich;** *b* 2 Nov. 1929; *s* of Rev. Canon Harold Spencer Goodrich and Gertrude Alice Goodrich; *m* 1960, Margaret Metcalfe Bennett; four *d*. *Educ:* Stamford Sch.; St John's Coll., Cambridge (MA); Cuddesdon Theological Coll. Curate, Rugby Parish Church, 1954-57; Chaplain, St John's Coll., Cambridge, 1957-61; Rector of the South Ormsby Group of Parishes, 1961-68; Vicar of Bromley, 1968-73; Diocesan Director of Ordinands, Rochester, 1974-. *Recreations:*

gardening, music, walking, looking at buildings. *Address:* Bishop's Lodge, St Botolph's Road, Sevenoaks, Kent. *T:* Sevenoaks 56070.

TONBRIDGE, Archdeacon of; *see* Mason, Ven. R. J.

TONČIĆ-SORINJ, Dr Lujo; Secretary-General, Council of Europe, 1969-74; *b* Vienna, 12 April 1915; *s* of Dušan Tončić-Sorinj (formerly Consul-Gen. in service of Imperial Ministry for Foreign Affairs), and Mabel (*née* Plason de la Woesthyne); *m* 1956, Renate Trenker; one *s* four *d*. *Educ:* Secondary sch. (Gymnasium), Salzburg. Studied law and philosophy at Univs of Vienna and Agram (Zagreb), 1934-41, also medicine and psychology (LLD Vienna); political science, Institut d'Etudes Politiques, Paris. Head of Polit. Dept of Austrian Research Inst. for Economics and Politics in Salzburg and Editor of Berichte und Informationen (political periodical published by Austrian Research Inst. for Economics and Politics), 1946-49. MP for Land Salzburg, 1949-66; Chairman: Legal Cttee of Austrian Parl., 1953-56; For. Affairs Cttee, 1956-59; in charge of For. Affairs questions, Austrian People's Party, 1959-66. Austrian Parly Observer to Consultative Assembly of Council of Europe, 1953-56; Austrian Mem., Consultative Assembly, 1956-66; Vice-Pres., Council of Europe; Vice-Pres., Political Commn, 1961-62; Minister for Foreign Affairs, Austria, 1966-68. Grand Cross of several orders including Order of St Michael and St George, Great Britain (Hon. GCMG). *Publications:* over 350 articles and essays on politics, economics, internat. law and history. *Recreations:* swimming, diving, history, geography. *Address:* 5020 Salzburg, Schloss Fürberg, Pausingerstrasse 11, Austria. *T:* 06222/73437.

TONG, Sir Walter (Wharton), Kt 1955; JP; MSc; *b* 26 February 1890; *e s* of William Tong and Bertha Tong (*née* Wharton), both of Bolton; *m* 1919, Anne (*d* 1972), 2nd *d* of Alfred Glaister, Bolton; three *d*. *Educ:* Bolton School; Giggleswick Sch.; Manchester Univ. Mem. Bolton Town Council, 1925-52; Alderman 1941; Mayor of Bolton, 1940-41; Chm. Housing Cttee, 1931-41; Chm. Finance Cttee, 1941-46 and 1948-52; Leader of Conservative Party in Town Council, 1942-52. Past Governor: Canon Slade Grammar Sch.; Bolton School; Bolton County Grammar School. Pres. Bolton Rotary Club, 1942-43; formerly Pres. and Trustee, Bolton Trustee Savings Bank. Formerly: Pres., Bolton Amateur Operatic Soc.; Chm., Bolton Little Theatre. JP, Bolton, 1935. Contested (C) Bolton West Division, 1950. *Address:* Greenleaves, Bromley Cross, Bolton BL7 9LZ. *T:* Bolton 53892.

TONGA, HM the King of; King Taufa'ahau Tupou IV, Hon. GCMG 1977 (Hon. KCMG 1968); Hon. GCVO 1970; Hon. KBE 1958 (Hon. CBE 1951); *b* 4 July 1918; *s* of Prince Uiliami Tupoulahi Tungi and Queen Salote Tupou of Tonga; *S* mother, 1966; *m* 1947, Halaevalu Mata'aho 'Ahome'e; three *s* one *d*. *Educ:* Tupou College, Tonga; Newington College, Sydney; Wesley College, Sydney University. Minister for Health and Education, Tonga, 1943-50; Prime Minister, 1950-65. *Heir: s* HRH Prince Taufa'ahau Manumataongo, *b* 4 May 1948. *Address:* The Palace, Nukualofa, Tonga. *T:* Nukualofa 1.

TONGE, George Edward, CBE 1960; JP; Chairman: Exmouth Docks Transit Co. Ltd; Devon Dock Pier and Steamship Co. Ltd; Exmouth Docks Co; Director, Westbrick Products Ltd; *b* 30 April 1910; bachelor. Mem. Council, Nat. Council of Social Service. Chairman: Trade Assoc. Management Services Ltd; London Port Employers, 1957-64; Nat. Assoc. of Port Employers, 1965-72; Oxford and Bermondsey Boys' Clubs; Governor, St Olave's and St Saviour's Grammar School Foundation and Schools; Trustee, Marshall's Charity; Area Chm., Devon Historic Churches Trust; Treasurer, Royal Society of Arts, 1958-62. JP London, 1965. *Recreations:* sailing, gardening, the arts. *Address:* Sherbrook Dene, Budleigh Salterton, Devon. *T:* Budleigh Salterton 3148. *Clubs:* Garrick, Royal Thames Yacht, Little Ship; Exe Sailing (Exmouth).

TONKIN, Derek; HM Diplomatic Service; Counsellor (Commercial), East Berlin, since 1976; *b* 30 Dec. 1929; *s* of Henry James Tonkin and Norah Wearing; *m* 1953, Doreen Rooke; two *s* two *d*. *Educ:* High Pavement Grammar Sch., Nottingham; St Catherine's Society, Oxford (MA). HM Forces, 1948-49; FO, 1952; Warsaw, 1955; Bangkok, 1957; Phnom Penh, 1961; FO, 1963; Warsaw, 1966; Wellington, 1968; FCO, 1972. *Publication:* Modern Cambodian Writing, 1962. *Recreations:* tennis, music. *Address:* Heathfields, Berry Lane, Worplesdon, Surrey. *T:* Worplesdon 2955. *Club:* United Oxford & Cambridge University.

TOOHEY, Mrs Joyce, CB 1977; Under-Secretary, Department of the Environment, 1970-77; *b* 20 Sept. 1917; *o d* of late Louis

and Lena Zinkin (*née* Daiches); *m* 1947, Monty I. Toohey, MD, MRCP, DCH (*d* 1960); two *d*. *Educ:* Brondesbury and Kilburn High Sch.; Girton Coll., Cambridge; London Sch. of Economics. BA 1938, MA 1945, Cambridge. Asst Principal, Min. of Supply, 1941; transferred to Min. of Works (later Min. of Public Building and Works, now Dept of the Environment), 1946; Principal, 1948; Asst Secretary, 1956; Under-Secretary, 1964. Harvard Business Sch., 1970. *Recreations:* reading, walking. *Address:* 11 Kensington Court Gardens, W8. *T:* 01-937 1559. *Club:* United Oxford & Cambridge University.

TOOKER, H. C. W.; *see* Whalley-Tooker.

TOOLEY, John; General Administrator, Royal Opera House, Covent Garden, since 1970; *b* 1 June 1924; *yr s* of late H. R. Tooley; *m* 1st, 1951, Judith Craig Morris (marr. diss., 1965); three *d*; 2nd, 1968, Patricia Janet Norah Bagshawe, 2nd *d* of late G. W. S. Bagshawe; one *s*. *Educ:* Repton; Magdalene Coll., Cambridge. Served The Rifle Brigade, 1943-47. Sec., Guildhall School of Music and Drama, 1952-55; Asst to Gen. Administrator, Royal Opera House, Covent Garden, 1955-60; Asst Gen. Administrator, Royal Opera House, Covent Garden, 1960-70. Chm., Nat. Music Council Executive, 1970-72. Hon. FRAM; Hon. GSM. Commendatore, Italian Republic, 1975. *Recreations:* sailing, theatre. *Address:* 12 Earl's Court Gardens, SW5. *Club:* Garrick.

TOOMEY, Ralph; Under-Secretary, Department of Education and Science, since 1969; *b* 26 Dec. 1918; *s* of late James and Theresa Toomey; *m* 1951, Patricia Tizard; two *d*. *Educ:* Cyfarthfa Grammar Sch., Merthyr Tydfil; University Coll., London; Univ. of Caen. Served British and Indian Army, 1940-46. Teacher, Enfield Grammar Sch., 1947; Lecturer, Univ. of London, at Sch. of Oriental and African Studies, 1948. Min. of Education, 1948-60 and 1963- (seconded to Govt of Mauritius, 1960-63, Principal Asst Sec. in Colonial Secretary's Office and Min. of Local Govt and Co-operative Develt). A UK Rep., High Council, European Univ. Inst., Florence, 1974-. *Address:* 8 The Close, Montreal Park, Sevenoaks, Kent. *T:* Sevenoaks 52553. *Club:* Knole Park Golf (Sevenoaks).

TOOTH, Hon. Sir Douglas; *see* Tooth, Hon. Sir S. D.

TOOTH, Geoffrey Cuthbert, MD, MRCP, DPM; Visiting Scientist, National Institute of Mental Health, USA, 1968-71; *b* 1 Sept. 1908; *s* of late Howard Henry Tooth, CB, CMG, MD, FRCP, and late Helen Katherine Tooth, OBE (*née* Chilver); *m* 1st, 1934, Princess Olga Galitzine (*d* 1955), *d* of Prince Alexander Galitzine, MD; 2nd, 1958, Princess Xenia Romanoff, *d* of Prince Andrew of Russia. *Educ:* Rugby Sch.; St John's Coll., Cambridge; St Bartholomew's Hosp.; Johns Hopkins Hosp., Baltimore, Md, USA. MRCS, LRCP 1934, MA Cantab 1935, MD Cantab 1946, DPM 1944; MRCP 1965. Asst Psychiatrist, Maudsley Hosp., 1937-39. Surg. Lt-Comdr, RNVR, Neuropsychiatric Specialist, 1939-45. Colonial Social Science Research Fellow, 1946-53; Comr, Bd of Control, 1954-60; transf. to Min. of Health, and retd as Sen. PMO, Head of Mental Health Section, Med. Div., 1960. Mem. Expert Advisory Panel (Mental Health), WHO. *Publications:* Studies in Mental Illness in the Gold Coast, 1950; various reports to learned societies; articles and papers in med. jls. *Recreations:* sailing, gardening, metal work, photography. *Address:* Grand Prouillac, Plazac, 24580 Rouffignac, France.

TOOTH, Sir Hugh; *see* Munro-Lucas-Tooth.

TOOTH, Hon. Sir (Seymour) Douglas, Kt 1975; retired from Government of Queensland; *b* 28 Jan. 1904; *s* of Percy Nash Tooth and Laura Tooth; *m* 1937, Eileen Mary O'Connor; one *d*. *Educ:* Univ. of Queensland (Teacher's Trng). Cl. 1 Teacher's Certif. Certificated Teacher, Qld Dept of Educn, 1922. Entered Qld Parlt as MP: Kelvin Grove, 1957; Ashgrove, 1960-74; apptd Minister for Health in Govt of Qld, 1964; retd from Parlt and Cabinet, 1974. Chm., Duke of Edinburgh Award Cttee, Qld, 1977. *Address:* Parmelia Close, 2/61 Bellevue Terrace, Clayfield, Queensland 4011, Australia. *T:* 262-4621.

TOOTHILL, Sir John (Norman), Kt 1964; CBE 1955; FRSE; retired 1975 as Director, Ferranti Ltd, Edinburgh; *b* 11 Nov. 1908; *s* of John Harold and Helena Toothill; *m* 1935, Ethel Amelia Stannard. *Educ:* Beaminster Grammar School. Apprenticed Tilling Stevens Ltd, Hoffman Manufacturing Co. Ltd, Harris Lebus Ltd. Joined Ferranti Ltd, Hollinwood, 1935, as Chief Cost Accountant; Gen. Manager, Ferranti Ltd, Edinburgh, 1943; Director: AI Welders Ltd, Inverness, 1963; Edinburgh Investment Trust, 1964; R. W. Toothill Ltd; W. A. Baxter & Sons Limited, Fochabers, Moray, 1971-; Brand-Rex Ltd, 1975. CompIEE, Comp. British IRE, Hon. Comp. Royal

Aeronautical Soc. Hon. LLD Aberdeen, 1966; Hon. DSc Heriot-Watt, 1968. *Publication:* Toothill Report on the Scottish Economy, 1961. *Recreations:* fishing, golf. *Address:* St Germains, Longniddry, East Lothian. *T:* Longniddry 2106; Lennoxbrae, Ordiequish, Fochabers, Morayshire. *T:* Fochabers 268. *Club:* Caledonian.

TOPE, Graham Norman; *b* 30 Nov. 1943; *s* of Leslie Tope, Plymouth and late Winifred Tope (*née* Merrick), Bermuda; *m* 1972, Margaret East; one *s*. *Educ:* Whitgift Sch., S Croydon. Company Sec., 1965-72; Insce Manager, 1970-72. Asst Gen. Sec., Camden Council of Social Service, 1975-. Pres., Nat. League of Young Liberals, 1973- (Vice-Chm., 1971-73); Mem., Liberal Party Nat. Council, 1970-; Councillor and Leader, Liberal Group, Sutton Council, 1974-. MP (L) Sutton and Cheam, 1972-Feb. 1974; Liberal Party spokesman on environment, Dec. 1972-1974; contested (L) Sutton and Cheam, Oct. 1974. *Publication:* (jtly) Liberals and the Community, 1974. *Address:* 14 Lindsay Court, Sherwood Park Road, Sutton, Surrey. *T:* 01-642 5010.

TOPHAM, Surgeon Captain Lawrence Garth, RN (Retd); Consultant Physician in Geriatric Medicine, Central Hampshire District Winchester and Andover Hospitals, since 1974; *b* 14 Nov. 1914; *s* of late J. Topham and late Mrs Topham; *m* 1943, Olive Barbara Marshall (VAD), *yr d* of late J. Marshall and late Mrs Marshall; one *s* one *d*. *Educ:* Bradford Grammar Sch.; Univ. of Leeds. MB, ChB 1937; MD 1946; MRCPE 1957; FRCPE 1967; MRCP 1969. Joined RN 1938. Served War: HMS Newcastle and HMS Milford, 1939-41; USN Flight Surgeon's Wings, 1943; RN Fleet Air Arm Pilot's Wings, 1944. Pres., Central Air Med. Bd, 1949; HMS Sheffield, 1951; Med. Specialist and Consultant in Medicine, at RN Hosps, Trincomalee, Haslar and Plymouth, 1952-66; Prof. of Med., RN, and RCP, 1966-71; QHP 1970; retd at own request, from RN, 1971. House Governor and Medical Superintendent, King Edward VII Convalescent Home for Officers, Osborne, IoW, 1971-74. Member: British Nat. Cttee, Internat. Soc. of Internal Medicine; British Geriatric Soc.; Wessex Physicians Club. OStJ (Officer Brother) 1970. *Publications:* several articles in med. jls, especially on subject of diseases of the chest. *Recreations:* Rugby football refereeing, rowing, photography, Oriental cookery. *Address:* Tilings, Holt Close, Wickham, Hants PO17 5EY. *T:* Wickham 832072.

TOPOLSKI, Feliks; Painter; *b* 14 Aug. 1907; *s* of Edward Topolski (actor) and Stanislawa Drutowska; *m* 1st, 1944, Marion Everall (marr. diss. 1975); one *s* one *d*; 2nd, 1975, Caryl J. Stanley. *Educ:* Mikolaj Rey Sch.; Acad. of Art, Warsaw; Officers' Sch. of Artillery Reserve, Wlodzimierz Wolynski; self-tutoring in Italy, Paris. Settled in England, 1935. Exhibited in London and provincial galleries, in Poland, USA, Canada, Eire, France, India, Australia, Italy, Argentine, Switzerland, Denmark, Norway, Israel, Germany, Brazil and Portugal; has contributed to numerous publications; to BBC television programmes; and designed theatrical settings and costumes; as War Artist (1940-45) pictured Battle of Britain, sea and air war, Russia, Middle East, India, Burma, China, Africa, Italy, Germany. British subject since 1947. Painted the Cavalcade of Commonwealth (60' x 20') for Festival of Britain, 1951 (later in Victoria Memorial Hall, Singapore, removed on Independence and returned to artist); four murals for Finsbury Borough Council, 1952 (since erased); Coronation of Elizabeth II (100' x 4') for Buckingham Palace, 1958-60; murals for Carlton Tower Hotel, London, 1960; St Regis Hotel, New York, 1965; twenty portraits of English writers for University of Texas, 1961-62. At present engaged on mural-environment, Memoir of the Century (600' × 12' to 20'), aided by GLC, 1975-. Film: Topolski's Moscow (for CBS TV), 1969. Works at British Museum, Victoria and Albert Museum, Imperial War Museum; Galleries: the Tate, Edinburgh, Glasgow, Aberdeen, Nottingham, Brooklyn, Toronto, Tel Aviv, New Delhi, Melbourne, Lisbon, Warsaw. Dr *hc*, Jagiellonian Univ. of Cracow, 1974. *Publications:* The London Spectacle, 1935; Illustrator of Bernard Shaw's Geneva, 1939, In Good King Charles's Golden Days, 1939, and Pygmalion, 1941; Penguin Prints, 1941; Britain in Peace and War, 1941; Russia in War, 1942; Three Continents, 1944-45; Portrait of GBS, 1946; Confessions of a Congress Delegate, 1949; 88 Pictures, 1951; Coronation, 1953; Sketches of Gandhi, 1954; The Blue Conventions, 1956; Topolski's Chronicle for Students of World Affairs, 1958; Topolski's Legal London, 1961; Face to Face, 1964; Holy China, 1968; (with Conor Cruise O'Brien) The United Nations: Sacred Drama, 1968; Shem Ham & Japheth Inc., 1971; Paris Lost, 1973; Topolski's Buckingham Palace Panoramas, 1977; prints for Christie's Contemporary Art, 1974, 1975; Topolski's Chronicle, 1953-. *Address:* Bridge Arch 158, opposite Artists' Entrance, Royal Festival Hall, SE1. *T:* 01-928 3405.

TOPP, Air Commodore Roger Leslie, AFC 1950 (Bar 1955, 2nd Bar 1957); Deputy General Manager, Multi-role Combat Aircraft Development Agency, Munich, since 1972; *b* 14 May 1923; *s* of William Horace Topp and Kathleen (*née* Peters); *m* 1945, Audrey Jane Jeffery; one *s* one *d*. *Educ:* North Mundham Sch.; RAF, Cranwell. Served War: Pilot trg, Canada, 1943-44, commissioned 1944; 'E' Sqdn Glider Pilot Regt, Rhine Crossing, 1945. Nos 107 and 98 Mosquito Sqdns, Germany, 1947-50; Empire Test Pilots' Sch. and RAE Farnborough, 1951-54; Commanded No 111 Fighter Sqdn (Black Arrows) Aerobatic Team, 1955-58; Allied Air Forces Central Europe, Fontainbleau, 1959; Sector Operational Centre, Brockzetel, Germany, 1959-61; jssc, Latimer, 1961-62; commanded Fighter Test Sqdn, Boscombe Down, 1962-64; Station Cmdr, RAF Coltishall, 1964-66; Nat. Def. Coll., Canada, 1966-67; Opl Requirements, MoD (Air), London, 1967-69; Multi-role Combat Aircraft Project, Munich, 1969-70; HQ No 38 Gp, Odiham, 1970; Commandant, Aeroplane and Armament Experimental Estabt, Boscombe Down, 1970-72. *Recreations:* golf, sailing. *Address:* Mayfield, Meadow Drive, Hoveton St John, Norfolk. *T:* Wroxham 2491. *Club:* Royal Air Force.

TOPP, Wilfred Bethridge, CMG 1949; retired; formerly London Technical Advisor to Diamond Producers Association; *b* 29 Aug. 1891; *s* of Joseph Bethridge Topp, Kimberley, S Africa; *m* 1918, Beatrice Maud Matthews, Port Elizabeth, S Africa. *Educ:* Kimberley, S Africa. Joined De Beers Consolidated Mines Ltd, 1909. Served with 7th S African Inf., 1914-17. Joined Consolidated Diamond Valuation Staff, 1920; one of valuators for famous Hans Merensky diamond finds at Orange River mouth, 1926; taken over by Union Govt for valuations of State Alluvial Diamonds, 1928. At amalgamation of all S African Diamond producers sent to Kimberley Central Office, until sent to England in 1934. At outbreak of War of 1939-45 joined a board of experts to control export of diamonds; after termination of hostilities examined all diamonds for export and import on two days each week (duties for the State honorary since 1939). *Recreations:* rifle shooting, golf. *Address:* Laughing Waters, Valley Road, Kenilworth, Cape, South Africa.

TOPPING, Prof. James, CBE 1977; MSc, PhD, DIC, FInstP; FIMA; Vice-Chancellor, Brunel University, 1966-71; Emeritus Professor, 1971; *b* 9 Dec. 1904; 3rd *s* of James and Mary A. Topping, Ince, Lancashire; *m* 1934, Muriel Phyllis Hall (*d* 1963); one *s*; *m* 1965, Phyllis Iles. *Educ:* Univ. of Manchester; Imperial Coll. of Science and Technology. BSc (Manchester), 1924; PhD (London), 1926; Beit Scientific Research Fellow, 1926-28. Asst Lectr, Imperial Coll., 1928-30; Lectr Chelsea Polytechnic, 1930-32; Lectr, Coll. of Technology, Manchester, 1932-37; Head, Dept of Maths and Physics, Polytechnic, Regent St, 1937-53; Principal, Technical Coll., Guildford, 1953-54; Principal, Brunel College, W3, 1955-66. Vice-Pres., Inst. of Physics, 1951-54, 1960-63; Chairman: Nuffield Secondary Science Consultative Cttee, 1965-71; Hillingdon Gp Hosp. Management Cttee, 1971-74; London Conf. on Overseas Students, 1971-; Council, Roehampton Inst. of Higher Educn, 1975-; Council, Polytechnic of the S Bank, 1975-; Vis. Cttee, Cranfield Inst. of Technol., 1970-; Member: Anderson Cttee on Student Grants, 1958-60; Nat. Council for Technological Awards, 1955-64; CNAA, 1964-70. Hon. DTech Brunel, 1967; Hon. DSc CNAA, 1969. *Publications:* Shorter Intermediate Mechanics (with D. Humphrey), 1949; Errors of Observation, 1955; papers in scientific jls. *Address:* 33 Harriotts Lane, Ashtead, Surrey. *T:* Ashtead 72168. *Club:* Athenæum.

TOPPING, Rt. Hon. Walter William Buchanan, PC (NI) 1957; QC (NI) 1946; **Rt. Hon. Judge Topping;** Recorder of Belfast, since 1960; Judge of County Court, Antrim, since 1960; *b* 13 Jan. 1908; *m* 1933, Maureen Gallaher; three *s*. *Educ:* Rossall School; Queen's University, Belfast. Called to Bar, NI, 1930; QC 1946. MP Larne Div. of Co. Antrim, Parliament of Northern Ireland, 1945; Chief Government Whip, Northern Ireland Parliament, 1947-56; Minister of Home Affairs, 1956-59. *Address:* Windy Ridge, Dunmurry, County Antrim, Northern Ireland.

TORLESSE, Rear-Adm. Arthur David, CB 1953; DSO 1946; retired; Regional Director of Civil Defence, North Midlands Region, 1955-Jan. 1967; *b* 24 Jan. 1902; *e s* of Captain A. W. Torlesse, Royal Navy, and H. M. Torlesse (*née* Jeans); *m* 1933, Sheila Mary Susan, *d* of Lt-Col Duncan Darroch of Gourock; two *s* one *d*. *Educ:* Stanmore Park; Royal Naval Colleges, Osborne and Dartmouth. Served as midshipman, Grand Fleet, 1918; specialised as observer, Fleet Air Arm, 1926; Commander, 1935; staff appointments in HMS Hood and at Singapore and Bangkok (Naval Attaché), 1936-39; Executive officer, HMS Suffolk, 1939-40; aviation staff appointments at Lee on Solent and Admiralty, 1940-44; Captain, 1942; commanded HMS

Hunter, 1944-45; Director of Air Equipment, Admiralty, 1946-48; Imperial Defence College, 1949; commanded HMS Triumph, Far East, 1950, taking part in first 3 months of Korean War (despatches); Rear-Admiral, 1951; Flag Officer, Special Squadron and in command of Monte Bello atomic trial expedition, 1952; Flag Officer, Ground Training, 1953-54, retired Dec. 1954. Officer, US Legion of Merit, 1954. *Recreations:* fishing, entomology. *Address:* 1 Sway Lodge, Sway, near Lymington, Hants. *T:* Sway 2550. *Club:* Naval and Military.

TORNARITIS, Criton George, QC (Cyprus); LLB (Hons, Athens); Attorney-General of the Republic of Cyprus since 1960 (Attorney-General, Cyprus, 1952); seconded as Commissioner for Consolidation of the Cyprus Legislation since 1956; *b* 27 May 1902; *m* 1934, Mary (*née* Pitta) (*d* 1973); one *s. Educ:* Gymnasium of Limassol; Athens University; Gray's Inn. Advocate of the Supreme Court of Cyprus, 1924; District Judge, Cyprus, 1940; President District Court, Cyprus, 1942; Solicitor-General, Cyprus, 1944; Attorney-General, Cyprus, 1952. Attached to Legal Div. of the Colonial Office, 1955. Legal Adviser to Greek-Cypriot Delegation on the Mixed Constitutional Commission, 1959; Greek-Cypriot delegate to Ankara for initialling of Constitution of Republic of Cyprus, 1960. *Publications:* The individual as a subject of international law, 1972; The Turkish invasion of Cyprus and legal problems arising therefrom, 1975; The European Convention of Human Rights in the Legal Order of the Republic of Cyprus, 1975; The Ecclesiastical Courts especially in Cyprus, 1976; Cyprus and its Constitutional and other Legal Problems, 1977; contributions to legal journals and periodicals; The Laws of Cyprus, rev. edn, 1959. *Recreations:* walking, reading. *Address:* Penelope Delta Street, Nicosia, Cyprus. *T:* 77242.

TORNEY, Thomas William; JP; MP (Lab) Bradford South since 1970; *b* London, 2 July 1915. *Educ:* elementary school. Joined Labour Party, 1930; Election Agent: Wembley North, 1945; Derbyshire West, 1964. Derby and Dist Area Organizer, USDAW, 1946-70. Mem. General Management Cttee, Derby Labour Party. Member: (Past Chm.) North Midland Regional Joint Apprenticeship Council for catering industry; Local Appeals Tribunal, Min. of Social Security, 1946-68; Parly Select Cttee on Race Relations and Immigration, 1970-; Chm., Parly Lab Party Gp on Agriculture, Fish and Food. Especially interested in education, social security, industrial relations, agriculture and food. JP Derby, 1969. Chevalier, Commanderie of GB, Confrérie des Chevaliers du Sacavan d'Anjou, 1976. *Address:* House of Commons, SW1; 76 The Hollow, Littleover, Derby. *T:* Derby 23705.

TORONTO, Archbishop of, (RC), since 1971; **Most Rev. Philip F. Pocock,** LLD. *Educ:* Univ. of Western Ontario; St Peter's Seminary, London, Can.; Catholic University of America, Washington, DC; Angelicum University, Rome. Ordination to Priesthood, 1930; Angelicum University, Rome, JCD, 1934; Professor of Moral Theology, St Peter's Seminary, 1934; consecrated Bishop of Saskatoon, 1944; Apostolic Administrator of Winnipeg, June 1951; Titular Archbishop of Apro and Coadjutor Archbishop of Winnipeg, Aug. 1951; Archbishop of Winnipeg, 1952-61; Coadjutor Archbishop of Toronto, 1961-71. Hon. LLD Univ. of Western Ontario, 1955; Univ. of Ottawa, 1958; Univ. of Manitoba, 1958; Assumption Univ. of Windsor, Ont., 1961; St Francis Xavier Univ., Antigonish, 1963; Hon. DD: Huron Coll., London, Ont., 1967. *Address:* 55 Gould Street, Toronto 2, Ontario, Canada.

TORONTO, Bishop of, since 1972; **Rt. Rev. Lewis Samuel Garnsworthy,** DD; *b* 18 July 1922; *m* 1954, Jean Valance Allen; one *s* one *d. Educ:* Univ. of Alberta (BA); Wycliffe Coll., Toronto (LTh). Asst Curate: St Paul's, Halifax, 1945; St John, Norway, Toronto, 1945-48; Rector: St Nicholas, Birchcliff, Toronto, 1948-56; Transfiguration, Toronto, 1956-59; St John's Church, York Mills, Toronto, 1960-68; Suffragan Bishop, Diocese of Toronto, 1968-72. Fellow, Coll. of Preachers, Washington, DC. DD *hc* : Wycliffe Coll., Toronto, 1969; Trinity Coll., Toronto, 1973; Huron Coll., 1976. *Address:* 135 Adelaide Street E, Toronto M5C 1L8. *T:* 363-6021. *Clubs:* Albany, York (Toronto).

TORPHICHEN, 15th Lord *cr* 1564; **James Andrew Douglas Sandilands;** *b* 27 Aug. 1946; *s* of 14th Lord Torphichen, and Mary Thurstan, *d* of late Randle Henry Neville Vaudrey; *S* father, 1975; *m* 1976, Margaret Elizabeth, *o d* of late William A. Beale and of Mrs Margaret Patten Beale, Peterborough, New Hampshire, USA. *Heir:* cousin Douglas Robert Alexander Sandilands [*b* 31 Aug. 1926; *m* 1949, Ethel Louise Burkitt; one *s*]. *Address:* Calder House, Mid-Calder, Midlothian.

TORRANCE, Rev. Professor James Bruce; Professor of Systematic Theology, King's College, University of Aberdeen, and Christ's College, Aberdeen, since 1977; *b* 3 Feb. 1923; *s* of late Rev. Thomas Torrance and Annie Elizabeth Sharp; *m* 1955, Mary Heather Aitken, medical practitioner; one *s* two *d. Educ:* Royal High School, Edinburgh; Edinburgh Univ. (MA Hons Philosophy, 1st Cl.); New Coll., Edinburgh (BD Systematic Theol., Distinction); Univs of Marburg, Basle and Oxford. Licensed Minister of Church of Scotland, 1950; parish of Invergowrie, Dundee, 1954; Lectr in Divinity and Dogmatics in History of Christian Thought, New Coll., Univ. of Edinburgh, 1961; Sen. Lectr in Christian Dogmatics, New Coll., 1972. Visiting Prof.: of New Testament, Union Theol. Seminary, Richmond, Va., 1960; of Theology, Columbia Theol. Seminary, Decatur, Ga., 1965, and Vancouver Sch. of Theology, BC, 1974-75. *Publications:* (trans. jtly) Oscar Cullmann's Early Christian Worship, 1953; contribs: Essays in Christology for Karl Barth (Karl Barth's Festschrift), 1956; Where Faith and Science Meet, 1954; articles to Biblical and Biographical Dictionaries, Scottish Jl of Theology, Interpretation, Church Service Society Annual, and other symposia. *Recreations:* beekeeping, fishing, gardening, swimming. *Address:* Don House, 46 Don Street, Old Aberdeen AB2 1UU. *T:* Aberdeen 41526.
See also Very Rev . Prof . T . F . Torrance .

TORRANCE, Very Rev. Prof. Thomas Forsyth, MBE 1945; DLitt, DTh, DThéol, Dr Teol, DD; Professor of Christian Dogmatics, University of Edinburgh, and New College, Edinburgh, since 1952; Moderator of General Assembly of Church of Scotland, May 1976-77; *b* 30 Aug. 1913; *e s* of late Rev. T. Torrance, then of Chengtu, Szechwan, China; *m* 1946, Margaret Edith, *y d* of late Mr and Mrs G. F. Spear, The Brow, Combe Down, Bath; two *s* one *d. Educ:* Chengtu Canadian School; Bellshill Academy; Univs of Edinburgh, Oxford, Basel. MA Edinburgh 1934; studies in Jerusalem and Athens, 1936; BD Edinburgh 1937; post-grad. studies, Basel, 1937-38; Prof. of Theology, Auburn, NY, USA, 1938-39; post-grad. studies, Oriel Coll., Oxford, 1939-40; ordained minister of Alyth Barony Parish, 1940; Church of Scotland chaplain (with Huts and Canteens) in MEF and CMF, 1943-45; returned to Alyth; DTh Univ. of Basel, 1946; minister of Beechgrove Church, Aberdeen, 1947; Professor of Church History, Univ. of Edinburgh, and New Coll., Edinburgh, 1950-52. Participant, World Conf. on Faith and Order, Lund, 1952; Evanston Assembly of WCC, 1954; Faith and Order Commn of WCC, 1952-62; Participant in Conversations between Church of Scotland and Church of England, 1950-58. Lectures: Hewett, 1959 (NY, Newton Center and Cambridge, Mass); Harris, Dundee, 1970; Anderson, Presbyterian Coll., Montreal, 1971; Taylor, Yale, 1971; Keese, Univ. of Mississippi, Chattanooga, 1971. Mem., Académie Internationale des Sciences Religieuses, 1965 (Pres., 1972-); For. Mem., Société de l'Histoire du Protestantisme Français, 1968; Mem. Soc. Internat. pour l'Etude de la Philosophie Médiévale, 1969; Hon. President: Soc. for Study of Theology, 1966-68; Church Service Soc. of the Church of Scotland, 1970-71; New Coll. Union, 1972-. Vice-Pres., Inst. of Religion and Theology of GB and Ireland, 1973-; Protopresbyter of Greek Orthodox Church (Patriarchate of Alexandria), 1973. DD (*hc*) Presbyterian Coll., Montreal, 1950; DThéol (*hc*) Geneva, 1959; DThéol (*hc*) Paris, 1959; DD (*hc*) St Andrews, 1960; Dr Teol (*hc*) Oslo, 1961; DLitt Edinburgh. Cross of St Mark (first class), 1970. *Publications:* The Modern Theological Debate, 1942; The Doctrine of Grace in the Apostolic Fathers, 1949; Calvin's Doctrine of Man, 1949; Royal Priesthood, 1955; Kingdom and Church, 1956; When Christ Comes and Comes Again, 1957; The Mystery of the Lord's Supper (Sermons on the Sacrament by Robert Bruce), 1958; ed Calvin's Tracts and Treatises, Vols I-III, 1959; The School of Faith, 1959; Conflict and Agreement in the Church, Vol. I, Order and Disorder, 1959; The Apocalypse Today, 1959; Conflict and Agreement in the Church, Vol. II, The Ministry and the Sacraments of the Gospel, 1960; Karl Barth: an Introduction to his Early Theology, 1910-1930, 1962; ed (with D. W. Torrance) Calvin's NT Commentaries, 1959-73; Theology in Reconstruction, 1965; Theological Science, 1969 (Collins Religious Book Award); Space, Time and Incarnation, 1969; God and Rationality, 1971; Theology in Reconciliation: essays towards Evangelical and Catholic Unity in East and West, 1975; The Centrality of Christ, 1976; Space, Time and Resurrection, 1976; Jt Editor, Church Dogmatics, Vols 1, 2, 3 and 4, by Karl Barth, 1956-69; Jt Editor: Scottish Jl Theology; SJT Monographs. *Recreations:* golf, fishing. *Address:* 37 Braid Farm Road, Edinburgh EH10 6LE. *T:* 031-447 3050.
See also Rev . Prof. J . B . Torrance .

TORRIE, Malcolm, *see* Mitchell, Gladys, M. W.

TORRINGTON, 11th Viscount, *cr* 1721; **Timothy Howard St George Byng;** Bt 1715; Baron Byng of Southill, 1721; Managing

Director, Attock Petroleum Ltd; *b* 13 July 1943; *o s* of Hon. George Byng, RN (*d* on active service, 1944; *o s* of 10th Viscount) and Anne Yvonne Wood (she *m* 2nd, 1951, Howard Henry Masterton Carpenter); *S* grandfather, 1961; *m* 1973, Susan, *d* of M. G. T. Webster, *qv*; one *d*. *Educ*: Harrow; St Edmund Hall, Oxford. *Recreation:* travel. *Heir: kinsman*, John Launcelot Byng, MC [*b* 18 March 1919; *m* 1955, Margaret Ellen Hardy; one *s* two *d*]. *Address:* 60 Cumberland Street, SW1. *Clubs:* White's; Muthaiga (Nairobi).

TORTELIER, Paul; Conductor; *b* 21 March 1914; *s* of Joseph Tortelier, cabinet maker; *m* 1946, Maud Martin; one *s* three *d*. *Educ:* Conservatoire National de Musique, Paris; gen. educn privately. Leading Cellist, Monte Carlo, 1935-37; Cellist, Boston Symphony Orch., 1937-40; Leading Cellist, Société des Concerts du Conservatoire de Paris, 1945-47; Internat. solo career began in Concertgebouw, Amsterdam, 1946, and London, 1947 (under Sir Thomas Beecham's baton). Concert tours: Europe, N America, North Africa, Israel, S America, USSR, Japan, etc. As a conductor: debut with Israel Philharmonic, 1956; Prof. of Violoncello: Conservatoire Nat. Supérieur de Musique, Paris, 1956-69; Folkwang Hochschule, Essen; conducts in Paris and in England. Master classes, for BBC TV, 1970. Hon. Mem., Royal Acad. of Music (England). Hon. DMus: Leicester, 1972; Oxon, 1975. *Publications:* Cello Sonata, Trois p'tits tours; Spirales for Cello and piano; Suite for unaccompanied cello; Elegie, Saxe, Toccata for cello and piano; Pièces en trio for oboe and 2 cellos; Edition of Sammartini Sonata; Cadenzas for classical concertos; The Great Flag (internat. anthem, written for UNO); Offrande, for string quartet or string orch.; (book) How I Play, How I Teach, 1973. *Recreations:* no time for these! *Address:* 24 avenue Germaine, 06 Nice, France.

TORY, Sir Geofroy (William), KCMG 1958 (CMG 1956); HM Diplomatic Service, retired; *b* 31 July 1912; *s* of William Frank Tory and Edith Wreghitt; *m* 1st, 1938, Emilia Strickland; two *s* one *d*; 2nd, 1952. Hazel Winfield. *Educ:* King Edward VII Sch., Sheffield; Queens' Coll., Cambridge. Apptd Dominions Office, 1935; Private Sec. to Perm. Under-Sec. of State, 1938-39; served War, 1939-43, in Royal Artillery; Prin. Private Sec. to Sec. of State, 1945-46; Senior Sec., Office of UK High Comr, Ottawa, 1946-49; Prin. Sec., Office of UK Rep. to Republic of Ireland, 1949-50; Counsellor, UK Embassy, Dublin, 1950-51; idc 1952; Dep. High Comr for UK in Pakistan (Peshawar), 1953-54, in Australia, 1954-57; Asst Under-Sec. of State, CRO, 1957; High Comr for UK in Fedn of Malaya, 1957-63; Ambassador to Ireland, 1964-66; High Commissioner to Malta, 1967-70. PMN (Malaysia) 1963. *Recreations:* fishing, painting, golf. *Address:* Rathclaren House, Kilbrittain, Co. Cork, Ireland.

TOTMAN, Grenfell William, CMG 1973; OBE 1963; FCA; Controller of Finance, Commonwealth Development Corporation, 1955-76; *b* 24 July 1911; *s* of William and Lilian Oldrieve Totman; *m* 1st, 1938, Eileen Joan Gidley (marr. diss. 1962); one *s*; 2nd, 1963, Barbara Florence Cannon. *Educ:* Selhurst Grammar Sch.; London Univ. (BCom). Served War, Royal Air Force, 1942-46. With Edward Moore & Sons, Chartered Accountants, 1931-50; Commonwealth Development Corp., 1950-76. *Recreations:* music, gardening. *Address:* Gayfere, East Hill, Otford, Kent. *T:* Otford 3256.

TOTNES, Archdeacon of; *see* Lucas, Ven. J. M.

TOTTENHAM, family name of Marquess of Ely.

TÖTTERMAN, Richard Evert Björnson, Hon. GCVO 1976 (Hon. KCVO 1969); Hon. OBE 1961; DPhil; Kt Comdr, Order of the White Rose of Finland; Finnish Ambassador to the Court of St James's, since 1975; *b* 10 Oct. 1926; *s* of Björn B. Tötterman and Katharine C. (*née* Wimpenny); *m* 1953, Camilla Susanna Veronica Huber; one *s* one *d*. *Educ:* Univ. of Helsinki (LLM); Brasenose Coll., Oxford (DPhil). Entered Finnish Foreign Service, 1952: served Stockholm, 1954-56; Moscow, 1956-58; Ministry for Foreign Affairs, Finland, 1958-62; First Sec., Berne, 1962-63; Counsellor, Paris, 1963-66; Dep. Dir, Min. for For. Affairs, Helsinki, 1966; Sec.-Gen., Office of the President of Finland, 1966-70; Sec.-Gen., Min. for For. Aff., 1970-75. Chm. or Mem. of a number of Finnish Govt Cttees, 1959-75, and participated as Finnish rep. in various internat. negotiations; Chm., Multilateral Consultations preparing Conf. on Security and Co-operation in Europe, 1972-73. Holds numerous foreign orders (Grand Cross, Kt Comdr, etc). *Recreations:* music, out-door life. *Address:* 14 Kensington Palace Gardens, W8. *T:* 01-221 4433. *Clubs:* White's, Hurlingham, Travellers'.

TOTTLE, Prof. Charles Ronald; Professor of Medical Engineering, University of Bath, 1975-78, a Pro Vice-Chancellor, 1973-77; Director, Bath Institute of Medical Engineering, 1975-78; *b* 2 Sept. 1920; *m* 1944, Eileen P. Geoghegan; one *s* one *d*. *Educ:* Nether Edge Grammar School; University of Sheffield (MMet). English Electric Co. Ltd, 1941-45; Lecturer in Metallurgy, University of Durham, King's College, 1945-50; Ministry of Supply, Atomic Energy Division, Springfields Works, 1950-51; Culcheth Laboratories, 1951-56 (UKAEA); Head of Laboratories, Dounreay, 1956-57; Deputy Director, Dounreay, 1958-59; Prof. of Metallurgy, Univ. of Manchester, 1959-67; Prof. and Head of School of Materials Science, Univ. of Bath, 1967-75; Man. Dir, South Western Industrial Research Ltd, 1970-75. Resident Research Associate, Argonne Nat. Laboratory, Illinois, USA, 1964-65. Vice-Pres., Instn of Metallurgists, 1968-70; Jt Editor, Institution of Metallurgists Series of Textbooks, 1962-70. FIM; FInstP, 1958. Hon. MSc Manchester. *Publications:* The Science of Engineering Materials, 1965; various contribs to metallurgical and engineering jls. *Recreations:* music, model making, gardening. *Address:* Thirdacre, Hilperton, Trowbridge, Wilts. *Clubs:* Science (Bath); Vintage Sports Car (Newbury).

TOUCH, Dr Arthur Gerald, CMG 1967; Chief Scientist, Government Communications Headquarters, 1961-71; *b* 5 July 1911; *s* of A. H. Touch, Northampton; *m* 1938, Phyllis Wallbank, Birmingham; one *s*. *Educ:* Oundle; Jesus College, Oxford. MA, DPhil 1937. Bawdsey Research Station, Air Ministry, 1936; Radio Dept, RAE, Farnborough, 1940; British Air Commn, Washington, DC, 1941; Supt, Blind Landing Experimental Unit, RAE, 1947; Director: Electronic R and D (Air), Min. of Supply, 1953; Electronic R and D (Ground), Min. of Supply, 1956-59; Imperial Defence College, 1957; Head, Radio Dept, RAE, 1959; Min. of Defence, 1960. *Recreations:* fly fishing, horticulture (orchids). *Address:* Yonder, Ideford, Newton Abbot, Devon TQ13 0BG. *T:* Chudleigh 852258.

TOUCHE, Sir Anthony (George), 3rd Bt *cr* 1920; Chairman of Touche, Remnant & Co., since 1971; Deputy Chairman, National Westminster Bank Ltd, since 1977; *b* 31 Jan. 1927; *s* of Donovan Meredith Touche (*d* 1952) (2nd *s* of 1st Bt) and of Muriel Amy Frances, *e d* of Rev. Charles R. Thorold Winckley; *S* uncle, 1977; *m* 1961, Hester Christina, *er d* of Dr Werner Pleuger; three *s* one *d*. *Educ:* Eton College. FCA. Partner in George A. Touche & Co. (now Touche Ross & Co.), 1951; Director of investment trust companies, 1952-; retired from Touche Ross & Co., 1968; Director, Westminster Bank Ltd, 1968; Chairman, Assoc. of Investment Trust Companies, 1971-73. *Recreations:* music, reading, walking. *Heir: s* William George Touche, *b* 26 June 1962. *Address:* Stane House, Ockley, Dorking, Surrey RH5 5TQ. *T:* Oakwood Hill 397. *Club:* Bath.

TOUCHE, Sir Rodney (Gordon), 2nd Bt *cr* 1962; President, Village Lake Louise Ltd, Alberta, Canada, since 1973; *b* 5 Dec. 1928; *s* of Rt Hon. Sir Gordon Touche, 1st Bt, and of Ruby, Lady Touche (formerly Ruby Ann Macpherson); *S* father 1972; *m* 1955, Ouida Ann, *d* of F. G. MacLellan, Moncton, NB, Canada; one *s* three *d*. *Educ:* Marlborough; University Coll., Oxford. Reporter for: Portsmouth Evening News, 1951-53; London Evening Standard, 1953-55; Toronto Financial Post, 1956-59. Subseq. career in oil industry, in a private investment company, and since 1966 as an investment consultant. *Heir: s* Eric MacLellan Touche, *b* 22 Feb. 1960. *Address:* 707 Prospect Avenue, Calgary, Alberta, Canada. *T:* 403-244-6097. *Club:* Royal Automobile.

TOULMIN, Stephen Edelston, MA, PhD; Professor in the Committee on Social Thought, University of Chicago, since 1973; *b* 25 March 1922; *s* of late G. E. Toulmin and of Mrs E. D. Toulmin. *Educ:* Oundle School; King's College, Cambridge. BA 1943; MA 1946; PhD 1948; MA (Oxon) 1948. Junior Scientific Officer, Ministry of Aircraft Production, 1942-45; Fellow of King's College, Cambridge, 1947-51; University Lecturer in the Philosophy of Science, Oxford, 1949-55; Acting Head of Department of History and Methods of Science, University of Melbourne, Australia, 1954-55; Professor of Philosophy, University of Leeds, 1955-59; Visiting Prof. of Philosophy, NY Univ. and Stanford Univ. (California) and Columbia Univ. (NY), 1959-60; Director, Nuffield Foundation Unit for History of Ideas, 1960-64; Prof. of Philosophy, Brandeis Univ., 1965-69, Michigan State Univ., 1969-72; Provost, Crown College, Univ. of California, Santa Cruz, 1972-73; Counsellor, Smithsonian Institution, 1966-75. *Publications:* The Place of Reason in Ethics, 1950; The Philosophy of Science: an Introduction, 1953; Metaphysical Beliefs (3 essays: author of one of them), 1957; The Uses of Argument, 1958; Foresight and Understanding, 1961; The Ancestry of Science, Vol. I (The Fabric of the Heavens) 1961, Vol. II (The Architecture of Matter), 1962, Vol. III (The Discovery of Time), 1965; Night Sky at Rhodes, 1963; Human Understanding, vol. 1, 1972; Wittgenstein's Vienna, 1973;

Knowing and Acting, 1976; also films, broadcast talks and contribs to learned jls and weeklies. *Address:* Committee on Social Thought, University of Chicago, Chicago, Ill 60637, USA.

TOURS, Kenneth Cecil, CMG 1955; *b* 16 Feb. 1908; *y s* of late Berthold George Tours, CMG, HM Consul-General in China; *m* 1934, Ruth Grace, *y d* of late Hugh Lewis; two *s. Educ:* Aldenham School; Corpus Christi College, Cambridge (MA). Administrative Service, Gold Coast, 1931; Gambia, 1935; Palestine, 1938; Malaya, 1945; Col (Food Control) and (Supplies), Brit. Mil. Administration, Malaya, 1945-46; Chm., Jt Supply Board, 1946; Establishment Office, Singapore, 1947; Permanent Sec., Min. of Finance, Gold Coast, 1950; Financial Sec. and Minister of Finance, 1954; Economic Adviser, Ghana, 1954; retd from Colonial Service, 1957. *Recreation:* gardening. *Address:* Ruskins, Lynwick Street, Rudgwick, Sussex. *T:* Rudgwick 2642.

TOUT, Herbert, CMG 1946; MA; Reader in Political Economy, University College, London, 1947-68, retired; *b* Manchester, 20 April 1904; *e s* of Professor T. F. Tout, Manchester University, and Mary Johnstone; unmarried. *Educ:* Sherborne School; Hertford College, Oxford. Instructor in Economics, University of Minnesota, USA, 1929-35; Assistant Lecturer, University College, London, 1936; Colston Research Fellow and Director of University of Bristol Social Survey, 1936-38; Lecturer, University of Bristol, 1938-47; Temp. Principal, Board of Trade, 1940-41; Assistant Secretary, 1941-45. *Recreations:* walking, farming, gardening. *Address:* Little Greeting, West Hoathly, East Grinstead, West Sussex RH19 4PW. *T:* Sharpthorne 810400.

TOVELL, Laurence, FCA, IPFA; Chief Inspector of Audit, Department of the Environment, since 1977; *b* 6 March 1919; *s* of William Henry Tovell and Margaret Tovell (née Mahoney); *m* 1945, Iris Joan (née Lee); two *s* one *d. Educ:* Devonport High School. Entered Civil Service as Audit Assistant, District Audit Service, 1938. Served War, 1940-46; Lieut RNVR, 1942-46. District Auditor, No 4 Audit District, Birmingham, 1962. *Recreation:* do-it-yourself. *Address:* White Lions, Links Road, Bramley, Guildford, Surrey. *T:* Bramley 2702.

TOWER, Maj.-Gen. Philip Thomas, CB 1968; DSO 1944; MBE 1942; National Trust Administrator, Blickling Hall, since 1973; County Commissioner (Norfolk), St John Ambulance, since 1975; *b* 1 March 1917; *s* of late Vice-Admiral Sir Thomas Tower, KBE, CB and late Mrs E. H. Tower; *m* 1943, Elizabeth, *y d* of late Thomas Ralph Sneyd-Kynnersley, OBE, MC and late Alice Sneyd-Kynnersley. *Educ:* Harrow; Royal Military Acad., Woolwich. 2nd Lt Royal Artillery, 1937; served in India, 1937-40; served War of 1939-45 (despatches); Middle East, 1940-42; POW Italy, 1942-43; escaped, 1943; Arnhem, 1944; Norway, 1945; Staff Coll., 1948; Instructor at RMA Sandhurst, 1951-53; comd J (Sidi Rezegh) Bty RHA in Middle East, 1954-55; Joint Services Staff Coll., 1955-56; GSO1 Plans, BJSM Washington, DC, 1956-57; comd 3rd Regt RHA, 1957-60; Imperial Defence Coll., 1961; Comd 51 Inf. Bde Gp, 1961-62; Comd 12 Inf. Bde Gp, BAOR, 1962-64; Director of Public Relations (Army), 1965-67; GOC Middle East Land Forces, 1967 (despatches); Comdt, RMA Sandhurst, 1968-72, retd 1972. Col Comdt, Royal Regt of Artillery, 1970-. *Recreations:* sailing, shooting, riding, gardening. *Address:* Blickling Hall, Norwich NR11 6NF. *T:* Aylsham 2439; Studio A, 414 Fulham Road, SW6. *T:* 01-385 8538. *Clubs:* Army and Navy, Pratt's; Royal Yacht Squadron.

TOWLER, Eric William, CBE 1971; farmer; farms 2,000 acres; *b* 28 April 1900; *s* of William Towler and Laura Mary (née Trew); *m* 1st, 1921, Isabel Edith Ina Hemsworth; two *s* (one *d* decd), 2nd, 1964, Stella Prideaux-Brune; two *s. Educ:* Morley Grammar Sch. Founder, Cawoods Holdings Ltd and Cawood Wharton & Co. Ltd, 1931; Managing Dir, Cawood Wharton & Co. Ltd, 1931-42, Chm., 1942-71; Chm., Cawoods Holdings Ltd, 1961-72, Dir, 1972-77, Hon. Pres., 1977-; Mining Director: Dorman Long & Co. Ltd, 1937-65; Pearson Dorman Long Ltd, 1937-65; Richard Thomas & Co. Ltd, 1929-31. MFH: Badsworth Hunt, 1938-43; South Shropshire Hunt, 1951-56. Chm., Nuffield Orthopaedic Centre, 1960-66; Chm., Bd of Governors, Oxford United Hosp., 1964-72. Hon. MA (Oxon) 1964. *Recreations:* hunting, gardening. *Address:* Glympton Park, near Woodstock, Oxon. *T:* Woodstock 811300; Willett House, Lydeard St Lawrence, Somerset. *T:* Lydeard St Lawrence 234. *Club:* Carlton.

TOWNDROW, Ven. Frank Noel; Archdeacon of Oakham, 1967-77, now Archdeacon Emeritus; Residentiary Canon of Peterborough, 1966-77, now Canon Emeritus; a Chaplain to the Queen, since 1975; *b* 25 Dec. 1911; *e s* of F. R. and H. A.

Towndrow, London; *m* 1947, Olive Helen Weinberger; one *d* (one *s* decd). *Educ:* St Olave's Grammar Sch.; King's Coll., Cambridge; Coll. of Resurrection, Mirfield. Curate, Chingford, E4, 1937-40; Chaplain, RAFVR, 1940-47; Rector of Grangemouth, Stirlingshire, 1947-51; Vicar of Kirton Lindsey, Lincs, 1951-53; Rector of Greenford, Middx, 1953-62; Vicar of Ravensthorpe, E Haddon and Rector of Holdenby, 1962-66. *Recreation:* modern history. *Address:* 2 Bourne Road, Swinstead, Grantham, Lincs. *T:* Corby Glen 422. *Clubs:* National Liberal; Town and Country (Northampton).

TOWNELEY, Simon Peter Edmund Cosmo William; Lord-Lieutenant and Custos Rotulorum of Lancashire, since 1976; *b* 14 Dec. 1921; *e s* of Col A. Koch de Gooreynd, OBE (who assumed surname of Worsthorne by deed poll, 1921), and of Baroness Norman, *qv*; assumed surname and arms of Towneley by royal licence, 1955, by reason of descent from *e d* and senior co-heiress of Col Charles Towneley of Towneley; *m* 1955, Mary, 2nd *d* of Cuthbert Fitzherbert, *qv*; one *s* six *d. Educ:* Stowe; Worcester Coll., Oxford (MA, DPhil). Served War of 1939-45, KRRC. Lectr in History of Music, Worcester Coll., Oxford, 1949-55. CC Lancs, 1961-64; JP 1956; DL 1970; High Sheriff of Lancashire, 1971. President: Community Council of Lancashire; Mid-Pennine Assoc. for the Arts; Chm., Northern Ballet Theatre; Member: Court and Council, Univ. of Manchester; Court and Council, Royal Northern Coll. of Music; Hallé Concerts Soc.; Hon. Rep. (Lancs), Nat. Trust; Vice-Pres., NW Arts Assoc. Hon. FRNCM. KStJ; KCSG. *Publications:* Venetian Opera in the Seventeenth Century, 1954 (repr. 1968); contribs to New Oxford History of Music. *Recreation:* playing chamber music. *Address:* Dyneley, Burnley, Lancs. *T:* Burnley 23322. *Clubs:* Turf, Pratt's, Beefsteak.
See also P. G. Worsthorne.

TOWNEND, Donald Thomas Alfred, CBE 1952; DSc London, PhD, DIC; FRIC; MIMinE; Fellow, Imperial College of Science and Technology; *b* Hackney, London, 15 July 1897; *s* of Charles Henry Townend; *m* 1924, Lilian (*d* 1974), *er d* of Samuel William Lewis, Bexley, Kent; one *s* one *d. Educ:* Bancroft's School, Woodford Green, Essex. East London (now Queen Mary) College, 1919-20; Imperial College of Science and Technology, 1920-38; Salters' Research Fellow, 1923-24; Rockefeller International Research Fellow, 1924-26; Livesey Prof. of Coal Gas and Fuel Industries, University of Leeds, 1938-46; Dir-Gen., British Coal Utilisation Research Assoc., 1946-62; formerly Research Fell. and Hon. Lectr in Roy. Coll. of Science. Jubilee Memorial Lectr, 1945, Brotherton Memorial Lecturer, 1946 and Hodsman Memorial Lectr, 1954, Soc. of Chemical Industry; Dalton Lecturer, Inst. of Chemistry, 1947; William Young Memorial Lectr, N Brit. Assoc. of Gas Managers, 1947; Des Vœux Memorial Lectr, Nat. Soc. for Clean Air, 1950; Melchett Lectr, Inst. of Fuel, 1952. Vice-Pres. 1957-61, Vice-Chm. 1961-64, Parly and Sci. Cttee. Gold Medallist, Institut Français des Combustibles et de l'Energie, 1958; BCURA Coal Science Medallist, 1963; Hon. FIGasE (Birmingham Medallist, IGasE); Hon. MInstF (Past Pres. and Melchett Medallist, InstF). Hon. DSc Tech Sheffield. *Publications:* (with late Professor W. A. Bone) Flame and Combustion in Gases, 1927; Gaseous Combustion at High Pressures, 1929; Papers in Proceedings of Royal Society, etc. *Recreations:* cricket, horticulture. *Address:* Uplands, Yarm Way, Leatherhead, Surrey. *T:* Leatherhead 73520. *Club:* Athenæum.

TOWNES, Charles Hard; University Professor, University of California, USA; *b* Greenville, South Carolina, 28 July 1915; *s* of Henry Keith Townes and Ellen Sumter (née Hard); *m* 1941, Frances H. Brown; four *d. Educ:* Furman Univ. (BA, BS); Duke Univ. (MA); California Institute of Technology (PhD). Assistant in Physics, California Inst. of Technology, 1937-39; Member Techn Staff, Bell Telephone Labs, 1939-47; Associate Prof. of Physics, Columbia Univ., 1948-50; Prof. of Physics, Columbia Univ., 1950-61; Exec. Director, Columbia Radiation Lab., 1950-52; Chairman, Dept of Physics, Columbia Univ., 1952-55; Vice-President and Director of Research, Inst. for Defense Analyses, 1959-61; Provost and Professor of Physics, MIT, 1961-66; Institute Professor, MIT, 1966-67. Guggenheim Fellow, 1955-56; Fulbright Lecturer, University of Paris, 1955-56, University of Tokyo, 1956; Lecturer, 1955, 1960, Dir, 1963, Enrico Fermi Internat. Sch. of Physics; Scott Lecturer, University of Cambridge, 1963. Centennial Lecturer, University of Toronto, 1967. Director: Perkin-Elmer Corp.; Bulletin of Atomic Scientists, 1964-69. Board of Editors: Review of Scientific Instruments, 1950-52; Physical Review, 1951-53; Journal of Molecular Spectroscopy, 1957-60; Columbia University Forum, 1957-59. Fellow: American Phys. Society (Richtmyer Lecturer, 1959; Member Council, 1959-62, 1965-71; President, 1967); Inst. of Electrical and Electronics Engrs;

Chairman, Sci. and Technology Adv. Commn for Manned Space Flight, NASA, 1964-69; Member: President's Science Adv. Cttee, 1966-69 (Vice-Chm., 1967-69); Scientific Adv. Bd, US Air Force, 1958-61; Soc. Française de Physique (Member Council, 1956-58); Nat. Acad. Scis (Mem. Council, 1969-72); American Acad. Arts and Sciences; American Philos. Society; American Astron. Society; American Assoc. of Physics Teachers; Société Royale des Sciences de Liège; Foreign Mem., Royal Society, 1976; Hon. Mem., Optical Soc. of America. Trustee: Salk Inst. for Biological Studies, 1963-68; Rand Corp., 1965-70; Carnegie Instn of Washington, 1965-. Chairman: Space Science Bd, Nat. Acad. of Sciences, 1970-73; Science Adv. Cttee, General Motors Corp., 1971-73; Bd of Dirs, General Motors, 1973-. Holds numerous honorary degrees. Nobel Prize for Physics (jointly), 1964. Research Corp. Annual Award, 1958; Comstock Prize, Nat. Acad. of Sciences, 1959; Stuart Ballantine Medal, Franklin Inst., 1959, 1962; Rumford Premium, Amer. Acad. of Arts and Sciences, 1961; Thomas Young Medal and Prize, Inst. of Physics and Physical Soc., England, 1963; Medal of Honor, Inst. of Electrical and Electronics Engineers, 1967; C. E. K. Mees Medal, Optical Soc. of America, 1968; Churchman of the Year Award, Southern Baptist Theological Seminary, 1967; Distinguished Public Service Medal, NASA, 1969; Michelson-Morley Award, 1970; Wilhelm-Exner Award, 1970; Medal of Honor, Univ. of Liège, 1971; Earle K. Plyler Prize, 1977. National Inventors Hall of Fame, 1976. *Publications:* (with A. L. Schawlow) Microwave Spectroscopy, 1955; (ed) Quantum Electronics, 1960; (ed with P. A. Miles) Quantum Electronics and Coherent Light, 1964; many scientific articles on microwave spectroscopy, molecular and nuclear structure, astrophysics and quantum electronics; fundamental patents on masers and lasers. *Address:* Department of Physics, University of California, Berkeley, California 94720, USA. *T:* 642-1128. *Club:* Cosmos (Washington, DC).

TOWNLEY, Sir John (Barton), Kt 1960; *b* 14 June 1914; *s* of Barton Townley and Margaret Alice, *d* of Richard Gorst; *m* 1939, Gwendoline May Ann, *d* of Arthur Simmonds; one *s* three *d*. *Educ:* Rydal Sch.; Downing Coll., Cambridge; Sorbonne. MA Cambridge, 1939. President: Preston Conservative Assoc., N and S Divisions, 1954-72 (Chairman, Preston S Conserv. Assoc., 1949-54); Preston Sea Cadet Corps, 1954-72; Preston Circle King George's Fund for Sailors, 1949-72; Preston Charities Assoc., 1949-; Life Vice-Pres., Preston, Chorley, Leyland Conservative Clubs Council (Pres. 1949-). Life Mem., North Western Industrial Assoc. Adv. Bd. Vice-Pres., RNLI. Chairman: Preston YMCA Special Appeals Cttee; Preston N Conservative Assoc., 1958; Founder Mem., Nat. Playing Fields Assoc.; Chm., Spastics Appeal, 1950-53. *Recreations:* a little golf and shooting and talking about all sports. *Address:* Flat 2, 33 East Beach, Lytham, Lancs. *Clubs:* Hawks, Union, Pitt (Cambridge).

TOWNLEY, Reginald Colin, CMG 1968; retired; *b* 5 April 1904; *s* of Reginald George and Susan Townley; *m* 1930, Irene Winifred Jones; three *s* one *d*. *Educ:* Hobart High Sch.; University of Tasmania. Chemist, 1927-64; Army, 1939-45, Middle East and Pacific. Tasmanian Parliament, 1946-64 (Leader of Opposition, 1950-56). *Recreation:* gardening. *Address:* 1 Carlton Street, Lenah Valley, Tasmania 7008, Australia. *T:* 281291. *Club:* Naval and Military (Hobart).

TOWNSEND, Albert Alan, FRS 1960; PhD; Reader (Experimental Fluid Mechanics), Cavendish Laboratory, University of Cambridge, since 1961 (Assistant Director of Research, 1950-61); Fellow of Emmanuel College, Cambridge, since 1947; *b* 22 Jan. 1917; *s* of A. R. Townsend and D. Gay; *m* 1950, V. Dees; one *s* two *d*. *Educ:* Telopea Park IHS; Melbourne and Cambridge Universities. PhD 1947. *Publications:* The Structure of Turbulent Shear Flow, 1956; papers in technical journals. *Address:* Emmanuel College, Cambridge.

TOWNSEND, Cyril David; MP (C) Bexley Bexleyheath since Feb. 1974; *b* 21 Dec. 1937; *s* of Lt-Col Cyril M. Townsend and Lois (née Henderson); *m* 1976, Anita, *d* of late Lt-Col F. G. W. Walshe and of Mrs Walshe. *Educ:* Bradfield Coll.; RMA Sandhurst. Commnd into Durham LI; served in Berlin and Hong Kong; active service in Cyprus, 1958 and Borneo, 1966; ADC to Governor and C-in-C Hong Kong, 1964-66; Adjt 1DLI, 1966-68. A Personal Asst to Edward Heath, 1968-70; Mem. Conservative Research Dept, 1970-74. Member: Select Cttee on Violence in the Family, 1975; Friends of Cyprus Cttee, 1976; SE London Industrial Consultative Gp; Chairman: Bow Gp Standing Cttee on Foreign Affairs; All-Party Freedom for Rudolf Hess Campaign; Jt Sec., Cons. Greater London MPs; Vice-Pres., Greater London Young Conservatives. Mem. Council, St Christopher's Fellowship. *Recreations:* books, music, exercise. *Address:* House of Commons, SW1A 0AA.

TOWNSEND, Brigadier Edward Philip, CBE 1957 (OBE 1951); DSO 1950; retired; *b* 24 July 1909; 2nd *s* of late Lt-Col E. C. Townsend, Indian Army; *m* 1952, Imogen Martin; two *d*. *Educ:* Haileybury; RMC, Sandhurst. Commissioned, 1929; joined 5th Royal Gurkha Rifles, 1930; Commanded: 2nd Bn 5th RGR, 1944-47; 1st Bn 6th Gurkha Rifles, 1948-51; 48th Gurkha Infantry Brigade, Aug. 1953-Feb. 1955; 99th Gurkha Infantry Brigade, Oct. 1955-Nov. 1957; British Gurkha L of C Nepal, July 1958-April 1961; retired, 1961. *Address:* Copleston, Peterstow, Ross-on-Wye, Herefordshire HR9 6LD.

TOWNSEND, Sir Lance; *see* Townsend, Sir S. L.

TOWNSEND, Mrs Lena Moncrieff, CBE 1974; Member, Race Relations Board, 1969-73; *b* 3 Nov. 1911; twin *d* of late Captain R. G. Westropp, Cairo, Egypt; *m* (twice); two *s* one *d*. *Educ:* Downe House, Newbury; Somerville Coll., Oxford; Heidelberg Univ., Germany. During War of 1939-45 was an Organiser in WVS and in Women's Land Army, and then taught at Downe House. Mem. for Hampstead, LCC, 1955-65; Alderman, London Borough of Camden, 1964-65; Mem. for Camden, GLC, 1967-70; Alderman, GLC, 1970-77, and Dep. Chm., 1976-77; Inner London Education Authority: Leader, 1969-70; Leader of the Opposition, 1970-71. Pres., Anglo-Egyptian Soc.; Exec. Member: British Council, European Movement; European Union of Women; Council of European Municipalities; Arkwright Arts Trust (Chm., 1971-73); Chairman: London Coll. of Fashion; Residence Cttee, Univ. of London; Mem., Council, Westfield Coll., London Univ. Patron, Lewis Carroll Soc. *Recreations:* foreign languages, travel, the arts, swimming, gardening, sewing. *Address:* 16 Holly Mount, NW3. *T:* 01-435 8555.

TOWNSEND, Rear-Adm. Michael Southcote, CB 1959; DSO 1942; OBE 1940; DSC 1940 (Bar, 1941); *b* 18 June 1908; *s* of Colonel Edward Coplestone Townsend and Gladys Hatt-Cook; *m* 1932, Joan Pendrill Charles; one *s* two *d*. *Educ:* Royal Naval Coll., Dartmouth. Rear-Admiral, 1956; Flag Officer, Admiralty Interview Boards and President, First Admiralty Interview Board, 1956-58; Commander Allied Naval Forces, Northern Area, Central Europe, 1958-61, retired; Admiralty Officer, Wales, 1962-68. *Address:* Tor-y-Mynydd Farm, Devauden, Chepstow, Gwent. *T:* Trellech 417.

TOWNSEND, Prof. Peter Brereton; Professor of Sociology, since 1963, Pro-Vice-Chancellor, since 1975, University of Essex; *b* 6 April 1928; *s* of Philip Brereton Townsend and Alice Mary Townsend (née Southcote); *m* 1st, 1949, Ruth (née Pearce); four *s*; 2nd, 1977, Joy (née Skegg); one *d*. *Educ:* Fleet Road Elementary Sch., London; University Coll. Sch., London; St John's Coll., Cambridge Univ.; Free Univ., Berlin. Research Sec., Political and Economic Planning, 1952-54; Research Officer, Inst. of Community Studies, 1954-57; Research Fellow and then Lectr in Social Administration, London Sch. of Economics, 1957-63. Chm., the Fabian Society, 1965-66 (Chm., Social Policy Cttee, 1970-); Pres., Psychiatric Rehabilitation Assoc., 1968-; Chairman: Child Poverty Action Gp, 1969-; Disability Alliance, 1974-; Member: Chief Scientist's Cttee, DHSS, 1976-; Govt Working Gp on Inequalities and Health, 1977-. *Publications:* The Family Life of Old People, 1957; National Superannuation (co-author), 1957; Nursing Homes in England and Wales (co-author), 1961; The Last Refuge: a survey of residential institutions and homes for the aged in England and Wales, 1962; The Aged in the Welfare State (co-author), 1965; The Poor and the Poorest (co-author), 1965; Old People in Three Industrial Societies (co-author), 1968; (ed) The Concept of Poverty, 1970; (ed) Labour and Inequality, 1972; The Social Minority, 1973; Sociology and Social Policy, 1975; Poverty in the United Kingdom: a survey of household resources and standards of living, 1978. *Recreation:* athletics. *Address:* Ferriers Farm Cottage, Bures, Suffolk. *T:* Bures 227370.

TOWNSEND, Group Captain Peter Wooldridge, CVO 1947; DSO 1941; DFC and Bar, 1940; *b* 22 Nov. 1914; *s* of late Lt-Col E. C. Townsend; *m* 1959, Marie Luce, *d* of Franz Jamagne, Brussels, Belgium; one *s* two *d* (two *s* by former marriage). *Educ:* Haileybury; Royal Air Force Coll., Cranwell. Royal Air Force, 1933; served War of 1939-45, Wing Commander, 1941 (despatches, DFC and Bar, DSO). Equerry to King George VI, 1944-52; Deputy Master of HM Household, 1950; Equerry to the Queen, 1952-53; Air Attaché, Brussels, 1953-56. *Publications:* Earth, My Friend, 1959; Duel of Eagles, 1970; The Last Emperor, 1975. *Address:* La Mare aux Oiseaux, 78116 Saint-Leger-en-Yvelines, France.

TOWNSEND, Sir (Sydney) Lance, Kt 1971; VRD 1955; Professor of Obstetrics and Gynaecology, 1951-78, Dean, Faculty of Medicine, 1971-78, University of Melbourne; *b* 17

Dec. 1912; s of Edward Henry and Muriel Constance Townsend; m 1943, Jean Campbell Smyth; one s three d (and one s decd). *Educ:* Bairnsdale High Sch.; Trinity Coll., Univ. of Melbourne. MD, BS; DTM&H; FRCSE; FACS; FRACS; FRCOG; Hon. FRCS(C); Hon. FACOG; Hon. FCOG (SA). Residential med. posts at Bendigo, Royal Women's Hosp. and Tenant Creek Hosp., 1936-38; Med. Off., W Middx Hosp., 1939; Med. Off., RN, 1940-46 (Surg. Comdr); Surg. Captain, RANVR, 1965; Hon. Obstetrician and Gynaecologist to Austin, Royal Women's, Royal Melbourne, Queen Victoria and Prince Henry's Hosps, 1948-78; Mem., Hon. Sec., Pres., Australian Council RCOG, 1951-69; Chm., Cons. Council on Maternal and Perinatal Mortality, 1955-; Mem. Bd of Management, Royal Women's Hosp., 1951-78; Sec., Victorian Bush Nursing Assoc., 1961-73; Chm., Victorian Cytology Service (Gynae.), 1965-; Chm. of Dirs, Australian and NZ Jl of Obstetrics and Gynaecology, 1961-76. *Publications:* High Blood Pressure and Pregnancy, 1959; Gynaecology for Students, 1964, 3rd edn 1969; Obstetrics for Students, 1964, 3rd edn 1978. *Recreations:* sailing, philately. *Address:* 28 Ryeburne Avenue, Hawthorn East, Victoria 3123, Australia. *T:* 823434. *Clubs:* Melbourne, Naval and Military (Melbourne).

TOWNSEND, Air Vice-Marshal William Edwin, CB 1971; CBE 1965 (OBE 1957); RAAF retired; Director of State Emergency Services and Chairman of Bush Fire Council, New South Wales, since 1973; b 25 April 1916; s of William Edwin Townsend (Senior) and Jessie May Lewry; m 1939, Linda Ruth Deakins; two s two d. *Educ:* Longerenong Coll., Vic, Australia. Grad. Pt Cook, 1937; Chief Flying Instr and 2nd i/c No 8 EFTS, 1940; Sen. Trg Staff Officer, 1941; Comdg Officer 67 and 22 Sqdns, 1942-43; shot down over enemy territory, escaped and returned to Aust., 1944; Comdg Officer, 5 Operational Trg Unit, 1944; SASO, NE Area, 1946; OC, Port Moresby, 1947-48; Sec., Australian Jt Staff, Washington, 1949-50; OC, East Sale, 1951-52; CO and Sen. Officer i/c Admin, Home Command, 1953-54; OC 78 Fighter Wing, 1955-56; Dir of Ops, 1957-60; OC, RAAF Williamtown, 1960-62; Dir Gen. Personnel, 1962-64; OC, RAAF, Butterworth, 1964-67; Dep. CAS, 1967-69; AOC Operational Comd, RAAF, 1969-72. Pres., Aust. Branch, RAF Escaping Soc.; Nat. Pres., Air Force Assoc. of Australia; Vice-Pres., St John Ambulance Assoc., NSW Centre. Councillor, Royal Humane Soc. of NSW. FAIM. *Address:* 8 Tutus Street, Balgowlah Heights, NSW 2093, Australia. *Clubs:* Royal Automobile; Imperial Service (Sydney).

TOWNSHEND, family name of **Marquess Townshend.**

TOWNSHEND, 7th Marquess cr 1787; **George John Patrick Dominic Townshend;** Bt 1617; Baron Townshend, 1661; Viscount Townshend, 1682; Chairman: Anglia Television Group Ltd; Anglia Television Ltd; Survival Anglia Ltd; Anchor Enterprises Ltd; AP Bank Ltd; Raynham Farm Co. Ltd; Executive Committee, Norfolk Agricultural Station; Vice-Chairman: Norwich Union Life Insurance Society Ltd; Norwich Union Fire Insurance Society Ltd; Royal Norfolk Agricultural Association; Director: Scottish Union & National Insurance Co.; Maritime Insurance Co. Ltd; East Coast Grain Ltd; London Merchant Securities; D. E. Longe & Co. Ltd; Napak Ltd; Anglia Radio Ltd; Trustee, East Anglian Trustee Savings Bank; b 13 May 1916; s of 6th Marquess and Gladys Ethel Gwendolen Eugenie (d 1959), d of late Thomas Sutherst, barrister; S father, 1921; m 1st, 1939, Elizabeth (marr. diss. 1960; she m 1960, Brig. Sir James Gault, KCMG, MVO, OBE), o d of Thomas Luby, Indian CS; one s two d; 2nd, 1960, Ann Frances, d of Arthur Pellew Darlow; one s one d. Norfolk Yeomanry TA, 1936-40; Scots Guards, 1940-45. DL Norfolk, 1951-61. *Heir:* s Viscount Raynham, qv. *Address:* Raynham Hall, Fakenham, Norfolk. *T:* Fakenham 2133. *Clubs:* White's, Pratt's, MCC; Norfolk (Norwich); Royal Yacht Squadron; House of Lords Yacht.

TOWNSING, Kenneth Joseph, CMG 1971; ISO 1966; Chairman, Salaries and Allowances Tribunal, since 1975; Director: Western Mining Corporation Ltd, since 1975; H.L. Brisbane and Wunderlich Ltd, since 1975; b 25 July 1914; s of J. W. and L. A. Townsing; m 1942, Frances Olive Daniel; two s one d. *Educ:* Perth Boys' Sch.; Univ. of Western Australia. Treasury Officer, 1933-39. Served War, AIF (Middle East), 1940-46, Major. Public Service Inspector, 1946-49; Sec., Public Service Commissioner's Office, 1949-52; Dep. Under Treasurer, 1952-57; Public Service Comr, 1958-59; Under Treasurer (Permanent Head), 1959-75. Mem. Senate, Univ. of Western Australia, 1954-70 (Chm. Finance Cttee, 1956-70; Pro-Chancellor, 1968-70); Comr, Rural and Industries Bank, 1959-65; Member: Jackson Cttee on Tertiary Educn, 1967; Tertiary Educn Commn, 1971-74; Past Mem. numerous other Bds and Cttees. Hon. LLD Univ. of W Australia, 1971; FASA. *Recreation:* gardening. *Address:*

22 Robin Street, Mount Lawley, WA 6050, Australia. *T:* 72 1393. *Club:* University House (Perth).

TOWNSVILLE, Bishop of, (RC), since 1967; **Most Rev. Leonard Anthony Faulkner;** b Booleroo Centre, South Australia, 5 Dec. 1926. *Educ:* Sacred Heart Coll., Glenelg; Corpus Christi Coll., Werribee; Pontifical Urban University, Rome. Ordained Propaganda Fide Coll., Rome, 1 Jan. 1950. Asst Priest, Woodville, SA, 1950-57; Administrator, St Francis Xavier Cathedral, Adelaide, 1957-67; Diocesan Chaplain, Young Christian Workers, 1955-67; Mem., Nat. Fitness Council of SA, 1958-67. *Address:* Bishop's House, Stanley Street, Townsville, Queensland 4810, Australia.

TOWRY, Peter; see Piper, D. T.

TOY, Francis Carter, CBE 1947; DSc, FInstP; b 5 May 1892; 2nd s of late Sir Henry Toy, CA, JP, Helston, Cornwall; m 1921, Gladys Marguerite, d of late James Thomas, CA, JP, Tregays, Lostwithiel, Cornwall; one d. *Educ:* Launceston Coll., Cornwall; University College, London. Fellow of University College, London. Served European War, 1914-18; Lieut, Cornwall Fortress Engineers, 1914-16; Lieut, First Army Field Survey Co. (Sound Ranging, Y section), BEF France, 1917-18. Physicist, British Photographic Research Association, 1919-29; Deputy Director of the Shirley Institute, Research Station of British Cotton Industry Research Association, 1930-43, Director, 1944-55. President: Manchester Fedn of Scientific Societies, 1953-55; Inst of Physics, 1948-50; Manchester Statistical Society, 1951-53; Manchester Literary and Philosophical Society, 1956-58; Past Chairman Cttee of Directors of Research Associations; Fellow of the Textile Institute; Past Member Court and Council, UMIST. *Publications:* numerous scientific. *Recreations:* travel, music and sport (cricket and golf). *Address:* 8 Fulshaw Court, Wilmslow, Cheshire. *T:* Wilmslow 25141. *Club:* Athenæum.

TOYE, Wendy; theatrical producer; film director; choreographer, actress, dancer. First professional appearance as Mustard-seed in A Midsummer Night's Dream, Old Vic, 1929; principal dancer in Hiawatha, Royal Albert Hall, 1931; Marigold, Phœbe in Toad of Toad Hall and produced dances, Royalty, Christmas, 1931-32; danced in C. B. Cochran's The Miracle, Lyceum, 1932; masked dancer in Ballerina, Gaiety, 1933; member of Ninette de Valois' original Vic Wells Ballet, principal dancer for Ninette de Valois in The Golden Toy, Coliseum, 1934; toured with Anton Dolin's ballet (choreog. for divertissements and short ballets), 1934-35; in Tulip Time, Alhambra, then Markova-Dolin Ballet as principal dancer and choreog., 1935; in Love and How to Cure It, Globe, 1937. Arranged dances and ballets for many shows and films including most of George Black's productions for next 7 years, notably Black Velvet in which also principal dancer, 1939. Shakespearean season, Open Air Theatre, 1939. *Theatre productions:* Big Ben, Bless the Bride, Tough at the Top (for C. B. Cochran), Adelphi; The Shepherd Show, Prince's; Co-Director and Choreographer, Peter Pan, New York; And So To Bed, New Theatre; Co-Director and Choreographer, Feu d'Artifice, Paris; Night of Masquerade, Q; Second Threshold, Vaudeville; Choreography for Three's Company in Joyce Grenfell Requests the Pleasure, Fortune; Wild Thyme, Duke of York's; Lady at the Wheel, Lyric, Hammersmith; Majority of One, Phœnix; Magic Lantern, Saville; As You Like It, Old Vic; Virtue in Danger, Mermaid and Strand; Robert and Elizabeth, Lyric; On the Level, Saville; Midsummer Night's Dream, Shakespeare quatercentenary Latin American tour, 1964; Soldier's Tale, Edinburgh Festival, 1967; Boots and Strawberry Jam, Nottingham Playhouse, 1968; The Great Waltz, Drury Lane, 1970; Showboat, Adelphi, 1971; She Stoops to Conquer, Young Vic, 1972; Cowardy Custard, Mermaid, 1972; Stand and Deliver, Roundhouse, 1972; R loves J, Chichester, 1973; The Confederacy, Chichester, 1974; The Englishman Amused, Young Vic, 1974; Follow The Star, Chichester, 1974, Westminster Theatre, 1976; Made in Heaven, Chichester, 1975; Make Me a World, Chichester, 1976; Once More with Music (with Cicely Courtneidge and Jack Hulbert), 1976; Oh, Mr Porter, Mermaid, 1977. *Opera Productions:* Bluebeard's Castle (Bartok), Sadler's Wells and Brussels; The Telephone (Menotti), Sadler's Wells; Russalka (Dvořák), Sadler's Wells; Fledermaus, Coliseum and Sadler's Wells; Orpheus in the Underworld, Sadler's Wells and Australia; La Vie Parisienne, Sadler's Wells; Seraglio, Bath Festival, 1967; The Impresario, Don Pasquale (for Phoenix Opera Group), 1968; The Italian Girl in Algiers, Coliseum, 1968. *Films directed:* The Stranger Left No Card; The Teckman Mystery; Raising a Riot; The Twelfth Day of Christmas; Three Cases of Murder; All for Mary; True as a Turtle; We Joined the Navy; The King's Breakfast; Cliff in Scotland; A Goodly Manor for a Song; Girls Wanted-Istanbul. Productions for TV, etc. Appeared with and was choreographer for Camargo Society; guest artist with Sadler's Wells Ballet and

Mme Rambert's Ballet Club; went to Denmark as principal dancer with British Ballet, organised by Adeline Geneé, 1932. Trained with Euphen MacLaren, Karsavina, Dolin, Morosoff, Legat, Rambert. *Address:* c/o London Management, 235 Regent Street, W1.

TOYN, Richard John; His Honour Judge Toyn; a Circuit Judge since 1972; *b* 24 Jan. 1927; *s* of Richard Thomas Millington Toyn and Ethel Toyn; *m* 1955, Joyce Evelyn Goodwin; two *s* two *d. Educ:* Solihull Sch.; Bristol Grammar Sch.; Bristol Univ. (LLB). Royal Army Service Corps, 1948-50. Called to the Bar, Gray's Inn, 1950. *Recreations:* music, drama, photography. *Address:* c/o Victoria Law Courts, Birmingham.

TOYNBEE, Prof. Jocelyn Mary Catherine, MA, DPhil; FSA; FBA; Laurence Professor Emerita of Classical Archæology, Cambridge University (Professor, 1951-62); Hon. Fellow of Newnham College; *b* 3 March 1897; *d* of late Harry Valpy Toynbee and late Sarah Edith (*née* Marshall). *Educ:* Winchester High School for Girls; Newnham Coll., Cambridge. Classical Tutor, St Hugh's Coll., Oxford, 1921-24; Lecturer in Classics, Reading University, 1924-27; Fellow and Director of Studies in Classics, Newnham Coll., Cambridge, and Lecturer in the Faculty of Classics, Cambridge Univ., 1927-51. Hon. Dlitt: University of Newcastle upon Tyne; University of Liverpool. *Publications:* The Hadrianic School: a Chapter in the History of Greek Art, 1934; Roman Medallions (American Numismatic Society, New York), 1944; Some Notes on Artists in the Roman World, (Brussels) 1951; The Shrine of St Peter and the Vatican Excavation (with John Ward Perkins), 1956; The Flavian Reliefs from the Palazzo della Cancelleria in Rome, 1957; Art in Roman Britain, 1962; Art in Britain under the Romans, 1964; The Art of the Romans, 1965; Death and Burial in the Roman World, 1971; Animals in Roman Life and Art, 1973; contribs to Journal of Roman Studies, Papers of British School, Rome, Numismatic Chronicle, Classical Review, Classical Quarterly, Antiquaries Journal, Archæologia, Antiquity, Gnomon, etc. *Recreation:* travelling. *Address:* 22 Park Town, Oxford. *T:* 57886.

TOYNBEE, (Theodore) Philip; Novelist; foreign correspondent of The Observer and member of editorial staff since 1950; *b* 25 June 1916; *s* of late Arnold Joseph Toynbee, CH, FBA, and Rosalind, *d* of late Prof. Gilbert Murray, OM; *m* 1st, 1939, Anne Barbara Denise Powell (marr. diss. 1950); two *d*; 2nd, 1950, Frances Genevieve Smith; one *s* two *d. Educ:* Rugby Sch.; Christ Church, Oxford. Editor of the Birmingham Town Crier, 1938-39; commission in Intelligence Corps, 1940-42; Ministry of Economic Warfare, 1942-44; on staff of SHAEF in France and Belgium, 1944-45; Literary Editor of Contact Publications, 1945-46. *Publications:* The Savage Days, 1937; School in Private, 1941; The Barricades, 1943; Tea with Mrs Goodman, 1947; The Garden to the Sea, 1953; Friends Apart, 1954; Pantaloon, 1961; (with Arnold Toynbee) Comparing Notes: a Dialogue across a Generation, 1963; (with Maurice Richardson) Thanatos: a Modern Symposium, 1963; Two Brothers, 1964; A Learned City, 1966; Views from a Lake, 1968; Towards the Holy Spirit, 1973; (ed) The Distant Drum, 1976; contrib.: New Statesman and Nation, Horizon, New Writing, Les Temps Modernes. *Recreations:* gardening, motor-bicycling. *Address:* Woodroyd Cottage, St Briavels, Lydney, Glos. *Club:* Oxford Union Society.

TRACY; *see* Hanbury-Tracy, family name of **Baron Sudeley.**

TRACY, Rear-Adm. Hugh Gordon Henry, CB 1965; DSC 1945; CEng; *b* 15 Nov. 1912; *e s* of Comdr A. F. G. Tracy, RN; *m* 1938, Muriel, *d* of Maj.-Gen. Sir R. B. Ainsworth, CB, DSO, OBE; two *s* one *d. Educ:* Nautical Coll., Pangbourne. Joined RN, 1929; Lieut, 1934; served in HMS Shropshire, Hawkins and Furious, in Admiralty and attended Advanced Engineering course before promotion to Lt-Comdr, 1942; Sen. Engineer, HMS Illustrious, 1942-44; Asst to Manager, Engineering Dept, HM Dockyard Chatham, 1944-46; Comdr 1946; served in HMS Manxman, Admiralty, RN Engineering Coll. and HM Dockyard Malta; Captain, 1955; Asst Director of Marine Engineering, Admiralty, 1956-58; CO HMS Sultan, 1959-60; Imperial Defence Coll., 1961; CSO (Tech.) to Flag Officer, Sea Training, 1962-63; Rear-Admiral, 1963; Director of Marine Engineering, Ministry of Defence (Navy), 1963-66; retired, 1966. FIMechE. *Recreations:* gardening, painting, plant ecology. *Address:* Orchard House, Claverton, Bath BA2 7BG. *T:* Bath 65650. *Club:* Army and Navy.

TRAFFORD; *see* de Trafford.

TRAFFORD, Dr (Joseph) Anthony (Porteous); Consultant Physician, Brighton and Lewes Group of Hospitals, since 1965; *b* 20 July 1932; *s* of Dr Harold Trafford, Warlingham, Surrey,

and late Laura Trafford; *m* 1960, Helen Chalk; one *s* one *d. Educ:* St Edmund's, Hindhead; Charterhouse; Guy's Hosp., Univ. of London. MB, BS Hons 1957; MRCP 1961. Various medical appts, 1957-63; Sen. Registrar, Guy's Hosp., 1963-66; Fulbright Scholar, Johns Hopkins Univ., 1963; Dir, Artificial Kidney Unit, Brighton, 1967. MP (C) The Wrekin, 1970-Feb. 1974. *Publications:* contribs to BMJ and Lancet. *Recreations:* golf, tennis, squash. *Address:* 103 The Drive, Hove, East Sussex. *T:* Brighton 731567.

TRAHAIR, John Rosewarne; Member South Western Regional Health Authority since 1974; *b* 29 March 1921; *s* of late Percy Edward Trahair and Edith Irene Trahair; *m* 1948, Patricia Elizabeth (*née* Godrich); one *s* one *d. Educ:* Leys Sch.; Christ's Coll., Cambridge (MA). FCIS. Served with Royal Artillery, 1941-46 (Captain). Finance Dir, Farleys Infant Food Ltd, 1948-73; Dir 1950-74, Dep. Chm. 1956-74, Western Credit Holdings Ltd; Chm., Moorhaven HMC, 1959-66; Chm., Plymouth and District HMC, 1966-74; Mem. SW Regional Hosp. Bd, 1965-74 (Vice-Chm. 1971-73, Chm. 1973-74). Mem., Devon CC, 1977-. *Recreations:* sailing, walking. *Address:* West Park, Ivybridge, South Devon. *T:* Ivybridge 2466. *Club:* Royal Western Yacht.

TRAHERNE, Sir Cennydd (George), KG 1970; Kt 1964; TD 1950; MA; HM Lord-Lieutenant of Mid, South and West Glamorgan, since 1974 (HM Lieutenant for Glamorgan, 1952-74); *b* 14 Dec. 1910; *er s* of late Comdr L. E. Traherne, RN, of Coedarhydyglyn, near Cardiff, and Dorothy, *d* of G. F. S. Sinclair; *m* 1934, Olivera Rowena, OBE, JP, DStJ, *d* of late James Binney, and late Lady Marjory Binney, Pampisford Hall, Cambridgeshire. *Educ:* Wellington; Brasenose Coll., Oxford. Barrister, Inner Temple, 1938. 81st Field Regt RA (TA), 1934-43; 102 Provost Coy, Corps of Military Police, 1943-45 (despatches); Dep. Asst Provost Marshal, Second British Army, 1945; 53rd Div. Provost Company, Royal Military Police, 1947-49, TA; Hon. Colonel, 53 Div. Signal Regt, 1953-58; Hon. Colonel 282 (Glamorgan Yeomanry) Field Regt RA (TA), 1958-61; Hon. Colonel: 282 (Glam and Mon) Regt RA (TA), 1962-67; 37 (Wessex and Welsh) Signal Regt, T&AVR, 1971-75. DL 1946, JP 1946, Glamorgan. Deputy Chairman Glamorgan Quarter Sessions, 1949-52; President, Welsh College of Advanced Technology, 1957-65. Chairman, Rep. Body of the Church in Wales, 1965-77; Pres., Welsh Nat. Sch. of Medicine, 1970. Director: Cardiff Building Society, 1953; Wales Gas Board, 1958-71; Commercial Bank of Wales, 1972-; Chm., Wales Gas Consultative Council, 1958-71; Advisory Local Dir, Barclays Bank Ltd. Member, Gorsedd of the Bards of Wales. Hon. Freeman, Borough of Cowbridge, 1971. Hon. LLD University of Wales. KStJ. *Address:* Coedarhydyglyn, near Cardiff, S Wales. *T:* Peterston-super-Ely 321. *Clubs:* Athenæum; Cardiff and County (Cardiff).

TRAINOR, James P.; Hon. Mr Justice Trainor; Justice of Supreme Court, Hong Kong, since 1972; *b* Belfast, 14 Oct. 1914; *s* of Owen Trainor and Mary Rose (*née* McArdle); *m* 1954, Angela (*née* O'Connor); one *s* two *d. Educ:* Mount St Joseph's, Monaghan, Ireland; University Coll., Dublin (BA). Admitted solicitor, Dublin, 1936; called to Irish Bar, King's Inn, 1950. Colonial Service: Magistrate, Singapore, 1954-55; Justice, Special Court, Cyprus, 1955-60; Called to English Bar, Gray's Inn, 1957; Comr, High Commissioner's Court, W Pacific High Commn, 1960-61; Co-Pres., Jt Court, Anglo-French Condominium of the New Hebrides, 1960-72; Judge, Fiji Court of Appeal, 1960-70; Judge, High Court of the Western Pacific, 1961-72. Commandeur de l'Ordre Nationale du Mérite (France), 1967. *Recreations:* golf, reading, music. *Address:* 23 Peak Mansions, The Peak, Hong Kong. *T:* Hong Kong 96979; 25 Nutgrove Park, Dublin. *Clubs:* Stephen's Green, United Services (Dublin).

TRANMIRE, Baron *cr* 1974 (Life Peer), of Upsall, North Yorkshire; **Robert Hugh Turton,** PC 1955; KBE 1971; MC 1942; JP; DL; *b* 8 Aug. 1903; *s* of late Major R. B. Turton, Kildale Hall, Kildale, York; *m* 1928, Ruby Christian, *d* of late Robert T. Scott, Beechmont, Sevenoaks; three *s* one *d. Educ:* Eton; Balliol Coll., Oxford. Called to Bar, Inner Temple, 1926; joined 4th Bn of Green Howards at outbreak of war, 1939; served as DAAG 50th (N) Division, AAG GHQ MEF. MP (C) Thirsk and Malton, 1929-Feb. 1974. Parly Sec., Min. of Nat. Insurance, 1951-53. Min. of Pensions and Nat. Insce, 1953-54; Joint Parly Under-Sec. of State for Foreign Affairs, Oct. 1954-Dec. 1955; Minister of Health, Dec. 1955-Jan. 1957; Chm., Select Cttee on Procedure, 1970-74. Chm., Commonwealth Industries Assoc., 1963-74. JP 1936, DL 1962, N Riding, Co. York. Hon. Colonel, 4/5th Bn The Green Howards (TA), 1963-67. *Address:* Upsall Castle, Thirsk, N Yorks YO7 2QJ. *T:* Upsall 202; 15 Grey Coat Gardens, SW1. *T:* 01-834 1535.

TRANT, Maj.-Gen. Richard Brooking; Commander, Land Forces Northern Ireland, since 1977; *b* 30 March 1928; *s* of Richard Brooking Trant and Dora Rodney Trant (*née* Lancaster); *m* 1957, Diana Clare, 2nd *d* of Rev. Stephen Zachary and Ruth Beatrice Edwards, Llystanwg, Harlech, N Wales; one *s* two *d*. Commissioned RA 1947; Defence Services Staff Coll., India, 1962-63; Jt Services Staff Coll., 1965; commanded 3rd Regt RHA, 1968-71, 5th Airportable Brigade, 1972-74; Dep. Mil. Sec., MoD (Army), 1975-76. Order of South Arabia, 3rd Class, 1965. *Recreations:* golf, field sports, natural history. *Address:* HQ Northern Ireland, BFPO 825. *Club:* Army and Navy.

TRANTER, Professor Clement John, CBE 1967 (OBE 1953); Bashforth Professor of Mathematical Physics, Royal Military College of Science, Shrivenham, 1953-74, now Emeritus; *b* 16 Aug. 1909; *s* of late Archibald Tranter, and Mrs Tranter, Cirencester, Glos.; *m* 1937, Joan Louise Hatton, *d* of late J. Hatton, MBE, and Mrs Hatton, Plumstead, SE18. *Educ:* Cirencester Grammar Sch.; Queen's Coll., Oxford (Open Math. Scholar; 1st Class Hons Mathematical Mods, 1929; 1st Class Hons Final Sch. of Maths, 1931; MA (Oxon) 1940; DSc (Oxon) 1953). Commissioned RA, TA, 1932; Captain, 1938. Junior Assistant Research Dept, Woolwich, 1931-34; Senior Lecturer, Gunnery and Mathematics Branch, Military College of Science, Woolwich, 1935-40; Asst Professor 1940-46; Assoc. Professor of Mathematics, Royal Military College of Science, Shrivenham, 1946-53. *Publications:* Integral Transforms in Mathematical Physics, 1951; Advanced Level Pure Mathematics, 1953; Techniques of Mathematical Analysis, 1957; (with C. G. Lambe) Differential Equations for Engineers and Scientists, 1961; Mathematics for Sixth Form Scientists, 1964; (with C. G. Lambe) Advanced Level Mathematics, 1966; Bessel Functions with some Physical Applications, 1968; mathematical papers in various journals. *Recreations:* painting, golf, fly-fishing. *Address:* Flagstones, Stanton Fitzwarren, near Swindon, Wilts SN6 7RZ. *T:* Highworth 762913.

TRANTER, Nigel; novelist and author since 1936; *b* Glasgow, 23 Nov. 1909; *yr s* of Gilbert T. Tranter and Eleanor A. Cass; *m* 1933, May Jean Campbell Grieve; one *d* (one *s* decd). *Educ:* St James Episcopal Sch., Edinburgh; George Heriot's Sch., Edinburgh. Served War of 1939-45, RASC and RA. Accountancy trng, then in small family insce co., until could live on writing, after war service; much and actively interested in Scottish public affairs; Chm., Scottish Convention, Edinburgh Br., 1948-51; Vice-Convener, Scottish Covenant Assoc., 1951-55; Pres., E Lothian Liberal Assoc., 1960-76; Chm., Nat. Forth Road Bridge Cttee, 1953-57; Pres., Scottish PEN, 1962-66, Hon. Pres., 1973-; Chm., Soc. of Authors, Scotland, 1966-72; Pres., E Lothian Wildfowlers' Assoc., 1952-73; Chm., St Andrew Soc. of E Lothian, 1966-; Chm., Nat. Book League, Scotland, 1972-; Mem., Cttee of Aberlady Bay Nature Reserve, 1953-76, etc. Hon. Mem., Mark Twain Soc. of Amer., 1976. Hon. MA Edinburgh, 1971. Chevalier, Order of St Lazarus of Jerusalem, 1961. *Publications: fiction:* 56 novels, from Trespass, 1937, including: Bridal Path, 1952; Macgregor's Gathering, 1957; the Master of Gray trilogy: The Master of Gray, 1961; The Courtesan, 1963; Past Master, 1965; Chain of Destiny, 1964; the Robert the Bruce trilogy: The Steps to the Empty Throne, 1969; The Path of the Hero King, 1970; The Price of the King's Peace, 1971; The Young Montrose, 1972; Montrose: the Captain General, 1973; The Wisest Fool, 1974; The Wallace, 1975; Lords of Misrule, 1976; A Folly of Princes, 1977; The Captive Crown, 1977; 12 children's novels; *non-fiction:* The Fortalices and Early Mansions of Southern Scotland, 1935; The Fortified House in Scotland (5 vols), 1962-71; Pegasus Book of Scotland, 1964; Outlaw of the Highlands: Rob Roy, 1965; Land of the Scots, 1968; Portrait of the Border Country, 1972; The Queen's Scotland Series: The Heartland: Clackmannan, Perth and Stirlingshire, 1971; The Eastern Counties: Aberdeen, Angus and Kincardineshire, 1972; The North East: Banff, Moray, Nairn, East Inverness and Easter Ross, 1974; Argyll and Bute, 1977; contribs to many jls, on Scots history, genealogy, topography, castellated architecture, knighthood, etc. *Recreations:* walking, wildfowling, historical research. *Address:* Quarry House, Aberlady, East Lothian. *T:* Aberlady 258. *Club:* PEN.

TRAPNELL, Alan Stewart; His Honour Judge Trapnell; a Circuit Judge, since 1969 (formerly Chairman of Middlesex Quarter Sessions); *b* 12 Jan. 1913; *s* of Francis C. Trapnell, MD, Beckenham, Kent. *Educ:* The Leys Sch., Cambridge; Jesus Coll., Cambridge. Served War of 1939-45, Queen Victoria's Rifles. Barrister-at-Law. Called to Bar, Inner Temple, 1936. Western Circuit, Hampshire Sessions. Member of Bar Council, 1958-62. Recorder of Barnstaple, 1962-64. Judge of: Bow County Court, 1964-66; Shoreditch County Court, 1966-67; Bromley County Court, 1968-69. *Address:* Francis Taylor Building, Temple,

EC4. *T:* 01-353 2182. *Clubs:* Athenæum, United Oxford & Cambridge University.

TRAPNELL, Barry Maurice Waller, MA, PhD Cantab; DL; Headmaster of Oundle School, since 1968; *b* 18 May 1924; *s* of Waller Bertram and late Rachel Trapnell; *m* 1951, Dorothy Joan, *d* of late P. J. Kerr, ICS; two *d*. *Educ:* University College Sch., Hampstead; St John's Coll., Cambridge (Scholar). Research in physical chemistry in Department of Colloid Science, Cambridge, 1945-46, and Royal Institution, London, 1946-50; Commonwealth Fund Fellow, Northwestern Univ., Ill., 1950-51; Lecturer in chemistry: Worcester Coll., Oxford, 1951-54; Liverpool Univ., 1954-57; Headmaster, Denstone Coll., 1957-68. Visiting Lecturer, American Association for Advancement of Science, 1961. Member: Adv. Cttee on Supply and Training of Teachers; C of E Commn on Religious Education. FRSA. DL: Staffs, 1967; Northants, 1974. *Publications:* Chemisorption, 1955 (Russian edition, 1958; 2nd English edition, 1964); Learning and Discerning, 1966; papers in British and American scientific journals. *Recreations:* several games (represented Cambridge *v* Oxford at cricket and squash rackets, and Gentlemen *v* Players at cricket; won Amateur Championships at Rugby Fives); English furniture and Silver. *Address:* Cobthorne, Oundle, Northants. *T:* Oundle 3536. *Club:* East India, Devonshire, Sports and Public Schools.

TRAPNELL, John Arthur; Under-Secretary, Departments of Trade and Industry, 1973-77; *b* 7 Sept. 1913; *s* of Arthur Westicote Trapnell and Helen Trapnell (*née* Alles); *m* 1939, Winifred Chadwick Rushton; two *d*. *Educ:* privately; Law Soc.'s Sch. of Law. Admitted Solicitor 1938; private practice until 1940; served HM Army, 1940-46: commnd Som. LI, 1943; served with 82nd W African Div. (Major). Civil Service from 1946: Board of Trade, Solicitors Dept. Mem. Law Soc. *Recreations:* golf, bridge. *Address:* 29 Connaught Road, New Malden, Surrey. *T:* 01-942 3183.

TRAPP, Rt. Rev. Eric Joseph; Hon. Assistant Bishop, Diocese of St Albans; *b* 17 July 1910; *s* of late Archibald Edward Trapp and Agnes Trapp, Leicester and Coventry; *m* 1937, Edna Noreen Thornton, SRN; two *d*. *Educ:* Alderman Newton's Sch., Leicester; Leeds Univ.; College of the Resurrection, Mirfield. BA 1st Class, philosophy. Asst Curate, St Olave's, Mitcham, Surrey, 1934-37; Director, Masite Mission, Basutoland, 1937-40; Rector, St Augustine's Bethlehem, Orange Free State, 1940-43; Rector, St John's, Maseru and Director of Maseru Mission, Basutoland, 1943-47; Canon of Bloemfontein Cathedral, 1944-47; Bishop of Zululand, 1947-57; Sec., Soc. for the Propagation of the Gospel, 1957-64, United Soc. for the Propagation of the Gospel, 1965-70; Bishop of Bermuda, 1970-75. Hon. DD Trinity College, Toronto, 1967. *Address:* 18 Sorrel Garth, Hitchin, Herts. *T:* Hitchin 4097.

TRAPP, Prof. Joseph Burney; Director, Warburg Institute (University of London) and Professor of the History of the Classical Tradition, since 1976; *b* 16 July 1925; *s* of H.M.B. and Frances M. Trapp; *m* 1953, Elayne M. Falla; two *s*. *Educ:* Dannevirke High Sch. and Victoria University Coll., Wellington, NZ (MA). Alexander Turnbull Library, Wellington, 1946-50; Jun. Lectr, Victoria University Coll., 1950-51; Asst Lectr, Reading Univ., 1951-53; Asst Librarian, Warburg Inst., 1953-66, Librarian, 1966-76. Visiting Prof., Univ. of Toronto, 1969. Mem. Adv. Council, V&A Museum, 1977-. *Publications:* articles in learned jls. *Address:* Warburg Institute, Woburn Square, WC1H 0AB. *T:* 01-580 9663.

TRASENSTER, Michael Augustus Tulk, CVO 1954; photographer; *b* 26 Jan. 1923; *er s* of late Major William Augustus Trasenster, MC, and Brenda de Courcy Trasenster; *m* 1950, Fay Norrie Darley, *d* of Thomas Bladworth Darley, Cantley Hall, Yorkshire; two *d*. *Educ:* Winchester. Served with 4th/7th Royal Dragoon Guards, 1942-; NW Europe, 1944; Middle East, 1946; ADC to Governor of South Australia, 1947-49; School of Tank Technology, 1951; retired, 1952. Military Secretary and Comptroller to the Governor General of New Zealand, 1952-55. Chevalier of Order of Leopold II of Belgium, 1944; Belgian Croix de Guerre, 1944. *Recreations:* painting, tennis. *Address:* c/o Williams & Glyn's Bank Ltd, High Street, Winchester, Hants.

TRATMAN, Edgar Kingsley, OBE 1949; retired; *b* 23 Feb. 1899; *s* of J. F. W. and E. S. Tratman. *Educ:* Clifton Coll.; University of Bristol. Prof. of Dental Surgery: King Edward VII College of Medicine, Singapore, 1929-49; University of Malaya, 1949-50; University of London (University College Hospital Med. Sch.), 1950-51. FDS, RCS 1949; MD University of Malaya, 1950; FDS, RCSE, 1951. FSA 1938. Hon. DSc Bristol, 1976. *Publications:* many contributions to dental and archæological journals. *Recreations:* cave exploring and prehistoric archæology. *Address:* Penrose Cottage, Burrington, Bristol BS18 7AA. *T:* Blagdon 62274.

TRAVANCORE, Rajpramukh of; Maj.-Gen. H. H. Sri Padmanabha Dasa Bala Rama Varma; GCSI 1946; GCIE 1935; *b* 1912. Founder of Travancore University and sometime Chancellor. Formerly: Colonel-in-Chief of Travancore State Forces; Hon. Major-General in British Army. Has introduced many reforms. Holds Hon. Doctorates. *Address:* Kaudiar Palace, Trivandrum 3, Kerala State, S India.

TRAVERS, Basil Holmes, OBE 1943; BA (Sydney); MA (Oxon); BLitt (Oxon); FACE; FRSA; FAIM; Headmaster of Sydney Church of England Grammar School, North Sydney, NSW, since 1959; *b* 7 July 1919; *m* 1942, Margaret Emily Marr; three *d. Educ:* Sydney Church of England Grammar Sch.; Sydney Univ.; New Coll., Oxford Univ. Rhodes Scholar for NSW, 1940. Served War of 1939-45 (despatches, OBE); AIF, 2/2 Australian Infantry Battalion; ADC to Maj.-Gen. Sir I. G. Mackay, 1940; Brigade Major, 15 Aust. Inf. Bde, 1943-44; psc 1944; GSO 2, HQ, 2 Aust. Corps, 1944-45. Assistant Master, Wellington Coll., Berks, England, 1948-49; Assistant Master, Cranbrook Sch., Sydney, 1950-52; Headmaster, Launceston Church Grammar Sch., Launceston, Tasmania, 1953-58. Chm., Headmasters' Conf. of Australia, 1971-73. Lt-Col commanding 12 Inf. Bn (CMF), 1955-58. Member: Soldiers' Children Education Board, 1959-; NSW Cttee, Duke of Edinburgh's Award Scheme in Australia. *Publications:* Let's Talk Rugger, 1949; The Captain General, 1952. *Recreations:* cricket (Oxford Blue, 1946, 1948), swimming, rugby (Oxford Blue, 1946, 1947), athletics (Half Blue, 1947); also Sydney Blue, football, cricket; Rugby Union International for England, 1947, 1948, 1949; represented NSW, 1950. *Address:* Sydney Church of England Grammar School, North Sydney, NSW 2060, Australia. *T:* 929 2263. *Clubs:* University, Rugby Union (Sydney).

TRAVERS, Ben, CBE 1976; AFC 1920; dramatist and novelist; *b* 1886; *e s* of W. F. Travers; *m* 1916, Violet (*d* 1951), *o c* of D. B. W. Mouncey; two *s* one *d. Educ:* Abbey Sch., Beckenham; Charterhouse. Served in RNAS, 1914-18, Squadron Commander; transferred RAF as Major, 1918; received Air Force Cross, 1920; rejoined RAF for War Service, Nov. 1939; Sqdn Leader, 1940; Prime Warden of Fishmongers' Company, 1946. Evening Standard special award for services to the theatre, 1976. *Publications: Plays, Novels and Films:* The Dippers, 1922; A Cuckoo in the Nest, 1925 (revived, 1964); Rookery Nook, 1926 (as musical, Popkiss, 1972); Mischief, 1926; Thark, 1927 (revived 1965); Plunder, 1928 (revived 1973 and 1976); The Collection To-day, 1928; A Cup of Kindness, 1929; A Night Like This, 1930; Turkey Time, 1931; The Chance of a Nighttime, 1931; Dirty Work, 1932; Just My Luck, 1932; A Bit of a Test, 1933; Hyde Side Up, 1933; Up to the Neck, Lady in Danger, 1934; Fighting Stock, 1935; Stormy Weather, 1935; Foreign Affairs, 1935; Pot Luck, 1936; Dishonour Bright, 1936; O Mistress Mine, 1936; For Valour, 1937; Second Best Bed, 1937; Old Iron, 1938; Banana Ridge, 1938 (revived 1976); Spotted Dick, 1939; She Follows Me About, 1943; Outrageous Fortune, 1947; Wild Horses, 1952; Nun's Veiling, 1956; Vale of Laughter (autobiography), 1957; Corker's End, 1969; The Bed Before Yesterday, 1975. Television Play, Potter, 1948. *Recreation:* watching cricket. *Address:* c/o Fishmongers' Company, Fishmongers' Hall, London Bridge, EC4R 9EL. *Clubs:* Garrick, Beefsteak, MCC.
See also P. T. H. Morgan.

TRAVERS, Rt. Rev. Mgr. Brendan; Rector of the Pontifical Beda College, Rome, since 1972; *b* 21 March 1931; *s* of Dr Charles Travers and Eileen Travers (*née* Gordon). *Educ:* Belmont Abbey Sch.; Venerable English College, Rome; Gregorian Univ., Rome. (STL, JCL, PhL). Ordained priest, 1955; Curate, Salford diocese, 1957-72; Bishop's Secretary, 1961-64; Chm., Manchester Catholic Marriage Adv. Council, 1966-71. *Recreation:* golf. *Address:* Pontifical Beda College, Viale di S Paolo 18, 00146 Rome, Italy. *T:* Rome 551700. *Club:* Worsley Golf (Manchester).

TRAVERS, Sir Thomas (à Beckett), Kt 1972; Consulting Ophthalmologist, Royal Melbourne Hospital, since 1962; *b* 16 Aug. 1902; *s* of late Walter Travers, Warragul, Vic and late Isabelle Travers; *m* Tone, widow of late R. S. Burnard; no *c. Educ:* Melbourne Grammar School. MB, BS 1925, DSc 1941, Melbourne; MRCP 1928; DOMS London 1928; FRACS. *Publications:* various on strabismus. *Recreation:* gardening. *Address:* 251 Grattan Street, Carlton, Victoria 3053, Australia. *T:* 347-4533. *Club:* Melbourne (Melbourne).

TREACHER, Adm. Sir John (Devereux), KCB 1975; Commander-in-Chief, Fleet, and Allied Commander-in-Chief, Channel and Eastern Atlantic, 1975-77; *b* Chile, 23 Sept. 1924; *s* of late Frank Charles Treacher, Bentley, Suffolk; *m* 1st, 1953, Patcie Jane (marr. diss. 1968), *d* of Dr F. L. McGrath, Evanston, Ill; one *s* one *d*; 2nd, 1969, Kirsteen Forbes, *d* of late D. F. Landale; one *s* one *d. Educ:* St Paul's School. Served in HM Ships Nelson, Glasgow, Keppel and Mermaid in Mediterranean, Russian convoys; qual. Fleet Air Arm pilot, 1947; CO: 778 Sqdn 1951, 849 Sqdn 1952-53; CO, HMS Lowestoft, 1964-66; CO, HMS Eagle, 1968-70; Flag Officer Carriers and Amphibious Ships and Comdr Carrier Striking Gp 2, 1970-72; Flag Officer, Naval Air Comd, 1972-73; Vice-Chief of Naval Staff, 1973-75. FRAeS 1973. *Recreations:* shooting, photography. *Club:* Naval and Military.

TREACY, Rt. Rev. Eric, MBE 1945; *b* 2 June 1907; *s* of George Treacy, Rangoon; *m* 1932, Mary Leyland, *d* of J. A. Shone, JP, Hoylake; no *c. Educ:* Haberdashers' School; King's Coll., London; St Aidan's, Birkenhead. Deacon, 1932, Priest, 1933; Curate of Liverpool Parish Church, 1932-34; Shrewsbury School Missioner, 1930-36; Vicar of Edge Hill, Liverpool, 1936-40; Chaplain to the Forces (EC), 1940-45; Senior Chaplain (NW Europe), 1944 (despatches, MBE); Rector of Keighley, 1945-49; Hon. Canon: of Bradford Cathedral, 1946; of Wakefield Cathedral, 1949; Rural Dean of South Craven, 1946; Proctor in Convocation, 1949; Examining Chaplain to Bishop of Wakefield, 1949; Canon of Wakefield Cathedral, 1956; Archdeacon of Halifax, 1949-61; Vicar and Rural Dean of Halifax, 1950-61; Bishop Suffragan of Pontefract, 1961-68; Archdeacon of Pontefract, 1961-68; Bishop of Wakefield, 1968-76. Hon. Chaplain, Duke of Wellington's Regt, 1961. Church Commissioner, 1963. Introduced House of Lords, 1972. Hon. Freeman, Co. Borough of Halifax, 1973. Hon. LLD (Leeds) 1968. *Publications:* Main Lines over the Border, 1960; The Lure of Steam, 1966; Portrait of Steam, 1967; Glory of Steam, 1969; Spell of Steam, 1973; Roaming the Northern Rail, 1975. *Recreations:* fell walking, photography, railways preservation. *Address:* The Ghyll, Applethwaite, Keswick, Cumbria. *Club:* Army and Navy.

TREADWELL, Charles James, CMG 1972; HM Diplomatic Service; Ambassador to Oman, since 1975; *b* 10 Feb. 1920; *s* of late C. A. L. Treadwell, OBE, Barrister and Solicitor, Wellington, NZ; *m* 1946, Philippa, *d* of late W. J. Perkins, CBE, MC; three *s. Educ:* Wellington Coll., NZ; University of New Zealand (LLB). Served with HM Forces, 1939-45. Sudan Political Service and Sudan Judiciary, 1945-55; FO, 1955-57; British High Commn, Lahore, 1957-60; HM Embassy, Ankara, 1960-62; HM Embassy, Jedda, 1963-64; British Dep. High Comr for Eastern Nigeria, 1965-66; Head of Joint Information Services Department, Foreign Office/Commonwealth Office, 1966-68; British Political Agent, Abu Dhabi, 1968-71; Ambassador, United Arab Emirates, 1971-73; High Comr to Bahamas, 1973-75. *Recreation:* fishing. *Address:* c/o Foreign and Commonwealth Office, SW1; Lindfield Gardens, London Road, Guildford, Surrey. *T:* Guildford 69380.

TREASE, Geoffrey; see Trease, R. G.

TREASE, Prof. George Edward, BPharm, Dr *hc* Strasbourg; Dr *hc* Clermont; FPS, FRIC; Professor of Pharmacognosy, Nottingham University, 1957-67, now Emeritus Professor; Head of Department of Pharmacy, University of Nottingham, 1944-67; *b* 8 July 1902; *e s* of George and Florence Trease; *m* 1928, Phyllis Thornton Wilkinson; two *d* (one *s* decd). *Educ:* Nottingham High Sch.; London College of Pharmacy. Lecturer in Pharmacognosy, University College, Nottingham, 1926. Served in Min. of Economic Warfare, 1939-40. Reader in Pharmacognosy, 1945; Examiner in Pharmacognosy to: Pharmaceutical Society, 1934-; University of London, 1937-; QUB, 1949, 1963-65; University of Glasgow, 1950-; University of Wales, 1945-; University of Nottingham, 1950-; University of Singapore, 1962; University of Bradford, 1966-; Pharmaceutical Society of Eire, 1959-. Vice-Pres., British Soc. for History of Pharmacy, 1967-70. Worshipful Society of Apothecaries of London, 1959. Dr *hc* Strasbourg University, 1954; Dr *hc* Clermont University, 1962. *Publications:* Chemistry of Crude Drugs, 1928 (with Prof. J. E. Driver); Textbook of Pharmacognosy, 1934, 11th edn 1977; Pharmacy in History, 1964; many papers and articles on pharmacognosy, pharmaceutical history and pharmaceutical education. *Recreation:* local history. *Address:* George Hill, Crediton, Devon. *T:* Crediton 2983.
See also R. G. Trease.

TREASE, (Robert) Geoffrey; Council, Society of Authors; *b* 11 Aug. 1909; *s* of George Albert Trease and Florence (*née* Dale);

m 1933, Marian Haselden Granger Boyer; one *d*. *Educ:* Nottingham High Sch.; Queen's Coll., Oxford. Chm., Cttee of Management, Society of Authors, 1972-73. *Publications:* Walking in England, 1935; Such Divinity, 1939; Only Natural, 1940; Tales Out of School, 1949; Snared Nightingale, 1957; So Wild the Heart, 1959; The Italian Story, 1963; The Grand Tour, 1967; (ed) Matthew Todd's Journal, 1968; Nottingham, a biography, 1970; The Condottieri, 1970; A Whiff of Burnt Boats, an early autobiography, 1971; Samuel Pepys and his World, 1972; Laughter at the Door, a continued autobiography, 1974; London, a concise history, 1975; *for young readers:* Bows Against the Barons, 1934; Cue for Treason, 1940; The Hills of Varna, 1948; No Boats on Bannermere, 1949; The Seven Queens of England, 1953; This Is Your Century, 1965; The Red Towers of Granada, 1966; Byron, A Poet Dangerous to Know, 1969; A Masque for the Queen, 1970; Horsemen on the Hills, 1971; D. H. Lawrence: the Phoenix and the Flame, 1973; Popinjay Stairs, 1973; Days to Remember, 1973; The Iron Tsar, 1975; The Chocolate Boy, 1975; When the Drums Beat, 1976; Violet for Bonaparte, 1976; The Field of the Forty Footsteps, 1977, and many others. *Recreations:* walking, the theatre. *Address:* The Croft, Colwall, Malvern, Worcs WR13 6EZ. *T:* Colwall 40366. *See also Prof. G. E. Trease.*

TREASURE, Col Kenneth David, CB 1972; CBE 1965; TD; DL; Solicitor; HM Coroner, County of Monmouth, since 1957; *b* 20 Sept. 1913; *s* of late David John Treasure, Maesycwmmer, and of Olive Treasure; *m* 1941, Jean Mitchell, Heathfield, Sussex; one *s* one *d*. *Educ:* Cranbrook; Univ. of Wales. Admitted Solicitor, 1937. Served War of 1939-45: Lt-Col, Monmouthshire Regt; (TA) in India and Burma. Legal Adviser, CCG, 1946-49; Col, Army Cadet Force, 1958; Chm., Monmouthshire T&AFA, 1960-68; a Rep. Chm. (Wales), Council of T&AF Assocs; Chm., Wales and Monmouthshire TA&VR Assoc., 1968-71; Mem. Council, TA&VR Assocs and TA Advisory Cttee, MoD. DL Monmouthshire, 1957. *Recreations:* golf, Rotary, field sports. *Address:* The Court, Lower Machen, Newport, Gwent. *T:* Machen 258. *Club:* Army and Navy.

TREATT, Hon. Sir Vernon (Haddon), KBE 1970; MM 1918; QC (Austr.) 1940; MA, BCL; private interests; *b* 15 May 1897; *s* of Frank Burford Treatt and Kate Ellen Treatt; *m* 1st, 1930, Dorothy Isobelle Henderson; one *s* one *d*; 2nd, 1960, Franki Embleton Wilson. *Educ:* Sydney C of E Grammar Sch.; St Paul's Coll., Sydney Univ.; New Coll., Oxford. Sydney Univ., 1915-16, 1919-20 (BA); AIF, 1916-18 (Gunner, MM); Rhodes Scholar, 1920; Oxford Univ., 1921-23. Called to Bar, Lincoln's Inn, 1923; Bar of NSW, 1924. NSW Legislative Assembly, 1938-62: Minister of Justice, 1939-41; Leader of Opposition, 1946-54; title of Honourable for life, 1955. Chm., Local Govt Boundaries Commn NSW, 1964-69. Chief Comr (in loco Lord Mayor), City of Sydney, 1967-69. *Publication:* Workers Compensation Law NSW. *Recreations:* swimming, reading, rural property. *Address:* 27 Waruda Street, Kirribilli, NSW 2061, Australia. *T:* 9292668; Riverview, O'Connell, NSW 2795. *T:* O'Connell 375762. *Clubs:* University, Royal Sydney Golf, Union, Australasian Pioneers' (Sydney).

TREDENNICK, Prof. (George) Hugh (Percival Phair); Professor Emeritus of Classics, University of London; *b* 30 June 1899; *yr s* of late Canon G. N. H. Tredennick, Sparkbrook, Birmingham; *m* 1924, Louella Margaret (*d* 1970), *o d* of late Canon E. E. M. Phair, Winnipeg, Canada; one *s* two *d*. *Educ:* King Edward's, Birmingham; Trinity Hall, Cambridge. War Service in France with Royal Artillery, 1918-19; Trinity Hall, Cambridge (Scholar and Prizeman), 1919-22; First Class Classical Tripos: Part I, 1921, Part II, 1922; BA, 1922; MA 1926. Assistant Master, Rossall School, 1923-24; Lecturer in Classics, University of Sheffield, 1924-36; Reader in Classics, Queen Mary College, University of London, 1936-46; Professor of Classics, Royal Holloway Coll., 1946-66. Dean of the Faculty of Arts, University of London, 1956-60; Editor (with C. J. Fordyce) The Classical Review, 1961-67. *Publications:* text and translation of Aristotle's Metaphysics, Vol. I, 1933, Vol. II, 1935; text and translation of Aristotle's Prior Analytics, 1938; The Last Days of Socrates (Penguin Classics), 1954; text and translation of Aristotle's Posterior Analytics, 1960; Memoirs of Socrates (Penguin Classics), 1970; contributions to classical journals. *Recreations:* genealogy, indoor gardening. *Address:* 705 Nelson House, Dolphin Square, SW1V 3PA. *T:* 01-834 4079.

TREDGOLD, Joan Alison, MA Cantab; Principal, Cheltenham Ladies' College, Sept. 1953-July 1964; *b* 6 Sept. 1903; *d* of Alfred Frank Tredgold, MD, FRCP, and Zoë B. T. Tredgold. *Educ:* Cheltenham Ladies' College; Newnham College, Cambridge. Mathematical Tripos part II, Class I, 1924; Fourth Year Scholarship, Newnham, 1924-25. Assistant Mistress, Sherborne School for Girls, 1925-29; Assistant Mistress, Cheltenham

Ladies' College, 1929-35. Senior Mathematical Mistress, 1935-53, Assistant House Mistress, 1938-39, Second Mistress, 1939-53, Roedean School. *Recreation:* foreign travel. *Address:* 12 Newcourt Park, Charlton Kings, Cheltenham, Glos. *T:* Cheltenham 59242. *Club:* University Women's.

TREFGARNE; family name of **Baron Trefgarne.**

TREFGARNE, 2nd Baron, *cr* 1947, of Cleddau; **David Garro Trefgarne;** Opposition Whip, House of Lords, since 1977; *b* 31 March 1941; *s* of 1st Baron Trefgarne and of Elizabeth (who *m* 1962, Comdr A. T. Courtney (from whom she obt. a divorce, 1966); *m* 1971, H. C. H. Ker, Dundee), *d* of C. E. Churchill; *S* father, 1960; *m* 1968, Rosalie, *d* of Peter Lane; two *s* one *d*. *Educ:* Haileybury; Princeton University, USA. Awarded Royal Aero Club Bronze Medal (jointly) for flight from England to Australia and back in light aircraft, 1963; formerly joint holder of Class C1d records London to New York, London to Reykjavik and Reykjavik to New York; also Class C1 records London to Reykjavik and Reykjavik to New York, (Fedn Aeronautique Internat.), 1964. *Recreations:* flying and photography. *Heir:* *s* Hon. George Garro Trefgarne, *b* 4 Jan. 1970. *Address:* House of Lords, SW1. *Club:* East India, Devonshire, Sports and Public Schools.

TREFUSIS; *see* Fane Trefusis, family name of **Baron Clinton.**

TREHANE, Sir (Walter) Richard, Kt 1967; Chairman of the Milk Marketing Board, 1958-77; *b* 14 July 1913; *s* of James Trehane and Muriel Yeoman Cowl; *m* 1948, Elizabeth Mitchell; two *s*. *Educ:* Monkton Combe School, Somerset; University of Reading (BSc (Agric.)). On staff of School of Agriculture, Cambridge, 1933-36; Manager of Hampreston Manor Farm, Dorset, 1936-. Member Dorset War Agric. Exec. Cttee, 1942-47; Mem. Milk Marketing Board, 1947- (Vice-Chm., 1952-58); Dep. Chm. Dorset Agric. Exec. Cttee, 1947-52; Mem. (later Vice-Chm.) Avon and Stour Catchment Bd, subseq. Avon & Dorset Rivers Bd, 1944-53; Mem. Dorset County Council and Chm. Secondary Education Cttee, 1946-49; Chm. Dorset National Farmers' Union, 1947-48; Member, Nat. Milk Publicity Council, 1954-77 (1st Pres. 1954-56); Chm. English Country Cheese Council, 1955-77; Pres. British Farm Produce Council, 1963- (Chm. 1960-63). Chm. Govg Body, Grassland Research Institute, Hurley, Berks, 1959-; Chm. and Pres. European Cttee on Milk/Butterfat Recording, 1957-60; Director of British Semen Exports Ltd, 1960-77; Vice-President: World Assoc. Animal Production, 1965-68; President: European Assoc. Animal Prodn, 1961-67; British Soc. Animal Prodn, 1954, 1961; British Friesian Cattle Soc., 1969-70; Royal Assoc. British Dairy Farmers, 1968, 1977; Internat. Dairy Fedn, 1968-72, Hon. Pres., 1972-76. Chm., UK Dairy Assoc., 1963-69. Director: Southern Television, 1969-; The Rank Organisation Ltd, 1970-. Trustee, UK Farming Scholarship Trust, 1970. Governor: Monkton Combe School, 1957- British Nutrition Foundn, 1975-77. FRAgSs 1970. Hon. DSc Reading, 1976. Justus-von-Liebig Prize, Kiel Univ., 1968; Gold Medal, Soc. of Dairy Technology, 1969; Massey-Fergusson Award, 1971. Comdr du Mérite Agricole, 1964. *Address:* Hampreston Manor Farm, Wimborne, Dorset. *Clubs:* Constitutional, Farmers', Travellers'; Royal Motor Yacht (Poole).

TREHERNE, John Edwin, ScD, PhD; Hon. Director of ARC Unit of Invertebrate Chemistry and Physiology, Department of Zoology, University of Cambridge, since 1969; University Reader in Invertebrate Physiology, since 1971; Fellow of Downing College, Cambridge, since 1966; *b* 15 May 1929; *s* of Arnold Edwin Wilson Treherne and Marion Grace Spiller; *m* 1955, June Vivienne Freeman; one *s* one *d*. *Educ:* Headlands Sch., Swindon, Wilts; Univ. of Bristol (BSc, PhD); Univ. of Cambridge (MA, ScD). Nat. Service, Lieut RAMC, 1953-55. Principal Sci. Officer, ARC Unit of Insect Physiology, Cambridge, 1955-67; Univ. Lectr in Zoology, Cambridge, 1968-71. Visiting Prof., Univ. of Virginia, 1963-64. Vice-Pres., Royal Entomological Soc., 1967-68. Scientific Medal of Zoological Soc., 1968. Dir, Company of Biologists Ltd, 1969-74; Editor: Advances in Insect Physiology, 1964; Jl of Experimental Biology, 1974. *Publications:* Neurochemistry of Arthropods, 1966; Insect Neurobiology, 1974; research papers in: Jl of Experimental Biology; Tissue and Cell; Nature. *Recreations:* domestic; military and naval Staffordshire figures; postcards of Edwardian actresses; marine insects. *Address:* Park End, Swaffham Bulbeck, Cambridge CB5 0NA. *T:* Cambridge 811404.

TREITEL, Guenter Heinz, DCL; FBA 1977; Fellow of Magdalen College, Oxford, since 1954; All Souls Reader in English Law, University of Oxford, since 1964; *b* 26 Oct. 1928; *s* of Theodor Treitel and Hannah Lilly Treitel (*née* Levy); *m* 1957, Phyllis

Margaret Cook; two s. *Educ:* Kilburn Grammar School; Magdalen College, Oxford. BA 1949, BCL 1951, MA 1953, DCL 1976. Called to the Bar, Gray's Inn, 1952. Asst Lecturer, London Sch. of Economics, 1951-53; Lectr, University Coll., Oxford, 1953-54; Vis. Lectr, Univ. of Chicago, 1963-64; Visiting Professor: Chicago, 1968-69 and 1971-72; W Australia, 1976; Houston, 1977; Southern Methodist, 1978. *Publications:* The Law of Contract, 1962, 4th edn 1975; An Outline of the Law of Contract, 1975; International Encyclopedia of Comparative Law, Vol. VII Ch. 16, on Remedies for Breach of Contract, 1976; edited jointly: Chitty on Contracts, 23rd edn, 1968 and 24th edn, 1977; Benjamin's Sale of Goods, 1974; Dicey's Conflict of Laws, 7th edn, 1958; Dicey and Morris, Conflict of Laws, 8th edn, 1967. *Recreations:* music, reading. *Address:* Magdalen College, Oxford OX1 4AU. *T:* Oxford 41781 and 40381.

TRELAWNY, Sir John Barry Salusbury-, 13th Bt *cr* 1628; JP; *b* 4 Sept. 1934; *s* of Sir John William Robin Maurice Salusbury-Trelawny, 12th Bt and of his 1st wife, Glenys Mary, *d* of John Cameron Kynoch; *S* father, 1956; *m* 1958, Carol Knox, *yr d* of late C. F. K. Watson, The Field, Saltwood, Kent; one *s* three *d. Educ:* HMS Worcester. Subseq. Sub-Lt RNVR (National Service). Dir, The Martin Walter Group Ltd, 1974-74; various directorships, 1974-. FInstM 1974. JP 1973. *Heir: s* John William Richard Salusbury-Trelawny, *b* 30 March 1960. *Address:* The Grange, Saltwood, Kent. *T:* 66476. *Club:* Army and Navy.

TRELFORD, Donald Gilchrist; Editor of The Observer, since 1975; a Director, The Observer Ltd, since 1975; *b* 9 Nov. 1937; *s* of Thomas Trelford and Doris Trelford (*née* Gilchrist); *m* 1963, Janice Ingram; two *s* one *d. Educ:* Bablake Sch., Coventry; Selwyn Coll., Cambridge (Open Exhibnr) (University rugby and cricket); MA Cantab. Pilot Officer, RAF, 1956-58. Reporter and Sub-Editor, Coventry Standard and Sheffield Telegraph, 1960-63; Editor, Nyasaland Times, 1963-66; Correspondent in Africa for The Observer, The Times, and BBC, 1963-66; Dep. News Editor, The Observer, 1966, Asst Man. Editor, 1968, Dep. Editor, 1969. Member: British Executive Cttee, IPI, 1976-; Council, Roehampton Inst. of Higher Educn, 1976. Patron, Milton Keynes Civic Forum, 1977. *Recreations:* golf, squash. *Address:* c/o The Observer, 8 St Andrew's Hill, EC4V 5JA. *T:* 01-236 0202. *Clubs:* Garrick, Press, Royal Air Force.

TREMAYNE, Air Marshal Sir John Tremayne, KCB 1942 (CB 1939); CBE 1934; DSO 1915; DL, JP; *b* 20 July 1891; *s* of C. H. Babington, 47 Lennox Gdns, SW1; renounced surname of Babington, 1945; *m* 1916, Cicely (*d* 1953), *y d* of Philip Beresford-Hope, Bedgebury; two *d.* Served European War, 1914-15 (DSO, Chevalier Legion of Honour); Air Representative to League of Nations, 1929-34; Air Officer Commanding RAF Halton, 1934-36; No 24 (Training) Group, 1936-38; Far East, 1938-41; Air Officer Commanding-in-Chief, Technical Training Command, 1941-43; Head of RAF Mission in Moscow, 1943; retired 1944. Cornwall: DL 1945, JP 1948, High Sheriff 1954. *Address:* Croan, Wadebridge, Cornwall. *T:* St Mabyn 368. *Club:* Army and Navy.

TREMELLEN, Norman Cleverton; FCIB; FRSA; *b* 8 March 1895; *s* of Henry Josiah and Elizabeth Tremellen; *m* 1923, Lorna, *o d* of Dr John McKeague and *g d* of Judge Purcell, Dublin. *Educ:* Villa Longchamp, Lausanne, Switzerland. Served European War, 1914-18 (4 General Service Medals). Former Member Common Council, City of London; Founder Chm. and Hon. Treas., City of London Sheriffs Society. Insurance Broker and Underwriting Member of Lloyd's; Fellow of the Corporation of Insurance Brokers; Past President, London Cornish Association. Past Governor of: The Bridewell and Bethlem Royal Hospitals; Archbishop Tenison's Grammar Sch. Pres., Insurance Debating Society. Sheriff of the City of London, 1953-54. Mem., Court, Worshipful Co. of Weavers; Mem. Worshipful Co. of Shipwrights; Past President: City Livery Club; Bishopsgate Ward Club; United Wards Club; Past Master, Lime Street Ward Club; Past Chm., Langbourn Ward Club; Mem., Three Rooms Club, Lloyd's; Governor (for 18 years), Bishopsgate Foundn. Past Dep. Gov. The Hon. The Irish Soc.; Fellow, Royal Soc. for Protection of Birds; FAMS. Mem. Anglo-Ethiopian Soc. Comdr Roy. Order of the North Star (Sweden). *Address:* Burlington, Orchehill Avenue, Gerrards Cross, Bucks. *T:* 83047. *Club:* City Livery.

TREMLETT, Rt. Rev. Anthony Paul; *see* Dover, Suffragan Bishop of.

TREMLETT, Maj.-Gen. Erroll Arthur Edwin, CB 1944; TD 1948; *b* 22 Dec. 1893; *s* of late Col E. J. Tremlett, RA; *m* Dorothy Mary, *d* of late H. W. Capper, 24 Suffolk St, Pall Mall;

one *s* one *d.* Served in European War, 1914-19, with RA, (despatches) (awarded Regular Commn in the "Field," Sept. 1916) and in France and Belgium 1940 (despatches); Comdr 44 AA Brigade, Nov. 1940; Major-General, Commander 10 AA Division, Feb. 1942; Commander AA Defences of London, 1942-44; Comdr Flying Bomb Deployment, 1945. Commander 2 AA Group, 1945-46; RARO 1946. Hon. Colonel 656 Light AA Regt RA (RB), 1947-57. Gold Staff Officer, Coronation of HM Queen Elizabeth II. *Address:* Clapham Cottage, Clapham, near Exeter, Devon. *T:* Kennford 832586. *Clubs:* Naval and Military, MCC.

TREMLETT, George William; author and journalist; Member of the Greater London Council; Director, National Association of Voluntary Hostels, since 1977; *b* 5 Sept. 1939; *s* of Wilfred George and Elizabeth Tremlett; *m* 1971, Jane, *o c* of late Benjamin James Mitchell and of Mrs P. A. Mitchell; one *s. Educ:* Taunton School; King Edward VI School, Stratford upon Avon. Member of Richmond upon Thames Borough Council, 1963-74; Chairman: Further Education Cttee, 1966-68; Barnes School Governors, 1967-73; Schools Cttee, 1972-73; Shene VIth Form Coll. Governors, 1973-74; Housing Cttee, 1972-74. Member of Greater London Council, 1970-: Opposition Housing Spokesman, 1974-77; Leader of Housing Policy Cttee, 1977-. Formerly: Governor, Kingston Polytechnic and Twickenham Coll. of Technology; Member, Thames Water Authority, 1973-74; Court of City Univ., 1968-74. *Publications:* 17 biographies of rock musicians, 1974-77—on John Lennon, David Bowie, 10cc, Paul McCartney, The Osmonds, Alvin Stardust, Cat Stevens, Cliff Richard, Slade, The Who, David Essex, Slik, Gary Glitter, Marc Bolan, Rod Stewart, Queen and the Rolling Stones (published in many different countries). *Recreations:* ornithology, exploring old churches, local history, rock 'n' roll music. *Address:* 7A Cambridge Park, East Twickenham TW1 2PF. *Clubs:* Carlton, Press.

TRENAMAN, Nancy Kathleen, (Mrs M. S. Trenaman); Principal of St Anne's College, Oxford, since 1966; *b* 1919; *d* of Frederick Broughton Fisher and Edith Fisher; *m* 1967, M. S. Trenaman. *Educ:* Bradford Girls' Grammar School; Somerville College, Oxford (Hon. Fellow, 1977). Board Board of Trade, 1941-51; Assistant Secretary, Ministry of Materials, 1951-54; Counsellor, British Embassy, Washington, 1951-53; Board of Trade, 1954-66, Under-Sec. 1962-66. Mem., Commn on the Constitution, 1969-73. *Address:* St Anne's College, Oxford; 4 Fairlawn End, Oxford OX2 8AR. *T:* Oxford 57723.

TRENCH, family name of **Baron Ashtown.**

TRENCH, Anthony C.; *see* Chenevix-Trench.

TRENCH, *see* Le Poer Trench, family name of Earl of Clancarty.

TRENCH, Sir David (Clive Crosbie), GCMG 1969 (KCMG 1962; CMG 1960); MC 1944; DL; Vice-Chairman, Advisory Committee on Distinction Awards, Department of Health and Social Security, since 1972; Chairman, Dorset Area Health Authority, since 1973; *b* 2 June 1915; *s* of late William Launcelot Crosbie Trench, CIE, and Margaret Zephanie (*née* Huddleston); *m* 1944, Margaret Gould; one *d. Educ:* Tonbridge School; Jesus College, Cambridge (MA). Cadet, British Solomon Islands Protectorate, 1938; seconded to W Pacific High Commission, 1941. Served War of 1939-45 (MC, US Legion of Merit); British Solomon Islands Defence Force, 1942-46, Lt-Col. Secretary to the Government, British Solomon Islands Protectorate, 1947; attended Joint Services Staff Coll., 1949; Asst Sec., Deputy Defence Sec., Hong Kong, 1950; Deputy Financial Sec., 1956; Commissioner of Labour and Mines, 1957; attended Imperial Defence College, 1958; Deputy Colonial Secretary, Hong Kong, 1959; High Commissioner for The Western Pacific, 1961-63; Governor and C-in-C, Hong Kong, 1964-71. Mem., new Dorset CC, 1973-. DL Dorset, 1977. Hon. LLD: Univ. of Hong Kong, 1968; Chinese Univ. of Hong Kong, 1968. Legion of Merit (US), 1944. *Recreation:* golf. *Address:* Church House, Church Road, Shillingstone, Blandford, Dorset DT11 0SL.

TRENCH, Sir Nigel (Clive Cosby), KCMG 1976 (CMG 1966); HM Diplomatic Service, retired; *b* 27 Oct. 1916; *s* of Clive Newcome Trench and Kathleen, 2nd *d* of Major Ivar MacIvor, CSI; *m* 1939, Marcelle Catherine Clotterbooke Patyn; one *s. Educ:* Eton; Univ. of Cambridge. Served in KRRC, 1940-46 (despatches). Appointed a Member of the Foreign (subseq. Diplomatic) Service, 1946; Lisbon, 1946; First Secretary, 1948; returned Foreign Office, 1949; First Secretary (Commercial) Lima, 1952; transf. Foreign Office, 1955; Counsellor, Tokyo, 1961; Counsellor, Washington, 1963; Cabinet Office, 1967; HM Ambassador to Korea, 1969-71; CS Selection Board, 1971-73; Ambassador to Portugal, 1974-76. *Address:* 4 Kensington Court Gardens, Kensington Court Place, W8 5QE. *Club:* Bath.

TRENCH, Peter Edward, CBE 1964 (OBE 1945); TD 1949; Chairman, Y. J. Lovell (Holdings) Ltd; *b* 16 June 1918; *s* of James Knights Trench and Grace Sim; *m* 1940, Mary St Clair Morford; one *s* one *d*. *Educ:* privately; London Sch. of Economics, London Univ.; St John's Coll., Cambridge Univ. BSc (Econ.) Hons. Served in The Queen's Royal Regt, 1939-46: Staff Coll., 1942; Mil. Raid Planner, Combined Ops HQ, 1943; AAG, HQ 21 Army Gp, 1944-45 (OBE). Man. Dir, Bovis Ltd, 1954-59; Dir, Nat. Fedn of Bldg Trades Employers, 1959-64; Dir, Nat. Bldg Agency, 1964-66; Part-time Mem., Nat. Bd for Prices and Incomes, 1965-68; Chm., Building Centre, 1970-73; Mem., Develt Control Rev. Panel, 1973-74; Mem., Tribunal to arbitrate on teachers' pay claim, 1971, 1972. Chairman: James Davies (Holdings) Ltd; Building Management & Marketing Consultants Ltd; Director: Capital & Counties Property Co. Ltd; The LEP Group Ltd; Nationwide Building Society; Crendon Concrete Ltd; The Builder Ltd; Chm., Construction and Housing Res. Adv. Council; Mem., Review of Housing Finance Adv. Gp, 1975-76; Conslt, Housing Res. Foundn; Vice-President: Modular Soc.; Building Centre; Hon. Mem., Architectural Assoc.; Member: Council, City and Guilds of London Inst.; PO Arbitration Tribunal; Employer Member, Advisory, Conciliation and Arbitration Service; Hon. Treasurer, St Mary's Hosp. Med. Sch. JP Inner London, 1963-71. FIOB; FIArb; FRSA; FBIM. *Recreations:* ski-ing, swimming, travelling. *Address:* 4 Napier Close, Napier Road, W14 8LG. *T:* 01-602 3936. *Club:* MCC.

TRENCHARD, family name of **Viscount Trenchard.**

TRENCHARD, 2nd Viscount, *cr* 1936, of Wolfeton; **Thomas Trenchard,** MC 1944; Baron, *cr* 1930; Bt, *cr* 1919; *b* 15 Dec. 1923; *o surv. s* of 1st Viscount Trenchard, GCB, OM, GCVO, DSO, first Marshal of the RAF, and of Katherine Viscountess Trenchard (*d* 1960); *S* father 1956; *m* 1948, Patricia, *d* of late Admiral Sir Sidney Bailey, KBE, CB, DSO and of Lady Bailey; three *s*. *Educ:* Eton. Served War of 1939-45, Captain, King's Royal Rifle Corps (MC). Mem., ARC, 1971-. *Heir:* *s* Hon. Hugh Trenchard, Captain 4th Royal Green Jackets, TA [*b* 12 March 1951; *m* 1975, Fiona, *d* of Hon. James Morrison]. *Address:* Abdale House, Warrengate Road, North Mymms, Hatfield, Herts AL9 7TX. *Club:* Brooks's.

TREND, family name of **Baron Trend.**

TREND, Baron *cr* 1974 (Life Peer), of Greenwich; **Burke St John Trend,** PC 1972; GCB 1968 (KCB 1962; CB 1955); CVO 1953; Rector, Lincoln College, Oxford since 1973; Pro-Vice-Chancellor, Oxford University, since 1975; *b* 2 Jan. 1914; *o s* of late Walter St John Trend and Marion Tyers; *m* 1949, Patricia Charlotte, *o d* of Rev. Gilbert Shaw; two *s* one *d*. *Educ:* Whitgift; Merton College, Oxford (Postmaster). 1st Cl. Honour Mods, 1934; 1st Cl. Lit. Hum., 1936; Hon. Fellow, Merton College, 1964. Home Civil Service Administrative Class, 1936; Min. of Education, 1936; transferred to HM Treasury, 1937; Asst Private Sec. to Chancellor of Exchequer, 1939-41; Principal Private Sec. to Chancellor of Exchequer, 1945-49; Under Secretary, HM Treasury, 1949-55; Office of the Lord Privy Seal, 1955-56; Deputy Secretary of the Cabinet, 1956-59; Third Secretary, HM Treasury, 1959-60, Second Secretary, 1960-62; Secretary of the Cabinet, 1963-73. Trustee, British Museum, 1973-; Managing Trustee, Nuffield Foundn, 1973-; Mem., Adv. Council on Public Records, 1974-. Hon. DCL Oxford, 1969; Hon. LLD St Andrews, 1974. *Address:* Lincoln College, Oxford. *Club:* Athenæum.

TRENDALL, Prof. Arthur Dale, AC 1976; CMG 1961; MA, LittD; FSA; FBA; FAHA; Resident Fellow, Menzies College, La Trobe University; Emeritus Professor, University of Sydney, 1954; *b* Auckland, NZ, 28 March 1909; *s* of late Arthur D. Trendall and late Iza W. Uttley-Todd; unmarried. *Educ:* King's College, Auckland; Univs of Otago (MA 1929, LittD 1936) and Cambridge (MA 1937, LittD 1968). NZ Post-Graduate Scholar in Arts, 1931; Rome Scholar in Archæology, 1934-35; Fellow of Trinity Coll., Cambridge, 1936-40; Librarian British School at Rome, 1936-38; FSA 1939; Professor of Greek, Univ. of Sydney, 1939-54; Dean, Faculty of Arts, 1947-50; Chairman Professorial Board, 1949-50, 1952; Acting Vice-Chancellor, 1953; Master of Univ. House, ANU, 1954-69, retd; Hon. Fellow, 1969. Hon. Curator, Greek and Roman Section, Nicholson Museum, 1954, and Hon. Consultant, National Gallery of Victoria, 1957; Deputy Vice-Chancellor, ANU, 1958-64; Mem. Royal Commn on Univ. of Tas., 1955. Geddes-Harrower Professor of Greek Art and Archæology, Aberdeen Univ., 1966-67. Chm. Aust. Humanities Research Council, 1957-59. Mem., Nat. Capital Planning Cttee, 1958-67; Mem. Australian Universities Commission, 1959-70. Member: Accademia dei Lincei, Rome, 1971; Athens Acad., 1973; Corresp. Mem., Pontifical Acad. of Archaeology, Rome, 1973; Life Mem., Nat. Gall. of Victoria, 1976; For. Mem., Royal Netherlands Acad., 1977. Hon. Fellow, Athens Archaeological Soc., 1975. FBA 1968. Hon. LittD: Melbourne, 1956; ANU 1970; Hon. DLitt: Adelaide, 1960; Sydney, 1972. For. Galileo Galilei Prize for Archaeology, 1971; Cassano Gold Medal for Magna Graecia Studies, 1971; Britannica Award (Australia), 1973. KCSG, 1956; Commendatore, Ordine al Merito, Republic of Italy, 1965 (Cav. Uff. 1961). *Publications:* Paestan Pottery, 1936; Frühitaliotische Vasen, 1938; Guide to the Cast Collection of the Nicholson Museum, Sydney, 1941; The Shellal Mosaic, 1942, 4th edn 1973; Handbook to the Nicholson Museum (editor), 2nd edn 1948; Paestan Pottery, Supplement, 1952; Vasi Italioti del Vaticano, vol. i, 1953; vol. ii, 1955; The Felton Greek Vases, 1958; Phlyax Vases, 1959, 2nd edn 1967; Paestan Addenda, 1960; Apulian Vase Painters of the Plain Style (with A. Cambitoglou), 1962; South Italian Vase Painting (British Museum Guide), 1966; The Red-figured Vases of Lucania, Campania and Sicily, 1967, Supplement I, 1970, Supplement II, 1973; Greek Vases in the Felton Collection, 1968, 2nd edn 1978; Greek Vases in the Logie Collection, Christchurch, NZ, 1971; Illustrations of Greek Drama (with T. B. L. Webster), 1971; Early South Italian Vase-painting, 1974; Eine Gruppe Apulischer Grabvasen in Basel (with M. Schmidt and A. Cambitoglou), 1976; several articles in learned periodicals. *Recreations:* travel, walking. *Address:* Menzies College, La Trobe University, Bundoora, Vic 3083, Australia.

TRENT, Group Captain Leonard Henry, VC 1946; DFC 1940; *b* 14 April 1915; *s* of Leonard Noel Trent, Nelson, New Zealand; British; *m* 1940, Ursula Elizabeth Woolhouse; one *s* two *d*. *Educ:* Nelson Coll., NZ. Entered firm of W. & R. Fletcher (New Zealand) Ltd 1935; joined RNZAF, 1937; joined RAF 1938. Arrived in England, 1938; served War, 1939-43, France and England (POW 1943); transferred to RNZAF, 1944; transferred back to RAF, 1947, Permanent Commission. Formerly: OC 214 Valiant Sqdn, RAF Marham; Trg HQ No. 3 Gp, Mildenhall, 1948-59; Comdg RAF Wittering, 1959-62; Asst Air Attaché, Washington, also SASO and Chief Intell. Officer (RAF), 1962-65. ADC to the Queen, 1962-65. *Recreations:* golf, carpentry, gardening, painting, oils and watercolours. *Address:* c/o Post Office, Leigh, Auckland, New Zealand.

TRESIDDER, Gerald Charles, FRCS; Senior Lecturer, Department of Human Morphology, University of Southampton, since 1976; *b* Rawalpindi, 5 Dec. 1912; *s* of late Lt-Col A. G. Tresidder, CIE, MD, MS, FRCS; *m* 1940, Ida Marguerite Livingstone Bell; one *s* two *d*. *Educ:* Haileybury College; University of London, Queen Mary College and The London Hospital Medical College. LRCP, MRCS 1937; MB, BS London 1938; FRCS 1946. Resident appointments at The London Hospital, 1937-39. Surgical Specialist, Major, Indian Medical Service, 1940-46. Postgraduate appointments at The London Hospital and Demonstrator of Anatomy at The London Hospital Medical College, 1946-48; Sen. Assistant to Surgical Unit, 1948-51; Surgeon, Dept of Urology, The London Hosp., Lectr in Surgery and part-time Sen. Lectr in Anatomy, The London Hosp. Med. Sch., 1951-76. Pres., Section of Urology, RSM; Member: Internat. Soc. of Urology; Council, British Assoc. of Urological Surgeons; Examr in Anatomy for Primary FRCS. *Publications:* contributions to: Rob and Smith's Clinical Surgery and Operative Surgery; British Jl of Surgery; British Jl of Urology; Lancet. *Recreations:* walking and talking. *Address:* Gowers, Burley Road, Brockenhurst, Hants SO4 7TB. *T:* Brockenhurst 2065.

TRESS, Ronald Charles, CBE 1968; BSc (Econ.) London, DSc Bristol; Director, Leverhulme Trust Fund, since 1977; Development Commissioner since 1959; Secretary-General, Royal Economic Society, since 1975; *b* Upchurch, Sittingbourne, Kent, 11 Jan. 1915; *er s* of S. C. Tress; *m* 1942, Josephine Kelly, *d* of H. J. Medland; one *s* two *d*. *Educ:* Gillingham (Kent) County School; Univ. College, Southampton. Gladstone Student, St Deiniol's Library, Hawarden, 1936-37; Drummond Fraser Research Fellow, Univ. of Manchester, 1937-38; Asst Lecturer in Economics, Univ. Coll. of the S West, Exeter, 1938-41; Economic Asst, War Cabinet Offices, 1941-45; Economic Adviser, Cabinet Secretariat, 1945-47; Reader in Public Finance, Univ. of London, 1947-51; Prof. of Political Economy, Univ. of Bristol, 1951-68; Master of Birkbeck Coll., 1968-77, Mem. Senate, 1968-77, and Court, 1976-77, London Univ. Managing Editor, London and Cambridge Economic Service, 1949-51; Member: Reorganisation Commn for Pigs and Bacon, 1955-56; Nigeria Fiscal Commn, 1957-58; Departmental Cttee on Rating of Charities, 1958; Financial Enquiry, Aden Colony, 1959; East Africa Economic and Fiscal Commn, 1960, Uganda Fiscal Commn, 1962; Kenya Fiscal Commn (Chm.), 1962-63; National Incomes Commn, 1963-65; Chm., SW

Economic Planning Council, 1965-68; Mem., Cttee of Inquiry into Teachers' Pay, 1974; Chm., Cttee for Univ. Assistance to Adult Educn in HM Forces, 1974-; Lay Mem., Solicitors' Disciplinary Tribunal, 1975-. Trustee, City Parochial Foundn, 1974-77. Governor: LSE, 1975-; Christ Church Coll., Canterbury, 1975-; Board of Management: London Sch. of Hygiene and Tropical Med., 1975-; Courtauld Inst. of Art, 1976-; British Inst. in Paris, 1977-. Mem. Council, Royal Econ. Soc., 1960-70, 1975-. Hon. LLD: Furman Univ., S Carolina, 1973; Exeter, 1976; DUniv. Open Univ., 1974. *Publications:* articles and reviews in Economic Journal, Economica, LCES Bulletin, etc. *Address:* Leverhulme Trust Fund, 15-19 New Fetter Lane, EC4A 1NR. *T:* 01-353 7474; 22 The Beach, Walmer, Deal, Kent CT14 7HJ. *T:* Deal 3254.

TRETHOWAN, (James) Ian (Raley); Director-General of the BBC, since 1977; *b* 20 Oct. 1922; *s* of late Major J. J. R. Trethowan, MBE and Mrs R. Trethowan; *m* 1963, Carolyn Reynolds; three *d. Educ:* Christ's Hospital. Entered Journalism, 1939. Fleet Air Arm, 1941-46. Political Corresp., Yorkshire Post, 1947-55; News Chronicle, 1955-57; Dep. Editor/Political Editor, Independent Television News, 1958-63; joined BBC, 1963, as Commentator on Politics and Current Affairs; Man. Dir, Radio, BBC, 1969-75; Man. Dir, Television, BBC, 1976-77. Political Commentator: The Economist, 1953-58, 1965-67; The Times, 1967-68. Mem., Cttee on Official Secrets Act, 1971. *Address:* c/o BBC, Broadcasting House, W1A 1AA. *T:* 01-580 4468. *Clubs:* Travellers', MCC.

TRETHOWAN, Prof. William Henry, CBE 1975; FRCP, FRACP, FRCPsych; Professor of Psychiatry, University of Birmingham, since 1962; Hon. Consultant Psychiatrist: Queen Elizabeth Hospital, Birmingham, since 1962; Hollymoor Hospital, since 1964; Midland Centre for Neurosurgery, since 1975; *b* 3 June 1917; *s* of William Henry Trethowan and Joan Durham Trethowan (*née* Hickson); *m* 1941, Pamela (*née* Waters); one *s* two *d. Educ:* Oundle Sch.; Clare Coll., Cambridge; Guy's Hosp. Med. Sch. MA, MB, BChir (Cantab) 1943; MRCP 1948; FRACP 1961; FRCP 1963; FRCPsych 1971. Served War, RAMC: Major, Med. Specialist, 1944-47. Psychiatric Registrar, Maudsley Hosp., 1948-50; Psychiatric Resident, Mass Gen. Hosp., and Hon. Teaching Fellow, Harvard, 1951; Lectr and Sen. Lectr in Psychiatry, Univ. of Manchester, 1951-56; Prof. of Psychiatry, Univ. of Sydney, and Hon. Consultant Psychiatrist, Royal Prince Alfred and Royal North Shore Hosps, Sydney, 1956-62. Mem. GMC, 1969-; Cons. Adviser in Psychiatry, DHSS, 1964-; Dean, Univ. of Birmingham Med. Sch., 1968-74; Chm., Standing Mental Health Adv. Cttee, 1968-74; Mem., UGC Med. Subcttee, 1974-. Member: Birmingham Reg. Hosp. Bd, 1964-74; Standing Med. Adv. Cttee, 1966- (Chm., 1976); Central Health Services Council, 1966- (Vice-Chm., 1976); W Midlands Regional Health Authority, 1974-76. Chm., Med. Acad. Adv. Cttee, Chinese Univ. of Hong Kong, 1976-. FRSocMed; Hon. Fellow, Aust. and NZ Coll. of Psychiatry (FANZCP), 1962. *Publications:* (with E. W. Anderson) Psychiatry, 3rd edn 1973; (with M. D. Enoch and J. Barker) Some Uncommon Psychiatric Syndromes, 1967, 2nd edn 1976; numerous scientific and other articles in various jls; book reviews, etc. *Recreations:* music, fishing. *Address:* 99 Bristol Road, Edgbaston, Birmingham B5 7TX. *T:* 021-440 3485.

TREVASKIS, Sir (Gerald) Kennedy (Nicholas), KCMG 1963 (CMG 1959); OBE 1948; *b* 1 Jan. 1915; *s* of late Rev. Hugh Kennedy Trevaskis; *m* 1945, Sheila James Harrington, *d* of Col F. T. Harrington; two *s* one *d. Educ:* Summer Fields; Marlborough; King's College, Cambridge. Entered Colonial Service, 1938, as Administrative Cadet, N Rhodesia. Enlisted N Rhodesia Regt 1939; captured by Italian Forces Tug Aqan, Br. Somaliland, 1940 and POW until 1941. Seconded British Military Administration, Eritrea, 1941-48 (Lt-Col) and British Administration, 1948-50; Senior Divisional Officer, Assab, 1943; Serae, 1944; Western Province, 1946; Political Secretary, 1950. Member British delegation four Power Commission ex-Italian Colonies, 1947-48 and Liaison Officer, United Nations Commission, Eritrea, 1950. N Rhodesia, 1950-51; District Commissioner, Ndola. Political Officer, Western Aden Protectorate, 1951; Deputy British Agent, 1952, Adviser and British Agent, 1954; High Commissioner for Aden and the Protectorate of South Arabia, 1963-65 (Deputy High Commissioner, Jan.-Aug. 1963). Member British Delegation, Anglo-Yemeni meeting in London, 1957. *Publications:* A Colony in transition: the British occupation of Eritrea, 1941-52, 1960; Shades of Amber: A South Arabian Episode, 1968. *Recreation:* beagling. *Address:* 20 Empire House, Thurloe Place, SW7. *Clubs:* Bath, MCC, RAC.

TREVELYAN, family name of **Baron Trevelyan.**

TREVELYAN, Baron *cr* 1968 (Life Peer); **Humphrey Trevelyan,** KG 1974; GCMG 1965 (KCMG 1955; CMG 1951); CIE 1947; OBE 1941; *b* 27 Nov. 1905; 2nd *s* of late Rev. George Philip Trevelyan; *m* 1937, Violet Margaret, *d* of late Gen. Sir William H. Bartholomew, GCB, CMG, DSO; two *d. Educ:* Lancing; Jesus College, Cambridge Univ. (Hon. Fellow, 1968). Entered Indian Civil Service, 1929; Indian Political Service, 1932-47. Served as Political Agent in the Indian States; Washington, 1944; Joint Sec. to Govt of India in External Affairs Dept, 1946; retired from Indian Political Service and entered Foreign (later Diplomatic) Service, 1947; Counsellor in Baghdad, 1948; Economic and Financial Adviser, UK High Commission for Germany, 1951-53; HM Chargé d'Affaires in Peking, 1953-55; Ambassador to Egypt, 1955-56; Under-Sec. at UN, 1958; Ambassador to Iraq, 1958-61; Deputy Under-Secretary of State, Foreign Office, 1962; Ambassador to the USSR, 1962-65, retd. High Commissioner in South Arabia, 1967. Director: British Petroleum Company Ltd, 1965-75; British Bank of the Middle East, 1965-77; General Electric Co. Ltd, 1967-76; President, Council of Foreign Bondholders. Chm. of Trustees, British Museum, 1970-; Chm., RIIA, 1970-77. Hon. LLD, Cambridge, 1970; Hon. DCL Durham, 1973; Hon. DLitt Leeds, 1975. *Publications:* The Middle East in Revolution, 1970; Worlds Apart, 1971; The India We Left, 1972; Diplomatic Channels, 1973. *Address:* 13 Wilton Street, SW1. *T:* 01-235 4503. *Clubs:* Pratt's, Beefsteak.

TREVELYAN, Dennis John; Assistant Under-Secretary of State, Broadcasting Department, Home Office, since 1976; *b* 21 July 1929; *s* of John Henry Trevelyan; *m* 1959, Carol Coombes; one *s* one *d. Educ:* Enfield Grammar Sch.; University Coll., Oxford. Entered Home Office, 1950; Treasury, 1953-54; Sec. to Parly Under-Sec. of State, Home Office, 1954-55; Principal Private Sec. to Lord President of Council and Leader of House, 1964-67; Asst Sec., 1966; Asst Under-Sec. of State, NI Office, 1972-76. Sec., Lord Radcliffe's Cttee of Privy Counsellors to inquire into D Notice Matters, 1967. *Recreations:* sailing, music. *Address:* 50 Russell Hill, Purley, Surrey CR2 2JA. *T:* 01-660 4049. *Clubs:* Athenæum; MCC.

TREVELYAN, Sir George (Lowthian), 4th Bt, *cr* 1874; retired; Founder and Director, Wrekin Trust, since 1971; *b* 5 Nov. 1906; *e s* of Rt Hon. Sir C. P. Trevelyan, 3rd Bt; *S* father 1958; *m* 1940, Editha Helen, *d* of Col John Lindsay-Smith; one adopted *d. Educ:* Sidcot School; Trinity College, Cambridge. Worked as artist-craftsman with Peter Waals workshops, fine furniture, 1930-31. Trained and worked in F. M. Alexander re-education method, 1932-36. Taught at Gordonstoun School and Abinger Hill School, 1936-41. Served War, 1941-45, Home Guard Training (Captain). Taught No 1 Army Coll., Newbattle Abbey, 1945-47. Warden, Shropshire Adult College, Attingham Park, Shrewsbury, 1947-71. *Heir: b* Geoffrey Washington Trevelyan [*b* 4 July 1920; *m* 1947, Gillian Isabel, *d* of late Alexander Wood; one *s* one *d*]. *Address:* May Tree Cottage, Upton Bishop, Ross-on-Wye, Herefordshire.

TREVELYAN, Julian Otto; painter and etcher; *b* 20 Feb. 1910; *s* of late R. C. Trevelyan; *m* 1934, Ursula Darwin (divorced, 1950); one *s*; *m* 1951, Mary Fedden. *Educ:* Bedales; Trinity College, Cambridge. Studied art in Paris, Atelier 17, 1930-33; has since lived and worked in Hammersmith. One man exhibns at Lefèvre Gall., 1935, 1938, 1942, 1943, 1944, 1946, 1948 and at Gimpel Fils, 1950, Redfern Gall., 1952, Zwemmer Gall., 1955, 1958, 1960, 1963, 1966, 1967, Galerie de France, Paris, 1947, St George's Gall., 1959; Alex Postan Gall., 1974, New Grafton Gall., 1977, Tate Gall., 1977. Pictures in public and private collections in England, America, Sweden, France, Eire and the USSR. Served War of 1939-45, as Camouflage Officer in Roy. Engineers, 1940-43. Engraving tutor at the Royal College of Art, 1955-63. *Publications:* Indigo Days, 1957; The Artist and His World, 1960; Etching (Studio Books), 1963; A Place, a State, 1975. *Recreation:* listening to music. *Address:* Durham Wharf, Hammersmith Terrace, W6. *T:* 01-748 2749.

TREVELYAN, Mary, CBE 1968 (OBE 1956); ARCM, ARCO; Founder and Governor, International Students' House, London; *e d* of late Rev. G. P. Trevelyan. *Educ:* Grovely College, Boscombe; Royal College of Music, London (Exhibitioner and George Carter Scholar). Musical posts included: organist and choirtrainer, St Barnabas, Oxford, music staff of Radley College and Marlborough College; conductor Chelsea Madrigal Society and Kensington Choral Society. Travelled from Ceylon to Kashmir, 1930-31; Warden of Student Movement House (international house for University students) London, 1932-46. Travelled to Far East, 1936-37, to study problems concerning migration of students from east to west for study and the effects on their return home; also visited USA to study work of the International Houses. Served on Programme Staff of YMCA with BLA in Belgium and France, Oct. 1944-June 1945; Head of Field Survey Bureau, Reconstruction Section, Paris, and made surveys on post-war priority needs in educn in Greece, the East and Far East, 1946-48; first Adviser to Overseas Students, Univ. of London, 1949-65; British Council Lecture Tour in W and E Africa, 1954; first Dir, Internat. Students House, London, 1965-67. Survey Tours, on Ford Foundn award, to univs and internat. centres in USA, Canada, Australia, NZ, the East, Far East and Middle East, 1967-69. *Publications:* From the Ends of the Earth, 1942; I'll Walk Beside You, 1946. *Recreation:* music. *Address:* Flat 5, 23 Embankment Gardens, Chelsea, SW3. *T:* 01-352 6773.

TREVELYAN, Sir Willoughby John, 9th Bt, *cr* 1662; *b* 16 April 1902; *s* of 8th Bt and Alice Edith Money, *y d* of late W. J. Money, CSI; *S* father, 1931. *Heir: kinsman* Norman Irving Trevelyan [*b* 29 Jan. 1915; *m* 1951, Jennifer Mary, *d* of Arthur E. Riddett, Burgh Heath, Surrey; two *s* one *d*]. *Address:* Old Manor House, Salisbury, Wilts.

TREVELYAN OMAN, Julia; *see* Oman.

TREVETHIN, 4th Baron AND OAKSEY, 2nd Baron; *see under* Oaksey, 2nd Baron.

TREVOR, 4th Baron *cr* 1880; **Charles Edwin Hill-Trevor,** JP; *b* 13 Aug. 1928; *e s* of 3rd Baron and Phyllis May, 2nd *d* of J. A. Sims, Ings House, Kirton-in-Lindsey, Lincolnshire; *S* father, 1950; *m* 1967, Susan Janet Elizabeth, *o d* of Dr Ronald Bence; two *s. Educ:* Shrewsbury. JP Clwyd (formerly Denbighshire) 1959. CStJ. *Heir: s* Hon. Marke Charles Hill-Trevor, *b* 8 Jan. 1970. *Address:* Brynkinalt, Chirk, Wrexham, Clwyd. *T:* Chirk 3425; Auch, Bridge of Orchy, Argyllshire. *T:* Tyndrum 282.

TREVOR, David; Hon. Consulting Orthopædic Surgeon: Charing Cross Hospital; St Bartholomew's Hospital; Hemel Hempstead General Hospital; Hon. Consulting Surgeon Royal National Orthopædic Hospital; *b* 24 July 1906; *m* 1935, Kathleen Fairfax Blyth; two *d. Educ:* Tregaron County School; St Bartholomew's Hospital Medical College; Charing Cross Hospital (Post Graduate). MRCS, LRCP 1931; MB, BS London 1931; FRCS 1932; MS London, University Medal, 1934. Past Mem., Internat. Soc. Orthop. and Traumatology, 1951. Past Pres., Orthopædic Section, RSocMed; late Examr in Surgery, Univ. of London; Mem. Council, RCS (Hunterian Prof., 1968; late Mem. Court of Examrs); Past Vice-Pres., British Orthopædic Assoc. Robert Jones Lectr, RCS, 1971. *Publications:* contributor to BMJ, Journal of Bone and Joint Surgery, Proc. RSM, Annals RCS. *Recreations:* golf, shooting. *Address:* Astridge Farm, Gustard Wood, Wheathampstead, Herts. *T:* 2200.

TREVOR, Elleston; author; *b* Bromley, Kent, 17 Feb. 1920; *m* 1947, Iris May Burgess (known as Jonquil); one *s. Educ:* Sevenoaks. Apprenticed as a racing driver upon leaving school, 1938. Served in Royal Air Force, War of 1939-45. Began writing professionally in 1945. Member: Writers' Guild of GB; Authors' Guild of America; British Interplanetary Soc. Amer. Mystery Writers' award, 1965; French Grand Prix de Littérature Policière, 1965. *Plays:* Touch of Purple, Globe, 1972; Just Before Dawn, Murder by All Means, 1972. *Publications:* Chorus of Echoes, 1950 (filmed); Tiger Street, 1951; Redfern's Miracle, 1951; A Blaze of Roses, 1952; The Passion and the Pity, 1953; The Big Pick-up, 1955 (filmed); Squadron Airborne, 1955; The Killing-Ground, 1956; Gale Force, 1956 (filmed); The Pillars of Midnight, 1957 (filmed); The VIP, 1959 (filmed); The Billboard Madonna, 1961; Flight of the Phœnix, 1964 (filmed); The Shoot, 1966; The Freebooters, 1967 (filmed); A Place for the Wicked, 1968; Bury Him Among Kings, 1970; The Theta Syndrome, 1977. Under pseudonym Warwick Scott: Image in the Dust, 1951; The Domesday Story, 1951; Naked Canvas, 1952. Under pseudonym Simon Rattray: Knight Sinister, Queen in Danger, Bishop in Check, Dead Silence, Dead Circuit (all 1951-53). Under pseudonym Adam Hall: Volcanoes of San Domingo, 1964; The Berlin Memorandum, 1964 (filmed as The Quiller Memorandum); The 9th Directive, 1966; The Striker Portfolio, 1969; The Warsaw Document, 1971; The Tango Briefing, 1973; The Mandarin Cypher, 1975; The Kobra Manifesto, 1976; The Sinkiang Executive, 1978. Under pseudonym Caesar Smith: Heatwave, 1957 (filmed). Under pseudonym Roger Fitzalan: A Blaze of Arms, 1967. Under pseudonym Howard North: Expressway, 1973; The Paragon (Night Stop, USA), 1974. *Recreations:* chess, reading, travelling, astronomy. *Address:* Ocotillo Grove, Fountain Hills, Arizona 85268, USA. *T:* (602)837-1484.

TREVOR, Kenneth Rowland Swetenham, CBE 1964 (OBE 1952); DSO 1945; Brigadier (retired 1966); *b* 15 April 1914; 2nd *s* of late Mr and Mrs E. S. R. Trevor, formerly of The Acres, Upton Heath, Chester; *m* 1941, Margaret Baynham, *er d* of late Reverend J. H. Baynham, ACG; two *s. Educ:* Rossall; RMC, Camberley. Joined 22nd (Cheshire) Regt, 1934; served in India and with RWAFF in Nigeria. War of 1939-45 (despatches and DSO): No. 1 Commando, N Africa and Burma, 1941-45, as CO, 1943-45; Staff College, Camberley, 1945-46; Bde Major, 29 Infantry Brigade Group, 1949-51; served Korea, 1950-51 (despatches, OBE); GSO1 and Chief Instructor, RMA, Sandhurst, 1954-56; Commanded 1st Bn Cheshire Regt, 1956-58; Malaya, 1957-58 (despatches); Deputy Commander, 50 Infantry Brigade Group/Central Area, Cyprus, 1959; Brigade Col Mercian Brigade, 1960-61; Commander, 2 Infantry Brigade Group and Devon/Cornwall Sub District, 1961-64; Commander, British Guiana Garrison, 1963; Inspector of Boys' Training (Army), 1964-66; Vice-Pres., The Commando Assoc. *Recreation:* golf. *Address:* Barrelwell Hill, Chester. *Club:* Army and Navy.

TREVOR, Meriol; Author; *b* 15 April 1919; *d* of Lt-Col Arthur Prescott Trevor and Lucy M. E. Trevor (*née* Dimmock). *Educ:* Perse Girls' Sch., Cambridge; St Hugh's Coll., Oxford. FRSL. *Publications:* novels: The Last of Britain, 1956; The New People, 1957; A Narrow Place, 1958; Shadows and Images, 1960; The City and the World, 1970; The Holy Images, 1971; The Fugitives, 1973; The Two Kingdoms, 1973; The Marked Man, 1974; The Enemy at Home, 1974; The Forgotten Country, 1975; The Fortunate Marriage, 1976; *poems:* Midsummer, Midwinter, 1957; *biography:* Newman: The Pillar of the Cloud, 1962; Newman: Light in Winter, 1962; Apostle of Rome, 1966; Pope John, 1967; Prophets and Guardians, 1969; The Arnolds, 1973; also books for children. *Address:* 70 Pulteney Street, Bath, Avon BA2 4DL.

TREVOR, William, (William Trevor Cox); writer; *b* 24 May 1928; *er s* of J. W. Cox; *m* 1952, Jane, *yr d* of C. N. Ryan; two *s. Educ:* St Columba's College, Co. Dublin; Trinity College, Dublin. Mem., Irish Acad. Letters. Television plays include: The Mark-2 Wife; O Fat White Woman; The Grass Widows; The General's Day; Love Affair, etc. Allied Irish Banks: Award for Literature, 1976. *Publications:* A Standard of Behaviour, 1956; The Old Boys, 1964 (Hawthornden Prize; as play, produced Mermaid, 1971); The Boarding-House, 1965; The Love Department, 1966; The Day We Got Drunk on Cake, 1967; Mrs Eckdorf in O'Neill's Hotel, 1969; Miss Gomez and the Brethren, 1971; The Ballroom of Romance, 1972; Going Home (play), 1972; A Night with Mrs da Tanka (play), 1972; Marriages (play), 1973; Elizabeth Alone, 1973; Angels at the Ritz, 1975 (RSL award); The Children of Dynmouth, 1976 (Whitbread Award). *Address:* Stentwood House, Dunkeswell, Honiton, Devon.

TREVOR COX, Major Horace Brimson, *o s* of late C. Horace Cox, Roche Old Court, Winterslow, Wilts and formerly of Whitby Hall, nr Chester; *m* 1957, Gwenda Mary, *d* of Alfred Ellis, Woodford, Essex; one *d. Educ:* Eton; Germany and USA. Major late Welsh Guards (SR); served in France with BEF, 1939-40, and on General Staff, 1940-44; Major AA Comd. HQ, 1944-46, RARO, 1946-61. Studied commercial and political conditions in Germany, 1927-29, in America and Canada, 1929-30, and in Near East (Egypt and Palestine), 1934; contested (C) NE Derbyshire, 1935, Stalybridge and Hyde, 1937; MP (C) County of Chester, Stalybridge and Hyde, 1937-45; Parliamentary Private Secretary to: Rt Hon. Sir Ronald Cross when Under-Secretary Board of Trade, 1938-39, and when Minister of Economic Warfare, 1939-40; Minister of Health Rt Hon. H. U. Willink, 1945. Hon. Treasr, Russian Relief Assoc., 1945-47. Contested (C) Stalybridge and Hyde, 1945, Birkenhead, 1950; Parly Candidate (C) for Romford and Brentwood, Essex, 1953-55; contested (Ind) Salisbury by-election, 1965; later joined Labour Party; contested (Lab): RDC, Wilts, 1970; Wilts CC, 1973. Mem. Fabian Soc. Member of Exec. County Committee, British Legion, Wilts, 1946-62; Chm., Salisbury and S Wilts Branch, English-Speaking Union, 1957-63; Mem. Exec. Cttee, CLA, for Wilts, Hants, IoW and Berks. Farmer and landowner. Lord of Manor of East Winterslow. *Address:* Roche Old Court, Winterslow, Wilts. *Club:* Brooks's.

TREVOR JONES, Alan; *see* Jones.

TREVOR-ROPER, Hugh Redwald; Regius Professor of Modern History, Oxford, since 1957; *b* 15 January 1914; *er s* of Dr B. W. E. Trevor-Roper, Glanton and Alnwick, Northumberland; *m* 1954, Lady Alexandra Howard-Johnston, *e d* of late Field-Marshal Earl Haig, KT, GCB, OM. *Educ:* Charterhouse; Christ Church, Oxford. Research Fellow Merton Coll., 1937-39.

Student of Christ Church, Oxford, 1946-57; Censor 1947-52. Dir, Times Newspapers Ltd, 1974-. Chevalier, Legion of Honour, 1975. *Publications:* Archbishop Laud, 1940; The Last Days of Hitler, 1947; The Gentry, 1540-1640, 1953; (ed) Hitler's Table Talk, 1953; (ed with J. A. W. Bennett) The Poems of Richard Corbett, 1955; Historical Essays, 1957; (ed) Hitler's War Directives, 1939-45, 1964; (ed) Essays in British History Presented to Sir Keith Feiling, 1964; The Rise of Christian Europe, 1965; Religion, The Reformation and Social Change, 1967; (ed) The Age of Expansion, 1968; The Philby Affair, 1968; The European Witch-Craze of the 16th and 17th Centuries, 1970; The Plunder of the Arts in the Seventeenth Century, 1970; Princes and Artists, 1976; A Hidden Life, 1976. *Address:* Oriel College, Oxford; 8 St Aldate's, Oxford; Chiefswood, Melrose. *Clubs:* Savile, Beefsteak; New (Edinburgh).
See also Earl Haig, P. D. Trevor-Roper.

TREVOR-ROPER, Patrick Dacre, MA, MD, BChir Cantab; FRCS, DOMS England; Consultant Ophthalmic Surgeon: Westminster Hospital, since 1947; Moorfields Eye Hospital; King Edward VII Hospital for Officers; Teacher of Ophthalmology, University of London; *b* 1916; *yr s* of Dr B. W. E. Trevor-Roper, Alnwick, Northumberland; unmarried. *Educ:* Charterhouse (senior classical schol.); Clare Coll., Cambridge (exhibitioner); Westminster Hospital Medical Sch. (scholar). Served as Captain, NZ Medical Corps, 1943-46, in Central Mediterranean Forces. Held resident appointments, Westminster Hospital and Moorfields Eye Hospital. Examiner for diploma of Ophthalmology, RCS. Member: Ophth. Group Cttee, BMA; Ophth. Services Cttee, London Exec. Council; London Med. Cttee; Chm., Ophth. Qualifications Cttee; Founder Mem., Internat. Acad. of Ophthalmology, 1976; FRSocMed (Pres., Ophthalmol Sect. June 1978-); FZS; FRGS; Hon. Member Brazilian Society of Ophthalmology, 1958; Hon. dipl., Peruvian and Columbian Societies of Otolaryngology and Ophthalmology, 1958; President, etc., of various clubs in connection with sports, music and drama, both hospital and county. *Publications:* (ed) Music at Court (Four 18th century studies by A. Yorke-Long), 1954; Ophthalmology, a Textbook for Diploma Students, 1955, new edn 1962; Lecture-notes in Ophthalmology, 1959, 5th rev. edn 1976; (ed) International Ophthalmology Clinics VIII, 1962; The World Through Blunted Sight: an inquiry into the effects of disordered vision on character and art, 1971, new edn 1972; The Eye and Its Disorders, 1973; (ed) Recent Advances in Opthalmology, 1975; miscellaneous articles in medical and other journals; Editor, Trans Ophthalmological Society UK, 1949-; Mem. Editorial Board, Modern Medicine, Annals of Ophth., The Broadway. *Recreations:* music, travel. *Address:* 3 Park Square West, Regent's Park, NW1. *T:* 01-935 5052; Long Crichel House, near Wimborne, Dorset. *Clubs:* Athenæum, Beefsteak.
See also H. R. Trevor-Roper.

TREW, Peter John Edward, MICE; Director, Rush & Tompkins Group Ltd, since 1973; *b* 30 April 1932; *s* of Antony Trew, DSC; *m* 1955, Angela, *d* of Kenneth Rush, CBE; two *s* one *d*. *Educ:* Diocesan Coll., Rondebosch, Cape. Royal Navy, 1950-54; served HMS Devonshire, Unicorn and Charity. Awarded Chartered Inst. of Secretaries Sir Ernest Clarke Prize, 1955. MP (C) Dartford, 1970-Feb. 1974; Jt Sec., Cons. Parly Finance Cttee, 1972-74; Mem., Select Cttee on Tax Credits, 1972-73. Contested (C) Dartford, Gen. Elec., 1966. Mem. Council, CBI, 1975-. ACIS. *Address:* Great Oaks, Shipbourne, Kent. *T:* Plaxtol 739. *Club:* Naval and Military.

TREWBY, Vice-Adm. Sir (George Francis) Allan, KCB 1974; Manager, Messrs Foster Wheeler Limited; *b* Simonstown, S Africa, 8 July 1917; *s* of late Vice-Admiral G. Trewby, CMG, DSO, and of Dorothea Trewby (*née* Allan); *m* 1942, Sandra Coleridge Stedham; two *s. Educ:* RNC, Dartmouth; RNEC, Keyham; RNC, Greenwich. Naval Cadet, Dartmouth, 1931 (King's Dirk, 1934). Served in HMS: Frobisher, Barham, Nelson, Duke of York, Dido, Cadiz, Albion. Comdg Officer, HMS Sultan, 1963-64; IDC, 1965; Captain of Naval Base, Portland, 1966-68; Asst Controller (Polaris), MoD, 1968-71; Chief of Fleet Support and Member of Board of Admiralty, 1971-74. Commander, 1950; Captain, 1959; Rear-Adm., 1968; Vice-Adm., 1971. Naval ADC to HM the Queen, 1968. CEng; FIMechE; FIMarE; FBIM; Akroyd Stuart Award of InstMarE for 1954-55. *Recreations:* swimming; Past Captain Navy Athletics Team. *Address:* 2 Radnor Close, Henley-on-Thames RG9 2DA. *T:* Henley 77260. *Clubs:* Ebury Court; Phyllis Court (Henley).

TREWIN, John Courtenay; FRSL; dramatic critic and author; *b* 4 Dec. 1908; *o s* of Captain John Trewin, The Lizard, Cornwall, and Annie (*née* James); *m* 1938, Wendy Monk; two *s. Educ:* Plymouth Coll. Editorial Staff: Western Independent, 1926-32;

The Morning Post, London, 1932-37; second dramatic critic, 1934-37. Contributor to The Observer, 1937-; editorial staff, 1942-53; Literary Editor, 1943-48; second dramatic critic, 1943-53. Dramatic critic: Punch, 1944-45; John o' London's, 1945-54; The Illustrated London News, 1946-; The Sketch, 1947-59; The Lady, 1949-; The Birmingham Post, 1955-; Radio-drama critic of The Listener, 1951-57; Editor: The West Country Magazine, 1946-52; Plays of the Year series (46 vols), 1948-; The Year's Work in the Theatre (for the British Council), 1949-51. President, The Critics' Circle, 1964-65; Chairman, W Country Writers' Assoc., 1964-73. Devised (with David Toguri) Farjeon Reviewed, Mermaid Theatre, 1975. *Publications:* Shakespeare Memorial Theatre, 1932; The English Theatre, 1948; Up From The Lizard, 1948; We'll Hear a Play, 1949; (with H. J. Willmott) London-Bodmin, 1950; Stratford-upon-Avon, 1950; The Theatre Since 1900, 1951; The Story of Bath, 1951; Drama 1945-50, 1951; Down To The Lion, 1952; (with E. M. King) Printer to the House, 1952; A Play To-night, 1952; (with T. C. Kemp) The Stratford Festival, 1953; Dramatists of Today, 1953; Edith Evans, 1954; (ed) Theatre Programme, 1954; Mr Macready, 1955; Sybil Thorndike, 1955; Verse Drama Since 1800, 1956; Paul Scofield, 1956; The Night Has Been Unruly, 1957; Alec Clunes, 1958; The Gay Twenties: A Decade of the Theatre, 1958; Benson and the Bensonians, 1960; The Turbulent Thirties, 1960; A Sword for A Prince, 1960; John Neville, 1961; The Birmingham Repertory Theatre, 1963; Shakespeare on the English Stage, 1900-1964, 1964; completion of Lamb's Tales, 1964; Drama in Britain, 1951-64, 1965; (with H. F. Rubinstein) The Drama Bedside Book, 1966; (ed) Macready's Journals, 1967; Robert Donat, 1968; The Pomping Folk, 1968; Shakespeare's Country, 1970; (with Arthur Colby Sprague) Shakespeare's Plays Today, 1970; Peter Brook, 1971; (ed) Sean: memoirs of Mrs Eileen O'Casey, 1971; I Call My Name (verse pamphlet), 1971; Portrait of Plymouth, 1973; Long Ago (verse pamphlet), 1973; Theatre Bedside Book, 1974; Tutor to the Tsarevich, 1975; (ed) Eileen, 1976; The Edwardian Theatre, 1976; Going to Shakespeare, 1977; A Cornish Name, 1978; (ed and revd) Nicoll, British Drama, 1978; ed several other books. *Recreation:* all things Cornish: a Bard of the Cornish Gorsedd (Den an Lesard). *Address:* 15 Eldon Grove, Hampstead, NW3. *T:* 01-435 0207. *Club:* Garrick.

TRIAS, Dr Juan Manuel S.; *see* Sucre-Trias.

TRIBE, Geoffrey Reuben, OBE 1968; Controller, Arts Division, British Council, since 1973; *b* 20 Feb. 1924; *s* of late Harry and Olive Tribe. *Educ:* Southern Grammar Sch., Portsmouth; University Coll. London (BA). Served War, Royal Hampshire Regt (Lieut), 1942-45. Teaching, 1948-58. Appointed to British Council, 1958; Asst Regional Rep., Madras, 1958-63; Regional Dir, Mwanza, 1963-65; Regional Rep., E Nigeria, 1965-67; Asst Controller, Personnel and Staff Recruitment, 1968-73. *Recreation:* sailing. *Address:* The British Council, 10 Spring Gardens, SW1A 2BN. *T:* 01-499 8011.

TRIBE, Rear-Admiral Raymond Haydn, CB 1964; MBE 1944; DL; *b* 9 April 1908; *s* of Thomas and Gillian Ada Tribe; *m* 1938, Alice Mary (*née* Golby); no *c.* Served War of 1939-45 (MBE, despatches twice). Commander, 1947; Captain, 1955; Rear-Admiral, 1962. Inspector-General, Fleet Maintenance, and Chief Staff Officer (Technical) to C-in-C Home Fleet, 1962-65; retired from Royal Navy, Sept. 1965. Distinguished Battle Service Medal of Soviet Union, 1943. CC Berks, 1970-. DL Berks, 1975. *Recreations:* gardening, painting. *Address:* Oak Cottage, Compton, near Newbury, Berks. *T:* Compton, Berks, 253. *Club:* Royal Naval and Royal Albert Yacht (Portsmouth).

TRICKER, Robert Ian; Director, Oxford Centre for Management Studies, since 1971; *b* 14 Dec. 1933; *s* of Ralph Edward Tricker, Coventry; *m* 1958, Doreen Murray; two *d. Educ:* King Henry VIII Sch., Coventry; Harvard Business Sch., USA. MA, JDipMA. Articled Clerk, Daffern & Co., 1950-55; Sub-Lt, RNVR, 1956-58; Controller, Unbrako Ltd, 1959-64; Directing Staff, Iron & Steel Fedn Management Coll., 1965; P. D. Leake Research Fellow, Oxford Centre for Management Studies, 1966-67; Barclays Bank Prof. of Management Information Systems, Univ. of Warwick, 1968-70. Vis. Fellow, Nuffield Coll., Oxford, 1971. Member: Council, ICMA, 1969-72; Management and Industrial Relations Cttee, SSRC, 1973-75; Chm., Independent Inquiry into Prescription Pricing Authority for Minister for Health, 1976. Mem., Nuffield Hosp. Management Cttee, 1972-74. FCA, FCMA. *Publications:* The Accountant in Management, 1967; Strategy for Accounting Research, 1975; Management Information and Control Systems, 1976. *Address:* Oxford Centre for Management Studies, Kennington, Oxford. *T:* Oxford 735422. *Club:* Naval.

TRICKETT, (Mabel) Rachel; Principal, St Hugh's College, Oxford, since Aug. 1973; *b* 20 Dec. 1923. *Educ:* Lady Margaret Hall, Oxford, 1942-45. BA Hons 1st Cl. in English; MA 1947. Asst to Curator, Manchester City Art Galleries, 1945-46; Asst Lectr in English, Univ. of Hull, 1946-49; Commonwealth Fund Fellow, Yale Univ., 1949-50; Lectr in English, Hull Univ., 1950-54; Fellow and Tutor in English, St Hugh's Coll., Oxford, 1954-73. *Publications:* The Honest Muse (a study in Augustan verse), 1967; *novels:* The Return Home, 1952; The Course of Love, 1954; Point of Honour, 1958; A Changing Place, 1962; The Elders, 1966; A Visit to Timon, 1970. *Address:* St Hugh's College, Oxford. *T:* Oxford 57341.

TRILLO, Rt. Rev. Albert John; *see* Chelmsford, Bishop of.

TRIMBLE, Brigadier (retired) Arthur Philip, CBE 1961; Deputy Surgeon, The Royal Hospital, Chelsea, 1964-76; Consultant Physician, Army Medical Services; *b* 21 Aug. 1909; *s* of Melville and Florence Trimble, Holywood, Co. Down, N Ireland; *m* 1952, Felicia, *d* of W. H. Friend, Bures, Suffolk; two *s*. *Educ:* St Columba's Coll., Co. Dublin; Queen's Univ., Belfast. MB 1931; MD; FRCPE. Joined RAMC, 1931. Served in Syrian, Western Desert, and Italian Campaigns, 1939-45; SMO 2nd Armoured Brigade. Consultant Physician: FarELF, 1953-56; BAOR, 1957-62; Near ELF, 1963. *Publications:* various articles on tropical diseases and diseases of children in Proc. Royal Society Med., Trans Royal Society of Tropical Med., Archives of Disease in Childhood and Journal of RAMC. *Recreation:* golf. *Address:* Sherbourne Cottage, Edwardstone, Suffolk.

TRIMLESTOWN, 19th Baron *cr* 1461; **Charles Aloysius Barnewall;** *b* 2 June 1899; *o* surv. *s* of 18th Baron and Margaret (*d* 1901), *d* of R. J. Stephens, Brisbane, Queensland; *S* father, 1937; *m* 1st, 1926, Muriel (*d* 1937), *o c* of Edward Oskar Schneider, Mansfield Lodge, Whalley Range, Manchester; two *s* one *d*; 2nd, 1952, Freda Kathleen Watkins, *d* of late Alfred Watkins, Ross-on-Wye. *Educ:* Ampleforth. Lieut, Irish Guards, 1918; served European War. *Heir: s* Hon. Anthony Edward Barnewall [*b* 2 Feb. 1928; *m* 1977, Mary W., *er d* of late Judge Thomas F. McAllister]. *Address:* Tigley, Dartington, Totnes, Devon.

TRINDER, Sir (Arnold) Charles, GBE 1969; Kt 1966; *b* 12 May 1906; *s* of Arnold Anderson Trinder, Oxshott; *m* 1st, 1929, Elizabeth Cairns; one *d*; 2nd, 1937, Elaine Chaytor; two *d*. *Educ:* Wellington Coll.; Clare Coll., Cambridge (MA (Hons)). Entered Trinder Anderson & Co., 1927; Sen. Partner, 1940-53; Chm., 1953-72; Consultant, 1972-76. Member, Baltic Exchange, 1928, Hon. Member, 1973. Common Councilman, 1951; Alderman of Aldgate, 1959-76; Sheriff, City of London, 1964; Lord Mayor of London for 1968-69. Chm., London Broadcasting Co. Ltd, 1972-74. Chairman: Family Welfare Assoc., 1967-73; Missions to Seamen (London Reg.), 1972-76. Member: Board of Governors, Museum of London; Court, The City University (Chancellor, 1968-69); Trustee, Morden Coll., Blackheath, 1972. Prime Warden, Worshipful Company of Shipwrights, 1973; Master, Worshipful Company of Fletchers, 1966. FICS 1963. Hon. DSc, City Univ., 1968. KStJ 1969. Order of Merit, Chile, 1965; Nat. Order of Niger, 1969; Order of Merit, Italy, 1969; Order of Lion of Finland, 1969. *Publication:* O Men of Athens, 1946. *Recreations:* gardening, astronomy, ancient history, logodaedaly. *Address:* Hoo End Farm, Whitwell, Herts. *Clubs:* Royal Automobile, City Livery, Guildhall.

TRINDER, Air Vice-Marshal Frank Noel, CB 1949; CBE 1944; psa; *b* 24 Dec. 1895; *s* of Alfred Probus Trinder, MRCS, LRCP, Parkstone, Dorset; *m* 1925, Marjorie Agnes Scott, *d* of Archie Scott Blake, Melrose, Scotland; one *s*. *Educ:* Epsom College. Served European War, 1914-18, with North Staffordshire Regt, 1915-17; France, 1915 (wounded); Lieut, 1916; transferred to RFC, 1917. Egypt, 1917-20; Iraq, 1920; Air Ministry, 1921-28; Staff College, 1929; Headquarters, India, 1930-35; Wing Commander, 1937; War of 1939-45 (despatches, CBE); Group Captain, 1940; Headquarters, Far East, 1938-40; USA, 1940-43; Air Commodore, 1943; Cossac Staff, 1943-44; SHAEF, 1944-45; Air Div. CCG, 1945-46; Senior Air Staff Officer, Headquarters Maintenance Command, 1947-49; Director-General of Equipment, Air Ministry, 1949-52; retired, 1952. *Address:* Broom Lodge, Teddington, Mddx. *Club:* Royal Air Force Yacht.

TRINDER, Thomas Edward, (Tommy Trinder), CBE 1975; comedian; Chairman, Fulham Football Club Ltd, 1955-76, Life President, since 1976; *b* 24 March 1909; *s* of Thomas Henry Trinder and Jean Mills. *Educ:* St Andrew's, Holborn. First London appearance, Collins's Music-hall, 1922; continued in variety, pantomimes and revues, including Band Waggon, Top of the World, Gangway, Best Bib and Tucker, Happy and Glorious, Here, There and Everywhere, Fancy Free; tours in Canada, NZ, South Africa, USA; numerous Royal Variety and Command performances; radio and TV shows. Films include: The Foreman Went to France; The Bells Go Down; Champagne Charlie. *Recreation:* Fulham Football Club.

TRING, A. Stephen; *see* Meynell, L. W.

TRIPP, John Peter, CMG 1971; HM Diplomatic Service; High Commissioner in Singapore, since 1974; *b* 27 March 1921; *s* of Charles Howard and Constance Tripp; *m* 1948, Rosemary Rees Jones; one *s* one *d*. *Educ:* Bedford Sch.; Sutton Valence Sch.; L'Institut de Touraine. Served War of 1939-45: Royal Marines, 1941-46. Sudan Political Service, 1946-54. Foreign (subsequently Diplomatic) Service, 1954-; Political Agent, Trucial States, 1955-58; Head of Chancery, Vienna, 1958-61; Economic Secretary, Residency Bahrain, 1961-63; Counsellor 1963; Political Agent, Bahrain, 1963-65; sabbatical year at Durham Univ., 1965; Amman, 1966-68; Head of Near Eastern Dept, FCO, 1969-70; Ambassador to Libya, 1970-74. *Recreations:* theatre, tennis. *Address:* c/o Foreign and Commonwealth Office, SW1. *Club:* Travellers'.

TRIPPE, Juan Terry; Hon. Director, Pan American World Airways Inc. (Chief Executive, 1926-68); Chairman or Director of other companies; *b* Seabright, New Jersey, USA, 27 June 1899; *s* of Charles White Trippe and Lucy Adeline (*née* Terry); *m* 1928, Betty Stettinius; three *s* one *d*. *Educ:* Yale Univ. (PhB). With Pan American World Airways Inc., 1927-. Member or Trustee of various organisations and societies. Holds 11 hon. degrees and has had numerous awards including United States Medal of Merit, and 26 from foreign nations. *Address:* Pan Am Building, New York, NY 10017, USA.

TRISTRAM, William John, CBE 1965; JP; Pharmaceutical Chemist; Liverpool City Council, 1934-55 (Alderman, 1944-55); appointed Hon. Alderman, 1964; *b* 6 Oct. 1896; *s* of late Rev. W. J. Tristram and Elizabeth Critchlow; *m* 1966, Philomena Mary Moylan, Drogheda. *Educ:* Scarborough High Sch.; Leeds Central High Sch.; Liverpool College of Pharmacy. Member Council Pharmaceutical Society of Great Britain, 1944-67 (President, 1952-53, FPS, 1966, Gold Medal, 1968); Hon. Treasurer and Member Executive National Pharmaceutical Union, 1936-68 (Chairman, 1943-44); Chairman, Joint Cttee for the Pharmaceutical Service, 1946-52; Member Central Health Services Council (Min. of Health), 1948-64. Vice-Chairman, Standing Pharmaceutical Advisory Cttee (Min. of Health), 1946-48 (Chairman, 1948-59); Chairman, Liverpool Licensing Cttee, 1965-70; Dep. Chairman, South Liverpool Hospitals Management Cttee, 1965-70; Liverpool Exec. Council (Min. of Health), 1948- (Chairman, 1960-64); Chairman, Liverpool Homœopathic Hospital, 1960-70. JP, Liverpool, 1938-; Lord Mayor of Liverpool, 1953-54; Dep. Lord Mayor, 1954-55. *Recreations:* cricket-watching, walking. *Address:* Childwall, 6 Westway, Heswall, Wirral, Merseyside L60 8PL. *T:* 051-342 1678. *Clubs:* National Liberal; Lyceum (Liverpool).

TRITTON, Major Sir Anthony (John Ernest), 4th Bt *cr* 1905; *b* 4 March 1927; *s* of Sir Geoffrey Ernest Tritton, 3rd Bt, CBE, and Mary Patience Winifred (*d* 1966), *d* of John Kenneth Foster; *S* father, 1976; *m* 1957, Diana, *d* of Rear-Adm. St J. A. Micklethwait, CB, DSO, and *d* of Clemence Penelope Olga Welby-Everard; one *s* one *d*. *Educ:* Eton. Commissioned 3rd Hussars, Oct. 1945; retired as Major, 1962, The Queen's Own Hussars. *Recreations:* shooting, fishing. *Heir: s* Jeremy Ernest Tritton, *b* 6 Oct. 1961. *Address:* Stanton House, Highworth, Wilts. *T:* Highworth 762923. *Club:* Cavalry and Guards.

TRITTON, Julian Seymour, FICE, FIMechE, MConsE; Consulting Engineer; retired from practice in the firm of Rendel, Palmer & Tritton (Partner, 1929-55; Consultant, 1955-65); *b* Calcutta, 31 Oct. 1889; *er s* of late Sir Seymour Tritton, KBE; *m* 1918, Theodora, *er d* of late Canon W. G. Kerr, Truro; one *s* one *d*. *Educ:* Rugby Sch.; King's Coll., University of London. Served European War, 1914-18; commissioned RE in Transportation Branch at WO, and later in Afghanistan Campaign; War of 1939-45: Technical Adviser to India Supply Mission in Washington. Was in charge of firm's Calcutta Branch, 1929-32. President, Instn of Locomotive Engineers, 1947 and 1951; Chairman, Assoc. of Consulting Engineers, 1953-54 and 1955-56; President International Federation of Consulting Engineers (FIDIC), 1955-63 (Hon. Member, 1963); President, Diesel Engineers' and Users' Association, 1962-63; Fellow and Silver Medallist, Royal Society of Arts. *Publications:* Presidential addresses and technical papers before Instn of Locomotive Engineers, Royal Society of Arts, and British Assoc. for Advancement of Science. *Recreations:* golf, bowls. *Address:* St Aubyn's, Oakshade Road, Oxshott, Surrey. *T:* Oxshott 2490. *Clubs:* Athenæum, Royal Automobile.

TRIVEDI, Sir Chandulal Madhavlal, KCSI 1945 (CSI 1941); Kt 1945; CIE, 1935; OBE 1931; LLD (hon. causa) Punjab University; Hon. DLitt Andhra University, 1955; Padma Vibhushan, 1956; *b* 2 July 1893; *m* 1906, Kusum Trivedi (Kaisar-i-Hind Gold Medal). *Educ:* Elphinstone Coll., Bombay; Bombay Univ. (BA, 1913); St John's Coll., Oxford. Entered Indian Civil Service, 1917; Under Sec. to Govt of CP and Berer; Dep. Sec. and Officiating Jt Sec. to Govt of India, Home Dept; Comr in various divs in CP and Berar; Chief Secretary to Government of CP and Berar; Addl. Secretary, Dept of Communications, Government of India, March-June 1942; Secretary, War Dept, Government of India, New Delhi, until 1946; Governor of Orissa, 1946-47; Governor of Punjab (India), 1947-53; Governor of Andhra, 1953-56; Governor of Andhra Pradesh, 1956-57; Member, Indian Planning Commission, 1957-Sept. 1963; Dep. Chairman, Planning Commission, Oct.-Dec. 1963; Arbitrator for UP and Bihar Boundary, Government of India, Jan.-Aug. 1964; Chairman, Madhya Pradesh Police Commn, 1964-65. Chancellor, Gujarat Ayurvedic Univ.; President, Bharat Scouts and Guides, 1967-73. *Address:* Chandra-Bhuvan, Kapadwanj, Gujarat State, India.

TROLLOPE, Sir Anthony Owen Clavering, 16th Bt, *cr* 1642; *b* 15 Jan. 1917; *s* of Sir Gordon Clavering Trollope, 15th Bt; *S* father, 1958; *m* 1942, Joan Mary Alexis, *d* of Alexis Robert Gibbs, Manly, New South Wales; two *s.* Served War of 1939-45: 2nd/5th Australian Field Regt, Royal Australian Artillery, Middle East and New Guinea. Director, Thomas C. Denton and Co. Pty Ltd. JP for State of NSW. *Heir: s* Anthony Simon Trollope, *b* 1945. *Address:* Clavering, 77 Roseville Avenue, Roseville, NSW 2069, Australia.

TROTMAN-DICKENSON, Dr Aubrey Fiennes; Principal, University of Wales Institute of Science and Technology, Cardiff, since 1968; Member, Welsh Council, since 1971; *b* 12 Feb. 1926; *s* of Edward Newton Trotman-Dickenson and Violet Murray Nicoll; *m* 1953, Danusia Irena Hewell; two *s* one *d.* *Educ:* Winchester Coll.; Balliol Coll., Oxford. MA Oxon, BSc Oxon; PhD Manchester; DSc Edinburgh. Fellow, National Research Council, Ottawa, 1948-50; Asst Lecturer, ICI Fellow, Manchester Univ., 1950-53; E. I. du Pont de Nemours, Wilmington, USA, 1953-54; Lecturer, Edinburgh Univ., 1954-60; Professor, University College of Wales, Aberystwyth, 1960-68; Vice-Chancellor, Univ. of Wales, 1975-77. Chm., Job Creation Programme, Wales, 1975-. Mem., Planning and Transport Res. Adv. Council, DoE, 1975-. Tilden Lectr, Chem. Soc., 1963. *Publications:* Gas Kinetics, 1955; Free Radicals, 1959; Tables of Bimolecular Gas Reactions, 1967; (ed) Comprehensive Inorganic Chemistry, 1973; contrib. to learned journals. *Address:* Radyr Chain, Llantrisant Road, Cardiff CF5 2PW. *T:* Cardiff 563263.

TROTT, Charles Edmund, MBE 1946; FIB, FCIS; Vice-Chairman, Banque Belge, since 1974; Director: Belgian and General Investments Ltd, since 1974; Midland Bank Ltd, since 1971; *b* 3 Dec. 1911; *s* of late Charles Edmund and Florence Katherine Trott; *m* 1938, Edith Maria Willson; two *d.* *Educ:* County Sch., Tottenham. BCom(London). Served War, RAF, 1941-46. Entered Midland Bank, 1929; Jt Gen. Manager, 1960; Asst Chief Gen. Manager, 1967; Dep. Chief Gen. Manager, 1969; Chief Gen. Manager, 1972-74. Dir, Midland Bank Executor and Trustee Co. Ltd, 1972-. Hon. Treas., British Drama League, 1950-58; Governor, Ashridge Management Coll., 1965-74; Member: Nat. Savings Cttee, 1968-74; Council, CBI, 1975-. *Recreations:* theatre, music, walking. *Address:* 61 Fairacres, Roehampton Lane, SW15 5LY. *T:* 01-876 1791. *Clubs:* Roehampton, Royal Air Force.

TROTTER, Neville Guthrie; MP (C) Tynemouth, since Feb. 1974; FCA; JP; *b* 27 Jan. 1932; *s* of Captain Alexander Trotter and Elizabeth Winifred Trotter (née Guthrie). *Educ:* Shrewsbury; King's Coll., Durham (BCom). Short service commn in RAF, 1955-58. Partner, Thornton Baker & Co., Chartered Accountants, 1962-74, now Consultant. Mem., Newcastle City Council, 1963-74 (Alderman, 1970-74; Chm., Finance Cttee, Traffic Highways and Transport Cttee, Theatre Cttee). Mem., Civil Aviation Authority Airline Users Cttee. JP Newcastle upon Tyne 1973. Mem., Tyne and Wear Metropolitan Council, 1973-74; Vice-Chm., Northumberland Police Authority, 1970-74. Vice-Chm., Cons. Parly Shipping and Shipbuilding Cttee; Mil. Sec., Cons. Parly Aviation Cttee; Mem., Industry Sub-Cttee, Select Cttee on Expenditure. Former Mem.: Northern Economic Planning Council; Tyne Improvement Commn; Tyneside Passenger Transport Authority; Industrial Relations Tribunal. Mem. Council, RUSI. *Recreation:* travel to outlandish places. *Address:* (home) Granville House, 12 Granville Road, Newcastle upon Tyne NE2 1TP. *T:* 812916; (office) Alliance House, Hood Street, Newcastle upon Tyne NE1 6LB. *T:* 612631. *Club:* Junior Carlton.

TROUBRIDGE, Sir Peter, 6th Bt, *cr* 1799; RN retired; Member of the Stock Exchange, since 1970; Partner with Hedderwick, since 1974; *b* 6 June 1927; *s* of late Vice-Admiral Sir T. H. Troubridge, KCB, DSO, and Lily Emily Kleinwort; *S* cousin, 1963; *m* 1954, Hon. Venetia Daphne Weeks; one *s* two *d.* *Educ:* Eton; Cambridge. Served Korean War, 1952-53, HMS Ocean; retired from RN (Lt-Comdr), 1967. OStJ 1973. *Recreations:* shooting, gardening, birdwatching. *Heir: s* Thomas Richard Troubridge, *b* 23 Jan. 1955. *Address:* The Manor House, Elsted, Midhurst, West Sussex. *T:* Harting 286. *Clubs:* White's, City of London, MCC.

TROUGHTON, Sir Charles (Hugh Willis), Kt 1977; CBE 1966; MC 1940; TD 1959; Chairman, British Council, since 1977; Chairman, Electric & General Investment Co., since 1977; Director, Wm Collins and Sons, since 1977; Member, Design Council, since 1975; *b* 27 Aug. 1916; *o s* of late Charles Vivian and Constance Scylla Troughton; *m* 1947, Constance Gillean Mitford, *d* of Colonel Philip Mitford, Berryfield House, Lentran, Inverness-shire; three *s* one *d.* *Educ:* Haileybury Coll.; Trinity Coll., Cambridge. BA 1938. Joined TA, 1938; served War of 1939-45, Oxford and Bucks Light Infantry; Prisoner of War, 1940-45. Called to the Bar, 1945. Dir, 1949-77 and Chm., 1972-77, W. H. Smith & Son (Holdings) Ltd; former Director: Equity & Law Life Assce Soc. Ltd; Barclays Bank UK Management Ltd; Thomas Tilling Ltd. Member Board of Management of NAAFI, 1953-73; Governor, LSE, 1976-. Mem. Council, RCA, 1977-. *Recreations:* reading, fishing, shooting. *Address:* Woolleys, Hambleden, Henley-on-Thames, Oxfordshire. *T:* Hambleden 244. *Clubs:* MCC, Boodles.

TROUGHTON, Henry Lionel, BSc(Eng), CEng, FIMechE, MIEE; Deputy Director, Projects and Research, Military Vehicles and Engineering Establishment, Ministry of Defence, 1970-74; *b* 30 March 1914; *o s* of late Henry James Troughton; *m* 1940, Dorothy Janet Louie (née Webb); one *d.* *Educ:* Mill Hill Sch.; University Coll., London. War of 1939-45: commissioned REME (Major), 1940-47; Fighting Vehicles Research and Development Estabt, 1947 (now Mil. Vehicles and Engineering Estabt); Asst Dir (Electrical), later Asst Dir (Power Plant), and Dep. Dir (Vehicles), 1960, retired 1974. *Recreations:* gardening, travel. *Address:* White Gable, Kingsley Avenue, Camberley, Surrey. *T:* Camberley 22422.

TROUP, Alistair Mewburn; a Recorder of the Crown Court, since 1977; *b* 23 Nov. 1927; *s* of William Annandale Troup, MC, MD, and Margaret Loïs Troup; *m* 1st, 1952, S. B. Wylde (marr. diss. 1963); three *d*; 2nd, 1963, C. F. Hancock (marr. diss. 1968); one *s*; 3rd, 1969, M. C. Hutchinson. *Educ:* Merchant Taylor's School; New College, Oxford; BA. Served Army, 1946-48. Called to the Bar, Lincoln's Inn, 1952; Overseas Civil Service (Legal), 1955-64; Member: Panel of Counsel for Courts Martial Appeals Court, 1970-; Panel of Counsel for Comrs of Customs and Excise at VAT Tribunals, 1973-; Inspector for DTI, Hartley-Baird Ltd Inquiry, 1974. *Recreations:* golf, gardening. *Address:* 109 Barkston Gardens, SW5. *T:* 01-370 2606.

TROUP, Sir Anthony; see Troup, Sir J. A. R.

TROUP, Vice-Adm. Sir (John) Anthony (Rose), KCB 1975; DSC and Bar; Flag Officer, Scotland and Northern Ireland and NATO Commander Norlant, 1974-77; *b* 18 July 1921; *s* of late Captain H. R. Troup, RN and N. M. Troup (née Milne-Thompson); *m* 1st, 1943, B. M. J. Gordon-Smith (marr. diss. 1952); two *s* one *d*; 2nd, 1953, C. M. Hope; two *s* one *d.* *Educ:* Naut. Trng Coll., HMS Worcester, 1934; RNC Dartmouth, 1936; served in HMS Cornwall, 1939; in submarines, 1941-45 (DSC and Bar, despatches), 1st Lieut Turbulent and i/c Strongbow; Staff Course, and Staff of Flag Officer Submarines, 1953-55; Exec. Officer Aircraft Carrier, HMS Victorious, 1956-59; Naval Asst to 1st Sea Lord, 1959-61; comd 3rd Submarine Sqdn, 1961-63; Dir of Naval Equipment, 1963-65; Captain of the Fleet (Home), 1965-66; comd HMS Intrepid, 1966-68; Flag Officer Sea Training and in comd HM Naval Base Portland, 1969-71; Comdr Far East Fleet, 1971; Flag Officer Submarines and NATO Comdr Submarines, Eastern Atlantic, 1972-74. Comdr 1953; Captain 1959; Rear-Adm. 1969; Vice-Adm. 1972. *Recreations:* sailing, shooting, painting. *Address:* Bridge Gardens, Hungerford, Berks. *T:* Hungerford 2742. *Clubs:* Army and Navy; Royal Yacht Squadron.

TROUT, Sir H(erbert) Leon, Kt 1959; FASA; Director of several Companies; Solicitor; *b* 12 Feb. 1906; *s* of late Walter John Trout and Margaret Alice Trout; *m* 1936, Peggy Elaine Hyland. *Educ:* Brisbane Grammar Sch. Fed. President, Australian Automobile Assoc., 1946; President, Brisbane Chamber of Commerce, 1953-56; Fed. President, Associated Chambers of Commerce of Australia, 1956-59; Member of Exports Payment

Insurance Corporation, 1958; Member of Manufacturers' Industries Advisory Council, 1958. President, Liberal Party of Queensland, 1953-57. President, Queensland National Art Gallery Society, 1951-54; Chairman of Trustees, Queensland Art Gallery; President, Queensland Musical Literary self-aid Society for the Blind, 1938-45. Active service overseas with RAAF, War of 1939-45; commissioned rank, Queensland Cameron Highlanders. *Recreations:* golf and bowls. *Address:* Everton House, Dargie Street, Everton Park, Brisbane, Queensland 4053, Australia. *Clubs:* Brisbane (President, 1955, 1956); Royal Queensland Yacht; (Hon. Life Member) Royal Automobile of Queensland (President, 1946, 1947, 1948).

TROWBRIDGE, George William Job, CBE 1969; CEng; Deputy Managing Director, Wickman Ltd, Coventry, since 1966; *b* 21 July 1911; *s* of George Clarke Trowbridge and Thirza Lampier Trowbridge (*née* Dingle); *m* 1938, Doris Isobel Morrison (decd); one *s*. *Educ:* Southall Technical Coll. Works Manager, Gays (Hampton) Ltd, 1938-45; Works Dir, Kingston Instrument Co. Ltd, 1945-52; Wickman Ltd, Coventry, 1952-: London Area Manager, 1952-57; General Sales Manager, 1957—62; General Sales Dir, 1962-64; Man. Dir, Machine Tool Sales Ltd, 1964-; Dep. Chm., Wickman Machine Tools (Overseas) Ltd, 1966-; Director: Wickman Machine Tool Mfg Co. Ltd, 1962-; Wickman Lang Ltd, Johnstone, 1964-; John Brown & Co. Ltd, 1969-; Machine Tools (India) Ltd, Calcutta, 1976-; W. Billinton & Co. Ltd, Calcutta, 1976-; Drury Wickman Ltd, Johannesburg, 1976-; Wickman (Australia) Ltd, Melbourne, 1976-; Chairman: Wickman Scrivener Ltd, Birmingham, 1966-; John Stirk & Sons Ltd, Halifax, 1966-; Kitchen & Walker Ltd, Halifax, 1966-; Coventry Machine Tool Works Ltd, Halifax, 1966-; Taylor & Challen Ltd, Birmingham, 1967-. President: Machine Tool Trades Assoc., 1975-77; Comité Européen de Coopération des Industries de la Machine-Outil, 1975-77; Member: Engrg Industries Council; Economic Develt Cttee for Machine Tools, 1968-. MIProdE. *Publications:* A Handbook for Marketing Machinery, 1970; A Financial Study of British Machine Tool Companies, 1974. *Recreations:* walking, fishing. *Address:* 100 Kenilworth Road, Coventry CV4 7AH. *T:* Coventry 62775. *Club:* Institute of Directors.

TROWBRIDGE, Martin Edward O'Keeffe, CEng; FIChemE; Director General, Chemical Industries Association, since 1973; *b* 9 May 1925; *s* of late Edward Stanley Trowbridge and Ida Trowbridge (*née* O'Keeffe); *m* 1946, Valerie Ann Glazebrook; one *s*. *Educ:* Royal College of Science and City and Guilds College, Imperial Coll., London; Amer. Management Assoc. Coll., NYC. BSc Eng (Chem. Eng), ACGI; Dip. Bus. Studies. FRSA. Technical Officer, ICI (Billingham Div.) Ltd, 1946-48; Division Manager, HWP/Fluor, 1948-53; Technical Dir, Sharples Centrifuges, 1953-57; Man. Dir, Sharples Centrifuges, 1957-59; Group Managing Director: Sharples International Corp., 1959-63; Pennwalt International Corp., 1963-72; Pegler-Hattersley Ltd, 1972-73. Member: Process Plant Working Party, NEDO, 1970-77; Chemicals EDC, NEDO, 1973-; Process Plant EDC, NEDO, 1977-; Conseil d'Administration/CEFIC, Brussels, 1973-. *Publications:* Centrifugal Purification of Oils for Marine Service, 1960; Scaling Up Centrifugal Separation Equipment, 1962; Centrifugation, 1966; Exhibiting for Profit, 1969; Market Research and Forecasting, 1969; The Financial Performance of Process and Plant Companies, 1970; contribs to Chemical Engineer, Chemistry in Britain, Gems, Engineering and Process Economics, etc. *Recreations:* shooting, mineralogy, gastronomic mycology. *Address:* Alembic House, Albert Embankment, SE1 7TU. *Clubs:* East India, Devonshire, Sports and Public Schools; Frensham Gun, Old Woking Gun (Surrey).

TROWBRIDGE, Rear-Adm. Sir Richard (John), KCVO 1975; Flag Officer Royal Yachts, 1970-75; *b* 21 Jan. 1920; *s* of A. G. Trowbridge, Andover, Hants; *m* 1955, Anne Mildred Perceval; two *s*. *Educ:* Andover Grammar Sch.; Royal Navy. Joined RN as Boy Seaman, 1935. War of 1939-45: commissioned as Sub Lieut, Dec. 1940 (despatches Aug. 1945). Comdr, 1953; commanded Destroyer Carysfort, 1956-58; Exec. Officer, HMS Bermuda, 1958-59, and HMS Excellent, 1959-60; Captain, 1960; commanded Fishery Protection Sqdn, 1962-64; completed course IDC, 1966; commanded HMS Hampshire, 1967-69; Rear-Adm., 1970. An Extra Equerry to the Queen, 1970-. Younger Brother of Trinity Hse, 1972. *Recreations:* fishing, sailing, golf; most outdoor pursuits. *Address:* Old Idsworth Garden, Finchdean, Portsmouth. *T:* Rowlands Castle 2714. *Club:* Army and Navy.

TROYAT, Henri; Légion d'Honneur; writer; Member of the French Academy, 1959; *b* Moscow, 1 Nov. 1911; *m* 1948, Marguerite Saintange; one *s* one *d*. *Educ:* Paris. *Publications:* novels: l'Araigne (Prix Goncourt, 1938); Les Semailles et les Moissons (5 vols); Tant que la Terre durera (3 vols); La Lumière

des Justes (5 vols); biographies: Pushkin, Dostoievsky, Tolstoi, Gogol. *Address:* Académie Française, Quai de Conti, Paris.

TRUBSHAW, (Ernest) Brian, CBE 1970 (OBE 1964); MVO 1948; FRAeS; Director of Flight Test, British Aircraft Corporation Ltd (Commercial Aircraft Division); *b* 29 Jan. 1924; *s* of late Major H. E. Trubshaw, DL, and Lumly Victoria (*née* Carter); *m* 1973, Mrs Yvonne Edmondson, *widow* of Richard Edmondson, and *d* of late J. A. Clapham, Harrogate, Yorks. *Educ:* Winchester College. Royal Air Force, 1942-50: Bomber Command, 1944; Transport Command, 1945-46; The King's Flight, 1946-48; Empire Flying School, 1949; RAF Flying Coll., 1949-50. Joined Vickers-Armstrongs (Aircraft) Ltd as Experimental Test Pilot, 1950; Dep. Chief Test Pilot, 1953; Chief Test Pilot, 1960; Company renamed British Aircraft Corp. (Operating) Ltd, Weybridge Division, 1964. Warden, Guild of Air Pilots, 1958-61; Fellow, Society Experimental Test Pilots, USA. FIWM. Derry and Richards Memorial Medal, 1961 and 1964; Richard Hansford Burroughs Memorial Trophy (USA), 1964; R. P. Alston Memorial Medal, 1964; Segrave Trophy, 1970; Air League Founders' Medal, 1971; Iven C. Kinchloe Award, USA, 1971; Harmon Aviation Trophy, 1971; Bluebird Trophy, 1973; French Aeronautical Medal, 1976. *Recreations:* cricket, golf. *Address:* Northland Cottage, Tetbury, Glos. *T:* Tetbury 52410. *Club:* Royal Air Force.

TRUDEAU, Rt. Hon. Pierre Elliott; PC, FRSC, QC; MP (Canada); Prime Minister of Canada and Leader of the Liberal Party of Canada, since April 1968; *b* Montreal, 8 Oct. 1919; *s* of Charles-Emile Trudeau and late Grace Elliott; *m* 1971, Margaret, *d* of James Sinclair and Kathleen Bernard; three *s*. *Educ:* Jean-de-Brébeuf College, Montreal; University of Montreal; Harvard University; Ecole des Sciences Politiques, Paris; London School of Economics. Called to Bar, Quebec, 1943; practised law, Quebec; co-founder of review Cité Libre; Associate Professor of Law, University of Montreal, 1961-65. Elected to House of Commons, 1965; Parliamentary Secretary to Prime Minister, Jan. 1966-April 1967; Minister of Justice and Attorney General, April 1967-July 1968. Mem., Bars of Provinces of Quebec and Ontario; QC 1969. Founding Member, Montreal Civil Liberties Union. Hon. LLD, Univ. of Alberta, 1968; Dr *hc* Duke Univ., 1974. Hon. Fellow, LSE, 1969; Freeman of City of London, 1975. *Publications:* La Grève de l'Amiante, 1956; (with Jacques Hébert) Deux Innocents en Chine Rouge, 1961 (Two Innocents in Red China, 1969); Le Fédéralisme et la Société canadienne-française, 1968 (Federalism and the French Canadians, 1968); Réponses, 1968. *Recreations:* swimming, ski-ing, flying, scuba diving, canoeing. *Address:* Prime Minister's Residence, 24 Sussex Drive, Ottawa, Canada.

TRUEMAN, Prof. Edwin Royden; Beyer Professor of Zoology, University of Manchester, since 1974; *b* 7 Jan. 1922; *s* of late Sir Arthur Trueman, KBE, FRS, and Lady (Florence Kate) Trueman (*née* Offler); *m* 1945, Doreen Burt; two *d*. *Educ:* Bristol Grammar Sch.; Univ. of Glasgow. DSc Glasgow, MSc Manchester. Technical Officer (Radar), RAF, 1942-46. Asst Lectr and Lectr, Univ. of Hull, 1946-58, Sen. Lectr and Reader, 1958-68; Dean, Faculty of Science, Univ. of Hull, 1954-57; Prof. of Zoology, Univ. of Manchester, 1969-74; R. T. French Vis. Prof., Univ. of Rochester, NY, 1960-61; Nuffield Travelling Fellowship in Tropical Marine Biology, Univ. of West Indies, Jamaica, 1968-69. *Publications:* Locomotion of Soft-bodied Animals, 1975; articles on animal locomotion, littoral physiology and Mollusca. *Address:* 31 Stoneheads, Whaley Bridge, Stockport SK12 7BB. *T:* Whaley Bridge 2222.

TRUFFAUT, François; Director of films; *b* Paris 17ème, France, 6 Feb. 1932; *s* of Roland Truffaut and Janine Truffaut (*née* de Monferrand); *m* 1957, Madeleine Morgenstern; two *d*. Reporter, film critic, 1954-58; Director of films, 1957, Producer, 1961; *productions include:* Les Mistons, 1958; Les Quatre Cents Coups, 1959 (prize, Cannes Film Festival); Tirez sur le Pianiste, 1960; L'Amour à 20 ans, 1962; Jules et Jim, 1961; La Peau Douce, 1963; Fahrenheit 451, 1966; La Mariée était en Noir, 1967; Baisers Volés, 1968; La Sirène du Mississipi, 1969; L'Enfant Sauvage, 1969; Domicile Conjugal, 1970; Les Deux Anglaises et le Continent, 1971; Une Belle Fille comme Moi, 1972; La Nuit Américaine, 1973; L'Histoire d'Adèle H., 1975; L'Argent de Poche, 1976; L'Homme qui aimait les femmes, 1977; La Chambre Verte, 1978. *Publications:* Hitchcock, 1966; Les Adventures d'Antoine Doinel, 1970; Les Films de ma Vie, 1975; L'Histoire d'Adèle H., 1975; L'Argent de Poche, 1976; L'Homme qui aimait les femmes, 1977. *Address:* 5 rue Robert-Estienne, Paris 8ème, France.

TRURO, Bishop of, since 1973; **Rt. Rev. Graham Douglas Leonard;** *b* 8 May 1921; *s* of late Rev. Douglas Leonard, MA; *m*

1943, Vivien Priscilla, *d* of late M. B. R. Swann, MD, Fellow of Gonville and Caius Coll., Cambridge; two *s*. *Educ:* Monkton Combe Sch.; Balliol Coll., Oxford. Hon. Sch. Nat. Science, shortened course. BA 1943, MA 1947. Served War, 1941-45; Captain, Oxford and Bucks Light Infantry; Army Operational Research Group (Ministry of Supply), 1944-45. Westcott House, Cambridge, 1946-47. Deacon 1947, Priest 1948; Vicar of Ardleigh, Essex, 1952-55; Director of Religious Education, Diocese of St Albans, 1955-58; Hon. Canon of St Albans, 1955-57; Canon Residentiary, 1957-58; Canon Emeritus, 1958; General Secretary, Nat. Society, and Secretary, C of E Schools Council, 1958-62; Archdeacon of Hampstead, Exam. Chaplain to Bishop of London, and Rector of St Andrew Undershaft *w* St Mary Axe, City of London, 1962-64; Bishop Suffragan of Willesden, 1964-73. Chairman: C of E Cttee for Social Work and the Social Services, 1967-76; C of E Board for Social Responsibility, 1976-; Mem., Churches Unity Commn, 1977-. An Anglican Mem., Commn for Anglican Orthodox Jt Doctrinal Discussions; one of Archbp of Canterbury's Counsellors on Foreign Relns, 1974. Elected delegate, 5th Assembly WCC, Nairobi, 1975. Entered House of Lords, 1977. Select Preacher to University of Oxford, 1968. President: Middlesex Assoc., 1970-73; Corporation of SS Mary and Nicholas (Woodard Schools), 1973-. DD (*hc*) Episcopal Seminary, Kentucky, 1974. *Publications:* Growing into Union (jt author), 1970; The Gospel is for Everyone, 1971; contrib. to: The Christian Religion Explained, 1960; Retreats Today, 1962; Communicating the Faith, 1969; A Critique of Eucharistic Agreement, 1975; various pamphlets and reviews. *Recreations:* reading, especially biographies; music. *Address:* Lis Escop, Truro, Cornwall. *T:* Devoran 862657. *Club:* Army and Navy.
See also Sir M. M. Swann.

TRURO, Dean of; *see* Lloyd, Very Rev. Henry Morgan.

TRUSCOTT, Sir Denis (Henry), GBE 1958; Kt 1953; TD 1950; President of Brown Knight and Truscott Ltd; *b* 9 July 1908; *s* of Henry Dexter Truscott, JP, and Evelyn Metcalf Truscott (*née* Gibbes); *m* 1932, Ethel Margaret, *d* of late Alexander Lyell, of Gardyne Castle, Guthrie, Angus, and Mrs Lyell; four *d*. *Educ:* Bilton Grange; Rugby Sch.; Magdalene Coll., Cambridge. Joined family firm of Jas. Truscott & Son Ltd, printers, 1929; Director, 1935; Chairman, 1951-66, of Brown, Knight & Truscott Ltd (amalgamation of Jas. Truscott & Son Ltd with Wm Brown & Chas. Knight Ltd, 1936). Director: Bedford General Insurance Co. Ltd; Zurich Life Assurance Society Ltd (Chm., 1974-). Elected to Court of Common Council, City of London, 1938, for Ward of Dowgate; Deputy, 1943; Alderman: Dowgate Ward, 1947-73; Bridge Without Ward, 1973-; Sheriff of City of London, 1951-52; Lord Mayor of London, 1957-58; one of HM Lieutenants, City of London, 1943-. Master Worshipful Company of Vintners, 1955-56; Master Worshipful Company of Musicians, 1956-57, 1970-71; Master, Guild of Freemen of the City of London, 1957; Master of Worshipful Company of Stationers and Newspaper Makers, 1959-60. Treasurer, St Bartholomew's Hospital Voluntary Bd; Mem., Bd of Governors, Royal Hospital and Home for Incurables, Putney; Chairman Trustees Rowland Hill Benevolent Fund; Member Exec. Cttee, Automobile Assoc.; President, Printing and Allied Trades Research Assoc., 1956-64; President, Institute of Printing, 1961-63; Chairman, Squash Racquets Assoc. of England, 1961-74. Grand Officer of Order of Merit, Italian Republic; Grand Cross of Merit of Order of Merit, Republic of Germany. *Recreations:* lawn tennis, golf. *Address:* Ivermark, 30 Drax Avenue, Wimbledon, SW20. *T:* 01-946 6111. *Clubs:* United Oxford & Cambridge University, Royal Automobile, City Livery, All England Lawn Tennis, MCC.

TRUSCOTT, Sir George (James Irving), 3rd Bt *cr* 1909; Company Director; *b* 24 Oct. 1929; *s* of Sir Eric Homewood Stanham Truscott, 2nd Bt, and Lady (Mary Dorcas) Truscott (*née* Irving) (*d* 1948); *S* father, 1973; *m* 1962, Yvonne Dora (*née* Nicholson); one *s* one *d*. *Educ:* Sherborne School. *Heir:* *s* Ralph Eric Nicholson Truscott, *b* 21 Feb. 1966. *Address:* BM QUILL, WC1V 6XX.

TRUSS, Leslie S.; *see* Seldon-Truss.

TRUSTED, Sir Harry Herbert, Kt 1938; QC; *b* 27 June 1888; *s* of the Rev. Wilson Trusted; *m* Mary, *d* of Sir Marshall Warmington, KC, 1st Bt; two *s* three *d*. *Educ:* Ellesmere Coll.; Trinity Hall, Cambridge. Called to Bar, Inner Temple, 1913; served overseas (Duke of Cornwall's Light Infantry and Staff), 1914-19; Puisne Judge, Supreme Court, Leeward Islands, 1925-27; Attorney-General, Leeward Islands, 1927-29; Attorney-General, Cyprus, 1929-32; Attorney-General, Palestine, 1932-37; Chief Justice, Palestine, 1937-41; Chief Justice, FMS, 1941-45; Chairman, Malayan Union and Singapore Salaries

Commission, 1947; Commissioner to inquire into disturbances at Aden, 1948; special duty with Foreign Office (FOAAT), 1951-53; sat as Divorce Commissioner, 1953-63. *Address:* Broomhill Court, Esher Close, Esher, Surrey. *T:* Esher 67368.

TRUSTRAM EVE; *see* Eve, family name of Baron Silsoe.

TRUSWELL, Prof. (Arthur) Stewart, MD, FRCP; Head of Department of Nutrition, Queen Elizabeth College, London University, since 1971; *b* 18 Aug. 1928; *s* of George Truswell and Molly Truswell (*née* Stewart-Hess); *m* 1956, Sheila Elspeth (*née* McGregor); four *s*. *Educ:* Ruthin Sch., Clwyd; Liverpool and Cape Town Univs. MB, ChB 1952, MD 1959; MFCM 1974, FRCP 1975. Registrar in Pathology, Cape Town Univ., 1954; Registrar in Med., Groote Schuur Hosp., 1955-57; Research Bursar, Clin. Nutrition Unit, Dept. of Med., Cape Town Univ., 1958 and 1959; Adams Meml Trav. Fellowship to London, 1960; Sen. Fellow, Clin. Nutrition, Tulane Univ., USA, 1961; Res. Officer, Clin. Nutrition Unit, Cape Town Univ., 1962; Sen. Mem., Scientific Staff, MRC Atheroma Research Unit, Western Infirmary, Glasgow, 1963 and 1964; full-time Lectr, then Sen. Lectr in Med. and Consultant Gen. Physician, Cape Town Univ. and Groote Schuur Hosp., 1965-71; Warden of Med. students' Residence, Cape Town Univ., 1967-69. Member, numerous cttees, working parties, editorial bds and socs related to nutrition; Mem., Royal Soc. Med. *Publications:* Human Nutrition and Dietetics, 6th edn (with S. Davidson, R. Passmore, J. F. Brock), 1975; numerous research papers in sci. jls on various topics in human nutrition and medicine. *Recreations:* gardening, walking (esp. on mountains), running. *Address:* 59 Hazlewell Road, Putney, SW15 6UT. *T:* 01-788 6396.

TRYON, family name of Baron Tryon.

TRYON, 3rd Baron *cr* 1940, of Durnford; **Anthony George Merrik Tryon;** Director of Lazard Bros & Co. Ltd and other companies; *b* 26 May 1940; *s* of 2nd Baron Tryon, PC, GCVO, KCB, DSO, and of Etheldreda Josephine, *d* of Sir Merrik Burrell, 7th Bt, CBE; *S* father, 1976; *m* 1973, Dale Elizabeth, *d* of Barry Harper; one *s* one *d*. *Educ:* Eton. Page of Honour to the Queen, 1954-56. Captain Wessex Yeomanry, 1972. Dir, Lazard Bros & Co. Ltd, 1976; Chairman, English & Scottish Investors Ltd, 1977. *Recreations:* fishing and shooting. *Heir:* *s* Hon. Charles George Barrington Tryon, *b* 15 May 1976. *Address:* 30 Walton Street, SW3 1RE. *T:* 01-589 0967. *Clubs:* Boodle's, Pratt's.

TRYPANIS, Constantine Athanasius, MA (Oxon); DLitt (Oxon) 1970; DPhil (Athens); FRSL; Minister of Culture and Science, Government of Greece, since 1974; *b* Chios, 22 Jan. 1909; *s* of Athanasius G. Trypanis and Maria Zolota; *m* 1942, Alice Macri; one *d*. *Educ:* Chios Gymnasium; Universities of Athens, Berlin and Munich. Classical Lecturer, Athens Univ., 1939-47; Bywater and Sotheby Professor of Byzantine and Modern Greek Language and Literature, and Fellow of Exeter Coll., Oxford, 1947-68; Emeritus Fellow, 1968-; Univ. Prof. of Classics, Chicago Univ., 1968-74. FRSL, 1958; Life Fellow, International Institute of Arts and Letters, 1958; Member Institute for Advanced Study, Princeton, USA, 1959-60; Visiting Professor: Hunter Coll., New York, 1963; Harvard Univ., 1963, 1964; Univ. of Chicago, 1965-66; Univ. of Cape Town, 1969. Corresp. Mem., Inst. for Balkan Studies (Greece); Member: Athens Academy, 1974 (Corres. Mem., 1971); Medieval Acad. of America. Hon. Fellow, Internat. Poetry Soc., 1977. Dr of Humane Letters *hc*: MacMurray Coll., USA, 1974; Assumption Coll., 1977. Archon Megas Hieromnemon of the Oekumenical Patriarchate. *Publications:* Influence of Hesiod upon Homeric Hymn of Hermes, 1939; Influence of Hesiod upon Homeric Hymn on Apollo, 1940; Alexandrian Poetry, 1943; Tartessos, 1945; Medieval and Modern Greek Poetry, 1951; Pedasus, 1955; Callimachus, 1956; The Stones of Troy, 1956; The Cocks of Hades, 1958; (with P. Maas) Sancti Romani Melodi Cantica, 1963, vol. II, 1970; Pompeian Dog, 1964; The Elegies of a Glass Adonis, 1967; Fourteen Early Byzantine Cantica, 1968; (ed) The Penguin Book of Greek Verse, 1971; The Glass Adonis, 1973; The Homeric Epics, 1975; articles in classical and literary periodicals. *Recreations:* walking, tennis, painting. *Address:* Ministry of Culture and Science, Athens, Greece.

TRYTHALL, Rear-Adm. John Douglas, CB 1970; OBE 1953; *b* 21 June 1914; *er s* of Alfonso Charles Trythall, Camborne, and Hilda Elizabeth (*née* Monson); *m* 1943, Elizabeth Loveday (*née* Donald); two *s* two *d*. *Educ:* Stretford Grammar Sch. Cadet, 1931; appointments in Home Fleet, America and West Indies, East Indies. Lent to RNZN, 1939; Battle of River Plate; Western Approaches; BJSM, Washington; Pacific; Hong Kong; Mediterranean. Secretary to: Second Sea Lord, C-in-C The

Nore, and C-in-C Plymouth; Asst Director of Plans, 1960-62; Captain of the Fleet, Medit., 1964-65; Head of Personnel Panel, MoD, 1966-67; subseq. on MoD Cttee; Asst Chief, Personnel and Logistics, MoD, 1969-72. JSSC, 1953; IDC, 1963. Commander, 1949; Captain, 1959; Rear-Admiral, 1968; retired 1972. FCIS 1956. Comr, St John Ambulance in Somerset, 1975. OStJ 1973. *Address:* The Old Vicarage, Corfe, Taunton, Som. *T:* Blagdon Hill 463. *Club:* MCC.

TSIBU DARKU, Nana Sir, Kt 1948; OBE 1945 (MBE 1941); *b* 19 March 1902; *s* of late Adrian Nicholas de Heer of Elmina, and late Effuah Tekyiwa (*née* Hagar Dadson), Cape Coast and Fanti Nyankumasi; *m* 1930, Maud, *d* of late Daniel Sackey, Accountant, PWD, Gold Coast; nine *s* nine *d. Educ:* African Methodist Episcopal Zion Mission Sch., Cape Coast; SPG Grammar Sch. (now Adisadel Coll.), Cape Coast. Served in Junior Service Political Administration, 1923-30; elected Paramount Chief of Asin Atandaso, Gold Coast (now Ghana), West Africa, 18 Nov. 1930; abdicated 18 Nov. 1951; re-elected Paramount Chief of Asin Atandaso Traditional Area, 13 Aug. 1962. Provincial Member Gold Coast Legislative Council, 1932-51; Sen. Unofficial Member of the Legislature, 1943-51; Member Governor's Exec. Council, Gold Coast, 1943-51. Served on various Government Cttees, including University Council of the Gold Coast and Coussey Cttee on Constitutional Reforms; attended African Conf., London, 1948. Dir, Messrs Guinness Ghana Ltd, 1969. Member: Adisadel College Board of Governors; Mfantsipim School Board of Management; Aggrey Secondary Sch. Board of Governors. Member, Cape Coast Municipal Council, 1954-59; Chairman, Tema Develt Corp., 1954-59; Chairman, Ghana Cocoa Marketing Board, 1959-66; Chairman, Kwame Nkrumah Trust Fund (Central Collection Cttee), 1959-66 (Chairman Trustees, 1960-66). Silver Jubilee Medal, 1935; Coronation Medal, 1937; King's Medal for African Chiefs, 1939. *Address:* PO Box 19, Fanti Nyankumasi, via Cape Coast, Ghana.

TS'ONG, Fou; *see* Fou Ts'ong.

TUAM, Archbishop of, (RC), since 1969; **Most Rev. Joseph Cunnane;** *b* 5 Oct. 1913; *s* of William and Margaret Cunnane, Knock, Co. Mayo. *Educ:* St Jarlath's Coll., Tuam; St Patrick's Coll., Maynooth. BA 1st Hons, Ancient Classics, 1935; DD 1941; Higher Dip. Educn 1941. Priest, 1939. Prof. of Irish, St Jarlath's Coll., 1941-57; Curate, Balla, Co. Mayo, 1957-67; Curate, Clifden, Co. Galway, 1967-69. Cross of Chaplain Conventual, SMO Malta, 1970. *Publications:* Vatican II on Priests, 1967; contribs to Irish Ecclesiastical Record, Furrow, Doctrine and Life, Studies in Pastoral Liturgy, etc. *Address:* Archbishop's House, Tuam, Co. Galway, Ireland. *T:* Tuam 24166.

TUAM, KILLALA and ACHONRY, Bishop of, since 1970; **Rt. Rev. John Coote Duggan;** *b* 7 April 1918; *s* of Rev. Charles Coote Whittaker Duggan, BD and Ella Thackeray Duggan (*née* Stritch); *m* 1948, Mary Elizabeth Davin; one *s* one *d* (and one *d* decd). *Educ:* High School, Dublin; Trinity Coll., Dublin (Schol.). Moderator (1st cl.) Men. and Moral Sci., 1940; Bernard Prize, Div. Test. (2nd cl.); BA 1940; BD 1946. Deacon 1941; Priest 1942. Curate Asst: St Luke, Cork, 1941-43; Taney, Dublin, 1943-48; Hon. Clerical Vicar, Christ Church Cath., 1944-48; Incumbent: Portarlington Union, Kildare, 1948-55; St Paul, Glenageary, Dublin, 1955-69; Westport and Achill Union, Tuam, 1969-70; Archdeacon of Tuam, 1969-70. Exam. Chaplain to Archbp of Dublin, 1958-69; Examiner in BD Degree, Univ. of Dublin, 1960-69. Editor, Irish Churchman's Almanack, 1958-69. *Publication:* A Short History of Glenageary Parish, 1968. *Recreation:* fishing. *Address:* Bishop's House, Knockglass, Crossmolina, Co. Mayo. *T:* Crossmolina 17. *Club:* Kildare Street and University (Dublin).

TUBBS, Francis Ralph, CBE 1960; MSc, PhD, ARCS, DIC, FIBiol; Leverhulme Research Fellow, John Innes Institute, since 1969; *b* 8 Oct. 1907; *s* of William Edward and Elizabeth Clara Tubbs; *m* 1939, Helen Beatrice Alice Green; two *s* two *d. Educ:* Hackney Downs School; Imperial College of Science. Forbes Medallist, 1928; Research at Rothamsted, 1928-30; Plant Physiologist, Tea Research Institute of Ceylon, 1930-48; Dir, East Malling Research Station, 1949-69. On active service, 1939-45, Lt-Col RARO, The Durham Light Infantry. Officer Order of Orange Nassau, 1946; Chevalier Order of Leopold II, avec Palme, 1946; Croix de Guerre, 1940, avec Palme, 1946. *Publications:* in scientific journals. *Recreations:* gardening and sailing. *Address:* Hayletts, Barton Turf, Norwich NR12 8AZ; The John Innes Institute, Colney, Norwich NR4 7UH.

TUBBS, Oswald Sydney, FRCS; Consulting Surgeon: in Cardiothoracic Surgery, St Bartholomew's Hospital; to Brompton Hospital; *b* 21 March 1908; *s* of late Sydney Walter Tubbs, The Glebe, Hadley Common, Hertfordshire; *m* 1934, Marjorie Betty Wilkins (*d* 1976); one *s* one *d. Educ:* Shrewsbury School; Caius College, Cambridge; St Bartholomew's Hospital. MA, MB, BCh, FRCS. Surgical training at St Bartholomew's Hosp. and Brompton Hosp. Dorothy Temple Cross Fellowship, spent as Surgical Fellow at Lahey Clinic, Boston, USA. Served War of 1939-45, in EMS. Consulting Chest Surgeon to Royal Navy, Papworth Village Settlement and to various Local Authorities. President: Soc. of Thoracic and Cardiovascular Surgeons of GB and Ireland, 1971-72; Thoracic Soc., 1973. *Publications:* papers on surgical subjects. *Recreations:* fishing and gardening. *Address:* The White Cottage, 136 Coast Road, West Mersea, Colchester, Essex CO5 8PA. *T:* Colchester 382355.

TUBBS, Ralph, OBE 1952; FRIBA; Architect; *b* 9 Jan. 1912; *s* of late Sydney W. Tubbs and Mabel Frost; *m* 1946, Mary Taberner; two *s* one *d. Educ:* Mill Hill School; Architectural Assoc. School (Hons Dip.). Sec. MARS Group (Modern Architectural Research), 1939; Member: Council and Executive Committee of RIBA, 1944-50, re-elected Council, 1951; Vice-Pres. Architectural Assoc., 1945-47; Associate Institute of Landscape Architects, 1942-. Member Presentation Panel and Design Group for 1951 Festival of Britain, and architect of Dome of Discovery in London Exhibn (then the largest dome in world, 365 ft diam.). Other works include: Baden-Powell House for Boy Scouts' Assoc., London; Indian Students' Union building, Fitzroy Sq., London; Granada TV Centre and Studios, Manchester; Cambridge Inst. Educn; Ramsay Hall for University Coll., London, Residential Areas at Harlow and Basildon New Towns; Industrial Buildings. Architect for new Charing Cross Hospital, London; Consultant for Hospital Develt, Jersey, CI. *Publications:* Living in Cities, 1942; The Englishman Builds, 1945. *Recreation:* keeping five senses alert. *Address:* 46 Queen Anne Street, W1. *T:* 01-935 0694.

TUCK, Sir Bruce (Adolph Reginald), 3rd Bt, *cr* 1910; *b* 29 June 1926; *o s* of Major Sir (William) Reginald Tuck, 2nd Bt, and Gladys Emily Kettle (*d* 1966), *d* of late N. Alfred Nathan, Wickford, Auckland, New Zealand, and *widow* of Desmond Fosberry Kettle, Auckland Mounted Rifles; *S* father 1954; *m* 1st, 1949, Luise (marr. diss., in Jamaica, 1964), *d* of John C. Renfro, San Angelo, Texas, USA; two *s*; 2nd, 1968, Pamela Dorothy Nicholson, *d* of Alfred Nicholson, London; one *d. Educ:* Canford School, Dorset. Lieutenant, Scots Guards, 1945-47. *Heir: s* Richard Bruce Tuck, *b* 7 Oct. 1952. *Address:* Montego Bay PO Box 274, Jamaica. *Club:* Lansdowne.

TUCK, Clarence Edward Henry; Director, Civil Service Selection Board, since 1977; *b* 18 April 1925; *s* of Frederick and May Tuck; *m* 1950, Daphne Robinson; one *s* one *d. Educ:* Rendcomb Coll., Cirencester; Merton Coll., Oxford. BA 1949. Served in Royal Signals, 1943-47. Inland Revenue, 1950; Min. of Supply, 1950-55; seconded to Nigerian Federal Govt, Lagos, 1955-57; Ministry of: Supply, 1957-59; Aviation, 1959-60; Defence, 1960-62; Aviation, 1962-66; IDC, 1967; Min. of Technology, 1968-70; Trade and Industry, 1970; CSD, 1971; Trade and Industry, 1973; Dept of Energy, 1974; Civil Service Dept, 1976. Asst Principal, 1950; Principal, 1953; Asst Sec., 1962; Under-Sec., 1970. *Address:* Civil Service Selection Board, Standard House, 28 Northumberland Avenue, WC2N 5AL. *Club:* Royal Commonwealth Society.

TUCK, Maj.-Gen. George Newsam, CB 1950; OBE 1944; retired; *b* 18 Dec. 1901; *s* of Harry Newman Tuck, Burma Commn; *m* 1929, Nell (*née* Winter); three *s. Educ:* Cheltenham Coll.; RMA, Woolwich. Commissioned Royal Engineers, 1921. Egypt, 1925-30; Instructor RMA, 1930-34; Staff Coll., 1935-36; Chief Instructor (RE), RMA, 1939; GSO1, Scapa Defences, 1939-40; DDRA, 1941; CRE 46 Div., 1942; Mil. Deputy to Scientific Adviser, War Office, 1943; Comdr Army Group RE, France and Germany, 1944-45; DSP, War Office, 1946; idc, 1947; DDSD, War Office, 1948; Chief of Staff, BAOR, 1949-Dec. 1951; Engineer-in-Chief, War Office, 1952-54; Deputy Controller of Munitions, Ministry of Supply, 1954-57; retired, 1957. Col Comdt, Corps of Royal Engineers, 1958-66. *Address:* c/o Lloyds Bank, Shaftesbury, Dorset.

TUCK, Prof. John Philip; Professor of Education, University of Newcastle upon Tyne (formerly King's College, University of Durham) 1948-76, now Emeritus; *b* 16 April 1911; *s* of late William John and Annie Tuck, Uplyme, Lyme Regis; *m* 1936, Jane Adelaide (*née* Wall); two *s. Educ:* Strand School; Jesus College, Cambridge. BA Hons English and History, Class I, 1933; Cambridge certificate in Education, 1934; Adelaide Stoll Bachelor Research Scholar, Christ's College, 1935; MA 1937. English Master: Gateshead Grammar School, 1936; Manchester

Central High School, 1938; Wilson's Grammar School, 1939 and 1946. Served War of 1939-45, East Surrey Regt, and Army Education Corps, N Africa, Sicily, Italy, Austria. Lecturer in Education, King's College, Newcastle upon Tyne, 1946-48. FRSA 1970. Hon. Fellow, Coll. of Speech Therapists, 1966. *Address:* Chillingham House, Church Street, Great Gransden, Sandy, Beds. *T:* Great Gransden 512.

TUCK, Raphael Herman; MP (Lab) Watford since 1964; *b* 5 April 1910; *er* and surv. *s* of late David Lionel Tuck and late Olive Tuck; *m* 1959, Monica J. L. Greaves. *Educ:* St Paul's School; London School of Economics; Trinity Hall, Cambridge; Harvard University, USA. BSc Econ. London 1936; MA Cantab 1939; LLM Harvard, 1940. British Embassy, Washington, 1940; Lecturer and later Professor of Law, University of Saskatchewan, Canada, 1941-45; Constitutional Adviser to Premier of Manitoba, 1943; Special Research, Dept of Labour, Ottawa, 1944; Prof. of Political Science, McGill Univ., Montreal, 1945-46; Prof. of Political Science, Tulane Univ., New Orleans, La, 1947-49. Barrister-at-Law, Gray's Inn, 1951. Member: Soc. of Labour Lawyers; "Justice"; Harvard Law Assoc. of UK; Harvard Club of London; Action for the Crippled Child (Watford Br.); Court, Reading Univ.; Hon. Member: Herts Chamber of Commerce; Watford Philharmonic Soc.; Vice-President: Herts Assoc.; Watford Soc. for Mentally Handicapped Children; Nat. Assoc. of Swimming Clubs for the Handicapped; Sea Lions Club of Watford for the Handicapped; Watford Community Relations Council; Watford Operatic Soc.; Abbots Langley Gilbert and Sullivan Soc. *Publications:* articles in University of Toronto Law Journal, Canadian Bar Review, Sask. Bar Review, Public Affairs, Canadian Jl of Econs and Polit. Science, Solicitor's Jl. *Recreations:* photography, music. *Address:* 10 King's Bench Walk, Temple, EC4. *T:* 01-353 3647.

TUCK, Wing Comdr Robert Roland S.; *see* Stanford-Tuck.

TUCK, Prof. Ronald Humphrey; Head of Department of Agricultural Economics, University of Reading, and Provincial Agricultural Economist (Reading Province), since 1965, now Department of Agricultural Economics and Management; *b* 28 June 1921; *s* of Francis Tuck and Edith Ann Tuck (*née* Bridgewater); *m* Margaret Sylvia Everley; one *s* two *d. Educ:* Harrow County Sch.; Corpus Christi Coll., Oxford. War Service, RAOC and REME, mainly N Africa and Italy, 1941-45 (despatches). Univ. of Reading, Dept of Agric. Economics: Research Economist, 1947-49; Lecturer, 1949-62; Reader, 1962-65; Dean, Faculty of Agriculture and Food, Univ. of Reading, 1971-74. *Publications:* An Essay on the Economic Theory of Rank, 1954; An Introduction to the Principles of Agricultural Economics, 1961 (Italian trans., 1970); reviews etc in Jl of Agric. Economics and Economic Jl. *Recreations:* reading, music, drawing, travelling, walking. *Address:* 211 Kidmore Road, Caversham, Reading, Berks. *T:* Reading 473426.

TUCKER, Prof. Archibald Norman; Professor of East African Languages, School of Oriental and African Studies, University of London, 1951-71, now Emeritus Professor; *b* Cape Town, 10 March 1904; *s* of Norman Tucker and Gertrude Sarah Tucker (*née* Matthews); *m* 1931, Elizabeth Berthe Hills; four *s* one *d. Educ:* South African College School; University of Cape Town; University of London. MA Cape Town 1926; PhD London 1929; DLit London 1949. Linguistic research in Basutoland and Transvaal for Univ. of Cape Town, 1926; Linguistic Expert to Sudan Govt for non-Arabic langs, 1929-31; joined staff of School of Oriental Studies, 1932; Linguistic Research in S Sudan and S Africa on Internat. African Inst. Fellowship, 1932-33; Dinka orthography unification for Sudan Govt, 1938. Conscientious objector during War of 1939-45; foundation member of Peace Pledge Union; served in Pacifist Service Unit in E End Hosp.; subseq. active Mem., Campaign for Nuclear Disarmament. Orthographic Research for Uganda and Kenya Govts in Luganda, Kikuyu and Nilotic langs, 1946-47; launched 1949 (and supervised, 1950-51) Bantu line expedition in Belgian Congo for Internat. African Inst.; research in Uganda, Kenya, and in Southern Sudan, 1949, 1950-51; organized and directed orthography conference, W Uganda, 1954; Vis Prof., Lovanium Univ., Kinshasa, 1963; research expedition in Tanzania, Kenya, Uganda, 1965-66, in which discovered grammatical resemblances between Ik (North Uganda) and Ancient Egyptian; visited and lectured at Univs and Instns in Cape Town, Pretoria, Salisbury, Nairobi, Jerusalem, 1973; Lecture tour, Nairobi and Khartoum Univs, for Inter-Univ. Council, 1975. Mem., Exec. Council, Internat. African Inst., 1951-71; Chm., Subcommission on Place-names in Africa south of Sahara. Hon. Fellow, SOAS, 1971. *Publications:* Comparative Phonetics of Suto-Chuana, 1929, rev. and expanded edn, 1969; Primitive Tribal Music and Dancing in the Southern Sudan, 1933; The Disappointed Lion and other stories from the Bari of

Central Africa, 1938; The Eastern Sudanic Languages, Vol. I, 1941; (with Mrs E. O. Ashton) Swahili Phonetics, 1943; (with Ashton, Mulira, Ndawula) a Luganda Grammar, 1954; (with J. T. Mpaayei) a Maasai Grammar, 1955; (with M. A. Bryan) Handbook of African Languages, Vol. III, 1956, Linguistic Survey of Northern Bantu Borderland, Vol. IV, 1957; Linguistic Analyses, 1966; (with P. E. Hackett), Le groupe linguistique zande, 1959; numerous articles in Bulletin School of Oriental and African Studies, Africa, African Studies, Kongo-Overzee, Afrika und Übersee, etc. *Recreations:* photography, African music. *Address:* 76 Granville Road, Sevenoaks, Kent. *T:* Sevenoaks 52572.

TUCKER, Brian George, CB 1976; OBE 1963; Deputy Secretary, Department of Energy; Member, UKAEA, since 1976; *b* 6 May 1922; *s* of late Frank Ernest Tucker and of May Tucker; *m* 1948, Marion Pollitt; three *d. Educ:* Christ's Hospital. Entered Home Civil Service, 1939, as Clerical Officer, Admty; successive postings at home, in Africa, the Middle East, Ceylon and Hong Kong till 1953; promoted Executive Officer, 1945; Higher Executive Officer, 1949. Min. of Power, Asst Principal, 1954, Principal, 1957; seconded to HMOCS, 1957-62, Asst Sec., Govt of Northern Rhodesia; returned to MOP, 1962, Principal Private Sec. to Minister, 1965-66, Asst Sec., 1966, Under-Sec., Ministry of Technology, 1969-70, Cabinet Office, 1970-72, DTI, 1972-73; Dep. Sec., 1973. *Recreations:* gardening, music. *Address:* 1 Sondes Place Drive, Dorking, Surrey. *T:* Dorking 4720.

TUCKER, Rt. Rev. Cyril James, CBE 1975; Bishop in the Falkland Islands, since 1963; *b* 17 Nov. 1911; British; *s* of Henry Castledine and Lilian Beatrice Tucker; *m* 1936, Kathleen Mabel, *d* of Major Merry; one *s* two *d. Educ:* Highgate Sch.; St Catharine's Coll., Cambridge (MA); Ridley Hall, Cambridge. MA Oxford (by Incorporation), 1951. Deacon, 1935; Priest, 1936; Curate, St Mark's, Dalston (in charge Highgate Sch. Mission), 1935; Curate, St Barnabas, Cambridge, 1937; Youth Sec., British and Foreign Bible Soc., 1938. Chaplain, RAFVR, 1939-46. Warden of Monmouth Sch., 1946; Chaplain, Wadham Coll., Oxford, and Chaplain of the Oxford Pastorate, 1949; Vicar of Holy Trinity, Cambridge, 1957-63; Rural Dean of Cambridge, 1959-63; Chaplain of the Cambridge Pastorate, 1957-63; Bishop in Argentina and Eastern S America, 1963-75. Hon. Exec. Dir, Argentine Dio. Assoc., 1976-. *Recreations:* sailing, fishing. *Address:* Gaydon House, Thriplow, Herts. *Clubs:* Hawks (Cambridge); Hurlingham (Buenos Aires).

TUCKER, Prof. David Gordon; Senior Fellow in History of Technology, University of Birmingham, since 1974; *b* 17 June 1914; *s* of John Ferry and Frances Tucker; *m* 1945, Florence Mary Barton; three *s* one *d. Educ:* Sir George Monoux Grammar School, London; University of London. BSc, 1936; PhD, 1943; DSc, 1948. On research staff of GPO, at the PO Research Station, Dollis Hill, 1934-50; Royal Naval Scientific Service (Senior Principal Scientific Officer), 1950-55; Prof. and Head of Dept of Electronic and Electrical Engrg, Univ. of Birmingham, 1955-73. Member: Gen. Council of IERE, 1958-62 and 1965-66, Educn Cttee, 1958-65, Research Cttee, 1962-; Council of British Acoustical Soc. 1965-73 (Vice-Pres., 1967-70; Pres., 1970-73); Council, Soc. for Underwater Technology, 1967-70; National Electronics Research Council, 1963-66; Treasury Cttee on Scientific Civil Service, 1964-65; Oceanography and Fisheries Cttee, NERC, 1965-70; Cttee on History of Technology, IEE, 1970-76 (Chm., 1973-75); Adv. Cttee for Nat. Archive in Electrical Sci. and Technol. (Chm., 1973-); and of various other Univ., Government, professional and educational committees. FIERE, 1953; FIEE, 1954. Clerk Maxwell Premium of IERE, 1961. *Publications:* Modulators and Frequency-Changers, 1953; Electrical Network Theory, 1964; Circuits with Periodically-Varying Parameters, 1964; Applied Underwater Acoustics (with B. K. Gazey) 1966; Underwater Observation Using Sonar, 1966; Sonar in Fisheries: A Forward Look, 1967; papers in professional and scientific journals. *Recreation:* history of technology. *Address:* 26 Twatling Road, Barnt Green, Birmingham B45 8HT. *T:* 021-445 1820.

TUCKER, Edward William, CB 1969; Head of Royal Naval Engineering Service, 1966-70; Director of Dockyards, Ministry of Defence, at Bath, 1967-70, retired; *b* 3 Nov. 1908; *s* of Henry Tucker, Plymouth; *m* 1935, Eva, *d* of Arthur Banks, Plymouth. *Educ:* Imperial Coll. of Science and Technology, London Univ.; Royal Naval Coll., Greenwich. BSc (Eng). Electrical Engineer in Admiralty service, at Plymouth, London, Hong Kong and Bath, 1935-64; General Manager of HM Dockyard, Chatham, 1964-66. *Recreations:* gardening, golf. *Address:* Gulls Cry, Thurlestone, Kingsbridge, Devon. *T:* Thurlestone 265. *Club:* Royal Western Yacht Club of England.

TUCKER, Hon. Sir Henry (James), KBE 1972 (CBE 1946); Kt 1961; Government Leader, Executive Council, Bermuda, 1968-71; General Manager, Bank of Bermuda Ltd, Hamilton, Bermuda, since 1938; *b* 14 March 1903; *s* of Henry James and Nella Louise Tucker; *m* 1925, Catherine Newbold Barstow; two *s* one *d*. *Educ*: Saltus Grammar School, Bermuda; Sherborne School, Dorset, England. New York Trust Co., 1924-26; Kelley, Drayton and Converse (Brokers), 1926-30; Milne Munro & Tucker (Brokers), 1930-34; joined Bank of Bermuda Ltd, 1934. Pres., Anglo Norness Shipping, 1968-. *Recreation*: golf. *Address*: The Lagoon, Paget, Bermuda. *T*: 2-1657. *Clubs*: Mid-Ocean Golf, Royal Bermuda Yacht, Royal Hamilton Dinghy, Riddells Bay Golf (all in Bermuda).

TUCKER, (Henry John) Martin, QC 1975; a Recorder of the Crown Court, since 1972; *b* 8 April 1930; *s* of late P. A. Tucker, LDS, RCS and Mrs Dorothy Tucker (*née* Hobbs); *m* 1957, Sheila Helen Wateridge, LRAM; one *s* four *d*. *Educ*: St Peter's Sch., Southbourne; Downside Sch.; Christ Church, Oxford (MA). Called to Bar, Inner Temple, 1954; Dep. Chm., Somerset QS, 1971. *Recreations*: walking occasionally; gardening gently; listening to music. *Address*: Chingri Khal, Sleepers Hill, Winchester, Hants. *T*: Winchester 3927. *Club*: Hampshire (Winchester).

TUCKER, Herbert Harold, OBE 1965; Counsellor (Information) and Director, British Information Services, Canberra, since 1974; *b* 4 Dec. 1925; *o s* of late Francis Tucker and late Mary Ann Tucker; *m* 1948, Mary Stewart Dunlop; three *s*. *Educ*: Queen Elizabeth's, Lincs; Rossington Main, Yorks. Western Morning News, Sheffield Telegraph, Nottingham Journal, Daily Telegraph, 1944-51; Economic Information Unit, Treasury, 1948-49; FO, later FCO, 1951. *Recreations*: gardening, reading. *Address*: c/o British High Commission, Commonwealth Avenue, Canberra, ACT, Australia. *Clubs*: National Press, Refugees (Canberra).

TUCKER, Norman Walter Gwynn, CBE 1956; a Governor of The Royal Ballet since 1957; *b* 24 April 1910; *s* of Walter Edwin and Agnes Janet Tucker. *Educ*: St Paul's School; New College, Oxford. Solo pianist, 1935-39. Civil servant, Treasury, 1939-45 (private sec. to Sir Kingsley Wood, Sir John Anderson (later *cr* Visc. Waverley) and Hugh Dalton). Director of Opera, Sadler's Wells, 1947; Director of Sadler's Wells Theatre, 1951-66. *Recreations*: playing the piano, squash racquets.

TUCKER, Peter Louis; Chief Executive, Commission for Racial Equality, since 1977; *b* 11 Dec. 1927; *s* of Peter Louis Tucker and Marion Tucker; *m* 1st, 1955, Clarissa Mary Harleston; three *s* one *d* (and one *d* decd); 2nd, 1972, Teresa Josephine Ganda; one *s*. *Educ*: Fourah Bay Coll., Sierra Leone (MA Latin, Dunelm); Jesus Coll., Oxford (MA Jurisp.); DipEd. Called to Bar, Gray's Inn, 1970. Teacher, 1952-57; Education Officer, 1957-61; Secretary, Training and Recruitment, Sierra Leone Civil Service, 1961-63; Establishment Sec., 1963-66; Sec. to the Prime Minister and Head of Sierra Leone Civil Service, 1966-67; Asst Director, UK Immigrants Advisory Service, 1970-72; Principal Admin. Officer, Community Relations Commn, 1972-74, Dir of Fieldwork and Admin., 1974-77; Dir of Legal and Gen. Services, and Sec., Commn for Racial Equality, 1977. Papal Medal Pro Ecclesia et Pontifice, 1966. *Publications*: miscellaneous booklets and articles for Community Relations Commission. *Recreations*: tennis, photography, listening to music. *Address*: 10 Dene Road, Northwood, Middlesex HA6 2AA. *T*: Northwood 23319. *Club*: United Oxford & Cambridge University.

TUCKER, Richard Howard, QC 1972; a Recorder of the Crown Court, since 1972; *b* 9 July 1930; *s* of Howard Archibald Tucker, later His Honour Judge Tucker, and Margaret Minton Tucker; *m* 1st, 1958, Paula Mary Bennett Frost (marr. diss. 1974); one *s* two *d*; 2nd, 1975, Wendy Kate Standbrook. *Educ*: Shrewsbury Sch.; The Queen's Coll., Oxford (MA). Called to Bar, Lincoln's Inn, 1954. *Recreations*: sailing, gardening. *Address*: Dormer House, Queen's Square, Winchcombe, Glos. *T*: Winchcombe 602372.

TUCKER, Robert St John P.; *see* Pitts-Tucker.

TUCKER, William Eldon, CVO 1954; MBE 1944; TD 1951; FRCS; Honorary Orthopædic Surgeon, Royal London Homœopathic Hospital; Director and Surgeon, The Clinic, Park Street, since 1936; *b* 6 Aug. 1903; *s* of late Dr W. E. Tucker, Hamilton, Bermuda; *m* 1931, Jean Stella (marr. diss. 1953), *d* of James Ferguson, Rudgwick, Sussex; two *s*; *m* 1956, Mary Beatrice Castle. *Educ*: Sherborne; Gonville and Caius Coll., Cambridge. MA 1931; FRCS 1930; MB, BCh 1946. St George's Hospital, 1925-34; Lt RAMC, TA, 1930-34; Major RAMC,

Orthopædic Specialist, 1939-45; Lt-Col, RAMC, TA, 1946-51; Col and Hon. Col 17th General Hospital, TA, 1951-63. Surgeon, St John's Hosp., Lewisham, 1931-37; Registrar, Royal Nat. Orthop. Hosp. 1933-34; Orthopædic Consultant, Horsham Hosp., 1945, Dorking Hosp., 1956. Hunterian Prof., RCS, Oct. 1958. Sen. Fellow, British Orthopædic Assoc. Corresp. Mem., Amer. Orthopædic Assoc.; Emeritus Mem., Société Internationale de Chirugie Orthopaedique et Traumatologie. Vice-President: Surrey CCC; Amateur Dancing Assoc. Master, Co. of Makers of Playing Cards, 1976. *Publications*: Active Alerted Posture, 1960; Home Treatment in Injury and Osteoarthritis, 1961, new edn, Home Treatment and Posture in Injury, Rheumatism and Osteoarthritis, 1969; (with J. R. Armstrong) Injury in Sport, 1964. *Recreations*: tennis, Rugby football exec. (formerly Cambridge XV, Captain 1925; England XV, 1926-30); ball-room dancing. *Address*: 71 Park Street, W1. *T*: 01-629 3763. *Club*: Pilgrims.

TUCKWELL, Barry Emmanuel, OBE 1965; horn soloist; *b* 5 March 1931; *s* of Charles Tuckwell, Australia; *m* Hilary Jane, *d* of James Warburton, Australia; two *s* one *d*. *Educ*: various schs, Australia; Sydney Conservatorium. Melbourne Symph. Orch., 1947; Sydney Symph. Orch., 1947-50; Hallé Orch., 1951-53; Scottish Nat. Orch., 1953-54; Bournemouth Symphony Orch., 1954-55; London Symph. Orch., 1955-68; founded Tuckwell Wind Quintet, 1968; Mem. Chamber Music Soc. of Lincoln Center, 1974-; Horn Prof., Royal Academy of Music, 1963-74; Pres., Internat. Horn Soc., 1969-. Plays annually as soloist throughout Europe, Gt Britain, USA and Canada; has appeared at many internat. festivals; took part in 1st Anglo-Soviet Music Exchange, Leningrad and Moscow, 1963; toured: Far East, 1964 and 1975; Australia, 1970, 1973, 1976, 1977; S America, 1976; USSR, 1977. Many works dedicated to him; has made numerous recordings. Editor, complete horn literature for G. Schirmer Inc. Hon. RAM, 1966; Hon. GSM, 1967. Harriet Cohen Internat. Award for Solo Instruments, 1968; Grammy Award Nominations, 1972 and 1974. *Recreations*: photography, sailing, archaeology. *Address*: 21 Lawford Road, NW5. *T*: 01-485 2274.

TUCKWELL, Sir Edward (George), KCVO 1975; MCh, FRCS; Serjeant-Surgeon to the Queen, 1973-75 (Surgeon to the Queen, 1969-73, to HM Household, 1964-73); Surgeon, St Bartholomew's Hospital, London, 1947-75; Surgeon, Royal Masonic Hospital, 1958-75; Consultant Surgeon, King Edward VII Convalescent Home, Osborne, since 1965; *b* 12 May 1910; *e s* of Edward Henry Tuckwell and Annie Clarice (*née* Sansom); *m* 1st, 1934, Phyllis Courthope Regester (*d* 1970); two *s* one *d*; 2nd, 1971, Barbara Gordon, *widow* of Major A. J. Gordon. *Educ*: Charterhouse; Magdalen College, Oxford; St Bartholomew's Hospital. BM, BCh Oxon 1936; MCh 1948; FRCS 1939. War Service in EMS and RAMC, Surgical Specialist, North-West Europe and South-East Asia, Lt.-Col. Examiner in Surgery to Univs of London, Manchester, Oxford, and in Pathology to Conjoint Board and Royal College of Surgeons; Dean of Medical School, St Bartholomew's Hospital, 1952-57; Surgeon, King Edward VII Hospital for Officers, 1961-75. Mem., Governing Body of Charterhouse School (Chm., 1973-) (London University representative); Governor, St Bartholomew's Hosp., 1954-74. Mem. Ct of Assts, 1973-, and Freeman, Barbers' Co. *Publications*: articles in medical journals. *Recreations*: gardening, shooting, travelling. *Address*: Berthorpe, Puttenham Heath Road, Guildford, Surrey GU3 1DU. *T*: Guildford 810217; 73 Harley Street, W1. *T*: 01-935 7288. *Clubs*: Oriental; Kennel.

TUDOR, James Cameron, CMG 1970; Permanent Representative of Barbados to the United Nations, since 1976; *b* St Michael, Barbados, 18 Oct. 1919; *e s* of James A. Tudor, JP, St Michael, Barbados; unmarried. *Educ*: Roebuck Boys' Sch.; Combermere Sch.; Harrison Coll., Barbados; Lodge Sch.; (again) Harrison Coll.; Keble Coll., Oxford, 1939-43. BA Hons (Mod. Greats), 1943, MA 1948; Pres., Oxford Union, 1942. Broadcaster, BBC: Lobby Correspondent (Parliament); Overseas Service, 1942-44; Lectr, Extra-Mural Dept, Reading Univ., 1944-45; History Master, Combermere Sch., Barbados, 1946-48; Civics and History Master, Queen's Coll., British Guiana, 1948-51; Sixth Form Master, Modern High Sch., Barbados, 1952-61, also free-lance Journalist, Lectr, Broadcaster, over the same period. Mem., Barbados Lab. Party, 1951-52; MLC, Barbados, 1954-72; Foundn Mem., Democratic Lab. Party, 1955 (Gen. Sec., 1955-63; Third Vice-Chm., 1964-65 and 1965-66). Minister: of Educn, 1961-67; of State for Caribbean and Latin American Affairs, 1967-71 (Leader of the House, 1965-71); of External Affairs, 1971-72 (Leader of the Senate, 1971-72); High Comr for Barbados in UK, 1972-75. Mem. Council, Univ. of the West Indies, 1962-65; awarded US State Dept Foreign Leader Grant, to study US Educn Instns, 1962. Silver Star, Order of Christopher Columbus (Dominican

Republic), 1969. *Recreations:* reading, lecturing; keen on Masonic and other fraternities. *Address:* Permanent Mission of Barbados to the United Nations, 866 United Nations Plaza, Suite 527, New York, NY 10017, USA; Lemon Grove, Westbury New Road, St Michael, Barbados.

TUDOR DAVIES, William; *see* Davies, W. T.

TUDOR EVANS, Hon. Sir Haydn, Kt 1974; Hon. Mr Justice Tudor Evans; a Judge of the High Court of Justice, Family Division, since 1974; *b* 20 June 1920; 4th *s* of John Edgar Evans and Ellen Stringer; *m* 1947, Sheilagh Isabella Pilkington; one *s*. *Educ:* West Monmouth School; Lincoln College, Oxford. RNVR, 1940-41. Open Scholar, Lincoln Coll., Oxford (Mod. History), 1940; Stewart Exhibitioner, 1942; Final Hons Sch., Mod. History, 1944; Final Hons Sch., Jurisprudence, 1945. Scholar, Lincoln's Inn, 1946; called to the Bar, Lincoln's Inn, 1947, Bencher 1970. QC 1962; Recorder of Crown Court, 1972-74. *Address:* 30 Stanford Road, W8. *T:* 01-937 1953. *Clubs:* Garrick, MCC.

TUDOR PRICE, David William; 7th Senior Prosecuting Counsel to the Crown at the Central Criminal Court, since 1975; *b* 29 Jan. 1931; *s* of Tudor Howell Price, OBE, and Mary Tudor Price; *m* 1956, Elspeth Patricia Longwell; two *s* one *d*. *Educ:* Rugby Sch.; Magdalene Coll., Cambridge (BA). Called to Bar, Inner Temple, 1955. Prosecuting Counsel to the Post Office, 1965-69; Junior Treasury Counsel, 1972; First Junior, 1974. Mem., Royal Commn on Gambling, 1976-. *Recreation:* golf. *Address:* The Old House, Aspley Guise, Milton Keynes MK17 8HH. *T:* Woburn Sands 583053. *Clubs:* Moor Park, Woking, and Aspley Guise Golf, Woburn Golf and Country.

TUDSBERY, Marmaduke Tudsbery, CBE 1941; FCGI 1950; FICE 1932; Fellow, Imperial College of Science and Technology, London University, 1953; Hon. Member Institution of Royal Engineers, 1937; President Smeatonian Society of Civil Engineers, 1956; *b* 4 Oct. 1892; 3rd *s* of late J. H. T. Tudsbery, DSc; unmarried. *Educ:* Westminster; Imperial College, London Univ.; engineering training under late John J. Webster, FICE, and at works of Yarrow & Co. Ltd, Glasgow. Commissioned, Special Reserve of Officers, RE: France, 1915 (9th Field Company); subsequently Army of the Rhine, Mesopotamia Expeditionary Force; staff of RE Board, War Office, 1920-25; Member, later Chairman, War Office Cttee on Army Building, 1940-44; Member: Home Office Committee on Structural Precautions against Air-Attack, 1936-39; Science Museum Adv. Council, 1959-69. Governor, Imperial Coll., London Univ., 1942-71. The Civil Engineer to BBC, 1926-52; Consulting Civil Engineer to BBC, 1952-60. *Address:* Littlebourne Nursing Home, Littlebourne, Canterbury, Kent CT3 1UN. *Clubs:* Athenæum, MCC, Royal Cruising, Royal Thames Yacht.

TUFNELL-BARRETT, Hugh, CIE 1943; K-i-H Gold Medal 1938; *b* 13 Jan. 1900; *s* of late Rev. Wilfrid Tufnell-Barrett, formerly of Court Lodge, Shorne, Kent; *m* 1929, Frances Eleanor (*d* 1971), *d* of late Julian Claude Platts, Melbourne, Australia; one *s* two *d*. *Educ:* St John's School, Leatherhead; Cadet College, Wellington, India. 2nd Lieut 31st Punjabis, IA, 1918; Temporary Captain and Staff Captain, Bushire Field Force, South Persia, 1920-21; Offg Bde Major, 3rd Ind. Inf. Bde, Peshawar, 1922; resigned, 1922; entered ICS, 1923; District Magistrate, Dacca, Bengal, 1931, Bakarganj, Bengal, 1935; Joint Sec. Commerce and Labour Dept, Bengal, 1939; Addl Sec. Home Dept, Bengal, 1939; Dep. Sec. to Govt of India, Dept of Labour, 1939-43; Joint Secretary to Govt of India, Dept of Labour, April 1943; Offg Sec. to Govt of India, Dept of Labour, June 1943; Civil Representative of Bengal Govt with Eastern Army and Additional Home Sec., Bengal, Dec. 1943; Director-General, Food, and Addtl Commissioner for Civil Supplies, Bengal, 1945; entered service of Pakistan Govt, Sept. 1947; Commissioner, Chittagong Division, E Pakistan, 1947-49; Secretary, Ministry of Kashmir Affairs, Government of Pakistan, 1949-50; Chief Warden, Westminster City Council Civil Defence Force, 1952-53. General Manager, Douglas Fraser & Sons (London) Ltd, 1953-74. *Recreation:* reading. *Address:* 9c Sunderland Terrace, W2 5PA.

TUFTON, family name of **Baron Hothfield.**

TUGENDHAT, Christopher Samuel; Member, Commission of the European Communities, since 1977; *b* 23 Feb. 1937; *er s* of late Dr Georg Tugendhat; *m* 1967, Julia Lissant Dobson; two *s*. *Educ:* Ampleforth Coll.; Gonville and Caius Coll., Cambridge (Pres. of Union). Financial Times leader and feature writer, 1960-70. MP (C) City of London and Westminster South, 1974-76 (Cities of London and Westminster, 1970-74); Opposition

spokesman: for Employment, 1974-75; on Foreign and Commonwealth Affairs, 1975-76. Director: Sunningdale Oils, 1971-76; Phillips Petroleum International (UK) Ltd, 1972-76; former Consultant to Wood Mackenzie & Co., Stockbrokers. *Publications:* Oil: the biggest business, 1968; The Multinationals, 1971 (McKinsey Foundn Book Award, 1971). *Recreations:* reading, following football, conversation. *Address:* 200 Rue de la Loi, 1049 Brussels, Belgium. *Club:* Carlton.

TUITE, Sir Dennis (George Harmsworth), 13th Bt *cr* 1622; MBE 1946; Major RE, retired; *b* 26 Jan. 1904; *s* of late Hugh George Spencer Tuite and late Eva Geraldine Tuite (*née* Hatton); *S* brother, 1970; *m* 1947, Margaret Essie, *o d* of late Col Walter Leslie Dundas, DSO, late 3rd QAO Gurkha Rifles; three *s*. *Educ:* St Paul's School; RMA Woolwich. Commissioned, Royal Engineers, 1925; served in India, North West Frontier, 1928-30, Burma, 1930-32 (medal). Served War, in Europe, 1939-45; Kenya, 1948-52; retired, 1959. *Recreations:* reading, travelling, fishing. *Heir: s* Christopher Hugh Tuite, BSc [*b* 3 Nov. 1949; *m* 1976, Deborah Anne, *o d* of A. E. Martz, Pittsburgh, Pa, USA; one *s*]. *Address:* Windhaven, Ladygate Drive, Grayshott, Hindhead, Surrey GU26 6DR. *T:* Hindhead 5026.

TUKE, Anthony Favill; Chairman: Barclays Bank Ltd, since 1973 (Director, since 1965, Vice-Chairman, 1972-73); Barclays Bank International, since 1972; *b* 22 Aug. 1920; *s* of late Anthony William Tuke; *m* 1946, Emilia Mila; one *s* one *d*. *Educ:* Winchester; Magdalene Coll., Cambridge. Scots Guards, 1940-46; Barclays Bank Ltd, 1946-. Vice-President: Inst. of Bankers, 1973-; British Bankers' Assoc., 1977-; Chm., Cttee of London Clearing Bankers, 1976- (Dep. Chm., 1974-76); Pres., Internat. Monetary Conference, 1977-. Mem., Stevenage Develt Corp., 1959-64; Mem. Council, Warwick Univ., 1966-73; Treas., English-Speaking Union, 1969-73. *Recreations:* gardening, lawn tennis. *Address:* 68 Frognal, NW3 6XD. *Club:* MCC.

TUKE, Comdr Seymour Charles, DSO 1940; Royal Navy; *b* 20 May 1903; 3rd *s* of late Rear-Adm. J. A. Tuke; *m* 1928, Marjorie Alice Moller; one *s* one *d*. *Educ:* Stonyhurst; RNC, Osborne and Dartmouth. Midshipman, 1921; Lieutenant, 1926; Acting Commander, 1945; FAA, 1927-29; Local Fishery Naval Officer, English Channel, 1935-37; served War of 1939-45 (DSO, 1939-45 Medal, Atlantic Star, Italy Star, War Medal); in command of SS Hannah Boge (first prize of the war), 1939; Senior Officer Res. Fleet, Harwich, 1946; Maintenance Comdr to Senior Officer Res. Fleet, 1947-48; retired, 1948. *Address:* Henstridge House, Crudwell, Malmesbury, Wiltshire. *T:* Crudwell 283.

TULL, Thomas Stuart, CBE 1963 (OBE (mil.) 1946); DSO 1946; HM Diplomatic Service, retired 1971; *b* 11 October 1914; *surv. yr s* of late Frank Stuart Tull and of Phyllis Mary Tull (*née* Back); *m* 1946, Constance Grace Townsend; one *s* two *d* (one *step s* one *step d*). *Educ:* Rossall School; Jesus College, Oxford. Entered Indian Civil Service, 1938; served in Punjab, 1939-41; ADC to the Governor, 1941; lent to War Department, Govt of India, for service with RAF, 1941; on active service in India and SE Asia Commands, 1941-46; retired from ICS and entered HM Diplomatic Service, 1947. Foreign Office, 1947-48; First Secretary at British Legation, Berne, 1948-51; Foreign Office, 1951-53; HM Consul at San Francisco, 1953-54; HM Consul at Denver, 1954-56; Press Counsellor at British Embassy: Cairo, 1956; Berne, 1957; HM Consul-General: Gothenburg, 1958-61; Philadelphia, 1961-66; Durban, 1966-67; High Comr, Malawi, 1967-71. Mem. UK Delegn to UN 12th Gen. Assembly, 1957. *Recreations:* sailing, photography. *Address:* Hunter's Moon, Charney Road, Longworth, Abingdon, Oxon OX13 5HW. *T:* Longworth 820234. *Clubs:* Royal Air Force, Travellers', Special Forces, Royal Commonwealth Society; Philadelphia (USA).

TULLIS, Major Ramsey; Vice Lord-Lieutenant of Clackmannanshire, since 1974; farmer; *b* 16 June 1916; *s* of late Major J. Kennedy Tullis, Tullibody, Clackmannanshire; *m* 1943, Daphne Mabon, *d* of late Lt-Col H. L. Warden, CBE, DSO, Edinburgh; three *s*. *Educ:* Trinity Coll., Glenalmond; Worcester Coll., Oxford (BA). 2nd Lieut, Cameronians, 1936. Served War, 1939-45: Cameronians, Parachute Regt; Major 1943; psc 1949; retired, 1958. County Comr for Scouts, Clackmannanshire, 1958-73; apptd: an Income Tax Comr, 1964; Activities Comr, Scottish HQ, Scout Assoc., 1974; Chm. Visiting Cttee, Glenochil Detention Centre, 1974. Clackmannanshire: JP 1960, DL 1962. *Address:* Woodacre, Pool of Muckhart, by Dollar, Clackmannanshire FK14 7KW.

TUMIM, Stephen; a Recorder of the Crown Court, since 1977; Chairman, National Deaf Children's Society, since 1974 (Vice-Chairman, 1966-74); *b* 15 Aug. 1930; *yr s* of late Joseph Tumim, CBE (late Clerk of Assize, Oxford Circuit) and late Renée Tumim; *m* 1962, Winifred, *er d* of late Col A. M. Borthwick;

three *d*. *Educ:* St Edward's Sch., Oxford; Worcester Coll., Oxford (Scholar). Called to Bar, Middle Temple, 1955; practises on Oxford Circuit. *Recreation:* second-hand book-shopping. *Address:* River House, Upper Mall, Hammersmith W6 9TA. *T:* 01-748 5238. *Clubs:* Garrick, Reform.

TUNBRIDGE, Sir Ronald (Ernest), Kt 1967; OBE 1944; JP; Professor of Medicine, University of Leeds, 1946-71, now Emeritus Professor; Chairman, Standing Medical Advisory Committee, Department of Health and Social Security, 1963-72; *b* 2 June 1906; *s* of Rev. W. J. Tunbridge and Norah (*née* Young); *m* 1935, Dorothy Gregg; two *s*. *Educ:* Kingswood School, Bath; University of Leeds. Research Fellowship in Physiology, 1928; Hons degree in Physiology, BSc, 1928, MSc, 1929; MB, ChB, Hons 1931; MD 1933; MRCP 1933; FRCP 1944; numerous resident appointments in Leeds. Clinical asst for one year at St Bartholomew's Hosp., under Sir Francis Fraser; Reader in Medicine, Univ. of Leeds; Consultant to Hosps in Leeds Region. Military Service, 1941-46; Adviser in Medicine, Malta Command; Cons. in Med., BLA and BAOR, 1945-46 (despatches). FRSocMed. Member: Assoc. of Physicians of GB and Ire. (Pres., 1977-78); Heberden Soc. (serving on Council of latter, Pres., 1954 and 1955); The Diabetic Assoc. (Banting Memorial Lectr, 1953); Vice-Pres., British Diabetic Assoc.; Chairman: Governing Body of 1st and 2nd International Gerontological Congresses (Member, Governing Body of Third Internat. Congress; Chm. Brit. Organizing Cttee of Third Congress); Leeds Regional Hosp. Bd, 1947-51; Mem. Bd of United Leeds Hosps, 1952-71; Chm., Educn Cttee, 1967-72, Mem. Management Cttee, 1967-, King Edward's Hospital Fund for London; Central Health Services Council: Mem., 1959-; Vice-Chm., 1963-72; Chm., Hosp. Records Cttee, 1964; Chm., Health of Hosp. Staff Cttee, 1968; Chm., Rehabilitation Cttee, 1972. Mem. Exec. Cttee, Nat. Old People's Welfare Council (Vice-Chm. Yorkshire Council); Pres., BMA 1974 (Chm. Bd of Science, 1968-72); Vice-President: Med. Defence Union; Age Concern; Chm., Leeds Local Broadcasting Council, 1968-72; Hon. Pres., British Dietetic Assoc.; Past Pres., Brit. Spas Fedn, 1955-63; Fellow, Coll. of Physicians of Ceylon, 1973. Heberden Orator, 1956; Lectures: Proctor Meml, 1958; Frederick Price, TCD, 1969; Founder, British Council for Rehabilitation of Disabled, 1972; Fernando, (and Prize), Ceylon Coll. of Physicians, 1973. Asst Editor, Gerontolgia. JP City of Leeds, 1958. Hon. DSc: Hull, 1974; Leeds, 1975. Bobst Award, Internat. Association of Gerontology, 1957; Osler Award, Canadian Med. Assoc., 1973. *Publications:* articles in Quarterly Jl of Medicine, Lancet, BMJ, etc. *Recreation:* walking. *Address:* 9 Ancaster Road, Leeds LS16 5HH. *Club:* Athenæum.

TUNC, Prof. André Robert; Croix de Guerre 1940; Chevalier de la Légion d'Honneur 1964; Professor, University of Paris, since 1958; *b* 3 May 1917; *s* of Gaston Tunc and Gervaise Letourneur; *m* 1941, Suzanne Fortin. *Educ:* Law Sch., Paris. LLB 1937, LLM 1941. Agrégé des Facultés de Droit, 1943. Prof., Univ. of Grenoble, 1943-47; Counsellor, Internat. Monetary Fund, 1947-50; Prof., Univ. of Grenoble, 1950-58; Legal Adviser, UN Economic Commn for Europe, 1957-58. Hon. Doctorates: Free Univ. of Brussels, 1958; Cath. Univ. of Louvain, 1968; DCL Oxford, 1970; MA Cantab, 1972; Corr. FBA (London), 1974. Officier de l'Ordre d'Orange-Nassau, 1965. *Publications:* Le contrat de garde, 1941; Le particulier au service de l'ordre public, 1942; (with Suzanne Tunc) Le Système constitutionnel des Etats-Unis d'Amérique, 2 vols, 1953, 1954; (with Suzanne Tunc) Le droit des Etats-Unis d'Amérique, 1955; (with François Givord) (tome 8) Le louage: Contrats civils, du Traité pratique de droit civil français de Planiol et Ripert, 2nd edn 1956; Traité théorique et pratique de la responsabilité civile de Henri et Léon Mazeaud, 3 vols, 1957, 1958, 1960, 5th edn, and 6th edn (Vol. I) 1965; Les Etats-Unis—comment ils sont gouvernés, 1958, 3rd edn 1974; Dans un monde qui souffre, 1962, 4th edn 1968; Le droit des Etats-Unis (Que sais-je?), 1964, 3rd edn 1973; La sécurité routière, 1965; Le droit anglais des sociétés anonymes, 1971 (supp. 1975); Traffic Accident Compensation: Law and Proposals (Internat. Encycl. of Comparative Law, Vol. XI: Torts, chap. 14), 1971; Le droit américain des sociétés anonymes (roneo.), 1972; Introd. to Vol. XI: Torts (Internat. Encycl. of Comparative Law), 1974; articles in various legal periodicals. *Address:* 112 rue de Vaugirard, 75006 Paris, France.

TUNNICLIFFE, Charles Frederick, RA 1954 (ARA 1944); RE 1934; ARCA; *b* 1 Dec. 1901; *s* of William and Margaret Tunnicliffe; *m* 1929, Winifred Wonnacott, ARCA (*d* 1969). *Educ:* St James School, Nr Macclesfield; Macclesfield and Manchester Schools of Art; Royal Exhibition Scholarship to Royal College of Art, 1921; Diploma of RCA in Painting, 1923; occupied in painting, engraving, book illustrating. Gold Medal, RSPB, 1975. *Publications:* My Country Book, 1942; Bird Portraiture, 1945; Shorelands Summer Diary, 1952. *Address:* Shorelands, Malltraeth Bay, Bodorgan, Gwynedd.

TUOHY, John Francis, (Frank Tuohy); novelist; short story writer; *b* 2 May 1925; *s* of late Patrick Gerald Tuohy and Dorothy Marion (*née* Annandale). *Educ:* Stowe Sch.; King's College, Cambridge. Prof. of English Language and Literature, Univ. of São Paulo, 1950-56; Contract Prof., Jagiellonian Univ., Cracow, Poland, 1958-60; Vis. Prof., Waseda Univ., Tokyo, 1964-67; Writer-in-Residence, Purdue Univ., Indiana, 1970-71, 1976. FRSL 1965. *Publications:* The Animal Game, 1957; The Warm Nights of January, 1960; The Admiral and the Nuns, short stories (Katherine Mansfield Memorial Prize), 1962; The Ice Saints (James Tait Black and Geoffrey Faber Memorial Prizes), 1964; Portugal, 1970; Fingers in the Door, short stories (E. M. Forster Meml Award, 1972), 1970; Yeats: a biographical study, 1976. *Recreation:* travel. *Address:* c/o Macmillan and Co. Ltd, Little Essex Street, WC2.

TUOHY, Thomas, CBE 1969; Managing Director, British Nuclear Fuels Ltd, 1971-73; *b* 7 Nov. 1917; *s* of late Michael Tuohy and Isabella Tuohy, Cobh, Eire; *m* 1949, Lilian May Barnes (*d* 1971); one *s* one *d*. *Educ:* St Cuthberts Grammar Sch., Newcastle; Reading Univ. (BSc). Chemist in various Royal Ordnance Factories, 1939-46. Manager: Health Physics, Springfields Nuclear Fuel Plant, Dept Atomic Energy, 1946; Health Physics, Windscale Plutonium Plant, 1949; Plutonium Piles and Metal Plant, Windscale, 1950; Works Manager: Springfields, 1952; Windscale, UKAEA, 1954; Windscale and Calder Hall: Dep. Gen. Manager, 1957; Gen. Manager, 1958; Man. Dir, Production Gp, UKAEA, 1964-71. Managing Director: Urenco, 1973-74; Vorsitzender der Geschäftsführung Centec GmbH, 1973-74; Dep. Chm., Centec, 1973-74; former Dir, Centec-Algermann Co. Mem. Council, Internat. Inst. for Management of Technology, 1971-73. *Publications:* various technical papers on reactor operation and plutonium manufacture. *Recreations:* golf, gardening, travel. *Address:* Ingleberg, Beckermet, Cumbria. *T:* Beckermet 226.

TUOMINEN, Leo Olavi; Finnish Ambassador to USA, since 1972; *b* 19 Jan. 1911; *s* of Johan Tuominen (until 1897 Seipel) and Johanna Johansson; *m* 1938, Johanna, *d* of Emil Habert; one *s* three *d*. *Educ:* Turku Univ. (MA). Joined Finnish Foreign Service, 1934; served abroad, 1934-39; Min. of For. Affairs, 1940-46; Legation in Brussels, 1946-48; Asst Under Sec., Min. of For. Affairs, 1948-50; Perm. Deleg. to Int. Orgns in Geneva, 1950-52; Envoy to Argentina, Chile and Uruguay, 1952-55. Min. of Foreign Affairs: Dep. Under Sec., 1955-56; Perm. Under-Sec. of State, 1956-57; Ambassador to Court of St James's, 1957-68, to Italy, 1968-69, to Sweden, 1969-72. Head of Delegn for econ. negotiations with many countries, incl. UK, 1945-56 (Pres. delegn at GATT Conf. Torquay, 1950). Hon. DrPhil Michigan, 1974. Hon. KBE, and holds other foreign decorations. *Publications:* articles and essays on economics. *Recreations:* athletics, ski-ing, reading, gardening. *Address:* 3001 Woodland Drive NW, Washington DC, USA. *Clubs:* Hurlingham, Travellers'.

TUPMAN, William Ivan, DPhil; Director General of Internal Audit, Ministry of Defence, since 1974; *b* 22 July 1921; *s* of Leonard and Elsie Tupman; *m* 1945, Barbara (*née* Capel); two *s* one *d*. *Educ:* Queen Elizabeth's Hosp., Bristol; New Coll., Oxford (Exhibnr; MA, DPhil). Served War, 1942-45, RN (Lieut RNVR). Entered Admiralty as Asst Principal, 1948; Private Sec. to Parly Sec., 1950-52; Principal, 1952; Civil Affairs Adviser to C-in-C, Far East Station, 1958-61; Private Sec. to First Lord of the Admiralty, 1963; Asst Sec., 1964; IDC, 1967. *Recreations:* golf, bridge. *Address:* 109 Seal Hollow Road, Sevenoaks, Kent TN13 3SE. *T:* Sevenoaks 55699.

TUPPER, Sir Charles Hibbert, 5th Bt *cr* 1888, of Armdale, Halifax, Nova Scotia; *b* 4 July 1930; *o s* of Sir James Macdonald Tupper, 4th Bt, formerly Assistant Commissioner, Royal Canadian Mounted Police, and of Mary Agnes Jean Collins; *S* father, 1967; *m* (marr. diss. 1976); one *s*. *Heir: s* Charles Hibbert Tupper, *b* 10 July 1964. *Address:* 9854 Stirling Arm Crescent, Sproat Lake RR3, Port Alberni, BC V9Y 7L7, Canada.

TURBERVILLE, Geoffrey, MA; Principal, Leulumoega High School, Samoa, 1959-62, (retired); *b* 31 Mar. 1899; *o s* of A. E. Turberville, FCA, Stroud Green, London; *m* Jane Campbell Lawson. *Educ:* Westminster Sch. (King's Scholar); Trinity College, Cambridge (Exhibitioner). 2nd Lieut, Queen's Royal West Surrey Regt, 1917-19; Senior Classical Master, Liverpool Collegiate School, 1921-25; Senior Classical Master, Epsom College, 1925-30; Headmaster of Eltham College, 1930-59. Chm. Dorset Congregational Assoc., 1970-71. *Publications:* Cicero and Antony; Arva Latina II; Translation into Latin. *Address:* Kingsbere, St James, Shaftesbury, Dorset.

TURBOTT, Sir Ian (Graham), Kt 1968; CMG 1962; CVO 1966; *b* Whangarei, New Zealand, 9 March 1922; *s* of late Thomas Turbott and late E. A. Turbott, both of New Zealand; *m* 1952, Nancy Hall Lantz, California, USA; three *d*. *Educ:* Takapuna Grammar School, Auckland, NZ; Auckland University; Jesus College, Cambridge; London University. NZ Forces (Army), 1940-46: Solomon Is area and 2 NZEF, Italy. Colonial Service (Overseas Civil Service): Western Pacific, Gilbert and Ellice Is, 1948-56; Colonial Office, 1956-58; Administrator of Antigua, The West Indies, 1958-64; also Queen's Representative under new constitution, 1960-64; Administrator of Grenada and Queen's Representative, 1964-67; Governor of Associated State of Grenada, 1967-68. Partner, Spencer Stuart and Associates Worldwide, 1973-; Chm. and Man. Dir, Spencer Stuart and Associates Pty Ltd (Sen. Vice-Pres., Internat. Co.); Chm., Spencer Stuart and Associates (Hong Kong) Ltd; Director: Chloride Batteries Australia Ltd, 1974; Hoyts Theatres Ltd; Suncoast Gp of Cos; Dep. Chm., Amer. Internat. Underwriting (Aust.) Ltd; Chairman: TNT Group 4 Total Security Pty Ltd; RSVP Consultants Pty Ltd, Sydney, 1974; RSVP Consultants (PTE) Ltd, Singapore, 1975; The Dance Co. (NSW); Internat. Piano Competition Ltd, Sydney. Governor, NSW Conservatorium of Music. FRSA, JP. Holds 1939-45 Star, Pacific Star, Italy Star, Defence Medal, War Medal, New Zealand Service Medal. CStJ 1964. *Publications:* various technical and scientific, 1948-51, in Jl of Polynesian Society (on Pacific area). *Recreations:* boating, farming, golf, fishing. *Address:* 27 Amiens Road, Clontarf, NSW 2093, Australia; Lazy B Ranch, Mangrove Creek Road, NSW 2255, Australia. *Clubs:* Australian (Sydney); Elanora Country; Royal Sydney Yacht.

TURECK, Rosalyn; concert artist (Bach specialist); conductor; writer; *b* Chicago, 14 Dec. 1914; *d* of Samuel Tureck and Monya (*née* Lipson); *m* 1964, George Wallingford Downs (*d* 1964). *Educ:* Juilliard Sch. of Music, NY. Member Faculty: Philadelphia Conservatory of Music, 1935-42; Mannes School, NYC, 1940-44; Juilliard School of Music, 1943-55; Lecturer in Music: Columbia University, NY, 1953-55; London Univ., 1955-56. Visiting Professor, Washington University, St Louis, 1963-64; Regents Professorship, University of California, San Diego, 1966; Prof. of Music, 4th Step, Univ. of California, San Diego, 1966-72; Vis. Fellow, St Hilda's Coll., Oxford, 1974 and 1976-, Hon. Life Fellow, 1974; Vis. Fellow, Wolfson Coll., Oxford, 1975. Has appeared as soloist and conductor of leading orchestras in US, Europe and Israel, and toured US, Canada, South Africa, South America; since 1947 has toured extensively in Europe, and played at festivals in Edinburgh, Venice, Holland, Wexford, Schaffhausen, Bath, Brussels World Fair, Glyndebourne, etc, and in major Amer. festivals including Mostly Mozart Festival, NY, Caramoor, Detroit, etc; extensive tours: India, Australia and Far East, 1971. Formed: Composers of Today, 1951-55; Tureck Bach Players, 1959; Internat. Bach Soc., Inc., 1966; Inst. for Bach Studies, 1968. Hon. Member, Guildhall School of Music and Drama, London, 1961; Member: Royal Musical Assoc., London; Inc. Soc. of Musicians, London; Amer. Musicological Soc. Numerous recordings. Hon. Dr of Music, Colby Coll., USA, 1964; Hon. DMus: Roosevelt Univ., 1968; Wilson Coll., 1968; Oxon, 1977. Has won several awards. *Publications:* An Introduction to the Performance of Bach, 1960; (ed) Bach-Sarabande, C minor, 1950; (transcribed) Paganini: Moto Perpetuo, 1950; many articles. *Address:* c/o Ibbs and Tillett Ltd, 124 Wigmore Street, London W1.

TURING, Sir John Leslie, 11th Bt *cr* 1638; MC; *b* 13 Sept. 1895; *s* of Sir James Walter Turing, 9th Bt and Mabel Rose, *d* of Andrew Caldecott; *S* twin brother, 1970. *Educ:* Wellington College. Formerly Lieut, Seaforth Highlanders; served European War, 1914-18 (wounded, MC). *Heir: kinsman* John Ferrier Turing [*b* 1 Sept. 1908; *m* 1st, 1934, Joan (marr. diss. 1960), *d* of Robert Humphreys; three *d* (one *s* decd); 2nd, 1960, Beryl Mary Ada, *d* of late Herbert Vaughan Hann; one *s*]. *Address:* Warren Farm House, Brandy Hole Lane, Chichester, Sussex.

TURNBULL, Prof. Alexander C., MD, FRCOG; Nuffield Professor of Obstetrics and Gynaecology, University of Oxford, since Oct. 1973; Fellow of Oriel College, Oxford, since 1973; *b* 18 Jan. 1925; *s* of George Harley and Anne White Turnbull, Aberdeen, Scotland; *m* 1953, Elizabeth Paterson Nicol Bell; one *s* one *d*. *Educ:* Merchant Taylors' Sch., Crosby; Aberdeen Grammar Sch. (Modern Dux, 1942); Aberdeen Univ. MB, ChB 1947; MD (with Hons and Thursfield Prize) 1966; MRCOG 1954; FRCOG 1966. Sen. Lectr and Hon. Cons. Obstetrician and Gynaecologist (with Prof. J. Walker), Univ. of Dundee, 1957-61; Sen. Lectr and Hon. Cons. Obstetrician and Gynaecologist (with Sir Dugald Baird), Univ. of Aberdeen, 1961-66; Prof. of Obst. and Gynaecol., Welsh Nat. Sch. of Med.,

Cardiff, and Hon. Cons. Gynaecologist, also Adviser in Obst. and Gynaecol., Welsh Hosp. Bd, 1966-73. Member: Med. Educn Sub-cttee of UGC, 1973-; Lane Commn, 1971-; Clinical Research Bd of MRC, 1969-72. Hon. MA Oxford, 1973. *Publications:* (co-ed) The Oxygen Supply to the Human Fetus, 1960; (chap. in) The Scientific Basis of Obstetrics and Gynaecology (ed R. R. Macdonald), 1969; contribs to: Brit. Jl Obstetrics and Gynaecol., Lancet, BMJ, Jl of Endocrinology and various others. *Recreations:* reading, travelling, occasionally playing golf. *Address:* Nuffield Department of Obstetrics and Gynaecology, University of Oxford, Oxford OX3 9DU; John Radcliffe Hospital, Headington, Oxford.

TURNBULL, Rev. (Anthony) Michael (Arnold); Chief Secretary, Church Army, since 1976; *b* 27 Dec. 1935; *s* of George Ernest Turnbull and Adeline Turnbull (*née* Awty); *m* 1963, Brenda Susan Merchant; one *s* two *d*. *Educ:* Ilkley Grammar Sch.; Keble Coll., Oxford (MA); St John's Coll., Durham (DipTh). Deacon, 1960; priest, 1961; Curate: Middleton, 1960-61; Luton, 1961-65; Domestic Chaplain to Archbishop of York, 1965-69; Rector of Heslington and Chaplain, York Univ., 1969-76. Mem., General Synod, 1970-75. *Publication:* (contrib.) Unity: the next step?, 1972. *Recreations:* early morning jogging, cricket, family life. *Address:* CSC House, North Circular Road, NW10 7UG. *T:* 01-903 3763. *Club:* Royal Commonwealth Society.

TURNBULL, Sir Frank (Fearon), KBE 1964; CB 1954; CIE 1946; HM Civil Service, retired; *b* 30 April 1905; *m* 1947, Gwynnedd Celia Marian Lewis; three *s*. *Educ:* Marlborough Coll.; Trinity Hall, Cambridge. Entered India Office, 1930; Principal Private Secretary to Secretary of State, 1941-46; Secretary to Cabinet Mission to India, 1946; Under-Secretary, HM Treasury, 1949-59; Secretary, Office of the Minister for Science, 1959-64; Deputy Under-Secretary of State, Dept of Education and Science, 1964-66. Member, Board of Governors, Imperial College, 1967-73. Hon. DSc Edinburgh, 1967. *Address:* 18 Aveley Lane, Farnham, Surrey. *T:* Farnham 21986.

TURNBULL, George Henry, BSc (Hons), CEng, FIMechE, FIProdE; Consultant Adviser to Chairman and Managing Director, Iran National Motor Company, Tehran, since 1977; Industrial Adviser, E. F. Hutton & Co. Inc., New York, since 1977; *b* 17 Oct. 1926; *m* 1950, Marion Wing; one *s* two *d*. *Educ:* King Henry VIII Sch., Coventry; Birmingham Univ. (BSc (Hons)). PA to Techn. Dir, Standard Motors, 1950-51; Liaison Officer between Standard Motors and Rolls Royce, 1951-53; Exec., i/c Experimental, 1954-55; Works Manager, Petters Ltd, 1955-56; Standard Motors: Divl Manager Cars, 1956-59; Gen. Man., 1959-62; Standard Triumph International: Dir and Gen. Man., 1962; Dep. Chm., 1969; British Leyland Motor Corporation Ltd: Dir, 1967; Dep. Man. Dir, 1968-73; Man. Dir, 1973; Man. Dir, BL Austin Morris Ltd, 1968-73; Chm., Truck & Bus Div., BL, 1972-73; Vice-Pres. and Dir, Hyundai Motors, Seoul, South Korea, 1974-77. Mem. Council, Birmingham Chamber of Commerce and Industry, 1972 (Vice-Pres., 1973); past Member: Careers Adv. Bd, Univ. of Warwick; Management Bd, Engineering Employers' Assoc.; Engineering Employers' Fedn; Engrg Industry Trng Bd. Governor, Bablake Sch., Coventry. FIMI; Fellow, Inst. of Directors. *Recreations:* golf, tennis, fishing. *Address:* c/o Iran National Industrial Manufacturing Co., 18 Karadj Road, Tehran, Iran.

TURNBULL, Gilbert Learmonth, CBE 1954; Deputy Chief Inspector of Taxes, 1952-Oct. 1960; *b* 22 Oct. 1895; *s* of late D. Lowe Turnbull, Edinburgh. *Educ:* George Watson's Coll. Entered Inland Revenue Department, 1914; retired as Dep. Chief Inspector of Taxes, Oct. 1960. *Address:* 5 Rowben Close, Totteridge, N20. *T:* 01-445 9555.

TURNBULL, Ven. John William; *b* 29 Aug. 1905; 2nd *s* of William and Elizabeth Turnbull; *m* 1938, Alice Trewick Atkinson; one *s* one *d*. *Educ:* Durham Univ.; Edinburgh Theological Coll. Deacon 1934, Priest 1935; Newcastle Cathedral. Curate of Horton, Northumberland, 1934-36; Curate of Alnwick, 1936-41; Vicar of Longbenton, 1941-48; Vicar of All Saints', Gosforth, 1948-62; Hon. Canon of Newcastle Cathedral, 1958-62; Canon Residentiary of Ripon Cathedral, 1962-72; Archdeacon of Richmond, 1962-76, now Archdeacon Emeritus. *Address:* St Anne's, High Saint Agnesgate, Ripon, North Yorkshire. *T:* Ripon 3270.

TURNBULL, Rev. Michael; *see* Turnbull, Rev. A. M. A.

TURNBULL, Reginald March; Director, Turnbull, Scott Shipping Co. Ltd; *b* 10 Jan. 1907; *s* of late Sir March and Lady (Gertrude) Turnbull; *m* twice; one *s*. *Educ:* Horton Sch.; Eton; Cambridge Univ. (MA). Family shipping firm, Turnbull, Scott & Co., 1928-. *Recreations:* teaching golf, motoring. *Address:*

Red Gables, Shrubbs Hill Lane, Sunningdale, Ascot, Berks SL5 0LD. *T:* Ascot 20753.

TURNBULL, Sir Richard (Gordon), GCMG 1962 (KCMG 1958, CMG 1953); *b* 7 July 1909; *s* of Richard Francis Turnbull; *m* 1939, Beatrice, *d* of John Wilson, Glasgow; two *s* one *d. Educ:* University College School, London; University College, London; Magdalene Coll., Cambridge. Colonial Administrative Service, Kenya: District Officer, 1931-48; Provincial Comr, 1948-53; Minister for Internal Security and Defence, 1954; Chief Secretary, Kenya, 1955-58; Governor and C-in-C, Tanganyika, 1958-61; Governor-General and Commander-in-Chief, 1961-62; Chairman, Central Land Board, Kenya, 1963-64; High Commissioner for Aden and the Protectorate of South Arabia, 1965-67. Fellow of University College, London; Hon. Fellow, Magdalene College, Cambridge, 1970-. KStJ 1958. *Address:* Queen Anne Cottage, Friday Street, Henley-on-Thames, Oxon.

TURNBULL, Sir Winton (George), Kt 1972; CBE 1968; *b* 13 Dec. 1899; *s* of Adam Turnbull, Winninburn Coleraine, and Georgiana Drummond; *g g s* of Adam Turnbull of Campbell Town, Tas; *m* 1941, Beryl Bradley; no *c. Educ:* being resident in country area, was chiefly tutored. Primary Producer until 1922; Live-stock Auctioneer, 1922-40. Served War: AIF (chiefly Malaya) 1940-46 (POW Selerang and Changi, 3 years). MHR for Wimmera, 1946-49, for Mallee, 1949-72; Australian Govt Dep. Whip, 1956-72; Aust. Parly Country Party Whip and Secretary, 1956-72. Holds undisputed world record for Parliamentary attendance, House of Representatives, Canberra ACT, Australia, of 26 years and 8 months without missing one sitting day; retired 1972. *Recreations:* various sports; now chiefly retired from football, cricket, show riding etc. *Address:* 41 Putnam Avenue, Bendigo, Victoria 3550, Australia. *T:* (054) 438104. *Clubs:* Australian country clubs only.

TURNER, family name of **Baron Netherthorpe.**

TURNER, Alan B.; *see* Brooke Turner.

TURNER, Sir Alan (George), Kt 1972; CBE 1965; Clerk of The House of Representatives, Canberra, Australia, 1959-71, retd; *b* 11 Dec. 1906; *m* 1931, Ina Arnot Maxwell; one *s. Educ:* Church of England Grammar Sch., Melbourne, Vic, Australia. An Officer of The House of Representatives, Canberra, Australia, 1924-71 (the Clerk, 1959-71). Hon. Sec., Australia Branch, Commonwealth Parliamentary Assoc. 1958-71. *Recreations:* golf, bowls. *Address:* 14 Fishburn Street, Red Hill, ACT 2603, Australia. *T:* 958583. *Clubs:* Canberra Bowling, Royal Canberra Golf (Canberra); Leagues (Queanbeyan, NSW).

TURNER, Rt. Hon. Sir Alexander (Kingcome), PC 1968; KBE 1973; Kt 1963; *b* Auckland, New Zealand, 18 Nov. 1901; *s* of J. H. Turner; *m* 1934, Dorothea F., *d* of Alan Mulgan; two *s* one *d. Educ:* Auckland Grammar Sch.; Auckland Univ. (Scholar). BA 1921; MA 1922; LLB 1923. Served War of 1939-45, National Military Reserve, New Zealand. Barrister and Solicitor, 1923; QC (NZ) 1952. Carnegie Travelling Fellowship, 1949. Judge of the Supreme Court of New Zealand, 1953-62; Senior Resident Judge at Auckland, 1958-62; Judge of Court of Appeal, 1962-71, Pres., 1972-73. President, Auckland University Students' Assoc., 1928; President, Auckland District Court of Convocation, 1933; Member, Auckland Univ. Council, 1935-51; Vice-President, Auckland Univ., 1950-51; a Governor, Massey Agricultural Coll., 1944-53. Hon. LLD Auckland, 1965. *Publications:* (with George Spencer Bower) The Law of Estoppel by Representation, 1966; Res Judicata, 1969; The Law of Actionable Misrepresentation, 1974. *Recreations:* gardening, golf, Bush conservation, agriculture. *Address:* 14 St Michael's Crescent, Kelburn, Wellington 5, New Zealand. *T:* 757768. *Clubs:* Wellington; Auckland.

TURNER, Amédée Edward, QC 1976; *b* 26 March 1929; *s* of Frederick William Turner and Ruth Hempson; *m* 1960, Deborah Dudley Owen; one *s* one *d. Educ:* Temple Grove, Heron's Ghyll, Sussex; Dauntsey Sch., Wilts; Christ Church, Oxford (MA). Called to Bar, Inner Temple, 1954; practised patent bar, 1954-57; Associate, Kenyon & Kenyon, patent attorneys, NY, 1957-60; returned to London practice, 1960. Contested (C) Norwich N, gen. elections, 1964, 1966, 1970. *Publications:* The Law of Trade Secrets, 1962, supplement, 1968; many Conservative Party study papers on defence, oil and Middle East. *Recreations:* garden design, art deco collection, fish keeping, Box M at Albery Theatre, oil painting. *Address:* 3 Montrose Place, SW1. *T:* 01-235 2894; 1 Essex Court, Temple, EC4. *T:* 01-353 8507; The Barn, Westleton, Saxmundham, Suffolk. *T:* Westleton 235. *Clubs:* Carlton, Coningsby, United & Cecil.

TURNER, Hon. Andrew; *see* Turner, Hon. James A.

TURNER, Adm. Sir (Arthur) Francis, KCB 1970 (CB 1966); DSC 1945; Chief of Fleet Support, Ministry of Defence, 1967-71; *b* 23 June 1912; *s* of Rear-Admiral A. W. J. Turner and Mrs A. M. Turner (*née* Lochrane); *m* 1963, Elizabeth Clare de Trafford; two *s. Educ:* Stonyhurst Coll. Entered RN, 1931; Commander, 1947; Captain, 1956; Rear-Admiral, 1964; Vice-Admiral, 1968; Admiral, 1970. Dir.-Gen. Aircraft (Navy), MoD, 1966-67. *Recreations:* cricket, golf. *Address:* Plantation House, East Horsley, Surrey. *Clubs:* Army and Navy; Union (Malta).

TURNER, Comdr Bradwell Talbot, CVO 1955; DSO 1940; OBE 1951; JP; RN, retired April 1957; *b* 7 April 1907; *s* of late A. F. and A. I. Turner; *m* 1937, Mary G. B., *d* of Professor W. Nixon; three *d. Educ:* Christ's Hospital; RN Colleges Osborne and Dartmouth. Joined Royal Navy, 1921; Barrister-at-Law, 1956; Naval Attaché, Oslo, Norway, 1954-57. With The Marconi Co., 1957-72. MIEE 1946. JP Chelmsford 1962 (Chm. Bench, 1974-). Officer, Legion of Merit (USA), 1945. *Recreation:* riding. *Address:* Delimara, Little Baddow, Essex.

TURNER, Air Vice-Marshal Cameron Archer, CB 1968; CBE 1960 (OBE 1947); Royal New Zealand Air Force, retired; *b* Wanganui, NZ, 29 Aug. 1915; *s* of James Oswald Turner and Vida Cathrine Turner; *m* 1941, Josephine Mary, *d* of George Richardson; two *s. Educ:* New Plymouth Boys' High Sch.; Victoria University of Wellington. CEng, FIEE, FRAeS. Commn RAF, 1936-39; commn RNZ Air Force, 1940; served War of 1939-45, UK, NZ, and Pacific; comd RNZAF Station Nausori, Fiji, 1944; comd RNZAF Station, Guadalcanal, Solomon Islands, 1944; Director of Signals, 1945-47; psa 1947; RNZAF Liaison Officer, Melbourne, Australia, 1948-50; comd RNZAF Station, Taieri, NZ, 1950-52; Director of Organization, HQ, RNZAF, 1953-56; comd RNZAF Station Ohakea, NZ, 1956-58; Asst Chief of Air Staff, HQ, RNZAF, 1958; Air Member for Personnel, HQ, RNZAF, 1959; idc 1960; AOC HQ, RNZAF, London, 1961-63; Air Member for Supply, HQ, RNZAF, 1964-65; Chief of Air Staff, HQ RNZAF, 1966-69. Dir, NZ Inventions Develt Authority, 1969-76. Pres., RNZAF Assoc., 1972-. *Recreations:* fishing, golf. *Address:* 37a Parkvale Road, Wellington 5, New Zealand. *T:* 766063. *Clubs:* Wellington, United Services Officers' (Wellington); Taranaki (New Plymouth).

TURNER, Sir Cedric Oban, Kt 1967; CBE 1958; Chief Executive and General Manager, Qantas Empire Airways Ltd, 1955-67; *b* 13 Feb. 1907; *s* of S. Turner, Gulgong, NSW; *m* 1935, Shirley (*d* 1972), *d* of late Sir Joseph Totterdell, sometime Lord Mayor of Perth, Western Australia; one *s* three *d. Educ:* Sydney High Sch. Chartered Accountant: Robert W. Nelson, 1924-29, UK and Europe, 1929-34. Joined Qantas Empire Airways, 1934; Chief Accountant; Assistant General Manager, 1949-51; General Manager, 1951-55. *Recreation:* golf. *Address:* 1 Tralee Avenue, Killarney Heights, NSW 2087, Australia.

TURNER, Brig. Charles Edward Francis, CBE 1944 (OBE 1941); DSO 1943; late RE; *b* 23 April 1899; *s* of late Lieut A. E. Turner, RE, and E. B., *d* of Maj.-Gen. Sir C. H. Scott, KCB; *m* 1930, Mary Victoria, *d* of H. Leeds Swift, York; one *s* two *d. Educ:* Twyford Sch., Winchester; Wellington Coll., Berks; Royal Military Academy, Woolwich. Regular Officer, Royal Engineers, Sept. 1917; BEF France, June-Nov. 1918; NREF Russia, July-Sept. 1919; India, 1920-23, including two years on North-West Frontier on service (despatches); Christ's Coll., Cambridge, 1923-24; Ordnance Survey, York and Edinburgh, 1925-30; Staff Coll., Camberley, 1931-32; Singapore, Egypt, Palestine, 1934-37, including service in Palestine (Bt Major, despatches); War Office, 1937-39; MEF 1940-43 (OBE, DSO, CBE, despatches twice); Malaya, 1948-50; retired pay, 1950. National Council of Social Service, 1950-58; Secretary, Iona Appeal Trust, 1958-61. *Address:* The Colleens, Cousley Wood, Wadhurst, East Sussex TN5 6HF. *T:* Wadhurst 2387.

TURNER, Christopher Gilbert; Headmaster, Dean Close School, since 1968; *b* 23 Dec. 1929; *s* of Theodore F. Turner, *qv*; *m* 1961, Lucia, *d* of late Prof. S. R. K. Glanville (Provost of King's Coll., Cambridge); one *s* two *d. Educ:* Winchester Coll. (Schol.); New Coll., Oxford (Exhibnr), MA. Asst Master, Radley Coll., 1952-61; Senior Classics Master, Charterhouse, 1961-68. Schoolmaster Student at Christ Church, Oxford, 1967. Foundation Member of Council, Cheltenham Colleges of Educn, 1968. Mem., HMC Cttee, 1974-75; Chm., Common Entrance Cttee, 1976. Lay Reader. FRSA. Rotarian. *Publication:* chapter on History, in Comparative Study of Greek and Latin Literature, 1969. *Recreations:* music (violin-playing), reading, walking, different forms of manual labour; OUBC 1951. *Address:* Dean Close House, Lansdown Road, Cheltenham,

Glos. *T:* Cheltenham 52537 (study 22640); Meadow House, Rhossili, near Swansea, Glam. *T:* Gower 582. *Club:* Vincent's (Oxford).
See also W. H. Hughes, M. J. Turner.

TURNER, Air Cdre Clifford John, CB 1973; MBE 1953; *b* 21 Dec. 1918; *s* of J. E. Turner; *m* 1942, Isabel Emily Cormack; two *s. Educ:* Parkstone Grammar Sch.; RAF Techn. College. CEng, FRAeS. Engrg Apprentice, 1935-38; various RAF engrg appts, 1938-64; Group Dir, RAF Staff Coll., 1965-67; Stn Comdr, RAF Colerne, 1968-69; AO Engineering, Training Comd, 1969-73.

TURNER, Colin Francis; Registrar, Family Division of High Court, since 1971; *b* 11 April 1930; *s* of Sidney F. and Charlotte C. Turner; *m* 1951, Josephine Alma Jones; two *s* one *d. Educ:* Beckenham Grammar Sch.; King's Coll., London. LLB 1955. Entered Principal Probate Registry, 1949; District Probate Registrar, York, 1965-68. *Publications:* (ed jtly) Rayden on Divorce, 9th, 11th and 12th edns. *Recreations:* ornithology, fishing. *Address:* 18 South Eden Park Road, Beckenham, Kent BR3 3BG. *T:* 01-777 0344.

TURNER, Colin William Carstairs, DFC 1944; *b* 4 Jan. 1922; *s* of late Colin C. W. Turner, Enfield; *m* 1949, Evelyn Mary, *d* of late Claude H. Buckard, Enfield; three *s* one *d. Educ:* Highgate Sch. Served War of 1939-45 with RAF, 1940-45, Air observer; S. Africa and E Africa, 223 Squadron; Desert Air Force, N. Africa, 1942-44; commissioned, 1943; invalided out as Flying Officer, 1945, after air crash; Chm., 223 Squadron Assoc., 1975-77. Member Enfield Borough Council, 1956-58. Managing Director, Colin Turner and W. Ager Group of Companies, International Media Representatives and Marketing Consultants. President, Overseas Press and Media Association, 1965-67 (Hon. Secretary, 1967; Hon. Treasurer, 1974-76; Editor, Overseas Media Guide, 1968, 1969, 1970, 1971, 1972, 1973, 1974); Chm., PR Cttee, Commonwealth Press Union, 1970-76; Chm., Cons. Commonwealth and Overseas Council, 1976 (Dep. Chm. 1975). Mem., Nat. Exec., Cons. Party, 1946-53, 1968-73, 1976. Contested (C) Enfield (East), 1950 and 1951; MP (C) Woolwich West, 1959-64. *Recreations:* gardening, do-it-yourself, sailing, fishing. *Address:* 55 Rowantree Road, Enfield, Mddx. *T:* 01-363 2403. *Clubs:* Royal Over-Seas League, RAF Reserves.

TURNER, Dr David Warren, FRS 1973; Fellow of Balliol College, Oxford, since 1967; University Lecturer in Physical Chemistry, Oxford, since 1968; *b* 16 July 1927; *s* of Robert Cecil Turner and Constance Margaret *m* 1954, Barbara Marion Fisher; one *s* one *d. Educ:* Westcliff High Sch.; Univ. of Exeter. MA, BSc, PhD, DIC. Lectr, Imperial Coll., 1958; Reader in Organic Chemistry, Imperial Coll., 1965. Kahlbaum Lectr, Univ. of Basle, 1971; Van Geuns Lectr, Univ. of Amsterdam, 1974; Harkins Lectr, Chicago Univ., 1974. Tilden Medal, Chemical Soc., 1967; Harrison Howe Award, Amer. Chem. Soc., 1973. Hon. DTech, Royal Inst., Stockholm, 1971. *Publications:* Molecular Photoelectron Spectroscopy, 1970; contrib. Phil. Trans Royal Soc., Proc. Royal Soc., Jl Chem. Soc., etc. *Recreations:* music, gardening, tinkering with gadgets. *Address:* Balliol College, Oxford.

TURNER, Donald William, CEng, FICE; Planning Director, British Airports Authority, since 1973; Full-time Member, British Airports Authority Board, since 1975; *b* 17 Aug. 1925; *s* of William John Turner and Agnes Elizabeth Jane (*née* Bristow); *m* 1947, Patricia (*née* Stuteley); one *s* one *d . Educ:* Wanstead County High Sch.; Birmingham Univ. Served War, Army, 1943-45. Subseq. completed engrg trng in Britain; then took up post in Australia with Qld Railways, 1949. Left Qld, 1954; joined firm of UK consulting engrs and then worked in W Africa on rly and highway construction until 1960. Returned to UK, but remained with consultants until 1966, when joined British Airports Authority as a Civil Engr; became Chief Engr of Heathrow Airport, 1970; Dep. Dir of Planning, 1972. *Recreations:* walking, reading, sketching, painting. *Address:* Peter's Cottage, New England Road, Haywards Heath, Sussex. *Club:* St Stephen's.

TURNER, Dudley Russell Flower, CB 1977; Secretary, Advisory, Conciliation and Arbitration Service, 1974-77; *b* 15 Nov. 1916; *s* of Gerald Flower Turner and Dorothy May Turner (*née* Gillard), Penang; *m* 1941, Sheila Isobel Stewart; one *s* one *d. Educ:* Whitgift Sch.; London Univ. (BA Hons). Served RA (Captain), 1940-46. Entered Ministry of Labour, 1935; HM Treasury, 1953-56; Principal Private Secretary to Minister of Labour, 1956-59; Assistant Secretary: Cabinet Office, 1959-62; Ministry of Labour, 1962-64, 1966; Under-Sec., Ministry of Labour, 1967; Asst Under-Sec. of State, Dept of Employment and Productivity, 1968-70; Under-Sec., Trng Div., 1970-72,

Manpower Gen. Div., 1972-73, Dept of Employment; Sec., Commn on Industrial Relations, 1973-74. Imperial Defence Coll., 1965. *Recreations:* tennis, music, gardening. *Address:* 10 Melville Avenue, South Croydon, Surrey. *Club:* Army and Navy.

TURNER, Elston Grey; see Grey-Turner.

TURNER, Eric, CBE 1968; FCA; Director: Iron Trades Employers Insurance Association Ltd; Iron Trades Mutual Insurance Co. Ltd; English & Scottish Investors Ltd; National Exhibition Centre Ltd; Underwriting Member of Lloyd's; *b* 18 July 1918; *o s* of William Edmund and Elsie Turner, Staveley, Derbyshire; *m* 1st, 1943, Zena Doreen Schellenberg (decd); 2nd, Eileen Laura Svrljuga; one *s* one *d. Educ:* Chesterfield Sch. Served India and Burma, War of 1939-45; demobilised, 1946, Lt-Col. Chairman (1955-59) and Managing Director (1951-59), The Blackburn Group; Chairman: BSA, 1961-71 (Chief Exec., 1960-71); Economic League, 1967-72. Member: Malta Industrial Development Board, 1959-65; Advisory Council, Export Credits Guarantee Dept, 1965-70; Pres., Birmingham Chamber of Commerce and Industry, 1971-72. Hon. Treasurer and Chairman of Finance Cttee, University of Aston, 1968-76. Hon. DSc Aston, 1976. *Recreation:* golf. *Address:* Dale Cross Grange, Barnt Green, Worcestershire. *T:* 021-445 1676. *Club:* Brooks's.

TURNER, Eric Gardner, CBE 1975; FBA; Professor of Papyrology, University College, London, since 1950; *b* 26 Feb. 1911; *s* of late William Ernest Stephen Turner; *m* 1940, Louise B. Taylor; one *s* one *d. Educ:* King Edward VII Sch., Sheffield; Magdalen Coll., Oxford (Demy). First Class Hons Classical Mods, 1932, and Lit Hum, 1934; Goldsmiths' Senior Scholar, 1935; Assistant in Humanity, University of Aberdeen, 1936; Lecturer in Classics, Aberdeen Univ., 1938-48; Reader in Papyrology, University of London, 1948-50; first Dir, Univ. of London Inst. of Classical Studies, 1953-63. Pres. Internat. Assoc. of Papyrologists, 1965-74; Vice-President: Hellenic Soc. (Pres., 1968-71); Roman Soc.; Chairman: Organising Cttee, Third Internat. Congress of Classical Studies, London, 1959; Organising Cttee, XIVth Internat. Congress of Papyrologists, Oxford, 1974; Cttee, Egypt Exploration Soc.; Jt Editor, Graeco-Roman publications. Visiting Member, Inst. for Advanced Study, Princeton, NJ, 1961, 1964, 1968. Pres., Union Académique Internationale, 1974-77 (Vice-Pres., 1970-73). Hon. Mem., Sociêtas Scientiarum Fennica (Humanities Section), 1969; For. Member: Accademia di Archeologia, Lettere e Belle Arti (Letters Section) of the Società Nazionale di Scienze, Lettere ed Arti, Naples, 1973; Det Kongelige Danske Videnskabernes Selskab (historisk-filosofiske klasse); Amer. Philosophical Soc., 1977; Corresp. Mem., Osterreichische Akademie der Wissenschaften, 1975; Sachsische Akademie der Wissenschaften, 1976; Deutsche Archäologisches Institut, 1976; Associate, Académie royale des Sciences, des Lettres et des Beaux-Arts de Belgique, 1974. Hon. Dr Phil et Lettres Brussels, 1956; Hon. Dès Geneva, 1976. *Publications:* Catalogue of Greek Papyri in University of Aberdeen, 1939; (with C. H. Roberts) Catalogue of Greek Papyri in John Rylands Library, Vol. IV, 1951; The Hibeh Papyri, Part II, 1955; (with others) The Oxyrhynchus Papyri Part XXIV, 1957, Part XXV, 1959, Part XXVII, 1962, Part XXXI, 1966, Part XXXIII, 1968, Part XXXVIII, 1971, Part XLI, 1972; (with H. I. Bell, V. Martin, D. van Berchem) The Abinnæus Papyri, 1962; New Fragments of the Misoumenos of Menander, 1965; Greek Papyri, an Introduction, 1968; Greek Manuscripts of the Ancient World, 1970; Menander: The Girl from Samos, 1972; The Papyrologist at Work, 1973; The Typology of the Early Codex, 1977; various papers in learned journals. *Recreations:* chamber music, playing the gramophone, walking, sailing. *Address:* c/o Greek Department, University College, Gower Street, WC1E 6BT; Thornheath, Cathedral Square, Fortrose, Ross and Cromarty. *Club:* United Oxford & Cambridge University.

TURNER, Dame Eva, DBE 1962; FRAM; prima donna; *b* Oldham, Lancashire; unmarried. Began to sing at an early age and, whilst in her teens, spent some years at the Royal Academy of Music; joined Royal Carl Rosa Opera Company in 1916, and became the Prima donna of the Company, remaining with it until 1924, when Toscanini engaged her for La Scala, Milan. Appeared all over Europe, USA, and S America; London, at Covent Garden in 1928 when she sang in Puccini's opera Turandot, Aida, and many others; for the Celebrations in connection with the commemoration of the Centenary of Bolivar, was specially chosen by President Gomez to be the Prima Donna. Visiting Professor of Voice to Music Faculty of University of Oklahoma, USA, 1949-59 (resigned); Professor of Voice Royal Academy of Music, London, 1959-66 (resigned). Pres., Wagner Soc., 1971-. Hon. Internat. Member Sigma Alpha Iota, 1951-; Hon. Internat. Soroptomist, 1955-. Member

National Assoc. of Teachers of Singing (USA). Hon. GSM 1968; FRCM 1974. *Recreations:* swimming, riding, motoring. *Address:* 26 Palace Court, W2; Junesca, Brusino-Arsizio, Lake of Lugano, Switzerland. *Club:* Royal Over-Seas League.

TURNER, Brig. Dame Evelyn Marguerite; *see* Turner, Brig. Dame Margot.

TURNER, Sir Francis; *see* Turner, Sir Arthur Francis.

TURNER, Francis McDougall Charlewood, MC; DFC; MA; Emeritus Fellow of Magdalene College, Cambridge; Bye Fellow, 1923; Fellow, 1926; President, 1957-62; *b* 17 March 1897; fifth *s* of late Charles Henry Turner, DD, Bishop of Islington, and Edith Emma, *d* of late Bishop McDougall; unmarried. *Educ:* Marlborough Coll.; Magdalene Coll., Cambridge. Royal Flying Corps, 1916-19 (MC, DFC). *Publication:* The Element of Irony in English Literature, 1926. *Recreation:* music. *Address:* 1 St Martin's Square, Chichester, West Sussex PO19 1NW. *Club:* United Oxford & Cambridge University.

TURNER, Harold Goodhew, CMG 1960; Malayan Civil Service (retired); *b* 23 Dec. 1906; *s* of George Prior Turner and Blanche Winifred Turner; *m* 1934, Aileen Mary Mace; one *s* one *d* (and one *s* decd). *Educ:* St Olave's and St Saviour's Grammar Sch., London; Trinity Coll., Cambridge. Cadet, Malayan CS, 1929; Principal Establishment Officer, 1958; Secretary to the Treasury, 1959. CRO (now FCO) 1962-68; Director of Studies, Royal Institute of Public Administration, 1969-73 (Associate Dir, 1961-62); *Recreation:* gardening. *Address:* 54 Robson Road, Goring-by-Sea, Worthing, West Sussex BN12 4EF. *T:* Worthing 41924. *Club:* Royal Commonwealth Society.

TURNER, Harold H.; *see* Horsfall Turner.

TURNER, Sir Harvey, Kt 1967; CBE 1953; Chairman of Directors of a number of Companies; *b* 11 Sept. 1889; *s* of Edward and Maude Turner; *m* 1914, Margaret Ethel Penman; three *s* two *d*. *Educ:* Huia Sch.; Giles Business College; Auckland Technical College. Served War of 1914-18, New Zealand; War of 1939-45 (Middle East, 1941-42; Major; despatches). Past President, Auckland Chamber of Commerce; Past Chairman, Auckland Harbour Board. *Publication:* (with Allan Kirk) Turners of Huia, 1966. *Recreations:* tennis, swimming, gardening. *Address:* PO Box 56, Auckland 1, New Zealand; Summit Drive, Auckland 3, New Zealand. *T:* Auckland 867-572.

TURNER, Rev. Professor Henry Ernest William, DD; Canon Residentiary, Durham Cathedral, 1950-73; Treasurer, 1956-73; Sub-Dean, 1959-73; Acting Dean, 1973; Van Mildert Professor of Divinity, Durham University, 1958-73, now Emeritus; *b* 14 Jan. 1907; *o s* of Henry Frederick Richard and Ethel Turner, Sheffield; *m* 1936, Constance Parker, *d* of Dr E. P. Haythornthwaite, Rowrah, Cumberland; two *s*. *Educ:* King Edward VII Sch., Sheffield; St John's Coll., Oxford; Wycliffe Hall, Oxford. MA 1933; BD 1940; DD 1955. Curate, Christ Church, Cockermouth, 1931-34; Curate, Holy Trinity, Wavertree, 1934-35; Fellow, Chaplain and Tutor, Lincoln Coll., Oxford, 1935-50; Chaplain, RAFVR, 1940-45; Librarian, Lincoln Coll., 1945-48; Senior Tutor, Lincoln Coll., 1948-50; Lightfoot Prof. of Divinity, Durham Univ., 1950-58. Select Preacher, Oxford Univ., 1950-51; Member: Anglican delegation to Third Conference of World Council of Churches, Lund, 1952; Anglican-Presbyterian Conversations, 1953-; Doctrine Commn of the Church of England, 1967-; Bampton Lecturer (Oxford), 1954. Theological Consultant to Anglican Roman Catholic Conversations, 1970. *Publications:* The Life and Person of Jesus Christ, 1951; The Patristic Doctrine of Redemption, 1952; Jesus Master and Lord, 1953; The Pattern of Christian Truth (Bampton Lectures), 1955; Why Bishops?, 1955; The Meaning of the Cross, 1959; (jt author with H. Montefiore) Thomas and the Evangelists, 1962; Historicity and the Gospels, 1963; Jesus the Christ, 1976; contributions to the Guardian, Theology and Church Quarterly Review. *Address:* Realands, Eskdale, near Holmrook, Cumbria CA19 1TW. *T:* Eskdale 321.

TURNER, Sir Henry Samuel Edwin, Kt 1946; *b* 18 Aug. 1887; *s* of Samuel Turner and Lillian, *d* of Henry Thorne; *m* 1912, Edith (*d* 1948), *d* of William Rose; two *d* ; *m* 1959, Louise (*d* 1975), *d* of late Ernest Kirk, Batley, Yorks, and *widow* of Marshal Shaw Lodge. *Educ:* Lower School of John Lyon, Harrow. English Civil Service, 1907-19; Board of Education, Ministry of Food; British Economic Section, Peace Conference, Paris; London Manager, NZ Refrigerating Co. Ltd, 1919-22; NZ Manager, NZ Refrigerating Co. Ltd, 1923-39; Controller of Meat and Livestock, Ministry of Food, London, 1940-50; Chairman, Towers & Co. Ltd, 1950-66; former Dir, Express Dairy Co. Ltd;

Past President, Canterbury Chamber of Commerce, NZ; Past Vice-President, Associated Chambers of Commerce of NZ. *Recreations:* reading and watching cricket. *Address:* White Lodge, 6 Oliver's Battery Road, Winchester, Hampshire. *Club:* Junior Carlton.
See also M . L . E . Fisher .

TURNER, Prof. Herbert Arthur (Frederick), BSc Econ London, PhD Manchester, MA Cantab; Montague Burton Professor of Industrial Relations, University of Cambridge, since 1963; Fellow of Churchill College, Cambridge; *b* 11 Dec. 1919; *s* of Frederick and May Turner. *Educ:* Henry Thornton Sch., Clapham; University of London. BSc (Econ) London, 1939; PhD Manchester, 1960. Member Trade Union Congress Research and Economic Department, 1944; Assistant Education Secretary, TUC, 1947; Lecturer, 1950, Senior Lecturer, 1959, University of Manchester; Montague Burton Professor of Industrial Relations, University of Leeds, 1961-63. Mem., NBPI, 1967-71. Visiting Professor: Harvard and MIT, 1971-72; Sydney Univ., 1976-77. Sometime Adviser to Govts of Congo, Zaire, Egypt, Tanzania, Fiji, Papua New Guinea, Iran, Zambia and other developing countries; Chm., Pay Policies Commn of E African Community, 1973. *Publications:* Trade Union Growth, Structure and Policy, 1962; Wages: the Problems for Underdeveloped Countries, 1965; Prices, Wages and Incomes Policies, 1966; Labour Relations in the Motor Industry, 1967; Is Britain Really Strike-Prone?, 1969; Do Trade Unions Cause Inflation?, 1972, 1974; Management Characteristics and Labour Conflict, 1976; various reports of ILO, monographs, papers and articles on labour economics and statistics, industrial relations. *Recreations:* minimal but mostly excusable. *Address:* Churchill College, Cambridge. *Club:* United Oxford & Cambridge University.

TURNER, Hugh Wason; Director General, Multi-Role Combat Aircraft, Ministry of Defence (Procurement Executive), since 1976; *b* 2 April 1923; *s* of Thomas W. Turner and Elizabeth P. Turner (*née* Pooley); *m* 1950, Rosemary Borley; two *s* two *d*. *Educ:* Dollar Academy; Glasgow University. BSc Hons (Mech. Eng); CEng; MRAeS. Aeroplane and Armament Experimental Establishment, 1943-52; Chief Tech. Instructor, Empire Test Pilots School, 1953; A&AEE (Prin. Scientific Officer), 1954-64; Asst Director, RAF Aircraft, Min. of Technology, 1965-68; Superintendent, Trials Management, A&AEE, 1968-69; Division Leader, Systems Engineering, NATO MRCA Management Agency (NAMMA), Munich, 1969-74; Chief Superintendent, A&AEE, 1974-75. *Recreation:* ski-ing. *Address:* 2 Wilmot Way, Camberley, Surrey GU15 1JA. *T:* Camberley 24383.

TURNER, Hon. (James) Andrew, FCA; Managing Director, Dalgety Ltd, since 1975 (Vice-Chairman and Executive Director, 1972-75); *b* 23 July 1936; *s* and *heir* of Baron Netherthorpe, *qv* ; *m* 1960, Belinda Nicholson; two *s* two *d*. *Educ:* Rugby Sch.; Pembroke Coll., Cambridge. Peat, Marwick, Mitchell & Co., Chartered Accountants, 1958-61; joined Lazard Brothers & Co. Ltd, 1961; seconded to Australian United Corp. Ltd, 1966-67; apptd Head of Lazards' Corporate Finance Dept, 1969; Dir, Lazards, 1971-; also Director: Dalgety Ltd; Dalgety UK Ltd; Dalgety Australia Ltd; Dalgety New Zealand Ltd; Dalgety, Inc.; Balfour Guthrie (Canada) Ltd; Babcock & Wilcox Ltd. Member: Covent Garden Market Authority; Council of British Australia Soc. *Address:* Boothby Hall, Boothby Pagnell, Grantham, Lincs NG33 4DQ. *T:* Ingoldsby 374.

TURNER, James Grant Smith, CMG 1949; *b* 7 Aug. 1897; *s* of Hector and Mary Turner; *m* 1st, 1930, Jemima Cunningham (*d* 1937); one *s* one *d* ; 2nd, 1947, Freda Gurling (*d* 1970); one *s*. *Educ:* Allan Glen's Sch., Glasgow; Glasgow Univ.; Liverpool Univ. MB, ChB, Glasgow, 1924; BSc, DPH, Glasgow, 1926; DTM, Liverpool, 1927. MO, Nigeria, 1927; Senior Health Officer, 1938; transferred to Sierra Leone, 1941; DDMS, Gold Coast, 1945, DMS, 1946-50; retired Jan. 1950. Military service: European War, 1915-18; War of 1939-45, 1940-41. *Recreations:* walking, fishing. *Address:* Castleweary, Teviothead, Hawick TD9 0LN.

TURNER, Hon. Joanna Elizabeth, (Hon. Mrs Turner), MA; Classics Teacher, Ellesmere College, Salop, since 1975; *b* 10 Jan. 1923; 2nd *d* of 1st Baron Piercy, CBE, and Mary Louisa, *d* of Hon. Thomas Pelham; *m* 1968, James Francis Turner, er *s* of late Rev. P. R. Turner. *Educ:* St Paul's Girls' Sch.; Somerville Coll., Oxford (Sen. Classics Schol.). Asst Classics Mistress: Downe House, Newbury, 1944-46; Gordonstoun Sch., 1947-48; Badminton Sch., Bristol, 1948-65, Headmistress, Badminton Sch., Bristol, 1966-69. JP Inner London (Juvenile Courts), 1970-75. *Recreations:* painting, foreign travel, reading. *Address:* The Old Rectory, Wem, Salop. *T:* Wem 32581.

TURNER, Hon. John Napier, PC (Can.) 1965; QC (Can.); lawyer; *b* 7 June 1929; *s* of Leonard Turner and Phyllis Turner (*née* Gregory); *m* 1963, Geills McCrae Kilgour; three *s* one *d*. *Educ:* Norman Model Public Sch., Ottawa, Ont.; Ashbury Coll., 1939-42; St Patrick's Coll., 1942-45; Univ. of BC; Oxford Univ. BA (PolSci, Hons) BC, 1949; Rhodes Scholar, Oxford Univ., BA (Juris.) 1951; BCL 1952; MA 1957. Joined Stikeman, Elliott, Tamaki, Mercier & Turner, Montreal, Quebec; practised with them after being called to English Bar, 1953, Bar of Quebec, 1954 and Bar of Ont., 1968; QC (Can.) 1968. MP for St Lawrence-St George, Montreal, 1962-68, Ottawa-Carleton, 1968-75; Parly Sec. to Minister of Nat. Affairs and Nat. Resources, 1963-65; Minister without Portfolio, Dec. 1965-April 1967; Registrar-Gen. of Canada April 1967-Jan. 1968; Minister of Consumer and Corporate Affairs, Jan.-July 1968; Solicitor-Gen., April-July 1968; Minister of Justice and Attorney-Gen. of Canada, July 1968-Jan. 1972; Minister of Finance, 1972-75. Joined law firm of McMillan Binch, Toronto, 1976. Barbados Bar, 1969; Yukon and Northwest Territories, 1969; Trinidad Bar, 1969; British Columbia, 1969. Hon. Dr of Laws: Univ. of New Brunswick, 1968; York Univ., Toronto, 1969. *Publications:* Senate of Canada, 1961; Politics of Purpose, 1968. *Recreations:* tennis, squash, canoeing; Canadian Track Field Champion 1950-51, Mem. English Track and Field Team. *Address:* (home) 435 Russell Hill Road, Toronto, Ont M5P 2S4, Canada. *T:* (416) 482-4330; (office) PO Box 38, 38th Floor, Royal Bank Plaza, Toronto, Ont M5P 2S4. *T:* (416) 865-7101.

TURNER, John Turnage; His Honour Judge Turner; a Circuit Judge, since 1976; *b* 12 Nov. 1929; *s* of Wilfred Edward and May Martha Turner; *m* 1956, Gillian Mary Rayner; two *d*. *Educ:* Earls Colne Grammar School. Called to the Bar, Inner Temple, 1952. *Address:* 23 Victoria Road, Colchester CO3 3NT. *T:* Colchester 5378.

TURNER, Dr J(ohn) W(illiam) Aldren, MA, DM Oxon; FRCP; Neurologist, St Bartholomew's Hospital, since 1946; Neurologist, St Alban's City Hospital and Finchley Memorial Hospital; *b* 13 Feb. 1911; *s* of W. Aldren Turner, CB, MD, FRCP; unmarried. *Educ:* Clifton Coll.; New Coll., Oxford; St Bartholomew's Hospital Medical Coll. BA (Oxon) 1932 (1st class honours Final School of Natural Science); Theodore Williams Scholarship in Anatomy and Gotch Medal in Physiology, University Entrance Scholarship, St Bart's. Walsham Prize in Pathology and Brackenbury Scholarship in Medicine; BM, BCh (Oxon), 1935; MRCP 1937; DM 1940; FRCP 1946. Resident house appointments at St Bart's, and at National Hospital for Nervous Diseases, Queen Square. Served War of 1939-45, Temp. Lt-Col, RAMC (adviser in Neurology, Southern Command, India). Sub-dean, St Bart's Medical Coll., 1946-50. Examiner in Neurology: University of London; Manchester and Conjoint Board. *Publications:* (joint) Clinical Neurology, 1952; papers on neurological subjects in medical journals. *Recreations:* philately, travel. *Address:* 149 Harley Street, W1. *T:* 01-935 4444; (home) 23 Malvern Court, Onslow Square, SW7. *T:* 01-589 1086. *Club:* Athenæum.

TURNER, Brig. Dame Margot, (E. M. Turner), DBE 1965 (MBE 1946); RRC 1956; Matron-in-Chief and Director Army Nursing Service, 1964-68; *b* 10 May 1910; *d* of late Thomas Frederick Turner and late Molly Cecilia (*née* Bryan). *Educ:* Finchley County Sch., Middlesex. Trained at St Bartholomew's Hospital, London, 1931-35. Joined QAIMNS, 1937 (became QARANC, 1949). Served in UK, India, Malaya, Hong Kong, Bermuda, Germany and Near East. POW Sumatra, Feb. 1942-Aug. 1945. Col Comdt, QARANC, 1969-74. CStJ 1966. *Relevant Publication:* Sir John Smyth, Will to Live: the story of Dame Margot Turner, 1970. *Recreations:* reading, photography, golf, tennis. *Address:* 2 Chantry Court, Frimley, Surrey. *T:* Camberley 22030. *Club:* United Nursing Services.

TURNER, Sir Mark; *see* Turner, Sir Ronald Mark Cunliffe.

TURNER, Michael John, QC 1973; a Recorder of the Crown Court, since 1972; *b* 31 May 1931; *s* of Theodore F. Turner, *qv*; *m* 1st, 1956, Hon. Susan Money-Coutts (marr. diss. 1965); one *s* one *d*; 2nd, 1965, Frances Deborah Croom-Johnson; two *s*. *Educ:* Winchester; Magdalene Coll., Cambridge (BA). Called to Bar, 1954. Dep. Chm., E Mids Agricultural Tribunal, 1972. *Recreations:* hunting, sailing, music. *Address:* Orchard House, Maidford, Towcester, Northants. *T:* Blakesley 391; 30 Shrewsbury House, Cheyne Walk, SW3. *T:* 01-352 2832.
    See also *C. G. Turner*.

TURNER, Sir Michael (William), Kt 1961; CBE 1957; Colonial Police Medal 1956; formerly Chairman and Chief Manager of The Hong-Kong and Shanghai Banking Corporation, retired 1962; *b* 25 April 1905; *s* of late Sir Skinner Turner, HBM

Supreme Court at Shanghai, and late Lady Turner; *m* 1938, Wendy Spencer, *d* of late Morris Stranack, Durban, SA; three *s*. *Educ:* Marlborough Coll.; University Coll., Oxford (MA). Joined The Hong-Kong and Shanghai Banking Corporation, 1926. Served in: Hong Kong, Shanghai, Singapore. Interned at Singapore, 1942-45. Former Dir, National Westminster Bank Ltd (Chm., W Midlands and Wales Regional Bd, 1973-75); Member, London Cttee, The Hong Kong and Shanghai Banking Corp., 1962-. Skinner and Citizen of the City of London; Master of the Skinners Company, 1967-68. FZS (London). Hon. LLD (Hong Kong), 1959. CStJ 1960; Commander, Order of Prince Henry the Navigator (Portugal), 1963. *Recreations:* shooting, fishing, walking, formerly hockey (Oxford Univ., Hockey XI, 1925, 1926). *Address:* Kirawin, Cliveden Mead, Maidenhead, Berks. *T:* Maidenhead 24718. *Clubs:* Overseas Bankers; Vincent's (Oxford); Hong Kong (Hong Kong).

TURNER, Norman Henry, CBE 1977; Official Solicitor to the Supreme Court of Judicature, since 1970; *b* 11 May 1916; *s* of late Henry James Turner, MA and Hilda Gertrude Turner; *m* 1939, Dora Ardella (*née* Cooper); three *s* two *d*. *Educ:* Nottingham High School. Articled, Nottingham, 1933; admitted Solicitor (Hons), 1938; joined Official Solicitor's Dept, 1948; Asst Official Solicitor, 1958. *Recreation:* caravanning. *Address:* 48 Rushington Avenue, Maidenhead, Berks. *T:* Maidenhead 22918.

TURNER, Patricia; National Woman Officer, General and Municipal Workers' Union; *b* 14 May 1927; *d* of John Richard and Maire Collins; *m* 1954, Donald Turner, BSc (Econ). *Educ:* London School of Economics (BSc (Econ), MSc (Econ)). Industrial Sociology Lectr, 1965-69; Consultant, Manpower and Productivity Service (Dept of Employment and Productivity), 1969-70; Sen. Industrial Relations Officer, Commn on Industrial Relations, 1970-71; Dir, Women's Dept, G&MWU, 1971. Member: Confedn of Shipbuilding and Engineering Unions Exec. Council, 1971-; Engineering Industry Training Bd, 1971-; Food, Drink and Tobacco Industry Training Bd, 1971-; Women's Nat. Commn, 1971-; Occupational Pensions Bd, 1973-. *Recreations:* reading, theatre. *Address:* (office) G&MWU, Thorne House, Ruxley Ridge, Claygate, Esher, Surrey KT10 0TL. *T:* Esher 62081.

TURNER, Peter; *see* Turner, T. P.

TURNER, Air Vice-Marshal Peter; Air Officer Administration, HQ RAF Support Command, since 1975, and Head of RAF Administrative Branch, 1976; *b* 29 Dec. 1924; *s* of late George Allen and of Emma Turner; *m* 1949, Doreen Newbon; one *s*. *Educ:* Tapton House Sch., Chesterfield. Served War of 1939-45; Air Signaller, 640 Sqdn, 1943-45; Nos 51, 242 and 246 Sqdns, 1945-48. RAF Staff Coll., 1960-61; HQ Comd Air EASTLANT (Logistics and Infrastructure Plans), 1963-67; jssc 1967; Chief Equipment and Secretarial Instructor, RAF Coll., Cranwell, 1967-68; Comd Accountant, HQ Air Support Comd, 1968-69; Station Comdr, RAF Uxbridge, 1969-71; RCDS, 1972; Dir of Personnel (Ground) (RAF), MoD, 1973-75. *Recreations:* walking, gardening, reading. *Address:* Park House, 35 Park Lane, Brampton, Huntingdon, Cambs PE18 8QL. *Club:* Royal Air Force.

TURNER, Peter William; Industrial Adviser to Department of Industry, since 1976 (seconded from Transport and General Workers' Union); *m* Maureen Ann Turner (*née* Hill), Councillor, JP. *Educ:* Bordesley Green Infant and Junior Sch.; Saltley Grammar Sch. (until 1940); various Trade Union weekend courses. District Officer, TGWU, 1969-; District Sec., CSEU, 1974-76. Member of various cttees including: Chemical Industry Area Productivity Cttee, 1969-76 (Vice-Chm., 1970-72, Chm., 1972-74); TUC Regional Educn Adv. Cttee, 1970-76; Birmingham Crime Prevention Panel, 1973-76; W Midlands Consultative Cttee on Race Relations, 1974-76; DoE Working Party on Race Relations, 1974-76. Member: Birmingham Trades Council, 1956-76; Local Appeals Tribunal, 1969-74. *Publications:* various booklets on industrial relations, industrial legislation and work study (for shop steward training). *Recreations:* motoring, boating, do-it-yourself, reading, electronics, music. *Address:* Department of Industry, 1 Victoria Street, SW1H 0ET. *T:* 01-215 5102.

TURNER, Philip, CBE 1975; LLB (London); temporary member of legal staff, Department of the Environment; Solicitor to the Post Office, 1972-75 (Principal Assistant Solicitor, 1962-72); *b* 1 June 1913; *er s* of late George Francis and late Daisy Louise Turner (*née* Frayn), Alverstoke, Hants; *m* 1938, Hazel Edith, *d* of late Douglas Anton and Edith Ada Benda; one *d* (one *d* decd). *Educ:* Peter Symonds, Winchester. Admitted Solicitor, 1935. Entered General Post Office Solicitor's Dept, 1935. Served in

Royal Navy, 1940-46 (Lt-Comdr). Asst Solicitor to General Post Office, 1953. Chm., Civil Service Legal Soc., 1957-58; Chm., Internat. Bar Assoc.'s Cttee on Public Utility Law. FRSA 1955. *Recreations:* piano, golf. *Address:* Well House, The Marld, Ashtead, Surrey. *T:* Ashtead 73656. *Clubs:* Naval; RAC Country (Epsom).
See also Rt Hon . John Adams .

TURNER, Surgeon Rear-Admiral (D) Philip Stanley, CB 1963; QHDS 1960-64; Director of Dental Services, RN, Admiralty, Nov. 1961-64; *b* 31 Oct. 1905; *s* of Frank Overy Turner and Ellen Mary Turner, Langton Green, Tunbridge Wells; *m* 1934, Marguerite Donnelly; one *d* (and one *s* decd). *Educ:* Cranbrook Coll.; Guy's Hospital. LDS, RCS 1927. Surgeon Lieut (D) Royal Navy, 1928; Surgeon Captain (D) 1955; Surgeon Rear-Admiral (D), 1961; Senior Specialist in Dental Surgery, 1946-61. Served in: HMS Ramillies, Vanguard, Implacable, Indomitable; HMHS Maine, Tjitjalengka; RN Hospitals Haslar, Plymouth; RN Barracks Portsmouth, etc; Naval HQ, Malta. Foundation Fellow, British Assoc. of Oral Surgeons, 1962. *Address:* Woodhurst, Warren Lane, Cross-in-Hand, Heathfield, East Sussex. *T:* Heathfield 3532.

TURNER, Sir Ralph Lilley, Kt 1950; MC; FBA 1942; MA, LittD, Hon. DLitt, Benares, 1951; Hon. DLit: Ceylon, 1958; London, 1967; Santiniketan, 1972; Kathmandu, 1977; Director of the School of Oriental and African Studies, 1937-57 (Hon. Fellow, 1957); Professor of Sanskrit, University of London, 1922-54, Emeritus Professor since 1954; *b* 5 Oct. 1888; *s* of George Turner, MA, JP, OBE, Cambridge; *m* 1920, Dorothy Rivers (*d* 1972), *d* of William Howard Goulty, Hale, Cheshire; one *s* three *d. Educ:* Perse Grammar Sch. and Christ's Coll., Cambridge (Senior Scholar). Classical Tripos Part I Class I, Div. 3; Oriental Languages Trip. Class I; Class. Trip. Part II Sect. E, Class I with distinction; Brotherton Memorial Sanskrit Prize; Fellow of Christ's Coll., 1912 (Hon. Fellow, 1950); Indian Educational Service, Lectr in Sanskrit at Queen's Coll., Benares, 1913; Wilson Philological Lectr, Bombay Univ., 1914; Indian Army R of O, attached 2/3rd QAO Gurkha Rifles, 1915-19 (despatches twice); Examiner Or. Lang. Trip. and Class. Trip. Part II Cambridge; Prof. of Indian Linguistics, Benares Hindu Univ., 1920; Wilson Philological Lectr, Bombay Univ., 1922; Hon. Treasurer (Pres., 1939-43) Philological Soc.; Pres., 1952-55, Royal Asiatic Soc. (Gold Medallist, 1953, Hon. Vice-Pres., 1963); 7th International Congress of Linguists, 1952; 23rd International Congress of Orientalists, 1954; Hon. Fellow, Deccan Coll., Poona. Formerly Member: Inter-Services Cttee on Language Training; Linguists' Cttee of Min. of Labour and National Service; Colonial Social Science Research Council; Adv. Cttee on the Humanities of the British Council; Adv. Cttee on Education in the Colonies; Treasury sub-cttee for studentships in foreign languages and cultures; sub-cttee University Grants Cttee on Oriental and African Studies; Corr. Member: Czecho-Slovakian Oriental Institute of Prag, Institut de France, Acad. des Inscriptions et Belles Lettres; Hon. Member: Norwegian Acad. of Science and Letters, Ceylon Acad. of Letters, Soc. Asiatique, Paris, American Oriental Soc., Deutsche Morgenländische Gesellschaft, Bihar Research Soc., Bhandarkar Oriental Research Inst., Ceylon Branch of Royal Asiatic Soc., Nagaripracarini Sabha, Banaras, Sanskrit Vishva Parishad, Vishveshvaranand Vedic Research Inst., Ganganatha Jha Research Inst., Linguistic Soc. of America, Linguistic Soc. of India, Ceylon Linguistic Soc., Mark Twain Soc. Campbell Gold Medallist, Asiatic Soc. of Bombay, 1967; Rabindranath Tagore Centenary Plaque, Asiatic Soc. of Bengal, 1971. Nepalese Order of Gorkha Dakshina Bahu, 2nd Class, 1951, 1st Class, 1960. *Publications:* Gujarati Phonology; The Position of Romani in Indo-Aryan; A Comparative and Etymological Dictionary of the Nepali Language; The Gavimath and Palkigundu Inscriptions of Asoka; ed. Indian Studies presented to Professor E. J. Rapson, Indian and Iranian Studies presented to Sir G. A. Grierson; Report to the Nuffield Foundation on a visit to Nigeria; Problems of Sound-change in Indo-Aryan; A Comparative Dictionary of the Indo-aryan Languages; Collected Papers, 1912-73; articles in Encyclopædia Britannica, etc. *Address:* Haverbrack, Bishop's Stortford, Herts. *T:* 54135.

TURNER, Raymond C.; *see* Clifford-Turner.

TURNER, Richard, CMG 1956; LRIBA; consultant architect; *b* 2 May 1909; *m* 1933, Annie Elizabeth, *d* of late Rev. R. W. Gair; one *d. Educ:* Dame Alice Owen's School. Entered Office of Works, 1929; in charge of ME Office, 1938-47, centred in Istanbul and, later, Cairo; Asst Chief Architect, Min. of Works, 1951; Dir of Works (Overseas), 1960-65; Dir, Overseas Svcs, MPBW, 1965-69, retired. Mem., Esher UDC, 1969-72. *Address:* Chestnuts, Knowle Drive, Sidmouth, Devon EX10 8HP. *T:* Sidmouth 3805. *Club:* Travellers'.

TURNER, Dr Richard Wainwright Duke, OBE 1945; Senior Research Fellow in Preventive Cardiology, University of Edinburgh, since 1974 (Reader in Medicine, 1960-74); Senior Physician and Physician in Charge of the Cardiac Department, Western General Hospital, Edinburgh, 1946-74; *b* Purley, Surrey, 30 May 1909; *s* of Sydney Duke Turner, MD (General Practitioner), and Lilian Maude, *d* of Sir James Wainwright; *m* Paula, *d* of Henry Meulen, Wimbledon; three *s* one *d. Educ:* Epsom Coll.; Clare Coll., Cambridge; St Thomas' Hosp., London. 1st Class Hons Nat. Sci. Tripos, Cambridge, 1934. MA, MB, BChir Cantab 1934; MRCS, LRCP 1935; MRCP 1936; MD Cantab 1940; FRCP 1950; FRCPE 1952. Served in RAMC, 1939-45: UK, Egypt and Italy (Lt-Col); officer i/c Med. Div. 31st and 92nd British General Hospitals. Examiner in Medicine: Univs of Edinburgh and Leeds; RCP; RCPE. Member: Assoc. Physicians of GB; British Cardiac Soc.; Hon. Member, Cardiol Socs of India and Pakistan. *Publications:* Diseases of Cardiovascular System in Davidson's Principles and Practice of Medicine, 1952-65; Electrocardiography, 1963; Auscultation of the Heart, 1963; contribs to British Heart Jl, Lancet, BMJ, Quarterly Jl of Med., American Heart Jl, etc. *Recreations:* travel, climbing, gardening, photography. *Address:* 15 Russell Place, Edinburgh EH5 3HQ. *T:* 031-552 5237; Department of Preventive Cardiology, 21 Buccleuch Place, Edinburgh EH8 9LN. *T:* 031-667 1011. *Clubs:* Royal Over-Seas League; University Staff (Edinburgh).

TURNER, Robert Noel, CMG 1955; retired; *b* 28 Dec. 1912; *s* of late Engr Rear-Adm. A. Turner and late Mrs V. E. Turner; *m* 1946, Evelyn Heynes Dupree (*d* 1976); two *s. Educ:* Dover Coll.; Wadham Coll., Oxford (MA). First Class Hons Modern History. Cadet, Malayan Civil Service, 1935; Third Asst Sec. to Govt, FMS, 1936; Asst District Officer, Lower Perak, FMS, 1938; Supernumerary Duty (Lower Perak), 1939; Asst Resident, Brunei, 1940 (interned by Japanese, Borneo, Dec. 1941-Sept. 1945); Asst Sec. to Governor-General, Malaya, May 1946; Prin. Asst Sec., Sarawak, Aug. 1946; First Asst Malayan Establishment Officer, 1948; Acting Dep. Malayan Establishment Officer, April 1950; Chief Sec., Barbados, 1950-56 (title changed from Colonial Sec., 1954); Acting Governor, Barbados, Nov. 1952-May 1953 and 1955, North Borneo, 1957-62 (commended by Sec. of State 'Hurricane Janet', 1955); Chief Sec., North Borneo, 1956-63 (Mem. Exec. Council and Legislative Council, 1950-63); State Sec., Sabah, Fedn of Malaysia, 1963-64 (Mem. State Cabinet, 1963-64). Hon. Mem., First Grade, Order of Kinabalu, Sabah (title: Datuk; lettering: SPDK), 1963. *Recreations:* reading history, watching cricket. *Address:* Kinabalu, The Rise, Brockenhurst, Hants SO4 7SJ. *T:* 3197.

TURNER, Sir (Ronald) Mark (Cunliffe), Kt 1946; Chairman and Chief Executive, Rio Tinto-Zinc Corporation, since 1975; Deputy Chairman, Kleinwort, Benson, Lonsdale Ltd, since 1969; Director: Whitbread Investment Co. Ltd, and other companies; *b* 29 March 1906; *s* of Christopher Rede Turner and Jill Helen Pickersgill Cunliffe; *m* 1st, 1931, Elizabeth Mary Sutton (marr. diss. 1936); one *d* decd; 2nd, 1939, Margaret Wake; three *s* two *d. Educ:* Wellington Coll., Berks. City, 1924, with M. Samuel & Co. Ltd, Merchant Bankers; Nov. 1934 until outbreak of war with Robert Benson & Co. Ltd, Merchant Bankers; with Ministry of Economic Warfare, 1939-44; Foreign Office, 1944-45; Under-Secretary Control Office for Germany and Austria, 1945-47. Chairman: Mercantile Credit Co. Ltd, 1957-72; British Home Stores Ltd, 1968-76; Dep. Chm., Kleinwort, Benson Ltd, 1966-71. Dir, Sotheby Parke Bernet Gp Ltd. *Address:* 3 The Grove, Highgate, N6. *T:* 01-340 3421. *Club:* Brooks's.

TURNER, Theodora, OBE 1961; ARRC 1944; retired as Matron of St Thomas' Hospital and Superintendent Nightingale Training School (1955-65); *b* 5 Aug. 1907; *er d* of H. E. M. Turner. *Educ:* Godolphin School, Salisbury; Edinburgh School of Domestic Economy. Ward Sister, St Thomas' Hosp., 1935-38; Administrative Course, Florence Nightingale Internat. Foundn, 1938-39. QAIMNS Reserve, 1939-45. Administrative Sister, St Thomas' Hosp., 1946-47; Matron Royal Infirmary, Liverpool, 1948-53; Education Officer, Educn Centre, Royal College of Nursing, Birmingham, 1953-55. President: Florence Nightingale Internat. Nurses Assoc., 1971-74; Royal Coll. of Nursing and Nat. Council of Nurses of UK, 1966-68. Mem., Argyll and Clyde Health Bd, 1974-75. *Recreations:* gardening and painting. *Address:* Achraich, Clachan Seil, by Oban, Argyll.

TURNER, Theodore Francis, QC 1943; Barrister-at-law; *b* 19 Nov. 1900; *s* of George Lewis and Mabel Mary Turner; *m* 1st, 1925, Elizabeth Alice, *o d* of 1st Baron Schuster, GCB, CVO, QC; two *s* one *d* ; 2nd, 1949, Ruth, 2nd *d* of late L. C. Ledyard, Jr, and late Mrs W. E. S. Griswold, NY. *Educ:* Downside;

Balliol Coll., Oxford (Exhibitioner). Called to Bar, 1924; joined South Eastern Circuit. Regional Controller, Ministry of Fuel and Power, North Midland Region, 1944-45; Recorder of Rochester, 1946-50; Chairman Mining Subsidence Cttee, 1947-48. Admitted New York Bar, 1962. *Address:* Windswept, East Norwich, Long Island, NY 11732, USA; 570 Park Avenue, New York City, NY 10021, USA. *Clubs:* Garrick; The Brook (NY). *See also W. H. Hughes, C. G. Turner, M. J. Turner.*

TURNER, (Thomas) Peter; Head of Operational Research, Civil Service Department, since 1977; *b* 8 May 1928; *s* of Thomas Turner and Laura Crawley; *m* 1952, Jean Rosalie Weston; one *s* one *d*. *Educ:* Ilford County High Sch.; London University. BSc (1st Class Hons), Maths and Physics. GEC, North Wembley, 1947-50; Armament Design Establishment, 1950-54; Air Ministry (Science 3), 1954-58 and 1962-63; Chief Research Officer, RAF Maintenance Command, 1958-62; Police Research and Development Branch, Home Office, 1963-68; Civil Service Dept (OR), 1968-73; Head of Treasury/CSD Joint Operational Research Unit, 1973-76. *Address:* 8 Waring Drive, Green St Green, Orpington, Kent BR6 6DW. *T:* Farnborough (Kent) 51189.

TURNER, Wilfred, CMG 1977; HM Diplomatic Service; High Commissioner to Botswana, since 1977; *b* 10 Oct. 1921; *s* of late Allen Turner and Eliza (*née* Leach); *m* 1947, June Gladys Tite; two *s* one *d*. *Educ:* Heywood Grammar Sch., Lancs; London Univ. BSc 1942 (external degree by private study). Min. of Labour, 1938-42. Served War, REME, 1942-47. Min. of Labour, 1947-55; Brit. High Commn, New Delhi (Asst Lab. Adviser), 1955-59; Min. of Labour, 1959-60; Min. of Health (Sec., Cttee on Safety of Drugs, 1963-66), 1960-66. Joined HM Diplomatic Service, 1966; Commonwealth Office, 1966; First Sec.: Kaduna, Nigeria, 1966-69; Kuala Lumpur, 1969-73; Dep. High Comr, and Commercial/Economic Counsellor, Accra, 1973-77. *Recreation:* hill walking. *Address:* c/o Foreign and Commonwealth Office, SW1; 44 Tower Road, Twickenham TW1 4PE. *T:* 01-892 1593. *Club:* Royal Commonwealth Society.

TURNER, Lt-Gen. Sir William (Francis Robert), KBE 1962; CB 1959; DSO 1945; Lord-Lieutenant of Dumfries, since 1972; *b* 12 Dec. 1907; *er s* of late Mr and Mrs F. R. Turner, Kelso, Roxburghshire; *m* 1938, Nancy Maude Stilwell, *er d* of late Lt-Col and Mrs J. B. L. Stilwell, Yateley, Hants; one *s*. *Educ:* Winchester College; RMC Sandhurst. 2nd Lieut, KOSB, 1928; served in Great Britain and India, 1928-39; Capt. 1938; BEF, 1939-40; Staff College, 1941; OC, 5 KOSB, 1942-45 (despatches), NW Europe; OC, 1 KOSB, 1945-46, NW Europe and Middle East; GSO1, Middle East and Great Britain, 1947-50. Colonel Brit. Military Mission to Greece, 1950-52; Comd 128 Inf. Bde (TA), 1952-54; BGS HQ Western Comd, 1954-56; GOC 44 (Home Counties) Infantry Div. (TA) and Home Counties District, and Deputy Constable of Dover Castle, 1956-59; President, Regular Commissions Board, 1959-61; GOC-in-C, Scottish Comd, and Governor of Edinburgh Castle, 1961-64; retd 1964; Colonel, King's Own Scottish Borderers, 1961-70; Ensign, Queen's Body Guard for Scotland (Royal Company of Archers). HM Comr, Queen Victoria School, Dunblane. DL, Dumfriesshire, 1970-72. Comdr with Star, Order of Saint Olav, Class II (Norway), 1962; Order of the Two Niles, Class II (Republic of the Sudan), 1963. *Address:* Milnhead, Kirkton, Dumfries. *T:* Dumfries 71319. *Clubs:* Naval and Military; New (Edinburgh).

TURNER, William Hovell, CIE 1947; CBE 1957; MC 1918; MA; Director of Audit, Indian Accounts in the UK, 1943-56; *b* 10 Sept. 1891; *s* of George Turner, OBE, JP, and Bertha, *d* of W. Eaden Lilley, Cambridge; *m* 1920, May Calder Scott, *d* of Mrs M. C. Turner, Godstowe Sch.; two *s* one *d*. *Educ:* Perse School and Christ's Coll., Cambridge; State Coll. of Washington, USA; Jena Univ., Germany. Served European War, 1914-19, RFA, Major (despatches twice). Junior clerk, India Office, 1919; Private Sec. to Earl of Lytton, Parly Under-Sec. of State, 1920-22; Sec. of Indian Delegn to League of Nations Assembly, 1932 and 1933; Asst Sec. Burma Office, 1940, Min. of Supply, 1943. Head of Indian Home Accounts for many years. *Address:* 26 Connaught Avenue, Loughton, Essex. *T:* 01-502 1108.

TURNER CAIN, Maj.-Gen. George Robert, CB 1967; CBE 1963; DSO 1945; Chairman: Anglia Maltings (Holdings) Ltd; Anglia Maltings Ltd; F. & G. Smith Ltd; Walpole & Wright Ltd; Director: Crisp Maltings Ltd; Crisp Malt Products Ltd; Edme Ltd; *b* 16 Feb. 1912; *s* of late Wing Comdr G. Turner Cain; *m* 1938, Lamorna Maturin, *d* of late Col G. B. Hingston; one *s* one *d*. *Educ:* Norwich Sch.; RMC Sandhurst. 2nd Lt Norfolk Regt, 1932; 1st Bn Royal Norfolk Regt, India, 1933-38; Waziristan Campaign, 1937. Served War of 1939-45 with 1st Royal Norfolk and 1st Hereford Regt, BLA, 1944-45. Comd 1st Royal Norfolk

Regt, Berlin, 1947-48; Hong Kong and UK, 1953-55; Comd Tactical Wing, School of Infantry, 1955-57; Comd 1st Fed. Inf. Bde, Malaya, in operations in Malaya, 1957-59; BGS, HQ, BAOR, 1961; Maj.-Gen. Administration, GHQ FARELF, 1964-67, retired; ADC, 1961-64. Dep. Col, Royal Anglian Regt, 1971-74. Croix de Guerre avec Palm, 1945; Star of Kedah (Malaya), 1959. *Recreation:* shooting. *Address:* Holbreck, Hollow Lane, Stiffkey, near Wells-next-the-Sea, Norfolk.

TURNER-SAMUELS, David Jessel, QC 1972; Barrister-at-Law; *b* 5 April 1918; *s* of late Moss Turner-Samuels, QC, MP, and Gladys Deborah Turner-Samuels (*née* Belcher); *m* 1939, Norma Turner-Samuels (*née* Verstone) (marr. diss. 1975); one *s* one *d*; *m* 1976, Norma Florence Negus (*née* Shellabear). *Educ:* Westminster Sch. Called to Bar, Middle Temple, 1939. Served War of 1939-45, in Army, 1939-46. *Publication:* (jointly) Industrial Negotiation and Arbitration, 1951. *Recreation:* getting away from it all. *Address:* Oak Cottage, The Lane, Thursley, Surrey. *T:* Elstead 2238; New Court, Temple, EC4Y 9BE. *T:* 01-353 7613.

TURNER-WARWICK, Prof. Margaret Elizabeth Harvey, MA, DM, PhD, FRCP; Professor of Medicine (Thoracic Medicine), Cardiothoracic Institute, Brompton Hospital, since 1972; *b* 19 Nov. 1924; *d* of William Harvey Moore, QC, and Maud Baden-Powell; *m* 1950, Richard Trevor Turner-Warwick, *qv*; two *d*. *Educ:* St Paul's Sch.; Lady Margaret Hall (Open Schol. 1943), Oxford. University Coll. Hosp., 1947-50: Tuke silver medal, Filliter exhibn in Pathology, Magrath Schol. in Medicine, Atchison Schol.; Postgrad. trng at UCH and Brompton Hosp., 1950-61; Cons. Physician: (Gen. Med.), Elizabeth Garrett Anderson Hosp., 1961-67; Brompton and London Chest Hosps, 1967-72. Sen. Lectr, Inst. of Diseases of the Chest, 1961-72. *Publications:* chapters in various textbooks, especially on immunology and thoracic medicine; contrib. original articles: Lancet, BMJ, Quarterly Jl Med., Thorax, Tubercle, Jl Clin. Experimental Immunology, etc. *Recreations:* her family and their hobbies, gardening, country life, music. *Address:* 55 Fitzroy Park, Highgate, N6 6JA. *T:* 01-340 6339.

TURNER-WARWICK, Richard Trevor, MA, BSc, DM Oxon, MCh, FRCS, MRCP, FACS; Surgeon and Senior Urologist to the Middlesex Hospital, W1; Urologist to King Edward VII Hospital for Officers, St Peter's Hospital Group and Royal National Orthopædic Hospital; Senior Lecturer, London University Institute of Urology; *b* 21 Feb. 1925; *s* of W. Turner Warwick, FRCS; *m* 1950, Prof. Margaret Elizabeth Turner-Warwick, *qv*; two *d*. *Educ:* Bedales School; Oriel Coll., Oxford; Middlesex Hosp. Medical School. Pres. OUBC, 1946; Mem. Univ. Boat Race Crew, Isis Head of River crew and Univ. fours, 1946; Winner OU Silver Sculls, 1946; BSc thesis in neuroanatomy, 1946. Sen. Broderip Schol., Lyell Gold Medallist and Freeman Schol., Middx Hosp., 1949; surgical trng at Middx Hosp. and St Paul's Hosp., London, and Columbia Presbyterian Med. Centre, NY, 1959. Hunterian Prof. of RCS, 1957, 1976; Moynihan Prize of Assoc. of Surgeons, 1957; Comyns Berkeley Travelling Fellowship to USA, 1959; FRSocMed; Fellow and Mem. Council, Assoc. of Surgeons of GB and Ireland; Fellow, British Assoc. of Urological Surgeons; Member: Internat. Soc. of Urology; European Soc. of Urology; Soc. of Pelvic Surgeons; Corresp. Member: Amer. Assoc. of Genito Urinary Surgeons; American, Australian and Belgian Urological Assocs. *Publications:* various articles on surgery, urodynamics and reconstructive urology in scientific journals. *Recreation:* water. *Address:* 61 Harley House, NW1. *T:* 01-935 2550; Tirnanog, 55 Fitzroy Park, Highgate, N6. *T:* 01-340 6339. *Clubs:* Vincent's (Oxford); Leander (Henley), Royal Motor Yacht (Poole).

TURNOUR, family name of Earl Winterton.

TURPIN, James Alexander, CMG 1966; HM Diplomatic Service, retired; *b* 7 Jan. 1917; *s* of late Samuel Alexander Turpin; *m* 1942, Kathleen Iris Eadie; one *d*. *Educ:* King's Hosp., Dublin; Trinity Coll., Dublin (MA). Asst Lectr, Trinity College, Dublin, 1940. Served Army (Royal Irish Fusiliers), 1942-46. Joined Foreign Service, 1947; Mem., UK Delegn to OEEC, Paris, 1948; 1st Sec., 1949; FO, 1950; Warsaw, 1953 (Chargé d'Affaires, 1953, 1954); Tokyo, 1955; Counsellor, 1960; seconded to BoT, 1960-63; Counsellor (Commercial), The Hague, 1963-67; Minister (Economic and Commercial), New Delhi, 1967-70; Asst Under-Sec. of State, FCO, 1971-72; Ambassador to the Philippines, 1972-76. *Recreations:* tennis, music, swimming. *Address:* 33 Elm Bank Mansions, Barnes, SW13. *Club:* Travellers'.

TURPIN, Kenneth Charlton; Provost, Oriel College, Oxford, since 1957; Pro-Vice Chancellor, Oxford University, 1964-66, and since 1969 (Vice-Chancellor, 1966-69); Member,

Hebdomadal Council, 1959-77; *b* 13 Jan. 1915; *e s* of late Henry John Turpin, Ludlow. *Educ:* Manchester Grammar Sch.; Oriel College, Oxford. Treasury, 1940-43; Asst Private Sec. to C. R. Attlee, Lord President and Dep. Prime Minister, 1943-45; 2nd Asst Registrar, University Registry, Oxford, 1945-47; Sec. of Faculties, Univ. of Oxford, 1947-57; professorial fellow, Oriel Coll., 1948; Hon. Fellow Trinity Coll., Dublin, 1968. *Recreations:* golf, walking. *Address:* Provost's Lodgings, Oriel College, Oxford. *T:* Oxford 41962; Copthorne, Knighton, Powys. *Clubs:* Athenæum; Vincent's (Oxford).

TURPIN, Maj.-Gen. Patrick George, CB 1962; OBE 1943; FCIT; *b* 27 April 1911; 3rd *s* of late Rev. J. J. Turpin, MA, BD, late Vicar of Misterton, Somerset; *m* 1947, Cherry Leslie Joy, *d* of late Major K. S. Grove, York and Lancaster Regiment; one *s* one *d*. *Educ:* Haileybury Coll., Hertford; Exeter College, Oxford (Sen. Classical Schol.). BA (Hons) Oxford (Lit. Hum.), 1933; MA 1963. Commd RASC, 2nd Lt, 1933; Lt 1936; Capt. 1941; Major 1946; Lt-Col 1949; Col 1953; Brig. 1959; Maj.-Gen. 1960. Served War of 1939-45 (despatches twice, OBE): Adjt, 1939-40; AQMG, 30 Corps, W Desert, 1943; AA&QMG, 5th Div., Italy, 1943-44; DA&QMG (Brig.), 1 Corps, BLA, 1945; Brig. A, 21 Army Gp, 1945-46; Comd 6 Training Bn, RASC, 1947; ADS&T, WO, 1948; AA&QMG (Plans), HQ, BTE (Egypt), 1950; GSO1 (instructor), Jt Services Staff Coll., 1951-53; ADS&T (Col), WO, 1953-54; DAG, HQ, BAOR, 1956-59; Brig. i/c Adm., 17 Gurkha Div., Malaya, 1959-60; DST, 1960-63; Dir of Movements, MoD (Army), 1963-66; psc 1941; jssc 1949; idc 1955; Col Comdt, Royal Corps of Transport, 1965-71; Col Gurkha Army Service Corps, 1960-65; Col Gurkha Transport Regt, 1965-73. Sec.-Gen., Assoc. of British Travel Agents, 1966-69. Governor, Royal Sch. for Daughters of Officers of the Army, Bath, 1963-. FCIT (MInsT 1961). *Recreations:* lawn tennis (Somerset County Champion, 1948, Army Colours, 1952); squash rackets (Bucks County Colours, 1952); golf. *Address:* Cottswood, West Clandon, Guildford, Surrey. *T:* Guildford 222580. *Clubs:* Royal Over-Seas League; Oxford Union Society; All England Lawn Tennis; International Lawn Tennis; Escorts Squash Rackets.

TURTON, family name of **Baron Tranmire.**

TURTON, Victor Ernest; Managing Director: V. E. Turton (Tools) Ltd; V. E. Turton (Motor Spares) Ltd; V. E. Turton (Wholesalers) Ltd; *b* 29 June 1924; *s* of H. E. Turton; *m* 1951, Jean Edith Murray; two *d*. *Educ:* Paget Secondary Modern Sch.; Aston Techn. Coll.; Birmingham Central Techn. Coll. Birmingham City Councillor (Lab) Duddeston Ward, 1945-63; Saltley Ward, 1970-71; Alderman, Birmingham, 1963-70 and 1971-74; Lord Mayor of Birmingham, 1971-72; Mem., W Midlands CC, 1974-77. Mem., Transportation Cttee, W Midlands CC; Chairman: Smallholdings and Agric. Cttee, 1954-58; Birmingham Airport, 1959-66; Airport Sub-Cttee, 1974-; Hall Green Div. Labour Party, 1957-59; West Midlands Regional Adv. Cttee for Civil Aviation, 1966-72; Heart of England Tourist Bd, 1975-; Jt Airports Cttee of Local Authorities, 1975-. Former Governor, Coll. of Technology (now Univ. of Aston in Birmingham). Mem., Inst. of Directors. *Recreations:* football, cricket, table tennis, philately. *Address:* 32 Tenbury Road, King's Heath, Birmingham B14 6AD.

TURTON-HART, Sir Francis (Edmund), KBE 1963 (MBE 1942); *b* 29 May 1908; *s* of David Edwin Hart and Zoe Evelyn Turton; *m* 1947, Margaret Greaves; one *d*. *Educ:* Uppingham. Served with Royal Engineers, 1939-46 (Hon. Major, 1946). East Africa, 1924-38; Portugal, 1939; West Africa, 1946-65; Federal House of Representatives, Nigeria, 1956-60; President, Lagos Chamber of Commerce, 1960-63. *Recreations:* shooting, fishing, golf. *Address:* Bagton, Kingsbridge, Devon. *Club:* Special Forces.

TURVEY, Ralph, DSc (Econ); economist; Economic Adviser, International Labour Office, since 1975; *b* 1 May 1927; *s* of John and Margaret Turvey; *m* 1957, Sheila Bucher, *d* of Otto and Doris Bucher; one *s* one *d*. *Educ:* Sidcot School; London School of Economics; Uppsala University. Lectr, then Reader in Economics, at London School of Economics, 1948-64, with interruptions. Vis. Lectr, Johns Hopkins Univ., 1953; Ford Foundation Vis. Res. Prof., Univ. of Chicago, 1958-59; Economic Section, HM Treasury, 1960-62; Center of Economic Research, Athens, 1963. Chief Economist, The Electricity Council, 1964-67. Member, NBPI, 1967-71, Jt Dep. Chm. 1968-71; Economic Adviser, Scientific Control Systems Ltd, 1971-75. Mem., Nat. Water Council, 1974-75. Vis. Prof. of Econs, LSE, 1973-75. Governor, Kingston Polytechnic, 1972-75. Mem., Inflation Accounting Cttee, 1974-75. *Publications:* The Economics of Real Property, 1957; Interest Rates and Asset Prices, 1960; Studies in Greek Taxation (joint author), 1964;

Optimal Pricing and Investment in Electricity Supply, 1968; Economic Analysis and Public Enterprises, 1971; Demand and Supply, 1971; (jtly) Electricity Economics, 1977; papers on applied welfare economics in Economic Jl, Amer. Economic Review, etc. *Recreations:* talking Swedish, alpine walking. *Address:* Case Postale 500, CH1211 Geneva 22, Switzerland. *Club:* Reform.

TURVILLE-PETRE, Prof. Edward Oswald Gabriel, FBA 1973; Professor of Ancient Icelandic Literature and Antiquities, Oxford University, 1953-75, now Professor Emeritus (Reader, 1941-53); Student of Christ Church, 1964-75; *b* 25 March 1908; *s* of late O. H. P. Turville-Petre and Margaret Lucy (*née* Cave); *m* 1943, Joan Elizabeth Blomfield; three *s*. *Educ:* Ampleforth; Christ Church, Oxford (MA, BLitt). Studied Icelandic language and literature in Iceland, Scandinavia and Germany. Lecturer, University of Iceland, 1936-38; Hon. Lectr in Modern Icelandic, Univ. of Leeds, 1935-50; Vis. Prof., Univ. of Melbourne, 1965. Corr. Mem. Icelandic Acad. of Sciences, 1959. Hon. DPh Univ. of Iceland, 1961. Kt of Falcon (Ice.), 1956, Comdr, 1963. *Publications:* Víga-Glúms Saga, 1940 (enlarged edn, 1960); The Heroic Age of Scandinavia, 1951; Origins of Icelandic Literature, 1953 (2nd edn 1967); Hervarar Saga, 1956; Myth and Religion of the North, 1964; Nine Norse Studies, 1972; Scaldic Poetry, 1976; (ed jtly) Iceland and the Mediaeval World, 1976; numerous articles in learned journals. *Address:* The Court, Old Headington, Oxford. *T:* Oxford 62502.

TUSHINGHAM, Rita; actress; *b* 14 March 1942; *d* of John Tushingham; *m* 1962, Terence William Bicknell (marr. diss. 1976); two *d*. *Educ:* La Sagesse Convent, Liverpool. Student, Liverpool Playhouse, 1958-60. *Stage appearances:* Royal Court Theatre: The Changeling, 1960; The Kitchen, 1961; A Midsummer Night's Dream, 1962; Twelfth Night, 1962; The Knack, 1962; The Giveaway, 1969; Lorna and Ted, 1970; Mistress of Novices, 1973. *Films:* A Taste of Honey, 1961 (Brit. Film Acad. and Variety Club awards for Most Promising Newcomer, 1961; NY Critics, Cannes Film Festival and Hollywood Foreign Press Assoc. awards); The Leather Boys, 1962; A Place to Go, 1963; Girl with Green Eyes, 1963 (Variety Club award); The Knack, 1964 (Silver Goddess award, Mexican Assoc. of Film Corresps); Dr Zhivago, 1965; The Trap, 1966; Smashing Time, 1967; Diamonds For Breakfast, 1967; The Guru, 1968; The Bed-Sitting Room, 1970; Straight on till Morning, 1972; Situation, 1972; Instant Coffee, 1973; Rachel's Man, 1974; The Human Factor, 1976; Pot Luck, 1977; State of Shock, 1977. *Recreation:* cooking. *Address:* c/o Jean Diamond, London Management, 235 Regent Street, W1.

TUSTIN, Arnold; Professor Emeritus, MSc, FIEE, retired; *b* 1899; *m* 1948; no *c*. *Educ:* King's Coll., Univ. of Durham. Subsequently Chief Asst Engineer, Metropolitan-Vickers Electrical Co., until 1945. Visiting Webster Prof., Massachusetts Inst. of Technology, 1953-54; Prof. of Electrical Engineering, Univ. of Birmingham, 1947-55; Prof. of Heavy Electrical Engineering, Imperial Coll., Univ. of London, 1955-64. Chm. Measurement and Control Section, IEE, 1959-60; Chm. Research Adv. Council, Transport Commn, 1960. Hon. DTech Bradford, 1968. *Publications:* Direct Current Machines for Control Systems, 1952; The Mechanism of Economic Systems, 1953; (ed) Automatic and Manual Control, 1951. *Address:* 1 Prospect Cottage, Lee Common, Great Missenden, Bucks.

TUTE, Warren Stanley; author; *b* 22 Feb. 1914; *s* of Stanley Harries Tute and Laura Edith Thompson; *m* 1st, 1944, Annette Elizabeth Neil (marr. diss. 1955); 2nd, 1958, Evelyn Mary Dalley; two *d*. *Educ:* Dragon Sch., Wrekin Coll. Entered RN 1932, served in HM Ships Nelson and Ajax; took part in N African, Sicilian and Normandy landings (despatches 1944), retired as Lt Comdr, 1946. Wrote for BBC, 1946-47; Dir, Random Film Productions Ltd, 1947-52; made films and trained scriptwriters for US Govt, 1952-54; Argentina, 1955; Dir, Theatrework (London) Ltd, 1960-, Kenway Theatre Co. Ltd, 1960-; produced (jtly) Little Mary Sunshine, Comedy, 1962; Head of Scripts, London Weekend TV, 1968-69. Visits USA and west and east Europe frequently. Chm., Whitefriars Club. *Publications:* novels: The Felthams, 1950; Lady in Thin Armour, 1951; Gentleman in Pink Uniform, 1952; The Younger Felthams, 1953; Girl in the Limelight, 1954; The Cruiser, 1955; The Rock, 1957; Leviathan, 1959; The Golden Greek, 1960; The Admiral, 1963; A Matter of Diplomacy, 1969; The Powder Train, 1970; The Tarnham Connection, 1971; The Resident, 1973; Next Saturday in Milan, 1975; Honours of War and Peace, 1976; The Cairo Sleeper, 1977; history: The Grey Top Hat, 1961; Atlantic Conquest, 1962; Cochrane, 1965; The Deadly Stroke, 1973; Hitler—The Last Ten Days, 1973; D Day, 1974; The North African War, 1976; plays: Jessica, 1956; A Time to be Born, 1956; Frost at Midnight (trans.), 1957; Quartet for Five,

1958; A Few Days in Greece, 1959; *other works:* Chico, 1950; Life of a Circus Bear, 1952; Cockney Cats, 1953; Le Petomane (trans.), 1967. *Recreations:* people, cats, wine, France. *Address:* 54 Rosemont Road, Richmond, Surrey. *T:* 01-940 3780; The Old Stables, 13 St Anne Junction, Mosta, Malta. *T:* 45736. *Club:* Garrick.

TUTIN, Dorothy, CBE 1967; actress (stage and films); *b* 8 April 1931; *d* of late John Tutin, DSc, and of Adie Evelyn Tutin; *m* 1963, Derek Barton-Chapple (stage name Derek Waring); one *s* one *d*. *Educ:* St Catherine's, Bramley, Surrey; RADA. Began career, 1950; Stratford Festival, 1958, 1960. *Parts include:* Rose, in The Living Room; Katherine, in Henry V; Sally Bowles, in I am a Camera; St Joan, in The Lark; Catherine, in The Gates of Summer; Hedwig, in The Wild Duck; Viola, in Twelfth Night; Juliet, in Romeo and Juliet; Ophelia, in Hamlet; during Shakespeare Memorial Theatre tour of Russia, 1958, played parts of Ophelia, Viola and Juliet; Dolly, in Once More, With Feeling (New), 1959; Portia, Viola, Cressida (S-on-A), 1960; Sister Jeanne, in The Devils (Aldwych), 1961, 1962; Juliet, Desdemona (S-on-A), 1961; Varya, in The Cherry Orchard (S-on-A, and Aldwych), 1961; Cressida, Prioress, in The Devils (Edinburgh), 1962; Polly Peachum, in The Beggar's Opera (Aldwych), 1963; The Hollow Crown (New York), 1963; Queen Victoria, in Portrait of a Queen, Vaudeville, 1965; Rosalind, in You Like It, Stratford, 1967, Los Angeles, 1968; Portrait of a Queen, NY, 1968; Play on Love, St Martin's, 1970; Old Times, Aldwych, 1971; Peter Pan, Coliseum, 1971, 1972; What Every Woman Knows, 1973, Albery, 1974; Natalya Petrovna, in A Month in the Country, Chichester, 1974, Albery, 1975; Cleopatra, in Antony and Cleopatra and in All For Love, Edinburgh, 1977. *Films:* Polly Peachum, in The Beggar's Opera; Cecily, in The Importance of Being Earnest; Lucie Manette, in A Tale of Two Cities; Henrietta Maria in Cromwell; Sophie Breska in Savage Messiah (Variety Club of GB Film Actress Award, 1972). Has appeared on television. *Recreations:* music; Isle of Arran. *Address:* c/o Peter Browne Management, 13 St Martin's Road, SW9.

TUTIN, Prof. Thomas Gaskell; Professor of Taxonomy, University of Leicester, 1967-73, now Emeritus; University Fellow, University of Leicester, 1974; *b* 21 April 1908; *o s* of Frank and Jane Tutin; *m* 1942, Winifred Pennington; one *s* three *d*. *Educ:* Cotham Sch., Bristol; Downing Coll., Cambridge. Expedition to British Guiana, 1933; Marine Laboratory, Plymouth, 1934-37; expedition to Lake Titicaca, 1937; part-time Demonstrator, KCL, 1938-39; Asst Lectr, Univ. of Manchester, 1939-42; Geographer, Naval Geological Div., 1942-44; Lectr, Univ. College of Leicester, 1944-47; Prof. of Botany, Univ. of Leicester, 1947-67. Foreign Member, Societas Scientiarum Fennica (Section for Natural Science), 1960. Linnean Medal, Linnean Soc., 1977. *Publications:* (with Clapham and Warburg) Flora of the British Isles, 1952, 2nd edn 1962; (with Clapham and Warburg) Excursion Flora of the British Isles, 1959, 2nd edn 1968; (with V. H. Heywood *et al*) Flora Europaea, Vol. I 1964, Vol. II 1968, Vol. III 1972, Vol. IV 1976; (with A. C. Jermy) British Sedges, 1968; papers in Annals of Botany, New Phytologist, Jl of Ecology, Watsonia, etc. *Recreations:* botany, music. *Address:* Home Farm, Knighton, Leicester LE2 3WG. *T:* Leicester 707356.

TUTTLE, Sir Geoffrey (William), KBE 1957 (OBE 1940); CB 1945; DFC 1937; FRAeS 1960; Air Marshal retired; Aerospace consultant; *b* 2 Oct. 1906; *s* of late Maj. E. W. Tuttle, Lowestoft. *Educ:* St Paul's School. Joined RAF, 1925; served war, 1939-45: France, Photo Reconnaissance Units, UK, Tunisia, Corsica, Sardinia, Italy, Greece; AOC RAF, Greece, 1944-46; Air Cdre 1948; Dir of Operational Requirements, Air Min., 1948-49; AOA, HQ Coastal Comd, 1950-51; Air Vice-Marshal 1952; ACAS (Operational Requirements), 1951-54; AOC No 19 Gp, RAF, 1954-56; Air Marshal 1957; DCAS, 1956-59, retd. British Aircraft Corp. Ltd, 1959-77. Order of Patriotic War, 2nd Class (Soviet), 1944; Grand Officer Royal Order of the Phœnix (Greece), 1945; Commandeur Légion d'Honneur (France); Croix de Guerre (France). *Recreation:* sailing. *Address:* Silver Waters, Kingswood Creek, Wraysbury, Bucks. *T:* Wraysbury 2346. *Club:* Royal Air Force.

TUZO, Gen. Sir Harry (Craufurd), GCB 1973 (KCB 1971); OBE 1961; MC 1945; Deputy Supreme Allied Commander, Europe, since 1976; Master Gunner, St James's Park, since 1977; *b* 26 Aug. 1917; *s* of John Atkinson Tuzo and Annie Katherine (*née* Craufurd); *m* 1943, Monica Patience Salter; one *d*. *Educ:* Wellington Coll.; Oriel Coll., Oxford. BA Oxon 1939, MA 1970. Regimental Service, Royal Artillery, 1939-45; Staff appts, Far East, 1946-49; Royal Horse Artillery, 1950-51 and 1954-58; Staff at Sch. of Infantry, 1951-53; GSO1, War Office, 1958-60; CO, 3rd Regt, RHA, 1960-62; Asst Comdt, Sandhurst, 1962-63;

Comdr, 51 Gurkha Infantry Bde, 1963-65; Imp. Def. Coll., 1966; Maj.-Gen. 1966; Chief of Staff, BAOR, 1967-69; Director, RA, 1969-71; Lt-Gen. 1971; GOC and Dir of Operations, NI, 1971-73; Gen. 1973: Comdr Northern Army Gp and C-in-C BAOR, 1973-76. ADC (Gen.) to the Queen, 1974-. Colonel Commandant: RA, 1971-; RHA, 1976-. Dato Setia Negeri Brunei, 1965. *Recreations:* sailing, music, shooting. *Address:* SHAPE, Mons, Belgium, BFPO 26. *Club:* Army and Navy.

TWEDDLE, Sir William, Kt 1977; CBE 1971 (OBE 1945); TD 1950; Partner in Simpson, Curtis & Co., Solicitors, Leeds, since 1940; Chairman, Yorkshire Regional Health Authority, since 1973; *b* 28 June 1914; *s* of late John Rippon Tweddle, and late Elizabeth Tweddle, Easingwold, Yorks; *m* 1941, Sheila Vartan; one *s* one *d*. *Educ:* Repton Sch.; Leeds Univ. (LLM). Solicitor, 1936. Asst Solicitor, Simpson, Curtis & Co., 1936-39. War Service, RA, TA, 1939-45: served overseas in France, 1940; Madagascar, 1942; NW Europe, 1944-45 (despatches twice, 1945); psc, 1943; Lt-Col., 1944. Chm., Leeds St James's Univ. (formerly Leeds A) HMC, 1957-74; Governor, United Leeds Hospitals, 1959-74; Member: Leeds Regional Hospital Bd, 1961-74; Central Health Services Council, 1974- (Chm. 1976-); Court and Council, Leeds Univ., 1970-; Chm., NHS Staff Cttee for Accomodation, Catering and other Support Services, 1975-; Governor: Pocklington Sch., 1950- (Chm., 1963-); Leeds Musical Festival, 1957- (Chm., 1972-); Pres., Leeds Law Soc., 1967-68; Warden, Leeds Parish Church, 1950-. Dir, Leeds Permanent Building Soc. (Pres., 1969-73), and other companies. *Recreations:* gardening, travel. *Address:* 3 The Drive, Roundhay, Leeds LS8 1JF. *T:* 662950. *Club:* Leeds (Leeds).

TWEEDDALE, 12th Marquis of, *cr* 1694; **David George Montagu Hay,** GC; Baron, 1488; Earl of Tweeddale, 1646; Earl of Gifford, Viscount Walden, 1694; Baron (UK), 1881; farmer and lobster fisherman since 1965; *b* Oct. 1921; *s* of Col Lord Edward Hay and Bridget Barclay; *S* kinsman, 1967; *m* 1st, 1946, Sonia Peake (marr. diss. 1958); three *s* (inc. twin *s*); 2nd, 1959, Nella Doreen Dutton; two *s* (twins). *Educ:* Eton. Merchant Service, 1939; Royal Naval Reserve, 1941; retired 1947. Worked in London various private enterprise jobs. Local Director, Martins Bank Ltd, 1955; retired, 1965. Albert Medal, 1941; Lloyd's Medal, 1942; Royal Life Saving Medal, 1943. *Recreations:* philately, entomology, ornithology; striving to exist after dynamic Socialism. *Heir: s* Earl of Gifford, *qv*. *Address:* Tweeddale House, Gifford, East Lothian. *T:* Gifford 217. *Club:* Puffins (Edinburgh).

TWEEDIE, Jill Sheila; Columnist with the Guardian newspaper, since 1969; *b* 1936; *d* of Patrick Graeme Tweedie, CBE and Sheila (*née* Whittall); *m* 1954, Count Bela Cziraky; one *s* one *d*; 1963, Robert d'Ancona; one *s*; *m* 1973, Alan Brien, *qv*. *Educ:* eight girls' schools, ranging from PNEU to GPDST; education unfinished at Swiss finishing school, since failed in objective of syllabus—trapping a rich husband. Advertising Copywriter, Lintas, 1953, later with J. Walter Thompson, Montreal; freelance journalist, London, 1965; contributor Farmer's Weekly, My Home, Woman's Mirror, New Statesman, Weekend Telegraph; Columnist, Daily Sketch, 1967; Asst Woman's Page Editor, Sunday Telegraph, 1968-69. Regular appearances on radio and television, incl. two years on Thames Television afternoon chat show. Women's Page Journalist of the Year, IPC Nat. Press Awards, 1971. *Publications:* contribs to various European and American anthologies, incl. annual Bedside Guardian. *Recreation:* changing mind. *Address:* 119 St Mary's Mansions, St Mary's Terrace, W2. *T:* 01-262 1893.

TWEEDIE, Brig. John William, CBE 1958; DSO 1944; DL; *b* 5 June 1907; *e s* of late Col William Tweedie, CMG, CBE; *m* 1937, Sheila Mary, *d* of Brig.-Gen. Thomas Hudson, CB; one *s* one *d*. *Educ:* Ampleforth; Royal Military College, Sandhurst. 2/Lt Argyll and Sutherland Highldrs, 1926; Adjutant, 1935-39; OC 2nd Bn, 1942-44; Brigade Commander, 39 Inf. Bde, 1951-54; ADC to the Queen, 1959-61; retired 1961. DL Dumfries, 1975. *Address:* Woodslee House, Canonbie, Dumfriesshire. *T:* 206. *Club:* Army and Navy.

TWEEDSMUIR, 2nd Baron, *cr* 1935, of Elsfield; **John Norman Stuart Buchan,** CBE 1964 (OBE (mil.) 1945); CD 1964; FRSE; Lt-Col Canadian Infantry Corps, retired; LLD (Hon.), Aberdeen, 1949, Queen's (Canada), 1955; *b* 25 November 1911; *e s* of 1st Baron and Susan Charlotte (*d* 1977), *d* of Hon. Norman Grosvenor; *S* father, 1940; *m* 1948, Priscilla Jean Fortescue (*see* Baroness Tweedsmuir of Belhelvie); one *d*. *Educ:* Eton; Brasenose Coll., Oxford (BA). Asst District Comr, Uganda Protectorate, 1934-36; joined Hudson's Bay Company, 1937; wintered in their service at Cape Dorset, Baffin Land, Canadian Arctic, 1938-39; served War of 1939-45 in Canadian Army (wounded, despatches twice, OBE (mil.) 1945, Order of Orange-

Nassau, with swords); comd Hastings and Prince Edward Regt in Sicily and Italy, 1943; Hon. Col, 1955-60. Rector of Aberdeen Univ., 1948-51; Chm., Joint East and Central African Board, 1950-52; UK Delegate: UN Assembly, 1951-52; Council of Europe, 1952; Pres., Commonwealth and British Empire Chambers of Commerce, 1955-57; a Governor: Commonwealth Inst., 1958-77, Trustee, 1977-; Ditchley Foundn; Pres., Inst. of Export, 1964-67; Mem. Board, BOAC, 1955-64; Chairman: Advertising Standards Authority, 1971-74; Council on Tribunals, 1973-. Mem., Scottish Cttee, Nature Conservancy, 1971-73. President: Institute of Rural Life at Home and Overseas, 1951-; British Schools Exploring Society, 1964-; Chm., British Rheumatism and Arthritis Assoc., 1971. Chancellor, Primrose League, 1969-75. FRSA. *Publications:* (part author) St Kilda papers, 1931; Hudson's Bay Trader, 1951; Always a Countryman, 1953; One Man's Happiness, 1968. *Recreations:* fishing, shooting, falconry. *Heir: b* Hon. William de l'Aigle Buchan, RAFVR [*b* 10 Jan. 1916; *m* 1st, Nesta (marr. diss. 1946), *o d* of Lt-Col C. D. Crozier; one *d*; 2nd, 1946, Barbara (marr. diss. 1960), 2nd *d* of E. N. Ensor, late of Hong Kong; three *s* three *d*; 3rd, 1960, Sauré Cynthia Mary, *y d* of late Major G. E. Tatchell, Royal Lincolnshire Regt; one *s*. *Educ:* Eton; New College, Oxford]. *Address:* 40 Tufton Court, Westminster, SW1. *T:* 01-222 6997; Potterton House, Balmedie, Aberdeenshire. *T:* Balmedie 2230. *Clubs:* Carlton, Travellers', Pratt's, Flyfishers'.
See also Lord James Douglas-Hamilton.

TWEEDSMUIR OF BELHELVIE, Baroness *cr* 1970 (Life Peer), of Potterton, Aberdeen; **Priscilla Jean Fortescue Buchan,** PC 1974; *b* 25 Jan. 1915; *d* of late Brig. Alan F. Thomson, DSO; *m* 1934, Major Sir Arthur Lindsay Grant, 11th Bt, Grenadier Guards (killed in action, 1944); two *d*; 2nd, 1948, 2nd Baron Tweedsmuir, *qv*; one *d*. *Educ:* England, Germany, France. Contested (C) N Div. of Aberdeen, July 1945; MP (C) Aberdeen South, 1946-66; Delegate Council of Europe, 1950-53; Mem. Commonwealth Parliamentary Delegation, West Indies, 1955; UK Delegate to UN General Assembly, 1960-61; Jt Party Under-Sec. of State, Scottish Office, 1962-64; Minister of State: Scottish Office, 1970-72; FCO, 1972-74; Principal Dep. Chm. of Cttees, 1974-77; Chm., Select Cttee on European Communities, 1974-77; a Deputy Speaker. Director: Factoryguards, 1966-70; Cunard Steam-ship Co., 1966-68; Cunard Line, 1968-70; Member, Cttee for Exports to Canada. Hon. Col (316 Scottish Command) Bn WRAC/TA, 1958-61. *Publications:* writes for TV and newspapers. *Recreations:* swimming, gardening, beekeeping. *Address:* 40 Tufton Court, Westminster, SW1. *T:* 01-222 6997; Potterton House, Balmedie, Aberdeenshire. *T:* Balmedie 230.
See also Lord James Douglas-Hamilton.

TWELVETREE, Eric Alan; County Treasurer, Essex County Council, since 1974; *b* 26 Dec. 1928; *m* 1953, Patricia Mary Starkings; two *d*. *Educ:* Stamford Sch., Lincs; qualif. IPFA and ACCA. Served with Borough Councils: Gt Yarmouth, Ipswich, Stockport, Southampton; County Councils: Gloucestershire, Kent. *Address:* County Hall, Chelmsford, Essex CM1 1JZ. *T:* Chelmsford 67222.

TWINING, Gen. Nathan Farragut, DSM (with two Oak Leaf Clusters), Navy DSM, Legion of Merit (with Oak Leaf Cluster), DFC; US Air Force (Retired); *b* Monroe, Wis., 11 October 1897; *s* of Clarence Walker Twining and Maize Barber; *m* 1932, Maude McKeever; two *s* one *d*. US Mil. Acad., 1918; student Inf. Sch., 1919-20, Air Corps Tactical Sch., 1935-36; Command and Gen. Staff Sch., 1936-37; rated command pilot. Served in Ore. Nat. Guard, 1916-17; comd 2nd Lt, Inf., Nov. 1918; transferred Air Corps, 1924, promoted through grades to Lt-Gen., 1945; Gen., USAF, 1950. Chief of Staff to Comdg Gen., USAFISPA, 1942-43; Comdg Gen., 13th Air Force, Solomon Is, 1943; 15th Air Force, Italy, and Mediterranean Allied Strategic Air Forces, 1943; 20th Air Force, Pacific, 1945; Air Materiel Command, Wright Field, Ohio, 1945-47; C-in-C Alaska, 1947-50; Vice-Chief of Staff, Air Force, 1950-53; Chief of Staff, Air Force, 1953-57; Chairman, Joint Chiefs of Staff, 1957-60. Has also numerous medals (US) and foreign decorations including Hon. KBE (Gt Brit.). *Recreations:* hunting, fishing, golf, carpentry. *Address:* 16 North Live Oak Road, Hilton Head Island, South Carolina 29928, USA.

TWINING, Richard Haynes, CBE 1959; Member of Council of Foreign Bondholders, 1948-75; *b* 3 Nov. 1889; *s* of Herbert Haynes Twining; *m* 1915, Ellen Irene Rosalind Tweed (*d* 1961); one *s* (killed in Tunisia, 1943). *Educ:* Eton; Magdalen Coll., Oxford. Served European War, 1914-18, in Queen's Royal West Surrey Regt; served War, 1939-46, Home Guard and Civil Defence. Deputy Chairman, The Stock Exchange, London, 1949-58. Trustee of MCC, President, 1964-65, Hon. Life Vice-President, 1969. *Recreations:* cricket (Eton XI, 1907-09, Captain 1909; Oxford University XI, 1910-13, Captain 1912); golf. *Address:* 114 Gloucester Road, SW7. *T:* 01-373 2320. *Clubs:* Buck's, MCC; I Zingari; Free Foresters.

TWINN, John Ernest; Director, Underwater Weapons Projects (Naval), Ministry of Defence, since 1976; *b* 11 July 1921; *s* of late Col Frank Charles George Twinn, CMG and Lilian May Twinn (*née* Tomlinson); *m* 1950, Mary Constance Smallwood; three *d*. *Educ:* Manchester Grammar Sch.; Christ's Coll., Cambridge (MA). MIEE. Air Min., 1941; Telecommunications Research Estabt (later Royal Radar Estabt), 1943; Head of Guided Weapons Gp, RRE, 1965; Head of Space Dept, RAE, 1968; Head of Weapons Dept, RAE, 1972; Asst Chief Scientific Advr (Projects), MoD, 1973. *Recreations:* sailing, music, genealogy. *Address:* Timbers, 9 Woodway, Merrow, Guildford, Surrey. *T:* Guildford 68993.

TWISLETON-WYKEHAM-FIENNES; *see* Fiennes.

TWISLETON-WYKEHAM-FIENNES, Gerard Francis Gisborne, OBE 1957; MA; *b* 7 June 1906; *s* of Gerard Yorke Twisleton-Wykeham-Fiennes, CBE, and Gwendolen; *m* 1st, 1934, Norah Davies (*d* 1960), Penymaes, Llangollen; three *s* two *d*; 2nd, 1962, Jean Kerridge. *Educ:* Horris Hill, Newbury; Winchester Coll.; Hertford Coll., Oxford. LNER 1928. Asst Yardmaster, Whitemoor, 1932; Chief Controller, Cambridge, 1934; appts at York, Liverpool Street, Edinburgh and Shenfield; District Supt; Nottingham, 1943; Stratford, 1944; Operating Supt, Eastern Region, 1956; Line Traffic Manager, King's Cross, 1957; Chief Operating Officer, BR, 1961; Chm., Western Railway Board, 1963; Lt-Col Railway Staff and Engrg Corps, 1963; Chm., Eastern Railway Board, and Gen. Manager, Eastern Region, British Railways, 1965-67. Dir, Hargreaves Gp, 1968-76. Broadcasts on radio and TV. FRSA 1966; FCIT (MInstT 1955). OStJ 1967. Mayor of Aldeburgh, 1976. *Publications:* I Tried to Run a Railway, 1967; various chapters and articles in railway technical press. *Recreations:* golf, sailing, fishing, railways. *Address:* Dartmouth, Aldeburgh, Suffolk. *T:* 2457. *Club:* MCC.

TWISLETON-WYKEHAM-FIENNES, Sir John (Saye Wingfield), KCB 1970 (CB 1953); QC 1972; First Parliamentary Counsel, 1968-72, retired; *b* 14 April 1911; *s* of Gerard Yorke Twisleton-Wykeham-Fiennes and Gwendolen (*née* Gisborne); *m* 1937, Sylvia Beatrice, *d* of Rev. C. R. L. McDowall; two *s* one *d*. *Educ:* Winchester; Balliol College, Oxford. Called to Bar, Middle Temple, 1936; Bencher, 1969. Joined parliamentary counsel office, 1939; Second Parly Coun., Treasury, 1956-68. Parliamentary Counsel, Malaya, 1962-63 (Colombo Plan). With Law Commission, 1965-66. Hon. JMN (Malaysia). *Address:* Mill House, Preston, Sudbury, Suffolk.

TWISS, Adm. Sir Frank (Roddam), KCB 1965 (CB 1962); DSC 1945; Gentleman Usher of the Black Rod, House of Lords, 1970-78; Serjeant-at-Arms, House of Lords, and Secretary to the Lord Great Chamberlain, 1971-78; *b* 7 July 1910; *s* of Col E. K. Twiss, DSO; *m* 1936, Prudence Dorothy Hutchison (*d* 1974); two *s* one *d*. *Educ:* RNC Dartmouth. Cadet 1924; Midshipman 1928; Lieut 1931; Comdr 1945; Captain 1950; Rear-Adm. 1960; Vice-Adm. 1963; Adm. 1967. Naval Sec., Admty, 1960-62; Flag Officer, Flotillas, Home Fleet, 1962-64; Comdr Far East Fleet, 1965-67; Second Sea Lord and Chief of Naval Personnel, 1967-70. Mem., Commonwealth War Graves Commn, 1970-. *Recreations:* fishing, walking. *Address:* Chalkstone House, Broad Hinton, near Swindon, Wilts. *Club:* Army and Navy.

TWISS, (Lionel) Peter; OBE 1957; DSC 1942 and Bar 1943; Test Pilot of Fairey Aviation Ltd, since 1946; Director, Fairey Marine Ltd, Hamble, since 1968; *b* 23 July 1921; *m* 1950, Mrs Vera Maguire (marr. diss.); one *d* (and one *d* decd), one step *s* one step *d*; *m* 1960, Cherry (marr. diss.), *d* of late Sir John Huggins, GCMG, MC; one *d*; *m* 1964, Mrs Heather Danby, Titchfield. *Educ:* Sherborne Sch. Joined Fleet Air Arm, 1939; served on catapult ships, aircraft-carriers, 1941-43; night fighter development, 1943-44; served in British Air Commn, America, 1944. Empire Test Pilots School, Boscombe Down, 1945; Test Pilot, Fairey Aviation Co. Ltd, 1946. Holder of World's Absolute Speed Record, 10 March 1956. *Publication:* Faster than the Sun, 1963. *Address:* Nettleworth, South Street, Titchfield, Hants. *T:* 43146. *Clubs:* Royal Southern Yacht, Island Sailing.

TWIST, George, CBE 1972; QPM; LLM; one of HM's Inspectors of Constabulary, London and South East Region, 1974-77, retired; *b* 12 March 1913; British; *m* 1947, Edith Kathleen Ibbotson; no *c*. *Educ:* Ormskirk Grammar Sch.; Liverpool University. Police Cadet, Liverpool, 1929-34; Liverpool City

Police, 1934-64 (Constable to Asst Chief Constable); Chief Constable, Bristol Constabulary, 1964-74. Mem., Home Secretary's Adv. Council on Penal Reform. OStJ 1969. Hon. MA Bristol, 1976. *Publications:* articles on police communications and crime prevention in Police Jl and Home Office Research and Planning Bulletin. *Recreations:* amateur radio (transmitting); music (organ). *Address:* Atlantic Lodge, Burnham, Dingle, Co. Kerry, Ireland.

TWIST, Henry Aloysius, CMG 1966; OBE 1947; Director of Studies, Royal Institute of Public Administration, since 1974; *b* 18 June 1914; *s* of John Twist, Preston; *m* 1941, Mary Monica, *yr d* of Nicholas Mulhall, Manchester; one *s* one *d. Educ:* Liverpool Univ. (BA). Senior Classics Master, St Chad's Coll., Wolverhampton, 1936-40; Lecturer in English, South Staffordshire High School of Commerce, 1939-40. Served War of 1939-45 with RASC and RAEC, 1940-46; released with rank of Lt-Col, 1946. Principal, Dominions Office, 1946; Official Secretary, Office of the British High Commissioner in Ceylon, 1948-49; Office of the British High Commissioner in Australia, 1949-52; Commonwealth Relations Office, 1952-54; Secretariat, Commonwealth Economic Conference, London, 1952; Deputy High Commissioner for the United Kingdom in Bombay, 1954-57; Assistant Secretary, Commonwealth Relations Office, 1957-60; British Deputy High Commissioner, Kaduna, Northern Region, Federation of Nigeria, 1960-62; Commonwealth Service representative on the 1963 Course at Imperial Defence College; Commonwealth Office, 1964; Asst Under-Sec., 1966; Dep High Comr, 1966-70, Minister (Commercial), 1968-70, Rawalpindi; retired 1970. *Recreation:* gardening. *Address:* Pine Lodge, Woodham Lane, Woking, Surrey. *Club:* Lighthouse.

TWITCHETT, Prof. Denis Crispin, FBA 1967; Professor of Chinese in the University of Cambridge, since 1968; *b* 23 Sept. 1925; *m* 1956, Umeko (*née* Ichikawa); two *s. Educ:* St Catharine's Coll., Cambridge. Lectr in Far-Eastern History, Univ. of London, 1954-56; Univ. Lectr in Classical Chinese, Univ. of Cambridge, 1956-60; Prof. of Chinese, SOAS, London Univ., 1960-68. Vis. Prof., Princetown Univ., 1973-74. Principal Editor, Cambridge History of China, 1977-. *Publications:* (ed with A. F. Wright) Confucian Personalities, 1962; The Financial Administration under the T'ang dynasty, 1963, 2nd edn 1971 (ed with A. F. Wright) Perspectives on the T'ang, 1973; (ed with P. J. M. Geelan) The Times Atlas of China, 1975. *Address:* St Catharine's College, Cambridge; 24 Arbury Road, Cambridge.

TYACKE, Maj.-Gen. David Noel Hugh, CB 1970; OBE 1957; Controller, Army Benevolent Fund; *b* 18 Nov. 1915; *s* of Capt. Charles Noel Walker Tyacke (killed in action, March 1918) and late Phoebe Mary Cicely (*née* Coulthard), Cornwall; *m* 1940, Diana, *d* of Aubrey Hare Duke; one *s. Educ:* Malvern Coll.; RMC Sandhurst. Commissioned DCLI, 1935; India, 1936-39; France and Belgium, 1939-40; India and Burma, 1943-46; Instructor, Staff Coll., Camberley, 1950-52; CO 1st Bn DCLI, 1957-59; Comdr 130 Inf. Bde (TA), 1961-63; Dir of Administrative Planning (Army), 1963-64; Brig. Gen. Staff (Ops), Min. of Defence, 1965-66; GOC Singapore Dist., 1966-70, retired. Col, The Light Infantry, 1972-77. *Recreations:* walking, motoring, bird-watching. *Address:* c/o Lloyds Bank Ltd, Cox's & King's Branch, 6 Pall Mall, SW1. *Club:* Naval and Military.

TYDEMAN, Col Frank William Edward, CMG 1966; CIE 1945; Port Consultant; Consulting Engineer, Ports and Harbours, Western Australian Government since 1946; General Manager, Fremantle Port Authority, 1950-65; *b* 20 January 1901; *s* of Harvey James and Kate Mary Anne Tydeman; *m* 1924, Jessie Sarah Mann (*d* 1947); two *s. Educ:* London University. BSc (Eng) London 1920. Chartered Civil Engineer. FICE, FIMechE, FIStructE, FIEAust, FCIT. Served Palestine; Haifa Harbour, 1930; Jaffa Port, 1934; Singapore Harbour Board, 1937; Colonel, Deputy Director Transportation, India and Burma, 1942. *Recreation:* golf. *Address:* c/o Australia & New Zealand Bank Ltd, Perth, WA 6000, Australia. *Clubs:* Naval and Military, West Australian Golf (Perth).

TYE, James; Director-General, British Safety Council, since 1968; *b* 21 Dec. 1921; *s* of late Benjamin Tye and Rose Tye; *m* 1950, Mrs Rosalie Hooker; one *s* one *d. Educ:* Upper Hornsey LCC Sch. Served War of 1939-45; RAF, 1940-46. Advertising Agent and Contractor, 1946-50; Managing Dir, 1950-62: Sky Press Ltd; Safety Publications Ltd; Press Transworld Ltd; Industrial Services Ltd. Joined British Safety Council as Exec. Dir, 1962. Chm., Bd of Governors, Internat. Inst. of Safety Management, 1975-. MBIM; Associate, Instn of Industrial Safety Officers; Member: Amer. Soc. of Safety Engineers; Amer. Safety Management Soc.; Vice-Pres., Jamaica Safety Council; Fellow, Inst. of Accident Prevention, Zambia. Freeman, City of London, 1976; Liveryman, Worshipful Co. of Basketmakers;

Mem., Guild of Freemen of City of London. *Publications:* Communicating the Safety Message, 1968; Management Introduction to Total Loss Control, 1971; Safety-Uncensored (with K. Ullyett, JP), 1971; handbooks, etc.: Industrial Safety Digest, 1953; Skilful Driving, 1952; Advanced Driving, 1954; Home Safety, 1956; International Nautical Safety Code (with Uffa Fox), 1961; Mothers' Safety Code, 1964; Papers and Reports to Parly Groups and British Safety Council Members on: vehicle seat belts, anti-jack knife devices for articulated vehicles, lifejackets and buoyancy aids, motorway safety barriers, Britain's filthy beaches, dangers of: mini fire extinguishers, safety in fairgrounds and drip feed oil heaters, children's flammable nightwear, etc. *Recreations:* squash, photography, sailing. *Address:* 55 Hartington Road, Chiswick, W4 3TS. *T:* 01-995 3206. *Clubs:* London Press, City Livery; New Grampians Squash.

TYE, Dr Walter, CBE 1966; CEng, FRAeS; Visiting Professor, Cranfield Institute of Technology, since 1975; *b* 12 Dec. 1912; *s* of Walter and Alice Tye; *m* 1939, Eileen Mary Whitmore; one *s* one *d. Educ:* Woodbridge Sch.; London Univ. (BScEng). Fairey Aviation Co., 1934; RAE, 1935-38; Air Registration Bd, 1938-39; RAE, 1939-44; Air Registration Bd, 1944-72 (Chief Techn. Officer, 1946, Chief Exec., 1969); Mem., CAA (Controller Safety), 1972-74. Hon. DSc Cranfield Inst. of Technology, 1972. *Publications:* articles, lectures and contrib. Jl RAeS. *Address:* The Spinney, Fairmile Park Road, Cobham, Surrey. *T:* Cobham 3692.

TYERMAN, Donald; journalist; Director, United City Merchants Ltd; Editor of The Economist, 1956-65; *b* 1 March 1908; *s* of late Joseph and late Catherine Tyerman, Middlesbrough, Yorks; *m* 1934, Margaret Charteris Gray; two *s* three *d. Educ:* Friends' School, Great Ayton; St Mary's College, Middlesbrough; Coatham Grammar Sch., Redcar; Gateshead Secondary Sch., Gateshead-on-Tyne; Brasenose College, Oxford. Lectr, University College, Southampton, 1930-36; Assistant and then Deputy Editor, The Economist, 1937-44; Deputy Editor, The Observer, 1943-44; Asst Editor, The Times, 1944-55. Chm., Exec. Bd of International Press Inst., 1961-62; Member: Press Council, 1963-69; Council, Commonwealth Press Union (Chm., Press Freedom Cttee, 1971-75); Council, Overseas Development Inst.; Council, Univ. of Sussex, 1963-75. Governor, LSE, 1951-75; Vice-Pres. and Hon. Associate of Council, Save the Children Fund; Life Vice-Pres., Ingatestone Cricket Club. *Recreations:* reading and watching games. *Address:* 41 Buckingham Mansions, West End Lane, NW6. *T:* 01-435 1030; Holly Cottage, Westleton, near Saxmundham, Suffolk. *T:* Saxmundham 73-261. *Club:* Reform.

TYLECOTE, Dame Mabel, DBE 1966; Vice-President of National Federation of Community Associations since 1961 (President, 1958-61); *b* 4 Feb. 1896; *d* of late John Ernest Phythian and Ada Prichard Phythian (*née* Crompton); *m* 1932, Frank Edward Tylecote (*d* 1965); one *s* (and one step *s* one step *d*). *Educ:* Univ. of Manchester; Univ. of Wisconsin (USA). BA, PhD (Manchester). Lectr in History, Huddersfield Techn. Coll., 1920-24; Asst Lectr in History, Univ. of Manchester, 1926-30; Warden of Elvington Settlement, 1930-32; part-time Lectr, Univ. of Manchester Joint Cttee for Adult Educn, 1935-51; Vice-Pres., WEA, 1960-68. Member: Pensions Appeal Tribunal, 1944-50; Manchester City Council, 1940-51; (co-opted) Manchester Educn Cttee, 1951-; Stockport Borough Council, 1956-63; Chm. of Council, Assoc. of Art Instns, 1960-61; Mem. Court, 1945-, Mem. Council, 1960-75, Univ. of Manchester; Mem. Court, Univ. of Manchester Inst. of Science and Technology, 1960-; Governor, Manchester Polytechnic, 1969- (Hon. Fellow, 1973); Vice-President: Manchester and Salford Council of Social Service, 1968-; Union of Lancashire and Cheshire Institutes, 1969-; Hon. Life Mem., Nat. Inst. of Adult Educn, 1974- (Chm., 1960-63). Contested (Lab): Fylde, 1938; Middleton and Prestwich, 1945; Norwich South, 1950, 1951, 1955. *Publications:* The Education of Women at Manchester University 1883-1933, 1941; The Mechanics' Institutes of Lancashire and Yorkshire before 1851, 1957; The Future of Adult Education (Fabian pamphlet), 1960; contrib., Artisan to Graduate, ed D. S. L. Cardwell, 1974; The Work of Lady Simon of Wythenshawe for Education in Manchester (address), 1974; articles in various social and educnl jls. *Address:* 1 Rusholme Gardens, Wilmslow Road, Manchester M14 5LG. *T:* 061-224 9366.

TYLER, Brig. Arthur Catchmay, CBE 1960; MC 1945; DL; Secretary, Council of Territorial Auxiliary and Volunteer Reserve Associations, 1967-72; *b* 20 Aug. 1913; 4th *s* of Hugh Griffin Tyler and Muriel Tyler (*née* Barnes); *m* 1938, Sheila, *d* of James Kinloch, Meigle, Perthshire; three *s* one *d. Educ:* Allhallows Sch.; RMC, Sandhurst. Commissioned, The Welch

Regt, 1933. Served War of 1939-45: Africa, India and Burma (despatches). Staff Coll., 1946; JSSC, 1951; Sec., BJSM, Washington, 1952-54; Bt Lt-Col, 1953; Comd 4th (Carms) Bn The Welch Regt, 1954-57; Col, 1957; AAG, War Office, 1957-60; Brig. 1960; Senior UK Liaison Officer and Military Adviser to High Commissioner, Canada, 1960; Asst Chief of Staff (Ops and Plans), Allied Forces Central Europe, 1963. Hon. Col., 7th(V) Bn, The Queen's Regt, T&AVR, 1971-75. Chm. Governors, Allhallows Sch. DL Surrey, 1968. *Address:* Higher Manor Cottage, Station Road, Sidmouth, Devon. *Club:* Army and Navy.

TYLER, Cyril, DSc, PhD, FRIC; Professor of Physiology and Biochemistry, University of Reading, 1958-76, now Emeritus; Deputy Vice-Chancellor, 1968-76; *b* 26 Jan. 1911; *er s* of John and Annie Tyler; *m* 1st, 1939, Myra Eileen (*d* 1971), *d* of George and Rosa Batten; two *s* one *d*; 2nd, 1971, Rita Patricia, *d* of Sidney and Lilian Jones. *Educ:* Ossett Grammar Sch.; Univ. of Leeds. BSc 1st Class Hons 1933, PhD 1935, DSc 1959, Leeds. Lectr in Agricultural Chemistry. RAC, Cirencester, 1935-39; Univ. of Reading: Lecturer in Agricultural Chemistry, 1939-47; Professor, 1947-58; Dean of the Faculty of Agriculture, 1959-62. Playing Mem., Glos CCC, 1936-39. *Publications:* Organic Chemistry for Students of Agriculture, 1946; Animal Nutrition (2nd edn), 1964; Wilhelm von Nathusius 1821-1899 on Avian Eggshells, 1964; numerous papers on poultry metabolism and egg shells in scientific journals. *Recreations:* gardening, history of animal nutrition. *Address:* 22 Belle Avenue, Reading, Berks.

TYLER, Froom, OBE 1969; *b* 30 Jan. 1904; *o s* of John Frederick Tyler, Bristol; *m* 1st, 1928, Doris May (*née* Chubb) (*d* 1963); one *d*; 2nd, Diana Griffiths (*née* Kirby) (*d* 1971). Editor of the Evening World, Bristol, 1936-40; Foreign Editor, Daily Mail, 1940-43; Staff Officer (Press) to Admiral (Submarines), 1943-45. Editor of Overseas Daily Mail, 1946-50; Editor of Leicester Evening Mail, 1950-57; Editor of South Wales Evening Post, 1957-69; Chm., Swansea Festival of Music and the Arts, 1970-. *Publications:* Cripps: A Portrait and a Prospect, 1942; His Majesty's Submarines (the Admiralty Account), 1945; News in Our Time (Daily Mail Jubilee Book), 1946; The Man Who Made Music, 1947. *Address:* 50 Harford Court, The Bryn, Sketty Green, Swansea.

TYLER, Ven. Leonard George; Rector of Easthampstead, since 1973; *b* 15 April 1920; *s* of Hugh Horstead Tyler and Mabel Adam Stewart Tyler; *m* 1946, Sylvia May Wilson; one *s* two *d*. *Educ:* Darwen Grammar School; Liverpool University; Christ's College, Cambridge; Westcott House. Chaplain, Trinity College, Kandy, Ceylon, 1946-48; Principal, Diocesan Divinity School, Colombo, Ceylon, 1948-50; Rector, Christ Church, Bradford, Manchester, 1950-55; Vicar of Leigh, Lancs, 1955-66 (Rural Dean, 1955-62); Chaplain, Leigh Infirmary, 1955-66; Archdeacon of Rochdale, 1962-66; Principal, William Temple College, Manchester, 1966-73. Anglican Adviser to ABC Television, 1958-68. *Publications:* contributor to Theology. *Address:* The Rectory, Easthampstead, Bracknell, Berks RG12 4ER. *T:* Bracknell 25205.

TYLER, Maj.-Gen. Sir Leslie (Norman), KBE 1961 (OBE 1942); CB 1955; BScEng; CEng; FIMechE; *b* 26 April 1904; *s* of late Major Norman Tyler, Addiscombe, Surrey; *m* 1st, 1930, Louie Teresa Franklin (*d* 1950); one *s* one *d*; 2nd, 1953, Sheila, *widow* of Maj.-Gen. L. H. Cox, CB, CBE, MC; two *s* two step *d*. *Educ:* RN Colleges Osborne and Dartmouth; King's College, Univ. of London. Commissioned Lieut, RAOC, 1927; served War of 1939-45, Malta and NW Europe; transferred to REME, 1942; DDME, Second Army, 1945; Comdt REME Training Centre, 1945-47; AAG, War Office, 1948-49; DME, MELF, 1949-50; DDME, War Office, 1950-53; DME, MELF, 1953-55; Commandant, Headquarters Base Workshop Group, REME, 1956-57; Director of Electrical and Mechanical Engineering, War Office, 1957-60; retd 1960. Regional Dir, MPBW, Central Mediterranean Region, 1963-69. Chm., Royal Hosp. and Home for Incurables, Putney, 1971-76. Colonel Commandant, REME, 1962-67. Freeman, City of London; Liveryman, 1961, Assistant, 1974, Worshipful Company of Turners. Fellow, King's Coll., London, 1969. *Address:* Higher Combe East, Haslemere, Surrey. *T:* Haslemere 3900. *Club:* Army and Navy.

TYLER, Paul Archer; politician and journalist; Executive Director, Cornwall Courier; *b* 29 Oct. 1941; *s* of Oliver Walter Tyler and Ursula Grace Gibbons Tyler (*née* May); *m* 1970, Nicola Mary Ingram; one *s* one *d*. *Educ:* Mount House Sch., Tavistock; Sherborne Sch.; Exeter Coll., Oxford (MA). Pres., Oxford Univ. Liberal Club, 1962. Royal Inst. of British Architects: Admin. Asst, 1966; Asst Sec., 1967; Dep. Dir Public Affairs, 1971; Dir Public Affairs, 1972. County Councillor, Devon, 1964-70; Mem., Devon and Cornwall Police Authority,

1965-70; Vice-Chm., Dartmoor Nat. Park Cttee, 1965-70; Chm., CPRE Working Party on the Future of the Village, 1974-77; Mem. Bd of Shelter (Nat. Campaign for the Homeless), and rep. in Devon and Cornwall, 1975-76. Contested (L): Totnes, 1966; Bodmin, 1970; MP (L) Bodmin, Feb.-Sept. 1974; Parly Liberal Spokesman on Housing and Transport, 1974; Parly Adviser to RIBA, 1974. *Recreations:* sailing, gardening, walking. *Address:* Tregrove House, Rilla Mill, Callington, Cornwall. *Clubs:* National Liberal; Liskeard Liberal (Cornwall); Saltash Sailing.

TYMMS, Sir Frederick, KCIE 1947 (CIE 1935); Kt 1941; MC; FRAeS; *b* 4 Aug. 1889; *s* of William Henry Tymms. *Educ:* Tenby; King's College, London. War Service: 4th Bn South Lancs Regt and Royal Flying Corps, France; British Aviation Mission to the USA, 1915-18 (MC, Chevalier de l'Ordre de la Couronne, Croix de Guerre, Belgium). Civil Aviation Dept, Air Min., 1920-27; Oxford Univ. Arctic Expedition to Spitsbergen, 1924; Air Min. Supt of Egypt-India air route, 1927; seconded to Govts of the Sudan, Kenya, Uganda and Tanganyika, 1928; Chief Technical Asst to Dir of Civil Aviation, Air Min., 1928-31; Air Min. Representative on the Commn to Africa, to organise the Cape to Cairo air route, 1929-30; Dir of Civil Aviation in India, 1931-42 and 1943-45; Man. Dir, Tata Aircraft Ltd, Bombay, 1942-43; Dir-Gen. of Civil Aviation in India, Sept. 1945-March 1947; UK Representative on Council of Internat. Civil Aviation Organisation, Montreal, 1947-54; retd from Civil Service, 1955. Govt of India delegate to Internat. Civil Aviation Conf., Chicago, 1944; Leader of UK Civil Aviation Mission to New Zealand, 1948. Master of Guild of Air Pilots and Air Navigators, 1957-58. Chm., Commn of Enquiry on Civil Aviation in West Indies, 1960. *Address:* High Thicket, Dockenfield, near Farnham, Surrey; c/o Lloyds Bank, Pall Mall, SW1. *Club:* Naval and Military.

TYMMS, Prof. Ralph Vincent, MA; Professor of German Language and Literature in the University of London (Royal Holloway College), since 1956; Head of German Department since 1948, Vice-Principal 1969-75, Royal Holloway College; *b* 9 Jan. 1913; *s* of Arthur Hugh Tymms and Janet Scott Coventon. *Educ:* Bradford Grammar Sch., Yorkshire; Magdalen Coll., Oxford; Univs of Vienna and Giessen. John Doncaster Scholar in German, Magdalen Coll., Oxford, 1931-34; 1st Class Hons, Oxford, 1934. Asst Lectr in German, Univ. of Manchester, 1936. Intelligence Corps, 1941-45; Major, 1945. Lecturer in German, Manchester Univ., 1945; Reader in German Language and Literature in Univ. of London, 1948. *Publications:* Doubles in Literary Psychology, 1949; German Romantic Literature, 1955. *Address:* Little Ormonde, Cooper's Hill Lane, Englefield Green, Egham, Surrey TW20 0JY. *T:* Egham 2125. *Club:* Athenæum.

TYNAN, Kenneth Peacock, FRSL; Literary Consultant of the National Theatre, 1969-73 (Literary Manager, 1963-69); *b* 2 April 1927; *s* of late Sir Peter Peacock and Letitia Rose Tynan; *m* 1951, Elaine Brimberg (marr. diss. 1964); one *d*; *m* 1967, Kathleen Halton; one *s* one *d*. *Educ:* King Edward's Sch., Birmingham; Magdalen Coll., Oxford. Dramatic Critic of: Spectator, 1951; Evening Standard, 1952-53; Daily Sketch, 1953-54; Observer, 1954-63; New Yorker, 1958-60. Script Ed., Ealing Films, 1955-57; Ed., TV programme Tempo, 1961-62; Film Critic of Observer, 1964-66. Member Drama Panel, British Council. Co-produced: Soldiers, New, 1968. Devised and part-wrote revues: Oh, Calcutta!, NY, 1969, London, 1970; Carte Blanche, Phoenix, 1976. *Publications:* He That Plays the King, 1950; Persona Grata, 1953; Alec Guinness, 1954; Bull Fever, 1955; The Quest for Corbett, 1960; Curtains, 1961; Tynan Right and Left, 1967; A View of the English Stage, 1975; The Sound of Two Hands Clapping, 1975; edited books on National Theatre productions of The Recruiting Officer, 1965, and Othello, 1966. *Recreations:* sex, eating. *Address:* 20 Thurloe Square, SW7.

TYNDALE-BISCOE, Rear-Adm. Alec Julian, CB 1959; OBE 1946; lately Chairman of Blaw Knox Ltd; *b* 10 Aug. 1906; *s* of late Lt-Col A. A. T. Tyndale-Biscoe, Aubrey House, Keyhaven, Lymington, Hants; *m* 1st, 1939, Emma Winifred Haselden (*d* 1974); four *d*; 2nd, 1974, Hugolyne Cotton Cooke, *widow* of Captain Geoffrey Cotton Cooke. *Educ:* RN Colleges Osborne and Dartmouth. Entered RN, 1920. Served War, 1939-46; HMS Vanguard, 1947-49; Captain, 1949; Asst Engineer-in-Chief, Fleet, 1950-53; Comdg RN Air Station, Anthorn, 1953-55; Fleet Engr Officer, Mediterranean, 1955-57; Rear-Adm. 1957; Flag-Officer Reserve Aircraft, 1957-59, retired. *Address:* Bunces Farm Gardens, Birch Grove, Haywards Heath, West Sussex.

TYNDALL, Sir Arthur, Kt 1955; CMG 1939; MInstCE; FASCE; FNZIE; ACA; Solicitor of the Supreme Court; Judge, Court of Arbitration, New Zealand, 1940-65; *b* Dunedin, Otago, NZ, April 1891; *s* of late A. W. Tyndall, Dunedin; *m* 1916, Gladys Muriel (*d* 1973), *d* of Col A. Stoneham, Gisborne, NZ. *Educ:*

Blue Spur Sch.; Lawrence District High Sch.; Otago Univ., Dunedin; Massachusetts Institute of Technology. Joined New Zealand Public Works Dept, 1909; Under-Secretary, Mines Dept, 1934-40; also Director Housing Construction, 1936-40. Hon. LLD Victoria Univ. of Wellington, 1973. Jubilee Medal, 1935; Coronation Medal, 1937 and 1953. *Address:* 5 Gilmer Terrace, Wellington, C1, New Zealand.

TYREE, Sir (Alfred) William, Kt 1975; OBE 1971; engineer and pastoralist; Chairman and Founder A. W. Tyree Foundation (incorporating Medicheck Referral Centre and Tyree Chair of Electrical Engineering, University of New South Wales); *b* 4 Nov. 1921; *m* 1946, Joyce, *d* of F. Lyndon; two *s* one *d* . *Educ:* Auckland Grammar Sch.; Sydney Technical Coll. Chairman and Founder: Tyree Industries Ltd; Westralian Transformers and subsids; Chairman: Tyree-Canada Wire Pty Ltd; Tyree Hldgs Pty Ltd; C. P. R. Constructions Pty Ltd; Reinhausen (Aust.) Pty Ltd. *Recreations:* ski-ing, private flying, water ski-ing; yachting, tennis, music, golf. *Address:* 3 Lindsay Avenue, Darling Point, NSW 2027, Australia. *Clubs:* Royal Aero, American National, Royal Automobile (NSW); Royal Prince Alfred Yacht, Royal Motor Yacht, Cruising Yacht, Kosciusko Alpine, Australian Alpine, RAC, Australian Golf.

TYRELL-KENYON; *see* Kenyon.

TYRONE, Earl of; Henry Nicholas de la Poer Beresford; *b* 23 March 1958; *s* and *heir* of 8th Marquess of Waterford, *qv* . *Educ:* Harrow School.

TYRRELL, Alan Rupert, QC 1976; a Recorder of the Crown Court, since 1972; Barrister-at-Law; *b* 27 June 1933; *s* of Rev. T. G. R. Tyrrell, and Mrs W. A. Tyrrell, MSc; *m* 1960, Elaine Eleanor Ware; one *s* one *d*. *Educ:* Bridport Grammar Sch.; London Univ. (LLB). Called to the Bar, Gray's Inn, 1956. *Publication:* (ed) Moore's Practical Agreements, 10th edn 1965. *Recreation:* bridge. *Address:* 15 Willifield Way, Hampstead Garden Suburb, NW11. *T:* 01-455 5798. *Clubs:* Hampshire (Winchester), Exeter and County (Exeter).

TYRRELL, Dr David Arthur John, FRS 1970; FRCP; Deputy Director of Clinical Research Centre, Northwick Park, Harrow, and Head of Division of Communicable Diseases, since 1970; *b* 19 June 1925; *s* of Sydney Charles Tyrrell and Agnes Kate (*née* Blewett); *m* 1950, Betty Moyra Wylie; one *s* two *d*. *Educ:* Sheffield University. Junior hosp. appts, Sheffield, 1948-51; Asst, Rockefeller Inst., New York, 1951-54; Virus Research Lab., Sheffield, 1954-57; Common Cold Research Unit, Salisbury, 1957-70. Stewart Prize, BMA, 1977. *Publications:* Common Colds and Related Diseases, 1965; Interferon and its Clinical Potential, 1976; numerous papers on infectious diseases and viruses. *Recreations:* music-making, gardening, sailing, walking; various Christian organizations. *Address:* 29 The Ridgeway, Stanmore, Mddx HA7 4BE.

TYRRELL, Gerald Fraser; former Buyer, Stewart Dry Goods Co., Louisville, USA, and London; retired 1974; *b* London, 7 March 1907; *s* of late Lt-Col G. E. Tyrrell, DSO, RA, and C. R. Tyrrell (*née* Fraser); *m* 1937, Virginia Lee Gettys, Louisville, Kentucky; three *s* one *d*. *Educ:* Eton; Magdalene Coll., Cambridge. Student Interpreter, China Consular Service, 1930; served in Tientsin, Chungking, Shanghai, Foochow, Canton; Vice-Consul at San Francisco, 1941; Vice-Consul, Boston, 1942, Acting Consul-General, 1944; 1st Secretary, Washington, 1945; Consul at Cincinnati, 1946; Acting Consul-General, New Orleans, 1947; Consul-General, Canton, 1948; Foreign Office, 1949, resigned, 1950. *Address:* 2333 Glenmary Avenue, Louisville, Kentucky 40204, USA.

TYRRELL, Sir Murray (Louis), KCVO 1968 (CVO 1954); CBE 1959; JP; Official Secretary to Governor-General of Australia, 1947-73; *b* 1 Dec. 1913; *s* of late Thomas Michael and Florence Evelyn Tyrrell; *m* 1939, Ellen St Clair, *d* of late E. W. St Clair Greig; one *s* two *d*. *Educ:* Orbost and Melbourne Boys' High Schools, Victoria. Central Office, Postmaster General's Department, Melbourne, 1929-39; Asst Private Secretary to Minister for Air and Civil Aviation, 1940; Private Secretary to Minister for Air, 1940, to Minister for Munitions, 1940; Personal Asst to Secretary, Min. of Munitions, 1942; Private Secretary: Commonwealth Treas. and Min. for Post-War Reconstruction, 1943, to Prime Minister and Treasurer, 1945; Official Secretary and Comptroller to Governor-General, 1947; resigned Comptrollership, 1953. Attached Royal Household, Buckingham Palace, May-Aug. 1962. Director: Nat. Heart Foundn of Australia, 1970-; Canberra C of E Girls' Grammar Sch., 1952-65; Canberra Grammar Sch., 1954-65; Registrar, Order of St John of Jerusalem in Australia, 1976-; Mem., Buildings and Grounds Cttee, ANU, 1974-. Alderman,

Queanbeyan CC, 1974; Mem., Southern Tablelands CC, 1974. CStJ 1969. *Recreation:* fishing. *Address:* 11 Blundell Street, Queanbeyan, NSW 2620, Australia.

TYRWHITT, Brig. Dame Mary (Joan Caroline), DBE 1949 (OBE 1946); TD; *b* 27 Dec. 1903; *d* of Admiral of the Fleet Sir Reginald Tyrwhitt, 1st Bt, GCB, DSO; unmarried. Senior Controller, 1946 (rank altered to Brigadier, 1950); Director, ATS, 1946-49, Women's Royal Army Corps, 1949-50, retired Dec. 1950; Hon. ADC to the King, 1949-50. *Address:* Constable's Cottage, Yatton Keynell, Chippenham, Wilts.

TYRWHITT, Sir Reginald (Thomas Newman), 3rd Bt, *cr* 1919; *b* 21 Feb. 1947; *er s* of Admiral Sir St John Tyrwhitt, 2nd Bt, KCB, DSO, DSC and Bar (*d* 1961), and of Nancy (Veronica) Gilbey (who *m* 1965, Sir Godfrey Agnew, *qv*); *S* father, 1961; *m* 1972, Sheila Gail, *d* of William Alistair Crawford Nicoll, Liphook, Hants. *Educ:* Downside. 2nd Lieut, RA, 1966, Lieut 1969; RARO 1969. *Recreations:* shooting, fishing. *Heir: b* John (Edward Charles) Tyrwhitt, *b* 27 July 1953. *Address:* Batch Cottage, Lower Street, Chewton Mendip, near Bath, Somerset. *See also Dame Mary Tyrwhitt* .

TYTLER, Christian Helen F.; *see* Fraser-Tytler.

TYTLER, Ven. Donald Alexander; Archdeacon of Aston, since 1977; *b* 2 May 1925; *s* of Alexander and Cicely Tytler; *m* 1948, Jane Evelyn Hodgson; two *d* . *Educ:* Eastbourne College; Christ's College, Cambridge (MA); Ridley Hall, Cambridge. Asst Curate of Yardley, Birmingham, 1949; SCM Chaplain, Univ. of Birmingham, 1952; Precentor, Birmingham Cathedral, 1955; Diocesan Director of Education, Birmingham, 1957; Vicar of St Mark, Londonderry and Rural Dean of Warley, Birmingham, 1963; Canon Residentiary of Birmingham Cathedral, 1972. *Publications:* Operation Think, 1963; (contrib.) Stirrings (essays), 1976. *Recreations:* music, gardening. *Address:* 51 Moor Green Lane, Birmingham B13 8NE. *T:* 021-449 0766.

TYZACK, Group Captain John Edward Valentine, CBE 1944; Chairman: John Tyzack & Partners Ltd, 1959-71; Dollar Land Holdings Ltd, 1970-72; *b* 11 Jan. 1904; *s* of late Ernest and Mildred Tyzack; *m* 1935, Carol, *d* of late Alfred and Caroline Davidson; two *s* one *d*. *Educ:* Harwich High Sch. RAF, 1929-46: served in Aden and Sudan, 1932-36; DAQMG, Palestine, 1936-37; Staff Coll., psa, 1938; HQ British Air Forces in France (despatches), 1939-40; Dep. Dir of Admin. Plans, Air Min., 1940-44; Dep. Dir, of Movements (Air), Air Min., 1944-45; retd at own request, 1946. Dir of Admin. Services, BEA, 1946-52; Man. Dir, Concrete Development Co. Ltd, 1953-56; Chm., Incomes Data Services Ltd, 1965-75. FBIM. *Recreations:* work, enjoyment of all the arts, gardening. *Address:* 50A Davenant Road, Oxford. *Club:* Savile.

TYZACK, Margaret Maud, OBE 1970; *b* 9 Sept. 1931; *d* of Thomas Edward Tyzack and Doris Moseley; *m* 1958, Alan Stephenson; one *s*. *Educ:* St Angela's Ursuline Convent; Royal Academy of Dramatic Art. Trained at RADA (Gilbert Prize for Comedy). First engagement, Civic Theatre, Chesterfield. Vassilissa in The Lower Depths, Royal Shakespeare Co., Arts Theatre, 1962; Lady MacBeth, Nottingham, 1962; Miss Frost in The Ginger Man, Royal Court Theatre, London, 1964; Madame Ranevsky in The Cherry Orchard, Exeter and Tour, 1969; Jacqui in Find Your Way Home, Open Space Theatre, London, 1970; Queen Elizabeth in Vivat! Vivat Regina!, Piccadilly, 1971; Tamora in Titus Andronicus, Portia in Julius Caesar and Volumnia in Coriolanus, Royal Shakespeare Co., Stratford-on-Avon, 1972; Portia in Julius Caesar and Volumnia in Coriolanus, RSC, Aldwych, 1973; Maria Lvovna in Summerfolk, RSC, Aldwych, and NY, 1974-75; Richard III, All's Well That Ends Well, Ghosts, Stratford, Ont., 1977. *Films:* Ring of Spies, 2001: A Space Odyssey, The Whisperers, A Clockwork Orange. *Television:* many appearances, incl. The Forsyte Saga series, The First Churchills, Cousin Bette, 1970-71; I, Claudius, 1976. Actress of the Year Award (Soc. of Film and Television Arts) for Queen Anne in The First Churchills, 1969. *Address:* c/o Representation Joyce Edwards, 8 Theed Street, SE1 8ST. *T:* 01-261 1488.

U

UBBELOHDE, Prof. Alfred R. J. P., CBE 1963; MA, DSc Oxon; FRS 1951; FRIC; FInstP; CEng; MIChemE; Hon. Laureate, Padua University, 1963; Senior Research Fellow, Imperial College of Science and Technology, since 1975; Professor of Thermodynamics, University of London (Imperial College), 1954-75, now Emeritus, and Head of Department of Chemical Engineering and Chemical Technology, 1961-75; *b* 14 Dec. 1907; 3rd *s* of F. C. Ubbelohde and Angele Verspreeuwen; unmarried. *Educ:* St Paul's Sch.; Christ Church, Oxford. Dewar Fellow of Royal Instn, 1935-40; research on explosives; Min. of Supply, 1940-45; Prof. of Chemistry, Queen's Univ., Belfast, 1945-54, Dean of the Faculty of Science, 1947-51. Chairman Fire Research Board, 1956-61; President of Council Institut Solvay, 1957-64, 1965-; Director of Salters' Institute, 1959-75; Past President, Faraday Society, 1963-; Past Vice-President, Society of Chemical Industry; Chairman, Science and Engineering Panel, British Council, 1964-; Member: Agricl Research Council, 1966-76; Pontifical Academy of Sciences, 1968. Hon. FCGI. Dr *hc* Faculty of Science, Univ. Libre, Brussels, 1962; Hon. DSc QUB, 1972. Messel Medal, 1972; George Skakl Award, 1975; Paul Lebeau Medal, 1975. *Publications:* Modern Thermodynamical Principles, 1937 (2nd edn 1952); Time and Thermodynamics, 1947; Man and Energy, 1954, 2nd edn 1963; Graphite and its crystal compounds, 1960; Melting and Crystal Structure, 1965; papers in Proceedings and Journals of scientific societies. *Address:* Imperial College, South Kensington, SW7; 48 Cottesmore Court, Stanford Road, W8; Platts Farm, Burwash, Sussex. *Clubs:* Athenæum, Royal Automobile.

UBEE, Air Vice-Marshal Sydney Richard, CB 1952; AFC 1939; Royal Air Force; retired as Air Officer Commanding, No 2 Group, 2nd Tactical Air Force, Germany (1955-58); *b* 5 March 1903; *s* of late Edward Joseph Ubee, London; *m* 1942, Marjorie Doris (*d* 1954), *d* of George Clement-Parker, Newport, Mon; two step *s. Educ:* Beaufoy Technical Institute. Joined RAF, 1927, with short service commission; permanent commission, 1932; test pilot, Royal Aircraft Establishment, Farnborough, 1933-37; served in India, Iraq, Iran, Burma, and Ceylon, 1937-43; Airborne Forces Experimental Establishment, 1943-47; Comdg Officer, Experimental Flying, RAE Farnborough, 1946-47; Commandant Empire Test Pilots' Sch., Cranfield, Bucks, and Farnborough, 1947-48; Deputy Director Operational Requirements, Air Min., 1948-51; Commandant RAF Flying Coll., Manby, 1951-54; Director-General of Personnel (II), Air Ministry, 1954-55. *Address:* Fresh Woods, Reading Road North, Fleet, Hants. *Club:* Royal Air Force.

UDOMA, Hon. Sir (Egbert) Udo, Kt 1964; Justice, Supreme Court of Nigeria, Lagos, since 1969; *b* 21 June 1917; *s* of Chief Udoma Inam of Ibekwe Ntanaran Akama of Opobo, Nigeria; *m* 1950, Grace Bassey; six *s* one *d. Educ:* Methodist Coll., Uzuakoli, Nigeria; Trinity Coll., Dublin; St Catherine's Coll., Oxford. BA 1942; LLB 1942; PhD 1944; MA 1945. President, Dublin Univ. Philosophical Society, 1942-43. Called to Bar, Gray's Inn, 1945; practised as Barrister-at-Law in Nigeria, 1946-61; Member, House of Representatives, Nigeria, 1952-59; Judge of High Court of Federal Territory of Lagos, Nigeria, 1961. Member Nigeria Marketing Board and Director Nigeria Marketing Co. Board, 1952-54; Member Managing Cttee, West African Inst. for Oil Palm Research, 1953-63; Nat. President, Ibibio State Union, 1947-63; Vice-President, Nigeria Bar Assoc., 1957-61; Member: Internat. Commn of Jurists; World Assoc. of Judges; Chief Justice, High Court, Uganda, 1963-69; Acting Gov.-Gen., Uganda, 1963; Vice-President, Uganda Sports Union, 1964; Chairman, Board of Trustees, King George V Memorial Fund, 1964-69; Chancellor, Ahmadu Bello Univ., Zaria, 1972-75. Patron, Nigerian Soc. of Internat. Law, 1968-. LLD (*hc*): Ibadan, 1967; Zaria, 1972; TCD, 1973. Awarded title of Obong Ikpa Isong Ibibio, 1961. *Publication:* The Lion and the Oil Palm and other essays, 1943. *Recreations:* billiards, tennis, gardening and walking. *Address:* Supreme Court, Lagos, Nigeria, West Africa. *T:* Lagos 21651, 55088. *Clubs:* Island, Metropolitan, Yoruba Tennis (Lagos, Nigeria).

UFFEN, Kenneth James, CMG 1977; HM Diplomatic Service; Ambassador to Colombia, since 1977; *b* 29 Sept. 1925; *s* of late Percival James Uffen, MBE, former Civil Servant, and late Gladys Ethel James; *m* 1954, Nancy Elizabeth Winbolt; one *s* two *d. Educ:* Latymer Upper Sch.; St Catharine's Coll., Cambridge. HM Forces (Flt-Lt, RAFVR), 1943-48; St Catharine's Coll., 1948-50; 3rd Sec., FO, 1950-52; Paris, 1952-55; 2nd Sec., Buenos Aires, 1955-58; 1st Sec., FO, 1958-61; 1st Sec. (Commercial), Moscow, 1961-63; seconded to HM Treasury, 1963-65; FCO, 1965-68; Counsellor, Mexico City,

1968-70; Economic Counsellor, Washington, 1970-72; Commercial Counsellor, Moscow, 1972-76; Res. Associate, IISS, 1976-77. *Recreation:* music. *Address:* c/o Foreign and Commonwealth Office, SW1A 2AH.

UGANDA, RWANDA, BURUNDI and BOGA ZAIRE, Archbishop of, since 1977; **Most Rev. Silvano Wani;** *b* July 1916; *s* of late Mana Ada Wani and late Daa Miriam; *m* 1936, Penina Yopa Wani; six *s* two *d* (and two *s* decd). *Educ:* Kampala Normal School, Makerere (Teacher's Cert.). Teaching, Arua Primary School, 1936-39; student, Buwalasi Theol. Coll., 1940-42; ordained as one of first two priests in West Nile District, 1943; Chaplain, King's African Rifles, 1944-46; Parish Priest: Arua, 1947-50; Koboko, 1951-60; Canon and Rural Dean, Koboko, 1953-60; attended Oak Hill Theological Coll., 1955-56; Diocesan Secretary/Treasurer, N Uganda Diocese, 1961-64; Asst Bishop, later full Bishop, N Uganda, 1964; Bishop of Madi/West Nile Diocese, 1969; Dean, Province of Church of Uganda, Rwanda, Burundi and Boga Zaire, 1974. Chaplain General to Uganda Armed Forces, 1964-. *Recreations:* reading, walking, gardening. *Address:* Provincial Secretariat, Church of Uganda, Rwanda, Burundi and Boga Zaire, PO Box 14123, Kampala, Uganda. *T:* Kampala (residence 70177, (office) 70218.

ULANOVA, Galina Sergeyevna; Order of Lenin, 1953; People's Artist of the USSR (1951); Order of Red Banner of Labour, 1939, 1951; Badge of Honour, 1940; Prima Ballerina, Bolshoi Theatre, Moscow, 1944-61, retired; ballet-mistress at the Bolshoi Theatre since 1963; *b* 10 Jan. 1910; *d* of Sergei Nikolaevich Ulanov and Maria Feodorovna Romanova (dancers at Mariinsky Theatre, Petersburg). *Educ:* State School of Choreography, Leningrad. Début Kirov Theatre of Opera and Ballet, Leningrad, 1928; danced Odette-Odile in Swan Lake, 1929; Raimonda, 1931; Solweig in The Ice Maiden, 1931; danced Diane Mirelle in first performance of Flames of Paris, 1932; Giselle, 1933; Masha in The Nutcracker Suite, 1933; The Fountain of Bakhchisarai, as Maria, 1934; Lost Illusions, as Coralie, 1936; Romeo and Juliet, as Juliet, 1940; Cinderella, as Cinderella, 1945; Parasha in The Bronze Horseman, 1949; Tao Hua in The Red Poppy, 1950; Katerina in The Stone Flower, 1954. Visited London with the Bolshoi Theatre Ballet, 1956. Awarded Stalin Prize, 1941; for Cinderella, 1945; for Romeo and Juliet, 1947; for Red Poppy, 1950. Awarded Lenin prize for outstanding achievement in ballet, 1957. FRAD, 1963. *Address:* Bolshoi Theatre, Moscow. *Clubs:* All-Russian Theatrical Society, Central House of Workers in the Arts.

ULLENDORFF, Prof. Edward, MA Jerusalem, DPhil Oxford; FBA 1965; Professor of Ethiopian Studies, School of Oriental and African Studies, University of London, since 1964 (Head of Africa Department, 1972-77); *b* 25 Jan. 1920; *s* of late Frederic and Cilli Ullendorff; *m* 1943, Dina Noack. *Educ:* Gymnasium Graues Kloster; Universities of Jerusalem and Oxford. Chief Examiner, British Censorship, Eritrea, 1942-43; Editor, African Publ., British Ministry of Information, Eritrea-Ethiopia, 1943-45; Assistant Political Secretary, British Military Admin., Eritrea, 1945-46; Asst Secretary, Palestine Government, 1947-48; Research Officer and Librarian, Oxford Univ. Inst. of Colonial Studies, 1948-49; Scarbrough Senior Research Studentship in Oriental Languages, 1949-50; Reader (Lectr, 1950-56) in Semitic Languages, St Andrews Univ., 1956-59; Professor of Semitic Languages and Literatures, University of Manchester, 1959-64. Carnegie Travelling Fellow to Ethiopia, 1958; Research Journeys to Ethiopia, 1964, 1966, 1969. Catalogued Ethiopian Manuscripts in Royal Library, Windsor Castle. Chairman: Assoc. of British Orientalists, 1963-64; Anglo-Ethiopian Soc., 1965-68 (Vice-Pres. 1969-77); Pres., Soc. for Old Testament Study, 1971; Vice-Pres., RAS, 1975-. Joint Organizer, 2nd Internat. Congress of Ethiopian Studies, Manchester, 1963. Chm., Editorial Bd, Bulletin of SOAS, 1968-; Mem., Adv. Bd, British Library, 1975-. Schweich Lectr, British Academy, 1967. FRAS. Imperial Ethiopian Gold Medallion, 1960; Haile Sellassie Internat. Prize for Ethiopian studies, 1972. MA Manchester; Hon. DLitt St Andrews, 1972. *Publications:* The definite article in the Semitic languages, 1941; Exploration and Study of Abyssinia, 1945; Catalogue of Ethiopian Manuscripts in the Bodleian Library, Oxford, 1951; The Semitic Languages of Ethiopia, 1955; The Ethiopians, 1959, 1973; (with Stephen Wright) Catalogue of Ethiopian MSS in Cambridge University Library, 1961; Comparative Semitics in Linguistica Semitica, 1961; (with S. Moscati and others) Introduction to Comparative Grammar of Semitic Languages, 1964; An Amharic Chrestomathy, 1965; The Challenge of Amharic, 1965; Ethiopia and the Bible, 1968; (with J. B. Pritchard and others) Solomon and Sheba, 1974; annotated and trans., Emperor Haile Sellassie, My Life and Ethiopia's Progress (autobiog.), 1976; Studies in Semitic Languages and Civilizations, 1977; Joint Editor of Studies in honour of G. R. Driver, 1962; Joint Editor of Ethiopian Studies, 1964; articles and reviews in journals of learned societies; contribs to Encyclopaedia Britannica, Encyclopaedia of Islam, etc; Joint Editor, Journal of Semitic Studies, 1961-64. *Recreations:* music, motoring in Scotland. *Address:* School of Oriental and African Studies, London University, WC1. *T:* 01-637 2388. *Club:* Athenæum.

ULLMANN, Liv (Johanne); actress; *b* Tokyo, 16 Dec. 1938; *d* of late Viggo Ullmann and of Janna (*née* Lund), Norway; *m* 1960, Dr Gappe Stang (marr. diss. 1965). *Educ:* Norway; London (dramatic trng). Stage début, The Diary of Anne Frank (title role), Stavanger, 1956; major roles, National Theatre and Norwegian State Theatre, Oslo; Amer. stage début, A Doll's House, New York Shakespeare Festival, 1974-75; Anna Christie, USA, 1977. *Films:* Pan, 1965; The Night Visitor, 1971; Pope Joan, 1972; The Emigrants, 1972 (Golden Globe Award); The New Land, 1973 (Best Actress, Nat. Soc. of Film Critics, USA); Lost Horizon, 1973; 40 Carats, 1973; Zandy's Bride, 1973; The Abdication, 1974; (*dir. by Ingmar Bergman*): Persona, 1966; The Hour of the Wolf, 1968 (Best Actress, Nat. Soc. of Film Critics, USA); Shame, 1968 (Best Actress, Nat. Soc. of Film Critics, USA); The Passion of Anna, 1969; Cries and Whispers, 1972; Scenes from a Marriage, 1974; Face to Face, 1976; The Serpent's Egg, 1977. Peer Gynt Award, Norway (1st female recipient). *Publication:* (autobiog.) Changing, 1977. *Address:* Drammensviens 91, Oslo, Norway.

ULLMANN, Walter, MA, LittD; FBA 1968; Professor of Medieval History, University of Cambridge, 1972-Sept. 1978 (Medieval Ecclesiastical History, 1966-72); Fellow of Trinity College, Cambridge, since 1959; *b* 29 Nov. 1910; *m* 1940, Mary Elizabeth Finnemore Knapp; two *s. Educ:* Universities of Vienna, Innsbruck (JUD), and Munich. Research at Cambridge University; Assistant Lecturer, University of Vienna, 1935-38. War service, 1940-43. History and Modern Languages Master, Ratcliffe Coll., Leicester, 1943-47; part-time Lecturer, Pol. Int. Dept, Foreign Office, 1944-46; Lecturer in Medieval History, University of Leeds, 1947-49; Maitland Mem. Lectr, Univ. of Cambridge, 1947-48; Univ. Lectr in Medieval History, Cambridge, 1949-57; Reader, 1957-65. Co-Editor Ephemerides Juris Canonici, 1951-64; Päpste & Papsttum, 1970-; Editor, Cambridge Studies in Medieval Life and Thought, 1968-. Prof. of Humanities, Johns Hopkins Univ., 1964-65. Birkbeck Lectr, Cambridge, 1968-69. Hon. Fellow, St Edmund's House, Cambridge, 1976. Hon. Dr *rerum politicarum* and Jubilee Medal for distinguished services, Univ. of Innsbruck, 1970. Corresp. Mem., Austrian and Bavarian Acads of Sciences. *Publications:* The Medieval Idea of Law, 1946, repr. 1969, 1972; The Origins of the Great Schism, 1948, repr. 1972 with new introd.; Medieval Papalism, 1949; The Growth of Papal Government in the Middle Ages, 1955 (rev. edn German: Die Machtstellung d. Papsttums im Mittelalter, 1960), 4th edn 1970; The Medieval Papacy, St Thomas and beyond (Aquinas lecture, 1958), 1960; Liber regie capelle, 1961; Principles of Government and Politics in the Middle Ages, 1961, 3rd edn 1974 (trans. into Spanish and Italian); Hist. Introd. to Lea's Inquisition, 1963; A History of Political Thought in The Middle Ages, 1965, rev. edn 1970; The Relevance of Medieval Eccles. History (inaug. lecture, 1966); Papst und König, 1966; The Individual and Society in the Middle Ages, 1967 (trans. into Japanese, German and Italian); The Carolingian Renaissance and the Idea of Kingship, 1969; A Short History of the Papacy in the Middle Ages, 1972, 2nd edn 1974, repr. 1977 (trans. into Italian and German); The Future of Medieval History, 1973; Law and Politics in the Middle Ages, 1975; The Church and the Law in the Earlier Middle Ages (Collected Studies I), 1975; The Papacy and Political Ideas in the Middle Ages (Collected Studies II), 1976; Medieval Foundations of Renaissance Humanism, 1977; contributed to English Historical Review, Jl of Ecclesiastical History, Jl of Theol Studies, Cambridge Hist. Jl, Law Quarterly Review, Trans. Royal Hist. Society, Studi Gregoriani, Studia Gratiana, Studi Federiciani, Studi Accursio, Misc. Hist. Pont., Rev. Bénédictine, Rev. hist. droit, Europa e il Diritto Romano, Arch. storico Pugliese, Savigny Z., Studia Patristica, Bartolo da Sassoferrato: studi e documenti; Acta Iuridica; Settimana studio Spoleto; Annali storia amministrativa; Recueils Soc. Bodin; Speculum Historiale; Historische Zeitschrift; Studies in Church History, Virginia Jl of Internat. Law, Hist. Jahrbuch, Annali di storia del diritto, Römische Hist. Mitteil. *Recreations:* music and travelling. *Address:* Trinity College, Cambridge CB2 1TQ.

ULLSWATER, 2nd Viscount *cr* 1921, of Campsea Ashe, Suffolk; **Nicholas James Christopher Lowther;** *b* 9 Jan. 1942; *s* of Lieut John Arthur Lowther, MVO, RNVR (*d* 1942), and Patricia Violet (*d* 1945), *yr d* of Reginald Everitt Lambert; *S* great-grandfather, 1949; *m* 1967, Susan, *d* of James Howard Weatherby; one *s* two *d. Educ:* Eton; Trinity Coll., Cambridge. Captain, Wessex Yeomanry, T&AVR, 1973. *Heir:* s Hon.

Benjamin James Lowther, *b* 26 Nov. 1975. *Address:* Knoyle Down Farm, Hindon, Salisbury, Wilts. *T:* Hindon 224.

ULSTER, Earl of; Alexander Patrick Gregers Richard Windsor; *b* 24 Oct. 1974; *s* of HRH the Duke of Gloucester and HRH the Duchess of Gloucester.
See under Royal Family.

UMFREVILLE, William Henry, CBE 1959; ISO 1951; retired as Accountant and Comptroller-General, Board of Inland Revenue (1954-58); *b* 7 June 1893; *e s* of William Henry Umfreville; *m* 1916, Daisy Catherine Colson; two *d. Educ:* Palmer's School. Post Office, 1909-12; Ministry of Agriculture and Fisheries, 1913-23; Inland Revenue, 1924-58, retired. *Address:* 2 Cumberland Avenue, Worthing, West Sussex.

UNDERHILL, (Henry) Reginall, CBE 1976; National Agent of the Labour Party, since 1972; *b* 8 May 1914; *s* of Henry James and Alice Maud Underhill; *m* 1937, Flora Janet Philbrick; two *s* one *d. Educ:* Norlington Road Elementary School; Tom Hood Central School, Leyton. Junior Clerk, C. A. Hardman & Sons Ltd, Lloyds Underwriters, 1929; joined Labour Party Head Office as Junior Accounts Clerk, 1933. National Fire Service, 1939-45. Assistant to Mr Morgan Phillips, Labour Party Gen. Sec., 1945; Admin. Assistant to National Agent, 1945; Propaganda Officer, 1947; Regional Organiser, W Midlands, 1948; Assistant National Agent, 1960. Joined Labour Party, 1930; Vice-Chm. 1933, Hon. Sec. 1937-48, Leyton West Constituency Labour Party. Hon. Sec., British Workers' Sports Assoc., 1935-37. *Recreations:* golf; life-long support of Leyton Orient FC; formerly cycling (club captain) and track and cross-country athletics. *Address:* 94 Loughton Way, Buckhurst Hill, Essex IG9 6AH. *T:* 01-504 1910.

UNDERHILL, Herbert Stuart; Publisher Victoria (BC) Daily Times, since 1971; *b* 20 May 1914; *s* of Canon H. J. Underhill and Helena (*née* Ross); *m* 1937, Emma Gwendolyn MacGregor; one *s* one *d. Educ:* University Sch., Victoria, BC. Correspondent and Editor, The Canadian Press, Vancouver, BC, Toronto, New York and London, 1936-50; Reuters North American Editor, 1950; Asst General Manager, Reuters, 1958 Managing Editor, 1965-68; Dep. Gen. Manager, with special responsibility for North and South America and Caribbean, 1963-70. Director: Canadian Daily Newspaper Publishers' Assoc., 1972-76; The Canadian Press, 1972-78. *Recreations:* travel, reading. *Address:* 308 Beach Drive, Victoria, BC, Canada.

UNDERHILL, Michael Thomas Ben, QC 1972; a Recorder of the Crown Court (formerly Recorder of Reading), since 1970; *b* 10 Feb. 1918; *s* of late Rev. P. C. Underhill and Viola Underhill; *m* 1950, Rosalie Jean Kinloch; three *s. Educ:* Radley Coll.; Brasenose Coll., Oxford (MA). Served Glos Regt, 1939-42; 2nd KEO Goorkha Rifles, 1942-46 (Major). Called to the Bar, Gray's Inn, 1947; Master of the Bench, Gray's Inn, 1978; Oxford Circuit; Dep. Chm., Salop QS, 1967-71. *Address:* Gore Lodge, Hampton-on-Thames, Mddx. *T:* 01-979 1260; 3 Pump Court, Temple, EC4. *Club:* Leander (Henley-on-Thames).

UNDERHILL, Reginall; see Underhill, H. R.

UNDERWOOD, Edgar Ashworth, MA, BSc, MD; Hon. DLitt Glasgow; DPH; FRCP, FLS, FSS; Chevalier de la Légion d'Honneur; Hon. Research Fellow, formerly Hon. Lecturer, Department of History and Philosophy of Science, University College, London; Member of Board of Studies in the History and Philosophy of Science, 1947-77, and formerly Examiner, University of London; Hunterian Trustee, Royal College of Surgeons, since 1953; President British Society for History of Science, 1957-62; Fellow, Royal Society Medicine (President, 1948-50, and Hon. Secretary, 1942-48, Section of History of Medicine, late Hon. Secretary Section of Epidemiology and Community Medicine; Member, Library Committee, since 1938); Hon. Fellow, American Medical Association; Corresponding Member of numerous foreign societies for history of medicine, etc; *b* Dumfries, 9 March 1899; *s* of David Underwood and Janet Milligan Grierson; *m* 1928, Embling Halliday, MA (marr. diss.); *m* 1949, Nancy W. Singer; two *d. Educ:* Dumfries Acad. (Modern dux, 1917); Univs of Glasgow (Cullen Medal in materia medica, Hunter Medals in midwifery and in clinical surgery; Vice-Pres., Glasgow Univ. Medico-Chirurgical Soc., 1923-24) and Leeds. Served European War (France), 1917-19, Cameron Highlanders. Hospital and public health posts in Glasgow and County of Lanark, 1925-29; Dep. MOH, Co. Borough of Rotherham, and Med. Supt of Oakwood Hall Sanatorium, 1929-31; Dep. MOH, City of Leeds, and Lectr in Public Health, Univ. of Leeds, 1932-34; MOH, Metrop. Borough of Shoreditch, 1934-37; MOH and Chief Sch. MO, Co. Borough of West Ham, 1937-45; Dir of the Wellcome Inst. of

History of Medicine, 1946-64. Thomas Vicary Lectr, RCS, 1946; Guest Lectr, Centenary Meeting of Amer. Med. Assoc., 1947; Fielding H. Garrison Lectr, Amer. Assoc. for History of Medicine, 1947; 2nd John Ash Lectr, Univ. of Birmingham, 1969; FitzPatrick Lectr, RCP, 1971, 1972. Hon. DLitt Glasgow, 1970. *Publications:* A Manual of Tuberculosis, Clinical and Administrative, 3rd edn, 1945; Science Medicine and History, Essays in honour of Charles Singer, 2 vols (ed), 1953; A Short History of Medicine (jt), 1962; memoir on Charles Creighton, the Man and his Work, 1965; (trans. and adapted) Pollak, The Healers (Die Jünger des Hippokrates), 1968; Boerhaave's Men at Leyden and After, 1977; individual essays on work of 21 Nobel Prizewinners in Encyclopedia of World Biography, 1973; contribs to Chambers's Encyclopædia and the Encyclopædia Britannica; publications on History of Society of Apothecaries of London, 1963 and in progress; papers on historical, epidemiological and statistical subjects in Proc. RSM, Annals of Science, and in other jls. *Recreations:* books, music, mountains. *Address:* Glenmerle, 36 Burwood Park Road, Walton-on-Thames, Surrey KT12 5LH. *T:* Walton-on-Thames 25725. *Club:* Athenæum.

UNDERWOOD, Prof. Eric John, AO 1976; CBE 1963; FRS 1970; FAA 1954; FTS; Emeritus Professor since 1971, and Hon. Research Fellow since 1976, University of Western Australia; *b* London, England, 7 Sept. 1905; 2nd *s* of James and Elizabeth Underwood; *m* 1934, Erica Reid Chandler; two *s* two *d. Educ:* Perth Modern Sch.; Univ. of Western Australia; Cambridge Univ.; Univ. of Wisconsin. Research Officer in Animal Nutrition, Dept of Agriculture, WA, 1931; Hackett Prof. of Agriculture, Dean of Faculty of Agric., and Dir, Inst. of Agric. in Univ. of Western Australia, 1946-70. Part-time Mem. Executive, CSIRO, 1966-75. Hon. degrees: DRurSci Univ. of New England, 1967; DScAgric Univ. of Western Australia, 1969; DAgricSc Univ. of Melbourne, 1973. *Publications:* Principles of Animal Production, 1946; Trace Elements in Human and Animal Nutrition, 1956, 4th edn 1977 (NY); The Mineral Nutrition of Livestock (FAO/CAB Pubn), 1966 (Aberdeen); about 100 pubns in Agricultural, Veterinary and Biological Research jls. *Recreations:* reading, gardening. *Address:* 3 Cooper Street, Nedlands, WA 6009, Australia.

UNDERWOOD, Michael; *see* Evelyn, J. M.

UNMACK, Randall Carter, MA, Docteur de l'Université, Sorbonne, Paris; Headmaster of King's College, Taunton, 1937-65, retired; *b* West Horsley, Surrey, 26 Aug. 1899; *s* of late Rev. E. C. Unmack, DD, formerly Rector of W Horsley, and of Emily, *d* of late Dean West, Ardagh, Ireland; *m* 1933, Anne Roberta (*d* 1972), *d* of late Dr Robert Stuart, Durham; one *s* one *d. Educ:* King's College Sch., Wimbledon; Queen's Coll., Oxford; Sorbonne, Paris. Served in RNAS and RAF, 2nd Lieut; Airship Pilot on Anti-submarine Patrol, 1918-19; taught at Oakham Sch., Rutland, Ecole Normale, Laval, Bristol Grammar Sch. and Mill Hill Sch. between 1921 and 1928; Senior Modern Language Master at Lancing Coll., 1928-33; Headmaster of Doncaster Grammar Sch,, 1933-37. Member Adv. Cttee on Religious Broadcasting, Western Region, 1952-56. Member, Governing Body St Audries Sch., 1960-66. Hon. Fellow, Woodard Corp., 1966; Governor, Cathedral School, Exeter, 1969-73. Order of Menelik II (Ethiopia), class IV, 1953. *Publications:* Education et Décentralisation, Paris, 1927; The Family and Education, London, 1962; articles on education and religious teaching. *Recreations:* travelling, sailing. *Address:* c/o Mrs Hill, Arundel, Victoria Road, Barnstaple, Devon EX32 9HP.

UNSTEAD, Robert John; author; *b* 21 Nov. 1915; *s* of Charles and Elizabeth Unstead; *m* 1939, Florence Margaret Thomas; three *d. Educ:* Dover Grammar Sch.; Goldsmiths' Coll., London. Schoolmaster, 1936-40. Served in RAF, 1940-46. Headmaster, Norton Road CP Sch., Letchworth, 1947-51, Grange Sch., Letchworth, 1951-57. Member, Herts Education Cttee, 1951-57; Chairman, Letchworth Primary Schools' Cttee of Management, 1960-64; Governor, Leiston Middle School, 1973-. Chm., Educational Writers' Group, Soc. of Authors, 1965-68. *Publications:* Looking at History, 1953; People in History, 1955; Teaching History in the Primary School, 1956; Travel by Road, 1958; A History of Houses, 1958; Looking at Ancient History, 1959; Monasteries, 1961; Black's Children's Encyclopædia (co-author), 1961; The Medieval Scene, 1962; Crown and Parliament, 1962; Some Kings and Queens, 1962; The Rise of Great Britain, 1963; A Century of Change, 1963; Royal Adventurers, 1964; Early Times, 1964; Men and Women in History, 1965; Britain in the Twentieth Century, 1966; The Story of Britain, 1969; Homes in Australia, 1969; Castles, 1970; Transport in Australia, 1970; Pioneer Homelife in Australia, 1971; History of the English-speaking World, 1972; The

Twenties, 1973; The Thirties, 1974; Living in Aztec Times, 1974; Living in Samuel Pepys' London, 1975; A Dictionary of History, 1976; general editor, Black's Junior Reference series, Looking at Geography. *Recreations:* golf, gardening, watching cricket. *Address:* Reedlands, Thorpeness, Suffolk. *T:* Aldeburgh 2665. *Club:* MCC.

UNSWORTH, Sir Edgar (Ignatius Godfrey), Kt 1963; CMG 1954; QC (N Rhodesia) 1951; Justice of Appeal, Gibraltar, since 1976; *b* 18 April 1906; *yr s* of John William and Minnie Unsworth; *m* 1964, Eileen, *widow* of Raymond Ritzema. *Educ:* Stonyhurst Coll.; Manchester Univ. (LLB Hons). Barrister-at-Law, Gray's Inn, 1930; private practice, 1930-37. Parly Cand. (C) for Farnworth, General Election, 1935. Crown Counsel: Nigeria, 1937; N Rhodesia, 1942; Solicitor-General: N Rhodesia, 1946; Fedn of Malaya, 1949; Chm. of Cttees, N Rhodesia, 1950; Attorney-General, N Rhodesia, 1951-56. Acting Chief Sec. and Dep. to Governor of N Rhodesia for periods during 1953, 1954 and 1955; Attorney-General, Fedn of Nigeria, 1956-60; Federal Justice of Federal Supreme Court of Nigeria, 1960-62; Chief Justice, Nyasaland, 1962-64; Director of a Course for Government Officers from Overseas, 1964-65; Chief Justice of Gibraltar, 1965-76. Member Rhodesia Railways Arbitration Tribunal, 1946; Chm., Commn of Enquiry into Central African Airways Corp., 1947. *Publication:* Laws of Northern Rhodesia (rev. edn), 1949. *Address:* The Little House, Charters Road, Sunningdale, Ascot, Berks SL5 9QF. *Club:* Royal Gibraltar Yacht.

UNTERMEYER, Louis; author, lecturer, editor; *b* New York City, 1 Oct. 1885; *s* of Emanuel Untermeyer and Julia Michael; *m* 1948, Bryna Ivens; no *c* ; (by previous marriages: three *s*, and one *s* decd). *Educ:* privately and abroad. Contributing Editor to The Masses and The Liberator. Editor of Publications at Office of War Information and Associate Editor of The Armed Services Editions during War of 1939-45. Lectr at various Univs throughout USA, including Michigan, Amherst, Knox, etc. Editor of Decca Records, 1945-58. Consultant in Poetry at Library of Congress in Washington, 1961-63. *Publications:* by 1969 author and editor of more than ninety volumes of prose and verse, including: Challenge, 1914; Roast Leviathan, 1923; Moses, a novel, 1928; Food and Drink, 1932; The Book of Living Verse, 1932; Rainbow in the Sky, 1935; Selected Poems and Parodies, 1935; Heinrich Heine: Paradox and Poet (2 vols), 1937; Play in Poetry, 1937; Modern American Poetry (10th edn 1969); Modern British Poetry (9th edn 1969); A Treasury of Great Poems, 1942; The Wonderful Adventures of Paul Bunyan, 1945; A Treasury of Laughter, 1946; The New England Poets, 1948; The Inner Sanctum, Walt Whitman, 1949; The Best Humor of 1949-50, 1950-51, 1951-52; The Magic Circle, 1952; Makers of the Modern World, 1955; A Treasury of Ribaldry, 1956; Lives of the Poets, 1959 (USA), 1960 (Eng.); The Golden Treasury of Poetry for Young People, 1959; The Britannica Library of Great American Writing, 1960; Collins Albatross Book of Verse, 1962; Long Feud: Selected Poems, 1962; An Uninhibited Treasury of Erotic Poetry, 1963; The Letters of Robert Frost to Louis Untermeyer, 1963; The World's Great Stories, 1964; Labyrinth of Love, 1965; Bygones: An Autobiography, 1965; The Paths of Poetry: Twenty-five Poets from Chaucer to Frost, 1966; Tales of the Ballets, 1968; The Firebringer and other Stories, 1968; The Pursuit of Poetry, 1969; Cat O'Nine Tales, 1971; A Treasury of Great Humor, 1972; 50 Modern American and British Poets, 1973. *Recreations:* piano-playing, gardening and cats. *Address:* Great Hill Road, Newtown, Conn 06470, USA.

UNWIN, Ven. Christopher Philip, TD 1963; MA; Archdeacon of Northumberland, since 1963; *b* 27 Sept. 1917; *e s* of Rev. Philip Henry and Decima Unwin. *Educ:* Repton Sch.; Magdalene Coll., Cambridge; Queen's Theological Coll., Birmingham. Deacon, 1940, Priest, 1941. Asst Curate of: Benwell, 1940-43; Sugley, 1944-47; Vicar of: Horton, Northumberland, 1947-55; Benwell, 1955-63. *Recreations:* reading, walking. *Address:* 80 Moorside North, Newcastle upon Tyne NE4 9DU. *T:* Newcastle upon Tyne 38245.

UNWIN, David Storr; author; *b* 3 Dec. 1918; *e s* of late Sir Stanley Unwin, KCMG; *m* 1945, Periwinkle, *yr d* of late Captain Sidney Herbert, RN; twin *s* and *d. Educ:* Abbotsholme. League of Nations Secretariat, Geneva, 1938-39; George Allen & Unwin Ltd, Publishers, 1940-44. *Publications:* The Governor's Wife, 1954; (Authors' Club First Novel Award, 1955); A View of the Heath, 1956; *for children:* (under pen name David Severn) Rick Afire!, 1942; A Cabin for Crusoe, 1943; Waggon for Five, 1944; Hermit in the Hills, 1945; Forest Holiday, 1946; Ponies and Poachers, 1947; Dream Gold, 1948; The Cruise of the Maiden Castle, 1948; Treasure for Three, 1949; My Foreign Correspondent through Africa, 1950; Crazy

Castle, 1951; Burglars and Bandicoots, 1952; Drumbeats!, 1953; The Future Took Us, 1958; The Green-eyed Gryphon, 1958; Foxy-boy, 1959; Three at the Sea, 1959; Clouds over the Alberhorn, 1963; Jeff Dickson, Cowhand, 1963; The Girl in the Grove, 1974; The Wishing Bone, 1977. *Recreations:* travel, gardening. *Address:* St Michael's, Helions Bumpstead, Haverhill, Suffolk. *T:* Steeple Bumpstead 316. *Club:* PEN. *See also R. S. Unwin.*

UNWIN, James Brian; Under Secretary, HM Treasury, since 1976; *b* 21 Sept. 1935; *s* of Reginald Unwin and Winifred Annie Walthall; *m* 1964, Diana Susan Scott; three *s*. *Educ:* Chesterfield School; New College, Oxford (1st class Mods; 2nd class Greats; MA); Yale University (MA). Asst Principal, CRO, 1960; Private Sec. to British High Commissioner, Salisbury, 1961-64; 1st Secretary, British High Commission, Accra, 1964-65; FCO, 1965-68; transferred to HM Treasury, 1968; Private Sec. to Chief Secretary to Treasury, 1970-72; Asst Secretary, 1972. *Recreations:* bird watching, Wellingtonia, cricket. *Address:* 25 Links Road, Epsom, Surrey. *T:* Epsom 24148. *Club:* Kingswood Village (Surrey).

UNWIN, Sir Keith, KBE 1964 (OBE 1937); CMG 1954; MA; Member, Human Rights Commission of United Nations, since 1970; *b* 3 Aug. 1909; *er s* of late Edwin Ernest Unwin and Jessie Magdalen Black; *m* 1935, Linda Giersé; one *s* two *d*. *Educ:* Merchant Taylors' Sch.; Lycée Condorcet, Paris; St John's Coll., Oxford; BA 1931. Department of Overseas Trade, 1932; Mem., Commercial Diplomatic Service, later HM Diplomatic Service, 1934-69; Madrid, 1934; Istanbul, 1937; San Sebastian (later Madrid), 1939; Mexico City, 1944; Paris, 1946; Prague, 1949; Buenos Aires, 1950; Rome, 1955-59; Foreign Service Inspector, 1959-62; UK Representative on Economic and Social Council of the United Nations, 1962-66; HM Ambassador to Uruguay, 1966-69. *Recreations:* gardening, reading. *Address:* Wildacres, Fleet, Hants. *T:* Fleet 7590. *Club:* Canning.

UNWIN, Nora Spicer, RE 1946 (ARE 1935); ARCA; artist, painter, print-maker, book-illustrator; *b* 22 Feb. 1907; *d* of George Soundy and Eleanor Mary Unwin. *Educ:* Surbiton High Sch. Studied at Leon Underwood's; Kingston School of Art; Royal College of Art, 1928-32; Diploma in Design, 1931; wood-engravings exhibited at Royal Academy; other galleries and international exhibitions in Europe and N and S America; Near and Far East; works purchased by Contemporary Art Society for British Museum; by Boston Public Library; by Library of Congress, Washington, DC; by Fitchburg Art Museum (Mass.); by New York Public Library for permanent collection; also represented in Metropolitan Museum, NY. One-man exhibitions held in Boston and cities in Eastern US, 1948-50, 1954-56, 1957, 1960, 1964, 1965, 1966, 1967, 1969, 1974, 1975. Exhibition Member: Royal Soc. Painter-Etchers and Engravers; Soc. of Wood-engravers; American Nat. Acad. (ANA 1954, NA 1976); Boston Print Makers; Print Club of Albany; Soc. of American Graphic Artists; NH Art Assoc.; Boston Watercolour Soc.; Cambridge Art Assoc. (CAA), etc. Awards: Soc. of American Graphic Artists, 1951; Boston Independent Artists, 1952; NHAA, 1952, 1975; NAWA, 1953; National Academy Design, 1958; Fitchburg Art Museum, 1965, 1973; BSWCP, 1965; Boston Printmakers Purchase, 1973. CAA 1967. *Publications:* author-illustrator of: Round the Year, 1939; Lucy and the Little Red Horse, 1942; Doughnuts for Lin, 1950; Proud Pumpkin, 1953; Poquito, the Little Mexican Duck, 1959; Two Too Many, 1962; The Way of the Shepherd, 1963; Joyful the Morning, 1963; The Midsummer Witch, 1966; Sinbad the Cygnet, 1970; The Chickerdees Come (poems), 1977; numerous books illustrated for English and American publishers. *Recreations:* music, swimming, walking, gardening, etc. *Address:* Pine-Apple Cottage, Old Street Road, Peterborough, NH 03458, USA.

UNWIN, Peter William; HM Diplomatic Service; Head of Personnel Policy Department, Foreign and Commonwealth Office, since 1976; *b* 20 May 1932; *s* of Arnold and Norah Unwin; *m* 1955, Monica Steven; two *s* two *d*. *Educ:* Ampleforth; Christ Church, Oxford (MA). Army, 1954-56; FO, 1956-58; British Legation, Budapest, 1958-61; British Embassy, Tokyo, 1961-63; FCO, 1963-67; British Information Services, NY, 1967-70; FCO, 1970-72; Bank of England, 1973; British Embassy, Bonn, 1973-76. *Address:* 30 Kew Green, Richmond, Surrey. *T:* 01-940 8037; 274 East Grafton, near Marlborough, Wilts.

UNWIN, Rayner Stephens, CBE 1977; Chairman, George Allen & Unwin Ltd, since 1968; *b* 23 Dec. 1925; *s* of late Sir Stanley Unwin and Mary Storr; *m* 1952, Carol Margaret, *d* of Harold Curwen; one *s* three *d*. *Educ:* Abbotsholme Sch.; Trinity Coll., Oxford (MA); Harvard, USA (MA). Sub-Lt, RNVR, 1944-47. Entered George Allen & Unwin Ltd, 1951. Mem. Council, Publishers' Assoc., 1965- (Treasurer, 1969; Pres., 1971; Vice-

Pres., 1973); Dir, The Australasian Publishing Co., 1969. *Publications:* The Rural Muse, 1954; The Defeat of John Hawkins, 1960. *Recreations:* skiing downhill, walking up-hill, birds and gardens. *Address:* (home) Limes Cottage, Little Missenden, near Amersham, Bucks. *T:* Great Missenden 2900; 28 Little Russell Street, WC1. *T:* 01-242 3781 *Club:* Garrick. *See also D. S. Unwin.*

UPDIKE, John Hoyer; freelance writer; *b* 18 March 1932; *s* of Wesley R. and Linda G. Updike; *m* 1953, Mary E. Pennington; two *s* two *d*. *Educ:* Harvard Coll. Worked as journalist for The New Yorker magazine, 1955-57. *Publications: poems:* Hoping for a Hoopoe (in America, The Carpentered Hen), 1958; Telephone Poles, 1968; Midpoint and other poems, 1969; Tossing and Turning, 1977; *novels:* The Poorhouse Fair, 1959; Rabbit, Run, 1960; The Centaur, 1963; Of the Farm, 1966; Couples, 1968; Rabbit Redux, 1972; A Month of Sundays, 1975; Marry Me, 1976; *short stories:* The Same Door, 1959; Pigeon Feathers, 1962; The Music School, 1966; Bech: A Book, 1970; Museums and Women, 1973; *miscellanies:* Assorted Prose, 1965; Picked-Up Pieces, 1976; *play:* Buchanan Dying, 1974. *Address:* West Main Street, Georgetown, Mass 01833, USA.

UPHAM, Captain Charles Hazlitt, VC 1941 and Bar, 1943; JP; sheep-farmer; *b* Christchurch, New Zealand, 21 Sept. 1908; *s* of John Hazlitt Upham, barrister, and Agatha Mary Upham, Christchurch, NZ; *m* 1945, Mary Eileen, *d* of James and Mary McTamney, Dunedin, New Zealand; three *d* (incl. twins). *Educ:* Waihi Prep. School, Winchester; Christ's Coll., Christchurch, NZ; Canterbury Agric. Coll., Lincoln, NZ (Diploma). Postgrad. course in valuation and farm management. Farm manager and musterer, 1930-36; govt valuer, 1937-39; farmer, 1945-. Served War of 1939-45 (VC and Bar, despatches): volunteered, Sept. 1939; 2nd NZEF (Sgt 1st echelon advance party); 2nd Lt; served Greece, Crete, W Desert (VC, Crete, Bar, Ruweisat); Captain; POW, released 1945. *Relevant Publication:* Mark of the Lion: The Story of Captain Charles Upham, VC and Bar (by Kenneth Sandford), 1962. *Recreations:* rowing, Rugby (1st XV Lincoln Coll., NZ). *Address:* Lansdowne, Hundalee, North Canterbury, NZ. *Clubs:* Canterbury, Christchurch, RSA (all NZ).

UPJOHN, Maj.-Gen. Gordon Farleigh, CB 1966; CBE 1959 (OBE 1955); *b* 9 May 1912; *e s* of late Dudley Francis Upjohn; *m* 1946, Rita Joan, *d* of late Major Clarence Walters; three *d*. *Educ:* Felsted School; RMC Sandhurst. 2nd Lieut, The Duke of Wellington's Regt; RWAFF, 1937; Adjt 3rd Bn The Nigeria Regt, 1940; Staff Coll., 1941; GSO2 Ops GHQ Middle East, 1941; Bde Maj. 3 WA Inf. Bde, 1942 (despatches); Lt-Col Comd 6 Bn The Nigeria Regt, 1944 (despatches); DAA&QMG Southern Comd India, 1946; GSO2 Mil. Ops Directorate WO, 1948; Lt-Col Chief Instructor RMA Sandhurst, 1951; Lt-Col Comd WA Inf. Bn, 1954; Bde Comdr 2 Inf. Bde Malaya, 1957 (despatches); Provost Marshal WO, 1960; GOC Yorkshire District, 1962-65. Automobile Assoc., 1965-76. *Recreations:* golf, cricket, field sports. *Address:* c/o Lloyds Bank Ltd, 62 Brook Street, W1. *Clubs:* Army and Navy, MCC.

UPJOHN, Sir William George Dismore, Kt 1958; OBE 1919; ED 1976; MD, MS, FRCS, FRACS, LLD (Melbourne), 1962; Hon. Surgeon to Inpatients and Clinical Lecturer in Surgery, Royal Melbourne Hospital, since 1927; Consulting Surgeon Royal Children's Hospital, Melbourne and Royal Melbourne Hospital; *b* Narrabri, NSW, 16 March 1888; *s* of George Dismore Upjohn; *m* 1927, Norma S., *d* of John Withers; two *s* two *d*. *Educ:* Wesley Coll.; Melbourne Univ.; Middlesex Hosp. Medical Sch.; London Hosp. Med. Sch. RMO, Clinical Asst and Hon. Surgeon to Outpatients, Melbourne Hosp., 1910-27; Lectr in Surgery and Stewart Lectr in Anatomy, Melbourne Univ., 1912-18. Served in both world wars: Dep. Chm. Central Coordination Cttee, War of 1939-45 (despatches). Lt-Col Australian Army Medical Corps, R of O. Chancellor, Melbourne Univ., 1966-37 (Council, 1958-74; Dep. Chancellor, 1962-66). Mem. Cttee, Greenvale Geriatric Centre, 1959- (Pres., 1959-77); Pres., Royal Melbourne Hosp., 1960. *Publication:* Human Osteology, 1913. *Recreations:* art, music, literature. *Address:* 12 Collins Street, Melbourne, Australia. *Club:* Melbourne (Melbourne).

UPTON, family name of Viscount Templetown.

UPTON, Leslie William Stokes, CBE 1967 (MBE 1954); JP; retired as Registrar of the Privy Council (1963-66); Barrister-at-law, Gray's Inn, 1952; *b* 29 June 1900; *yr s* of late Alfred Charles Upton; *m* 1927, Frances, *yr d* of late Richard John Snowden Jesson; one *s*. *Educ:* Coopers' Company's School. Served with Hon. Artillery Company, 1918; Asst Clerk, War Office, 1918; transferred to Treasury, 1921; 3rd Clerk, 1925; 2nd Clerk, 1937, to the Judicial Cttee of the Privy Council; Chief Clerk, Judicial

Cttee of the Privy Council, 1954-63. JP Kent, 1956. *Publications:* contribs to legal jls. *Recreations:* music, motoring. *Address:* 114 Copse Avenue, West Wickham, Kent. *T:* 01-777 3162. *Clubs:* Civil Service, Royal Commonwealth Society.

URE, James Mathie, OBE 1969; Controller, Home Division, British Council, since 1975; *b* 5 May 1925; *s* of late William Alexander Ure, and of Helen Jones; *m* 1950, Martha Walker Paterson; one *s* one *d*. *Educ:* Shawlands Acad., Glasgow; Glasgow Univ. (MA); Trinity Coll., Oxford (BLitt). Army Service, 1944-47. Lectr, Edinburgh Univ., 1953-59; British Council: Istanbul, 1956-57; India, 1959-68; Dep. Controller, Arts Div., 1968-71; Rep., Indonesia, 1971-75. *Publications:* Old English Benedictine Office, 1952; (with L. A. Hill) English Sounds and Spellings, 1962; (with L. A. Hill) English Sounds and Spellings—Tests, 1963; (with J. S. Bhandari and C. S. Bhandari) Read and Act, 1965; (with C. S. Bhandari) Short Stories, 1966. *Address:* Southlands, Downs Side, Belmont, Surrey. *T:* 01-642 7241. *Club:* Royal Commonwealth Society.

URE, John Burns, MVO 1968; HM Diplomatic Service; Head of South America Department, Foreign and Commonwealth Office, since 1977; *b* 5 July 1931; *s* of late Tam Ure; *m* 1972, Caroline, *d* of Charles Allan, Chesterknowes, Roxburghshire. *Educ:* Uppingham Sch.; Magdalene Coll., Cambridge (MA); Harvard Business Sch. (AMP). Active Service as 2nd Lieut with Cameronians (Scottish Rifles), Malaya, 1950-51; joined Foreign (subseq. Diplomatic) Service, 1956; 3rd Sec. and Private Sec. to Ambassador, Moscow, 1957-59; Resident Clerk, FO, 1960-61; 2nd Sec., Leopoldville, 1962-63; FO, 1964-66; 1st Sec. (Commercial), Santiago, 1967-70; FCO, 1971-72; Counsellor, Lisbon, 1972-77. FRGS. Comdr, Mil. Order of Christ, Portugal, 1973. *Publications:* Cucumber Sandwiches in the Andes, 1973 (Travel Book Club Choice); Prince Henry the Navigator, 1977 (History Guild Choice); articles on S America in The Times, etc. *Recreation:* travelling uncomfortably in remote places and reading and writing about it comfortably afterwards. *Address:* Little Horden Farmhouse, Goudhurst, Kent TN17 2NE. *T:* Goudhurst 396. *Clubs:* White's, Travellers', Beefsteak.

UREN, Reginald Harold, FRIBA; private practice of architecture, 1933-68; *b* New Zealand, 5 March 1906; *s* of Richard Ellis and Christina Uren; *m* 1930, Dorothy Marion Morgan; one *d*. *Educ:* Hutt Valley High School, New Zealand; London University. Qualified as Architect in New Zealand, 1929; ARIBA, London, 1931; won open architectural competition for Hornsey Town Hall (281 entries), 1933; joined in partnership with J. Alan Slater and A. H. Moberly, 1936; architectural practice includes public buildings, department stores, domestic, commercial and school buildings. Works include: John Lewis Store, Oxford Street; Arthur Sanderson & Sons Building, Berners Street; Norfolk County Hall. Freeman of City of London, 1938; Master, Tylers and Bricklayers Company, 1966. War service, 1942-46, Capt. Royal Engineers. Council, RIBA, 1946-65; London Architecture Bronze Medal, 1935; Tylers and Bricklayers Company Gold Medal, 1936; Min. of Housing and Local Govt Medal for London Region, 1954; New Zealand Inst. of Architects Award of Merit, 1965. *Recreation:* debate. *Address:* PO Box 102, Thames, New Zealand. *Club:* Reform.

UREY, Harold Clayton; Emeritus Professor of Chemistry, University of California, La Jolla, California, since 1958; Eastman Professor, Oxford University, 1956-June 1957; Foreign Member of the Royal Society, 1947; *b* 29 April 1893; *s* of Samuel Clayton Urey and Cora Rebecca Reinoehl; *m* 1926, Frieda Daum; one *s* three *d*. *Educ:* University of Montana (BS); Univ. of California (PhD); American Scandinavian Foundation Fellow to Denmark, 1923-24. Research Chemist, Barrett Chemical Co., 1918-19; Instructor in Chemistry, University of Montana, 1919-21; Associate in Chemistry, Johns Hopkins University, 1924-29; Associate Professor of Chemistry, Columbia University, 1929-34; Professor of Chemistry, 1934-45; Distinguished Service Prof. of Chem., Univ. of Chicago, 1945-52; Martin A. Ryerson Distinguished Service Professor of Chemistry, University of Chicago, Chicago, Illinois, 1952-58; Executive Officer, Department of Chem., Columbia, 1939-42; Dir of War Research Atomic Bomb Project, Columbia, 1940-45. Editor, Jl of Chemical Physics, 1933-40; Board of Directors, Amer.-Scandinavian Foundation; Mem., many scientific and other learned socs; ARAS, 1960. Willard Gibbs Medal, 1934; Nobel Prize in Chemistry, 1934; Davy Medal, Royal Society of London, 1940; Franklin Medal, Franklin Inst., 1943; Medal for Merit, 1946; Cordoza Award, 1954; Honor Scroll, Amer. Inst. Chemists, 1954; Joseph Priestley Award, Dickinson Coll., 1955; Alexander Hamilton Award, Columbia Univ., 1961; J. Lawrence Smith Award, National Academy of Science, 1962; Remsen Memorial Award, Amer. Chem. Soc., Baltimore, 1963;

Univ. Paris Medal, 1964; National Sci. Medal, 1964; Gold Medal, RAS, 1966; Chemical Pioneer Award, Amer. Inst. of Chemists, 1969; Leonard Medal, Meteoritical Soc., 1969; Arthur L. Day Award, Geological Soc. of America, 1969; Linus Pauling Award, Oregon State Univ., 1970; Johann Kepler Medal, AAAS, 1971; Gold Medal Award, Amer. Inst. Chemists, 1972; Priestley Award, ACS, 1973; NASA Exceptional Scientific Achievement Award, 1973; Headliner Award, San Diego Press Club, 1974; V. M. Goldschmidt Medal, Geochem. Soc. of Amer., 1975. Hon. DSc of many universities. *Publications:* Atoms, Molecules and Quanta, with A. E. Ruark, 1930; The Planets, 1952; numerous articles in Chemical journals on the structure of atoms and molecules, discovery of heavy hydrogen and its properties, separation of isotopes, measurement of paleotemperatures, origin of the planets, origin of life. *Address:* c/o University of California, PO Box 109, La Jolla, California 92037, USA.

URGÜPLÜ, Ali Suad Hayri; Turkish diplomat and lawyer; a Senator of the Presidential Contingent, since 1966; Prime Minister of Turkey, Jan.-Oct. 1965; nominated for second time, April 1972, resigned after 15 days; Scheik-ul-Islam of the Ottoman Empire; *b* 13 Aug. 1903; *s* of Mustafa Hayri Urgüplü; *m* 1932, Z. Nigàr Cevdet; one *s*. *Educ:* Galatasaray Grammar Sch., Istanbul; Faculty of Law of Istanbul Univ. Turkish Sec. to Mixed Courts of Arbitration (Treaty of Lausanne), 1926-29. Magistrate, Supreme Commercial Court, Istanbul, 1929-32; Lawyer at Courts of Istanbul and Member Administrative Council, 1932-39. Deputy for Kayseri, Grand Nat. Assembly of Turkey, 1939-46 and from 1950; Minister of Customs and Monopolies, 1943-46; Turkish rep. and Pres. of Turkish Delegn to Cons. Assembly of Council of Europe, Strasbourg and Vice-Pres. of Consultative Assembly, 1950, 1951 and 1952; rep. Turkey at Conf. of Inter-parly Union, Dublin and Istanbul, 1950 and 1951; re-elected Member 9th Legislative Period, 1950, Turkey; Ambassador of Turkey to German Federal Republic, 1952-55; Ambassador of the Turkish Republic to the Court of St James's, 1955-57; Turkish Delegate to: Tripartite Conf. on Eastern Mediterranean and Cyprus, London, 1955, Suez Canal, London, 1956; Turkish Ambassador to the United States, 1957-60, to Spain, 1960; Chm., Foreign Relations Cttee of Senate, 1966-69. Elected as Indep. Senator from Kayseri, then elected from all parties, as Speaker to Senate of the Republic for 2 yrs. Chm., Culture and Art Foundn; Pres., European League for Economic Cooperation, Turkish Section. Gold Medal, Mark Twain Soc.; Grand Cross of Order of Merit with Star and Sash (Fed. Repub. of Germany). *Publications:* articles and studies in various judicial reviews. *Recreation:* reading. *Address:* Sahil Cad, No 19, Yesilyurt, Istanbul, Turkey; (office) Yapi ve Kredi Bankasi, Istanbul, Turkey.

URIE, Wing Comdr John Dunlop; Vice Lord-Lieutenant, Strathclyde Region (Dunbartonshire), since 1976; *b* 12 Oct. 1915; *s* of late John Urie, OBE, Glasgow; *m* 1939, Mary Taylor, *d* of Peter Bonnar, Dunfermline; one *s* two *d*. *Educ:* Sedbergh; Glasgow Univ. Served War of 1939-45: with RAuxAF, in Fighter Command and Middle East Command; Wing Comdr, 1942. DL Co. of Glasgow, 1963. OStJ. *Address:* 55 West Regent Street, Glasgow C2; Ardlarich, Rhu, Dunbartonshire. *Clubs:* Western (Glasgow); Royal Northern Yacht.

URMSON, James Opie, MC 1943; Fellow and Tutor in Philosophy, Corpus Christi College, Oxford, since 1959, and Stuart Professor of Philosophy, Stanford University, since 1975; *b* 4 March 1915; *s* of Rev. J. O. Urmson; *m* 1940, Marion Joyce Drage; one *d*. *Educ:* Kingswood School, Bath; Corpus Christi College, Oxford. Senior Demy, Magdalen College, 1938; Fellow by examination, Magdalen College, 1939-45. Served Army (Duke of Wellington's Regt), 1939-45. Lecturer of Christ Church, 1945-46; Student of Christ Church, 1946-55; Professor of Philosophy, Queen's College, Dundee, University of St Andrews, 1955-59; Visiting Associate Prof., Princeton Univ., 1950-51. Visiting Lectr, Univ. of Michigan, 1961-62, 1965-66, and 1969. *Publications:* Philosophical Analysis, 1956; The Emotive Theory of Ethics, 1968; edited: Encylopedia of Western Philosophy, 1960; J. L. Austin: How to Do Things with Words, 1962; (with G. J. Warnock) J. L. Austin: Philosophical Papers, 2nd edn, 1970; articles in philosophical jls. *Recreations:* gardening, music. *Address:* Standfast, Tumbledown Dick, Cumnor, Oxford. *T:* Cumnor 2769.

URQUHART, Sir Andrew, KCMG 1963 (CMG 1960); MBE 1950; Principal, St Godric's College, since 1975 (Vice-Principal, 1970-75); *b* 6 Jan. 1918; *s* of late Rev. Andrew Urquhart and of J. B. Urquhart; *m* 1956, Jessie Stanley Allison; two *s*. *Educ:* Greenock Academy; Glasgow University. Served War of 1939-45, Royal Marines, 1940-46. Cadet, Colonial Administrative Service, 1946; Senior District Officer, 1954; Admin. Officer,

Class I, 1957; Permanent Sec., 1958; Deputy Governor, Eastern Region, Nigeria, 1958-63; Gen. Manager, The Housing Corp., 1964-70. *Address:* The Old House, Balcombe, Sussex.

URQUHART, Brian Edward, MBE 1945; an Under-Secretary-General, United Nations, since 1974; *b* 28 Feb. 1919; *s* of Murray and Bertha Urquhart; *m* 1st, 1944, Alfreda Huntington (marr. diss. 1963); two *s* one *d*; 2nd, 1963, Sidney Damrosch Howard; one *s* one *d. Educ:* Westminster; Christ Church, Oxford. British Army: Dorset Regt and Airborne Forces, N Africa, Sicily and Europe, 1939-45; Personal Asst to Gladwyn Jebb, Exec. Sec. of Preparatory Commn of UN, London, 1945-46; Personal Asst to Trygve Lie, 1st Sec.-Gen. of UN, 1946-49; Sec., Collective Measures Cttee, 1951-53; Mem., Office of Under-Sec.-Gen. for Special Political Affairs, 1954-71; Asst Sec.-Gen., UN, 1972-74; Exec. Sec., 1st and 2nd UN Conf. on Peaceful Uses of Atomic Energy, 1955 and 1958; active in organization and direction of UN Emergency Force in Middle East, 1956; Dep. Exec. Sec., Preparatory Commn of Internat. Atomic Energy Agency, 1957; Asst to Sec.-Gen.'s Special Rep. in Congo, July-Oct. 1960; UN Rep. in Katanga, Congo, 1961-62; currently involved in organization and direction of UN peacekeeping ops and special political assignments. *Publications:* Hammarskjold, 1972; various articles and reviews on internat. affairs. *Address:* 131 East 66th Street, New York, NY 10021, USA; Howard Farm, Tyringham, Mass 01264. *T:* LE 5-0805. *Club:* Century (New York).

URQUHART, Donald John, CBE 1970; Director General, British Library Lending Services, 1973-74; *b* 27 Nov. 1909; *s* of late Roderick and Rose Catherine Urquhart, Whitley Bay; *m* 1939, Beatrice Winefride, *d* of late W. G. Parker, Sheffield; two *s. Educ:* Barnard Castle School; Sheffield University (BSc, PhD). Research Dept, English Steel Corp., 1934-37; Science Museum Library, 1938-39; Admiralty, 1939-40; Min. of Supply, 1940-45; Science Museum Library, 1945-48; DSIR Headquarters, 1948-61; Dir, Nat. Lending Library for Science and Technology, 1961-73. Hon. Lectr, Postgrad. Sch. of Librarianship and Information Science, Sheffield Univ., 1970-; Vis. Prof., Loughborough Univ. Dept of Library and Information Studies, 1973-. Chm., Standing Conf. of Nat. and Univ. Libraries, 1969-71. FLA (Pres., Library Assoc., 1972). Hon. DSc: Heriot-Watt, 1974; Sheffield, 1974; Salford, 1974. *Publications:* papers on library and scientific information questions. *Recreation:* gardening. *Address:* Wood Garth, First Avenue, Bardsey, near Leeds. *T:* Collingham Bridge 3228. *Club:* Athenæum.

URQUHART, James Graham, FCIT; Executive Member (Operations), British Railways Board, since 1977; *b* 23 April 1925; *s* of James Graham Urquhart and Mary Clark; *m* 1949, Margaret Hutchinson; two *d. Educ:* Berwickshire High Sch. Served War, RAF, 1941-44. Management Trainee, Eastern Region, BR, 1949-52; Chief Controller, Fenchurch Street, 1956-59; Dist Traffic Supt, Perth, 1960-62; Divl Operating Supt, Glasgow, 1962-64; Divl Manager, Glasgow and SW Scotland, 1964-67; Asst Gen. Man., Eastern Reg., 1967-69; BR Bd HQ: Chief Ops Man., 1969-72; Exec. Dir, Personnel, 1972-75; Gen. Manager, London Midland Reg., BR, 1975-76. MIPM, MInstM. *Recreations:* golf, travel, gardening. *Address:* 222 Marylebone Road, NW1 6JJ. *T:* 01-262 3232.

URQUHART, Maj.-Gen. Robert Elliott, CB 1944; DSO 1943; *b* 28 Nov. 1901; *e s* of Alexander Urquhart, MD; *m* 1939, Pamela Condon; one *s* three *d. Educ:* St Paul's, West Kensington; RMC Sandhurst. 2nd Lt HLI 1920; Staff Coll., Camberley, 1936-37; Staff Capt., India, 1938; DAQMG, AHQ, India, 1939-40; DAAG, 3 Div., 1940; AA&QMG, 3 Div., 1940-41; commanded 2nd DCLI, 1941-42; GSO1, 51st Highland Div. N Africa, 1942-43; commanded 231 Malta Brigade, Sicily, 1943, and in landings Italy, 1943 (DSO and Bar); BGS 12 Corps, 1943; GOC 1st Airborne Div., 1944-45 (CB); Col 1945; Maj.-Gen. 1946; Director Territorial Army and Army Cadet Force, War Office, 1945-46; GOC 16th Airborne Division, TA, 1947-48; Commander, Lowland District, 1948-50; Commander Malaya District and 17th Gurkha Division, Mar.-Aug. 1950; GOC Malaya, 1950-52; GOC-in-C British Troops in Austria, 1952-55; retired, Dec. 1955. Col Highland Light Infantry, 1954-58. Dir, Davy and United Engineering Co. Ltd, 1957-70. Netherlands Bronze Lion, 1944; Norwegian Order of St Olaf, 1945. *Publication:* Arnhem, 1958. *Recreation:* golf. *Address:* Bigram, Port of Menteith, Stirling. *T:* Port of Menteith 267. *Club:* Naval and Military.

See also *Sir G. P. Grant-Suttie, Bt, Sir John Kinloch, Bt.*

URQUHART, Sir Robert William, KBE 1950 (OBE 1923); CMG 1944; *b* 14 August 1896; *s* of late Robert Urquhart and Margaret Stewart; *m* 1925, Brenda Gertrude Phillips (*d* 1975);

four *d*; *m* 1977, Jane Gibson. *Educ:* Aberdeen; Cambridge. Entered Levant Consular Service, 1920; Consul at Tabriz, 1934; transferred to Foreign Office, 1938; Inspector-General of Consulates, 1939; seconded to the Home Office, 1940-41; Consul-General, Tabriz, 1942, transferred to New Orleans, La, USA, 1943; reappointed Inspector-General of HM Consular Establishment, 1945; HM Minister at Washington, 1947; HM Consul-General at Shanghai, 1948-50; British Ambassador to Venezuela, 1951-55; retired from Foreign Service, 1955. Chairman of the Crofters' Commission, 1955-63. Hon. LLD Aberdeen, 1954. *Address:* 35 Falcon Gardens, Edinburgh EH10 4AR.

URS, Devaraj Vijayadevaraj; Vice-Chancellor, University of Mysore, India, since 1976; *b* 19 Dec. 1927; *s* of late Devaraj Urs and of Laxammanni Urs; *m* Srimati A. R. Jayalakshammanni. *Educ:* Maharaja's Coll., Univ. of Mysore (BA Hons Social Philosophy). Lectr in Logic, Univ. of Mysore, 1949 (resigned to go abroad for higher studies, 1949); Harvard Univ. and New Sch. for Social Res., USA, 1949-54; Univ. of Mysore: Lectr in Internat. Relations and Polit. Theory, Maharaja's Coll., 1959-65; Sec. to Vice-Chancellor, 1965, full-time Sec., 1969; Sec., Students' Information Bureau, 1965-69; Dep. Dir, Inst. of Correspondence Course and Continuing Educn, Oct. 1969, Dir 1973 (also part-time Sec. to Vice-Chancellor); Registrar, Univ. of Mysore, 1973-76; Actg Vice-Chancellor 1973-75 (three times). Life Mem., Mysore Music Assoc. Editor: Kautilya (biannual of internat. affairs), 1962-74; Report on University Examinations, 1966-74. *Publications:* (ed) University, Society and State, 1973; (ed) Regional Planning and National Development and Strategies for Regional Development, 1977; papers on law and polit. develt. *Address:* Vice-Chancellor, University of Mysore, Crawford Hall, Mysore 570005, S India. *T:* (office) 23555, (home) 20150 or 23658 *Clubs:* Century (Bangalore); Sri Kanteerava Narasimharaja Sports, Films (Mysore).

URSELL, Prof. Fritz Joseph, FRS 1972; Beyer Professor of Applied Mathematics, Manchester University, since 1961; *b* 28 April 1923; *m* 1959, Katharina Renate (*née* Zander); two *d. Educ:* Clifton; Marlborough; Trinity College, Cambridge. BA 1943, MA 1947, ScD 1957, Cambridge. Admiralty Service, 1943-47; ICI Fellow in Applied Mathematics, Manchester Univ., 1947-50. Fellow (Title A), Trinity Coll., Cambridge, 1947-51; Univ. Lecturer in Mathematics, Cambridge, 1950-61; Stringer Fellow in Natural Sciences, King's Coll., Cambridge, 1954-60. FIMA 1964. MSc (Manchester), 1965. *Address:* 28 Old Broadway, Withington, Manchester M20 9DF. *T:* 061-445 5791.

URTON, Sir William (Holmes Lister), Kt 1960; MBE 1943; TD 1952; *b* 30 June 1908; *s* of late Capt. Edgar Lister Urton; *m* 1946, Kirsten Hustad, *d* of late Einar Hustad, Narvos, Norway; two *d. Educ:* Chesterfield Grammar Sch. Conservative Agent: Chesterfield, 1930; Howdenshire, 1935. TA, 1936; HQ 150 Inf. Bde, 1939-41. HQ 50 (Northumbrian) Division, 1941-46. Conservative Central Office Agent: Yorkshire, 1946; London, 1952. Electoral Adviser, WEU Saar Commission, 1955. General Director, Conservative and Unionist Central Office, 1957-66. *Recreations:* walking, gardening. *Address:* Namsos, The Way, Reigate, Surrey RH2 0LD. *T:* Reigate 46343. *Clubs:* Constitutional, Junior Carlton.

URWICK, Alan Bedford; HM Diplomatic Service; Minister, Madrid, since 1977; *b* 2 May 1930; *s* of Col Lyndall Fownes Urwick, *qv; m* 1960, Marta, *o d* of Adhemar Montagne; three *s. Educ:* Dragon Sch.; Rugby (Schol.); New Coll., Oxford (Exhibr). 1st cl. hons Mod. History 1952. Joined HM Foreign (subseq. Diplomatic) Service, 1952; served in: Brussels, 1954-56; Moscow, 1958-59; Baghdad, 1960-61; Amman, 1965-67; Washington, 1967-70; Cairo, 1971-73; seconded to Cabinet Office as Asst Sec., Central Policy Review Staff, 1973-75; Head of Near East and N Africa Dept, FCO, 1975-76. *Address:* The Moat House, Slaugham, Sussex. *T:* Handcross 400458. *Club:* Garrick.

URWICK, Lyndall Fownes, OBE, MC; MA; Hon. DSc; CIMechE, MASME, MIPE, FBIM, FRSA; Hon. Associate Manchester College of Technology and College of Technology, Birmingham; President Urwick, Orr & Partners Ltd, since 1963; *b* 3 March 1891; *o c* of late Sir Henry Urwick; *m* 1923, Joan Wilhelmina Bedford; one *s* one *d*; *m* 1941, Betty, *o d* of late Major H. M. Warrand; one *s* one *d. Educ:* Boxgrove School, Guildford; Repton School; New College, Oxford (Hist. Exhibitioner). Duke of Devonshire Prize, 1910; BA 1913; MA 1919. War Service, 1914-18 (despatches thrice); Employers' Sec., Joint Industrial Council of Glove-making Industry, 1919-20; employed by Rowntree & Co. Ltd, York, 1922-28; Hon. Sec., Management Research Groups, 1926-28; Dir Internat.

Management Inst., Geneva, 1928-33; Gen. Sec., Internat. Cttee of Scientific Management, 1932-35; Consultant to HM Treasury, 1940-42; Mem., Mitcheson Cttee on Min. of Pensions, 1940-41; Lt-Col Petroleum Warfare Dept, 1942-44. Chm., Cttee on Educn for Management, 1946; Vice-Chm. Coun., BIM, 1947-52; Chm., Anglo-Amer. Productivity Team on Educn for Management in USA, 1951; Dir, American Management Assoc. Study of Management Education, 1952-53; Pres., Institutional Management Assoc., 1956-59; Colombo Plan Adviser to Indian Govt, 1956; Pres., European Fedn of Management Consultants' Assocs., 1960-61; Hon. Vis. Prof., Univ. of York, Toronto, 1967. Life Member: American Management Assoc., 1957; American Soc. Mechanical Engineers, 1952. Past Master, Company of Glovers. Hon. DSc Aston Univ., 1969; Hon. LLD York Univ., Toronto, 1972. Kt, 1st Cl. Order of St Olaf (Norway); Silver Medal, RSA, 1948; Gold Medal, Internat. Cttee for Scientific Management, 1951; Wallace Clark Internat. Management Award, 1955; Henry Laurence Gantt Gold Medal, 1961; Taylor Key, 1963; Bowie Medal, 1968. *Publications:* Factory Organisation, 1928; Organising a Sales Office, 1928, 2nd edn 1937; The Meaning of Rationalisation, 1929; Problems of Distribution in Europe and the United States, 1931; Management of To-Morrow, 1933; Committees in Organisation, 1937; Papers on the Science of Administration, 1937; The Development of Scientific Management in Great Britain, 1938; Dynamic Administration, 1941; The Elements of Administration, 1943; The Making of Scientific Management, vol. i, Thirteen Pioneers, 1945, vol. ii, British Industry, 1946, vol. iii, The Hawthorne Experiments, 1948; Freedom and Coordination, 1949; Management Education in American Business, 1955; The Pattern of Management, 1956; Leadership in the XXth Century, 1957; Organisation, 1964; articles on rationalisation, and scientific management. *Address:* Poyntington, 83 Kenneth Street, Longueville, NSW 2066, Australia. *T:* Sydney 42102; Urwick House, 50 Doughty Street, WC1N 2LS. *Clubs:* Savile, Reform.
See also A. B. Urwick.

URWIN, Harry, (Charles Henry); Member, TUC General Council, since 1969; Deputy General-Secretary, Transport and General Workers Union, since 1969; Member: National Enterprise Board, since 1975; Manpower Services Commission, since 1973; Chairman, TUC Employment Policy and Organisation Committee; *b* 24 Feb. 1915; *s* of Thomas and Lydia Urwin; *m* 1941, Hilda Pinfold; one *d. Educ:* Durham County Council Sch. Convenor, Machine Tool Industry, until 1947; Coventry Dist Officer, TGWU, 1947-59; Coventry Dist Sec., Confedn of Shipbuilding and Engineering Unions, 1954-59; Regional Officer, TGWU, 1959-69; Member: Industrial Develt Adv. Bd, Industry Act, 1972; Sir Don Ryder Inquiry, British Leyland Motor Corp., 1974-75; Central Arbitration Cttee; Energy Commn, 1977-. *Recreation:* swimming. *Address:* 4 Leacliffe Way, Aldridge, Walsall WS9 0PW; Transport House, Smith Square, SW1.

URWIN, Thomas William; MP (Lab) Houghton-le-Spring since 1964; *b* 9 June 1912; *s* of a miner; *m* 1934, Edith Scott, *d* of a miner; three *s* one *d. Educ:* Brandon Colliery and Easington Lane Elementary Schools and NCLC. Bricklayer, 1926-54; full-time Organiser, Amalgamated Union of Building Trade Workers, 1954-64. Minister of State, DEA, 1968-69; Minister of State, with responsibilities for regional policy, and special responsibility for the Northern Region, Oct. 1969-June 1970. Leader, British Parly delegn to Council of Europe and WEU, 1976-; Chm., Socialist Group, Council of Europe, 1976-. Member Houghton-le-Spring Urban District Council, 1949-65, Chm. 1954-55, Chm. Planning and Housing, 1950-65. *Recreations:* football (local soccer), cricket. *Address:* 28 Stanhope Close, Houghton-le-Spring, Tyne and Wear. *T:* Houghton-le-Spring 3139.

USBORNE, Henry Charles, MA; JP; President, Nu-Way Heating Plants Ltd, Droitwich; Chairman, UA Engineering Ltd, Sheffield; *b* 16 Jan. 1909; *s* of Charles Frederick Usborne and Janet Lefroy; *m* 1936; two *s* two *d. Educ:* Bradfield; Corpus Christi, Cambridge. MP (Lab) Yardley Div. of Birmingham, 1950-59 (Acock's Green Div. of Birmingham, 1945-50). JP Worcs, 1964. *Address:* Totterdown, The Parks, Evesham, Worcs.
See also R. A. Usborne.

USBORNE, Richard Alexander; Custodian, National Trust, since 1974; *b* 16 May 1910; *s* of Charles Frederick Usborne, ICS, and Janet Muriel (*née* Lefroy); *m* 1938, Monica, *d* of Archibald Stuart MacArthur, Wagon Mound, New Mexico, USA; one *s* one *d. Educ:* Summer Fields Preparatory Sch.; Charterhouse; Balliol Coll., Oxford. BA Mods and Greats. Served War, 1941-45: Army, SOE and PWE, Middle East, Major, Gen. List.

Advertising agencies, 1933-36; part-owner and Editor of What's On, 1936-37; London Press Exchange, 1937-39; BBC Monitoring Service, 1939-41; Asst Editor, Strand Magazine, 1946-50; Dir, Graham & Gillies Ltd, Advertising, retd, 1970. *Publications:* Clubland Heroes, 1953 (rev. 1975); (ed) A Century of Summer Fields, 1964; Wodehouse at Work, 1961, rev. edn, as Wodehouse at Work to the End, 1977; (ed) Sunset at Blandings, 1977. *Recreations:* reading, writing verse. *Address:* Fenton House, Windmill Hill, NW3 6RT. *T:* 01-435 3471.
See also H . C . Usborne .

USHER, Col Charles Milne, DSO 1940; OBE 1919; MA (Edinburgh); Director of Physical Education, Edinburgh University, 1946-59; *b* 6 September 1891; *s* of Robert Usher, Edinburgh; *m* 1919, Madge Elsa, *d* of F. Carbut Bell, London; two *s. Educ:* Merchiston Castle School, Edinburgh; RMC Sandhurst. Joined Gordon Highlanders, 1911; Lt-Col 1938; actg Brig. 1940; served European War, 1914-18 (OBE, Mons Star, 2 Medals); War of 1939-45 (despatches, DSO, Chevalier Legion of Honour, Croix de Guerre with Palm); Citoyen d'honneur of the town of Caen (Calvados). Captained Mother Country, Scotland, Army, and London Scottish at Rugby Football, also Captained Scotland versus USA at Fencing (Sabre and Epée), and British Empire Games, New Zealand, 1950. Hon. Pres., Scottish Amateur Fencing Union, Scottish Univs Rugby Club; Vice Patron, Army Rugby Union; Hon. Pres., Piobaireachd Soc. Grand Prix du Dirigeant Sportif, 1958. *Publications:* The Usher Family in Scotland, 1956; The Story of Edinburgh University Athletic Club, 1966. *Recreations:* hunting and shooting. *Address:* The White House, North Berwick, East Lothian. *T:* 2694. *Clubs:* Caledonian; New (Edinburgh).

USHER, Sir Peter Lionel, 5th Bt *cr* 1899, of Norton, Midlothian, and of Wells, Co. Roxburgh; *b* 31 Oct. 1931; *er s* of Sir (Robert) Stuart Usher, 4th Bt, and Gertrude Martha, 2nd *d* of Lionel Barnard Sampson, Tresmontes, Villa Valeria, Prov. Cordoba, Argentina; *S* father, 1962. *Educ:* privately. *Heir:* b Robert Edward Usher, *b* 18 April 1934. *Address:* (Seat) Hallrule, Hawick, Roxburghshire. *T:* Bonchester Bridge 216.

USHER, Brig. Thomas Clive, CBE 1945; DSO and Bar 1943; RA, retired 1958; now farming; *b* 21 June 1907; *s* of Sir Robert Usher, 2nd Bt, of Norton and Wells; *m* 1939, Valentine Sears Stockwell; one *d. Educ:* Uppingham; RMA. Served War of 1939-45: North Africa, Sicily and Italy (DSO and Bar, CBE); Temp. Brig. 1944. Lt-Col 1950; Col 1951; Temp. Brig. 1953; ADC, 1957-58. Formerly Military Adviser to UK High Comr in India; OC 18 Trg Bde, RA, 1955-57; Brig. RA, Scottish Comd, 1958. *Recreations:* riding, sailing, fishing, shooting. *Address:* Wells Stables, Hawick, Roxburghshire. *T:* Denholm 235.

USHER-WILSON, Rt. Rev. Lucian Charles, CBE 1961; MA; Honorary Assistant Bishop of Bristol, since 1972; Hon. Canon of Guildford Cathedral, 1965; *b* 10 Jan. 1903; *s* of Rev. C. Usher-Wilson; *m* 1929, Muriel Constance Wood; one *s* three *d. Educ:* Christ's Hospital; Lincoln College, Oxford; St Augustine's College, Canterbury. Asst Master, King William's College, Isle of Man; Asst Master, King's College, Budo, Kampala, Uganda; CMS Missionary at Jinja, Busoga, Uganda; Rural Dean, Busoga District, Uganda; Bishop on Upper Nile, 1936-61, Bishop of Mbale, 1961-64 (name of Dio. changed, 1961); an Asst Bishop of Guildford and Vicar of Churt, 1964-72. *Recreation:* gardening. *Address:* 58 The Dell, Westbury-on-Trym, Bristol BS9 3UG. *Clubs:* Old Blues, Royal Commonwealth Society.

USHERWOOD, Kenneth Ascough, CBE 1964; Director, Prudential Assurance Co. Ltd (General Manager, 1961-67, Deputy Chairman, 1969-70, Chairman, 1970-75); *b* 19 Aug. 1904; *s* of late H. T. Usherwood and late Lettie Ascough; *m* 1st, 1933, Molly Tidbeck (marr. diss. 1945), Johannesburg; one *d* ; 2nd, 1946, Mary, *d* of T. L. Reepmaker d'Orville; one *s. Educ:* City of London School; St John's College, Cambridge (MA). Prudential Assurance Co. Ltd, 1925-: South Africa, 1932-34; Near East, 1934-37; Deputy General Manager, 1947-60. Director of Statistics, Ministry of Supply, 1941-45. Chm., Industrial Life Offices Assoc., 1966-67. Institute of Actuaries: Fellow (FIA) 1925; Pres. 1962-64. Mem. Gaming Board, 1968-72; Treasurer, Field Studies Council, 1969-77. *Address:* 24 Litchfield Way, NW11. *T:* 01-455 7915; Laurel Cottage, Walberswick, Suffolk. *T:* Southwold 723265. *Club:* Oriental.

USTINOV, Peter Alexander, CBE 1975; FRSA; actor, dramatist, film director; Rector of the University of Dundee, 1968-74; Goodwill Ambassador for UNICEF, 1969; *b* London, 16 April 1921; *s* of late Iona Ustinov and Nadia Benois, painter; *m* 1st, 1940, Isolde Denham (marr. diss. 1950); one *d* ; 2nd, 1954, Suzanne Cloutier (marr. diss. 1971); one *s* two *d* ; 3rd, 1972, Hélène du Lau d'Allemans. *Educ:* Westminster School. Served in Army, Royal Sussex Regt and RAOC, 1942-46. Author of plays: House of Regrets, 1940 (prod Arts Theatre 1942); Blow Your Own Trumpet, 1941 (prod Playhouse [Old Vic] 1943); Beyond, 1942 (prod Arts Theatre, 1943); The Banbury Nose, 1943 (prod Wyndham's 1944); The Tragedy of Good Intentions, 1944 (prod Old Vic, Liverpool, 1945); The Indifferent Shepherd (prod Criterion, 1948); Frenzy (adapted from Swedish of Ingmar Bergman, (prod and acted in St Martin's, 1948); The Man in the Raincoat (Edinburgh Festival, 1949); The Love of Four Colonels (and acted in, Wyndham's, 1951); The Moment of Truth (Adelphi, 1951); High Balcony, 1952 (written 1946); No Sign of the Dove (Savoy, 1953); The Empty Chair (Bristol Old Vic, 1956); Romanoff and Juliet (Piccadilly, 1956, film, 1961; musical, R loves J, Chichester, 1973); Photo Finish (prod and acted in it, Saville, 1962); The Life in My Hands, 1963; The Unknown Soldier and his Wife, 1967 (prod and acted in it, Chichester, 1968, New London, 1973); Halfway up the Tree (Queen's), 1967. Co-Author of film: The Way Ahead, 1943-44. Author and Director of films: School for Secrets, 1946; Vice-Versa, 1947. Author, director, producer and main actor in film Private Angelo, 1949; acted in films: Odette, Quo Vadis, Hotel Sahara, 1950; Beau Brummell, The Egyptian, We're No Angels, 1954; An Angel Flew Over Brooklyn, 1957; Spartacus, 1960; The Sundowners, 1961; Topkapi, 1964; John Goldfarb, Please Come Home; Blackbeard's Ghost; The Comedians, 1968; Hot Millions, 1968; Viva Max, 1969; Treasure of Matecumbe, 1977; Un Taxi Mauve, 1977; director, producer and actor in film Billy Budd, 1961; director and actor in film Hammersmith is Out, 1971. Produced operas at Covent Garden, 1962, and Hamburg Opera, 1968. Acted in: revues: Swinging the Gate, 1940, Diversion, 1941; plays: Crime and Punishment, New Theatre, 1946; Love in Albania, St James's, 1949; directed Lady L, 1965; TV Series, The Mighty Continent, 1974. Member, British Film Academy. Mem., British USA Bicentennial Liaison Cttee, 1973-. Benjamin Franklin Medal, Royal Society of Arts, 1957; Order of the Smile (for dedication to idea of internat. assistance to children), Warsaw, 1974. *Publications:* House of Regrets, 1943; Beyond, 1944; The Banbury Nose, 1945; Plays About People, 1950; The Love of Four Colonels, 1951; The Moment of Truth, 1953; Romanoff and Juliet (Stage and Film); Add a Dash of Pity (short stories), 1959; Ustinov's Diplomats (a book of photographs), 1960; The Loser (novel), 1961; The Frontiers of the Sea, 1966; Krumnagel, 1971; Dear Me (autobiog.), 1977; contributor short stories to Atlantic Monthly. *Recreations:* lawn tennis, squash, collecting old masters' drawings, music. *Address:* c/o Christopher Mann Ltd, 140 Park Lane, W1. *Clubs:* Garrick, Savage, Royal Automobile, Arts Theatre, Queen's.

UTIGER, Ronald Ernest, CBE 1977; Managing Director, The British Aluminium Co. Ltd, since 1968; Director, British National Oil Corporation, since 1976; *b* 5 May 1926; *s* of Ernest Frederick Utiger and Kathleen Utiger (*née* Cram); *m* 1953, Barbara Anna von Mohl; one *s* one *d* . *Educ:* Worcester Coll., Oxford (2nd cl. Hons PPE 1950; MA). Economist, Courtaulds Ltd, 1950-61; British Aluminium Ltd: Financial Controller, 1961-64; Commercial Dir, 1965-68. Chm., Internat. Primary Aluminium Inst.; Pres. European Primary Aluminium Assoc., 1976-77. FRSA; FBIM 1975. *Recreations:* music, gardening. *Address:* 9 Ailsa Road, St Margaret's-on-Thames, Twickenham, Mddx. *T:* 01-892 5810.

UTLEY, Clifton Maxwell; commentator, television and radio newspaper columnist, USA; *b* 31 May 1904; *m* 1931, Frayn Garrick; three *s*. *Educ:* Univs of Chicago, Munich, and Algiers. Director, Chicago Council on Foreign Relations, 1931-59; commentator, NBC, USA, 1941-59; American commentator, British Broadcasting Corporation, 1945-53. Dupont award for TV and radio commentaries, 1957. Hon. DHL, Illinois Coll., 1946; Hon. LLD, Lawrence Coll., 1945. *Address:* SR Box 110, Hana, Hawaii 96713, USA. *Clubs:* Quadrangle, Commonwealth, Wayfarers' (Chicago).

UTLEY, Thomas Edwin; Leader writer, The Daily Telegraph, since 1964; *b* 1 Feb. 1921; adopted *s* of late Miss Anne Utley; *m* 1951, Brigid Viola Mary, *yr d* of late D. M. M. Morrah, and of Ruth Morrah, *qv* ; two *s* two *d* . *Educ:* privately; Corpus Christi Coll., Cambridge (1st cl. Hons Hist. Tripos; Foundn Schol.; MA). Sec., Anglo-French Relations post-War Reconstruction Gp, FIIA, 1942-44; temp. Foreign Leader writer, The Times, 1944-45; Leader writer, Sunday Times, 1945-47; Editorial staff, The Observer, 1947-48; Leader writer, The Times, 1948-54; Associate Editor, Spectator, 1954-55; freelance journalist and broadcasting, 1955-64. A Governor, House of Citizenship, Hartwell House, Aylesbury, 1957-76. Contested (U) North Antrim, Feb. 1974. Chm., Paddington Cons. Assoc., 1977. *Publications:* Essays in Conservatism, 1949; Modern Political Thought, 1952; The Conservatives and the Critics, 1956; (ed jtly) Documents of Modern Political Thought, 1957; Not Guilty,

1957; Edmund Burke, 1957; Occasion for Ombudsmen, 1963; Your Money and Your Life, 1964; Enoch Powell: the man and his thinking, 1968; What Laws May Cure, 1968; Lessons of Ulster, 1975. *Address:* 60 St Mary's Mansions, St Mary's Terrace, W2. *T:* 01-723 1149.

UTTING, William Benjamin; Chief Social Work Officer, Department of Health and Social Security, since 1976; *b* 13 May 1931; *s* of John William Utting and Florence Ada Utting; *m* 1954, Mildred Jackson; two *s* one *d* . *Educ:* Great Yarmouth Grammar Sch.; New Coll., Oxford; Barnett House, Oxford. MA Oxon. Probation Officer: Co. Durham, 1956-58; Norfolk, 1958-61; Sen. Probation Officer, Co. Durham, 1961-64; Principal Probation Officer, Newcastle upon Tyne, 1964-68; Lectr in Social Studies, Univ. of Newcastle upon Tyne, 1968-70; Dir of Social Services, Kensington and Chelsea, 1970-76. *Publications:* contribs to professional jls. *Recreations:* literature, music, art, idleness. *Address:* 76 Great Brownings, College Road, SE21 7HR. *T:* 01-670 1201.

UTTLEY, Prof. Albert Maurel, PhD; Research Professor of Experimental Psychology, University of Sussex, 1966-73, now Emeritus; *b* 14 Aug. 1906; *s* of George Uttley and Ethel Uttley (*née* Player), London; *m* 1941, Gwendoline Lucy Richens; two *d. Educ:* King's College, London University. BSc Mathematics; PhD Psychology. Dep. Chief Scientific Officer (Individual Merit Post), Royal Radar Establishment, 1940-56; Superintendent of Autonomics Div., NPL, 1956-66. Fellow, Center for Advanced Studies in Behavioral Sciences, Univ. of Stanford, Calif, 1962-63. Pres., Biological Engineering Soc., 1964-66. Kelvin Premium, IEE, 1948; Simms Gold Medal, RAeS, 1950. *Publications:* papers in various scientific journals on theory of control and of computers and on theoretical neurophysiology of brain function. *Recreations:* formerly mountaineering, now painting, travel. *Address:* Dunnocks, Lewes Road, Ditchling, Sussex.

UVAROV, Olga, DSc, FRCVS; Adviser on Technical Information, British Veterinary Association, since 1976; President, Royal College of Veterinary Surgeons, 1976-77; *d* of Nikolas and Elena Uvarov. *Educ:* Royal Vet. Coll (Bronze Medals for Physiol. and Histol.). MRCVS 1934; FRCVS 1973. Asst in gen. mixed practice, 1934-43; own small animal practice, 1944-53; licence to practice and work at greyhound stadium, 1945-68; clinical res., Pharmaceutical industry, 1953-70; Head of Vet. Adv. Dept, Glaxo Laboratories, 1967-70; BVA Technical Inf. Service, 1970-76; Mem. MAFF Cttees under Medicines Act (1968), 1971-. RCVS: Mem. Council, 1968-; Chm. Parly Cttee, 1971-74; Jun. Vice-Pres., 1975; President: Soc. Women Vet. Surgeons, 1947-49 (Sec., 1946); Central Vet. Soc., 1951-52; Assoc. Vet. Teachers and Res. Workers, 1967-68 (Pres. S Reg., 1967-68); Section of Comparative Medicine, RSocMed, 1967-68 (Sec., 1965-67; Sec. for Internat. Affairs, 1971-); Member Council: BVA, 1944-67; RSocMed, 1968-70; Res. Defence Soc., 1968-; Member: Vet. Res. Club, 1967-; British Small Animal Vet. Assoc.; British Codex Sub-Cttee, Pharmaceutical Soc., 1970-71; Senior Vice-Pres., RCVS, 1977-. Hon. DSc Guelph, 1976. Victory Gold Medal, Central Vet. Soc., 1965. *Publications:* contribs to: The Veterinary Annual; International Encyclopaedia of Veterinary Medicine, 1966; also papers in many learned jls. *Recreations:* work, travel, literature, flowers, the arts. *Address:* 39 Rodney Gardens, Eastcote, Pinner, Mddx HA5 2RT. *T:* 01-866 3359. *Club:* Royal Society of Medicine.

UXBRIDGE, Earl of; Charles Alexander Vaughan Paget; *b* 13 Nov 1950; *s* and *heir* of 7th Marquess of Anglesey, *qv. Educ:* Dragon School, Oxford; Eton; Exeter Coll., Oxford. *Address:* Plâs-Newydd, Llanfairpwll, Gwynedd.

V

VACHON, Most Rev. Louis-Albert, CC (Canada) 1969; FRSC 1974; Officier de l'Ordre de la fidélité française, 1963; Auxiliary Bishop of Quebec, since 1977; *b* 4 Feb. 1912; *s* of Napoléon Vachon and Alexandrine Gilbert. *Educ:* Laval Univ. (PhD Philosophy, 1947); PhD Theology, Angelicum, Rome, 1949. Superior, Grand Séminaire de Québec, 1955-59; Superior General, 1960-77; Vice-Rector of Laval Univ , 1959-60, Rector, 1960-72. Hon. doctorates: Montreal, McGill and Victoria, 1964; Guelph, 1966; Moncton, 1967; Queen's, Bishop's and Strasbourg, 1968; Notre-Dame (Indiana), 1971; Carleton, 1971. Mem., Royal Canadian Soc. of Arts. Hon. Fellow, Royal Coll. Physicians and Surgeons of Canada, 1972. *Publications:*

Espérance et Présomption, 1958; Vérité et Liberté, 1962; Unité de l'Université, 1962; Apostolat de l'universitaire catholique, 1963; Mémorial, 1963; Communauté universitaire, 1963; Progrès de l'université et consentement populaire, 1964; Responsabilité collective des universitaires, 1964; Les humanités aujourd'hui, 1966; Excellence et loyauté des universitaires, 1969. *Address:* 2 Port-Dauphin, PO Box 459, Quebec G1R 4R6. *T:* 692-3935. *Club:* Cercle Universitaire.

VAEA, Baron of Houma; Minister for Labour, Commerce and Industries, Tonga, since 1973; *b* 15 May 1921; *s* of Viliami Vilai Tupou and Tupou Seini Vaea; *m* 1952, Tuputupu Ma'afu; three *s* three *d*. *Educ:* Wesley College, Auckland, NZ. RNZAF, 1942-45; Tonga Civil Service, 1945-53; ADC to HM Queen Salote, 1954-59; Governor of Haapai, 1959-68; Commissioner and Consul in UK, 1969; High Comr in UK, 1970-72. Given the title Baron Vaea of Houma by HM The King of Tonga, 1970. *Recreations:* Rugby, cricket, fishing. *Heir: e s* Albert Tuivanuavou Vaea, *b* 19 Sept. 1957. *Address:* PO Box 110, Nuku'alofa, Tonga.

VAES, Robert, Hon. KCMG 1966; LLD; Grand Officer, Order of Leopold II; Grand Officer, Order of the Crown, Belgium; Belgian Ambassador to the Court of St James's, since 1976; *b* Antwerp, 9 Jan. 1919; *m* 1947, Anne Albers; one *d*. *Educ:* Brussels Univ. (LLD; special degree in Commercial and Maritime Law). Joined Diplomatic Service, 1946: postings to Washington, Paris, Hong Kong, London and Rome; Personal Private Sec. to Minister of Foreign Trade, 1958-60; Dir-Gen. of Polit. Affairs, 1964-66; Permanent Under-Sec., Min. of For. Affairs, For. Trade and Develt Cooperation, 1966-72; Ambassador to Spain, 1972-76. Formerly, Chairman: Council, Benelux Union; Belgian-Luxemburg Admin. Commn. Foreign decorations from The Netherlands, Italy, Norway, Niger, Luxemburg, Tunisia, Cameroon, Denmark, Austria, Senegal, France, Japan, Peru, and Spain. *Recreations:* tennis, golf, bridge. *Address:* 36 Belgrave Square, SW1X 8QB. *T:* 01-235 1752. *Clubs:* Travellers', White's, Royal Automobile, Anglo-Belgian, Hurlingham; Swinley Forest (Berks); Royal Yacht of Belgium.

VAGHJEE, Sir Harilal Ranchhordas, Kt 1970; Speaker, Legislative Assembly, Mauritius, since 1960; *b* 10 Jan. 1912, Mauritius; *s* of Ranchhordas Vaghjee. *Educ:* Port Louis High Sch., Mauritius. Called to Bar, Middle Temple, 1937. MLC, Mauritius, 1948-59; Vice-Pres., Legislative Council, 1951-57; Minister of Educn and Cultural Affairs, 1957-59. *Address:* Government House, Port Louis, Mauritius.

VAIZEY, family name of Baron Vaizey.

VAIZEY, Baron *cr* 1976 (Life Peer), of Greenwich; **John Ernest Vaizey;** Professor of Economics, since 1966 and Head of School of Social Sciences, since 1973, Brunel University; *b* 1 Oct. 1929; *s* of late Ernest and Lucy Butler Vaizey; *m* 1961, Marina (*see* Lady Vaizey); two *s* one *d*. *Educ:* Queen Mary's Hosp. Sch.; Queens' Coll., Cambridge (Schol.). MA Cantab, MA Oxon, DSc Brunel, DLitt Adelaide. Econs Tripos, Cambridge, 1951; Gladstone Prizeman, 1954. UN, Geneva, 1952-53; Fellow of St Catharine's Coll., Cambridge, 1953-56; Univ. Lectr, Oxford, 1956-60; Dir, Research Unit, Univ. of London, 1960-62; Fellow and Tutor, Worcester Coll., Oxford, 1962-66. Director, Bumpus Ltd, 1962-67. Prof., Univ. of California, 1965-66; Eleanor Rathbone Lectr, Univs of Liverpool and Durham, 1966; O'Brien Lectr, UCD, 1968; Centenary Prof., Univ. of Adelaide, 1974-75; Hoover Prof., Univ. of NSW, 1977. Member: Nat. Adv. Council on Trng and Supply of Teachers, 1962-66; UNESCO Nat. Commn, 1965-72; Exec., Fabian Soc., 1959-66; Public Schools Commn, 1966-68; Nat. Council on Educn Technology, 1967-73; Inner London Educn Authority, 1970-72; Commn on Educn, Spain, 1968-72; Adv. Council, Radio London, 1970-73; Governing Body, Internat. Inst. for Educnl Planning, 1971-; Adv. Cttee, Gulbenkian Foundn, 1971-77; Chairman: Cttee on Trng for the Drama, 1974-75; Cttee on Dance, 1974-; Cttee on Music Training, 1975-77; British-Irish Assoc., 1976-; Vice-Pres., Greater London Arts Assoc., 1974-; Pres., Blackheath Soc., 1975-. Trustee: Acton Soc. Trust, 1968- (Dir 1960-68); St Catharine's, Cumberland Lodge, 1972-. Governor, Ditchley Foundn, 1973-. Consultant, UN, etc. *Publications:* The Costs of Education, 1958; Scenes from Institutional Life, 1959; (with P. Lynch) Guinness's Brewery in the Irish Economy, 1961; The Economics of Education, 1962; Education for Tomorrow, 1962, 5th edn 1970; The Control of Education, 1963; (ed) The Residual Factor and Economic Growth, 1965; (ed with E. A. G. Robinson) The Economics of Education, 1965; Barometer Man, 1967; Education in the Modern World, 1967, 2nd edn, 1975; (with John Sheehan) Resources for Education, 1968; The Sleepless Lunch, 1968; (with colleagues) The Economics of Educational Costing, 4 vols, 1969-71; The Type to Succeed,

1970; Capitalism, 1971; Social Democracy, 1971; The Political Economy of Education, 1972; (with Keith Norris) The Economics of Research and Technology, 1973; History of British Steel, 1974; (ed) Economic Sovereignty and Regional Policy; (ed) Whatever Happened to Equality, 1975; (with C. F. O. Clarke) Education: the state of the debate, 1976; (with Keith Norris) Teach Yourself Economics, 1977. *Recreations:* arts, travel. *Address:* 24 Heathfield Terrace, W4 4JE. *T:* 01-994 7994. *Clubs:* Garrick; Kildare Street and University (Dublin).

VAIZEY, Lady; Marina Vaizey; Art Critic of the Sunday Times, since 1974; *b* 16 Jan. 1938; *o d* of Lyman Stansky and late Ruth Stansky; *m* 1961, Baron Vaizey, *qv*; two *s* one *d*. *Educ:* Brearley Sch., New York; Putney Sch., Putney, Vermont; Radcliffe Coll., Harvard Univ. (BA Medieval History and Lit.); Girton Coll., Cambridge (BA, MA). Art Critic, Financial Times, 1970-74; Mem. Arts Council, 1976- (Mem. Art Panel, 1973-, now Dep. Chm.); Member: Advisory Cttee, DoE, 1975-; Paintings for Hospitals, 1974-; Cttee, Contemporary Art Soc., 1974-; Governor, Camberwell Coll. of Arts and Crafts, 1971-. Broadcaster, occasional exhibition organiser and lecturer; organised Critic's Choice, Tooth's, 1974. Co-Sec., Radcliffe Club of London, 1968-74. *Publications:* articles in various periodicals, exhibition catalogues. *Recreation:* reading thrillers. *Address:* 24 Heathfield Terrace, W4 4JE. *T:* 01-994 7994.

VAJPAYEE, Atal Behari; Minister of External Affairs, India, since 1977; *b* 25 Dec. 1926. *Educ:* Victoria Coll., Gwalior; D.A.V. Coll., Kanpur (MA). Member, Rashtriya Swayamsewak Sangh, 1941; Sec. to Dr Shayama Prasad Mukherjee, 1952-53; Member: Lok Sabha, 1957-62, 1967-; Rajya Sabha, 1962; Founder Mem., Bharatipa Jana Sangh; Pres., 1968-74; Chm., Public Accounts Cttee, 1969-70; Nationalist (chiefly Hindu) Parliamentary Leader (in Opposition, 1976-77). *Publications:* Amar Balidan; Mrityuya Hatya; Jana Sangh our Musalman. *Address:* 1 Ferozeshah Road, New Delhi 1, India. *T:* 387-446.

VALANTINE, Louis Francis, CBE 1964 (MBE 1956); JP; High Commissioner for The Gambia in London, 1965-68; *b* 7 July 1907; *s* of late René Charles Valantine, JP, Banjul; *m* 1940, Priscilla Ellen, *d* of late Sir John Mahoney, OBE, JP, Banjul; three *s* two *d*. *Educ:* Hagan St Sch.; Boys' High Sch., Banjul; Fourah Bay Coll., Sierra Leone. BA (Durham), 1930. Joined The Gambia Civil Service, 1933; Administrative Officer, 1949-59; Asst Postmaster General, 1959-60; Postmaster General, 1960-62; Chm. of Public Service Commn, 1962-64; Gambia Comr in London, 1964. JP Banjul, 1960. *Recreations:* reading, walking. *Address:* 9 Picton Street, Banjul, The Gambia.

VALDAR, Colin Gordon; Consultant Editor and Chairman, Bouverie Publishing Co. Ltd, since 1964; *b* 18 Dec. 1918; 3rd *s* of Lionel and Mary Valdar; *m* 1st, 1940, Evelyn Margaret Barriff (marr. diss.); two *s*; 2nd, Jill, (*née* Davis). *Educ:* Haberdashers' Aske's Hampstead School. Free-lance journalist, 1936-39. Served War of 1939-45, Royal Engineers, 1939-42. Successively Production Editor, Features Editor, Asst Editor Sunday Pictorial, 1942-46; Features Editor, Daily Express, 1946-51; Asst Editor, Daily Express, 1951-53; Editor, Sunday Pictorial, 1953-59; Editor, Daily Sketch, 1959-62. Director, Sunday Pictorial Newspapers Ltd, 1957-59; Director, Daily Sketch and Daily Graphic Ltd, 1959-62. *Address:* 94 Clifford's Inn, Fleet Street, EC4. *T:* 01-242 0935.

VALENTIA, 14th Viscount (Ireland) *cr* 1621 (Dormant 1844-1959); **Francis Dighton Annesley,** Baron Mountnorris (Ireland) 1628; Bt 1620; MC 1918; MRCS, LRCP; Brigadier retired, late RAMC; *b* 12 Aug. 1888; *o s* of late George Dighton Annesley (uncle of *de jure* 13th Viscount); *S* cousin, 1951, established his succession, 1959; *m* 1925, Joan Elizabeth, 2nd *d* of late John Joseph Curtis; one *s* three *d*. *Educ:* St Lawrence Coll.; Guy's Hospital. Lieut, RAMC, 1914; served European War, France, Belgium, Aug. 1914-March 1919; Afghanistan, 1919; Waziristan, 1922-23; War of 1939-45, India, Iraq, Persia, Egypt, France, Germany, Lt-Col 1936; Col 1941; Brig. 1942; retd 1948. Croix de Guerre (Belge), 1918. *Heir: s* Hon. Richard John Dighton Annesley, Captain, RA, retd [*b* 15 Aug. 1929; *m* 1957, Anita Phyllis, *o d* of W. A. Joy; three *s* one *d*]. *Address:* St Michael's, Lea, Malmesbury, Wilts. *T:* Malmesbury 2312.

VALENTINE, Sir Alec, (Alexander Balmain Bruce), Kt 1964; MA; OStJ; *b* 22 Dec. 1899; *o s* of late Mr and Mrs Milward Valentine (and *g s* of late Prof. A. B. Bruce, DD, of Glasgow); *m* 1936, Beryl, *o c* of late Eng. Capt. F. Barter, RN, and Mrs Barter; one *s* two *d*. *Educ:* Highgate School; Worcester Coll., Oxford (Scholar, 1918). Dep. Editor, British Commercial Gas Assoc., 1922-27; entered service of Underground Group of Companies, 1928; transferred to London Passenger Transport

Board, 1933; Personal Asst to late Frank Pick, 1928-36; Chief Supplies Officer, 1943-47; Chief Commercial Officer, 1945-47; Operating Manager (Railways), 1946-47; Member: Railway (London Plan) Cttee, 1946-48; Railway Executive Cttee, 1947; London Transport Executive, 1947-54; British Transport Commission, 1954-62, and its Southern Area Board, 1955-59; Chairman: London Transport Executive, 1959-62; London Transport Board, 1963-65. Mem., Supervisory Cttee, Channel Tunnel Study Group, 1957-62; Dir, Channel Tunnel Co., 1956-69. Colonel (Commanding) Engineer and Railway Staff Corps, RE, 1963-64. Mem., Oxford University Appointments Cttee, 1955-69. Governor of Highgate School, 1963-69. Pres., Design and Industries Assoc., 1963-64. FCIT (Pres., 1951-52). *Publication:* Tramping Round London by "Fieldfare" (of the Evening News), 1933. *Recreations:* exploring wild country, bird watching, fishing. *Address:* Balmain, Borders Lane, Etchingham, E Sussex TN19 7AE. *T:* Etchingham 220. *Club:* United Oxford & Cambridge University.

VALENTINE, Rt. Rev. Barry; see Rupert's Land, Bishop of.

VALENTINE, Prof. David Henriques; George Harrison Professor of Botany, University of Manchester, since 1966; *b* 16 Feb. 1912; *s* of Emmanuel and Dora Valentine; *m* 1938, Joan Winifred Todd; two *s* three *d*. *Educ:* Manchester Grammar Sch.; St John's Coll., Cambridge. MA 1936, PhD 1937. Curator of the Herbarium and Demonstrator in Botany, Cambridge, 1936; Research Fellow of St John's Coll., Cambridge, 1938; Ministry of Food (Dehydration Division), 1941; Reader in Botany, Durham, 1945, Prof., 1950-66. Trustee, BM (Natural History), 1975-. Foreign Mem., Societas Scientiarum Fennica (Section for Natural Sciences), 1964. *Publications:* Flora Europaea, Vol. 1, 1964, Vol. 2, 1968, Vol. 3, 1972, Vol. 4, 1976; Taxonomy, Phytogeography and Evolution, 1972; papers on experimental taxonomy in botanical journals. *Recreation:* reading novels. *Address:* 4 Pine Road, Didsbury, Manchester M20 0UY. *T:* 061-445 7224.

VALLANCE, Michael Wilson; Headmaster of Durham School since 1972; *b* 9 Sept. 1933; *er s* of late Vivian Victor Wilson Vallance and of Kate Vallance, Wandsworth and Helston; *m* 1970, Mary Winifred Ann, *d* of John Steele Garnett; one *s* two *d*. *Educ:* Brighton Coll.; St John's Coll., Cambridge (MA). On staff of United Steel Companies Ltd, 1952-53; awarded United Steel Companies Scholarship (held at Cambridge), 1953; Asst Master, Abingdon School, 1957-61; Asst Master, Harrow School, 1961-72. Chm., Cttee of Northern Isis, 1976-77. *Recreations:* reading, cricket, gardening, the sea. *Address:* Durham School, Durham City DH1 4SZ. *T:* Durham 2977. *Clubs:* MCC, Jesters; County (Durham).

VALLANCE-OWEN, Prof. John, MA, MD, FRCP, FRCPath; Professor of Medicine, Queen's University, Belfast; Consultant Physician to Royal Victoria Hospital and Belfast City Hospital since 1966; *b* 31 Oct. 1920; *s* of late Prof. E. A. Owen; *m* 1950, Renee Thornton; two *s* two *d*. *Educ:* Friar's Sch., Bangor; Epsom Coll.; St John's Coll., Cambridge (de Havilland Schol. from Epsom); London Hosp. (Schol.). BA 1943; MA, MB, BChir Cantab, 1946; MD Cantab 1951; FRCP 1962; Hon. FRCPI 1970; FRCPath 1971. Various appts incl. Pathology Asst and Med. 1st Asst, London Hosp., 1946-51; Med. Tutor, Royal Postgrad. Med. Sch., Hammersmith Hosp., 1952-55 and 1956-58; Rockefeller Trav. Fellowship, at George S. Cox Med. Research Inst., Univ. of Pennsylvania, 1955-56; Cons. Phys. and Lectr in Medicine, Univ. of Durham, 1958-64; Cons. Phys., Royal Victoria Infirmary and Reader in Medicine, Univ. of Newcastle upon Tyne, 1964-66. Member: Standing Med. Adv. Cttee, Min. of Health and Social Services, NI, 1970-73; Specialist Adv. Cttee (General Internal Medicine) to the Govt; Northern Health and Social Services Bd, Dept of Health and Soc. Services, NI; Mem., Exec. Cttee, Assoc. of Physicians of GB and Ireland; Regional Adviser for N Ire, to RCP, 1970-75 and Councillor, RCP, 1976- (Oliver-Sharpey Prize, RCP, 1976); Mem. Research Cttee, Brit. Diabetic Assoc.; Brit. Council Lectr, Dept Medicine, Zürich Univ., 1963; 1st Helen Martin Lectr, Diabetic Assoc. of S Calif, Wm H. Mulberg Lectr, Cincinnati Diabetes Assoc., and Lectr, Brookhaven Nat. Labs, NY, 1965; Brit. Council Lectr, Haile Selassie Univ., Makerere UC and S African Univs, 1966; Guest Lectr: Japan Endocrinological Soc., 1968; Madrid Univ., 1969; Endocrine Soc. of Australia, 1970, Bologna Univ., 1976. *Publications:* Essentials of Cardiology, 1961 (2nd edn 1968); Diabetes: its physiological and biochemical basis, 1976; papers in biochem., med., and scientific jls on carbohydrate and fat metabolism and aetiology of diabetes mellitus and related conditions, with special reference to insulin antagonism. *Recreations:* tennis, golf, music. *Address:* Department of Medicine, Queen's University, Belfast, Northern Ireland; (home) 74 Osborne Park, Belfast BT9 6JP. *T:* Belfast

667882. *Clubs:* East India, Devonshire, Sports and Public Schools; Fitzwilliam Lawn Tennis, Royal County Down Golf.

VALLAT, Prof. Sir Francis Aimé, KCMG 1962 (CMG 1955); QC 1961; Professor of International Law, King's College, University of London, 1970-76 (Reader, 1969-70); Director of International Law Studies, King's College, since 1968; *b* 25 May 1912; *s* of Col Frederick W. Vallat, OBE; *m* 1939, Mary Alison Cockell; one *s* one *d*. *Educ:* University College, Toronto (BA Hons); Gonville and Caius Coll., Cambridge (LLB). Called to Bar, Gray's Inn, 1935, Bencher, 1971; Assistant Lecturer, Bristol Univ., 1935-36; practice at Bar, London, 1936-39; RAFVR (Flt Lieut), 1941-45; Asst Legal Adviser, Foreign Office, 1945-50; Legal Adviser, UK Permanent Deleg. to UN, 1950-54; Deputy Legal Adviser, FO, 1954-60, Legal Adviser, 1960-68. (On leave of absence) Actg Director, Inst. of Air and Space Law, and Vis. Prof. of Law, McGill Univ., 1965-66. Dir of Studies, Internat. Law Assoc., 1969-73. UK Mem., UN Fact Finding Panel, 1969-. Associate Member, Institut de Droit international, 1965; Mem., Internat. Law Commn, 1973. *Publications:* International Law and the Practitioner, 1966; Introduction to the Study of Human Rights, 1972; articles in British Year Book of International Law and other journals. *Recreation:* restoration of antiques. *Address:* 17 Ranelagh Grove, SW1. *T:* 01-730 6656; 3 Essex Court, Temple, EC4. *T:* 01-353 2624. *Clubs:* Athenæum, Hurlingham.

VALOIS, Dame Ninette de; see de Valois.

VAN ALLEN, Prof. James Alfred; Professor of Physics and Head of Department of Physics (of Physics and Astronomy since 1959), since 1951, Carver Professor of Physics, since 1972, University of Iowa, USA; *b* Iowa, 7 Sept. 1914; *s* of Alfred Morris and Alma Olney Van Allen; *m* 1945, Abigail Fithian Halsey II; two *s* three *d*. *Educ:* Public High School, and Iowa Wesleyan Coll., Mount Pleasant, Iowa (BSc); State University of Iowa, Iowa City (MSc, PhD). Research Fellow, then Physicist, Carnegie Instn of Washington, 1939-42; Physicist, Applied Physics Lab., Johns Hopkins Univ., Md, 1942. Ordnance and Gunnery Officer and Combat Observer, USN, 1942-46, Lt-Comdr 1946. Supervisor of High-Altitude Research Group and of Proximity Fuze Unit, Johns Hopkins Univ., 1946-50. Leader, various scientific expeditions to Central and S Pacific, Arctic and Antarctic, for study of cosmic rays and earth's magnetic field, using Aerobee and balloon-launched rockets, 1949-57. Took part in promotion and planning of International Geophysical Year, 1958-59; worked on radiation measuring equipment of first American satellite, Explorer I, and subseq. satellites (discoverer of Van Allen Radiation Belts of the earth, 1958); has continued study of earth's radiation belts, aurorae, cosmic rays, energetic particles in interplanetary space, etc. Research Fellow, Guggenheim Memorial Foundation, 1951; Research Associate (controlled thermonuclear reactions), Princeton Univ., Project Matterhorn, 1953-54. Associate Editor; Physics of Fluids, 1958-62; Jl of Geophys. Research, 1959-67. Mem., Space Science Bd of Nat. Acad. of Sciences, 1958-70; Consultant, President's Science Advisory Cttee; Mem., Rocket and Satellites Research Panel, and other technical cttees, etc. Fellow, American Phys. Society, etc; Member, Nat. Acad. of Sciences; Founder Member, International Acad. of Astronautics, etc. Holds many awards and hon. doctorates. *Publications:* numerous articles in learned journals and contribs to scientific works. *Address:* Department of Physics and Astronomy, University of Iowa, Iowa City, Iowa 52242, USA; 5 Woodland Mounds Road, RFD 6, Iowa City, Iowa 52240, USA.

VANCE, Cyrus Robert; Secretary of State, USA, since 1977; barrister-at-law; *b* Clarksburg, W Va, 27 March 1917; *m* 1947, Grace Elsie Sloane; one *s* four *d*. *Educ:* Kent Sch.; Yale Univ. (BA 1939); Yale Univ. Law Sch. (LLB 1942). Served War, USNR, to Lieut (s.g.), 1942-46. Asst to Pres., The Mead Corp., 1946-47; admitted to New York Bar, 1947; Associate and Partner of Simpson Thacher & Bartlett, New York, 1947-60 (Partner, Jan. 1967-77). Special Counsel, Preparedness Investigation Sub-cttee of Senate Armed Services Cttee, 1957-60; Consulting Counsel, Special Cttee on Space and Astronautics, US Senate, 1958; Gen. Counsel, Dept of Defense, 1961-62; Sec. of the Army, 1962-64; Dep. Sec. of Defense, 1964-67; Special Rep. of the President: in Civil Disturbances in Detroit, July-Aug. 1967; in Cyprus, Nov.-Dec. 1967; in Korea, Feb. 1968; one of two US Negotiators, Paris Peace Conf. on Vietnam, May 1968-Feb. 1969; Mem., Commn to Investigate Alleged Police Corruption in NYC, 1970-72; Pres., Assoc. of Bar of City of New York, 1974-76. Hon. degrees: Marshall, 1963; Trinity Coll., 1966; Yale, 1968; West Virginia, 1969; Brandeis, 1971. Medal of Freedom (US), 1969. *Address:* Office of the Secretary of State, Washington, DC 20520, USA.

VANCOUVER, Archbishop of, (RC), since 1969; **Most Rev. James F. Carney,** DD; *b* Vancouver, BC, 28 June 1915. *Educ:* Vancouver College; St Joseph's Seminary, Edmonton, Alta. Ordained, 1942; Vicar-General and Domestic Prelate, 1964; Auxiliary Bishop of Vancouver, 1966. *Address:* 150 Robson Street, Vancouver, BC V6B 2A7, Canada. *T:* 683-0281.

VANDEN-BEMPDE-JOHNSTONE; see Johnstone.

VAN DEN BERGH, James Philip, CBE 1946; Director of Unilever Ltd, 1937-65, retired; Vice-Chairman of Lindustries, 1965-75; Deputy Chairman, William Baird & Co., 1965-75; Chairman, National Cold Stores (Management Ltd), 1965-70; *b* 26 April 1905; *s* of Albert Van den Bergh; *m* 1929, Betty D'Arcy Hart; one *s* one *d*. *Educ:* Harrow; Trinity Coll., Cambridge. Entered Van den Berghs Ltd, 1927; subseq. Man. Dir; Chm., 1942. Min. of Food: Dir of Margarine and Cooking Fats, 1939; Dir of Dehydration, 1940; Dir of Fish Supplies, 1945. Government Director, British Sugar Corp., 1956-58, retired. Member Exec. Council, Food Manufacturers' Federation, 1957 (President, 1958-61); Member Food Research Advisory Cttee, 1960-65 (Chairman, 1963); Member Council, Queen Elizabeth Coll., London Univ., 1961-; Hon. Fellow, 1968. *Recreations:* shooting, gardening. *Address:* Field House, Cranleigh, Surrey. *Clubs:* Bath; Leander (Henley).

VAN DEN BOGAERDE, Derek Niven, (Dirk Bogarde); actor; *b* 28 March 1921. *Educ:* University College School; Allan Glen's (Scotland). Served War of 1939-45: Queen's Royal Regt, 1940-46, Europe and Far East, and Air Photographic Intelligence. *Films* include (since 1947): Hunted, Appointment in London, They Who Dare, The Sleeping Tiger, Doctor in the House, Doctor at Sea, Doctor at Large, Simba, The Spanish Gardener, Cast a Dark Shadow, Ill Met by Moonlight, The Blue Lamp, So Long at the Fair, Quartet, A Tale of Two Cities (Sidney Carton), The Wind Cannot Read, The Doctor's Dilemma, Libel, Song Without End, The Angel Wore Red, The Singer Not The Song, Victim, HMS Defiant, The Password is Courage, The Lonely Stage, The Mindbenders, The Servant, Doctor in Distress, Hot Enough for June, The High Bright Sun, King and Country, Darling..., Modesty Blaise, Accident, Our Mother's House, Mister Sebastian, The Fixer, Oh What A Lovely War, Götterdämmerung, Justine, Death in Venice, Upon This Rock, Le Serpent, The Night Porter, Permission To Kill, Providence, A Bridge Too Far, Despair. *Theatre:* Cliff, in Power Without Glory, 1947; Orpheus, in Point of Departure, 1950; Nicky, in The Vortex, 1953; Alberto, in Summertime, 1955-56; Jezebel, Oxford Playhouse, 1958, etc. *Publication:* A Postillion Struck by Lightning (autobiog.), 1977. *Recreations:* gardening, painting, motoring. *Address:* 06 Châteauneuf de Grasse, France.

VAN DEN HOVEN, Helmert Frans; see Hoven.

VANDERFELT, Sir Robin (Victor), KBE 1973 (OBE 1954); Secretary-General, Commonwealth Parliamentary Association, since 1961; *b* 24 July 1921; *y s* of late Sydney Gorton Vanderfelt, OBE, and Ethel Maude Vanderfelt (*née* Tremayne); *m* 1962, Jean Margaret Becker, *d* of John and Eve Steward; two *s* (and one step *s* one step *d*). *Educ:* Haileybury; Peterhouse, Cambridge. Served War in India and Burma, 1941-45. Asst Secretary, UK Branch, CPA, 1949-59; Secretary, 1960-61. Secretary, UK Delegn, Commonwealth Parly Conf., India, 1957; as Sec.-Gen., CPA, has served as Secretary to Parliamentary Conferences throughout Commonwealth, 1961-, also attended many area and regional confs; Conf. of Speakers and Clerks of Parliaments of East and Central African States, Nairobi, 1964; Conf. of Commonwealth Speakers and Clerks, Ottawa, 1969. *Recreation:* gardening. *Address:* Commonwealth Parliamentary Association, General Council, 7 Old Palace Yard, SW1. *T:* 01-219 4281; Penridge House, Penselwood, Wincanton, Som. *T:* Bourton (Dorset) 479.

VAN DER KISTE, Wing Commander Robert Edgar Guy, DSO 1941; OBE 1957; Royal Auxiliary Air Force, retired; Director, Plymouth Incorporated Chamber of Trade and Commerce, since 1974 (Secretary, 1964-74); *b* 20 July 1912; *y s* of late Lt-Col F. W. Van der Kiste, DSO; *m* 1939, Nancy Kathleen, *er d* of Alec George Holman, MRCS, LRCP, and Grace Kathleen Brown; one *s* two *d* (and one *s* decd). *Educ:* Cheltenham College. Commissioned Royal Air Force, Nov. 1936. Served War of 1939-45 (despatches, DSO); retired, 1959. Commanded No 3 MHQ Unit, Royal Auxiliary Air Force. *Recreations:* sailing, caravanning. *Address:* Yonder Cross, South Brent, Devon TQ10 9DR.

van der LOON, Prof. Piet; Professor of Chinese, University of Oxford, since 1972; Fellow of University College, Oxford, since 1972; *b* 7 April 1920; *m* 1947, Minnie C. Snellen; two *d*. *Educ:*

Univ. of Leiden. Litt. Drs Leiden, MA Cantab. Univ. Asst Lectr, Cambridge, 1948; Univ. Lectr, Cambridge, 1949. *Publications:* articles in Asia Major, T'oung Pao, Jl Asiatique. *Recreation:* travel. *Address:* University College, Oxford.

VANDERMEER, (Arnold) Roy; a Recorder of the Crown Court, since 1972; *b* London, 26 June 1931; *o s* of late William Arnold Vandermeer and Katherine Nora Vandermeer; *m* 1964, Caroline Veronica (*née* Christopher); one *s* two *d*. *Educ:* Dame Alice Owen's Sch., Islington; King's Coll., London (LLB). Called to Bar, Gray's Inn, 1955. Flt-Lt, RAF, 1955-58. *Recreations:* reading, cricket. *Address:* The Field House, Barnet Lane, Elstree, Herts. *T:* 01-953 2244.

VAN DER MEULEN, Daniel; Netherlands Indies civil servant and diplomat; Arabist author and traveller; *b* 4 Sept. 1894; *m* 1st, 1917, A. C. E. Kelling; three *s* (and one *s* murdered in Germany) two *d*; 2nd, 1959, Dr H. M. Duhm; one *s*. *Educ:* Leyden Univ. Netherlands Indies Civil Service, North of Sumatra in Toba-lake district of Toba Batak country, 1915-23; studied Arabic and Islam under Prof. Dr C. Snouck Hurgronje, Leyden Univ.; consular and diplomatic service, Jeddah, Sa'oudi-Arabia, 1926-31; first exploration in South Arabia, 1931; Netherlands Indies Civil Service, Pajakumbuh, Central Sumatra, Palembang, South Sumatra, 1932-38; second exploration in South Arabia, 1939; Netherlands Indies Civil Service, Makassar, South Celebes, 1939-41; Minister in Jeddah, Sa'oudi-Arabia, 1941-45; Resident Adviser to Netherlands East India Government at Batavia, 1945-48; Chief of the Arabic Section of Radio Netherland World-broadcast at Hilversum, 1949-51. Hon. Mem., Royal Netherlands Geographical Soc., 1956. Officer, Oranje Nassau; Patron's Medal, Royal Geographical Society, London, 1947. *Publications:* Hadhramaut, some of its mysteries unveiled (with map by Prof. Dr H. von Wissmann), 1932; Aden to the Hadhramaut, 1947 (numerous trans.); Onbekend Arabië, 1947; Ontwakend Arabië, 1954; Mÿn weg naar Arabië en de Islaam, 1954; The Wells of Ibn Sa'ud, 1954; Verdwijnend Arabië, 1959; Faces in Shem, 1961; Ik Stond Erbÿ, het einde van ons koloniale rÿk, 1965; Hoort Ge de donder niet? (autobiog.), 1977. *Address:* 9 Flierder Weg, Gorssel, Holland. *T:* 05759-1684.

VAN DER POST, Laurens Jan, CBE 1947; writer, farmer, explorer; *b* Philippolis, S Africa, 13 Dec. 1906; *s* of late C. W. H. Van Der Post, Chairman of Orange Free State Republic Volksraad, and late M. M. Lubbe, Boesmansfontein, Wolwekop, and Stilton; *m* 1928, Marjorie Wendt; one *s* one *d*; *m* 1949, Ingaret Giffard. Served War of 1939-45: Ethiopia; North Africa; Syria; Dutch East Indies; Java; commanded 43 Special Military Mission, Prisoner of War 1943-45, thereafter attached to British Minister, Batavia, until 1947. Since then has undertaken several missions for British Government and Colonial Development Corp. in Africa, including Government Mission to Kalahari, 1952. FRSL. Hon. DLitt: Univ. of Natal, 1964; Univ. of Liverpool, 1976; DUniv Surrey, 1971. *Films:* Lost World of Kalahari, 1956; A Region of Shadow, 1971; The Story of Carl Gustav Jung, 1971; All Africa Within Us, 1975. *Publications:* In a Province, 1934; Venture to the Interior, 1952 (Book Society choice and Amy Woolf Memorial Prize); A Bar of Shadow, 1952 (repr., 1972); The Face Beside the Fire, 1953; Flamingo Feather, 1955 (German Book Society choice); The Dark Eye in Africa, 1955; Creative Pattern in Primitive Man, 1956; The Lost World of the Kalahari, 1958 (American Literary Guild Choice); The Heart of the Hunter, 1961; The Seed and the Sower, 1963 (South African CNA Award for best work published in 1963); Journey into Russia, 1964; A Portrait of all The Russias, 1967; The Hunter and the Whale, 1967 (CNA and Yorkshire Post Fiction Awards); A Portrait of Japan, 1968; The Night of the New Moon, 1970; A Story like the Wind, 1972; A Far Off Place, 1974; A Mantis Carol, 1975; Jung and the Story of Our Time, 1976; First Catch Your Eland: a taste of Africa, 1977. *Recreations:* walking, climbing, ski-ing, tennis, studying grasses and cooking in winter. *Address:* 27 Chelsea Towers, SW3; Turnstones, Aldeburgh, Suffolk; Wolwekop, Philippolis, South Africa.

VANE, family name of **Baron Barnard.**

VANE, Dr John Robert, FRS 1974; Group Research and Development Director, The Wellcome Foundation, since 1973; *b* 29 March 1927; *s* of Maurice Vane and Frances Florence Vane (*née* Fisher); *m* 1948, Elizabeth Daphne Page; two *d*. *Educ:* Univs of Birmingham and Oxford. BSc Chemistry Birmingham, 1946; BSc Pharmacology Oxon, 1949; DPhil 1953; DSc 1970. Stothert Research Fellow of Royal Soc., 1951-53; Asst Prof. of Pharmacology, Yale Univ., 1953-55; Sen. Lectr in Pharmacology, Inst. of Basic Medical Sciences, RCS, 1955-61; Reader in Pharmacology, RCS, Univ. of London, 1961-65; Prof.

of Experimental Pharmacology, RCS, Univ. of London, 1966-73. Vis. Prof., King's Coll., London, 1976. British Pharmacological Soc.: Meetings Sec., 1967-70; Gen. Sec., 1970-73. Hon. Mem., Polish Pharmacological Soc., 1973; Hon. DM Krakow, 1977. *Publications:* (ed jtly) Adrenergic Mechanisms, 1960; (ed jointly) Prostaglandin Synthetase Inhibitors, 1974; numerous papers in learned jls. *Recreations:* photography, travel, archaeology, underwater swimming. *Address:* White Angles, 7 Beech Dell, Keston Park, Kent BR2 6EP. *T:* Farnborough 53128. *Club:* Athenæum.

VANE, (FLETCHER-); family name of **Baron Inglewood.**

VANE-TEMPEST-STEWART, family name of **Marquess of Londonderry.**

van HASSELT, Marc; Headmaster, Cranleigh School, since 1970; *b* 24 April 1924; *s* of Marc and Helen van Hasselt; *m* 1949, Geraldine Frances Sinclair; three *s* one *d. Educ:* Sherborne; Selwyn Coll., Cambridge (MA). Served War of 1939-45 (despatches): commissioned in Essex Yeomanry, RHA, 1944; served North-West Europe. Lecturer in Commonwealth Studies, RMA, Sandhurst, 1950-58; Asst Master, Oundle School, 1959-70 (Housemaster, Sanderson House, 1963-70). *Publications:* occasional articles in Yachting World. *Recreation:* cruising under sail. *Address:* Headmaster's House, Cranleigh School, Cranleigh, Surrey. *T:* Cranleigh 4640; Kilbronogue, Ballydehob, Co. Cork, Ireland. *Club:* Royal Cruising.

van HEYNINGEN, William Edward, MA Oxon, ScD Cantab; Master of St Cross College, Oxford, since 1965; Reader in Bacterial Chemistry, University of Oxford, since 1966; *b* 24 Dec. 1911; *s* of late George Philipus Stephanus van Heyningen and late Mabel Constance (*née* Higgs); *m* 1940, Ruth Eleanor Treverton; one *s* one *d. Educ:* Village schools in S Africa; Univs of Stellenbosch and Cambridge. Commonwealth Fund Fellow, Harvard Univ., and College of Physicians and Surgeons, Columbia Univ., 1936-38; Senior Student of Royal Commn for Exhibn of 1851, 1938-40. Staff Member, Wellcome Physiological Research Laboratories, 1943-46; Sen. Res. Officer, Sir William Dunn School of Pathology, Oxford Univ., 1947-66; Sec., Soc. for Gen. Microbiology, 1946-52; Curator of the Bodleian Library, 1961-; Mem. Hebdomadal Council, Oxford Univ., 1963-69. Vis. Prof., State Univ. of New York, 1967. Visitor of the Ashmolean Museum, 1969-. Trustee, Ruskin Sch. of Drawing, 1975-77. Consultant, Cholera Adv. Cttee, Nat. Insts of Health, USA, 1968-73. *Publications:* Bacterial Toxins, 1950; papers mainly concerned with bacterial toxins in various books and journals. *Address:* St Cross College, Oxford. *Club:* Reform.

van LENNEP, Jonkheer Emile; Knight, Order of the Netherlands Lion; Commander, Order of Orange Nassau; Secretary-General, OECD, since Oct. 1969; *b* 20 Jan. 1915; *s* of Louis Henri van Lennep and Catharina Hillegonda Enschede; *m* 1941, Alexa Alison Labberton; two *s* two *d. Educ:* Univ. of Amsterdam. Foreign Exchange Inst., 1940-45; Netherlands Bank, 1945-48; Financial Counsellor, High Representative of the Crown, Indonesia, 1948-50; Netherlands Bank, 1950-51. Treasurer-General, Ministry of Finance, The Netherlands, 1951-69. Chairman: Monetary Cttee, EEC, 1958; Working Party No 3, OECD, 1962; Mem., Board Directors, KLM (Airline), 1951. KStJ. Grand Officer or Comdr in various foreign orders. *Address:* (office) OECD, 2 rue André Pascal, 75116 Paris, France; (private) 92 avenue Henri Martin, 75116 Paris, France. *Clubs:* Haagsche (The Hague); Union Interalliée (Paris).

van MAURIK, Ernest Henry, OBE 1944; HM Diplomatic Service, retired; *b* 24 Aug. 1916; *s* of Justus van Maurik and Sybil van Maurik (*née* Ebert); *m* 1945, Winifred Emery Ritchie Hay; one *s* one *d. Educ:* Lancing Coll.; Ecole Sup. de Commerce, Neuchatel, Switzerland. Worked in Tea Export, Mincing Lane, 1936-39. Commnd as 2nd Lt, in Wiltshire Regt, 1939; seconded to Special Ops Exec., 1941-46; demob. with hon. rank of Lt-Col (subst. Major), 1946. Joined Foreign Office, 1946; Moscow, 1948-50; West Germany and West Berlin, 1952-56; Buenos Aires, 1958-62; Copenhagen, 1965-67; Rio de Janeiro, 1968-71; FCO, 1971-75. Officier de la Couronne (Belgium), 1944. *Recreations:* golf, gardening, languages. *Address:* Parkside, The Common, Sevenoaks, Kent. *T:* Sevenoaks 52173. *Club:* Special Forces.

van MEERBEKE, René Louis Joseph Marie; Grand Officier, Orders of the Crown and of Léopold II (Belgium); Commander, Order of Leopold II (with swords); Officer, Orders of Léopold and of the Crown (with swords); Croix de Guerre (Belgium), 1914-18 (with palms); Croix de Feu; Civil Cross (1st Class); *b* 15 Nov. 1895; *m* 1926, Léonor Restrepo del Corral; two *s* one *d. Educ:* University of Ghent (Licentiate of Faculty of Law in

Commercial and Consular Sciences). Entered Diplomatic Service, 1920; Secretary, Legation, Lima, 1921; Chargé d'Affaires a.i. Bogota, 1924; Chargé d'Affaires, 1936; Minister, Bogota, 1945; Ambassador, Rio de Janeiro, 1954; Ambassador to the Court of St James's, 1957-61, and concurrently Belgian Perm. Rep. to Council of WEU. Entrusted with special missions as Representative of the Belgian Government at the investitures of new Presidents of the Republic: in Colomb.a, in 1946, 1950 and 1958; in Ecuador in 1948 and 1952, and in Brazil in 1956. Grand Cross Orders of Merit (Ecuador), Southern Cross (Brazil), Boyaca and San Carlos (Colombia); Grand Officer of Aztec Eagle (Mexico); Commander, Legion of Honour; Commander, Order of the Liberator (Venezuela); Officer, Order of the Sun (Peru); Golden Medal of the French Reconnaissance, etc. *Recreation:* horse riding. *Clubs:* Cercle Royal Gaulois (Vice-Pres.) (Brussels); Royal Golf Club de Belgique.

VANNECK, family name of **Baron Huntingfield.**

VANNECK, Air Commodore Hon. Sir Peter Beckford Rutgers, GBE 1977 (OBE 1963); CB 1973; AFC 1955; AE 1954; DL; Gentleman Usher to the Queen since 1967; Lord Mayor of London for 1977-78; *b* 7 Jan. 1922; *y* s of 5th Baron Huntingfield, KCMG and Margaret Eleanor, *d* of Judge Ernest Crosby, NY; *m* 1943, Cordelia, *y d* of Captain R. H. Errington, RN (retd); one *d* (and one *d* decd). *Educ:* Geelong Grammar Sch.; Stowe Sch.; Trinity Coll., Cambridge (MA); Harvard. MIAgrE; TEng (CEI). Cadet, RN, 1939; served in Nelson, King George V, Eskimo, 55th LCA Flot., Wren, MTB 606 (in comd), 771 Sqdn and 807 Sqdn FAA, resigned 1949; Cambridge Univ. Air Sqdn, 1949; 601 (Co. of London) Sqdn RAuxAF, 1950-57 (101 Sqdn Mass. Air Nat. Guard, 1953); 3619 (Co. of Suffolk) Fighter Control Unit, 1958-61 (in comd 1959-61); No 1 Maritime HQ Unit, 1961-63; Group Captain, 1963; Inspector RAuxAF, 1963-73, Hon. Inspector-General 1974-; ADC to the Queen, 1963-73; Hon. Air Cdre, No 1 (Co. Hertford) Maritime HQ Unit, RAuxAF, 1973-. Mem. Court of Assts, Fishmongers' Co.; Master, Gunmakers' Co., 1977; Past Master, Guild of Air Pilots and Air Navigators; Alderman of Cordwainer Ward, City of London, 1969. Member: Ipswich Gp Hosps Bd, 1956-62; Gov. Body Brit. Post Graduate Medical Fedn. Univ. of London, 1963-71; St Bartholomew's Hosp. Bd of Governors, 1971-73; Special Trustee, St Bartholomew's Hosp., 1974-; Trustee, RAF Museum, 1976-; Governor, Royal Shakespeare Theatre, 1974-. Mem., City and E London AHA, 1973-77. KStJ (Mem. Chapter General). DL Greater London, 1970; Sheriff City of London, 1974-75. Churchwarden of St. Mary-le-Bow. *Recreations:* sailing, shooting, ski-ing, bad bridge. *Address:* White Lodge, Waldringfield, Suffolk. *T:* Waldringfield 244; 25 Elvaston Place, SW7 5NL. *T:* 01-584 6994; Moulin de Tressange, Mercoeur, 19 Correze, France. *Clubs:* White's, Pratt's; Royal Yacht Squadron, Royal London Yacht (Commodore); Seawanhaka Corinthian Yacht (US).
See also Baron Huntingfield, H. D. Stevenson.

VAN OSS, (Adam) Oliver, MA; FSA; Master of the London Charterhouse, since 1973; *b* 28 March 1909; *s* of S. F. Van Oss, The Hague, newspaper proprietor; *m* 1945, Audrey (*d* 1960), *widow* of Capt. J. R. Allsopp; two *d. Educ:* Dragon Sch., Oxford; Clifton; Magdalen Coll., Oxford. Housemaster and Head of Modern Language Dept, Eton Coll.; Lower Master, and Acting Headmaster, Eton Coll., 1959-64; Headmaster of Charterhouse, 1965-73. Formerly Hon. Editor Transactions English Ceramic Circle. Mem. Council, City Univ.; Governor: Highgate; Sherborne. Chevalier de la Legion d'Honneur. *Publications:* articles on ceramics, travel and education. *Recreations:* all forms of art and sport except racing; formerly Rugby football (played for Berkshire). *Address:* The Master's Lodge, The Charterhouse, Charterhouse Square, EC1. *T:* 01-253 0272. *Clubs:* Athenæum, Beefsteak.

VAN PRAAGH, Dame Peggy, DBE 1970 (OBE 1966); Dance Consultant to, and Member Council, Victorian Ministry for the Arts, since 1975; Member of Council and Guest Teacher, Australian Ballet School, since 1975; director and producer of ballet in UK and many other countries; *b* London, 1 Sept. 1910; *d* of Harold John Van Praagh, MD, and Ethel Louise Shanks. *Educ:* King Alfred Sch., Hampstead. Studied and trained in the Cecchetti Method of classical ballet with Margaret Craske; passed Advanced Cecchetti Exam., 1932; danced in Tudor's Adam and Eve, Camargo Society, 1932. Joined Ballet Rambert and danced at Ballet Club, 1933-38; created rôles in Tudor's Ballets: Jardin aux Lilas, Dark Elegies, Gala Performance, Soirée Musicale, etc; joined Tudor's Co., the London Ballet, as a Principal Dancer, 1938. Examiner and Cttee member, Cecchetti Society, 1937-. Joined Sadler's Wells Ballet as dancer and teacher, 1941; danced Swanhilda in Coppelia, Blue Girl in Patineurs, etc. Producer and Asst Director to Ninette De Valois,

Sadler's Wells Theatre Ballet, and worked with that company, 1946-56. Produced many TV ballets for BBC. Guest Teacher and Producer for National Ballet of Canada, 1956; Guest Producer: Munich, Bavarian Opera House, 1956; Theatre Royal, Stockholm, 1957; Director: Norsk Ballet, 1957-58; Edinburgh International Festival Ballet, 1958; Borovansky Ballet in Australia, 1960; Guest Teacher: Jacob's Pillow, USA, 1959; Ballet of Marquis de Cuevas, 1961; Artistic Dir, Australian Ballet, 1962-74. Brought Australian Ballet to Commonwealth Festival, London, 1965; to Expo '67 Montreal, followed by tour of S America, 1967. Hon. DLitt, Univ. of New England, NSW, 1974. Queen Elizabeth II Coronation Award, Royal Academy of Dancing, 1965; Distinguished Artist Award, Australia Council, 1975. *Publications:* How I Became a Ballet Dancer, 1954; The Choreographic Art (with Peter Brinson), 1963. *Recreations:* motoring, swimming. *Address:* 24/248 The Avenue, Parkville, Victoria 3052, Australia.

van **RIEMSDIJK, John Theodore;** Keeper of Mechanical and Civil Engineering, Science Museum, since 1976; *b* 13 Nov. 1924; *s* of Adrianus K. van Riemsdijk and Nora P. van Riemsdijk (*née* James); *m* 1957, Jocelyn Kilma Arfon-Price. *Educ:* University College Sch.; Birkbeck Coll. (BA). Served SOE, 1943-46. Manufacturer of gearing, 1946-54; Science Museum: Asst, 1954; Lectr, 1961; Educn Officer, 1969. *Publications:* Science Museum Books; contribs to: BBC Publications; Newcomen Soc. Trans. *Recreations:* oil painting, making models. *Address:* 2 Farquhar Street, Hertford. *T:* Hertford 52750.

VANSITTART, Guy Nicholas; *b* 8 Sept. 1893; *y s* of late Capt. Robert Arnold Vansittart and late Alice (*née* Blane). *Educ:* Eton; Trinity Coll., Oxford. BA (Oxon), Honour School of History. Captain, Indian Army, Central India Horse, 1913-22. *Address:* Flat 7, 20 Charles Street, W1X 7HD.

van **STRAUBENZEE, William Radcliffe,** MBE 1954; MP (C) Wokingham since Oct. 1959; *b* 27 Jan. 1924; *o s* of late Brig. A. B. van Straubenzee, DSO, MC and of Margaret Joan, 3rd *d* of A. N. Radcliffe, Kensington Square, W8, and Bag Park, Widecombe-in-the-Moor, Newton Abbot, S Devon. *Educ:* Westminster. Served War of 1939-45: five years with Royal Artillery (Major); Regimental and Staff Appointments, including two years in Far East. Admitted a Solicitor, 1952. Chairman, Young Conservative Nat. Advisory Cttee, 1951-53; contested Wandsworth (Clapham), 1955; PPS to Minister of Educn (Sir David Eccles), 1960-62; Jt Parly Under-Sec. of State, Dept of Educn and Science, 1970-72; Minister of State, NI Office, 1972-74; Chm., Select Cttee on Assistance to Private Members, 1975. Member of Richmond (Surrey) Borough Council, 1955-58. Chairman: United and Cecil Club, 1965-68 (Hon. Sec., 1952-59); Westminster House Boys' Club, Camberwell, 1965-68 (Hon. Sec., 1952-65); Nat. Council for Drama Training, 1976-; Mem., Court of Reading Univ. Hon. Sec., Fedn of Conservative Students, 1965-71, Vice-Pres., 1974. A Church Comr; Mem. House of Laity, Church Assembly, 1965-70, Mem. General Synod, 1975-; Patron of Living of Rockbourne, Hants. Hon. Vice-Pres., National Union of Students. *Recreations:* walking, swimming, reading. *Address:* 199 Westminster Bridge Road, SE1. *T:* 01-928 6855; 30 Rose Street, Wokingham, Berkshire. *T:* Wokingham 784464. *Club:* Carlton.

VAN VLECK, Prof. John Hasbrouck; Hollis Professor of Mathematics and Natural Philosophy, Harvard University, 1951-69, now Professor Emeritus; *b* 13 March 1899; *s* of Edward Burr Van Vleck and Hester Raymond Van Vleck; *m* 1927, Abigail Pearson; no *c. Educ:* Wisconsin Univ.; Harvard Univ. AB Wisconsin, 1920; AM 1921, PhD 1922, Harvard. Instructor, Harvard Univ., 1922-23; Asst Prof., then Prof., Minnesota Univ., 1923-28; Prof., Wisconsin Univ., 1928-34; Harvard Univ.; Assoc. Prof., 1934-35; Prof., 1935-69; Head of Theory Group, Radio Res. Lab., 1943-45; Dean of Engineering and Applied Physics, 1951-57. Guggenheim Fellow, 1930; Lorentz Visiting Prof., Leiden Univ., 1960; Eastman Prof., Oxford Univ., 1961-62; Visiting Lecturer, various universities; member numerous scientific societies; President, American Phys. Soc., 1952-53; MNAS; Member: Amer. Philosoph. Soc.; Amer. Acad. of Arts and Sciences; Internat. Acad. of Quantum Chem.; Foreign Member: Royal Society, London; Royal Netherlands Acad. of Science; Royal Swedish Acad. of Science; Royal Uppsala Acad. of Science; Foreign Associate, Académie des Sciences, France; Hon. Member, Phys. Soc. of France. Hon. ScD: Wesleyan, 1936; Wisconsin, 1947; Maryland, 1955; Oxford, 1958; Rockford Coll., 1962; Harvard, 1966; Chicago, 1968; Minnesota, 1971; Dr *hc*: Grenoble, 1950; Paris, 1960; Nancy, 1961. Michelson Prize, Case Inst. of Technology, 1963; Langmuir Award, American Phys. Society, 1965; National Medal of Science, US, 1966; Cresson Medal, Franklin Inst., 1971; Lorentz Medal,

Netherlands Acad., 1974; (jtly) Nobel Prize for Physics, 1977. Chevalier, Légion d'Honneur, 1970. *Publications:* Quantum Principles and Line Spectra, 1926; The Theory of Electric and Magnetic Susceptibilities, 1932. *Address:* Lyman Laboratory of Physics, Harvard University, Cambridge, Mass 02138, USA. *T:* 547-1427. *Clubs:* Harvard (New York and Boston).

van **WACHEM, Lodewijk Christiaan,** CBE (Hon.) 1977; mechanical engineer, Netherlands; Managing Director, Royal Dutch Petroleum Co.; Member, Presidium of Board of Directors of Shell Petroleum N.V.; Managing Director, The Shell Petroleum Co. Ltd; Co-ordinator, Exploration and Production, Shell Internationale Petroleum Maatschappij B.V.; *b* Pangkalan Brandan, Indonesia, 31 July 1931; *m* 1958, Elisabeth G. Cristofoli; two *s* one *d. Educ:* Technological Univ., Delft (mech. engr). Joined BPM, The Hague, 1953; Mech. Engr, Compania Shell de Venezuela, 1954-63; Shell-BP Petr. Develt Co. of Nigeria: Chief Engr, 1963-66; Engrg Manager, 1966-67; Brunei Shell Petr. Co. Ltd: Head of Techn. Admin., 1967-69; Techn. Dir, 1969-71; Head of Prod. Div., SIPM, The Hague, 1971-72; Chm. and Managing Dir, Shell-BP Petr. Develt Co. of Nigeria, 1972-76; Co-ordinator, Exploration and Prod., SIPM, The Hague, 1976-. *Address:* (home) Groot Haesebroekseweg 21, Wassenaar, Holland. *T:* 01751-78767; (office) Carel van Bylandtlaan 30, The Hague, Holland. *T:* 070-773766.

VARAH, (Doris) Susan, OBE 1976; Central President of The Mothers' Union, 1970-76; *b* 29 Oct. 1916; *d* of Harry W. and Matilda H. Whanslaw; *m* 1940, Rev. (Edward) Chad Varah, *qv*; four *s* (three of them triplets) one *d. Educ:* Trinity Coll. of Music. Mothers' Union: Diocesan Pres., Southwark, 1956-64; Vice-Chm., Central Young Members' Cttee, 1962-64; Central Vice-Pres., 1962-70; Vice-Chm., Central Social Problems Cttee, 1965-67, Chm., 1970-76; Chm., Central Overseas Cttee, 1968-70. *Recreations:* music, gardening, motoring. *Address:* 42 Hillersdon Avenue, SW13. *T:* 01-876 5720.

VARAH, Rev. Preb. (Edward) Chad, OBE 1969; Founder, The Samaritans (to befriend the suicidal and despairing), 1953, President of London Branch, since 1974 (Director, 1953-74), Chairman, Befrienders International (Samaritans Worldwide), since 1970; Rector, Lord Mayor's Parish Church of St Stephen Walbrook, in the City of London, since 1953; a Prebendary of St Paul's Cathedral, since 1975; *b* 12 Nov. 1911; *e s* of Canon William Edward Varah, Vicar of Barton-on-Humber, and Mary (*née* Atkinson); *m* 1940, Doris Susan Whanslaw (*see* D. S. Varah); four *s* (three of them triplets) one *d. Educ:* Worksop Coll., Notts; Keble Coll., Oxford; Lincoln Theol. Coll. Exhibnr in Nat. Sci. (Keble); BA Oxon (Hons in PPE), 1933, MA 1943. Deacon, 1935, Priest, 1936. Curate of: St Giles, Lincoln, 1935-38; Putney, 1938-40; Barrow-in-Furness, 1940-42; Vicar of: Holy Trinity, Blackburn, 1942-49; St Paul, Clapham Junction, 1949-53. Staff Scriptwriter-Visualiser for Eagle and Girl, 1950-61; Sec., Orthodox Churches Aid Fund, 1952-69; Pres., Cttee for Publishing Russian Orthodox Church Music, 1960-76; Chm., The Samaritans (Inc.), 1963-66; Pres., Internat. Fedn for Services of Emergency Telephonic Help, 1964-67. Hon. Liveryman, Worshipful Co. of Carmen, 1977. Roumanian Patriarchal Cross, 1968. Albert Schweitzer Gold Medal, 1972; Louis Dublin Award, Amer. Assoc. Suicidology, 1974. *Publications:* Notny Sbornik Russkogo Pravoslavnogo Tserkovnogo Peniya, vol. 1 Bozhestveniya Liturgia, 1962, vol. 2 Pt 1 Vsenoshchnaya, 1975; (ed) The Samaritans in the 70s, 1973, rev. edn, 1977; Telephone Masturbators, 1976; Befriending, 1977. *Recreations:* opposing censorship, photography, growing dahlias. *Address:* St Stephen's Church, Walbrook, EC4N 8BN; 39 Walbrook, EC4N 8BP. *T:* 01-283 4444 and 01-626 2277. *Clubs:* Sion College (EC4); Oxford Union.

VARAH, Susan; *see* Varah, Doris S.

VARLEY, Rt. Hon. Eric Graham, PC 1974; MP (Lab) Chesterfield, since 1964; Secretary of State for Industry, since 1975; *b* 11 Aug. 1932; *s* of Frank Varley, retired miner, and Eva Varley; *m* 1955, Marjorie Turner; one *s. Educ:* Secondary Modern and Technical Schools; Ruskin Coll., Oxford. Apprentice Engineer's Turner, 1947-52; Engineer's Turner, 1952-55; Mining Industry (Coal) Craftsman, 1955-64. National Union of Mineworkers: Branch Sec., 1955-64; Mem. Area Exec. Cttee, Derbyshire, 1956-64. Asst Govt Whip, 1967-68; PPS to the Prime Minister, 1968-69; Minister of State, Min. of Technology, 1969-70; Chm., Trade Union Gp of Labour MPs, 1971-74; Sec. of State for Energy, 1974-75. *Recreations:* reading, gardening, music, sport. *Address:* House of Commons, SW1. *T:* 01-219 3000.

VARLEY, George Copley, MA, PhD Cantab, MA Oxon; Hope Professor of Zoology (Entomology), Oxford, 1948-77; *b* 19 Nov.

1910; s of late George Percy Varley and Elsie Mary Varley (née Sanderson); m 1955, Dr Margaret Elizabeth Brown; one s one d. Educ: Manchester Grammar Sch.; Sidney Sussex Coll., Cambridge. Scholar of Sidney Sussex Coll., 1929-33; First Class in both parts of Nat. Sci. Tripos, Frank Smart Prizeman in Zoology, 1933; Research Student, 1933-35; Research Fellow, Sidney Sussex Coll., 1935-38; Hon. Research Fellow, University of California, 1937-38. Supt of Entomological Field Station, Cambridge, 1933-37; University Demonstrator in Zoology, Cambridge, and Curator of Insects in the University Museum of Zoology, 1938-45. Experimental Officer, and later Senior Experimental Officer in Army Operational Research Gp, Min. of Supply, studying centimetric radar on South Coast, 1941-45. Reader in Entomology, King's Coll., Newcastle upon Tyne, 1945-48; Fellow of Jesus Coll., Oxford, 1948-. Publications: (with G. R. Gradwell and M. P. Hassell) Insect Population Ecology, 1973; various papers on insects and population dynamics in scientific periodicals. Recreations: games included squash racquets, tennis, etc; sedentary pastimes included sailing, gliding, ski-ing; now reduced to gardening. Address: 18 Apsley Road, Oxford OX2 7QY. T: Oxford 56988.

VARNAM, Ivor, CEng, FIEE; Deputy Director, Royal Armament Research and Development Establishment, since 1974; b 12 Aug. 1922; s of Walter Varnam and Gertrude Susan Varnam (née Vincent); m 1942, Doris May Thomas; two s. Educ: Alleyn's Coll., Dulwich; University Coll., Cardiff; Birkbeck Coll., London. BSc Wales 1944; BSc (Hons) London 1952; CEng, FIEE 1973. Served War, RAF, 1940-46 (commnd 1944). Joined Tannoy Products, 1946; Atomic Energy Research Estabt, 1947; Siemens Bros., 1948; Royal Armament Research and Development Estabt, 1953-60 and 1962- (Defence Research Staff, Washington, USA, 1960-62), as: Supt Mil. ADP Br., 1964; Supt GW Br., 1967; Prin. Supt Systems Div., 1969; Head, Applied Physics Dept, 1972. Publications: official reports. Recreations: gardening, photography, bridge, music. Address: Fort Halstead, Sevenoaks, Kent TN14 7BP. T: Sevenoaks 55211.

VARVILL, Michael Hugh, CMG 1959; b 29 Sept. 1909; s of Dr Bernard and Maud Varvill; unmarried. Educ: Marlborough; New Coll., Oxford (Scholar; BA). Appointed to Colonial Service, Nigeria, 1932; seconded to Colonial Office, 1943-47; Senior District Officer, 1951; Nigeria, Permanent Secretary: Ministry of Transport, 1952; Ministry of Works, 1953-54; and again (Federal) Ministry of Transport, 1955, retired 1960. With G. Bell & Sons, publishers, 1960-73 (Dir, 1963-73). Recreations: tennis, hockey, chess. Address: 125 Marsham Court, Marsham Street, SW1. Club: Travellers'.

VASARY, Tamàs; pianist and conductor; b 8 Nov. 1933; s of Jozsef Vàsàry and Elizabeth (née Baltazàr); m 1967, Ildiko (née Kovàcs). Educ: Franz Liszt Music Academy, Budapest. First concert at age of 8 in Debrecen, Hungary; First Prize, Franz Liszt Competition, Budapest, 1947; prizes at internat. competitions in Warsaw, Paris, Brussels, Rio de Janeiro; Bach and Paderewski medals, London, 1961; début in London, 1961, in Carnegie Hall, NY, 1961; plays with major orchestras and at festivals in Europe, USA, Australasia and Far East; 3 world tours. Conducting debut, 1970; conducts in Europe and USA. Records Chopin, Debussy, Liszt, Rachmaninov (in Germany). Recreations: yoga, writing, sports. Address: 9 Village Road, N3. T: 01-346 2381.

VASCONCELLOS, Josephina de, FRBS; Founder Member, Society of Portrait Sculptors; Founder, Outpost Emmaus; Hon. Liaison for New Projects for Offenders (Combined Action Now—CAN: Beached Trawler adapted for Nature-observation Base for Young Disabled), under Church of England Council for Social Aid; d of late H. H. de Vasconcellos, Brazilian Consul-General in England, and Freda Coleman; m 1930, Delmar Banner, painter. Educ: sculpture: London, Paris, Florence; Royal Academy Schools. Works: High Altar and Statue, Varengeville, Normandy, 1925; Bronze St Hubert, Nat. Gall. of Brazil, 1926; Music in Trees, in stone, Southampton Gall., 1933; Ducks, in marble, Glasgow Art Gall., 1946; Refugees, in stone, Sheffield Art Gall., 1949; Episcopal Crozier in Perspex, for Bishop of Bristol, 1948. Exhibits RA, Leicester Galls. Exhibn with husband, of 46 sculptures in 20 materials at RWS Gall., 1947; Last Chimera, Canongate Kirk, Edinburgh; 8ft Christ (in Portland Stone), Nat. War Meml to Battle of Britain, Aldershot, 1950. Two works, Festival of Britain, Lambeth Palace, 1951; Sculpture Exhibn, with husband, RWS Galls, 1955; War Memorial, St Bees School, 1955; two figures, St Bees Priory, 1955; life-size Mary and Child and design group of 11 sculptures by 11 collaborators, for Nativity, St Paul's Cathedral, Christmas 1955; Mary and Child bought for St Paul's, 1956; life-size Resurrection for St Mary, Westfield, Workington, 1956-57;

Madonna and Child, St James's, Piccadilly, 1957; Rising Christ in St Bartholomew the Great, Smithfield; Winter, carving in Perspex, Oldham Gallery, 1958; Nativity (for ruins of Coventry Cathedral), 1958; Flight into Egypt, for St Martin-in-the-Fields, 1958 (now in Cartmel Priory); War Memorial, Reredos of carved oak, Rossall School Chapel, 1959; Nativity Set, life-size figures, St Martin-in-the-Fields, annually in Trafalgar Sq.; Winged Victory Crucifix, Clewer Church, 1964, and Canongate Kirk, Edinburgh; life-size Holy Family, Liverpool Cathedral and Gloucester Cathedral, 1965; life-size Virgin and Child, Blackburn Cathedral, 1974; Reunion, Bradford Univ., 1977; sculptures at Dallas, Tulsa, Chicago, USA; Portraits: bronze of Lord Denning, 1969; Bishop Fleming; Rev. Austen Williams and Mario Borelli. Documentary film Out of Nature (on her work), 1949; BBC programme, Viewpoint TV, 1968. Pres., Guild of Lakeland Craftsmen, 1971-73. Hon. Member, Glider Pilots Regimental Assoc. Prize for Track Gliding for the Disabled (gear based on climbing and sailing to enable more scope in movement), Cognitive Res. Trust, Cambridge and Perstorp Res. Foundn, Sweden, 1975. Hon. DLitt Bradford, 1977. Publications: Woodcut illustrations for The Cup (Poems by F. Johnson), 1938; contrib. to They Became Christians (ed Dewi Morgan), 1966. Recreation: working on Jeu Libre (new methods of movements for blind and handicapped children). Address: The Bield, Little Langdale, Ambleside, Cumbria LA22 9PD. T: Langdale 254. Club: Reynolds.

VASEY, Sir Ernest (Albert), KBE 1959; CMG 1945; Financial and Economic Adviser, World Bank Development Service, 1962-66; Resident Representative, IBRD, Pakistan, 1963-66; b 27 Aug. 1901; m 1st, 1923, Norah May Mitchell; one s; 2nd, 1944, Hannah Strauss; one s. Member Shrewsbury Town Council, England. Mayor of Nairobi, 1941-42, 1944-46; Member Kenya Legislative Council for Nairobi North, 1945-50; Member for Education, Health and Local Government for Kenya, 1950; Minister for Finance and Development, Kenya, 1951-59; Minister for Finance and Economics, Tanganyika, 1959-60; Minister for Finance, Tanganyika, 1960-62. Brilliant Star of Zanzibar, 2nd Class, 1955; Hilal-i-Quaid-i-Azam (Pakistan), 1966. Address: Box 14235, Nairobi, Kenya.

VASSAR-SMITH, Major Sir Richard Rathborne, 3rd Bt, cr 1917; TD; RA; Partner at St Ronan's Preparatory School, since 1957; b 24 Nov. 1909; s of late Major Charles Martin Vassar-Smith (2nd s of 1st Bt); S uncle, 1942; m 1932, Mary Dawn, d of late Sir Raymond Woods, CBE; one s one d. Educ: Lancing; Pembroke College, Cambridge. Employed by Lloyds Bank Ltd, 1932-37; Schoolmaster, 1938-39. War of 1939-45, Major, RA. Recreation: Association football (Cambridge, 1928-31). Heir: s John Rathborne Vassar-Smith [b 23 July 1936; m 1971, Roberta Elaine, y d of Wing Comdr N. Williamson; one s]. Address: Orchard House, Hawkhurst, Kent. T: Hawkhurst 2300. Clubs: Royal Automobile; Hawks (Cambridge); Rye Golf.

VAUGHAN, family name of **Earl of Lisburne.**

VAUGHAN, Viscount; David John Francis Malet Vaughan; b 15 June 1945; e s of 8th Earl of Lisburne, qv. Educ: Ampleforth Coll. Address: The Old Church House, Cross, Isle of Lewis.

VAUGHAN, Rt. Rev. Benjamin Noel Young; see Swansea and Brecon, Bishop of.

VAUGHAN, David Wyamar, CBE 1962; b 15 July 1906; s of late Dr W. W. Vaughan, MVO, DLitt and Margaret, d of J. Addington Symonds; m 1st, 1928, Norah (d 1963), d of late J. H. Burn; two s one d; 2nd, 1966, Mrs Joy Beebee. Educ: Rugby. Joined Barclays Bank, 1930, Director, London Board, 1953-77; Local Director: Shrewsbury, 1934; Cardiff, 1939-72; Swansea, 1945-57; Windsor, 1972-77. Served War of 1939-45, with Welsh Guards, 1940-45, resigned with rank of Major. Treas., Univ. Coll. of S Wales and Monmouthshire, 1951-67; Mem. Court, Univ. of Wales, 1957-67; Hon. Treas., Welsh Nat. Sch. of Medicine, 1962-67. Dir and Treas., Empire and Commonwealth Games, 1958. Chm. Finance Cttee, Representative Body Church in Wales, 1955-76; Trustee, Historic Churches Preservation Trust; Mem., Churches Main Cttee. JP County Glamorgan, 1956-66. High Sheriff of Glamorgan, 1963. LLD Univ. of Wales, 1965. Recreations: shooting, fishing and all country pursuits. Address: The Old Rectory, Wherwell, Hants. T: Chilbolton 270. Club: Boodle's.

VAUGHAN, Sir Edgar; see Vaughan, Sir G. E.

VAUGHAN, Elizabeth, (Mrs Ray Brown), FRAM; international operatic soprano; b Llanfyllin, Montgomeryshire, 12 March 1937; m 1968, Ray Brown; one s one d. Educ: Llanfyllin Grammar Sch.; RAM. ARAM, LRAM; Kathleen Ferrier Prize.

Mem., Incorp. Soc. of Musicians. Has sung leading roles in: Benvenuto Cellini; La Bohème; Midsummer Night's Dream; Madame Butterfly; Otello; Rigoletto; Simon Boccanegra; La Traviata; Il Trovatore; Turandot; Don Giovanni; Un Ballo in Maschera; Ernani; Nabucco; Aida; Cassandra. Has appeared with: Royal Opera; Vienna State Opera; Berlin State Opera; Hamburg State Opera; Metropolitan Opera, NY. Has toured in: Europe; S Africa; USA; Australia; Canada and Japan. *Recreations:* tennis, driving, cookery. *Address:* c/o S. A. Gorlinsky Ltd, 35 Dover Street, W1; Plas Dyffryn, Oswestry, Salop. *T:* Oswestry 3445.

VAUGHAN, Ernest James, CBE 1961; retired as Director of Materials Research, Royal Naval Scientific Service; *b* 19 Oct. 1901; 3rd *s* of late James and Helena Vaughan; *m* 1927, Marjorie Solly; one *s* decd. *Educ:* Brockley; London University. BSc, MSc London; ARCS; DIC. Jun. Chemist, War Dept; Chemist, 1925-27; Chemist, Chemical Dept, Portsmouth Dockyard, 1927-36; Dep. Supt, then Supt, Bragg Laboratory, 1936-49; Dep. Dir, then Dir of Materials Research, Royal Naval Scientific Service, 1949-66. Hon. Treas., Royal Inst. of Chemistry, 1963-72. *Publications:* Protective Coatings for Metals, 1946; (monograph) Metallurgical Analysis; papers in learned jls. *Address:* Flat 2, Ashmede, 56 West Cliff Road, Bournemouth, Dorset BH4 8BE. *T:* Bournemouth 764232. *Club:* Savage.

VAUGHAN, Sir (George) Edgar, KBE 1963 (CBE 1956; OBE 1937); *b* 24 Feb. 1907; *s* of late William John Vaughan, BSc, of Cardiff, and Emma Kate Caudle; *m* 1933, Elsie Winifred Deubert; one *s* two *d. Educ:* Cheltenham Grammar Sch.; Jesus Coll., Oxford (Exhibitioner and later Hon. Scholar; Hon. Fellow, 1966). 1st Cl. Honour School of Mod. Hist., 1928; 1st Cl. Honour School of Philosophy, Politics and Economics, 1929; Laming Travelling Fellow of the Queen's College, Oxford, 1929-31. Entered Consular Service, 1930; Vice-Consul at: Hamburg, 1931; La Paz, 1932-35; Barcelona, 1935-38; Buenos Aires, 1938-44; Chargé d'Affaires, Monrovia, 1945-46; Consul at Seattle, Washington, 1946-49; Consul-General at Lourenço Marques, 1949-53, Amsterdam, 1953-56; Minister and Consul-General at Buenos Aires, 1956-60; Ambassador, 1960-63 and Consul-General, 1963, at Panama; Ambassador to Colombia, 1964-66. Retired from Diplomatic Service, 1966. Univ. of Saskatchewan, Regina Campus: Special Lectr, 1966-67; Prof. of History, 1967-74; Dean of Arts and Science, 1969-73. FRHistS 1965. *Recreation:* golf. *Address:* 27 Birch Grove, W3 9SP. *Club:* Travellers'.

VAUGHAN, Gerard Folliott, FRCP; MP (C) Reading South, since 1974 (Reading, 1970-74); Physician, Guy's Hospital; *b* Xinavane, Portuguese E Africa, 11 June 1923; *s* of late Leonard Vaughan, DSO, DFC, and Joan Vaughan (née Folliott); *m* 1955, Joyce Thurle (née Laver); one *s* one *d. Educ:* privately in E Africa; London Univ.; Guy's Hosp. MB, BS 1947; MRCP 1949; Academic DPM London 1952; FRCP 1966; FRCPsych 1972. Consultant Staff, Guy's Hosp., 1958. Mem., MRC, 1973-76; Alderman: LCC, 1955-61; LCC Streatham, 1961-64; GLC Lambeth, 1966-70; GLC, 1970-72; Chm., Strategic Planning Cttee GLC, 1968-71; Mem., SE Economic Planning Council, 1968-71. Governor, UCL, 1959-68. Liveryman, Worshipful Co. of Barbers. Contested (C) Poplar, 1955. *Publications:* various professional and general literary publications. *Recreation:* painting. *Address:* House of Commons, SW1. *Club:* Carlton.

VAUGHAN, Henry William Campbell, JP; Lord Provost of the City of Dundee, since 1977; *b* 15 March 1919; *s* of Harry Skene Vaughan and Flora Lamont Campbell Blair; *m* 1947, Margaret Cowie Flett; one *s* one *d. Educ:* Dundee Training Coll.; Logie and Stobswell Secondary Schools. Apprentice Stationer, Burns & Harris, 1934-39; RAF (Volunteer Reserve), 1939-46; Chief Buyer, Messrs Valentine & Son, Fine Art Publishers, Dundee, 1946-64; Group Purchasing Officer, Scott & Robertson (Tay Textiles Ltd), 1964-75; Stationery Manager, Burns & Harris Ltd, Dundee, 1975-. Mem., Inst. of Purchasing and Supply. JP Dundee, 1969. Silver Jubilee Medal, 1977. *Recreations:* cine photography, fishing, water colour painting, sketching. *Address:* 15 Fraser Street, Dundee. *T:* Dundee 86175.

VAUGHAN, Hilda, (Mrs Charles Morgan); novelist; *b* Builth, Breconshire, 1892; *d* of late Hugh Vaughan Vaughan; *m* 1923, Charles Morgan, LLD, FRSL (*d* 1958); one *s* one *d. Educ:* privately. FRSL 1963. *Publications:* The Battle to the Weak; Here Are Lovers; The Invader; Her Father's House; The Soldier and the Gentlewoman; A Thing of Nought; The Curtain Rises; Harvest Home; Pardon and Peace; Iron and Gold; The Candle and the Light. *Plays:* She, too, was Young; Forsaking All Other (both with Laurier Lister); Introduction to Thomas Traherne's Centuries. *Address:* c/o Roger Morgan, 30 St Peter's Square, W6 9UH.

See also Marchioness of Anglesey, Roger H. V. C. Morgan.

VAUGHAN, Dame Janet (Maria), DBE 1957 (OBE 1944); DM, FRCP; Principal of Somerville College, Oxford, 1945-67, Hon. Fellow since 1967; *b* 18 October 1899; *d* of William Wyamar Vaughan and Margaret Symonds; *m* 1930, David Gourlay (*d* 1963); two *d. Educ:* North Foreland Lodge; Somerville College, Oxford; University College Hospital (Goldsmith Entrance Scholar). Asst Clinical Pathologist, Univ. Coll. Hosp.; Rockefeller Fellowship, 1929-30; Beit Memorial Fellowship, 1930-33; Leverhulme Fellow, RCP, 1933-34; Asst in Clinical Pathology, British Post-Graduate Medical School, 1934-39; Mem. Inter-Departmental Cttee on Medical Schools, 1942; Nuffield Trustee, 1943; late Medical Officer in charge North-West London Blood Supply Depot for Medical Research Council. Mem., Royal Commn on Equal Pay, 1944; Chm., Oxford Regional Hosp. Board, 1950-51 (Vice-Chm. 1948); Member: Cttee on Economic and Financial Problems of Provision for Old Age, 1953-54; Medical Adv. Cttee of University Grants Cttee; University Grants Cttee on Libraries; Commonwealth Scholarship Commn in the UK. Fogarty Scholar, NIH, 1973. Osler Meml Medal, Univ. of Oxford. Hon. DSc: Wales, 1960; Leeds, 1973; Hon. DCL: Oxford, 1967; London, 1968; Bristol, 1971. *Publications:* The Anæmias, 1st edn 1934, 2nd edn 1936; The Physiology of Bone, 1969, 2nd edn 1975; The Effects of Irradiation on the Skeleton, 1973; numerous papers in scientific jls on blood diseases, blood transfusion and metabolism of strontium and plutonium isotopes; section on leukæmias, Brit. Encyc. Med. Pract.; section on blood transfusion in British Surgical Practice, 1945. *Recreations:* travel, gardening. *Address:* 1 Fairlawn End, First Turn, Wolvercote, Oxford. *T:* Oxford 54111.

VAUGHAN, John Godfrey, FCA; Chairman, The Charterhouse Group Ltd, 1971-77; *b* 2 May 1916; *s* of Charles Godfrey Vaughan and Mabel Rose Hart; *m* 1st, 1948, Barbara Josephine Knowles (*d* 1967); one *d*; 2nd, 1969, Lucia Maria Boer. *Educ:* Bedford Sch. Served War: with 4th Queens Own Hussars in Greece, N Africa, Italy and Austria, 1939-45 (2nd i/comd, 1944). Joined The Charterhouse Group Ltd, 1946; Dir, 1953; Dep. Chm., 1968-71; Chm., 1971-; Dir, George Kent Ltd, 1961, Dep. Chm., 1963, Chm., 1970-74; Chm., Brown Boveri Kent Ltd, 1974-; Dir, Slough Estates, 1968-. *Recreations:* racing, tennis, reading, theatre. *Address:* 55 Cumberland Terrace, NW1. *Clubs:* Cavalry and Guards, City of London.

VAUGHAN, (John) Keith, CBE 1965; painter, designer, illustrator; Tutor at Slade School of Art, London; *b* 23 Aug. 1912; *e s* of E. G. S. Vaughan, civil engineer, and Gladys Regina Marion (née Mackintosh); unmarried. *Educ:* Christ's Hospital. Mem. Faculty of Painting, British School at Rome, 1962; Advisory Cttee for Painting, Gulbenkian Foundation, 1964; Hon. Fellow Royal Coll. of Art, 1964. First exhibited at Lefevre Gallery, 1942. One-man shows at following galleries: Lefevre, 1944, 1946, 1948, 1951; Redfern, 1950, 1952; Hanover, 1951; Durlacher, New York, 1948, 1952, 1955, 1957, 1966; Inst. of Modern Art, Buenos Aires, 1950; Leicester Galls, London, 1953, 1955, 1956, 1958, 1959; Matthiesen Gall., London, 1960; Whitechapel Art Gall., 1962; Sao Paulo Bienal, 1963; Marlborough Gall., London, 1964, 1965, 1969; Waddington Galls, 1973, 1974. Works in many public collections of UK, USA, Australia, New Zealand, and Israel. Executed, central mural in Dome of Discovery, Festival of Britain, 1951; mural for Aboyne Estate, Wandsworth, 1963 (LCC Commn). Member of Arts Panel, Arts Council of Great Britain, 1956, 1959. *Publications:* books illustrated: Tom Sawyer, 1947; Rimbaud, Une Saison en Enfer, 1949; Journal and Drawings, 1939-65, 1966. *Address:* 9 Belsize Park, NW3; Harrow Hill, Toppesfield, Halstead, Essex.

VAUGHAN, Keith; see Vaughan, John Keith.

VAUGHAN, William Randal; Founder and Proprietor, W.R. Vaughan Ltd, and Vaughan Associates Ltd, since 1945; *b* 11 March 1912; *m* 1945, K. A. Headland; three *s* and *d. Educ:* Centaur Trade School, Coventry. FIProdE. Apprenticed, Alfred Herbert Ltd, 1926; Coventry Gauge & Tool Co. Ltd, 1933; A. C. Wickman Ltd, 1934; A. Pattison Ltd, 1942; C. G. Wade Ltd, London, 1943. Chairman, Machine Tool Industry Research Assoc., 1974; President, Machine Tool Trades Assoc., 1977-79. Member of Lloyds. *Recreations:* squash, skiing, sailing, flying. *Address:* 4 Queen Street, Mayfair, W1. *T:* 01-499 8362. *Clubs:* Lansdowne, RAC.

VAUGHAN-HUGHES, Brig. Gerald Birdwood, MC 1918; DL; JP; retired 1948; *b* 14 April 1896; *s* of Gerald Mainwaring Vaughan-Hughes and Isabel Bridget Crawford (née Birdwood); *m* 1927, Violet Mary Jessie (*d* 1968), *d* of Maj.-Gen. W. H. Kay, CB, DSO; two *s. Educ:* Wellington College; RMA Woolwich. Served European War, 1914-18 (wounded thrice, despatches,

MC); RHA and RFA, 2nd Lt, 1914; RHA, 1916; India, RFA, 1919-28; Capt. 1926; ADC to C-in-C India, 1927-28; RHA, 1930; Staff Coll., 1931-32; Maj. 1934; SO: RA Southern Comd, 1934-35; Aldershot, 1936-37; GSO2, Palestine, 1939. War of 1939-45, AAG, Palestine, Greece and Crete, 1941; GSO1 RA, ME, 1941; Comdg Northumberland Hussars and II RHA, 1941-42; CRA (Brig.) 7th Armoured Div., 1942 (despatches twice), retired. DL 1958, JP 1956, High Sheriff, 1960, Monmouthshire. *Address:* Wyelands, Chepstow, Gwent. *T:* Chepstow 2127.

VAUGHAN-JACKSON, Oliver James, VRD 1951; FRCS; Visiting Professor in Orthopaedics, Memorial University of Newfoundland, 1971-73; Senior Consultant in Orthopaedics at St John's General Hospital, St Clare Mercy Hospital and Janeway Child Health Centre, St John's, Newfoundland, 1971-73; Consulting Orthopaedic Surgeon to London Hospital, since 1971; *b* 6 July 1907; *e s* of Surgeon Captain P. Vaughan-Jackson, RN, Carramore, Ballina, County Mayo; *m* 1939, Joan Madeline, *er d* of E. A. Bowring, CBE, St Johns, Newfoundland; two *s*. *Educ:* Berkhamsted School; Balliol Coll., Oxford; The London Hospital. Kitchener Scholar; BA, BM, BCh Oxon, 1932; MRCS, LRCP, 1932; FRCS 1936. House Physician, Demonstrator of Pathology, House Surgeon, Resident Accoucheur, and Surgical Registrar at The London Hosp. Surgeon Lieut-Comdr RNVR, Retd, Surgical specialist, Roy. Naval Hosp., Sydney, Australia. Sen. Registrar (Orthopædic), The London Hosp.; Orthopaedic Surgeon to: The London Hosp., 1946-71; St Bartholomew's Hosp., Rochester, 1947-70; Medway Hosp., 1970-71; Claybury Mental Hosp., 1946-64; Halliwick Cripples Sch., 1946-71; Cons. In Orthopaedics to Royal Navy, 1956-71. Fellow: British Orthopædic Assoc.; RSM (Pres., Section of Orthopædics, 1968-69); Med. Soc. London; Member: Soc. Internat. de Chirurgie Orthopédique et de Traumatologie; British Soc. for Surgery of the Hand. Former Mem., Editorial Board of Jl of Bone and Joint Surgery. Hon. DSc Memorial Univ. of Newfoundland, 1973. *Publications:* Sections on: Arthrodesis (Maingot's Techniques in British Surgery), 1950; Arthrodesis of the Hip, and Osteotomy of the Upper End of Femur (Operative Surgery, ed Rob and Smith), 1958; Surgery of the Hand; Orthopædic Surgery in Spastic conditions; Peripheral Nerve Injuries (Textbook of British Surgery, ed Sir Henry Souttar and Prof. J. C. Goligher), 1959; The Rheumatoid Hand; Carpal Tunnel Compression of the Median Nerve (Clinical Surgery, ed Rob and Smith), 1966; Surgery in Arthritis of the Hand, in Textbook of Rheumatic Diseases, 1968; The Rheumatoid Hand, in Operative Surgery, 2nd edn, 1971; contribs to Jl of Bone and Joint Surgery, etc. *Recreations:* gardening, photography. *Address:* The White Cottage, Bowesden Lane, Shorne, near Gravesend, Kent DA12 3LA. *T:* Shorne 2321. *Club:* Naval and Military.

VAUGHAN-MORGAN, family name of **Baron Reigate.**

VAUGHAN-THOMAS, (Lewis John) Wynford, OBE 1974; MA Oxon; radio and television commentator since 1937; author, journalist; Director, Harlech Television Ltd; *b* 15 Aug. 1908; *s* of Dr David Vaughan-Thomas and Morfydd Vaughan-Thomas; *m* 1946, Charlotte Rowlands, MBE; one *s*. *Educ:* Swansea Grammar Sch.; Exeter College, Oxford. Keeper of MSS and Records, National Library of Wales, 1933; Area Officer, S Wales Council of Social Service, 1934-37; joined BBC, 1937. Dir of Programmes, Harlech Television Ltd, 1968-71. Commentator, Royal Commonwealth Tours, BBC War Correspondent, 1942-45; Governor, BFI, 1977-. Croix de Guerre, 1945. *Publications:* Royal Tour, 1953-54, 1954; Anzio, 1961; Madly in all Directions, 1967; (with Alun Llewellyn) The Shell Guide to Wales, 1969; The Splendour Falls, 1973; Gower, 1975. *Recreations:* mountaineering, sailing. *Address:* (home) 51 Belsize Avenue, NW3. *T:* 01-794 3525. *Clubs:* Climbers', Savile.

VAUTELET, Renée G., (Mme H. E.), CBE 1943; *b* 27 July 1897; *d* of Aimé Geoffrion, KC; *m* Lt-Col Henri Vautelet (*d* 1964), lately head of Insurance Brokerage firm of O'Halloran & Vautelet; two *d*. *Educ:* private. Hon. LLD Concordia Univ., 1975. *Recreations:* painting, writing. *Address:* 16 Bellevue Avenue, Westmount, Montreal 6, Quebec, Canada. *T:* Hunter 8-1622.

VAUX OF HARROWDEN, 10th Baron *cr* 1523; **John Hugh Philip Gilbey;** *b* 4 Aug. 1915; 2nd *s* of William Gordon Gilbey (*d* 1965) and Grace Mary Eleanor, 8th Baroness Vaux of Harrowden (*d* 1958); *S* brother, 1977; *m* 1939, Maureen Pamela, *e d* of Hugh Gilbey; three *s* one *d*. *Educ:* Ampleforth College; Christ Church, Oxford (BA 1937). Formerly Major, Duke of Wellington's Regt; served War of 1939-45. *Heir: s* Hon. Anthony William Gilbey [*b* 25 May 1940; *m* 1964, Beverley Anne, *o d* of Charles Alexander Walton; two *s* one *d*]. *Address:* Cholmondeley Cottage, 2 Cholmondeley Walk, Richmond, Surrey.

VAVASOUR, Comdr Sir Geoffrey William, 5th Bt *cr* 1828; DSC 1943; RN (retired); a Director of W. M. Still & Sons; *b* 5 Sept. 1914; *s* of Captain Sir Leonard Vavasour, 4th Bt, RN, and Ellice Margaret Nelson; *S* father, 1961; *m* 1st, 1940, Joan Robb (marr. diss. 1947); two *d*; 2nd, 1971, Marcia Christine, *d* of late Marshall Lodge, Batley, Yorks. *Educ:* RNC Dartmouth. *Heir: kinsman* Hugh Bernard Moore Vavasour [*b* 4 July 1918; *m* 1950, Monique Pauline Marie Madeleine, *d* of Maurice Erick Beck; one *s* one *d*]. *Address:* 8 Bede House, Manor Fields, Putney, SW15. *Clubs:* Hurlingham; MCC, Royal Wimbledon Golf, All England Lawn Tennis.

VEAL, Group Captain John Bartholomew, CBE 1956; AFC 1940; Civil Aviation Safety Adviser, Department of Trade and Industry, 1972-74, retired; *b* 28 September 1909; *er s* of John Henry and Sarah Grace Veal; *m* 1933, Enid Marjorie Hill; two *s*. *Educ:* Christ's Hosp. Special trainee, Metropolitan-Vickers, 1926-27; commissioned in RAF as pilot officer, 1927; served in Nos 4 and 501 Squadrons and as flying Instructor at Central Flying School, transferring to RAFO, 1932; Flying-Instructor, Chief Flying Instructor, and Test Pilot, Air Service Training Ltd, 1932-39; recalled to regular RAF service, 1939; commanded navigation and flying training schools, 1939-43; Air Staff No. 46 Transport Group, 1944 and Transport Command, 1945-46 (despatches); released from RAF, 1946, to become Deputy Director of Training, Ministry of Civil Aviation; Director of Air Safety and Training, 1947; Director of Operations, Safety and Licensing, 1952; Deputy Director-General of Navigational Services, Ministry of Transport and Civil Aviation, 1958; Director-General of Navigational Services, Ministry of Aviation, 1959-62; Chief Inspector of Accidents, Civil Aviation Department, Board of Trade (formerly Min. of Aviation), 1963-68; Dir Gen. of Safety and Operations, DTI (formerly BOT), 1968-72. FRAeS 1967 (AFRAeS 1958). *Recreation:* trout fishing. *Address:* Woodacre, Horsham Road, Cranleigh, Surrey GU6 8DZ. *T:* Cranleigh 4490. *Club:* Royal Air Force.

VEALL, Harry Truman, CB 1963; Controller of Death Duties, Board of Inland Revenue, 1960-64, retired; *b* 19 Feb. 1901; 2nd *s* of late Wright Veall, Ewyas Harold, Herefs, and late Bertha Veall; *m* 1926, Lily Kershaw, *yr d* of Joshua E. Ryder, Alverthorpe, Wakefield, Yorks; two *d*. *Educ:* Wakefield Grammar Sch. LLB (external) London, 1926. Entered Civil Service, 1916; Asst Controller of Death Duties, 1953, Dep. Controller, 1957. *Address:* 20 Wincombe Drive, Ferndown, Dorset BH22 8HX. *T:* Ferndown 874726.

VEASEY, Brig. Harley Gerald, DSO 1939; late The Queen's Royal Regiment; a Vice-President, Surrey County British Legion; *b* 29 Jan. 1896; *o s* of late H. C. Veasey, Ranchi, Bihar; *m* 1922, Iris, *o d* of late W. P. Morrison, Reigate, Surrey; two *d*. *Educ:* Haileybury College. Commissioned TA 1915, 2/5th Battalion The Queen's Royal Regiment, served European War, 1914-18, France (wounded); Regular Commission The Queen's Royal Regiment, 1916; Ireland, 1920-22; adjt 5th Bn The Queen's Royal Regiment, 1922-25; Hong-Kong, 1927; Malta, 1929; North China, 1930-34; Palestine, 1939 (DSO, despatches); Commanding 2nd Bn Northern Rhodesia Regt, Northern Rhodesia and Madagascar, 1940-43; MEC and MLC, Mauritius (as OC Troops), 1943; Temp. Col, Temp. Brig., Comdr 28th EA Inf. Bde, Kenya and Ceylon, 1943-44; commanded 1/7th Bn The Queen's Royal Regt, 1945; 13th Infantry Training Centre, 1946-47; No. 2 PTC 1947-48; retired Sept. 1948, with Hon. rank of Brig. Organising Director of Conservative and Unionist Films Association, 1948-51; Sector Commander, Home Guard (West Surrey), 1952-57. *Address:* Woodhill Cottage, Shamley Green, Guildford, Surrey.

VEASEY, Josephine, CBE 1970; opera singer (mezzo soprano); *b* London, 10 July 1930; *m* (marr. diss.); one *s* one *d*. *Educ:* coached by Audrey Langford, ARCM. Joined chorus of Royal Opera House, Covent Garden, 1949; a Principal there, 1955- (interval on tour, in opera, for Arts Council). Operatic Roles include: Royal Opera House: Octavian in Der Rosenkavalier, 1966; subseq. Cherubino in Figaro (Glyndebourne also); name role in Iphigenie (Peru also); Dorabella in Cosi fan Tutte; Amneris in Aida (Germany also); 1968-69: Fricka in Die Walküre (Metropolitan, New York, and Scala, Milan also); Fricka in Das Rheingold (Met., NY, also); name role in Carmen; Dido and Cassandra in the Trojans (Dido in Paris also); Marguerite in The Damnation of Faust (Geneva), 1969; Charlotte in The Sorrows of Werther (Glyndebourne and Paris also) 1969; Eboli, Don Carlos (Royal Opera House; Berlin and Munich also), 1970; name role, Orfeo (Barcelona), 1970; Kundry in Parsifal, Paris Opera, 1973; name role in Norma, Geneva and Orange Festival. Concerts, 1960-70 (Conductors included Giulini, Bernstein, Solti, Mehta, Sargent). Verdi's

Requiem; Monteverdi's Combattimento di Tancredi e Clorinda, Aix Festival, 1967; various works of Mahler; two tours of Israel (Solti); subseq. sang in Los Angeles (Mehta); then Berlioz: Death of Cleopatra, Royal Festival Hall, and L'enfance dù Christ, London and Paris; Rossini's Petite Messe Solennelle, London and Huddersfield (with late Sir Malcolm Sargent); Handel's Messiah, England, Munich, Oporto, Lisbon; Berlioz' Romeo and Juliette, London, and Bergen Festival; Rossini's Stabat Mater, Festival d'Angers and London. 1971; some of above, and also Berlioz' Beatrice and Benedict, NY, and London; Emperor in 1st perf. Henze's We Come to the River, Covent Garden, 1976. Has sung Elgar's Dream of Gerontius all over England. Frequently makes recordings. Hon. RAM, 1972. *Recreations:* reading, gardening. *Address:* 13 Ballards Farm Road, South Croydon, Surrey CR2 7JB. *T:* 01-657 8158.

VEIL, Simone Annie, Chevalier de l'Ordre national du Mérite; Magistrate; Minister of Health, France, since 1974; *b* Nice, 13 July 1927; *d* of André Jacob and Yvonne (*née* Steinmetz); *m* 1946, Antoine Veil, Inspecteur des Finances, Director General of UTA; three *s*. *Educ:* Lycée de Nice; Lic. en droit, dipl. de l'Institut d'Etudes Politiques, Paris; qualified as Magistrate, 1956. Deported to Auschwitz and Berjen-Belsen, Belsen, March 1944-May 1945. Ministry of Justice, 1957-69; Technical Advr to Office of Keeper of the Seals, 1969; Gen.-Sec., Conseil Supérieur de la magistrature, 1970-74. Mem., Administrative Council: ORTF, 1972; Foundation de France, 1972. Médaille Pénitentiaire; Médaille de l'Education Surveillée. Dhc: Princeton, 1975; Institut Weizmann, 1976. *Publication:* (jtly) L'Adoption, données médicales, psychologiques et sociales, 1969. *Address:* 11 place Vauban, 75007 Paris, France.

VENABLES, Sir Peter (Percy Frederick Ronald), Kt 1963; PhD, BSc, FRIC; *b* 5 Aug. 1904; British; *m* 1932, Ethel Craig Howell, MSc (PhD 1956); two *s* two *d*. *Educ:* Liverpool University. BSc 1st Cl. Hons, 1925; Education Diploma, 1926; PhD 1928; Research Fellowship, 1928-30. Lectr and Sen. Lectr, Leicester Coll. of Technology, 1930-36; Head of Science Dept, SE Essex Tech. Coll., 1936-41; Principal: Municipal Coll., Southend-on-Sea, 1941-47; Royal Technical College, Salford, 1947-56; Coll. Advanced Technology, Birmingham, 1956-66; Vice-Chancellor, 1966-69, Univ. Fellow, 1969-72, Univ. of Aston in Birmingham; Chm., Planning Cttee to establish Open Univ., 1967-69; Pro-Chancellor and Chm. of Council, Open Univ., 1969-74. Leverhulme Research Fellowship, 1955-56. Commonwealth Senior Visiting Fellowship, Australia, 1960. President: Assoc. of Principals of Technical Instns, 1952-53; Manchester Literary and Philosophical Soc., 1954-56; Birmingham and Midland Inst., 1969-71; Vice-Pres., BACIE, 1969-73; Pres., Nat. Inst. of Adult Educn, 1971-77; Chairman: Council of Assoc. of Technical Institutions, 1953-54; ITA Adult Education Adv. Cttee, 1965-69; BBC Further Education Adv. Council for the UK, 1965-69; Member: Central Advisory Council for Education (England), 1956-60; Adv. Council on Scientific Policy, 1962-64; Cttee on Manpower Resources, 1965-68; Northern Ireland Cttee on Univ. and Higher Tech. Educn, 1963-64; West Midlands Economic Planning Council, 1965-68; Midlands Electricity Board (part-time), 1967-73. Hon. Fellow: UMIST, 1970; Chelsea Coll., 1973. Hon. DSc: Aston, 1969; Sussex, 1971; DUniv Open Univ., 1973. *Publications:* Technical Education, 1956; Sandwich Courses for training Technologists and Technicians, 1959; British Technical Education, 1959; The Smaller Firm and Technical Education, 1961; papers in educational jls. *Recreations:* varied. *Address:* 15 Forest Road, Moseley, Birmingham B13 9DL. *T:* 021-449 3462. *Club:* Athenæum.

VENABLES-LLEWELYN, Sir John (Michael) Dillwyn-, 4th Bt *cr* 1890; farmer, since 1975; *b* 12 Aug. 1938; *s* of Sir Charles Michael Dillwyn-Venables-Llewelyn, 3rd Bt, MVO, and of Lady Delia Mary Dillwyn-Venables-Llewelyn, *g d* of 1st Earl St Aldwyn; *S* father, 1976; *m* 1st, 1963, Nina (marr. diss. 1972), *d* of late Lt J. S. Hallam; two *d*; 2nd, 1975, Nina Gay Richardson Oliver. *Recreation:* racing vintage cars. *Address:* Talwen Uchaf Farm, Garthbrengy, Brecon, Powys LD3 9TE. *T:* Brecon 4263.

VENEZUELA, Bishop of, since 1976; **Rt. Rev. Haydn Harold Jones;** Dean of St Mary's Cathedral, Caracas; *b* 22 Aug. 1920; *s* of Charles Samuel and Blodwen Jones, Penarth, Glam. *Educ:* Brotherhood of Saint Paul, Barton. RAF, 1941-44. Deacon 1947, priest 1948, Diocese of Bradford. Curate of St Barnabas, Heaton, Bradford, 1947-49; Tor Mohun, Torquay, 1949-51; Chaplain RN, 1951-53; Licence to Officiate, Diocese of London, 1954-62, Diocese of Coventry, 1962-63; Curate of St Peter's, Coventry, 1963-64; Rector of Clutton, Diocese of Bath and Wells, 1964-76, with Cameley, 1975-76; Surrogate, 1972-76. *Recreations:* bridge, films, theatre. *Address:* Bishop's House, Apartado 61, 116 del Este, Caracas, Venezuela. *T:* Caracas 91.47.27.

VENN, Air Commodore George Oswald, CBE 1945; *b* 15 Sept. 1892; *er s* of George Venn, Warrington; *m* 1st, 1923, Betty (*d* 1953), *d* of Alderman T. Stopher, Winchester; two *s* one *d*; 2nd, 1960, Monica, *d* of Rev. J. B. Cholmeley. *Educ:* Boteler Grammar Sch., Warrington. Architecture, 1909-14 (Student RIBA); served European War, 1914-16, Royal Fusiliers (University Public Sch. Bn), 1916-45, RFC and RAF (despatches twice). War of 1939-45, Iraq, Abyssinia, Western Desert, Fighter Command; Director of Personal Services, Air Ministry, 1943-45; retired, 1945. Executive Director Remploy Ltd, 1945-61. *Address:* Great Glenham, Saxmundham, Suffolk. *Club:* Royal Air Force.

VENTRY, 7th Baron, *cr* 1800; **Arthur Frederick Daubeney Olav Eveleigh-de-Moleyns;** *b* Norton Malreward, Som, 28 July 1898; *er s* of 6th Baron and Evelyn Muriel Stuart (*d* 1966), *y d* of Lansdowne Daubeney, Norton Malreward, Somerset; *S* father, 1936. *Educ:* Old Malthouse, Swanage; Wellington Coll., Berks. Served Irish Guards, 1917-18 (wounded); afterwards in RAF; served RAF, 1939-45. Certificated Aeronaut. *Publications:* on aerostation and scouting. *Recreations:* music, travelling, airship piloting. *Heir: nephew* Andrew (Harold) Wesley Daubeny de Moleyns [*b* 28 May 1943; *m* 1963, Nelly Edouard Renée, *d* of Abel Chaumillon, Torremolinos, Spain; one *s* two *d*]. *Address:* Lindsay Hall, Lindsay Road, Bournemouth. *Clubs:* Naval and Military, Norwegian, Balloon and Airship.

VERCO, Walter John George, CVO 1970 (MVO 1952); Secretary of the Order of the Garter, since 1974; Norroy and Ulster King of Arms, since 1971; Secretary to the Earl Marshal, since 1961; *b* 18 January 1907; *s* of late John Walter Verco, Chelsea; *m* 1929, Ada Rose, *d* of late Bertram Leonard Bennett, Lymington, Hants; one *s* one *d*. Served War, 1940-45, with RAFVR, Flight Lt. Secretary to Garter King of Arms, 1949-60; Rouge Croix Pursuivant of Arms, 1954-60; Chester Herald, 1960-71. Hon. Genealogist to Order of the British Empire, 1959-, to Royal Victorian Order, 1968-; Inspector, RAF Badges, 1970-, RAAF Badges, 1971-; Adviser on Naval Heraldry, 1970-. Fellow, Royal Commonwealth Soc. OStJ. *Address:* College of Arms, Queen Victoria Street, EC4. *T:* 01-248 6185; 53 Alington Crescent, Kingsbury, Mddx. *T:* 01-205 7553.

VERCORS; (pen-name of Jean Bruller); writer; designer-engraver (as Jean Bruller); Légion d'honneur; médaille de la Résistance; *b* Paris, 26 February 1902; *s* of Louis Bruller and E. Bourbon; *m* 1931, Jeanne Barusseaud (marr. diss.); three *s*; *m* Rita Barisse. *Educ:* Ecole Alsacienne, Paris. Dessinateur-graveur: publié, 1926-39; Albums: 21 Recettes de Mort Violente, 1926; Hypothèses sur les Amateurs de Peinture, 1927; Un Homme Coupé en tranches, 1929; Nouvelle Clé des Songes, 1934; L'enfer, 1935; Visions intimes et rassurantes de la guerre, 1936; Silences, 1937. Décor et costumes pour L'Orphelin de la Chine, de Voltaire, à la Comédie Française, 1965; Hamlet (adapt.) prod. Lyons, 1977; Macbeth (adapt.) prod. Festival d'Anjou, etc, 1977. *Publications:* Les Relevés Trimestriels, planches dont l'ensemble (160 planches) forme La Danse des Vivants, 1932-38; Nombreuses illustrations pour livres de luxe; expositions retrospectives: Vienne, 1970; Budapest, Cologne, 1971. En 1941, fondation des Editions de Minuit clandestines; Publication, sous le nom de Vercors, Le Silence de la Mer, 1942; depuis, sous le même nom, La Marche à l'Etoile, 1943; Le Songe, 1944; Les Armes de la Nuit, 1946; Le Sable du Temps, 1945; Les Yeux et la Lumière, 1948; Plus ou Moins Homme, 1950; La Puissance du jour, 1951; Les Animaux dénaturés (Borderline), 1952; Les Pas dans le Sable; Portrait d'une Amitié, 1954, Divagations d'un Français en Chine; Colères (The Insurgents), 1956; PPC, 1957; Sur Ce Rivage (I Le Périple, II Monsieur Prousthe, 1958, III Liberté de Décembre, 1959); Sylva, 1961; Zoo (comedy) Prod. Carcassonne, 1963, Théâtre National Populaire, Paris, 1964; et dans de nombreux pays d'Europe et d'Amérique; Hamlet (trad. et illus.), 1965; Les Chemins de l'Etre (en coll. av. P. Misraki), 1965; Quota ou les Pléthoriens (en coll. av. Coronel), 1966; La Bataille du Silence, 1967; Oedipe-Roi (drame d'après Sophocle) prod. La Rochelle, 1967, Paris, 1970; Le Radeau de la Méduse (novel), 1969; Le Fer et le Velours (play), prod. Nîmes, 1969; Oedipe et Hamlet, 2 plays, 2 dossiers, 1970; Contes des Cataplasmes, 1971; Sillages (novel), 1972; Sept Sentiers du Désert (short stories), 1972; Questions sur la vie à MM les Biologistes (essay), 1973; Comme un Frère (novel), 1973; Tendre Naufrage (novel), 1974; Ce que je crois (essay), 1976; Je cuisine comme un chef (cook book), 1976. Nombreux articles dans les periodiques. *Address:* Moulin des Iles, 77120 St Augustin, France. *Clubs:* PEN, section française; Comité National des Ecrivains (Hon. Pres.).

VERDIN, Lt-Col Sir Richard Bertram, Kt 1962; OBE 1954; TD; DL; JP; Deputy Chairman, Meat and Livestock Commission, 1967-73; *b* 1912; *e s* of late Lt-Col Richard Norman Harrison

Verdin, DL, JP, Garnstone, Weobley, Herefordshire; *m* 1950, Helen Margaret, *e d* of Sir Watkin Williams-Wynn, 8th Bt; one *s*. *Educ:* Harrow; Magdalen Coll., Oxford. Barrister, Inner Temple 1937. Liaison Officer, Ministry of Agriculture, Fisheries and Food, 1958-71; Chairman: Pig Industrial Develt Authority (PIDA), 1962-69; Lawes Trust Cttee, Rothamstead, 1964-. Served with Cheshire Yeomanry, 1931-54; Lt-Col 1952. Chm., County Agric. Exec. Cttee, 1955-72; Pres., Country Landowners' Assoc., 1959-61. DL, JP, Cheshire, 1955. *Publication:* History of the Cheshire (Earl of Chester's) Yeomanry, 1971. *Address:* Stoke Hall, Nantwich, Cheshire.

VERDON-SMITH, Sir (William) Reginald, Kt 1953; DL; Deputy Chairman, Lloyds Bank Ltd, since 1967; Chairman, Lloyds Bank International Ltd, since 1973; Director, Lloyds Bank California, since 1975; Partner, George White, Evans, Tribe & Co., Stockbrokers, since 1952; Pro-Chancellor, Bristol University, since 1965; *b* 5 Nov. 1912; *s* of late Sir William G. Verdon Smith, CBE, JP; *m* 1946, Jane Margaret, *d* of late V. W. J. Hobbs; one *s* one *d*. *Educ:* Repton School; Brasenose College, Oxford (Scholar), 1st class School of Jurisprudence, 1935; BCL 1936 and Vinerian Law Scholar; Barrister-at-law, Inner Temple. Bristol Aeroplane Co., 1938-68: Dir., 1942; Jt Asst Man. Dir., 1947; Jt Man. Dir., 1952; Chm. 1955. Vice-Chm., Rolls Royce Ltd, 1966-68; Chm., British Aircraft Corp. (Hldgs) Ltd, 1969-72. Pres. SBAC, 1946-48; Chm., Fatstock and Meat Marketing Committee of Enquiry, 1962-64; Mem. of Council, Univ. of Bristol (Chm., 1949-56). Mem. Cttee on the Working of the Monetary System (Radcliffe Cttee), 1957-59. Mem., Review Body on Remuneration of Doctors and Dentists, 1964-68. Master, Worshipful Co. of Coachmakers and Coach Harness Makers, 1960-61; Master, Soc. of Merchant Venturers, 1968-69. FRSA. DL Avon, 1974, Hon. LLD Bristol, 1959; Hon. DSc, Cranfield Inst. of Technology, 1971; Hon. Fellow, Brasenose Coll., Oxford, 1965. *Recreations:* golf and sailing. *Address:* 13 Redcliffe Parade West, Bristol BS1 6SP. *Clubs:* Athenæum; Royal Yacht Squadron, Royal Cruising.

VERE OF HANWORTH, Lord; Charles Francis Topham de Vere Beauclerk; *b* 22 Feb. 1965; *s* and *heir* of Earl of Burford, *qv*.

VERE-LAURIE, Lt-Col George Halliburton Foster Peel, DL; JP; High Sheriff of Notts, 1957-58; *b* 22 Aug. 1906; *er s* of Lt-Col George Laurie (killed in action, 1915), and Florence, Viscountess Masserene and Ferrard; *m* 1932, Caroline Judith (from whom he obtained a divorce, 1968), *yr d* of Edward Francklin, JP, Gonalston Hall, Notts; one *s* one *d*. *Educ:* Eton; RMC Sandhurst. 2nd Lieut 9th Lancers, 1927; Captain and Adjutant, Notts Yeomanry, 1934-38; Capt. 1938; Maj. 1940; Lt-Col Royal Military Police, 1946; retired pay, 1947. Served War of 1939-45, France and Palestine. Gold Staff Officer, Coronation, 1953. Chairman: Southwell RDC, 1951 and 1956; Governors of Newark Technical Coll., 1952-61; Bd of Visitors, Lincoln Prison, 1973- (Mem., 1963-73); Mem., Newark DC, 1973- (Chm., 1976-77). A General Commissioner of Income Tax, 1956. Freeman City of London. Court of Assistants, Saddlers' Co., 1959, Master, 1965; Lord of the Manors of Carlton-on-Trent and Willoughby-in-Norwell. DL Notts 1948, JP Notts 1952. *Recreations:* hunting and shooting (Hon. Sec. Rufford Foxhounds, 1949-55; Joint Master and Huntsman, South Notts Foxhounds, 1956-58, Joint Master, 1959-68; Chm., Grove and Rufford Hunt, 1970-76). *Address:* Carlton Hall, Carlton-on-Trent, Newark, Notts. *T:* Sutton-on-Trent 288. *Club:* Cavalry.

VEREKER, family name of **Viscount Gort.**

VEREY, David Cecil Wynter; retired as Senior Investigator, Historic Buildings, Ministry of Housing and Local Government (1946-65); architectural historian and writer; *b* 9 Sept. 1913; *o s* of Rev. Cecil Henry Verey and Constance Lindaraja Dearman Birchall; *m* 1939, Rosemary Isabel Baird, *d* of Lt-Col Prescott Sandilands, DSO; two *s* two *d*. *Educ:* Eton; Trinity Coll., Cambridge (MA). ARIBA 1940. Capt., Royal Fusiliers, 1940; seconded SOE 1943, N Africa and Italy. Chm., Gloucester Diocesan Adv. Cttee on Churches; President: Bristol and Gloucestershire Archæological Soc., 1972; Cirencester Arch. and Hist Soc.; Glos Soc. for Industrial Archaeology; Member: Severn Regional Cttee of Nat. Trust; Gen. Cttee, Inc. Church Building Soc. High Sheriff of County of Gloucester, 1966. FSA. *Publications:* Shell Guides to six counties, England and Wales; The Buildings of England (Gloucestershire Vols), 1970; Cotswold Churches, 1976; Seven Victorian Architects, 1976; articles on architectural history. *Recreations:* private museum, Arlington Mill, Bibury; gardening. *Address:* Barnsley House, Cirencester, Glos. *T:* Bibury 281.

VEREY, Michael John, TD 1945; Chairman of Trustees, Charities Official Investment Fund, since 1974; *b* 12 Oct. 1912; *yr s* of late Henry Edward and late Lucy Alice Verey; *m* 1947, Sylvia Mary, *widow* of Charles Bartlet and *d* of late Lt-Col Denis Wilson and late Mrs Mary Henrietta Wilson; two *s* one *d*. *Educ:* Eton; Trinity College, Cambridge (MA). Joined Helbert, Wagg & Co. Ltd, 1934. Served War of 1939-45, Middle East, Italy, Warwickshire Yeomanry (Lt-Col). Chairman: J. Henry Schroder Wagg & Co. Ltd, 1972-73 (Dep. Chm., 1966-72); Schroders Ltd, 1973-77; Accepting Houses Cttee, 1974-77; Broadstone Investment Trust Ltd; Brixton Estate Ltd; Director: British Petroleum Co. Ltd; Boots Pure Drug Co. Ltd; Commercial Union Assurance Co. Ltd (Vice-Chm., 1975-); NEGIT SA; Sviluppo e Gestione Investimenti Mobiliari, SpA, and other cos; Mem., Covent Garden Market Authority, 1961-66. High Sheriff of Berkshire, 1968. Pres., Royal Worcestershire and Warwickshire Regtl Assoc., 1976. *Recreations:* gardening, travel. *Address:* Little Bowden, Pangbourne, Berks. *T:* Pangbourne 2210. *Club:* Boodle's.

VERITY, Group Captain Conrad Edward Howe, OBE 1943; JP; Engineering Consultant; *b* 18 February 1901; *s* of Edward Storr Verity and Annie Amelia Verity (*née* Howe); *m* 1931, Doreen Louise Bishop; one *s* one *d*. *Educ:* Wellingborough Sch. Engrg Trg, W. H. Allen Sons & Co. Ltd, Bedford, and Bedford Tech. Coll., 1917-22; Contracts Engr, W. H. Allen Sons & Co. Ltd, Bedford, 1922-24; Tech. Engr, Contraflo Engrg Co. Ltd, 1924-27; Tech. Engr (Mech.), London Power Co., 1927-40. Served War, 1940-45: RAF, finishing as Gp Capt.; service in England, USA, NW Africa, Pacific, India, China, etc. Chief Development and Testing Engineer, London Power Co., 1945-48; Generation Constr Engr, Brit. Elec. Authority, 1948-50; Dep. Chief Engr, Brit. Elec. Authority, and later Central Elec. Authority, 1950-55; Dir, Foster Wheeler Ltd and Manager Steam Div., 1955-59, Managing Dir, 1960-62, Chm., 1962-66; Dep. Chm., Foster Wheeler John Brown Boilers Ltd, 1966-67; Dir, Rolls-Royce and Associates, Derby, 1959-67. JP Surrey, 1960. American Legion of Merit (Officer), 1945. *Publications:* technical papers to: Institution Civil Engrs; Electrical Power Engrs Assoc.; Instn of Mech. Engrs, etc. *Recreations:* rowing, and sport generally. *Address:* Farthings, Earleydene, Sunninghill, Berks. *T:* Ascot 22033. *Clubs:* Naval and Military; Twickenham Rowing (Hon. Life Mem.); Burway Rowing (Vice-Pres.).

VERNEY, family name of **Baron Willoughby de Broke.**

VERNEY, Sir John, 2nd Bt, *cr* 1946; MC 1944; TD 1970; painter, illustrator, author; *b* 30 Sept. 1913; *s* of Sir Ralph Verney, 1st Bt (Speaker's Secretary, 1921-55); *S* father, 1959; *m* 1939, Lucinda, *d* of late Major Herbert Musgrave, DSO; one *s* five *d* (and one *s* decd). *Educ:* Eton; Christ Church, Oxford. Served War of 1939-45 with N. Somerset Yeomanry, RAC and SAS Regt in Palestine, Syria, Egypt, Italy, France and Germany (despatches twice, MC). Exhibitor: RBA; London Group; Leicester, Redfern, AIA and Zwemmer Galleries. Légion d'Honneur, 1945. *Publications:* Verney Abroad, 1954; Going to the Wars, 1955; Friday's Tunnel, 1959; Look at Houses, 1959; February's Road, 1961; Every Advantage, 1961; The Mad King of Chichiboo, 1963; ismo, 1964; A Dinner of Herbs, 1966; Fine Day for a Picnic, 1968; Seven Sunflower Seeds, 1968; Samson's Hoard, 1973; periodic contributor to Cornhill etc; annually, The Dodo Pad (the amusing telephone diary). *Heir:* *s* John Sebastian Verney, *b* 30 Aug. 1945. *Address:* Runwick House, Farnham, Surrey. *T:* Farnham 6323.

VERNEY, Lawrence John, TD 1955; DL; His Honour Judge Verney; a Circuit Judge (formerly Deputy Chairman, Middlesex Sessions) since 1971; *b* 19 July 1924; *y s* of Sir Harry Verney, 4th Bt, DSO; *m* 1972, Zoë Auriel, *d* of Lt-Col P. G. Goodeve-Docker. *Educ:* Harrow; Oriel Coll., Oxford. Called to Bar, Inner Temple, 1952. Dep. Chm., Bucks QS, 1962-71. Editor, Harrow School Register, 1948-; Governor, Harrow Sch., 1972-. DL Bucks 1967. *Recreation:* squash rackets. *Address:* The Old Rectory, Middle Claydon, Buckingham MK18 2EU. *T:* Steeple Claydon 557.

See also Bishop Suffragan of Repton, Sir R . B . Verney, Bt.

VERNEY, Sir Ralph (Bruce), 5th Bt *cr* 1818; KBE 1974; JP; Landowner; Vice-Lord-Lieutenant (formerly Vice-Lieutenant) of Buckinghamshire since 1965; Member, Royal Commission on Environmental Pollution, since 1973; *b* 18 Jan. 1915; *e s* of Sir Harry Calvert Williams Verney, 4th Bt, DSO, and Lady Rachel Bruce (*d* 1964), *d* of 9th Earl of Elgin; *S* father, 1974; *m* 1948, Mary Vestey; one *s* three *d*. *Educ:* Canford; Balliol Coll., Oxford. 2nd Lieut Bucks Yeomanry, 1940; Major, Berks Yeomanry, 1945 and Bucks Yeomanry, 1946. Pres., Country Landowners' Assoc., 1961-63; Vice-President for Great Britain, Confédération Européenne de L'Agriculture, 1965-71,

Counsellor, 1971-; Chairman, Forestry Commn Cttee for England, 1967; Forestry Comr, 1968-; Member: Nature Conservancy, 1966-71; Milton Keynes New Town Corporation, 1967-74; BBC Adv. Cttee on Agriculture, 1970-; Chm., Sec. of State for the Environment's Adv. Cttee on Aggregates for Construction Industry, 1972-77. Trustee: Radcliffe Trust; Ernest Cook Trust; Chequers Trust. Buckinghamshire County Council: Member, 1951; Chairman, Finance Cttee, 1957; Planning Cttee, 1967; CA 1961; JP Bucks, 1954; High Sheriff of Buckinghamshire, 1957-58; DL Bucks, 1960; High Steward of Buckingham, 1966. Prime Warden, Worshipful Co. of Dyers, 1969-70. Hon. Fellow, RIBA, 1977. *Recreation:* shooting. *Heir:* s Edmund Ralph Verney, *b* 28 June 1950. *Address:* Claydon House, Middle Claydon, Buckingham MK18 2EX. *T:* Steeple Claydon 297; Plas Rhôscolyn, Holyhead LL65 2NZ. *T:* Treaddur Bay 860288. *Clubs:* Brooks's, Cavalry and Guards, Farmers'.
See also Bishop Suffragan of Repton , L . J . Verney .

VERNEY, Rt. Rev. Stephen Edmund; *see* Repton, Bishop Suffragan of.

VERNEY-CAVE, family name of **Baron Braye.**

VERNIER-PALLIEZ, Bernard Maurice Alexandre; Officier de la Légion d'Honneur; Croix de Guerre; Médaille de la Résistance; Président Directeur Général de la Régie Nationale des Usines Renault, since Dec. 1975; *b* 2 March 1918; *s* of Maurice Vernier and Marie-Thérèse Palliez; *m* 1952, Denise Silet-Pathe; one *s* three *d* . *Educ:* Ecole des Hautes Etudes Commerciales; Ecole Libre des Sciences Politiques. Licencié en Droit. Joined Régie Nationale des Usines, Renault, 1945 (dealing with personnel and trade unions); Sécretaire Général, RNUR, 1948-67; Directeur Général Adjoint, RNUR, 1967-71; Président Directeur Général, SAVIEM, 1967-74; Délégué Général aux Vehicules Industriels, Cars et Bus à la RNUR, Président du Directoire de Berliet, and Vice-Président du Conseil de Surveillance de SAVIEM, Jan.-Dec. 1975. *Address:* Régie Nationale des Usines Renault, 34 Quai du Point du Jour, 92109 Boulogne Billancourt, France. *T:* 609 64 14.

VERNON, family name of **Barons Lyveden** and **Vernon.**

VERNON, 10th Baron, *cr* 1762; **John Lawrance Vernon;** *b* 1 Feb. 1923; *s* of 9th Baron, and Violet, *d* of Colonel Clay; *S* father, 1963; *m* 1955, Sheila Jean, *d* of W. Marshall Clark, Johannesburg; two *d*. *Educ:* Eton; Magdalen Coll., Oxford. Served in Scots Guards, 1942-46, retiring with rank of Captain. Called to Bar, Lincoln's Inn, 1949. Served in various Government Departments, 1950-61; attached to Colonial Office (for service in Kenya), 1957-58. Mem., Peak Park Planning Bd, 1974-77. JP Derbyshire 1965. *Heir: kinsman,* 2nd Viscount Harcourt, *qv. Address:* Sudbury House, Sudbury, Derbyshire.

VERNON, David Bowater; Under Secretary, Inland Revenue, since 1975; *b* 14 Nov. 1926; *s* of Lt-Col Herbert Bowater Vernon, MC, and Ivy Margaret Vernon; *m* 1954, Anne de Montmorency Fleming; three *s* three *d* . *Educ:* Marlborough Coll.; Oriel Coll., Oxford (MA). RA, 1945-48 (Lieut). Inland Revenue, 1951-. *Recreation:* gardening. *Address:* Birches, Penshurst, Tonbridge, Kent. *T:* Penshurst 349.

VERNON, Sir James, Kt 1965; CBE 1962 (OBE 1960); Director: CSR Ltd; Commercial Banking Company of Sydney Ltd; MLC Ltd; United Telecasters Sydney Ltd; Westham Dredging Co. Pty Ltd; Martin Corporation Group Ltd (Chairman); *b* 1910; *s* of Donald Vernon, Tamworth, New South Wales; *m* 1935, Mavis, *d* of C. Lonsdale Smith; two *d. Educ:* Sydney Univ. (BSc); University College, London (PhD). Colonial Sugar Refining Co. Ltd: Chief Chemist, 1938-51; Senior Exec. Officer, 1951-56; Asst General Manager, 1956-57; Gen. Manager, 1958-72. Chairman: Commonwealth Cttee of Economic Enquiry, 1963-65; Australian Post Office Commn of Inquiry, 1973; President: Australia/Japan Business Co-operation Cttee; Australian Nat. Cttee, Pacific Basin Econ. Council; Mem., Internat. Adv. Cttee, Chase Manhattan Bank. Leighton Medal, Royal Australian Chemical Inst., 1965; John Storey Medal, Aust. Inst. of Management, 1971. Hon. DSc: Sydney, 1965; Newcastle, 1969. FRACI. *Address:* 27 Manning Road, Double Bay, NSW 2028, Australia. *Clubs:* Australian, Union, Royal Sydney Golf (Sydney).

VERNON, James William, CMG 1964; barrister-at-law; *b* 1915; *s* of late John Alfred Vernon; *m* 1941, Betty Désirée, *d* of Gordon E. Nathan; one *s* one *d. Educ:* Wallasey Grammar Sch.; Emmanuel Coll., Cambridge (Scholar). BA 1937, MA 1940. Entered Civil Service, Ministry of Food, 1939; Flt Lieut, RAF, 1943; Wing Comdr (despatches), 1945; Principal Scientific

Officer, Ministry of Works, 1945; Assistant Secretary, Colonial Office, 1954-64; Economic Adviser, British High Commission, Lusaka, 1966; Asst Under-Sec. of State, DEA, 1966-69; Under-Sec., Min. of Housing and Local Govt, later DoE, 1969-72. Called to Bar, Inner Temple, 1975. Queen's Commendation for Brave Conduct, 1955. *Recreations:* gardening, photography, reading. *Address:* 43 The Crescent, Belmont, Sutton, Surrey.

VERNON, Kenneth Robert; Deputy Chairman and Chief Executive, North of Scotland Hydro-Electric Board, since 1973; *b* 15 March 1923; *s* of late Cecil W. Vernon and Jessie McGaw, Dumfries; *m* 1946, Pamela Hands, Harrow; one *s* four *d. Educ:* Dumfries Academy; Glasgow University. BSc, CEng, FIEE, FIMechE. BTH Co., Edinburgh Corp., British Electricity Authority, 1948-55; South of Scotland Electricity Bd, 1955-56; North of Scotland Hydro-Electric Bd, 1956: Chief Electrical and Mech. Engr, 1964; Gen. Man., 1966; Bd Mem., 1970. *Publications:* various papers to technical instns. *Recreation:* fishing. *Address:* 10 Keith Crescent, Edinburgh EH4 3NH. *T:* 031-332 4610. *Club:* Royal Commonwealth Society.

VERNON, Prof. Magdalen Dorothea, MA (Cantab) 1926; ScD (Cantab) 1953; Professor of Psychology in the University of Reading, 1956-67; *b* 25 June 1901; *d* of Dr Horace Middleton Vernon and Katharine Dorothea Ewart. *Educ:* Oxford High Sch.; Newnham Coll., Cambridge. Asst Investigator to the Industrial Health Research Board, 1924-27; Research Investigator to the Medical Research Council, in the Psychological Laboratory, Cambridge, 1927-46; Lecturer in Psychology, 1946-51, Senior Lecturer in Psychology, 1951-55, Reader in Psychology, 1955-56, University of Reading. President, British Psychological Society, 1958 (Hon. Fellow, 1970); President, Psychology Section, British Assoc., 1959. *Publications:* The Experimental Study of Reading, 1931; Visual Perception, 1937; A Further Study of Visual Perception, 1952; Backwardness in Reading, 1957; The Psychology of Perception, 1962; Experiments in Visual Perception, 1966; Human Motivation, 1969; Perception through Experience, 1970; Reading and its Difficulties, 1971; numerous papers on Perception, etc. in British Journal of Psychology and British Journal of Educational Psychology. *Recreations:* walking, gardening. *Address:* 50 Cressingham Road, Reading, Berks. *T:* Reading 81088. *Club:* University Women's.

VERNON, Michael; *see* Vernon, William M.

VERNON, Sir Nigel (John Douglas), 4th Bt, *cr* 1914; Director: Robert Barrow (Insurance Services) Ltd; Travel Finance Ltd; *b* 2 May 1924; *s* of Sir (William) Norman Vernon, 3rd Bt, and Janet Lady Vernon (*d* 1973); *S* father, 1967; *m* 1947, Margaret Ellen (*née* Dobell); two *s* one *d. Educ:* Charterhouse. Royal Naval Volunteer Reserve (Lieutenant), 1942-45. Spillers Ltd, 1945-65; Director: Castle Brick Co Ltd, 1965-71; Deeside Merchants Ltd, 1971-74. *Recreations:* golf, gardening. *Heir: s* James William Vernon, ACA, *b* 2 April 1949. *Address:* Top-y-Fron Hall, Kelsterton, near Flint, N Wales. *T:* Deeside 812129. *Club:* Naval.

VERNON, Prof. Philip Ewart, MA, PhD, DSc; Professor of Educational Psychology and Senior Research Consultant, University of Calgary, since 1968; Emeritus Professor, University of London; *b* 6 June 1905; *e s* of late Horace Middleton Vernon; *m* 1st, 1938, Annie C. Gray; 2nd, 1947, Dorothy Anne Fairley Lawson, MA, MEd; one *s. Educ:* Oundle Sch.; St John's Coll., Cambridge; Yale and Harvard Universities. First Class Hons in Nat. Sci. Tripos, Part I, 1926, and Moral Sci. Tripos, Part II, 1927; John Stewart of Rannoch Scholarship in Sacred Music, 1925; Strathcona Research Studentship, 1927-29; Laura Spelman Rockefeller Fellowship in Social Sciences, 1929-31; Fellowship of St John's Coll., Cambridge, 1930-33; Pinsent-Darwin Studentship in Mental Pathology, 1933-35. Psychologist to LCC at Maudsley Hospital Child Guidance Clinic, 1933-35; Head of Psychology Dept, Jordanhill Training Centre, Glasgow, 1935-38; Head of Psychology Dept, University of Glasgow, 1938-47; Psychological Research Adviser to Admiralty and War Office, 1942-45; Prof. of Educational Psychology, Inst. of Education, University of London, 1949-64; Prof. of Psychology, 1964-68. Fellow, Centre for Advanced Studies in Behavioural Scis, Stanford, Calif, 1961-62, Vis. Canada Council Fellow, 1975. Visiting Professor: Princeton Univ. and Educnl Testing Service, 1957; Teachers' Coll., Sydney, 1977; numerous internat. educnl consultancies and lect. tours for British Council, 1953-68. Mem., Bd of Directors, Calgary Philharmonic Soc., 1976-. President: Psych. Sect., British Assoc. Advancement of Science, 1952; BPsS, 1954-55. Govt of Alberta Achievement Award, 1972. *Publications:* (with G. W. Allport) Studies in Expressive Movement, 1933; The Measurement of Abilities, 1940, 2nd edn, 1956; (with J. B. Parry) Personnel Selection in the British

Forces, 1949; The Structure of Human Abilities, 1950, 2nd edn, 1961; Personality Tests and Assessments, 1953; Secondary School Selection, 1957; Intelligence and Attainment Tests, 1960; Personality Assessment: A Critical Survey, 1963; Intelligence and Cultural Environment, 1969; Readings in Creativity, 1971; (with G. Adamson and Dorothy F. Vernon) Psychology and Education of Gifted Children, 1977; numerous papers in British and American psychological journals. *Recreations:* music, snowshoeing. *Address:* 4107 53rd Street NW, Calgary, Alberta, Canada.

VERNON, (William) Michael; Chairman and Chief Executive of Spillers Ltd, since 1968; *b* 17 April 1926; *o* surv. *s* of late Sir Wilfred Vernon; *m* 1952, Rosheen O'Meara (marr. diss. 1977); one *s*; *m* 1977, Mrs Jane Colston. *Educ:* Marlborough Coll.; Trinity Coll., Cambridge. MA 1948. Lieut, Royal Marines, 1944-46. Joined Spillers Ltd, 1948: Dir 1960; Jt Man. Dir 1962; Dir, EMI Ltd. Pres., Nat. Assoc. of British and Irish Millers, 1965; Vice-Chm., Millers' Mutual Assoc.; Pres., British Food Export Council, 1977-; Mem., Management Cttee, RNLI (Vice-Pres.). *Recreations:* sailing, shooting, ski-ing. *Address:* Fyfield Manor, Andover, Hants. *Clubs:* Royal Ocean Racing (Cdre 1964-68); Royal Yacht Squadron.

VERNON-HUNT, Ralph Holmes, DFC; Managing Director, Pan Books Ltd, since 1970; *b* 23 May 1923; *m* 1946, Elizabeth Mary Harris; four *s* two *d* (and one *s* decd). *Educ:* Malvern College. Flt-Lt RAF, 1941-46; Bookseller, 1946-47; Sales Dir, Pan Books Ltd, 1947-62; Sales Dir, Paul Hamlyn Ltd, 1963-69. *Address:* Gordon House, Ham Common, Richmond, Surrey. *T:* 01-940 9090.

VERONESE, Dr Vittorino; Cavaliere di Gran Croce della Repubblica Italiana; Gold Medal Awarded for Culture (Italian Republic); Doctor of Law (Padua, 1930); lawyer, banker, administrator; Chairman, Board of Directors, Banco di Roma, 1961-76 (Auditor, 1945-53; Director, 1953-57); *b* Vicenza, 1 March 1910; *m* 1939, Maria Petrarca; four *s* three *d*. General Secretary: Catholic Movement Graduates, 1939; Italian Catholic Action, 1944-46 (President, 1946-52); Vice-President, Internat. Movement of Catholic Intellectuals of Pax Romana, 1947-55. Vice-President, Banca Cattolica del Veneto, 1952-57; President, Consorzio di Credito per le Opere Pubbliche and Istituto di Credito per le Imprese di Pubblica Utilitá, 1957-58; Italian Deleg. to General Conf. of UNESCO, Beirut, 1950, Paris, 1952-53; Member Italian Nat. Commn, 1953-58; Vice-President, Exec. Board, 1954-56; President, 1956-58. Director-General of UNESCO, 1958-61, resigned; Member, Comité Consultatif International pour l'Alphabétisation, UNESCO, 1967; Vice-President: Comité Consultatif International pour Venise, UNESCO; Societa Italiano per l'Organizzazione Internationale (SIOI); Pres., Italian Consultative Cttee for Human Rights, 1965. Pres., Circolo di Roma, 1968. Lay Observer in Concilio Ecumenico Vaticano II; Member, Pontificia Commissione Justitia et Pax, 1967. Cav. di Gran Groce dell' Ordine di S Silvestro Papa; Commendatore dell' Ordine Piano. Holds several foreign orders. *Address:* c/o Banco di Roma, Via del Corso 307, Rome, Italy; 21 Via Cadlolo, Rome, Italy.

VERRY, Frederick William, CMG 1958; OBE 1948; Assistant Secretary, Air Ministry, 1953-62, retired; *b* 15 Feb. 1899; *s* of late Herbert William Verry; *m* 1926, Phyllis (*d* 1972), *d* of late William Pitt MacConochie. *Educ:* Stockport Secondary Sch.; Northern Polytechnic Sch., London. Joined Civil Service as Boy Clerk, War Office, 1914. Served in RN Airship Service and RAF, 1917-19. Air Ministry, 1920. Financial Adviser, Middle East Air Force, 1946-49. *Recreation:* painting. *Address:* 17 The Tracery, Park Road, Banstead, Surrey SM7 3DD. *T:* Burgh Heath 55550.

VERSEY, Henry Cherry; Emeritus Professor of Geology, University of Leeds, since 1959; *b* 22 Jan. 1894; *s* of Charles Versey, Welton, East Yorkshire; *m* 1923, Hypatia Ingersoll, *d* of Greevz Fysher, Leeds; two *s* two *d*. *Educ:* Hymers Coll., Hull; University of Leeds. Service with RAOC, European War, 1916-19. Lecturer in Geology, University of Leeds, 1919-49; Reader in Applied Geology, 1949-56; Professor of Geology, 1956-59, University of Leeds. Hon. LLD (Leeds), 1967. Phillips Medal, Yorkshire Geological Society, 1964. *Publications:* Geology of the Appleby District, 1941; Geology and Scenery of the Countryside round Leeds and Bradford, 1948. Many papers on Yorkshire geology. *Recreation:* philately. *Address:* 1 Stainburn Terrace, Leeds LS17 6NJ. *T:* Leeds 682244.

VERULAM, 7th Earl of, *cr* 1815; **John Duncan Grimston;** Bt 1629; Baron Forrester (Scot.), 1633; Baron Dunboyne and Viscount Grimston (Ire.), 1719; Baron Verulam (Gt. Brit.),

1790; Viscount Grimston (UK), 1815; *b* 21 April 1951; *s* of 6th Earl of Verulam, and of Marjorie Ray, *d* of late Walter Atholl Duncan; *S* father, 1973; *m* 1976, Dione Angela, *e d* of Jeremy Smith, Balcombe House, Sussex. *Educ:* Eton; Christ Church, Oxford (MA 1976). *Heir: kinsman* Baron Grimston of Westbury, *qv. Address:* Gorhambury, St Albans, Herts AL3 6AH. *T:* St Albans 55000. *Clubs:* Beefsteak, Turf, Bath.

VERYKIOS, Dr Panaghiotis Andrew; Kt Commander of Order of George I, of Greece, and of Order of the Phoenix; MM (Greece); Greek Ambassador, retired; *b* Athens, 1910; *m* 1939, Mary (*née* Dracoulis); three *s*. *Educ:* Athens and Paris. Law (Dr) and Political Sciences. Greek Diplomatic Service, 1935. Served in the Army, 1939-40. Various diplomatic posts until 1946; Secretary of Embassy, London, 1947-51; Counsellor, Dep. Representative of NATO, Paris, 1952-54; Counsellor of Embassy, Paris, 1954-56; Head of NATO Div., Min. of Foreign Affairs, Athens, 1956-60; Ambassador to: The Netherlands, 1960-64; Norway, 1961-67; Denmark, 1964-67; Iceland, 1967; Court of St James's, 1967-69; Spain, 1969-70. Holds foreign decorations. *Publication:* La Prescription en Droit International, 1934 (Paris). *Recreation:* music. *Address:* 6 Iras Street, Ekali, Athens. *T:* 8031216; 7 Avenue Jurigoz, 1006 Lausanne, Switzerland. *T:* (021)-264690. *Club:* Athenian (Athens).

VESEY, family name of **Viscount de Vesci.**

VESEY, Sir Henry; *see* Vesey, Sir N. H. P.

VESEY, Sir (Nathaniel) Henry (Peniston), Kt 1965; CBE 1953; Chairman, H. A. & E. Smith Ltd, since 1939; Chairman, Bank of N. T. Butterfield & Son Ltd, since 1970; Member of House of Assembly, Bermuda, 1938-72; *b* 1 June 1901; *s* of late Hon. Nathaniel Vesey, Devonshire, Bermuda; *m* 1920, Louise Marie, *d* of late Captain J. A. Stubbs, Shelly Bay, Bermuda; two *s*. *Educ:* Saltus Grammar Sch. Chairman: Food and Supplies Control Board, 1941-42; Board of Trade, 1943; Finance Cttee of House of Assembly, 1943-44; Bermuda Trade Development Board, 1945-56, 1960-69; Board of Civil Aviation, 1957-59; Board of Agriculture, 1957-59. MEC, 1948-57, Mem. Executive Council for Tourism and Trade, 1968-69. *Recreations:* fishing, golf. *Address:* Windward, Shelly Bay, Bermuda. *T:* 3-0186. *Clubs:* Naval and Military; Royal Bermuda Yacht, Mid Ocean (Bermuda); Bankers (New York).

VESEY-FITZGERALD, Brian Seymour; Author; Member Honourable Society of Cymmrodorion; President of the British Fairground Society, 1953-63; Editor-in-Chief of The Field, 1938-46; Chairman of Preliminary Enquiry into Cause of Canine Hysteria, 1938; Chairman, Association of School Natural History Societies, 1947-48; Member of Institute for the Study of Animal Behaviour; Member of Gypsy Lore Society. Field Fare Broadcasts, 1940-45; There and Back Broadcasts, 1947-49. Editor of Country Books since 1943. FRSA. *Publications:* Amateur Boxing, Professional Boxing (Lonsdale Library, Sporting Records), 1936; Badgers Funeral, 1937; A Book of British Waders, 1939; Hampshire Scene, 1940; The Noctule, 1941; Programme for Agriculture, 1941; A Country Chronicle, 1942; Farming in Britain, 1942; Hedgerow and Field, 1943; Gypsies of Britain, 1944, rev. edn 1964; British Countryside, 1946; British Game, 1946; The Book of the Horse, 1946; It's My Delight, 1947; British Bats, 1947; A Child's Biology, 1948; Bird Biology for Beginners, 1948; The Book of the Dog, 1948; Background to Birds, 1949; Hampshire, 1949; Rivermouth, 1949; (co-ed) Game Fish of the World, 1950; The River Avon, 1951; Gypsy Borrow, 1953; Winchester, 1953; British Birds and their Nests, 1953; More British Birds and their Nests, 1954; Nature Recognition, 1955; Cats, 1956; A Third Book of British Birds and their Nests, 1956; The Domestic Dog, 1957; A Book of Wildflowers, 1958; Instructions to Young Naturalists, 1959; The Beauty of Cats, 1959; A Book of Garden Flowers, 1960; The Beauty of Dogs, 1960; A Book of Trees, 1962; About Dogs, 1963; The Cat Lover's Encyclopædia, 1963; Foxes in Britain, 1964; Animal Anthology, 1965; The Dog-Owners Encyclopædia, 1965; Portrait of the New Forest, 1966; Garden Alive, 1967; The World of Reptiles, 1968; The Vanishing Wild Life of Britain, 1969; The World of Ants, Bees and Wasps, 1969; The Domestic Cat, 1969. *Recreations:* bird-watching, gardening. *Address:* Long Croft, Wrecclesham, Surrey.

VESSEY, Prof. Martin Paterson; Professor of Social and Community Medicine, University of Oxford, since Oct. 1974; *b* 22 July 1936; *s* of Sidney J. Vessey and Catherine P. Vessey (*née* Thomson); *m* 1959, Anne Platt; two *s* one *d*. *Educ:* University College Sch., Hampstead; University Coll. London; University Coll. Hosp. Med. Sch., London. MB, BS London 1959; MD London 1971; FFCM RCP 1972; MA Oxon 1974. Scientific Officer, Dept of Statistics, Rothamsted Exper. Stn, 1960-65;

House Surg. and House Phys., Barnet Gen. Hosp., 1965-66; Mem. Sci. Staff, MRC Statistical Research Unit, 1966-69; Lectr in Epidemiology, Univ. of Oxford, 1969-74. *Publications:* many sci. articles in learned jls, notably on med. aspects of fertility control, safety of drugs, and epidemiology of cancer. *Recreations:* motoring, singing, conservation. *Address:* Hill House, Swan Hill, Tetsworth, Oxford OX9 7AB. *T:* Tetsworth 360.

VESTEY, family name of **Baron Vestey.**

VESTEY, 3rd Baron, *cr* 1922, of Kingswood; **Samuel George Armstrong Vestey;** Bt, *cr* 1913; *b* 19 March 1941; *s* of late Captain the Hon. William Howarth Vestey (killed in action in Italy, 1944; *o s* of 2nd Baron Vestey and Frances Sarah Howarth) and of Pamela Helen Fullerton, *d* of George Nesbitt Armstrong; *S* grandfather, 1954; *m* 1970, Kathryn Mary, *er d* of John Eccles, Moor Park, Herts; one *d. Educ:* Eton. Lieut, Scots Guards. Director, Union International Co. Ltd, and associated companies. Dep. Pres., Glos Assoc. of Boys' Clubs; County Vice-Pres., St John Ambulance Brigade (Glos); Liveryman, Butchers' Co.; Pres., London Meat Trade and Drovers Benevolent Assoc., 1973. *Recreations:* polo, shooting. *Heir:* b Hon. Mark William Vestey [*b* 16 April 1943; *m* 1975, Rose Amelia, *d* of Lt-Col Peter Thomas Clifton, *qv*; one *d. Educ:* Eton]. *Address:* Stowell Park, Northleach, Glos. *Clubs:* White's; Melbourne (Melbourne).

VESTEY, Edmund Hoyle; Chairman: Blue Star Line; Lamport & Holt Line; Albion Insurance Co.; Director, Union International Co. and associated companies; *b* 1932; *o s* of Ronald Arthur Vestey, *qv*; *m* 1960, Anne Moubray, *yr d* of Gen. Sir Geoffrey Scoones, KCB, KBE, CSI, DSO, MC; four *s. Educ:* Eton. 2nd Lieut Queen's Bays, 1951; Lieut, City of London Yeomanry. Joint Master, Puckeridge and Thurlow Foxhounds. High Sheriff, Essex, 1977. *Address:* Waltons, Ashdon, Saffron Walden, Essex; Glencanisp Lodge, Lochinver, Sutherland; Sunnyside Farmhouse, Hawick, Roxburghshire. *Clubs:* Cavalry and Guards, Carlton; Highland (Inverness).

VESTEY, Sir (John) Derek, 2nd Bt, *cr* 1921; *b* 4 June 1914; *s* of John Joseph Vesey (*d* 1932) and Dorothy Mary (*d* 1918), *d* of John Henry Beaver, Gawthorpe Hall, Bingley, Yorkshire; *g s* of Sir Edmund Vestey, 1st Bt; *S* grandfather 1953; *m* 1938, Phyllis Irene, *o d* of H. Brewer, Banstead, Surrey; one *s* one *d. Educ:* Leys Sch., Cambridge. Served War of 1939-45: Flt-Lieut, RAFVR, 1940-45. *Heir: s* Paul Edmund Vestey [*b* 15 Feb. 1944; *m* 1971, Victoria Anne Scudamore, *d* of John Salter, Tiverton, Devon; three *d. Educ:* Radley]. *Address:* 5 Carlton Gardens, SW1. *T:* 01-930 1610; Harcombe House, Ropley, Hants. *T:* Ropley 2394. *Clubs:* MCC, Farmers', Royal Automobile.

See also R. A. Vestey.

VESTEY, Ronald Arthur; DL; Director: Blue Star Line; Lamport & Holt Line; Albion Insurance Co.; Union International Co. and Associated Companies, and other Companies; *b* 10 May 1898; 4th but *e surv s* of Sir Edmund Hoyle Vestey, 1st Bt; *m* 1923, Florence Ellen McLean (*d* 1966), *o d* of Colonel T. G. Luis, VD, Broughty Ferry, Angus; one *s* three *d. Educ:* Malvern Coll. Travelled extensively throughout world, with interests in many countries. High Sheriff of Suffolk, 1961; DL Suffolk, 1970. *Recreations:* shooting, fishing. *Address:* Great Thurlow Hall, Suffolk. *T:* Thurlow 240. *Clubs:* Carlton, MCC.

See also E. H. Vestey.

VEYSEY, Geoffrey Charles, CB 1948; *b* 20 Dec. 1895; *e s* of late Charles Veysey, Exeter; *m* 1925, Eileen Agnes, *d* of late Charles Henry Byers, Gunnersbury. *Educ:* Latymer Upper Sch., Hammersmith. Served European War, 1914-18. Lieut, RGA. Entered Ministry of Labour, 1919; Private Secretary to Parliamentary Secretaries and Permanent Secretaries of Ministry, 1929-32; Assistant Secretary, 1938; Principal Assistant Secretary, 1944; Under-Secretary, Ministry of Labour and National Service, 1946-60. *Address:* 8 Stokes House, Sutherland Avenue, Bexhill-on-Sea, East Sussex TN39 3QT. *T:* Bexhill-on-Sea 214320. *Club:* Athenæum.

VIBERT, McInroy Este; Consular Service, retired; *b* Chiswick, 6 June 1894; *o s* of late Arthur Reginald Vibert and Margaret Eleanor Fraser; *m* 1st, Joyce Havell; one *s* one *d*; 2nd, Ellen Fiebiger-Guermanova. *Educ:* Taunton Sch.; France and Germany. Served European War, 1914-18, 10th Royal Fusiliers; Vice-Consul at Brussels, 1919, and subsequently at Philadelphia, Stettin, Koenigsberg, Memel, Frankfort-on-Main, Punta Arenas, Cologne, and Tunis; Consul at Sarajevo, 1936-39, and Split, 1939-41, Lisbon, 1941-44; Barcelona, 1944, Curacao, 1944-45; Consul-General (local rank) and Counsellor of Legation at Havana, 1945-47; Chargé d'Affaires, July 1946;

Foreign Office, 1947-48; Consul at Vigo; retired, 1950, on pension. *Recreations:* water-colour painting, philately. *Address:* Camino Vecinal la Vileta 215, Apartamento No 104, Palma, Mallorca, Spain. *T:* 67-14-48.

VICARS-HARRIS, Noël Hedley, CMG 1953; *b* 22 Nov. 1901; *o s* of late C. F. Harris and Evelyn C. Vicars, The Gate House, Rugby; *m* 1st, 1926, Maria Guimarães of Sao Paulo, Brazil (marr. dissolved, 1939); two *s*; 2nd, 1940, Joan Marguerite Francis; one *s. Educ:* Charterhouse; St John's Coll., Cambridge. BA Agric., 1924. Employed in Brazil by Brazil Plantations Syndicate Ltd, 1924-27; HM Colonial Service, Tanganyika, 1927-55; Official Member of Legislative and Executive Councils, Tanganyika, 1950-Nov. 1953; Member for Lands and Mines, Tanganyika, 1950-55. *Recreation:* gardening. *Address:* Bampfylde Cottage, Sparkford, Somerset. *T:* North Cadbury 454.

VICARY, Rev. Canon Douglas Reginald; Canon Residentiary and Precentor of Wells Cathedral, since 1975; Chaplain to the Queen, since 1977; *b* 24 Sept. 1916; *e s* of R. W. Vicary, Walthamstow; *m* 1947, Ruth, *y d* of late F. J. L. Hickinbotham, JP, and of Mrs Hickinbotham, Edgbaston; two *s* two *d. Educ:* Sir George Monoux Grammar Sch., Walthamstow; Trinity Coll., Oxford (Open Scholar), Wycliffe Hall, Oxford. 1st Class Nat. Sci. 1939; BSc 1939, MA 1942; Diploma in Theology with distinction, 1940; deacon, 1940; priest, 1941. Curate of St Peter and St Paul, Courteenhall, and Asst Chaplain and House Master, St Lawrence Coll., Ramsgate, while evacuated at Courteenhall, Northampton, 1940-44; Chaplain, Hertford Coll., Oxford, 1945-48; Tutor at Wycliffe Hall, 1945-47, Chaplain 1947-48; Dir of Religious Education, Rochester Diocese, 1948-57; Sec., CACTM Exams Cttee and GOE, 1952-57; Dir, Post-Ordination Training, 1952-57, Headmaster of King's School, Rochester, 1957-75. Minor Canon, Rochester Cathedral, 1949-52; Canon Residentiary and Precentor, 1952-57; Hon. Canon, 1957-75. Exam. Chaplain to Bishop of Rochester, 1950-, to Bishop of Bath and Wells, 1975-. FRSA 1970. *Publication:* contrib. Canterbury Chapters, 1976. *Recreations:* music, architecture, hill-walking, reading. *Address:* 4 The Liberty, Wells, Somerset BA5 2SU. *T:* Wells 73188.

VICK, A(rnold) O(ughtred) Russell; a Recorder of the Crown Court, since 1972; *b* 14 Sept. 1933; *yr s* of late His Honour Judge Sir Godfrey Russell Vick, QC; *m* 1959, Zinnia Mary, *e d* of Thomas Brown Yates, Godalming; two *s* one *d. Educ:* The Leys Sch., Cambridge; Jesus Coll., Cambridge (MA). Pilot, RAF, 1952-54. Called to Bar, Inner Temple, 1958; Mem. Gen. Council of the Bar, 1964-68; Prosecuting Counsel to the Post Office, 1964-69; Dep. Recorder, Rochester City QS, 1971. Mem., Lord Chancellor's County Court Rules Cttee, 1972-. Master, Curriers' Co., 1976-77. *Recreations:* golf, cricket. *Address:* Ameroak, Seal, Sevenoaks, Kent. *T:* Sevenoaks 61686; 2 Harcourt Buildings, Temple, EC4. *T:* 01-353 4746. *Clubs:* MCC; Hawks (Cambridge); Wildernesse (Sevenoaks).

VICK, Sir (Francis) Arthur, Kt 1973; OBE 1945; DSc, PhD; FIEE, FInstP; MRIA; President and Vice-Chancellor, Queen's University of Belfast, 1966-76; Pro-Chancellor and Chairman of Council, University of Warwick, since 1977; *b* 5 June 1911; *s* of late Wallace Devenport Vick and late Clara (*née* Taylor); *m* 1943, Elizabeth Dorothy Story; one *d. Educ:* Waverley Grammar School, Birmingham; Birmingham Univ. Asst Lectr in Physics, University Coll., London, 1936-39, Lectr, 1939-44; Asst Dir of Scientific Research, Min. of Supply, 1939-44; Lectr in Physics, Manchester Univ., 1944-47, Sen. Lectr, 1947-50; Prof. of Physics, University Coll. of N Staffs, 1950-59 (Vice-Principal, 1950-54, Actg Principal, 1952-53); Dep. Dir, AERE, Harwell, 1959-60, Dir, 1960-64; Dir of Research Group, UKAEA, 1961-66; Mem. for Research, 1964-66. Institute of Physics: Mem. Bd, 1946-51; Chm., Manchester and District Branch, 1948-51; Vice-Pres., 1953-56; Hon. Sec., 1956-60. Chairman: Manchester Fedn of Scientific Societies, 1949-51; Naval Educn Adv. Cttee, 1964-70; Academic Adv. Council, MoD, 1969-76. Pres., Assoc. of Teachers in Colls and Depts of Educn, 1964-72, Hon. Mem., 1972; Vice-Pres., Arts Council of NI, 1966-76. Member: Adv. Council on Bldg Research, Min. of Works, 1955-59; Scientific Adv. Council, Min. of Supply, 1956-59; UGC, 1959-66; Colonial Univ. Grants Adv. Cttee, 1960-65; Adv. Council on Research and Develt, Min. of Power, 1960-63; Nuclear Safety Adv. Cttee, Min. of Power, 1960-66; Governing Body, Nat. Inst. for Research in Nuclear Science, 1964-65. MRIA 1973. Hon. DSc: Keele, 1972; NUI, 1976; Hon. LLD: Dublin, 1973; Belfast, 1977; Hon. DCL Kent, 1977. Kt Comdr, Liberian Humane Order of African Redemption, 1962. *Publications:* various scientific papers and contributions to books. *Recreations:* music, gardening, using tools. *Address:* Fieldhead Cottage, Fieldhead Lane, Myton Road, Warwick CV34 6QF. *T:* Warwick 41822. *Clubs:* Athenæum, Savile.

VICK, Richard (William); His Honour Judge Vick; a Circuit Judge (formerly County Court Judge, since 1969, and Deputy Chairman of Quarter Sessions for Middlesex Area of Greater London, since 1965); Honorary Recorder of Guildford, since 1973; *b* 9 Dec. 1917; *s* of late Richard William Vick, JP, and Hilda Josephine (*née* Carlton), Windsor, Berks; *m* 1st, 1947, Judith Jean (*d* 1974), *d* of Denis Franklin Warren; one *s* two *d*; 2nd, 1975, Mrs Joan Chesney Frost, BA, *d* of Arthur Blaney Powe, MA, Sydney, Australia. *Educ:* Stowe; Jesus Coll., Cambridge (BA). Served in RNVR, 1939-46 (Lieut). Called to Bar, Inner Temple, 1940. Dep. Chairman, W Kent QS, 1960-62; Dep. Chairman, Kent QS, 1962-65. Vice-Chm., Surrey Magistrates Soc., 1972; Member: Magistrates' Courts Cttee; Probation Cttee. Mem. Court, Surrey Univ. *Publication:* The Administration of Civil Justice in England and Wales, 1967. *Recreations:* sailing, shooting, swimming, bridge. *Address:* The Town House, Godalming, Surrey. *Clubs:* Bath; Hawks (Cambridge).

VICKERS, family name of **Baroness Vickers.**

VICKERS, Baroness *cr* 1974 (Life Peer), of Devonport; **Joan Helen Vickers,** DBE 1964 (MBE 1946); *e d* of late Horace Cecil Vickers and late Lilian Monro Lambert Grose. *Educ:* St Monica's Coll., Burgh Heath, Surrey. Member, LCC, Norwood Division of Lambeth, 1937-45. Contested (C) South Poplar, 1945. Served with British Red Cross in SE Asia (MBE); Colonial Service in Malaya, 1946-50. MP (C) Plymouth, Devonport, 1955-Feb. 1974; UK Delegate (C), Council of Europe and WEU, 1967-74. Chairman: Anglo-Indonesian Society; UK Delegate, UK Status of Women Commn, 1960-64; President: Internat. Cttee for Suppression of Traffic in Persons; Status of Women Cttee; Internat. Friendship League; Inst. of Qualified Private Secretaries; Women's Corona Soc. Netherlands Red Cross Medal. *Address:* The Manor House, East Chisenbury, Pewsey, Wilts.

VICKERS, Sir (Charles) Geoffrey, VC 1915; Kt 1946; Solicitor, Administrator and Author; *b* 13 Oct. 1894; *y s* of C. H. Vickers, Nottingham; *m* 1st, 1918, Helen Tregoning (marr. diss. 1934), *y d* of A. H. Newton, Bexhill, Sussex; one *s* one *d*; 2nd, 1935, Ethel Ellen (*d* 1972), *d* of late H. R. B. Tweed, Laindon Frith, Billericay, Essex; one *s*. *Educ:* Oundle Sch.; Merton Coll., Oxford (MA). Served World War I with the Sherwood Foresters and other regts (2nd Lt-Major, 1915-18). Admitted Solicitor, 1923; Partner, Slaughter & May, 1926-45. World War II, re-commissioned (Colonel), specially employed; seconded as Deputy Dir.-Gen., Ministry of Economic Warfare, in charge of economic intelligence, and Member, Joint Intelligence Cttee of Chiefs of Staff, 1941-45. Legal adviser to National Coal Board, 1946-48, Board Member in charge of manpower, training, education, health and welfare, 1948-55; Director, Parkinson Cowan Ltd, 1955-65. Member, many public and professional bodies including: London Passenger Transport Board, 1941-46; Council of Law Society, 1944-48; Med. Research Council, 1952-60; Chairman, Research Cttee of Mental Health Research Fund, 1951-67. Hon. FRCPsych. *Publications:* (1953-) 50 papers and 6 books on application of system theory to management, government, medicine and human ecology, including The Art of Judgement, 1965, Value Systems and Social Process, 1968, Freedom in a Rocking Boat, 1970; Making Institutions Work, 1974. *Address:* Little Mead, Goring-on-Thames, Reading, Berks. *T:* Goring 2933.

VICKERS, Eric; Director of Defence Services, Department of the Environment, since 1972; *b* 25 April 1921; *s* of late Charles Vickers and late Ida Vickers; *m* 1945, Barbara Mary Jones; one *s* one *d*. *Educ:* King's School, Grantham. Joined India Office, 1938; RAF (Fl/Lt Coastal Command), 1941-46; Ministry of Works, 1948; Principal, 1950; Assistant Secretary, 1962; Imperial Defence College, 1969; Dir of Home Estate Management, DoE, 1970-72. *Recreation:* photography. *Address:* 16 Place House Lane, Old Coulsdon, Surrey. *T:* Downland 54303.

VICKERS, James Oswald Noel, OBE 1977; General Secretary, Civil Service Union, 1963-77 (Deputy General Secretary, 1960-62); *b* 6 April 1916; *s* of Noel Muschamp and Linda Vickers; *m* 1940, Winifred Mary Lambert; one *s* one *d*. *Educ:* Stowe Sch.; Queens' Coll., Cambridge. Exhibnr, BA Hons Hist., MA. Served War, HM Forces, 1939-45. Warden, Wedgwood Memorial Coll., 1946-49; Educn Officer, ETU, and Head of Esher Coll., 1949-56. Member: Civil Service Nat. Whitley Council, 1962-77 (Chm. Staff Side, 1975-77); TUC Inter-Union Disputes Panel, 1970-77; TUC Non-Manual Workers Adv. Cttee, 1973-75; Fabian Soc. Trade Union and Industrial Relations Cttee, 1964- (Chm. 1973-); co-opted Exec. Cttee, 1975; UCL Coll. Cttee, 1974-; Council, Tavistock Inst., 1976-. *Publications:* contrib. to

Fabian pamphlets. *Recreations:* bird-watching, gardening, travel. *Address:* 5 The Butts, Brentford, Mddx TW8 8BJ. *T:* 01-560 3482. *Club:* Royal Commonwealth Society.

VICKERS, Jon, CC (Canada) 1968; dramatic tenor; *b* Prince Albert, Saskatchewan, 1926; *m* 1953, Henrietta Outerbridge; three *s* two *d*. Studied under George Lambert, Royal Conservatory of Music, Toronto. Made debut with Toronto Opera Company, 1952; Stratford (Ontario) Festival, 1956. Joined Royal Opera House, Covent Garden, 1957. First sang at: Bayreuth Festival, 1958; Vienna State Opera, San Francisco Opera, and Chicago Lyric, 1959; Metropolitan, New York, and La Scala, Milan, 1960; Buenos Aires, 1962; Salzburg Festival, 1966. *Films:* Carmen; Pagliacci; Otello. Has made many recordings. Presbyterian. Hon. Dr: University of Saskatchewan, 1963; Bishop's Univ., 1965; Univ. West Ontario, 1970. Canada Centennial Medal, 1967. *Address:* c/o John Coast, 1 Park Close, SW1.

VICKERS, Prof. Michael Douglas Allen; Professor of Anaesthetics, Welsh National School of Medicine, since 1976; *b* 11 May 1929; *s* of George and Freda Vickers; *m* 1959, Ann Hazel Courtney; two *s* one *d*. *Educ:* Abingdon Sch.; Guy's Hosp. Med. Sch. MB, BS; FFARCS; FRSM. Lectr, RPMS, 1965-68; Consultant Anaesthetist, Birmingham AHA, 1968-76. Mem. Bd, Faculty of Anaesthetists, 1971-; Hon. Sec., Assoc. of Anaesthetists, 1974-76. Hon. FFARACS. *Publications:* (jtly) Principles of Measurement for Anaesthetists, 1970; (jtly) Drugs in Anaesthetic Practice, 5th edn 1978; Medicine for Anaesthetists, 1977. *Recreations:* music, theatre. *Address:* Department of Anaesthetics, Welsh National School of Medicine, Heath Park, Cardiff CF4 4XN. *T:* Cardiff 755944.

VICKERS, Maj.-Gen. Richard Maurice Hilton, OBE 1970 (MBE 1964); MVO 1959; GOC 4th Armoured Division, since 1977; *b* 21 Aug. 1928; *s* of Lt-Gen. W. G. H. Vickers, *qv*; *m* 1957, Gaie, *d* of Maj.-Gen. G. P. B. Roberts, *qv*; three *d*. *Educ:* Haileybury and Imperial Service Coll.; RMA. Commissioned Royal Tank Regt, 1948; 1st RTR, BAOR, Korea, Middle East, 1948-54; Equerry to HM The Queen, 1956-59; Brigade Major, 7 Armd Bde, 1962-64; 4th RTR, Borneo and Malaysia, 1964-66; CO The Royal Dragoons, 1967-68, The Blues and Royals, 1968-69; Comdr, 11th Armd Brigade, 1972-74; Dep. Dir of Army Training, 1975-77. *Recreations:* squash, flyfishing. *Address:* Little Minterne Farm House, near Dorchester, Dorset. *T:* Cerne Abbas 392. *Club:* Cavalry and Guards.

VICKERS, Thomas Douglas, CMG 1956; *b* 25 Sept. 1916; 2nd *s* of late Ronald Vickers, Scaitcliffe, Englefield Green, Surrey; *m* 1951, Margaret Awdry, *o c* of late E. A. Headley, Wagga, NSW; one *s* one *d*. *Educ:* Eton; King's Coll., Cambridge (MA Hons). Cadet, Colonial Administrative Service, 1938. Served War of 1939-45; Coldstream Guards, 1940-45. Colonial Office, 1938-40 and 1945-50; Gold Coast, 1950-53; Colonial Secretary, British Honduras, 1953-60; Chief Secretary, Mauritius, 1960-67, Dep. Governor, 1967-68; retired from HMOCS, Oct. 1968. Head of Staff Dept, Imperial Cancer Research Fund, 1969-. *Address:* Wood End, Worplesdon, Surrey. *T:* Worplesdon 3468. *Club:* Army and Navy.

VICKERS, William John, CMG 1950; MRCS, LRCP, DPH Cambridge; DTM&H Cambridge; Barrister-at-Law (Inner Temple); Deputy Coroner for East Staffordshire and County Borough of Burton-on-Trent, 1959-74; *b* 21 March 1898; *s* of late William Vickers; *m* 1939, Elizabeth Rachel, *d* of late S. Vernon Jackson; one *s* one *d*. *Educ:* Privately; Birmingham Medical Sch. Served European War, 1917-19, 2nd Lieut, RFA; resident Staff, General Hospital, Birmingham, 1923-25; Colonial Medical Service, 1925-54 (retired 1954); Malaya, 1925-38; Medical Officer, Health Officer, Acting Senior Health Officer, Kedah; Palestine, 1938-44: Senior Medical Officer, Acting Dep. Director of Medical Services; British West Indies, 1944-45: Adviser on Human Nutrition to Development and Welfare Organisation. British Military Administration, Singapore (Temporary Colonel), 1945-46; gazetted Hon. Colonel. Director of Medical Services, Colony of Singapore, 1946-54; MLC, Colony of Singapore, 1948-54. CStJ, 1951. *Publications:* (Government): (jointly) Health Survey of the State of Kedah, 1936; A Nutritional Economic Review of War-Time Palestine, 1944. *Address:* 174 Ashby Road, Burton-on-Trent, Staffs DE15 0LG. *T:* Burton-on-Trent 68899.

VICKERS, Lt.-Gen. Wilmot Gordon Hilton, CB 1942; OBE 1919; DL; *b* 8 June 1890; *s* of late Lt-Col Hilton Vickers, IA; *m* Mary Catherine (*decd*) *d* of Dr A. E. Nuttall; two *s*. *Educ:* United Services Coll., Westward Ho!, and Windsor (now Haileybury and Imperial Service Coll.). Commissioned Indian Army (Unattached List), 1910; 2nd Lieut, Indian Army, 1911;

Captain, 1915; Major, 1926; Bt Lt-Col, 1931; Col, 1935; Maj.-Gen., 1940; Lt-Gen., 1943; Comdt and Chief Instructor, Equitation Sch., India, 1934-35; Dep. Dir of Staff Duties, India, 1935-37; Brigade Comdr, India, 1939-40; Dir of Supplies and Transport, India, 1940-41; Maj.-Gen. i/c Administration, Iraq-Persia, 1941-42; Quarter-master-General, India, 1942-44; retired, 1944. DL County of Gloucestershire, 1946. County Cadet Commandant, Gloucestershire, Army Cadet Force, 1946-55. County Chief Warden, Civil Defence, Gloucestershire, 1949-60. *Address:* 4 Oakhurst Court, Parabola Road, Cheltenham, Glos. *Clubs:* Cavalry and Guards; New (Cheltenham).
See also R . M . H . Vickers .

VICKERY, Prof. Brian Campbell, FLA, FIInfSc; Professor of Library Studies and Director, School of Library Archive and Information Studies, University College London, since 1973; *b* 11 Sept. 1918; *s* of Adam Cairns McCay and Violet Mary Watson; *m* 1st, 1945, Manuletta McMenamin; one *s* one *d* ; 2nd, 1970, Alina Gralewska. *Educ:* King's Sch., Canterbury; Brasenose Coll., Oxford. MA. Chemist, Royal Ordnance Factory, Somerset, 1941-45; Librarian, ICI Ltd, Welwyn, 1946-60; Principal Scientific Officer, Nat. Lending Library for Sci. and Technology, 1960-64; Librarian, UMIST, 1964-66; Head of R&D, Aslib, 1966-73. *Publications:* Classification and Indexing in Science, 1958, 3rd edn 1975; On Retrieval System Theory, 1961, 2nd edn 1965; Techniques of Information Retrieval, 1970; Information Systems, 1973; articles in professional jls. *Recreations:* reading history, poetry, philosophy; music and theatre. *Address:* 138 Midhurst Road, W13 9TP. *T:* 01-567 6544.

VICKERY, Sir Philip Crawford, Kt 1948; CIE 1939; OBE 1923; *b* 23 Feb. 1890; *s* of late John Evans Vickery and Alice Maud Mary Vickery; *m* 1920, Phyllis Field Fairweather; one *s* (*yr s,* Coldstream Guards, died of wounds in Italy, April 1945). *Educ:* Portora Royal Sch., Enniskillen; Dean Close Sch., Cheltenham; Trinity Coll., Dublin. Joined Indian Police, 1909; Coronation Durbar, Delhi, 1911; served European War, 1915-21 and War of 1939-45; Acting Lieut-Colonel, Sept. 1939, and Colonel, 1942. Commonwealth Relations Office, 1952-65. *Clubs:* East India, Devonshire, Sports and Public Schools, Royal Automobile.

VIDAL, Gore; author; *b* 3 Oct. 1925; *s* of Eugene and Nina Gore Vidal. *Educ:* Phillips Exeter Academy, New Hampshire, USA (grad. 1943). Army of the US, 1943-46: Private to Warrant Officer (jg) and First Mate, Army FS-35, Pacific Theatre Ops. Democratic-Liberal candidate for US Congress, 1960; apptd to President Kennedy's Adv. Council of the Arts, 1961-63. *Publications: novels:* Williwaw, 1946; In a Yellow Wood, 1947; The City and the Pillar, 1948; The Season of Comfort, 1949; A Search for the King, 1950; Dark Green, Bright Red, 1950; The Judgment of Paris, 1952; Messiah, 1954; Julian, 1964; Washington, DC, 1967; Myra Breckinridge, 1968 (filmed 1969); Two Sisters, 1970; Burr, 1973; Myron, 1975; 1876, 1976; *essays:* Rocking the Boat, 1962; Reflections upon a Sinking Ship, 1969; Homage to Daniel Shays (collected essays 1952-72), 1972; Matters of Fact and of Fiction, 1977; *short stories:* A Thirsty Evil, 1956; *plays:* Visit to a Small Planet (NY prod.), 1957; The Best Man (NY prod.), 1960; Romulus (adapted from F. Dürrenmatt) (NY prod.), 1962; Weekend (NY prod.), 1968; On the March to the Sea (German prod.), 1962; An Evening with Richard Nixon, 1972; *screenplays,* from 1955: Wedding Breakfast, 1957; Suddenly Last Summer, 1958; The Best Man, 1964, etc; *television plays:* 1954-56: The Death of Billy the Kid (translated to screen as The Lefthanded Gun, 1959), etc; *literary and political criticism for:* NY Review of Books, Esquire, Partisan Review, TLS, etc. *Recreations:* as noted above. *Address:* Via di Torre Argentina 21, Rome, Italy.

VIDIC, Dobrivoje, Order of Yugoslav Flag 1st class; Order of Service to the People; Order of Brotherhood and Unity 1st class; Order for Bravery; Partisan Remembrance Medal 1941; Member, Executive Committee of the Presidium, Central Committee of the League of Communists of Yugoslavia, since 1974; *b* 24 Dec. 1918; *m* 1941, Mrs Vukica; one *s.* *Educ:* Skoplje University. Joined Diplomatic Service, 1951; served as: Minister Counsellor, London; Ambassador to Burma; Ambassador to USSR; Under-Sec. of State for Foreign Affairs; Perm. Rep. to UN, New York; Chm., Commn for Internat. Relations of Socialist Alliance of Yugoslavia; Ambassador to USSR; Ambassador of Yugoslavia to the Court of St James's, 1970-73. *Address:* Central Committee of the League of Communists of Yugoslavia, Belgrade, Yugoslavia.

VIDLER, Rev. Alexander Roper, LittD; Dean of King's College, Cambridge, 1956-66; Fellow of King's College, 1956-67, Hon. Fellow since 1972; *b* 1899; *s* of late Leopold Amon Vidler, JP, Rye, Sussex; unmarried. *Educ:* Sutton Valence Sch.; Selwyn

Coll., Cambridge. BA 2nd Class Theol. Tripos, 1921; MA 1925; Norrisian Prize, 1933; BD 1938; LittD 1957; University of Edinburgh, DD, 1946; Hon. DD: University of Toronto, 1961; College of Emmanuel and St Chad, Saskatoon, 1966. Wells Theological Coll.; Deacon, 1922; Priest, 1923; Curate of St Philip's, Newcastle upon Tyne, 1922-24; of St Aidan's, Birmingham, 1925-31; on staff of the Oratory House, Cambridge, 1931-38; Warden of St Deiniol's Library, Hawarden, 1939-48; Hon. Canon of Derby Cathedral, 1946-48; Canon of St George's Chapel, Windsor, 1948-56; licensed by Cambridge Univ. to preach throughout England, 1957; University Lecturer in Divinity, 1959-67; Commissary for Bishop of New Guinea, 1936-62; Hale Lecturer (USA), 1947; Birkbeck Lecturer (Trinity Coll., Cambridge), 1953; Firth Lecturer (Nottingham Univ.), 1955; Robertson Lecturer (Glasgow Univ.), 1964; Sarum Lecturer (Oxford Univ.), 1968-69. Sec., Christian Frontier Council, 1949-56. Mayor of Rye, 1972-74. Editor, Theology, 1939-64; Co-editor of The Frontier, 1950-52. *Publications:* Magic and Religion, 1930; Sex, Marriage and Religion, 1932; The Modernist Movement in the Roman Church, 1934; A Plain Man's Guide to Christianity, 1936; God's Demand and Man's Response, 1938; God's Judgement on Europe, 1940; Secular Despair and Christian Faith, 1941; Christ's Strange Work, 1944; The Orb and the Cross, 1945; Good News for Mankind, 1947; The Theology of F. D. Maurice, 1949; Christian Belief, 1950; Prophecy and Papacy, 1954; Christian Belief and This World, 1956; Essays in Liberality, 1957; Windsor Sermons, 1958; The Church in an Age of Revolution, 1961; A Century of Social Catholicism, 1964; 20th Century Defenders of the Faith, 1965; F. D. Maurice and Company, 1966; A Variety of Catholic Modernists, 1970; Scenes from a Clerical Life, 1977; (jointly): The Development of Modern Catholicism, 1933; The Gospel of God and the Authority of the Church, 1937; Natural Law, 1946; Editor, Soundings: Essays concerning Christian Understanding, 1962; Objections to Christian Belief, 1963; (with Malcolm Muggeridge) Paul: envoy extraordinary, 1972. *Recreations:* gardening, golf, beekeeping. *Address:* Friars of the Sack, Rye, East Sussex TN31 7HE.

VIDOR, King (Wallis); Independent Film Director and Producer (US); *b* Galveston, Texas, 8 Feb. 1896; *s* of Chas S. Vidor and Kate (*née* Wallis); *m* 1st, 1919, Florence Vidor; one *d* ; 2nd, 1927, Eleanor Boardman; two *d* ; 3rd, 1937, Elizabeth Hill. *Educ:* Peacock Military College, Texas; Jacob Tome Institute, Maryland. Directed films when aged 19, in Texas, 1914; in film industry worked as cameraman, writer and actor; directed again from 1918. Films directed include: Turn in the Road; The Jack Knife Man; Peg O' My Heart; Wild Oranges; The Big Parade; La Bohème; The Crowd; Hallelujah; Street Scene; The Champ; Bird of Paradise; Our Daily Bread; The Texas Rangers; Stella Dallas; The Citadel; Northwest Passage; HM Pulham Esq.; American Romance; Duel in the Sun; The Fountainhead; Ruby Gentry; Man Without a Star; War and Peace; Solomon and Sheba. D. W. Griffith award by Screen Directors Guild (for outstanding contributions in film direction over a long period of years), 1957; many awards for various films throughout America and Europe. Golden Thistle Award, Edinburgh Festival, 1964. Cavaliere Ufficiale, Italy, 1970. *Publications:* A Tree is a Tree (autobiography), 1953 (New York), also published in England; Guerra e Pace, 1956 (Italy); King Vidor on Film-making, 1972 (New York). *Recreations:* golf; plays classical Spanish Guitar; paints in oils. *Address:* c/o General Management Association, PO Box 49993, Los Angeles, Calif 90049, USA. *Clubs:* Academy Motion Picture Arts and Sciences, Bel Air Country, Screen Directors Guild, PEN (USA).

VIELER, Geoffrey Herbert, FCA; Member of Board, Post Office Corporation, 1969-71; *b* 21 Aug. 1910; *s* of late Herbert Charles Stuart Vieler, Huddersfield, and Emily Mary; *m* 1934, Phyllis Violet; one *d. Educ:* Fairway Sch., Bexhill-on-Sea. With Vale & West, Chartered Accountants, Reading, 1927-41 (qual. 1932); War Service, 1941-46: commnd RAOC, 1943, Major 1945; joined Binder Hamlyn, Chartered Accountants, 1946, Partner 1959-69; Managing Dir, Posts and National Giro, 1969-71. Mem. Techn. Adv. Cttee, Inst. of Chartered Accountants in England and Wales, 1967-74. Chm., London Chartered Accountants, 1976-77. *Address:* Robins Wood, Monks Drive, South Ascot, Berks SL5 9BB; Riversmeet, Mill Lane, Lower Shiplake RG9 3LY.

VIERTEL, Deborah Kerr; see Kerr, D. J.

VIGARS, Robert Lewis; Leader of the Opposition, Inner London Education Authority, since 1974; *b* 26 May 1923; *s* of Francis Henry Vigars and Susan Laurina May Vigars (*née* Lewis); *m* 1962, Margaret Ann Christine, *y d* of late Sir John Walton, KCIE, CB, MC, and of Lady Walton; two *d. Educ:* Truro

Cathedral Sch.; London Univ. (LLB (Hons)). Served War of 1939-45: RA and Royal Corps of Signals, 1942-47; attached Indian Army (Captain), 1944-47; Captain, Princess Louise's Kensington Regt, TA, 1951-54. Qualified as solicitor (Hons), 1948. Partner, Simmons & Simmons, London, EC2, 1951-75. Young Conservative deleg. to World Assembly of Youth at Dakar (W Africa), 1952. Member: Kensington Borough Council, 1953-59; London and Home Counties Traffic Adv. Cttee, 1956-58; London Roads (Nugent) Cttee, 1958-59; LCC and GLC Kensington (formerly South Kensington), 1955-; Environmental Planning Cttee, GLC, 1967-71 (Chm.); Strategic Planning Cttee, GLC, 1971-73 (Chm.); Standing Conf. on London and SE Regional Planning and SE Economic Planning Council, 1968-75. *Publication:* Let Our Cities Live (Bow Gp, jointly). *Recreation:* mountain walking. *Address:* 24 Cope Place, Kensington, W8 6AA. *Club:* Hurlingham.

VIGGERS, Peter John; MP (C) Gosport, since Feb. 1974; *b* 13 March 1938; *s* of late J. S. Viggers and E. F. Viggers, Gosport; *m* 1968, Jennifer Mary McMillan, MB, BS, LRCP, MRCS, DA, *d* of late Dr R. B. McMillan, MD, FRCP, Guildford, and late Mrs J. T. C. McMillan, MA, MIB; two *s* one *d*. *Educ:* Portsmouth Grammar Sch.; Trinity Hall, Cambridge (MA). Solicitor 1967. Trained as RAF Pilot with Royal Canadian Air Force, awarded Wings 1958. Cambridge, 1958-61; Chm. Cambridge Univ. Conservative Assoc., 1960. Commnd in 457 (Wessex) Regt Royal Artillery (TA), 1963. Director: Energy, Finance and General Trust Ltd; Premier Consolidated Oilfields Ltd; The Sangers Group Ltd. Underwriting Member of Lloyds. *Recreations:* beagling, walking and messing about in boats. *Address:* House of Commons, SW1.

VILE, Prof. Maurice John Crawley; Professor of Political Science since 1968, and Pro-Vice-Chancellor since 1975, University of Kent at Canterbury; *b* 23 July 1927; *s* of Edward M. and Elsie M. Vile; two *s*. *Educ:* London Sch. of Economics. BSc (Econ) 1951; PhD London, 1954; MA Oxford, 1962. Lectr in Politics, Univ. of Exeter, 1954-62; Fellow of Nuffield Coll., Oxford, 1962-65; Reader in Politics and Govt, Univ. of Kent, 1965-68; Dean of Faculty of Social Scis, 1969-75. Visiting Professor: Univ. of Massachusetts, 1960; Smith College, Mass., 1961. Royer Lectr, Univ. of Calif., Berkeley, 1974. *Publications:* The Structure of American Federalism, 1961; Constitutionalism and the Separation of Powers, 1967; Politics in the USA, 1970, rev. edn 1976; Federalism in the United States, Canada and Australia (Res. Paper No 2, Commn on the Constitution), 1973; The Presidency (Amer. Hist. Documents Vol. IV), 1974. *Address:* Keynes College, The University, Canterbury, Kent. *T:* Canterbury 66822.

VILLIERS, family name of **Earls of Jersey** and **Clarendon.**

VILLIERS; see De Villiers.

VILLIERS, Viscount; George Henry Child Villiers; *b* 29 Aug. 1948; *s* and *heir* of 9th Earl of Jersey, *qv; m* 1st, 1969, Verna (marr. diss. 1973), 2nd *d* of K. A. Stott, St Mary, Jersey; one *d;* 2nd, 1974, Sandra, step *d* of H. Briginshaw, Feremina, St Martin, Guernsey; one *s*. *Educ:* Eton; Millfield. Late The Royal Hussars (PWO), now Army Reserve. *Heir: s* Hon. George Francis William Child-Villiers, *b* 5 Feb. 1976. *Address:* Bel Respiro, Trinity Hill, St Helier, Jersey, CI. *Clubs:* Brooks's, Royal Automobile.

VILLIERS, Alan John, DSC; *b* 23 Sept. 1903; *s* of Leon Joseph Villiers and Anastasia Hayes; *m* 1940, Nancie, *o d* of Alban Henry and Mabel Wills, Melbourne; two *s* one *d*. *Educ:* State Schools, Essendon High School, Melbourne. Went to sea 1919 in sail, whaling in Antarctic with Norwegian Carl Anton Larsen's first Ross Sea Expedition in whaler Sir James Clark Ross, 1923-24; joined Captain De Cloux in purchase of four-masted barque Parma, 1931; bought Danish schoolship Georg Stage June 1934, renamed her Joseph Conrad and sailed 58,000 miles round world, 1934, 1935, 1936; sailing in Kuweit dhows in Persian Gulf-Zanzibar trade, 1938-39; Lieut, RNVR, 1940-42; Lt Cdr 1943; Comdr 1944. Commanded 'A' Squadron of Landing Craft (Infantry) in the invasions of Italy and Normandy (DSC) and at the occupation of Rangoon, Malaya, and East Indies; Master, training ship Warspite, Outward Bound Sea School, Aberdovey, N Wales, 1949; sailed with Portuguese Arctic codfishing fleet in schooner Argus, 1950. Commendador of Portuguese Order of St James of the Sword. Volunteered as Master of Mayflower replica, 1956, and sailed the vessel to the USA, 1957. In command of square-rigged ships for films: Moby Dick, 1955; John Paul Jones, 1958; Billy Budd, 1961; Hawaii, 1965. Vice-President, Soc. for Nautical Research; FRGS; Trustee of National Maritime Museum, 1948-74; Governor Cutty Sark Preservation Soc.; Member: HMS Victory Technical Advisory

Committee; Ships Cttee, Maritime Trust. *Publications:* Whaling in the Frozen South; Falmouth for Orders; By Way of Cape Horn; The Sea in Ships; Sea Dogs of To-day; Voyage of the Parma; Vanished Fleets; The Last of the Windships; Cruise of the Conrad; Stormalong; The Making of a Sailor, 1938; Sons of Sinbad, 1940; The Set of the Sails, 1949; The Coral Sea, 1950; The Quest of the Schooner Argus, 1951 (Camões Prize, Portugal); The Indian Ocean, 1952; The Way of a Ship, 1954; Posted Missing, 1956; Pioneers of the Seven Seas, 1956; The Western Ocean, 1957; Give Me a Ship to Sail, 1958; The New Mayflower, 1959; The Oceans, 1963; The Battle of Trafalgar, 1965; Captain Cook, the Seamen's Seaman, 1967; The War with Cape Horn, 1971; (with H. Picard) The Bounty Ships of France, 1972. *Recreations:* sailing, photography. *Address:* 1a Lucerne Road, Oxford. *T:* Oxford 55632. *Clubs:* Naval; Royal Harwich Yacht (Harwich); Royal Cruising; Circumnavigators (New York).

VILLIERS, Sir Charles (Hyde), Kt 1975; MC 1945; Chairman, British Steel Corporation, since 1976; Member, National Economic Development Council, since 1976; *b* 14 Aug. 1912; *s* of Algernon Hyde Villiers (killed in action, 1917) and of Beatrix Paul (now Dowager Lady Aldenham); *m* 1st, 1938, Pamela Constance Flower (*d* 1943); one *s*; 2nd, 1946, Marie José, *d* of Count Henri de la Barre d'Erquelinnes, Jurbise, Belgium; two *d*. *Educ:* Eton; New Coll., Oxford. Asst to Rev. P. B. Clayton, of Toc H, 1931; Glyn Mills, Bankers, 1932. Grenadier Guards (SRO), 1936; served at Dunkirk, 1940 (wounded, 1942); Special Ops Exec., London and Italy, 1943-45; parachuted into Yugoslavia and Austria, 1944; Lt-Col and Comd 6 Special Force Staff Section, 1945 (MC). A Man. Dir, Helbert Wagg, 1948, and J. Henry Schroder Wagg, 1960-68; Managing Director, Industrial Reorganisation Corporation, 1968-71; Chm., Guinness Mahon & Co. Ltd, 1971-76; Exec. Dep. Chm., Guinness Peat Gp, 1973-76. Director: Bass Charrington; Courtaulds; Sun Life Assurance; Banque Belge; Financor SA; Darling & Co. (Pty); Formerly Chm., Ashdown Trans-Europe and Trans-Australian Investment Trusts. Chairman: Federal Trust Gp on European Monetary Integration, 1972; Northern Ireland Finance Corp., 1972-73. Co-Chm., Europalia Festival, 1973; Chm., Theatre Royal, Windsor; Trustee, Royal Opera House Trust, 1974-. Member: Inst. Internat. d'Etudes Bancaires, 1959-76 (Pres. 1964); Minister of Labour's Resettlement Cttee for London and SE, 1958 (Chm. 1961-68); Review Body for N Ireland Economic Develt, 1971. Lubbock Meml Lectr, Oxford, 1971. Mem., Chelsea Borough Council, 1950-53. Order of the People, Yugoslavia, 1970; Grand Officier de l'Ordre de Léopold II (Belgium), 1974; Gold Medal of IRI, Italy, 1975. *Recreations:* gardening and ciné. *Address:* 54 Eaton Square, SW1. *T:* 01-235 7634; Blacknest House, Sunninghill, Berks. *T:* Ascot 22137. *Club:* Anglo-Belgian.
See also Baron Aldenham.

VILLIERS, Vice-Adm. Sir (John) Michael, KCB 1962 (CB 1960); OBE 1943; *b* 22 June 1907; 3rd *s* of late Rear-Adm. E. C. Villiers, CMG and of Mrs Villiers; *m* 1936, Rosemary, CStJ, 2nd *d* of late Lt-Col B. S. Grissell, DSO, and late Lady Astley-Cubitt; two *d. Educ:* Oundle School; Royal Navy. Served War of 1939-45 (despatches, OBE). Comd HMS Ursa, 1945, and HMS Snipe, 1946-47; directing staff of Joint Services Staff College, 1948-49; Assistant Director of Plans Admiralty, 1950-51; Queen's Harbour Master, Malta, 1952-54; comd HMS Bulwark, 1954-57; Chief of Naval Staff, New Zealand, 1958-60; a Lord Commissioner of the Admiralty, Fourth Sea Lord and Vice-Controller, 1960-63; Lt-Governor and C-in-C Jersey, 1964-69. KStJ 1964. *Address:* Decoy House, Melton, Woodbridge, Suffolk IP13 6DJ. *Club:* Army and Navy.

VINAVER, Eugène, MA, DLitt, D ès L; Emeritus Professor in the University of Manchester; *b* St Petersburg, 18 June 1899; *s* of Maxime Vinaver; *m* 1939, Alice Elisabeth Malet Vaudrey; one *s. Educ:* Univs of Paris and Oxford. Lectr in French Language and Literature at Lincoln College, Oxford, 1924-28; Lecturer in French, University of Oxford, 1928-31; Reader in French Literature, 1931-33; Professor of French Language and Literature, Univ. of Manchester, 1933-66; Gregynog Lectr, Univ. of Wales, 1957; Zaharoff Lectr, Univ. of Oxford, 1960; Alexander White Professor, Univ. of Chicago, 1960; Visiting Professor of French, Stanford Univ., 1962; Herbert F. Johnson Professor, Univ. of Wisconsin, 1964-65; Phi Beta Kappa Visiting Scholar, 1967-68; Visiting Professor: Univ. of Wisconsin, 1966-70; Northwestern Univ., 1970-74; Univ. of Victoria, BC, 1972-73, 1974-75; Univ. of Toronto, 1975-76; Univ. of Texas, 1977; Hon. Prof. of French, Univs of Hull and Kent, 1977-; Lord Northcliffe Lectr in Literature, London Univ., 1971. President: Soc. Study of Medieval Langs and Lit., 1939-48; Modern Language Assoc., 1961; Modern Humanities Research Association, 1966; Internat. Arthurian Soc., 1966-69 (Hon.

Pres., 1969-). BLitt 1922. MA 1927, Oxford; Docteur ès Lettres at Paris, 1925; DLitt, Oxford, 1950; Hon. DHL, Chicago, 1960; Hon. DLitt: Hull, 1964; Univ. of Wales, 1969; Hon. LLD Univ. of Victoria, 1976; Hon. Fellow, Lincoln College, Oxford; Corresp. Fellow: British Academy, 1972; Medieval Acad. of America, 1973; Laureate, French Acad. (Prix Broquette-Gonin, 1971); Foreign Mem. Belgian Roy. Acad. of French Language and Literature; Hon. Mem., Modern Language Assoc. of America; Chevalier of the Legion of Honour. *Publications:* The Love Potion in the Primitive Tristan Romance, 1924; Le Roman de Tristan et Iseut dans l'œuvre de Malory, 1925; Etudes sur le Tristan en prose, 1925; Malory, 1929, 2nd imp. 1970; Principles of Textual Emendation, 1939; Hommage à Bédier, 1942; Le Roman de Balain (Introduction) 1942; Racine et la poésie tragique, 1951 (Eng. trans. 1955; revised French edn, 1963); L'Action poétique dans le théâtre de Racine, 1960; Tristan et Iseut à travers le temps, 1961; Form and Meaning in Medieval Romance, 1966; A la Recherche d'une poétique médiévale, 1970; The Rise of Romance, 1971; critical editions of Renan, Prière sur l'Acropole (with T. B. L. Webster), 1934; Racine, Principes de la Tragédie, 1944, 2nd edn, 1951; The Works of Sir Thomas Malory, 3 vols, 1947 (reprinted 1948; one vol. edn, 1954, 1970; 2nd rev. edn 1967); Malory's Tale of the Death of King Arthur, 1955, 1967; King Arthur and His Knights, 1956, 1968, 1975; articles in Medium Aevum, French Studies, Bulletin of the John Rylands Library, Revue d'Histoire littéraire de la France, Cahiers de Civilisation médiévale, etc.; Editor of Arthuriana, 1929-31. *Address:* 20 Fordwich Road, Sturry, Canterbury, Kent; 4 Rue des Eaux, Paris, 16e.

VINCENT, Maj.-Gen. Douglas, CB 1969; OBE 1954; Director, Standard Telephones & Cables Pty Ltd, since 1973; *b* Australia, 10 March 1916; *s* of William Frederick Vincent, civil engineer, and Sarah Jane Vincent; *m* 1947, Margaret Ector, *d* of N. W. Persse, Melbourne; two *s* one *d. Educ:* Brisbane State High School; Royal Military Coll., Duntroon. Commissioned, Dec. 1938; Middle East (7 Div.), 1940-42; BLA, 1944; NW Europe (30 Corps); Borneo Campaign, 1945; Brit. Commonwealth Forces, Korea, 1954; Dir of Signals, 1954-58; Dir of Staff Duties, 1958-60; Chief of Staff, Eastern Command, 1960-62; Commander, Aust. Army Force, 1962-63 (Singapore, Malaya); idc 1964; Commander: 1 Task Force, 1965; 1st Div., 1966; Aust. Force, Vietnam, 1967-68; Head, Aust. Jt Services Staff, Washington, DC, USA, 1968-70; Adjutant General, Australian Army, 1970-73. MIREE(Aust). *Recreations:* golf, swimming. *Address:* 41 Hampton Circuit, Yarralumla, Canberra, ACT 2600, Australia. *Club:* Imperial Services (Sydney).

VINCENT, Prof. Eric R. P., CBE 1947; LittD; DPhil; MA; Professor Emeritus of Italian, Cambridge University, since 1962 (Professor, 1935-62); Fellow of Corpus Christi College, Cambridge; President, 1954-59; *b* 10 Dec. 1894; *s* of Charles Vincent, MusDoc Oxon., and Hannah Phillips; *m* 1923, Ivy, 3rd *d* of Lt-Col W. Barrow-Simonds, JP; one *d. Educ:* Berkhamsted School; Christ Church, Oxford (Heath-Harrison travelling scholar. First class honours in the School of Modern and Medieval languages, 1921). Studying in Germany at outbreak of war, 1914, and interned as a civil prisoner of war in Ruhleben Camp until Nov. 1918. Lecturer in Italian at King's College, University of London, 1922; Univ. Lecturer in Italian language and literature at Oxford, 1927-34; Assistant Dir in a Department of Foreign Office, 1939-45. British Academy Serena Medal, 1973. Commendatore, Order Al merito della Repubblica Italiana, 1955. *Publications:* Ardengo Soffici, Six Essays on Modern Art, Preface and Notes, 1922; The Italy of the Italians, 1927; R. B. Adam Library Publication, trans. and editing of Italian MSS in this collection, 1930; Enciclopedia Italiana, many articles, 1932-34; Machiavelli, Il Principe, Preface and revision of text 1935; Gabriele Rossetti in England, 1936; The Commemoration of the Dead (Foscolo's Sepolcri), 1936; British Academy Lecture on Dante, 1945; Byron, Hobhouse and Foscolo, 1949; Ugo Foscolo, An Italian in Regency England, 1953; contributions to learned periodicals; translations, etc. *Address:* Sandhills Cottage, Salcombe, S Devon; Corpus Christi College, Cambridge.

VINCENT, Prof. Ewart Albert; Professor of Geology, and Fellow of University College, Oxford, since 1967; *b* 23 Aug. 1919; *o s* of Albert and Winifred Vincent, Aylesbury; *m* 1944, Myrtle Ablett; two *d. Educ:* Reading Sch.; Univ. of Reading. BSc (Reading) 1940; PhD 1951; MA (Oxon) 1952; MSc (Manch.) 1966. FRIC, FGS. Chemist, Min. of Supply, 1940-45; Geologist, Anglo-Iranian Oil Co., 1945-46; Lectr in Mineralogy and Crystallography, Univ. of Durham, 1946-51; Lectr in Geology, Oxford Univ., 1951-56; Reader in Mineralogy, Oxford Univ., 1956-62; Prof. of Geology, Manchester Univ., 1962-66. Mem. NERC, 1975-. Vice-Pres., Internat. Assoc. of Volcanology, 1968-71; Pres., Mineralogical Soc. of GB, 1974-76; Mem.

Council, Geol Soc., 1973-76. Fellow, Mineralogical Soc. of Amer. Hon. Corresp. Mem., Soc. Géol. de Belgique. Awarded Wollaston Fund, Geol Soc. London, 1961. *Publications:* scientific papers in learned jls. *Recreations:* music, photography. *Address:* 10a Bardwell Road, Oxford; Department of Geology and Mineralogy, Parks Road, Oxford. *T:* Oxford 54511.

VINCENT, Sir (Harold) Graham, KCMG 1953; CB 1935; CVO 1932; *b* 1891; *s* of late William Vincent; *m* 1921, Brenda (*d* 1973), *d* of late Edward Wood-White, MD, BS; one *d. Educ:* Haileybury; Jesus College, Cambridge. First Class, Mathematical Tripos, 1914; served European War, 1914-18, in London Rifle Bde and Army Signal Service (Captain); entered HM Treasury, 1919; Private Sec. to the Parliamentary Sec. to the Treasury, 1924; Private Secretary to successive Prime Ministers, 1928-36; Principal Private Secretary, 1934-36; Principal Assistant Secretary Committee of Imperial Defence, 1936-39; Ministry: of Food, 1939-40; of Works and Buildings, and of Town and Country Planning, 1940-44; of Production, 1944-46; of Civil Aviation, 1946-49; Secretary, Government Hospitality, 1949-56. *Recreation:* golf. *Address:* Windrush, Coles Lane, Brasted, Kent.

VINCENT, Ivor Francis Sutherland, CMG 1966; MBE 1945; HM Diplomatic Service, retired; *b* 14 Oct. 1916; *s* of late Lt-Col Frank Lloyd Vincent and Gladys Clarke; *m* 1949, Patricia Mayne; three *d* (and one *d* decd). *Educ:* St Peter's Coll., Radley; Christ Church, Oxford. Served Indian Army, Royal Garhwal Rifles, 1941-46. Entered HM Foreign Service, 1946; Second Secretary, Foreign Office, 1946-48; First Sec., Buenos Aires, 1948-51; UK Delegn, NATO, Paris, 1951-53; FO, 1954-57; Rabat, 1957-59; Geneva (Disarmt Delegn), 1960; Paris (UK Delegn to OECD), 1960-62; Counsellor, FO, 1962-66; Baghdad, Jan.-June, 1967; Caracas, Oct. 1967-70; Ambassador to Nicaragua, 1970-73; Consul-Gen., Melbourne, 1973-76, retired. *Recreations:* music, walking. *Address:* 101 Barkston Gardens, SW5. *T:* 01-373 5273. *Club:* Travellers'.

VINCENT, Prof. John Joseph, MSc, MSc Tech., FTI; Professor of Textile Technology, University of Manchester Institute of Science and Technology, 1957-74, now Emeritus; *b* 29 June 1907; 2nd *s* of J. H. Vincent, MA, DSc; *m* 1935, M. Monica Watson, MSc, PhD, of Sheffield; one *s* one *d. Educ:* County Grammar Sch., Harrow; University Coll., London. Mathematics Dept, University Coll., London, 1927-29; Shirley Inst., Manchester, 1929-42 and 1945-57. Ministry of Aircraft Production, 1942-45. Hon. Life Mem., Textile Institute, 1976 (Mem. Council, 1959-74; Vice-Pres., 1971-74); Pres., British Assoc. of Managers of Textile Works, 1963-64; Mem., Cotton and Allied Textiles Industry Training Bd, 1966-74. Textile Inst. Medal, 1968; Leverhulme Emeritus Fellowship, 1976. *Publications:* papers on textile technology. *Recreations:* gardening, reading, listening to music. *Address:* The White House, Perranarworthal, Truro, Cornwall TR3 7QE. *T:* Devoran 863504.

VINCENT, Leonard Grange, CBE 1960; FRIBA, FRTPI, Distinction Town Planning (RIBA); formerly architect and town planner, and Principal Partner, Vincent and Gorbing, Architects and Planning Consultants; *b* 13 April 1916; *s* of late Godfrey Grange Vincent; *m* 1942, Evelyn (*née* Gretton); twin *s* one *d. Educ:* Forest House School. Trained as architect in London, 1933, and subsequently as a town planner; experience in private practice and local government. Served War of 1939-45: Royal Engineers (Major); mostly overseas, in Western Desert, and Italian campaigns with 8th Army, 1940-45. Formerly Chief Architect and Planner, Stevenage Development Corporation. *Publications:* various technical and planning articles in technical press. *Recreations:* archaeology, painting. *Address:* Medbury, Rectory Lane, Stevenage, Hertfordshire. *T:* Stevenage 51175.

VINCENT, Sir William (Percy Maxwell), 3rd Bt, *cr* 1936; *b* 1 February 1945; *o s* of Sir Lacey Vincent, 2nd Bt, and of Helen Millicent, *d* of Field Marshal Sir William Robert Robertson, 1st Bt, GCB, GCMG, GCVO, DSO; *S* father, 1963; *m* 1976, Christine Margaret, *d* of Rev. E. G. Walton. *Educ:* Eton College. 2nd Lieutenant, Irish Guards, 1964-67. *Recreations:* water ski-ing, sailing. *Heir:* none. *Address:* Whistlers, Buriton, Petersfield, Hampshire. *T:* Petersfield 3532.

VINCENT BROWN, Kenneth; see Brown, Kenneth V.

VINCENT-JONES, Captain Desmond, DSC; Royal Navy; retired 1964; *b* 13 Feb. 1912; *s* of late Sir Vincent Jones, KBE; *m* 1944, Jacqueline, *e d* of Col Sloggett, DSO; two *d. Educ:* Beacon School, Crowborough; Royal Naval College, Dartmouth. Served in Royal Navy, 1929-64; War of 1939-45, in aircraft carrier operations in Atlantic and Mediterranean (DSC and Bar); Served in Air Staff appointments and in Command of HM Ships, 1946-64. Graduate of US Armed Forces and British Services Staff Colleges. Naval and Military Attaché to Buenos Aires and Montevideo, 1958-60. On retirement from RN joined Marine Consortiums as consultant. *Recreations:* golf, tennis, fishing, cruising. *Address:* Holiday House, Sunningdale, Berks SL5 7RM. *T:* Ascot 21866. *Clubs:* White's, MCC, Free Foresters; Sunningdale Golf.

VINCZE, Paul, FRBS, FRNS; *b* Hungary, 15 August 1907; *s* of Lajos Vincze; British subject, 1948; *m* 1958, Emilienne Chauzeix. *Educ:* High School of Arts and Crafts, Budapest, later under E. Telcs. Won a travelling scholarship to Rome, 1935-37; came to England, 1938. *Exhibited:* Royal Academy, Rome, Budapest, Paris, etc; *works represented in:* British Museum, London; Museum of Fine Arts, Budapest; Ashmolean Museum, Oxford; Swedish Historical Museum; Danish Nat. Museum; Museum of Amer. Numismatic Soc.; Smithsonian Instn, Washington; Cabinet des Medailles, Paris, etc. *Works include:* Aga Khan Platinum Jubilee Portrait; Sir Bernard Pares Memorial Tablet, Senate House, London Univ.; President Truman, portrait medallion; Pope Paul VI, portrait medallion; official medal to commemorate 400th Anniversary of birth of William Shakespeare; medal to commemorate Independence of Ghana; official seal of Ghana Govt; (designed) Smithsonian Instn Award Medal (1965); Nat. Commemorative Society (USA) Winston Churchill Medal; Florence Nightingale Medal for Société Commemorative de Femmes Célèbres; E. and J. De Rothschild Medal for inauguration of Knesset, 1966; Yehudi Menuhin 50th Birthday Medal, 1966; Prince Karim Aga Khan 10th Anniversary Medal, 1968; Cassandra Memorial Tablet for Internat. Publishing Corp. Bldg, 1968; Shakespeare-Garrick Medal, 1969; Medal to commemorate 100th Anniversary of birth of Sir Henry J. Wood, 1969; Dickens 100th Anniversary Medal for Dickens Fellowship, 1970; Medal to commemorate J. B. Priestley's 80th birthday, 1974; Internat. Shakespeare Assoc. Congress Medal, USA, 1976; *coin designs:* obverse and reverses, Libya, 1951; obverses, Guatemala, 1954; reverses, threepence, sixpence and shilling, Cen. African Fedn, 1955; obverses, Ghana, 1958; reverses, Guernsey, 1957; threepence and florin, Nigeria, 1960; Guinea, obverse and reverses, Malawi, 1964; reverse, Uganda crown, 1968; Bustamante Portrait for obverse of Jamaican Dollar, 1969; reverses for decimal coins, Guernsey, 1970, etc. Awarded Premio Especial, Internat. Exhib., Madrid, 1951; Silver Medal, Paris Salon, 1964; first gold Medal of Amer. Numismatic Assoc., 1966. *Address:* 5 Rossetti Studios, Flood Street, Chelsea, SW3. *T:* 01-352 3975; Villa La Meridienne, Domaine Bastide, avenue La Bastide, 06520 Magagnosc, France. *T:* 36.47.54. *Club:* Art Workers Guild.

VINE, Prof. Frederick John, FRS 1974; Professor of Environmental Sciences, University of East Anglia, since 1974; *b* 17 June 1939; *s* of Frederick Royston Vine and Ivy Grace Vine (née Bryant); *m* 1964, Susan Alice McCall; one *s* one *d. Educ:* Latymer Upper Sch., Hammersmith; St John's Coll., Cambridge (BA, PhD). Instructor, 1965-67, and Asst Professor, 1967-70, Dept of Geological and Geophysical Sciences, Princeton Univ., NJ, USA; Reader, School of Environmental Sciences, Univ. of E Anglia, 1970-74. *Publications:* articles in Nature, Science, Phil. Trans Roy. Soc. London, etc. *Recreations:* walking, camping. *Address:* 144 Christchurch Road, Norwich NR2 3PG. *T:* Norwich 53875.

VINE, Philip Mesban; DL; Town Clerk and Chief Executive Officer, Nottingham, 1966-74; *b* 26 Oct. 1919; *s* of late Major George H. M. Vine and Elsie Mary (née Shephard); London; *m* 1944, Paulina, JP, *d* of late Arthur Oyler, Great Hormead Hall, Herts; one *s* one *d. Educ:* Sherborne Sch.; Taft Sch., USA; Sidney Sussex Coll., Cambridge (MA, LLB). Served in Royal Artillery, 1939-45; Adjutant 90th Field Regt, RA. Articled to W. H. Bentley, Town Clerk of Paddington; admitted Solicitor, 1948; Asst Solicitor, Paddington, 1948-50; Chief Asst Solicitor, Birkenhead, 1950-53; Deputy Town Clerk: Wallasey, 1953-59; Southend-on-Sea, 1959-62; Town Clerk, Cambridge, 1963-66. Mem. Court, Nottingham Univ., 1966-74; Chm., Notts Local Valuation Panel, 1974-; Mem., Local Radio Council for BBC Radio Nottingham, 1970-76; Indep. Chm., Home Sec.'s Adv. Cttee, Wireless and Telegraphy Act 1949, 1975-; Member: Panel of Asst Comrs of Local Govt Boundary Commn, 1974-; Panel of Inspectors, DoE, 1974-; Bd Telford (New Town) Develt Corp., 1975-; New Towns Staff Commn, 1976-; Police Complaints Bd, 1977-. Gen. Comr of Income Tax, 1975-. Liveryman, Clockmakers' Co. DL Notts, 1974. *Recreations:* fishing, archaeology, enjoyment of music. *Address:* 42 Magdala Road, Mapperley Park, Nottingham NG3 5DF. *T:* Nottingham 621269. *Club:* United Services (Nottingham).

VINE, Col (Roland) Stephen, FRCPath, FZS; Chief Inspector, Cruelty to Animals Act (1876), Home Office, 1962-75; *b* 26 Dec. 1910; *s* of late Joseph Soutter Vine and of Josephine Vine (née Moylan); *m* 1935, Flora Betty, *d* of Charles Strutton Brookes, MBE, Dovercourt; three *d. Educ:* Southend-on-Sea High Sch.; Guy's Hosp. BSc; MRCS, LRCP, FRCPath, FZS(Scientific). Royal Army Medical Corps, 1934-60 (incl. War of 1939-45). Home Office, 1960-75. *Publications:* articles in RAMC Jl; chapter in Biomedical Technology in Hospital Diagnosis. *Recreations:* gardening, swimming. *Address:* Bryher, Fielden Road, Crowborough, Sussex TN6 1TR. *T:* Crowborough 61381. *Club:* Civil Service.

VINELOTT, John Evelyn, QC 1968; *b* 15 Oct. 1923; *s* of George Frederick Vine-Lott and Vera Lilian Vine-Lott (née Mockford); *m* 1956, Sally Elizabeth, *d* of His Honour Sir Walker Kelly Carter, *qv*; two *s* one *d. Educ:* Queen Elizabeth's Gram. Sch., Faversham, Kent; Queens' Coll., Cambridge (MA). War Service, Sub-Lieut RNVR, 1942-46. Called to Bar, Gray's Inn, 1953, Bencher, 1974; in practice at the Chancery Bar. *Publications:* articles on Revenue Law, in specialist periodicals. *Address:* 9 Campden Hill Square, W8. *T:* 01-727 4778; 7 New Square, Lincoln's Inn, WC2. *T:* 01-405 1266/8. *Club:* Royal Ocean Racing.

VINEN, William Frank, FRS 1973; Poynting Professor, and Head of the Department of Physics, University of Birmingham, since 1974 (Professor of Physics, 1962-74); *b* 15 Feb. 1930; *o s* of Gilbert Vinen and Olive Maud Vinen (née Roach); *m* 1960, Susan-Mary Audrey Master; one *s* one *d. Educ:* Watford Grammar Sch.; Clare College, Cambridge. Research Fellow, Clare College, 1955-58. Royal Air Force, 1948-49. Demonstrator in Physics, Univ. of Cambridge and Fellow of Pembroke Coll., 1958-62. *Recreation:* good food. *Address:* 52 Middle Park Road, Birmingham B29 4BJ.

VINES, Eric Victor, OBE 1971; HM Diplomatic Service; Counsellor (Commercial), Stockholm, since 1977; *b* 28 May 1929; *s* of Henry E. Vines; *m* 1953, Ellen-Grethe Ella Küppers; one *s. Educ:* St Dunstan's Coll., London; St Catharine's Coll., Cambridge (MA). Army service, 1947-49. Joined Commonwealth Relations Office, 1952; Colombo, 1954-55; 1st Sec., Singapore, 1958-61; Canberra, 1961-65; Diplomatic Service Administration Office, 1965-68; 1st Sec., Information, Mexico City, 1968-70; Counsellor, Exec. Sec.-Gen., SEATO Conf., London, 1971; Head, Cultural Exchange Dept, FCO, 1971-74; Counsellor (Commercial), Tel Aviv, 1974-77. *Recreations:* opera, travel, walking. *Address:* c/o Foreign and Commonwealth Office, King Charles Street, SW1.

VINES, Prof. Howard William Copland, MA, MD retired; *b* 10 March 1893; *yr s* of late Emer. Prof. S. H. Vines; *m* 1st, 1921, Dorothy Mary Beatrice Brindley (*d* 1951); one *s* one *d*; 2nd, 1953, Ingrid Gertrud Hedwig Apel; two *d. Educ:* Rugby School; Christ's Coll., Cambridge; St Bartholomew's Hosp. 1st Cl. Nat. Sci. Tripos 1 and Bachelor Schol. Christ's Coll., 1914; MB, BCh (Cantab.) 1920; MD (Cantab.) and Horton-Smith Prize, 1922; Fellow of Christ's Coll. and Director of Med. Studies, 1919-26; Beit Memorial Fellow, 1921-23; Foulerton Research Student, 1923-27. Sector Pathologist EMS, 1939-44; Professor of Pathology, University of London, 1948-53; Pathologist, Charing Cross Hospital, 1928-53; Dean, Charing Cross Hospital Medical School, 1945-50; Mem. Charing Cross Hosp. Council, 1945-48; Bd of Governors, 1948-55; Chm., Charing Cross Hosp. and Med. Sch. Planning Cttees, 1948-55; Mem. West Cornwall Hosp. Management Cttee, 1954-64; Member North West Metropolitan Regional Board, 1948-50. *Publications:* The Parathyroid Glands, 1924; (jointly) The Adrenal Cortex and Intersexuality, 1938; Green's Pathology, 15th edn 1934; 16th edn 1940, 17th edn 1949; Background to Hospital Planning, 1952. Papers on endocrinology in Pathol and Med. journals; papers on Hospital Planning. *Recreation:* gardening. *Address:* Gull Rock House, Carlyon Bay, St Austell, Cornwall. *T:* Par 2632.

VINES, Sir William (Joshua), Kt 1977; CMG 1969; ACIS; psc; Chairman, Dalgety Australia Ltd; Chairman, Carbonless Papers (Wiggins Teape) Pty Ltd; Director: Commercial Union Assurance Co. of Australia Ltd; Conzinc Rio Tinto of Australia Ltd; Port Phillip Mills Pty Ltd; Tubemakers of Australia Ltd; Associated Pulp & Paper Mills Ltd; Dalgety Limited (London); Dalgety New Zealand Ltd; Wiggins Teape Limited (London); Grazier at Old Southwood, Tara, Queensland, since 1966; *b* 27 May 1916; *s* of P. V. Vines, Canterbury, Victoria, Australia; *m* 1939, Thelma J., *d* of late F. J. Ogden; one *s* two *d. Educ:* Haileybury College, Brighton Beach, Victoria. Managing Director: Internat. Wool Secretariat, 1961-69 (Board Mem., 1969-); Berger, Jenson & Nicholson Ltd, 1960 (Dir, 1961-69);

Dalgety Australia Ltd, 1971-76; Group Managing Director, Lewis Berger & Sons Ltd, 1955; Director: Lewis Berger & Sons (Aust.) Pty Ltd & Sherwin Williams Co. (Aust.) Pty Ltd, 1952-55; Goodlass Wall & Co. Pty Ltd, 1947-49; Vice-President Melbourne Legacy, 1949-51; Pres. Building Industry Congress, Vic., 1954-55. Mem. Exec., CSIRO, 1973-; Chm. Council, Hawkesbury Agric. Coll., 1975-. FASA. Served War of 1939-45 (despatches), 2nd AIF, 2/23 Aust. Inf. Bn, Middle East, New Guinea and Borneo, Capt. *Recreation:* swimming. *Address:* 73 Yarranabbe Road, Darling Point, Sydney, NSW 2027, Australia. *T:* 328.7970. *Clubs:* Junior Carlton, Royal Automobile; Union, Royal Sydney Golf (Sydney); Australian, Melbourne (Melbourne).

VINEY, Hon. Anne Margaret, (Hon. Mrs Viney), JP; Chairman, Consumer Protection Advisory Committee, since 1973; *b* 14 June 1926; *d* of late Baron Morton of Henryton, PC, MC, and of Lady Morton of Henryton; *m* 1947, Peter Andrew Hopwood Viney; one *s* two *d*. *Educ:* Priorsfield, Godalming, Surrey. Left school after matriculation, 1943; clerk in Min. of Economic Warfare, 1943-45; worked in publicity dept of Internat. Wool Secretariat, 1945-47. Councillor, Kensington and Chelsea BC (Health and Children's Cttees), 1960-62. JP, 1961; apptd to Inner London Juvenile Court panel, 1961 (Chm. 1970); currently Jt Co-Chm., Hammersmith Juvenile Court. Helped to found London Adventure Playground Assoc., 1962 (Sec. 1962-69). *Recreations:* conversation, playing poetry game. *Address:* 4 Lansdowne Road, W11 3LW. *T:* 01-727 4884; Worth House, Worth Matravers, near Swanage, Dorset.

VINEY, Elliott (Merriam), DSO 1945; MBE 1946; TD; JP; DL; FSA; Director: British Printing Corporation Ltd, 1964-75; Hazell, Watson & Viney Ltd, since 1947; *b* 21 Aug. 1913; *s* of late Col. Oscar Viney, TD, DL, and Edith Merriam; *m* 1950, Rosamund Ann Pelly; two *d*. *Educ:* Oundle; Univ. Coll., Oxford. Bucks Bn, Oxford and Bucks Light Infantry (TA), 1932-46. Governor and Trustee, Museum of London, 1972-. Pres., British Fedn of Master Printers, 1972-73. Master, Grocers' Company, 1970-71. County Dir, Bucks St John Amb. Assoc., 1953-55; Hon. Sec., Bucks Archaeol. Soc., 1954-. JP 1950, DL 1952, High Sheriff, 1964, Buckinghamshire. OStJ 1953. Editor: Oxford Mountaineering, 1935; Climbers' Club Jl, 1936-39; (jt) Records of Bucks, 1947-. *Publications:* The Sheriffs of Buckinghamshire, 1965; (jtly) Old Aylesbury, 1976. *Recreations:* conversation, music, walking. *Address:* Green End House, Aylesbury, Bucks. *T:* Aylesbury 3091. *Clubs:* Army and Navy, Alpine.

VINING, Rowena Adelaide, MBE 1964; HM Diplomatic Service; HM Consul at Florence and HM Consul-General to San Marino, since Oct. 1974; *b* 25 Sept. 1921; *er d* of late Col Percival Llewellyn Vining and Phyllis Servante Vining. *Educ:* privately, and at Chiddingstone Castle, Edenbridge, Kent. Foreign Office, 1941-52 (war service in Italy, Indonesia, 1943-45). Commonwealth Relations Office, 1952-55; Second Secretary: Karachi, 1955-58; Sydney, 1958-62; First Sec.: CRO, 1962-65; Canberra, 1965-67; Commonwealth Office (later Foreign and Commonwealth Office), 1967-71; Vienna, 1972-74. *Recreations:* gardening, music. *Address:* c/o Foreign and Commonwealth Office, SW1; Dorchester Cottage, Greywell, near Basingstoke RG25 1BT. *Club:* Royal Commonwealth Society.

VINSON, Nigel; Inventor; Chairman, Industrial Participation Association, since 1971; *b* Nettlestead Place, Kent, 27 Jan. 1931; *s* of late Ronald Vinson and of Bettina Vinson (*née* Southwell-Sander); *m* 1972, Yvonne Ann Collin; two *d*. *Educ:* Pangbourne Naval Coll. Lieut, Queen's Royal Regt, 1949-51. Chm. and Founder, Plastic Coatings Ltd (started in a Nissen hut, 1952, flotation, 1969; Queen's Award to Industry, 1971). Dir, Sugar Bd, 1968-75; Member: BoT Investment Grants Adv. Cttee, 1967-71; NHS Pharmaceutical Services Cttee, 1971-76; Crafts Adv. Cttee, 1971-; Design Council, 1973- (Chm., 1976 Awards Cttee); Trustee, Inst. of Economic Affairs, 1971-; Dir, Centre for Policy Studies, 1974-; Mem. Council: Inst. of Directors, 1971-; King George VI Jubilee Trust, 1974-; Hon. Dir, Queen's Silver Jubilee Appeal Council, 1977; Director: Kentish Times, 1971-73; Techn. Investment Trust, 1972-; Electra Investment Trust, 1975-; British Airports Authority, 1973-. Chm., CBI Surrey Area, 1965-68; Mem. CBI Grand Council, Taxation and Membership Cttee, 1967-. FRSA, FBIM. *Publications:* financial articles in Spectator, Director, Crossbow, etc. *Recreations:* fine art and craftmanship, horses, conservation (foundation donor Martin Mere Wildfowl Trust). *Address:* 34 Kynance Mews, SW7. *T:* (office) Long Sutton (Hants) 431. *Club:* Boodle's.

VINTER, (Frederick Robert) Peter, CB 1965; Director, Vickers Ltd, since 1974; Overseas Adviser to Central Electricity

Generating Board, since 1973; *b* 27 March 1914; *m* 1938, Margaret, *d* of S. I. Rake, Pembroke; two *s*. *Educ:* Haileybury Coll.; King's Coll., Cambridge (2nd cl. hons English Tripos Pt I, 1st cl. hons Hist. Tripos Pt II); MA. Min. of Economic Warfare, 1939; Cabinet Office, 1943; HM Treasury, 1945-69, Third Sec., 1965-69; Dep. Sec., Min. of Technology and DTI, 1969-73. Nuffield Travelling Fellowship (in India), 1950-51. *Address:* 3 Sunnyside, Wimbledon, SW19 4SL. *T:* 01-946 4137. *Club:* Athenæum.

VINTER, Geoffrey Odell; JP; Director of Companies; Underwriting Member of Lloyd's; *b* 29 April 1900; *s* of Harold Skelsey Vinter; *g s* of James Odell Vinter, High Sheriff Cambridgeshire and Huntingdonshire, 1921; *m* 1925, Mary Margaret Hardy (novelist: Mary Vinter); one *d*. *Educ:* Clifton; University Coll., Oxford (MA). Chm., Papworth Village Settlement, 1974-. High Sheriff of Cambridgeshire and Huntingdonshire, 1948-49; JP Cambs 1951. *Recreations:* shooting, fishing. *Address:* Thriplow Manor, Royston, Herts. *T:* Fowlmere 255.

VINTER, Peter; *see* Vinter, F. R. P.

VIRTUE, Sir John (Evenden), KBE 1975; Judge of Supreme Court of Western Australia, 1951-75 (retd); Senior Puisne Judge, 1969-75; *b* 25 April 1905; *s* of Ernest Evenden Virtue and Mary Hamilton Virtue; *m* 1938, Mary Joan, *d* of Reginald and Mary Lloyd. *Educ:* Hale Sch., Perth, WA; Univs of Melbourne and Western Australia. LLM (Melb), BA (WA). Barrister and solicitor, admitted to practise in Supreme Courts of Western Australia and Victoria; in practice as barrister and solicitor, Supreme Court of W Australia, 1928-50. Lectured (part-time) in Torts and Criminal Law, Univ. of WA, 1930-49. Served War, AIF (Major), 1940-43. Pres., Law Soc. of WA, 1950. *Recreations:* lawn bowls, contract bridge. *Address:* 74 Kingsway, Nedlands, Western Australia. *T:* 86-1856. *Clubs:* Weld, Royal Perth Yacht (Perth, WA).

VISHNEVSKAYA, Galina; principal soprano of the Bolshoi Theatre, Moscow; *b* 25 Oct. 1926; *m* 1955, Mstislav Rostropovich, *qv*; two *d*. *Educ:* studied with Vera Garina. Toured with Leningrad Light Opera Co., 1944-48, with Leningrad Philharmonic Soc., 1948-52; joined Bolshoi Theatre, 1952. Concert appearances in Europe and USA, 1950-; first appeared at Metropolitan Opera, NY, 1961. Rôles include: Leonora in Fidelio and Tatiana in Eugene Onegin. Has sung in Britain at Festival Hall, Aldeburgh Festival, Edinburgh Festival, Covent Garden. Makes concert tours with her husband. Has made many recordings. *Address:* c/o Victor Hochhauser, 4 Holland Park Avenue, W11 3QU.

VISSER, John Bancroft; Director of Administration, Science Research Council, since 1974; *b* 29 Jan. 1928; *o s* of late Gilbert and Ethel Visser; *m* 1955, Astrid Margareta Olson; two *s* one *d*. *Educ:* Mill Hill Sch.; New Coll., Oxford (Exhibnr). Entered Civil Service, Asst Principal, Min. of Supply, 1951; Principal, 1956; Min. of Aviation, 1959; Admin. Staff Coll., 1965; Asst Sec., 1965; Min. of Technology, 1967; Royal Coll. of Defence Studies, 1970; Civil Service Dept, 1971; Procurement Exec., MoD, 1971; Under-Sec., 1974; Sec. of Nat. Defence Industries Council, 1971-74. Dir, Construction Holdings Ltd, 1976. *Recreations:* sport, music, gardening, walking. *Address:* Rosslyn, 3 Berkeley Road, Cirencester, Glos GL7 1TY. *T:* Cirencester 2626. *Club:* Old Millhillians.

VISSER 't HOOFT, Dr Willem Adolf; Commander, Order of the Lion (Netherlands); Officer, Legion of Honour (France); Grand Cross, Order of Merit, with ribbon and star (Federal Republic of Germany); Cross of Great Commander of Holy Sepulchre; Order of St Vladimir, Orthodox Church of Russia; Commander, Order of St Andrew (Ecumenical Patriarchate); Hon. CStJ; General Secretary of World Council of Churches, 1938-66, Hon. President, 1968; *b* 20 Sept. 1900; *m* 1924, Henriette Philippine Jacoba Boddaert (*d* 1968); two *s* one *d*. *Educ:* Leyden University. Secretary, World Committee of YMCA, 1924-31; General Secretary, World Student Christian Federation, 1931-38. Hon. Professor: Theolog. Faculty, Budapest, 1947; Theolog. Acad., Moscow, 1964. Hon. Fellow, Hebrew Univ. of Jerusalem, 1972. Hon. DD: Aberdeen, 1939; Princetown, USA; Trinity Coll., Toronto, 1950; Geneva, 1951; Yale, 1954; Oberlin Coll., 1954; Oxford, 1955; Harvard, 1958; St Paul's, Tokyo, 1959; Faculté Libre de Théologie, Paris, 1963; Kirchliche Hochschule, Berlin, 1964; Brown Univ., Providence, RI, 1965; Theol Faculty, Zürich, 1966; Univ. Catholique, Louvain, 1967; Open Univ., 1974. Cardinal Bea Prize, 1975; Louise Weiss Foundn Prize, 1976; Hanseatic Goethe Prize, 1977. *Publications:* The Background of the Social Gospel in America, 1928; Anglo-Catholicism and Orthodoxy, 1933; None other Gods, 1937; The

Church and its Function in Society (with J. H. Oldham), 1937; Wretchedness and Greatness of the Church, 1943; The Struggle of the Dutch Church, 1946; Kingship of Christ, 1948; Rembrandt et la Bible, 1947; The Meaning of Ecumenical, 1953; The Ecumenical Movement and the Racial Problem, 1954; The Renewal of the Church (Eng. edn 1956); Rembrandt and the Gospel, 1957; The Pressure of our Common Calling, 1959; No Other Name, 1963; Hauptschriften, Bd 1 and 2, 1967; (with Cardinal Bea) Peace Among Christians, 1967; Memoirs, 1973; Has the Ecumenical Movement a Future?, 1974. *Address:* 150, route de Ferney, 1211 Geneva 20, Switzerland. *T:* 33 34 00.

VIVENOT, Baroness de (Hermine Hallam-Hipwell), OBE 1967; free lance writer; *b* Buenos Aires; *d* of late Humphrey Hallam-Hipwell and Gertrude Hermine Isebrée-Moens tot Bloois; *m* 1931, Baron Raoul de Vivenot (*d* 1973), *e s* of Baron de Vivenot and Countess Kuenburg, Vienna; one *s*. *Educ:* Northlands, Buenos Aires. Joined Min. of Information, 1941; transferred Foreign Office, 1946; appointed to Foreign (subseq. Diplomatic) Service, Jan. 1947; Vice-Consul, Bordeaux, 1949-52, Nantes, 1952-53; Foreign Office, 1953-55; First Secretary (Information), HM Embassy, Brussels, 1955-59; Foreign Office, 1959-62; First Secretary (Information), HM Embassy, The Hague, 1962-66; retired 1967. External Examiner in Spanish, Univ. of London. *Publications:* The Ninas of Balcarce, a novel, 1935; Younger Argentine painters; Argentine Art Notes; Buenos Aires Vignettes; Poems, etc. *Recreations:* Whippet racing and coursing, gardening, grandchildren. *Address:* Coppinghall, Uckfield, East Sussex TN22 1BT. *T:* Uckfield 2778.

VIVIAN, family name of **Barons Swansea** and **Vivian**.

VIVIAN, 5th Baron, *cr* 1841; **Anthony Crespigny Claude Vivian;** Bt *cr* 1828; *b* 4 March 1906; *e s* of 4th Baron and Barbara, *d* of William A. Fanning; *S* father 1940; *m* 1930, Victoria, *er d* of late Captain H. G. L. Oliphant, DSO, MVO; two *s* one *d*. *Educ:* Eton. Served RA. *Heir: s* Lt-Col Nicholas Crespigny Laurence Vivian, 16/5 Lancers [*b* 11 Dec. 1935; *m* 1st, 1960, Catherine Joyce (marr. diss. 1972), *y d* of James Kenneth Hope, *qv*; one *s* one *d*; 2nd, 1972, Carol, *d* of F. Alan Martineau; two *d*]. *Address:* 154 Coleherne Court, SW5; Boskenna Ros, St Buryan, near Penzance, Cornwall.
See also *Marquess of Bath, Earl of Glasgow, Earl Haig.*

VIVIAN, Arthur Henry Seymour; Clerk of the Skinners' Company, 1941-59; Hon. Freeman and Member of Court of the Company, 1959; *b* 30 June 1899; *o s* of late Henry Chester Vivian, Cardiff; *m* 1927, Elizabeth, *yr d* of late Maj. R. H. Hood-Haggie; one *d*. *Educ:* Harrow and Magdalen Coll., Oxford (MA). RFA, 1918; called to the Bar, Inner Temple, 1923; Assistant to Clerk of Skinners' Company, 1933. Commissioned London Welsh AA Regiment, 1939-43. Hon. Secretary Governing Bodies' Association, 1953-67; Hon. Member, Committee, 1967. *Recreation:* golf (played for Oxford, 1921 and 1922). *Address:* 24 Sandy Lodge Road, Moor Park, Rickmansworth, Herts. *T:* Rickmansworth 74055. *Clubs:* Royal Automobile, MCC; Royal Porthcawl Golf; Moor Park Golf (Pres., 1971-).

VIVIAN, Graham Linsell, CSI 1946; CIE 1944; *b* 1 Aug. 1887; *s* of late Richard Thomas Vivian; *m* 1923, Norah, *d* of late E. H. Ashworth; two *s* one *d*. *Educ:* Epsom Coll.; Selwyn Coll., Cambridge. Entered Indian Civil Service, 1911; held various administrative posts in United Provinces, rising to Commissioner, 1941; Adviser to the Governor, 1945; retired, 1946. *Address:* Middlemead, Rectory Close, Burwash, Sussex. *T:* Burwash 882436.

VIVIAN, Michael Hugh; Controller Safety, Civil Aviation Authority, since Dec. 1974; *b* 15 Dec. 1919; *s* of Hugh Vivian and Mary (*née* Gilbertson); *m* 1951, June Stiven; one *s* one *d*. *Educ:* Uppingham; Oxford. Served War: RAF (139 Sqdn), Flying Instructor, Test Pilot, 1940-44. Min. of Civil Aviation, 1945; Private Sec. to Parly Sec. for Civil Aviation, 1945-46; various operational appts, 1947-61; Dep. Dir of Flight Safety, 1961-66; Dir of Flight Safety, 1966-67; Dir of Advanced Aircraft Ops, 1967-71; Civil Aviation Authority, 1972; Dir-Gen. Safety Ops, 1972-74; Controller Safety and Full-time Member, Civil Aviation Authority, 1974-. *Recreations:* golf, vintage cars. *Address:* 14 Roland Way, SW7 3RE. *T:* 01-373 1620. *Club:* Royal Air Force.

VIVIAN, Richard P. G.; see Graham-Vivian.

VLASTO, Michael, MB, BS, FRCS; Officier de l'Instruction Publique; late Consulting Throat and Ear Surgeon to West London Hospital and Consulting Surgeon to Throat and Ear Departments of Queen's Hospital for Children; Fellow of Royal Society of Medicine; *b* 1888; *o s* of Ernest and Helen Vlasto; *m* 1919, Chrissy Mitchell Croil, Aberdeen; three *d* (one *s* decd). *Educ:* Winchester Coll.; University College Hospital. Surgeon-Lieut, 1914-19; late Surgeon-in-Chief of Ear, Nose and Throat Dept of Royal Naval Hospitals of Portsmouth and Malta; Registrar Golden Square Nose and Throat Hospital. *Publications:* Diseases of the Ear, Nose, Throat, for Nurses, and various papers in medical journals. *Recreation:* chess. *Address:* Gresham Lodge, Limpsfield, Oxted, Surrey. *T:* Oxted 3961.

VOCKLER, Rt. Rev. John Charles, (Rt. Rev. Brother John Charles, SSF); Minister Provincial, Pacific Province, Society of St Francis, since 1976; Warden: The Community of St Clare, Newcastle, NSW, since 1975; Society of The Sacred Advent, since 1976; *b* 22 July 1924; *e s* of John Thomas Vockler and Mary Catherine Vockler (*née* Widerberg), Dee Why, New South Wales. *Educ:* Sydney Boys' High Sch.; University of Queensland; Moore Theological Coll.; St John's Theological College, Morpeth, NSW; General Theological Seminary, New York. LTheol, Australian College of Theology, 1948. Deacon, 1948; priest, 1948; Asst Deacon, Christ Church Cathedral, Newcastle, 1948; Asst Priest, 1948-50; Vice-Warden of S John's Coll., within University of Queensland, 1950-53; Acting Chaplain, C of E Grammar School for Boys, Brisbane, 1953. BA (1st Class Hons History) University of Queensland, 1953; University Gold Medal for outstanding achievement, 1953; BA University of Adelaide, aegr, 1961; Walter and Eliza Hall Foundation Travelling Scholarship, University of Queensland, 1953; Fulbright Scholar, 1953. Acting Vice-Warden, S John's Coll., Morpeth and Lecturer in Old Testament, 1953; Graduate Student, General Theological Seminary, New York, 1954. STB (General Seminary), 1954. Asst Priest, Cathedral of S John the Divine, NY and Chaplain, St Luke's Home for Aged Women and the Home for Old Men and Aged Couples, 1954; Australian Delegate to Anglican Congress, 1954; Fellow and Tutor Gen. Theol. Seminary, 1954-56; MDiv (formerly STM) Gen. Theol. Seminary, 1956. Asst Priest, St Stephen's Church, West 69th Street, NY, 1955; Priest-in-charge, St Stephen's, New York, 1956; Asst Priest, parish of Singleton, NSW, 1956-59; Lecturer in Theology, St John's Theological College, Morpeth, NSW, 1956-59; Secretary, Newcastle Diocesan Board of Education, 1958-59. Titular Bishop of Mount Gambier and Assistant Bishop of Adelaide (Coadjutor, 1959; title changed to Assistant, 1961), until 1962; also Archdeacon of Eyre Peninsula, 1959-62; Vicar-General, Examining Chaplain to Bishop of Adelaide, 1960-62; Bishop of Polynesia, 1962-68. President, Harry Charman's All Races Sports and Social Club, Suva, Fiji, 1962-68, Hon. Life Vice-Pres., 1968; Chairman: S Pacific Anglican Council, 1963-68; Council of Pacific Theological Coll., 1963-68; President: Fiji Council of Social Services, 1964-68; Fiji Branch, Royal Commonwealth Soc., 1966-68. Entered Soc. of St Francis, 1969, to test vocation to religious life; professed, 1972; Chaplain to Third Order, Soc. of St Francis (European Province), 1972-74; made life profession in Soc. of St Francis, 1975; Permission to officiate: dio. Salisbury, 1969-70; dio. Fulham and Gibraltar, with Episcopal Commn, 1971-73; dio. Newcastle, NSW, 1975; Vice-Pres. and Mem. Council, USPG, 1973-74; Assistant Bishop: Chelmsford, 1973-74; Southwark, 1974-75; Hon. Canon of Southwark, 1975, Canon Emeritus 1975; Hon. Mission Chaplain, dio. Brisbane, 1975; Guardian, Friary of St Francis, Brisbane, 1975-77. Examnr for Aust. Coll. of Theology, 1975-76. ThD (*lure dig*.) ACT, 1961; STD (*hc*) Gen. Theological Seminary, NY, 1961; BD (*ad eund*.) Melbourne College of Divinity, 1960. *Publications:* Can Anglicans Believe Anything— The Nature and Spirit of Anglicanism, 1961 (NSW); Forward Day by Day, 1962; (ed) Believing in God (by M. L. Yates), 1962 (Australian edn); One Man's Journey, 1972; contributions to: Preparatory Volume for Anglican Congress, Toronto, 1963; Mutual Responsibility: Questions and Answers, 1964; All One Body (ed T. Wilson), 1968; Australian Dictionary of Biography; St Mark's Review, Australian Church Quarterly, The Anglican, The Young Anglican, Pacific Journal of Theology, New Zealand Theological Review. *Recreations:* classical music, detective stories, theatre, films, prints and engravings. *Address:* The Friary of S Francis, 131 Brookfield Road, Brookfield, Queensland 4069, Australia. *T:* Brisbane 78-2160. *Club:* Tonga (Nukualofa).

VOGT, Dr Marthe Louise, FRS 1952; Dr med Berlin, Dr phil Berlin; PhD Cantab; *b* 1903; *d* of Oskar Vogt and Cécile Vogt (*née* Mugnier). *Educ:* Auguste Viktoria-Schule, Berlin; University of Berlin. Research Assistant, Department of Pharmacology, Berlin Univ., 1930; Research Assistant and head of chemical division, Kaiser Wilhelm Institut für Hirnforschung, Berlin, 1931-35; Rockefeller Travelling Fellow, 1935-36; Research Worker, Dept of Pharmacology, Cambridge Univ., 1935-40; Alfred Yarrow Research Fellow, of Girton Coll., 1937-40; Member Staff of College of Pharmaceutical

Society, London, 1941-46; Lecturer, later Reader, in Pharmacology, University of Edinburgh, 1947-60; Head of Pharmacology Unit, Agricultural Research Council, Institute of Animal Physiology, 1960-68. Vis. Associate Prof. in Pharmacology, Columbia Univ., New York, 1949; Vis. Prof., Sydney 1965, Montreal 1968. Life Fellow, Girton Coll., Cambridge, 1970. Hon. DSc Edinburgh, 1974. *Publications:* papers in neurological, physiological and pharmacological journals. *Address:* Agricultural Research Council Institute of Animal Physiology, Babraham, Cambridge.

VOKES, Maj.-Gen. Christopher, CB 1945; CBE 1944; DSO 1943; retired from the Canadian Army in 1960; *b* 13 April 1904; *e s* of late Major F. P. Vokes, Kingston, Ontario, and Elizabeth Briens; *m* 1932, Constance Mary Waugh (*d* 1969), Winnipeg; two *s. Educ:* RMC, Kingston; McGill Univ., Montreal. 1st Commission Royal Canadian Engineers, 1925; Staff Coll., Camberley, 1934-35; Brigadier Comd 2 Cdn Inf. Bde, 1942-43; Maj.-Gen. GOC 1 Cdn Div., 1943-44; GOC 4 Cdn Armd Div., 1944-45. Campaigns: Sicily, Italy, NW Europe (despatches twice, DSO, CBE, CB); GOC Cdn Occupation Force, Germany, 1945; Officer of Legion of Honour (France); Croix de Guerre avec Palme (France); Order of Golden Ariston Andrias (Greece); Commander Mil. Order of Italy. *Address:* 42 First Street, Oakville, Ontario L6J 3R3, Canada.

VOLLRATH, Prof. Lutz Ernst Wolf; Professor of Histology and Embryology, University of Mainz, Germany, since 1974; *b* 2 Sept. 1936; *s* of Pastor Richard Hermann Vollrath and Rita (*née* Brügmann); *m* 1963, Gisela (*née* Dialer); three *d. Educ:* Ulrich von Hutten-Schule, Berlin; Univs of Berlin, Kiel and Tübingen. Dr med Kiel, 1961. Wissenschaftlicher Assistent, Dept of Anatomy, Würzburg, Germany, 1963; Res. Fellow, Dept of Anatomy, Birmingham, 1964; Wissenschaftlicher Assistent, Dept of Anatomy, Würzburg, 1965-71 (Privatdozent, 1968; Oberassistent, 1969; Universitätsdozent, 1970); King's College London: Reader in Anatomy, 1971; Prof. of Anatomy, 1973-74. *Publications:* (co-editor) Neurosecretion: the final neuroendocrine pathway, 1974; research publications on histochemistry and ultrastructure of organogenesis and various aspects of neuroendocrinology, in Z Zellforsch., Histochemie, Phil. Trans Royal Society B, Erg. Anat. Entw.gesch. *Recreations:* gardening, tennis. *Address:* c/o Anatomisches Institut, 65 Mainz, Saarstr. 19/21, Germany.

von BITTENFELD; *see* Herwarth von Bittenfeld.

von EULER, Prof. Ulf Svante; Comdr North Star of Sweden (1st cl.) 1970; Professor of Physiology, Karolinska Institute, 1939-71; *b* 7 Feb. 1905; *s* of Hans von Euler and Astrid von Euler (*née* Cleve); *m* 1st, 1930, Jane Sodenstierna; two *s* two *d* ; 2nd, 1958, Dagmar Cronstedt. *Educ:* Karolinska Institute, Stockholm. MD 1930. For. Mem., Royal Soc., 1973. Nobel Prize in Physiology or Medicine (jt), 1970. Hon. degrees, Univs of: Umea, 1958; Dijon, 1962; Ghent, 1963; Tübingen, 1964; Buenos Aires, 1971; Edinburgh, 1971; Manchester, 1973; Madrid, 1973. Cross of the Sun (Brazil), 1952. *Publications:* Noradrenaline, 1956; Prostaglandins (with R. Eliasson), 1967; articles in jls of physiology and pharmacology. *Address:* Sturegatan 14, Stockholm S-11436, Sweden. *T:* S-08-636559.

von FRISCH, Dr Karl; retired but doing scientific work; *b* Vienna, 20 Nov. 1886; *s* of Dr Anton Ritter von Frisch, Prof., Surgeon and Urologist and Marie (*née* Exner); *m* 1917, Margarete (*née* Mohr) (*d* 1964); one *s* three *d. Educ:* Schottengymnasium, Vienna; Univs of Munich and Vienna. Dr Phil Vienna 1910. Asst, Zoolog. Inst., Univ. of Munich, 1910; Lectr in Zoology and Comparable Anatomy, Univ. of Munich, 1912; Prof. and Dir of Zoolog. Inst., Univ. of Rostock, 1921; Univ. of Breslau, 1923; Univ. of Munich, 1925; Univ. of Graz (Austria), 1946; returned to Munich, 1950 and retired 1958. Member: Bayer Acad. Science, 1926; Copenhagen, 1931; Leopoldina Halle, 1935; Acad. of Science, Vienna, 1938 (Hon. Mem. 1954) and Göttingen, 1947; (Hon.) Royal Entomological Soc., London, 1949; Acad. of Science and Lit., Mainz, 1949; Nat. Acad. Sciences, Washington, 1951; (Hon.) Amer. Physiol Soc., 1952; Acad. of Arts and Scis, Boston, 1952; Swedish Acad. of Sci., 1952; Royal Soc., 1954; Amer. Entomological Soc., 1955; Linnaean Soc., 1956, etc. Pour le Mérite (Peace Class), 1952; Kalinga Prize (Unesco), 1959; Austrian Award for Science and Art, 1960; Balzan Prize for Biology, 1963; Nobel Prize for Medicine or Physiology, 1973. Hon. Dr: Bern, 1949; Zürich Polytechnic, 1955; Graz, 1957; Harvard, 1963; Tubingen, 1964; Rostock, 1969. *Publications:* Aus dem Leben der Bienen, 1927 (The Dancing Bees, 1954); Du und das Leben, 1936 (Man and the Living World, 1963); Bees, 1950, rev. edn 1971; Biologie, 1952 (Biology, 1964); Erinnerungen eines Biologen, 1957 (A Biologist Remembers, 1967, 1973); Tanzsprache und Orientierung der Bienen, 1965 (The Dance Language and Orientation of Bees, 1967); Animal Architecture, 1974. *Address:* Ueber der Klause 10, 8000 Munich 90, West Germany. *T:* 644948.

VON HAGEN, Victor Wolfgang, FZS; FRGS; Organiser-Leader, Persian Royal Road Expedition, 1972, American Geographical Society Expedition, 1973-75, explorations in Iran, Iraq and Turkey; Leader, Roman Road Expeditions, 1962; Director: Inca High Expedition; American Geographical Society; History of Science Society; Latin American Adviser, Encyclopedia Americana; Contributor: Encyclopædia Britannica; Geographical Magazine, London; Research Associate Museum of the American Indian, New York; Consultant UN Guggenheim Fellowship for creative writing, 1949, renewed 1950-51; American Philosophical Society (Research Fellow); *b* Saint Louis, Mo., 29 Feb. 1908; *s* of Henry von Hagen and Eleanor Josephine Stippe-Hornbach; *m* 1933, Christine Inez Brown (marr. diss.); one *d; m* 1951, Silvia Hofmann-Edzard (marr. diss. 1962); two *d. Educ:* Morgan Park Military Acad.; New York Univ.; Univ. de Quito, S America. Served US Army, War of 1941-45, 13th Inf. Regt, Texas. Explorer, naturalist, ethnographer. Expedition Mexico, 1931-33; Ecuador, Amazon, Peru, Galapagos Islands, 1934-36; Honduras, Mosquito Coast, Guatemala, 1937-38, to study quetzal bird for Zoo, Regent's Park; Panama, Costa Rica, 1940; Colombia, Peru, 1947-48; resided BWI, 1949-50; expedition to Peru, 1952-54; studied Roman Roads, Lubeck to Africa, 1955; expedition to Mexico, 1957; Yucatan, 1958-59; Study of Roman Roads in Italy, 1961; exploration of Roman Roads: throughout Tunisia, Libya, Egypt, Arabia, Petra, 1963; Spain and Yugoslavia, 1965; Egyptian Eastern Desert, Sinai, Turkey, Bulgaria and Greece, 1966; exploration and excavation of Roman Alpine roads in Austria, Italy, France and Germany, 1968-70; physically traversed and mapped the Persian Road from Troy and Istanbul, through Turkey, Iraq and Iran to river Indus, 1973-75. Founder, Charles Darwin Res. Station, Galápagos Is. Professor (*hc*) Universidad Catolica del Peru. Member, Academia de Historia de Bogota (Columbia), Centro de historia de Pasto (Columbia), Instituto Investigaciones Historicas (Peru). Discovered "extinct" tribe of Jicaque Indians in Honduras. Orden al Merito, Ecuador; Comdr, Orden al Merito, Peru. *Publications:* Off With their Heads, 1937; Ecuador the Unknown, 1939; Quetzal Quest (with Hawkins), 1940 (repr. 1968); Tsátchela Indians of Western Ecuador, 1939; The Encantadas of Herman Melville, 1940; Treasure of Tortoise Islands, 1940; Riches of South America, 1941; Riches of Central America, 1942; The Jicaque Indians of Honduras, 1943; Natural History of Termites, 1943; Paper and Civilisation, 1943; The Aztec and Maya Papermakers, 1943, 2nd edn, 1944; Jungle in the Clouds, 1945 (American edition, 1940); La Fabricación del Papel entre los aztecas y los Mayas, Mexico, 1945; South America Called Them, a biography, 1945; Maya Explorer, the life of John Lloyd Stephens, 1947; The Green World of the Naturalists (Anthology), 1948; Ecuador and the Galapagos Islands, 1949; Regional Guides to Peru, 1949; Frederick Catherwood, Architect (with Introduction by Aldous Huxley), 1950; El Dorado, The Golden Kingdoms of Colombia, 1951; The Four Seasons of Manuela (biography), 1952, repr. 1973; Highway of the Sun, 1956; The High Voyage, 1956; (Trans.) The Journals of J. B. Boussingault, 1957; Realm of the Incas, 1957; The Aztec: Man and Tribe, 1958; The Sun Kingdom of the Aztecs, 1958; The World of the Maya, 1960; The Ancient Sun Kingdom of The Americas, 1961, repr. 1973; The Desert Kingdoms of Peru, 1965; The Story of the Roman Roads, 1966 (for children; two book awards); F. Catherwood: Architect-Explorer of Two Worlds, 1967; The Roads that Led to Rome (in 6 languages), 1967; Roma nel Mundo, le grande stradi, 1969; The Road Runner (autobiog.), 1970; The German Peoples in the History of the Americas, German edn 1970, Amer. edn 1976; Il Sistema Stradale dell'Impero Romano, 1971; Search for the Mayas, the story of Stephens and Catherwood, 1973; The Golden Man, 1974; The Royal Road of the Incas, 1976; Ecuador: a history, 1976; The Gateways to Persia, 1978; (ed) The Incas (Chronicles) of Pedro de Cieza de Leon, 1959; (ed) Stephens' Incidents of Travel in Yucatan, 1961; (ed) Stephens' Incidents of Travel in Arabia Petraea, 1970. *Recreation:* watching moods of Lago Bracciano. *Address:* Trevignano Romano, Rome 00069, Italy.

von HASE, Karl-Günther, Hon. GCVO 1972; Hon. KCMG 1965; Director-General, Zweites Deutsches Fernsehen, since 1977; *b* 15 Dec. 1917; *m* 1945, Renate Stumpff; five *d. Educ:* German schools. Professional Soldier, 1936-45; War Academy, 1943-44; Training College for Diplomats, 1950-51; Georgetown Univ., Washington DC, 1952. German Foreign Service: German Embassy, Ottawa, 1953-56; Spokesman, Foreign Office Bonn, 1958-61; Head, West European Dept, 1961-62; Spokesman of German Federal Government, 1962-67; State Secretary, Min. of

Defence, German Federal Govt, 1968-69; German Ambassador to the Court of St James's, 1970-77. Holds German and other foreign decorations. *Recreations:* shooting, music. *Address:* Zweites Deutsches Fernsehen, Essenheimer Landstrasse, D-6500 Mainz-Lerchenberg, West Germany.

VON KARAJAN, Herbert; Conductor; Director: Salzburg Festival, since 1964; Vienna State Opera, since 1976 (Artistic Manager, 1956-64); Life Director Gesellschaft der Musikfreunde, Vienna; Artistic Director, Berlin Philharmonic Orchestra; *b* Salzburg, 5 April 1908; *s* of Ernest van Karajan and Martha v. Karajan Cosmâc. *Educ:* Salzburg Hochschule and Mozarteum; Vienna Univ. Conductor: Ulm Opernhaus, 1927-33; Aachen Opernhaus, 1933-40; Berlin Staatsoper, 1938-42; Festivals: Salzburg; Bayreuth; Edinburgh, 1953-54; Lucerne, 1947-56; Conductor and régisseur, La Scala, Milan, 1948-55; Musical Director, Berlin Philharmonic Orchestra, 1955-56. First European Tour with Philharmonia Orchestra, 1952; Director, Salzburg Festival, 1957. Films directed and conducted include: Bajazzo, Carmen, Beethoven's 9th Symphony. *Recreations:* ski-ing, mountaineering, flying, yachting, motoring, theatre, acoustical research. *Address:* Festspielhaus, Salzburg, Austria.

von WEIZSÄCKER, Freiherr Carl-Friedrich, Dr Phil; University Professor; Director, Max-Planck-Institut for study of the conditions of life in the Modern World, since 1970; *b* Kiel, 28 June 1912; *m* 1937, Gundalena (*née* Wille); three *s* one *d*. *Educ:* Universities of Leipzig, Göttingen, Copenhagen, 1929-33. Dr.phil 1933, Dr.phil.habil, 1936, Univ. Leipzig; Asst., Inst. of Theor. Physik, Univ. of Leipzig, 1934-36; Wissenschaftl. Mitarb., Kaiser Wilhelm Inst., Berlin, 1936-42; Dozent, Univ. of Berlin, 1937-42; pl. ao. Prof. Theor. Physik, Univ. of Strassburg, 1942-44; Kaiser-Wilhelm-Inst., Berlin and Hechingen, 1944-45; Hon. Prof., Univ. Göttingen and Abt. Leiter, Max Planck Inst. für Physik, Göttingen, 1946-57; Hon. Prof. of Theor. Physik, Univ. of Göttingen, 1946-57; Ord. Prof. of Philosophy, Univ. of Hamburg, 1957-69. Hon. Prof., Univ. of Munich, 1970-. Gifford Lecturer, Glasgow Univ., 1959-61. Member: Deutsche Akademie der Naturforscher Leopoldina, Halle (DDR); Akademie der Wissenschaften, Göttingen; Joachim-Jungius-Gesellschaft der Wissenschaften, Hamburg; Bayerische Akademie der Wissenschaften, München; Deutsche Akademie für Sprache und Dichtung, Darmstadt; Deutsches PEN-Zentrum der Bundesrepublik Deutschland, Darmstadt; Österreichische Akademie der Wissenschaften, Wien; Sächsische Akademie der Wissenschaften zu Leipzig. Verdienstorden der Bundesrepublik Deutschland, 1959-73; Orden Pour le Mérite für Wissenschaften und Künste, 1961; Wiss. Mitglied der Max-Planck-Gesellschaft, Göttingen. Max Planck Medal, 1957; Goethe Prize (Frankfurt) 1958; Friedenspreis des deutschen Buchhandels, 1963; Erasmus Prize (with Gabriel Marcel), 1969. *Publications:* Die Atomkerne, 1937; Zum Weltbild der Physik, 11th edn, 1970 (English, London, 1952); Die Geschichte der Natur, 7th edn, 1970 (English, Chicago, 1949); Physik der Gegenwart (with J. Juilfs), 2nd edn, 1958 (Engl., 1957); Die Verantwortung der Wissenschaft im Atomzeitalter, 5th edn, 1969; Atomenergie und Atomzeitalter, 3rd edn, 1958; Bedingungen des Friedens, 1963, 5th edn, 1970; Die Tragweite der Wissenschaft, 1964; Der ungesicherte Friede, 1969; Die Einheit der Natur, 1971, 3rd edn, 1972; (ed) Kriegsfolgen und Kriegsverhütung, 1970, 3rd edn, 1971; Voraussetzungen der naturwissenschaftlichen Denkens, 1972, 2nd edn, 1972; Fragen zur Weltpolitik, 1975; Wege in der Gefahr, 1976; Der Garten des Menschlichen, Beiträge zur geschichtlichen Anthropologie, 1977. *Relevant Publications:* bibliography in Einheit und Vielheit, Festschrift...ed Scheibe and Süssmann, 1973. *Recreations:* hiking, chess. *Address:* 813 Starnberg, Riemerschmidstrasse 7, Germany. *Club:* PEN.

VORSTER, Hon. Balthazar Johannes, BA, LLB; MP for Nigel in the Parliament of South Africa; Prime Minister of the Republic of South Africa, since 1966; Leader of the National Party of South Africa, since 1966; *b* 13 Dec. 1915; *s* of late William Carel Vorster; *m* 1941, Martini, *d* of P. A. Malan; two *s* one *d*. *Educ:* Sterkstroom High Sch.; Stellenbosch Univ. LLB 1938. Attorney, Port Elizabeth and Brakpan, until 1953; Member, Johannesburg Bar, practising 1953-58. Contested Brakpan, 1948; MP Nigel, 1953; Deputy Minister of Education, Arts, Science, Social Welfare and Pensions, 1958-61; Minister of Justice, 1961-66; Minister of Justice, of Police and of Prisons, 1966. DPhil (*hc*) Stellenbosch Univ., 1966; LLD (*hc*); University of Pretoria; Univ. of OFS, 1967; Univ. of Potchefstroom. *Recreations:* golf, chess. *Address:* (office) Union Buildings, Pretoria, South Africa. *T:* 20851; H. F. Verwoerd Buildings, Cape Town, South Africa. *T:* 457300; (residence) Libertas, Pretoria, South Africa; Groote Schuur, Cape Town, South Africa. *Clubs:* Zwartkops Golf; Rondebosch Golf.

VOS, Geoffrey Michael; a Recorder of the Crown Court, since 1976; *b* 18 Feb. 1927; *s* of Louis and Rachel Eva Vos; *m* 1955, Marcia Joan Goldstone (marr. diss. 1977); two *s* two *d*. *Educ:* St Joseph's College, Blackpool; Gonville and Caius College, Cambridge. MA, LLB. Called to the Bar, Gray's Inn, 1950. *Recreations:* badminton, tennis, walking. *Address:* Cheriton, 1 Wainwright Road, Altrincham, Cheshire. *T:* 061-928 2190.

VOUEL, Raymond; Member, Commission of the European Communities, responsible for Competition Policy, since 1977; *b* 1923; *m*; three *c*. Journalist on Socialist daily newspaper, Tageblatt; Admin. Dir, Esch Hosp., 1954-64; Mem. Town Council, Esch (Chm. Bldgs Cttee), 1973. Member, Chamber of Deputies, 1964-76; Sec. of State: for Public Health; for Employment; for Social Security; for Mining Industry, 1964-69. Chm., Parly Socialist Group, 1970-74; Gen. Sec., Parti Ouvrier Socialiste Luxembourgeois (Socialists), 1970; Dep. Prime Minister, Minister for Finance and Land Develt, 1974-76; Mem., Commission of European Communities with responsibility for Competition, Personnel, and Admin., July-Dec. 1976. *Address:* Commission of the European Communities, 200 rue de la Loi, 1040 Brussels, Belgium.

VOWDEN, Desmond Harvey Weight, QC 1969; His Honour Judge Vowden; a Circuit Judge, since 1975; *b* 6 Jan. 1921; *s* of late Rev. A. W. J. Vowden, MBE, TD; *m* 1964, Iris, *d* of L. A. Stafford-Northcote. *Educ:* Clifton Coll. Served in RN and RM, 1938-50; Captain RM, retired 1950. Called to the Bar, 1950; Dep. Chm., Wiltshire Quarter Sessions, 1968-71; Recorder of Devizes, later a Recorder of Crown Court, 1971-75. Comr, CCC, 1969-72. Steward of Appeal, BBB of C, 1967-. *Recreations:* music, gardening. *Address:* Orchard Cottage, Worton, Devizes, Wilts. *T:* Devizes 2877. *Club:* Garrick.

VOWLES, Paul Foster; Academic Registrar, University of London, since 1973; *b* 12 June 1919; *s* of late E. F. Vowles and G. M. Vowles, Bristol; *m* 1948, Valerie Eleanor Hickman; one *s* two *d*. *Educ:* Bristol Grammar Sch.; Corpus Christi Coll., Oxford (schol.; MA). Served Gloucestershire Regt and King's African Rifles, 1939-46, (despatches, Major). Asst Secretary: Appts Bd, Univ. of Birmingham, 1947-48; Inter-University Council for Higher Educn Overseas, 1948-51; Registrar, Makerere University Coll., E Africa, 1951-63; Sen. Asst to Principal, Univ. of London, 1964-68; Warden, Lillian Penson Hall, 1965-69; External Registrar, 1968-73. *Address:* 30 Torrington Square, WC1E 7JL. *T:* 01-734 5801.

VOYSEY, Charles C.; *see* Cowles-Voysey.

VOYSEY, Reginald George, FIMechE; Deputy Director, National Physical Laboratory, since 1970; *s* of Richard Voysey and Anne Paul; *m* 1943, Laidley Mary Elizabeth Barley; one *s* three *d* (and one *s* decd). *Educ:* Royal Dockyard Sch., Portsmouth; Imperial Coll. of Science. ACGI, DIC, WhSch. Dep. Develt Manager, Power Jets Ltd, 1940-45; Gas Turbine Dept Manager, C. A. Parsons & Co., 1945-48; Engineering Asst to Chief Scientist, Min. of Fuel and Power, 1948-66; IDC 1963; Scientific Counsellor, British Embassy, and Dir, UK Sci. Mission to Washington, 1966-69. *Publications:* patents and articles in jls. *Recreations:* swimming, sailing, painting. *Address:* 16 Beauchamp Road, East Molesey, Surrey. *T:* 01-979 3762. *Club:* Athenæum.

VREDELING, Hendrikus, (Henk); Member, Commission of the European Communities for Employment and Social Affairs and for the Tripartite Conference, since 1977; *b* 20 Nov. 1924. *Educ:* Agricultural Univ., Wageningen. Member: Second Chamber of States-General, Netherlands, 1956-; European Parl.; Socio-Economic Adviser to Agricultural Workers' Union, Netherlands, and Minister of Defence, 1973-76. *Address:* Commission of the European Communities, 200 rue de la Loi, 1040 Brussels, Belgium.

VYNER, Clare George; *b* 1894; 2nd *s* of late Lord Alwyne Frederick Compton and Mary Evelyn, *e d* of Robert Charles de Grey Vyner, of Newby Hall, Yorks, and Gautby, Lincs; *m* 1923, Lady Doris Gordon-Lennox, 2nd *d* of 8th Duke of Richmond and Gordon; one *s* (and one *s* one *d* decd). Formerly Lieut, RN, serving war of 1939-45, Commander. Assumed surname of Vyner, 1912. Formerly DL, W Riding of Yorkshire and City and Co. of York. *Address:* 41a Hays Mews, W1. *T:* 01-499 1431; Keanchulish, Ullapool, Ross-shire. *T:* Ullapool 2100; Fountains Hall, Ripon, North Yorks. *T:* Sawley 675.
See also Marquess of Northampton.

VYSE, Lt-Gen. Sir Edward D. H.; *see* Howard-Vyse.

VYVYAN, Sir Richard Philip, 11th Bt, *cr* 1645; *b* 21 Nov. 1891; *s* of late Major Richard Walter Comyn Vyvyan, 2nd *s* of 9th Bt; *S* uncle, 1941. *Heir: cousin* John Stanley Vyvyan [*b* 20 Jan. 1916; *m* 1st, 1941, Joyce Lilia (marr. diss. 1946), 2nd *d* of late Frederick Marsh; one *d*; 2nd, 1948, Marie (marr. diss. 1958), *o d* of late Dr O'Shea; 3rd, 1959, Jonet Noël, *e d* of Lt-Col Alexander Barclay, DSO, MC; one *s* one *d*].

W

WAAL; *see* De Waal.

WACHER, David Mure; Metropolitan Stipendiary Magistrate, 1962-74, retired; *b* 9 Oct. 1909; *s* of late Dr Harold Wacher, FSA, and Violet Amy Wacher (*née* Peebles); *m* 1935, Kathleen Margaret Roche, *yr d* of late Rev. George Ralph Melvyrn Roche; one *s* one *d*. *Educ:* Charterhouse. Called to Bar, Middle Temple, 1935. Served in Royal Artillery, 1939-43. Acting Attorney-General, Gibraltar, 1943; Stipendiary Magistrate, Gibraltar, 1943-49; Acting Chief Justice, Gibraltar, 1948. Vice-Chairman, Mental Health Review Tribunal for SW Metropolitan RHB Area, 1960-62. *Recreations:* music and the theatre. *Address:* 19 Belgrave Crescent, Edinburgh EH4 3AJ. *T:* 031-332 5893. *Club:* New (Edinburgh).

WACKETT, Air Vice-Marshal Ellis Charles, CB 1957; CBE 1951 (OBE 1941); CEng; FRAeS; psa; Royal Australian Air Force; *b* 13 Aug. 1901; *yr s* of James Wackett, Townsville, Queensland; *m* 1928, Doreen I., *d* of Thomas S. Dove, Mildura, Victoria; two *s* one *d*. *Educ:* Jervis Bay Royal Australian Naval Coll.; Keyham Engineering College, England; Imperial College of Science and Technology, London. Joined Australian Navy, 1914; commissioned, 1921. Transferred to Royal Australian Air Force, 1923; graduated RAF Staff Coll., 1933. Air Vice-Marshal, 1948. Air Member for Engineering and Maintenance, 1942; Air Member for Technical Service, RAAF, 1948; retired 1959. Member, Australian Nat. Airlines Commn (TAA), 1960-68. *Recreation:* angling. *Address:* 13/32 Berkeley Street, Hawthorn, Victoria 3122, Australia. *Club:* Naval and Military (Victoria).

WACKETT, Sir Lawrence (James), Kt 1954; DFC 1918, AFC 1919; BSc; Founder, Manager, and a Director of Commonwealth Aircraft Corporation Ltd, 1936-61, retired; Director, Joseph Lucas (Australia) Ltd, 1960-69; *b* 2 Jan. 1896; *s* of James Wackett, Townsville, Queensland; *m* 1919, Letitia Emily Florence, *d* of Fred B. Wood, Townsville, Queensland; one *d* (one *s* decd). *Educ:* Royal Military Coll. (Duntroon); Melbourne University (BSc). Officer, Australian Regular Army, 1913-20; served in Australian Flying Corps in France and Palestine (despatches twice); Officer, RAAF, 1921, retired a Wing Commander, 1930; Aeronautical Engineer, 1930-35. Designed: Widgeon flying boat; Gannet; Wackett trainer; Boomerang; pioneered aircraft construction in Australia, 1936. Commodore, Beaumaris Motor Yacht Squadron, 1962-68. Kernot Memorial Medallist, 1959; Finlay National Award, 1967; Kingsford Smith Meml Medal, RAeS; Oswald Watt Meml Medal, Royal Aero Club of Australia. FIProdE; Hon. FRAeS 1977. *Publications:* My Hobby is Trout Fishing, 1944; Studies of an Angler, 1949; Aircraft Pioneer, 1972. *Recreations:* became quadriplegic in 1970; now developing aids for disabled. *Address:* 55 Fiddens Wharf Road, Killara, Sydney, NSW 2071, Australia.

WADDELL, Sir Alexander (Nicol Anton), KCMG 1959 (CMG 1955); DSC 1944; United Kingdom Commissioner, British Phosphate Commissioners, since 1965; *b* 8 Nov. 1913; *yr s* of late Rev. Alexander Waddell, Eassie, Angus, Scotland, and late Effie Thompson Anton Waddell; *m* 1949, Jean Margot Lesbia, *d* of late W. E. Masters. *Educ:* Fettes Coll., Edinburgh; Edinburgh Univ. (MA); Gonville and Caius Coll., Cambridge. Colonial Administrative Service, 1937; British Solomon Islands Protectorate: Cadet, 1937; District Officer, 1938; District Commissioner, 1945; Acting Resident Commissioner, 1945; Malayan Civil Service, 1946; Principal Asst Secretary, North Borneo, 1947-52 (Acting Dep. Chief Secretary, periods, 1947-51). Colonial Secretary, Gambia, 1952-56; Colonial Secretary, Sierra Leone, 1956-58; Dep. Governor, Sierra Leone, 1958-60; Governor and Commander-in-Chief of Sarawak, 1960-63. On Naval Service, 1942-44. Lieut, RANVR; on Military Service, 1945-47, Lt-Col, Gen. List (British Mil. Administration). *Recreations:* golf, gardening. *Address:* Pilgrim Cottage, Ashton Keynes, Wilts. *Clubs:* Naval, Royal Commonwealth Society, East India, Devonshire, Sports and Public Schools.

WADDELL, Sir James (Henderson), Kt 1974; CB 1960; Deputy

Chairman, Police Complaints Board, since 1977; *b* 5 Oct. 1914; *s* of D. M. Waddell and J. C. Fleming; *m* 1940, Dorothy Abbie Wright; one *s* one *d*. *Educ:* George Heriot's Sch.; Edinburgh Univ. Assistance Board, 1936; Ministry of Information, 1940; Reconnaissance Corps, 1942; Ministry of Housing and Local Government, 1946; Under-Secretary, 1955; Under-Secretary, Cabinet Office, 1961-63; Dep.-Secretary, Min. of Housing and Local Government, 1963-66; Dep. Under-Sec., Home Office, 1966-75. *Recreation:* sailing. *Address:* Oakwood, East Lavant, Chichester, Sussex. *T:* Chichester 527129.

WADDILOVE, Lewis Edgar, OBE 1965; JP; Director, Joseph Rowntree Memorial Trust, since 1961 (Executive Officer of the Trust, 1946-61); *b* 5 Sept. 1914; *s* of Alfred and Edith Waddilove; *m* 1st, 1940, Louise Power (*d* 1967); one *s* one *d*; 2nd, 1969, Maureen Piper. *Educ:* Westcliff High Sch.; Univ. of London (DPA). Admin. Officer, LCC Educn Dept, 1936-38; Govt Evacuation Scheme, Min. of Health, 1938-43; Friends Ambulance Unit, Middle East, 1943-45 (Exec. Chm., 1946); Chairman, Friends Service Council, 1961-67. Member: Cttee on Housing in Greater London (Milner Holland), 1963-65; Nat. Fedn of Housing Societies, 1965-73, 1977- (Chm.); Nat. Cttee for Commonwealth Immigrants, 1966-68; Social Science Research Council, 1967-71; Public Schools Commn, 1968-70; Central Housing Advisory Cttee, 1960-75; Housing Corp., 1968-; Standing Cttee, Centre for Socio-Legal Studies at Oxford, 1972-75; Legal Aid Advisory Cttee, 1972-; Adv. Cttee on Rent Rebates and Rent Allowances, 1975-; Cttee on Voluntary Organisations, 1974-; Working Party on Housing Cooperatives, 1974-76; Chairman: Advisory Cttee on Fair Rents, 1973-74; Advisory Cttee on Housing Cooperatives, 1976-; York City Charities, 1957-65 and 1972-; York Univ. Council, 1977-; Personal Social Services Council, 1977-; Trustee, Shelter, 1966-74 (Chm. 1970-72). Presiding Clerk, 4th World Conf. of Friends, in N Carolina, 1967. Governor, Co. of Merchant Adventurers, City of York, 1978-. Governor: Leighton Park Sch., 1951-71; Bootham and The Mount Schs., 1972- (Chm. 1974-). JP York, 1968. *Publications:* One Man's Vision, 1954; Housing Associations (PEP), 1962; various articles in technical jls. *Address:* Clifton Lodge, York YO3 6NP. *T:* York 53151. *Club:* Reform.

WADDINGTON, David Charles; QC 1971; a Recorder of the Crown Court, since 1972; *b* 2 Aug. 1929; *o s* of late Charles Waddington and of Mrs Minnie Hughan Waddington; *m* 1958, Gillian Rosemary, *d* of Alan Green, *qv*; three *s* two *d*. *Educ:* Sedbergh; Hertford Coll., Oxford. President, Oxford Univ. Conservative Assoc., 1950. 2nd Lieut, XII Royal Lancers, 1951-53. Called to Bar, Gray's Inn, 1951. Contested (C): Farnworth Div., 1955; Nelson and Colne Div., 1964; Heywood and Royton Div., 1966; MP (C) Nelson and Colne, 1968-Sept. 1974. Director: Wolstenholme Bronze Powders Ltd; Progress Mills Ltd; J. & J. Roberts Ltd; Padiham Room & Power Co. Ltd. *Address:* Whins House, Sabden, near Blackburn, Lancs. *T:* Padiham 71070. *Club:* Cavalry and Guards.

WADDINGTON, Gerald Eugene, CBE 1975; QC (Cayman Islands) 1971; Attorney General of the Cayman Islands, 1970-April 1977; *b* 31 Jan. 1909; *o s* of Walter George Waddington and Una Blanche Waddington (*née* Hammond); *m* 1935, Hylda Kathleen (*née* Allen); one *s* one *d*. *Educ:* Jamaica Coll.; Wolmer's Schl., Jamaica. Solicitor, Supreme Court, Jamaica, 1932; LLB (London) 1949; Solicitor, Supreme Court, England, 1950; called to the Bar, Gray's Inn, 1957. Deputy Clerk of Courts, Jamaica, 1939; Asst Crown Solicitor, Jamaica, 1943-48; Resident Magistrate, 1948-58; Puisne Judge, 1959-64; Judge of the Court of Appeal, Jamaica, 1964-70, retired. Joint ed. West Indian Law Reports. Vice-Pres. Nat. Rifle Assoc. Chm. St John Council for Jamaica. CStJ 1962, KStJ 1970. *Recreation:* shooting (Member of Jamaica Rifle Team to Bisley, 1937, 1950, 1953, 1956, 1957, 1960, 1963, 1965, 1967, 1968; Captain, 1950, 1953, 1957, 1967; Captain, WI Rifle Team, 1960). *Address:* PO Box 438, Stittsville, Ontario K0A 3G0, Canada. *Clubs:* Royal Commonwealth Society, Royal Over-Seas League.

WADDINGTON, Very Rev. John Albert Henry, MBE 1945; TD 1951; MA (Lambeth) 1959; Provost of Bury St Edmunds, 1958-76, now Provost Emeritus; a Church Commissioner, 1972-76; *b* 10 Feb. 1910; *s* of H. Waddington, Tooting Graveney, Surrey; *m* 1938, Marguerite Elisabeth, *d* of F. Day, Wallington, Surrey; two *d*. *Educ:* Wandsworth Sch.; London Univ.; London College of Divinity. BCom London Univ., 1929. Deacon, 1933; priest, 1934; Curate of St Andrew's, Streatham, 1933-35; Curate of St Paul's, Furzedown, 1935-38; Rector of Great Bircham, 1938-45; Vicar of St Peter Mancroft, Norwich, 1945; Chaplain to High Sheriff of Norfolk, 1950; Proctor in Convocation of Canterbury, 1950; Hon. Canon of Norwich, 1951. Chaplain to Forces (TA) 1935-58; Staff Chaplain, Eighth Army, 1943 (despatches twice);

DACG XIII Corps, 1945, Eastern Command TA, 1951. *Recreations:* travel, theatre and cinema, religious journalism. *Address:* Three Ways, Maypole Green, Bradfield St George, Bury St Edmunds, Suffolk. *T:* Sicklesmere 352.

WADDINGTON, Leslie; Managing Director, Waddington and Tooth Galleries (formerly Waddington Galleries), since 1966; *b* 9 Feb. 1934; *s* of Victor and Zelda Waddington; *m* 1966, Ferriel (*née* Lyle); two *d*. *Educ:* Portora Royal School; École du Louvre (Diplômé). *Recreations:* chess, ping pong, reading. *Address:* 1 Elm Tree Road, NW8. *T:* 01-286 6338.

WADDINGTON, Rev. Canon Robert Murray; General Secretary of Church of England Board of Education and National Society for Promoting Religious Education, since 1977; *b* 24 Oct. 1927; *s* of Percy Nevill and Dorothy Waddington. *Educ:* Dulwich Coll.; Selwyn Coll., Cambridge; Ely Theological Coll. MA (2nd cl. Theol.). Asst Curate St John's, Bethnal Green, 1953-55; Chaplain, Slade Sch., Warwick, Qld, Aust., 1955-59; Curate, St Luke's, Cambridge, 1959-61; Headmaster, St Barnabas Sch., Ravenshoe, N Qld, Aust., 1961-70; Oxford Univ. Dept of Education, 1971-72; Residentiary Canon, Carlisle Cathedral, and Bishop's Adviser for Education, 1972-77. *Recreations:* cooking, films, sociology. *Address:* 22 Wincott Street, SE11; Church House, Westminster, SW1P 3NZ. *T:* 01-222 9011. *Club:* United Oxford & Cambridge University.

WADDY, Rev. Lawrence Heber; Lecturer, University of California, San Diego, since 1970; Hon. Assistant, St James', La Jolla, since 1974; *b* 5 Oct. 1914; *s* of late Archdeacon Stacy Waddy, Secretary of SPG, and Etheldred (*née* Spittal). *Educ:* Marlborough Coll.; Balliol Coll., Oxford. Domus Exhibitioner in Classics, Balliol, 1933; 1st Class Hon. Mods., Oxford, 1935; de Paravicini Scholar, 1935; Craven Scholar, 1935; 2nd Class Lit. Hum., 1937; BA 1937; MA 1945; Asst Master: Marlborough Coll., 1937-38; Winchester Coll., 1938-42 and 1946-49 (Chaplain, 1946). Headmaster, Tonbridge Sch., 1949-62. Select Preacher, Cambridge Univ., 1951; Oxford Univ., 1954-56. Examining Chaplain to the Bishop of Rochester, 1959-63; Hon. Canon of Rochester, 1961-63; Hon. Chaplain to the Bishop of Rochester, 1963. Deacon, 1940; Priest, 1941; Chaplain, RNVR, 1942-46. Lecturer in Classics, University of California, 1961. Education Officer, School Broadcasting Council, 1962-63; Chaplain to The Bishop's School, La Jolla, California, 1963-67; Headmaster, Santa Maria Internat. Acad., Chula Vista, Calif, 1967-70; Vicar, Church of the Good Samaritan, University City, 1970-74. *Publications:* Pax Romana and World Peace, 1950; The Prodigal Son (musical play), 1963; The Bible as Drama, 1974; Faith of Our Fathers, 1975; Symphony, 1977. *Recreations:* cricket and other games. *Address:* 5910 Camino de la Costa, La Jolla, California 92037, USA.

WADE, family name of **Baron Wade.**

WADE, Baron, *cr* 1964 (Life Peer); **Donald William Wade,** DL; MA, LLB; *b* 16 June 1904; *s* of William Mercer and Beatrice Hemington Wade; *m* 1932, Ellenora Beatrice (*née* Bentham); two *s* two *d. Educ:* Mill Hill; Trinity Hall, Cambridge. Admitted Solicitor, 1929. MP (L) Huddersfield West, 1950-64; Liberal Whip, 1956-62; Deputy Leader, Liberal Parliamentary Party, 1962-64; Deputy Liberal Whip, House of Lords, 1965-67; President, Liberal Party, 1967-68. DL, W Riding, Yorks, 1967, N Yorks, 1974. *Publications:* Democracy, 1944; Way of the West, 1945; Our Aim and Purpose, 1961; Yorkshire Survey: a report on community relations in Yorkshire, 1972; Europe and the British Health Service, 1974. *Address:* High Houses, Wath-in-Nidderdale, Pateley Bridge, Yorks HG3 5PL. *T:* Harrogate 711431. *Clubs:* National Liberal, Reform.

WADE, Maj.-Gen. (Douglas) Ashton (Lofft), CB 1946; OBE 1941; MC 1918; BA; CEng; MIEE; *b* 13 March 1898; 2nd *s* of C. S. D. Wade, Solicitor, Saffron Walden, Essex; *m* 1st, 1926, Heather Mary Patricia Bulmer (*d* 1968), Sowerby, Thirsk, Yorkshire; one *d*; 2nd, 1972, Cynthia Halliday (*née* Allen). *Educ:* St Lawrence Coll., Ramsgate; Royal Military Acad., Woolwich; Clare Coll., Cambridge. Commnd into Royal Artillery, 1916; served European War, France and Italy; seconded RE 1918-21; transferred to Royal Signals, 1921; Staff Coll., Camberley, 1933-34; DAQMG India, 1937-40; GSO 1, GHQ, BEF and GHQ Home Forces, 1940-41; AA and QMG 2nd Division, 1941-42; Dep. Ajt.-General, India, 1942-44; Comdr, Madras Area, India, 1944-47; GOC Malaya District, 1947-48; Mem., Indian Armed Forces Nationalisation Cttee, 1947; Special Appointment War Office, 1948-49; retired, 1950; Telecommunications Attaché, British Embassy, Washington, 1951-54; Sen. Planning Engineer, Independent Television

Authority, 1954-60; Regional Officer, East Anglia, Independent Television Authority, 1960-64. Technical Consultant: Inter-University Research Unit, Cambridge, 1965-69; WRVS Headquarters, 1970-75. Chm., South East Forum for closed circuit TV in educn, 1967-73. Chm., Royal Signals Institute, 1957-63; National Vice-Chairman Dunkirk Veterans' Association, 1962-67, National Chairman, 1967-74. *Publications:* contributed to various Services publications, including RUSI Journal, United Services Journal (India), and Brassey's Annual. *Recreation:* gardening. *Address:* 24 Highway Road, Leicester LE5 5RD. *T:* Leicester 737563.

WADE, Emlyn Capel Stewart, QC 1959; JP; MA, LLD (Cantab); Hon. DCL (Durham); FBA; Downing Professor of the Laws of England, Cambridge University, 1945-62, Professor Emeritus, since 1962; Fellow of Gonville and Caius College since 1931; Reader in Constitutional Law, Council of Legal Education, 1945-66; Member of the Law Reform Committee, 1952-63; Hinkley Visiting Professor, Johns Hopkins University, Baltimore, 1962-63; Barrister-at-Law; Hon. Bencher, Inner Temple; *b* 31 Aug. 1895; *er s* of late Charles Stewart Douglas Wade; *m* 1924, Mary Esmé, *yr d* of late Rev. W. B. Cardew; four *d. Educ:* St Lawrence Coll., Ramsgate; Gonville and Caius Coll., Cambridge. Served with British Salonika Force, and in France, 1916-19; Temp. Major, RA (TA), 1940-42; employed in offices of War Cabinet and Home Office, 1942-45; Lecturer-in-Law, Armstrong Coll., University of Durham, 1923-24; Vice-Principal, 1924-26, Principal, 1926-28. Law Society's School of Law; Fellow of St John's Coll., Cambridge, 1928-31; Member of the Council of the Senate, Cambridge Univ., 1936-40; Hon. Secretary, Society of Public Teachers of Law, 1925-38, President, 1950-51. Member of Lord Chancellor's Committees on Law of Defamation and Limitation of Actions; Cttee on Electoral Law Reform. JP Cambridge, 1946. *Publications:* (with late G. Godfrey Phillips) Constitutional Law, 1931, 8th edn (with A. W. Bradley), 1970; edited Dicey, Law of the Constitution, 10th edn, 1959; articles in Law Quarterly Review, and various legal publications. *Address:* 17 Sculthorpe Road, Fakenham, Norfolk. *T:* Fakenham 2565.

WADE, Col Sir George Albert, Kt 1955; MC; JP; Director: Wade Potteries Ltd; Wade (Ireland) Ltd; George Wade & Son Ltd; A. J. Wade Ltd; Wade Heath & Co. Ltd; *b* 1891; *s* of George Wade, JP, Burslem; *m* 1915, Florence (*d* 1971), *d* of Samuel Johnson, JP, Burslem; one *s* two *d. Educ:* Newcastle-under-Lyme High Sch., Staffordshire. Served European War, 1914-18, with S Staffs Regt (MC and Bar); served War of 1939-45, with his Regiment and on General Staff; Colonel (retired) late S Staffs Regiment. Contested (C) Newcastle-under-Lyme, General Election, 1945. Past President: North Staffordshire Political Union; North Staffs Chamber of Commerce. Chairman: Pottery and Glass Trades Benevolent Institution, 1949-54; Machine Gun Corps Old Comrades Association. Pres. N Staffs Medical Inst. Fellow Corporation of Secretaries. JP Stoke-on-Trent. *Publications:* Minor Tactics Training Manual (issued to Home Guard) and a series of 12 books on Military Training, during War of 1939-45. *Recreations:* painting, photography, ornithology. *Address:* Brand Hall, Norton-in-Hales, Market Drayton, Salop. *T:* Market Drayton 3006.

WADE, Henry William Rawson, QC 1968; FBA 1969; MA; LLD (Cantab); DCL (Oxon); Master of Gonville and Caius College, Cambridge, since 1976; Rouse Ball Professor of English Law, University of Cambridge, from Oct. 1978; Barrister-at-Law; *b* 16 Jan. 1918; *s* of late Colonel H. O. Wade and of E. L. Rawson-Ackroyd; *m* 1943, Marie, *d* of late G. E. Osland-Hill; two *s. Educ:* Shrewsbury Sch.; Gonville and Caius Coll., Cambridge. Henry Fellow, Harvard Univ., 1939; temp. officer, Treasury, 1940-46. Called to the Bar, Lincoln's Inn, 1946; Hon. Bencher, 1964. Fellow of Trinity Coll., Cambridge, 1946-61; University Lecturer, 1947; Reader, 1959; Prof. of English Law, Oxford Univ., 1961-76; Fellow, St John's College, Oxford, 1961-76, Hon. Fellow, 1976. Lectr, Council of Legal Education, 1957; British Council Lectr in Scandinavia, 1958, and Turkey, 1959; Cooley Lectr, Michigan Univ., 1961; Vithalbai Patel Lectr, New Delhi, 1971; Chettyar Lectr, Madras, 1974. Member: Council on Tribunals, 1958-71; Relationships Commn, Uganda, 1961; Royal Commn on Tribunals of Inquiry, 1966. *Publications:* The Law of Real Property, 1957 (with Hon. Mr Justice Megarry), 4th edn, 1975; Administrative Law, 1961, 4th edn, 1977; Towards Administrative Justice, 1963; (with Prof. B. Schwartz) Legal Control of Government, 1972; Editor, Annual Survey of Commonwealth Law; articles in legal journals; broadcast talks. *Recreations:* climbing, gardening. *Address:* Master's Lodge, Caius College, Cambridge. *T:* Cambridge 312211. *Club:* Alpine.

WADE, John Charles, OBE 1959; JP; Lord-Lieutenant of Cumbria, since 1974 (of the County of Cumberland, 1968-74); *b*

15 Feb. 1908; unmarried. *Educ:* St Bees School. Midland Bank Ltd, 1925-27. West Cumberland Farmers Ltd, 1927-68 (General Manager, 1931-64; Managing Director, 1964-68). Director: W Cumberland Farmers Ltd; Border Television Ltd; Chicpac Ltd. President: Cumbria Assoc. of Boys Clubs; Cumbria Scouts; Whitehaven Rugby Club; Whitehaven Cricket Club; Chm., Gosforth Agricultural Soc.; Chm., Whitehaven Harbour Comrs. Chm. of Governors, St Bees Sch.; Governor, Sedbergh Sch.; Dir, Eskdale Outward Bound Mountain Sch. JP Cumberland, 1956, Cumbria, 1974. Freeman, Borough of Whitehaven. KStJ 1974 (Chm. Cumbria Council of St John). *Recreations:* shooting, fishing. *Address:* Hillcrest, Whitehaven, Cumbria. *T:* Whitehaven 2844. *Club:* Cumberland County (Carlisle).

WADE, John Roland, CB 1942; retired as Director of Remploy Ltd (1960-63); *b* 11 Oct. 1890; *e s* of late George Alfred Wade; *m* 1928, Penelope Dorothy Haig, *y d* of late Dr Haig Ferguson, Edinburgh; two *s. Educ:* Westminster School (King's Scholar); Queens' Coll., Cambridge (Scholar). Entered War Office, 1914; Director of Establishments, War Office, 1939-53; retired Dec. 1953. Financial Director (part-time), Remploy Ltd, 1954-Oct. 1960. *Address:* 15 St Catherine's Court, Bedford Road, W4.

WADE, Joseph Frederick; General Secretary, National Graphical Association, since 1976; *b* 18 Dec. 1919; *s* of James and Ellen Wade; *m*; two *s. Educ:* elementary sch., Blackburn, Lancs. Trained as compositor, The Blackburn Times, 1934-40; served UK and overseas, East Lancs Regt and RAOC, 1940-46; newspaper compositor, 1946-56. Full-time Trade Union official, Typographical Assoc., 1956; Nat. Officer, NGA, 1964; Asst Gen. Sec., NGA, 1968. Member: Exec. Cttee, Printing and Kindred Trades Fedn, 1971-74; Exec. Cttee, Internat. Graphical Fedn, 1976- (Vice-Pres.); TUC Printing Industries Cttee, 1976-; Printing and Publishing Industry Training Bd, 1977-. Mem., Blackburn County Borough Council, 1952-56. *Recreations:* walking, Scrabble, swimming. *Address:* National Graphical Association, 63-67 Bromham Road, Bedford MK40 2AG. *T:* Bedford 51521.

WADE, Prof. Owen Lyndon, MD, FRCP; Professor of Therapeutics and Clinical Pharmacology, University of Birmingham, since 1971; *b* 17 May 1921; *s* of J. O. D. Wade, MS, FRCS, and Kate Wade, Cardiff; *m* 1948, Margaret Burton, LDS; three *d. Educ:* Repton; Cambridge; University College Hospital, London. Senior Scholar, Emmanuel Coll., Cambridge, 1941; Achison and Atkinson Morley Schol., UCH, 1945; Resident Medical Officer, UCH, 1946; Clinical Assistant, Pneumoconiosis Research Unit of the Medical Research Council, 1948-51; Lecturer and Sen. Lecturer in Medicine, Dept of Medicine, University of Birmingham, 1951-57; Whitla Prof. of Therapeutics and Pharmacology, Queen's Univ., Belfast, 1957-71. Rockefeller Travelling Fellowship in Medicine, 1954-55; Research Fellow, Columbia Univ. at Department of Medicine, Presbyterian Hospital, New York, 1954-55; Consultant, WHO. Member: Medicines Commn, DHSS; Clinical Res. Bd, MRC. Dep. Chm., Jt Formulary Cttee for British Nat. Formulary. *Publications:* (with J. M. Bishop) The Cardiac Output and Regional Blood Flow, 1962; Adverse Reactions to Drugs, 1970, 2nd edn with L. Beeley, 1976; papers on cardiorespiratory research, adverse reactions to drugs and drug use in the community, in Jl Physiology, Clinical Science, Brit. Med. Bull., Jl Clin. Invest. *Recreations:* books, travel and sailing. *Address:* Department of Therapeutics and Clinical Pharmacology, The Medical School, University of Birmingham, Birmingham B15 2TJ. *T:* 021-472 1301.

WADE, R(obert) Hunter; New Zealand Ambassador to the Federal Republic of Germany and to Switzerland, since 1975; *b* 14 June 1916; *s* of R. H. Wade, Balclutha, NZ; *m* 1941, Avelda Grace Petersen; two *s* two *d. Educ:* Waitaki; Otago Univ. NZ Treasury and Marketing Depts, 1939; NZ Govt diplomatic appts, Delhi, Simla, Sydney, Canberra, 1941-49; Head of Eastern Political Div., Dept of External Affairs, Wellington, NZ, 1949; NZ Embassy, Washington, 1951; NZ High Commn, Ottawa, 1956; Director of Colombo Plan Bureau, Colombo, 1957; Dir, External Aid, Wellington, 1959; Comr for NZ in Singapore and British Borneo, 1962; High Comr in Malaya/Malaysia, 1963-67; Dep. High Comr in London, 1967-69; NZ Ambassador to Japan and Korea, 1969-71; Dep. Sec.-Gen. of the Commonwealth, 1972-75. Represented New Zealand at Independence of: Uganda, 1962; Botswana, 1966; Lesotho, 1966. Pres., Asiatic Soc. of Japan, 1971. *Address:* New Zealand Embassy, Turmstrasse 4, Bonn, Germany. *Clubs:* Brooks's; Wellington (Wellington, NZ).

WADE, Major-General Ronald Eustace, CB 1961; CBE 1956; retired; *b* 28 Oct. 1905; *s* of late Rev. E. V. Wade and Marcia Wade; *m* 1933, Doris, *d* of late C. K. Ross, Kojonup, WA; one *s*

one *d. Educ:* Melbourne Church of England Grammar Sch.; RMC, Duntroon. ACT. Commissioned, 1927; attached 4/7 DG (India), 1928-29; Adjutant 10 LH and 9 LH, 1930-38; Captain, 1935; Major, 1940; served War of 1939-45, Lieut-Colonel (CO 2/10 Aust. Armd Regt), 1942; Colonel (Colonel A, Adv. LHQ, Morotai), 1945; Colonel Q, AHQ, Melbourne, 1946; idc 1948; Director of Cadets, 1949; Director of Quartering, 1950-51; Director of Personal Services, 1951-52; Military Secretary, 1952-53; Comd 11 Inf. Bde (Brig.), 1953-55; Maj.-General (Head Aust. Joint Service Staff, Washington), 1956-57; Adjutant-General, 1957-60; GOC Northern Command, 1961-62, retired, 1962. *Recreations:* fishing, mechanical handicrafts. *Address:* Friendship, Albany, WA 6330, Australia.

WADE, Rosalind (Herschel), (Mrs R. H. Seymour); novelist; Editor, Contemporary Review, since 1970; *d* of Lieut-Colonel H. A. L. H. Wade and Kathleen Adelaide Wade; *m* William Kean Seymour, FRSL (*d* 1975); two *s. Educ:* Glendower Sch., London; privately, abroad and Bedford Coll., London. Member: Society of Women Writers and Journalists (Chairman, 1962-64, Vice President, 1965-); Committee West Country Writers Assoc., 1953-65; General and Exec. Councils, The Poetry Society Inc., 1962-64, 1965-66; Guildford Centre of Poetry Soc. (Chm. 1969-71); Alresford Historical and Literary Soc. (Chm. 1968-70, 1972-73); Literature Panel, Southern Arts Assoc., 1973-77; conducting Writing and Literary Courses at Moor Park College, Farnham (jointly with William Kean Seymour, 1962-74), Writers' Workshop, 1976-. Vice-Pres., W Country Writers' Assoc., 1975-. Editor, PEN Broadsheet, 1975-77. *Publications: novels:* Children, Be Happy, 1931; Kept Man, 1933; Pity the Child, 1934; Shadow Thy Dream, 1934; A Fawn in a Field, 1935; Men Ask for Beauty, 1936; Treasure in Heaven, 1937; Fairweather Faith, 1940; The Man of Promise, 1941; Bracelet for Julia, 1942; Pride of the Family, 1943; Present Ending, 1946; As the Narcissus, 1946; The Widows, 1948; The Raft, 1950; The Falling Leaves, 1951; Alys at Endon, 1953; The Silly Dove, 1953; Cassandra Calls, 1954; Come Fill The Cup, 1955; Morning Break, 1956; Mrs Jamison's Daughter, 1957; The Grain Will Grow, 1959; The Will of Heaven, 1960; A Small Shower, 1961; The Ramerson Case, 1962; New Pasture, 1964; The Vanished Days, 1966; Ladders, 1968; The Umbrella, 1970; The Golden Bowl, 1970; Mrs Medlend's Private World, 1973; *as Catharine Carr:* English Summer, 1954; Lovers in the Sun, 1955; The Richest Gift, 1956; Heart Tide, 1956; A Dream Come True, 1957; It Must Be Love, 1959; In Search of a Dream, 1960; The Shining Heart, 1961; The Golden City, 1963; Mountain Glory, 1967; *contributor to:* The Fourth Ghost Book, 1965; The Unlikely Ghosts, 1967; Happy Christmas, 1968; Haunted Cornwall, 1973; People Within, 1974; Cornish Harvest, 1974; Tales from the Macabre, 1976; My Favourite Story, 1977; Contemporary Review, Poetry Review, Books and Bookmen, Cornish Review, etc. *Recreations:* walking and historical research. *Address:* 4 Dollis Drive, Guildford Road, Farnham, Surrey. *T:* Farnham 3883. *Clubs:* Royal Commonwealth Society, PEN.

WADE, Air Chief Marshal Sir Ruthven (Lowry), KCB 1974 (CB 1970); DFC 1944; Chief of Personnel and Logistics, Ministry of Defence, since 1976; *b* 1920; *Educ:* Cheltenham Coll.; RAF Coll., Cranwell. RAF, 1939; served War of 1939-45, UK and Mediterranean (DFC); psa, 1953; HQ 2nd Tactical Air Force, Germany; RAF Flying Coll.; Gp Captain 1960; Staff Officer, Air HQ, Malta; Comdr, Bomber Comd station, RAF Gaydon, 1962-65; Air Cdre, 1964; idc 1965; Air Exec. to Deputy for Nuclear Affairs, SHAPE, 1967-68; AOC No 1 (Bomber) Gp, Strike Comd, 1968-71; Air Vice-Marshal, 1968; Dep. Comdr, RAF Germany, 1971-72; ACAS (Ops), 1973; Vice Chief of Air Staff, 1973-76; Air Marshal, 1974; Air Chief Marshal, 1976. *Address:* c/o Ministry of Defence (Main Building), Whitehall, SW1.

WADE-GERY, Robert Lucian; HM Diplomatic Service; Minister, Moscow, since 1977; *b* 22 April 1929; *o s* of late Prof. H. T. Wade-Gery; *m* 1962, Sarah, *er d* of A. D. Marris, *qv*; one *s* one *d. Educ:* Winchester; New Coll., Oxford. 1st cl. Hon. Mods 1949 and Lit. Hum. 1951. Fellow, All Souls Coll., Oxford, 1951-73. Joined HM Foreign (now Diplomatic) Service, 1951; FO (Economic Relations Dept), 1951-54; Bonn, 1954-57; FO (Private Sec. to Perm. Under-Sec., later Southern Dept), 1957-60; Tel Aviv, 1961-64; FO (Planning Staff), 1964-67; Saigon, 1967-68; Cabinet Office (Sec. to Duncan Cttee), 1968-69; Counsellor 1969; on loan to Bank of England, 1969; Head of Financial Policy and Aid Dept, FCO, 1969-71; Under-Sec., Central Policy Review Staff, Cabinet Office, 1971-73; Minister, Madrid, 1973-77. *Recreations:* walking, sailing, travel. *Address:* c/o Foreign and Commonwealth Office, SW1; 7 Rothwell Street, NW1. *T:* 01-722 4754. *Club:* Athenæum.

WADLEY, Sir Douglas, Kt 1969; solicitor; Consultant to O'Shea, Corser & Wadley; *b* 9 Nov. 1904; *s* of John and Honora Wadley; *m* 1928, Vera Joyce Bodman; two *s* two *d. Educ:* various state schools in Qld; Central Technical Coll. High Sch., Brisbane. Admitted Solicitor, Supreme Court of Queensland, 1926. Chm. of Dirs, Carlton and United Breweries (Queensland) Ltd; Chm. of Dirs, Queensland Television Ltd. Pres., Royal National Agricultural and Industrial Assoc. of Queensland. *Recreation:* racing. *Address:* 18 Nindethana Street, Indooroopilly, Brisbane, Queensland 4068, Australia. *T:* 70-2737. *Clubs:* Brisbane, Tattersalls, Johnsonian, Queensland Turf (Chm.) (Brisbane).

WADLEY, Walter Joseph Durham, CMG 1959; *b* 21 June 1903; *o s* of late Joseph Wadley, Stanbrook Croft, Callow End, Worcester; *m* 1946, Marie Ivy Louise, *er d* of late Arthur Dunnett, St Andrew, Jamaica; one *d. Educ:* City of London Sch.; Lincoln Coll., Oxford. Classical scholar, Lincoln Coll., Oxford, 1922; BA 1926, MA 1930. Inspector of Schools, Ghana (then Gold Coast), 1926; Senior Education Officer, 1935; Assistant Director of Education, 1944; Deputy Director of Education, Kenya, 1946; Director of Education, Kenya, 1951; retired from Colonial Education Service, 1959. Dep. General Manager, E. Africa Tourist Travel Assoc., 1959-64; Chief Executive Officer of the Association, 1965. Now retired. Coronation Medal, 1953. *Recreations:* travel, photography, woodwork, gardening. *Address:* The Old Brewhouse, Shutford, Banbury, Oxon. *T:* Swalcliffe 478.

WADSWORTH, George; *b* 10 Dec. 1902; *s* of Arnold Holroyd Wadsworth, Halifax; *m* 1930, Guinivere Shepherd; one *d. Educ:* Heath Grammar Sch., Halifax; Willaston Coll., Nantwich. Director: G. Wadsworth & Sons Ltd, Wadsworth White Lead Co. Ltd, G. Wadsworth & Son (London) Ltd. Founder Chairman Halifax Round Table. Vice-Chairman Halifax Watch, Safety First, Lighting Committee. Member of Halifax Town Council, 1938-45. MP (L), Buckrose Division of E Riding of Yorks, 1945-50; Member, Public Accounts Cttee, 1945-49. Past Master Lodge of Probity No 61. *Recreations:* golf, yachting, swimming. *Address:* Kingston Grange, Halifax, West Yorks. *T:* Halifax 61216.

WAECHTER, Sir (Harry Leonard) d'Arcy, 2nd Bt, *cr* 1911; Lieut, RASC; *b* 22 May 1912; *s* of 1st Bt and Josephine (*d* 1955), *o d* of late John d'Arcy, of Corbetstown, Westmeath; *S* father, 1929; *m* 1939, Philippa Margaret (marr. diss. 1957), *y d* of late James Frederick Twinberrow, Suckley, Worcestershire. *Educ:* Pangbourne Nautical School. Lieut, East Yorkshire Regt (SR), 1931-35; Lieut, RASC, 1942-47; Captain, Worcestershire Regt, GSO 3 159 Inf. Bde (TA), 1947-48; Captain, TARO, 1949. Joint MFH North Ledbury. *Heir: b* John d'Arcy Waechter [*b* 16 Nov. 1915; *m* 1952, Caroline Dymond, *yr d* of Ven. E. F. Hall; two *d*]. *Recreation:* hunting.

WAGNER, Sir Anthony (Richard), KCVO 1961 (CVO 1953); DLitt, MA, Oxon; FSA; Garter Principal King of Arms, since 1961; Inspector of Regimental Colours, since 1961; Kt Principal, Imperial Society of Knights Bachelor, since 1962; Secretary of Order of the Garter, 1952-61; Joint Register of Court of Chivalry, since 1954; Editor, Society of Antiquaries' Dictionary of British Arms, since 1940; *b* 6 Sept. 1908; *o s* of late Orlando Henry Wagner, 90 Queen's Gate, SW7, and late Monica, *d* of late Rev. G. E. Bell, Henley in Arden; *m* 1953, Gillian Mary Millicent (*see* G. M. M. Wagner); two *s* one *d. Educ:* Eton (King's Scholar); Balliol Coll., Oxford (Robin Hollway Scholar). Portcullis Pursuivant, 1931-43. Richmond Herald, 1943-61; served in WO, 1939-43; Ministry of Town and Country Planning, 1943-46; Private Secretary to Minister, 1944-45; Secretary (1945-46), member, 1947-66, Advisory Cttee on Buildings of special architectural or historic interest. Registrar of College of Arms, 1953-60; Genealogist: the Order of the Bath, 1961-72; the Order of St John, 1961-75. President: Chelsea Soc., 1967-73; Aldeburgh Soc., 1970-. Mem. Council, Nat. Trust, 1953-74; Trustee, Nat. Portrait Gallery, 1973-; Chm. of Trustees, Marc Fitch Fund, 1971-77. Master, Vintners' Co., 1973-74. Hon. Fellow, Heraldry Soc. of Canada, 1976. KStJ. *Publications:* Catalogue of the Heralds' Commemorative Exhibition, 1934 (compiler); Historic Heraldry of Britain, 1939, repr. 1972; Heralds and Heraldry in the Middle Ages, 1939; Heraldry in England, 1946; Catalogue of English Mediæval Rolls of Arms, 1950; articles, Heraldry, Genealogy, etc., Chambers's Encyclopædia; The Records and Collections of the College of Arms, 1952; English Genealogy, 1960; English Ancestry, 1961; Heralds of England, 1967; Pedigree and Progress, 1975; Heralds and Ancestors, 1978; genealogical and heraldic articles. *Address:* College of Arms, Queen Victoria Street, EC4. *T:* 01-248 4300; 68 Chelsea Square, SW3. *T:* 01-352 0934; Wyndham Cottage, Aldeburgh, Suffolk. *T:* Aldeburgh 2596. *Clubs:* Athenæum, Beefsteak.

WAGNER, Prof. Franz William; Professor of Education, and Director of Institute of Education, University of Southampton, 1950-71, now Emeritus; *b* 26 Oct. 1905; *s* of Franz Henry and Adelaide Wagner; *m* 1934, Maria Schiller; one *s* one *d. Educ:* University of Adelaide, (Rhodes Scholar for S. Austr., 1928) Christ Church, Oxford. Asst Master, Christ's Hospital, 1931-39; Tutor and Lecturer, Oxford Univ., Department of Education, 1939-50. *Recreation:* gardening. *Address:* Avonmore, Southdown Road, Shawford, Winchester, Hants SO21 2BY.

WAGNER, Gerrit Abram, KBE (Hon.) 1977; Kt, Order of Netherlands Lion, 1969; Commander, Order of Oranje Nassau, 1977; Chairman Supervisory Board, Royal Dutch Petroleum Co., since 1977 (President, 1971-77); Chairman, Committee of Managing Directors, Royal Dutch/Shell Group, 1972-77; *b* 21 Oct. 1916; *m* 1946, M. van der Heul; one *s* three *d. Educ:* Leyden Univ. LLM 1939. After a period in a bank in Rotterdam and in Civil Service in Rotterdam and The Hague, joined Royal Dutch Shell Group, 1946; assignments in The Hague, Curaçao, Venezuela, London and Indonesia; apptd Man. Dir, Royal Dutch Petroleum Co. and Shell Petroleum Co. Ltd; Mem. Presidium of Bd of Directors of Shell Petroleum NV, 1964; Dir, Shell Canada Ltd, 1971-; Hon. CBE (Gt Britain) 1964; Order of Francisco de Miranda (Venezuela), 1965; Officier Légion d'Honneur (France), 1974. *Address:* c/o Royal Dutch Petroleum Company, 30 Carel van Bylandtlaan, The Hague, The Netherlands. *T:* 77.37.48 The Hague; Teylingerhorstlaan 13, Wassenaar, The Netherlands.

WAGNER, Gillian Mary Millicent, OBE 1977, (Lady Wagner); Chairman, Executive/Finance Committee, Dr Barnardo's, since 1973; Member of Council, Dr Barnardo's, since 1976; *b* 25 Oct. 1927; *e d* of late Major Henry Archibald Roger Graham, and of Hon. Margaret Beatrix, *d* of 1st Baron Roborough; *m* 1953, Sir Anthony Wagner, *qv*; two *s* one *d. Educ:* Cheltenham Ladies' Coll.; Geneva Univ. (Licence ès Sciences Morales); London Sch. of Economics (Dip. Social Admin.). Governor, Thomas Coram Foundation for Children; Mem. Exec. Cttee, Georgian Group; Governor, Felixstowe Coll. *Recreations:* sailing, gardening, travelling. *Address:* 68 Chelsea Square, SW3. *T:* 01-352 0934; Wyndham Cottage, Crespigny Road, Aldeburgh, Suffolk. *T:* Aldeburgh 2596. *Club:* Aldeburgh Yacht.

WAGSTAFF, Charles John Leonard; *b* 3 March 1875; *s* of late Rev. J. Wagstaff, Rector of Whittonstall, Northumberland; *m* 1913, Marjorie Bloomer (*d* 1972); one *s* two *d. Educ:* Emmanuel Coll., Cambridge; 16th Wrangler, 1897; 1st Class Natural Sciences Tripos, 1898; Senior Science Master at Bradford Grammar Sch., 1899-1903; Oundle Sch., 1904-09; Headmaster at Haberdashers' Aske's Hampstead Sch., 1910-19; Headmaster King Edward VII Sch., King's Lynn, 1920-39. *Publications:* Electricity; Properties of Matter. *Recreations:* turning ivory, etc. *Address:* 13 Nizells Avenue, Hove, East Sussex. *T:* Brighton 736132.

WAGSTAFF, David St John Rivers; a Recorder of the Crown Court, since 1974; barrister; *b* 22 June 1930; *s* of Prof. John Edward Pretty Wagstaff and Dorothy Margaret (*née* McRobie); *m* 1970, Dorothy Elizabeth Starkie; two *d. Educ:* Winchester Coll. (Schol.); Trinity Coll., Cambridge (Schol., MA, LLB). Called to Bar, Lincoln's Inn, 1954. *Recreations:* mountaineering, fencing. *Address:* 37 Park Square, Leeds LS1 2PD. *T:* Leeds 452702. *Clubs:* Alpine; Fell and Rock Climbing (Lake District), Leeds (Leeds).

WAGSTAFF, Colonel Henry Wynter, CSI 1945; MC 1917; FCIT; RE (retired); *b* 19 July 1890; *s* of Edward Wynter Wagstaff and Flora de Smidt; *m* 1st, 1918, Jean, MB, BS, *d* of George Frederick Mathieson; two *s* ; 2nd, 1967, Margaret, *o d* of late Sir John Hubert Marshall, CIE. *Educ:* Woodbridge; RMA, Woolwich. Commissioned RE 1910; served in India and Mesopotamia in European War, 1914-18 (despatches, MC); Captain, 1916; seconded Indian State Railways, 1921; Major, 1927; Lieut-Colonel, 1934; Colonel, 1940. 1929-46, employed on problems connected with Labour in general and Railway Labour in particular. Member, Railway Board, Government of India, New Delhi, 1942-46; retired, 1948. *Publication:* Operation of Indian Railways in Recent Years, 1931. *Recreations:* reading and writing. *Address:* c/o Lloyds Bank Ltd, 6 Pall Mall, SW1.

WAIAPU, Bishop of, since 1971; **Rt. Rev. Paul Alfred Reeves;** *b* 6 Dec. 1932; 2nd *s* of D'Arcy Lionel and Hilda Mary Reeves; *m* 1959, Beverley Gwendolen Watkins; three *d. Educ:* Wellington Coll., New Zealand; Victoria Univ. of Wellington (MA); St John's Theol. Coll., Auckland (LTh); St Peter's Coll., Univ. of Oxford (MA). Deacon, 1958; Priest, 1960; Curate, Tokoroa, NZ, 1958-59; Curate: St Mary the Virgin, Oxford, 1959-61; Kirkley St Peter, Lowestoft, 1961-63; Vicar, St Paul, Okato, NZ,

1964-66; Lectr in Church History, St John's Coll., Auckland, NZ, 1966-69; Dir of Christian Educn, Dio. Auckland, 1969-71. Chm., Environmental Council, 1974-76. *Publications:* Life is Liturgy, 1966; contrib. NZ Theological Review. *Recreations:* tennis, squash, swimming. *Address:* 8 Cameron Terrace, Napier, NZ. *T:* 57846.

WAIGHTS, Rev. Kenneth (Laws); Member, Methodist World Council; Ex-President of the Methodist Conference (1971-72); *b* 15 May 1909; *s* of Rev. William Waights and Selina Waights; *m* 1935, Dorothy Margaret Rowe. *Educ:* Stationers' Company Sch.; George Watson's Coll., Edinburgh; Handsworth Theological Coll., Birmingham. Served in the following Methodist Churches: Ilfracombe, Exeter, Birmingham Mission, Winson Green Prison (as Chaplain), Hastings, Liverpool, Scarborough, Nottingham (Chm. of District), Bristol, Sunderland, Newcastle upon Tyne; Chairman, Newcastle District of Methodist Church. *Recreations:* golf, walking, travel; formerly: played Rugby football for Devon County, Moseley and Exeter Rugby Clubs. *Address:* 40 St James, Shaftesbury, Dorset.

WAIKATO, Bishop of; *see* New Zealand, Primate and Archbishop of.

WAIN, John Barrington; author; Professor of Poetry, University of Oxford, since 1973; Fellow of Brasenose College, since 1973; *b* 14 March 1925; *e* surv. *s* of Arnold A. Wain and Anne Wain, Stoke-on-Trent; *m* 1960, Eirian, *o d* of late T. E. James; three *s*. *Educ:* The High Sch., Newcastle-under-Lyme; St John's Coll., Oxford. Fereday Fellow, St John's Coll., Oxford, 1946-49; Lecturer in English Literature, University of Reading, 1947-55; resigned to become freelance author and critic. Churchill Visiting Prof., University of Bristol, 1967; Vis. Prof., Centre Universitaire Expérimentale de Vincennes, Paris, 1969. First Fellow in creative arts, Brasenose College, Oxford, 1971-72. FRSL 1960, resigned 1961. *Publications include: fiction:* Hurry On Down, 1953; Living in the Present, 1955; The Contenders, 1958; A Travelling Woman, 1959; Nuncle and other stories, 1960; Strike the Father Dead, 1962; The Young Visitors, 1965; Death of the Hind Legs and other stories, 1966; The Smaller Sky, 1967; A Winter in the Hills, 1970; The Life Guard and Other Stories, 1971; *play:* Harry in the Night, 1975; *poetry:* A Word Carved on a Sill, 1956; Weep Before God, 1961; Wildtrack, 1965; Letters to Five Artists, 1969; Feng, 1975; *criticism:* Preliminary Essays, 1957; Essays on Literature and Ideas, 1963; The Living World of Shakespeare, 1964; A House for the Truth, 1972; Professing Poetry, 1977; *biography:* Samuel Johnson, 1974 (James Tait Black Meml Prize; Heinemann Award, 1975); *autobiography:* Sprightly Running, 1962; much work as editor, anthologist, reviewer, broadcaster, etc. *Recreations:* canoeing, walking. *Address:* c/o Macmillan & Co. Ltd, Little Essex Street, WC2.

WAIN, Prof. Ralph Louis, CBE 1968; FRS 1960; DSc, PhD, FRIC; Professor of Agricultural Chemistry, University of London, since 1950, and Head of Department of Physical Sciences at Wye College (University of London) since 1945; Hon. Director, Agricultural Research Council Unit on Plant Growth Substances and Systemic Fungicides, since 1953; *b* 29 May 1911; 2nd *s* of late G. Wain, Hyde, Cheshire; *m* 1940, Joan Bowker; one *s* one *d*. *Educ:* County Grammar Sch., Hyde, Cheshire; University of Sheffield (First Class Hons Chemistry, 1932; MSc 1933; PhD 1935; Hon. DSc 1977); DSc London, 1949; Town Trustees Fellow, University of Sheffield, 1934; Research Assistant, University of Manchester, 1935-37; Lecturer in Chemistry, Wye Coll., 1937-39; Research Chemist, Long Ashton Research Station (University of Bristol), 1939-45. Vice-President, Royal Institute of Chemistry, 1961-64, 1975-; Mem., E African Natural Resources Res. Council, 1963-; Manager, Royal Instn, 1971-74. Hon. Prof. of Chemistry, Univ. of Kent, 1977-; Nuffield Vis. Prof., Ibadan Univ., 1959; Vis. Prof., Cornell Univ., 1966; NZ Prestige Fellowship, 1973. Lectures: Sir Thomas Middleton Meml, London, 1955; Frankland Meml, Birmingham, 1965; Benjamin Minge Duggar Meml, Alabama, 1966; Amos Meml, E Malling, 1969; Sir Jesse Boot Foundn, Nottingham, 1974; Ronald Slack Meml, London, 1975; Extramural Centenary, London Univ., 1976; Vis. Lectr, Pontifical Acad. Scis, 1976; Douglas Wills Bristol, 1977. Royal Soc. Vis. Prof. to Czechoslovakia, 1968, Mexico, 1971, China, 1973, Romania, 1974, Poland, 1976. Pruthivi Gold Medal, 1957; RASE Research Medal, 1960; John Scott Award, 1963; Flintoft Medal, Chem. Soc., 1969; Internat. Award, Amer. Chem. Soc., 1972; Internat. Medal for Research on Plant Growth Substances, 1973; John Jeyes Gold Medal and Award, Chem. Soc., 1976; Royal Instn Actonian Award, 1977. Hon. DAgricSci, Ghent, 1963; Hon. DSc: Kent, 1976; Lausanne, 1977. *Publications:* numerous research publications in Annals of

Applied Biology, Journal of Agric. Science, Journal of Chemical Society, Berichte der Deutschen Chemischen Gesellschaft, Proc. Royal Society, etc. *Recreations:* painting, travel. *Address:* Staple Farm, Hastingleigh, near Ashford, Kent. *T:* Elmsted 248.

WAINE, Rt. Rev. John; *see* Stafford, Bishop Suffragan of.

WAINWRIGHT, Edwin, BEM 1957; MP (Lab) Dearne Valley Division of West Yorkshire, since Oct. 1959; *b* 12 Aug. 1908; *s* of John Wainwright and Ellen (*née* Hodgson); *m* 1938, Dorothy Metcalfe; two *s* two *d*. *Educ:* Darfield Council School; Wombwell and Barnsley Technical Colleges. WEA student for 20 years. Started work at 14, at Darfield Main Colliery; Nat. Union of Mineworkers: Member Branch Cttee, 1933-39; Delegate, 1939-48; Branch Sec., 1948-59; Member, Nat. Exec. Cttee, 1952-59. Member, Wombwell UDC, 1939-59. Sec./Agent, Dearne Valley Labour Party, 1951-59. Sec. Parly Lab. Party Trade Union Gp, 1966-; Sec. Yorkshire Gp of Parly Lab. Party, 1966-; Chm., Sub-Cttee B, Select Cttee on Nationalised Industries. *Recreations:* gardening, reading. *Address:* 20 Dovecliffe Road, Wombwell, near Barnsley, South Yorks. *T:* Wombwell 2153.

WAINWRIGHT, Richard Scurrah; MP (L) Colne Valley, 1966-70 and since Feb. 1974; Chairman, Liberal Party National Standing Committee, since 1976; *b* 11 April 1918; *o s* of late Henry Scurrah and Emily Wainwright; *m* 1948, Joyce Mary Hollis; one *s* two *d* (and one *s* decd). *Educ:* Shrewsbury Sch.; Clare Coll., Cambridge (Open Scholar). BA Hons Cantab. (History), 1939. Friends Ambulance Unit, NW Europe, 1939-46. Retired Partner, Peat Marwick Mitchell & Co., Chartered Accountants. Pres., Leeds/Bradford Society of Chartered Accountants, 1965-66. Chm., Liberal Party Research Dept, 1968-70; Chm., Liberal Party, 1970-72. Dir, Rowntree Social Service Trust. *Recreations:* gardening, swimming. *Address:* The Heath, Adel, Leeds LS16 8EG. *T:* Leeds 673938. *Clubs:* Reform, National Liberal; Golcar Liberal, Honley Liberal, Linthwaite Liberal.

WAINWRIGHT, Robert Everard, CMG 1959; *b* 24 June 1913; *s* of Dr G. B. Wainwright, OBE, MB; *m* 1939, Bridget Alan-Williams; two *s*. *Educ:* Marlborough; Trinity College, Cambridge (BA). District Officer, Kenya, 1935; Provincial Commissioner, Rift Valley Province, 1953-58. Imperial Defence College, 1959. Chief Commissioner, Kenya, 1960-63; Administrator, Turks and Caicos Is, WI, 1967-71. *Recreations:* sailing, tennis, shooting, cabinet-making. *Address:* 42 Cecily Hill, Cirencester, Glos. *T:* Cirencester 2856. *Club:* Mombasa (Mombasa).

WAINWRIGHT, Rear-Adm. Rupert Charles Purchas, CB 1966; DSC 1943; Vice Naval Deputy to Supreme Allied Commander Europe, 1965-67; retired 1967; with Redditch Development Corporation, 1968-77; *b* 16 Oct. 1913; *s* of late Lieut Comdr O. J. Wainwright and Mrs S. Wainwright; *m* 1937, Patricia Mary Helen, *d* of late Col F. H. Blackwood, DSO and late Mrs Blackwood; two *s* two *d*. *Educ:* Royal Naval College, Dartmouth. Commanded HM Ships Actaeon, Tintagel Castle, Zephyr, 1952-54; Captain HMS Cambridge, 1955-57; Chief of Staff, S Atlantic and S America Station, 1958-60; Director Naval Recruiting, 1960-62; Commodore Naval Drafting, 1962-64. Comdr 1949; Capt. 1955; Rear-Adm. 1965. Mem. Council, Missions to Seamen. Vice-President: Stratford-upon-Avon Soc. DC, Stratford-on-Avon, 1973-; Assoc. District Councils, 1976-. *Publications:* two Prize Essays, RUSI Jl. *Recreations:* hockey (Combined Services; a Vice-Pres., England Hockey Assoc.), swimming (Royal Navy), tennis. *Address:* Regency Cottage, Maidenhead Road, Stratford-upon-Avon, Warwicks. *Club:* Royal Navy.

WAINWRIGHT, Sammy; Member of Board, Post Office Corporation, since 1977; Managing Director, National Giro, since 1977; *b* 2 Oct. 1924; *m* Ruth Strom; three *s* one *d*. *Educ:* Regent Street Polytechnic; LSE (MSc Econ). Financial journalist, Glasgow Herald, 1950; Deputy City Editor, 1952-55; Director: Rea Brothers Ltd (Merchant Bankers), 1960-77 (Managing Dir, 1965-77); Furness Withy & Co. Ltd, 1971-77; Stothert & Pitt Ltd, 1970-77 (Chm., 1975-77); Aeronautical & General Instruments Ltd, 1968-77; Manders (Holdings) Ltd, 1972-; Lancashire & London Investment Trust Ltd, 1963-77; Scottish Cities Investment Trust Ltd, 1961-77; Scottish & Mercantile Investment Co. Ltd, 1964-77. Mem. Council, Soc. of Investment Analysts, 1961-75. Hon. Editor, The Investment Analyst, 1961-74. *Publications:* articles in various Bank Reviews. *Recreations:* reading, bridge. *Address:* 6 Heath Close, NW11 7DX. *T:* 01-455 4448. *Clubs:* Reform, Overseas Bankers'.

WAITE, John Douglas, QC 1975; *b* 3 July 1932; *s* of late Archibald Harvey Waite, Coleshill, Bucks, and Betty, *d* of late Ernest Bates; *m* 1966, Julia Mary, *er d* of late Joseph Tangye, Bellington, Kidderminster, Worcs; three *s* two step *s*. *Educ:* Sherborne Sch.; Corpus Christi Coll., Cambridge (MA). President of Cambridge Union, 1955. Nat. Service, 2nd Lieut, RA, 1951-52. Called to Bar, Gray's Inn, 1956; Mem., General Council of the Bar, 1968-69; Junior Counsel to Registrar of Trade Unions, 1972-74. *Recreations:* keeping weeds down, boats afloat, and children happy. *Address:* 54 Church Street, Orford, Woodbridge, Suffolk IP12 2NT; 7 Brunswick Gardens, W8 4AS; 1 New Square, Lincoln's Inn, WC2A 3SA.
See also Maj.-Gen. Sir (E.) J. (H.) Bates.

WAKE, Sir Hereward, 14th Bt *cr* 1621; MC 1942; DL; Major (retired) King's Royal Rifle Corps; *b* 7 Oct. 1916; *e s* of Sir Hereward Wake, 13th Bt, CB, CMG, DSO, and Margaret W. (*d* 1976), *er d* of R. H. Benson; *S* father, 1963; *m* 1952, Julia Rosemary, JP, *yr d* of late Capt. G. W. M. Lees, Falcutt House, Nr Brackley, Northants; one *s* three *d*. *Educ:* Eton; RMC, Sandhurst. Served War of 1939-45 (wounded, MC). Retired from 60th Rifles, 1947, and studied Estate Management and Agriculture. High Sheriff, 1955, DL 1969, Northants. *Heir: s* Hereward Charles Wake [*b* 22 Nov. 1952; *m* 1977, Lady Doune Ogilvy, *e d* of Earl of Airlie, *qv*]. *Address:* Courteenhall, Northampton. *Club:* Brooks's.

WAKE, Hereward Baldwin Lawrence; Headmaster of St John's School, Leatherhead, Surrey, 1948-60, retired; *b* Aug. 1900; *s* late Rev. Preb. Hereward Eyre Wake and Mary Frances, *d* of late James Sealy Lawrence; *m* 1926, Sheila, *d* of late Captain Henry Harris; two *s*. *Educ:* Marlborough (Classical Exhibnr); Keble College, Oxford (Classical Scholar). Oxford Rugby XV (blue 1922); Capt. Somerset Rugby XV, 1923-29 (Captain 1927). Asst Housemaster, 1923, Housemaster, 1934-39, 1945-48, Cheltenham College. 7th Bn Gloucester Regt (TA), 1939; War Office, 1941-45 (Lt-Col, GSO1). *Recreations:* ornithology, reading, attempting The Times crossword. *Address:* High Ridge, Knoll Wood, Knoll Road, Godalming, Surrey. *T:* Godalming 22622. *Club:* East India, Devonshire, Sports and Public Schools.

WAKEFIELD, family name of Baron Wakefield of Kendal.

WAKEFIELD OF KENDAL, 1st Baron, *cr* 1963, of Kendal; William Wavell Wakefield, Kt 1944; Company Director; *b* Beckenham, Kent, 10 March 1898; *s* of late Roger William Wakefield, MB, JP, and Ethel May Knott; *m* 1919, Rowena Doris, *d* of late Llewellyn Lewis, MD, OBE, JP; three *d*. *Educ:* The Craig Preparatory School; Sedbergh School; Pembroke College, Cambridge. In the RNAS then RAF European War (rose to rank of Captain, despatches); retired from the RAF as Flight-Lieutenant, 1923; transferred to Reserve; rejoined RAF at outbreak of war for flying duty; Director of the Air Training Corps, 1942-44; MP (Nat C) Swindon division of Wiltshire, 1935-45; (C) St Marylebone, 1945-63. Parliamentary Private Sec. to the Marquess of Hartington, 1936-38; to Rt Hon. R. H. Hudson, 1939-40; to Capt. Rt Hon. Harold Balfour, 1940-42; Chm. Parliamentary and Scientific Cttee, 1952-55; Director: Lake District Estates Co. Ltd; Shapland & Petter, Ltd; Portman Building Society, and other companies; Member of Executive Committee, YMCA; Member Executive Committee and Council, the National Playing Fields Assoc.; formerly Mem. Nature Conservancy; Member, Council of Royal National Mission to Deep Sea Fishermen; President, Metropolitan Assoc. of Building Societies; former Pres., Industrial Transport Assoc.; Vice-Pres., Council of The Roy. Albert Hall. Captained England, Cambridge Univ., Middlesex, Royal Air Force, Harlequins, at Rugby football; Past President: Rugby Football Union; Ski Club of Great Britain; British Sub-Aqua Club; Pres., British Water Ski Fedn. *Publication:* Rugger. *Recreation:* skiing. *Heir:* none. *Address:* 71 Park Street, W1; The Old House, Kendal, Cumbria. *T:* Kendal 20861. *Clubs:* Carlton, MCC.
See also R. C. Wakefield.

WAKEFIELD, Bishop of, since 1977; Rt. Rev. Colin Clement Walter James; *b* 20 Sept. 1926; *yr s* of late Canon Charles Clement Hancock James and of Mrs Gwenyth Mary James; *m* 1962, Margaret Joan Henshaw; one *s* two *d*. *Educ:* Aldenham School; King's College, Cambridge (MA, Hons History); Cuddesdon Theological College. Assistant Curate, Stepney Parish Church, 1952-55; Chaplain, Stowe School, 1955-59; BBC Religious Broadcasting Dept, 1959-67; Religious Broadcasting Organizer, BBC South and West, 1960-67; Vicar of St Peter with St Swithin, Bournemouth, 1967-73; Bishop Suffragan of Basingstoke, 1973-77; Canon Residentiary of Winchester Cathedral, 1973-77. Member of General Synod, 1970-; Chm., Church Information Cttee, 1976-. *Recreations:* theatre,

travelling. *Address:* Bishop's Lodge, Woodthorpe Lane, Wakefield, W Yorks WF2 6JJ.

WAKEFIELD, Provost of; *see* Lister, Very Rev. J. F.

WAKEFIELD, Sir (Edward) Humphry (Tyrrell), 2nd Bt *cr* 1962; *b* 11 July 1936; *s* of Sir Edward Birkbeck Wakefield, 1st Bt, CIE, and of Constance Lalage, *e d* of late Sir John Perronet Thompson, KCSI, KCIE; *S* father, 1969; *m* 1st, 1960, Priscilla (marr. diss. 1964), *e d* of O. R. Bagot; 2nd, 1966, Hon. Elizabeth Sophia (from whom he obt. a divorce, 1971), *e d* of Viscount De L'Isle, VC, KG, PC, GCMG, GCVO, and former wife of G. S. O. A. Colthurst; one *s*; 3rd, 1974, Hon. Katharine Mary Alice Baring, *d* of 1st Baron Howick of Glendale, KG, GCMG, KCVO, and of Lady Mary Howick; one *s* one *d* (and one *s* decd). *Educ:* Gordonstoun; Trinity Coll., Cambridge. Formerly Lieut, 10th Royal Hussars. Exec. Vice-Pres., Mallett, America Ltd, 1970-75; Chm., Tyrrell and Moore Ltd; Director: Mallett & Son (Antiques), London; Mallett at Bourdon House Ltd; Enterprise, Republic of Ireland; F. William Free Advertising (UK); Multinational Business Communications, USA; Save Piccadilly Foundn. Dir, Spoleto Fest. of Two Worlds, USA and Italy. Fellow, Pierrepont Morgan Library. *Recreations:* riding, writing, music, shooting. *Heir: s* Maximilian Edward Vereker Wakefield, *b* 22 Feb. 1967. *Address:* c/o Barclays Bank, St James' Street, Derby DE1 1QU. *Clubs:* Cavalry and Guards, Turf.

WAKEFIELD, Hubert George; *see* Wakefield, Hugh.

WAKEFIELD, Hugh, (Hubert George); MA Cantab; Hon. FMA; FRSA; Keeper of the Department of Circulation, Victoria and Albert Museum, 1960-75; *b* 6 March 1915; *o s* of late George Wakefield; *m* 1939, Nora Hilary Inglis; one *s* one *d*. *Educ:* King Edward's Sch., Birmingham; Trinity Coll., Cambridge. Joined staff of Royal Commission on Historical Monuments (England), 1938. Served War of 1939-45, Temp. Captain (Instructor in Gunnery), RA, 1942-46. Asst Keeper, Victoria and Albert Museum, 1948. Governor of the National Museum of Wales, 1960-75; Mem. Council, Museums' Assoc., 1960-63; Mem., DES Crafts Advisory Cttee, 1971-75; Chm., Cttee for Museums of Applied Art, Internat. Council of Museums, 1974-75; Corresp. Mem., Finnish Soc. of Crafts and Design, 1965-. *Publications:* (ed) Victorian Collector (series); Nineteenth Century British Glass, 1961; Victorian Pottery, 1962; Contributor to: Connoisseur Early Victorian Period Guide, 1958; World Ceramics (ed R. J. Charleston), 1968; Das Pompöse Zeitalter, 1970; Encyc. Brit. *Recreation:* travel. *Address:* 32 Strand-on-the-Green, W4. *T:* 01-994 6355.

WAKEFIELD, Sir Humphry; *see* Wakefield, Sir E. H. T.

WAKEFIELD, Sir Peter (George Arthur), KBE 1977; CMG 1973; HM Diplomatic Service; HM Ambassador to the Lebanon, since 1975; *b* 13 May 1922; *s* of John Bunting Wakefield and Dorothy Ina Stace; *m* 1951, Felicity Maurice-Jones; four *s* one *d*. *Educ:* Cranleigh Sch.; Corpus Christi Coll., Oxford. Army Service, 1942-47; Military Govt, Eritrea, 1946-47; Hulton Press, 1947-49; entered Diplomatic Service, 1949; Middle East Centre for Arab Studies, 1950; 2nd Sec., Amman, 1950-52; Foreign Office, 1953-55; 1st Sec., British Middle East Office, Nicosia, 1955-56; 1st Sec. (Commercial), Cairo, 1956; Administrative Staff Coll., Henley, 1957; 1st Sec. (Commercial), Vienna, 1957-60; 1st Sec. (Commercial), Tokyo, 1960-63; Foreign Office, 1964-66; Consul-General and Counsellor, Benghazi, 1966-69; Econ. and Commercial Counsellor, Tokyo, 1970-72; Econ. and Commercial Minister, Tokyo, 1973; seconded as Special Adviser on the Japanese Market, BOTB, 1973-75. *Recreations:* ceramics and restoring ruins; tennis, swimming. *Address:* c/o Foreign and Commonwealth Office, SW1; Lincoln House, Montpelier Row, Twickenham, Mddx. *T:* 01-892 6390; La Molineta, Frigiliana, near Malaga, Spain. *Club:* Travellers'.

WAKEFIELD, Roger Cuthbert, CMG 1953; OBE 1950; DL; retired; *b* Cark-in-Cartmel, Lancs, 27 June 1906; 4th and *y s* of late Roger William Wakefield, MB, BCh, Kendal, and Ethel May Knott; *m* 1936, Elizabeth Rhoda, *yr d* of late Sidney R. Davie and Margaret Preston Lawson, West Byfleet, Surrey; one *d*. *Educ:* Sedbergh School; Trinity College, Cambridge (BA 1928). Joined Sudan Civil Service, 1929; Survey of the Arc of the Thirtieth Meridian, 1935-40. War of 1939-45; Civil Defence Duties and desert navigation, 1940-43; Director of Surveys, Sudan, 1946-54; Survey Consultant to Sudan Government, 1954-55. Director, Equatoria Projects Board, 1949; Chairman, Unclassified Staff Wages Commn, 1951; Councillor without Portfolio on Governor-Gen.'s Exec. Council and Member Legislative Assembly, 1952. Member: British-Argentine Rugby

football touring team, 1927; Cambridge East Greenland Exped., 1929; Lake Rudolf Rift Valley Exped., 1934. Chm., Highland Div., Scottish Community Drama Assoc., 1975-. FRICS, 1949. DL Ross and Cromarty, 1976. *Publication:* (with D. F. Munsey) The Arc of the Thirtieth Meridian between the Egyptian Frontier and Latitude 13° 45′, 1950. *Recreations:* mountaineering, sailing, fishing. *Address:* Glendrynoch Lodge, Carbost, Isle of Skye. *Club:* Alpine.
See also Baron *Wakefield of Kendal.*

WAKEFIELD, William Barry; Assistant Director, Central Statistical Office, Cabinet Office, since 1975; *b* 6 June 1930; *s* of Stanley Arthur and Evelyn Grace Wakefield; *m* 1953, Elizabeth Violet (*née* Alexander); three *s* one *d*. *Educ:* Harrow County Grammar Sch.; University Coll., London. BSc; FSS. Statistician, NCB, 1953-62; DES, 1962-67; Chief Statistician, MoD, 1967-72. Member, United Reformed Church. *Recreations:* horse racing, gardening. *Address:* 7 The Spinneys, Hockley, Essex. *T:* Hockley 3514.

WAKEFORD, Geoffrey Michael Montgomery; Clerk to the Worshipful Company of Mercers, since 1974; Barrister-at-Law; *b* 10 Dec. 1937; *o s* of Geoffrey and late Helen Wakeford; *m* 1966, Diana Margaret Loy Cooper; two *s* two *d*. *Educ:* Downside; Clare Coll., Cambridge (Classical Schol., MA, LLB). Called to Bar, Gray's Inn and South Eastern Circuit, 1961; practised at Common Law Bar until 1971. Apptd Dep. Clerk to the Mercers Co., 1971. Clerk to: Governors St Paul's Schs; Joint Grand Gresham Cttee; City & Metropolitan Welfare Trustees; Collyers Foundn Trustees; Mem., City of London National Savings Cttee. *Address:* Mercers Hall, Ironmonger Lane, EC2V 8HE. *T:* 01-606 2433.

WAKEFORD, John Chrysostom Barnabas, CMG 1948; *b* 23 Aug. 1898; *o s* of Rev. John Wakeford, Anfield, Liverpool; *m* 1st, 1921, Grace (*d* 1965), *d* of Charles Cooke, Church Coppenhall; one *d*; 2nd, 1970, Dorothy May, *d* of Frederick Ward, Aldeburgh, Suffolk. *Educ:* Malvern College; RMA, Woolwich; Clare College, Cambridge. Commissioned Royal Engineers, 1917; served European War, France and Belgium, 1917-18; N Russia Campaign (despatches). Dep. Dir Transportn, W Africa, 1941-43; Ceylon, 1943-44 (Col); Dir of Transportn, SE Asia, 1944-45 (Brig.). Chief Railway Commissioner, Burma; General Manager, Burma Railways and Technical Adviser to Government of Burma, 1945-48; Chief Engineer, Cameroons Development Corporation, W Africa, 1948-50; with Rendel Palmer & Tritton, 1950-63; FICE, FIMechE, FCIT, FRSA. *Address:* 41 South Road, Saffron Walden, Essex. *T:* Saffron Walden 22010.

WAKEFORD, Air Marshal Sir Richard (Gordon), KCB 1976; MVO 1961; OBE 1958; AFC 1952; Deputy Chief of Defence Staff (Intelligence), 1975-78; *b* 20 April 1922; *s* of Charles Edward Augustus Wakeford, property owner; *m* 1948, Anne Butler; two *s* two *d*. *Educ:* Montpelier Sch., Paignton; Kelly Coll., Tavistock. Joined RAF, 1941; flying Catalina flying boats, Coastal Comd, operating out of India, Scotland, N Ireland, 1942-45; flying Liberator and York transport aircraft on overseas routes, 1945-47; CFS 1947; Flying Instructor, RAF Coll. Cranwell; CFS Examining Wing; ground appts, incl. 2½ years on staff of Dir of Emergency Ops in Malaya, 1952-58; comdg Queen's Flight, 1958-61; Directing Staff, RAF Staff Coll., 1961-64; subseq.: comdg RAF Scampton; SASO, HQ 3 Group Bomber Comd; Asst Comdt (Cadets), RAF Coll. Cranwell; idc 1969; Comdr N Maritime Air Region, and Air Officer Scotland and N Ireland, 1970-72; Dir of Service Intelligence, MoD, 1972-73; ANZUK Force Comdr, Singapore, 1974-75. *Recreations:* golf, fishing. *Address:* Earlston House, Forgandenny, Perth. *T:* Bridge of Earn 2392. *Clubs:* Royal Air Force, Flyfishers'.

WAKEHAM, John, FCA; JP; MP (C) Maldon since Feb. 1974; *b* 22 June 1932; *s* of late Major W. J. Wakeham and late Mrs E. R. Wakeham; *m* 1965, Anne Roberta Bailey; two *s*. *Educ:* Charterhouse. Chartered Accountant in practice from 1960; Company Director. JP Inner London 1972. *Publications:* The Case against Wealth Tax, 1968; A Personal View, 1969. *Recreations:* farming, sailing, racing, reading. *Address:* House of Commons, SW1. *Club:* St Stephen's.

WAKEHURST, 3rd Baron *cr* 1934, of Ardingly; **(John) Christopher Loder;** Chairman, Continental Illinois Ltd, since 1973; Deputy Chairman, London and Manchester Assurance Company Ltd; Director: Anglo-American Securities Corporation Ltd; Oil & Gas Enterprises (NS) Ltd; *b* 23 Sept. 1925; *s* of 2nd Baron Wakehurst, KG, KCMG, and of Dowager Lady Wakehurst, *qv*; *S* father, 1970; *m* 1956, Ingeborg Krumbholz-Hess (*d* 1977); one *s* one *d*. *Educ:* Eton; King's

School, nr Sydney, NSW; Trinity College, Cambridge (BA 1948, LLB 1949, MA 1953). Served War as Sub Lieut RANVR and RNVR; West Pacific, 1943-45. Barrister, Inner Temple, 1950. CStJ. *Heir:* *s* Hon. Timothy Walter Loder, *b* 28 March 1958. *Address:* c/o 14 Moorfields Highwalk, EC2Y 9DL. *T:* 01-638 6060.

WAKEHURST, Dowager Lady; Dame Margaret Wakehurst, DBE 1965; *b* 4 Nov. 1899; *d* of Sir Charles Tennant, Bt and of Marguerite (*née* Miles); *m* 1920, John de Vere Loder (later 2nd Baron Wakehurst, KG, KCMG) (*d* 1970); three *s* one *d*. Vice-Pres., Nat. Assoc. for Mental Health; Founder, Northern Ireland Assoc. for Mental Health; Vice-Pres., Royal College of Nursing. Hon. LLD Queen's Univ., Belfast; Hon. DLitt New Univ. of Ulster, 1973. DStJ 1959; GCStJ 1970. *Address:* 31 Lennox Gardens, SW1. *T:* 01-589 0956.

WAKELEY, Sir Cecil (Pembrey Grey), 1st Bt *cr* 1952; KBE 1946; CB 1941; DSc (London); MCh; Consulting Surgeon: King's College Hospital; Belgrave Hospital for Children; West End Hospital for Nervous Diseases; Royal Masonic Hospital; Petersfield Hospital; Senior Consulting Surgeon, Royal Navy; Senior Lecturer in Anatomy, King's College, University of London, since 1919; *b* Rainham, Kent, 5 May 1892; *s* of Percy and Mary Wakeley, West Dulwich; *m* 1925, Elizabeth Muriel, *d* of James Nicholson-Smith, Blackheath; three *s*. *Educ:* Dulwich Coll.; King's Coll. Hosp. (Tanner Prizeman, Jelf Medal for surgery and other surgical prizes). Temp. Surgeon, RN, 1915-19, and 1939-46 (Rear-Adm.); Mem., War Wounds and Burns Cttee, MRC. President: Bible League; Chartered Soc. of Physiotherapy; RCS, 1949-54 (formerly Vice-Pres. and Mem. Court of Examiners); Med. Soc. of London; Hunterian Soc. Past President: Harveian Soc. of London; Listerian Soc.; Clinical, United Services and Children's Sections of Roy. Soc. Med.; Royal Life Saving Soc.; Alleyn Club. Vice-President: British Empire Cancer Campaign (also Chm. Council) Imperial Cancer Research Fund, 1949-67. Past Vice-Pres., Council, Med. Defence Union. Chairman: Med. Sickness Finance Corp.; Internat. Wine Soc.; Wakeley Bros, Rainham, Kent. Pres., Med. Sickness Soc. Member: Cttee of Management, Conjoint Bd, 1942-54; Council (also Treas.), Gen. Med. Council, 1942-55; Council, Med. Defence Union. Treas., Assoc. of Independent Hospitals. Examiner in Surgery to Univs of London, Cambridge, Durham, Sheffield, Glasgow, Wales and Dublin. Royal College of Surgeons: Hunterian Prof., 1929, 1934, 1937, 1940, 1942; Arris and Gale Lectr, 1924, 1925; Erasmus Wilson Lectr, 1928, 1930-33, 1935-36; Bradshaw Lectr, 1947; Hunterian Orator, 1955; Thomas Vicary Lectr, 1957; Arnott Demonstrator, 1934. Harveian Lectr, Harveian Soc., 1934; Sheen Memorial Lectr, Cardiff, 1953. Legg Lectr, King's Coll. Hosp. Med. Sch., 1957; Sir Thomas and Lady Edith Dixon Memorial Lectr, Queen's Univ. of Belfast, 1957. Past Grand Warden, United Grand Lodge of England; Past Master and Mem. Court of Assistants: Worshipful Co. of Barbers; Worshipful Soc. of Apothecaries. Hon. Convener, Professional Nurses and Midwives' Yearly Conference. Pres., St John's Ambulance Cadets, Chatham. FRSE, FRCS, FRSA, FKC, FZS. Hon. FRCSE, Hon. FRFPS, Hon. FFR, Hon. FRCSI, Hon. FRACS, Hon. FACS. Hon. LLD: Glasgow; Leeds; Lahore. Hon. DSc: Delhi; Colombo. KStJ; Mem., Chapter Gen., Order of St John; Order of the Nile, 2nd Class, 1938; Legion of Merit (USA), 1946; Chevalier, Légion d'honneur, 1950; Order of Southern Cross, Brazil, 1951. Editorial Sec., British Jl of Surgery, 1940-72. *Publications:* A Textbook of Surgical Pathology; The Life of Sir George Buckston Browne; ed Rose and Carless' Manual of Surgery, 1922-; ed Surgical Diagnosis; ed Treeves' and Wakeley's Handbook of Surgical Operations; ed Aids to Surgery; ed The Pineal Gland; ed Neuro-radiology; ed Synopsis of Surgery; ed Medical Dictionary; ed Surgery for Nurses; ed Annals of Roy. Coll. of Surgeons, 1947-69; ed Medical Press, 1932; articles on surgery, cancer and cancer research, and surgical subjects, in med. and sci. jls. *Recreations:* gardening and photography. *Heir:* *s* John Cecil Nicholson Wakeley, *qv*. *Address:* 240 Maidstone Road, Chatham, Kent. *T:* Medway 45946.

WAKELEY, John Cecil Nicholson, FRCS; Consultant Surgeon, West Cheshire Group of Hospitals, since 1961; *b* 27 Aug. 1926; *s* and *heir* of Sir Cecil Pembrey Grey Wakeley, Bt, *qv*; *m* 1954, June Leney; two *s* one *d*. *Educ:* Canford School. MB, BS London 1950; LRCP 1950, FRCS 1955 (MRCS 1950). Lectr in Anatomy, Univ. of London, 1951-52. Sqdn Ldr, RAF, 1953-54. Councillor, RCS, 1971; Member: Mersey Regional Health Authority, 1974-; Editorial Bd, Health Trends, DHSS, 1968-71; Examiner for Gen. Nursing Council for England and Wales, 1954-59. Liveryman: Worshipful Soc. of Apothecaries; Worshipful Co. of Barbers; Freeman of City of London. FACS 1973. CStJ 1959. *Publications:* papers on leading med. jls, incl. British Empire Cancer Campaign Scientific Report, Vol. II: Zinc

65 and the prostate, 1958; report on distribution and radiation dosimetry of Zinc 65 in the rat, 1959. *Recreations:* music, photography, bird-watching. *Address:* Mickle Lodge, Mickle Trafford, Chester CH2 4EB. *T:* Mickle Trafford 300316. *Club:* Council Club of Royal College of Surgeons.

WAKELING, Rt. Rev. John Denis; *see* Southwell, Bishop of.

WAKELY, Leonard John Dean, CMG 1965; OBE 1945; *b* 18 June 1909; *s* of Sir Leonard Wakely, KCIE, CB; *m* 1938, Margaret Houssemayne Tinson; two *s. Educ:* Westminster School; Christ Church, Oxford; School of Oriental Studies, London. Indian Civil Service, 1932-47. Served in the Punjab and in the Defence Co-ordination, Defence and Legislative Departments of the Government of India. Appointed to Commonwealth Relations Office, 1947; Office of UK High Commissioner in the Union of South Africa, 1950-52; Dep. UK High Comr in India (Madras), 1953-57; Asst Sec., 1955; Dep. UK High Comr in Ghana, 1957-60; Dep. British High Comr in Canada, 1962-65; British Ambassador in Burma, 1965-67. *Address:* Long Meadow, Forest Road, East Horsley, Surrey.

WAKEMAN, Sir (Offley) David, 5th Bt *cr* 1828; *b* 6 March 1922; *s* of Sir Offley Wakeman, 4th Bt, CBE, and Winifred (*d* 1924), 2nd *d* of late Col C. R. Prideaux-Brune; *S* father, 1975; *m* 1946, Pamela Rose Arabella, *d* of late Lt-Col C. Hunter Little, DSO, MBE. *Educ:* Canford School. *Heir:* half-brother Edward Offley Bertram Wakeman, *b* 31 July 1934. *Address:* Peverey House, Bomere Heath, Shrewsbury, Salop. *T:* Montford Bridge 561. *Clubs:* Lansdowne; Salop (Shrewsbury).

WAKLEY, Bertram Joseph, MBE 1945; **His Honour Judge Wakley;** a Circuit Judge, since 1973; *b* 7 July 1917; *s* of Major Bertram Joseph Wakley and Hon. Mrs Dorothy Wakley (*née* Hamilton); *m* 1953, Alice Margaret Lorimer. *Educ:* Wellington Coll.; Christ Church, Oxford. BA 1939, MA 1943. Commnd S Lancs Regt, 1940; Captain 1941; Major 1943; served N Africa, Italy, Greece (despatches). Called to Bar, Gray's Inn, 1948. A Recorder of the Crown Court, 1972-73. *Publications:* History of the Wimbledon Cricket Club, 1954; Bradman the Great, 1959; Classic Centuries, 1964. *Recreations:* cricket, golf. *Address:* Hamilton House, Kingston Hill, Surrey. *T:* 01-546 9961. *Clubs:* Junior Carlton, MCC, Roehampton.

WALBANK, Frank William, FBA 1953; MA; Rathbone Professor of Ancient History and Classical Archæology in the University of Liverpool, 1951-77, now Professor Emeritus; Dean, Faculty of Arts, 1974-77; *b* 10 Dec. 1909; *s* of A. J. D. Walbank, Bingley, Yorks; *m* 1935, Mary Woodward, *e d* of O. C. A. Fox, Shipley, Yorks; one *s* two *d. Educ:* Bradford Grammar School; Peterhouse, Cambridge. Scholar of Peterhouse, 1928-31; First Class, Parts I and II Classical Tripos, 1930-31; Hugo de Balsham Research Student, Peterhouse, 1931-32; Senior Classics Master at North Manchester High School, 1932-33; Thirlwall Prize, 1933; Asst Lecturer, 1934-36; Lecturer, 1936-46, in Latin, Professor of Latin, 1946-51, University of Liverpool; Public Orator, 1956-60; Hare Prize, 1939. Andrew Mellon Vis. Prof., Univ. Pittsburgh, 1964; Myres Memorial Lectr, Univ. of Oxford, 1964-65. Mem. of Coun.: Classical Assoc., 1944-48, 1958-61 (Pres. 1969-70); Roman Soc., 1948-51 (Vice-Pres., 1953-; President, 1961-64); Hellenic Soc., 1951-54; 1955-56; Classical Journals Bd, 1948-66; British Acad., 1960-63; J. H. Gray Lecturer, University of Cambridge, 1957; Sather Prof., Univ. of California (Berkeley), 1971. *Publications:* Aratos of Sicyon, 1933; Philip V of Macedon, 1940; Latin Prose Versions contributed to Key to Bradley's Arnold, Latin Prose Composition, ed. J. F. Mountford, 1940; The Decline of the Roman Empire in the West, 1946; Chapters on Greek History, in The Year's Work in Classical Studies, special vol., 1938-45, 1948; vol. 34, 1949; contributions to the Oxford Classical Dictionary, 1949, to Chambers's Encyclopædia, 1950 and to Encyclopædia Britannica, 1960 and 1974; Chapters in The Cambridge Economic History of Europe, Vol. II, 1952, and A Scientific Survey of Merseyside, 1953; A Historical Commentary on Polybius, Vol. i, 1957, Vol. ii, 1967; The Awful Revolution, 1969; Polybius, 1972; contributor to English and foreign classical books and periodicals. *Address:* 64 Grantchester Meadows, Cambridge. *T:* Cambridge 64350.

WALD, Prof. George; Higgins Professor of Biology, Harvard University, since 1968; *b* 18 Nov. 1906; *s* of Isaac Wald and Ernestine (*née* Rosenmann); *m* 1st, 1931, Frances Kingsley (marr. diss.); two *s*; 2nd, 1958, Ruth Hubbard; one *s* one *d. Educ:* Washington Square Coll. of New York Univ. (BS); Columbia Univ. (PhD). Nat. Research Coun. Fellowship, 1932-34. Harvard University: Instr and Tutor in Biology, 1934-39; Faculty Instr, 1939-44; Associate Prof., 1944-48; Prof. of Biology, 1948-68. Nobel Prize in Physiology and Medicine

(jointly), 1967. Has many hon. doctorates from univs in USA and abroad; Guest, China Assoc. for Friendship with Foreign Peoples, Jan.-Feb. 1972; US/Japan Distinguished Scientist Exchange, 1973. *Publications:* (co-author) General Education in a Free Society; (co-author) Twenty-six Afternoons of Biology. Many sci. papers (on the biochemistry and physiology of vision and on biochem. evolution) in: Jl of Gen. Physiology, Nature, Science, Jl of Opt. Soc. of Amer., etc. *Recreations:* art, archæology, ski-ing, horseback riding. *Address:* Biological Laboratories, Harvard University, Cambridge, Mass 02138, USA. *T:* (617) 495-2311.

WALDEGRAVE, family name of Earl Waldegrave.

WALDEGRAVE, 12th Earl, *cr* 1729, **Geoffrey Noel Waldegrave,** KG 1971; GCVO 1976; TD; DL; Bt 1643; Baron Waldegrave, 1685; Viscount Chewton, 1729; Member of the Prince's Council of the Duchy of Cornwall, 1951-58 and 1965-76, Lord Warden of the Stannaries, 1965-76; Director: Lloyds Bank Ltd, 1964-76 (Chairman, Bristol Regional Board, 1966-76); Bristol Waterworks Co.; *b* 21 Nov. 1905; *o s* of 11th Earl and Anne Katharine (*d* 1962), *d* of late Rev. W. P. Bastard, Ashburton and Kitley, Devon; *S* father, 1936; *m* 1930, Mary Hermione, *d* of Lt-Col A. M. Grenfell, DSO; two *s* five *d. Educ:* Winchester; Trinity Coll., Cambridge (BA). Served War of 1939-45, Major RA (TA). Chm., Som AEC, 1948-51; Liaison Officer to Min. of Agriculture, Fisheries and Food (formerly Min. of Agriculture and Fisheries), for Som, Wilts and Glos, 1952-57; Jt Parly Sec., Min. of Agriculture, Fisheries and Food, 1958-62; Chairman: Forestry Commn, 1963-65; Adv. Cttee on Meat Research, 1969-73. Pres., Somerset Trust for Nature Conservation. Member: BBC Gen. Adv. Council, 1963-66; Bristol Univ. Court and Council (former Chm., Agricultural Cttee). Mem. Council and Trustee, Bath and W Southern Counties Soc. (Pres., 1974); Trustee, Partis Coll., Bath; Chm., Friends of Wells Cathedral. Hon. LLD Bristol, 1976. Former Governor: Wells Cathedral Sch.; Nat. Fruit and Cider Inst., Long Ashton. Mem. Som CC, 1937-58; CA, 1949-58; DL Somerset, 1951; Vice-Lieutenant Somerset, 1955-60. Officer, Legion of Merit, USA. *Heir:* s Viscount Chewton, *qv. Address:* Chewton House, Chewton Mendip, Bath BA3 4LQ. *T:* Chewton Mendip 264. *Clubs:* Travellers', Farmers'.
See also J . D. Boles, Baron Forteviot, M. J. Hussey, Lady Susan Hussey, Baron Strathcona and Mount Royal.

WALDEN, Brian Alastair; Presenter, Weekend World, London Weekend Television, since 1977; *b* 8 July 1932; *s* of W. F. Walden; *m* Hazel Downes, *d* of William A. Downes; three *s* of former marriages. *Educ:* West Bromwich Grammar School; Queen's College and Nuffield College, Oxford. University Lecturer. Joined Labour party, 1951. Contested Oswestry by-election, November 1961. MP (Lab): Birmingham, All Saints, 1964-74; Birmingham, Ladywood, 1974-77; *Recreations:* chess, gardening. *Address:* 29 Warwick Avenue, W9.

WALDEN, Stanley Arthur, CMG 1956; FRPS(L) 1960; MA Cantab; Chairman, Overseas Service Pensioners' Benevolent Society; Member, Council and Executive Committee, Overseas Service Pensioners' Association, since 1969 (Secretary, 1960-71); *b* 17 June 1905; *s* of late Alfred Walden, Rotherfield, Henley-on-Thames; unmarried. *Educ:* Royal Grammar Sch., Henley-on-Thames; Selwyn College, Cambridge. Cadet, Colonial Service, Tanganyika, 1929; Assistant District Officer, 1931; District Officer, 1941; Deputy Provincial Comr, 1948; Provincial Commissioner, 1951; Sen. Provincial Commissioner, 1953-59; Provincial Comr in charge of Lake Province, 1954-59. Mem., House of Laity, General Synod of Church of England, 1970-75; Chm. Wage Structure Cttee of Joint Council of Sisal Industry, Tanganyika, 1960. Chm., Bd of Visitors, HM Borstal, Huntercombe. *Recreations:* philately, music, rowing. *Address:* Laund, Henley-on-Thames, Oxon RG9 1NG. *T:* 4715. *Clubs:* Royal Commonwealth Society; Leander.

WALDEN, Trevor Alfred, CBE 1974; Director, City of Glasgow Museums and Art Galleries, since 1972; *b* 15 April 1916; *s* of Alfred Walden, Peterborough; *m* 1941, Annie Chalmers Nicoll, Dundee; two *s. Educ:* Wyggeston Sch., Leicester. Trained Leicester Museums, 1934-38; Asst Keeper, Halifax Museums, 1938-41; War Service, Royal Navy, 1941-46; Leicester Museums: Keeper of Biology, 1947-49; Dep. Dir, 1949-51; Dir, 1951-72. Chm. of Educn, Museums Assoc., 1959-64, Pres. 1970. Hon. MSc Leicester 1965. *Publications:* papers in Museums Jl, etc. *Address:* Machrimore, Manse Road, Bowling, Glasgow G60 5AA. *T:* Duntocher 72747. *Clubs:* Glasgow Art, Royal Scottish Automobile (Glasgow).

WALDER, (Alan) David; ERD 1965; MP (C) Clitheroe since 1970; Barrister and Author; *b* 13 Nov. 1928; *o s* of late James

Walder, Chailey, Sussex, and of Helen Walder (*née* McColville); *m* 1956, Elspeth Margaret, *y d* of late Rt Hon. Lord Milligan; one *s* three *d* (including twin *d*). *Educ:* Latymer School; Christ Church, Oxford (Scholar), MA. Served Malaya, 1948-49; AER of 4th Queen's Own Hussars until 1958, of Queen's Royal Irish Hussars until 1965. Served as a Reservist in Germany, Aden and Borneo, Major. Called to the Bar, Inner Temple, 1956; Forster-Boulton Prize; Paul Methven Scholar; Midland Circuit. Chairman, Wembley South Conservative Assoc., 1959. Contested (C) Leicester SW Division, 1959. MP (C) High Peak Division of Derbyshire, 1961-66. PPS to Jt Under-Secs of State, Scottish Office, 1963-64; PPS to Minister for Trade, 1970-72; an Asst Govt Whip, 1973-74. Mem., UK Parly Delegn to Chinese Republic, 1972; UK Parly Deleg. to Council of Europe and Assembly of WEU, 1972, 1973; Vice-Chm., Cons. Home Affairs Cttee, 1973. Vice-Chm., Conservative Defence Cttee; Mem. Exec., 1922 Cttee. Exec., National Book League, 1976-. *Publications:* Stability and Survival (with Julian Critchley), 1961; Bags of Swank, 1963; The Short List, 1964; The House Party, 1966; The Gift Bearers (USA), 1967; The Fair Ladies of Salamanca, 1967; The Chanak Affair, 1969; The Short Victorious War, 1973; Nelson, 1978; (contrib.) Purnell's History of the First World War. *Recreations:* shooting, ornithology, opera. *Address:* The White House, Grimsargh, near Preston, Lancs PR2 5JR. *T:* Longridge 3618; 45 Courtenay Street, SE11 5PH. *T:* 01-735 8281. *Club:* Cavalry and Guards.

WALDER, Edwin James, CMG 1971; President, Metropolitan Water Sewerage and Drainage Board, Sydney, NSW, since 1965; *b* 5 Aug. 1921; *s* of Edwin James Walder and Dulcie Muriel Walder (*née* Griffiths); *m* 1944, Norma Cheslin; two *d*. *Educ:* North Newtown High Sch.; Univ. of Sydney (BEc). Apptd NSW Civil Service, 1938; NSW State Treasury: 1945; Asst Under-Sec. (Finance), 1959-61; Dep. Under-Sec., 1961-63; Under-Sec. and Comptroller of Accounts, 1963-65. Member: State Pollution Control Commn, 1971-; Metropolitan Waste Disposal Authority (Sydney), 1971-; NSW Technical Educn Adv. Council, 1966-. *Recreations:* lawn bowls, fishing, swimming. *Address:* 7 Adina Place, Beverly Hills, NSW 2209, Australia. *T:* 269-5000. *Clubs:* Royal Automobile; Roselands Bowling, St George Leagues (all in Sydney).

WALDER, Ruth Christabel, (Mrs Wesierska), OBE 1956; *b* 15 Jan. 1906; *d* of Rev. Ernest Walder; *m* 1955, Maj.-Gen. George Wesierski (*d* 1967), formerly Judge Advocate General of the Polish Forces. *Educ:* Cheltenham Ladies' College. General Organiser, National Federation of Women's Institutes, 1934-40; Admiralty, 1940-41; Relief Department, Foreign Office, 1942-44; UNRRA, Sec. Food Cttee of Council for Europe, 1944-47; Secretary United Nations Appeal for Children (in the UK), 1948; National General Secretary, YWCA of Great Britain, 1949-67. Lectr for the European Community, 1970-. Defence Medal, 1946. Polish Gold Cross of Merit, 1969. *Address:* Westhope, Langton Herring, Weymouth, Dorset. *T:* Abbotsbury 233. *Club:* Naval and Military.

WALDHEIM, Dr Kurt; Secretary-General of the United Nations since Jan. 1972; *b* 21 Dec. 1918; *m* 1944, Elisabeth Ritschel Waldheim; one *s* two *d*. *Educ:* Consular Academy, Vienna; Univ. of Vienna (Dr Jr 1944). Entered Austrian foreign service, 1945; served in Min. of Foreign Affairs; Mem., Austrian Delegn to Paris, London and Moscow for negotiations on Austrian State Treaty, 1945-47; 1st Sec., Embassy, Paris, 1948-51; apptd Counsellor and Head of Personnel Div., Min. of Foreign Affairs, 1951-55; Permanent Austrian Observer to UN, 1955-56; Minister Plenipotentiary to Canada, 1956-58; Ambassador to Canada, 1958-60; Dir-Gen. for Political Affairs, Min. of Foreign Affairs, 1960-64; Permanent Rep. of Austria to UN, 1964-68 (Chm., Outer Space Cttee of UN 1965-68 and 1970-71); Federal Minister for Foreign Affairs, 1968-70; Candidate for the Presidency of Republic of Austria, 1971; Permanent Rep. of Austria to UN, 1970-Dec. 1971. Hon. LLD: Chile, 1972; Carleton, Canada, 1972; Rutgers, 1972; Fordham, 1972; Jawaharlal Nehru, 1973; Bucharest, 1973; Wagner Coll., NY, 1974; Catholic Univ. of America, 1974; Wilfrid Laurier, 1974; Catholic Univ. of Leuven, 1975; Charles Univ., 1975; Hamilton Coll., Clinton, NY, 1975; Denver, 1976; Philippines, 1976; Nice, 1976; American Univ., 1977; Kent State, 1977; Warsaw, 1977. George Marshall Peace Award, USA, 1977. *Publication:* The Austrian Example, 1971, English edn 1973. *Recreations:* sailing, swimming, skiing, horseback riding. *Address:* United Nations, New York, NY 10017, USA.

WALDMAN, Ronald Hartley; Managing Director, Visnews Ltd, 1963-77; Trustee, International Institute of Communications, since 1975; *b* 13 May 1914; *e s* of late Michael Ernest Waldman, OBE, JP; *m* 1953, Lana Morris; one *s*. *Educ:* Owen's School; Pembroke College, Oxford. Actor and Producer, 1935-38.

Producer, BBC Variety Dept, 1938; wartime service in RAFVR. Assistant Head of Variety (Productions), 1948; Senior Producer, Television Light Entertainment, 1950; Head of Light Entertainment, BBC Television, 1950; Business Manager, BBC TV Programmes, 1958-60; General Manager, BBC TV Enterprises, 1960-63. *Recreations:* music, cricket, watching and listening to experts being expert. *Address:* 60 Wolsey Road, Moor Park, Mddx. *Clubs:* MCC, Lord's Taverners'.
See also S . J . Waldman .

WALDMAN, Stanley John; Master of the Supreme Court, Queen's Bench Division, since 1971; *b* 18 Sept. 1923; *s* of late Michael Ernest Waldman, OBE, JP; *m* 1951, Naomi Sorsky; one *s* two *d*. *Educ:* Owen's School, London; Pembroke College, Oxford. BA; MA 1948. RAF, 1942-46; called to the Bar, Gray's Inn, 1949; practised in London and on SE Circuit. *Address:* 80 South Hill Park, NW3.
See also R . H . Waldman .

WALDOCK, Sir (Claud) Humphrey (Meredith), Kt 1961; CMG 1946; OBE 1942; QC 1951; DCL; MA; a Judge of the International Court of Justice, since 1973; *b* 13 Aug. 1904; *s* of Frederic William Waldock and Lizzie Kyd Souter; *m* 1934, Ethel Beatrice Williams; one *s* one *d*. *Educ:* Uppingham School; Brasenose Coll., Oxford. Hockey Blue, 1926; BA 1927; BCL 1928; Barrister-at-Law, Gray's Inn, 1928, Bencher, 1957, Treasurer, 1971, Vice-Treasurer, 1972; Midland Circuit, 1928-30; Fellow and Lectr in Law, Brasenose, 1930-47; Tutor, 1937; Hon. Fellow, 1960. Lecturer in Law, Oriel College, 1930-39; Pro-Proctor, 1936. Temp. Principal Admiralty, 1940; Assistant-Secretary, 1943; Principal Assistant Secretary, 1944. UK Commissioner on Italo-Yugoslav Boundary Commission; Commission for Free Territory of Trieste, Council of Foreign Ministers, 1946. Trustee, Uppingham Sch., 1947-59. Chichele Prof. of Public Internat. Law, Univ. of Oxford, and Fellow, All Souls Coll., 1947-72; Assessor in the Chancellor's Court, 1947; Mem. Hebdomadal Council, 1948-61; European Commn of Human Rights, 1954-61 (Pres. 1955-61); Judge, European Court of Human Rights, 1966-74 (Vice-Pres., 1968-71, Pres., 1971-74). Chm., Cttee of Inquiry into Oxford University Press, 1967-70. Editor, British Year Book of International Law, 1955-74; Member: Inst. of Internat. Law; Swedish-Finnish Conciliation Commn, 1957; Swedish-Swiss Conciliation Commn, 1960; Swedish-Turkish and German-Swiss Conciliation Commns, 1963; US-Danish Conciliation Commn, 1964; Chilean-Italian Conciliation Commn, 1965; Danish-Norwegian Conciliation Commn, 1967; Swedish-Spanish Conciliation Commn, 1968; UN Internat. Law Commn, 1961-72 (Special Rapporteur on Law of Treaties, 1962-66, on Succession of States in respect of Treaties, 1968-72; President 1967); UN Expert on Law of Treaties, Vienna Conf., 1968, 1969; Member: Permanent Court of Arbitration, 1965-; Council of Legal Education, 1965-; Curatorium of the Hague Academy, 1977-. *Publications:* Law of Mortgages; Regulation of the Use of Force by Individual States (Hague Recueil), 1952; General Course on Public International Law (Hague Recueil), 1962; Editor, Brierly's Law of Nations (6th edn), 1963. Articles on International Law. *Recreations:* cricket, tennis, shooting, fishing. *Address:* 6 Lathbury Road, Oxford. *T:* 58227. *Club:* United Oxford & Cambridge University.

WALDRON, Brig. John Graham Claverhouse, CBE 1958 (OBE 1944); DSO 1945; *b* 15 Nov. 1909; *s* of William Slade Olver (*d* 1909), Falmouth; *m* 1933, Marjorie, *d* of Arthur Waldron (*d* 1953), Newbury; one *s* one *d*. *Educ:* Marlborough; RMC, Sandhurst. jssc, psc. 2nd Lieut, Gloucestershire Regt, 1929. Served War of 1939-45 (OBE, DSO): 5 British Division and 1st Bn Green Howards, in India, Middle East, Italy, NW Europe. Lt-Col, 10th Gurkha Rifles, 1951; Brigadier, 1958; ADC to the Queen, 1960-61; retired, 1961. *Address:* c/o Banco Hispano Americano, Avenida Ramón y Cajal 12, Marbella, Spain. *Clubs:* Army and Navy, Royal Cruising.

WALDRON-RAMSEY, Waldo Emerson; Ambassador and Permanent Representative for Barbados to the United Nations, 1971-76; *b* 1 Jan. 1930; *s* of Wyatt and Delcina Waldron-Ramsey; *m* 1954, Shiela Pamella Beresford, Georgetown, Guyana; one *s* two *d*. *Educ:* Barbados; Hague Academy; London Sch. of Economics; Yugoslavia. LLB Hons; BSc (Econ) Hons; PhD. Called to Bar, Middle Temple; practised London Bar and SW Circuit, 1957-60; Marketing Economist, Shell International, 1960-61; Tanzanian Foreign Service, 1961-70; High Comr for Barbados in UK, and Ambassador to France, Netherlands and Germany, 1970-71. UN Legal Expert: in field of human rights, 1967-71; on Israel, 1968-71. Member: Amer. Acad. of Political and Social Sciences; Amer. Soc. of Internat. Law; Amer. Inst. of Petroleum (Marketing Div.). Hon. Fellow, Hebrew Univ. of Jerusalem, 1972; Hon. LLD: Univ. of Phnom-Penh, 1973;

Chung-Ang Univ., Republic of Korea, 1975. Grand Officer (1st Class), Nat. Order of Honneur et Mérite, Republic of Haiti, 1968; Grand Officier, Ordre Nat. de l'Amitié et Mérite, Khymèr, 1973; Order of Distinguished Diplomatic Service Merit, Gwangwha (1st Class), Republic of Korea, 1974. *Recreations:* cricket, tennis, bridge, travel. *Address:* c/o Ministry of Foreign Affairs, Bridgetown, Barbados. *Clubs:* Royal Automobile; Lincoln Lodge (Connecticut).

WALES, Archbishop of, since 1971; **Most Rev. Gwilym Owen Williams,** DD Lambeth 1957; Bishop of Bangor since 1957; *b* 23 March 1913; *s* of Owen G. Williams; *m* 1941, Megan (*d* 1976), *d* of T. D. Jones; one *s. Educ:* Llanberis Gram. Sch.; Jesus Coll., Oxford, Hon Fellow, 1972. BA 1st Class Hons English, 1933; 1st Class Hons Theol. 1935; Gladstone Student at St Deiniol's Library, Hawarden, 1935; St Stephen's House, Oxford, 1936; MA 1937. Curate of Denbigh, 1937; Reader in Theology, St David's Coll., Lampeter, 1940; Warden of Church Hostel, Bangor; Lecturer in Theology, University Coll., Bangor; Canon of Bangor Cathedral, 1947. Warden and Headmaster, Llandovery Coll., 1948-56. Chaplain and Sub-Prelate of Order of St John of Jerusalem, 1965. *Publication:* The Church's Work, 1959. *Recreations:* fishing and walking. *Address:* Tŷ'r Esgob, Bangor, Gwynedd LL57 2SS. *Club:* Reform.

WALES, Geoffrey, RE 1961 (ARE 1948); ARCA 1936; wood engraver; Lecturer, Norwich School of Art, 1953-77; *b* 26 May 1912; *s* of Ernest and Kathleen Wales; *m* 1940, Marjorie Skeeles; two *d. Educ:* Chatham House School, Ramsgate; Thanet School of Art; Royal College of Art. Served War of 1939-45, in Royal Air Force, 1940-46. Member of the Norwich Twenty Group, 1953 (Chairman, 1957). Prints and drawings in Victoria and Albert Museum; Whitworth Gallery, Manchester; Kunsthaus, Graz; and private collections. Exhibits with: Royal Society of Painter Etchers and Engravers; Norwich Twenty Group. Illustrated books for Golden Cockerel Press, Kynoch Press, Folio Soc. and general graphic work. Engravings produced in publications and articles on wood-engraving. *Address:* 15 Heigham Grove, Norwich, Norfolk NR2 3DQ. *T:* Norwich 29066.

WALES, Horace Geoffrey Quaritch, MA, PhD, LittD; Orientalist and Archæologist; *b* 17 Oct. 1900; *s* of late E. Horace Wales; *g s* of late Bernard Quaritch; *m* 1931, Dorothy Clementina Johnson, LLB. *Educ:* Charterhouse; Queens' College, Cambridge. Siamese Government Service, 1924-28; travelled widely in India, Burma, Indochina and Indonesia in connection with Oriental research; during 1934-36, as Field Director of the Greater-India Research Committee, carried out archæological investigations in Siam, and during 1937-40 in Malaya, excavating ancient sites and exploring early trade routes; conducted excavations at early Buddhist sites in Siam, 1955-56, 1964, 1968. Chairman, Bernard Quaritch Ltd, 1951-75 (Director, 1939-75); served IA (Gen. Staff), 1940-41; in USA writing and speaking on Pacific affairs and publicizing India's war effort, 1942-45. Member Council, Royal Asiatic Society, 1947-58, 1964-68 (Vice-President, 1958-62); Hon. Member Royal Asiatic Soc., Malayan Branch. *Publications:* Siamese State Ceremonies, 1931; Ancient Siamese Government and Administration, 1934; Towards Angkor, 1937; Archæological Researches on Ancient Indian Colonization in Malaya, 1940; The Making of Greater India, 1951; Ancient South-East Asian Warfare, 1952; The Mountain of God, 1953; Prehistory and Religion in South-east Asia, 1957; Angkor and Rome, 1965; The Indianization of China, 1967; Dvāravatī, the Earliest Kingdom of Siam, 1969; Early Burma—Old Siam, 1973; The Malay Peninsula in Hindu Times, 1976; The Universe around Them, 1977; contrib. to The Cambridge History of India, many articles in various learned journals. *Club:* East India, Devonshire, Sports and Public Schools.

WALEY, (Andrew) Felix, VRD 1960 and Clasp 1970; QC 1973; a Recorder of the Crown Court, since 1974; *b* 14 April 1926; *s* of Guy Felix Waley and Anne Elizabeth (*née* Dickson); *m* 1955, Petica Mary, *d* of Sir Philip Rose, Bt, *qv*; one *s* three *d* (and one *d* decd). *Educ:* Charterhouse; Worcester Coll., Oxford (MA). RN, 1944-48; RNR, 1951-70, retd as Comdr. Oxford, 1948-51; called to the Bar, Middle Temple, 1953. Conservative Councillor, Paddington, 1956-59. Contested (C) Dagenham, 1959. *Recreations:* yachting, gardening. *Address:* 24 Manor Way, Blackheath, SE3 9EF. *T:* 01-852 0437. *Clubs:* Garrick; Island Sailing (IoW).

WALEY, Daniel Philip, PhD; Keeper of Manuscripts, British Library, since 1973 (Keeper of Manuscripts, British Museum, 1972-73); *b* 20 March 1921; *er s* of late Hubert David Waley and of Margaret Hendelah Waley; *m* 1945, Pamela Joan Griffiths; one *s* two *d. Educ:* Dauntsey's Sch.; King's Coll., Cambridge

(MA, PhD). Historical Tripos, Cambridge, 1939-40 and 1945-46 (cl. 1). Served War, 1940-45. Fellow of King's Coll., Cambridge, 1950-54. Asst Lectr in Medieval History, London School of Economics and Political Science, Univ. of London, 1949-51, Lectr, 1951-61, Reader in History, 1961-70, Prof. of History, 1970-72. British Acad. Italian Lectr, 1975. *Publications:* Mediaeval Orvieto, 1952; The Papal State in the 13th Century, 1961; Later Medieval Europe, 1964 (2nd edn 1975); The Italian City Republics, 1969, 2nd edn, 1978; British Public Opinion and the Abyssinian War, 1935-36, 1975; contributor to: Dizionario Biografico degli Italiani, English Hist. Review, Trans Royal Hist. Soc., Papers of British Sch. at Rome, Jl of Ecclesiastical Hist., Jl of the History of Ideas, Rivista Storica Italiana, Rivista di Storia della Chiesa in Italia, Procs Brit. Acad., etc. *Recreations:* walking, tennis. *Address:* Flat 5, 24 Park Road, NW1 4SH.

WALEY, Felix; *see* Waley, A. F.

WALEY-COHEN, Sir Bernard (Nathaniel), 1st Bt *cr* 1961; Kt 1957; Director: Matthews Wrightson Pulbrook Ltd; Lloyds Bank Ltd Central London Region; Kleeman Industrial Holdings Ltd, and other companies; *b* 29 May 1914; *er s* of late Sir Robert Waley Cohen, KBE and Alice Violet, *d* of Henry Edward Beddington, London and Newmarket; *m* 1943, Hon. Joyce Constance Ina, MA, JP, *o d* of 1st Baron Nathan of Churt, PC, TD, two *s* two *d. Educ:* HMS Britannia (RNC Dartmouth); Clifton College; Magdalene Coll., Cambridge (MA). Mem. of staff, Duke of York's Camp, Southwold, 1932-36; Mem. of Public School Empire Tour, New Zealand, 1932-33; Liveryman, Clothworkers' Company, 1936, Court 1966, Chm., Finance Cttee, 1971, Master, 1975. Gunner, HAC, 1937-38; Underwriting Member of Lloyd's 1939; Principal Ministry of Fuel and Power 1940-47. Alderman, City of London Portsoken Ward, 1949; Sheriff, City of London, 1955-56; Lord Mayor of London, 1960-61; one of HM Lieutenants, City of London, 1949-. Mem. Council and Board of Governors, Clifton Coll., 1952; Mem., College Cttee, University College London, 1953, Treasurer 1962; Vice-Chm. 1970; Chm., 1971; Mem. Senate, 1962; Court, 1966, London Univ.; Governor, Wellesley House Prep. Sch., 1965, Chm., 1965-77. Hon. Sec. and Treasurer, Devon and Somerset Staghounds, 1940, Chm. 1953; Mem. Finance and General Purposes Cttee, British Field Sports Soc., 1957, Treasurer 1965; President: Bath and West and Southern Counties Show, 1963; Devon Cattle Breeders' Soc., 1963; W of England Hound Show, Honiton, 1974. Mem., Marshall Aid Commemoration Commn, 1957-60; Treasurer, Jewish Welfare Board, 1948-53; Vice-Pres., United Synagogue, 1952-61; Vice-Pres., Anglo-Jewish Assoc., 1962; Pres., Jewish Museum, 1964; Vice-Chairman: Palestine Corp., 1947-53; Union Bank of Israel Ltd, 1950-53; Chm., Simo Securities Trust Ltd, 1955-70; Mem., Nat. Corporation for Care of Old People, 1965; Mem., Executive Cttee and Central Council, Probation and After Care Cttees, 1965-69; Mem., Club Facilities Cttee, MCC, 1965; Trustee, Coll. of Arms Trust, 1970; Mem., Exec. Cttee, St Paul's Cathedral Appeal, 1970-72. Comr and Dep. Chm., Public Works Loan Board, 1971-72, Chm. 1972-. Governor, Hon. Irish Soc., 1973-76. Hon. Liveryman of Farmers' Company 1961. Assoc. KStJ 1961. Hon. LLD London, 1961. *Recreations:* hunting, racing, shooting. *Heir: s* Stephen Harry Waley-Cohen [*b* 22 June 1946; *m* 1972, Pamela Elizabeth Doniger; one *s* one *d. Educ:* Eton (Oppidan Scholar); Magdalene Coll., Cambridge (BA 1968). Financial Journalist, Daily Mail, 1968-73; Exec. Dir, Euromoney, 1973-]. *Address:* 11 Little St James's Street, SW1A 1DP. *T:* 01-629 1615; Honeymead, Simonsbath, Minehead, Somerset. *T:* Exford 242; *TA:* 247JX. *Clubs:* Boodle's, Pratts, MCC, Harlequins RFC, City Livery; Jockey Club Rooms (Newmarket); University Pitt (Cambridge).

WALFORD, Major-General Alfred Ernest, CB 1946; CBE 1944; MM 1916; ED; Legion of Merit (USA); CA; FCIS; *b* Montreal, 20 Aug. 1896; *s* of Alfred G. S. and Phoebe Anne Walford, Montreal; *m* 1922, Olive Marjorie, *d* of James A. Dyke, Westmount Province of Quebec; one *s. Educ:* Westmount Acad. Served European War, 1914-19, with Royal Canadian Artillery, and War of 1939-45, HQ 1st Canadian Div., 1st Canadian Corps and as DA&QMG 1st Canadian Army in NW Europe; Adjutant-General Canadian Forces, Nat. Defence Headquarters, Ottawa, 1944-46. Partner, Alfred Walford & Sons, Chartered Accountants, 1923-29; Dir, Sec. and Treasurer, of James A. Ogilvy Ltd, 1929-39, of Henry Morgan & Co. Ltd, 1946-61; Pres., Morgan Trust Co., 1946-65; Chairman: E. G. M. Cape & Co. Ltd, 1965-68; Canadian Vickers Ltd, 1959-67; Dir and Chm., Montreal Adv. Bd of Canada Trust Co., 1961-72; Hon. Dir, Canada Trust, 1972-. Member: Metropolitan Adv. Bd, YMCA; Nat Adv. Bd, Salvation Army; Past President: Fedn Commonwealth Chambers of Commerce; National Cttee, English-Speaking Union; Montreal Board of Trade; Past

Chairman, Exec. Development Institute. Fellow, Royal Commonwealth Society; Fellow, Canadian Chartered Inst. of Secretaries; Life Mem., Order of Chartered Accountants of Quebec. *Address:* (office) Suite 1400, 635 Dorchester Boulevard West, Montreal PQ H3B 1S3, Canada; (home) E90, The Chateau Apartments, 1321 Sherbrooke West, Montreal, PQ H3G 1J4. *Clubs:* St James's, Forest and Stream (Montreal).

WALKER; *see* Gordon Walker.

WALKER, Sir Alan, Kt 1975; President, Bass Charrington Ltd, since 1976 (Chairman, 1967-76); Member, British Railways Board, since 1969 (Chairman, Western Region Advisory Board, since 1977); a Deputy Chairman, Midland Bank, since 1977; Director: Bass Charrington Vintners (Chairman, 1974-76); Crest Hotels Ltd; Eagle Star Insurance Co. Ltd; Standard Broadcasting Corp. (UK) Ltd; Capital Radio; Hogg Robinson Group Ltd; Chm., Thos Cook Group Ltd, 1976-. Chm., Midland Western Region, BR, 1972-77. Trustee, Glyndebourne Festival. Liveryman, Shipwrights' Co.; Liveryman, Ct, Brewers' Co. *Recreations:* fishing, ballet, opera. *Address:* 7 Grosvenor Gardens, SW1. *T:* 01-834 3121; Poachers, Alcester Heath, Warwickshire. *T:* Alcester 2291. *Clubs:* Brooks's, MCC.

WALKER, Alexander Neilson Strachan, CMG 1974; with Conservative Research Department; *b* 8 March 1921; *s* of Col W. O. Walker, IMS and Janet Cormack (*née* Strachan); *m* 1947, Elizabeth Anne (*née* Ireland); two *s* three *d*. *Educ:* Oundle Sch.; Gonville and Caius Coll., Cambridge (BA). Royal Artillery, 1941-46 (despatches twice); served Africa, France, Italy and SE Asia. HM Foreign (subseq. Diplomatic) Service, 1949-77; served in Paris, 1950; FO, 1952; Düsseldorf, 1954; Rangoon, 1957; Singapore, 1959; FO, 1961; Brussels, 1964; FCO, 1968; Rome, 1971; Washington, 1973; FCO, 1975-77. Croix de Guerre with Palm 1944. *Recreations:* fishing, gardening. *Address:* Puck Hill, Wadhurst, East Sussex. *T:* Wadhurst 2586. *Club:* Travellers'.

WALKER, Sir Allan (Grierson), Kt 1968; QC (Scotland); Sheriff Principal of Lanarkshire, 1963-74; *b* 1 May 1907; *er s* of late Joseph Walker, merchant, London, and Mary Grierson; *m* 1935, Audrey Margaret, *o d* of late Dr T. A. Glover, Doncaster; one *s*. *Educ:* Whitgift Sch., Croydon; Edinburgh Univ. Practised at Scottish Bar, 1931-39; Sheriff-Substitute of Roxburgh, Berwick, and Selkirk at Selkirk and of the County of Peebles, 1942-45; Sheriff-Substitute of Stirling, Dumbarton and Clackmannan at Dumbarton, 1945-50; Sheriff-Substitute of Lanarkshire at Glasgow, 1950-63; Member, Law Reform Cttee for Scotland, 1964-70; Chm., Sheriff Court Rules Council, 1972-74. Hon. LLD Glasgow, 1967. *Publications:* The Law of Evidence in Scotland (joint author); Purves' Scottish Licensing Laws (7th, 8th edns). *Recreations:* walking, gardening. *Address:* Davington Cottage, Eskdalemuir, by Langholm, Dumfriesshire. *T:* Eskdalemuir 250; 2 Franklin Place, Troqueer Road, Dumfries. *T:* Dumfries 2510.

WALKER, Angus Henry; Director, School of Slavonic and East European Studies, London University, since 1976; *b* 30 Aug. 1935; *s* of late Frederick William Walker, and of Esther Victoria Nicholas; *m* 1968, Beverly Phillpotts (marr. diss. 1976). *Educ:* Erith Grammar Sch., Kent; Balliol Coll., Oxford (Domus Scholar; BA Mod. Hist.; Stanhope Prize, 1958; MA). Nat. Service, 1954-56. Senior Scholar, St Antony's Coll., Oxford, 1959-63; HM Diplomatic Service, 1963-68: FO, 1963-65; First Sec., Washington, 1965-68. Lectr, SSEES, London Univ., 1968-70; Univ. Lectr in Russian Social and Political Thought, Oxford, and Lectr, Balliol Coll., 1971-76; Fellow, Wolfson Coll., Oxford, 1972-76. *Publications:* trans. from Polish: Political Economy, by Oskar Lange, vol 1, 1963; Marx: Capitalism Transcended, 1978. *Address:* School of Slavonic and East European Studies, London University, WC1E 7HU. *T:* 01-637 4934.

WALKER, Arthur Geoffrey, FRS 1955; Professor of Pure Mathematics, Liverpool University, 1952-74, now Emeritus; *b* 17 July 1909; 2nd *s* of late A. J. Walker, Watford, Herts; *m* 1939, Phyllis Ashcroft, *d* of late Sterry B. Freeman, CBE. *Educ:* Watford Grammar Sch.; Balliol Coll., Oxford. MA (Oxon); PhD, DSc (Edinburgh); FRSE; Lectr at Imperial Coll. Science and Technology, 1935-36; at Liverpool Univ., 1936-47; Prof. of Mathematics in the Univ. of Sheffield, 1947-52. Mem. of Council, Royal Soc., 1962-63. Pres., London Mathematical Soc., 1963-65. Junior Berwick Prize of London Mathematical Soc., 1947; Keith Medal of Royal Society of Edinburgh, 1950. *Publication:* Harmonic Spaces (with H. S. Ruse and T. J. Willmore), 1962. *Address:* Beechcroft, Roundabout Lane, West Chiltington, Pulborough, W Sussex RH20 2RL. *T:* West Chiltington 2412.

WALKER, Air Chief Marshal Sir Augustus; *see* Walker, Air Chief Marshal Sir G. A.

WALKER, Sir Baldwin Patrick, 4th Bt, *cr* 1856; *b* 10 Sept. 1924; *s* of late Comdr Baldwin Charles Walker, *o s* of 3rd Bt and Mary, *d* of F. P. Barnett of Whalton, Northumberland; *S* grandfather, 1928; *m* 1948, Joy Yvonne (marr. diss., 1954); *m* 1954, Sandra Stewart; *m* 1966, Rosemary Ann, *d* of late Henry Hollingdrake; one *s* one *d*. *Educ:* Gordonstoun. Served Royal Navy, Fleet Air Arm, 1943-58. Lieut, RN, retired. *Heir: s* Christopher Robert Baldwin Walker, *b* 25 Oct. 1969. *Address:* Eikerus, Bo Daljosaphat, near Paarl, CP, South Africa.

WALKER, Bobby; *see* Walker, W. B. S.

WALKER, Brian Wilson; Director General of Oxfam since 1974; *b* 31 Oct. 1930; *s* of Arthur Walker and Eleanor (*née* Wilson); *m* 1954, Nancy Margaret Gawith; one *s* five *d*. *Educ:* Heversham Sch., Westmorland; Leicester Coll. of Technology; Faculty Technology, Manchester Univ. Management Trainee, Sommerville Bros, Kendal, 1952-55; Personnel Man., Pye Radio, Larne, 1956-61; Bridgeport Brass Ltd, Lisburn: Personnel Man., 1961-66; Gen. Man. (Develt), 1966-69; Gen. Man. (Manufrg), 1969-74. Founder Chm., New Ulster Movt, 1969-74; Founder Pres., New Ulster Movt Ltd, 1974. Mem., Standing Adv. Commn on Human Rights for NI, 1975-77. Kt, Sov. Order of St Thomas of Acre; Kentucky Colonel, 1966. *Publications:* various political/religious papers on Northern Ireland problem and Third World subjects. *Recreations:* gardening, Irish politics, classical music, active Quaker. *Address:* 14 Upland Park Road, Oxford.

WALKER, Carl, GC 1972; Police Inspector, since 1976; *b* 31 March 1934; English; *m* 1955, Kathleen Barker; one *s*. *Educ:* Kendal Grammar Sch., Westmorland. RAF Police, 1952-54 (Corporal). Lancashire Police, Oct. 1954-March 1956, resigned; Blackpool Police, 1959- (amalgamated with Lancashire Constabulary, April 1968); Sergeant, 1971. *Recreations:* Rugby; Cumberland and Westmorland wrestling.

WALKER, Sir (Charles) Michael, GCMG 1976 (KCMG 1963; CMG 1960); HM Diplomatic Service, retired; Chairman, Commonwealth Scholarship Commission in the UK; *b* 22 Nov. 1916; *s* of late Col C. W. G. Walker, CMG, DSO; *m* 1945, Enid Dorothy, *d* of late W. A. McAdam, CMG; one *s* one *d*. *Educ:* Charterhouse; New Coll., Oxford. Clerk of House of Lords, June 1939. Enlisted in Army, Oct. 1939, and served in RA until 1946 when released with rank of Lt-Col. Dominions Office, 1947; First Sec., British Embassy, Washington, 1949-51; Office of United Kingdom High Comr in Calcutta and New Delhi, 1952-55; Establishment Officer, Commonwealth Relations Office, 1955-58. Imperial Defence Coll., 1958; Asst Under-Sec. of State and Dir of Establishment and Organisation, CRO, 1959-62; British High Commissioner in: Ceylon, 1962-65 (concurrently Ambassador to Maldive Islands, July-Nov. 1965), Malaysia, 1966-71; Sec., ODA, FCO, 1971-73; High Comr, India, 1974-76. *Recreations:* fishing, gardening, golf. *Address:* Herongate House, West Chiltington Common, Pulborough, Sussex. *Clubs:* Travellers', Oriental.

WALKER, Vice-Adm. Sir (Charles) Peter (Graham), KBE 1967; CB 1964; DSC 1944; *b* 23 Feb. 1911; *s* of Charles Graham Walker and Lilla Geraldine (*née* Gandy); *m* 1938, Pamela Marcia Hawley, *d* of late George W. Hawley, Cape, SA; one *s* one *d*. *Educ:* Worksop College. Entered Royal Navy, 1929; Royal Naval Engineering Coll., 1930-34; Advanced Engineering Course at RN Coll., Greenwich, 1935-37. War service in HM Ships Cornwall, Georgetown, Duke of York and Berwick and at the Admiralty; Vice-Admiral, 1965; Dir-Gen., Dockyards and Maintenance, MoD (Navy), 1962-67; Chief Naval Engr Officer, 1963-67; retired 1967. *Address:* Brookfield Coach House, Weston Lane, Bath. *T:* Bath 23863. *Club:* Army and Navy.

WALKER, Charls E., PhD; Consultant, Washington, DC, since 1973; *b* Graham, Texas, 24 Dec. 1923; *s* of Pinkney Clay and Sammye McCombs Walker; *m* 1949, Harmolyn Hart, Laurens, S Carolina; one *s* one *d*. *Educ:* Univ. of Texas (MBA); Wharton Sch. of Finance, Univ. of Pennsylvania (PhD). Instructor in Finance, 1947-48, and later Asst and Associate Prof., 1950-54, at Univ. of Texas, in the interim teaching at Wharton Sch. of Finance, Univ. of Pennsylvania; Associate Economist, Fed. Reserve Bank of Philadelphia, 1953, of Dallas, 1954 (Vice-Pres. and Economic Advr, 1958-61); Economist and Special Asst to Pres. of Republic Nat. Bank of Dallas, 1955-56 (took leave to serve as Asst to Treasury Sec., Robert B. Anderson, April 1959-Jan. 1961); Exec. Vice-Pres., Amer. Bankers Assoc., 1961-69. Under-Sec. of the Treasury, 1969-72, Dep. Sec., 1972-73. Chm., American Council for Capital Formation; Vice-Chm., Jt

Council on Economic Educn. Hon. LLD Ashland Coll., 1970. *Publications:* Co-editor of The Banker's Handbook; contribs to learned jls, periodicals. *Recreations:* golf, fishing, music. *Address:* 1661 Crescent Place, NW, Washington, DC 20009, USA. *T:* 232-3437. *Clubs:* Union League (NYC); Burning Tree Golf (Bethesda, Md); Federal City (Washington, DC).

WALKER, Sir Clive Radzivill Forestier-, 5th Bt *cr* 1835; *b* 30 April 1922; *s* of Radzivill Clive Forestier-Walker (*g s* of 2nd Bt) (*d* 1973) and of Kathleen Rose, *d* of late William George Tinkler, King's Lynn; *S* cousin, Sir George Ferdinand Forestier-Walker, 4th Bt, 1976; *m* 1948, Pamela Mercy, *d* of Clifford Leach; three *d*. *Heir: cousin* Michael Leolin Forestier-Walker, *b* 24 April 1949. *Address:* 28 Grove Road, Rayleigh, Essex SS6 8PX.

WALKER, Prof. Daniel Pickering, FBA 1974; Professor of the History of the Classical Tradition, in the University of London at the Warburg Institute, since 1975; *b* 30 June 1914; *s* of Frederick Pickering Walker and Miriam Laura Walker (*née* Crittall). *Educ:* Westminster Sch.; Christ Church, Oxford. BA 1935 (1st cl. French), MA, DPhil 1940, Oxon. Corporal, Infantry and Intell. Corps, 1940-43; Foreign Office, 1943-45. Lectr, then Reader, French Dept, UCL, 1945-61; Reader in Renaissance Studies, Warburg Inst., Univ. of London, 1961-75, Sen. Fellow, 1953-56. Sen. Fellow, Cornell Univ. (Soc. for Humanities), 1971. *Publications: Musikalischer Humanismus,* 1947; *Spiritual and Demonic Magic,* 1958; *The Decline of Hell,* 1964; *The Ancient Theology,* 1972; articles in Jl of Warburg and Courtauld Insts, etc. *Recreations:* chamber music, gardening. *Address:* 2 Regent's Park Terrace, NW1. *T:* 01-485 1699.

WALKER, David Harry, MBE 1946; Author; *b* 9 Feb. 1911; *s* of Harry Giles Walker and Elizabeth Bewley (*née* Newsom); *m* 1939, Willa Magee, Montreal; four *s*. *Educ:* Shrewsbury; Sandhurst. The Black Watch, 1931-47 (retired); ADC to Gov.-Gen. of Canada, 1938-39; Comptroller to Viceroy of India, 1946-47. Member: Royal Company of Archers; Canada Council, 1957-61; Chm., Roosevelt-Campobello Internat. Park Commn, 1970-72 (Canadian Comr, 1965). Hon. DLitt, Univ. of New Brunswick, 1955. FRSL. *Publications: novels:* The Storm and the Silence, 1950 (USA 1949); Geordie, 1950 (filmed 1955); The Pillar, 1952; Digby, 1953; Harry Black, 1956 (filmed, 1957); Sandy was a Soldier's Boy, 1957; Where the High Winds Blow, 1960; Storms of Our Journey and Other Stories, 1962; Dragon Hill (for children), 1962; Winter of Madness, 1964; Mallabec, 1965; Come Back, Geordie, 1966; Devil's Plunge (USA, Cab-Intersec), 1968; Pirate Rock, 1969; Big Ben (for children), 1970; The Lord's Pink Ocean, 1972; Black Dougal, 1973 (USA 1974); Ash, 1976; Pot of Gold, 1977. *Address:* Strathcroix, St Andrews, New Brunswick, Canada. *Club:* Royal and Ancient.

WALKER, Prof. David Maxwell, QC; FBA 1976; Regius Professor of Law, Glasgow University, since 1958; Dean of the Faculty of Law, 1956-59; Senate Assessor on University Court, 1962-66; *b* 9 April 1920; *o s* of James Mitchell Walker, Branch Manager, Union Bank of Scotland, and Mary Paton Colquhoun Irvine; *m* 1954, Margaret Knox, MA, *yr d* of Robert Knox, yarn merchant, Brookfield, Renfrewshire. *Educ:* High School of Glasgow (Mackindlay Prizeman in Classics); Glasgow, Edinburgh and London Universities. MA (Glasgow) 1946; LLB (Distinction), Robertson Schol., 1948; Faulds Fellow in Law, 1949-52; PhD (Edinburgh), 1952; Blackwell Prize, Aberdeen Univ., 1955; LLB (London), 1957; LLD (Edinburgh), 1960; LLD (London), 1968. Served War of 1939-45, NCO Cameronians; commissioned HLI, 1940; seconded to RIASC, 1941; served with Indian Forces in India, 1942, Middle East, 1942-43, and Italy, 1943-46, in MT companies and as Brigade Supply and Transport Officer (Captain). HQ 21 Ind. Inf. Bde, 8 Ind. Div. Advocate of Scottish Bar, 1948; Barrister, Middle Temple, 1957; QC (Scotland) 1958; practised at Scottish Bar, 1948-53; studied at Inst. of Advanced Legal Studies, Univ. of London, 1953-54; Prof. of Jurisprudence, Glasgow Univ., 1954-58. Dir, Scottish Univs' Law Inst., 1974-. Trustee, Hamlyn Trust, 1954-. Governor Scottish College of Commerce, 1957-64. Hon. Sheriff of Lanarkshire at Glasgow, 1966-. FSA Scotland. Hon. LLD Edinburgh, 1974. *Publications:* (ed) Faculty Digest of Decisions, 1940-50, Supplements, 1951 and 1952; Law of Damages in Scotland, 1955; The Scottish Legal System, 1959 (4th edn, 1976); Law of Delict in Scotland, 1966; Scottish Courts and Tribunals, 1969 (3rd edn, 1975); Principles of Scottish Private Law, 1970 (2nd edn, 1975); Law of Prescription and Limitation in Scotland, 1973 (2nd edn, 1976); Law of Civil Remedies in Scotland, 1974; Scottish Part of Topham and Ivamy's Company Law, 12th to 16th edns; contribs to collaborative works; articles in legal periodicals. *Recreations:* motoring, book collecting, Scottish history. *Address:* 1 Beaumont Gate, Glasgow G12 9EE. *T:* 041-339 2802.

WALKER, Maj.-Gen. Derek William Rothwell, CEng, FIMechE, FIEE; Director, Equipment Engineering, since 1977; *b* 12 Dec. 1924; *s* of Frederick and Eileen Walker; *m* 1950, Florence Margaret Panting; two *s* (and one *s* decd). *Educ:* Mitcham County Grammar Sch.; Battersea Polytechnic. Commissioned REME, 1946; served: Middle East, 1947-50 (despatches 1949); BAOR, 1951-53; Far East, 1954-56 (despatches 1957); Near East, 1960-62; Far East, 1964-67; psc 1957. Lt-Col 1964, Col 1970, Brig. 1973. Appts include: ADEME FARELF, 1964-67; OC Ac. Tech. Service Unit, 1967-70; Asst Dir and Dep. Dir HQ; Dir, Elec. and Mech. Engrg (Army), 1970-76; Comdr, REME Support Group, 1976-77. Mem. Council, IEE, 1975-. *Recreations:* fishing, caravanning, wine-making. *Address:* 26 Cranford Drive, Holybourne, Alton, Hants GU34 4HJ. *T:* Alton 84737.

WALKER, Sir E(dward) Ronald, Kt 1963; CBE 1956; Australian economist and diplomat; *b* 26 Jan. 1907; *s* of Rev. Frederick Thomas Walker; *m* 1933, Louise Donckers; one *s* one *d*. *Educ:* Sydney Univ. (MA, DSc Econ); Cambridge Univ. (PhD, LittD). Lecturer in Economics, Sydney Univ., 1927-30, 1933-39; Fellow of Rockefeller Foundation, 1931-33; Economic Adviser: NSW Treasury, 1938-39; Govt of Tasmania, 1939-41; Prof. of Economics, Univ. of Tasmania, 1939-46; Chief Economic Adviser and Dep. Dir-Gen., Australian Dept of War Organisation of Industry, 1941-45; UNRRA HQ, Washington, 1945; Counsellor, Australian Embassy, Paris, 1945-50; Exec. Member, Nat. Security Resources Board, Prime Minister's Dept, Canberra, 1950-52; Australian Ambassador to Japan, 1952-55; Ambassador and Permanent Representative of Australia at United Nations, 1956-59 (Aust. Rep., Security Council, 1956-57); Ambassador: to France, 1959-68; to the Federal Republic of Germany, 1968-71; to OECD, Paris, 1971-73. Delegate to many confs and cttees connected with UN, ILO, Unesco, etc; Pres., UN Economic and Social Council, 1964. *Publications:* An Outline of Australian Economics, 1931; Australia in the World Depression, 1933; Money, 1935; Unemployment Policy, 1936; Wartime Economics, 1939; From Economic Theory to Policy, 1943; The Australian Economy in War and Reconstruction, 1947. *Address:* 1 rue de Longchamp, Paris 16e, France. *T:* 553.0300.

WALKER, Frank Stockdale, MC 1919; Chairman, Lever Brothers, Port Sunlight Limited, 1954-60, retired; Director, Thames Board Mills Limited (until 1960); Director, Glycerine Limited; *b* 24 June 1895; *s* of Frank and Mary Elizabeth Walker; *m* 1921, Elsie May Nicholas (*d* 1974); one *s*. *Address:* 10 Knowle Grange, Knowle Drive, Sidmouth EX10 8HN. *T:* Sidmouth 5470.

WALKER, Geoffrey Basil W.; *see* Woodd Walker.

WALKER, Air Chief Marshal Sir (George) Augustus, GCB 1969 (KCB 1962; CB 1959); CBE 1945; DSO 1941; DFC 1941; AFC 1956; Director, Philips Electronic & Associated Industries Ltd; *b* 24 Aug. 1912; *s* of G. H. Walker, Garforth, Leeds; *m* 1942, Brenda Brewis; one *s* one *d*. *Educ:* St Bees' Sch.; St Catharine's, Cambridge. Entered RAF Univ. Commission, 1934; Air Min. (R&D), 1938-39; commanded Bomber Sqdns, Stations and Base, 1940-45; SASO No 4 Group, 1945-46; Air Min., Dep. Dir, Operational Training, 1946-48; SASO Rhodesian Air Training Group, 1948-50; JSSC 1950; IDC 1953; Commandant, Royal Air Force Flying Coll., 1954-56; AOC No 1 Group, 1956-59; Chief Information Officer, Air Min., 1959-61; AOC-in-C, Flying Training Command, 1961-64; Inspector-General, RAF, 1964-67; Dep. C-in-C Allied Forces, Central Europe, 1967-70, retd. ADC to the Queen, 1952-56, to King George VI, 1943-52; Air ADC to the Queen, 1968-70. Hon. Col, 33rd (Lancashire and Cheshire) Signal Regt, Royal Corps of Signals, T&AVR, 1970-75. Pres., RFU, 1965-66; Chairman: Royal Air Forces Assoc., 1973-; Nat. Sporting Club, 1974-; Scholarship Cttee, Lord Kitchener Nat. Meml Fund, 1974-. Governor and Commandant, Church Lads Brigade, 1970-. *Recreations:* Rugby (played for England, Barbarians, RAF, Blackheath, Yorkshire; Captained RAF, 1936-39), golf, sailing. *Address:* c/o Barclays Bank, 28/30 Park Row, Leeds LS1 1PA. *Club:* Royal Air Force.

WALKER, Dr George Patrick Leonard, FRS 1975; Reader in Geology, Imperial College of Science and Technology, London, since 1964; *b* 2 March 1926; *s* of Leonard Richard Thomas Walker and Evelyn Frances Walker; *m* 1958, Hazel Rosemary (*née* Smith); one *s* one *d*. *Educ:* Wallace High Sch., Lisburn, N Ire.; Queen's Univ., Belfast (BSc, MSc); Univ. of Leeds (PhD). Research, Univ. of Leeds, 1948-51; Asst Lectr and Lectr, Imperial Coll., 1951-64. Awarded moiety of Lyell Fund of Geological Soc. of London, 1963. Hon. Mem., Vísindafjelag Islendinga, (Iceland), 1968. *Publications:* scientific papers on mineralogy, the geology of Iceland, and volcanology.

Recreation: visiting volcanoes. *Address:* Imperial College of Science and Technology, SW7 2BP.

WALKER, Prof. Gilbert James, MA Oxon, DLitt Birmingham; Professor of Commerce and Head of Department of Industrial Economics and Business Studies, University of Birmingham, 1955-74, now Emeritus; *b* 6 Jan. 1907; *s* of James MacFarlane Walker and Margaret Theresa Burrows; *m* 1943, Mavis Foyle; one *s. Educ:* Abbotsholme, Rocester, Staffs; University College Sch., London; New Coll., Oxford. Senior George Webb Medley Schol., Oxford Univ., 1928; Madden Prizeman and Meritorious Disappointed Candidate, TCD, 1930. Asst Lectr in Economics, Birmingham Univ., 1930; Rockefeller Fellow, USA, 1934; Consultant, Economics of Transport, Nova Scotia Govt, 1929; Sen. Investigator Man-power Survey, Min. of Labour, 1940; Asst Dir and Dep. Dir of Statistics, Min. of Supply, 1941; Dir of Statistics, British Supply Mission, Washington, DC, 1942; Reader in Economics of Transport, Univ. of Birmingham, 1945, Professor of Economics 1947; Dean of Faculty of Commerce and Social Science, Birmingham, 1956. Lectr in Harvard Summer Sch., July 1949 and 1953. Consultant Economics of Transport, CO and Nigeria, 1950. Pres. of Section F (Economics and Statistics) of British Assoc. for the Advancement of Science, 1956; Consultant, Economics of Transport in W Africa for UN, 1957-58. *Publications:* Survey of Transportation in Nova Scotia, 1941; Road and Rail, an enquiry into the economics of competition and state control, 1942, 2nd edn, 1947; Traffic and Transport in Nigeria, 1956; Economic Planning by Programme and Control, 1957. Contrib. to Econ. Jl, Modern Law Review, Economica and Jl of Political Econ.; proc. Inst. Transport; British Transport Review, etc. *Address:* 78 Wellington Road, Edgbaston, Birmingham B15 2ET.

WALKER, Harold; MP (Lab) Doncaster, since 1964; Minister of State, Department of Employment, since 1976; *b* 12 July 1927; *s* of Harold and Phyllis Walker; *m* 1956, Barbara Hague; one *d. Educ:* Manchester College of Technology. An Assistant Government Whip, 1967-68; Jt Parly Under-Sec. of State, Dept of Employment and Productivity, 1968-70; Opposition Front-Bench spokesman on Industrial Relations, 1970-74; Parly Under-Sec. of State, Dept of Employment, 1974-76. *Recreations:* reading, gardening. *Address:* House of Commons, SW1. *Clubs:* Westminster, Clay Lane, Doncaster Trades, RN, Catholic (all Doncaster).

WALKER, Harold Berners; HM Diplomatic Service; Head of Personnel Operations Department, Foreign and Commonwealth Office, since 1976; *b* 19 Oct. 1932; *s* of late Admiral Sir Harold Walker, KCB, RN, and of Lady Walker (*née* Berners); *m* 1960, Jane Bittleston; one *s* two *d. Educ:* Winchester (Exhibition 1946); Worcester Coll., Oxford (Exhibition 1952). BA 1955. 2nd Lieut RE, 1951-52. Foreign Office, 1955; MECAS, 1957; Asst Political Agent, Dubai, 1958; Foreign Office, 1960; Principal Instructor, MECAS, 1963; First Sec., Cairo, 1964; Head of Chancery and Consul, Damascus, 1966; Foreign Office (later FCO), 1967; First Sec. (Commercial), Washington, 1970; Counsellor, Jedda, 1973; Dep. Head, Personnel Operations Dept, FCO, 1975-76. *Recreation:* tennis. *Address:* Mapledown, Wych Hill Lane, Woking, Surrey. *Club:* United Oxford & Cambridge University.

WALKER, Sir (Horace) Alan; *see* Walker, Sir Alan.

WALKER, Major Sir Hugh (Ronald), 4th Bt, *cr* 1906; *b* 13 Dec. 1925; *s* of Major Sir Cecil Edward Walker, 3rd Bt, DSO, MC, and Violet (*née* McMaster); *S* father, 1964; *m* 1971, Norna, *er d* of Lt-Cdr R. D. Baird, RNR; two *s. Educ:* Wellington Coll., Berks. Joined Royal Artillery, 1943; commissioned Sept. 1945; 2 iC, RA Range, Benbecula, Outer Hebrides, 1964-66; Commanding No 1 Army Information Team, in Aden and Hong Kong, 1966-68; Larkhill, 1969-73, retired. Mem., Assoc. of Supervisory and Executive Engineers. *Recreation:* horses. *Heir:* *s* Robert Cecil Walker, *b* 26 Sept. 1974. *Address:* Ballinamona, Hospital, Kilmallock, Co. Limerick, Ireland.

WALKER, Sir Hugh Selby N.; *see* Norman-Walker.

WALKER, Prof. James, CBE 1971; BSc, MD, FRCPGlas, FRCOG; Professor of Obstetrics and Gynæcology, University of Dundee, since 1967 (University of St Andrews, 1956-67); Consultant, Eastern Regional Hospital Board, Scotland, since 1956; *b* 8 March 1916; *s* of James Walker, FEIS; *m* 1940, Catherine Clark Johnston, *d* of George R. A. Johnston; one *s* two *d. Educ:* High Schs of Falkirk and Stirling; Univ. of Glasgow. BSc 1935; MB, ChB (Hons) 1938; Brunton Memorial Prize; MRCOG 1947; MD (Hons) 1954; FRCOG 1957; MRCPGlas 1963, FRCPGlas 1968. Blair Bell Memorial Lectr, Royal Coll. Obstetrics and Gynæcology, 1953. Served War of

1939-45, RAFVR, UK and India, 1941-46. Hon. Surgeon to Out Patients, Royal Infirmary, Glasgow, Hall Tutor in Midwifery, Univ. Glasgow, 1946; Sen. Lectr in Midwifery and Gynæcology, Univ. of Aberdeen, Consultant NE Regional Hospital Board (Scotland), 1948; Reader in Obst. and Gynæcology, Univ. of London, Consultant, Hammersmith Hospital, 1955. Visiting Professor: Univ. of New York State, 1957, 1970; Univ. of Florida, 1965, 1970; McGill Univ., 1967. *Publications:* senior editor, Combined Textbook of Obstetrics and Gynæcology, 9th edn, 1976; contrib. on Obstetrics and Gynæcology to textbooks and learned jls. *Address:* Beechlea, 1 Ellieslea Road, Dundee DD5 1JG. *T:* Dundee 79238. *Club:* Royal Air Force.

WALKER, James Arthur H.; *see* Higgs-Walker.

WALKER, James Findlay, QPM 1964; Commandant, National Police College, 1973-76; *b* 20 May 1916; *m* 1941, Gertrude Eleanor Bell; one *s. Educ:* Arbroath High Sch., Angus, Scotland. Joined Metropolitan Police, 1936. Served War, 1943-46: commissioned Black Watch; demobilised rank Captain. Served in Metropolitan Police through ranks to Chief Supt, 1963; Staff of Police Coll., 1963-65; Asst Chief Constable: W Riding Constabulary, 1965-68; W Yorks Constabulary, 1968-70; Dep. Chief Constable, W Yorks Constabulary, 1970-73. *Recreations:* gardening, golf. *Address:* Mayfield, Quarry Hill, Horbury, Wakefield, W Yorks.

WALKER, Sir James (Graham), Kt 1972; MBE 1963; Part Owner of Cumberland Santa Gertrudis Stud and Wakefield Merino Sheep Property; Chairman, Central Western Electricity Board, 1966-76, Capricornia Electricity Board, since 1977; *b* Bellingen, NSW, 7 May 1913; *s* of late Albert Edward Walker and Adelaide Walker, Sydney, NSW; *m* 1939, Mary Vivienne Maude Poole; two *s* three *d. Educ:* New England Grammar Sch., Glen Innes, NSW. Councillor, Longreach Shire Council, 1953- (Chm., 1957-); Vice-Pres., Local Authorities of Qld, 1966, Sen. Vice-Chm., 1972. Dep. Chm., Longreach Pastoral Coll., since inception, 1966-; Exec. Mem., Central Western Queensland Local Authorities' Assoc. and Queensland Local Authorities' Assoc., 1964-. Dir, Longreach Printing Co. Chm., Santa Gertrudis Assoc., Australia, 1976. Past Asst Grand Master, United Grand Lodge of Qld, 1970. Session Clerk, St Andrews Church, Longreach, 1948-. Fellow, Internat. Inst. of Community Service, 1975. *Recreations:* bowls, clay bird shooting, surfing, oil painting. *Address:* Camden Park, Longreach, Queensland 4730, Australia. *T:* Longreach 331. *Clubs:* Queensland (Brisbane); Longreach, Longreach Rotary (Longreach).

WALKER, Sir James Heron, 5th Bt, *cr* 1868; *b* 7 April 1914; *s* of 4th Bt and Synolda, *y d* of late James Thursby-Pelham; *S* father, 1930; *m* 1st, 1939, Angela Margaret, *o d* of Victor Alexandre Beaufort; one *s* (one *d* decd); 2nd, 1972, Sharrone, *er d* of David Read; one *s. Educ:* Eton Coll.; Magdalene Coll., Cambridge. *Recreations:* long haired Dachshunds and music. *Heir:* *s* Victor Stewart Heron Walker [*b* 8 Oct. 1942; *m* 1969, Caroline Louise, *d* of late Lt-Col F. E. B. Wignall; two *s*]. *Address:* Ringdale Manor, Faringdon, Oxon.
See also Baron Cornwallis.

WALKER, Sir John, KCMG 1959 (CMG 1951); OBE 1947; *b* 27 June 1906; *s* of late Rupert Walker; *m* 1934, Muriel Winifred (*d* 1976) *d* of Henry John Hill; one *s* (and one *s* decd). *Educ:* Ashby Grammar Sch.; London Univ.; Sorbonne. Passed examination and entered Dept of Overseas Trade, 1929; Asst Commercial Sec., Santiago, 1931; transf. to Buenos Aires, 1933; Commercial Sec., Bagdad, 1938, 1943; transf. to Madrid, 1944, Counsellor, (Commercial), 1947; transf. to Tehran, 1948; HM Inspector of Foreign Service Establishments, Foreign Office, 1953-55; Ambassador to Venezuela, 1955-60; Ambassador to Norway, 1961-62. Dir-Gen., Hispanic and Luso-Brazilian Councils, 1963-69. Knight Grand Cross, Order of St Olav (Norway), 1962. Fellow, University College, London, 1968-. *Publications:* Economic Survey of Iraq, 1944; Economic Survey of Spain, 1948. *Recreations:* golf, shooting, fishing. *Address:* Primrose Cottage, Lodsworth, Petworth, West Sussex GU28 9DA. *T:* Lodsworth 350.

WALKER, John; Director, National Gallery of Art, Washington, DC, 1956-69, now Director Emeritus; *b* 24 Dec. 1906; *s* of Hay Walker and Rebekah Jane Friend; *m* 1937, Lady Margaret Gwendolen Mary Drummond; one *s* one *d. Educ:* Harvard Univ. (AB). Associate in charge Dept Fine Arts American Acad., Rome, 1935-39 (now Trustee); Chief Curator, National Gall., Washington DC, 1939-56. Connected with protection and preservation of artistic and historic monuments; John Harvard Fellow, Harvard Univ., 1930-31; American Federation of Arts; Board of Advisers, Dumbarton Oaks; Trustee: Andrew W.

Mellon Educational and Charitable Trust; American Federation of Arts; Wallace Foundation, NY; National Trust for Historic Preservation; Mem., Art Adv. Panel, National Trust (UK); Member Advisory Council: Univ. of Notre Dame; New York Univ.; Hon. Dr Fine Arts: Tufts Univ., 1958; Brown Univ., 1959; La Salle Coll., 1962; LittD: Notre Dame, 1959, Washington and Jefferson Univs, 1960; LHD: Catholic Univ. of America, 1964; Univ. of New York, 1965; Maryland Inst.; Georgetown Univ., 1966; William and Mary Univ., 1967. Holds foreign decorations. *Publications:* (with Macgill James) Great American Paintings from Smibert to Bellows, 1943; (with Huntington Cairns) Masterpieces of Painting from National Gallery of Art, 1944; Paintings from America, 1951; (with Huntington Cairns) Great Paintings from the National Gallery of Art, 1952; National Gallery of Art, Washington, 1956; Bellini and Titian at Ferrara, 1957; Treasures from the National Gallery of Art, 1963; The National Gallery of Art, Washington, DC, 1964; (with H. Cairns) Pageant of Painting, 1966; Self-Portrait with Donors, 1974; National Gallery of Art, 1976; Turner, 1976. *Address:* 1729 H Street, NW, Washington, DC 20006, USA. *T:* 965-2253. *Clubs:* Turf, Dilettanti, Pilgrims'; Century Association, The Brook (New York City); Chevy Chase, Metropolitan (Washington, DC).

WALKER, John David; His Honour Judge Walker; a Circuit Judge, since 1972; *b* 13 March 1924; *y s* of late L. C. Walker, MA, MB (Cantab), BCh, and late Mrs J. Walker, Malton; *m* 1953, Elizabeth Mary Emma (*née* Owbridge); one *s* two *d. Educ:* Oundle (1937-42); Christ's Coll., Cambridge (1947-50); BA 1950, MA 1953. War of 1939-45: commissioned Frontier Force Rifles, Indian Army, 1943; demob., Captain, 1947. Called to the Bar, Middle Temple, 1951; a Recorder, 1972. *Recreations:* shooting, fishing. *Address:* Molescroft Close, Beverley, North Humberside. *T:* Beverley 881359. *Clubs:* Lansdowne; Pacific (Hull).

WALKER, John Riddell Bromhead, MVO 1953; MC 1944; Clarenceux King of Arms, since 1968; Lieutenant-Colonel (retired), late 14th Sikhs; *b* 21 June 1913; *s* of late Col P. G. Walker, IA, and Judith Dorothy Gonville, *d* of late Col Sir Benjamin Bromhead, Bt, CB, Thurlby Hall, Lincoln; *m* 1939, Marjorie, *d* of late Col Frank Fleming, DSO, TD; two *s* one *d. Educ:* Dover; Royal Military Coll., Sandhurst. Attached 2nd Bn York and Lancaster Regt, 1933; 1/11th Sikh Regt (14th Sikhs) and 7/11th Sikh Regt, 1934-47; adjutant, 1938-41; various staff appointments in India, 1942-47; Instructor Staff Coll., Haifa, 1944-45; NWF (India), Waziristan, 1937; Ahmedzai, 1940; Datta Khel Relief, 1942; Arakan and Imphal, 1944; Rouge Croix Pursuivant of Arms, 1947-53; Lancaster Herald, 1953-68; Registrar of College of Arms, 1960-67. *Address:* College of Arms, Queen Victoria Street, EC4. *T:* 01-236 6231. *Club:* Flyfishers'.

WALKER, Julian Fortay, MBE 1960; HM Diplomatic Service; Director, Middle East Centre for Arab Studies, Lebanon, since 1977; *b* 7 May 1929; *s* of Kenneth Macfarlane Walker, FRCS, and Eileen Marjorie Walker (*née* Wilson); unmarried. *Educ:* Harvey Sch., Hawthorne, New York; Stowe; Bryanston; Cambridge Univ. (MA). National Service, RN, 1947-49; Cambridge, 1949-52; London Univ. Sch. of African and Oriental Studies, 1952. Foreign Service: MECAS, 1953; Asst Political Agent, Trucial States, 1953-55; 3rd and 2nd Sec., Bahrain Residency, 1955-57; FCO and Frontier Settlement, Oman, 1957-60; 2nd and 1st Sec., Oslo, 1960-63; FCO News Dept Spokesman, 1963-67; 1st Sec., Baghdad, 1967; 1st Sec., Morocco (Rabat), 1967-69; FCO, 1969-71; Political Agent, Dubai, Trucial States, 1971, Consul-Gen. and Counsellor, British Embassy, Dubai, United Arab Emirates, 1971-72; Cambridge Univ. on sabbatical leave, 1972-73; Political Advr and Head of Chancery, British Mil. Govt, Berlin, 1973-76. *Recreations:* skiing, sailing, tennis, music, cooking. *Address:* c/o Foreign and Commonwealth Office, SW1; MECAS, Shemlan, 6530 Lebanon. *Club:* Royal Automobile.

WALKER, Malcolm Thomas, CBE 1964; HM Diplomatic Service, retired; *b* 8 April 1915; *s* of late Major Herbert Thomas Walker and Caroline Dorothy Clerk; *m* 1949, Jean Rosemary Edith Mair; two *s* one *d. Educ:* Sherborne Sch.; Worcester Coll., Oxford. Entered HM Foreign Service, 1938; served at Beirut, 1938; Jedda, 1940; Bagdad, 1943; First Secretary in Foreign Office, 1947; Benghazi, 1949; Amman, 1950; Foreign Office, 1953; Counsellor at Khartoum, 1956; Consul-General, Hanoi, 1958; Consul-General, Seville, Spain, 1960-63; British Ambassador in Liberia, 1963-67; Consul-General, Cape Town, 1967-70; retd. *Recreations:* sailing and gardening. *Address:* The Manor House, Plush, Dorchester, Dorset DT2 7RJ. *T:* Piddletrenthide 280. *Club:* Royal Ocean Racing.

WALKER, Sir Michael; *see* Walker, Sir C. M.

WALKER, Michael; a Recorder of the Crown Court, since 1972; *b* 13 April 1931; *m* 1959, Elizabeth Mary Currie; two *s. Educ:* Chadderton Grammar Sch.; Sheffield Univ. (LLM). Called to the Bar, Gray's Inn, 1956. Joined North Eastern Circuit, 1958.

WALKER, Prof. Nigel David, MA Oxon, PhD Edinburgh, DLitt Oxon; Wolfson Professor of Criminology, Cambridge University, Director of Institute of Criminology and Fellow of King's College, Cambridge, since 1973; *b* 6 Aug. 1917; *s* of David B. Walker and Violet Walker (*née* Johnson); *m* 1939, Sheila Margaret Johnston; one *d. Educ:* Tientsin Grammar Sch.; Edinburgh Academy; Christ Church, Oxford (Hon. Scholar). Served War, Infantry officer (Camerons and Lovat Scouts), 1940-46. Scottish Office, 1946-61; Gwilym Gibbon Fellow, Nuffield Coll., 1958-59; University Reader in Criminology and Fellow of Nuffield Coll., Oxford, 1961-73. Chairman: Home Secretary's Adv. Council on Probation and After-care, 1972-76 (Mem., 1962-76); Study Gp on Legal Training of Social Workers, 1972-73; Vice-Pres., Howard League for Penal Reform, 1971-; Member: Home Sec.'s TV Research Cttee, 1963-69; Adv. Council on Penal System, 1969-; Cttee on Mentally Abnormal Offenders, 1972-75; Working Party on Judicial Training and Information, 1975-. Hon. LLD Leicester, 1976. *Publications:* Delphi, 1936; A Short History of Psychotherapy, 1957 (various trans); Morale in the Civil Service, 1961; Crime and Punishment in Britain, 1965; Crime and Insanity in England, 2 vols, 1968 and 1972; Sentencing in a Rational Society, 1969 (various trans.); Crimes, Courts and Figures, 1971; Explaining Misbehaviour (inaug. lecture), 1974; Treatment and Justice (Sandor lecture), 1976; Behaviour and Misbehaviour, 1977; reports, articles, etc. *Recreations:* chess, hill-climbing. *Address:* Institute of Criminology, 7 West Road, Cambridge. *T:* Cambridge 68511. *Club:* Royal Society of Medicine.

WALKER, Sir Peter; *see* Walker, Sir C. P. G.

WALKER, Rt. Hon. Peter Edward, PC 1970; MBE 1960; MP (C) Worcester since March 1961; *b* 25 March 1932; *s* of Sydney and Rose Walker; *m* 1969, Tessa, *d* of G. I. Pout; two *s* one *d. Educ:* Latymer Upper Sch. Member, National Executive of Conservative Party, 1956-; Nat. Chairman, Young Conservatives, 1958-60; Parliamentary Candidate (C) for Dartford, 1955 and 1959. Chairman, Rose, Thomson, Young & Co. Ltd (Lloyd's Brokers), 1956-70; Dep. Chairman, Slater, Walker Securities Ltd, 1964-70; Director: Hugh Paul & Co. Ltd, Lloyd's Brokers, 1960; Adwest Ltd, 1963-70 and 1975-; Mem., Lloyd's, 1969. PPS to Leader of House of Commons, 1963-64; Opposition Front Bench Spokesman: on Finance and Economics, 1964-66; on Transport, 1966-68; on Local Government, Housing, and Land, 1968-70; Minister of Housing and Local Govt, June-Oct. 1970; Secretary of State for: the Environment, 1970-72; Trade and Industry, 1972-74; Opposition Spokesman on Trade, Industry and Consumer Affairs, Feb.-June 1974, on Defence, June 1974-Feb. 1975. *Publication:* The Ascent of Britain, 1977. *Address:* Deer Park, Droitwich, Worcs. *Clubs:* Buck's City of London, Turf; Worcestershire County Cricket, Union and County (Worcester).

WALKER, Rt. Rev. Peter Knight; *see* Ely, Bishop of.

WALKER, Prof. Peter Martin Brabazon, CBE 1976; FRSE; Honorary Professor and Director, MRC Mammalian Genome Unit, since 1973; *b* 1 May 1922; *e s* of Major Ernest Walker and Mildred Walker (*née* Heaton-Ellis), Kenya; *m* 1943, Violet Norah Wright; one *s* three *d. Educ:* Haileybury Coll.; Trinity Coll., Cambridge, 1945. BA, PhD. Tool and instrument maker, 1939 (during War); Scientific Staff, MRC Biophysics Research Unit, King's Coll., London, 1948; Royal Society Research Fellow, Edinburgh, 1958; Univ. of Edinburgh: Lectr in Zoology, 1962; Reader in Zoology, 1963; Professor of Natural History, 1966-73. Member: Biological Research Bd, MRC, 1967; Mem. MRC, 1970; Chief Scientist Cttee, Scottish Home and Health Dept, 1973-; Chm., Equipment Res. Cttee, Scottish Home and Health Dept, 1973-. *Publications:* contribs to the molecular biology of the genetic material of mammals in: Nature; Jl of Molecular Biology, etc. *Recreations:* gardening, design of scientific instruments, railway history. *Address:* House of Ross, Comrie, Perthshire. *T:* Comrie 303; 5 Grange Terrace, Edinburgh EH9 2LD. *T:* 031-667 3060.

WALKER, Philip Gordon, FCA; Chairman and Chief Executive: Sun Life Assurance Society Ltd; Sun Life Pensions Management Ltd; Solar Artagen Properties Ltd; Chairman: Chapman & Co. (Balham) Ltd; Chapman & Co. Engineers (Balham) Ltd; The New Waterside Paper Mills Ltd; Chapman Cartons Ltd; Chapman Envelopes Ltd; Weir Waterside Paper Mills Ltd; *b* 9

June 1912; *s* of late William and Kate Blanche Walker; *m* 1st, 1938, Anne May (marr. diss.); one *s* two *d* ; 2nd, 1962, Elizabeth Oliver. *Educ:* Epworth Coll., Rhyl, North Wales. Bourner, Bullock & Co., Chartered Accountants, 1929-35; Walkers (Century Oils) Ltd, 1935-40; Layton Bennett, Billingham & Co., Chartered Accountants, 1940, Partner, 1944-51 (now Josolyne Layton-Bennett & Co.); Albert E. Reed & Co Ltd (now Reed International), Man. Dir, 1951-63. Part-time Mem. Monopolies Commn, 1963-65; Member: Performing Right Tribunal, 1971-; Restrictive Practices Court, 1973-. *Recreation:* golf. *Address:* Dunwood, East Drive, Wentworth, Virginia Water, Surrey GU25 4JT. *T:* Wentworth 2520. *Clubs:* Brooks's; Wildernesse (Sevenoaks); Rye; Berkshire.

WALKER, Philip Henry Conyers; a Recorder of the Crown Court since 1972; Solicitor; *b* 22 Dec. 1926; *o c* of Philip Howard and Kathleen Walker; *m* 1953, Mary Elizabeth Ross; two *s* two *d*. *Educ:* Marlborough; Oriel Coll., Oxford. MA, BCL (Oxon); DipTh (London). Army (6 AB Sigs), 1944-48 (despatches, 1948). Solicitor in private practice, 1954-. Mem., Church Assembly, Nat. Synod of C of E, 1960-. *Recreations:* fishing, shooting, sailing, walking. *Address:* Pond House, Askwith, Otley, West Yorks. *T:* Otley 3196.

WALKER, Raymond St John, CBE 1970; Secretary, Science Research Council, since 1972 (Director, Establishment and Finance, later Administration, 1965-72); *b* 11 April 1917; *o s* of late William and Sybil MacLaren Walker; *m* 1941, Eva Mary, *e d* of late Walter Lionel and Ethel Marion Dudley; three *s*. *Educ:* Leeds Grammar Sch.; St Peter's Coll., Oxford. Royal Artillery, 1939-46. Min. of Supply, 1947-58 (Private Sec. to Minister, 1950-53); Imperial Defence Coll., 1959; Min. of Aviation, 1960-61; DSIR, 1962-64. *Recreation:* sailing. *Address:* 63 Rayleigh Road, Hutton, Essex. *T:* Brentwood 210179. *Club:* Athenæum.

WALKER, Richard Alwyne F.; *see* Fyjis-Walker.

WALKER, Richard John Boileau, MA; FSA; National Portrait Gallery Cataloguer, since 1976; *b* 4 June 1916; *s* of Comdr Kenneth Walker and Caroline Livingstone-Learmonth; *m* 1946, Margaret, *d* of Brig. Roy Firebrace, CBE; one *s* two *d*. *Educ:* Harrow; Magdalene Coll., Cambridge (MA); Courtauld Institute of Art. Active service, RNVR, 1939-45. British Council, 1946; Tate Gallery, 1947-48; Min. of Works Picture Adviser, 1949-76; Curator of the Palace of Westminster, 1950-76. Trustee, Nat. Maritime Museum, 1977-. *Publications:* Catalogue of Pictures at Audley End, 1950 and 1973; articles in Apollo, Connoisseur, Walpole Soc. Jl, etc. *Recreations:* looking at pictures and hunting quotations. *Address:* 31 Cadogan Place, SW1X 9RX. *T:* 01-235 1801; Ashbrook House, Blewbury, Oxfordshire OX11 9QA. *Clubs:* Athenæum, United Oxford & Cambridge University.

WALKER, Robert; HM Diplomatic Service, retired; Deputy Registrar, Hull University, since 1972; *b* 1 May 1924; *s* of Young and Gladys Walker, Luddendenfoot, Yorks; *m* 1949, Rita Thomas; one *s* one *d*. *Educ:* Sowerby Bridge Grammar Sch.; Peterhouse, Cambridge. Commissioned RNVR 1944; served in minesweepers in home waters. Cambridge, 1942-43 and 1946-48; BA Hons History, 1948; MA 1963. Joined CRO, 1948; served Peshawar and Karachi, 1949-51; New Delhi, 1955-59; Sen. First Sec., Accra, 1962-64; Dep. British High Comr, in Ghana, 1964-65; FCO, 1965-68. IDC, 1969; Commercial Counsellor, Ankara, 1970-71; Dep. High Comr, Nairobi, 1971-72. Contested (L) Haltemprice, Feb. and Oct. 1974; Mem., Liberal Party Council; Chm., Yorkshire and Humberside Liberal Fedn. Mem., N Humberside VSO Cttee. *Recreations:* coarse golf, country wine making, interior decorating. *Address:* c/o University of Hull, Hull HU6 7RX. *Club:* Naval.

WALKER, Robert Milnes, CBE 1964; Director of Surgical Studies, Royal College of Surgeons, 1968-71; Director, Cancer Records Bureau, SW Regional Hospital Board, 1965-71; Professor of Surgery, University of Bristol, 1946-64, Emeritus since 1964; Hon. Surgeon, Bristol Royal Hospital; Member of the Medical Research Council, 1959-63; *b* 2 Aug. 1903; *s* of J. W. Walker, FSA, FRCS, Wakefield, Yorks; *m* 1931, Grace Anna McCormick; two *s* four *d*. *Educ:* Oundle Sch.; University College Hospital, London. Hon. Surgeon, Royal Hospital, Wolverhampton, 1931-46; Rock Carling Fellow, Nuffield Hospital Trust, 1965. Editor, Medical Annual, 1954-74. Member Council, RCS, 1953-69; Vice-Pres., 1966-68; President: Assoc. Surgeons of GB, 1961; Surgical Research Soc., 1962-64. Fellow of University Coll., London, 1953. Mem., Medical Sub-Cttee, UGC, 1959-67. Master, Worshipful Co. of Barbers, 1974 (Upper Warden, 1973). Hon. FACS; Hon. FRCSE. Hon. Gold Medal, RCS, 1972. *Publications:* Portal Hypertension, 1959; Medical Education in Britain, 1965; Cancer in South West

England, 1973. *Recreations:* gardening, bird watching, travel. *Address:* Wergs Copse, Kintbury, Newbury, Berks.

WALKER, Robert Scott, FRICS; City Surveyor, City of London Corporation, 1955-75; *b* 13 June 1913; *s* of Harold and Mary Walker; *m* 1946, Anne Armstrong; no *c*. *Educ:* West Buckland Sch., North Devon. War Service, 1939-45, Major RA. Assistant City Surveyor, Manchester, 1946-55. *Address:* 10 Woodcote Close, Epsom, Surrey. *T:* Epsom 21220.

WALKER, Sir Ronald; *see* Walker, Sir E. R.

WALKER, Col Ronald Draycott S.; *see* Sherbrooke-Walker.

WALKER, Ronald Leslie, CSI 1946; CIE 1942; *b* 9 April 1896; *m* 1948, Joyce Edwina Collins, OBE, 1946, Kaisar-i-Hind Gold Medal, 1939, *e d* of late G. Turville Brown. *Educ:* Bedford Sch.; Hertford Coll., Oxford. European War, 1914-18, Northamptonshire Regt, 1915; Machine-Gun Corps, 1916-18. Entered Indian Civil Service, 1920; Finance Secretary, Bengal, 1939-45; Adviser to Governor of Bengal, 1945; Chief Secretary, Bengal, 1946. *Address:* Little Coombe, Coombe Hill Road, East Grinstead, West Sussex. *T:* East Grinstead 25616. *Club:* East India, Sports and Public Schools.

WALKER, Samuel Richard, CBE 1955; DL; Founder and Hon. President, Walker & Rice (Walric Fabrics) Ltd; *b* 6 Jan. 1892; *s* of Samuel Reuben and Elizabeth Louise Walker; *m* 1923, Marjorie Jackson Clark, *d* of A. J. Clark, Hove, Sussex; one *s* two *d*. *Educ:* William Ellis's. Queen Victoria Rifles, 1909-13; served European War, 1914-19, in France: 1st King Edward's Horse and RFA; Home Guard, 1939-45. City of London: DL 1951; Member Common Council (Bread Street Ward, 1937-76; Deputy, 1951-76), Chief Commoner, 1953-54; Chairman: Officers and Clerks Cttee, 1952; Privileges Cttee, 1957-73; Comr of Income Tax, 1960-66. Sheriff of City of London, 1957-58; one of HM Lieutenants, City of London. Master, Worshipful Company of Farriers, 1954-55; Master, Worshipful Company of Founders, 1962-63, Liveryman of Worshipful Company of Weavers, 1964-; Chairman: Cattle Markets Cttee, 1945-46; Central Criminal Court Extension Cttee, 1964-75; Benevolent Assoc. of Corporation of London, 1970-76; Reconstruction of Guildhall Cttee, 1953; various Cttees, City of London, 1950-54. Vice-Pres., Mid Sussex Assoc. for Mentally Handicapped Children, 1970-. Governor, Bridewell Royal Hosp., 1942-; Life Governor and Vice-Chm., City of London Sheriffs' and Recorders' Fund Soc., 1957-; Chm., Thomas Carpenter and John Lane Trust, 1951-; Governor and Almoner, Christ's Hosp., 1966-; Trustee and Pres., Seaforth Hall, Warninglid. Commendatore of Order Al Merito della Repubblica (Italy), 1957. *Recreations:* golf, riding. *Address:* Copyhold Rise, Copyhold Lane, Cuckfield, Sussex. *Clubs:* City Livery (President, 1955-56), Guildhall, Oriental; West Hove Golf (Life Pres.), West Sussex Golf.

WALKER, Mrs Sheila Mosley, JP; Chief Commissioner, Girl Guides Association, since 1975; *b* 11 Dec. 1917; *yr d* of late Charles Eric Mosley Mayne, Indian Cavalry, and Evelyn Mary, *d* of Sir Thomas Skewes-Cox, MP; *m* 1st, 1940, Major Bruce Dawson, MC, Royal Berkshire Regt (killed, Arnhem, 1944); one *s* one *d* ; 2nd, 1955, Henry William Owen, *s* of late Sir Henry Walker, CBE; one step *s* one step *d*. *Educ:* St Mary's Hall, Brighton; St James' Secretarial Coll., London. JP Nottingham City, 1970. *Recreations:* children, animals, all country and nature preservation. *Address:* The Old Schoolhouse, Kinoulton, Nottingham. *T:* Kinoulton 268.

WALKER, Dame Susan (Armour), DBE 1972 (CBE 1963); Vice-Chairman, Women's Royal Voluntary Service, since 1969; *d* of James Walker, Bowmont, Dunbar; unmarried. *Educ:* Grammar School, Dunbar. Conservative Central Office Agent, Yorkshire, 1950-56; Deputy Chief Organisation Officer, Conservative Central Office, 1956-64; Vice-Chm., Cons. Party Organisation, 1964-68, retired 1968. *Recreations:* golf, walking. *Address:* 25 Chester Row, SW1. *T:* 01-730 8778; Hownam, Kelso, Roxburghshire. *T:* Morebattle 277. *Club:* Constitutional.

WALKER, Terence William, (Terry Walker); MP (Lab) Kingswood, since Feb. 1974; Second Church Estates Commissioner, since Nov. 1974; *b* 26 Oct. 1935; *s* of William Edwin and Lilian Grace Walker; *m* 1959, Priscilla Dart; two *s* one *d*. *Educ:* Grammar Sch. and Coll. of Further Educn, Bristol. Employed by Courage (Western) Ltd at Bristol for 23 yrs, Mem. Chief Accountant's Dept. *Recreations:* cricket, football. *Address:* 19 Forest Edge, Hanham, Bristol BS15 3PP. *T:* Bristol 672301.

WALKER, Prof. Thomas William, ARCS; DSc; DIC; Professor of Soil Science, Lincoln College, New Zealand, since 1961; *b* 22 July 1916; *m* 1940, Edith Edna Bott; four *d*. *Educ:* Loughborough Grammar School; Royal College of Science. Royal Scholar and Kitchener Scholar, 1935-39; Salter's Fellow, 1939-41; Lecturer and Adviser in Agricultural Chemistry, Univ. of Manchester, 1941-46. Provincial Advisory Soil Chemist, NAAS, 1946-51; Prof. of Soil Science, Canterbury Agric. Coll., New Zealand, 1952-58; Prof. of Agric., King's Coll., Newcastle upon Tyne, 1958-61. *Publications:* numerous research. *Recreations:* fishing, gardening. *Address:* Lincoln College, Christchurch, New Zealand.

WALKER, Walter Basil Scarlett, (Bobby Walker), MA; FCA; Partner in charge of London office of Peat, Marwick, Mitchell & Co., since 1974; *b* 19 Dec. 1915; *s* of James and Hilda Walker, Southport); *m* 1945, Teresa Mary Louise John; one *d* (and one *s* decd). *Educ:* Rugby Sch.; Clare Coll., Cambridge (MA). Joined Peat, Marwick, Mitchell & Co., 1937, leaving temporarily, 1939, to join RNVR; service in Home Fleet, incl. convoys to Russia and Malta, 1940-42; finally, Asst Sec. to British Naval C-in-C in Germany; Lt-Comdr. Returned to Peat, Marwick, Mitchell & Co., 1946, becoming a partner, 1956. Mem. (part-time), UKAEA, 1972-. *Recreations:* ballet, gardening, golf. *Address:* 11 Sloane Avenue, SW3 3JD. *T:* 01-589 4133; Coles, Privett, near Alton, Hants GU34 3PH. *T:* Privett 223. *Clubs:* Junior Carlton, Royal Automobile.

WALKER, Gen. Sir Walter (Colyear), KCB 1968 (CB 1964); CBE 1959 (OBE 1949); DSO 1946 and Bars, 1953 and 1965; Commander-in-Chief, Allied Forces Northern Europe, 1969-72, retired; *b* 11 Nov. 1912; *s* of late Arthur Colyear Walker; *m* 1938, Beryl, *d* of late E.N.W. Johnston; two *s* one *d*. *Educ:* Blundell's; RMC, Sandhurst. Waziristan, 1939-41 (despatches twice); Burma, 1942, 1944-46 (despatches, DSO); Malaya, 1949-59 (despatches twice, OBE, Bar to DSO, CBE); Atomic Trials, Maralinga, SA, 1956; Dir of Operations, Borneo, 1962-65 (CB, Bar to DSO); Deputy Chief of Staff, HQ ALFCE, 1965; Acting Chief of Staff, 1966-67; GOC-in-C, Northern Command, 1967-69. jssc 1950; idc 1960. Colonel, 7th Duke of Edinburgh's Own Gurkha Rifles, 1964-. Dato Seri Setia, Order of Paduka Stia Negara, Brunei, 1964; Hon. Panglima Mangku Nagara, Malaysia, 1965. *Recreations:* shooting, tennis. *Address:* Charlton House, Charlton All Saints, Salisbury, Wilts SP5 4HQ. *Club:* Army and Navy.

WALKER, Prof. William; FRCP, FRCPE; Regius Professor of Materia Medica, University of Aberdeen, since 1973; *b* 1 Jan. 1920; *s* of William Sharp Walker and Joan Strachan Gloak; *m* 1948, Mary Cathleen Kenny; one adopted *s* one adopted *d*. *Educ:* Harris Academy, Dundee; Univ. of St Andrews. MA, MB, ChB; FRCP, FRCPE. Served War: commissioned Royal Scots, 1939; wounded, 1940; invalided, 1941. Lecturer in Pathology, Univ. of St Andrews, 1947; Medical Registrar, Newcastle, 1948. Research Fellow, Haematology, Boston Univ. Mass, 1954-55; Lectr in Therapeutics, St Andrews, 1952, Sen. Lectr, 1955; Consultant Physician, Aberdeen, 1964; Clinical Reader in Medicine, 1971. Mem., Cttee on the Review of Medicines, 1975-. *Publications:* various medical, chiefly in thrombotic and haemorrhagic disease, and drug therapy. *Recreations:* gardening, philosophy, social and political controversy. *Address:* Woodhill, Kinellar, Aberdeenshire AB5 0RZ. *T:* Aberdeen 79314.

WALKER, Sir William (Giles Newsom), Kt 1959; TD 1942; DL; *b* 20 Nov. 1905; *e s* of late H. Giles Walker, Over Rankeillour, Cupar, Fife and of late Mrs Elizabeth Bewley Newsom (Walker), Cork, Eire; *m* 1930, Mildred Brenda, 3rd *d* of Sir Michael Nairn, 2nd Bt, Elie House, Fife, and Pitcarmick, Blairgowrie; one *s* two *d*. *Educ:* Shrewsbury Sch.; Jesus Coll., Cambridge (BA). War of 1939-45: Lt-Col comdg 1st Fife and Forfar Yeomanry, 1943-45 (mobilised Aug. 1939; despatches, TD). Jute Industries Ltd, Dundee: entered 1927; rejoined after War, 1945; Director, 1946-71; Managing Director, 1947-69; Chairman, 1948-70; Hon. Pres., 1971. Director: Nairn & Williamson (Holdings) Ltd, 1954-75; Clydesdale Bank Ltd; Scottish Television Ltd, 1964-74; Alliance Trust Co. Ltd, 1963-76; Second Alliance Trust Co. Ltd, 1963-76. Formerly: Jute Working Party (Employer Mem.); Dundee Chamber of Commerce (Dir); Scottish Industrial Estates Ltd. (Dir); Member, Scottish Railway Bd, Hon. Colonel: Fife and Forfar Yeomanry/Scottish Horse, 1967-69; Highland Yeomanry, 1969-71. DL Fife, 1958. USA Bronze Star, 1945. *Recreations:* shooting and golf. *Address:* Pitlair, Cupar, Fife. *T:* Ladybank 413. *Clubs:* Cavalry and Guards; Eastern (Dundee); Royal and Ancient Golf (Capt. 1962-63) (St Andrews); The Honourable Company of Edinburgh Golfers (Muirfield).

WALKER, William MacLelland, QC (Scot.) 1971; *b* 19 May 1933; *s* of late Hon. Lord Walker; *m* 1957, Joan Margaret, *d* of late Charles Hutchison Wood, headmaster, Dundee; one *d*. *Educ:* Edinburgh Academy; Edinburgh Univ. (MA, LLB). Advocate, 1957; Flying Officer, RAF, 1957-59; Standing Junior Counsel: Min. of Aviation, 1963-68; BoT (Aviation), 1968-71; Min. of Technology, 1968-70; Dept of Trade and Industry (Power), 1971; Min. of Aviation Supply, 1971. Chm. Industrial Tribunals in Scotland, 1972-. *Recreations:* shooting, travel. *Address:* 17 India Street, Edinburgh EH3 6HE. *T:* 031-225 3846; Edenside, Gordon, Berwickshire TD3 6LB. *T:* Gordon 271. *Clubs:* Royal Air Force; New (Edinburgh).

WALKER LEE, Rev. William; *see* Lee, Rev. W. W.

WALKER-OKEOVER, Colonel Sir Ian Peter Andrew Monro, 3rd Bt, *cr* 1886; DSO and Bar 1945; TD; JP; Lord-Lieutenant of Derbyshire since 1951; *b* 30 Nov. 1902; *e s* of Sir Peter Walker, 2nd Bt, and Ethel Blanche, *d* of late H. C. and Hon. Mrs Okeover, *d* of 3rd Baron Waterpark; granted royal licence and authority to use surname of Okeover in addition to that of Walker, 1956; *S* father, 1915; *m* 1938, Dorothy Elizabeth, *yr d* of Capt. Josceline Heber-Percy, Guy's Cliffe, Warwick; one *s* two *d*. Served War of 1939-45 (DSO). Formerly Hon. Col, Derbyshire Yeomanry (subsequently Hon. Col Leicestershire and Derbyshire Yeomanry, retired 1962); Col Comdt, Yeomanry, RAC, TA, 1962-65. Derbyshire: JP 1932, High Sheriff 1934, DL 1948. Mem., Queen's Body Guard for Scotland (The Royal Company of Archers). KStJ 1974. *Heir:* s Captain Peter Ralph Leopold Walker-Okeover, Blues and Royals, retd [*b* 22 July 1947; *m* 1972, Catherine, *d* of Col George Maule Ramsay; one *d*]. *Address:* Okeover Hall, Ashbourne, Derbyshire; House of Glenmuick, Ballater, Aberdeenshire. *Clubs:* White's, Boodle's.

WALKER-SMITH, Rt. Hon. Sir Derek Colclough, 1st Bt, *cr* 1960; PC 1957; QC 1955; TD; MP (C) East Division of Hertfordshire since 1955 (Hertford Division, 1945-55); Member, British Delegation to European Parliament, since 1973; *b* April 1910; *y s* of late Sir Jonah Walker-Smith; *m* 1938, Dorothy, *d* of late L. J. W. Etherton, Rowlands Castle, Hants; one *s* two *d*. *Educ:* Rossall; Christ Church, Oxford. 1st Class Hons Modern History, Oxford Univ., 1931. Called to Bar, Middle Temple, 1934, Bencher 1963. Chm. Conservative Advisory Cttee on Local Govt, 1954-55; Chm. Conservative Members (1922) Cttee, 1951-55. Parly Sec. to the Board of Trade, 1955-Nov. 1956; Economic Secretary to the Treasury, Nov. 1956-Jan. 1957; Minister of State, Board of Trade, 1957; Minister of Health, 1957-60. Chm., Soc. of Conservative Lawyers, 1969-75. Associate of Royal Institution of Chartered Surveyors. *Heir:* s John Jonah Walker-Smith [*b* 6 Sept. 1939; *m* 1974, Aileen Marie, *d* of late Joseph Smith; one *d*]. *Address:* 25 Cavendish Close, NW8 9JB. *T:* 01-286 1441. *Club:* Carlton.

WALKEY, Maj.-Gen. John Christopher, CB 1953; CBE 1943; *b* 18 Oct. 1903; *s* of late S. Walkey, Dawlish, Devon; *m* 1947, Beatrice Record Brown; one *d* decd. *Educ:* Newton College, Devon. Commissioned into Royal Engineers from RMA Woolwich, 1923; Chief Engineer, 13 Corps, 1943-47; Asst Comdt, RMA Sandhurst, 1949-51; Chief Engineer, Middle East Land Forces, 1951-54; Engineer-in-Chief, War Office, 1954-57; retired, 1957. Col Comdt RE, 1958-68. Hon. Col RE Resources Units (AER), 1959-64. Officer Legion of Merit (USA), 1945. *Recreations:* usual country pursuits. *Address:* Linden Spinney, Chagford, Devon. *Club:* Naval and Military.

WALKLING, Maj.-Gen. Alec Ernest, CB 1973; OBE 1954; *b* 12 April 1918; *s* of late Ernest George Walkling; *m* 1940, Marian Harris; one *s* one *d*. *Educ:* Weymouth Grammar School; Keble College, Oxford. BA (Oxon) Mod. Langs, 1939; BA (Oxon) Hons Nat. Science, 1949. Commissioned 2nd Lieut RA, 1940; served War of 1939-45, N Africa and Burma (despatches). Staff Coll., Quetta, 1944; Min. of Supply, 1949-53; British Joint Services Mission, Washington, 1956-58; Comd Regt in BAOR, 1961-63; Comd Brigade (TA), 1963-64; Imperial Defence Coll., 1965; Dep. Commandant, RMCS, 1966-68; Dir-Gen. of Artillery, 1969-70; Dep. Master-Gen. of the Ordnance, 1970-73, retired; Col Comdt, RA, 1974-. *Recreations:* golf, oil and water colour painting. *Address:* Brackenhurst, Brackendale Road, Camberley, Surrey. *T:* Camberley 21016. *Club:* Army and Navy.

WALL, family name of Baron Wall.

WALL, Baron *cr* 1976 (Life Peer), of Coombe in Greater London; John Edward Wall, Kt 1968; OBE 1944; Director: Laporte Industries (Holdings) Ltd, since 1968; The Exchange Telegraph Co. (Holdings) Ltd, since 1972; Grundy (Teddington) Ltd, since 1972; Chairman: Charterhouse Development Capital Ltd, since

1976; Nurdin and Peacock, since 1977; *b* 15 Feb. 1913; *s* of late Harry Arthur Fitzgerald and Marie Louise Wall; *m* 1939, Gladys Evelyn (*née* Wright); two *s* one *d*. *Educ:* Wandsworth School; London School of Economics, BCom 1933, Hon. Fellow, 1970. O. T. Falk & Co., 1933-39; Min. of Food, 1939-52; Under-Sec., 1948-52. Dep. Head, Finance Dept, Unilever Ltd, 1952-56; Head of Organisation Div., Unilever Ltd, 1956-58; Man. Dir, Electric & Musical Industries, 1960-66 (Dir, 1958); Dep. Chm., Post Office Board, 1966-68; Chairman: International Computers (Holdings) Ltd and International Computers Ltd, 1968-72; Burrup Mathieson (Holdings) Ltd, 1973-76. Mem. (part-time), Sugar Bd, 1964-77. Officer, Order of Orange Nassau, 1947. *Recreation:* golf. *Address:* Wychwood, Combe End, Kingston-upon-Thames, Surrey. *T:* 01-942 3873. *Club:* Royal Autumobile.

WALL, (Alice) Anne, CVO 1972 (MVO 1964); **Mrs Michael Wall;** Assistant Press Secretary to HM The Queen, since 1958; *b* 1928; *d* of Admiral Sir Geoffrey Hawkins, *qv*; *m* 1975, Commander Michael St Q. Wall. *Educ:* Miss Faunce's PNEU School. *Address:* 2 Chester House, 231 Kennington Road, SE11.

WALL, Prof. Charles Terence Clegg, FRS 1969; Professor of Pure Mathematics, Liverpool University, since 1965; *b* 14 Dec. 1936; *s* of Charles Wall, schoolteacher, Woodfield, Dursley, Glos; *m* 1959, Alexandra Joy, *d* of Prof. Leslie Spencer Hearnshaw, *qv*; two *s* two *d*. *Educ:* Marlborough Coll.; Trinity Coll., Cambridge. PhD Cantab 1960. Fellow, Trinity Coll., 1959-64; Harkness Fellow, Princeton, 1960-61; Univ. Lectr, Cambridge, 1961-64; Reader in Mathematics, and Fellow of St Catherine's Coll., Oxford, 1964-65. Royal Soc. Leverhulme Vis. Prof., CIEA, Mexico, 1967. *Publications:* Surgery on Compact Manifolds, 1970; A Geometric Introduction to Topology, 1972; papers on various problems in geometric topology, and related algebra. *Recreations:* gardening, home winemaking. *Address:* 5 Kirby Park, West Kirby, Wirral, Merseyside L48 2HA. *T:* 051-625 5063.

WALL, David (Richard); Principal Dancer, Royal Ballet Company; *b* 15 March 1946; *s* of Charles and Dorothy Wall; *m* 1967, Alfreda Thorogood; one *s* one *d*. *Educ:* Royal Ballet Sch. Joined Royal Ballet Co., Aug. 1964. Promotion to: Soloist, Aug. 1966; Junior Principal Dancer, Aug. 1967; Senior Principal Dancer, Aug. 1968. During period of employment has danced all major roles and has had many ballets created for him. *Recreations:* music, theatre. *Address:* 70 Elmbourne Road, SW17.

WALL, Rt. Rev. Eric St Quintin; see Huntingdon, Bishop Suffragan of.

WALL, John William, CMG 1953; HM Diplomatic Service, retired 1966; *b* 6 Nov. 1910; *m* 1950, Eleanor Rosemary Riesle; one *d*. *Educ:* Grammar Sch., Mexborough; Jesus Coll., Cambridge. Probationer Vice-Consul, Levant Consular Service, 1933; Vice-Consul, Cairo, 1936; in charge of Vice-Consulate, Suez, 1937; transferred to Jedda as 2nd Sec. in Diplomatic Service, 1939; acting Consul, Jedda, 1942, 1943; transferred to Tabriz, 1944, Isfahan, 1946, Casablanca, 1947; Brit. Middle East Office, Cairo: Head of Polit. Div., 1948, in charge 1949, 1950; Oriental Counsellor, Cairo, 1951; Political Agent, Bahrein, 1952-54; Consul-General at Salonika, 1955-57; HM Ambassador and Consul-General to Paraguay, 1957-59; Counsellor, Foreign Office, 1959-63; Consul-General at Alexandria, 1963-66. *Address:* c/o Barclays Bank Ltd, 1 Pall Mall East, SW1; Pen-y-Fan, Monmouth, Gwent.

WALL, Prof. Patrick David, MA, DM; Professor of Anatomy and Director, Cerebral Functions Research Group, University College, London, since 1967; *b* 5 April 1925; *s* of T. Wall, MC, and R. Wall (*née* Cresswell); *m* 1976, Vera Ronnen, enamellist, *d* of Ernst Bischitz. *Educ:* St Paul's; Christ Church, Oxford. MA 1947; BM, BCh 1948; DM 1960. Instructor, Yale School of Medicine, 1948-50; Asst Prof., Univ. of Chicago, 1950-53; Instructor, Harvard Univ., 1953-55; Assoc. Prof., 1957-60, Professor 1960-67, MIT. Vis. Prof., Hebrew Univ., Jerusalem, 1973-. *Publications:* many papers on Anatomy and Physiology of the Nervous System; (novel) Trio, The revolting intellectuals' organizations, 1966 (US 1965). *Recreation:* kibbitzing. *Address:* Cerebral Functions Research Group, Department of Anatomy, University College, Gower Street, WC1.

WALL, Major Patrick Henry Bligh, MC 1945; VRD 1957; RM (retd) MP (C) Haltemprice Division of East Yorkshire, since 1955 (Haltemprice Division of Hull, Feb. 1954-55); *b* 19 Oct. 1916; *s* of Henry Benedict Wall and Gladys Eleanor Finney; *m* 1953, Sheila Elizabeth Putnam; one *d*. *Educ:* Downside. Commissioned in RM 1935 (specialised in naval gunnery).

Served in HM Ships, support craft, with RM Commandos and US Navy. Actg Major, 1943; RN Staff Coll., 1945; Joint Services Staff Coll., 1947; Major, 1949. Contested Cleveland Division (Yorks), 1951 and 1952. Parliamentary Private Secretary to: Minister of Agriculture, Fisheries and Food, 1955-57; Chancellor of the Exchequer, 1958-59. Westminster City Council, 1953-62; CO 47 Commando RMFVR, 1951-57; Comr for Sea Scouts for London, 1950-66; Pres. Yorks Area Young Conservatives, 1955-60; Chm. Mediterranean Group of Conservative Commonwealth Council, 1954-67; Chm. Cons. Parly East and Central Africa Cttee, 1956-59; Vice-Chairman: Conservative Commonwealth Affairs Cttee, 1960-68; Cons. Overseas Bureau, 1963-73; Cons. Defence Cttee, 1965-; IPU, 1974- (Vice-Chm., British, Anglo-Maltese, Anglo-Bahrain, Anglo-Portuguese Groups; Chm., Anglo-South African Group). Rapporteur, Mil. Cttee, N Atlantic Assembly (Chm., Cons./Christian Democrat Gp); Chm., Pro Fide Movement, 1970-; Mem. Defence Cttee, WEU and Council of Europe, 1972-75. Chairman: Cons. Fisheries Sub-Cttee, 1962-; Africa Centre, 1961-65; Joint East and Central Africa Board, 1965-75; Cons. Southern Africa Group, 1970-; British Rep. at 17th General Assembly of UN, 1962. Vice-Pres., British Sub-Aqua Club; Chm., Nat. Underwater Instructors Assoc.; Vice-Pres., Urban District Councils Assoc. Kt, SMO Malta; USA Legion of Merit, 1945. *Publications:* Royal Marine Pocket Book, 1944; Student Power, 1968; Defence Policy, 1969; Overseas Aid, 1969; The Soviet Maritime Threat, 1973; The Indian Ocean and the Threat to the West, 1975; Prelude to Detente, 1975; co-author of a number of political pamphlets. *Recreations:* messing about in boats, ship models, foreign birds. *Address:* 8 Westminster Gardens, Marsham Street, SW1. *T:* 01-828 1803; Brantinghamthorp, Brantingham, near Brough, North Humberside. *T:* Brough 667248. *Clubs:* Naval and Military; Royal Yacht Squadron; Royal Naval Sailing Association.

WALL, Maj.-Gen. Robert Percival Walter; Chief of Staff to Commandant General Royal Marines, since 1976; *b* 23 Aug. 1927; *s* of Frank Ernest and Ethel Elizabeth Wall; *m* 1953, Patricia Kathleen O'Brien; two *s* one *d*. Joined Royal Marines, 1945; regimental soldiering in Commandos, and Commando trng, followed by service at sea and on staff of HQ 3 Commando Bde RM, 1945-54; psc(M) 1959; jssc 1961; Asst Sec., Chiefs of Staff Secretariat, 1962-65; 43 Commando RM, 1965-66; Naval Staff, 1966-68; Directing Staff, JSS Coll., 1969-71; Col GS Commando Forces and Dept of Commandant General Royal Marines, 1971-74; course at RCDS, 1975. Mem. Council, River Thames Soc. *Recreations:* cricket, walking, reading. *Address:* Department of Commandant General Royal Marines, Ministry of Defence, Main Building, Whitehall, SW1A 2HB. *Club:* Army and Navy, MCC.

WALL, Ronald George Robert, CB 1961; *b* 25 Jan. 1910; *s* of George Thomas and Sophia Jane Wall; *m* 1st, 1936, Winifred Evans (marr. diss., 1950); one *s*; 2nd, 1960, Mrs Muriel Sorrell (*née* Page). *Educ:* Alleyn's School, Dulwich; St John's College, Oxford (MA). Administrative Civil Service; entered Ministry of Agriculture and Fisheries, 1933; Fisheries Sec., 1952-59. Gwilym Gibbon Research Fellow, Nuffield College, Oxford, 1951-52. President of Permanent Commission under Internat. Fisheries Convention of 1946, 1953-56; Chairman of the International Whaling Commission, 1958-60; Dep. Sec., Min. of Agriculture, Fisheries and Food, 1961-70. Chm., Sugar Bd, 1970-77. *Address:* 201 London Road, Twickenham, Mddx. *T:* 01-892 7086. *Clubs:* United Oxford & Cambridge University, Arts Theatre.

WALL, Prof. William Douglas, PhD; Professor of Educational Psychology, Institute of Education, University of London, since 1972; *b* 22 Aug. 1913; *s* of late John Henry Wall and Ann McCulloch Wall, Wallington, Surrey; *m* 1st, 1936, Doris Margaret (*née* Satchel) (marr. diss. 1960); two *s* one *d*; 2nd, 1960, Ursula Maria (*née* Gallusser); one *s*. *Educ:* Univ. Coll. London, 1931-34 (BA Hons); Univ. Coll. London/Univ. of Birmingham, 1944-48 (PhD (Psychol.)). Mem. BPsS, Cttee of Prof. Psychologists, Social Psych. Sect., Child and Educnl Psych. Sect. Univ. of Birmingham Educn Dept, 1945-51; Reader, 1948-53; Head, Educn and Child Develt Unit, UNESCO, Paris, 1951-56; Dir, Nat. Foundn for Educnl Res. in England and Wales, 1956-68; Dean, Inst. of Educn, Univ. of London, 1968-73. Visiting Professor: Univ. of Michigan, 1957; Univ. of Jerusalem, 1962; Univ. of Tel Aviv, 1967. Chm., Internat. Project Evaluation of Educnl Attainment, 1958-62; Mem., Police Trng Council, 1970-; Co-Dir, 1958-75, and Chm., Nat. Child Develt Study, 1958-; Mem. Council, Internat. Children's Centre, Paris, 1970-. *Publications:* (many trans. various langs): Adolescent Child, 1948 (2nd edn, 1952); Education and Mental Health, 1955; Psychological Services for Schools, 1956; Child of our Times, 1959; Failure in School, 1962;

Adolescents in School and Society, 1968; Longitudinal Studies and the Social Sciences, 1970; Constructive Education for Children, 1975; Constructive Education for Adolescents, 1977; contrib: British Jl Educnl Psych.; British Jl Psych., Educnl Res. (Editor, 1958-68), Educnl Rev., Enfance, Human Develt, Internat. Rev. Educn. *Recreations:* painting, gardening. *Address:* La Geneste, Rose Hill, Burnham, Bucks. *T:* Burnham 4242.

WALLACE; see Hope-Wallace.

WALLACE, family name of **Baroness Dudley** and **Barons Wallace of Campsie** and **Wallace of Coslany.**

WALLACE OF CAMPSIE, Baron *cr* 1974 (Life Peer), of Newlands, Glasgow; **George Wallace,** JP; DL; President, Wallace, Cameron (Holdings) Ltd, since 1977; Director, Smith & Nephew Associated Companies Ltd, 1973-77; *b* 13 Feb. 1915; *s* of John Wallace and Mary Pollock; *m* 1977, Irene Alice Langdon Phipps, *er d* of Ernest Phipps, Glasgow. *Educ:* Queen's Park Secondary Sch., Glasgow; Glasgow Univ. Estd Wallace, Cameron & Co. Ltd, 1948, Chm., 1950-77. Solicitor to the Supreme Courts, 1950-; Hon. Sheriff at Hamilton, 1971-. Chm., E Kilbride and Stonehouse Develt Corp., 1969-75. Pres., Glasgow Chamber of Commerce, 1974-76; Vice-Pres., Scottish Assoc. of Youth Clubs, 1971-; Chm., Adv. Bd (Glasgow) Salvation Army, 1972-; Mem. Court, Univ. of Strathclyde, 1973-74; Hon. Pres., Town and Country Planning Assoc. (Scottish Sect.), 1969-; Chm., Scottish Exec. Cttee, Brit. Heart Foundn, 1973-76; Chm., Britannia Cttee, British Sailors' Soc., 1967-77. FRSA 1970; FInstM 1968; MBIM 1969. JP 1968, DL 1971, Glasgow. KStJ 1976. *Recreation:* reading. *Address:* 14 Fernleigh Road, Newlands, Glasgow G43 2UE. *T:* 041-637 3337. *Clubs:* Caledonian; Royal Scottish Automobile (Glasgow).

WALLACE OF COSLANY, Baron *cr* 1974 (Life Peer), of Coslany in the City of Norwich; **George Douglas Wallace;** a Lord in Waiting (Government Whip), since 1977; *b* 18 April 1906; *e s* of late George Wallace, Cheltenham Spa, Gloucestershire; *m* 1932, Vera Randall, Guildford, Surrey; one *s* one *d*. *Educ:* Central School, Cheltenham Spa. Mem. of Management Cttee, in early years, of YMCA at East Bristol and Guildford; Mem. Chislehurst-Sidcup UDC, 1937-46; has been Divisional Sec. and also Chm., Chislehurst Labour Party; also Chm. of Parks and Cemeteries Cttee of UDC, Schools Manager and Member of Chislehurst, Sidcup and Orpington Divisional Education Executive; Mem., Cray Valley and Sevenoaks Hosp. Management Cttee; Chm., House Cttee, Queen Mary's Hosp.; Vice-Chm., Greenwich and Bexley AHA, 1974-77. Joined Royal Air Force, reaching rank of Sergeant. Served in No 11 Group Fighter Command, 1941-45. MP (Lab) Chislehurst Div. of Kent, 1945-50; Junior Govt Whip, 1947-50; MP (Lab) Norwich North, Oct. 1964-Feb. 1974; PPS: to Lord President of the Council, Nov. 1964-65; to Sec. of State for Commonwealth Affairs, 1965; to Minister of State, Min. of Housing and Local Govt, 1967-68; Mem. Speaker's Panel of Chairmen, 1970-74; Delegate to Council of Europe and WEU, 1975-. Member: Labour Parly Assoc. and Transport and General Workers' Union; Commonwealth Parly Assoc.; Commonwealth War Graves Commn, 1970-; Kent CC, 1952-57. *Recreations:* interested in Youth Movements and social welfare schemes. *Address:* 44 Shuttle Close, Sidcup, Kent. *T:* 01-300 3634.

WALLACE, Very Rev. Alexander Ross; Dean of Exeter, 1950-60, retired; *b* 27 Sept. 1891; *s* of late Maj.-Gen. Sir Alexander Wallace, KCB; *m* 1915, Winifred, *d* of late Rev. H. C. Sturges; two *s* two *d*. *Educ:* Clifton Coll. (Scholar); Corpus Christi Coll., Cambridge (Scholar). Classical Tripos, 1913, Class II, Div. I; entered ICS, 1914; served in the IARO att. 17th Cavalry; Special Service Officer, Patiala I. S. Lancers; retired from ICS, 1922; Asst Master and Tutor, Wellington Coll., Berks; Headmaster, Cargilfield School, Edinburgh, 1925-30; Blundell's School, Tiverton, 1930-33; Sherborne School, 1934-July 1950; ordained Deacon, 1938; Priest, 1939. Canon and Prebendary of Salisbury Cathedral, 1942-50. *Publications:* The Three Pillars, 1940; Conversation about Christianity, 1946; Christian Focus, 1956. *Recreations:* golf, fishing. *Address:* c/o I. A. Wallace, Steeple Close, Hindon, Salisbury, Wilts.
See also I. A. Wallace.

WALLACE, Charles William, CVO 1975; Ambassador to Paraguay, since 1976; *b* 19 Jan. 1926; *s* of Percival Francis and Julia Wallace; *m* 1957, Gloria Regina de Ros Ribas (*née* Sanz-Agero); two step *s*. *Educ:* privately and abroad. HM Foreign (later Diplomatic) Service, 1949; served: Asuncion; Barcelona; Bari; Bahrain; Tegucigalpa; Guatemala; Panama; Foreign Office; Baghdad; Buenos Aires; Montevideo; FO, later FCO, Asst Head of American Dept; Counsellor 1969; Rome and

Milan; Mexico City. Order of Aztec Eagle, 1975. *Recreations:* sailing, fishing. *Address:* c/o Foreign and Commonwealth Office, SW1A 2AH; 17 Old Court House, Old Court Place, W8. *Club:* Travellers'.

WALLACE, Col the Hon. Clarence, CBE 1946; CD; LLD; Lieutenant-Governor of British Columbia, Canada, 1950-55; *b* 22 June 1894; *s* of Alfred Wallace and Eliza E. Wallace (*née* Underhill), both of Vancouver, BC; *m* 1916, Charlotte Hazel (*d* 1974), *d* of Edward Chapman, Vancouver, BC; two *s* (and one *s* killed on active service, RCAF, 1942; one *s* decd 1956); *m* 1975, Hilda Ernestine McLennan. *Educ:* St Andrews Coll., Toronto, Ontario. Served overseas as Private, 5th Bn, 1914-16; Hon. Col BC Regt (Duke of Connaught's Own Rifles), 13th Armd Regt. Director of companies; Hon. Member of Council, Canadian Industrial Preparedness Association. KStJ 1951. *Recreations:* shooting, golf. *Address:* Plaza del Mar, 1575 Beach Avenue, Vancouver 5, BC, Canada. *T:* MU-2-2300. *Clubs:* Vancouver, Royal Vancouver Yacht, Vancouver Rowing, Capilano Golf (Vancouver); Union (Victoria); Washington Athletic (Seattle).

WALLACE, David Mitchell, OBE 1942; MS, FRCS; Professor of Urology, Riyadh Medical School, Saudi Arabia; *b* 8 May 1913; *s* of F. David Wallace and M. I. F. Wallace; *m* 1940, Noel Wilson; one *s* three *d*. *Educ:* Mill Hill; University Coll., London, BSc 1934; MB, BS 1938; FRCS 1939; MS 1948. Served War of 1939-45, Wing Comdr, RAF (despatches). Hunterian Prof., Royal Coll. of Surgeons, London, 1956. Formerly: Surgeon, St Peter's Hospital; Urologist, Royal Marsden Hospital, Chelsea Hospital for Women, and Manor House Hospitals; Lecturer, Institute of Urology; Adviser on Cancer to WHO. Mem., Amer. Radium Soc., 1968. *Publications:* Tumours of the Bladder, 1957; contrib. to Cancer, British Jl of Urology, Proc. Royal Soc. Med. *Recreations:* cine photography, pistol shooting. *Address:* Box 2925, Medical School, Riyadh, Saudi Arabia.

WALLACE, Doreen, (Mrs D. E. A. Rash), MA; novelist; *b* 18 June 1897; *d* of R. B. Agnew Wallace and Mary Elizabeth Peebles; *m* 1922, Rowland H. Rash (*d* 1977), Wortham, Suffolk; one *s* two *d*. *Educ:* Malvern Girls' College; Somerville College, Oxford. Honours in English 1919; taught English in a grammar school for three years, then married; first novel published, 1931. *Publications:* -Esques (with E. F. A. Geach), 1918; A Little Learning; The Gentle Heart; The Portion of the Levites; Creatures of an Hour; Even Such is Time; Barnham Rectory, 1934; Latter Howe, 1935; So Long to Learn 1936; Going to the Sea, 1936; Old Father Antic, 1937; The Faithful Compass, 1937; The Time of Wild Roses, 1938; A Handful of Silver, 1939; East Anglia, 1939; The Spring Returns, 1940; English Lakeland, 1941; Green Acres, 1941; Land from the Waters, 1944; Carlotta Green, 1944; The Noble Savage, 1945; Billy Potter, 1946; Willow Farm, 1948; How Little We Know, 1949; Only One Life, 1950; (non-fiction) In a Green Shade, 1950; Norfolk (with R. Bagnall-Oakeley), 1951; Root of Evil, 1952; Sons of Gentlemen, 1953; The Younger Son, 1954; Daughters, 1955; The Interloper, 1956; The Money Field, 1957; Forty Years on, 1958; Richard and Lucy, 1959; Mayland Hall, 1960; Lindsay Langton and Wives, 1961; Woman with a Mirror, 1963; The Mill Pond, 1966; Ashbury People, 1968; The Turtle, 1969; Elegy, 1970; An Earthly Paradise, 1971; A Thinking Reed, 1973; Changes and Chances, 1975; Landscape with Figures, 1976. *Recreations:* painting, gardening. *Address:* Wortham Manor, Diss, Norfolk.

WALLACE, Sir Gordon, Kt 1968; President, Court of Appeal, New South Wales, 1966-70; Acting Chief Justice of New South Wales, Oct. 1968-Feb. 1969; *b* 22 Jan. 1900; *s* of A. C. Isaacs, Sydney; *m* 1927, Marjorie, *d* of A. E. Mullins, Chepstow, Mon.; one *s* one *d*. *Educ:* Sydney High School; RMC Duntroon; Sydney University. Lt, Australian Staff Corps; AMF and AIF, 1939-44 (Col). KC 1940. Judge of Supreme Court, NSW, 1960-70. Pres., NSW Bar Assoc., 1957-58; Vice-Pres., Australian Law Council, 1957; Pres., Internat. Law Assoc., Aust. Br., 1959-65. Mem., Commonwealth Commn of Enquiry into Income Tax, 1952-53. Chm., Royal Commn on Great Barrier Reef Petroleum Drilling, 1970-74. *Publications:* (jtly with Sir Percy Spender) Company Law, 1937; (jtly with J. McI. Young, QC) Australian Company Law, 1965. *Recreations:* bowls, music. *Address:* 6 Lynwood Avenue, Killara, NSW 2071, Australia. *T:* 498 1818. *Clubs:* University, Pioneers (Sydney); Elanora Country.

WALLACE, Ian Alexander; JP; Headmaster, Canford School, 1961-76; *b* 5 Oct. 1917; *s* of Very Rev. A. R. Wallace, *qv*; *m* 1947, Janet Glossop; two *s* two *d*. *Educ:* Clifton; Corpus Christi College, Cambridge (open scholar). Classical Tripos, Part I, 1st Cl.; Theological Tripos Part I, 2nd Cl. Div. One. Served War of 1939-45, Mountain Artillery, NW Frontier, India, 1941; School of Artillery, India, 1942-43; Arakan, 1944; Mandalay, 1945 (despatches). Rossall School: Assistant Master, 1946;

Housemaster, 1951-61. SW Regional Sec., Independent Schools Careers Organisation, 1976-. Governor: Portsmouth Grammar Sch., 1977; King's Sch., Bruton, 1977. JP Poole Borough, 1966. *Address:* Steeple Close, Hindon, Salisbury, Wilts.

WALLACE, Ian Bryce; singer, actor and broadcaster; *b* London, 10 July 1919; *o s* of late Sir John Wallace, Kirkcaldy, Fife (onetime MP for Dunfermline), and of Mary Bryce Wallace (*née* Temple), Glasgow; *m* 1948, Patricia Gordon Black, Edenwood, Cupar, Fife; one *s* one *d. Educ:* Charterhouse; Trinity Hall, Cambridge (MA). Served War of 1939-45, (invalided from) RA, 1944. London stage debut in The Forrigan Reel, Sadlers Wells, 1945. Opera debut, as Schaunard, in La Bohème, with New London Opera Co., Cambridge Theatre, London, 1946. Sang principal roles for NLOC, 1946-49, incl. Dr Bartolo in Il Barbiere di Siviglia. Glyndebourne debut, Masetto, Don Giovanni, Edin. Fest., 1948. Regular appearances as principal *buffo* for Glyndebourne, both in Sussex and at Edin. Fest., 1948-61, incl. perfs as Don Magnifico in La Cenerentola, at Berlin Festwoche, 1954. Italian debut: Masetto, Don Giovanni, at Parma, 1950; also Don Magnifico, La Cenerentola, Rome, 1955, Dr Bartolo, Il Barbiere di Siviglia, Venice, 1956, and Bregenz Fest., 1964-65. Regular appearances for Scottish Opera, 1965-, incl. Leporello in Don Giovanni, Don Pasquale, Welsh Nat. Opera, 1967, Dr Dulcamara, L'Elisir d'Amore, Glyndebourne Touring Opera, 1968. Devised, wrote and presented three series of adult education programmes on opera, entitled Singing For Your Supper, for Scottish Television (ITV), 1967-70. Recordings include: Gilbert and Sullivan Operas with Sir Malcolm Sargent, and humorous songs by Flanders and Swann. Theatrical career includes: a Royal Command Variety Perf., London Palladium, 1952; Cesar in Fanny, Theatre Royal, Drury Lane, 1956; Toad in Toad of Toad Hall, Queen's, 1964. Regular broadcaster, 1944-: radio and TV, as singer, actor and compere: a regular panellist on radio musical quiz game, My Music. Principal concert activity, An Evening With Ian Wallace. *Publication:* Promise Me You'll Sing Mud (autobiog.), 1975. *Recreations:* golf, elementary sailing, photography; singing a song about a hippopotamus to children of all ages. *Address:* 18 Denewood Road, Highgate, N6 4AJ. *T:* 01-340 5802. *Clubs:* Garrick, MCC; Stage Golfing Society.

WALLACE, Ian James, CBE 1971 (OBE 1942); Director, Wraxall Hydraulics Ltd; Chairman, SNR (Bearings) UK Ltd; *b* 25 Feb. 1916; *s* of John Madder Wallace, CBE; *m* 1942, Catherine Frost Mitchell, *e d* of Cleveland S. Mitchell; one *s* one *d. Educ:* Uppingham Sch.; Jesus Coll., Cambridge (BA). Underwriting at Lloyd's, 1935-39. War Service, Fleet Air Arm: Cmdr (A) RNVR, 1939-46. Harry Ferguson Ltd from 1947: Dir 1950; later Massey Ferguson Ltd, Dir Holdings Board until 1970. Commercial consultant, TRW Valves Ltd; Chm., Coventry Cons. Assoc., 1968- (Treas., 1956-68); Chm., W Midlands Cons. Council, 1967-70 (Treas., 1962-67); Pres., W Midlands Area Cons. Council. Member: Severn-Trent Water Authy; W Midlands Econ. Planning Council, 1965-75; Vice-Chm., Midland Regional Council, CBI, 1964, Chm., 1967-69; Pres., Coventry Chamber of Commerce, 1972-74. *Recreations:* flying, golf, shooting (rifle and game). *Address:* Bridge House, Hunningham, Leamington Spa, Warwicks. *T:* Marton 632282. *Clubs:* Carlton, Naval and Military.

WALLACE, Ian Norman Duncan, QC 1973; *b* 21 April 1922; *s* of late Duncan Gardner Wallace, HBM Crown Advocate in Egypt, Paymaster-Comdr RNR and Eileen Agnes Wallace. *Educ:* Loretto; Oriel Coll., Oxford (MA). Served War of 1939-45: Ordinary Seaman RN, 1940; Lieut RNVR, 1941-46. Called to Bar, Middle Temple, 1948; Western Circuit, 1949. Vis. Scholar, Berkeley Univ., Calif., 1977. *Publications:* (ed) Hudson on Building and Civil Engineering Contracts, 8th edn 1959, 9th edn 1965 and 10th edn 1970; Building and Civil Engineering Standard Forms, 1969; Further Building and Engineering Standard Forms, 1973; The International Civil Engineering Contract, 1974; contrib. Law Qly Review, Jl of Internat. Law and Commerce. *Recreations:* keeping fit, foreign travel. *Address:* 53 Holland Park, W11 3RS. *T:* 01-727 7640. *Clubs:* Lansdowne, Hurlingham.

WALLACE, Irving; free-lance author; *b* 19 March 1916; *s* of Alexander Wallace and Bessie (*née* Liss); *m* 1941, Sylvia Kahn Wallace; one *s* one *d. Educ:* Kenosha (Wisc.) Central High Sch.; Williams Inst., Berkeley, Calif.; Los Angeles City College. Served USAAF and US Army Signal Corps, 1942-46. Magazine writer, Saturday Evening Post, Reader's Digest, Collier's, etc., 1931-54; film scenarist, 1955-58, Exploration: Honduras jungles, Wisconsin Collegiate Expedn, 1934-35. Member: PEN; Soc. of Authors; Authors League of America. Supreme Award of Merit, George Washington Carver Memorial Inst., Washington, DC, 1964; Commonwealth Club of Calif. Lit. Award for 1964; Nat.

Bestsellers Inst. Paperback of the Year Award, 1965; Popular Culture Assoc. Award, 1974. *Publications:* The Fabulous Originals, 1955; The Square Pegs, 1957; The Fabulous Showman, 1959; The Sins of Philip Fleming, 1959; The Chapman Report, 1960; The Twenty-Seventh Wife, 1961; The Prize, 1962; The Three Sirens, 1963; The Man, 1964; The Sunday Gentleman, 1965; The Plot, 1967; The Writing of One Novel, 1968; The Seven Minutes, 1969; The Nympho and Other Maniacs, 1971; The Word, 1972; The Fan Club, 1974; The People's Almanac, 1975; The R Document, 1976; The Book of Lists, 1977; The Two, 1978; The People's Almanac II, 1978; contribs to Collier's Encyclopædia, American Oxford Encyclopædia, Encyclopædia Britannica. *Relevant publication:* Irving Wallace: a writer's profile, 1974. *Recreations:* tennis and table tennis, hiking, billiards, travel abroad, collecting autographs, French Impressionist art, canes. *Address:* c/o Paul Gitlin, Counsellor at Law, 7 West 51st Street, New York, NY 10019, USA.

WALLACE, Air Cdre James, DSO 1944; MVO 1962; DFC 1942; AFC 1953; *b* 28 July 1918; *s* of late Frederick George Wallace and late Isobel May (*née* Wickham), Limerick, Ireland; *m* 1948, Irene Maria (*née* Heilbuth), Copenhagen (marr. diss. 1971); one *s* one *d. Educ:* Mountjoy School; Limerick, Ireland. Joined RAF, 1938; served in: Middle East, 1939-41; Desert Air Force, 1941-43; psa 1942; Italy, 1943-44; NE Europe, 1944-48; Fighter Comd, OC 41 Sqdn, 1949-51; Fighter Comd, Duxford wing, 1951-53; jssc 1953; British Joint Staff, Washington, DC, 1954-56; NATO (France), 1956-58; Fighter Comd, 1958-60; Deputy Capt. The Queen's Flight, 1960-63; Director of Public Relations (RAF), Ministry of Defence, 1964-67; retired. Spitfire Productions Ltd, 1967-70; Director, Promotor (Europe) Ltd, 1970-73. Area Warden, Wilts Nat. Trust, 1974-75. Walsh Security Service, London Hilton, 1976-77. Légion d'Honneur, Croix de Guerre (French), 1945. *Recreations:* military history, swimming, walking. *Address:* c/o National Westminster Bank, 14 Minster Street, Salisbury, Wilts. *Clubs:* London Irish Rugby, Lord's Taverners'.

WALLACE, Air Vice-Marshal John Brown, CB 1963; OBE 1945; RAF retired; Deputy Director-General of Medical Services, Royal Air Force, 1961-66; *b* 4 Sept. 1907; *s* of late James Wallace, Cambuslang, near Glasgow; *m* 1937, Gwendolen Mary Shorthouse; two *d. Educ:* Hamilton Academy; Glasgow University. MB, ChB (Glasgow), 1931, MD (Glasgow), 1940. Joined RAF, 1935; served in Southern Rhodesia, 1941-45. Dep. Principal MO, Coastal Command, 1950, appointment in USA, 1950-54; Dep. Principal MO, Home Command, 1955; Principal MO: Fighter Command, 1958; Near East Air Force (Cyprus), 1961. QHS, 1962-66. *Recreation:* gardening. *Address:* 3 Wakehams Hill, Pinner, Mddx. *T:* 01-866 8345.

WALLACE, Lawrence James, OC 1972; Agent-General for British Columbia in the United Kingdom and Europe, since Aug. 1977; *b* Victoria, BC, Canada, 24 April 1913; *s* of John Wallace and Mary Wallace (*née* Parker); *m* 1942, Lois Leeming; three *d. Educ:* Univ. of British Columbia (BA); Univ. of Washington, USA (MEd). Served War, Lt-Comdr, Royal Canadian Navy Voluntary Reserve, 1941-45. Joined British Columbia Govt, as Dir of Community Programmes and Adult Educn, 1953; apptd Dep. Provincial Sec., 1959; Dep. to Premier, 1969-72. General Chairman: four centennial celebrations, marking founding of Crown Colony of British Columbia in 1858, union of Crown Colonies of Vancouver Is. and British Columbia, 1866, Canadian Confedn, 1867, and joining into confedn by British Columbia in 1871. Past Chm., Inter-Provincial Lottery Corp., Queen Elizabeth II Schol. Cttee, and Nancy Green Schol. Cttee; Hon. Trustee, British Columbia Sports Hall of Fame. Director: Duke of Edinburgh Awards Cttee; BC Forest Museum; Adv. Bd, Salvation Army; Canadian Council of Christians and Jews. Canadian Centennial Medal, 1967; Comdr Brother, OStJ, 1969. Named British Columbia Man of the Year, 1958, and Greater Vancouver Man of the Year, 1967; City of Victoria Citizenship Award, 1971; Hon. Member: BC High Sch. Basketball Assoc.; BC Recreation Assoc. Hon. Chief: Alberni, Gilford and Southern Vancouver Is Indian Bands. *Recreations:* gardening, community activities. *Address:* Agent-General for British Columbia, 1 Regent Street, SW1Y 4NS.

WALLACE, Sir Martin (Kelso), Kt 1963; *b* 3 May 1898; *s* of William Henry and Mary May Wallace; *m* 1926, Eileen Bertha (*née* Marshall), OBE, BA, LLB, HDipEd. *Educ:* Methodist College, Belfast. Served RNVR European War, 1914-18 (General Service and Victory Medals). High Sheriff, 1960, Lord Mayor, 1961-63, Belfast. Rep. Windsor Ward as Councillor, later Alderman, in Belfast Corporation, for 19 years. Served on various boards, hospital cttees, etc. *Recreation:* angling.

Address: 23 Cranmore Avenue, Belfast, Northern Ireland BT9 6JH. *T:* Belfast 665531.

WALLACE, Robert, CBE 1970; BL; JP; Chairman, Highland Health Board, since 1973; *b* 20 May 1911; *s* of late John Wallace, Glespin, Lanarkshire, and late Elizabeth Brydson; *m* 1940, Jane Maxwell, *d* of late John Smith Rankin, Waulkmill, Thornhill, Dumfriesshire and late Jane Maxwell; no *c. Educ:* Sanquhar Sch.; Glasgow University. Solicitor 1932; BL (Dist.) 1933. Private legal practice, 1932-40; Depute Town Clerk, Ayr Burgh, 1940-44; Civil Defence Controller, Ayr Burgh, 1941-44; Depute County Clerk and Treas., Co. Inverness, 1944-48; County Clerk, Treasurer and Collector of the County of Inverness, 1948-73; Temp. Sheriff, Grampian, Highland and Islands, 1976-. Hon. Sheriff at Inverness, 1967-. JP Co. Inverness, 1951-. *Recreations:* fishing, gardening, walking. *Address:* Eildon, 29 Old Edinburgh Road, Inverness IV2 3HJ. *T:* Inverness 31969. *Clubs:* Royal Commonwealth Society; Caledonian (Edinburgh).

WALLACE, Walter Ian James, CMG 1957; OBE 1943; retired; *b* 18 Dec. 1905; *e s* of late David Wallace, Sandgate, Kent; *m* 1940, Olive Mary (*d* 1973), 4th *d* of late Col Charles William Spriggs, Southsea; no *c. Educ:* Bedford Modern School; St Catharine's College, Cambridge. Entered ICS 1928, posted to Burma; Dep. Commissioner, 1933; Settlement Officer, 1934-38; Dep. Commissioner, 1939-42; Defence Secretary, 1942-44; Military Administration of Burma (Col and Dep. Director Civil Affairs), 1944-45 (despatches); Commissioner, 1946; Chief Secretary, 1946-47. Joined Colonial Office, 1947, Asst Sec., 1949-62; Asst Under-Sec. of State, 1962-66, retired. *Publication:* Revision Settlement Operations in the Minbu District of Upper Burma, 1939. *Recreation:* local history. *Address:* 61 Windfield, Leatherhead, Surrey. *T:* Leatherhead 4022. *Club:* East India, Devonshire, Sports and Public Schools.

WALLACE, Walter Wilkinson, CBE 1973 (OBE 1964); DSC 1944; Governor, British Virgin Islands, since 1974; *b* 23 Sept. 1923; *s* of late Walter Wallace and of Helen Wallace (*née* Douglas); *m* 1955, Susan Blanche, *d* of Brig. F. W. B. Parry, CBE; one *s* one *d. Educ:* George Heriot's, Edinburgh. Served War, Royal Marines, 1942-46 (Captain). Joined Colonial Service, 1946; Asst Dist Comr, Sierra Leone, 1948; Dist Comr, 1954; seconded to Colonial Office, 1955-57; Sen. Dist Comr, 1961; Provincial Comr, 1961; Develt Sec., 1962-64; Estabt Sec., Bahamas, 1964-67; Sec. to Cabinet, Bermuda, 1968-73; HM Commissioner, Anguilla, 1973. *Recreation:* golf. *Address:* Government House, Tortola, British Virgin Islands; Becketts, Itchenor, Sussex. *T:* Birdham 512438. *Club:* Army and Navy.

WALLACE, William, CMG 1961; Assistant Comptroller of Patent Office and Industrial Property and Copyright Department, Department of Trade and Industry (formerly Board of Trade (Patent Office)), 1954-73, retired; *b* 8 July 1911; *s* of A. S. Wallace, Wemyss Bay, Renfrewshire; *m* 1940, Sheila, *d* of Sydney Hopper, Wallington, Surrey; one *s* two *d. Educ:* Mill Hill School; St Edmund Hall, Oxford. Barrister, Inner Temple, 1936-39. Served War of 1939-45, Royal Artillery with final rank of Major. Board of Trade legal staff, 1945-54. UK Delegate, Internat. Confs on Copyright and Patents; Chm. Intergovernmental Cttee on Rights of Performers, Record Makers and Broadcasting Orgns, 1967-69; Actg Chairman: Intergovernmental Copyright Cttee, 1970; Exec. Cttee, Berne Copyright Union, 1970; Vice-Chm., Whitford Cttee on Copyright and Designs, 1974. Jean Geiringer Meml Lectr, USA, 1971. *Address:* Weavers, Capel, Surrey. *T:* Dorking 711205. *Clubs:* Athenæum, Old Millhillians.

WALLACE-HADRILL, Prof. John Michael, DLitt; FBA 1969; Chichele Professor of Modern History, and Fellow of All Souls College, Oxford, since 1974; *b* 29 Sept. 1916; *e s* of late Frederic and Norah Wallace-Hadrill, Bromsgrove, Worcs; *m* 1950, Anne, *e d* of late Neville Wakefield, DSO, and of Violet Wakefield (*née* Dewar); two *s. Educ:* Cheltenham College; Corpus Christi College, Oxford (Scholar, and Fellow). Lothian Prize, 1938. Served War of 1939-45, (latterly Major, Gen. Staff, attached to a dept of Foreign Office). Fellow and Tutor, 1947-55, Sen. Res. Fellow, 1961-74, Sub-Warden, 1964-66, Merton Coll., Oxford; Professor of Mediæval History, University of Manchester, 1955-61; Editor, English Historical Review, 1965-74. Lectures: Ford's, Oxford, 1969-70; Birkbeck, Cambridge, 1973-74; Stenton, Reading, 1974; Prothero, RHistS, 1974; Raleigh, British Acad., 1978. Delegate, Oxford Univ. Press, 1971-. Vice-Pres., Royal Hist. Soc., 1973-76; Publications Sec., British Academy, 1978-. Hon. Fellow, Merton Coll., Oxford, 1974. *Publications:* The Barbarian West, 400-1000, 1952; (with J. McManners) France, Government and Society, 1957; The Chronicle of Fredegar, 1960; The Long-Haired Kings, 1962; Early Germanic Kingship, 1971; Early Medieval History, 1976. *Address:* All Souls College, Oxford. *Club:* Athenæum.

WALLEN, Ella Kathleen, MA (Oxon); Headmistress, St Mary's School, Wantage, since April 1977; *b* 15 Feb. 1914. *Educ:* Camden School for Girls; St Hugh's College, Oxford. History Mistress, Queen Victoria High School, Stockton-on-Tees, 1937-41; Senior History Mistress, High School for Girls, Gloucester, 1942-59; Headmistress: Queen Victoria High School, Stockton-on Tees, 1959-65; Bedford High Sch., 1965-76. *Address:* St Mary's School Wantage, Oxon OX12 8BZ.

WALLER, Rt. Hon. Sir George (Stanley), PC 1976; Kt 1965; OBE 1945; **Rt. Hon. Lord Justice Waller;** a Lord Justice of Appeal, since 1976; *b* 3 Aug. 1911; *s* of late James Stanley and late Ann Waller; *m* 1936, Elizabeth Margery, *d* of 1st Baron Hacking; two *s* one *d. Educ:* Oundle; Queens' Coll., Cambridge (Hon. Fellow 1974). Called to the Bar, Gray's Inn, 1934, Bencher, 1961. RAFO, 1931-36; served War of 1939-45, in RAFVR, Coastal Command; 502 Sqdn, 1940-41; Wing Comdr, 1943 (despatches). Chm., Northern Dist Valuation Bd, 1948-55; QC 1954; Recorder of Doncaster, 1953-54, of Sunderland, 1954-55, of Bradford, 1955-57, of Sheffield, 1957-61, and of Leeds, 1961-65; a Judge of the High Court, Queen's Bench Div., 1965-76; Presiding Judge, NE Circuit, 1973-76. Solicitor-General of the County Palatine of Durham, 1957-61; Attorney-General of the County Palatine of Durham, 1961-65; Member: Criminal Injuries Compensation Board, 1964-65; General Council of the Bar, 1958-62 and 1963-65; Parole Bd, 1969-72 (Vice-Chm., 1971-72); Adv. Council on the Penal System, 1970-73 and 1974-; Criminal Law Revision Cttee, 1977; Chm., Policy Adv. Cttee, 1977-. *Address:* Hatch Hill, Kingsley Green, near Haslemere, Surrey. *T:* Haslemere 4629. *Clubs:* Army and Navy; Hawks (Cambridge).

WALLER, Sir (John) Keith, Kt 1968; CBE 1961 (OBE 1957); Secretary, Department of Foreign Affairs, Canberra, 1970-74, retired; *b* 19 Feb. 1914; *s* of late A. J. Waller, Melbourne; *m* 1943, Alison Irwin Dent; two *d. Educ:* Scotch Coll., Melbourne; Melbourne Univ. Entered Dept of External Affairs, Australia, 1936; Private Sec. to Rt Hon. W. M. Hughes, 1937-40; Second Sec., Australian Legation, Chungking, 1941; Sec.-Gen., Australian Delegn, San Francisco Conf., 1945; First Sec., Australian Legation, Rio de Janeiro, 1945; Chargé d'Affaires, 1946; First Sec., Washington, 1947; Consul-Gen., Manila, 1948; Officer-in-Charge, Political Intelligence Div., Canberra, 1950; External Affairs Officer, London, 1951; Asst Sec., Dept of External Affairs, Canberra, 1953-57; Ambassador to Thailand, 1957-60; Ambassador to USSR, 1960-62; First Asst Sec., Dept of External Affairs, 1963-64; Ambassador to US, 1964-70. Member: Australian Council for the Arts, 1973; Interim Film Board, 1974. Chm., Radio Australia Inquiry, 1975. *Address:* 17 Canterbury Crescent, Deakin, ACT 2600, Australia. *Club:* Commonwealth (Canberra).

WALLER, Sir John Stanier, 7th Bt, *cr* 1815; author, poet, and journalist; *b* 27 July 1917; *s* of Capt. Stanier Edmund William Waller (*d* 1923), and of Alice Amy (who *m* 2nd, 1940, Gerald H. Holiday), *d* of J. W. Harris, Oxford; *S kinsman* Sir Edmund Waller, 6th Bt, 1954; *m* 1974, Anne Eileen Mileham. *Educ:* Weymouth Coll.; Worcester Coll., Oxford (BA). Founder-Editor of Quarterly, Kingdom Come, first new literary magazine of war, 1939-41. Served 1940-46 with RASC (in Middle East, 1941-46); Adjt RASC, HQ, Cairo Area; Capt. 1942; Features Editor, Brit. Min. of Inf., Middle East, 1943-45; Chief Press Officer, Brit. Embassy, Bagdad, 1945; News and Features Editor, MIME, Cairo, 1945-46. Dramatic Critic Cairo Weekly, The Sphinx, 1943-46; Founder-Mem. Salamander Soc. of Poets, Cairo, 1942; lectured in Pantheon Theatre, Athens, 1945; Greenwood Award for Poetry, 1947; Keats Prize, 1974; FRSL 1948; Lectr and Tutor in English and Eng. Lit. at Carlisle and Gregson (Jimmy's), Ltd, 1953-54; Asst Master, London Nautical Sch., May-June 1954; Information Officer, Overseas Press Services Div., Central Office of Information, 1954-59. Director: Literature Ltd, 1940-42; Richard Congreve Ltd, 1948-50; Export Trade Ships Ltd, 1956; Bristol Stone and Concrete Ltd, 1974. *Publications:* The Confessions of Peter Pan, 1941; Fortunate Hamlet, 1941; Spring Legend, 1942; The Merry Ghosts, 1946; Middle East Anthology (Editor), 1946; Crusade, 1946; The Kiss of Stars, 1948; The Collected Poems of Keith Douglas (Editor), 1951 and 1966; Shaggy Dog, 1953; Alamein to Zem Zem by Keith Douglas (Editor), 1966; Goldenhair and the Two Black Hawks, 1971. Contrib. to numerous anthologies and periodicals at home and abroad. *Recreations:* portrait photography, teaching. *Heir:* none. *Address:* 99 The Grove, Isleworth, Middlesex. *T:* 01-560 8142.

WALLER, Sir Keith; see Waller, Sir J. K.

WALLER, Sir Robert William, 9th Bt, *cr* 1780, of Newport, Co. Tipperary; employed by the General Electric Co. of America as an Industrial Engineer, since 1957; *b* 16 June 1934; *s* of Sir Roland Edgar Waller, 8th Bt, and Helen Madeline, *d* of Joseph Radl, Matawan, New Jersey, USA; *S* father 1958; is a citizen of the United States; *m* 1960 (marr. diss.); two *s* one *d* (and one *s* decd). *Educ:* St Peter's Prep. Sch.; Newark Coll. of Engrg; Fairleigh Dickinson University. *Heir: s* John Michael Waller, *b* 14 May 1962. *Address:* 5 Lookout Terrace, Lynnfield, Mass 01940, USA.

WALLER, Prof. Ross Douglas, CBE 1958 (MBE 1945); Director of Extra-Mural Studies, 1937-60, and Professor of Adult Education, 1949-66 (Professor Emeritus, 1966), Manchester University; *b* 21 Jan. 1899; *m* 1928, Isobel May Brown; three *s* one *d*. *Educ:* Manchester Central High School for Boys; Manchester University. Served European War, KOYLI, and NF, 1917-19. BA, 1920; MA 1921; post-graduate studies in Florence, 1921-22; Schoolmaster, 1922-24; Lecturer in English Literature, Manchester Univ., 1924-37. Chm. North-Western Dist, WEA, 1943-57; Pres., Educational Centres Association, 1948-65; OECD Consultant on Adult Educn in Sardinia, 1961-62. Cavaliere Ufficiale, Order of Merit, Italy, 1956. *Publications:* The Monks and the Giants, 1926; The Rossetti Family, 1932; Marlowe, Edward II (with H. B. Charlton), 1933; Learning to Live, 1947; Harold Pilkington Turner, 1953; Residential College, 1954; Design for Democracy (Introductory Essay), 1956. Articles in Adult Education, Highway, Times Educational Supplement, etc. *Recreations:* recorder playing, painting, and visiting Italy. *Address:* 46 Appleby Lodge, Wilmslow Road, Manchester M14 6HY. *T:* 061-224 9944.

WALLEY, Francis; Under-Secretary, Director of Civil Engineering Services, Department of the Environment, since 1973; *b* 30 Dec. 1918; *s* of late Reginald M. Walley and Maria M. Walley; *m* 1946, Margaret, *yr d* of late Rev. Thomas and Margaret J. Probert; two *d*. *Educ:* Cheltenham Grammar Sch.; Bristol Univ. MSc, PhD; FICE; FIStructE. Entered Min. of Home Security as Engr, 1941; Min. of Works, 1945; Suptg Civil Engr, 1963; Dep. Dir of Building Develt, 1965; Dir of Estate Management Overseas, 1969; Dir of Post Office Services, 1971. *Publications:* Prestressed Concrete Design and Construction, 1954; (with Dr S. C. C. Bate) A Guide to the Code of Practice CP 115, 1960; several papers to ICE and techn. jls. *Recreations:* gardening, furniture-making. *Address:* 13 Julien Road, Coulsdon, Surrey CR3 2DN. *T:* 01-660 3290.

See also R. P. Probert, Sir John Walley.

WALLEY, Sir John, KBE 1965; CB 1950; retired as Deputy Secretary, Ministry of Social Security, 1966 (Ministry of Pensions and National Insurance, 1958-66); *b* Barnstaple, Devon, 3 April 1906; *e s* of late R. M. Walley; *m* 1934, Elisabeth Mary, *e d* of late R. H. Pinhorn, OBE; two *s* two *d*. *Educ:* Hereford High Sch.; Hereford Cathedral Sch.; Merton Coll., Oxford; Postmaster, 1924-28; Hons Maths and Dip., Pol. and Econ. Sci. Ministry of Labour: Asst Principal, 1929; Sec., Cabinet Cttee on Unemployment, 1932; Principal, 1934; Asst Sec., Min. of Labour and National Service, 1941; Transf. Under-Sec., Min. of National Insurance, 1945; Chm., Dental Benefit Council, 1945-48. Chm., Hampstead Centre, National Trust, 1969-. *Publications:* Social Security-Another British Failure?, 1972; contribs: to The Future of the Social Services, ed Robson and Crick, 1970; on Children's Allowances, in Family Poverty, ed David Bull, 1971; articles in the press on Social Security matters. *Address:* 46 Rotherwick Road, NW11. *T:* 01-455 6528.

See also F. Walley.

WALLINGER, Sir Geoffrey (Arnold), GBE 1963; KCMG 1953 (CMG 1947); *b* 2 May 1903; *s* of late William A. Wallinger, OBE, IFS; *m* 1st, 1939, Diana Peel Nelson; one *s*; 2nd, 1950, Alix de la Faye Lamotte (*d* 1956); 3rd, 1958, Stella Irena, *d* of late Konni Zilliacus. *Educ:* Sherborne; Clare Coll., Cambridge. Entered Diplomatic Service, 1926; Secretary: at Cairo, 1927-29, at Vienna, 1929-31, at Foreign Office, 1931-34; Political Sec. to UK High Comr in S Africa, 1935-38; First Sec., Buenos Aires, 1938-42; First Sec., Foreign Office, 1943; Counsellor in China, 1943-47 (Minister-local rank, 1945); Counsellor in Foreign Office, 1947-49; Minister to Hungary, 1949-51; Ambassador to Thailand, 1951-54; Ambassador to Austria, 1954-58; Ambassador to Brazil, 1958-63; retired from Foreign Service, 1963. Director: Lloyds Bank International, 1972-75; Bank of London and South America, 1963-75. *Address:* 10 Baskerville Road, SW18. *T:* 01-870 4474. *Club:* Brooks's.

WALLINGFORD, Air Cdre Sidney, CB 1951; CBE 1944; RNZAF, retired; *b* 12 July 1898; *s* of late Major Jesse Alfred Wallingford, MC, and Alice Wallingford; *m* 1929, Kathleen Matilda Jamieson; one *s* one *d*. *Educ:* Auckland Grammar Sch., New Zealand. Served European War, 1916-20, with Artists' Rifles, Rifle Brigade, and RAF; First Commissioned, Dec. 1916;

Fiji Constabulary, 1921-23; Royal Air Force, 1924-29; NZ Permanent Air Force, 1929; PSA 1937; NZ Liaison Officer, Air Ministry, 1938-40; Air Force Member for Personnel, Air Dept, Wellington, NZ, 1941-42; RNZAF Staff Officer to Commander Aircraft South Pacific and AOC No. 1 (Islands) Group, RNZAF, 1942-43; AOC Northern Group, RNZAF, 1944; Air Member for Supply at Air Dept, Wellington, NZ, 1945-46; idc 1947; Air Member for Personnel at Air Dept, NZ, 1948-52; AOC HQ Task Force, RNZAF at Hobsonville, Auckland, NZ, 1952-53; retired 1954. Pres. Nat. Rifle Assoc. of NZ, 1954-58. US Legion of Merit (Degree of Officer). *Recreations:* trout fishing, rifle and pistol shooting; winner Queen Mary's Prize at Bisley in 1928; RAF Rifle Championship, 1927, 1929. *Address:* Opito Bay, Whitianga, New Zealand. *Club:* Officers' (Auckland, NZ).

WALLIS, Captain Arthur Hammond, CBE 1952; RN (retired); Chief of Naval Information, Admiralty, 1957-64; *b* 16 Sept. 1903; *s* of late Harold T. Wallis; *m* 1940, Lucy Joyce (*d* 1974), *er d* of late Lt-Col L. E. Becher, DSO; one *s* one *d*. *Educ:* Wixenford; Osborne and Dartmouth. Entered Royal Navy as Cadet, 1917; specialised as Torpedo Officer, 1930; staff of Rear-Adm. Destroyers, 1936-38; Torpedo Officer, HMS Nelson, 1938-41; Comdr, 1941; i/c Torpedo Experimental Dept, HMS Vernon, 1941-43; Exec. Officer, HMS Illustrious, 1943-45; Captain, 1947; in command HM Underwater Detection Establishment at Portland, 1948-50; Sen. Naval Officer, Persian Gulf and in command HMS Wild Goose, 1950-51; Cdre, HMS Mauritius, 1951; UK Naval Delegate, Military Agency for Standardisation, NATO, 1952-53; Director of Under-water Weapons, Admiralty, 1953-56. Naval ADC to the Queen, 1956. *Recreations:* golf, gardening. *Address:* Compton's Barn, Woodstreet, near Guildford, Surrey. *T:* Normandy 3143. *Clubs:* Naval and Military; Worplesdon Golf.

WALLIS, Sir Barnes (Neville), Kt 1968; CBE 1943; FRS 1945; Hon. DSc Eng London and Bristol; Hon. ScD Cambridge; Hon. DSc Loughborough, Oxford and Heriot-Watt; FICE; Hon. MIMechE; Hon. FRAeS; FRSA; FSE; RDI, 1943; Chief of Aeronautical Research and Development, British Aircraft Corporation Ltd, Weybridge Division, Weybridge, Surrey, 1945-71; *b* 26 Sept. 1887; *s* of Charles George Wallis, BA (Oxon), MRCS, LRCP, and Edith Eyre Ashby; *m* 1925, Mary Frances, *d* of Arthur George Bloxam, FIC; two *s* two *d*. *Educ:* Christ's Hospital. Trained as Marine Engineer at J. S. White & Co. Ltd, Cowes, 1905-1913; Designer, Airship Dept, Vickers Ltd, 1913-15; served European War, Artists' Rifles and RNVR, 1915; Chief Designer, Vickers Ltd, Airship Dept, Barrow-in-Furness, 1916-22; Chief Engineer, Airship Guarantee Co., London and Howden, Yorks, 1923-30; Chief Designer, Structures, Vickers Aviation Ltd, Weybridge, 1930-37; Asst Chief Designer, Vickers-Armstrongs Ltd, Aviation Section, 1937-45. Designer of HMA R100; Inventor of Geodetic Construction; Inventor of weapon which destroyed Moehne and Eder Dams, and penetration bombs, 1940-45; Inventor of Variable Geometry Aircraft. Vice-Pres., Bath Inst. of Medical Engineering, 1968-. Master of Faculty, RDI, 1965-67. Hon. Fellow, Churchill Coll., Cambridge, 1965-; Senior Fellow, RCA, 1966; Hon. Fellow: UMIST; Manchester Coll. Art and Design. Hon. FRAeS 1967; Hon. Life Mem. and Fellow, Inst. of Patentees and Inventors, 1968. Treasurer, Christ's Hosp., and Chm., Council of Almoners, 1957-70. Freeman and Liveryman, Worshipful Co. of Shipwrights and Guild of Air Pilots and Navigators; Freeman of City of London. Founders' Medal, Air League, 1963; Kelvin Gold Medal, ICE, 1968; Albert Medal, RSA, 1968; Royal Medal, Royal Society, 1975. *Publications:* Some Technical Aspects of the Commercial Airship (Lloyd's Register of Shipping, 1925); The Design and Construction of HMA R100; *relevant publication:* Barnes Wallis, by J. E. Morpurgo, 1972. *Address:* White Hill House, Effingham, Surrey. *T:* Bookham 52027. *Clubs:* Athenæum, Royal Air Force.

WALLIS, Claude (Edgar), MBE 1944; retired as Chairman and Managing Director Associated Iliffe Press Ltd (1945-60) and Chairman Kelly's Directories Ltd (1954-60); *b* Madras, India, 21 Jan. 1886; *s* of late Charles and Constance Walder-Wallis. *Educ:* City of Westminster and Emanuel Schools. Associated with motoring journalism for 60 years; joined late Lord Montague in 1905 on staff of Car Illustrated and transf. to Iliffe & Sons Ltd, publishers of The Autocar, Automobile Engineer, and other motoring and aviation journals, 1911; Managing Director Associated Iliffe Press, 1939. Special Reserve of Officers, 1912-20, rank Captain. Served European War: 1st Bn Loyal North Lancashire Regt during retreat from Mons (wounded, prisoner, Sept. 1914; despatches, 1914 Star, GS and Victory Medals); War of 1939-45 (MBE); served on numerous government cttees relating to publishing, paper rationing, etc.;

was instrumental in organising special appeals in motor and other industries which raised £250,000 for BRCS. President: Motor & Cycle Trades Benevolent Fund, 1947-48; Periodical Proprietors Assoc., 1953-56; Fellowship of the Motor Industry. *Recreations:* motoring, sailing. *Address:* 25 Manchester Square, W1. *T:* 01-935 9375. *Clubs:* Royal Automobile; Royal Motor Yacht (Poole).

WALLIS, Frederick Alfred John E.; *see* Emery-Wallis.

WALLIS, Col Hugh Macdonell, OC 1969; DSO 1919; OBE 1945; MC, VD, CD, KCLJ; *b* 7 Dec. 1893; *s* of John McCall Wallis, Peterborough, Ont, and Gertrude Thornton, *d* of Lt-Col Samuel Smith Macdonell, QC, LLD, DCL, Windsor, Ont; *m* 1st, 1935, Leslie (marr. diss., 1953), *d* of late Mr and Mrs K. K. Carson, London; 2nd 1969, Corinne de Boucherville, *widow* of Hon. Jean Desy. *Educ:* Lakefield Preparatory Sch.; Toronto Univ. Enlisted 1st CEF, Sept. 1914; served France, Belgium, Germany, 1915-19; Bde Major 4th Can. Inf. Bde, 1918 (DSO, MC, despatches twice); Colonel Comdg The Black Watch, Royal Highlanders of Canada, then Permanent Active Militia, 1930; VD 1930; CD 1967; R of O, 1931; Hon. ADC to Earl of Bessborough, Gov.-Gen. of Canada, 1931-35; Active Service, Canadian Forces, 1940-45; Colonel Asst DAG Nat. Defence HQ (OBE); Hon. Lt-Col 3rd Bn The Black Watch of Canada, 1961-68. Chartered Accountant, with McDonald, Currie & Co., 1923. Past President: Canadian Citizenship Council, St Andrews Soc. of Montreal, Canadian Club of Montreal, Montreal Museum of Fine Arts. Man. Dir and Pres., Mount Royal Rice Mills Ltd, Montreal, 1924-53. Governor: Canada Cttee, Lakefield College Sch.; Montreal General Hosp.; Montreal Children's Hosp. (Past Chm. of Exec.); l'Hôpital Marie Enfant; Chm., Adv. Bd, Canadian Centenary (1967) Council (past Chm. Org. and Exec. Cttees). Hon. Sponsor, Trent Univ., Ont., 1963; Associate, McGill Univ. and l'Univ. de Montréal. FRSA 1959. Kt Comdr, Order of St Lazarus of Jerusalem. Outstanding Citizen Award, Montreal Citizenship Council, 1967. Canada Centennial Medal, 1967. *Recreations:* travel, fine arts, Canadiana books and history. *Address:* Apartment 505, 3768 Drummond Street, Montreal, PQ, Canada. *Clubs:* Canadian, United Services (Montreal); Braeside Golf (Senneville).

WALLIS, Peter Ralph; Director General Guided Weapons and Electronics, Ministry of Defence, since 1975; *b* 17 Aug. 1924; *s* of Leonard Francis Wallis and Molly McCulloch Wallis (*née* Jones); *m* 1949, Frances Jean Patricia Cowie; three *s* one *d*. *Educ:* University College Sch., Hampstead; Imperial Coll. of Science and Technology, London (BSc(Eng)). Henrici and Siemens Medals of the College, 1944. Joined Royal Naval Scientific Service 1944; work at Admty Signal and Radar Estab. till 1959, Admty Underwater Weapons Estab. till 1968; Asst Chief Scientific Advr (Research), MoD, 1968-71; Dir Gen. Research Weapons, MoD, 1971-75. Marconi Award, IERE, 1964; ACGI, CEng, FIEE, FIMA. *Publications:* articles in Jl of IEE, IERE and Op. Res. Quarterly. *Recreations:* skiing, mountain walking, swimming, tennis, amateur dramatics, gen. Sec., Hampstead Scientific Soc. *Address:* 22 Flask Walk, NW3 1HE.

WALLIS-JONES, Ewan Perrins; His Honour Judge Wallis-Jones; a Circuit Judge (formerly County Court Judge), since 1964; *b* 22 June 1913; *s* of late William James Wallis-Jones, MBE, and late Ethel Perrins Wallis-Jones; *m* 1940, Veronica Mary (*née* Fowler); one *s* two *d*. *Educ:* Mill Hill Sch.; University Coll. of Wales, Aberystwyth; Balliol Coll., Oxford. LLB Hons Wales, 1934; BA Oxon 1936; MA Oxon 1941. Qualified Solicitor, 1935; called to Bar, Gray's Inn, 1938. Chm., Carmarthenshire QS, 1966-71. ARPS. *Recreations:* music, reading and photography. *Address:* 25 Cotham Grove, Bristol BS6 6AN. *T:* Bristol 48908; 28 Quay Street, Carmarthen. *T:* Carmarthen 5106. *Club:* Royal Photographic Society.

WALLIS-KING, Maj.-Gen. Colin Sainthill, CBE 1975 (OBE 1971); Director of Service Intelligence, since 1977; *b* 13 Sept. 1926; *s* of late Lt-Col Frank King, DSO, OBE, 4th Hussars, and of Colline Ammabel, *d* of late Lt-Col C. G. H. St Hill; *m* 1962, Lisabeth, *d* of late Swan Swanstrøm, Oslo, Norway; two *d*. *Educ:* Stowe. Commissioned Coldstream Guards, 1945; Liaison Officer with Fleet Air Arm, 1954; Staff Coll., 1960; Regtl Adjutant, Coldstream Guards, 1961; seconded to Para. Regt, 1963; ACOS HQ Land Norway, 1965; Comdr 2nd Bn Coldstream Guards, 1969; Dep. Comdr 8 Inf. Brigade, 1972; Comdr 3 Inf. Brigade, 1973; BGS Intell., MoD, 1975. *Recreations:* equitation, sailing, music, cross-country skiing. *Address:* Director of Service Intelligence, Ministry of Defence, Whitehall, SW1A 2HB. *Club:* Cavalry and Guards.

WALLOP, family name of **Earl of Portsmouth.**

WALLROCK, John; Chairman, Minet Holdings Ltd, since 1972; *b* 14 Nov. 1922; *s* of Samuel and Marie Kate Wallrock; *m* 1967, Audrey Louise Ariow; two *d*. *Educ:* Bradfield Coll., Berks. Apprentice, Merchant Navy, 1939; Lieut RNR, 1943; Master Mariner, 1949; J. H. Minet & Co. Ltd, 1950, Dir, 1955, Chm., 1972; Underwriting Mem. of Lloyds, 1951. *Recreations:* yachting, shooting. *Address:* Cleeve Lodge, 42 Hyde Park Gate, SW7 5DU. *T:* 01-584 4476. *Clubs:* Boodle's; Royal London Yacht, Royal Southern Yacht.

WALLS, Prof. Eldred Wright; Emeritus Professor of Anatomy in the University of London at Middlesex Hospital Medical School (Dean, Medical School, 1967-74); Hon. Consultant Anatomist, St Mark's Hospital; *b* 17 Aug. 1912; 2nd *s* of late J. T. Walls, Glasgow; *m* 1939, Jessie Vivien Mary Robb, MB, ChB, DPH, *o d* of late R. F. Robb and late M. T. Robb; one *s* one *d*. *Educ:* Hillhead High Sch.; Glasgow Univ. BSc, 1931; MB, ChB (Hons), 1934; MD (Hons), 1947, FRSE, FRCS; Struthers Medal and Prize, 1942. Demonstrator and Lectr in Anatomy, Glasgow Univ., 1935-41; Senior Lectr in Anatomy, University Coll. of S Wales and Monmouthshire, 1941-47; Reader in Anatomy, Middlesex Hospital Medical Sch. 1947-49, S. A. Courtauld Prof. of Anatomy, 1949-74. Past President: Anatomical Soc. of GB and Ireland; Chartered Soc. of Physiotherapy. *Publications:* (co-editor) Rest and Pain (by John Hilton) (6th edn), 1950; (co-author) Sir Charles Bell, His Life and Times, 1958; contrib. Blood-vascular and Lymphatic Systems, to Cunningham's Textbook Anat., 1972; contrib. to Journal of Anatomy, Lancet, etc. *Recreations:* golf and gardening. *Address:* Chesterhall, Ancrum, Jedburgh TD8 6UN. *T:* Ancrum 258. *Club:* MCC.

WALLS, Henry James, BSc, PhD; Director, Metropolitan Police Laboratory, New Scotland Yard, 1964-68; *b* 1907; *s* of late William Walls, RSA, and late Elizabeth Maclellan Walls; *m* 1940, Constance Mary Butler; one *s* one *d*. *Educ:* George Watson's Boys' Coll., Edinburgh; Melville Coll., Edinburgh; Edinburgh Univ. BSc 1930; PhD 1933. Postgrad. research in physical chemistry, Munich, Edinburgh and Bristol, 1930-35; ICI (Explosives), 1935-36; Staff of Metropolitan Police Lab., 1936-46; Staff Chemist, Home Office Forensic Science Lab., Bristol, 1946-58; Director of Home Office Forensic Science Lab., Newcastle upon Tyne, 1958-64. *Publications:* Forensic Science, 1968; (with Alistair Brownlie) Drink, Drugs and Driving, 1969; Expert Witness, 1972; two books on photography; papers in journals dealing with forensic science. *Recreations:* reading, plays and films, talking, people. *Address:* 65 Marmora Road, SE22 0RY.

WALLS, Rev. Brother Roland Charles; Member, Community of the Transfiguration, since 1965; *b* 7 June 1917; *s* of late Roland William Walls and late Tina Josephine Hayward. *Educ:* Sandown Grammar Sch.; Corpus Christi Coll., Cambridge; Kelham Theological Coll. Curate of St James', Crossgates, Leeds, 1940-42; Curate of St Cecilia's, Parson Cross, Sheffield, 1942-45; Licensed preacher, Diocese of Ely, 1945-48; Fellow of Corpus Christi Coll., Cambridge, 1948-62; Lecturer in Theology, Kelham Theological Coll., 1948-51; Chaplain and Dean of Chapel, Corpus Christi Coll., Cambridge, 1952-58; Canon Residentiary, Sheffield Cathedral, 1958-62; Chaplain of Rosslyn Chapel, Midlothian, 1962-68. Examining Chaplain to Bishop of Edinburgh. Lecturer at Coates Hall Theological Coll.; Lecturer in Dogmatics Dept, New Coll., Edinburgh, 1963-74. *Publication:* (contrib.) Theological Word Book (ed A. Richardson), 1950. *Recreations:* walking, music, etc. *Address:* Community House, 23 Manse Road, Roslin, Midlothian.

WALLWORK, John Sackfield; Director, Associated Newspapers Group Ltd, London, since 1973; Managing Director, Northcliffe Newspapers Group Ltd, since 1972 (General Manager, 1967-71); *b* 2 Nov. 1918; *s* of Peter Wallwork and Clara Cawthorne Wallwork; *m* 1945, Bessie Bray; one *s* one *d*. *Educ:* Leigh Grammar Sch., Leigh, Lancs. FCISA. General Manager, Scottish Daily Mail, Edinburgh, 1959-62; Asst Gen. Man., Associated Newspapers Gp Ltd, London, 1962-66; Director of many newspaper companies and of news radio and publishing companies, in the UK. Chm., Press Association Ltd, 1973-74 (Dir, 1969-76); Dir, Reuters Ltd, 1973-76; Member Press Council, 1974-75; Newspaper Society: Mem. Council, 1967-; Jun. Vice-Pres. 1975; Sen. Vice-Pres., 1976, Pres., 1977-. Commander, Order of Merit, Republic of Italy, 1973. *Recreations:* golf, motoring. *Address:* 49 Westbury Road, Northwood, Mddx HA6 3DB. *T:* Northwood 23069. *Clubs:* Wellington, Sandy Lodge Golf (Northwood).

WALLWORTH, Cyril; Assistant Under-Secretary of State, Ministry of Defence, 1964-74; *b* 6 June 1916; *s* of Albert A.

Wallworth and Eva (*née* Taylor); unmarried. *Educ:* Oldham High Sch.; Manchester Univ. BA (Hons) History, 1937. Asst Principal, Admiralty, 1939; Asst Private Secretary to First Lord, 1941-45, Principal, 1943; Asst Secretary, 1951; Under-Secretary, 1964. Gwilym Gibbon Res. Fellow, Nuffield Coll., Oxford, 1975-76. *Recreations:* music, wine, cooking, photography. *Club:* Hurlingham.

WALMESLEY WHITE, Brigadier Arthur, CBE 1972; Planning Inspectorate, Department of the Environment, since 1972; Chairman, Palestine Exploration Fund, since 1973 (Member, Executive Committee, since 1949); *b* 10 Sept. 1917; *s* of late Walter Walmesley White, MA, and late Jessie Beswick; *m* 1951, Jocelyn Mary Beale, *d* of late Captain G. H. Beale, DSO, RN; one *s* three *d*. *Educ:* Eastbourne Coll.; Royal Military Academy; Pembroke Coll., Cambridge (MA). Commissioned, Royal Engineers, 1937; RE Field Units and Staff, 1939-45; Military Survey Staff and Units, 1946-49; Ordnance Survey, 1949-52; School of Military Survey, 1952-56 (Chief Instr, 1954-56); Directorate of Mil. Survey, 1956-59; CO, 42 Survey Engr Regt, Cyprus, 1959-62; Chief Survey Officer, Northern Army Gp/TWOATAF, Germany, 1962-63; Chief Geographic Officer, AFCENT, France, 1963-65; Ordnance Survey, 1965-69 (Dir of Map Publication, 1966-69). Brigadier 1966. Dir of Military Survey, and Chief of Geographical Section, Gen. Staff. MoD, 1969-72; retired, 1972. FRGS (Mem. Council, 1969-72); FRICS; MIOP. *Publications:* various papers on cartographic subjects in learned jls. *Recreations:* gardening, wood-working, hill-walking. *Address:* Old Barton, Whitestone, Exeter, Devon EX4 2LF. *T:* Longdown 232. *Club:* Army and Navy.

WALMSLEY, Arnold Robert, CMG 1963; MBE 1946; HM Diplomatic Service, retired; *b* 29 Aug. 1912; *s* of late Rev. Canon A. M. Walmsley; *m* 1944, Frances Councell de Mouilped. *Educ:* Rossall Sch.; Hertford Coll., Oxford. 1st Class Maths Mods, 1st Class Modern Greats. Private Sec. to Julius Meinl, Vienna, 1935-38; Foreign Office, 1939-45; established in Foreign Service, 1946; Foreign Office, 1946-50; British Consul in Jerusalem, 1950-54; Foreign Office, 1954-63; Head of Arabian Dept, 1961; Counsellor, Khartoum, 1963-65; Dir, Middle East Centre of Arab Studies, Lebanon, 1965-69. *Publications:* (as Nicholas Roland) The Great One, 1967; Natural Causes, 1969; Who Came by Night, 1971. *Address:* Manor Farm, Dunmow Road, Bishop's Stortford, Herts. *Club:* Travellers'.

WALMSLEY, Air Marshal Sir Hugh Sydney Porter, KCB 1952 (CB 1944); KCIE 1947; CBE 1943 (OBE 1937); MC 1918; DFC 1922; *b* 6 June 1898; 3rd *s* of late James Walmsley, Broughton, near Preston; *m* 1928, Audrey Maude, 3rd *d* of late Dr Pim, Sleaford; three *s*. *Educ:* Old Coll., Windermere; Dover Coll. 2nd Lieut, Loyal North Lancs Regt, 1915-16; seconded to RFC 1916; Captain, RFC, 1917; permanent commission RAF 1919 as Flying Officer; Flt Lt, 1921; Sqdn Ldr, 1931; Wing Comdr, 1937; Gp Capt., 1939; Air Cdre, 1942; Air Vice-Marshal, 1943; Acting Air Marshal, 1947-48; Air Marshal, 1949. 55 Sqdn, BEF, 1917-18 (MC); Iraq, 1921-23; OC 33 Sqdn Bicester, 1933-34, 8 Sqdn, Aden, 1935-37; War of 1939-45 (despatches 5 times); OC 71 Wing AASF, 1939-40; OC RAF Station, Scampton, 1940-41; HQ Bomber Command, 1941-42; AOC 91 Group, 1942-43; SASO, HQ Bomber Command, 1944-45; AOC 4 Group, Transport Command, 1945-46; Air Officer, Transport Command, SE Asia, 1946; AOC-in-C, Air HQ, India, 1946-47; Deputy Chief of the Air Staff, 1948-50; AOC-in-C, Flying Training Command, 1950-52; Retired from Active List, 1952. Managing Director of Air Service Training Ltd, 1952-59; Principal of College of Air Training, Hamble, 1960, resigned July 1960. *Recreations:* represented RAF Inter-Service Athletics in 1919, 1924 and 1926; all games; gardening, sailing. *Address:* Upwood, Tiptoe, Lymington, Hants. *Club:* Royal Air Force.

WALMSLEY, Prof. Robert, MD; DSc; FRCPE, FRCSE, FRSE; formerly Bute Professor of Anatomy, University of St Andrews, 1946-73; *b* 24 Aug. 1906; *s* of late Thomas Walmsley, Supt Marine Engr; *m* 1939, Isabel Mary, *e d* of James Mathieson, Aberdeen; two *s*. *Educ:* Greenock Acad.; Univ. of Edinburgh; Carnegie Inst. of Embryology, Baltimore, USA. MB, ChB (Edinburgh); MD (Edinburgh) with Gold Medal, 1937. Demonstrator, Lectr and Senior Lectr on Anatomy, Univ. of Edinburgh, 1931-46; Goodsir Fellowship in Anatomy, 1933; Rockefeller Fellowship, 1935-36; served as Pathologist in RAMC in UK and MEF, 1939-44. Struthers Lectr, Royal Coll. of Surgeons, Edinburgh, 1952; Fulbright Advanced Scholarship, 1960; Pres., Edinburgh Harveian Soc., 1963-64. Vis. Prof. of Anatomy: George Washington Univ., USA, 1960; Auckland, NZ, 1967. Formerly: Master, St Salvator's Coll.; Chm., Council St Leonard's and St Katherine's Schs; Hon. Pres., British Medical Students Assoc.; External Examiner in Anatomy, Cambridge, Edinburgh, Durham, Glasgow, Aberdeen,

Liverpool, Singapore, Kingston (WI), Accra, etc. Mem. Anatomical Soc. Hon. DSc St Andrews, 1972. First Farquharson Teaching Award, RCSEd., 1974. *Publications:* Co-author Manual of Surgical Anatomy, 1964. Revised section of Arthrology, Cunningham's Textbook of Anatomy, 1972; co-reviser, Jamieson's Illustrations Regional Anatomy, 1971; (jtly) Clinical Anatomy of the Heart, 1977; contribs to various jls, on Heart, Bone and Joints, and on Whales. *Recreations:* gardening, golf. *Address:* 45 Kilrymont Road, St Andrews, Fife. *T:* St Andrews 2879.

WALPOLE, family name of **Baron Walpole.**

WALPOLE, 9th Baron, of Walpole, *cr* 1723; 7th Baron Walpole of Wolterton, *cr* 1756; **Robert Henry Montgomerie Walpole,** TD; Captain, RA; *b* 25 April 1913; *s* of late Horatio Spencer Walpole and Dorothea Frances, *o d* of Frederick Butler Molyneux Montgomerie; *S* to baronies at the death of his cousin, 5th Earl of Orford, 1931; *m* 1937, Nancy Louisa, OBE, *y d* of late Frank Harding Jones, Housham Tye, Harlow, Essex; one *s* one *d* (and one *s* one *d* decd). *Educ:* Eton; South Eastern Agricultural Coll., Wye; Royal Agricultural Coll., Cirencester. *Recreations:* curling, shooting, golf. *Heir: s* Hon. Robert Horatio Walpole [*b* 8 Dec. 1938; *m* 1962, Judith, *yr d* of T. T. Schofield, Stockingwood House, Harpenden; two *s* two *d*. *Educ:* Eton; King's Coll., Cambridge]. *Address:* Wolterton Hall, Norwich NR11 7LY. *T:* Hanworth 210, Matlaske 274. *Clubs:* Bath; Norfolk (Norwich).

WALPOLE, Kathleen Annette, MA; Head Mistress of Wycombe Abbey School, Bucks, from 1948 until Dec. 1961; *b* Ootacamund, S India, 1899; *e d* of Major A. Walpole, RE. *Educ:* Southlands Sch., Exmouth; Westfield Coll., University of London. BA Hons London, 1921; History Mistress, The Church High Sch., Newcastle upon Tyne, 1922-27; Research Student, Westfield Coll., 1927-28; MA London, 1929; Alexander Prize of RHistSoc, 1931; History Mistress, The Royal Sch., Bath, 1928-34; Head Mistress, The Red Maids Sch., Bristol, 1934-47. *Publications:* articles in the Trans. of Historic Society of Lancashire and Cheshire, and of the RHistSoc, 1929 and 1931, on Emigration to British North America. *Recreations:* gardening, walking, study of antiques. *Address:* 7 Springfield Place, Lansdown, Bath. *T:* Bath 64389. *Club:* Royal Commonwealth Society.

WALSH, family name of **Baron Ormathwaite.**

WALSH, Sir Alan, Kt 1977; DSc; FRS 1969; Assistant Chief of Division, Division of Chemical Physics, Commonwealth Scientific and Industrial Research Organization, 1961-77; *b* 19 Dec. 1916; *s* of late Thomas Haworth and Betsy Alice Walsh, Hoddlesden, Lancs; *m* 1949, Audrey Dale Hutchinson; two *s*. *Educ:* Darwen Grammar Sch.; Manchester Univ. BSc 1938; MSc (Tech.) 1946; DSc 1960. FAA 1958. British Non-Ferrous Metals Research Assoc., 1939-42 and 1944-46; Min. of Aircraft Production, 1943; Div. of Chemical Physics, CSIRO, Melbourne, 1946-77. Einstein Memorial Lectr, Australian Inst. of Physics, 1967; Pres., Australian Inst. of Physics, 1967-69. Hon. Member: Soc. of Analytical Chemistry, 1969; Royal Soc. NZ, 1975. Foreign Mem., Royal Acad. of Sciences, Stockholm, 1969. Hon. Fellow, Chemical Soc., London, 1973. Hon. DSc Monash, 1970. Britannica Australia Science Award, 1966; Research Medal, Royal Soc. of Victoria, 1968; Talanta Gold Medal, 1969; Maurice Hasler Award, Soc. of Applied Spectroscopy, USA, 1972; James Cook Medal, Royal Soc. of NSW, 1975; Torbern Bergman Medal, Swedish Chem. Soc., 1976; Royal Medal, Royal Soc., 1976. *Publications:* papers in learned jls. *Address:* 11 Dendy Street, Brighton, Victoria 3168, Australia. *T:* Melbourne 92 4897. *Club:* Metropolitan Golf (Melbourne).

WALSH, Brian, QC 1977; a Recorder of the Crown Court, since 1972. Called to the Bar, Middle Temple, 1961. Prosecuting Counsel, DHSS. *Address:* 37 Park Square, Leeds LS1 2PD.

WALSH, Sir David (Philip), KBE 1962; CB 1946; retired as Deputy Secretary, Ministry of Housing and Local Government (1960-63). Formerly: Principal Asst Secretary (Director of Establishments), Admiralty; Under Secretary, Ministry of Town and Country Planning; Under-Secretary, Ministry of Housing and Local Government (formerly Min. of Local Government and Planning), 1951-60. *Address:* Lantern House, 3 Chapel Hill, Budleigh Salterton, Devon. *T:* Budleigh Salterton 2777.

WALSH, Surgeon Rear-Adm. (retired) Dermot Francis, CB 1960; OBE 1952; FRCSE; *b* 21 Jan. 1901; *s* of Dr J. A. Walsh. *Educ:* Belvedere Coll., Dublin; Trinity Coll., Dublin. BA 1927; MB, BCh, BAO, 1928; FRCSE 1943, QHS 1958. CStJ 1958.

Recreations: golf, gardening, music. *Address:* Latona, Torquay Road, Foxrock, Dublin 18. *T:* Dublin 893164.

WALSH, Maj.-Gen. Francis James, CB 1948; CBE 1945; psc†; *b* 12 Jan. 1900; *s* of F. J. Walsh, Wexford, Eire; *m* 1931, Marjorie Olive Watney; two *s. Educ:* Clongowes Coll., Eire. RMC, Sandhurst, 1918; Royal Irish Regt, 1918-22; King's African Rifles, 1922-28; South Lancashire Regt, 1928-31; Indian Army, 1931-48; Staff Coll., Camberley, 1933-34; staff employment, India, Burma, Malaya, 1935-48; DA&QMG 33 Corps, 1943; DQMG 11 Army Group, 1943-44; DA&QMG 4 Corps and 14 Army, 1944-45; MGA N Comd, India, 1945-47. Maj.-Gen. (Temp.) 1945; Subst., 1947; retired, 1948. *Recreation:* sailing. *Address:* Orchard House, Turpins Lane, Frinton-on-Sea, Essex. *T:* 4472. *Club:* Naval and Military.

WALSH, Lt-Gen. Geoffrey, CBE 1944; DSO 1943; CD; *b* 1909; *s* of late H. L. Walsh; *m* 1935, Gwynn Abigail Currie; one *s. Educ:* Royal Military Coll., Kingston; McGill Univ. (BEngEE). DSc(Mil) RMC, Kingston, 1971. Chief Engineer, 1st Canadian Army, 1944-45; DQMG, 1945-46; Comdr Northwest Highway System, 1946-48; Comdr Eastern Ontario Area, 1948-51; Comdr 27 Bde (Europe), 1951-52; DGMT 1953-55; QMG 1955-58; GOC, Western Command, 1958-61; Chief of the General Staff, Canada, 1961-64; Vice Chief of the Defence Staff, Canada, 1964-65. Col Comdt, Royal Canadian Army Cadets and Cadet Services of Canada, 1970-73. Legion of Merit (US); Comdr of Orange Order of Nassau (Netherlands). *Recreations:* golf, fishing, philately. *Address:* 201 Northcote Place, Rockcliffe Park, Ottawa, Canada. *Clubs:* RMC, Royal Ottawa Golf (Ottawa); USI (Ottawa and Edmonton).

WALSH, Ven. Geoffrey David Jeremy; Archdeacon of Ipswich, since 1976; Rector of Elmsett with Aldham, since 1976; *b* 7 Dec. 1929; *s* of late Howard Wilton Walsh, OBE and of Helen Maud Walsh (*née* Lovell); *m* 1961, Cynthia Helen, *d* of F. P. Knight, FLS, VMH, and late H. I. C. Knight, OBE; two *s* one *d. Educ:* Felsted Sch., Essex; Pembroke Coll., Cambridge (MA Econ.); Lincoln Theological Coll. Curate, Christ Church, Southgate, London, 1955-58; Staff Sec., SCM, and Curate, St Mary the Great, Cambridge, 1958-61; Vicar, St Matthew, Moorfields, Bristol, 1961-66; Rector of Marlborough, Wilts, 1966-76; Hon. Canon, Salisbury Cathedral, 1973-76. *Recreations:* gardening, golf, bird-watching. *Address:* The Rectory, Elmsett, Ipswich IP7 6NA. *T:* Offton 219.

WALSH, James Mark, CMG 1956; OBE 1948; Consul-General, Zürich, 1962-68; *b* 18 Aug. 1909; *s* of Mark Walsh and Emily (*née* Porter); *m* 1st, 1937, Mireille Loir (*d* 1966); one *s*; 2nd, 1967, Bertha Hoch. *Educ:* Mayfield Coll., Sussex; King's Coll., London; Lincoln's Inn, London. BA (Hons), 1929; LLB, 1932; Barrister, 1932; passed an examination and appointed to Foreign Service, 1932; Vice-Consul: Paris, 1932-33, Rotterdam, 1933-34; Judge of HBM Provincial Court, Alexandria, Egypt, 1934-38; Acting Consul-General, Barcelona, 1939; Vice-Consul, Philadelphia, 1939-44; Consul, Antwerp, 1944-45. First Secretary, British Legation: Helsinki, 1945-46, Budapest, 1946-48; Dep. Consul-General, New York, 1948-50; Counsellor (Commercial), Ankara, 1950-54, and Berne, 1954-59; Consul-General, Jerusalem, 1959-62. *Recreations:* painting, golf. *Address:* Eleonorenstrasse 9, 8032 Zürich, Switzerland.

WALSH, Dr John James; Consultant to Paddocks Private Clinic, Aylesbury Road, Princes Risborough; *b* 4 July 1917; *s* of Dr Thomas Walsh and Margaret (*née* O'Sullivan); *m* 1946, Joan Mary, *d* of Henry Teasdale and Nita Birks; three *s* one *d. Educ:* Mungret Coll.; University Coll., Cork. MB, BCh 1940; MD 1963; MRCP 1968, FRCP 1975; FRCS 1969. Various hospital appointments, including Medical Officer, Spinal Injuries Centre, Stoke Mandeville Hospital, Aylesbury, 1947; Deputy Director, National Spinal Injuries Centre, Stoke Mandeville Hospital, 1957-66, Dir, 1966-77. *Publications:* Understanding Paraplegia, 1964; a number of publications on subjects pertaining to paraplegia in medical journals. *Recreation:* shooting. *Address:* Wayside, Station Road, Princes Risborough, Bucks. *T:* Princes Risborough 3347.

WALSH, Sir John (Patrick), KBE 1960; Professor of Dentistry and Dean and Director, University of Otago Dental School, 1946-72; *b* 5 July 1911; *s* of John Patrick Walsh and Lillian Jane (*née* Burbidge), Vic, Australia; *m* 1934, Enid Morris; one *s* three *d. Educ:* Ormond Coll.; Melbourne Univ. BDSc 1st Cl. Hons Melbourne; LDS Victoria, 1936; MB, BS Melbourne, 1943; DDSc Melbourne, 1950; FDSRCS 1950; FDSRCS Edinburgh, 1951; MDS NUI, 1952; FRSNZ 1961; FACD 1962; Hon. FACDS, 1967; Hon. DSc Otago, 1975. Hosp. and teaching appointments in Melbourne till 1946. MO, RAAF, 1945-46. Consultant, WHO Dental Health Seminars: Wellington, 1954;

Adelaide, 1959. Speaker: 11th and 12th Internat. Dental Congresses, London and Rome; Centennial Congress of Amer. Dental Assoc., New York, 1959; 12th, 14th and 15th Australian Dental Congresses. Chairman: Dental Council of NZ, 1956-72; Mental Health Assoc. of Otago, 1960. Dominion Pres., UNA, 1960-64. Member: MRC of NZ, 1950-72 (Chm. Dental Cttee, 1947-60); Scientific Commn; Fedn Dentaire Internat., 1954-61; Council, Univ. of Otago, 1958-63; Nat. Commn for UNESCO, 1961-69; Educn Commn, 1961-; Expert Panel on Dental Health, WHO, 1962; Nat. Council, Duke of Edinburgh's Award, 1963-68. CC, Dunedin, 1968-73. Pres., Dunedin Rotary Club, 1960, Governor Dist 298, 1966-67. Hon. Mem., American Dental Assoc., 1969-; List of Honour, FDI, 1969-. Holds hon. degrees. *Publications:* A Manual of Stomatology, 1957; Living with Uncertainty, 1968; Psychiatry and Dentistry, 1976; numerous articles in scientific literature. *Recreation:* Retirement. *Address:* 108 Cannington Road, Dunedin, New Zealand. *T:* Dunedin 69-943.

WALSH, Leslie; Stipendiary Magistrate, for Greater Manchester, 1974-75 (for Salford, 1951-74); *b* 6 May 1903; *s* of Rt Hon. Stephen and Anne Walsh; *m* 1934, Katharine de Hoghton Birtwell. *Educ:* Wigan Grammar Sch.; Victoria Univ., Manchester (LLB); St John's Coll., Oxford (BCL). Called to Bar, Gray's Inn, 1927; practised Northern Circuit. RAF, 1940-45. Deputy Licensing Authority NW Area, 1946-51; Chairman, Salford and District Rent Tribunal, 1946-51. Hon. MA Salford, 1976. *Address:* 4 Grange Road, Urmston, Manchester M31 1HU. *Club:* St James's (Manchester).

WALSH, Maj.-Gen. Michael John Hatley, DSO 1968; General Officer Commanding 3rd Division, since 1976; *b* 10 June 1927; *s* of Captain Victor Michael Walsh, late Royal Sussex, and Audrey Walsh; *m* 1952, Angela, *d* of Col Leonard Beswick; two *d. Educ:* Sedbergh Sch. Commnd, KRRC, 1946; served in Malaya, Germany, Cyprus, Suez, Aden, Australia and Singapore; Bde Maj. 44 Parachute Bde, 1960-61; GSO1 Defence Planning Staff, 1966; CO 1 Para Bn, 1967-69; Col AQ 1 Div., 1969-71; Comdr, 28 Commonwealth Bde, 1971-73; BGS HQ BAOR, 1973-76. *Recreations:* athletics, boxing (Chm., Army Boxing Assoc., 1976), sailing, Australian Rules football. *Address:* c/o Barclays Bank Ltd, James Street, Harrogate. *Club:* Royal Corinthian Yacht (Cowes).

WALSH, Lt-Col Noel Perrings, FIOB; Under Secretary, and Director of Home Regional Services, Department of the Environment, since 1976; *b* 25 Dec. 1919; *s* of late John and Nancy Walsh; *m* 1945, Olive Mary, *y d* of late Thomas Walsh, Waterford; three *s* one *d. Educ:* Purbrook Park Grammar Sch. Served Regular Army, 1940-66; India, 1941-44; Arakan Campaign, 1944-45; DAQMG, 52 (L) Div., 1951-53; GSO2 RA, HQ BAOR, 1955-57; GSO1 PR, MoD Army, 1964-66; retired Lt-Col, RA, 1966. Entered Home Civil Service as Principal, MPBW, 1966; Regional Director: Far East, 1969-70; Midland Region, 1970-75. *Recreations:* gardening, squash, gauge O railway modelling. *Address:* 25 Oakfield Road, Selly Park, Birmingham B29 7HH. *T:* 021-472 2031. *Clubs:* Naval and Military; Edgbaston Priory (Birmingham).

WALSH, Prof. William, FRSA; Professor of Commonwealth Literature, University of Leeds, since 1972; Douglas Grant Fellow in Commonwealth Literature in the School of English, since 1969; Chairman, School of English, since 1973; Director, Yorkshire Television, since 1967; *b* 23 Feb. 1916; *e s* of William and Elizabeth Walsh; *m* 1945, May Watson; one *s* one *d. Educ:* Downing Coll., Cambridge; University of London. Schoolmaster, 1943-51; Senior English Master, Raynes Park County Grammar Sch., 1945-51; Lecturer in Education, University Coll. of N' Staffordshire, 1951-53; Lecturer in Education, Univ. of Edinburgh, 1953-57; Prof. of Education, and Head of Dept. of Education, Univ. of Leeds, 1957-72; Chm., Sch. of Education, 1969-72; Chm., Bd of combined Faculties of Arts, Economics, Social Studies and Law, Univ. of Leeds, 1964-66; Pro-Vice-Chancellor, Univ. of Leeds, 1965-67; Chm. Bd of Adult Educn, 1969-; Member: IBA Adult Educn Cttee, 1974-76; IBA Educn Adv. Cttee, 1976-. Vis. Prof., ANU, 1968; Australian Commonwealth Vis. Fellow, 1970; Vis. Prof., Canadian Univs, 1973. FRSA 1970. *Publications:* Use of Imagination, 1959; A Human Idiom, 1964; Coleridge: The Work and the Relevance, 1967; A Manifold Voice, 1970; R. K. Narayan, 1972; V. S. Naipaul, 1972; Commonwealth Literature, 1973; Readings in Commonwealth Literature, 1973; D. J. Enright: poet of humanism, 1974; Patrick White: Voss, 1976; contributions to: From Blake to Byron, 1957; Young Writers, Young Readers, 1960; Speaking of the Famous, 1962; F. R. Leavis-Some Aspects of his Work, 1963; The Teaching of English Literature Overseas, 1963; Higher Education: patterns of change in the 1970s, 1972; Literatures of the World in

English, 1974; papers and essays on literary and educational topics in British and American journals. *Address:* 27 Moor Drive, Headingley, Leeds LS6 4BY. *T:* Leeds 755705. *Club:* United Oxford & Cambridge University.

WALSH, Prof. William Henry; FBA 1969; Professor of Logic and Metaphysics in the University of Edinburgh, since 1960; Vice Principal, University of Edinburgh, since 1975; *b* 10 Dec. 1913; *s* of Fred and Mary Walsh, Leeds; *m* 1938, Frances Beatrix Ruth (*née* Pearson); one *s* two *d*. *Educ:* Leeds Grammar Sch.; Merton Coll., Oxford. Class I, Classical Mods., 1934, Class I, Lit. Hum., 1936; Gaisford Greek Prose Prize, 1934; Junior Research Fellow, Merton Coll., 1936. Served War of 1939-45, Royal Corps of Signals, 1940-41; subsequently employed in branch of Foreign Office. Lecturer in Philosophy, Univ. Coll., Dundee (University of St Andrews), 1946; Fellow and Tutor in Philosophy, Merton Coll., Oxford, 1947-60. Sub-Warden, 1948-50, Senior Tutor, 1954-60; Lecturer in Philosophy, University of Oxford, 1947-60; Dean of Faculty of Arts, University of Edinburgh, 1966-68; Senatus Assessor, Univ. Ct, Edinburgh, 1970-73. Dawes Hicks Lecturer, British Academy, 1963. Visiting Professor: Ohio State Univ., USA, 1957-58; Dartmouth Coll., NH, USA, 1965; Univ. of Maryland, 1969-70. Pres. Aristotelian Soc., 1964-65. *Publications:* Reason and Experience, 1947; An Introduction to Philosophy of History, 1951; Metaphysics, 1963; Hegelian Ethics, 1969; Kant's Criticism of Metaphysics, 1975; articles in philosophical periodicals. *Address:* 19 Great Stuart Street, Edinburgh EH3 7TP. *T:* 031-225 1471.

WALSH, William Joseph; National Secretary, Association of Clerical, Technical and Supervisory Staffs, since 1961; *b* 28 Aug. 1919; *m* 1942, Doreen Mary Garton; three *s*. *Educ:* Tonysguboriau Sch., Llantrisant, Glam. Regional Officer, Assoc. of Clerical, Technical and Supervisory Staffs, 1951. Member: Nat. Jt Council for Local Authorities APT&C Grades, 1961-; TUC Non-Manual Adv. Cttee, 1962-; TUC Steel Cttee, 1964-; Nat. Jt Council for Non-Manual Staff of National Bus Co., 1968-; Petroleum Trng Bd, 1970-; Nat. Council for Passenger Transport Exec. Staff, 1970-; Business Studies Bd, British Educn Council, 1976-. *Recreations:* Rugby Union football, cricket, National Hunt racing. *Address:* 171 Clapham Road, SW9. *T:* 01-274 5906.

WALSH ATKINS, Leonard Brian, CMG 1962; CVO 1961; Consultant, The Abbeyfield Society, since 1975, General Secretary, 1971; *b* 15 March 1915; *o c* of late Leonard and Gladys Atkins; step *s* of late Geoffrey Walsh, CMG, CBE; *m* 1st, 1940, Marguerite Black (marr. diss. 1968); three *s*; 2nd, 1969, Margaret Lady Runcorn. *Educ:* Charterhouse (Scholar); Hertford Coll., Oxford (Scholar). BA, Lit. Hum., Class II, 1937. Asst Principal, India Office, 1937. Fleet Air Arm, Nov. 1940-July 1945; Lieut-Comdr (A), RNVR (despatches). Principal: Burma Office, 1945-47; Commonwealth Relations Office, 1947; Asst Secretary, 1949; Counsellor, British Embassy, Dublin, 1953-56 (sometime Chargé d'Affaires); Student, Imperial Defence Coll., 1957; Dep. High Comr, Karachi, 1959-61 (sometime Actg High Comr); Asst Under-Sec. of State, 1962; seconded to Civil Service Selection Bd, 1967; retired 1970. *Recreation:* sailing. *Address:* Wood Cottage, Mundon, Maldon, Essex.

WALSHAM, Rear-Adm. Sir John Scarlett Warren, 4th Bt, *cr* 1831; CB 1963; OBE 1944; RN, retired; Admiral Superintendent HM Dockyard, Portsmouth, 1961-64; *b* 29 Nov. 1910; *s* of Sir John S. Walsham, 3rd Bt, and Bessie Geraldine Gundreda (*d* 1941), *e d* of late Vice-Admiral John B. Warren; *S* father, 1940; *m* 1936, Sheila Christina, *o d* of Comdr B. Bannerman, DSO; one *s* two *d*. Rear-Admiral, 1961. *Heir:* *s* Timothy John Walsham [*b* 26 April 1939. *Educ:* Sherborne]. *Address:* Ash Beacon, Churchill, Axminster, Devon.

WALSINGHAM, 9th Baron, *cr* 1780; **John de Grey,** MC 1952; Lieut-Colonel, Royal Artillery, retired, 1968; *b* 21 Feb. 1925; *s* of 8th Baron Walsingham, DSO, OBE, and Hyacinth (*d* 1968), *o d* of late Lt-Col Lambart Henry Bouwens, RA; *S* father, 1965; *m* 1963, Wendy, *er d* of E. Hoare, Southwick, Sussex; one *s* two *d*. *Educ:* Wellington Coll.; Aberdeen Univ.; Magdalen Coll., Oxford; RMCS. BA Oxon, 1950; MA 1959. Army in India, 1945-47; Palestine, 1947; Oxford Univ., 1947-50; Foreign Office, 1950; Army in Korea, 1951-52; Hong Kong, 1952-54; Malaya, 1954-56; Cyprus, Suez, 1956; Aden, 1957-58; Royal Military Coll. of Science, 1958-60; Aden, 1961-63; Malaysia, 1963-65. *Heir:* *s* Hon. Robert de Grey, *b* 21 June 1969. *Address:* Merton Hall, Thetford, Norfolk IP25 6QJ. *T:* Watton (Norfolk) 881226. *Clubs:* Army and Navy, Special Forces, Farmers'; Norfolk County (Norwich).

WALSTON, family name of Baron Walston.

WALSTON, Baron *cr* 1961 (Life Peer), of Newton; **Henry David Leonard George Walston,** JP; farmer; *b* 16 June 1912; *o s* of late Sir Charles Walston, LittD, LHD, PhD, and Florence, *d* of David Einstein; *m* 1935, Catherine Macdonald, *d* of late D. H. Crompton and late Mrs Charles Tobey; three *s* two *d*. (and one *s* decd). *Educ:* Eton; King's Coll., Cambridge (MA). Research Fellow in Bacteriology, Harvard, USA, 1934-35; Mem., Hunts War Agricultural Cttee, 1939-45; Dir of Agriculture, British Zone of Germany, 1946-47; Agricultural Adviser for Germany to FO, 1947-48; Counsellor, Duchy of Lancaster, 1948-54. Contested: (L) Hunts, 1945; (Lab) Cambridgeshire, 1951 and 1955; (Lab) Gainsborough, 1957 (by-election), and 1959. Parly Under-Sec. of State, FO, 1964-67; Parly Sec., BoT, Jan.-Aug. 1967; Member: UK Delegn to Council of Europe and WEU, 1970-75; European Parlt, 1975-77. HM Special Ambassador to inauguration of Presidents of Mexico, 1964, of Columbia, 1966, and of Liberia, 1968. Crown Estate Comr, 1968-76; Chm., Inst. of Race Relations, 1968-71; Mem., Commonwealth Development Corp., 1975-. Minister of Agriculture's Liaison Officer, 1969-70; Chairman: East Anglia Regional Planning Council, 1969-; GB/East Europe Centre, 1974-; Centre of E Anglian Studies, 1975-; Harwich Harbour Conservancy Bd, 1975-; Member: Cambs Agricultural Cttee, 1948-50; Home Office Cttee on Experiments on Animals, 1961-62. Chm., Harlow Group Hosp. Management Cttee, 1962-64; Dep. Chm., Council, Royal Commonwealth Soc., 1963-64 (Vice-Pres., 1970-); Trustee, Rural Industries Bureau 1959-64; Governor, Guy's Hosp., 1944-47. JP Cambridge, 1944. *Publications:* From Forces to Farming, 1944; Our Daily Bread, 1952; No More Bread, 1954; Life on the Land, 1954; (with John Mackie) Land Nationalisation, for and against, 1958; Agriculture under Communism, 1961; The Farmer and Europe, 1962; The Farm Gate to Europe, 1970; Dealing with Hunger, 1976; contribs to Proc. of Experimental Biology and Medicine, Jl of Hygiene, Observer, Economist, New Statesman, Spectator. *Recreations:* shooting, sailing. *Address:* Town's End Springs, Thriplow, near Royston, Herts; A14 Albany, Piccadilly, W1; Marquis Estates, St Lucia, West Indies. *Clubs:* Brooks's, MCC; County (Cambridge); House of Lords Yacht.

WALTARI, Mika; Author since 1928, Finland; Member of Academy of Finland since 1957; *b* 19 Sept. 1908; *s* of Toimi Armas Waltari and Olga Maria (*née* Johansson); *m* 1931, Marjatta Luukkonen; one *d*. *Educ:* Helsinki Univ. (MA). Literary critic for Maaseudun Tulevaisuus, 1932-42; Literary reviewer for Finnish Broadcasting Company, 1937-38; Editor for Suomen Kuvalehti, weekly illustrated magazine, 1936-38; with editorial office of Finnish State Information Bureau, 1939-40 and 1941-44. DrPhil *hc* Turku Univ., 1970. Awarded literary prizes, Finland 1934, 1935, 1950 and 1954; Pro Finlandia, 1952; Commander of Finnish Lion, 1960. *Publications:* The Egyptian, 1949; Michael the Finn, 1950; The Sultan's Renegade, 1951; The Dark Angel, 1953; A Nail Merchant at Nightfall, 1954; Moonscape, 1955; The Etruscan, 1957; The Secret of the Kingdom, 1961; The Roman, 1966. *Recreation:* detective stories. *Address:* Tunturikatu 13, Helsinki 10, Finland. *Club:* PEN (Finland).

WALTER, Hon. Sir Harold (Edward), Kt 1972; MLA since 1959, Minister of External Affairs, Tourism and Emigration, since 1976, Mauritius; *b* 17 April 1920; *e s* of Rev. Edward Walter and Marie Augusta Donat; *m* 1942, Yvette Nidza, MBE, *d* of James Toolsy; no *c*. *Educ:* Royal Coll., Mauritius. Served in HM Forces, 1940-48, Mauritius Sub-Area; E Africa Comd, GHQ MELF. Called to Bar, Lincoln's Inn, 1951. Village Councillor, 1952; Municipal Councillor, Port Louis, 1956. Minister: of Works and Internal Communications, 1959-65; of Health, 1965-67 and 1971-76; of Labour, 1967-71; mem. numerous ministerial delegns. Chm., Commonwealth Med. Conf., 1972-74; Dep. Leader, UN General Assembly, NY, 1973, 1974; Pres., WHO, 1976-77. Chm., Council of Ministers, Organisation of African Unity, 1976-77. Commandeur de l'Ordre National Français des Palmes Acadèmiques, 1974. *Recreations:* shooting, fishing, swimming, gardening. *Address:* La Rocca, Eau Coulée, Mauritius. *T:* 65500. *Clubs:* Wings, Racing (Mauritius).

WALTER, Kenneth Burwood; Full-time Member, British Airports Authority, since 1975; *b* 16 Oct. 1918; *s* of late Leonard James Walter and of Jesse Florence Walter; *m* 1940, Elsie Marjorie Collett; two *s*. *Educ:* St Dunstan's Coll., SE6. Dept of Civil Aviation, Air Ministry, 1936. Served War, Royal Artillery (Anti Aircraft and Field), home and Far East, 1940-46. Ministries of: Civil Aviation; Transport and Civil Aviation; Aviation, 1946-66; British Airports Authority: Dep. Dir Planning, 1966; Dir Planning, 1972; Airport Dir, Heathrow, 1973-77. MCIT, ARAeS. *Publications:* various papers on airports. *Recreations:* music, swimming, fishing, gardening. *Address:* D'Albiac House, Heathrow Airport, Hounslow, Mddx TW6 1JH. *T:* 01-759 7241.

WALTER, Captain Philip Norman, DSO 1940; RN; Commandant, Corps of Commissionaires, 1950-60; Director of The Times, 1958-64; *b* 12 Dec. 1898; *s* of Captain Philip Walter, RN, and *g s* of John Walter III, of The Times; *m* 1946, Sylvia (*d* 1976), *d* of J. C. M. Ogilvie-Forbes, Boyndlie, Aberdeenshire; one *s. Educ:* RN Colleges Osborne and Dartmouth. Served European War, 1914-18, Dardanelles and North Sea; Commander, 1932; Captain, 1940; War of 1939-45, Norway; commanded Inshore Squadron, N Africa, 1942; wounded, PoW; Assistant Chief of Staff to Allied Naval Commander-in-Chief, 1944; invalided, 1948. Chevalier of Légion d'Honneur, Croix de Guerre (France). *Address:* c/o Barclays Bank Ltd, 1 Pall Mall East, SW1.

WALTERS, Prof. Alan Arthur; Professor of Political Economy, Johns Hopkins University, Maryland, since 1977; *b* 17 June 1926; *s* of James Arthur Walters and Claribel Walters (*née* Heywood); *m* ; one *d. Educ:* Alderman Newton's Sch., Leicester; University Coll., Leicester (BSc (Econ) London); Nuffield Coll., Oxford. Lectr in Econometrics, Univ. of Birmingham, 1951; Visiting Prof. of Economics, Northwestern Univ., Evanston, Ill, USA, 1958-59; Prof. of Econometrics and Social Statistics, Univ. of Birmingham, 1961; Vis. Prof. of Economics, Massachusetts Inst. of Technology, 1966-67; Cassel Prof. of Economics, LSE, 1968-77. Mem. Commission on Third London Airport (the Roskill Commission), 1968-70. Fellow, Econometric Soc., 1971. *Publications:* Growth Without Development (with R. Clower and G. Dalton), 1966 (USA); Economics of Road User Charges, 1968; An Introduction to Econometrics, 1969 (2nd edn 1971); Economics of Ocean Freight Rates (with E. Bennathan), 1969 (USA); Money in Boom and Slump, 1970 (3rd edn 1971); Noise and Prices, 1974; (with R. G. Layard) Microeconomic Theory, 1977. *Recreations:* music, Thai porcelain. *Address:* 2820 P Street NW, Washington, DC 20007, USA. *Club:* Political Economy.

WALTERS, Rev. David John, MC, MA; *b* Ammanford, Carmarthenshire, 13 Jan. 1893; *s* of T. Watkyn Walters, Tirydail, Neath; *m* 1917, Frances, *d* of Mrs F. Atkinson, Daleside, Sleights, Yorks; one *s* one *d. Educ:* Christ College, Brecon; Brasenose College, Oxford (Junior Hulme Scholar), 2nd Class Hons School of Natural Science. Assistant Master at Haileybury College, 1914-19; Assistant Master and Housemaster at Uppingham School, 1919-31; Headmaster of Bromsgrove School, 1931-53; Vicar of Lindridge, dio. of Worcester, 1953-57; Rector of All Saints', Worcester, 1957-64; Rural Dean of Worcester, 1960-64. On active service as Lieutenant in RGA, 1915-18 (despatches, MC). *Publications:* (Joint) History of 135th Siege Battery, RGA, 1921; Bromsgrove in Exile, 1971. *Recreation:* walking. *Address:* 138 Graham Road, Malvern, Worcs.

WALTERS, Dennis, MBE 1960; MP (C) Westbury Division of Wiltshire since 1964; *b* Nov. 1928; *s* of late Douglas L. Walters; *m* 1st, 1955, Vanora McIndoe (marr. diss. 1969); one *s* one *d* ; 2nd, 1970, Mrs Celia Kennedy, *yr d* of Rt Hon. Lord Duncan-Sandys, *qv,* and of late Mrs Diana Churchill; one *s. Educ:* Downside; St Catharine's College (Exhibitioner), Cambridge (MA). War of 1939-45: interned in Italy; served with Italian Resistance Movement behind German lines after Armistice; repatriated and continued normal educn, 1944. Chm., Fedn of Univ. Conservative and Unionist Assocs, 1950; Personal Asst to Lord Hailsham throughout his Chairmanship of Conservative Party; Chm., Coningsby Club, 1959. Contested (C) Blyth, 1959 and Nov. 1960. Jt Hon. Sec., Conservative Parly Foreign Affairs Cttee, 1965-71; Jt Vice-Chm., 1974-. Dir, Specialised Travel Service Ltd. AFI Group Ltd. Chm., Asthma Research Council, 1969-; Jt Chm., Council for Advancement of Arab British Understanding, 1970- (jt Vice-Chm., 1967-70). Comdr, Order of Cedar of Lebanon, 1969. *Address:* 63 Warwick Square, SW1. *T:* 01-821 0377. Orchardleigh, Corton, Warminster, Wilts. *T:* Codford St Mary 369. *Club:* Boodle's.

WALTERS, Geraint Gwynn, CBE 1958; Director for Wales, Ministry of Public Building and Works and Department of the Environment, 1966-72, retired; *b* in the Welsh Colony in Patagonia, 6 June 1910; *s* of Rev. D. D. Walters; *m* 1st, 1942, Doreena Owen (*d* 1959); 2nd, 1968, Sarah Ann Ruth Price; no *c. Educ:* various schools in Argentina and Wales; University Coll., Bangor (BA). Gladstone Prizeman, Foyle Prizeman. Schoolmaster, 1933-35; political organizer on staff of Rt Hon. David Lloyd George, 1935-40; Min. of Information, 1940-45; Dep. Regional Dir of Inf., Bristol and Plymouth, 1942-45; Principal, Min. of Works HQ, 1945-48; Dir for Wales, Min. of

Works, 1948-63; Dir, Far East Region, Min. of Public Building and Works, 1963-66. Chm., Royal Inst. of Public Admin (S Wales Br.), 1960-61; Hon. Mem. of Gorsedd, 1961; Pres., St David's Soc. of Singapore, 1965; Leader of Welsh Overseas, at Nat. Eisteddfod of Wales, 1965; Chm., Argentine Welsh Soc., 1976-77. Chm., Civil Service Sports Council for Wales, 1970-72. Member: Welsh Bd for Industry, 1948-62; Housing Production Bd for Wales; Cttee of Inquiry on Welsh Television, 1963; Mem. Council, Univ. of Wales Inst. of Science and Technology; Govt Housing Comr for Merthyr Tydfil, 1972-73. *Recreations:* golf, Rugby football, broadcasting, travel. *Address:* 29 The Rise, Llanishen, Cardiff. *T:* Cardiff 752070. *Clubs:* Civil Service; Cardiff and County (Cardiff).

WALTERS, Peter Ernest, CMG 1965; Group Staff Manager, Courage Ltd, since 1967; *b* 9 Oct. 1913; *s* of Ernest Helm Walters and Kathleen Walters (*née* Farrer-Baynes); *m* 1943, Ayesha Margaret, *d* of Alfred and Winifred Bunker; three *d. Educ:* Windlesham House Sch. Emigrated to Kenya, 1931. Army Service, 1939-45; commissioned KAR, 1940; Major 1944. Cadet, Colonial Admin. Service, Kenya, 1945; Dist Comr, 1948; Provincial Comr, Northern Prov., 1959; Civil Sec., Eastern Region, Kenya, 1963-65; retd from Colonial Service, 1965. Principal, Min. of Aviation (London), 1965-67. Staff Manager, Courage, Barclay and Simonds Ltd, 1967. *Address:* Cherry Orchard, Ockley, near Dorking, Surrey RH5 5NS. *T:* Dorking 711119. *Club:* Nairobi (Kenya).

WALTERS, Peter (Hugh Bennetts) Ensor, OBE 1957; Public Relations and Fund Raising Consultant since 1959; *b* 18 July 1912; *yr s* of late Rev. C. Ensor Walters, a President of the Methodist Conference, and late Muriel Havergal, *d* of late Alderman J. H. Bennetts, JP, Penzance; *m* 1936, Marcia, *er d* of Percival Burdle Hayter; no *c. Educ:* Manor House Sch.; St Peter's Coll., Oxford. On staff of late Rt Hon. David Lloyd George, 1935-39; enlisted as volunteer in Army, 1940; commissioned in Royal Army Pay Corps, 1942; National Organizer, National Liberal Organization, 1944-51. General Sec., National Liberal Organization, Hon. Sec. and Treas., National Liberal Party Council, and Dir, National Liberal Forum, 1951-58. Vice-Chm., Nat. Liberal Club, 1972-74. *Recreation:* travel. *Address:* 10 Windlesham Court, Grand Avenue, West Worthing, West Sussex BN11 5AE. *T:* Worthing 42600. *Club:* Union Society (Oxford).

WALTERS, Peter Ingram; a Managing Director, British Petroleum Co. Ltd, since 1973; *b* 11 March 1931; *s* of Stephen Walters and Edna Walters (*née* Redgate); *m* 1960, Patricia Anne (*née* Tulloch); two *s* one *d. Educ:* King Edward's Sch., Birmingham; Birmingham Univ. (BCom). RASC, 1952-54; British Petroleum Co. Ltd, 1954-: Vice-Pres., BP North America, 1965-67; Dir, BP Trading Ltd, 1971-; Chm., BP Chemicals, 1976-. Mem., Indust. Soc. Council, 1975-; Pres., Gen. Council of British Shipping, 1977-. Vice Pres., Inst. of Manpower Studies, 1977-. *Recreations:* golf, gardening. *Address:* 10 Stormont Road, Highgate, N6 4NL. *T:* 01-340 4029.

WALTERS, Sir Roger (Talbot), KBE 1971 (CBE 1965); FRIBA, FIStructE; Architect and Controller of Construction Services, Greater London Council, since 1971; *b* 31 March 1917; 3rd *s* of Alfred Bernard Walters, Sudbury, Suffolk; *m* 1976, Claire Myfanwy Chappell. *Educ:* Oundle; Architectural Association School of Architecture; Liverpool University. Diploma in Architecture, 1939. Served in Royal Engineers, 1943-46. Office of Sir E. Owen Williams, KBE, 1936; Directorate of Constructional Design, Min. of Works, 1941-43; Architect to Timber Development Assoc., 1946-49; Principal Asst Architect, Eastern Region, British Railways, 1949-59; Chief Architect (Development), Directorate of Works, War Office, 1959-62; Dep. Dir-Gen., R&D, MPBW, 1962-67; Dir-Gen., Production, 1967-69; Controller General, 1969-71. Hon. FAIA. *Address:* 46 Princess Road, NW1. *T:* 01-722 3740. *Club:* Reform.

WALTERS, Stuart Max, MA, PhD; Director, University Botanic Garden, Cambridge, since 1973; *b* 23 May 1920; *s* of Bernard Walters and Ivy Dane; *m* 1948, Lorna Mary Strutt; two *s* one *d. Educ:* Penistone Grammar Sch.; St John's Coll., Cambridge. 1st cl. hons Pt I Nat. Scis Tripos 1940 and Pt II Botany 1946; PhD 1949. Research Fellow, St John's Coll., 1947-50; Curator of Herbarium, Botany Sch., Cambridge, 1948-73; Lectr in Botany 1962-73; Fellow of King's Coll., Cambridge, 1964-. *Publications:* (with J. S. L. Gilmour) Wild Flowers, 1954; (with J. Raven) Mountain Flowers, 1956; (ed, with F. H. Perring) Atlas of the British Flora, 1962; (with F. H. Perring, P. D. Sell and H. L. K. Whitehouse) A Flora of Cambridgeshire, 1964; (with D. Briggs) Plant Variation and Evolution, 1969. *Address:* Cory Lodge, University Botanic Garden, Cambridge. *T:* Cambridge 58145.

WALTON, Anthony Michael, QC 1970; *b* 4 May 1925; *y s* of Henry Herbert Walton and Clara Martha Walton, Dulwich; *m* 1955, Jean Frederica, *o d* of William Montague Hey, Bedford; one *s*. *Educ:* Dulwich College (sometime Scholar); Hertford College, Oxford (sometime Scholar); pupil to W. L. Ferrar (maths) and C. H. S. Fifoot (law). BA 1946; BCL 1950; MA 1950. Pres., Oxford Union Society, Trinity Term 1945. Nat. Service as physicist. Called to the Bar, Middle Temple, 1950; pupil to Lord Justice Winn. Interested in education. Liveryman, Worshipful Co. of Gunmakers. Freeman, City of London, 1968. *Publications:* (ed) (Asst to Hon. H. Fletcher-Moulton) Digest of the Patent, Design, Trade Mark and Other Cases, 1959; (ed) Russell on Arbitration, 17th edn, 1963, 18th edn, 1970. *Address:* 62 Kingsmead Road, SW2.
See also Hon. Sir Raymond Walton.

WALTON, Arthur Halsall, FCA; Partner in Lysons, Haworth & Sankey since 1949; *b* 13 July 1916; *s* of Arthur Walton and Elizabeth Leeming (*née* Halsall); *m* 1958, Kathleen Elsie Abram; three *s*. *Educ:* The Leys School. Articled in Lysons & Talbot, 1934; ACA 1940. Military Service, 1939-48: commnd Lancs Fusiliers, 1940. Inst. of Chartered Accountants: Mem. Council 1959; Vice-Pres., 1969; Dep. Pres. 1970; Pres. 1971. *Recreation:* reading. *Address:* Epping Cottage, 4 Kennerleys Lane, Wilmslow, Cheshire. *Club:* St James's (Manchester).

WALTON, Ernest Thomas Sinton, MA, MSc, PhD; Fellow of Trinity College, Dublin, 1934-74, Fellow emeritus 1974; Erasmus Smith's Professor of Natural and Experimental Philosophy 1947-74; *b* 6 October 1903; *s* of Rev. J. A. Walton, MA; *m* 1934, Winifred Isabel Wilson; two *s* two *d*. *Educ:* Methodist College, Belfast; Trinity College, Dublin; Cambridge University. 1851 Overseas Research Scholarship, 1927-30; Senior Research Award of Dept of Scientific and Industrial Research, 1930-34; Clerk Maxwell Scholar, 1932-34; Awarded Hughes Medal by Royal Society, 1938. (With Sir John Cockcroft) Nobel prize for physics, 1951. Hon. DSc, Queen's Univ. of Belfast, 1959. *Publications:* Papers on hydrodynamics, nuclear physics and micro-waves. *Address:* Trinity College, Dublin; 26 St Kevin's Park, Dartry Road, Dublin 6. *T:* 971328.

WALTON, Prof. John Nicholas, TD 1962; FRCP; Dean of Medicine, since 1971, and Professor of Neurology since 1968, University of Newcastle upon Tyne; *b* 16 Sept. 1922; *s* of Herbert Walton and Eleanor Watson Walton; *m* 1946, Mary Elizabeth Harrison; one *s* two *d*. *Educ:* Alderman Wraith Grammar Sch., Spennymoor, Co. Durham; Med. Sch., King's Coll., Univ. of Durham. MB, BS (1st Cl. Hons) 1945; MD (Durham) 1952; DSc (Newcastle) 1972; FRCP 1963 (MRCP 1950). Ho. Phys., Royal Victoria Inf., Newcastle, 1946-47; service in RAMC, 1947-49; Med. Registrar, Royal Vic. Inf., 1949-51; Research Asst, Univ. of Durham, 1951-56; Nuffield Foundn Fellow, Mass. Gen. Hosp. and Harvard Univ., 1953-54; King's Coll. Fellow, Neurological Res. Unit, Nat. Hosp., Queen Square, 1954-55; First Asst in Neurology, Newcastle upon Tyne, 1956-58; Cons. Neurologist, Newcastle Univ. Hosps, 1958-. Mem. MRC, 1974-; Mem., GMC, 1971- (Chm. Educn Cttee, 1975-); UK Rep., EEC Adv. Cttee, Med. Educn, 1975-; Editor-in-Chief, Jl of Neurological Sciences, 1966-77; Chm., Muscular Dystrophy Gp of GB, 1970-, etc. Col (late RAMC) and OC 1 (N) Gen. Hosp. (TA), 1963-66; Hon. Col 201(N) Gen. Hosp. (T&AVR) 1971-77. Dr de l'Univ. (Hon.) Aix-Marseille, 1975; Hon. Corresponding For. Member: Amer. Neurological Assoc., Amer. Acad. of Neurology, and of French, German, Australian, Spanish, Polish, Venezuelan and Brazilian Neurological Assocs. Numerous named lectureships and overseas visiting professorships. *Publications:* Subarachnoid Haemorrhage, 1956; (with R. D. Adams) Polymyositis, 1958; Essentials of Neurology, 1961, 4th edn 1975; Disorders of Voluntary Muscle, 1964, 3rd edn 1974; Brain's Diseases of the Nervous System, 7th edn 1969, 8th edn 1977, etc; numerous chapters in books and papers in sci. jls. *Recreations:* golf and other sports, reading, music. *Address:* Holmwood, 9 Beechfield Road, Gosforth, Newcastle upon Tyne NE3 4EP. *T:* Newcastle upon Tyne 858871. *Clubs:* Athenæum, East India, Devonshire, Sports and Public Schools.

WALTON, Sir John Robert, Kt 1971; retired; Director, Waltons Ltd Group, Australia (Managing Director, 1951-72, Chairman, 1961-72); Chairman, FNCB-Waltons Corp. Ltd, Australia, 1966-75; *b* 7 Feb. 1904; *s* of John Thomas Walton; *m* 1938, Peggy Everley Gamble; one *s* one *d*. *Educ:* Scots Coll., Sydney. National Cash Register Co. Pty Ltd, 1930: NSW Manager, 1934, Managing Director in Australia, 1946-51. *Recreations:* gardening, swimming, golf, reading. *Address:* Yarranabbe, 71 Yarranabbe Road, Darling Point, NSW 2027, Australia. *Clubs:* Rotary, Royal Sydney Golf, American National, Tattersall's (all in Sydney).

WALTON, John William Scott; Director of Statistics, Board of Inland Revenue, since 1977; *b* 25 Sept. 1925; *s* of Sir John Charles Walton, KCIE, CB, MC, and of Nelly Margaret, Lady Walton. *Educ:* Marlborough; Brasenose Coll., Oxford. Mutual Security Agency, Paris, 1952; Inland Revenue, 1954; Central Statistical Office, 1958, Chief Statistician, 1967, Asst Dir, 1972. *Publications:* (contrib. jtly) M. Perlman, The Organization and Retrieval of Economic Knowledge, 1977; articles in Economic Trends, Business Economist, Statistical News. *Address:* 70 Gloucester Terrace, W2 3HH. *T:* 01-262 1346. *Club:* United Oxford & Cambridge University.

WALTON, Prof. Kenneth, FRSE, FRSGS; Professor of Geography, since 1965, Vice-Principal, since 1977, University of Aberdeen; *b* 9 March 1923; *s* of Albert Walton and Annie Constance (*née* Burton); *m* 1949, Sheila Burrows; two *s*. *Educ:* King's Sch., Macclesfield; Univ. of Edinburgh. Univ. of Edinburgh, 1941-42. Commissioned in RA, 1942-46. Univ. of Edinburgh, 1946-48. Grad. 1st Class Hons with MA in Geography. Univ. of Aberdeen: Research Fellow, 1948; Lectr, 1949 (PhD 1951); Sen. Lectr, 1960; Reader, 1965. *Publications:* The Highlands and Islands of Scotland, 1961; The Arid Zones, 1969; papers in Scottish Geographical Magazine, Trans. Inst. British Geographers, etc. *Recreations:* compulsive sailor, watching the family gardening, photography. *Address:* 23 Baillieswells Road, Bieldside, Aberdeen AB1 9BL. *T:* 48387.

WALTON, Hon. Sir Raymond (Henry), Kt 1973; Hon. Mr Justice Walton; a Judge of the High Court of Justice, Chancery Division, since 1973; *b* 9 Sept. 1915; *e s* of Henry Herbert Walton and Clara Martha Walton, Dulwich; *m* 1940, Helen Alexandra, *e d* of Alexander Dingwall, Jedburgh; one *s* two *d*. *Educ:* Dulwich College; Balliol College, Oxford. Open Math. Schol., Balliol, 1933; BA 1937; MA 1942. Pres., Oxford Union Soc., Feb. 1938; BCL 1938. Called to Bar, Lincoln's Inn, 1939; Bencher, 1970. War service in Anti-Aircraft Artillery (including Instructor in Gunnery and Experimental Officer), 1940-46. Contested (L) North Lambeth, 1945. Returned to practice at Bar, 1946; QC 1963. Legal corresp., Financial Times, 1953-72. Mem., Lord Chancellor's Law Reform Cttee, 1959-; Chm., Insolvency Rules Adv. Cttee, 1977-. Church Comr for England, 1969-73; Dep. Chm., Boundaries Commn for England, 1973-. Hon. Fellow, Coll. of Estate Management, 1977. *Publications:* An introduction to the law of Sales of Land, 1949, 3rd edn 1969; (edited) Kerr on Receivers, 12th edn (with A. W. Sarson), 13th and 14th edns; Adkin's Law of Landlord and Tenant, 13th, 14th and (with Michael Essayan) 15th to 17th edns. *Recreation:* philately. *Address:* Royal Courts of Justice, WC2.
See also A. M. Walton.

WALTON, Prof. William Stanley, GM; MD, BHy; Emeritus Professor of Public Health, London School of Hygiene and Tropical Medicine, University of London; *b* 9 Nov. 1901; *s* of William and Mary Walton; *m* 1930, Anne Dorothy Margaret, *e d* of Edward Robson, Hexham. *Educ:* Gateshead Grammar Sch.; Univ. of Durham. MB, BS, Durham, 1925; BHy and DPH, 1927; MD (Commend.), 1932. Medical Officer of Health, West Bromwich; Dep. Medical Officer of Health for the City and Port of Plymouth; Dep. MOH, Middlesbrough; Medical Officer and School Medical Officer for the City of Newcastle upon Tyne, and Head of Department of Public Health, Durham University; also sometime External Examiner in Public Health to 12 British universities; Consultant to WHO; Fellow of the Society of Medical Officers of Health; Member Soc. Middle Temple. *Publications:* (joint) A Thousand Families in Newcastle upon Tyne, 1954; One Hundred Years in History of The Society of Medical Officers of Health, 1956; (joint) Growing up in Newcastle upon Tyne, 1960. *Address:* Kingstreet End, Little Missenden, Amersham, Bucks HP7 0RA. *T:* Great Missenden 2857. *Club:* Athenæum.

WALTON, Sir William (Turner), OM 1967; Kt 1951; MusD; Composer; *b* 29 March 1902; *s* of Charles Alexander and Louisa Maria Walton; *m* 1949, Susana Gil Passo. *Educ:* Cathedral Choir School and Christ Church, Oxford. Hon. Student Christ Church, Oxford; Hon. MusD (Oxon, Dunelm, TCD, Manchester); Hon. DMus (Cantab, London); Hon. FRCM; Hon. FRAM; Gold Medal Royal Philharmonic Society, 1947; Gold Medal Worshipful Company of Musicians 1947; Benjamin Franklin Medal, RSA, 1972. Mem. Royal Swedish Acad. of Music; Accademico onorario di Santa Cecilia, Rome; Hon. Mem., Royal Manchester Coll. of Music, 1972. *Compositions:* Pianoforte Quartet (Carnegie award), 1918, rev. 1974; String Quartet (unpublished), 1921; Façade (with Edith Sitwell), 1923 and 1926, Siesta for small orchestra, 1926; Portsmouth Point, 1926; Sinfonia Concertante for piano and orchestra, 1928; Viola Concerto, 1929; Belshazzar's Feast, 1931; Three Songs for Soprano, 1932; Symphony, 1935; Crown Imperial (Coronation

March), 1937; In Honour of the City of London, 1937; Violin Concerto, 1939; Music for Children, 1940; Scapino (comedy overture), 1940; & (ballet), 1943; Henry V (film), 1945; Quartet, 1947; Hamlet (film), 1948; Sonata for Violin and Pianoforte, 1949; Te Deum, 1953; Orb and Sceptre (Coronation March), 1953; Troilus and Cressida (opera), 1954; Richard III (film), 1955; Johannesburg Overture, 1956; Violoncello Concerto, 1956; Partita, 1957; Anon in Love, 1960; Symphony No. 2, 1960; Gloria, 1961; A Song for the Lord Mayor's Table, 1962; Prelude for Orchestra, 1962; Variations on a Theme by Hindemith, 1963; The Twelve (anthem), 1964; Missa Brevis, 1966; The Bear (comic opera) 1967; Capriccio Burlesco, 1968; Improvisations on an Impromptu by Benjamin Britten, 1970; Jubilate, 1972; Five Bagatelles (guitar), 1972; Sonata for String Orchestra, 1972; Cantico del Sole, 1974; Magnificat and Nunc Dimittis, 1974; Varii Capricci, 1976. *Address:* c/o Oxford University Press, 44 Conduit Street, W1. *Clubs:* Athenæum, Savile, Garrick.

WALWYN, Rear-Adm. James Humphrey, CB 1964; OBE 1944; retirement consultant, since 1975; *b* 21 Aug. 1913; *o s* of late Vice-Admiral Sir Humphrey Walwyn, KCSI, KCMG, CB, DSO and Lady Walwyn, DBE; *m* 1945, Pamela Digby Bell; one *s* two *d. Educ:* The Old Malthouse and RN College, Dartmouth. Entered RN, 1931; Lieut 1935; ADC to Governor of Newfoundland, 1936-37; specialised in Gunnery, 1938; HMS Renown, 1939-41; HMS Newcastle, 1942-44; Staff of C-in-C Home Fleet, 1945-47; Comdr 1948; Naval Staff Course, 1948; Admiralty, 1948-50; Comdg HMS Chevron, 1951-52; Captain 1953; Staff of SHAPE, Paris, 1954-56; Captain Inshore Flotilla, Mediterranean, 1956-58; Dir, RN Tactical School, 1958-59; Dir of Officer Appts, Admiralty, 1960-62; Rear-Adm. 1962; Flag Officer Flotillas, Mediterranean, 1962-65; retired, 1965. Chief Exec., Personnel, British Oxygen Co., 1965-75. FIPM. SBStJ 1972. *Recreations:* fishing, tennis. *Address:* 40 Jubilee Place, SW3. *T:* 01-352 7802. *Clubs:* Army and Navy, Hurlingham.

WALWYN, Peter Tyndall; racehorse trainer, since 1960; *b* 1 July 1933; *s* of late Lt-Col Charles Lawrence Tyndall Walwyn, DSO, OBE, MC, Moreton in Marsh, Glos; *m* 1960, Virginia Gaselee, *d* of A. S. Gaselee, MFH; one *s* one *d. Educ:* Amesbury Sch., Hindhead, Surrey; Charterhouse. Leading trainer on the flat, 1974, 1975; a new record in earnings (£373,563), 1975. Major races won include: One Thousand Guineas, 1970, Humble Duty; Oaks Stakes, 1974, Polygamy; Irish Derby, 1974, English Prince, and 1975, Grundy; King George VI and Queen Elizabeth Stakes, Ascot, 1975, Grundy; Epsom Derby, 1975, Grundy. *Recreations:* foxhunting, shooting. *Address:* Seven Barrows, Lambourn, Berks RG16 7UJ. *T:* Lambourn 71347. *Club:* Turf.

WANAMAKER, Sam; Actor; Director, Theatrical Producer; *b* Chicago, 14 June 1919; *s* of Morris Wanamaker and Molly (*née* Bobele); *m* 1940, Charlotte Holland; three *d. Educ:* Drake University, Iowa, USA. Studied for the stage at Goodman Theatre, Chicago. Appeared in summer theatres, Chicago (acting and directing), 1936-39; joined Globe Shakespearian Theatre Group; first New York Appearance, Café Crown, 1941; Counter Attack, 1942. Served in United States Armed Forces, 1943-46. In several parts on New York stage, 1946-49; appeared in This, Too, Shall Pass, 1946; directed and played in: Joan of Lorraine, 1946-47; Goodbye My Fancy, 1948-49; directed: Caeser and Cleopatra, 1950; The Soldier and the Lady, 1954; created Festival Repertory Theatre, New York, 1950. First performance (also producer) on London stage as Bernie Dodd, in Winter Journey, St James's, 1952; presented and appeared in The Shrike, Prince's, 1953; produced: Purple Dust, Glasgow, 1953; Foreign Field, Birmingham, 1954; directed and appeared in One More River, Cat on a Hot Tin Roof, and The Potting Shed, 1957. In Liverpool, 1957, created New Shakespeare Theatre Cultural Center, where produced (appearing in some): Tea and Sympathy, A View from the Bridge, 1957; The Rose Tattoo, Finian's Rainbow, Bus Stop, The Rainmaker, and Reclining Figure (all in 1958). *Presented, prod and appeared in:* The Big Knife, Duke of York's 1954; The Lovers, Winter Garden, 1955; The Rainmaker, St Martin's 1956; A Hatful of Rain, Prince's, 1957; The Rose Tattoo, New, 1959; Iago, Stratford-on-Avon, 1959; Dr Breuer, in A Far Country, New York, 1961; The Watergate Tapes, Royal Court, 1974; *produced:* The World of Sholom Aleichem, Embassy, 1955; King Priam, Coventry Theatre and Royal Opera House, Covent Garden, 1962, 1967, and 1972; Verdi's La Forza del Destino, Royal Opera House, Covent Garden, 1962; John Player season, Globe, 1972-73; Southwark Summer Festival, 1974; Shakespeare Birthday Celebrations, 1974; *directed:* Children from their Games, New York, 1963; A Case of Libel, New York, 1963; A Murder Among Us, New York, 1964; Defenders, 1964; The File of the Golden Goose, 1968; The Executioner, 1969; Catlow, 1971; War and Peace (première), Sydney Opera House, 1973;

The Ice Break, Royal Opera House, Covent Garden, 1977; *acted and directed* Macbeth, Goodman Theater, Chicago, 1964; *acted (films):* Give Us This Day; Taras Bulba; Those Magnificent Men in Their Flying Machines, 1964; The Winston Affair, 1964; The Spy Who Came in from the Cold, 1964; Warning Shot; The Law, 1974; Spiral Staircase, 1974; The Sell-Out, 1975; The Voyage, 1975; Billy Jack goes to Washington, 1976; Blind Love (TV), 1976; *films directed:* Hawk, 1965; Lancer, 1966; Custer, 1967; File of the Golden Goose, 1968; The Executioner, 1969; Catlow, 1970; Sinbad and the Eye of the Tiger, 1975; *directed (television):* Colombo, 1977; The Holocaust, 1977; Founder and Executive Director: Globe Playhouse Trust Ltd, 1971; World Centre for Shakespeare Studies Ltd. Directs and acts in TV productions, in UK and USA. *Address:* 99 Aldwych, WC2B 4JY.

WAND, Dr Solomon; Treasurer of British Medical Association, 1963-72 (Chairman of Council, 1956-61); *b* 14 January 1899; *s* of Louis and Jane Wand; *m* 1st, 1921, Claire Cohen (*d* 1951); one *s* one *d*; 2nd, 1960, Shaunagh Denison Crew, *o d* of Major Robert Douglas Crew and Irene Crew, Milford-on-Sea, Hants. *Educ:* Manchester Grammar School; Manchester University. Qualified 1921, MB, ChB (Manchester), with distinction in medicine; in general practice in Birmingham. FRCGP. Member of: Council BMA, 1935-72 (Pres. Midland Branch, 1969-70); Gen. Medical Council, 1961-71; Advertising Advisory Cttee of IBA (formerly ITA), 1961-74; Court of Governors, Univ. of Birmingham, 1969-70; Board, General Practice Finance Corporation, 1969-76; Chairman: Gen. Medical Services Cttee, BMA, 1948-52; Representative Body, BMA, 1951-54; Gold Medallist, BMA, 1954; formerly Member Central Health Services Council, Medical Advisory Cttee of Min. of Health; formerly Mem. Health Education Cttee. Hon. Vice-Pres. British Medical Students Assoc., 1959; Chm., British Medical Students Trust, 1968-; formerly Examng MO, Dept of Health and Social Security; Member: Study Cttee of World Medical Assoc., 1959-; Management Cttee, Medical Insurance Agency, 1964-; Birmingham Central District Medical Cttee, 1974-; Chm., Med. Adv. Cttee, Allied Investments Ltd. Hon. DCL, Durham, 1957; Hon. LLD Queen's Univ., Belfast, 1962. *Publications:* contribs to Encyclopædia of General Practice. *Address:* D 5 Kenilworth Court, Hagley Road, Edgbaston, Birmingham B16 9NU. *T:* 021-454 3997.

WANDSWORTH, Archdeacon of; see Coombs, Ven. P. B.

WANGARATTA, Bishop of, since 1975; **Rt. Rev. Maxwell McNee Thomas,** ThD; *b* 23 Aug. 1926; *s* of Rev. Charles Elliot Thomas, ThL, and Elsie Frances Thomas (*née* McNee); *m* 1952, Elaine Joy Walker; two *s* one *d. Educ:* St Paul's Coll., Univ. of Sydney (MA, BD); General Theological Seminary, New York (ThD). Lectr in Theology and Greek, St John's Coll., Morpeth, NSW, 1950; deacon, 1950; priest, 1952; Curate: St Peter's, E Maitland, 1951-52; St Mary Magdalene, Richmond, Surrey, 1952-54; All Saints', Singleton, NSW, 1955. Priest-in-Charge and Rector, The Entrance, NSW, 1955-59; Fellow and Tutor, General Theol. Seminary, NY, 1959-63; Hon. Chaplain to Bishop of New York, 1959-63, Chaplain, 1963-64; Chaplain, Univ. of Melbourne and of Canterbury Fellowship, 1964-68; Consultant Theologian to Archbishop of Melbourne, Stewart Lectr in Divinity, Trinity Coll. and Chaplain of Canterbury Fellowship, 1968-75. *Address:* Bishop's Lodge, Wangaratta, Victoria 3677, Australia. *T:* Wangaratta 21.3643.

WANI, Most Rev. Silvano; *see* Uganda, Rwanda, Burundi and Boga Zaire, Archbishop of.

WANSBROUGH, George, MA; CompIEE; *b* Oxford, 23 April 1904; *s* of Rev. H. A. Wansbrough, Rector of South Warnborough, and of Uliana, *d* of Bishop Tufnell; *m* 1st, 1928, Elizabeth (marr. diss. 1938), *d* of Sir George Lewis, 2nd Bt; one *s* one *d*; 2nd, 1939, Kathleen Barbara Rawdon (marr. diss. 1955), *d* of C. G. H. R. Macnamara, Indian Civil Service; one *s*; 3rd, 1955, Nancy, *d* of F. D. H. Joy, Marelands, Bentley, Hampshire. *Educ:* Cheam School; Eton (King's Scholar, Capt. of the School); King's College, Cambridge (Minor Scholar). Class I Mathematical Tripos Part I, 1924; Class II Div. I Economics Tripos Part II, 1926; Second Winchester Reading Prize, 1926; stroked Cambridge VIII, 1925; with Selfridge & Co. Ltd, intermittently, 1923-27; played rôle of The Poet in Anmer Hall's production of Sierra's Cradle Song, Little Theatre and Fortune Theatre, 1926-27; Robert Benson & Co. Ltd, Merchant Bankers, 1927-35, Dir, 1932-35; Sec., Anglo-French Timber Production Cttee, 1939-40; Member of Pottery Working Party, 1946; Cttee of Inquiry into Tudor Aircraft, 1947; Cttee to advise Govt on methods of purchase of aircraft for airways corporations, 1948; Director: A. Reyrolle & Co. Ltd, 1934-49, Chm. 1945-59; Mercantile Credit Co. Ltd, 1934-75; Bank of England, 1946-49;

Chm., Morphy-Richards Ltd, 1943-54; investment consultant, 1952-73. Member: National Advisory Council for Motor Manufacturing Industry, 1946-49; Development Areas Treasury Advisory Cttee, 1945-49; Public Works Loan Bd, 1946-49; Mem. Council, Institution of Electrical Engineers, 1946-49. Member: St Marylebone Borough Council, 1934-37; Holborn Borough Council, 1937-38. Financial Adviser to New Philharmonia Orchestra, 1968-69. Joint Treas. Fabian Soc., 1936-37; contested (Lab) West Woolwich, 1935. Mem. Governing Body, Bedales Sch., 1965-74. MSAE 1967. *Publications:* various articles, reviews, etc, signed and unsigned in The Times, Economist, Economic Journal, motoring and yachting press, etc. *Recreations:* reading, writing, arithmetic. *Address:* Udimore Cottage, Otterbourne Hill, Winchester. *T:* Chandler's Ford 66525. *Club:* Leander, Political Economy (Hon. Member).

WANSBROUGH-JONES, Sir Owen (Haddon), KBE 1955 (OBE 1946; MBE 1942); CB 1950; MA, PhD (Cantab); FRIC; Chairman, Albright & Wilson Ltd, 1967-69 (Executive Vice-Chairman, 1965-67); Director, British Oxygen International, 1960-76; *b* 25 March 1905; *y s* of late Arthur Wansbrough-Jones, BA, LLB, Long Stratton, Norfolk, and Beatrice (*d* 1972), *d* of late Thomas Slipper, JP, Bradeston Hall, Norfolk; unmarried. *Educ:* Gresham's School, Holt; Trinity Hall, Cambridge (Open Schol.). 1st Cl., Natural Sciences Tripos Part I and Part II (Chemistry); Research Student of Trinity Hall, and of Goldsmiths' & Salters' Company; Ramsay Memorial Fellow; studied Physical Chemistry at Cambridge under Prof. Sir Eric Rideal, and in Berlin under Professor Fritz Haber; Fellow of Trinity Hall, 1930-46; Assistant Tutor, 1932-34; Tutor, 1934-40; Hon. Fellow, 1957; Departmental Demonstrator, Dept of Colloid Science, University of Cambridge, 1932-40; Emergency Commission, 1940; France, 1940; Brig. 1945; Dir of Special Weapons and Vehicles, War Office, 1946; Scientific Adviser to Army Council, 1946-51; Principal Dir of Scientific Research (Defence) Min. of Supply, 1951-53; Chief Scientist of Min. of Supply, 1953-59. Mem., Natural Environment Research Council, 1968-74. Treasurer of Faraday Soc., 1949-60; Pres., Jesters Club, 1958-77. Prime Warden, Goldsmiths' Company, 1967; Hon. Freeman, Fishmongers' Co., 1973. *Publications:* scientific papers on physical chemistry in British and German scientific journals, 1929-38. *Recreations:* gardening, shooting. *Address:* 7 King Street, St James's, SW1. *T:* 01-930 8608; Orchardleigh, Long Stratton, Norfolk NR15 2XQ. *T:* Long Stratton 30410. *Club:* United Oxford & Cambridge University.

WANSTALL, Hon. Sir Charles Gray, Kt 1974; Hon. Mr Justice Wanstall; Senior Puisne Judge of Supreme Court, Queensland, Australia; *b* 17 Feb. 1912; *m* 1938, Olwyn Mabel, *d* of C. O. John; one *d. Educ:* Roma and Gympie State Schs; Gympie High Sch., Queensland, Australia. Called to Queensland Bar, 1933. High Court, 1942. MLA (Liberal) for Toowong, 1944-50; Dep. Leader of Liberal Party of Australia (Qld Div.), 1950-53. QC 1956; Judge, Supreme Court, Qld, 1958. *Recreations:* reading, photography. *Address:* Judge's Chambers, Supreme Court, Brisbane, Qld, Australia; Gra-wyn, Sandford Street, St Lucia, Brisbane, Queensland 4067, Australia. *Clubs:* Queensland (Brisbane); St Lucia Bowling.

WARBEY, William Noble; Executive Director, Organisation for World Political and Social Studies, since 1965; Secretary, World Studies Trust, since 1966; Chairman, Rossetti House Group, since 1968; *b* 16 August 1903; *s* of Charles Noble Warbey and Alice May Symons; *m* 1931, Audrey Grace Wicks; no *c. Educ:* Grocers' Company's School, Hackney Downs; King's College, London; London School of Economics. Language Teacher and Interpreter, France and Germany, 1925-26; Secondary School Master, Derby Municipal Secondary School, 1927-28; Secretary and Tutor, University Tutorial College, London, 1929-37; Tutor-Organiser, National Council of Labour Colls, 1937-40; Chief English Press Officer to Norwegian Govt (London), 1941-45. MP (Lab) for Luton Div. of Beds, 1945-50; Broxtowe Div. of Notts, (Sept.) 1953-55; Ashfield Div. of Notts, 1955-66, resigned. Travel organiser, 1950-51; Editor of Look and Listen, 1952-55. *Publications:* Look to Norway, 1945; (jt) Modern Norway, 1950; Vietnam: The Truth, 1965; Ho Chi Minh: Life and Achievements, 1970. *Recreations:* music, travel, organic horticulture.

WARBURG, Fredric John; President, Secker and Warburg Ltd, Publishers (Chairman, 1936-71); *b* 27 Nov. 1898; *s* of late John Cimon Warburg and Violet Amalia Warburg; *m*; three *s*; *m* 1933, Pamela de Bayou; (one *s* decd). *Educ:* Westminster School; Christ Church, Oxford (Exhibnr). 2nd Cl. Lit. Hum. (Greats); MA 1922. Served as 2nd Lieut with 284th Siege Battery, Belgium and France, 1917-19. Joined George Routledge & Sons Ltd as apprentice, 1922; Joint Man. Dir, 1931;

resigned, 1935. Bought publishing firm Martin Secker, Ltd, 1936; name changed to Martin Secker & Warburg, 1936, with himself as Chairman. Served as Corporal in St John's Wood Co., Home Guard under Sergeant George Orwell (Eric Blair), 1941-45. Joined Heinemann Group of Publishers, 1951. Tried at Central Criminal Court (Old Bailey) for publishing an allegedly obscene novel, and acquitted, 1954. Elected Director of Heinemann Group of Publishers, 1961-71. *Publications:* An Occupation for Gentlemen, 1959; A Slight Case of Obscenity (9000 words) in New Yorker Magazine, 20 April 1957; All Authors are Equal, 1973. *Recreations:* replaying chess games of the masters, window box gardening, reading, writing. *Address:* 29 St Edmund's Court, Regent's Park, NW8. *T:* 01-722 5641.

WARBURG, Sir Siegmund G(eorge), Kt 1966; President, S. G. Warburg & Co. Ltd, London, since 1970 (Director, 1946-69); *b* 30 Sept. 1902; *s* of George S. Warburg and Lucie (*née* Kaulla); *m* 1926, Eva Maria Philipson; one *s* one *d. Educ:* Gymnasium, Reutlingen, Germany; Humanistic Seminary, Urach, Germany, 1920-30; training periods in Hamburg, London, Boston and New York; Partner M. M. Warburg & Co., Hamburg, 1930-38; Director, New Trading Co. Ltd, London, 1938-46. *Recreations:* reading and walking. *Address:* 30 Gresham Street, EC2. *T:* 01-600 4555.

WARBURTON, Col Alfred Arthur, CBE 1961; DSO 1945; DL; JP; Chairman, SHEF Engineering Ltd, 1970-75; Company Director since 1953; *b* 12 April 1913; *s* of late A. V. Warburton. *Educ:* Sedbergh. Served War of 1939-45, with Essex Yeomanry; Lt-Col comdg South Notts Hussars Yeomanry, 1953-58; Hon. Col 1966-76; Col DCRA 49th Inf. Div. TA, 1958-60; ADC to the Queen, 1961-66; Chm., Notts Cttee TA&VR Assoc. for E Midlands. Director, John Shaw Ltd, Worksop, 1953-66. DL 1966, High Sheriff 1968, JP 1968, Notts. *Recreations:* shooting, fishing. *Address:* Wigthorpe House, near Worksop, Notts. *T:* Worksop 730357. *Clubs:* Cavalry and Guards; Nottinghamshire County (Nottingham).

WARBURTON, Anne Marion, CMG 1977; CVO 1965; HM Ambassador to Denmark, since 1976; *b* 8 June 1927; *d* of Captain Eliot Warburton, MC and Mary Louise (*née* Thompson), US. *Educ:* Barnard Coll.; Columbia Univ. (BA); Somerville Coll., Oxford (BA, MA); Hon. Fellow, 1977. Economic Cooperation Administration, London, 1949-52; NATO Secretariat, Paris, 1952-54; Lazard Bros, London, 1955-57; entered Diplomatic Service, Nov. 1957; 2nd Sec., FO, 1957-59; 2nd, then 1st Sec., UK Mission to UN, NY, 1959-62; 1st Sec., Bonn, 1962-65; 1st Sec., DSAO, London, 1965-67; 1st Sec., FO, then FCO, 1967-70; Counsellor, UK Mission to UN, Geneva, 1970-75; Head of Guidance and Information Policy Dept, FCO, 1975-76. Verdienstkreuz, 1st Class (West Germany), 1965. *Recreations:* ski-ing, theatre, travel. *Address:* British Embassy, Bredgade 26, Copenhagen, Denmark; c/o Foreign and Commonwealth Office, SW1. *Clubs:* United Oxford & Cambridge University, Ski Club of Great Britain, English-Speaking Union.

WARBURTON, Eric John Newnham, CBE 1966; a Vice-Chairman, Lloyds Bank Ltd, 1967-75; *b* 22 Nov. 1904; *o s* of late E. and H. R. Warburton, Bexhill-on-Sea, Sussex; *m* 1933, Louise, *er d* of late C. J. and L. R. Martin, Crowborough, Sussex; one *s* one *d. Educ:* Eastbourne Grammar School. Entered Lloyds Bank Ltd, 1922; Jt General Man., 1953; Dep. Chief Gen. Man., 1958; Chief Gen. Man., 1959-66; Dir, 1965-75; Dep. Chm., Lloyds Bank International Ltd, 1971-75; Director: Lloyds Bank Unit Trust Managers Ltd, 1966-75; First Western Bank Trust Co., Calif., 1974-75; Lewis's Bank Ltd, 1967-75; Intercontinental Banking Services Ltd, 1968-75. Chairman: Exec. Cttee, Banking Information Service, 1965-71; Bank Education Service, 1966-71; Dep. Chairman: City of London Savings Cttee, 1962-74; Exports Credit Guarantee Dept Adv. Council, 1968-71 (Member, 1966-71); Member: Decimal Currency Bd, 1967-71; Nat. Savings Cttee, 1963-74; Council, CBI, 1971-75. Member Board: Trinity Coll. of Music, 1968-; Management Cttee, Sussex Housing Assoc. for the Aged, 1970-; American Bankers Assoc. Internat. Monetary Conf., 1970-72. FRSA 1970; Hon. FTCL 1969. *Recreations:* golf, gardening, music. *Address:* 9 Denmans Close, Lindfield, Haywards Heath, West Sussex RH16 2JX. *T:* Lindfield 2351. *Club:* Bath.

WARBURTON, Prof. Geoffrey Barratt; Professor of Applied Mechanics, University of Nottingham, since 1961; *b* 9 June 1924; *s* of Ernest McPherson and Beatrice Warburton; *m* 1952, Margaret Coan; three *d. Educ:* William Hulme's Grammar School, Manchester; Peterhouse, Cambridge. Cambridge: Open Exhibition in Mathematics, 1942; 1st cl. Hons in Mechanical Sciences Tripos, 1944; BA 1945; MA 1949; Junior Demonstrator, 1944-46. Asst Lecturer in Engineering, Univ.

Coll. of Swansea, 1946-47; Dept of Engineering, Univ. of Edinburgh; Assistant, 1947-48, Lecturer, 1948-50 and 1953-56; ICI Research Fellow, 1950-53; Head of Post-graduate School of Applied Dynamics, 1956-61; PhD (Edinburgh) 1949. FRSE 1960; FIMechE 1968. Associate Editor, Internat. Jl of Earthquake Engineering and Structural Dynamics; Member, Editorial Boards: Internat. Jl of Mechanical Sciences; Internat. Jl for Numerical Methods in Engineering; Jl of Sound and Vibration. *Publications:* The Dynamical Behaviour of Structures, 1964, 2nd edn 1976; research on mechanical vibrations, in several scientific journals. *Address:* University of Nottingham, Nottingham NG7 2RD.

WARD, family name of **Earl of Dudley,** of **Viscounts Bangor** and **Ward of Witley,** and of **Baroness Ward of North Tyneside.**

WARD OF NORTH TYNESIDE, Baroness *cr* 1974 (Life Peer), of North Tyneside; **Irene Mary Bewick Ward,** CH 1973; DBE 1955 (CBE 1929); JP; *d* of late Alfred Ward, London, and late Elvina Mary Ward. Contested (C) Morpeth, 1924 and 1929, Wallsend, 1945; MP (C) Wallsend-on-Tyne, 1931-45; MP (C) Tynemouth, 1950-Feb. 1974. Hon. Fellow, Lucy Cavendish Collegiate Soc., Cambridge, 1972; Hon. FRSA, 1972. JP Newcastle upon Tyne, 1949. *Publication:* FANY Invicta, 1955. *Address:* 4 Roseworth Terrace, Gosforth, Newcastle upon Tyne NE3 1AA. *T:* 51863. *Club:* Sloane.

WARD OF WITLEY, 1st Viscount, *cr* 1960; **George Reginald Ward,** PC 1957; *b* 20 Nov. 1907; 4th *s* (twin) of 2nd Earl of Dudley; *m* 1st, 1940, Anne Capel (marr. diss., 1951); one *s* one *d*; 2nd, 1962, Hon. Mrs Barbara Astor (who *m* 1st, 1942. Hon. Michael Langhorne Astor, *qv*). *Educ:* Eton; Christ Church, Oxford. AAF, 1929; RAF, 1932-37 and 1939-45. MP (C) for Worcester City, 1945-60. Parly Under-Sec. of State, Air Min., 1952-55; Parly and Financial Sec., Admiralty, Dec. 1955-Jan. 1957; Secretary of State for Air, 1957-60. *Heir: s* Hon. Anthony Giles Humble Ward, *b* 10 June 1943. *Address:* 23 Queens Gate Gardens, SW7 5LZ. *Clubs:* White's, Pratt's.

WARD, Prof. Alan Gordon, CBE 1972 (OBE 1959); Procter Professor of Food and Leather Science, Leeds University, 1961-77, now Emeritus; *b* 18 April 1914; *s* of Lionel Howell Ward and Lily Maud Ward (*née* Morgan); *m* 1938, Cicely Jean Chapman; one *s* two *d*. *Educ:* Queen Elizabeth's Grammar Sch., Wimborne; Trinity Coll., Cambridge (schol.). BA (Cantab) 1935; MA (Cantab) 1940; FInstP 1946; FIFST 1966. Lectr in Physics and Mathematics, N Staffs Technical Coll., 1937-40; Experimental Officer, Min. of Supply, 1940-46; Sen. Scientific Officer, Building Research Station, 1946-48; Principal Scientific Officer, 1948-49; Dir of Research, The British Gelatine and Glue Research Assoc., 1949-59; Prof. of Leather Industries, Leeds Univ., 1959-61. Chm., Food Standards Cttee set up by Minister of Agriculture, 1965-. *Publications:* Nature of Crystals, 1938; Colloids, Their Properties and Applications, 1945; The Science and Technology of Gelatin, 1977; papers in Trans. Far. Soc., Jl Sci. Instr, Biochem. Jl, etc. *Recreation:* music. *Address:* 35 Templar Gardens, Wetherby, West Yorkshire. *T:* Wetherby 64177. *Club:* Savage.

WARD, Ven. Arthur Frederick, BA; Archdeacon of Exeter and a Canon Residentiary of Exeter Cathedral since 1970, Precentor since 1972; *b* 23 April 1912; *s* of William Thomas and Annie Florence Ward, Corbridge, Northumberland; *m* 1937, Margaret Melrose, Tynemouth, Northumberland; two *d*. *Educ:* Durham Choir School; Newcastle upon Tyne Royal Grammar School; Durham University; Ridley Hall, Cambridge. Curate, Byker Parish Church, Newcastle, 1935-40; Rector of Harpurhey, North Manchester, 1940-44; Vicar of Nelson, 1944-55; Vicar of Christ Church, Paignton, 1955-62; Archdeacon of Barnstaple and Rector of Shirwell with Loxhore, Devon, 1962-70. *Recreations:* gardening, cricket, touring. *Address:* 12 The Close, Exeter EX1 1EZ. *T:* Exeter 75745.

WARD, Sir Aubrey (Ernest), Kt 1967; JP; DL; *b* 17 April 1899; *s* of Edward Alfred Ward; *m* 1919, Mary Jane Davidson Rutherford, MB, ChB; one *d*. *Educ:* Royal Veterinary College, London. Served War of 1914-18; Night FO, RFC (now RAF). Veterinary Practice, 1923-66. Vice-Chm., Thames Conservancy Bd, 1964-74. Mayor of Slough, 1940-45, Hon. Freeman, 1961. JP 1957, DL 1963, Chm., CC, 1963-74, Buckinghamshire. *Address:* 54 Pound Lane, Marlow, Bucks. *T:* Marlow 5250.

WARD, Barbara; *see* Jackson of Lodsworth, Baroness.

WARD, Christopher John Ferguson; solicitor; with Arthur F. Clark & Son, Reading, since 1965; *b* 26 Dec. 1942; *m* Elizabeth Ward; two *s* one *d*. *Educ:* Magdalen College Sch.; Law Society Sch. of Law. MP (C) Swindon, Oct. 1969-June 1970. Member:

Berks CC, 1965- (Dep. Leader of the Council, 1976-); Standing Conf. on London and SE Regional Planning, 1967-70; Mem., Young Conservatives, 1958- (former Chm., Young Cons. Wessex Adv. Cttee). *Address:* Endfield House, Sandisplatt Road, Maidenhead, Berks. *T:* Maidenhead 70146; (office) Reading 585321.

WARD, David, CBE 1972; FRCM; Opera Singer; *b* 3 July 1922; *s* of James Ward and Catherine Bell; *m* 1960, Susan E. V. Rutherford; no *c*. *Educ:* St Patrick's School, Dumbarton; Royal College of Music. Royal Navy, 1940-43; Royal Indian Navy, 1943-46. Sadler's Wells, 1953-59; Covent Garden, 1960-64; now international free-lance singer, Germany, USA, Italy, France, etc. Hon. RAM 1973; FRCM 1973. Hon. LLD Strathclyde, 1974. *Recreation:* golf. *Address:* 14 Clarence Terrace, Regent's Park, NW1.

WARD, David Conisbee; Under Secretary, War Pensions and Industrial Injury Benefits Division, Department of Health and Social Security, since 1976; *b* 7 Jan. 1933; *s* of late Sydney L. Ward and Ivy A. Ward; *m* 1958, Patricia Jeanette (*née* Nobes); one *s* one *d*. *Educ:* Kingston Grammar Sch.; St John's Coll., Cambridge (Scholar, MA). Asst Principal, Nat. Assistance Bd, 1956; Asst Private Sec. to Lord President of the Council and Minister for Science, 1960-61; Principal, Nat. Assistance Bd, 1961, Min. of Social Security, 1966, DHSS, 1968; Asst Sec., DHSS, 1970. Reader, St Matthew, Surbiton, 1960-. *Recreations:* philately, Chelsea FC, allotmenteering. *Address:* 5 St Matthew's Avenue, Surbiton, Surrey KT6 6JJ. *T:* 01-399 3323. *Club:* Royal Commonwealth Society.

WARD, Sir Deighton (Harcourt Lisle), GCMG 1976; QC (Barbados) 1959; Governor-General, Barbados, since 1976; *b* 16 May 1909; *s* of Edmund Lisle Ward and Ellen Ward; *m* 1936, Audrey Doreen Ramsey; three *d*. *Educ:* Boys' Foundation Sch.; Harrison Coll., Barbados. Called to the Bar, Middle Temple, 1933; practised at Barbados Bar, 1934-63; Mem., Legislative Council of Barbados, 1955-58; Mem., House of Representatives, Fedn of West Indies, 1958-62; High Court of Barbados, 1963-76. Pres., Barbados Football Assoc., 1954-75. *Recreations:* reading, bridge, billiards. *Address:* Government House, Barbados. *T:* 92646. *Clubs:* Spartan (Barbados); (Hon.) Summerhays; (Hon.) Bridgetown; (Hon.) Barbados Turf.

WARD, Denzil Anthony Seaver, CMG 1967; Barrister, New Zealand; *b* Nelson, NZ, 26 March 1909; 3rd *s* of late Louis Ernest Ward, Civil Servant NZ Government and Secretary Geographic Board, and Theresa Ward (*née* Kilgour); *m* 1938, Mary Iredale Garland, *d* of late John Edwin Garland, Christchurch, NZ; three *d*. *Educ:* Christ's College and Cathedral Grammar Sch., Christchurch, NZ; Victoria Univ. of Wellington, NZ. BA 1928; LLB 1938; practised law as barrister and solicitor, 1938-42; Asst Law Draftsman, Law Drafting Office, 1942; First Asst, 1947; Law Draftsman, 1958-66; Counsel to Law Drafting Office and Compiler of Statutes, 1966-74. Lecturer in law subjects, Victoria Univ. of Wellington, NZ, 1944-45, 1949-55. Member: NZ Law Revision Commn, 1958-74; Public and Administrative Law Reform Cttee, 1966-; Criminal Law Reform Cttee, 1971-; Vice-Patron, Legal Research Foundation, 1965-68. Mem. Otaki and Porirua Trusts Bd, 1952-71, Chm., 1965-71; Mem. Papawai and Kaikokirikiri Trusts Bd, 1965-, Chm., 1972-. Foundation mem. and mem. Council, NZ Founders Soc., 1939-42; elected hon. life mem., 1941. Chm., Royal Wellington Choral Union, 1949-50; mem. Schola Cantorum, 1951-55. *Publications:* (jointly) Ward and Wild's Mercantile Law in New Zealand, 1947; (ed) NZ Statutes Reprint, 1908-57, vols 3-16; articles in legal periodicals. *Recreations:* music, reading, gardening, watching rugby and cricket. *Address:* 15 Plymouth Street, Karori, Wellington 5, New Zealand. *T:* 768-096.

WARD, Donald Albert; Secretary General, International Union of Credit and Investment Insurers (Berne Union), since 1974; *b* 30 March 1920; *s* of Albert and Rosie Ward; *m* 1948, Maureen Molloy; five *s*. *Educ:* Brewery Road Elementary Sch.; Southend-on-Sea High Sch.; The Queen's Coll., Oxford. BA(Hons)(Maths). Served War, Indian Army (RIASC), 10th Indian Div., Middle East and Italy, 1940-45 (despatches). Min. of Food, 1946-53; Export Credits Guarantee Dept, 1953-74 (Under-Sec., 1971-74). *Address:* Lindisfarne, St Nicholas Hill, Leatherhead, Surrey.

WARD, General Sir Dudley, GCB 1959 (KCB 1957; CB 1945); KBE 1953 (CBE 1945); DSO 1944; DL; *b* 27 Jan. 1905; *s* of L. H. Ward, Wimborne, Dorset; *m* 1st, 1933, Beatrice Constance (*d* 1962), *d* of Rev. T. F. Griffith, The Bourne, Farnham, Surrey; one *d*; 2nd, 1963, Joan Elspeth de Pechell, *d* of late Colonel D. C. Scott, CBE, Netherbury, Dorset. *Educ:* Wimborne Grammar

Sch.; Royal Military Coll., Sandhurst. 2nd Lieut, Dorset Regt, 1929; Captain, The King's Regt, 1937. Served War of 1939-45 (DSO, CBE, CB); Director of Military Operations, War Office, 1947-48; Commandant, Staff Coll., Camberley, 1948-51; Commander of the 1st Corps, 1951-52; Deputy Chief of Imperial General Staff, 1953-56; Commander, Northern Army Group and Commander-in-Chief, British Army of the Rhine, 1957-Dec. 1959; Comdr in Chief, British Forces, Near East, 1960-62; Governor and Commander in Chief of Gibraltar, 1962-65. Colonel, King's Regt, 1947-57; Colonel Commandant, REME, 1958-63; ADC General to the Queen, 1959-61. DL Suffolk, 1968. *Recreation:* golf. *Address:* Wynney's Farmhouse, Dennington, Woodbridge, Suffolk. *T:* Badingham 663. *Club:* Army and Navy.

WARD, Edmund Fisher, CBE 1972; Architect; Member, Royal Fine Art Commission, since 1974; Design Consultant, Royal Opera House, Covent Garden; Consultant (formerly Partner), Gollins Melvin Ward Partnership. *Address:* White Cottage, The Street, Chipperfield, near King's Langley, Hertfordshire WD4 9BH.

WARD, Edward; *see* Bangor, 7th Viscount.

WARD, Edward Rex, CMG 1948; *b* 19 May 1902; *y s* of late Daniel Ward, FSI, Tavistock; *m* 1st, 1934, Mary Nell (from whom he obtained a divorce, 1941); 2nd, 1947, Molly Owen Jones, *née* Money (*d* 1971), widow of Flying Officer Owen Jones, RAF; one *s* two step *d. Educ:* King's Coll., Taunton; Coll. of Estate Management, Lincoln's Inn Fields, WC1. Colonial Administrative Service, Nigeria, 1926; transferred to The Gambia, 1942; Actg Governor on several occasions since 1945; Colonial Secretary, The Gambia, 1945-52; retired, 1952. *Recreation:* gardening. *Address:* Cairnbrook, Fairy Road, Seaview, Isle of Wight. *T:* Seaview 2478. *Club:* Seaview Yacht.

WARD, Ven. Edwin James Greenfield, MVO 1963; Archdeacon of Sherborne since 1967; Rector of West Stafford since 1967; *b* 26 Oct. 1919; *er s* of Canon F. G. Ward, MC, lately of Canberra, Australia; *m* 1946, Grizell Evelyn Buxton; one *s* two *d. Educ:* St John's, Leatherhead; Christ's Coll., Cambridge (MA). Served King's Dragoon Guards, 1940; Reserve, 1946. Ordained 1948; Vicar of North Elmham, Norfolk, 1950-55; Chaplain to the Queen, 1955; Chaplain, Royal Chapel, Windsor Great Park, 1955-67. *Recreations:* shooting, fishing, golf. *Address:* The Rectory, West Stafford, Dorchester, Dorset. *T:* Dorchester 4637. *Club:* Norfolk (Norwich).

WARD, Air Cdre Ellacott Lyne Stephens, CB 1954; DFC 1939; RAF, retired; *b* 22 Aug. 1905; *s* of late Lt-Col E. L. Ward, CBE, IMS; *m* 1929, Sylvia Winifred Constance Etheridge (*d* 1974), *d* of late Lt-Col F. Etheridge, DSO, IA, and late Mrs Etheridge; one *s* one *d. Educ:* Bradfield; Cranwell. No 20 Sqdn, India, 1926-30; Engineering Course, and Engineering duties, UK, 1930-34; student, Army Staff Coll., Quetta, 1936-37; comd No 28 Sqdn, RAF, 1938-39; MAP, 1940-42; Instructor, RAF Staff Coll., 1942-43; Bomber Comd, 1943-44; Dep. Head, RAF Mission to Chinese Air Force Staff Coll., Chengtu, China, 1945-46; SASO, Burma, 1946-47; Air Ministry, 1947-49; Flying Training Comd, 1949-52; Head of British Services Mission to Burma, 1952-54; AOC No 64 (N) Group, Royal Air Force, 1954-57. Chinese Cloud and Banner, 1946; Chinese Chenyuan, 1946. *Recreation:* bookbinding. *Address:* Carousel, 37 Brownsea Road, Sandbanks, Poole, Dorset. *T:* Canford Cliffs 709455. *Club:* Royal Motor Yacht (Poole).

WARD, Francis Alan Burnett, CBE 1964; PhD; Keeper, Department of Physics, Science Museum, London, SW7, 1945-March 1970; *b* 5 March 1905; *o s* of late Herbert Ward, CBE, and late Eva Caroline (*née* Burnett); *m* 1953, E. Marianne Brown, Ilkley. *Educ:* Highgate Sch.; Sidney Sussex Coll., Cambridge. MA, PhD (Cantab), 1931. Research on atomic physics at Cavendish Laboratory, Cambridge, 1927-31; Asst Keeper, The Science Museum, 1931; seconded to Air Ministry (Meteorological Office), 1939. Flt-Lieut, RAFVR (Meteorological Branch), 1943-45. In charge of Atomic Physics and Time Measurement sections, Science Museum, 1931-70. FBHI; FInstP; FMA. *Publications:* official Science Museum Handbooks on Time Measurement, 1936 and 1937, and later edns. Various papers on atomic physics in Proc. Royal Society and Proc. Physical Soc. *Recreations:* bird-watching, gardening, photography, music. *Address:* Wendover, 8 Parkgate Avenue, Hadley Wood, Barnet, Herts EN4 0NR. *T:* 01-449 6880.

WARD, Frederick John; Under-Secretary, Department of the Environment (formerly Ministry of Housing and Local Government), 1968-76. *Address:* 29 Groveside, Great Bookham, Leatherhead, Surrey. *T:* Bookham 52282. *Club:* MCC.

WARD, Hubert, MA; JP; Headmaster of the King's School, Ely, since 1970; *b* 26 Sept. 1931; *s* of Allan Miles Ward and Joan Mary Ward; *m* 1958, Elizabeth Cynthia Fearn Bechervaise; one *s* two *d. Educ:* Westminster Sch.; Trinity Coll., Cambridge. Asst Master (Maths), Geelong C of E Grammar Sch., Victoria, 1955-66; Asst Master (Maths), Westminster Sch., London, 1966-69. *Publication:* (with K. Lewis) Starting Statistics, 1969. *Recreations:* rowing, sailing, bird-watching. *Address:* The King's School, Ely, Cambridgeshire. *T:* Ely 2824.

WARD, Ivor William, OBE 1968; Deputy Managing Director, Associated Television (Network) Ltd, 1974-77, retired; *b* 19 Jan. 1916; *s* of Stanley James Ward and Emily Ward; *m* 1st, 1940, Patricia Aston; two *s* one *d*; 2nd, 1970, Betty Nichols; one step *s*. *Educ:* Hoe Grammar Sch., Plymouth. Asst Engr, BBC Radio Plymouth, 1932; Technical Asst, BBC Experimental TV Service, Alexandra Palace, 1936; Maintenance Engr, BBC TV London, 1937. Instructor Radar, REME and Military Coll. of Science, 1939-45. Studio Manager, BBC TV, 1946; Producer, BBC TV, 1947-55; Head of Light Entertainment, ATV (Network) ITV, 1955-61; Production Controller, ATV, 1961-63; Executive Controller and Production Controller, ATV, 1963-67; Director of Programmes, ATV, 1968-76. Chm., ITV Network Sports Cttee, 1972-; Head of Ops Gp World Cup 1978, EBO, 1977-. FRSA. *Recreations:* sport, golf, fishing, motor sport and motor cars, photography, music. *Address:* The Anchorage, Old Church Road, Mawnan, near Falmouth, Cornwall. *T:* Mawnan Smith 535.

WARD, Prof. John Clive, FRS 1965; Professor, Macquarie University, Sydney, NSW, since 1967; *b* 1 Aug. 1924; *s* of Joseph William Ward and Winifred Palmer. *Educ:* Bishops Stortford Coll.; Merton Coll., Oxford. Member, Inst. for Advanced Study, Princeton, 1951-52, 1955-56, 1960-61; Professor of Physics, Carnegie Inst. of Technology, Pittsburgh, 1959-60; The Johns Hopkins University, Baltimore, 1961-66. *Publications:* various articles on particle theory and statistical mechanics. *Recreations:* ski-ing, music. *Address:* School of Mathematics and Physics, Macquarie University, 171-7 Epping Road, North Ryde, NSW 2113, Australia; 16 Fern Street, Pymble, NSW 2073.

WARD, Sir John (Guthrie), GCMG 1967 (KCMG 1956; CMG 1947); *b* 3 March 1909; *o s* of late Herbert John Ward and Alice Ward (*née* Guthrie); *m* 1st, 1933, Bettine (*d* 1941), *d* of late Col Sydney Hankey; one *s* one *d*; 2nd, 1942, Daphne, *d* of late Captain Hon. A. S. E. Mulholland and of Joan, Countess of Cavan; two *d. Educ:* Wellington Coll.; Pembroke Coll., Cambridge (History School). BA 1929, Hon. Fellow 1976; Member of University Air Squadron. Entered Diplomatic Service, 1931; served Foreign Office and British Embassies, Baghdad (1932-34) and Cairo (1938-40); British Representative on League of Nations Cttee for settlement of Assyrians, 1935-37. Second Sec., 1936; First Sec., 1941; Mem. of UK Delegns to Moscow confs, 1943-44-45 and Potsdam conf., 1945; Counsellor and Head of UN Dept, Foreign Office, 1946; Counsellor, British Embassy, Rome, 1946-49; Civilian Member of Directing Staff of Imperial Defence Coll., London, 1950; Dep. UK High Comr in Germany, 1951-54; Dep. Under-Sec. of State, Foreign Office, 1954-56; British Ambassador to Argentina, 1957-61; British Ambassador to Italy, 1962-66; retired from HM Diplomatic Service, 1967. Chairman, British-Italian Soc., 1967-74. Mem. Council, RSPCA, 1970-75; Pres., ISPA. *Recreations:* history, gardening. *Address:* Lenox, St Margarets Bay, near Dover; Flat 5, 15 Herbert Crescent, SW1. *Club:* Royal Automobile.

WARD, John Stanton, RA 1965 (ARA 1956); RP; *b* 10 Oct. 1917; *s* of Russell Stanton and Jessie Elizabeth Ward; *m* 1950, Alison Christine Mary Williams; four *s* twin *d. Educ:* St Owen's School, Hereford; Royal College of Art. Royal Engineers, 1939-46. Vogue Magazine, 1948-52. Has held exhibitions at Trafford Gallery, Arthur Jeffress Gallery and Maas Gallery. *Recreation:* book illustration. *Address:* Bilting Court, Bilting, Ashford, Kent. *T:* Wye 812478. *Club:* Athenæum.

WARD, Sir Joseph James Laffey, 4th Bt *cr* 1911; *b* 11 Nov. 1946; *s* of Sir Joseph George Davidson Ward, 3rd Bt, and of Joan

Mary Haden, *d* of Major Thomas J. Laffey, NZSC; *S* father, 1970; *m* 1968, Robyn Allison, *d* of William Maitland Martin, Rotorua, NZ. *Heir: b* Roderic Anthony Ward, *b* 23 April 1948.

WARD, Leslie M.; *see* Ward, Philip Leslie M.

WARD, Martyn Eric; His Honour Judge Ward; a Circuit Judge since 1972; *b* 10 Oct. 1927; 3rd *s* of Arthur George Ward, DSM and Dorothy Ward (*née* Perkins); *m* 1st, 1957, Rosaleen Iona Soloman; one *d*; 2nd, 1966, Rosanna Maria; two *s*. Royal Navy, 1945-48. Called to Bar, Lincoln's Inn, 1955. *Recreations:* skiing, swimming, the cinema, sitting on the beach. *Address:* The House on the Heath, Fordham Heath, Colchester, Essex CO3 5TL. *T:* Colchester 240624.

WARD, Michael Jackson; British Council Representative in Italy, since 1977; *b* 16 Sept. 1931; *s* of Harry Ward, CBE, and of late Dorothy Julia Ward (*née* Clutterbuck); *m* 1955, Eileen Patricia Foster; one *s* one *d*. *Educ:* Drayton Manor Grammar Sch.; University Coll. London (BA); Univ. of Freiburg; Corpus Christi Coll., Oxford. HM Forces, 1953-55; 2nd Lieut Royal Signals. Admin. Officer, HMOCS, serving as Dist Comr and Asst Sec. to Govt, Gilbert and Ellice Is; British Council, 1961-: Schs Recruitment Dept, 1961-64; Regional Rep., Sarawak, 1964-68; Dep. Rep., Pakistan, 1968-70; Dir, Appointments Services Dept, 1970-72; Dir, Personnel Dept, 1972-75; Controller, Personnel and Appts Div., 1975-77. *Recreation:* music. *Address:* Palazzo del Drago, Via delle Quattro Fontane 20, 00184 Rome. *T:* 4750018/20. *Club:* National Liberal.

WARD, Michael John; MP (Lab) Peterborough, since Oct. 1974; *b* 7 April 1931; *s* of Stanley William Ward and Margaret Annie Ward; *m* 1953, Lilian Lomas; two *d*. *Educ:* Mawney Road Jun. Mixed Sch., Romford; Royal Liberty Sch., Romford; Bungay Grammar Sch.; Univ. of Manchester. BA (Admin). MIPR. Education Officer, RAF, 1953-57; Registrar, Chartered Inst. of Secretaries, 1958-60; S. J. Noel-Brown & Co. Ltd: O&M consultant to local authorities, 1960-61; Local Govt Officer, 1961-65; Public Relns consultant to local authorities, 1965-70; Press Officer, ILEA, 1970-74. PPS to Sec. of State for Educn and Science, 1975-76, Minister for Overseas Develt, 1976, Minister of State, FCO, 1976-. Sponsored Unfair Contract Terms Act, 1977. Councillor, Borough of Romford, 1958-61 and 1962-65; London Borough of Havering: Councillor, 1964; Alderman, 1971-; Leader of Council, 1971-74. Contested (Lab) Peterborough, 1966, 1970, Feb. 1974. Labour Chief Whip, London Boroughs Assoc., 1968-71; Mem. Essex River Authority, 1964-71; Hon. Treas., Greater London Arts Assoc., 1969-71. *Recreations:* music, reading, travel. *Address:* House of Commons, SW1A 0AA. *T:* 01-219 3436.

WARD, Maj.-Gen. Sir Philip (John Newling), KCVO 1976; CBE 1972; Commandant, Royal Military Academy Sandhurst, since 1976; *b* 10 July 1924; *s* of George William Newling Ward and Mary Florence Ward; *m*; two *s* two *d*. *Educ:* privately and at Monkton Combe School. Adjt, RMA Sandhurst, 1960-62; Bde Major, Household Bde, 1962-65; Comdg 1st Bn Welsh Guards, 1965-67; Comdr Land Forces, Gulf, 1969-71; GOC London Dist and Maj.-Gen. comdg Household Div., 1973-76. *Recreations:* gardening, fishing. *Address:* Government House, Royal Military Academy Sandhurst, Camberley, Surrey; The Old Rectory, Patching, near Worthing, West Sussex. *Clubs:* Cavalry and Guards, Buck's.

WARD, (Philip) Leslie Moffat, RE 1936 (ARE 1916); artist; formerly Senior Assistant, Southern College of Art, Bournemouth; retired, 1953; *b* 2 April 1888; *s* of Charles James and Charlotte Maud Ward, Worcester; *m* 1st, 1925, Nellie Ethel Robinson; one *s*; 2nd, 1939, Eleanor Glassford Roberts. Gold Medallist (Pictorial Composition and Illustration) National Competition of School of Art, 1909-10. Hon. Member Society of Graphic Art; exhibitor at RA in most years since 1915. Pictures in public art galleries: Southampton, Rochdale, Bournemouth, Eastbourne, Hastings; also at Worcester, Mass, USA, and at Los Angeles, California, USA. One man shows, Red House Art Gallery, Christchurch, Hants, and Eastbourne and Hastings Municipal Galleries, 1956. Senior Fellow, Royal Society of Painter Etchers, 1963. *Address:* 47 Wellington Road, Bournemouth, Dorset.

WARD, Gen. Sir Richard (Erskine), GBE 1976; KCB 1971 (CB 1969); DSO 1943 and Bar, 1943; MC 1942; Chief of Personnel and Logistics, Ministry of Defence, 1974-76, retired; *b* 15 Oct. 1917; *o s* of late John Petty Ward and Gladys Rose Ward (*née* Marsh-Dunn); *m* 1947, Stella Elizabeth, 2nd *d* of late Brig. P. N. Ellis, RA, and Mrs Rachel Ellis; two *s* two *d*. *Educ:* Marlborough Coll.; RMC, Sandhurst. Commissioned Royal Tank Corps, 1937; served War of 1939-45 (despatches thrice);

5th Royal Tank Regt, 1939-43; Staff Coll., Camberley, 1944; Bde Major, 4th Armoured Bde, 1944; CO Westminster Dragoons, 1945; Korea with 1st Royal Tank Regt, 1952 (despatches); Lt-Col Chiefs of Staff Secretariat, 1955; CO 3 Royal Tank Regt, 1957; idc 1961; on staff of Chief of Defence Staff, 1962; comd 20 Armoured Bde, 1963; GOC 1st Division 1965-67; Vice-Adjutant-General, 1968-70; Cmdr British Forces, Hong Kong, 1970-73. Maj.-Gen., 1965; Lt-Gen., 1970; Gen., 1974. Col Comdt RTR, 1970-75. Croix de Guerre, with palm, 1940; Chevalier, Order of Leopold II, with palm, 1945. *Address:* Little Sheldons, Hook, Hants RG27 9LD. *Club:* Army and Navy.

WARD, Roy Livingstone, QC 1972; a Recorder of the Crown Court, since 1972; *b* 31 Aug. 1925; *m* 1972, Barbara Anne (*née* Brockbank); one *s* one *d*. *Educ:* Taunton Sch.; Pembroke Coll., Cambridge. BA(Hons). Served RAF, 1943-47. Called to Bar, Middle Temple, 1950. *Address:* The Chase, Burton, Wirral, Merseyside. *Club:* United Oxford & Cambridge University.

WARD, Rev. Simon B.; *see* Barrington-Ward.

WARD, Prof. Stacey George; Professor and Senior Fellow, Department of Minerals Engineering, University of Birmingham, 1973-74, now Emeritus; *b* 3 Sept. 1906; *s* of George Richard Ward; *m* 1950, Helen, *d* of Samuel Thomas Windsor. *Educ:* Queen Elizabeth's Grammar Sch., Kingston-upon-Thames; Imperial College of Science, London. PhD, MSc, ARCS, DIC. Research Dept, Powell Duffryn Associated Collieries Ltd, 1930-34; Field Research and Liaison Officer, British Iron and Steel Federation, 1935-37; University of Birmingham: Lecturer, Mining Dept, 1937-42; Acting Prof. of Mining, 1942-46 and 1947-48; Prof. of Chemical Engineering, 1946-48; Prof. and Head of Dept of Minerals Engineering, 1948-73; Dean of the Faculty of Science, 1960-63. *Publications:* various technical papers connected with coal, fuel, minerals Engineering, extractive metallurgy and rheology of suspensions. *Address:* 5 Birnam, 56 Harborne Road, Edgbaston, Birmingham B15 3HE.

WARD, Sir Terence George, Kt 1971; CBE 1961 (MBE 1945); Dean of the Faculty of Dental Surgery, Royal College of Surgeons, 1965-68; *b* 16 Jan. 1906; *m* 1931, Elizabeth Ambrose Wilson; one *s* one *d*. *Educ:* Edinburgh. Mem., SE Metropolitan Regional Hosp. Bd; Exmr, DSRCSEd, FDRCSIre. Pres., Internat. Assoc. Oral Surgeons; Past Pres., British Association of Oral Surgeons; Consulting Oral Surgeon to the Royal Navy; Consulting Dental Surgeon: to the British Army, 1954-71; Emeritus 1971; to the Royal Air Force; to Dept of Health and Social Security; to the Queen Victoria Hospital, East Grinstead. LRCP, LRCSEd 1928; LRFPS, 1930; LDS (Edinburgh) 1928; FDSRCS 1948; FACD (USA) 1959; FACDSurgeons; FFDRCS Ire., 1964; Hon. FDSRCSE, 1966; Hon. FRCCD, 1966. DDSc, Melbourne, 1963. Mem., SA Dental Assoc.; Hon. Member: Amer. Soc. Oral Surgeons; Dutch Soc. Oral Surgeons; Hon. Fellow: Scandinavian Assoc. Oral Surgeons; Spanish Assoc. Oral Surgeons. *Publication:* The Dental Treatment of Maxillofacial Injuries, 1956. *Recreation:* golf. *Address:* 22 Marina Court Avenue, Bexhill-on-Sea, East Sussex. *T:* Bexhill-on-Sea 4760.

WARD, Thomas William, ARCA 1949; RE 1955; RWS 1957; Course Director, Illustration, Harrow College of Technology and Art; painter in water colour and oil colour; *b* 8 Nov. 1918; *s* of John B. Ward, Master Stationer, and Lillee B. Ward (*née* Hunt), Sheffield; *m* Joan Palmer, ARCA, *d* of F. N. Palmer, Blackheath; one *s* one *d*. *Educ:* Nether Edge Grammar Sch., Sheffield; Sheffield Coll. of Art (part-time); Royal Coll. of Art. Cadet, Merchant Service, 1935-36; stationer, W. H. Smith & Son Ltd, 1936-39; Military service, 1939-46: commissioned N Staffs Regt, 1942; GSO3 1945-46. Post graduate schol., RCA, 1949-50, silver medal for engraving, 1949. *Exhibitions include:* one-man, Walker Gall., 1957, 1960; Wakefield City Art Gall., 1962; Shipley Art Gall., Newcastle, 1962; Middlesbrough Art Gall., 1963; St John's Coll., York, 1965. *Group Exhibitions:* Leicester Gall., 1951; Kensington Gall., 1953; Zwemmer Gall., 1955. *Open Exhibitions:* RA, NEAC, London Group; Roy. Soc. of Marine Artists, and in Japan, USA, S Africa, NZ. *Works purchased:* S London Art Gall.; V&A; Nat. Gall. of NZ; Leicester, Oxford and Durham Univs; Arts Council; Contemp. Art Soc.; Bowes Mus.; Graves Art Gall.; Rochdale Art Gall.; Sir Kenneth Clark. *Illustrations for:* Colman Prentis Varley; Shell Mex; Editions Lausanne; D. R. MacGregor. *Designed:* maritime properties for Tom Arnold Ice Show. *Recreation:* sailing. *Address:* 20 The Grove, W5 5LH.

WARD, Wilfrid Arthur, CMG 1948; MC 1918; *b* 9 May 1892; *s* of late Arthur Henry Ward; *m* 1922, Norah Anne Phelps; one *s*. *Educ:* Christ's Hospital. Served European War; mobilised with

Civil Service Rifles, 1914, France; commissioned in Lancashire Fusiliers (SR) 1915, France, Salonika, Palestine; Captain, 1917. Cadet Malayan Civil Service, 1920; various District posts in FMS, Kedah and Kelantan; Secretary to Resident, Selangor, 1936; Under-Secretary, Straits Settlements, 1941; interned in Singapore, 1942-45; Resident Commissioner, Selangor, 1946-48; Commissioner for Malaya in the UK, 1948-53. *Address:* Beckleys, Lymington, Hants.

WARD, William Alec; HM Diplomatic Service; High Commissioner, Mauritius, since 1977; *b* 27 Nov. 1928; *s* of William Leslie Ward and Gladys Ward; *m* 1955, Sheila Joan Hawking; two *s* two *d*. *Educ:* King's Coll. Sch., Wimbledon; Christ Church, Oxford. HM Forces, 1947-49. Colonial Office, 1952; Private Sec. to Permanent Under-Sec., 1955-57; Singapore, 1960-64; seconded to CRO, 1963; Karachi, 1964-66; Islamabad, 1966-68; joined HM Diplomatic Service, 1968; FCO, 1968-71; Salisbury, 1971-72; Dep. High Comr, Colombo, 1973-76. *Recreations:* music, walking. *Address:* c/o Foreign and Commonwealth Office, SW1; Nyewoods, Elm Road, Horsell, Woking, Surrey. *Club:* Royal Commonwealth Society.

WARD, William Ernest Frank, CMG 1945; *b* 24 Dec. 1900; *s* of W. H. Ward, Borough Treasurer, Battersea; *m* 1926, Sylvia Grace, *d* of Arthur Clayton Vallance, Mansfield, Notts; no *c*. *Educ:* LCC elementary school; Mercers' Sch.; Dulwich Coll.; Lincoln Coll., Oxford (BLitt, MA); Ridley Hall, Cambridge (Diploma in Education). Master, Achimota Coll., Gold Coast, 1924; Director of Education, Mauritius, 1940; Deputy Educational Adviser, Colonial Office, 1945-56. Editor, Oversea Education, 1946-63. Member of UK delegation to seven general conferences of UNESCO and many other international meetings on education. *Publications:* History of Ghana, 1967 (originally published as History of the Gold Coast, 1948); Educating Young Nations, 1959; Fraser of Trinity and Achimota, 1965; The Royal Navy and the Slavers, 1969; various historical works and educational textbooks. *Recreations:* music, walking. *Address:* 59 Beresford Road, Cheam, Surrey. *T:* 01-642 1749.

WARD, William Kenneth, CMG 1977; Under-Secretary, Department of Trade, since 1974; *b* 20 Jan. 1918; *e s* of late Harold and Emily Ward; *m* 1949, Victoria Emily, *d* of late Ralph Perkins, Carcavelos, Portugal; three *s* one *d*. *Educ:* Queen Elizabeth's Grammar Sch., Ashbourne; Trinity Coll., Cambridge. 1st class Hons Modern and Medieval Langs Tripos. Entered Ministry of Supply, 1939; Board of Trade, 1955; HM Principal Trade Commissioner, Vancouver, BC, 1959-63; Under-Sec., BoT, 1966-69; Min. of Technology, later DTI and Dept of Trade, 1969-; Sec., BOTB, 1973. *Recreation:* gardening. *Address:* 31 Plough Lane, Purley, Surrey. *T:* 01-660 2462.

WARD-BOOTH, Maj.-Gen. John Antony, OBE 1971; Director, Army Air Corps, since 1976; *b* 18 July 1927; *s* of Rev. J. Ward-Booth and Mrs E. M. Ward-Booth; *m* 1952, Margaret Joan Hooper; two *s* two *d*. *Educ:* Worksop College, Notts. Joined Army, 1945; commnd into Worcestershire Regt in India, 1946; served India and Middle East, 1946-48; trans. to Bedfordshire and Hertfordshire Regt, 1948; served BAOR, Far East, Nigeria and Congo, 1950-63, trans. to Parachute Regt, 1963; commanded 3rd Bn, Parachute Regt, 1967-69; Hong Kong, 1969-70; Comdr, 16 Parachute Bde, 1970-73; Nat. Defence Coll., Canada, 1973-74; DAG, HQ BAOR, 1974-75. *Recreations:* sailing, golf, squash, cricket. *Address:* Longthatch, Hurstbourne Priors, near Andover, Hants. *T:* Whitchurch 2461. *Club:* Army and Navy.

WARD-HARRISON, Maj.-Gen. John Martin Donald, OBE 1962; MC and bar 1945; *b* 18 April 1918; *s* of Commander S. J. Ward-Harrison, Haughley House, Suffolk; *m* 1945, June Amoret, *d* of late Major C. A. Fleury Teulon, Inniskilling Dragoons; one *d* (one *s* decd). *Educ:* Shrewsbury Sch. Commnd Suffolk and Norfolk Yeomanry, 1936-39; 5th Royal Inniskilling Dragoon Guards, 1939-45; Staff Coll., S Africa, 1945; Staff appts and regimental duty, 1946-56; GSO1, 7 Armoured Div., 1956-58; comd 10th Royal Hussars (PWO), 1959-62; Col Gen. Staff, 1962-63; Brig., Royal Armoured Corps, E and S Commands, 1964; Imperial Defence Coll., 1965; Dep. Comdt, Staff Coll., Camberley, 1966-68; GOC Northumbrian District, 1968-70; COS, HQ Northern Comd, 1970-72; GOC NE District, 1973; retd 1973. President: Royal Soc. of St George (York and Humberside), 1973; Flaxton Branch, CPRE, 1975. Dir, York Minster Fund, 1975. Manager, Thirsk Racecourse Co. Ltd, 1976. *Recreations:* field sports. *Address:* Hazel Bush House, Stockton-on-the-Forest, York YO3 9TP. *T:* Flaxton Moor 239. *Club:* Army and Navy.

See also Sir I. G. Bosville Macdonald of Sleat, Bt.

WARD-JACKSON, Mrs (Audrey) Muriel; *b* 30 Oct. 1914; *d* of late William James Jenkins and Alice Jenkins (*née* Glyde); *m* 1946, George Ralph Norman Ward-Jackson; no *c*. *Educ:* Queenswood, Hatfield, Herts; Lady Margaret Hall, Oxford (MA). Home Civil Service (Ministries of Works, Town and Country Planning, Housing and Local Government, and HM Treasury): Asst Principal, 1937; Principal, 1942; Asst Sec., 1946-55. A Director (concerned mainly with Finance), John Lewis Partnership, 1955-74; John Lewis Partnership Ltd: Dir, 1957-74; Dir, John Lewis Properties Ltd, 1969-74; Chm., John Lewis Partnership Pensions Trust, 1964-74. On Civil Service Arbitration Tribunal, 1959-64; Chm., Consumers Cttees (Agric. Marketing), 1971-75; Member: Nat. Savings Review Cttee, 1971-73; Royal Commn on Standards of Conduct in Public Life, 1974-76. A Governor, British Film Inst., 1962-65; Mem. Council, Bedford Coll., London Univ., 1967-72. *Recreations:* swimming, gardening. *Address:* Beacon Hill, Heddington, Calne, Wilts. *T:* Bromham 390. *Clubs:* Lansdowne, Naval and Military.

WARD-PERKINS, John Bryan, CMG 1975; CBE 1955; MA; FBA 1951; FSA; Director of the British School at Rome, 1946-74; *b* 1912; *s* of late Bryan Ward-Perkins, Indian Civil Service (retired); *m* 1943, Margaret Sheilah Long; three *s* one *d*. *Educ:* Winchester (Schol.); New Coll., Oxford; Senior Demy of Magdalen Coll., Oxford; Craven Travelling Fellow, 1934-36. Asst, London Museum, 1936-38; Prof. of Archæology, Royal Univ. of Malta, 1939; war service (TA), 1939-45, England, Africa, and Italy (despatches); Lt-Col, Royal Artillery; organised military government antiquities dept in Tripoli and Cyrenaica; Dir of Monuments and Fine Arts Subcommission in Italy. Directed archæological excavations at Welwyn, 1937, Ightham, Kent, 1938, Tripolitania, 1948-53, Istanbul, 1953, Italy, 1957-71, and Cyrenaica, 1969-71. Member: Pontificia Accademia Romana di Archeologia; German Archæological Inst. Corresp. Mem., Royal Acad. of History, Antiquity and Letters, Stockholm; Acad. of Archaeology, Letters and Fine Arts of Naples. President: Internat. Union of Institutes, Rome, 1953, 1964, 1976; Tabula Imperii Romani. Pres., Internat. Assoc. for Classical Archæology, 1974-78. Visiting Professor: New York Univ., 1957; Univ. of Sydney, 1977; Vis. Mem., Inst. for Advanced Study, Princeton, 1974-75; Lectures: Carl Newell Jackson Harvard Univ., 1957; Rhind Soc. of Antiquaries of Scotland, 1960; Myres Memorial Oxford Univ., 1963; M. V. Taylor Memorial 1968; Jerome Rome and Ann Arbor, 1969; Mortimer Wheeler, British Acad., 1971; Shuffrey Meml, Lincoln Coll., Oxford, 1976. Hon. DLitt, Birmingham; Hon. LLD Alberta, 1969. Medaglia d'oro per i Benemeriti della Cultura (Italian Govt), 1958; Serena Medallist of the British Academy, 1962. *Publications:* London Museum Medieval Catalogue; Inscriptions of Roman Tripolitania, 1952; The Shrine of St Peter, 1955; (jointly) The Great Palace of the Byzantine Emperors, 1959; The Historical Topography of Veii, 1961; The Northeastern Ager Veieintanus, 1969; (jtly) Etruscan and Roman Architecture, 1970; The Cities of Ancient Greece and Italy: planning in classical antiquity, 1974; Architettura Romana, 1975; Pompeii AD79, 1976; papers on archæological subjects. *Address:* Old Barn, Stratton, Cirencester, Glos. *Club:* Athenæum.

WARD THOMAS, Gwyn Edward, CBE 1973; DFC; Chairman since 1976 and Managing Director since 1970, Trident Television Ltd (Deputy Chairman, 1972-76); Deputy Chairman, Yorkshire Television Ltd, since 1973 (Managing Director 1967-73); Chairman: Trident Management Ltd; Trident Television Holdings (Australia) Pty Ltd; Trident Television Pty Ltd; Trident Films Ltd; Trident Leisure Ltd; *b* 1 Aug. 1923; *o s* of William J. and Constance Thomas; *m* 1945, Patricia Cornelius; one *d*. *Educ:* Bloxham Sch.; The Lycée, Rouen. Served RAF, 1 Group Bomber Command and 229 Group Transport Command, 1941-46. Granada Television, 1955-61; Man. Dir, Grampian Television, 1961-67. Chairman: Castlewood Investments Ltd; Don Robinson Holdings Ltd; Watts & Corry Ltd; President: Trident Independent Television Enterprises SA, 1969-; Trident Anglia Sales SA, 1977-. British Bureau of Television Advertising: Dir, 1966; Chm., 1968-70; Mem. Council, Independent Television Companies Assoc., 1961-76 (Chairman: Labour Relations Cttee, 1967; Network Programme Cttee, 1971). *Recreations:* ski-ing, boats, photography. *Address:* Sefton, Old Avenue, St George's Hill, Weybridge, Surrey.

WARDALE, Geoffrey Charles, CB 1974; Deputy Secretary, Department of the Environment, since 1972; *b* 29 Nov. 1919; *m* 1944, Rosemary Octavia Dyer; one *s* one *d*. *Educ:* Altrincham Grammar Sch.; Queens' Coll., Cambridge (Schol.). Army Service, 1940-41. Joined Ministry of War Transport as Temp. Asst Princ., 1942; Private Sec. to Perm. Sec., 1946; Princ., 1948; Asst Sec., 1957; Under-Sec., Min. of Transport, later DoE, 1966.

Recreations: transport history, painting, listening to music. *Address:* 4 Cranedown, Lewes, East Sussex. *T:* Lewes 3468; 6 Karen Court, Dilwyn, Herefordshire. *Club:* United Oxford & Cambridge University.

WARDE, John Robins; His Honour Judge John Warde; a Circuit Judge, since 1977; *b* 25 April 1920; (Guardian) A. W. Ormond, CBE, FRCS; *m* 1941, Edna Holliday Gipson; three *s. Educ:* Radley Coll., Abingdon, Berks; Corpus Christi Coll., Oxford (MA). Served War, 1940-45: Lieut, RA; awarded C-inC's certif. for outstanding good service in the campaign in NW Europe. Member: Devon CC, 1946-49; Devon Agricl Exec. Cttee, 1948-53; West Regional Advisory Council of BBC, 1950-53. Admitted a solicitor, 1950; Partner in Waugh and Co., Solicitors, Haywards Heath and East Grinstead, Sussex, 1960-70. A Recorder of the Crown Court, 1972-77. Registrar of Clerkenwell County Court, 1970-77. *Recreations:* mountaineering, watching cricket, listening to music. *Address:* 20 Clifton Terrace, Brighton, East Sussex BN1 3HA. *T:* Brighton 26642. *Clubs:* Law Society, MCC, Forty; Swiss Alpine (Lauterbrunnen Section).

WARDEN, Mrs Roy; *see* Grenfell, A.

WARDER, John Arthur, CBE 1957; General Managing Director, Oil Operating Companies in Iran, 1963-67, retired; *b* 13 Nov. 1909; *s* of John William Warder and Blanche Longstaffe, Bournemouth; *m* 1936, Sylvia Mary Hughes; two *s* one *d. Educ:* Kent Coll., Canterbury. Joined Asiatic Petroleum Co., 1927; practical training in oilfields and refinery operations in Argentina. Pres. and Gen. Man., Cia. Mexicana de Petroleo El Aguila, 1950; Gen. Man., Shell Cos in Colombia, 1953; Vice-Pres., Cia. Shell de Venezuela, 1957, Pres., 1959; Shell's Regional Co-ordinator (Oil), Middle East, 1961-63; Dir, Shell Internat. Petroleum Co. Ltd, and Mem. of Bds, Iranian Oil Participants Ltd and Iraq Petroleum Co. Ltd, 1961-63. Officer, Order of Arts and Culture (France), 1966; Order of Taj, 3rd degree (Iran), 1966. *Recreations:* yachting, golf. *Address:* Byways, Village de Putron, Guernsey, CI. *T:* 36935. *Clubs:* American; Larchmont Yacht (New York); Chapultepec Golf (Mexico); Royal Channel Islands Yacht; Royal Guernsey Golf. *See also* W. J. M. Shelton.

WARDINGTON, 2nd Baron, *cr* 1936, of Alnmouth in the County of Northumberland; **Christopher Henry Beaumont Pease;** *b* 22 Jan. 1924; *s* of 1st Baron and Hon. Dorothy Charlotte, *er d* of 1st Baron Forster; *S* father, 1950; *m* 1964, Margaret Audrey Dunfee, *d* of John and Eva White; one *s* two *d* (adopted). *Educ:* Eton. Served War of 1939-45, in Scots Guards, 1942-47, Captain. Partner in Stockbroking firm of Hoare Govett Ltd. Alderman of Broad Street Ward, City of London, 1960-63. Comr, Public Works Loan Bd, 1969-73. *Recreations:* cricket, golf, squash racquets. *Heir: b* Hon. William Simon Pease [*b* 15 Oct. 1925; *m* 1962, Hon. Elizabeth Jane Ormsby-Gore, *d* of 4th Baron Harlech, KG, PC, GCMG]. *Address:* Wardington Manor, Banbury, Oxon. *T:* Cropredy 202; 29 Moore Street, SW3. *T:* 01-584 4793. *Club:* Royal Automobile.

WARDLAW, Claude Wilson, PhD, DSc, MSc, FRSE; FLS; George Harrison Professor of Botany, University of Manchester, 1958-66, now Emeritus Professor; *b* 4 Feb. 1901; *s* of Major J. Wardlaw, HLI, and Mary Hood Wardlaw; *m* 1928, Jessie Connell (*d* 1971); two *s. Educ:* Paisley Grammar Sch.; Glasgow Univ. Demonstrator and Lecturer in Botany, Glasgow Univ., 1921-28; Pathologist and Officer-in-Charge, Low Temperature Research Station, Imperial College of Tropical Agriculture, Trinidad, BWI, 1928-40; Professor of Cryptogamic Botany, University of Manchester, 1940-58; wide travel in United States, Central and South America and in West Indies, Africa and East Indies. Prather Lecturer, Harvard Univ.; Hon. Foreign Mem., American Academy of Arts and Sciences; Hon. Foreign Correspondent, Académie d'Agriculture de la France; Hon. For. Associate, Royal Academy of Belgium; Corresp. Mem., American Botanical Soc., 1967; Sen. For. Scientist Fellowship, Nat. Sci. Foundation, Univ. of California, 1968. Vis. Prof., NY State Univ., Buffalo, 1967. Hon. DSc McGill. Pelton Award, Amer. Botanical Soc., 1970. Trinidad Volunteer Regt, 1937-40; Lt-Col TA, retired. *Publications:* Diseases of the Banana, 1935; Green Havoc, 1935; Tropical Fruits and Vegetables: Storage and Transport, 1937; Phylogeny and Morphogenesis; Morphogenesis in Plants, 1952; Embryogenesis in Plants, 1955; Banana Diseases, 1961, new enl. edn 1972; Organization and Evolution in Plants, 1965; Morphogenesis in Plants: A Contemporary Study, 1968; Essays on Form in Plants, 1968; Cellular Differentiation in Plants and Other Essays, 1969; A Quiet Talent: Jessie Wardlaw, 1903-1971, 1971; Enchantment in Iere, 1974; Scientific Papers published in Phil. Trans. Royal Society Edinburgh, Royal Soc., Annals of Botany, Nature, etc;

relevant publication: Festschrift: Trends in Plant Morphogenesis, ed E. G. Cutter, 1966. *Address:* 6 Robins Close, Bramhall, Cheshire.

WARDLAW, Sir Henry, 20th Bt of Pitreavie, *cr* 1631; *b* 30 Aug. 1894; *o s* of Sir Henry Wardlaw, 19th Bt, and Janet Montgomerie, *d* of James Wylie; *S* father 1954; *m* 1929, Ellen, *d* of John Francis Brady; four *s* one *d. Heir: s* Henry John Wardlaw, MB, BS [*b* 30 Nov. 1930; *m* 1962, Julie-Ann, *d* of late Edward Patrick Kirwan; five *s* two *d*]. *Address:* 82 Vincent Street, Sandringham, Vic 3191, Australia.

WARDLE, Air Cdre Alfred Randles, CBE 1945; AFC 1929; MRAeS; RAF, retired; *b* 29 Oct. 1898; *s* of William Wardle, Stafford; *m* 1926, Sarah, *d* of David Brindley, Cotes Heath; one *s* one *d.* Joined Hon. Artillery Co., 1916; RFC 1917; RAF 1918; Director of Operational Requirements, Air Ministry, 1943-46; AOC Ceylon, 1947-49; AOC No. 66 (Scottish) Group, 1950-52. Air Commodore, 1943; retired 1952. Secretary: Corby Develt Corp., 1954-67; Milton Keynes Develt Corp., 1967-68; Peterborough Develt Corp., 1968-69; Northampton Develt Corp., 1969; Central Lancs Develt Corp., 1971-72. *Address:* 88 Gipsy Lane, Kettering, Northants. *T:* Kettering 85780. *Club:* Royal Air Force.

WARDLE, (John) Irving; Drama Critic, The Times, since 1963; *b* 20 July 1929; *s* of John Wardle and Nellie Partington; *m* 1958, Joan Notkin (marr. diss.); *m* 1963, Fay Crowder (marr. diss.); two *s* ; *m* 1975, Elizabeth Grist; one *s* one *d . Educ:* Bolton Sch.; Wadham Coll., Oxford (BA); Royal Coll. of Music (ARCM). Joined Times Educational Supplement as sub-editor, 1956; Dep. Theatre Critic, The Observer, 1960. Editor, Gambit, 1973-75. Play: The Houseboy, prod Open Space Theatre, 1974. *Publication:* biography: The Theatres of George Devine, 1978. *Recreation:* piano playing. *Address:* 51 Richmond Road, New Barnet, Herts. *T:* 01-440 3671.

WARDLE, Sir Thomas (Edward Jewell), Kt 1970; Lord Mayor of Perth, Western Australia, 1967-72; *b* 18 Aug. 1912; *s* of Walter Wardle and Lily Wardle (*née* Jewell); *m* 1940, Hulda May Olson; one *s* one *d. Educ:* Perth Boys' Sch., Western Australia. Member: King's Park Bd, 1970-; Bd, Churchland Teachers Coll., 1973-; Chairman: Trustees, WA Museum, 1973-; Aboriginal Loans Commn, 1974-; Pres., Nat. Trust of WA, 1971-. Hon. LLD Univ. of WA, 1973. Commendator, Order of Merit (Italy), 1970. *Recreations:* boating, fishing. *Address:* 3 Kent Street, Bicton, Western Australia 6157. *Clubs:* Tattersalls, Commercial Travellers', Perth, Returned Services League, Western Australian (all in Western Australia).

WARDLE, Ven. Walter Thomas; Archdeacon of Gloucester since 1949; Canon Residentiary of Gloucester Cathedral, since 1948; *b* 22 July 1900; *s* of late James Thomas Wardle, Southsea, Hants; unmarried. *Educ:* Pembroke Coll., Oxford; Ripon Hall, Oxford. 3rd Class History BA 1924, MA 1932. Deacon, 1926; Priest, 1927; Curate of Weeke, Winchester, 1926-28; SPG Chaplain, Montana, Switzerland, 1928; Rector of Wolferton with Babingley, Norfolk, 1929-38; Vicar of Great and Little Barrington with Taynton, 1938-43; Vicar of Charlton Kings, Cheltenham, 1943-48. *Address:* 7 College Green, Gloucester. *T:* Gloucester 24948.

WARDS, Brig. George Thexton, CMG 1943; OBE 1935; late IA; Historian, Cabinet Office, 1951-69. *Educ:* Heversham Sch., Westmorland. Served European War, 1914-18, with 7 London Regt, France and Belgium, 1917-18; 2nd Lieut, Indian Army, 1918; attached to HM Embassy, Tokyo, 1923-28; NW Frontier of India, 1930; Bt Major, 1933; Staff Officer to British Troops in North China, 1932-36; Lt-Col and Asst Military Attaché, Tokyo, 1937-41; Brig., Military Attaché, Tokyo, 1941; GSO1, GHQ India, 1942; Commandant Intelligence Sch., India, 1943-45; Commandant Intelligence Corps, Training Centre, India, 1945-47. Lt-Col, 1944; Col, 1945. Official Interpreter in Japanese to Govt of India, 1928-32, 1936, and 1944-47. Information Officer, Min. of Food, 1949; Chief Enforcement Officer, Min. of Food, 1950. Chm., Nat. Anti-Vivisection Soc., 1954-57; Mem. Council, RSPCA, 1956-67; Official visit to Japan, 1966. *Publications:* Joint author, Official History, The War against Japan, Vol. I 1955, Vol. II 1958, Vol. III 1962, Vol. IV 1965, Vol. V 1969. *Club:* Army and Navy.

WARE, Cyril George; Under-Secretary, Inland Revenue, since 1974; *b* 25 May 1922; *s* of Frederick George Ware and Elizabeth Mary Ware; *m* 1946, Gwennie (*née* Wooding); two *s* one *d. Educ:* Leyton County High Sch. Entered Inland Revenue as Tax Officer, 1939; Inspector of Taxes, 1949; Sen. Principal Inspector, 1969. *Recreations:* music, woodwork, gardening, swimming. *Address:* 86 Tycehurst Hill, Loughton, Essex. *T:* 01-508 3588.

WARE, Sir Henry (Gabriel), KCB 1972 (CB 1971); HM Procurator-General and Treasury Solicitor, 1971-75; *b* 23 July 1912; *o s* of late Charles Martin Ware and Dorothy Anne Ware (*née* Gwyn Jeffreys); *m* 1939, Gloria Harriet Platt; three *s* (and one *s* decd). *Educ:* Marlborough; St John's Coll., Oxford. Admitted solicitor, 1938; entered Treasury Solicitor's Dept, 1939; Dep. Treasury Solicitor, 1969-71. Served War of 1939-45 with Royal Artillery. *Recreations:* fly fishing, gardening. *Address:* The Little House, Tilford, Farnham, Surrey. *T:* Frensham 2151. *Clubs:* Athenæum; Frensham Fly Fishers (Frensham).

WARE, Martin, MB, FRCP; research student in micropalæontology, University College of Wales, Aberystwyth; *b* 1 Aug. 1915; *o s* of late Canon Martin Stewart Ware and late Margaret Isabel (*née* Baker, later Baker Wilbraham); *m* 1938, Winifred Elsie Boyce; two *s* three *d*. *Educ:* Eton; St Bartholomew's Hospital. MB, BS (London) 1939; MRCP 1945; FRCP 1967. Editor, St Bartholomew's Hosp. Jl, 1937-38. House-surgeon, St Bartholomew's Hosp., 1939; served with RAMC, attached to Royal W African Frontier Force (Captain, graded physician), 1940-45; Publications Officer, Medical Research Council, 1946-50; Asst Editor, British Medical Jl, 1950; Editor, 1966-75. Vice-President: BMA; Soc. for Relief of Widows and Orphans of Medical Men; Internat. Union of Med. Press, 1966-75; Member: Council of Res. Defence Soc., 1960-65; Med. Panel of British Council, 1966-75. *Recreations:* palaeontology, country life. *Address:* 35 Rhos Hendre, Waun Fawr, Aberystwyth, Dyfed SY23 3PT. *T:* Aberystwyth 4059.

WARE, Michael John; barrister-at-law; Under Secretary (Legal), Department of Trade, since 1977; *b* 7 May 1932; *s* of Kenneth George Ware and Phyllis Matilda (*née* Joynes); *m* 1966, Susan Ann Maitland; three *d*. *Educ:* Cheltenham Grammar Sch.; Trinity Hall, Cambridge (BA(Law), LLB). Called to Bar, Middle Temple. Nat. Service, 2/Lieut RASC, 1954-56. Board of Trade (later Dept of Trade and Industry): Legal Asst, 1957-64; Sen. Legal Asst, 1964-72; Asst Solicitor, 1972-73; Dir, Legal Dept, Office of Fair Trading, 1973-77. *Recreation:* gardening. *Address:* 14 College Hill, Haslemere, Surrey. *T:* Haslemere 4699.

WAREHAM, Arthur George; *b* 24 April 1908; *y s* of late George Wareham and of Elizabeth Wareham; *m* 1936, Kathleen Mary, *d* of H. E. and Mabel Tapley; one *s* one *d*. *Educ:* Queen's Coll., Taunton. Joined Western Morning News, 1926; Daily Mail, 1935; Editor, Daily Mail, 1954-59. Chm., Arthur Wareham Associates Ltd, 1961-77. *Address:* Three Corners, Forest Ridge, Keston, Kent. *T:* Farnborough (Kent) 53606. *Club:* Garrick.

WAREING, Prof. Philip Frank, PhD, DSc London; FRS 1969, FLS; Professor of Botany, University College of Wales, Aberystwyth, since 1958; *b* 27 April 1914; *e s* of late Frank Wareing; *m* 1939, Helen Clark; one *s* one *d* (and one *d* decd). *Educ:* Watford Grammar School; Birkbeck Coll., Univ. of London. Exec. Officer, Inland Revenue, 1931-41. Captain, REME, 1942-46. Lectr, Bedford Coll., Univ. of London, 1947-50; Lectr, then Sen. Lectr, Univ. of Manchester, 1950-58. Member: Nature Conservancy, 1965-68; Water Resources Board, 1968-71; Chm. Res. Adv. Cttee, Forestry Commn, 1972. Pres., Sect. K, British Assoc., 1970; Mem. Council, Royal Soc., 1972. Mem., Leopoldina Acad. of Science, 1971. *Publications:* Control of Plant Growth and Differentiation, 1970; various papers on plant physiology in scientific journals. *Recreations:* gardening, hill walking. *Address:* Brynrhedyn, Cae Melyn, Aberystwyth, Dyfed SY23 3DA. *T:* Aberystwyth 3910.

WARHURST, Alan; Director, Manchester Museum, since 1977; *b* 6 Feb. 1927; *s* of W. Warhurst; *m* 1953, Sheila Lilian Bradbury; one *s* two *d*. *Educ:* Canon Slade Grammar Sch., Bolton; Manchester Univ. BA Hons History 1950. Asst, Grosvenor Museum, Chester, 1950-51; Asst Curator, Maidstone Museum and Art Gallery, 1951-55; Curator, Northampton Museum and Art Gallery, 1955-60; Director, City Museum, Bristol, 1960-70; Director, Ulster Museum, 1970-77. FSA 1958; FMA 1958. Pres., S Western Fedn Museums and Galleries, 1966-68; Chm., Irish Nat. Cttee, ICOM, 1973-75; Pres., Museums Assoc., 1975-76. *Publications:* various archaeological and museum contribs to learned jls. *Address:* The Manchester Museum, The University, Manchester M13 9PL. *T:* 061-273 3333.

WARING, Sir Alfred Harold, 2nd Bt, *cr* 1935; BA, BSc, AMIMechE; *b* 14 Feb. 1902; *o s* of Sir Holburt Jacob Waring, 1st Bt, CBE, MS, FRCS, and Annie Cassandra (*d* 1948), *d* of Charles Johnston Hill, Holland Park, W; *S* father, 1953; *m* 1930, Winifred, *d* of late Albert Boston, Stockton-on-Tees; one *s* two *d*. *Educ:* Winchester; Trinity Coll., Cambridge; London Univ. BA Cambridge, 1924; BSc(Eng) London, 1924. AMIMechE 1932. *Heir: s* Alfred Holburt Waring [*b* 2 Aug. 1933; *m* 1958, Anita, *d* of late Valentin Medinilla, Madrid; one *s* two *d*]. *Address:* Pen Moel, Tidenham, near Chepstow, Gwent. *T:* Chepstow 2448.

WARING, Sir Douglas (Tremayne), Kt 1957; CBE 1953; retired; *b* 16 April 1904; *s* of late Rev. C. T. Waring, Oxted, Surrey. *Educ:* Rossall Sch. Chartered Accountant, 1927. Joined London Tin Corp., London, 1927; Director, Anglo-Oriental (Malaya) Ltd, 1934; Chairman of Anglo-Oriental (Malaya) Ltd, 1952-59, and of other Tin Mining Companies operating and registered in Malaya. Pres., FMS Chamber of Mines, Ipoh, Malaya, 1952, 1955, and 1956. Served with FMS Volunteer Force, 1939-46 (POW Malaya and Siam, 1942-45). MLC and Mem. Exec. Council, Federation of Malaya, 1948-59; Chairman: London Tin Corporation, 1961-72 (Dep. Chm., 1958); Malayan Chamber of Mines, London, 1963-73; Amalgamated Tin Mines of Nigeria (Holdings), Ltd, 1961-74; Southern Kinta Consolidated Ltd, 1961-74; Kamunting Tin Dredging Ltd, 1966-74. Past Pres., Overseas Mining Assoc. Hon. Panglima Mangku Negara (Malaya), 1961. *Recreation:* retirement. *Address:* 93 Whitehall Court, SW1. *T:* 01-930 5073. *Clubs:* City of London, Farmers'; Roehampton.

WARK, Sir Ian (William), Kt 1969; CMG 1967; CBE 1963; PhD (London); DSc (Melbourne); Hon. Consultant, CSIRO Minerals Research Laboratories, since 1971; *b* 8 May 1899; *s* of William John Wark and Florence Emily (*née* Walton); *m* 1927, Elsie Evelyn, *d* of late W. E. Booth; one *d*. *Educ:* Scotch Coll., Melbourne; Univs of Melbourne, London and California (Berkeley). Exhibn of 1851 Science Research Scholarship, 1921-24; Lectr in Chemistry, Univ. of Sydney, 1925; Research Chemist, Electrolytic Zinc Co. of Australasia Ltd, 1926-39; CSIRO: Chief, Div. of Industrial Chemistry, 1940-58; Dir, Chemical Research Laboratories, 1958-60; Mem. Exec., 1961-65. Chm., Commonwealth Adv. Cttee on Advanced Educn., 1965-71. Gen. Pres., Royal Australian Chem. Inst., 1957-58; Treas., Australian Acad. of Science, 1959-63. FAA 1954; FTS 1976; Hon. Mem., Australasian Inst. of Mining and Metallurgy, 1960-; Fellow, UCL, 1965. ANZAAS Medal, 1973. *Publications:* (monograph) Principles of Flotation, 1938 (revised, with K. L. Sutherland, 1955); Why Research?, 1968; numerous papers in scientific jls. *Recreations:* golf, fishing. *Address:* 31 Linum Street, Blackburn, Victoria 3130, Australia. *T:* Melbourne 8772878. *Club:* Sciences (Melbourne).

WARMAN, Ven. Francis Frederic Guy; Archdeacon of Aston, 1965-77, Emeritus since 1977; Canon Residentiary of Birmingham, 1965-77, Emeritus since 1977; *b* 1 Dec. 1904; *er s* of Frederic Sumpter Guy Warman, one time Bishop of Manchester, and Gertrude Warman (*née* Earle); *m* 1932, Kathleen Olive, *d* of O. C. Phillips; one *s* one *d*. *Educ:* Weymouth Coll.; Worcester Coll., Oxford; Ridley Hall, Cambridge. Ordained as Curate of Radford, Coventry, 1927; Curate of Chilvers Coton, Nuneaton, 1930; Vicar of: St James, Selby, 1932; Beeston, Leeds, 1936; Ward End, Birmingham, 1943; Aston-juxta-Birmingham, 1946. Rural Dean of East Birmingham, 1944-46; Proctor in Convocation, 1945-75; Hon. Canon of Birmingham, 1948-65. *Recreations:* music, golf. *Address:* 76 Winterbourne Close, Lewes, Sussex BN7 1JZ. *T:* Lewes 2440. *Club:* Royal Over-Seas League.

WARMINGTON, Eric Herbert, MA; FRHistS; Professor Emeritus of Classics, University of London; Fellow of Birkbeck College; Vice-Master, Birkbeck College, 1954-65, Vice-President, since 1966; Acting Master, 1950-51, 1965-66; *b* 15 March 1898; *s* of John Herbert Warmington, MA, and Maud Lockhart; *m* 1922, Marian Eveline Robertson, Kinsale, Co. Cork; one *s* two *d*. *Educ:* Perse School, Cambridge; Peterhouse, Cambridge (Scholar). Served in Garrison Artillery and King's Own Yorkshire Light Infantry, 1917-19; Cambridge University, 1919-22; First Class, Classical Tripos, Part I, 1921; First Class, Part II, 1922; BA 1922; Assistant master at Charterhouse, 1922-23; Classical Sixth Form master, Mill Hill School, 1923-25; Reader in Ancient History, University of London, 1925-35; Le Bas Prize, Cambridge University, 1925; MA 1925; FRHistS, 1928; Editor, Loeb Classical Library, 1937-74. Dean of Faculty of Arts, University of London, 1951-56; Member of Senate, University of London, 1956-66; Acting Director Univ. of London Inst. of Education, 1957-58; Chairman, Goldsmiths' College Delegacy, 1958-75; President London Branch Classical Assoc. 1963-66. *Publications:* The Commerce between the Roman Empire and India, 1928; Athens, 1928; The Ancient Explorers (with M. Cary), 1929; Greek Geography, 1934; Africa in Ancient and Medieval Times, in the Cambridge History of the British Empire, 1936; Remains of Old Latin, Vol. I, 1935; Vol. II, 1936; Vol. III, 1938, Vol. IV, 1940; articles in The Oxford Classical Dictionary, 1949; A History of Birkbeck College,

University of London, during the second World War, 1939-1945, 1954; (ed) Great Dialogues of Plato (trans. by W. H. D. Rouse), 1956; various articles and reviews. *Recreations:* music, gardening and natural history. *Address:* 48 Flower Lane, Mill Hill, NW7. *T:* 01-959 1905.

WARMINGTON, Lt-Comdr Sir Marshall George Clitheroe, 3rd Bt, *cr* 1908; Royal Navy, retired; *b* 26 May 1910; *o s* of Sir Marshall Denham Warmington, 2nd Bt, and Alice Daisy Ing; *S* father, 1935; *m* 1st, 1933, Mollie (from whom he obtained a divorce, 1941), *er d* of late Capt. M. A. Kennard, RN (retired); one *s* one *d* ; 2nd, 1942, Eileen Mary (*d* 1969), *o d* of late P. J. Howes; two *s*. *Educ:* Charterhouse. *Heir: s* Marshall Denham Malcolm Warmington, *b* 5 Jan. 1934. *Address:* Swallowfield Park, near Reading, Berks RG7 1TG. *T:* Reading 882210. *Clubs:* Army and Navy; MCC.
See also Sir H. H. Trusted.

WARNE, Ernest John David; Under-Secretary, Establishment Personnel Division, Department of Industry, since 1975; *b* 4 Dec. 1926; *m* 1953, Rena Wolfe; three *s*. *Educ:* Univ. of London (BA(Hons)). Civil Service Commission, 1953; Asst Comr and Principal, Civil Service Commn, 1958; BoT, later DTI and Dept of Industry: Principal, 1962; Asst Sec., 1967; Under-Sec., 1972; Dir for Scotland, 1972-75. *Recreations:* reading, collecting prints, languages. *Address:* 3 Woodville Road, Ealing, W5. *T:* 01-998 0215.

WARNE, Rear-Adm. Robert Spencer, CB 1953; CBE 1945; retired; *b* 26 June 1903; *s* of E. S. Warne, London; *m* 1925, Dorothy Hadwen Wheelwright (*d* 1976); three *s*. *Educ:* RN Colleges, Osborne and Dartmouth. Joined Submarine Branch, 1925; Commander, 1936; Captain, 1941; Rear-Admiral 1951; Deputy Chief of Naval Personnel, Admiralty, 1951-53; Flag Officer, Germany and Chief British Naval Representative in the Allied Control Commission, 1953-55; retired 1955. *Recreations:* sailing, golf. *Address:* Tra Ley, High Street, Prestwood, Bucks. *T:* Great Missenden 5158. *Club:* Royal Naval and Royal Albert Yacht (Portsmouth).

WARNER, Sir (Edward Courtenay) Henry, 3rd Bt, *cr* 1910; Chairman, Law Land Company, since 1975; *b* 3 Aug. 1922; *s* of Colonel Sir Edward Courtenay Thomas Warner, 2nd Bt, DSO, MC, and Hon. Nesta Douglas-Pennant (*d* 1970), *yr d* of 2nd Baron Penrhyn; *S* father, 1955; *m* 1949, Jocelyn Mary, *d* of Commander Sir Thomas Beevor, 6th Bt, RN, Hargham Hall, Norfolk, and of Mrs Robert Currie, and *sister* of Sir Thomas Beevor, 7th Bt, *qv* ; three *s*. *Educ:* Eton; Christ Church, Oxford. Served War of 1939-45 in France, Lieut Scots Guards (wounded). *Heir: s* Philip Courtenay Thomas Warner, *b* 3 April 1951. *Address:* The Grove, Great Baddow, Essex. *Club:* Cavalry and Guards.

WARNER, Sir Edward (Redston), KCMG 1965 (CMG 1955); OBE 1948; HM Diplomatic Service, retired; *b* 23 March 1911; *s* of Sir George Redston Warner, *qv* ; *m* 1943, Grizel Margaret Clerk Rattray; three *s* one *d*. *Educ:* Oundle; King's College, Cambridge. Entered Foreign Office and Diplomatic Service, 1935; UK Delegation to OEEC, Paris, 1956-59; Minister at HM Embassy, Tokyo, 1959-62; Ambassador to the Federal Republic of Cameroon, 1963-66; UK Rep., Econ. and Social Council of UN, 1966-67; Ambassador to Tunisia, 1968-70. *Address:* 10D Compton Road, Canonbury, N1 2PA. *Clubs:* United Oxford & Cambridge University, Royal Commonwealth Society.

WARNER, Sir Frederick Archibald, (Sir Fred Warner), GCVO 1975; KCMG 1972 (CMG 1963); HM Diplomatic Service, retired; Chairman: Guinness Peat (Overseas) Ltd; Yard Farms Ltd; Director: Guinness Peat Group; Mercantile and General Reinsurance Co. Ltd; Chloride Group Ltd; *b* 2 May 1918; *s* of Frederick A. Warner, Chaguanas, Trinidad, and Marjorie Miller Winants, New Jersey, USA; *m* 1971, Mrs Simone Georgina de Ferranti, *d* of late Col. Hubert Jocelyn Nangle; two *s* and one step *d*. *Educ:* Wixenford; RNC Dartmouth; Magdalen Coll., Oxford. Served War of 1939-45. Asst Principal, Foreign Office, Feb. 1946; Member of Foreign Service, April 1946; promoted 2nd Sec., May 1946; promoted 1st Sec., and transferred to Moscow, 1950; Foreign Office, Dec. 1951; Rangoon, 1956 (acted as Chargé d'Affaires, 1956); transferred to Athens, 1958; Head of South-East Asia Dept, Foreign Office, 1960; Imperial Defence College, 1964; Ambassador to Laos, 1965-67; Minister, NATO, 1968; Under-Secretary of State, FCO, 1969; Ambassador and Dep. Permanent UK Rep. to UN, 1969-72; Ambassador to Japan, 1972-75. *Address:* Laverstock, Bridport, Dorset. *T:* Broadwindsor 543; L6 Albany, Piccadilly, W1. *T:* 01-734 2856. *Clubs:* Beefsteak, Puffin's, Turf.

WARNER, Prof. Sir Frederick (Edward), Kt 1968; FRS 1976; Senior Partner, Cremer and Warner, since 1963; Visiting Professor: School of Environmental Studies, University College London, since 1970; Department of Chemical Engineering, Imperial College, since 1970; *b* 31 March 1910; *s* of Frederick Warner; *m* 1st, Margaret Anderson McCrea; two *s* two *d* ; 2nd, Barbara Ivy Reynolds. *Educ:* Bancrofts Sch.; University Coll., London. Pres., Univ. of London Union, 1933. Chemical Engr with various cos, 1934-56; self-employed, 1956-. Inst. of Chemical Engrs: Hon. Sec., 1953; Pres., 1966; Mem. Council, Engrg Instns, 1962; President: Fedn Européenne d'Assocs nationales d'Ingénieurs, 1968-71; Brit. Assoc. for Commercial and Industrial Educn, 1977; Vice Pres., BSI, 1976- (Chm., Exec. Bd, 1973-76). Missions and Consultations in India, Russia, Iran, ARE, Greece, France. Assessor, Windscale Inquiry, 1977. Chairman: Cttee on Detergents, 1970-74; Process Plant Working Party, 1971-77; Sch. of Pharmacy, Univ. of London, 1971-; Member: Royal Commn on Environmental Pollution, 1973-76; Adv. Council for Energy Conservation, 1974-. Pro-Chancellor, Open Univ., 1974-; Member Court: Cranfield Inst. of Technology; Essex Univ.; Westfield Coll. Fellow UCL, 1967. Ordinario, Accademia Tiberina, 1969. Hon. DTech, Bradford, 1969; Hon. DSc, Aston, 1970. Gold Medal, Czecho-Slovak Soc. for Internat. Relations, 1969; Medal, Insinöö-riliitto, Finland, 1969. Hon. Mem., Koninklijk Instituut van Ingenieurs, 1972. *Publications:* Problem in Chemical Engineering Design (with J. M. Coulson), 1949; Technology Today (ed de Bono), 1971. Papers on nitric acid, heat transfer, underground gasification of coal, air and water pollution, contracts, planning, safety, professional and continuous education. *Recreations:* monumental brasses, ceramics, gardens. *Address:* 140 Buckingham Palace Road, SW1. *T:* 01-730 0777. *Clubs:* Athenæum, Anglo-Belgian, Chemical.

WARNER, Frederick Sydney, LDS RCS, 1926; LRCP, MRCS, 1928; FDS RCS, 1947; Dental Surgeon, Guy's Hospital, 1949-68, Emeritus since 1968; Sub-Dean, 1946-65; Lecturer in Oral Surgery, 1954-61, Guy's Hospital Dental School, SE1; Dean of Dental Studies, 1965-68; Member of Board of Examiners in Dental Surgery, Royal College of Surgeons of England, 1947-64, and University of London, 1953-57. *b* 14 April 1903; *s* of Frederick Watkin Warner; *m* 1937, Cicely Florence Michelson. *Educ:* Guy's Hospital Medical School. Asst Dental Surgeon, Guy's Hospital, 1936-49. Member of Board of Faculty of Dental Surgery, Royal College of Surgeons of England, 1946-65; Vice-Dean, 1954-55. *Recreations:* philately, photography. *Address:* Flat 11, 115A Ridgway, SW19.

WARNER, Sir George (Redston), KCVO 1934; CMG 1927; *b* 18 July 1879; *s* of late Sir Joseph Warner; *m* 1910, Margery Catherine (*d* 1963), *e d* of late W. E. Nicol, Ballogie, Aberdeenshire; three *s*. *Educ:* Eton; Balliol College, Oxford. Entered Foreign Office, 1903; served at HM Legations at Tangier and Oslo; Minister at Berne, 1935-39. *Address:* Inholmes, Cliff Way, Compton Down, near Winchester, Hants. *Club:* Travellers'.
See also Sir Edward Redston Warner.

WARNER, Gerald Chierici; HM-Diplomatic Service; Counsellor, Foreign and Commonwealth Office, since 1976; *b* 27 Sept. 1931; *s* of Howard Warner and Elizabeth (*née* Chierici-Kendall); *m* 1956, Mary Wynne Davies, DMath, Lectr, City Univ; one *s* two *d*. *Educ:* Univ. of Oxford (BA). 3rd Sec., Peking, 1956-58; 2nd Sec., Rangoon, 1960-61; 1st Sec., Warsaw, 1964-66, Geneva, 1966-68; Counsellor, Kuala Lumpur, 1974-76. *Address:* c/o Foreign and Commonwealth Office, SW1A 2AH; Bruton Cottage, Kemerton, Tewkesbury, Glos. *T:* Overbury 242.

WARNER, Sir Henry; *see* Warner, Sir E. C. H.

WARNER, Jack, (Jack Waters), OBE 1965; MSM 1918; film and variety artiste; *b* 24 Oct. *Educ:* Coopers' Company School; University of London. Films include: The Captive Heart; Hue and Cry; Dear Murderer; Holiday Camp; It Always Rains on Sunday; Against the Wind; Easy Money; My Brother's Keeper; Here Come the Huggetts; Vote for Huggett; The Huggetts Abroad; Train of Events; Boys in Brown; The Blue Lamp; Scrooge; Emergency Call; Meet Me To-night; The Final Test; The Square Ring; Now and forever; Carve Her Name with Pride; appeared on television as Dixon of Dock Green, 1955-76. RAF Meritorious Service Medal, 1918. Variety Club of GB Special Award, 1972. *Publication:* Jack of all Trades (autobiog.), 1975. *Recreations:* golf, swimming. *Address:* Porsea Cottage, Kingsgate, Thanet. *Clubs:* Savage, Green Room, Royal Automobile.

WARNER, Jean-Pierre Frank Eugene, QC 1972; Advocate-General, Court of Justice of the European Communities, since

1973; *b* 24 Sept. 1924; *s* of late Frank Cloudesley ffolliot Warner and of Louise Marie Blanche Warner (*née* Gouet); *m* 1950, Sylvia Frances, *d* of Sir Ernest Goodale, *qv* ; two *d. Educ:* Sainte Croix de Neuilly; Ecole des Roches; Harrow; Trinity Coll., Cambridge (MA). Served in Rifle Bde, 1943-47, Actg Major, GSO2 (Ops) GHQ Far East. Called to Bar, Lincoln's Inn, 1950 (Cassel Schol.), Bencher 1966; Mem. Gen. Council of Bar, 1969-72. Junior Counsel: to Registrar of Restrictive Trading Agreements, 1961-64; to Treasury (Chancery), 1964-72. Councillor: Royal Borough of Kensington, 1959-65 (Chm., Gen. Purposes Cttee, 1963-65); Royal Borough of Kensington and Chelsea, 1964-68. Dir, Warner & Sons Ltd and subsids, 1952-70. Liveryman, Worshipful Co. of Weavers, 1957. Chevalier du Tastevin, 1952, Commandeur 1960. *Recreation:* sitting in the sun with a cool drink. *Address:* 32 Abingdon Villas, W8 6BX. *T:* 01-937 7023; 15 Avenue Guillaume, Luxembourg GD. *T:* Luxembourg 47-17-11.

WARNER, Rt. Rev. Kenneth Charles Harman, DSO 1919; DD (Edinburgh) 1950; Assistant Bishop in Diocese of Canterbury, since 1962; *b* 6 April 1891; *e s* of late Charles Edward Warner and Ethel Constantia Catharine Cornfoot, Tonbridge, Kent; *m* 1st, 1916, Constance Margaret (*d* 1968), 2nd *d* of Arnold F. Hills, Penshurst, Kent; two *s* two *d* ; 2nd, 1970, Angela Margaret, *widow* of Rev. Edward Prescott-Decie. *Educ:* Tonbridge Sch.; Trinity Coll., Oxford; Cuddesdon Theological Coll. 2nd Cl. Jurisp., 1912; MA 1921; Solicitors' Articles, 1912; served European War, 1914-19; Major, Kent Cyclist Bn, 1917 (DSO); partner in firm of Warner Son and Brydone, Solicitors, Tonbridge, Kent, 1919-22; Cuddesdon, 1923; Deacon, 1923; Priest, 1924; Curate of St George's, Ramsgate, 1923-26; Chaplain Royal Air Force, 1927-33; Rector and Provost of St Mary's Cathedral, Glasgow, 1933-38; Archdeacon of Lincoln and 4th Canon in Lincoln Cathedral; Prebendary of Gretton, 1938-47; Bishop of Edinburgh, 1947-61, retired. Select Preacher: Cambridge University, 1939; Oxford University, 1950-51. *Address:* Perry Wood House, Sheldwich, near Faversham, Kent. *T:* Selling 263.

WARNER, Rex; author; University Professor, University of Connecticut, 1964-74, retired 1974; *b* 9 March 1905; *s* of Rev. F. E. Warner and Kathleen Luce; *m* 1929, Frances Chamier Grove; two *s* one *d* ; *m* 1949, Barbara, Lady Rothschild; one *d* ; *m* 1966, Frances Chamier Warner. *Educ:* St George's Harpenden; Wadham College, Oxford (Open Classical Scholar, First Class Classical Hon. Mods, degree in English Literature); Hon. Fellow 1973. Schoolmaster in Egypt and in England; Director of The British Institute, Athens, 1945-47. Tallman Prof., Bowdoin Coll., 1962-63. Has written poems, novels, and critical essays; also has done work on films and broadcasting. Hon. DLitt Rider Coll., 1968. Comdr, Royal Order of Phœnix (Greece), 1963. *Publications:* Poems, 1937; The Wild Goose Chase, 1937; The Professor, 1938; The Aerodrome, 1941; Why was I killed?, 1943; Translation of the Medea of Euripides, 1944; English Public Schools, 1945; The Cult of Power, 1946; Translation of Aeschylus' Prometheus Bound, 1947; Xenophon's Anabasis, 1949; Men of Stones, 1949; John Milton, 1949; Translation of Euripides' Hippolytus, 1950; Men and Gods, 1950; Translation of Euripides' Helen, 1951; Greeks and Trojans, 1951; Views of Attica, 1951; Escapade, 1953; (with Martin Hürlimann) Eternal Greece, 1953 (new edn 1962); Translation of Thucydides, 1954; The Vengeance of the Gods, 1954; The Young Cæsar, 1958; The Greek Philosophers, 1958; The Fall of the Roman Republic (trans. from Plutarch), 1958; Cæsar's War Commentaries (trans.), 1959; Poems of Seferis (trans.), 1960; Imperial Cæsar, 1960; Confessions of St Augustine (trans.), 1962; Pericles the Athenian, 1963; History of my Times (Hellenica), Xenophon (trans.), 1966; The Greek Style, by Seferis (trans.), 1966; The Converts, 1967; Athens at War, 1970; Plutarch: Moral Essays (trans.), 1971; Men of Athens, 1972. *Address:* Anchor House, St Leonard's Lane, Wallingford, Oxon. *Club:* Savile.

WARNER, Sydney Jeannetta, CBE 1946 (OBE 1918); Director, Dominion and Foreign Relations Department British Red Cross, retired 1949; *b* 13 June 1890; *d* of Frederick Ashton Warner, FRCS, and Sydney Anne Grove. *Educ:* home and in Germany. British Red Cross Commandant, 1910-17; Area VAD Commandant in France, 1915-17; Dep. Asst Dir Personnel in WRNS (OBE), 1917-19. Worked for LNU, rep. them at Geneva at various cttees of the League of Nations, 1919-28; Mem. staff of Internat. Office of World Assoc. of Girl Guides and Girl Scouts, 1928-36; rejoined British Red Cross for the War, 1939. 1st Class Knight of Order of St Olav (Norwegian), 1946; Chevalier de la Légion d'Honneur, 1946; Danish Médaille Royale de Récompense de première classe avec couronne, avec l'autorisation de la porter dans le ruban de l'ordre de Dannebrog, 1947; Commander of Order of Orange Nassau (Netherlands), 1948; Commander of Order of Phœnix (Greece),

1950. *Recreation:* travelling. *Address:* 33 Moore Street, Chelsea, SW3. *T:* 01-589 6816.

WARNER, Sylvia Townsend, FRSL; Hon. AAAL; Author; *b* 1893. Prix Menton, 1969. *Publications:* The Espalier, 1925; Lolly Willowes, 1926; Mr Fortune's Maggot, 1927; Time Importuned, 1928; The True Heart, 1929; Opus 7, 1931; The Salutation, 1932; Whether a Dove or Seagull (with Valentine Ackland), 1934; Summer Will Show, 1936; After the Death of Don Juan, 1938; A Garland of Straw, 1943; The Museum of Cheats, 1947; The Corner That Held Them, 1948, repr. 1972; The Flint Anchor, 1954; Winter in the Air, 1956; (with Reynolds Stone) Boxwood, 1960; The Cat's Cradle Book, 1960; A Spirit Rises, 1962; A Stranger with a Bag, 1966; T. H. White: a biography, 1967; The Innocent and the Guilty, 1971; Kingdoms of Elfin (short stories), 1977. *Address:* c/o Chatto & Windus, 40 William IV Street, WC2.

WARNOCK, Geoffrey James; Principal, Hertford College, Oxford, since 1971; *b* 16 Aug. 1923; *s* of James Warnock, OBE, MD; *m* 1949, Helen Mary Wilson (*see* Mrs H. M. Warnock); two *s* three *d. Educ:* Winchester Coll.; New Coll., Oxford, Hon. Fellow, 1973. Served War of 1939-45: Irish Guards, 1942-45 (Captain). Fellow by Examination, Magdalen Coll., 1949; Fellow and Tutor, Brasenose Coll., 1950-53; Fellow and Tutor in Philosophy, Magdalen Coll., 1953-71, Emeritus Fellow, 1972. Visiting Lectr, Univ. of Illinois, 1957; Visiting Professor: Princeton Univ., 1962; Univ. of Wisconsin, 1966. *Publications:* Berkeley, 1953; English Philosophy since 1900, 1958; Contemporary Moral Philosophy, 1967; (ed with J. O. Urmson) J. L. Austin: Philosophical Papers, 2nd edn, 1970; The Object of Morality, 1971; articles in: Mind, Proc. Aristotelian Soc., etc. *Recreations:* golf, cricket. *Address:* Hertford College, Oxford. *T:* Oxford 42947.

WARNOCK, Mrs (Helen) Mary; Senior Research Fellow, St Hugh's College, Oxford, since 1976; *b* 14 April 1924; *d* of late Archibald Edward Wilson, Winchester; *m* 1949, Geoffrey James Warnock, *qv* ; two *s* three *d. Educ:* St Swithun's, Winchester; Lady Margaret Hall, Oxford. Fellow and Tutor in Philosophy, St Hugh's Coll., Oxford, 1949-66; Headmistress, Oxford High Sch., GPDST, 1966-72; Talbot Res. Fellow, Lady Margaret Hall, Oxford, 1972-76. Mem., IBA, 1973-; Chm., Cttee of Inquiry into Special Educn, 1974-. *Publications:* Ethics since 1900, 1960; J.-P. Sartre, 1963; Existentialist Ethics, 1966; Existentialism, 1970; Imagination, 1976; Schools of Thought, 1977; (with T. Devlin) What Must We Teach?, 1977. *Recreations:* music, golf. *Address:* Hertford College, Oxford; St Hugh's College, Oxford.
See also Sir A. D. Wilson.

WARR, George Michael, CBE 1966; HM Diplomatic Service, retired; *b* 22 Jan. 1915; *s* of late Sir Godfrey Warr, and of Lady Warr; *m* 1950, Gillian Addis (*née* Dearmer); one *s* two *d* (one step *s*). *Educ:* Winchester; Christ Church, Oxford. Entered Foreign Service, 1938; served in Chile, Germany, Soviet Union, Uruguay; Counsellor, British Embassy, Brussels, 1959-62; British Consul-General, Istanbul, Turkey, 1962-67; Ambassador to Nicaragua, 1967-70. *Recreation:* gardening. *Address:* Woodside, Frant, Tunbridge Wells TN3 9HW. *T:* Frant 496.

WARRACK, Guy Douglas Hamilton; Hon. ARCM; composer; conductor; *b* Edinburgh, 8 Feb. 1900; *s* of John Warrack, LLD, and Jean Hamilton (*née* Dunlop); *m* 1st, 1926, Jacynth Ellerton (marr. diss.); one *s* one *d* ; 2nd, 1933, Valentine Clair Jeffrey; two *s. Educ:* Winchester; Magdalen College, Oxford; Royal College of Music. BA Oxon, 1923; Hon. ARCM, 1926. Teaching staff of RCM, 1925-35; Examiner for Associated Board of Royal Schools of Music, 1926-; Conductor: Oxford Orchestral Society and Oxford City Concerts for Children, 1926-30; Handel Society, 1934-35; BBC Scottish Orchestra, 1936-45; Musical Director, Sadler's Wells Theatre Ballet, 1948-51; Chairman of Composers' Guild of Great Britain, 1952, 1956; Pres. Internat. Council of Composers, 1955-59; General Council of PRS, 1958-75. Chairman: Sherlock Holmes Soc. of London, 1955-57; Intimate Opera Soc. Ltd, 1969-76; Conducted Concerts, Opera, Ballet, etc in London, Ceylon, New Zealand, South Africa and Provinces. Compositions include: Variations for Orchestra, 1924; Symphony in C minor (The "Edinburgh"), 1932; Divertimento Pasticciato, 1938; music for many films, including Theirs is the Glory, 1946; XIVth Olympiad, 1948; The Story of Time, 1949; A Queen is Crowned, 1953; also many arrangements. *Publications:* Sherlock Holmes and Music, 1947. Articles in The Times, Daily Telegraph, Music and Letters, Musical Times, etc. *Address:* 72 Courtfield Gardens, SW5. *T:* 01-370 1758. *Clubs:* Savile; New (Edinburgh).

WARRELL, Ernest Herbert; Organist and Director of Music, Southwark Cathedral, 1968-76; Lecturer in Music, King's College, London, since 1953; Musical Director, Gregorian Association, since 1969; *b* 23 June 1915; *er s* of Herbert Henry Warrell and Edith Peacock; *m* 1952, Jean Denton Denton; two *s* one *d. Educ:* Loughborough School. Articled pupil (Dr E. T. Cook), Southwark Cath., 1938; Asst Organist, Southwark Cath., 1946-54; Organist, St Mary's, Primrose Hill, 1954-57; Lectr in Plainsong, RSCM, 1954-59; Organist, St John the Divine, Kennington, SW9, 1961-68. *Publications:* Accompaniments to the Psalm Tones, 1942; Plainsong and the Anglican Organist, 1943. *Recreation:* walking. *Address:* 41 Beechhill Road, Eltham, SE9. *T:* 01-850 7800. *Clubs:* Special Forces; Royal Scots (Edinburgh).

WARREN, Alastair Kennedy, TD 1953; Regional Editor, Scottish and Universal Newspapers Ltd, since 1974; Editor, Dumfries and Galloway Standard, since 1976; *b* 17 July 1922; *s* of John Russell Warren, MC, and Jean Coscal Warren; *m* 1952, Ann Lindsay Maclean; two *s. Educ:* Glasgow Acad.; Loretto; Glasgow Univ. (MA Hons). Served War of 1939-45; HLI, 1940-46; Major, 1946. Served 5/6th Bn HLI (TA) 1947-63. Sales Clerk, Stewarts & Lloyds Ltd, 1950-53; joined editorial staff of The Glasgow Herald as Sub-Editor, 1954; Leader Writer, 1955-58; Features Editor, 1958-59; Commercial Editor, 1960-64; City Editor, 1964-65; Editor, 1965-74. *Publications:* contribs to various periodicals. *Recreations:* swimming, hill walking. *Address:* Rathan, New Galloway, Kirkcudbrightshire. *T:* New Galloway 257.

WARREN, Alec Stephen, CMG 1950; *b* 27 June 1894; *s* of James Herbert Warren, Hatch End, Middlesex; *m* 1958, Beryl May Cheese. *Educ:* Aldenham School. Director, Warren Sons & Co. Ltd, 1920; Chairman, Warren & Reynolds Ltd, 1935. Joined Ministry of Food, 1939; Director of Canned Fish, Fruit and Vegetables Division, Ministry of Food, 1944-52; Director of Bacon and Ham Division, 1952-56; Mem. Potato Marketing Board, 1956-59. *Publication:* The Warren Code, 1964. *Recreation:* billiards. *Address:* Maison Pommier, Sark, Channel Islands. *T:* Sark 35.

WARREN, Sir Alfred Henry, (Sir Freddie Warren), Kt 1976; CBE 1970 (MBE 1957); Secretary to the Government Chief Whip, since 1958; *b* 19 Dec. 1915; *s* of William Warren and Clara Wooff; *m* 1940, Margaret Ann; one *s* one *d. Educ:* Sir Walter St John's Grammar Sch., SW11. Asst Private Secretary to the Secretary to the Cabinet, 1951-58. *Address:* 12 Downing Street, SW1.

WARREN, Dame (Alice) Josephine (Mary Taylor); see Barnes, Dame A. J. M. T.

WARREN, Rt. Rev. Alwyn Keith, CMG 1967; MC 1945; *b* 23 Sept. 1900; 2nd *s* of Major T. J. C. Warren, JP, Penlee House, Te Aute, Hawkes Bay, NZ, and Lucy, *d* of Ven. Samuel Williams, Archdeacon of Hawkes Bay, NZ; *m* 1928, Doreen Eda, *d* of Capt. C. F. Laws; one *s* two *d. Educ:* Marlborough College; Magdalen College, Oxford (BA 1922, Hons Nat. Sci.; MA 1926); Cuddesdon Theological College. Ordained, 1925; Curate of Ashford, Kent, 1925-29; Vicar of Ross and South Westland, NZ, 1929-32; Vicar of Waimate, South Canterbury, NZ, 1932-34; Vicar of St Mary's, Merivale, Christchurch, NZ, 1934-40; Archdeacon of Christchurch, 1937-44; Dean of Christchurch, 1940-51; Vicar-General, 1940-44 and 1946-51; Bishop of Christchurch, 1951-66. Chaplain to 2nd NZ Exped. Force (NZ Divisional Cavalry), Italy, 1944-45 (wounded, MC). Member Council, University Canterbury, 1946-73, Pro-Chancellor, 1961, Chancellor, 1965-69; Member Senate, University of New Zealand, 1948-61; Warden or Chm. Bds various colleges, schools and social service organisations. Chairman National Council of Churches of NZ, 1949-51; Member Central Committee of World Council of Churches, 1954-66. Chaplain and Sub-Prelate, Order of St John; Chaplain, Priory of St John in NZ, 1966-72; formerly Pres., Canterbury and West Coast Centre, St John Ambulance Assoc.; Vice-President: Christchurch Civic Music Council; Christchurch Harmonic Soc.; Pres., Royal Christchurch Musical Soc.; Trustee, NZ National Library. *Publications:* Prayers in Time of War, 1940; Christianity Today: section on Churches in NZ, 1947. Contrib. to Stimmen aus der ökumene, 1963 (Berlin). *Recreations:* formerly rowing, tennis, now people, reading biographies, music, gardening. *Address:* Littlecourt, 193 Memorial Avenue, Christchurch 5, New Zealand. *Clubs:* Leander; Christchurch, University of Canterbury, University Staff (Christchurch).

See also W. D. J. *Cargill Thompson*.

WARREN, Sir Brian; see Warren, Sir H. B. S.

WARREN, Sir Brian Charles Pennefather, 9th Bt *cr* 1784; *b* 4 June 1923; *o s* of Sir Thomas Richard Pennefather Warren, 8th Bt, CBE; *S* father, 1961; *m* 1976, Cola, *d* of Captain E. L. Cazenove, Great Dalby, Leics. *Educ:* Wellington College. Served War of 1939-45; Lt, 1943-45, 2nd Bn Irish Guards. *Recreations:* hunting, squash. *Heir: uncle,* William Robert Vaughton Warren, OBE, MC [*b* 23 Feb. 1889; *m* 1st, 1914, M. M. Briggs (marr. diss., 1926); two *s* one *d*; 2nd, 1926, V. E. Gill (*d* 1963)]. *Address:* The Wilderness, Castle Oliver, Kilmallock, Co. Limerick. *T:* Kilfinane 89. *Club:* Cavalry and Guards.

WARREN, Rt. Rev. Cecil Allan; see Canberra and Goulburn, Bishop of.

WARREN, Douglas Ernest, CMG 1973; Director of Overseas Surveys and Survey Adviser, Ministry of Overseas Development, since 1968; *b* 8 June 1918; *s* of late Samuel Henry Warren; *m* 1945, Constance Vera (*née* Nix); two *d. Educ:* High Storrs Grammar Sch., Sheffield; Sheffield Univ. (BSc). FRICS. Royal Corps of Signals, 1940-46 (Captain): POW Thailand, 1942-45. Joined Colonial Service (later HMOCS), Tanganyika, as Surveyor, 1946: Supt of Surveys, 1955; transf. to Kenya as Asst Dir of Surveys, 1957; Dir of Survey of Kenya, 1961-65; retd from HMOCS, 1965; joined UK Civil Service as Dep. to Dir of Overseas Surveys, Min. of Overseas Develt, 1965. Member: Land Surveyors Council, RICS, 1965-72; Council, RGS, 1968-71; various Royal Society cttees, 1968-; Pres., Photogrammetric Soc., 1969-71. *Recreations:* travel, golf. *Address:* Brockstones, Bear's Den, Kingswood, Surrey. *T:* Mogador 2653. *Club:* Kingswood Golf.

WARREN, Hon. Sir Edward (Emerton), KCMG 1969 (CMG 1956); KBE 1959; MSM 1918; Member Legislative Council, New South Wales Parliament, since 1954; *b* Broken Hill, NSW, 26 Aug. 1897; *s* of John T. Warren, Derbyshire, England; *m* 1926, Doris, *d* of Charles F. Schultz; two *s. Educ:* Broken Hill, NSW. Served European War, 1914-18: 18th Bn AIF, Gallipoli and France. Chairman: NSW Combined Colliery Proprietors' Assoc., 1949; Northern Colliery Proprietors' Assoc., 1949; Aust. Coal Assoc., 1956; Aust. Coal Assoc. (Research) Ltd, 1956; Aust. Coal Industry Research Laboratories Ltd, 1965; Brown's Coal Pty Ltd (Victoria); Coal & Allied (Sales) Pty Ltd; Dowsett Engineering (Australia) Pty Ltd. Man. Dir, The Wallarah Coal Co. Ltd; Governing Dir, Thomas Brown Ltd (Wellington, NZ). Director and Chief General Manager: Coal & Allied Industries Ltd; Coal & Allied Industries KK (Tokyo-Japan); J. & A. Brown & Abermain Seaham Collieries Ltd; Caledonian Collieries Ltd; Cessnock Collieries Ltd; Liddell Collieries Pty Ltd; Durham Coal Mines Pty Ltd; South Maitland Railways Pty Ltd; Hexham Engineering Pty Ltd; Jones Bros Coal Pty Ltd; Director: Westinghouse Brake (A/sia) Pty Ltd; McKenzie & Holland (Australia) Pty Ltd. Member: Coal Conservation Cttee, NSW Govt, 1951; C'wealth Govt Mission investigating overseas coal-mining methods, 1952; Dep. Chm., Aust. Nat. Cttee, World Power Conf., 1960; Vice-Chm., Internat. Exec. Council, World Power Conf., 1962; Chm., Coal Trades Section, Aust. Trade Mission to S America, 1962; Pres., Australia/Japan Business Co-operation Cttee, 1964-; rep. Aust. Employers, ILO, Geneva, 1964; Mem., Nat. Coal Research Adv. Cttee, 1965; launched Malaysia/Australia Business Co-operation Cttee, Kuala Lumpur, 1965; led Aust. Delegn, Hawaii, 1968 (resulted in Pacific Basin Econ. Co-op. Cttee); Australian Pres., 1970-71, and Internat. Pres., 1970-71, Pacific Basin Econ. Co-op. Council; Mem., C'wealth Govt Adv. Cttee, Expo 70, 1968; Pres., Australia/Korea Business Co-operation Cttee, 1969. Has travelled extensively. Member: Council, Univ. of NSW, 1965-; Med. Foundn, Univ. of NSW, 1968-. Rising Sun with Grand Cordon, Japan, 1967. *Address:* 16 Morella Road, Clifton Gardens, NSW 2088, Australia. *T:* (home) 969 4662; (office) 27 8641. *Clubs:* American, Tattersall's, New South Wales, Royal Automobile of Australia, NSW Sports, Manly Golf (Sydney); Newcastle (Newcastle, NSW).

WARREN, Frederick Lloyd, MA, BSc (Oxon), PhD, DSc (London); Professor of Biochemistry, London Hospital Medical College, since 1952; *b* 2 Oct. 1911; *s* of Frederick James and Edith Agnes Warren; *m* 1st, 1949, Natalia Vera Peierls (*née* Ladan) (marriage dissolved, 1958); two *s* one *d*; 2nd, 1961, Ruth Natallé Jacobs. *Educ:* Bristol Grammar Sch.; Exeter Coll., Oxford. Demonstrator, Biochem. Dept, Oxford, 1932-34; Sir Halley Stewart Res. Fellow, Chester Beatty Research Institute, Royal Cancer Hospital, 1934-46; Laura de Saliceto Student, University of London, 1937-42; Anna Fuller Research Student, 1942-46; Senior Lecturer in Biochemistry, St Mary's Hospital Medical School, 1946-48; Reader in Biochemistry, University College, London, 1948-52. *Publications:* papers and articles in scientific journals. *Address:* London Hospital Medical College, Turner Street, E1. *T:* 01-247 0644.

WARREN, Sir (Harold) Brian (Seymour), Kt 1974; physician; *b* 19 Dec. 1914; *er s* of late Harold Warren, St Ives, Hunts and Marian Jessie Emlyn; *m* 1st, 1942, Dame Alice Josephine Mary Taylor Barnes, *qv* (marr. diss. 1964); one *s* two *d*; 2nd, 1964, Elizabeth Anne, *y d* of late Walter William Marsh, Wordsley, Staffs; two *s. Educ:* Bishop's Stortford Coll.; University Coll. London; University Coll. Hosp. MRCS, LRCP. Pres., Univ. of London Union, 1937-38. House Phys. and House Surg., UCH, 1942. War service with RAMC, RMO 1st Bn Gren. Gds and DADMS Gds Div., 1942-46 (despatches). Mem., Westminster City Council, 1955-64 and 1968-; rep. West Woolwich on LCC, 1955-58, County Alderman 1961-62. Contested (C) Brixton Div. of Lambeth, 1959. Personal Phys. to Prime Minister, 1970-74. Mem., Westminster, Chelsea and Kensington AHA, 1975-77. Visitor and Mem. Emergency Bed Service Cttee, King Edward's Hosp. Fund for London, 1966-72; Mem. Governing Body, Westminster Hosp., 1970-74; Mem. Council, King Edward VII's Hosp. for Officers (Surg.-Apothecary, 1952-). Pres., Chelsea Clinical Soc., 1955-56. Liveryman, Apothecaries' Soc., 1950; Freeman, City of London. *Publications:* contrib. Encycl. Gen. Practice. *Recreations:* shooting, gardening, travel, listening to music. *Address:* 2 Kingston House South, SW7 1NF. *T:* 01-581 1018; King Edward VII's Hospital for Officers, Beaumont Street, W1N 2AA. *T:* 01-487 5244. *Clubs:* Boodle's, Pratt's. *See also M. G. J. Neary.*

WARREN, Ian Scott; Master of the Supreme Court (Queen's Bench Division) since 1970; *b* 30 March 1917; *e s* of Arthur Owen Warren and Margaret Cromarty Warren; *m* 1943, Barbara, *er d* of Walter Myrick; four *s* one *d. Educ:* Charterhouse; Magdalene Coll., Cambridge. Colonial Administrative Service, 1938-41; RAF, 1942-46. Called to Bar, Lincoln's Inn, 1947, Bencher 1967. *Recreations:* ski-ing, poetry. *Address:* 28 Consort House, Queensway, W2. *T:* 01-229 0213. *Clubs:* Garrick, MCC, Hurlingham.

WARREN, Jack Hamilton; Canadian Co-ordinator for the Multilateral Trade Negotiations, 1977; *b* 10 April 1921; *s* of Tom Hamilton Warren and Olive Sykes (*née* Horsfall); *m* 1953, Hilary Joan Titterington; two *s* two *d. Educ:* Queen's Univ., Kingston, Ont, Canada (BA). Served War, with Royal Canadian Navy (VR) as Lieut (Exec.), 1941-45. Joined Dept of Extl Affairs, 1945; served at Canadian High Commn, London, 1948-51; transf. to Dept of Finance, 1954; Financial Counsellor, Canadian Embassy, Washington, 1954-57, and as alternate Canadian Dir of Internat. Bank for Reconstruction and Devolt, and of Internat. Monetary Fund; returned to Extl Affairs and joined Canadian Delegn to Council of NATO and OEEC, 1957; apptd Asst Dep. Minister of Dept of Trade and Commerce, 1958; elected Chm. of GATT Contracting Parties, 1962-65; apptd Dep. Minister of Trade and Commerce, 1964; Dep. Minister of Dept of Industry, Trade and Commerce, 1968; High Comr for Canada in London, 1971-74; Ambassador to USA, 1975-77. Hon. LLD Queen's, Ont, 1974. Outstanding Achievement Award, Public Service of Canada, 1975. *Recreations:* fishing, golf, skiing. *Address:* Canadian Co-ordinator for Multilateral Trade Negotiations, 4th Floor West, 240 Sparks Street, Ottawa, Ont K1A 0H5, Canada. *Clubs:* Chevy Chase (Washington); White Pine Fishing, Larrimac Golf (Canada).

WARREN, Dame Josephine; *see* Barnes, Dame A. J. M. T.

WARREN, Kenneth Robin; CEng, FRAeS; FCIT; MP (C) Hastings since 1970; Consultant in Aeronautical Engineering, Warren Woodfield Associates Ltd, since 1970; Partner, Parsons, Tozero Newton Ltd (formerly, before amalgamation, Warren, Cook & Partners), since 1971; Director, Ventek Ltd, since 1972; *b* 15 Aug. 1926; *s* of Edward Charles Warren and Ella May Warren (*née* Adams); *m* 1962, Elizabeth Anne Chamberlain, MA Cantab; one *s* two *d. Educ:* Midsomer Norton; Aldenham; London Univ.; De Havilland Aeronautical Technical Sch. Research Engineer, BOAC, 1951-57; Personal Asst to Gen. Manager, Smiths Aircraft Instruments Ltd, 1957-60; Elliott Automation Ltd, 1960-69; Military Flight Systems: Manager, 1960-63; Divisional Manager, 1963-66; Marketing Manager, 1966-69. Mem., Select Cttee on Science and Technology, 1970-; Mem., Council of Europe, 1973-; Chm., WEU, Science, Technology and Aerospace Cttee. *Publications:* various papers to technical confs on aeronautical engineering and operations, in USA, UK, Netherlands and Japan. *Recreations:* mountaineering, flying, gardening. *Address:* Woodfield House, Goudhurst, Kent. *T:* Goudhurst 590.

WARREN, Prof. Raymond Henry Charles, MusD; Stanley Hugh Badock Professor of Music, University of Bristol, since 1972; *b* 7 Nov. 1928; *m* 1953, Roberta Lydia Alice Smith; three *s* one *d. Educ:* Bancroft's Sch.; Corpus Christi Coll., Cambridge (MA, MusD). Music Master, Wolverstone Hall Sch., 1952-55; Queen's University Belfast: Lectr in Music, 1955-66; Prof. of Composition, 1966-72; Resident Composer, Ulster Orchestra, 1967-72. Compositions incl. 2 symphonies and 4 operas. *Publications: compositions:* The Passion, 1964; String Quartet No 1, 1967; Violin Concerto, 1967; Songs of Old Age, 1971. *Recreation:* walking. *Address:* 7 Redland Terrace, Redland, Bristol BS6 6TD. *T:* Bristol 37689.

WARREN, Robert Penn; writer; Member of: American Academy of Arts and Letters; American Philosophical Society; Professor of English, Yale University, 1962-73, now Emeritus; *b* 24 April 1905; *s* of Robert Franklin Warren and Anna Ruth Penn; *m* 1930, Emma Brescia (*d* 1951); *m* 1952, Eleanor Clark; two *c. Educ:* Vanderbilt University, Univ. of California; Yale University; Oxford University. Asst Professor: Southwestern Coll., Tennessee, 1930-31; Vanderbilt Univ., 1931-34; Assoc. Prof., Univ. of Louisiana, 1934-42; Founder and an editor Southern Review, 1935-42; Prof., Univ. of Minnesota, 1942-50; Prof. of Drama, Yale University, 1951-56. Houghton Mifflin Fellow (fiction), 1936; Guggenheim Fellow 1939, 1947; Shelley Memorial Award (poetry), 1942; Chair of Poetry, Library of Congress, 1944-45; Pulitzer Prize (fiction), 1947; Meltzer Award for screen play, 1949; Sidney Hillman Award for Journalism, 1957; Millay Prize (Amer. Poetry Society), 1958; National Book Award (Poetry), 1958; Pulitzer Prize (poetry), 1958; Irita Van Doren Award (Herald Tribune), 1965; Bollingen Prize for Poetry, 1967; Nat. Arts Foundn Award, 1968; Nat. Medal for Literature, 1970; Emerson-Thoreau Medal (Amer. Acad. of Arts and Sciences), 1975; Copernicus Award for Poetry, 1976. Chancellor, Acad. of American Poets, 1972; Jefferson Lectr, Nat. Endowment for Humanities, 1974. Hon. DLitt: University of Louisville, 1949; Kenyon College, 1952; Colby College, 1956; University of Kentucky, 1957; Swarthmore College, 1959; Yale University, 1960; Fairfield Univ., 1969; Wesleyan Univ., 1970; Harvard Univ., 1973; New Haven, 1973; South Western Coll., 1974; Univ. of the South, 1974; Johns Hopkins Univ., 1977; Hon. LLD, Univ. of Bridgeport, 1965. *Publications:* John Brown: Making of a Martyr, 1929; XXXVI Poems, 1936; Night Rider (novel), 1939; At Heaven's Gate (novel), 1943; Eleven Poems on Same Theme, 1942; Selected Poems, 1944; All the King's Men (novel), 1946, 2nd edn, 1973 (film, 1949); Coleridge's Ancient Mariner, 1947; Blackberry Winter (Novelette), 1947; Circus in the Attic (stories), 1947; World Enough and Time (novel), 1950, 2nd edn, 1974; Brother to Dragons (poem), 1953; Band of Angels (novel), 1955, (film, 1957); Segregation: The Inner Conflict of the South, 1956; Promises: Poems 1954-56, 1957; Selected Essays, 1958; The Cave (novel), 1959; You, Emperors, and Others: Poems 1957-60, 1960; Legacy of the Civil War: A meditation on the centennial, 1961; Wilderness (novel), 1961; Flood: a romance of our time (novel), 1964; Who Speaks for the Negro?, 1965; Selected Poems, Old and New, 1923-1966, 1966; Incarnations: Poems 1966-68, 1968; Audubon: a vision (poems), 1969; Homage to Theodore Dreiser, 1971; Meet Me in the Green Glen (novel), 1971; Or Else—Poem/Poems, 1968-74, 1974; Democracy and Poetry, 1975; Selected Poems 1923-75, 1977; A Place to Come To (novel), 1977; various collections and anthologies. *Recreations:* swimming, walking. *Address:* 2495 Redding Road, Fairfield, Conn, USA. *Club:* Century (New York).

WARREN, Stanley Anthony T., CEng, FRINA, FIMechE; RCNC; Deputy Director of Submarines (Polaris), Ministry of Defence (Procurement Executive), since 1976; *b* 26 Sept. 1925; *s* of Stanley Howard Warren and Mabel Harriett (*née* Ham); *m* 1950, Sheila Gloria May (*née* Rowe); two *s* one *d. Educ:* King's Coll., Univ. of London (BSc 1st Cl. Hons Engrg); RNC, Greenwich (1st Cl. Naval Architecture). FRINA 1967; FIMechE. Sub-Lieut, RN, 1945-47; Constructor Lieut, RCNC, 1947-51; Royal Yacht Britannia design, 1951-54; frigate modernisations, 1954-57; Constructor, HM Dockyard, Malta, 1957-60; Admiralty Constructor Overseer, John Brown and Yarrow, 1960-64; Polaris Submarine design, 1964-67; Chief Constructor and Principal Naval Overseer, Birkenhead, 1967-72; Asst Dir and Through Deck Cruiser Proj. Manager, 1972-76. *Publications:* contribs to learned societies. *Recreations:* golf, motoring, gardening. *Address:* 4 Kenton Drive, Trowbridge, Wilts. *T:* Trowbridge 5113.

WARREN, Dr Wilfrid, FRCP, FRCPsych; Physician, Bethlem Royal Hospital and the Maudsley Hospital, 1948-75, now Emeritus; *b* 11 Oct. 1910; *s* of Frank Warren, FSA, JP, and Maud Warren; *m* 1938, Elizabeth Margaret Park; one *s* one *d. Educ:* Sherborne Sch.; Sidney Sussex Coll., Cambridge (MA; MD 1948); St Bartholomew's Hosp., London. DPM 1946. FRCP 1972; FRCPsych 1971. Served War, 1939-45: Surgeon Lt Comdr, RNVR. Consultant Adviser, Child and Adolescent Psychiatry, DHSS (formerly Min. of Health), 1961-76; Hon.

Consultant in Child Psych. to Army, 1969-75. President: Sect. of Mental Health, Soc. of Med. Officers of Health, 1962-63; Sect. of Psych., RSM, 1970-71. Treasurer, Royal Coll. of Psychiatrists (formerly Royal Medico-Psychol Soc.), 1962- (Vice-Pres., 1974-76). Distinguished Hon. Fellow, Amer. Psychiatric Assoc., 1968. *Publications:* articles in learned jls on child and adolescent psychiatry. *Recreations:* gardening, literature, music. *Address:* 76 West Common Road, Hayes, Bromley, Kent BR2 7BY. *T:* 01-462 2676.

WARREN EVANS, (John) Roger, FIOB; Managing Director, Barratt Developments (London), since 1977; *b* 11 Dec. 1935; *s* of Thomas and Mary Warren Evans; *m* 1966, Elizabeth M. James; one *s* one *d*. *Educ:* Leighton Park Sch., Reading; Trinity Coll., Cambridge (BA History, 1st Cl.); London Sch. of Economics. Called to Bar, Gray's Inn, 1962. Television Interviewer, Anglia Television, 1960-61; Research Officer, Centre for Urban Studies, London, 1961; practice at Bar, 1962-69; Legal Correspondent, New Society, 1964-68; general management functions with Bovis Gp, in construction and develt, 1969-74, incl. Man. Dir, Bovis Homes Southern Ltd, 1971-74; Under-Secretary, DoE, 1975; Industrial Advr on Construction, DoE, 1975-76. London Borough Councillor (Hackney), 1971-73. FIOB 1976. *Recreations:* golf, squash, talking, playing the guitar. *Address:* 47 Calton Avenue, Dulwich SE21. *T:* 01-693 0146.

WARRENDER, family name of **Baron Bruntisfield.**

WARRENDER, Col the Hon. John Robert, OBE 1963; MC 1943; TD 1967; DL; Chairman, Thistle Industrial Holdings Ltd, since 1973; *b* 7 Feb. 1921; *s* and *heir* of Baron Bruntisfield, *qv*; *m* 1st, 1948, (Anne) Moireen Campbell (*d* 1976), 2nd *d* of Sir Walter Campbell, KCIE; two *s* two *d*; 2nd, 1977, Shirley (former wife of J. J. Crawley, from whom she obtained a divorce 1977), *o d* of E. J. L. Ross; three step *s*. *Educ:* Eton; RMC, Sandhurst. Royal Scots Greys (2nd Dragoons), 1939-48; ADC to Governor of Madras, 1946-48; comd N Somerset Yeomanry/44th Royal Tank Regt, 1957-62; Dep. Brigadier RAC (TA), Southern and Eastern Commands, 1962-67. Brig., Queen's Body Guard for Scotland (Royal Co. of Archers), 1973. Mem. Council, Nat. Trust for Scotland, 1972-. DL Somerset 1965. *Recreations:* shooting, fishing. *Address:* Whitelaws, Garvald, Haddington, East Lothian EH41 4LN. *Club:* Cavalry and Guards.

WARRINGTON, Bishop Suffragan of, since 1976; **Rt. Rev. Michael Henshall;** *b* 29 Feb. 1928; *m* Ann Elizabeth (*née* Stephenson); two *s* one *d*. *Educ:* Manchester Grammar Sch.; St Chad's Coll., Durham (BA 1954, DipTh 1956). Deacon 1956, priest 1957, dio. York; Curate of Holy Trinity, Bridlington and of Sowerby, 1956-59; Priest-in-charge, All Saints, Conventional District of Micklehurst, 1959-62; Vicar, 1962-63; Vicar of Altrincham, 1963-75; Proctor in Convocation, 1964-75; Hon. Canon of Chester, 1972-75; Secretary, Chester Diocesan Advisory Board for Ministry, 1968-75. Editor for 12 years of local newspaper, Spearhead. *Recreations:* military history, old battlefields, etc. *Address:* Martinsfield, Elm Avenue, Great Crosby, Liverpool, Merseyside L23 2SX.

WARRINGTON, Archdeacon of; *see* Lawton, Ven. J. A.

WARRINGTON, Anthony; Under-Secretary, Air Division, Department of Industry, since 1973; *b* 15 Aug. 1929; *s* of Stanley Warrington and Gladys (*née* Sutcliffe); *m* 1955, Lavinia Lord; three *s*. *Educ:* Welwyn Garden City Grammar Sch.; London School of Economics. Asst Statistician: Admiralty, 1953; British Electricity Authority, 1954-55; Economist, British Transport Commn, 1956-58; Statistician, Min. of Power, 1958-66; Asst Secretary: Petroleum Div., Min. of Power (later Min. of Technology), 1966-72; Atomic Energy Div., DTI, 1972-73; Dir-Gen., Concorde Div. DoI, 1976-77. *Recreations:* education, theatre, hockey. *Address:* 9 Fern Grove, Welwyn Garden City, Herts AL8 7ND. *T:* Welwyn Garden 26110.

WARTIOVAARA, Otso Uolevi, Hon. GCVO; Ambassador of Finland to the Court of St James's, 1968-74; *b* Helsinki, 16 Nov. 1908; *s* of J. V. Wartiovaara, Dir-Gen. of Finnish Govt Accounting Office, and Siiri Nystén; *m* 1936, Maine Alanen, three *s*. *Educ:* Helsinki Univ. Master of Law, 1932; Asst Judge, 1934. Entered Foreign Service, 1934: Attaché, Paris, 1936-39; Sec. and Head of Section, Min. for For. Affairs, 1939-42; Counsellor, Stockholm, 1942-44; Consul, Haaparanta, Sweden, 1944-45; Head of Section, Min. for For. Affairs, 1945-49; Counsellor, Washington, 1949-52; Head of Admin. Dept, Min. for For. Affairs, 1952-54; Envoy and Minister, 1954; Head of Legal Dept, Min. for For. Affairs, 1954-56; Minister, Belgrade and Athens, 1956-58; Ambassador, Belgrade, and Minister to Athens, 1958-61; Ambassador to Vienna, 1961-68, and to Holy See, 1966-68, also Perm. Rep. to Internat. Atomic Energy Organization, 1961-68. Grand Cross, Order of Lion of Finland; Kt Comdr, Order of White Rose of Finland; Cross of Freedom; Silver Cross of Sport, Finland. Grand Gold Cross of Austria; Grand Cross, Orders of Phœnix (Greece), Pius IX, Flag (Yugoslavia); Comdr, Orders of Northern Star (Sweden), St Olav (Norway) and Vasa (Sweden). *Recreations:* golf, shooting. *Address:* Lutherinkatn 6. A, 00100 Helsinki 10, Finland. *Club:* Travellers'.

WARTNABY, Dr John; Keeper, Department of Astronomy, Mathematics and the Earth Sciences, Science Museum, South Kensington, since 1969; *b* 6 Jan. 1926; *o s* of Ernest John and Beatrice Hilda Wartnaby; *m* 1962, Kathleen Mary Barber, MD, MRCP, DPM; one *s* one *d*. *Educ:* Chiswick Grammar Sch.; Chelsea Coll. (BSc 1946); Imperial Coll. of Science and Technology (DIC 1950); University Coll., London (MSc 1967; PhD 1972). FInstP 1971. Asst Keeper, Dept of Astronomy and Geophysics, Science Museum, 1951; Deputy Keeper, 1960. Dir, E. & B. Wartnaby Ltd. *Publications:* Seismology, 1957; The International Geophysical Year, 1957; Surveying, 1968; papers in learned jls. *Recreations:* country walking, reading, painting, minority languages. *Address:* Greenway, 11 Greenhurst Lane, Oxted, Surrey RH8 0LD. *T:* Oxted 4461.

WARWICK; *see* Turner-Warwick.

WARWICK, 7th Earl of, *cr* 1759; **Charles Guy Fulke Greville;** Baron Brooke, 1621; Earl Brooke, 1746; DL; Lieut, Reserve of Officers, Grenadier Guards; *b* 4 March 1911, *e s* of 6th Earl and Marjorie (*d* 1943), *d* of Sir W. Eden, 7th Bt; *S* father, 1928; *m* 1st, 1933, Rose (from whom he obtained a divorce, 1938), *d* of late D. C. Bingham, Coldstream Guards, and Lady Rosabelle Brand; one *s*; 2nd, 1942, Mary (from whom he obtained a divorce, 1949), *d* of P. C. Hopkinson, Kingston Gorse, Sussex; 3rd, 1963, Mme Janine Angele Josephine Detry de Marès. Merchant Navy, Admiralty Small Vessels Pool, 1943. Warwickshire CC, 1934-36; a Governor of Birmingham Univ.; Mayor of Warwick, 1951; Alderman 1952; DL, Warwickshire. Governor: Warwick Kings Schools; Royal Shakespeare Theatre. *Heir:* s Lord Brooke, *qv*. *Address:* Warwick Castle.

WARWICK, Archdeacon of; *see* Taylor, Ven. E.

WARWICK, Cyril Walter; Chairman: Warwick & Esplen Ltd, since 1971; Houlder Bros & Co. Ltd, 1962-69 (President since 1970); *b* 30 Sept. 1899; 2nd *s* of late J. W. Warwick; *m* 1925, Dorothy Fitzgerald, *d* of late John Miller; one *s* one *d*. *Educ:* Tollington Sch.; King's Coll., London Univ. Served RFC and RAF, 1917-19. Joined Kaye Son & Co., shipbrokers, 1919; elected Baltic Exchange, 1920; joined Houlder Bros & Co. Ltd, 1938; Director Hadley Shipping Co. Ltd, 1938, Chm. 1962; Director: Houlder Line, 1944-69; Furness Withy & Co. Ltd, 1962-69; Royal Mail Lines Ltd, 1965-75; and various other shipping companies; Dep. Chairman, Houlder Bros, 1957; Director, Baltic Mercantile and Shipping Exchange, 1951; Vice-Chairman, 1959; Chairman, 1961-63; Hon. Mem., 1970. President: Cereals and Baltic Friendly Society, 1966-68; Baltic Exchange Benevolent Soc., 1973-77; Mem. Council, Chamber of Shipping of UK, 1949-75; Fellow, Inst. Chartered Shipbrokers; Liveryman, Worshipful Company of Shipwrights. Freight Market Rep. of Ministry of Transport, 1958-67. *Recreations:* riding, ski-ing, fishing. *Address:* Witley Court, Wormley, Witley, Surrey. *T:* Wormley 2626. *Clubs:* Bath, Canning.

WARWICK, Prof. Roger; Professor of Anatomy and Director of Department of Anatomy, Guy's Hospital Medical School, University of London, since 1955. *Educ:* Victoria University of Manchester. BSc, 1935; MB, ChB, Manchester, 1937; MD (Gold Medal), 1952; PhD, 1955. House Physician and House Surgeon, Professorial Unit, Manchester Royal Infirmary, 1938-39; Surgeon Lieut, RNVR, 1939-45; Demonstrator and Lecturer in Anatomy, University of Manchester, 1945-55. Member Anatomical Society of Great Britain (Symington Memorial Prize, 1953); Scientific Fellow of Zoological Society; Fellow, Linnean Soc.; Hon. Sec., Internat. Anat. Nomenclature Commn; Member Society for Human Biology, etc. *Publications:* (co-ed) Gray's Anatomy, 35th edn, 1973; (ed) Wolff's Anatomy of the Eye and Orbit, 7th edn, 1977; contributions to Brain, Journal Anat., Journal Comp. Neurol., etc. *Recreations:* Natural history, especially Lepidoptera, radio communication, archæology. *Address:* Department of Anatomy, Guy's Hospital Medical School, St Thomas's Street, London Bridge, SE1.

WARWICK, Captain William Eldon, CBE 1971; RD, RNR retired; Commodore, Cunard Line Ltd, 1970-75; First Master, RMS Queen Elizabeth 2, 1966-72; *b* 12 Nov. 1912; *e s* of Eldon Warwick, architect and Gertrude Florence Gent; *m* 1939, Evelyn King (*née* Williams); three *s*. *Educ:* Birkenhead Sch.;

HMTS Conway. Joined Merchant Service, 1928, serving in Indian Ocean and Red Sea; awarded Master Mariner's Certificate, 1936; joined Cunard White Star as Jun. Officer (Lancastria), 1937; commissioned in RNR, 1937. Mobilized in RN War Service, 1939, in Coastal Forces and Corvettes in North Atlantic, Russian Convoys and Normandy Landings, 1939-46 (despatches, 1946). First cargo command, Alsatia, 1954; first passenger command, Carinthia, 1958; followed by command of almost all the passenger liners in Cunard fleet. Promoted Captain RNR, 1960; retd RNR, 1965. Younger Brother of Trinity House; Liveryman, Hon. Co. of Master Mariners (Master, 1976-77); Freeman of City of London; MIN. *Recreations:* reading, music, walking. *Address:* Greywell Cottage, Callow Hill, Virginia Water, Surrey. *T:* Wentworth 3361. *Clubs:* Naval and Military, Naval.

WASHBOURN, Rear-Admiral Richard Everley, CB 1961; DSO 1940; OBE 1950; Chief of Naval Staff, RNZN, 1963-65, retired; *b* 14 Feb. 1910; *s* of H. E. A. Washbourn, Nelson, NZ; *m* 1943, June, *d* of L. M. Herapath, Auckland, NZ; one *s* one *d. Educ:* Nelson Coll., New Zealand. Entered Royal Navy by Special Entry from New Zealand, 1927; HMS Erebus, 1928; HMS London, 1929-31; Courses, 1932; HMS Warspite, 1933; HMS Diomede, 1934-35; Specialised in Gunnery, 1936-37; HMS Excellent, 1938; HMS Achilles, 1939-42; Battle of the Plate, 13 Dec. 1939 (DSO); HMS Excellent, 1942; HMS Anson, 1943. Admiralty Gunnery Establishment, 1944-45; Exec. Officer, HMNZS, Bellona, 1946-48; Comdr Supt HMNZ Dockyard, Devonport, 1950; Dep. Director of Naval Ordnance, 1950-53; HMS Manxman, 1953; Chief Staff Officer to Flag Officer (Flotillas), Mediterranean, 1954-55; Director of Naval Ordnance, Admiralty, 1956-58; HMS Tiger, 1959; Director-General, Weapons, 1960-62; retired Royal Navy, 1962; entered RNZN, 1963; retired RNZN, 1965. *Recreation:* beachcombing. *Address:* Onekaka, RD2, Takaka, Golden Bay, Nelson, New Zealand.

WASS, Dr Charles Alfred Alan; Director of Safety in Mines Research Establishment, Sheffield, 1970-74; *b* 20 July 1911; *s* of William and Louise Wass, Sutton-in-Ashfield, Nottinghamshire; *m* 1936, Alice Elizabeth Carpenter; two *d. Educ:* Brunt's Sch., Mansfield; Nottingham Univ. Post Office Radio Research Station, 1934-46; Royal Aircraft Establishment, 1946-55; Safety in Mines Research Establishment, 1955-74. *Publications:* Introduction to Electronic Analogue Computers, 1955 (2nd edn, with K. C. Garner, 1965); papers on electrical communication subjects and mine safety. *Recreations:* music making, reed instruments. *Address:* The Old School House, Swine, Hull, North Humberside, Hull 4JE. *T:* Hull 811227.

WASS, Sir Douglas (William Gretton), KCB 1975 (CB 1971); Permanent Secretary to HM Treasury, since 1974; *b* 15 April 1923; *s* of Arthur W. and Elsie W. Wass; *m* 1954, Dr Milica Pavičić; one *s* one *d. Educ:* Nottingham High Sch.; St John's Coll., Cambridge (MA). Served War, 1943-46: Scientific Research with Admiralty, at home and in Far East. Entered HM Treasury as Asst Principal, 1946; Principal, 1951; Commonwealth Fund Fellow in USA, 1958-59; Vis. Fellow, Brookings Instn, Washington, DC, 1959; Private Sec.: to Chancellor of the Exchequer, 1959-61; to Chief Sec. to Treasury, 1961-62; Asst Sec., 1962; Alternate Exec. Dir, Internat. Monetary Fund, and Financial Counsellor, British Embassy, Washington, DC, 1965-67; HM Treasury: Under-Sec., 1968; Dep. Sec., 1970-73; Second Permanent Sec., 1973-74. *Address:* 6 Dora Road, SW19 7HH. *T:* 01-946 5556. *Club:* Reform.

WASSERSTEIN, Prof. Abraham; Professor of Greek, Hebrew University of Jerusalem, since 1969; *b* Frankfurt/Main, Germany, 5 Oct. 1921; *s* of late Berl Bernhard Wasserstein and late Czarna Cilla (*née* Laub); *m* 1942, Margaret Eva (*née* Ecker); two *s* one *d. Educ:* Schools in Berlin and Rome; privately in Palestine; Birkbeck Coll., London Univ. BA 1949, PhD 1951. Assistant in Greek, 1951-52, Lecturer in Greek, 1952-60, Glasgow Univ.; Prof. of Classics, Leicester Univ., 1960-69, and Dean of Faculty of Arts, 1966-69. Vis. Fellow, Centre for Postgraduate Hebrew Studies, Oriental Inst., Univ. of Oxford, 1973-74. Mem. Inst. for Advanced Study, Princeton, 1975-76. FRAS 1961; Pres., Classical Assoc. of Israel, 1971-74. *Publications:* Flavius Josephus, 1974; contrib. to learned journals. *Recreations:* theatre, travel. *Address:* Department of Classics, The Hebrew University, Jerusalem, Israel.

WASTELL, Cyril Gordon, CBE 1975; Secretary General of Lloyd's, 1967-76, retired; *b* 10 Jan. 1916; *s* of Arthur Edward Wastell and Lilian Wastell; *m* 1947, Margaret Lilian (*née* Moore); one *d. Educ:* Brentwood Sch., Essex. Joined Staff of Corporation of Lloyd's, 1932; apart from war service (Lieut Royal Corps of Signals), 1939-46, progressed through various depts and positions at Lloyd's, until retirement. *Recreations:* sailing, reading, gardening under duress. *Address:* Candys, Burgmann's Hill, Lympstone, Devon EX8 5HP.

WASTIE, Winston Victor, CB 1962; OBE 1946 (MBE 1937); Under-Secretary, Ministry of Public Building and Works, Scotland, 1959-62, retired; *b* 5 March 1900; *s* of H. Wastie; *m* 1924, Charmbury Billows; one *d. Educ:* Greenwich Secondary Sch. Civil Service, New Scotland Yard, 1915-42; Chief Licensing Officer, Civil Building Control, Ministry of Works, 1942-46; Assistant Secretary, Scottish HQ, Ministry of Works, 1946-59; Under-Secretary, 1959. *Recreations:* bridge, gardening and sport. *Address:* Dirleton, Hazelbank Close, Petersfield, Hants.

WATERFIELD, John Percival; Principal Establishments and Finance Officer, Northern Ireland Office, since 1973; *b* Dublin, 5 Oct. 1921; *er s* of late Sir Percival Waterfield, KBE, CB; *m* 1950, Margaret Lee Thomas; two *s* one *d. Educ:* Dragon Sch.; Charterhouse (schol.); Christ Church, Oxford (schol.). Served War of 1939-45: 1st Bn, The King's Royal Rifle Corps (60th Rifles), Western Desert, Tunisia, Italy and Austria (despatches). Entered HM Foreign (subseq. Diplomatic) Service, 1946; Third Secretary, Moscow, 1947; Second Secretary, Tokyo, 1950; Foreign Office, 1952; First Secretary, Santiago, Chile, 1954; HM Consul (Commercial), New York, 1957; FO, 1960; Ambassador to Mali Republic, 1964-65, concurrently to Guinea, 1965; duties connected with NATO, 1966; Counsellor and Head of Chancery, New Delhi, 1966-68; Head of Western Organizations Dept, FCO, 1969. Man. Dir, BEAMA, 1971. *Address:* 30 Kelso Place, W8. *T:* 01-937 2826; 5 North Street, Somerton, Somerset. *T:* Somerton 72389. *Club:* Boodles.

WATERFORD, 8th Marquess of, *cr* 1789; **John Hubert de la Poer Beresford;** Baron La Poer, 1375; Baronet, 1668; Viscount Tyrone, Baron Beresford, 1720; Earl of Tyrone, 1746; Baron Tyrone (Great Britain), 1786; *b* 14 July 1933; *er s* of 7th Marquess and Juliet Mary (who *m* 2nd, 1946, Lieut-Colonel John Silcock), 2nd *d* of late David Lindsay; *S* father, 1934; *m* 1957, Lady Caroline Wyndham-Quin, *yr d* of 6th Earl of Dunraven and Mount-Earl, CB, CBE, MC; three *s* one *d. Educ:* Eton. Lieut, RHG Reserve. *Heir: s* Earl of Tyrone, *qv. Address:* Curraghmore, Portlaw, Co. Waterford. *T:* Waterford 87102. *Club:* White's.

WATERHOUSE, Dr Douglas Frew, CMG 1970; FRS 1967; FAA 1954; FRACI 1951; Chief of Division of Entomology, Commonwealth Scientific and Industrial Research Organization, since 1960; *b* 3 June 1916; *s* of E. G. Waterhouse, *qv; m* 1944, Allison D., *d* of J. H. Calthorpe; three *s* one *d. Educ:* Sydney C. of E. Grammar Sch.; Universities of Sydney and Cambridge. BSc Hons, University Medal, MSc, DSc, Sydney. Served War of 1939-45, Captain, AAMC Medical Entomology. Joined Research Staff, CSIRO, 1938; Asst Chief, Div. of Entomology, 1953-59. Biological Secretary, Australian Acad. of Science, 1961-66; Chm. Council, Canberra Coll. of Advanced Educn, 1969-. Corresp. Mem., Brazilian Acad. of Sciences, 1974. Hon. FRES 1972. David Syme Research Prize, 1953; Mueller Medal, 1972; Farrer Medal, 1973. *Publications:* numerous articles on insect physiology, biochemistry, ecology and control of insects. *Recreations:* gardening, fishing, gyotaku. *Address:* 60 National Circuit, Deakin, ACT 2600, Australia. *T:* 731772.

WATERHOUSE, Eben Gowrie, CMG 1976; OBE 1962; MA, Officier d'Académie; Cavaliere of the Order of the Crown of Italy; Professor of German, Sydney University, 1937-46, now Emeritus Professor; *b* 29 April 1881; *s* of Australian parents; *m* 1912, Janet Frew Kellie, MA (*d* 1973), Kilmarnock, Scotland; four *s. Educ:* Sydney Grammar Sch.; Sydney Univ.; Leipzig Univ.; Paris. BA (Sydney) with First Class Honours in English, French, German, and MacCallum prize for English; MA with First Class Honours in French; Master of Modern Languages at Sydney Grammar Sch. (for 4 years); Senior Lecturer in Modern Languages at Teachers' Coll., Sydney (for 11 years); acting Professor of French at Sydney Univ., 1921; Associate Professor of German and Comparative Literature, 1925-37; President of the Sydney University Union, 1928; Trustee Art Gallery of New South Wales, 1938-62. President Internat. Camellia Society, 1975. Gold Medal of Goethe Institute, 1957. *Publications:* The Teaching of the French Verb by the Direct Method; (with J. A. Snowden) The Initial Stages in French by the Direct Method, Parts I and II; French Phonetic and Fluency Exercises; Goethe (Centenary lecture), 1932; Camellia Quest, 1947; Camellia Trail, with 21 colour plates, 1952; (with Norman Sparnon) The Magic of Camellias, 1968. *Recreations:* landscape gardening; special hobby: the propagation and cultivation of camellias. *Address:* Eryldene, 17 McIntosh Street, Gordon, Sydney, NSW 2072, Australia. *T:* 498-2271.

See also D. F. Waterhouse.

WATERHOUSE, Sir Ellis (Kirkham), Kt 1975; CBE 1956 (MBE 1943); FBA 1955; *b* 16 Feb. 1905; *s* of P. Leslie Waterhouse and Eleanor Margetson; *m* 1949, Helen, *d* of F. W. Thomas; two *d*. *Educ:* Marlborough; New Coll., Oxford (Scholar; MA; Hon. Fellow 1976). Commonwealth Fund Fellow (Department of Art and Archæology, University of Princeton, USA), 1927-29 (AM); Assistant, National Gallery, 1929-33; Librarian, British School at Rome, 1933-36; selected and catalogued pictures for RA Exhibition of 17th Century Art (1938), 1937; Fellow of Magdalen Coll., Oxford, 1938-47; served with Army and Foreign Office (mainly in Middle East), 1939-45; temp. editor, Burlington Magazine, 1946; Reader in History of Art, Manchester Univ., 1947-48; Director of National Galleries of Scotland, 1949-52; Slade Professor of Fine Arts, University of Oxford, 1953-55; Clark Visiting Professor, Williams Coll., Mass, 1962-63; Mellon Visiting Professor, University of Pittsburgh, 1967-68; Barber Professor of Fine Arts and Dir of Barber Inst., Birmingham Univ., 1952-70; Dir of Studies, Paul Mellon Centre for Studies in British Art, 1970-73; Kress Prof. in Residence, Nat. Gallery of Art, Washington DC, 1974-75. Mem., Exec. Cttee, Nat. Art Collections Fund, 1972-. FRHistSoc. Hon. DLitt: Nottingham, 1968; Leicester, 1970; Birmingham, 1973; Oxon, 1976. Officer of Order Orange Nassau. Cavaliere ufficiale, Ordine al Merito della Repubblica italiana, 1961. *Publications:* El Greco's Italian Period, 1930; Roman Baroque Painting, 1937, rev. edn 1976; Sir Joshua Reynolds, 1941; British Painting, 1530-1790, 1953; Gainsborough, 1958; Italian Baroque Painting, 1962; Jayne Lectures, 1964, 1965; Catalogue of Pictures at Waddesdon Manor, 1967; Reynolds, 1973; numerous articles and catalogues. *Address:* Overshot, Hinksey Hill, Oxford. *T:* Oxford 735320.

WATERHOUSE, Keith Spencer; writer; *b* 6 Feb. 1929; 4th *s* of Ernest and Elsie Edith Waterhouse; *m* 1951, Joan Foster (marr. diss. 1968); one *s* two *d*. *Educ:* Leeds. Journalist in Leeds and London, 1950-; Columnist with Daily Mirror, 1970-; Contributor to Punch, 1966-. Granada Columnist of the Year Award, 1970; IPC Descriptive Writer of the Year Award, 1970; IPC Columnist of the Year Award, 1973; Gold Medal International Award (Italy), 1974. Films (with Willis Hall) include: Billy Liar; Whistle Down the Wind; A Kind of Loving; Lock Up Your Daughters. Plays (with Willis Hall) include: Billy Liar, 1960 (from which musical Billy was adapted, 1974); Celebration, 1961; All Things Bright and Beautiful, 1963; Say Who You Are, 1965; Whoops-a-Daisy, 1968; Children's Day, 1969; Who's Who, 1972; The Card (musical), 1973; Saturday, Sunday, Monday (adaptation from de Filippo), 1973. TV series: Budgie, Queenie's Castle, The Upper Crusts, Billy Liar, The Upchat Line, etc. *Publications: novels:* There is a Happy Land, 1957; Billy Liar, 1959; Jubb, 1963; The Bucket Shop, 1968; Billy Liar on the Moon, 1975; *plays:* (all with Willis Hall) include: Billy Liar, 1960; Celebration, 1961; All Things Bright and Beautiful, 1963; Say Who You Are, 1965; Who's Who, 1974; Saturday, Sunday, Monday (adaptation from de Filippo), 1974; *general:* (with Guy Deghy) Café Royal, 1956; (ed) Writers' Theatre, 1967; The Passing of The Third-floor Buck, 1974; Mondays, Thursdays, 1976. *Address:* 70 St Paul Street, N1. *Clubs:* Garrick, PEN.

WATERHOUSE, Ronald Gough, QC 1969; a Recorder of the Crown Court, since 1972; Chairman, Local Government Boundary Commission for Wales, since 1974; *b* Holywell, Flintshire, 8 May 1926; *s* of late Thomas Waterhouse, CBE, and of Doris Helena Waterhouse (*née* Gough); *m* 1960, Sarah Selina, *d* of late Captain E. A. Ingram; one *s* two *d*. *Educ:* Holywell Grammar Sch.; St John's Coll., Cambridge. RAFVR, 1944-48. McMahon Schol., St John's Coll., 1949; Pres., Cambridge Union Soc., 1950; MA, LLB; called to Bar, Middle Temple, 1952 (Harmsworth Schol.); Bencher 1977. Mem. Bar Council, 1961-65. Deputy Chairman: Cheshire QS, 1964-71; Flintshire QS, 1966-71. Contested (Lab) West Flintshire, 1959. Chm., Inter-departmental Cttee of Inquiry on Rabies, 1970; Chm. Cttees of Investigation for GB and England and Wales, under Agricultural Mkting Act, 1971-. Mem. Council, Zoological Soc. of London, 1972-, a Vice-Pres., 1976-. *Recreations:* music, golf. *Address:* 12 Cavendish Avenue, NW8. *T:* 01-286 7609; Farrar's Building, Temple, EC4. *T:* 01-583 9241. *Clubs:* Garrick, MCC; Cardiff and County (Cardiff); Bristol Channel Yacht (Mumbles).

WATERLOW, Sir Christopher Rupert, 5th Bt *cr* 1873; *b* 12 Aug. 1959; *s* of (Peter) Rupert Waterlow (*d* 1969) and Jill Elizabeth (*d* 1961), *e d* of E. T. Gourlay; *S* grandfather 1973. *Heir: great-uncle* Derek Vaudrey Waterlow, *b* 19 Feb. 1902. *Address:* Grenville Manor, Haddenham, Bucks.

WATERLOW, Prof. John Conrad, CMG 1970; MD, ScD; FRCP; FRGS; Professor of Human Nutrition, London School of Hygiene and Tropical Medicine, since 1970; *b* 13 June 1916; *o s* of Sir Sydney Waterlow, KCMG, CBE, HM Diplomatic Service; *m* 1939, Angela Pauline Cecil Gray; two *s* one *d*. *Educ:* Eton Coll.; Trinity Coll., Cambridge (MD, ScD); London Hosp. Med. College. Mem., Scientific Staff, MRC, 1942; Dir, MRC Tropical Metabolism Research Unit, Univ. of the West Indies, 1954-70. Chm., Adv. Cttee on Medical Research, Pan-American Health Organization, 1969-. *Publications:* numerous papers on protein malnutrition and protein metabolism. *Recreation:* mountain walking. *Address:* Oare, Marlborough, Wilts. *Club:* Savile.

WATERLOW, Sir Thomas Gordon, 3rd Bt *cr* 1930; CBE 1946; Director: Royal Bank of Scotland, since 1951 (Deputy Chairman, 1967-75); Director: Standard Life Assurance Company, since 1948 (Chairman, 1960-63); Williams & Glyn's Bank, 1974-77; *b* 2 Jan. 1911; *yr s* of late Sir William A. Waterlow, 1st Bt, KBE, Lord Mayor of London, 1929-30, and late Lady Waterlow; *S* brother, 1969; *m* 1938, Helen Elizabeth (*d* 1970), *yr d* of late Gerard A. H. Robinson, Bix, Henley-on-Thames; three *s*. *Educ:* Marlborough Coll., Trinity Coll., Cambridge. Joined Whitehead Morris Ltd, 1932; Joint Managing Director, 1937-39. Commissioned in Auxiliary Air Force, 601 (County of London) Squadron, 1937. Served RAF, War of 1939-45 (despatches, Battle of Britain, 1940); released with rank of Group Captain. Chairman, British Carton Assoc., 1953-55; Director: British Investment Trust Ltd, 1960; R. and R. Clark Ltd, 1957-70; Deputy Chairman, Livingston Development Corp., 1965-68; Member: Scottish Aerodromes Board, 1947-59; Exec. Cttee Scottish Council (Development and Industry), 1946-48; Scottish Cttee, Council of Industrial Design, 1949-50; Exec. Council, Assoc. of British Chambers of Commerce, 1952-54, 1963-65 (Vice-Pres., 1971-75); President, Edinburgh Chamber of Commerce, 1963-65. FBIM. Hon. DLitt Heriot-Watt, 1972. *Recreation:* golf. *Heir: s* (James) Gerard Waterlow [*b* 3 Sept. 1939; *m* 1965, Diana Suzanne, *yr d* of Sir W. T. C. Skyrme, *qv*; one *s* one *d*]. *Address:* 1 Lennox Street, Edinburgh EH4 1QB. *T:* 031-332 2621. *Clubs:* MCC; Caledonian, New (Edinburgh); Hon. Company of Edinburgh Golfers.

WATERMAN, Sir Ewen McIntyre, Kt 1963; Chairman, Onkaparinga Textiles Ltd; Director: Elder Smith Goldsbrough Mort Ltd; F. & T. Industries Ltd; Waterman Brothers Holdings Pty Ltd; B.E.A. Motors Pty Ltd; *b* Semaphore, South Australia, 22 Dec. 1901; *s* of late Hugh McIntyre Waterman, Echunga, SA; *m* 1928, Vera, *d* of late J. G. Gibb; one *d*. *Educ:* Woodville High Sch.; Adelaide School of Mines and Industries. Australian Member, International Wool Secretariat, 1948-55 (Chairman, 1952-54); Chairman Exec. Cttee, Wool Bureau Inc. (USA), 1952-54; Commonwealth Member, Australian Wool Board, 1955-63; Consultant, FAO Livestock Survey, E Africa, 1965; Chairman, Australian Wool Industry Conference, 1966-71; President: Royal Flying Doctor Service (SA Section), 1960-62; South Australian Adult Deaf Society, 1947-; Member Council, South Australian Institute of Technology, 1962-69; Member Board of Governors, Adelaide Festival of Arts; Pres., Postgraduate Foundation in Medicine, University of Adelaide. *Address:* Blackwood Park, Strathalbyn, South Australia 5255. *Clubs:* Oriental; Adelaide (Adelaide).

WATERMAN, Rt. Rev. Robert Harold; *b* 11 March 1894; *s* of Canon Robert B. Waterman and Annabella Hughton; *m* 1921, Frances Isabel Bayne; three *s* two *d* (and one *s* decd). *Educ:* University of Bishop's Coll., Lennoxville, PQ. BA 1914, BD 1933, Deacon, 1920; priest, 1921; Curate of Bearbrook, 1920-21, Rector, 1921-27; Rector of Pembroke, 1927-33; Rector of Smith's Falls, 1933-37; Rector of Christchurch Cathedral, Hamilton, Diocese of Niagara, 1937-48; Dean of Niagara, 1938-48; Bishop Coadjutor of Nova Scotia, 1948-50; Bishop of Nova Scotia, 1950-63, retired. *Address:* 40 Vaudry Street, Lennoxville, PQ J1M 1B3, Canada.

WATERPARK, 7th Baron *cr* 1792; **Frederick Caryll Philip Cavendish**, Bt 1755; Sales Director, CSE Aviation Ltd, since 1962; *b* 6 Oct. 1926; *s* of Brig.-General Frederick William Laurence Sheppard Hart Cavendish, CMG, DSO (*d* 1931) and Enid, Countess of Kenmare (she *m* 3rd, 1933, as his 3rd wife, 1st Viscount Furness, who *d* 1940; 4th, as his 2nd wife, 6th Earl of Kenmare), *d* of Charles Lindeman, Sydney, New South Wales, and *widow* of Roderick Cameron, New York; *S* uncle 1948; *m* 1951, Daniele, *e d* of Monsieur Guirche, Paris; one *s* two *d*. *Educ:* Eton. Lieut, 4th and 1st Bn Grenadier Guards, 1944-46. Served as Assistant District Commandant Kenya Police Reserve, 1952-55, during Mau Mau Rebellion. *Heir: s* Hon. Roderick Alexander Cavendish, *b* 10 Oct. 1959. *Address:* (office) CSE Aviation, Oxford Airport, Kidlington, Oxford; (home) 74 Elm Park Road, SW3. *Club:* Cavalry and Guards.

WATERS, Alwyn Brunow, CBE 1971 (MBE 1943) GM 1944; Senior Partner, The Waters Jamieson Partnership, Architects and Engineers, London and Edinburgh; *b* 18 Sept. 1906; *s* of Samuel Gilbert Waters and Gertrude Madeleine Brunow; *m* 1933, Ruby Alice Bindon; one *s* one *d*. *Educ:* Regent Street Polytechnic; Central Sch. of Arts and Crafts; Royal Academy Schs; Imperial College. ARIBA 1933; FRIBA 1945; FRIAS; FIArb. War service, RE (bomb disposal), 1940-46 (Major). Asst in various London offices, 1927-32; teaching at LCC Hammersmith Sch. of Bldg and private practice, 1932-46; founded Llewellyn Smith & Waters, 1937, Senior Partner 1946-70. Member: various cttees, RIBA, 1945-; Council, Inst. of Arbitrators, 1958-70 (Pres. 1965); Nat. Jt Consultative Cttee of Architects, Quantity Surveyors and Builders, 1965-74 (Chm. 1972). Governor, Willesden Coll. of Technology, 1946-71; Chm., Jt Contracts Tribunal, 1960-73. Bossom Lectr, RSA, 1970. Asst, Worshipful Co. of Masons. *Publications:* Story of a House, 1948; contrib. Building, Architects Jl, etc, primarily on warehousing and distribution. *Recreations:* architecture, fly fishing. *Address:* Long Ridge, North Park, Gerrards Cross, Bucks. *T:* Gerrards Cross 82116. *Club:* Royal Automobile.

WATERS, Major (Hon. Colonel) Sir Arnold (Horace Santo), VC 1919; Kt 1954; CBE 1949; DSO 1918; MC; JP; DL; FInstCE; FIMechE; FGS; MInstWE; Consulting Engineer; *b* 1886; *y s* of Rev. Richard Waters, Plymouth; *m* 1924, Gladys, *d* of Rev. C. D. Barriball, Birmingham; three *s*. President InstStructE, 1933, 1943; Divisional Food Officer, W Midland Div., 1941-42. JP Sutton Coldfield, 1930; DL Warwicks, 1957. Hon. FInstStructE; Hon. Mem. Instn Royal Engrs; Hon. FInstPHE. Chm., South Staffs Waterworks Co., 1946-59. *Address:* St Winnow, Ladywood Road, Four Oaks, Sutton Coldfield, West Midlands. *T:* 021-308 0060.

WATERS, Prof. David Watkin, Lt-Comdr RN; Deputy Director, National Maritime Museum, since 1971; *b* 2 Aug. 1911; *s* of Eng. Lt William Waters, RN, and Jessie Rhena (*née* Whitemore); *m* 1946, Hope Waters (*née* Pritchard); one step *s* one step *d*. *Educ:* RN Coll., Dartmouth. Joined RN, 1925; specialised in Aviation (Pilot), 1935. Served War of 1939-45: Fleet Air Arm, Malta (PoW, Italy, Germany, 1940-45). Admlty, 1946-50; retd, 1950. Admlty Historian (Defence of Shipping), 1946-60; Head of Dept of Navigation and Astronomy, Nat. Maritime Museum, 1960-76, and Sec. of Museum, 1968-71. Pres., British Soc. for Hist. of Sci., 1976-78; Vis. Prof. of History, Simon Fraser Univ., Burnaby, BC, 1978. Gold Medal, Admiralty Naval History, 1936, and Special Award, 1946; FRHistS 1951; FRIN 1959; Fellow., Inst. Internac. da Cultura Portuguesa, 1966; FSA 1970. *Publications:* The True and Perfect Newes of Syr Francis Drake, 1955; The Art of Navigation in England in Elizabethan and Early Stuart Times, 1958; The Sea—or Mariner's Astrolabe, 1966; The Rutter of the Sea, 1967; (with Hope Waters) The Saluki in History, Art, and Sport, 1969, 2nd edn 1978; (with G. P. B. Naish) The Elizabethan Navy and the Armada of Spain, 1975; Science and the Techniques of Navigation in the Renaissance, 1976; contrib.: Jl RIN; RUSI; Mariners' Mirror; American Neptune; Jl RN Scientific Service; Jl British Soc. of History of Science. *Recreations:* living with and judging Salukis; growing apples; history of technology (especially in the Renaissance and Chinese sailing craft). *Address:* Robin Hill, Bury, near Pulborough, West Sussex. *T:* Bury (Sussex) 687. *Clubs:* Kennel, English-Speaking Union.

WATERS, Mrs Frank; see Brown, D. L.

WATERS, Jack; see Warner, Jack.

WATERS, Montague, QC 1968; *b* 28 Feb. 1917; *s* of Elias Wasserman, BSc, and Rose Waters; *m* 1940, Jessica Freedman; three *s*. *Educ:* Central Foundation Sch., City of London; London University. LLB (Hons) London, 1938. Solicitor of the Supreme Court, 1939. Military Service, KRRC, Intelligence Corps and Dept of HM Judge Advocate General, 1940-46 (Defence and Victory Medals, 1939-45 Star). Called to the Bar, Inner Temple, 1946; released from HM Forces with rank of Major (Legal Staff), 1946. Governor, Central Foundation Schools, 1968. Freeman, City of London, 1962. *Recreations:* theatre, sport. *Address:* Arlington, The Bishops Avenue, N2. *T:* 01-883 3255.

WATERS, William Alexander, FRS 1954; Professor of Chemistry, Dyson Perrins Laboratory, Oxford University, 1967-70, now Professor Emeritus; Fellow, Balliol College, Oxford, 1945-70, now Fellow Emeritus; *b* Cardiff, 8 May 1903; *o s* of William Waters, schoolmaster, Cardiff; *m* 1932, Elizabeth, *y d* of William Dougall, Darlington; no *c*. *Educ:* Cardiff High Sch.; Gonville and Caius Coll., Cambridge. Rhondda Schol.; MA; PhD; ScD; MA Oxon (by incorporation). Lecturer in Chemistry, Durham Univ. (Durham Div.), 1928-45; University

Demonstrator in Organic Chemistry, Oxford, 1945-60; Reader in Physical Organic Chemistry, 1960-67; Chemistry Tutor, Balliol Coll., 1945-67. Sir C. V. Raman Vis. Prof., Univ. of Madras, 1976-77. Leverhulme Research Fellow, 1939; Ministry of Supply: Scientific Officer, 1939-42; Senior Scientific Officer, 1942-44. Goldsmiths' Company's Exhibitioner (Chem.) 1923. FRIC (Member, Council 1968-71); Chem. Soc. Council, 1948-51, 1959-62; Member DSIR Road Tar Research Cttee, 1950-60. Hon. DSc Warwick, 1977. Chem. Soc. medal, 1973. *Publications:* Physical Aspects of Organic Chemistry, 5th edn, 1954; The Chemistry of Free Radicals, 2nd edn, 1948; (Editor and part author) Methods of Quantitive Micro-analysis, 1949, 2nd edn, 1955; (ed) Vistas in Free Radical Chemistry, 1959; Mechanisms of Oxidation of Organic Compounds, 1964; (ed) Free Radical Reactions, 1973, 1975; publications in Proc. Royal Society, Journal Chem. Society, Trans. and Discussions of Faraday Society. *Address:* 5 Field House Drive, Oxford; Dyson Perrins Laboratory, Oxford. *T:* 59601.

WATERSON, Prof. Anthony Peter, MD, FRCP; Professor of Virology, Royal Postgraduate Medical School, London, since 1967; *b* 23 Dec. 1923; *m* 1958, Ellen Ware; one *s* two *d*. *Educ:* Epsom Coll.; Emmanuel Coll., Cambridge; London Hospital Medical Coll. MD (Cantab) 1954; MRCP 1950; FRCP 1970. House appointments, London Hospital, 1947-48; MO, Headquarters Unit, BAFO, Germany, 1948-50; Ho. Phys. and Clin. Pathologist, Addenbrooke's Hospital, Cambridge, 1950-52; Demonstrator in Path., 1953-58, Lecturer in Path., 1958-64, University of Cambridge; Fellow of Emmanuel Coll., 1954-64, Asst Tutor, 1957-64; Professor of Med. Microbiology, St Thomas's Hospital Medical Sch., 1964-67. Spent year 1962-63 on sabbatical leave at Max-Planck Institut für Virusforschung, Tübingen. *Publications:* Introduction to Animal Virology, 1961, 2nd edn, 1968. Papers on viruses and virus diseases. *Recreations:* mountain walking; European history; gardens; browsing in Who's Who. *Address:* Department of Virology, Royal Postgraduate Medical School, Ducane Road, W12. *T:* 01-743 2030; 17 Queen's Road, Richmond, Surrey. *T:* 01-940 2325.

WATERSTON, David James, CBE 1972 (MBE 1940); FRCS; FRCSE; Consultant Surgeon, Hospital for Sick Children, Great Ormond Street, since 1951; *b* 1910; *s* of late Prof. David Waterston, the University of St Andrews; *m* 1948, Anne, widow of Lieut H. C. C. Tanner, RN, and *d* of late Rt Rev. A. A. Markham, sometime Bishop of Grantham; one *s* two *d* (and one *s* decd). Educ: Craigflower Sch.; privately; Universities of St Andrews and Edinburgh. Ho. Surg., Royal Infirmary, Edinburgh, 1934; Ho. Surg., Surgical Registrar and Res. Medical Supt, Hospital for Sick Children, Great Ormond Street, London, 1934-38, 1948-51. Hunterian Professor, RCS, 1961; President British Association Pædiatric Surgeons, 1961. Consulting Pædiatric Surgeon to the Army, to 1975. Served RAMC, 1939-45 (despatches twice, MBE); Captain, Field Ambulance and Field Transfusion Unit, Major (Surgical Specialist). Hon. MD Genoa, 1970. *Publications:* Chapters in: Paediatric Surgery, 2nd edn 1970; Operative Surgery, 2nd edn 1971; Surgery of the Oesophagus, 1972; articles in medical journals. *Address:* Richard Reynolds House, Old Isleworth, Middlesex. *T:* 01-560 2873. *Club:* Royal and Ancient (St Andrews).

WATERSTONE, David George Stuart; Board Member, British Steel Corporation, since 1976; Executive Chairman, BSC Chemicals, and Redpath Dorman Long, since 1977; *b* 9 Aug. 1935; *s* of Malcolm Waterstone and Sylvia Sawday; *m* 1960, Dominque Viriot; one *s* two *d*. *Educ:* Tonbridge; St Catharine's Coll., Cambridge (MA). HM Diplomatic Service, 1959-70: Japan, 1959-64; Switzerland, 1968-70; Sen. Exec., IRC, 1970-71; BSC, 1971-: Man. Dir, Commercial Affairs, 1972-77. Dir, Bridon Gp, 1977-. *Recreations:* sailing, walking. *Address:* 4 Millers Court, Chiswick Mall, W4 2PF. *T:* 01-741 0261. *Clubs:* Canning; Royal Harwich Yacht.

WATERTON, Sqdn Leader William Arthur, GM 1952; AFC 1942, Bar 1946; *b* Edmonton, Canada, 18 March 1916. *Educ:* Royal Military College of Canada; University of Alberta. Cadet Royal Military College of Canada, 1934-37; Subaltern and Lieut, 19th Alberta Dragoons, Canadian Cavalry, 1937-39; served RAF, 1939-46: Fighter Squadrons; Training Command; Transatlantic Ferrying Command; Fighter Command; Meteorological Flight; Fighter Experimental Unit; CFE High Speed Flight World Speed Record. Joined Gloster Aircraft Co. Ltd, 1946. 100 km closed circuit record, 1947; Paris/London record (618.5 mph), 1947; "Hare and Tortoise" Helicopter and jet aircraft Centre of London to Centre of Paris (47 mins), 1948. Chief Test Pilot Gloster Aircraft Co. Ltd, 1946-54. Prototype trials on first Canadian jet fighter, Canuck and British first operational delta wing fighter, the Javelin. *Publications:* The

Comet Riddle, 1956; The Quick and The Dead, 1956; aeronautical and meteorological articles. *Recreations:* sailing, riding, photography, motoring, shooting. *Address:* c/o Williams & Glyn's Bank Ltd, Kirkland House, Whitehall, SW1. *Club:* Royal Military College of Canada (Kingston, Ont.).

WATES, Sir Ronald (Wallace), Kt 1975; JP; President, Wates Ltd, since 1973 (Chairman, 1969-73); *b* 4 June 1907; *s* of Edward Wates and Sarah (*née* Holmes); *m* 1931, Phyllis Mary Trace; four *s. Educ:* Emanuel Sch. FRICS; FIOB. Became a Director of Wates Ltd, 1931; Vice-Chm., 1937-69. Trustee, Historic Churches Preservation Trust. JP Inner London, 1947. Hon. Fellow, University Coll. London, 1972. DUniv Surrey, 1975. *Recreation:* field sports. *Address:* Manor House, Headley, near Epsom, Surrey KT18 6NA. *T:* Leatherhead 77346. *Clubs:* Royal Automobile, City Livery.

WATKIN, Rt. Rev. Abbot Christopher Aelred Paul; titular Abbot of Glastonbury; Headmaster of Downside School, 1962-75; *b* 23 Feb. 1918; *s* of Edward Ingram Watkin and late Helena Watkin (*née* Shepheard). *Educ:* Blackfriars Sch., Laxton; Christ's Coll., Cambridge (1st class Parts I and II, historical Tripos). Housemaster at Downside Sch., 1948-62. FRHistS, 1946; FSA, 1950; FRSA, 1969. *Publications:* Wells Cathedral Miscellany, 1943; (ed) Great Chartulary of Glastonbury, 3 vols, 1946-58; (ed) Registrum Archidiaconatus Norwyci, 2 vols, 1946-48; Heart of the World, 1954; The Enemies of Love, 1958; articles in Eng. Hist. Rev., Cambridge Hist. Journal, Victoria County History of Wilts, etc. *Address:* St Benet's, Grange Road, Beccles, Suffolk. *T:* Beccles 713179.

WATKIN WILLIAMS, Sir Peter, Kt 1963; non-resident Chief Justice of St Helena and President of Anguilla Court of Appeal, since 1972; *b* 8 July 1911; *s* of late Robert Thesiger Watkin Williams, late Master of the Supreme Court, and Mary Watkin Williams; *m* 1938, Jane Dickinson (*née* Wilkin); two *d. Educ:* Sherborne; Pembroke Coll., Cambridge. Partner in Hansons, legal practitioners, Shanghai, 1937-40; served War of 1939-45, Rhodesia and Middle East, 1940-46. Resident Magistrate, Uganda, 1946-55; Puisne Judge, Trinidad and Tobago, 1955-58; Puisne Judge, Sierra Leone, 1958-61; Plebiscite Judge, Cameroons, 1961; Chief Justice of Basutoland, Bechuanaland and Swaziland, and President of the Court of Appeal, 1961-65; High Court Judge, Malawi, 1967-69; Chief Justice of Malawi, 1969-70. *Recreation:* fishing. *Address:* Lower East Horner, Stockland, Honiton, Devon.

WATKINS, family name of **Baron Watkins.**

WATKINS, Baron *cr* 1972 (Life Peer), of Glyntawe, Brecknock; **Tudor Elwyn Watkins;** Chairman, Powys County Council, 1973-76; Lieutenant of Powys, since 1975; *b* 9 May 1903; *e s* of late County Councillor Howell Watkins, JP, Abercrave, Swansea Valley; *m* 1936, Bronwen R., 3rd *d* of late T. Stather, Talgarth; no *c. Educ:* local elementary schools; evening continuation classes; University Tutorial, WEA and NCLC classes; Coleg Harlech, N Wales (Bursary). Began working at local collieries at age of 13½; miner for 8 years; political agent for Brecon and Radnor, 1928-33; MP (Lab) Brecon and Radnor, 1945-70; PPS to Sec. of State for Wales, 1964-68. Alderman, Breconshire CC, 1940-74. General Secretary Breconshire Assoc. of Friendly Societies, 1937-48. Hon. Freeman, Brecon Borough; Chm., Brecon Beacons Nat. Park Cttee, 1974. *Recreations:* served as Secretary of Abercrave Athletic Club, Cricket Club, Ystalyfera Football League, Horticultural Society and Show. *Address:* Bronafon, Penyfan Road, Powys. *T:* 2961.

WATKINS, Alan (Rhun); journalist; Political Columnist, Observer, since 1976; *b* 3 April 1933; *o c* of D. J. Watkins, schoolmaster, Tycroes, Dyfed, and Violet Harris; *m* 1955, Ruth Howard; one *s* two *d. Educ:* Amman Valley Grammar Sch.; Queens' Coll., Cambridge. Chm., Cambridge Univ. Labour Club, 1954. National Service, RAF, Educn Br., 1955-57 (FO). Called to Bar, Lincoln's Inn, 1957. Research Asst, Dept of Govt, LSE, 1958-59; Editorial Staff, Sunday Express, 1959-64 (New York Corresp., 1961; Actg Political Corresp., 1963; Cross-Bencher Columnist, 1963-64); Political Corresp., Spectator, 1964-67; Script-Writer, BBC 3 and The Late Show, 1966-67; Political Corresp., New Statesman, 1967-76; Political Columnist, Sunday Mirror, 1968-69; Columnist, Evening Standard, 1974-75. Mem. (Lab) Fulham Bor. Council, 1959-62. Dir, The Statesman and Nation Publishing Co. Ltd, 1973-76. Granada Award, Political Columnist of the Year, 1973. *Publications:* The Liberal Dilemma, 1966; (contrib.) The Left, 1966; (with A. Alexander) The Making of the Prime Minister 1970, 1970. *Recreations:* reading, drinking wine, sleeping, watching cricket and Rugby. *Address:* 12 Battishill Street, N1 1TE. *T:* 01-359 7816.

WATKINS, Prof. Arthur Goronwy, CBE 1967; Professor of Child Health, Welsh National School of Medicine, 1950-68, Emeritus Professor, since 1968; Dean of Clinical and Post-Graduate Studies, 1947-68; *b* 19 March 1903; *s* of Sir Percy Watkins; *m* 1933, Aileen Llewellyn; one *s* three *d. Educ:* Sidcot Sch.; University Coll., Cardiff; University Coll. Hospital, London. BSc (Wales) 1925; MD (London) 1930; FRCP 1943. Res. Hosp. appts, University Coll. Hosp., 1927-29, West London Hosp., 1929, Hosp. for Sick Children, Gt Ormond Street, 1930; First Asst, Dept of Pædiatrics, University Coll. Hosp., 1930-32; Lectr In Pædiatrics, Welsh Nat. Sch. of Medicine, 1932-50; Cons. Pædiatrician, Royal Infirmary and Llandough Hosp., Cardiff, 1932. Former Mem. Bd of Govs, United Cardiff Hosps; Consultant and Adviser in Pædiatrics, Welsh Hosp. Bd; Hon. Treas. Brit. Pædiatric Assoc., 1958-63, Pres., 1966-67; Pres. Children's Sect., Roy. Soc. Med., 1953, Hon. Mem. 1970; Pres. Cardiff Div., BMA, 1953; Corr. Mem. Soc. de Pédiatrie, Paris; Hon. Fellow, Amer. Academy of Pediatrics, 1967; Mem. Albemarle Cttee on Youth Service; Mem. Central Coun. of Educ. (Wales), 1954-56; External Examr, Univs of Bristol, Birmingham, Manchester, Leeds; Colonial Office Visitor to W Indies, 1956 and Far East, 1959. President Cardiff Medical Soc., 1963-64. *Publications:* (with W. J. Pearson) The Infant, 1932; Pædiatrics for Nurses, 1947; articles in BMJ, Lancet, Archives of Disease in Childhood, etc. *Recreation:* golf. *Address:* 181 Cyncoed Road, Cardiff, S Wales. *T:* 751262.

WATKINS, David John; MP (Lab) Consett since 1966; Engineer; *b* 27 Aug. 1925; *s* of Thomas George Watkins and Alice Elizabeth (*née* Allen); unmarried. *Educ:* Bristol. Member: Bristol City Council, 1954-57; Bristol Educn Cttee, 1958-66; Labour Party, 1950-; Amalgamated Union of Engineering Workers (formerly AEU), 1942-; Sec., AUEW Gp of MPs, 1968-77. Contested Bristol NW, 1964. Sponsored Employers Liability (Compulsory Insurance) Act, 1969, and Industrial Common Ownership Act, 1976 as Private Member's Bills; introd Drained Weight Bill, 1973; Chm., Labour Middle East Council, 1974-. *Publication:* Labour and Palestine, 1975. *Recreations:* reading, listening to music, swimming. *Address:* House of Commons, SW1; 1 Carisbrooke House, Courtlands, Sheen Road, Richmond, Surrey. *T:* 01-940 8732.

WATKINS, Harold James; Managing Director, CANUSA Ltd, since 1956; Director other subsidiaries (home and overseas) Montague L. Meyer Ltd; *b* 1914; *s* of late J. W. Watkins, Aberystwyth; *m* 1940, Jean, *d* of Frank Morris, OBE; one *s* (and one *s* decd). *Educ:* Ardwyn Grammar Sch., Aberystwyth; Univ. of Wales (BSc). Forestry and Forest Botany, 1935; Forest Products Research Laboratory, 1936. Joined Montague L. Meyer Ltd, 1937. Served War, 1940-45: India, Burma; Capt. 1st Royal Welch Fusiliers. Concerned with development of Malaysian Timber Industry, 1948-. A Forestry Comr, 1967-73; Mem., Nat. Cttee for Wales, Forestry Commn, 1967-73 (England, 1967-70). *Recreations:* poetry; the art of doing nothing. *Address:* 6 The Green, Woodford Green, Essex. *T:* 01-504 1181; Pen y banc, Cwmystwyth, Dyfed. *T:* Pontrhydygroes 219.

WATKINS, Lt-Col Hubert Bromley, OBE 1945; MC 1917; DCM 1916; DL; Vice-Lieutenant of Radnorshire, 1958-74; Chairman, Radnorshire Co. Ltd, 1966-70; Chairman, Bates & Hunt (Agric.) Ltd, 1952-70; *b* 9 July 1897; *s* of Hubert and Helen Watkins, Ludlow; *m* 1936, Mary (*née* Edwards); one *s* two *d. Educ:* Monmouth. King's Shropshire Light Infantry, 1914-19; Radnorshire Rifles (HG), 1940-45. Deputy Lieutenant, Powys (formerly Radnorshire), 1948; High Sheriff, 1952. President, National Assoc. Corn and Agricultural Merchants, 1949-50. *Recreations:* fishing, previously Rugby football and cricket. *Address:* Dunvegan, Kingsland, Leominster, Herefordshire. *T:* Kingsland 571. *Club:* Cardiff and County (Cardiff).

WATKINS, Mary Gwendolen, MA Oxon; Headmistress, Bedford High School, 1949-65, retired; *b* 1905; *d* of late M. J. Watkins, CBE. *Educ:* Newland High School, Hull; Penrhos College; St Hugh's College, Oxford (open scholar). Headmistress, Erdington Grammar School, Birmingham, 1940-49. Member of Staff of Martyrs Memorial School, Papua/New Guinea, Jan.-Dec. 1966. *Recreations:* music, travel. *Address:* 5 South Avenue, Kidlington, Oxford.

WATKINS, Hon. Sir Tasker, Kt 1971; VC 1944; DL; **Hon. Mr Justice Watkins;** Major, the Welch Regiment; Judge of the High Court of Justice, Queen's Bench Division, since 1974 (Family Division, 1971-74); Presiding Judge, Wales and Chester Circuit, since 1975; *b* 18 Nov. 1918; *s* of late Bertram and Jane Watkins, Nelson, Glam; *m* 1941, Eirwen Evans; one *s* one *d. Educ:* Pontypridd Grammar Sch. Called to Bar, Middle Temple, 1948, Bencher 1970; QC 1965; Deputy Chairman: Radnor QS, 1962-

71; Carmarthenshire QS, 1966-71. Recorder: Merthyr Tydfil, 1968-70, Swansea, 1970-71; Leader, Wales and Chester Circuit, 1970-71. Counsel (as Deputy to Attorney-General) to Inquiry into Aberfan Disaster, 1966. Chairman, Mental Health Review Tribunal, Wales Region, 1960-71. DL Glamorgan, 1956. *Address:* Royal Courts of Justice, Strand, WC2A 2LL; Fairwater Lodge, Fairwater Road, Llandaff, Glamorgan. *T:* Cardiff 563558. *Clubs:* Army and Navy; Cardiff and County (Cardiff).

WATKINS, Thomas Frederick; Director, Chemical Defence Establishment, Porton, 1972-74; *b* 19 Feb. 1914; *s* of late Edward and late Louisa Watkins; *m* 1939, Jeannie Blodwen Roberts; two *d. Educ:* Cowbridge Grammar Sch.; Univ. of Wales, Cardiff. BSc Hons Wales 1935; MSc Wales 1936; FRIC 1947. Joined Scientific Staff of War Dept, 1936; seconded to Govt of India, 1939-44; seconded to Dept of Nat. Defence, Canada, 1947-49; Head of Research Section, CDRE, Sutton Oak and Min. of Supply CDE, Nancekuke, 1949-56; Supt Chemistry Research Div., CDE, Porton, 1956; Asst Dir Chemical Research, CDE, Porton, 1963; Dep. Dir, CDE, Porton, 1966. *Publications:* various papers on organic chemistry. *Recreation:* gardening. *Address:* 34 Harnwood Road, Salisbury, Wilts. *T:* Salisbury 5135.

WATKINS, Dr Winifred May, FRS 1969; Head of Division of Immunochemical Genetics, Clinical Research Centre, Medical Research Council, since 1976; *b* 6 Aug. 1924; *d* of Albert E. and Annie B. Watkins. *Educ:* Godolphin and Latymer Sch., London; Univ. of London. PhD 1950; DSc 1963. Research Asst in Biochemistry, St Bartholomew's Hosp. Med. Sch., 1948-50; Beit Memorial Research Fellow, 1952-55; Mem. of Staff of Lister Inst. of Preventive Medicine, 1955-76; Wellcome Travelling Research Fellow, Univ. of California, 1960-61; Reader in Biochemistry, 1965; Prof. of Biochemistry, Univ. of London, 1968-76; William Julius Mickle Fellow, London Univ. 1971. Landsteiner Memorial Award (jtly), 1967; Paul Ehrlich-Ludwig Darmstädter Prize (jtly), 1969. *Publications:* various papers in biochemical and immunological jls. *Address:* MRC Clinical Research Centre, Watford Road, Harrow, Middlesex HA1 3UJ.

WATKINS-PITCHFORD, Denys James, FRSA; ARCA; author and artist; *b* 25 July 1905; *s* of Rev. Walter Watkins-Pitchford, BA, and Edith Elizabeth (*née* Wilson); *m* 1939, Cecily Mary Adnitt (*d* 1974); one *d* (one *s* decd). *Educ:* privately; studied art in Paris, 1924, and at Royal Coll. of Art, London (Painting Schs), 1926-28. Asst Art Master, Rugby Sch., 1930-47. Served City of London Yeomanry RHA, 1926-29. Captain, Home Guard, 1940-46. Carnegie Medal, 1942. *Publications:* (under pseudonym 'BB'): Sportsman's Bedside Book, 1937; Wild Lone, 1939; Manka, 1939; Countryman's Bedside Book, 1941; Little Grey Men, 1941; The Idle Countryman, 1943; Brendon Chase, 1944; Fisherman's Bedside Book, 1945; The Wayfaring Tree, 1945; Down the Bright Stream, 1948; Shooting Man's Bedside Book, 1948; Meeting Hill, 1948; Confessions of a Carp Fisher, 1950; Tides Ending, 1950; Dark Estuary, 1952; The Forest of Boland Light Railway, 1955; Mr Bumstead, 1958; The Wizard of Boland, 1958; Autumn Road to the Isles, 1959; The Badgers of Bearshanks, 1961; The White Road Westwards, 1961; September Road to Caithness, 1962; Lepus the Brown Hare, 1962; The Summer Road to Wales, 1964; Pegasus Book of the Countryside, 1964; The Whopper, 1967; A Summer on the Nene, 1967; At the Back o' Ben Dee, 1968; The Tyger Tray, 1971; Pool of the Black Witch, 1974; Lord of the Forest, 1975; Recollections of a Longshore Gunner, 1976; Unforgettable Unforgotten (autobiog.), 1978; contribs to Field, Country Life, Shooting Times. *Recreations:* natural history, fishing, shooting. *Address:* The Round House, Sudborough, Kettering, Northants. *T:* Thrapston 3215.

WATKINS-PITCHFORD, Dr John, CB 1968; Chief Medical Adviser, Department of Health and Social Security (formerly Ministry of Social Security and Ministry of Pensions and National Insurance), 1965-73; retired 1973; *b* 20 April 1912; *s* of Wilfred Watkins Pitchford, FRCS, first Director of South African Institute of Medical Research, and Olive Mary (*née* Nichol); *m* 1945, Elizabeth Patricia Wright; one *s. Educ:* Shrewsbury School; St Thomas's Hospital. MRCS, LRCP 1937; MB, BS 1939 (London); MD 1946 (London); DPH 1946; DIH 1949. Various hosp. appts War of 1939-45: served RAFVR, Sqdn Ldr. Med. Inspector of Factories, 1947-50; Sen. Med. Off., Min. of Nat. Insce, 1950. Mem., Industrial Injuries Adv. Council, 1975-. QHP 1971-74. *Publications:* articles on occupational medicine. *Recreation:* gardening. *Address:* Whitewoods, Brasted Chart, Westerham, Kent. *T:* Westerham 62347. *Club:* Athenæum.

WATKINSON, family name of Viscount Watkinson.

WATKINSON, 1st Viscount *cr* 1964, of Woking; **Harold Arthur Watkinson,** PC 1955; CH 1962; President, Confederation of British Industry, 1976-77; Chairman of Cadbury Schweppes Ltd, 1969-74 (Group Managing Director, Schweppes Ltd, 1963-68); Director: British Insulated Callender's Cables, 1968-77; Midland Bank Ltd; *b* 25 Jan. 1910; *e s* of A. G. Watkinson, Walton-on-Thames; *m* 1939, Vera, *y d* of John Langmead, West Sussex; two *d. Educ:* Queen's College, Taunton; King's College, London. Family business, 1929-35; technical and engineering journalism, 1935-39. Served War of 1939-45, active service, Lieut-Comdr RNVR. Chairman Production Efficiency Panel for S England, Machine Tool Trades Association, 1948; Chairman (first) Dorking Div. Conservative Assoc., 1948-49. MP (C) Woking Division of Surrey, 1950-64; Parliamentary Private Secretary to the Minister of Transport and Civil Aviation, 1951-52; Parliamentary Secretary to Ministry of Labour and National Service, 1952-55; Minister of Transport and Civil Aviation, Dec. 1955-59; Minister of Defence, 1959-62; Cabinet Minister, 1957-62. Mem., Brit. Nat. Export Council 1964-70; Chairman: Cttee for Exports to the United States, 1964-67; Nat. Advisory Cttee on the Employment of Older Men and Women, 1952-55; Companies Cttee, CBI, 1972-; a Vice-Pres., Council, BIM, 1970-73, Pres., 1973- (Chm., 1968-70). President: Grocers' Inst., 1970-71; Inst. of Grocery Distribution, 1972-73; Member: Council, RSA, 1972-; NEDC, 1976-. Pres., RNVR Officers' Assoc., 1973-. Chairman: Council, Cranleigh and Bramley Schools, 1973-; Recruitment Working Party, Duke of Edinburgh's 1974 Study Conf., 1972-74. *Publication:* Blueprint for Industrial Survival, 1976. *Recreations:* mountaineering, walking, sailing. *Heir:* none. *Address:* Tyma House, Bosham, near Chichester, Sussex. *Clubs:* Naval; Royal Southern Yacht (Southampton).

WATKINSON, John Taylor; MP (Lab) Gloucestershire West, since Oct. 1974; barrister; *b* 25 Jan. 1941; *s* of William Forshaw Watkinson; *m* 1969. *Educ:* Bristol Grammar Sch.; Worcester Coll., Oxford. Schoolmaster, 1964-71. Called to Bar, Middle Temple, 1971. Contested (Lab) Warwick and Leamington, 1970. PPS to Sec. of State, Home Office, 1975-. Member: Fabian Soc.; Soc. of Labour Lawyers; TGWU. Mem. and Rapporteur, Council of Europe and WEU, 1976-. *Recreations:* theatre, cinema, opera, sport. *Address:* House of Commons, SW1A 0AA.

WATLING, (David) Brian; Senior Treasury Counsel, since 1975; *b* 18 June 1935; *o s* of late Vernon Russell Watling and of Edith Stella (*née* Ridley); *m* 1964, Second Officer Noelle Louise Bugden, WRNS. *Educ:* Charterhouse; King's Coll., London (LLB). Called to Bar, Middle Temple, 1957. Nat. Service, Sub-Lieut RNR, 1957. Temporary Dep. Chm., QS, 1969-71; Jun. Prosecuting Counsel: to Inland Revenue, 1970; Inner London Sessions, 1971; Prosecuting Counsel to the Crown, Mddx Sessions, 1972; Jun. Prosecuting Counsel to the Crown, Central Criminal Court, 1972, Sen. Prosecuting Counsel, 1975. Extra-mural Lectr in Criminal Law, Univ. Coll. at Buckingham, 1978. *Recreations:* sailing, theatre and ballet, fireside reading, the company of old friends. *Address:* Queen Elizabeth Building, Temple, EC4Y 9BS. *T:* 01-353 6453.

WATSON; see Milne-Watson.

WATSON, family name of Baron Manton.

WATSON, Adam; see Watson, John Hugh A.

WATSON, Alan; see Watson, W. A. J.

WATSON, Rear-Adm. Alan George, CB 1975. Joined Royal Navy as Dartmouth Cadet, 1941. Served War of 1939-45; HMS Jaguar, 1942; later HMS Dulverton and HMS Duke of York; joined HMS Swift, serving in Home Fleet, on Russian convoys and in Normandy, 1943-44; Dir-Gen., Personal Services and Training (Naval), MoD, Aug. 1972-74; Asst Chief of Naval Staff, 1974-77, retired.

WATSON, Alan John; Head of the Audio-Visual Division, Directorate-General Information, European Commission; Chief Executive, European Commission TV and Radio Studios; Supervisory Editor, European Community Newsreel Service to Lomé Convention Countries; *b* 3 Feb. 1941; *s* of Rev. John William Watson and Edna Mary (*née* Peters); *m* 1965, Karen Lederer; two *s. Educ:* Diocesan Coll., Cape Town, SA; Kingswood Sch., Bath, Somerset; Jesus Coll., Cambridge (Open Schol. in History 1959, State Schol. 1959) (MA Hons). Vice-Pres., Cambridge Union; Pres., Cambridge Univ. Liberal Club; Chm., Cambridge Univ. European Gp. Research Asst to

Cambridge Prof. of Modern History on post-war history of Unilever, 1962-64. General trainee, BBC, 1965-66; Reporter, BBC TV, The Money Programme, 1966-68; Chief Public Affairs Commentator, London Weekend Television; own series, For the Record, 1968-69; Political and Economic Reporter, BBC TV: The Money Programme, Party Political Confs, Documentaries in UK and abroad, 1969-72; Reporter, Panorama, 1972-74; Presenter, The Money Programme, 1974-75. Special TV series for BBC TV: Who Runs Europe?, 1967; The Six and Britain, 1971; These Young People, 1973; Party Lines, 1974. Radio work includes: It's Your Line, Today, and Overseas Services. Prospective Parly Cand. (L) Richmond, Surrey; contested (L) Richmond, Oct. 1974. Mem., EEC Comité Audiovisuel Européen, 1973-. Grand Prix Eurodiaporama of European Community for Common Market coverage, 1974. *Publication:* Europe at Risk: an analysis of the politics and economics of European integration, 1972. *Recreation:* historical biography. *Address:* Rue de la Loi 200, Brussels 1040; 2 Retreat Road, Richmond, Surrey TW9 1NN. *Clubs:* Reform, National Liberal.

WATSON, Sir Andrew; see Watson, Sir J. A.

WATSON, Maj.-Gen. Andrew Linton; General Officer Commanding Eastern District, since 1977; *b* 9 April 1927; *s* of Col W. L. Watson, OBE, and Mrs D. E. Watson (*née* Lea); *m* 1952, Mary Elizabeth, *d* of Mr and Mrs A. S. Rigby, Warrenpoint, Co. Down; two *s* one *d*. *Educ:* Wellington Coll., Berks. psc, jssc, rcds. Commnd The Black Watch, 1946; served, 1946-66: with 1st and 2nd Bns, Black Watch, in UK, Germany, Cyprus and British Guiana; with UN Force, Cyprus; as GSO 2 and 3 on Staff, UK and Germany; GSO 1 HQ 17 Div./Malaya Dist, 1966-68; CO 1st Bn The Black Watch, UK, Gibraltar and NI, 1969-71; Comdr 19 Airportable Bde, Colchester, 1972-73; RCDS, 1974; Comdr British Army Staff, and Military Attaché, Washington, DC, 1975-77. *Recreations:* tennis, shooting, walking, classical music, pipe music, Scottish country dancing. *Address:* c/o Royal Bank of Scotland, 18 South Methven Street, Perth, Scotland. *T:* Perth 31441. *Clubs:* Army and Navy; Puffins (Edinburgh); Highland Brigade.

WATSON, Anthony Heriot, CBE 1965; *b* 13 April 1912; *s* of William Watson and Dora Isabel Watson (*née* Fisher); *m* 1946, Hilary Margaret Fyfe. *Educ:* St Paul's Sch.; Christ Church, Oxford; University Coll., London. Statistical Officer, British Cotton Industry Research Assoc., 1936. Min. of Supply, 1940: Statistician; Asst Dir of Statistics; Min. of Aircraft Production, 1942; Statistician, Dept of Civil Aviation, Air Ministry, 1945; Chief Statistician: Min. of Civil Aviation, 1951; Min. of Transport and Civil Aviation, 1954; Min. of Aviation, 1959; Min. of Transport, 1964, Dir of Statistics, 1966; DoE, 1970; retired 1973. *Recreations:* music, garden. *Address:* 9 Kirk Park, Edinburgh EH16 6HZ. *T:* 031-664 7428.

WATSON, Arthur Christopher, CMG 1977; Governor, Turks and Caicos Islands, since 1975; *b* 2 Jan. 1927; *s* of late Dr A. J. Watson and Dr Mary Watson, Kunming, China, and Chinnor; *m* 1956, Mary Cecil Candler (*née* Earl); one *d*; and one step *s* one step *d*. *Educ:* Norwich Sch.; St Catharine's Coll., Cambridge. Naval Service, 1945-48 (commissioned RNVR, 1946). Colonial Administrative Service, Uganda, 1951; District Commissioner, 1959; Principal Asst Sec., 1960; Principal, Commonwealth Relations Office, 1963; HM Diplomatic Service, 1965; Karachi, 1964-67; Lahore, 1967; FCO, 1967-71; HM Comr in Anguilla, 1971-74. *Recreations:* boats, birds. *Address:* Government House, Turks and Caicos Islands, West Indies; Holmesdale, Oval Way, Gerrards Cross, Bucks. *Club:* Royal Commonwealth Society.

WATSON, (Daniel) Stewart, CB 1967; OBE 1958; *b* 30 Dec. 1911; *s* of Reverend Dr William Watson, DD, DLitt, and Mary Mackintosh Watson; *m* 1939, Isabel (*née* Gibson); one *s*. *Educ:* Robert Gordon's Coll.; Aberdeen University. Student Apprentice, British Thomson Houston, Rugby, 1933, Research Engr, 1936. Scientific Officer, Admiralty, 1938-; Dir, Admiralty Surface Weapons Establishment, 1961-68; Dep. Chief Scientist (Naval), MoD, 1968-72; Dir Gen. Establishments, Resources Programme A, MoD, 1972-73. *Publications:* contribs to IEEJ. *Recreations:* thoroughbred cars; caravanning. *Address:* The Cedars, Jumps Road, Churt, Surrey.

WATSON, Captain Sir Derrick William Inglefield Inglefield-, 4th Bt, *cr* 1895; TD 1945; 4th Battalion Queen's Own Royal West Kent Regimental Reserve of Officers (TA); Active List 3 Sept. 1939; now retired; *b* 7 Oct. 1901; *s* of Sir John Watson, 2nd Bt, and Edith Jane, *e d* of W. H. Nott, Liverpool; *S* brother, 1918; changed name by Deed Poll to Inglefield-Watson, Jan. 1946; *m* 1925, Margrett Georgina (who obtained a divorce, 1939), *o d* of late Col T. S. G. H. Robertson-Aikman, CB; one *s*

one *d*; *m* 1946, Terezia (Terry), *d* of late Prof. Charles Bodon, Budapest. *Educ:* Eton; Christ Church, Oxford. County Councillor, Kent (No 4 Tonbridge Division), 1931-37. *Heir: s* John Forbes Watson, Lt-Col Royal Engineers, *b* 16 May 1926. *Address:* Ringshill House, Wouldham, near Rochester, Kent. *T:* Medway 61514.

WATSON, Sir Duncan; see Watson, Sir N. D.

WATSON, Vice-Adm. Sir Dymock; see Watson, Vice-Adm. Sir R. D.

WATSON, Sir Francis (John Bagott), KCVO 1973 (CVO 1965; MVO 1959); BA Cantab; MA Oxon 1969, FBA 1969, FSA; Director, Wallace Collection, 1963-74; Surveyor of The Queen's Works of Art, 1963-72, retired; Advisor for Works of Art, since 1972; *b* 24 Aug. 1907; *s* of Hugh Watson, Blakedown, and Helen Marian Bagott, Dudley; *m* 1941, Mary Rosalie Gray (*d* 1969), *d* of George Strong, Bognor; one adopted *s*. *Educ:* Shrewsbury School; St John's College, Cambridge. Registrar, Courtauld Inst. of Art, 1934-38; Asst Keeper (later Dep. Dir), Wallace Collection, 1938-63; Deputy Surveyor of The Queen's (until 1952 The King's) Works of Art, 1947-63; Trustee, Whitechapel Art Gallery, 1949-74; Chairman: Furniture History Society, 1966-74; Walpole Society, 1970-; Slade Prof. of Fine Art, Oxford, 1969-70; Wrightsman Prof., NY Univ., 1970-71; Vis. Lectr, Univ. of California, 1970; Kress Prof., National Gallery, Washington DC, 1975-76. Uff. del Ord. al Merito della Repubblica Italiana, 1961. New York University Gold Medal, 1966. *Publicatons:* Canaletto, 1949 (rev. 2nd edn, 1954); Southill, A Regency House (part author), 1951; Wallace Collection: Catalogue of Furniture, 1956; Louis XVI Furniture, 1959 (rev. French edn, 1963); The Choiseul Gold Box (Charlton Lecture), 1963; Great Family Collections (pt-auth.), 1965; The Guardi Family of Painters (Fred Cook Memorial Lecture), 1966; Eighteenth Century Gold Boxes (pt-author), 1966; The Wrightsman Collection Catalogue, Vols 1 and 2: Furniture, 1966, Vols 3 and 4: Furniture, Goldsmith's Work and Ceramics, 1970, Vol. 5: Paintings and Sculpture; Giambattista Tiepolo, 1966; Fragonard, 1967; numerous contribs to learned journals, in Europe, America and Asia. *Recreations:* sinology, Western Americana. *Address:* c/o Whittingstall Road, SW6. *Club:* Beefsteak.

WATSON, George Hugh Nicholas; see Seton-Watson.

WATSON, Gilbert, CBE 1947; HM Senior Chief Inspector of Schools in Scotland, retired; *b* 1882; *er s* of John Watson, Edinburgh; *m* 1st, 1911, Annie Macdonald (decd); 2nd, 1974, Christian M. Kennedy. *Educ:* Royal High School, Edinburgh; Edinburgh and Oxford Universities. Rector, Inverness Royal Academy, 1909; entered inspectorate of Scottish Education Department, 1910; HM Senior Chief Inspector, 1944. *Publications:* Theriac and Mithridatium: a study in Therapeutics (Wellcome Historical Medical Library), 1966; A Short History of Craigmillar Park Golf Club, Edinburgh, 1974; co-author of books on Latin Grammar and Latin prose composition. *Recreation:* golf. *Address:* 38 Granby Road, Edinburgh EH16 5NL. *T:* 031-667 5744.

WATSON, Henry, CBE 1969; QPM 1963; Chief Constable of Cheshire, 1963-74; *b* 16 Oct. 1910; *s* of John and Ann Watson, Preston, Lancs; *m* 1933, Nellie Greenhalgh; two *d*. *Educ:* Preston Victoria Junior Technical Coll. Admitted to Inst. of Chartered Accountants, 1934; joined Ashton-under-Lyne Borough Police, 1934; King's Lynn Borough Police, 1942; Norfolk County Constabulary, 1947; Asst Chief Constable, Cumberland and Westmorland, 1955, Chief Constable, 1959. CStJ 1973. *Recreation:* golf. *Address:* Gorgate Road, Hoe, Dereham, Norfolk.

WATSON, Maj.-Gen. Henry Stuart Ramsay, CBE 1973 (MBE 1954); *b* 9 July 1922; *yr s* of Major H. A. Watson, CBE, MVO and Mrs Dorothy Bannerman Watson, OBE; *m* 1965, Susan, *o d* of Col W. H. Jackson, CBE, DL; two *s* one *d*. *Educ:* Winchester College. MBIM. Commnd 2nd Lieut 13th/18th Royal Hussars, 1942; Lieut 1943; Captain 1945; Adjt 13/18 H, 1945-46 and 1948-50; psc 1951; GSO2, HQ 1st Corps, 1952-53; Instr RMA Sandhurst, 1955-57; Instr Staff Coll. Camberley, 1960-62; CO 13/18 H, 1962-64; GSO1, MoD, 1964-65; Col GS, SHAPE, 1965-68; Col, Defence Policy Staff. MoD, 1968; idc 1969; BGS HQ BAOR, 1970-73; Dir Defence Policy, MoD, 1973-74; Sen. Army Directing Staff, RCDS, 1974-76. *Recreation:* golf. *Address:* Longhope, Great Missenden, Bucks. *T:* Great Missenden 2179. *Club:* Cavalry and Guards.

WATSON, Herbert Edmeston, DSc (London); FRIC; FIChemE; Emeritus Professor of Chemical Engineering, University of

London; b 17 May 1886; s of late A. E. Watson, London; m 1917, Margaret Kathleen (d 1951), d of late William Rowson, Liverpool; one s one d. Educ: Marlborough College; London, Berlin, Geneva, Cambridge Universities. BSc 1st Class Hons Chemistry, 1907; DSc 1912; 1851 Exhibition Scholar, 1909; Fellow University College, London, 1914; Assistant Professor Indian Institute of Science, 1911-16; Professor of Inorganic and Physical Chemistry, Indian Institute of Science, Bangalore, 1916-34; Professor of Chemical Engineering, University College, 1934-51 (services lent to Admiralty, 1939-45); invented neon glow lamp, 1911. Publications: numerous papers in scientific journals. Recreation: Fluoride research. Address: Westside, Knowl Hill, Woking, Surrey GU22 7HL. T: Woking 5411.

WATSON, Herbert James, CB 1954; b 9 Aug. 1895; s of Thomas Francis Watson, Inverness; m 1929, Elsie May Carter; two s one d. Educ: Royal Naval College, Greenwich. Entered Royal Corps of Naval Constructors, 1918; Chief Constructor: Admiralty, 1940-43; Chatham, 1943-45; Manager: Malta, 1945-46; Devonport, 1946-47; Asst Director of Dockyards, 1947-49; Deputy Director of Dockyards, 1949-56. Recreation: sailing. Address: 145 Currie Street, Warnbro, WA 6169, Australia.

WATSON, Rev. Hubert Luing; retired as General Superintendent of the Baptist Union, North Western Area (1949-60); President of the Baptist Union of Great Britain and Ireland, 1963 (Vice-President, 1962); Chairman, Baptist Minister Fellowship, 1960-63; b 30 Nov. 1892; s of Austin and Margaret M. Watson; m 1914, Mercy (née Harwood); one d. Educ: Winslow School. Baptist Union Exams, External student, Manchester Coll. Pastor of: Milton and Little Leigh, 1918-23; Enon, Burnley, 1923-29; Ansdell, Lytham, 1929-35; Richmond, Liverpool, 1935-49. Recreations: gardening and motoring. Address: Cartref, Spurlands End Road, Gt Kingshill, High Wycombe, Bucks. T: Holmer Green 2062.

WATSON, Hugh Gordon; Barrister-at-Law; one of the Special Commissioners of Income Tax, 1952-76; b 3 Feb. 1912; o s of late Andrew Gordon Watson, Physician, 21 The Circus, Bath, and late Clementina (née Macdonald); m 1940, Winefride Frances (d 1973), d of late Clement Brand, Westfield, Reigate, and late Winefride Denise (née Casella); three s. Educ: Ampleforth College; Pembroke College, Oxford. Insurance Broker, 1935-39. Served War of 1939-45 in RNVR. Called to the Bar, Lincoln's Inn, 1947. Address: 24 Evesham Close, Reigate, Surrey.

WATSON, Sir (James) Andrew, 5th Bt, cr 1866; b 30 Dec. 1937; s of 4th Bt and Ella Marguerite, y d of late Sir George Farrar, 1st Bt; S father, 1941; m 1965, Christabel Mary, e d of K. R. M. Carlisle and Hon. Mrs Carlisle; two s one d. Educ: Eton. Barrister-at-law. Contested (L) Sutton Coldfield, Feb. and Oct. 1974. Heir: s Roland Victor Watson, b 4 Mar. 1966. Address: Talton House, Newbold on Stour, Stratford-upon-Avon, Warwickshire. T: Alderminster 212.

WATSON, Prof. James Dewey; Director, Cold Spring Harbour Laboratory, since 1969; b 6 April 1928; s of James D. and Jean Mitchell Watson; m 1968, Elizabeth Lewis; two s. Educ: Univ. of Chicago (BS); Indiana Univ. (PhD); Clare Coll., Cambridge. Senior Res. Fellow in Biology, California Inst. of Technology, 1953-55; Harvard University: Asst Prof. of Biology, 1955-57; Associate Prof., 1958-61; Prof. of Molecular Biology, 1961-76. Member: US National Acad. Sciences, 1962-; Amer Acad. of Arts and Sciences, 1957; Royal Danish Acad. 1962. Hon. DSc: Chicago, 1961; Indiana, 1963; Long Island, 1970; Adelphi, 1972; Brandeis, 1973; Albert Einstein Coll. of Medicine, 1974; Hofstra, 1976; Hon. LLD Notre Dame, 1965. Hon. Fellow, Clare Coll., Camb., 1967. Nobel Award in Medicine and Physiology (jointly), 1962. Publications: Molecular Biology of the Gene, 1965, 3rd edn 1976; The Double Helix, 1968; scientific papers on the mechanism of heredity. Recreation: mountain walking. Address: Bungtown Road, Cold Spring Harbor, New York 11724, USA.

WATSON, Prof. James Patrick; Professor of Psychiatry, Guy's Hospital Medical School, since 1974; b 14 May 1936; e s of Hubert Timothy Watson and Grace Emily (née Mizen); m 1962, Dr Christine Mary Colley; four s. Educ: Roan Sch. for Boys, Greenwich; Trinity Coll., Cambridge; King's Coll. Hosp. Med. Sch., London. MA, MD; MRCP, FRCPsych, DPM, DCH. Qualified, 1960. Hosp. appts in Medicine, Paediatrics, Pathology, Neurosurgery, at King's Coll. Hosp. and elsewhere, 1960-64; Registrar and Sen. Registrar, Bethlem Royal and Maudsley Hosps, 1964-71; Sen. Lectr in Psychiatry, St George's Hosp. Med. Sch., and Hon. Consultant Psychiatrist, St George's Hosp., 1971-74. Member: Inst. of Group Analysis; British Assoc. for Behavioural Psychotherapy; British Psychological

Soc. Mem., various bodies concerned with interfaces between counselling and psychotherapy, religion and medicine. Publications: papers on gp psychotherapy, treatment of phobic anxiety, psychiatry in gen. hosps, in BMJ, Lancet, British Jl of Psychiatry, British Jl of Med. Psychology, Behaviour Research and Therapy. Recreations: mountains; music, especially opera, especially Mozart. Address: 36 Alleyn Road, SE21 8AL. T: 01-670 0444.

WATSON, Prof. James Wreford; Professor of Geography, since 1954, and Convenor, Centre of Canadian Studies, since 1973, Edinburgh University; b 8 Feb. 1915; s of Rev. James Watson; m 1939, Jessie W. Black; one s one d. Educ: George Watson's College, Edinburgh; Edinburgh Univ. (MA); Toronto Univ. (PhD). Asst Lecturer in Geography, Sheffield Eng., 1937-39; Prof. of Geography, and founder of Geog. Dept, McMaster University, Canada, 1945-49; Chief Geographer, Canada, and Director of the Geographical Branch, Department of Mines and Technical Surveys, Canada, 1949-54; Prof. and founder of Geog. Dept, Carleton Univ., Ottawa, 1952-54; Head of Dept of Geography, 1954, Convenor, Sch. of Scottish Studies, 1956-59, Dean, Faculty of Social Science, 1964-68, Edinburgh Univ. Visiting Professor: Queen's Univ., Kingston, Ont, 1959-60; Univ. of Manitoba, 1968-69; Columbia Univ., 1971; Simon Fraser Univ., BC. Editor: Scottish Studies, 1957-64; Atlas of Canada; Hon. Ed., Scot. Geog. Magazine, 1975-. Member: Brit. Nat. Cttee for Geog., 1960-; Geog. Cttee, SSRC, 1965-68; Council SSRC, and Chm., Geog. Planning Jt Cttee, 1972-75; President: Geog. Section, Brit. Assoc. for Advancement of Science, 1971; British Assoc. for Canadian Studies, 1975-77; RSGS, 1977-. Hon. LLD McMaster Univ., 1977. Award of Merit, Amer. Assoc. of Geogrs, 1949; Murchison Award, RGS, 1956; Research Medal, RSGS, 1965; Gov. General's Medal, Canada (literary), 1953. FRSC; FRSE. Publications: geographical: General Geography, 1957 (Toronto); North America: Its Countries and Regions, 1963 (London); A Geography of Bermuda, 1965 (London); Canada: Problems and Prospects, 1968 (Toronto); Geographical Essays (co-editor with Prof. R. Miller); (ed) The British Isles, A Systematic Geography, 1964 (London); (ed) Collins-Longmans Advanced Atlas, 1968; (ed with T. O'Riordan) The American Environment: perceptions and policies, 1975; (jtly with Jessie Watson) The Canadians: how they live and work, 1977; A Social Geography of the United States, 1978; articles on historical and social geography in Geography, Scottish Geographical Magazine, Geographical Review, Jl of Geography, Canadian Jl of Economics and Political Science, etc; literary: Unit of Five, 1947; Of Time and the Lover, 1953; Scotland, the Great Upheaval, 1972; verse in Canadian and British literary jls. Address: Centre of Canadian Studies, The University, Edinburgh.

WATSON, John, FRCS, FRCSE; Consultant Plastic Surgeon to: Queen Victoria Hospital, East Grinstead, and Tunbridge Wells Group of Hospitals, 1950-77; London Hospital, 1963-77; King Edward VII's Hospital for Officers; b 10 Sept. 1914; s of late John Watson; m 1941, June Christine Stiles; one s three d. Educ: Leighton Park, Reading; Jesus Coll., Cambridge; Guy's Hospital. MRCS, LRCP 1938; MA, MB, BChir (Cantab) 1939; FRCS(Ed.) 1946; FRCS 1963. Served as Sqdn Ldr (temp.) RAF, 1940-46 (despatches twice). Marks Fellow in Plastic Surgery, Queen Victoria Hosp., E Grinstead, 1947-50. Exec. Trustee and Sec., E Grinstead Research Trust for McIndoe Memorial Research Unit; Gen. Sec., Internat. Confedn for Plastic and Reconstructive Surgery, 1971-75; Mem. Brit. Assoc. of Plastic Surgeons (Hon. Sec., 1960-62, Pres., 1969); FRSM. Publications: numerous articles on plastic surgery in techn. jls and scientific periodicals. Chapters in: Textbook of Surgery, Plastic Surgery for Nurses, Modern Trends in Plastic Surgery, Clinical Surgery. Recreations: fishing, contemplation. Address: Clock Court, Hartfield, East Sussex. T: 412; 122 Harley Street, W1. T: 01-935 5608.

WATSON, John Arthur Fergus, CBE 1965; PPRICS; JP; Member, Lands Tribunal, 1957-69; retired Juvenile Court Magistrate; b 24 July 1903; s of late Capt. J. G. Maitland Watson, Royal Artillery, and Mabel (née Weir); m 1948, Joan, d of late Claude Leigh; one s one d. Educ: Uppingham. Passed into RMA, Woolwich, 1921, but declined cadetship. Chartered surveyor, 1926; partner in Ferris & Puckridge, 1928-47; and in Alfred Savill & Sons, 1947-56. A Chm., Inner London Juvenile Courts, 1936-68. Member: Central Housing Advisory Cttee to Minister of Health, 1936-47; Inter-departmental Cttee on New Towns, 1945-46; Prime Minister's Cttee on Regent's Park Terraces, 1946-47; Pres., RICS, 1949-50; Mem., Stevenage Development Corp., 1952-56. Worked voluntarily for some years in prisons and borstals; Vice-Pres., Nat. Assoc. of Prison Visitors, 1938- (Hon. Sec., 1928-38; Chm., 1941-44); Mem.

Youth Advisory Council to Minister of Education, 1942-45; advised CCG on problems of juvenile delinquency in British Zone, 1947-48; Mem., Royal Commission on Justices of the Peace, 1946-48; Mem. Nat. Adv. Council on Training of Magistrates, 1967-73. JP Inner London Area (formerly County of London) 1935. *Publications:* The Housing Act 1935, 1936; Meet the Prisoner, 1939; The Child and the Magistrate, 1942 (revd 1950, 1965); British Juvenile Courts, 1948; Which is the Justice?, 1969; The Juvenile Court-1970 Onward, 1970; Nothing but the Truth: expert evidence in principle and practice, 1971 (rev. edn 1975); The Incompleat Surveyor, 1973; (with P. M. Austin) The Modern Juvenile Court, 1975; Savills: a Family and a Firm 1652-1977, 1977. *Address:* Elmdon Old Vicarage, Saffron Walden, Essex. *T:* Chrishall (via Cambridge) 346.

WATSON, Rear-Adm. John Garth, CB 1965; BScEng; CEng, FICE, FIEE; Secretary, Institution of Civil Engineers, since 1967; *b* 20 February 1914; *er s* of Alexander Henry St Croix Watson and Gladys Margaret Watson (*née* Payne); *m* 1943, Barbara Elizabeth Falloon; two *s* one *d. Educ:* Univ. Coll. School, Hampstead; Northampton Engineering Coll., Univ. of London. BSc (Eng.). MIEE 1948; AMICE 1944; MAmerIEE 1946; Amer. Soc. of Naval Engrs 1947. 2nd Lieut, 1st Bn Herts Regt (TA), 1932; resigned on joining Admiralty, 1939; Student and Asst Elec. Engr, Northmet Power Co.; HMS Vernon, 1939; Development of Magnetic Minesweepers, Dec. 1939; wounded, 1941; Warship Electrical Supt, London and SE Area, 1943; BJSM, Washington, DC, 1945; Admlty, 1948; transf. to Naval Elec. Branch, 1949; HMS Collingwood, 1950; 6th Destroyer Flot., HMS Broadsword, Battleaxe, Nov. 1950; Staff of Flag Officer, Flot., Home Fleet, HMS Superb, Switsure, 1951; Admlty, 1952; HM Dockyard Devonport, 1953; Capt. 1955; Staff of C-in-C Home Fleet, Fleet Elec. Officer, HMS Tyne, Maidstone, 1955; Suptg Elec. Engr, HM Dockyard Gibraltar, 1957; Sen. Officers' War Course, 1960; Admlty, 1961; Asst Dir of Elec. Engineering, Admlty, Nov. 1961; Adm. Superintendent, Rosyth, 1963-66; retired. ADC to the Queen, 1962. *Recreations:* sailing and light gardening. *Address:* Little Hall Court, Shedfield, near Southampton. *T:* Wickham 833216; 58 Iverna Court, W8. *T:* 01-937 2508. *Clubs:* Athenæum, Royal Thames Yacht; Royal Naval and Royal Albert Yacht (Portsmouth).
See also Vice-Adm. Sir P. A. Watson.

WATSON, (John Hugh) Adam, CMG 1958; Director General, International Association for Cultural Freedom, since 1974; *b* 10 Aug. 1914; *er s* of Joseph Charlton Watson and Alice (*née* Tate); *m* 1950, Katharine Anne Campbell; two *s* one *d. Educ:* Rugby; King's Coll., Camb. Entered the Diplomatic Service, 1937; Brit. Legation, Bucharest, 1939; Brit. Embassy, Cairo, 1940; Brit. Embassy, Moscow, 1944; FO, 1947; Brit. Embassy, Washington, 1950; Head of African Dept, Foreign Office, 1956-59; appointed British Consul-General at Dakar, 1959; British Ambassador: to the Federation of Mali, 1960-61; to Senegal, Mauritania and Togo, 1960-62; to Cuba, 1963-66; Under-Secretary, Foreign Office, 1966-68; Diplomatic Adviser, British Leyland Motor Corp., 1968-73. Gwilym Gibbon Fellow, Nuffield Coll., Oxford, Oct. 1962-Oct. 1963. Vis. Fellow, ANU, 1973. *Publications:* The War of the Goldsmith's Daughter, 1964; Nature and Problems of Third World, 1968; various plays broadcast by BBC. *Address:* 53 Hamilton Terrace, NW8. *T:* 01-286 6330; Sharnden Old Manor, Mayfield, East Sussex. *T:* Mayfield 2441. *Club:* Brooks's.

WATSON, John Parker, CBE 1972; TD 1945; partner, Lindsays, WS (formerly Lindsay Howe & Co., WS), since 1935; *b* 22 Aug. 1909; *s* of John Parker Watson, WS, and Rachel Watson (*née* Henderson); *m* 1936, Barbara Parkin Wimperis; two *s* one *d. Educ:* Merchiston Castle Sch., Edinburgh; Corpus Christi Coll., Oxford (scholar); Edinburgh Univ. MA Oxon; LLB Edin. Served War, 1939-45, RA; Adjt, 94th (City of Edinburgh) HAA Regt; Staff Capt., JAG'S Dept; Bde Major, 12th AA Bde (8th Army); Staff Coll., Haifa; GSO2 HQ 9th Army. Admitted Mem., WS Soc., 1934. Lectr in Public Internat. Law, Edinburgh Univ., 1937-39. Chairman: Edinburgh Marriage Guidance Council, 1951-54; Scottish Marriage Guidance Council, 1962-65; Scottish Solicitors' Discipline Tribunal, 1974; Mem., SE Scotland Regional Hosp. Bd, 1952-55. Mem. Council, Law Soc. of Scotland, 1950- (Vice-Pres., 1957-58, Pres., 1970-72). *Recreations:* travel, hill walking, listening to music, golf. *Address:* 66 Murrayfield Gardens, Edinburgh EH12 6DQ. *T:* 031-337 3405. *Clubs:* Travellers'; New (Edinburgh).

WATSON, (John) Steven, MA; FRSE; FRHistS; Principal, University of St Andrews, since 1966; *b* Hebburn-on-Tyne, 20 March 1916; *o s* of George Watson and Elizabeth Layborn Gall, Newcastle upon Tyne; *m* 1942, Heba Sylvia de Cordova Newbery; two *s. Educ:* Merchant Taylors' Sch.; St John's Coll., Oxford (Andrew Schol.). 1st cl. hons Mod. Hist., 1939.

Harmsworth Sen. Schol., Merton Coll., 1939-42, for research into Speakership of House of Commons; unfit, owing to loss of leg in road accident, for mil. service. Admin Asst to Controller-General, Min. of Fuel and Power, 1942; Private Sec. to Ministers of Fuel and Power, 1942-45; Lectr, Student and Tutor, Christ Church, Oxford, 1945-66 (Censor, 1955-61); Chm. Bd of Modern History, Oxford, 1956-58; Editor, Oxford Historical series, 1950-66; Chm., Scottish Academic Press. Mem., British Library Bd, 1973-. Wiles Lectr, 1968. Member: Franks Commission of University Inquiry, 1964-66; Cttee to examine operation of Section 2 of Official Secrets Act, 1971. TV Scripts and Performances. Hon. DLitt, DePauw, 1967; DHL: St Andrews, Laurinburg, NC, 1972; Philadelphia; Doctor of Humanities, Simpson Coll., Iowa. Medal of City of Paris, 1967. *Publications:* (with Dr W. C. Costin) The Law and Working of the Constitution 1660-1914, 2 vols, 1952; The Reign of George III 1760-1815 (vol. XII, Oxf. Hist. of England), 1960; A History of the Salters' Company, 1963; essays in various collections and jls. *Address:* University House, The Scores, St Andrews, Fife. *T:* St Andrews 3117; 37 Flask Walk, NW3. *Clubs:* Caledonian; New (Edinburgh); Royal and Ancient (St Andrews).

WATSON, Rev. John T., BA (London); LTCL; General Secretary, British and Foreign Bible Society, 1960-69, retired; *b* 13 Jan. 1904; *s* of late F. Watson, Sutton Bridge, Lincs; *m* 1933, Gertrude Emily Crossley, Farsley, Leeds; two *s* one *d. Educ:* Moulton Grammar School; Westminster Training College, London; Didsbury Training College, Manchester. Schoolmaster, 1924-26. Missionary (under Methodist Missionary Soc.) in Dahomey, W Africa, 1929-34; Methodist Minister: Plymouth, 1935-38; Golders Green, 1938-46; Bible Society: Secretary for Schools and Colleges, 1946-49; Asst Home Sec., 1949-54; Asst Gen. Sec., 1954-60. Hon. DD, West Virginia Wesleyan Coll., 1966. *Publications:* Seen and Heard in Dahomey, 1934; Daily Prayers for the Methodist Church, 1951. *Recreation:* music. *Address:* 16 Beverington Road, Eastbourne, East Sussex. *T:* Eastbourne 29838.

WATSON, Joseph Stanley, MBE 1946; QC 1955; National Insurance and Industrial Injuries Commissioner since 1965; *b* 13 Sept. 1910; *er s* of late Joseph Watson and late Gertrude Ethel (*née* Catton); *m* 1951, Elizabeth Elliston, *d* of late Col G. Elliston Allen, TD; four *d. Educ:* Rossall Sch.; Jesus Coll., Cambridge (MA). Barrister, Inner Temple, 1933. Served War of 1939-45 (MBE): RA (Field), UK, MEF, Force 281, Dodecanese in Unit and on G Staff (Greek Military Cross), rank of Major. No 7 (NW) Legal Aid Area Cttee, 1949-55. Mem. Gen. Council of the Bar, 1959-64; Master of the Bench, Inner Temple, 1961; Recorder of Blackpool, 1961-65. *Address:* 6 Grosvenor Gardens, SW1. *T:* 01-730 9236; The Old Dairy, Mickleham, Surrey. *T:* Leatherhead 74387.

WATSON, Air Cdre (retired) Michael, CB 1952; CBE 1945 (OBE 1942); *b* 12 Aug. 1909; *s* of late William Watson, Kew. *Educ:* St Paul's Prep. School; Saffron Walden School. Joined RAF 1929, and qualified as Pilot; trained as Signals Officer, 1933. Served War of 1939-45 (despatches twice); Air Min. Combined Ops Signals Plans 1942; HQ, AEAF, 1943; SHAEF 1944; HQ Middle East, 1946; Air Ministry, 1947; Comdg RAF Welford, 1949; HQ, Fighter Comd, 1950-53; Director of Signals, Air Ministry, 1953-54; retired from RAF at own request, 1954. Rolls Royce Representative with N American Aviation Inc., Calif., 1956-60; Asst Gen. Man., Sales and Service, Rolls Royce, Ltd, 1961-62; Space Div., N American Rockwell Inc., Calif, 1964-71, retired. Chevalier de la Légion d'Honneur, 1944; Officer US Legion of Merit, 1945. *Recreations:* fishing, sailing. *Address:* 3524 Rose Avenue, Long Beach, Calif 90807, USA.

WATSON, Sir (Noel) Duncan, KCMG 1967 (CMG 1960); HM Diplomatic Service, retired; *b* 16 Dec. 1915; *s* of late Harry and Mary Noel Watson, Bradford, Yorks; *m* 1951, Aileen Bryans, *d* of late Charles Bell, Dublin. *Educ:* Bradford Grammar School; New College, Oxford. Colonial Administrative Service: Admin. Officer, Cyprus, 1938-43; Assistant Colonial Secretary, Trinidad, 1943-45; Principal, Colonial Office (secondment), 1946; transferred to Home Civil Service, 1947; Principal Private Sec. to Sec. of State for the Colonies, 1947-50; Asst Sec.: CO, 1950-62, Cent. Af. Office, 1962-63; Under-Secretary, 1963; Asst Under-Sec. of State, CO and CRO, 1964-67; Political Adviser to C-in-C Far East, 1967-70; High Comr in Malta, 1970-72; Dep. Under-Sec. of State, FCO, 1972-74. *Address:* Sconce, Steels Lane, Oxshott, Surrey. *Clubs:* Travellers'; Royal Commonwealth Society; Leander.

WATSON, Sir Norman James, 2nd Bt, *cr* 1912; late Flying Officer, RAFVR; late KRRC and RAF; FRGS; *b* 17 March 1897; *er s* of Sir George Watson, 1st Bt, and Bessie, *d* of T. Atkinson; *S* father, 1930; *m* 1974, Lady (Beryl) Rose. *Educ:*

Eton. Sheriff of Berkshire, 1940. *Publication:* (with Edward J. King) Round Mystery Mountain, 1935. *Heir:* none. *Address:* Flat 132, 55 Park Lane, W1. *Clubs:* Royal Air Force, Alpine.

WATSON, Vice-Adm. Sir Philip (Alexander), KBE 1976; MVO 1960; with GEC-Marconi Ltd, since 1977; *b* 7 Oct. 1919; *yr s* of A. H. St C. Watson; *m* 1948, Jennifer Beatrice Tanner; one *s* two *d. Educ:* St Albans School. FIEE 1963; FIERE 1965; FBIM 1973. Mem. Council IEE, 1975. Sub-Lt RNVR, 1940; qual. Torpedo Specialist, 1943; transf. to RN, 1946; Comdr 1955; HM Yacht Britannia, 1957-59; Captain 1963; MoD (Ship Dept), 1963; Senior Officers' War Course, 1966; comd HMS Collingwood, 1967; Dep. Dir of Engrg (Ship Dept), MoD, 1969; Dir Gen. Weapons (Naval), MoD, 1970-77; Chief Naval Engineer Officer, 1974-77. Rear-Adm. 1970; Vice-Adm. 1974. *Address:* Ashley Farm House, Box, Wilts. *T:* Box 2353. *Clubs:* Army and Navy; Bath and County (Bath). *See also Rear-Adm. J. G. Watson.*

WATSON, Rt. Rev. Richard Charles Challinor; *see* Burnley, Suffragan Bishop of.

WATSON, Richard (Eagleson Gordon) Burges; HM Diplomatic Service; Counsellor (Commercial), Brussels, since 1976; *b* 23 Sept. 1930; *er s* of late Harold Burges Watson and Marjorie Eleanor (*née* Gordon); *m* 1966, Ann Rosamund Clarke; two *s* three *d. Educ:* King Edward VI Sch., Bury St Edmunds; St John's Coll., Cambridge (MA); Ecole des Langues Orientales, Paris. RA, 1948-50 (2nd Lieut). Joined HM Foreign (subseq. Diplomatic) Service, 1954; 3rd, later 2nd Sec., Tokyo, 1954-60; FO, 1960-63; 1st Sec., Bamako (Mali), 1963-66; British Delegn to OECD, 1966-69; FCO, 1969-71; Vis. Student, Woodrow Wilson Sch., Princeton, 1971-72; Counsellor (Economic), Tokyo, 1972-76. *Recreations:* ski-ing, tennis, swimming, walking. *Address:* c/o Foreign and Commonwealth Office, SW1A 2AH. *Club:* Hurlingham.

WATSON, Vice-Adm. Sir (Robert) Dymock, KCB 1959 (CB 1956); CBE 1948; DL; *b* 5 April 1904; *e s* of Robert Watson, FRIBA, Farnham, Surrey; *m* 1st, 1939, Margaret Lois (*d* 1968), *d* of late Rev. F. R. Gillespy; one *s* three *d* ; 2nd, 1977, Elizabeth Evelyn Petronella, *widow* of Amyas Chichester, MC. *Educ:* Royal Naval Colls Osborne and Dartmouth. Captain; Asst Dir of Plans, Joint Planning Staff, Min. of Defence, 1944-46; Capt. (D) 1st Destroyer Flotilla Medit., 1947-48; idc, 1949; Dir of Plans, Admty, 1950-52; CO, HMS Illustrious, 1953; Rear-Adm., 1954; Flag Officer Flotillas, Medit., 1954-55, Vice-Adm. 1957; a Lord Commissioner of the Admiralty, Fourth Sea Lord, Chief of Supplies and Transport, 1955-58; Commander-in-Chief, South Atlantic and South America, 1958-60; retired, 1961. DL County of Brecknock, 1965, Powys 1974. *Address:* Trebinshwn House, near Brecon, Wales.

WATSON, Roderick Anthony, QC 1967. Called to the Bar, Lincoln's Inn, 1949, Bencher, 1975. *Address:* Merton House, The Promenade, Castletown, Isle of Man.

WATSON, Steven; *see* Watson, J. S.

WATSON, Stewart; *see* Watson, D. S.

WATSON, Sydney, OBE 1970; MA; DMus; FRCO; FRCM; Student, Organist and Lecturer in Music, Christ Church, Oxford, 1955-70; Professor, Royal College of Music, 1946-71; Examiner, Royal Schools of Music; *b* Denton, Lancashire, 3 Sept. 1903; *s* of W. T. Watson; unmarried. *Educ:* Warwick Sch.; Royal College of Music; Keble Coll., Oxford (Organ Scholar). Assistant music master, Stowe School, 1925-28; Precentor of Radley Coll., 1929-33; Conductor of Abingdon Madrigal Society, 1931-36; Organist of New Coll., Oxford, 1933-38; Organist of Sheldonian Theatre, Conductor of Oxford Harmonic Society, 1933-38; Oxford Orchestral Society, 1936-38; Director of Concerts, Balliol Coll., 1933-38, 1962-69; Choragus to Oxford Univ., 1963-68; Master of Music, Winchester Coll., and Conductor Winchester Music Club, 1938-45; Precentor and Director of Music, Eton Coll., 1946-55; Conductor Petersfield Festival, 1946-64, Slough Philharmonic Society, 1946-55; Windsor and Eton Choral Society, 1949-55; Conductor, Oxford Bach Choir, 1955-70; Oxford Orchestral Society, 1956-70. *Publications:* Church Music. *Address:* Aynhoe Park, Aynho, Banbury, Oxon. *Club:* Athenæum.

WATSON, Thomas Frederick; Chairman, Board of Governors, since 1974, and Chairman, Finance Committee, since 1975, Governor since 1971, National Society for Epileptics; *b* 18 April 1906; *s* of late Frederick Watson and Jane Lucy (*née* Britton); *m* 1932, Eveline Dorothy Strang; one *d* . *Educ:* Tiffins Sch., Kingston-on-Thames. FCIS 1957; FCA 1960. With Deloitte

Co., Chartered Accountants, 1925-45; qual. as Chartered Sec., 1930; Incorporated Accountant, 1935. Exchange Telegraph Co. Ltd; Chief Acct, 1945; Secretary, 1949; Asst Man. Dir and Dep. Chm., 1954; Jt Man. Dir, 1958; Man. Dir, 1959; Chm. and Man. Dir, 1961-68. Mem. Council, Commonwealth Press Union, 1959-68. *Recreations:* gardening, bridge, theatre, charity work. *Address:* Rose Cottage, Hoggeston, Buckingham MK18 3LQ. *T:* Winslow 2251.

WATSON, Thomas Yirrell, CMG 1955; MBE 1943; *b* 27 May 1906; *s* of William Scott Watson and Edith Rose Watson (*née* Yirrell); *m* 1935, Margaret Alice, *d* of late J. J. Watson; one *d. Educ:* Aberdeen Grammar Sch.; Aberdeen Univ. (BSc); Cambridge Univ. (Diploma in Agricultural Science); Pretoria Univ., South Africa. Colonial Agricultural Scholar, 1929-31; Agricultural Officer, Kenya, 1931-43; Senior Agricultural Officer, Kenya, 1943-48; Dep. Director of Agriculture, Uganda, 1948-51; Director of Agriculture, Uganda, 1951-53; Secretary for Agriculture and Natural Resources, Uganda, 1954-55; Minister of Natural Resources, 1955-56. General Manager, Uganda Lint Cotton Marketing Board, 1951-53; MEC and MLC, Uganda, 1951-56. Member: Commission of Inquiry into Land and Population Problems, Fiji, 1959-60; Economic Development Commn, Zanzibar, 1961; Commission of Inquiry into Cotton Ginning Industry, Uganda, 1962; Commissioner, Burley Tobacco Industry Inquiry, Malawi, 1964. Coronation Medal, 1953. *Address:* Marchwood, 19 Seafield Road, Southbourne, Bournemouth, Dorset BH6 3JE.

WATSON, Sir William, Kt 1962; Director, Standard Life Assurance Company, 1941-75 (Chairman, 1966-69); *b* 23 Nov. 1902; *s* of late Knight Watson, SSC; *m* 1929, Elizabeth Margaret Dods; two *s* one *d. Educ:* Edinburgh Institution (now Melville College). Member of the Institute of Chartered Accountants of Scotland (Council, 1950-52). Partner Messrs Baillie Gifford & Co., 1930-47. Director: Bank of Scotland 1944-71 (Treasurer, 1952-66); Standard Life Assurance Co.; Member Edinburgh Southern Hospitals Group Board of Management, 1948, Chairman, 1950-52; Member Jenkins Cttee on Company Law Amendment, 1960; President Inst. of Bankers in Scotland, 1963-65; Member Academic Adv. Cttee, Universities of St Andrews and Dundee, 1964-66. *Recreation:* golf. *Address:* 1 Hope Terrace, Edinburgh EH9 2AP. *T:* 031-447 2752. *Clubs:* Caledonian; New (Edinburgh); Hon. Co. of Edinburgh Golfers.

WATSON, Prof. William, MA; FBA 1972; FSA; Professor of Chinese Art and Archaeology in University of London, at the School of Oriental and African Studies, and Head of the Percival David Foundation of Chinese Art, since 1966; *b* 9 Dec. 1917; *s* of Robert Scoular Watson and Lily Waterfield; *m* 1940, Katherine Sylvia Mary, *d* of Mr and Mrs J. H. Armfield, Ringwood, Hants; four *s. Educ:* Glasgow High Sch.; Herbert Strutt Sch.; Gonville and Caius Coll., Cantab (Scholar; tripos in Modern and Medieval Langs). Served Intelligence Corps, 1940-46, Egypt, N Africa, Italy, India, ending as Major. Asst Keeper, British Museum, first in Dept of British and Medieval Antiquities, then in Dept of Oriental Antiquities, 1947-66. Slade Prof. of Fine Art, Cambridge University, 1975-76. Sir Percy Sykes Meml Medal, 1973. *Publications:* The Sculpture of Japan, 1959; Archaeology in China, 1960; China before the Han Dynasty, 1961; Ancient Chinese Bronzes, 1961; Jade Books in the Chester Beatty Library, 1963; Cultural Frontiers in Ancient East Asia, 1971; The Genius of China (catalogue of Burlington House exhibn), 1973; Style in the Arts of China, 1974; contrib. to Jl RAS, Oriental Art, Burlington Mag., BM Quarterly, etc. *Recreations:* exploring Romanesque France and N Wales, opera, claret. *Address:* 17 Lichfield Road, Kew Gardens, Richmond, Surrey. *T:* 01-940 3027.

WATSON, Prof. William Alexander Jardine; Professor of Civil Law, University of Edinburgh, since 1968; *b* 27 Oct. 1933; *s* of James W. and Janet J. Watson; *m* 1958, Cynthia Betty Balls, MA,BLitt; one *s* one *d* . *Educ:* Univ. of Glasgow (MA 1954, LLB 1957); Univ. of Oxford (BA (by decree) 1957, MA 1958, DPhil 1960, DCL 1973). Lectr, Wadham Coll., Oxford, 1957-59; Lectr, 1959-60, Fellow, 1960-65, Oriel Coll., Oxford; Pro-Proctor, Oxford Univ., 1962-63; Douglas Prof. of Civil Law, Univ. of Glasgow, 1965-68. Visiting Professor of Law: Tulane Univ., 1967; Univ. of Virginia, 1970 and 1974; Univ. of Cape Town, 1974 and 1975; Univ. of Michigan, 1977. Mem. Council, Stair Soc., 1970- ; Hon. Mem., Speculative Soc., 1975. *Publications:* (as Alan Watson): Contract of Mandate in Roman Law, 1961; Law of Obligations in Later Roman Republic, 1965; Law of Persons in Later Roman Republic, 1967; Law of Property in Later Roman Republic, 1968; Law of the Ancient Romans, 1970; Roman Private Law Around 200 BC, 1971; Law of Succession in Later Roman Republic, 1971; Law Making in Later Roman Republic, 1974; Legal Transplants, An Approach to Comparative Law, 1974; (ed) Daube Noster, 1974; Rome of the Twelve Tables, 1975; Society and Legal Change, 1977; The Nature of Law; various articles. *Recreations:* Roman numismatics, shooting. *Address:* 10 Bright's Crescent, Edinburgh EH9 2DD. *T:* 031-667 6609.

WATSON-ARMSTRONG, family name of **Baron Armstrong.**

WATT, Sir Alan (Stewart), Kt 1954; CBE 1952; Hon. Fellow, Australian National University, since 1965; Director, The Canberra Times, 1964-72; *b* 13 April 1901; *s* of George Watt and Susan Stewart Robb Gray; *m* 1927, Mildred Mary Wait; three *s* one *d*. *Educ:* Sydney Boys' High Sch.; Sydney and Oxford Universities. Rhodes Scholar for NSW, 1921; practised as Barrister-at-Law, Sydney; appointed to Dept of External Affairs, Canberra, 1937; First Secretary, Australian Legation, Washington, 1940-45; Adviser, Australian Deleg. to San Francisco, UN Conf., 1945; Alternate Deleg., UN General Assembly, London, 1946; Asst Secretary (Political), Dept of External Affairs, 1946; Del. to UN Gen. Assemblies, New York, 1946 and 1947, Paris, 1948; Leader, Australian Deleg. to Conf. on Freedom of Information, Geneva, 1948. Australian Minister to USSR, 1947-48; Australian Ambassador to USSR, 1949-50; Secretary, Department of External Affairs, Canberra, ACT, 1950-53; Australian Commissioner in SE Asia, 1954-56; Australian Ambassador: to Japan, 1956-60; to Federal Republic of Germany, 1960-62. Australian Delegate, Colombo Plan Cons. Cttee Meeting, Sydney, 1950; Member Deleg. accompanying Prime Minister to Prime Ministers' Conf., London, 1951 and 1953; Member Australian Delegation to ANZUS Council Meeting, Honolulu, 1952, and Geneva, 1954; alternate Leader, Australian Deleg. to Conf. on Indo-China and Korea, Geneva, 1954, Manila Treaty Conf., Manila 1954. Bangkok 1955. Retired from Commonwealth Public Service, July 1962. Visiting Fellow, Australian National Univ., 1963-64; Dir, Australian Inst. of Internat. Affairs, 1963-69. *Publications:* Evolution of Australian Foreign Policy 1938-1965, 1967; Vietnam, 1968; Memoirs, 1972; United Nations, 1974. *Recreation:* lawn tennis. *Address:* 1 Mermaid Street, Red Hill, Canberra, ACT 2603, Australia. *Club:* Commonwealth (Canberra).

WATT, Alexander Stuart, PhD; FRS 1957; retired as Lecturer in Forest Botany, Cambridge University (1933-59); *b* 21 June 1892; *s* of George Watt and Maggie Jean Stuart; *m* 1929, Annie Constable Kennaway; two *s* one *d*. *Educ:* Turriff Secondary Sch.; Robert Gordon's Coll., Aberdeen; Aberdeen and Cambridge Universities. BA 1919, PhD 1924, Cambridge. Lecturer in Forest Botany and Forest Zoology, 1915-29; Gurney Lecturer in Forestry, Cambridge, 1929-33. Visiting Lecturer, University of Colorado, 1963; Visiting Prof., University of Khartoum, 1965. *Publications:* papers in Journal of Ecology, New Phytologist, etc. *Recreation:* hill walking. *Address:* 38 Chesterton Hall Crescent, Cambridge. *T:* Cambridge 59371.

WATT, Very Rev. Alfred Ian; Provost of St Ninian's Cathedral, Perth, since 1969; *b* 1934. *Educ:* Edinburgh Theological College. Deacon, 1960, priest 1961, Diocese of Brechin; Curate, St Paul's Cathedral, Dundee, 1960-63; Precentor, 1963-66; Rector of Arbroath, 1966-69. *Address:* St Ninian's House, 47 Balhousie Street, Perth PH1 5HJ. *T:* Perth 26874.

WATT, Andrew, CBE 1963; Forestry Commissioner, 1965-69; *b* 10 Nov. 1909; 2nd *surv. s* of late James Watt, LLD, WS, and of late Menie Watt; *m* 1943, Helen McGuffog (*d* 1969); two *s* one *d*. *Educ:* Winchester; Magdalen Coll., Oxford. BA 1931. District Officer, Forestry Commn, 1934; Divisional Officer, 1940; Conservator, 1946; Director of Forestry for Scotland, 1957-63; Director of Forest Research, 1963-65. *Address:* Greenways, 4 Ravelston Dykes Lane, Edinburgh EH4 3NY. *T:* 031-337 7986.

WATT, Very Rev. Dr Archibald; Minister, Edzell-Lethnot Parish Church, 1957-69, retired; Moderator of the General Assembly of the Church of Scotland, May 1965-66; *b* 1 Aug. 1901; *s* of Archibald Watt and Elsie Cormack; *m* 1933, Mary Swapp; two *s*. *Educ:* Robert Gordon's Coll., Aberdeen Univ. (MA) and Christ's Coll., Aberdeen; Union Theolog. Seminary, NY (STM *magna cum laude*). Hugh Black Fellowship for Union Theological Seminary, 1926-27; Assistant Minister: North Church, Aberdeen, 1927-29; St Serf's Church, Almondbank, Perthshire, 1929-34; Chalmers Church, Uddingston, 1934-42; Stonelaw Church, Rutherglen, 1942-57. Convener, Social Service Cttee of Church of Scotland, 1957-62. Hon. DD Aberdeen, 1959. *Publications:* 10 pamphlets on the Reformed Faith. *Recreation:* fishing. *Address:* 44 Springfield Avenue, Aberdeen. *T:* Aberdeen 36059. *Club:* Royal Over-Seas League.

WATT, David; Director, Royal Institute of International Affairs, since 1978; *b* Edinburgh, 9 Jan. 1932; *s* of Rev. John Hunter

Watt; *m* 1968, Susanne, *d* of Dr Frank Burchardt; three *s* . *Educ:* Marlborough; Hertford Coll., Oxford. Dramatic Critic, Spectator, 1956-57; Diplomatic Corresp., Scotsman, 1958-60; Common Market Corresp., Daily Herald, 1960-61; Polit. Corresp., Spectator, 1962-63; Washington Corresp., Financial Times, 1964-67, Polit. Editor, 1968-77. Vis. Fellow, All Souls Coll., Oxford, 1972-73. *Recreations:* music, chess, golf. *Address:* 18 Groveway, SW9 0AR. *T:* 01-582 9829. *Club:* Travellers'.

WATT, Prof. Donald Cameron; *see* Cameron Watt.

WATT, George Percival Norman, CMG 1957; CBE 1951; *b* 2 June 1890; *s* of Edmund J. Watt, Melbourne, Australia; *m* 1916, Nellie V. M. Hough (decd); one *s* one *d*. *Educ:* Wesley Coll., Melbourne, Victoria. Clerk, Victorian Railways and State Treasury, 1905-08; Navy Finance Branch, 1911; Accountant, Navy Department, 1917; Secretary, HMA Naval Establishments, Sydney, 1923; Commonwealth Public Service Inspector, 1928-40; First Assistant Secretary, Defence Division Treasury, Melbourne, 1940; Deputy Secretary, Treasury, Canberra, 1947-48; Secretary, Commonwealth Treasury, Canberra, 1948-51, retired. Chairman, Australian National Airlines Commission, 1950-57; Chairman, British Commonwealth Pacific Airlines, 1950-54; Director, Qantas Empire Airways, 1947-62; Chairman and Director, Volkswagen (Australasia) Ltd, 1959-66. *Recreation:* golf. *Address:* 23 Through Road, Burwood, Victoria 3125, Australia. *Club:* Athenæum (Melbourne).

WATT, Sir G. S. H.; *see* Harvie-Watt.

WATT, Hamish; MP (SNP) Banff, since Feb. 1974; *b* 27 Dec. 1925; *s* of Wm Watt and Caroline C. Allan; *m* 1948, Mary Helen Grant; one *s* two *d*. *Educ:* Keith Grammar Sch.; St Andrews Univ. Engaged in farming (dairy and sheep). Subseq. company director, restaurants, quarries. Contested (C), Caithness, 1966; contested (SNP), Banff, 1970. *Address:* Netherton, Keith, Scotland. *T:* Keith 2861. *Clubs:* Farmers', Whitehall Court.

WATT, Rt. Hon. Hugh, PC 1974; Member, Accident Compensation Commission, New Zealand, since 1976; *b* 19 March 1912; *m* 1st, 1935; 2nd, 1968; two *s* two *d*. *Educ:* Remuera Primary Sch.; Techn. College. Engineer. Founded own engineering business, 1947. MP for Onehunga, New Zealand, 1953; Minister of Works, also Minister of Electricity, 1957-60; Deputy Prime Minister, 1972-74; Minister of Works, Development and Labour, 1972-74; High Comr for NZ in UK, 1975-76. *Recreations:* football, racing, swimming, fishing. *Address:* c/o Accident Compensation Commission, Private Bag, Wellington, New Zealand.

WATT, Ian Buchanan, CMG 1967; HM Diplomatic Service, retired; now with Grindlay Brandt Ltd; *b* 3 Aug. 1916; *s* of John Watt and Margaret Gibson Watt, Perth; *m* 1963, Diana Susan, *d* of Captain R. A. Villiers, Royal Navy (retired) and late Mrs R. A. Villiers; two *s* one *d* (one *d* decd). *Educ:* Perth Academy; St Andrews Univ. MA 1939. Asst Principal, Government of N. Ireland, 1939. Naval Service, 1942-46; Lieut, RNVR. Principal, Colonial Office, 1946; Asst Secretary, 1956; Dep. UK Commissioner, Malta, 1962; Dep. High Commissioner, Malta, 1964; transf. to Diplomatic Service, 1964; Counsellor, CRO, 1965; British High Commissioner, Lesotho, 1966-70; Counsellor, FCO, 1970-72; High Comr, Sierra Leone, 1972-76. *Recreations:* riding, swimming. *Address:* Rosewood House, Weston Park, Thames Ditton, Surrey. *T:* 01-398 5728; Grindlay Brandt Ltd, 23 Fenchurch Street, EC3. *Club:* Travellers'.

WATT, Surgeon Vice-Adm. Sir James, KBE 1975; MS, FRCS; Medical Director-General (Navy), 1972-77; *b* 19 Aug. 1914; *s* of Thomas Watt and Sarah Alice Clarkson. *Educ:* King Edward VI Sch., Morpeth; Univ. of Durham. MB, BS 1938; MS 1949; FRCS 1955; MD 1972; FRCP 1975. Surgical Registrar, Royal Vic. Infirm., Newcastle upon Tyne, 1947; Surgical Specialist: N Ire., 1949; RN Hosp., Hong Kong, 1954; Consultant in Surgery, RN Hospitals: Plymouth, 1956; Haslar, 1959; Malta, 1961; Haslar, 1963; Jt Prof. of Naval Surgery, RCS and RN Hosp., Haslar, 1965-69; Dean of Naval Medicine and MO i/c, Inst. of Naval Medicine, 1969-72. Chm., RN Clin. Research Working Party, 1969-77; Chm. Bd of Trustees, Naval Christian Fellowship, 1968-75; Pres., Royal Naval Lay Readers Soc., 1974. QHS 1969-77. Surg. Comdr 1956; Surg. Captain 1965; Surg. Rear-Adm. 1969; Surg. Vice-Adm. 1972. Mem., Environmental Medicine Res. Policy Cttee, MRC, 1974-77. Thomas Vicary Lectr, RCS, 1974. FICS 1964; Fellow: Assoc. of Surgeons of Gt Brit. and Ire.; Med. Soc. of London (Mem. Council, 1976); FRSM; Hon. FRCSE; Member: Brit. Soc. for Surgery of the Hand; Internat. Soc. for Burns Injuries; Société Internat. de Chirurgie; Corr. Mem., Surgical Research Soc.,

1966-77; Mem. Editorial Bd, Brit. Jl of Surgery, 1966-77. Examiner in Surgery, Aberdeen Univ. Errol-Eldridge Prize, 1968; Gilbert Blane Medal, 1971. CStJ 1972. *Publications:* papers on: burns, cancer chemotherapy, peptic ulceration, hyberbaric oxygen therapy. *Recreations:* mountain walking, music. *Address:* 7 Cambisgate, Church Road, Wimbledon, SW19 5AL. *Club:* English-Speaking Union.

WATT, Rt. Hon. (James) David G.; *see* Gibson-Watt.

WATT, Prof. John Mitchell, ED; MB, ChB (Edinburgh), Hon. LLD (Witwatersrand); FRCP (Edinburgh), FRSE, FLS, FRSSAf; CStJ; Emeritus Professor of Pharmacology and Therapeutics, University of the Witwatersrand, Johannesburg; Priory Surgeon-in-Chief (Reserve), St John Ambulance Brigade, Southern Africa; *b* Port Elizabeth, South Africa, 1 Dec. 1892; Scottish parentage; *m* 1st, 1920, Yelena T. Nikonova; two *s* two *d*; 2nd, 1942, Betty Gwendoline Lory; one *s* one *d. Educ:* Grey Institute High Sch., Port Elizabeth; Stirling High Sch., Scotland; University of Edinburgh. Graduated MB, ChB 1916; commissioned in the RAMC (Special Reserve) 4 Aug. 1914; on Active Service until 1919; Assistant in Materia Medica to Professor Cushny of Edinburgh Univ.; medical author, and member various medical societies; Foreign Corresponding Member, Royal Flemish Academy of Medicine, Belgium. Twice President of the Royal Medical Society of Edinburgh. Selected by Universities' Bureau of British Empire for a Carnegie Corporation Grant, 1933-34. Served as Head of Section M3 on the staff of Medical Headquarters, Union Defence Forces, South Africa, 1941-45; Major, RAMC (Militia) (retired); Colonel, South African Medical Corps (Retired List). *Publications:* numerous articles on medical and natural history subjects in medical and scientific journals; The Medicinal and Poisonous Plants of Southern and Eastern Africa (with Maria G. Breyer-Brandwijk), 2nd edn, 1962. Editor, Formulary of the South African Railways and Harbours Sick Fund, 1st edn, 1935, 2nd edn, 1943, 3rd edn, 1952; Practical Notes on Pharmacology, Therapeutics, and Prescription Writing, 1940. Editor with F. J. Todd of The South African Pharmaceutical Formulary, 1943; Practical Pharmacology and Prescription Writing (with Margaret Brown), 1949. *Recreations:* gardening, ornithology, philately. *Address:* 36 Ludlow Street, Chapel Hill, Qld 4069, Australia.

WATT, Robert; His Honour Judge Watt; County Court Judge since 1971; *b* 10 March 1923; *s* of John Watt, schoolmaster, Ballymena, Co. Antrim; *m* 1951, Edna Rea; one *d. Educ:* Ballymena Academy; Queen's Univ., Belfast (LLB). Called to Bar, Gray's Inn; called to Bar of Northern Ireland, 1946; QC (NI) 1964; subseq. Sen. Crown Prosecutor Counties Fermanagh and Tyrone. *Recreation:* sailing. *Address:* 12 Deramore Drive, Belfast BT9 5JQ. *Club:* Royal North of Ireland Yacht.

WATT, Robert Cameron; *b* 4 Aug. 1898; *s* of Rev. J. Gordon Watt; *m* 1925, Barbara (*d* 1977), *d* of late Rt Rev. E. J. Bidwell, former Bishop of Ontario; three *s. Educ:* Fettes Coll., Edinburgh; Oriel Coll., Oxford. Lecturer in History, Queen's Univ., Kingston, Ontario, 1922-24; Asst Master, Clifton Coll., 1924-26; Senior History Master, Rugby Sch., 1926-51, Housemaster, 1944-51; Rector, Edinburgh Acad., 1951-62; Assistant Master: St George's Sch., Newport, RI, 1963-66; Fettes Coll., 1967-. *Recreations:* gardening, walking. *Address:* 9 Wardie Avenue, Edinburgh EH5 2AB.
See also D . Cameron Watt.

WATT, William, OBE 1969; FRS 1976; Senior Research Fellow, Department of Materials Science, University of Surrey, since 1975; *b* 14 April 1912; *o c* of Patrick Watt, Aberdeen, and Flora (*née* Corsar), Arbroath; *m* 1946, Irene Isabel Corps; two *d. Educ:* George Heriot's Sch., Edinburgh; Heriot-Watt Coll., Edinburgh BSc (1st Cl. Hons, Chem.); AH-WC. ARIC 1935. Research Chemist, Royal Aircraft Establishment, 1936-75, retiring as Sen. Principal Scientific Officer, (Merit). Consultant to Dir, RAE, 1975-. Hon. DSc Heriot-Watt, 1977. Gold Medal, Congrès des Matériaux Résistant à Chaud, Paris, 1951; (jtly) Civil Service Wolfe Award for Carbon Fibre Research, 1968; Silver Medal, RAeS, 1969; C. Pettinos Award for Res. and Innovation in Carbon, viz, Pyrolytic Graphite and Carbon Fibres, Amer. Carbon Cttee, 1971. *Publications:* (jtly) 57th Thomas Hawksley Lecture, IMechE (public lecture), 1970; Pettinos Award Lecture, Carbon Work at the RAE, 10th US Carbon Conf., Bethlehem (public lecture), 1971; many papers in Proc. of Confs and in scientific jls. *Recreations:* gardening, golf, continental travel. *Address:* Eilean Donan, Avenue Road, Farnborough, Hants GU14 7BL. *T:* Farnborough Hants 42560. *Club:* North Hants Golf (Fleet, Hants).

WATT, Prof. W(illiam) Montgomery; Professor of Arabic and Islamic Studies, University of Edinburgh, since 1964; *b* Ceres, Fife, 14 March 1909; *o c* of late Rev. Andrew Watt; *m* 1943, Jean Macdonald, *er d* of late Prof. Robert Donaldson; one *s* four *d. Educ:* George Watson's Coll., Edinburgh; University of Edinburgh; Balliol Coll., Oxford; University of Jena; Cuddesdon Coll. Warner Exhibition (Balliol), 1930; Ferguson Schol. in Classics, 1931; MA, PhD (Edinburgh); MA, BLitt (Oxon). Asst Lecturer, Moral Philosophy, University of Edinburgh, 1934-38; Curate, St Mary Boltons, London, 1939-41; Curate, Old St Paul's, Edinburgh, 1941-43; Arabic specialist to Bishop in Jerusalem, 1943-46; Lecturer, Ancient Philosophy, University of Edinburgh, 1946-47; Lectr, Sen. Lectr and Reader in Arabic, Univ. of Edinburgh, 1947-64; Visiting Prof. of Islamic Studies, University of Toronto, 1963; Visiting Prof., Collège de France, Paris, 1970. Chairman, Assoc. of British Orientalists, 1964-65. Hon. DD Aberdeen, 1966. *Publications:* Free Will and Predestination in Early Islam, 1949; The Faith and Practice of al-Ghazali, 1953; Muhammad at Mecca, 1953; Muhammad at Medina, 1956; The Reality of God, 1958; The Cure for Human Troubles, 1959; Islam and the Integration of Society, 1961; Muhammad Prophet and Statesman, 1961; Islamic Philosophy and Theology, 1962; Muslim Intellectual, 1963; Truth in the Religions, 1963; Islamic Spain, 1965; Islam (in Propyläen Weltgeschichte, XI), 1965; A Companion to the Qur'an, 1967; What is Islam?, 1968; Islamic Political Thought, 1968; Islamic Revelation and the Modern World, 1970; Bell's Introduction to the Qur'ān, 1970; The Influence of Islam on Medieval Europe, 1972; The Formative Period of Islamic Thought, 1973; The Majesty that was Islam, 1974; (ed) Islamic Surveys; contribs learned journals. *Address:* The Neuk, Dalkeith, Midlothian EH22 1JT. *T:* 031-663 3197.

WATT, Prof. William Smith, MA (Glasgow and Oxon); Regius Professor of Humanity in the University of Aberdeen since 1952, Vice-Principal, 1969-72; *b* 20 June 1913; *s* of John Watt and Agnes Smith; *m* 1944, Dorothea, *e d* of R. J. Codrington Smith; one *s. Educ:* University of Glasgow; Balliol Coll., Oxford (Snell Exhibitioner and Hon. Scholar). First Class Hons in Classics, Glasgow Univ., 1933; Ferguson Schol., 1934; Craven Schol., 1934; First Class, Classical Moderations, 1935; Hertford Schol., 1935; Ireland Schol., 1935; First Class, Lit. Hum., 1937. Lecturer in Greek and Greek History, University of Glasgow, 1937-38; Fellow and Tutor in Classics, Balliol Coll., Oxford, 1938-52. Civilian Officer, Admiralty (Naval Intelligence Div.), 1941-45. Convener, Scottish Univs Council on Entrance, 1973-77. Governor, Aberdeen Coll. of Educn, 1958-75 (Chm. of Governors 1971-75). *Publications:* (ed) Ciceronis Epistulae ad Quintum fratrem, etc, 1958, 1965; (ed) Ciceronis Epistularum ad Atticum Libri I-VIII, 1965; articles and reviews in classical periodicals. *Address:* Department of Humanity, King's College, Aberdeen; 38 Woodburn Gardens, Aberdeen AB1 8JA. *T:* Aberdeen 34369. *Club:* Business and Professional (Aberdeen).

WATTON, Most Rev. James Augustus; *see* Moosonee, Archbishop of.

WATTS, Arthur Desmond, CMG 1977; Legal Counsellor, Foreign and Commonwealth Office, since 1977; *b* 14 Nov. 1931; *o s* of Col A. E. Watts, MA (Cantab); *m* 1957, Iris Ann Collier, MA (Cantab); one *s* one *d. Educ:* Haileybury and Imperial Service College; Royal Military Academy, Sandhurst; Downing Coll., Cambridge (Schol.). BA 1954; LLB (First Cl.) 1955; Whewell Schol. in Internat. Law, 1955; called to Bar, Gray's Inn, 1957; MA. Legal Asst, Foreign Office, 1957-59; Legal Adviser, British Property Commn (later British Embassy), Cairo, 1959-62; Asst Legal Adviser, FO, 1962-67; Legal Adviser, British Embassy, Bonn, 1967-69; Asst Solicitor, Law Officers Dept, 1969-70; Legal Counsellor, FCO, 1970-73; Counsellor (Legal Advr), Office of UK Permanent Rep. to EEC, 1973-77. *Publications:* Legal Effects of War, 4th edn (with Lord McNair), 1966; contribs to: British Year Book of Internat. Law; Internat. and Comparative Law Quarterly; Egyptian Review of Internat. Law. *Recreation:* cricket (County Cap, Shropshire, 1955). *Address:* 2 Manor Lodge, Manor Park, Chislehurst, Kent.

WATTS, Helen Josephine, Hon. FRAM; concert, lieder and opera singer (contralto); *b* 7 Dec. 1927; *d* of Thomas Watts and Winifred (*née* Morgan). *Educ:* St Mary and St Anne's Sch., Abbots Bromley; Royal Academy of Music (LRAM). Hon. FRAM 1961 (Hon. ARAM 1955). *Recreation:* gardening. *Address:* c/o Harold Holt Ltd, 134 Wigmore Street, W1H 0DJ. *Club:* English-Speaking Union.

WATTS, Colonel John Cadman, OBE 1959; MC 1946; FRCS 1949; Consultant Surgeon, Bedford General Hospital, 1966-76, retired; *b* 13 April 1913; *s* of John Nixon Watts, solicitor, and

Amy Bettina (née Cadman); m 1938, Joan Lillian (née Inwood); three s one d. Educ: Merchant Taylors' Sch.; St Thomas's Hospital. MRCS, LRCP, 1936; MB, BS, 1938. Casualty Officer, Resident Anæsthetist, House Surgeon, St Thomas's Hospital, 1937; Surgical Specialist, RAMC, 1938-60, serving in Palestine, Egypt, Libya, Syria, Tunisia, Italy, France, Holland, Germany, Malaya, Java, Japan, and Cyprus. Hunterian Professor, RCS, 1960; Professor of Military Surgery, RCS, 1960-64; Chm., N Beds Div. BMA, 1971; Mem. Council, BMA, 1972-74. Co. Comr, St John Ambulance Brigade, 1970. OStJ 1970. *Publications:* Surgeon at War, 1955; Clinical Surgery, 1964; Exploration Medicine, 1964. *Recreations:* sailing, ski-ing, shooting. *Address:* Lowood Lodge, Hasketon, near Woodbridge, Suffolk. *T:* Grundisburgh 326. *Clubs:* Royal Automobile; Deben Yacht (Woodbridge).

WATTS, John Francis, BA; Principal, Countesthorpe College, Leicestershire, since 1972; Chairman, National Association for Teaching of English (NATE), 1974-76; *b* 18 Oct. 1926; *s* of John Weldon Watts and Norah K. Watts; *m* 1950, Elizabeth Hamilton; four *s* one *d*. *Educ:* West Buckland Sch.; Univ. of Bristol (BA). First Headmaster, Les Quennevais Sch., Jersey, CI, 1964-69; Lectr, Univ. of London, 1969-72. *Publications:* Encounters, 1965; Contact, 1970 (Australia); Interplay, 1972; Teaching, 1974; contrib. to various publications. *Address:* Countesthorpe College, Leicester LE8 3PR. *T:* Leicester 771555.

WATTS, Ronald George, CBE 1962; *b* 15 May 1914; *m* 1940, Ruth Hansen (*d* 1970); one *s* two *d*. *Educ:* Latymer Sch., Edmonton; St John's Coll., Cambridge. Foreign Service from 1937; appointed Counsellor, Foreign Office, 1958; Consul-Gen., Osaka-Kobe, 1958-63; Head of Consular Dept, FO, 1963-65; Consul-Gen., Paris, 1966-67; FCO 1967-69, retired. *Recreation:* music. *Address:* 14 Arlington Road, Petersham, Richmond, Surrey. *T:* 01-940 6137.

WATTS, Roy; Member, British Airways Board, since 1974; Director, Commercial Operations, British Airways, since 1977; *b* 17 Aug. 1925; *m* 1951, Jean Rosaline; one *s* two *d*. *Educ:* Doncaster Grammar Sch.; Edinburgh Univ. (MA). FIMTA, FRAeS, FCIT. Accountant in local govt until 1955; joined BEA, 1955: Head of Systems Study Section (O&M Br.); Chief Internal Auditor; Area Man., Sweden and Finland; Fleet Planning Man.; Regional Gen. Man., North and East Europe; Dir, S1-11 Div; Chief Exec. BEA British Airways, 1972-74 (Chm., Jan.-March 1974); Chief Exec., European Div., British Airways, 1974-77. *Recreations:* squash, cricket. *Address:* Scotswood, Penn Road, Beaconsfield, Bucks. *T:* Beaconsfield 3755.

WATTS, Rev. Sidney Maurice, DD (St Andrews), BD (London); Minister of Union Church, Mill Hill, NW7, 1942-61, retired; Moderator, International Congregational Council, 1953-58; *b* Bishops Stortford, 1892; *y s* of James Watts, Lowestoft; *m* 1917, Winifred Chambers; one *s* two *d*. *Educ:* Lowestoft; Hackney Coll. (University of London). President, London University Debating Society, 1915; Asst Minister, Bromley Congregational Church, 1916-18; Supt Minister (Congregational), Whitefield's Central Mission, Tottenham Court Road, W1, 1918-24; Minister of Warwick Road Congregational Church, Coventry, 1924; of Elgin Place Congregational Church, Glasgow, 1937-42. Chairman Congregational Union of England and Wales, 1948-49; Moderator Free Church Federal Council, 1952-53. *Publications:* The Garden of God, a volume of Sermons; Liberty to the Captives, a short history of Slavery; Thinking Again About the Future Life, 1948. *Recreation:* gardening. *Address:* Fen Place, Turner's Hill, Crawley, East Sussex.

WATTS, Victor Brian; a Recorder of the Crown Court, since 1972; barrister-at-law; *b* 7 Jan. 1927; *o s* of Percy William King Watts and Doris Millicent Watts; *m* 1965, Patricia Eileen (née Steer); one *s* one *d*. *Educ:* Colfe's Grammar Sch.; University Coll., Oxford. MA(Oxon); BCL. Called to the Bar, Middle Temple, 1950; subseq. Western Circuit. Flying Officer, Royal Air Force, 1950-52. *Publications:* Landlord and Tenant Act, 1954; Leading Cases on the Law of Contract, 1955; occasional articles of a legal nature. *Recreations:* walking, tennis. *Address:* 28 Abinger Road, W4. *T:* 01-994 4435. *Club:* Hurlingham.

WATTS, William John, OBE 1969; HM Diplomatic Service; Counsellor (Economic), Nairobi, since 1976; *b* 11 March 1923; *s* of William Thomas Watts and Beatrice (née Vickers); *m* 1949, Anne Brown Watt; one *s* one *d*. RAF, 1941-46. HMOCS, Malaya, 1947-59: retd as Dep. Sec., Min. of Interior and Justice; HM Diplomatic Service, 1960-: served in Colombo, Bangkok and Singapore. *Recreations:* tennis, reading, current affairs. *Address:* c/o British High Commission, PO Box 30465, Nairobi, Kenya; Robinwood, 35 Gregories Road, Beaconsfield, Bucks.

Clubs: Pathfinder; Royal Bangkok Sports (Thailand); Muthaiga (Nairobi, Kenya).

WAUCHOPE, Sir Patrick (George) Don-, 10th Bt, *cr* 1667; Horticulturist; *b* 7 May 1898; *o s* of late Patrick Hamilton Don-Wauchope (3rd *s* of 8th Bt) and late Georgiana Renira; *S* uncle 1951; *m* 1936, Ismay Lilian Ursula (marr. diss.), *d* of late Sidney Hodges, Edendale, Natal, South Africa; two *s*. *Educ:* The Edinburgh Academy. Served European War, 1914-18, with RFA, France and Belgium (wounded); War of 1939-46, Egypt and Italy. *Recreations:* cricket, golf. *Heir: s* Roger (Hamilton) Don-Wauchope [Chartered Accountant, S Africa; *b* 16 Oct. 1938; *m* 1963, Sallee, *yr d* of Lt-Col H. Mill Colman, OBE, AMICE, Durban; two *s* one *d*]. *Address:* Private Bag 729, Margate, Natal, South Africa.

WAUD, Christopher Denis George Pierre; a Recorder of the Crown Court, since Dec. 1974; barrister-at-law; *b* 5 Dec. 1928; *s* of late Christopher William Henry Pierre Waud and Vera Constance Mavia Waud; *m* 1954, Rosemary Paynter Bradshaw Moorhead; one *s* four *d* (and one *s* decd). *Educ:* Charterhouse; Christ Church, Oxford. Called to Bar, Middle Temple, 1956. Part-time Chm. of Industrial Tribunals, 1977-. *Recreations:* sailing, walking. *Address:* Lamb Building, Temple, EC4Y 7AS. *Clubs:* Royal Lymington Yacht (Lymington), Bar Yacht.

WAUGH, Alec; *b* Hampstead, 8 July 1898; *er s* of late Arthur Waugh; *m* 1932, Joan (*d* 1969), *d* of Andrew Chirnside, Victoria, Australia; two *s* one *d*; *m* 1969, Virginia Sorensen, *d* of Claude Eggertsen, Provo, Utah, USA. *Educ:* Sherborne; Sandhurst. Gazetted to Dorset Regt, 1917; BEF France, 1917-18; prisoner of war, 1918; has travelled extensively; rejoined Dorset Regt, 1939; BEF France, 1940; Staff Captain, Ministry of Mines, 1940; MEF, 1941; Paiforce, 1942-45; retired with rank of Major, 1945. Writer in Residence at Central State Coll., Edmond, Oklahoma, 1966-67. *Publications:* has written fifty books which include: The Loom of Youth, 1917; Kept, 1925; Nor Many Waters, 1928; Hot Countries, 1930; Most Women..., 1931; So Lovers Dream, 1931; The Balliols, 1934; Jill Somerset, 1936; Eight Short Stories, 1937; Going Their Own Ways, 1938; No Truce with Time, 1941; His Second War, 1944; Unclouded Summer, 1948; The Lipton Story, 1951; Where the Clocks Chime Twice, 1952; Guy Renton, 1953; Island in the Sun, 1956 (produced as film, 1957); The Sugar Islands, 1958; In Praise of Wine, 1959; Fuel for the Flame, 1960; My Place in the Bazaar, 1961; The Early Years of Alec Waugh, 1962; A Family of Islands, 1964; The Mule on the Minaret, 1965; My Brother Evelyn and Other Profiles, 1967; Wines and Spirits of the World, 1968; A Spy in the Family, 1970; Bangkok: the story of a city, 1970; The Fatal Gift, 1973; A Year to Remember: a reminiscence of 1931, 1975; Married to a Spy, 1976. *Recreation:* watching life go by. *Address:* c/o A. D. Peters & Co., 10 Buckingham Street, WC2. *Clubs:* Athenæum, Beefsteak, Pratt's, Savage; Century, Coffee House (New York).

WAUGH, Auberon Alexander; Columnist: Private Eye, since 1970; The Spectator, since 1976; Chief Fiction Reviewer, Evening Standard, since 1973; *b* 17 Nov. 1939; *e s* of late Evelyn Waugh, writer, and late Laura Waugh, Combe Florey House, Somerset; *m* 1961, Teresa, *o d* of 6th Earl of Onslow, KBE, MC, and *sister* of 7th Earl of Onslow, *qv*; two *s* two *d*. *Educ:* Downside (schol. in Classics); Christ Church, Oxford (exhibn in English, read PPE). Editorial staff, Daily Telgraph, 1960-63. Commissioned Royal Horse Guards, 1957; served Cyprus; retd with wounds, 1958. Weekly Columnist, Catholic Herald, 1963-64; special writer, Mirror group, 1964-67; Political Correspondent: Spectator, 1967-70; Private Eye, 1970-; Weekly Columnist, The Times, 1970-71; Chief Fiction Reviewer, Spectator, 1970-73; Weekly Columnist, New Statesman, 1973-76; monthly contributor, Books and Bookmen, 1973-. Pres., British Croatian Soc., 1973-. Nat. Press 'Critic of the Year' commendation, 1976. *Publications:* novels: The Foxglove Saga, 1960; Path of Dalliance, 1963; Who are the Violets Now?, 1966; Consider the Lilies, 1968; A Bed of Flowers, 1972; *non-fiction:* (with S. Cronje) Biafra: Britain's Shame, 1969; Four Crowded Years: the Diaries of Auberon Waugh, 1976; *essays:* Country Topics, 1974. *Recreation:* gossip. *Address:* Combe Florey House, near Taunton, Somerset; La Pesegado, 11320 Montmaur, France. *Clubs:* Beefsteak, Le Petit Club Français.

WAVERLEY, 2nd Viscount, *cr* 1952, of Westdean; **David Alastair Pearson Anderson;** Consultant Physician, Reading Group of Hospitals, since 1951; *b* 18 Feb. 1911; *s* of 1st Viscount Waverley, PC, GCB, OM, GCSI, GCIE, FRS, and Christina Anderson; *S* father, 1958; *m* 1948, Myrtle Ledgerwood; one *s* one *d* (and one *d* decd). *Educ:* Malvern Coll.; Universities of Frankfurt A/Main and Cambridge (Pembroke Coll.); St Thomas's Hospital, London. MB, BChir (Cantab), 1937; MRCP (London), 1946; FRCP (London), 1957. Appointments at St

Thomas's Hospital, 1938-39. Served War of 1939-45, RAF Med. Br. Med. Registrar, Res. Asst Physician and Registrar Dept Clin. Pathology, St Thomas's Hospital, 1946-50. *Publications:* various communications to medical journals. *Recreations:* golf and fishing; formerly athletics and Association football (rep. Cambridge *v* Oxford, in Inter-Varsity Relays, etc). *Heir: s* Hon. John Desmond Forbes Anderson, *b* 31 Oct. 1949. *Address:* Path Hill House, Whitchurch, Oxon. *T:* Pangbourne 2417. *Clubs:* Travellers'; Hawks (Cambridge).
See also Brig. Hon. Dame Mary Pihl.

WAY, Sir Richard (George Kitchener), KCB 1961 (CB 1957); CBE 1952; Principal, King's College London, since 1975; *b* 15 Sept. 1914; *s* of Frederick and Clara Way; *m* 1947, Ursula Joan Starr; one *s* two *d. Educ:* Polytechnic Secondary Sch., London. Joined Civil Service as Exec. Officer, 1933; Higher Executive Officer, 1940; Principal, 1942; Asst Secretary, 1946; Asst Under-Secretary of State, 1954; Deputy Under-Secretary of State, War Office, 1955-57; Dep. Secretary, Ministry of Defence, 1957-58; Dep. Secretary, Ministry of Supply, 1958-59; Permanent Under-Secretary of State, War Office, 1960-63; Permanent Secretary, Ministry of Aviation, 1963-66. Dep. Chm., Lansing Bagnall Ltd, 1966-67, Chm. 1967-69; Chm., LTE, 1970-74. Chairman, EDC Machine Tool Industry, 1967-70; Member (part-time) Board of: BOAC, 1967-73; Dobson Park Industries Ltd, 1975-. Chm., Council of Roedean Sch., 1969-74; Mem. Council, London Zoological Soc., 1977-. FKC 1975. Coronation Medal, 1953. American Medal of Freedom (with bronze palm), 1946. CStJ 1974. *Address:* Manor Farm, Shalden, Alton, Hants. *T:* Alton 82383. *Clubs:* Brooks's, MCC.

WAY, Rt. Rev. Wilfrid Lewis Mark; *b* 12 May 1905; *s* of late Rev. C. C. L. Way and Margaret (*née* Corser); *m* 1960, Marion Crosbie, *d* of late Sir Robert Robinson, OM, FRS, and late Lady (Gertrude M.) Robinson; one *s* one *d. Educ:* Rossall Sch.; Trinity Coll., Cambridge (Classical Scholar); Westcott House. 1st Cl. Class. Tripos, part I, 1925; BA 2nd Cl. Class. Tripos, part II, 1927; MA 1935; Deacon, 1928; Priest, 1929, Liv. Curate of St Faith, Great Crosby, 1928-34; St Bartholomew, Brighton, 1934-37; UMCA Dio., Zanzibar, 1937; Curate of Korogwe, 1937-38; Priest i/c Zanzibar, 1938-40; Msalabani, 1940-44; Mkuzi, 1944-45; Kideleko, 1948-51; Warden of Kalole Theol. Coll., Dio. of Zanzibar, 1951-52; Bishop of Masasi, 1952-59; Rector of Averham with Kelham, 1960-71. *Address:* Clifford's House, Quebec, Durham DH7 9DN. *T:* Esh Winning 284.

WAYMOUTH, Charity, BSc (London), PhD (Aberdeen); Senior Staff Scientist, since 1963, Assistant Director (Research), since 1976, The Jackson Laboratory, Bar Harbor, Maine, USA (Staff Scientist, 1952-63; Assistant Director (Training), 1969-72); *b* 29 April 1915; *o d* of Charles Sydney Herbert Waymouth, Major, The Dorsetshire Regt, and Ada Curror Scott Dalgleish; unmarried. *Educ:* Royal School for Daughters of Officers of the Army, Bath; University of London; University of Aberdeen. Biochemist, City of Manchester General Hospitals, 1938-41; Research Fellow, University of Aberdeen, 1944; Beit Memorial Fellow for Medical Research, 1944-46; Member of scientific staff and head of tissue culture dept, Chester Beatty Research Institute for Cancer Research (University of London), 1947-52; British Empire Cancer Campaign-American Cancer Society Exchange Fellow, 1952-53. Rose Morgan Vis. Prof., Univ. of Kansas, 1971. Member Tissue Culture Association (President, 1960-62, Editor-in-Chief 1968-75). Member of various British and American professional and learned societies; Hon. Life member and Hon. Director, Psora Society (Canada); Episcopal Church of the USA: Vice-Chm., Clergy Deployment Bd, 1971-, and Exec. Council, 1967-70; Deputy, Gen. Convention, 1970, 1973, 1976; Member, Diocesan Council, Diocese of Maine, 1962-70, 1971-76; Chm., Cttee on the State of the Church, 1976-. *Publications:* numerous papers in scientific journals, on nucleic acids and on tissue culture and cell nutrition. *Recreations:* reading, gardening; lawn tennis. *Address:* 10 Atlantic Avenue, Bar Harbor, Maine 04609, USA. *T:* (207) 288-4008.

WAYNE, Sir Edward (Johnson), Kt 1964; MD, MSc, PhD, FRCP (London and Edinburgh); FRCP (Glasgow); Regius Professor of Practice of Medicine, Glasgow University, 1954-67; Physician to Western Infirmary, Glasgow; Hon. Physician to the Queen in Scotland, 1954-67; *b* 3 June 1902; *s* of late William Wayne, Leeds, Yorks, and late Ellen Rawding, Leadenham, Lincs; *m* 1932, Honora Nancy Halloran; one *s* one *d. Educ:* Leeds Univ. and Medical School (Akroyd Scholar and Sir Swire Smith Fellow); Manchester Univ. BSc Leeds (1st Class Hons Chemistry) 1923; MB, ChB (Leeds), 1st Class Hons, 1929; MD 1938; Hey Gold Medallist; Demonstrator in Physiology, University of Leeds, 1930-31; Assistant in Dept Clinical Research, University College Hospital, London, 1931-34; Professor of Pharmacology and Therapeutics, University of

Sheffield, 1934-53 (formerly Physician to Royal Infirmary and Children's Hospital, Sheffield). Member Scottish Secretary of State's Advisory Cttee on Medical Research, 1958-67; Member of the Medical Research Council, 1958-62; Chairman, Clinical Research Board, 1960-64; Chairman, British Pharmacopœia Commn, 1958-63; Chairman, Advisory Cttee on Drug Dependence, 1967-69. Sims Commonwealth Travelling Professor, 1959. Bradshaw Lecturer, 1953; Lumleian Lecturer, RCP, 1959; Crookshank Lecturer and Medallist, Faculty of Radiol., 1966. Hon. DSc Sheffield, 1967. *Publications:* Papers in scientific and medical journals. *Recreation:* walking. *Address:* Green Dragon Close, Chipping Campden, Glos GL55 6AR. *T:* Evesham 840453. *Club:* Athenæum.

WEATHERALL, Prof. David John, MD, FRCP; FRS 1977; Nuffield Professor of Clinical Medicine, University of Oxford, since 1974; Fellow, Magdalen College, Oxford, since 1974; *b* 9 March 1933; *s* of Harry and Gwendoline Weatherall; *m* 1962, Stella Mayorga Nestler; one *s. Educ:* Calday Grange Grammar Sch.; Univ. of Liverpool. MB, ChB, MD, FRCP, MRCPath; MA Oxon 1974. Ho. Officer in Med. and Surg., United Liverpool Hosps, 1956-58; Captain, RAMC, Jun. Med. Specialist, BMH, Singapore, and BMH, Kamunting, Malaya, 1958-60; Research Fellow in Genetics, Johns Hopkins Hosp., Baltimore, USA, 1960-62; Sen. Med. Registrar, Liverpool Royal Infirmary, 1962-63; Research Fellow in Haematology, Johns Hopkins Hosp., 1963-65; Consultant, WHO, 1966-70; Univ. of Liverpool: Lectr in Med., 1965-66; Sen. Lectr in Med., 1966-69; Reader in Med., 1969-71; Prof. of Haematology, 1971-74; Consultant Physician, United Liverpool Hosps, 1966-74. Mem. Soc. of Scholars, and Centennial Schol., Johns Hopkins Univ., 1976. Watson Smith Lectr, RCP, 1974. Hon. Mem., Assoc. of Amer. Physicians, 1976. *Publications:* The Thalassaemia Syndromes, 1965 (2nd edn 1972); Blood and its Disorders, 1973; many papers on Abnormal Haemoglobin Synthesis and related disorders. *Recreations:* music, oriental food. *Address:* 8 Cumnor Rise Road, Cumnor Hill, Oxford. *T:* Cumnor 2467.

WEATHERALL, Miles, MA, DM, DSc; FIBiol; Director of Establishments, Wellcome Research Laboratories, since 1974 (Deputy Director, 1969-74); *b* 14 Oct. 1920; *s* of Rev. J. H. and Mary Weatherall; *m* 1944, Josephine A. C. Ogston; three *d. Educ:* Dragon School and St Edward's School, Oxford; Oriel College, Oxford. BA, BSc 1941; BM 1943; MA 1945; DM 1951; DSc 1966. Open Schol. in Nat. Sci., Oriel Coll., 1938. Lecturer in Pharmacology, Edinburgh University, 1945; Head of Dept of Pharmacology, London Hosp. Med. Coll., 1949-66; Prof. of Pharmacology, Univ. of London, 1958-66; Head, Therapeutic Res. Div., Wellcome Res. Labs, 1967-75. Member: Adv. Cttee on Pesticides and other Toxic Chemicals, 1964-66. Council, Pharmaceutical Soc., 1966-70; Cttee, Internat. Exhibn Coop. Wine Soc., 1964-72. Chairman Council: Chelsea Coll., Univ. of London, 1970-; RSM, 1972- (Hon. Sec. 1974-). *Publications:* Statistics for Medical Students (jointly with L. Bernstein), 1952; Scientific Method, 1968; papers in scientific and medical journals. *Recreations:* gardening, walking. *Address:* 17 Tollgate Drive, SE21.

WEATHERHEAD, Sir Arthur (Trenham), Kt 1960; CMG 1957; *b* 19 May 1905; *s* of late Canon A. S. Weatherhead; *m* 1938, Sylvia Mary, *d* of late A. Lace, Eastbourne; one *s* two *d. Educ:* St Bees School; Queen's College, Oxford. Sudan Plantations Syndicate, 1927; Colonial Administrative Service, Nigeria, 1930-60. Dep. Governor, Northern Region, Nigeria, 1958-60, retired. *Recreations:* gardening, chess. *Address:* Wood Rise, Amberley, Stroud, Glos. *T:* Amberley 2584.

WEATHERILL, (Bruce) Bernard; MP (C) Croydon North-East since 1964; Opposition Deputy Chief Whip, since 1974; *b* 25 Nov. 1920; *s* of late Bernard Weatherill, Spring Hill, Guildford, and Annie Gertrude (*née* Creak); *m* 1949, Lyn, *d* of late H. T. Eatwell; two *s* one *d. Educ:* Malvern College. Served War of 1939-45; commissioned 4/7th Royal Dragoon Guards, 1940; transferred to Indian Army, 1941 and served with 19th King George V's Own Lancers, 1941-45 (Captain). Man. Dir, Bernard Weatherill Ltd, 1957-70. First Chm., Guildford Young Conservatives, 1946-49; Chm., Guildford Cons. Assoc., 1959-63; Vice-Chm., SE Area Prov. Council, 1962-64; Member National Union of Cons. Party, 1963-64. An Opposition Whip, 1967; a Lord Comr of HM Treasury, 1970-71; Vice-Chamberlain, HM Household, 1971-72; Comptroller of HM Household, 1972-73; Treasurer of HM Household and Dep. Chief Govt Whip, 1973-74. Freeman of City of London. *Recreations:* golf, tennis. *Address:* 98 Lupus Street, SW1. *T:* 01-828 6040. *Clubs:* Carlton, City Livery; Conservative (Croydon).

WEATHERLEY, Prof. Paul Egerton, FRS 1973; Regius Professor of Botany in the University of Aberdeen since 1959; *b*

6 May 1917; *o s* of Leonard Roger Weatherley and late Ethel Maude (*née* Collin), Leicester; *m* 1942, Margaret Logan, *o d* of late John Pirie, JP, Castle of Auchry, Aberdeenshire; one *s* three *d. Educ:* Wyggeston School; Keble College (Open Schol.), Oxford. Final Sch. of Nat. Sci. (Hons Botany) 1939; Keble Research Schol., 1939-40, elected to Colonial Agric. Schol., 1940. Trained in RE, then Colonial Office cadet at Imperial Coll. of Tropical Agric. Trinidad, 1940-42. Govt Botanist in Dept of Agriculture, Uganda Protectorate, 1942-47; Asst Lectr, Univ. of Manchester, 1947-49; Lecturer in Botany, 1949-59 (Sen. Lectr 1956), Univ. of Nottingham. *Publications:* papers in (mainly) botanical journals. *Recreations:* music, sketching. *Address:* 8 The Chanonry, Old Aberdeen.

WEAVER, Sir Tobias Rushton, (Sir Toby Weaver), Kt 1973; CB 1962; Professor of Educational Studies, Open University, since 1976; *b* 19 July 1911; *s* of late Sir Lawrence Weaver, KBE, and late Lady Weaver (*née* Kathleen Purcell); *m* 1941, Marjorie, *d* of Rt Hon. Sir Charles Trevelyan, 3rd Bt, PC; one *s* three *d. Educ:* Clifton College; Corpus Christi College, Cambridge. Bank clerk, Toronto, 1932; teaching at Barking, 1935, Eton, 1936; Asst Director of Education: Wilts CC 1936, Essex CC 1939. Admiralty, 1941; War Office, 1942; Dept of Education and Science, 1946-73; Under-Secretary, 1956; Deputy Secretary, 1962. Visiting Professor of Education: Univ. of Southampton, 1973; Univ. of London Inst of Educn, 1974; Open Univ., 1976. *Address:* 13 Vicarage Gardens, W8. *T:* 01-229 3217.

WEAVER, Warren; Medal for Merit (US), 1946; Vice-President, Alfred P. Sloan Foundation until 1964, when resigned, but continues as consultant on scientific affairs; *b* 17 July 1894; *s* of Isaiah and Kittie Belle Stupfell Weaver; *m* 1919, Mary Hemenway; one *s* one *d. Educ:* Univ. of Wisconsin. 2nd Lieut Air Service, 1917-19. Asst Prof. Mathematics: Throop Coll., 1917-18; Cal. Inst. of Technology, 1919-20; Univ. of Wisconsin, 1920-25, Assoc. Prof. Mathematics, 1925-28, Prof. of Mathematics and Chairman of Dept, 1928-32; Lecturer, Univ. of Chicago, summer, 1928; Dir, Div. of Natural Sciences: Gen. Educn Bd, 1932-37; Rockefeller Foundation, 1932-55; Vice-Pres., Rockefeller Foundation, 1955-59. Chief, Applied Mathematics Panel, Office of Scientific Research and Devel., 1943-46; Chm., Naval Research Adv. Cttee, 1946-47. Sloan-Kettering Inst.: Trustee, 1954-67; Chairman Board, 1959-60; Vice-President, 1958-59; Trustee: Eastman Fund; Alfred P. Sloan Foundation, 1956-67; Member: Nat. Science Board, Nat. Science Foundation, 1956-60; Board of Directors, Coun. on Library Resources, 1956-59; Nat. Advisory Cancer Council, US Public Health Service, 1957-60; Councillor, Amer. Philos. Soc., 1957-60; Bd of Managers, Memorial Center for Cancer and Allied Diseases, 1958-60; Mem. Bd of Managers and Exec. Cttee, Mem. Hosp. for Cancer and Allied Diseases, 1960-67; Mem. and Vice-Chm., Health Res. Council, C., NY, 1958-60; Mem. Gov. Coun., Courant Inst. of Mathematical Sciences, 1962-72; Bd of Dirs, Scientists' Inst. for Public Information, 1963-67; Mem., Gov. Rockefeller's Cttee on Hosp. Costs, 1964-65. Fellow Amer. Acad. of Arts and Scis., 1958-; Assoc. Trustee, Univ. of Pennsylvania, 1959-63; Acad. of Religion and Mental Health (Mem. Bd of Trustees, 1959-63); Vice-Pres., 1961-63, Hon. Vice-Pres., 1963-); Memorial Sloan-Kettering Cancer Center (Vice-Chm. of Board, 1960-67; Chm. Cttee on Scientific Policy; Public Health Research Inst. of City of New York, Inc. (Pres. 1961-63); Salk Inst. for Biological Studies, San Diego, Calif. (Trustee, Chm. Bd, Non-Res. Fellow, 1962-). Holds several hon. degrees and awards. King's Medal for Service in Cause of Freedom (Gt Brit.), 1948; Public Welfare Medal, National Academy of Sciences, USA, 1957. Kalinga Prize, 1964; Arches of Science Award, 1964. Officer, Legion of Honor (France), 1950. *Publications:* (with Max Mason) The Electromagnetic Field, 1929; (with Claude Shannon) Mathematical Theory of Communication, 1949; Lady Luck-The Theory of Probability, 1963; Alice in Many Tongues, 1964; US Philanthropic Foundations: Their History, Structure, Management and Record, 1967; Science and Imagination, 1967; Scene of Change (autobiography), 1970. Editor: The Scientists Speak, 1947; mathematical and general articles, on science, in journals. *Recreation:* collector of Lewis Carroll. *Address:* 40 Lillis Road, RR3, New Milford, Conn 06776, USA. *T:* New Milford, Elgin 4-4177. *Club:* Century Association (NY City).

WEBB, Mrs Allan Bourne; *see* Gibbons, Stella Dorothea.

WEBB, Anthony Michael Francis, CMG 1963; QC (Kenya) 1961; JP; *b* 27 Dec. 1914; *s* of late Sir (Ambrose) Henry Webb; *m* 1948, Diana Mary, *e d* of late Capt. Graham Farley, Indian Army, and Mrs Herbert Browne (*née* Pyper); one *s* one *d. Educ:* Ampleforth; Magdalen Coll., Oxford (MA). Barrister-at-Law, Gray's Inn, 1939. Served War, 1939-46, Maj. GSO2, The Queen's Bays. Colonial Legal Service (HMOCS), 1947-64

(Malaya; Kenya; MLC 1958-63; Attorney-General and Minister for Legal Affairs, 1961-63); Sec., Nat. Adv. Council on Trng of Magistrates, and Trng Officer, 1964-73, Dep. Sec. of Commns, 1969-75, Head of Court Business, 1975-77, Lord Chancellor's Office; retd 1977. Member of Council of Kenya Lawn Tennis Association, 1957-63. JP, Kent, 1966. *Publication:* The Natzweiler Trial (ed). *Address:* 10 Royal Chase, Tunbridge Wells, Kent. *T:* 30016. *Club:* Special Forces.

WEBB, Rear-Adm. Arthur Brooke, CB 1975; retired; *b* 13 June 1918; 2nd *s* of late Captain A. B. H. Webb and Mrs G. Webb; *m* 1949, Rachel Marian Gerrish; three *d. Educ* St John's Coll., Southsea, Hants. Joined Royal Navy, 1936; served in Alexandria, 1939-42, HMS Howe, 1942-46, Egypt, 1946-49. Secretary: to Deputy Chief of Naval Personnel, (Manpower) Admiralty, 1951-53; to Flag Officer Germany, 1953-55; to Director of Naval Intell., 1955-58; HM Ships Belfast, 1958-60; Hermes, 1962-64. Staff of Chief of Defence Staff, 1964-67; Chief Staff Officer (Administration) to Fleet Commander, Far East Fleet, 1967-69, and Flag Officer Plymouth, 1970-72; Flag Officer, Admiralty Interview Bd, 1973-75. Comdr 1954, Captain 1963, Rear-Adm. 1973. *Recreations:* DIY, gardening, camping, walking, sailing. *Address:* Sorrel Cottage, Burrell Way, Balsham, Cambridge CB1 6DY. *T:* West Wratting 810.

WEBB, Douglas Edward, CVO 1961; OBE 1947; Deputy Commissioner of Police of the Metropolis, 1961-66; retired; *b* 8 Oct. 1909; *yr s* of late Supt O. C. Webb, KPM, Metropolitan Police; *m* 1935, Mary McMillan, *yr d* of late Capt. J. S. Learmont, Trinity House; one *s* one *d. Educ:* Bordon Grammar School; Devonport High School. Joined Metropolitan Police, 1929; Metropolitan Police Coll., Hendon, 1935-36. Allied Commission, Italy and Austria, 1945-47. Chief Supt, Bow Street, 1952-53, West End Central, 1953-54; Dep. Commander, New Scotland Yard, 1954-55; Commander, No 3 District (E London), 1955-57; Asst Commissioner (Traffic), 1957-58; Assistant Commissioner, Administration and Operations, New Scotland Yard, Dec. 1958-61. Officer, Legion of Honour, 1961; Order of Merit, Chile, 1965. *Address:* Tanglewood, 5 Deer Park Close, Tavistock, Devon PL19 9HE. *T:* Tavistock 2377.

WEBB, Prof. Edwin Clifford, PhD; Vice-Chancellor, Macquarie University, since 1976; *b* 21 May 1921; *s* of William Webb and Nellie Webb; *m* 1942, Violet Sheila Joan (*née* Tucker); one *s* four *d* (and one *s* decd). *Educ:* Poole Grammar Sch.; Cambridge Univ. (BA, MA, PhD). FRACI 1968. Cambridge University: Beit Meml Res. Fellow, 1944-46; Univ. Demonstrator in Biochem., 1946-50; Univ. Lectr in Biochem., 1950-62; University of Queensland: Foundn Prof. of Biochem. and Head of Dept, 1962-70, now Emeritus Prof.; Dep. Vice-Chancellor (Academic), 1970-76. *Publications:* Enzymes, 1959 (2nd edn 1964); 56 scientific papers. *Recreations:* photography, music, fishing, motoring, coin collecting. *Address:* 3 Norfolk Street, Killara, Sydney, NSW 2071, Australia. *T:* Sydney 4981369.

WEBB, James; Commissioner of Inland Revenue, since 1968; *b* 11 Nov. 1918; 2nd *s* of late James Webb and late Lucy Webb (*née* McGorrin); *m* 1957, Kathleen Veronica, 3rd *d* of late Catherine Downey (*née* McDaid) and of late James Downey, Londonderry. *Educ:* St Francis Xavier's, Liverpool; King's Coll., London Univ. (LLB 1940, 1st Cl. Hons). Entered Inland Revenue Dept (Estate Duty Office), 1937. Served War of 1939-45: W Africa, India and Burma; HM Forces, South Lancashire Regt, 1940; Sandhurst, 1942; Nigeria Regt, 1942-45 (Temp. Major, 1945). Assistant Principal Inland Revenue, 1947; Principal Establishment Officer and Dir of Personnel, 1971-75. *Address:* 3 Avondale Avenue, Hinchley Wood, Esher, Surrey. *T:* 01-398 6330.

WEBB, Prof. John Stuart; Professor of Applied Geochemistry in the University of London, at Imperial College of Science and Technology, since 1961; *b* 28 Aug. 1920; *s* of Stuart George Webb and Caroline Rabjohns Webb (*née* Pengelly); *m* 1946, Jean Millicent Dyer; one *s. Educ:* Westminster City School; Royal School of Mines, Imperial College of Science and Technology, BSc, ARSM, 1941. Served War of 1939-45, Royal Engineers, 1941-43. Geological Survey of Nigeria, 1943-44; Royal School of Mines, Imperial Coll., 1945-; Beit Scientific Research Fellow, 1945-47; PhD, DIC, in Mining Geology, 1947; Lecturer in Mining Geology, 1947-55; Reader in Applied Geochemistry, 1955-61. DSc, 1967. Mem., Home Office Forensic Science Cttee, 1969-75. Mem. Council, Instn of Mining and Metallurgy, 1964-71, and 1974-, Vice Pres., 1971-73, Pres., 1973-74; Mem. Bd, Council Engineering Instns, 1973-74; Hon. Sec., Rowhook Medical Soc., 1975-; Hon. Mem., Assoc. Exploration Geochemists, USA, 1977. Consolidated Goldfields of SA Gold Medal, Instn of Mining and Metallurgy, 1953. *Publications:* (with H. E. Hawkes) Geochemistry in Mineral

Exploration, 1962; (jtly) Geochemical Atlas of Northern Ireland, 1973; (jtly) Wolfson Geochemical Atlas of England and Wales, 1977; contrib. to scientific and technical jls. *Recreations:* fishing, amateur radio. *Address:* Stone Cottage, Slinfold, Horsham, Sussex RH13 7QT. *T:* Slinfold 790243.

WEBB, Prof. Joseph Ernest, PhD (London) 1944, DSc (London) 1949; FIBiol; Professor of Zoology, since 1960, and Vice-Principal, since 1976, Westfield College, University of London; *b* 22 March 1915; *s* of Joseph Webb and Constance Inman Webb (*née* Hickox); *m* 1940, Gwenlilian Clara Coldwell; three *s. Educ:* Rutlish School; Birkbeck College, London. Research Entomologist and Parasitologist at The Cooper Technical Bureau, Berkhampsted, Herts, 1940-46; Lecturer, Univ. of Aberdeen, 1946-48; Senior Lecturer, 1948-50; Professor of Zoology, 1950-60, University Coll., Ibadan, Nigeria. FIBiol. *Publications:* various on insect physiology, insecticides, systematics, populations, tropical ecology and marine biology. *Recreations:* art, music, photography. *Address:* 43 Hill Top, NW11. *T:* 01-458 2571. *Club:* Athenæum.

WEBB, Kaye, MBE 1974; Director, Children's Division, Penguin Books Ltd; Director, Penguin Books Ltd; Chairman and Founder of Puffin Club (for children); Director and Trustee, Unicorn Children's Theatre; Member Executive, National Book League; *b* 26 Jan. 1914; *d* of Arthur Webb and Kathleen Stevens, journalists; *m* 1st, Christopher Brierley; 2nd, Andrew Hunter; 3rd, 1946, Ronald Searle, *qv* ; one *s* one *d. Educ:* Hornsey High Sch.; Ashburton Grammar Sch.; France. Entered journalism via Picturegoer, 1931; joined staff of Picture Post, 1938; Asst Editor, Lilliput, 1941-47; Theatre Corresp., The Leader, 1947-49; Feature Writer, News Chronicle, 1949-55; Editor of children's magazine Elizabethan, 1955-58; Theatre Critic to National Review, 1957-58; Children's Editor, Puffin Books, 1961-. Eleanor Farjeon Award for services to Children's Literature, 1969. *Publications:* (ed) C. Fry: Experience of Critics; (ed) Penguin Patrick Campbell; (ed) The Friday Miracle; (ed) The St Trinian's Story; (with Ronald Searle): Looking at London; Paris Sketchbook; Refugees 1960; (with Treld Bicknell) 1st and 2nd Puffin Annuals; Puffins Pleasure. *Recreations:* children and other people, gardening, theatre. *Address:* 8 Lampard House, Maida Avenue, W2. *T:* 01-262 4695. *Club:* Puffin.

WEBB, Maysie (Florence), BSc; Deputy Director, British Museum, since 1971 (Assistant Director 1968-71); *b* 1 May 1923; *d* of Charles and Florence Webb. *Educ:* Kingsbury County School; Northern Polytechnic. Southwark Public Libraries, 1940-45; A. C. Cossor Ltd, 1945-50; British Non-Ferrous Metals Research Assoc., 1950-52; Mullard Equipment Ltd, 1952-55; Morgan Crucible Co. Ltd, 1955-60; Patent Office Library, 1960-66; Keeper, National Reference Library of Science and Invention, 1966-68. A General Comr of Income Tax, 1976-. Mem. Council, RSA, 1971-76 (Chm., Membership Cttee, 1974-76); Manager, Royal Instn, 1975-; Governor: Eltham Coll., 1975-; Walthamstow Hall, 1975-. *Publications:* articles on scientific libraries. *Recreations:* family and friends, country life. *Address:* British Museum, Bloomsbury, WC1.

WEBB, Pauline Mary, AKC; Chairman, Community and Race Relations Unit, British Council of Churches, since 1976; Area Secretary, Methodist Missionary Society, since 1973; author; *b* 28 June 1927; *d* of Rev. Leonard F. Webb. *Educ:* King's Coll., London Univ. (BA, AKC); Union Theological Seminary, New York (STM). BA English Hons (King's), 1948; Teacher's Diploma, London Inst. of Educn, 1949. Asst Mistress, Thames Valley Grammar Sch., 1949-52; Editor, Methodist Missionary Soc., 1955-66; Vice-Pres., Methodist Conf., 1965-66; Dir, Lay Training, Methodist Church, 1967-73. Vice-Chm., Central Cttee, WCC, 1968-75. *Publications:* Women of Our Company, 1958; Women of Our Time, 1966; Operation-Healing, 1964; All God's Children, 1964; Are We Yet Alive?, 1966; Agenda for the Churches, 1968; Salvation Today, 1974; Eventful Worship, 1975. *Address:* 25 Marylebone Road, NW1. *T:* 01-935 2541.

WEBB, Lt-Gen. Sir Richard (James Holden), KBE 1974 (CBE 1970, MBE 1952); CB 1972; *b* 21 Dec. 1919; *s* of late George Robert Holden Webb and Jessie Muriel Hair; *m* 1950, Barbara, *d* of Richard Griffin; one *s* one *d. Educ:* Nelson Coll., NZ; Royal Military Coll., Duntroon (Aust.); Staff Coll., Haifa; Joint Services Staff Coll., Latimer; Imperial Defence Coll. Commissioned NZ Army 1941. Served War, with Divisional Artillery, 2nd NZ Expeditionary Force, in Middle East and Italy, 1942-45, and Korea, 1950-51 (despatches twice). Quartermaster-Gen., NZ Army, 1967; Dep. Chief of Gen. Staff, NZ Army, 1969-70; Chief of Gen. Staff, NZ Army, 1970-71; Chief of Defence Staff, NZ, 1971-76. Comdr, Legion of Merit (US), 1971. *Recreation:* golf. *Address:* MacMurray Road, Paihia, Bay of Islands, New Zealand. *Clubs:* Wellington (Wellington, NZ).

WEBB, Dr Robert Alexander, AB (Southwestern, Tenn); MD (Johns Hopkins); MRCS; LRCP; PhD (Cambridge); Demonstrator in Bacteriology, Oxford University; Hon. Consultant Pathologist, Royal Free Hospital; Professor Emeritus University of London since 1956; *b* Charleston, SC, USA, 26 July 1891; *s* of Robert A. Webb, Prof. of Theology, Presbyterian Theological Seminary of Kentucky, and Roberta C. Beck; *m* 1918, May Barrow, Edgbaston; one *s* two *d.* Demonstrator in Pathology, University of Manchester, 1921-22; University Demonstrator in Pathology and MRC. Research Grant, Cambridge University, 1922-29; Lecturer in Pathology, Cambridge University, 1929-33; Capt. US Medical Corps (attached RAMC, England and BEF), 1917-18. *Publications:* various papers in scientific journals. *Recreations:* golf, tennis, squash. *Address:* Wyck Rissington, Glos GL54 2PN. *T:* Bourton-on-The-Water 20262; Dunn School of Pathology, Oxford University. *T:* Oxford 57321.

WEBB, Sir Thomas (Langley), Kt 1975; Chairman, Commercial Bank of Australia Ltd, since 1970; *b* 25 April 1908; *s* of Robert Langley Webb and Alice Mary Webb; *m* 1942, Jeannette Alison Lang; one *s* one *d. Educ:* Melbourne Church of England Grammar Sch. Joined Huddart Parker Ltd, 1926 (Man. Dir, 1955-61). Served War, AIF, 1940-45. Dir, Commercial Bank of Aust., 1960-; Director: Alliance Oil Development NL (Chm.); Bulkships Pty Ltd; Email Ltd; ESC Tools (OL) (Chm.); Lamson Industries Australia Ltd (Chm.); McIlwraith McEacharn Ltd; Metals Exploration Ltd; Trustees Executors & Agency Co. Ltd (Chm.). Vice-Pres., Royal Victorian Eye and Ear Hosp. *Recreations:* golf, tennis. *Address:* 6 Yarradale Road, Toorak, Victoria 3142, Australia. *T:* Melbourne 24 5259. *Clubs:* Australian, Melbourne, Royal Melbourne Golf (all Melbourne); Royal South Yarra Tennis.

WEBBER; see Lloyd Webber.

WEBBER, Fernley Douglas, CMG 1959; MC 1942; TD 1954; HM Diplomatic Service, retired; Secretary, Committee for Environmental Conservation; *b* 12 March 1918; *s* of Herbert Webber; *m* 1947, Veronica Elizabeth Ann, *d* of Major F. B. Hitchcock, MC; two *s* two *d. Educ:* Cotham School, Bristol; Jesus College, Cambridge. Entered Colonial Office after open competition, 1939; Diplomatic Service, 1965. Served War of 1939-45, Burma, 1940-45; Comd 624 LAA Regt RA (RF) TA, 1952-54, Bt-Col, 1954. Principal, CO, 1946; Asst Sec. 1950; Establishment Officer, 1952-58; Head of E Af. Dept, 1958-63; idc 1964; Deputy High Commissioner in Eastern Malaysia during part of 1965; High Commissioner in Brunei, 1965-67; Minister, British High Commn in Canberra, 1967-68; FCO, 1969-70. *Address:* 6 Mills Lane, Rodbridge Corner, Long Melford, Suffolk. *Club:* Royal Commonwealth Society.

WEBBER, Lt-Col G. S. I.; see Incledon-Webber.

WEBBER, Sir William (James Percival), Kt 1968; CBE 1962; MA; Member, National Coal Board, 1962-67; *b* 1901; *s* of James Augustus Webber, Swansea, Glam; *m* 1929, Evelyn May, *d* of Thomas Rees, Swansea; one *s. Educ:* Elementary; Swansea Grammar Sch. Entered Great Western Railway Service, 1917, Clerk until 1944; Divl Sec. Railways Clerks' Assoc. (now Transport Salaried Staffs' Assoc.), 1944, Asst Gen. Sec., 1949. Swansea Borough Councillor, 1932-44, Dep. Mayor, 1942-43; Chm. Nat. Jt Council for Local Authorities Clerical, Administrative, Professional and Technical Grades, 1940-44; Member, Labour Party Nat. Exec., 1949-53. Part-time Member, Nat. Coal Bd, 1958-62; served on Govt Cttees and Courts of Inquiry; Member: Royal Commission on the Press, 1961-62; Transport Advisory Council, 1965; General Secretary, Transport Salaried Staffs Association, 1953-62; Mem., General Council, Trades Union Congress, 1953-62. Visiting Fellow, Nuffield College, Oxford, 1954-62. *Address:* 76 Thames Village, Hartington Road, Chiswick, W4 3UE. *T:* 01-994 4563.

WEBER, (Edmund) Derek (Craig); Editor, The Geographical Magazine, since 1967; *b* 29 April 1921; 3rd *s* of late R. J. C. and of B. M. Weber; *m* 1953, Molly Patricia, *d* of the late R. O. and Ellen Podger; one *s* four *d. Educ:* Bristol Grammar School. Journalist on newspapers in Swindon, Bristol and Bath, and on magazines in London from 1937 until 1953, except for War Service in RAF, 1940-46. Art Editor, The Geographical Magazine, 1953; Assoc. Editor, 1965. *Address:* 31 Beeleigh Road, Maldon, Essex. *T:* Maldon 53216. *Club:* Savage.

WEBSTER, Very Rev. Alan Brunskill; Dean of St Paul's, since 1978; *b* 1918; *s* of Reverend J. Webster; *m* 1951, M. C. F. Falconer; two *s* two *d. Educ:* Shrewsbury School; Queen's College, Oxford. MA, BD. Ordained, 1942; Curate of Attercliffe Parishes, Sheffield, 1942; Curate of St Paul's, Arbourthorne,

Sheffield, 1944; Chaplain of Westcott House, 1946-48, Vice-Principal, 1948-53; Vicar of Barnard Castle, 1953; Warden, Lincoln Theol Coll., 1959-70; Canon and Prebendary of Lincoln Cathedral, 1964-70; Dean of Norwich, 1970-78. Mem., Church Commn on Crown Appts, 1977-. *Publications:* Joshua Watson, 1954; Broken Bones May Joy, 1968; Julian of Norwich, 1974. Contributor to The Historic Episcopate, 1954. *Recreations:* family life, travel, writing. *Address:* St Paul's, EC4A 5VA.

WEBSTER, Dr Cyril Charles, CMG 1966; Chief Scientific Officer, Agricultural Research Council, 1971-75 (Scientific Adviser, 1965-71); *b* 28 Dec. 1909; *s* of Ernest Webster; *m* 1947, Mary, *d* of H. R. Wimhurst; one *s* one *d. Educ:* Beckenham County Sch.; Wye Coll.; Selwyn Coll., Cambridge; Imperial Coll. of Tropical Agriculture, Trinidad. Colonial Agricultural Service, 1936-57: Nigeria, 1936-38; Nyasaland, 1938-50; Kenya (Chief Research Officer), 1950-55; Malaya (Dep. Dir of Agriculture), 1956-57; Prof. of Agriculture, Imperial Coll. of Tropical Agriculture, Univ. of W Indies, 1957-60; Dir, Rubber Research Inst. of Malaya, 1961-65. JMN, 1965. *Publications:* (with P. N. Wilson) Agriculture in the Tropics, 1966; scientific papers in agricultural jls. *Address:* 5 Shenden Way, Sevenoaks, Kent. *T:* Sevenoaks 53984.

WEBSTER, David; Director of Public Affairs, British Broadcasting Corporation, since 1977; *b* 11 Jan. 1931; *s* of Alec Webster and Clare Webster; *m* 1955, Lucy Law, Princeton, NJ; two *s. Educ:* Taunton Sch.; Ruskin Coll., Oxford. British Broadcasting Corporation: Sub-Editor, External Services News Dept, 1953-59; Producer, Panorama, 1959-64; Exec. Producer, Enquiry, and Encounter, BBC-2, 1964-66; Dep. Editor, Panorama, 1966, Editor, 1967-69; Exec. Editor, Current Affairs Group, 1969, Asst Head, 1970; Rep. in USA, 1971-76; Controller, Information Services, 1976-77. Chm., Internat. Council of National Acad. of Television Arts and Sciences, USA, 1974 and 1975. *Recreation:* coarse tennis. *Address:* Broadcasting House, W1A 1AA. *Club:* Savile.

WEBSTER, Derek Adrian; Chairman and Editorial Director, Daily Record and Sunday Mail Ltd, since 1974; *b* 24 March 1927; *s* of James Tulloch Webster and Isobel Webster; *m* 1966, Dorothy Frances Johnson; two *s* one *d. Educ:* St Peter's, Bournemouth. Served RN, 1944-48. Reporter, Western Morning News, 1943; Staff Journalist, Daily Mail, 1949-51; joined Mirror Group, 1952; Northern Editor, Daily Mirror, 1964-67; Editor, Daily Record, 1967-72; Dir, Mirror Gp Newspapers, 1974-. Vice-Chm., Age Concern (Scotland), 1977-. *Recreations:* boating, gardening. *Address:* Gateside, Blanefield, by Glasgow. *T:* Blanefield 70252. *Club:* Oil (Glasgow).

WEBSTER, Rev. Canon Douglas, MA, DD; Canon Residentiary and Precentor of St Paul's Cathedral since 1969; *b* 15 April 1920; *s* of Robert and Annie Webster; unmarried. *Educ:* Dulwich Coll.; St Peter's Coll., Oxford; Wycliffe Hall, Oxford. BA 1942, MA 1946. Curate: St Helens Parish Church, Lancs, 1943-46; Christ Church, Crouch End, London, 1946-47; Lectr, London Coll. of Divinity, 1947-52; Educn Sec., CMS, 1953-61; Theologian-Missioner, CMS, 1961-65; Chavasse Lectr in World Mission, Wycliffe Hall, Oxford, 1963-65; Prof. of Mission, Selly Oak Colls, Birmingham, 1966-69. Hon. Canon of Chelmsford, 1963-69; Exam. Chap. to Bp of Chelmsford, 1962-. Mem. Court, Worshipful Co. of Cutlers, Master 1974-76. Lectures: Godfrey Day, Dublin, 1967; Moorhouse, Melbourne, 1969. Hon. DD Wycliffe Coll., Toronto, 1967. Sub-ChStJ 1977. *Publications:* In Debt to Christ, 1957; What is Evangelism?, 1959; Local Church and World Mission, 1962; Pentecostalism and Speaking with Tongues, 1964; Unchanging Mission, 1965; Yes to Mission, 1966; Not Ashamed, 1970; Good News from John, 1974; contribs. to: Charles Simeon, Bicentenary Essays, 1959; The Parish Communion Today, 1962; Lambeth Essays on Ministry, 1968. *Recreations:* walking, gardening, music. *Address:* 1 Amen Court, EC4. *T:* 01-248 1817; The Moat House, Weston-sub-Edge, Chipping Campden, Glos. *T:* Evesham 840695. *Clubs:* Athenæum, Royal Commonwealth Society.

WEBSTER, Henry George, CBE 1974; FSAE; Group Engineering Director, Automotive Products, since 1974; *b* Coventry, 27 May 1917; *s* of William George Webster; *m* 1943, Margaret, *d* of H. C. Sharp; one *d. Educ:* Welshpool County Sch.; Coventry Technical Coll. Standard Motor Co. Ltd: apprenticed, 1932; Asst Technl Engr, 1938-40; Dep. Chief Inspector, 1940-46; Asst Technl Engr, 1946-48; Chief Chassis Engr, 1948-55; Chief Engr, 1955-57; Dir and Chief Engr, Standard-Triumph Internat., 1957-68; Technical Dir, Austin Morris Div., British Leyland UK Ltd, 1968-74. Joined original Instn of Automobile Engrs, as a grad., 1937 (Sec. of Grad. Section, Coventry Br. of Instn, 1941-45); transf. to Associate Mem., 1946, Mem., 1964. MSAE, 1958; FSAE, 1976. Freeman,

City of Coventry. *Recreation:* golf. *Address:* The Old School House, Barrowfield Lane, Kenilworth, Warwickshire CV8 1EP. *T:* Kenilworth 53363.

WEBSTER, Herman Armour, RE 1914; (ARE 1907); painter-etcher; *b* New York City, 6 April 1878; *s* of George Huntingdon Webster and Ellen F. Pickford; *m* 1st, 1909, Doriane Delors (*d* 1950), Paris; one *s*; 2nd, 1951, Charlotte Huard. *Educ:* St Paul's School, Concord; PhB Yale Univ., 1900. Editorial Staff of the Chicago Record-Herald, 1902; began study of art in the Académie Julian under Jean-Paul Laurens, 1904; Mem. Corresp. de la Société des Peintres-Graveurs Français, 1909; Mem. Titulaire, 1953; Associé de la Société Nationale des Beaux-Arts, 1912; Sociétaire, 1933; Mem. Soc. of American Graphic Artists; Gold Medal, San Francisco International Exposition, 1915; Noyes Prize, Brooklyn, USA, 1930; Grand Prix (gravure), Paris Exposition, 1937; Co-founder Société des Amis des Vieux Moulins (France); entered French Army, 1914; American Field Service, 1915; transferred to American Expeditionary Force, 1st Lieut, SC, 1917; Captain, 1918; Major, 1919; Croix de Guerre, Verdun, 1916; Médaille de la France Libérée; Officier de la Légion d'Honneur. *Address:* 38 rue Boileau, Paris 16e, France. *T:* 288.73.43.

WEBSTER, Prof. Hugh Colin, CMG 1959; Emeritus Professor of Physics, University of Queensland, 1970, and Counsellor (Scientific), Australian Embassy, Washington, 1970-72; *b* 24 Oct. 1905; *s* of Edwin Herbert Webster and Edith Maud Webster (*née* Hudspeth); unmarried. *Educ:* Hutchins School, Hobart; Universities of Tasmania, Melbourne, and Cambridge. Exhibn of 1851 Sci. Research Scholar, 1928-31; PhD (Cantab), 1932; Research Physicist Radio Research Bd (Australia), 1933-37; Lectr in Biophysics, Univ. of Qld, 1937-45; DSc (Tas) 1941; seconded to CSIR (Australia), 1940-45; Austr. Sci. Research Liaison Officer, London, 1941-43; Lectr (later Associate Prof.) in Radiation Physics, Univ. of Qld, 1945-49; Prof. of Physics, Univ. of Qld, 1949-70. Chm. Radio Research Board, 1963-70. *Publications:* Medical Physics (with D. F. Robertson), 1948; Medical and Biological Physics (with D. F. Robertson), 1961; several papers in scientific jls. *Recreations:* gardening, bushwalking. *Address:* 12 Tarcoola Street, St Lucia, Brisbane, Qld 4067, Australia. *Club:* Queensland (Brisbane).

WEBSTER, Ian Stevenson; Chairman, Industrial Tribunals for Manchester, since 1976; *b* 20 March 1925; *s* of late Harvey Webster and late Annabella Stevenson Webster (*née* MacBain); *m* 1951, Margaret (*née* Sharples); two *s. Educ:* Rochdale Grammar Sch.; Manchester Univ. Sub. Lieut (A), RNVR, 1944. Called to the Bar, Middle Temple, 1948. Asst Recorder: of Oldham, 1970; of Salford, 1971; a Recorder of the Crown Court, 1972-76. *Recreations:* golf, dinghy-racing. *Address:* Alexandra House, 14-22 The Parsonage, Manchester. *T:* 061-833 0581; 39 Midge Hall Drive, Bamford, Rochdale, Lancs.

WEBSTER, John Alexander R.; see Riddell-Webster.

WEBSTER, John Lawrence Harvey, CMG 1963; *b* 10 March 1913; *s* of late Sydney Webster, Hindhead, and Elsie Gwendoline Webster (*née* Harvey); *m* 1st, 1940, Elizabeth Marshall Gilbertson (marr. diss., 1959); two *d*; 2nd, 1960, Jessie Lillian Royston-Smith. *Educ:* Rugby Sch.; Balliol College, Oxford (MA). District Officer, Colonial Administrative Service, Kenya, 1935-49; Secretary for Development, 1949-54; Administrative Sec., 1954-56; Sec. to Cabinet, 1956-58; Permanent Sec., Kenya, 1958-63; on retirement from HMOCS, with the British Council in Thailand, Ceylon, Hong Kong, Istanbul and London. *Recreations:* badminton, swimming, golf. *Address:* Timbercroft, 11 Pevensey Road, West Worthing, Sussex. *Clubs:* Royal Commonwealth Society; Leander; Nairobi (Kenya).

WEBSTER, Prof. John Roger, MA, PhD; DipEd; Professor of Education, University College of North Wales, Bangor, since 1966; *b* 24 June 1926; *s* of Samuel and Jessie Webster; *m* 1963, Ivy Mary Garlick; one *s* one *d. Educ:* Llangefni Secondary Sch.; University College of Wales, Aberystwyth. Lectr, Trinity Coll., Carmarthen, 1948; Lectr in Educn, University Coll., Swansea, 1951. Director for Wales, Arts Council of GB, 1961; Member: Lloyd Cttee on Nat. Film Sch., 1965-66; James Cttee on Teacher Educn and Trng, 1971; Venables Cttee on Continuing Educn, 1974-76; Mem. Council, Open Univ., 1969-; Chm., Standing Conf. on Studies in Educn, 1972-76; Mem., CNAA, 1976-. *Publications:* (monograph) Ceri Richards, 1961; (monograph) Joseph Herman, 1962; contribs on educn and the arts to collective works and learned jls. *Address:* Awelfryn, Llandegfan, Anglesey. *T:* Menai Bridge 712303.

WEBSTER, Prof. Keith Edward, PhD; Professor of Anatomy, King's College, University of London, since 1975; *b* 18 June

1935; *e s* of Thomas Brotherwick Webster and Edna Pyzer; *m* 1959, Doreen Andrew; two *s*. *Educ:* UCL (BSc 1957, PhD 1960); UCH Med. Sch. (MB, BS 1962). University Coll. London: Lectr in Anatomy, 1962-66; Sen. Lectr in Anat., 1966-74; Reader in Anat., 1974-75. Symington Prize, British Anatomical Soc., 1966. *Publications:* A Manual of Human Anatomy, Vol. 5: The Central Nervous System (with J. T. Aitken and J. Z. Young), 1967; papers on the nervous system in Brain Res., Jl of Comp. Neurol., and Neurocytology. *Recreations:* Richard Wagner and myself. *Address:* Department of Anatomy, King's College London, Strand, WC2R 2LS. *T:* 01-836 5454.

WEBSTER, Michael George Thomas, DL; Chairman, Fitch Lovell Ltd, since 1977 (Vice-Chairman, 1976); Director: National Provident Institution, since 1973; Dickinson, Robinson Group Ltd, since 1976; *b* 27 May 1920; *s* of late J. A. Webster, CB, DSO, and late Constance A. Webster, 2nd *d* of late Richard and Lady Constance Combe; *m* 1947, Mrs Isabel Margaret Bucknill, *d* of late Major J. L. Dent, DSO, MC; three *d*. *Educ:* Stowe; Magdalen Coll., Oxford (MA). Commnd Grenadier Guards, 1940-46: NW Europe Campaign, 1944-45 (despatches); DAAG Guards Div., 1946. Joined Watney Combe Reid & Co. Ltd, 1946; Chm., Watney Combe Reid, 1963-68; Watney Mann Ltd: Vice-Chm., 1965-70; Chm., 1970-72; Deputy Chm., 1972-74; Chm., Watney Mann & Truman Holdings, 1974; Dir, Grand Metropolitan Ltd, 1972-74. Master of Brewers' Co., 1964-65. Chm., Aldenham School Governing Body, 1977- (Vice-Chm., 1968); a Vice-Pres., The Brewers' Soc. (formerly Vice-Chm.). High Sheriff, Berks, 1971. *Recreations:* fishing, shooting, golf. *Address:* The Vale, Windsor Forest, Berks. *Clubs:* Cavalry and Guards, MCC.
See also Viscount Torrington.

WEBSTER, Patrick; Barrister-at-Law; a Recorder of the Crown Court, since 1972; Chairman, Industrial Tribunals, Cardiff Region, since 1976 (a part-time Chairman, 1965-75); *b* 6 January 1928; *s* of Francis Glyn Webster and Ann Webster; *m* 1955, Elizabeth Knight; two *s* four *d*. *Educ:* Swansea Grammar Sch.; Rockwell Coll., Eire; St Edmund's Coll., Ware; Downing Coll., Cambridge (BA). Called to Bar, Gray's Inn, 1950. Practised at bar, in Swansea, 1950-75; Chm., Medical Appeals Tribunal (part-time), 1971-75. *Recreations:* listening to music; bringing up six children. *Address:* 103 Plymouth Road, Penarth, South Glam. *T:* Penarth 704758. *Clubs:* Challoner; Penarth Yacht; Beechwood (Swansea).

WEBSTER, Peter (Edlin), QC 1967; a Recorder of the Crown Court, since 1972; *b* 16 Feb. 1924; *s* of Herbert Edlin Webster and Florence Helen Webster; *m* 1955, Susan Elizabeth Richards (marr. diss.); one *s* two *d*; *m* 1968, Avril Carolyn Simpson, *d* of Dr John Ernest McCrae Harrisson. *Educ:* Haileybury; Merton Coll., Oxford (MA). RNVR, 1943-46 and 1950, Lieut (A). Imperial Tobacco Co., 1949; Lectr in Law, Lincoln Coll., Oxford, 1950-52; called to Bar, Middle Temple, 1952; Bencher, 1972; Standing Jun. Counsel to Min. of Labour, 1964-67. Member of Bar Council, 1968-70, 1971-74; Chm., Senate of the Inns of Court and the Bar, 1976-77 (Vice-Chm. 1975-76); Chm., London Common Law Bar Assoc., 1975-76. *Address:* Fountain Court, EC4.

WEBSTER, Sir Richard James, Kt 1971; DSO 1945; Director of Organisation, Conservative Central Office, 1966-76; *b* 15 July 1913; *e s* of late Gerald Webster and late Violet Webster; *m* 1940, Sheila, *y d* of late Jack Marston and of Geraldine Marston; two *d*. *Educ:* Sandroyd Sch.; Shrewsbury Sch. Conservative Agent: West Willesden, 1946-47; Aldershot, 1948-57; Central Office Agent, North West Provincial Area, 1958-66. *Recreations:* all spectator sports, sunbathing. *Address:* 1a Holland Place, W8. *Clubs:* Carlton, Constitutional.

WEBSTER, Sir Robert (Joseph), Kt 1963; CMG 1959; CBE 1956; MC; Hon. DSc: University NSW; Wollongong University; Fellow, International Academy of Management; FASA; Chairman, 1936-40 and 1960-76, General Manager, 1936-40, Managing Director, 1940-67, Bradmill Industries Ltd; *b* 10 June 1891; *s* of Alexander J. Webster; *m* 1st, 1921, May (*d* 1949), *d* of Charles Twigg; one *s* three *d* (and one *s* decd); 2nd, 1954, Daphne, *d* of Edward Kingcott. *Educ:* Charters Towers School, Qld. In Commonwealth Public Service, 1906-19. Chancellor, 1970-76 and Mem. Council, 1947-76, Univ. of NSW, now Chancellor Emeritus; JP Qld and NSW Gen. Manager, Qld Cotton Board, 1926-36, and Commonwealth Controller of Cotton, 1942-46; President: The Sydney Div. Australian Institute of Management, 1947-50, 1958-62 (Federal Pres., 1962-64); NSW Chamber of Manufactures, 1950 and 1951, and Assoc. Chamber of Manufactures of Aust., 1950-51; Textile Council of Australia, 1960-73; Member: Aust. Nat. Airlines Commn, 1952-

55; Australia-Japan Business Co-operation Cttee. Served European War, 1914-19, with AIF and on Staff (first Australian to be apptd to Staff at GHQ, France) in Egypt, Gallipoli and France (despatches, MC). Companion of the Textile Institute 1967. *Recreation:* golf. *Address:* 2 Buena Vista Avenue, Clifton Gardens, Sydney, New South Wales, Australia. *T:* (home) 969 6714 (business) 516 1188. *Clubs:* Union, Imperial Service; American National; Australian Golf.

WECK, Richard, CBE 1969; PhD; FRS 1975; Visiting Independent Professor, Imperial College of Science and Technology, 1968-74 and since 1975; *b* 5 March 1913; *s* of Francis and Katie Weck; *m* 1933, Katie (*née* Bartl). *Educ:* Tech. Univ., Prague (degree in Civ. Engrg). FICE, FIMechE, FInstW. Site Engr, 1936-38 (Prague); Design Project Leader, 1938-43; Research Asst to Sir John Baker, 1943-46; Head of Fatigue Laboratory, British Welding Research Assoc., 1946-51; Lectr in Engineering, Cambridge Univ., 1951-57; Dir of Research, British Welding Res. Assoc., 1957-68; Dir-Gen., Welding Inst., 1968-77. Bessemer Gold Medal, 1975. *Publications:* papers on welded structures, fatigue, res. stresses. *Recreations:* gardening, listening to music. *Address:* Abington Hall, Cambridge CB1 6AH. *T:* Cambridge 891339 or Cambridge 891162. *Club:* Athenæum.

WEDD, George Morton; Under Secretary, Departments of Transport and of the Environment, since 1976; *b* 30 March 1930; *s* of Albert Wedd and Dora Wedd; *m* 1953, Kate Pullin; two *s* one *d*. *Educ:* various schs in Derbyshire; St John's Coll., Cambridge (BA 1951). Joined Min. of Housing and Local Govt (later DoE), 1951; Principal, 1957; Asst Sec., 1966; Reg. Dir for S-E Region, 1976. *Address:* Rowan Cottage, Herington Grove, Brentwood, Essex. *T:* Brentwood 224000; 1 Horsebrook Cottages, Avonwick, Devon.

WEDDELL, Prof. Alexander Graham McDonnell, MA (Oxon), MD, DSc (London); Professor of Anatomy, University of Oxford, 1973-1975; *b* 18 Feb. 1908; *s* of Alexander George Weddell and Maud Eileen McDonnell; *m* 1937, Barbara Monica Mills; two *d*. *Educ:* Cheltenham Coll.; St Bartholomew's Hosp. Med. Sch., London. Demonstrator in Anatomy, St Bart's, London, 1933-34; Commonwealth Fund Fellow in Neuroanatomy and Neurological Surgery, USA, 1935-37; Demonstrator in Anatomy, University Coll. London, 1937-39. Served War: Neurosurgery, RAMC, until 1943; then Anatomical Research for Royal Naval Personnel Cttee of MRC, 1943-45. Apptd Demonstrator in Human Anatomy, Univ. of Oxford, with leave of absence, 1945. Reader in Human Anatomy, Univ. of Oxford, 1947-73; Fellow and Med. Tutor, Oriel Coll., Oxford, 1947; Sen. Proctor, Univ. of Oxford, 1951; elected Mem., Hebdomadal Council, 1952. WHO study team investigating neurological rehabilitation in leprosy, 1960; Harold Chaffer Lectureship, Dunedin Univ., NZ, 1961; Mem., MRC Leprosy Sub-Cttee, 1967; Designated WHO Leprosy Ref. Lab. (under dir of Dr R. J. W. Rees), 1967. Pres., Anatomical Soc. of GB and Ire., 1973-75. *Publications:* papers in learned jls on cutaneous sensibility and leprosy. *Recreations:* photography, swimming. *Address:* 7 Mill Street, Islip, Oxford OX5 2SZ. *T:* Kidlington 6326.

WEDDERBURN; *see* Scrymgeour-Wedderburn.

WEDDERBURN, family name of **Baron Wedderburn of Charlton.**

WEDDERBURN OF CHARLTON, Baron *cr* 1977 (Life Peer), of Highgate; **Kenneth William Wedderburn;** Cassel Professor of Commercial Law, London School of Economics, University of London, since 1964; *b* 13 April 1927; *o s* of Herbert J. and Mabel Wedderburn, Deptford; *m* 1st, 1951, Nina Salaman; one *s* two *d*; 2nd 1962, Dorothy E. Cole; 3rd, 1969, Frances Ann Knight; one *s*. *Educ:* Aske's Hatcham School; Whitgift School; Queens' College, Cambridge. BA 1948; LLB 1949 (Chancellor's Medallist); MA 1951. Royal Air Force, 1949-51. Called to the Bar, Middle Temple, 1953. Fellow, 1952-64, Tutor, 1957-60, Clare College, Cambridge; Asst Lectr, 1953-55, Lectr 1955-64, Faculty of Law, Cambridge University. Vis. Prof., Harvard Law Sch., 1969-70. Staff Panel Mem., Civil Service Arbitration Tribunal; Chm., Independent Review Cttee, 1976-; Mem., Cttee on Industrial Democracy, 1976-; Independent Chm., London and Provincial Theatre Councils. Gen. Editor, Modern Law Review. *Publications:* The Worker and the Law, 1965, 2nd edn, 1971; Cases and Materials on Labour Law, 1967; (with P. Davies) Employment Grievances and Disputes Procedures in Britain, 1969; (ed) Contracts, Sutton and Shannon, 1956, 1963; Asst Editor: Torts, Clerk and Lindsell, 1975; Modern Company Law, Gower, 1969; (ed with B. Aaron) Industrial Conflict, 1972; articles in legal and other jls. *Recreations:* pop music and

Charlton Athletic Football Club. *Address:* London School of Economics, Aldwych, WC2. *T:* 01-405 7686.

WEDDERBURN, Sir Andrew John Alexander O.; *see* Ogilvy-Wedderburn.

WEDDERBURN, Prof. Dorothy Enid Cole; Director of Industrial Sociology Unit, since 1973, and Professor of Industrial Sociology, since 1977, Imperial College of Science and Technology; *b* 18 Sept. 1925; *d* of Frederick C. Barnard and Ethel C. Barnard; *m* 1st, 1947, William A. Cole; 2nd, 1962, Kenneth W. Wedderburn (marr. diss. 1969). *Educ:* Walthamstow High Sch. for Girls; Girton Coll., Cambridge (MA). Research Officer, subseq. Sen. Res. Officer, Dept of Applied Economics, Cambridge, 1950-65; Lectr in Industrial Sociology, Imperial College of Science and Technology, 1965-70, Reader, 1970-77; Vis. Prof., Sloan Sch. of Management, MIT, 1969-70. Mem. SSRC, 1976. Mem., Govt Cttee on the Pay and Condition of Nurses, 1974-75; part-time Mem., Royal Commn on the Distribution of Income and Wealth, 1974-; Mem. Council, Advisory Conciliation and Arbitration Service, 1976-. *Publications:* White Collar Redundancy, 1964; Redundancy and the Railwayman, 1964; Enterprise Planning for Change, 1968; (with J. E. G. Utting) The Economic Circumstances of Old People, 1962; (with Peter Townsend) The Aged in the Welfare State, 1965; (jtly) Old Age in Three Industrial Societies, 1968; (with Rosemary Crompton) Workers' Attitudes and Technology, 1972; (ed) Poverty, Inequality and Class Structure, 1974; contrib. Jl of Royal Statistical Soc.; Sociological Review; New Society, etc. *Recreations:* politics, walking, cooking. *Address:* Flat 5, 65 Ladbroke Grove, W11 2PD.

WEDDERSPOON, Sir Thomas (Adam), Kt 1955; JP; *b* 4 August 1904; *s* of late Thomas and Margaret Wedderspoon; *m* 1936, Helen Catherine Margaret MacKenzie; one *s* two *d*. *Educ:* Seafield House, Broughty Ferry, Angus; Trinity College, Glenalmond, Perthshire; Trinity Hall, Cambridge. JP Angus, 1928. *Address:* Shielhill House, Forfar, Angus, Scotland. *T:* Foreside 209.

WEDELL, Prof. (Eberhard Arthur Otto) George; Head of Community Employment Policy Division, European Commission, since 1973; Hon. Visiting Professor of Employment Policy, Manchester University, since 1975; *b* 4 April 1927; *er s* of Rev. Dr H. Wedell and Gertrude (*née* Bonhoeffer); *m* 1948, Rosemarie (*née* Winckler); three *s* one *d*. *Educ:* Cranbrook; London School of Economics (BSc Econ., 1947). Ministry of Education, 1950-58; Sec., Bd for Social Responsibility, Nat. Assembly of Church of England, 1958-60; Dep. Sec., ITA, 1960-61, Secretary, 1961-64; Prof. of Adult Educn and Dir of Extra-Mural Studies, Manchester Univ., 1964-75; seconded to European Commn, 1973-75. Member: IBA Educnl Adv. Council, 1973-; Health Educn Council, DHSS, 1973-. Consultant: ABC, 1964-68; ODM, 1968; GPO, 1969; UNESCO, 1970-71; IBRD, 1971-72; Internat. Broadcast Inst., 1972-75. Trustee: William Temple Foundn, 1969-; Beatrice Hankey Foundn, 1971-; Director, Royal Exchange Theatre Company, 1968-. FRSA; Mem., Royal Television Soc. Hon. MEd Manchester, 1968. *Publications:* The Use of Television in Education, 1963; Broadcasting and Public Policy, 1968; (with H. D. Perraton) Teaching at a Distance, 1968; (ed) Structures of Broadcasting, 1970; (with R. Glatter) Study by Correspondence, 1971; Correspondence Education in Europe, 1971; Teachers and Educational Development in Cyprus, 1971; (ed) Education and the Development of Malawi, 1973; (with E. Katz) Broadcasting and National Development, 1977. *Recreations:* gardening, theatre, reading. *Address:* 18 Cranmer Road, Manchester M20 0AW. *T:* 061-445 5106; 335 Avenue Louise, 1050 Brussels. *T:* 640.36.45. *Clubs:* Athenæum, Reform; Ski.

WEDGWOOD, family name of **Baron Wedgwood.**

WEDGWOOD, 4th Baron *cr* 1942, of Barlaston; **Piers Anthony Weymouth Wedgwood;** *b* 20 Sept. 1954; *s* of 3rd Baron Wedgwood and of Lady Wedgwood (Jane Weymouth, *d* of W. J. Poulton, Kenjockety, Molo, Kenya); *S* father, 1970. *Educ:* Marlborough College. Commissioned into the Royal Scots, 1973. GSM for N Ireland. *Heir: cousin* John Wedgwood, MD, FRCP [*b* 28 Sept. 1919; *m* 1st, 1943, Margaret (marr. diss. 1971), *d* of A. S. Mason; three *s* two *d*; 2nd, 1972, Joan, *d* of J. Ripsher]. *Address:* c/o RHQ, The Royal Scots, The Castle, Edinburgh.

WEDGWOOD, Dame (Cicely) Veronica, OM 1969; DBE 1968 (CBE 1956); FRHistS; FBA 1975; Hon. LLD Glasgow; Hon. LittD Sheffield; Hon. DLitt: Smith College; Harvard; Oxford; Keele; Sussex; Liverpool; Historian; Member, Royal Commission on Historical MSS since 1953; Trustee, National

Gallery, 1962-68 and 1969-76; *b* 20 July 1910; *d* of Sir Ralph Wedgwood, 1st Bt, CB, CMG. *Educ:* privately; Lady Margaret Hall, Oxford. 1st Class Mod. Hist. 1931. President: English Assoc., 1955-56; English Centre of Internat. Pen Club, 1951-57; Society of Authors, 1972-77; Member: Arts Council, 1958-61; Arts Council Literature Panel, 1965-67; Institute for Advanced Study, Princeton, 1953-68; Adv. Council, V&A Museum, 1960-69; Hon. Member: American Academy of Arts and Letters, 1966; American Acad. of Arts and Scis, 1973. Special Lecturer, UCL, 1962-70. Hon. Fellow: Lady Margaret Hall, Oxford, 1962; UCL, 1965. Officer, Order of Orange-Nassau, 1946; Goethe Medal, 1958. *Publications:* Strafford, 1935 (revd edn, as Thomas Wentworth, 1961); The Thirty Years' War, 1938; Oliver Cromwell 1939, rev. edn 1973; Charles V by Carl Brandi (trans.), 1939; William the Silent, 1944 (James Tait Black Prize for 1944); Auto da Fé by Elias Canetti (translation), 1946; Velvet Studies, 1946; Richelieu and the French Monarchy, 1949; Seventeenth Century Literature, 1950; Montrose, 1952; The King's Peace, 1955; The King's War, 1958; Truth and Opinion, 1960; Poetry and Politics, 1960; The Trial of Charles I, 1964 (in USA as A Coffin for King Charles, 1964); Milton and his World, 1969; The Political Career of Rubens, 1975. *Address:* c/o Messrs Collins, 14 St James's Place, SW1.
See also Sir John Wedgwood, Bt.

WEDGWOOD, Geoffrey H., RE 1934; ARCA; Artist Engraver; *b* 16 April 1900; *s* of Frank and Jane Wedgwood. *Educ:* Liverpool Institute; Liverpool School of Art; Royal College of Art; British School at Rome. ARE 1925; ARCA (London) 1925; awarded Rome Scholarship in Engraving; Member of The Chicago Society of Etchers 1926; Exhibitor Royal Academy since 1923; Exhibited Prague, Bucharest, Vienna and Empire Exhibition, South Africa, 1936; works in the following Permanent Collections: British Museum; Victoria and Albert Museum; Rutherston Collection, Manchester; Walker Art Gallery; Wakefield Collection; several English towns; Art Museum Boston, USA; Art Institute of Chicago, USA. Hon. Retired Fellow, Royal Soc. of Painter-Etchers and Engravers, 1971. *Publications:* Original Engravings. *Address:* Kingsley, 85 Rupert Road, Roby, Liverpool. *Club:* Sandon Society (Liverpool).

WEDGWOOD, John Alleyne, FCIS; Chairman, Southern Electricity Board, since 1977; *b* 26 Jan. 1920; *s* of Rev. Charles Henry Wedgwood and Myrtle Winifred Perry; *m* 1st, 1942, Freda Mary Lambert (*d* 1963); 2nd, 1974, Lilian Nora Forey; one *s*. *Educ:* Monkton Combe Sch.; Queens' Coll., Cambridge (MA Hons Hist. Tripos). CompIEE; FCIS. Served War, Lincs Regt and Durham LI, 1940-46 (Actg Major). Asst Principal, Min. of Fuel and Power, 1946-48; Admin. Officer, British Electricity Authority, 1948-55; Dep. Sec., London Electricity Bd, 1955-58; Dep. Sec., Electricity Council, 1958-65, Sec., 1965-74; Dep. Chm., S Eastern Elec. Bd, 1974-77. Pres., Inst. of Chartered Secs and Administrators, 1976-. Chm. Bd of Management, Electrical and Electronics Industries Benevolent Assoc., 1977-. Member: Worshipful Co. of Scriveners, 1973-; SE Econ. Planning Council, 1975-. Freeman, City of London, 1973. *Recreations:* gardening, music, railways, ornithology. *Address:* Pengethley, 16 Rotherfield Road, Henley-on-Thames, Oxon RG9 1NY. *T:* Henley-on-Thames 6804. *Club:* Royal Commonwealth Society.

WEDGWOOD, Sir John Hamilton, 2nd Bt, *cr* 1942; TD 1948; Chairman, Artistic Framing Ltd, Holsworthy, Devon, since 1970; Deputy-Chairman of Josiah Wedgwood and Sons Ltd, until 1966; Member, British National Export Council, 1964-66; *b* 16 Nov. 1907; *s* of Sir Ralph L. Wedgwood, 1st Bt, CB, CMG, TD, and of Iris, Lady Wedgwood (*née* Pawson); *S* father 1956; *m* 1933, Diana Mildred (*d* 1976), *d* of late Col Oliver Hawkshaw, TD; three *s* one *d* (and one *s* decd). *Educ:* Winchester College; Trinity College, Cambridge; and abroad. Served War of 1939-45, Major GSO2 (1b). Chm., Anglo-American Community Relations, Lakenheath Base, 1972-76. FRSA 1968; FRGS 1973. Liveryman, Worshipful Co. of Painter-Stainers, 1971. Hon. LLD Birmingham, 1966. *Recreations:* mountaineering, caving, foreign travel. *Heir: s* (Hugo) Martin Wedgwood [*b* 27 Dec. 1933; *m* 1963, Alexandra Mary Gordon Clark, *er d* of late Judge Alfred Gordon Clark, and Mrs Gordon Clark; one *s* two *d*. *Educ:* Eton; Trinity College, Oxford]. *Address:* c/o Artistic Framing Ltd, Dobles Lane, Holsworthy, N Devon.
See also Dame C. V. Wedgwood.

WEDGWOOD, Dame Veronica; *see* Dame C. V. Wedgwood.

WEE CHONG JIN, Hon. Mr Justice; Chief Justice of the Supreme Court, Singapore; *b* 28 Sept. 1917; *s* of late Wee Gim Puay and Lim Paik Yew; *m* 1955, Cecilia Mary Henderson; three *s* one *d*. *Educ:* Penang Free Sch.; St John's Coll.,

Cambridge. Called to Bar, Middle Temple, 1938; admitted Advocate and Solicitor of Straits Settlement, 1940; practised in Penang and Singapore, 1940-57; Puisne Judge, Singapore, 1957, Chief Justice, 1963. *Recreation:* golf. *Address:* c/o Chief Justice's Chambers, Supreme Court, Singapore.

WEEDON, Dr Basil Charles Leicester, CBE 1974; DSc; PhD; FRS 1971; FRIC; Vice-Chancellor, Nottingham University, since 1976; *b* 18 July 1923; *s* of late Charles William Weedon; *m* 1959, Barbara Mary Dawe; one *s* one *d. Educ:* Wandsworth Sch.; Imperial Coll. of Science and Technology (ARCS; DIC). Research Chemist, ICI Ltd (Dyestuffs Div.), 1943-47; Lecturer in Organic Chemistry, Imperial Coll., 1947-55, Reader, 1955-60; Prof. of Organic Chemistry, QMC, 1960-76. Chm., Food Additives and Contaminants Cttee, 1968-; Mem., EEC Scientific Cttee for Food, 1974-; Scientific Editor, Pure and Applied Chemistry, 1960-75. Mem., UGC, 1974-76. Tilden Lecturer, Chemical Society, 1966. Hon. DTech Brunel Univ., 1975. Meldola Medal, Roy. Inst. of Chemistry, 1952. *Publications:* A Guide to Qualitative Organic Chemical Analysis (with Sir Patrick Linstead), 1956; scientific papers, mainly in Jl Chem. Soc. *Address:* c/o Nottingham University, University Park, Nottingham NG7 2RD. *T:* Nottingham 56101.

WEEKES, Rt. Rev. Ambrose Walter Marcus, CB 1970; FKC; Assistant Bishop, Diocese of Gibraltar, since 1977; *b* 25 April 1919; *s* of late Capt William Charles Tinnoth Weekes, DSO, RNVR, and Ethel Sarah Weekes, JP. *Educ:* Cathedral Choir Sch., Rochester; Sir Joseph Williamson's Sch., Rochester; King's Coll., London; AKC 1941, FKC 1972; Scholae Cancellarii, Lincoln. Chaplain, RNVR, 1944-46, RN 1946-72; HMS: Ganges, 1946-48; Ulster, 1948-49; Triumph, 1949-51; Royal Marines, Deal, 1951-53; 3 Commando Bde, RM, 1953-55; HMS: Ganges, 1955-56; St Vincent, 1956-58; Tyne, 1958-60; Ganges, 1960-62; 40 Commando, RM, 1962-63; MoD, 1963-65; HMS: Eagle, 1965-66; Vernon, 1966-67; Terror, and Staff of Comdr Far East Fleet, 1967-68; HMS Mercury, 1968-69; Chaplain of the Fleet and Archdeacon for the Royal Navy, 1969-72; Dean of Gibraltar, 1973-77. QHC, 1969-72; Hon. Canon, dio. of Gibraltar, 1971; Chaplain of St Andrew, Tangier, 1972-73. *Recreations:* yachting, music. *Address:* Fig Tree House, Queenborough, Kent. *Clubs:* Athenæum, Naval and Military, Royal Automobile.

WEEKLEY, Charles Montague, FSA; Officer-in-Charge of Bethnal Green Museum, 1946-64; *b* 15 June 1900; *o s* of late Prof. Ernest Weekley, DLitt and Frieda (afterwards Mrs D. H. Lawrence), 2nd *d* of Baron Friedrich von Richthofen; *m* 1930, Vera (*d* 1973), artist, *er d* of late P. Murray Ross, Dornoch, Sutherlandshire; one *s* one *d. Educ:* St Paul's School (scholar and leaving exhibitioner); St John's College, Oxford (scholar). BA (Oxon), 1922; MA (Oxon) 1967. Assistant, Department of Circulation, V&A Museum, 1924; Dep. Keeper, 1938; General Finance Branch, Ministry of Supply, 1939-43; Southern Dept, Foreign Office, 1943-44; Ministry of Education, 1944-46; Trustee of Whitechapel Art Gallery, 1946-74; a Governor of Parmiter's School, 1946-64; Hon. Mem., Art Workers Guild, 1954. *Publications:* William Morris, 1934; Thomas Bewick, 1953; General Editor of The Library of English Art; (ed) A Memoir of Thomas Bewick, 1961; contributor to Chambers's Encyclopædia, DNB, Times, Country Life, Architectural Review, etc. *Recreations:* Oxford University Athletic Team (1 mile) *v* Cambridge, 1922; Oxford University Relay Team (4 miles) *v* Cambridge, 1920. *Address:* 45 Gibson Square, Islington, N1. *T:* 01-226 8307. *Club:* Achilles.

WEEKS, Alan Frederick; Director, Sports Aid Foundation, since 1976; *b* 8 Sept. 1923; *s* of late Captain Frederick Charles Weeks, MN, and Ada Frances Weeks; *m* 1947, Barbara Jane (*née* Huckle); two *s* one *d. Educ:* Brighton, Hove and Sussex Grammar School. Served RNR, Midshipman to Lieut, 1939-46. PRO, Sports Stadium, Brighton, 1946-65; Sec., Brighton Tigers Ice Hockey Club, 1946-65; Dir, London Lions Ice Hockey Club, 1973-74. BBC Commentator: Ice Hockey, Ice Skating, 1951-76; Football, 1956-74; Presenter, Summer Grandstand, 1959-62; BBC Commentator: Winter Olympics: 1964, 1968, 1972, 1976; Olympics: 1960, 1968, 1972, 1976; World Cup: 1966, 1970, 1974; Commonwealth Games: 1970, 1974. *Recreation:* swimming. *Address:* Old Fort Road, Shoreham-by-Sea, West Sussex BN4 5HL.

WEEKS, Edward A.; Senior Editor and Consultant, Atlantic Monthly Press, since 1966; Trustee: University of Rochester (Hon.); United Negro College Fund; American Field Service (Croix de Guerre, 1918); Fellow American Academy Arts and Sciences; *b* 19 Feb. 1898; *s* of Edward Augustus Weeks and Frederika Suydam; *m* 1925, Frederica Watriss (decd); one *s* one *d*; *m* 1971, Phœbe Adams. *Educ:* Pingry and Battin High School, Elizabeth, NJ; Cornell Univ.; BS Harvard, 1922; Camb. Univ. (Fiske Schol.). Hon. LittD: Northeastern Univ., Boston, 1938; Lake Forest Coll. (Illinois), 1939; Williams Coll., Mass., 1942; Middlebury College, Vt, 1944; University of Alabama, 1945; Dartmouth Coll., 1950; Bucknell Univ., 1952; Boston Univ., 1953; Hobart Coll., 1956; Univ. of Richmond, 1957; New York Univ., 1958; further hon. degrees from: Clark Univ., Massachusetts, 1958 (Humane Letters); Pomona Coll., Calif., 1958 (LittD); Univ. of Pittsburgh, 1959 (Humane Letters); Univ. of Akron, 1961 (LittD); Northwestern Univ., 1961 (Humane Letters); Rutgers, 1962 (Dr Letters); Union College, 1962 (DCL); Washington and Jefferson, 1962 (Dr Laws). Began as manuscript reader and book salesman with Horace Liveright, Inc., New York City, 1923; Associate Editor, Atlantic Monthly, 1924-28; Editor: Atlantic Monthly Press, 1928-37; Atlantic Monthly, 1938-66. Overseer, Harvard Coll., 1945-51. Henry Johnson Fisher Award, 1968; Irita Van Doren Award, 1970. *Publications:* This Trade of Writing, 1935; The Open Heart, 1955; In Friendly Candour, 1959; Breaking into Print, 1962; Boston, Cradle of Liberty, 1965; The Lowells and their Institute, 1966; Fresh Waters, 1968; The Moisie Salmon Club, a chronicle, 1971; My Green Age: a memoir, 1974; Myopia: 1875-1975, 1975; Editor: Great Short Novels (Anthology), 1941; Jubilee, One Hundred Years of the Atlantic (with Emily Flint), 1957; contrib. essays, articles, and book reviews to magazines. *Recreations:* fishing, preferably with a light rod; golf; poker. *Address:* 59 Chestnut Street, Boston 02108, USA; 8 Arlington Street, Boston, Mass 02116, USA. *Cable address:* Lanticmon. *Clubs:* Tavern (Boston); Myopia Hunt (Hamilton, Mass.); Century (New York).

WEEKS, Major-Gen. Ernest Geoffrey, CB 1946; CBE 1944; MC (and bar); MM (and bar); CD; retired; *b* Charlottetown, PEI, 30 May 1896; *s* of William Arthur and Fanny Weeks; *m* 1930, Vivian Rose Scott, Toronto, Canada; one *s. Educ:* Prince of Wales Coll., Charlottetown, PEI. Canadian Militia, 1910-14; European War, Belgium and France, 1915-19; Canadian Permanent Force from 1920; War of 1939-45, Italy; Maj.-Gen. i/c Administration Canadian Military, HQ, London, England, 1944-45; Adjutant-General Canadian Army, 1946-49; retired, 1949. *Recreations:* gardening, fishing. *Address:* 46 Prince Charles Drive, Charlottetown, PEI, C1A 3C2, Canada.

WEEKS, Sir Hugh (Thomas), Kt 1966; CMG 1946; Chairman: Leopold Joseph Holdings Ltd, since 1966; London American Finance Corporation Ltd, since 1970; Electrical Industrial Securities, 1971-77; *b* 27 April 1904; *m* 1929; one *s* one *d*; *m* 1949, Constance Tomkinson; one *d. Educ:* Hendon Secondary and Kilburn Grammar Schools; Emmanuel College, Cambridge (MA). Research and Statistical Manager, Cadbury Bros, till 1939; Director of Statistics, Min. of Supply, 1939-42; Director-General of Statistics and Programmes and Member of Supply Council, 1942-43; Head of Programmes and Planning Division, Ministry of Production, 1943-45. Represented Ministries of Supply and Production on various Missions to N America, 1941-45; Managing Director J. S. Fry & Sons, 1945-47; Mem. Economic Planning Bd, 1947-48, 1959-61; Joint Controller of Colonial Development Corporation, 1948-51; Chm., NIESR, 1970-74. Director: Finance Corp. for Industry, 1956-74; Industrial and Commercial Finance Corp., 1960-74. UK Representative, UN Cttee for Industrial Development, 1961-63. Dep. Chm., Richard Thomas & Baldwins, 1965-68; Dir, S Wales and Strip Mill Bds, BSC, 1968-72. Chairman: EDC for Distributive Trades, 1964-70; Econ. Cttees, FBI and CBI, 1957-72. Pres., British Export Houses Assoc., 1972-74. Medal of Freedom with Silver Palm (US). *Publications:* Market Research (with Paul Redmayne); various articles. *Address:* 8 The Grove, Highgate Village, N6. *T:* 01-340 9517; (office) 01-588 2323. *Club:* United Oxford & Cambridge University.

WEETCH, Kenneth Thomas; MP (Lab) Ipswich, since Oct. 1974; *b* 17 Sept. 1933; *s* of Kenneth George and Charlotte Irene Weetch; *m* 1961, Audrey Wilson; two *d. Educ:* Newbridge Grammar Sch., Mon; London School of Economics. MSc(Econ), DipEd (London Inst. of Educn). National Service: Sgt, RAEC, Hong Kong, 1955-57; Walthamstow and Ilford Educn Authorities and Research at LSE, 1957-64; Head of History Dept, Hockerill Coll. of Educn, Bishop's Stortford, 1964-74. Contested (Lab) Saffron Walden, 1970. *Recreations:* walking, reading, watching Association football, playing the piano in pubs. *Address:* 12 Appleby Close, Ipswich, Suffolk. *Club:* Silent Street Labour (Ipswich).

WEEVERS, Theodoor, LitD (Leyden); Officier in de Orde van Oranje-Nassau; Professor of Dutch Language and Literature, University of London, 1945-71; *b* Amersfoort, 3 June 1904; *e s* of Prof. Theodorus Weevers and Cornelia Jeannette, *d* of J. de Graaff; *m* 1933, Sybil Doreen, 2nd *d* of Alfred Jervis; two *s.*

Educ: Gymnasia at Amersfoort and Groningen; Universities of Groningen and Leyden; Lecturer in Dutch at University College and Bedford College, London, 1931-36; Reader in Dutch Language and Literature in University of London, 1937-45; Lecturer in Dutch at Birkbeck College (Univ. of London), 1942-45. During War of 1939-45 Language Supervisor and Announcer-Translator in European News Service of BBC (Dutch Section), 1940-44. Corr. mem. Koninklijke Nederlandse Akademie van Wetenschappen te Amsterdam; hon. mem. Koninklijke Academie voor Nederlandse Taal en Letterkunde, Gent; mem. Maatschappij der Nederlandse Letterkunde. *Publications:* Coornhert's Dolinghe van Ulysse, 1934; De Dolinge van Ulysse door Dierick Volckertsz Coornhert, 1939; The Idea of Holland in Dutch Poetry, 1948; Poetry of the Netherlands in its European Context, 1170-1930, 1960; Mythe en Vorm in de gedichten van Albert Verwey, 1965; Albert Verwey's Portrayal of the Growth of the Poetic Imagination, in Essays in German and Dutch Literature, 1973; articles and reviews in Modern Language Review, Mededelingen Kon. Nederlandse Akademie van Wetenschappen, Tijdschrift v. Nederl. Taal en Letterkunde, De Nieuwe Taalgids, Neophilologus, Journal of English and Germanic Philology, Publications of the English Goethe Society, English Studies. *Recreations:* music, walking. *Address:* 10 Devonshire Road, Harpenden, Herts.

WEIDENFELD, family name of **Baron Weidenfeld.**

WEIDENFELD, Baron *cr* 1976 (Life Peer), of Chelsea; **Arthur George Weidenfeld,** Kt 1969; Chairman: Weidenfeld & Nicolson Ltd since 1948, and associated companies; *b* 13 Sept. 1919; *o s* of late Max and of Rosa Weidenfeld; *m* 1st, 1952, Jane Sieff; one *d* ; 2nd, 1956, Barbara Connolly (*née* Skelton) (marr. diss. 1961); 3rd, 1966, Sandra Payson Meyer (marr. diss. 1976). *Educ:* Piaristen Gymnasium, Vienna; University of Vienna (Law); Konsular Akademie (Diplomatic College). BBC Monitoring Service, 1939-42; BBC News Commentator on European Affairs on BBC Empire & North American service, 1942-46. Wrote weekly foreign affairs column, News Chronicle, 1943-44; Founder: Contact Magazine and Books, 1945; Weidenfeld & Nicolson Ltd, 1948. One year's leave as Political Adviser and Chief of Cabinet of President Weizmann of Israel. Vice-Chm., Bd of Governors, Ben Gurion Univ. of the Negev, Beer-Sheva. *Publication:* The Goebbels Experiment, 1943 (also publ. USA). *Recreations:* travel, opera. *Address:* 9 Chelsea Embankment, SW3. *T:* 01-351 0042.

WEIDLEIN, Edward Ray, MA, ScD, EngD, LLD; President Mellon Institute, 1921-56, retired; Technical Adviser of Rubber Reserve Company (now Synthetic Rubber Division of National Science Foundation), 1941-70; Director, Allegheny County Council West of the Boy Scouts of America; National Council of the Boy Scouts of America; Advisory Committee, Oakland Office, Mellon National Bank; President, Regional Industrial Develt Corp. Fund, 1962-71; registered professional engineer in Pa; *b* Augusta, Kansas, 14 July 1887; *s* of Edward Weidlein and Nettie Lemon; *m* 1915, Hazel Butts; three *s. Educ:* University of Kansas. Developed processes for the use of sulphur dioxide in hydrometallurgy; Chief of Chemicals Branch War Production Board, 1940-42; Senior Consultant of Chemical Division of War Production Board, Feb. 1942-Mar. 1946; Head Technical Consultant in War Production Board, Mar. 1942-Mar. 1946; Technical Adviser, R&D Div., Quartermaster Corps, US Army, 1943-46; Member: Special Cttee for examination of enemy war materials and supplies under War Metallurgy Cttee of Nat. Research Council and Nat. Acad. of Sciences; Research Cttee in Co-operation with Chemical Warfare Service of American Chemical Society; Cttee on Co-operation with National Defense Research Cttee of Office of Sc. Research and Development; Studies, Reports, and Seminars Cttee of Army Ordn. Assoc.; Nat. Engineers Cttee of Engineers Jt Council; Exec. Cttees, Allegheny Conf. on Community Develt and Pittsburgh Regional Planning Assoc.; Board of Directors Western Pennsylvania Hosp.; Bd of Trustees, Rolling Rock Club; Trustee (emer.) Univ. of Pittsburgh and of Shadyside Academy, Pittsburgh. Member, leading chemical and scientific societies. Various awards have been obtained for distinguished service in his field; Edward R. Weidlein Professorship established, 1967, by Bd of Trustees, Univ. of Pittsburgh. Holds numerous hon. degrees in Science, Laws and Engineering. *Publications:* (joint) Science in Action; Glances at Industrial Research; many articles on industrial research. *Recreations:* golf, hunting and fishing. *Address:* Weidacres, PO Box 45, Rector, Pennsylvania 15677, USA. *Clubs:* University, Pitt Faculty, Pittsburgh Golf, Rolling Rock, Duquesne, Authors' (Pittsburgh); Chemists' (New York); Chemists' (Pittsburgh).

WEIGALL, Peter Raymond; Managing Director, P. R. Weigall & Co. Ltd, 1976; Chairman, Nimbus Conversions Ltd, 1977; *b* 24 Feb. 1922; *s* of Henry Stuart Brome Weigall and Madeleine Bezard; *m* 1950, Nancy, *d* of Alexander Webster, CIE, and Margaret Webster; one *s* one *d. Educ:* Lycée Janson, Paris; Edinburgh Univ. (BSc). Served War, Captain, RE, 1942-46. Henry Wiggin & Co. Ltd, Birmingham, 1949-51; Petrochemicals Ltd, London, 1951-54; Chemical Industry Admin, Shell Petroleum Co., London, 1954-58; Chemicals Manager, Shell Sekiyu, Tokyo, 1958-63; Shell Internat. Chemical Co., London, 1964-69; Managing Dir, Monteshell, Milan, 1970-73; Industrial Advr to HM Govt, DTI, 1973-75. Member: Movement of Exports EDC, 1974-75; Chemicals EDC, 1974-75; Motor Vehicle Distribution and Repair EDC, 1974-75; Mergers Panel, Office of Fair Trading, 1974-75. *Recreation:* walking in the mountains. *Address:* 35 Cottenham Drive, SW20. *T:* 01-946 9514.

WEIGHELL, Sidney; General Secretary, National Union of Railwaymen, since Feb. 1975; Member, Trades Union General Council, since 1975; *b* 31 March 1922; *s* of John Thomas and Rose Lena Weighell; *m* 1st, 1949, Margaret Alison Hunter (killed, 1956); one *s* (one *d,* killed, 1956); 2nd, 1959, Joan Sheila Willets. *Educ:* Church of England Sch., Northallerton, Yorks. Joined LNER, Motive Power Dept, 1938. Elected to: NUR Exec., 1953; full-time NUR Official, 1954; Asst Gen. Sec., 1965. Labour Party Agent, 1947-52; Mem., Labour Party Exec., 1972-75. *Recreations:* trout fishing, swimming, gardening; professional footballer, Sunderland FC, 1945-47. *Address:* 7 The Chase, Bishop's Stortford, Herts CM23 3HT. *T:* Bishop's Stortford 53175.

WEIGHILL, Air Cdre Robert Harold George, CBE 1973; DFC 1944; Secretary, Rugby Football Union, since 1973; *b* 9 Sept. 1920; *s* of Harold James and late Elsie Weighill, Heswall, Cheshire; *m* 1946, Beryl, *d* of late W. Y. Hodgson, Bromborough, Cheshire; two *s* one *d. Educ:* Wirral Grammar Sch., Bebington, Cheshire. Served War: RAF, 1941; No 2 F R Sqdn, 1942-44; No 19 F Sqdn, 1944-45. Sqdn Comdr, RAF Coll., Cranwell, 1948-52; Student, RAF Staff Coll., 1952; CO, No 2 FR Sqdn and 138 F Wing, 1953-57; Student, JSSC, 1959; Directing Staff, Imperial Defence Coll., 1959-61; CO, RAF, Cottesmore, 1961-64; Gp Captain Ops, RAF Germany, 1964-67; Asst Comdt, RAF Coll. of Air Warfare, 1967-68; Comdt, RAF Halton, 1968-73. ADC to the Queen, 1968-73. *Recreations:* Rugby (Harlequins, Barbarians, Cheshire, RAF, Combined Services, England), squash, swimming. *Address:* South View, Whitton Road, Twickenham, Mddx. *Clubs:* Royal Air Force, East India, Devonshire, Sports and Public Schools.

WEIGHT, Prof. Carel Victor Morlais, CBE 1961; RA 1965 (ARA 1955); Hon. RBA 1972 (RBA 1934); practising artist (painter); Hon. Fellow and Professor Emeritus, Royal College of Art, since 1973; Trustee RA, since 1975; *b* London, 10 Sept. 1908; *s* of Sidney Louis and Blanche H. C. Weight; British. *Educ:* Sloane School; Goldsmiths' Coll., Univ. of London (Sen. County Scholarship, 1933). First exhibited at Royal Acad., 1931; first one-man show, Cooling Galls, 1934; 2nd and 3rd exhibns, Picture Hire Ltd, 1936 and 1938. Official War Artist, 1945. Royal College of Art: Teacher of Painting, 1947; Fellow, 1956; Prof. of Painting, 1957-73. One-man Shows: Leicester Galls, 1946, 1952, 1968; Zwemmer Gall., 1956, 1959, 1961, 1965; Agnew's, 1959; Russell Cotes Gall., Bournemouth, 1962; Fieldbourne Galleries, 1972; New Grafton Gall., 1974, 1976; exhibited in: 60 Paintings for 1951; (by invitation) exhibns of Contemporary British Art in provinces and overseas, incl. USSR, 1957; Retrospective Exhibns: Reading Museum and Art Gallery, 1970; RCA, 1973. Work purchased by: Chantry Bequest for Tate Gall., 1955, 1956, 1957, 1963, 1968; Walker Art Gall., Liverpool; Southampton, Hastings and Oldham Art Galls, etc; Art Gall., Melbourne; Nat. Gall., Adelaide; Arts Council; New Coll., Oxford; Contemporary Art Soc.; V & A Museum. Mural for: Festival of Britain, 1951; Manchester Cathedral, 1963. Picture, Transfiguration, presented by Roman Catholics to the Pope, 1970. Vice-Pres., Greater London Arts Assoc., 1968. Member: London Group, 1950; West of England Acad.; Fine Arts Panel, Arts Council, 1951-57; Rome Faculty of Art. 1960. *Recreations:* music, reading. *Address:* 33 Spencer Road, SW18. *T:* 01-228 6928. *Club:* Arts.

WEILER, Terence Gerard; Assistant Under-Secretary of State, Home Office, since 1967 (Prison Department since 1971); *b* 12 Oct. 1919; *s* of Charles and Clare Weiler; *m* 1952, Truda, *d* of Wilfrid and Mary Woollen; two *s* two *d. Educ:* Wimbledon College; University College, London. Army (RA and Queen's Royal Regiment), 1940-45; UCL, 1937-39 and 1946-47; Home Office: Asst Principal, 1947; Principal, 1948; Asst Sec., 1958; Mem., Prisons Board, 1962-66, 1971-; Chm., Working Party: on

Habitual Drunken Offenders, 1967-70; on Adjudication Procedures in Prisons, 1975. *Recreations:* cinema, crime fiction. *Address:* 372 Jersey Road, Osterley, Mddx. *T:* 01-560 7822.

WEINER, Prof. Joseph Sidney, MA, DSc, MRCP, FIBiol, FRAI, FSA; Director, Medical Research Council Environmental Physiology Unit, London School of Hygiene and Tropical Medicine, since 1962; Professor of Environmental Physiology, University of London, since 1965; *b* S Africa, 29 June 1915; *s* of Robert Weiner and Fanny Weiner (*née* Simon); *m* 1943, Marjorie Winifred Daw; one *s* one *d. Educ:* High Sch. for Boys, Pretoria; Univ. of Witwatersrand (MSc 1937); St George's Hosp. Med. Sch. (LRCP, MRCS 1947); Univ. of London (PhD 1946). Physiologist, Rand Mines Ltd, 1935-38; Demonstrator, Dept of Applied Physiology, London Sch. of Hygiene and Tropical Medicine, 1940; Mem., Scientific Staff, MRC, 1942; Reader in Physical Anthropology, Univ. of Oxford, 1945; Hon. Dep. Dir, MRC Unit Dept of Human Anatomy, Oxford, 1955. Chm., Ergonomics Res. Soc., 1961-63; Pres., Royal Anthropological Inst., 1963-64; world convener, Human Adaptability Section, Internat. Biol Programme, 1964-74; Pres., Section H (Anthropology), Brit. Assoc., 1966; Chm., Soc. for Study of Human Biology, 1968-71; Bureau Mem., Scientific Cttee on Problems of the Environment (ICSU), 1973; Cons. Physiologist to Sports Council, 1975-. Vis. Fellow, Australian Acad. of Scis, 1971. Vernon Prize and Medal for Industrial Physiology, 1956; Rivers Meml Medal, RAI, 1969; Huxley Medal, RAI, 1978. *Publications:* (jtly) One Hundred Years of Anthropology, 1952; The Piltdown Forgery, 1955; (jtly) Human Biology, 1964; (jtly) The Taxonomic Status of the Swanscombe Skull, 1964; (ed and co-author) The Biology of Human Adaptability, 1966; (ed) Human Biology: a guide to field methods, 1969; The Natural History of Man, 1971; (ed jtly) Case Studies in Ergonomics; (jtly) Human Adaptability in the International Biological Programme, 1976; (ed) Physiological Variation and its Genetic Basis, 1977; numerous papers on climatic physiology, human evolution and human biology. *Recreation:* gardening. *Address:* 56 Oxford Street, Woodstock, Oxon OX7 1TT. *T:* Woodstock 812392. *Club:* Athenæum.
See also R . O . Miles .

WEINSTOCK, Sir Arnold, Kt 1970; BSc (Econ), FSS; Managing Director, General Electric Co. Ltd, since 1963; *b* 29 July 1924; *s* of Simon and Golda Weinstock; *m* 1949, Netta, *d* of Michael Sobell; one *s* one *d. Educ:* University of London. Degree in Statistics. Junior administrative officer, Admiralty, 1944-47; engaged in finance and property development, group of private companies, 1947-54; Radio & Allied Industries Ltd (later Radio & Allied Holdings Ltd), 1954-63 (Managing Director); General Electric Co. Ltd, Director 1961. Dir, Rolls-Royce (1971) Ltd, 1971-73. Hon. FRCR. Hon. DSc: Salford, 1975; Aston, 1976. *Recreations:* racing and music. *Address:* 7 Grosvenor Square, W1.

WEIPERS, Prof. Sir William (Lee), Kt 1966; Director of Veterinary Education, 1949-68; Dean of the Faculty of Veterinary Medicine, 1968-74, University of Glasgow Veterinary School, retired 1974; *b* 21 Jan. 1904; *s* of Rev. John Weipers, MA, BD and Evelyn Bovelle Lee; *m* 1939, Mary MacLean; one *d. Educ:* Whitehill Higher Grade School, Dennistoun, Glasgow; Glasgow Veterinary College (MRCVS). General practice, 1925-27; on staff of Royal (Dick) Veterinary College, 1927-29. DVSM 1927; general practice, 1927-49. Member Council of Royal College of Veterinary Surgeons, 1949-74, President, 1963-64. BSc (Glasgow), 1951; FRSE 1953; FRCVS 1958. *Publications:* in professional papers. *Recreation:* tree culture. *Address:* The Snab, Duntocher, Dunbartonshire. *T:* Duntocher 73216. *Club:* Royal Scottish Automobile.

WEIR, family name of Baron Inverforth and Viscount Weir.

WEIR, 3rd Viscount *cr* 1938; **William Kenneth James Weir;** Chairman and Chief Executive, The Weir Group Ltd, since 1972; Chairman, Great Northern Investment Trust Ltd, since 1975 (Director, since 1970); Director: BICC Ltd, since 1977; British Bank of the Middle East, since 1977; Member, Court of Bank of England, since 1972; *b* Nov 1933; *e s* of 2nd Viscount Weir CBE, and Lucy (*d* 1972), *d* of late James F. Crowdy, MVO; *S* father, 1975; *m* 1st, 1964, Diana (marr. diss.), *o d* of Peter L. MacDougall; one *s* one *d*; 2nd, 1976, Mrs Jacqueline Mary Marr, *er d* of late Baron Louis de Chollet. *Educ:* Eton; Trinity Coll., Cambridge (BA). Dir, BSC, 1972-76. Mem., Engineering Industries Council, 1975-. *Recreations:* shooting, golf, fishing. *Heir: s* Hon. James William Hartland Weir, *b* 6 June 1965. *Address:* Rodinghead, Mauchline, Ayrshire. *T:* Fiveways 233. *Club:* White's.

WEIR, Very Rev. Andrew John, MSc, DD; Clerk of Assembly and General Secretary, The Presbyterian Church in Ireland, since 1964; *b* 24 March 1919; *s* of Rev. Andrew Weir and Margaret Weir, Missionaries to Manchuria of the Presbyterian Church in Ireland. *Educ:* Campbell Coll., Belfast; Queen's Univ., Belfast; New Coll., Edinburgh; Presbyterian Coll., Belfast. Ordained, 1944; Missionary to China, 1945-52; Minister, Trinity Presbyterian Church, Letterkenny, Co. Donegal, 1952-62; Asst Clerk of Assembly and Home Mission Convener, The Presbyterian Church in Ireland, 1962-64. Moderator of the General Assembly, The Presbyterian Church in Ireland, 1976-77. *Address:* (official) Church House, Belfast BT1 6DW. *T:* Belfast 22284; (home) 16 Harberton Drive, Belfast BT9 6PF. *T:* Belfast 667901.

WEIR, Rev. Cecil James Mullo, MA, DD, DPhil; Professor of Hebrew and Semitic Languages, University of Glasgow, 1937-68; *b* Edinburgh, 4 Dec. 1897; *e s* of late James Mullo Weir, SSC, FSAScot, Solicitor, Edinburgh; unmarried. *Educ:* Royal High School, Edinburgh; Universities of Edinburgh, Marburg, Paris and Leipzig; Jesus College, Oxford. Served European War, 1917-19, with Expeditionary Force in France, Belgium and Germany; Tutor in Hebrew, University of Edinburgh, 1921-22; MA Edinburgh with 1st Class Honours in Classics, 1923; 1st Class Honours in Semitic Languages, 1925; BD Edinburgh, 1926; DPhil Oxford, 1930; Minister of Orwell, Kinross-shire, 1932-34; Rankin Lecturer and Head of Department of Hebrew and Ancient Semitic Languages, University of Liverpool, 1934-37; Lecturer in the Institute of Archæology, Liverpool, 1934-37. President, Glasgow Archæological Soc., 1945-48; Dean of Faculty of Divinity, Univ. of Glasgow, 1951-54; Hon. DD (Edinburgh), 1959; FRAS, FSAScot. *Publications:* A Lexicon of Accadian Prayers in the Rituals of Expiation, 1934; contributed to A Companion to the Bible (ed Manson), 1939; Fortuna Domus, 1952; Documents from Old Testament Times (ed Thomas), 1958; Hastings's Dictionary of the Bible, 1963; A Companion to the Bible (ed Rowley), 1963; Archæology and Old Testament Study (ed Thomas), 1967; edited Transactions of Glasgow University Oriental Soc., Studia Semitica et Orientalia, Transactions of Glasgow Archæological Soc.; articles and reviews of books. *Recreations:* golf, travel. *Address:* 3 Inchgarry Court, North Berwick. *T:* North Berwick 2812.

WEIR, David Bruce, QC (Scot.) 1971; *b* 19 Dec. 1931; *yr s* of James Douglas Weir and late Kathleen Maxwell Weir (*née* Auld); *m* 1964, Katharine Lindsay, *yr d* of Hon. Lord Cameron, *qv*; three *s. Educ:* Kelvinside Academy; Glasgow Academy; The Leys Sch., Cambridge; Glasgow Univ. (MA, LLB). Royal Naval Reserve, 1955-64, Lieut RNR. Admitted to Faculty of Advocates, 1959; Advocate Depute for Sheriff Court, 1964; Hon. Sheriff of Lothians and Peebles, 1964; Standing Junior Counsel: to MPBW, 1969; to DoE, 1970. Chairman: Medical Appeal Tribunal, 1972-77; Pensions Appeals Tribunal, 1976-; Mem., Criminal Injuries Compensation Bd, 1974-. *Recreations:* sailing, music. *Address:* 9 Russell Place, Edinburgh EH5 3HQ. *T:* 031-552 2015. *Clubs:* New (Edinburgh); Royal Highland Yacht.

WEIR, Michael Scott, CMG 1974; HM Diplomatic Service; Assistant Under-Secretary of State, Foreign and Commonwealth Office, since 1974; *b* 28 Jan. 1925; *s* of Archibald and Agnes Weir; *m* 1953, Alison Walker; two *s* two *d*; *m* 1976, Hilary Reid; one *s. Educ:* Dunfermline High School; Balliol College, Oxford. Served RAF (Flt Lt), 1944-47; subseq. HM Diplomatic Service; Foreign Office, 1950; Political Agent, Trucial States, 1952-54; FO, 1954-56; Consul, San Francisco, 1956-58; 1st Secretary: Washington, 1958-61; Cairo, 1961-63; FO, 1963-68; Counsellor, Head of Arabian Dept, 1966; Dep. Political Resident, Persian Gulf, Bahrain, 1968-71; Head of Chancery, UK Mission to UN, NY, 1971-73. *Recreations:* golf, music. *Address:* c/o Foreign and Commonwealth Office, SW1.

WEIR, Robert Hendry, CB 1960; Engineering Consultant; *b* Glasgow, 18 Feb. 1912; *s* of Peter and Malcolmna Weir; *m* 1934, Edna Frances Lewis; three *s. Educ:* Allan Glen's Glasgow; Glasgow University (BSc Hons). Engineering Apprenticeship, Wm Denny & Bros, Dumbarton, 1928-33; Royal Aircraft Establishment, 1933-39; Air Ministry HQ, 1939-40; Aircraft and Armament Experimental Establishment, 1940-42; Ministry of Aircraft Production and Ministry of Supply, 1942-; Asst Director, 1948-50; Director of Industrial Gas Turbines, 1950-52; Director of Engine Research and Development, 1952-53; Deputy Director-General, Engine Research and Development, 1954-59 (Min. of Supply); Dir-Gen. of Engine Research and Development 1959-60 (Min. of Aviation); Dir, Nat. Gas Turbine Establishment, Pyestock, near Farnborough, 1960-70; Dir, Nat. Engineering Laboratory, East Kilbride, 1970-74. FRAeSoc. Coronation Medal, 1953. *Publications:* various. *Recreations:*

golf, painting; keen interest in Association Football. *Address:* Broom Cliff, 30 Castleton Drive, Newton Mearns, Glasgow G77 5LG. *T:* 041-639 5388.

WEISKRANTZ, Lawrence; Professor of Psychology, Oxford University, since 1967; Fellow, Magdalen College, Oxford; *b* 28 March 1926; *s* of Dr Benjamin Weiskrantz and Rose (*née* Rifkin); *m* 1954, Barbara Collins; one *s* one *d. Educ:* Girard College; Swarthmore; Univs of Oxford and Harvard. Part-time Lectr, Tufts University, 1952; Research Assoc., Inst. of Living, 1952-55; Sen. Postdoctoral Fellow, US Nat. Res. Coun., 1955-56; Research Assoc., Cambridge Univ., 1956-61; Asst Dir of Research, Cambridge Univ., 1961-66; Reader in Physiological Psychology, Cambridge Univ., 1966-67. *Publications:* (jtly) Analysis of Behavioural Change, 1967; articles in Science, Nature, Quarterly Jl of Experimental Psychology, Jl of Comparative and Physiological Psychology, Animal Behaviour, Brain. *Recreations:* music, walking. *Address:* Department of Experimental Psychology, South Parks Road, Oxford OX1 3UD.

WEISS, Mrs Althea McNish; see McNish, A. M.

WEISS, Eric; Chairman, Foseco Minsep Ltd, since 1969; *b* 30 Dec. 1908; *s* of late Solomon Weiss and Ada Weiss; *m* 1934, Greta Kobaltzky; two *s* two *d. Educ:* Augustinus Gymnasium, Weiden, Germany; Neues Gym., Nurnberg, Germany. Founder, Foundry Services Ltd (original co. of Foseco Group), 1932; Chm., Minerals Separation Ltd, 1964; Chm., Foseco Minsep Ltd, 1969-, when co. formed by merger of Foseco Ltd with Minerals Separation Ltd. Underwriting Mem., Lloyd's, 1976-. United World Colleges: Dep. Pres., 1973-76; Mem., UK Commn of United World Colls Project, 1968-74; Mem., Internat. Council, 1969-76; Mem., Bd of Dirs, 1970-; Mem. Bd Governors, United World Coll. of Atlantic, 1976-. Mem., Inst. of British Foundrymen. Trustee: Inst. for Archaeo-Metallurgical Studies, 1976-; Oakham Sch., 1963-. *Recreations:* golf, travel. *Address:* The Manor House, Little Marlow, Bucks SL7 3RZ. *T:* Marlow 2824. *Clubs:* Garrick, Royal Automobile.

WEISS, Peter; writer, painter, film producer; *b* Germany, 8 Nov. 1916; *s* of Eugene and Frieda Weiss; *m* 1952, Gunilla Palmstierna. *Educ:* Art Academy, Prague. Left Germany, 1934, lived in England 1934-36, Czechoslovakia, 1936-38, Sweden since 1939. Awarded Charles Veillon prize for Literature, 1963, Lessing Prize, Hamburg, 1965, Heinrich Mann Prize, Academy of Arts, East Berlin, 1966. Illustrated Swedish edn of Thousand and One Nights, 1957. *Films:* Hallucinations, 1953; Faces in Shadow, 1956; The Mirage, 1958. *Plays:* The Persecution and Assassination of Marat, 1964 (filmed 1967); Mockinpott, 1964; The Investigation, 1965; The Song of the Lusitanian Bogey, 1966; Vietnam Discourse, 1967; The Song of the Scarecrow, 1968; Trotsky in Exile, 1970; The Trial (after Kafka's novel), 1975. *Publications:* The Shadow of the Coachman's Body, 1960; The Leavetaking, 1961; Point of Escape, 1962; The Conversation of the Three Walkers, 1963; Night with Guests (play), 1963; Vanishing Point (novel); Notes on the Cultural Life of the Democratic Republic of Vietnam, 1971; Hölderlin, 1971; Die Asthetik des Widerstands Roman, 1976. *Address:* Suhrkamp Verlag, Lindenstrasse 29-35, Frankfurt-am-Main, Germany.

WEISSKOPF, Prof. Victor Frederick; Professor of Physics at Massachusetts Institute of Technology, Cambridge, Mass, USA, since 1946 (on leave, 1961-65); Chairman, Department of Physics, MIT, since 1967; *b* 19 Sept. 1908; *m* 1934, Ellen Margrete Tvede; one *s* one *d. Educ:* Göttingen, Germany. PhD 1931. Research Associate: Berlin Univ., 1932; Eidgenossiche Technische Hochschule (Swiss Federal Institute of Technology), Zürich, 1933-35; Inst. for Theoretical Physics, Copenhagen, 1936; Asst Professor of Physics, Univ. of Rochester, NY, USA, 1937-43; Dep. Division Leader, Manhattan Project, Los Alamos, USA, 1943-45; Director-Gen., CERN, Geneva, 1961-65. Chm., High Energy Physics Adv. Panel, AEC, 1967-. Mem., Nat. Acad. of Sciences, Washington, 1954; Corresp. Member: French Acad. of Sciences, 1957; Scottish Acad. of Scis, 1959; Royal Danish Scientific Soc., 1961; Bavarian Acad. of Scis, 1962; Austrian Acad. of Scis, 1963; Spanish Acad. of Scis, 1964; Soviet Acad. of Scis, 1976; Pontifical Acad. of Scis, 1976. Hon. Fellow, Weizmann Inst., Rehovot, Israel, 1962. Hon. PhD: Manchester, 1961; Uppsala, 1964; Yale, 1964; Chicago, 1967; Hon. DSc: Montreal, 1959; Sussex, 1961; Lyon, 1962; Basle, 1962; Bonn, 1963; Genève, 1964; Oxford, 1965; Vienna, 1965; Paris, 1966; Copenhagen, 1966; Torino, 1968. Cherwell-Simon Memorial Lecturer, Oxford, 1963-64. Planck Medal, 1956; Gamov Award, 1969; Prix Mondial Del Duca, 1972; Killian Award, 1973. Légion d'Honneur (France), 1959. *Publications:* Theoretical Nuclear Physics, 1952; Knowledge and Wonder, 1962; Physics in the XX Century, 1972; papers on theoretical

physics in various journals. *Address:* 36 Arlington Street, Cambridge, Mass 02140, USA.

WEITNAUER, Dr Albert; Secretary General of the Swiss Foreign Ministry, since 1976; *b* 30 May 1916; *s* of Albert Weitnauer and Stephanie (*née* Hoeschl); unmarried. *Educ:* Basle Gymnasium; Basle Univ. (Dr of Laws). Entered Swiss Govt Service, 1941; Legal Adviser to Central Office of War Economy, 1941-46; transf. to Div. of Foreign Trade, 1946; 1st Head of Section, 1951; attached to Swiss Embassy in London, 1953-54 and in Washington, 1954-58 as Counsellor i/c Econ. Affairs; Delegate of Swiss Govt for Trade Agreements and Special Missions, 1959-71; Minister, 1961; Ambassador, 1966; Ambassador to the Court of St James's, 1971-75. *Publications:* articles on problems of Swiss foreign policy, European integration and world trade. *Recreations:* golf, reading, study of languages. *Address:* c/o Palais Fédéral, Berne, Switzerland.

WEITZ, Prof. Bernard George Felix, OBE 1965; DSc; MRCVS; FIBiol; Chief Scientist, Ministry of Agriculture, Fisheries and Food, since 1977; *b* London, 14 Aug. 1919; *m* 1945, Elizabeth Shine; one *s* one *d. Educ:* St Andrew, Bruges, Belgium; Royal Veterinary College, London. MRCVS 1942; DSc London 1961. Temp. Research Worker, ARC Field Station, Compton, Berks, 1942; Research Officer, Veterinary Laboratory, Min. of Agric. and Fisheries, 1942-47; Asst Bacteriologist, Lister Inst. of Preventive Medicine, Elstree, Herts, 1947; Head of Serum Dept, 1952; Dir, Nat. Inst. for Res. in Dairying, Univ. of Reading, Shinfield, Berks, 1967-77. Hon. FRASE, 1977. *Publications:* many contribs to scientific journals on Immunology and Tropical Medicine. *Recreations:* music, croquet. *Address:* Ministry of Agriculture, Fisheries and Food, Whitehall Place, SW1.

WEITZMAN, David, QC 1951; MP (Lab) for Hackney North and Stoke Newington, since 1950 (for Stoke Newington, 1945-50); Barrister-at-Law; *b* 18 June 1898; *s* of Percy Weitzman; *m* 1st, 1925 (wife *d* 1950); one *s* one *d*; 2nd, 1955, Lena (*d* 1969), widow of Dr S. H. Dundon, Liverpool; 3rd, 1972, Vivienne Hammond. *Educ:* Hutchesons' Grammar School, Glasgow; Manchester Central School; Manchester University. Private, 3rd Battalion Manchester Regiment, 1916; BA (History Honours), 1921; called to Bar (Gray's Inn), 1922; member of Northern Circuit. Member of Labour Party since 1923. Contested (Lab) Stoke Newington, 1935. *Recreation:* golf. *Address:* Devereux Chambers, Devereux Court, Temple, WC2R 3JJ. *T:* 01-353 7534.

See also P. Weitzman.

WEITZMAN, Peter, QC 1973; a Recorder of the Crown Court, since 1974; *b* 20 June 1926; *s* of David Weitzman, *qv*, and late Fanny Weitzman; *m* 1954, Anne Mary Larkam; two *s* two *d. Educ:* Cheltenham Coll.; Christ Church, Oxford (MA). Royal Artillery, 1945-48. Called to Bar, Gray's Inn, 1952. *Recreations:* hedging and ditching. *Address:* 21 St James's Gardens, W11; Little Leigh, Kingsbridge, Devon.

WELBORE KER, Keith R.; see Ker.

WELBOURN, Prof. Richard Burkewood, MA, MD, FRCS; Professor of Surgery, University of London; Director, Department of Surgery, Royal Post-graduate Medical School and Hammersmith Hospital, since 1963; *b* 1919; *y s* of late Burkewood Welbourn, MEng, MIEE, and Edith Welbourn, Rainhill, Lancs; *m* 1944, Rachel Mary Haighton, BDS, Nantwich, Cheshire; one *s* four *d. Educ:* Rugby School; Emmanuel College, Cambridge; Liverpool University. MB, BChir 1942; FRCS 1948; MA, MD Cambridge, 1953. War of 1939-45: RAMC. Senior Registrar, Liverpool Royal Infirmary, 1948; Research Asst, Dept of Surgery, Liverpool Univ., 1949. Fellow in Surgical Research, Mayo Foundation, Rochester, Minn., 1951. Professor of Surgical Science, Queen's University of Belfast, 1958-63; Surgeon, Royal Victoria Hospital, Belfast, 1951-63 and Belfast City Hosp., 1962-63. Consultant Adviser in Surgery to Dept of Health and Social Security, 1971-. Member: Council, MRC, 1971-75; Council, Royal Postgraduate Med. Sch. Hunterian Professor, RCS of England, 1958. Member: Society of Sigma XI; British Medical Association; Moynihan Chirurgical Club. Formerly: Mem. Council: British Soc. of Gastro-enterology and Assoc. of Surgeons; 58th Member King James IV Surgical Association Inc.; Fellow, West African Coll. of Surgeons; FRSM (Former Mem. Council, Section of Endocrinology, former Vice-Pres., Section of Surgery); Hon. Fellow Amer. Surgical Assoc.; Hon. Mem., Soc. for Surgery of the Alimentary Tract; formerly: Pres., Surgical Res. Soc.; Chm., Assoc. of Profs of Surgery; Mem., Jt Cttee for Higher Surgical Training; Examr in Surgery: Univs of Newcastle, Glasgow, Oxford, Sheffield; Queen's Univ. of Belfast; Edinburgh; RCS;

Mem., Editorial Cttee, Gut. James Berry Prize (RCS), 1970. Mem., Exec. Cttee, British Journal of Surgery. Former Pres., Prout Club. Hon. MD Karolinska Inst., Stockholm, 1974. *Publications:* (with D. A. D. Montgomery): Clinical endocrinology for Surgeons, 1963; Medical and Surgical Endocrinology, 1975; contrib. chaps to Textbook of British Surgery, ed Souttar & Goligher; Surgery of Peptic Ulcer, ed Wells & Kyle; Progress in Clinical Surgery, ed Rodney Smith; British Surgical Practice, ed Rock-Carling & Ross; Scientific Basis of Surgery, ed Wells & Kyle; Scientific Basis of Oncology, ed Symington and Carter; Recent Advances in Surgery, etc; papers, mainly on gastro-intestinal and endocrine surgery and physiology, in med. and surg. jls. *Recreations:* reading, writing, gardening, music. *Address:* 6 Broomfield Road, Kew Gardens, Richmond, Surrey TW9 3HR. *T:* 01-940 2906. *Club:* Athenæum.

WELBY, Sir Bruno; see Welby, Sir R. B. G.

WELBY, Euphemia Violet, CBE 1944; JP Somerset; late Superintendent Women's Royal Naval Service; *b* 28 Sept. 1891; *d* of Admiral H. Lyon, CB; *m* 1917, Lt-Comdr R. M. Welby; two *s* one *d* (and one *d* decd). *Educ:* Private. Hon. Sec. SS&AFA Devonport, 1914-16; Red Cross Cook, Malta, 1916-19; later Hon. Sec. SS&AFA; served in WRNS, 1939-45; social work on committees in Plymouth and Chairman Astor Institute. *Recreation:* riding. *Address:* College Farm, Tintinhull, near Yeovil. *T:* Martock 3536; Milton Lodge, Freshwater Bay, Isle of Wight. *T:* Freshwater 3139.

WELBY, Sir (Richard) Bruno (Gregory), 7th Bt *cr* 1801; *b* 11 March 1928; *s* of Sir Oliver Charles Earle Welby, 6th Bt, TD, and of Barbara Angela Mary Lind, *d* of late John Duncan Gregory, CB, CMG; *S* father, 1977; *m* 1952, Jane Biddulph, *y d* of late Ralph Wilfred Hodder-Williams, MC; three *s* one *d*. *Educ:* Eton; Christ Church, Oxford (BA 1950). *Heir: s* Charles William Hodder Welby, *b* 6 May 1953. *Address:* The Leys House, Denton, Grantham, Lincs.

WELBY-EVERARD, Maj.-Gen. Sir Christopher Earle, KBE 1965 (OBE 1945); CB 1961; DL; *b* 9 Aug. 1909; *s* of late E. E. E. Welby-Everard, Gosberton House, near Spalding, Lincolnshire; *m* 1938, Sybil Juliet Wake Shorrock; two *s. Educ:* Charterhouse; CCC, Oxford. Gazetted The Lincolnshire Regt, 1930; OC 2 Lincolns, 1944; GSO1, 49 (WR) Inf. Div., 1944-46; GSO1 GHQ, MELF, 1946-48; OC 1 Royal Lincolnshire Regt, 1949-51; Comd 264 Scottish Beach Bde and 157 (L) Inf. Bde, 1954-57. BGS (Ops), HQ, BAOR, and HQ Northern Army Group, 1957-59; Chief of Staff, HQ Allied Forces, Northern Europe, 1959-61; GOC Nigerian Army, 1962-65; retd. DL Lincolnshire, 1966; High Sheriff of Lincolnshire, 1974. *Recreations:* shooting, cricket. *Address:* The Manor House, Sapperton, Sleaford, Lincolnshire NG34 0TB. *T:* Ingoldsby 273. *Clubs:* Army and Navy; Free Foresters.

WELCH, Anthony Edward, CB 1957; CMG 1949; formerly Under-Secretary, Board of Trade, 1946-66 (Ministry of Materials, 1951-54); *b* 17 July 1906; *s* of late Francis Bertram Welch; *m* 1946, Margaret Eileen Strudwick; no *c. Educ:* Cheltenham College; New College, Oxford. *Address:* Brandon Lodge, Walberswick, Suffolk. *T:* Southwold 2582.

WELCH, Sir Cullum; see Welch, Sir G. J. C.

WELCH, Air Vice-Marshal Edward Lawrence C.; see Colbeck-Welch.

WELCH, Col Sir (George James) Cullum, 1st Bt, *cr* 1957; Kt 1952; OBE 1944; MC 1918; Alderman of City of London, Ward of Bridge Within, 1947-70; *b* 20 Oct. 1895; *o s* of late James Reader Welch, Beckenham and Croydon, and late Harriet Welch; *m* 1st, 1921, Gertrude Evelyn Sladin (*d* 1966), *o d* of late John William Harrison, Stubbins, Lancs and Eastbourne, and late Evelyn Harrison; one *s* one *d*; 2nd, 1969, Irene Avril, *d* of late John Foster, OBE. *Educ:* Alleyn's School, Dulwich. Served European War, 1914-18, in France in Royal Berkshire Regt and on Staff of 18th Div. Admitted Solicitor, 1920. Member of Court of Common Council (Ward of Candlewick), 1931-47; Chief Commoner, 1946; Sheriff of the City of London, 1950-51; Lord Mayor of London, 1956-57. War of 1939-45 commanded 3rd HGAA Regt; Member City of London TA&AFA, 1941-65 and City Lieutenancy; Hon. Colonel City of London Battalion Royal Fusiliers (TA), 1956-65; and City of London Army Cadet Force, 1953-65; Liveryman and Member, Court of Assistants, Co. of Haberdashers (Warden, 1963, 1964, 1965, 1966; Master, 1966-67); Liveryman: Co. of Spectaclemakers; Co. of Solicitors of the City of London (Past Master); Co. of Parish Clerks (Past Master); Co. of Paviors (Past Master); Member Council, Law

Society, 1951-63; Registrar Archdeaconry of London, 1953-67; Chairman, Florence Nightingale Hosp., 1954-63; Vice-Chm. Bd of Govs, Bethlem Royal Hosp. and Maudsley Hosp., 1953-66; Chm. Lord Mayor of London's Nat. Hungarian and Cent. European Relief Fund, 1956-60; Dep. Chm. George VI Foundn Exec. Cttee; Pres., London Homes for the Elderly; Governor, Irish Soc., 1967-70; Hon. Treas., UK Cttee, UN Children's Fund, 1963-67; Chm. of Trustees, Morden Coll.; Trustee, Wakefield (Tower Hill Trinity Sq.) Trust, to 1972; Pres. City Livery Club, 1943-44. Freedoms: Bangor, County Down, 1957; Chard, Somerset, 1957; London, Ontario, 1957; Granby, Canada, 1957; New Orleans, 1957. K of Justice St J. Order of Mercy; Officer of Orange Nassau (Netherlands); Commander Dannebrog (Denmark). Commander (1st Class) of Order of The Lion of Finland; Grand Ufficiale Al Merito Della Repubblica Italiana. *Heir: s* John Reader Welch, MA Oxon, OStJ, Mem. Ct of Common Council [*b* 26 July 1933; *m* 1962, Margaret Kerry, *o d* of K. Douglass, formerly of Killara, NSW; one *s* twin *d*]. *Address:* 43 St Margarets, Rottingdean, East Sussex BN2 5HS; 6 Stone Buildings, Lincoln's Inn, WC2A 3YG. *T:* 01-242 2882. *Club:* City Livery.

WELCH, Rt. Rev. William Neville, MA; *b* 30 April 1906; *s* of Thomas William and Agnes Maud Welch; *m* 1935, Kathleen Margaret Beattie; two *s* two *d. Educ:* Dean Close Sch., Cheltenham; Keble Coll., Oxford; Wycliffe Hall, Oxford. Asst Curate: Kidderminster, 1929-32; St Michael's, St Albans, 1932-34; Organising Sec., Missions to Seamen, 1934-39; Vicar of Grays, 1939-43; Officiating Chaplain, Training Ship Exmouth, 1939-40; Vicar of Ilford, 1943-53; Rural Dean of Barking, 1948-53; Vicar of Great Burstead, 1953-56; Archdeacon of Southend, 1953-72; Bishop Suffragan of Bradwell, 1968-73. Proctor in Convocation, 1945 and 1950; Hon. Canon of Chelmsford, 1951-53. *Address:* 112 Earlham Road, Norwich. *T:* Norwich 618192.

WELCH, William Tom, OBE 1973; JP; Vice-Chairman, Co-operative Wholesale Society Ltd, 1973-75; *b* 13 June 1910; *s* of Alfred Henry Welch and Mary (*née* Topp); *m* 1935, Audrey D. Moxham; one *s. Educ:* Queen Elizabeth Grammar Sch., Wimborne. Gen. Man., Bournemouth Co-operative Soc., 1947; Dir, Co-operative Wholesale Soc. Ltd, 1957; Chm., Shoefayre Ltd, 1966-75; Dir, Co-operative Insce Soc., 1962-75. Mem. EDC for Distributive Trades, 1966-76. JP Dorset 1951. *Recreations:* music (especially church organs), Dorset history, gardening, angling. *Address:* Stourton, Redcotts Road, Wimborne, Dorset BH21 1ET. *T:* Wimborne 882667.

WELD, Col Sir Joseph William, Kt 1973; OBE 1946; TD 1947 (two Bars); JP; Lord-Lieutenant of Dorset, since 1964; Chairman, Wessex Regional Health Authority (formerly Wessex Regional Hospital Board), 1972-75; *b* 22 Sept. 1909; *s* of Wilfrid Joseph Weld, Avon Dassett, Warwickshire; *m* 1933, Elizabeth, *d* of E. J. Bellord; one *s* six *d. Educ:* Stonyhurst; Balliol College, Oxford. Served with Dorset Regt, TA, 1932-41; Staff College, Camberley, 1941; GSO2, General Headquarters Home Forces, 1942; Instructor, Staff College, Camberley, 1942-43; GSO1, Headquarters SEAC, 1943-46; commanded 4th Battalion Dorset Regt, 1947-51; Colonel, 1951. Hon. Colonel, 4th Battalion Dorset Regiment (TA). Chairman of Dorset Branch, County Landowners' Assoc., 1949-60; Chm. S Dorset Conservative Assoc., 1952-55 (Pres., 1955-59); Privy Chamberlain of Sword and Cape to Pope Pius XII. JP 1938, High Sheriff 1951, DL 1952, CC 1961, Dorset. KStJ 1967. *Address:* Lulworth Manor, Dorset. *T:* West Lulworth 259. *Club:* Royal Dorset Yacht.

WELD FORESTER, family name of **Baron Forester.**

WELDON, Brig. Hamilton Edward Crosdill, CBE 1961 (OBE 1951); DL; Regional Organiser, Army Benevolent Fund (Eastern Region), since 1975; *b* 14 September 1910; *s* of late Lt-Col Henry Walter Weldon, DSO, and Helen Louise Victoria Weldon (*née* Cowan); *m* 1st, 1935, Margaret Helen Katharine Passy (whom he divorced, 1946); one *d*; 2nd, 1948, Elwyne Priscilla Chaldecott; two *s* one *d. Educ:* Bilton Grange Preparatory School; Charterhouse; Royal Military Academy, Woolwich. Commissioned into RA as 2nd Lieut, 1930; Lieut 1933; Capt. 1938. Served War of 1939-45 (despatches, 1943, 1945): Adjutant, 1939-40; Bde Major, Malta, 1941; GSO1, RA Malta (Lt-Col), 1941-43. Staff Coll., Camberley, 1943-44; Lt-Col on Staff of SHAEF and 21 Army Group and various appointments in BAOR, 1944-47; AQMG (Lt-Col) HQ Southern Command, 1948; BAOR, 1951-52; Col on Staff of SHAPE, 1952-53; Command of 22 LAA Regt in Germany, 1953-55; Administrative Staff Coll., Greenlands, Henley, May-August 1955; Col at WO, 1955-58; Comdr, (Brig.) 33 AA Bde, 1958-60; Commandant, School of Artillery, Manorbier, 1960-62, retired. ADC to the Queen, 1961-62; Secretary, County of

London T&AFA, 1962-68, Greater London TA&VRA, 1968-74. Croix-de-Guerre with Palm (Fr.), 1945. Hon. Col: 265 Light Air Defence Regt, RA (TA), 1965-67; London and Kent Regt, RA (T), 1967-69; London and Kent Regt RA Cadre, 1969-; a Dep. Hon. Col, 6th Bn Queen's Regt, T&AVR, 1971-72. Vice-Pres., Fedn of Old Comrades Assocs of London, 1963-; Pres., Windsor and District Gun Club, 1970-74; Hon. Treasurer, Nat. Canine Defence League, 1975-; Mem. Council, Nat. Artillery Assoc., 1976-. DL Greater London, 1967. *Publications:* Drama in Malta, 1946; compiled Official Administrative History of 21 Army Group in NW Europe, 1945. *Recreations:* racing, shooting, theatre and writing. *Address:* Duke of York's Headquarters, Chelsea, SW3. *T:* 01-930 4466; Loaders, 23 Echo Barn Lane, Wrecclesham, Farnham, Surrey. *T:* Farnham 21783. *Clubs:* Royal Over Seas League, Army and Navy.

WELDON, Sir Thomas (Brian), 8th Bt *cr* 1723; retired; *b* 19 May 1905; 2nd *s* of Col Sir Anthony Arthur Weldon, 6th Bt, CVO, DSO, and Winifred Bruce Blakeney (OBE) (later Mrs. Wilfred Fitzgerald) (*d* 1951), *d* of Col Varty Rogers; *S* brother, 1971; *m* 1942, Marie Isobel, *d* of Hon. William Joseph French; one *s* one *d. Recreations:* shooting, fishing. *Heir: s* Anthony William Weldon, *b* 11 May 1947. *Address:* The Fighting Cocks, West Amesbury, Salisbury, Wilts SP4 7BH. *T:* Amesbury 2239. *Club:* White's.

WELENSKY, Rt. Hon. Sir Roy, (Roland), PC 1960; KCMG 1959 (CMG 1946); Kt 1953; *b* Salisbury, Southern Rhodesia, 20 January 1907; *s* of Michael and Leah Welensky; *m* 1st, 1928, Elizabeth Henderson (*d* 1969); one *s* one *d* ; 2nd, 1972, Valerie Scott; one *d. Educ:* Salisbury, S Rhodesia. Joined Railway service, 1924; Member National Council of the Railway Workers Union; Director of Manpower, Northern Rhodesia, 1941-46; formed N Rhodesia Labour Party, 1941; Member of Sir John Forster's commission to investigate the 1940 riots in Copperbelt; Chairman of various conciliation Boards and member of the Strauss (1943) and Grant (1946) Railway Arbitration Tribunals. Member of delegn to London to discuss Mineral Royalties (1949) and Constitution (1950 and 1951); Member of Northern Rhodesia delegation to Closer Association Conference at Victoria Falls, 1951. MLC, N Rhodesia, 1938, MEC 1940-53. Chm. Unofficial Members Assoc. 1946-53. Federation of Rhodesia and Nyasaland: Minister of Transport, Communications and Posts, 1953-56; Leader of the House and Deputy Prime Minister, 1955-56; Prime Minister and Minister of External Affairs, 1956-63 (also Minister of Defence, 1956-59). Heavy-weight boxing champion of the Rhodesias, 1926-28. *Publication:* Welensky's 4000 Days, The Life and Death of the Federation of Rhodesia and Nyasaland, 1964. *Relevant Publications:* The Rhodesian, by Don Taylor; Welensky's Story, by Garry Allighan. *Recreation:* gardening. *Address:* PO Box 804, Salisbury, Rhodesia. *T:* (Office) 23338. *Club:* Farmers'.

WELLAND, Colin, (Colin Williams); actor, playwright; *b* 4 July 1934; *s* of John Arthur Williams and Norah Williams; *m* 1962, Patricia Sweeney; one *s* two *d. Educ:* Newton-le-Willows Grammar Sch.; Bretton Hall Coll.; Goldsmiths' Coll., London (Teacher's Dip. in Art and Drama). Art teacher, 1958-62; entered theatre, 1962; Library Theatre, Manchester, 1962-64; television, films, theatre, 1962-. Films (actor): Kes; Villain; Straw Dogs; Sweeney. Play (author): Say Goodnight to Grandma, St Martin's, 1973. Best TV Playwright, Writers Guild, 1970, 1973 and 1974; Best TV Writer, and Best Supporting Film Actor, BAFTA Awards, 1970; Broadcasting Press Guild Award (for writing), 1973. *Publications:* plays: Roomful of Holes, 1972; Say Goodnight to Grandma, 1973. *Recreations:* cricket, watching Rugby and soccer, films, dining out; enjoys travel. *Address:* c/o Clive Goodwin Associates, 79 Cromwell Road, SW7.

WELLBELOVED, James; MP (Lab) Bexley, Erith and Crayford, since 1974 (Erith and Crayford, Nov. 1965-1974); Parliamentary Under-Secretary of State for Defence (RAF), Ministry of Defence, since 1976; Commercial Consultant; writer and broadcaster on foreign and domestic affairs; *b* 29 July 1926; *s* of Wilfred Henry Wellbeloved, Sydenham and Brockley (London), and Paddock Wood, Kent; *m* 1948, Mavis Beryl Ratcliff; two *s* one *d. Educ:* South East London Technical College. Boy seaman, 1942-46. Parly Private Secretary: Minister of Defence (Admin), 1967-69; Sec. of State for Foreign and Commonwealth Affairs, 1969-70; an Opposition Whip, 1972-74. Dep. Chm., London MPs Parly Gp, 1970-; Chairman: River Thames Gp; All Party Parly Camping and Caravanning Gp, 1967-74; Mem., Ecclesiastical Cttee, 1971-. Member: RACS Political Purposes Cttee, 1973-; PLP Liaison Cttee, 1974-; Vice Chm., Labour Party Defence Gp, 1970-. Governor, Greenwich Hosp. Sch. *Publication:* Local Government, 1971. *Recreations:* camping, travel. *Address:* House of Commons, SW1. *T:* 01-219 4563.

WELLBY, Rear-Adm. Roger Stanley, CB 1958; DSO 1940; DL; Retired; lately Head of UK Services Liaison Staff in Australia and Senior Naval Adviser to UK High Commissioner, 1956-59; *b* 28 Apr. 1906; *o s* of Dr Stanley Wellby and Marian Schwann; *m* 1936, Elaine, *d* of late Sir Clifford Heathcote-Smith; three *s. Educ:* RNC, Dartmouth. Qualified as Torpedo Officer, 1931; Commander, 1939; Special Service in France, 1940 (DSO, Croix de Guerre); Captain, 1947; Imperial Defence College; Rear-Adm. 1956. Dep. Comr-in-Chief, St John Ambulance Brigade, 1963-71; Comr, St John Ambulance Brigade, Bucks, 1971-75. DL Bucks 1972. KStJ 1966. *Recreation:* hockey, for Navy. *Address:* Oakengrove, Hastoe, Tring, Herts. *T:* Tring 3233.

WELLER, Dr Thomas Huckle; Richard Pearson Strong Professor of Tropical Public Health, and Head, Department of Tropical Public Health, Harvard, since 1954; Director Center for Prevention of Infectious Diseases, Harvard School of Public Health, since 1966; *b* 15 June 1915; *s* of Carl V. and Elsie H. Weller; *m* 1945, Kathleen R. Fahey; two *s* two *d. Educ:* University of Michigan (AB, MS); Harvard (MD). Fellow, Departments of Comparative Pathology and Tropical Medicine and Bacteriology, Harvard Medical School, 1940-41; Intern, Children's Hosp., Boston, 1941-42. Served War, 1942-45: 1st Lieut to Major, Medical Corps, US Army. Asst Resident in Medicine, Children's Hosp., 1946; Fellow, Pediatrics, Harvard Medical School, 1947; Instructor, Dept Tropical Public Health, Harvard School of Public Health, 1948; Assistant Professor, 1949; Associate Professor, 1950. Asst Director, Research Div. of Infectious Diseases, Children's Medical Center, Boston, 1949-55; Dir, Commission on Parasitic Diseases, Armed Forces Epidemiological Bd, 1953-59, Mem. 1959-72; Mem. Trop. Med. and parasitology study sect., US Public Health Service, 1953-56. Diplomate, American Board of Pediatrics, 1948; Amer. Acad. of Arts and Sciences, 1955; National Academy of Sciences, USA. Mead Johnson Award of Amer. Acad. of Pediatrics (jointly), 1954; Kimble Methodology Award (jointly), 1954; Nobel Prize Physiology or Medicine (jointly), 1954; Ledlie Prize, 1963; United Cerebral Palsy Weinstein-Goldenson Award, 1974. Hon. LLD Michigan, 1956; Hon. DSc Gustavus Adolphus Coll., 1975; Hon. LHD Lavell, 1977. *Publications:* numerous scientific papers on *in vitro* cultivation of viruses and on helminth infections of man. *Recreations:* gardening, photography. *Address:* (home) 56 Winding River Road, Needham, Mass, USA; (office) 665 Huntington Avenue, Boston, Mass 02115. *Club:* Harvard (Boston).

WELLES, (George) Orson; Director, Mercury Productions (films, theatre, radio, play publishing); Columnist; *b* Kenosha, Wisc., 6 May 1915; *s* of Richard Head Welles, inventor-manufacturer, and Beatrice Ives, pianist; *m* Virginia Nicholson, Chicago (whom he divorced, 1940); one *d* ; *m* Rita Hayworth (who obtained a divorce, 1947); one *d* ; *m* 1955, Paola Mori; one *d. Educ:* Todd School, Woodstock, Ill. Directed eight productions a year at Todd School, also doing some scene sketching; studied drawing at Chicago Art Inst., 1931; appeared at Gate Theatre, Dublin, 1931, in Trilby, Jew Suss, and Hamlet; returned to America, 1932; trip to Africa; toured US with Katharine Cornell, 1933; went into radio work as an actor, 1934; produced for Federal Theatre Macbeth with negro cast, Doctor Faustus and Horse Eats Hat; later formed Mercury Theatre, which produced The Cradle Will Rock, Heartbreak House, Shoemakers' Holiday, Danton's Death, Caesar and Five Kings; also made a series of Columbia educational recordings of Shakespearean plays for schoolroom use; came to Hollywood, 1939; produced, directed, wrote, and acted in his first picture, Citizen Kane; wrote, directed, and produced film, The Magnificent Ambersons; co-author, producer, and actor in Journey Into Fear. Produced Native Son in New York, 1939; co-starred Jane Eyre, 1943; appeared in Follow the Boys, 1943; produced, directed, starred in Mercury Wonder Show, a magic show for Army and Navy personnel, 1943; co-starred in Tomorrow is Forever, 1945; wrote, produced, acted and directed, The Lady From Shanghai, 1946; wrote screenplay, produced, directed and acted in screenplay, Macbeth, 1947; acted in Cagliostro (screenplay made in Italy), 1947; produced, and acted name-part in Othello, St James's, 1951; acted in film, Three Cases of Murder, 1955; adapted, produced, and acted in play, Moby Dick, Duke of York's, 1955; wrote, directed, and acted in film, Confidential Report, 1955; produced and acted name-part in King Lear, New York, 1956; adapted, directed and acted in film, Othello, 1956; acted in films: The Long, Hot, Summer, 1958, Compulsion, 1959, Ferry to Hong Kong, 1959, David and Goliath, 1961, The VIP's, 1963; (produced and acted) The Trial, 1963; Oedipus The King, 1968, Catch 22, 1970; The Kremlin Letter, 1970; Ten Days' Wonder, 1972; F for Fake, 1976. Directed The Immortal Story, 1968, Southern Star, 1969 (films); adapted and acted in play, Chimes at Midnight, 1960 (filmed 1966). Prod play, Rhinoceros, Royal Court Theatre,

London, 1960. Associate Editor of Free World Magazine. Special Oscar Award, 1971. Life Achievement Award, American Film Institute, 1975. *Publications:* Illustrated edns of Macbeth, Julius Cæsar, Twelfth Night, and the Merchant of Venice with editing, illustrations, and stage directions (Mercury Shakespeare); Mr Arkadin, 1957. *Recreations:* prestidigitating, cartooning, swimming, reading. *Clubs:* Advertising, Lotos (New York); National Variety (Los Angeles).

WELLESLEY, family name of **Earl Cowley** and of **Duke of Wellington.**

WELLINGS, Sir Jack (Alfred), Kt 1975; CBE 1970; Chairman and Managing Director, The 600 Group Ltd, since 1968; Member, National Coal Board, since 1971; *b* 16 Aug. 1917; *s* of Edward Josiah and Selina Wellings; *m* 1946, Greta, *d* of late George Tidey; one *s* two *d. Educ:* Selhurst Grammar Sch.; London Polytechnic. Vice-Pres., Hawker Siddeley (Canada) Ltd, 1952-62; Dep. Man. Dir, 600 Group Ltd, 1962. Mem., NEB, 1977-. *Address:* Boundary Meadow, Collum Green Road, Stoke Poges, Bucks. *T:* Fulmer 2978.

WELLINGS, Victor Gordon, QC 1973; Member of the Lands Tribunal, since 1973; *b* 19 July 1919; *e s* of late Gordon Arthur Wellings, solicitor, and Alice Adelaide Wellings (now Mrs Alice Adelaide Poole); *m* 1948, Helen Margaret Jill Lovell; three *s. Educ:* Reading Sch.; Exeter Coll., Oxford (MA). Called to Bar, Gray's Inn, 1949; practised 1949-73. War service, 1940-46; Captain Indian Army, 17th Dogra Regt; Intell. Corps, India; Captain, TARO, 1949-. *Publications:* Joint Editor, 26th and 27th edns of Woodfall, The Law of Landlord and Tenant, 1963 and 1968, and other works on same subject. *Recreations:* golf, fishing. *Address:* Cherry Tree Cottage, Whitchurch Hill, Pangbourne, Berks RG8 7PT. *T:* Pangbourne 2779. *Clubs:* United Oxford & Cambridge University; Phyllis Court (Henley); Goring and Streatley Golf.

WELLINGTON, 8th Duke of, *cr* 1814; **Arthur Valerian Wellesley,** MVO 1952; OBE 1957; MC; DL; Baron Mornington, 1746; Earl of Morningham, Viscount Wellesley, 1760; Viscount Wellington of Talavera and Wellington, Somersetshire, Baron Douro, 1809; Earl of Wellington, Feb. 1812; Marquess of Wellington, Oct. 1812; Marquess Douro, 1814; Prince of Waterloo, 1815, Netherlands; Count of Vimeiro, Marquess of Torres Vedras and Duke of Victoria in Portugal; Duke of Ciudad Rodrigo and a Grandee of Spain, 1st class; *b* 2 July 1915; *s* of 7th Duke of Wellington, KG, and Dorothy Violet (*d* 1956), *d* of Robert Ashton, Croughton, Cheshire; *S* father, 1972; *m* 1944, Diana Ruth, *o d* of Maj.-Gen. D. F. McConnel; four *s* one *d. Educ:* Eton; New Coll., Oxford. Served War of 1939-45 in Middle East (MC), CMF and BLA. Lt-Col Comdg Royal Horse Guards, 1954-58; Silver Stick-in-Waiting and Lt-Col Comdg the Household Cavalry, 1959-60; Comdr 22nd Armoured Bde, 1960-61; Comdr RAC 1st (Br.) Corps, 1962-64; Defence Attaché, Madrid, 1964-67, retired; Col-in-Chief, The Duke of Wellington's Regt, 1974-; Hon. Col 2nd Bn, The Wessex Regt, 1974. Director: Massey Ferguson Holdings Ltd, 1967; Motor Iberica SA, Spain, 1967; Massey Ferguson Ltd, 1973. Pres., Game Conservancy, 1976; Member Council: Zool Soc., 1974-; RASE, 1976-. Hampshire CC 1967-74; DL Hants, 1975. Governor of Wellington Coll., 1964-. OStJ. Officier, Légion d'Honneur (France). *Heir:* s Marquess of Douro, *qv. Address:* Stratfield Saye House, Reading; Apsley House, 149 Piccadilly, W1V 9FA. *Clubs:* Turf, Buck's, Cavalry and Guards.

WELLINGTON (NZ), Archbishop of, (RC), since 1974; **His Eminence Reginald John Cardinal Delargey;** *b* Timaru, NZ, 1914. *Educ:* Holy Cross College, Dunedin; Pontificio Collegio Urbano de Propaganda Fide, Rome. Titular Bishop of Hirina, 1957; Auxiliary Bishop of Auckland, 1958; Bishop of Auckland, 1970-74. Cardinal, 1976. *Address:* PO Box 198, Wellington, NZ; (residence) 21 Eccleston Hill, Wellington.

WELLINGTON (NZ), Bishop of, since 1973; **Rt. Rev. Edward Kinsella Norman,** MC 1943; DSO 1945; *b* 1916. *Educ:* Univ. of New Zealand (BA 1939); St John's Coll., Auckland; Westcott House, Cambridge. Served War of 1939-45 (despatches, MC, DSO). Deacon 1947, priest 1948, Newcastle upon Tyne; Curate of Berwick-on-Tweed, 1947-49; Vicar of Waiwhetu, 1949-52; Levin, 1952-59; Tauranga, 1959-65; Karori, 1965-73; Chaplain to Samuel Marsden Coll. Sch., 1965-73; Chaplain to RNZNVR, 1966-73; Archdeacon of Wellington, 1969-73. Legion of Merit (US), 1945. *Address:* Bishopscourt, 28 Eccleston Hill, Wellington 1, New Zealand.

WELLINGTON, Sir Lindsay; *see* Wellington, Sir R. E. L.

WELLINGTON, Peter Scott, DSC; PhD; ARCS; FLS; Director, National Institute of Agricultural Botany, since 1970; *b* 20 March 1919; *er s* of late Robert Wellington, MBE, MC; *m* 1947, Kathleen Joyce, *widow* of E. H. Coombe; one *s* one *d. Educ:* Kelly Coll.; Imperial Coll. of Science. BSc 1946. Observer, Fleet Air Arm, 1940-45 (Lt-Comdr (A) RNVR). Research Asst 1948-52, Chief Officer 1953-61, Official Seed Testing Stn for England and Wales; Asst Dir 1961-68, Dep. Dir 1968-69, Nat. Inst. of Agricultural Botany. Vice-Pres., Internat. Seed Testing Assoc., 1953-56 (Chm. Germination Cttee, 1956-70); Chief Officer, UK Variety Classification Unit, 1965-70; Chm., Technical Working Group, Internat. Convention for Protection of Plant Varieties, 1966-68. *Publications:* papers on germination of cereals and weeds, seed-testing and seed legislation. *Recreations:* gardening, walking, reading. *Address:* College Farm, 41 High Street, Teversham, Cambs. *T:* Teversham 2308. *Club:* Farmers'.

WELLINGTON, Sir (Reginald Everard) Lindsay, Kt 1963; CBE 1944; Retired from BBC, 1963; *b* 10 August 1901; *s* of Hubert Lindsay Wellington and Nancy Charlotte Boughtwood; *m* 1st, 1928, Evelyn Mary Ramsay; one *s* one *d* ; 2nd, 1952, Margot Osborn. *Educ:* Queen Elizabeth Grammar School, Wakefield; The Queen's College, Oxford. BBC Programme Staff since 1924; Director Broadcasting Division, Ministry of Information, 1940-41; N American Director, BBC, 1941-44; Controller (Programmes), BBC, 1944-45; Controller BBC Home Service, 1945-52; Director of Sound Broadcasting, BBC, 1952-63. *Recreations:* reading, music. *Address:* Witheridge, near Henley-on-Thames, Oxon. *T:* Nettlebed 214. *Club:* Savile.

WELLS, Dean of; *see* Mitchell, Very Rev. P. R.

WELLS, Archdeacon of; *see* Haynes, Ven. P.

WELLS, Dr Alan Arthur, FRS 1977; Director-General, The Welding Institute, since 1977; *s* of Arthur John Wells and Lydia Wells; *m* 1950, Rosemary Edith Alice Mitchell; four *s* one *d* . *Educ:* City of London Sch.; Univ. of Nottingham (BScEng); Clare Coll., Cambridge (PhD). MIMechE, Hon. FWeldI. British Welding Res. Association: Asst Dir, 1956; Dep. Dir (Scientific), 1963; Queen's Univ. of Belfast: Prof. of Struct. Science, 1964; Head of Civil Engrg Dept, 1970-77; Dean, Faculty of Applied Science and Technol., 1973-76. MRIA 1976. Hon. Dr, Faculty of Engrg, Univ. of Gent, 1972. *Publications:* Brittle Fracture of Welded Plate (jtly), 1967; res. papers on welding technol. and fracture mechanics. *Recreation:* handyman about the house and garden. *Address:* The Welding Institute, Abington Hall, Abington, Cambs CB1 6AL. *T:* Cambridge 891162.

WELLS, Charles Alexander, CBE 1963; SPk (Sitara-i-Pakistan) 1961; FRCS; Emeritus Professor of Surgery, University of Liverpool; Hon. Surgeon Royal Liverpool United Hospital and Consultant to Royal Prince Alfred, Sydney, NSW, and other hospitals; FRSocMed (President, Section of Surgery and Past President Section of Urology); Corresponding member Société Franc. d'Urologie; *b* 9 Jan, 1898; *o s* of late Percy M. and late Frances L. Wells, Liverpool; *m* 1928, Joyce Mary Rivett Harrington; two *s. Educ:* Merchant Taylors', Crosby; Liverpool University (MB, ChB, 1st Hons). Active service, RFA, 1916-18. Lately surgeon and urologist to various hospitals; Resident Surgical Officer Ancoats Hospital, Manchester; Demonstrator in Anatomy McGill University, Montreal; Clinical Assistant St Peter's Hospital, London. Mem. Council RCS (Vice-Pres., 1965-66, Bradshaw Lectr, 1966); Mem. Med. Adv. Council, ODM, and Chm. Recruitment Panel; Chairman: Merseyside Conf. for Overseas Students; Cttee on Surgical Educn, Internat. Fedn Surgical Colls. Ex-Council of British Association of Urological Surgeons (Home and Overseas); Past President Liverpool Medical Institution; Pakistan Health Reforms Commn, 1960; Adrian Committee (Ministry of Health) on Radiation Hazards, 1958-; Medical Research Council's Committee, Pressure Steam Sterilisation. Litchfield Lectr, Oxford, 1953; Luis Guerrero Meml Lectr, Santo Tomas Univ., Manila, 1957; McIlraith Guest Prof., Univ. of Sydney, 1957; Murat Willis Orator, Richmond, Va, 1963. Hon. FACS 1968. Hon. LLD (Panjab), 1960. *Publications:* Surgery for Nurses, 1938; Text Book of Urology (ed Winsbury-White); Treatment of Cancer in Clinical Practice, 1960; contrib. to textbooks and symposia, various chapters, Prostatectomy (monograph), 1952; (with J. Kyle) Peptic Ulceration, 1960; (ed with J. Kyle) Scientific Foundations of Surgery, 1967, 2nd edn, 1974; numerous articles in scientific jls. *Recreations:* shooting, painting in oils. *Address:* 11 Curzon Road, Hoylake, Wirral, Merseyside L47 1HB. *T:* Hoylake 4326. *Club:* Junior Carlton.

WELLS, Sir Charles Maltby, 2nd Bt *cr* 1944; TD 1960; *b* 24 July 1908; *e s* of 1st Bt, and Mary Dorothy Maltby (*d* 1956); *S* father,

1956; *m* 1935, Katharine Boulton, *d* of Frank Boteler Kenrick, Toronto; two *s*. *Educ:* Bedford School; Pembroke College, Cambridge. Joined RE (TA), 1933; Capt. 1939; served War of 1939-45: 54th (EA) Div., 1939-41; Lt-Col 1941; 76th Div., 1941-43; British Army Staff, Washington, 1943-45. *Heir: s* Christopher Charles Wells [*b* 12 Aug. 1936; *m* 1960, Elizabeth Florence Vaughan, *d* of I. F. Griffiths, Outremont, Quebec; two *s* two *d*]. *Address:* 37 Duggan Avenue, Toronto, Canada.

WELLS, Rear-Adm. David Charles, CBE 1971; Flag Officer Commanding Her Majesty's Australian Fleet, 1974-75; *b* Inverell, NSW, Australia, 19 Nov. 1918; *s* of C. V. T. Wells; *m* 1940, J. Moira A., *d* of Rear-Adm. C. J. Pope, CBE; two *s* two *d*. *Educ:* St Peter's Coll., Adelaide, SA; Royal Australian Naval Coll. Joined RAN, 1933. Served War of 1939-45: Atlantic, Mediterranean, Arctic, Indian and Pacific Oceans. Comdr, 1953; in comd HMAS Queenborough, 1953-56; Exec. Off., HMAS Cerberus, 1956-58; Capt. 1959; Dir of Plans, Navy Office, 1958-60; ADC to Governor-Gen., 1960-63; in comd HMAS Voyager, 1960-62; RN Exchange Service, and Dep. Dir, RN Staff Coll., 1962-64; IDC, 1965; in comd HMAS Melbourne, 1965-66; in comd HMAS Albatross, 1967; Rear-Adm. 1968; Flag Officer-in-Charge, E Australia Area, 1968-70; Dep. Chief of Naval Staff, Australia, 1970-71; ANZUK Force Comdr, Malaysia/Singapore, 1971-73. *Address:* Pine Ridge, Leadville, NSW 2744, Australia.

WELLS, Doreen Patricia, (Marchioness of Londonderry); Ballerina of the Royal Ballet, 1955-74; *b* 25 June 1937; *m* 1972, 9th Marquess of Londonderry, *qv*; two *s*. *Educ:* Walthamstow; Bush Davies School; Royal Ballet School. Engaged in Pantomime, 1952 and 1953. Joined Royal Ballet, 1955; became Principal Dancer, 1960; has danced leading roles in Noctambules, Harlequin in April, Dance Concertante, Sleeping Beauty, Coppelia, Swan Lake, Sylvia, La Fille mal Gardée, Two Pigeons, Giselle, Invitation, Rendezvous, Blood Wedding, Raymonda, Concerto, Nutcracker, Romeo and Juliet, Concerto No 2 (Ballet Imperial); has created leading roles in Toccata, La Création du Monde, Sinfonietta, Prometheus, Grand Tour. Adeline Genée Gold Medal, 1954. *Recreations:* classical music, reading, theatre-going. *Address:* Wynyard Park, Billingham, Cleveland TS22 5NF. *T:* Wolviston 310; 29 First Street, SW3.
See also Viscount Castlereagh.

WELLS, Prof. George Philip, FRS 1955; ScD; Emeritus Professor of Zoology in the University of London; *b* 17 July 1901; *er s* of Herbert George and Amy Catherine Wells; *m* 1927, Marjorie Stewart Craig (marr. diss., 1960); one *s* one *d*. *Educ:* Oundle; Trinity Coll., Cambridge. Temp. Asst, Dept of Zoology, University College, London, 1928; Lecturer, 1931; Reader, 1943; Professor, 1954-68. Hon. Associate, Dept of Zoology, British Museum (Natural History), 1953; Zoological Soc., Soc. for Experimental Biology, 1929-36, Hon. Member 1964; a Vice-Pres., Freshwater Biolog. Assoc., 1966-. *Publications:* (with H. G. Wells and Julian Huxley) The Science of Life, 1929-30 (in fortnightly parts); (various subseq. revisions); many scientific papers and popular writings and broadcasts. *Address:* University College, WC1E 6BT. *Club:* Savile.

WELLS, Lt-Col Herbert James, CBE 1958; MC 1918; FCA 1934; JP; DL; *b* 27 March 1897; *s* of late James J. Wells, NSW; *m* 1926, Rose Hamilton, *d* of late H. D. Brown, Bournemouth; no *c*. *Educ:* NSW. Chartered Accountant; Sen. Partner, Amsdon Cossart & Wells. Surrey CC: Alderman, 1960; Vice-Chm., 1959-62; Chm., 1962-65. JP Surrey 1952 (Chm., Magistrates' Ct, Wallington, 1960-70); DL 1962, High Sheriff 1965, Surrey. A General Comr for Income Tax. Freeman, City of London. Pres. Brit. Red Cross, Carshalton and Sutton Division; former Member, Surrey T&AFA, retired 1968; Chairman, Queen Mary's Hospital for Children, Carshalton, 1958-60; Member, Carshalton UDC, 1945-62 (Chm. 1950-52 and 1955-56). Served European War, 1914-18 with Aust. Inf. and Aust. Flying Corps in Egypt and France (MC); served War of 1939-45. DUniv Surrey, 1975. *Recreations:* football, hockey, tennis, squash, now golf. *Address:* 17 Oakhurst Rise, Carshalton Beeches, Surrey. *T:* 01-643 4125. *Club:* Royal Automobile.

WELLS, John Julius; MP (C) Maidstone since October 1959; *b* 30 March 1925; *s* of A. Reginald K. Wells, Marlands, Sampford Arundel, Som; *m* 1948, Lucinda Meath-Baker; two *s* two *d*. *Educ:* Eton; Corpus Christi College, Oxford (MA). War of 1939-45: joined RN as ordinary seaman, 1942; commissioned, 1943, served in submarines until 1946. Contested (C) Smethwick Division, General Election, 1955. Chairman: Cons. Party Horticulture Cttee, 1965-71; Horticultural sub-Cttee, Select Cttee on Agriculture, 1968; Parly Waterways Group, 1974-; Vice-Chm., Cons. Party Agriculture Cttee, 1970; Mem., Mr Speaker's Panel of Chairmen, 1974. Master, Worshipful Co. of

Fruiterers, 1977. Kt Comdr, Order of Civil Merit (Spain), 1972. *Recreations:* country pursuits. *Address:* Mere House, Mereworth, Kent.

WELLS, Malcolm Henry Weston, FCA; Chairman, Charterhouse Japhet Ltd, since 1973; *b* 26 July 1927; *s* of Lt-Comdr Geoffrey Weston Wells; *m* 1952, Elizabeth A. Harland, *d* of Rt. Rev. M. H. Harland, *qv*; one *s* one *d*. *Educ:* Eton Coll. ACA 1951, FCA 1961. Served RNVR, 1945-48. Peat, Marwick Mitchell Ltd, 1948-58; Siebe Gorman and Co. Ltd, 1958-63; Charterhouse Japhet, 1963-. Director: Charterhouse Group, 1971-; Civil Aviation Authority, 1974-. Mem., Solicitors' Disciplinary Tribunal, 1975-. *Recreation:* sailing. *Address:* Holmbush, Findon, West Sussex. *T:* Findon 3630. *Clubs:* City of London; West Wittering Sailing.

WELLS, Ronald Alfred, OBE 1965; BSc, FRIC, FIMM; Managing Director, Alternative Materials and Fibres Unit, Turner & Newall Ltd, since 1977; Joint Managing Director, TBA Industrial Products Ltd, since 1970; *b* 11 February 1920; *s* of Alfred John Wells and Winifred Jessie (*née* Lambert); *m* 1953, Anne Brebner Lanshe; two *s*. *Educ:* Birkbeck College, London; Newport Technical College. Service with Government Chemist, 1939-40; Royal Naval Scientific Service, 1940-47; Joined Nat. Chemical Laboratory, 1947; Mem. UK Scientific Mission, Washington, 1951-52; Head of Radio-chemical Group, 1956; Head of Div. of Inorganic and Mineral Chemistry, 1963; Deputy Director, Nov. 1963; Director of National Chemical Laboratory, 1964; Dir of Research, TBA Industrial Products Ltd, 1965-70. Mem. Council, Royal Inst. Chemistry, 1965-68. *Publications:* numerous contribs to Inorganic Chromatography and Extractive Metallurgy. *Recreations:* gardening, golf. *Address:* Barberton, 4 Moorgate Avenue, Bamford, Rochdale, Lancs. *T:* Rochdale 49940.

WELLS, Mrs Stanley; *see* Hill, S. E.

WELLS, Thomas Umfrey, MA; Headmaster, Wanganui Collegiate School, New Zealand, since 1960; *b* 6 Feb. 1927; *s* of Athol Umfrey and Gladys Colebrook Wells; *m* 1953, Valerie Esther Brewis; two *s* one *d*. *Educ:* King's College, Auckland, New Zealand; Auckland University (BA); (Orford Studentship to) King's College, Cambridge. BA 1951; MA 1954. Assistant Master, Clifton College, 1952-60 (Senior English Master, 1957-60). Pres., NZ Assoc. of Heads of Independent Secondary Schs., 1972-75. *Recreations:* reading, theatre, cricket (Cambridge Blue, 1950), tennis, fishing; formerly Rugby football (Cambridge Blue, 1951). *Address:* The Collegiate School, Wanganui, New Zealand. *T:* 8097. *Clubs:* MCC; Hawks (Cambridge); Wanganui (NZ).

WELLS, William Thomas, QC 1955; a Recorder of the Crown Court, since 1972; Member, Magistrates Courts Rules Committee, since 1954; A Governor, Bedford College, since 1963; Editorial Adviser on English Law, Encyclopædia Britannica; Director: Provincial Insurance Co. Ltd (London Board); Frank O'Shanohun Associates Ltd; *b* 10 Aug. 1908; *s* of late William Collins Wells (formerly of Clare Coll., Cambridge, and Bexhill-on-Sea) and Gertrude Wells; *m* 1936, Angela, 2nd *d* of late Robert Noble, formerly of HM Colonial Legal Service; two *s* two *d*. *Educ:* Lancing Coll.; Balliol Coll., Oxford (BA 1930). Joined Fabian Society, 1930; called to Bar, Middle Temple, 1932, Bencher 1963. QC Hong Kong, 1968. Dep. Chm., Hertfordshire QS, 1961-71; Recorder of King's Lynn, 1965-71. Formerly Mem., Internat. Adv. Committee of Labour Party and of Political Committee and Local Government Committee of the Fabian Society. Army, 1940-45: a General Staff Officer, 2nd grade, Directorate of Military Training, War Office, with temp. rank of Major, 1942-45. MP (Lab) Walsall, 1945-55, Walsall North, 1955-Feb. 1974; Member of Lord Chancellor's Cttee on Practice and Procedure of Supreme Court, 1947-53; Mem. of Chm.'s Panel, House of Commons, 1948-50; Mem. Departmental Cttee on Homosexual Offences and Prostitution, 1954-57; Chm., Legal and Judicial Gp (Parly Labour Party), 1964-70. Governor, Polytechnic of North London, 1971-74 (formerly Northern Polytechnic, 1938-71). Hon. Freeman, Borough of Walsall, 1974. *Publications:* How English Law Works, 1947; former contributor to The Fortnightly, Spectator, Times Literary Supplement, etc, mainly on political and military subjects. *Address:* Little Court, Conyngham Road, Beltinge, near Herne Bay, Kent CT6 6PT. *T:* Herne Bay 64257; 4 King's Bench Walk, Temple, EC4. *T:* 01-353 4716. *Club:* Athenæum.

WELLS-PESTELL, family name of **Baron Wells-Pestell**.

WELLS-PESTELL, Baron *cr* 1965 (Life Peer), of Combs in the County of Suffolk; **Reginald Alfred Wells-Pestell**, MA, LLD, FPhS; sociologist; a Lord in Waiting (Government Whip), and a

Spokesman in the House of Lords for the Department of Health and Social Security, since 1974; *b* 27 Jan. 1910; *o s* of Robert Pestell and Mary (*née* Manning); *m* 1935, Irene, *y d* of late Arthur Wells; two *s*. *Educ*: elementary and grammar schs; Univ. of London. Formerly London Probation Service; Vice-Pres., Nat. Assoc. of Probation Officers, 1974-. A Founder, Nat. Marriage Guidance Coun. (now a Vice-Pres.). Magistrate for London, 1946-; a Chm., Chelsea and E London Matrimonial Courts. Mem. LCC, 1946-52; Leader of Council, 1946, Mayor, 1947-49, Stoke Newington Borough; Mem. E Suffolk County Council, 1964-67. Contested (Lab) Taunton, 1955 and 1956, Hornsey, 1950 and 1951. Member: Church of England Council for Social Aid; Bridgehead Cttee (appointed by Home Office); Cttee and Council of Outcasts (providing help for the socially inadequate), and Chm. of Trustees; Wireless for the Bedridden (Chm.); delegations to Far East, Africa and Israel. Captain KRRC, 9th Bn City of London HG, 1940-45. *Publications*: articles and pamphlets on marriage and family life, delinquency and social problems for press and jls. *Recreations*: music, opera. *Address*: 88 Southfield Park, Bartlemas Close, Oxford OX4 2BA.

WELMAN, Douglas Pole, CBE 1966; *b* 22 June 1902; *s* of late Col Arthur Pole Welman and late Lady (Percy) Scott; *m* 1st, 1929, Denise, *d* of Charles Steers Peel; one *d*; 2nd, 1946, Betty Marjorie, *d* of late Henry Huth. *Educ*: Tonbridge Sch.; Faraday House Engineering Coll. DFH, CEng, FIMechE, FIEE, CIGasE. Electrical and Mechanical Engineering career at home and abroad, West Indies, 1928-32; Consulting Practice, 1932-37; Man. Dir of Foster, Yates and Thom Limited, Heavy Precision Engineers, 1937-50; Chairman or Member of number of wartime committees in Lancashire including Armaments Production, Emergency Services Organisation, and Ministry of Production; went to Ministry of Aircraft Production at request of Minister as Director of Engine Production, 1942; Deputy Director-General, 1943; Control of Directorate-Gen. including Propeller and Accessory Production, 1944; Part Time Member North Western Gas Board, 1949, Chairman, 1950-64; Chairman, Southern Gas Board, 1964-67; Member, Gas Council, 1950-67; Chm. and Man. Dir, Allsported Holdings Ltd, 1967-72. Member, Ct of Govs, Univ. of Manchester Inst. of Sci. and Techn., 1956-64, 1968-72 (Mem. Coun., 1960-64, 1968-72). FRSA. CStJ 1968 (OStJ 1964). *Publications*: articles and papers on company management. *Recreations*: sailing, fishing. *Address*: 11 St Michael's Gardens, St Cross, Winchester SO23 9JD. *T*: Winchester 68091. *Clubs*: Royal Automobile; Royal Thames Yacht.

WELSH, Andrew; MP (SNP) South Angus, since Oct. 1974; *b* 19 April 1944; *s* of William and Agnes Welsh; *m* 1971, Sheena Margaret Cannon. *Educ*: Univ. of Glasgow. MA (Hons) History and Politics. Teacher of History, 1972-74. SNP Parly Dep. Whip; SNP Spokesman on: Housing; Self Employed Affairs and Small Businesses; Agriculture. *Recreations*: music, horse riding, languages. *Address*: Olympia Buildings, Market Place, Arbroath, Angus DD11 1HR. *T*: Arbroath 4522. *Club*: Glasgow University Union.

WELSH, Brig. David, CBE 1959; DSO 1944; late Royal Artillery; Retired; *b* 10 April 1908; *s* of late Capt. Tom Welsh, Earlshaugh, Peebleshire; *m* 1947, Maud Elinor Mitchell (*d* 1977), *d* of late Major M. I. M. Campbell, MC, of Auchmannoch; one *s*. *Educ*: Winchester; RMA. Commissioned 2nd Lieut, RA, 1928. Served War of 1939-45 (DSO): with Royal Horse Artillery and Royal Artillery in France, N Africa and Italy. Lt-Col, 1950; Brigadier, 1958; Brigadier, RA, FarELF, 1957-60; retd, 1961. *Address*: Abbeyfield, Tarvin, Chester. *Club*: Army and Navy.

WELSH, Frank Reeson, MA; FBIM; FRSA; Director: Grindlays Bank Ltd, since 1971; Henry Ansbacher & Co., since 1976; Chairman: Hadfields Ltd, since 1967; Dunford & Elliott Ltd, since 1972; Underwriting Member of Lloyd's; *b* 16 Aug. 1931; *s* of F. C. Welsh and D. M. Welsh; *m* 1954, Agnes Cowley; two *s* two *d*. *Educ*: Gateshead and Blaydon Grammar Schools; Magdalene Coll., Cambridge (MA). With John Lewis Partnership, 1954-1958; CAS Group, 1958-64; Man. Dir, William Brandt's Sons & Co. Ltd, 1965-72; Chm., Jensen Motors Ltd, 1968-72. Member: British Waterways Board, 1975-; Gen. Adv. Council, Independent Broadcasting Authority, 1976-; Royal Commn on Nat. Health Service, 1976-. *Address*: Flass, Maulds Meaburn, Penrith, Cumbria. *T*: Ravensworth 278; 23 Montagu Square, W1. *T*: 01-486 4380. *Club*: United Oxford & Cambridge University.

WELSH, Prof. Harry Lambert, OC 1971; FRS 1962; FRSC 1952; Professor of Physics, University of Toronto, since 1954; *b* 13 March 1910, Canadian; *s* of Israel Welsh and Harriet Collingwood; *m* 1942, Marguerite Hazel Ostrander; no *c*. *Educ*: University of Toronto; University of Göttingen. Demonstrator in Physics, Univ. of Toronto, 1935-42; Asst Professor, 1942-48; Assoc. Professor, 1948-54; Chm., Dept of Physics, 1962-68; Chm., Research Bd, 1971-73. Lt-Comdr, RCNVR (Operational Research at Navy HQ, Ottawa), 1944-45. Pres., Canadian Assoc. of Physicists, 1973; Medal of Cdn Assoc. of Physicists, 1961; Tory Medal, Royal Society of Canada, 1963. Hon. DSc: Univ. of Windsor, Ont., 1964; Memorial Univ., St John's, Newfoundland, 1968. Meggers Medal, Optical Soc. of America, 1974. *Publications*: many papers on infra-red and Raman spectroscopy and high-pressure physics in various scientific jls. *Recreation*: music. *Address*: Department of Physics, University of Toronto, Toronto M5S 1A7, Ontario, Canada. *T*: 978-2939.

WELSH, Dame (Ruth) Mary (Eldridge), DBE 1946; TD 1976; Legion of Merit, USA; *d* of late Dr William Dalzell; *m* 1922, Air Marshal Sir William Welsh, KCB, DSC, AFC (marr. diss. 1947; he *d* 1962); one *s*. Director WAAF, 1943-46. Air Chief Comdt, WRAF. *Address*: 3 Webb House, The Bury, Odiham, Hampshire.

WELTY, Eudora. *Publications*: A Curtain of Green, 1943; The Robber Bridegroom, 1944; The Wide Net, 1945; Delta Wedding, 1947; Golden Apples, 1950; The Ponder Heart, 1954; The Bride of Innisfallen, 1955; The Shoe Bird, 1964; Losing Battles, 1970; One Time, One Place, 1971; The Optimist's Daughter, 1972 (Pulitzer Prize, 1973). *Address*: 1119 Pinehurst Street, Jackson, Miss 39202, USA.

WEMYSS, 12th Earl of *cr* 1633, and **MARCH, 8th Earl of** *cr* 1697; **Francis David Charteris**, KT 1966; Lord Wemyss of Elcho, 1628; Lord Elcho and Methil, 1633; Viscount Peebles, Baron Douglas of Neidpath, Lyne and Munard, 1697; Baron Wemyss of Wemyss (UK), 1821; Lord-Lieutenant of East Lothian since 1967; President, The National Trust for Scotland (Chairman of Council, 1947-69); Chairman, Royal Commission on Ancient and Historical Monuments and Constructions of Scotland; Lord Clerk Register of Scotland and Keeper of the Signet, since 1974; *b* 19 Jan. 1912; *s* of late Lord Elcho (killed in action, 1916) and Lady Violet Manners (she *m* 2nd, 1921, Guy Holford Benson (decd), and *d* 1971), 2nd *d* of 8th Duke of Rutland; *S* grandfather, 1937; *m* 1940, Mavis Lynette Gordon, BA, *er d* of late E. E. Murray, Hermanus, Cape Province; one *s* one *d* (and one *s* and one *d* decd). *Educ*: Eton; Balliol College, Oxford. Assistant District Commissioner, Basutoland, 1937-44. Served with Basuto Troops in Middle East, 1941-44. Ensign, Queen's Body Guard for Scotland, Royal Company of Archers; Lord High Comr to Gen. Assembly of Church of Scotland, 1959, 1960, 1977; Chairman: Scottish Cttee, Marie Curie Meml Foundn; Scottish Churches Council, 1964-71; Pres., The Thistle Foundn; Former Mem., Central Cttee, WCC; Mem., Royal Commn on Historical Manuscripts, 1975-; Director: Wemyss and March Estates Management Co. Ltd; Standard Life Assurance Co. Ltd; Scottish Television. Hon. LLD St Andrews, 1953. *Heir*: *s* Lord Neidpath, *qv*. *Address*: Gosford House, Longniddry, East Lothian. *Club*: New (Edinburgh).
See also Rt Hon. Sir Martin Charteris.

WEMYSS, Rear-Adm. Martin La Touche; Flag Officer, Second Flotilla, since 1977; *b* 5 Dec. 1927; *s* of Comdr David Edward Gillespie Wemyss, DSO, DSC, RN, and late Edith Mary Digges La Touche; *m* 1st, 1951, Ann Hall (marr. diss. 1973); one *s* one *d*; 2nd, 1973, Elizabeth Loveday Alexander; one *s* one *d*. *Educ*: Shrewsbury School. CO HMS Sentinel, 1956-57; Naval Intell. Div., 1957-59; CO HMS Alliance, 1959-60; CO Commanding Officers' Qualifying Course, 1961-63; Naval Staff, 1963-65; CO HMS Cleopatra, 1965-67; Naval Asst to First Sea Lord, 1967-70; CO 3rd Submarine Sqdn, 1970-73; CO HMS Norfolk, 1973-74; Dir of Naval Warfare, 1974-76; Rear-Adm., 1977. *Recreations*: sailing, shooting, skiing. *Address*: 67 Chiswick Staithe, Hartington Road, W4. *T*: 01-994 2678. *Clubs*: White's, Army and Navy.

WENBAN-SMITH, William, CMG 1960; CBE 1957; *b* 8 June 1908; *o s* of Frederick Wenban-Smith, Worthing; *m* 1935, Ruth Orme, *e d* of S. B. B. McElderry, *qv*; three *s* two *d*. *Educ*: Bradfield; King's Coll., Cambridge (MA). Colonial Administrative Service, 1931-61: Cadet, Zanzibar, 1931; Administrative Officer, Grade II, 1933; Asst DO, Tanganyika, 1935; DO, 1943; Sen. DO, 1951 (acted on various occasions as Resident Magistrate, Comr for Co-op. Development, Provincial Comr, and Sec. for Finance); Dir of Establishments, 1953; Minister for Social Services, 1958; Minister for Education and Labour, 1959-61. Chairman, Public Service Commission and Speaker, Legislative Council, Nyasaland, 1961-63. HM Diplomatic Service, Kuala Lumpur, 1964-69. *Publication*: Walks in the New Forest, 1975. *Recreations*: music, gardening, walking. *Address*: Crossways, Milford on Sea, Lymington,

Hants. *T:* Milford on Sea 3207. *Club:* Royal Commonwealth Society.

WENGER, Marjorie Lawson; *b* 10 Sept. 1910; *d* of late Rev. W. J. L. and Mrs A. M. Wenger. *Educ:* Walthamstow Hall, Sevenoaks, Kent. Nursing training, The Middlesex Hospital, 1930-34, SRN 1933; Midwifery training, SCM, 1935; Ward Sister, Night Sister; Sister Tutor, 1940-47. Editor, Nursing Times (Journal of the Royal College of Nursing), 1948-60; Editor, International Nursing Review (Jl of the International Council of Nurses), 1960-65; Nursing Editor, Pitman Medical Publishing Co., 1965-67; Sen. Tutor, SEN Sch. of Nursing, St Francis Hosp., SE22, 1967-70. *Recreations:* reading, theatre, travel. *Address:* Farthings, Wallcrouch, Wadhurst, E Sussex.

WENNER, Michael Alfred; HM Diplomatic Service, retired; President, Micron West Ltd; *b* 17 March 1921; *s* of Alfred E. Wenner and of Simone Roussel; *m* 1950, Gunilla Cecilia Ståhle, *d* of Envoyé Nils K. Ståhle, CBE, and of Birgit Olsson; four s. *Educ:* Stonyhurst; Oriel College, Oxford (Scholar). Served E Yorks Regt, 1940; Lancs Fusiliers and 151 Parachute Bn, India, 1941-42; 156 Bn, N Africa, 1943; No 9 Commando, Italy and Greece, 1944-45. Entered HM Foreign Service, 1947; 3rd Sec., Stockholm, 1948-51; 2nd Sec., Washington, 1951-53; Foreign Office, 1953-55; 1st Sec., Tel Aviv, 1956-59; Head of Chancery, La Paz, 1959-61, and at Vienna, 1961-63; Inspector of Diplomatic Establishments, 1964-67; Ambassador to El Salvador, 1967-70. *Recreations:* fly-fishing, old maps. *Address:* 8705 Katy Freeway, Suite 400, Houston, Texas 77024, USA; Laythams Farm, Slaidburn, Clitheroe, Lancs.

WENTWORTH, Maurice Frank Gerard, CMG 1957; OBE 1946; *b* 5 Nov. 1908; *s* of F. B. Wentworth, Finchley, N3; *m* 1962, Belinda Margaret, *d* of late B. S. Tatham and Mrs Tatham, Mickleham, Surrey; one s one d. *Educ:* Haileybury; University Coll., London (BA). Military Service, 1939-46, Lieutenant-Colonel. Gold Coast: Inspector of Schools, 1930; Sen. Education Officer, 1945; Principal, Teacher Training Coll., Tamale, 1946; Administrative Officer Class I, 1951; Permanent Secretary, 1953; Establishment Secretary, 1954-57 (Ghana Civil Service); Chairman: Public Service Commission: Sierra Leone, 1958-61; E African High Commn, 1961-64; Appointments Officer, ODM, 1964-73. *Address:* Quarry Hill, Todber, Sturminster Newton, Dorset.

WENTWORTH-FITZWILLIAM; *see* Fitzwilliam.

WERNER, Alfred Emil Anthony; Chairman, Pacific Regional Conservation Center, since 1975; *b* 18 June 1911; *o s* of late Professor Emil Alphonse Werner, Dublin; *m* 1939, Marion Jane Davies; two d. *Educ:* St Gerard's School, Bray; Trinity College, Dublin. MSc (Dublin Univ.) and ARIC 1936; MA (Dublin) and DPhil (Univ. of Freiburg im Breisgau) 1937; Hon. ScD (Dublin) 1971. Lecturer in Chemistry, TCD, 1937; Reader in Organic Chemistry, TCD, 1946; Research Chemist, National Gallery, 1948; Principal Scientific Officer, British Museum Research Laboratory, 1954, Keeper, 1959-75. Prof. of Chemistry, Royal Acad., 1962-75. FSA 1958; FMA 1959 (President, 1967); MRIA 1963. Pres., International Institute for the Conservation of Artistic and Historic Works, 1971 (Hon. Treasurer, 1962). *Publications:* The Scientific Examination of Paintings, 1952; (with H. Roosen-Runge) Codex Lindisfarnensis, Part V, 1961; (with H. J. Plenderleith) The Conservation of Antiquities and Works of Art, 1972; articles in scientific and museum journals. *Recreations:* chess, travelling. *Address:* Millwood House, Groton, Colchester, Essex. *T:* Boxford 210231; c/o Bishop Museum, PO Box 6037, Honolulu, Hawaii 96818, USA. *Club:* Athenæum.

WERNHAM, Prof. Archibald Garden, MA Aberdeen, BA Oxford; Regius Professor of Moral Philosophy in the University of Aberdeen since 1960; *b* 4 March 1916; *e s* of Archibald Garden Wernham and Christina Noble; *m* 1944, Hilda Frances Clayton; two s. *Educ:* Robert Gordon's College, Aberdeen; Aberdeen University; Balliol College, Oxford. 1st Class Hons Classics, Aberdeen, 1938, Croom Robertson Fellow, Aberdeen, 1939; 1st Cl. Hons Classical Mods, Oxford, 1939, 1st Cl. Lit. Hum., Oxford, 1943. Served in RA, 1940-42. Lecturer in Moral and Political Philosophy, St Andrews Univ., 1945-53; Sen. Lecturer, 1953-59; Reader, 1959-60. *Publications:* Benedict de Spinoza-The Political Works, 1958; reviews and articles. *Recreations:* music, swimming, walking. *Address:* Department of Moral Philosophy, King's College, Old Aberdeen. *T:* 40241.

WERNHAM, Prof. Richard Bruce, MA Oxon; Professor of Modern History, Oxford University, 1951-72; Fellow of Worcester College, Oxford, 1951-72; now Professor and Fellow Emeritus; *b* 11 Oct. 1906; *o s* of Richard George and Eleanor

Mary Wernham; *m* 1939, Isobel Hendry Macmillan, Vancouver BC; one d. *Educ:* Newbury Grammar School; Exeter College, Oxford. Research Asst, Inst. of Historical Research, London Univ., 1929-30; Temp. Asst, Public Record Office, 1930-32; Editor, PRO, State Papers, Foreign Series. 1933-; Lecturer in Modern History, University Coll., London, 1933-34; Fellow of Trinity College, Oxford, 1934-51, Senior Tutor, 1940-41 and 1948-51; University Lecturer in Modern History, Oxford, 1941-51; Examiner in Final Honour School of Modern History, Oxford, 1946-48. Served in RAF, 1941-45. *Publications:* Before the Armada: the Growth of English Foreign Policy 1485-1558, 1966; Calendars of State Papers, Foreign Series, Elizabeth; (ed) Vol III, New Cambridge Modern History: The Counter-Reformation and Price Revolution, 1559-1610, 1968. Articles in English Hist. Review, History, Trans Royal Hist. Soc., Encyclopædia Britannica. *Address:* 63 Hill Head Road, Hill Head, Fareham, Hants.

WESIERSKA, Mrs George; *see* Walder, Ruth C.

WESIL, Dennis; *b* 18 Feb. 1915; *e s* of Jack and Polly Wesil, London; *m* 1941, Kathleen, *d* of H. S. McAlpine; two d. *Educ:* Central Foundation Sch.; University Coll., London. Entered London telephone service as Asst Supt of Traffic, 1937; PO Investigation Branch, 1941; Asst Postal Controller, 1947; Principal, PO Headqrtrs, 1953; Dep. Chief Inspector of Postal Services, 1961; Asst Sec. in charge of Postal Mechanisation Branch (GPO), 1963; Dep. Dir, NE Region (GPO), 1966; Director: NE Postal Region, 1967; London Postal Region, 1970-71; Sen. Dir, Posts, PO, 1971-75. Mem., PO Management Bd, 1975. *Recreations:* music, theatre, reading, open air. *Address:* 2 Stoneleigh, Martello Road South, Poole, Dorset BH13 7HQ. *T:* Canford Cliffs 707304.

WESKER, Arnold; playwright; Founder Director of Centre 42, 1961 (dissolved 1970); *b* 24 May 1932; *s* of Joseph Wesker and Leah Perlmutter; *m* 1958, Dusty Bicker; two s one d. *Educ:* Upton House School, Hackney. Furniture Maker's Apprentice, Carpenter's Mate, 1948; Bookseller's Asst, 1949 and 1952; Royal Air Force, 1950-52; Plumber's Mate, 1952; Farm Labourer, Seed Sorter, 1953; Kitchen Porter, 1953-54; Pastry Cook, 1954-58. Former Member, Youth Service Council. Author of plays: The Kitchen, produced at Royal Court Theatre, 1959, 1961; (filmed, 1961); Trilogy of plays (Chicken Soup with Barley, Roots, I'm Talking about Jerusalem) produced Belgrade Theatre (Coventry), 1958-60, Royal Court Theatre, 1960; Chips with Everything, Royal Court, 1962, Vaudeville, 1962 and Plymouth Theatre, Broadway, 1963; The Four Seasons, Belgrade Theatre (Coventry) and Saville, 1965; Their Very Own and Golden City, Royal Court, 1966; The Friends, Stockholm and London, 1970 (also dir); The Old Ones, Royal Court, 1972; The Wedding Feast, Stockholm, 1974, Leeds 1977; The Journalists, Coventry (amateur), 1977, Yugoslav TV, 1978; The Merchant, Stockholm and Aarhus, 1976, Broadway, 1977. *Television:* (first play) Menace, 1963. *Publications:* Chicken Soup with Barley, 1959; Roots, 1959; I'm Talking about Jerusalem, 1960; The Wesker Trilogy, 1960; The Kitchen, 1961; Chips with Everything, 1962; The Four Seasons, 1966; Their Very Own and Golden City, 1966 (Marzotto Drama Prize, 1964); Fears of Fragmentation, 1970; The Friends, 1970; Six Sundays in January, 1971; The Old Ones, 1972; The Journalists, 1974; Love Letters on Blue Paper, 1974; (with John Allin) Say Goodbye! You May Never See Them Again, 1974; Words—as definitions of experience, 1976; The Wedding Feast, 1977; Journey Into Journalism, 1977; Fatlips, 1978; Said the Old Man to the Young Man, 1978; The Merchant, 1978; Collected Plays, vol. 1, 1976, vol. 2, 1977. *Address:* 27 Bishops Road, N6 4HR.

WESSEL, Robert Leslie, OBE 1969; *b* 21 Oct. 1912; *s* of late H. L. Wessel, Copenhagen, Denmark; *m* 1936, Dora Elizabeth, *d* of G. C. G. Gee, Rothley, Leics; two s two d. *Educ:* Malvern College. Entered N. Corah & Sons Ltd, 1932, Chm., 1957-69, retired. Served War of 1939-45, 44th Searchlight Regt RATA, 1939-41. Chairman: Nat. Youth Bureau, 1972-76; Youth Service Information Centre, 1968-72; Nat. Coll. for training Youth Leaders, 1960-70. Member: Council of Industrial Soc. (Chm., 1969-72); Cttee of Management, RNLI, 1974; Pro-Chancellor, Loughborough University of Technology; Group Chairman, Duke of Edinburgh's Conference, 1956. Mem., N and E Midlands Regional Bd, Lloyds Bank Ltd; Director: Loughborough Consultants Ltd; Ambelia Management Co. FBIM; FIWM. Mem., Worshipful Co. of Framework Knitters (Master, 1969-70). *Recreations:* painting, photography, music, travel. *Address:* The Mill House, 3 Home Farm Close, Old Woodhouse, Loughborough, Leics. *T:* Woodhouse Eaves 890529.

WEST, family name of Baron Granville-West.

WEST; see Sackville-West, family name of Baron Sackville.

WEST, Anthony Panther; author; *b* Hunstanton, Norfolk, 4 Aug. 1914; *m* 1936, Katharine Church; one *s* one *d*; *m* 1952, Lily Dulany Emmet; one *s* one *d*. *Educ:* in England. Became a breeder of registered Guernsey cattle and a dairy farmer, 1937. During war was with BBC's Far Eastern Desk, Home News Div., 1943-45, and then with their Japanese Service, 1945-47. Went to USA and joined staff of the New Yorker Magazine, 1950. Houghton Mifflin Fellow, 1947. *Publications:* Another Kind, (USA) 1949, (UK) 1951; One Dark Night, (UK) 1949, (as Vintage, USA, 1950); D. H. Lawrence (a critical biography), (UK) 1951, 2nd edn 1966; Gloucestershire, (UK) 1952; The Crusades, (USA) 1954 (as All About the Crusades, UK, 1967); Heritage, (USA) 1955; Principals and Persuasions, (USA) 1957, (UK) 1958, new edn 1970; The Trend Is Up, (USA) 1960; Elizabethan England, (USA) 1966, (UK) 1966; David Rees Among Others, (USA) 1970, (UK) 1970; Mortal Wounds, (USA) 1973, (UK) 1975. *Address:* c/o The New Yorker, 25 W 43rd Street, New York City, NY, USA.

WEST, David Thomson; Head of Economic Policy (Manpower) Branch, Department of Employment, since 1977; *b* 10 March 1923; *m* 1958, Marie Sellar; one *s* one *d*. *Educ:* Malvern Coll.; St John's Coll., Oxford. Served in RNVR, 1942-45; HM Diplomatic Service, 1946-76; served in Foreign Office, Office of Comr General for UK in SE Asia, HM Embassies, Paris, Lima, and Tunis; Counsellor, 1964; Commercial Inspector, 1965-68; Counsellor (Commercial) Berne, 1968-71; Head of Export Promotion Dept, FCO, 1971-72; seconded to Civil Service Dept as Head of Manpower Div., 1972-76; transf. to Home Civil Service, 1976; Dep. Head, Finance Div., Dept of Employment, 1976-77. *Address:* 7 St Paul's Place, N1. *T:* 01-226 7505. *Club:* Garrick.

WEST, Air Commodore Ferdinand, VC 1918; CBE 1945; MC; *b* London, 29 Jan. 1896; *s* of late Francis West and late Countess De la Garde de Saignes; *m* 1922, Winifred, *d* of John Leslie; one *s*. *Educ:* Xaverian Coll., Brighton; Lycée Berchet; Univ. of Genoa. 2nd Lieutenant, Lieutenant, and Acting Captain in the Royal Munster Fusiliers, 1914-17; attached to the Flying Corps, 1917-18; transferred to the Royal Air Force as a Captain, 1919 (wounded three times, MC, VC, despatches twice, Cavaliere Crown of Italy); Commanded 4 Squadron, RAF, Farnborough, 1933-36; Air Attaché, British Legations, Helsingfors, Riga, Tallin, Kovno, 1936-38; Commanded, RAF Station, Odiham, 1938-40; Air Attaché, British Embassy, Rome, 1940; Air Attaché, British Legation, Berne, 1940; retired from RAF, 1946. Man. Dir, J. Arthur Rank Overseas Film Distributors, 1947-58. Retired as Chairman: Hurst Park Syndicate, 1963-71; Continental Shipyard Agencies Ltd; Technical Equipment Supplies Ltd; Dir, Tokalon Ltd, 1963-73; Terravia Trading Services. Comdr Order of Orange Nassau, 1949; Chevalier Legion of Honour, 1958. First Class Army Interpreter (Italian) Second Class (French). *Address:* Zoar, Devenish Road, Sunningdale, Berks. *T:* Ascot 20579. *Club:* Royal Air Force.

WEST, Rt. Rev. Francis Horner, MA; *b* 9 Jan. 1909; *o s* of Sydney Hague and Mary West, St Albans, Herts; *m* 1947, Beryl Elaine, 2nd *d* of late Rev. W. A. Renwick, Smallbridge, Rochdale; one *s* one *d*. *Educ:* Berkhamsted School; Magdalene Coll. and Ridley Hall, Cambridge. Exhibitioner, Magdalene, Cambridge; MA 1934; Curate St Agnes, Leeds, 1933-36; Chaplain, Ridley Hall, Cambridge, 1936-38; Vicar of Starbeck, Yorks, 1938-42. Served War of 1939-45, as CF with BEF, MEF, CMF and SEAC, 1939-46 (despatches, 1945); Director of Service Ordination Candidates, 1946-47; Vicar of Upton, Notts, 1947-51; Archdeacon of Newark, 1947-62; Vicar of East Retford, 1951-55; Bishop Suffragan of Taunton, 1962-77; Prebendary of Wells, 1962-77; Rector of Dinder, Somerset, 1962-71. Select Preacher, Cambridge Univ., 1962. Visitor, Croft House School. *Publications:* Rude Forefathers, The Story of an English Village, 1600-1666, 1949; The Great North Road in Nottinghamshire, 1956; Sparrows of the Spirit, 1957; The Country Parish Today and Tomorrow, 1960. *Recreation:* writing. *Address:* 11 Castle Street, Aldbourne, Marlborough, Wilts. *T:* Aldbourne 630.

WEST, Rt. Rev. George Algernon, MM; MA; *b* 17 Dec. 1893; *s* of George Algernon and Marion West; *m* 1st, 1923, Helen Margaret Scott Moncrieff (deceased); 2nd, 1943, Grace Hay. *Educ:* S Bees School; Lincoln College, Oxford. Served in Serbia with Serbian Relief Fund, 1915; in France with Royal Garrison Artillery, Corporal; MM 1918. Went to Burma under SPG 1921; Bishop of Rangoon, 1935-54. Asst Bishop of Durham, 1965-68, resigned. *Publications:* Jungle Folk (with D. C. Atwool); Jungle Friends, 1937; The World that Works, 1944. *Address:* Lever Flat, Sherburn House, Durham.

WEST, Rt. Hon. Henry William, PC (N Ire) 1960; Leader, Ulster Unionist Party, since Jan. 1974; *b* 27 March 1917; *s* of late W. H. West, JP; *m* 1956, Maureen Elizabeth Hall; three *s* three *d*. *Educ:* Enniskillen Model School; Portora Royal School. Farmer. MP for Enniskillen, NI Parlt, 1954-72; Mem. (U), Fermanagh and S Tyrone, NI Assembly, 1973-75; Parly Sec. to Minister of Agriculture, 1958; Minister of Agriculture, 1960-67, and 1971-72; MP (UUUC) Fermanagh and South Tyrone, Feb.-Sept. 1974; Mem. (UUUC), for Fermanagh and South Tyrone, NI Constitutional Convention, 1975-76. N Ireland representative on British Wool Marketing Board, 1950-58; President, Ulster Farmers' Union, 1955-56. High Sheriff, Co. Fermanagh, 1954. *Address:* Rossahilly House, Enniskillen. *T:* Killadeas 231.

WEST, Mrs James; see McCarthy, Mary.

WEST, Prof. John Clifford, CBE 1977; PhD, DSc; CEng; FIEE; Professor of Electrical and Control Engineering, University of Sussex, since 1965; Director of the Phillips' Philatelic Unit, since 1970; *b* 4 June 1922; *s* of J. H. West and Mrs West (*née* Ascroft); *m* 1946, Winefride Mary Turner; three *d*. *Educ:* Hindley and Abram Grammar School; Victoria Univ., Manchester. PhD 1953, DSc 1957. Matthew Kirtley Entrance Schol., Manchester Univ., 1940. Electrical Lieutenant, RNVR, 1943-46. Lecturer, University of Manchester, 1946-57; Professor of Electrical Engineering, The Queen's University of Belfast, 1958-65; Founder Dean, Sch. of Applied Scis, 1965-73, Pro-Vice-Chancellor, 1967-71, Univ. of Sussex. Director, A. C. E. Machinery Ltd, 1966-. Member: UGC, 1973- (Chm., Technology Sub-Cttee, 1973-); Science Res. Council Cttee on Systems and Electrical Engineering, 1963-67; Science Res. Council Engrg Bd, 1976-; Vis. Cttee, Dept of Educn and Science, Cranfield; Civil Service Commn Special Merit Promotions Panel, 1966-72; Naval Educn Adv. Cttee, 1965-72; Crawford Cttee on Broadcasting Coverage, 1973-74; Inter-Univ. Inst. of Engrg Control, 1967- (Dir, 1967-70). Chm., Automation and Control Div., IEE, 1970-71 (Vice-Chm., 1967-70). Member: Royal Philatelic Soc., 1960-; Sociedad Filatélica de Chile, 1970-; FRPSL, 1970-. *Publications:* Textbook of Servomechanisms, 1953; Analytical Techniques for Non-Linear Control Systems, 1960; papers in Proc. IEE, Trans Amer. IEE, Brit. Jl of Applied Physics, Jl of Scientific Instruments, Proc. Soc. of Instrument Technology. *Recreation:* philately. *Address:* 17 Eldred Avenue, Withdean, Brighton, East Sussex BN1 5EB. *T:* Brighton 554819. *Club:* Athenæum.

WEST, Martin Litchfield, DPhil; FBA 1973; Professor of Greek, Bedford College, University of London, since 1974; *b* 23 Sept. 1937; *s* of Maurice Charles West and Catherine Baker West (*née* Stainthorpe); *m* 1960, Stephanie Roberta Pickard; one *s* one *d*. *Educ:* St Paul's Sch.; Balliol Coll., Oxford. Chancellor's Prizes for Latin Prose and Verse, 1957; Hertford and de Paravicini Schols, 1957; Ireland Schol., 1957; Woodhouse Jun. Research Fellow, St John's Coll., Oxford, 1960-63; Fellow and Praelector in Classics, University Coll., Oxford, 1963-74; MA (Oxon) 1962, DPhil (Oxon) 1963; Conington Prize, 1965. Editor of Liddell and Scott's Greek-English Lexicon, 1965; Visiting Lectr, Harvard, 1967-68. *Publications:* Hesiod, Theogony, 1966; Fragmenta Hesiodea (ed with R. Merkelbach), 1967; Early Greek Philosophy and the Orient, 1971; Sing Me, Goddess, 1971; Iambi et Elegi Graeci (ed), 1971-72; Textual Criticism and Editorial Technique, 1973; Studies in Greek Elegy and Iambus, 1974; articles in classical periodicals. *Recreations:* music, old Germanic languages. *Address:* Bedford College, Inner Circle, Regents Park, NW1 4NS. *T:* 01-486 4400; 42 Portland Road, Oxford. *T:* 56060.

WEST, Michael Charles B.; see Beresford West.

WEST, Gen. Sir Michael (Montgomerie Alston Roberts), GCB 1964 (KCB 1959; CB 1951); DSO and Bar 1945, 2nd Bar, 1953; *b* 27 Oct. 1905; *s* of Capt. H. C. J. Alston-Roberts-West, RN; *m* 1935, Christine Sybil Oppenheim; one *d*. *Educ:* Uppingham; Royal Military College, Sandhurst. 2nd Lt Oxford and Bucks Light Infantry, 1925. Served War of 1939-45; Brigade Major, 165 Brigade; Commanding 2nd South Lancashire Regt; Dep. Comdr 72 Indian Infantry Brigade; Commander 5 Infantry Brigade; Commandant, School of Infantry, 1946-48; Dep. Director, Man Power Planning, War Office, 1949-50; GOC-in-C British Troops in Austria, 1950-52; Commander, Commonwealth Division, Korea, 1952-53; Director, Territorial Army, War Office, 1955-57; Commander 1st British Corps, BAOR, 1958-59; GOC-in-C, Northern Command, 1960-62; Head of British Defence Staff, Washington, and UK Representative on the NATO Standing Group, 1962-65. Commander, US Legion of Merit, 1954. *Recreations:* undisclosed. *Address:* The Garland, Bembridge, Isle of Wight. *Clubs:* White's, Ronnie Scott's.

WEST, Morris (Langlo); author; *b* Melbourne, 26 April 1916; *s* of Charles Langlo West and Florence Guilfoyle Hanlon; *m* 1953; three *s* one *d*. *Educ:* Melbourne Univ. (BA 1937). Taught modern langs and maths, NSW and Tas, 1933-39. Served, Lieutenant, AIF, South Pacific, 1939-43. FRSL; Fellow World Acad. of Art and Science. Hon. DLitt, Univ. of Santa Clara, 1969. *Publications:* Gallows on the Sand, 1955; Kundu, 1956; Children of the Sun, 1957; The Crooked Road, 1957 (Eng.: The Big Story); The Concubine, 1958 (Eng.: McCreary Moves In); Backlash, 1958 (Eng.: Second Victory); The Devil's Advocate, 1959 (National Brotherhood Award, National Council of Christians and Jews 1960; James Tait Black Memorial Prize, 1960; RSL Heinemann Award, 1960); The Naked Country, 1960; Daughter of Silence, 1961; The Shoes of the Fisherman, 1963; The Ambassador, 1965; The Tower of Babel, 1968; The Heretic (stage drama), 1970; (jt author) Scandal in the Assembly, 1970; Summer of the Red Wolf, 1971; The Salamander, 1973; Harlequin, 1974; The Navigator, 1976. *Address:* (office) c/o Paul R. Reynolds Inc., 12 East 41st Street, New York, NY 10017, USA. *Clubs:* Wentworth Golf; Royal Prince Alfred Yacht (Sydney).

WEST, Peter; television and radio commentator/anchorman, since 1947; Rugby Football Correspondent of The Times, since 1971; Chairman, West & Nally Group (Public Relations), since 1971; *b* 12 Aug. 1920; *s* of Harold William and Dorcas Anne West; *m* 1946, Pauline Mary Pike; two *s* one *d*. *Educ:* Cranbrook Sch.; RMC, Sandhurst. Served War of 1939-45: Duke of Wellington's Regt. TV/Radio commentaries every year: on Test matches, 1952-77; Wimbledon, 1955-77; on Rugby Union, 1950-77; Olympics, 1948-60-64-68-72-76. TV shows: Chairman of: Why?, 1963; Guess my Story, 1953-54-55. Introduced: At Home, 1955; First Hand and It's Up to You, 1956-57; Box Office, 1957; Come Dancing, 1957-72 (incl.); Be Your Own Boss and Wish You Were Here, 1958; Get Ahead, 1958-62; Good Companions, 1958-62; First Years at Work (Schs TV), 1958-69 (incl.); Miss World, 1961-66 (incl.). Children's TV: introd.: Question Marks, 1957; Ask Your Dad, 1958; What's New?, 1962-63-64. Radio: introd.: What Shall We Call It?, 1955; Sound Idea, 1958; Morning Call, 1960-61; Treble Chance, 1962; Sporting Chance, 1964; Games People Play, 1975-76-77. *Publications:* The Fight for the Ashes, 1953; The Fight for the Ashes, 1956. *Recreation:* gardening. *Address:* Torches Cross, Hartfield, Sussex TN7 4DJ. *T:* Hartfield 409.

WEST, Dame Rebecca, DBE 1959 (CBE 1949); CLit 1968; *b* Christmas, 1892; Cicily Isabel, *y d* of late Charles Fairfield, Co. Kerry; *m* 1930, Henry Maxwell Andrews (*d* 1968). *Educ:* George Watson's Ladies' College, Edinburgh. Joined Staff of Freewoman as reviewer, 1911; joined staff of The Clarion as political writer, 1912; has since contributed to many leading English and American newspapers as literary critic and political writer. Fellow, Saybrook Coll., Yale Univ. Member American Academy of Arts and Sciences. Hon. DLitt, New York University, USA. Benson Medal (RSL), 1966. Order of Saint Sava, 1937; Chevalier of the Legion of Honour, 1957. *Publications:* Henry James, 1916; The Return of the Soldier, 1918; The Judge, 1922; The Strange Necessity, 1928; Lions and Lambs (pseudonym Lynx in collaboration with Low); Harriet Hume, 1929; D. H. Lawrence, an Elegy, 1930; Ending in Earnest, 1931 (published in America only); St Augustine, 1933; The Rake's Progress (in collaboration with Low), 1934; The Harsh Voice, 1935; The Thinking Reed, 1936; Black Lamb and Grey Falcon (a book about Yugoslavia), 1942; The Meaning of Treason, 1949; A Train of Powder, 1955; The Fountain Overflows, 1957; The Court and the Castle, 1958; The Vassall Affair, 1963; The New Meaning of Treason, 1964; The Birds Fall Down, 1966; Rebecca West: A Celebration, 1977. *Address:* c/o Messrs Macmillan, 4 Little Essex Street, WC2R 3LF.

WEST, Prof. Richard Gilbert, FRS 1968; FGS; Fellow of Clare College, Cambridge, since 1954; Professor of Botany, University of Cambridge, since 1977, and Director, Subdepartment of Quaternary Research, since 1966; *b* 31 May 1926; *m* 1st, 1958; one *s*; 2nd, 1973, Hazel Gristwood; two *d*. *Educ:* King's School, Canterbury; Univ. of Cambridge. Univ. Demonstrator in Botany, 1957-60; Univ. Lecturer in Botany, 1960-67; Reader in Quaternary Research, 1967-75, Prof. of Palaeoecology, 1975-77, Univ. of Cambridge. Darwin Lecturer to the British Association, 1959; Lyell Fund, 1961, Bigsby Medal, 1969, Geological Society of London. *Publications:* Pleistocene Geology and Biology, 1968, 2nd edn 1977; (jtly) The Ice Age in Britain, 1972. *Address:* Woodlands, 3A Woollards Lane, Great Shelford, Cambs. *T:* Shelford 2578; Clare College, Cambridge.

WEST, Prof. William Dixon, CIE 1947; ScD, FGS, FNA (Geol.); Emeritus Professor of Applied Geology, Director of Centre for Advanced Research in Geology, University of Saugar; *b* 1901; *s* of Arthur Joseph West. *Educ:* King's Sch., Canterbury; St John's Coll., Cambridge (BA; ScD). Former Director, Geological Survey of India; Former Dean of Pharmaceutical and Earth Sciences, Univ. of Saugar. Lyell Medal, Geological Soc. of London, 1950. *Address:* Department of Applied Geology, University of Saugar, Gour Nagar, Madhya Pradesh, India.

WEST AFRICA, Archbishop of, since 1969, and Bishop of Sierra Leone since 1961; **Most Rev. Moses Nathanael Christopher Omobiala Scott,** Commander of the Rokel, 1974; CBE 1970; Hon. DD Durham; *b* 18 Aug. 1911; *s* of late Christopher Columbus Scott, Hastings Village, Sierra Leone, and Cleopatra Eliza Scott, York Village; *m* 1941, Cordelia Elizabeth Deborah Maddy, Gloucester Village; three *s* two *d*. *Educ:* CMS Grammar School and Fourah Bay Coll., Freetown, Sierra Leone. Deacon 1943; Priest, 1946. Curate of: Lunsar, 1943-44; Yongro, Bullom, 1944-46; Missionary-in-charge of Makeni, 1946-48, of Bo, 1948-50; studied at London College of Divinity for DipTheol, 1950-51; Curate of Grappenhall, Cheshire, 1951-53; returned to Bo, 1954; Priest in charge, Bo District, 1954-57; Archdeacon of Missions, Sierra Leone, 1957-59; Archdeacon of Bonthe and Bo, 1959-61. Hon. DD Durham, 1962. *Recreations:* playwriting, croquet. *Address:* Bishopscourt, PO Box 128, Freetown, Sierra Leone. *T:* Freetown 50555.

WEST CUMBERLAND, Archdeacon of; *see* Hardie, Ven. A. G.

WEST HAM, Archdeacon of; *see* Taylor, Ven. J. B.

WEST INDIES, Archbishop of, since 1950, and Bishop of Guyana, since 1937; **Most Rev. Alan John Knight,** CMG 1954; DD; Sub-Prelate of The Venerable Order of St John of Jerusalem; *s* of John William Knight and Henrietta E. A. Shillito. *Educ:* Owen's School; Cambridge (MA, LLB). DD (Lambeth) 1950. Asst Master University College School (Junior School), 1923; Bishop's College, Cheshunt, 1924; Deacon, 1925; Priest, 1926; Curate at St James', Enfield Highway, 1925-28; Headmaster of Adisadel College, Gold Coast, 1928-37. FCP 1966. *Address:* Austin House, Georgetown, Guyana. *T:* Georgetown 02-64239; c/o National Westminster Bank Ltd, Felixstowe, Suffolk.

WEST-RUSSELL, David (Sturrock); His Honour Judge West-Russell; a Circuit Judge (formerly Deputy Chairman, Inner London Quarter Sessions), since 1966; *b* 17 July 1921; *o s* of late Sir Alexander West-Russell and late Agnes West-Russell; *m* Christine, *y d* of Sidney and Gladys Tyler; one *s* two *d*. *Educ:* Rugby; Pembroke Coll., Cambridge. Commissioned Queen's Own Cameron Highlanders, 1941; Parachute Regt, 1942-46; served in N Africa, Italy, France, Greece, Norway and Palestine (despatches, Maj.). Harmsworth Law Scholar, 1952; called to Bar, Middle Temple, 1953; SE Circuit; Mem., Departmental Cttee on Legal Aid in Criminal Proceedings, 1964-65. Comr (NI Emergency Provisions Act), 1974-; Chm., Adv. Cttee on Appts of JPs for Inner London, 1976-. *Address:* The Crown Court, Inner London, SE1 6A2. *Club:* Garrick.

WESTALL, Gen. Sir John Chaddesley, KCB 1954 (CB 1952); CBE 1951; *b* 2 July 1901; *s* of late John Chaddesley Westall, Hawkes Bay, NZ; *m* 1st, 1930, Maud Marion Bushe (*d* 1971); two *s* one *d*; 2nd, 1977, Mrs Margaret Boyle. *Educ:* Dulwich College. Entered Royal Marines, Oct. 1919; Capt. 1930; Major 1939; Naval Staff College, 1938. Served War of 1939-45: Malaya, India and Burma; promoted Bt Lt-Col for War Service, 1944. Staff Officer Intelligence, South Africa, 1947. Comd Royal Marine Barracks, Plymouth, 1949; Comd Royal Marines, Deal, 1950; Maj.-Gen. 1951; Chief of Staff, Royal Marines, 1951; Commandant General, Royal Marines, 1952-55; retired, 1955. Col Comdt, Royal Marines, 1961-64. *Recreations:* fishing, shooting. *Address:* Gorse Cottage, Petworth Road, Haslemere.

WESTALL, Rupert Vyvyan Hawksley, MA Cantab; Lieutenant Commander RN (retired); Head Master, Kelly College, Tavistock, Devon, 1939-59; *b* 27 July 1899; *s* of late Rev. William Hawksley Westall and Adela Clara Pope; *m* 1925, Sylvia G. D. Page; two *s* three *d*. *Educ:* RN Colleges Osborne and Dartmouth; Queens' College, Cambridge. Royal Navy, 1912-22; served European War, 1914-18; served in HMS Goliath, HMS Canada, HMS Ure and four years in The Submarine Service; Service on East African Station and Gallipoli, 1914-15, Jutland, China Station; Queens' College, Cambridge, 1922-26 (Exhibitioner in History, MA 1926, 1st division 2nd class both parts History Tripos); Training College for Schoolmasters, Cambridge, 1925-26; VI form and Careers Master, Blundell's School, 1926-34; Head Master West Buckland School, 1934-38. *Address:* Penrose, Kimberley Place, Falmouth, Cornwall TR11 3QL. *T:* Falmouth 313238.

WESTALL, Rt. Rev. Wilfrid Arthur Edmund; an Assistant Bishop, Diocese of Exeter; *b* 20 Nov. 1900; *s* of Rev. A. St Leger and Jessie Margaret Westall; *m* 1927, Ruth, *d* of Frank and Beatrice Evans; one *s* three *d. Educ:* Merchant Taylors' Sch.; St Chad's Coll., Durham Univ. (BA). Priest, 1925; Asst Curate, St Aidan's, Birmingham, 1925-27, of the Church of the Good Shepherd, Brighton, 1927-30; Vicar of St Wilfrid's, Brighton, 1930-41; Rector of Hawnby-with-Old Byland, Yorks, 1941-45; Vicar of Shaldon, Devon, 1945-51; Archdeacon of Exeter and Canon Residentiary of Exeter Cathedral, 1951-58. Prebendary of Exeter Cathedral, 1951-60; Bishop Suffragan of Crediton, 1954-74. Proctor in Convocation, 1949-64; Select Preacher to Oxford Univ., 1967; Examining Chaplain to Bishop of Exeter; Chaplain and Sub-Prelate of the Order of St John of Jerusalem; Vice-Pres., Additional Curates' Soc.; Fellow, Corp. of St Mary & St Nicholas (Woodard Schs); Pres., Exeter Civic Soc. Hon. DD Exeter, 1971. *Recreations:* sketching, railways and travel. *Address:* Ford House, Broadclyst, Exeter, Devon.
See also C. T. Evans, C. F. Evans.

WESTBROOK, Neil Gowanloch; Chairman, Trafford Park Estates Ltd; *b* 21 Jan. 1917; *s* of Frank and Dorothy Westbrook; *m* 1945, Hon. Mary Joan Fraser, *o d* of 1st Baron Strathalmond, CBE; one *s* one *d. Educ:* Oundle Sch.; Clare Coll., Cambridge (MA). FRICS. Served War of 1939-45: Sapper, 1939; Actg Lt-Col 1945 (despatches). Treas., Manchester Area Conservative Assoc., 1964-73, Dep. Chm., 1973-74, Chm., 1974-, Chm., Greater Manchester Co-ordinating Cttee, 1977; Manchester City Council, 1949-70; Dep. Leader 1967-69; Lord Mayor 1969-70. Chm., North Western Art Galleries and Museums Service, 1965-68; Mem., Exec. Cttee, Museums Assoc., 1965-69. *Recreations:* football, fishing, horse racing. *Address:* White Gables, Prestbury, Cheshire. *T:* Prestbury 49337. *Club:* St James's (Manchester).

WESTBROOK, Trevor Cresswell Lawrence, CBE 1945; FRAeS; MIPE; MInstM; Production Consultant since 1945; Chairman: Kenure Development Ltd; Action Engineering Ltd (since inception, 1965); Director of a number of companies; *b* 14 January 1901; *s* of late Dr Ernest Westbrook; *m* 1942, Shielah Gillham; one *s* one *d. Educ:* Epsom College. Gen. Man. Vickers Supermarine, 1929-36; Gen. Man. Vickers Aviation Section, 1937-40; joined MAP 1940, Director of Aircraft Repairs and all American Aircraft Purchases and later in charge of Aircraft Programme; Member of Minister's Council, June 1941; Adviser to Intendant-General, Sept. 1941; Production Adviser to Ministry of Supply, Sept. 1941-Jan. 1942; Member first Churchill mission to USA, 1942; Production Controller de Havilland Aircraft, 1942-45; responsible for production of Schneider Spitfire and Wellington aircraft. Also productionising Mosquito; Production adviser to De Havillands Canada temporary war assignment. *Address:* Little Brockhurst, Lurgashall, near Petworth, W Sussex. *Clubs:* Royal Thames Yacht, Royal Air Force.

WESTBURY, 5th Baron, *cr* 1861; **David Alan Bethell,** MC 1942; DL; *b* 16 July 1922; *s* of Captain The Hon. Richard Bethell (*d* 1929; *o c* of 3rd Baron); *S* brother, 1961; *m* 1947, Ursula Mary Rose James; two *s* one *d. Educ:* Harrow. 2nd Lieut 1940, Capt. 1944, Scots Guards. Equerry to the Duke of Gloucester, 1946-49. DL N Yorks, formerly NR Yorks, 1973. KStJ 1977. *Heir: s* Hon. Richard Nicholas Bethell [*b* 29 May 1950; *m* 1975, Caroline Mary, *d* of Richard Palmer. *Educ:* Harrow; RMA Sandhurst. Captain Scots Guards, 1975]. *Address:* Barton Cottage, Malton, North Yorkshire. *T:* Malton 2293. *Club:* Cavalry and Guards.

WESTBURY, (Rose) Marjorie; Singer and Actress; *b* 18 June 1905; *o d* of George and Adella Westbury, Langley, Near Birmingham. Won 4 year scholarship to RCM, London, 1927. Sang Gretel at Old Vic as operatic debut for Lilian Baylis, 1932. Began broadcasting (as singer), 1933; joined BBC Drama Repertory, 1942; Solveig in Peer Gynt; Ylena (Lorca); Miles and Flora in Turn of the Screw; Nora in The Doll's House; Elsa Strauss in the Henry Reed series (Emily Butter); Steve Temple in Paul Temple series; Susan Grantly in Barchester Chronicles. *Recreations:* gardening, cooking, sewing, croquet. *Address:* The Hundred House, Framfield, near Uckfield, East Sussex. *T:* Framfield 377.

WESTCOTT, George Foss, MA, MIMechE; freelance, since 1957; *b* 6 Feb. 1893; *e s* of Rev. Arthur Westcott, 2nd *s* of Brooke Foss Westcott, Bishop of Durham; *m* 1938, Anne Esther Anderberg; two *d. Educ:* Sherborne; GNR Locomotive Works, Doncaster (Premium Apprentice); Queens' College, Cambridge (Exhibitioner). Served in European War, 1914-19, in ASC (MT) and RFC; Hons Mechanical Science Tripos, 1920; worked for Scientific and Industrial Research Department, 1920; Assistant at Science Museum, 1921; Keeper, 1937; on loan to Admiralty Engineering Lab., 1939; Emergency Commn in RASC, 1941-42; Science Museum, 1942; Keeper of Dept of Land And Water Transport, 1950; retired 1953; re-engaged as Asst Keeper, 1953; finally retired from Civil Service, 1957; worked for Intercontinental Marketing Services Ltd, 1963; Reader, Acad. of Visual Arts, 1964; founded Basic Ideology Research Unit, 1967. *Publications:* Science Museum Handbooks; Pumping Machinery, 1932; Mechanical and Electrical Engineering, 1955 (new edn, 1960); The British Railway Locomotive, 1803-1853, 1958; Various historical Synopses of Events Charts, 1922-56; The Conflict of Ideas, 1967; Christianity, Freethinking and Sex, 1968; Towards Intellectual Freedom: the development of a basic ideology, 1972, rev. edn 1974; The Science of Man, 1975, rev. edn 1976. *Recreations:* sociological research, reading. *Address:* 1 Netherlands Court, Eaton Road, Sutton, Surrey. *T:* 01-643 2837.

WESTCOTT, Prof. John Hugh, DSc(Eng), PhD, DIC, CEng, FIEE, FBCS, FInstMC; Professor of Control Systems and Head of Computing and Control Department, Imperial College of Science and Technology, since 1970; Chairman, Feedback Ltd; *b* 3 Nov. 1920; *s* of John Stanley Westcott and Margaret Elisabeth Westcott (*née* Bass); *m* 1950, Helen Fay Morgan; two *s* one *d. Educ:* Wandsworth Sch.; City and Guilds Coll., London; Massachusetts Inst. of Technology. Royal Commission for the Exhibition of 1851 Senior Studentship; Apprenticeship BTH Co., Rugby. Radar Research and Develt Estabt, 1941-45; Lectr, Imperial Coll., 1951; Reader, 1956; Prof., 1961. Control Commn for Germany, 1945-46. Consultant to: Bataafsche Petroleum Maatschappij (Shell), The Hague, Holland, 1953-58; AEI, 1955-69; ICI, 1965-69; George Wimpey & Son, 1975-. Chm., Control and Automation Div., Instn of Electrical Engrs, 1968-69. Member: Exec. Council of Internat. Fedn of Automatic Control; Manuftrg Technology Cttee, Science Research Council; Comité de Direction of Laboratoire d'Automatique et d'Analyse des Systèmes, Toulouse, France; Chm., United Kingdom Automation Council; Governor, Kingston Polytechnic. *Publications:* An Exposition of Adaptive Control, 1962; monographs and papers, mainly on Control Systems and related topics. *Recreations:* gardening, reading. *Address:* Department of Computing and Control, Imperial College, SW7 2BT. *T:* 01-589 5111; (home) 3 Sharon Close, Long Ditton, Surrey KT6 5HD. *T:* 01-398 6808.

WESTENRA, family name of **Baron Rossmore.**

WESTERMAN, Sir (Wilfred) Alan, Kt 1963; CBE 1962 (OBE 1957); EdD; MAEcon; Chairman, Australian Industry Development Corporation, since 1971; *b* NZ, 25 March 1913; *s* of W. J. Westerman, Sydney, NSW. *Educ:* Knox Grammar School; Universities of Tasmania, Melbourne and Columbia. Chairman, Commonwealth Tariff Board, 1958-60; Sec., Dept of Trade and Industry, Canberra, 1960-71. Director: Ampol Petroleum Ltd; Philips Industries Holdings Ltd. *Recreation:* tennis. *Address:* Australian Industry Development Corporation, PO Box 1483, Canberra, ACT 2601, Australia. *Clubs:* Commonwealth (Canberra); Athenæum (Melbourne); Union (Sydney).

WESTERN, Prof. John Henry, BSc, PhD (Wales); Emeritus Professor of Agricultural Botany, University of Leeds, since 1971; *b* Ide, Devon, 29 Sept. 1906; *s* of late Henry Toogood and Emma Western, Dawlish, Devon; *m* 1940, Rachel Elizabeth Harries; one *s. Educ:* University College of Wales, Aberystwyth; University of Minnesota, USA. Research on diseases of pasture plants, Welsh Plant Breeding Station, Aberystwyth, 1937-39; Lecturer and Adviser in Agricultural Botany and Mycology, University of Manchester, 1939-46; Provincial Plant Pathologist, Ministry of Agriculture and Fisheries, Newcastle upon Tyne, 1946-50; Senior Lecturer in Agricultural Botany, 1951-59, Prof., 1959-71, Dept of Agricultural Sciences, University of Leeds. Pres., Assoc. Applied Biologists, 1964-65. *Publications:* papers on mycology, plant pathology and agricultural botany in various scientific journals. *Address:* Westhide, North Drive, Bramhope, near Leeds.

WESTLAKE, Alan Robert Cecil, CSI 1947; CIE 1943; *b* 18 July 1894; *s* of late Robert Hole and of Gertrude Westlake; *m* 1916, Dorothy Louise Turner (*d* 1966); one *s* three *d*; *m* 1966, Isabel Flora Beck. *Educ:* at a Council School; University College School; Brasenose College, Oxford. DCLI (TF), 1914-18, retiring with rank of Capt.; Political Dept, Iraq, 1919-21; entered ICS 1921. Collector and District Magistrate. Director of Agriculture, 1948. Secretary Revenue, Development Depts. Member Board of Revenue, Madras; retd. *Address:* Chanctonbury, Fuller's Road, Rowledge, Farnham, Surrey. *T:* Frensham 2658.
See also P. A. G. Westlake.

WESTLAKE, Prof. Henry Dickinson; Hulme Professor of Greek in the University of Manchester, 1949-72, now Professor Emeritus; b 4 Sept. 1906; s of C. A. Westlake and Charlotte M. Westlake (née Manlove); m 1940, Mary Helen Sayers; one s one d. Educ: Uppingham School; St John's College, Cambridge (Scholar). Strathcona Student, 1929; Assistant Lecturer, University College, Swansea, 1930-32; Fellow of St John's College, Cambridge, 1932-35; Assistant Lecturer, University of Bristol, 1936-37; Lecturer, King's College, Newcastle, 1937-46; Administrative Assistant, Ministry of Home Security, 1941-44; Reader in Greek, University of Durham, 1946-49; Dean of the Faculty of Arts, Univ. of Manchester, 1960-61; Pro-Vice-Chancellor, 1965-68. Publications: Thessaly in the Fourth Century BC, 1935; Timoleon and his relations with tyrants, 1952; Individuals in Thucydides, 1968; Essays on the Greek Historians and Greek History, 1969. Articles and reviews in learned periodicals. Recreation:' walking. Address: 1 High Street, Wrestlingworth, Sandy, Bedfordshire. T: Sandy 23254.

WESTLAKE, Peter Alan Grant, CMG 1972; MC 1943; b 2 Feb. 1919; s of A. R. C. Westlake, qv; m 1943, Katherine Spackman; two s. Educ: Sherborne; Corpus Christi Coll., Oxford; Military College of Science. Served with 1st Regt RHA (Adjt 1942), and on the staff (despatches). HM Foreign Service (now Diplomatic Service), 1946-76: served in Japan and at Foreign Office; Joint Services Staff College, 1954; Israel, 1955; Japan, 1957; Administrative Staff Coll., 1961; Counsellor: Foreign Office, 1961; Washington, 1965; British High Commn, Canberra, 1967-71; Minister, Tokyo, 1971-76. Pres., Asiatic Soc. of Japan, 1972-74. UK Commr-General, Internat. Ocean Expo, Okinawa, 1975. FRAS. Order of the Rising Sun, Japan. Address: 53 Church Street, Beaumaris, Anglesey.

WESTMEATH, 13th Earl of, cr 1621; **William Anthony Nugent;** Baron Delvin, by tenure temp. Henry II; by summons, 1486; Captain, RA, retired; b 21 Nov. 1928; s of 12th Earl of Westmeath and Doris (d 1968), 2nd d of C. Imlach, Liverpool; S father, 1971; m 1963, Susanna Margaret, o d of J. C. B. W. Leonard, qv; two s. Educ: Marlborough Coll. Heir: s Hon. Sean Charles Weston Nugent, b 16 Feb. 1965. Address: Farthings, Rotten Row Hill, Bradfield, Berks. T: Bradfield 426.

WESTMINSTER, 5th Duke of, cr 1874; **Robert George Grosvenor,** TD, DL, JP; Bt 1622; Baron Grosvenor, 1761; Earl Grosvenor and Viscount Belgrave, 1784; Marquess of Westminster, 1831; Lord-Lieutenant of Co. Fermanagh, since 1977; b 24 April 1910; yr s of Captain Lord Hugh William Grosvenor, 1st Life Guards (killed in action, 1914), and Lady Mabel Hamilton-Stubber, MBE (d 1944); S brother, 4th Duke of Westminster, 1967; m 1946, Hon. Viola Maud Lyttelton, e surv. d of 9th Viscount Cobham, KCB, TD, Hagley Hall, Worcestershire; one s two d. Educ: Eton. 2nd Lt City of London Yeo., 1938; served 1939-45 with RA (Middle East), Lt-Col, 1943; Maj., City of London Yeo., 1946-49; Maj. North Irish Horse, 1949, Lt-Col, 1953-56, Hon. Col, 1971-75. MP (UU) Fermanagh and South Tyrone, 1955-64; PPS to the Foreign Secretary (Mr Selwyn Lloyd), 1957-59; Senator, NI Parlt, 1964-67. Chm., Maritime Trust, 1970-75, Vice-Pres., 1975-. Freeman: The Goldsmiths' Company; City of London; City of Chester. A Younger Brother of Trinity House, 1970-. Joint Master, Fermanagh Harriers, 1959-62. JP 1950, DL 1953, Vice-Lieutenant, 1971-76, Co. Fermanagh; High Sheriff, 1952; DL Cheshire, 1970. Hon. ADC to Governor of N Ireland, 1953-55. KStJ 1976. Heir: s Earl Grosvenor, qv. Address: Eaton Hall, Chester. T: Chester 674489; Ely Lodge, Enniskillen, Co. Fermanagh, Northern Ireland. T: Springfield 224. Clubs: Cavalry and Guards; MCC, Royal Ocean Racing; Royal Yacht Squadron; Ulster (Belfast); Vancouver (BC).
See also Earl of Lichfield, Duke of Roxburghe.

WESTMINSTER, Archbishop of, (RC), since 1976; **His Eminence (George) Basil Cardinal Hume;** b 2 March 1923; s of Sir William Hume, CMG, FRCP. Educ: Ampleforth Coll.; St Benet's Hall, Oxford; Fribourg Univ., Switzerland. Ordained priest 1950. Ampleforth College: Senior Modern Language Master, 1952-63; Housemaster, 1955-63; Prof. of Dogmatic Theology, 1955-63; Magister Scholarum of the English Benedictine Congregation, 1957-63; Abbot of Ampleforth, 1963-76. Cardinal, 1976. Hon. Bencher, Inner Temple, 1976. Publication: Searching for God, 1977. Address: Archbishop's House, Westminster, SW1P 1QJ.

WESTMINSTER, Auxiliary Bishops of, (RC); see Butler, Rt Rev. B. C., Guazzelli, Rt Rev. V., Harvey, Rt Rev. P. J. B., Konstant, Rt Rev. D. E., and Mahon, Rt Rev. G. T.

WESTMINSTER, Dean of; see Carpenter, Very Rev. E. F.

WESTMINSTER, Archdeacon of; see Knapp-Fisher, Rt. Rev. and Ven. E. G.

WESTMORLAND, 15th Earl of cr 1624, **David Anthony Thomas Fane,** KCVO 1970; Baron Burghersh, 1624; late RHG; a Lord in Waiting to the Queen since 1955; b 31 March 1924; e s of 14th Earl of Westmorland and Hon. Diana Lister, widow of Capt. Arthur Edward Capel, CBE, and y d of 4th Baron Ribblesdale; S father 1948; m 1950, Jane, d of Lt-Col Sir Roland Lewis Findlay, Bt, qv; two s one d. Served War of 1939-45 (wounded); resigned from RHG with hon. rank of Captain, 1950. Heir: s Lord Burghersh, qv. Address: Kingsmead, Didmarton, Glos; 23 Chester Row, SW1. Clubs: Buck's, White's.

WESTMORLAND AND FURNESS, Archdeacon of; see Attwell, Ven. A. H.

WESTOBY, Jack Cecil, CMG 1975; retired, 1974; b 10 Dec. 1912; s of John William Westoby and Rose Ellen Miles; m 1941, Florence May Jackson; two s. Educ: Wheeler Street Council Sch., Hull; Hymers Coll., Hull; University Coll., Hull, BScEcon (London); FSS; FIS. Railway clerk, LNER, 1936-45; Statistician, BoT, 1945-52. Food and Agriculture Organisation of United Nations: Economist/Statistician, 1952-58; Chief, Forest Economics Br., 1958-62; Dep. Dir, Forestry Div., 1962-69; Dir of Program Co-ordination and Ops, Forestry Dept, 1970-74. Regents' Prof., Univ. of California, 1972. Foreign Member: Royal Agriculture and Forestry Acad. of Sweden, 1968; Italian Acad. of Forest Science, 1971; Finnish Forestry Soc., 1964; Soc. of Amer. Foresters, 1971; Hon. Life Mem., Commonwealth Forestry Soc. Publications: many studies and articles in official publications of FAO and in a wide variety of professional forestry jls. Recreations: music, theatre. Address: Calcioli, Via Collegalle 12, 50022 Greve-in-Chianti (FI), Italy. T: (055) 853.283.

WESTOLL, James, DL; b 26 July 1918; s of late James Westoll, Glingerbank, Longtown; m 1946, Sylvia Jane Luxmoore, MBE, d of late Lord Justice Luxmoore, Bilsington, Kent; two s two d. Educ: Eton; Trinity College, Cambridge (MA). Served War of 1939-45: Major, The Border Regiment (despatches). Called to Bar, Lincoln's Inn, 1952. Member, NW Electricity Board, 1959-66; a Deputy Chm., Cumberland Quarter Sessions, 1960-71; Cumberland County Council: CC 1947; CA 1959-74; Chm., 1958-74; Chm., Cumbria Local Govt Reorganisation Jt Cttee, 1973; Chm., Cumbria CC, 1973-76. DL 1963, High Sheriff 1964, Cumberland. Warden, Clothworkers' Company, 1973-75. CStJ 1977. Recreations: gardening, shooting. Address: Dykeside, Longtown, Carlisle, Cumbria CA6 5ND. T: Longtown 235; 5 Royal Avenue, SW3. T: 01-730 2354. Clubs: Boodle's, Farmers'; County and Border (Carlisle).

WESTOLL, Prof. Thomas Stanley, FRS 1952; FRSE, FGS; BSc, PhD (Dunelm), DSc (Aberdeen); J. B. Simpson Professor of Geology, University of Newcastle upon Tyne (formerly King's College, Newcastle upon Tyne, University of Durham), 1948-77, now Emeritus; b W Hartlepool, Durham, 3 July 1912; e s of Horace Stanley Raine Westoll; m 1st, 1939, Dorothy Cecil Isobel Wood (marr. diss. 1951); one s; 2nd, 1952, Barbara Swanson McAdie. Educ: West Hartlepool Grammar School; Armstrong (later King's) Coll., Univ. of Durham; University College, London. Senior Research Award, DSIR, 1934-37; Lecturer in Geology, Univ. of Aberdeen, 1937-48. Leverhulme Emeritus Res. Fellow, 1977. Alexander Agassiz Visiting Professor of Vertebrate Paleontology, Harvard University, 1952; Huxley Lectr, Univ. of Birmingham, 1967. J. B. Tyrell Fund, 1937, and Daniel Pidgeon Fund, 1939, Geological Soc. of London. President: Palæontological Assoc., 1966-68; Section C, British Assoc. for Advancement of Science, Durham, 1970; Geological Soc., 1972-74; Mem. Council, Royal Soc., 1966-68. Corr. Mem., Amer. Museum of Natural History; Hon. Life Mem., Soc. of Vertebrate Paleontology, USA, 1976. Murchison Medal, Geol. Soc. London, 1967; Clough Medal, Geol Soc. of Edinburgh, 1977. Publications: (ed) Studies on Fossil Vertebrates, 1958; (ed, with D. G. Murchison) Coal and Coal-bearing Strata, 1968; (ed, with N. Rast) Geology of the USSR, by D. V. Nalivkin, 1973; numerous papers and monographs on vertebrate anatomy and palæontology and geological topics, in several journals. Recreations: photography and numismatics. Address: Department of Geology, The University, Newcastle upon Tyne NE1 7RU; 21 Osborne Avenue, Newcastle upon Tyne NE2 1JQ. T: 81-1622.

WESTON, Bertram John, CMG 1960; OBE 1957; retired from the public service; now Estate Factor to British Union Trust Ltd; b 30 March 1907; o s of late J. G. Weston, Kennington, Kent; m 1932, Irene Carey; two d. Educ: Ashford Grammar School; Sidney Sussex College, Cambridge (MA); Pretoria University,

SA (MSc, Agric); Cornell University, USA (Post Grad.). Horticulturist, Cyprus, 1931; Asst Comr, Nicosia (on secondment), 1937; Administrative Officer, 1939. War Service, 1940-43 (Major). Commissioner for development and post-war construction, Cyprus, 1943; Commissioner, 1946; Administrative Officer Class I, 1951; Senior Administrative Officer, 1954; Senior Commissioner, 1958; Government Sec., St Helena, 1960-63; acted as Governor and C-in-C, St Helena, at various times during this period. *Recreations:* lawn tennis, gardening. *Address:* Redbraes, Marchmont, Greenlaw, Berwickshire. *Club:* Royal Commonwealth Society.

WESTON, Rear-Adm. Charles Arthur Winfield; Admiral President, RN College, Greenwich, since 1976; *b* 12 July 1922; *s* of late Charles Winfield Weston and of Edith Alice Weston; *m* 1946, Jeanie Findlay Miller; one *s* one *d* . *Educ:* Merchant Taylors' Sch. Entered RN as Special Entry Cadet, 1940; HM Ships: Glasgow, 1940; Durban, 1942; Staff of C-in-C Mediterranean, as Sec. to Captain of the Fleet, 1944-45 (despatches 1945); Sec. to Cdre in Charge Sheerness, 1946-47, to Flag Captain Home Fleet, HMS Duke of York, 1947-48; Loan Service, RAN, 1948-50; HM Ships: St Vincent, 1952-53; Ceres, 1954-55; Decoy, 1956; Sec. to DCNP (Trng and Manning), 1957-58, to DG Trng, 1959; CO HMS Jufair, 1960; Supply Officer, St Vincent, 1961-62; Sec. to Fleet Comdr Far East Fleet, 1963-64, to Second Sea Lord, 1965-67; sowc 1968; Chief Staff Officer (Q) to C-in-C Naval Home Comd, 1969-70; DNPTS, 1971; Director Defence Admin Planning Staff, 1972-74; Dir of Quartering (Navy), 1975. Rear-Adm. 1976. FBIM. *Recreations:* cricket, golf, gardening, music. *Address:* Westacre, Liphook, Hants GU30 7NY. *T:* Liphook 723337. *Clubs:* MCC, Army and Navy.

WESTON, Rev. Canon Frank Valentine; Principal and Pantonian Professor, Edinburgh Theological College, since 1976; *b* 16 Sept. 1935; *s* of William Valentine Weston and Gertrude Hamilton Weston; *m* 1963, Penelope Brighid, *d* of Marmaduke Carver Middleton Athorpe, formerly of Dinnington, Yorks; one *s* two *d* . *Educ:* Christ's Hospital; Queen's Coll., Oxford; Lichfield Theological Coll. BA 1960, MA 1964. Curate, St John the Baptist, Atherton, Lancs, 1961-65; Chaplain, 1965-69, Principal, 1969-76, College of the Ascension, Selly Oak, Birmingham; Vice-Pres., Selly Oak Colls, 1973-76. *Publications:* (contrib.) Quel Missionnaire, 1971; contribs to Faith and Unity, Sobornost, Eglise Vivante. *Recreations:* wine, persons and song; exploring the countryside. *Address:* The Theological College, Rosebery Crescent, Edinburgh EH12 5JT. *T:* 031-337 3838.

WESTON, Garfield; *see* Weston, W. G.

WESTON, Garfield Howard; Chairman, Associated British Foods, since 1967; *b* 28 April 1927; *s* of Willard Garfield Weston, *qv*; *m* 1959, Mary Ruth, *d* of late Major-Gen. Sir Howard Kippenberger; three *s* three *d* . *Educ:* Sir William Borlase School, Marlow; New College, Oxford; Harvard University (Economics). Man. Director: Ryvita Co. Ltd, 1951; Weston Biscuit Co., Aust., 1954; Vice-Chairman, Associated British Foods Ltd, 1960; Chairman, Weston Holdings Pty Ltd, Australia, 1965. *Recreation:* squash. *Address:* Weston Centre, 40 Berkeley Square, W1. *T:* 01-499 8931. *Club:* Lansdowne.

WESTON, Garry; *see* Weston, G. H.

WESTON, Geoffrey Harold, CBE 1975; FHA; Deputy Health Service Commissioner, since 1977; *b* 11 Sept. 1920; *s* of George and Florence Mary Weston; *m* 1953, Monica Mary Grace Comyns; three *d* . *Educ:* Wolverhampton Sch. War Service, 1940-46. Gp Sec., Reading and Dist Hosp. Management Cttee, 1955-65; Board Sec., NW Metropolitan Regional Hosp. Bd, 1965-73; Regional Administrator, NW Thames RHA, 1973-76. Member: Salmon Cttee, 1963-65; Whitley Councils: Mem. Management side of Optical Council, 1955-65, and of Nurses and Midwives Council, 1966-76; Mem., Working Party on Collab. between Local Govt and re-organised Nat. Health Service, 1973-74. Inst. of Health Service Administrators: Mem., Nat. and Reg. Councils, 1959- (Vice-Chm. of Council, 1968, Chm. 1969, Pres. of Inst., 1970). Assisted in forming first Work Study Sch. for Hosp. Service; travelled for study of hosps and health care org. in Europe, Canada and USA. *Recreations:* lawn tennis, gardening, travel, dining with friends. *Address:* Ferriby, Goring on Thames, near Reading, Berks. *T:* Goring on Thames 2881. *Club:* Royal Air Force.

WESTON, John; *see* Weston, P. J.

WESTON, Dr John Carruthers; General Manager, Northampton Development Corporation, 1969-77. *Educ:* Univ. of Nottingham. Admiralty Research, 1940-46; Plessey Co., 1946-

47; Building Research Station, 1947-64; Chief Exec. Operational Div., Nat. Building Agency, 1964-65; Dir, Building Research Station, MPBW, 1966-69. *Recreations:* gardening, music, theatre, walking, sailing, reading and living.

WESTON, Air Vice-Marshal Sir John (Gerald Willsley), KBE 1964 (OBE 1942); CB 1947; *b* 15 Nov. 1908; *e s* of late Col Edward Thomas Weston and Constance Alice Weston (née Turpin); *m* 1932, Eileen Margaret Gwendoline (*d* 1966), *o d* of late H. E. Rose, Bristol; one *s* one *d* . *Educ:* Cranbrook Sch.; RAF Coll., Cranwell. 207 (B) Sqdn, 1929; 60 (B) Sqdn, 1930-32; Signals Specialist Course, 1932-33; 99 (B) Sqdn, 1934; seconded RCAF, 1935-36; Air Ministry staff duties, 1938-41 (despatches, 1940); Chief Signals Officer, Ferry Command, 1941; Dep. Director Signals, Air Ministry, 1942-43; Director of Signals, Air Ministry, 1943-45; Comdt Central Signals Establishment, 1946-47; idc, 1948; Director of Policy (AS), Air Ministry, 1949-51; Commandant RAF, Halton, 1952-53; AOC No 90 (Signals) Group, 1954-55; Assistant Chief of Air Staff (Signals), Air Ministry, 1956-59; Senior Directing Staff, Imperial Defence College, 1959-61; Director-General of Manning, Air Ministry, 1961-64, retd. Chm., National Small-bore Rifle Assoc., 1965-68. *Recreations:* cricket, shooting. *Address:* c/o Williams & Glyn's Bank Ltd, Whitehall, SW1. *Club:* Royal Air Force.

WESTON, John Pix, BSc(Eng), BSc(Econ); CEng, FIEE, MBIM; Director General, Royal Society for the Prevention of Accidents, since 1975; *b* 3 Jan. 1920; *s* of John Pix Weston and Margaret Elizabeth (née Cox); *m* 1948, Ivy (née Glover); three *s* . *Educ:* King Edward's Sch., Birmingham; Univ. of Aston, 1946-50 (BSc(Eng), Hons); Univ. of London (LSE), 1954-57 (BSc(Econ), Hons). CEng 1953, FIEE 1966; FSS 1958; FREconS 1958; MBIM 1973. City of Birmingham: Police Dept, 1936-39; Electricity Supply Dept, 1939-48; Midlands Electricity Bd, 1948-50; English Electricity Co., 1950-51; NW Elec. Bd, 1951-58; Eastern Elec. Bd, 1958-60; Dep. Operating Man., Jamaica Public Services Co., 1960-61; Principal Asst Engr, Midlands Elec. Bd, 1961-64; Asst Ch. Commercial Officer, S of Scotland Elec. Bd, 1964-66; Sen. Econ. Adviser to Mrs Barbara Castle, MoT, 1966-68; Sen. Econ. and Chartered Engr, IBRD, 1968-70; Michelin Tyre Co., France, 1970-72; Dir of Post Experience Courses, Open Univ., 1972-75. MIES 1963; Mem., Assoc. of Public Lighting Engrs, 1962. Page Prize, IEE, 1950; Rosebery Prize, Univ. of London, 1957. SBStJ 1962. *Publications:* papers, reports and other contribs on electricity, highways, educn (espec. function and progress of the Open University), etc, to public bodies, congresses and conferences, UK and abroad. *Recreations:* cine photography, gardening, swimming. *Address:* The Bungalow, Marlbrook Lane, Upper Marlbrook, Bromsgrove, Worcs. *T:* 021-445 2393. *Clubs:* Farmers', St John House; Birmingham Press.

WESTON, John William; Principal Assistant Solicitor, Board of Inland Revenue, since 1967; *b* 3 Feb. 1915; *s* of Herbert Edward Weston, MA, and Emma Gertrude Weston; *m* 1943, Frances Winifred (née Johnson); two *s* one *d* . *Educ:* Berkhamsted Sch., Herts. Solicitor, 1937. Joined Inland Revenue, 1940; Sen. Legal Asst, 1948; Asst Solicitor, 1954. *Recreations:* tennis, golf. *Address:* 5 Dickerage Road, Kingston Hill, Surrey. *T:* 01-942 8130.

WESTON, Margaret Kate, BScEng (London); MIEE; FMA; Director of the Science Museum, since 1973; *b* 7 March 1926; *o c* of late Charles Edward and Margaret Weston. *Educ:* Stroud High School; College of Technology, Birmingham (now Univ. of Aston). Engineering apprenticeship with General Electric Co. Ltd, followed in 1949 by development work, very largely on high voltage insulation problems. Joined Science Museum as an Assistant Keeper, Dept of Electrical Engineering and Communications, 1955; Deputy Keeper, 1962; Keeper, Dept of Museum Services, 1967-72. Member: Design Council, 1975-; Ancient Monuments Bd for England, 1977-. Fellow, Imperial Coll. London, 1975. FMA 1976. Hon. DSc Aston, 1974. *Address:* 7 Shawley Way, Epsom, Surrey. *T:* Burgh Heath 55885.

WESTON, (Philip) John; HM Diplomatic Service; Visiting Fellow, All Souls College, Oxford, 1977-78; *b* 13 April 1938; *s* of late Philip George Weston and Edith Alice Bray (née Ansell); *m* 1967, Margaret Salley Ehlers; two *s* one *d* . *Educ:* Sherborne (major scholar); Worcester Coll., Oxford (major scholar). 1st Cl. Hons, Honour Mods Classics and Lit. Hum. Served with Royal Marines, 1956-58. Entered Diplomatic Service, 1962; FO, 1962-63; Treasury Centre for Admin. Studies, 1964; Chinese Language student, Hong Kong, 1964-66; Peking, 1967-68; FO, 1969-71; Office of UK Permanent Representative to EEC, 1972-74; Asst Private Sec. to Sec. of State for Foreign and Commonwealth Affairs (Rt Hon. James Callaghan, Rt Hon.

Anthony Crosland), 1974-76; Counsellor, Head of EEC Presidency Secretariat, FCO, 1976-77. *Recreations:* poems, chess, running. *Address:* c/o Foreign and Commonwealth Office, SW1; 13 Denbigh Gardens, Richmond, Surrey. *T:* 01-940 0388.

WESTON, (Willard) Garfield; Chairman: George Weston Holdings, Ltd and its associated companies; Weston Foods, Ltd; Fortnum & Mason Ltd; Director of other companies in Britain; President, Associated British Foods Ltd; Chairman of George Weston Ltd, Toronto, and of its associated companies; also of Weston Bakeries Ltd, Toronto; Wm Paterson, Ltd, Brantford, Ontario, and Weston Biscuit Co., Passaic, New Jersey, USA; *b* Toronto, Ontario, 1898; *e s* of George and Emma Maude Weston; *m* 1921, Reta Lila Howard (*d* 1967); three *s* six *d*. *Educ:* Harbord Collegiate Inst., Toronto. Joined Canadian Engrs on leaving sch. and served in France during European War; with George Weston Ltd (Toronto) since 1919, becoming Vice-President in 1921 and Manager in 1922; came to Great Britain in 1934; founded the Weston Biscuit Companies and erected new plants in many parts of the country; founded Allied Bakeries, Ltd. MP (Nat U) for Macclesfield Division, 1939-45. *Recreations:* riding, tennis. *Address:* Weston Centre, 40 Berkeley Square, W1. *T:* 01-499 8931. *TA:* Garwest; London. *Club:* Carlton.
See also G. H. Weston.

WESTON, William Guy, CMG 1945; Governing Director, W. G. Weston Ltd; Director: Maritime International Consultancy Research Ltd; Common Brothers Shipping Services Ltd; *b* 30 Jan. 1907; *o s* of late W. H. Weston, Quorn Lodge, Melton Mowbray; *m* 1st, 1930, Joan (marriage dissolved, 1953), *d* of J. P. Chettle, RBA; three *s* one *d* ; 2nd, 1955, Evelyn Mary, *er d* of late T. G. Marriott. *Educ:* Melton Mowbray Grammar School; Manchester Univ.; St John's College, Cambridge. Lightfoot Scholar in Ecclesiastical History, Cambridge, 1929; Historical Tripos, 1929-30; Dep. Sec. Minister of Transport, 1946-48; General Manager Marine Dept Anglo-Saxon Petroleum Co., 1948-52. *Recreation:* painting. *Address:* Little Meadow House, Highmoor, Henley-on-Thames RG9 5DH. *T:* Nettlebed 316. *Clubs:* Reform, Travellers'.

WESTON, Rear-Adm. William Kenneth, CB 1956; OBE 1945; RN retired; *b* 8 November 1904; *s* of late William Weston; *m* 1934, Mary Ursula Shine; one *s* two *d*. *Educ:* RNC Osborne and Dartmouth. RNEC Keyham; RNC Greenwich. Served on staff of Flag Officer Destroyers, Pacific, 1945-46; Admiralty District Engineer Overseer, NW District, 1951-54; Staff of C-in-C Plymouth, 1954-58; retired, 1958. Court of Assistants of the Worshipful Company of Salters, 1959, Master, 1963. *Address:* Brackleyways, Hartley Wintney, Hants. *T:* Hartley Wintney 2546. *Club:* Naval and Military.

WESTROP, Brigadier Sidney A., CBE 1946; DSO 1917; MC 1915; FIMechE; Consulting Engineer; *b* 25 May 1895; *s* of A. W. Westrop; *m* 1918, Eileen M. Alton; one *s* three *d*. *Educ:* Bridgnorth Grammar School; Birmingham Univ. (BSc). Served European War, 1914-18 (despatches twice, MC, DSO); on active service in France, England, Iraq, India and Burmah, 1939-46 (despatches twice, CBE); Chief Engineer and Brig. 1943; was Director of Open Cut Coal Mining for India, 1944-45. *Recreations:* fishing, shooting. *Address:* Old Rectory, Brattleby, Lincoln, *T:* Scampton 221. *Club:* East India, Devonshire, Sports and Public Schools.

WESTWOOD, family name of **Baron Westwood.**

WESTWOOD, 2nd Baron, *cr* 1944, of Gosforth; **William Westwood;** Company Director; *b* 25 Dec. 1907; *s* of 1st Baron and Margaret Taylor Young (*d* 1916); *S* father 1953; *m* 1937, Marjorie, *o c* of Arthur Bonwick, Newcastle upon Tyne; two *s*. *Educ:* Glasgow; JP Newcastle upon Tyne, 1949. Dir of several private and public companies. Pres., Football League, and a Vice-Pres., Football Assoc., 1974-. FRSA; FCIS. *Recreations:* golf, football. *Heir: s* Hon. William Gavin Westwood [*b* 30 Jan. 1944; *m* 1969, Penelope, *er d* of Dr C. E. Shafto, Newcastle upon Tyne; two *s*]. *Address:* 12 Westfield Drive, Newcastle upon Tyne NE3 4XU. *T:* Newcastle upon Tyne 857020.

WESTWOOD, Earle Cathers; Agent-General for British Columbia in London, Oct. 1964-Oct. 1968; *b* 13 September 1909; *s* of Joseph Arthur Westwood and Mary Smith; *m* 1956, Sheila Blackwood Maxwell; one *d*. *Educ:* Nanaimo and Vancouver, BC, Canada. Pres. of Chamber of Commerce, Nanaimo, 1940; Chm. of Sch. Bd, 1942 and 1943; Mem. City Coun., 1944; Finance Chm. for five years; Mayor of City of Nanaimo, 1950, 1951, 1952, 1956. Provincial politics, 1956-63: Minister of Industrial Development, Trade and Commerce;

Minister of Recreation and Conservation; Minister of Commercial Transport. *Recreations:* golf, sailing, fishing. *Address:* 2540 Lynburn Crescent, Nanaimo, BC, Canada. *Clubs:* Royal Automobile; Hendon Golf; Nanaimo Yacht; Union (Victoria, BC).

WESTWOOD, Rt Rev. William John; *see* Edmonton, Bishop Suffragan of.

WETHERALL, Lt-Gen. Sir (Harry) Edward de Robillard, KBE 1946 (OBE 1937); CB 1941; DSO 1917; MC; *b* 22 Feb. 1889; 2nd *s* of late Major H. A. Wetherall, Coldstream Guards; *m* 1923, Vera G., *o d* of George de Lisle Bush, of Eastington Park, Stonehouse, Gloucestershire. Gloucester Regt; served European War, 1914-18 (wounded, despatches, MC, DSO); accelerated promotion, Captain to Major, 1927; GSO for Weapon Training, Scottish Command, 1930-34 (Brevet Lt-Col); commanded 1st Bn York and Lancaster Regiment, 1936-38; Commander 19th Infantry Brigade, 1938-40; Commander 11th African Div. in Abyssinia, 1941; GOC-in-C E Africa, 1941; GOC Ceylon, 1943-45; C-in-C Ceylon, 1945-46; retired pay, 1946. Colonel, The Gloucestershire Regiment, 1947-54. *Address:* Littlecourt, Bagborough, Taunton, Somerset. *Club:* Army and Navy.

WETHERALL, Rev. Canon Theodore Sumner; *b* 31 May 1910; *s* of late Rev. A. S. Wetherall and Mrs G. V. M. Wetherall (*née* Bennett-Powell); *m* 1939, Caroline, 4th *d* of Dr Charles Milne; one *s* three *d*. *Educ:* St Edward's School, Oxford; Oriel College, Oxford. Exhibitioner at Oriel College, 1929; 1st Class Classical Mods, 1931; BA (2nd Class Lit. Hum.), 1933. Preparatory Schoolmaster, Wellesley House, Broadstairs, 1933-35; MA 1936; Liddon Student, 1936; Cuddesdon College, 1936-37; Asst Curate, St John's, Greengates, Bradford, 1937-39; Fellow and Chaplain, Corpus Christi College, Oxford, 1939-47, Dean, 1940-45, Vice-Pres., 1947; Principal of St Chad's College, Durham, 1948-65. Vicar of St Edward the Confessor, Barnsley, 1965-69; Vicar of Huddersfield, 1969-76. Select Preacher to the Univ. of Oxford, 1945-47; Chaplain in the Univ. of Oxford to Bishop of Derby, 1940-47, Examining Chaplain to Bishop of Oxford, 1946-47, to Bishop of Durham, 1948-65, to Bishop of Bradford, 1949-55; to Bishop of Wakefield, 1969-76; Surrogate for Marriages, 1969-76; Rural Dean of Huddersfield, 1969-76. Hon. Canon: Durham, 1958-65, Wakefield, 1970-76; Hon. Canon Emeritus, Wakefield, 1976-. *Address:* 2 Lomas Cottages, Litton, Buxton, Derbyshire SK17 8QR. *T:* Tideswell 871042.

WETHERELL, Alan Marmaduke, PhD; FRS 1971; Senior Physicist, CERN (European Organisation for Nuclear Research), Geneva, since 1963; *b* 31 Dec. 1932; *s* of Marmaduke and Margaret Edna Wetherell; *m* 1957, Alison Morag Dunn (*d* 1974); one *s*. *Educ:* Univ. of Liverpool (BSc, PhD). Demonstrator in Physics, Univ. of Liverpool, 1956-57; Commonwealth Fund Fellow, California Inst. of Technology, Pasadena, Calif., 1957-59; Physicist, CERN, 1959-63. *Publications:* scientific papers in: Proc. Phys. Soc. (London), Proc. Roy. Soc. (London), Physical Review, Physical Review Letters, Physics Letters, Nuovo Cimento, Nuclear Physics, Yadernaya Fizika, Uspekhi Fizicheski Nauk. *Recreations:* skiing, water skiing. *Address:* 27 Chemin de la Vendee, 1213 Petit Lancy, Geneva, Switzerland. *T:* 022 928742.

WEYER, Deryk Vander, FIB, FBIM; Vice-Chairman: Barclays Bank Ltd, since 1977; Barclays Merchant Bank Ltd, since 1977; Director, Barclays Bank International Ltd, since 1977; *b* 21 Jan. 1925; *s* of Clement Weyer and Harriet Vander Weyer; *m* 1950, Margeurite (*née* Warden); one *s* one *d* . *Educ:* Bridlington Sch. FIB 1972; FBIM 1976. Joined Barclays Bank Ltd, 1941; Asst Manager, Liverpool, 1956; Man., Chester Br., 1961; Local Dir, Liverpool, 1965; Asst Gen. Man., 1968; Gen. Man., 1969; Sen. Gen. Man., 1973. Mem., Royal Commn on Distribn of Income and Wealth, 1977-. *Recreations:* painting, music. *Address:* 96 Old Church Street, Chelsea, SW3 6EP. *T:* 01-352 0312.

WEYMOUTH, Viscount; Alexander George Thynn; *b* 6 May 1932; *s* of Marquess of Bath, *qv* ; *m* 1969, Anna Gyarmathy; one *s* one *d*. *Educ:* Eton College; Christ Church, Oxford. Lieutenant in the Life Guards, 1951-52, and in Royal Wilts Yeomanry, 1953-57. Contested (Wessex Regionalist), Westbury, 1974. Permanent exhibn of murals (painted 1964-69, opened to public 1973), in private apartments at Longleat House. Record, I Play the Host, singing own compositions, 1974. *Publications:* (as Alexander Thynn) (before 1976 Alexander Thynne) The Carry-cot, 1972; Lord Weymouth's Murals, 1974; A Regionalist Manifesto, 1975; The King is Dead, 1976. *Heir: s* Hon. Ceawlin Henry Laszlo Thynn, *b* 6 June 1974. *Address:* Longleat, Warminster, Wilts. *T:* Maiden Bradley 300.

WHALE, Rev. John Seldon, MA (Oxon); DD (Glasgow); *b* 19 Dec. 1896; *s* of Rev. John Whale and Alice Emily Seldon; *m* Mary, *d* of Rev. H. C. Carter, MA; two *s* two *d* (and one *s* decd). *Educ:* Caterham School, Surrey; St Catherine's Society and Mansfield College, Oxford; 1st Class Hons Sch. of Mod. Hist. 1922; Magdalene College, Cambridge, 1933. Minister of Bowdon Downs Congregational Church, Manchester, 1925-29; Mackennal Professor of Ecclesiastical History, Mansfield College, Oxford, and Tutor in Modern History, St Catherine's, 1929-33; President of Cheshunt College, Cambridge, 1933-44; Headmaster of Mill Hill School, 1944-51; Visiting Professor of Christian Theology, Drew Univ., Madison, NJ, USA, 1951-53. Moderator of Free Church Federal Council, 1942-43; Select Preacher, Univ. of Cambridge, 1943, 1957; Warrack Lecturer, 1944; Russell Lecturer (Auburn and New York), 1936 and 1948; Alden Tuthill Lecturer, Chicago, 1952; Greene Lecturer, Andover, 1952; Currie Lecturer, Austin, Texas, 1953; Hill Lectr, St Olaf Coll., Minnesota, 1954; Visiting Lecturer, Univ. of Toronto, 1957; Danforth Scholar, USA, 1958; Sir D. Owen Evans Lectures, Aberystwyth, 1958. Visiting Professor, Univ. of Chicago, 1959; Senior Fellow of Council of Humanities, Princeton Univ., 1960. *Publications:* The Christian Answer to the Problem of Evil, 1936; What is a Living Church?, 1937; This Christian Faith, 1938; Facing the Facts, 1940; Christian Doctrine, 1941; The Protestant Tradition, 1955; Victor and Victim: the Christian doctrine of Redemption, 1960; Christian Reunion: historic divisions reconsidered, 1971; The Coming Dark Age, 1973 (Eng. trans. of Roberto Vacca's Il Medioevo Prossimo Venturo, 1972). *Address:* Wild Goose, Widecombe-in-the-Moor, Newton Abbot, S Devon. *T:* Widecombe-in-the-Moor 260.

WHALLEY, Prof. William Basil; Professor of Chemistry and Head of Department of Pharmaceutical Chemistry, School of Pharmacy, University of London, since 1961; *b* 17 Dec. 1916; *s* of William and Catherine Lucy Whalley; *m* 1945, Marie Agnes Alston; four *s* one *d*. *Educ:* St Edward's College, Liverpool; Liverpool University. BSc Hons 1938; PhD 1940; DSc 1952; FRIC 1950. MOS and ICI 1940-45. Lecturer, 1946-55, Sen. Lectr, 1955-57, Reader, 1957-61, in Organic Chemistry, at Liverpool University. *Publications:* contrib. on organic chemistry to several books: eg Heterocyclic Compounds, Vol. 7, Edited R. C. Elderfield, Wiley (New York); many pubns in Jl of Chem. Soc., Jl Amer. Chem. Soc., etc. *Recreations:* music and mountaineering. *Address:* 9 Peaks Hill, Purley, Surrey. *T:* 01-668 2244.

WHALLEY-TOOKER, Hyde Charnock, MA, LLM (Cantab); MA (Oxon); Emeritus Fellow of Downing College, Cambridge (Fellow, 1927-67, and Senior Tutor, 1931-47); University Lecturer in Law, 1931-67; *b* 1 Sept. 1900; *o s* of Edward Whalley-Tooker; *m* 1935, Frances, *er d* of late Thomas Halsted; one *d*. *Educ:* Eton; Trinity Hall, Cambridge; Balliol College, Oxford; Law Tripos Part I, Class I, 1921; Part II, Class I, 1922. *Address:* 5 Wilberforce Road, Cambridge. *T:* Cambridge 50073.

WHARNCLIFFE, 4th Earl of, *cr* 1876; **Alan James Montagu-Stuart-Wortley-Mackenzie;** Viscount Carlton, 1876; Baron Wharncliffe, 1826; National Service, RNVR, 1953; *b* 23 March 1935; *o s* of 3rd Earl and Lady Elfrida Wentworth Fitzwilliam, *d* of 7th Earl Fitzwilliam; *S* father 1953; *m* 1957, Aline, *d* of late R. F. D. Bruce, Wharncliffe Side, near Sheffield; two *d*. *Educ:* Eton. *Recreation:* shooting. *Heir: cousin,* Alan Ralph Montagu-Scott-Wortley [*b* 27 July 1927; *m* 1952, Virginia Anne, *d* of W. Martin Claybaugh; two *s* one *d*]. *Address:* Wharncliffe House, Wortley, Sheffield S30 4DG. *T:* Stocksbridge 2331.
   See also D. C. Mansel Lewis, Duke of Newcastle.

WHARTON, Barony *cr* 1544-5; in abeyance. *Co-heiresses:* Hon. Myrtle Olive Felix Robertson [*b* 20 Feb. 1934; *m* 1958, Henry MacLeod Robertson; three *s* one *d*]; Hon. Caroline Elizabeth Appleyard-List [*b* 28 Aug. 1935; *m* 1970, Commander Jonathon Cecil Appleyard-List, RN; one *d*].

WHARTON, Sir (George) Anthony, Kt 1977; CBE 1969 (MBE 1944); TD 1946; DL; solicitor; Under Sheriff of Nottinghamshire, since 1952; *b* 22 Sept. 1917; *s* of George Leslie Wharton and Beatrice Alice Wharton. *Educ:* Oakham; E Midlands Law Sch. (University Coll., Nottingham). Solicitor, 1947. Clerk of the Peace, Notts, 1956-76. Chairman: Notts T&AFA, 1956-68; E Midlands TA&VRA, 1968-; a Vice-Chm. Council, TA&VRAs, 1972-. Pres., RFU, 1977-78 (formerly Vice-Pres.). DL Notts 1958. *Recreations:* Volunteer Forces, Rugby football, young people. *Address:* The Old House, Edwalton, Notts. *T:* (office) Nottingham 42042. *Clubs:* Brooks's, Army and Navy, Naval and Military.

WHATELEY, Dame Leslie Violet Lucy Evelyn Mary, DBE 1946 (CBE 1943); TD 1951; *b* 28 Jan. 1899; *d* of late Ada Lilian Hutton and late Col Evelyn F. M. Wood, CB, DSO, OBE; *m* 1st, 1922, W. J. Balfour; one *s*; 2nd, 1939, H. Raymond Whateley, Squadron-Leader, RAFVR. *Educ:* Convents of Society of HCJ, St Leonards-on-Sea and Cavendish Square. Private Secretary up to marriage, and then Social Welfare Work, including District Nursing Associations and Village Institutes. Director of Auxiliary Territorial Service, 1943-46; Hon. Col 668 (bn) HAA Regt RA (TA), 1948-53. Director World Bureau of Girl Guides/Girl Scouts, 1951-64; Administrator of Voluntary Services, Queen Mary's Hosp., Roehampton, 1965-74. Chevalier Légion d'Honneur, 1945; Order of Merit (USA), 1946. *Publications:* As Thoughts Survive, 1949; Yesterday, Today and Tomorrow, 1974. *Recreations:* gardening, writing. *Address:* c/o Lloyds Bank, 6 Pall Mall, SW1.

WHATLEY, Prof. Frederick Robert, FRS 1975; Sherardian Professor of Botany, Oxford University, since 1971; Fellow of Magdalen College, Oxford, since 1971; *b* 26 Jan. 1924; *s* of Frederick Norman Whatley and Maud Louise (*née* Hare); *m* 1951, Jean Margaret Smith Bowie; two *d*. *Educ:* Bishop Wordsworth's Sch., Salisbury; (Scholar) Selwyn Coll., Cambridge University (BA, PhD). Benn W. Levy Student, Cambridge, 1947. Sen. Lectr. in Biochemistry, Univ. of Sydney, 1950-53; Asst Biochemist, Univ. of California at Berkeley, 1954-58; Associate Biochemist, 1959-64; Guggenheim Fellowship (Oxford and Stockholm), 1960; Prof. of Botany, King's Coll., London, 1964-71. *Publications:* numerous articles and reviews in scientific jls. *Address:* Botany School, South Parks Road, Oxford OX1 3RA. *T:* Oxford 53391.

WHEARE, Sir Kenneth Clinton, Kt 1966; CMG 1953; FBA 1952; DLitt (Oxon); Fellow, All Souls College, Oxford, 1944-57, and since 1973; Chancellor of Liverpool University, since 1972; *b* Warragul, Vict., Australia, 26 March 1907; *e s* of Eustace Leonard Wheare and Kathleen Frances Kinahan; *m* 1st, 1934, Helen Mary Allan; one *s*; 2nd, 1943, Joan Randell; two *s* two *d*. *Educ:* Scotch College, Melbourne; University of Melbourne; Oriel College, Oxford. BA Univ. of Melbourne, 1929, MA, 1949; Rhodes Scholar from Victoria, Australia, 1929; Oriel College, Oxford, 1929-32; 1st class Hons, School of Philosophy, Politics and Economics, 1932; BA Oxford, 1932, MA 1935, DLitt 1957; Lecturer, Christ Church, Oxford, 1934-39; Beit Lecturer in Colonial History, Oxford, 1935-44; Fellow of University Coll., Oxford, 1939-44, and Dean, 1942-45; Gladstone Prof. of Government and Public Administration, Univ. of Oxford, 1944-57; Fellow of Nuffield College, 1944-58; Rector, Exeter Coll., Oxford, 1956-72; Vice-Chancellor, 1958-64, 1966-72. Hon. Fellow of Nuffield, Oriel, University, Wolfson and Exeter Colls, Oxford. Member of Oxford City Council, 1940-57. Member of Hebdomadal Council, 1947-67; Constitutional Adviser to Nat. Convention of Newfoundland, 1946-47, and to Confs on Central African Federation, 1951, 1952, 1953; a Rhodes Trustee, 1948-77; Chm. Departmental Cttee on Children and the Cinema, 1947-50; Member: Franks Cttee on Administrative Tribunals and Inquiries, 1955-57; University Grants Committee, 1959-63; Governing Body, Sch. of Oriental and African Studies, Univ. of London, 1970-74; Nuffield Trustee, 1966-75; Pres. Brit. Acad., 1967-71. Rede Lectr, Cambridge, 1967; Hamlyn Lectr, 1973. Hon. Admiral, Herring Fishery Fleet, IOM, 1973-75. Hon. LHD Columbia, 1954; Hon. LittD Cambridge, 1969; Hon. LLD: Exeter, 1970; Liverpool, 1972; Manchester, 1975. Queen's Silver Jubilee Medal, 1977. *Publications:* The Statute of Westminster, 1931, 1933; The Statute of Westminster and Dominion Status, 1938 (5th edn 1953); Federal Government, 1946 (4th edn 1963); Abraham Lincoln and the United States, 1948; Modern Constitutions, 1951; Government by Committee, 1955; The Constitutional Structure of the Commonwealth, 1960; Legislatures, 1963; Maladministration and its Remedies, 1973; Walter Bagehot (lecture), 1974. *Recreations:* walking, cooking. *Address:* 55 Park Town, Oxford. *T:* Oxford 53775. *Clubs:* Vincent's (Oxford); Athenæum (Liverpool).

WHEATCROFT, Edward Lewis Elam, MA, FIMechE, FIEE; *b* 17 July 1896; *s* of late W. H. Wheatcroft, LLD, Cambridge; *m* Ethel Margaret, *d* of late Dr A. E. L. Wear, Harrogate; three *d*. *Educ:* Oundle; Cambridge. Switchboard Engineer with the British Thomson-Houston Co.; Calculation Engineer with the Commonwealth Power Corporation of Michigan; Professor of Electrical Engineering at Leeds University, 1926-40; Member of Council: of IEE, 1934-36, 1948-51, and 1954-57; of Hydromechanics Research Association, 1950. Freeman of City of London; Liveryman, Worshipful Co. of Makers of Playing Cards. *Publications:* Gaseous Electrical Conductors, 1938; papers in Phil. Mag., Proceedings of IEE, etc. *Recreation:* motoring. *Address:* 3 Regent Road, Surbiton, Surrey KT5 8NN.

WHEATCROFT, George Shorrock Ashcombe, JP; Professor of English Law, University of London, 1959-68, now Professor Emeritus; First Editor, British Tax Review, 1956-71, now Consulting Editor; first Editor of British Tax Encyclopedia, 1962-71, now Consulting Editor; Consulting Editor, Encyclopedia of Value Added Tax; Vice-Chairman, Hambro Life Assurance Ltd, since 1971; Chairman, G. S. A. & M. Wheatcroft (Advisory Services) Ltd; Adviser to HM Customs and Excise on Value Added Tax, 1971-72; *b* 29 Oct. 1905; *s* of Hubert Ashcombe Wheatcroft and Jane (*née* Eccles); *m* 1930, Mildred Susan, *d* of late Canon Walter Lock, DD, formerly Warden of Keble College, Oxford; two *s* one *d. Educ:* Rugby; New College, Oxford (MA). Qualified as Solicitor, 1929; partner in Corbin Greener and Cook, Solicitors, of 52 Bedford Row, London, 1930-51; Master of the Supreme Court (Chancery Division), 1951-59. Served as an officer in RASC, 1940-45; released in 1945 with hon. rank of Lt-Col (despatches twice). Mem., Payne Cttee on enforcement of civil debts. Past President British Chess Federation; Fellow, Inst. of Taxation. JP County of London, 1955. Consulting Editor, Hambro Tax Guide, 1972-. Hon. Fellow, LSE, 1976. *Publications:* The Taxation of Gifts and Settlements, 1953 (3rd edn 1958); The Law of Income Tax, Surtax and Profits Tax, 1962; Estate and Gift Taxation, 1965; Capital Gains Tax, 1965; Wheatcroft on Capital Gains Taxes (with A. E. W. Park), 1967; Corporation Tax (with J. E. Talbot), 1968; Sweet & Maxwell's Guide to the Estate Duty Statutes, 1969 (2nd edn 1972); Whiteman and Wheatcroft on Income Tax and Surtax, 1971; (with G. D. Hewson) Capital Transfer Tax, 1975; titles Discovery, Execution, Judgments and Orders and Practice and Procedure in Halsbury's Laws of England (3rd edn); articles on taxation and legal procedure in periodicals. *Recreations:* golf, bridge, chess (represented England at Stockholm in 1937). *Address:* Blewburton Hall, Aston Upthorpe, Didcot, Oxon. *Club:* Reform.

WHEATCROFT, Stephen Frederick, OBE 1974; Member, since 1972 and Director of Subsidiaries, since 1977, British Airways Board; Chairman: International Aeradio Ltd; British Airways Helicopter Ltd; British Airways Associated Companies Ltd; *b* 11 Sept. 1921; *s* of late Percy and Fanny Wheatcroft; *m* 1st, 1943, Joy (*d* 1974), *d* of late Cecil Reed; two *s* one *d* ; 2nd, 1974, Alison, *d* of late Arnold Dessau; one *s . Educ:* Latymer Sch., N9; London Sch. of Economics. BSc(Econ) 1942. Served War, Pilot in Fleet Air Arm, 1942-45. Commercial Planning Manager, BEA, 1946-53; Simon Research Fellow, Manchester Univ. 1953-55; private practice as Aviation Consultant, 1956-72; retained as Economic Adviser to BEA; Gp Planning Dir, British Airways, 1972-74; Commns for Govts of: Canada, India, W Indies, E African Community, Afghanistan; Consultant to World Bank; Assessor to Edwards Cttee on British Air Transport in the Seventies. Mem., EDC for Exports; Governor, London Sch. of Economics. FRAeS, FCIT. *Publications:* Economics of European Air Transport, 1956; Airline Competition in Canada, 1958; Air Transport Policy, 1966; articles in professional jls. *Recreations:* travel. *Address:* 20 Mallord Street, SW3. *T:* 01-351 1511. *Club:* Reform.

WHEATLEY, family name of **Baron Wheatley**.

WHEATLEY, Baron *cr* 1970 (Life Peer), of Shettleston, Glasgow; **Rt. Hon. Lord Justice-Clerk; John Wheatley**, PC 1947; one of the Senators of the College of Justice in Scotland since 1954; Lord Justice-Clerk since 1972; *b* 17 Jan. 1908; *s* of Patrick Wheatley and Janet Murphy; *m* 1935, Agnes Nichol; four *s* one *d. Educ:* St Aloysius Coll., Glasgow; Mount St Mary's Coll., Chesterfield; Glasgow Univ. MA 1928; LLB 1930; called to Scottish Bar, 1932; Advocate-Depute, 1945-47. War of 1939-45, RA (Field) and later with Judge Advocate-General's Branch; Chm. Scottish Nurses' Salaries Cttee, 1945-47; Chm. Milk Enquiry in Scotland, 1946-47; Chm., Cttee on Teaching Profession (Scotland), 1961-63; Mem., Royal Commn on Penal Reform (England and Wales), 1964-66; Chairman: Exec. Cttee Royal Scottish Soc. for Prevention of Cruelty to Children; Royal Commn on Local Govt in Scotland, 1966-69; conducted enquiry into crowd safety at sports grounds, 1971-72. Solicitor-General for Scotland, March-Oct. 1947; QC (Scotland) 1947; Lord Advocate, 1947-51; MP (Lab) East Edinburgh, 1947-54. Hon. LLD Glasgow, 1963; DUniv Stirling, 1976; Hon. FEIS. *Recreation:* golf. *Address:* 3 Greenhill Gardens, Edinburgh EH10 4BN. *T:* 031-447 1671.
    See also T. Dalyell.

WHEATLEY, Sir Andrew; *see* Wheatley, Sir G. A.

WHEATLEY, Dennis Yates, Bronze Star (Mil., US), 1945; FRSA; FRSL; Novelist, Inventor (with J. G. Links) of Crime Dossier Murder Fiction; *b* 8 January 1897; *o s* of late Albert David Wheatley and Florence, Lady Newton; *m* 1st, 1923,

Nancy Madelaine Leslie Robinson; one *s* ; 2nd, 1931, Joan Gwendoline, *d* of late Hon. Louis Johnstone. *Educ:* HMS Worcester; Germany. Entered his father's Mayfair wine business, 1914; Commissioned RFA (T), Sept. 1914 (City of London Brigade); President, Old Comrades Association, 1961; transferred to 36th (Ulster) Division, 1917; invalided from the Service, 1919; re-entered his father's business; became sole owner, 1926; bought and dispersed many famous cellars; director of numerous companies; sold business, 1931; commenced writing, 1932. Toured England as member of Sir John Anderson's panel of voluntary speakers on National Service, 1939. Recommissioned in RAFVR Dec. 1941 to fill specially created post; only non-regular officer to be commissioned direct to Joint Planning Staff; worked for following three years in Offices of the War Cabinet; Wing Comdr, 1944. Invented war games, Invasion, 1938, Blockade, 1939, Alibi, 1953. Livery of Vintners' Company, 1918, and of Distillers' Company, 1922. Pres. New Forest Agricultural Show, 1968. *Publications:* The Forbidden Territory (filmed); Such Power is Dangerous; Old Rowley (a Private Life of Charles II), 1933; Black August; The Fabulous Valley, 1934; The Devil Rides Out (filmed); The Eunuch of Stamboul (filmed), 1935; They Found Atlantis; Murder Off Miami (with J. G. Links); Contraband, 1936; The Secret War; Who Killed Robert Prentice (with J. G. Links); Red Eagle (story of the Russian Revolution), 1937; Uncharted Seas (filmed as The Lost Continent); The Malinsay Massacre (with J. G. Links); The Golden Spaniard, 1938; The Quest of Julian Day; Herewith the Clues! (with J. G. Links); Sixty Days to Live; Those Modern Musketeers, 1939; Three Inquisitive People; The Scarlet Impostor; Faked Passports; The Black Baroness, 1940; Strange Conflict; The Sword of Fate; Total War, 1941; V for Vengeance; Mediterranean Nights (Short Stories), 1942; Gunmen, Gallants and Ghosts (Short Stories), 1943; The Man Who Missed the War, 1945; Codeword Golden Fleece; Come into my Parlour, 1946; The Launching of Roger Brook, 1947; The Shadow of Tyburn Tree; The Haunting of Toby Jugg, 1948; The Rising Storm; The Seven Ages of Justerini (privately printed for bi-centenary of firm of Justerini & Brooks), 1949; The Second Seal, 1950; The Man Who Killed the King, 1951; Star of Ill Omen, 1952; To the Devil a Daughter (filmed); Curtain of Fear, 1953; The Island where Time Stands Still, 1954; The Dark Secret of Josephine, 1955; The Ka of Gifford Hillary, 1956; The Prisoner in the Mask, 1957; Traitors' Gate, 1958; Stranger than Fiction; The Rape of Venice, 1959; The Satanist, 1960; Saturdays with Bricks, 1960; A Vendetta in Spain, 1961; Mayhem in Greece, 1962; The Sultan's Daughter, 1963; Bill for the Use of a Body, 1964; They Used Dark Forces, 1964; Dangerous Inheritance, 1965; The Wanton Princess, 1966; Unholy Crusade, 1967; The White Witch of the South Seas, 1968; Evil in a Mask, 1969; Gateway to Hell, 1970; The Ravishing of Lady Mary Ware, 1971; The Devil and all his Works, 1971; The Strange Story of Linda Lee, 1972; The Irish Witch, 1973; (ed) Dennis Wheatley's Library of the Occult, 1974; Desperate Measures, 1974; The Time Has Come (memoirs), vol. 1, 1977, vol. II, 1978. Writings published in 31 languages. *Recreations:* collecting books, stamps, coins, Georgian furniture and Oriental rugs; travel, building. *Address:* 60 Cadogan Square, SW1. *Clubs:* White's, Pratt's, Saintsbury, Paternosters.

WHEATLEY, Derek Peter Francis; Legal Adviser to Lloyds Bank; Member, Commercial Court Committee; Barrister-at-Law; *b* 18 Dec. 1925; 3rd *s* of late Edward Pearse Wheatley, company director, and Gladys Wheatley; *m* 1955, Elizabeth Pamela, *d* of John and Gertrude Reynolds; two *s* one *d. Educ:* The Leys Sch., Cambridge; University Coll., Oxford (MA). Served War of 1939-45, Army, 1944-47: (short univ. course, Oxford, 1944); commissioned into 8th King's Royal Irish Hussars, 1945, Lieut. University Coll., Oxford, 1947-49; called to the Bar, Middle Temple, 1951; Mem., Senate of Inns of Court and the Bar, 1975; Western Circuit and Devon Sessions. Deputy Coroner: to the Royal Household, 1959-64; for London, 1959-64; for Middlesex, 1960-64; Asst Dep.-Coroner for Surrey and for Essex, 1957-64; Recorder of the Crown Court, 1972-74. *Recreation:* sailing. *Address:* 6 Pump Court, Temple, EC4Y 7AR. *T:* 01-353 7242; Cheriton, Berwyn Road, Richmond, Surrey. *T:* 01-876 2182. *Club:* Bar Yacht.

WHEATLEY, Sir (George) Andrew, Kt 1967; CBE 1960; MA; BCL; Clerk of the Peace and Clerk of Hampshire County Council, 1946-67; *b* 1908; *s* of late Robert Albert Wheatley; *m* 1937, Mary Vera Hunt; three *s* two *d. Educ:* Rugby and Exeter Coll., Oxford. Asst Solicitor: Pembrokeshire CC, 1932-34; East Suffolk CC, 1934-36; N Riding, Yorks, 1936-39; Dep. Clerk of the Peace and Dep. Clerk of Cumberland CC, 1939-42; Clerk of the Peace and Clerk of the Cumberland CC, 1942-46. Hon. Sec., Society of Clerks of the Peace of Counties and of Clerks of County Councils, 1961; former Member: Local Government

Advisory Panel, Dept of Technical Co-operation; Home Office Adv. Council on Child Care; Central Training Council in Child Care; Min. of Housing and Local Govt Departmental Cttee on Management in Local Govt; Royal Commn on Assizes and Quarter Sessions; Mem., English Local Govt Boundary Commn, 1971-. DL Hants, 1967-70. *Clubs:* Royal Lymington Yacht, Royal Solent Yacht.

WHEATLEY, Maj.-Gen. Mervyn Savile, CB 1953; CBE 1945; CEng, FIEE; retired 1957; *b* 18 April 1900; *s* of late Major S. G. Wheatley and Mrs Savile Wheatley, Parkstone, Dorset; *m* 1936, Iris Veronica Margaret Kenyon; one *d* (by previous marriage). *Educ:* Blundell's; RMC Sandhurst. 2nd Lt Dorset Regt, 1918; Lt Royal Signals, 1925, Adjutant, Captain 1926-29; Instructor, RMA, Woolwich, 1929-33; DAAG War Office (Major), 1939-40; Commander, Royal Signals, 1st Armoured Division (Lieutenant-Colonel), 1940-41; Chief Signal Officer, SE Comd (Colonel), 1941-42; GSO1 Home Forces and 21 Army Group (Colonel), 1942-43; Chief Signal Officer, 13 Corps, Italy (Brig.), 1943-44; DD Signals, War Office, 1944-46; Comdr STC, 1946-47; Comdr Canal South District, 1947-49; Dep. Comdr Mid West District, 1949-51; Maj.-Gen. 1951; Chief Signal Officer, MELF, 1951-54; Signal Officer-in-Chief, War Office, 1954-57. Col Comdt Royal Signals, 1957-62. Hon. Col 41st Signal Regt (Princess Louise's Kensington Regt TA), 1957-62. *Recreations:* tennis, golf, sailing. *Address:* 5 Heathfield Court, Fleet, Hants. *Club:* Army and Navy.

WHEATLEY, Maj.-Gen. Percival Ross, DSO 1943; late RAMC, retired; Surgeon, P&O Lines Ltd, 1969-77; *b* Westbury, Wilts, 4 May 1909; *s* of late Rev. Percival Wheatley, Congregational Minister, and late Margaret Lettice Wheatley (*née* Wallis); *m* 1939, Dorothy Joan Fellows (*née* Brock); one *s*. *Educ:* St Dunstan's Coll., Catford; Guy's Hosp. Med. School. MB, BS (London), MRCS, LRCP, 1933; FRCS 1940. Commissioned Lieut RAMC, 1939; BEF as Surgical Specialist, Sept. 1939; 2nd in comd 16 Para. Field Ambulance, 1942, comdg, 1943; N Africa, 1942; Sicily and Italy, 1943; ADMS, 2nd Indian Airborne Div., 1944-46; Surgical Specialist, 1946-60: Catterick, Hamburg, Singapore, Japan, Millbank; seconded to Ghana Army, Surgical Specialist, 1960-61; Consultant Surgeon: FARELF, 1963-66; BAOR, 1966-67; Dir of Army Surgery and Consulting Surgeon to the Army, 1967-69. FRSocMed; Senior Fellow: Brit. Orthopædic Assoc.; Assoc. of Surgeons of Great Britain and Ireland. QHS 1967-69. *Publication:* contrib. to Basic Surgery. *Recreation:* sailing. *Address:* Sherwood, High Park Avenue, East Horsley, Surrey. *T:* East Horsley 2151. *Club:* Army and Navy.

WHEATON, Rev. Canon David Harry; Principal, Oak Hill Theological College, since 1971; *b* 2 June 1930; *s* of Harry Wheaton, MBE, and Kathleen Mary (*née* Frost); *m* 1956, Helen Joy Forrer; one *s* two *d*. *Educ:* Abingdon Sch.; St John's Coll., Oxford (Exhibnr; MA); London Univ. (BD (London Bible Coll.)); Oak Hill Theol Coll. NCO, Wiltshire Regt, 1948-49. Deacon, 1959; priest, 1960; Tutor, Oak Hill Coll., 1954-62; Rector of Ludgershall, Bucks, 1962-66; Vicar of St Paul, Onslow Square, S Kensington, 1966-71; Chaplain, Brompton Chest Hosp., 1969-71. Hon. Canon, Cathedral and Abbey Church of St Alban, 1976. *Publications:* (contrib.) Baker's Dictionary of Theology, 1960; (contrib.) New Bible Dictionary, 1962; (contrib.) New Bible Commentary (rev.), 1970. *Recreations:* walking, carpentry and do-it-yourself. *Address:* Oak Hill College, Southgate, N14 4PS. *T:* 01-449 0467.

WHEELDON, Edward Christian, CBE 1959; *b* 12 May 1907; *s* of Edward Wheeldon, Manchester; *m* 1935, Alice Willan; one *s*. *Educ:* Openshaw Technical College; Manchester College of Technology. Served apprenticeship at Metropolitan-Vickers Ltd, Manchester, 1923-28; Process Engineer, 1928-34; Group Production Engineer, Parkinson and Cowan, 1934-38; joined Westland Aircraft Ltd as Planning Engineer, 1938; Works Supt, 1939; Works Manager, 1943; Works Dir 1944; Dep. Man. Dir, 1946; Man. Dir, 1950; Dep. Chm. and Man. Dir, 1960; Dep. Chm. and Chief Executive, 1965; Chm., 1968-70. Pres., Soc. of British Aerospace Cos Ltd, 1964-65; Treasurer, 1968-72. FIProdE; FRAeS; FInstAT. *Recreations:* golf, Association football. *Address:* 88 Ilchester Road, Yeovil, Somerset. *T:* Yeovil 24799. *Clubs:* Golf (Yeovil); Golf (Sherborne).

WHEELDON, Rt. Rev. Philip William, OBE 1946; *b* 20 May 1913; *e s* of late Alfred Leonard Wheeldon and late Margaret Proctor Wheeldon (*née* Smith); *m* 1966, Margaret Redfearn. *Educ:* Clifton Coll., Bristol; Downing Coll., Cambridge; Westcott House Theological Coll. BA 1935, MA 1942. Deacon, 1937; Priest, 1938; Farnham Parish Church, Dio. Guildford, 1937-39; Chaplain to the Forces, 1939-46; Chaplain, 1st Bn Coldstream Guards, 1939-42; Senior Chaplain, 79th Armoured

Div., 1942-43; Dep. Asst Chaplain-Gen. 12th Corps, 1943-45; 8th Corps, 1945-46; Hon. Chaplain to the Forces, 1946-; Domestic Chaplain to Archbishop of York, 1946-49, Hon. Chaplain, 1950-54; General Sec., CACTM, 1949-54; Prebendary of Wedmore II in Wells Cathedral, 1952-54; Suffragan Bishop of Whitby, 1954-61; Bishop of Kimberley and Kuruman, 1961-65; resigned, 1965; an Asst Bishop, Dio. Worcester, 1965-68; Bishop of Kimberley and Kuruman, 1968-76. Hon. Asst Bishop, Diocese of Worcester, 1976-. *Recreations:* music, sport, gardening. *Address:* Westgate Close, Clifton, Brighouse, West Yorks HD6 4HJ. *Clubs:* Brooks's, Royal Automobile.

WHEELER, Lt-Comdr Ernest Richard, CVO 1969 (MVO 1965); MBE 1943; RN retd; Clerk of the Council and Keeper of Records, Duchy of Lancaster, since 1970; *b* 21 July 1917; *s* of late Rev. Harold W. Wheeler, Burton Bradstock and Weston Turville, and Margaret Laura Wheeler; *m* 1st, 1939, Yvonne Burns (*d* 1973); one *d*; 2nd, 1974, Auriel Clifford. *Educ:* Marlborough Coll.; HMS Frobisher. Paymaster Cadet, RN, 1935; Lieut 1939; served: HM Ships Devonshire, Emerald, Office of C-in-C Med., 1940-42; Sec. to Chief of Staff, C-in-C Med., 1942-43; HMS Daedalus and Admty, 1944-47; Lt-Comdr 1947; retd (invalided), 1949. Asst Bursar, Epsom Coll., 1949-52; Chief Clerk, Duchy of Lancaster, 1952-70. *Address:* Duchy of Lancaster Office, WC2.

WHEELER, Sir Frederick (Henry), Kt 1967; CBE 1962 (OBE 1952); Secretary to the Treasury, Commonwealth of Australia, since 1971; *b* 9 Jan. 1914; *s* of late A. H. Wheeler; *m* 1939, Peggy Hilda (*d* 1975), *d* of Basil P. Bell; one *s* two *d*. *Educ:* Scotch College; Melbourne University (BCom). State Savings Bank of Victoria, 1929-39; Treasury: Research Officer, 1939; Economist, 1944; Asst Sec., 1946; First Asst Sec., 1949-52; Treasurer Comptroller, ILO, Geneva, 1952-60; Chm., Commonwealth Public Service Bd, Canberra, 1961-71. Member: Aust. delegn to various British Commonwealth Finance Ministers' Conferences; Austr. Delegn Bretton Woods Monetary Conf.; UN Civil Service Adv. Bd, 1969-72. *Address:* 9 Charlotte Street, Red Hill, ACT 2603, Australia. *T:* 959 888. *Clubs:* (Pres. 1966-69) Commonwealth (Canberra); Royal Canberra Golf.

WHEELER, Geoffrey, CB 1952; *b* 22 Nov. 1909; *s* of late A. E. Wheeler; *m* 1937, Dorothy Mary Wallis; one *s* one *d*. *Educ:* Clay Cross School, Derbyshire; St John's Coll., Cambridge (Scholar). First Class Part I Historical Tripos, 1930; First Class Part II Historical Tripos, 1931. Entered Civil Service, 1932, and appointed to Board of Customs and Excise; Private Sec. to Sir Evelyn Murray, 1936; Principal, 1937; Assistant Secretary, 1943; Under-Secretary (Ministry of Defence), 1948; Under-Secretary: Min. of Aviation, 1964-67; Min. of Technology (Principal Estabt Officer), 1967-70; Min. of Aviation Supply, 1970-71; Asst Under Sec. of State (Personnel), Procurement Exec., MoD, 1971-72; Asst Dir, Civil Service Selection Bd, 1972-76. Pres., Groupe Statut EEC, 1977. Chm., London Derbyshire Soc., 1973-. *Recreations:* music; amateur theatre. *Address:* 63 Woodcote Valley Road, Purley, Surrey. *T:* 01-660 2858.

WHEELER, Lt-Col Geoffrey Edleston, CIE 1943; CBE 1948; Hon. MA University of Durham, 1955; Director of Central Asian Research Centre, 1953-68; *b* 22 June 1897; *s* of late Capt. Owen Wheeler, Leicestershire Regiment; *m* 1927, Irena Nicolaevna Boulatoff (*d* 1973); one *s*. *Educ:* Eastbourne Coll. Commissioned Queen's Regt 1915; served in France, 1915-17; transferred to Indian Army, 1918, 6th Gurkha Rifles; various Intelligence appointments in Turkey, Malta, and Palestine to 1925; Military Attaché, Meshed, 1926; Intelligence duties in Iraq, 1928-31; 7th Rajput Regt to 1936; General Staff, Army HQ, India, 1936-41; Director, Publications Division, Govt of India, 1941-46; Counsellor, British Embassy, Teheran, 1946-50. Sir Percy Sykes Memorial Medal, RCAS, 1967. *Publications:* Racial Problems in Soviet Muslim Asia; The Modern History of Soviet Central Asia; The Peoples of Soviet Central Asia. *Address:* 5 Sandown Lodge, Avenue Road, Epsom, Surrey.

WHEELER, Rt. Rev. Monsignor Gordon; *see* Wheeler, W. G.

WHEELER, Harry Anthony, OBE 1973; RSA, FRIBA; Senior Partner, Wheeler & Sproson, Architects, Engineers, Town Planners, Kirkcaldy and Edinburgh, since 1954; *b* 7 Nov. 1919; *s* of Herbert George Wheeler and Laura Emma Groom; *m* 1944, Dorothy Jean Campbell; one *d*. *Educ:* Stranraer High Sch.; Royal Technical Coll., Glasgow; Glasgow School of Art; Univ. of Strathclyde (BArch). RIBA, DipTP, MRTPI. Glasgow Sch. of Architecture, 1937-48 (war service, Royal Artillery, 1939-46); John Keppie Scholar and Sir Rowand Anderson Studentship, 1948; RIBA Grissell Gold Medallist, 1948, and Neale Bursar, 1949. Assistant: to City Architect, Oxford, 1948; to Sir Herbert

Baker & Scott, London, 1949; Sen. Architect, Glenrothes New Town, 1949-51; Sen. Lectr, Dundee Sch. of Arch., 1952-58; commenced private practice in Fife, 1952. Principal works include: Woodside Shopping Centre and St Columba's Parish Church, Glenrothes; Reconstruction of Giles Pittenweem; Redevelopment of Dysart and of Old Buckhaven; Town Centre Renewal, Grangemouth; Students' Union, Univ. of St Andrews; Extension to Edinburgh Coll. of Art; St Peter's Episcopal Ch., Kirkcaldy. Member: Royal Fine Art Commn for Scotland; Scottish Housing Adv. Cttee; Trustee, Scottish Civic Trust; Pres., RIAS, 1973-75; Vice-Pres., RIBA, 1973-75. RSA 1975 (ARSA 1963). 13 Saltire Soc. Awards for Housing and Reconstruction; 4 Civic Trust Awards. *Publications:* articles on civic design and housing in technical jls. *Recreations:* making gardens, sketching and water colours, fishing, music and drama. *Address:* Hawthornbank House, Dean Village, Edinburgh EH4 3BH. *T:* 031-225 2334. *Clubs:* Caledonian, Scottish Arts (Edinburgh).

WHEELER, Air Chief Marshal Sir (Henry) Neil (George), GCB 1975 (KCB 1969; CB 1967); CBE 1957 (OBE 1949); DSO 1943; DFC 1941 (Bar 1943); AFC 1954; Director: Rolls-Royce Ltd; Flight Refuelling Ltd; *b* 8 July 1917; *s* of T. H. Wheeler, South African Police; *m* 1942, Elizabeth, *d* of late W. H. Weightman, CMG; two *s* one *d*. *Educ:* St Helen's College, Southsea, Hants. Entered Royal Air Force College, Cranwell, 1935; Bomber Comd, 1937-40; Fighter and Coastal Comds, 1940-45; RAF and US Army Staff Colls, 1943-44; Cabinet Office, 1944-45; Directing Staff, RAF Staff Coll., 1945-46; FEAF, 1947-49; Directing Staff, JSSC, 1949-51; Bomber Comd, 1951-53; Air Min., 1953-57. Asst Comdt, RAF Coll., 1957-59; OC, RAF Laarbruch, 1959-60; IDC, 1961; Min. of Defence, 1961-63; Senior Air Staff Officer, HQ, RAF Germany (2nd TAF), Sept. 1963-66; Asst Chief of Defence Staff (Operational Requirements), MoD, 1966-67; Deputy Chief of Defence Staff, 1967-68; Commander, FEAF, 1969-70; Air Mem. for Supply and Organisation, MoD, 1970-73; Controller, Aircraft, MoD Procurement Exec., 1973-75. ADC to the Queen, 1957-61. FRAeS; FBIM. *Address:* Boundary Hall, Cooksbridge, Lewes, East Sussex. *Clubs:* Hurlingham, Royal Air Force, Flyfishers'. *See also Maj.-Gen. T. N. S. Wheeler.*

WHEELER, Sir John (Hieron), 3rd Bt *cr* 1920; formerly Chairman, Raithby, Lawrence & Co. Ltd, retired 1973; *b* 22 July 1905; 2nd *s* of Sir Arthur Wheeler, 1st Bt; *S* brother, Sir Arthur (Frederick Pullman) Wheeler, 1964; *m* 1929, Gwendolen Alice (*née* Oram); two *s*. *Educ:* Charterhouse. Engaged in Print. Served War of 1939-45, Trooper, RTR, 1941-45. After the war, returned to printing. *Recreations:* whittling, dry stone walling. *Heir: s* John Frederick Wheeler [*b* 3 May 1933; *m* 1963, Barbara Mary, *d* of Raymond Flint, Leicester; two *s* one *d*]. *Address:* 39 Morland Avenue, Leicester LE2 2PF. *Club:* Wig and Pen.

WHEELER, Hon. Sir Kenneth (Henry), Kt 1976; Speaker of the Victorian Parliament, Australia, since 1973; *b* 7 Sept. 1912; *s* of William Henry Wheeler and Alma Nellie Wheeler; *m* 1934, Hazel Jean Collins; one *s* one *d*. *Educ:* Mernda State Sch., Vic. Grazier and retail dairyman for 19 years. Municipal Councillor, 1950-59; Mayor, City of Coburg, Vic., 1955-56; elected to Parliament of Victoria for Essendon, 1958. *Recreations:* golf, football, exhibition of horses. *Address:* 13 Downes Street, Strathmore, Vic 3041, Australia. *T:* 379-8281. *Clubs:* Essendon; Gisborne Golf.

WHEELER, Michael Mortimer, QC 1961; *b* Westminster, 8 Jan. 1915; *o s* of late Sir Mortimer Wheeler, CH, CIE, MC, TD, and late Tessa Verney Wheeler, FSA; *m* 1939, Sheila, *e d* of late M. S. Mayou, FRCS; two *d*. *Educ:* Dragon School, Oxford; Rugby School; Christ Church, Oxford. Barrister: Gray's Inn, 1938; Lincoln's Inn, 1946 (Bencher 1967). Served throughout War of 1939-45, with RA (TA) in UK and Italy (Lt-Col 1945; despatches); TD 1961. *Address:* 114 Hallam Street, W1. *T:* 01-580 7284. *Clubs:* Garrick, MCC.

WHEELER, Sir Neil; *see* Wheeler, Sir H. N. G.

WHEELER, Maj.-Gen. (retd) Richard Henry Littleton, CB 1960; CBE 1953; Maj.-Gen. RA, HQ, Northern Army Group (Northag), 1958-61; *b* 2 Nov. 1906; *s* of Maj. Henry Littleton Wheeler, CB, DSO, and Vera Gillum Webb; *m* 1941, Iris Letitia Hope; one *d*. *Educ:* Uppingham; RMA, Woolwich. 2nd Lt RA, 1926. Served War of 1939-45, 50th Division. Lt-Col 1942; Brigadier 1950; Temp. Maj.-Gen. 1958; Maj.-Gen. 1959. Col Comdt RA, 1963-71. *Recreations:* riding, music. *Address:* Manor Farm, Knighton, Sherborne, Dorset DT9 6QU. *Club:* Army and Navy.

WHEELER, Maj.-Gen. Thomas Norman Samuel, CB 1967; CBE 1964 (OBE 1958); Deputy Managing Director, Associated Independent Stores Ltd, since 1976; *b* 16 June 1915; *e s* of late Thomas Henry Wheeler, S African Police; *m* 1939, Helen Clifford, *y d* of F. H. E. Webber, Emsworth, Hants; one *s* one *d*. *Educ:* South Africa; St Helen's College, Southsea; RMC Sandhurst. Commissioned Royal Ulster Rifles, 1935; Palestine Rebellion, 1937-39 (despatches). Served War of 1939-45 (despatches twice): Bde Major, 38 Irish Bde, 1941-42; MEF, 1942-43; British Military Mission to Albania, 1943-44; 2nd Bn Royal Ulster Rifles, 1944-45. AA & QMG 6th Airborne Div., 1945-46; Airborne Establishment, 1946-47; Mil. Asst to Adj.-Gen. to the Forces, 1949-50; UK Services Liaison Staff, Australia, 1951-52; GSO1 and Col GS, HQ Northern Army Group and HQ, BAOR, 1954-57; comd 1st Bn Royal Ulster Rifles Cyprus Rebellion, 1958-59 (despatches); comd 39 Inf. Bde Group, N Ireland, 1960-62; Chief of Staff 1st (British) Corps, BAOR, 1962-63; General Officer Commanding Second Division, 1964-66; Chief of Staff, Contingencies Planning, SHAPE, 1966-69; Chief of Staff, HQ, BAOR, 1969-71; retired, 1971. Dir and Sec., Independent Stores Assoc., 1971-76. *Recreations:* travel, tennis, water ski-ing. *Address:* Glebe House, Liston, Sudbury, Suffolk. *Clubs:* Army and Navy, Airborne. *See also Sir Neil Wheeler.*

WHEELER, Rt. Rev. (William) Gordon; *see* Leeds, Bishop of, (RC).

WHEELER, William Henry, CMG 1959; PhD (London); Managing Director since 1961, and Deputy Chairman since 1968, Urquhart Engineering Co. Ltd, Perivale and Bristol; Deputy Chairman, Steam & Combustion Engineering Ltd; Chairman: Mark Laboratories Ltd; Process Combustion Corporation (USA); Urquhart Engineering GmbH; *b* Petersfield, Hants, 5 March 1907; *s* of John William and Ellen Wheeler; *m* 1937, Mary Inkpen; no *c*. *Educ:* St Catharine's Coll., Cambridge (BA); Imperial Coll. of Science (DIC). Beit Memorial Research Fellow, Imperial Coll., 1931. Man. British Automatic Refrigerators, London, 1935; Government Scientific Service, 1937; Dir, Guided Weapons Research & Development, 1950; Head of UK Ministry of Supply Staff and Scientific Adviser to UK High Commission, Australia, 1955; Director of Explosives Research, Waltham Abbey, 1959. *Publications:* papers on Combustion and Detonation in Proc. and Trans. Royal Society, and on Rocket Propellants in Nature, Proc. of Inst. of Fuel and Instn of Chemical Engineers; papers on the Mechanism of Cavitation Erosion for DSIR and American Soc. of Mechanical Engineers. *Recreation:* private research laboratory. *Address:* Mark House, Ashmead Lane, Denham, Bucks.

WHEEN, Rear-Adm. Charles Kerr Thorneycroft, CB 1966; Director, Cement Makers Federation, since 1967; *b* 28 Sept. 1912; *s* of late F. T. Wheen, Holmbury, Chislehurst, Kent; *m* 1940, Veryan Rosamond, *d* of late William Acworth, Chobham; three *s* one *d*. *Educ:* RN College, Dartmouth. Entered RN as Cadet, 1926. Served War of 1939-45: China, The Nore, Admiralty, Normandy Landings, East Indies. Naval Attaché, Beirut, Amman and Addis Ababa, 1958-60; Director of Officers' Appointments (S), Admiralty, 1960-63; Flag Officer Admiralty Interview Board, 1964-66. Capt. 1956; Rear-Adm. 1964; retd 1966. Chm., Bd of Governors, Gordon Boys School, 1971-. *Recreation:* golf. *Address:* Donnystone, Chobham, Surrey. *T:* Chobham 8118. *Clubs:* Army and Navy; MCC.

WHELAN, Air Cdre James Roger, CBE 1968; DSO 1944; DFC 1940 (Bar 1943); RAF retired; with Echo & Post Ltd, Hemel Hempstead, since 1969; *b* Saskatoon, Sask, Canada, 29 April 1914; *s* of James P. Whelan; *m* 1946, Irene, *d* of late P. Rennie, Bathurst, NB, Canada; two *d*. *Educ:* Bathurst High School; Univ. of St Francis Xavier, Antigonish, NS, Canada. Commissioned, RAF, 1937. Served War of 1939-45: France, Egypt, Germany, Italy. Commanded RAF St Eval, 1957-58; Base Comdr, Christmas Island, 1959; Dir of Intelligence (B), Air Min., 1961-64; AO i/c A, HQ Coastal Command, 1965-68. RAF Staff Coll., 1949; jssc, 1952; idc, 1960. *Recreations:* ski-ing, tennis, photography. *Address:* 26 Laburnum Court, Dennis Lane, Stanmore, Mddx. *T:* 01-954 2255. *Club:* Royal Air Force.

WHELAN, Michael John, FRS 1976; MA, PhD, DPhil; Reader in the Physical Examination of Materials, Department of Metallurgy and Science of Materials, University of Oxford, since 1966; Fellow of Linacre College, Oxford, since 1967; *b* 2 Nov. 1931; *s* of William Whelan and Ellen Pound. *Educ:* Farnborough Grammar Sch.; Gonville and Caius Coll., Cambridge. FInstP. Fellow of Gonville and Caius Coll., 1958-66; Demonstrator in Physics, Univ. of Cambridge, 1961-65; Asst Dir of Research in Physics, Univ. of Cambridge, 1965-66.

Publications: (co-author) Electron Microscopy of Thin Crystals, 1965; numerous papers in learned jls. *Recreation:* gardening. *Address:* 18 Salford Road, Old Marston, Oxford OX3 0RX. *T:* Oxford 44556.

WHELAN, Prof. Robert Ford, MD, PhD, DSc; FRACP, FACE, FAA; Vice-Chancellor, University of Liverpool, since 1977; *b* Belfast, NI, 22 Dec. 1922; *s* of Robert Henry Whelan and Dorothy Ivy Whelan; *m* 1951, Helen Elizabeth Macdonald Hepburn; two *s* one *d*. *Educ:* private schs; QUB (MB, BCh, BAO 1946; MD 1951; PhD 1955; DSc 1960). MD Adelaide, 1958. FRACP 1962; FAA 1966; FACE 1974. RMO, Belfast City Hosp., 1947; Sen. Ship's Surg., Glen Line, Alfred Holt & Co., Far East and Australia, 1948; Jun. Lectr and Asst Lectr in Physiol., QUB, 1949-51; Res. Fellow, Sherrington Sch. of Physiol., St Thomas's Hosp. Med. Sch., 1951-52; Lectr in Physiol., QUB and NI Hosps Authority, 1952-57; Univ. of Adelaide: Prof. and Head of Dept of Human Physiol. and Pharmacol., 1958-71; Associate Dean, Faculty of Med., 1960 and 1961, Dean, 1964 and 1965; Mem., Standing Sub-Cttee, Educn Cttee (Professorial Bd), 1963-66, Chm. Educn Cttee, 1971; Hon. Cons. Physiologist, Royal Adelaide Hosp., 1959-71; Vice-Chancellor, Univ. of Western Australia, 1971-76. Vis. Prof., Sherrington Sch. of Physiol., St Thomas's Hosp. Med. Sch., 1962; Carnegie Trav. Fellow, USA, 1962; Vis. Prof., Dept. of Physiol., Univ. of Southern Calif, 1962; Vis. Lectr, Univ. of Queensland, 1964; (jtly) Demonstration, Royal Soc. Conversazione, 1966; Edward Stirling Lectr, Postgrad. Cttee, Univ. of Adelaide, 1967; Vis. Prof. of Physiol., Univ. of Singapore, 1970. Aust. Delegate, Internat. Congress of Pharmacology: Basle, 1969; San Francisco, 1972; Chm., Aust. Nat. Cttee, Internat. Union of Pharmacologists, 1968-75. Mem. Council, (new) Flinders Univ. of SA, 1966-71; Mem. Bd of Dirs, Walter and Eliza Hall Inst. for Med. Res., 1968-71; Mem. Bd of Governors: Collegiate Sch. of St Peter, Adelaide, 1967-71; Walford Sch. for Girls, Adelaide, 1969-71. Fellow: Royal Acad. of Med. in Ireland, 1953; Royal Soc. of SA, 1959. Member: Brit. Physiol Soc., 1951; Med. Res. Soc., 1953; Pharmacol Soc., 1956; Med. Sciences Club of SA, 1958 (Vice Pres. 1961, Pres. 1963); Extraord. Mem., Cardiac Soc. of Aust. and NZ, 1960; Foundn Mem. and Mem. Council, Aust. Physiol Soc., 1960. Hon. Member: Royal Adelaide Hosp. Med. Officers' Assoc., 1962; Aust. Soc. of Clin. and Expmtl Pharmacol., 1971 (first Pres., 1966); Aust. Physiol and Pharmacol Soc., 1972. *Publications:* Control of the Peripheral Circulation in Man, 1967; over 100 pubns in med. and sci. jls. *Address:* The Vice-Chancellor's Lodge, Sefton Park Road, Liverpool L8 3SL.

WHELDON, Sir Huw (Pyrs), Kt 1976; OBE 1952; MC 1944; broadcaster; Chairman, Court of Governors, London School of Economics and Political Science, since 1975; consultant, NBC of America, since 1977; *b* 7 May 1916; *e s* of late Sir Wynn Wheldon KBE, DSO, LLD; *m* Jacqueline Mary (*née* Clarke); one *s* two *d*. *Educ:* Friars Sch., Bangor, Wales; London Sch. of Economics, BSc(Econ), 1938. Kent Educn Cttee staff, 1939. Commnd Royal Welch Fusiliers, 1940; served NW Europe and Middle East with 1st and 6th Airborne Divs (Major, 1st Bn Roy. Ulster Rifles), 1941-45. Arts Council Dir for Wales, 1946; Festival of Britain Directorate, 1949; BBC Television, 1952-77; producer, director, commentator, author; credits include: All Your Own, Opera for Everybody, Men in Battle, Portraits of Power, Orson Welles Sketchbook, 1952-57; Monitor, magazine of the arts, 1958-64; Royal Heritage, 1977. Head of Documentary Programmes, 1962; Head of Music and Documentary Programmes, 1963-65; Controller of Programmes, 1965-68; Man. Dir, 1968-75; Special Adviser, BBC, 1975-76. Vice-Pres., Royal TV Soc., 1973; Trustee, Nat. Portrait Gall., 1976-; Governor, Nat. Film Sch.; Member: Youth Develt Council, 1959-62; Design Council, 1970-75; Council: RCA, 1974-; Brunel Univ., 1973-; Hon. Soc. of Cymmrodorion, 1950-. Hon. Fellow: LSE, 1973; Manchester Coll. of Art, 1969; Hon. DLitt, Ulster, 1975; Gold Medal, Royal TV Soc., 1976. *Address:* 120 Richmond Hill, Richmond, Surrey. *Clubs:* Garrick, Savile.

WHELER, Captain Sir Trevor Wood, 13th Bt, *cr* 1660; late Captain Royal Sussex Regiment, TF, 1914-20, and Royal Engineers, 1940-47; *b* 20 Sept. 1889; *s* of Lt-Col Sir Edward Wheler, 12th Bt, 1st Bn Royal Sussex Regt, and Mary Leontine, *d* of Sir Richard Wood, GCMG; *S* father, 1903; *m* 1915, Margaret Idris, *y d* of late Sir Ernest Birch, KCMG; one *s* two *d*. Served War of 1914-18, 6th Bn, Royal Sussex Regt; Waziristan, NW Frontier, 1917; attached IA, 1918-20. A principal Game Farmer between the wars, and Pres., Gamefarmers' Assoc., throughout that period. War of 1939-45: Home Guard (LDV), 1940; recalled Army 1940; RE (Movement Control), Scottish Comd, and BAOR, 1940-46. CCG, 1947-50; served in Kenya Police Reserve throughout Mau Mau Emergency, 1953 (General Service Medal). *Heir: s* Edward Woodford Wheler, late Captain Royal Sussex Regt [*b* 13 June 1920; *m* 1945, Molly Ashworth, *e d* of Thomas Lever, Devon; one *s* one *d*]. *Address:* 19 Knole Court, Knole Road, Bexhill-on-Sea, East Sussex. *T:* Bexhill 211333.

WHETTON, Prof. John Thomas, DSO 1943; OBE 1941; MC 1919; TD 1951; Professor of Mining, University of Leeds, 1945-60, now Emeritus; Private Consultant, Mining, Surveying, Geophysical Surveying, since 1960; *b* 27 Oct. 1894; *m* no *c*. *Educ:* Universities of Leeds and Durham. MSc (Leeds); MSc (Durham); 1st Class Colliery Manager's Certificate. Practical Mining experience West and South Yorks, Durham, Northumberland, Germany, France, Belgium, Poland and Canada. Visited oil fields of the Middle East, Venezuela and Trinidad. Army service France and Russia, 1914-19. Reader in Mining, King's Coll., Univ. of Durham, 1924-39. Comd 4th Survey Regt RA TA, 1937-48; service in Balkans, Middle East, North Africa, Sicily and NW Europe. Mining Advr (Tech.), Ruhr, Germany, 1945. Pro-Vice-Chancellor, University of Leeds, 1955-57. Founder Member, International Organising Mining Committee, 1957. Nuffield Foundn and Research Coun. of Canada Lectr, 1960; Engineers Jt Coun., Lectr, American Inst. of Mining Engineers, 1964. Hon. Col, Leeds Univ. Officers' Training Corps T & AVR, 1968-69. President, Midland Institute of Mining Engineers, 1960-61. Russian Order of St Stanislav 2nd class with swords, 1919; Belgian Order of the Crown with Palm, 1945; Belgian Croix de Guerre, 1945. *Publications:* contrib. Prospecting, Boring, and Sinking sections in Coal Mining Practice, 1958; numerous research and general papers on mining and allied sciences to technical press and instns in UK, Canada, USA, Holland, Poland and Czechoslovakia, from 1925. *Recreations:* cricket and bowls. *Address:* Westbourne House, 16 Westbourne Grove, Scarborough, North Yorks. *T:* Scarborough 72432.

WHEWELL, Prof. Charles Smalley, PhD; Professor of Textile Industries, University of Leeds, 1975-77, Emeritus Professor 1977; (Professor of Textile Technology, 1954-63, Head of Department, 1963-75); *b* 26 April 1912; *m* 1937, Emma Stott, PhD; one *s*. *Educ:* Grammar School, Darwen, Lancs; University of Leeds (BSc, PhD). Research Chemist, Wool Industries Research Association, 1935-37. University of Leeds, 1937-77: Lecturer in Textile Chemistry; Lecturer in Textile Finishing; Senior Lecturer in Textile Chemistry; Reader in Textile Finishing; Pro-Vice-Chancellor, 1973-75. Pres., Textile Inst., 1977-. Hon. Liveryman, Clothworkers' Company, 1970. Textile Institute Medal, 1954; Warner Memorial Medal, 1960; Textile Institute Service Medal, 1971. *Publications:* contrib. to: Chambers's Encyclopædia; Encyclopædia Britannica; British Wool Manual; Waterproofing and Water-repellency; Chemistry of Natural Fibres, ed Asquith, 1977; Jl Soc. of Dyers and Colourists; Jl Textile Inst. *Recreations:* music (organ), travel. *Address:* Department of Textile Industries, The University of Leeds, Leeds LS2 9JT. *T:* Leeds 31751.

WHICKER, Alan Donald; television broadcaster (Whicker's World); writer; *b* 2 Aug. 1925; *o s* of late Charles Henry Whicker and late Anne Jane Cross. *Educ:* Haberdashers' Aske's Sch. Capt., Devonshire Regt; Dir, Army Film and Photo Section, with 8th Army and US 5th Army. War Corresp. in Korea, For. Corresp., novelist, writer and radio Broadcaster. Joined BBC TV, 1957: Tonight programme (appeared nightly in filmed reports from around the world, studio interviews, outside broadcasts, Eurovision, and Telstar, incl. first Telstar two-way transmission at opening of UN Assembly, NY, 1962); TV Series: Whicker's World, 1959-60; Whicker Down Under, 1961; Whicker on Top of the World!, 1962; Whicker in Sweden, Whicker in the Heart of Texas, Whicker down Mexico Way, 1963; Alan Whicker Report series: The Solitary Billionaire (J. Paul Getty), etc; wrote and appeared in own series of monthly documentaries on BBC 2, subseq. repeated on BBC 1, under series title, Whicker's World, 1965-67 (31 programmes later shown around the world); BBC radio programmes and articles for The Listener, etc; left BBC, 1968. Various cinema films, incl. The Angry Silence. Mem., successful consortium for Yorkshire Television, 1967. Contrib. a documentary series to ITV, 1968. Completed 16 Documentaries for Yorkshire TV during its first year of operation, incl. Whicker's New World Series, and Specials on Gen. Stroessner of Paraguay, Count von Rosen, and Pres. Duvalier of Haiti; Whicker in Europe; Whicker's Walkabout; Broken Hill—Walled City; Gairy's Grenada; documentary series, World of Whicker; Whicker's Orient; Whicker within a Woman's World, 1972; Whicker's South Seas, Whicker way out West, 1973; Whicker's World, series on cities, 1974-; Whicker's World—Down Under, 1976. Various awards, 1963-, incl. Screenwriters' Guild, best Documentary Script, 1963; Guild of Television Producers and Directors Personality of the Year, 1964; Silver Medal, Royal Television Soc., 1968; Dumont Award, Univ. of California, 1970; Best Interview Prog. Award, Hollywood Festival of TV, 1973. FRSA 1970. *Publications:* Some Rise by Sin, 1949; Away—with Alan Whicker, 1963; Sunday newspaper columns; contrib. various internat. pubns. *Recreations:* people, photography, writing, travel, and reading (usually airline timetables). *Address:* Le Gallais Chambers, Bath Street, St Helier, Jersey.

WHIFFEN, David Hardy, MA, DPhil (Oxon), DSc (Birmingham); FRS 1966; FRIC; Professor of Physical Chemistry, since 1968, University of Newcastle upon Tyne; *s* of Noël H. and late Mary Whiffen; *m* Jean P. Bell; four *s. Educ:* Oundle School; St John's College, Oxford (Scholar). Sometime Commonwealth Fund Fellow, Sen. Student of Commn for 1851 Exhibition. Formerly: Lectr in Chemistry, Univ. of Birmingham; Supt, Molecular Science Div., NPL. *Publications:* papers in scientific jls. *Address:* Department of Physical Chemistry, The University, Newcastle upon Tyne NE1 7RU. *T:* Newcastle 28511.

WHINNEY, Ven. Michael Humphrey Dickens; Archdeacon of Southwark and Borough Dean of Southwark, since 1973; *b* 8 July 1930; *s* of Humphrey Charles Dickens Whinney and Evelyn Lawrence Revell Whinney (*née* Low); great-great-grandson of Charles Dickens; *m* 1958, Veronica (*née* Webster); two *s* one *d. Educ:* Charterhouse; Pembroke Coll., Cambridge (BA 1955, MA 1958); Ridley Hall, Cambridge. National Service commission, RA, 1949 (served in 5th Regt, RHA and Surrey Yeo. Queen Mary's Regt). Articled clerk to Chartered Accountants, Whinney Smith & Whinney (now Whinney Murray), 1950-52. Curate, Rainham Parish Church, Essex, 1957-60; Head, Cambridge University Mission Settlement, Bermondsey, 1960-67, Chaplain, 1967-72; Vicar, St James' with Christ Church, Bermondsey, 1967-73. *Recreations:* mountaineering, sailing, squash. *Address:* 17 Stradella Road, Herne Hill, SE24.

WHIPPLE, Prof. Fred Lawrence; Senior Scientist, Smithsonian Astrophysical Observatory, since 1973; Director, Smithsonian Institution Astrophysical Observatory, since 1955-73; Phillips Professor of Astronomy, Harvard University, since 1968; *b* 5 Nov. 1906; *s* of Harry Lawrence Whipple and Celestia Whipple (*née* MacFarland); *m* 1st, 1928, Dorothy Woods (divorced 1935); one *s* ; 2nd, 1946, Babette Frances Samelson; two *d. Educ:* Long Beach High School, Calif; UCLA; Univ. of California, Berkeley. Lick Observatory Fellow, 1930-31; Staff Member, Harvard Univ., 1931-; Instructor, 1932-38; Lecturer, 1938-45; Assoc. Prof., 1945-50; Professor, 1950-; Chm. Dept of Astronomy, 1949-56. US Nat. Cttee of Internat. Geophysical Year: Chm. Techn. Panel on Rocketry, 1955-59; Member: Techn. Panel on Earth Satellite Program, 1955-59; Working Group on Satellite Tracking and Computation, 1955-58; Scientific Advisory Bd to USAF, 1953-62; Cttee on Meteorology, Nat. Acad. of Sciences, Nat. Research Coun., 1958-; Special Cttees on Space Techn., Nat. Advisory Cttee for Aeronautics, 1958- (now NASA), US; Space Sciences Working Group on Orbiting Astronomical Observatories, Nat. Acad. of Sciences (Mem. Nat. Acad. of Sciences, 1959-); Advisory Panel to Cttee on Sci. and Astronautics of US House of Representatives, 1960-73; Amer. Philosophical Soc., Philadelphia; Amer. Acad. of Arts and Sciences, Boston; New York Acad. of Science, NY; several technical societies. Associate, Royal Astronomical Soc., 1970-. Benjamin Franklin Fellow, RSA, 1968-. Editor: Smithsonian Contributions to Astrophysics, 1956-73; Planetary and Space Science, 1958-. Hon. degrees: MA, Harvard Univ., 1945; DSc, Amer. Internat. Coll., 1958; DLitt, North-eastern Univ., 1961; DS, Temple Univ., 1961; LLD, CW Post Coll. of Long Island Univ., 1962. J. Lawrence Smith Medal of Nat. Acad. of Sciences, 1949; Donohue Medals, 1932, 1933, 1937, 1940, 1942 (received two medals that year); Presidential Certificate of Merit, 1948; Exceptional Service Award, US Air Force Scientific Adv. Bd, 1960; Space Flight Award, Amer. Astron. Soc., 1961; President's Award for Distinguished Federal Civilian Service, 1963; Space Pioneers Medallion, 1968; NASA Public Services Award, 1969; Kepler Medal, AAAS, 1971; Nat. Civil Service League's Civil Service Award, 1972; Henry Medal, Smithsonian Instn, 1973; Alumnus of the Year Award, UCLA, 1976; also has foreign awards. *Publications:* Earth, Moon and Planets, 1942, 3rd edn 1968. Many technical papers in various astronomical and geophysical journals and books; popular articles in magazines and in Encyclopædia Britannica. *Recreation:* cultivation of roses. *Address:* Smithsonian Astrophysical Observatory, 60 Garden Street, Cambridge, Mass 02138, USA. *T:* Boston University 4-7383.

WHISHAW, Sir Charles (Percival Law), Kt 1969; Trustee, Calouste Gulbenkian Foundation, since 1956; Director: Molin's Ltd; Solicitors' Law Stationery Society; *b* 29 October 1909; 2nd *s* of late Montague Law Whishaw and Erna Louise (*née* Spies); *m* 1936, Margaret Joan, *e d* of late Col T. H. Hawkins, CMG, RMLI; one *s* two *d. Educ:* Charterhouse; Worcester College, Oxford. Called to Bar, Inner Temple, 1932; Solicitor, 1938; Partner in Freshfields, 1943-74. Member: Iron and Steel Holding and Realisation Agency, 1953-67; Council, Law Soc., 1967-76. *Address:* Westcott Hill House, Westcott, Surrey. *T:* Dorking 5315. *Club:* Savile.

WHISTLER, Maj.-Gen. Alwyne Michael Webster, CB 1963; CBE 1959; retired, 1965; *b* 30 Dec. 1909; *s* of Rev. W. W. Whistler and Lilian Whistler (*née* Meade), Elsted, Sussex; *m* 1936, Margaret Louise Michelette, *d* of Brig.-Gen. Malcolm Welch, CB, CMG, JP, Stedham, Sussex; one *s* two *d. Educ:* Gresham's Sch., Holt; RMA Woolwich. 2nd Lt Royal Signals, 1929; served in India, 1932-44; War of 1939-45: Staff Coll., Camberley, 1944; Burma Campaign, 19 and 25 Indian Divs and XII Army, 1944-45 (despatches twice). ADPR, Berlin, 1946; GSO1 (Military Adviser), Military Governor of Germany, 1946-48; AQMG, War Office, 1949-50; JSSC 1950; Comdg Royal Signals, 3 Div., 1951-54; Col GS, War Office, 1955-57; Col Q Far ELF, 1957-58; Comdr Corps Royal Signals, 1 (British) Corps, BAOR, 1959-60; Signal Officer-in-Chief, War Office, 1960-62; Chairman, British Joint Communications Board, Ministry of Defence, 1962-64; Assistant Chief of the Defence Staff (Signals), 1964-65. Hon. Col Princess Louise's Kensington Regt (41st Signals) TA, 1963-66; Col Commandant, Royal Corps of Signals, 1964-68; Hon. Col 32nd (Scottish) Signal Regiment (V), 1967-72. Master of Fox Hounds, Nerbudda Vale Hunt, 1938-40. *Recreations:* field sports, particularly fishing. *Address:* Tigh-na-Leven, by Tarbert, Argyll. *T:* Tarbert 610.

WHISTLER, Laurence, CBE 1973 (OBE 1955); FRSL; engraver on glass; writer; *b* 21 Jan. 1912; *s* of Henry Whistler and Helen (*née* Ward); *yr b* of late Rex Whistler; *m* 1st, 1939, Jill (*d* 1944), *d* of Sir Ralph Furse, KCMG, DSO; one *s* and 2nd, 1950, Theresa, *yr sister* of Jill Furse; one *s* one *d. Educ:* Stowe; Balliol College, Oxford (Hon. Fellow 1974). BA Oxon. Chancellor's Essay Prize, 1934. Served War of 1939-45: private soldier, 1940; commissioned in The Rifle Brigade, 1941. King's Gold Medal for Poetry, 1935 (first award); Atlantic Award for Literature, 1945. First Pres., Guild of Glass Engravers, 1975. *Work on glass includes:* goblets, etc, in point-engraving and drill, and engraved church windows and panels at: Sherborne Abbey; Moreton, Dorset; Checkendon, Oxon; Ilton, Som; Eastbury, Berks (window to Edward and Helen Thomas); Guards' Chapel, London; Stowe, Bucks; St Hugh's Coll., Oxford; Ashmansworth, Berks. *Exhibitions:* Agnews, Bond Street, 1969; Marble Hill, Twickenham, 1972; Corning Museum, USA, 1974; Ashmolean, 1976. *Publications include:* Sir John Vanbrugh (biography), 1938; The English Festivals, 1947; Rex Whistler, His Life and His Drawings, 1948; The World's Room (Collected Poems), 1949; The Engraved Glass of Laurence Whistler, 1952; Rex Whistler: The Königsmark Drawings, 1952; The Imagination of Vanbrugh and his Fellow Artists, 1954; The View From This Window (poems), 1956; Engraved Glass, 1952-58; The Work of Rex Whistler (with Ronald Fuller), 1960; Audible Silence (poems), 1961; The Initials in the Heart: the story of a marriage, 1964, rev. edn 1975; To Celebrate Her Living (poems), 1967; Pictures on Glass, 1972; The Image on the Glass, 1975. *Address:* Little Place, Lyme Regis, Dorset. *T:* Lyme Regis 2355.

WHITAKER, Benjamin Charles George; author; Director, Minority Rights Group, since 1971 (Deputy Director, 1970-71); *b* 15 Sept. 1934; 3rd *s* of Maj.-Gen. Sir John Whitaker, 2nd Bt, CB, CBE (*d* 1957), Retford, Notts; *m* 1964, Janet Alison Stewart; two *s* one *d. Educ:* Eton; New Coll., Oxford. BA (Modern History). Called to Bar, Inner Temple, 1959 (Yarborough-Anderson Scholar). Vice-Chm., Danilo Dolci Trust, 1960-69; Extra-mural Lectr in Law, London Univ., 1963-64. Practised as Barrister, 1959-67. MP (Lab) Hampstead, 1966-70; PPS to Minister of: Overseas Development, 1966; Housing and Local Govt, 1966-67; Parly Sec., ODM, 1969-70. Member: College Cttee, University Coll., London Univ.; UN Sub-Commn on Prevention of Discrimination and Protection of Minorities, 1975-; Goodman Cttee on Charity Law Reform, 1974-76; Chairman: UN Working Gp on Slavery, 1976-; Defence of Literature and Arts Soc.; City Poverty Cttee. *Publications:* The Police, 1964; (ed) A Radical Future, 1967; Crime and Society, 1967; Participation and Poverty, 1968; Parks for People, 1971; (ed) The Fourth World, 1972; The Foundations, 1974; Gen. Editor, Sources for Contemporary Issues series (7 vols), 1973-75. *Address:* 13 Elsworthy Road, NW3.
See also Sir James Whitaker, Bt.

WHITAKER, Charles Kenneth; Controller, Newcastle Central Office, Department of Health and Social Security, since Dec. 1974; *b* Snaith, 15 May 1919; *o s* of late Charles Henry Whitaker and Elsie (*née* Austwick); *m* 1972, Dorothy (*née* Grimster). *Educ:* Drax Grammar School. Served with Cameronians (Scottish Rifles), 1939-46. Entered Min. of Health, 1936; Finance Officer and Dep. Sec., Public Health Laboratory Service Bd, 1960-65; Head of Health Services Superannuation Div., 1966-74; Controller, Blackpool Central Office, 1972-74. *Recreation:* walking. *Address:* Department of Health and Social Security, Newcastle upon Tyne NE98 1YX; The Gables, 19 Leamington Road, Blackpool, Lancs. *T:* Blackpool 24600.

WHITAKER, Frank Howard, CMG 1969; OBE 1946; Secretary of the Metrication Board, 1969-74; *b* 9 Jan. 1909; *er s* of late Frank Harold Whitaker and late Edith Whitaker, Bradford; *m* 1937, Marjorie Firth; no *c*. *Educ:* Thornton Grammar Sch.; Leeds University. LLB (1st cl. hons) 1929; Solicitor (1st cl. hons, D. Reardon and Wakefield and Bradford Prizeman), 1931. Legal Practice until 1939. Royal Air Force, 1940-46 (Sqdn Leader). Entered Civil Service as Principal, Board of Trade, 1946; Asst Sec., 1955; Export Credits Guarantee Dept, 1957, Under-Secretary, 1966. *Recreation:* mountaineering. *Address:* Tavistock, The Rowans, Gerrards Cross, Bucks.

WHITAKER, Mrs Geoffrey Charles Francis; *see* Love, Enid Rosamond.

WHITAKER, Sir James Herbert Ingham, 3rd Bt, *cr* 1936; Vice-Chairman, Halifax Building Society, since 1973, Chairman, London Board, since 1974; *b* 27 July 1925; *s* of late Maj.-Gen. Sir John Whitaker, 2nd Bt, CB, CBE, and Lady Whitaker (*née* Snowden); *S* father 1957; *m* 1948, Mary Elisabeth Lander Urling Clark (*née* Johnston), *widow* of Captain D. Urling Clark, MC; one *s* one *d*. *Educ:* Eton. Coldstream Guards, 1944. Served in North West Europe. Retired, 1947. Director: National Carbonising Co.; Updown Investment Trust; Member, Board of Economic Forestry (Holdings), 1965-; The Moorside Trust; Dep. Chm., Governing Body, Atlantic College. High Sheriff of Notts, 1969-70. *Recreation:* shooting. *Heir: s* John James Ingham Whitaker, *b* 23 October 1952. *Address:* Babworth Hall, Retford, Notts. *T:* Retford 3454; Auchnafree, Dunkeld, Perthshire. *Club:* Boodle's.
See also B. C. G. Whitaker.

WHITAKER, Thomas Kenneth; Chancellor, National University of Ireland, since 1976; *b* 8 Dec. 1916; *s* of Edward Whitaker and Jane O'Connor; *m* 1941, Nora Fogarty; five *s* one *d*. *Educ:* Christian Brothers' Sch., Drogheda; London Univ. (External Student; BScEcon, MScEcon). Irish CS, 1934-69 (Sec., Dept of Finance, 1956-69); Governor, Central Bank of Ireland, 1969-76; Dir, Bank of Ireland, 1976-. Dir, Arthur Guinness Son & Co. Ltd, 1976-. Chairman: Bord na Gaeilge, 1975-; Agency for Personal Service Overseas, 1973-. Pres., Econ. and Social Res. Inst.; Mem. Council, Dublin Inst. for Advanced Studies. MRIA. Hon. DEconSc National Univ. of Ireland, 1962; Hon. LLD Univ. of Dublin, 1976. Commandeur de la Légion d'Honneur, France, 1976. *Publications:* Financing by Credit Creation, 1947; Economic Development, 1958. *Recreations:* fishing, golf, music. *Address:* 148 Stillorgan Road, Donnybrook, Dublin 4, Ireland. *T:* Dublin 693474.

WHITBREAD, Major Simon; Lord-Lieutenant and Custos Rotulorum for Bedfordshire, since 1957; *b* 12 Oct. 1904; *s* of late Samuel Howard Whitbread, CB, JP, Southill, Biggleswade, Beds; *m* 1936, Helen Beatrice Margaret, *d* of Hon. Robert Trefusis, 27 Coleherne Court, SW7; one *s* one *d*. *Educ:* Eton; Trinity College, Cambridge. Joined KRRC, 1925; Captain, 1937; retired, 1937. Re-employed War of 1939-45, served in Africa and Italy (despatches). Director of Whitbread & Co. Ltd; Gov. and mem. Bd of Management, Middlesex Hosp., 1937-; Mem., General Nursing Council for England and Wales, 1958-65. DL 1946, JP 1939. County Councillor, 1938, CA 1949, Chm. CC 1967, Beds; High Sheriff of Beds, 1947. Pres., E Anglia TA&AFA, 1973-. Hon. Col 286 Field Regt RA (TA) (The Hertfordshire and Bedfordshire Yeomanry), 1965-67. KStJ 1977 (OStJ 1941). *Recreations:* shooting and fishing. *Address:* The Mallowry, Riseley, Bedford. *T:* Riseley 248; 31 Egerton Gardens, SW3. *T:* 01-584 1763. *Clubs:* Buck's, MCC.

WHITBREAD, William Henry, TD; MA Cantab; President, Whitbread and Company, Ltd since 1972 (Chairman, 1944-71, Managing Director, 1927-68); Director, Whitbread Investment Co. Ltd (Chairman, 1956-77); Vice-President of the Brewers' Society (Chairman, 1952-53); Past-Master, Brewers' Company; Vice-Pres. Inst. of Brewing (Chm. Res. Cttee, 1948-52); *b* 22 Dec. 1900; *s* of late Henry William Whitbread, Norton Bavant, Wiltshire; *m* 1st, 1927, Ann Joscelyne (*d* 1936), *d* of late Samuel

Howard Whitbread, CB, Southill, Beds; two *s* one *d*; 2nd, 1941, Betty Parr, *d* of Samuel Russell, ICS; one *s* two *d*. *Educ:* Eton; Corpus Christi College, Cambridge. Lovat Scouts, 1920-41; served War of 1939-45: Lovat Scouts, 1939-41; Reconnaissance Corps, 1941-45; Parachutist. Chm. Parliamentary Cttee, Brewers' Society, 1948-52. Director: Barclays Bank Ltd, 1958-73; Eagle Star Insurance Co., 1958-74. Member Governing Body Aldenham School, 1929-61 (Chairman, 1948-58). President: BSJA, 1966-68; Shire Horse Soc., 1971-72; Member: National Hunt Committee, 1956-68; Jockey Club, 1968-; Hurlingham Club Polo Committee, 1932-45; Master, Trinity Foot Beagles, 1921-23. *Recreations:* shooting, fishing and sailing. *Address:* Warren Mere, Godalming, Surrey; Letterewe, Ross-shire; Farleaze, Near Malmesbury, Wilts. *Clubs:* Brooks's, Pratt's, Royal Thames Yacht; Royal Yacht Squadron.
See also Sir H. T. Tollemache, Bt.

WHITBY, Bishop Suffragan of, since 1976; **Rt. Rev. Clifford Conder Barker,** TD 1970; *b* 22 April 1926; *s* of Sidney and Kathleen Alice Barker; *m* 1952, Marie Edwards; one *s* two *d*. *Educ:* Oriel Coll., Oxford (BA 1950, MA 1955); St Chad's Coll., Durham (Dip. in Theol. 1952). Emergency Commn, The Green Howards, 1944-48; deacon 1952, priest 1953; Curate: All Saints', Scarborough, 1952-55; Redcar, 1955-57; Vicar: All Saints', Sculcoates, Hull, 1957-63; Rudby-in-Cleveland, 1963-70; RD of Stokesley, 1965-70; Vicar, St Olave with St Giles, York, 1970-76; RD of York, 1971-76; Canon of York, 1973-76. CF (TA), 1958-74. *Recreations:* golf, gardening, music. *Address:* 60 West Green, Stokesley, Middlesbrough, Cleveland TS9 5BD. *T:* Stokesley 710390.

WHITBY, Charles Harley, QC 1970; a Recorder of the Crown Court, Western Circuit, since 1972; *b* 2 April 1926; *s* of Arthur William Whitby and Florence Whitby. *Educ:*, St John's, Leatherhead; Peterhouse, Cambridge. Open Schol., Peterhouse, 1943; served RAFVR, 1944-48; BA (History) 1st cl. 1949, MA 1951. Called to Bar, Middle Temple, 1952; Mem. Bar Council, 1969-71, 1972-. Mem., Criminal Injuries Compensation Bd, 1975-. *Publications:* contrib. to Master and Servant in Halsbury's Laws of England, 3rd edn, Vol. 25, 1959 and Master and Servant in Atkin's Encyclopaedia of Court Forms, 2nd edn, Vol. 25, 1962. *Recreations:* golf, swimming, theatre, cinema. *Address:* 12 King's Bench Walk, Temple, EC4. *T:* 01-583 0811. *Clubs:* United Oxford & Cambridge University, Royal Automobile, Garrick.

WHITBY, Harry, CB 1965; Government-appointed Member, Potato Marketing Board, since 1972; *b* 19 June 1910; *er s* of Edward Whitby, Hatfield, Herts, and Sarah Alice (*née* Booth); *m* 1937, Ruby Josephine, *yr d* of Charles J. Dyer, East Runton, Norfolk; two *s* two *d*. *Educ:* Ardingly College, Sussex; University of Manitoba. Student Asst, Agricultural Economics Research Institute, Univ. of Oxford, 1933-36; Asst to Advisory Officer in Agricultural Economics, Dept of Agriculture, Univ. of Leeds, 1936-38; Economist, Min. of Agriculture and Fisheries, 1938-47; Adviser on Farm Economics, 1947-50, Asst Sec. 1950-58, Under-Sec., 1958-68, Sec., 1968-71, Dept of Agriculture and Fisheries for Scotland. *Recreations:* gardening, cricket. *Address:* Cutlers Cottage, East Runton, Cromer, Norfolk. *Club:* Royal Commonwealth Society.

WHITBY, Professor Lionel Gordon, FRCP, FRCPE, FRSE, FRCPath; Professor of Clinical Chemistry, University of Edinburgh, since 1963; *b* 18 July 1926; *s* of late Sir Lionel Whitby, CVO, MC, MD, FRCP, Regius Prof. of Physic and Master of Downing Coll., Cambridge; *m* 1949, Joan Hunter Sanderson; one *s* two *d*. *Educ:* King's Coll., Cambridge; Middlesex Hosp. MA, PhD, MD, BChir. Fellow of King's College, Cambridge, 1951-55; W. A. Meek Schol., Univ. of Cambridge, 1951; Murchison Schol., RCP, 1958; Rockefeller Trav. Res. Fellow, Nat. Insts of Health Bethesda, Md, USA, 1959. Registrar and Asst Lectr in Chem. Path., Hammersmith Hosp. and Postgrad. Med. Sch. of London, 1958-60; Univ. Biochemist to Addenbrooke's Hosp., Cambridge, 1960-63; Dean of Faculty of Medicine, Univ. of Edinburgh, 1969-72; Member: Scientific Services Adv. Gp, SHHD, 1975-77; Laboratory Develt Adv. Group, DHSS, 1972-76; Screening Sub-Cttee of Standing Medical Adv. Cttee, 1975-. Guest Lectr, Amer. Chem. Soc., 1966; Vis. Prof. of Chemical Pathology, RPMS, 1974. Examr for RCPath. *Publications:* (ed jointly) Principles and Practice of Medical Computing, 1971; (jointly) Lecture Notes on Clinical Chemistry, 1975; scientific papers on flavinglucosides, catecholamines and metabolites, several aspects of clin. chem., and early detection of disease by chemical tests. *Recreations:* gardening, photography. *Address:* 51 Dick Place, Edinburgh EH9 2JA. *T:* 031-667 4358; The Royal Infirmary, Edinburgh. *T:* 031-229 2477, ext. 2319.

WHITCOMBE, Maj.-Gen. Philip Sidney, CB 1944; OBE 1941; *b* 3 Oct. 1893; *e s* of late Rt Rev. Robert Henry Whitcombe, DD, Bishop of Colchester; *m* 1919, Madeline Lelia Brydges, *d* of Canon Arthur Symonds, Over Tabley, Knutsford; two *s. Educ:* Winchester. Gazetted to ASC from Durham LI (Spec. Res.), June 1914; served with BEF in France and Flanders, Aug. 1914-18; DAD Transport, 1918-19; psc 1926; Bde Major, Madras, 1928-32; Bt Major, 1933; DAAG, N Comd, York, 1934-36; GSO 2 War Office, 1936-38; Bt Lt-Col 1939; served in France as ADS and T 1939-40 (despatches); AA and QMG 1940-41 (OBE); Gibraltar, Brig. i/c Admin., 1941-42; Col 1942; DA and QMG, BTNI, 1942-43; MGA Eastern Command, 1943-47; retired, 1947. JP for Wilts, 1948. *Recreations:* cricket, fishing. Played cricket for Essex, 1922, the Army, 1925, and Berkshire, 1925-32. *Address:* The Grange, Lake, Amesbury, Wilts. *T:* Amesbury 3175. *Clubs:* Army and Navy, MCC.

WHITE; *see* Blanco White.

WHITE, family name of **Baron Annaly** and **Baroness White.**

WHITE, Baroness *cr* 1970 (Life Peer), of Rhymney, Monmouth; **Eirene Lloyd White;** Chairman, Land Authority for Wales, since 1975; Member, Royal Commission on Environmental Pollution, since 1974; Member, British Waterways Board, since 1974; *b* 7 Nov. 1909; *d* of late Dr Thomas Jones, CH; *m* 1948, John Cameron White (*d* 1968). *Educ:* St Paul's Girls' Sch.; Somerville Coll., Oxford. Ministry of Labour officer, 1933-37 and 1941-45; Political Correspondent, Manchester Evening News, 1945-49; contested (Lab) Flintshire, 1945; MP (Lab) East Flint, 1950-70. Nat. Exec. Cttee of the Labour Party, 1947-53, 1958-72, Chm. 1968-69; Parly Secretary, Colonial Office, 1964-66; Minister of State for Foreign Affairs, 1966-67; Minister of State, Welsh Office, 1967-70. Governor: National Library of Wales; Brit. Film Inst. and National Film Theatre, 1959-64; Indep. Mem. Cinematograph Films Council, 1946-64. Chairman, Fabian Society, 1958-59; President: Nursery School Assoc., 1964-66; Nat. Council of Women (Wales); Council for Protection of Rural Wales; Lord President's nominee, Court of UCW, Aberystwyth and of UCNW, Bangor; Mem., UGC, 1977-; Chm., Internat. Cttee, Nat. Council of Social Service, 1973-77; Chairman: Coleg Harlech; Adv. Cttee on Oil Pollution at sea; Dep. Chm., Metrication Bd, 1972-76; Vice-Pres.: Commonwealth Countries League; Commonwealth Youth Exchange Council. Hon. Fellow, Somerville College, Oxford, 1966. *Address:* 36 Westminster Gardens, Marsham Street, SW1. *T:* 01-828 3320; Panteg, Ceinws, Machynlleth, Powys SY20 9HE. *T:* Corris 679. *Club:* Royal Commonwealth Society.

WHITE, Adrian N. S.; *see* Sherwin-White.

WHITE, Alan, OBE 1973; HM Diplomatic Service; Counsellor (Commercial), Madrid, since 1976; *b* 13 Aug. 1930; *s* of William White and Ida (*née* Hall); *m* 1954, Cynthia Maidwell; two *s* one *d*. WO, 1950; Germany, 1954-57; Hong Kong, 1959-63; MoD (Central), 1965; First Sec., FO (later FCO), 1966; Mexico City, 1969; First Sec., UK Disarmament Delegn, Geneva, 1974. *Recreations:* mountaineering, travel. *Address:* c/o Foreign and Commonwealth Office, SW1; c/o British Embassy, Madrid, Spain. *T:* Madrid 419-0200. *Club:* Royal Automobile.

WHITE, Prof. Alan Richard, BA, PhD; Ferens Professor of Philosophy in the University of Hull, since 1961; *b* Toronto, Canada, 9 Oct. 1922; *s* of late George Albert White and Jean Gabriel Kingston; *m* 1948, Eileen Anne Jarvis; one *s* two *d*. *Educ:* Midleton College and Presentation College, Cork; Trinity College, Dublin. Dublin: Schol. and 1st class Moderator in Classics, 1st class Moderator in Mental and Moral Science; Boxing Pink; President of the 'Phil'; Univ. Student in Classics and Dep. Lecturer in Logic, 1945-46; Asst Lecturer, Lecturer, Sen. Lecturer in Philosophy, Univ. of Hull, 1946-61; Visiting Professor: Univ. of Maryland, 1967-68; Temple Univ., 1974; Secretary, Mind Assoc., 1960-69, Pres., 1972. 42nd Dublin Rifles (LDF), 1941-45. *Publications:* G. E. Moore: A Critical Exposition, 1958; Attention, 1964; The Philosophy of Mind, 1967; (ed) The Philosophy of Action, 1968; Truth, 1970; Modal Thinking, 1975; articles in philosophical journals. *Recreations:* dilettantism and odd-jobbery. *Address:* The University, Hull HU6 7RX. *T:* Hull 46311.

WHITE, Hon. Sir Alfred (John), Kt 1971; Tasmanian Agent-General in London, 1959-71; *b* 2 Feb. 1902; British; *m* 1939, Veronica Louisa Punch; two *s* two *d*. Elected to Tasmanian Parliament, 1941; Minister for Health and Chief Secretary, 1946-48, then Chief Secretary and Minister for Labour and Industry, Shipping and Emergency Supplies until Jan. 1959. JP since 1934, and Territorial JP for the State of Tasmania in London, 1959. Appointed Agent-General for Tasmania in London for period of 3 years, Jan. 1959, re-appointed for a further period of 3 years, Jan. 1962; re-appointed 1967; granted title of "Honourable" for life. *Recreations:* ski-ing, gardening, bowls and fishing. *Address:* 18 Clarke Avenue, Battery Point, Hobart, Tasmania 7000, Australia.

WHITE, Antonia, FRSL; author; *b* 31 Mar. 1899; *d* of Cecil George Botting, MA, and Christine Julia Botting (*née* White); *m* 1930, H. T. Hopkinson (marr. diss., 1938); two *d. Educ:* Convent of the Sacred Heart, Roehampton; St Paul's Girls' School. Copywriter, W. S. Crawford Ltd, 1924-31; Assistant Editor, Life and Letters, 1928-29; Freelance Journalist, 1931-34; Copywriter, J. Walter Thompson, 1934-35; Fashion Editor, Daily Mirror, 1935-37; Fashion Editor, Sunday Pictorial, 1937-39; BBC 1940-43; Political Intelligence Dept (French Section), FO, 1943-45. Occupied in writing novels, short stories and occasional critical articles and reviews, also translating from the French. Denyse Clairouin prize for translation, 1950. Visiting Lecturer in English, St Mary's College, Notre Dame, Indiana, 1959. *Publications:* Frost in May, 1933; The Lost Traveller, 1950; The Sugar House, 1952; Beyond the Glass, 1954; Strangers (short stories), 1954; Minka and Curdy, 1957; The Hound and the Falcon, 1966; Life with Minka and Curdy, 1970; over 30 trans from the French including Maupassant's Une Vie, 1949, Colette's La Chatte, 1953, Claudine à L'Ecole, 1956, Claudine à Paris, 1958, Claudine en Ménage, 1960; Claudine s'en va, 1961; Le Tendron (Selected Short Stories), 1959; L'Entrave, 1966; L'Ingénue Libertine, 1968; Loys Masson, Le Notaire des Noirs, 1962; H. Fabre-Luce, Haute Cour, 1963; Christine Arnothy, Le Cardinal Prisonnier, 1964; Mémoires du Chevalier d'Eon, 1970; Simenon, La Cage de Verre, 1973; Paul-Gabriel Bouclé, Les Romans de Smollett, 1974; Voltaire, Histoire de Charles XII, 1976. *Recreations:* reading, seeing friends, crosswords. *Address:* 42D Courtfield Gardens, SW5. *T:* 01-370 2661.

WHITE, Arthur John Stanley, CMG 1947; OBE 1932; *b* 28 Aug. 1896; *s* of A. R. White, DL, OBE, and of Minnie B. White, OBE (*née* Beauchamp); *m* 1932, Joan, *d* of R. O. Davies and *niece* of Lord Waring; four *s* one *d. Educ:* Marlborough College; Clare College, Cambridge (Scholar), MA 1930. Served European War, Wiltshire Regt, 1915-20, France and Ireland; Indian Civil Service, Burma, 1922; Under-Secretary, Home and Political Dept, 1924; Deputy Commissioner, 1928 (Burma Rebellion 1931-32, OBE); Secretary to Government of Burma, 1934; appointed to British Council as Dep. Sec.-Gen., 1937, Sec.-Gen. 1940-47, Controller, 1947-62. Retired 1962. Director, OPOS (Office for placing overseas boys and girls in British Schs), 1964-67. *Recreations:* hockey (International Trials, 1921 and 1922), cricket, tennis, shooting. *Address:* The Red House, Burkes Road, Beaconsfield, Bucks. *T:* 3244. *Club:* East India, Devonshire, Sports and Public Schools.

WHITE, Arthur W.; *see* Walmesley White.

WHITE, Rev. Barrington Raymond; Principal, Regent's Park College, Oxford, since 1972; *b* 28 Jan. 1934; *s* of Raymond Gerard and Lucy Mildred White; *m* 1957, Margaret Muriel Hooper; two *d. Educ:* Chislehurst and Sidcup Grammar Sch.; Queens' Coll., Cambridge (BA Theol, MA); Regent's Park Coll., Oxford (DPhil). Ordained, 1959; Minister, Andover Baptist Church, 1959-63; Lectr in Ecclesiastical History, Regent's Park Coll., Oxford, 1963-72. First Breman Prof. of Social Relations, Univ. of N Carolina at Asheville, 1976. FRHistS 1973. *Publications:* The English Separatist Tradition, 1971; Association Records of the Particular Baptists to 1660, Part I, 1971, Part II, 1973, Part III, 1974; contrib. to Baptist Qly, Jl of Theological Studies, Jl of Ecclesiastical History, Welsh Baptist Studies. *Recreation:* recorded music. *Address:* The Principal's Lodging, Regent's Park College, Oxford. *T:* Oxford 56093.

WHITE, Sir Bruce Gordon, KBE 1944 (CBE 1943; MBE 1919); FCGI; FICE; FIMechE; FIEE; Senior Partner, Sir Bruce White, Wolfe Barry & Partners, Chartered Civil and Consulting Engineers; *b* 5 Feb. 1885; *m* 1912, Margery Gertrude (*d* 1965), *d* of C. W. Hodson, CSI; one *s* one *d. Educ:* Marlborough. Served European War, 1914-18 (MBE); War of 1939-45 as Brig. Director of Ports and IWT, War Office (KBE). *Address:* Reydon, Midway, Walton-on-Thames, Surrey.

WHITE, Byron R(aymond); Associate Justice of the Supreme Court of the United States since 1962; *b* Fort Collins, Colorado, 8 June 1917; *s* of Alpha White, Wellington, Colorado; *m* 1946, Marion Lloyd Stearns, *d* of Dr Robert L. Stearns; one *s* one *d. Educ:* Wellington High Sch.; Univ. of Colorado; Oxford Univ. (Rhodes Scholar); Yale Univ. Law Sch (before and after War). Served War of 1939-45: USNR, Naval Intell., Pacific (two Bronze Stars). Law Clerk to Chief Justice of US Supreme Court, 1946-47; law practice in Denver, Colorado, 1947-60, with firm of

Lewis, Grant, Newton, Davis and Henry (later Lewis, Grant and Davis). Dep. Attorney-Gen., 1961-62. Phi Beta Kappa, Phi Gamma Delta. As a Democrat, he was a prominent supporter of John F. Kennedy in the Presidential campaign of 1960. *Recreations:* ski-ing, paddle tennis, fishing. *Address:* US Supreme Court, 1 First Street NE, Washington, DC 20543, USA.

WHITE, Maj.-Gen. Cecil Meadows Frith, CB 1945; CBE 1943 (OBE 1941); DSO 1940; late Royal Signals; retired; Colonel Commandant, Royal Corps of Signals, 1950-60; *b* 29 Aug. 1897; *s* of late Herbert Meadows Frith White and late Annie Laura Borrett; *m* 1925, Elizabeth Rennie Robertson; one *d. Educ:* Eton College; RMA, Woolwich. Commissioned RFA 1915; served 1915-19 in Egypt, Serbia, Greece, and Palestine (despatches); transferred to Royal Signals, 1925; Brigade Major Signal Training Centre, 1934-36; Lt-Col 1939; served War of 1939-45 (despatches five times, DSO, OBE, CBE, CB); commanded 4th Indian Divisional Signals in Wavell's advance in Western Desert, 1940; CSO East Africa during East Africa Campaign, 1941; CSO 8th Army, 1941; Temp. Brig. 1941; Col 1943; acting Maj.-Gen. Jan. 1944 as SO in C 21 Army Group; Temp. Maj.-Gen. 1945; Maj.-Gen. 1949; CSO, GHQ, MELF, Nov. 1945-July 1949; GOC Catterick District, 1949-51; retired, 1951. Deputy Controller, Civil Defence, Southdown Group, 1958. Civil Defence Officer, County Borough of Brighton, 1960-65. *Recreations:* fishing, gardening; formerly polo and rugger, show-jumping, hunting, sailing. *Address:* Hansdown House, Maesbury Wells, Somerset. *TA and T:* Oakhill 498.

WHITE, Prof. Cedric Masey, DSc(Eng.), PhD; Professor Emeritus, University of London, 1966; Consultant for River and Coastal projects; *b* 19 Oct. 1898; *s* of Joseph Masey White, Nottingham; *m* 1st, 1921, Dorothy F. Lowe; 2nd, 1946, Josephine M. Ramage; one *d. Educ:* privately; University College, Nottingham. Served European War, in Tank Corps, 1917-19. Lecturer in Civil Engineering, Univ. of London, King's Coll., 1927-33; Reader in Civil Engineering, and Asst Prof. in Imperial Coll. of Science and Technology, 1933-45; Responsible for work of Hawksley Hydraulic Lab., 1933-66; Professor of Fluid Mechanics and Hydraulic Engineering, 1946-66. Completed various investigations for Admiralty, WO, MAP, etc, during War of 1939-45, and investigations of proposed river-structures for Hydro-Power here and abroad, 1946-56. Founder Member, Hydraulic Research Bd, 1946-51, 1959-67; sometime member of Research Committees of Instn of Civil Engineers; delegation on Hydrology to Internat. Union of Geodesy and Geophysics, 1939, 1948, 1951; Member: Council of British Hydromechanics Research Assoc., 1949-59; Internat. Assoc. for Hydraulic Research, 1947-59. Hon. ACGI, 1951. *Publications:* various engineering reports and scientific papers, chiefly on the motion of air and water. *Address:* 8 Orchard Close, East Budleigh, Devon. *T:* Budleigh Salterton 3559.

WHITE, Christopher John, PhD; Director of Studies, Paul Mellon Centre for Studies in British Art, since 1973, and Associate Director, Yale Center for British Art and British Studies, New Haven, since 1976; *b* 19 Sept. 1930; *s* of Gabriel Ernest Edward Francis White, *qv; m* 1957, Rosemary Katharine Desages; one *s* two *d . Educ:* Downside Sch.; Courtauld Institute of Art, London Univ. BA (Hons) 1954, PhD 1970. Served Army, 1949-50; commnd. RA, 1949. Asst Keeper, Dept of Prints and Drawings, British Museum, 1954-65; Director, P. and D. Colnaghi, 1965-71; Curator of Graphic Arts, Nat. Gall. of Art, Washington, 1971-73. Dutch Govt Schol., 1956; Hermione Lectr, Alexandra Coll., Dublin, 1959; Adjunct Prof., Inst. of Fine Arts, New York Univ., 1973 and 1976; Conference Dir, European-Amer. Assembly on Art Museums, Ditchley Park, 1975; Visiting Prof., Dept of History of Art, Yale Univ., 1976. Reviews Editor, Master Drawings, 1967-. *Publications:* Rembrandt and his World, 1964; The Flower Drawings of Jan van Huysum, 1965; Rubens and his World, 1968; Rembrandt as an Etcher, 1969; (jtly) Rembrandt's Etchings: a catalogue raisonné, 1970; Dürer: the artist and his drawings, 1972; English Landscape 1630-1850; film (script and commentary), Rembrandt's Three Crosses, 1969; various exhibn catalogues; contribs to Burlington Mag., Master Drawings, etc. *Address:* 20 Regent's Park Terrace, NW1 7ED. *T:* 01-485 9148; Shingle House, St Cross, Harleston, Norfolk IP20 0NT. *T:* St Cross 264.

WHITE, Sir Christopher (Robert Meadows), 3rd Bt *cr* 1937, of Boulge Hall, Suffolk; engaged in care of adult mentally sub-normal and maladjusted, Hill House, Northrepps; *b* 26 Aug. 1940; *s* of Sir (Eric) Richard Meadows White, 2nd Bt, and Lady Elizabeth Mary Gladys (*d* 1950), *o d* of 6th Marquess Townshend; *S* father, 1972; *m* 1st, 1962, Anne Marie Ghislaine (marr. diss. 1968), *yr d* of Major Tom Brown, OBE; 2nd, 1968, Dinah Mary Sutton (marr. diss. 1972), Orange House,

Heacham, Norfolk; 3rd, 1976, Ingrid Carolyn Jowett, *e d* of Eric Jowett, Great Baddow; two step *s . Educ:* Bradfield Coll., Berks. Imperial Russian Ballet School, Cannes, France, 1961; schoolmaster, 1961-72; Professore, Istituto Shenker, Rome, and Scuola Specialisti Aeronauta, Macerata, 1962-63; Housemaster, St Michael's Sch., Ingoldisthorpe, Norfolk, 1963-69. Dir, Agripharm Ltd. Hon. Pres., Warnborough House, Oxford, 1973-. Hon. Aux. Sec., Cromer and Dist RSPCA. Lieutenant, TA, Norfolk, 1969. *Recreations:* dogs, vintage cars, antiques. *Address:* The Hill House, Northrepps, Cromer, Norfolk. *T:* Overstrand 242. *Clubs:* Raffles, Frère Jacques.

WHITE, Christopher Stuart Stuart-; *see* Stuart-White.

WHITE, Cyril Grove C.; *see* Costley-White.

WHITE, Cyril Montgomery, CMG 1972; QC 1946; MA; Chairman, Foreign Compensation Commission, 1958-72; *b* 10 August 1897; *o s* of William Montgomery White and Mary Augusta Mourilyan; *m* 1950, Jessie Thompson (OBE 1945), *d* of late James Kidd of Linlithgow; one *d. Educ:* Colet Court; St Paul's School; Corpus Christi College, Oxford. Served in European War (Royal Flying Corps and Royal Air Force) July 1916-Jan. 1919. Called to Bar, Lincoln's Inn, 1923; Bencher, 1952; Treasurer, 1971. Served War of 1939-45 (RAFVR) Aug. 1939-Jan. 1944; Pres. (except for Scottish Proceedings) Transport Arbitration Tribunal, 1947-57. *Publications:* The Conveyancers' Year Book 1947. Senior Editor, Underhill on Trusts and Trustees, 10th edn, 1950, 11th edn, 1959. Has contributed to Halsbury's Laws of England, 3rd edition (Titles: Landlord and Tenant, 1958; Real Property, 1960). *Recreation:* travel. *Address:* Bartlemas, 7 Dover Road, Sandwich, Kent. *T:* Sandwich 3336; 2 Stone Buildings, Lincoln's Inn, WC2. *T:* 01-242 7637. *Club:* United Oxford & Cambridge University.

WHITE, Lt-Col David A. P.; *see* Price-White.

WHITE, Sir Dennis (Charles), KBE 1962 (OBE 1953); CMG 1959; Brunei Government Agent in the United Kingdom, since 1967; *b* 30 July 1910; unmarried. *Educ:* Bradfield College. Joined service of HH the Rajah of Sarawak, 1932. Civilian Prisoner of War, Dec. 1941-Sept. 1945. HM Overseas Civil Service: Senior Resident, 1955; British Resident, Brunei, 1958; HM High Comr for Brunei, 1959-63. Star of Sarawak (Officer) 1946. Esteemed Family Order of Brunei, 1st Class. *Recreations:* general. *Address:* Virginia Cottage, Emery Down, Lyndhurst, Hants. *Club:* Travellers'.

WHITE, Sir Dick (Goldsmith), KCMG 1960; KBE 1955 (CBE 1950; OBE 1942); formerly attached to Foreign and Commonwealth Office, retired 1972; *b* 20 Dec. 1906; *s* of Percy Hall White and Gertrude White (née Farthing); *m* 1945, Kathleen Bellamy; two *s. Educ:* Bishops Stortford Coll.; Christ Church, Oxford; Universities of Michigan and California, USA. US Legion of Merit, Croix de Guerre (France). *Address:* The Leat, Burpham, near Arundel, West Sussex. *T:* Arundel 883030. *Club:* Garrick.
    See also J. A. White.

WHITE, Prof. Edwin George, PhD, DSc, BSc (Vet. Sci.), BSc (Physiol.), FRCVS; William Prescott Professor of Veterinary Preventive Medicine, University of Liverpool, 1950-76; Pro-Vice-Chancellor, 1966-70; *b* 26 March 1911; *s* of Edwin White and Alice Maud White; *m* 1st, 1936, Grace Mary Adlington; two *d*; 2nd, 1974, Winefred Wright. *Educ:* Newport (Mon.) High School; Royal Veterinary College, London; University College, London. Studentship for Research in Animal Health, 1933-35, for postgraduate study in Germany and England; Lecturer in Pathology, Royal Veterinary College, London, 1935; Reader in Pathology, 1939; Principal Scientific Officer, Rowett Research Inst., Bucksburn, Aberdeenshire, 1946; Director of East African Veterinary Research Organisation, 1947; Dean of Faculty of Vet. Sci., Univ. of Liverpool, 1961-65. Pres., RCVS, 1967-68. Chm., Granada Schs Adv. Cttee. *Publications:* articles in various scientific journals since 1934. *Recreation:* gardening. *Address:* Afton, Neston Road, Burton-in-Wirral, Merseyside L64 5SY. *T:* 051-336 4210. *Club:* Royal Commonwealth Society.

WHITE, Elwyn Brooks; Contributor to The New Yorker; *b* 11 July 1899; *s* of Samuel T. White and Jessie Hart; *m* 1929, Katharine Sergeant Angell; one *s. Educ:* Cornell University, USA. Newspaper reporting, advertising, and editorial work as staff member of New Yorker Magazine, to which he has contributed verse, satirical essays, and editorials; wrote a monthly department for Harper's Magazine called One Man's Meat, 1938-43. Hon. degrees: Dartmouth Coll.; Univs of Maine, Yale, Bowdoin, Hamilton, Harvard, Colby. Fellow, Amer. Acad. of Arts and Sciences; Mem., AAAL, 1974. Gold Medal

Nat. Inst. of Arts and Letters, 1960; Presidential Medal of Freedom, 1963; Laura Ingalls Wilder Award, 1970; Nat. Medal for Literature, 1971. *Publications:* The Lady is Cold, 1929; (with J. Thurber) Is Sex Necessary, 1929; Every Day is Saturday, 1934; The Fox of Peapack, 1938; Quo Vadimus?, 1939; One Man's Meat, 1942 (enlarged) 1944; Stuart Little, 1945; The Wild Flag, 1946; Here Is New York, 1949; Charlotte's Web, 1952; The Second Tree from the Corner, 1954; The Points of My Compass, 1962; The Trumpet of the Swan, 1970; (ed, with Katharine S. White) A Subtreasury of American Humor, 1941; rev. and enl. Strunk, The Elements of Style, 1959. *Address:* North Brooklin, Maine, USA. *TA:* care The New Yorker Magazine, 25 W.43.

WHITE, Sir Eric (Henry) W.; *see* Wyndham White.

WHITE, Brig. Eric Stuart, DSO 1918; OStJ; late RASC; *b* 15 Nov. 1888; *o s* of late W. W. White of Lee, Kent; *m* 1st, 1914; one *d*; 2nd, 1939, Ysobel Dora (*d* 1959), *d* of Lt-Col W. P. Murray, DSO, Farnham. *Educ:* Felsted; Sandhurst. Served European War, 1914-18, NW Persia, Iraq (DSO, despatches, Officer, Order of Crown of Belgium; Belgian Croix de Guerre, with two palms); retired, 1944. *Address:* The Cottage, Donnington, Chichester, West Sussex.

WHITE, Erica, FRBS (retired); Sculptor and Painter; *d* of Frederic Charles White, solicitor and Mildred S. Hutchings. *Educ:* St George's School, Harpenden; Slade School of Art (Sculpture Scholarship two years and Painting Prize); gained London University Diploma in Fine Arts; studied at Central School of Arts and Crafts; gained British Institution Scholarship in Sculpture; studied at Royal Acad. Schools (Silver and Bronze Medallist); awarded Feodora Gleichen Memorial Fund Grant; exhibited at Royal Academy and at Glasgow, Brighton, Bournemouth and other Art Galleries. *Recreations:* outdoor sports and music. *Address:* South Cliff Cottage, 3 South Cliff, Bexhill-on-Sea, Sussex TN39 3EJ. *T:* Bexhill 211013.

WHITE, Sir Ernest (Keith), Kt 1969; CBE 1967; MC; Chairman, R. J. White & Co. (Sydney) Pty Ltd, since 1935; *b* 1892; *s* of late Robert John White; *m* 1915, Pauline Marjory, *d* of J. J. Mason; one *s* two *d. Educ:* Gosford Public Sch., NSW. Served European War, 1914-18 (Sir Douglas Haig's despatches, MC): Captain 4th Bn AIF, in Egypt and France (Ypres, Somme, Broodsiend Ridge, Bullecourt, Strrozeel). Pres., Liberal Democratic Party, Australia, 1943; Delegate to Prelim. and Plenary Conf. which founded Liberal Party of Australia, and apptd to Provisional State and Federal Council, 1943. Vice-Pres., Australian American Assoc. (Founder and 1st Federal Pres., 1936). *Address:* Baden House, Baden Road, Kurraba Point, Neutral Bay, NSW 2089, Australia. *T:* 90 5741. *Clubs:* Royal Commonwealth Society; Tattersall's; Australian Jockey; American National.

WHITE, Errol Ivor, CBE 1960; DSc, PhD (London); FRS 1956; FGS, FLS, FKC; retired as Keeper of Department of Palæontology (formerly of Geology), British Museum (Natural History), 1955-66 (Deputy Keeper, 1938-55); *b* 1901; *y s* of late Felix E. White and Lilian Daniels; *m* 1st, 1933, Barbara Gladwyn Christian (marr. diss. 1940, she *d* 1969); 2nd, 1944, Margaret Clare (Jane), BCom (Leeds), *y d* of late T. C. Fawcett, Bolton Abbey, Yorks; one *s. Educ:* Highgate School (Senior Foundationer); King's Coll., London Univ. (Tennant Prizeman). BSc 1921; PhD 1927; DSc 1936. Entered British Museum (Natural History), 1922; Geological Expeditions to Madagascar, 1929-30, and Spitsbergen, 1939; temp. Principal, Min. of Health, 1940-April 1945; Hon. Sec. Ray Society, 1946-51, Vice-Pres., 1951-54, 1959-, Pres., 1956-59; Council, Geological Soc., 1949-53, 1956-60; Vice-Pres., 1957-60 (Murchison Medal, 1962); President, Linnean Soc., 1964-67 (Linnean Gold Medal, 1970); Chm. Systematics Assoc., 1955-58; Coun., Zool. Soc., 1959-63. *Publications:* Technical memoirs and papers in various scientific jls, chiefly relating to extinct agnatha and fishes. *Recreations:* ornithology, philately, bridge. *Address:* Prospect House, North Stoke, Oxford OX9 6BL. *T:* Wallingford 37342.

WHITE, Frank John; His Honour Judge White; a Circuit Judge, since 1974; *b* 12 March 1927; *s* of late Frank Byron White; *m* 1953, Anne Rowlandson, MBE, *d* of late Sir Harold Gibson Howitt, GBE, DSO, MC; two *s* two *d. Educ:* Reading Sch.; King's Coll., London. LLB, LLM (London). Sub-Lt, RNVR, 1945-47; called to the Bar, Gray's Inn, 1951; Mem., General Council of the Bar, 1969-73; Dep. Chm., Berkshire QS, 1970-72; a Recorder of the Crown Court, 1972-74. *Recreation:* photography. *Address:* 8 Queen's Ride, SW13 0JB. *T:* 01-788 8903; Blauvac, Vaucluse, France. *Clubs:* Athenæum, Roehampton.

WHITE, Frank Richard, JP; MP (Lab) Bury and Radcliffe, since Oct. 1974; industrial relations adviser; *b* Nov. 1939; *m*; three *c*. *Educ:* Bolton Tech. Coll. Member: Bolton CC, 1963-74; Greater Manchester CC, 1973-75. Member: NUGMW; IPM; IWSP. Contested (Lab) Bury and Radcliffe, Feb. 1974. PPS to Minister of State, Dept of Industry, 1975-76. *Address:* House of Commons, SW1A 0AA; 36 Parkdale Road, Tonge Moor, Bolton, Lancs BL2 2QU.

WHITE, Sir Frederick William George, KBE 1962 (CBE 1954); PhD; FAA 1960; FRS 1966; Chairman, Commonwealth Scientific and Industrial Research Organization, 1959-70 (Deputy Chairman, 1957, Chief Executive Officer, 1949-57); *b* 26 May 1905; *s* of late William Henry White; *m* 1932, Elizabeth Cooper; one *s* one *d. Educ:* Wellington College, New Zealand; Victoria University College, Univ. of New Zealand (MSc 1928); Cambridge Univ. (PhD 1932). Postgrad. School. in Science, Univ. of NZ and Strathcona Schol., St John's Coll., Cambridge; Research in Physics, Cavendish Laboratory, 1929-31; Asst Lecturer in Physics, Univ. of London, King's Coll., 1931-36; Professor of Physics, Canterbury University Coll., NZ, 1937; Member, British Empire Cancer Campaign Soc., Canterbury Branch Cttee, 1938; Radio Research Cttee, DSIR NZ, 1937; Advisor to NZ Govt on radar research, 1939; seconded to Aust. CSIR, 1941; Chm., Radiophysics Adv. Bd, 1941; Chief, Div. of Radiophysics, 1942. Exec. Officer, 1945, Mem., Exec. Cttee, 1946, CSIR Aust. Radio Research Bd, 1942; Scientific Adv. Cttee, Aust. Atomic Energy Commn, 1953; FInstP; Fellow Aust. Instn of Radio Engrs. Hon. DSc: Monash Univ.; ANU; Univ. of Papua and New Guinea. *Publications:* scientific papers on nature of ionosphere over NZ and on propagation of radio waves; Electromagnetic Waves, 1934. *Recreation:* fishing. *Address:* 57 Investigator Street, Red Hill, Canberra, ACT 2603, Australia. *T:* 957424.

WHITE, Gabriel Ernest Edward Francis, CBE 1963; Director of Art, Arts Council of Great Britain, 1958-70; *b* 29 Nov. 1902; *s* of late Ernest Arthur White and Alice White; *m* 1st, 1928, Elizabeth Grace (*d* 1958), *d* of late Auguste Ardizzone; two *s*; 2nd, 1963, Jane, *d* of late J. R. Kingdon and of Mrs Kingdon, Minehead; one *s* one *d. Educ:* Dnoriside Sch.; Trinity Coll., Oxford. Staff Officer RE Camouflage, 1940-45; Asst Art Director, Arts Council of Great Britain, 1945-58. Order of the Aztec Eagle, 2nd class (Mexico). *Publication:* Sickert Drawings (in Art and Technics), 1952. *Recreations:* drawing, painting. *Address:* 88 Holmdene Avenue, SE24. *T:* 01-274 9643.

See also C. J. White.

WHITE, Sir George (Stanley Midelton), 3rd Bt, *cr* 1904; *b* 11 April 1913; *s* of 2nd Bt and late Kate Muriel, *d* of late Thomas Baker, Bristol; *S* father, 1964; *m* 1939, Diane Eleanor, *d* of late Bernard Abdy Collins, CIE; one *s* one *d. Educ:* Harrow; Magdalene College, Cambridge. Member of the firm of George White, Evans, Tribe & Co., Bristol (formerly George White, Evans & Co.). *Heir:* *s* George Stanley James White [*b* 4 November 1948; *m* 1974, Susan Elizabeth, *d* of late John Langmaid Ford]. *Address:* Pypers, Rudgeway, near Bristol. *T:* Thornbury 412312.

WHITE, Maj.-Gen. Gilbert Anthony, MBE 1944; Managing Director, White Maud & Warner Ltd, since 1971; *b* 10 June 1916; *s* of Cecil James Lawrence White and Muriel (*née* Collins); *m* 1939, Margaret Isabel Duncan Wallet; two *d. Educ:* Christ's Hosp., Horsham. Member of Lloyd's, 1938. Joined TA Artists Rifles, 1937; TA Commn, E Surrey Regt, 1939; served BEF, 1940, N Africa, 1943-44, Italy, 1944-45; Staff Coll., 1944; Instructor, Staff Coll., Haifa, 1946; with UK Delegn to UN, 1946-48; served on Lord Mountbatten's personal staff in MoD, 1960-61; idc 1965; BAOR, 1966-69; Chief, Jt Services Liaison Orgn, Bonn, 1969-71; retd 1971. Hon. Treasurer, S Regional Assoc. for the Blind, 1972-. *Recreations:* golf, racing. *Address:* Speedwell, Tekels Avenue, Camberley, Surrey. *T:* Camberley 23812. *Club:* Army and Navy.

WHITE, Harold Clare, MBE 1967; Consul-General, Seattle, since 1976; *b* 26 Oct. 1919; *s* of Alfred John White and Nora White; *m* 1951, Marie Elizabeth Richardson; two *d. Educ:* Grammar Sch., Warrington. Served War, Royal Signals, 1939-45. GPO, 1937-39 and 1946; FO, 1947; Third Sec., Djakarta, 1951; FO, 1955; Vice-Consul, Piraeus, Kirkuk, San Francisco, and Durban, 1957-64; 1st Secretary: Kinshasa, 1964; Kuala Lumpur, 1968; FCO, 1972; Dep. Consul-Gen., Chicago, 1974. *Recreations:* cricket, golf. *Address:* c/o Foreign and Commonwealth Office, SW1; 65 The Ridgeway, Tonbridge, Kent TN10 4NL. *T:* Tonbridge 354651. *Clubs:* Civil Service; Rainier, Harbour (Seattle).

WHITE, Sir Harold (Leslie), Kt 1970; CBE 1962; MA; FLAA; FAHA; FASSA; National Librarian, National Library of Australia, Canberra, 1947-70; *b* Numurkah, Vic, 14 June 1905; *s* of late James White, Canterbury, Vic; *m* 1930, Elizabeth (MBE), *d* of Richard Wilson; two *s* two *d. Educ:* Wesley College, Melbourne; Queen's College, University of Melbourne. Commonwealth Parliamentary Library, 1923-67; National and Parliamentary Librarian, 1947-67. Visited US as Carnegie Scholar, 1939, and as first Australian under "Leaders and Specialists programme" of Smith Mundt Act, 1950. Represented Australia at various overseas Conferences, 1939-69. Chairman, Standing Cttee, Aust. Advisory Council on Bibliographical Services, 1960-70; Member: various Aust. cttees for UNESCO; Aust. Nat. Film Bd; UNESCO Internat. Cttee on Bibliography, Documentation and Terminology, 1961-64; Nat. Meml Cttee, 1975-; Chm., Adv. Cttee, Australian Encyclopaedia, 1970-; Governor, Australian Film Inst., 1958-77; Hon. Vice Pres., Library Assoc. of Australia, 1970-. *Publications:* (ed) Canberra: A Nation's Capital; contribs to various jls. *Address:* 27 Mugga Way, Canberra, ACT 2603, Australia.

WHITE, Sir Henry Arthur Dalrymple D.; *see* Dalrymple-White.

WHITE, Hugh Fortescue Moresby, CMG 1943; *b* 15 Sept. 1891; *s* of Lt-Col R. F. Moresby White, OBE, VD, Grantham; *m* Betty Sophia Pennington, *d* of Capt. Frank Brandt, RN; one *s. Educ:* Malvern College; St John's College, Oxford. Administrative Service, Nigeria, 1915-45; Acting Chief Commissioner, Southern Provinces, 1938, Western Provinces 1939 and 1944; Senior Resident, Oyo Province, 1940-44. *Address:* Le Clos D'Avranche, St Mary, Jersey, Channel Islands. *T:* Central 61631.

WHITE, Air Vice-Marshal Hugh Granville, CB 1952; CBE 1944; CEng; FIMechE; retired; *b* 1 Mar. 1898; *s* of Herbert White, The Poplars, Maidstone, Kent; *m* 1926, Mabel Joyce Hickman; two *s* one *d. Educ:* HMS Conway; Eastbourne College; Royal Military College, Sandhurst; Jesus College, Cambridge. Commissioned in East Kent Regt, attached RFC, 1916; served as pilot in France, 1916-18; permanent commission on formation of RAF, 1918; comd Nos 29, 64 and 501 Squadrons; Staff appointments as Technical Officer, Royal Air Force College, Cranwell, 1930-33; HQ Air Defence, Gt Britain, 1933-35; STSO, HQ Far East, 1936-39; SASO No 24 Group, 1939-42; AOC Halton, 1942-46; STSO, HQ, BAFO, Germany, 1946-48; AOC No 43 Group, 1948-50; AOC No 41 Group, 1950-53; AOA HQ Maintenance Cmd, 1953-55; retired 1955. *Recreations:* played rugby for RAF, 1922-23; gardening. *Address:* 30 Hillside, Eastdean, Eastbourne, East Sussex BN20 0HE. *T:* Eastdean 3151. *Club:* Royal Over-Seas League.

WHITE, Prof. James; Dyson Professor of Refractories Technology, University of Sheffield, 1956-73, now Emeritus; Dean of Faculty of Metallurgy, 1958-62; *b* 1 April 1908; *s* of late John White and Margaret E. White (*née* Laidlaw), Langholm, Dumfriesshire; *m* 1936, Elizabeth Kelly, Glasgow; one *s. Educ:* Langholm Acad. (Dux Medallist); Dumfries Acad. (Science Dux); Glasgow University. BSc 1st Cl. Hons Physical Chemistry, 1931; PhD 1935; DSc 1939. DSIR Research Scholarship, Roy. Technical Coll., Glasgow, 1931; Dr James McKenzie Prize for Research, 1933; Research Asst in Metallurgy, Roy. Technical Coll., 1933; Associateship of Roy. Technical Coll., 1934; Lectr in Metallurgy, Roy. Tech. Coll., 1935; Andrew Carnegie Research Scholarship of Iron and Steel Inst., 1936-38; Andrew Carnegie Gold Medallist of Iron and Steel Inst., 1939; Research Technologist in Refractories Industry, 1943; Lectr in Refractory Materials, Sheffield Univ., 1946; Reader in Ceramics, Sheffield Univ., 1952. FIM 1952; Founder FICeram 1955; FRSA 1972. Silver Jubilee Lectr, Glass and Ceramic Res. Inst., Calcutta. President: Sheffield Metallurgical Assoc., 1950; Refractories Assoc. of Great Britain, 1959-60; Chm. Clay Minerals Group, Mineralogical Society, 1959-61; First Chm. Basic Science Section, British Ceramic Soc.; Pres., British Ceramic Soc., 1961-62; Hon. Mem. Council, Iron and Steel Inst., 1961-62. Visiting Prof., Nat. Research Centre, Cairo, 1962; Student's Trust Fund Visiting Lectr, Univ. of the Witwatersrand, SA, 1964; Visiting Prof., Univ. of Illinois, 1966; Nat. Sci. Foundn Senior Foreign Scientist Fellowship, Univ. of Alfred, NY, 1968. Fellow, Mineralogical Soc. of America, 1960; Hon. Mem., Iron and Steel Inst., 1973. Griffith Medal, Materials Science Club, 1971. *Publications:* numerous scientific papers on ferrous metallurgy and refractory materials (some jointly). *Recreations:* sketching, motor-cars, walking. *Address:* 1 Chequers Close, Ranby, Retford DN22 8JX.

WHITE, James; MP (Lab) Glasgow (Pollok) since 1970; *b* 10 April 1922; *m* 1948, Mary E. Dempsey; one *s* two *d. Educ:* Knightswood Secondary School. Served War of 1939-45: African and Italian Stars; Defence Medal. Managing Director, Glasgow Car Collection Ltd, 1959-. Mem., Commonwealth Parly Assoc. Delegn, Bangladesh, 1973. *Recreations:* reading, golf, swimming. *Address:* House of Commons, SW1; 23 Alder Road, Glasgow G43 2UU. *T:* 041-637 6412.

WHITE, James; Director, National Gallery of Ireland, since 1964; Professor of the History of Painting, Royal Hibernian Academy, since 1968; External Lecturer in the History of Art, University College, Dublin, and Trinity College, Dublin, since 1955; *b* 16 Sept. 1913; *s* of Thomas John White and Florence Coffey; *m* 1941, Agnes Bowe; three *s* two *d. Educ:* Belvedere Coll., Dublin; privately in European museums and collections. Art Critic: Standard, 1940-50; Irish Press, 1950-59; Irish Times, 1959-62. Curator, Municipal Gallery of Modern Art, Dublin, 1960-64. Visiting Lectr in Univs and Socs in GB, Italy, USA, Canada. Radio and Television contribs: BBC, RTE, and in the USA. Irish Comr to Biennale at Venice and at Paris on various occasions; Organiser of Exhibns in Dublin, London, Paris, etc., incl. Paintings from Irish Collections, 1957. Hon. LLD NUI, 1970. Silver Medal of the Italian Govt Dept of Foreign Affairs, 1967; Arnold K. Henry Medal of RCS of Ireland. Chevalier, Légion d'Honneur, 1974. *Publications:* Irish Stained Glass, 1963; The National Gallery of Ireland, 1968; Jack B. Yeats, 1971; John Butler Yeats and the Irish Renaissance, 1972; contributor to: Apollo, Art News, Studio, Connoisseur, Blackfriars, Manchester Guardian, The Furrow, Doctrine and Life, Art Notes, Merian, Werk, Das Munster, Hollandsche Art, La Biennale, La Revue Française, Il Milione, Encyclopedia of Art, etc. *Recreations:* golf, swimming, gardening, bridge. *Address:* (office) National Gallery of Ireland, Merrion Sq., Dublin 2. *T:* 761699; (private) 15 Herbert Park, Ballsbridge, Dublin 4. *T:* 683723. *Club:* Kildare Street and University (Dublin).

WHITE, John Alan; Deputy Chairman, Associated Book Publishers Ltd, 1963-68 (Managing Director, 1946-62); former Director: British Publishers Guild Ltd; Eyre & Spottiswoode Ltd; *b* 20 June 1905; *e s* of Percy Hall White and Gertrude (*née* Farthing); *m* 1st, Marjorie Lovelace Vincent (*d* 1958); two *s*; 2nd, Vivienne Rosalie Musgrave. *Educ:* Bishops Stortford College. President, Publishers' Association, 1955-57; Chairman, National Book League, 1963-65. *Recreations:* reading, gardening. *Address:* Hayfield House, College Road, Cork, Ireland. *T:* Cork 21519. *Clubs:* Athenæum, Garrick.
See also Sir Dick Goldsmith White.

WHITE, Lt-Col John Baker, TD 1950; JP; *b* West Malling, Kent, 12 Aug. 1902; *s* of late J. W. B. White, Street End House, Canterbury; *m* 1925, Sybil Irene Erica, *d* of late C. B. Graham, Onslow Gardens, SW1; one *s* one *d. Educ:* Stubbington House, Fareham; Malvern College. Worked on farms in Kent and Sussex to gain a basic knowledge of agriculture, 1920-22; worked in a circus to gain a wider knowledge of human nature, 1922; studied the structure of industry and social science in London and various industrial centres, 1922-24; worked as a voluntary helper in canteens for the unemployed and among distressed ex-service men; employed in the coal industry, 1924-26; Director Economic League, 1926-45, Publicity Adviser, 1945-76. Joined Territorial Army, London Rifle Brigade, 1934; served in Army as regimental soldier, on War Office staff with Political Intelligence Dept of FO, and Political Warfare Mission in the Middle East, 1939-45; Lieut-Colonel 1941. MP (C) Canterbury division of Kent, 1945-53. JP Kent, 1954. Pres., E Kent Fruit Show Soc.; Vice Pres., Canterbury Soc.; Pres., Scour Valley Soc. *Publications:* Red Russia Arms, 1934; It's Gone for Good, 1941; The Soviet Spy System, 1948; The Red Network, 1953; The Big Lie, 1955; Pattern for Conquest, 1956; Sabotage is Suspected, 1957; True Blue, 1970. *Address:* Street End Place, near Canterbury, Kent CT4 5NP. *T:* Petham 265. *Club:* Royal Automobile.

WHITE, Prof. John Edward Clement Twarowski; Durning-Lawrence Professor of the History of Art, University College, London, since 1971; Chairman, Reviewing Committee on Export of Works of Art, since 1976 (Member since 1975); *b* 4 Oct. 1924; *s* of Brigadier A. E. White and Suzanne Twarowska; *m* 1950, Xenia Joannides. *Educ:* Ampleforth College; Trinity College, Oxford; Courtauld Institute of Art, University of London. Served in RAF, 1943-47. BA London 1950; Junior Research Fellow, Warburg Inst., 1950-52; PhD Lond. 1952; MA Manchester 1963. Lectr in History of Art, Courtauld Inst., 1952-58; Alexander White Vis. Prof., Univ. of Chicago, 1958; Reader in History of Art, Courtauld Inst., 1958-59; Pilkington Prof. of the History of Art and Dir of The Whitworth Art Gallery, Univ. of Manchester, 1959-66; Vis. Ferens Prof. of Fine Art, Univ. of Hull, 1961-62; Prof. of the History of Art and

Chm., Dept of History of Art, Johns Hopkins Univ., USA, 1966-71. Member: Adv. Council of V&A, 1973-76; Exec. Cttee, Assoc. of Art Historians, 1974- (Chm., 1976-); Art Panel, Arts Council, 1974-. Trustee, Whitechapel Art Gall., 1976-. *Publications:* Perspective in Ancient Drawings and Painting, 1956; The Birth and Rebirth of Pictorial Space, 1957; Art and Architecture in Italy, 1250-1400, 1966; articles in Burlington Magazine, Jl of Warburg and Courtauld Institutes, Art Bulletin. *Address:* Department of The History of Art, University College, Gower Street, WC1; (home) 25 Cadogan Place, SW1.

WHITE, John Sampson, CMG 1970; Secretary to the Governor, South Australia, since 1976; *b* 9 June 1916; *s* of late W. J. White; *m* 1941, Dorothy G., *d* of late E. J. Griffin; one *s* one *d*. *Educ:* Black Forest Primary and Adelaide High Schs. AASA. Attorney-General's Dept, 1933-61. Served War, 2nd AIF, 1941-45, Captain. Asst Sec., Industries Develt Cttee, 1950, Sec., 1951-61; Sec., Land Agents' Bd, 1951-61; Sec. to Premier, SA, 1961-65; Mem., SA Superannuation Fund Bd, 1961-74; Sec., Premier's Dept, SA, 1965-74; Agent-Gen. for SA, 1974-76; Comr of Charitable Funds, 1964-74. Mem., Council of Governors, Presb. Girls' Coll., 1958-73. Freeman, City of London. *Recreations:* swimming, tennis. *Address:* Peppertree Cottage, Government House, North Terrace, Adelaide, SA 5000, Australia. *Clubs:* Adelaide, Naval, Military and Air Force (Adelaide); Sturt.

WHITE, Sir John (Woolmer), 4th Bt *cr* 1922; *b* 4 Feb. 1947; *s* of Sir Headley Dymoke White, 3rd Bt and of Elizabeth Victoria Mary, *er d* of late Wilfrid Ingram Wrightson; *S* father, 1971. *Educ:* Hurst Court, Hastings; Cheltenham College. *Heir:* uncle Lynton Stuart White, MBE, TD [*b* 11 Aug. 1916; *m* 1945, Phyllis Marie Rochfort, *d* of Sir Newnham Worley, KBE, and late Marie Forlong; four *s* one *d*]. *Address:* Salle Park, Salle, Norwich, Norfolk NOR 73X.

WHITE, Lawrence John, CMG 1972; formerly Assistant Secretary, Board of Customs and Excise, 1961-75, retired; *b* 23 Feb. 1915; *s* of Arthur Yirrell White and Helen Christina White; *m* 1936, Ivy Margaret Coates; one *s*. *Educ:* Banbury Grammar Sch. Joined Customs and Excise, 1933; Commonwealth Relations Office, 1948-50; Customs and Excise, 1951-75. *Recreations:* reading, walking. *Address:* Peach Tree Cottage, Fifield, Oxon. *T:* Shipton under Wychwood 830806.

WHITE, Leslie Gordon, CBE 1949; retired; *b* 1889; *s* of late Henry Tom White; *m* 1919, Dorothy Morgan (*d* 1961). *Educ:* Eastbourne Grammar School; Entered Inland Revenue Department, 1908; Dep. Chief Inspector of Taxes, 1947-50; retired 1950. *Address:* Ashdene, 277 Dyke Road, Hove BN3 6PB. *T:* Brighton 552954.

WHITE, Michael James Denham; FRS 1961; FAA; Visiting Fellow, Australian National University, since 1976; *b* 20 August 1910; *s* of James Kemp White and Una Theodora Chase; *m* 1938, Isobel Mary Lunn; two *s* one *d*. *Educ:* University College, London. Asst Lecturer, 1933-35; Lecturer, 1936-46, Reader, 1947, University Coll., London; Guest Investigator, Carnegie Instn of Washington, 1947; Professor of Zoology, Univ. of Texas, 1947-53; Senior Research Fellow, CSIRO, Canberra, Australia, 1953-56; Prof. of Zoology, Univ. of Missouri, 1957-58; Univ. of Melbourne: Prof. of Zoology, 1958-64; Prof. of Genetics, 1964-75. Foreign Member, Amer. Acad. of Arts and Sciences; Pres., Genetics Soc. of Australia, 1971-73. Mueller Medallist, Aust. and NZ Assoc. for the Advancement of Science, 1965. *Publications:* (Monograph) The Chromosomes, 1937, 6th edn 1973 (trans into French, Italian, Polish, Portuguese, and Spanish); Animal Cytology and Evolution, 1945, 3rd edn 1973; Modes of Speciation, 1978; many papers in learned journals. *Address:* Department of Population Biology, Australian National University, PO Box 475, Canberra City, ACT 2601, Australia.

WHITE, Air Vice-Marshal Michael William Langtry; Principal Medical Officer, RAF Support Command, 1973-74; retired 1974; *b* 6 March 1915; *s* of Frederick William White, solicitor, and Pauline Marie White; *m* 1940, Mary Seton Dury Arnould, Battle, Sussex; one *s* one *d*. *Educ:* Dauntsey's; St Bartholomew's Hosp. MFCM, MRCS, LRCP, DPH. Qualified as doctor, 1940. Served War, Mediterranean Theatre, 1942-45 (despatches 1943). Air Vice-Marshal, 1971; PMO RAF Training Comd, 1971-73. psc 1955. QHP 1972-74. *Recreations:* shooting, fishing, gardening. *Address:* Owl Cottage, Netheravon, Wilts. *T:* Netheravon 396. *Club:* Royal Air Force.

WHITE, Maj.-Gen. Napier; *see* White, Maj.-Gen. P. N.

WHITE, Norman Lewis, MD, FRCS, FRCOG; retired as Obstetrician, University College Hospital; Gynæcological Surgeon, Royal Northern Hospital; Gynæcologist, Ministry of Pensions Hospital, Roehampton, and West Herts Hospital. *Educ:* University of Cambridge; University College Hospital, London. MRCS, LRCP 1923; BA Cambridge (1st Cl. Nat. Sci. Tripos), MA, BChir, 1929; FRCS 1929; MD 1933; FRCOG 1943. Examiner in Midwifery, Society of Apothecaries; Fellow of the Royal Society of Medicine. Formerly: Associate Examiner in Obstetrics and Gynæcology, University of London; First Assistant, Obstetrical Unit, University College Hospital; Examiner, Midwives Conjoint Board. *Address:* Fern Cottage, Norton Green, Freshwater, Isle of Wight.

WHITE, Patrick Victor Martindale; Author; *b* 28 May 1912; *s* of Victor Martindale White and Ruth Withycombe. *Educ:* Cheltenham Coll.; King's Coll., Cambridge. Brought up partly in Australia, partly in England. First published while living in London before War of 1939-45. Served War with RAF, as Intelligence Officer, mainly in Middle East. Returned to Australia after War. Nobel Prize for Literature, 1973. *Publications: novels:* Happy Valley, 1939; The Living and the Dead, 1941 (new edn 1962); The Aunt's Story, 1946; The Tree of Man, 1954; Voss, 1957 (1st annual literary award of £1000 from W. H. Smith & Son, 1959); Riders in the Chariot, 1961; The Solid Mandala, 1966; The Vivisector, 1970; The Eye of the Storm, 1973; A Fringe of Leaves, 1976; *plays:* The Ham Funeral, 1947; The Season at Sarsaparilla, 1961; A Cheery Soul, 1962; Night on Bald Mountain, 1962; Big Toys, 1977; *short stories:* The Burnt Ones, 1964; The Cockatoos, 1974. *Recreations:* friendship, cooking, gardening, listening to music, keeping dogs. *Address:* 20 Martin Road, Centennial Park, Sydney, NSW 2021, Australia.

WHITE, Maj.-Gen. (Percival) Napier, CB 1951; CBE 1946; psc; late Infantry; *b* 1901; *s* of A. J. White, Norton, Evesham, Worcestershire; *m* 1st, 1928, Dorothy Usticke Kemp (*d* 1946), *d* of Rev. Canon Bater, Derby; one *d* (and one *d* decd); 2nd, 1947, Geraldine Margaret Joan Brooking, *d* of late Captain Guy Lushington Coleridge, Royal Navy; two *s*. *Educ:* Cathedral School, Worcester; Royal Military College, Sandhurst. 2nd Lieutenant Sherwood Foresters, 1921; Lt-Colonel, 1941; acting Brigadier, 1943; Colonel, 1946. Served War of 1939-45: in France, 1939-40. Middle East, 1941-45 (despatches twice). Colonel The Sherwood Foresters, 1947-58. Chief of Staff, Northern Command, 1951-53; Assistant Chief of Staff (Organisation and Training), SHAPE, 1953-55; Commandant Joint Services Staff College, 1956-58, retired. Controller, Army Benevolent Fund, 1960-71. *Address:* Little Langley, Chobham, Surrey. *Club:* Army and Navy.

WHITE, Adm. Sir Peter, GBE 1977 (KBE 1976; CBE 1960; MBE 1944); Chief of Fleet Support, 1974-77; *b* 25 Jan. 1919; *s* of William White, Amersham, Bucks; *m* 1947, Audrey Eileen, *d* of Ernest Wallin, Northampton; two *s*. *Educ:* Dover College. Secretary: to Chief of Staff, Home Fleet, 1942-43; to Flag Officer Comdg 4th Cruiser Sqdn, 1944-45; to Asst Chief of Naval Personnel, 1946-47; to Flag Officer, Destroyers, Mediterranean, 1948-49; to Controller of the Navy, 1949-53; to C-in-C Home Fleet and C-in-C Eastern Atlantic, 1954-55; Naval Asst to Chm. BJSM, Washington, and UK Rep. of Standing Group, NATO, 1956-59; Supply Officer, HMS Adamant, 1960-61; Dep. Dir of Service Conditions and Fleet Supply Duties, Admty, 1961-63; idc 1964; CO HMS Raleigh, 1965-66; Principal Staff Officer to Chief of Defence Staff, 1967-69; Dir-Gen. Fleet Services, 1969-71; Port Admiral, Rosyth, 1972-74. *Address:* White Pines, Denbigh Road, Haslemere, Surrey. *Club:* Army and Navy.

WHITE, Raymond Walter Ralph; Governor, Reserve Bank of New Zealand, since 1977; *b* 23 June 1923; *s* of Henry Underhill White and Ethel Annie White; *m* 1946, Nola Colleen Adin; one *s* two *d*. *Educ:* Palmerston North Technical High Sch.; Victoria Univ. ACA; FCIS 1968. Dep. Governor, Reserve Bank of NZ, 1967. *Recreations:* golf, tennis, gardening. *Address:* 63 Chatsworth Road, Silverstream, New Zealand. *T:* Upper Hutt 82084. *Club:* Wellington (NZ).

WHITE, Captain Richard Taylor, DSO 1940 (Bars 1941 and 1942); RN retired; *b* 29 Jan. 1908; *s* of Sir Archibald White, 4th Bt and *heir-pres.* to Sir Thomas White, *qv*; *m* 1936, Gabrielle Ursula Style; three *s* two *d*. *Educ:* RN College, Dartmouth. Served War of 1939-45 (DSO and two Bars). Retired 1955. *Address:* Wateringbury Place, near Maidstone, Kent.

WHITE, Prof. Robert George, FRSEd; Gardiner Professor and Head of Department of Bacteriology and Immunology, University of Glasgow, since 1963; Hon. Consultant in Bacteriology, Western Infirmary, Glasgow; *b* 18 July 1917; *s* of

Thomas Percy White and Alice Robina Fewkes; *m* 1953, Joan Margaret Horsburgh; one *s* two *d. Educ:* King Edward VI Sch., Nuneaton; The Queen's Coll., Oxford (Open Schol.). BA 1939; qual. in med., Oxford and London Hosp., BM, BCh 1942; MA 1953; DM 1953; MRCP 1964; FRSEd 1968; FRCPath 1970; FRCP 1972. Surg. Lt-Comdr, RNVR, 1945-47; Freedom Research Fellow, Lond. Hosp., 1948-52; MRC Trav. Fellow, at Harvard Med. Sch., USA, 1952-53; Reader in Bacteriology, Lond. Hosp., 1954-63. Trav. Prof., Univ. of Florida, 1960. WHO Adv. in Immuno-pathology, 1964-; Meetings Sec., Br. Soc. for Immunology, 1957-63; Mem. Coun., Hannah Dairy Research Inst., Ayr, 1964-. Past Pres., Sect. Allergy and Clin. Immunology, RSM, 1964-66; Chm., Sci. Adv. Council, Lady Tata Memorial Trust, 1976- (Mem., 1968). Examiner: Trinity College Dublin; Univ. of Edinburgh. FRSocMed. *Publications:* (with J. H. Humphrey) Immunology for Students of Medicine, 1963 (3rd edn 1970); (with Morag Timbury) Immunology and Microbiology, 1973; articles in sci. jls: Nature, Jl Exptl Med., Lancet, Immunology, Br. Jl Exptl Path. *Recreations:* skating, ski-ing, sailing, painting in oils. *Address:* Dunarden, Campbell Street, Helensburgh, Scotland. *T:* Helensburgh 2201 and 041-339 8822 (ext. 222). *Club:* RNVR (Scotland).

WHITE, Roger Lowrey, JP; Managing Director, Research Information Services (Westminster) Ltd; Director: Williamson Tea Holdings Ltd, since 1972; Majuli Tea Co. Ltd, since 1973; Romai Tea Holdings Ltd, since 1977; Security Lorry Parks Ltd, since 1977; *b* 1 June 1928; *o s* of late George Frederick White and Dorothy Jeanette White; *m* 1962, Angela Mary (*née* Orman), company director. *Educ:* St Joseph's Coll., Beulah Hill. National Vice-Chm., Young Conservatives, 1958-59; Founder Mem., Conservative Commonwealth Council; Mem. Council, London Borough of Bromley, 1964-68. MP (C) Gravesend, 1970-Feb. 1974. Member: British Bd of Boxing Control (1929) Ltd; Asthma Research Council, 1973-. Freeman, City of London, 1953; Liveryman, Worshipful Co. of Makers of Playing Cards, 1975-; JP Inner London Area, 1965. *Recreations:* golf, tennis, painting. *Address:* 74 Clifton Court, Aberdeen Place, NW8. *Clubs:* Carlton, St Stephen's.

WHITE, Rt. Rev. Russell Berridge; MA (Oxon), Dipl. Theology (Oxon); *b* 13 Dec. 1896; *yr s* of late Benjamin Beeson, Poplar, London; *m* 1926, Sarah Margaret, *e d* of Rev. J. A. Bunch, Manby, Lincs; two *s* one *d* (and one *s* decd). *Educ:* City of Oxford School; St Edmund Hall, Oxford (1919-22); Wycliffe Hall, Oxford (1922-23). Served European War, 1914-18 (Mons Star, etc.); Queen's Own Oxfordshire Hussars. Curate St Philemon, Toxteth, 1923-27; Clerical Supt, Liverpool CE Scripture Readers Society, 1927-29, Secretary from 1932; Vicar of St Chrysostom, Everton, 1929-33; Secretary, Evangelical Churchmen's Ordination Council, 1933-59; Curate of St Mary Woolnoth, London and offg Chap. Mercer's Co., 1934-37; Vicar of St Stephen, E Twickenham, 1937-45; Vicar of Tonbridge, 1945-59; Rural Dean of Tonbridge, 1946-59; Suffragan Bishop of Tonbridge, 1959-68. Proctor in Convocation, 1947-64. *Recreations:* music, gardening. *Address:* 11 Sondes Place Drive, Dorking, Surrey. *T:* Dorking 3445.

WHITE, Terence de Vere; Literary Editor, The Irish Times, since 1961; *b* 29 April 1912; *s* of Frederick S. de Vere White, LLD, and Ethel (*née* Perry); *m* 1941, Mary O'Farrell; two *s* one *d. Educ:* St Stephen's Green Sch., Dublin; Trinity Coll., Dublin (BA, LLB). Admitted solicitor, 1933. Mem. Council, Incorporated Law Society, retd 1961. Vice-Chm., Board of Governors, National Gallery of Ireland; Trustee: National Library; Chester Beatty Library; Dir, Gate Theatre, 1969-. Mem., Irish Academy of Letters, 1968; Hon. RHA 1968; Hon. Prof. of Literature, RHA, 1973. *Publications:* The Road of Excess, 1945; Kevin O'Higgins, 1948; The Story of the Royal Dublin Society, 1955; A Fretful Midge, 1957; A Leaf from the Yellow Book, 1958; An Affair with the Moon, 1959; Prenez Garde, 1962; The Remainder Man, 1963; Lucifer Falling, 1965; The Parents of Oscar Wilde, 1967; Tara, 1967; Leinster, 1968; Ireland, 1968; The Lambert Mile, 1969; The March Hare, 1970; Mr Stephen, 1971; The Anglo-Irish, 1972; The Distance and the Dark, 1973; The Radish Memoirs, 1974; Big Fleas and Little Fleas, 1976; Chimes at Midnight, 1977; Tom Moore, 1977; contribs to 19th Century, Cambridge Review, Horizon. *Recreation:* formerly riding. *Address:* The Cottage, Dartmouth Lane, Dublin 6, Ireland. *T:* 684863. *Club:* Kildare Street and University (Dublin).

WHITE, Sir Thomas Astley Woollaston, 5th Bt, *cr* 1802; JP; Hon. Sheriff for Wigtownshire, since 1963; *b* 13 May 1904; *s* of Sir Archibald Woollaston White, 4th Bt, and late Gladys Becher Love, *d* of Rev. E. A. B. Pitman; *S* father, 1945; *m* 1935, Daphne Margaret, *er d* of late Lt-Col F. R. I. Athill, CMG; one *d. Educ:* Wellington College. FRICS. JP Wigtownshire, 1952. *Heir: b*

Capt. Richard T. White, *qv. Address:* Torhousemuir, Wigtown, Wigtownshire. *T:* Wigtown 2138.

WHITE, Prof. Thomas Cyril, CBE 1977; Professor of Orthodontics, 1961-76, and Director of Dental Studies, University of Glasgow, 1964-76; Director of Dental Hospital, Glasgow, 1964-76; *b* 11 March 1911; *s* of Thomas William White, MPS, and Edith Weldon; *m* 1940, Catherine Elizabeth Hunter, LDS; no *c. Educ:* Glasgow Acad.; Glasgow Dental Sch. LDS 1933; LRCP, LRCS (Edin.), LRFPS (Glasgow) 1935; BSc, FRCS, FDS, FFD, DDO. Lectr in Orthodontics, in charge Orthodontic Dept, Glasgow Dental School, 1938-48; Cons. Dental Surgeon, Western Regional Hosp. Bd, 1948-61. Past President: Glasgow Odontological Society; W of Scotland Branch, Brit. DA; Mem., Forth Valley Area Health Bd, 1977-. Past Member: Gen. Dental Council; Dental Education Adv. Council; Past Chm., Nat. Dental Consultative Cttee (Scotland). Past Convener, Dental Council, Roy. Coll. of Phys and Surg. of Glasgow; Dental Consultant to RN, 1967-76; *Publications: Text-Books:* Orthodontics for Dental Students, 1954 (Joint), 3rd edn 1976; Manual de Ortodoncia, 1958 (Joint). Contributions to Dental Journals. *Recreations:* gardening. *Address:* Five Acres, Buchlyvie, Stirlingshire. *T:* Buchlyvie 255. *Clubs:* Royal Commonwealth Society; Royal Scottish Automobile (Glasgow).

WHITE, Wilfrid H.; *see* Hyde White.

WHITE, William Kelvin Kennedy; HM Diplomatic Service; Counsellor, British High Commission, New Delhi, 1974-77; *b* 10 July 1930; *y s* of Kennedy White, JP, Caldy, Cheshire, and Violet White; *m* 1957, Susan Margaret, *y d* of late R. T. Colthurst, JP, Malvern, Worcs; three *s. Educ:* Birkenhead Sch.; Merton Coll., Oxford. 2nd Lieut, 1st Bn, Manchester Regt, 1949-50; Lieut, 13th (Lancs) Bn, Parachute Regt (TA), 1950-54. Entered HM Foreign (later Diplomatic) Service, 1954; Foreign Office, 1954-56, attending UN Gen. Assemblies, 1954 and 1955; 3rd Sec., Helsinki, 1956-57; 2nd Sec., Commissioner-General's Office, Singapore, 1957-61; 2nd Sec., then 1st Sec., FO, 1961-66; 1st Sec. (Commercial), Stockholm, 1966-69; 1st Sec., then Counsellor, FCO, 1969-74. *Address:* c/o Foreign and Commonwealth Office, SW1. *Clubs:* Travellers'; Moreton CC.

WHITE-THOMSON, Very Rev. Ian Hugh; Dean of Canterbury, 1963-76; *b* 18 December 1904; *m* 1954, Wendy Ernesta Woolliams; two *s* two *d. Educ:* Harrow; Oxford. Deacon, 1929; Priest, 1930; Curacy, St Mary's, Ashford, Kent, 1929-34; Rector of S Martin's with St Paul's, Canterbury, 1934-39; Chaplain to Archbishop of Canterbury, 1939-47; Vicar of Folkestone, 1947-54; Archdeacon of Northumberland and Canon of Newcastle, 1955-63; Chaplain to King George VI, 1947-52, to the Queen, 1952-63; Examining Chaplain to Bishop of Newcastle, 1955-63. Hon. Canon of Canterbury Cathedral, 1950. Governor, Harrow School, 1965-69. Hon. DCL Univ. of Kent at Canterbury, 1971. *Address:* Camphill, Harville Road, Wye, Ashford, Kent. *T:* Wye 812210.

WHITEHEAD, Commander Edward, CBE 1967 (OBE 1961); on board of Bahamas Development Corporation and other Bahamian companies; *b* 20 May 1908; *s* of Walter and Amy Whitehead; *m* 1940, Adinah (known as Tommy) (*d* 1976); one *s* one step *d. Educ:* Aldershot County High School. General Accident Assurance Company, 1925-39. Served RNVR, 1939-46. General Secretary, British Assoc. for Commercial and Industrial Educn, 1946; HM Treasury, 1947-50; joined Schweppes Ltd, 1950; Pres., Schweppes (USA) Ltd, 1953-67, later Chm. Former Director: Cadbury Schweppes Ltd; Cunard Steam-Ship Co. Ltd; General Cigar Co. Inc., etc. *Publications:* How to Live the Good Life, 1977; various articles. *Recreations:* sailing, swimming, walking, beagling, fox hunting, ski-ing. *Address:* Lyford Cay Club, PO Box N7776, Nassau, Bahamas. *Clubs:* Lansdowne; RN Sailing Assoc.; Lyford Cay (Nassau).

WHITEHEAD, Edward Anthony; *see* Whitehead, T.

WHITEHEAD, Garnet George Archie, DFC 1944; His Honour Judge Whitehead; a Circuit Judge, since 1977; *b* 22 July 1916; *s* of late Archibald Payne Whitehead and Margaret Elizabeth Whitehead; *m* 1946, Monica (*née* Watson); two *d. Educ:* Wisbech. Admitted Solicitor, 1949. Served War, 1939-45, RAF, Pilot, Bomber Comd and Transport Comd; demob. as Flt Lt, 1 Jan. 1947. Articled to Edmund W. Roythorne, MBE, Solicitor, Spalding. Formerly Senior Partner, Roythorne & Co., Solicitor, Boston, Lincs (Partner, 1950-77); a Recorder of the Crown Court, 1972-77. Formerly Alderman, Boston Borough Council; Mayor of Boston, 1969-70. *Recreations:* photography, walking. *Address:* 150 Spilsby Road, Boston, Lincs. *T:* Boston 64977.

WHITEHEAD, George Sydney, CMG 1966; MVO 1961; HM Diplomatic Service, retired; re-employed in Foreign and Commonwealth Office (Security Department), since 1976; *b* 15 Nov. 1915; *s* of William George and Annie Sabina Whitehead; *m* 1948, Constance Mary Hart (*née* Vale); one *d* (and one step *d*). *Educ:* Harrow County Sch.; London Sch. of Economics. India Office, 1934. Armed Forces (Royal Artillery), 1940-45. Private Sec. to Parly Under-Sec. of State for India and Burma, 1945-46; British Embassy, Rangoon, 1947; CRO 1948-52; British High Commn, Canberra, 1952-55; Counsellor, British High Commn, Calcutta, 1958-61; Inspector, Commonwealth Service, 1961-64; Inspector, Diplomatic Service, 1965; Head of Asia Economic Dept, CO, 1966-67; Head of Commonwealth Trade Dept, CO, 1967-68; Head of Commodities Dept, FCO, 1968-69; Dep. High Comr and Minister (Commercial), Ottawa, 1970-72; Asst Under-Sec. of State, 1972-75, Dep. Chief Clerk, 1973-75, FCO. *Recreations:* golf, tennis. *Address:* 399 Pinner Road, Harrow, Mddx. *T:* 01-427 5872. *Clubs:* Civil Service, Royal Commonwealth Society; Middlesex County Cricket.

WHITEHEAD, Col James Buckley, CBE 1957; MC 1918; TD 1934 (three bars); DL; JP; Cotton Spinner; *b* 1898; *s* of Edwin Whitehead, Oldham, Lancs; *m* 1926, Florence, *d* of J. R. Thomason, Oldham; one *s* one *d*. *Educ:* Oldham High School. Served European War, 1916-19, in France and Flanders with 10th Manchester Regt; War of 1939-45 with Roy. Tank Regt and Yorkshire Hussars. Hon. Col 40/41 Royal Tank Regt. DL for Co. Lancaster, 1956; JP WR Yorks, 1948. *Address:* Staghurst, Grasscroft, near Oldham, Lancs. *T:* Saddleworth 2112. *Club:* Army and Navy.

WHITEHEAD, John Stainton, CMG 1976; HM Diplomatic Service; Counsellor and Head of Chancery, British Embassy, Bonn, since 1976; *b* 20 Sept. 1932; *s* of late John William and of Kathleen Whitehead; *m* 1964, Mary Carolyn (*née* Hilton); two *s* two *d*. *Educ:* Christ's Hospital; Hertford Coll., Oxford (MA). HM Forces, 1950-52; Oxford, 1952-55; FO, 1955-56; 3rd Sec., later 2nd Sec., Tokyo, 1956-61; FO, 1961-64; 1st Sec., Washington, 1964-67; 1st Sec. (Economic), Tokyo, 1968-71; FCO, 1971-76, Head of Personnel Services Dept, 1973-76. *Recreations:* music, travel, tree-felling, walking, chess. *Address:* Im Etzental 21, Bonn-Bad Godesberg, Germany. *T:* 36.41.74; Bracken Edge, High Pitfold, Hindhead, Surrey. *T:* Hindhead 4162.

WHITEHEAD, Phillip; MP (Lab) Derby North, since 1970; *b* 30 May 1937; adopted *s* of late Harold and Frances Whitehead; *m* 1967, Christine, *d* of T. G. Usborne; two *s* one *d*. *Educ:* Lady Manners' Grammar Sch., Bakewell; Exeter Coll., Oxford. President, Oxford Union, 1961. BBC Producer, 1961-67, and WEA Lecturer, 1961-65; Editor of This Week, Thames TV, 1967-70. Guild of TV Producers Award for Factual Programmes, 1969. Vice-Chm., Young Fabian Group, 1965; a founder of 76 Group for Broadcasting Reform, 1969; elected to Parly Labour Party Liaison Cttee, 1975. Mem., Annan Cttee on Future of Broadcasting, 1974-77. Mem., NUJ; Mem., Co-operative Party; contested (Lab) W Derbyshire, Gen. Elec., 1966. *Recreations:* walking, cinema, old model railways. *Address:* Mill House, Rowsley, Matlock, Derbys. *T:* Darley Dale 2659; House of Commons, SW1.

WHITEHEAD, Sir Rowland (John Rathbone), 5th Bt, *cr* 1889; *b* 24 June 1930; *s* of Major Sir Philip Henry Rathbone Whitehead, 4th Bt, and 1st wife Gertrude, *d* of J. C. Palmer, West Virginia, USA; *S* father, 1953; *m* 1954, Marie-Louise, *d* of Arnold Christian Gausel, Stavanger, Norway; one *s* one *d*. *Educ:* Radley; Trinity Hall, Cambridge (BA). Late 2nd Lieutenant RA. *Heir:* *s* Philip Henry Rathbone Whitehead, *b* 13 Oct. 1957. *Recreations:* poetry and rural indolence. *Address:* Sutton House, Chiswick Mall, W4 2PR. *T:* 01-994 2710; Walnut Tree Cottage, Fyfield, Lechlade, Glos GL7 3NT. *Clubs:* Reform, City University.

WHITEHEAD, Ted, (Edward Anthony); playwright, since 1971; theatre reviewer, since 1976; *b* 3 April 1933; *s* of Edward Whitehead and Catherine Curran; *m* 1st, 1958, Kathleen Horton (marr. diss. 1976); two *d*; 2nd, 1976, Gwenda Bagshaw. *Educ:* Christ's Coll., Cambridge (MA). Military Service, King's Regt (Infantry), 1955-57. Bus conductor, copywriter, pharmaceutical salesman, and teacher, 1958-65; advertising exec., 1965-71. Evening Standard Award, and George Devine Award, 1971. *Publications:* The Foursome, 1972; Alpha Beta, 1972; The Sea Anchor, 1975; Old Flames, 1976; The Punishment (Hutchinson's Prompt series), 1976; Mecca, 1977. *Recreations:* soccer, pubs, music. *Address:* c/o Margaret Ramsay Ltd, 14A Goodwin's Court, St Martin's Lane, WC2N 4LL. *T:* 01-240 0691.

WHITEHEAD, Prof. Thomas Patterson, MCB, MRCPath, FRIC; Professor of Clinical Chemistry, University of Birmingham, since 1968; Consultant Biochemist, Queen Elizabeth Medical Centre, since 1960; Director of Wolfson Research Laboratories, since 1972; *b* 7 May 1923; *m* 1947, Doreen Grace Whitton; two *s* one *d*. *Educ:* Salford Royal Technical Coll.; Univ. of Birmingham (PhD). Biochemist to S Warwickshire Hospital Gp, 1950-60. Council Mem., Med. Research Council, 1972-76; Mem., Health Service Research Bd, 1973-75. Consultant to WHO, Geneva, 1974-. Wellcome Prize, 1972; Dade Award, Geneva, 1975. *Publications:* Quality Control in Clinical Chemistry, 1976; papers in med. and scientific jls. *Recreation:* growing and exhibiting sweet peas. *Address:* 70 Northumberland Road, Leamington Spa CV32 6HB. *T:* Leamington Spa 21974. *Club:* Athenæum.

WHITEHEAD, Comdr Walter Edward; *see* Whitehead, Comdr E.

WHITEHEAD, Lieut-Col Wilfrid Arthur, DSO 1941; IA (retired 1947); *b* 28 Jan. 1898; *e s* of late Rev. Arthur Whitehead, Rector of Keinton-Mandeville; *m* 1930, Constance Dulcie (*d* 1967), *e d* of W. W. Crouch, MA; two *s*. *Educ:* St John's Leatherhead. Entered IA (76th Punjabis), 1915; Mesopotamia and Palestine, 1917-19; NW Frontier of India, 1924-25, 1929-30, 1937; Western Desert and Eritrea, 1940-41 (severely wounded, despatches twice, DSO); Burma 1943. Comdt 3rd Bn 1st Punjab Regt; GSO1 GHQ(I); Comdt Ind. Small Arms School. Patron of Living of Keinton-Mandeville, Somersetshire. *Address:* The Corner House, Instow, North Devon. *Club:* Naval and Military.

WHITEHORN, John Roland Malcolm, CMG 1974; a Deputy Director-General, Confederation of British Industry, since Aug. 1966; *b* 19 May 1924; *s* of Alan and Edith Whitehorn; *m* 1st, 1951, Josephine (*née* Plummer) (marr. diss. 1973); no *c*; 2nd, 1973, Marion FitzGibbon (*née* Gutmann). *Educ:* Rugby Sch. (Exhbnr); Trinity Coll., Cambridge (Exhbnr). Served War, 1943-46, RAFVR (Flying Officer). Joined FBI, 1947; Dep. Overseas Dir, 1960; Overseas Dir, 1963; Overseas Dir, CBI, 1965-68; Director, Industrial and Trade Fairs Internat. Ltd; Member: BOTB, 1975-; Design Council; Bd, British Council; Council, BIM; Academic Council, Wilton Park; European Discussion Centre. *Address:* 42 Ordnance Hill, NW8. *T:* 01-722 4665. *Clubs:* Reform, MCC.
See also Katharine Whitehorn.

WHITEHORN, Katharine Elizabeth, (Mrs Gavin Lyall); Columnist, The Observer, since 1960; *b* London; *d* of A. D. and E. M. Whitehorn; *m* 1958, Gavin Lyall, *qv*; two *s*. *Educ:* Blunt House; Roedean; Glasgow High School for Girls, and others; Newnham Coll., Cambridge. Publisher's Reader, 1950-53; Teacher-Secretary in Finland, 1953-54; Grad. Asst, Cornell Univ., USA, 1954-55; Picture Post, 1956-57; Woman's Own, 1958; Spectator, 1959-61. Member: Latey Cttee on Age of Majority, 1965-67; BBC Adv. Gp on Social Effects of Television, 1971-72; Board, British Airports Authority, 1972-77. *Publications:* Cooking in a Bedsitter, 1960; Roundabout, 1961; Only on Sundays, 1966; Whitehorn's Social Survival, 1968; Observations, 1970; How to Survive in Hospital, 1972; How to Survive Children, 1975; Sunday Best, 1976. *Recreation:* gardening. *Address:* c/o The Observer, 8 St Andrew's Hill, EC4. *T:* 01-236 0202.
See also J. R. M. Whitehorn.

WHITEHOUSE, Cyril John Arthur, OBE 1951; Controller of Operational Services, Greater London Council, 1974-77; *b* 15 May 1913; *s* of F. A. S. and F. A. Whitehouse; *m* 1st, 1937, Elsie Eleanor Reed (*d* 1949); 2nd, 1950, Isobel Mary Lickley; two *d*. *Educ:* Gillingham County School. Clerical Officer, Air Ministry, 1930; Exec. Officer, Inland Revenue, 1932; Higher Exec. Officer, Air Min., 1939; Min. of Aircraft Production: Sen. Exec. Officer, 1942; Asst Dir, 1945; Min. of Supply: Principal, 1946; Asst Sec., 1951; Controller, Scotland, BoT, 1960; Under-Sec., BoT, 1966-69; Under-Sec., Min. of Technology, 1969-71; Dir of Housing, GLC, 1971-74. *Recreations:* golf, gardening. *Address:* Catherston, Pine Ridge Drive, Farnham, Surrey. *Club:* Camberley Heath Golf.

WHITEHOUSE, Dr David Bryn; Director, British School at Rome, since Oct. 1974; *b* 15 Oct. 1941; *s* of Brindley Charles Whitehouse and Alice Margaret Whitehouse; *m* 1st, 1963, Ruth Delamain Ainger; one *s* two *d*; 2nd, 1975, Elizabeth-Ann Ollemans; one *d*. *Educ:* King Edward's Sch., Birmingham; St John's Coll., Cambridge. MA, PhD; FSA. Scholar, British Sch. at Rome, 1963-65; Wainwright Fellow in Near Eastern Archaeology, Univ. of Oxford, 1966-73; Dir, Sīrāf Expedn, 1966-73; Dir, British Inst. of Afghan Studies, 1973-74. *Publications:* (jtly) Background to Archaeology, 1973; (jtly) The

Origins of Europe, 1974; (with .Ruth Whitehouse) Archaeological Atlas of the World, 1975; many papers in Iran, Antiquity, Med. Archaeol., Papers of Brit. Sch. at Rome, etc. *Address:* Accademia Britannica, Via Gramsci 61, 00197 Roma, Italy. *T:* 06-877 312.

WHITEHOUSE, Mary; Honorary General Secretary, National Viewers' and Listeners' Association, since Nov. 1965; free lance journalist, broadcaster; *b* 13 June 1910; *d* of James and Beatrice Hutcheson; *m* 1940, Ernest R. Whitehouse; three *s. Educ:* Chester City Grammar Sch.; Cheshire County Training Coll. Art Specialist: Wednesfield Sch., Wolverhampton, 1932-40; Brewood Grammar Sch., Staffs, 1943; Sen. Mistress, and Sen. Art Mistress, Madeley Sch., Shropshire, 1960-64. Co-founder, "Clean up TV campaign", 1964. *Publications:* Cleaning Up TV, 1966; "Who Does She Think She Is?", 1971; Whatever Happened to Sex?, 1977. *Recreations:* reading, gardening, walking. *Address:* Blachernae, Ardleigh, Colchester, Essex. *T:* Colchester 230123.

WHITEHOUSE, Walter Alexander; Professor of Theology, University of Kent, 1965-77; Master of Eliot College, University of Kent, 1965-69, and 1973-75; *b* 27 Feb. 1915; *e s* of Walter and Clara Whitehouse, Shelley, near Huddersfield; *m* 1st, 1946, Beatrice Mary Kent Smith (*d* 1971); 2nd, 1974, Audrey Ethel Lemmon. *Educ:* Penistone Gram. Sch.; St John's Coll., Cambridge; Mansfield Coll., Oxford. Minister of Elland Congregational Church, 1940-44; Chaplain at Mansfield College, Oxford, 1944-47; Reader in Divinity, Univ. of Durham, 1947-65. Principal of St Cuthbert's Soc., Univ. of Durham, 1955-60; Pro-Vice-Chancellor of Univ., and Sub-Warden, 1961-64. Hon. DD Edinburgh, 1960. *Publications:* Christian Faith and the Scientific Attitude, 1952; Order, Goodness, Glory (Riddell Memorial Lectures), 1959. *Address:* The Manse, Ravenstonedale, Kirby Stephen, Cumbria.

WHITELAW, Billie; actress; *b* 6 June 1932; *d* of Perceval and Frances Whitelaw; *m* Robert Muller, writer; one *s. Educ:* Thornton Grammar Sch., Bradford. Appeared in: *plays:* Hotel Paradiso, Winter Garden, 1954 and Oxford Playhouse, 1956; Progress to the Park, Theatre Workshop and Saville, 1961; England our England, Prince's, 1962; Touch of the Poet, Venice and Dublin, 1962; National Theatre, 1963-65: Othello, London and Moscow; Hobson's Choice; Beckett's Play; Trelawny of the Wells; The Dutch Courtesan; After Haggerty, Criterion, 1971; Not I, Royal Court, 1973 and 1975; Alphabetical Order, Mayfair, 1975; Footfalls, Royal Court, 1976; *films:* No Love for Johnny; Charlie Bubbles; Twisted Nerve; The Adding Machine; Start the Revolution Without Me; Leo the Last; Eagle in a Cage; Gumshoe; Frenzy; Night Watch; The Omen; The Water Babies; *television:* No Trams to Lime Street; Lena Oh My Lena; Resurrection; The Skin Game; Beyond the Horizon; Anna Christie; Lady of the Camelias; The Pity of it all; Love on the Dole; A World of Time; You and I; Poet Game; Sextet (8 plays); Napoleon and Love (9 plays: Josephine); The Fifty Pound Note (Ten from the Twenties); The Withered Arm (Wessex Tales); The Werewolf Reunion (2 plays); Two Plays by Samuel Beckett; Not I; Eustace and Hilda (2 plays), etc; *radio plays:* The Master Builder; Marching Song; Jane Eyre; The Female Messiah; Alpha Beta. Silver Heart Variety Club Award, 1961; TV Actress of Year, 1971, 1972; British Academy Award, 1968; US Film Critics Award, 1968. *Recreation:* pottering about the house. *Address:* c/o Joy Jameson, 7 West Eaton Place Mews, SW1X 8LY.

WHITELAW, Rt. Hon. William (Stephen Ian), PC 1967; CH 1974; MC; DL; MP (C) Penrith and the Border Division of Cumberland, since 1955; Deputy Leader of the Opposition, and spokesman on home affairs, since 1975; is a farmer and landowner; *b* 28 June 1918; *s* of late W. A. Whitelaw and Mrs W. A. Whitelaw, Monkland, Nairn; *m* 1943, Cecilia Doriel, 2nd *d* of late Major Mark Sprot, Riddell, Melrose, Roxburghshire; four *d. Educ:* Winchester Coll.; Trinity Coll., Camb. Reg. Officer, Scots Guards; Emergency Commn, 1939; resigned Commn, 1947. PPS to Chancellor of the Exchequer, 1957-58 (to Pres. of BOT, 1956); Asst Govt Whip, 1959-61; a Lord Comr of the Treasury, 1961-62; Parly Sec., Min. of Labour, July 1962-Oct. 1964; Chief Opposition Whip, Nov. 1964-70; Lord Pres. of Council and Leader, House of Commons, 1970-72; Secretary of State for: N Ireland, 1972-73; Employment, 1973-74; Chm., Conservative Party, 1974-75. Visiting Fellow, Nuffield Coll., Oxford, 1970-. DL Dunbartonshire, 1952-66; DL Cumbria, formerly Cumberland, 1967. *Recreations:* golf, shooting. *Address:* Ennim, Penrith, Cumbria. *Clubs:* Carlton; County (Carlisle); Royal and Ancient (Captain 1969-70).
See also Earl of Swinton.

WHITELEY, family name of **Baron Marchamley.**

WHITELEY, Maj.-Gen. Gerald Abson, CB 1969; OBE 1952; *b* 4 March 1915; *s* of late Harry Whiteley, Walton Park, Bexhill; *m* 1943, Ellen Hanna (*d* 1973). *Educ:* Worksop Coll.; Emmanuel Coll., Cambridge (MA). Solicitor, 1938. Commissioned, RA, 1940; Maj., DJAG's Staff, ME, 1942-45. AAG, Mil. Dept, JAG's Office, WO, 1945-48; Asst Dir of Army Legal Services: FARELF, 1948-51; WO, 1952-53; Northern Army Gp, 1953-54; MELF, 1954-57; BAOR, 1957-60; Dep. Dir of Army Legal Services, BAOR, 1960-62; Col, Legal Staff, WO, 1962-64; Dir of Army Legal Services, MoD, 1964-69. *Recreations:* photography, walking. *Address:* 8 Kemnal Park, Haslemere, Surrey. *T:* Haslemere 2803. *Club:* Army and Navy.

WHITELEY, Sir Hugo Baldwin Huntington-; *see* Huntington-Whiteley, Sir H. B.

WHITELEY, Gen. Sir Peter (John Frederick), KCB 1976; OBE 1960; Commander-in-Chief Allied Forces Northern Europe, since 1977; *b* 13 Dec. 1920; *s* of late John George Whiteley; *m* 1948, Nancy Vivian, *d* of late W. Carter Clayden; two *s* two *d. Educ:* Bishop's Stortford Coll.; Bembridge Sch.; Ecole des Roches. Joined Royal Marines, 1940; 101 Bde, 1941; HMS: Resolution, 1941; Renown, 1942; HMNZS Gambia, 1942; seconded to Fleet Air Arm, 1946-50; Adjt 40 Commando, 1951; Staff Coll., Camberley, 1954; Bde Major 3rd Commando Bde, 1957; Instructor, Staff Coll., Camberley, 1960-63; CO 42 Commando, 1965-66 (despatches, Malaysia, 1966); Col GS Dept of CGRM, 1966-68; Nato Defence Coll., 1968; Comdr 3rd Commando Bde, 1968-70; Maj.-Gen. Commando Forces, 1970-72; C of S, HQ Allied Forces Northern Europe, 1972-75; Commandant General, Royal Marines, 1975-77. FBIM. *Recreations:* music (Mem. Glyndebourne Festival Soc.), photography, painting, wood carving, sailing, dogs. *Address:* Stoneycross Farm, Yealmpton, Devon. *Clubs:* Anchorites, Royal Marines Sailing, Royal Naval Sailing Assoc., Royal Norwegian Sailing.

WHITELEY, Samuel Lloyd; Legal Assistant to the Clerk to the Haberdashers' Company, since 1973; formerly Deputy Chief Land Registrar; *b* 30 April 1913; *s* of Rev. Charles Whiteley and Ann Letitia Whiteley; *m* 1939, Kathleen Jones; two *d. Educ:* George Dixon Sch.; Birmingham Univ. LLB (Hons) 1933. Admitted Solicitor, 1935; HM Land Registry, 1936; seconded Official Solicitor's Dept, 1939; RAF, 1940-46; HM Land Registry, 1946-73. *Recreations:* sport, as a reminiscent spectator; amateur theatre. *Address:* 8 Stonehaven Court, Knole Road, Bexhill, Sussex. *T:* Bexhill 213191.

WHITELOCK, Prof. Dorothy, CBE 1964; MA, LittD (Cambridge), MA (Oxford); FBA, FSA, FRHistS; Elrington and Bosworth Professor of Anglo-Saxon, Cambridge University, 1957-69; Professorial Fellow, Newnham College, Cambridge, 1957-69, Hon. Fellow since 1970; Hon. Fellow, St Hilda's College, Oxford, since 1957; *b* 11 Nov. 1901; *d* of Edward Whitelock and Emmeline (*née* Dawson). *Educ:* Leeds Girls' High School; Newnham College, Cambridge. 1st Class, English Tripos, section B, 1923, 2nd Class, section A, 1924; Marion Kennedy Student, Newnham Coll., 1924-26; Cambridge Univ. Student, Univ. of Uppsala, 1927-29; Allen Scholar, Univ. of Cambridge, 1929-30. Lecturer in English Language at St Hilda's College, Oxford, 1930-36, Fellow and Tutor in English Language, 1936-57, Vice-Principal, 1951-57; Lecturer in Old English in the University of Oxford, 1946-55, Senior Lecturer, 1955-57. Leverhulme Fellow, 1939-40; Pres. Viking Soc. for Northern Research, 1939-41; Co-Editor of Saga-Book of the Viking Society, 1940-59; Pres., English Place-Name Soc., 1967-. Hon. LittD Leeds, 1971. *Publications:* Anglo-Saxon Wills, 1930; Sermo Lupi ad Anglos, 1939; The Audience of Beowulf, 1950; The Beginnings of English Society (Pelican Books), 1952; The Peterborough Chronicle (Copenhagen), 1954; English Historical Documents, c 500-1042, 1955; The Anglo-Saxon Chronicle: A Revised Translation, 1961; The Genuine Asser, 1968; The Will of Æthelgifu (Roxburghe Club), 1968; articles in English Historical Review, Medium Aevum, etc. *Address:* Newnham College, Cambridge. *T:* 62273; 30 Thornton Close, Cambridge. *T:* Cambridge 76592. *Club:* University Women's.

WHITEMAN, Elizabeth Anne Osborn, DPhil; FRHistS, FSA; JP; Tutor in Modern History since 1946, Fellow since 1948, and Vice-Principal since 1971, Lady Margaret Hall, Oxford; *b* 10 Feb. 1918; *d* of Harry Whitmore Whiteman and Dorothy May (*née* Austin). *Educ:* St Albans High Sch.; Somerville Coll., Oxford (MA 1945, DPhil 1951). FRHistS 1954; FSA 1958. Served War, WAAF, 1940-45: served in N Africa and Italy (mentioned in despatches, 1943). Rep. of Women's Colls, Oxford Univ., 1960-61. Member: Hebdomadal Council, Oxford

Univ., 1968-; Academic Planning Bd, Univ. of Warwick, 1961-65; UGC, 1976-. Trustee, Ruskin Sch. of Drawing, 1974-. JP City of Oxford, 1962. *Publications:* (contrib.) Victoria County History, Wilts, Vol. III, 1956; (contrib.) New Cambridge Modern History, Vol. V, 1961; (contrib.) From Uniformity to Unity, ed Chadwick and Nuttall, 1962; (ed with J. S. Bromley and P. G. M. Dickson, and contrib.) Statesmen, Scholars and Merchants: Essays in eighteenth-century History presented to Dame Lucy Sutherland, 1973; contrib. hist. jls. *Address:* Lady Margaret Hall, Oxford. *T:* Oxford 54353.

WHITEMAN, Peter George, QC 1977; barrister-at-law; *b* 8 Aug. 1942; *s* of David Whiteman and Betsy Bessie Coster; *m* 1971, Katherine Ruth (*née* Ellenbogen); one *d*. *Educ:* Warwick Secondary Modern Sch.; Leyton County High Sch.; LSE (LLB, LLM with Distinction). Called to the Bar, Lincoln's Inn, 1967. Lectr, London Univ., 1966-70. Head of Chambers, 1977. FRSA. *Publications:* Wheatcroft and Whiteman on Capital Gains Tax, 1967 (2nd edn 1973); Whiteman and Wheatcroft on Income Tax, 1971 (2nd edn 1976); contrib. British Tax Encyc. *Recreations:* tennis, squash, mountain-walking, jogging. *Address:* 26 Clapham Common Northside, SW4 0RL. *T:* 01-622 5055, (chambers) 01-353 9076.

WHITEMAN, William Meredith; MA; FRSA; writer, and consultant on caravanning and the countryside; Vice-President: British Caravanners Club; Camping Club; *b* 29 May 1905; *m* 1931, Patricia Aileen Thornton (*d* 1954); three *d*; *m* 1965, Mary Moore (*née* Hall). *Educ:* St Albans School; St John's College, Cambridge. President National Picture Print Society, 1938. Founder National Caravan Council. Hon. Secretary, 1939-49, Hon. Director, 1949-52. Director, Caravan Club, 1938-60. Organiser, Moveable Dwelling Conference, 1947-49. Editor, The Caravan, 1938-61. Man. Editor, Link House Publications Ltd, 1942-70; UK Mem., Internat. Caravan Commn, 1947-70, Pres., 1957-70; Countryside Commn transit site study group, 1969-70; Chm., Rural Cttee, Hampshire Council of Community Service; served on more than 50 cttees, working parties etc, on caravanning and camping. Hon. Life Mem., Caravan Club; Hon. Mem., Fédération Internationale de Camping et de Caravanning. *Publications:* books on camping and caravanning. *Address:* Northfield Cottage, Steep, Petersfield, Hants GU32 2DQ. *T:* Petersfield 3915.

WHITESIDE, Dr Derek Thomas, FBA 1975; University Reader in History of Mathematics, Cambridge, since 1976; *b* 23 July 1932; *s* of Ernest Whiteside and Edith (*née* Watts); *m* 1962, Ruth Isabel Robinson; one *s* one *d*. *Educ:* Blackpool Grammar Sch.; Bristol Univ. (BA); Cambridge Univ. (PhD). Leverhulme Research Fellow, 1959-61; DSIR Research Fellow, 1961-63; Research Asst, 1963-72, Asst Dir of Research, 1972-76, Univ. of Cambridge. Médaille Koyré, Académie Internat. d'Histoire des Sciences, 1968; Sarton Medal, Amer. History of Sci. Soc., 1977. *Publications:* Patterns of Mathematical Thought in the later Seventeenth Century, 1961; (ed) The Mathematical Papers of Isaac Newton (7 vols), 1967-77; articles in Brit. Jl Hist. Science, Jl for Hist. of Astronomy, etc. *Recreations:* a diversity of things unenergetic. *Address:* Whipple Science Museum, Free School Lane, Cambridge.

WHITFIELD, family name of **Baron Kenswood.**

WHITFIELD, Prof. Charles Richard, MD; FRCOG; Regius Professor of Midwifery in the University of Glasgow, since Oct. 1976; *b* 21 Oct. 1927; *s* of Charles Alexander and Aileen Muriel Whitfield; *m* 1953, Marion Douglas McKinney; one *s* two *d*. *Educ:* Campbell Coll., Belfast; Queen's Univ., Belfast (MD). House Surg. and Ho. Phys. appts in Belfast teaching hospitals, 1951-53; Specialist in Obstetrics and Gynaecology, RAMC (Lt-Col retd), 1953-64; Sen. Lectr/Hon. Reader in Dept of Midwifery and Gynaecology, Queen's Univ., Belfast, 1964-74; Consultant to Belfast teaching hosps, 1964-74; Prof. of Obstetrics and Gynaecology, Univ. of Manchester, 1974-76. *Publications:* papers on perinatal medicine, pregnancy anaemia and other obstetric and gynaec. topics in med. and scientific jls. *Recreations:* food, travel, sun-worship. *Address:* Queen Mother's Hospital, Glasgow G3 8SH.

WHITFIELD, George; poet, artist, and (retired) journalist; former art critic, film critic, and sub-editor Liverpool Echo; *b* 1891; *m* Beatrix, *d* of Jacob and Makrouhi Yanekian, Chanak, Dardanelles; one *d*. *Educ:* privately and at Jesuit College. Studied art under Fred V. Burridge, RE, in Liverpool. Political, sporting, and comic-strip cartoons in London, provincial and overseas papers; former correspondent motoring journals and film publicity, British and American companies. Served Royal Naval Air Service (aerial and service drawings). Founder-member of one-time Liverpool Pickwickians (their first Mr Pickwick) and Liverpool First-Nighters Society. On selection and hanging committees of World Cartoons Exhibn, first Liverpool Festival. *Publications:* poetry and signed articles on art, architecture, cinema, radio, boxing. *Recreations:* poetry, pictures, and people. *Address:* Rockley House, Rossett, Clwyd. *Club:* Press.

WHITFIELD, Rev. George Joshua Newbold; General Secretary, Church of England Board of Education, 1969-74; *b* 2 June 1909; *s* of late Joshua Newbold and Eva Whitfield; *m* 1937, Dr Audrey Priscilla Dence, *d* of late Rev. A. T. Dence; two *s* two *d*. *Educ:* Bede Gram. Sch., Sunderland; King's Coll., Univ. of London; Bishops' Coll., Cheshunt. BA 1st cl. Hons, Engl. and AKC 1930 (Barry Prizeman); MA 1935. Asst Master, Trin. Sch., Croydon, 1931-34; Sen. Engl. Master: Doncaster Gram. Sch., 1934-36; Hymers Coll., Hull, 1937-43; Headmaster: Tavistock Gram. Sch., 1943-46; Stockport Sch., 1946-50; Hampton Sch., 1950-68. Chief Examr in Engl., Univ. of Durham Sch. Exams Bd, 1940-43. Deacon, 1962; Priest, 1963. Member: Duke of Edinburgh's Award Adv. Cttee, 1960-66; Headmasters' Conf., 1964-68; Corporation of Church House, 1974-; Pres., Headmasters' Assoc., 1967. *Publications:* (ed) Teaching Poetry, 1937; An Introduction to Drama, 1938; God and Man in the Old Testament, 1949; (ed) Poetry in the Sixth Form, 1950; Philosophy and Religion, 1955; (jtly) Christliche Erziehung in Europa, Band I, England, 1975. *Recreations:* gardening, photography. *Address:* Hampton House, 31 Foxholes Hill, Exmouth, Devon EX8 2DQ. *T:* Exmouth 74162. *Club:* Athenæum.

WHITFIELD, Professor John Humphreys; Serena Professor of Italian Language and Literature in the University of Birmingham, 1946-Oct. 1974; *b* 2 Oct. 1906; *s* of J. A. Whitfield; *m* 1936, Joan Herrin, ARCA; two *s*. *Educ:* Handsworth Grammar School; Magdalen College, Oxford. William Doncaster Scholar, Magdalen Coll., 1925-29; Double First Class Hons in Mod. Langs, 1928, 1929; Paget Toynbee Prizeman, 1933. Asst Master, King Edward VII School, Sheffield, 1930-36; University Lecturer in Italian, Oxford University, 1936-46; Awarder to Oxford and Cambridge Schools Examination Bd, 1940-68. Part-time Temporary Assistant Civil Officer, Naval Intelligence Department, 1943. Chairman, Society for Italian Studies, 1962-74; Senior editor of Italian Studies, 1967-74. President: Dante Alighieri Society (Comitato di Birmingham), 1957-75; Assoc. of Teachers of Italian, 1976-77. Barlow Lecturer on Dante, University College, London, 1958-59. Edmund G. Gardner Memorial Prize, 1959; Amedeo Maiuri Prize (Rome), 1965. Commendatore, Ordine al Merito della Repubblica Italiana, 1972 (Cavaliere Ufficiale, 1960). *Publications:* Petrarch and the Renascence, 1943 (NY, 1966); Machiavelli, 1947 (NY, 1966); Petrarca e il Rinascimento (tr. V. Capocci, Laterza), 1949; Dante and Virgil, 1949; Giacomo Leopardi, 1954 (Italian tr. 1964); A Short History of Italian Literature, 1962 (Pelican, 1960, 2nd edn 1970, Westport, Conn, 1976); The Barlow Lectures on Dante, 1960; Leopardi's Canti, trans. into English Verse, 1962; Leopardi's Canti, ed with Introduction and notes, 1967; Discourses on Machiavelli, 1969; The Charlecote Manuscript of Machiavelli's Prince, facsimile edn with an Essay on the Prince, 1969; Castiglione: The Courtier, ed with introduction, 1974; Guarini: Il Pastor Fido, ed bilingual edn with introduction, 1976; articles and reviews contrib. to Modern Language Review, Italian Studies, History, Medium Aevum, Comparative Literature, Problemi della Pedagogia, Le parole e le Idee, Encyclopædia Britannica, Chambers's Encyclopædia, Hutchinson's Encyclopædia, etc. *Festschrift:* Essays in Honour of John Humphreys Whitfield, 1975. *Address:* 2 Woodbourne Road, Edgbaston, Birmingham B15 3QH. *T:* 021-454 1035.

WHITFIELD LEWIS, Herbert John; *see* Lewis, H. J. W.

WHITFORD, Hon. Sir John (Norman Keates), Kt 1970; Hon. Mr Justice Whitford; a Judge of the High Court, Chancery Division, since 1970; *b* 24 June 1913; *s* of Harry Whitford and Ella Mary Keates; *m* 1946, Rosemary, *d* of John Barcham Green and Emily Paillard; four *d*. *Educ:* University College School; Munich University; Peterhouse, Cambridge. President, ADC. Called to the Bar: Inner Temple, 1935; Middle Temple, 1946 (Bencher 1970). Served with RAFVR, 1939-44: Wing Comdr, 1942; Chief Radar Officer and Dep. Chief Signals Officer, Air Headquarters Eastern Mediterranean; Advisor on patents and information exchanged for war purposes, HM Embassy, Washington, 1944-45. QC 1965. Member of Bar Council, 1968-70. Chm., Departmental Cttee on Law Relating to Copyright and Designs, 1974-76. *Address:* Royal Courts of Justice, WC2.

WHITHAM, Prof. Gerald Beresford, FRS 1965; Professor of Applied Mathematics, at the California Institute of Technology, Pasadena, Calif, since 1962; *b* 13 Dec. 1927; *s* of Harry and

Elizabeth Ellen Whitham; *m* 1951, Nancy (*née* Lord); one *s* two *d. Educ:* Elland Gram. Sch., Elland, Yorks; Manchester University. PhD Maths, Manchester, 1953. Lectr in Applied Mathematics, Manchester Univ., 1953-56; Assoc. Prof., Applied Mathematics, New York Univ., 1956-59; Prof., Mathematics, MIT, 1959-62. FAAAS 1959. *Publications:* Linear and Nonlinear Waves, 1974; research papers in Proc. Roy. Soc., Jl Fluid Mechanics, Communications on Pure and Applied Maths. *Address:* California Institute of Technology, Pasadena, California 91125, USA.

WHITING, Maurice Henry, OBE; MA, MB, BCh Cantab; FRCS; Consulting Surgeon, Royal London Ophthalmic Hospital; Emeritus Ophthalmic Surgeon, Middlesex Hospital; *b* 12 Oct. 1885; *s* of William Henry Whiting, CB; *m* 1st, 1916, Blanche Beatrice (*d* 1952), *d* of Edward Aggas; (*o s* killed in action, RAF, 1942); 2nd, 1953, Dorothy Miller, *d* of William Gilford. *Educ:* Mill Hill School; Downing College, Cambridge; The Middlesex Hospital, House Surgeon, Middlesex Hospital; House Surgeon and Pathologist, Royal London Ophthalmic Hospital; Capt. RAMC 1914-19; at Boulogne as Ophthalmic Specialist, 1915-19 (despatches); engaged in work in London as Ophthalmic surgeon since 1919; late Hon. Sec. Ophthalmological Soc. of the UK; late Ophthalmic Surgeon, Paddington Green Children's Hosp.; Member of Board of Governors Middlesex Hospital; President of Ophthalmological Society of UK, 1950-51; Pres. Old Millhillians Club, 1950-51; Pres. Downing College Assoc., 1953-54. *Publications:* Modern Developments in Cataract Extraction, Montgomery Lecture, RCSI, 1933; Ophthalmic Nursing; Concussion Changes in the Crystalline Lens; Technique of the Haab and Small Magnets, and other articles in medical and ophthalmic journals. *Address:* 32 Abbey Gardens, NW8. *T:* 01-624 8010.

WHITING, Winifred Ada, MA (London); retired, 1958; *b* 6 Jan. 1898; *d* of Harry Whiting and Ada Elizabeth Kent. *Educ:* County School, Putney; King's College, London. Teaching posts at Kesteven and Sleaford High School, Lincs; William Gibb's School, Faversham, Kent; St Paul's Girls' School; Headmistress, Girls' County Grammar School, Bromley, Kent; Principal, CF Mott Training College, Liverpool; Principal, Nonington Coll. of Physical Educn, near Dover, Kent, retd.

WHITLAM, Hon. (Edward) Gough, QC 1962; MP for Werriwa, NSW, since 1952; Leader of the Opposition, Australia, since 1976; *b* 11 July 1916; *s* of late H. F. E. Whitlam, Australian Crown Solicitor and Aust. rep. on UN Human Rights Commission; *m* 1942, Margaret Elaine, *d* of late Mr Justice Dovey, NSW Supreme Court; three *s* one *d. Educ:* University of Sydney. BA 1938; LLB 1946. RAAF Flight Lieut, 1941-45. Barrister, 1947; Joint Committee on Constitutional Review, 1956-59; Deputy Leader, Aust. Labor Party, 1960, Leader, 1967; Leader of the Opposition, 1967-72; Prime Minister of Australia, 1972-75; Minister for Foreign Affairs, 1972-73. Silver Plate of Honour, Socialist Internat., 1976. *Publications:* The Constitution *versus* Labor, 1957; Australian Foreign Policy, 1963; Socialism within the Constitution, 1965; Australia, Base or Bridge?, 1966; Beyond Vietnam: Australia's Regional Responsibility, 1968; An Urban Nation, 1969; A New Federalism, 1971; Urbanised Australia, 1972; Australian Public Administration and the Labor Government, 1973; Australia's Foreign Policy: New Directions, New Definitions, 1973; Road to Reform: Labor in Government, 1975; The New Federalism: Labor's Programs and Policies, 1976; On the Constitution, 1977. *Address:* Parliament House, Canberra, ACT, Australia.

WHITLEY, Elizabeth Young, (Mrs H. C. Whitley); social worker and journalist; *b* 28 Dec. 1915; *d* of Robert Thom and Mary Muir Wilson; *m* 1939, Henry Charles Whitley (Very Rev. Dr H. C. Whitley, CVO; *d* 1976); two *s* two *d* (and one *s* decd). *Educ:* Laurelbank School, Glasgow; Glasgow University. MA 1936; courses: in Italian at Perugia Univ., 1935, in Social Science at London School of Economics and Glasgow School of Social Science, 1938-39. Ran Girls' Clubs in Govan and Plantation, Glasgow, and Young Mothers' Clubs in Partick and Port Glasgow; Vice-Chm. Scottish Association of Girls' Clubs and Mixed Clubs, 1957-61, and Chm. of Advisory Cttee, 1958-59. Broadcast regular programme with BBC (Scottish Home Service), 1953. Member: Faversham Committee on AID, 1958-60; Pilkington Committee on Broadcasting, 1960-62. Columnist, Scottish Daily Express. Adopted as Parly candidate for SNP by West Perth and Kinross, 1968. *Publications:* Plain Mr Knox, 1960; The Two Kingdoms: the story of the Scottish covenanters, 1977; descriptive and centenary articles for Scottish papers, particularly Glasgow Herald and Scotland's Magazine. *Recreations:* reading, gardening. *Address:* The Glebe, Southwick, by Dumfries. *T:* Southwick 276.

WHITLEY, Air Marshal Sir John R., KBE 1956 (CBE 1945); CB 1946; DSO 1943; AFC 1937, Bar, 1956; *b* 7 September 1905; *s* of late A. Whitley, Condette, Pas de Calais, France; *m* 1932, Barbara Liscombe (*d* 1965); four *s* ; *m* 1967, Mrs Alison Russell. *Educ:* Haileybury. Entered Royal Air Force with a short-service commission, 1926; Permanent Commission, 1931; served in India, 1932-37; served in Bomber Command, 1940-45, as a Squadron Comdr, Station Comdr, Base Comdr and AOC a Group; Director of Organisation (Establishments), Air Ministry, 1948 and 1949; Imperial Defence College, 1950; AOA, 2nd Tactical Air Force, 1951 and 1952; AOC No 1 (Bomber) Group, 1953-56; Air Member for Personnel, 1957-59; Inspector-General, RAF, 1959-62; Controller, RAF Benevolent Fund, 1962-68, retd. *Address:* Little Salterns, Bucklers Hard, Beaulieu, Hampshire. *Clubs:* Royal Air Force; Royal Lymington Yacht, Island Sailing (IoW).

WHITLEY, Oliver John; Managing Director, External Broadcasting, British Broadcasting Corporation, 1969-72, retired; *b* 12 Feb. 1912; *s* of Rt Hon. J. H. Whitley, PC, and Marguerite (*née* Marchetti); *m* 1939, Elspeth Catherine (*née* Forrester-Paton); four *s* one *d. Educ:* Clifton Coll.; New Coll., Oxford. Barrister-at-Law, 1935; BBC, 1935-41. Served in RNVR, 1942-46; Coastal Forces and Combined Ops. BBC 1946-: seconded to Colonial Office, 1946-49; Head of General Overseas Service, 1950-54; Assistant Controller, Overseas Services, 1955-57; Appointments Officer, 1957-60; Controller, Staff Training and Appointments, 1960-64; Chief Assistant to Dir-Gen., 1964-68. *Recreations:* reading and gardening. *Address:* Greenacre, Ganavan Road, Oban, Argyll PA34 5TU. *T:* Oban 2555.

WHITLOCK, William Charles; MP (Lab) Nottingham North since October 1959; *b* 20 June 1918; *s* of late George Whitlock and of Sarah Whitlock, Sholing, Southampton; *m* 1943, Jessie Hilda, *d* of George Reardon of Armagh; five *s. Educ:* Itchen Gram. Sch.; Southampton Univ. Army Service, 1939-46. Apptd full-time Trade Union Officer, Area Organiser of Union of Shop, Distributive and Allied Workers, 1946. President, Leicester and District Trades Council, 1955-56; President, Leicester City Labour Party, 1956-57; President, North-East Leicester Labour Party, 1955-56, and 1958-59. Member East Midlands Regional Council of Labour Party, 1955-67, Vice-Chairman 1961-62, Chairman 1962-63. Opposition Whip, House of Commons, 1962-64; Vice-Chamberlain of the Household, 1964-66; Lord Comr of Treasury, March 1966-July 1966; Comptroller of HM Household, July 1966-March 1967; Dep. Chief Whip and Lord Comr of the Treasury, March-July 1967; Under Sec. of State for Commonwealth Affairs, 1967-68; Parly Under-Sec. of State, FCO, 1968-69. *Address:* House of Commons, SW1; 51 Stoughton Road, Leicester. *T:* 703367.

WHITMARSH, Gerald Edward Leaman, CBE 1972; DL; FCA; Vice-President, formerly Chairman, West Country Tourist Board, since 1974; Chairman: Poron Insulation Ltd; Capital Securities Ltd; Toptown Printers Ltd, since 1973; Director: Dartington Hall Ltd, since 1975; Armada Investments Ltd, since 1976; Founder (and original Director), Western Credit Ltd, 1935; *b* 10 Oct. 1908; *s* of Edward Whitmarsh, Plymouth; *m* 1938, Phyllis May, *d* of William T. Allchin, Charlton, SE; two *s* one *d. Educ:* Plymouth Coll.; Rippon Hall, Oxford. Contested (L): Truro, 1950; St Ives, 1959 and 1964. Chm., Devon CC, 1966-71 (Chm. Finance Cttee, 1965-67); Mem., SW Economic Planning Council, 1967-72. DL Co. Devon, 1969. Mem. Council, 1965-77, Finance Cttee, 1958-, Univ. of Exeter. Hon. MA, Exeter, 1965. *Recreation:* walking on Dartmoor. *Address:* South Winds, Crapstone, Yelverton, Devon. *T:* Yelverton 2316.

WHITMORE, Clive Anthony; Under Secretary, Cabinet Office, since 1977; *b* 18 Jan. 1935; *s* of Charles Arthur Whitmore and Louisa Lilian Whitmore; *m* 1961, Jennifer Mary Thorpe; one *s* two *d. Educ:* Sutton Grammar Sch., Surrey; Christ's Coll., Cambridge (BA). Asst Principal, WO, 1959; Private Sec. to Permanent Under-Sec. of State, WO, 1961; Asst Private Sec. to Sec. of State for War, 1962; Principal, 1964; Private Sec. to Permanent Under-Sec. of State, MoD, 1969; Asst Sec., 1971; Asst Under-Sec. of State (Defence Staff), MoD, 1975. *Recreations:* gardening, listening to music. *Address:* Hempstead, Whitemans Green, Cuckfield, West Sussex. *T:* Haywards Heath 54248.

WHITMORE, Sir John (Henry Douglas), 2nd Bt *cr* 1954; *b* 16 Oct. 1937; *s* of Col Sir Francis Henry Douglas Charlton Whitmore, 1st Bt, KCB, CMG, DSO, TD, and of Lady Whitmore (*née* Ellis Johnsen); *S* father 1961; *m* 1962, Gunilla (marr. diss. 1969), *e d* of Sven A. Hansson, OV, KLH, Danderyd, and *o d* of Mrs Ella Hansson, Stockholm, Sweden; one *d. Educ:* Stone House, Kent; Eton; Sandhurst; Cirencester.

Occupation: tax exile. *Recreations:* flying, ski-ing, etc. *Address:* 1267 Vich, Vaud, Switzerland. *Club:* British Racing Drivers.

WHITNEY, John Hay; Bronze Star and Legion of Merit (US); CBE (Hon.; UK), 1948; Chairman: Whitney Communications Corporation; The International Herald Tribune; *b* 17 Aug. 1904; *s* of Payne and Helen Hay Whitney; *m* 1942, Betsey Cushing. *Educ:* Groton School; Yale University; Oxford University. BA and MA Yale. Served American Air Force in War, 1941-45 (Colonel). American Ambassador to the Court of St James's, 1957-61. Senior Partner J. H. Whitney & Co.; Editor-in-Chief, and Publisher New York Herald Tribune, 1961-66; Chm., John Hay Whitney Foundation; Life Governor: New York Hospital; Yale Corporation (Fellow, 1955-70, Sen. Fellow, 1970-73); Former Trustee, Museum of Modern Art; Trustee and Vice-Pres., Nat. Gallery of Art. Formerly special adviser and consultant on public affairs, Department of State; Commission on Foreign Economic Policy; Secretary of State's Public Committee on Personnel, and President's Committee on Education beyond High School; Jockey Club; Graduate Mem. Business Council. Mem., Corp. for Public Broadcasting, 1970-72. Private collection of Impressionist and post-Impressionist paintings shown at Tate Gallery, London, 1960-61. Hon. Fellow, New College, Oxford, 1957. Hon. Degrees: MA Yale University; Doctorate of Humane Letters, Kenyon College; Doctor of Laws: Colgate Univ.; Brown Univ.; Exeter College, Oxford; Columbia Univ.; Colby Coll. Benjamin Franklin Medal, 1963. *Address:* 110 West 51st Street, New York, NY 10020, USA. *Clubs:* White's; Buck's; Royal and Ancient.

WHITNEY, John Norton Braithwaite; Managing Director and Programme Controller, Capital Radio, since 1973; *b* 20 Dec. 1930; *s* of Willis Bevan Whitney and Dorothy Anne Whitney; *m* 1956, Roma Elizabeth; one *s* one *d*. *Educ:* Leighton Park Friends' Sch., Reading, Berks. Radio producer, 1951-64; wrote, edited and devised numerous television series, 1956-76. *Recreations:* chess, sculpture, looking at sunrises. *Address:* Capital Radio Ltd, Euston Tower, NW1 3DR. *T:* 01-288 1288; 10 Wadham Gardens, NW3 3DP. *Clubs:* Garrick, Pilgrims.

WHITNEY, Raymond William, OBE 1968; HM Diplomatic Service; Head of Overseas Information Department, Foreign and Commonwealth Office, since 1977; *b* 28 Nov. 1930; *o s* of late George Whitney, Northampton; *m* 1956, Sheila Margot Beswick Prince; two *s*. *Educ:* Wellingborough Sch.; RMA, Sandhurst; London Univ. (BA (Hons) Oriental Studies). Commnd Northamptonshire Regt, 1951; served in Trieste, Korea, Hong Kong, Germany; seconded to Australian Army HQ, 1960-63; resigned and entered HM Diplomatic Service, 1964; First Sec., Peking, 1966-68; Head of Chancery, Buenos Aires, 1969-72; FCO, 1972-73; Dep. High Comr, Dacca, 1973-76; FCO, 1976-. *Publications:* articles on Chinese and Asian affairs in professional jls. *Recreations:* theatricals (performing, producing and writing), tennis, bridge, walking. *Address:* The Dial House, Sunninghill, Berks SL5 0AG. *T:* Ascot 23164. *Club:* Royal Automobile.

WHITSEY, Fred; Editor, Popular Gardening, since 1967; Gardening Correspondent, Daily Telegraph, since 1971; *b* 18 July 1919; *m* 1947, Patricia Searle. *Educ:* outside school hours, and continuously since then. Assistant Editor, Popular Gardening, 1948-64, Associate Editor, 1964-67. Gardening correspondent, Sunday Telegraph, 1961-71. Broadcaster on BBC and independant radio programmes. *Publications:* Sunday Telegraph Gardening Book, 1966; contribs to Country Life and Homes & Gardens. *Recreations:* gardening, music. *Address:* Avens Mead, Oast Road, Oxted, Surrey RH8 9DV.

WHITSEY, Rt. Rev. Hubert Victor; *see* Chester, Bishop of.

WHITTAKER, Arnold, CSI 1947; CIE 1938; ICS, retired; Chairman Somerset County Council, 1956-59 (County Alderman, 1953); *b* 27 July 1900; *m* 1934, Hilda Lucy, *d* of late O. W. Street, MA; one *d*. *Educ:* Colne Grammar School; London School of Economics; Christ Church, Oxford. Joined ICS 1924; retired, 1939; Political Adviser to Indian Tea Association and Member, Assam Legislative Assembly; Secretary to Planting and Commerce Group, Assam Legislature, 1939-46. Director: Commonwealth Trust Ltd, 1948; Bridgwater Building Society, 1961. *Address:* Hey House, Somerton, Somerset. *T:* Somerton 72447.

WHITTAKER, John Macnaghten, FRS 1949; MA, DSc, FRSE; Vice-Chancellor of Sheffield University, Sept. 1952-65, retired; *b* 7 March 1905; *s* of late Sir Edmund Whittaker, FRS; *m* 1933, Iona, *d* of J. S. Elliot; two *s*. *Educ:* Fettes; Edin. Univ.; Trinity College, Cambridge (Scholar). Wrangler, 1927; Smith's Prize, 1929; Adams Prize, 1949; Lecturer in Mathematics, Edinburgh

Univ., 1927-29; Fellow and Lecturer, Pembroke Coll., Cambridge, 1929-33; Prof. of Pure Mathematics, Liverpool Univ., 1933-52. Senior Fellow, Birmingham University, 1965-66. Vis. Professor: Ain Shams Univ., Cairo, 1967; Inst. of Mathematics, Teheran, 1968-69; Univ. of West Indies, Barbados, 1970-71. Served in RA, 1940-45 (AA Command, Western Desert, Tunisia, and as GSO1, War Office); Lt-Col RA, 1944; Dep. Scientific Adviser to the Army Council, 1944. Chairman: Joint Standing Cttee of Universities and Accountancy Profession, 1953-64; Commn on Royal University of Malta, 1957. A Capital Burgess of the Town and Parish of Sheffield, 1956-70; Freedom of City of Sheffield, 1965. Hon. LLD (Sheffield). *Publications:* Interpolatory Function Theory, 1935; Les séries de base de polynomes quelconques, 1949; Memoirs in various journals. *Address:* 11B Endcliffe Crescent, Sheffield S10 3EB. *T:* Sheffield 663712.

WHITTAKER, Sir (Joseph) Meredith, Kt 1974; TD 1950; DL; Chairman of Scarborough and District Newspapers Ltd; *b* 28 Sept. 1914; *s* of late Francis Croyden Whittaker; *m* 1939, Gwenllian Enid, *d* of F. W. Allen, Scarborough; one *s* one *d*. *Educ:* Scarborough Coll.; Queen's Coll., Oxford (MA). Mem. NR Yorks CC, 1949-74, and North Yorkshire CC, 1973-. Vice-Chm. of Exec. Council, County Councils Assoc., 1969-72; Chairman of Executive Council: County Councils Assoc., 1972-74; Assoc. of County Councils, 1973-76; Chairman: British Sections: Internat. Union of Local Authorities; Council of European Municipalities. DL Yorks 1971. *Address:* High Dalby House, Thornton Dale, Pickering, North Yorkshire YO18 7LP. *T:* (home) Lockton 214, (business) Scarborough 63631. *Club:* Anglo-Belgian.

WHITTALL, Lionel Harry; Foreign Books Buyer, Globe Book Shops, Washington DC, USA; *b* 1907; *s* of H. A. Whittall; *m* 1937, Elizabeth Morris; no *c*. *Educ:* privately, in W Europe; Oxford (MA); Inst. of Education, London; Agric. Dept Grad. Sch. HM Foreign Service, 1929-56; latterly Consul-Gen., Berlin. Translations for World Bank, Berlitz, Govt of Chile, Sec. of Treasury, etc. *Publications:* contrib. to official surveys of foreign press; unsigned trans. for official use: Rumanian Forces Uniforms; Surinam Pilot, and other manuals. *Recreations:* reading, travel. *Address:* 5410 Connecticut Avenue, Washington, DC 20015, USA. *Clubs:* Old Greshamian (Holt); Union (Oxford).

WHITTAM, Prof. Ronald, FRS 1973; Professor of Physiology, The University, Leicester, since 1966; *b* 21 March 1925; *e s* of Edward Whittam and May Whittam (*née* Butterworth), Oldham, Lancs; *m* 1957, Christine Patricia Margaret, 2nd *d* of Canon J. W. Lamb, Bridlington, Yorks; one *s* one *d*. *Educ:* Council and Technical Schools, Oldham; Univs of Manchester, Sheffield and Cambridge. BSc 1st Class Hons (Manchester); PhD (Sheffield and Cambridge). Served War of 1939-45, RAF, 1943-47. John Stokes Fellow, Dept of Biochem., Univ. of Sheffield, 1953-55; Beit Memorial Fellow, Physiological Lab., Cambridge, 1955-58; Mem. Scientific Staff, MRC Cell Metabolism Research Unit, Oxford, 1958-60; Univ. Lectr in Biochemistry, Oxford, 1960-66; Bruno Mendel Fellow of Royal Society, 1965-66; Mem. Editorial Bd of Biochem. Jl, 1963-67; Hon. Sec., Physiological Soc., 1969-74; Mem. Biological Research Bd of MRC, 1971-74, Co-Chm., 1973-74; Mem., Biological Sciences Cttee, UGC, 1974-; Chm., Biological Educn Cttee, Royal Soc. and Inst Biol., 1974-. *Publications:* Transport and Diffusion in Red Blood Cells, 1964; scientific papers dealing with cell membranes. *Recreation:* walking. *Address:* Department of Physiology, The University, Leicester LE1 7RH. *T:* Leicester 23271.

WHITTAM SMITH, Andreas; City Editor, Daily Telegraph, since 1977; *b* 13 June 1937; *s* of Canon J. E. Smith and Mrs Smith (*née* Barlow); *m* 1964, Valerie Catherine, *d* of late Wing Comdr J. A. Sherry and of Mrs N. W. H. Wyllys; two *s*. *Educ:* Birkenhead Sch., Cheshire; Keble Coll., Oxford (BA). With N. M. Rothschild, 1960-62; Stock Exchange Gazette, 1962-63; Financial Times, 1963-64; The Times, 1964-66; Dep. City Editor, Daily Telegraph, 1966-69; City Editor, The Guardian, 1969-70; Editor, Investors Chronicle and Stock Exchange Gazette, and Dir, Throgmorton Publications, 1970-77. Wincott award, 1975. *Recreations:* music, history. *Address:* 2 Holly Bush Hill, Hampstead, NW3. *T:* 01-435 4310. *Club:* Garrick.

WHITTEMORE, Ernest William, MM 1944 and Bar 1945; Under-Secretary, Department of Health and Social Security, 1973-76; *b* 31 Aug. 1916; *s* of late Ernest William Whittemore and Hilda Whittemore; *m* 1942, Irene Mollie Hudson; two *d*. *Educ:* Raine's Sch., Stepney; King's Coll., London. BA Hons English. Receiver's Office, New Scotland Yard, 1934-35; Min. of Health, 1935-45; Royal Artillery, 1942-46; Min. of Nat. Insce (and successor depts), 1945-76. *Recreations:* bibliomania, travel. *Address:* 39 Montalt Road, Woodford Green, Essex IG8 9RS. *T:* 01-504 7028.

WHITTERIDGE, Prof. David, FRS 1953; Waynflete Professor of Physiology, University of Oxford, since 1968; *b* 22 June 1912; 2nd *s* of Walter and Jeanne Whitteridge; *m* 1938, Gweneth, *d* of S. Hutchings; three *d. Educ:* Whitgift School, Croydon; Magdalen College, Oxford (1st cl. Physiology Finals, 1934); King's College Hospital. BSc 1936; BM, BCh 1937; DM 1945; Beit Memorial Fellowship, 1940; Schorstein Research Fellow, 1944; Fellow by Special Election, Magdalen College, Oxford, 1945-50; University Demonstrator in Physiology, Univ. of Oxford, 1944-50; Prof. of Physiology, Univ. of Edinburgh, 1950-68. Leverhulme Vis. Prof., Univ. Delhi, 1967 and 1973; Sherrington Lectr, RSM, 1972; Victor Horsley Meml Lectr, BMA, 1972; Bowman Lectr, OSUK, 1977. Mem. Bd of Trustees, Nat. Lib. of Scotland, 1966-70. Feldberg Prize, 1962. FRCP London, 1966. *Publications:* papers on physiological topics in Jl Physiol., Brain, etc. *Address:* University Laboratory of Physiology, Parks Road, Oxford OX1 3PT; Winterslow, Lincombe Lane, Boar's Hill, Oxford OX1 5DZ. *T:* Oxford 735211.
See also R. A. Furtado, Sir G. C. Whitteridge.

WHITTERIDGE, Sir Gordon (Coligny), KCMG 1964 (CMG 1956); OBE 1946; *b* 6 Nov. 1908; *s* of late Walter Randall Whitteridge and of Jeanne Whitteridge, Croydon; *m* 1st, 1938, Margaret Lungley (*d* 1942; one *s* one *d* decd 1942); 2nd, 1951, Jane, twin *d* of Frederick J. Driscoll, Brookline, Mass, USA; one *s. Educ:* Whitgift School, Croydon; University of Cambridge. Joined Consular Service, 1932; one of HM Vice-Consuls, Siam, 1933; Vice-Consul, Batavia, 1936; Acting Consul, Batavia, 1937, 1938, and 1939; Acting Consul, Medan, Sept. 1941-Feb. 1942. Employed at Foreign Office from June, 1942; promoted Consul (Grade II), Foreign Office, 1944, Consul, 1945. 1st Secretary, Moscow, 1948-49; Consul-General Stuttgart, 1949-51; Counsellor/Consul-Gen., 1950; Counsellor, Bangkok, 1951-56 (Chargé d'Affaires in 1952, 1953, 1954, 1955); Consul-Gen., Seattle, Wash, 1956-60; HM Consul-General, Istanbul, 1960-62; Ambassador: to Burma, 1962-65; to Afghanistan, 1965-68; retired, 1968. Chm., Anglo-Thai Soc., 1971-76; Hon. Treasurer, Soc. for Afghan Studies, 1972-. *Recreations:* tennis, music. *Address:* 13 Grimwade Avenue, Croydon, Surrey. *Club:* Royal Commonwealth Society.
See also R. A. Furtado, Prof. D. Whitteridge.

WHITTET, Dr Thomas Douglas, CBE 1977; Chief Pharmacist, Department of Health and Social Security, since 1967; *b* 4 Jan. 1915; *s* of late Thomas Douglas Whittet and Ellen Sloan Whittet (*née* Scott); *m* 1942, Doreen Mary Bowes; two *s. Educ:* Rosebank Sch., Hartlepool; Sunderland Polytechnic; University Coll., London. PhC (now FPS) 1938; BSc (London) 1953; FRIC 1955; CChem 1975; PhD (London) 1958. Chief Chemist, Numol Ltd, 1939-41; hospital pharmacy, 1941-43; Chief Pharmacist and Lectr in Pharmacy: Charing Cross Hosp., 1943-47; University Coll. Hosp. and Med. Sch., 1947-65; Dep. Chief Pharmacist, Min. of Health, 1965-67. Member: Brit. Pharm. Codex Revis. Cttee, 1967-75; Joint Formulary Cttee, 1967-; European Pharmacopoeia Commn, 1967-71; WHO Expert Adv. Cttee on Internat. Pharmacopoeia, 1948-; Council of Europe (Partial Agreement) Pharmaceutical Cttee, 1967-; EEC Pharmaceutical Ctte and working parties, 1977-. Mem., Ct of Assts, Soc. of Apothecaries of London (Sydenham Lectr, 1965; Delaune Lectr, 1977; Chm., Faculty of Hist. and Philos. of Medicine and Pharmacy, 1975-). Wright Meml Lectr, Sydney, 1972; Winch Meml Lectr, 1973; Harrison Meml Lectr and Medallist, 1973. Hon. Member: Royal Spanish Acad. of Pharmacy, 1958; Internat. Acad. of Pharmacy, 1965. Hon. DSc: Bath, 1968; Aston, 1974. Evans Gold Medal (Guild of Public Pharmacists), 1960. FRSocMed. *Publications:* Hormones, 1946; Diagnostic Agents, 1947; Sterilisation and Disinfection, 1965; The Apothecaries in the Great Plague of London of 1665, 1971; many papers on medical and pharmaceutical history; numerous papers in Jl of Pharmacy and Pharmacology and in Pharmaceutical Jl on pyrogens and fever and on drug stability. *Recreations:* overseas travel, especially Commonwealth; medical and pharmaceutical history. *Address:* Woburn Lodge, 8 Lyndhurst Drive, Harpenden, Herts. *T:* Harpenden 4376. *Clubs:* Royal Commonwealth Society; MCC.

WHITTICK, Richard James; Assistant Under-Secretary of State, Home Office, 1967-72; *b* 21 August 1912; *s* of Ernest G. Whittick and Grace M. Shaw; *m* 1938, Elizabeth Mason; two *s. Educ:* George Heriot's School; Edinburgh University. British Museum (Natural History), 1936; Home Office, 1940; Principal Private Secretary to Home Secretary, 1952-53; Assistant Secretary, 1953. *Recreation:* gardening. *Address:* Coombe

Cottage, Coombe, Sherborne, Dorset DT9 4BX. *T:* Sherborne 4488.

WHITTINGHAM, Charles Percival, BA, PhD Cantab; Head of Department of Botany, Rothamsted Experimental Station, since 1971; *b* 1922; *m* 1946, Alison Phillips; two *d. Educ:* St John's College, Cambridge. Professor of Botany, London University, at Queen Mary College, 1958-64; Head of Dept of Botany, 1967-71, and Prof. of Plant Physiology, 1964-71, Imperial Coll., Univ of London; Dean, Royal Coll. of Science, 1969-71; Hon. Dir, ARC Unit for Plant Physiology, 1964-71. Vis. Prof., Imperial College, 1971-. *Publications:* Chemistry of Plant Processes, 1964; (with R. Hill) Photosynthesis, 1955; The Mechanism of Photosynthesis, 1974; contrib. to scientific journals. *Recreations:* music, travel. *Address:* Rothamsted Experimental Station, Harpenden, Herts.

WHITTINGHAM, Air Marshal Sir Harold (Edward), KCB 1945; KBE 1941 (CBE 1930); MB, ChB (Glasgow); FRCP; FRCPE; FRFPS; FRSTM&H; DPH, DTM&H; LLD (Hon.) Glasgow; FRCS (Hon.) Edinburgh; KStJ, 1945; Hon. FRSM; Hon. FRIPHH; Hon. Fellow Aerospace Med. Assoc.: Hon. Mem. Assoc. Mil. Surgeons of USA; Hon. Civil Consultant in Aviation Medicine to RAF; Member, World Health Organisation Expert Advisory Panels on International Quarantine and on Environmental Sanitation, and Member, Expert Committee on Sanitation of International Airports, 1953-74; Medical Consultant to the Commonwealth Development Corp. (Adviser, 1956-66); Member, Internat. Acad. of Astronautics; *b* 1887; 2nd *s* of late Engineer Rear-Admiral Wm Whittingham, CB; *m* 1st, 1912, Agnes Kerr (*d* 1966), *d* of late William Seright, MD, FRFPS; one *s* one *d*; 2nd, 1966, Rita C. J., *d* of late W. Harold White, MPS. *Educ:* Christ's Hosp.; Greenock Acad.; Glasgow Univ. Pathologist and Assistant Director of Research, Royal Cancer Hosp., Glasgow, 1910-15; Pathologist, Scottish National Red Cross, 1914-15; served European War, 1915-18, with RAMC in India and Mesopotamia (despatches); attached Royal Flying Corps, 1917-18; transferred RAF, 1918, as Pathologist; in charge of RAF Sandfly Fever Commn, Malta, 1921-23; Director of Pathology, RAF, 1925-30; Lecturer, Bio-Chemistry, London School of Tropical Medicine, 1926-30; Pathologist, Royal Bucks Hosp., 1927-39; Consultant in Pathology and Tropical Medicine, RAF, 1930-35; OC RAF Central Medical Establishment, 1934-39; Consultant in Hygiene, Pathology and Tropical Medicine, RAF, 1935-39; Hon. Physician to the King, 1938-46; Director of Hygiene, Air Ministry, 1939-41; Chief Executive Officer, Flying Personnel Research Committee, 1939-41; DGMS, RAF, 1941-46; Medical Adviser, British Red Cross Soc., 1946-48; DMS, BOAC, 1948-56. Group Capt., 1932; Air Commodore, 1936; Air Vice-Marshal, 1940; Air Marshal, 1941. Royal Society of Tropical Medicine and Hygiene: Fellow, 1921; Mem. Council, 1924-43 and 1945-47; Vice-Pres., 1943-45; Hon. Mem., Assoc. Clinical Pathologists, 1921-. Chairman: Flying Personnel Res. Cttee, 1949-67; IATA Med. Cttee, 1950-57. Harveian Lectr, RCS, 1946. Duncan and Lalcaca Medals, London Sch. of Tropical Medicine, 1920; N Persian Memorial Medallist, 1923; Chadwick Gold Medal, 1925; John Jeffries Award of Institute of Aeronautical Sciences, USA, 1944; Stewart Meml Award, 1970. Commander of the Legion of Merit, USA, 1945; Cross and Star of the Order of Polonia Restituta, 1945; Knight Grand Cross of the Order of St Olaf of Norway; Czechoslovak Military Medal, 1st Class. Hon. Freeman of Barber-Surgeon's Co. *Publications:* include numerous scientific papers and reports on aviation medicine, cancer, influenza, malaria, dysentery, sandfly fever, cerebrospinal fever, scarlet fever, diphtheria, tonsillitis and first aid. *Address:* 26 Marlborough Gardens, Lovelace Road, Surbiton, Surrey KT6 6NF. *T:* 01-399 8648.

WHITTINGTON, Charles Richard, MC 1944; Chamberlain of London, 1964-1973; *b* 8 March 1908; *er s* of late Charles Henry Whittington, Stock Exchange, and of Vera Whittington; *m* 1938, Helen Irene Minnie, *d* of late Lieutenant-Colonel J. E. Hance, RHA; one *s* four *d. Educ:* Uppingham School. Commissioned in Queen's Royal Regiment, TA, 1928; Captain, 1931; TARO, 1937. Served War of 1939-45 with Queen's, East Surrey, and Dorset Regts in Sicily, Italy, and NW Europe (D-Day landing, wounded, MC); demobilised with rank of Captain, 1945. Member of The Stock Exchange, London, 1931-64. Liveryman Mercers' Company, 1931; Mem. of Court of Common Council for Ward of Broad Street, 1939-64; one of HM Lieutenants, City of London, 1964-73. *Recreation:* gardening. *Address:* Park Cottage, Bramptor. Bryan, Bucknell, Salop. *T:* Bucknell 291.

WHITTINGTON, Prof. Harry Blackmore, FRS 1971; Woodwardian Professor of Geology, Cambridge University, since 1966; *b* 24 March 1916; *s* of Harry Whittington and Edith M. (*née* Blackmore); *m* 1940, Dorothy E. Arnold; no *c. Educ:*

Handsworth Gram. Sch.; Birmingham University. Commonwealth Fund Fellow, Yale Univ., 1938-40; Lectr in Geology, Judson Coll., Rangoon, 1940-42; Prof. of Geography, Ginling Coll., Chengtu, W China, 1943-45; Lectr in Geology, Birmingham Univ., 1945-49; Harvard Univ.: Vis. Lectr, 1949-50; Assoc. Prof. of Geology, 1950-58; Prof. of Geology, 1958-66. Hon. AM, Harvard Univ., 1950. *Publications:* articles in Jl of Paleontology, Bulletin Geol. Soc. of Amer., Quarterly Jl Geol. Soc. London, etc. *Address:* 20 Rutherford Road, Cambridge CB2 2HH. *Club:* Geological.

WHITTINGTON, Thomas Alan, CB 1977; Circuit Administrator, North Eastern Circuit, since 1974; *b* 15 May 1916; *o s* of late George Whittington, JP and Mary Elizabeth Whittington; *m* 1939, Audrey Elizabeth, *y d* of late Craven Gilpin, Leeds; four *s. Educ:* Uppingham Sch.; Leeds Univ. (LLB). Commnd W Yorks Regt (Leeds Rifles) TA, 1937, serving War of 1939-45 in UK and 14th Army in India (Major). Solicitor of Supreme Court, 1945; Clerk of the Peace, Leeds, 1952-70; Senior Partner, Marklands, Solicitors, Leeds, 1967-70; Under-Sec., Lord Chancellor's Office, 1970; Circuit Administrator, Northern Circuit, 1970-74. *Recreations:* fishing, shooting, holiday golf. *Address:* The Cottage, School Lane, Collingham, Wetherby LS22 5BQ. *T:* Collingham Bridge 3881. *Club:* Leeds (Leeds).

WHITTLE, Dr Claude Howard, MA, MD Cantab; FRCP; Associate Lecturer in Clinical Medicine, University of Cambridge; Physician, and later Physician to the Skin Department of the United Cambridge Hospitals, 1930-61; Consultant Member, Medical Appeal Tribunal; Consultant Dermatologist, Ministry of Social Security, 1945-72; Hon. Consultant Physician; *b* 2 May 1896; *s* of Tom Whittle and Edith Annie Thompson; *m* 1923, Phyllis Lena Fricker, LRAM; three *s. Educ:* The Masonic School, Bushey, Herts; Queens' College, Cambridge (Foundation Scholar in Natural Science); King's Coll. Hosp., London. Clinical Pathologist, 1923. Pres. Dermatological Sec. RSM, 1961-62, Hon. Sec., 1945-6-7; Pres. British Assoc. of Dermatology, 1953-54, Hon. Mem. 1968; Member; Assoc. of Physicians; Path. Soc. of Gt Britain; British Allergy Soc.; Hon. Mem. British Soc. Mycopath., 1968, Pres., 1973-75. *Publications:* Vitamin A in psoriasis, Candida skin infections, Fungous infections in Cambridge, Paronychia, Kerato-acanthoma, in Brit. Jl Dermatology, Lancet, etc.; articles on skin diseases in Modern Treatment in General Practice, 1934 and 1938, and in Progress in Biological Sciences, 1960; many others in Proc. Roy. Soc. Medicine, Brit. Jl Dermatology, BMJ, Sabouraudia, Lancet, etc. *Recreations:* painting, sailing, music. *Address:* 41 Newton Road, Cambridge. *T:* 59237.

WHITTLE, Air Cdre Sir Frank, KBE 1948 (CBE 1944); CB 1947; Comdr, US Legion of Merit, 1946; FRS 1947; CEng; MA Cantab; RAF, retired; Navair Research Professor, US Naval Academy, Annapolis, Maryland, since 1977; *b* 1 June 1907; *s* of M. Whittle; *m* 1930, Dorothy Mary Lee (marr. diss. 1976); two *s*; *m* 1976, Hazel S. Hall. *Educ:* Leamington Coll.; No 4 Apprentices' Wing, RAF Cranwell; RAF Coll., Cranwell; Peterhouse, Cambridge (Mechanical Sciences Tripos, BA 1st Cl. Hons). No 4 Apprentices' Wing, RAF Cranwell, 1923-26; Flight Cadet, RAF Coll., Cranwell, 1926-28 (Abdy-Gerrard-Fellowes Memorial Prize); Pilot Officer, 111 (Fighter) Sqdn, 1928-29; Flying Instructors' Course, Central Flying Sch., 1929; Flying Instructor, No 2 Flying Training Sch., RAF Digby, 1930; Test Pilot, Marine Aircraft Experimental Estab., RAF Felixstowe, 1931-32; RAF Sch. of Aeronautical Engrg, Henlow, 1932-34; Officer i/c Engine Test, Engine Repair Section, Henlow, 1934 (6 mths); Cambridge Univ., 1934-37 (Post-Graduate year, 1936-37); Special Duty List, attached Power Jets Ltd for devel of aircraft gas turbine for jet propulsion, 1937-46; War Course, RAF Staff Coll., 1943; Technical Adviser to Controller of Supplies (Air), Min. of Supply, 1946-48; retd RAF, 1948. Hon. Technical Adviser: Jet Aircraft, BOAC, 1948-52; Shell Gp, 1953-57; Consultant, Bristol Siddeley Engines/Rolls Royce on turbo drill project, 1961-70. Partnered late Flt-Lt G. E. Campbell in Crazy Flying RAF Display, Hendon, 1930; 1st flights of Gloster jet-propelled aeroplane with Whittle engine, May 1941. Freeman of Royal Leamington Spa, 1944. Hon. FRAeS; Hon. FAeSI; Hon. FIMechE; Founder Fellow, Fellowship of Engineering, 1976. Hon. Mem., Franklin Inst.; Hon. FAIAA; Hon. Mem., Société Royale Belge des Ingénieurs; Hon. Foreign Mem., Amer. Acad. Arts and Scis, 1976; Hon. Fellow, Soc. of Experimental Test Pilots, USA; Hon. MEIC. Hon. Fellow, Peterhouse. Hon. DSc: Oxon; Manchester; Leicester; Bath; Warwick; Exeter; Hon. LLD Edinburgh; Hon. ScD Cantab; Hon. DTech Trondheim. James Alfred Ewing Medal, ICE, 1944; Gold Medal, RAeS, 1944; James Clayton Prize, IMechE, 1946; Daniel Guggenheim Medal, USA, 1946;

Kelvin Gold Medal, 1947; Melchett Medal, 1949; Rumford Medal, Royal Soc., 1950; Gold Medal, Fedn Aeronautique Internat., 1951; Churchill Gold Medal, Soc. of Engineers, 1952; Albert Gold Medal, Soc. of Arts, 1952; Franklin Medal, USA, 1956; John Scott Award, 1957; Goddard Award, USA, 1965; Coventry Award of Merit, 1966; International Communications (Christopher Columbus) Prize, City of Genoa, 1966; Tony Jannus Award, Greater Tampa Chamber of Commerce, 1969; James Watt Internat. Gold Medal, IMechE, 1977. *Publication:* Jet, 1953.

WHITTLE, Kenneth Francis, CEng, FIEE; Chairman, South Western Electricity Board, since 1977; *b* 28 April 1922; *s* of Thomas Whittle and May Whittle; *m* 1945, Dorothy Inskip; one *s* one *d. Educ:* Kingswood Sch., Bath; Faculty of Technol., Manchester Univ. (BScTech). FIEE 1943. Served War, Electrical Lieut, RNVR, 1943-46. Metropolitan Vickers Elec. Co. Ltd, 1946-48; NW Div., CEGB, 1948-55; North West Electricity Board: various posts, 1955-64; Area Commercial Officer, Blackburn, 1964-68; Manager, Peak Area, 1969-71, Manchester Area, 1971-74; Chief Commercial Officer, 1974-75; Dep. Chm., Yorks Elec. Bd, 1975-77. *Recreation:* golf. *Address:* 8 Cambridge Road, Clevedon, Avon BS21 7HX. *T:* Clevedon 874017.

WHITTLE, Prof. Peter; Churchill Professor of Mathematics of Operational Research, University of Cambridge, since 1967; *b* 27 Feb. 1927; *s* of Percy Whittle and Elsie Tregurtha; *m* 1951, Käthe Hildegard Blomquist; three *s* three *d. Educ:* Wellington Coll., New Zealand. Docent, Uppsala Univ., 1951-53; employed New Zealand DSIR, 1953-59, rising to Senior Principal Scientifc Officer; Lectr, Univ. of Cambridge, 1959-61; Prof. of Mathematical Statistics, Univ. of Manchester, 1961-67. *Publications:* Hypothesis Testing in Time Series Analysis, 1951; Prediction and Regulation, 1963; Probability, 1970; Optimisation under Constraints, 1971; contribs to Biometrika, Jl Roy. Statistical Soc., Proc. Camb. Phil. Soc., Proc. Roy. Soc. *Recreation:* guitar. *Address:* 268 Queen Edith's Way, Cambridge; Statistical Laboratory, University of Cambridge.

WHITTON, Cuthbert Henry; *b* 18 Feb. 1905; *s* of Henry and Eleanor Whitton; *m* 1938, Iris Elva Moody; one *d. Educ:* St Andrew's College, Dublin; Dublin University. Malayan Civil Service, 1929; Colonial Legal Service, 1939; Puisne Judge, Federation of Malaya, 1951; Puisne Judge, Supreme Court, Singapore, 1954; Foreign Compensation Commn, Legal Dept, 1959-71. *Recreations:* golf, gardening. *Address:* Far End, Hill Waye, Gerrard's Cross, Bucks. *T:* 85608. *Clubs:* Royal Commonwealth Society; Kildare Street and University (Dublin).

WHITTUCK, Gerald Saumarez, CB 1959; *b* 13 Oct. 1912; *s* of late Francis Gerald Whittuck; *m* 1938, Catherine McCrea; two *s. Educ:* Cheltenham; Clare Coll., Cambridge. Air Ministry, 1935; Private Secretary to Secretary of State, 1944-46; Asst Under-Secretary of State: Air Ministry, 1955-63; War Office, 1963-64; MoD, 1964-71; Dir, Greenwich Hosp., 1971-74. Mem., Royal Patriotic Fund Corp., 1971-74. *Address:* 15A Greenaway Gardens, NW3. *T:* 01-435 3742.

WHITWELL, Stephen John, CMG 1969; MC; HM Diplomatic Service, retired; *b* 30 July 1920; *s* of Arthur Percy Whitwell and Marion Whitwell (*née* Greenwood). *Educ:* Stowe; Christ Church, Oxford. Coldstream Guards, 1941-47 (demobilised with hon. rank Capt.). Joined HM Foreign Service (now Diplomatic Service), 1947; served: Tehran, 1947; FO, 1949; Belgrade, 1952; New Delhi, 1954; FO, 1958; Seoul, 1961. Polit. Adv. to C-in-C Middle East, Aden, 1964; Counsellor, Belgrade, 1965; Ambassador to Somalia, 1968-70; Head of East-West Contacts Dept, FCO, 1970-71. *Recreations:* reading, painting, looking at buildings. *Address:* Jervis Cottage, Aston Tirrold, Oxon. *Club:* Travellers'.

WHITWORTH, Clifford, MSc; PhD; FRIC; Vice-Chancellor of the University of Salford, 1967-74; *b* 6 Nov. 1906; *s* of late Joseph and Lucy Whitworth; *m* 1941, Ada Alice Belfit. *Educ:* Manchester Grammar School; Manchester University. Senior Research Assistant to Prof. H. S. Taylor, 1931-33; Industrial Research Chemist, 1933-35; Senior Lecturer in Chemistry, 1935-38, and Head of Dept of Pure and Applied Science, 1939-49, Loughborough College; Asst Education Officer for Further Education, Middlesex CC, 1949-57; Principal, Royal Coll. of Advanced Technology, Salford, 1959-67; Mem., Nat. Council for Technological Awards, 1955-60; Mem. Educn Cttee, Inst. of Fuel, 1951-73, Chm. 1968-73; Chm. NW Section, Inst. of Fuel, 1966-68; Vice-Pres., Inst. of Fuel, 1969-71. Mem. Council, Brit. Assoc. for the Advancement of Science, 1963-72; Chm., North-Western Regional Adv. Council Academic Bd, 1969-71. Member: Nat. Adv. Council on Educn for Industry and

Commerce, 1970-72; Cttee for Industrial Technologies, DTI, 1972-74. Mem. Governing Body, Hornsey Coll. of Art, 1966-72; Vice-Pres., Union of Lancs and Cheshire Insts, 1967-. Hon. DSc Salford, 1971. *Publications:* contrib. to sci. jls. *Address:* 6 Highfield Road, Bramhall, Cheshire SK7 3BE. *Club:* Athenæum.

WHITWORTH, Group Captain Frank, QC 1965; Judge of Courts of Appeal of Jersey and Guernsey, since 1971; a Recorder of the Crown Court, since 1972; *b* 13 May 1910; *o s* of late Daniel Arthur Whitworth, Didsbury, Manchester; *m* 1939, Mary Lucy, *o d* of late Sir John Holdsworth Robinson, JP, Bingley, Yorks; no *c. Educ:* Shrewsbury Sch.; Trinity Hall, Cambridge. Served with RAFVR (Special Duties), 1940-45, retired. Called to Bar, Gray's Inn, 1934. Member of Dorking and Horley RDC, 1939-68. Contested (C) St Helens, 1945. Master, Clockmakers' Co., 1962 and 1971. Trustee, Whiteley Village Homes, 1963. *Publications:* miscellaneous verse and articles. *Recreation:* farming. *Address:* Anstie Grange, South Holmwood, near Dorking, Surrey. *T:* Dorking 67136; 13 King's Bench Walk, Temple, EC4. *T:* 01-353 7204. *Club:* United Oxford & Cambridge University.

WHITWORTH, Hugh Hope Aston, MBE 1945; Lay Assistant to the Archbishop of Canterbury, since 1969; *b* 21 May 1914; *s* of Sidney Alexander Whitworth and Elsie Hope Aston; *m* 1st, 1944, Elizabeth Jean Boyes (*d* 1961); two *s* one *d*; 2nd, 1961, Catherine Helen Bell. *Educ:* Bromsgrove Sch.; Pembroke Coll., Cambridge (BA). Indian Civil Service, Bombay Province, 1937-47; Administrator, Ahmedabad Municipality, 1942-44; Collector and District Magistrate, Nasik, 1945-46; Board of Trade, 1947-55; Scottish Home Dept, 1955; Asst Sec., 1957; Under-Sec., Scottish Home and Health Dept, 1968-69. *Recreations:* travel, theatre, gardening. *Address:* 47 Orford Gardens, Strawberry Hill, Twickenham, Mddx. *T:* 01-892 4672. *Club:* United Oxford & Cambridge University.

WHITWORTH, Maj.-Gen. Reginald Henry, CB 1969; CBE 1963; MA; Bursar and Official Fellow, Exeter College, Oxford, since 1970; *b* 27 Aug. 1916; 2nd *s* of late Aymer William Whitworth and late Alice (*née* Hervey), Eton College; *m* 1946, June Rachel, *o d* of Sir Bartle Edwards, CVO, MC, and of Daphne, MBE, *d* of Sir Cyril Kendall Butler, KBE; two *s* one *d*. *Educ:* Eton; Balliol College, Oxford, 1st cl. Hons, Modern History, 1938; Laming Travelling Fellow, Queen's Coll., Oxford, 1938-39. 2nd Lt Grenadier Guards, 1940; GSO2, 78 Division, 1944; Bde Major, 24 Guards Brigade, 1945-46; GSO2, Staff College, Camberley, 1953-55; comdg 1st Bn Grenadier Guards, 1955-57; GSO1, SHAPE, 1958-59; Sen. Army Instructor, Jt Services Staff Coll., 1959-61; Comdr Berlin Infantry Bde Gp, 1961-63; DMS 1, Ministry of Defence, 1964-66; GOC: Yorkshire District, 1966-67; Northumbrian District, 1967-68; Chief of Staff, Southern Command, 1968-70. Bronze Star, USA, 1947. Governor: Felsted Sch.; St Mary's, Wantage; Mem. Exec. Cttee, Gordon Boys Sch. Trustee: Army Museum; Ogilby Trust. *Publications:* Field Marshal Earl Ligonier, 1958; Famous Regiments: the Grenadier Guards, 1974. *Recreations:* riding, fishing, military history. *Address:* The Old Manor, Letcombe Regis, Wantage, Oxon. *T:* Wantage 2259. *Club:* Army and Navy.

WHITWORTH, Thomas; Master of Hatfield College, Durham, since 1956; *b* 7 April 1917; *o s* of late Leonard and Elizabeth Whitworth, Oldham, Lancs; *m* 1941, Joan Mohene, *er d* of late Sir Clifford Agarwala; one *s* two *d*. *Educ:* Manchester Grammar School; Oriel College, Oxford. Royal Engineers, 1939-45. Burdett-Coutts Scholar, Oxford University, 1947-49. MA (Oxon) 1947, DPhil (Oxon) 1950. University Demonstrator in geology at Oxford and Lecturer of Oriel College, 1949-56. *Publications:* in various scientific journals. *Recreations:* painting; refereeing (Rugby Union); geological expeditions to East Africa. *Address:* The Master's Lodging, Hatfield College, Durham. *T:* Durham 65008.

WHYATT, Sir John, Kt 1957; *b* 13 April 1905; *o s* of late George Whyatt; *m* 1936, Margaret (*d* 1976), *er d* of Kenneth Stewart; one *s. Educ:* Stonyhurst; Balliol Coll., Oxford. Entered Colonial Legal Service, 1937; Crown Counsel, Hong Kong; Hong Kong Deleg. to Eastern Group Conference, New Delhi, 1940; Secretary, Eastern Group Supply Council, New Delhi, 1941; Adviser to British Representative, UNRRA Council Meeting, Sydney, 1945; Attorney-General, Barbados, 1948; Attorney-General and Minister for Legal Affairs, Kenya, 1951-55; Chief Justice of Singapore, 1955-58, retd. Judge of the Chief Court for the Persian Gulf, 1961-66; Director of Studies, Overseas Government Legal Officers Course, 1966-67. KC (Barbados) 1949; QC (Kenya) 1952. *Recreations:* travel, fishing, walking. *Address:* Boxwood, Amberley, Arundel, West Sussex. *Club:* Travellers'.

WW83

WHYTE, Gabriel Thomas; *b* 25 June 1925; *s* of Alexander and Margit Whyte; *m* 1951, Agnes Kalman; one *s. Educ:* Highgate Sch.; London Univ. (BSc Hon.). Founder and Man. Dir, Airfix Plastics Ltd, 1945-60; Dir, Airfix Industries, 1961-63; Man. Dir, Triumph Investment Trust, 1964-74; Pres., Atlantic Materials, 1975. *Recreations:* riding and dressage, hunting, fishing. *Address:* 910 Fifth Avenue, New York, NY 10021, USA.

WHYTE, Hamilton; *see* Whyte, W. E. H.

WHYTE, Rev. James Aitken; Professor of Practical Theology and Christian Ethics, St Mary's College, University of St Andrews, since 1958; Dean of Faculty of Divinity, 1968-72; *b* 28 Jan. 1920; 2nd *s* of late Andrew Whyte, Leith, and late Barbara Janet Pittillo Aitken; *m* 1942, Elisabeth, *er d* of Rev. G. S. Mill, MA, BSc, Kalimpong, India; two *s* one *d. Educ:* Daniel Stewart's Coll., Edinburgh; University of Edinburgh (Arts and Divinity), MA 1st Cl. Hons Phil., 1942. Ordained, 1945; Chaplain to the Forces, 1945-48; Minister of: Dunollie Road, Oban, 1948-54; Mayfield North (subseq. Mayfield and Fountainhall), 1954-58. Guest Lectr, Inst. for the Study of Worship and Religious Architecture, Birmingham, 1965-66; Lectures: Kerr, Univ. of Glasgow, 1969-72; Croall, Univ. of Edinburgh, 1972-73. *Publications:* (ed jtly) Worship Now, 1972; contributor to Towards a Church Architecture, 1962; Preparing for the Ministry of the 1970's, 1965; A Dictionary of Christian Ethics, 1967; Duty and Discernment, 1975; articles in journals, etc. *Address:* 56 South Street, St Andrews, Fife. *Club:* New (Edinburgh).

WHYTE, John Stuart, CBE 1976; MSc(Eng); CEng; FIEE; Senior Director of Development, Post Office Telecommunications Headquarters, since 1977; *b* High Wycombe, 20 July 1923; *s* of late William W. Whyte and of Ethel K. Whyte; *m* 1951, E. Joan M. (*née* Budd); one *s* one *d. Educ:* The John Lyon Sch., Harrow; Northampton Polytechnic, London Univ. BSc(Eng) (Hons), MSc(Eng). Post Office Radio Laboratory, Castleton, Cardiff, 1949-57; PO Research Station, Dollis Hill: Sen. Exec. Engr, 1957-61; Asst Staff Engr, 1961-65. Asst Sec., HM Treasury, 1965-68; Dep. Dir of Engrg, PO, 1968-71; Dir, Operational Programming, PO, 1971-75; Dir of Purchasing and Supply, PO Telecommunications HQ, 1975-76. Manager, Royal Instn, 1971-74 (Vice-Pres., 1972, 1973, 1974), Mem. Cttee of Visitors, 1975-, Chm., Membership Cttee, 1975-. *Publications:* various articles and papers in professional telecommunications jls. *Recreations:* mountaineering, photography, opera, church activity. *Address:* 40 Cassiobury Drive, Watford, Herts WD1 3AB. *T:* Watford 24104. *Clubs:* Alpine; Swiss Alpine (Berne).

WHYTE, (John) Stuart Scott; Under Secretary, Cabinet Office, since 1974; *b* 1 April 1926; *er s* of late Thomas and Mysie Scott Whyte, Sandycove, Co. Dublin; *m* 1950, Jocelyn Margaret, *o d* of late George Hawley, CBE, Edinburgh; two *s* one *d. Educ:* St Andrew's Coll., Dublin; Trinity Coll., Univ. of Dublin. BA 1947; LLB 1948. Asst Principal, Dept of Health for Scotland, 1948; Principal, 1955; Principal Private Sec. to Sec. of State for Scotland, 1959; Asst Sec., Scottish Develt Dept, 1962; Asst Sec., Cabinet Office, 1969; Asst Under-Sec. of State, Scottish Office, 1969-74. *Address:* 26 Langley Hill, Kings Langley, Herts. *T:* Kings Langley 64745; 26 Coppershell, Gastard, Corsham, Wilts. *T:* Corsham 713738.

WHYTE, Lewis Gilmour, CBE 1973; FFA; Chairman: London and Manchester Assurance Co. Ltd, 1961-78; New York & Gartmore Investment Trust Ltd, since 1972; Welfare Insurance Co. Ltd, 1974-78; Director: Associated Commercial Vehicles Ltd, since 1953; Broadstone Investment Trust Ltd, since 1953; *b* 9 Oct. 1906; *s* of Robert Whyte and Florence Smith; *m* 1st, 1935, Ursula Frances Ware (marr. diss. 1971); one *s* three *d*; 2nd, 1971, Diana Mary Campbell. *Educ:* Trinity Coll., Glenalmond. FFA 1929. Investment Manager, later Dir, Equity & Law Life Assurance Company Ltd, 1940-1953; Dir, Save & Prosper Group Ltd, 1950-63; Member: NCB, 1963-66; NFC, 1971-74; Dep. Chm., British Leyland Motor Corporation Ltd, 1968-72; Chm., Transport Holding Company, 1971-73. Receiver-General, Order of St John of Jerusalem, 1955-68. GCStJ 1969. *Publications:* Principles of Finance and Investment, vol. 1, 1949, vol. 2, 1950. *Recreations:* golf, gardening. *Address:* Appletrees, Wyre Piddle, near Pershore, Worcs.

WHYTE, Air Commandant Dame Roberta (Mary), DBE, cr 1955; RRC 1949; *b* 6 June 1897; *d* of Robert Whyte and Mary Whyte (formerly Lumsden). Trained at King's College Hospital, SE5, 1923-28. Princess Mary's Royal Air Force Nursing Service, 1929-56; Matron-in-Chief Princess Mary's Royal Air Force Nursing Service, 1952-56, retired; QHNS 1952. *Club:* United Nursing Services.

WHYTE, Stuart Scott; *see* Whyte, J.S.S.

WHYTE, William Erskine Hamilton; HM Diplomatic Service; Head of News Department, Foreign and Commonwealth Office, since 1976; *b* 28 May 1927; *s* of late William Hamilton Whyte; *m* 1953, Sheila Annie Duck; three *d*. *Educ:* King's Sch., Bruton; The Queen's Coll., Oxford. Served, Royal Navy, 1945-48. Civil Asst, War Office, 1952-55; HM Foreign (later Diplomatic) Service, 1955; Vienna, 1956; Bangkok, 1959; UK Mission to UN, New York, 1963; Foreign Office, 1966; Counsellor, HM Embassy, Kinshasa, Democratic Republic of the Congo, 1970-71; Dir-Gen., British Information Services, and Dep. Consul-General (Information), NY, 1972-76. *Recreations:* gardening, photography. *Address:* c/o Foreign and Commonwealth Office, SW1; The Lodge, Ford, West Sussex.

WIBBERLEY, Prof. Gerald Percy, CBE 1972; Ernest Cook Professor of Countryside Planning in the University of London, University College/Wye College, since 1969; *b* 15 April 1915; *m* 1943, Helen Yeomans; one *d*. *Educ:* King Henry VIII Grammar Sch., Abergavenny; Univs of Wales, Oxford, and Illinois, USA. BSc, MS, PhD. Asst Lectr, Univ. of Manchester, 1940-41; E Sussex Agricultural Cttee: Dist Officer, 1941-43; Asst Exec. Officer, 1943-44; Min. of Agriculture: Asst Rural Land Utilisation Officer, 1944-49; Research Officer, Land Use, 1949-54; Univ. of London, Wye Coll.: Head of Dept of Economics, 1954-69, also Reader in Agricultural Economics, 1958-62; Prof. of Rural Economy, 1963-69. Dir, Council for Small Industries in Rural Areas, 1968-; Mem., Nature Conservancy Council, 1973-; Pres., British Agricl Econs Soc., 1975-76. Hon. Associate Mem. TPI, 1949-67; Hon. Mem., RTPI, 1967-. *Publications:* Agriculture and Urban Growth, 1959; (part author): The Agricultural Significance of the Hills, 1956; Land Use in an Urban Environment, 1960; Outdoor Recreation in the British Countryside, 1963; An Agricultural Land Budget for Britain 1965-2000, 1970; The Nature and Distribution of Second Homes in England and Wales, 1973; (jtly) Planning and the Rural Environment, 1976; contributor to Jls of: Agricl Economics, Land Economics, Town and Country Planning. *Recreations:* music, altering old houses, arguing about rural affairs. *Address:* Vicarage Cottage, 7 Upper Bridge Street, Wye, near Ashford, Kent. *T:* Wye 812377. *Club:* Farmers'.

WICKBERG, Gen. Erik E.; Comdr of the Order of Vasa (Sweden), 1970; General of the Salvation Army, 1969-74; *b* 6 July 1904; *s* of David Wickberg, Commissioner, Salvation Army, and Betty (*née* Lundblad); *m* 1932, Captain Margarete Dietrich (*d* 1976); two *s* two *d*; *m* 1977, Major Eivor Lindberg. *Educ:* Uppsala; Berlin; Stockholm. Salvation Army Internat. Training Coll., 1924-25, and Staff Coll., 1926; commissioned, 1925; appts in Scotland, Berlin, London; Divisional Commander, Uppsala, 1946-48; Chief Secretary, Switzerland, 1948-53; Chief Secretary, Sweden, 1953-57; Territorial Commander, Germany, 1957-61; Chief of the Staff, Internat. HQ, London, 1961-69; elected General of the Salvation Army, July 1969; assumed international leadership, Sept. 1969. Hon. LLD Choong Ang Univ., Seoul, 1970. Order of Moo-Koong-Wha, Korea, 1970; Commander, Order of Vasa, Sweden, 1970; Grosses Verdienstkreuz, Germany, 1971. *Publications:* In Darkest England Now, 1974; articles in Salvation Army periodicals and Year Book. *Recreations:* reading, fishing, chess. *Address:* c/o The Salvation Army, Östermalmsgatan 71, Stockholm 5, Sweden.

WICKENDEN, Keith David; Chairman: European Ferries Ltd, since 1972; Felixstowe Dock & Railway Co., 1976; *b* 22 Nov. 1932; 3rd *s* of Joseph Robert Wickenden and Elsie Alice Wickenden (*née* Miller); *m* 1956, Brenda Paice; four *s*. *Educ:* East Grinstead Grammar Sch. FCA. Partner, Thornton Baker & Co., 1958. Jt Liquidator, Rolls Royce Ltd, 1971. Prospective Parly Cand. (C), Dorking, 1976-. *Recreations:* cricket, flying, being a Director of Brighton and Hove Albion Football Club. *Address:* 11 Waterloo Place, SW1. *T:* 01-930 0952. *Club:* Junior Carlton.

WICKHAM, Rt. Rev. Edward Ralph; *see* Middleton, Suffragan Bishop of.

WICKHAM, Glynne William Gladstone; Professor of Drama, University of Bristol, since 1960; Dean of Faculty of Arts, 1970-72; *b* 15 May 1922; *s* of W. G. and Catherine Wickham; *m* 1954, Marjorie Heseltine (*née* Mudford); two *s* one *d*. *Educ:* Winchester College; New College, Oxford. Entered RAF, 1942; commissioned as Navigator, 1943; discharged as Flt Lt, 1946. BA, 1947; DPhil, 1951 (Oxon); President of OUDS, 1946-47. Asst Lecturer, Drama Dept, Bristol Univ., 1948; Senior Lecturer and Head of Dept, 1955. Worked sporadically as actor, script-writer and critic for BBC, from 1946; attended General

Course in Broadcasting, BBC Staff Trg Sch., 1953. Travelled in America on Rockefeller Award, 1953. Visiting Prof., Drama Dept, State Univ. of Iowa, 1960; Ferens Vis. Prof. of Drama, Hull Univ., 1969; Vis. Prof. of Theatre History, Yale Univ., 1970; Killam Res. Prof., Dalhousie Univ., 1976-77. Lectures: G. F. Reynolds Meml, Univ. of Colorado, 1960; Judith E. Wilson, in Poetry and Drama, Cambridge, 1960-61; Festvortrag, Deutsche Shakespeare Gesellschaft, 1973; British Council, in Europe, annually 1969-. Directed: Amer. première, The Birthday Party, for Actors' Workshop, San Francisco, 1960; world première, Wole Soyinka's Brother Jero's Metamorphosis, 1974. Consultant to Finnish National Theatre and Theatre School on establishment of Drama Department in Univ. of Helsinki, 1963. Governor of Bristol Old Vic Trust, 1963. Consultant to Univ. of E Africa on establishment of a Sch. of Drama in University Coll., Dar-es-Salaam, Tanzania, 1965; Dir, Theatre Seminar, for Summer Univ., Vaasa, Finland, 1965; External Examr to Sch. of Drama in Univ. of Ibadan, Nigeria, 1965-68. Chm., Nat. Drama Conf., Nat. Council of Social Service, 1970-76; Pres., Soc. for Theatre Research, 1976-; Member: English Panel, NCAA, 1968-72; Internat. Adv. Cttee, World Shakespeare Congress, Vancouver, 1971 (Chm. Elizabethan Theatre Panel); Adv. Cttee, British Theatre Museum, 1974-; Edit. Cttee, Shakespeare Survey, 1974-; Chm., Adv. Bd, Theatre Research International, 1975-. *Publications:* Early English Stages 1300-1660, Vol. I (1300-1576), 1959; Vol. II (1576-1660, Pt 1), 1962; Vol II (Pt 2), 1972; Editor: The Relationship between Universities and Radio, Film and Television, 1954; Drama in a World of Science, 1962; Gen. Introd. to the London Shakespeare, 6 vols (ed J. Munro), 1958; Shakespeare's Dramatic Heritage, 1969; The Medieval Theatre, 1974; English Moral Interludes, 1975. *Recreations:* gardening and travel. *Address:* 6 College Road, Clifton, Bristol BS8 3JB. *T:* Bristol 34918. *Club:* Garrick.

WICKHAM, William Rayley; His Honour Judge Wickham; a Circuit Judge, since 1975; *b* 22 Sept. 1926; *s* of late Rayley Esmond Wickham and late Mary Joyce Wickham; *m* 1957, Elizabeth Mary (*née* Thompson); one *s* two *d*. *Educ:* Sedbergh Sch.; Brasenose Coll., Oxford (MA, BCL). Served War of 1939-45, Army, 1944-48. Called to Bar, Inner Temple, 1951. Magistrate, Aden, 1953; Chief Magistrate, Aden, 1958; Crown Counsel, Tanganyika, 1959; Asst to Law Officers, Tanganyika, 1961-63; practised on Northern Circuit, 1963-75; a Recorder of the Crown Court, 1972-75. *Recreations:* fell walking, music, amateur dramatics. *Address:* 115 Vyner Road South, Birkenhead. *T:* 051-652 2095.

WICKLOW, 8th Earl of, *cr* 1793; **William Cecil James Philip John Paul Howard;** Baron of Clonmore; Captain Royal Fusiliers; Director, Sun Insurance Company, Dublin; *b* 30 Oct. 1902; *o s* of 7th Earl of Wicklow and Lady Gladys Mary Hamilton (*d* 1917), *y d* of 2nd Duke of Abercorn; *S* father, 1946; *m* 1959, Eleanor, *d* of Prof. R. M. Butler. *Educ:* Eton; Merton College, Oxford (BA Hons). Roman Catholic. Editor, Dublin Review, 1937-40. *Publications:* Pope Pius XI and World Peace, 1937; More about Dom Marmion, 1949; Fireside Fusilier, 1959; and various translations. *Heir: cousin* Cecil Aymar Forward-Howard, *b* 13 Sept. 1909. *Address:* Sea Grange, Sandycove, Dun Laoghaire, Co. Dublin. *Club:* Royal Irish Yacht (Dun Laoghaire).

WICKREME, A. S. K.; *see* Kohoban-Wickreme.

WICKREMESINGHE, Dr Walter Gerald, CMG 1954; OBE 1949; *b* 13 Feb. 1897; *s* of Peter Edwin Wickremesinghe and Charlotte Catherine Goonetilleka; *m* 1931, Irene Amelia Goontilleka; two *s* two *d*. *Educ:* Royal College, Colombo; Ceylon Medical College; London University (the London Hospital); Harvard University (School of Public Health). Licentiate in Medicine and Surgery (Ceylon), 1921; MRCS, LRCP, 1923; Master of Public Health (Harvard), 1926; Dr of Public Health (Harvard), 1927. Director of Medical and Sanitary Services, Ceylon, 1948-53. Chief Delegate from Ceylon at WHO. Assembly and Executive board, Geneva, 1952; Mem. UN Health Planning Mission to Korea, 1952; WHO Consultant, Manila, 1965; Chairman, Committee of Inquiry into Mental Health Services, Ceylon, 1966. (Hon.) FAPHA 1952. OStJ. *Publications:* contributions to Brit. Med. Jl; Ceylon Med. Jl; Trans. Soc. of Med. Officers of Health, Ceylon; Amer. Jl of Public Health. *Recreations:* golf, tennis, riding, swimming. *Address:* 48 Buller's Lane, Colombo 7, Sri Lanka. *T:* Colombo 81374. *Clubs:* Otter Aquatic, Royal Colombo Golf (Colombo); Nuwara Eliya Golf, Nuwara Eliya Hill; (Life Mem.) Health Dept Sports.

WICKS, Allan; Organist, Canterbury Cathedral, since 1961; *b* 1923; *s* of Edward Kemble Wicks, Priest, and Nancie (*née*

Murgatroyd); *m* 1955, Elizabeth Kay Butcher; two *d. Educ:* Leatherhead; Christ Church, Oxford. Sub-organist, York Minster, 1947; Organist, Manchester Cathedral, 1954. MusDoc Lambeth, 1974. *Address:* The Old Farm House, Lower Hardres, Canterbury, Kent. *T:* Petham 253.

WICKS, David Vaughan, RE 1961 (ARE 1950); Technical Artist, Bank of England Printing Works, since 1954; *b* 20 Dec. 1918; British; *m* 1948, Margaret Gwyneth Downs; one *s* one *d* (and one *s* decd). *Educ:* Wychwood, Bournemouth; Cranleigh School, Surrey. Polytechnic School of Art, 1936, silver medal for figure composition, 1938, 1939. Radio Officer, Merchant Navy, 1940-46. Royal College of Art, Engraving School, 1946-49, Diploma, ARCA Engraving. Taught Processes of Engraving at RCA, 1949-54. *Recreations:* archery and tennis. *Address:* 56 Rous Road, Buckhurst Hill, Essex. *T:* 01-504 8087.

WICKS, Hon. Sir James, Kt 1972; Chief Justice of Kenya, since 1971; *b* 20 June 1909; *s* of late James Wicks and late Mrs Wicks; *m* 1960, Doris Mary, *d* of late G. F. Sutton; no *c. Educ:* Royal Grammar Sch., Guildford; King's Coll., London (LLB); Christ Church, Oxford (MA, BLitt). Chartered Surveyor (PASI) 1931; called to the Bar, Gray's Inn, 1939; practised at Bar, 1939-40 and 1945-46. Served War: RAF (Sqdn Ldr), 1940-45 (despatches thrice). Crown Counsel Palestine, 1946-48; Magistrate, Hong Kong, 1948-53; Actg Additional Judge, Supreme Court, Hong Kong, 1948-49; Dist Judge, Hong Kong, 1953-58; Actg Puisne Judge, Hong Kong, 1953, 1955, 1957; High Court, Kenya: Puisne Judge, 1958-69; Sen. Puisne Judge, 1969-71. *Publication:* The Doctrine of Consideration, 1939. *Recreation:* golf. *Address:* High Court of Kenya, Box 30041, Nairobi, Kenya. *Clubs:* Mombasa, Nairobi (Kenya).

WICKS, Rt. Rev. Ralph Edwin, ED 1964; Assistant Bishop of Brisbane, Australia, since 1973; *b* 16 Aug. 1921; *s* of Charles Thomas Wicks and Florence Maud Wicks (*née* White); *m* 1946, Gladys Hawgood; one *s* one *d. Educ:* East State Sch. and State High Sch., Toowoomba, Qld; St Francis Theological Coll., Brisbane, Qld (LTh). Mem., Qld Public Service (Educn Dept), 1936-41; Theological Student, 1941-44; Asst Curate: Holy Trinity Ch., Fortitude Valley, Brisbane, 1944-47; St James' Ch., Toowoomba, Qld, 1947-48; Rector: Holy Trinity Ch., Goondiwindi, Qld, 1949-54; Holy Trinity Ch., Fortitude Valley, Brisbane, 1954-63; St James' Church, Toowoomba, Qld, 1963-72. Hon. Canon of St John's Cath., Brisbane, 1968; Archdeacon of Darling Downs, Qld, 1973. Chaplain to the Australian Army, 1949-70. *Recreations:* reading, gardening, music. *Address:* Church House, Ann Street, Brisbane, Queensland 4001, Australia. *T:* Brisbane 294766; (home) 211 Taringa Parade, Taringa, Qld 4068. *T:* Brisbane 785604.

WIDDAS, Prof. Wilfred Faraday, MB, BS; BSc; PhD; DSc; Professor of Physiology in the University of London, Bedford College, since 1960; *b* 2 May 1916; *s* of late Percy Widdas, BSc, mining engineer, and Annie Maude (*née* Snowdon); *m* 1940, Gladys Green; one *s* two *d. Educ:* Durham School; University of Durham College of Medicine and Royal Victoria Infirmary, Newcastle upon Tyne. MB, BS 1938; BSc 1947; PhD 1953; DSc 1958. Assistant in General Practice, 1938-39. Served in RAMC, 1939-47; Deputy Assistant Director-General Army Medical Services, War Office (Major), 1942-47. Research Fellow, St Mary's Hospital Medical School, 1947-49; Lecturer and Sen. Lecturer in Physiology, St Mary's Hospital Medical School, 1949-55; Senior Lecturer in Physiology, King's College, 1955-56; University Reader in Physiology at King's College, 1956-60. FRSocMed. Member: Royal Institution of Gt Britain; Physiological Society; Society of Experimental Biology. *Publications:* Membrane Transport of Sugars, chapter in Carbohydrate Metabolism and its Disorders; Permeability, chapter in Recent Advances in Physiology; also papers on similar topics in (chiefly) Jl of Physiology. *Recreations:* tennis, golf. *Address:* 67 Marksbury Avenue, Kew Gardens, Richmond, Surrey. *T:* 01-876 6374. *Club:* Queen's.

WIDDECOMBE, James Murray, CB 1968; OBE 1959; General Secretary, Civil Service Retirement Fellowship; *b* 7 Jan. 1910; *s* of late Charles Frederick Widdecombe and late Alice Widdecombe; *m* 1936, Rita Noreen Plummer; one *s* one *d. Educ:* Devonport High Sch. Asst Naval Armament Supply Officer, Portsmouth, Holton Heath and Chatham, 1929-35; Dep. Naval Armt Supply Officer, Chatham, 1936; OC, RN Armt Depot, Gibraltar, 1936-40; Naval Armt Supply Officer: Admty, 1940-43; Levant, 1943-44. Capt. (SP) RNVR. Sen. Armt Supply Officer: Staff of C-in-C, Med., 1944-46; Admty, 1946-50; Asst Dir of Armt Supply, Admty, 1950-51, and 1956-59; Suptg Naval Armt Supply Officer, Portsmouth, 1951-53; Prin. Naval Armt Supply Officer, Staff of C-in-C, Far East, 1953-56; Dep. Dir of Armt Supply, Admiralty, 1959-61; Dir of Victualling, Admty,

1961-66; Head of RN Supply and Transport Service, MoD, 1966-68; Dir-Gen. of Supplies and Transport (Naval), MoD, 1968-70; special duties, Management Services, MoD, 1970-73. FInstPS; MBIM. *Recreations:* golf, gardening, amateur dramatics. *Address:* 1 Manor Close, Haslemere, Surrey GU27 1PP. *T:* Haslemere 2899. *Clubs:* Hindhead Golf, Navy Department Golfing Society.

WIDDESS, Rev. Canon Arthur Geoffrey; Canon Treasurer of York Minster, since 1976; *b* 1920; *s* of David Charles and Florence Widdess; *m* 1948, Doris May Henderson; one *s* one *d. Educ:* Bradford Grammar Sch.; Christ's Coll., Cambridge (MA); Ridley Hall, Cambridge; School of Oriental and African Studies, London Univ. Curate of St Helens, Lancs, 1945-47; Lectr, Central Theol Sch., Shanghai, 1949-50; Asst Master, St Stephen's Coll., Stanley, Hong Kong, 1950-51; Prof. of OT Studies, United Theol Coll., Bangalore, S India, 1951-52; Tutor, St John's Coll., Durham, 1952-55, Vice-Principal, 1955-56; Lectr in Theology, Univ. of Durham, 1952-56; Vicar of St Nicholas, Leicester, and Chaplain to Anglican Students, Univ. of Leicester, 1956-63; Hon. Canon of Leicester, 1961-63; Principal of St Aidan's Coll., Birkenhead, 1963-70; Vicar of Huntington, York, 1970-76. *Publications :* (contrib.) Worship in a Changing Church, ed R. S. Wilkinson, 1965; contribs to various theol jls. *Recreations:* gardening, motoring. *Address:* 10 Precentor's Court, York YO1 2EJ. *T:* York 20877.

WIDDICOMBE, David Graham, QC 1965; *b* 7 Jan. 1924; *s* of Aubrey Guy Widdicombe and Margaret (*née* Puddy); *m* 1961, Anastasia Cecilia (*née* Leech); two *s* one *d. Educ:* St Albans Sch.; Queen's Coll., Cambridge. Called to the Bar, Inner Temple, 1950, Bencher, 1973. Mem., Cttee on Local Govt Rules of Conduct, 1973-74; Chm., Oxfordshire Structural Plan Examination in Public, 1977. *Publication:* (ed) Ryde on Rating, 1968-. *Address:* 2 Mitre Court Buildings, Temple, EC4. *T:* 01-353 4488; 8 Park Village East, NW1. *T:* 01-387 4288. *Clubs:* Athenæum, Garrick.

WIDDOWS, Air Commodore (Stanley) Charles, CB 1959; DFC 1941; RAF Retired; People's Deputy, States of Guernsey, since 1973; *b* 4 Oct. 1909; *s* of P. L. Widdows, Southend, Bradfield, Berkshire; *m* 1939, Irene Ethel, *d* of S. H. Rawlings, Ugley, Essex; two *s. Educ:* St Bartolomew's School, Newbury; No 1 School of Technical Training, RAF, Halton; Royal Air Force College, Cranwell. Commissioned, 1931; Fighting Area, RAF, 1931-32; RAF Middle East, Sudan and Palestine, 1933-37; Aeroplane and Armament Experimental Estab., 1937-40; OC 29 (Night Fighter) Sqdn, 1940-41; OC RAF West Malling, 1941-42; Gp Capt., Night Ops, HQ 11 and 12 Gp, 1942; SASO, No 85 (Base Defence) Gp, 1943; Gp Capt. Organisation, Supreme HQ, Allied Expeditionary Air Force, 1944; OC, RAF Wahn, Germany, 1944-46; RAF Instructor, Sen. Officers War Course, RNC, Greenwich, 1946-48; Fighter Command, 1948-54: SASO HQ No 12 Gp; Chief Instructor, Air Defence Wing, School of Land/Air Warfare; Sector Commander, Eastern Sector. Imperial Defence College, 1955; Director of Operations (Air Defence), Air Ministry, 1956-58. *Address:* Les Granges de Beauvoir, Rohais, St Peter Port, Guernsey, CI. *T:* Guernsey 20219.

WIDDOWSON, Dr Elsie May, FRS 1976; Medical Research Council Grant-Holder in Department of Medicine, Addenbrooke's Hospital, Cambridge, since 1972; *b* 21 Oct. 1906; *d* of Thomas Henry Widdowson and Rose Widdowson. *Educ:* Imperial Coll., London (BSc, PhD); DSc London 1948. Courtauld Inst. of Biochemistry, Mddx Hosp., 1931-33; KCH, London, 1933-38; Cambridge University: Dept of Exper. Medicine, 1938-66; Infant Nutrition Res. Div., 1966-72. President: Nutrition Soc., 1977-; Neonatal Soc., 1978-. Hon. DSc Manchester, 1974. *Publications:* (with R. A. McCance) The Composition of Foods, 1940 (2nd edn 1967); (with R. A. McCance) Breads White and Brown: Their Place in Thought and Social History, 1956; contrib. Proc. Royal Soc., Jl Physiol., Biochem. Jl, Brit. Jl Nut., Arch. Dis. Child., Lancet, BMJ, Nature, Biol. Neonate, Nut. Metabol., and Ped. Res. *Address:* Orchard House, Barrington, Cambridge. *T:* Cambridge 870219.

WIDDUP, Malcolm; Under-Secretary, HM Treasury, since 1971; *b* 9 May 1920; *s* of John and Frances Ellen Widdup; *m* 1947, Margaret Ruth Anderson; one *s* one *d. Educ:* Giggleswick Sch.; Trinity Coll., Oxford (MA). Served War, Army, RA and Staff, 1940-45. Ministry of Food, 1946-53; HM Treasury, 1953-55; Cabinet Office, 1955-57; HM Treasury, 1957-60; Min. of Health, 1960-62; HM Treasury, 1962-66; UK Delegn to OECD, 1966-68; HM Treasury, 1968-. *Recreations:* sailing, gardening, music. *Address:* c/o HM Treasury, Parliament Street, SW1.

WIDGERY, family name of **Baron Widgery.**

WIDGERY, Baron *cr* 1971 (Life Peer), of South Molton; **John Passmore Widgery,** PC 1968; Kt 1961; OBE 1945; TD; Lord Chief Justice of England, since 1971; *b* 24 July 1911; *s* of Samuel Widgery, South Molton, Devon; *m* 1948, Ann, *d* of William Edwin Kermode, Peel, Isle of Man. *Educ:* Queen's Coll., Taunton. Solicitor (John Mackrell Prizeman), 1933. Served War of 1939-45, Roy. Artillery, North-West Europe, Lieut-Col, 1942; Brigadier (TA) 1952. Called to Bar, Lincoln's Inn, 1946, Bencher, 1961, Treasurer, 1977; practising South-Eastern circuit; QC 1958; Recorder of Hastings, 1959-61; Judge of the High Court of Justice (Queen's Bench Division), 1961-68; a Lord Justice of Appeal, 1968-71. Chairman, Deptl Cttee on Legal Aid in Criminal Cases, 1964-65. First Pres. Senate of the Inns of Court, 1966-70. Vice-Chm. Home Office Adv. Council on the Penal System, 1966-70. DL Co. London, 1951; Freeman: S Molton, Devon, 1971; Exeter, 1975. Hon. LLD: Exeter, 1971; Leeds, 1976; Columbia, USA, 1976. *Address:* Royal Courts of Justice, WC2. *Clubs:* Boodle's, Garrick.

WIEN, Hon. Sir Phillip, Kt 1970; **Hon. Mr Justice Wien;** a Judge of the High Court, Queen's Bench Division, since 1970; Presiding Judge, Wales and Chester Circuit, since 1976; *b* 7 August 1913; *y s* of Samuel Wien, Cyncoed, Cardiff; *m* 1947, Anita Hermer; two *d. Educ:* Canton High School, Cardiff; University College of S Wales and Monmouthshire; University College, London. Solicitor, 1938-46; LLM Exhibitioner in Law. Served War of 1939-45, North Western Europe with 79 Armd Division; Major, 22nd Dragoons, 1940-46 (despatches). Barrister, Inner Temple, 1946; QC 1961; Master of Bench, 1969; Mem. Bar Council, 1969-70; Leader of Wales and Chester Circuit, 1969-70; Recorder of Birkenhead, 1965-69; Recorder of Swansea, 1969-70. Chairman of Medical Appeals Tribunal, 1961-70. *Address:* Royal Courts of Justice, WC2A 2LL; 13 King's Bench Walk, Temple, EC4Y 7EN. *T:* 01-353 5115. *Club:* Army and Navy.

WIESNER, Dr Jerome Bert; President of the Massachusetts Institute of Technology, since 1971 (Provost, 1966-71); *b* 30 May 1915; *s* of Joseph and Ida Friedman Wiesner; *m* 1940, Laya Wainger; three *s* one *d. Educ:* University of Michigan, Ann Arbor, Michigan. PhD in electrical engineering, 1950. Staff, University of Michigan, 1937-40; Chief Engineer, Library of Congress, 1940-42; Staff, MIT Radiation Lab., 1942-45; Staff, Univ. of Calif Los Alamos Lab., 1945-46; Asst Prof. of Electrical Engrg, MIT, 1946; Associate Prof. of Electrical Engrg, 1947; Prof. of Electrical Engrg, 1950-64; Dir, Res. Lab. of Electronics, 1952-61. Special Assistant to the President of the USA, for Science and Technology, The White House, 1961-64; Director, Office of Science and Technology, Exec. Office of the President, 1962-64; Chm., Tech. Assessment Adv. Council, Office of Tech. Assessment, US Congress, 1976-. Dean of Science, MIT, 1964-66. *Publications:* Where Science and Politics Meet, 1965; contrib.: Modern Physics for the Engineer, 1954; Arms Control, Disarmament and National Security, 1960; Arms Control, issues for the Public, 1961; Lectures on Modern Communications, 1961; technical papers in: Science, Physical Rev., Jl Applied Physics, Scientific American, Proc. Inst. Radio Engineers, etc. *Recreations:* photography, boating. *Address:* Massachusetts Institute of Technology, Cambridge, Mass 02139, USA. *T:* 253-4665. *Clubs:* Cosmos (Washington, DC); Commercial, St Botolph's (Boston); Century, Harvard Club of New York City (NY).

WIESNER, Prof. Karel František, OC 1975; FRS 1969; Research Professor, University of New Brunswick, since 1964; *b* 25 Nov. 1919; *s* of Karel Wiesner, industrialist, Chrudim, Czechoslovakia, and Eugenie Storová, Prague; *m* 1942, Blanka Pevná; one *s* (and one *d* decd). *Educ:* Gymnasium Chrudim; Charles Univ., Prague. Asst, Dept of Physical Chem., Charles Univ., Prague, 1945-46; Post-doctoral Fellow, ETH Zürich, 1946-48; Prof. of Organic Chem., Univ. of New Brunswick, 1948-62; Associate Dir of Research, Ayerst Laboratories, Montreal, 1962-64. Hon. DSc: New Brunswick, 1970; Western Ontario, 1972; Montreal, 1975. *Publications:* about 162 research papers in various scientific periodicals. *Recreations:* tennis, skiing, hunting. *Address:* 814 Burden Street, Fredericton, New Brunswick, Canada. *T:* 4544007.

WIGAN, Sir Frederick Adair, 4th Bt, *cr* 1898; *b* 13 April 1911; *e s* of Sir Roderick Grey Wigan, 3rd Bt, and Ina (*d* 1977), *o c* of late Lewis D. Wigan, Glenalmond, Perthshire; *S* father 1954. *Educ:* privately; Heir: *b* Alan Lewis Wigan [*b* 19 Nov. 1913; *m* 1950, Robina, *d* of Lt-Col Sir Iain Colquhoun, 7th Bt, KT, DSO; one *s* one *d. Educ:* Eton; Magdalen Coll., Oxford. Captain, King's Royal Rifle Corps (Reserve of Officers); served War of 1939-45 (prisoner)]. *Address:* Borrobol, Kinbrace, Sutherland.

WIGDOR, Lucien Simon, CEng, MRAeS; Deputy Chairman and Chief Executive, Leslie & Godwin (Holdings) Ltd, since 1977; Managing Director, L. S. Wigdor Ltd, since 1976; *b* Oct. 1919; *s* of William and Adèle Wigdor; *m* 1951, Marion Louise, *d* of Henry Risner; one *s* one *d. Educ:* Highgate Sch.; College of Aeronautical Engineering. Served War, RAF, 1940-46; Operational Research, BEA: Research Engr, 1947-51; Manager, Industrial and Corporate Develt, Vertol Corp., USA, 1951-55; Managing Dir, Tunnel Refineries Ltd, 1955-69, Vice-Chm., 1969-72; Corporate Consultant, The Boeing Company, 1960-72; Dep. Dir-Gen., CBI, 1972-76. Dir, Rothschild Investment Trust Ltd, 1977-. *Publications:* papers to: Royal Aeronautical Soc., American Helicopter Soc. *Recreations:* ski-ing, model engineering. *Address:* Wallingford, Leas Green, Chislehurst, Kent. *T:* 01-300 1519; 3 Westminster Gardens, Marsham Street, SW1. *T:* 01-834 2021. *Clubs:* Junior Carlton, Royal Air Force.

WIGG, family name of **Baron Wigg.**

WIGG, Baron *cr* 1967 (Life Peer), of the Borough of Dudley; **George Edward Cecil Wigg,** PC 1964; President, Betting Office Licensees' Association, since 1973; *b* 28 Nov. 1900; *m* ; three *d. Educ:* Fairfields Council Schs and Queen Mary's Sch., Basingstoke, Hants. Served in Regular Army, 1919-37, 1940-46. MP (Lab) Dudley, 1945-67; PPS to Rt Hon. E. Shinwell when Minister of Fuel and Power, Sec. of State for War and Minister of Defence; an Opposition Whip, 1951-54; Paymaster-General, 1964-67. Member: Racecourse Betting Control Bd, 1957-61; Totalisator Bd, 1961-64; Chm., Horserace Betting Levy Bd, 1967-72. *Publication:* George Wigg, 1972. *Address:* 117 Newcastle Road, Trent Vale, Stoke-on-Trent.

WIGGIN, Alfred William, (Jerry Wiggin); TD 1970; MP (C) Weston-super-Mare since 1969; *b* 24 Feb. 1937; *e s* of late Col Sir William H. Wiggin, KCB, DSO, TD, DL, JP, and late Lady Wiggin, Worcestershire; *m* 1964, Rosemary Janet, *d* of David L. D. Orr; two *s* one *d. Educ:* Eton; Trinity Coll., Cambridge. 2nd Lieut, Queen's Own Warwickshire and Worcestershire Yeomanry (TA), 1959; Major, Royal Yeomanry, 1975. Contested (C), Montgomeryshire, Gen. Elections, 1964 and 1966. PPS to Lord Balniel, at MoD, later FCO, 1970-74, and to Ian Gilmour, MoD, 1971-72. Promoted Hallmarking Act, 1973. Jt Hon. Sec., Conservative Defence Cttee, 1974-75; Vice-Chm., Conservative Agricultural Cttee, 1975-. General Rapporteur, Economic Cttee, North Atlantic Assembly, 1976-. *Address:* House of Commons, SW1. *T:* 01-219 4522; The Court, Axbridge, Somerset. *T:* Axbridge 732527. *Clubs:* Cavalry and Guards, Farmers'.

WIGGIN, Jerry; see Wiggin, A. W.

WIGGIN, Sir John (Henry), 4th Bt *cr* 1892; MC 1946; Major, Grenadier Guards, retired; *b* 3 March 1921; *s* of Sir Charles Richard Henry Wiggin, 3rd Bt, TD, and Mabel Violet Mary (*d* 1961), *d* of Sir William Jaffray, 2nd Bt; *S* father, 1972; *m* 1st, 1947, Lady Cecilia Evelyn Anson (marr. diss. 1961; she *d* 1963), *yr d* of 4th Earl of Lichfield; two *s*; 2nd, 1963, Sarah, *d* of Brigadier Stewart Forster; two *s. Educ:* Eton; Trinity College, Cambridge. Served War of 1939-45 (prisoner-of-war). High Sheriff Warwicks, 1976. *Heir: s* Charles Rupert John Wiggin, Captain, Grenadier Guards [*b* 2 July 1949. *Educ:* Eton]. *Address:* Honington Hall, Shipston-on-Stour, Warwicks. *T:* Shipston-on-Stour 61434. *Club:* Cavalry and Guards.

WIGGINS, Rt. Rev. Maxwell Lester; Assistant Bishop of Wellington, NZ, since 1976; *b* 5 Feb. 1915; *s* of Herbert Lester and Isobel Jane Wiggins; *m* 1941, Margaret Agnes (*née* Evans); one *s* two *d. Educ:* Christchurch Boys' High Sch., NZ; Canterbury University College, NZ (BA). Asst Curate, St Mary's, Merivale, NZ, 1938; Vicar of Oxford, NZ, 1941; CMS Missionary, Diocese Central Tanganyika, 1945; Head Master, Alliance Secondary Sch., Dodoma, 1948; Provost, Cathedral of Holy Spirit, Dodoma, 1949; Principal, St Philip's Theological Coll., and Canon of Cathedral of Holy Spirit, Dodoma, 1954; Archdeacon of Lake Province, 1956; Asst Bishop of Central Tanganyika, 1959; Bishop of Victoria Nyanza, 1963-76. *Address:* 18A Hill Street, Wellington, New Zealand.

WIGGLESWORTH, Gordon Hardy; Housing Architect, Greater London Council, since 1974; *b* 27 June 1920; *m* 1952, Cherry Diana Heath; three *d. Educ:* Highgate; University Coll., London; Architectural Association. ARIBA; AADipl. Served War of 1939-45: Royal Engineers, 1941-46. Architectural Assoc., 1946-48; private practice and Univ. of Hong Kong, 1948-52; private practice: London, 1952-54; Hong Kong, 1954-56; London, 1956-57. Asst Chief Architect, Dept of Education and Science, 1957-67; Dir of Building Develt, MPBW, later DoE, 1967-72; Principal Architect, Educn, GLC (ILEA), 1972-

74. *Address:* 53 Canonbury Park South, N1 2JL. *T:* 01-226 7734. *Club:* Reform.

WIGGLESWORTH, Sir Vincent (Brian), Kt 1964; CBE 1951; FRS 1939; MA, MD, BCh Cantab, FRES; Retired Director, Agricultural Research Council Unit of Insect Physiology (1943-67); Quick Professor of Biology, University of Cambridge, 1952-66; Fellow of Gonville and Caius College; *b* 17 April 1899; *s* of late Sidney Wigglesworth, MRCS; *m* 1928, Mabel Katherine, *d* of late Col Sir David Semple, IMS; three *s* one *d*. *Educ:* Repton; Caius Coll., Cambridge (Scholar); St Thomas' Hosp. 2nd Lt RFA, 1917-18, served in France; Frank Smart Student of Caius College, 1922-24; Lecturer in Medical Entomology in London School of Hygiene and Tropical Medicine, 1926; Reader in Entomology in University of London, 1936-44; Reader in Entomology, in University of Cambridge, 1945-52. Fellow, Imperial College, London, 1977. Hon. Member: Royal Entomological Soc.; Physiological Soc.; Soc. Experimental Biology; Assoc. Applied Biology; International Confs of Entomology; Soc. of European Endocrinologists; Royal Danish Academy of Science; US Nat. Academy of Sciences; American Academy of Arts and Sciences; Kaiserliche Deutsche Akademie der Naturforscher, Leopoldina; Deutsche Entomologische Gesellschaft; American Entomol. Soc.; USSR Acad. of Sciences; All-Union Entomol. Soc.; Entomol. Soc. of India; Société Zoologique de France; Société Entomologique de France, Société Entomologique d'Egypte; Entomological Society of the Netherlands; Schweizerische Entomologische Gesellschaft; Indian Academy of Zoology; Corresponding Member: Accademia delle Scienze dell' Istituto di Bologna; Société de Pathologie Exotique; Entomological Soc. of Finland; Dunham Lecturer, Harvard, 1945; Woodward Lecturer, Yale, 1945; Croonian Lecturer, Royal Society, 1948; Messenger Lecturer, Cornell, 1958; Tercentenary Lecturer, Royal Society, 1960. Royal Medal, Royal Society, 1955; Swammerdam Medal, Soc. Med. Chir., Amsterdam, 1966; Gregor Mendel Gold Medal, Czechoslovak Acad. of Science, 1967. DPhil (*hc*) University, Berne; DSc (*hc*): Paris, Newcastle and Cambridge. *Publications:* Insect Physiology, 1934; The Principles of Insect Physiology, 1939; The Physiology of Insect Metamorphosis, 1954; The Life of Insects, 1964; Insect Hormones, 1970; Insects and the Life of Man, 1976; numerous papers on comparative physiology. *Address:* 14 Shilling Street, Lavenham, Suffolk. *T:* Lavenham 293.

WIGHAM, Eric Leonard, CBE 1967; Labour Correspondent, The Times, 1946-69; *b* 8 Oct. 1904; *s* of Leonard and Caroline Nicholson Wigham; *m* 1929, Jane Dawson; one *d*. *Educ:* Ackworth and Bootham Schools; Birmingham University (MA). Reporter on Newcastle upon Tyne papers, 1925-32; Manchester Evening News, 1932-45; War Correspondent, The Observer and Manchester Evening News, 1944-45; Labour Correspondent, Manchester Guardian, 1945-46. Member, Royal Commission on Trade Unions and Employers' Associations, 1965-68. Order of King Leopold II (Belgium), 1945. *Publications:* Trade Unions, 1956; What's Wrong with the Unions?, 1961; The Power to Manage: a history of the Engineering Employers' Federation, 1973; Strikes and the Government 1893-1974, 1976. *Recreation:* gardening. *Address:* Link View, The Avenue, West Wickham, Kent. *T:* 01-776 0397. *Club:* National Liberal.

WIGHT, James Alfred, MRCVS; practising veterinary surgeon, since 1939; author, since 1970; *b* 3 Oct. 1916; *s* of James Henry and Hannah Wight; *m* 1941, Joan Catherine Danbury; one *s* one *d*. *Educ:* Hillhead High Sch.; Glasgow Veterinary Coll. Started in general veterinary practice in Thirsk, Yorks, 1940, and has been there ever since with the exception of war-time service with the RAF. Began to write at the ripe age of 50 and quite unexpectedly became a best-selling author of books on his veterinary experiences which have been translated into all European languages and many others, incl. Japanese. Hon. Mem., British Vet. Assoc., 1975. *Publications:* (as James Herriot): If Only They Could Talk, 1970; It Shouldn't Happen to a Vet, 1972; All Creatures Great and Small, (USA) 1972; Let Sleeping Vets Lie, 1973; All Things Bright and Beautiful, (USA) 1973; Vet in Harness, 1974; Vets Might Fly, 1976. *Recreations:* music, dog-walking. *Address:* Mire Beck, Thirlby, Thirsk, Yorks YO7 2DJ.

WIGHTWICK, Charles Christopher Brooke, MA; Headmaster, King's College School, Wimbledon, since Sept. 1975; *b* 16 Aug. 1931; *s* of Charles Frederick Wightwick and Marion Frances Wightwick (*née* Smith); *m* 1955, Pamela Layzell; one *s* two *d*. *Educ:* St Michael's, Otford Court; Lancing Coll.; St Edmund Hall, Oxford. BA 1954, MA 1958. Asst Master, Hurstpierpoint Coll., 1954-59; Head of German, Denstone Coll., 1959-65; Head of Languages, then Director of Studies, Westminster Sch., 1965-

75. *Publication:* (co-author) Longman Audio-Lingual German, 1974. *Recreations:* photography, judo, language. *Address:* King's College School, Southside, Wimbledon Common, SW19 4TT. *T:* 01-946 3542.

WIGLEY, Dafydd; MP (Plaid Cymru) Caernarvon since Feb. 1974; industrial economist; *b* April 1943; *s* of Elfyn Edward Wigley, former County Treasurer, Caernarfonshire CC; *m* Elinor Bennett (*née* Owen), *d* of Emrys Bennett Owen, Dolgellau; two *s* one *d*. *Educ:* Caernarvon Grammar Sch.; Rydal Sch., Colwyn Bay; Manchester Univ. Ford Motor Co., 1964-67; Chief Cost Accountant and Financial Planning Manager, Mars Ltd, 1967-71; Financial Controller, Hoover Ltd, Merthyr Tydfil, 1971-74. Vice-Chairman, Plaid Cymru and party spokesman on industry and economic affairs. Member Merthyr Tydfil Borough Council. *Publication:* An Economic Plan for Wales, 1977. *Address:* House of Commons, SW1A 0AA.

WIGLEY, Sir Henry (Rodolph), KBE 1976 (CBE 1968; OBE (mil.) 1944); Managing Director and Chairman of Board, Mount Cook & Southern Lakes Tourist Co. Ltd, since 1946; *b* 2 Feb. 1913; *s* of Rodolph L. Wigley and Jessie Christie Grant; *m* 1939, Isabella Jessie Allport; one *s* four *d*. *Educ:* Christ's Coll., Christchurch, NZ. FCIT; FRAeS. RNZAF, 1940-45 (mentioned in despatches). Joined Mount Cook & Southern Lakes Tourist Co. Ltd, 1930. *Publication:* Ski-Plane Adventure, 1965 (2nd edn 1965). *Recreations:* skiing, tennis, golf, photography, gardening. *Address:* 46 Balmoral Lane, Redcliffs, Christchurch 8, New Zealand. *T:* 849-659. *Club:* Christchurch.

WIGNER, Prof. Eugene P(aul); Thomas D. Jones Professor of Mathematical Physics of Princeton University, 1938-71, retired; *b* 17 Nov. 1902; *s* of Anthony and Elizabeth Wigner; *m* 1st, 1936, Amelia Z. Frank (*d* 1937); 2nd, 1941, Mary Annette Wheeler; one *s* one *d*. *Educ:* Technische Hochschule, Berlin, Dr Ing. 1925. Mem. Gen. Adv. Cttee to US Atomic Energy Commn, 1952-57, 1959-64; Director: Nat. Acad. of Sciences Harbor Project for Civil Defense, 1963; Civil Defense Project, Oak Ridge Nat. Lab., 1964-65. Pres., Amer. Physical Soc., 1956 (Vice-Pres., 1955); Mem. Royal Netherlands Acad. of Science and Letters, 1960; Foreign Mem., Royal Soc., 1970; Corresp. Mem. Acad. of Science, Göttingen, 1951; Austrian Acad. Sciences, 1968; Nat. Acad. Sci. (US); Amer. Philos. Soc.; Amer. Acad. Sci. Citation, NJ Sci. Teachers' Assoc., 1951. US Government Medal for Merit, 1946; Franklin Medal, 1950; Fermi Award, 1958; Atoms for Peace Award, 1960; Max Planck Medal of German Phys. Soc., 1961; Nobel Prize for Physics, 1963; Semmelweiss Medal, Amer. Hungarian Med. Assoc., 1965; US Nat. Medal for Science, 1969; Albert Einstein Award, 1972. Holds numerous hon. doctorates. *Publications:* Nuclear Structure (with L. Eisenbud), 1958; The Physical Theory of Neutron Chain Reactors (with A. M. Weinberg), 1958; Group Theory (orig. in German, 1931), English trans., NY, 1959; Symmetries and Reflections, 1967. *Address:* 8 Ober Road, Princeton, NJ 08540, USA. *T:* 609-924-1189. *Club:* Cosmos (Washington, DC).

WIGODER, family name of **Baron Wigoder.**

WIGODER, Baron *cr* 1974 (Life Peer), of Cheetham in the City of Manchester; **Basil Thomas Wigoder,** QC 1966; a Recorder of the Crown Court, since 1972; Chief Liberal Whip, House of Lords, since 1977 (Deputy Whip, 1976-77); Chairman, Health Services Board, since 1977; *b* 12 Feb. 1921; *s* of late Dr P. I. Wigoder and of Mrs R. R. Wigoder, JP, Manchester; *m* 1948, Yoland Levinson; three *s* one *d*. *Educ:* Manchester Gram. Sch.; Oriel Coll., Oxford. Served RA, 1942-45. Pres. Oxford Union, 1946. Called to Bar, Gray's Inn, 1946, Master of the Bench, 1972; Mem., Gen. Council of the Bar, 1970-; Mem., Crown Court Rules Cttee, 1971-. BoT Inspector, Pinnock Finance (GB) Ltd, 1967. Chm., Liberal Party Exec., 1963-65; Chm., Liberal Party Organising Cttee, 1965-66. Contested (L): Bournemouth, 1945; Westbury, 1959 and 1964. *Recreation:* cricket. *Address:* 3 Temple Gardens, EC4. *T:* 01-353 1662. *Clubs:* National Liberal, MCC.

WIGRAM, family name of **Baron Wigram.**

WIGRAM, 2nd Baron, *cr* 1935, of Clewer; **George Neville Clive Wigram,** MC 1945; JP; DL; *b* 2 Aug. 1915; *s* of Clive, 1st Baron Wigram, PC, GCB, GCVO, CSI, and Nora Mary (*d* 1956), *d* of Sir Neville Chamberlain, KCB, KCVO; *S* father 1960; *m* 1941, Margaret Helen, *yr d* of late General Sir Andrew Thorne, KCB, CMG, DSO; one *s* two *d*. *Educ:* Winchester and Magdalen College, Oxford. Page of Honour to HM King George V, 1925-32; served in Grenadier Guards, 1937-57; Military Secretary and Comptroller to Governor-General of New Zealand, 1946-49;

commanded 1st Bn Grenadier Guards, 1955-56. Governor of Westminster Hospital, 1967. JP Gloucestershire, 1959, DL 1969. *Heir: s* Captain Hon. Andrew (Francis Clive) Wigram, Grenadier Guards [*b* 18 March 1949; *m* 1974, Gabrielle Diana, *y d* of late R. D. Moore; one *s*]. *Address:* Poulton Fields, Cirencester, Gloucestershire. *T:* Poulton 250. *Club:* Cavalry and Guards.

WIGRAM, Rev. Canon Sir Clifford Woolmore, 7th Bt, *cr* 1805; Vicar of Marston St Lawrence with Warkworth in Banbury, since 1945, also of Thenford, since 1975; Non-Residentiary Canon of Peterborough Cathedral, since 1973; *b* 24 Jan. 1911; *er s* of late Robert Ainger Wigram and Evelyn Dorothy, *d* of C. W. E. Henslowe; *S* uncle, 1935; *m* 1948, Christobel Joan Marriott, *d* of late William Winter Goode. *Educ:* Winchester; Trinity Coll., Cambridge. Asst Priest at St Ann's, Brondesbury, 1934-37; Chaplain Ely Theological College, 1937. *Heir: b* Maj. Edward Robert Woolmore Wigram, Indian Army [*b* 19 July 1913; *m* 1944, Viva Ann, *d* of late Douglas Bailey, Laughton Lodge, near Lewes, Sussex; one *d*. *Educ:* Winchester; Trinity Coll., Cambridge. Attached 2nd Batt. South Staffordshire Regt, Bangalore, 1935; Major, 19th KGO Lancers, Lahore, 1938]. *Address:* The Vicarage, Marston St Lawrence, Banbury, Oxon OX17 2DA.

WIGRAM, Derek Roland, MA, BSc (Econ.); Headmaster of Monkton Combe School, near Bath, 1946-68; *b* 18 Mar. 1908; *er s* of late Roland Lewis Wigram and of Mildred (*née* Willock); *m* 1944, Catharine Mary, *d* of late Very Rev. W. R. Inge, KCVO, DD, former Dean of St Paul's; one *s* one *d*. *Educ:* Marlborough Coll.; Peterhouse, Cambridge (Scholar). 1st Class Hons Classical Tripos, 1929; 2nd Class Hons Economics and Political Science, London, 1943; Assistant Master and Careers Master, Whitgift School, Croydon, 1929-36; House Master and Careers Master, Bryanston School, 1936-46. Hon. Associate Mem., Headmasters' Conf. (Chm., 1963-64); Vice-Pres., CMS (Chm., Exec. Cttee, 1956-58, 1969-72); Patron, Oxford Conf. in Education; Member: Council and Exec. of Coll. of Preachers; Council of Lee Abbey; Exec. Cttee of Christian Orgns Research and Adv. Trust. Bishops' Inspector of Theological Colls (Mem. Archbishops' Commn, 1970-71); Dir and part-time consultant, Sch. and Charity Consultants. Governor: Walhampton Sch. (Chm.); Centre for International Briefing. *Publication:* (Jt Editor) Hymns for Church and School, 1964. *Address:* Housels Field, Westwood, Bradford on Avon, Wilts. *T:* Bradford on Avon 2362.

WIKELEY, Thomas, CMG 1955; OBE 1944; *b* 9 Oct. 1902; *s* of late Col J. M. Wikeley (Indian Army, retired) and late Christine Wikeley (*née* Duns); unmarried. *Educ:* Loretto; Pembroke Coll., Cambridge. MA Mod. Langs. Levant Consular Service, 1926. Served at Alexandria, Cairo, Jedda, Rabat, Genoa, Harar, Addis Ababa, Port Said. Transferred to Foreign Office, 1944; Consul-General, Athens, Dec. 1946; Consul-General, Leopoldville, 1948-51; Consul-General, Tetuan (Spanish Morocco), 1952-54; Consul-General, Jerusalem, 1954-57; HM Minister and Consul-Gen., Guatemala, 1957-60; Foreign Office, 1962-69 (British Delegate to Internat. Exhibitions Bureau); retired 1969. *Publications:* trans. Eugène Pepin: The Loire and its Chateaux, 1971; trans. Jean Chesneaux: The Political and Social Ideas of Jules Verne, 1972. *Address:* 19 Cromwell Court, Hove, East Sussex BN3 3EF.

WILBERFORCE, family name of **Baron Wilberforce**.

WILBERFORCE, Baron, *cr* 1964 (Life Peer); **Richard Orme Wilberforce**, PC 1964; Kt 1961; CMG 1956; OBE 1944; a Lord of Appeal in Ordinary since 1964; Fellow, All Souls College, Oxford, since 1932; *b* 11 Mar. 1907; *s* of late S. Wilberforce; *m* 1947, Yvette, *d* of Roger Lenoan, Judge of Court of Cassation, France; one *s* one *d*. *Educ:* Winchester; New College, Oxford. Served War, 1939-46; returned to Bar, 1947; QC 1954; Senior UK Representative on Legal Committee of International Civil Aviation Organisation, 1947-. Judge of the High Court of Justice (Chancery Division), 1961-64; Bencher, Middle Temple, 1961. Chm. Exec. Council, Internat. Law Assoc.; Mem., Permanent Court of Arbitration. High Steward of Oxford University, 1967-; Visitor, Wolfson Coll., Oxford, 1974. Hon. Fellow, New Coll., Oxford, 1965. Hon. FRCM. Hon. Comp. Royal Aeronautical Society. Hon. DCL Oxon, 1968; Hon. LLD: London, 1972; Hull, 1973. Diplôme d'Honneur, Corp. des Vignerons de Champagne. US Bronze Star, 1944; Gran Cruz San Raimondo de Peñafort, 1976. *Publications:* The Law of Restrictive Trade Practices, 1956; articles and pamphlets on Air Law and International Law. *Recreations:* the turf, travel, opera. *Address:* 8 Cambridge Place, W8. *T:* 01-937 4895. *Club:* Athenæum.

WILBERFORCE, Robert, CBE 1924; retired; *b* 8 Dec. 1887; 2nd *s* of H. E. Wilberforce; *m* 1914, Hope Elizabeth (*d* 1970), *d* of Schuyler N. Warren, New York. *Educ:* Beaumont and Stonyhurst; Balliol College, Oxford. BA 1912, Honour School of Modern History; War Trade Intelligence Department, 1915-16; Attaché HM Legation to Holy See, 1917-19; called to Bar, Inner Temple, 1921; Member of British Delegation to Washington Disarmament Conference, 1921-22; Carnegie Endowment International Mission to Vatican Library, 1927; British Delegation to Geneva Disarmament Conference, 1932 and 1933; Director British Information Services, New York; retired 1952. *Publications:* The Church and Slavery; Meditations in Verse; articles and reviews in various periodicals. *Address:* St Teresa's, Corston, near Bath. *T:* Saltford 2607.

WILBERFORCE, William John Antony; HM Diplomatic Service; Head of Defence Department, Foreign and Commonwealth Office, since 1975; *b* 3 Jan. 1930; *s* of late Lt-Col W. B. Wilberforce and Cecilia (*née* Dormer); *m* 1953, Laura Lyon, *d* of late Howard Sykes, Englewood, NJ; one *s* two *d*. *Educ:* Ampleforth; Christ Church, Oxford. Army National Service, 2nd Lieut KOYLI, 1948-49. HM Foreign Service, 1953; served: Oslo, 1955-57; Berlin, 1957-59; Ankara, 1962-64; Abidjan, 1964-67; Asst Head of UN (Econ. and Social) Dept, 1967-70, and of Southern European Dept, 1970-72; Counsellor, 1972-74, and Head of Chancery, 1974-75, Washington. Hon. DHum Wilberforce, 1973. *Recreations:* the turf, travel, gardening. *Address:* Markington Hall, Harrogate, North Yorks. *T:* Bishop Monkton 356. *Club:* Athenæum.

WILBRAHAM; *see* Bootle-Wilbraham, family name of Baron Skelmersdale.

WILBRAHAM, Sir Randle (John) Baker, 7th Bt, *cr* 1776; FRICS; DL; JP; Consultant partner in firm of John German Ralph Pay, Land Agents; *b* 31 March 1906; *o s* of Sir Philip W. Baker Wilbraham, 6th Bt, KBE, DCL; *S* father 1957; *m* 1930, Betty Ann, CBE (*d* 1975), *e d* of W. Matt Torrens, The Grove, Hayes, Kent; one *s* one *d*. *Educ:* Harrow; Balliol College, Oxford. Entered the Land Agency profession, 1928; served War of 1939-45 as Squadron-Leader, Royal Auxiliary Air Force; resumed practice, 1945. President of the Chartered Land Agents' Society, 1958-59; High Steward of Congleton, 1957-; High Sheriff, 1953, JP 1954, DL 1959, Cheshire. *Heir: s* Richard Baker Wilbraham, late Lieut Welsh Guards [*b* 5 Feb. 1934; *m* 1962, Anne Christine Peto Bennett; one *s* three *d*. *Educ:* Harrow. A Dir, Schroder Wagg & Co.]. *Address:* Rode Hall, Scholar Green, Cheshire. *T:* Alsager 3237. *Clubs:* MCC, United Oxford & Cambridge University.

WILBY, John Ronald William, CMG 1961; Professor of International Trade and Finance, Seattle University, since 1967; *b* 1 Sept. 1906; *s* of Thomas Wilby and Gertrude Snowdon; *m* 1944, Winifred Russell Walker; no *c*. *Educ:* Batley School; University of Leeds. Board of Inland Revenue, 1928-46; Board of Trade (Principal), 1946-49; First Secretary (Commercial), British Embassy, Washington, 1949-53; British Trade Commissioner, Ottawa, 1953-55; Principal British Trade Commissioner in Ontario, Canada, 1955-64; Consul-General in Seattle, 1964-67. *Recreations:* sailing, music. *Address:* 185 34th Avenue E, Seattle, Wash 98112, USA. *T:* EA5-6999.

WILCHER, Lewis Charles, CBE 1955; MA, BLitt; *b* 9 December 1908; *s* of L. G. Wilcher, Middle Swan, W Australia; *m* 1935, Vere Wylie; one *s* one *d*. *Educ:* St Peter's College, Adelaide; University of Adelaide; Balliol College, Oxford (Rhodes Scholar). Dean, Trinity College, Melbourne, 1934-37; Lecturer in Modern History, Univ. of Melbourne, 1935-40; AIF 1940-47; Lieut-Col; Asst Dir of Army Education, 1942-47; Principal, Univ. Coll., Khartoum, 1947-56; Warden, Queen Elizabeth House, Oxford, 1956-68. *Publication:* Education, Press, Radio, 1947. *Recreation:* walking. *Address:* 12 Staunton Road, Oxford.

WILCOX, Albert Frederick, CBE 1967; QPM 1957; Chief Constable of Hertfordshire, 1947-69, retired; *b* 18 April 1909; *s* of late Albert Clement Wilcox, Ashley Hill, Bristol; *m* 1939, Ethel, *d* of late E. H. W. Wilmott, Manor House, Whitchurch, Bristol; one *s* two *d*. *Educ:* Fairfield Grammar School, Bristol. Joined Bristol City Police, 1929; Hendon Police Coll., 1934; Metropolitan Police, 1934-43. Served Allied Mil. Govt, Italy and Austria (Lt-Col), 1943-46. Asst Chief Constable of Buckinghamshire, 1946. Cropwood Fellowship, Inst. of Criminology, Cambridge, 1969. Pres. Assoc. of Chief Police Officers, Eng. and Wales, 1966-67; Chm. of Management Cttee, Police Dependents' Trust, 1967-69. Regional Police Commander (designate), 1962-69. Member, Parole Board, 1970-73. Criminological Res. Fellowship, Council of Europe, 1974-76. Barrister-at-Law, Gray's Inn, 1941. Mem. Edit. Bd, Criminal

Law Review. *Publication:* The Decision to Prosecute, 1972. *Address:* 34 Roundwood Park, Harpenden, Herts.

WILCOX, Bernard Herbert, OBE 1967; HM Diplomatic Service, retired; Consul-General, Lille, France, 1973-77; *b* 4 May 1917; *s* of late Herbert Wilcox, and of Elsie May Wilcox; *m* 1946, Mary Cameron Rae; one *d. Educ:* King Edward's High Sch., Birmingham; Birmingham Univ. (BA). Served War, with S Staffords, RA, and British Mil. Mission to Italian Army, 1939-46. British Vice-Consul, Lisbon, 1947-49; Pro-Consul, Berlin, 1949-50; 2nd Sec., British Embassy, Belgrade, 1950-52; Vice-Consul: Los Angeles, 1952-54; Kansas City, 1954-56; Consul, Philadelphia, 1956-58; FO, 1958-60; 1st Sec., British Embassy, Rangoon, 1960-63; Consul, Los Angeles, 1963-67; 1st Sec., British Embassy, Paris, 1967-72; Consul-General, Casablanca, 1972-73. *Recreations:* tennis, chess, gardening. *Address:* 4 Randolph Close, Stoke D'Abernon, Cobham, Surrey KT11 2SW.

WILCOX, Claude Henry Marwood; *b* 10 January 1908; *s* of late Harry Robert Wilcox, Sherborne; *m* 1934, Winifred, *d* of late William Francis, Diss; two *s* two *d. Educ:* Sherborne School; Pembroke College, Cambridge (Scholar). Wrangler, 1929; MA 1947. Entered Ministry of Agriculture and Fisheries through Home Civil Service Administrative Examination, 1930; seconded to HM Treasury, 1939-47; Under-Secretary, Ministry of Agriculture, Fisheries and Food, 1948-68. Mem., Guildford Council of Churches, 1969-. Hon. Sec., Probus Club of Guildford, 1974-. *Address:* Blythburgh, 57 Pewley Hill, Guildford, Surrey GU1 3SW. *T:* Guildford 65794.

WILCOX, Rev. Canon David Peter; Principal of Ripon College, Cuddesdon, Oxford, since 1977; *b* 29 June 1930; *s* of John Wilcox and Stella Wilcox (*née* Bower); *m* 1956, Pamela Ann Hedges; two *s* two *d. Educ:* Northampton Grammar School; St John's Coll., Oxford (2nd cl. Hons Theol., MA); Lincoln Theological Coll. Deacon 1954, priest 1955; Asst Curate, St Peter's, St Helier, Morden, Surrey, 1954-56; Asst Curate, University Church, Oxford and SCM Staff Secretary in Oxford, 1956-59; Tutor, Chaplain, then Sub-Warden, Lincoln Theological Coll., 1959-64; USPG Missionary on staff of United Theological Coll., Bangalore, and Presbyter in Church of S India, 1964-70; Vicar of Great Gransden with Little Gransden, dio. Ely, 1970-72; Canon Residentiary, Derby Cathedral and Warden, E Midlands Joint Ordination Training Scheme, 1972-77; Proctor in Convocation, 1973-77; Canon Emeritus, Derby Cathedral, 1977. *Recreations:* walking, music. *Address:* The Old Vicarage, Cuddesdon, Oxford OX9 9HJ. *T:* Wheatley 4368.

WILCOX, Desmond John; Head of General Features, BBC Television, since 1972; *b* 21 May 1931; *e s* of John Wallace Wilcox and Alice May Wilcox; *m* (marr. diss.); one *s* two *d. Educ:* Cheltenham Grammar Sch.; Christ's Coll., London; Outward Bound Sea Sch. Sail training apprentice, 1947; Deckhand, Merchant Marine, 1948; Reporter, weekly papers, 1949; commissioned Army, National Service, 1949-51; News Agency reporter, 1951-52; Reporter and Foreign Correspondent, Daily Mirror, incl. New York Bureau and UN, 1952-60; Reporter, This Week, ITV, 1960-65; joined BBC 1965; Co-Editor/Presenter, Man Alive, 1965; formed Man Alive Unit, 1968. SFTA Award for best factual programme series, 1967; Richard Dimbleby Award, SFTA, for most important personal contrib. in factual television, 1971. *Publication:* Explorers, 1975. *Recreations:* offshore sail cruising, ski-ing, television. *Address:* BBC-TV, Kensington House, Richmond Way, W14 0AX. *T:* 01-743 1272. *Clubs:* Arts, BBC.

WILCOX, Malcolm George, MBE (mil.) 1943; Director and Chief General Manager, Midland Bank Ltd, since 1974; *b* 3 June 1921; *s* of George Harrison and Edith Mary Wilcox; *m* 1958, Sheila Mary Hewitt; one *s* one *d. Educ:* Wallasey Grammar Sch. TA, 1939; served war 1939-45: RA, RHA and General Staff. Entered Midland Bank Ltd, Liverpool, 1938: Jt General Manager, 1967-72; Asst Chief General Manager, 1972-74; Managing Director, and later Vice Chm., Forward Trust Ltd, 1967-75; Director: Euro-Pacific Finance Corp. Ltd, 1974-77; Midland Bank Finance Corp., 1967- (formerly Man. Dir and Vice-Chm.); Samuel Montagu & Co. Ltd, 1970-; Thomas Cook Gp Ltd, 1972- (Dep. Chm. 1972-75); Midland Bank Insurance Services Ltd, 1972-; Midland Bank Trust Co. Ltd, 1974-; Bland Payne Holdings Ltd, 1974-; European Banking Co. Ltd, 1974-; Midland and International Banks Ltd, 1974-; European Banks' International Co., 1975-; European-American Bank and Trust Co. NY, 1975-; Banque Européenne de Crédit, 1975-; Standard and Chartered Banking Gp Ltd, 1975-; Dir, Midland Bank Group Unit Trust Managers, 1975-. Pres., Brit. Junior Chambers of Commerce, 1960-61; Chm., Finance Houses Assoc., 1970-72; Mem. Council, Inst. of Bankers, 1970-, Vice-

Chm., 1976-77, Pres., 1977-; Mem., Export Guarantees Adv. Council, 1976-, Dep. Chm., 1976-77, Chm., 1977-. Member: Bd of Management, Royal Alexandra and Albert Sch., Reigate, 1972-; Adv. Panel to Graduate Business Centre, City Univ., 1971- (Chm.). FIB, FBIM. *Publications:* contributor to banking jls. *Recreations:* theatre, gardening, reading, golf. *Address:* Woodland Chase, Blackhall Lane, Sevenoaks, Kent TN15 0HU. *T:* Sevenoaks 61215. *Club:* Wildernesse (Seal, Kent).

WILCOX, Dame Marjorie; see Neagle, Dame Anna.

WILD, David Humphrey; His Honour Judge Wild; a Circuit Judge (Crown Court, Cambridge), since 1972; *b* 24 May 1927; *s* of John S. Wild and Edith Lemarchand; *m* 1st, 1950, Joy Josephine, *d* of A. C. Nesbitt, Lincoln's Inn; one *d*; 2nd, 1963, Estelle Grace Prowett, *d* of James Marshall, Aberdeen and Malaya; one *s. Educ:* Whitgift Middle Sch., Croydon. Served War of 1939-45, Royal Navy, 1944-48. Called to Bar, Middle Temple, 1951. Practised, London and SE Circuit, 1951-58, Midland Circuit, 1958-72. Councillor, Oundle and Thrapston RDC, 1968-72. *Publication:* The Law of Hire Purchase, 1960 (2nd edn, 1964). *Address:* 6 Pump Court, Temple, EC4; College Farm House, Fotheringhay, Peterborough. *Clubs:* Bath, Savile; Northampton and County (Northampton); Luffenham Heath Golf.

WILD, Rt. Rev. Eric; see Reading, Suffragan Bishop of.

WILD, Captain Geoffrey Alan, CBE 1963; retired as Commodore Captain, P&O Steam Navigation Company (1961-63), and Captain of the Canberra; *b* 21 Feb. 1904; *s* of Rev. Harry Wild, formerly Vicar, St Annes, Clifton, near Manchester, and of Susan Wild (*née* Holt); *m* 1932, Dorothy Louisa Bickell; no *c. Educ:* St Bees, Cumberland; Nautical College, Pangbourne. One year in Barquentine St George, then two years as Cadet, New Zealand Shipping Co. Joined P&O as 4th Officer, 1923; Staff Captain, 1949. First command in Shillong, 1951; commanded Iberia, 1956, also Strathnaver, Canton, Corfu, Chusan, Strathaird, Arcadia and Himalaya. *Recreation:* all sports. *Address:* 1 Valentine Court, South Street, Eastbourne, East Sussex.

WILD, Major Hon. Gerald Percy, MBE 1941; Company Director; Agent-General for Western Australia in London, 1965-71; *b* 2 Jan. 1908; *m* 1944, Virginia Mary Baxter; two *s* one *d. Educ:* Shoreham Gram. Sch., Sussex; Chivers Acad., Portsmouth, Hants. Served War of 1939-45 (despatches, MBE): Middle East, Greece, Crete, Syria, New Guinea and Moratai, Netherlands East Indies (Major). Elected MLA for Western Australia, 1947; Minister for Housing and Forests, 1950-53; Minister for Works and Water Supplies and Labour (WA), 1959-65. JP Perth (WA), 1953. *Recreations:* golf, tennis, cricket, football. *Address:* 2/41 Park Street, Como, WA 6152, Australia. *T:* 601910. *Clubs:* East India, Devonshire, Sports and Public Schools, MCC; Naval and Military, Western Australia, West Australian Turf (WA).

WILD, Rt. Hon. Sir (Herbert) Richard (Churton), PC 1966; KCMG 1966; Chief Justice of New Zealand since 1966; *b* 1912; *s* of Dr L. J. Wild; *m* 1940, Janet Grainger; two *s* two *d. Educ:* Feilding High Sch.; Victoria Univ. Private practice, 1939-57 (absent on War Service with NZ Div. in ME, 1940-45). Apptd Judge Advocate Gen., 1955; QC 1957. Solicitor-Gen., 1957-65. Hon. LLD, Victoria Univ., 1969. Hon. Bencher, Inner Temple, 1969. *Address:* Chief Justice's Chambers, Supreme Court, Wellington, NZ. *Club:* Wellington (NZ).

WILD, Very Rev. John Herbert Severn, MA Oxon; Hon. DD Durham, 1958; Dean of Durham, 1951-73, Dean Emeritus, since 1973; *b* 22 Dec. 1904; *e s* of Right Rev. Herbert Louis Wild and Helen Christian, *d* of Walter Severn; *m* 1945, Margaret Elizabeth Everard, *d* of G. B. Wainwright, OBE, MB. *Educ:* Clifton Coll.; Brasenose College, Oxford (Scholar); represented Oxford against Cambridge at Three Miles, 1927; Westcott House, Cambridge. Curate of St Aidan, Newcastle upon Tyne, 1929-33; Chaplain-Fellow of University College, Oxford, 1933-45; Domestic Bursar, 1936-45; Dean, 1939-42; Vice-Master, 1942-43; Pro-Master, 1943-45; Master, 1945-51; Hon. Fellow, 1951-; Select Preacher, Univ. of Oxford, 1948-49. Church Comr, 1958-73. ChStJ, 1966-. Chm. of Governors, Durham Sch., 1951-73. *Recreations:* fishing, walking. *Address:* Deacons Farmhouse, Rapps, Ilminster, Somerset TA19 9LG. *T:* Ilminster 3398. *Club:* United Oxford & Cambridge University.

WILD, Dr John Paul, FRS 1970; FAA 1962; Chief, Division of Radiophysics, Commonwealth Scientific and Industrial Research Organization, since 1971; *b* 1923; *s* of late Alwyn Howard Wild and late Bessie Delafield (*née* Arnold); *m* 1948,

Elaine Poole Hull; two s one d. *Educ:* Whitgift Sch.; Peterhouse, Cambridge. ScD 1962. Radar Officer in Royal Navy, 1943-47; joined Research Staff of Div. of Radiophysics, 1947, working on problems in radio astronomy, esp. of the sun. For. Hon. Mem., Amer. Acad. of Arts and Scis, 1961; For. Mem., Amer. Philos. Soc., 1962; Corresp. Mem., Royal Soc. of Scis, Liège, 1969; For. Sec., Australian Acad. of Science, 1973-. Edgeworth David Medal, 1958; Hendryk Arctowski Gold Medal, US Nat. Acad. of Scis; Balthasar van der Pol Gold Medal, Internat. Union of Radio Science, 1969. *Publications:* numerous research papers and reviews on radio astronomy in scientific jls. *Address:* 3 Strathfield Avenue, Strathfield, NSW 2135, Australia. *T:* Sydney 76-6880.

WILD, John Vernon, CMG 1960; OBE 1955; Colonial Administrative Service, retired; Lecturer, Exeter College, 1971-76; *b* 26 April 1915; *m* 1942, Margaret Patricia Rendell (*d* 1975); one s one d ; *m* 1976, Marjorie Mary Lovatt Robertson. *Educ:* Taunton School; King's College, Cambridge. Senior Optime, Cambridge Univ., 1937. Colonial Administrative Service, Uganda: Assistant District Officer, 1938; Assistant Chief Secretary, 1950; Establishment Secretary, 1951; Administrative Secretary, 1955-60; Chairman, Constitutional Committee, 1959. Teacher and Lectr in Mathematics, 1960-76. *Publications:* The Story of the Uganda Agreement; The Uganda Mutiny; Early Travellers in Acholi. *Recreations:* cricket (Cambridge Blue, 1938), golf, music. *Address:* Maplestone Farm, Broad Oak, Brede, near Rye, East Sussex TN31 6EP. *Club:* Hawkhurst Golf and Country.

WILD, Rt. Hon. Sir Richard; *see* Wild, Rt Hon. Sir H. R. C.

WILDE, Derek Edward; Vice Chairman, 1972-77, and Director since 1969, Barclays Bank Ltd; Chairman, Keyser Ullmann Holdings, since 1975; *b* 6 May 1912; *s* of late William Henry Wilde and Ethel May Wilde; *m* 1940, Helen, *d* of William Harrison; (one d decd). *Educ:* King Edward VII School, Sheffield. Entered Barclays Bank Ltd, Sheffield, 1929; General Manager, 1961; Sen. General Manager, 1966-72. Dir, Yorkshire Bank Ltd. Governor, Midhurst Med. Res. Inst. Fellow, Inst. of Bankers (Hon. Fellow 1975). *Recreation:* gardening. *Address:* Ranmoor, Smarts Hill, Penshurst, Kent. *T:* Penshurst 228.

WILDE, Peter Appleton; HM Diplomatic Service, retired; *b* 5 April 1925; *m* 1950, Frances Elisabeth Candida Bayliss; two s. *Educ:* Chesterfield Grammar Sch.; St Edmund Hall, Oxford. Army (National Service), 1943-47; Temp. Asst Lectr, Southampton, 1950; FO, 1950; 3rd Sec., Bangkok, 1951-53; Vice-Consul, Zürich, 1953-54; FO, 1954-57; 2nd Sec., Baghdad, 1957-58; 1st Sec., UK Delegn to OEEC (later OECD), Paris, 1958-61; 1st Sec., Katmandu, 1961-64; FO (later FCO), 1964-69; Consul-Gen., Lourenço Marques, 1969-71; Dep. High Comr, Colombo, 1971-73. Mem., Llanfihangel Rhosycorn Community Council, 1974-. Mem. Management Cttee, Carmarthenshire Pest Control Soc. Ltd, 1974-. *Recreation:* Forestry. *Address:* Nantyperchyll, Gwernogle, Carmarthen, Dyfed SA32 7RR. *T:* Brechfa 241.

WILDENSTEIN, Daniel Leopold; art historian; President, Wildenstein Foundation Inc., since 1964; Chairman, Wildenstein & Co Inc., New York, since 1968 (Vice-President, 1943-59, President, 1959-68); *b* Verrières-le-Buisson, France, 11 Sept. 1917; *s* of Georges Wildenstein; *m* 1939, Martine Kapferer (marr. diss. 1968); two s. *Educ:* Cours Hattemer; Sorbonne (LèsL 1938). Gp Sec., French Pavilion, World's Fair, 1937; went to US, 1940; with Wildenstein & Co. Inc., New York, 1940-; Director: Wildenstein & Co. Inc., London, 1963-; Wildenstein Arte, Buenos Aires, 1963-. Dir, Gazette des Beaux Arts, 1963-; Dir of Activities, Musée Jacquemart-André, Paris, 1956-62; Musée Chaalis, Institut de France, Paris, 1956-62; organiser of art competitions (Hallmark art award). Mem., French Chamber of Commerce in US (Conseiller), 1942-; Founder (1947) and Mem, Amer. Inst. of France (Sec.). Mem., Institut de France (Académie des Beaux-Arts), 1971; Membre du Haut Comité du Musée de Monaco. *Publications:* Claude Monet, vol. 1, 1975; Edouard Manet, 1976-77. *Recreation:* horse racing (leading owner, 1976). *Address:* case postale 152, 1000 Lausanne, 12 Chailly, Switzerland; (office) 57 rue La Boétie, Paris 8ème, France. *T:* 359-22-36. *Clubs:* Brooks's; Turf and Field, Madison Square Garden (New York); Cercle de Deauville, Tir au Pigeon (Paris); Jockey (Buenos Aires).

WILDING, Michael; Actor (stage and films); *b* Westcliff-on-Sea, Essex, 23 July 1912; *s* of late Henry Wilding, MBE and Ethel Thompson; *m* 1937, Kay Young (marr. diss. 1952); *m* 1952, Elizabeth Taylor (marr. diss. 1957); two s ; *m* 1958, Mrs Susan Nell (marr. diss.); *m* 1964, Margaret Leighton, CBE (*d* 1976). *Educ:* Christ's Hospital. Began career painting portraits and

working at commercial art in Brussels. First West End appearance, Daly's, 1935; toured with Fay Compton in Australia and New Zealand, playing leading parts in Victoria Regina, To-Night at 8-30, and George and Margaret; played Denys Royd in Quiet Week-End, Wyndham's, 1941-43; went to Gibraltar and Malta, with John Gielgud and Company, entertaining HM Forces, Jan. 1943; succeeded John Mills as Lew in Men in Shadow, Vaudeville, 1943; played the Earl of Harpenden in While the Sun Shines, Dec. 1943 until 1945; succeeded Sir John Gielgud in Nude With Violin, 1957; Mary Mary, Broadway, 1961. First appeared in films, 1940. Films include: Piccadilly Incident, Carnival, The Courtneys of Curzon Street, An Ideal Husband, Spring in Park Lane, Maytime in Mayfair, Under Capricorn, Stage Fright, The Law and The Lady, The Lady With a Lamp, Derby Day, Trent's Last Case, Torch Song, The Law and the Lady, The Egyptian, The Glass Slipper, The World of Suzie Wong, The Naked Edge, The Two Enemies, Waterloo, Lady Caroline Lamb, Dr Frankenstein. *Address:* c/o Green & Underwood, 11 Garrick Street, WC2.

WILDING, Richard William Longworth; Deputy Secretary, Civil Service Department, since 1976; *b* 22 April 1929; *er s* of late L. A. Wilding; *m* 1954, Mary Rosamund de Villiers; one s two d. *Educ:* Dragon Sch.; Oxford; Winchester Coll.; New Coll., Oxford (MA). HM Foreign Service, 1953-59; transf. to Home Civil Service, 1959; Principal, HM Treasury, 1959-67; Sec., Fulton Cttee on Civil Service, 1966-68; Asst Sec., Civil Service Dept, 1968-70; Asst Sec., Supplementary Benefits Commn, DHSS, 1970-72; Under-Sec., Management Services, 1972-76, Pay, 1976, CSD. *Publications:* (with L. A. Wilding) A Classical Anthology, 1954; Key to Latin Course for Schools, 1966; articles in Jl Public Administration, Social Work Today, Studies. *Recreations:* music, gardening. *Address:* 16 Middleway, NW11. *T:* 01-455 6245. *Club:* Civil Service.

WILDISH, Vice-Adm. Denis Bryan Harvey, CB 1968; Director General of Personal Services and Training (Naval), 1970-72, retired; *b* 24 Dec. 1914; *s* of late Rear-Adm. Sir Henry William Wildish, KBE, CB; *m* 1941, Leslie Henrietta Jacob; two d. *Educ:* RNC Dartmouth; RNEC. Entered Royal Navy, 1928; Comdr 1948; Capt. 1957; Rear-Adm. 1966; Vice-Adm. 1970. Dir of Fleet Maintenance, 1962-64; Commodore Naval Drafting, 1964-66; Adm. Supt, HM Dockyard, Devonport, 1966-70. *Recreations:* cricket, painting. *Address:* Deans Farm, Weston, near Petersfield, Hants. *Clubs:* Army and Navy, MCC.

WILDSMITH, Brian Lawrence; artist and maker of picture books for young children; *b* 22 Jan. 1930; *s* of Paul Wildsmith and Annie Elizabeth Oxley; *m* 1955, Aurelie Janet Craigie Ithurbide; one s three d. *Educ:* de la Salle Coll.; Barnsley Sch. of Art; Slade Sch. of Fine Arts. Art Master, Selhurst Grammar School for Boys, 1954-57; freelance artist, 1957-. Production design, illustrations, titles and graphics for first USA-USSR Leningrad film co-production of the Blue Bird. Kate Greenaway Medal, 1962. *Publications:* ABC, 1962; The Lion and the Rat, 1963; The North Wind and the Sun, 1964; Mother Goose, 1964; The Rich Man and the Shoemaker, 1965; The Hare and the Tortoise, 1966; Birds, 1967; Animals, 1967; Fish, 1968; The Miller the Boy and the Donkey, 1969; The Circus, 1970; Puzzles, 1970; The Owl and the Woodpecker, 1971; The Twelve Days of Christmas, 1972; The Little Wood Duck, 1972; The Lazy Bear, 1973; Squirrels, 1974; Pythons Party, 1974; The Blue Bird, 1976; The True Cross, 1977. *Recreations:* squash, tennis, music (piano). *Address:* 11 Castellaras, 06370 Mouans-Sartoux, France. *T:* (93) 90.24.11.

WILDY, Prof. (Norman) Peter (Leete); Professor of Pathology, and Fellow of Gonville and Caius College, University of Cambridge, since 1975; *b* 31 March 1920; *s* of late Eric Lawrence and of Gwendolen Wildy, Hinxton, Cambs; *m* 1945, Joan Audrey Kenion; one s two d. *Educ:* Eastbourne College; Caius Coll., Cambridge; St Thos Hosp., London. MRCS, LRCP 1944; MB, BChir 1948. RAMC, 1945-47. St Thomas's Hospital Medical School: Michael and Sydney Herbert and Leonard Dudgeon Res. Fellow, 1949-51; Lecturer in Bacteriology, 1952-57; Sen. Lectr in Bacteriology, 1957-58; Brit. Memorial Fellow in Virology, 1953-54; Asst Director, MRC Unit for Experimental Virus Research, Glasgow, 1959-63; Prof. of Virology, Univ. of Birmingham, 1963-75. FRSE 1962; FRCPath 1975. *Publications:* articles on bacteria and viruses. *Address:* The Old Parsonage, Hinxton, Cambs.

WILEMAN, Margaret Annie, MA; Honorary Fellow since 1973 (President (formerly Principal), 1953-73), Hughes Hall, Cambridge; *b* 19 July 1908; *e d* of Clement Wileman and Alice (*née* Brinson). *Educ:* Lady Margaret Hall, Oxford, and the University of Paris. Scholar of Lady Margaret Hall, Oxford, 1927; First in Hons School of Mod. Langs, 1930; Zaharoff

Travelling Scholar, 1931; Assistant, Abbey School, Reading, 1934; Senior Tutor, Queen's College, Harley Street, 1937; Lecturer, St Katherine's coll., Liverpool, 1940; Resident Tutor, Bedford College, Univ. of London, 1944-53; Univ. Lectr, and Dir of Women Students, Dept of Educn, Cambridge Univ., 1953-73. *Address:* 5 Drosier Road, Cambridge. *T:* Cambridge 51846. *Club:* University Women's.

WILES, Donald Alonzo, CMG 1965; OBE 1960; Administrative Secretary, Da Costa & Musson Ltd, Barbados, since 1965; *b* 8 Jan. 1912; *s* of Donald Alonzo Wiles and Millicent Wiles; *m* 1938, Amelie Elsie Pemberton; two *d. Educ:* Harrison Coll., Barbados; Univs of London, Toronto, Oxford. Member of Staff of Harrison College, Barbados, 1931-45; Public Librarian, Barbados, 1945-50; Asst Colonial Secretary, Barbados, 1950-54; Permanent Secretary, Barbados, 1954-60; Administrator, Montserrat, 1960-64. Member, West Indies Committee. Pres., Barbados Nat. Trust. *Recreations:* swimming, hiking, tennis. *Address:* Casa Loma, Pine Gardens, St Michael, Barbados. *T:* 66875. *Clubs:* Barbados Yacht, Bridgetown (Barbados).

WILES, Rev. Prof. Maurice Frank; Canon of Christ Church, Oxford, and Regius Professor of Divinity, since 1970; *b* 17 Oct. 1923; *s* of late Sir Harold Wiles, KBE, CB, and of Lady Wiles; *m* 1950, Patricia Margaret (*née* Mowll); two *s* one *d. Educ:* Tonbridge School; Christ's College, Cambridge. Curate, St George's, Stockport, 1950-52; Chaplain, Ridley Hall, Cambridge, 1952-55; Lectr in New Testament Studies, Ibadan, Nigeria, 1955-59; Lectr in Divinity, Univ. of Cambridge, and Dean of Clare College, 1959-67; Prof. of Christian Doctrine, King's Coll., Univ. of London, 1967-70. FKC 1972. *Publications:* The Spiritual Gospel, 1960; The Christian Fathers, 1966; The Divine Apostle, 1967; The Making of Christian Doctrine, 1967; The Remaking of Christian Doctrine, 1974; (with M. Santer) Documents in Early Christian Thought, 1975; Working Papers in Doctrine, 1976; What is Theology?, 1976. *Address:* Christ Church, Oxford.

WILES, Prof. Peter John de la Fosse; Professor of Russian Social and Economic Studies, University of London, since 1965; *b* 25 Nov. 1919; *m* 1st, 1945, Elizabeth Coppin (marr. diss., 1960); one *s* two *d*; 2nd, 1960, Carolyn Stedman. *Educ:* Lambrook Sch.; Winchester Coll.; New Coll., Oxford. Royal Artillery, 1940-45 (despatches twice). Fellow, All Souls Coll., Oxford, 1947-48; Fellow, New Coll., Oxford, 1948-60; Prof., Brandeis Univ., USA, 1960-63; Research Associate, Institutet för Internationell Ekonomi, Stockholm, 1963-64. Vis. Prof.: Columbia Univ., USA, 1958; City Coll. of New York, 1964 and 1967. *Publications:* The Political Economy of Communism, 1962; Price, Cost and Output (2nd edn), 1962; Communist International Economics, 1968; (ed) The Prediction of Communist Economic Performance, 1971; Economic Institutions Compared, 1977. *Recreations:* simple. *Address:* 23 Ridgmount Gardens, WC1.

WILFORD, Sir (Kenneth) Michael, KCMG 1976 (CMG 1967); HM Diplomatic Service; Ambassador to Japan, since 1975; *b* Wellington, New Zealand, 31 Jan. 1922; *yr s* of late George McLean Wilford and late Dorothy Veronica (*née* Wilson); *m* 1944, Joan Mary, *d* of Captain E. F. B. Law, RN; three *d. Educ:* Wrekin College; Pembroke College, Cambridge. Served in Royal Engineers, 1940-46 (despatches). Entered HM Foreign (subseq. Diplomatic) Service, 1947; Third Sec., Berlin, 1947; Asst Private Secretary to Secretary of State, Foreign Office, 1949; Paris, 1952; Singapore, 1955; Asst Private Sec. to Sec. of State, Foreign Office, 1959; Private Sec. to the Lord Privy Seal, 1960; served Rabat, 1962; Counsellor (Office of British Chargé d'Affaires) also Consul-General, Peking, 1964-66; Visiting Fellow of All Souls, Oxford, 1966-67; Counsellor, Washington, 1967-69; Asst Under Sec. of State, FCO, 1969-73; Dep. Under Sec. of State, FCO, 1973-75. *Recreations:* golf, gardening. *Address:* Brook Cottage, Abbotts Ann, Andover, Hants. *T:* Abbotts Ann 509.

WILHELM, Most Rev. Joseph Lawrence; *see* Kingston (Ontario), Archbishop of (RC).

WILKES, Rev. John Comyn Vaughan, MA Oxon; Rector of Great Kimble, Aylesbury, 1967-72, retired; *b* 30 March 1902; *s* of L. C. Vaughan Wilkes, St Cyprian's, Eastbourne; *m* 1940, Joan, *y d* of late Very Rev. C. A. Alington, DD; six *s* one *d. Educ:* Fonthill, East Grinstead; St Cyprian's, Eastbourne; Eton Coll. (King's Schol.); Trinity Coll. Oxford (Classical Schol.). 1st Class Classical Moderations, 1923; 1st Class Lit. Hum., 1925; Half Blue for Golf (played *v* Cambridge, 1924, 1925); subsequently Assistant Master, Eton College 1925-37; Master in College, Eton College, 1930-37; Warden, Radley College, Abingdon, 1937-54; Vicar of Hunslet, Leeds, 1954-58; Vicar of Marlow, 1958-65; Rector of Preston Bissett, Buckingham, 1965-

67. Ordained deacon (C of E) 1945; priest, 1945. *Recreations:* golf, gardening. *Address:* The Old Stables, Burghill, Hereford. *T:* Hereford 760209. *Clubs:* Sussex Martlets, Eton Ramblers, Oxford and Cambridge Golfing Society.
See also Baron Home of the Hirsel .

WILKES, Prof. John Joseph, FSA; Professor of Archaeology of the Roman Provinces, University of London, since 1974; *b* 12 July 1936; *s* of Arthur Cyril Wilkes and Enid Cecilia Eustance. *Educ:* King Henry VIII Grammar Sch., Coventry; Harrow County Grammar Sch.; University Coll. London (BA); Univ. of Durham (St Cuthbert's Society) (PhD). FSA 1969. Research Fellow, Univ. of Birmingham, 1961-63; Asst Lectr in History and Archaeology, Univ. of Manchester, 1963-64; Lectr in Roman History, 1964-71, Sen. Lectr 1971-74, Univ. of Birmingham. Visiting Fellow, Inst. of Humanistic Studies, Pennsylvania State Univ., 1971; Corr. Mem., German Archaeological Inst., 1976. *Publications:* Dalmatia (Provinces of Roman Empire series), 1969; (jtly) Diocletian's Palace: joint excavations in the southeast quarter, Pt 1, Split, 1972; papers, excavation reports and reviews in learned jls of Britain, Amer., and Europe. *Recreations:* listening to music, watching Association football. *Address:* Institute of Archaeology, 31-4 Gordon Square, WC1H 0PY. *T:* 01-387 6052.

WILKES, Lyall; His Honour Judge Lyall Wilkes; a Circuit Judge (formerly Judge of the County Courts), since 1964; *b* 19 May 1914; *e s* of George and Doris Wilkes, Newcastle upon Tyne; *m* 1946, Margaret Tait; four *d. Educ:* Newcastle Grammar School; Balliol Coll., Oxford (MA). Secretary Oxford Union Society, 1937. Joined Middlesex Regiment 1940; active service North Africa, Italy and German-occupied Greece, attached force 133; Major, 1944 (despatches). Called to Bar, Middle Temple, 1947; practised North-Eastern Circuit, 1947-64; Dep. Chm., County of Durham QS, 1961-64; Asst Recorder, Sheffield and Newcastle upon Tyne, 1960-62; MP (Lab) for Newcastle Central, 1945-51. Mem., Laing Art Gallery Cttee, Newcastle upon Tyne, 1957-64. *Publications:* (with Gordon Dodds) Tyneside Classical: the Newcastle of Grainger, Dobson and Clayton, 1964; Tyneside Portraits: studies in Art and Life, 1971; Old Jesmond and other poems (limited edn), 1975. *Club:* Northern Counties (Newcastle-upon-Tyne).

WILKES, Maurice Vincent, FRS 1956; MA, PhD; FIEE; FBCS; Head of the Computer Laboratory, Cambridge (formerly Mathematical Laboratory), since 1970; Professor of Computer Technology, 1965; Fellow of St John's College, 1950; *b* 26 June 1913; *s* of late Vincent J. Wilkes, OBE; *m* 1947, Nina Twyman; one *s* two *d. Educ:* King Edward's School, Stourbridge; St John's College, Cambridge. Mathematical Tripos (Wrangler). Research in physics at Cavendish Lab.; Univ. Demonstrator, 1937. Served War of 1939-45, Radar and Operational Research. Univ. Lecturer and Acting Dir of Mathematical Laboratory, Cambridge, 1945; Dir of Mathematical Laboratory, 1946-70. Member: Measurement and Control Section Committee, IEE, 1956-59; Council, IEE, 1973-76; First President British Computer Soc., 1957-60, Distinguished Fellow 1973. Mem. Council, IFIP, 1960-63; Chm. IEE E Anglia Sub-Centre, 1969-70; Turing Lectr Assoc. for Computing Machinery, 1967; Harry Goode Award, Amer. Fedn of Information Processing Socs, 1968. Foreign Hon. Mem., Amer. Acad. of Arts and Sciences, 1974; Foreign Associate, US Nat. Acad. of Engrg, 1977. Hon. DSc: Newcastle upon Tyne, 1972; Hull, 1974; Kent, 1975; City, 1975; Hon. DTech Linköping, 1975. *Publications:* Oscillations of the Earth's Atmosphere, 1949; (joint) Preparations of Programs for an Electronic Digital Computer, Addison-Wesley (Cambridge, Mass), 1951, 2nd edn 1958; Automatic Digital Computers, 1956; A Short Introduction to Numerical Analysis, 1966; Time-sharing Computer System, 1968, 3rd edn 1975; papers in scientific jls. *Address:* The Computer Laboratory, Corn Exchange Street, Cambridge CB2 3QG. *T:* Cambridge 52435. *Club:* Constitutional.

WILKIE, Prof. Douglas Robert, FRS 1971; Jodrell Professor of Physiology, in the University of London, since 1969; *b* 2 Oct. 1922; *m* 1949, June Rosalind Hill; one *s. Educ:* Medical Student, University Coll. London, 1940-42 (Fellow, 1972); Yale Univ. (MD), 1942-43; University Coll. Hosp., MB, BS, 1944, MRCP 1945; FRCP 1972. Lectr, Dept of Physiology, UCL, 1948; Inst. of Aviation Medicine, Farnborough (Mil. Service), 1948-50; Locke Research Fellowship (Royal Soc.), 1951-54; Readership in Experimental Physiology, UCL, 1954-65; Prof. of Experimental Physiology, 1965-69. *Publications:* Muscle, 1968; contribs to learned jls, etc, mainly research on energetics of muscular contraction, and attempts to make thermodynamics simpler. *Recreations:* sailing, friends, photography. *Address:* 4 Grange Road, Highgate, N6. *T:* 01-348 0145.

WILKIE, James, MA, FRSE; Secretary Carnegie United Kingdom Trust, 1939-54; *b* Manchester, 1 June 1896; *er s* of late James Wilkie, Glasgow; *m* 1930, Ethel Susan, *er d* of late W. H. Moore, JP, Killough, Co. Down; three *d. Educ:* Whitgift School; Brasenose College, Oxford (Dist. Litt. Hum. 1920). Served European War, 1914-19 (Captain, Machine Gun Corps, despatches twice, wounded, Order of Crown of Rumania) and War of 1939-45 (Major, Home Guard). Entered Board of Education, 1921 (Asst Private Sec. to President, 1924-27), transferred to Empire Marketing Board, 1927-33; returned to Board of Education, 1933-39 (in charge of Metropolitan Div. and Sec. to Adult Education Cttee). Mem. Exec. Cttee: Newbattle Abbey Coll., 1939-54; Scottish Council of Social Service, 1944-54; Land Settlement Assoc., 1939-48; Nat. Central Library, 1939-50; Scottish Leadership Training Assoc., 1945-50; Member: NHS Executive Council for E Sussex, 1955-71; Advisory Council on Education in Scotland, 1948-51; Council of Nat. Federation of Young Farmers' Clubs, 1939-51; Vice-Pres.: Sussex Rural Community Council, Sussex Assoc. of Parish Councils; Irish Library Assoc., 1940-48; Pres., Library Assoc., 1951. *Address:* The Red Cottage, Fletching Common, Newick, Lewes, East Sussex BN8 4QS. *T:* Newick 2677.

WILKINS, Charles Timothy, OBE 1952; CEng; FRAeS; Director of Hawker Siddeley Dynamics Limited, in charge of Space Projects, 1963; *s* of G. C. A. Wilkins and A. N. Berg; *m* 1940, Gladys Marie Alexander; one *s* one *d. Educ:* Cordwalles; Brighton College. With Vickers Armstrongs Ltd, Weybridge, 2 years Shops and 1 year Drawing Office; Drawing Office, de Havilland Aircraft Co. Ltd, 1928-30; Drawing Office of Cierva Autogiro Co. for 1½ years and of Handley Page Ltd for six months; rejoined de Havilland Aircraft Co. Ltd, Drawing Office, 1932; appointed Director, 1958. "A" Licence (Pilot's), 1929. FRAeS 1950. Fellow, British Interplanetary Society. *Address:* Brook Hill Cottage, Brook Hill, Woodstock, Oxon. *T:* Woodstock 812071.

WILKINS, Frederick Charles, CB 1963; *b* 10 July 1901; *s* of Richard Charles Wilkins; *m* 1926, Winifred Bertha Denham; one *d. Educ:* Portsmouth. Entered Admiralty Service, 1917; Naval Store Officer, 1939 (Asst 1923; Dep. 1936); Asst Dir of Stores, 1942; Capt. RNVR (attached to Brit. Pacific Fleet, 1944-46); Dep. Dir of Stores, 1955; Dir of Stores, Admiralty, 1960-64. *Recreation:* reading (Theology). *Address:* 6 Spurwood Road, Turramurra, NSW 2074, Australia.

WILKINS, Graham John; Chairman and Chief Executive, Beecham Group Ltd, since 1975; *b* 22 Jan. 1924; *s* of George William and Anne May Wilkins; *m* 1945, Daphne Mildred Haynes. *Educ:* Yeovil Sch.; University Coll., South West of England, Exeter (BSc). Dir and Vice-Pres., Beecham (Canada) Ltd, 1954-59; C. L. Bencard Ltd, and Beecham Research Labs Ltd: Asst Man. Dir, 1959; Man. Dir, 1960; Dir, Beecham Pharmaceutical Div., 1962-64; Beecham Group Ltd: Dir and Chm., Pharmaceutical Div., 1964-72; Man. Dir (Pharmaceuticals), 1972; Exec. Vice-Chm., 1974; Director: Beecham Inc., 1967-; Beecham AG, 1973-; Courtaulds Ltd, 1975-; Hill Samuel Gp Ltd, 1977-. Vice-Chm., Proprietary Assoc. of Gt Brit., 1966-68; Pres., Assoc. of Brit. Pharmaceutical Industry, 1969-71 (Vice-Pres., 1968-69); Chm., Medico-Pharmaceutical Forum, 1971-73 (Vice-Chm., 1969-70). *Publications:* various papers on pharmaceutical industry. *Recreations:* golf, theatre-going, motor yacht cruising. *Address:* Alceda, Walton Lane, Shepperton-on-Thames, Mddx TW17 8LQ. *T:* Walton 27714.

WILKINS, Prof. Malcolm Barrett; FRSE 1972; Regius Professor of Botany, Glasgow University, since 1970; *b* 27 Feb. 1933; *s* of Barrett Charles Wilkins and Eleanor Mary Wilkins (*née* Jenkins); *m* 1959, Mary Patricia Maltby; one *s* one *d. Educ:* Monkton Home Sch., Cardiff; King's Coll., London. BSc 1955; PhD London 1958; AKC 1958; DSc 1972. Lectr in Botany, King's Coll., London, 1958-64; Rockefeller Foundn Fellow, Yale Univ., 1961-62; Research Fellow, Harvard Univ., 1962-63; Lectr in Biology, Univ. of East Anglia, 1964-65; Prof. of Biology, Univ. of East Anglia, 1965-67; Prof. of Plant Physiology, Univ. of Nottingham, 1967-70. Darwin Lectr, British Assoc. for Advancement of Science, 1967. Member: Biol. Sci. Cttee of SRC, 1971-74; Governing Body: Scottish Horticultural Research Inst; Hill Farming Research Orgn; Exec. Cttee, Scottish Field Studies Assoc.; British Nat. Cttee for Biology; Cons. Editor in Plant Biology, McGraw-Hill Publishing Co.; Editorial Board, Planta. *Publications:* (ed) The Physiology of Plant Growth and Development; papers in Jl of Experimental Botany, Plant Physiology, Planta, Nature, Proc. Royal Soc. *Recreation:* sailing. *Address:* Department of Botany, The University, Glasgow G12 8QQ. *T:* 041-339 8855.

WILKINS, Maurice Hugh Frederick, CBE 1963; FRS 1959; MA, PhD; Professor of Bio-physics, since 1970, and Fellow, since 1973, King's College, University of London; Director, Medical Research Council Cell Biophysics Unit, since 1974 (Deputy Director, 1955-70, Director, 1970-72, Biophysics Unit; Director Neurobiology Unit, 1972-74); *b* 15 Dec. 1916; *s* of late Edgar Henry Wilkins and of Eveline Constance Jane (*née* Whittaker), both of Dublin; *m* 1959, Patricia Ann Chidgey; two *s* two *d. Educ:* King Edward's Sch., Birmingham: St John's College, Cambridge (Hon. Fellow, 1972). Research on luminescence of solids at Physics Department, Birmingham University, with Ministry of Home Security and Aircraft Production, 1938; PhD 1940; Manhattan Project (Ministry of Supply), Univ. of California (research on separation of uranium isotopes by mass spectrograph), 1944; Lectr in Physics, St Andrews Univ., 1945; MRC Biophysics Unit in Physics Department, King's College, London, 1946; Hon. Lecturer in the sub-department of Biophysics, 1958; Prof. of Molecular Biology, King's Coll., 1963-70. Pres., British Soc. for Social Responsibility in Science, 1969. Hon. Mem., Amer. Soc. of Biological Chemists, 1964; For. Hon. Mem., Amer. Acad. of Arts and Scis, 1970. Albert Lasker Award, Amer. Public Health Assoc., 1960. Hon. LLD Glasgow, 1972. (Jt) Nobel Prize for Medicine, 1962. *Publications:* papers in scientific journals on luminescence and topics in bio-physics, *eg* molecular structure of nucleic acids and structure of nerve membranes. *Address:* 30 St John's Park, SE3. *T:* 01-858 1817.

WILKINS, William Albert, CBE 1965; *b* 17 Jan. 1899; *m* 1923, Violet Florrie Reed; three *s* one *d. Educ:* Whitehall Elementary School, Bristol. Linotype operator; commenced work at 13½ as an errand boy. Apprenticed to Thos Goulding, Printer, 6 Nelson St, Bristol. Later employed by Bristol Evening Times and Echo and Bristol Evening World. Actively engaged in politics since 1922; MP (Lab) Bristol South, 1945-70; Assistant Govt Whip (unpaid), 1947-50; a Lord Comr of the Treasury, 1950-51. Member Typographical Association (now National Graphical Association), 1919-. Past member of Typographical Association Nat. Executive, Past President Bristol Branch, Past Pres. South-Western Group TA. Member of Bristol City Council, 1936-46. *Address:* 37 King Street, Two Mile Hill, Kingswood, Bristol. *T:* 673779.

WILKINSON, Rev. Canon Alan Bassindale, PhD; Lecturer in Theology and Ethics, Crewe and Alsager College of Higher Education, since 1975; *b* 26 Jan. 1931; *s* of Rev. J. T. Wilkinson, DD; *m* 1975, Fenella Holland; two *s* one *d* of first marriage. *Educ:* William Hulme's Grammar Sch., Manchester; St Catharine's Coll., Cambridge; College of the Resurrection, Mirfield. MA 1958, PhD 1959 (Cambridge). Deacon, 1959; Priest, 1960; Asst Curate, St Augustine's, Kilburn, 1959-61; Chaplain, St Catharine's Coll., Cambridge, 1961-67; Vicar of Barrow Gurney and Lecturer in Theology, College of St Matthias, Bristol, 1967-70; Principal, Chichester Theol. Coll., 1970-74; Canon and Prebendary of Thorney, 1970-74, Canon Emeritus, 1975; Warden of Verulam House, Dir of Training for Auxiliary Ministry, dio. of St Albans, 1974-75. Hulsean Preacher, 1967-68. *Publications:* The Church of England and the First World War, 1978; contributor to: Cambridge Sermons on Christian Unity, 1966; Catholic Anglicans Today, 1968; also to: Faith and Unity, Sobornost, Preacher's Quarterly, London Quarterly Holborn Review, Theology, Clergy Review, New Fire. *Recreations:* gardening, walking, cinema, Victorian architecture. *Address:* 9 Fairview Avenue, Alsager, Stoke-on-Trent ST7 2NW. *T:* Alsager 4261.

WILKINSON, Prof. Alexander Birrell; Professor of Private Law, since 1972 and Dean of the Faculty of Law, 1974-76, University of Dundee; *b* 2 Feb. 1932; *o s* of late Captain Alexander Wilkinson, MBE, The Black Watch and Isabella Ball Birrell; *m* 1965, Wendy Imogen, *d* of late Ernest Albert Barrett, Belfast; one *s* one *d. Educ:* Perth Academy; Univs of St Andrews and Edinburgh. Walker Trust Scholar 1950, Grieve Prizeman in Moral Philosophy 1952, MA(Hons Classics) 1954, Univ. of St Andrews. National Service, RAEC, 1954-56. Balfour Keith Prizeman in Constitutional Law 1957, LLB (with distinction) 1959, Univ. of Edinburgh. Admitted to Faculty of Advocates, 1959; in practice at Scottish bar, 1959-69; Lecturer in Scots Law, Univ. of Edinburgh, 1965-69; Sheriff of Stirling, Dunbarton and Clackmannan at Stirling and Alloa, 1969-72. Chm., Central Scotland Marriage Guidance Council, 1970-72; Chm., Scottish Marriage Guidance Council, 1974-77. *Publications:* articles in legal periodicals. *Recreations:* collecting books and pictures, reading, travel. *Address:* Invergowrie House, Dundee DD2 1UA. *T:* Dundee 68939. *Clubs:* New (Edinburgh); University (Dundee).

WILKINSON, Prof. Andrew Wood, ChM (Edinburgh); PRCSE; FRCS; Nuffield Professor of Pædiatric Surgery, Institute of

Child Health, Great Ormond Street, and Surgeon, Hospital for Sick Children, Great Ormond Street, since 1958; Hon. Consultant Pædiatric Surgeon, Post-graduate Medical School, Hammersmith, and Queen Elizabeth Hospital for Children; Civilian Consultant in Pediatric Surgery to RN; *b* 19 April 1914; *s* of Andrew W. and Caroline G. Wilkinson; *m* 1941, Joan Longair Sharp; two *s* two *d. Educ:* Univ. of Edinburgh. MB, ChB, Edin., 1937; ChM; (1st cl. hons and gold medal for thesis), 1949; FRCS Edin. 1940; FRCS Eng. 1959. Syme Surgical Fellowship, Univ. of Edinburgh, 1946-49; Senior University Clinical Tutor in Surgery, 1946-51; Lecturer in Surgery, University of Edinburgh and Assistant Surgeon, Deaconess Hosp., Edinburgh, 1951-53; Sen. Lectr in Surgery, Univ.of Aberd. and Asst Surg., Roy. Inf. and Roy. Aberd. Hosp. for Sick Children, 1953-58. Mem. Council, RCSE, 1964-73, Vice-Pres., 1973-76, Pres., 1976-; Member: Armed Forces Med. Adv. Bd; Nat. Med. Consultative Cttee; Hunterian Prof., RCSEng, 1965. Examr Primary and Final FRCS Ed.; Past Examiner: Univ. Glasgow, DCH London; Primary FRCSEng. Tisdall Lectr, Canadian Med. Assoc., 1966; Mason Brown Meml Lectr, 1972. Visiting Prof. Univ. of Alexandria, 1965, Albert Einstein Coll. of Medicine, 1967. Late Temp. Lt-Col RAMC. Founder Member: Scottish Surgical Pædiatric Soc.; Neonatal Soc.; Past pres., British Assoc. of Pediatric Surgeons (1970-72). FRSocMed (Pres. Open Section, 1974-76). Hon. FRACS. Hon. Fellow: Brasilian Soc. Pædiatric Surgery; Greek Pædiatric Surgical Soc.; Amer. Acad. Pediatrics; Italian Pediatric Surgical Soc.; Pediatric Surgical Soc. of Ecuador; Hong Kong Surgical Soc.; Hon. Mem. Peruvian Socs Pediatrics and Pædiatric Surgery; Corresp. Member: Scandinavian Pediatric Surgical Assoc. Sicilian Calabrian Soc. of Pædiatric Surgery. *Publications:* Body Fluids in Surgery, 1955, 4th edn 1973; Recent Advances in Pædiatric Surgery, 1963, 3rd edn 1974; Parenteral Feeding, 1972; (jtly) Research in Burns, 1966; (jtly) Metabolism and the Response to Injury, 1976; Early Nutrition and Later Development, 1976; chapters, articles and reviews in various books, and surgical and other jls. *Recreations:* fishing and gardening. *Address:* Institute of Child Health, Great Ormond Street, WC1. *T:* 01-242 9789. *Club:* New (Edinburgh).

WILKINSON, Rt. Rev. (Charles Robert) Heber; Assistant Bishop of Niagara, 1960-70; *b* 28 Dec. 1900; *s* of late Rev. Frederick Wilkinson; *m* 1926, Rowena Victoria Stringer; two *s* one *d. Educ:* University of Toronto Schools; University of Toronto. MA (Toronto) and grad. Wycliffe Coll., Toronto, 1926. Priest, 1926, and appointed to Kangra Mission, Punjab Missionary Society, C of E in Canada. Secretary-Treasurer, Kangra Mission, 1930; Canon, Lahore Cathedral, 1942; Archdeacon, East Punjab, 1949; Assistant Bishop of Lahore, 1950; first Bishop of Amritsar, 1953-59. Hon. DD: Wycliffe Coll., 1946; Huron Coll., 1962. Jubilee Medal, 1935; Coronation Medal, 1937; Kaisar-i-Hind (Silver), 1942. *Address:* 2211 New Street, Burlington, Ont, Canada.

WILKINSON, Christopher Richard; Division Chief, Directorate General for Regional Policy, Commission of the European Communities, since 1973; *b* 3 July 1941; *s* of Rev. Thomas Richard Wilkinson and Winifred Frances Wilkinson (*née* Steel); *m* 1965, Marie-Françoise Courthieu; one *s* one *d. Educ:* Hymers Coll., Kingston upon Hull; Heath Grammar Sch., Halifax; Selwyn Coll., Cambridge (MA). Commonwealth Economic Cttee, 1963-65; OECD, Paris, 1965-66; IBRD, Washington and Lagos, 1966-73. Vice-Pres., European School Parents Assoc., Brussels, 1974, 1976-77. *Recreations:* mountain walking, gardening. *Address:* Avenue des Frères Legrain 23, 1150 Brussels, Belgium. *T:* 734-72-65; 81 Old Bank Road, Mirfield, West Yorkshire.

WILKINSON, Sir (David) Graham Brook, 3rd Bt *cr* 1941; *b* 18 May 1947; *s* of Sir (Leonard) David Wilkinson, 2nd Bt, DSC, and of Sylvia Ruby Eva Anne, *d* of Professor Bosley Alan Rex Gater; *S* father, 1972; *m* 1977, Sandra Caroline, *d* of Dr Richard Rossdale. *Educ:* Millfield; Christ Church, Oxford.

WILKINSON, David Lloyd; General Secretary, Cooperative Union, since 1975; *b* 28 May 1937; *m* 1960; one *s* one *d. Educ:* Royds Hall Grammar Sch. ACIS; CSD. *Address:* 29 Mountfield Road, Waterloo, Huddersfield HD5 8RA. *T:* Huddersfield 27419.

WILKINSON, Sir Denys (Haigh), Kt 1974; FRS 1956; Vice-Chancellor, University of Sussex, since 1976; *b* Leeds, Yorks, 5 September 1922; *o s* of Charles and Hilda Wilkinson; *m* 1st, 1947, Christiane Andrée Clavier (marriage dissolved, 1967); three *d*; 2nd, 1967, Helen Sellschop; two step *d. Educ:* Loughborough Gram. Sch.; Jesus Coll. Cambridge (Fellow, 1944-59, Hon Fellow, 1961). BA 1943, MA, PhD 1947, ScD 1961. British and Canadian Atomic Energy Projects, 1943-46;

Univ. Demonstrator, Cambridge, 1947-51; Univ. Lecturer, 1951-56; Reader in Nuclear Physics, Univ. of Cambridge, 1956-57; Professor of Nuclear Physics, Univ. of Oxford, 1957-59; Prof. of Experimental Physics, Univ. of Oxford, 1959-76, Head of Dept of Nuclear Physics, 1962-76; Student, Christ Church, Oxford, 1957-76, Emeritus Student, 1976. Mem. Governing Board of National Institute for Research in Nuclear Science, 1957-63 and 1964-65; Member, Science Research Council, 1967-70; Chairman: Nuclear Physics Board of SRC, 1968-70; Physics III Cttee, CERN, Geneva, 1971-75. Lectures: Welch, Houston, 1957; Scott, Cambridge Univ., 1961; Rutherford Meml, Brit. Physical Soc., 1962; Graham Young, Glasgow Univ., 1964; Queen's, Berlin, 1966; Silliman, Yale Univ., 1966; Cherwell-Simon, Oxford Univ., 1970; Goodspeed-Richard, Pennsylvania Univ., 1973; Welsh, Toronto Univ., 1975; Tizard Meml, Westminster Sch., 1975; Lauritsen Meml, Cal. Tech., 1976; Herbert Spencer, Oxford Univ., 1976; Schiff Meml, Stanford Univ., 1977; Racah Meml, Hebrew Univ. Jerusalem, 1977. Walker Ames Prof., Univ. of Washington, 1968; Battelle Distinguished Prof., Univ. of Washington, 1970-71. Holweck Medallist of the British and French Physical Socs, 1957; Hughes Medallist of the Royal Society, 1965; Bruce-Preller Prize, RSE, 1969; Bonner Prize, American Physical Soc., 1974. Hon. DSc: Univ. of Saskatchewan, 1964; Utah State Univ., 1975. Comm. Bontemps Médoc et Graves, 1973. *Publications:* Ionization Chambers and Counters, 1951; (ed) Isospin in Nuclear Physics, 1969; papers on nuclear physics and bird navigation. *Recreations:* mediæval church architecture and watching birds. *Address:* Ashcombe House, St Ann-without-Lewes, East Sussex. *T:* Lewis 4794. *Clubs:* Athenæum, Achilles.

WILKINSON, Edgar Riley, CMG 1956; FIMechE; FIEE; *b* 14 April 1898; *s* of late James Driver Wilkinson, Ashton-on-Ribble, Preston, Lancashire; *m* 1945, Frances Elizabeth, *d* of late Dr George Lambright, Shaker Heights, Ohio, USA; two *d. Educ:* Technical College, Preston. Power Station design engineer, English Electric Co., 1919-24; Cons. Engineer, Merz and McLellan, 1924-28; Deputy Commercial Manager, Central Electricity Board, 1928-37. Commercial Manager, 1937-48; Commercial Manager, British Electricity Authority, 1948-55. Dep. Chm. Balfour Beatty & Co. Ltd, 1956-67; Dir, Power Securities Corp. Ltd, 1956-68; Deputy Chairman (London Board): East African Power & Light Co., 1966-72; Kenya Power Co. Ltd, 1966-72. Pres. Assoc. of Supervising Electrical Engineers, 1944-46; Technical Adviser, Four-Power Conf., Paris, 1946; Chm. Br. Electrical Develt Assoc., 1950-51; Special rep. of IBRD (Mexico), 1954-55. *Address:* 2 Alington House, Lilliput, Poole, Dorset. *T:* Canford Cliffs 708038. *Club:* Reform.

WILKINSON, Elizabeth Mary, PhD; FBA 1972; Professor of German, University College London, 1960-76, now Emeritus; *b* 17 Sept. 1909; *d* of Frank Wilkinson and Martha E. Gilleard, Keighley, Yorks. *Educ:* Whalley Range High Sch., Manchester; Bedford Coll., London. Prof.-at-Large of Cornell Univ., 1967-. President: English Goethe Soc., 1974-; Modern Language Assoc., GB, 1964; Hon. Mem., Modern Language Assoc. of America, 1965. Korresp. Mitglied, Akademie der Wissenschaften zu Göttingen, 1973; Deutsche Akad. für Sprache und Dichtung, 1976. Hon. LLD Smith Coll., Mass, 1966; Hon. DLitt Kent, 1971. Medaille in Gold des Goethe-Instituts, 1965; Preis für Germanistik im Ausland der Deutsche Akad. für Sprache und Dichtung, 1974. *Publications:* J. E. Schlegel: A German Pioneer in Aesthetics, 1945; (with L. A. Willoughby) Goethe: Poet and Thinker, 1962; with L. A. Willoughby) Schiller: On the Aesthetic Education of Man, 1967 (German edn 1977); Models of Wholeness, 1978. *Recreations:* housekeeping and scholarship at a civilized pace at last. *Address:* 33 Queen Court, Queen Square, WC1.

WILKINSON, Prof. Frank Clare, CBE 1956; LLD; MD; ChB, BDS, DDSc, MSc; FRCS, FDS; Hon. Consultant Dental Surgeon, Eastman Dental Hospital, 1959-64, retired; Dean and Dir of Studies of Institute of Dental Surgery in British Post-graduate Medical Federation, Univ. of London, and Dir of Eastman Dental Hospital, 1950-59; Prof. of Dental Surgery, London Univ., 1952-57; Consultant Dental Surgeon to the Royal Navy, 1944; Member, Board of the Faculty of Dental Surgery, Roy. Coll. of Surgeons, 1947, Dean, 1953-56; *b* Cheshire, 31 Aug. 1889; *s* of Frank Wilkinson and Annie A. Clare; *m* 1917, Gladys Eveline Tweedie; one *d. Educ:* Wallasey Grammar School; Univ. of Liverpool. Prizes in Operative Dental Surgery and in Orthodontia; House Surgeon, Liverpool Dental Hospital, 1912; Senior Demonstrator in Operative Dental Surgery, University of Liverpool, 1919-23; Dental Tutor, University of Liverpool, 1923; Hon. Dental Surgeon, David Lewis Northern Hospital; Lecturer for the Dental Board of UK; Member, Board Dental Studies University of Liverpool; Professor of Dental Science, Dean of the Faculty of Dental

Science, and Director Dental Research Depart, University of Melbourne; Principal of the Australian College of Dentistry, 1925-33; Captain RAMC, attached Liverpool Merchants Mobile Hosp., France, 1915-19; Hon. Major AMC, 1928-33; Professor of Dental Surgery, Dean of the Turner Dental School, and Director of Dental Hospital, Manchester University, 1933-50; Hon. Adviser in Dental Surgery, Manchester Royal Infirmary, 1934-50, and St Mary's Hospitals, 1946-50; Hon. Consultant Dental Surgeon Christie Hospital and Holt Radium Institute, 1934-50; Director, Maxillo-facial Centre, NW Area, 1939-50; Surgical Specialist, EMS; Member: Dental Advisory Cttee, MEd. Research Council, 1947-60; Standing Dental Services Advisory Cttee, Central Health Council, 1948-60; Medical Sub cttee of Univ. Grants Cttee, 1952-60; Inter-departmental Cttee on Recruitment of Dental Students, 1955; Council Roy. Soc. Med. (Pres. Odont. Sect. 1959-60); General Dental Council (Chm. Educ. Cttee), 1956-59; Mem. NW Metropolitan Regional Hospital Board, 1954-60. Colyer Gold Medal, 1965. Hon. FRACDS. *Publications:* numerous articles in British Dental Journal, etc. *Recreation:* yachting. *Address:* 33 Craigmore Tower, Guildford Road, Woking, Surrey.

WILKINSON, Frederick, OBE 1968; MA; Head Master, Latymer Upper School, Hammersmith, 1937-57; *b* 18 Apr. 1891; *m* 1924, Edith Mary Previté (*d* 1968), *e d* of Professor Kennedy Orton, DSc, FRS. *Educ:* Grammar School, Dudley; Sidney Sussex College, Cambridge. Historical Tripos, Second Class; Assistant Master, Laxton School, Oundle; Senior History and House Master, Liverpool College, 1920-26; Head Master, Grammar School, Wallasey, 1927-34; Polytechnic School, W1, 1934-37; Active Service 1914-19 in France, Egypt and Italy; Captain 5th South Staffs Regt, Captain and Wing Adjutant RAF (Observers' Badge, R Aero Club Certificate, despatches); Producer of Plays and Operas to various Societies-specialised in the work of Purcell and Holst. Hon. Fellow, Roy. Commonwealth Society. *Publications:* Various articles in English and foreign periodicals on subjects connected with education, drama and film. *Recreation:* walking. *Address:* 5 The Mall, East Sheen, SW14. *T:* 01-876 6186.

WILKINSON, Prof. Sir Geoffrey, Kt 1976; FRS 1965; Professor of Inorganic Chemistry, University of London, since 1956; *b* 14 July 1921; *s* of Henry and Ruth Wilkinson; *m* 1951, Lise Sølver, *o d* of Rektor Prof. Svend Aa. Schou, Copenhagen; two *d. Educ:* Todmorden Gram. Sch (Royal Scholar, 1939); Imperial Coll., London; USA. Junior Scientific Officer, Nat. Res. Council, Atomic Energy Div., Canada, 1943-46; Research Fellow: Radiation Lab., Univ. of Calif, Berkeley, Calif, USA, 1946-50; Chemistry Dept, Mass Inst. of Technology, Cambridge, Mass, USA, 1950-51; Asst Prof. of Chemistry, Harvard Univ., Cambridge, Mass, 1951-56; Arthur D. Little Visiting Prof., MIT, 1967; William Draper Harkins' Memorial Lectr, Univ. of Chicago, 1968; Leermakers Lectr, Wesleyan Univ., 1975; John Simon Guggenheim Fellow, 1954. Foreign Member: Roy. Danish Acad. of Science and Arts (math.-phys section), 1968; Amer. Acad. of Arts and Sciences, 1970; Foreign Assoc., Nat. Acad. of Scis, 1975; Centennial Foreign Fellow, Amer. Chem. Soc., 1976. Hon. DSc: Edinburgh, 1975; Granada, 1976. American Chem. Soc. Award in Inorganic Chemistry, 1965; Lavoisier Medal, Société Chimique de France, 1968; Chem. Soc. Award for Transition Metal Chemistry, 1972; (jtly) Nobel Prize for Chemistry, 1973; Consejero de Honor, Spanish Council for Scientific Res., 1974. *Publications:* (jtly) Advanced Inorganic Chemistry: a Comprehensive Text, 1962, 3rd edn 1972; Basic Inorganic Chemistry, 1976; numerous in Physical Review, Journal of the American Chemical Society, etc. *Address:* Chemistry Department, Imperial College, SW7. *T:* 01-589 5111.

WILKINSON, Sir Graham Brook; *see* Wilkinson, Sir D. G. B.

WILKINSON, Sir Harold, Kt 1964; CMG 1946; retired as: Managing Director, The "Shell" Transport and Trading Co. Ltd; Director: The Shell Petroleum Co. Ltd; Shell Petroleum NV; Guinness Mahon Holdings; *b* 24 Feb. 1903; *s* of Charles Robert Wilkinson, MA Oxon, ICS, Ramsey, Isle of Man; *m* 1939, Marie Frances Elie; three *s* one *d* (and one *step-d*). *Educ:* King William's Coll., Isle of Man. Joined Royal Dutch/Shell Group of Cos, 1922; formerly: Man. Dir and Dep. Chm., The "Shell" Transport and Trading Co. Ltd; Man. Dir, Shell Petroleum Co. Ltd; Principal Dir, Bataafse Petroleum Mij. NV; Pres., Asiatic Petroleum Corp., USA; Chm., Shell Caribbean Petroleum Co., USA; Pres., Canadian Shell; Chm., Shell Tankers; Dir, Shell Oil Co., USA; retd 1964. Petroleum Rep. in Washington of UK Govt, 1941-45. US Medal of Freedom with Bronze Palm, 1951; Kt Comdr Order of Merit, Ecuador; Comdr Order of Oranje-Nassau, 1964. *Recreations:* golf, sailing and shooting. *Address:* La Sologne en Ballègue, Epalinges 1066, Vaud, Switzerland. *Clubs:* Hurlingham; Sunningdale; St

Andrews; Royal Yacht Squadron; Royal Bermuda Yacht (Bermuda).

WILKINSON, Rt. Rev. Heber; *see* Wilkinson, Rt Rev. C. R. H.

WILKINSON, Ven. Hubert Seed; Archdeacon of Liverpool, 1951-70; Archdeacon Emeritus, since 1971; Residentiary Canon, 1968-70; *e s* of late Rev. John and Margaret Wilkinson; *m* Frances Elizabeth, 4th *d* of Dr J. Staveley Dick; two *d. Educ:* St John's Coll., Durham Univ. (Exhibnr). MA (2nd cl. Hons English Lit.; 2nd cl. Hons Modern Hist.). Curate of Colne, 1925-29; Rector of Harpurhey, Manchester, 1929-36; Rector of Chester-le-Street, 1936-40; Rural Dean of Chester-le-Street, 1937-40; Vicar of Allerton, Liverpool, 1940-47; Canon Diocesan of Liverpool Cathedral, 1945-47, and 1951-68; Examining Chaplain to Bishop of Liverpool, 1945-47 and 1955-70; Vicar of Winster, 1947-48; Archdeacon of Westmorland, 1947-51; Vicar of: Ambleside with Rydal, 1948-50; St Mary's, Grassendale, 1951-68; late Hon. Canon of Carlisle Cathedral and Director of Religious Education. *Address:* Hammer Cottage, Warborough, Oxon OX9 8DJ. *T:* Warborough 8558.

WILKINSON, James Hardy, FRS 1969; MA Cantab, ScD; Individual Merit Chief Scientific Officer, National Physical Laboratory, Teddington, since 1974; *b* 27 Sept. 1919; *s* of J. W. and K. C. Wilkinson; *m* 1945, Heather Nora Ware; one *s* one *d. Educ:* Sir Joseph Williamson's Mathematical Sch., Rochester; Trinity Coll., Cambridge. Major Scholar (Maths) Trinity Coll., 1935; Pemberton Prize, 1937; Mathison Prize, 1939; BA 1939, MA Cantab 1942; ScD 1962. War service: Mathematical Laboratory, Cambridge, 1940-43; Armament Research Dept, Fort Halstead, 1943-46. Mathematics Div., Nat. Physical Lab. (working on design, construction and use of electronic computers), 1946-; DCSO, 1962-74. Visiting Professor: Univ. of Michigan, numerous occasions, 1957-73; Stanford Univ., 1961, 1967, 1969. Founder Fellow: Inst. of Mathematics and its Applications (Vice-Pres., 1973-75, Hon. Fellow 1977); British Computer Society (Distinguished FBCS, 1973). Mem. Council, Royal Soc., 1974-. Visited USSR Academy of Sciences, as a leading scientist, 1968. Hon. DTech Brunel, 1971; Hon. DSc Heriot-Watt, 1973; DUniv Essex, 1977. A. M. Turing award, Assoc. for Computing Machinery, 1970; J. von Neumann award, Soc. for Applied Maths, 1970; Engineer of Distinction, Engineers Jt Council, 1974; Distinguished Lectr, Univ. of Waterloo, 1976; G. E. Forsythe Award, Stanford Univ., 1977. Foreign Hon. Mem., Amer. Acad. of Arts and Sciences, 1974. *Publications:* Rounding Errors in Algebraic Processes, 1963; The Algebraic Eigenvalue Problem, 1965; Linear Algebra, 1971; chapters in six books on computers and numerical analysis; numerous papers in learned jls. *Recreations:* music, travel. *Address:* 40 Atbara Road, Teddington, Mddx. *T:* 01-977 1207.

WILKINSON, John Arbuthnot Ducane; Senior Sales Executive, Eagle Aircraft Services Ltd, since 1977; *b* 23 Sept. 1940; 2nd *s* of late Denys Wilkinson and Gillian Wilkinson, Eton College; *m* 1969, Paula Adey, *o d* of Joseph Adey, East Herrington, Co. Durham. *Educ:* Eton (King's Scholar); RAF Coll., Cranwell; Churchill Coll., Cambridge (2nd cl. Hons Mod. Hist.; MA). Flight Cadet, RAF Coll., Cranwell, 1959-61 (Philip Sassoon Meml Prize, qualified French Interpreter); commnd 1961; Flying Instructor, No 8 FTS, Swinderby, 1962; resigned Oct. 1962. Churchill Coll., Cambridge, Oct. 1962-65. Trooper, 21st Special Air Service Regt (Artists'), TA, 1963-65; rejoined RAF 1965; Flying Instructor, RAF Coll., Cranwell, 1966-67; Tutor, Stanford Univ.'s British Campus, 1967; ADC to Comdr 2nd Allied Tactical Air Force, Germany, 1967; resigned RAF, 1967. Head of Universities' Dept, Conservative Central Office, 1967-68; Aviation Specialist, Cons. Research Dept, 1969; Senior Administration Officer (Anglo-French Jaguar Project), Preston Div., British Aircraft Corp., 1969-70; Tutor, Open Univ., 1970-71; Vis. Lectr, OCTU RAF Henlow, 1971-75; aviation consultant, 1972-74; Chief Flying Instructor, Skywork Ltd, Stansted, 1974-75; Gen. Manager, General Aviation Div., Brooklands Aviation Ltd, 1975-76; PA to Chm., BAC, 1976-77. MP (C) Bradford W, 1970-Feb. 1974; Jt Sec., Cons. Parly Aviation Cttee, 1972-74; Sec., Cons. Parly Defence Cttee, 1972-74; Member Select Committee on: Race Relations and Immigration, 1972-74; Sci. and Technol., 1972-74. Contested (C) Bradford W, Oct. 1974; Prospective Parly Cand. (C) Ruislip, Northwood, 1975-. *Publications:* various pamphlets and articles on defence and politics. *Recreation:* flying. *Address:* c/o Lloyds Bank Ltd, Trinity Street, Cambridge. *Club:* Royal Air Force.

WILKINSON, Dr John Frederick, FRCP, MD (Gold Medal), ChB, BSc (1st Cl. Hons Chem.), MSc, PhD Manchester, CChem; FRIC; author; Consulting Physician; Consulting Physician, United Manchester Hospitals; late Director of Department of Hæmatology, University and Royal Infirmary of

Manchester; late Reader in Hæmatology, and Lecturer in Systematic Medicine, Univ. of Manchester; late Hon. Consulting Hæmatologist, The Christie Cancer Hospital, Holt Radium Institute and The Duchess of York Hospital for Babies, Manchester; Hon. Editor, Manchester Medical Society; formerly President, European Hæmatological Soc.; Life Councillor and Founder, International Hæmatological Soc.; *b* Oldham, 10 June 1897; *s* of John Frederick Wilkinson, Oldham and Stockport, and Annie, *d* of late Reverend E. Wareham, DD, Rector of Heaton Mersey; *m* 1964, Marion Crossfield, Major, WRAC. *Educ:* Arnold School, Blackpool; University of Manchester; Manchester Royal Infirmary. Served European War, 1916-19, RNAS, RN, and later attached Tank Corps, France; also served on Vindictive at Zeebrugge, 1918, and ballotted for Victoria Cross award; Chemical Research Manchester University, 1919-28; Medical Research since 1929; Regional Transfusion Officer, and Regional Adviser on Resuscitation, Ministry of Health, NW Region, 1940-46. Graduate Scholarship (Chemistry), 1920; Dalton Research Scholarship; Sir Clement Royds Research Fellowship; Medical (Graduate) Scholarship, 1923; Hon. Demonstrator in Crystallography; Research Asst in Physiology; Sidney Renshaw Physiology Prizeman; Gold Medal for Dissertation in Med., 1931, University of Manchester. Oliver Sharpey Lectr, 1948, and Samuel Gee Lectr, 1977, Royal College of Physicians, London; Liveryman Worshipful Society of Apothecaries, London; Freeman City of London. Hon. DSc Bradford, 1976. *Publications:* scientific and medical publications since 1920 in English and foreign journals, etc. Sections on Blood Diseases, Anæmias and Leukæmias in British Encyclopædia of Medical Practice, 1936, 1950 and yearly supplements since 1951, and in Encyclopædia of General Practice, 1964; Section on Emergencies in Blood Diseases, in Medical Emergencies, 1948 to date; ed Modern Trends in Diseases of the Blood, 1955, 1975; The Diagnosis and Treatment of Blood Diseases, 1973; ed, Section in Clinical Surgery, 1967; articles on antiques, Old English and continental apothecaries' drug jars, etc, in miscellaneous medical and art jls, 1970-77. *Recreations:* motoring, antiques, travel, zoos, tropical fish keeping, lecturing. *Address:* Mobberley Old Hall, Knutsford, Cheshire WA16 7AB. *T:* Mobberley 2111; 5 Lorne Street, Manchester M13 0EZ. *T:* 061-273 4253. *Clubs:* Savage, Lansdowne.

WILKINSON, Kenneth Grahame, Hon. DSc, BSc, CEng, FCGI, FRAeS, FCIT, FSLAET, FRSA; Member, British Airways Board, 1971-72 and since 1976; Engineering Director, British Airways, since 1976; Director, Airways Aero Associations Ltd; *b* 14 July 1917; *s* of Bertie and Dorothy Wilkinson; *m* 1941, Mary Holman Victory; one *s* one *d*. *Educ:* Shooter's Hill; Imperial Coll. (BSc, DIC). Sen. Scientific Officer, RAE, Farnborough, 1945; Performance and Analysis Supt, BEA, 1946-52; Manager, Fleet Planning Br., BEA, 1960; Chief Engr, BEA, 1964; Mem. Bd, BEA, 1968-72; Dep. Chief Exec. and Man. Dir (BEA Mainline), BEA, 1971-72, Chm. and Chief Exec., BEA, Sept.-Nov. 1972; Mem. Bd, BOAC, 1972; Rolls Royce (1971) Ltd: Man. Dir, 1972-74; Vice-Chm., 1974-76. Chm., BGA Techn. Cttee, 1946-48; Chm., BGA, 1970, Vice-Pres., 1972; Pres. RAeS, 1972. Member: Cranwell Adv. Bd, 1970-; Council, Cranfield Inst of Technology, 1971. *Publications:* Sailplanes of the World (with B. S. Shenstone): Vol. 1, 1960; Vol. 2, 1963; articles and papers to: Jl of Royal Aeronautical Soc.; Aircraft Engineering. *Recreations:* gliding, swimming, gardening, travel. *Address:* Speedbird House, London (Heathrow) Airport, Hounslow, Mddx.

WILKINSON, (Lancelot) Patrick, MA; FRSL; Fellow, King's College, Cambridge; Lecturer in Classics, 1936-67, Reader in Latin Literature, 1967-69, Brereton Reader in Classics, 1969-74, Orator, 1958-74, Cambridge University; *b* 1 June 1907; *s* of late Lancelot George William and Kate Wilkinson; *m* 1944, Sydney Alix, *d* of late Sir Herbert Eason, CB, CMG; two adopted *s*. *Educ:* Charterhouse; King's College, Cambridge, 1st Class Classical Tripos, Parts I and II; Craven Scholar, 1929; Chancellor's Classical Medallist, 1930; Craven Student, 1930; Fellow of King's College, Cambridge, 1932; Dean, 1934-45; attached to Foreign Office, 1939-45; Asst Tutor, 1945-46; Senior Tutor, 1946-56; Vice-Provost, 1961-65. Chm., Cambridge Greek Play Cttee, 1973- (Sec., 1938-63); Dep. for Public Orator, 1950-51, 1957; Member of the Council of the Senate, 1952-56; Chm. of Classical Faculty, 1969, 1970; Foundation Mem. Council, New Hall, Cambridge, 1954-65; Governor, Queen Mary Coll., London, 1954-57; Mem. Governing Body, Charterhouse School, 1954-69. Mem. Conseil Consultatif de Fondation Hardt, Geneva, 1959-63. A Vice-Pres., Classical Assoc. (Pres., 1971-72). Lord Northcliffe Meml Lectr, UCL, 1976; Donald Dudley Meml Lectr, Univ. of Birmingham, 1976. *Publications:* Horace and his Lyric Poetry, 1945; Letters of Cicero, 1949; Ovid Recalled, 1955 (abr. as Ovid Surveyed, 1962); Golden Latin Artistry, 1963;

(with R. H. Bulmer) Register of King's College, Cambridge, 1919-58, 1963; words for Benjamin Britten's *Cantata Misericordium,* 1963; The Georgics of Virgil, 1969; The Roman Experience, 1974; (with R. H. Bulmer) Register of King's College, Cambridge, 1945-70, 1974; articles in classical jls. *Recreations:* reading, travel. *Address:* King's College, Cambridge. *T:* 50411; 21 Marlowe Road, Cambridge. *T:* 63188.

WILKINSON, Sir Martin; see Wilkinson, Sir R. F. M.

WILKINSON, Nicolas Christopher Henry B.; see Browne-Wilkinson.

WILKINSON, Patrick; see Wilkinson, L. P.

WILKINSON, Peter; HM Diplomatic Service; Foreign and Commonwealth Office, since 1971; *b* 25 May 1918; *s* of late Fred and Doris Wilkinson; *m* 1944, Anne Sutherland; two *s*. *Educ:* Barnsley Holgate Grammar School. Inland Revenue, 1936-38; Air Min., 1938-40; RAF, 1940-46; Control Office for Germany and Austria, 1946-47; FO, 1947-48; 2nd Sec., British Embassy, Bangkok, 1948-50; Asst Political Adviser to Allied Mil. Govt, Trieste, 1950-52; FO, 1952-55; 1st Sec., Baghdad, 1955-58; FO, 1958-61; 1st Sec., Washington, 1961-64; Counsellor, Tehran, 1964-68; Inspector of Diplomatic Service Establishments, 1968-69; seconded to Board of Trade, 1969-71. *Recreations:* ski-ing, travel, music. *Address:* 65 Cornwall Gardens, SW7. *T:* 01-937 2936. *Club:* Travellers'.

WILKINSON, Sir Peter (Allix), KCMG 1970 (CMG 1960); DSO 1944; OBE 1944; HM Diplomatic Service, retired; *b* 15 April 1914; *s* of late Captain Osborn Cecil Wilkinson; *m* 1945, Mary Theresa, *d* of late Algernon Villiers; two *d*. *Educ:* Rugby; Corpus Christi Coll., Cambridge. Commissioned in 2nd Bn Royal Fusiliers, 1935; active service in Poland (despatches), France, Italy and Balkans; retired with rank of Lieut-Colonel, 1947. Entered HM Foreign Service, appointed 1st Secretary at British Legation, Vienna, 1947; 1st Secretary at British Embassy, Washington, 1952; Secretary-General of Heads of Government Meeting at Geneva, 1955; Counsellor, HM Embassy, Bonn, 1955; Counsellor, Foreign Office, 1960-63; Under-Secretary, Cabinet Office, 1963-64; Senior Civilian Instructor at the Imperial Defence Coll., 1964-66; Ambassador to Vietnam, 1966-67; Under-Secretary, Foreign Office, 1967-68; Chief of Administration, HM Diplomatic Service, 1968-70; Ambassador to Vienna, 1970-71. Cross of Valour (Poland), 1940; Order of White Lion (IV Class) (Czechoslovakia), 1945. *Recreations:* gardening, sailing, fishing. *Address:* Mill House, Charing, Kent. *T:* Charing 2306. *Clubs:* White's, Army and Navy.

WILKINSON, Sir (Robert Francis) Martin, Kt 1969; Chairman: the Stock Exchange, London, 1965-March 1973; The Stock Exchange, March-June 1973 (Deputy Chairman, 1963-65); Chairman, Federation of Stock Exchanges in Great Britain and Ireland, 1965-73; *b* 4 June 1911; *e s* of late Sir Robert Pelham Wilkinson and Phyllis Marion Wilkinson; *m* 1936, Dora Esme, *d* of late William John Arendt and late Mrs Arendt; three *d*. *Educ:* Repton. Member, Stock Exchange, 1933; Partner in de Zoete & Gorton, 1936; Senior Partner, de Zoete & Bevan, 1970-76; Member of Council, Stock Exchange, 1959. Chairman: Altifund, 1976-; City of London Brwery Trust, 1977-. One of HM Lieutenants, City of London, 1973-. Served with RAF 1940-45. *Recreations:* cricket, gardening. *Address:* Kixes, Sharpthorne, Sussex. *T:* Sharpthorne 810370. *Clubs:* City of London, Gresham.

WILKINSON, Sydney Frank, CB 1951; Director of Administration, National Research Development Corporation, 1955-65; *b* 14 Dec. 1894; *s* of Charles James Carey Wilkinson; *m* 1924, Gladys Millicent Boorsma; one *s*. *Educ:* Strand Sch.; King's Coll., London. Entered Civil Service, National Health Insurance Commission, 1913; Commissioned RFA, 1918; Private Secretary to Minister of Food, 1920; Secretary to Parliamentary Conference on Reform of Licensing Law, 1921; Assistant Private Secretary to Sir Kingsley Wood, 1935; loaned to National Fitness Council, 1937; Private Secretary to Mr Walter Elliot and Mr Malcolm MacDonald, 1938-40; Security Executive, 1940-41; Director of Public Relations, Ministry of Health, 1941-43. Under-Secretary for Housing, Ministry of Housing and Local Government, 1951-54 (Ministry of Local Government and Planning, 1951; Ministry of Health, 1947-51). *Recreation:* golf. *Address:* 51 Cornwall Road, Cheam, Surrey SM2 6DU. *T:* 01-642 0374.

WILKINSON, Sir Thomas Crowe S.; see Spenser-Wilkinson.

WILKS, Jean Ruth Fraser, CBE 1977; Mistress, King Edward VI High School for Girls, Birmingham, 1965-77; *b* 14 April 1917; *d* of Mark Wilks. *Educ:* North London Collegiate Sch.; Somerville Coll., Oxford (MA). Assistant Mistress: Truro High Sch., 1940-43; James Allen's Girls' Sch., Dulwich, 1943-51; Head Mistress, Hertfordshire and Essex High Sch., Bishop's Stortford, Hertfordshire, 1951-64. Pres., Assoc. of Head Mistresses, 1972-74; Chm., Academic Staffing Cttee, 1976-; Member: Public Schools Commn, 1968-70; Council, Univ. of Birmingham, 1971-; Governing Council of Schools Council, 1972-75; Adv. Council on Supply and Trng of Teachers, 1973-; Educn Cttee, Royal Coll. of Nursing, 1973-. *Address:* 4 Haywood Road, Oxford OX2 8LW. *Club:* Naval and Military.

WILKS, Stanley David; Chief Executive, British Overseas Trade Board, since 1975; *b* 1 Aug. 1920; *s* of Walter Arthur and Sarah Wilks; *m* 1947, Dorothy Irene Adamthwaite; one *s* one *d. Educ:* Polytechnic Sch., London. Royal Armoured Corps, 1939-46; service with 48th Bn, Royal Tank Regt; 3rd Carabiniers, Imphal, 1944. Home Office, 1946-50; Board of Trade: Asst Principal, 1950; Principal 1951; Asst Sec. 1961; Under-Secretary: ECGD, 1969-72; DTI, later Dept of Trade, 1972-75, airports policy, 1974-75. Vice-Chm., Internat. Tin Council, 1968-69; Mem. Exec. Cttee, British Council, 1975-. *Recreations:* sailing, music. *Address:* 6 Foxgrove Avenue, Beckenham, Kent. *T:* 01-650 7728. *Club:* Medway Yacht.

WILL, Ronald Kerr; Deputy Keeper of Her Majesty's Signet, since 1975; Partner, Dundas & Wilson, CS, Edinburgh; *b* 22 March 1918; 3rd *s* of late James Alexander Will, WS and late Bessie Kennedy Salmon, Dumfries; *m* 1964, Margaret Joyce, *d* of late D. Alan Stevenson, BSc, FRSE; two *s. Educ:* Merchiston Castle Sch.; Edinburgh Univ. Commnd King's Own Scottish Borderers, 1940; served with 1st Bn and in Staff appts (despatches); psc; GSO2. Writer to the Signet, 1950. Director: Scottish Equitable Life Assce Soc.; Scottish Investment Trust Co. Ltd and other companies; Mem. Council on Tribunals, 1971-76 and Chm. of Scottish Cttee, 1972-76. Governor, Merchiston Castle Sch., 1953-76. *Recreations:* shooting, fishing. *Address:* 31 Heriot Row, Edinburgh EH3 6ES. *T:* 031-225 4169. *Club:* New (Edinburgh).

WILLAN, Edward Gervase, CMG 1964; HM Diplomatic Service, retired; Ambassador to Czechoslovakia, 1974-77; *b* 17 May 1917; *er s* of late Captain F. G. L. Willan, RNR; *m* 1944, Mary Bickley Joy, *d* of late Lieut-Colonel H. A. Joy, IAOC. *Educ:* Radley; Pembroke Coll., Cambridge (Exhibitioner, MA). Indian Civil Service, 1939-47; 2nd Secretary (from 1948, 1st Secretary) on staff of UK High Commissioner, New Delhi, 1947-49; appointed to HM Diplomatic Service, 1948; Foreign Office, 1949-52; 1st Secretary, HM Embassy, The Hague, 1953-55; 1st Secretary, HM Legation, Bucharest, 1956-58 (Chargé d'Affaires, 1956, 1957 and 1958); Head of Communications Dept, FO, 1958-62; Political Adviser to Hong Kong Government, 1962-65; Head of Scientific Relations Dept, FO, 1966-68; Minister, Lagos, 1968-70; Ambassador at Rangoon, 1970-74. *Recreations:* travel, walking, gardening. *Address:* 14 Markham Street, SW3. *Club:* United Oxford & Cambridge University.

WILLAN, Group Captain Frank Andrew, CBE 1960; DFC 1940; DL; RAF (retd); Chairman, Wiltshire County Council; *b* 21 Dec. 1915; *s* of late Brig. Robert Hugh Willan, DSO, MC; *m* 1945, Joan, *d* of late L. G. Wickham Legg, New College, Oxford; two *s* one *d. Educ:* Eton; Magdalen Coll., Oxford. Served War of 1939-45, RAF Bomber Command. CO, Oxford Univ. Air Sqdn, 1951-53; CO, RAF Feltwell, 1958-60; retd, 1960. Mem., Wilts County Council, 1961 (Chm. Educn Cttee, 1965-68; Vice-Chm., CC, 1968; Chm., 1973); DL Wilts, 1968. Mem. Wessex Regional Hosp. Bd, 1970-74; Vice-Chm., Wessex RHA, 1974-; Chm., Salisbury Diocesan Bd of Finance, 1970-; Chm., Jt Advisory Cttee, Local Authorities' Purchasing, 1970-. *Recreations:* shooting, gardening. *Address:* Bridges, Teffont, Salisbury SP3 5RG. *T:* Teffont 230. *Clubs:* Army and Navy; Leander (Henley).

WILLAN, Prof. Thomas Stuart, MA, BLitt, DPhil; Professor of Economic History, University of Manchester, 1961-73, now Emeritus; *b* 3 Jan. 1910; 3rd *s* of Matthew Willan and Jane (*née* Stuart); unmarried. *Educ:* Queen Elizabeth's Sch., Kirkby Lonsdale; The Queen's Coll., Oxford. Asst Lecturer, School of Economics and Commerce, Dundee, 1934-35; University of Manchester: Asst Lecturer in History, 1935-45; Lecturer in History, 1945-47; Senior Lecturer in History, 1947-49; Reader in History, 1949-61. *Publications:* River Navigation in England, 1600-1750, 1936; The English Coasting Trade, 1600-1750, 1938; (ed with E. W. Crossley) Three Seventeenth-century Yorkshire Surveys, 1941; The Navigation of the Great Ouse between St Ives and Bedford in the Seventeenth Century, 1946; The

Navigation of the River Weaver in the Eighteenth Century, 1951; The Muscovy Merchants of 1555, 1953; The Early History of the Russia Company, 1553-1603, 1956; Studies in Elizabethan Foreign Trade, 1959; (ed) A Tudor Book of Rates, 1962; The Early History of the Don Navigation, 1965; An Eighteenth-Century Shopkeeper, Abraham Dent of Kirkby Stephen, 1970; The Inland Trade, 1976; articles in English Historical Review, Economic History Review, etc. *Address:* 3 Raynham Avenue, Didsbury, Manchester M20 0BW. *T:* 061-445 4771. *Club:* Penn.

WILLASEY-WILSEY, Maj.-Gen. Anthony Patrick, CB 1970; MBE 1948; MC 1956; Major-General, Commando Forces Royal Marines, Plymouth, 1968-70, retired; *b* 20 Sept. 1920; *e s* of late Colonel F. H. Willasey-Wilsey, MC, 8th Gurkha Rifles; *m* 1948, Dorothy, *y d* of Dr R. B. M. Yates, Market Drayton, Salop; two *s. Educ:* Repton Sch. Commissioned in RM, Jan. 1939; HMS Rodney, 1940-42; HMS Howe, 1943; 47 Commando, Belgium and Holland, 1944-45. Instructor, RMA, Sandhurst, 1948-50; 40 Commando, Malayan Emergency, 1951-52 (despatches); Staff Coll., Camberley, 1954; 40 Commando, Cyprus and Suez, 1956-58; DAA and QMG, HQ 3 Commando Bde, ME, 1958; jssc, 1961; CO, 43 Commando, 1962-63; G 1 Plans, MoD, 1964-65; Comdr, 3 Commando Bde, Far East, 1965-66. IDC, 1967. MBIM 1970. *Address:* The Dun Cow Cottage, Market Drayton, Salop. *T:* Market Drayton 2360. *Club:* Army and Navy.

WILLATT, Sir (Robert) Hugh, Kt 1972; Member Council and Management Committee, Royal Court Theatre (English Stage Company), since 1976; *b* 25 April 1909; *m* 1945, Evelyn Gibbs, ARE, ARCA, (Rome Scholar); no *c. Educ:* Repton; Pembroke Coll., Oxford (MA). Admitted a Solicitor, 1934; Partner in family firm of Hunt, Dickins and Willatt, Nottingham, and later Partner in Lewis, Silkin & Partners, Westminster. Served War of 1939-45, in RAF. Member BBC Midland Regional Adv. Council, 1953-58; Member Arts Council Drama Panel, 1955-68 (Chairman, 1960-68); Arts Council of Great Britain: Member, 1958-68; Secretary-General, 1968-75; (at various times) Member Board: National Theatre; Mercury Trust Ltd (Ballet Rambert); Nottingham Theatre Trust Ltd. FRSA 1974. Hon. MA, University of Nottingham. *Address:* St Peter's Wharf, Hammersmith Terrace, W6. *Club:* Garrick.

WILLCOCK, Kenneth Milner, QC 1972; His Honour Judge Willcock; a Circuit Judge, since 1972. MA; BCL. Called to Bar, Inner Temple, 1950. Dep. Chm., Somerset QS, 1969-71; a Recorder of the Crown Court, 1972. *Address:* Queen Elizabeth Building, Temple, EC4Y 9BS.

WILLCOCKS, Sir David (Valentine), Kt 1977; CBE 1971; MC 1944; MA, MusB (Cantab), FRCO, FRCM, FRSCM; Director, Royal College of Music, since 1974; Musical Director of the Bach Choir since 1960; General Editor, OUP Church Music, since 1961; *b* 30 Dec. 1919; *s* of late T. H. Willcocks; *m* 1947, Rachel Gordon, *d* of late Rev. A. C. Blyth, Fellow of Selwyn Coll., Cambridge; two *s* two *d. Educ:* Clifton Coll.; King's Coll., Cambridge. Chorister, Westminster Abbey, 1929-33; Scholar, Clifton Coll., 1934-38; FRCO, 1938; Scholar at College of St Nicolas (RSCM), 1938-39; Organ Scholar, King's Coll., Cambridge, 1939-40; Open Foundation Scholarship, King's Coll., Cambridge, 1940; Stewart of Rannoch Scholarship, 1940. Served War of 1939-45, 5th Bn DCLI, 1940-45. Organ Scholar, King's Coll., Cambridge, 1945-47; Fellow of King's Coll., Cambridge, 1947-51; Organist of Salisbury Cathedral, 1947-50; Master of the Choristers and Organist, Worcester Cathedral, 1950-57; Fellow and Organist, King's Coll., Cambridge, 1957-73; Univ. Lectr in Music, Cambridge Univ., 1957-74; Univ. Organist, Cambridge Univ., 1958-74. Conductor: Cambridge Philharmonic Soc., 1947; City of Birmingham Choir, 1950-57; Bradford Festival Choral Soc., 1957-74; Cambridge Univ. Musical Soc., 1958-73. President, Royal College of Organists, 1966-68. Hon. RAM; Hon. FRNCM 1977; Hon. FTCL; Hon. Fellow, Royal Canadian College of Organists, 1967. Hon. MA Bradford, 1973; Hon. DMus: Exeter, 1976; Leicester, 1977. *Recreation:* golf. *Address:* 2 Ennismore Gardens, SW7. *Club:* Athenæum.

WILLEBRANDS, His Eminence Cardinal Johannes Gerardus Maria; President, Secretariat for Promoting Christian Unity, since 1969; Archbishop of Utrecht and Primate of Holland, since 1975; *b* Netherlands, 4 Sept. 1909. *Educ:* Warmond Seminary, Holland; Angelicum, Rome (Dr Phil.). Priest, 1934; Chaplain, Begijnhof Church, Amsterdam, 1937-40; Prof. of Philosophy, Warmond, 1940; Director, 1945; Pres., St Willibrord Assoc., 1946; organised Catholic Conf. on Ecumenical Questions, 1951; Sec., Vatican Secretariat for Promoting Christian Unity, 1960; Titular Bishop of Mauriana, 1964; Cardinal, 1969; Cardinal with the Title of St Sebastian, Martyr, 1975. Hon. Dr of Letters: Notre Dame Univ.; St Louis

Univ.; St Olaf Coll., USA; Hon. Dr of Theology: Catholic Univ. of Louvain; Leningrad Theological Acad. *Publications:* Oecuménisme et Problèmes Actuels; reports on the ecumenical situation and articles on inter-church relationships. *Address:* Via dell'Erba 1, Rome 00193, Italy; Maliebaan 40, PO Box 13000, Utrecht, Netherlands.

WILLESDEN, Bishop Suffragan of, since 1974; **Rt. Rev. Geoffrey Hewlett Thompson;** *b* 14 Aug. 1929; *o s* of Lt-Col R. R. Thompson, MC, RAMC; *m* 1954, Elisabeth Joy Fausitt, *d* of Col G. F. and Dr Frances Taylor; two *s* two *d. Educ:* Aldenham Sch.; Trinity Hall, Cambridge (MA); Cuddesdon Theol College. 2nd Lieut, Queen's Own Royal West Kent Regt, 1948-49 (Nat. Service). Ordained 1954. Curate, St Matthew, Northampton, 1954; Vicar: St Augustine, Wisbech, 1959; St Saviour, Folkestone, 1966. Vice-Chm., Community and Race Relations Unit, BCC, 1976-. *Recreations:* fell walking, reading, singing. *Address:* 173 Willesden Lane, NW6 7YN. *T:* 01-451 0189

WILLESEE, Senator the Hon. Donald Robert; Member of Senate for Western Australia since 1949; *b* 14 April 1916; *m;* four *s* two *d. Educ:* Carnarvon, Western Australia. Special Minister of State, Minister assisting Prime Minister, Minister assisting Minister for Foreign Affairs and Vice-Pres. of Exec. Council, 1972-73; Minister for Foreign Affairs, 1973-75; Leader of Opposition in the Senate, 1966-67; Deputy Leader of Opposition in Senate, 1969-72; Deputy Leader of Govt in Senate, 1972. *Recreation:* swimming. *Address:* 25 Walton Place, Quinns Rocks, Western Australia 6065.

WILLETT, Archibald Anthony; Bursar, St Antony's College, Oxford, since 1977; Director, Eurotech Group of Companies; Director and Counsellor, Arab-British Chamber of Commerce; *b* 27 Jan. 1924; *s* of Reginald Beckett Willett and Mabel Alice (*née* Plaister); *m* 1948, Doris Marjorie Peat; one *s* one *d. Educ:* Oswestry High Sch.; Southall Grammar School. Lloyds Bank Ltd, 1940; Great Western Railway Co., 1941-42 and 1947-48; RAF (Signals Branch), 1942-47; Cable & Wireless Ltd, 1948-77; Dir, 1967-77; Dep. Man. Dir, 1971-72; Man. Dir, 1973-77. MA Oxon 1977; FCIS 1963; FBIM 1975. *Recreations:* home and garden, local community affairs, walking. *Address:* (office) St Antony's College, Oxford. *T:* Oxford 59651; (home) The Forge, 55 Corn Street, Witney, Oxon. *T:* Witney 2521. *Clubs:* Royal Automobile; Exiles' (Twickenham).

WILLETT, Prof. Frederick John, DSC 1944; Vice-Chancellor, Griffith University, Queensland, since 1972; *b* 26 Feb. 1922; *s* of E. Willett; *m* 1949, Jane Cunningham Westwater; one *s* two *d. Educ:* Fitzwilliam House, Cambridge. MA (Cantab), MBA (Melb.). Asst Director of Research in Industrial Management, Univ. of Cambridge, 1957-62; Sidney Myer Prof. of Commerce and Business Administration, Univ. of Melbourne, 1962-72, now Emeritus. Pro Vice-Chancellor, University of Melbourne, 1966-72. Hon. LLD Melbourne 1973; FAIM. *Publications:* many articles and papers. *Address:* Griffith University, Nathan, Queensland 4111, Australia. *T:* Brisbane 275 7111. *Clubs:* Melbourne (Melbourne); Queensland (Brisbane).

WILLETT, Guy William; a Recorder of the Crown Court, since 1971; *b* 10 June 1913; *y s* of late William and late Florence Mary Anne Willett; *m* 1945, Elizabeth Evelyn Joan Radford; one *s* two *d. Educ:* Malvern; Gonville and Caius Coll., Cambridge (BA). Called to Bar, 1937; Western Circuit, 1938; Head of Chambers, 1961. Chm., Halstead Sch., 1958-74. *Recreations:* cricket, sailing, golf, visiting Alderney. *Address:* Trevarno, Danes Hill, Woking, Surrey GU22 7HQ. *T:* Woking 60877; Francis Taylor Building, Temple, EC4. *T:* 01-353 2182. *Clubs:* Hampshire (Winchester); Royal Albert Yacht, Woking Golf, Westfield and District Cricket (Pres. 1946-74), Admiralty Ferry Crew Assoc., Alderney Golf, Alderney Sailing, Alderney Society, Bar Yacht, Bar Golf.

WILLEY, family name of **Baron Barnby.**

WILLEY, Prof. Basil, MA (Cantab); FBA 1947; FRSL 1950; Hon. LittD (Manchester), 1948; King Edward VII Professor of English Literature, University of Cambridge, 1946-64; Hon. Fellow, Pembroke College, 1964 (Fellow, 1935); President, 1958-64; *b* 25 July 1897; *s* of William Herbert Willey and Alice Ann Le Gros; *m* 1923, Zélie Murlis Ricks; two *s* two *d. Educ:* University College Sch., Hampstead. History Scholarship at Peterhouse, 1915; Lieut, West Yorkshire Regt, 1916-18; 1st Class Historical Tripos, 1920; 1st Class English Tripos, 1921; Hugo de Balsham Student at Peterhouse and Le Bas Prize, 1922; Lecturer in English at Cambridge from 1923; University Lecturer, 1934. Visiting Professor: Columbia Univ., New York, 1948-49; Cornell Univ., 1953; Vis. Fellow, University Coll., Cardiff, 1970-71; Chairman, Dove Cottage Trustees, 1961-72;

Lectures: Hibbert, 1959; Ballard Mathews, UC N Wales, 1964; Drew, New Coll., Univ. of London, 1967. *Publications:* Tendencies in Renaissance Literary Theory (Le Bas Prize Essay), 1922; The Seventeenth Century Background, 1934; The Eighteenth Century Background, 1940; Collected Essays and Studies by Members of the Eng. Assoc., Vol. XXXII, 1946, XLIV, 1958; Coleridge on Imagination and Fancy (British Acad. Warton Lecture, 1946); Chapter on English Thought in The Character of England (ed Sir Ernest Barker, 1947); Richard Crashaw Memorial Lecture, 1949; Nineteenth Century Studies, 1949; Introduction to Thoreau's Walden, 1951; Christianity Past and Present, 1952; (ed) Bacon and Donne in Major British Writers (New York), 1953; More Nineteenth Century Studies, 1956; The Religion of Nature (Essex Hall Lecture), 1957; Darwin and Butler: Two Versions of Evolution, 1959; The English Moralists, 1964; Centenary Introductions to Newman's Apologia and Quiller-Couch's Troy Town, 1964; Spots of Time, 1965; Cambridge and Other Memories, 1920-1953, 1969; Introduction to Mark Rutherford's Autobiography and Deliverance, 1969; Religion Today, 1969; Samuel Taylor Coleridge, 1972; various articles and reviews. *Relevant publication:* The English Mind (essays presented to Basil Willey, ed by H. S. Davies and G. Watson), 1964. *Recreations:* music; the English countryside. *Address:* 18 Adams Road, Cambridge. *Club:* Athenæum.

WILLEY, Rt. Hon. Frederick Thomas, PC 1964; MP (Lab) Sunderland North since 1950 (Sunderland, 1945-50); Member Council, Save the Children Fund; Barrister; *b* 1910; *s* of late Frederick and Mary Willey; *m* 1939, Eleanor, *d* of late William and Elizabeth Snowdon; two *s* one *d. Educ:* Johnston Sch.; St John's Coll., Cambridge Univ. (Full blue Soccer; 1st Class Hons Law; Blackstone Prizeman, Harmsworth Studentship, McMahon Studentship, etc.). Called to Bar, Middle Temple, 1936. PPS to Rt Hon. J. Chuter Ede, 1946-50; Chm., Select Cttee on Estimates and Mem. Select Cttees on Statutory Instruments and Public Accounts until 1950; Parly Sec. to Ministry of Food, 1950-51; Dir, North-Eastern Trading Estates Ltd, until 1950; River Wear Commr until 1950; Former Mem., Consultative Assembly of the Council of Europe and Assembly of WEU; Minister of Land and Natural Resources, 1964-67; Minister of State, Ministry of Housing and Local Government, 1967; Chairman, Select Committee on: Members' Interests; Race Relations and Immigration; Selection; Abortion (Amendment) Bill; Chm., Parly and Scientific Cttee; Mem., Select Cttee on Privileges; Vice-Chm., Parly Lab. Party. *Publications:* Plan for Shipbuilding, 1956; Education, Today and Tomorrow, 1964; An Enquiry into Teacher Training, 1971; The Honourable Member, 1974; articles in various periodicals, legal and political. *Address:* 11 North Square, NW11.

WILLIAM-POWLETT, Vice-Admiral Sir Peveril (Barton Reibey Wallop), KCB 1953 (CB 1949); KCMG 1959; CBE 1945; DSO 1942; DL; RN retired; Governor of Southern Rhodesia, Nov. 1954-Dec. 1959; Vice-Chairman, Appledore Shipbuilders Ltd, 1974 (Chairman 1962-74); *b* 5 March 1898; 2nd *s* of Major Barton William-Powlett; *m* 1923, Helen Constance (*d* 1965), *d* of James Forbes Crombie, Aberdeen; three *d*; *m* 1966, Mrs Barbara Patience William-Powett, *d* of Sir Bernard Greenwell, 2nd Bt, MBE, and *widow* of Captain Newton William-Powlett, RN. *Educ:* Cordwalles Sch.; Osborne and Dartmouth. Midshipman, 1914; served European War, 1914-18, Gallipoli, Jutland; Lieut, 1918; specialised in signals; Commander 1931; Captain, 1938; commanded HMS Frobisher, 1938-39; Director of Manning, 1939-40; comd HMS Fiji, 1941 (DSO); Chief of Staff Force 'H', 1941-42; comd HMS Newcastle, 1942-44; Captain of Fleet, Home Fleet, 1944-45 (CBE); Captain in command of Royal Naval Coll., Dartmouth, 1946-48; Naval Secretary to First Lord of the Admiralty, 1948-50; Flag Officer (destroyers), Mediterranean Fleet, 1950-51; Commander-in-Chief, South Atlantic, 1952-54; retired, 1954; Rear-Admiral, 1948; Vice-Admiral, 1950. High Sheriff 1972, DL 1973, Devon. KStJ. *Recreations:* Rugby (played for England, 1922); golf, shooting, and fishing. *Address:* 80 Old Church Street, Chelsea, SW3. *T:* 01-352 2624; Cadhay, Ottery St Mary, Devon. *T:* Ottery St Mary 2432. *Clubs:* Naval and Military, Chelsea Arts.
See also Sir Michael Colman, Bt.

WILLIAMS; see Garnons Williams.

WILLIAMS; see Rees-Williams, family name of Baron Ogmore.

WILLIAMS, A. Franklyn, CMG 1960; Member, Welsh Council, since 1971; *b* 5 Feb. 1907; *s* of Benjamin Williams and Katherine Williams (*née* Thomas); *m* 1st, Doris May (marr. diss., 1952), *d* of David I. and Sarah Jane Munro; one *s* decd; 2nd, 1952, Nancy, MBE, *d* of Evan John and Edith David. *Educ:* Ferndale

Secondary Sch., Rhondda; University College, Cardiff. BSc University of Wales, 1927. HM Inspector of Taxes, Inland Revenue, 1929-45; Ministry of Power, 1946-. Chairman, Coal Cttee of Economic Commn for Europe (ECE), 1952-55. Petroleum Attaché, HM Embassy, Washington, 1956-60; Senior Officer for Wales, Ministry of Power, 1960-61; Chairman, Welsh Bd of Health, 1962-69. Mem., General Optical Council, 1974-. CStJ 1968. *Recreation:* wood turning. *Address:* 45 Cyncoed Road, Cardiff. *T:* Cardiff 32334; *Clubs:* Royal Air Force; Cardiff and County (Cardiff).

WILLIAMS, Rt. Hon. Alan John, PC 1977; MP (Lab) Swansea West since 1964; Minister of State, Department of Industry, since 1976; *b* 14 Oct. 1930; *m* 1957, Mary Patricia Rees, Blackwood, Mon; two *s* one *d. Educ:* Cardiff High Sch.; Cardiff College of Technology; University College, Oxford. BSc (London); BA (Oxon). Lecturer in economics, Welsh College of Advanced Technology; Free-lance Journalist. Joined Labour Party, 1950. Member: Association of Teachers at Technical Institutes, 1958-; Fabian Society; Co-operative Party; National Union of Students delegation to Russia, 1954. Contested (Lab) Poole. 1959. PPS to Postmaster General, 1966-67; Parly Under-Sec., DEA, 1967-69; Parly Sec., Min. of Technology, 1969-70; Opposition Spokesman on Consumer Protection, Small Businesses, Minerals, 1970-74; Minister of State, Dept of Prices and Consumer Protection, 1974-76. Chairman, Welsh Parly Labour Party, 1966-67; Delegate, Council of Europe and WEU, 1966-67; Mem. Public Accts Cttee, 1966-67. *Address:* House of Commons, SW1; Hill View, 96 Plunch Lane, Limeslade, Swansea. *Club:* Clyne Golf.

WILLIAMS, Alan (Lee), OBE 1973; MP (Lab) Havering, Hornchurch, since Feb. 1974 (Hornchurch, 1966-70); *b* 29 Nov. 1930. *Educ:* Roan Sch., Greenwich; Ruskin Coll., Oxford. Freeman of Company of Watermen and Lightermen, 1945-51; National Service, RAF, 1951-53; Oxford, 1954-56; National Youth Officer, Labour Party, 1956-62; Dir, British Atlantic Cttee, 1972-74. PPS to Sec. of State for Defence, 1969-70, 1976; PPS to Sec. of State for NI, 1976-. Chm., Parly Lab. Party Defence Cttee, 1976-; Member: FO Adv. Cttee on Disarmament and Arms Control, 1975-; Adv. Council of European Discussion Centre, Wilton Park, 1975-; Chm., Delegn to 4th Cttee of UN, NY, 1969; European Co-Chm., Transatlantic Policy Panel on Standardisation, Georgetown Univ., 1976-; Chm., All Party Parly River Thames Group; Chm., Transport on Water Assoc.; Mem., Thames Riparian Housing Assoc.; Mem., Cttee, Royal Hosp. Sch.; Governor, Royal Greenwich Hosp. Sch., 1976-; Deputy Director, European Movement, 1970-71, Treasurer, 1972-. Mem., RUSI. Freeman, City of London. *Publications:* Radical Essays, 1966; Europe or the Open Sea?, 1971; Crisis in European Defence, 1973; UN Assoc. pamphlet, UN and Warsaw and Nato Pacts; Fabian Soc. pamphlet on East/West Détente. *Recreations:* reading, history and novels, walking, camping. *Address:* House of Commons, SW1. *T:* 01-219 3000. *Clubs:* Reform, Travellers'.

WILLIAMS, (Albert) Clifford, BEM 1957; JP; Member: Welsh National Water Development Authority; Sports Council for Wales (Vice-Chairman, Centre Committee; Chairman, Water Recreation Committee); *b* 28 June 1905; British; *s* of Daniel Williams, Blaina, Mon; *m* 1929, Beatrice Anne, *d* of Charles Garbett; one *d. Educ:* Primary Sch., Blaina, Mon. Trade Union Official, 1935-50. Mem. 21 years, Chm. 10 years, Usk Rivers Authority; Vice-Pres., former Assoc. of River Authorities. Administrator of Voluntary Hospitals, 40 years until 1969; Vice-Chm., N Monmouthshire HMC. County Councillor, Monmouthshire; Alderman, 1964-74; MP (Lab) Abertillery, April 1965-1970. *Recreations:* watching sports, Rugby football. *Address:* Brodawel, Abertillery Road, Blaina, Gwent NP3 3DZ. *T:* Blaina 379.

WILLIAMS, Sir Alexander (Thomas), KCMG 1958 (CMG 1950); MBE 1936; *b* 13 July 1903; *s* of late John Williams and Mary Williams (*née* Kennedy); *m* 1931, Madeline O'Connor; two *s. Educ:* Bishop Foy Sch., Waterford; Trinity Coll., Dublin; Downing Coll., Cambridge. BA (Dublin). Cadet, Northern Rhodesia, 1928; District Officer, 1930; Assistant Chief Secretary, 1944; Administrative Secretary, 1947-52; Chief Secretary and Governor's Deputy, 1952-57; Governor and Commander-in-Chief of the Leeward Islands, 1957-59. Hon. LLD Dublin. KStJ 1958. *Recreation:* golf. *Address:* West Dormers, Cowes, Isle of Wight. *T:* Cowes 3657. *Clubs:* Travellers'; Kildare Street and University (Dublin).

WILLIAMS, Alfred Martyn, CBE 1957; DSC; Commander RN retired; *b* 14 May 1897; *s* of J. C. Williams of Caerhays Castle, Cornwall; *m* 1920, Audrey Hester (*d* 1943), 2nd *d* of C. Coltman Rogers, Stanage Park, Radnorshire; two *s* one *d*; *m* 1945,

Dorothea Veronica, *widow* of Major F. F. Robins and *yr d* of Colonel W. H. Carver; one *s. Educ:* RN Colleges, Osborne and Dartmouth. MP (U) North Cornwall, 1924-29; High Sheriff of Cornwall, 1938; DL Cornwall, 1956. *Address:* Pollards Hill, Torrington, Devon EX38 8JA. *T:* Torrington 3119. *Club:* Brooks's.
See also F. J. Williams.

WILLIAMS, Dr Alwyn, FRS 1967; FRSE, MRIA, FGS, PhD (Wales); Principal and Vice-Chancellor of University of Glasgow, since 1976; *b* 8 June 1921; *s* of D. D. and E. M. Williams; *m* 1949, E. Joan Bevan; one *s* one *d. Educ:* Aberdare Boys' Grammar Sch.; University College of Wales, Aberystwyth. Harkness Fund Fellow at US National Museum, Washington, DC, 1948-50; Lecturer in Geology in University of Glasgow, 1950-54; Prof. of Geology, 1954-74, Pro-Vice-Chancellor, 1967-74, Queen's Univ. of Belfast; Lapworth Prof. of Geology, and Head of Dept, Univ. of Birmingham, 1974-76. Pres., Palaeontological Assoc., 1968-70. Trustee, British Museum (Nat. History), 1971-, Chm. of Trustees, 1974-. Member: Equip. and Phys. Sci. sub-cttee, UGC, 1974-76; NERC, 1974-76; Adv. Council, British Library. Hon. Fellow, Geol Soc. of America, 1970-. Hon. DSc: Wales, 1974; Belfast, 1975. Bigsby Medal, 1961, Murchison Medal, 1973, Geol Soc.; Clough Medal, Edin. Geol. Soc., 1976. *Publications:* contrib. to Trans Royal Soc., Jl Geological Society; Geological Magazine; Washington Acad. of Sciences; Geological Society of America; Palaeontology; Journal of Paleontology, etc. *Address:* The Principal's Lodging, 12 The University, Glasgow G12 8QG. *T:* 041-339 0383.

WILLIAMS, Anthony James, CMG 1971; HM Diplomatic Service; Ambassador to the Libyan Arab Jamahariya since 1977; *b* 28 May 1923; *s* of late Bernard Warren Williams, FRCS, and of Hon. Muriel B. Buckley; *m* 1955, Hedwig Gabrielle, Gräfin Neipperg; two *s* two *d. Educ:* Oundle; Trinity Coll., Oxford. Entered Foreign Service, 1945; served in: Prague; Montevideo; Cairo; UK Permanent Mission to UN, New York; Buenos Aires; UK Permanent Mission to 18 Nation Disarmament Conf., Western, United Nations and South East Asian Depts of Foreign Office. Counsellor, Head of Chancery, Moscow, 1965-67; IDC, 1968; Counsellor (Political), Washington, 1969-70; Ambassador at Phnom Penh, 1970-73; Minister, Rome, 1973-76. *Address:* c/o Foreign and Commonwealth Office, SW1; Jolly's, Salehurst, Sussex. *Clubs:* Beefsteak, United Oxford & Cambridge University.

WILLIAMS, Maj.-Gen. Arthur Nicholl, CBE 1945 (OBE 1941); *b* 28 Oct. 1894; *y s* of late Rev. Canon W. H. Williams and Mrs Williams, Mathern, Mon; *m* 1919, Effie (*d* 1975), *d* of late Englesbe Seon; one *s* one *d. Educ:* Stancliffe Hall, Matlock; Hereford Cathedral Sch. Entered RM, 2nd Lieut, 1913; served European War, 1914-18, and War of 1939-45 (despatches); retired, 1946; Manager, Conservative Central Board of Finance, 1951-65. *Address:* 901 Hood House, Dolphin Square, SW1. *T:* 01-834 9701. *Club:* Athenæum.

WILLIAMS, Arthur Vivian, CBE 1969; General Manager and Solicitor, Peterlee (New Town) Development Corporation, 1948-74, and of Aycliffe (New Town) Development Corporation, 1954-74; *b* 2 Jan. 1909; *s* of N. T. and Gwendolen Williams; *m* 1937, Charlotte Moyra, *d* of Dr E. H. M. Milligan; three *s* one *d. Educ:* William Hulme's Grammar Sch., Manchester; Jesus Coll., Oxford. BA (Oxon), Final Honour Sch. of Mod. Hist. Admitted as Solicitor, 1936; Dep. Town Clerk of Finchley, 1938-41; Town Clerk of Bilston, 1941-46; Town Clerk and Clerk of the Peace, Dudley, 1946-48. *Recreation:* angling. *Address:* The Bryn, Newton Aycliffe, Co. Durham. *T:* Aycliffe 2987.

WILLIAMS, Rev. Austen; *see* Williams, Rev. S. A.

WILLIAMS, Prof. Bernard Arthur Owen, FBA 1971; Knightbridge Professor of Philosophy, University of Cambridge, and Fellow of King's College, Cambridge, since 1967; *b* 21 Sept. 1929; *s* of late O. P. D. Williams, OBE and of H. A. Williams; *m* 1955, Shirley Vivienne Teresa Brittain Catlin (*see* Mrs S. V. T. B. Williams) (marr. diss. 1974); one *d*; *m* 1974, Patricia Law Skinner; one *s. Educ:* Chigwell Sch., Essex; Balliol Coll., Oxford. BA (Oxon) 1951; MA 1954. Fellow of All Souls Coll., Oxford, 1951-54; RAF (Gen. Duties Br.), 1951-53; Fellow of New Coll., Oxford, 1954-59; Vis. Lectr, Univ. Coll. of Ghana, 1958-59; Lectr in Philosophy, Univ. Coll., London, 1959-64; Professor of Philosophy, Bedford College, London, 1964-67. Visiting Professor: Princeton Univ., USA, 1963; Harvard Univ., 1973; Vis. Fellow, Inst. of Advanced Studies, ANU, 1969; Mem., Institut International de Philosophie. Member: Public Schools Commn, 1965-70; Royal Commn on Gambling, 1976-;

Chm., Cttee on Obscenity and Film Censorship, 1977-. Dir, English Nat. Opera. *Publications:* (ed with A. C. Montefiore) British Analytical Philosophy, 1966; Morality, 1972; Problems of the Self, 1973; A Critique of Utilitarianism, 1973; Descartes: The Project of Pure Enquiry, 1978; articles in philosophical jls, etc. *Recreation:* music, particularly opera. *Address:* Kent House, Swaffham Prior, Cambs. *T:* Newmarket 741443.

WILLIAMS, Sir Brandon M. R.; *see* Rhys Williams.

WILLIAMS, Prof. Bruce Rodda; Vice-Chancellor and Principal of the University of Sydney since 1967; Chairman of the New South Wales State Cancer Council since 1967; Member, Reserve Bank Board, since 1969; Chairman, Australian Government Committee of Enquiry into Education and Training, 1976-78; *b* 10 January 1919; *s* of late Reverend W. J. Williams; *m* 1942, Roma Olive Hotten; five *d. Educ:* Wesley College; Queen's College, University of Melbourne. Lecturer in Economics, University of Adelaide, 1939-46 and at Queen's University of Belfast, 1946-50; Professor of Economics, University College of North Staffordshire, 1950-59; Robert Otley Prof., 1959-63, and Stanley Jevons Prof., 1963-67, Univ. of Manchester; Secretary and Joint Director of Research, Science and Industry Committee, 1952-59. Member National Board for Prices and Incomes, 1966-67; Econ. Adviser to Minister of Technology, 1966-67; Mem. Central Advisory Council on Science and Technology, 1967; Chm., Australian Vice Chancellors Cttee, 1972-74. Editor, The Sociological Review, 1953-59, and the Manchester Sch., 1959-67. President Economics Section of British Assoc., 1964. *Publications:* The Socialist Order and Freedom, 1942; (with C. F. Carter): Industry and Technical Progress, 1957, Investment in Innovation, 1958, and Science in Industry, 1959; Investment Behaviour, 1962; Investment Proposals and Decisions, 1965; Investment, Technology and Growth, 1967; Science and Technology in Economic Growth, 1973. *Address:* The University of Sydney, Sydney, NSW 2006, Australia.

WILLIAMS, Campbell (Sherston); *see under* Smith, Campbell (Sherston).

WILLIAMS, Carrington Bonsor, FRS 1954, MA, ScD (Cambridge); Chief Entomologist, Rothamsted Experimental Station, 1932-55; retired; *b* Liverpool, 7 Oct. 1889; *s* of Alfred and Lilian B. Williams; *m* 1920, Ellen Margaret Bain; three *s. Educ:* Birkenhead School; Clare Coll., Cambridge. Entomologist at John Innes Horticultural Institution, Merton, Surrey, 1911-16; Sugar Cane Entomologist, Dept of Agriculture, Trinidad, BWI, 1916-21. Sub-Dir and Dir Entomological Service, Ministry of Agriculture, Egypt, 1921-27; Entomologist to East African Agricultural Research Station, Amani, Tanganyika, 1927-29; Steven Lecturer in Agricultural and Forest Zoology, Edinburgh Univ., 1929-32; Guest Professor of Entomology, University of Minnesota, USA, 1932 and 1958. *Publications:* Migration of Butterflies, 1930; Insect Migration, 1958; Patterns in the Balance of Nature, 1964; Style and Vocabulary, numerical studies, 1970; numerous scientific papers on ecology, statistics and related sciences. *Address:* 8 The Crofts, Kirkcudbright, Scotland. *T:* Kirkcudbright 30015.

WILLIAMS, Cecil Beaumont, OBE 1963; High Commissioner for Barbados in the UK, since 1976; *b* 8 March 1926; *s* of George Cuthbert and Violet Irene Williams; *m* 1952, Dorothy Marshall; two *s* one *d. Educ:* Harrison Coll., Barbados; Durham Univ.; Oxford Univ. BA, DipEd. Asst Master, Harrison Coll., 1948-54. Asst Sec., Govt Personnel Dept, and Min. of Trade, Industry and Labour (Barbados), 1954-56; Permanent Secretary: Min. of Educn, 1958; Min. of Trade, Industry and Labour, 1958-63; Dir, Economic Planning Unit, 1964—65; Manager, Industrial Develt Corp., 1966-67; High Comr to Canada, 1967-70; Permanent Sec., Min. of External Affairs, 1971-74; Ambassador to USA and Perm. Rep. to OAS, 1974-75. *Recreations:* music, tennis, reading, gardening. *Address:* Iverta, Boyle Farm, Burtenshaw Road, Thames Ditton, Surrey.

WILLIAMS, Charles Cuthbert Powell; Chairman, Price Commission, since 1977; *b* 9 Feb. 1933; *s* of Dr Norman Powell Williams, DD, and Mrs Muriel de Lérisson Williams (*née* Cazenove); *m* 1975, Jane Gillian (*née* Portal); one step *s . Educ:* Westminster Sch.; Christ Church, Oxford (MA); LSE. British Petroleum Co. Ltd, 1958-64; Bank of London and Montreal, 1964-66; Eurofinance SA, Paris, 1966-70; Baring Brothers and Co. Ltd, 1970-77 (Man. Dir, 1971-77). Parly Candidate (Lab), Colchester, 1964. Founder Mem., Labour Econ. Finance and Taxation Assoc. (Vice-Chm., 1975-77). *Recreations:* cricket (Oxford Univ. CC, 1953-55, Captain 1955; Essex CCC, 1953-59); music, real tennis. *Address:* 48 Thurloe Square, SW7 2SX. *T:* 01-581 1783. *Clubs:* MCC, Hurlingham.

WILLIAMS, Charles Frederick Victor, CIE 1944; late ICS; *b* 1898; Director, National Union of Manufacturers, 1953-56, retired Nov. 1956. *Educ:* Pembroke College, Oxford. Joined ICS 1923; Under-Sec. Madras Govt 1928; Sec., 3rd Round Table Conference, London, 1932; Under-Sec., Govt of India, 1933; Dep. Secretary, Govt of India, 1934; Secretary, Agent-General for India in South Africa, 1935; Home Secretary, Madras Govt, 1941; Jt Sec., Home Dept, Govt of India, 1945; Sec. to Governor-General (Public), 1947. *Address:* 16 Egerton Gardens, SW3. *Club:* East India, Devonshire, Sports and Public Schools.

WILLIAMS, Charles Harold, MA; Emeritus Professor of History in the University of London (Head, Department of History, and Assistant Principal, 1945-63, King's College); Fellow of King's College, London; *b* 12 May 1895; *s* of Charles and Margaret Williams; *m* 1930, Clare Ruth, *e d* of Justin E. Pollak; one *s* one *d. Educ:* Sidney Sussex Coll., Cambridge; University Coll., London. Asst Lecturer, University Coll., London, 1924; Reader in Constitutional History in the University of London, 1931; Asst Editor of History, 1928, Editor, 1934-47. Member of the Council of the Historical Assoc. *Publications:* England under the Early Tudors, 1925; The Making of the Tudor Despotism, 1928; Year Book 1 Henry VI (Vol. L of the Selden Soc. Publications, 1933); The Yorkist Kings, in Cambridge Medieval History, Vol. VIII, 1936; The Modern Historian, 1938; English Historical Documents, 1485-1558, 1967; William Tyndale, 1969; papers, reviews, etc, in historical periodicals. *Recreations:* walking, music. *Address:* 9 Blackfriars Street, Canterbury, Kent. *T:* Canterbury 63392. *Club:* Athenæum.

WILLIAMS, Sir Charles Henry Trelease, (Sir Harry), Kt 1970; CBE 1964; FIMechE, FIProdE; *b* 11 May 1898; *s* of James Morgan Williams, Consett, Co. Durham and Letitia, *d* of John Henry and Lavinia Dwight Trelease; *m* 1925, Florence Alice, *d* of John William and Mary Ann Exley. *Educ:* Doncaster Road and South Grove Schs, Rotherham. Entered works of The Park Gate Iron & Steel Co. Ltd, as apprentice electrical fitter, 1912; Dir and Gen. Manager, 1945; Jt Man. Dir, 1948; Man. Dir, 1953; Chm., 1960; Director: The Steetley Co. Ltd, 1959-71; Tube Investments Ltd, 1960; Chairman: Renishaw Iron Co. Ltd, 1960; Round Oak Steel Works Ltd, 1960; retired, March 1966. Chairman: British Iron and Steel Fedn Training Cttee, 1952-66; Iron and Steel Ind. Trng Bd, 1964-72. Master of The Company of Cutlers in Hallamshire, 1960-61. JP Rotherham, 1948-70. Hon. Freeman, Co. Borough of Rotherham, 1971. *Recreations:* music, golf, cricket. *Address:* Overdales, 4 Brunswick Road, Rotherham S60 2RH. *T:* Rotherham 2463.

WILLIAMS, Dr Cicely Delphine, CMG 1968; retired (except on demand); *b* 2 Dec. 1893; *d* of James Rowland Williams, Kew Park, Jamaica (Dir of Educn, Jamaica) and Margaret E. C. Williams (*née* Farewell). *Educ:* Bath High Sch. for Girls; Somerville Coll., Oxford (Hon. Fellow, 1977); King's Coll. Hosp. DM, FRCP, DTM&H. Colonial Med. Service: appts, 1929-48. WHO Adv. in Maternal and Child Health, 1948-51; Research on Vomiting Sickness, 1951-53; Sen. Lectr in Nutrition, London, 1953-55; consulting visits to various countries, 1955-59; Visiting Professor: of Maternal and Child Health, Amer. Univ. of Beirut, 1959-64; Tulane Sch. of Public Health, New Orleans, 1971-; Adv. in Trng Progrs, Family Planning Assoc., 1964-67. Lectures: Milroy, RCP, 1958; Blackfan, Harvard Med. Sch., 1973. Emeritus Professor of Maternal and Child Health, Nursing and Nutrition, Tulane Sch. of Public Health, 1974. Hon. FRSM 1976. Hon. DSc: Univ. of WI; Univ. of Maryland; Univ. of Tulane; Smith Coll., Northampton, Mass. James Spence Meml Medal, Br. Paed. Assoc., 1965; Goldberger Award in Clin. Nutrition, Amer. Med. Assoc., 1967; Dawson-Williams Award in Paediatrics, BMA (jt), 1973. Order of Merit, Jamaica, 1975. *Publications:* chapters in: Diseases of Children in the Tropics, 1954; Sick Children, 1956; The Matrix of Medicine, 1958; (with D. B. Jelliffe) Mother and Child Health: delivering the services, 1972; contrib. to: The Lancet, Archives of Diseases in Childhood, Tropical Pediatrics, etc. *Recreations:* people and solitude. *Address:* 57 Poplar Walk, SE24. *T:* 01-733 1678. *Club:* Royal Commonwealth Society.

WILLIAMS, Clifford; *see* Williams, A. C.

WILLIAMS, Clifford; Associate Director, Royal Shakespeare Company, since 1963; *b* 30 Dec. 1926; *s* of George Frederick Williams and Florence Maud Williams (*née* Gapper); *m* 1st, 1952, Joanna Douglas (marr. diss. 1959); no *c*; 2nd, 1962, Josiane Eugenie Peset; two *d. Educ:* Highbury County Grammar Sch. Acted in London (These Mortals, Larissa, Wolves and Sheep, Great Catherine), and repertory theatres, 1945-48; founded and directed Mime Theatre Company, 1950-53; Dir of

Productions: at Marlowe Theatre, Canterbury, 1955-56; at Queen's Theatre, Hornchurch, 1957. Directed at Arts Theatre, London: Yerma, 1957; Radio Rescue, 1958; Dark Halo, Quartet for Five, The Marriage of Mr Mississippi (all in 1959); Moon for the Misbegotten, The Shepherd's Chameleon, Victims of Duty (all in 1960); The Race of Adam, Llandaff Festival, 1961. Joined Royal Shakespeare Company, 1961; Directed: Afore Night Come, 1962; The Comedy of Errors, 1963. Prods for RSC in Stratford and London: The Tempest, The Representative, The Comedy of Errors (revival), 1963; Richard II, Henry IV Pts I and II (co-dir), Afore Night Come (revival), The Jew of Malta, 1964; The Merchant of Venice, The Jew of Malta (revival), The Comedy of Errors (revival), 1965; The Meteor, Twelfth Night, Henry IV Pts I and II (co-dir, revivals), 1966; Doctor Faustus, 1968; Major Barbara, 1970; The Duchess of Malfi, 1971; The Comedy of Errors (revival), 1972; The Taming of the Shrew, A Lesson in Blood and Roses, 1973; Cymbeline, 1974; The Mouth Organ, Too True to be Good, 1975; Wild Oaks, 1976; Man and Superman, 1977. Other productions include: Our Man Crichton, 1964, and The Flying Dutchman, 1966, in London; The Gardener's Dog, 1965, and The Merry Wives of Windsor, 1967, for the Finnish National Theatre; Volpone at Yale Univ., 1967; Othello, for Bulgarian Nat. Theatre, 1968; Soldiers, New York and London, 1968; Dido and Aeneas, Windsor Festival, 1969; Famine, English Stage Soc., 1969; As You Like It, 1967, and Back to Methuselah, 1969, both for the Nat. Theatre of Gt Britain; The Winter's Tale, 1969, for Yugoslav Nat. Theatre; Sleuth, London, NY and Paris, 1970; Oh! Calcutta!, London and Paris, 1970; Emperor Henry IV, New York, 1973; As You Like It (revival), New York, 1974; What Every Woman Knows, London, 1974; Emperor Henry IV, London, 1974; Murderer, London, 1975; Mardi-Gras, London, 1976; Carte Blanche, London, 1976; Stevie, The Old Country, Rosmerholm, London, 1977. Also directed plays for the Arena Theatre, Theatre Workshop, Guildford, Oxford, Coventry, Toronto, Los Angeles, Washington, Johannesburg, Edinburgh Festival. Mem. Welsh Arts Council, 1963-72; Chairman: Welsh Nat. Theatre Co, 1968-72; British Theatre Assoc.; Advisory Editor to: Theatre Quarterly, and Drama; Chm., British Children's Theatre Assoc., 1968-71. Associate Artist of Yugoslav Nat. Theatre, 1969; FTCL. *Publications:* plays: The Disguises of Arlecchino, 1951; The Sleeping Princess, 1953; The Goose Girl, 1954; The Secret Garden, 1955; (with Donald Jonson) Stephen Dedalus, 1956. *Recreations:* motor boating, water-ski-ing. *Address:* 43 Onslow Square, SW7 3NJ; The Vineyard, Domaine du Chateauneuf, 06560 Valbonne, France. *Club:* Garrick.

WILLIAMS, Colin; see Welland, C.

WILLIAMS, Cyril Herbert, CMG 1956; OBE 1949; *b* 27 Dec. 1908; *s* of T. E. Williams; *m* 1936, Patricia Joy Collyer; one *s* two *d. Educ:* Bedford Modern Sch.; Jesus Coll., Camb. (MA). Colonial Service, Kenya, 1931; Provincial Commissioner, Nyanza Province, Kenya, 1951-56, retd; farming in Kenya, 1956-65; Mem., Kenya Council of State, 1961-64; Chm., Naivasha CC, 1961-64; Mem., Nyandarua CC, 1963; Deputy Chairman Appeal Tribunal, 1962-63, apptd under the Public Security (Restriction) Regulations. Master: Westerleigh School, 1965-66; Great Sanders School, 1966-69; Claremont School, 1969-74, retired. *Recreations:* reading, watching sport. *Address:* Nortons Farm, New House, Sedlescombe, East Sussex. *Club:* East India, Devonshire, Sports and Public Schools.

WILLIAMS, Cyril Robert, CBE 1945; *b* 11 May 1895; *s* of Rev. F. J. Williams, MA; *m* 1928, Ethel Winifred Wise; two *d. Educ:* Wellington College, Berks; New College, Oxford. Dist Loco. Supt, Khartoum, Sudan Rlys, 1923; Asst Mech. Engineer (Outdoor), 1924; Loco. Running Supt, 1927; Works Manager, 1932; Asst Chief Mech. Engineer, 1936; Deputy General Manager, 1939; General Manager, 1941. JP Somerset, 1947-69. *Recreation:* philately. *Address:* Ballacree, Somerton, Somerset. *T:* Somerton 72408.

WILLIAMS, Dafydd Wyn J.; see Jones-Williams.

WILLIAMS, Prof. David; Professor of Mining Geology in the University of London (Imperial College), 1950-66, Emeritus Professor, since 1966; Geological Consultant; *b* 12 Oct. 1898; *s* of William and Laura Williams, Caernarvonshire, N Wales; *m* 1929, Dorothy Welland Shepard; two *d. Educ:* Holt Secondary School, Liverpool; University of Liverpool; Imperial College, London. DSc 1952, PhD 1925, MSc 1923, BEng 1921, Univ. of Liverpool; DIC. Geophysical Prospecting, N Rhodesia, 1926-28; Geologist, Rio Tinto Company, Spain, 1928-32; Lecturer in Geology, Imperial College, 1932-47, Reader in Mining Geology, 1947-50. Dean, Royal School of Mines, 1952-59. Secretary, Geological Society of London, 1942-51, Vice-Pres., 1951-53, 1964-65, Foreign Secretary, 1970-73; Council, Institution of

Mining and Metallurgy, 1948-70, Vice-President, 1954-57, President, 1960-61; Pres., Geologists' Assoc., 1958-60. Fellow, Imp. Coll. of Science and Technology, 1968. Hon. FIMM, 1969. Consolidated Gold Fields of SA Gold Medal, InstMM, 1934; Lyell Medal, Geological Soc. of London, 1959. *Publications:* (with W. R. Jones) Minerals and Mineral Deposits, 1948; scientific papers in geological and mining journals. *Address:* Downsway, 315 Fir Tree Road, Epsom Downs, Surrey. *T:* Burgh Heath 52655.

WILLIAMS, Prof. David; Sir John Williams Professor of Welsh History, University College of Wales, 1945-67, retired, 1967; *b* 9 Feb. 1900; *y s* of David and Anne Williams, Llan-y-cefn, Pembrokeshire; *m* 1st, 1930, Irene Muriel Fothergill (*d* 1942); 2nd, 1952, Hilarie Margaret Waddington. *Educ:* University of Wales; Columbia University; Paris and Berlin. AM (Columbia); MA, DLitt (Wales). Lecturer, University College, Cardiff, 1930-45. Served European War of 1914-18, army; War of 1939-45, Man Power Officer for south-east Wales, Min. of Labour. *Publications:* John Frost: A Study in Chartism, 1939; A History of Modern Wales, 1950; The Rebecca Riots, a Study in Agrarian Discontent, 1955; John Penry: Three Treatises concerning Wales, 1960; contrib. Eng. Hist. Rev., American Hist. Rev., etc. *Address:* 2 Laura Place, Aberystwyth. *T:* Aberystwyth 7407.

WILLIAMS, Adm. Sir David, GCB 1977 (KCB 1975); Commander-in-Chief, Naval Home Command, since 1977; Flag ADC to the Queen, since 1977; *b* 22 Oct. 1921; 3rd *s* of A. E. Williams, Ashford, Kent; *m* 1947, Philippa Beatrice Stevens; two *s. Educ:* Yardley Court Sch., Tonbridge; RN College, Dartmouth. Cadet, Dartmouth, 1935. Served War of 1939-45 at sea in RN. Qual. in Gunnery, 1946; Comdr, 1952; Captain, 1960; Naval Asst to First Sea Lord, 1961-64; HMS Devonshire, 1964-66; Dir of Naval Plans, 1966-68; Captain, BRNC, Dartmouth, 1968-70; Rear-Adm. 1970; Flag Officer, Second in Command Far East Fleet, 1970-72; Vice-Adm. 1973; Dir-Gen. Naval Manpower and Training, 1972-74; adm. 1974; Chief of Naval Personnel and Second Sea Lord, 1974-77. Grad. of US Naval War Coll., Newport, RI, USA. *Recreations:* sailing, tennis, gardening. *Address:* Brockholt, Strete, Dartmouth, Devon. *Clubs:* Royal Dart Yacht; RN Sailing Association (Cdre); Royal Yacht Squadron.

WILLIAMS, Rear-Adm. David Apthorp, CB 1965; DSC 1942; *b* 27 Jan. 1911; *s* of Thomas Pettit Williams and Vera Frederica Dudley Williams (*née* Apthorp); *m* 1951, Susan Eastlake, 3rd *d* of late Dr W. H. Lamplough and widow of Surg. Cdr H. de B. Kempthorne, RN; one *s* two step *d. Educ:* Cheltenham College; Royal Naval Engineering College, Keyham. Joined RN, 1929. Served War, Engineer Officer, HMS Hasty, 1939-42 (DSC, despatches four times), 2nd Destroyer Flotilla, Med. Fleet, S Atlantic Stn, Home Fleet, E Med. Fleet; Sen. Engineer, HMS Implacable, 1942-45, Home Fleet, and 1st Aircraft Carrier Sqdn, British Pacific Fleet, Comdr (E) 1945; Capt. 1955; Rear-Adm. 1963; Dir Gen. Aircraft, Admiralty, 1962-64; Dir Gen., Aircraft (Naval), Ministry of Defence, 1964-65; retired list, 1965. Member, Civil Service Commn Panel of Interviewers for Professional and Technology Officers. CEng, MIMechE. *Recreations:* various. *Address:* 3 Ellachie Gardens, Alverstoke, Hants PO12 2DS. *T:* Gosport 83375. *Club:* Army and Navy.

WILLIAMS, David Barry, TD 1964; QC 1975; a Recorder of the Crown Court, since 1972; *b* 20 Feb. 1931; *s* of Dr W. B. Williams and Mrs G. Williams, Garndiffaith, Mon; *m* 1961, Angela Joy Davies; three *s* one *d. Educ:* Cardiff High Sch. for Boys; Wellington Sch., Somerset; Exeter Coll., Oxford (MA). Called to Bar, Gray's Inn, 1955; Wales and Chester Circuit, 1957. Asst Comr, Local Govt Boundary Commn for Wales, 1976-. *Recreations:* mountain walking, Rugby football. *Address:* 52 Cyncoed Road, Cardiff. *T:* Cardiff 498189. *Clubs:* Army and Navy; Cardiff and County (Cardiff).

WILLIAMS, David Carlton, PhD; retired; President and Vice-Chancellor, University of Western Ontario, 1967-77; *b* 7 July 1912; *s* of John Andrew Williams and Anna Williams (Carlton); *m* 1943, Margaret Ashwell Carson; one *s* one *d. Educ:* Gordon Bell and Kelvin High Schs; Univ. of Manitoba, Winnipeg (BA); Univ. of Toronto (MA, PhD, Psych.). Special Lectr in Psychology, Univ. of Toronto, 1946; Associate Prof. of Psychology, Univ. of Manitoba, 1947; Prof. and Head, Dept of Psychology, Univ. of Manitoba, 1948; Prof. of Psychology, Univ. of Toronto, 1949-58 (Cons. to Toronto Juvenile Ct Clinic, 1951-58); Dir of Univ. Extension, Univ. of Toronto, 1958; a Dir, John Howard Soc., Toronto, 1956-67; Mem., Royal Commn on Govt Organization, 1961; Chm., Ontario Commn on Freedom of Information and Individual Privacy, 1977. Vice-Pres., Univ. of Toronto, for Scarborough and Erindale Colls, 1963-67. Principal of Scarborough Coll., Univ. of Toronto, 1963;

Principal of Erindale Coll., Univ. of Toronto, 1965. Chm., Council of Ontario Univs, 1970-73; Dir, Assoc. of Univs and Colls of Canada, 1970-. Hon. LLD: Univ. of Manitoba, 1969; Univ. Windsor, 1977; Univ. Ontario, 1977. *Publications:* The Arts as Communication, 1963; University Television, 1965. *Recreations:* photography, music, swimming, fishing. *Address:* 252 Sydenham Street, London, Ontario, Canada N6A 1WJ. *T:* 433-8344. *Clubs:* University, London, London Hunt and Country (all London, Ont); Arts and Letters, University, York (Toronto).

WILLIAMS, David Claverly, CVO 1970; CBE 1977; *b* 31 July 1917; *s* of late Rev. Canon Henry Williams, OBE, and late Ethel Florence Williams; *m* 1944, Elizabeth Anne Fraser; three *d.* *Educ:* Christ's Coll., Christchurch, NZ; Victoria Univ. of Wellington. Professional Exam. in Public Administration. Inland Revenue Dept, 1936-39. Served War, 2NZEF, Pacific and Middle East, 1939-46. NZ Forest Service, 1946-60; Official Sec. to the Governor-General of NZ, 1960-77. *Address:* 34A Karn Crescent, Waikanae, New Zealand. *Club:* United Services Officers' (Wellington).

WILLIAMS, David Glyndwr Tudor; Reader in Public Law, Cambridge University, since 1976; Fellow of Emmanuel College, since 1967; *b* 22 Oct. 1930; *s* of late Tudor Williams, OBE (Headmaster of Queen Elizabeth Grammar Sch., Carmarthen, 1929-55), and of Anne Williams; *m* 1959, Sally Gillian Mary Cole; one *s* two *d.* *Educ:* Queen Elizabeth Grammar Sch., Carmarthen; Emmanuel Coll., Cambridge (MA, LLB). LLM Calif. Called to the Bar, Lincoln's Inn, 1956. Commonwealth Fund Fellow of Harkness Foundn, Berkeley and Harvard, 1956-58; Lecturer: Univ. of Nottingham, 1958-63; Univ. of Oxford, 1963-67 (Fellow of Keble Coll.); Sen. Tutor and Tutor for Admissions, Emmanuel Coll., Cambridge, 1970-76. Vis. Fellow, ANU, 1974. Member: Council on Tribunals, 1972-; Clean Air Council, 1971-; Royal Commn on Environmental Pollution, 1976-. *Publications:* Not in the Public Interest, 1965; Keeping the Peace, 1967; (ed jtly) Administrative Law, in Halsbury's Laws of England, Vol. 1, 4th edn 1973; articles in legal jls. *Address:* 29 Sedley Taylor Road, Cambridge. *T:* Cambridge 46232.

WILLIAMS, D(avid) Innes, MD, MChir Cambridge, FRCS; Urologist, Hospital for Sick Children, Great Ormond Street, since 1952; Senior Surgeon, St Peter's Hospital, since 1950; Civilian Consultant Urologist to Royal Navy; Dean, Institute of Urology, University of London; *b* 12 June 1919; *s* of late Gwynne E. O. Williams, MS, FRCS; *m* 1944, Margaret Eileen Harding; two *s.* *Educ:* Sherborne Sch.; Trinity Hall, Cambridge; Univ. College Hospital. Pres., British Assoc. of Urological Surgeons; Vice-Pres., Internat. Soc. of Urology; Member Council: RCS; Imperial Cancer Res. Fund; Mem., Central Cttee for Hosp. Medical Services. *Publications:* Urology of Childhood, 1958; Paediatric Urology, 1968; Scientific Foundations of Urology, 1976; various contributions to medical journals. *Address:* 15c Heath Drive, NW3 7SN. *T:* 01-435 4926; The Old Rectory, East Knoyle, Salisbury, Wilts. *T:* 255.

WILLIAMS, Dr David Iorwerth, FRCP, AKC; Dean, King's College Hospital Medical School, 1966-77; Consultant in Dermatology, King's College Hospital, since 1947; *b* 7 May 1913; *s* of William Tom Williams and Mabel Williams (*née* Edwards); *m* 1939, Ethel Margaret Wiseman; one *s* (one *d* decd). *Educ:* Dulwich Coll. (Jun. and Sen. Scholar); King's College Hosp. Med. Sch. Warneford and Raymond Gooch Scholar; MB, BS 1938; FRCP 1953; AKC 1934; FKC 1977. RAMC, 1940-46, Lt-Col. Member: BMA; Brit. Assoc. of Dermatology (Past Pres. and Past Sec.); Royal Soc. of Med. (Past Pres. Dermatology Section); West Kent Medico-Chirurgical Soc. (Past Pres.); Hon. (or Foreign) Member: American, Austrian, Danish, French and S African Dermatological Socs. Gold Medal of Brit. Assoc. of Dermatology, 1965. *Publications:* articles in various med. jls over last 30 yrs. *Recreations:* golf, music. *Address:* 28 South Row, SE3 0RY. *T:* 01-852 7060.

WILLIAMS, David John; Lord Chancellor's Office, since 1966; *b* 10 July 1914; *s* of late James Herbert Williams and of Ethel (*née* Redman); unmarried. *Educ:* Lancing College; Christ Church, Oxford (MA). Called to Bar, Inner Temple, 1939. Served War of 1939-45, Royal Artillery. Practised as Barrister, Norwich, 1946-51; Resident Magistrate, Tanganyika, 1951-56; Senior Resident Magistrate, 1956-60; Judge of High Court of Tanganyika, 1960-62; retired, 1962. Postgrad. Dip. in Social Anthropology, LSE, 1965. *Recreations:* the arts and travelling. *Address:* Hillfield, 27 Crawley Hill, Camberley, Surrey GU15 2DA; 94 Thomas More House, Barbican, EC2Y 8BU.

WILLIAMS, David Wakelin, MSc, PhD, FInstBiol; retired as Director, Department of Agriculture and Fisheries for Scotland, Agricultural Scientific Services, 1963-73; *b* 2 Oct. 1913; *e s* of John Thomas Williams and Ethel (*née* Lock); *m* 1948, Margaret Mary Wills, BSc, *d* of late Rev. R. H. Wills; one *s.* *Educ:* Rhondda Grammar School, Porth; University College, Cardiff. Demonstrator, Zoology Dept, Univ. Coll., Cardiff, 1937-38; Lectr in Zoology and Botany, Tech. Coll., Crumlin, Mon., 1938-39; research work on nematode physiology, etc. (MSc, PhD), 1937-41; biochemical work on enzymes (Industrial Estate, Treforest), 1942-43. Food Infestation Control Inspector (Min. of Food), Glasgow; Sen. Inspector, W Scotland, 1945; Scotland and N Ireland, 1946. Prin. Scientific Officer, Dept Agriculture for Scotland, 1948; Sen. Prin. Scientific Officer, 1961; Dep. Chief Scientific Officer (Director), 1963. Chairman, Potato Trials Advisory Cttee, 1963-; FInstBiol 1966 (Council Mem. Scottish Br., 1966-69). *Publications:* various on the environment and pest control. *Recreations:* music, writing, electronics, photography, golf. *Address:* 8 Hillview Road, Edinburgh EH12 8QN. *T:* 031-334 1108.

WILLIAMS, Dr Denis (John), CBE 1955; DSc; MD; FRCP; Hon. Consulting Neurologist, St George's Hospital; Hon. Consulting Physician, National Hospital, Queen Square; Senior Neurologist, King Edward VII Hospital for Officers; Hon. Neurologist, Star and Garter Home, Richmond; Hon. Civil Consultant in Neurology, RAF, British Airways; Civil Consultant in Electro-encephalography, RAF and Army; Lecturer in Neurology, London University, 1946-75; Editor of Brain and of Modern Trends in Neurology, 1954-75; *b* 4 Dec. 1908; *s* of Rev. Daniel Jenkin Williams, MA, BD, Aberayron; *m* 1937, Joyce Beverley Jewson, MBE, JP, MB, BS, DPH; one *s* two *d.* *Educ:* Manchester Univ.; Harvard University. DSc (Physiol.), Manchester 1942 (MSc 1938, BSc 1929); MD (Gold Medal) Manchester 1935 (MB, ChB 1932); FRCP 1943 (MRCP 1937). After resident appts in Manchester and London, Prof. Tom Jones Mem. Fellow in Surgery; Halley Stewart Research Fellow, Med. Research Council; Rockefeller Travelling Fellow in Neurology. Hon. Research Fellow, Harvard Univ. Wing Comdr RAF; Air Crew Research and Clinical Neurology in Royal Air Force, 1939-45, and seconded to Royal Navy; then Physician, Departments of Applied Electrophysiology, St George's and National Hosps. Consultant Advr, DHSS, 1966-73. Chm., Academic Bd, Inst. of Neurology, 1965-74. Bradshaw Lecturer, Royal College of Physicians, 1955; Scott-Heron Lecturer, Belfast, 1960; Guest Lecturer, Canadian Medical Assoc., 1963; Hugh Cairns Lecturer, Adelaide, 1965; Bruce Hall Lecturer, Sydney, 1965; Guest Lecturer, RACP, 1965; Richardson Lectr, Toronto, 1974. Visiting Professor: Univ. of Cincinnati, 1963, 1969; St Vincent's Hosp. Sydney (Hon. Phys.), 1965. Mem. Council, 1960-63, 2nd Vice-Pres., 1976, 1977, RCP (Chm., Cttee on Neurology, 1965-74); Pres., Sect. of Neurology, Roy Soc Med, 1967; Pres., Assoc. of British Neurologists 1972-74 (Sec., 1952-60); Hon. Member: American, Canadian and German Neurological Assocs; EEG Soc., London. Examr in Neurology: RCP; various Univs. Governor, Nat. Hosp.; Trustee, Brain Res. Trust. Gowers Medal, UC and Nat. Hosps, London, 1974. *Publications:* scientific articles dealing mainly with brain function, epilepsy, abnormal behaviour and electro-encephalography, in Brain, Modern Trends in Neurology, and other journals; Neurology, in Price's Medicine; Contrib. to Handbook of Neurology. *Recreations:* farming, gardening. *Address:* 149 Harley Street, W1. *T:* 01-935 4444; 11 Frognal Way, Hampstead, NW3. *T:* 01-435 4030; Woodlands House, Mathry, Dyfed. *T:* St Nicholas 220. *Clubs:* Wayfarers', Royal Air Force.

WILLIAMS, Derek Alfred H.; *see* Hutton-Williams.

WILLIAMS, Donald; *see* Williams, W. D.

WILLIAMS, Sir Donald Mark, 10th Bt *cr* 1866; *b* 7 Nov. 1954; *s* of Sir Robert Ernest Williams, 9th Bt, and of Ruth Margaret, *d* of Charles Edwin Butcher, Hudson Bay, Saskatchewan, Canada; *S* father, 1976. *Educ:* West Buckland School, Devon. *Heir: b* Barton Matthew Williams, *b* 20 Nov. 1956. *Address:* Upcott House, Barnstaple, N Devon.

WILLIAMS, Dorian; Director, Pendley Centre of Adult Education, Tring, since 1945; BBC, TV, Equestrian Commentator since 1951; *b* 1 July 1914; *er s* of late Col Williams and Mrs V. D. S. Williams, Farnham Royal, Bucks; *m* 1st, 1938, Hon. Moyra Lubbock (marr. diss. 1946); 2nd, 1956, Jennifer Neale; one *s* one *d.* *Educ:* Harrow; Guildhall Sch. of Music and Drama. Schoolmaster, 1936-45. Founded Pendley Centre of Adult Education, Tring, 1945. MFH, Whaddon Chase, 1954-. Chairman: National Equestrian Centre, 1967-74; BHS, 1974-. Master, Farriers' Co., 1977-78. *Publications:* Clear Round,

1954; Pendley and a Pack of Hounds, 1956; Batsford Book of Horses, 1959; Every Child's Book of Riding, 1960; The Girl's Book of Riding and Horses, 1961; Show Pony, 1961; A Gallery of Riders, 1963; Pony to Jump, 1963; Working with Horses as a Career, 1963; Learning to Ride, 1964; Ponies and Riding, 1966; Showing Horse Sense, 1967; The Horseman's Companion, 1967; Pancho, The Story of a Horse (novel), 1967; Show Jumping, 1968; Famous Horse Stories, 1968; Show Jumping: The Great Ones, 1970; Dorian Williams' World of Show Jumping, 1970; Kingdom for a horse (novel), 1971; Great Moments in Show Jumping, 1972; Lost (novel), 1974; Great Riding Schools of the World, 1975; The Horse of the Year, 1976. *Recreations:* hunting, riding; Shakespeare. *Address:* Foscote Manor, Buckingham. *T:* Buckingham 3152; (office) *T:* Buckingham 3981. *Clubs:* Buck's, Sportsman's, Anglo-Belgian.

WILLIAMS, Douglas, CB 1977; CVO 1966; Deputy Secretary, Ministry of Overseas Development (formerly Overseas Development Administration), 1973-77, retired; *b* 14 May 1917; *s* of James E. Williams and late Elsie Williams; *m* 1948, Marie Jacquot; no *c. Educ:* Wolverhampton Sch.; Exeter Coll., Oxford. Served War, 1939-46 (despatches): Major, RA. Colonial Office, 1947; Principal, 1949; Colonial Attaché, Washington, 1956-60; Asst Sec., Colonial Office, 1961; transferred to ODM (later ODA), 1967, Under-Sec., 1968-73; Dep.-Sec., 1973-77. *Address:* 14 Gomshall Road, Cheam, Sutton, Surrey. *T:* 01-393 7306.

WILLIAMS, Sir Dudley; *see* Dudley-Williams, Sir Rolf Dudley.

WILLIAMS, Sir Edgar (Trevor), Kt 1973; CB 1946; CBE 1944; DSO 1943; DL; Rhodes Trust since 1951; Fellow of Balliol College, Oxford, since 1945; a Pro-Vice-Chancellor, University of Oxford, since 1968; Editor, Dictionary of National Biography, since 1949; Chairman, Nuffield Provincial Hospitals Trust, since 1966; a Radcliffe Trustee, since 1960; Trustee, Nuffield Medical Benefaction, Oxford, since 1975; a Freeman of Chester; *b* 20 Nov. 1912; *e s* of late Rev. J. E. Williams; and *m* 1946, Monica, *d* of late Professor P. W. Robertson; one *d*; *m* 1946, Gillian, *yr d* of late Major-General M. D. Gambier-Parry, MC; one *s* one *d. Educ:* Tettenhall College; KES, Sheffield; Merton College, Oxford (Chambers Postmaster, 1931-34; First Class, Modern History, 1934; Harmsworth Senior Scholar, 1934-35; Junior Research Fellow, 1937-39; MA 1938; Hon. Fellow, 1964-); Asst Lectr, Univ. of Liverpool, 1936. Served War of 1939-45 (despatches thrice); 2nd Lieut (SRO), 1st King's Dragoon Guards, 1939; Western Desert, 1941; GSO1, Eighth Army (North Africa, 1942-43, Sicily and Italy, 1943); Brig., Gen. Staff I, 21st Army Gp, 1944-45; Rhine Army, 1945-46; Officer, US Legion of Merit, 1945. UN Security Council Secretariat, 1946-47. FRHistS 1947. Mem., Devlin Nyasaland Commn, 1959. DL Oxfordshire, 1964-. President, OUCC, 1966-68 (Sen. Treasurer, 1949-61); a Governor, St Edward's Sch., Oxford. Hon. Mem., American Hosp. Assoc., 1971. Hon. Fellow, Queen Elizabeth House, Oxford, 1975. Hon. LLD: Waynesburg Coll., Pa, 1947; Univ. of Windsor, Ontario, 1969; Hon. LHD, Williams Coll., Mass, 1965; Hon. PdD, Franklin and Marshall Coll., Pa, 1966; Hon. DLitt: Warwick, 1967; Hull, 1970; Hon. LittD Swarthmore Coll., Pa, 1969. *Address:* Rhodes House, Oxford. *T:* 55745. *Clubs:* Savile; MCC; Vincent's (Oxford).

WILLIAMS, Maj.-Gen. Edward Alexander Wilmot, CB 1962; CBE 1958; MC 1940; DL; *b* 8 June 1910; *s* of late Captain B. C. W. Williams, DL, JP, Herringston, Dorchester and late Hon. Mrs W. M. Williams (*er d* of 2nd Baron Addington); *m* 1943, Sybilla Margaret, *er d* of late Colonel O. A. Archdale, MBE, late The Rifle Brigade, West Knighton House, Dorchester; one *s* three *d. Educ:* Eton; Royal Military College. 2nd Lieut 60th Rifles, 1930; Adjutant, 2nd Battalion (Calais), 1938-39. Served War of 1939-45; commanded 1st Bn 60th Rifles, 1944. Bt Lieut-Col, 1950; Directing Staff, Joint Services Staff College, 1950-52; commanded 2nd Bn 60th Rifles, 1954-55; Comdr 2nd Infantry Brigade, 1956-57; Imperial Defence College, 1958; Brigadier Author, War Office, 1959. GOC 2nd Div. BAOR, 1960-62; Chief of Staff, GHQ Far East Land Forces, May-Nov. 1962; General Officer Commanding Singapore Base District, 1962-63; Chairman, Vehicle Cttee, Min. of Defence, 1964; retired 1965; Colonel Commandant, 2nd Bn The Royal Green Jackets (The King's Royal Rifle Corps), 1965-70. DL Dorset, 1965; High Sheriff of Dorset, 1970-71. *Recreations:* fishing, shooting. *Address:* Herringston, Dorchester, Dorset. *T:* Dorchester 4122. *Clubs:* Lansdowne, Pratt's; Royal Dorset Yacht.

WILLIAMS, Edward Taylor, CMG 1962; MICE; retired as General Manager, Malayan Railway; civil engineering railway consultant with Henderson, Hughes and Busby, consulting engineers and economists, since 1965; *b* Bolton, Lancashire, 15 October 1911; *s* of Edward and Harriet Williams; *m* 1940, Ethel

Gertrude Bradley; one step *s* one step *d. Educ:* Accrington Grammar School; Manchester College of Technology. LMS Rly, pupil engineer, 1929-36; Sudan Rly, Asst Civil Engr, 1936-38; Metropolitan Water Board, Civil Engr, 1939-41; Malayan Rly, 1941-62 (Gen. Man. 1959-62); Rly Advr, Saudi Govt Railroad, 1963-65. Interned in Singapore, in Changi and Sime Road, 1941-45. *Recreation:* travel. *Address:* (until June 1978) 400 Santa Maria Estate, Mellieha, Malta GC; (from June 1978) Gatchell House, Trull, Taunton, Somerset. *T:* Taunton 83641.

WILLIAMS, Emlyn, CBE 1962; Hon. LLD Bangor; *b* 1905; *m* Molly O'Shann (*d* 1970); two *s. Educ:* County School, Holywell; Geneva; Christ Church, Oxford (MA). *Plays:* A Murder has been Arranged; Glamour; Full Moon; Vigil; Vessels Departing; Spring, 1600; Night Must Fall; He Was Born Gay; The Corn is Green; The Light of Heart; The Morning Star; adaptation of A Month in the Country; The Druid's Rest; The Wind of Heaven; Trespass; Accolade; Someone Waiting; Beth; adaptation of The Master Builder. In addition to acting in most of these, has acted at the Old Vic, also in The Winslow Boy, Lyric, 1947; The Wild Duck, Saville, 1955; Season at Stratford-on-Avon, 1956. Shadow of Heroes, Piccadilly, 1958. As Charles Dickens (solo performance), Lyric (Hammersmith), Criterion, Duchess, 1951, Golden Theatre (New York), Ambassadors, 1952. As Dylan Thomas (A Boy Growing up: solo performance), Globe, 1955 and 1958, also Long Acre Theatre (New York), Oct. 1957; as Saki (solo performance), Apollo, 1977. Acted in: Three, Criterion, 1961; Daughter of Silence, New York, 1961; A Man For All Seasons, New York, 1962; The Deputy, New York, 1964; World Tour as Dickens, 1964-65; as Charles Dickens, Globe, 1965, and Haymarket, 1975; acted in A Month in the Country, Cambridge, 1965; Forty Years On, Apollo, 1969. *Films include:* The Last Days of Dolwyn (author, co-director, and star), 1948; Ivanhoe, 1950; Deep Blue Sea, 1955; I Accuse, 1957; The Wreck of the Mary Deare, 1959; The L-Shaped Room, 1962; Eye of the Devil, 1966; The Walking-Stick, 1969; David Copperfield, 1969. *Publications:* (autobiog.) George, 1961; Beyond Belief, 1967; (autobiog.) Emlyn, 1973. *Address:* 123 Dovehouse Street, SW3. *T:* 01-352 0208.

WILLIAMS, Eric, MC 1944; writer; *b* 13 July 1911; *m* 1st, 1940, Joan Mary Roberts (decd); 2nd, 1948, Sibyl Grain, MBE; no *c. Educ:* Christ's College, Finchley. Served War of 1939-45, RAF, 1940-46; shot down over Germany as Flt Lt Dec. 1942; captured, and imprisoned in Stalag-Luft III; escaped Oct. 1943; returned to England Dec. 1943. Book buyer Lewis's Ltd, 1946-49; Scriptwriter, Wessex Film Productions Ltd, 1949-50. Set out on Twenty-year Slowest Expedition round the World, 1959. *Publications:* Goon in the Block, 1945; The Wooden Horse, 1949; The Tunnel, 1951; The Escapers, 1953; Complete and Free, 1957; Great Escape Stories, 1958; Dragoman Pass, 1959 (rev. edn, Dragoman, 1970); The Borders of Barbarism, 1961; More Escapers, 1968; Great Air Battles, 1971. *Recreations:* travel, seafaring, fishing, shooting, fighting officiousness in all its forms. *Address:* Union Bank of Switzerland, Bern, Switzerland.

WILLIAMS, Rt. Hon. Eric, PC 1964; CH 1969; Prime Minister, Trinidad and Tobago, since 1961; Minister of Finance, since 1976; *b* Trinidad, 25 Sept. 1911; *e s* of T. H. Williams. *Educ:* Tranquillity Boys' School and Queen's Royal College, Trinidad; St Catherine's Society, Oxford. BA 1932, Cl. I Hist., DPhil 1938. Howard University, Washington, DC; Assistant Professor of Social and Political Science, 1939; Associate Prof., 1944; Prof., 1947. Worked with Caribbean Commn and Research Council (Dep. Chm. latter, 1948-55). Founder and Polit. Leader, Peoples' National Movement, 1956; first Chief Minister and Minister of Finance, 1956; first Premier, 1959; Minister of: External Affairs, 1961-64; Finance Planning and Develt, 1967-71; National Security, 1967-71; Tobago Affairs, 1967-71; led Trinidad and Tobago Delegns, London (US Bases Talks, 1960; WI Fedn Conf., 1961; Indep. Conf., 1961; Commonwealth PM's Conf., 1962), and at discussions with European Economic Commn, Brussels, 1962. Pro-Chancellor, Univ. of WI; Hon. Fellow, St Catherine's College, Oxford, 1964. Hon. DCL, Oxford, 1965. *Publications:* The Negro in the Caribbean, 1942; (Jt) The Economic Future of the Caribbean, 1943; Capitalism and Slavery, 1944; Education in the British West Indies, 1950; History of the People of Trinidad and Tobago, 1962; Documents of West Indian History, Vol. I, 1492-1655, 1963; Inward Hunger: the Education of a Prime Minister, 1969; From Columbus to Castro: the history of the Caribbean 1492-1969, 1970; articles in learned jls. *Address:* Prime Minister's Residence, La Fantasie Road, St Anns, Port-of-Spain, Trinidad.

WILLIAMS, Eric Charles, CB 1969; Chief Inspector of Nuclear Installations, 1971-75; *b* 15 May 1915; *s* of Charles Henry Williams and Agnes (*née* Turner); *m* 1946, Elisabeth Ruby Alice Bryan; one *s* one *d. Educ:* King Edward VI School, Stratford upon Avon; University of Birmingham. BSc (Hons 1st Cl.) 1935, MSc 1936. Joined Civil Service, 1936, at Bawdsey Research Station, Air Ministry; Hon. Wing Commander, RAF, 1943-45; attended Imperial Defence Coll., 1947; Asst Scientific Adviser, Air Ministry, 1948-49; Director of Operational Research, Admiralty, 1949-54; Scientific Adviser, Intelligence, Min. of Defence, 1955-60; Director, SHAPE Technical Centre, 1960-64; Chief Scientific Adviser, MoT, 1964-67; Chief Scientist, Min. of Power, then Chief Scientist (Energy), Min. of Technology (later DTI), 1968-74. *Recreations:* cricket, gardening. *Address:* 4 Sandringham Drive, Bangor, Co. Down, N Ireland. *T:* Bangor 55261. *Clubs:* Athenæum, Royal Air Force.

WILLIAMS, Brig. Eric Llewellyn Griffith G.; *see* Griffith-Williams.

WILLIAMS, Evelyn Faithfull M.; *see* Monier-Williams.

WILLIAMS, Sir Francis (John Watkin), 8th Bt *cr* 1798; QC 1952; *b* Anglesey, 24 Jan. 1905; *s* of Col Lawrence Williams, OBE, DL, JP (*d* 1958) (*gs* of 1st Bt); *S* brother, 1971; *m* 1932, Brenda, *d* of Sir John Jarvis, 1st Bt; four *d. Educ:* Malvern College; Trinity Hall, Cambridge. Barrister of Middle Temple, 1928. Served War of 1939-45; Wing Comdr, RAFVR. Recorder of Birkenhead, 1950-58; Recorder of Chester, 1958-71; Chm., Anglesey QS, 1960-71 (Dep. Chm., 1949-60); Chm., Flint QS, 1961-71 (Dep Chm., 1953-61); Dep. Chm., Cheshire QS, 1952-71; a Recorder of the Crown Court, 1972-74. JP Denbighshire, 1951-74; Chm. Medical Appeal Tribunal for N Wales Areas, 1954-57; High Sheriff: of Denbighshire, 1957, of Anglesey, 1963. Chancellor, Diocese of St Asaph, 1966. Freeman of City of Chester, 1960. *Heir: half-b* Lawrence Hugh Williams [*b* 25 Aug. 1929; *m* 1952, Sara Margaret Helen, 3rd *d* of Sir Harry Platt, Bt, *qv*; two *d*]. *Address:* Llys Meirchion, Denbigh, Clwyd. *T:* 69. *Clubs:* United Oxford & Cambridge University; Grosvenor (Chester).
See also Sir Charles Kimber, Bt.

WILLIAMS, Francis Julian, JP; DL; Member of Prince of Wales' Council, Duchy of Cornwall, since 1969; *b* 16 April 1927; 2nd *s* of Alfred Martyn Williams, *qv*; *m* Delia Fearne Marshall, *e d* of Captain Campbell Marshall; two *s. Educ:* Eton; Trinity Coll., Cambridge (BA). RAF, 1945-48. Chm., Cambridge Univ. Conservative Assoc;, 1950; Pres., Cambridge Union, 1951. Contested (C) All Saints Div. of Birmingham, 1955. Mem., Devon and Cornwall Cttee, Lloyds Bank, 1971-. Succeeded to Caerhays, 1955. Pres., Cornwall Cricket Club. Mem., Cornwall CC, 1967- (Vice-Chm., 1974-). JP 1970, DL 1977, Cornwall. *Recreation:* gardening. *Address:* Caerhays Castle, Gorran, St Austell, Cornwall. *T:* Veryan 250. *Clubs:* Brooks's, White's.

WILLIAMS, Frank Denry Clement, CMG 1956; *b* 3 May 1913; *s* of Frank Norris Williams and Joanna Esther Williams; *m* 1941, Traute Kahn; no *c. Educ:* Leighton Park School, Reading; London School of Economics (BSc Econ.). Cadet, Colonial Administrative Service, 1946; Asst Financial Sec., Nigeria, 1952; Financial Secretary: Jamaica, 1954; Federation of Nigeria, 1956; Economic Adviser, Federation of Nigeria, 1957-58; Permanent Secretary, Prime Minister's Dept, Fedn of The W Indies, 1958-62; Financial Sec., The Gambia, 1962-65. *Recreations:* walking, languages. *Address:* Siggiewi, Malta, GC.

WILLIAMS, Prof. Gareth Howel; Professor of Chemistry, University of London, and Head of Department of Chemistry, Bedford College, University of London, since 1967; *b* 17 June 1925; *s* of Morgan John and Miriam Williams, Treherbert, Glam; *m* 1955, Marie, BA, *yr d* of William and Jessie Mary Mitchell, Wanlockhead, Dumfriesshire; one *s* one *d. Educ:* Pentre Grammar Sch.; University Coll., London. BSc, PhD, DSc London; FRIC. Asst Lectr, then Lectr in Chemistry, King's Coll., Univ of London, 1947-60; Research Fellow, Univ. of Chicago, 1953-54; Reader in Organic Chemistry, Birkbeck Coll., Univ. of London, 1960-67. Vis. Lectr, Univ. of Ife, Nigeria, 1965; Rose Morgan Vis. Prof., Univ. of Kansas, 1969-70. External Examr: Univ. of Rhodesia, 1967-70; Univ. of Khartoum, 1967-73, 1976-; City Univ., 1968-74; Univ. of Surrey, 1974-76. *Publications:* Homolytic Aromatic Substitution, 1960; (Editor) Advances in Free-Radical Chemistry, Vol. I, 1965, Vol. II, 1967, Vol. III, 1969, Vol. IV, 1972, Vol. V, 1975; numerous papers in Jl Chem. Soc. and other scientific jls. *Recreation:* music. *Address:* Hillside, Watford Road, Northwood, Mddx. *T:* Northwood 25297; Department of Chemistry, Bedford College, Regent's Park, NW1 4NS. *T:* 01-486 4400.

WILLIAMS, Geoffrey Guy; Deputy Chairman, J. Henry Schroder Wagg & Co. Ltd, since 1977; *b* 12 July 1930; *s* of late Captain Guy Williams, OBE, and Mrs Margaret Williams (*née*

Thomas). *Educ:* Blundell's Sch.; Christ's Coll., Cambridge (MA, LLB). Slaughter and May, Solicitors, 1952-66, Partner 1961; Dir, J. Henry Schroder Wagg & Co. Ltd, 1966, Vice-Chm. 1974. Chm., National Film Finance Corp., 1976- (Dir, 1970-). Director: Bass Charrington Ltd, 1971-; Schroders Ltd, 1976-; John Brown and Co. Ltd, 1977-. *Recreations:* reading, theatre, cinema. *Address:* 18G Eaton Square, SW1W 9DD. *T:* 01-235 5212. *Club:* Brooks's.

WILLIAMS, George W.; *see* Wynn-Williams.

WILLIAMS, Gerald Wellington, JP; *b* 1903; *s* of Wellington Archbold Williams, JP, Shernfold Park, Frant, Sussex; *m* 1930, Mary Katharine Victoria, *d* of Captain Joscelyn Heber-Percy, DL, JP, East Lymden, Ticehurst, Sussex; one *s* two *d. Educ:* Eton; Christ Church, Oxford (MA). RNVR, 1939 (Lt-Comdr 1942). MP (C) Tonbridge division of Kent, 1945-56, resigned. JP Tunbridge Wells, 1957; High Sheriff of Kent, 1968-69. *Address:* Crockham House, Westerham, Kent. *T:* Crockham Hill 215. *Clubs:* Carlton, MCC.

WILLIAMS, Lady, (Gertrude), CBE 1963; Professor of Social Economics, University of London, 1955, Professor Emeritus since 1964; *b* 11 January 1897; *d* of I. Rosenblum; *m* 1919, Sir William Emrys Williams, CBE; no *c. Educ:* Manchester University; London School of Economics. Apptd to Dept of Social Studies and Economics, Bedford Coll., Univ. of London, 1919, since when has been attached to this dept as: Special Lecturer in Economics, Reader in Social Economics, now Professor, Min. of Home Security and Min. of Labour and Nat. Service, 1940-42. Member of many Govt cttees of Enquiry. Member Central Training Council, 1964. *Publications:* The State and the Standard of Living, 1936; The Price of Social Security, 1946; Women and Work, 1946; Economics of Everyday Life (Pelican), 1950, rev. and enl. edn 1972, rev. and rewritten, 1976; Recruitment to Skilled Trades, 1957; Apprenticeship in Europe: The Lesson for Britain, 1963; The Coming of the Welfare State, 1967; articles in Economic Jl, etc. *Recreations:* travel; ballet, opera. *Address:* Grenville Paddock, Haddenham, Bucks. *T:* Haddenham 291464.

WILLIAMS, Gilbert Milner, CB 1956; CBE 1950; retired from Civil Service, 1961; *b* London, 27 May 1898; *o s* of late H. Noel Williams; *m* 1927, Vera, *y d* of Carl Salling; one *d* (one *s* one *d* decd). *Educ:* Merchant Taylor's School. Barrister-at-law (Gray's Inn). Served European War, 1915-19 (RE); Admty, 1919-28; Min. of Labour, 1928-44; Assistant Secretary, Ministry of National Insurance, 1945-53; Under-Secretary for Finance and Accountant-General, Ministry for Pensions and National Insurance, 1953-57, and Director of Establishments and Organisation, 1957-61. Public Inquiries for Min. of Transport, 1962-70. *Address:* 61 The Avenue, Watford, Herts. *T:* Watford 26761. *Club:* Royal Commonwealth Society.

WILLIAMS, Prof. Glanmor; Professor of History, since 1957, and a Vice-Principal, since 1975, University College of Swansea; *b* 5 May 1920; *s* of Daniel and Ceinwen Williams, Dowlais, Glam; *m* 1946, Margaret Fay Davies; one *s* one *d. Educ:* Cyfarthfa Grammar Sch., Merthyr Tydfil; Univ. Coll. of Wales, Aberystwyth. MA 1947; DLitt 1962. Univ. Coll. of Swansea: Asst Lectr in History, 1945; Sen. Lectr, 1952. Nat. Governor, BBC, for Wales, 1965-71; Member: Royal Commn on Ancient and Historical Monuments in Wales, 1962-; Historic Bldgs Council for Wales, 1962-; British Library Bd, 1973-; Adv. Council on Public Records, 1974-. Chm., Pantyfedwen Foundations, 1973-. FRHistS 1954. *Publications:* Yr Esgob Richard Davies, 1953; The Welsh Church, 1962; Owen Glendower, 1966; Welsh Reformation Essays, 1967; Editor, Glamorgan County History, vol. III 1971, vol. IV 1974; contrib. to: History, Welsh History Review, etc. *Recreations:* walking, gramophone, cine-photography. *Address:* 11 Grosvenor Road, Swansea. *T:* Swansea 24113. *Club:* National Liberal.

WILLIAMS, Glanville Llewelyn, QC 1968; FBA 1957; Fellow of Jesus College, Cambridge, since 1955, and Rouse Ball Professor of English Law in the University of Cambridge, 1968-Oct. 1978; (Reader, 1957-65; Professor, 1966); *b* 15 Feb. 1911; *s* of late B. E. Williams, Bridgend, Glam; *m* 1939, Lorna Margaret, *d* of late F. W. Lawfield, Cambridge; one *s. Educ:* Cowbridge; University College of Wales, Aberystwyth; St John's Coll., Cambridge. Called to the Bar, 1935; PhD (Cantab), 1936; Research Fellow of St John's Coll., 1936-42; LLD (Cantab), 1946; Reader in English Law and successively Professor of Public Law and Quain Professor of Jurisprudence, University of London, 1945-55; Carpentier Lecturer in Columbia Univ., 1956; Cohen Lecturer in Hebrew University of Jerusalem, 1957; first Walter E. Meyer Visiting Research Professor, New York Univ., 1959-60; Charles Inglis Thompson Guest Professor, University of

Colorado, 1965. Special Consultant for the American Law Institute's Model Penal Code, 1956-58; Member: Standing Cttee on Criminal Law Revision, 1959-; Law Commn's Working Party on Codification of Criminal Law, 1967-; Cttee on Mentally Abnormal Offenders, 1972-. Pres., Abortion Law Reform Assoc., 1962-. Ames Prize, Harvard, 1963; (joint) Swiney Prize, RSA, 1964. Hon. LLD: Nottingham, 1963; Wales, 1974. *Publications:* Liability for Animals, 1939; chapters in McElroy's Impossibility of Performance, 1941; The Law Reform (Frustrated Contracts) Act (1943), 1944; Learning the Law, 1st edn 1945, 9th edn 1973; Crown Proceedings, 1948; Joint Obligations, 1949; Joint Torts and Contributory Negligence, 1950; Criminal Law; The General Part, 1st edn 1953, 2nd edn 1961; The Proof of Guilt, 1st edn 1955, 3rd edn 1963; The Sanctity of Life and the Criminal Law, American edn 1956, English edn 1958; The Mental Element in Crime, 1965; (with B. A. Hepple) Foundations of the Law of Tort, 1976; articles in legal periodicals. *Address:* Merrion Gate, Gazeley Road, Cambridge CB2 2HB. *T:* Trumpington 3175.

WILLIAMS, Rev. Dr Glen Garfield; General Secretary, Conference of European Churches, since 1968; *b* 14 Sept. 1923; *s* of John Archibald Douglas Williams and Violet May (*née* Tucker); *m* 1945, Velia Cristina (*née* Baglio). *Educ:* Newport High Sch.; Universities of Wales (Cardiff), London, Tübingen. Military Service, 1943-47. Univ. studies, 1947-55. Minister, Dagnall Street Baptist Church, St Albans, 1955-59; European Area Secretary, World Council of Churches, Geneva, 1959-68. Hon. DTh Budapest, 1975. Order of St Vladimir, Russian Orthodox Church, 1976. *Publications:* contrib. to Handbook on Western Europe, 1967, etc.; numerous articles, mainly in Continental journals. *Recreations:* travel, reading, archæology. *Address:* c/o 150 Route de Ferney, 1211 Geneva 20, Switzerland. *T:* (022)33.34.00. *Club:* Athenæum.

WILLIAMS, Most Rev. Gwilym Owen; see Wales, Archbishop of.

WILLIAMS, Sir Gwilym (Tecwyn), Kt 1970; CBE 1966; Director, Dalgety (UK) Ltd, since 1975; *b* 1913; *s* of David and Margaret Williams; *m* 1936, Kathleen, *d* of John and Maria Edwards; two *s* one *d. Educ:* Llanfyllin CSS; Llysfasi Farm Inst.; Harper Adams Agric. Coll. Leader, Employers' side, Agricultural Wages Board, 1960-66; Director, FMC Ltd, 1962. Potato Marketing Board: Member, 1954-58; Chairman, 1955-58; Special Member, 1961-66. Member: Agric. NEDO, 1968-76; Econ. and Social Cttee, EEC, 1972-; Adv. Council for Agriculture and Horticulture in England and Wales, 1973-. National Farmers' Union: Mem. Council, 1948-; Vice-Pres., 1953, 1954, 1960-62; Dep. Pres., 1955, 1963-65; Pres., 1966-70. *Recreations:* trout fishing, shooting. *Address:* Longford Grange, Newport, Salop. *T:* Lilleshall 4229. *Club:* Farmers'.

WILLIAMS, Very Rev. Harold Claude Noel; Provost of Coventry Cathedral since 1958; *b* 6 Dec. 1914; *s* of Charles Williams and Elizabeth Malherbe, Grahamstown, S Africa; *m* 1940, Pamela Marguerite Taylor, Southampton; two *s* two *d* (and one *d* decd). *Educ:* Graeme Coll., S Africa; Durham Univ.; Southampton Univ. Ordained, 1938; Curate of Weeke, Winchester, 1938-40; Principal, St Matthew's Coll., S Africa, 1941-49; Vicar of Hyde, Winchester, 1950-54; Rector of St Mary's, Southampton, 1954-58. Hon. LLD Valparaiso Univ., USA. Grosse Verdienstkreuz des Verdienst Ordens, Federal Republic of Germany, 1967. *Publications:* African Folk Songs, 1948; (ed) Vision of Duty, 1963; Twentieth Century Cathedral, 1964; Coventry Cathedral and its Ministry, 1965; Nothing to Fear, 1967; Coventry Cathedral in Action, 1968; Basics and Variables, 1970. *Recreations:* mountaineering and fishing. *Address:* The Provost's House, Coventry. *T:* Coventry 74868. *Club:* Alpine.

WILLIAMS, Air Vice-Marshal Harold Guy L.; see Leonard-Williams.

WILLIAMS, Harri Llwyd H.; see Hudson-Williams.

WILLIAMS, Sir Harry; see Williams, Sir Charles H. T.

WILLIAMS, Rev. Harry Abbott; Community of the Resurrection, since 1969; *b* 10 May 1919; *s* of late Captain Harry Williams, RN, and Annie Williams. *Educ:* Cranleigh Sch.; Trinity Coll., Cambridge; Cuddesdon Coll., Oxford. BA 1941; MA 1945. Deacon, 1943; Priest, 1944. Curate of St Barnabas, Pimlico, 1943-45; Curate of All Saints, Margaret Street, 1945-48; Chaplain and Tutor of Westcott House, Cambridge, 1948-51; Fellow of Trinity Coll., Cambridge, 1951-69; Dean of Chapel, 1958-69, and Tutor, 1958-68; Exam. Chaplain to Bishop of London, 1948-69. Mem., Anglican delegation to Russian

Orthodox Church, Moscow, 1956; Select Preacher, Univ. of Cambridge, 1950, 1958, 1975; Hulsean Preacher, 1962, 1975; Select Preacher, Univ. of Oxford, 1974. Licensed to officiate in Dio. of Ely, 1948-. *Publications:* Jesus and the Resurrection, 1951; God's Wisdom in Christ's Cross, 1960; The Four Last Things, 1960; The True Wilderness, 1965; True Resurrection, 1972; Poverty, Chastity and Obedience: the true virtues, 1975; Tensions, 1976; Becoming What I Am, 1977; contribs to: Soundings, 1962; Objections to Christian Belief, 1963; The God I Want, 1967. *Recreations:* idleness and religion. *Address:* House of the Resurrection, Mirfield, West Yorks.

WILLIAMS, Rev. Dr (Henry) Howard; Minister, Bloomsbury Central Baptist Church, since 1958; *b* 30 April 1918; *s* of Rev. Henry James Williams and Edith Gwenllian Williams; *m* 1950, Athena Mary (*née* Maurice); three *s* one *d. Educ:* Mountain Ash Grammar Sch.; Rawdon Coll.; Leeds Univ. BA, BD, PhD. Minister: Blenheim Baptist Church, Leeds, 1943-53; Beechen Grove, Watford, 1953-58; Member: Baptist Union Council, 1954-; Central Religious Advisory Council, BBC, 1962-65; Religious Advisory Panel, ITA, 1965-70. Pres., Baptist Union of Great Britain and Ireland, 1965; Director: Baptist Times Ltd; Central YMCA, London; Mem. Editorial Bd, New Christian, 1965-70. *Publications:* Down to Earth, 1964; Noughts and Crosses, 1965; Old Memories and New Ways, 1965; The Song of the Devil, 1972; My Word, 1973; contributor to Expository Times. *Recreations:* now reduced to viewing the activity of others. *Address:* 162 Hendon Way, NW2 2NE. *T:* 01-455 6628.

WILLIAMS, Ven. Henry Leslie; Archdeacon of Chester, since 1975; Vicar of Barnston, Wirral, since 1953; *b* 26 Dec. 1919; *m* 1949, Elsie Marie; one *s. Educ:* Bethesda Gram. Sch.; St David's Coll., Lampeter (BA); St Michael's Coll., Llandaff. Deacon 1943, priest 1944, Bangor; Curate of Aberdovey, 1943-45; St Mary's, Bangor, 1945-48; Chaplain, HMS Conway, 1948-49; Curate, St Mary-without-the-Walls, Chester, 1949-53. RD of Wirral North, 1967-75; Hon. Canon of Chester Cathedral, 1972-75. CF (TA), 1953-62. *Recreation:* fly-fishing. *Address:* The Vicarage, Barnston, Wirral, Merseyside. *T:* 051-648 1776.

WILLIAMS, Sir Henry Morton Leech, Kt 1961; MBE 1945; farmer; Managing Director, Guest, Keen, Williams Ltd, 1952-62; President, Bengal Chamber of Commerce and Industry, and President, Associated Chambers of Commerce, India, 1960; *b* 1913; *s* of late O. R. Williams; *m* 1945, Bridget Mary, *d* of late C. G. Dowding; two *s* two *d. Educ:* Harrow; Corpus Christi Coll., Cambridge. Served War of 1939-45 (despatches, MBE), becoming Major, REME. CC Berkshire, 1967. *Address:* Grounds Farm, Uffington, Oxon SN7 7RD. *Club:* Oriental.

WILLIAMS, Howard; see Williams, Henry H.

WILLIAMS, Hubert Glyn, AE 1944; a Recorder of the Crown Court, since 1974; Senior Partner, Blake, Lapthorn, Rea & Williams, Solicitors, Portsmouth and District; *b* 18 Dec. 1912; *s* of John Christmas Williams and Florence Jane Williams (*née* Jones); *m* 1952, Audrey Elizabeth Righton; one *s* one *d. Educ:* Ruthin. Admitted solicitor, 1934 (2nd cl. Hons). Served War of 1939-45 (Sqdn Ldr; AE): AAF, 1939-41; RAFVR, 1941-45; UK, Egypt, E Africa, Palestine. Vice-Pres., Hampshire Inc. Law Soc., 1976-77. *Recreation:* cricket. *Address:* Twenty Nine, The Avenue, Alverstoke, Hants PO12 2JS. *T:* Gosport 83058. *Clubs:* MCC; Fareham and County (Fareham).

WILLIAMS, Ian Malcolm Gordon, CBE 1960 (OBE 1954; MBE 1945); Programme Director, United Nations/Thai Programme for Drug Abuse Control in Thailand; *b* 7 May 1914; *s* of late Thomas and Mabel Williams. *Educ:* Tatterford Sch., Norfolk; Leeds Univ.; Gonville and Caius Coll., Cambridge. President, Leeds University Students' Union, 1939. Volunteered Military Service, Sept. 1939; Officer Cadet, 123 OCTU; Commnd Royal Regt of Artillery, March 1940; NW Frontier of India and Burma, 1940-45, as Major, RA, and Mountain Artillery, Indian Army (despatches, MBE). Staff Officer, Hong Kong Planning Unit, 1946; Adjutant, Hong Kong Defence Force, 1946. Entered Colonial Administrative Service, 1946; was District Officer and Asst Colonial Secretary, Hong Kong, 1946-49; at Colonial Office, 1949-51; Senior Asst Secretary, Secretariat, Cyprus, 1951-53; Commissioner: of Paphos, 1953-55, of Larnaca, 1955-57, of Limassol, 1957-60; Chief Officer, Sovereign Base Areas of Akrotiri and Dhekelia, 1960-64. Member Administrator's Advisory Board; UK Chairman, Joint Consultative Board, 1960-64. *Recreations:* art, Cypriot archæology, swimming. *Address:* White House, Adderbury, near Banbury, Oxfordshire; UN/Thai Programme for Drug Abuse Control in Thailand (UNPDAC), 2948 Soi Somprasong 3, Petchburi Road, Bangkok, Thailand. *Club:* East India, Devonshire, Sports and Public Schools.

WILLIAMS, (James) Vaughan, DSO 1942; OBE 1959; TD 1947; JP; HM Lieutenant for the County of West Glamorgan since 1974; b 25 Oct. 1912; s of James Vaughan Williams, Merthyr Tydfil; m 1938, Mary Edith Jones (d 1972), d of G. Bryn Jones, OBE, JP, Merthyr Tydfil; two d. CEng, FICE, FIOB. Local Govt Service, 1930-39. Commnd RE (TA), 1934; served War of 1939-45, BEF, France, Egypt, Italy, Berlin (despatches 1942 and 1943); psc 1946; Lt-Col TA, 1947-59; Hon. Col 53rd (W) Div. RE, 1959-67. Mem. Wales TA&VRA, 1968; Vice-Chm. Glam TA&VR Cttee, 1968; President, Swansea Branch: Royal British Legion; Royal Engrs Assoc.; Dunkirk Veteran Assoc.; Scout Council West Glamorgan; West Glam Branch Red Cross Soc.; Mem., West Glam Council St John of Jerusalem. Past Chm., S Wales Assoc. ICE. Trustee, S Wales and Border Counties TSB. DL Glam 1959, JP Glamorgan 1975. CStJ 1974. Recreations: sailing, sea fishing, travel, gardening. Address: 5 The Grove, Mumbles, Swansea, West Glamorgan. T: Swansea 68551. Clubs: Army and Navy, St Stephen's; Cardiff and County (Cardiff); Bristol Channel Yacht.

WILLIAMS, John; guitarist; b Melbourne, 24 April 1941. Studied with Segovia and at RCM. London début, Wigmore Hall, 1958; since when has given many recitals and concerts, and made recordings of both solo guitar, and chamber and orchestral music. Recreations: people, living, chess, table-tennis, music. Address: c/o Harold Holt Ltd, 122 Wigmore Street, W1H 0AX.

WILLIAMS, (John Bucknall) Kingsley; solicitor; Chairman, Wessex Regional Health Authority, since 1975; b 28 July 1927; s of Charles Kingsley Williams and Margaret Elizabeth (née Bucknall); m 1961, Brenda (née Baldwin); two s. Educ: Kingswood Sch., Bath; Trinity Hall, Cambridge (MA, LLB). Admitted solicitor, 1954; Mem., Fowey Borough Council, 1954-56; Partner, Dutton Gregory & Williams, Solicitors, Winchester, 1956-. Member: Winchester City Council, 1966-73 (Chm. Planning Cttee and Leader of Lab. Gp, 1970-73); Hampshire Exec. Council of Nat. Health Service; ex-officio Mem., Hampshire CC Planning and Health Cttees, 1971-73; Leader of Labour Gp on Hampshire CC, 1973-75; Jt Sec., and Convenor Planning and Transportation Cttee, Labour Gp, Assoc. of County Councils, 1973-75; Mem., Council, Southampton Univ., 1976-. Address: Danesacre, Worthy Road, Winchester, Hants SO23 7AD. T: (home) Winchester 2594; (office) Winchester 66363.

WILLIAMS, Ven. John Charles; Archdeacon of Worcester, since 1975; Residentiary Canon of Worcester Cathedral, since 1975; b 17 July 1912; s of William and Edith Williams; m 1940, Agnes Mildred Hutchings, MA; one s one d. Educ: Cowbridge Sch.; St David's, Lampeter; University College, Oxford. Asst Curate, Christ Church, Summerfield, Birmingham, 1937-39; Asst Curate, Hales Owen, in charge of St Margaret's, Hasbury, 1939-43; Vicar: Cradley Heath, Staffs, 1943-48; Redditch, Worcs, 1948-59. Surrogate, 1951-71; Rural Dean of Bromsgrove, 1958-59; Rector, Hales Owen, 1959-70; Archdeacon of Dudley, 1968-75; Vicar of Dodderhill, 1970-75. Hon. Canon, Worcester Cathedral, 1965-75; Examng Chaplain to Bishop of Worcester, 1969-; Dir, Worcester Diocesan Central Services, 1974-75; Director of Ordination Candidates, 1975-. Publication: One Hundred Years, 1847-1947; A History of Cradley Heath Parish. Recreations: history of architecture, sailing. Address: 12 College Green, Worcester WR1 2LH. T: Worcester 23538. Clubs: Oxford University Occasionals, United Oxford & Cambridge University.

WILLIAMS, John Eirwyn F.; see Ffowcs Williams.

WILLIAMS, John Elwyn; His Honour Judge Williams; a Circuit Judge, since 1974; b 16 June 1921; s of Benjamin and Maria Williams; m 1st, Gwladys Margaret Vivian; two s; 2nd, Nancy Hilda. Educ: Cyfarthfa Castle Grammar Sch.; Aberystwyth University Coll.; University College London (LLB). Called to the Bar, Gray's Inn, 1950. Recreations: music, climbing. Address: 6 Langford Close, St John's Wood, NW8. T: 01-624 4377.

WILLIAMS, Sir John (Francis), Kt 1958; journalist and company director; retired 1973; b Grafton, New South Wales, 16 June 1901; s of Edward and Susan Williams; m 1931, Mabel Gwendoline Dawkins, Adelaide, SA; one s. Educ: Sydney High Sch. Managing Editor, Barrier Miner, Broken Hill, NSW, 1933-35; Managing Director, Queensland Newspapers Pty Ltd, Brisbane, 1937-46; Editor-in-Chief, Herald and Weekly Times Ltd, Melbourne, 1946-55, Managing Director, 1955-67; Chm., 1964-69. Address: Herald-Sun Office, Melbourne, Victoria 3000, Australia.

WILLIAMS, Very Rev. John Frederick; b 9 March 1907; s of John Abraham and Lydia Miriam Williams; m Millicent Jones (JP 1951); one d. Educ: Friars' School, Bangor; University of Wales. Curate: Portmadoc, Caerns, 1930; Aberdare, Glam, 1933; Vicar: Miskin, Glam, 1937; Skewen, Glam, 1953; Rector, Neath, Glam, 1962; Canon, Llandaff Cathedral, 1963; Precentor, 1966; Archdeacon of Llandaff and Priest-in-Charge, Penmark, 1969-71; Dean of Llandaff, 1971-77. Recreation: calligraphy. Address: 3a Park Road, Barry, S Glam.

WILLIAMS, John Haulfryn; Hon. Secretary, Honourable Society of Cymmrodorion, since 1973; b 1 Nov. 1908; s of Morgan and Elizabeth Williams; m 1938, Mary Gertrude Snowden; one s. Educ: Rhondda Grammar Sch.; Univ. of Wales (University Coll., Cardiff). BA (Hons Classics). Entered Inland Revenue Dept as Asst Inspector of Taxes, 1930; retd as Sen. Principal Inspector of Taxes, 1973. Mem. Council, Honourable Soc. of Cymmrodorion, 1973-. Publications: contribs to Qly Jl of HM Inspectors of Taxes on Taxation of Insurance Companies and on Double Taxation. Recreations: music, archaeology, bookbinding, walking. Address: 52 Harrow Road, Carshalton, Surrey SM5 3QQ. T: 01-642 6393.

WILLIAMS, (John) Kyffin, RA 1974 (ARA 1970); b 9 May 1918; s of Henry Inglis Wynne Williams and Essyllt Mary Williams (née Williams). Educ: Shrewsbury Sch.; Slade Sch. of Art. Sen. Art Master, Highgate Sch., 1944-73. One-man shows: Leicester Galleries, 1951, 1953, 1956, 1960, 1966, 1970; Colnaghi Galleries, 1948, 1949, 1965, 1970; Thackeray Gall., 1975. Pres., Royal Cambrian Acad., 1969. Winston Churchill Fellow, 1968. Hon. MA Wales, 1973. Publication: Across the Straits (autobiog.), 1973. Recreations: the countryside, sport. Address: Pwllfanogl, Llanfairpwll, Gwynedd. T: Llanfairpwll 693.

WILLIAMS, Sir (John) Leslie, Kt 1974; CBE 1970; Chairman, Civil Service Appeal Board, since 1977 (Deputy Chairman, 1973-77); Secretary General, Civil Service National Whitley Council (Staff Side), 1966-73; b 1 Aug. 1913; s of Thomas Oliver Williams and Mary Ellen Williams; m 1937, Florrie Read Jones; one s. Educ: Grove Park Grammar Sch., Wrexham, N. Wales. Civil Servant, 1931-46. Society of Civil Servants: Asst Secretary, 1947-49; Dep. General Secretary, 1949-56; General Secretary, 1956-66. Royal Institute of Public Administration: Executive Council Member, 1955-74; Chairman, 1968; Vice-Pres., 1974-. Member Board of Governors, Nat. Hospitals for Nervous Diseases, 1962- (Chm., 1974-); Member: NW Metropolitan Regional Hospital Board, 1963-65; (part-time) UKAEA, 1970-; Adv. Council, Civil Service Coll., 1970-76; (part-time) Pay Bd, 1974; Royal Commn on Standards of Conduct in Public Life, 1974-76; Armed Forces Pay Review Body, 1975-; (part-time) Independent Chm., Conciliation Cttees NJC for Civil Air Transport, 1974-77. Recreatopms: cricket, gardening, music. Address: 26 Russell Green Close, Purley, Surrey. T: 01-660 9666.

WILLIAMS, John Melville, QC 1977; b 20 June 1931; o s of late Baron Francis-Williams and late Lady (Jessie Melville) Francis-Williams; m 1955, Jean Margaret, d of Harold and Hilda Lucas, Huddersfield; three s one d. Educ: St Christopher Sch., Letchworth; St John's Coll., Cambridge (BA). Called to the Bar, Inner Temple, 1955. Recreations: mountain scrambling and walking, indifferent golf. Address: Deers Hill, Sutton Abinger, near Dorking, Surrey. T: Dorking 730331; 15 Old Square, Lincoln's Inn, WC2A 3UH. T: 01-831 7517.

WILLIAMS, Captain Sir John (Protheroe), Kt 1967; CMG 1960; OBE 1950; b 1896; m 1st, 1921, Gladys Grieves (d 1962); one s three d; 2nd, 1964, Mrs Althea Florence Carr (widow). Educ: Queen Elizabeth's Grammar Sch., Carmarthen. Master Mariner; Chairman: Australian National Line, 1956-71; United Salvage Pty Ltd; City Ice & Cold Storage Pty Ltd; Penmore Pty Ltd; Snr Partner, graziers J. P. Williams & Associates; Underwriting Mem. of Lloyd's of London. Officer in Charge on behalf of Bank of England, Salvage Operations of RMS Niagara, sunk in 438 ft of water, 1941, when £2,396,000 worth of gold bullion weighing 8½ tons was recovered. Address: 77 St Georges Road, Toorak, Victoria 3142, Australia. T: 24.2440; Penmore, Bolinda, Victoria. Clubs: Australian (Melbourne and Sydney); Melbourne (Melbourne).

WILLIAMS, John Robert, CMG 1973; HM Diplomatic Service; Minister, British High Commission, Lagos, since 1974; Ambassador (non-resident) to Benin, since 1976; b 15 Sept. 1922; s of late Sydney James Williams, Salisbury; m 1958, Helga Elizabeth, d of Frederick Konow Lund, Bergen; two s two d. Educ: Sheen County School; Fitzwilliam House, Cambridge. Served War of 1939-45, with 1st Bn King's African Rifles in

East Africa and Burma Campaign (Captain). Joined Colonial Office as Asst Principal, 1949; First Secretary, UK High Commission, New Delhi, 1956; Commonwealth Relations Office, 1958; Deputy High Commissioner in North Malaya, 1959-63; Counsellor, New Delhi, 1963-66; Commonwealth Office, 1966; Private Sec. to Commonwealth Secretary, 1967; Diplomatic Service Inspectorate, 1968; High Comr, Suva, 1970-74. *Recreations:* music, golf, gardening. *Address:* c/o Foreign and Commonwealth Office, SW1; British High Commission, Lagos, Nigeria. *Clubs:* Roehampton, Royal Commonwealth Society.

WILLIAMS, John Trevor; HM Diplomatic Service, retired; *b* 12 Nov. 1921; *yr s* of Dr Griffith Williams and Monica Johnson; *m* 1953, Ena Ferguson Boyd (*d* 1974); two *d. Educ:* St Paul's Sch.; Jesus Coll., Oxford. Joined Royal Armoured Corps, 1941; served with 14th/20th King's Hussars in Middle East and Italy, 1943-45. Home Civil Service, 1947-67; joined HM Diplomatic Service, 1967; Counsellor, High Commn, Wellington, NZ, 1967-69; Nato Defence Coll., Rome, 1970; Counsellor, Dublin, 1970-72; Head of Commodities Dept, FCO, 1972; seconded to: N Ireland Office, 1972-73; DoE, 1973-76. *Recreations:* riding, theatre, looking for good restaurants. *Address:* 29 Astell Street, Chelsea, SW3. *T:* 01-352 3945. *Club:* Hurlingham.

WILLIAMS, Maj.-Gen. John William C.; *see* Channing Williams.

WILLIAMS, Kingsley; *see* Williams, J. B. K.

WILLIAMS, Kyffin; *see* Williams, John K.

WILLIAMS, L(aurence) F(rederic) Rushbrook, CBE 1923 (OBE 1919); MA, BLitt; JP; formerly Chairman of Petty Sessions and a Commissioner for Income Tax (Basingstoke); Adviser to Maharao of Kutch; Membre Associé de l'Académie Diplomatique Internationale; Corresponding Hon. Member of the Institut Historique et Heraldique de France; Vice-President, Indo-British Historical Association; Editorial Adviser, Pakistan Society; *b* 10 July 1890; *m* 1923, Freda May, *d* of Frederick H. Chance, of Coward, Hawksley Sons and Chance; two *s* one *d. Educ:* private; University College, Oxford. Linton Exhibitioner at University College, 1909; Leicester Exhibitioner, 1910; Plumptre Prizeman, 1912; Gladstone Memorial Prizeman, 1912; 1st Class Final Honour School of Modern History, 1912; BLitt 1913; Lecturer in Medieval History at Queen's University, Canada, 1913-14; Fellow of All Souls Coll., Oxford, 1914-21; University Professor of Modern Indian History in the University of Allahabad, India, 1914-19; Royal Society of Arts Silver Medal, 1937; on Special Duty in connection with the Indian Constitutional Reforms, 1918; on Special Duty in the Home Department, Government of India, 1919; Director, Central Bureau of Information, 1920-26; Secretary to the Indian Delegation at the Imperial Conference, 1923; Political Secretary to the Maharaja of Patiala, and Substitute-Delegate, League of Nations Assembly, 1925; Secretary to the Chancellor of the Chamber of Princes, 1926-30; Foreign Minister of Patiala State, India, 1925-31, MLA 1924-25; Joint Director, Indian Princes' Special Organisation, 1929-31; Adviser to Indian States Delegn, Round Table Conf., 1930-31; Delegate Round Table Conf., 1932; CO 1935-38; FO 1938-39; Adviser, ME Affairs, MOI 1939-41; Eastern Service Dir, BBC, 1941-44; Editorial Staff, The Times, 1944-55. LFRSA. JP Hants, 1935. *Publications:* (with J. K. Fotheringham, DLitt) Marco Sanudo, or The Conquest of the Archipelago; History of the Abbey of St Albans; Four Lectures on the Handling of Historical Material; Students' Supplement to the Ain Akbari: A Sixteenth-Century Empire-Builder; A Primer of Indian Administration; Moral and Material Progress Reports of India (Parliamentary Papers), 1917-25; Report of Lord Chelmsford's Administration (Official Document); History of the Tour of the Prince of Wales (Official Document); India's Parliament, Vols I-IV *et seq*; A History of India under the Company and the Crown; What About India?; India (Oxford Pamphlet); The State of Israel (World Jewish Congress Book of the Year for 1957). The Black Hills: Kutch in History and Legend; The State of Pakistan, 1962, 1966; The East Pakistan Tragedy, 1972; Sufi Studies East and West, 1973; (ed) A Handbook for Travellers in India, Pakistan, Nepal, Bangladesh and Sri Lanka, 1975; contribs to: The Times; The Times Literary Supplement; The Round Table; Encyclopædia Britannica; Asian Affairs. *Recreation:* colour photography. *Address:* Bodgers Chance Mews, Great Kimble, Aylesbury HP17 9TN. *T:* Princes Risborough 5256.

WILLIAMS, Leonard, CB 1975; Director-General for Energy, Commission of the European Communities, since 1976; *b* 19 Sept. 1919; *m* Anne Taylor Witherley; three *d. Educ:* St Olave's

Grammar Sch.; King's Coll., London. Inland Revenue, 1938. War Service (RA), 1940-47. Ministry of Defence, 1948; NATO, 1951-54; Min. of Supply (later Aviation), 1954: Asst Sec., 1959; Min. of Technology (later DTI), 1964; IDC 1966; Dep. Sec., 1973; Dept of Energy, 1974-76. *Address:* 200 rue de la Loi, 1049 Brussels, Belgium.

WILLIAMS, Leonard Edmund Henry, DFC 1944; Director and Chief General Manager, Nationwide Building Society; *b* 6 Dec. 1919; *s* of William Edmund Williams; *m* 1946, Marie Harries-Jones; four *s* one *d. Educ:* Acton County Grammar School. FCA, FBS, IPFA. RAF, 1939-46. Acton Borough Council, 1935-39, Chief Internal Auditor 1946-49; Asst Accountant, Gas Council, 1949-53; Nationwide Building Society: Finance Officer, 1954-61; Dep. Gen. Man., 1961-67; Gen. Man., 1967-71; Chief Gen. Manager, 1971-; Dir, 1975-. Chm., Metrop. Assoc. of Building Socs, 1972-73; Dep. Chm., Building Socs Assoc., 1977-; Member Council: Building Socs Inst. (Pres. 1969-70); Industrial Soc.; Mem., Housing Corp., 1976-; Mem. Council of Management, European Fedn of Building Socs; Chm., Develt Cttee, Internat. Union of Building Socs and Savings Assocs. FBIM; FRSA. *Publication:* Building Society Accounts, 1966. *Recreations:* golf, sailing, reading. *Address:* The Romanys, Albury Road, Burwood Park, Walton-on-Thames, Surrey KT12 5DY. *T:* Walton-on-Thames 42758.

WILLIAMS, Sir Leslie; *see* Williams, Sir J. L.

WILLIAMS, Ven. Leslie Arthur, MA; Archdeacon of Bristol since 1967; *b* 14 May 1909; *s* of Arthur and Susan Williams; *m* 1937, Margaret Mary, *d* of Richard Crocker; one *s* one *d. Educ:* Knutsford; Downing Coll., Cambridge. Curate of Holy Trinity, Bristol, 1934-37; Licensed to officiate, St Andrew the Great, Cambridge, 1937-40; Curate in Charge, St Peter, Lowden, Chippenham, 1940-42; Chaplain, RAFVR, 1942-46; Curate: Stoke Bishop, 1946-47; Vicar: Corsham, Wilts, 1947-53; Bishopston, Bristol, 1953-60; Stoke Bishop, Bristol, 1960-67. Rural Dean of Clifton, 1966-67; Hon. Canon of Bristol, 1958. *Recreation:* gardening. *Address:* 29 Old Sneed Avenue, Stoke Bishop, Bristol BS9 1SD. *T:* 683747. *Clubs:* Hawks (Cambridge); Savage, Rotary (Bristol).

WILLIAMS, Leslie Harry; Member, British Railways Board, 1962-66 (Member, British Transport Commission, 1961-62); *b* 30 July 1909; *s* of late Harold Williams; Cosham, Hants, and of late Ivy Williams, Reigate, Surrey; *m* 1946, Margaret, *o d* of late H. T. Gerrard, Goring-by-Sea, Sussex; one *s. Educ:* Portsmouth Grammar Sch.; Jesus Coll., Cambridge. Joined Shell Petroleum Co., 1930; served Kenya and Uganda, 1931-41; Adviser on oil supplies to Occupied Enemy Territories Administration, Addis Ababa, 1941; West Africa, 1942-45; General Manager, Shell Chemicals, Johannesburg, 1948-50; Managing Director, Petrochemicals Ltd and Shell Chemical Co. Ltd, London, 1955-60. *Recreations:* fishing, gardening, music. *Address:* 18 Woodland Rise, Sevenoaks, Kent. *T:* Sevenoaks 61166. *Clubs:* MCC, Catalysts.

WILLIAMS, Leslie Henry; Deputy Chairman, Imperial Chemical Industries Ltd, 1960-67; Chairman, ICI Fibres Ltd, 1965-67; *b* 26 Jan. 1903; *s* of late Edward Henry Williams; *m* 1930, Alice, *d* of late Henry Oliver Harrison; one *s. Educ:* Highbury County Sch.; London Univ. (BSc). Joined ICI Ltd, Paints Division, 1929; appointed Director, 1943; Managing Director, 1946; Chairman, 1947; Director of ICI Main Board, 1957, Dep. Chm., 1960; Director, British Nylon Spinners Ltd, 1957-64; Director Ilford Ltd, 1958-67. FRIC 1945; President, Royal Institute of Chemistry, 1967-70. Member, Monopolies Commission, 1967-73. Hon. DSc Salford, 1972. *Recreations:* golf, gardening, music. *Address:* Penny Green, West End Lane, Stoke Poges, Bucks. *T:* Farnham Common 3423.

WILLIAMS, Mrs Michael; *see* Dench, J. O.

WILLIAMS, Prof. Michael Maurice Rudolph, Professor of Nuclear Engineering, Queen Mary College, University of London, since 1970; *b* 1 Dec. 1935; *s* of late M. F. Williams and G. M. A. Denton; *m* 1958, Ann Doreen Betty; one *s* one *d. Educ:* Ewell Castle Sch.; Croydon Polytechnic; King's Coll., London; Queen Mary Coll., London. BSc, PhD, DSc; Fellow, Instn Nuclear Engrs (Vice-Pres., 1971); FInstP. Engr with Central Electricity Generating Board, 1962; Research Associate at Brookhaven Nat. Lab., USA, 1962-63; Lectr, Dept of Physics, Univ. of Birmingham, 1963-65; Reader in Nuclear Engrg, Queen Mary Coll., London Univ., 1965-70. Exec. Editor, Annals of Nuclear Energy. Fellow American Nuclear Soc. *Publications:* The Slowing Down and Thermalization of Neutrons, 1966; Mathematical Methods in Particle Transport Theory, 1971; Random Processes in Nuclear Reactors, 1974; contribs to Proc.

Camb. Phil. Soc., Nucl. Science and Engrg, Jl Nuclear Energy, Jl Physics. *Address:* Nuclear Engineering Department, Queen Mary College, Mile End Road, E1. *T:* 01-980 4811.

WILLIAMS, Sir Michael O.; *see* Williams, Sir Osmond.

WILLIAMS, Sir Michael (Sanigear), KCMG 1968 (CMG 1954); HM Diplomatic Service, retired 1970; *b* 17 Aug. 1911; *s* of late Rev. F. F. S. Williams; *m* 1942, Joy Katharine Holdsworth Hunt (*d* 1964); two *d*; *m* 1965, Mary Grace Lindon (*née* Harding). *Educ:* Rugby; Trinity Coll., Cambridge. Entered Foreign Office, 1935; served at HM Embassy in Spain, 1938-39; Foreign Office, 1939-47; HM Embassy, Rome, 1947-50; HM Embassy, Rio de Janeiro, 1950-52; Foreign Office, 1952-56; Minister at Bonn, 1956-60; Minister to Guatemala, 1960-62; Ambassador to Guatemala, 1962-63; Assistant Under-Secretary of State, Foreign Office, 1963-65; Minister to the Holy See, 1965-70. *Recreations:* golf, gardening, motoring. *Address:* Wentways, Waldron, Heathfield, East Sussex.
See also Baron Dunboyne.

WILLIAMS, Nicholas James Donald; Managing Director and Chief Executive, Don Engineering, since 1977; *b* 21 Oct. 1925; *s* of late Nicholas Thomas Williams and Daisy Eustace (*née* Hollow); *m* 1st, 1947, Dawn Vyvyan (*née* Hill); one *s* one *d*; 2nd, 1955, Sheila Mary (*née* Dalgety); two *s* one *d*. *Educ:* St Erbyn's Sch., Penzance; Rugby Sch. (Scholar). Admitted Solicitor 1949. Served Royal Marines, 1943-47 (Captain). Partner, Nicholas Williams & Co., Solicitors, London, 1950; Senior Partner, Surridge & Beecheno, Solicitors, Karachi, 1955; Burmah Oil Co. Ltd: Legal Adviser, 1961; Co-ordinator for Eastern ops, 1963; Dir, 1965; Asst Man. Dir, 1967; Man. Dir and Chief Exec., 1969-75. *Recreation:* sailing. *Address:* Charlton House, Tetbury, Glos. *Clubs:* Oriental, MCC, Royal Cornwall Yacht.

WILLIAMS, Nigel Christopher Ransome; HM Diplomatic Service; Counsellor (Economic), Tokyo, since 1976; *b* 29 April 1937; *s* of Cecil Gwynne Ransome Williams and Corinne Belden (*née* Rudd). *Educ:* Merchant Taylors' Sch.; St John's Coll., Oxford. Joined Foreign Service and posted to Tokyo, 1961; FO, 1966; Private Secretary: to Minister of State, 1968; to Chancellor of Duchy of Lancaster, 1969; UK Mission to UN, New York, 1970; FCO, 1973. *Address:* c/o Foreign and Commonwealth Office, SW1.

WILLIAMS, Noel Ignace B.; *see* Bond-Williams.

WILLIAMS, Norman; *see* Williams, R. N.

WILLIAMS, Sir Osmond, 2nd Bt, *cr* 1909; MC 1944; JP; Chairman, Quarry Tours Ltd, since 1973; *b* 22 April 1914; *s* of late Captain Osmond T. D. Williams, DSO, 2nd *s* of 1st Bt, and Lady Gladys Margaret Finch-Hatton, *o d* of 13th Earl of Winchilsea; *S* grandfather, 1927; *m* 1947, Benita Mary, *yr d* of late G. Henry Booker, and of Mrs Michael Burn; two *d*. *Educ:* Eton; Freiburg Univ. Royal Scots Greys, 1935-37, and 1939-45; served Palestine, Africa, Italy and NW Europe. Exec. Mem., Amnesty Internat. (British Sect.). Mem., Merioneth Park Planning Cttee, 1971-74. Governor, Rainer Foundn Outdoor Pursuits Centre. JP 1960 (Chairman of the Bench, Penrhyndeudraeth, Gwynedd). Chevalier, Order of Leopold II with Palm; Croix de Guerre with Palm (Belgium), 1940. *Recreations:* music, travelling. *Heir:* none. *Address:* Borthwen, Penrhyndeudraeth, Gwynedd. *Club:* Travellers'.

WILLIAMS, Owen Lenn; Regional Financial and Development Adviser, St Vincent, West Indies, since 1976; *b* 4 March 1914; *s* of Richard Owen Williams and Frances Daisy Williams (*née* Lenn); *m* 1959, Gisela Frucht. *Educ:* St Albans Sch.; London University. Asst Principal, Export Credit Guarantee Dept, 1938; Asst Principal, Treasury, 1939; UK High Commn, Ottawa, 1941; Principal, Treasury, 1945; Asst Treasury Representative, UK High Commn, New Delhi, 1953; Treasury Rep., UK High Commn, Karachi, 1955; Economic and Financial Adviser, Leeward Islands, 1957; Perm. Sec., Min. of Finance, Eastern Nigeria, 1959; Asst Sec., Treasury, 1962; Counsellor, UK Delegn to OECD, 1968-73; Gen. Fiscal Adviser to Minister of Finance, Sierra Leone, 1974-75. *Recreations:* music, travel. *Address:* c/o National Westminster Bank Ltd, Caxton House, SW1; Ministry of Finance, Kingstown, St Vincent, West Indies. *Club:* Reform.

WILLIAMS, Paul; Chairman and Managing Director: Mount Charlotte Investments Ltd, 1966-77; Mount Charlotte Catering Ltd; Grand Hotel Co. Bristol Ltd; Mount Charlotte Hotels Ltd; Knightsbridge Cake (Manchester) Ltd; and all their subsidiary companies; Director, Greenwing Ltd; *b* 14 Nov. 1922; *s* of late

Samuel O. Williams and Esmée I. Williams (*née* Cail); *m* 1947, Barbara Joan Hardy (marr. diss. 1964); two *d*; *m* 1964, Gillian Foote, *e d* of A. G. Howland Jackson, Elstead, Surrey, and of Mrs E. J. Foote, and *step d* of E. J. Foote, Cascais, Portugal; one *d*. *Educ:* Marlborough; Trinity Hall, Cambridge (MA). MP (C) Sunderland South, (C 1953-57, Ind. C 1957-58, C 1958-64). Chairman, Monday Club, 1964-69. FInstD. *Address:* 6 Elm Park Road, SW3. *T:* 01-352 5527. *Club:* Institute of Directors.

WILLIAMS, Paul H.; *see* Hodder-Williams.

WILLIAMS, Dr Peter Orchard, FRCP; Director, and Secretary to the Trustees, The Wellcome Trust, since 1965; *b* 23 Sept. 1925; *s* of Robert Orchard Williams, CBE, and Agnes Annie Birkinshaw; *m* 1949, Billie Innes Brown; two *d*. *Educ:* Caterham Sch.; Queen's Royal College, Trinidad; St John's Coll., Cambridge (MA); St Mary's Hospital Medical School. MB, BChir 1950; MRCP 1952; FRCP 1970. House Physician, St Mary's Hospital, 1950-51; Registrar, Royal Free Hospital, 1951-52; Medical Specialist, RAMC, BMH Iserlohn, 1954; Medical Officer, Headquarters, MRC, 1955-60; Wellcome Trust: Asst and Dep. Scientific Secretary, 1960-64; Scientific Secretary, 1964-65. Vice-Pres., Royal Soc. of Tropical Med. and Hygiene, 1975-77; Mem., Nat. Council of Soc. Services Cttee of Enquiry into Charity Law and Practice, 1974-76; Chm., Foundations Forum, 1977-. *Publications:* Careers in Medicine, 1952; papers in scientific journals. *Recreations:* gardening, travel, tennis. *Address:* Fairlie House, The Grove, Epsom, Surrey. *T:* Epsom 21403. *Club:* Athenæum.

WILLIAMS, Sir Peter W.; *see* Watkin Williams.

WILLIAMS, Sir Philip; *see* Williams, Sir R. P. N.

WILLIAMS, Sir Ralph D. D.; *see under* Dudley-Williams, Sir Rolf (Dudley).

WILLIAMS, Prof. Raymond Henry; Professor of Drama, University of Cambridge, since 1974; Fellow of Jesus College, Cambridge, since 1961; *b* 31 Aug. 1921; *s* of Henry Joseph Williams and Gwendolene Williams (*née* Bird); *m* 1942, Joyce Mary Dalling; two *s* one *d*. *Educ:* Abergavenny Grammar Sch.; Trinity Coll., Cambridge; MA, LittD. War service (ending as Captain), 21st Anti-Tank Regt, Guards Armoured Div., 1941-45; Staff Tutor in Literature, Oxford University Extra-Mural Delegacy, 1946-61; Univ. Reader in Drama, Cambridge, 1967-74. Mem., Arts Council, 1976-. Vis. Prof. of Political Science, Stanford Univ., USA, 1973; General Editor, New Thinkers' Library, 1962-70. Editor: Politics and Letters, 1946-47; May Day Manifesto, 1968. *Publications:* Reading and Criticism, 1950; Drama from Ibsen to Eliot, 1952; Drama in Performance, 1954 (rev. edn 1968); Culture and Society, 1958; Border Country, 1960; The Long Revolution, 1961; Communications, 1962 (rev. edn, 1976); Second Generation, 1964; Modern Tragedy, 1966; Public Inquiry, 1967; Drama from Ibsen to Brecht, 1968; The English Novel from Dickens to Lawrence, 1970; A Letter from the Country, 1971; Orwell, 1971; The Country and the City, 1973; Television: technology and cultural form, 1974; (ed) George Orwell, 1975; Keywords, 1976; Marxism and Literature, 1977. *Recreation:* gardening. *Address:* Jesus College, Cambridge.

WILLIAMS, (Reginald) Norman; Under Secretary, Department of Health and Social Security, since 1977; *b* 23 Oct. 1917; *s* of Reginald Gardnar Williams and Janet Mary Williams; *m* 1956, Hilary Frances West; two *s*. *Educ:* Neath Grammar Sch.; Swansea Univ. Served War: Captain RA and later Staff Captain HQ 30 Corps, 1940-46. Solicitor in private practice, 1947-48. Dept of Health and Social Security (formerly Min. of Nat. Insurance): Legal Asst, 1948; Sen. Legal Asst, 1959; Asst Solicitor, 1966; Principal Asst Solicitor, 1974. Member of Law Society. *Recreations:* golf, photography, reading. *Address:* Brecon, 23 Castle Hill Avenue, Berkhamsted, Herts HP4 1HJ. *T:* Berkhamsted 5291.

WILLIAMS, Air Marshal Sir Richard, KBE 1954 (CBE 1927; OBE 1919); CB 1935; DSO 1917; RAAF (retired); Director-General of Civil Aviation in Australia, 1946-56, retired; *b* 1890; *s* of late Richard Williams, Grant Avenue, Rose Park, Adelaide; *m* 1st, 1915, Constance Esther Griffiths; 2nd, 1950, Lois V. Cross. Served European War, 1914-19 (despatches, DSO, OBE, Order of El Nahda of the Hedjaz). Formerly Chief of Air Staff, RAAF, and later RAAF Representative, Washington, DC. *Publication:* These are Facts (autobiog.), 1977. *Address:* 5 Ardgour Street, North Balwyn, Victoria 3104, Australia.

WILLIAMS, Richard Aelwyn Ellis, CIE 1945; late ICS; *b* 5 Dec. 1901; *s* of Rev. Richard Ellis Williams; *m* 1933, Fay Muriel

Boylan; two s one d. Educ: Taunton School; University College of Wales, Aberystwyth (graduate); Lincoln Coll., Oxford (graduate). Appointed to ICS 1925; posted to province of Bihar and Orissa; Under-Secretary, Political Department, Bihar and Orissa Government, 1930; District Magistrate, Shahabad, 1933; Rent Settlement Officer, 1937; Secretary to Bihar Government, Revenue Dept and Controller of Prices and Supplies, 1939; Chief Secretary to Orissa Government, 1944; retired from India, 1946; with Ministry of Agriculture, London, 1947-67. *Recreation:* gardening. *Address:* 9 Clareville Road, Caterham, Surrey.

WILLIAMS, Richard Derrick, MA (Cantab); Director, Gloucestershire Institute of Higher Education, since 1977; b 30 March 1926; s of Richard Leslie Williams and Lizzie Paddington; m 1949, Beryl Newbury Stonebanks; four s. *Educ:* St John's Coll., Cambridge. Asst Master, Lawrence Sherrif Sch., Rugby, 1950-51; Lectr, University Coll., Ibadan, Nigeria, 1951-52; Adult Tutor, Ashby-de-la-Zouch Community Coll., Leicestershire, 1952-54; Further Educn Organising Tutor, Oxfordshire, 1954-60; Asst Educn Officer: West Suffolk, 1960-65; Bristol, 1965-67; Dep. Chief Educn Officer, Bristol, 1967-73; Chief Educn Officer, County of Avon, 1973-76. *Recreations:* cricket, coaching cricket to sons, watching cricket. *Address:* Westbury House, 18 Eldorado Road, Cheltenham, Glos. *T:* Cheltenham 24314.

WILLIAMS, Richard Tecwyn, FRS 1967; (first) Professor of Biochemistry at St Mary's Hospital Medical School (University of London), 1949-76, now Emeritus Professor; Deputy Dean, St Mary's Hospital Medical School, 1970-76; sometime Examiner, Universities of Wales, the West Indies, and Royal Veterinary College, Universities of Glasgow, Liverpool, St Andrews, Ibadan, Nigeria, Ghana, and Royal College of Physicians; b Abertillery, Mon, South Wales, 20 Feb. 1909; e s of Richard and Mary Williams, North Wales; m 1937, Josephine Teresa Sullivan; two s three d. *Educ:* Abertillery County Sch.; University College, Cardiff. BSc (Wales) 1929; Research Assistant to Dr J. Pryde at Physiology Institute, Cardiff, 1930-34; PhD (Wales) 1932; Lecturer in Biochemistry, University of Birmingham, 1934-42; DSc (Birmingham) 1939; Senior Lecturer in Biochemistry, University of Liverpool, 1942-48. Visiting Scientist, National Institutes of Health, Bethesda, Md, USA, 1956; Member: Jt FAO/WHO Expert Cttee on Food Additives, Geneva, 1961; WHO Sci. Gp on safety of food additives, Geneva, 1966; Food Additives and Contaminants Cttee, Min. of Agriculture, 1965-72; Horserace Anti-Doping Cttee, 1970-; Toxicity Sub-Cttee of Cttee on Med. Aspects of Chemicals in Food and Environment, 1972-. Vis. Professor: NY Univ. Med. Sch., 1965-66; Indian Inst. of Science, 1975; Howard Fox Meml Lectr, NY Univ. Med. Sch., 1969. Hon. Member: Society of Toxicology (USA), 1966; Societé Française de Toxicologie, 1976; Hon. Life Member, Pan American Medical Assoc., 1968. DUniv Paris, 1966; Hon. MD Tübingen Univ., 1972; Hon. DSc: Univ. Ibadan, Nigeria, 1974; Wales, 1976. Merit award, Society of Toxicology (USA), 1968; CIBA Medal and Prize, Biochem. Soc., 1972; 1922 Medal, Univ. of Turku, Finland, 1975; Medal of Acad. de Pharmacie, Paris, 1970. *Publications:* Detoxication Mechanisms-The Metabolism of Drugs and Allied Organic Compounds, 1947 (2nd edn, 1959). Ed. Biochemical Society Symposia, 1947-55. Numerous research papers published mainly in Biochemical Journal and Journal of Chemical Society. *Recreations:* walking on Welsh mountains, Welsh Culture and History. *Address:* 95 Vernon Drive, Stanmore, Mddx. *T:* 01-427 5554.

WILLIAMS, Robert Emmanuel; b 1 Jan. 1900; o s of David Williams; m 1st, 1928, Rosamund May Taylor (d 1929); 2nd, 1938, Audrey Forbes Higginson; three s one d. *Educ:* Liverpool Institute; Liverpool Univ. (MSc); Brasenose Coll., Oxford (MA). Assistant Master: Ilkeston, Rugby, Lawrence Sheriff Sch., Repton, 1922-36; Lecturer, Oxford Univ. Department of Education, 1936-39; HM Inspector of Schools, 1939; Staff Inspector, 1945; Chief Inspector of Schools, Ministry of Education, 1952-61; Simon Senior Research Fellow, Manchester Univ., 1961-62; Lecturer in Education, London Univ. Institute of Education, 1962-67. *Publications:* contributions to School Science Review, Religion in Education. *Address:* Sea Crest, 10 Ryder's Avenue, Westgate-on-Sea, Kent.

WILLIAMS, Sir Robert (Evan Owen), Kt 1976; MD, FRCP, FRCPath; FFCM; Director, Public Health Laboratory Service, since 1973; b 30 June 1916; s of Gwynne Evan Owen Williams and Cicely Mary (née Innes); m 1944, Margaret (née Lumsden); one s two d. *Educ:* Sherborne Sch., Dorset; University College, London and University College Hospital. Assistant Pathologist, EMS, 1941-42; Pathologist, Medical Research Council Unit, Birmingham Accident Hospital, 1942-46; on staff Public Health

Laboratory Service, 1946-60 (Director, Streptococcus, Staphylococcus and Air Hygiene Laboratory, 1949-60); Prof. of Bacteriology, Univ. of London, at St Mary's Hosp. Med. Sch., 1960-73, Dean 1967-73. Mem. MRC, 1969-73. Pres., RCPath, 1975. Fellow, UCL, 1968. Hon. FRCPA, 1977; Hon. MD Uppsala, 1972; Hon. DSc Bath, 1977. *Publications:* (jt author) Hospital Infection, 1966; numerous publications in journals on bacteriological and epidemiological subjects. *Recreation:* horticulture. *Address:* 26 Brampton Grove, Hendon, NW4 4AQ. *T:* 01-202 9774; Little Platt, Plush, Dorset. *Club:* Athenæum.

WILLIAMS, Prof. Robert Joseph Paton, DPhil; FRS 1972; Royal Society Napier Research Professor at Oxford, since 1974; Fellow of Wadham College, Oxford, since 1955; b 25 Feb. 1926; m 1952, Jelly Klara (née Büchli); two s. *Educ:* Wallasey Grammar Sch.; Merton Coll., Oxford (MA, DPhil). ARIC. Rotary Foundn Fellow, Uppsala, 1950-51; Jun. Res. Fellow, Merton Coll., Oxford, 1951-55; Lectr, 1955-73, Reader in Inorganic Chemistry, 1973-74, Univ. of Oxford. Associate, Peter Bent Brigham Hosp., Boston, USA; Commonwealth Fellow, Mass, 1965-66. Tilden Medal, Chem. Soc., 1970; Keilin Medal, Biochem. Soc., 1972. *Publications:* (with C. S. G. Phillips) Inorganic Chemistry, 1965; papers in Jl Chem. Soc., biochemical jls, etc. *Recreation:* walking in the country. *Address:* Wadham College, Oxford. *T:* Oxford 42564. *Club:* Climbers'.

WILLIAMS, Robert Martin, CBE 1973; Chairman, State Services Commission, New Zealand, since 1975; b 30 March 1919; s of late Canon Henry Williams; m Mary Constance, d of late Rev. Francis H. Thorpe; one s two d. *Educ:* Christ's Coll., NZ; Canterbury University College, NZ; St John's Coll., Cambridge. MA. 1st Class Hons Mathematics, Univ. Sen. Schol., Shirtcliffe Fellow, NZ, 1940; BA, 1st Class Hons Mathematics Tripos, Cantab, 1947; PhD Math. Statistics, Cantab, 1949. Mathematician at Radar Development Laboratory, DSIR, NZ, 1941-44; Member UK Atomic Group in US, 1944-45; Member, 1949-53, Director, 1953-62, Applied Mathematics Laboratory, DSIR, NZ; Harkness Commonwealth Fellow and Vis. Fellow, at Princeton Univ., 1957-58; State Services Commissioner, NZ Public Service, 1963-67; Vice-Chancellor: Univ. of Otago, Dunedin, 1967-73; ANU, 1973-75. Mem., NZ Metric Adv. Bd, 1969-73. Mem., Internat. Statistical Inst., 1961-. Chm., Cttee of Inquiry into Educnl TV, 1970-72. Carnegie Travel Award, 1969. Hon. LLD Otago, 1972. *Publications:* papers mainly on mathematical statistics and related topics. *Address:* 21 Wadestown Road, Wellington, New Zealand.

WILLIAMS, Sir (Robert) Philip (Nathaniel), 4th Bt cr 1915; b 3 May 1950; s of Sir David Philip Williams, 3rd Bt and of Elizabeth Mary Garneys, d of late William Ralph Garneys Bond; S father, 1970. *Educ.:* Marlborough; St Andrews Univ. MA Hons. *Heir:* b David Michael Ralph Williams, b 1 Feb. 1955. *Address:* Bridehead, Dorchester, Dorset. *T:* Long Bredy 232. *Club:* MCC.

WILLIAMS, Sir Robin (Philip), 2nd Bt, cr 1953; Insurance Broker since 1952; Lloyd's Underwriter, 1961; 2nd Lieut, retired, RA; b 27 May 1928; s of Sir Herbert Geraint Williams, 1st Bt, MP, MSc, MEngAssoc, MInstCE; S father 1954; m 1955, Wendy Adèle Marguerite, o d of late Felix Joseph Alexander, London and Hong Kong; two s. *Educ:* Eton Coll.; St John's Coll., Cambridge (MA). 2nd Lieut, Royal Artillery, 1947. Vice-Chairman, Federation of Univ. Conservative and Unionist Assocs, 1951-52; Acting Chairman, 1952; Chairman of Bow Group (Conservative Research Society), 1954. Called to Bar, Middle Temple, 1954; Chm., Anti-Common Market League, 1969; Dir, Common Market Safeguards Campaign, 1973-76. Councillor, Haringey, 1968-74. *Publication:* Whose Public Schools?, 1957. *Heir:* s Anthony Geraint Williams, b 22 Dec. 1958. *Address:* 1 Broadlands Close, Highgate, N6.

WILLIAMS, Sir Rolf D. D.; see Dudley-Williams.

WILLIAMS, Rt. Rev. Ronald Ralph; see Leicester, Bishop of.

WILLIAMS, Roy; Under Secretary, Posts and Telecommunications, Department of Industry, since 1976; b 31 Dec. 1934; s of Eric Williams and Ellen Williams; m 1959, Shirley, d of Captain and Mrs O. Warwick; one s one d. *Educ:* Liverpool Univ. (BA Econs). Asst Principal, Min. of Power, 1956; Principal, 1961; Harkness Commonwealth Fellow, Univs of Chicago and Berkeley, 1963-64; Principal Private Sec., Minister of Power and subseq. Paymaster Gen., 1969; Asst Sec., DTI, 1971; Principal Private Sec., Sec. of State for Industry, 1974. *Address:* 4 The Glade, Sevenoaks, Kent. *T:* Sevenoaks 53369.

WILLIAMS, Sir Roy E. H.; see Hume-Williams.

WILLIAMS, Rt. Hon. Shirley Vivien Teresa Brittain, PC 1974; MP (Lab) Hertford and Stevenage, since 1974 (Hitchin, 1964-74); Secretary of State for Education and Science, since 1976; also Paymaster General, since 1976; *b* 27 July 1930; *d* of Prof. Sir George Catlin, *qv* and late Mrs Catlin (Vera Brittain); *m* 1955, Prof. Bernard Arthur Owen Williams (marr. diss. 1974), *qv*; one *d*. *Educ:* St Paul's Girls' Sch.; Somerville Coll., Oxford (MA), Hon. Fellow, 1970; Columbia Univ., New York. General Secretary, Fabian Soc., 1960-64. Contested (Lab) Harwich, Essex, 1954 and 1955, and Southampton Test, 1959; Parliamentary Private Secretary, Minister of Health, 1964-66; Parly Sec., Min. of Labour, 1966-67; Minister of State: Education and Science, 1967-69; Home Office, 1969-70; Opposition spokesman on: Social Services, 1970-71, on Home Affairs, 1971-73; Prices and Consumer Protection, 1973-74; Sec. of State for Prices and Consumer Protection, 1974-76. Mem., Labour Party Nat. Exec. Cttee, 1970-. Visiting Fellow, Nuffield College, Oxford, 1967-75. Hon. DEd CNAA, 1969; Hon. Dr Pol. Econ., Univ. of Leuven, 1976. *Publications:* (with B. A. O. Williams) chapter in What the Human Race is Up To, 1962; chapter in Christian Order and World Poverty, 1964; *pamphlets:* The Common Market and Its Forerunners, 1958; The Free Trade Area, 1958; Central Africa: The Economics of Inequality, 1960. *Recreations:* music and walking. *Address:* House of Commons, SW1.

WILLIAMS, Rev. (Sidney) Austen; Vicar of St Martin-in-the-Fields, since 1956; Chaplain to the Queen's Household since 1961; a Prebendary of St Paul's Cathedral, since 1973; *b* 23 Feb. 1912; *s* of Sidney Herbert and Dorothy Williams; *m* 1945, Daphne Joan McWilliam; one *s* one *d*. *Educ:* Bromsgrove School; St Catharine's College, Cambridge (MA); Westcott House, Cambridge. Curate of St Paul, Harringay, 1937-40. Chaplain, Toc H, France and Germany (POW), 1940-48. Curate of: All Hallows, Barking by the Tower, 1945-46; St Martin-in-the-Fields, 1946-51; Vicar of St Albans, Westbury Park, Clifton, Bristol, 1951-56. Freeman of the City of London, 1977. *Publication:* What Jesus Really Said, 1958. *Recreations:* photography, ornithology. *Address:* 5 St Martin's Place, WC2N 4JJ. *T:* 01-930 1862.

WILLIAMS, Stanley; solicitor; Member, Mental Health Review Tribunal (Wales Region), since 1972; *b* 6 April 1911; *s* of Thomas and Sarah Elizabeth Williams; *m* 1948, Lily Ceridwen Evans; three *s* one *d*. *Educ:* Froncysyllte; Llangollen County Sch. (Schol.); Liverpool Univ. (LLB). Admitted Solicitor, 1934. Served War of 1939-45: ranks, 1940-43; commnd RAMC, 1943. Contested (Lab) Denbigh Division, 1959 and 1964. A Recorder of the Crown Court, 1972-75. Member: Bootle Corporation, 1934-38 and 1946-50; Denbighshire County Council, 1960-63; Wrexham Corporation, 1966-68; Noise Adv. Council, 1970. *Recreations:* music, walking, gardening. *Address:* Liddington, Wynnstay Lane, Marford, Wrexham, Clwyd. *T:* Gresford 2715.

WILLIAMS, Stuart Graeme, OBE 1949; Controller, Television Administration, BBC, 1956-74; a Director of Studies, Royal Institute of Public Administration, since 1975; part-time Member, Civil Service Commission Appointment Boards; Business Consultant; *b* 5 October 1914; *y s* of late Graeme Douglas Williams, author and journalist, and of Winifred Maud Williams (now Mrs Sydney A. Moseley); *m* 1938, Catherine Anne, *d* of Charles Thomas and Florence Hutchison; one *d*. *Educ:* Alleyn Court, Westcliff-on-Sea; Wallingbrook, Chulmleigh. Joined BBC as Programme Sub-Editor, Radio Times, 1931; particularly concerned with war-time and post-war develt, BBC Overseas, European and Monitoring Services, and with develt of BBC and Internat. TV. Principal appointments: Executive: Outside Broadcasting, 1938; Monitoring Service, 1939; Empire Service, 1940; Asst Head, Overseas Programme Admin., 1941; Overseas Services, 1942; visited Middle and Far East for negotiations concerning future of British Far Eastern Broadcasting Service, Singapore and Radio SEAC, Ceylon, 1947 and 1948; Head of External Broadcasting Admin., 1948; BBC Staff Admin. Officer, 1952; Asst Controller, Staff Admin., 1955; visited Nigeria to advise Nigeria Govt concerning incorporation of Nigeria Broadcasting Service, 1955; visited Malta as member of a BBC Working Party to report on possible introduction of television in Malta, 1959; advised on organisation of Broadcasting in Singapore, 1968. Dir, Visnews Ltd, the international Newsfilm Agency, 1957-74 (Dep. Chm., 1962-74); Chm., European Broadcasting Union Cost-Sharing Gp, 1965-74. Mem., Exec. Council, Roy. Inst of Public Administration, 1951-68, Chm., 1957; Mem., Asian Broadcasting Union Finance Gp, 1971-74. *Address:* 4 Hardwick Green, Clevelands, Ealing, W13. *T:* 01-998 7191.

WILLIAMS, Tennessee, (Thomas Lanier Williams); Playwright; *b* 26 March 1911; *s* of Cornelius Coffin Williams and Edwina Dakin. *Educ:* University of Missouri; University of Iowa; Washington University. Awarded Rockefeller Fellowship 1940 (playwriting); Grant from National Institute of Arts and Letters ($1000), 1943; New York Drama Critics Circle Award, 1944-45, 1947-48, 1955, 1960-61; Pulitzer Prize, 1948, 1955. Member Alpha Tau Omega. *Publications: plays:* Battle of Angels; The Glass Menagerie, 1944; (with Donald Windham) You Touched Me, 1945; A Streetcar Named Desire, 1947; Summer and Smoke, 1948; The Rose Tattoo, 1951; Camino Real, 1953; Cat on a Hot Tin Roof, 1955; Orpheus Descending, 1957; Garden District (2 plays: Suddenly Last Summer and Something Unspoken), 1958; Sweet Bird of Youth, 1959; Period of Adjustment, 1960 (filmed, 1963); The Night of the Iguana, 1961 (filmed, 1964); The Milk Train Doesn't Stop Here Any More, 1963 (revised, 1964; filmed, as Boom, 1968); Slapstick Tragedy, 1966; The Seven Descents of Myrtle, 1968; In the Bar of a Tokyo Hotel, 1969; Small Craft Warnings, 1972; Out Cry, 1973; The Red Devil Battery Sign, 1975; The Eccentricities of a Nightingale, 1976; *film:* Baby Doll, 1957; *screen plays for:* The Glass Menagerie, A Street Car Named Desire, The Rose Tattoo; (with Meade Roberts) The Fugitive Kind (Orpheus Descending); (with Gore Vidal) Suddenly Last Summer; Boom; *volumes:* volume of one-act plays, 1945; vols of short stories, 1948, 1960 (Three Players of a Summer Game); vol. of verse, 1944; Hard Candy and other Stories, 1954; Dragon Country (plays), 1970; Eight Mortal Ladies Possessed (short stories), 1975; *novels:* The Roman Spring of Mrs Stone, 1950; Moise and the World of Reason, 1976; *novella:* The Knightly Quest, 1966; *autobiography:* Memoirs, 1975. *Recreations:* swimming, travelling. *Address:* c/o Bill Barnes, International Creative Management, 40 West 57th Street, New York, NY 10019, USA.

WILLIAMS, Sir Thomas; see Williams, Sir W. T.

WILLIAMS, Prof. Thomas Eifion Hopkins; Professor of Civil Engineering, University of Southampton, since 1967; *b* 14 June 1923; *s* of David Garfield Williams and Annie Mary Williams (*née* Hopkins), Cwmtwrch, Brecon; *m* 1947, Elizabeth Lois Davies; one *s* two *d*. *Educ:* Ystradgynlais Grammar Sch.; Univ. of Wales (BSc, MSc); Univ. of Durham (PhD). FICE, MIStructE, FInstHE, MCIT. Research Stressman, Sir W. G. Armstrong-Whitworth Aircraft, 1945; Asst Engr, Trunk Roads, Glam CC, 1946; Asst Lectr Civil Engrg, UC Swansea, 1947; Lectr in Civil Engrg, King's Coll., Univ. of Durham, 1948; Resident Site Engr, R. T. James & Partners, 1952; Post-doctoral Visitor, Univ. of California at Berkeley, 1955; Vis. Prof., Civil Engrg, Northwestern Univ., 1957; Sen. Lectr, Reader and Prof. of Civil and Transport Engrg, King's Coll., Univ. of Durham (Subseq. Univ. of Newcastle upon Tyne), 1958-67. Chm., Civil Engrg Economic Develt Cttee, 1970-; Member: EDC Civil Engrg, Nat. Econ. Develt Office; Transport Cttee, SRC; Roads Engrg Bd, ICE; British Nat. Cttee, PIARC; Council and Transp. Engrg Bd, Inst. Highway Engrs; Adv. Cttee on Trunk Rd Assessment, Dept of Transport, 1977-; Adv. Cttee on Traffic and Safety, TRRL, 1977-. *Publications:* (Editor) Urban Survival and Traffic, 1961; Capacity, in Traffic Engineering Practice, 1963; Prediction of Traffic in Industrial Areas, 1966; Autostrade: Strategia, di sviluppo industriale e la vitalita delle nostre citta, 1965; Inter-City VTOL: Potential Traffic and Sites, 1969; Mobility and the Environment, 1971; (ed) Transportation and Environment: policies, plans and practice, 1973; Integrated Transport: developments and trends, 1976; Air, Rail and Road Inter-City Transport Systems, 1976; Land Use, Highways and Traffic, 1977; contribs to Proc. ICE, Highway Engrs, IMunE, Road International, Traffic Engrg and Control, Segnalazioni Stradali, OTA/PIARC Confs. *Recreation:* music. *Address:* Willowdale, Woodlea Way, Ampfield, Romsey, Hants SO5 9DA. *T:* Chandler's Ford 3342. *Club:* Royal Automobile.

WILLIAMS, Thomas Lanier; see Williams, Tennessee.

WILLIAMS, Trevor Illtyd, MA, BSc, DPhil, FRIC, FRHistS; scientific consultant and writer; *b* 16 July 1921; *s* of Illtyd Williams and Alma Mathilde Sohlberg; *m* 1st, 1945 (marriage dissolved, 1952); 2nd, 1952, Sylvia Irène Armstead; four *s* one *d*. *Educ:* Clifton College; Queen's College, Oxford. Nuffield Research Scholar, Sir William Dunn Sch. of Pathology, Oxford, 1942-45; Endeavour: Deputy Editor, 1945-54; Editor, 1954-74, 1977- (Consulting Scientific Editor, 1974-76). Academic Relations Advr, ICI Ltd, 1962-74. Chm., Soc. for the Study of Alchemy and Early Chemistry, 1967-; Jt Editor, Annals of Science, 1966-74; Chm., World List of Scientific Periodicals, 1966-; Mem. Adv. Council, Science Museum, 1972-; Mem. Council, University Coll., Swansea, 1965-. Dexter Award, Amer. Chem. Soc., for contribs to the history of chemistry, 1976. *Publications:* An Introduction to Chromatography, 1946; Drugs from Plants, 1947; (ed) The Soil and the Sea, 1949; The Chemical Industry Past and Present, 1953; The Elements of Chromatography, 1954; (ed, jtly) A History of Technology, 1954-58; (with T. K. Derry) A Short History of Technology, 1960; Science and Technology (Ch. III, Vol. XI, New Cambridge Mod. History); (rev. edn) Alexander Findlay's A Hundred Years of Chemistry, 1965; (ed) A Biographical Dictionary of Scientists, 1968; Alfred Bernhard Nobel, 1973; James Cook, 1974; Man the Chemist, 1976; (ed) A History of Technology, the twentieth century, 1978; numerous articles on scientific subjects, especially history of science and technology. *Recreations:* fishing, trade tokens. *Address:* 20 Blenheim Drive, Oxford. *T:* Oxford 58591. *Club:* Athenæum.

WILLIAMS, Vaughan; *see* Williams, J. V.

WILLIAMS, Prof. William David, MA, DPhil; Professor of German, Liverpool University, since 1954; *b* 10 March 1917; *s* of William Williams and Winifred Ethel Williams (*née* Anstey); *m* 1946, Mary Hope Davis; one *s* one *d. Educ:* Merchant Taylors' School; St John's Coll., Oxford (MA, DPhil). Served War of 1939-45, with Sudan Defence Force, Middle East, and as Liaison Officer with Polish Army in Italy; Asst Lecturer in German, Leeds Univ., 1946; Lecturer in German, Oxford Univ., 1948-54; Pro-Vice-Chancellor, Liverpool Univ., 1965-68. *Publications:* Nietzsche and the French, 1952; The Stories of C. F. Meyer, 1962; reviews, etc, in Modern Language Review, and Erasmus. *Recreation:* gardening. *Address:* 20 Menlove Gardens South, Liverpool L18 2EL.

WILLIAMS, (William) Donald; *b* 17 Oct. 1919; 2nd *s* of Sidney Williams, Malvern; *m* 1945, Cecilia Mary (*née* Hirons); one *s. Educ:* Royal Grammar Sch., Worcester. Served War of 1939-45: Volunteer, 8th Bn Worcestershire Regt, May 1939; POW 1940 (Germany); escaped to Russia and was repatriated, 1945. Qualified as a Chartered Accountant, 1949. In practice as a Partner of firm Kendall, Wadley & Co., 1950-; Dir, Fiesta Foods Ltd; Malvern Instruments Ltd. Contested (C) Dudley, (Gen. Elec.), 1966; MP (C) Dudley, March 1968-70. By invitation, Prospective Parly Cand. (C) Dudley East, 1977. CC Hereford/Worcester, 1973-, re-elected 1977; Chairman: Public Accounts Cttee, 1977; Financial Adv. Panel, 1977; Mem., Gen. Purposes, Policy Resources and Financial Cttees. *Recreation:* reading. *Address:* Sexton Barns, 2 Cockshot Road, Malvern, Worcs. *T:* Malvern 5635.

WILLIAMS, William Penry, JP Caernarvon; Bank Manager, Midland Bank Ltd, Caernarvon, 1938-52; retired 1952; *b* 7 Sept. 1892; *s* of Capt. R. Jones Williams, Gwydryn, Abersoch, Caerns; *m* 1918, Elizabeth, *d* of John Hughes, Liverpool; one *s* one *d*; *m* 1949, Mrs Margaret Ellen Roberts. *Educ:* County Secondary School, Pwllheli. Entered Midland Bank Ltd, 1909. High Sheriff Caernarvonshire, 1944. Certificated Associate Inst. of Bankers. Commission First RWF, European War, 1914-18. Mem. Council, University Coll. of North Wales, Bangor; Vice-Chm. and Trustee of Port of Caernarvon. *Recreations:* golf and shooting. *Address:* Tyddyn Hen, Clynnog, Caernarvon. *T:* Clynnog 238. *Club:* Royal Welsh Yacht.

WILLIAMS, Col William Picton B.; *see* Bradley-Williams.

WILLIAMS, William Thomas, ARCS; PhD, DSc (London); DIC; FIBiol; FLS; with Townsville Laboratory, Division of Tropical Agronomy, CSIRO, since 1973; pianoforte teacher (LMus Australia), since 1973; *b* 18 Apr. 1913; *o s* of William Thomas and Clara Williams. *Educ:* Stationers' Company's School, London; Imperial College of Science and Technology. Demonstrator in Botany, Imperial College, 1933-36; Lecturer in Biology, Sir John Cass' College, 1936-40. Served War, 1940-46; RA (Sjt), RAOC (2/Lt), REME (T/Major). Lecturer in Botany, Bedford College, London, 1946-51; Professor of Botany, University of Southampton, 1951-65; CSIRO Division of Computing Research, Canberra, Australia, 1966-68; Div. of Tropical Pastures, Brisbane, 1968-73; Chief Res. Scientist, CSIRO, 1970-73. Sometime Secretary of Society for Experimental Biology, and of Sherlock Holmes Society of London. Past Editor, Journal of Experimental Botany. Hon. DSc Queensland, 1973. *Publications:* The Four Prisons of Man, 1971; (ed) Pattern Analysis in Agricultural Science, 1976; over 100 papers on plant physiology, numerical taxonomy and statistical ecology in scientific journals. *Recreations:* music, drinking beer. *Address:* 10 Surrey Street, Hyde Park, Townsville, Qld 4812, Australia.

WILLIAMS, Sir (William) Thomas, Kt 1976; QC 1964; MP (Lab and Co-op) Warrington since 1961; a Recorder of the Crown Court, since 1972; *b* 22 Sept. 1915; *s* of David John Williams, Aberdare, and Edith Williams; *m* 1942, Gwyneth, *d* of Rev. D.

G. Harries, Aberdare; one *s* one *d. Educ:* University Coll., Cardiff; St Catherine's, Oxford; University of London; Lincoln's Inn. President, Students' Union, University of Wales, 1939. Baptist Minister, 1941-46; Chaplain and Welfare Officer, RAF, 1944-46; Tutor, Manchester College, Oxford, 1946-49. Called to the Bar, Lincoln's Inn, 1951, Bencher, 1972. Recorder of Birkenhead, 1969-71. MP (Lab & Co-op) Hammersmith South, Feb. 1949-55, Barons Court, 1955-59; Parliamentary Private Secretary: Minister of Pensions, 1950-51; Minister of Health, 1951; Attorney General, 1965-67. Chm., IPU, 1974. Member: Advisory Council on Public Records, 1965-71; Adv. Council on Statute Law, 1974-; SE Metropolitan Regional Hospital Board, 1965-71; Select Cttee for Parly Comr, 1974-; Chm., Select Cttee on Parly Procedure, 1976-. Governor, King's Coll. Hosp., 1968-; Chm., Cray Valley Hosp. Management Cttee, 1968-69. *Address:* 20 Alleyn Park, Dulwich, SE21. *T:* 01-670 4554.

WILLIAMS, Yvonne Lovat; Secretary, Monopolies and Mergers Commission, since 1974; *b* 23 Feb. 1920; *d* of Wendros Williams, CBE and Vera Lovat Williams. *Educ:* Queenswood Sch., Hatfield; Newnham Coll., Cambridge. BA History 1941, MA 1946. Temp. Civil Servant, BoT, 1941-46; Asst Principal, BoT, 1946-48, Principal 1948-56; Treasury, 1956-58; BoT, 1958-63; Asst Sec., BoT, Min. Tech., DTI, 1963-73; Asst Sec., Monopolies and Mergers Commn, 1973-74. *Recreations:* visiting friends, theatres and old places. *Address:* Flat 16, The Limes, Linden Gardens, W2 4ET. *T:* 01-727 9851.

WILLIAMS-BULKELEY, Sir Richard Harry David, 13th Bt, *cr* 1661; TD; JP; Lord Lieutenant of Gwynedd, since 1974 (HM Lieutenant for the County of Anglesey, 1947-74); Member: Anglesey County Council, 1946-74 (Chairman, 1955-57); Mayor of Beaumaris, 1949-51; *b* 5 Oct. 1911; *s* of late Maj. R. G. W. Williams-Bulkeley, MC, and late Mrs V. Williams-Bulkeley; *S* grand-father, 1942; *m* 1938, Renée Arundell, *yr d* of Sir Thomas L. H. Neave, 5th Bt; two *s. Educ:* Eton. Served with 9th and 8th Bns Royal Welch Fusiliers, 1939-44, 2nd in Command of both Battalions and with Allied Land Forces South East Asia, specially employed, 1944-Sept. 1945, Lt-Col Comdt, Anglesey and Caernarvonshire Army Cadet Force, 1946-47 (resigned on appointment as HM Lieut). CStJ. *Recreations:* shooting, golf, hunting. *Heir: s* Richard Thomas Williams-Bulkeley [*b* 25 May 1939; *m* 1964, Sarah Susan, *er d* of Rt Hon. Sir Henry Josceline Phillimore, OBE; twin *s* one *d*]. *Address:* Plâs Meigan, Beaumaris, Gwynedd. *T:* Beaumaris 810345. *Club:* Boodles'.

WILLIAMS-ELLIS, Amabel, (Lady Williams-Ellis); Author and Journalist; *b* Newlands Corner, near Guildford; *d* of late J. St Loe Strachey, of the Spectator; *m* 1915, Sir Clough Williams-Ellis, *qv*; (son killed in action, 1944) two *d. Educ:* home. Literary editor Spectator, 1922-23. *Publications:* An Anatomy of Poetry; The Pleasures of Architecture (with Clough Williams-Ellis); But We Know Better; Noah's Ark; The Wall of Glass; How You Began; The Tragedy of John Ruskin; The Beagle in S America; Men Who Found Out; How You Are Made; Volcano; What Shall I Be; To Tell the Truth; The Big Firm; Good Citizens; Learn to Love First; Women in War Factories; Princesses and Trolls; A Food and People Geography; The Art of being a Woman; Headlong down the Years; The Art of Being a Parent; Changing the World; Seekers and Finders; Modern Scientists at Work; Darwin's Moon (A Life of Alfred Russel Wallace); Life in England, a pictorial history; Gypsy Folk Tales; Out of This World (10 vols SF anthology); The Raingod's Daughter, 1977. *Recreation:* travel. *Address:* Plâs Brondanw, Llanfrothen, Gwynedd. *TA:* Penrhyndeudraeth.

WILLIAMS-ELLIS, Sir (Bertram) Clough, Kt 1972; CBE 1958; MC; JP; FRIBA; architect; Past-President Design and Industry Association; Vice-Pres., Council for the Preservation of Rural Wales; Member Town Planning Institute; Member National Parks Committee; Chairman Glass Industry Working Party; Member National Trust Committee for Wales; Member Government Committee on Art and Industry; Member of Art Committee, University of Wales; Member Grand Council, British Travel Association; Vice-President Institute Landscape Architects; Member Advisory Council for Welsh Reconstruction; First Chairman First New Town Development Corporation (Stevenage); Member Festival of Britain 1951 Committee (Wales); Member Trunk Road Advisory Committee; late Welsh Guards, served in France, 1915-18 (despatches); *b* 28 May 1883; *m* 1915, Amabel (*see* Amabel Williams-Ellis), *o d* of late J. St Loe Strachey, Newlands Corner, Surrey; (son Christopher, killed in action—Welsh Guards—1944) two *d. Educ:* Oundle; Trinity College, Cambridge. Larger works include sections of the Wembley Exhibitions, Llangoed and Bolesworth Castles, Moynes Park, Oare House, Caversham Place, Kilve Court, Stowe School, Hurtwood School, Bishop's Stortford College Chapel, Great Hundridge Manor, Cornwell

Manor and Village, conversion of Ashridge Park (Bonar Law College), Lloyd George Mausoleum, Museum, Westminster Abbey Memorial and Memorial County College, Rhiwlas, Voelas, Nantclwyd Hall, Dalton Hall, etc; other works include churches, schools and village schemes in England, Ireland and Wales, a number of smaller houses, hotels, monuments and gardens, several London houses, including Dartmouth House and Ladies' Carlton Club, Oxford and Cambridge Club Annexe, also residences in China, S Africa and New Zealand; owns and is designer and builder of the new model resort of Portmeirion, North Wales; Town Planning Consultant to various Municipalities. Hon. LLD Wales, 1971. *Publications:* Cottage Building; England and the Octopus; the Architect; The Face of the Land; Sir Laurence Weaver (with his wife); The Tank Corps (a War History); The Pleasures of Architecture; (with John Summerson) Architecture here and now; (Editor) Britain and the Beast, 1937; (with Lord Rosse) The Protection of Ancient Buildings, 1939; Plan for Living; On Trust for the Nation; (2 Vols) An Artist in North Wales; The Adventure of Building; Town and Country Planning; Portmeirion—the place and its meaning, rev. and updated edn 1973; Trunk Roads in the landscape; Architect Errant (autobiog.). *Recreations:* travelling, building. *Address:* Plâs Brondanw, Penrhyndeudraeth, Gwynedd. *T:* Penrhyndeudraeth 292. *Clubs:* Athenæum, Lansdowne; Royal Welsh Yacht (Caernarvon).

WILLIAMS-THOMAS, Lt-Col Reginald Silvers, DSO 1940; TD; JP; DL; Commander of Crown (Belgium); Croix de Guerre; RA; Queen's Own Worcestershire Hussars; Glass Manufacturer; Director, Stevens and Williams Ltd; Lloyd's Underwriter; *b* 11 February 1914; *s* of late Hubert Silvers Williams-Thomas, Broome, Stourbridge, Worcestershire; *m* 1938, Esmée Florence Taylor; two *s* one *d*; *m* 1963, Sonia Margot Jewell, *d* of Major M. F. S. Jewell, CBE, DL, Birdham, near Chichester. *Educ:* Shrewsbury School. JP Staffs, 1947; DL Worcestershire, 1954. Freeman of the City of London; Mem., Worshipful Co. of Glass-Sellers. *Recreations:* shooting, archery, fishing, gardening. *Address:* The Tythe House, Broome, near Stourbridge, West Midlands. *T:* Kidderminster 700632.

WILLIAMS-WYNN, Col Sir (Owen) Watkin, 10th Bt, *cr* 1688; CBE 1969; FRAgSs 1969; Lord Lieutenant of Clwyd, since 1976; *b* 30 Nov. 1904; *s* of Sir Robert William Herbert Watkin Williams-Wynn, 9th Bt, KCB, DSO; *S* father 1951; *m* 1st, 1939, Margaret Jean (*d* 1961), *d* of late Col William Alleyne Macbean, RA, and Hon. Mrs Gerald Scarlett; one *s* (and one *s* decd); 2nd, 1968, Gabrielle Haden Matheson, *d* of late Herbert Alexander Caffin. *Educ:* Eton; RMA, Woolwich. Commnd RA, 1925; RHA, Instructor at Equitation Sch., Weedon; Adj. 61st (Carnarvon and Denbigh Yeo.) Medium Regt RA (TA), 1936-40; Major, 1940. Served with Regt as 2nd in command, France and Dunkirk; served with 18th Division, Singapore (despatches twice); Prisoner of War, Siam and Burmah Railway; Lt-Col comdg 361st Med. Regt RA (TA), 1946; Hon. Col 361 Med. Regt RA (TA), 1952-57. Liaison Officer to Min. of Agriculture for N Wales, 1961-70; Mem., Nature Conservancy for Wales, 1963-66. Master Flint and Denbigh Foxhounds, 1946-61; Joint Master, Sir W. W. Wynn's Hounds, 1925. JP 1937, DL 1947, Denbighshire; High Sheriff of Denbighshire, 1954; Vice-Lieutenant, Denbighshire, 1957-66, Lord Lieutenant 1966-74; Lieutenant of Clwyd, 1974-76. KStJ 1972. *Heir: s* David Watkin Williams-Wynn [*b* 18 Feb. 1940; *m* 1968, Harriet Veryan Elspeth, *d* of Gen. Sir Norman Tailyour, *qv*; two *s* twin *d*]. *Address:* Llangedwyn, Oswestry, Salop. *T:* Llanrhaiadr 269. *Club:* Army and Navy.

WILLIAMS-WYNNE, Col John Francis, CBE 1972; DSO 1945; JP; FRAgSs; Lieutenant of Gwynedd, since 1974 (HM Lieutenant of Merioneth, 1957-74); Constable of Harlech Castle since 1964; *b* 9 June 1908; *s* of late Major F. R. Williams-Wynn, CB, and late Beatrice (*née* Cooper); *m* 1938, Margaret Gwendolen, *d* of late Rev. George Roper and late Mrs G. S. White; one *s* two *d*. *Educ:* Oundle; Magdalene College, Cambridge (MA Mech. Sciences). Commissioned in RA 1929; served NW Frontier, 1936; served War of 1939-45; psc Camberley; Brigade Major, RA 2 Div., 1940-41; GSO2 HQ Ceylon Comd, 1942; comd 160 Jungle Field Regt, RA, 1943-44; GSO1, GHQ India, 1945; GSO1, War Office, 1946-48; retd 1948; comd 636 (R Welch) LAA Regt, RA, TA, 1951-54; Subs. Col 1954. Hon. Col 7th (Cadet) Bn RWF, 1964-74. JP 1950, DL 1953, VL 1954, Merioneth. Chairman, Advisory Cttee, Min. of Agric. Experimental Husbandry Farm, Trawscoed, 1955-76. Part-time mem., Merseyside and N Wales Electricity Bd, 1953-65; National Parks Comr, 1961-66; Forestry Comr, 1963-65; Member: Regional Adv. Cttee N Wales Conservancy Forestry Commission, 1950-63; County Agric. Exec. Cttee, 1955-63 and 1967-71; Gwynedd River Board, 1957-63; Forestry Cttee of GB, 1966-76; Home Grown Timber Advisory Cttee, 1966-76; Prince

of Wales's Cttee for Wales, 1970-; President: Timber Growers Organisation, 1974-76; Royal Welsh Agric. Soc., 1968 (Chm. Council, 1971-77); Chairman: Agricl Adv. Cttee, BBC Wales, 1974-; Flying Farmers' Assoc., 1974-. Mem., Airline Users Cttee of Civil Aviation Authority, 1973. Chairman and Man. Dir, Cross Foxes Ltd. *Recreations:* farming, forestry and flying. *Address:* Peniarth Towyn, Gwynedd. *T:* Towyn 328. *Clubs:* Army and Navy, Pratt's.
See also Hon . D . A . C . Douglas -Home .

WILLIAMSON, family name of **Barons Forres** and **Williamson.**

WILLIAMSON, Baron *cr* 1962, of Eccleston (Life Peer); **Thomas Williamson,** Kt 1956; CBE 1950; JP; General Secretary National Union of General and Municipal Workers, 1946-61; a Director of Securicor Ltd since 1964; (part-time) member, Iron and Steel Board, 1960-67; Member of ITA, 1961-64; Chairman British Productivity Council, 1953-54; Director of the Daily Herald, 1953-62; *b* 2 September 1897; *s* of James and Selina Williamson; *m* 1925, Hilda Hartley, St Helens; one *d*. *Educ:* Knowsley Road, St Helens; Workers' Educational Association, Liverpool University. Member Liverpool City Council, 1929-35; Member National Executive British Labour Party, and Chm. of Finance and General Purposes Cttee, 1940-47; Mem. TUC General Council, 1947-62; Chm. TUC, 1956-57; MP (Lab) Brigg Div. of Lincoln and Rutland, 1945-48. Trustee: Thomson Foundn, 1962-; Liverpool Vic. Friendly Soc., 1967-. Hon. Associate, College of Technology, Birmingham. Served as non-commissioned officer, Royal Engineers, 1915-19, two years' active service, France and Belgium. JP Liverpool, 1933. Hon. LLD (Cambridge), 1959. *Address:* 13 Hurst Lea Court, Alderley Edge, Cheshire.

WILLIAMSON, Air Commandant Dame Alice Mary, DBE 1958; RRC 1948 (ARRC 1941); retired as Matron-in-Chief, Princess Mary's Royal Air Force Nursing Service (1956-59); *d* of John William and Theodosia Williamson (*née* Lewis). *Educ:* Mells Girls Sch., near Frome, Somerset. Training Sch., Manchester Royal Infirmary, 1924-27; Post Graduate Courses, SCM, 1928-29; X-Ray Course, 1929-30; PMRAFNS, 1930-59. Promoted to Matron, Dec. 1944; Senior Matron, Wing Officer, 1951; Group Officer, 1952; Air Commandant, 1956; QHNS, 1956-59. Chief Nursing Officer, Kuwait Govt Nursing Service, 1959-62. *Recreations:* tennis, swimming, needlework. *Address:* 4 Essex Place, Westlands, Newcastle-under-Lyme, Staffs. *Club:* United Nursing Services.

WILLIAMSON, Bruce, MD Edinburgh; FRCP; Hon. Consulting Physician: Royal Northern Hospital, N7; Prince of Wales General Hospital, N15; Barnet General Hospital; Enfield War Memorial Hospital; Brentwood and District Hospital; Hornsey Central Hospital; Ex-Member Medical Appeals Tribunal; Trustee Edinburgh University Club; *b* South Shields, 1893; 5th *s* of Captain David Williamson, Ladybank, and Jane Theresa Short, Edinburgh; *m* 1936, Margaret Stewart, *d* of William Gibson, Broughty Ferry; one *s*; *m* 1959, Yvonne, *d* of Arthur Carlebach. *Educ:* Newcastle; Bruges; Royal Colleges and University of Edinburgh. Senior Pres., Royal Medical Society, Edinburgh, 1921; Hons MD Edinburgh University, 1925; Lt, Bucks Bn Oxford and Bucks LI, seconded Machine Gun Corps. Founder, Hon. Mem. and former Pres., Scottish Med. Golfing Soc. *Publications:* Text Books: Diseases of Children, 9th edn 1964; Vital Cardiology: A New Outlook on the Prevention of Heart Failure; Diastole (Honeyman Gillespie lecture, Edin. Univ.); The Autonomic Nervous System, 1972; The Executive and the Seventies (lay physiology), 1972; articles in medical journals; The Future and The Fighting General (political-economy); contrib. to The Statist. *Recreation:* golf. *Address:* 45 Cumberland Terrace, NW1. *T:* 01-935 5657. *Club:* Edinburgh Univ. of London.

WILLIAMSON, David, OBE 1971; QPM 1968; Chief Constable of Renfrew and Bute Constabulary, 1967-75, retired; *b* 16 Jan. 1916; *s* of Walter Williamson, fisherman, Havera, Shetland and Margaret Ann Fraser, Havera; *m* 1944, Mary Gwendoline Price, Warley, Staffs; one *s*. *Educ:* Anderson Educational Inst., Lerwick. Joined Greenock Burgh Police, 1937; Flt-Lt, RAF Bomber Comd, 1941-45; rejoined Greenock Burgh Police, 1945; Chief Constable, Greenock Burgh Police, 1958. *Recreations:* gardening, cabinetmaking, reading. *Address:* Havera, Lawmarnock Crescent, Bridge of Weir, Renfrewshire. *T:* Bridge of Weir 612121.

WILLIAMSON, David Francis; Deputy Director General, Agriculture, European Commission, since 1977; *b* 8 May 1934; *s* of Samuel Charles Wathen Williamson and Marie Eileen Williamson (*née* Denney); *m* 1961, Patricia Margaret Smith; two *s*. *Educ:* Tonbridge Sch.; Exeter Coll., Oxford (MA). Entered

Min. of Agriculture, Fisheries and Food, 1958; Private Sec. to Permanent Sec. and to successive Parly Secs, 1960-62. HM Diplomatic Service, as First Sec. (Agric. and Food), Geneva, for Kennedy Round Trade Negotiations, 1965-67. Principal Private Sec. to successive Ministers of Agric., Fisheries and Food, 1967-70; Head of Milk and Milk Products Div., Marketing Policy Div. and Food Policy Div., 1970-74; Under-Sec., Gen. Agricultural Policy Gp, 1974-76, EEC Gp, 1976-77. *Address:* 147 avenue des Statuaires, Uccle, 1180 Brussels, Belgium. *T:* 374 29 59.

WILLIAMSON, David Theodore Nelson, DSc; FRS 1968; Group Director of Engineering, Rank Xerox Ltd, 1974-76; Director, Xerox Research (UK) Ltd, 1975-76; retired; *b* 15 Feb. 1923; *s* of David Williamson and Ellie (*née* Nelson); *m* 1951, Alexandra Janet Smith Neilson; two *s* two *d. Educ:* George Heriot's Sch., Edinburgh; Univ. of Edinburgh. MO Valve Co. Ltd, 1943-46; Ferranti Ltd, Edinburgh, 1946-61; pioneered numerical control of machine tools, 1951; Manager, Machine Tool Control Div., 1959-61; Work on sound reproduction: Williamson amplifier, 1947, Ferranti pickup, 1949; collab. with P. J. Walker in develop't of first wide-range electrostatic loud-speaker, 1951-56; Dir of Res. and Develt, Molins Ltd, 1961-74. Member: NEL Metrology and Noise Control Sub cttee, 1954-57; NEL Cttee on Automatic Design and Machine Tool Control, 1964-66; Min. of Technology Working Party on Computer-Aided Design, 1967; Penny Cttee on Computer-Aided Design, 1967-69; Steering Cttee, IAMTACT, 1967-69; SRC Mech. and Prod. Engrg Cttee, 1965-69; SRC Control Panel, 1966-69; Mech. Engrg EDC, 1968-74; SRC Engrg Bd, 1969-73; Adv. Cttee for Mech. Engrg, 1969-71; Court, Cranfield Inst. of Technology, 1970-; Council and Exec. Cttee, British Hydrodynamics Research Assoc., 1970-73; Design Council (formerly CoID) Engrg Design Adv. Cttee, 1971-75; Council for Scientific Policy, 1972-73; Science Mus. Adv. Cttee, 1972-; SRC Manufrg Technology Cttee, 1972-75 (Chm.); Mech. Engrg and Machine Tool Requirements Bd, DTI subseq DoI, 1973-76. *Publications:* contrib. to: Electronic Engineers' Reference Book, 1959; Progress in Automation, 1960; Numerical Control Handbook, 1968. Papers and articles on engrg subjects. James Clayton Lecture, IMechE, 1968. *Recreations:* music, photography. *Address:* Home Farm House, Mentmore Road, Leighton Buzzard, Beds. *T:* Leighton Buzzard 71305.

WILLIAMSON, Dame (Elsie) Marjorie, DBE 1973; MSc, PhD (London); Principal, Royal Holloway College, University of London, 1962-73; *b* 30 July 1913; *d* of late Leonard Claude Williamson and Hannah Elizabeth Cary. *Educ:* Wakefield Girls' High School; Royal Holloway College. Demonstrator in Physics, Royal Holloway College, University of London, 1936-39; Lecturer in Physics, University College of Wales, Aberystwyth, 1939-45; Lecturer in Physics, Bedford Coll., Univ. of London, 1945-55; Principal, St Mary's Coll., Univ. of Durham, 1955-62; Deputy Vice-Chancellor, Univ. of London, 1970-71, 1971-72. Fellow, Bedford Coll., Univ. of London, 1975. A Manager, The Royal Instn, 1967-70, 1971-74. Mem., Commonwealth Scholarship Commn, 1975-. *Publications:* Papers in various scientific periodicals. *Address:* Forge Cottage, Pillerton Hersey, Warwick. *T:* Stratford on Avon 740243. *Club:* University Women's.

WILLIAMSON, Frank Edger, QPM 1966; *b* 24 Feb. 1917; *s* of John and late Mary Williamson; *m* 1943, Margaret Beaumont; one *d. Educ:* Northampton Grammar Sch. Manchester City Police, 1936-61; Chief Constable: Carlisle, 1961-63; Cumbria Constabulary, 1963-67; HM Inspector of Constabulary, 1967-72. OStJ 1967. *Address:* Drake Lane Farm, Acton, Nantwich, Cheshire. *T:* Nantwich 65530.

WILLIAMSON, Sir Hedworth; *see* Williamson, Sir N. F. H.

WILLIAMSON, Group Captain Hugh Alexander, CMG 1919; AFC; *b* 1885; *s* of Andrew Williamson. Served European War, 1914-19 (despatches, CMG); Iraq command, 1923-24; retired 1928. Calshot Pembroke Dock and Air Ministry, 1939-43. *Address:* Mill Park House, Witheridge, Tiverton, Devon.

WILLIAMSON, Hugh R.; *see* Ross Williamson.

WILLIAMSON, John; Editor, The Press Association Ltd, 1966-69; *b* 19 April 1915; *s* of late William Williamson and Jemima Williamson; *m* 1942, Queenie Myfanwy Pearl Bennett; two *d. Educ:* Holy Trinity School, Ashton-under-Lyne, Lancs. Junior Reporter, Manchester Evening News, 1933-34; Reporter, Morecambe & Heysham Visitor, 1934-36; Chief Reporter, East Ham Echo, 1936-38; News Sub-Editor, Press Assoc., 1938; Army, 1940-46, including service as Official Court Shorthand Writer in JAG's Office at Courts Martial and War Crime Trials;

rejoined Press Assoc. as Sub-Editor, 1946; held various editorial appointments until 1958, when became Chief News Editor; Acting Man. Editor, Oct. 1965. *Recreations:* gardening, reading, walking. *Address:* 51 Carbery Avenue, W3. *T:* 01-992 7941. *Club:* Press.

WILLIAMSON, Air Vice-Marshal Keith Alec, AFC 1968; Assistant Chief of Staff (Plans and Policy), Supreme HQ Allied Powers Europe, since 1977; *b* 25 Feb. 1928; *s* of Percy and Gertrude Williamson; *m* 1953, Patricia Anne, *d* of W/Cdr F. M. N. Watts; two *s* two *d. Educ:* Bancroft's Sch., Woodford Green; Market Harborough Grammar Sch.; RAF Coll., Cranwell. Commissioned, 1950; flew with Royal Australian Air Force in Korea, 1953; OC 23 Sqdn, 1966-68; Command, RAF Gütersloh, 1968-70; RCDS 1971; Dir, Air Staff Plans, 1972-75; Comdt, RAF Staff Coll., 1975-77. W/Cdr 1964; Gp Captain 1968; Air Cdre 1973; Air Vice-Marshal 1975. *Recreations:* squash, golf; listening to opera. *Address:* c/o Midland Bank Ltd, 25 Notting Hill Gate, W11. *Club:* Royal Air Force.

WILLIAMSON, Malcolm Benjamin Graham Christopher, CBE 1976; composer, pianist, organist; Master of the Queen's Music, since 1975; *b* 21 Nov. 1931; *s* of Rev. George Williamson, Sydney, Australia; *m* 1960, Dolores Daniel; one *s* two *d. Educ:* Barker Coll., Hornsby, NSW; Sydney Conservatorium. Composer-in-Residence, Westminster Choir Coll., Princeton, NJ, 1970-71. Pres., Royal Philharmonic Orch., 1977-. *Publications:* ballets, symphonic, chamber, choral and keyboard works, film scores; operas: Our Man in Havana, 1963; The Happy Prince, 1965; The Violins of Saint-Jacques, Julius Caesar Jones, 1966; The Moonrakers, Dunstan and the Devil, 1967; The Growing Castle, The Snow Wolf, Knights in Shining Armour, 1968; Lucky-Peter's Journey, 1969; Genesis, The Stone Wall, 1971; The Red Sea, 1972; The Winter Star, 1973. *Recreations:* reading, children. *Address:* Josef Weinberger Ltd, 10-16 Rathbone Street, W1P 2BJ.

WILLIAMSON, Dame Marjorie; *see* Williamson, Dame E. M.

WILLIAMSON, Sir (Nicholas Frederick) Hedworth, 11th Bt, *cr* 1642; *b* 26 Oct. 1937; *s* of late Maj. William Hedworth Williamson (killed in action, 1942) and Diana Mary, *d* of late Brig.-Gen. Hon. Charles Lambton, DSO (she *m* 2nd, 1945, 1st Baron Hailes, PC, GBE, CH); *S* uncle, 1946. *Address:* The Lane House, Mortimer, Reading, Berks RG7 3PP.

WILLIAMSON, Nicol; actor; *b* Hamilton, Scotland, 14 Sept. 1938. Dundee Rep. Theatre, 1960-61; Royal Court: That's Us, Arden of Faversham, 1961; A Midsummer Night's Dream, Twelfth Night, 1962; Royal Shakespeare Company, 1962; Nil Carborundum, The Lower Depths, Women Beware Women; Royal Court: Spring Awakening, 1962; Kelly's Eye, The Ginger Man, 1963; Inadmissable Evidence, 1964, Wyndham's 1965 (Evening Standard Best Actor Award), NY 1965 (NY Drama Critics Award); A Cuckoo in the Nest, Waiting for Godot, Miniatures, 1964; Sweeney Agonistes, Globe, 1965; Diary of a Madman, Duchess, 1967; Plaza Suite, NY, 1968; Hamlet, Round House, 1969 (Evening Standard Best Actor Award), NY and US tour, 1969; Midwinter Spring, Queen's, 1972; Circle in the Square, Uncle Vanya, NY, 1973; Royal Shakespeare Company: Coriolanus, Midwinter Spring, Aldwych, 1973; Twelfth Night, Macbeth, Stratford 1974, Aldwych 1975; dir and title role, Uncle Vanya, Other Place, Stratford, 1974. *Films:* Inadmissable Evidence, 1967; The Bofors Gun, 1968; Laughter in the Dark, 1968; The Reckoning, 1969; Hamlet, 1970; The Jerusalem File, 1971; The Wilby Conspiracy, 1974; The Seven Per Cent Solution, 1975; The Cheap Detective, The Goodbye Girl, Force Ten From Navarone, 1977. *Address:* c/o ICM, 22 Grafton Street, W1X 3LD.

WILLIAMSON, Air Vice-Marshal Peter Greville Kaye, CB 1977; CBE 1970; DFC 1943, and Bar 1944; AOC 38 Group, RAF, 1974-77; *b* 28 Feb. 1923; *s* of Maurice Kaye Williamson and Laura Elizabeth (*née* Clare); *m* 1953, Jill Anne Catherine Harvey; two *s* three *d. Educ:* Winchester House, Brackley; Dauntsey's Sch. Served War of 1939-45: N Africa and NW Europe (DFC and Bar); OC 219 Sqdn, 1945-46, OC 23 Sqdn, 1946-48, and OC 4 Sqdn, 1951-53; HQ NATO, Izmir, 1958, and Naples, 1959-61; OC 25 Sqdn, 1962; jssc 1963; Air Adviser to British High Comr, Pakistan, 1963-64; Gp Capt, Air Plans, RAF Germany, 1965-68; OC RAF Wittering, 1969-70; Dir of Establishments and Management Services, MoD (Air), 1970-72; SASO, HQ RAF Training Comd, 1972-74. MBIM 1971. Order of St Olav, 1962. *Recreations:* sailing (cruising), flying, shooting, fishing, aqualung diving, golf, bee-keeping. *Address:* South Lombard, Lanteglos-by-Fowey, Cornwall. *Clubs:* Royal Air Force, Royal Cruising, Cruising Association; RAF Yacht (Hamble).

WILLIAMSON, Thomas Bateson; Assistant Secretary, Department of Health and Social Security, 1969-75, retired; *b* 17 April 1915; *y s* of late George Williamson and Dora May Williamson; *m* 1st, 1944, Winifred Mary Johnstone (decd); two *s*; 2nd, 1953, Pauline Mary Luard; four *d. Educ:* Barrow Gram. Sch.; Gonville and Caius Coll., Cambridge. 1st Cl. Hons, Mod. Langs Tripos, 1937. Entered War Office as Asst Principal, 1938. Served with HM Forces, 1940-45. Asst Principal, Min. of Health, 1945; Principal, 1946; Asst Secretary, 1954; Commonwealth Fund Fellowship, 1958-59; Under-Secretary, 1965; retired (health grounds), 1969; Asst Secretary, 1969. *Recreations:* fell-walking, music. *Address:* 1 St Mary's Grove, Barnes, SW13. *T:* 01-788 4274.

WILLINGDON, 2nd Marquess of, *cr* 1936, **Inigo Brassey Freeman-Thomas;** Earl of Willingdon, *cr* 1931; Viscount Ratendone of Willingdon, *cr* 1931; Viscount Willingdon, *cr* 1924; Baron Willingdon of Ratton, *cr* 1910; *b* 25 July 1899; 2nd and *o* surv. *s* of 1st Marquess and Lady Marie Adelaide (*d* 1960) (Marie, Marchioness of Willingdon, CI, GBE), *d* of 1st Earl Brassey; *S* father, 1941; *m* 1943, Daphne, *er d* of late Seymour Cadwell. *Educ:* Eton. President of: St John's, Berkshire; The Fauna Preservation Society; The Feathers Clubs Association. Late Capt. 3rd Skinners Horse, Indian Cavalry; Major Sussex Yeomanry; Sqdn Ldr RAFVR. KStJ. *Address:* Kilbees Farm, Windsor Forest. *T:* Winkfield Row 2645. *Clubs:* Turf, White's.

WILLINK, Sir Charles (William), 2nd Bt *cr* 1957; Assistant Master at Eton College, since 1954; *b* 10 Sept. 1929; *s* of Rt Hon. Sir Henry Urmston Willink, 1st Bt, MC, QC (*d* 1973), and Cynthia Frances (*d* 1959), *d* of H. Morley Fletcher, MD, FRCP; *S* father, 1973; *m* 1954, Elizabeth, *d* of Humfrey Andrewes, Highgate, London; one *s* one *d. Educ:* Eton College (scholar); Trinity College, Cambridge (scholar). MA Cantab. Assistant Master, Marlborough College, 1952-54; Housemaster, Eton College, 1964-77. *Publications:* articles on Euripidean drama in Classical Quarterly, 1966, 1968, 1971. *Recreations:* bridge, field botany, music (bassoon). *Heir: s* Edward Daniel Willink, *b* 18 Feb. 1957. *Address:* 22 High Street, Eton, Windsor SL4 6AZ. *T:* Windsor 60675.

WILLIS, family name of **Baron Willis.**

WILLIS, Baron, *cr* 1963, of Chislehurst (Life Peer); **Edward Henry Willis;** FRSA; playwright (as Ted Willis); Director: World Wide Pictures, since 1967; Capital Radio Ltd; *b* London, 13 Jan. 1918; *m* 1944, Audrey Hale; one *s* one *d. Educ:* Tottenham Central School. *Plays include:* Hot Summer Night, New, 1957; God Bless the Guv'nor, Unity, 1959; Woman in a Dressing Gown, 1962; A Slow Roll of Drums, 1964; Queenie, 1967; Mr Polly, 1977; TV Scriptwriter: Dixon of Dock Green Series, 1953-; Sergeant Cork, 1963-67; Knock on any Door, 1964; Crime of Passion, 1970; Hunter's Walk, 1973. *Films include:* Woman in a Dressing Gown, 1958 (Berlin Award); Flame in the Streets (play, Hot Summer Night), 1961; Bitter Harvest, 1963; A Long Way to Shiloh, 1969. President, Screenwriters' Guild, 1958-68. Mem., Sports Council, 1971-73. *Publications:* Woman in a Dressing Gown and other TV plays, 1959; Whatever Happened to Tom Mix? (autobiography), 1970; novels Death May Surprise Us, 1974; The Left-Handed Sleeper, 1975; Man-eater, 1976; The Churchill Commando, 1977. *Recreations:* tennis, Association football. *Address:* 5 Shepherds Green, Chislehurst, Kent BR7 6PB. *Club:* Wig and Pen.

WILLIS, Charles Reginald; Director, Tiverton Gazette & Associated Papers Ltd, since 1971; Member, Press Council, 1967; *b* 11 June 1906; *s* of Charles and Marie Willis, Tiverton, Devon; *m* 1929, Violet Stubbs; one *d. Educ:* Tiverton Grammar Sch. Tiverton Gazette, 1922-27; North Western Daily Mail, 1927-29; Evening Chronicle, Newcastle upon Tyne, 1929-1935; Evening Chronicle, Manchester, 1935-42; Empire News, London, 1942-43; The Evening News, London, 1943 (Editor, 1954-66); Dir, Associated Newspapers Ltd, 1961-71; Editorial Dir, Harmsworth Publications, 1967-70. *Recreation:* cricket. *Address:* Howden Heyes, Ashley, Tiverton, Devon. *T:* Tiverton 4829. *Club:* Saints and Sinners.

WILLIS, Hon. Sir Eric (Archibald), KBE 1975; CMG 1974; Leader of the Opposition, New South Wales Parliament, since 1976; *b* 15 Jan. 1922; *s* of Archibald Clarence Willis and Vida Mabel Willis (*née* Buttenshaw); *m* 1951, Norma Dorothy, *d* of L. E. Knight; two *s* one *d. Educ:* Murwillumbah High Sch., NSW; Univ. of Sydney (BA Hons). MLA (Liberal) for Earlwood, NSW, 1950; Dep. Leader, NSW Parly Liberal Party, 1959-75, Leader, 1976-; Minister for Labour and Industry, Chief Secretary and Minister for Tourism, 1965-71; Chief Sec. and Minister for Sport, 1971-72; Minister for Education, 1972-76; Premier and Treasurer, 1976. *Recreation:* politics. *Address:* 16 Crewe Street, Bardwell Park, NSW 2207, Australia. *T:* 59.1835.

WILLIS, Rt. Hon. Eustace George, PC 1967; *b* 7 March 1903; *s* of Walter Willis and Rose Jane Eaton; *m* 1929, Mary Swan Ramsay Nisbet; one *d. Educ:* City of Norwich Sch. Engine Room Artificer, Royal Navy, 1919-30. Served Royal Artillery, 1942-45. Political Organiser, 1930-32; Bookseller and Lecturer for NCLC, 1932-64. MP (Lab), North Edinburgh, 1945-50, East Edinburgh, April 1954-70. Member: Select Cttee on Estimates, 1945-50, 1954-59; Central Adv. Cttee to Min. of Pensions, 1945-50; Mineral Development Cttee, 1946-48. Chairman: Edinburgh City Labour Party, 1952-54; Scottish Labour Party, 1954-55; Scottish Parliamentary Labour Party, 1961-63. Parliamentary Deleg. to Atlantic Congress, 1959, NATO, 1960-62. Minister of State, Scottish Office, 1964-67. Gen. Comr, Bd of Inland Revenue, 1972-; Mem., Scottish Parole Bd. Member, NUGMW. *Recreations:* book-collecting, music. *Address:* 31 Great King Street, Edinburgh EH3 6QR. *T:* 031-556 6941.

WILLIS, Harold Infield, QC 1952; *b* 28 March 1902; *yr s* of late Sir Frederick James Willis, KBE, CB, and Lady Willis; *m* 1943, Eileen Burnett Murray; three *s. Educ:* Berkhamsted; New Coll., Oxford. Called to the Bar, 1926, Middle Temple; Bencher, Middle Temple, 1948, Treasurer, 1969. Served War of 1939-45, RAFVR, 1940-45. Dep. Chm., Hampshire QS, 1966-71. *Recreations:* gardening and fishing. *Address:* Homington House, Coombe Bissett, near Salisbury, Wilts.

WILLIS, Dr Hector Ford, CB 1960; Scientific Adviser, Ministry of Defence, 1962-70, retired; *b* 3 March 1909; *m* 1936, Marie Iddon (*née* Renwick). *Educ:* Howard Gardens High Sch.; University College, Cardiff; Trinity Coll., Cambridge. British Cotton Industry Research Association, 1935-38; Admiralty, 1938; Chief of the Royal Naval Scientific Service, 1954-62. US Medal of Freedom (Silver Palm), 1947. *Publications:* Papers in Proceedings of Royal Society, Philosophical Magazine, Proceedings of the Faraday Society. *Address:* Fulwood, Eaton Park, Cobham, Surrey.

WILLIS, John Brooke; His Honour Judge Brooke Willis; a Circuit Judge (formerly County Court Judge), since 1965; Barrister-at-Law; *b* 3 July 1906; *yr s* of William Brooke Willis and Maud Mary Willis, Rotherham; *m* 1929, Mary Margaret Coward (marr. diss., 1946); one *s* one *d*; *m* 1964, Terena Ann Steel (formerly Hood); two *d. Educ:* Bedford Modern Sch.; Sheffield Univ. Called to the Bar, Middle Temple, 1938, North Eastern Circuit. Served War of 1939-45. RAFVR, 1940-45, Sqdn Leader. Recorder, Rotherham, 1955-59, Huddersfield, 1959-65; Dep. Chm., W Riding of Yorks QS, 1958-71. Chairman, Medical Appeal Tribunal under the National Insurance (Industrial Injuries) Acts, 1953-65. *Address:* The Ivies, Etwall, near Derby DE6 6LR.

WILLIS, John Henry, RBA, ARCA (London); artist; *b* Tavistock, 9 Oct. 1887; *s* of R. Willis, art dealer; *m* Eleanor Rushton (*née* Claughton); one *s* by a former marriage. *Educ:* Armstrong Coll., Durham Univ.; Royal College of Art, South Kensington. Portrait and Landscape Painter. *Principal works:* Kiwi Hut, on the line RA, 1921; 'Twixt Devon and Cornwall, on the line RA, 1923; The Nant Francon Pass, on the line RA, 1924; *portraits:* M. C. Oliver, RA, 1922; Stanley, son of E. J. Miles, RA, 1923. *Recreations:* tennis, golf. *Address:* 20 Titchfield Gardens, Paignton, Devon.

WILLIS, Hon. Sir John (Ramsay), Kt 1966; **Hon. Mr Justice Willis;** Judge of the High Court of Justice, Queen's Bench Division, since 1966; *b* 1908; *s* of Dr and Mrs J. K. Willis, Cranleigh, Surrey; *m* 1st, 1935, Peggy Eileen Branch; two *s*; 2nd, 1959, Barbara Ringrose. *Educ:* Lancing; Trinity Coll., Dublin (BA, LLB). Called to Bar, Gray's Inn, 1932; QC 1956. Royal Signals (TA), 1938-45; served War of 1939-45; GSO 1 14th Army. Bencher, Gray's Inn, 1953, Treasurer, 1969. Recorder of Southampton, 1965-66; Dep. Chairman, E Suffolk QS, 1965-71. *Recreation:* mountaineering. *Address:* 1 Verulam Buildings, Gray's Inn, WC1. *T:* 01-242 7722; Waterfields, Snape, near Saxmundham, Suffolk. *Clubs:* Garrick, Alpine.

WILLIS, John Robert, CB 1951; MC 1917; Under Secretary, Ministry of Transport, 1948-57; *b* 28 June 1896; *s* of late Professor A. R. Willis; *m* 1925, Alice Mary, *o d* of late R. F. Clarke; one *s* one *d. Educ:* St Paul's Sch.; Balliol Coll., Oxford. Inns of Court OTC, Worcestershire Regt (Lieut) and RAF, 1916-19; entered Board of Trade, 1920; Secretary, Food Council, 1932; Assistant Secretary, Industrial Supplies Dept, 1939; Commercial Relations and Treaties Dept, 1940; British Middle East Office, Cairo, 1946. *Address:* 39 Sheen Common Drive, Richmond, Surrey. *T:* 01-876 6022.

WILLIS, John Trueman, DFM 1942; Director of Castle Rock Housing Association, Edinburgh, since 1976; *b* 27 Oct. 1918; *s* of

Gordon and Ethel Willis, Headington, Oxford; *m* 1947, Audrey Joan, *d* of Aubrey and Gertrude Gurden, Headington, Oxford; one *s* one *d*. *Educ:* Oxford High Sch., Oxford. Estates Management, Magdalen Coll., Oxford, 1935-36; Industrial Trng, Lockheed Hydraulic Brake Co., Leamington Spa, 1937-38. Served War of 1939-45: Pilot on 14 Sqdn RAF Middle East, 1940-42; PoW Stalag Luft III, Germany, 1943-45. Estates Management, 1946-64, Estates Sec., 1953-, Magdalen Coll., Oxford; Rent Officer for Oxford, 1965-67; Sec. Housing Societies Charitable Trust, 1968-69; Housing Dir, 1969-70, Dir, 1971-72, Shelter. Mem., NEDO Housing Strategy Cttee, 1975-. ACIS, FRVA. *Publications:* Housing and Poverty Report, 1970; contrib. to architectural and housing jls as Dir of Shelter. *Recreations:* Rugby football, community action. *Address:* 1/3 Fettes Rise, Edinburgh EH4 1QH. *T:* 031-552 6423. *Clubs:* Bluecoats (Liverpool); Oxford Sports.

WILLIS, Joseph Robert McKenzie, CB 1952; CMG 1946; Deputy Chairman, Board of Inland Revenue, 1957-71; *b* 18 March 1909; 2nd *s* of Charles Frederick Willis and Lucy Alice McKenzie; *m* 1945, Elizabeth Browning, *er d* of James Ewing; one *s* one *d*. *Educ:* Eton; Christ Church, Oxford. Entered Inland Revenue Dept, 1932; Under Secretary, Central Economic Planning Staff, Treasury, 1948-49; Commissioner of Inland Revenue, 1949; Student of Imperial Defence Coll., 1948. Bath University: Professorial Res. Fellow, 1972-73; Vis. Prof., 1973. Specialist advr to Select Cttee on Wealth Tax, 1975. *Publications:* (with C. T. Sandford and D. J. Ironside): An Accessions Tax, 1973; An Annual Wealth Tax, 1975. *Address:* Bunbury, Lower Shiplake, Henley-on-Thames, Oxon. *T:* Wargrave 2726.

WILLIS, Norman David; Deputy General Secretary, Trades Union Congress, since 1977 (Assistant General Secretary, 1974-77); *b* 21 Jan. 1933; *s* of Victor J. M. and Kate E. Willis; *m* 1963, Maureen Kenning; one *s* one *d*. *Educ:* Ashford County Grammar Sch.; Ruskin and Oriel Colls, Oxford. Employed by TGWU, 1949; Nat. Service, 1951-53; Oxford, 1955-59; Personal Research Asst to Gen. Sec., TGWU, 1959-70; Nat. Sec., Research and Educn, TGWU, 1970-74. Mem., SSRC, 1977-. Councillor (Lab) Staines UDC, 1971-74. *Recreations:* reading novels, watching television, going to jumble sales, looking at beautiful buildings. *Address:* 13 Links Road, Ashford, Mddx.

WILLIS, Lady; Olive Christine, CBE 1951; *b* 20 Nov. 1895; *d* of late Henry Edward Millar, Hampstead; *m* 1916, Lieut Algernon Usborne Willis (Admiral of the Fleet Sir Algernon U. Willis, GCB, KBE, DSO) (*d* 1976); two *d*. *Educ:* St Felix Sch., Southwold, Suffolk; Newnham Coll., Cambridge. Officer (Sister) Order of St John of Jerusalem, 1948. *Recreation:* gardening. *Address:* Monks Lea, Tilmore, Petersfield, Hampshire. *T:* Petersfield 4135. *Club:* English-Speaking Union.

WILLIS, Robert William Gaspard, MA; Founder and Headmaster of Copford Glebe School, 1958-69, Principal, 1969-72 (now Copford College); *b* 22 Nov. 1905; *s* of Rev. W. N. Willis, founder and Headmaster for 38 years, of Ascham St Vincent's, Eastbourne, and Sophia Caroline Baker; *m* 1930, Ernestine Ruth Kimber; two *s* two *d*. *Educ:* Ascham St Vincent's, Eastbourne; Eton Coll. (Foundation Scholar); Corpus Christi Coll., Cambridge (Scholar). Assistant Master at Malvern Coll., Worcs, 1927-39 (Mathematics and Classics); Senior Mathematical Master at The King's School, Macclesfield, Cheshire, 1939-41; Headmaster of Sir William Turner's School (Coatham School), Redcar, 1941-53; Headmaster of English High School for Boys, Istanbul, Turkey, 1953-57. Hon. Fellow, Huguenot Soc. of London. Hon. Sec., Gainsborough's House Soc., Sudbury. *Recreation:* golf. *Address:* 8 Links View, Newton Green, Sudbury, Suffolk. *T:* Sudbury 72522. *Clubs:* Royal Over-Seas League; Newton Green Golf.

WILLIS, Roger Blenkiron, TD; **His Honour Judge Willis;** a Circuit Judge (formerly County Court Judge), since 1959; *b* 22 June 1906; *s* of late William Outhwaite Willis, KC, and Margaret Alice (*née* Blenkiron); *m* 1933, Joan Eleanor Amy Good; two *d*. *Educ:* Charterhouse School; Emmanuel Coll., Cambridge. Barrister, Inner Temple, Nov. 1930. Joined Middlesex Yeomanry (TA), 1938. Served War of 1939-45. *Recreation:* golf. *Address:* 18 Turners Reach House, 9 Chelsea Embankment, SW3. *T:* 01-352 6041. *Clubs:* Garrick, MCC.

WILLIS, Prof. Rupert A., DSc, MD, FRCP, FRCS; FRACP; Consultant Pathologist, Imperial Cancer Research Fund, London; Emeritus Professor and Research Fellow in Pathology, University of Leeds; *b* 24 Dec. 1898; Australian; *m* 1924, Alice Margaret Tolhurst; one *s* one *d*. *Educ:* Melbourne Univ. Medical Superintendent, Austin Hospital, Melbourne, 1927-30; Pathologist: Alfred Hospital, Melbourne, 1930-45; Royal

College of Surgeons, London, 1945-48; Royal Cancer Hospital, London, 1948-50. Professor of Pathology, University of Leeds, 1950-55; Macfarlane Professor of Experimental Medicine, University of Glasgow, 1963-64. Hon. LLD Glasgow, 1962; Hon. MD Perugia, 1975. *Publications:* The Spread of Tumours in the Human Body, 1934; Pathology of Tumours, 1948; Principles of Pathology, 1950; Borderland of Embryology and Pathology, 1958; Pathology of Tumours of Children, 1962; contrib. to Journal Path. Bact., Medical Journal Australia, etc. *Recreation:* gardening. *Address:* Inverdee, Delavor Road, Heswall, Wirral, Merseyside.

WILLIS, Ted; *see* Willis, Baron.

WILLIS, Comdr William John Adlam, CBE 1953 (OBE 1937); MVO 1936; CGM 1916; KPM 1944; RN retired; DL; HM Inspector of Constabulary, 1953-64, retired; *b* 27 June 1894; *s* of Thomas Willis, RN, retired, Gillingham, Kent; *m* 1929, Kate Constance, *d* of Henry Sanders, Gillingham; two *s* one *d*. *Educ:* Royal Navy Hospital Sch., Greenwich. Joined RN 1909; wounded at Battle of Jutland 1916 (CGM); Lt-Comdr 1929; HMS Pembroke 1933-37. Chief Constable of Rochester, 1937-40; Chief Constable of Bedfordshire, 1940-53; DL: Bedfordshire, 1951-61; Suffolk, 1964-. French Médaille Militaire, 1916. *Address:* Cross Green Cottage, Cockfield, near Bury St Edmunds, Suffolk. *T:* Cockfield Green 376. *Club:* Reform.

WILLISON, Lt-Gen. Sir David (John), KCB 1973; OBE 1958; MC 1945; Director General of Intelligence, Ministry of Defence, since 1975; *b* 25 Dec. 1919; *s* of Brig. A. C. Willison, DSO, MC; *m* 1941, Betty Vernon Bates; one *s* two *d*. *Educ:* Wellington; RMA Woolwich. 2/Lt RE, 1939; OC 17 and 246 Field Cos, 1944-45; Staff Coll., Camberley 1945; Indian Inf. Brigade, 1946; Malaya; WO, 1948-50; OC 16 Field Co., Egypt, 1950-52; GHQ MELF, 1952-53; OC, RE Troops, Berlin, 1953-55; Directing Staff, Staff Coll., Camberley, 1955-58; AQMG (Ops), HQ British Forces Aden, 1958-60; CO, 38 Engr Regt, 1960-63; Col GS MI/DI4, MoD, 1963-66; idc 1966; BGS (Intell.), MoD, 1967-70; BGS (Intell. and Security)/ACOS, G2, HQ NORTHAG, 1970-71; Dir of Service Intelligence, MoD, 1971-72; Dep. Chief Defence Staff (Int.), 1972-75. Col Comdt RE, 1973-. *Recreations:* sailing, ski-ing. *Address:* 32 Eaton Mews South, SW1. *Club:* Royal Thames Yacht.

WILLISON, Sir John (Alexander), Kt 1970; OBE 1964; QPM 1968; DL; *b* 3 Jan. 1914; *s* of John Willison Gow Willison and Mabel Willison, Dalry, Ayrshire; *m* 1947, Jess Morris Bruce. *Educ:* Sedbergh School. Joined City of London Police, 1933; served with RNVR, 1943-46; Chief Constable: Berwick, Roxburgh and Selkirk, 1952-58; Worcestershire Constabulary, 1958-67; West Mercia Constabulary, 1967-74. DL Worcs 1968. KStJ 1973. *Address:* Ravenhills Green, Lulsley, near Worcester.

WILLMER, Prof. Edward Nevill, ScD; FRS 1960; Emeritus Professor of Histology, University of Cambridge, since 1969; Fellow of Clare College since 1936; *b* 15 Aug. 1902; 5th *s* of Arthur W. Willmer, Birkenhead; *m* 1939, Henrietta Noreen (Penny), 2nd *d* of H. Napier Rowlatt; two *s* two *d*. *Educ:* Birkenhead Sch.; Corpus Christi Coll., Oxford. BA (Oxon) 1924; MA (Oxon) 1965; MSc (Manchester) 1927; ScD (Cambridge) 1944. Demonstrator and Assistant Lecturer in Physiology, Manchester, 1924-29; Lecturer in Histology, Cambridge, 1930-48; Reader, 1948-65, Prof., 1966-69. Editor, Biological Reviews, 1969-. *Publications:* Tissue Culture, 1934; Retinal Structure and Colour Vision, 1946; Cytology and Evolution, 1960, 2nd edn 1970; (ed) Cells and Tissues in Culture, 1965; Old Grantchester, 1976; contrib. physiological and biological journals. *Recreations:* painting, gardening, walking. *Address:* Yew Garth, Grantchester, Cambridge. *T:* Trumpington 2360.

WILLMER, Rt. Hon. Sir (Henry) Gordon, PC 1958; Kt 1945; OBE 1945; TD; a Lord Justice of Appeal, 1958-Jan. 1969; *b* 1899; 4th *s* of late A. W. Willmer, JP, Birkenhead; *m* 1928, Barbara, *d* of late Sir Archibald Hurd; one *s* two *d*. *Educ:* Birkenhead Sch.; Corpus Christi Coll., Oxford. Hon. Fellow of Corpus Christi Coll., 1949. Called to Bar, 1924; KC 1939. Joined Territorial Army in 1925, and served with 53rd Medium Bde, RA (TA), till 1938, when retired on to TA Reserve of Officers, from which called up for service during the war; served with Coast Artillery, 1940-43, and with AMG, CMF, 1943-45. A Justice of the High Court. Probate, Divorce and Admiralty Division, 1945-58. President, Shipping Claims Tribunal, 1946; Member Supreme Court Cttee on Practice and Procedure, 1947; Member, General Claims Tribunal, 1950; Chm., NI Detention Appeals Tribunal, 1973-75. Chairman, Inns of Court Mission, 1950-63; Treasurer, Inner Temple, 1969; Chm., Statutory Cttee, Pharmaceutical Soc. of GB, 1970; Mem., London Maritime

Arbitrators' Assoc., 1970. Trustee, Thalidomide Children's Trust, 1973. Hon. LLD Liverpool, 1966. *Recreation:* golf. *Address:* Flat 1, 34 Arkwright Road, Hampstead, NW3 6BH. *T:* 01-435 0690.
See also J. F. *Willmer.*

WILLMER, John Franklin, QC 1967; *b* 30 May 1930; *s* of Rt Hon. Sir (Henry) Gordon Willmer, *qv; m* 1958, Nicola Ann Dickinson; one *s* three *d. Educ:* Winchester; Corpus Christi Coll., Oxford. National Service, 2nd Lieut, Cheshire Regt, 1949-50; TA Cheshire Regt, 1950-51; Middlesex Regt, 1951-57 (Captain). Called to Bar, Inner Temple, 1955, Bencher, 1975. Member: panel of Lloyd's Arbitrators in Salvage Cases, 1967; panel from which Wreck Commissioners appointed, 1967. *Recreation:* walking. *Address:* 45 Lyndale Avenue, NW2 2QB. *T:* 01-435 6540. *Club:* United Oxford & Cambridge University.

WILLMOTT, Prof. Peter; Co-Director, Institute of Community Studies, since 1964; Visiting Professor, School of Environmental Studies, University College, London, since 1972; *b* 18 Sept. 1923; *s* of Benjamin Merriman Willmott and Dorothy Willmott (*née* Waymouth); *m* 1948, Phyllis Mary Noble; two *s. Educ:* Tollington Sch., London; Ruskin Coll., Oxford. BSc (Soc) (external) London. Research Asst, Labour Party, 1948-54; Res. Officer, Inst. of Community Studies, 1954-60; Dep. Dir, Inst. of Community Studies, 1960-64; Vice-Chm., Planning Cttee, SSRC, 1971-74. Vis. Prof., Ecole Pratique des Hautes Etudes, Univ. of Paris, 1972; Chm., Organising Gp of Jt Working Party on Transmitted Deprivation (DHSS/SSRC), 1974-; Governor, Centre for Environmental Studies, 1975-. *Publications:* (with Michael Young) Family and Kinship in East London, 1957; (with Michael Young) Family and Class in a London Suburb, 1960; The Evolution of a Community, 1963; Adolescent Boys of East London, 1966; (with Michael Young) The Symmetrical Family, 1973; (ed) Sharing Inflation? Poverty Report, 1976; (with Graeme Shankland and David Jordan) Inner London: policies for dispersal and balance, 1977. *Address:* 18 Victoria Park Square, E2 9PF. *T:* 01-980 6263.

WILLOCHRA, Bishop of, since 1970; **Rt. Rev. Stanley Bruce Rosier;** *b* 18 Nov. 1928; *s* of S. C. and A. Rosier; *m* 1954, Faith Margaret Alice Norwood; one *s* three *d. Educ:* Univ. of WA; Christ Church, Oxford. Asst Curate, Ecclesall, Dio. of Sheffield, 1954; Rector of: Wyalkatchem, Dio. of Perth, 1957; Kellerberrin, Dio. of Perth, 1964; Auxiliary Bishop in Diocese of Perth, Western Australia, 1967-70. *Recreation:* natural history. *Address:* Bishop's House, Gladstone, SA 5473, Australia. *T:* 622057.

WILLOTT, Lt-Col Roland Lancaster, DSO 1940; OBE 1945; TD 1946; BSc; CEng, FIMechE; Director and Vice Chairman, Summers Building Society, since 1970; *b* 1 May 1912; *s* of Frederick John Willott and Gertrude May Leese; *m* 1960, Elisabeth Petersen. *Educ:* Wellington Sch. (Somerset); University of Wales. College Apprentice Metropolitan Vickers Electrical Co., Trafford Park, Manchester, 1931-33; Mechanical Engineer Metropolitan Vickers Co., 1933-36; Major RE 1939-41; Lt-Col CRE 1941-45; Colonel Commander Army Group RE, 1945 (despatches, DSO, OBE, Order of Leopold of Belgium, Croix de Guerre). Chief Engineer, John Summers & Sons Ltd, 1945-69, Dir, 1965-71; Group Chief Engineer, Shotton Works, BSC, 1969-72. *Address:* Lea Croft, Yeld Lane, Kelsall Hill, Tarporley, Cheshire CW6 0TE. *T:* Kelsall 51344.

WILLOUGHBY, family name of **Baron Middleton.**

WILLOUGHBY, HEATHCOTE-DRUMMOND-; family name of **Earl of Ancaster.**

WILLOUGHBY, Rear-Admiral Guy; CB 1955; *b* 7 Nov. 1902; *s* of Rev. Nesbit E. Willoughby, Vicar of Bickington, Devon, and of Marjorie Helen Willoughby (*née* Kaye); *m* 1923, Mary, *d* of J. G. W. Aldridge, AMICE, Wimbledon; one *s* one *d. Educ:* Osborne and Dartmouth. Joined Osborne, 1916; Sub-Lieut, 1923; qualified as a naval pilot 1925, and thereafter flew as a pilot in Naval and RAF Squadrons, embarked in various Carriers until 1936; Commander, 1937; Commander (Air) in Glorious, 1938-39; served on naval staff, Admiralty, 1940-41; comd HM Carrier Activity, 1942-43; Captain, 1943; Chief Staff Officer to Admiral Comdg Carriers in Eastern Fleet, 1944; Director of Air Warfare and Training (Naval Staff, Admiralty), 1945-46; Imperial Defence Coll., 1947; 4th Naval Member of Australian Commonwealth Navy Board and Cdre (Air), 1948-50; comd HM Carrier Eagle, 1951-52; Rear-Admiral 1953; Flag Officer, Flying Training, 1953-56, retired, 1956. *Address:* High Croft, South Woodchester, near Stroud, Glos. *T:* Amberley 2594. *Club:* Naval and Military.

WILLOUGHBY, Maj.-Gen. Sir John (Edward Francis), KBE 1967 (CBE 1963; OBE 1953); CB 1966; *b* 18 June 1913; *s* of Major N. E. G. Willoughby, The Middlesex Regt, and Mrs B. A. M. Willoughby, Heytesbury, Wiltshire; *m* 1938, Muriel Alexandra Rosamund Scott; three *d.* Commissioned, Middlesex Regt, 1933. Served War of 1939-45 with Middlesex Regt, BEF, 1940-41; OC 2 Middlesex Regt, 1943; GSO 1 220 Military Mission, USA, Pacific, Burma and UK, 1943-44; OC 1 Dorsets Regt, NW Europe, 1944; served with Middlesex Regt, FARELF, Korea, 1950-51; GSO1, 3 Inf. Div., UK and MELF, 1951-53; OC 1 Middlesex Regt, British Troops Austria, UK and MELF, 1954-56; Colonel, The Middlesex Regt, 1959-65; Chief of Staff, Land Forces, Hong Kong, 1961; GOC, 48 Inf. Div. (TA) and W Midland District, 1963-65; GOC Land Forces ME Comd, Inspector-Gen. of Federal Regular Army of S Arabia and Security Comdr Aden State, 1965-67; Adviser on Defence to Fedn of Arab Emirates, 1968-71. *Address:* Overton House, Codford St Peter, Wilts.

WILLOUGHBY, Kenneth James; *b* 6 Nov. 1922; *y s* of late Frank Albert Willoughby and late Florence Rose (*née* Darbyshire); *m* 1943, Vera May Dickerson; one *s* one *d. Educ:* Hackney Downs (Grocers') Sch.; Selwyn Coll., Cambridge. Tax Officer, Inland Revenue, 1939; Royal Engineers, UK, Egypt, Italy, Austria, Greece, 1941-47 (despatches, Captain); Asst Auditor, Exchequer and Audit Dept, 1947; Asst Prin., Min. of Civil Aviation, 1949; Asst Private Sec. to Minister of Civil Aviation, 1950; Private Sec. to Perm. Sec., 1951; Principal, Min. of Transport (and later, Civil Aviation), 1951; Sec., Air Transport Adv. Council, 1957-61; Asst Sec., Min. of Aviation, 1962; Under-Secretary: Min. of Technology, 1968-70; DTI, 1970-74. *Address:* 67 Pine Hill, Epsom, Surrey. *T:* Epsom 25107.

WILLOUGHBY DE BROKE, 20th Baron, *cr* 1492; **John Henry Peyto Verney,** MC 1918; AFC 1940; AE; KStJ 1948; JP; Lord Lieutenant of Warwickshire, 1939-68; Air Commodore, Auxiliary Air Force, retired; *b* 21 May 1896; *o c* of 19th Baron and Marie Frances Lisette, OBE (*d* 1941), *y d* of C. A. Hanbury, Strathgarve, Ross-shire; *S* father, 1923; *m* 1933, Rachel, *d* of Sir Bouchier Wrey, 11th Bt, and Mrs Godfrey Heseltine; one *s* one *d. Educ:* Eton; Sandhurst. Served European War (MC); ADC to Governor of Bombay, 1919-22; late Captain, 17-21st Lancers; Adjutant, Warwickshire Yeomanry, 1925-29; Joint Master Warwickshire Hounds, 1929-35; commanded No. 605 (County of Warwick) AAF Squadron, 1936-39 (AFCAEA) Staff Officer 11 Fighter Group, 1940 (despatches); Deputy Director Public Relations, Air Ministry, 1941-44; Director Public Relations, 1945-46. Member: National Hunt Cttee, 1940 (Steward, 1942-44, 1950-53, and 1964-67); Jockey Club, 1941 (Steward, 1944-47 and 1954-56). Chm., Tattersall's Cttee, 1948-53. Chairman: Birmingham Racecourse Co. Ltd, 1952-65 (Dir, 1932-65); The Steeplechase Co. (Cheltenham) Ltd, 1953-71 (Dir, 1944-71); Wolverhampton Racecourse Co. Ltd, 1947-71; Race-Finish Recording Co. Ltd, later Racecourse Technical Services Ltd, 1959-70 (Dir, 1947-70). Mem., Bloodstock Industry Cttee, Animal Health Trust, 1944- (Chm., 1964-77). President: Hunters' Improvement Society, 1957-58; Warwickshire Association of Boys' Clubs; Scouts Association; Council for Order of St John, 1946-68. Hon. Colonel, Warwickshire Yeomanry, 1942-63. *Heir: s* Hon. Leopold David Verney [*b* 14 Sept. 1938; *m* 1965, Petra, 2nd *d* of Sir John Aird, 3rd Bt, MVO, MC; three *s*]. *Address:* 2 Upper Phillimore Gardens, W8 7HA. *T:* 01-937 8548; Fox Cottage, Kineton, Warwickshire CV35 0LP. *T:* Kineton 640318. *Clubs:* White's, Cavalry and Guards.

WILLS, family name of **Baron Dulverton.**

WILLS, Arthur William, DMus (Dunelm), FRCO (CHM), ADCM; composer; Organist, Ely Cathedral, since 1958; *b* 19 Sept. 1926; *s* of Violet Elizabeth and Archibald Wills; *m* 1953, Mary Elizabeth Titterton; one *s* one *d. Educ:* St John's Sch., Coventry. Sub. Organist, Ely Cathedral, 1949; Director of Music, King's School, Ely, 1953-65; Prof., Royal Academy of Music, 1964. Mem. Council, RCO, 1966-; Examr to Royal Schs of Music, 1966-. Recital tours in Canada, Europe, USA; recording artist. Hon. RAM, Hon. FLCM, FRSCM. *Publications:* The Art of Organ Improvisation, 1974; (contrib.) English Church Music, 1976; numerous musical compositions. *Recreations:* travel, antique collecting, Eastern philosophy. *Address:* The Old Sacristy, The College, Ely, Cambs. *T:* Ely 2084. *Club:* Savage.

WILLS, Lt-Col Sir Edward; see Wills, Lt-Col Sir E. E. de W.

WILLS, Lt-Col Sir (Ernest) Edward (de Winton), 4th Bt, *cr* 1904, of Hazlewood and Clapton-in-Gordano; *b* 8 Dec. 1903; *s* of Sir Ernest Salter Wills, 3rd Bt, and Caroline Fanny Maud de

Winton (d 1953); S father 1958; m 1st, 1926, Sylvia Margaret (d 1946), d of late William Barker Ogden; two d; 2nd, 1949, Juliet Eve, d of late Captain John Eagles Henry Graham-Clarke, JP, Frocester Manor, Glos. Educ: Eton. Formerly Lieut, Scots Guards; Lieut-Colonel late Middlesex Regt; Lieut-Colonel Comdg 5th Bn, Manchester Regt; served European War, 1939-45. Is a member of Lloyd's. Recreations: stalking, shooting, fishing, yachting. Heir: b Major George Seton Wills [b 18 May 1911; m 1st, 1935, Lilah Mary (marr. diss. 1946), d of late Captain Percy Richard Hare; one s; 2nd, 1961, Victoria Allbut]. Address: Meggernie Castle, Glenlyon, Perthshire PH15 2PR. T: Bridge of Balgie 200 and 205; Mount Prosperous, Hungerford, Berks RG17 0RP. T: Hungerford 2624. Clubs: Cavalry and Guards; Household Division Yacht.
See also A. C. N. Hopkins.

WILLS, Helen; see Roark, H. W.

WILLS, Sir John Spencer; Kt 1969; FCIT; Chairman: British Electric Traction Co. Ltd, since 1966 (Managing Director, 1946-73, Deputy Chairman, 1951-66); Birmingham and District Investment Trust Ltd; Electrical & Industrial Investment Co. Ltd; Rediffusion Ltd; Rediffusion Television Ltd; Wembley Stadium Ltd; Chairman or Director of numerous other companies; b 10 Aug. 1904; s of Cedric Spencer Wills and Cécile Charlotte; m 1936, Elizabeth Drusilla Alice Clare Garcke; two s. Educ: Cleobury Mortimer Coll., Shropshire; Merchant Taylors' Sch., London. General Manager of E Yorkshire Motor Services Ltd, 1926-31, Dir 1931, and Chm., 1939-68; Chm., Birmingham & Midland Motor Omnibus Co. Ltd, 1946-68; Dir, 1947-73, Dep. Chm., 1953-71, Monotype Corp. Ltd; Director of Public Companies, 1931-. Chairman Hull and Grimsby Section of Incorporated Secretaries' Assoc. (now Chartered Inst. of Secretaries), 1929-31; President, BET Federation Ltd; Member of Council: Public Road Transport Assoc. (formerly Public Transport Assoc.), 1943-68 (Chairman, 1945-46; Hon. Mem., 1969), subseq. Confedn of British Road Passenger Transport Ltd (Hon. Mem., 1975); FCIT (Henry Spurrier Meml Lecturer, 1946, President, 1950-51); Chairman, Omnibus Owners' Assoc., 1943-44; Member: Nat. Council for Omnibus Industry, 1940-66 (Chairman, 1944-45); Standing Cttee of Air Transport Sect., London Chamber of Commerce. Vice-Patron, The Theatre Royal Windsor Trust, 1965-; Governor, Royal Shakespeare Theatre, Stratford upon Avon, 1946-74; Member, Council, The Society of the Royal Opera House, 1962-74; Trustee, The London Symphony Orchestra Trust, 1962-68; Member, UK Council, European Movement, 1966-. Recreations: complete idleness; formerly: flying, swimming, ski-ing, tennis, riding, shooting. Address: 1 Campden House Terrace, Kensington Church Street, W8. T: 01-727 5981; Beech Farm, Battle, East Sussex. T: Battle 2950. Clubs: Naval and Military, East India, Devonshire, Sports, and Public Schools.

WILLS, Sir John Vernon, 4th Bt, cr 1923; TD; FRICS; JP; Lord-Lieutenant and Custos Rotulorum of Avon, since 1974; Chairman, Wessex Water Authority, since 1973; Member, National Water Council, since 1973; Director: Bristol and West Building Society, since 1969; Bristol Evening Post, since 1973; b 3 July 1928; s of Sir George Vernon Proctor Wills, 2nd Bt, and Lady Nellie Jeannie, ARRC, JP, y d of late J. T. Rutherford, Abergavenny; S brother 1945; m 1953, Diana Veronica Cecil (Jane), o d of Douglas R. M. Baker, Winsford, Somerset; four s. Educ: Eton. Served Coldstream Guards, 1946-49; Lt-Col Comdg N Somerset and Bristol Yeomanry, 1965-67; Bt Col 1967; now TARO. Hon. Col, 37th (Wessex and Welsh) Signal Regt, T&AVR, 1975-. Dep. Chm., Bristol Waterworks Co., 1962-73. Member of Somerset CC. JP 1962, DL 1968, High Sheriff, 1968, Somerset. Heir: s David James Vernon Wills, b 2 Jan. 1955. Address: Langford Court, near Bristol, Avon. T: Wrington 862338. Club: Cavalry and Guards.

WILLS, Joseph Lyttleton; Hon. Mr Justice Wills, CBE 1965; FSA; Judge, Supreme Court, Windward Islands and Leeward Islands, WI, since 1955; b 24 June 1899; m 1940, Dorothy Cather; one d. Educ: Middle School, Georgetown, British Guiana; Queen's Coll., British Guiana; King's Coll., London. Barrister-at-law, Inner Temple, 1928; admitted to practice as Barrister-at-Law, British Guiana, 1930; Magistrate, 1947; Additional Puisne Judge of Supreme Court of British Guiana, 1953-55. Councillor of Georgetown, 1933; Deputy Mayor, 1942-43; Hon. Member of Legislative Council, British Guiana, 1933; President, British Guiana Labour Union and British Guiana Workers League; Chairman and Member of several public committees; Member Judicial Service Commn, British Guiana, 1963; Chairman, Income Tax (Appeal) Board of Review, Guyana, 1966. Chairman of British Guiana Congregational Union, 1949-53 and 1974-75. Jubilee Medal, 1935; Coronation Medal, 1953. Recreations: horse-riding, motoring and cricket.

Address: Lyttleton House, 57 Chalmers Place, Stabroek, Georgetown, Guyana. Clubs: Royal Commonwealth Society (West Indian); Guyana Cricket, Maltenoes Sports (Guyana); Castries (WI).

WILLS, Leonard Johnston; MA, ScD (Cambridge), PhD (Birmingham); FGS; Emeritus Professor, formerly Professor of Geology and Geomorphology, Birmingham University (1932-49); b 27 Feb. 1884; s of W. Leonard Wills; m 1910, Maud Janet (d 1952), d of late Sir Alfred Ewing, KCB; one s one d. Educ: Uppingham Sch.; King's Coll., Cambridge. Hon. Fellow, Geolog. Soc., 1975. Publications: The Physiographical Evolution of Britain, a Palæogeographical Atlas, Concealed Coalfields, Palæogeological Maps, and scientific papers. Address: Brockencote, Romsley, Halesowen B62 0LY.

WILLS, Philip Aubrey, CBE 1945; President, George Wills & Sons (Holdings) Ltd, since 1977 (Chairman, 1959-77); b 26 May 1907; s of C. P. Wills; m 1931, Katharine Fisher; three s one d. Educ: Harrow. Learnt to fly 1928, owned a light aeroplane and in 1932 took up gliding. Took part in rapid development of British sail-flying from that date; second British holder of international "Silver C" in 1934, held British records for height and distance on and off since 1934. First British holder of International Gold Badge (No. 3) for flights of over 3000 metres and 300 kms distance on a sailplane. Senior pilot British team at seven World Gliding Championships; World Champion, 1952 (single-seaters), Madrid. Joined ATA in 1939, became 2nd in command and Director of Operations. Qualified to ferry all types of single-, twin- and multi-engined aircraft. General Manager (Technical) British European Airways Corporation, 1946-48; President of the British Gliding Association; Chm., Royal Aero Club, 1975-77. AFRAeS; Coronation Medal, 1953; British gold medal for aeronautics, 1960. Publications: On Being a Bird, 1953; Where No Birds Fly, 1961; Free as a Bird, 1973; The Inevitability of Confrontation, Part 1, 1974, Part 2, 1975; contributions to the technical and non-technical press on motorless flight, aircraft accident prevention, etc. Recreation: sail-flying. Address: 54 Holland Park Mews, W11.

WILLSON, Douglas James, CBE 1953; TD; b 30 Oct. 1906; s of late Ernest Victor Willson and late Mary Willson; m 1942, Morna Josephine, d of Stanley Hine; one d. Educ: Bishop's Stortford Coll., Herts. Admitted Solicitor, 1928; joined Customs and Excise, 1928. Served War, 1939-45, Lieut-Colonel, RA. Solicitor for Bd of Customs and Excise, 1963-71. Publications: Titles Purchase Tax and Excise in Halsbury's Encyclopædia of Laws of England, 3rd edn; Willson & Mainprice on Value Added Tax. Recreations: gardening and bird watching. Address: Smith's Croft, West Farleigh, Kent. T: Maidstone 812203.

WILLSON, Dr Francis Michael Glenn; Principal of the University of London, since 1975; b 29 Sept. 1924; s of late Christopher Glenn Willson and late Elsie Katrine (née Mattick); m 1945, Jean (née Carlyle); two d. Educ: Carlisle Grammar Sch.; Manchester Univ. (BA Admin); Balliol and Nuffield Colls, Oxford (DPhil, MA). Merchant Navy, 1941-42; RAF, 1943-46; BOAC 1946-47. Research Officer, Royal Inst. of Public Admin, 1953-60; Res. Fellow, Nuffield Coll., Oxford, 1955-60; Lectr in Politics, St Edmund Hall, Oxford, 1958-60; Prof. of Govt, UC Rhodesia and Nyasaland, 1960-64; Dean, Faculty of Social Studies, UC Rhodesia and Nyasaland, 1962-64; Univ. of California, Santa Cruz: Prof. of Govt/Politics, 1965-74; Provost of Stevenson Coll., 1967-74; Vice-Chancellor, College and Student Affairs, 1973-74; Warden, Goldsmiths' Coll., London, 1974-75. Publications: (with D.N. Chester) The Organization of British Central Government 1914-56, 2nd edn 1914-64, 1968; Administrators in Action, 1961; contrib. Public Admin, Polit. Studies, Parly Affairs, etc. Address: The University of London, Senate House, WC1E 7HU. T: 01-636 8000.

WILLWAY, Brig. Alfred Cedric Cowan, CB 1953; CBE 1944; TD 1940; Chairman, Surrey Quarter Sessions, 1955-69; b 1898; o s of late Rev. A. P. Willway and late Laura Elizabeth (née Cowan); m 1922, Frances Mary, y d of late C. A. Crane; one s one d. Educ: privately; Oriel Coll., Oxford (BA 1921, 2nd Class Honours Mod Hist.). Barrister, Inner Temple, 1924; practised till 1932; Deputy Clerk of the Peace (Surrey), 1932-46; Member, Social Services Committee (Home Office), 1934-36; Probation Advisory Committee and Probation Training Board, 1936-39; Chm. Surrey Probation Cttee, 1948-69, Magistrates Courts Cttee, 1957-69; Vice-Chm. Surrey Standing Jt Cttee JP (Surrey) 1946; Chairman, Surrey Quarter Sessions (formerly Deputy Chairman), 1955; DL (Surrey) 1950-72; CC (Surrey) 1952-59. Mem. Standing Cttee on Criminal Law Revision, 1959-69. Vice-Pres., Magistrates' Assoc., 1969. Served European War (2nd Lt RE), Palestine; commissioned R Signals TA, 1922; War of 1939-45, comd 56 Div. Signals, 1936-41; Dep. CSO, SE Command,

1941; CSO, 5 Corps (N Africa and Italy), 1942-44 (despatches, CBE); CSO, Northern Command, 1945-46; Hon. Col 56 (Lond.) Armd Div. Sig. Regt, 1945-56; Chairman Surrey T&AFA, 1949-52. *Publication:* Willway's Quarter Sessions Practice, 1940 (Supplement, 1952). *Recreation:* gardening. *Address:* Wilgate Farm House, Throwley, near Faversham, Kent. *T:* Eastling 244. *Club:* Junior Carlton.

WILMERS, John Geoffrey, QC 1965; a Recorder of the Crown Court, since 1972; *b* 27 Dec. 1920; *m* 1946, June I. K. Mecredy; one *s* two *d. Educ:* Leighton Park Sch., Reading; St John's Coll., Cambridge. Called to the Bar, Inner Temple, 1948, Bencher, 1972. Dep. Chm., Hants QS, 1970-71. *Recreation:* ski-ing. *Address:* 1 Harcourt Buildings, Temple, EC4. *T:* 01-353 2214.

WILMINGTON, Lord; Daniel Bingham Compton; *b* 16 Jan. 1973; *s* and *heir* of Earl Compton, *qv.*

WILMINGTON, Joseph (Robert); Lord Mayor of Liverpool, 1974-75; *b* 21 April 1932; *s* of Joseph R. Wilmington. *Educ:* Alsop High Sch., Liverpool; London Sch. of Economics. Mem., Liverpool City Council, 1962; Past Chm., Liverpool Liberal Party, 1965-67; Chairman: Personnel Cttee, Liverpool City Council; Markets Cttee, Liverpool City Council; Chief Whip. Chm., NW Fedn of Employment Consultants; Mem. Nat. Exec., Fedn of Employment Consultants; Mem. Inst. Employment Consultants. *Recreations:* football, music and the arts. *Address:* 30 Utting Avenue East, Liverpool L11 1DQ. *T:* 051-226 4834.

WILMOT, Air Vice-Marshal Aubrey S.; *see* Sidney-Wilmot.

WILMOT, Sir Henry Robert, 9th Bt *cr* 1759; *b* 10 April 1967; *s* of Sir Robert Arthur Wilmot, 8th Bt, and of Juliet Elvira, *e d of* Captain M. N. Tufnell, RN (who *m* 2nd, 1976, Richard James Stanes); *S* father, 1974. *Heir: b* Charles Sacheverel Wilmot, *b* 13 Feb. 1969. *Address:* Pitters Farmhouse, Sandy Lane, Chippenham, Wilts.

WILMOT, Sir John Assheton E.; *see* Eardley-Wilmot.

WILSEY, Maj.-Gen. Anthony Patrick W.; *see* Willasey-Wilsey.

WILSON; *see* McNair-Wilson.

WILSON, family name of Barons Moran, Nunburnholme, Wilson, Wilson of High Wray, Wilson of Langside and Wilson of Radcliffe.

WILSON, 2nd Baron, *cr* 1946, of Libya and of Stowlangtoft; **Patrick Maitland Wilson;** *b* 14 Sept. 1915; *s* of Field-Marshal 1st Baron Wilson, GCB, GBE, DSO, and Hester Mary, *d* of Philip James Digby Wykeham, Tythrop House, Oxon; *S* father 1964; *m* 1945, Violet Storeen, *d* of late Major James Hamilton Douglas Campbell, OBE. *Educ:* Eton; King's College, Cambridge. Served War of 1939-45 (despatches). Lt-Col, Rifle Brigade. *Heir:* none. *Address:* c/o Barclays Bank Ltd, Cambridge.

WILSON OF HIGH WRAY, Baron *cr* 1976 (Life Peer), of Kendal, Cumbria; **Paul Norman Wilson,** OBE 1959; DSC 1945; MA (Cantab); FSA; FICE; FIMechE; JP; Lieut-Commander RNVR (retired); HM Lieutenant of Cumbria, since 1974 (Lord Lieutenant of Westmorland, 1965-74); *b* 24 Oct. 1908; *y s* of late Norman Forster Wilson, CE, Kendal, and H. G. M. Wilson (*née* Harris); *m* 1935, Valerie Frances Elizabeth, *d* of late William Baron Fletcher, Cape Town; no *c. Educ:* Gresham's Sch.; Clare Coll., Cambridge. MA (Mech. Sci.) Cantab, 1934. Served War of 1939-45: mainly at sea in capital ships; temp. Lt-Comdr RN. Worked in S Africa, 1930-34; Gilbert Gilkes & Gordon Ltd, Water Turbine & Pump Manufacturers, Kendal: Man. Dir, 1934-67; Chairman, 1954-. Chairman: Kendal & District Local Employment Cttee, 1954-69; Westmorland Youth Employment Cttee, 1946-69; Mem., Nat. Youth Employment Council, 1959-69; Member Council: Newcomen Soc., 1958-77 (Vice-Pres., 1968-77, Pres, 1973-75); and Patron, Cumberland & Westmorland Antiquarian and Archaeological Soc., 1965- (Pres., 1975-78); Dep. Chm., Exec. Cttee, British Hydromechanics Res. Assoc., 1973-75; Science Museum: Mem. Adv. Council, 1968-72, 1973-; Chm., Fund for Preservation of Technol and Scientific Material, 1973-. Chairman of Governors, Kendal Coll. of Further Educn, 1958-74; Governor, Sedbergh Sch., 1965-74; Chairman of Trustees and Governors: Lake District Museum Trust, 1968-; Heron Corn Mill Beetham Trust, 1973-; Governor of BBC, 1968-72. JP 1958, DL 1964, Cumbria, formerly Westmorland. KStJ 1966. *Publications:* Watermills, an introduction, 1956, 2nd edn 1973; Watermills with Horizontal Wheels, 1960; Water Turbines (Sci. Mus. Pubn), 1974; Water and other forms of Motive Power, in History of Technology, 1900-1950, 1977; contributions to journals on history of water power, local history and technical matters. *Recreation:* industrial archæology (especially water power). *Address:* Gillinggate House, Kendal, Cumbria LA9 4JB. *T:* Kendal 20209. *Clubs:* Army and Navy, Beefsteak.

WILSON OF LANGSIDE, Baron *cr* 1969 (Life Peer); **Henry Stephen Wilson,** PC 1967; QC (Scot.) 1965; Sheriff Principal of Glasgow and Strathkelvin, 1975-77; *b* 21 March 1916; *s* of James Wilson, Solicitor, Glasgow, and Margaret Wilson (*née* Young); *m* 1942, Jessie Forrester Waters; no *c. Educ:* High School, Glasgow; Univ. of Glasgow (MA, LLB). Joined Army, 1939; Commd 1940; Regl Officer, HLI and RAC, 1940-46. Called to Scottish Bar, 1946; Advocate-Depute, 1948-51. Sheriff-Substitute: Greenock, 1955-56; Glasgow, 1956-65; Solicitor-General for Scotland, 1965-67; Lord Advocate, 1967-70; Sheriff of Glasgow, 1971-75; Dir, Scottish Courts Administration, 1971-74. Contested (Lab) Dumfriesshire, 1950, 1955, W Edinburgh, 1951. *Recreations:* hill walking, gardening. *Address:* Dunallan, Kippen, Stirlingshire. *T:* Kippen 210. *Club:* Western (Glasgow).

WILSON OF RADCLIFFE, Baron *cr* 1974 (Life Peer), of Radcliffe, Lancs; **Alfred Wilson;** *b* 10 June 1909; *s* of late William Barnes Wilson and Jane; *m* 1st, 1932, Elsie Hulton (*d* 1974); one *d* (one *s* decd); 2nd, 1976, Freda Mather. *Educ:* Technical Sch., Newcastle upon Tyne. CWS Ltd: Dep. Sec. and Exec. Officer, 1953; Sec., 1965; Chief Exec. Officer, 1969-74. Dir, Estate and General Investments Ltd. FCIS. *Recreations:* photography, walking, gardening. *Address:* 58 Ringley Road, Whitefield, Manchester.

WILSON, Rear-Adm. Alan Christopher Wyndham, CB 1972; retired, 1975; Senior Naval Member, Directing Staff, Royal College of Defence Studies, 1972-Jan. 1975; *b* 7 Sept. 1919; *s* of Alan Christopher Hill-Wilson and Nancy Green; *m* 1958, Joan Rhoda Landale, Deniliquin, Australia; one step *d. Educ:* St Bee's, Cumberland. Served at sea during War of 1939-45; Malta Dockyard, 1946-49; HMS Diamond, 1949-52; Admty, 1952-55; Australia, 1956-58; HMS Ark Royal, 1959-61; Admty, 1962-64; with Flag Officer, Aircraft Carriers, 1964-66; with Comdr, Far East Fleet, 1966-69; idc 1969; Hd of British Defence Liaison Staff, Canberra, 1970-72. *Recreations:* golf, fishing. *Address:* Church Farm House, Wellow, near Bath. *T:* Combe Down 832051. *Clubs:* Army and Navy, Royal Automobile.

WILSON, Prof. Alan Geoffrey; Professor of Urban and Regional Geography, University of Leeds, since 1970; *b* 8 Jan. 1939; *s* of Harry Wilson and Gladys (*née* Naylor); *m* 1965, Christine Diane Snow. *Educ:* Corpus Christi Coll., Cambridge (MA). Scientific Officer, Rutherford High Energy Lab., 1961-64; Res. Officer, Inst. of Econs and Statistics, Univ. of Oxford, 1964-66; Math. Adviser, MoT, 1966-68; Asst Dir, Centre for Environmental Studies, London, 1968-70. *Publications:* Entropy in Urban and Regional Modelling, 1970; Papers in Urban and Regional Analysis, 1972; Urban and Regional Models in Geography and Planning, 1974; (with M. J. Kirkby) Mathematics for Geographers and Planners, 1975; (with P. H. Rees) Spatial Population Analysis, 1977; (ed with P. H. Rees and C. M. Leigh) Models of Cities and Regions, 1977. *Recreations:* golf, walking. *Address:* 5 Hydro Close, Ben Rhydding, Ilkley, West Yorks LS29 8RZ. *T:* Ilkley 66852.

WILSON, Sir Alan (Herries), Kt 1961; FRS 1942; Part-time Member and Deputy Chairman, Electricity Council, 1966-76; *b* 2 July 1906; *o s* of H. and A. Wilson; *m* 1934, Margaret Constance Monks (*d* 1961); two *s. Educ:* Wallasey Gram. Sch.; Emmanuel College, Cambridge. Smith's Prize, 1928; Adams Prize, 1931-32; Fellow of Emmanuel College, Cambridge, 1929-33; Fellow and Lecturer of Trinity College, Cambridge, 1933-45; University Lecturer in Mathematics in the University of Cambridge, 1933-45; joined Courtaulds Ltd, 1945; Man. Dir, 1954; Dep. Chm., 1957-62. Dir, Internat. Computers (Hldgs) Ltd, 1962-72; Chm., Glaxo Group Ltd, 1963-73. Chairman: Committee on Coal Derivatives, 1959-60; Committee on Noise, 1960-63; Nuclear Safety Adv. Committee, 1965-66; Central Adv. Water Cttee, 1969-74; Member: Iron and Steel Board, 1960-67; UGC, 1964-66; President: Inst. of Physics and Physical Soc., 1963-64; Nat. Society for Clean Air, 1965-66; Aslib, 1971-73. Chm. Governing Body, Nat. Inst. of Agricultural Engrg, 1971-76; Chm., Bd of Governors, Bethlem Royal and Maudsley Hosps., 1973-. Prime Warden, Goldsmiths Co., 1969-70. Hon. Fellow: Emmanuel College, Cambridge; St Catherine's College, Oxford; UMIST. Hon. FIChemE; Hon. FInstP. Hon. DSc: Oxford; Edinburgh. *Publications:* The Theory of Metals, 1936, 2nd edition 1953; Semi-conductors and Metals, 1939; Thermo-dynamics and Statistical Mechanics, 1957; many papers on atomic physics. *Address:* 65 Oakleigh Park South, Whetstone, N20. *T:* 01-445 3030. *Club:* Athenæum.

WILSON, Alexander; MP (Lab) Hamilton since 1970; Member, Scottish National Union of Mineworkers; *b* Wilsontown, Lanarkshire, 5 June 1917; *s* of James and Elizabeth Wilson; *m* 1941; one *s* one *d. Educ:* Forth Grammar School. Became a Miner. Joined Labour Party, 1946. Member, 3rd District Council, Lanarkshire, 11 years. Contested (Lab) Hamilton, by-election 1967. Especially interested in welfare of the disabled, sick and elderly persons, and in Trade Unionism. *Publication:* The Chartist Movement in Scotland, 1971. *Address:* House of Commons, SW1.

WILSON, Alexander, FLA; Director, Cheshire Libraries and Museums Service, since 1972; Member, British Library Board, since 1974; *b* 12 Feb. 1921; *s* of late William Wilson and Amelia Wilson; *m* 1949, Mary Catherin Traynor; two *s*. *Educ:* Bolton County Grammar Sch. FLA 1950. Served War, RAF, 1941-46. Librarian at Bolton, Harrogate, Taunton, and Swindon, 1946-52; Dir of Library and Cultural Services, Dudley and later Coventry, 1952-72. CNAA Assessor to Library Sch.; Liverpool Polytechnic, 1974-. Mem., Library Adv. Council (England), 1971-74. *Publications:* (contrib.) British Librarianship Today, 1976; contrib. books and periodicals on libraries and other cultural services. *Recreations:* walking, listening to music, lecturing and writing on professional subjects. *Address:* 1 Brockway West, Tattenhall, near Chester.

WILSON, Lt-Gen. Sir (Alexander) James, KBE 1974 (CBE 1966; MBE 1948); MC 1945; Chairman, Tobacco Advisory Committee, since 1977; *b* 13 April 1921; *s* of Maj.-Gen. Bevil Thomson Wilson, CB, DSO, and of Florence Erica, *d* of Sir John Starkey, 1st Bt; *m* 1958, Hon. Jean Margaret Paul, 2nd *d* of 2nd Baron Rankeillour; two *s. Educ:* Winchester Coll.; New Coll., Oxford (BA, Law). Served War of 1939-45, North Africa and Italy, Rifle Bde (despatches); Adjt, IMA Dehra Dun, 1945-47; PS to C-in-C Pakistan, 1948-49; Co. Comdr, 1st Bn Rifle Bde, BAOR 1949 and 1951-52, Kenya 1954-55 (despatches); psc 1950; Bde Major 11th Armd Div., BAOR, 1952-54; Instr, Staff Coll. Camberley, 1955-58; 2nd in comd 3rd Green Jackets, BAOR, 1959-60; GSO1 Sandhurst, 1960-62; CO 1st Bn XX Lancs Fus, 1962-64; Chief of Staff, UN Force in Cyprus, 1964-66 (Actg Force Comdr, 1965-66); Comdr, 147 Inf. Bde TA, 1966-67; Dir of Army Recruiting, MoD, 1967-70; GOC NW District, 1970-72; Vice Adjutant General, MoD, 1972-74; GOC SE District, 1974-77. Dep. Col (Lancashire), RRF, 1973-77, Col, 1977-. Col Commandant: Queen's Division, 1974-77; RAEC, 1975-; Royal Greenjackets, 1977-. Chm., Council, RUSI, 1973-75. Mem., Sports Council, 1973-; Pres., Army Cricket Assoc., 1973-76; Vice-Pres., Army Football Assoc., 1973-76, Chm., 1976-77, Pres., 1977-; Hon. Vice-Pres., FA, 1976-. Association Football Correspondent, Sunday Times, 1957-. *Publications:* articles and book reviews on mil. subjects and peacekeeping. *Recreations:* cricket, Association football. *Address:* Tobacco Advisory Committee, Glen House, Stag Place, SW1; Flat 4, 33 Wilton Place, SW1; Goldhill Farm House, Edingley, near Newark, Notts. *T:* Southwell 3308. *Clubs:* Travellers', MCC; Notts CC.

WILSON, Alfred Harold, CB 1949; CBE 1946; *b* 9 March 1895; *er s* of late Alfred Henry Wilson; *m* 1925, Edythe Rose, *d* of late Philip Richard Snewin; no *c. Educ:* Tottenham Grammar School. Associate of Assoc. of Certified Accountants, 1922. Board of Trade, Central Office for Labour Exchanges, 1913; GPO, Accountant-General's Department, 1914. Served European War, Royal Marine Artillery, 1916-19. Assistant Surveyor, General Post Office, 1923; Principal, Air Ministry, Dept of Civil Aviation, 1937; Assistant Secretary, Air Ministry, i/c Organisation and Methods Division, 1941; Assistant Secretary (with title Director of Home Civil Aviation) Air Ministry, Dept of Civil Aviation, 1943; transferred to new Ministry of Civil Aviation on its formation and promoted Principal Asst Secretary, 1945; Under Secretary, Ministry of Civil Aviation, 1946; during this period was Chairman London Airport lay-out Panel, which was responsible for runway layout design of the Airport; Deputy Secretary, Ministry of Transport and Civil Aviation, 1956-58; Adviser on Commercial Air Transport to the Ministry of Transport and Civil Aviation, 1958-60; Member of the Air Transport Licensing Board, 1960-65. *Address:* Cornerways, Epsom Road, Guildford, Surrey. *T:* Guildford 75046. *Club:* Royal Automobile.

WILSON, Rev. Canon Andrew; Canon Residentiary of Newcastle, and Director of Ordinands and Post-Ordination Studies, since 1964; Examining Chaplain to the Bishop of Newcastle, since 1969; *b* 27 April 1920; *o s* of late Stewart and of Isobel Wilson. *Educ:* Salt's High School, Shipley; Univ. of Durham. Scholar of St Chad's Coll., Durham, 1939; BA Hons Mod. Hist., 1941; Lightfoot Scholar, 1941; Dip. Theol. (Dist.), 1943; MA 1944; Deacon, 1943; Priest, 1944. Asst Curate: of St

Cuthbert's, Newcastle, 1943-45; of St John's, Wallsend, 1945-48; Priest-in-charge of Backworth, 1948-55; Vicar of Horton, 1955-58; Rector of St John's, Ballachulish, 1958-64. *Address:* 1 Mitchell Avenue, Jesmond, Newcastle upon Tyne NE2 3JY. *T:* Newcastle 812075.

WILSON, Angus Frank Johnstone, CBE 1968; CLit 1972; FRSL 1958; author; Professor of English Literature, University of East Anglia, since 1966; *b* 11 Aug. 1913; *s* of William Johnstone-Wilson, Dumfriesshire, and of Maude (*née* Caney), Durban, Natal, South Africa. *Educ:* Westminster School; Merton College, Oxford. Foreign Office, 1942-46. Deputy to Superintendent of Reading Room, British Museum, 1949-55. Began to write in 1946. Lectr, Internat. Assoc. of Professors of English, Lausanne, 1959; Ewing Lectr, Los Angeles, 1960; Bergen Lectr, Yale Univ., 1960; Wm Vaughan Moody Lectr, Chicago, 1960; Northcliffe Lectrs, Lond., 1961; Leslie Stephen Lectr, Cambridge, 1962-63; Lectr, Sch. of Eng. Studies, E Anglia Univ., 1963; Beckman Prof., Univ. of California, Berkeley, 1967; John Hinkley Vis. Prof., Johns Hopkins Univ., Baltimore, 1974; Vis. Prof., Univ. of Delaware, 1977. Mem. Cttee, Royal Literary Fund, 1966. Mem. Arts Council, 1967-69; Chm., NBL, 1971-74. President: Powys Soc., 1970-; Dickens Fellowship, 1974-75. Hon. DLitt Leicester, 1977. Chevalier de l'Ordre des Arts et des Lettres, 1972. *Publications:* (short stories, novels, etc); The Wrong Set, 1949; Such Darling Dodos, 1950; Emile Zola, 1950; Hemlock and After (novel), 1952; For Whom The Cloche Tolls, 1953, 2nd edn, 1973; The Mulberry Bush (play) (prod Bristol, 1955, Royal Court Theatre, London, 1956); Anglo-Saxon Attitudes (novel), 1956; A Bit off the Map, 1957; The Middle Age of Mrs Eliot (novel), 1958 (James Tait Black Meml Prize; Prix du Meilleur Roman Etranger, Paris); The Old Men at the Zoo (novel), 1961; The Wild Garden, 1963; Late Call (novel), 1964 (adapted for TV, 1975); No Laughing Matter (novel), 1967; The World of Charles Dickens, 1970 (Yorkshire Post Book of the Year, 1970); (with Edwin Smith and Olive Cook) England, 1971; As If By Magic (novel), 1973; The Naughty Nineties, 1976; The Strange Ride of Rudyard Kipling, 1977. TV plays: After the Show (perf. 1959); The Stranger (perf. 1960); The Invasion (perf. 1963). *Recreations:* gardening, travel. *Address:* Felsham Woodside, Bradfield St George, Bury St Edmund's, Suffolk. *T:* Rattlesden 200. *Club:* Athenæum.

WILSON, Sir (Archibald) Duncan, GCMG 1971 (KCMG 1965; CMG 1955); HM Diplomatic Service, retired; Master of Corpus Christi College, Cambridge, since 1971; *b* 12 August 1911; *s* of late Archibald Edward Wilson and late Ethel Mary (*née* Schuster); *m* 1937, Elizabeth Anne Martin Fleming; two *d* (one *s* decd). *Educ:* Winchester; Balliol College, Oxford 1st Class Hon. Mods, Lit. Hum., Oxford; Craven schol., Oxford Univ., Jenkyns Exhibitioner, Balliol Coll.; Laming Fellow, Queen's Coll. Taught at Westminster School, 1936-37; Asst Keeper, British Museum, 1937-39; Min. of Economic Warfare, 1939-41; empl. FO, 1941-45; CCG, 1945-46; entered Foreign Service, 1947; served Berlin, 1947-49; Yugoslavia, 1951-53; Director of Research and Acting Librarian, 1955-57; Chargé d'Affaires, Peking, 1957-59; Assistant Under-Secretary, Foreign Office, 1960-64; Ambassador to: Yugoslavia, 1964-68; the USSR, 1968-71. Fellow, Center of International Affairs, Harvard Univ. (on Secondment, 1959-60). Hon. Vice-Pres., UK Council for Overseas Student Affairs. Mem., Standing Commn on Museums and Galls, 1973-. Mem. Bd of Governors, King's Sch., Canterbury. *Publication:* Life and Times of Vuk Stefanović Karadzić, 1970. *Recreations:* music, tennis, golf, walking. *Address:* The Master's Lodge, Corpus Christi College, Cambridge. *T:* Cambridge 59418. *Club:* Royal Commonwealth Society.
See also Mrs H. M. Warnock.

WILSON, Maj.-Gen. Arthur Gillespie, CBE 1955; DSO 1946; *b* 29 Sept. 1900; *s* of late Charles Wilson, originally of Glasgow, Scotland; *m* 1st, 1927, Edna D. L. Gibson (*d* 1940); no *c*; 2nd, 1953, Shirley H. Cruickshank, *d* of late Colin Campbell, Queenscliff, Victoria, Australia; no *c. Educ:* North Sydney Boys' High School, NSW, Australia; Royal Military College, Duntroon, Australia. Commissioned Aust. Staff Corps, 1921; served India with various Brit. and IA Artillery Units, 1924; commanded Roy. Aust. Artillery, Thursday Island, 1926-28; Staff College, Quetta, 1935-36; GSO3, AHQ 1938; continued to serve in various appts at AHQ until joined AIF 1940; GSO1 HQ AIF UK and then Assistant Mil. Liaison Officer, Australian High Commissioner's Office, UK, until 1943, when returned to Australia; served with AIF New Guinea Philippines and Borneo, 1943-45; DDDS(o) Land Headquarters, 1944-45; commanded British Commonwealth Base BCOF Japan, 1946-47; served various appts AHQ and HQ Eastern Command, 1947-52; Aust. Army Rep., UK, 1953-54; GOC, Central Command, Australia, 1954-57; retired 1957. *Address:* Leahurst

Cottage, Craters, South Australia 5152, Australia. *Club:* Naval, Military and Air Force (Adelaide).

WILSON, Prof. Arthur James Cochran, FRS 1963; Professor of Crystallography, Department of Physics, Birmingham University, since 1965; *b* 28 November 1914; *o s* of Arthur A. C. and Hildegarde Gretchen (*née* Geldert) Wilson, Springhill, Nova Scotia, Canada; *m* 1946, Harriett Charlotte, BSc, PhD, Sociologist (*née* Friedeberg); two *s* one *d. Educ:* King's Collegiate School, Windsor, Nova Scotia, Canada; Dalhousie University, Halifax, Canada (MSc); Massachusetts Institute of Technology (PhD); Cambridge University (PhD). 1851 Exhibition Scholar, 1938-41. Res. Asst, Cavendish Lab., Cambridge, 1941-45; Lecturer, 1945, and Senior Lecturer, 1946, in Physics, University College, Cardiff; Professor of Physics, University College, Cardiff, 1954-65. Visiting Professor: Georgia Inst. of Technology, 1965, 1968, 1971; Univ. of Tokyo, 1972. Editor of Structure Reports, 1948-59; Editor of Acta Crystallographica, 1960-. Member: Exec. Cttee, Internat. Union of Crystallography, 1954-60; ICSU Abstracting Bd, 1971-. *Publications:* X-ray Optics, 1949 (Russian edn 1951, 2nd edn 1962); Mathematical Theory of X-ray Powder Diffractometry, 1963 (French edn 1964, German edn 1965); Elements of X-ray Crystallography, 1970; (with L. V. Azároff and others) X-ray Diffraction, 1974; numerous papers in Proc. Phys. Soc., Proc. Roy. Soc., Acta Cryst., etc. *Address:* The University of Birmingham, Birmingham B15 2TT.

WILSON, Lt-Col Blair Aubyn S.; *see* Stewart-Wilson.

WILSON, Brian Harvey, CBE 1972 (MBE 1944); solicitor; Hon. Clerk to Housing and Works Committee, London Boroughs Association, since 1965; *b* 4 Sept. 1915; *o s* of Sydney John Wilson, MC, and Bessie Mildred (*née* Scott); *m* 1941, Constance Jane (*née* Gee); one *s. Educ:* Manchester Grammar Sch.; (Exhibitioner) Corpus Christi Coll., Cambridge (MA, LLB). Chief Asst Solicitor, Warrington, 1946-48; Dep. Town Clerk: Grimsby, 1948-53; Ilford, 1953-56; Town Clerk, Hampstead, 1956-65 (now Camden); Town Clerk and Chief Exec., London Borough of Camden, 1965-77. Chm., Royal Inst. of Public Administration, 1973-75. Mem., Uganda Resettlement Board, 1972-73. *Address:* Old Housing, Fifield, Oxon. *T:* Shipton-under-Wychwood 830695.

WILSON, Col Campbell Aubrey Kenneth I.; *see* Innes-Wilson.

WILSON, Sir Charles Haynes, Kt 1965; MA Glasgow and Oxon; Principal and Vice-Chancellor of University of Glasgow, 1961-76; *b* 16 May 1909; 2nd *s* of late George Wilson and Florence Margaret Hannay; *m* 1935, Jessie Gilmour Wilson; one *s* two *d. Educ:* Hillhead High School; Glasgow Univ.; Oxford Univ. Glasgow University Faulds Fellow in Political Philosophy, 1932-34. Lecturer in Political Science, London School of Economics, 1934-39; Fellow and Tutor in Modern History, Corpus Christi College, Oxford, 1939-52. Junior Proctor, 1945; Faculty Fellow, Nuffield College. Visiting Professor in Comparative Government at Ohio State Univ., 1950; Principal, The University College of Leicester, 1952-57; Vice-Chancellor, Univ. of Leicester, 1957-61. Chairman: Commn on Fourah Bay Coll., Sierra Leone, 1957; Miners' Welfare Nat. Schol. Scheme Selec. Cttee, 1959-64; Acad. Planning Bd for Univ. of E Anglia, 1960; Member: Academic Planning Cttee and Council of UC of Sussex, 1958; Acad. Adv. Cttee, Royal Coll. of Science and Technology, Glasgow (now Univ. of Strathclyde), 1962; British Cttee of Selection for Harkness Fellowships of Commonwealth Fund, 1962-67; Heyworth Cttee on Social Studies, 1962; Acad. Planning Bd, Univ. of Stirling, 1964; Chairman, Cttee of Vice-Chancellors and Principals, 1964-67; Chm., Assoc. of Commonwealth Univs, 1966-67 and 1972-74. Mem., Standing Commn on Museums and Galleries, 1976-. Hon. Fellow: Corpus Christi Coll., Oxford, 1963; LSE, 1965-. Hon. LLD: Glasgow, 1957; Leicester, 1961; Rhodes Univ., 1964; Queen's Univ., Kingston, Ont, 1967; Ohio State Univ., 1969; Pennsylvania, 1975; Hon. DLitt: Strathclyde, 1966; NUU, 1976; Heriot-Watt, 1977; Hon. DCL East Anglia, 1966. Chevalier, Legion of Honour. *Address:* Whinnymuir, Dalry, Castle Douglas DG7 3TT. *T:* Dalry 218. *Clubs:* Naval and Military; Royal Scottish Automobile.

WILSON, Prof. Charles Henry, LittD; FBA 1966; Fellow of Jesus College, Cambridge, since 1938; Professor of Modern History, Cambridge University, since 1965; seconded as Professor of History and Civilization, European University Institute, Florence, since 1975; *b* 16 Apr. 1914; *s* of Joseph Edwin Wilson and Louisa Wilson; *m* 1st 1939, Angela (marr. diss.), *d* of John Marshman; one *d*; 2nd, 1972, Alena, *d* of Dr Vladimir Kouril, Ostrava, Czechoslovakia. *Educ:* De Aston Grammar Sch., Lincs; Jesus Coll., Cambridge. DLitt

Cambridge, 1976. Studied in Holland and Germany, 1937-38. Served in RNVR and Admiralty, 1940-45. Univ. Lecturer in History, 1945-64, Reader in Modern Economic History, 1964-65, Cambridge Univ.; Bursar of Jesus Coll., 1945-55. Ford Lecturer in English History, Oxford Univ., for 1968-69. Vis. Prof., Univ. of Tokyo, 1974. Mem., Lord Chancellor's Adv. Council on Public Records, 1972-77; British Govt Representative, Anglo-Netherlands Cultural Commn, 1956. Jt Ed., Econ. Hist. Review, 1960-67. Corres. Fellow: Royal Danish Acad. of Arts and Science, 1970; Royal Belgian Acad., 1973. Manager, Istituto Datini, Prato, 1971. LittD (*hc*) Univ. of Groningen, 1964; Univ. of Louvain, 1977. Comdr, Order of Oranje-Nassau, 1973. *Publications:* Anglo-Dutch Commerce and Finance in 18th Century, 1940; Holland and Britain, 1945; History of Unilever, 1954; Profit and Power, 1957; (with William Reader) Men and Machines, 1958; England's Apprenticeship 1603-1763, 1965; Unilever, 1945-65, 1968; The Dutch Republic and the Civilization of the Seventeenth Century, 1968; Queen Elizabeth and the Revolt of the Netherlands, 1970; The Transformation of Europe, 1976; (ed with E. E. Rich) Cambridge Economic History of Europe, vol V, 1977; (ed with N. G. Parker) The Sources of European Economic History, 1977; numerous articles. *Recreation:* music. *Address:* The European University Institute (Badia Fiesolana), 50016 San Domenico di Fiesole, Florence, Italy.

WILSON, (Christopher) David, CBE 1968; MC 1945; Chairman: Southern Television Ltd, since 1976 (Managing Director, 1959—76); Southstar Television International, since 1976; *b* 17 Dec. 1916; *s* of late Anthony James Wilson, Highclere, Worplesdon, Surrey; *m* 1947, Jean Barbara Morton Smith; no *c. Educ:* St George's Sch., Windsor; Aldenham. Served War of 1939-45: Captain RA, in India, Middle East and Italy. Business Manager, Associated Newspapers Ltd, 1955-57; Dir, Associated Rediffusion Ltd, 1956-57; Gen. Manager, Southern Television Ltd, 1957-59; Vice-Pres., Southern Arts Assoc.; Mem. Exec. Cttee, South East Arts Assoc.; Trustee, Chichester Festival Theatre Trust Ltd. FCA 1947. *Recreations:* sailing, music. *Address:* Little Croft, Upham, Hants. *T:* Durley 204. *Clubs:* MCC; Royal Southern Yacht.

WILSON, Clifford; Professor of Medicine, University of London, at the London Hospital and Director, Medical Unit, The London Hospital, 1946-71, now Emeritus Professor; *b* 27 Jan. 1906; *m* 1936, Kathleen Hebden; one *s* one *d. Educ:* Balliol College, Oxford. Brackenbury Scholar, Balliol Coll., Oxford, 1924; 1st Class Oxford Final Hons School of Nat. Sciences, 1928; House Physician, etc., London Hospital, 1931-34; Rockefeller Travelling Fellow, 1934-35; Research Fellow, Harvard Univ.; Asst Director, Medical Unit, London Hosp., 1938; Univ. Reader in Medicine, London Hosp., 1940; Major RAMC, Medical Research Section, 1942-45. President Renal Association, 1963-64. Examiner MRCP, 1960-; Censor, RCP, 1964-66; Senior Censor and Senior Vice-Pres., 1967-68. Dean, Faculty of Medicine, Univ. of London, 1968-71. *Publications:* sections on renal diseases and diseases of the arteries in Price's Text Book of Medicine; papers on renal disease, hypertension, arterial disease and other medical subjects, 1930-70. *Address:* The White Cottage, Woodgreen, Fordingbridge, Hants.

WILSON, Prof. Colin Alexander St John, FRIBA; Professor of Architecture, Cambridge University, since 1975; Fellow, Pembroke College, Cambridge, since 1977; Architect (own private practice); *b* 14 March 1922; *yr s* of late Rt Rev. Henry A. Wilson, CBE, DD; *m* 1st, 1955, Muriel Lavender (marr. diss. 1971); 2nd, 1972, Mary Jane Long; one *s* one *d . Educ:* Felsted Sch.; Corpus Christi Coll., Cambridge, 1940-42 (MA); Sch. of Architecture, London Univ., 1946-49 (Dip. Lond.). Served War, RNVR, 1942-46. Asst in Housing Div., Architects Dept, LCC, 1950-55; Lectr at Sch. of Architecture, Univ. of Cambridge, 1955-69; Fellow, Churchill Coll., Cambridge, 1962-71. Practised in assoc. with Sir Leslie Martin, 1955-64: on bldgs in Cambridge (Harvey Court, Gonville and Caius Coll.; Stone Building, Peterhouse); Univ. of Oxford, Law Library; Univ. of Leicester, Science Campus; Univ. of London, Royal Holloway Coll. In own practice Buildings include: Extension to Sch. of Architecture, Cambridge; Research Laboratory, Babraham; Extension to British Museum; Project for Liverpool Civic and Social Centre; Project for Brit. Museum and Science Ref. Libraries, Bloomsbury. Vis. Critic to Yale Sch. of Architecture, USA, 1960 and 1964; Bemis Prof. of Architecture MIT, USA, 1970-72. Trustee, Tate Gall, 1974-. *Publications:* articles in: The Observer; professional jls in UK, USA, France, Spain, Japan, Germany, Norway, Italy, Switzerland, etc. *Address:* 31A Grove End Road, NW8. *T:* 01-286 8306; 2 Grantchester Road, Cambridge. *T:* Cambridge 57776; (office) Colin St John Wilson & Partners, 9-11 Wilson Street, EC2M 2TQ. *T:* 01-628 4851. *Club:* Athenæum.

WILSON, Colin Henry; author; *b* Leicester, 26 June 1931; *s* of Arthur Wilson and Annetta Jones; *m* Dorothy Betty Troop; one *s*; *m* Joy Stewart; two *s* one *d. Educ:* The Gateway Secondary Technical School, Leicester. Left school at 16. Laboratory Asst (Gateway School), 1948-49; Civil Servant (collector of taxes), Leicester and Rugby, 1949-50; national service with RAF, AC2, 1949-50. Various jobs, and a period spent in Paris and Strasbourg, 1950; came to London, 1951; various labouring jobs, long period in plastic factory; returned to Paris, 1953; labouring jobs in London until Dec. 1954, when began writing The Outsider: has since made a living at writing. Visiting Professor: Hollins Coll., Va, 1966-67; Univ. of Washington, Seattle, 1967; Dowling Coll., Majorca, 1969; Rutgers Univ., NJ, 1974. Plays produced: Viennese Interlude; The Metal Flower Blossom; Strindberg. *Publications:* The Outsider, 1956; Religion and the Rebel, 1957; The Age of Defeat, 1959; Ritual in the Dark, 1960; Adrift in Soho, 1961; An Encyclopædia of Murder, 1961; The Strength to Dream, 1962; Origins of the Sexual Impulse, 1963; The Man without a Shadow, 1963; The World of Violence, 1963; Rasputin and the Fall of the Romanovs, 1964; The Brandy of the Damned (musical essays), 1964; Necessary Doubt, 1964; Beyond the Outsider, 1965; Eagle and Earwig, 1965; The Mind Parasites, 1966; Introduction to The New Existentialism, 1966; The Glass Cage, 1966; Sex and the Intelligent Teenager, 1966; The Philosopher's Stone, 1968; Strindberg (play), 1968; Bernard Shaw: A Reassessment, 1969; Voyage to a Beginning, 1969; Poetry and Mysticism, 1970; The Black Room, 1970; A Casebook of Murder, 1970; The God of the Labyrinth, 1970; Lingard, 1970; (jtly) The Strange Genius of David Lindsay, 1970; The Occult, 1971; New Pathways in Psychology, 1972; Order of Assassins, 1971; Tree by Tolkien, 1973; Hermann Hesse, 1973; Strange Powers, 1973; The Schoolgirl Murder Case, 1974; Return of the Lloigor, 1974; A Book of Booze, 1974; The Craft of the Novel, 1975; The Space Vampires, 1976; The Geller Phenomenon, 1977; contribs to: The Spectator, Audio, Books and Bookmen, Hi-Fi News, Sunday Times, Sunday Telegraph, etc. *Recreations:* collecting gramophone records, mainly opera; mathematics. *Address:* Tetherdown, Trewallock Lane, Gorran Haven, Cornwall. *Clubs:* Savage; The Club (St Austell).

WILSON, Maj.-Gen. Dare; *see* Wilson, Maj.-Gen. R. D.

WILSON, David; *see* Wilson, C. D.

WILSON, Sir David, 3rd Bt *cr* 1920; solicitor; *b* 30 Oct. 1928; *s* of Sir John Mitchell Harvey Wilson, 2nd Bt, KCVO, and of Mary Elizabeth, *d* of late William Richards, CBE; *S* father, 1975; *m* 1955, Eva Margareta, *e d* of Tore Lindell; two *s* one *d. Educ:* Deerfield Acad., Mass., USA; Harrow School; Oriel Coll., Oxford (Brisco Owen Schol.). Barrister, Lincoln's Inn, 1954-61; admitted Solicitor, 1962; Partner in Simmons & Simmons, EC2, 1963-. *Heir: s* Thomas David Wilson, *b* 6 Jan. 1959. *Address:* Tandem House, Queen's Drive, Oxshott, Leatherhead, Surrey KT22 0PH. *Club:* Arts.

WILSON, David Mackenzie; Director of the British Museum, since 1977; *b* 30 Oct. 1931; *e s* of Rev. Joseph Wilson; *m* 1955, Eva, *o d* of Dr Gunnar Sjögren, Stockholm; one *s* one *d. Educ:* Kingswood Sch.; St John's Coll., Cambridge (LittD); Lund Univ., Sweden. Research Asst, Cambridge Univ., 1954; Asst Keeper, British Museum, 1954-64; Reader in Archaeology of Anglo-Saxon Period, London Univ., 1964-71; Prof. of Medieval Archaeology, Univ. of London, 1971-76; Jt Head of Dept of Scandinavian Studies, UCL, 1973-76. Mem., Ancient Monuments Bd for England, 1976-. Governor, Museum of London, 1976-. Crabtree Orator 1966, Jarrow Lectr 1969, Dalrymple Lectr, Glasgow Univ., 1971; Rafn Lectr, Odense Univ., 1974. Member: German Archaeological Inst.; Royal Gustav Adolf's Acad. of Sweden; Vetenskapssocieteten, Lund, Sweden; FSA; Hon. MRIA; Hon. Mem., Polish Archaeological and Numismatic Soc.; Sec., Soc. for Medieval Archaeology, 1957-67; Pres., Viking Soc., 1968-70; Pres., Brit. Archaeological Assoc., 1962-68. *Publications:* The Anglo-Saxons, 1960 (2nd edn 1970); Anglo-Saxon Metalwork 700-1100 in British Museum, 1964; (with O. Klindt-Jensen) Viking Art, 1966; (with G. Bersu) Three Viking Graves in the Isle of Man, 1969; The Vikings and their Origins, 1970; (with P. G. Foote) The Viking Achievement, 1970 (Dag Strömbäck Prize, Royal Gustav Adolf's Acad., 1975); Reflections on the St Ninian's Isle Treasure (Jarrow Lecture), 1970; (with A. Small and C. Thomas) St Ninian's Isle and its Treasure, 1973; The Viking Age in the Isle of Man, 1974; (ed) Anglo-Saxon Archaeology, 1976; contrib. Archaeologia, Antiquaries Jl, Acta Archaeologica, Medieval Archaeology. *Address:* 25 Stratford Villas, NW1 9SE. *T:* 01-267 3489; 1 Parliament Lane, Castletown, Isle of Man. *Club:* Athenæum.

WILSON, Des; Editor, Social Work Today, since 1976; *b* 5 March 1941; *s* of Albert H. Wilson, Oamaru, New Zealand; *m* 1962, Rita Claire Williams (marr. diss. 1977); one *s* one *d. Educ:* Waitaki Boys' High Sch., New Zealand. Journalist-Broadcaster, 1957-67; Director, Shelter, Nat. Campaign for the Homeless, 1967-71; Head of Public Affairs, RSC, 1974-76. Member: Nat. Exec., Nat. Council for Civil Liberties, 1971-73; Cttee for City Poverty, 1972-73. Columnist, The Guardian, 1968-70; Columnist, The Observer, 1971-75; regular contributor, Illustrated London News, 1974-77. Contested (L) Hove, 1973, 1974; Mem., Liberal Party Council, 1973-74 and 1977. *Publications:* I Know It Was the Place's Fault, 1970; Des Wilson's Minority Report (a diary of protest), 1973. *Address:* 55 Wyre Hill, Bewdley, Worcs.

WILSON, Rt. Rev. Douglas John, MA; *b* 22 June 1903; *e s* of late Canon J. K. Wilson, Vicar of Bromley, Kent, and late Mrs E. L. Wilson; *m* 1946, Mary Theodora, *er d* of late Rev. A. F. Bliss; one *s* one *d. Educ:* King's School, Rochester; Haileybury College; Queens' College, Cambridge; Westcott House, Cambridge. Hist. Tripos, BA Cantab 1924; MA Cantab 1928; ordained 1927, to Curacy of Dartford Parish Church; Curate Walsall Parish Church, 1931; Vicar of Kingswinford, Staffs, 1935; Asst Bishop of British Honduras, 1938-44; Archdeacon in Central America, 1939-44; Asst Bishop of Southwell, 1944-45; Bishop of British Honduras, 1945-50; Bishop of Trinidad, 1950-56; Asst Bishop of Bath and Wells and Canon Residentiary and Treasurer of Wells Cathedral, 1956-73; Proctor in Convocation for Dean and Chapter, Wells Cathedral, 1961-63. Fellow of Woodard Corporation (Western Division), 1958, Vice-Provost, 1976; Chairman of Governors, King's Coll., Taunton, 1958-75. Coronation Medal, 1953. *Recreation:* reading Who's Who. *Address:* 3 St Mary Well Street, Beaminster, Dorset. *T:* Beaminster 862616.

WILSON, Sir Duncan; *see* Wilson, Sir A. D.

WILSON, Prof. Edward Meryon, FBA 1964; MA, PhD; Professor of Spanish, Cambridge University, 1953-73; Vice-Master of Emmanuel College, 1961-65; *b* Kendal, 1906; *s* of Norman F. Wilson, Kendal, and Henrietta Gwendolen Meryon Harris. *Educ:* Windermere Grammar School; Trinity Coll., Cambridge. Modern Languages Tripos, Part II, 1928; Esmé Howard Studentship at Residencia de Estudiantes, Madrid, 1929-30; Rouse Ball Studentship at Trinity College, Cambridge, 1930-31; Jane Eliza Proctor Visiting Fellowship at University of Princeton (NJ), 1932-33; PhD Cambridge, 1934; Assistant Lecturer in Spanish at Cambridge, 1933-39; University Lecturer there, 1939-45 (absent on national service, 1941-44); Cervantes Prof. of Spanish, Univ. of London, 1945-53. Fellow of Emmanuel College, Cambridge, Jan.-Sept. 1945. Visiting Professor: Indiana Univ., Bloomington, 1966; Univ. of Calif., Berkeley, 1968-69; Univ. of Texas, 1975; Johnson Prof., Inst. of Res. in Humanities, Univ. of Wisconsin, 1977. Pres. Assoc. of Hispanists of Great Britain and Ireland, 1971-73; Provisional Pres. First Internat. Congress of Hispanists, Oxford, 1962; Pres., Internat Assoc. of Hispanists, 1971-74; Pres., Cambridge Bibliographical Soc., 1975-. Corresp. Member: Hispanic Soc. of America, 1963; Royal Spanish Acad., 1964; Royal Acad. of Good Letters, Barcelona, 1974. Hon. DLitt Southampton, 1972. *Publications:* The Solitudes of Don Luis de Gongora, 1931, 2nd edn, 1965; (with Jack Sage) Poesias liricas en las obras dramáticas de Calderón, 1964; (with F. J. Norton) Two Spanish Verse Chap-books, 1968; Entre las jarchas y Cernuda, 1977; also articles in various reviews. *Address:* Emmanuel College, Cambridge CB2 3AP.

WILSON, Ellis; *see* Wilson, H. E. C.

WILSON, Lt-Col Eric Charles Twelves, VC 1940; retired; *b* 2 October 1912; *s* of Rev. C. C. C. Wilson; *m* 1943, Ann (from whom he obtained a divorce, 1953), *d* of Major Humphrey Pleydell-Bouverie, MBE; two *s*; *m* 1953, Angela Joy, *d* of Lt-Col J. McK. Gordon, MC; one *s. Educ:* Marlborough; RMC, Sandhurst. Commissioned in East Surrey Regt, 1933; seconded to King's African Rifles, 1937; seconded to Somaliland Camel Corps, 1939; Long Range Desert Gp, 1941-42; Burma, 1944; seconded to N Rhodesia Regt, 1946; retd from Regular Army, 1949; Admin Officer, HM Overseas Civil Service, Tanganyika, 1949-61; Dep. Warden, London House, 1962, Warden, 1966-77. Hon. Sec., Anglo-Somali Soc., 1972-77. *Recreation:* country life. *Address:* Woodside Cottage, Stowell, Sherborne, Dorset. *T:* Templecombe 264.

WILSON, Frank Richard, CMG 1963; OBE 1946; Controller of Administration, Commonwealth Development Corporation; retired HMOCS Oct. 1963; *b* 26 Oct. 1920; *er s* of Sir Leonard Wilson, *qv* and the late Muriel Wilson; *m* 1947, Alexandra

Dorothy Mary (*née* Haigh); two *s*. *Educ:* Oundle Sch.; Trinity Hall, Cambridge (1939-40 only). Commnd Indian Army, 1941; retired as Lieut-Col, 1946. Joined Colonial Administrative Service (later HMOCS) in Kenya, 1947; District Comr, 1950-56; Private Sec. to the Governor, 1956-59; Provincial Comr, Central Province, 1959-63; Civil Sec., Central Region, 1963; joined CDC, 1964. *Address:* The Old Lodge, Firbank Lane, Woking, Surrey.

WILSON, Geoffrey; Chairman, Wells, O'Brien & Co., since 1972; Managing Director, Dunkeld Holdings Ltd, since 1974 (Director since 1972); Director: Irish Intercontinental Bank since 1973; William Murray and Associates, since 1972; *b* 11 July 1929; *m* 1962, Philomena Mary Kavanagh; one *s* one *d*. *Educ:* Bolton County Grammar Sch.; Univ. of Birmingham. PE Consulting Group, 1958-63; British Railways, 1963-71; Mem., BR Bd, 1968-71, Chief Exec. (Railways), 1971; Member: Council, Royal Inst. of Public Admin, 1970-71; Council, Inst. of Transport, 1970-71. *Recreation:* golf. *Address:* The Gables, Barnsley, Cirencester, Glos. *Club:* Royal Dublin Golf.

WILSON, Sir Geoffrey Masterman, KCB 1969 (CB 1968); CMG 1962; Chairman, Oxfam, since 1977; *b* 7 April 1910; 3rd *s* of late Alexander Cowan Wilson and Edith Jane Brayshaw; *m* 1946, Julie Stafford Trowbridge; two *s* two *d*. *Educ:* Manchester Grammar School; Oriel College, Oxford. Chairman, Oxford Univ. Labour Club, 1930; Pres., Oxford Union, 1931. Harmsworth Law Scholar, Middle Temple, 1931; called to Bar, Middle Temple, 1934. Served in HM Embassy, Moscow, and Russian Dept of Foreign Office, 1940-45. Cabinet Office, 1947; Treasury, 1948; Director, Colombo Plan Technical Co-operation Bureau, 1951-53; Under-Secretary, Treasury, 1956-58; Deputy Head of UK Treasury Delegn and Alternate Exec. Dir for UK, Internat. Bank, Washington, 1958; Vice-President, International Bank, Washington, 1961; Deputy Secretary, ODM, 1966-68, Permanent Secretary, 1968-70; Dep. Sec.-Gen. (Economic), Commonwealth Secretariat, 1971. Chm., Race Relations Bd, 1971-76. Hon. Fellow, Wolfson Coll., Cambridge, 1971. *Address:* Hansteads, East Hanney, Oxon.
See also Prof. J. E. Meade, Prof. R. C. Wilson and S. S. Wilson.

WILSON, Geoffrey Studholme, CMG 1961; Commissioner of Police, Tanganyika Police Force, 1958-62; *b* 5 June 1913; *s* of late J. E. S. Wilson; *m* 1936, Joy Noel, *d* of Capt. C. st G. Harris-Walker; two *s*. *Educ:* Radley College. Joined Hong Kong Police, 1933; Commissioner of Police, Sarawak Constabulary, 1953-58. King's Police Medal, 1950. OStJ 1961. *Recreations:* golf, fishing, sailing. *Address:* c/o The Hong Kong & Shanghai Banking Corporation, 9 Gracechurch Street, EC3. *Clubs:* Royal Commonwealth Society; Hong Kong (Hong Kong).

WILSON, Sir George, KBE 1959; Kt 1944; Hon. LLD; Chairman of Governors of West of Scotland Agricultural College, 1942-71; *b* 24 Nov. 1900; 3rd *s* of Sir David Wilson, 1st Bt of Carbeth, Killearn; unmarried. *Educ:* Harrow; Trinity College, Cambridge (MA, Nat. Sci. Tripos). Hon. LLD (Glasgow), 1950; DUniv Stirling, 1973. Post-graduate study, then farming. Member: Scottish Milk Marketing Bd, 1935-50 (Chm.); Balfour of Burleigh Committee on Hill Sheep Farming in Scotland, 1941-44; Herring Industry Bd, 1945-63; Director British Linen Bank, 1950-71. Mem., Stirling CC, 1930-75. *Recreations:* fishing, walking. *Address:* King's Mile, Killearn, by Glasgow. *TA:* King's Mile, Killearn. *T:* Killearn 50363. *Club:* Athenæum.

WILSON, George Ambler, CBE 1967; CEng, FICE, FIMechE; Consultant Engineer and Director of Land Reclamation and Development; *b* 16 May 1906; *s* of Frederick Coe Wilson and Betsey Alice (*née* Pickles), Halifax, Yorks; *m* 1950, Audry Beryl (*née* Vernon); two *d*. *Educ:* Wrekin Coll.; Liverpool Univ. MEng 1932, FICE 1944, FIMechE 1951. Leyland Motors Apprentice; Anglo-Iranian Oil Co.; MoT, Bridge Section; Admty, Civil Engr-in-Chief's Dept; Port of London Authority, 1948-69 (Dir, 1965-69). Pres., Council of Instn of Civil Engrs, 1971-72; Hon. Member: Perm. Internat. Assoc. of Navig. Congresses; Hydraulic Research Bd, Wallingford (Chm., 1959-63); British Hydromechanics Research Assoc. (Vice-Chm., 1968); Thames Survey Cttee, 1948-63; Nat. Economic Develt Cttee for Civil Engrg Industry, 1965-70; Smeatonian Soc. of Civil Engineers. Pres., Société des Ingénieurs Civils de France, 1969. OC, Engr and Rly Staff Corps, RE T&AVR, 1964-69. *Recreation:* a little gardening. *Address:* Amblers, Lanchard Lane, Shillingstone, Dorset. *Clubs:* Athenæum, Royal Automobile.

WILSON, George Pritchard Harvey, CMG 1966; JP; Chairman, Victorian Inland Meat Authority, since 1973 (Deputy Chairman, 1970-73); *b* 10 March 1918; *s* of late G. L. Wilson; *m* 1945, Fay Hobart Duff; two *s* one *d*. *Educ:* Geelong Grammar School. Nuffield Scholar (Farming), 1952. Council Member, Monash University, 1961-69; Royal Agricultural Society of Victoria: Councillor, 1950-; President, 1964-73; Trustee, 1968-. Mem., Victoria Promotion Cttee, 1968-. JP 1957. *Recreation:* fishing. *Address:* Wilson House, Berwick, Victoria 3806, Australia. *T:* Berwick 7071271. *Clubs:* Melbourne, Amateur Sports, Royal Automobile Club of Victoria (all Melbourne).

WILSON, Gilbert; *b* 2 March 1908; *s* of J. E. Wilson; *m* 1934, Janet Joy Turner; two *d*. *Educ:* Auckland Grammar School. Served with 2nd NZEF, Middle East, 1940-43. Joined National Bank of New Zealand, 1924; joined Reserve Bank of New Zealand, 1935; Dep. Chief Cashier, 1948-53; Chief Cashier, 1953-56; Dep. Governor, 1956-62; Governor, 1962-67; also Alternate Governor for New Zealand of International Monetary Fund, 1962-67. *Recreations:* golf, gardening. *Address:* 41 Mere Road, Taupo, New Zealand. *Club:* Taupo Golf (NZ).

WILSON, Gordon; *see* Wilson, Robert G.

WILSON, Gordon Wallace; Under Secretary, Ministry of Agriculture, Fisheries and Food, since 1975; *b* 14 July 1926; *s* of late John Wallace Wilson and of Mrs Joyce Elizabeth Grace Sherwood-Smith; *m* 1951, Gillian Maxwell (*née* Wood); three *s*. *Educ:* King's Sch., Bruton; Queen's Coll., Oxford (BA PPE). Entered Civil Service (War Office), 1950; Principal Private Sec. to Sec. of State for War, 1962; Asst Sec., MoD, 1964; Dir, Centre of Admin Studies, HM Treasury, 1965; Asst Sec., DEA, 1968; HM Treasury, 1969. *Recreations:* tennis, carpentry, gardening, camping. *Address:* 61 Ottways Lane, Ashtead, Surrey. *T:* Ashtead 72898.

WILSON, Graeme McDonald, CMG 1975; British Civil Aviation Representative (Far East), since 1964; *b* 9 May 1919; *s* of Robert Linton McDonald Wilson and Sophie Hamilton Wilson (*née* Milner); *m* 1968, Yabu Masae; three *s*. *Educ:* Rendcomb Coll., Glos; Schloss Schule Salem, Germany; Lincoln Coll., Oxford; Gray's Inn, London. Served in Fleet Air Arm, 1939-46. Joined Home Civil Service, 1946. Private Sec. to Parly Sec., Min. of Civil Aviation, 1946-49; Planning 1, 1949-53; Dep. UK Rep. on Council of ICAO, 1953-56; Lt-Comdr (A) (O) (Ph) (q) RCNR, 1954; Internat. Relations 1, Min. of Transport and Civil Aviation, 1956-61; Asst Sec. Interdependence, Exports and Electronics, Min. of Aviation, 1961-64; seconded to Foreign Service as Counsellor and Civil Air Attaché, at twelve Far Eastern posts, 1964. Ford Foundn Fellow, Nat. Translation Center, Austin, Texas, 1968-69. *Publications:* Face At The Bottom Of The World: translations of the modern Japanese poetry of Hagiwara Sakutaro, 1969; (trans., with Ito Aiko) I Am a Cat, 1971; (trans., with Atsumi Ikuko) Three Contemporary Japanese Poets, 1972; (trans., with Ito Aiko) Heredity of Taste, 1973; Nihon no Kindaishi to Gendaishi no Dai Yon-sho: Hagiwara Sakutaro, 1974; articles on East Asian literature and poems (mostly Japanese, Chinese, Vietnamese and Korean trans). *Address:* H7, Repulse Bay Towers, Repulse Bay, Hong Kong. *T:* Hong Kong 920454. *Clubs:* Naval; PEN Club of Japan (Tokyo).

WILSON, Sir Graham (Selby), Kt 1962; MD, FRCP, DPH (London); late Captain Royal Army Medical Corps (Special Reserve); Hon. Lecturer, Department of Bacteriology and Immunology, London School of Hygiene and Tropical Medicine, 1964-70; Director of the Public Health Laboratory Service, 1941-63; KHP, 1944-46; *b* 10 Sept. 1895; *m* Mary Joyce (*d* 1976), *d* of Alfred Ayrton, Chester; two *s*. *Educ:* Epsom College; King's Coll., London; Charing Cross Hospital, London; Governors' Clinical Gold Medal, Charing Cross Hospital, and Gold Medal, University of London, MB, BS; Specialist in Bacteriology, Royal Army Med. Corps, 1916-20; Demonstrator in Bacteriology, Charing Cross Hospital Medical School, 1919-22; Lecturer in Bacteriology, University of Manchester, 1923-27; Reader in Bacteriology, University of London, 1927-30; Prof. of Bacteriology as applied to Hygiene, London School of Hygiene and Tropical Medicine, 1930-47; William Julius Mickle Fellowship, University of London, 1939. Member: Council, RCP, 1938-40; of several cttees on tuberculosis, poliomyelitis and other infectious diseases; Weber-Parkes prize, RCP 1942; Milroy Lecturer, RCP, 1948; Hon. Fellow, Amer. Public Health Assoc., 1953; Hon. Fellow: Royal Soc. of Health, 1960; London Sch. of Hygiene and Tropical Medicine, 1976; Hon. FRSocMed, 1971; Hon. FRCPath, 1972. Czechoslovak Medical Society, Jan Evangelista Purkyně, 1963; Bisset Hawkins Medal, RCP, 1956; Marjory Stephenson Memorial Prize, 1959; Stewart Prize, 1960; Buchanan Medal, Royal Society, 1967; Harben Gold Medal, 1970; Jenner Meml Medal, 1975. Hon. LLD (Glasgow) 1962. *Publications:* The Principles of Bacteriology and Immunity (with late Professor W. W. C. Topley and Sir Ashley Miles), 6th edn 1975; The Hazards of Immunization, 1967; The

Bacteriological Grading of Milk (with collaborators), 1935; The Pasteurization of Milk, 1942; numerous papers on bacteriological subjects. *Recreation:* cycling. *Address:* 65 Hillway, N6 6AB. *Club:* Athenæum.

WILSON, Rear-Adm. Guy Austen Moore, CB 1958; Breeder and Voluntary Organiser, Guide Dogs for the Blind Association; *b* 7 June 1906; *s* of Ernest Moore Wilson, Buenos Aires, and Katharine Lawrence; *m* 1932, Dorothy, *d* of Sir Arthur Watson, CBE; two *s* three *d*. *Educ:* Royal Naval Colleges, Osborne and Dartmouth. Joined Royal Navy, 1920; Engineering Specialist Course, 1924-28. Advanced Engineering Course, Royal Naval College, Greenwich, 1928-30; served War of 1939-45, at Admiralty and in HMS Berwick; Portsmouth Dockyard, 1946-49; Comdr, 1940; Captain, 1948; Dep. Director Aircraft Maintenance and Repair, Admiralty, 1950-52; Supt, RN Aircraft Yard, Fleetlands, 1952-55; Rear-Admiral, 1955; Deputy Engineer-in-Chief for Fleet Maintenance and Administration, 1955-57; Rear-Admiral Nuclear Propulsion and Deputy Engineer-in-Chief (Nuclear Propulsion), 1957-59, retired 1960; Chief Executive, Dracone Developments Ltd, 1960-63. *Recreations:* swimming, motoring, gardening. *Address:* Barn Acre, Saxstead Green, Woodbridge, Suffolk. *T:* Earl Soham 365.

WILSON, Rt. Hon. Sir Harold; *see* Wilson, Rt Hon. Sir J. H.

WILSON, Harold; Chairman of Industrial Tribunals, Birmingham, since 1976; *b* 19 Sept. 1931; *s* of Edward Simpson Wilson, Harpenden; *m* 1973, Jill Ginever, *d* of late Charles Edward Walter Barlow; one step *s* one step *d* ; three *s* one *d* by previous marriage. *Educ:* St Albans Sch.; Sidney Sussex Coll., Cambridge (MA). Commnd service, RAF, RAFVR, RAuxAF, 1950-disbandment. Called to the Bar, Gray's Inn, 1958; Oxford Circuit, 1960-70; Midland and Oxford Circuit, 1971-75; Dep. Chm., Monmouthshire Quarter Sessions, 1970; a Recorder, Midland and Oxford Circuit, 1971-75. *Recreations:* sailing; Vice-Chm., Friends of Abingdon Civic Trust, 1974. *Address:* 2 Harcourt Buildings, Temple, EC4Y 9DB. *T:* 01-353 8549; Struan Court, 17 Park Crescent, Abingdon OX14 1DF. *T:* Abingdon 29500.

WILSON, Harold Arthur Cooper B.; *see* Bird-Wilson.

WILSON, Harold Fitzhardinge Wilson; Solicitor and Parliamentary Officer, Greater London Council, 1970-77 (Dep. Solicitor and Dep. Parly Officer, 1965); *b* 6 Jan. 1913; *s* of Walter James Wilson and Aileen Wilson (*née* Scrivens), Broadway, Worcs; *m* 1939, Deb Buckland; one *s* one *d*. Law Clerk, LCC, 1935. Company Officer, then Senior Company Officer, Nat. Fire Service, 1939-45. Principal Asst, LCC, 1951; Asst Parly Officer, LCC, 1960. Hon. Solicitor, RoSPA, 1970-77. Liveryman, Glaziers' Co. *Recreations:* the theatre, walking, gardening, reading. *Address:* 10 Courtenay Square, SE11.

WILSON, Harry; *see* Wilson of Langside, Baron.

WILSON, (Harry) Ellis (Charter), MB, ChB; DSc; FRCPGlas; retired as Lecturer in Pathological Biochemistry at Royal Hospital for Sick Children, Glasgow; *b* 26 July 1899; *s* of Harry James and Margaret Williaminia Wilson. *Educ:* Glasgow Academy and University. Carnegie Scholar, 1923; studied in Würzburg, 1926; Assistant in Institute of Physiology, Glasgow University, 1924; a Rockefeller Fellowship tenable in USA, 1926; carried out research in New York and the Mayo Clinic, Rochester; Carnegie Teaching Fellow in Institute of Physiology, Glasgow University, 1930; studied (research) in Germany, 1931; Professor of Biochemistry and Nutrition, The All-India Institute of Hygiene and Public Health, Calcutta, 1934-37, and Professor of Chemistry, The Medical College, Calcutta, 1935-37. *Publications:* papers on biochemical subjects in various journals. *Recreations:* golf, travel. *Address:* Redholm, 5 West Chapelton Avenue, Bearsden, Glasgow; The Royal Hospital for Sick Children, Yorkhill, Glasgow.

WILSON, Harry Lawrence L.; *see* Lawrence-Wilson.

WILSON, Henry Braithwaite; Assistant Under-Secretary of State, Home Office, 1963-71; *b* 6 Aug. 1911; *s* of Charles Braithwaite Wilson and Ellen Blanche Hargrove; *m* 1936, Margaret Bodden; two *s* two *d*. *Educ:* Leighton Park School; Lincoln College, Oxford. Editorial work for Joseph Rowntree Social Service Trust, 1933-40; Sub-Warden, Toynbee Hall, 1940-41; Home Office: Temp. Administrative Asst, 1941-44; Sec., Departmental Cttee on War Damaged Licensed Premises and Reconstruction, 1942-44; Principal, 1944 (estab. 1946); Asst Sec., 1956. *Recreations:* gardening, walking. *Address:* Arran, Yew Tree Road, Grange over Sands, Cumbria. *T:* Grange 3488.

WILSON, Col Henry James, CBE 1963 (OBE 1943); TD 1944; Farmer since 1949; Hon. Treasurer, NFU; Chairman, NFU Trust Co.; Member, British Agricultural Export Council; *b* 10 June 1904; *s* of late James Wilson; *m* 1930, Anita Gertrude Petley; three *s*. *Educ:* Mercers' School. Westminster Bank, 1921-39. Served London Scottish, 1923-44; Commanded 1st Bn London Scottish, 1941-44; AAG, 8th Army HQ, 1944; DDPS, AFHQ, 1944-45; War Office, 1945-49. Joined NFU, 1947; Council Member, 1954; Vice-Pres., 1958; Dep. Pres., 1959-62. Chairman: Bacon Consultative Council, 1957-64; Industry Panel, Bacon Mkt Council, 1964-72. *Recreations:* shooting, and fishing. *Address:* Hamsey, Caldbec Hill, Battle, East Sussex. *Clubs:* Farmers'; Highland Brigade.

WILSON, Henry Moir, CB 1969; CMG 1965; MBE 1946; PhD, BSc, FRAeS; *b* 3 Sept. 1910; 3rd *s* of late Charles Wilson, Belfast; *m* 1937, Susan Eveline Wilson; one *s* three *d*. *Educ:* Royal Belfast Academical Institution, Queen's Univ., Belfast. Apprentice in Mech. Eng, Combe Barbour, Belfast, 1927-31; QUB, 1927-31 (part-time) and 1931-34 (full-time); BSc with 1st Class Hons in Elect. Eng, 1932; PhD 1934 (Thesis on High Voltage Transients on Power Transmission Lines). College Apprentice, Metropolitan-Vickers, Manchester, 1934-35. Joined RAF Educational Service, 1935; commissioned RAFVR, 1939; Senior Tutor, RAF Advanced Armament Course, Ft. Halstead, 1943-46; Senior Educ. Officer, Empire Air Armament School, Manby (Acting Wing Comdr), 1946-47. Joined Ministry of Supply, 1947, as Senior Principal Sci. Officer, Supt Servo Div., Guided Projectile Estab., Westcott, 1947; Supt Guidance and Control Div. Guided Weapons Dept, RAE, 1947-49; Head of Armament Dept, RAE, 1949-56. Dep. Chief Sci. Officer, 1952; Chief Scientific Officer, 1956; Director-General, Aircraft Equipment Research and Devel., Ministry of Aviation, 1956-62; Head, Defence Research and Development Staff, British Embassy, Washington, DC, 1962-65; Dep. Chief Scientist (Army), 1965-66, Chief Scientist (Army), 1967-70; Dir, SHAPE Tech. Centre, 1970-75. Hon. DSc QUB, 1971. *Recreations:* golf, gardening. *Address:* 7 Carlinwark Drive, Camberley, Surrey.

WILSON, Sir Hubert Guy M. M.; *see* Maryon-Wilson.

WILSON, Sir Hugh; *see* Wilson, Sir L. H.

WILSON, Ian D.; *see* Douglas-Wilson.

WILSON, Ian Matthew; Under Secretary, Scottish Education Department, since 1977; *b* 12 Dec. 1926; *s* of Matthew Thomson Wilson and Mary Lily Barnett; *m* 1953, Anne Chalmers; three *s*. *Educ:* George Watson's Coll.; Edinburgh Univ. (MA). Asst Principal, Scottish Home Dept, 1950; Private Sec. to Perm. Under-Sec. of State, Scottish Office, 1953-55; Principal, Scottish Home Dept, 1955; Asst Secretary: Scottish Educn Dept, 1963; SHHD, 1971; Asst Under-Sec. of State, Scottish Office, 1974-77. *Address:* 1 Bonaly Drive, Edinburgh EH13 0EJ. *T:* 031-441 2541. *Club:* Royal Commonwealth Society.

WILSON, Isabel Grace Hood, CBE 1961; MD, FRCP; Principal Medical Officer, Ministry of Health, retired; *b* 16 Sept. 1895; *d* of late Dr George R. Wilson and Susan C. Sandeman. *Educ:* privately; University of Edinburgh. MB, ChB, Edinburgh, 1921; DPM London, 1924; MD, Edinburgh, 1926; MRCP London, 1937, FRCP 1947. Formerly: Asst Medical Officer, Severalls Mental Hospital, Colchester; Physician, Tavistock Square Clinic for Functional Nervous Disorders; Medical Commissioner, Board of Control, 1931-49; Senior Medical Commissioner, Board of Control, 1949-60. Member BMA; President, Royal Medico Psychological Assoc., 1962-63. Founder Mem., Royal College of Psychiatrists. *Publications:* A Study of Hypoglycæmic Shock Treatment in Schizophrenia (Report), 1936; (jointly) Report on Cardiazol Treatment, 1938; various contributions to journals. *Recreations:* water-colour painting, travel. *Address:* 48 Redcliffe Gardens, SW10 9HB. *T:* 01-352 5707.

WILSON, James, JP; DSc, BCom, CEng, FIMechE; Industrial Training Consultant, retired; *b* 15 July 1899; *s* of late James Wilson, JP, Lugar and Glasgow; *m* 1930, Jesmar Smith, Clarkston, Glasgow; one *s* two *d*. *Educ:* Cumnock Academy; Kilmarnock Academy; Glasgow Univ.; Royal Technical Coll. Mech. and Electr. Engrg with Andrew Barclay Sons & Co. Ltd, Kilmarnock (sandwiched with University studies) and Gen. Electric Co., Coventry, 1914-21; Assistant and Lecturer: Royal Technical Coll., Glasgow, 1921, Glasgow Univ., 1921-35; part-time supervisor of science and technology classes, Corp. of Glasgow, 1931-35; Coventry Technical Coll., Vice-Principal, 1935-36; Principal, 1936-46; Principal, Birmingham College of Tech., 1946-56; Director of Education and Training, British Motor Corp. Ltd, 1962-65. OC engineer unit, Glasgow Univ.,

OTC, 1933-35; OC 71st LAA Battery (TAR), 122 LAA Regt, RA, 1939; Army Welfare Officer, Warwicks, TA, 1940-45; Chairman No. 84 (2nd City of Coventry) ATC, 1945-48; estab. Midland Theatre Company at College Theatre, Coventry, 1945 (in co-operation with Arts Council); founded Playgoers Circle. Member Anglo-American Prod. Assoc. Team "Education for Management", 1951; Mem. Council, Birmingham Productivity Assoc.; Mem., Jt Commn, Nat. Diplomas and Cert. in Business Studies. Ed. The Torch, Glasgow Education Cttee, 1932-35. Hon. MIPlantE; Hon. DSc Aston. *Publications:* (jointly) Gaining Skill; various on education and training, management education, humanism in tech. education. *Recreations:* golf, cinematography, magic. *Address:* 33 Dovehouse Lane, Solihull, West Midlands. *T:* 021-706 5333.

WILSON, Sir James; *see* Wilson, Sir A. J.

WILSON, Rt. Hon. Sir (James) Harold, KG 1976; PC 1947; OBE 1945; FRS 1969; MP (Lab) Huyton Division of Lancs since 1950 (Ormskirk Division, 1945-50); Chancellor of Bradford University, since 1966; Chairman, Committee to Review the Functioning of Financial Institutions, since 1976; *b* 11 March 1916; *s* of late James Herbert and Ethel Wilson, Huddersfield, Yorks (formerly of Manchester); *m* 1940, Gladys Mary, *d* of Rev. D. Baldwin, The Manse, Duxford, Cambridge; two *s.* *Educ:* Milnsbridge Council Sch. and Royds Hall Sch. Huddersfield; Wirral Grammar Sch., Bebington, Cheshire; Jesus Coll., Oxford (Gladstone Memorial Prize, Webb Medley Economics Scholarship, First Class Hons Philosophy, Politics and Economics). Lecturer in Economics, New Coll., Oxford, 1937; Fellow of University Coll., 1938; Praelector in Economics and Domestic Bursar, 1945. Dir of Econs and Stats, Min. of Fuel and Power, 1943-44; Parly Sec. to Ministry of Works, 1945- March 1947; Sec. for Overseas Trade, March-Oct. 1947; Pres., BoT, Oct. 1947-April 1951; Chairman: Labour Party Exec. Cttee, 1961-62; Public Accounts Cttee, 1959-63; Leader, Labour Party, 1963-76; Prime Minister and First Lord of the Treasury, 1964-70, 1974-76; Leader of the Opposition, 1963-64, 1970-74. Pres., Royal Statistical Soc., 1972-73. An Elder Brother of Trinity House, 1968. Hon. Fellow, Jesus and University Colleges, Oxford, 1963. Hon. Freeman, City of London, 1975. Hon. Pres., Great Britain-USSR Assoc., 1976-. Pres., Royal Shakespeare Theatre Co., 1976-. Hon. LLD: Lancaster, 1964; Liverpool, 1965; Nottingham, 1966; Sussex, 1966; Hon. DCL, Oxford, 1965; Hon. DTech., Bradford, 1966; DUniv: Essex, 1967; Open, 1974. *Publications:* New Deal for Coal, 1945; In Place of Dollars, 1952; The War on World Poverty, 1953; The Relevance of British Socialism, 1964; Purpose in Politics, 1964; The New Britain (Penguin), 1964; Purpose in Power, 1966; The Labour Government 1964-70, 1971; The Governance of Britain, 1976. *Recreation:* golf. *Address:* House of Commons, SW1.

WILSON, Dr James Maxwell Glover, FRCP, FFCM; Senior Principal Medical Officer, Department of Health and Social Security, 1972-76; Nuffield Senior Research Fellow, Information Services Division, Common Services Agency, Scottish Health Service; *b* 31 Aug. 1913; *s* of late James Thomas Wilson and Mabel Salomons; *m* Lallie Methley; three *s.* *Educ:* King's College Choir Sch., Cambridge; Oundle Sch.; St John's Coll., Cambridge; University College Hosp., London. MA, MB, BChir (Cantab). Clinical appts, London and Cambridge, 1937- 39. Served War, RAMC (Major, 6th Airborne Div.), 1939-45. Hospital appts, London and Edinburgh, 1945-54; medical work on tea estates in India, 1954-57. Medical Staff, Min. of Health (later DHSS), concerned with the centrally financed research programme, 1957-76. Lectr (part-time), Public Health Dept, London Sch. of Hygiene and Tropical Med., 1968-72. *Publications:* (with G. Jungner) Principles and Practice of Screening for Disease (WHO), 1968; contribs to med. jls, mainly on screening for disease. *Recreations:* reading, walking, fishing. *Address:* 1 Darnaway Street, Edinburgh EH3 6DW. *T:* 031-226 2903.

WILSON, James Noel, ChM, FRCS; Consultant Orthopædic Surgeon: Royal National Orthopædic Hospital, London, National Hospitals for Nervous Diseases, Queen Square and Maida Vale, since 1962; and Surgeon i/c of Accident Unit, RNOH, Stanmore, since 1955; Teacher of Orthopædics, Institute of Orthopædics, University of London; *b* Coventry, 25 Dec. 1919; *s* of Alexander Wilson and Isobel Barbara Wilson (*née* Fairweather); *m* 1945, Patricia Norah McCullough; two *s* two *d.* *Educ:* King Henry VIII Sch., Coventry; University of Birmingham. Peter Thompson Prize in Anatomy, 1940; Sen. Surgical Prize, 1942; Arthur Foxwell Prize in Clinical Medicine, 1943; MB, ChB 1943; MRCS, LRCP, 1943; FRCS 1948; ChM (Birmingham) 1949; House Surgeon, Birmingham General Hospital, 1943; Heaton Award as Best Resident for 1943. Service in RAMC, Nov. 1943-Oct. 1946, discharged as Captain;

qualified as Parachutist and served with 1st Airborne Division. Resident surgical posts, Birmingham General Hospital and Coventry and Warwickshire Hospital, 1947-49; Resident Surgical Officer, Robert Jones and Agnes Hunt Orthopædic Hospital, Oswestry, 1949-52; Consultant Orthopædic Surgeon to Cardiff Royal Infirmary and Welsh Regional Hospital Board, 1952-55. Member BMA; Mem. Brit. Editorial Bd, Jl of Bone and Joint Surgery; Editorial Sec. and Fellow British Orthopædic Assoc. (BOA Travelling Fellowship to USA, 1954); FRSocMed. *Publications:* Sections in Butterworth's Operative Surgery; (ed) Watson Jones Fractures and Joint Injuries, 5th edn, 1976; articles on orthopædic subjects to various journals. *Recreations:* golf, gardening and photography. *Address:* The Chequers, Waterdale, near Watford, Herts. *T:* Garston 72364. *Club:* Airborne.

WILSON, Air Vice-Marshal James Stewart, CBE 1959; Lecturer, in Epidemiology and Preventive Medicine, Institute of Community Medicine, RAF Halton, since 1965; *b* 4 Sept. 1909; *s* of late J. Wilson, Broughty Ferry, Angus, and late Helen Fyffe Wilson; *m* 1937, Elizabeth Elias; one *s* (and one *s* decd). *Educ:* Dundee High Sch.; St Andrews Univ. (MB, ChB). DPH (London) 1948; FFCM(RCP) 1974. House Surgeon, Dundee Royal Infirmary, 1933; House Surgeon, Arbroath Infirmary, 1934; Commissioned Royal Air Force, 1935. Served North Africa, 1942-45. Director Hygiene and Research, Air Ministry, London, 1956-59; Principal Medical Officer, Flying Training Command, 1959-61; Director-General of Medical Services, Royal Australian Air Force, 1961-63. QHP 1961; Principal Medical Officer, Bomber Command, 1963-65, retired. *Publications:* articles (jointly) on respiratory virus infections, in medical journals. *Recreations:* golf, fishing, shooting. *Address:* Eucumbene, Buckland, Aylesbury, Bucks. *T:* Aylesbury 630062. *Club:* Royal Air Force.

WILSON, Sir John (Foster), Kt 1975; CBE 1965 (OBE 1955); Director, Royal Commonwealth Society for the Blind, since 1950; *b* 20 Jan. 1919; *s* of late Rev. George Henry Wilson, Buxton, Derbys; *m* 1944, Chloe Jean McDermid; two *d.* *Educ:* Worcester College for the Blind; St Catherine's, Oxford (MA Jurisprudence, Dipl. Public and Social Administration). Asst Secretary, Royal National Inst. for the Blind, 1941-49; Member, Colonial Office Delegation investigating blindness in Africa and Near East, 1946-47. Proposed formation of Royal Commonwealth Society for Blind; became its first Director, 1950; extensive tours in Africa, Asia, Near and Far East, Caribbean and N. America, 1952-67; world tours, 1958 and 1963; formulated Asian plan for the Blind 1963, and African Plan for the Blind, 1966. Chairman, Ghana Cabinet Cttee on Rehabilitation of Disabled, 1961; Internat. Member of World Council for Welfare of Blind (Chairman, Prevention of Blindness Cttee, 1958-, of Overseas Aid Cttee, 1972-); Member Exec. Cttee of World Braille Council; Founder Member, National Fedn of Blind (President, 1955-60); Pres., Internat. Agency for Prevention of Blindness, 1974-. Helen Keller International Award, 1970. *Publications:* Blindness in African and Middle East Territories, 1948; Ghana's Handicapped Citizens, 1961; Travelling Blind, 1963; various on Commonwealth affairs, rehabilitation and blindness. *Recreations:* current affairs, travel, writing, tape-recording, wine-making. *Address:* 22 The Cliff, Roedean, Brighton, East Sussex. *T:* Brighton 67667. *Club:* Royal Commonwealth Society.

WILSON, Prof. John Graham; Cavendish Professor of Physics, 1963-76 (Professor, 1952-63), Pro-Vice-Chancellor, 1969-71, University of Leeds; now Emeritus Professor; *b* 28 April 1911; *er s* of J. E. Wilson, Hartlepool, Co. Durham; *m* 1938, Georgiana Brooke, *o d* of Charles W. Bird, Bisley, Surrey; one *s* one *d.* *Educ:* West Hartlepool Secondary Sch.; Sidney Sussex Coll., Cambridge. Member of Teaching staff, University of Manchester, 1938-52; Reader in Physics, 1951. University of York: Member, Academic Planning Board, 1960-63; Member of Council, 1964-; Chairman, Joint Matriculation Board, 1964-67. DUniv York, 1975; Hon. DSc Durham, 1977. *Publications:* The Principles of Cloud Chamber Technique, 1951. Editor of Progress in Cosmic Ray Physics, 1952-71; (with G. D. Rochester), Cloud Chamber Photographs of the Cosmic Radiation, 1952. Papers on cosmic ray physics, articles in jls. *Recreations:* fell-walking, gardening. *Address:* 23 Newall Hall Park, Otley, West Yorks LS21 2RD. *T:* Otley 51251.

WILSON, J(ohn) Greenwood, MD, FRCP, DPH; Fellow of King's College, University of London; Group Medical Consultant, Health and Hygiene, FMC Ltd; formerly Medical Officer of Health, Port and City of London (first holder of dual appointment; MOH Port of London, 1954, MOH, City of London, in addition, 1956); *b* 27 July 1897; 2nd *s* of late Rev. John Wilson, Woolwich; *m* 1st, 1929, Wenda Margaret

Hithersay Smith (marr. diss. 1941); one *s* two *d*; 2nd, 1943, Gwendoline Mary Watkins (*d* 1975); one *d*. *Educ:* Colfe Grammar Sch.; Westminster Hospital, University of London. Served European War, S. Lancashire Regt, RFC and RAF, 1916-19 (wounded). Various hospital appointments, London and provinces and some general practice, 1923-28; subseq. MOH and Sch. Medical Officer posts; then MOH City and Port of Cardiff, Sch. MO, Cardiff Education Authority, and Lecturer in Preventive Medicine, Welsh Nat. School of Medicine, 1933-54. President, Welsh Br. Society of Med. Officers of Health, 1940-45, Member Nat. Adv. Council for recruitment of Nurses and Midwives, 1943-56. Governor, St Bart's Hospital Medical College. Formerly Examiner in Public Health, RCPS (London); Vice-President (Past Chairman of Council) and Hon. Fellow, Royal Society of Health. Hon. Sec., Assoc. of Sea and Air Port Health Authorities of British Isles, 1936-43; Member, Central Housing Advisory Cttee, 1936-56; Member Royal Commission on Mental Health, 1954-57; Chairman, City Division, BMA, 1962-63; Vice-President (Past Chairman), National Housebuilders Council. Hon. Fellow American Public Health Association. OStJ 1953. *Publications:* Diptheria Immunisation Propaganda and Counter Propaganda, 1933; Public Health Law in Question and Answer, 1951; numerous contributions to med., scientific and tech. publications. *Recreations:* theatre, music, swimming. *Address:* Flat 2, 10 Beckenham Grove, Bromley BR2 0JU. *T:* 01-460 1532. *Club:* Wig and Pen.

WILSON, Ven. John Hewitt, CB 1977; QHC 1973; Chaplain-in-Chief, Royal Air Force, since June 1973; *b* 14 Feb. 1924; *s* of John Joseph and Marion Wilson; *m* 1951, Gertrude Elsie Joan Weir; three *s* two *d*. *Educ:* Kilkenny Coll., Kilkenny; Mountjoy Sch., Dublin; Trinity Coll., Dublin. BA 1946, MA 1956. Curate, St George's Church, Dublin, 1947-50. Entered RAF, 1950: RAF Coll., Cranwell, 1950-52; Aden, 1952-55; RAF Wittering, 1955-57; RAF Cottesmore, 1957-58; RAF Germany, 1958-61; Staff Chaplain, Air Ministry, 1961-63; RAF Coll., Cranwell, 1963-66; Asst Chaplain-in-Chief: Far East Air Force, 1966-69; Strike command, 1969-73. *Recreations:* Rugby football, tennis, driving, theatre. *Address:* (home) Wing House, North Weald, Epping, Essex. *T:* North Weald 2244. *Club:* Royal Air Force.

WILSON, Sir John (Martindale), KCB 1974 (CB 1960); Chairman, Crown Housing Association, since 1975; Deputy Chairman, Civil Service Appeal Board, since 1975; *b* 3 Sept. 1915; *e s* of late John and Kate Wilson; *m* 1941, Penelope Beatrice, *e d* of late Francis A. Bolton, JP, Oakamoor, Staffs; one *s* one *d*. *Educ:* Bradfield Coll.; Gonville and Caius Coll., Cambridge. BA (Cantab), 1st Class Law Trip., 1937; MA 1946. Asst Principal, Dept of Agriculture for Scotland, 1938; Ministry of Supply, 1939; served War, 1939-46 (despatches) with Royal Artillery in India and Burma; Private Sec. to Minister of Supply, 1946-50; Asst Sec., 1950; Under-Sec., 1954; Cabinet Office, 1955-58; MoD, 1958-60; Dep. Sec., Min. of Aviation, 1961-65; Dep. Under-Sec. of State, MoD, 1965-72; Second Permanent Under-Sec. of State (Admin), MoD, 1972-75. *Recreations:* gardening and golf. *Address:* Bourne Close, Bourne Lane, Twyford, near Winchester, Hants. *T:* Twyford 713488. *Club:* Army and Navy.

WILSON, John Spark, OBE 1969; Assistant Commissioner, Traffic Department, Metropolitan Police, since 1977; *b* 9 May 1922; *s* of John Wilson and Elizabeth Kidd Wilson; *m* 1948, Marguerite Chisholm Wilson; two *s* one *d*. *Educ:* Logie Central Sch., Dundee. Joined Metropolitan Police, 1946; Special Branch, 1948-67; Detective Chief Supt, 1968; Comdr, 1968; went to Wales re Investiture of Prince of Wales, 1969; Dep. Asst Comr (CID), 1972; Asst Comr (Crime), 1975. *Recreations:* football, Rugby, boxing. *Address:* New Scotland Yard, Broadway, SW1H 0BG.

WILSON, Prof. John Stuart Gladstone, MA, DipCom; Professor of Economics and Commerce in the University of Hull; Head of Department, 1959-71, and 1974-77; *b* 18 Aug. 1916; *s* of Herbert Gladstone Wilson and Mary Buchanan Wilson (*née* Wylie); *m* 1943, Beryl Margaret Gibson, *d* of Alexander Millar Gibson and Bertha Noble Gibson; no *c*. *Educ:* University of Western Australia. Lecturer in Economics: University of Tasmania, 1941-43; Sydney, 1944-45; Canberra, 1946-47; LSE, 1948-49. Reader in Economics, with special reference to Money and Banking, Univ. of London, 1950-59; Dean, Faculty of Social Sciences and Law, Univ. of Hull, 1962-65; Chairman, Centre for S-E Asian Studies, Univ. of Hull, 1963-66. Hackett Research Student, 1947; Leverhulme Research Award, 1955 (to visit US and Canada). Economic Survey of New Hebrides on behalf of Colonial Office, 1958-59; Consultant, Trade and Payments Dept, OECD, 1965-66; Consultant with Harvard Advisory Development Service in Liberia, 1967; headed Enquiry into Sources of Capital and Credit to UK Agriculture, 1970-73;

Consultant, Directorate Gen. for Agric., EEC, 1974-75; Specialist Adviser, H of C Select Cttee on Nationalised Industries, 1976; SSRC Grant for comparative study of banking policy and structure, 1977; Cttee of Management, Inst. of Commonwealth Studies, London, 1960-77; Governor, SOAS, London, 1963-. Member: Yorkshire Council for Further Education, 1963-67; Nat. Advisory Council on Education for Industry and Commerce, 1964-66; Sec.-General, Société Universitaire Européenne de Recherches Financières, 1968-72, Pres., 1973-75, Vice-Pres., 1977-. Editor, Yorkshire Bulletin of Economic and Social Research, 1964-67; Mem., Editorial Adv. Bd, Modern Asian Studies, 1966-. *Publications:* French Banking Structure and Credit Policy, 1957; Economic Environment and Development Programmes, 1960; Monetary Policy and the Development of Money Markets, 1966; Economic Survey of the New Hebrides, 1966; (ed with C. R. Whittlesey) Essays in Money and Banking in Honour of R. S. Sayers, 1968, repr. 1970; Availability of Capital and Credit to United Kingdom Agriculture, 1973; (ed with C. F. Scheffer) Multinational Enterprises—Financial and Monetary Aspects, 1974; Credit to Agriculture—United Kingdom, 1975; The London Money Markets, 1976; (ed with J. E. Wadsworth and H. Fournier) The Development of Financial Institutions in Europe, 1956-1976; contribs. to Banking in the British Commonwealth (ed R. S. Sayers), 1952 and to Banking in Western Europe (ed R. S. Sayers), 1962; A Decade of the Commonwealth, 1955-64, ed W. B. Hamilton and others, 1966; to International Encyclopaedia of the Social Sciences; Encyclopaedia Britannica, 15th edn; Economica, Economic Journal, Journal of Political Econ., Economic Record. *Recreations:* squash rackets, gardening, theatre, art galleries. *Address:* Department of Economics and Commerce, The University, Hull, North Humberside. *Club:* Reform.

WILSON, John Tuzo, CC (Canada) 1974; OBE 1946; FRS 1968; FRSC 1949; Professor of Geophysics, University of Toronto, 1946-74, Emeritus Professor, 1977; Director-General, Ontario Science Centre, since 1974; *b* Ottawa, 24 Oct. 1908; *s* of John Armitstead Wilson, CBE, and Henrietta L. Tuzo; *m* 1938, Isabel Jean Dickson; two *d*. *Educ:* Ottawa; Universities of Toronto (Governor-General's medal, Trinity Coll., 1930; Massey Fellow, 1930), Cambridge (ScD) and Princeton (PhD). Asst Geologist, Geological Survey of Canada, 1936-46; Principal, Erindale Coll., Univ. of Toronto, 1968-74. Regimental service and staff appointments, Royal Canadian Engrs, UK and Sicily, 1939-43; Director, Opl. Research, Nat. Defence HQ, Ottawa (Colonel), 1944-46. President, International Union of Geodesy and Geophysics, 1957-60; Visiting Prof.: Australian Nat. Univ., 1950 and 1965; Ohio State Univ., 1968; California Inst. of Technology, 1976. Member Nat. Research Council of Canada, 1957-63; Member Defence Res. Board, 1958-64. Canadian Delegation to Gen. Ass., UNESCO, 1962, 1964, 1966. Pres., Royal Society of Canada, 1972-73. Overseas Fellow, Churchill Coll., Cambridge, 1965; Trustee, Nat. Museums of Canada, 1968-74. Hon. Fellow, Trinity Coll., University of Toronto, 1962. Foreign Associate, Nat. Acad. of Sciences, USA, 1968; Foreign Hon. Mem., Amer. Acad. of Arts and Sciences. Holds hon. doctorates and hon. or foreign memberships and medals, etc, in Canada and abroad. OC (Canada) 1970. *Publications:* One Chinese Moon, 1959; Physics and Geology (with J. A. Jacobs and R. D. Russell), 1959; IGY Year of the New Moons, 1961; (ed) Continents Adrift, 1972; Unglazed China, 1973; (ed) Continents Adrift and Continents Aground, 1976; scientific papers. *Recreations:* travel, sailing Hong Kong junk. *Address:* 27 Pricefield Road, Toronto M4W 1Z8, Canada. *T:* 923-4244. *Club:* Arts and Letters (Toronto).

WILSON, Joseph Albert; Secretary to the Cabinet, Sierra Leone Government, 1968; Barrister-at-Law; *b* 22 Jan. 1922; *e s* of late George Wilson; *m* 1947, Esther Massaquoi; two *s* four *d* (and one *s* decd). *Educ:* St Edward's Secondary Sch., Freetown, Sierra Leone; University of Exeter, (DPA); Middle Temple. Graded Clerical Service, Sierra Leone Government, 1941-47; family business, 1948-51; Secretary, Bonthe District Council, 1951-59; Administrative Officer, Sierra Leone Government, rising to rank of Cabinet Secretary, 1959-; High Comr from Sierra Leone to UK, 1967-68. Manager (Special Duties), SLST Ltd, 1959; Dir, National Diamond Mining Co. (Sierra Leone) Ltd. Mem., Court of Univ. of Sierra Leone. *Recreations:* tennis, golf. *Address:* 14 Syke Street, Brookfields, Freetown, Sierra Leone. *T:* 2590.

WILSON, Joseph Vivian; retired as New Zealand Ambassador to France, 1959; *b* 14 July 1894; *s* of J. H. Wilson; *m* 1929, Valentine, *d* of H. van Muyden, Geneva; two *s*. *Educ:* Christchurch Boys' High Sch.; Canterbury University College, NZ; Trinity Coll., Cambridge (MA). Craven Scholar and Porson Prizeman, Cambridge. Served in first New Zealand

Expeditionary Force, 1915-18. International Labour Office, Geneva, 1921-23; Secretariat, League of Nations, Geneva, 1923-40 (Chief of Central section, 1933-40); Assistant Director of Research, Chatham House, London, 1940-44; Member NZ delegation to San Francisco Conference, 1945, and to several sessions of the General Assembly of the United Nations; Assistant Secretary of External Affairs, New Zealand, 1944-56; HM New Zealand Minister at Paris, 1956, Ambassador, 1957. *Address:* 2 Mahina Road, Eastbourne, NZ. *Club:* United Oxford & Cambridge University.

WILSON, Sir Keith (Cameron), Kt 1966; Member of House of Representatives for Sturt, South Australia, 1949-54, 1955-66; *b* 3 Sept. 1900; *s* of Algernon Theodore King Wilson; *m* 1930, Elizabeth H., *d* of late Sir Lavington Bonython; two *s* one *d*. *Educ:* Collegiate School of St Peter, Adelaide; University of Adelaide. LLB 1922. Admitted to Bar, 1922. Served War of 1939-45: Gunner, 2nd AIF, 1940; Middle East, 1940-43; Major. Senator for South Australia, 1938-44. Chairman: Aged Cottage Homes Inc., 1952-71; War Blinded Welfare Fund; President: Good Neighbour Council of SA, 1968-72; Queen Elizabeth Hosp. Research Foundn; Past President Legacy. *Publication:* Wilson-Uppill Wheat Equalization Scheme, 1938. *Address:* 79 Tusmore Avenue, Tusmore, SA 5065, Australia. *T:* 315578. *Club:* Adelaide (Adelaide).

WILSON, Sir Leonard, KCIE 1945; Kt 1941; BEng; MICE; *b* Birkenhead, 12 March 1888; *s* of late G. R. Wilson, Birkenhead; *m* 1919, Muriel (*d* 1926), *d* of John Smethurst; two *s*; *m* 1947, Annis, *d* of late Rev. J. C. Abdy. *Educ:* Birkenhead Sch.; Liverpool Univ. Went to India, 1910; employed GIP Railway, Chief Engineer, 1930-34; General Manager, 1934-40; Chief Commissioner of Railways, India, 1940-46. *Address:* Lowbury, Compton, Berks. *Club:* East India, Devonshire, Sports and Public Schools.
See also F. R. Wilson.

WILSON, Sir (Leslie) Hugh, Kt 1967; OBE 1952; RIBA; FRTPI; Architect and Town Planner; Partner, Hugh Wilson & Lewis Womersley, Chartered Architects and Town Planners, since 1962; *b* 1 May 1913; *s* of Frederick Charles Wilson and Ethel Anne Hughes; *m* 1938, Monica Chrysavye Nomico (*d* 1966); one *s* two *d*. *Educ:* Haberdashers' Aske's Sch. Asst Architect, private practices, 1933-39; Asst Architect, Canterbury, 1939-45; City Architect and Planning Officer, Canterbury, 1945-56; Chief Architect and Planning Officer, Cumbernauld New Town, 1956-62. Techn. Adviser on Urban Development to Min. of Housing and Local Government, 1965-67. Works include housing, churches, central area develt; Master Plans for Irvine, Skelmersdale, Redditch, and Northampton New Towns; central area plans for Oxford, Brighton, Exeter, Lewes, Cardiff, Torbay. Dir (part-time), Property Services Agency, DoE, 1973-74. Mem. EDC for Building, NEDO, 1970-; Mem., Royal Fine Art Commn, 1971-; Mem., Environmental Bd, 1975-; Chm., Docklands Jt Cttee, GLC, 1977-. Vice-President, RIBA, 1960-61, 1962-64, Sen. Vice-President, 1966-67, President, 1967-69. DistTP 1956. Hon. FRAIC; Hon. FAIA; Hon. FIStructE; Hon. FIOB; Hon. Mem., Akademie der Künste, Berlin. Hon. DSc Aston, 1969. *Recreations:* travel, music. *Address:* 2 Kings Well, Heath Street, Hampstead, NW3 1EN. *T:* 01-435 3637. *Club:* Athenæum.

WILSON, Canon Leslie Rule; *b* 19 July 1909; *y s* of Rev. John and Mary Adelaide Wilson. *Educ:* Royal Grammar Sch., Newcastle upon Tyne; University College, Durham; Edinburgh Theological College. Asst Priest, Old St Paul's, Edinburgh, 1934-36; Rector of Fort William, 1936; Canon of Argyll and The Isles, 1940-42; Education Officer, 1942-45; Welfare Officer, SEAC (Toc H), 1945-46; Vicar of Malacca, Malaya, 1946-50; Principal Probation Officer, Federation of Malaya, 1950-52; Vicar of Kuching, Sarawak, 1952-55; Provost and Canon of St Thomas' Cathedral, Kuching, 1955-59; Rector of Geraldton, W Australia, 1960-64; Dean of Geraldton, 1964-66; Archdeacon of Carpentaria, 1966-67; Rector of Winterbourne Stickland with Turnworth and Winterbourne Houghton, 1967-70; Vicar of Holmside, 1970-74. Hon. Canon, Holy Cross Cathedral, Geraldton, 1966. Founder and Chairman, Parson Woodforde Society, 1968-75 (Hon. Life Pres., 1975). *Recreations:* reading, geneaology. *Address:* 10 Falkous Terrace, Witton Gilbert, Durham DH7 6TA. *T:* Sacriston 711234.

WILSON, Rt. Rev. Lucian C. U.; *see* Usher-Wilson.

WILSON, Sir (Mathew) Martin, 5th Bt, *cr* 1874; *b* 2 July 1906; *s* of Lieut-Colonel Sir Mathew Richard Henry Wilson, 4th Bt, and Hon. Barbara Lister (*d* 1943), *d* of 4th Baron Ribblesdale; *S* father, 1958. *Educ:* Eton. *Heir: b* Anthony Thomas Wilson [*b* 15 Nov. 1908; *m* 1st 1934, Margaret (Motion) (marr. diss. 1938), *d*

of late Alfred Holden; one *s*; 2nd, 1939, Emily May, *d* of late J. T. Milliken, St Louis, USA]. *Address:* 1 Sandgate Esplanade, Folkestone, Kent.

WILSON, Sir Michael (Thomond), Kt 1975; MBE 1945; a Vice-Chairman: Lloyds Bank Ltd, since 1973 (a Director, since 1968; Chief General Manager, 1967-73); Lloyds & Scottish Ltd, since 1976; Director: Lloyds Bank International Ltd, since 1973; Yorkshire Bank Ltd, since 1973; *b* 7 Feb. 1911; *e s* of late Sir Roy Wilson, Pyrford, near Woking; *m* 1933, Jessie Babette, *o d* of late John Winston Foley Winnington, Malvern, Worcs; two *s* one *d*. *Educ:* Rugby Sch.; Oriel Coll., Oxford. War Service with RA and on Staff in UK and India, 1939-45. Entered Lloyds Bank, 1932; Assistant General Manager, 1958; Dep. Chief General Manager, 1963. Chm., Export Guarantees Adv. Council, 1972-77. JP Berks, 1952-66. *Address:* Clytha, South Ascot, Berks. *T:* Ascot 20833.

WILSON, Norman George, CMG 1966; Commercial Director, ICI of Australia Ltd, 1972-73; Deputy Chairman, Fibremakers Ltd, 1972-73; *b* 20 Oct. 1911; *s* of P. Wilson; *m* 1939, Dorothy Gwen, *d* of late Sir W. Lennon Raws; one *s* two *d*. *Educ:* Melbourne University (BCE). Joined ICI Australia Ltd, 1935: Exec. positions, 1936-48; General Manager, Dyes and Plastics Group, 1949-54; Director, 1959-73; Managing Director: Dulux Pty Ltd, 1954-62; Fibremakers Ltd, 1962-72. Business Adviser to Dept of Air, and Dep. Chm. Defence Business Board, Commonwealth Government, 1957-; Chairman Production Board, Dept of Manufacturing Industries, Commonwealth Government, 1960. Mem., Export Develt Council, Dept of Trade and Industry, Commonwealth Govt, 1966-72. Mem. Bd, Victorian Railways, 1973-; Dep. Chm., Victorian Conservation Trust, 1973-. FInstD, FAIM. *Recreations:* golf, farming. *Address:* Apartment 14, 18 Lansell Road, Toorak, Victoria 3142, Australia. *T:* Melbourne 24-4438. *Clubs:* Australian (Melbourne); Royal Melbourne Golf, Melbourne Cricket, Victoria Racing.

WILSON, Percy, CB 1955; Director of Education, Bank Education Service, since 1965; *b* 15 Dec. 1904; *s* of Joseph Edwin and Louisa Wilson; *m* 1st, 1929, Beryl Godsell (decd); 2nd, 1943, Dorothy Spiers; one *s* one *d*. *Educ:* Market Rasen Grammar Sch.; Jesus Coll., Cambridge. Schoolmaster, 1927-35; HM Inspector of Schools, 1935-45 (seconded to war duties, 1939-42); Staff Inspector for English, 1945-47; a Chief Inspector, Ministry of Education, 1947-57; Sen. Chief Inspector, Dept of Education and Science, 1957-65. Hon. FCP, 1965. A Governor, Wellington Coll., 1966-75. *Recreation:* painting. *Address:* The Cottage, Walcot Lane, Drakes Broughton, Pershore, Worcs. *T:* Worcester 840265. *Club:* Athenæum.

WILSON, Peter Cecil, CBE 1970; Chairman, Sotheby & Co., since 1958 (Director, since 1938); *b* 8 March 1913; 3rd *s* of Sir Mathew Wilson, 4th Bt, CSI, DSO, Eshton Hall, Gargrave, Yorkshire; *m* 1935, Grace Helen Ranken (marr. diss.); two *s*. *Educ:* Eton; New Coll., Oxford. Benjamin Franklin Medal, RSA 1968. *Address:* 4 Green Street, W1.
See also Sir M. M. Wilson.

WILSON, Peter Humphrey St John, CB 1956; CBE 1952; Deputy Under Secretary of State, Department of Employment and Productivity, 1968-69, retired (Deputy Secretary, Ministry of Labour, 1958-68); *b* 1 May 1908; *e s* of late Rt Rev. Henry A. Wilson, CBE, DD; *m* 1939, Catherine Laird (*d* 1963), *d* of late H. J. Bonser, London; three *d*. *Educ:* Cheltenham Coll. (Schol.); Corpus Christi Coll., Cambridge (Foundation Schol.). Assistant Principal, Ministry of Labour, 1930; Principal, 1936; Regional Controller, Northern Region, 1941; Controller, Scotland, 1944; Under Secretary, 1952. *Recreations:* reading, music, grand-children. *Address:* Thorntree Cottage, Blackheath, near Guildford, Surrey. *T:* Bramley 3758.

WILSON, Prof. Raymond; Professor of Education, University of Reading, since 1968; *b* 20 Dec. 1925; *s* of John William Wilson and Edith (*née* Walker); *m* 1950, Gertrude Mary Russell; two *s* one *d*. *Educ:* London Univ. (BA English, 1st Cl.). Teacher, secondary schs, 1950-57; English Master, subseq. Chief English Master, Dulwich Coll., 1957-65; Lectr, Southampton Univ., 1965-68. Chm., Sch. of Educn, Reading Univ., 1969-76. *Publications:* ed textbooks; papers on English and related studies; occasional poet. *Address:* Roselawn, Shiplake, Henley-on-Thames, Oxon. *T:* Wargrave 2528.

WILSON, Sir Reginald (Holmes), Kt 1951; BCom; FCIT; FBIM; Scottish Chartered Accountant; Chairman, Board for Simplification of International Trade Practices, since 1976; Director of business and finance companies; *b* 1905; *o s* of Alexander Wilson and Emily Holmes Wilson; *m* 1st, 1930, Rose

Marie von Arnim; one *s* one *d*; 2nd, 1938, Sonia Havell. *Educ:* St Peter's Sch., Panchgani; St Lawrence, Ramsgate; London Univ. BCom. Partner in Whinney Murray & Co., 1937-72; HM Treasury, 1940; Principal Assistant Secretary, Ministry of Shipping, 1941; Director of Finance, Ministry of War Transport, 1941; Under-Secretary, Ministry of Transport, 1945; returned to City, 1946; Joint Financial Adviser, Ministry of Transport, 1946; Member of Royal Commission on Press, 1946; Vice-Chairman, Hemel Hempstead Development Corporation, 1946-56; Adviser on Special Matters, CCG, 1947. Comptroller BTC, 1947, Member BTC, 1953, Chm. E Area Board, 1955-60, Chm. London Midland Area Board, 1960-62; Dep. Chm. and Man. Dir, Transport Holding Co., 1962-67; Chairman: Transport Holding Co., 1967-70; Nat. Freight Corp., 1969-70; Transport Develt Gp, 1971-74 (Dep. Chm., 1970-71); Thos Cook & Son Ltd, 1967-76. Mem., Cttee of Enquiry into Civil Air Transport, 1967-69. Award of Merit, Inst. Transport, 1953; President, Inst. Transport, 1957-58. Chairman, Board of Governors: Hospitals for Diseases of the Chest, 1960-71; National Heart Hospital, 1968-71; National Heart and Chest Hospitals, 1971-. UK Rep., Council of Management, Internat. Hosp. Fedn, 1973-. *Publications:* various papers on transport matters. *Recreations:* music, walking. *Address:* 13 Gloucester Square, W2 2TB. *Clubs:* Athenæum, Oriental.

WILSON, Prof. Richard Middlewood; Professor of English Language, University of Sheffield, 1955-73; *b* 20 Sept. 1908; *e s* of late R. L. Wilson, The Grange, Kilham, Driffield, E Yorks; *m* 1938, Dorothy Muriel, *y d* of late C. E. Leeson, Eastgate House, Kilham, Driffield; one *d. Educ:* Woodhouse Grove School; Leeds University. Asst Lecturer, Leeds Univ., 1931, Lecturer, 1936; Senior Lecturer and Head of Dept of English Language, Sheffield Univ., 1946. *Publications:* Sawles Warde, 1939; Early Middle English Literature, 1939; (with B. Dickins) Early Middle English Texts, 1951; The Lost Literature of Medieval England, 1952; (with D. J. Price) The Equatorie of the Planetis, 1955; articles and reviews. *Recreation:* cricket. *Address:* 9 Endcliffe Vale Avenue, Sheffield S11 8RX. *T:* Sheffield 663431.

WILSON, Prof. Robert, FRS 1975; Perren Professor of Astronomy and Director of the Observatories, University College London, since 1972; *b* 16 April 1927; *s* of Robert Graham Wilson and Anne Wilson; *m* 1952, Eileen Flora (*née* Milne); two *s* one *d. Educ:* King's Coll., Newcastle upon Tyne; Univ. of Edinburgh. BSc (Physics), Newcastle, 1948; PhD (Astrophysics), Edin., 1952. SSO, Royal Observatory, Edinburgh, 1952-57; Research Fellow, Dominion Astrophysical Observatory, Canada, 1957-58; Leader of Plasma Spectroscopy Gp, CTR Div., Harwell, 1959-61; Head of Spectroscopy Div., Culham Laboratory, 1962-68; Head of Science Research Council's Astrophysics Research Unit, Culham, 1968-72. Foreign Mem., Société Royale des Sciences, Liège; Mem. Overseas Cttee, Dept of Astronomy, Harvard Univ. *Publications:* papers in many jls on: optical astronomy, plasma spectroscopy, solar physics, ultraviolet astronomy. *Recreations:* history, sport. *Address:* 3 Fitzharry's Road, Abingdon, Oxon.

WILSON, Robert Andrew, CB 1962; Principal Keeper, Department of Printed Books, British Museum, 1959-66; *b* 18 July 1905; *s* of Robert Bruce Wilson; *m* 1967, Rosemary Ann, *d* of Sydney Joseph Norris. *Educ:* Westminster School; Trinity College, Cambridge. Assistant Keeper, Department of Printed Books, British Museum, 1929-48, Deputy Keeper, 1948-52; also Superintendent of the Reading Room, British Museum, 1948-52; Keeper, 1952-59. *Address:* 33 Denmark Avenue, Wimbledon, SW19.

WILSON, Hon. Sir Robert (Christian), Kt 1966; CMG 1952; Chairman: Australian Guarantee Corporation Ltd; Country Television Services Ltd; Sydney Board, Union Fidelity Trustee Co. Ltd; a Director of other companies; *b* 11 Nov. 1896; *s* of late Henry Christian Wilson, Blayney; *m* 1932, Gertrude, *d* of Clayton K. Brooks, Boston, Mass., USA; one *s* two *d. Educ:* Fort Street High School, Australia. Served European War, 1914-18; on active service, 1st LH Regt, AIF in Palestine, 1915-18. MLC New South Wales, 1949-61. General Manager, Grazcos Co-op. Ltd, 1924-61; Chm., Tooheys Ltd, 1962-72; formerly Director: Bank of NSW; Scottish Australian Co. Ltd. *Address:* 25 Bushlands Avenue, Gordon, Sydney, NSW 2072, Australia. *Club:* Australian, Elanora Country (Sydney).

WILSON, (Robert) Gordon; MP (SNP) Dundee East since Feb. 1974; formerly solicitor in private practice; *b* 16 April 1938; *s* of R. G. Wilson; *m* 1965, Edith M. Hassall; two *d. Educ:* Douglas High Sch.; Edinburgh Univ. (BL). Nat. Sec., SNP, 1963-71; Exec. Vice-Chm., 1972-73; Sen. Vice-Chm., 1973-74. SNP Parly Spokesman: on Energy, 1974-; on Home Affairs, 1975-76; on Devolution (jt responsibility), 1976-. Dep. Leader, SNP, 1974-.

Recreations: gardening, sailing. *Address:* 48 Monifieth Road, Broughty Ferry, Dundee DD5 2RX. *T:* Dundee 79009.

WILSON, Robert Graham, MBE 1956; Regional Director, Chairman Economic Planning Board, Yorkshire and Humberside Region of Department of the Environment, 1973-77; retired; *b* 7 Aug. 1917; 2nd *s* of late John Wilson and late Kate Benson Wilson (*née* Martindale); *m* 1943, Winifred Mary (*née* Elson); one *s* three *d. Educ:* Bradfield Coll.; Gonville and Caius Coll., Cambridge. BA Pt 1 Geog., Pt 2 History. Joined Burma Frontier Service, 1939; War Service in Burma (Captain; despatches 1945); left Burma on Independence, 1948 (Asst Resident); joined Colonial Admin. Service, as District Officer, Kenya, 1949 (despatches, Mau Mau, 1957); left Kenya on Independence, Dec. 1963 (Provincial Comr); joined Home Civil Service, MPBW, 1964; Regional Dir, MPBW, Malta, 1968-71; Regional Dir (Works) Leeds, DoE, 1971-73. *Recreations:* golf, gardening, water colour painting. *Address:* Westbrook, 5 Shorefield Way, Milford-on-Sea, Hampshire. *T:* Milford-on-Sea 2006. *Club:* Hawks (Cambridge).

WILSON, Very Rev. Professor-Emeritus Robert John, MA, BD, DD; retired as Principal of the Presbyterian College, Belfast (1961-64), and Professor of Old Testament Language, Literature and Theology (1939-64); also Principal of the Presbyterian Theological Faculty, Ireland (1962-64); *b* 23 September 1893; *s* of Robert Wilson; *m* 1917, Margaret Mary Kilpatrick; one *s* two *d. Educ:* Mayo St National School, Belfast; Trade Preparatory School, Municipal Technical Inst.; Kelvin House, Botanic Ave; Methodist Coll.; Queen's Univ. and Presbyterian Coll., Belfast. BA 1913, QUB 1st Hons (Philosophy) with Special Prize; MA 1914; BD 1925 London; BD Hons London, 1930, in Hebrew, Aramaic and Syriac; Univ. of London GCE, Classical Hebrew Advanced Level, Grade A, Special Paper, Grade 1 (Distinction), 1968, Ordinary Level Grade A, 1969. Minister of Presbyterian Churches: Raffrey, Co. Down, 1917, First Donaghadee, Co. Down, 1921; Waterside, Londonderry, 1923; First Carrickfergus, Co. Antrim, 1928. Presbyterian College, Belfast: part-time Lecturer in Hebrew, 1933-34; Warden, 1941-49; Carey Lecturer, 1942; Secretary of Faculty, 1945-61; Convener of Coll. Bd of Management, 1946-62; Vice-Principal of Faculty, 1951-61. Recognised Teacher in Faculty of Theology, in Hebrew and Old Testament Theology, and Internal Examiner for BD, QUB, 1939-64; Internal Examiner for BA in Hebrew, 1948-64; Part-time Lecturer in Hebrew in Faculty of Arts, QUB, 1946-64. Moderator of the General Assembly of the Presbyterian Church in Ireland, 1957-58. Hon. DD Knox College, Toronto, 1961. *Recreations:* walking, motoring, lawn-verging. *Address:* 18 Mount Eden Park, Belfast BT9 6RA. *T:* Belfast 668830.

WILSON, Prof. Robert McLachlan, PhD; FBA 1977; Professor of New Testament Language and Literature, University of St Andrews, since 1969; *b* 13 Feb. 1916; *e r s* of Hugh McL. Wilson and Janet N. (*née* Struthers); *m* 1945, Enid Mary, *d* of Rev. and Mrs F. J. Bomford, Bournemouth, Hants; two *s. Educ:* Greenock Acad.; Royal High Sch., Edinburgh; Univ. of Edinburgh (MA 1939, BD 1942); Univ. of Cambridge (PhD 1945). Minister of Rankin Church, Strathaven, Lanarkshire, 1946-54; Lectr in New Testament Language and Literature, St Mary's Coll., Univ. of St Andrews, 1954, Sen. Lectr, 1964. Vis. Prof., Vanderbilt Divinity Sch., Nashville, Tenn, 1964-65. Hon. Mem., Soc. of Biblical Literature, 1972-. Associate Editor, New Testament Studies, 1967-77, Editor 1977-; Mem., Internat. Cttee for publication of Nag Hammadi Codices, and of Editorial Bd of Nag Hammadi Studies monograph series. *Publications:* The Gnostic Problem, 1958; Studies in the Gospel of Thomas, 1960; The Gospel of Philip, 1962; Gnosis and the New Testament, 1968; (ed) English trans., Hennecke-Schneemelcher, NT Apocrypha: vol. 1, 1963 (2nd edn 1973); vol. 2, 1965 (2nd edn 1974); (ed) English trans., Haenchen, The Acts of the Apostles, 1971; (ed) English trans., Foerster, Gnosis: vol. 1, 1972; vol. 2, 1974; (ed and trans., jtly) Jung Codex treatises: De Resurrectione, 1963; Epistula Jacobi Apocrypha, 1968; Tractatus Tripartitus, pars 1 1973, pars 2 1975; articles in British, Amer. and continental jls. *Recreation:* golf. *Address:* 10 Murrayfield Road, St Andrews, Fife. *T:* St Andrews 4331.

WILSON, Prof. Roger Cowan; Professor of Education, University of Bristol, 1951-71, Emeritus 1971; Visiting Professor: University of Malawi, 1966; Harvard University, 1968; *b* 3 August 1906; 2nd *s* of Alexander Cowan Wilson and Edith Jane Brayshaw; *m* 1931, Margery Lilian, *y d* of late Rev. C. W. Emmet, Fellow of University College, Oxford, and Gertrude Weir; one *s* one *d. Educ:* Manchester Grammar School; The Queen's College, Oxford (Exhibitioner); Manchester College of Technology. Chairman, OU Labour Club, 1927; President, Oxford Union, 1929; First Cl. in Philosophy, Politics and Economics, 1929. Apprentice in Cotton

Industry, 1929-35; Talks Staff of BBC, 1935-40; dismissed from BBC as conscientious objector; General Secretary, Friends Relief Service, 1940-46; head of Dept of Social Studies, University College, Hull, 1946-51. Senior Adviser on Social Affairs, United Nations Operation in the Congo, 1961-62. Chm., Bd of Visitors, Shepton Mallet Prison, 1966-70; Chm., Council for Voluntary Action, South Lakeland, 1974-; Clerk, London Yearly Meeting of Society of Friends, 1975-. JP Bristol, 1954-67. Médaille de la Reconnaisance Française, 1948. *Publications:* Frank Lenwood, a biography, 1936; Authority, Leadership and Concern, a study of motive and administration in Quaker relief work, 1948; Quaker Relief, 1940-48, 1952; (with Kuenstler and others) Social Group Work in Gt Britain, 1955; Difficult Housing Estates, 1963; (with Lomas and others) Social Aspects of Urban Development, 1966. *Recreations:* walking, Quaker interests. *Address:* Peter Hill House, Yealand Conyers, near Carnforth, Lancs. *T:* Carnforth 3519.
See also *D. M. Emmet, J. E. Meade, Sir Geoffrey Wilson and S. S. Wilson.*

WILSON, Rt. Rev. Roger Plumpton, KCVO 1974; DD (Lambeth), 1949; Clerk of the Closet to the Queen, 1963-75; *b* 3 Aug. 1905; *s* of Canon Clifford Plumpton Wilson, Bristol, and Hester Marion Wansey; *m* 1935, Mabel Joyce Avery, Leigh Woods, Bristol; two *s* one *d*. *Educ:* Winchester Coll. (Exhibitioner); Keble Coll., Oxford (Classical Scholar). Hon. Mods in Classics 1st Class, Lit. Hum. 2nd Class, BA 1928; MA 1932. Classical Master, Shrewsbury Sch., 1928-30, 1932-34; Classical Master, St Andrew's Coll., Grahamstown, S Africa, 1930-32. Deacon, 1935; Priest, 1936; Curacies: St Paul's, Prince's Park, Liverpool, 1935-38; St John's, Smith Square, SW1, 1938-39; Vicar of South Shore, Blackpool, 1939-45; Archdeacon of Nottingham and Vicar of Radcliffe on Trent, 1945-49; also Vicar of Shelford (in plurality), 1946-49; Bishop of Wakefield, 1949-58; Bishop of Chichester, 1958-74. Chm., Church of England Schools Council, 1957-71; Mem., Presidium, Conf. of European Churches, 1967-74. *Recreations:* Oxford University Authentics Cricket Club, Oxford University Centaurs Football Club, golf. *Address:* Kingsett, Wrington, Bristol. *Club:* Royal Commonwealth Society.

WILSON, Sir Roland, KBE 1965 (CBE 1941); Kt 1955; Chairman: Commonwealth Banking Corporation, 1966-75; Qantas Airways Ltd, 1966-73; Director: The MLC Ltd; Wentworth Hotel (Chairman 1966-73); economic and financial consultant; *b* Ulverstone, Tasmania, 7 April 1904; *s* of Thomas Wilson; *m* 1930, Valeska (*d* 1971), *d* of William Thompson; *m* 1975, Joyce, *d* of Clarence Henry Chivers. *Educ:* Devonport High School; Univ. of Tasmania; Oriel College, Oxford; Chicago University. Rhodes Scholar for Tasmania, 1925; BCom 1926, Univ. of Tasmania; Dipl. in Economics and Political Science 1926, and DPhil 1929, Oxon; Commonwealth Fund Fellow, 1928, and PhD 1930, Chicago. Pitt Cobbett Lecturer in Economics, Univ. of Tasmania, 1930-32; Director of Tutorial Classes, Univ. of Tasmania, 1931-32; Asst Commonwealth Statistician and Economist, 1932; Economist, Statistician's Branch, Commonwealth Treasury, 1933; Commonwealth Statistician and Economic Adviser to the Treasury, Commonwealth of Australia, 1936-40 and 1946-51; Sec. to Dept Labour and Nat. Service, 1941-46; Chairman Economic and Employment Commission, United Nations, 1948-49. Secretary to Treasury, Commonwealth of Australia, 1951-66; Member Bd: Commonwealth Bank of Australia, 1951-59; Reserve Bank of Australia, 1960-66; Qantas Empire Airways, 1954-66; Commonwealth Banking Corp., 1960-66. Hon. LLD Tasmania, 1969. *Publications:* Capital Imports and the Terms of Trade, 1931; Public and Private Investment in Australia, 1939; Facts and Fancies of Productivity, 1946. *Address:* 64 Empire Circuit, Forrest, Canberra, ACT 2603, Australia. *T:* 73-1848. *Club:* Commonwealth (Canberra).

WILSON, Maj.-Gen. (Ronald) Dare, CBE 1968 (MBE 1949); MC 1945; MA Cantab; retired; Exmoor National Park Officer, since 1974; additional interests farming and forestry; *b* 3 Aug. 1919; *s* of Sydney E. D. Wilson and Dorothea, *d* of George Burgess; *m* 1973, Sarah, *d* of Sir Peter Stallard, *qv*. *Educ:* Shrewsbury Sch.; St John's Coll. Cambridge (Pt I 1939, BA 1972). Commissioned into Royal Northumberland Fusiliers, 1939; served War, 1939-45: BEF 1940, ME and NW Europe (MC, despatches 1946); 6th Airborne Div., 1945-48; 1st Bn Parachute Regt, 1949; MoD, 1950; Royal Northumberland Fusiliers: Korea, 1951; Kenya, 1953; GSO2, Staff Coll. Camberley, 1954-56; AA&QMG, 3rd Div., 1958-59; comd 22 Special Air Service Regt, 1960-62; Canadian Nat. Defence Coll., 1962-63; Col GS 1(BR) Corps BAOR, 1963-65; comd 149 Infantry Bde (TA), 1966-67; Brig. 1966; Brig., AQ ME Comd, 1967; Maj.-Gen. 1968; Dir, Land/Air Warfare, MoD, 1968-69; Dir, Army Aviation, MoD, 1970-71. Helicopter and light

aircraft pilot; Mem., Army Cresta Run Team and Army Rifle VIII; captained British Free-Fall Parachute Team, 1962-65; Chm., British Parachute Assoc., 1962-65. FRGS. Royal Aero Club Silver Medal, 1967. *Publications:* Cordon and Search, 1948; contribs to military jls. *Recreations:* country pursuits, travelling, winter sports. *Address:* Combeland, Dulverton, Somerset. *Club:* Flyfishers'.

WILSON, Sheriff Roy Alexander, WS; Sheriff of Grampian, Highlands and Islands at Elgin and Aberdeen, since 1975; *b* 22 Oct. 1927; *s* of Eric Moir Wilson and Jean Dey Gibb; *m* 1954, Alison Mary Craig; one *s* one *d*. *Educ:* Drumwhindle Sch.; Aberdeen Grammar Sch.; Merchiston Castle Sch.; Lincoln Coll., Oxford Univ. (BA); Edinburgh Univ. (LLB); Thaw Scholarship in Scots Law; 1952. WS; NP. Solicitor, 1953. Partner, subseq. Sen. Partner, Messrs Allan McNeil & Son, WS, Edinburgh, 1957-75. Chm., indust. relations tribunals, 1971-75. *Recreations:* golf, curling, spectator sports, reading. *Address:* Deansford, Bishopmill, Elgin, Moray. *T:* Elgin 7339. *Clubs:* Royal Northern (Aberdeen); Elgin.

WILSON, Sir Roy (Mickel), Kt 1962; QC; President of the Industrial Court, 1961-71, and of the Industrial Arbitration Board, 1971-76; *b* 1903; *e s* of late Rev. Robert Wilson and Jessie, *d* of Robert Mickel, JP; *m* 1935, Henrietta Bennett, *d* of late Dean Willard L. Sperry, DD of Harvard University, USA. *Educ:* Glasgow High School; Glasgow University; Balliol Coll., Oxford (Lit. Hum. and BCL). Called to Bar, Gray's Inn, 1931, Bencher 1956, Treas. 1973; S-E Circuit. KC 1950. Commissioned QO Cameron Highlanders, 1940; served War of 1939-45; DAAG 2nd Division, 1942; GHQ, India, 1942-45; Lt-Col, 1943; Brigadier, 1944. Recorder: Faversham, 1950-51; Croydon, 1957-61. Mem., Industrial Disputes Tribunal, 1958-59; Chairman: Cttee of Inquiry into arrangements at Smithfield Market, 1958; Cttee of Inquiry into differences in the Electrical Contracting Industry on the Shell Centre site, 1959; Railway Staff National Tribunal, 1961-62; London Transport Rly Wages Bd, 1961-; Cttee of Inquiry into strikes by Winding Engineers in the Yorkshire Coalmining Area, 1964; Cttee of Inquiry into Provincial Bus Dispute, 1964; Court of Inquiry into stevedore/docker demarcation in the Port of London, 1966; Cttee on Immigration Appeals, 1966; Cttee of Inquiry into Bristol Siddeley Contracts, 1967-68; Arts Council Inquiry into industrial relations at the Coliseum Theatre, 1975. Mem., Race Relations Bd, 1968-77 (Acting Chairman of Bd, Jan.-Oct. 1971; Chm. Employment Cttee, 1968-77). FRSA, 1968. *Recreations:* fishing, golf, bird-watching. *Address:* 4 Gray's Inn Square, WC1. *T:* 01-405 7789; The Cottage on the Green, Plaistow, Sussex. *T:* Plaistow 279. *Clubs:* Reform; Union (Oxford).

WILSON, Sandy; composer, lyric writer, playwright; *b* 19 May 1924; *s* of George Walter Wilson and Caroline Elsie (*née* Humphrey). *Educ:* Elstree Preparatory School; Harrow School; Oriel College, Oxford (BA Eng. Lit.). Contributed material to Oranges and Lemons, Slings and Arrows, 1948; wrote lyrics for touring musical play Caprice, 1950; words and music for two revues at Watergate Theatre, 1951 and 1952; (musical comedy) The Boy Friend for Players' Theatre, 1953, later produced in West End and on Broadway, 1954, directed revival (Comedy), 1967; (musical play) The Buccaneer, 1955; Valmouth (musical play, based on Firbank's novel), Lyric, Hammersmith and Savile Theatre, 1959, New York, 1960; songs for Call It Love, Wyndham's Theatre, 1960; Divorce Me, Darling! (musical comedy), Players' Theatre, 1964, Globe, 1965; music for TV series, The World of Wooster, 1965-66; music for As Dorothy Parker Once Said, Fortune, 1969; songs for Danny la Rue's Charley's Aunt (TV), 1969; wrote and performed in Sandy Wilson Thanks the Ladies, Hampstead Theatre Club, 1971; His Monkey Wife, Hampstead, 1971. *Publications:* This is Sylvia (with own illustrs), 1954; The Boy Friend (with own illustrs), 1955; Who's Who for Beginners (with photographs by Jon Rose), 1957; Prince What Shall I Do (illustrations, with Rhoda Levine), 1961; The Poodle from Rome, 1962; I Could Be Happy (autobiog.), 1975; Ivor, 1975; Caught in the Act, 1976; The Roaring Twenties, 1977. *Recreations:* reading, painting, theatre and cinema-going, travel. *Address:* 2 Southwell Gardens, SW7. *T:* 01-373 6172. *Club:* Players' Theatre.

WILSON, Stanley John, FCIS; Managing Director, The Burmah Oil Co. Ltd, since 1975; *b* 23 Oct. 1921; *s* of Joseph Wilson and Jessie Cormack; *m* 1952, Molly Ann (*née* Clarkson); two *s*. *Educ:* King Edward VII Sch., Johannesburg; Witwatersrand Univ. CA (SA); ASAA, ACWA; FCIS 1945. 1945-73: Chartered Accountant, Savory & Dickinson; Sec. and Sales Man., Rhodesian Timber Hldgs; Chm. and Chief Exec. for S Africa, Vacuum Oil Co.; Reg. Vice Pres. for S and E Asia, Mobil Petroleum; Pres., Mobil Sekiyu; Pres., subseq. Reg. Vice Pres. for Europe, Mobil Europe Inc.; Pres., Mobil East Inc., and Reg.

Vice Pres. for Far East, S and SE Asia, Australia, Indian Sub-Continent, etc, 1973-75. *Recreations:* golf, shooting, fishing. *Address:* Leigh Hill, Savernake, near Marlborough, Wilts SN8 3BH. *T:* Burbage 230. *Clubs:* City of London, Royal Automobile; Royal Mid-Surrey Golf; Tidworth Garrison Golf; City (Cape Town); Rand (Johannesburg); Heresewentien (SA).

WILSON, Stanley Livingstone, CMG 1966; DSO 1943; Visiting Surgeon, Dunedin Hospital, 1937-66, Hon. Consulting Surgeon, Dunedin Hospital, since 1966; *b* 17 April 1905; *s* of Robert and Elizabeth Wilson; *m* 1930, Isabel, *d* of William Kirkland; two *s* one *d. Educ:* Dannevirke High School; University of Otago. Univ. Entrance Schol., 1923; MB, ChB 1928; FRCS 1932; FRACS 1937. Resident Surgeon, Dunedin Hosp., Royal Northern and St Mary's Hosps, London, 1929-37. NZ Medical Corps, Middle East; Solomons, 1940-44; OC 2 NZ Casualty Clearing Station, Pacific, 1943-44. President, Otago BMA, 1948; Council, RACS 1951-63 (President, 1961-62). Examiner in Surgery, Univ. of Otago, 1952-65; Court of Examiners, RACS, 1948-60; Mem., Otago Hosp. Bd, 1965-74. Hon. Fellow, American Coll. of Surgeons, 1963. Hon. DSc Otago, 1975. *Recreation:* golf. *Address:* 27 Burwood Avenue, Dunedin, NW1, NZ. *T:* 60925; Maypark, Middlemarch, Otago, NZ. *Clubs:* Dunedin (Dunedin); Otago Officers' (Dunedin).

WILSON, Stephen Shipley, CB 1950; Keeper of Public Records, 1960-66; *b* 4 Aug. 1904; *s* of late Alexander Cowan Wilson and Edith Jane Brayshaw; *m* 1933, Martha Mott, *d* of A. B. Kelley and Mariana Parrish, Philadelphia, Pa; two *s* one *d. Educ:* Leighton Park; Queen's Coll., Oxford. Fellow, Brookings Inst., Washington, DC, 1926-27; Instructor, Columbia University, New York City, 1927-28; Public Record Office, 1928-29; Ministry of Transport, 1929-47; Ministry of Supply, 1947-50; Secretary, Iron and Steel Corporation of Great Britain, 1950-53, and Secretary, Iron and Steel Holding and Realisation Agency, 1953-60. Historical Section, Cabinet Office, 1966-77. *Address:* 3 Willow Road, NW3 1TH. *T:* 01-435 0148. *Club:* Reform.
See also J. E. Meade, Sir Geoffrey Wilson, R. C. Wilson.

WILSON, Prof. Thomas, CBE 1959; Professor of Tropical Hygiene, Liverpool School of Tropical Medicine, University of Liverpool, 1962-71; *b* 5 Nov. 1905; *s* of R. H. Wilson, OBE, Belfast; *m* 1930, Annie Cooley; two *s* one *d. Educ:* Belfast Royal Academy; Queen's Univ., Belfast. MB, BCh, BAO (Belfast) 1927; DPH (Belfast) 1929; DTM, DTH (Liverpool) 1930; MD (Belfast) 1952. MO, Central Health Bd, FMS 1930; Health Officer, Malayan Med. Service, 1931; Lieut and Capt., RAMC (POW in Malaya and Thailand), 1942-45; Sen. Malaria Research Officer, Inst. for Med. Res., Fedn of Malaya, 1949; Dir, Inst. for Med. Res., Fedn of Malaya, 1956; Sen. Lectr in Tropical Hygiene, Liverpool Sch. of Trop. Med., Univ. of Liverpool, 1959. *Publications:* (with T. H. Davey) Davey and Lightbody's Control of Disease in the Tropics, 1965, 4th edn 1971; contrib. to Hobson's Theory and Practice of Public Health, 3rd edn 1969, 4th edn 1975; articles in medical journals on malaria and filariasis. *Recreation:* golf. *Address:* 77 Strand Road, Portstewart, N Ireland.

WILSON, Prof. Thomas, OBE 1945; FBA 1976; Adam Smith Professor of Political Economy, University of Glasgow, since 1958; *b* 23 June 1916; *s* of late John Bright and Margaret G. Wilson, Belfast; *m* 1943, Dorothy Joan Parry; one *s* two *d. Educ:* Queen's University, Belfast; London School of Economics. Mins of Economic Warfare and Aircraft Production, 1940-42; Prime Minister's Statistical Branch, 1942-45. Fellow of University College, Oxford, 1946-58; Faculty Fellow of Nuffield College, Oxford, 1950-54; Vis. Fellow, All Souls Coll., Oxford, 1974-75; Editor, Oxford Economic Papers, 1948-58. Vice-Chm., Scottish Council's Cttee of Inquiry into the Scottish Economy, 1960-61; Nuffield Foundation Visiting Prof., Univ. of Ibadan, 1962. Economic Consultant to Govt of N Ireland, 1964-65, 1968-70; to Sec. of State for Scotland, 1963-64 and 1970-; Shipbuilding Industry Cttee, 1965. Mem., SSRC Economics Cttee, 1969-73. *Publications:* Fluctuations in Income and Employment, 1941; (ed) Ulster under Home Rule, 1955; Inflation, 1960; Planning and Growth, 1964; (ed) Pensions, Inflation and Growth, 1974; (ed with A. S. Skinner) Essays on Adam Smith, 1975; (ed with A. S. Skinner) The Market and the State, 1976; The Political Economy of Inflation (British Acad. Keynes Lecture), 1976. *Recreations:* sailing and walking. *Address:* 8 The University, Glasgow G12 8QQ. *T:* 041-339 8344.

WILSON, Captain Sir Thomas (Douglas), 4th Bt, *cr* 1906; MC 1940; *b* (posthumous) 10 June 1917; *s* of Thomas Douglas Wilson (*s* of 1st Bt), 2nd Lieut 7th Bn Argyll and Sutherland Highlanders (killed in action, 1917), and Kathleen Elsie, *d* of Henry Edward Grey; *S* uncle, 1968; *m* 1947, Pamela Aileen, 2nd *d* of Sir Edward Hanmer, 7th Bt, and late Aileen Mary, *er d* of

Captain J. E. Rogerson; one *s* three *d. Educ:* Marlborough and Sandhurst. Commissioned 15th/19th Hussars, 1937; served in France, 1939-40 (MC); Western Desert, 1942-43; retired, 1947. Contested (C) Dudley and Stourbridge, 1955. *Recreations:* hunting, racing. *Heir: s* James William Douglas Wilson, *b* 8 Oct. 1960. *Address:* Lillingstone Lovell Manor, Buckingham MK18 5BQ. *T:* Lillingstone Dayrell 237. *Club:* Cavalry and Guards.

WILSON, Thomas Marcus; Assistant Under-Secretary, Ministry of Defence (Procurement Executive), 1971-73; retired; *b* 15 April 1913; *s* of Reverend C. Wilson; *m* 1939, Norah Boyes (*née* Sinclair); no *c. Educ:* Manchester Grammar School; Jesus College, Cambridge. Asst Principal, Customs and Excise, 1936; Private Secretary: to Board of Customs and Excise, 1939; to Chm. Bd, 1940; Principal, 1941; lent to Treasury, 1942; lent to Office of Lord President of Council, 1946; Asst Sec., 1947; seconded: Min. of Food, 1949; Min. of Supply, 1953, Under-Sec., 1962, and Prin. Scientific and Civil Aviation Adv. to Brit. High Comr in Australia, also Head of Defence Research and Supply Staff, 1962-64; Under-Secretary: Min. of Aviation, 1964-67; Min. of Technology, 1967-70; Min. of Aviation Supply, 1970-71; MoD, 1971-73. Consultant, IMF, 1974-. *Recreations:* reading, music, painting and travel, especially in France. *Address:* 5 Fir Tree Close, Coronation Road, South Ascot, Berks.

WILSON, Sir T. George; *see* Wilson, Sir George.

WILSON, William; DL; MP (Lab) Coventry South East, since 1974 (Coventry South, 1964-74); *b* 28 June 1913; *s* of Charles and Charlotte Wilson; *m* 1939, Bernice Wilson; one *s. Educ:* Wheatley St Sch.; Cheylesmore Sch.; Coventry Jun. Technical School. Qual. as Solicitor, 1939. Entered Army, 1941; served in N Africa, Italy and Greece; demobilised, 1946 (Sergeant). Contested (Lab) Warwick and Leamington, 1951, 1955, March 1957, 1959. Member: Commons Select Cttee on Race Relations and Immigration, 1970-; Warwicks CC, 1958-70 (Leader Labour Group), re-elected 1972. DL County of Warwick, 1967. *Recreations:* gardening, theatre, watching Association football. *Address:* Avonside House, High Street, Barford, Warwickshire. *T:* Barford 624278.

WILSON, Prof. William Adam; Lord President Reid Professor of Law, University of Edinburgh, since 1972; *b* 28 July 1928; *s* of Hugh Wilson and Anne Adam. *Educ:* Hillhead High Sch., Glasgow; Glasgow Univ. MA 1948, LLB 1951. Solicitor, 1951. Lectr in Scots Law, Edinburgh Univ., 1960, Sen. Lectr 1965. *Publications:* articles in legal jls. *Address:* 2 Great Stuart Street, Edinburgh EH3 6AW. *T:* 031-225 4958.

WILSON, William Desmond, OBE 1964 (MBE 1954); MC 1945; DSC (USA) 1945; HM Diplomatic Service; Deputy High Commissioner, Kaduna, Nigeria, since 1975; *b* 2 Jan. 1922; *s* of late Crozier Irvine Wilson and Mabel Evelyn (*née* Richardson); *m* 1949, Lucy Bride; two *s. Educ:* Royal Belfast Acad. Instrn; QUB; Trinity Coll., Cambridge. Joined Indian Army, 1941; served with 10 Gurkha Rifles, India and Italy, 1942-46 (Major). Colonial Admin. Service: Northern Nigeria, 1948-63; retd as Permanent Sec.; joined Foreign (subseq. Diplomatic) Service, 1963; First Sec., Ankara, 1963-67; UN (Polit.) Dept, FO, 1967; First Sec. and Head of Chancery, Kathmandu, 1969-74; Counsellor, 1975; Sen. Officers' War Course, RNC Greenwich, 1975. *Recreations:* shooting, riding. *Address:* c/o Foreign and Commonwealth Office, SW1; Spinneyhem, Forge Hill, Pluckley, Kent. *T:* Pluckley 300. *Clubs:* East India, Golfers'.

WILSON, William George, OBE 1960; Assistant Secretary, Department of Health and Social Security, since 1975; *b* 19 Feb. 1921; *s* of late William James Wilson and late Susannah Wilson; *m* 1948, Freda Huddleston; three *s. Educ:* Blaydon Secondary Sch., Co. Durham. Exec. Officer, Min. of Health, 1939. Served War, Army, in India and Ceylon, 1940-46. Higher Exec. Officer, Min. of Nat. Insurance, 1947; asst Principal, Colonial Office, 1947; Principal, CO, 1950-57 (Adviser, UK Delegn to UN Gen. Assembly, 1951); Financial Sec., Mauritius, 1957-60; Principal, Dept of Technical Co-operation, 1960; Asst Sec., MoH, 1962; Consultant, Hosp. Design and Construction, Middle East and Africa, 1968-70; Asst Sec., DHSS, 1971; Under-Sec., DHSS, 1972-75. *Recreations:* book collecting, archaeology of Hadrian's Wall. *Address:* 4 Priors Terrace, Tynemouth, Tyne and Wear. *Clubs:* Wig and Pen; Society of Antiquaries (Newcastle upon Tyne).

WILSON, William Joseph Robinson, CMG 1961; Grazier; *b* 2 April 1909; *s* of late Alexander William Wilson and Marion Ferris Wilson; *m* 1937, Mary Weir, *d* of late Arthur Maurice and Elizabeth Reid. *Educ:* Scotch Coll., Melbourne. Member: Faculty of Veterinary Science, Univ. of Melbourne; Australian

Cattle and Beef Research Cttee, 1962-64; Australian Woolgrowers' Council, 1952-54 and 1955-60; Graziers' Federal Council, 1954-60; Australian Overseas Transport Assoc., 1955-58; President, Graziers' Assoc. of Victoria, 1958-60; Vice-Pres. Graziers' Federal Council, 1958-60. Major, AIF, Middle East and New Guinea, 1940-44. *Address:* 17 Nareeb Court, Toorak, Victoria 3142, Australia. *Clubs:* Australian, Melbourne, Naval and Military, Victorian Racing (Melbourne).

WILSON, William Lawrence, CB 1967; OBE 1954; retired as Deputy Secretary, Department of the Environment, now Consultant; *b* 11 Sept. 1912; *s* of Joseph Osmond and Ann Wilson; *m* C. V. Richards; two *s*. *Educ:* Stockton on Tees Secondary School; Constantine College, Middlesbrough. BSc (London), FIMechE, Whitworth Prizeman. Apprentice, ICI Billingham 1928-33; Technical Asst, ICI, 1933-36; Assistant Engineer, HMOW, 1937; subsequently Engineer, 1939; Superintending Engineer, (MOW) 1945; Assistant Chief Engineer, 1954; Chief Engineer, 1962; Deputy Secretary, MPBW later DoE, 1969-73. Pres., Assoc. of Supervising Electrical Engineers. FRSA; Hon. FCIBS. Coronation Medal. *Publications:* papers on Radioactive Wastes; contrib. to World Power Conference, USSR and USA. *Recreations:* cricket, fishing, watching all forms of sport. *Address:* Oakwood, Chestnut Avenue, Rickmansworth, Herts. *T:* Rickmansworth 74419. *Club:* Civil Service.

WILSON, Group Captain William Proctor, CBE (mil.) 1943; (RAFVR); *b* 14 Jan. 1902; *e c* of late Canon C. E. Wilson, MA, BD; *m* 1st, 1926, Evelyne Christiana Cornet-Auquier; two *s*; 2nd, 1947, Agnes Christian Gillan, OBE, MB, ChB (*d* 1975); one *s*. *Educ:* St Lawrence College, Ramsgate; City and Guilds; Imperial Coll. (University of London). BSc (Eng); FCGI; CEng, FIEE; RAF (Signals Branch), 1939-45; RAF Supplementary Reserve (Signals Branch), 1946-54; Head of Research Department, BBC, 1950-64. Member, Radio Research Board, 1962-64; Mullard Ltd, 1964-72. Hon. Research Fellow, Dept of Electrical Engineering, University College, London, 1964-73. *Address:* c/o Barclays Bank, Langham Place, W1. *Clubs:* Athenæum, RAF Reserves.

WILSON-HAFFENDEN, Maj.-Gen. Donald James, CBE 1945; *b* 26 November 1900; *s* of late Rev. L. A. Wilson-Haffenden, Seaford, Sussex; *m* 1923, Isabella Sutherland (*d* 1968); one *d*; *m* 1969, Ruth Lea Douglass, late of CMS. *Educ:* Christ's Hosp.; Victoria Coll., Jersey. Commissioned 91st Punjabis (LI), 1920; served Waziristan, 1921-24; psc 1936; AA and QMG, 1st Division, 1941; DA and QMG 110 Force, 1941-42; DA and QMG 33 Corps, 1943; DQMG, GHQ, India, 1944. Hon. Treasurer, Eddystone Housing Assoc. *Address:* Quinnettes, Churt, near Farnham, Surrey. *Club:* Royal Commonwealth Society.

WILSON SMITH, Sir Henry, KCB 1949; KBE 1945; Director: Guest Keen and Nettlefolds Ltd, 1951-72 (Deputy Chairman, 1962-72); Powell Duffryn Ltd, 1951-69 (Chairman, 1957-69); Doxford & Sunderland Ltd, 1961-72; HAT Group Ltd, 1969-74; *b* 30 Dec. 1904; *e s* of J. Wilson Smith, Newcastle upon Tyne; *m* 1931, Molly, *d* of A. W. G. Dyson, Wylam, Northumberland; two *s*. *Educ:* Royal Grammar School, Newcastle upon Tyne; Peterhouse, Cambridge. 1st Class, 1st Div. History Tripos, Parts I and II; Administrative Class, Home Civil Service, 1927; Secretary's Office, General Post Office, 1927-29; HM Treasury, 1930; Asst Private Secretary to Chancellor of Exchequer, 1932, Prin. Private Sec., 1940-42; Under-Sec., HM Treasury, 1942-46; Permnt Sec., Min. of Defence, 1947-48; addtl Second Sec., HM Treasury, 1948-51. Chm. Doxford and Sunderland Shipbuilding & Engineering Co. Ltd, 1962-68; Formerly Part-time Mem. Nat. Coal Board; Dir, Bank of England, 1964-70. A Vice-Chm., Council BIM, 1963-67. *Address:* 68 Colinas Verdes, Bensafrim, Lagos, Algarve, Portugal. *Club:* United Oxford & Cambridge University.

WILTON, 7th Earl of, *cr* 1801; **Seymour William Arthur John Egerton;** Viscount Grey de Wilton, 1801; *b* 29 May 1921; *s* of 6th Earl and Brenda (*d* 1930), *d* of late Sir William Petersen, KBE; *S* father, 1927; *m* 1962, Mrs Diana Naylor Leyland. *Heir:* (by special remainder) *kinsman* Baron Ebury, *qv*. *Address:* 27 Egerton Terrace, SW3. *Club:* White's.

WILTON, Arthur John, CMG 1967; MC 1945; HM Diplomatic Service; Ambassador to Saudi Arabia, since 1976; *b* 21 Oct. 1921; *s* of late Walter Wilton, and of Annetta Irene Wilton (*née* Perman); *m* 1950, Maureen Elizabeth Alison Meaker; four *s* one *d*. *Educ:* Wanstead High School; St John's Coll., Oxford. Open Schol., St John's Coll., Oxford, 1940. Commissioned, Royal Ulster Rifles, 1942; served with Irish Brigade, N Africa, Italy and Austria, 1943-46. Entered HM Diplomatic Service, 1947;

served Lebanon, Egypt, Gulf Shaikhdoms, Roumania, Aden, and Yugoslavia; Ambassador to Kuwait, 1970-74; Asst Under-Sec. of State, FCO, 1974-76. Director, Middle East Centre for Arabic Studies, Shemlan, 1960-65. *Recreation:* whatever is available. *Address:* Summersdale House, The Drive, Chichester. *Club:* Athenæum.

WILTON, Gen. Sir John Gordon Noel, KBE 1964 (CBE 1954; OBE 1946); CB 1962; DSO 1944; idc; psc; retired; *b* Sydney, 22 Nov. 1910; *s* of late Noel V. S. Wilton, Grafton, New South Wales; *m* 1938, Helen Thelma, *d* of Robert Marshall; two *s* one *d*. *Educ:* Grafton High School, NSW; RMC, Duntroon, Canberra. Served in British Army, in UK, India and Burma, 1931-39. Served War of 1939-45 (DSO, OBE); AIF; Middle East, 1940-41; New Guinea, 1942-43; GSO Aust. Military Mission to Washington, 1944; Col, Gen. Staff Advance HQ, AMF, SW Pacific Area, 1945. Deputy Director, Military Operations, AHQ, Melbourne, 1946; Director, Military Operations and Plans, 1947-51; Comdg 28th Commonwealth Bde, Korea (CBE), 1953; Brig. i/c Administration, HQ Eastern Command, NSW, 1954-55; Brig. Gen. Staff AHQ, 1955-56; Comdt, RMC, Duntroon, Canberra, 1957-60; Head of SEATO, Military Planning Office, Bangkok, 1960-63; Chief of the Australian General Staff, 1963-66; Chm., Australian Chiefs of Staff Cttee, 1966-70; Australian Consul General, New York, 1973-75. Has the American Legion of Merit. *Recreation:* golf. *Address:* 11 Melbourne Avenue, Forrest, ACT 2603, Australia. *Club:* Imperial Service (Sydney).

WILTS, Archdeacon of; *see* Ramsbury, Bishop Suffragan of.

WILTSHIRE, Earl of; Christopher John Hilton Paulet; *b* 30 July 1969; *s* and *heir* of Marquess of Winchester, *qv*.

WILTSHIRE, Edward Parr, CBE 1965; HM Diplomatic Service, retired; *b* 18 Feb. 1910; 2nd *s* of late Major Percy Wiltshire and Kathleen Olivier Lefroy Parr Wiltshire, Great Yarmouth; *m* 1942, Gladys Mabel Stevens; one *d*. *Educ:* Cheltenham College; Jesus College, Cambridge. Entered Foreign Service, 1932. Served in: Beirut, Mosul, Baghdad, Tehran, Basra, New York (one of HM Vice-Consuls, 1944); promoted Consul, 1945; transf. Cairo, 1946 (Actg Consul-Gen., 1947, 1948); transf. Shiraz (having qual. in Arabic, and subseq. in Persian); Consul, Port Said, 1952; 1st Sec. and Consul: Baghdad, 1952, Rio de Janeiro, 1957; promoted Counsellor, 1959; Political Agent, Bahrain, 1959-63; Consul-General, Geneva, 1963-67; Dir, Diplomatic Service Language Centre, London, 1967-68; worked for Council for Nature (Editor, Habitat), 1968-69; Consul, Le Havre, 1969-75. *Publication:* The Lepidoptera of Iraq, 1957. *Recreations:* music, entomology, tennis, swimming. *Address:* 140 Marsham Court, Marsham Street, SW1.

WILTSHIRE, Sir Frederick Munro, Kt 1976; CBE 1970 (OBE 1966); FTS 1976; Managing Director: Wiltshire File Co. Pty Ltd, Australia, since 1938; Wiltshire Cutlery Co. Pty Ltd, since 1959; Director: Repco Ltd, since 1966; Australian Paper Manufacturers Ltd, since 1966; *b* 1911; *m* 1938, Jennie L., *d* of F. M. Frencham; one *d*. Chm., Dept of Trade and Industry Adv. Cttee on Small Businesses, 1968; Chm., Cttees of Inquiry, etc. Mem., Executive, CSIRO, 1974. Past Pres., Aust. Industries Develt Assoc.; Member, Manufacturing Industries Adv. Council, 1957- (Vice-Pres. 1972); Industrial Member, Science and Industry Forum of Aust. Acad. of Science, 1967-; FAIM (Councillor, 1955-69). *Address:* 38 Rockley Road, South Yarra, Vic 3141, Australia. *Clubs:* Athenæum (Melbourne); Kingston Heath Golf (Aust.).

WIMBERLEY, Maj.-Gen. Douglas Neil, CB 1943; DSO 1942; MC 1918; DL Dundee, 1947-75, Perthshire 1975; Hon. LLD Aberdeen, 1948, Dundee, 1967; *b* 15 Aug. 1896; *s* of late Colonel C. N. Campbell Wimberley, CMG, Inverness, and Lesmoir Gordon Wimberley; *m* 1925, E. Myrtle L., *d* of late Capt. F. L. Campbell, RN, Achalader, Perthshire, and Lady Dobell; one *s* one *d*. *Educ:* Alton Burn, Nairn; Wellington; Emmanuel College, Cambridge; RMC, Sandhurst. 2nd Lieut Cameron Highlanders, 1915; served European War as Regimental officer, France and Belgium, 1st and 51st Highland Divs, 1915-16 and 1917-18 (wounded, MC), including battles of Loos, Somme, Ypres, Cambrai and St Quentin; Acting and Temp. Major, 1918-19; North Russia, with MGC, 1919; Adjutant, 2nd Camerons, 1921; psc 1927; Bde Major 1st (Ghurkha) Inf. Bde, 1929; Operations NWFP India, 1930; Brevet Major, 1933; DAAG and GSO II, WO, 1934-37; Brevet Lt-Col 1936; Lt-Col Commanding 1st Cameron Highlanders, 1938; France, 1939; GSO1 and Chief Instructor Senior Officers' School, 1940; Temp. Brigadier 1941; Temp. Major-General 1942; Major-General 1943; Brig. Comdr 13th and 152nd Seaforth and Cameron Bde, 1940-41; GOC 46th Div., 1941; Div. Comdr, 51st Highland Div., 1941-43; including battles Alamein, Mareth, Medinine, Akarit, Enfidaville and Adrano; 8th Army campaign N Africa, Sicily, 1942-43 (despatches, slightly wounded, DSO, CB), Comdt Staff Coll., Camberley, 1943-44; Dir of Infantry, WO, 1944-46; retd at own request; Principal of University College, Dundee, in the Univ. of St Andrews, 1946-54. Governor, Dundee Colls of Art and Technol., 1946-54; Founder Governor, Scottish Horticultural Res. Inst., 1952-62. Member Royal Company of Archers, Queen's Body Guard for Scotland; Gentleman Usher of the Scarlet Rod in the Order of the Bath, 1948-54; Registrar and Secretary, 1954-64. Hon. Col St Andrews Univ. OTC 1951-63; Col of the Queen's Own Cameron Highlanders, 1951-61. Pres. Royal Celtic Soc., 1971-74; Hon. Vice Pres., Angus and Perthshire British Legion, 1965, Hon. Pres., 1976. *Publications:* military articles in service jls and Chambers's Encyclopædia; Army Quarterly prize essay, 1933. *Recreations:* once athletics (mem. Army AA; second, half mile, 1922); now genealogy, angling. *Address:* Foxhall, Coupar Angus, Perthshire. *T:* 384. *Club:* Naval and Military (Hon. Mem.).

WIMBLE, Ernest Walter, CBE 1946; *b* 23 Sept. 1887; 4th *s* of Charles Wimble, Old Romney, Kent, and Annie Elizabeth Wimble (*née* Aylward); *m* 1912, Daisy Edith Robarts (*d* 1961); one *s* one *d. Educ:* Elementary Sch.; St Dunstan's, Catford; King's College, London. 4 years Civil Service, 1903-06; 6 years Commercial, 1906-12; served European War, 1914-19; 11 years WEA, 1912-23; 25 years Secretary and Gen. Man. Workers' Travel Assoc. Ltd, 1923-47; Dir of Students Bookshops Ltd, 1924-65; Member Management Committee Travel Assoc. of Great Britain and Northern Ireland, 1945-49; Member British Tourist and Holidays Board, 1947-50. Chm. Creative Tourist Agents Conf., 1947-48; Chm. Home Holidays Division British Tourist and Holidays Board, 1947-50; Pres. International Union of Official Travel Organisations, 1948-49; Chm. Olympic Games (Overseas) Visitors Accommodation Bureau, 1948; Member: Hôtels Executive (British Transport), 1948-52; British Travel and Holidays Assoc., 1950; National Parks Commission, 1950-51; Founder-member of Youth Hostels Assoc. *Publications:* European Recovery, 1948-51 and the Tourist Industry, 1948; Western Europe's Tourist Trade, 1948, 1949, 1950. Editor and founder of The Travel Log. *Recreation:* travel. *Address:* Flat 5, 67 St Aubyns, Hove BN3 2TL.

WIMBORNE, 3rd Viscount, *cr* 1918; **Ivor Fox-Strangways Guest;** Baron Wimborne, 1880; Baron Ashby St Ledgers, 1910; Bt 1838; *b* 2 Dec. 1939; *s* of 2nd Viscount and of Dowager Viscountess Wimborne; *S* father, 1967; *m* 1966, Victoria Ann, *o d* of late Col Mervyn Vigors, DSO, MC; one *s. Educ:* Eton. Chairman, Harris & Dixon Group of Cos, 1972-76 (Man. Dir, 1967-71). Jt Master, Pytchley Hounds, 1968-76. *Heir:* *s* Hon. Ivor Mervyn Vigors Guest, *b* 19 Sept. 1968. *Club:* Travellers' (Paris).

WIMBUSH, Rt. Rev. Richard Knyvet; Priest-in-charge of Etton with Dalton Holme, dio. York, since 1977; an Assistant Bishop, Diocese of York, since 1977; *b* 18 March 1909; *s* of late Rev. Canon J. S. Wimbush, Terrington, Yorks, and late Judith Isabel Wimbush, *d* of Sir Douglas Fox; *m* 1937, Mary Margaret, *d* of Rev. E. H. Smith; three *s* one *d. Educ:* Haileybury Coll.; Oriel Coll., Oxford; Cuddesdon Coll. 2nd cl. Classical Mods 1930; BA 1st cl. Theol. 1932; MA 1935. Deacon, 1934; Priest, 1935; Chaplain, Cuddesdon Coll., Oxon, 1934-37; Curate: Pocklington, Yorks, 1937-39; St Wilfrid, Harrogate, 1939-42. Rector, Melsonby, Yorks, 1942-48; Principal, Edinburgh Theological Coll., 1948-63; Bishop of Argyll and the Isles, 1963-77; Primus of the Episcopal Church in Scotland, 1974-77. Canon of St Mary's Cathedral, Edinburgh, 1948-63; Exam. Chap. to Bp of Edinburgh, 1949-62; Select Preacher, Oxford Univ., 1971. *Recreations:* gardening, walking. *Address:* Etton Rectory, Beverley, Yorks HU17 7PQ. *Club:* New (Edinburgh).

WINCHESTER, 18th Marquess of, *cr* 1551; **Nigel George Paulet;** Baron St John of Basing, 1539; Earl of Wiltshire, 1550; Premier Marquess of England; *b* 23 Dec. 1941; *s* of George Cecil Paulet (*g g g s* of 13th Marquess) (*d* 1961), and Hazel Margaret, *o d* of late Major Danvers Wheeler, RA, Salisbury, Rhodesia; *S* kinsman, 1968; *m* 1967, Rosemary Anne, *d* of Major Aubrey John Hilton; two *s*. Director: Rhodesia Mineral Ventures (Pvt) Ltd; Sani-Dan Services (Pvt) Ltd; Rhodesian Prospectors (1969) (Pvt) Ltd. *Heir:* *s* Earl of Wiltshire, *qv. Address:* Lydford Cottage, 35 Whyte Ladies Lane, Borrowdale, Salisbury, Rhodesia.

WINCHESTER, Bishop of, since 1975; **Rt. Rev. John Vernon Taylor;** *b* 11 Sept. 1914; *s* of late Bishop J. R. S. Taylor and Margaret Irene Taylor (*née* Garrett); *m* 1940, Margaret Wright; one *s* two *d. Educ:* St Lawrence Coll., Ramsgate; Trinity Coll., Cambridge; St Catherine's Soc., Oxford; Wycliffe Hall, Oxford;

Institute of Education, London. Curate, All Souls, Langham Place, W1, 1938-40; Curate in Charge, St Andrew's Church, St Helens, Lancs, 1940-43; Warden, Bishop Tucker College, Mukono, Uganda, 1945-54; Research Worker, Internat. Missionary Council, 1955-59; Africa Sec., CMS, 1959-63; Gen. Sec., CMS, 1963-74. Examng Chap. to Bishop of Truro, 1974-75. Hon. Canon of Namirembe Cathedral, 1963-74. Hon. DD (Wycliffe Coll., Toronto), 1964. *Publications:* Man in the Midst, 1955; Christianity and Politics in Africa, 1957; The Growth of the Church in Buganda, 1958; African Passion, 1958; Christians of the Copperbelt, 1961; The Primal Vision, 1963; For All the World, 1966; Change of Address, 1968; The Go-Between God, 1972; Enough is Enough, 1975; *Recreations:* theatre, music. *Address:* Wolvesey, Winchester, Hants.

WINCHESTER, Dean of; *see* Stancliffe, Very Rev. M. S.

WINCHESTER, Archdeacon of; *see* Cartwright, Ven. E. D.

WINCHESTER, Clarence; Editor and Author; *s* of Arthur William and Elizabeth Alice Clark; *m* Constance Katherine Groves; one *s* (and one *d* decd). *Educ:* privately; technical schools. Has been variously associated with stage, aeronautics, and journalism in England and abroad, on newspapers and periodicals; learned to fly, 1913-14; formerly with Allied Newspapers, Daily Mail, etc; special correspondent, Kemsley Newspapers, Ltd; Assistant Chief Editor to Cassell's and Chief Editor of group of Amalgamated Press publications; Assistant Editor The Daily Sketch; edited: Railway Wonders of the World; Wonders of World Engineering; Shipping Wonders of the World; Wonders of World Aviation; World Film Encyclopædia; The King's Navy (in co-operation with Admiralty); The King's Army (in co-operation with War Office); The King's Air Force (in co-operation with Air Ministry); British Legion Poppy Annual, 1941; The Queen Elizabeth, Winchester's Screen Encyclopedia, 1948; Mind and Matter, etc; also formerly Director and Managing Editor, Dropmore Press Ltd; Consulting Editor, Law Society's Gazette; Managing Director and Chief Editor, Winchester Publications, Ltd; correspondent on European affairs to the Argonaut weekly, San Francisco, USA; Editor, England (quarterly). Associate, Amer. Museum of Natural History. *Publications:* Sonnets and Some Others; Aerial Photography (with F. L. Wills); The Devil Rides High; An Innocent in Hollywood; Let's Look at London; Earthquake in Los Angeles; Three Men in a Plane; The Captain Lost his Bathroom; City of Lies; Airman Tomorrow (with Alfred Kerr); The Black Poppy; A Great Rushing of Wings and Other Poems; Signatures of God; Editor and designer of The Royal Philatelic Collection, by Sir John Wilson, Bt (by permission of HM King George VI); The Crown Jewels, by Major General H. D. W. Sitwell, CB, MC, Keeper of the Jewel House (by permission of the Lord Chamberlain and the Resident Governor of the Tower), etc. *Address:* 60 Jireh Court, Haywards Heath, West Sussex. *T:* Haywards Heath 54804. *Club:* Savage.

WINCHESTER, Ian Sinclair; HM Diplomatic Service; Head of Southern European Department, Foreign and Commonwealth Office, since 1976; *b* 14 March 1931; *s* of Dr Alexander Hugh Winchester, FRCS(Ed), and late Mary Stewart (*née* Duguid); *m* 1957, Shirley Louise Milner; three *s. Educ:* Lewes County Grammar Sch., Sussex; Magdalen Coll., Oxford. Foreign Office, 1953; Third Sec. (Oriental), Cairo, 1955-56; FO, 1956-60; Asst Political Agent, Dubai, 1960-62; Actg Political Agent, Doha, 1962; First Sec. (Inf.), Vienna, 1962-65; First Sec. (Commercial), Damascus, 1965-67; FO (later FCO), 1967-70; Counsellor, Jedda, 1970-72; Counsellor (Commercial), Brussels, 1973-76. *Address:* c/o Foreign and Commonwealth Office, SW1A 2AH.

WINCHILSEA, 16th Earl of, *cr* 1628, **and NOTTINGHAM, 11th Earl of,** *cr* 1675; **Christopher Denys Stormont Finch Hatton,** Bart 1611; Viscount Maidstone, 1623; Bart English, 1660; Baron Finch, 1674; Hereditary Lord of Royal Manor of Wye; *b* 17 Nov. 1936; *er s* of 15th Earl and Countess Gladys Széchényi (who obtained a divorce, 1946; she *m* 1954, Arthur Talbot Peterson), 3rd *d* of Count László Széchényi; *S* father, 1950; *m* 1962, Shirley, *e d* of late Bernard Hatfield, Wylde Green, Sutton Coldfield; one *s* one *d. Heir:* *s* Viscount Maidstone, *qv. Address:* South Cadbury House, Yeovil, Somerset.

See also W. W. Straight.

WINDER, Col John Lyon C.; *see* Corbett-Winder.

WINDEYER, Sir Brian (Wellingham), Kt 1961; FRCP, FRCS, FRCSE, FRSM, FRCR, DMRE; Vice-Chancellor, University of London, 1969-72; Professor of Radiology (Therapeutic), Middlesex Hospital Medical School, University of London, 1942-69; Dean, Middlesex Hospital Medical School, 1954-67;

formerly Director: Meyerstein Institute of Radiotherapy, Middlesex Hospital; Radiotherapy Department, Mount Vernon Hospital; Cons. Adviser in Radiotherapy to Ministry of Health; *b* 7 Feb. 1904; *s* of Richard Windeyer, KC, Sydney, Australia; *m* 1st, 1928, Joyce Ziele, *d* of Harry Russell, Sydney; one *s* one *d*; 2nd, 1948, Elspeth Anne, *d* of H. Bowry, Singapore; one *s* two *d*. *Educ:* Sydney C of E Grammar Sch.; St Andrew's Coll., Univ. of Sydney. Sydney Univ. Rugby Team, 1922-27; combined Australian and NZ Univs Rugby Team, 1923; coll. crew, 1922-26. MB, BS Sydney, 1927; FRCSE 1930; DMRE Cambridge, 1933; FFR 1940; FRCS (ad eundem) 1948; MRCP 1957. Formerly House Physician, House Surgeon and Radium Registrar, Royal Prince Alfred Hosp., Sydney; Asst, Fondation Curie, Paris, 1929-30; Middlesex Hospital: Radium Officer, 1931; MO i/c Radiotherapy Dept, 1936; Medical Comdt, 1940-45; Dir, EMS Radiotherapy Dept, Mt Vernon Hosp., 1940-46; Dean, Faculty of Medicine, Univ. of London, 1964-68. Skinner Lectr, Faculty of Radiologists, 1943 (Pres. of Faculty, 1949-52); Hunterian Prof., RCS, 1951. Pres., Radiology Section, RSM, 1958-59. Chairman: Radio-active Substances Adv. Cttee, 1961-70; Nat. Radiological Protection Bd, 1970-; Academic Council, Univ. of London, 1967-69; Matilda and Terence Kennedy Inst. of Rheumatology, 1970-; Inst. of Educn, Univ. of London, 1974-; Council, RSA, 1973-. Member: Royal Commn on Med. Educn; Grand Council and Exec. Cttee, British Empire Cancer Campaign; British Inst. of Radiology (late Mem. Council); Med. Soc. of London; MRC, 1958-62 and 1968-71; Clinical Research Bd, 1954-62 (Chm., 1968). Co-opted Mem. Council, RCS, to rep. radiology, 1948-53. Hon. Mem., Amer. Radium Soc., 1948. Hon. FRACS, 1951; Hon. FCRA 1955. Hon. DSc: British Columbia, 1952; Wales, 1965; Cantab, 1971; Hon. LLD Glasgow, 1968. *Publications:* various articles on cancer and radiotherapy. *Recreations:* golf, gardening. *Address:* Moreton Gap, Thame Park Road, Thame, Oxon. *T:* Thame 2371. *Club:* Athenæum.

WINDEYER, Rt. Hon. Sir (William John) Victor, PC 1963; KBE 1958 (CBE 1944); CB 1953; DSO (and bar), 1942; ED; Justice of the High Court of Australia, 1958-72, retired; *b* 28 July 1900; *s* of W. A. Windeyer, Sydney, NSW; *m* 1934, Margaret Moor Vicars; three *s* one *d*. *Educ:* Sydney Grammar Sch., University of Sydney (MA, LLB). Admitted to Bar of NSW, 1925; KC (NSW) 1949; sometime lecturer in Faculty of Law, University of Sydney. Lieut AMF (Militia), 1922; War of 1939-45; Lieut-Colonel comdg 2/48 Bn, AIF, 1940-42 (including siege of Tobruk); Brig. comdg 20th Australian Inf. Bde, AIF, 1942-46 (El Alamein, New Guinea, Borneo); Major-General and CMF Member, Australian Military Board, 1950-53; Retired List, 1957. Member of Senate, University of Sydney, 1949-59, Dep. Chancellor, 1953-58; Hon. Col, Sydney University Regiment, 1956-66; Member Council Australian National University, 1951-55. Director: Colonial Sugar Refining Co., 1953-58; Mutual Life and Citizens Assurance Co., 1954-58. Chairman Trustees, Gowrie Scholarship Fund, 1964-. Vice-President, Selden Society, 1965-; Pres., NSW Branch, Australian Scouts Assoc., 1970-. Hon. Member, Society Public Teachers of Law; Hon. Bencher, Middle Temple, 1972. Hon. LLD Sydney, 1975. *Publications:* The Law of Wagers, Gaming and Lotteries, 1929; Lectures on Legal History, 1938, 2nd edn, 1949, rev. 1957; numerous articles and lectures on legal and historical subjects. *Address:* Peroomba, Turramurra, NSW 2074, Australia. *Clubs:* Australian, Pioneers (Sydney); Elanora Country (Narrabeen).

WINDHAM, Sir Ralph, Kt 1960; Commissioner, Foreign Compensation Commission, 1965-77, Vice-Chairman, 1969, Chairman, 1972-77; *b* 25 March 1905; *er s* of Major Ashe Windham and Cora E. S. Middleton, Waghen Hall, East Yorkshire; *m* 1946, Kathleen Mary, *o d* of Captain Cecil Henry FitzHerbert, DSC, Latimerstown, Wexford, Eire; two *s* two *d*. *Educ:* Wellington Coll.; Trinity Coll., Cambridge, 1st class Part II, Law Tripos; MA, LLB, 1928; Barrister-at-Law, Lincoln's Inn (Buchanan Prizeman), 1930. Legal Draftsman, Government of Palestine, 1935; Judge of Dist Court, Palestine, 1942; Puisne Judge, Supreme Court, Ceylon, 1947; Puisne Judge, Supreme Court, Kenya, 1950-55; Chief Justice, Zanzibar, 1955-59; Justice of Appeal, Court of Appeal for Eastern Africa, 1959-60; Chief Justice, Tanganyika (later Tanzania), 1960-65; Actg Gov.-Gen., Tanganyika, Feb.-May 1962. Order of the Brilliant Star of Zanzibar (2nd class), 1959; Grand Commander, Star of Africa (Liberia), 1964. *Recreations:* music and tennis. *Address:* Hook's Cottage, Kingscote, near Tetbury, Gloucestershire.

WINDHAM, William Evan; *b* 1 May 1904; *o s* of late Sir William Windham, CBE; *m* 1932, Constance (*d* 1939), *d* of late J. H. Loudon, Olantigh, Wye, Kent; two *d*; *m* 1962, Dorothy Muir, *widow* of Carl Davis (MInstMM, Gold Medallist), Villa Berg, Bishopscourt, Cape Town. *Educ:* Wellington Coll.; London University. Barrister at Law, Gray's Inn, 1936. Served AAF,

1928. Administration, Fiji and Western Pacific, 1930-34; practised on South Eastern circuit, 1936-39. Served War of 1939-45 in Fighter Command, RAFVR (despatches), Sqdn Leader. Sen. Res. Magistrate, N Rhodesia, 1952; Commissioner, Emergency Regulations, 1956-57; Puisne Judge, High Court of Northern Rhodesia, 1956-63; Chief Justice, St Helena and Dependencies, 1969-71. *Recreations:* tennis, golf. *Address:* De Goede Verwachting, Cavalcade Road, Green Point, Cape, S Africa. *Clubs:* Royal Air Force, Royal Commonwealth Society.

WINDHAM, Brig. William Russell S.; *see* Smijth-Windham.

WINDLESHAM, 3rd Baron, *cr* 1937; **David James George Hennessy;** PC 1973; Bt 1927; Managing Director, ATV Network, since 1975 (Joint Managing Director, 1974-75); Director, Associated Television Corporation, since 1975; Chairman, Independent Television Companies Association, since 1976; *b* 28 Jan. 1932; *s* of 2nd Baron Windlesham; *S* father, 1962; *m* 1965, Prudence Glynn, *qv*; one *s* one *d*. *Educ:* Ampleforth; Trinity Coll., Oxford (MA). Chairman, Bow Group, 1959-60, 1962-63; Member, Westminster City Council, 1958-62. Dir, Rediffusion Television, 1965-67; Man. Dir, Grampian Television, 1967-70. Minister of State, Home Office, 1970-72; Minister of State for Northern Ireland, 1972-73; Lord Privy Seal and Leader of the House of Lords, 1973-74. Mem., Cttee of Privy Counsellors on Ministerial Memoirs, 1975. Jt Dep. Chm., Queen's Silver Jubilee Appeal, 1976-77; Dep. Chm., Queen's Silver Jubilee Trust, 1977-. *Publications:* Communication and Political Power, 1966; Politics in Practice, 1975. *Heir:* *s* Hon. James Rupert Hennessy, *b* 9 Nov. 1968. *Address:* House of Lords, SW1A 0PW.

WINDSOR, Viscount; Ivor Edward Other Windsor-Clive; Director, Fine Art Consultants Ltd; *b* 19 Nov. 1951; *s* and *heir* of 3rd Earl of Plymouth, *qv*. *Educ:* Harrow. Co-founder, and Dir, Centre for the Study of Modern Art, 1973. *Recreations:* cricket, frisbee. *Address:* 90B Addison Road, W14. *T:* 01-602 2507.

WINDSOR, Dean of; *see* Mann, Rt. Rev. M. A.

WINDSOR, Robert, CB 1974; Assistant Under Secretary of State, Department of Health and Social Security (formerly Ministry of Social Security), 1966-76, retired; *b* 9 April 1916; *s* of late Henry and Alice Windsor; *m* 1939, Eleanor Malone; two *s* one *d*. *Educ:* Liverpool Collegiate Sch.; University of Liverpool. BA 1937, MA 1940. Served in S Lancs Regt and Intelligence Corps, 1940-45. Asst Principal, Assistance Board, 1947; Principal, National Assistance Board, 1949; Asst Secretary, National Assistance Board, 1962; Under-Secretary, National Assistance Board, 1965. *Recreation:* listening to music. *Address:* Berfra-Mont, Armscote, Stratford-upon-Avon, Warwickshire CV37 8DE. *T:* Ilmington 302.

WINDSOR-AUBREY, Henry Miles; Puisne Judge, Supreme Court, Ghana, from 1949, retired; Chairman: Industrial Tribunal; Rent Tribunal; Rent Assessment Panel; *b* 1901; *m* 1928, Dorothy Dagmar Montrose; one *s*. *Educ:* Clifton College. Called to the Bar, Inner Temple, 1925. Served in Uganda, 1934-49. Magistrate, 1934-36; Crown Counsel, 1936-43; Solicitor-General, 1943-49. *Recreations:* golf and gardening. *Address:* Bogside House, Irthington, near Carlisle, Cumbria.

WINDSOR-CLIVE, family name of **Earl of Plymouth.**

WINDWARD ISLANDS, Bishop of, since 1969; **Rt. Rev. George Cuthbert Manning Woodroffe,** CBE 1973; MA, LTh; *b* 17 May 1918; *s* of James Manning Woodroffe and Evelyn Agatha (*née* Norton); *m* 1947, Aileen Alice Connell; one *s* one *d* (and one *s* decd). *Educ:* Grenada Boys' Secondary School; Codrington Coll., Barbados. Clerk in Civil Service, 1936-41; Codrington Coll. (Univ. of Durham), 1941-44; Deacon 1944; Priest 1945; Asst Priest, St George's Cath., St Vincent, 1944-47; Vicar of St Simon's, Barbados, 1947-50; Rector: St Andrew, 1950-57; St Joseph, 1957-62; St John, 1962-67; Rural Dean of St John, Barbados, 1965-67; Sub-Dean and Rector of St George's Cathedral, St Vincent, Windward Islands, 1967-69. Vice-Chm., Anglican Consultative Council, 1974. Mem., Bd of Educn, Barbados, 1964-67. Chm., Bd of Governors, Alleyne Sch., Barbados, 1951-57. *Recreations:* music, driving, detective tales and novels, military band music. *Address:* Bishop's House, PO Box 128, St Vincent, West Indies. *T:* St Vincent 61895. *Club:* Royal Commonwealth Society.

WINEGARTEN, Prof. Asher, CBE 1968; Deputy Director General, National Farmers' Union, since 1970; Visiting Professor of Agricultural Policy, Wye College, University of London, since 1973; *b* 26 March 1922; *s* of Emanuel and Sally

Winegarten; *m* 1946, Renee Cecile Aarons. *Educ:* Highbury County Secondary Sch.; London Sch. of Economics. 1st cl. hons BCom and BScEcon; Farr Medallist 1942; FSS; FRAgSs. Admty, 1942-47: Sec., Chain Cable Control (Temp. Admin. Asst). Chief Economist, NFU, 1947. Employer Mem., Agricultural Wages Bd, 1957-77; a Mem. for NFU on Council of CBI; Mem. Council for Internat. Develt, 1977-. *Publications:* (contrib.) Agriculture and the British Economy, 1956; (contrib.) Economic Change and Agriculture, 1967; (contrib.) US Agriculture in a World Context, 1974; various lectures and papers; contrib. Jls of Ag. Econ. Soc., Royal Soc. of Arts, Farmers' Club, etc. *Recreations:* opera, theatre, travel, gardening. *Address:* 12 Heather Walk, Edgware, Mddx HA8 9TS. *T:* 01-958 9365. *Clubs:* Reform, Farmers'.

WINGATE, Henry Smith; International Nickel Co. of Canada Ltd and International Nickel Co. Inc., New York: Director since 1942, Chairman, Advisory Committee; Chairman of the Board and Chief Officer, 1960-72; Member, Advisory Committee, International Nickel Ltd, 1954-72; Director: United States Steel Corporation; American Standard Inc.; Canadian Pacific Ltd; JP Morgan & Co., Inc.; Morgan Guaranty Trust Co. of New York; Peoples' Symphony Concerts, Inc., New York; Société de Chimie Industrielle, Paris; *b* Talas, Turkey, 8 Oct. 1905; *s* of Henry Knowles Wingate and Jane Caroline Wingate (*née* Smith), US citizens; *m* 1929, Ardis Adeline Swenson; two *s*. *Educ:* Carleton Coll.; University of Michigan. BA Carleton Coll., 1927; JD Michigan 1929. Admitted to New York bar, 1931. Associated with Sullivan & Cromwell, NYC, 1929-35. Internat. Nickel Co. of Canada, Ltd: Asst Secretary, 1935-39; Secretary, 1939-49; Vice-President and Secretary, 1949-52; Vice-President, 1952-54; President, 1954-60. Assistant to the President, International Nickel Co., Inc., NY, 1935-54; President, 1954-60; former Dir, Bank of Montreal. Trustee: Seamen's Bank for Savings, NY; Foundn for Child Develt; Sen. Mem., The Conference Board; Member: The Business Council, Washington, DC; Canadian-American Cttee, National Planning Association, Washington, DC, and C. D. Howe Res. Inst., Montreal; US Steel Foundation, Inc.; Canadian Inst. of Mining and Metallurgy; Canadian Society of NY; Council on Foreign Relations, Inc., NY; Economic Club of NY; Mining and Metallurgical Society of America; Pilgrims of the United States; Vice-Pres., Amer. Friends of Canada Cttee, Inc. Formerly Trustee: Legal Aid Soc. of NY; Public Health Inst., City of NY; Manhattan Eye, Ear and Throat Hosp.; US Council, Internat. Chamber of Commerce; Annuity Fund for Congregational Ministers; Retirement Fund for Lay Workers. Hon. LLD: Manitoba, 1957; Marshall, 1967; York, 1967; Laurentian, 1968; Colby Coll., 1970; Hon. LHD Carleton Coll., 1973. *Address:* (business) One New York Plaza, New York, NY 10004, USA. *T:* 742-4000; (home) 520 East 86th Street, New York, NY 10028. *T:* Regent 4-3568. *Clubs:* Recess, Union, Cold Spring Harbor Beach, Huntington Country, New York Plaza, Links, University (New York); International (Washington).

WINGATE, Captain Miles Buckley; Deputy Master of Trinity House, London, since 1976; *b* 17 May 1923; *s* of Terrence Wingate and Edith Wingate; *m* 1947, Alicia Forbes Philip; three *d*. *Educ:* Taunton Grammar Sch.; Southampton and Prior Park Coll., Somerset. Master Mariner. Apprenticed to Royal Mail Lines Ltd, 1939; first Comd, 1957; elected to Bd of Trinity House, 1968. *Recreation:* golf. *Address:* Trinity House, Tower Hill, EC3N 4DH. *T:* 01-480 6601. *Club:* Royal Thames Yacht.

WINGATE, Sir Ronald (Evelyn Leslie), 2nd Bt, *cr* 1920; CB 1959; CMG 1952; CIE 1931; OBE 1945; ICS, retired; *b* 30 Sept. 1889; *o* surv. *s* of Sir F. Reginald Wingate, 1st Bt, GCB, GCVO, GBE, KCMG, DSO; *S* father 1953; *m* 1916, Mary Harpoth, *d* of Lady Vinogradoff, Oxford. *Educ:* Bradfield; Balliol Coll., Oxford (MA). Entered ICS 1912; Indian Political Service; retired, 1939; served Mesopotamia, 1917-19 (despatches). Served War of 1939-45, in Africa, South-East Asia and with Joint Planning Staff in Offices of the War Cabinet. *Publications:* Wingate of the Sudan, 1955; Not in the Limelight, 1959; Lord Ismay, 1970. *Recreations:* shooting, fishing, golf. *Heir:* none. *Address:* Barford Manor, Barford St Martin, Salisbury, Wilts. *T:* Wilton 2252. *Club:* Brooks's.

WINGATE, William Granville, QC 1963; **His Honour Judge Wingate;** a Circuit Judge (formerly a County Court Judge), since 1967; *b* 28 May 1911; *s* of Colonel George and Mary Ethel Wingate; *m* 1960, Judith Rosemary Evatt; one *s* one *d*. *Educ:* Brighton Coll.; Lincoln Coll., Oxford (BA). Called to Bar, Inner Temple, 1933; Western Circuit. Served Army, 1940-46. Dep. Chm., Essex QS, 1965-71. Member: Bar Council, 1961-67; County Court Rule Cttee, 1971-; Lord Chancellor's Legal Aid Adv. Cttee, 1971-; Lord Chancellor's Law Reform Cttee, 1974-. *Recreation:* sailing. *Address:* 2 Garden Court, Temple, EC4. *T:*

01-353 4741; Cox's Mill, Dallington, Heathfield, Sussex. *Clubs:* Royal Corinthian Yacht (Commodore, 1965-68), Bar Yacht (Commodore, 1972-).

WINGFIELD, family name of **Viscount Powerscourt.**

WINGFIELD DIGBY; *see* Digby.

WINGFIELD DIGBY, Ven. Stephen Basil, MBE 1944; Archdeacon of Sarum, since 1968; Canon Residentiary since 1968, and Treasurer since 1971, Salisbury Cathedral; *b* 10 Nov. 1910; *m* 1940, Barbara Hatton Budge; three *s* one *d*. *Educ:* Marlborough Coll.; Christ Church, Oxford; Wycliffe Hall, Oxford. Asst Master, Kenton Coll., Kenya, 1933-36; Curate, St Paul's, Salisbury, 1936-38; Priest-in-Charge, St George's, Oakdale, Poole, 1938-47. CF (temp.), 1939-45; SCF, 7th Armoured Div., 1943-45. Vicar of Sherborne with Castleton and Lillington, 1947-68. RD of Sherborne and Canon of Salisbury Cathedral, 1954-68. *Recreations:* fishing, shooting, cricket. *Address:* 23 The Close, Salisbury, Wilts.

WINKS, Prof. Robin W(illiam Evert), MA, PhD; Professor of History, Yale University, since 1957; *b* 5 Dec. 1930; *s* of Evert McKinley Winks and Jewell Sampson; *m* 1952, Avril Flockton, Wellington, NZ; one *s* one *d*. *Educ:* Univ. of Colorado (BA Hons 1952, MA 1953); Victoria Univ., NZ (MA Cert. 1952); Johns Hopkins Univ. (PhD 1957). Instructor, Yale Univ., 1957; Dir, Office of Special Projects and Foundns, Yale Univ., 1974-76. Smith-Mundt Prof., Univ. of Malaya, 1962; Vis. Prof., Univ. of Sydney, 1963; Vis. Fellow, Inst. of Commonwealth Studies, 1966-67. Cultural Attaché, Amer. Embassy, London, 1969-71; Advisor to Dept of State, 1971-. Mem. RHistS. Hon. MA Yale 1967; Hon. DLitt Univ. of Nebraska, 1976. *Publications:* Canada and the United States, 1960 (2nd edn 1973); The Cold War, 1964 (2nd edn 1977); Historiography of the British Empire-Commonwealth, 1966; Age of Imperialism, 1969; Pastmasters, 1969; The Historian as Detective, 1969; The Blacks in Canada, 1971; Slavery, 1972; An American's Guide to Britain, 1977; articles in Amer. Hist. Rev. *Recreations:* travel, old maps, detective fiction. *Address:* 648 Yale Station, New Haven, Conn 06520, USA. *Clubs:* Athenæum, Reform, Royal Commonwealth Society; Yale (NY); Mory's (New Haven).

WINLAW, Ashley William Edgell, OBE 1968; TD 1953; English Master, Mangochi Secondary School, Mangochi, Malaŵi, since April 1975; *b* 8 Feb. 1914; *s* of Rev. G. P. K. Winlaw, Morden, Surrey, and Minnie Ashley, Kidlington, Yorks. *Educ:* Winchester Coll.; St John's Coll., Cambridge (MA). Master, Aldenham Sch., 1936-39; Master, Shrewsbury Sch., 1939-40; served War, 1940-46; Intelligence Corps, Special Forces, Airborne (Lt-Col; retired as Hon. Major). Master, Rugby Sch., 1946-54; Master, Kent Sch., Connecticut, USA, 1950-51; Headmaster, Achimota Sch., Accra, Ghana, 1954-59; Principal, Government Cadet Coll., Hasan Abdal, W Pakistan, 1959-65; Director of Studies, British Inst., Santiago, Chile, 1965-66; Principal, Federal Govt Coll., Warri, Nigeria, 1966-69; English Master: Bishops Senior Sch., Mukono, Uganda, 1969-72; Blantyre Secondary Sch., Blantyre, Malaŵi, 1972-75. Tamgha-i-Pakistan (TPk), Pakistan, 1964. *Recreations:* sports, sailing, drama, painting. *Address:* c/o Barclays Bank Ltd, Rugby, Warwickshire. *Clubs:* Special Forces, MCC, Free Foresters, I Zingari.

WINN, family name of **Barons Headley** and **St Oswald.**

WINN, Air Vice-Marshal Charles Vivian, CBE 1963; DSO 1945; OBE 1950; DFC 1941; AOC Scotland and Northern Ireland 1972-73; *b* 20 April 1918; *s* of C. A. Winn, Cardiff, Past Pres. of Shipping Fedn, and D. B. Winn (*née* Thomas); *m* 1946, Suzanne Patricia (*née* Baily); one *s* one *d*. *Educ:* St Peter's Sch., Weston-super-Mare; Wycliffe Coll. Station Comdr, Felixstowe, 1951 (Queen's Commendation for Bravery, 1953); DP2, Air Ministry, 1953; Station Comdr: Weston Zoyland, 1955; Laarbruch, 1957; SASO, 38 Gp, 1960; Chief of Plans and Ops, Far East, Nov. 1962; Dir of Ops, MoD (Air), 1965; Air Comdr, Malta, 1968; Chief of Plans, SHAPE, 1971. Chief Recreation Officer, Anglian Water Authority, 1974. MBIM. *Address:* The Cottage, Green End, Great Stukeley, Huntingdon, Cambs. *Clubs:* Royal Air Force; Union (Malta).

WINNEKE, Hon. Sir Henry (Arthur), KCMG 1966; KCVO 1977; Kt 1957; OBE 1944; QC (Australia); Governor of Victoria, Australia, since 1974; *b* 29 Oct. 1908; *s* of Henry Christian Winneke, Judge of County Courts, Victoria, and Ethel Janet Winneke; *m* 1933, Nancy Rae Wilkinson; two *s*. *Educ:* Ballarat Grammar Sch.; Scotch Coll., Melbourne; University of Melbourne. Master of Laws, 1st Class Hons, Melbourne, 1929; Hockey Blue, Melbourne Univ. Called to Victorian Bar, 1931.

Served with Royal Australian Air Force, 1939-46, Group Captain, Director of Personal Services. Resumed practice Victorian Bar, 1946; KC 1949; Senior Counsel to Attorney-General and Prosecutor for the King, 1950; Solicitor-General of Victoria, 1951-64; Chief Justice, Supreme Court of Victoria, 1964-74; Lieutenant-Governor of Victoria, 1972-74. Member: Council Scotch Coll., Melbourne, 1947-56; Council Victoria Bar, 1948, 1949. President: Literary Council of Victoria, 1966; Boy Scouts Assoc., Victoria Br.; Victoria Law Foundn; Victorian Council Legal Educn. KStJ 1974. *Recreations:* golf, gardening, racing. *Address:* Government House, Melbourne, Victoria 3004, Australia; *Clubs:* Athenæum, Melbourne Cricket, Savage, Metropolitan Golf (Melbourne); Royal Automobile, Moonee Valley Racing (Victoria).

WINNER, Dame Albertine (Louise), DBE 1967 (OBE 1945); Linacre Fellow, Royal College of Physicians, 1967-78; Chairman, St Christopher's Hospice; *b* 4 March 1907; *d* of Isidore and Annie Winner, 4k Portman Mansions, W1. *Educ:* Francis Holland Sch., Clarence Gate; University College, London, and University College Hospital. BSc (Hons Physiology) 1929; MRCS, LRCP, 1932; MBBS London, 1933 (University Gold Medal); MD (London), 1934; MRCP (London) 1935; FRCP (London) 1959; FFCM 1973. Hon. Assistant Physician, Elizabeth Garrett Anderson Hospital, 1937; Hon. Physician, Mothers' Hospital, Clapton, 1937. Service with RAMC, 1940-46 (Lieut-Colonel). Service with Ministry of Health, 1947-67. Hon. Consultant for Women's Services to the Army, 1946-70. Visiting Lecturer, London School of Economics, 1951-63. Fellow, University College, London, 1965. QHP 1965-68. *Publications:* articles in Lancet, Public Health, etc. *Recreations:* gardening, Japanese prints, music, people, opera. *Address:* 35 Gordon Mansions, Torrington Place, WC1. *T:* 01-636 1921. *Clubs:* Lansdowne, New Arts.

WINNER, Prof. Harold Ivor, MA, MD, FRCP, FRCPath; Professor of Medical Microbiology (formerly of Bacteriology), University of London, at Charing Cross Hospital Medical School, since 1965; Consultant Bacteriologist, Charing Cross Hospital, since 1954; *b* 1 June 1918; *y s* of late Jacob Davis and Janet Winner; *m* 1945, Nina, *e d* of Jacques and Lily Katz; two *s.* *Educ:* St Paul's Sch.; Downing Coll., Cambridge (Maj. Schol.); University College Hospital Medical School. 1st class hons, Nat. Scis Tripos Cambridge, 1939. House Surgeon, Addenbrooke's Hospital, Cambridge, 1942; served RAMC, 1942-44; Asst Pathologist, EMS, 1945-48 and NW Group Laboratory, Hampstead, 1948-50; Lecturer, Sen. Lecturer, and Reader in Bacteriology, Charing Cross Hospital Medical Sch., 1950-64; Examiner: Examining Board in England, 1962-; Royal Coll. of Surgeons, 1971; Royal Coll. of Pathologists, 1975; universities at home and overseas. Founder Fellow and Archivist, RCPath; Vice-Pres., Sect. of Comparative Medicine, formerly Pres. and Hon. Editor, Section of Pathology, RSM; Vis. Prof., Guest Lectr and corresp. Mem., various univs and medical insts overseas. FRSA. *Publications:* Candida albicans (jointly), 1964; Symposium on Candida Infections (jointly), 1966; Microbiology in Modern Nursing, 1969; Microbiology in Patient Care, 1973; Louis Pasteur and Microbiology, 1974; chapters in medical books; papers in medical, scientific and nursing journals. *Recreations:* listening to music, looking at pictures and buildings, gardening, travel. *Address:* 48 Lyndale Avenue, NW2 2QA. *T:* 01-435 5959; Charing Cross Hospital Medical School, W6 8RF. *T:* 01-748 2050.

WINNER, Michael Robert; Chairman: Scimitar Films Ltd, Michael Winner Ltd, Motion Picture and Theatrical Investments Ltd, since 1957; *b* 30 Oct. 1935; *s* of George Joseph and Helen Winner. *Educ:* St Christopher's Sch., Letchworth; Downing Coll., Cambridge Univ. (MA). Film critic and Fleet Street journalist and contributor to: The Spectator, Daily Express, London Evening Standard, etc. Entered Motion Pictures, 1956, as Screen Writer, Asst Director, Editor. Films include: Play It Cool, (Dir), 1962; The Cool Mikado (Dir and Writer), 1962; West Eleven (Dir), 1963; The System (Prod. and Dir), 1963; You Must Be Joking (Prod., Dir, Writer), 1965; The Jokers (Prod., Dir, Writer), 1966; I'll Never Forget What's 'isname (Prod. and Dir), 1967; Hannibal Brooks (Prod., Dir, Writer), 1968; The Games (Prod. and Dir), 1969; Lawman (Prod. and Dir), 1970; The Nightcomers (Prod. and Dir), 1971; Chato's Land (Prod. and Dir), 1971; The Mechanic (Dir), 1972; Scorpio (Prod. and Dir), 1972; The Stone Killer (Prod. and Dir), 1973; Death Wish (Prod. and Dir), 1974; Won Ton Ton The Dog That Saved Hollywood (Prod. and Dir), 1975; The Sentinel (Prod. Dir, Writer), 1976; The Big Sleep (Prod. Dir, Writer), 1977. *Recreations:* walking around art galleries, museums, antique shops. *Address:* 6/8 Sackville Street, W1. *T:* 01-734 8385.

WINNICK, David Julian; *b* Brighton, 26 June 1933; *s* of Eugene and Rose Winnick; *m* 1968, Bengi Rona, *d* of Tarik and Zeynep Rona. *Educ:* secondary school; London Sch. of Economics (Dip. in Social Admin). Army National Service, 1951-53. Branch Secretary, Clerical and Administrative Workers' Union, 1956-62; Advertisement Manager, Tribune, 1963-66. Contested (Lab) Harwich, 1964; MP (Lab) Croydon South, 1966-70; contested (Lab): Croydon Central, Oct. 1974; Walsall N, Nov. 1976; Prospective Parly Cand. (Lab), Walsall N, 1976. Member Willesden Borough Council, 1959-64; Member London Borough of Brent Council, 1964-66 (Chairman, Children Cttee, 1965-66). Active in local community relations. Contributor to socialist and trade union journals. *Recreations:* walking, cinema, theatre, reading. *Address:* 11A Chichele Mansions, Chichele Road, NW2.

WINNIFRITH, Sir (Alfred) John (Digby), KCB 1959 (CB 1950); *b* 16 Oct. 1908; *s* of Rev. B. T. Winnifrith; *m* 1935, Lesbia Margaret, *d* of late Sir Arthur Cochrane, KCVO; two *s* one *d.* *Educ:* Westminster School; Christ Church, Oxford. Entered Board of Trade, 1932; transferred to HM Treasury, 1934; Third Secretary, HM Treasury, 1951-59; Permanent Secretary, Ministry of Agriculture, Fisheries and Food, 1959-67; Dir-Gen., National Trust, 1968-70. Trustee, British Museum (Natural History), 1967-72; Member: Royal Commn on Environmental Pollution, 1970-73; Commonwealth War Graves Commn, 1970-; Hops Marketing Board, 1970-. Hon. ARCVS 1974. *Address:* Hallhouse Farm, Appledore, Kent. *T:* Appledore 264.

WINNING, Most Rev. Thomas J.; *see* Glasgow, Archbishop of, (RC).

WINNINGTON, Sir Francis Salwey William, 6th Bt, *cr* 1755; Lieut, late Welsh Guards; *b* 24 June 1907; *er s* of late Francis Salwey Winnington, *e s* of 5th Bt and Blanch, *d* of Commander William John Casberd-Boteler, RN; *S* grandfather, 1931; *m* 1944, Anne, *o d* of late Captain Lawrence Drury-Lowe; one *d.* *Educ:* Eton. Served War of 1939-45 (wounded, prisoner). Owns 4700 acres. *Heir: b* Colonel Thomas Foley Churchill Winnington, Grenadier Guards [*b* 16 Aug. 1910; *m* 1944, Lady Betty Marjorie Anson, *er d* of 4th Earl of Lichfield; two *s* two *d*]. *Address:* Brockhill Court, Shelsley Beauchamp, Worcs. *Club:* Cavalry and Guards.
See also Viscount Campden.

WINNINGTON-INGRAM, Prof. Reginald Pepys, FBA 1958; Professor of Greek Language and Literature in the University of London (King's College), 1953-71, now Professor Emeritus; Fellow of King's College, since 1969; *b* 22 Jan. 1904; *s* of late Rear-Admiral and late Mrs C. W. Winnington-Ingram; *m* 1938, Mary, *d* of late Thomas Cousins. *Educ:* Clifton Coll., Trinity Coll., Cambridge. BA 1925; MA 1929; Scholar of Trinity Coll., 1922, Fellow, 1928-32; 1st Class Classical Tripos, Part I, 1923; Waddington Schol., 1924; 1st Class Classical Tripos, Part II, 1925; Charles Oldham Classical Schol., 1926. Asst Lecturer and Lecturer, University of Manchester, 1928, 1930 and 1933; Reader in Classics, University of London (Birkbeck College), 1934-48. Temp. Civil Servant, Ministry of Labour and National Service, 1940-45 (Asst Secretary, 1944); Professor of Classics in the University of London (Westfield Coll.) 1948; J. H. Gray Lectures, Cambridge Univ., 1956. Vis. Prof., Univ. of Texas at Austin, 1971, 1973; Vis. Aurelio Prof., Boston Univ., 1975. President, Society for the Promotion of Hellenic Studies, 1959-62 (Hon. Secretary, 1963). Director, University of London Inst. of Classical Studies, 1964-67. Hon. DLitt Glasgow, 1969. *Publications:* Mode in Ancient Greek Music, 1936; Euripides and Dionysus, 1948. Contributions to classical and musical journals, dictionaries, etc. *Recreation:* music. *Address:* 7 Ladywell Court, East Heath Road, NW3 1AH. *T:* 01-435 6843. *Club:* Athenæum.

WINNIPEG, Archbishop of, (RC), since 1961; **His Eminence Cardinal George Bernard Flahiff,** CC (Canada) 1974; CSB, DD; *b* Paris, Ontario, 26 Oct. 1905; *s* of John James Flahiff and Eleanor (*née* Fleming). *Educ:* St Michael's Coll. (BA); St Basil's Seminary; University of Strasbourg; Ecole des Chartes and Ecole des Hautes Etudes, Paris, 1931-35; Professor of Mediæval History, University of Toronto Graduate School and Pontifical Institute of Mediæval Studies, 1935-54; Superior General, Basilian Fathers, 1954-61; Cardinal, 1969. Member: Sacred Congregation of Religious, Rome, 1969; Société de l'Ecole des Chartes (Paris); American Catholic Historical Society; Mediæval Academy of America. Hon. LLD: St John Fisher Coll., Rochester, NY, 1964; Seattle, 1965; Notre Dame, 1969; Manitoba, 1969; Windsor, 1970; Toronto, 1972; Hon. DD: Winnipeg, 1972; St Francis Xavier, 1973; Laval, 1974; Univ. of St Thomas, Houston, 1977. *Address:* 50 Stafford Street, Winnipeg, Manitoba R3M 2V7, Canada.

WINSER, (Cyril) Legh, CMG 1928; MVO; Private Secretary to Governors of South Australia, 1915-40; *b* 27 Nov. 1884; *s* of Rev. C. J. Winser, MA; *m* 1912, Agnes Dorothy Mayura Langhorne; one *s* two *d. Educ:* Oundle. *Recreations:* cricket, golf. *Address:* Bostock Avenue, Barwon Heads, Victoria 3227, Australia. *Club:* Royal Adelaide Golf (Adelaide).

WINSKILL, Air Commodore Archie Little, CVO; CBE; DFC and Bar; AE; Captain of the Queen's Flight and Extra Equerry to the Queen, since 1968; *b* 24 Jan. 1917; *s* of late Dr Sydney A. Winskill; *m* 1947, Christiane Amilie Pauline, *d* of M. Bailleux, Calais, France; one *s* one *d*. War of 1939-45: Fighter Pilot: Battle of Britain; European and North African Theatres. Post-war: Air Adviser to Belgian Govt; Station Cmdr, RAF Turnhouse and Duxford; Gp Capt. Ops Germany; Air Attaché, Paris; Dir of Public Relations, MoD (RAF). MRAeS. *Recreation:* golf. *Address:* Brook House, North Stoke, Oxon. *T:* Wallingford 37606; (office) The Queen's Flight, Royal Air Force Benson, Oxon. *T:* 01-636 0844. *Club:* Royal Air Force.

WINSTANLEY, family name of **Baron Winstanley.**

WINSTANLEY, Baron *cr* 1975 (Life Peer), of Urmston in Greater Manchester; **Michael Platt Winstanley;** TV and radio broadcaster, author, journalist, columnist, medical practitioner; *b* Nantwich, Cheshire, 27 Aug. 1918; *e s* of late Dr Sydney A. Winstanley; *m* 1st, 1945, Nancy Penney (marr. diss. 1952); one *s*; 2nd, 1955, Joyce M. Woodhouse; one *s* one *d. Educ:* Manchester Grammar Sch.; Manchester Univ. President, Manchester Univ. Union, 1940-41; Captain, Manchester Univ. Cricket Club, 1940-42; Captain Combined English Univs Cricket Team, 1941; Ed. University magazine, 1941-42. MRCS LRCP, 1944. Resident Surgical Officer, Wigan Infirmary, 1945; Surgical Specialist, RAMC, 1946; GP, Urmston, Manchester, 1948-66; MO, Royal Ordnance Factory, Patricroft, 1950-66; Treasury MO and Admiralty Surgeon and Agent, 1953-66; Member Lancs Local Med. Cttee, 1954-66; Member Lancs Exec. Council, 1956-65. Spokesman for Manchester Div. of BMA, 1957-65. Member Liberal Party Council, 1962-66. Contested (L) Stretford, 1964; MP (L) Cheadle, 1966-70; MP (L) Hazel Grove, Feb.-Sept. 1974. Chairman Liberal Party Health Cttee, 1965-66; Liberal Party Spokesman on health, Post Office and broadcasting. TV and radio broadcaster, 1957-; own series on Indep. TV and BBC. Mem., BBC Gen. Adv. Council, 1967-70. *Publications:* Home Truths for Home Doctors, 1963; The Anatomy of First-Aid, 1966; The British Ombudsman, 1970; Tell Me, Doctor, 1972; Know Your Rights, 1975; cricket columnist, Manchester Evening News, 1964-65; weekly personal column, Manchester Evening News, 1970-; articles on current affairs, health, etc. *Recreations:* cricket; golf; playing the bagpipes. *Address:* Heather Hill, Broad Lane, Hale, Cheshire. *T:* 061-980 8608. *Clubs:* National Liberal, Authors'.

WINSTON, Charles Edward, CMG 1974; FRACS; Consulting Surgeon: Sydney Hospital, Australia, and Crown Street (Women's) Hospital, since 1958; Royal South Sydney Hospital, since 1963; *b* 3 June 1898; *s* of James Percival and Annie Elizabeth Winston; *m* 1933; one *d. Educ:* Sydney Boys' High Sch.; Univ. of Sydney. MB, ChM. Director, Bd of Sydney Hosp., 1958, Vice Pres. 1968-; Mem. Council, War Memorial Hosp., Sydney; Med. Mem. Council, ATNA, 1940-; Chm. Cttee, Royal South Sydney Hosp. Rehabil. Cttee, 1963-. *Publications:* papers on surgical problems to MJA. *Recreations:* golf, bowls, fishing. *Address:* 683 New South Head Road, Rose Bay, NSW 2029, Australia. *T:* 371-7728; 135 Macquarie Street, Sydney, NSW 2000, Australia. *T:* 27-1770. *Clubs:* Australian, Royal Sydney Golf (NSW).

WINSTONE, Frank Reece, FRPS; self employed, since 1925; illustrative photographer, since 1937; book designer, publisher and distributor, since 1957; *b* 3 Sept. 1909; *s* of John Ephraim Winstone and Lillian Kate (*née* Reece); *m* 1937, Dorothy Agnes Attrill; one *s. Educ:* Bristol Cathedral Sch. FRPS 1976. Partner, father's menswear business, 1925-36. *Publications:* Bristol As It Was, 1939-1914, 1957 (4th edn 1969); Bristol As It Was, 1914-1900, 1957 (3rd edn 1972); Bristol Today, 1958 (4th edn 1971); Bristol in the 1890's, 1960 (3rd edn 1973); Bristol in the 1940's, 1961 (2nd edn 1970); Bristol in the 1880's, 1962; Bristol As It Was, 1950-1953, 1964 (2nd edn 1970); Bristol As It Was, 1879-1874, 1965 (2nd edn 1968); Bristol As It Was, 1874-1866, 1966 (2nd edn 1971); Bristol As It Was, 1866-1860, 1967 (2nd edn 1972); Bristol Fashion, 1968; Bristol in the 1850's, 1968; Bristol As It Was, 1953-1956, 1969; Bristol's Earliest Photographs, 1970 (2nd edn 1975); Bristol Tradition, 1970; Bristol in the 1920's, 1971 (2nd edn 1977); Bristol As It Was, 1956-1959, 1972; Bristol Blitzed, 1973 (2nd edn 1976); Bristol Trams, 1974; Bristol As It Was, 1913-1921, 1976; (ed) Bristol's History: Vol. 1, 1966 (2nd edn 1969); Vol. 2, 1975; (ed) Miss Ann Green, 1974; (ed) History of Bristol's Suburbs, 1977. *Recreations:* local preservation societies, motoring, the gramophone, serious broadcast programmes, reading. *Address:* 23 Hyland Grove, Henbury Hill, Bristol 9. *T:* Bristol 503646.

WINT, Dr Arthur Stanley, CD 1973; MBE 1954; FRCS; Jamaican High Commissioner in the United Kingdom, since 1974; *b* 25 May 1920; *s* of John Samuel Wint and Hilda Wint; *m* 1949, Norma Wint (*née* Marsh); three *d. Educ:* Calabar High School; Excelsior College, Jamaica; St Bartholomew's Medical School. MB BS; FRCS. Served RAF, 1942-47; Medical School, 1947-53. Medical Practitioner, 1953-73. FICS 1972; DMJ (Clin), 1975. *Recreations:* badminton, swimming, walking. *Address:* 50 St James's Street, SW1. *T:* 01-499 8600. *Club:* Polytechnic Harriers.

WINTER, Rt. Rev. Allen Ernest; *b* 8 Dec. 1903; *o s* of Ernest Thomas and Margaret Winter, Malvern, Vic; *m* 1939, Eunice Eleanor, 3rd *d* of Albert and Eleanor Sambell; three *s* two *d. Educ:* Melbourne C of E Grammar School; Trinity Coll., Univ. of Melbourne (BA 1926, MA 1928); University Coll., Oxford (BA 1932, MA 1951); Australian College of Theology (ThL 1927, ThD 1951 iur. dig.). Deacon, 1927, priest, 1928, Melbourne; Curate, Christ Church, S Yarra, 1927-29; on leave, Oxford, 1929-32; Curate, St James', Ivanhoe, 1932-35; Minister of Sunshine, 1935-39; Incumbent of St Luke's, Brighton, Melb., 1939-48; Chaplain, AIF, 1942-46; Incumbent of Christ Church, Essendon, 1948-49; Canon-Residentiary and Rector of All Saints' Cathedral, Bathurst, 1949-51; Bishop of St Arnaud, 1951-73; Chaplain, St John's Coll., Morpeth, NSW, 1974. *Address:* Lis Escop, 62 Patterson Street, Middle Park, Vic 3206, Australia. *T:* 03-94-2055.

WINTER, Frederick Thomas, CBE 1963; racehorse trainer since 1964; *b* 20 Sept. 1926; *s* of Frederick Neville Winter and Ann (*née* Flanagan); *m* 1956, Diana Pearson; three *d* (incl. twins). *Educ:* Ewell Castle. Served as Lieut, 6th Bn Para. Regt, 1944-47. Jockey, Flat, 1939-42; National Hunt jockey, 1947-64. *Recreations:* golf, gardening. *Address:* Uplands, Lambourn, Berks. *T:* Lambourn 71438.

WINTER, Keith, Novelist and Dramatist; *b* 22 Oct. 1906; *s* of Thomas Winter, Professor of Agriculture, Bangor University, N Wales, and Margaret Baron. *Educ:* Berkhamsted Sch.; Lincoln Coll., Oxford. After leaving school spent six months in the American Express Co., London; then became a preparatory school master for two and a half years; went to Oxford and published first novel while still there; has been writing ever since. *Publications: novels:* Other Man's Saucer; The Rats of Norway; Impassioned Pygmies; *plays:* The Rats of Norway; Ringmaster; The Shining Hour; Worse Things happen at Sea; Old Music; Weights and Measures; We at the Cross Roads; Miss Hallelujah; The Passionate Men; Round the Corner; *Musicals:* Nell; Say When! (with Arnold Goland); Pegasus (with Arnold Goland); *Films:* The Red Shoes, Above Suspicion, Devotion, Uncle Harry. *Recreations:* tennis, swimming, travel. *Address:* c/o Jo Stewart, International Creative Management, 40 West 57th Street, New York, NY 10019, USA.

WINTERBOTHAM, Group Captain Frederick William, CBE 1943; author; *b* 16 April 1897; *s* of late F. Winterbotham, Painswick, Gloucestershire; *m* 1st, 1921; one *s* two *d*; *m* 1947; one *d. Educ:* Charterhouse; Christ Church, Oxon. Royal Gloucestershire Hussars, 1915; RFC and RAF, 1916-19; Pedigree Stock Breeder, 1920-29; Air Staff and Foreign Office, 1929-45; BOAC 1945-48. *Publications:* Secret and Personal, 1969; The Ultra Secret, 1974. *Address:* Frittiscombe, Chillington, Kingsbridge, S Devon. *T:* Torcross 281. *Club:* Royal Air Force.

WINTERBOTTOM, family name of **Baron Winterbottom.**

WINTERBOTTOM, Baron, *cr* 1965 (Life Peer); **Ian Winterbottom;** a Lord in Waiting (Government Whip), since Oct. 1974; *b* 6 April 1913; *s* of G. H. Winterbottom, Horton House, Northants; *m*; three *s* one *d. Educ:* Charterhouse; Clare Coll., Cambridge. Worked in Textile and Engineering Trades in Manchester, Derby and Germany. Captain Royal Horse Guards; served War of 1939-45, NW European Campaign; ADC and subsequently Personal Assistant to Regional Commissioner, Hamburg, 1946-49. MP (Lab) Nottingham Central, 1950-55; Parly Under Sec. of State, Royal Navy, MoD, 1966-67; Parly Sec., MPBW, 1967-68; Parly Under-Sec. of State, RAF, MoD, 1968-70. Chm., Venesta International, 1972-74. *Address:* Woodland Place, St Briavels, near Lydney, Glos.

WINTERBOTTOM, Walter, CBE 1972 (OBE 1963); Director, The Sports Council, 1965-78; *b* 31 March 1913; *s* of James

Winterbottom and Frances Holt; *m* 1942, Ann Richards; one *s* two *d. Educ:* Chester Coll. of Educn; Carnegie Coll. of Physical Educn. Schoolmaster, Oldham; Lectr, Carnegie Coll. of Phys. Educn; Wing Comdr, RAF, 1939-45; Dir of Coaching and Manager of England Team, Football Assoc., 1946-62; Gen. Sec., Central Council of Physical Recreation, 1963-72. *Publications:* technical, on association football. *Recreations:* association football, cricket, squash rackets. *Address:* Shockleigh House, Holland Walk, Stanmore, Mddx. *T:* 01-954 1277. *Club:* Royal Automobile.

WINTERSGILL, Dr William; Senior Principal Medical Officer, Department of Health and Social Security (Medical Group OS3), since 1977; *b* 20 Dec. 1922; *s* of Fred Wintersgill and May Wintersgill; *m* 1952, Iris May Holland; three *d. Educ:* Barnsley Holgate Grammar Sch.; Leeds Medical Sch., Univ. of Leeds (MB, ChB). MRCGP, MFCM. House Surgeon, 1948, and Registrar, 1948-49, Pontefract Infirmary; Principal, Gen. Practice, Snaith, Yorks, 1950-66; Dept of Health and Social Security (formerly Min. of Health): Reg. MO, 1967-70; SMO, 1970-72; PMO, 1972-76; SPMO 1976. *Recreations:* gardening, antique collecting (silver especially), playing the piano, painting, old buildings. *Address:* Juniper Hill, Stoatley Rise, Haslemere, Surrey. *T:* Haslemere 51042.

WINTERTON, 7th Earl, *cr* 1766 (Ireland); **Robert Chad Turnour;** Baron Winterton, *cr* 1761 (Ireland); Viscount Turnour, 1766 (Ireland); Royal Canadian Air Force; *b* 13 Sept. 1915; *s* of Cecil Turnour (*d* 1953), Saskatoon, Sask.; *S* kinsman, 1962; *m* 1st, 1941, Kathleen Ella (*d* 1969), *d* of D. B. Whyte; 2nd, 1971, Marion Eleanor, *d* of late Arthur Phillips. *Educ:* Nutana Coll., Canada. Joined RCAF, 1940; with Canadian NATO Force Sqdn, Sardinia, 1957-58. *Heir: b* Noel Cecil Turnour, DFM, CD [*b* 11 Dec. 1919; *m* 1941, Evelyn Isobel, *d* of J. C. A. Oulton; three *s.* Formerly Flt Lieut, RCAF]. *Address:* 1326 55th Street, Delta, BC, Canada.

WINTERTON, Maj.-Gen. Sir John; *see* Winterton, Maj.-Gen. Sir (Thomas) John.

WINTERTON, Nicholas Raymond; MP (C) Macclesfield since Sept. 1971; *b* 31 March 1938; *o s* of late N. H. Winterton, Lysways House, Longdon Green, near Rugeley, Staffs; *m* 1960, Jane Ann, *e d* of J. R. Hodgson, Langley Gorse, Fox Hollies Road, Walmley, Sutton Coldfield, Warwicks; two *s* one *d. Educ:* Bilton Grange Prep. Sch.; Rugby Sch. Commnd 14th/20th King's Hussars, 1957-59. Sales Exec. Trainee, Shell-Mex and BP Ltd, 1959-60; Sales and Gen. Manager, Stevens and Hodgson Ltd, Birmingham (Co. engaged in sale and hire of construction equipment), 1960-71. Chairman: CPC Cttee, Meriden Cons. Assoc., 1966-68; Midland Branch, Contractors Mech. Plant Engrs Assoc., 1968-69. Member: W Midlands Cons. Council, 1966-69, 1971-72; Central Council, Nat. Union of Cons. and Unionist Assocs, 1971-72. Contested (C) Newcastle-under-Lyme, Oct. 1969, 1970; Jt Vice-Chm., Anglo Danish Parly Gp; Vice-Chm., All Party Parly Textile Gp; Jt Sec., Cons. Parly Agric. Cttee; Jt Sec., Cons. Parly Educn Cttee; Chm., British-Sri Lanka Parly Gp, 1976 and 1977. County Councillor, Atherstone Div. Warwickshire CC, 1967-72. President: Macclesfield Boys Club; Poynton Community Centre; N Staffs Polytechnic Conservative Assoc.; Wigan Young Conservatives; Vice-President: NW Area Young Conservative Assoc.; Macclesfield and Congleton District Scout Council; Cheshire Scout Assoc.; Hon. Mem., Macclesfield Lions Club; Patron, Macclesfield and District Sheep Dog Trials Assoc. *Recreations:* Rugby football, hockey, tennis, swimming, horse riding. *Address:* Whitehall Farm, Mow Lane, Newbold Astbury, Congleton, Cheshire.

WINTERTON, Maj.-Gen. Sir (Thomas) John (Willoughby), KCB 1955 (CB 1946); KCMG 1950; CBE 1942 (OBE 1940); DL; retired; *b* 13 April 1898; *e s* of H. J. C. Winterton, Lichfield, Staffs; *m* 1921, Helen (*d* 1976), *d* of late H. Shepherd Cross, Hamels Park, Herts; three *s. Educ:* Oundle; RMA, Woolwich. Served European War, 1917-18; Burma, 1930-32; War of 1939-45; Dep. Comr Allied Commission for Austria, 1945-49; British High Commissioner and C-in-C in Austria, 1950; Military Governor and Commander, British/US Zone Free Territory of Trieste, 1951-54, retired Jan. 1955. ADC to the King, 1948-49. Colonel Comdt 1st Green Jackets 43rd and 52nd (formerly the Oxfordshire and Buckinghamshire Light Infantry), 1955-60. Formerly President, S Berks Conservative and Unionist Assoc. (Chairman, 1958-65). Formerly Member St John Council for Berkshire (Chairman, 1962-64); a Vice-Pres., Royal Humane Society, 1973- (Cttee Mem., 1962-73). DL, Berkshire, 1966. CStJ 1969. *Address:* Craven Lodge, Speen, Newbury, Berks. *T:* Newbury 40525. *Club:* Army and Navy.

WINTERTON, William Ralph, FRCS, FRCOG; Consultant Gynaecological Surgeon Emeritus, Middlesex Hospital; Surgeon, Hospital for Women, Soho Square; Obstetric Surgeon, Queen Charlotte's Maternity Hospital; Archivist to the Middlesex Hospital; *b* 24 June 1905; *o s* of late Rev. William Charles Winterton; *m* 1934, Kathleen Margaret, 2nd *d* of late Rev. D. Marsden; two *s* two *d. Educ:* Marlborough Coll.; Gonville and Caius Coll., Cambridge; Middlesex Hospital. MA; MB, BChir. House appointments, Middlesex Hospital, 1929-31; Gynæcological Registrar, Middlesex Hospital, 1934-36. Examr in Obstetrics to Universities of Cambridge, London, Glasgow, Ibadan, Dar-es-Salaam, and to Royal College of Obstetricians and Gynæcologists. Fellow of the Royal Society of Medicine, President Obstetric Section, 1960-61. Governor: Bancroft's Sch., Woodford Green, 1960-75; Howell's Sch., Denbigh (Vice-Chairman). Court of Assistants of the Drapers' Company (Master, 1964-65). Past President, Guild of Med. Bellringers. *Publications:* Aids to Gynæcology; (jointly) Queen Charlotte's Textbook of Obstetrics. Contributions to Medical Journals. *Recreations:* fishing, gardening, change ringing, and Do-it-yourself. *Address:* 95 Harley Street, W1N 1DF. *T:* 01-580 3733; 26 De Walden Street, W1; Youngloves, Rushden, Herts SG9 0SP. *T:* Broadfield 217.

WINTON, Frank Robert, MA, MD Cambridge, DSc London; FInstBiol, FIST; Consultant, May and Baker Ltd, etc; Emeritus Professor of Pharmacology, University of London, 1961; *b* 1894; *m* 1922, Bessie Rawlins; one *d. Educ:* Oundle Sch.; Clare Coll., Cambridge; St Bartholomew's and University College Hospitals. Assistant, Dept of Pharmacology, University College, London, 1924; Lecturer, Dept of Physiology, University College, London, 1927; Beit Memorial Research Fellow; Lecturer in Physiology, University of Cambridge, 1931; Reader in Physiology, University of Cambridge, 1933; Professor of Pharmacology, University College, London, 1938-61. Hon. Member, Harvey Society of New York. Hon. DEd CNAA, 1976. *Publications:* (joint) Human Physiology, 1930, 6th edn, 1968; Modern Views on the Secretion of Urine (ed F. R. Winton), 1956; Scientific Papers in Journal of Physiology, and other journals on the kidney, plain muscle, etc. *Recreations:* chamber music, wine. *Address:* 32 Arkwright Road, NW3 6BH. *T:* 01-435 2412.

WINTON, Walter; Keeper Department of Electrical Engineering, Telecommunications and Loan Circulation, Science Museum, since 1976; *b* 15 May 1917; *m* 1942, Dorothy Rickard; two *s* one *d . Educ:* Glossop Grammar Sch.; Manchester Univ. (BSc and Teacher's Diploma). Royal Ordnance Factories, Chemist, 1940-45. Taught Science, Harrow County and Greenford, 1945-50; Assistant and Deputy Keeper, Science Museum, 1950-67; Keeper: Dept of Loan Circulation, Mining and Marine Technol., 1968-73; Dept of Museum Services, 1973; Dept of Mechanical and Civil Engrg and Loan Circulation, 1973-76. *Publications:* contrib. to journals. *Recreations:* Scottish dancing, breeding waterfowl. *Address:* The Old Workhouse, Harefield, Middlesex. *T:* 01-420 2103.

WINTOUR, Charles Vere, MBE 1945; Chairman, Evening Standard, since 1968; Managing Director, Daily Express, since 1977; Director, Beaverbrook Newspapers Ltd, since 1964; *b* 18 May 1917; *s* of late Maj.-Gen. F. Wintour, CB, CBE; *m* 1940, Eleanor Trego Baker, *er d* of Prof. R. J. Baker, Harvard Univ.; two *s* two *d* (and one *s* decd). *Educ:* Oundle Sch.; Peterhouse, Cambridge. BA 1939; MA 1946. Royal Norfolk Regt, 1940; GSO2 Headquarters of Chief of Staff to the Supreme Allied Commander (Designate) and SHAEF, 1943-45 (despatches). Joined Evening Standard, 1946; Political Editor, Evening Standard, 1952; Assistant Editor, Sunday Express, 1952-54; Deputy Editor, Evening Standard, 1954-57; Managing Editor, Daily Express, 1957-59; Editor, Evening Standard, 1959-76. Croix de Guerre (France) 1945; Bronze Star (US) 1945. *Publication:* Pressures on the Press, 1972. *Recreations:* theatre-going, reading newspapers. *Address:* 27 Gerrard Road, N1 8AY.

WINTRINGHAM, Col John Workman, CBE 1943; MC; DL, JP; *b* 24 Sept. 1894; *s* of late John Fildes Wintringham, LLB, and of late Eliza Mapson; *m* 1920, Caroline Howe; two *s* one *d. Educ:* Mill Hill Sch. Lincs Yeomanry, 1913-19, Egypt and Palestine (MC, despatches); retired as Hon. Colonel. Asst County Commissioner, Lincs Boy Scouts, 1934; HG, 1940, Zone Commander, 1941, Lincs. JP Lindsey (Lincs) 1929; DL Lincs 1944. *Recreation:* Boy Scouts Association. *Address:* 63 Humberstone Avenue, Humberstone DN36 45R. *T:* Grimsby 812134.

WIPPELL, Rev. Canon John Cecil, MA; BD; Hon. DD; Chaplain to Deaconess House, Farquharson House and Nuttall Hospital, 1957-63; Warden, St Peter's Theological College, West

Indies, 1961-63 (Tutor, 1956-59); retired; *b* 6 June 1883; *s* of late William Joseph Wippell. *Educ:* Exeter Sch. (Oxford and Cambridge Higher Certificate); Exeter Coll., Oxford (2nd Class Hons Theology); BD (London) Pass 1911, 1st Class Hons, 1913. Tutor of St Boniface Coll., Warminster, 1905-11; Deacon, 1907; Priest, 1908; Assistant Curate of Warminster, 1907-10; Prof. of Theology, Codrington Coll., Barbados, 1911-18; Principal of Codrington Coll., 1918-45; Principal Rawle Training Institute for Elementary Teachers; Chaplain of SPG Estates, Barbados; CF to 4 BWI Regt, France, 1917-18; Hon. CF; Examining Chaplain to the Bishop of Barbados, 1918-45, and to the Bishop of the Windward Islands; Canon of Barbados, 1932. General License, Diocese of Jamaica, 1945; Canon Emeritus of Barbados, 1946; Rector of Brown's Town, 1947-49; Rector of St Michael's, Kingston, 1949-52; Asst Master, Kingston Coll., 1952-53; Asst Master and Chaplain, Jamaica Coll., 1954-56. Hon. Chaplain to Univ. of WI, 1960-; Lectr, United Theol Coll. of WI, 1967-70. Hon. DD Trinity Coll., Toronto, 1934; Hon. LLD Univ. of West Indies, 1972. Coronation Medal, 1937. *Address:* 16 Phoenix Avenue, Kingston 10, Jamaica.

WIRKKALA, Tapio; Knight of White Rose of Finland; designer; *b* 2 June 1915; *s* of Ilmari Wirkkala, artist, and Selma Wirkkala; *m* 1945, Rut Bryk, artist; one *s* one *d. Educ:* Industrial Art Inst., Helsinki. Mil. rank of Lt, Finnish Army. Glass designer for Karhula-Iittala, Finland, 1947-; designer for firms in Finland and abroad, 1955-. Art director, Industrial Art Inst., Helsinki, 1951-54. *One-man exhibitions:* Oslo, 1952; England, Germany, Switzerland, Italy, 1962-64; Czechoslovakia, 1967-, etc. Architect of numerous exhibns (or sections of these) abroad, including Ambulatory Finnish Art and Industrial Arts Exhibn, Gt Brit., 1952. *Works included in:* Museum of Modern Art and Metropolitan Museum of Art, New York; Victoria and Albert Museum, London; Kunstgewerbemuseum, Zürich; National Museum, Stockholm; Nordenfjellske Museum, Trondheim; Stedelijk Mus., Amsterdam; Die Neue Sammlung, München; Nat. Gall. of Vic., Melbourne; Mus. Universitaria de Ciencias y Arte, Mexico City. Cross of Freedom (4th class; twice, once with oak leaves), Finland; Pro Finlandia Medal. SIA Medal, 1958; Cultural Foundn of Finland Honorary Prize, 1968; 7 Grande Premios at Milan Triennale and various other prizes and medals for design (ceramics, glass, wood, bank notes, stamps, etc); Academician, Helsinki, 1972; Hon. RDI (GB), 1964, Hon. Dr RCA 1971, and other foreign awards. *Recreation:* fishing. *Address:* Itäranta 24, Tapiola, Finland. *T:* 46 44 14.

WISBECH, Archdeacon of; *see* Fox, Ven. B. G. B.

WISDOM, Prof. Arthur John Terence Dibben, MA; Professor of Philosophy, University of Oregon, 1968-72; Fellow of Trinity College, Cambridge; *b* 1904; *s* of Rev. H. C. Wisdom and Edith S. Wisdom. *Educ:* Aldeburgh Lodge School; Fitzwilliam House, Cambridge. BA 1924; MA 1934. Lecturer in Moral Sciences, Trinity Coll., Cambridge; Prof. of Philosophy, Cambridge Univ., 1952-68. *Publications:* Other Minds, 1952; Philosophy and Psycho-Analysis, 1952; Paradox and Discovery, 1966. Contributions to Mind and to Proceedings of the Aristotelian Society. *Address:* 154 Stanley Road, Cambridge.

WISDOM, Norman; Actor/Comedian; *b* 4 Feb. 1925; has starred regularly in West End, since 1952. First film in 1953 (winning an Academy Award) since which has starred in 19 major films in both England and America; two Broadway awards for stage musical, Walking Happy; numerous Royal Performances, film and stage. *Recreations:* all sports. *Address:* c/o 235 Regent Street, W1. *Club:* Eccentric.

WISE, family name of **Baron Wise.**

WISE, 2nd Baron, *cr* 1951, of King's Lynn; **John Clayton Wise;** farmer; *b* 11 June 1923; *s* of 1st Baron Wise and of Kate Elizabeth, *e d* of late John Michael Sturgeon; *S* father, 1968; *m* 1946, Margaret Annie, *d* of Frederick Victor Snead, Banbury; two *s. Heir:* *s* Hon. Christopher John Clayton Wise, BSc Hons, *b* 19 March 1949. *Address:* Ramsley Farm, North Elmham, Norfolk. *Club:* Farmers'.

WISE, Mrs Audrey; MP (Lab) Coventry South West since Feb. 1974; *d* of George and Elsie Crawford Brown; *m* John Wise; one *s* one *d.* Shorthand typist. *Publications:* Women and the Struggle for Workers' Control, 1973; Eyewitness in Revolutionary Portugal, 1975. *Recreations:* family life, camping, walking, reading. *Address:* 99 Wolverhampton Road, Stafford. *T:* Stafford 59490.

WISE, Rear-Adm. Cyril Hubert Surtees, CB; MBE; Voluntary Services Organiser, St Stephen's Hospital, Fulham; *b* 20 Feb. 1913; *s* of H. P. S. Wise; *m* 1948, Margaret Isobel Phelps

McKenzie; one *s. Educ:* RN College, Dartmouth. Student RN Staff College, 1953; Imperial Defence College, 1958; Captain, HMS Collingwood, 1963-65; Inspector-Gen., Fleet Maintenance, and Chief Staff Officer (Technical), Western Fleet, 1965-67, retd. Principal, Technical Training Inst., Royal Saudi Air Force, Dhahran, 1968-70; Gen. Manager, Airwork Services Ltd, Dhahran, 1970. *Address:* c/o National Westminster Bank Ltd, Broadway, Chesham, Bucks. *Club:* Army and Navy.

WISE, Ernie; *see* Wiseman, Ernest.

WISE, Sir John (Humphrey), KCMG 1943; CBE 1939; Indian Civil Service, retired; *b* 11 March 1890; *s* of late William Wise, Ashbourne, Derbyshire, and St Servan, France; *m* 1918, Edith Frances Anne, *d* of late Lt-Col L. G. Fischer, IMS; one *s* (one *d* decd). *Educ:* Christ's Hospital; University College, Oxford. Entered ICS, 1914; IARO, 1915-19, served in India, Mesopotamia, Egypt and Palestine (92nd Punjabis) (despatches); Deputy Commissioner, Toungoo, 1924; Secretary Public Service Commission, India, 1926; Deputy Commissioner, Pegu, 1931; Secretary to Govt of Burma, 1932-39; Member of Burma Railway Board, 1937; Controller of Supplies, Burma, 1939; Counsellor to Governor of Burma, 1940-46; Adviser to the Secretary of State for Burma, 1946-47; Leader of British Mission to Brazil, 1948; Deputy Chairman, Raw Cotton Commission, 1949-53. *Recreations:* chess, walking. *Address:* 5 Cressy House, Queen's Ride, SW13. *T:* 01-789 3745. *Club:* Roehampton.

WISE, Prof. Michael John, MC 1945; PhD; FRGS; Professor of Geography in the University of London, at the London School of Economics and Political Science, since 1958; *b* Stafford, 17 August 1918; *s* of Harry Cuthbert and Sarah Evelyn Wise; *m* 1942, Barbara Mary, *d* of C. L. Hodgetts, Wolverhampton; one *s* one *d. Educ:* Saltley Grammar School, Birmingham; University of Birmingham. BA (Hons Geography) Birmingham, and Mercator Prize in Geography, 1939; PhD Birmingham, 1951. Served War, Royal Artillery, 80th LAA Regt, 1941-44, 5th Bn The Northamptonshire Regt, 1944-46, in Middle East and Italy; commissioned, 1941, Major, 1944. Assistant Lecturer, Univ. of Birmingham, 1946-48, Lecturer in Geography, 1948-51; Lecturer in Geography, London School of Economics, 1951-54; Sir Ernest Cassel Reader in Economic Geography, 1954-58. Chm., Departmental Cttee of Inquiry into Statutory Smallholdings, 1963-67; Mem., Dept of the Environment Adv. Cttee on Landscape Treatment of Trunk Roads, 1971-. Mem., UGC for Hong Kong, 1966-73. Recorder, Sect. E, Brit. Assoc. for Advancement of Science, 1955-60 (Pres., 1965); President: Inst. of British Geographers, 1974; IGU, 1976- (Vice-Pres., 1968-76); Geographical Assoc., 1976-77 (Hon. Treasurer, 1967-76); Mem., SSRC, 1976-; Mem. Council and Chm., Exec. Cttee, Assoc. of Agriculture; Hon. Sec., RGS, 1963-73, Vice-Pres., 1975-. Governor, Birkbeck Coll., 1968-. Erskine Fellow, Univ. of Canterbury, NZ, 1970. Hon. Life Mem., Univ. of London Union, 1977. Received Gill Memorial award of RGS, 1958; RGS Founder's Medal, 1977. *Publications:* Hon. Editor, Birmingham and its Regional Setting, 1951; A Pictorial Geography of the West Midlands, 1958; numerous articles on economic and urban geography. *Recreation:* music. *Address:* 45 Oakleigh Avenue, N20. *T:* 01-445 6057. *Club:* Athenæum.

WISEMAN, C. L., MA; Headmaster, Queen's College, Taunton, 1926-53; retired, 1953; *b* 20 April 1893; *s* of late Rev. F. L. Wiseman and Elsie Daniel; *m* 1946, Christine Irene, *d* of Sir William Savage, MD; *m* 1972, Patricia Joan Wragge, *d* of Prebendary R. Wragge-Morley. *Educ:* King Edward's School, Birmingham; Peterhouse, Cambridge (Scholar). Instructor Lt RN, 1915-19; Senior Mathematical Master, Kingswood School, Bath, 1921-26. *Recreation:* music. *Address:* 11 Park Lane, Milford-on-Sea, Lymington, Hants.

WISEMAN, Gen. Clarence D., OC 1976; General of the Salvation Army, 1974-77; *b* Moreton's Harbour, Newfoundland; *m* Janet Kelly; one *s* one *d. Educ:* Salvation Army Officers Training Coll., Toronto, Canada (grad.). In comd chief Salvation Army evangelistic centres in Canada. Served overseas, War of 1939-45, as Chaplain, Canadian Forces; after 3 yrs directed all Salvation Army Welfare Services on various fighting fronts. After the war held some senior admin. posts in Canada. Transferred to E Africa to direct work of SA in Kenya, Tanzania and Uganda, 1960. Principal, Internat. Training Coll., London, Eng., 1962; Mem., General's Adv. Council at National Headquarters, Toronto; Head of Salvation Army in Canada and Bermuda, 1967-74. Holds hon. doctorates. *Address:* 170 Oakmeadow Boulevard, Scarborough, Ontario M1E 4H3, Canada.

WISEMAN, Prof. Donald John, OBE 1943; DLit; FBA 1966; FSA; Professor of Assyriology in the University of London since

1961; b 25 Oct. 1918; s of late Air Cdre Percy John Wiseman, CBE, RAF; m 1948, Mary Catherine, d of P. O. Ruoff; three d. Educ: Dulwich College; King's College, London. BA (London); AKC, McCaul Hebrew Prize, 1939. Served War of 1939-45, in RAFVR. Ops, 11 Fighter Group, 1939-41; Chief Intelligence Officer, Mediterranean Allied Tactical Air Forces with Rank of Group Capt., 1942-45. Heap Exhibitioner in Oriental Languages, Wadham Coll., Oxford, 1945-47; MA 1949. Asst Keeper, Dept of Egyptian and Assyrian, later Western Asiatic, Antiquities, British Museum, 1948-61. Epigraphist on archæological excavations at Nimrud, Harran, Rimah; Jt Dir of British School of Archæology in Iraq, 1961-65, Chm. 1970-. Corresp. Mem., German Archæological Inst., 1961. Ed. of Journal IRAQ, 1953-; Joint Ed. of Reallexion der Assyriologie, 1959-. Bronze Star (USA), 1944. Publications: The Alalakh Tablets, 1953; Chronicles of Chaldaean Kings, 1956; Cuneiform Texts from Cappadocian Tablets in the British Museum, V, 1956; Cylinder-Seals of Western Asia, 1958; Vassal-Treaties of Esarhaddon, 1958; Illustrations from Biblical Archæology, 1958; Catalogue of Western Asiatic Seals in the British Museum, 1963; Peoples of Old Testament Times, 1973; contrib. to journals. Address: 16 Downs Side, Sutton, Surrey SM2 7EQ. T: 01-642 4805.

WISEMAN, Ernest, OBE 1976; (Ernie Wise); b 27 Nov. 1925; s of Harry and Connie Wiseman; m 1953, Doreen Blyth. Educ: Council School. Career in show business: radio, variety, TV, films. First double act (with E. Morecambe), at Empire Theatre, Liverpool, 1941; first broadcast, 1943; BBC and ITV television series, 1955- (Soc. of Film and Television Arts Best Light Entertainment Award, 1973). Awards: SFTA, 1963, 1971, 1972, 1973; Silver Heart, 1964; Water Rats, 1970; Radio Industries, 1971, 1972; Sun Newspaper, 1973; Sun, 1974; Water Rats Distinguished Services, 1974. Films: The Intelligence Men, 1964; That Riviera Touch, 1965; The Magnificent Two, 1966. Publications: (with E. Morecambe) Eric and Ernie: an autobiography of Morecambe and Wise, 1973; Scripts of Morecambe and Wise, 1974. Recreation: boating. Address: BBC, London W1A 1AA.

WISEMAN, Sir John William, 11th Bt, cr 1628; b 16 March 1957; o s of Sir William George Eden Wiseman, 10th Bt, and Joan Mary, d of late Arthur Phelps, Harrow; S father, 1962. Educ: Millfield Sch.; Univ. of Hartford, Conn, USA. Heir: kinsman Thomas Alan Wiseman [b 8 July 1921; m 1946, Hildemarie Domnik; (one s one d decd)]. Address: 32 Victoria Road, W8.

WISHART, Maureen; see Lehane, M.

WISTRICH, Ernest, CBE 1973; Director, European Movement (British Council), since 1969; b 22 May 1923; s of Dr Arthur and Mrs Eva Wistrich; m 1950, Enid Barbara (née Heiber); one s one d (and one s decd). Educ: Poland; University Tutorial Coll., London. Served in RAF, 1942-46; Timber Merchant, 1946-67; Dir, Britain in Europe, 1967-69; Councillor, Hampstead Borough Council, 1959-65; Camden Borough Council, Alderman 1964-71, Councillor 1971-74; Chm., Camden Cttee for Community Relations, 1964-68; Mem., Skeffington Cttee on Public Participation in Planning, 1968-69. Contested (Lab): Isle of Thanet, 1964; Hendon North, 1966. Editor of various jls. Publications: contrib. Into Europe, Facts, New Europe and other jls. Recreations: music, walking, ski-ing. Address: 37B Gayton Road, NW3. T: 01-435 8796. Club: National Liberal.

WITHERS, Googie, (Mrs John McCallum); Actress since 1932; b Karachi, India, 12 March 1917; d of late Captain E. C. Withers, CBE, CIE, RIM, and late Lizette Catherine Wilhelmina van Wageningen; m 1948, John Neil McCallum, qv; one s two d. Educ: Fredville Park, Nonnington, Kent; Convent of the Holy Family, Kensington. Started as dancer in Musical Comedy. First film contract at age of 17; has acted in over 50 pictures, starring in 30. Films include: One of our Aircraft is Missing; The Silver Fleet; On Approval; Loves of Joanna Godden; It Always Rains on Sunday; White Corridors; Nickel Queen. Plays include: They Came to a City; Private Lives; Winter Journey; The Deep Blue Sea; Waiting for Gillian; Janus. Stratford on Avon Season, 1958: Beatrice in Much Ado About Nothing; Gertrude in Hamlet. The Complaisant Lover, New York, 1962; Exit the King, London, 1963; Getting Married, Strand, 1967; Madame Renevsky in The Cherry Orchard, Mrs Cheveley in An Ideal Husband, 1972; Lady Kitty in The Circle, Chichester Festival Theatre, 1976, Haymarket, 1977. Tours: 1959, Australia and NZ with: Roar Like a Dove, The Constant Wife and Woman in a Dressing Gown; 1964, excerpts Shakespeare (Kate, Margaret of Anjou, Beatrice, Portia, Rosalind, Cleopatra); 1965, Australia and NZ, with Beekman Place; 1968, Australia, with Relatively Speaking; 1969-70, Australia and NZ, with Plaza Suite. TV appearances in

drama including series Within These Walls, 1974-76 (Best Actress of the Year, 1974); also Last Year's Confetti, Court Circular, 1971; Knightsbridge, 1972; The Cherry Orchard, 1973. Recreations: music, travel, reading, interior decorating. Address: 1740 Pittwater Road, Bay View, NSW 2104, Australia; c/o Coutts & Co., 440 Strand, WC2.

WITHERS, John Keppel Ingold D.; see Douglas-Withers.

WITHERS, Senator Rt. Hon. Reginald (Greive), PC 1977; Vice-President of Executive Council, Leader of Government in Senate, and Minister for Administrative Services, Government of Australia, since 1975; Senator (L) for Western Australia, since 1966; b 26 Oct. 1924; s of late F. J. Withers and I. L. Greive; m 1953, Shirley Lloyd-Jones; two s one d. Educ: Banbury; Univ. of WA (LLB). Barrister-at-law 1953. Served War, RAN, 1942-46. Councillor, Bunbury Municipal Council, 1954-56; Mem., Bunbury Diocesan Council, 1958-59, Treasurer, 1961-68. State Vice-Pres., Liberal and Country League of WA, 1958-61, State Pres., 1961-65; Mem., Federal Exec. of Liberal Party, 1961-65; Fed. Vice-Pres., Liberal Party, 1962-65. Govt Whip in Senate, 1969-71; Leader of Opposition in Senate, 1972-75; Special Minister of State, Minister for Capital Territory, Minister for Media, and Minister for Tourism and Recreation, Nov.-Dec. 1975. Sec., SW Law Soc., 1955-68. Recreations: swimming, reading, painting. Address: 23 Malcolm Street, West Perth, WA 6005, Australia. T: 092-214608.

WITHERS, Rupert Alfred; Director, Dalgety Ltd (Deputy Chairman and Managing Director, 1969-71; Chairman, 1972-77; b 29 Oct. 1913; o s of late Herbert Withers, FRAM and Marguerite (née Elzy); m; three d. Educ: University College School. Fellow Institute of Chartered Accountants, 1938. Secretary and Chief Accountant, Gloster Aircraft Co. Ltd, 1940-44; a Senior Partner of Urwick Orr & Partners Ltd until 1959; Man. Dir, Ilford Ltd, 1959-64; Chm. and Chief Executive, 1964-68. Mem. Council, Cheltenham Coll. 1964. Recreations: music, books, theatre, golf. Address: Flat 24, 100 Lancaster Gate, W2 3NY. T: 01-262 7141; Epwell Mill Cottage, Banbury, Oxon. T: Swalcliffe 327. Clubs: Savile, Buck's.

WITHY, George; Assistant Editor (night), Liverpool Echo, since 1972; b Birkenhead, 15 May 1924; er s of George Withy and Alma Elizabeth Withy (née Stankley); m 1950, Dorothy Betty, e c of Bertram Allen and Dorothy Gray, Northfield, Birmingham; two d. Educ: Birkenhead Park High Sch. Served War, Royal Artillery, Britain and NW Europe, 1942-47. Trainee and Reporter, Birkenhead News, 1940; Chief Reporter, Redditch Indicator, 1948; District Reporter, Birmingham Post and Mail, 1950; Editor, Redditch Indicator, 1952. Joined Liverpool Daily Post 1960: successively Sub-Editor, Dep. Chief Sub-Editor, Asst News Editor, Chief Sub-Editor. Chief Sub-Editor, Liverpool Echo, 1970. Inst. of Journalists, 1962: successively Sec. and Chm., Liverpool District; Convenor, NW Region; Chm., Salaries and Conditions Bd, 1973-; Vice-Pres. and then Pres., 1975; Fellow 1975. Chm., Nat. Council for the Trng of Journalists, 1974 (Mem., 1970; Vice-Chm., 1973; Chm., North-West Adv. Trng Cttee, 1974-76); Mem., Newspaper Trng Cttee, Printing and Publishing Industry Trng Bd; Mem., Gen. Council of the Press, 1973-. Recreations: writing on Rugby Union football, gardening, reading, philately. Address: 3 Woodside Road, Irby, Wirral, Merseyside L61 4UL. T: 051-648 2809.

WITNEY, Kenneth Percy, CVO 1976; Special Consultant to Royal Commission on Gambling, since 1976; b 19 March 1916; s of late Rev. Thomas and of Dr Myfanwy Witney, S India; m 1947, Joan Tait; one s one d. Educ: Eltham Coll.; Wadham Coll., Oxford (Schol.). BA Hons Mod. History, 1938; MA 1975. Min. of Home Security, 1940; Private Sec. to Parly Under-Sec., 1942-44; Home Office, 1945; Asst Private Sec. to Home Sec., 1945-47; Colonial Office (Police Div.), 1955-57; Asst Sec., Home Office, 1957; Asst Under-Sec. of State, Home Office, 1969-76. Publication: The Jutish Forest, 1976. Recreations: local history, gardening. Address: 61 Hadlow Road, Tonbridge, Kent. T: Tonbridge 352971. Club: United Oxford & Cambridge University.

WITT, Rt. Rev. Howell Arthur John; see Australia, North-West, Bishop of.

WITT, Sir John (Clermont), Kt 1967; FSA; Solicitor; lately Senior Partner in firm of Stephenson Harwood & Tatham, Saddlers' Hall, Gutter Lane, Cheapside EC2; Member, Management Committee of Courtauld Institute of Art, since 1952 (Chairman, since 1975); Director, Equity & Law Life Assurance Society Ltd (Chairman, 1964-77); b 5 November 1907; s of Sir Robert Clermont Witt, CBE, and Mary Helene Marten; m 1931, Margaret, d of Henry S. Bowers, Scotland, Conn, USA; one s one *d. Educ:* Eton; New Coll., Oxford (BA); Harvard, USA. Admitted Solicitor, 1934. Served War, 1941-45; 1st Bn The Rifle Brigade, Middle East, Italy, France, and Germany (Major; despatches). Independent Member, Reviewing Committee on Export of Works of Art, 1952-59, 1963-67; Member: Standing Commn on Museums and Galleries, 1958-73; Arts Council, 1962-76 (Vice-Chm., 1970-76). Trustee: Tate Gall., 1959-62; National Gall., 1955-62, 1965-72 (Chm. 1959-62, 1967-72); Theatres Trust, 1977-. Cavaliere, Order of S Gregorio Magno, 1965. *Address:* 15 Dorset Square, NW1 6QB. *T:* 01-723 5589; Down Mead, Boro Marsh, Wargrave, Berks. *Clubs:* Travellers', City University.

WITT, Maj.-Gen. John Evered, CB 1952; CBE 1948; MC 1918; retired from Army, 1953; *b* 15 Jan. 1897; *s* of late Rev. A. R. Witt, Royal Army Chaplains' Department; *m* 1st, 1924, Kathleen Phyllis Outram (*d* 1968); one *s*; 2nd, 1969, Mrs Cynthia Myrtle Margaret Reynolds, *yr d* of late Dr Geoffrey Eden, FRCP. *Educ:* King's Sch., Canterbury. RMC Sandhurst, 1914; 2nd Lt ASC, Dec. 1914; BEF, 1915-19; BAOR, 1919-21; UK, 1921-23; BAOR, 1923-26; UK, 1926; India, 1927; Egypt, 1927-32; UK, 1932-46; Director of Supplies and Transport, BAOR, 1946-48; FarELF, 1948-49 (despatches); Director of Supplies and Transport, Middle East Land Forces, 1950-53. *Recreations:* fishing, golf. *Address:* Gledswood, Liss, Hants.

WITTE, Prof. William; Professor of German in the University of Aberdeen, 1951-77; *b* 18 Feb. 1907; *o s* of W. G. J. and E. O. Witte; *m* 1937, Edith Mary Stenhouse Melvin; one *s* one *d. Educ:* Universities of Breslau, Munich, Berlin. MA, DLit (London); PhD (Aberdeen). Assistant, Department of German: Aberdeen, 1931-36; Edinburgh, 1936-37; Lecturer, Department of German, Aberdeen, 1937; Head of Dept, 1945; Reader in German, 1947. Gold Medal, Goethe Inst., 1971. Cross of the Order of Merit (Federal Republic of Germany), 1974. *Publications:* Modern German Prose Usage, 1937; Schiller, 1949; ed Schiller's Wallenstein, 1952; ed Two Stories by Thomas Mann, 1957; Schiller and Burns, and Other Essays, 1959; ed Schiller's Wallensteins Tod, 1962; ed Schiller's Maria Stuart, 1965; ed Goethe's Clavigo, 1973; contributions to collective works; articles in Modern Language Review, German Life and Letters, Oxford German Studies, Publications of the English Goethe Society, Publications of the Carlyle Soc., Aberdeen Univ. Rev., Wisconsin Monatshefte, Schiller-Jahrbuch, Forum for Modern Language Studies, Encyclopædia Britannica, etc. *Recreations:* gardening, motoring. *Address:* 41 Beechgrove Terrace, Aberdeen. *T:* 53799.

WITTEVEEN, Prof. Dr (Hendrik) Johannes, Kt Order of Netherlands Lion; Comdr Order of Orange Nassau; Managing Director, International Monetary Fund, 1973-Aug. 1978; *b* Zeist, Netherlands, 12 June 1921; *m* 1949, Liesbeth de Vries Feyens; three *s* one *d. Educ:* Univ. Rotterdam (DrEcons). Central Planning Bureau, 1947-48; Prof., Univ. Rotterdam, 1948-63; Minister of Finance, Netherlands, 1963-65 and 1967-71; Adviser and Mem. Bd of internat. investment trusts and business corps, incl. Royal Dutch Petroleum Co., Robeco and Unilever, 1971-73; Mem. Netherlands Parlt, First Chamber, 1959-63 and 1971-73, and Second Chamber, 1965-67. Grand Cross, Order of Crown (Belgium); Order of Oak Wreath (Luxemburg); Order of Merit (Fed. Republic Germany). *Publications:* Loonshoogte en Werkgelegenheid, 1947; Growth and Business Cycles, 1954; articles in Economische Statistische Berichten, Euromoney. *Recreation:* hiking. *Address:* 2335 49th Street NW, Washington, DC 20007, USA. *T:* (office) 477-3057; Wassenaar, Waldeck Pyrmontlaan 15, The Netherlands.

WITTEWRONGE, Sir J. C. B. L.; *see* Lawes, Sir J. C. B.

WITTON-DAVIES, Ven. Carlyle; Archdeacon of Oxford and Canon of Christ Church, Oxford, since 1957; Sub Dean, since 1972; Examining Chaplain to the Bishop of Oxford since 1965; *b* 10 June 1913; *s* of late Prof. T. Witton Davies, DD, and Hilda Mabel Witton Davies (*née* Everett); *m* 1941, Mary Rees, BA, *o d* of late Canon W. J. Rees, St Asaph, Clwyd; three *s* four *d. Educ:* Friars School, Bangor; University College of N Wales, Bangor; Exeter College, Oxford; Cuddesdon College, Oxford; Hebrew University, Jerusalem. Exhib., University Coll. of N Wales, Bangor, 1930-34; BA (Wales), 1st Cl. Hons Hebrew, 1934; BA (Oxon), 2nd Cl. Hons Theology, 1937; Junior Hall Houghton Septuagint Prize, Oxford, 1938, Senior, 1939; MA (Oxon), 1940; Deacon, 1937, Priest, 1938, St Asaph; Assistant Curate, Buckley, 1937-40; Subwarden, St Michael's College, Llandaff, 1940-44; Examining Chaplain to Bishop of Monmouth, 1940-44; Adviser on Judaica to Anglican Bishop in Jerusalem, 1944-49; Examining Chaplain to Bishop in Jerusalem, 1945-49; Canon Residentiary of Nazareth in St George's Collegiate Church, Jerusalem, 1947-49; Dean and Precentor of St David's Cathedral, 1949-57; Examining Chaplain to Bishop of St

David's, 1950-57; Chaplain, Order of St John of Jerusalem, 1954-; Surrogate. Chairman: Council of Christians and Jews, 1957-; Clergy Friendly Society, 1961-63. Mem., Archbishops' Commn on Crown Appointments, 1962-64; Censor Theologiae, Christ Church, 1972-75; Member, Convocation of Canterbury, and Church Assembly/General Synod of C of E, 1957-75. *Publications:* Journey of a Lifetime, 1962; (part translated) Martin Buber's Hasidism, 1948; (translated) Martin Buber's The Prophetic Faith, 1949; contrib. to Oxford Dictionary of the Christian Church, 1957; contrib. to The Mission of Israel, 1963. *Recreations:* music, lawn tennis, swimming. *Address:* Archdeacon's Lodging, Christ Church, Oxford. *T:* Oxford 43847.

WITTRICK, Prof. William Henry; Beale Professor and Head of Department of Civil Engineering, University of Birmingham, since 1969; *b* 29 Oct. 1922; *s* of late Frank Wittrick; *m* 1945, Joyce Farrington, *d* of late Arthur Farrington; two *d. Educ:* Huddersfield Coll.; St Catharine's Coll., Cambridge (Scholar). Mech. Scis Tripos 1942, Archibald Denny Prize. MA, ScD Cantab; PhD Sydney; FAA 1958; FRAeS; MICE; AFAIAA; CEng. Temp. Demonstrator in Engrg, Univ. of Cambridge, 1942-44; Scientific Officer, RAE, 1944-45; Univ. of Sydney: Sen. Lectr, 1945-54; Reader, 1954-56; Lawrence Hargrave Prof. of Aeronautical Engrg, 1956-64; Dean of Faculty of Engrg, 1962-63; Prof. of Structural Engrg, Univ. of Birmingham, 1964-69. Vis. Research Fellow, California Inst. of Technology, 1953; Vis. Prof., Coll. of Aeronautics, Cranfield, 1960; Pres., Australian Div. RAeS, 1961-62; Mem. 1956-61, Chm. 1961-64, Australian Aeronautical Research Cttee; Mem., Aeronautical Research Council, 1970-73. *Publications:* numerous contribs to theory of structures and mechanics of solids in learned jls. *Recreations:* bookbinding, carpentry, theatre. *Address:* 39 Meadow Hill Road, Kings Norton, Birmingham B38 8DF. *T:* 021-458 7575.

WITTS, Leslie John, CBE 1959; MD Manchester; FRCP; DM Oxford; Hon. ScD Dublin; Hon. MD Bristol; Hon. DSc Belfast; Hon. DSc Manchester; Fellow of Magdalen College and Nuffield Professor of Clinical Medicine, Oxford, 1938-65; now Emeritus Fellow and Professor; *b* 1898; *s* of Wyndham John Witts, Warrington, Lancs; *m* 1929, Nancy Grace, *y d* of L. F. Salzman; one *s* three *d. Educ:* Boteler Grammar Sch., Warrington; Victoria Univ. of Manchester; Sidney Sussex Coll., Cambridge. Served with Inns of Court OTC and RFA, 1916-18; Dickenson Travelling Scholar, 1925; John Lucas Walker Student, 1926; Edmonds Research Fellow, 1929. Lectures: Goulstonian, RCP, 1932; Frederick Price, Dublin, 1950; Schorstein Meml, London Hosp., 1955; Sidney Watson Smith, Edinburgh, 1956; Gwladys and Olwen Williams, Liverpool, 1957; Shepherd, Montreal, 1959; Lumleian, RCP, 1961; Heath Clark, Univ. of London, 1964; Litchfield, Oxon, 1969; Harveian, RCP, 1971. Late Asst to Med. Unit, London Hospital; Director, Medical Professorial Clinic and Physician St Bartholomew's Hospital; Assistant Physician to Guy's Hospital; Member of Medical Research Council, 1938-42, 1943-47; Hon. Secretary and Treasurer Assoc. Physicians of Great Britain and Ireland, 1933-48; Second Vice-Pres. Royal Coll. of Physicians, 1965-66. Mem., Min. of Health Committee on Safety of Drugs, 1963-68. McIlrath Guest Professor, Sydney, 1956. Hon. Fellow, Royal Coll. of Physicians and Surgeons of Canada. Hon. Member, Assoc. of American Physicians, and Danish Soc. of Internal Med. *Publications:* Anæmia and the Alimentary Tract, 1956; The Stomach and Anaemia, 1966; Hypochromic Anaemia, 1969. Editor of Medical Surveys and Clinical Trials, 2nd edn, 1964. Contributions to medical and scientific journals. *Recreations:* walking, play-going. *Address:* 293 Woodstock Road, Oxford. *T:* 58843.

WITTY, (John) David; Chief Executive, Westminster City Council, since 1977; *b* 1 Oct. 1924; *s* of late Harold Witty and Olive Witty, Beverley; *m* 1955, Doreen Hanlan; one *s*. *Educ:* Beverley Grammar Sch.; Balliol Coll., Oxford (MA). Served War, RN, 1943-46. Asst Town Clerk, Beverley, 1951-53; Asst Solicitor: Essex CC, 1953-54; Hornsey, 1954-60; Dep. Town Clerk: Kingston upon Thames, 1960-65; Merton, 1965-67; Asst Chief Exec., Westminster, 1967-77. *Recreation:* golf. *Address:* 95 Richmond Hill Court, Richmond, Surrey TW10 6BG.

WODEHOUSE, family name of **Earl of Kimberley.**

WODEHOUSE, Lord; John Armine Wodehouse; Research Chemist, Glaxo, since 1974; *b* 15 Jan. 1951; *s* and *heir* of 4th Earl of Kimberley, *qv*; *m* 1973, Hon. Carol Palmer, MA, *er d* of Baron Palmer, *qv*; one *d. Educ:* Eton; Univ. of East Anglia. BSc (Chemistry) 1973; MSc (Physical Organic Chemistry) 1974. FRSA. *Address:* 36 Pottery Lane, W11.

WODEN, George; *see* Slaney, G. W.

WOLEDGE, Brian; Emeritus Professor of French Language and Literature, University of London; Fielden Professor of French, University College, London, 1939-71; Hon. Research Fellow, University College London; *b* 16 Aug. 1904; *m* 1933, Christine Mary Craven; one *s* one *d. Educ:* Leeds Boys' Modern School; University of Leeds. BA (Leeds) 1926; MA (Leeds) 1928; Docteur de l'Université de Paris, 1930; Asst Lecturer in French, University College, Hull, 1930-32; Lecturer in French, University of Aberdeen, 1932-39. Visiting Andrew Mellon Professor of French, University of Pittsburg, 1967. Docteur *hc* de l'Université d'Aix-Marseille, 1970. *Publications:* L'Atre périlleux; études sur les manuscrits, la langue et l'importance littéraire du poème, 1930; L'Atre périlleux, roman de la Table ronde (Les Classiques français du moyen âge 76), 1935; Bibliographie des romans et nouvelles en prose française antérieurs à 1500, 1954, repr. 1975, Supplement 1975; The Penguin Book of French Verse, Vol. I, To the Fifteenth Century, 1961; Répertoire des premiers textes en prose française, 842-1210 (with H. P. Clive), 1964. *Address:* 28a Dobbins Lane, Wendover, Aylesbury, Bucks. *T:* Wendover 622188.

WOLFE, Very Rev. Charles William; Dean of Cashel, 1961-73; *b* 15 July 1914; *s* of Charles and Rose Wolfe, Cork; *m* 1938, Violet Millicent McCollum; one *d. Educ:* The King's Hosp. and Trinity Coll., Dublin. Sen. Exhibn, 1934; Schol. of the Hse, 1935; Bernard, Wray and Oratory Prize; Moderatorship, 1936, with Large Gold Medal in Mental and Moral Science. BA 1936; BLitt 1938; MLitt 1960; 1st Cl. Divinity Testimonial, 1937; Theolog. Exhibn, 1938. Deacon, 1938; Priest, 1939; Curate, Kinsale, 1938; Rector: Berehaven, 1940; Fermoy, 1943; Tramore, 1949. Archdeacon of Waterford, 1960. Exam. Chap. to Bp of Cashel. *Publications:* A Memoir of Christ Church, Tramore, 1951; Cashel: its Cathedrals and Library, 1965; Catalogue of Cashel Diocesan Library, 1974. *Address:* Church Road, Carrigaline, Co. Cork, Ireland.

WOLFE, William Cuthbertson; Chairman, Scottish National Party, since 1969; *b* 22 Feb. 1924; *s* of Major Tom Wolfe, TD, and Katie Cuthbertson; *m* 1953, Arna Mary, *d* of late Dr Melville Dinwiddie, CBE, DSO, MC; two *s* two *d. Educ:* Bathgate Academy; George Watson's Coll., Edinburgh. CA. Army service, 1942-47, NW Europe and Far East; Air OP Pilot. Hon. Publications Treas., Saltire Society, 1953-60; Scout County Comr, West Lothian, 1960-64; Hon. Pres. (Rector), Students' Assoc., Heriot-Watt Univ., 1966-69. Contested (SNP) West Lothian, 1962, 1964, 1966, 1970, Feb. and Oct. 1974. *Publication:* Scotland Lives, 1973. *Address:* Craigpark, Torphichen, Bathgate, West Lothian. *T:* Bathgate 52981.

WOLFENDALE, Prof. Arnold Whittaker; PhD, DSc; FRS 1977; FInstP, FRAS; Professor of Physics, University of Durham, since 1965; *b* 25 June 1927; *s* of Arnold Wolfendale and Doris Wolfendale; *m* 1951, Audrey Darby; twin *s*. *Educ:* Univ. of Manchester (BSc Physics 1st Cl. Hons 1948, PhD 1953, DSc 1970). FInstP 1958; FRAS 1973. Asst Lectr, Univ. of Manchester, 1951, Lectr, 1954; Univ. of Durham: Lectr, 1956; Sen. Lectr, 1959; Reader in Physics, 1963; Head of Dept, 1973-77. Chm., Northern Reg. Action Cttee, Manpower Services Commn's Job Creation Prog., 1975-. *Publications:* Cosmic Rays, 1963; (ed) Cosmic Rays at Ground Level, 1973; (ed) Origin of Cosmic Rays, 1974; original papers on studies of cosmic radiation. *Recreations:* fell walking, foreign travel. *Address:* 15 Surtees Drive, Crossgate Moor, Durham. *T:* Durham 2714.

WOLFENDEN, family name of **Baron Wolfenden.**

WOLFENDEN, Baron *cr* 1974 (Life Peer), of Westcott; **John Frederick Wolfenden,** Kt 1956; CBE 1942; President, Chelsea College, University of London, since 1972; Chairman, Alleyn's College of God's Gift, since 1973; *b* 26 June 1906; *s* of late G. Wolfenden, Halifax; *m* 1932, Eileen Le Messurier, 2nd *d* of late A. J. Spilsbury; one *s* two *d* (one *s* decd). *Educ:* Wakefield School; Queen's College, Oxford (Hastings Scholar, Akroyd Scholar; Hon. Fellow 1959); 2nd Class Classical Mods, 1926; 1st Class Literae Humaniores, 1928; Henry P. Davison Scholar Princeton University, USA, 1928-29; Fellow and Tutor in Philosophy, Magdalen College, Oxford, 1929-34; Headmaster of Uppingham School, 1934-44; Headmaster of Shrewsbury School, 1944-50; Vice-Chancellor of Reading University, 1950-63; Chm., UGC, 1963-68; Dir and Principal Librarian, British Museum, 1969-73. Director of Pre-Entry Training, Air Ministry, 1941; Chairman: Ministry of Education's Youth Advisory Council, 1942-45; Headmasters' Conference, 1945, 1946, 1948, 1949; Departmental Cttee on Employment of National Service Men, 1956; Secondary School Examinations Council, 1951-57; Departmental Cttee on Homosexual Offences

and Prostitution, 1954-57; National Council of Social Service, 1953-60; CCPR Sport Enquiry, 1957-60; Family Service Units, 1957-63; National Association of Youth Clubs, 1958-63; Local Government Examinations Board, 1958-63; Councils for the Training of Health Visitors and for Training in Social Work, 1962-63; Carnegie UK Trust, 1969-74; Cttee on Voluntary Organisations, 1974-77. President: Section L British Association, 1955; Aslib, 1969-71. Hon. DLitt: Reading, 1963; Warwick, 1977; Hon. LLD: Hull, 1969; Wales, 1971; Manchester, 1972; Williams Coll., Mass., 1973; Hon. LHD Hamilton Coll., NY, 1972; DUniv York, 1973. Oxford University Hockey XI, 1927, 1928, English Hockey XI, 1930-33. Provost, Order of the Buffalo Hunt (Manitoba). *Publications:* The Approach to Philosophy, 1932; The Public Schools To-Day, 1948; How to Choose Your School, 1952; Chapters in The Prospect Before Us, 1948; Education in a Changing World, 1951; Turning Points (memoirs), 1976; occasional articles, named lectures, and reviews. *Recreation:* weeding. *Address:* The White House, Westcott, near Dorking, Surrey. *T:* Dorking 5475. *Clubs:* United Oxford & Cambridge University; Vincent's (Oxford).

WOLFF, Hon. Sir Albert (Asher), KCMG 1959; Chief Justice of Western Australia, 1959-69; Lieutenant-Governor of Western Australia, 1968-74; *b* 30 April 1899; *s* of Simon and Bertha Clara Wolff; *m* 1st, 1924, Ida Violet Jackson (*d* 1953); one *s* one *d*; 2nd, 1956, Mary Godwin. *Educ:* Perth Modern School. Admitted Bar Supreme Court of Western Australia, 1921; Crown Prosecutor, 1926; Crown Solicitor and Parliamentary Draughtsman, 1929; KC 1936; Justice Supreme Court of Western Australia, 1938. President Public Library, Museum and Art Gallery Trust, WA, 1954-58. Author and draughtsman W Aust. Matrimonial Causes Code and Rules. Official Visitor Harvey Internment Camp, War of 1939-45. *Address:* c/o Home of Peace, Thomas Street, Subiaco, WA 6008, Australia.

WOLFF, Frederick Ferdinand, CBE 1975; TD 1945; Chairman, Rudolf Wolff & Co. Ltd, since 1965; *b* 13 Oct. 1910; *s* of Philip Robert Wolff and Irma Wolff; *m* 1937, Natalie Winifred Virginia Byrne; two *s* three *d* (incl. twin *s* and *d*). *Educ:* Shirley House Prep. Sch., Watford, Herts; Beaumont Coll., Old Windsor, Berks. Oxfordshire and Bucks LI, 1939-45 (Captain). Joined Rudolf Wolff & Co., 1929; Partner, 1951. Chairman: London Metal Exchange Committee, 1970- (Mem. Cttee, 1961-; Mem. Bd, 1963-); Fedn of Commodity Assocs, 1971-; Mem., Cttee on Invisible Exports, 1971-. AAA Champion 440 yards, 1933; British Gold Medallist, 4×400 metres relay team, Olympic Games, Berlin, 1936. *Recreations:* golf, racing. *Address:* Parsonage Farm, Pauls Hill, Penn, Bucks. *T:* Penn 3349. *Clubs:* London Athletic, Gresham, Naval and Military; Beaconsfield Golf.

WOLFF, Henry D.; *see* Drummond-Wolff.

WOLFF, John Arnold Harrop, CMG 1963; *b* 14 July 1912; *er s* of late Arnold H. Wolff, Halebarns, Cheshire; *m* 1939, Helen Muriel McCracken, Howth, Co. Dublin; one *s* one *d. Educ:* Haileybury College; Peterhouse, Cambridge. Colonial Administrative Service, Kenya: District Officer, 1935-59; Provincial Commissioner, 1959-63; Civil Secretary, Rift Valley Region, 1963; retired, Nov. 1963. *Recreations:* gardening, golf. *Address:* Wallflowers, Bloxham, Oxon.

WOLFF, Prof. Otto Herbert, MD, FRCP; Nuffield Professor of Child Health, University of London, since 1965; *b* 10 Jan. 1920; *s* of Dr H. A. J. Wolff; *m* 1952, Dr Jill Freeborough; one *s* one *d. Educ:* Peterhouse, Cambridge; University College Hospital, London. Lieut and Capt. RAMC, 1944-47. Resident Medical Officer, Registrar and Sen. Med. Registrar, Birmingham Children's Hospital, 1948-51; Lecturer, Sen. Lectr, Reader, Dept of Pædiatrics and Child Health, Univ. of Birmingham, 1951-64. Pres., British Pædiatric Assoc.; Member: Royal Society of Medicine; American Pædiatric Society; New York Academy of Sciences; Amer. Academy of Pediatrics; European Soc. for Paediatric Research; European Soc. for Paediatric Gastroenterology. Corresp. Member: Société Française de Pédiatrie; Société Suisse de Pédiatrie; Osterreichische Gesellschaft fur Kinderheilkunde. *Publications:* chapter on Disturbances of Serum Lipoproteins in Endocrine and Genetic Diseases of Childhood (ed L. I. Gardner); chapter on Obesity in Recent Advances in Paediatrics (ed David Hull); articles in Lancet, British Medical Journal, Archives of Disease in Childhood, Quarterly Jl of Medicine, etc. *Recreation:* music. *Address:* 53 Danbury Street, N1 8LE. *T:* 01-226 0748.

WOLFF, Rosemary Langley; Member, Police Complaints Board, since 1977; *b* 10 July 1926; *er d* of late A. C. V. Clarkson; *m* 1956, Michael Wolff, JP (*d* 1976); two *d. Educ:* Haberdashers'

Aske's Sch. Mem., Community Relations Commn, 1973-77. Manager of various primary schs in North Kensington and Tower Hamlets, 1963-; Governor, City College; Chm., Conservative Contact Group, 1973-77. *Address:* 13 Holland Park, W11 3TH. *T:* 01-727 9051.

WOLFSON, Sir Isaac, 1st Bt *cr* 1962; FRS 1963; Hon. Fellow: Weizmann Institute of Science, Israel; St Edmund Hall, Oxford; Jews' College; Founder Fellow, Wolfson College, Oxford; Chairman (since 1946), The Great Universal Stores Ltd; *b* 17 Sept. 1897; *m* 1926, Edith Specterman; one *s. Educ:* Queen's Park School, Glasgow. Joined The Great Universal Stores Ltd, 1932. Member, Worshipful Company of Pattenmakers; Member, Grand Council, Cancer Research Campaign; Hon. Pres., Weizmann Institute of Science Foundation; Trustee, Religious Centre, Jerusalem; Patron, Royal College of Surgeons; Founder, and Pres., 1975- (formerly Chm.), and Trustee, Wolfson Foundation which was created in 1955 mainly for the advancement of health, education and youth activities in the UK and Commonwealth. Fellow, Royal Postgrad. Med. Sch., 1972; Hon. FRCP 1959; Hon. FRCS 1969; Hon. FRCP&S Glasgow. Hon. DCL Oxford, 1963; Hon. LLD: London, 1958; Glasgow, 1963; Cambridge, 1966; Manchester, 1967; Strathclyde, 1969; Brandeis Univ., US 1969; Nottingham, 1971; Hon. PhD Jerusalem, 1970. Einstein Award, US, 1967; Herbert Lehmann Award, US, 1968. Freeman, City of Glasgow, 1971. *Recreation:* golf. *Heir: s* Sir Leonard Gordon Wolfson, *qv. Address:* 74 Portland Place, W1.

WOLFSON, Sir Leonard (Gordon), Kt 1977; Chairman and a Founder Trustee, Wolfson Foundation; Managing Director, Great Universal Stores, since 1962 (Director, 1952); Chairman, Great Universal Stores Merchandise Corporation, since 1966; *b* 11 Nov. 1927; *s of* Sir Isaac Wolfson, 1st Bt, *qv*; *m* 1949, Ruth, *d* of E. A. Sterling; four *d. Educ:* King's School, Worcester. Pres., Jewish Welfare Bd. Trustee, Wolfson Coll., Oxford; Hon. Fellow: St Catherine's Coll., Oxford; Wolfson Coll., Cambridge; Wolfson Coll., Oxford; Worcester Coll., Oxford. Patron, Royal College of Surgeons, 1976. Trustee, Civic Trust. Hon. FRCP, 1977. Hon. PhD Tel Aviv, 1971; Hon. DCL Oxon, 1972; Hon. LLD Strathclyde, 1972; Hon. DSc Hull, 1977. *Recreations:* history, economics, bridge, golf. *Address:* Universal House, 251 Tottenham Court Road, W1A 1BZ. *Clubs:* MCC, Carlton, Eccentric.

WOLLEN, Sir (Ernest) Russell (Storey), KBE 1969 (CBE 1962; OBE 1953); retired; *b* 9 June 1902; *s* of Cecil Storey Wollen, Glengariffe, Torquay, Devon; *m* 1924, Maise, *d* of Robert Adamson, Neville's Cross, Co. Durham; two *s* two *d. Educ:* Marlborough. Coffee Planter, 1922-39; Chm., Coffee Bd of Kenya, 1933-40; Mem., Kenya Supply Bd, 1940-44; E African Manager, Dalgety & Co., 1944-55; Chm., Kenya Coffee Marketing Bd, 1955-67. Retired to reside in Western Australia, 1967. *Recreations:* sailing, riding, golf. *Address:* 9 Dunkley Avenue, Applecross, Western Australia 6153, Australia. *T:* Perth 643193. *Clubs:* Farmers' (London); Muthaiga Country (Nairobi).

WOLLHEIM, Prof. Richard Arthur, FBA 1972; Grote Professor of Philosophy of Mind and Logic in the University of London since 1963; *b* 5 May 1923; *s* of Eric Wollheim; *m* 1st, 1950, Anne, *yr d* of Lieutenant-Colonel E. G. H. Powell (marr. diss. 1967); two *s* ; 2nd, 1969, Mary Day, *er d* of Robert S. Lanier, NYC. *Educ:* Westminster School; Balliol College, Oxford (MA). Assistant Lecturer in Philosophy, University College, London, 1949; Lecturer, 1951; Reader, 1960; Visiting Professor: Columbia Univ., 1959-60, 1970; Visva-Bharati Univ., Santiniketan, India, 1968; Univ. of Minnesota, 1972; Graduate Centre, City Univ. of NY, 1975. Power Lectr, Univ. of Sydney, 1972. Pres., Aristotelian Soc., 1967-68; Vice-Pres., British Soc. of Aesthetics, 1969-. Served in the Army, Northern Europe, 1942-45 (prisoner of war during August 1944). *Publications:* F. H. Bradley, 1959, rev. edn 1969; Socialism and Culture, 1961; On Drawing an Object (Inaugural Lecture), 1965; Art and its Objects, 1968; A Family Romance (fiction), 1969; Freud, 1971; On Art and the Mind (essays and lectures), 1973; edited: F. H. Bradley, Ethical Studies, 1961; Hume on Religion, 1963; F. H. Bradley, Appearance and Reality, 1968; Adrian Stokes, selected writings, 1972; Freud, a collection of critical essays, 1974; J. S. Mill, Three Essays, 1975; articles in anthologies, philosophical and literary jls. *Address:* 20 Ashchurch Park Villas, W12.

WOLMER, Viscount; William Lewis Palmer; *b* 1 Sept. 1971; *s* and *heir* of 4th Earl of Selborne, *qv.*

WOLRIGE-GORDON, Patrick; *b* 10 Aug. 1935; *s* of late Captain Robert Wolrige-Gordon, MC and Joan Wolrige-Gordon; *m* 1962, Anne, *o d* of late Peter D. Howard and Mrs

Howard; one *s* two *d. Educ:* Eton; New College, Oxford. MP (C) Aberdeenshire East, Nov. 1958-Feb. 1974. Liveryman Worshipful Company of Wheelwrights, 1966. *Recreations:* reading, walking, music. *Address:* Ythan Lodge, Newburgh, Aberdeenshire. *Club:* Royal Over-Seas League.

WOLSELEY, Sir Charles Garnet Richard Mark, 11th Bt, *cr* 1628; Associate Partner, Smiths Gore, Chartered Surveyors, since 1974; *b* 16 June 1944; *s* of Capt. Stephen Garnet Hubert Francis Wolseley, Royal Artillery (*d* 1944, of wounds received in action), and of Pamela, *yr d* of late Capt. F. Barry and of Mrs Power, Wolseley Park, Rugeley, Staffs; *S* grandfather, Sir Edric Charles Joseph Wolseley, 10th Bt, 1954; *m* 1968, Anita Maria, *er d* of H. J. Fried, Epsom, Surrey; three *d . Educ:* St Bede's School, Nr Stafford; Ampleforth College, York. FRICS. *Recreations:* shooting, fishing, gardening. *Heir: uncle* Basil Charles Daniel Rudolph Wolseley [*b* 16 Nov. 1921; *m* 1950, Ruth Key, *d* of Lt-Col William Tom Carter, OBE; four *d*]. *Address:* Wolseley Park, Rugeley, Staffs. *T:* Rugeley 2346; Hilliers, Petworth, West Sussex. *T:* Petworth 42414. *Clubs:* Farmers'; N London Rifle, English XX Rifle (Bisley Camp, Brookwood).

WOLSELEY, Sir Garnet, 12th Bt, *cr* 1745 (Ireland); emigrated to Ontario, Canada, 1951; *b* 27 May 1915; *s* of late Richard Bingham and Mary Alexandra Wolseley; *S* cousin (Rev. Sir William Augustus Wolseley), 1950; *m* 1950, Lillian Mary, *d* of late William Bertram Ellison, Wallasey. *Educ:* New Brighton Secondary Sch. Served War of 1939-45, Northants Regt, Madagascar, Sicily, Italy and Germany. Boot Repairer Manager, 1946. *Address:* 73 Dorothy Street, Brantford, Ontario, Canada. *T:* 753-7957.

WOLSTENCROFT, Alan, CB 1961; *b* 18 Oct. 1914; *yr s* of late Walter and Bertha Wolstencroft; *m* 1951, Ellen, *d* of late W. Tomlinson. *Educ:* Lancaster Royal Grammar Sch.; Caius Coll., Cambridge (MA 1st Cl. Classical Tripos). Assistant Principal, GPO, 1936. Served War of 1939-45: Royal Engineers (Postal Section), France and Middle East. Principal GPO, 1945; Assistant Secretary, GPO, 1949; Secretary, Independent Television Authority, 1954; General Post Office: Director of Personnel, 1955; Director of Postal Services, 1957; Director of Radio Services, 1960-64; Deputy Director General, 1964-67; Man. Dir Posts, 1967, Posts and GIRO, 1968; Adviser on Special Projects to Chm. of Post Office Corporation, 1969-70; Sec. to Post Office, 1970-73; retired. *Address:* Green Court, 161 Long Lane, Tilehurst, Reading RG3 6YW.

WOLSTENHOLME, Sir Gordon (Ethelbert Ward), Kt 1976; OBE (mil.) 1944; MA, MB, BChir; MRCS, FRCP, FIBiol; Director, The Ciba Foundation, 1949-Dec. 1978; Chairman, Genetic Manipulation Advisory Group, since 1976; Member, General Medical Council, since 1973; *b* Sheffield, 28 May 1913; *m* 1st, one *s* two *d* ; 2nd, two *d. Educ:* Repton; Corpus Christi Coll., Cambridge; Middlesex Hosp. Med. Sch. Served with RAMC, 1940-47 (OBE); France, UK, ME and Central Mediterranean; specialist and advr in transfusion and resuscitation; OC Gen. Hosp. in Udine and Trieste. Founder Mem. 1954, Treasurer 1955-61, Mem. Exec. Bd 1961-70, UK Cttee for WHO; Organizer and Advr, Haile Selassie I Prize Trust, 1963-74; Advr, La Trinidad Med. Centre, Caracas, 1969-. Royal Society of Medicine: FRSocMed; Hon. Sec. 1964-70; Pres. Library (Sci. Res) Sect., 1968-70; Chm. Working Party on Soc's Future, 1972-73; Chm. Building Cttee, 1974-; Pres., 1975-77; Royal College of Physicians: FRCP 1964; Member: Library Cttee, 1966-69; Journal Cttee, 1969-75; Zoological Society: Scientific Fellow; Member: Finance Cttee, 1962-69; Council, 1962-66, 1967-70, 1976-; Chm., Nuffield Inst. for Comparative Medicine, 1969-70; Chm. Governors, Inst. for Res. into Mental and Multiple Handicap, 1973-77. Founder Mem. 1950, Hon. Treasurer 1956-69, Renal Assoc. of GB; Chm. Congress Prog. Cttee, 1962-64, Mem. Finance Cttee 1968-72, Internat. Soc. for Endocrinology; Trustee and Mem. Res. Bd, Spastics' Soc., 1963-67; Chm. 1965-69, Trustee 1965-76, Developmental Scis Trust; Founder Chm., European Soc. for Clinical Investigation, 1966-67 (Boerhaave Lectr, 1976); Mem. Council 1969-75, Sponsor 1976-, Inst. for Study of Drug Dependence. Member: Council, Westfield Coll., London Univ., 1965-73; Planning Bd, University College at Buckingham, 1969. Chm., Anglo-Ethiopian Soc., 1967-70. Mem. Ct of Assistants, Soc. of Apothecaries, 1969- (Warden, 1977; Chm., Faculty of Hist. and Philosophy of Med. and Pharmacy, 1973-75; Visitor, 1975-). Hon. Life Governor, Middlesex Hosp., 1978. Hon. FACP, 1975; Hon. Fellow: Hunterian Soc., 1975 (Orator 1976); Royal Acad. of Med. in Ireland, 1976. Hon. Member: Swedish Soc. of Endocrinology, 1955; Soc. of Endocrinology, 1959; Swiss Acad. of Med. Sciences, 1975; Foreign Mem., Swedish Med. Soc., 1959. Linnaeus medal, Royal Swedish Acad. Sci., 1977. Hon. LLD Cambridge, 1968. Gold Medal: Perugia Univ., 1961; (class

1A) Italian Min. of Educn, 1961. Tito Lik, 1945; Chevalier, Légion d'Honneur, 1959; Star of Ethiopia, 1966. *Publications:* (ed) Ciba Foundation vols, 1950-; Royal College of Physicians: Portraits, vol. I (ed with David Piper), 1964, vol. II (ed with John Kerslake), 1977. *Recreations: walking, simple gardening. Address:* The Ciba Foundation, 41 Portland Place, W1N 4BN. *T:* 01-636 9456; The Dutch House, 77a Fitzjohn's Avenue, NW3 6NY. *T:* 01-435 3074. *Club:* Athenæum.

WOLTERS, Very Rev. Conrad Clifton; Chaplain to the Society of St Margaret, since 1976; Provost Emeritus of Newcastle, since 1976; *b* 3 April 1909; *e s* of Frederick Charles and Gertrude Elizabeth Wolters; *m* 1937, Joyce Cunnold; one *s. Educ:* privately; London College of Divinity; St John's College, Durham. ALCD 1932; LTh 1932; BA 1933; MA 1936. Curate: Christ Church, Gipsy Hill, SE19, 1933-37; Christ Church, Beckenham, 1937-41; Vicar, St Luke's, Wimbledon Park, 1941-49; Rector, Sanderstead, Surrey, 1949-59; Canon of Newcastle, 1959-62; Vicar of Newcastle and Provost of the Cathedral, 1962-76. *Publications:* (ed) Cloud of Unknowing, 1960; (ed) Revelations of Divine Love, 1966; (ed) The Fire of Love, 1971. *Address:* The Cottage, St Margaret's Convent, East Grinstead, West Sussex RH19 3LE. *T:* East Grinstead 22406.

WOLTERS, Gwyneth Eleanor Mary; a Commissioner of Inland Revenue since 1971; *d* of late Prof. and Mrs A. W. Wolters. *Educ:* Abbey Sch., Reading; Reading Univ.; Newnham Coll., Cambridge. Entered Inland Revenue Dept, 1947. *Address:* 45 Albert Road, Caversham, Reading. *T:* Reading 472605.

WOLVERSON COPE, F.; see Cope, F(rederick) Wolverson.

WOLVERTON, 5th Baron *cr* 1869; **Nigel Reginald Victor Glyn;** Captain RA, TA; *b* 23 June 1904; *o* surv. *s* of 4th Baron and Lady Edith Amelia Ward, CBE (*d* 1956), *o d* of 1st Earl of Dudley; *S* father, 1932. *Educ:* Eton. *Heir:* kinsman Jeremy Christopher Glyn [*b* 1 Oct. 1930; *m* 1956, Robina Elspeth, *o d* of Sir George Arthur Harford, 2nd Bt; one *d*]. *Address:* Queensberry House, Newmarket, Suffolk.
See also Baron Rhyl.

WOMBWELL, Sir George (Philip Frederick), 7th Bt *cr* 1778; *b* 21 May 1949; *s* of Sir (Frederick) Philip (Alfred William) Wombwell, 6th Bt, MBE, and of Ida Elizabeth, *er d* of Frederick J. Leitch; *S* father, 1977; *m* 1974, (Hermione) Jane, *e d* of T. S. Wrightson; one *s. Educ:* Repton. *Heir: s* Stephen Philip Henry Wombwell, *b* 12 May 1977. *Address:* Oulston Hall, Oulston, York.

WOMERSLEY, Denis Keith, CBE 1974; HM Diplomatic Service, retired; *b* 21 March 1920; *s* of late Alfred Womersley, Bradford, Yorks, and late Agnes (*née* Keighley); *m* 1955, Eileen Georgina, *d* of late George and Margaret Howe. *Educ:* Christ's Hospital; Caius Coll., Cambridge (Hons, MA). Served War, HM Forces, 1940-46. Entered Foreign (later Diplomatic) Service, 1946; Foreign Office, 1948, Control Commn Germany, 1952; Vienna, 1955; Hong Kong, 1957, FO, 1960; Baghdad, 1962; FO, 1963; Aden, 1966; Beirut, 1967; FCO, 1969-71; Bonn, 1971-74; Counsellor, FCO, 1974-77. FRSA 1976. *Recreations:* violin-playing, photography, film-making. *Address:* High Timbers, Fryern Road, Storrington, Sussex. *Club:* Christ's Hospital (Horsham).

WOMERSLEY, J(ohn) Lewis, CBE 1962; RIBA; FRTPI; FRSA; Consultant, Hugh Wilson and Lewis Womersley, Chartered Architects and Town Planners (Partner, 1964-77); *b* 12 Dec. 1910; *s* of Norman Womersley and Elizabeth Margaret Lewis; *m* 1936, Jean Roberts; two *s. Educ:* Huddersfield College. Asst Architect, private practices in London and Liverpool, 1933-38; Borough Architect and Town Planning Officer, Northampton, 1946-53; City Architect, Sheffield, 1953-64. Past Member Council, RIBA (Vice-President, 1961-62). Member: Central Housing Adv. Cttee, 1956-61, Parker Morris Cttee on Housing Standards, 1958-60, Min. of Housing and Local Govt; North West Econ. Planning Council, 1965-72; Manchester Conservation Areas and Historic Buildings Panel, 1970-77 (Chm., 1974-77); Chm., Manchester's Albert Meml Restoration Appeal Cttee, 1976-. Works include housing, Manchester Education Precinct Plan, Huddersfield Polytechnic, Develt Plan and Central Services Building, central area redevelopment. RIBA DistTP, 1956. Hon. LLD Sheffield, 1966. *Publication:* Traffic Management in the Lake District National Park, 1972. *Recreations:* reading, gardening. *Address:* Wall Nook, Ferney Green, Bowness-on-Windermere, Cumbria. *T:* Windermere 3458. *Clubs:* Reform; St James's (Manchester).

WOMERSLEY, Sir Peter (John Walter), 2nd Bt *cr* 1945; Personnel Manager, Beecham Group; *b* 10 November 1941; *s* of

Capt. John Womersley (*o s* of 1st Bt; killed in action in Italy, 1944), and of Betty, *d* of Cyril Williams, Elstead, Surrey; *S* grandfather, 1961; *m* 1968, Janet Margaret Grant; two *s* two *d. Educ:* Aldro; Charterhouse; RMA, Sandhurst. Entered Royal Military Academy (Regular Army), 1960; Lt, King's Own Royal Border Regt, 1964, retd 1968. *Heir: s* John Gavin Grant Womersley, *b* 7 Dec. 1971. *Address:* Sunnycroft, The Street, Bramber, near Steyning, Sussex.

WONTNER, Sir Hugh (Walter Kingwell), GBE 1974; Kt 1972; CVO 1969 (MVO 1950); JP; Chairman of The Savoy, Claridge's and Berkeley Hotels, London, and other undertakings associated with The Savoy, since 1948 (Managing Director since 1941); Clerk of the Royal Kitchens, since 1953, and a Catering Adviser in the Royal Household, since 1938; Alderman of City of London (Broad Street Ward), since 1963; Underwriting Member of Lloyd's, since 1937; *b* 22 Oct. 1908; *er s* of Arthur Wontner, actor-manager; *m* 1936, Catherine, *o d* of Lieut T. W. Irvin, Gordon Highlanders (*d* of wounds, France, 1916); two *s* one *d. Educ:* Oundle and in France. On staff of London Chamber of Commerce, 1927-33; Asst Sec., Home Cttee, Associated Chambers of Commerce of India and Ceylon, 1930-31; Sec., London Cttee, Burma Chamber of Commerce, 1931; Gen. Sec., Hotels and Restaurants Assoc. of Great Britain, 1933-38; Asst to Sir George Reeves-Smith at The Savoy, 1938-41; Director, The Savoy Hotel Ltd, 1940; Sec., Coronation Accommodation Cttee, 1936-37, Chm., 1953; a British delegate, Internat. Hotel Alliance, 1933-38; Pres., Internat. Hotel Assoc., 1961-64, Mem. of Honour, 1965-. Chairman: Exec. Cttee, British Hotels and Rests Assoc., 1957-60 (Vice-Chm., 1952-57; Vice-Chm. of Council, 1961-68; Chm., London Div., 1949-51); Chm. of Council, British Hotels, Restaurants and Caterers Assoc., 1969-73; London Hotels Information Service, 1952-56; Working Party, Owners of Historic Houses open to the public, 1965-66; Historic Houses Cttee, BTA, 1966-77. Member: Historic Buildings Council, 1968-73; Board of BTA, 1950-69; LCC Consultative Cttee, Hotel and Restaurant Technical School, 1933-38; Court of Assistants, Irish Soc., 1967-68, 1971-73; Vis. Cttee, Holloway Prison, 1963-68. Governor: University Coll. Hosp., 1945-53 (Chm., Nutrition Cttee, 1945-52); Christ's Hosp., 1963-. Trustee: College of Arms Trust; Southwark Cathedral Develt Trust; D'Oyly Carte Opera Trust; Chm., Temple Bar Trustees; Vice Pres., The Pilgrims; Chairman: The Savoy Theatre, 1948-; Lancaster Hotel, Paris, 1973-. Liveryman: Worshipful Co. of Feltmakers, 1934- (Master, 1962-63 and 1973-74); Clockmakers, 1967- (Warden, 1971-; Master, 1975-76); Hon. Liveryman: Launderers' Co., 1970; Worshipful Co. of Plaisterers, 1975; Chancellor, The City Univ., 1973-74; one of HM Lieuts and a JP for the City of London, 1963-, Chief Magistrate, 1973-74; Freeman, 1934, Sheriff, 1970-71; Lord Mayor of London, 1973-74. Hon. Citizen, St Emilion, 1974; Freeman of the Seychelles, 1974. Order of Cisneros, Spain, 1964; Officer, L'Etoile Equatoriale, 1970; Médaille de Vermeil, City of Paris, 1972; Ordre de l'Etoile Civique, 1972; Officier du Mérite Agricole, 1973; Comdr, Nat. Order of the Leopard, Zaire, 1974; Knight Comdr, Order of the Dannebrog, 1974; Order of the Crown of Malaysia, 1974. KStJ 1973 (OStJ 1971). Hon. DLitt 1973. *Recreations:* genealogy, acting. *Address:* 1 Savoy Hill, WC2. *T:* 01-836 1533. *Clubs:* Garrick, City Livery.

WOOD; see Hill-Wood.

WOOD, family name of **Earl of Halifax.**

WOOD, Alan John, CBE 1971; Tan Sri (Malaysia) 1972; Executive Vice-President, Sowers, Lewis, Wood Inc., PO Box 241, Greenwich, Conn 06870, USA; *b* 16 Feb. 1925; *s* of Lt-Col Maurice Taylor Wood, MBE; *m* 1950, June (*née* Barker); one *s* one *d. Educ:* King Edward VI Royal Grammar Sch., Guildford, Surrey, UK. Served War, Army: with HM Forces, 1943-47; demobilised rank Captain. Various exec. and managerial positions with Borneo Motors Ltd, Singapore and Malaya, 1947-64 (Dir, 1964); Director: Borneo Bhd, 1968-73; Inchcape Bhd, 1968-73. Pres., Malaysian Internat. Chamber of Commerce, 1968-72; Chm., Nat. Chambers of Commerce of Malaysia, 1968 and 1972; Dep. Chm., Inchcape Bhd Malaysia and Singapore, 1973-74. Panglima Setia Mahkota (Hon.) (Malaysia), 1972. *Recreation:* golf. *Address:* c/o Lloyds Bank Ltd, 32 Commercial Road, Woking, Surrey GU21 1ER. *Clubs:* Oriental, Naval and Military (London); Lake, Royal Selangor Golf (Kuala Lumpur); Penang (Penang); Tanglin, Singapore Island Country (Singapore).

WOOD, Alan Marshall M.; see Muir Wood.

WOOD, Sir Anthony John P.; see Page Wood.

WOOD, Canon Cecil Thomas; Provincial Archivist, South Africa, since 1957; *b* 1903; *s* of Henry Mathew Wood and Letitia Maud Cannon. *Educ:* Uppingham Sch.; Lincoln Coll., Oxford; Cuddesdon Theological Coll. MA (Oxford) 1926. Deacon 1927, priest 1928, Southwark diocese. Curate, St John the Divine, Kennington, 1927-32; Chaplain to Archbp of Cape Town, 1933-38; SPG Candidates Sec., 1938-41; actg Archdeacon of Bloemfontein, 1942-46; Warden of St John's Hostel, Cape Town, 1946-51; Director of South African Church Institute, London, 1952-55; Rector of Hermanus, Cape, 1955-58; Archdeacon of Cape Town, 1958-65; Canon Emeritus, 1965; Senior Chaplain to Archibishop of Cape Town, 1965-72. Vicar General of Diocese of Cape Town, 1963, 1968. Hon. Associate in Theology (SA), 1963. *Publications:* Short History of Bloemfontein Cathedral, 1945; Cathedral Sermons, 1962. *Recreations:* travel, book collecting. *Address:* Taunton House, Cape Town, South Africa. *Clubs:* United Oxford & Cambridge University; Vincent's (Oxford); Leander (Henley); Civil Service (Cape Town).

WOOD, Charles Gerald; writer for films, television and the theatre, since 1962; *b* 6 Aug. 1932; *s* of John Edward Wood, actor and Catherine Mae (*née* Harris), actress; *m* 1954, Valerie Elizabeth Newman, actress; one *s* one *d*. *Educ:* King Charles I Sch., Kidderminster; Birmingham Coll. of Art. Soldier, 1950-55; Factory worker, 1955-57; Stage Manager and Theatre Designer, 1957-59; Layout Artist, 1959-62. Wrote plays: Prisoner and Escort, John Thomas, Spare, (Cockade), Arts Theatre, 1963; Meals on Wheels, Royal Court, 1965; Don't Make Me Laugh, Aldwych, 1966; Fill the Stage with Happy Hours, Nottingham Playhouse, 1967; Dingo, Bristol Arts Centre, 1967; H., National Theatre, 1969; Welfare, Liverpool Everyman, 1971; Veterans, Lyceum, Edinburgh, 1972; Jingo, RSC, Aldwych, 1975; The Script, Hampstead Theatre, 1976. Screenplays, television and radio. *Publications:* plays: Cockade, 1965; Fill the Stage with Happy Hours, 1967; Dingo, 1967; H., 1970; Veterans, 1972. *Recreations:* military and theatrical studies; supporting Bristol Rovers FC. *Address:* The Manor House, Milton, near Banbury, Oxon. *Club:* Dramatists'.

WOOD, Maj.-Gen. Denys Broomfield; Director of Army Quartering, since 1975; *b* 2 Nov. 1923; *s* of late Percy Neville Wood and Meryl Broomfield; *m* 1948, Jennifer Nora Page, *d* of late Air Cdre William Morton Page, CBE; one *s* two *d*. *Educ:* Radley; Pembroke Coll., Cambridge. MA, FIMechE. Commissioned into REME, 1944; war service in UK and Far East, 1944-47; Staff Captain, WO, 1948-49; Instructor, RMA, Sandhurst, 1949-52; Staff Coll., 1953; DAA&QMG, 11 Infantry Bde, 1955-57; OC, 10 Infantry Workshop, Malaya, 1958-60; jssc 1960; Directing Staff, Staff Coll., 1961-63; Comdr, REME, 3rd Div., 1963-65; Operational Observer, Viet Nam, 1966-67; Col GS, Staff Coll., 1967-69; idc 1970; Dir, Administrative Planning, 1971-73; Dep. Military Sec. (2), 1973-75. *Recreations:* walking, gardening, reading. *Address:* Elmtree House, Hurtmore, Godalming, Surrey. *T:* Godalming 6936. *Club:* Army and Navy.

WOOD, Prof. Edward James; Professor of Latin, University of Leeds, 1938-67, Professor Emeritus, 1967; Pro-Vice-Chancellor, University of Leeds, 1957-59; *b* 3 Sept. 1902; *s* of James M. A. Wood, Advocate in Aberdeen; *m* 1933, Marion Grace Chorley; one *s* one *d*. *Educ:* Aberdeen Grammar School; Aberdeen University; Trinity College, Cambridge. Lectr in Classics, Manchester University, 1928; Professor of Latin, Aberystwyth, 1932. *Publications:* contributions to: Classical Review, Gnomon. *Address:* 35 Barleyfields Road, Wetherby, West Yorks. *T:* Wetherby 62488.

WOOD, Franklin Garrett, MA, MB, BCh, DMRE Cantab; Hon. Consulting Radiologist to: Hospital for Diseases of the Chest, German Hospital, London, and Black Notley Hospital; Fellow of Royal Society of Medicine; 2nd *s* of late James Wood, LLD, Grove House, Southport. *Educ:* Rydal School; Jesus Coll., Cambridge; St Thomas' Hospital, London. Late House Physician and Casualty Officer, St Thomas' Hospital; Temporary Surgeon Lt RN. *Publications:* Contributions to Medical Press. *Recreations:* riding and music. *Address:* 14 Upper Park Road, NW3.

WOOD, Sir Frederick (Ambrose Stuart), Kt 1977; Chairman, National Bus Company, since 1972; Chairman since 1960, and Managing Director since 1953, Croda International Ltd; Member, National Research Development Corporation, since 1973; *b* 30 May 1926; *s* of Alfred Phillip Wood, Goole, Yorkshire, and Patras, Greece, and Charlotte Wood (*née* Barnes), Goole, Yorkshire, and Athens, Greece; *m* 1947, June R. King; two *s* one *d*. *Educ:* Felsted Sch., Essex; Clare Coll., Cambridge. Served War, Sub-Lt (A) Observer, Fleet Air Arm, 1944-47. Trainee Manager, Croda Ltd, 1947-50; Pres., Croda Inc., New York, 1950-53. Mem., Nationalised Industries Chms'

Gp, 1975-. Chm. British Sect., Centre Européen d'Entreprise Publique, 1976-. *Address:* 33 Cheyne Place, Chelsea, SW3. *T:* 01-352 3036; Casa del Pozzo, Porto Maratea, Italy. *T:* Maratea 76178. *Club:* Junior Carlton.

WOOD, Prof. Emer. Frederick Lloyd Whitfeld, CMG 1974; Professor Emeritus, Victoria University, 1969; *b* 29 Sept. 1903; *s* of Prof. G. A. Wood and Eleanor Madeline Wood (*née* Whitfeld), Sydney; *m* 1932, Joan Myrtle, *d* of E. L. Walter, Sydney; one *s* one *d* (and one *s* one *d* decd). *Educ:* Sydney Grammar Sch.; Univ. of Sydney (BA); Balliol Coll., Oxford (MA). Univ. Medals History and Philos., Sydney. Frazer Scholar, Univ. of Sydney, 1925; Goldsmith Sen. Student, Oxford, 1929; Lectr in History, Univ. of Sydney, 1930-34; Actg Lectr in History, Balliol Coll., 1929 and 1937; Prof. of History, Victoria Univ., Wellington, NZ, 1935-69. Carnegie Vis. Fellow, Royal Inst. of Internat. Affairs, London, 1952-53. Res. Dir, NZ Inst. of Internat. Affairs, 1974. *Publications:* The Constitutional Development of Australia, 1933; Concise History of Australia, 1935; New Zealand in the World, 1940; Understanding New Zealand, 1944; revised edns as This New Zealand, 1946, 1952 and 1958; The New Zealand People at War, Political and External Affairs, 1958; contrib. NZ Jl of History, DNB. *Recreation:* walking. *Address:* 4 Gladstone Terrace, Wellington, New Zealand. *T:* Wellington 726-818. *Club:* University (Wellington).

WOOD, Sir George (Ernest Francis), KBE 1975 (OBE 1946); ISO 1958; retired Director, Reserve Bank of New Zealand (1959-1964); *b* 13 July 1900; *s* of George Francis Wood and Margaret Wood (*née* Blewman); *m* 1928, Eileen Alice Oudaille; one *s* one *d*. *Educ:* Greymouth District High Sch.; Waitaki Boys' High Sch.; Victoria Univ., Wellington, NZ. MA Hons in Economics. Statistician, Dept of Statistics, Wellington, NZ, 1921-38; Govt Statistician: Palestine, 1938-45; New Zealand, 1946-58. Chm., Consumer Council, 1959-75. *Publications:* The Wordsmiths: a study of advertising, 1964; Consumers in Action, 1973. *Recreations:* gardening, reading, following Rugby football. *Address:* 116 Morningside Road, Whangarei, New Zealand. *T:* 87-274.

WOOD, Maj.-Gen. George Neville, CB 1946; CBE 1945; DSO 1945; MC; *b* 4 May 1898; *o s* of Frederick Wood, Newnham-on-Severn, Glos; *m* 1928, Mary, *d* of Ven. H. C. Izard, late Archdeacon of Singapore; one *s* one *d*. *Educ:* Colston's School; Royal Military College, Sandhurst. First Commission Dorset Regt 1916; active service France, Russia, Turkey, 1916-20 (despatches twice, wounded, OBE, MC); regimental service Near East and Sudan, 1921-25; Staff College, Camberley, 1926-27; Staff employment War Office, and Aldershot, 1928-31; regimental service and Staff employment, India, 1932-38; commanded Oxford University OTC 1938-39; MA Oxon (hon.); Staff employment, home theatre, 1939-40; commanded 12th Bn West Yorkshire Regt 1941; commanded 2nd Bn Dorset Regt 1941-42; commanded 4th Infantry Brigade, 1942; BGS Ceylon Army Command, 1943; BGS 33rd Indian Corps in Assam-Burma operations, 1943-44; GOC 25th Indian Division in Arakan operations and re-occupation of Malaya, 1944-46 (despatches twice, CBE, DSO, CB); President No 6 Reg. Commissions Board, 1946; GOC Mid-West District and 53rd (Welsh) Div. TA, 1947-50; Director of Quartering, War Office, 1951-52; retired 1952. Col, The Devonshire and Dorset Regt, 1952-62. *Recreations:* cricket, history. *Address:* 6 Elsworthy Terrace, Hampstead, NW3.

WOOD, Maj.-Gen. Harry Stewart, CB 1967; TD 1950; Military Sales Manager, Hunting Hivolt Ltd (formerly Miles Group of Companies), since 1967; *b* 16 Sept. 1913; *e s* of late Roland and Eva M. Wood; *m* 1939, Joan Gordon, *d* of Gordon S. King; two *s* (and one *s* decd). *Educ:* Nautical Coll., Pangbourne. Civil Engineer (inc. articled trg), 1931-39. Commnd RA (TA), 1937. Served War of 1939-45: Regimental Service, Sept. 1939-June 1944; subseq. Technical Staff. Dep. Dir of Artillery, Min. of Supply (Col), 1958-60; Dep. Dir of Inspection (Brig.), 1960-62; Sen. Mil. Officer, Royal Armament Research and Development Estab. (Brig.), 1962-64; Vice-President, Ordnance Board, 1964-66, President, 1966-67. Maj.-Gen. 1964; retd, 1967. Legion of Merit, degree of Legionnaire (USA), 1947. *Recreations:* home and garden, motor sport. *Address:* Brook House, Faygate, near Horsham, Sussex. *T:* Faygate 342.

WOOD, Sir Henry (Peart), Kt 1967; CBE 1960; Principal, Jordanhill College of Education, Glasgow, 1949-71, retired; *b* 30 Nov. 1908; *s* of T. M. Wood, Bedlington, Northumberland; *m* 1937, Isobel Mary, *d* of W. F. Stamp, Carbis Bay, Cornwall; one *s* two *d*. *Educ:* Morpeth Grammar Sch.; Durham University. BSc 1930, MSc 1934, Durham; MA 1938, MEd 1941, Manchester. Lecturer, Manchester University, 1937-44;

Jordanhill College of Education: Principal Lecturer, 1944-46; Vice-Principal, 1947-49. Hon. LLD Glasgow, 1972. *Address:* 51 Whittingehame Drive, Glasgow G12 0YH. *T:* 041-334 3647.

WOOD, Hubert Lyon-Campbell, MS London; FRCS; retired; former Professor of Clinical Orthopaedics, Ahmadu Bello University, Zaria, Nigeria; Senior Orthopædic Surgeon, King's College Hospital, 1952-68, retired from National Health Service, 1968; Orthopædic Surgeon, Royal Masonic Hospital, since 1952; *b* 3 Nov. 1903; *s* of Dr H. M. Wood and Lola Lyon-Campbell; *m* 1935, Dr Irene Parker Murray, MB, BS London (*d* 1966); two *d*. *Educ:* Marlborough Coll., Wilts; King's Coll., London Univ. MRCS, LRCS, 1926; MB, BS London (Hons), 1927; FRCS 1930; MS London, 1934. Orthopædic Surgeon, EMS, 1939-48; Assistant Surgeon: King's College Hosp., 1932; Evelina Hosp., 1934; Orthopædic Surgeon, Leatherhead Hosp., 1940. *Publications:* Chapters in Post Graduate Surgery, 1937; chapters in Rose and Carless, 1958; Operative Surgery, 1957; articles in Br. Jl Bone and Joint Surgery (past member of editorial board). *Recreations:* gardening, riding, photography. *Address:* South House, 95 Dulwich Village, SE21 7BJ.

WOOD, Sir Ian (Jeffreys), Kt 1976; MBE 1942; MD; FRCP, FRACP; Consultant Physician, Royal Melbourne Hospital, since 1963; *b* 5 Feb. 1903; *s* of Dr Jeffreys Wood and Mrs Isla Wood; *m* 1939, Edith Mary Cooke; two *d*. *Educ:* Melbourne C of E Grammar Sch.; Univ. of Melbourne (MD, BS). FRCP 1943; FRACP 1937. War Service, 1939-45: RAAMC, ME and Pacific Zone; Col Comdg 2/7 Aust. Gen. Hosp., New Guinea, 1944-45. Med. Supt, Children's Hosp., Melbourne, 1930-31; House Phys., Hosp. for Sick Children, Great Ormond Street, London, 1932; Royal Melbourne Hospital: Phys., 1939-63; Asst Dir, Walter and Eliza Hall Inst. of Med. Res., 1946-63. Neil Hamilton Fairley Medal, for Outstanding Contributions to Medicine, RCP and RACP, 1974; Stawell Oration, The Great and Glorious Masterpiece of Man, Melbourne, 1975. Univ. of Melbourne Blue for Cricket and Hockey, 1926; Victorian State Hockey Team, 1927. *Publications:* Diffuse Lesions of the Stomach (with Dr L. I. Taft), 1958; contribs in field of gastroenterology in BMJ, Lancet and Med. Jl of Aust. *Recreations:* book collecting, cricket and tennis. *Address:* Flat 1, 27 Tintern Avenue, Toorak, Vic 3142, Australia. *T:* 24 9622. *Clubs:* Melbourne, Melbourne Cricket.

WOOD, James Maxwell, (Max Wood), OBE 1975; Chairman, Metrication Board, since 1977 (Deputy Chairman, 1976-77); *b* 24 June 1914; *s* of Arthur Henry and Emily Louisa Wood; *m* 1943, Olive Margaret Musk; one *s* two *d*. *Educ:* Technical colls; Ruskin Coll., Oxford; Co-operative Coll., Loughborough. Dip. Econ. and Pol. Sci. (Oxon). Private Sec. to Rt Hon. A. V. Alexander, MP (later Earl Alexander of Hillsborough) to 1940. Served War, 1940-46: RAF, and Embassies in S America. Asst Parly Sec., Co-op. Union, to 1951; Organising Sec., Co-op. Dry Goods Trade Assoc., 1951-56; Parly Sec., Co-op. Union, 1956-74. Member: Retail Consortium, 1968-74; Consumers' Cttee under Agricultural Marketing Acts, 1966-; Food Hygiene Adv. Council (DHSS); Consumers' Consultative Cttee of EEC, 1973-76; Nat. Consumer Council, 1975-; Policyholders Protection Bd, 1975-; Chm., Consumer Working Party of Internat. Co-op. Alliance, 1963-73; Hon. Sec., Parly All-Party Retail Trade Gp; Pres., Co-op. Congress, 1974. *Publications:* numerous pamphlets and articles, over period of many years, on: consumer affairs, monopolies and restrictive practices, distributive trades. *Recreations:* music, water-colour painting. *Address:* 20 Ena Road, Norbury SW16 4JB. *T:* 01-764 2982.

WOOD, John; actor. *Educ:* Bedford Sch.; Jesus Coll., Oxford. Old Vic Co., 1954-56; Camino Real, Phoenix, 1957; The Making of Moo, Royal Court, 1957; Brouhaha, Aldwych, 1958; The Fantasticks, Apollo, 1961; Rosencrantz and Guildenstern are Dead, NY, 1967; Exiles, Mermaid, 1970; joined Royal Shakespeare Company, 1971; Enemies, The Man of Mode, Exiles, The Balcony, Aldwych, 1971; The Comedy of Errors, Stratford, 1972; Julius Caesar, Titus Andronicus, Stratford, 1972, Aldwych, 1973; Collaborators, Duchess, 1973; A Lesson in Blood and Roses, The Place, 1973; Sherlock Holmes, Travesties (Evening Standard Best Actor Award, 1974; Tony Award, 1976), Aldwych, 1974, NY, 1974; The Devil's Disciple, Ivanov, Aldwych, 1976. Television: A Tale of Two Cities, Barnaby Rudge, 1964-65; The Victorians, 1965; The Duel, 1966. Films: Nicholas and Alexandra, 1971; Slaughterhouse Five, 1972. *Address:* c/o Royal Shakespeare Company, Aldwych Theatre, Aldwych, WC2.

WOOD, Hon. Sir John (Kember), Kt 1977; MC 1944; **Hon. Mr Justice Wood;** a Judge of the High Court of Justice, Family Division, since 1977; *b* 8 Aug. 1922; *s* of John Rosskruge Wood; *m* 1952, Kathleen Ann Lowe; one *s* one *d*. *Educ:* Shrewsbury Sch.; Magdalene Coll., Cambridge. Served War of 1939-45: Rifle Brigade, 1941-46. Magdalene Coll., 1946-48. Barrister (Lincolns Inn), 1949, Bencher, 1977. QC 1969. A Recorder of the Crown Court, 1975-77. *Recreations:* sport, travel. *Address:* Royal Courts of Justice, WC2. *Clubs:* MCC; Hawks (Cambridge).

WOOD, John Laurence; Keeper, Department of Printed Books, British Library (formerly British Museum), 1966-76; *b* 27 Nov. 1911; *s* of J. A. Wood and Clara Josephine (*née* Ryan); *m* 1947, Rowena Beatrice Ross; one *s* one *d*. *Educ:* King James I Sch., Bishop Auckland; Merton Coll., Oxford (BA); Besançon; Paris. Lecteur, Univ. of Besançon, 1934-35; Asst Cataloguer, British Museum, 1936; seconded to Foreign Office, 1941-45; Asst Keeper, British Museum, 1946; Deputy Keeper, 1959. *Publications:* (trans.) The French Prisoner, Garneray, 1957; (trans.) Contours of the Middle Ages, Genicot, 1967. *Recreations:* eating, do-it-yourself, reading detective stories, bookbinding. *Address:* 88 Hampstead Way, NW11. *T:* 01-455 4395.

WOOD, John Peter; Editor, Amateur Gardening, since 1971; *b* 27 March 1925; *s* of Walter Ralph Wood and Henrietta Martin; *m* 1956, Susan Maye White; one *s* one *d*. *Educ:* Grove Park Grammar Sch.; Seale Hayne Agricultural Coll. (NDH and Dip. in Hort., of College). Served War, 1943-46. Horticultural studies, 1946-52; Amateur Gardening: Asst Editor, 1952-66; Dep. Editor, 1966-71. *Publications:* Amateur Gardening Handbook—Bulbs, 1957; Amateur Gardening Picture Book— Greenhouse Management, 1959. *Recreations:* gardening, music appreciation. *Address:* West House, Wych Hill Lane, Woking, Surrey. *T:* Woking 63339.

WOOD, Joseph Neville; Director General, The General Council of British Shipping, since 1975; *b* 25 October 1916; *o s* of late Robert Hind Wood and Emily Wood, Durham; *m* 1st, 1944, Elizabeth May (*d* 1959); three *d*; 2nd, 1965, Josephine Samuel. *Educ:* Johnston School, Durham; London School of Economics. Entered Civil Service (Board of Trade), 1935; Ministry of War Transport, 1940; jssc 1950; Ministry of Transport: Asst Sec., 1951; Far East Representative, 1952-55; Under-Sec., 1961; Chief of Highway Administration, 1967-68. Joined Chamber of Shipping of the UK, 1968, Dep. Dir, 1970, Dir, 1972-. Mem., Baltic Exchange, 1968-. FCIT 1976. Officier, Ordre de Mérite Maritime, 1950. *Recreation:* gardening. *Address:* Barbers Cottage, Heyshott, Midhurst, Sussex. *T:* Midhurst 4282.

WOOD, Kenneth Maynard; Chairman and Managing Director, Dawson-Keith Ltd, since 1971; Chairman: Rowlands Castle Hotels Ltd, since 1968; Hipley Developments Ltd, since 1971; Director, Stocklands Equestrian Ltd; *b* 4 Oct. 1916; *s* of late Frederick Cavendish Wood and Agnes Maynard; *m* 1944, Laurie Marion McKinlay; two *s* two *d*. *Educ:* Bromley County School. Cadet, Merchant Navy, 1930-34; electrical and mechanical engineering, 1934-37; started own company radio, television and radar development, 1937-39; sold business and joined RAF, transferred for development of electronic equipment, 1939-46; started Kenwood Manufacturing Co. Ltd, 1946; Managing Director, 1946-68. Fellow, Inst. of Ophthalmology; FInstMSM. *Recreations:* golf, riding. *Address:* Camelot, Shipton Green, Itchenor, Sussex. *T:* Birdham 512259. *Clubs:* Constitutional, Royal Automobile.

WOOD, Sir Kenneth (Millns), Kt 1970; FCA; Chairman, Bison Group (formerly Concrete Ltd), Hounslow; *b* 25 April 1909; *s* of Sydney Wood and Edith Wood (*née* Barker); *m* 1939, Julia Mary, *d* of John and Mary Ambrose; one *d*. *Educ:* Barnstaple Grammar Sch.; Trinity Coll., Cambridge (BA). Wrangler in Maths Tripos, Trinity Coll., 1930. Chartered Accountant, 1933. Served War of 1939-45 (Lt-Col). Concrete Ltd: Dir 1946; Man. Dir 1950; Chm. 1958. Seconded to Min. of Housing and Local Govt as Industrial Adviser on House-Building to Minister, 1966-67; Dir, National Building Agency, 1966. FBIM 1971. *Recreations:* golf, ski-ing, sailing, tennis. *Address:* Ridge End, Finchampstead, Berks. *T:* Eversley (Hants) 733294. *Club:* East Berks Golf.

WOOD, Rt. Rev. Mark; *see* Wood, Rt. Rev. S. M.

WOOD, Rt. Rev. Maurice Arthur Ponsonby; *see* Norwich, Bishop of.

WOOD, Norman, CBE 1965; Director: Co-operative Wholesale Society Ltd, 1942-64; Manchester Ship Canal Co., 1954-64; Associated British Foods Ltd, 1964-75, retired; *b* 2 Oct. 1905; *m* 1st, 1933, Ada Entwisle (*d* 1974); two *s* one *d*; 2nd, 1976, Nita Miller. *Educ:* Bolton Co. Grammar Sch.; Co-operative Coll. Nat. Exec. Co-operative Party, and Central Board of Co-operative Union, 1934; Ministry of Information, 1939;

Chocolate and Sugar Confectionery War-time Assoc., 1942; British Tourist and Holidays Board (later BTA), 1947-70 (Dep. Chm., 1964-67); Plunkett Foundation, 1948- (Vice-Pres. 1972-); Cake and Biscuit Alliance, 1948; Wheat Commission, 1950; Domestic Coal Consumers Council, 1950; Coronation Accommodation Cttee, 1952. Member: British and Irish Millers, 1950-64; White Fish Authority, 1959-63; Food Res. Adv. Cttee, 1961-65; DTI Japan Trade Adv. Cttee, 1971-; Exec. Mem., British Food Export Council, 1970-75. Chairman: Food and Drink Cttee, British Week, Toronto, 1967, Tokyo, 1969; Chm., ten Food and Drink Missions to Hong Kong and Japan, 1968-76; Dir, Fedn of Agricl Co-ops (UK) Ltd, 1975-; Mem., Lab Party Study Gp on Export Services and Organisation, 1974. *Recreations:* walking, music. *Address:* 17 Wallace Fields, Epsom, Surrey; The Croft, Kettlebaston, Ipswich, Suffolk. *T:* (office) 01-393 9052. *Club:* Oriental.

WOOD, Peter (Lawrence); theatrical and television director; *b* 8 Oct. 1928; *s* of Frank Wood and Lucy Eleanor (*née* Meeson). *Educ:* Taunton School; Downing College, Cambridge. Resident Director, Arts Theatre, 1956-57; The Iceman Cometh, Arts, 1958; The Birthday Party, Lyric, Hammersmith, 1958; Maria Stuart, Old Vic, 1958; As You Like It, Stratford, Canada, 1959; Winter's Tale, Stratford, England, 1960; The Devils, Stratford, Aldwych, 1961; Hamlet, Stratford, England, 1961; The Private Ear and The Public Eye, Globe, 1962; The Devils, Aldwych, 1962; The Beggar's Opera, Aldwych, 1963; The Private Ear and The Public Eye, Morosco, New York, 1963; Co-Director, History Cycle, Stratford-on-Avon, 1964; The Master Builder, National Theatre, 1964; Carving a Statue, Haymarket, 1964; Poor Richard, Helen Hayes Theatre, New York, 1964; Love for Love, Moscow, and National Theatre, 1965; Incident at Vichy, Phœnix, 1966; The Prime of Miss Jean Brodie, Wyndham's, 1966; White Liars, and Black Comedy 1968; In Search of Gregory (film), 1968-69; Hamlet, NBC TV, 1970; Design for Living, Los Angeles, 1971; Jumpers, National Theatre, 1972, Burgtheater, Vienna, 1973; Billy Rose Theatre, NY, 1974; Dear Love, Comedy, 1973; Long Day's Journey into Night, ABC TV, 1973; Travesties, Aldwych, 1974, NY, 1975; Macbeth, LA, 1975; The Mother of us All (opera), Sante Fe, 1976; Shakespeare, episode I, ATV, 1976; Long Day's Journey into Night, LA, 1977; Cosi Fan Tutte, Santa Fe, 1977. *Recreations:* swimming, sailing, travelling. *Address:* 11 Warwick Avenue, W9.

WOOD, Ralph; His Honour Judge Wood; a Circuit Judge since 1972; *b* 26 April 1921; *o s* of Harold and Dorothy Wood, Wilmslow, Cheshire. *Educ:* King's Sch., Macclesfield; Exeter Coll., Oxford. Served War of 1939-45: commissioned Somerset LI, and served in England, India and Manipur, 1941-46. Called to Bar, Gray's Inn, 1948; practised on Northern Circuit; JP Co. Lancs, 1970; Dep. Chm., Lancashire QS, 1970-71. *Address:* 38 Hawthorn Lane, Wilmslow, Cheshire. *T:* Wilmslow 22673.

WOOD, (René) Victor; Chief Executive since 1969, and Chairman since 1974, Hill Samuel Insurance and Shipping Holdings Ltd; Director, Hill Samuel Group Ltd, and Hill Samuel & Co. Ltd; Chairman: Hill Samuel Life Assurance Ltd; Lowndes Lambert Group; Lambert Brothers Shipping Ltd; Lowndes-Ajax Computer Service Ltd; Elizabethan Marine & General Insurance Co Ltd; Director, Haslemere Estates Ltd; *b* 1925. *Educ:* Jesus Coll., Oxford (BA). FFA. *Publications:* (with Michael Pilch): Pension Schemes, 1960; New Trends in Pensions, 1964; Pension Scheme Practice, 1967; Company Pension Schemes, 1971; Managing Pension Schemes, 1974. *Address:* (office) 53 Eastcheap, EC3. *T:* 01-283 2000; (home) Little Woodbury, Newchapel, near Lingfield, Surrey. *T:* Lingfield 832054.

WOOD, Rt. Hon. Richard Frederick, PC 1959; DL; MP (C) Bridlington Division of Yorkshire since 1950; *b* 5 Oct. 1920; 2nd surv. *s* of 1st Earl of Halifax, KG, PC, OM, GCSI, GCMG, GCIE, TD; *m* 1947, Diana, *d* of late Col E. O. Kellett, DSO, MP, and of Hon. Mrs W. J. McGowan; one *s* one *d. Educ:* Eton; New College, Oxford. Hon. Attaché, British Embassy, Rome, 1940; served War of 1939-45 as Lieutenant, KRRC, 1941-43; retired, wounded, 1943; toured US Army hospitals, 1943-45; New College, Oxford, 1945-47; Parliamentary Private Secretary: to Minister of Pensions, 1951-53; to Minister of State, Board of Trade, 1953-54; to Minister of Agriculture and Fisheries, 1954-55; Joint Parliamentary Secretary: Ministry of Pensions and National Insurance, 1955-58; Ministry of Labour, 1958-59; Minister of Power, October 1959-63, of Pensions and National Insurance, Oct. 1963-64; Minister of Overseas Develt, ODM, June-Oct. 1970, FCO, 1970-74. Dir, Hargreaves Group Ltd, 1974-. Mem., Hansard Soc. Commn on Electoral Reform, 1975-76. DL E Riding Yorks, 1967. Hon. LLD Sheffield Univ., 1962; Hon. Colonel: Queen's Royal Rifles, 1962; 4th (Volunteer) Bn

Royal Green Jackets, 1967-. *Address:* Flat Top House, Bishop Wilton, York YO4 1RY. *T:* Bishop Wilton 266; 49 Cadogan Place, SW1 9RT. *T:* 01-235 1597.
See also Col Sir E. W. Brooksbank, Bt.

WOOD, Robert Eric, CBE 1972; Director, City of Leicester Polytechnic, 1969-73; *b* 6 May 1909; *e s* of Robert and Emma Wood; *m* 1935, Beatrice May Skinner; one *s* one *d. Educ:* Birkenhead Inst.; Liverpool Univ. BSc 1st cl. hons, MSc; FInstP. Lectr and Demonstrator, Liverpool Univ., 1930; Lecturer: Borough Road Trng Coll., 1931; Kingston Techn. Coll., 1934; Woolwich Polytechnic, 1939; Head of Physics Dept, Wigan Techn. Coll., 1942; Principal: Grimsby Techn. Coll., 1947; Leicester Regional Coll. of Technology, 1953. Assoc. of Principals of Technical Instns: Hon. Sec., 1960-65; Pres., 1965-66; Chm., Interim Cttee of Polytechnic Directors, 1969-70; Mem. Council, CNAA, 1964-70; Mem., Council for Techn. Educn and Trng in Overseas Countries, 1962-66; Vice-Chm., Nat. Adv. Council on Educn for Industry and Commerce, 1967-72. Hon. FBSI. *Address:* Capler, Peppers Lane, Burton Lazars, Melton Mowbray, Leics. *T:* Melton Mowbray 4576.

WOOD, Robert Noel; Director, Overseas Development Institute, since 1974; *b* 25 Dec. 1934; *s* of Ernest Clement Wood, CIE and Lucy Eileen Wood; *m* 1962, Sarah Child; one *s* one *d. Educ:* Sherborne Sch.; New Coll., Oxford (BA Hons PPE); LSE (Rockefeller Student; Certif. in Internat. Studies). Nat. Service Commn, RHA, 1953-55. Dep. Res. Dir, Internat. Div., Economist Intelligence Unit Ltd, 1959-65; Inst. of Econs and Statistics, Oxford, 1965-70; Sen. Economist, Min. of Econ. Affairs and Develt Planning, Tanzania, 1966-69; Dir of Studies, Overseas Develt Inst., 1970-74; Adviser to House of Commons Select Cttee on Overseas Develt, 1973-74. *Publications:* contrib. Bull. Oxford Inst. of Econs and Statistics, ODI Rev. *Recreations:* Victorian painters and wood engravers, jazz, singing, swimming. *Address:* 55 Carlton Hill, NW8. *T:* 01-624 1768. *Club:* Le Petit Club Français.

WOOD, Roger L.; *see* Leigh-Wood.

WOOD, Prof. Ronald Karslake Starr, ARCS, BSc, DIC, PhD, FRS 1976; FIBiol; Professor of Plant Pathology, Imperial College, University of London, since 1964; *b* 8 April 1919; *s* of Percival Thomas Evans Wood and Florence Dix Starr; *m* 1947, Marjorie Schofield; one *s* one *d. Educ:* Ferndale Grammar Sch.; Imperial College. Royal Scholar, 1937; Forbes Medal, 1941; Huxley Medal, 1950. Research Asst to Prof. W. Brown, 1941; Directorate of Aircraft Equipment, Min. of Aircraft Production, 1942; Lectr, Imperial Coll., 1947; Commonwealth Fund Fellow, 1950; Univ. Reader in Plant Pathology, 1955; Research Fellow, Connecticut Agric. Experiment Stn, 1957. Mem. Council, British Mycological Soc., 1948; Sec., Assoc. of Applied Biologists; Mem., Parly and Sci. Cttee; Mem., Biological Council, 1949; Consultant, Nat. Fedn of Fruit and Potato Trades, 1955; Mem. council, Inst. of Biology, 1956; Chm., Plant Pathology Cttee, British Mycological Soc.; Mem. Governing Body, Nat. Fruit and Cider Inst., Barnes Memorial Lectr, 1962; Sec., First Internat. Congress of Plant Pathology, 1965; Mem. Governing Body, East Malling Research Stn, 1966; Pres., Internat. Soc. for Plant Pathology, 1968; Dean, RCS, 1975. Scientific Dir, NATO Advanced Study Inst., Pugnochiuso, 1970, Sardinia, 1975; Consultant, FAO/UNDP, India, 1976. Fellow, Amer. Phytopathological Soc., 1972; Corres. Mem., Deutsche Phytomedizinische Gesellschaft, 1973. *Publications:* Physiological Plant Pathology, 1967; (ed) Phytotoxins in Plant Diseases, 1972; (ed) Specifity in Plant Diseases, 1976; numerous papers in Annals of Applied Biology, Annals of Botany, Phytopathology, Trans British Mycological Soc. *Recreation:* gardening. *Address:* Pyrford Woods, Pyrford, near Woking, Surrey. *T:* Byfleet 43827.

WOOD, Russell Dillon, MVO 1975; VRD 1964; Lt-Comdr, RNR; Deputy Treasurer to the Queen since 1969; *b* 16 May 1922; *s* of William G. S. Wood, Whitstable, Kent, and Alice Wood; *m* 1948, Jean Violet Yelwa Davidson, *d* of Alan S. Davidson, Yalding, Kent; one *s* three *d. Educ:* King's Sch., Canterbury. Fleet Air Arm Pilot, 1940-46 (despatches twice). Qual. as Chartered Accountant, 1951; financial Management career with major public companies, 1951-68. *Recreations:* private flying, sailing. *Address:* Cleves Cottage, Westleton, Suffolk. *T:* Westleton 325; 4 The Old Barracks, Kensington Palace, W8. *Clubs:* Army and Navy; East Anglian Flying, Aldeburgh Yacht.

WOOD, Sam, MSc; Director of Statistics and Business Research, Post Office, 1965-72, retired; *b* 10 Oct. 1911; *m* 1940, Lucy Greenhalgh Whittaker; two *d. Educ:* Glossop Grammar School, Derbyshire; University of Manchester. Gaskell Open

Scholarship, Derbyshire Major Scholarship, 1929; BSc (1st cl. Hons) Maths; Bishop Harvey Goodwin Research Scholarship, 1932; MSc 1933. Civil Service: GPO, 1933-34; National Assistance Board, 1934-43; Min. of Aircraft Production, 1943-46; Treasury, 1946-50; GPO: Statistician, 1950; Chief Statistician, 1954. *Publications:* articles in JL of Inst. of Statisticians, British Jl of Industrial Relations. *Address:* Boxhedge House, Astwood Road, Cranfield, Beds. *T:* Bedford 750392.

WOOD, Rt. Rev. (Stanley) Mark; Assistant Bishop of Hereford, since 1977; *b* 21 May 1919; *s* of Arthur Mark and Jane Wood; *m* 1947, Winifred Ruth, *d* of Edward James Toase; three *s* two *d*. *Educ:* Pontypridd County School; University College, Cardiff; College of the Resurrection, Mirfield. BA (2nd cl. Greek and Latin), Wales. Curate at St Mary's, Cardiff Docks, 1942-45; Curate, Sophiatown Mission, Johannesburg, 1945-47; Rector of Bloemhof, Transvaal, 1947-50; Priest in charge of St Cyprian's Mission, Johannesburg, 1950-55; Rector of Marandellas, Rhodesia, 1955-65; Dean of Salisbury, Rhodesia, 1965-70; Bishop of Matabeleland, 1971-77. *Address:* How Caple Rectory, Hereford HR1 4TE. *T:* How Caple 231.

WOOD, Rev. Prof. Thomas; D. J. James Professor of Pastoral Theology, St David's University College, Lampeter, since 1957; Deputy Principal, 1971-77; *b* 30 April 1919; *o s* of Willie Wood and Mabel (*née* Gaffey), Batley, Yorks; *m* 1945, Joan Ashley Pollard; three *s*. *Educ:* Batley Grammar Sch.; Univ. of Leeds (BA 1st Cl. Hons English 1941; BD 1945; MA with Dist. 1947); Coll. of the Resurrection, Mirfield. Deacon 1943, priest 1944. Asst Curate, St Anne's, Worksop, 1943-47; Sen. Asst Curate, Mansfield Parish Church, 1947-52; Vicar of Seascale, 1952-57. Chm., Ch. in Wales Working Party on Marriage and Divorce, 1972-75. Member: Southwell Dioc. Cttee for Post-ordination Trng, 1948-52; Social and Indust. Commn of Ch. Assembly, 1949-50; Churches' Council on Gambling, 1965-; Doctrinal Commn of Ch. in Wales, 1969-; Ch. in Wales Adv. Commn on Ch. and Society, 1973-. An Ecclesiastical Judge, Provincial Ct of Ch. in Wales, 1976-. Bishop's Selector, CACTM, 1955-66; Select Preacher, Univ. of Cambridge, 1961. *Publications:* English Casuistical Divinity during the Seventeenth Century, 1952; The Pastoral Responsibility of the Church Today, 1958; Five Pastorals, 1961; Some Moral Problems, 1961; Chastity Not Outmoded, 1965; (contrib.) A Dictionary of Christian Ethics, 1967; articles and revs in Theol., Ch. Qtly Rev., Jl Theol Studies, Ch. in Wales Qtly, Trivium. *Address:* College House, St David's University College, Lampeter, Dyfed SA48 7ED.

WOOD, Victor; *see* Wood, R. V.

WOOD, Walter; Town Clerk, City of Birmingham, 1972-74; *b* Bolton, 11 Jan. 1914; *s* of Walter Scott Wood; *m* 1939, Hilda Maude, *d* of Albert Forrester; two *s*. *Educ:* Canon Slade Sch., Bolton; Victoria Univ., Manchester (LLB). Served with RAF, 1940-45. Admitted solicitor, 1937 (Daniel Reardon and Clabon prizeman); legal associate member, RTPI, 1948; Asst Solicitor, Bradford, 1937. Swansea, 1939; Dep. Town Clerk, Grimsby, 1947; Principal Asst Solicitor, Sheffield, 1948; Asst Town Clerk, Birmingham, 1952; Dep. Town Clerk, Birmingham, 1960. Panel Inspector, DoE, 1974. Governor, Solihull Sch., 1974. Pres., Birmingham Law Soc., 1976. *Recreations:* swimming, philately. *Address:* 43 Sandgate Road, Hall Green, Birmingham B28 0UN. *T:* 021-744 1195.

WOOD, William Alan, CB 1970; Second Crown Estate Commissioner since 1968; *b* 8 Dec. 1916; *m* 1943, Zoë, *d* of Rev. Dr D. Frazer-Hurst; two *s* two *d*. *Educ:* Dulwich Coll.; Corpus Christi Coll., Cambridge (Scholar). Ministry of Home Affairs, N. Ireland, 1939. Lieut, RNVR, 1942-46. Ministry of Town and Country Planning, 1946; Minister's Private Secretary, 1951; Principal Regional Officer (West Midlands), Ministry of Housing and Local Government, 1954; Asst Secretary, 1956; Under-Secretary, 1964-68. Chm. Council, King Alfred Sch., 1966-. *Address:* 654 Finchley Road, NW11. *T:* 01-458 2684. *Club:* Farmers'.

WOOD, William Walter, FRIBA, CEng, FIStructE; *b* Arnold, Notts, 24 Nov. 1896; *e s* of Uriah and Georgina Maria Wood; *m* 1920, Frances Agnes Irene, *d* of Samuel Edwin and Emma Jane Varney, Nottingham; two *s*. *Educ:* Nottingham High Sch. Articled to late Frederick Ball, Nottingham, and trained at Nottingham University College and School of Art, Architectural Association School of Architecture, London, and in the atelier of the late Fernand Billerey in London; Asst Professor of Architecture and Senior Lecturer in Architectural Design in the Royal School of Engineering, Cairo, 1926-28; Head of the Dept of Architecture at Plymouth Central School of Arts and Crafts, 1928-32; Head of the Dept of Building at

Plymouth and Devonport Technical Colleges, 1931-32; Principal, Mid-Essex Technical College and School of Art, Chelmsford, 1932-40; Founder and Principal, Delhi Polytechnic, Delhi, 1940-46. Member of the Schools Cttee of the Board of Architectural Education, RIBA, 1929-31; Founder-President, Association of Principals of Technical Institutions (India), 1941-46. Chairman, National Service Labour Tribunal, President Technical Training Selection Cttee and Regional Inspector of Technical Training, Delhi, Ajmer-Merwara and Rajputana, 1941-42; served in Egypt, Palestine, France, Belgium, and Germany, 1915-19; works: University of Rajasthan; Government House of South-West Africa; factories, mills, offices, showrooms, banks, hotels, airports, schools, hostels, flats, houses in England, Egypt, India, Southern Africa. Works exhibited at Royal Academy, RIBA, RSA, and Architectural Association, London, also Salon d'Automne, Paris. *Publications:* articles in technical periodicals, with translations in French and French Colonial architectural reviews; former English Correspondent of L'Architecture d'Aujourd'hui. *Recreations:* bowls, photography, and travel. *Address:* PO Box 5154, Walmer 6065, Port Elizabeth, South Africa.

WOODALL, Alec; MP (Lab) Hemsworth since Feb. 1974; *b* 20 Sept. 1918; *m* 1950; one *s* one *d*. *Educ:* South Road Elementary School. Colliery official. PPS to Sec. of State for Trade, 1976-. *Address:* 2 Grove Terrace, Hemsworth, West Yorkshire WF9 4BQ. *T:* Hemsworth 613897.

WOODALL, Lt.-Gen. Sir John (Dane), KCMG 1959; KBE 1953 (OBE 1942; MBE 1919); CB 1947; MC 1917; Governor and Commander-in-Chief, Bermuda, 1955-60; *b* 19 April 1897; *s* of late Colonel F. Woodall, CMG; *m* 1st, 1920, Helen (Nischan-I-Schefakat), *o d* of late Sir Adam Block, KCMG; one *d*; 2nd, 1935, Marion, CStJ, *d* of late Alfred Aitkin Thom; one *s* two *d*. *Educ:* St Columba's; RMA, Woolwich; Staff Colleges, Camberley and RAF. Served European War, 1914-18, Major, Royal Artillery (despatches, MBE, MC); DAAG Turkey, 1922-24; Instructor in Gunnery; Brigade Major; commanded battery RA; Instructor RAF Staff College; commanded regt RA; GSO1; Brigadier, General Staff, 1940; DDSD, War Office; Director Man Power, War Office; served War of 1939-46 (despatches, CB, OBE); Vice-Adjutant-General to the Forces, 1949-52; GOC, N. Ireland, 1952-55; retired, 1955. Colonel Comdt, RA, 1954-62. KStJ 1958. *Recreations:* lawn tennis and squash. *Address:* Whitewell Lodge, near Whitchurch, Salop. *Club:* Army and Navy.

WOODALL, Mary, CBE 1959; PhD; DLitt; FSA; FMA; London Adviser to Felton Trust, Melbourne, 1965-75; *b* 6 March 1901. *Educ:* Cheltenham Ladies' Coll.; Somerville Coll., Oxford. Voluntary, British Museum Dept of Prints and Drawings. WRVS Regional Administrator, 1938-42; Temp. Principal, Ministry of Health and Ministry of Supply, 1942-45; Keeper, Dept of Art, 1945-56, Director, 1956-64, City Museum and Art Gallery, Birmingham. Trustee, Nat. Gallery, 1968-76. Fellow of University College, London, 1958. *Publications:* Gainsborough's Landscape Drawings, 1939; Thomas Gainsborough, 1949; The Letters of Thomas Gainsborough, 1962. *Recreations:* travelling, painting. *Address:* Red House, Clifton Hampden, Abingdon-on-Thames, Oxon. *Club:* University Women's.

WOODBINE PARISH, David Elmer; *see* Parish.

WOODBURN, Rt. Hon. Arthur, PC 1947; DLitt; *b* Edinburgh, 25 Oct. 1890; *s* of Matthew Woodburn (Brassfounder) and Janet Brown Woodburn; *m* 1919, Barbara Halliday. *Educ:* Bruntsfield and Boroughmuir Public Schools, Edinburgh; Heriot-Watt Coll., Edinburgh. For 25 years in Engineering and Ironfounding Administration, specialised in languages and costing; Hon. Secretary, Edinburgh Labour College till 1932; Secretary, Scottish Labour College, till 1939; President National Council of Labour Colleges, 1937-; Lectured in History, Economics and Finance in Labour College, 1919 onwards; gave evidence before MacMillan Cttee on Finance and Industry, 1929; contested (Lab) S Edinburgh, 1929, Leith, 1931; Scottish Secretary, Labour Party, 1932-39; MP (Lab) Clackmannan and East Stirling, 1939-70; Parliamentary Private Secretary to Rt Hon. Thomas Johnston, Secretary of State for Scotland, 1941-45; Parliamentary Secretary, Ministry of Supply, 1945-47; Secretary of State for Scotland, 1947-50. Member of Select Cttee on National Expenditure and Chairman Sub-Committee on Finance and Establishments, 1939-45; Administrative Cttee and Front Bench of Parliamentary Labour Party, 1943-45; Member of Speaker's Conference on Electoral Reform, 1944; led first Inter-Parliamentary Union Delegn to West German Bundestag at Bonn; Member: Select Cttee on Clergy Disqualification, 1952-53; Select Cttee on Delegated Legislation, 1952-53; Select Cttee on House of Commons Procedure, 1956-68; Historic Buildings Council for Scotland. Trustee, Scottish National Library, 1962. Led British Inter-Parliamentary Union Delegations to Uruguay, 1957, to Spain, 1960 and House of Commons Delegn to Uganda, 1964, to Kenya, 1966; has visited numerous countries in Europe and S America; Jt Pres., Brit. Section, Council of European Municipalities, 1971-. *Publications:* Banks and the Workers, 1924; Mystery of Money, 1929; Outline of Finance, 1930 (4 editions). *Recreation:* golf. *Address:* 83 Orchard Road, Edinburgh EH4 2EX. *T:* 031-332 1961.

WOODCOCK, Eric Charles, MA; Professor of Latin in the University of Durham (late Durham Colleges), 1948-66; now Professor Emeritus; *b* 20 May 1904; *s* of Charles T. Woodcock; *m* 1933, Ruth Mary Ball; two *s. Educ:* King Edward's Sch., Birmingham; St John's Coll., Cambridge. First class in both parts of Classical Tripos, Cambridge (Part I, 1925; Part II, 1927); Instructor in Department of Ancient Languages, Harvard, 1927-28; Asst Lecturer in Classics, University of Reading, 1928-30; Asst Lecturer in Classics, University of Manchester, 1930-32; Lecturer in Latin, 1932-47; Senior Lecturer in Latin, 1947-48. *Publications:* Tacitus, Annals XIV (edited with Introduction and notes), 1939; A New Latin Syntax, 1959; various articles and reviews in Harvard Studies in Classical Philology, in Classical Review and in Greece and Rome. *Recreation:* reading. *Address:* 25 Dingle Road, Boscombe, Bournemouth BH5 2DP.

WOODCOCK, Rt. Hon. George, PC 1967; CBE 1953; *b* 20 Oct. 1904; 2nd *s* of Peter Woodcock, Bamber Bridge, Lancashire; *m* 1933, Laura M. McKernan; one *s* one *d. Educ:* Brownedge Elementary; Ruskin College and New Coll., Oxford. Cotton Weaver, 1916-27; 1st Class Hons Philos. and Polit. Economy, Oxford, 1933; Jessie Theresa Rowden Senior Scholarship, New Coll., 1933; Civil Servant, 1934-36; Secretary to TUC Research and Economic Dept, 1936-47; Assistant General Secretary, TUC, 1947-60, General Secretary, 1960-69. Member Royal Commn: on Taxation of Profits and Income, 1950; on Trade Unions and Employers' Assocs, 1965-68; Member British Guiana Constitutional Commission, 1954; Member Committee on the Working of the Monetary System, 1957; Vice-Chairman, National Savings Cttee, 1952-75; Mem., NEDC, 1962-69; Chm., Commn on Industrial Relations, 1969-71. Hon. Fellow, New Coll., Oxford, 1963; Hon. Fellow, LSE, 1964. Hon. LLD: Sussex, 1963; Manchester, 1968; Lancaster, 1970; London, 1970; Hon. DCL: Oxford Univ., 1964; Kent Univ., 1968; Hon. DSc, University of Aston in Birmingham, 1967. *Address:* Lower Hill Road, Epsom, Surrey. *T:* Epsom 22694.

WOODCOCK, Dr George, FRSC, FRGS; Editor, Canadian Literature, since 1959; author; *b* 8 May 1912; *s* of Samuel Arthur Woodcock and Margaret Gertrude Woodcock (*née* Lewis); *m* 1949, Ingeborg Hedwig Elisabeth Linzer. *Educ:* Sir William Borlase's Sch., Marlow. Editor, Now, London, 1940-47; freelance writer, 1947-54; Lectr in English, Univ. of Washington, 1954-56; Lectr, Asst Prof. and finally Associate Prof. of English, Univ. of British Columbia, 1956-63; Lectr in Asian Studies, Univ. of British Columbia, 1966-67. At the same time continued writing books and talks; also plays and documentaries for Canadian Broadcasting Corporation. Prepared a series of nine documentary films for CBC, on South Pacific, 1972-73. Hon. LLD: Victoria, 1967; Winnipeg, 1975; Hon. DLitt: Sir George Williams Univ., 1970; Univ. of Ottawa, 1974. John Simon Guggenheim Fellow, 1950; Canadian Govt Overseas Fellow, 1957; Canada Council: Killam Fellow, 1970; Senior Arts Fellow, 1975. Governor-General's Award for Non-Fiction, 1967; Molson Prize, 1973; UBC Medal for Popular Biography, 1973. FRSC 1968, FRGS 1971. *Publications:* William Godwin, 1946; The Anarchist Prince, 1950; Proudhon, 1956; To the City of the Dead, 1956; Selected Poems, 1967; Anarchism, 1962; Faces of India, 1964; The Greeks in India, 1966; The Crystal Spirit: a study of George Orwell, 1966; Canada and the Canadians, 1970; Dawn and the Darkest Hour, 1971; Gandhi, 1971; Rejection of Politics, 1972; Herbert Read, 1972; Who Killed the British Empire?, 1974; Gabriel Dumont, 1975; Notes on Visitations, 1975; South Sea Journey, 1977; also many articles. *Recreation:* travel. *Address:* 6429 McCleery Street, Vancouver, BC V6N 1G5, Canada. *T:* 266-9393. *Club:* Faculty (Vancouver).

WOODCOCK, Gordon, FCA, CIPFA; County Treasurer of Staffordshire, since 1973. Served War, Royal Navy, 1942-46. City Treasurer's Dept: Birmingham, 1937-42 and 1946-54; Stoke-on-Trent, 1954-73; City Treasurer of Stoke-on-Trent, 1971-73. *Address:* PO Box 10, County Buildings, Eastgate Street, Stafford ST16 2NF. *T:* Stafford 3121.

WOODCOCK, John, TD (with 2 bars) 1958; a Recorder of the Crown Court since 1972; Solicitor since 1948; *b* 1 Sept. 1920; *e s* of late Lt-Col F. A. Woodcock and Margaret (*née* Murphy); *m* 1951, Catherine Deirdre Ryan; two *s. Educ:* Bury Grammar Sch.; Prior Park Coll., Bath; Victoria Univ., Manchester. Royal Humane Soc. Hon. Testimonial, 1936; commissioned Lancs Fusiliers, TA, 1938. Served War: BEF, France, 1940, and with Kenya Armoured Car Regt, E Africa, 1940-43, and SEAC, 1943-45. Councillor, Tottington UDC, 1957-74 (Chm., 1963-64); Chm., Bury and Radcliffe Conservative Assoc., 1965-71; County Comr for Scouts, SE Lancashire, 1966-74; Pres., Bury and Dist. Law Soc., 1967; Chm., Bury and Rochdale Legal Aid Cttee, 1966-71; Pres., Tottington Ex-Service Mens' Assoc., 1947-; Pres., British Legion, Bury, 1969-. *Recreation:* gardening, when time! *Address:* Tonge Fold, Hawkshaw, near Bury, Lancashire. *T:* Tottington 2796, (business) 061-761 4611. *Club:* Conservative (Tottington).

WOODD WALKER, Geoffrey Basil, FRCS; retired as a Consultant Surgeon (West London Hospital, 1930-65); *b* 9 June 1900; *s* of Basil Woodd Walker, MD, and Margaret Jane Routledge; *m* 1932, Ulla Troili; two *s. Educ:* Rugby Sch.; King's Coll., Cambridge; St Mary's Hospital. MA Cambridge; MB, BCh; MRCS, LRCP London; FRCS 1928. *Recreation:* zoology (FZS). *Address:* 33 Lexden Road, Colchester, Essex CO3 3PX. *Club:* Athenæum.

WOODESON, Sir James (Brewis), Kt 1977; CBE 1972 (OBE 1945); TD; Executive Chairman, Clarke Chapman Ltd, since 1949; Chairman, Reyrolle Parsons Ltd, since 1974; Director, British Steel Corporation, since 1976; *b* 14 Oct. 1917; *s* of William Armstrong Woodeson and Ethel Margaret Woodeson (formerly Brewis); *m* 1957, Joyce Doreen Burrows; one *d* decd. *Educ:* Oundle Sch., Northants. Commenced with Clarke Chapman Ltd, 1933; Dir, 1938. Mem., Engineering Industries Council, 1975-; Mem (part time), BSC, 1976-. Hon. DCL Newcastle upon Tyne 1971. *Recreations:* golf, shooting, ornithology. *Address:* Overcliffe, Foxton, Alnmouth, Northumberland. *T:* Alnmouth 284. *Club:* Northern Counties (Newcastle).

WOODFIELD, Philip John, CB 1974; CBE 1963; Deputy Secretary, Home Office, since 1974; *b* 30 Aug. 1923; *s* of Ralph Woodfield; *m* 1958, Diana Margaret, *d* of Sydney Herington; three *d. Educ:* Alleyn's Sch., Dulwich; King's Coll., London. Served War of 1939-45: Royal Artillery, 1942-47 (captain). Entered Home Office, 1950; Asst Private Secretary to Home Secretary, 1952; Federal Government of Nigeria, 1955-57; Home Office, 1957-60; Private Secretary to the Prime Minister, 1961-65; Asst Sec. 1965-67, Asst Under-Sec. of State, 1967-72, Home Office; Deputy Sec., NI Office, 1972-74. Secretary to Commonwealth Immigration Mission, 1965; Secretary to Lord Mountbatten's inquiry into prison security, Nov.-Dec. 1966. *Recreation:* music. *Address:* 5 Erskine Hill, NW11. *T:* 01-458 4655. *Clubs:* Garrick, Beefsteak.

WOODFIELD, Ven. Samuel Percy, MA; Rector of Waterval Boven (African and European), 1964-72 (Priest-in-charge, Waterval Boven Missions, 1959-72); Archdeacon of Barberton, 1960-63, Archdeacon Emeritus from 1964; Canon S Alban's Cathedral, Pretoria, South Africa, 1932-64; Hon. Canon, 1964; *b* 19 April 1889; *s* of Samuel Robinson Woodfield and Emma Utting. *Educ:* Great Yarmouth Grammar Sch.; Selwyn Coll., Cambridge. Asst Priest, St Mary's, Hitchin, 1915-19; Headmaster, Norton Sch., Letchworth, 1917-19; Asst Priest, Sawbridgeworth, 1919-21; Vice-Principal, Diocesan Training Coll., Pietersburg, N Transvaal, 1922-24, Principal, 1924-38, 1954-57; Priest-in-Charge, Pietersburg West Native Mission, 1936-38; Priest-in-charge, Pretoria Native Mission, 1938-53, and Coloured Mission, 1943-53; Archdeacon of Pretoria (City) Native Mission, 1945-53; Archdeacon of W Transvaal, 1953-60; Archdeacon of E Transvaal, 1958-60. Exam. Chaplain to Bishop of Pretoria, 1922-50; Member: Advisory Board for Native Education in the Transvaal, 1924-37, 1940-43, 1946-50; Chaplain Westfort Leper Inst., 1938-53; Div. Pathfinder Scout Commissioner for the Transvaal, 1931-50; Deputy Chief Scouts' African Commissioner for S Africa, 1943-53; Chief Scout's Commissioner for African Scouts, S Africa, 1953-61; Emeritus Comr, 1961. King George V Jubilee Medal; Coronation Medals, 1937, 1953. *Address:* Irene Homes, 1675 Irene, Transvaal, South Africa. *T:* 65116.

WOODFORD, Brigadier Edward Cecil James, CBE 1946; DSO 1943; *b* 1901; *s* of late Major Edward Francis Woodford, York and Lancaster Regt; *m* 1949, Joanne Eileen, *d* of Peter Charles Mayer, Washington, DC, USA; one *s* two *d. Educ:* Bedford Sch.; RMC Sandhurst. 2nd Lieut, York and Lancaster Regt, 1920. Served War of 1939-45, N Africa, Iraq, Persia, Sicily, Italy,

Burma, French Indo-China; Lieut-Colonel, 1942, Brigadier, 1945. Commander, Lubbecke District, BAOR, 1952-55, retired 1955. *Address:* Hamlet House, 3535 Chevy Chace Lake Drive, Chevy Chace, Md 20015, USA.

WOODGATE, Joan Mary, CBE 1964; RRC 1959; Matron-in-Chief, Queen Alexandra's RN Nursing Service, 1962-66, retired; *b* 30 Aug. 1912; *d* of Sir Alfred Woodgate, CBE, and Louisa Alice (*née* Digby). *Educ:* Surbiton High Sch., Surrey. Trained at St George's Hospital, 1932-36, Sister, 1937-38; Queen Charlotte's Hospital, 1936. Joined QARNNS, 1938; served Middle East and Far East; HM Hospital Ship, Empire Clyde, 1945-47; HM Hospital Ship, Maine, 1953-54; Principal Matron: RNH Haslar, 1959-61; RNH Malta, 1961-62. OStJ 1959; QHNS, 1962-64. Member Commonwealth War Graves Commn, 1966-. *Recreations:* gardening, country pursuits. *Address:* Tiptoe, near Lymington, Hants. *Club:* English-Speaking Union.

WOODGER, Professor Joseph Henry; Emeritus Professor of Biology, University of London; *b* 2 May 1894; *s* of N. L. Woodger, Great Yarmouth, Norfolk; *m* 1921, Doris Eden, *d* of late Major-General C. R. Buckle, CB, CMG, DSO; three *s* one *d*. *Educ:* Felsted Sch.; University College, London. Graduated in Zoology, 1914. 2nd Lieut, Norfolk Regt, 1915; served European War, 2nd Bn Norfolk Regt, in Mesopotamia, 1916-18. Protozoologist in Central Lab. Amara, 1918-19; Derby Scholar, UCL, 1919; Assistant in Zoology Department, University College, London, 1919-22; Reader in Biology, 1922; Professor of Biology, 1947, University of London (Middlesex Hosp. Med. Sch.); retired 1959. Tarner Lecturer, Trinity Coll., Cambridge, 1949-50. *Publications:* Elementary Morphology and Physiology, 1924; Biological Principles, 1929; The Axiomatic Method in Biology, 1937; The Technique of Theory Construction, 1939; Biology and Language, 1952; Physics, Psychology and Medicine, 1956. Papers in Quart. Journal Micro. Sci.; Proc. Arist. Soc., Phil. Trans. Royal Society; Quart. Review Biology, British Journal Phil. Sci., etc. *Recreations:* reading the Bible and Shakespeare; viticulture. *Address:* Tanhurst, Epsom Downs, Surrey. *T:* Ashtead (Surrey) 76469.

WOODHAM, Professor Ronald Ernest; Professor of Music, Reading University, 1951-77; *b* 8 Feb. 1912; *s* of Ernest Victor Woodham, Beckenham, Kent; *m* 1949, Kathleen Isabel, *e d* of P. J. Malone; three *s*. *Educ:* Sherborne Sch.; Royal College of Music, London; Christ Church, Oxford. BA, DMus; FRCO, ARCM. Assistant Director of Music, Bradfield Coll., 1936. Served in RASC, in Middle East and Italy, 1939-45 (despatches). Acting Director of Music, Bradfield Coll., 1946; Director of Music, Sherborne Sch., 1946; Cramb Lecturer in Music, Glasgow Univ., 1947-51. *Address:* Lorien, Admoor Lane, Southend Bradfield, Reading RG7 6HT.

WOODHAMS, Ven. Brian Watson; Archdeacon of Newark since 1965; Hon. Canon of Southwell Minster since 1960; Rector of Staunton with Flawborough and Kilvington, since 1971; *b* 16 Jan. 1911; *s* of Herbert and Florence Osmond Woodhams; *m* 1941, Vera Charlotte White; one *s*. *Educ:* Dover Coll.; Oak Hill Theological Coll.; St John's Coll., University of Durham. LTh 1934, BA 1936, Durham. Deacon, 1936; Priest, 1937. Curate: St Mary Magdalene, Holloway, 1936-39; St James-the-Less, Bethnal Green, 1939-41; Christ Church, New Malden, i/c of St John, New Malden, 1941-43; Vicar: St Mark, Poplar, 1943-45; St James-the-Less, Bethnal Green, 1945-50; St Jude's, Mapperley, Nottingham, 1950-65; Farndon with Thorpe-by-Newark, 1965-71. Proctor in York Convocation, 1955-65. Chairman, Southwell Diocesan Board of Women's Work, 1966-. *Recreations:* children's and refugee work (Chairman, Nottingham Branch Save the Children Fund); interested in sport (local FA football referee). *Address:* 10 Lunn Lane, Collingham, Newark, Notts. *T:* Newark 892207.

WOODHOUSE, family name of **Baron Terrington.**

WOODHOUSE, Ven. Andrew Henry, DSC 1945; MA; Archdeacon of Ludlow since 1970; *b* 30 Jan. 1923; *s* of H. A. Woodhouse, Dental Surgeon, Hanover Square, W1, and Woking, Surrey, and Mrs P. Woodhouse; unmarried. *Educ:* Lancing Coll.; The Queen's Coll., Oxford. MA 1949. Served War, RNVR, 1942-46 (Lieut). Oxford, 1941-42 and 1946-47; Lincoln Theological Coll., 1948-50. Deacon, 1950; Priest, 1951; Curate of All Saints, Poplar, 1950-56; Vicar of St Martin, West Drayton, 1956-70; Rural Dean of Hillingdon, 1967-70. *Recreations:* photography, walking. *Address:* Wistanstow Rectory, Craven Arms, Salop. *T:* Craven Arms 3244. *Club:* Naval.

WOODHOUSE, Rt. Hon. Sir (Arthur) Owen, PC 1974; Kt 1974; DSC 1944; **Rt. Hon. Mr Justice Woodhouse;** a Judge of the Supreme Court, New Zealand, since 1961; a Judge of the Court of Appeal, since 1974; *b* Napier, 18 July 1916; *s* of A. J. Woodhouse: *m* 1940, Margaret Leah Thorp; four *s* two *d*. *Educ:* Napier Boys' High Sch.; Auckland Univ. (LLB). Served War of 1939-45, Lt-Comdr in RNZNVR on secondment to RN; service in MTBs; liaison officer with Yugoslav Partisans, 1943; Asst to Naval Attaché, HM Embassy Belgrade, 1945. Joined Lusk, Willis & Sproule, barristers and solicitors, 1946; Crown Solicitor, Napier, 1953; appointed Judge of Supreme Court, 1961. Chairman: Royal Commn on Compensation and Rehabilitation in respect of Personal Injury in NZ, 1966-67; Inquiry into similar questions in Australia, 1973-74. *Recreations:* music, golf. *Address:* 45 Portland Road, Auckland 5, New Zealand. *Clubs:* Northern (Auckland); Hawkes Bay (Napier); Wellesley, Wellington (Wellington).

WOODHOUSE, Admiral (retired) Sir Charles (Henry Lawrence), KCB, *cr* 1949 (CB 1940); *b* 9 July 1893; *s* of Rev. A. P. Woodhouse and F. D. Woodhouse; *m* 1928, Barbara Margaret, *d* of Dr H. M. Brownfield, Petersfield; three *d*. *Educ:* RN Colleges, Osborne and Dartmouth. Commanded HMS Ajax in Battle of the River Plate 1939 (CB); C-in-C East Indies Station, 1948-50; retired, 1950; Admiral, retired list, 1952. *Address:* Flat 2, 98 Westhall Road, Warlingham, Surrey CR3 9HD.

WOODHOUSE, Hon. (Christopher) Montague, DSO 1943; OBE 1944; MA (Oxon); *b* 11 May 1917; 2nd *s* of 3rd Baron Terrington, KBE; *b* and *heir-pres.* to 4th Baron Terrington, *qv*; *m* 1945, Lady Davina, *d* of 2nd Earl of Lytton, KG, PC, GCSI, GCIE, and *widow* of 5th Earl of Erne; two *s* one *d*. *Educ:* Winchester; New Coll., Oxford (Craven and Hertford Schols, Gaisford Prizeman). First Cl. Hon. Mods, 1937; First Class Lit. Hum., 1939; MA 1947; Lord Justice Holker Schol. Gray's Inn, 1939; enlisted RA, 1939, commissioned 1940; Colonel, Aug. 1943, in command of Allied Military Mission to Greek Guerillas in German-occupied Greece (despatches twice, DSO, OBE, Officer of Legion of Merit (USA), Commander of Order of the Phoenix, with Swords (Greece)). Served in HM Embassy, Athens, 1945, Tehran, 1951; Secretary-General, Allied Mission for Observing Greek Elections, 1946; worked in industry 1946-48; Asst Secretary, Nuffield Foundation, 1948-50; Foreign Office, 1952; Director-General, RIIA, and Dir. of Studies, 1955-59; MP (C) Oxford, 1959-66 and 1970-Sept. 1974; Parliamentary Secretary, Ministry of Aviation, 1961-62; Joint Under-Secretary of State, Home Office, July 1962-Oct. 1964. Dir, Educn and Training, CBI, 1966-70. President, Classical Assoc., 1968. Fellow of Trinity Hall, Cambridge, 1950; FRSL, 1951; Visiting Fellow, Nuffield Coll., Oxford, 1956. *Publications:* Apple of Discord, 1948; One Omen, 1950; Dostoievsky, 1951; The Greek War of Independence, 1952; Britain and the Middle East, 1959; British Foreign Policy since the Second World War, 1961; Rhodes (with late J. G. Lockhart), 1963; The New Concert of Nations, 1964; The Battle of Navarino, 1965; Post-War Britain, 1966; The Story of Modern Greece, 1968; The Philhellenes, 1969; Capodistria: the founder of Greek independence, 1973; The Struggle for Greece (1941-1949), 1976; numerous articles, translations, broadcasts. *Address:* Willow Cottage, Latimer, Bucks. *T:* Little Chalfont 2627.

WOODHOUSE, Henry, CB 1975; Principal Assistant Solicitor; Head of Transport Branch of Legal Directorate, Departments of the Environment and Transport, since 1969; *b* 12 July 1913; *s* of Frank and Florence A. Woodhouse, Cradley Heath, Warley, W Midlands; *m* 1941, Eileen Mary, *d* of Harry and Florence C. Roach, Cradley Heath; two *d*. *Educ:* King Edward's Sch., Birmingham; St John's Coll., Oxford (MA). Solicitor, 1938; served in HM Forces, 1940-46: Lt-Col in Legal Div., Control Commn for Germany, 1945-46; entered Treasury Solicitor's Dept, 1946; Asst Treasury Solicitor, 1955-69; Principal Asst Treasury Solicitor, 1969-71; Principal Asst Solicitor, DoE, 1972. *Publications:* articles in The Conveyancer. *Recreations:* Methodist local preacher, photography, gardening. *Address:* 16 Abbots Close, Onslow Village, Guildford, Surrey. *T:* Guildford 66467; (office) 2 Marsham Street, SW1P 3EB. *T:* 01-212 3434. *Club:* Athenæum.

WOODHOUSE, James Stephen; Headmaster of Rugby School since 1967; *b* 21 May 1933; *s* of late Rt Rev. J. W. Woodhouse, sometime Bishop of Thetford, and late Mrs K. M. Woodhouse; *m* 1957, Sarah, *d* of Major Hubert Blount, Cley, Norfolk; three *s* one *d*. *Educ:* St Edward's Sch.; St Catharine's Coll., Cambridge. BA (English) Cantab, 1957; MA 1961. Nat. Service, 14th Field Regt RA, 1953. Asst Master, Westminster Sch., 1957; Under Master and Master of the Queen's Scholars, 1963. Chairman: NABC Religious Adv. Cttee, 1971; Bloxham Project, 1974; Vice-Chm., E-SU Schoolboy Scholarship Cttee. *Recreations:* sailing, listening to music, hill walking. *Address:* School House, Rugby, Warwickshire.

WOODHOUSE, Hon. Montague; see Woodhouse, Hon. C. M.

WOODHOUSE, Ven. Samuel Mostyn Forbes; Archdeacon of London and Canon Residentiary of St Paul's since 1967; b 28 April 1912; s of Rev. Major James D. F. Woodhouse, DSO, and Elsie Noel Woodhouse, Water, Manaton, Devon; m 1939, Patricia Daniel; two s one d. Educ: Shrewsbury; Christ Church, Oxford; Wells Theological Coll. BA 1934; MA 1942. Deacon, 1936, Priest, 1937, Diocese of Blackburn; Curate, Lancaster Priory, 1936-39. Chaplain to the Forces (Army), 1939-45 (despatches thrice). Vicar, Holy Trinity, South Shore, Blackpool, 1945-49; Vicar of Leominster, 1949-57; Rural Dean of Leominster, 1956-57; Rector of Bristol City Parish Church (St Stephen's), 1957-67. Recreations: golf, fishing, walking, painting, architecture. Address: 9 Amen Court, EC4. T: 01-248 3312. Clubs: Cavalry and Guards; Leander; Vincent's (Oxford).

WOODIFIELD, Rear-Admiral Anthony, CB 1965; CBE 1961; MVO 1953; b 5 Aug. 1912; s of late Colonel A. H. Woodifield, CB, CMG, OBE, St Leonards-on-Sea, Sussex; m 1947, Elizabeth, d of late E. J. Stevens, Sutton, Surrey; two s. Educ: Cheltenham College. Joined RN, 1929. Served 1939-45 in Home Fleet and on East Indies Station. On Staff of Commander-in-Chief, Portsmouth and for Coronation Naval Review, 1951-53; Secretary to Flag Officer, Second-in-Command, Mediterranean, 1954-55; Secretary to Third Sea Lord and Controller of the Navy, 1956-61; Comdg Officer, HMS Phœnicia, 1961-63; Director General of Naval Personal Services and Officer Appointments, 1964-66. Comdr, 1947; Captain, 1955; Rear-Admiral, 1963; retired list, 1966. Recreation: fishing. Address: Stocks Cottage, Kington Langley, Chippenham, Wilts. T: Kington Langley 281. Club: Army and Navy.

WOODLAND, Austin William, CBE 1975; PhD; FGS; Director, Institute of Geological Sciences, since 1976; Director, Geological Survey of Northern Ireland, since 1976; Geological Adviser to Minister of Overseas Development, since 1976; b Mountain Ash, Mid Glamorgan, 4 April 1914; er s of William Austin Woodland and Sarah Jane (née Butler); m 1939, Nesta Ann Phillips; one s one d. Educ: Mountain Ash Co. Sch.; University Coll. of Wales, Aberystwyth (BSc Hons Geol., PhD). Lyell Fund, Geol Soc., 1947; FGS 1937. Temp. Asst Lectr in Geol., Manchester Univ., 1937; Demonstrator in Geol., QUB, 1937-39; Geologist, Geol Survey of GB (now incorp. in Inst. of Geol Sciences), 1939; Dist Geologist, 1957-62; Asst Dir (Northern England), 1962-71; Dep. Dir, 1971-75. President: Yorks Geol Soc., 1966-68; Sect. C (Geol.), BAAS, Swansea, 1971 (Mem. Council, 1970-73; Mem. Gen. Cttee, 1973-); Vice-Pres., Geol Soc., 1968-70 (Mem. Council, 1967-70). Sec.-Gen., 6th Internat. Congress of Carboniferous Stratigraphy and Geol., Sheffield, 1967; Geol Adviser, Aberfan Disaster Tribunal, 1966-67. Major, Special Geol Sect., RE (AER), 1948-57. Publications: Geology of district around Pontypridd and Maesteg, 1964; (ed) Petroleum and the Continental Shelf of North West Europe, 1975; papers on geol aspects of manganese, coal, water supply, engrg applications. Recreations: golf, stamp collecting, gardening (in abeyance). Address: 2 Chiltern House, Hillcrest Road, W5. T: 01-998 6950. Club: Athenæum.

WOODLOCK, Jack Terence; Under-Secretary, Department of Health and Social Security, since 1969; b 10 July 1919; s of late James Patrick and Florence Woodlock; m 1941, Joan Mary Taylor; three s one d. Educ: Bromley Grammar School. Entered Civil Service, 1936; served in Royal Artillery, 1939-45; Ministry of Health, 1945; Asst Principal 1946; Principal 1950; Principal Private Sec. to Minister, 1958-59; Asst Sec. 1959. Recreations: gardening, camping. Address: 9 Berens Way, Chislehurst, Kent. T: Orpington 22895.

WOODROFFE, Rt. Rev. George Cuthbert Manning; see Windward Islands, Bishop of.

WOODROOFE, Sir Ernest (George), Kt 1973; PhD, FInstP, FIChemE; Chairman, Review Body on Doctors' and Dentists' Remuneration, since 1975; b 6 Jan. 1912; s of late Ernest George Woodroofe and Ada (née Dickinson); m 1st, 1938, Margaret Downes (d 1961); one d; 2nd, 1962, Enid Grace Hutchinson Arnold. Educ: Cockburn High Sch.; Leeds Univ. Staff of Loders & Nucoline Ltd, 1935-44; Staff of British Oil & Cake Mills Ltd, 1944-50; Mem., Oil Mills Executive of Unilever Ltd, 1951-55; Director of British Oil & Cake Mills Ltd, 1951-55; Head of Research Division of Unilever Ltd, 1955-61; Director: United Africa Co. Ltd, 1961-63; Unilever NV, 1956-74; Chm., Unilever Ltd, 1970-74 (Dir, 1956-74; Vice-Chm., 1961-70). President, International Society for Fat Research, 1962. Member Cttee of Enquiry into the Organisation of Civil Science, 1962-63; A Vice-Pres., Soc. of Chemical Industry, 1963-66; Member: Tropical Products Inst. Cttee, 1964-69; Council for Nat. Academic

Awards, 1964-67; Cttee of Award of the Commonwealth Fund, 1965-70; Royal Commn for the Exhbn of 1851, 1968-; British Gas Corp., 1973-. Director: Schroders Ltd, 1974-; Burton Group Ltd, 1974-; Guthrie Corp. Ltd, 1974-. Chairman: Leverhulme Trust; CBI Research Cttee, 1966-69. Governor, London Business Sch., 1970-75 (Dep. Chm., 1973-75). Hon. ACT Liverpool, 1963; Hon. Fellow, University of Manchester Inst. of Science and Technology, 1968; Hon. LLD Leeds, 1968; DUniv Surrey, 1970; Hon. DSc Cranfield, 1974. Vis. Fellow, Nuffield Coll., Oxford, 1972-. Comdr, Order of Orange Nassau (Netherlands), 1972. Recreations: fishing, golf. Address: The Crest, Berry Lane, Worplesdon, Surrey. T: Worplesdon 2666. Club: Athenæum.

WOODROW, Maj.-Gen. Albert John, MBE 1949; Director of Army Security, since 1973; b 3 June 1919; s of Frederick Henry Woodrow, Portsmouth; m 1944, Elizabeth, d of late Major Sir John Theodore Prestige, Bourne Park, Bishopsbourne, Kent; two s one d. Educ: Nunthorpe; Sheffield University. Commd Royal Signals, 1940; served War of 1939-45 in NW Europe and Burma (despatches); British Mission to Burma, 1948-49; exchange duty Canada, 1954-56; CO 1 Div. Sigs, 1961-63; British Army Staff, Washington, 1963-65; Comdr Trng Bde Royal Signals, 1965-68; Dir of Public Relations Army, 1968-70; GOC Wales, 1970-73. Bt Lt-Col 1960; Brig. 1965; Maj.-Gen. 1970. Col Comdt, Royal Corps of Signals, 1970-77. Recreations: sailing, shooting. Address: Hookers Green, Bishopsbourne, Canterbury, Kent. Club: Army and Navy.

WOODROW, David; solicitor; Chairman: Oxford Regional Health Authority, since 1973; National Staff Committee, Administrative and Clerical Staff, since 1975; b 16 March 1920; s of Sydney Melson Woodrow and Edith Constance (née Farmer); m 1950, Marie-Armande, d of late Benjamin Barrios, KBE, and late Lady Ovey; two d. Educ: Shrewsbury; Trinity Coll., Oxford (MA). Commnd Royal Artillery, 1940; served SE Asia; POW Java and Japan, 1942-45. Admitted Solicitor, 1949. Chairman: Reading and District HMC, 1966-72; Oxford Regional Hosp. Bd, 1972-74. Recreation: pottering (mainly making things). Address: King's Pool House, Ewelme, Oxon. T: Ewelme 275. Club: Leander (Henley-on-Thames).

WOODRUFF, Prof. Alan Waller; Wellcome Professor of Clinical Tropical Medicine, London School of Hygiene and Tropical Medicine, University of London, since 1952; Lecturer in Tropical Medicine, Royal Free Hospital School of Medicine, since 1952; Physician, Hospital for Tropical Diseases, University College Hospital, London, since 1952; Hon. Consultant in Tropical Diseases to: the Army, since 1956; British Airways, since 1962; b 27 June 1916; s of late William Henry Woodruff, Sunderland, and Mary Margaret Woodruff; m 1946, Mercia Helen, d of late Leonard\Frederick Arnold, Dorking, and Amy Elizabeth Arnold; two s one d. Educ: Bede Collegiate Sch., Sunderland; Durham Univ. MB, BS 1939, MD 1941, Durham; DTM&H England, 1946; PhD London, 1952; FRCP 1953; FRCPE 1960. House Physician and House Surgeon, Royal Victoria Infirmary, Newcastle upon Tyne, 1939-40; MO and Med. Specialist, RAFVR, 1940-46; Med. Registrar, Royal Victoria Infirmary, Newcastle upon Tyne, 1946-48; Sen. Lectr in Clinical Tropical Medicine, London Sch. of Hygiene and Trop. Medicine, and First Asst, Hosp. for Tropical Diseases, University Coll. Hosp., London, 1948-52; William Julius Mickle Fellow, Univ. of London, 1959. Lectures: Goulstonian, RCP, 1954; Lettsomian, Med. Soc. of London, 1969; Watson-Smith, RCP, 1970. Orator, Reading Pathological Soc., 1976. Member: WHO Expert Adv. Panel on Parasitic Diseases, 1963-; Med. Cttee of Overseas Develt Administration; Assoc. of Physicians of GB and Ireland. President: Durham Univ. Soc., 1963-73; Royal Soc. of Tropical Medicine and Hygiene, 1973-75; Medical Soc. of London, 1975-76; Section of History of Medicine, Royal Soc. Med., 1977-. Hon. Mem., Burma Med. Assoc., 1966; Hon. Mem., Société de Pathologie Exotique, Paris; Hon. Associate Mem., Soc. Belge de Médicine Tropicale, 1965; Hon. Mem., Brazilian Soc. of Tropical Medicine. Katherine Bishop Harman Prize, BMA, 1951. Publications: (with J. Ungar) Antibiotics and Sulphonamides in Tropical Medicine, 1965; (with S. Bell) A Synopsis of Infectious and Tropical Diseases, 1968; (ed) Alimentary and Haematological Aspects of Tropical Disease, 1970; (ed) Medicine in the Tropics, 1974; sections in: Paediatrics for the Practitioner (ed Gaisford and Lightwood); Medicine (ed Richardson); contribs to BMJ, Lancet, Trans Royal Soc. Trop. Medicine and Hygiene, W African Med. Jl, E African Med. Jl, Newcastle Med. Jl, Practitioner, Trans Assoc. Industrial Medical Officers, Proc. Nutrition Soc., etc. Address: 157 Denmark Hill, SE5. T: 01-274 3578. Club: Athenæum.

WOODRUFF, Douglas; see Woodruff, J. D.

WOODRUFF, Harry Wells, CMG 1966; Assistant Secretary, Department of Trade and Industry (formerly Board of Trade), 1968-72; *b* 31 Oct. 1912; *s* of Leonard Wells Woodruff and Rosina Woodruff; *m* 1938, Margaret Bradley; one *d. Educ:* Reigate Grammar Sch.; London Univ. Trade Comr, Johannesburg, 1946-51; Trade Comr and Economic Adviser to High Commissioner: Salisbury, 1951-55; Kuala Lumpur, 1957-61; Commercial Counsellor, Canberra, 1962-66; Economic Adviser to Foreign Office, 1966-68. *Publication:* (jointly) Economic Development in Rhodesia and Nyasaland, 1955. *Recreation:* painting. *Address:* Old Oak Cottage, Chetnole, Sherborne, Dorset.

WOODRUFF, (John) Douglas, CBE 1962; Chairman, BOW Holdings, 1959-70; Chairman, Associated Catholic Newspapers, 1953-70; Editor of The Tablet, 1936-67; *b* 8 May 1897; *s* of late Cumberland Woodruff, BCL, FSA, of the Public Record Office, and late Emily Louisa, *d* of William Hewett, Norton Fitzwarren, Somerset; *m* 1933, Hon. Marie Immaculée, *d* of 2nd Lord Acton. *Educ:* St Augustine's, Ramsgate; Downside Sch.; New Coll., Oxford (Lothian prizeman, 1921, 1st class Hon. Modern History, 1923, President of the Union). Served under Foreign Office in Holland, 1917-19; Lecturer in History at Sheffield Univ., 1923-24; Editorial staff of The Times, 1926-38; in charge of Press Publicity for Empire Marketing Board, 1931-33; on staff of BBC, 1934-36; Dep. Chairman Burns and Oates, Publishers, 1948-62; Director, Hollis & Carter, 1948-62; Chairman of Allied Circle, 1947-62. Grand Cross, Order of St Gregory the Great, 1968. *Publications:* Plato's American Republic, 1926; The British Empire, 1929; Plato's Britannia, 1930; Charlemagne, 1934; Contributor to Early Victorian England, 1934; Great Tudors, 1935; European Civilisation, The Grand Tour, 1935; (Editor) Dear Sir, 1936; The Story of the British Colonial Empire, 1939; Talking at Random, 1941; More Talking at Random, 1944; Still Talking at Random, 1948; Walrus Talk, 1954; The Tichborne Claimant, 1957; Church and State in History, 1961; The Life and Times of Alfred the Great, 1974; contrib. to current periodicals. *Address:* Marcham Priory, Abingdon, Oxon. *T:* Frilford Heath 391260. *Club:* Athenæum.

WOODRUFF, Keith Montague Cumberland, MB, BS (London); MRCS; LRCP; FFARCS; *b* 18 June 1891; *s* of Rev. A. W. Woodruff and Emily (*née* Hamilton), Testwood, Hants; *m* 1934, Beatrice Evelyn, *d* of late Colonel C. C. O. Whiteley and of Mrs Whiteley; one *s. Educ:* Eastmans Royal Army and Navy Academy, Winchester; St Edward's Sch., Oxford; Guy's Hospital. Consulting Anæsthetist: Royal National Orthopædic Hospital, 1924; Chelsea Hospital for Women, 1925; Queen Charlotte's Maternity Hospital, 1938; Charing Cross Hospital, 1935; Royal Masonic Hospital, 1937. 1914-15 Medal, 1914-18 Medal, Victory Medal, 1914-18. *Recreations:* golf, sailing. *Address:* Mount Cottage, Rhodes Minnis, Elham, near Canterbury, Kent. *T:* Lyminge 862445.

WOODRUFF, Prof. Sir Michael (Francis Addison), Kt 1969; FRS 1968; FRCS; DSc, MS (Melbourne); Professor of Surgery (formerly of Surgical Science), University of Edinburgh, and Surgeon, Edinburgh Royal Infirmary, 1957-76; now Professor Emeritus; Director, Nuffield Transplantation Surgery Unit, Edinburgh, 1968-76; *b* 3 April 1911; *s* of late Prof. Harold Addison Woodruff and Margaret Ada (*née* Cooper); *m* 1946, Hazel Gwenyth Ashby; two *s* one *d. Educ:* Wesley Coll., Melbourne; Queen's Coll., University of Melbourne. MB, BS (Melbourne) 1937, MD 1940, MS 1941; FRCS 1946. Captain, Australian Army Medical Corps, 1940-46. Tutor in Surgery, Univ. of Sheffield, 1946-48; Lecturer in Surgery, Univ. of Aberdeen, 1948-52; Hunterian Prof., RCS, 1952; Travelling Fellow, WHO, 1949; Prof. of Surgery, Univ. of Otago, Dunedin, NZ, 1953-56. Associé Etranger, Académie de Chirurgie, 1964; Hon. Member American Surgical Assoc., 1965; Korrespondierendem Mitglied, Deutsche Gesellschaft für Chirurgie. Hon. FACS 1975. Lister Medal, 1969; Gold Medal, Soc. of Apothecaries, 1974. *Publications:* (Joint) Deficiency Diseases in Japanese Prison Camps, 1951; Surgery for Dental Students, 1954; Transplantation of Tissues and Organs, 1960; (essays) On Science and Surgery, 1977; articles on surgical topics and on experimental tissue transplantation. *Recreations:* music, sailing. *Address:* The Bield, 506 Lanark Road, Juniper Green, Edinburgh EH14 5DH. *Club:* Athenæum.

WOODRUFF, Philip; see Mason, Philip.

WOODRUFF, William Charles; Controller, National Air Traffic Services, since 1977 (Deputy Controller, 1974-77); *b* 14 Aug. 1921; *s* of late Thomas and Caroline Woodruff; *m* 1946, Ethel May Miles; one *s* one *d. Educ:* St George's, Ramsgate. RAF, 1941-46: Navigator/Observer, 1409 Flight; POW Germany, 1943-45. Seconded Air Min., 1945, and later Min. of Civil

Aviation for Air Traffic Control planning; various air traffic control appts at Hurn, Northolt, Southern Centre, Heston and MTCA Hdqrs, 1946-56; Air Traffic Control Officer i/c Heathrow, 1956-62; Sec. of Patch Long-term Air Traffic Control Planning Group, 1960-61; Dep. Dir, 1962-67, Dir, 1967-69, Civil Air Traffic Ops; Jt Field Comdr, NATS, 1969-74. Guild of Air Traffic Control Officers: Clerk, 1952-56; Master, 1956. *Publications:* articles on aviation subjects. *Recreations:* gardening, wine-making, photography. *Address:* National Air Traffic Services, Space House, 43-59 Kingsway, WC2B 6TE. *T:* 01-379 7311; 25 Chichester Avenue, Ruislip, Mddx HA4 7EJ. *T:* Ruislip 73567.

WOODS, Brian; His Honour Judge Woods; a Circuit Judge, since 1975; *b* 5 Nov. 1928; *yr s* of late E. P. Woods, Woodmancote, Cheltenham; *m* 1957, Margaret, *d* of late F. J. Griffiths, Parkgate, Wirral; three *d. Educ:* City of Leicester Boys' Sch.; Nottingham Univ. (LLB 1952). National Service, RAF, 1947-49. Called to the Bar, Gray's Inn, 1955; Midland Circuit; Dep. Chm., Lincs (Lindsey) QS, 1968. Anglican Lay Reader, 1970-; Chancellor, Diocese of Leicester, 1977-. Mem. Council, S Mary and S Anne's Sch., Abbots Bromley, 1977-. *Recreations:* daughters, musical music, taking photographs. *Address:* The Old Vicarage, Hanbury, Burton-on-Trent, Staffordshire. *Club:* Leicestershire Far and Near.

WOODS, Maj.-Gen. Charles William, CB 1970; MBE 1952; MC 1944; Chairman: Royal Engineers Association, since 1971; Douglas Haig Memorial Homes, since 1975; *b* 21 March 1917; *s* of late Captain F. W. U. Woods and of Mrs M. E. Woods, Gosbrook House, Binfield Heath, Henley-on-Thames; *m* 1940, Angela Helen Clay; one *d* (one *s* decd). *Educ:* Uppingham Sch.; Trinity Coll., Cambridge (MA). Commnd into Corps of Royal Engineers, 1938; served War of 1939-45, N Africa, Sicily, Italy, NW Europe (D Landings with 50th Div.); Staff Coll., Camberley, 1946; served in Korea, 1951-52; comd 35 Corps Engineer Regt, BAOR, 1959-60; Dep. Military Secretary, 1964-67; Dir of Manning (Army), 1967-70. Col Comdt, RE, 1973-. *Recreations:* sailing, ski-ing. *Address:* Riversdale Cottage, Boldre, Lymington, Hants SO4 8PE. *T:* Lymington 3445. *Clubs:* Naval and Military, Royal Ocean Racing, Ski Club of Great Britain; Royal Lymington Yacht, Royal Engineer Yacht.

WOODS, Sir Colin (Philip Joseph), KCVO 1977; CBE 1973; HM Chief Inspector of Constabulary, since 1977; *b* London, 20 April 1920; *s* of late Michael Woods, Sub-divisional Inspector, Metropolitan Police; *m* 1941, Gladys Ella May (*née* Howell); one *d. Educ:* LCC Primary and Secondary Schs; Finchley Grammar Sch. Served War, in 60th Rifles and RUR, 1939-46. Metropolitan Police: Constable, through ranks, to Dep. Comdr; Commander, Traffic Dept, 1966-67; Head of Management Services, 1968; Comdt, National Police Coll., 1969-70; Asst Comr (Traffic Dept), 1970; Asst Comr (Crime), 1972; Dep. Comr, 1975-77. *Recreations:* walking, music, cabinet making, gardening. *Address:* Home Office, 50 Queen Anne's Gate, SW1H 9AT. *T:* 01-213 4037.

WOODS, Most Rev. Frank, KBE 1972; Archbishop of Melbourne, 1957-77; Primate of Australia, 1971-77; *b* 6 April 1907; *s* of late Rt Rev. E. S. Woods, DD, Bishop of Lichfield; *m* 1936, Jean Margaret Sprules; two *s* two *d. Educ:* Marlborough; Trinity Coll., Cambridge. Deacon, 1931; priest, 1932; Curate of Portsea Parish Church, 1932-33; Chaplain, Trinity Coll., Cambridge, 1933-36; Vice-principal, Wells Theological Coll., 1936-39; Chaplain to the Forces, 1939-45; Vicar of Huddersfield, 1945-52; Suffragan Bishop of Middleton, 1952-57. Proctor in Convocation, 1946-51; Chaplain to the King, 1951-52; Chaplain, Victoria Order St J, 1962. *Recreation:* walking. *Address:* 2 Hughes Street, N Balwyn, Victoria 3104, Australia. *See also Bishop of Worcester.*

WOODS, George David; banker; with The First Boston Corporation, New York City, 1934-62 and since 1968 (Chairman of Board, 1951-62); Chairman: Henry J. Kaiser Family Foundation (also Trustee), since 1968; International Executive Service Corps, 1968-74, Executive Committee, since 1974; Director since 1970, President since 1971, Foreign Bondholders Protective Council Inc.; Director Emeritus, Lincoln Center for the Performing Arts, Inc.; *b* 27 July 1901; *s* of John Woods and Laura A. Woods (*née* Rhodes); *m* 1935, Louise Taraldson; no *c. Educ:* New York public schools; American Institute of Banking; New York Univ. Investment Banking: Harris Forbes & Co., NY City, 1918-34. Pres. and Chm. of Exec. Dirs, IBRD and IDA, 1963-68; Chm. of Board and Pres., IFC, 1963-68. Holds honorary doctorates from Universities and Colleges. Legion of Merit, US Army, 1945. *Address:* 277 Park Avenue, New York, NY 10017, USA; (home) 825 Fifth Avenue, New York, NY 10021, USA. *Clubs:* Links, Pinnacle, Players,

Racquet & Tennis, World Trade Center (New York); Duquesne (Pittsburgh); Federal City (Washington, DC).

WOODS, Maj.-Gen. Henry Gabriel, MBE 1965; MC 1945; General Officer Commanding North East District, since 1976; *b* 7 May 1924; *s* of late G. S. Woods and F. C. F. Woods (*née* McNevin); *m* 1953, Imogen Elizabeth Birchenough Dodd; two *d*. *Educ:* Highgate Sch.; Trinity Coll., Oxford (MA 1st Cl. Hons Mod. History). AMBIM. psc, jssc, rcds. Commnd 5th Royal Inniskilling Dragoon Guards, 1944; served NW Europe, 1944-45; Korea, 1951-52; Adjt, 1952-53; Sqdn Leader, 1954-55 and 1960-62; Army Staff Coll., 1956; Jt Services Staff Coll., 1960; Mil. Asst to Vice CDS, MoD, 1962-64; comd 5th Royal Inniskilling Dragoon Gds, 1965-67; Asst Mil. Sec. to C-in-C BAOR, 1968-69; Comdt, RAC Centre, 1969-71; RCDS, 1972; Mil. Attaché, Brit. Embassy, Washington, 1973-75. Officier, Ordre, Ordre de Léopold, Belgium, 1965. *Recreations:* hunting, fencing, sailing, military history. *Address:* c/o National Westminster Bank Ltd, 208 Piccadilly, W1A 2DG. *Clubs:* Cavalry and Guards; Ends of the Earth (UK section), Trinity Society.

WOODS, Ivan; *see* Woods, W. I.

WOODS, Very Rev. John Mawhinney; Provost, St Andrew's Cathedral, Inverness, since 1975; *b* 16 Dec. 1919; *s* of Robert and Sarah Hannah Woods. *Educ:* Edinburgh Theological College. Deacon 1958, for St Peter's, Kirkcaldy, Fife; priest, 1959; Rector of Walpole St Peter, Norfolk, 1960-75. *Address:* St Andrew's House, 15 Ardross Street, Inverness IV3 5QP. *T:* Inverness 33535.

WOODS, Prof. Leslie Colin, BE, MA, DPhil, DSc; Professor of Mathematics (Theory of Plasma), University of Oxford, and Fellow of Balliol College, Oxford, since 1970; *b* Reporoa; NZ, 6 Dec. 1922; *s* of A. B. Woodhead, Sandringham, NZ; *m* 1943, Gladys Elizabeth Bayley; five *d*. *Educ:* Auckland Univ. Coll.; Merton Coll., Oxford. Fighter pilot, RNZAF, Pacific Area, 1942-45. Rhodes Schol., Merton Coll., Oxford, 1948-51; Scientist (NZ Scientific Defense Corps) with Aerodynamics Div., NPL Mddx, 1951-54; Senior Lectr in Applied Maths, Sydney Univ., 1954-56; Nuffield Research Prof. of Engineering, Univ. of New South Wales, 1956-60; Fellow and Tutor in Engrg Science, Balliol Coll., Oxford, 1960-70; Reader in Applied Maths, Oxford, 1964-70. *Publications:* The Theory of Subsonic Plane Flow, 1961; Introduction to Neutron Distribution Theory, 1964; The Thermodynamics of Fluid Systems, 1975; many research papers in aerodynamics and plasma physics in Proc. Royal Soc., Physics of Fluids, etc. *Recreations:* music, sailing. *Address:* Balliol College, Oxford.

WOODS, Reginald Salisbury, (Rex Woods), MA; MD, BCh (Cantab); FRCS; Médaille d'Honneur de l'Education Physique et des Sports, République Française, 1946; in General Practice; Hon. Life Member, British Association of Sport and Medicine; Surgical Specialist to numerous insurance companies; Cambridgeshire Warden King George's Jubilee Trust; Past Assistant of Glazier's Company, Freeman of City of London; a Patron of Cambridge Branch, Old Contemptibles and of British Legion; Past President, Downing College Association, 1962; *b* London, 15 Oct. 1891; *o s* of late H. T. Woods, Galway; *m* 1918, Irene, CBE, TD (*d* 1976), *y d* of late T. Pickering; one *s* two *d*. *Educ:* Dulwich Coll.; Downing Coll., Cambridge (Entr. Exh.); St George's Hospital (Senior Univ. Entrance Scholar, Research Exhib., etc.). HS, HP, and Surg. Registrar. Captain, RAMC, BEF, 1916-19 (despatches); late Surg. Spec. Ministry of Pensions; Surg. EMS (Cambridge County Hospital), 1939-43; Major, RAMC 1943-45 (Surg. Spec. E Africa Command). Formerly: Hon. Demonstrator Anatomy, Cambridge Univ. Med. Schs; Pres., Cambridge Med. Soc., County Dir BRCS, and Chm., Nat. Playing Fields Assoc. and Cambs AAA. Hon. Treasurer and Co-Manager, 5 Oxford/Cambridge Athletic Tours *v* USA Univs, 1925-49. *Publications:* Cambridge Doctor, 1962; many contribs on sports injuries in British and US med. jls. *Recreations:* represented England 1914 and 1920-29; Great Britain at Olympic Games, 1924 and 1928, and British Empire *v* USA, 1924 and 1928, in Putting the Weight. President (1914), Hon. Treasurer (1919-39) and Chairman (1939-52), of CUAC. AAA Champion, 1924 and 1926; Captained Public Schools Past and Present at Rugby Football, 1919; golf, bridge. *Address:* 4 Manor Court, Grange Road, Cambridge; 40 Green Street, Cambridge. *Clubs:* British Sportsman's; Cambridge County, Hawks, Pitt, Cambridge, Achilles; Oxford and Cambridge Golfing Society.

See also Sir F. W. W. Pemberton.

WOODS, Rt. Rev. Robert Wilmer; *see* Worcester, Bishop of.

WOODS, Maj.-Gen. Thomas Frederic Mackie, CB 1960; OBE 1945; MD; FRCP(I); retired; *b* 14 July 1904; *s* of Dr Annesley Woods, Birr, Ireland; *m* 1930, Juliet Frances, *d* of D. L. Rogers, Dublin; two *d*. *Educ:* St Paul's Sch.; Trinity Coll., Dublin. BA, MB, Dublin, 1926; MD, Dublin, 1932; MRCP Ireland, 1934. Joined RAMC 1927; served in India, Malta and UK until 1940. Served War of 1939-45: in UK, Madagascar, India, Middle East, Burma, Malaya. Seconded to Ministry of Food, 1946-48, as Chief Health Officer E. African Groundnut Scheme; 2 Div., RAMC Depot, HQ London Dist, HQ 1 (BR) Corps; HQ Southern Command. Brigadier, 1956; Maj.-Gen., 1957. QHP 1959-61. Colonel Comdt, RAMC, 1965-69. OStJ. *Address:* White Lodge, Berwick St James, near Salisbury, Wilts.

WOODS, (William) Ivan; Secretary, Milbern Trust, since 1976; 3rd *s* of late William and Anna Woods, Annaghmore, Co. Armagh; *m* (1st wife *d* 1965); one *s* one *d*; 2nd, 1966, Florence Margaret, *o d* of William and Florence Sloan, Ach-na-mara, Donaghadee, Co. Down; one *s* two *d*. *Educ:* Ranelagh Sch., Athlone; Mountjoy Sch., Dublin. Clerical Officer, Min. of Finance for N Ire., 1934; Accountant to Ministry, 1962; N Ire. Govt Liaison Officer in London, 1963; Dir of Office of Parliamentary Commissioner for Administration for Northern Ireland, 1969; Dir of Office of Commissioner for Complaints, Dec. 1969; Dep. Sec., Dept of Finance of NI, 1973-76. *Recreations:* golf, sailing. *Address:* 22 Cabin Hill Park, Belfast, Northern Ireland. *T:* Belfast 650666. *Clubs:* Royal Commonwealth Society; Clandeboye Golf, Kircubbin Sailing (Co. Down).

WOODS BALLARD, Lt-Col Basil, CIE 1943; MBE 1935; *b* 28 Sept. 1900; *s* of Frederick George Ballard; *m* 1931, Eileen Rose Molesworth; two *s*. *Educ:* Dulwich Coll. Commissioned 5th Royal Gurkha Rifles, FF, IA, 1920; Indian Political Service, 1925; Political Agent, Loralai, 1936-39; Secretary to Resident, Punjab States, 1939-41; Political Agent, Quetta, 1941-45; Political Agent, Bhopal, 1945-47; Resident in Kolhapur, 1947; retired, Aug. 1947. Employed in Persian Gulf, 1948-53; served on local councils and managing and governing bodies of schools in E Sussex, 1955-72. *Address:* Shepherds Oak, Crawley Down, West Sussex. *T:* Copthorne 712314.

WOODWARD, Prof. C(omer) Vann; Sterling Professor of History, Yale University, since 1961; *b* 13 Nov. 1908; *s* of Hugh Allison Woodward and Bess (*née* Vann); *m* 1937, Glenn Boyd MacLeod; one *s*. *Educ:* Emory Univ. (PhB); Universities of Columbia (MA), North Carolina (PhD). Asst Professor of History, University of Florida, 1937-39; Visiting Asst Professor of History, University of Virginia, 1939-40; Assoc. Professor of History, Scripps Coll., 1940-43; Assoc. Professor of History, Johns Hopkins University, 1946; Professor of American History, Johns Hopkins Univ., 1947-61. Served with US Naval Reserve, 1943-46. Commonwealth Lecturer, UCL, 1954; Harold Vyvyan Harmsworth Professor of American History, University of Oxford, 1954-55; Literary Award, Nat. Inst. of Arts and Letters, 1954, etc. Corresp. Fellow, British Academy, 1972. Member: American Academy of Arts and Sciences; American Philosophical Society; Nat. Inst. of Arts and Letters; American Historical Assoc. (President, 1969); Orgn of American Historians (President, 1968-69). Hon. degrees: MA Oxon, 1954; LLD: N Carolina, 1959; Arkansas, 1961; Michigan, 1971; LittD: Emory, 1963; William and Mary, 1964; Princeton, 1971; Columbia, 1972; DLitt Cambridge, 1975. *Publications:* Tom Watson: Agrarian Rebel, 1938; The Battle for Leyte Gulf, 1947; Origins of the New South (1877-1913), 1951 (Bancroft Prize, 1952); Reunion and Reaction, 1951; The Strange Career of Jim Crow, 1955; The Burden of Southern History, 1960; American Counterpoint, 1971; (ed) The Comparative Approach to American History, 1968. *Address:* History Department, Yale University, New Haven, Conn 06520, USA.

WOODWARD, Edward; actor and singer, since 1946; *b* 1 June 1930; *s* of Edward Oliver Woodward and Violet Edith Woodward; *m* 1952, Venetia Mary Collett; two *s* one *d*. *Educ:* Kingston Coll.; RADA. Castle Theatre, Farnham, 1946; appeared for some years in rep. cos throughout England and Scotland; first appearance on London stage, Where There's a Will, Garrick, 1955; Stratford Memorial Theatre Co., 1958: Mercutio in Romeo and Juliet, and Laertes in Hamlet; National Theatre Co., 1971: Cyrano in Cyrano de Bergerac, and Flamineo in The White Devil; has appeared in over 25 prodns on London stage, incl.: The Wolf, 1973; Male of the Species, Piccadilly, 1975; On Approval, Theatre Royal and Haymarket, 1976; has appeared in 3 prodns in NY. Over 200 TV prodns; 7 films; 9 long-playing records (singing) and 3 records (poetry). 9 national and internat. acting awards. *Recreations:* boating, geology. *Address:* c/o Eric Glass Ltd, 28 Berkeley Square, W1X 6HD. *T:* 01-629 7162. *Clubs:* Green Room, Macreadys, Wellington.

WOODWARD, (Foster) Neville, CBE 1956; FRSE; FRIC; Technology policy adviser to government in developing countries; Research Policy Adviser, Scottish Council: Development and Industry, since 1974; *b* 2 May 1905; *s* of Foster Woodward; *m* 1932, Elizabeth Holme Siddall; one *s* one *d. Educ:* Bradford; University Coll., London (PhD, gold medallist). After ten years in industry, and two as Res. Asst (to Prof. Sir Robert Robinson, FRS), Oxford Univ., became Head of Res. and Develt Div., HM Chem. Defence Res. Estabt, Sutton Oak, 1937-42. During War of 1939-45 served on Govt Sci. Cttees and Missions; subseq. served on scientific missions to foreign countries concerned with natural resources develt, internat. scientific relations, and management of R&D in co-operative, contract and industrial research insts in developing countries. Officer in Charge, Min. of Supply Res. Estabt, Leamington Spa, 1943; Dep. Sci. Adv. to Min. of Production, 1944-46; Dir, Inst. of Seaweed Research, 1946-56 (Mem. Bd Inst., 1956-69); seconded to FO as Dir UK Sci. Mission, Washington DC; Attaché for Sci. Questions, Brit. Embassy, Washington DC, and Sci. Adv. to UK High Comr in Canada, 1947-48; Hon. Sci. Adv. to Sec. of State for Scotland, 1951-56; Sci. Attaché to European Productivity Agency, OEEC, Paris, 1956-61; Sen. Sci. Counsellor, Directorate of Scientific Affairs, OECD, Paris, 1961-70. Dir, Arthur D. Little Res. Inst., 1956-70; Man. Dir, Arthur D. Little Ltd, 1963-68. Chm., Inveresk Res. Internat. Management Cttee, 1970-73. Vice-President: Soc. of Chemical Industry, 1968-71; RIC, 1969-71; Chm., Assoc. of Consulting Scientists, 1967-69. Ramsay Meml Fellowship Trustee, 1969-. *Publications:* A Survey of Agricultural, Forestry and Fishery Products in the United Kingdom and their Utilisation (with J. Maxton and A. B. Stewart), 1953; Structure of Industrial Research Associations, 1964; (with T. S. Chung and R. D. Lalkaka) Guidelines for Development of Industrial Technology in Asia and the Pacific, 1976; about 50 publications in scientific press. *Recreations:* mountains, foreign travel, reading, writing. *Address:* St Margaret's Lodge, Gullane, East Lothian. *T:* Gullane 842210; Cuil Moss, Ardgour, Argyll. *Club:* New (Edinburgh).

WOODWARD, Geoffrey Royston; Under-Secretary, Ministry of Agriculture, Fisheries and Food, since 1970; *b* 26 June 1921; *o s* of James Edward Woodward and Gwendolen May (*née* Dodridge); *m* 1st, 1947, Marjorie Beatrice Bishop (marr. diss. 1974); three *s* ; 2nd, 1974, Doreen Parker, MBE. *Educ:* Bradford Grammar Sch. Entered Civil Service, 1938; served RAFVR, 1941-46 (Flt-Lt, despatches). Joined Min. of Agriculture and Fisheries, 1948. *Recreation:* armchair archaeology. *Address:* 3 Gilbert Court, Green Vale, W5 3AX. *Club:* Reform.

WOODWARD, Joan; see Woodward, (W.) J.

WOODWARD, Rev. Max Wakerley; Methodist Minister, retired 1973; *b* 29 Jan. 1908; *s* of Alfred Woodward, Methodist Minister, and Mabel Woodward; *m* 1934, Kathleen May Beaty; three *s* one *d. Educ:* Orme Sch., Newcastle; Kingswood Sch., Bath; Handsworth Coll., Birmingham. Missionary to Ceylon, 1929-42; Chaplain, Royal Navy, 1942-46; Minister: Leamington Spa, 1946-50; Finsbury Park, 1950-54; Harrow, 1954-58; Wesley's Chapel, London, 1958-64; Secretary, World Methodist Council, 1964-69; Minister, Bromley, Kent, 1969-73. Exchange Preacher, Univ. Methodist Church, Baton Rouge, La, 1957. *Publication:* One At London, 1966. *Recreations:* gardening, chess. *Address:* 3 Godfrey Close, Radford Semele, Leamington Spa, Warwicks. *T:* Leamington Spa 20756.

WOODWARD, Neville; see Woodward, F. N.

WOODWARD, Prof. R(obert) B(urns), BS; PhD; Donner Professor of Science, Harvard University, since 1960; Director of the Woodward Research Institute, Basel, since 1963; Member of Corporation, Massachusetts Institute of Technology, 1966-71; *b* Boston, 10 April 1917; *s* of Arthur Chester Woodward and Margaret (*née* Burns); *m* 1st, 1938, Irja Pullman; two *d* ; 2nd, 1946, Eudoxia M. M. Muller; one *s* one *d. Educ:* Massachusetts Institute of Technology. BS, 1936; PhD, 1937. Post-Doctoral Fellow, Harvard Univ., 1937-38; Mem., Soc. of Fellows, 1938-40; Instructor in Chemistry, 1941-44; Asst Prof., 1944-46; Assoc. Prof., 1946-50; Prof., 1950-53; Morris Loeb Prof. of Chem., 1953-60. Todd Prof. of Chem. and Fellow, Christ's Coll., Cambridge Univ., 1973-74. Consultant: Polaroid Corp., 1942-; Cttee on Medical Research, Office of Scientific Research and Development, 1944-45; War Production Bd, 1944-45; Pfizer & Co. Inc., 1951-70. Dir, CIBA-GEIGY Ltd, Basel, 1970-. Mem. Bd of Governors, Weizmann Inst. of Science, 1968-. Hon. Lecturer to many organisations in America, Europe, Australia and Asia. Member, National Academy of Sciences; Fellow, Amer. Acad. of Arts and Sciences; Foreign Member: Royal Society; Accademia Nazionale dei Lincei; Acad. of Scis of

USSR; For. Fellow, Indian Nat. Sci. Acad.; Hon. Fellow: Chemical Society; Indian Academy of Sciences; Weizmann Inst. of Science; Indian Chem. Soc.; Hon. Member: German Chemical Society; Royal Irish Academy; Belgian Chemical Society; Swiss Chemical Society; Pharmaceutical Soc. of Japan; Pharmaceutical Soc. of GB; Royal Instn of GB; Hon. Life Mem., NY Acad. of Scis; Member: American Philosophical Society; Deutsche Akademie der Naturforscher (Leopoldina); Harvey Soc. of NY; Corresponding Member: Austrian Academy of Sciences; Yugoslav Acad. of Scis and Arts. Hon. AM Harvard Univ., 1946; Hon. LLD Glasgow, 1966; Hon. Dr tech. wiss. Zurich; Hon. DSc: Wesleyan; Manchester; Bucknell; New Brunswick; Yale, Harvard; S California; Chicago; New England Coll. of Pharmacy; Colby; Cambridge; Brandeis; Stonehill; Sheffield; Haifa; Brooklyn; W Ontario; Columbia; Louvain; Paris; St Andrews; London. John Scott Medal, 1945; Baekeland Medal, 1955; Ledlie Prize, 1955; Research Corp. Award, 1955; Nichols Medal, 1956; Amer. Chem. Soc. Synthetic Organic Chemistry Award, 1957; T. W. Richards Medal, 1958; Davy Medal, Royal Soc., 1959; Roger Adams Medal, 1961; Pius XI Gold Medal of Pontifical Acad. of Sciences, 1961; Scientific Achievement Medal, 1961; Priestley Medallion, 1962; Stas Medal, 1962; Gold Medal for Creative Res. in Synthetic Organic Chem., 1962; Nat. Medal of Science, USA. 1964; Nobel Prize for Chemistry, 1965; Kirkwood Medal, 1965; Willard Gibbs Medal, 1967; Lavoisier Medal, 1968; Hanbury Meml Medal, 1970; Pierre Bruylants Medal, 1970; Scientific Achievement Award, 1971; Dr B. C. Law Gold Medal, 1972; Arthur C. Cope Award, 1973. Order of the Rising Sun, 2nd cl. (Japan), 1970. *Address:* Dept of Chemistry, Harvard University, 12 Oxford Street, Cambridge, Mass 02138, USA.

WOODWARD, (Winifred) Joan; Assistant Principal Probation Officer, Inner London Probation and After-care Service, 1950-72; *b* 14 Sept. 1907; *d* of late Brig.-Gen. J. A. H. Woodward, IA, and Winifred Mary Strahan. *Educ:* Princess Helena Coll., Ealing. Appointed to Probation Service, 1936; served at: North London and Edmonton, Apr.-Nov. 1936; Marylebone, Nov. 1936-June 1940; appointed to Bow Street, 1940; Senior Probation Officer, Bow Street Magistrates Court, Nov. 1948. *Address:* 2 Queen Anne's Grove, Ealing, W5. *T:* 01-567 8571.

WOODWARD-NUTT, Arthur Edgar; *b* 19 Aug. 1902; *m* 1st, 1928, Dorothy Muriel Linzell (*d* 1974); one *s* ; 2nd, 1975, Gladys Alexandra MacBain. *Educ:* King Edward's, Birmingham; Gonville and Caius Coll., Cambridge (MA). Seely Prizeman, Cambridge, 1923. De Havilland Aircraft Co., 1924-25; at Royal Aircraft Estabt, Farnborough, 1925-27 and 1934-38, Aeroplane and Armament Experimental Estabt, Martlesham Heath, 1927-31, Marine Aircraft Experimental Estabt, Felixstowe, 1931-34; in charge of Air Defence Res. Section, Air Ministry, 1938-41; Sec. to Brit. Technical Mission to USA, 1940; various directing appointments at Min. of Aircraft Production and Min. of Supply, 1941-58; Dir.-Gen. of Aircraft General Services, Ministry of Aviation, 1958-65; Technical Adviser (Civil) to Ministry of Aviation, 1965-66; British Exec. Deleg. and Chm. of Central Secretariat, Commonwealth Adv. Aeronautical Res. Council, 1957-66; retired 1966. CEng; FRAeS. *Publications:* various Reports and Memoranda of Aeronautical Research Council, and articles in Technical Press. *Recreations:* lawn tennis, gardening. *Address:* Badgers, 5 Woodland Way, Crowhurst, Sussex. *T:* Crowhurst 286.

WOOF, Robert Edward; MP (Lab) Blaydon, Co. Durham, since Feb. 1956; Member and official, National Union of Mineworkers; *b* 24 Oct. 1911; *m* Mary Bell (*d* 1971); one *d. Educ:* Elementary School. Began work in the mines at an early age, subsequently coal face worker. Member of the Labour Party, 1937-; Member Durham County Council, 1947-56. *Address:* House of Commons, SW1A 0AA; Laburnum House, Dipwood Road, Rowlands Gill, Tyne and Wear NE39 1BY.

WOOKEY, Eric Edgar, MC 1916; Dental Surgeon in private practice at Wimpole Street, 1933-68, retired, 1968; Senior Dental Surgeon, Royal Free Hospital, 1936-Sept. 1958, Hon. Consulting Dental Surgeon, since 1958; *b* 11 January 1892; *s* of Edgar Wookey, Shipham, Somerset, and Clara (*née* Davidson); *m* 1927, Doris Kathleen Fenner (*d* 1976); one *s* two *d. Educ:* Haverfordwest Grammar School; Clevedon College; Bristol University; Royal Dental Hospital, London. Bristol Univ. Student, medical and dental, 1909-14; Infantry commission in 4th Glos Regt TF, 1914; served overseas, France (wounded, despatches, MC); Italy, BEF (despatches twice); Bt Major, Comd 4th Glos Regt at Armistice, Nov. 1918. LDS, RCS 1919, and after a period of hospital practice commenced private practice at Hendon, 1920; Asst Dental Surgeon, Royal Free Hosp., 1921; full-time practice in Wimpole Street, 1933. During War of 1939-45, served in EMS. Member of Representative Bd,

British Dental Assoc., 1946-54 and 1958-61; Pres. Metropolitan Branch, 1949-50; Founder Member, Past-President, and Past Chm. of Council, Brit. Soc. of Med. and Dental Hypnosis (formerly Dental and Med. Soc. for Study of Hypnosis); Fellow Internat. Soc. of Clinical and Experimental Hypnosis (PP Brit. Section). Member: Council, Soc. for Psychical Research; British Archæological Soc. Liveryman, Tallow Chandlers' Co. Ecclesiological Soc. Silver Medal for Valour (Italy), 1918. *Publications:* articles in British Dental Jl and British Jl of Clinical Hypnosis. *Recreations:* music (piano), golf, numismatics (FRNS), philately, horology. *Address:* 51 Lake View, Canons Park, Edgware, Middx. *T:* 01-958 6029.

WOOLF, Harry Kenneth; a Recorder of the Crown Court, since 1972; Treasury Junior Counsel (Common Law), since 1974; *b* 2 May 1933; *s* of Alexander Woolf and Leah Woolf (*née* Cussins); *m* 1961, Marguerite Sassoon, *d* of George Sassoon; three *s*. *Educ:* Fettes Coll.; University Coll., London (LLB). Pres., University College Union Debating Soc., 1953. Called to Bar, Inner Temple, 1954; Bencher, 1976. Commnd (Nat. Service), 15/19th Royal Hussars, 1954; seconded Army Legal Services, 1955; Captain 1955. Started practice at Bar, 1956. Jun. Counsel, Inland Revenue, 1973-74. *Recreations:* riding, gardening, theatre. *Address:* (chambers) 1 Crown Office Row, Temple, EC4Y 7HH.

WOOLF, Sir John, Kt 1975; film and television producer; Chairman, Romulus Films; Executive Director, Anglia TV; Managing Director, British and American Film Holdings; *s* of Charles M. and Vera Woolf; *m* 1955, Ann; two *s*. *Educ:* Institut Montana, Switzerland. War, 1939-45 (Bronze Star (USA), 1945): Asst Dir, Army Kinematography, War Office, 1944-45. Member: Cinematograph Films Council; Bd of Governors, Services Kinema Corp. Special awards for contribution to British film industry from: Cinematograph Exhibitors Assoc., 1969; Variety Club of GB, 1974. Films produced by Romulus Group include: The African Queen, Pandora and the Flying Dutchman, Moulin Rouge, I am a Camera, Carrington VC, Beat the Devil, Story of Esther Costello, Room at the Top (British Film Academy Award for Best Film, 1958), Wrong Arm of the Law, The L-Shaped Room, Term of Trial, Life at the Top, Oliver! (Oscar and Golden Globe Award for Best Film, 1969), Day of the Jackal, The Odessa File. *Address:* Brook House, Park Lane, W1Y 4JN. *T:* 01-493 7741.

WOOLF, John Moss, CB 1975; Deputy Chairman of the Board of Customs and Excise, and Director-General (Customs and Establishments), since 1973; *b* 5 June 1918; *o s* of Alfred and Maud Woolf; *m* 1940, Phyllis Ada Mary Johnson; one *d*. *Educ:* Drayton Manor Sch.; Honourable Society of Lincoln's Inn. Barrister-at-law, 1948. War Service, 1939-46 (Captain, RA). Inland Revenue, 1937. Asst Principal, Min. of Fuel and Power, 1948; HM Customs and Excise, 1950: Principal, 1951; Asst Sec., 1960; Chm., Valuation Cttee, Customs Cooperation Council, Brussels, 1964-65; National Bd for Prices and Incomes, 1965; Under-Secretary, 1967; Asst Under-Sec. of State, Dept of Employment and Productivity, 1968-70; HM Customs and Excise: Comr, 1970; Dir of Establishments and Organisation, 1971-73. Assoc. of First Div. Civil Servants: Mem. of Exec. Cttee, 1950-58 and 1961-65; Hon. Sec., 1952-55; Chm., 1955-58 and 1964-65; Mem., Civil Service National Whitley Council (Staff Side), 1953-55. Commandeur d'Honneur, Ordre du Bontemps de Médoc et des Graves, 1973; Hon. Borgenerális (Hungary), 1974. *Publication:* Report on Control of Prices in Trinidad and Tobago (with M. M. Eccleshall), 1968. *Recreations:* reading, gardening. *Address:* West Lodge, 113 Marsh Lane, Stanmore, Mddx HA7 4TH. *T:* 01-952 1373. *Club:* Reform.

WOOLFORD, Harry Russell Halkerston, OBE 1970; Consultant, formerly Chief Restorer, National Gallery of Scotland; *b* 23 May 1905; *s* of H. Woolford, engineer; *m* 1932, Nancy Philip; one *d*. *Educ:* Edinburgh. Studied art at Edinburgh Coll. of Art (Painting and Drawing) and RSA Life School (Carnegie Travelling Scholarship, 1928), London, Paris and Italy; afterwards specialized in picture restoration. FMA; FIIC. Hon. MA Dundee, 1976. *Address:* Dean Park, Golf Course Road, Bonnyrigg, Midlothian EH19 2EU. *T:* 031-663 7949. *Club:* Scottish Arts.

WOOLFSON, Mark; Consultant and Director of Consortium, Pollution Control Consultants, since 1972; *b* 10 Nov. 1911; *s* of Victor Woolfson and Sarah (*née* Kixman); *m* 1940, Queenie Carlis; two *d*. *Educ:* City of London. Student Engr, Lancashire Dynamo & Crypto, until 1936; Engr, ASEA Electric Ltd, 1936-40; War Service, RNVR, 1940-46 (Lt-Comdr); MPBW, later DoE, 1946-71, Chief Mech. and Electr. Engineer, 1969-71. FIMechE, FIEE, Sen. Mem. IEE, IEEE. *Publications:* papers in

Jls of Instns of Civil, Mechanical and Elect. Engrs. *Recreations:* tennis, gardening, golf. *Address:* 3 Runnelfield, Harrow, Mddx. *T:* 01-422 1599.

WOOLLAM, John Victor; Barrister-at-Law; *b* 14 Aug. 1927; *s* of Thomas Alfred and Edie Moss Woollam; *m* 1964, Lavinia Rosamund Ela, *d* of S. R. E. Snow; two *s*. *Educ:* Liverpool Univ. Called to the Bar, Inner Temple. Contested (C) Scotland Div. of Liverpool, 1950; MP (C) W Derby Div. of Liverpool, Nov. 1954-Sept. 1964; Parliamentary Private Sec. to Minister of Labour, 1960-62. *Recreation:* philately. *Address:* 3 South Hill Grove, Oxton, Merseyside.

WOOLLCOMBE, Dame Jocelyn May, DBE 1950 (CBE 1944); *b* 9 May 1898; *d* of late Admiral Maurice Woollcombe and Ella Margaret Roberts; unmarried. *Educ:* Moorfield, Plymouth. Admiralty, NID as Clerk, 1916-19. Joined WRNS, enrolled as Chief Officer, Aug. 1939; Superintendent, 1940; Deputy Director, 1943-46; Director, 1946-50; Hon. ADC to the King, 1949. General Secretary, British Council for Aid to Refugees (Hungarian Section), 1957-58. Governor, The Sister Trust, 1956-65; Gov., WRNS Benevolent Trust, 1942-67; Pres., Assoc. of Wrens 1959-. *Recreation:* drama. *Address:* 2 Thorn Park, Plymouth PL3 4TG.

WOOLLCOMBE, Rt. Rev. Kenneth John; Assistant Bishop, Diocese of London, since 1978; *b* 2 Jan. 1924; *s* of late Rev. E. P. Woollcombe, OBE, and Elsie Ockenden Woollcombe; *m* 1950, Gwendoline Rhona Vyvien Hodges (*d* 1976); three *d*. *Educ:* Haileybury Coll., Hertford; St John's Coll., Oxford; Westcott House, Cambridge. Sub-Lieut (E) RNVR, 1945. Curate, St James, Grimsby, 1951; Fellow, Chaplain and Tutor, St John's Coll., Oxford, 1953, Hon. Fellow, 1971; Professor of Dogmatic Theology, General Theological Seminary, New York, 1960; Principal of Episcopal Theological Coll., Edinburgh, 1963; Bishop of Oxford, 1971-78. Chm., SPCK, 1973-78. Mem., Central Cttee, World Council of Churches, 1975-. STD Univ. of the South, Sewanee, USA, 1963; Hon. DD Hartford, Conn., 1975. *Publications:* (contrib.) The Historic Episcopate, 1954; (jointly) Essays on Typology, 1957. *Address:* c/o London Diocesan House, Causton Street, SW1P 4AU.

WOOLLER, Arthur, CBE 1967; HM Diplomatic Service, retired; *b* 23 May 1912; *s* of Joseph Edward Wooller and Sarah Elizabeth (*née* Kershaw); *m* 1944, Frances, *e d* of Justice A. L. Blank, ICS; three *s*. *Educ:* Bradford Grammar School; Corpus Christi College, Oxford. ICS, Bengal, 1935; Indian Foreign and Political Service, 1939; UK Trade Comr, New Zealand, 1947; First Sec. (Commercial), Ottawa, 1953; UK Trade Comr, Toronto, 1959; British Trade Comr, Hong Kong, 1960; Principal British Trade Comr, Bombay, 1963; British Deputy High Commissioner in Western India, Bombay, 1965-68; High Comr in Mauritius, 1968-70; Economic Advr, FCO, 1970-72. *Recreations:* fishing, golf, gardening. *Address:* 22 Browning Road, Harpenden, Herts. *T:* Harpenden 5076. *Club:* United Oxford & Cambridge University.

WOOLLETT, Maj.-Gen. John Castle, CBE 1957 (OBE 1955); MC 1945; MA Cantab; FICE; Principal Planning Inspector, Department of the Environment, since 1971; *b* 5 Nov. 1915; *o s* of John Castle Woollett and Lily Bradley Woollett, Bredgar, Kent; *m* 1st, 1941, Joan Eileen Stranks (marr. diss., 1957); two *s* (and one *s* decd); 2nd, 1959, Helen Wendy Willis; two step *s*. *Educ:* St Benedict's Sch.; RMA Woolwich; St John's Coll., Cambridge. Joined RE, 1935; 23 Field Co., 1938-40 (BEF, 1939-40); 6 Commando, 1940-42; Major Comdg 16 Field Sqdn and 16 Assault Sqdn RE, 1942-45 (BLA, 1944-45); Student, Staff Coll., Camberley, 1946; DAAG and GSO2, Brit. Service Mission to Burma, 1947-50; Major Comdg 51 Port Sqdn RE, 1950; Instructor, Staff Coll., Camberley, 1950-53; Lt-Col Comdg 28 Field Engr Regt, 1954-55 (Korea); Bt Lt-Col 1955; Comdr Christmas Is, 1956-57; GSO1, Northern Army Gp, 1957-59; Col GS, US Army Staff Coll., Fort Leavenworth, 1959-61; DQMG (Movements), BAOR, 1962-64; Brig. Comdg Hants Sub District and Transportation Centre, RE, 1964-65; Sch. of Transport, 1965-66; Dep. Engr-in-Chief, 1966-67; Maj.-Gen., Chief Engineer, BAOR, 1967-70, retired. Col Comdt, RE, 1973-. Pres., Instn of RE, 1974. *Recreations:* cruising, ski-ing, shooting. *Address:* 19 Shepherds Way, Liphook, Hants. *Clubs:* Army and Navy, Royal Ocean Racing, Ski Club of Great Britain, Royal Cruising; Island Sailing (Cowes), Bosham Sailing.

WOOLLEY, family name of **Baron Woolley.**

WOOLLEY, Baron *cr* 1967 (Life Peer), of Hatton; **Harold Woolley,** Kt 1964; CBE 1958; DL; President of National Farmers' Union of England and Wales 1960-66; *b* 6 Feb. 1905; *s* of William Woolley, JP and Eleanor Woolley; *m* 1st, 1926,

Martha Annie Jeffs (d 1936); four s; 2nd, 1937, Hazel Eileen Archer Jones (d 1975); two d. Educ: Woodhouse Grove School, Yorkshire. Farmer. Cheshire Deleg. to NFU Council, 1943; Chairman: NFU Parliamentary Cttee, 1947-57; Employers' Reps of Agricultural Wages Bd, 1947-57; Agricultural Apprenticeship Council for England and Wales, 1951-60. National Farmers' Union: Vice-Pres. 1948 and 1955; Dep. Pres., 1949-50 and 1956; Director: NFU Mutual Insurance Society, 1965-; NW Regional Adv. Bd, Abbey Nat. Building Soc. Member Nat. Jt Advisory Council to Ministry of Labour, 1950-58. DL Cheshire, 1969. Recreations: hunting, golf; interested in all sport. Address: Hatton House Farm, Hatton Heath, Chester. T: Tattenhall 356. Club: MCC.
See also W. E. Woolley.

WOOLLEY, Rev. (Alfred) Russell; MA; Rector, St Lawrence, IoW, 1967-74; b 10 Sept. 1899; e s of late A. W. Woolley, Moseley, and Margaret A. Russell, Shrewsbury; m 1933, Lina Mariana, 3rd d of late Prof. Bertram Hopkinson, CMG, FRS, Fellow of King's College, Cambridge; four s three d. Educ: King Edward's Camp Hill Grammar School; Wadham College, Oxford (Symons Exhibitioner). 2nd Class Hons Modern History, 1922; incorporated MA Cantab. (Trinity College), 1929. One year Inns of Court OTC and 6th OC Bn; Bromsgrove School, 1922-26; Repton School, 1927-28; The Leys School (Chief History Master, House-Master, Librarian, OC, OTC), 1929-33; Headmaster of Scarborough Coll., 1933-37, and of Wellingborough Gram. Sch., 1937-45; Educnl Sec. to the Oxford Univ. Appts Cttee, 1945-62. Ordained 1960. Rector of Gestingthorpe, Essex, 1962-67. Mem. Coun. IAHM, 1945; of Oxfordshire Educn Cttee, 1955-62; of Govng Body of Milton Abbey Sch., 1955-74; of Lindisfarne Coll., 1961-77; ex-Sec. Oxford Union Soc. Publications: Oxford University and City, 1951; Clarendon Guide to Oxford, 1963, 3rd edn 1975. Recreations: walking, travel. Address: Gestingthorpe Hall, Halstead, Essex CO9 3BB. T: Hedingham 60638.

WOOLLEY, Sir Charles (Campbell), GBE 1953 (OBE 1934); KCMG 1943 (CMG 1937); MC; LLD; b 1893; 3rd s of Henry Woolley; m 1921, Ivy (d 1974), d of late David Howells, Cwmbarry, Barry, Glamorgan; two s. Educ: Univ. Coll., Cardiff. Served European War, 1914-20; Captain S Wales Borderers; various staff appts; Active Service, France, Salonika, Constantinople, Caucasus (despatches, MC); Ceylon Civil Service, 1921-35; Secretary to the Governor; Colonial Secretary, Jamaica, 1935-38; Chief Secretary Nigeria, 1938-41; administered Govt of Jamaica and Nigeria at various times; Governor and C-in-C, Cyprus, 1941-46; Governor and Commander-in-Chief, British Guiana, 1947-53; retired Jan. 1953. Pres., Internat. Soc. for Protection of Animals, 1969-71; Vice-Pres., Southern Counties Orchestral Soc. KJStJ. Recreations: bridge, music. Address: Orchard Hill, Liss, Hants. T: Liss 2317.

WOOLLEY, Frank Edward; cricketer, retired; b Kent, 27 May 1887; 4th s of Charles William Woolley and Louise Lewis Woolley; m 1st, Sibyl Fordham (d 1962), Ashford, Kent; two d (one s decd); 2nd, Martha Wilson Morse, Chester, NS, widow of Major Sydney J. Morse. Educ: in Tonbridge, Kent. Professional, Kent County Cricket Club, 1903; subseq. played 67 times for England in 32 years; scored over 60,000 runs in 1st cl. cricket, took over 2,500 wickets, made 1,007 catches (world record) and 156 centuries; played in 54 consecutive Test Matches (world record); scored over 2000 runs and took 100 wickets in 4 successive seasons (world record); on 8 occasions, scored over a century and took 10 wickets in same match (world record); in Tasmania, 1912, scored highest-ever (305) in 4 hrs 15 mins not out (unequalled record); played greatest innings at Lords against Australia (93-95), 1921; scored 50 runs and 5 wickets, Gravesend, 1937; captained The Players at Lords for last time, Sept. 1938, then retd. Served War of 1914-18, HMS King George V. Publications: The King of Games; Early Memoirs of Frank Woolley as told to Martha Woolley, 1976. Relevant publications: Encyclopædia Britannica (under Cricket); Woolley, the Pride of Kent, by Ian Peebles; Great Men of Kent, by A. A. Thompson; Good Days, Full Score, etc, by Neville Cardus; A Sort of Cricketer, by E. W. Swanton; Frank Woolley, by Oliver Warner; Cricket Scores of Frank E. Woolley, by A. K. Nowill. Address: Chester, Nova Scotia, Canada. T: 902 275-3866. Clubs: (Hon. Life Mem.) MCC; (Hon. Life Mem.) Band of Brothers; Men of Kent; Kent County Cricket; Royal Nova Scotia Yacht Squadron.

WOOLLEY, John Maxwell, MBE 1945; TD 1946; Clerk, Merchant Taylors' Company, and Clerk to The Governors, Merchant Taylors' School, since 1962; b 22 March 1917; s of Lt-Col Jasper Maxwell Woolley, IMS (Retd) and Kathleen Mary Woolley (née Waller); m 1952, Esme Adela Hamilton-Cole; two

s. Educ: Cheltenham College; Trinity College, Oxford. BA (Oxon) 1938, MA (Oxon) 1962. Practising Solicitor, 1950-55; Asst Clerk, Merchant Taylors' Company, 1955-62. Governor: Merchant Taylors' Schs, Crosby; Wolverhampton Grammar Sch. Address: 26 Vallance Gardens, Hove, East Sussex BN3 2DD. T: Brighton 733200.

WOOLLEY, Sir Richard (van der Riet), Kt 1963; OBE 1953; FRS 1953; Director, South African Astronomical Observatory, 1972-76; Hon. Fellow, University House, Australian National University, since 1955; Hon. Fellow, Gonville and Caius College, Cambridge, since 1956; b Weymouth, Dorset, 24 April 1906; s of Paymaster Rear-Admiral Charles E. A. Woolley, CMG, RN; m 1932, Gwyneth Jane Margaret (née Meyler). Educ: Allhallows School, Honiton; University of Cape Town; Gonville and Caius College, Cambridge; MSc Cape Town; MA, ScD Cantab; Hon. LLD Melbourne. Commonwealth Fund Fellow, at Mt Wilson Observatory, California, 1929-31; Isaac Newton Student, Cambridge Univ., 1931-33; Chief Assistant, R Observatory, Greenwich, 1933-37; John Couch Adams Astronomer, Cambridge, 1937-39; Commonwealth Astronomer, 1939-55; Astronomer Royal, 1956-71. Hon. Professor of Astronomy in Australian National University, 1950-. Visiting Prof. of Astronomy, Univ. of Sussex, 1966-. Pres., Royal Astronomical Soc., 1963-65. Vice-Pres., International Astronomical Union, 1952-58; Pres., Australian and New Zealand Assoc. for the Advancement of Science, Melbourne meeting, 1955. Hon. DrPhil Uppsala, 1956; Hon. DSc: Cape Town, 1969; Sussex, 1970. Corresp. Mem. de la Société Royale des Sciences de Liège, 1956. Master, Worshipful Co. of Clockmakers, 1969. Gold Medal, RAS, 1971. Publications: (with Sir Frank Dyson) Eclipses of the Sun and Moon, 1937; (with D. W. N. Stibbs) The Outer Layers of a Star, 1953. Address: Magnolia House, Hankham, near Pevensey, East Sussex. Club: Athenæum.

WOOLLEY, Roy Gilbert; His Honour Judge Woolley; a Circuit Judge, since 1976; b 28 Nov. 1922; s of John Woolley and Edith Mary Woolley; m 1953, Doreen, d of Humphrey and Kathleen Morris; two s two d. Educ: Overton and Marchwiel Primary Schs; Deeside Secondary Sch.; UCL (LLB Hons 1949). Served War, 1939-45, Air Gunner, RAF. Christopher Tancred Student, Lincoln's Inn, 1948; called to the Bar, 1951; Wales and Chester Circuit; Recorder, 1975. Reader: Diocese of Chester, 1955-; Diocese of Lichfield, 1977-. Recreations: outdoor pursuits, incl. horse riding, gardening, shooting; interested in music, poetry, art and antique furniture. Address: Henlle Hall, St Martins, Oswestry, Salop SY10 7AX. T: Gobowen 257.

WOOLLEY, Russell; see Woolley, A. R.

WOOLLEY, William Edward, CBE 1974; DL; Chairman, Cupal Ltd, since 1947; Director, Secto Co. Ltd, since 1947; b 17 March 1901; s of William Woolley, JP, and Eleanor Woolley; m 1929, Marion Elizabeth Aspinall; one s one d. Educ: Woodhouse Grove School, Yorkshire; Edinburgh University. MP (Nat L) for Spen Valley Division of Yorkshire, 1940-45; Parliamentary Private Secretary to Minister of Health, 1943, to Minister of Aircraft Production, 1945. JP; Chairman: Blackburn Borough Magistrates, 1967-72; Gen. Comrs Income Tax, Lancs Adv. Cttee, 1974-76; Gen Comrs Income Tax, Blackburn District, 1960-76; Blackburn and District Hosp. Management Cttee, 1952-74; Manchester Regional Hosp. Staff Cttee, 1966-74; Pres., Blackburn and District Council of Social Service. Contested (Nat L) Brighouse and Spenborough, General elections, 1950, 1951. DL Lancs, 1975. Address: Billinge Crest, Billinge End Road, Blackburn, Lancs BB2 6PY. TA and T: Blackburn 53449. Club: National Liberal.
See also Baron Woolley.

WOOLNER, Maj.-Gen. Christopher Geoffrey, CB 1942; MC; b 18 Oct. 1893; m 1923, Anne, d of Sydney Pitt; two d. Educ: Marlborough; RMA, Woolwich. 2nd Lt RE, 1912; Captain, 1917; Bt Major, 1919; Major, 1928; Bt Lt-Col, 1933; Lt-Col, 1936; Col, 1939; Maj.-Gen., 1941. Survey Duty, Gold Coast, 1920-23; Officer Company of Gentlemen Cadets Royal Military Academy, 1924-27; GSO2 India, 1930-32; Bde Major, India, 1932-34; Deputy Inspector and Deputy Comdt School of Military Engineering, Aug.-Sept. 1939; GSO1, BEF, 1939-40; Bde Comdr, Feb.-Nov. 1940; Comdr, 1940. Served European War, 1914-18 (wounded, despatches twice, Bt Major, MC and two Bars); War of 1939-45 (despatches thrice, CB); Commander 81st (West African) Div.; Commander Mid-West District and 53 (Welsh) Infantry Division TA; retired, 1947. Clubs: Army and Navy, Naval and Military.

WOOLTON, 3rd Earl of, cr 1956; **Simon Frederick Marquis;** Baron Woolton, 1939; Viscount Woolton, 1953; Viscount

Walberton, 1956; *b* 24 May 1958; *s* of 2nd Earl of Woolton and Cecily Josephine (now Lady Forres), *e d* of Sir Alexander Gordon Cumming, 5th Bt; *S* father, 1969. *Address:* 31 Tite Street, SW3; Strone House, Bridge of Cally, Blairgowrie, Perthshire.
See also Baron Forres.

WOOLWICH, Bishop Suffragan of, since 1975; **Rt. Rev. Michael Eric Marshall,** MA; *b* Lincoln, 14 April 1936. *Educ:* Lincoln Sch.; Christ's Coll., Cambridge (Tancred Scholar, Upper II: Hist. Pt 1 and Theol Pt 1a, MA); Cuddesdon Theological Coll. Deacon, 1960; Curate, St Peter's, Spring Hill, Birmingham, 1960-62; Tutor, Ely Theological Coll. and Minor Canon of Ely Cath., 1962-64; Chaplain in London Univ., 1964-69; Vicar of All Saints', Margaret Street, W1, 1969-75. Founder and Dir, Inst. of Christian Studies, 1970; Member: Gen. Synod, 1970, also Diocesan and Deanery Synods; Liturgical Commn; Anglican/Methodist Liaison Commn until 1974; SPCK Governing Body; USPG Governing Body. Exam. Chap. to Bp of London, 1974. Has frequently broadcast on BBC and commercial radio; also lectured, preached and broadcast in Canada and USA. *Publications:* (co-author) A Pattern of Faith, 1966; Founder and co-editor, Christian Quarterly. *Recreations:* music, cooking. *Address:* 4 College Gardens, SE21 7BE. *T:* 01-693 2726. *Club:* Naval and Military.

WOOSTER, Clive Edward Doré, FRIBA; MBIM; consultant; *b* 3 Nov. 1913; *s* of Edward Doré Wooster; *m*; two *s*; *m* 1970, Patricia Iris (formerly Dewey). *Educ:* Private School, Southend-on-Sea. Private offices, 1930-40; War Service, Captain RA, 1940-46. Local Authority Offices and LCC, 1946-51; Ministry of Education, 1951-58; University Grants Cttee, 1958-59; Works Directorate, War Office, 1959-63; Dep. Chief Architect, Min. of Housing and Local Govt, 1969; Dir, Housing Develt, DoE, 1972-74, retired. RIBA Technical Standards Cttee, 1960-64; RIBA Building Controls Panel Chairman, 1960-63; RIBA Management Handbook Cttee, 1963-67; RIBA Council, 1970-72. *Publications:* Lectures on architectural and building management subjects; contrib. to professional journals. *Address:* 141 Harefield Road, Rickmansworth, Herts WD3 1PB. *T:* Rickmansworth 75401.

WOOTTEN, Maj.-Gen. Richard Montague, CB 1940; MC; *b* 19 June 1889; *s* of William Montague Wootten, Headington House, Oxon; *m* 1st, 1915, *d* of Sir John Wormald, KBE; two *d*; 2nd, *d* of William Percival. *Educ:* Rugby; RMC Sandhurst; Staff College, Camberley. 2nd Lieut 6th Dragoons, 1909; Major Queen's Bays, 1921; served European War, France and Belgium, 1914-18 (MC); Instructor Staff Coll., 1928-31; CO The Queen's Bays, 1932-36; Dep. Dir-Gen., TA, 1938-39, Dep. QMG for US Forces; Palestine and Egypt, 1936-39; War of 1939-45 (CB, Commander Legion of Merit, USA). Retired, 1945. *Address:* Little Court, Cromwell Gardens, Marlow, Bucks. *T:* 4246.

WOOTTON OF ABINGER, Baroness *cr* 1958 (Life Peer), of Abinger Common, (**Barbara Frances**), CH 1977; MA; *b* Cambridge, 1897; *d* of late Dr James Adam, Senior Tutor of Emmanuel Coll., Cambridge and Mrs Adam, sometime Fellow of Girton Coll., Cambridge; *m* 1st, 1917, John Wesley Wootton (*d* of wounds, 1917), Earl of Derby Research Student, Trinity College, Cambridge; 2nd, 1935, George Percival Wright (*d* 1964). *Educ:* Perse High School for Girls, Cambridge; Girton Coll., Cambridge (MA Cantab). Director of Studies and Lecturer in Economics, Girton Coll., 1920-22; Research Officer Trades Union Congress and Labour Party Joint Research Department, 1922-26; Principal, Morley College for Working Men and Women, 1926-27; Director of Studies for Tutorial Classes, University of London, 1927-44; Professor of Social Studies, University of London, 1948-52; Nuffield Research Fellow, Bedford College, University of London, 1952-57. A Governor of the BBC, 1950-56; a Deputy-Speaker in House of Lords, 1967-. Member: Royal Commission on Workmen's Compensation, 1938; Royal Commn on the Press, 1947; Royal Commn on the Civil Service, 1954; Royal Commn on Penal System, 1964-66; Penal Adv. Council, 1966-; Adv. Council on Misuse of Drugs, 1971-74; Chm., Countryside Commn, 1968-70 (Nat. Parks Commn, 1966-68). JP in the Metropolitan Courts, 1926-70 (on the Panel of Chairmen in the Metropolitan Juvenile Courts, 1946-62). Hon. degrees from one US and eleven British Universities. Hon. Fellow: Girton Coll., Cambridge, 1965-; Bedford Coll., London, 1964-. *Publications:* (as *Barbara Wootton*): Twos and Threes, 1933; Plan or No Plan, 1934; London's Burning, 1936; Lament for Economics, 1938; End Social Inequality, 1941; Freedom Under Planning, 1945; Testament for Social Science, 1950; The Social Foundations of Wage Policy, 1955; Social Science and Social Pathology, 1959; Crime and the Criminal Law, 1964; In a World I Never Made,

1967; Contemporary Britain, 1971; Incomes Policy: an inquest and a proposal, 1974; Reflections on the Penal System, 1978. *Recreation:* country life. *Address:* High Barn, Abinger Common, Dorking, Surrey. *T:* Dorking 730180.

WOOTTON, Godfrey; see Wootton, N. G.

WOOTTON, Gordon Henry; a Recorder of the Crown Court, since 1975; *b* 23 April 1927; *s* of William Henry Wootton and Winifred Beatrice Wootton; *m* 1953, Camilla Bowes; two *s*. LLB Hons. Captain, RE, 1947. Called to the Bar, Middle Temple, 1952; Resident Magistrate, Uganda, 1954-62. *Address:* Southcot, Cog Road, Sully, South Glamorgan. *T:* Sully 530248.

WOOTTON, Harold Samuel, CMG 1942; FCIS; JP; Town Clerk of Melbourne, 1935-54, retired; *b* Ballan, Vic, 13 Dec. 1891; *s* of late John Richard Wootton, Tatura, Goulburn Valley, Victoria; *m* 1914, Anne, *d* of late Joseph Biggs; one *s* one *d*. *Educ:* State School, Waranga, Victoria; Central Business College, Melbourne. Junior Clerk, Melbourne Town Hall, 1909; Deputy Town Clerk, 1923. *Recreation:* bowls. *Address:* Noosa River Units, 104 Gympie Terrace, Noosaville, Qld 4566, Australia. *Clubs:* St Kilda Bowling, Tewantin Bowling (Queensland).

WOOTTON, Ian David Phimester, MA, MB, BChir, PhD, FRIC, FRCPath, FRCP; Professor of Chemical Pathology, Royal Postgraduate Medical School, University of London, since 1963; *b* 5 March 1921; *s* of D. Wootton and Charlotte (*née* Phimester); *m* 1946, Veryan Mary Walshe; two *s* two *d*. *Educ:* Weymouth Grammar School; St John's College, Cambridge; St Mary's Hospital, London. Research Assistant, Postgraduate Med. School, 1945; Lecturer, 1949; Sen. Lecturer, 1959; Reader, 1961. Consultant Pathologist to Hammersmith Hospital, 1952. Member of Medical Research Council Unit, Cairo, 1947-48; Major, RAMC, 1949; Smith-Mundt Fellow, Memorial Hosp., New York, 1951. Chief Scientist (Hosp. Scientific and Technical Services), DHSS, 1972-73. *Publications:* Microanalysis in Medical Biochemistry, 1964, ed 5th edn, 1974; Biochemical Disorders in Human Disease, 1970; papers in medical and scientific journals on biochemistry and pathology. *Recreations:* carpentry, boating. *Address:* 16 River Reach, Broomwater, Teddington, Mddx. *T:* 01-977 1033.

WOOTTON, (Norman) Godfrey; Stipendiary Magistrate for Merseyside, since 1976; *b* 10 April 1926; *s* of H. N. and E. Wootton, Crewe, Cheshire. *Educ:* The Grammar Sch., Crewe; Liverpool Univ. (LLB). Called to Bar, Gray's Inn, 1951. Joined Northern Circuit, 1951. A Recorder of the Crown Court, 1972-76. *Recreations:* travel, photography. *Address:* Magistrates' Court, Dale Street, Liverpool L2.

WOOZLEY, Prof. Anthony Douglas, MA; Professor of Philosophy, University of Virginia, since 1966, Commonwealth Professor of Philosophy, since 1974; *b* 14 Aug. 1912; *o s* of David Adams Woozley and Kathleen Lucy Moore; *m* 1937, Thelma Suffield, *e d* of late Frank Townshend, Worcester; one *d*. *Educ:* Haileybury College; Queen's College, Oxford. Open Scholar, Queen's College, 1931-35; 1st Cl. Class. Hon. Mods, 1933; 1st Cl. Lit. Hum., 1935; John Locke Schol., 1935. Fellow of All Souls College, 1935-37; Fellow and Praelector in Philosophy, Queen's Coll., 1937-54; Librarian, 1938-54; Professor of Moral Philosophy, Univ. of St Andrews, 1954-67. Served War, 1940-46 (despatches), in Army; commissioned King's Dragoon Guards, 1941; served North Africa, Italy, Greece, Egypt, Syria, Palestine; Major. Tutor, Queen's College, 1946-54; University Lecturer in Philosophy, 1947-54; Senior Proctor, 1953-54. Editor of The Philosophical Quarterly, 1957-62; Editor, Home University Library, 1962-68. Visiting Professor of Philosophy: Univ. of Rochester, USA, 1965; Univ. of Arizona, 1972. *Publications:* (ed) Thomas Reid's Essays on the Intellectual Powers of Man, 1941; Theory of Knowledge, 1949; (with R. C. Cross) Plato's Republic: a Philosophical Commentary, 1964; (ed) John Locke's Essay Concerning Human Understanding, 1964. Articles and reviews in Mind, etc. *Address:* RFD 3, Kearsarge, Charlottesville, Va 22901, USA.

WORCESTER, Bishop of, since 1970; **Rt. Rev. Robert Wilmer Woods,** KCVO 1971; MA; Prelate of the Most Distinguished Order of St Michael and St George, since 1971; *b* 15 Feb. 1914; *s* of late Edward Woods, Bishop of Lichfield, and Clemence (*née* Barclay); *m* 1942, Henrietta Marion (JP 1966), *d* of late K. H. Wilson; two *s* three *d*. *Educ:* Gresham's Sch., Holt; Trinity Coll., Cambridge. Asst Sec., Student Christian Movement, 1937-42; Chaplain to the Forces, 1942-46 (despatches, 1944); Vicar of South Wigston, Leicester, 1946-51; Archdeacon of Singapore and Vicar of St Andrew's Cathedral, 1951-58; Archdeacon of Sheffield and Rector of Tankersley, 1958-62; Dean of Windsor, 1962-70; Domestic Chaplain to the Queen, 1962-70; Register of

the Most Noble Order of the Garter, 1962-70. Secretary, Anglican/Methodist Commn for Unity, 1965-74; Member: Council, Duke of Edinburgh's Award Scheme, 1968; Public Schools Commn, 1968-70; Governor, Haileybury Coll.; Pres, Queen's Coll., Birmingham, and Chm. Council, 1970-; Chairman: Windsor Festival Co., 1969-71; Churches Television Centre, 1969-; Dir, Christian Aid, 1969. Visitor, Malvern Coll., 1970-. *Recreations:* sailing, shooting, painting. *Address:* Bishop's House, Hartlebury Castle, Kidderminster, Worcs. *Clubs:* Brooks's, English-Speaking Union.
See also Most Rev . F . Woods .

WORCESTER, Dean of; see Baker, Very Rev. T. G. A.

WORCESTER, Archdeacon of; see Williams, Ven. J. C.

WORDEN, Prof. Alastair Norman; Professor of Toxicology, University of Bath, since 1973; Chairman, Huntingdon Research Centre, since 1951; *b* 23 April 1916; *s* of Dr C. Norman and Elizabeth Worden; *m* 1st, 1942, Agnes Marshall Murray; one *s*; 2nd, 1950, Dorothy Mary Jensen (*née* Peel), MA (Fellow and Steward, Lucy Cavendish Coll., Cambridge); two *s* one *d*. *Educ:* Queen Elizabeth's Sch., Barnet; St John's Coll., Cambridge (MA, PhD); Royal Veterinary, Birkbeck and University Colls, London (DVetMed, DSc). DrVetMed Zurich; FRCPath; FRCVS; FACVT; FRIC; FIBiol. Research Student, Lister Inst. of Preventive Medicine and Univ. Cambridge, 1938-41; Res. Officer, Univ. Cambridge, 1941-45; Milford Res. Prof., Univ. Wales, 1945-50; Fellow and Co-ordinator of Environmental Studies, Wolfson (formerly University) Coll., Cambridge, 1971-; Student, Cambridge Univ. Sch. of Clinical Medicine, 1975-. Expert Pharmacologue-Toxicologue du Ministère de la Santé Publique, France, 1974-. Member: ARC Tech. Cttees on Calf and Pig Diseases, 1944; Jt ARC Agricl Improvement Council Cttee on Grassland Improvement Station, 1946; ARC Res. (Frazer) Cttee on Toxic Chemicals, 1961; MAFF British Agrochemicals Jt Medical Panel, 1961; Zool Soc. Lond. Animal Husbandry and Welfare Cttee, 1954-; Royal Society Study Gp on Long Term Toxic Effects, 1975-; Governor, Taverham Hall Educnl Trust, 1968; Mem. Papworth-Huntingdon HMC, 1970-74; Trustee, Lucy Cavendish Coll., Cambridge, 1975-. President: Hunts Br., Historical Assoc.; Hunts Fauna and Flora Soc., 1965-; Beds and Hunts Naturalist Trust; Chm., Mammal Soc. British Isles, 1953-54; Vice-President: Hunts CCC, FA, Football League and Referees' Assoc.; Life Member: CUCC; CURUFC. Mem. Worshipful Soc. Apothecaries, 1971. Freeman, City of London, 1974. Editor: Animal Behaviour, 1950-65; Toxicology Letters, 1977-. *Publications:* Laboratory Animals, 1947; (with Harry V. Thompson) The Rabbit, 1956; Animal Health, Production and Pasture, 1964; numerous papers on nutrition, biochemistry and toxicology. *Recreations:* history, natural history, sport, travel. *Address:* Cross Keys Orchard, Hemingford Abbots, Cambs PE18 9AE. *T:* Huntingdon 62434. *Clubs:* Athenæum, United Oxford & Cambridge University, Farmers', No 10; MCC, Surrey CCC.

WORDIE, John Stewart, CBE 1975; VRD 1963; barrister-at-law; *b* 15 Jan. 1924; *s* of late Sir James Mann Wordie, CBE, Hon. LLD, and of Lady Wordie (*née* Henderson); *m* 1955, Patricia Gladys Kynoch, Keith, Banffshire, *d* of Lt-Col G. B. Kynoch, CBE, TD, DL; four *s*. *Educ:* Winchester Coll.; St John's Coll., Cambridge (MA; LLB). Served RNVR, 1942-46. Comdr RNR, 1967; Comdr London Div. RNR, 1969-71. Cambridge, 1946-49; Called to the Bar, Inner Temple, 1950; in practice at the Bar, 1951-. Chairman: Burnham, Pelham and Soulbury Cttees, 1966-; Wages Councils; Mem., Agricultural Wages Bd for England and Wales, 1974-; Dep. Chm. and Mem., Central Arbitration Cttee, 1976-. Mem. Court of Assistants, Salters' Co., 1971-, Master, 1975. *Recreations:* shooting, sailing and boating, athletics, tennis. *Address:* Oakfield, 45 Ormond Avenue, Hampton, Mddx. *T:* 01-979 1018; Shallows Cottage, Breamore, Fordingbridge, Hants. *T:* Breamore 432. *Clubs:* Travellers'; RORC, Hawks, Royal Tennis Court, Clyde Corinthian Yacht.

WORDSWORTH, Maj.-Gen. Robert Harley, CB 1945; CBE 1943; late IA; Administrator, Norfolk Island, 1962-64; *b* 21 July 1894; *s* of W. H. Wordsworth; *m* 1928, Margaret Joan Ross-Reynolds; one *s* one *d*. Served European War, 1914-18, AIF (despatches); Waziristan, 1919-21; NW Frontier of India, 1930; Persia-Iraq, 1943 (CBE); Middle East, 1945 (CB); retired, 1947. Senator Commonwealth Parlt of Australia, 1949-59. *Recreation:* trout fishing. *Address:* 23 Warragul Street, Norwood, Launceston, Tasmania 7250, Australia. *Club:* Launceston (Launceston, Tasmania).

WORKMAN, Robert Little, CB 1974; Under-Secretary, HM Treasury, 1967-74; *b* 30 Oct. 1914; *s* of late Robert Workman

and Jesse Little; *m* 1940, Gladys Munroe Foord; two *d*. *Educ:* Sedbergh Sch.; Clare Coll., Cambridge. Economist, Export Credits Guarantee Dept, 1938-49; HM Treasury: Principal, 1949-59; Asst Secretary, 1959-66. Member, St Pancras Borough Council, 1945-49. *Recreations:* building and the visual arts. *Address:* Flatts Farm, Hawstead, Suffolk. *T:* Sicklesmere 497.

WORLOCK, Most Rev. Derek John Harford; see Liverpool, Archbishop of, (RC).

WORMALD, Brian Harvey Goodwin, MA; University Lecturer in History, Cambridge, since 1948; Fellow of Peterhouse since 1938; *b* 24 July 1912; *s* of late Rev. C. O. R. Wormald and Mrs A. W. C. Wormald (*née* Brooks); *m* 1946, Rosemary, *d* of E. J. B. Lloyd; four *s*. *Educ:* Harrow; Peterhouse, Cambridge (Scholar). BA 1934 (1st Class Hons Hist. Tripos, Parts I and II); Members Prize (English Essay), 1935; Strathcona Research Student, St John's College, 1936-38; Prince Consort Prize, 1938; MA 1938. Chaplain and Catechist, Peterhouse, 1940-48; Dean, 1941-44; Tutor, 1952-62. Select Preacher, Cambridge, 1945 and 1954. Junior Proctor, 1951-52. Received into Catholic Church, 1955. *Publication:* Clarendon: Politics, History and Religion, 1951. *Address:* Peterhouse, Cambridge. *Club:* Travellers'.

WORMALD, Maj.-Gen. Derrick Bruce, DSO 1944; MC 1940, Bar 1945; Director-General of Fighting Vehicles and Engineer Equipment, Ministry of Defence, 1966-70, retired; *b* 28 April 1916; 2nd *s* of Arthur and Veronica Wormald; *m* 1953, Betty Craddock; two *d*. *Educ:* Bryanston Sch.; RMA Sandhurst. Commnd into 13/18 Royal Hussars (QMO), 1936; served in India, 1936-38, BEF, 1939-40 and BLA, 1944-45; Comd, 25th Dragoons, India, 1945-47; Staff Coll., Quetta, 1947; War Office, 1948-50; Comdr, 1st Armoured Car Regt of Arab Legion, 1951-52; Comdr Arab Legion Armoured Corps, 1953-54; jssc 1955; GSO1, 11th Armoured Div., 1956; Comd, 3rd The King's Own Hussars, 1956, and The Queen's Own Hussars, 1958; Comdr, Aden Protectorate Levies, 1959-61; Comdr, Salisbury Plain Sub District, 1962-65. Col, 13th/18th Royal Hussars (QMO), 1974-. Order of El Istiqlal (Jordan), 1953. *Recreations:* shooting, fishing, sailing. *Address:* Ballards, Wickham Bishops, Essex. *T:* Maldon 891218. *Club:* Cavalry and Guards.

WORMALD, Dame Ethel (May), DBE 1968; JP; DL; *b* 19 Nov. 1901; *d* of late John Robert Robinson, Journalist, Newcastle upon Tyne; *m* 1923, Stanley Wormald, MA, MEd, BSc (decd); two *s*. *Educ:* Whitley Bay High Sch.; Leeds Univ. (BA, DipEd). Liverpool City Councillor, 1953-67; Lord Mayor of Liverpool, 1967-68. President, Assoc. of Education Cttees, 1961-62; Chairman, Liverpool Education Cttee, 1955-61, and 1963-67; Chairman: Liverpool Coll. of Higher Educn; Burton Manor Residential Coll. of Further Educn, Wirral; Mem. Court and Council, Liverpool Univ.; Governor, Liverpool Polytechnic. JP Liverpool, 1948-; DL Lancaster, 1970, Merseyside, 1974. *Recreations:* theatre, foreign travel. *Address:* 26 Princes Park Mansions, Liverpool L8 3SA. *T:* 051-728 8670.

WORMELL, Prof. Donald Ernest Wilson; Professor of Latin, University of Dublin, since 1942; Senior Fellow, Trinity College, Dublin; *b* 5 Jan. 1908; *yr s* of Thomas Wilson and Florence Wormell; *m* 1941, Daphne Dillon Wallace; three *s* one *d*. *Educ:* Perse School. Schol., St John's Coll., Cambridge, 1926; 1st Class Classical Tripos, Parts I and II; Sandys Student, 1930; Henry Fund Fellow, 1931; Sterling Research Fellow, Yale, 1932; PhD Yale, 1933; Fellow, St John's Coll., Cambridge, 1933-36; Asst Lecturer in Classics, University College, Swansea, 1936-39. Leverhulme Research Fellowship, 1958. Employed by Air Ministry and Foreign Office, 1942-44. Public Orator, University of Dublin, 1952-69; Vice-Provost, Trinity Coll., Dublin, 1973-74. MRIA; Mem., Inst. for Advanced Study, Princeton, USA, 1967-68. *Publications:* (with H. W. Parke) The Delphic Oracle, 1956; articles on classical literature and ancient history in learned periodicals. *Recreation:* music. *Address:* Gatineau, Sandyford Road, Dundrum, Dublin 14. *T:* Dublin 983932.

WORRALL, Air Vice-Marshal John, CB 1963; DFC 1940; retired; Managing Director, The Advertising Agency Poster Bureau Ltd, 1964-65; *b* 9 April 1911; *o s* of late J. R. S. Worrall, Thackers, Bombay, India; *m* 1967, Barbara Jocelyne, *er d* of late Vincent Ronald Robb. *Educ:* Cranleigh; Royal Air Force Coll., Cranwell. Commission Royal Air Force, 1931; flying duties No 1 Sqdn, 1932, No 208 Sqdn, 1933-36; language study, Peking, 1936-39; commanded No 32 (F) Sqdn Biggin Hill, 1940; Fighter Control, Biggin Hill, 1940; Fighter and Transport Staff and Unit, 1941-45; RAF Staff Coll., 1945; Senior Personnel Staff Officer, HQ Transport Command, 1945-48; OC, RAF West Malling and Metropolitan Sector, 1948-49; OC, RAF Kai Tak, Hong Kong, 1949-51; HQ Home Command, 1952-53; Air Ministry, Organisation Branch, 1953-54; OC Eastern Sector,

1954-56; AOA, HQ Flying Training Command, 1956-58; Assistant Chief of Air Staff (Training), 1958-60; SASO, NEAF, 1960-63; retired from RAF, 1963. Chairman RAF Ski and Winter Sports Assoc., 1953-60, Vice-President, 1960-68; Chairman, Battle of Britain Fighter Assoc., 1958-60. *Recreations:* ski-ing, sailing. *Address:* Es Muli den Cosme, Calle Ramón Llull 49, Alqueria Blanca, Mallorca, Spain. *T:* Mallorca 65.38.73; c/o National Westminster Bank Ltd, 155 North Street, Brighton, East Sussex. *Club:* RAF Reserves.

WORSFOLD, Reginald Lewis; Member for Personnel, British Gas Corporation (formerly Gas Council), since 1973; *b* 18 Dec. 1925; *s* of Charles S. and Doris Worsfold; *m* 1952, Margot Kempell; one *s* one *d. Educ:* School of Technology, Art and Commerce, Oxford; London Sch. of Economics. MIPM. Served War of 1939-45: Lieut 44 Royal Marine Commandos, 1943-46. Organising Commissioner, Scout Council of Nigeria, 1947-49; Personnel Manager: British European Airways, 1953-65; W Midlands Gas Bd, 1965-69; Gas Council: Dep. Personnel Dir, 1969-70; Personnel Dir, 1970-72. *Recreations:* sailing, camping, music. *Address:* 59 Blenheim Gardens, Kingston Hill, Kingston-upon-Thames, Surrey. *T:* 01-549 2827.

WORSKETT, Prof. Roy, RIBA; City Architect and Senior Planning Officer, Bath City Council, since 1974; Professor of Urban Conservation, School of Architecture, Bath University, since 1974; *b* 3 Sept. 1932; *s* of Archibald Ellwood Worskett and Dorothy Alice Roffey; two *s* one *d. Educ:* Collyer's Sch., Horsham; Portsmouth Sch. of Architecture. MRTPI 1975; RIBA 1955. Architect's Dept, LCC, 1957-60; Architect, Civic Trust, London, 1960-63; Historic Areas Div., DoE (formerly MPBW), 1963-74. Chm., Conservation Cttees, Crafts Adv. Cttee, 1974-; Member: Heritage Educn Group, 1976-; Council for Urban Study Centres, TCPA, 1977-; Council of Management, Architectural Heritage Fund, 1977-. Vis. Prof., UNESCO Internat. Centre for Conservation, Rome, 1972-. *Publications:* The Character of Towns, 1968; articles in architect. and planning magazines. *Recreation:* looking and listening in disbelief. *Address:* 24 Richmond Place, Bath, Avon. *T:* Bath 28411.

WORSLEY, Lord; Charles John Pelham; *b* 5 Nov. 1963; *s* and heir of 7th Earl of Yarborough, *qv.*

WORSLEY, Air Cdre G. N. E. T. C.; *see* Tindal-Carill-Worsley.

WORSLEY, Very Rev. Godfrey Stuart Harling; Dean Emeritus of Gibraltar, and Rector of Pen Selwood, since 1969; *b* 4 Dec. 1906; *o s* of late Rev. A. E. Worsley, Rector of Georgeham; *m* 1933, Stella Mary, *o c* of late H. S. Church, Croyde Manor, N Devon; two *s* one *d. Educ:* Dean Close, Cheltenham; London College of Divinity. Deacon, 1929; Priest, 1931; Asst Curate, Croydon Parish Church, 1930-33; CF, Ireland, Malta, Catterick, 1933-43; SCF, W Africa, Greece, Cyprus, 1943-49; DACG, N Midland District and Malta, 1949-54; Rector of Kingsland, 1954-60; Rural Dean of Leominster, 1956-60; Prebendary de Cublington in Hereford Cathedral, and Proctor in Convocation, Diocese of Hereford, 1959-60; Dean of Gibraltar and Rural Dean of Southern Spain, and officiating chaplain RN, 1960-69. *Address:* Pen Selwood Rectory, Wincanton, Somerset. *T:* Bourton (Dorset) 325.

WORSLEY, Lt-Gen. Sir John (Francis), KBE 1966 (OBE 1951); CB 1963; MC 1945; retired, 1968; *b* 8 July 1912; *s* of Geoffrey Worsley, OBE, ICS, and Elsie Margaret (*née* Macpherson); *m* 1942, Barbara Elizabeth Jarvis (*née* Greenwood); one *s* three *d* (and two step *d*). *Educ:* Radley; Royal Military Coll., Sandhurst. Unattached List, Indian Army (attached Queen's Own Cameron Highlanders), 1933; 3rd Bn 2nd Punjab Regt, 1934; served NW Frontier, India, 1935 and 1936-37; War of 1939-45, Middle East and SE Asia; Staff Coll., Quetta, 1941; Comd 2nd Bn 1st Punjab Regt, 1945; York and Lancaster Regt, 1947; Joint Services Staff Coll., 1951; Comd 1st Bn The South Lancashire Regt (Prince of Wales's Volunteers), 1953; Secretary, Joint Planning Staff, Ministry of Defence, 1956; Comd 6th Infantry Brigade Group, 1957; Imperial Defence Coll., 1960; General Officer Commanding 48 Division (Territorial Army) and West Midland District, 1961-63; Commandant, Staff Coll., Camberley, 1963-66; Commander, British Forces, Hong Kong, 1966-68. Mem. Exec. Cttee, Nat. Army Museum; Chm., Indian Services Museum Cttee. *Address:* Haydon Farmhouse, Sherborne, Dorset. *Clubs:* Army and Navy.

WORSLEY, Sir Marcus; *see* Worsley, Sir W. M. J.

WORSLEY, Lt-Gen. Sir Richard (Edward), KCB 1976; OBE 1964; GOC 1 (British) Corps, 1976-July 1978; *b* 29 May 1923; *s*

of H. H. K. Worsley, Grey Abbey, Co. Down; *m* 1959, Sarah Anne Mitchell; one *s* one *d. Educ:* Radley Coll. Served War: commissioned into Rifle Bde, 1942, Middle East and Italian Campaigns, 1942-45. Instr, RMA Sandhurst, 1948-51; Malayan Emergency, 1956-57; Instr, Staff Coll., Camberley, 1958-61; CO, The Royal Dragoons, 1962-65; Comdr, 7th Armoured Bde, 1965-67; Imperial Defence Coll., 1968; Chief of Staff, Far East Land Forces, 1969-71; GOC 3rd Div., 1972-74; Vice-QMG, MoD, 1974-76. *Recreations:* shooting, ornithology. *Address:* c/o Barclays Bank Ltd, 27 Regent Street, SW1. *Club:* Cavalry and Guards.

WORSLEY, Sir (William) Marcus (John), 5th Bt *cr* 1838; *b* 6 April 1925; *s* of Colonel Sir William Arthington Worsley, 4th Bt, and of Joyce Morgan, *d* of Sir John Fowler Brunner, 2nd Bt; *S* father, 1973; *m* 1955, Hon. Bridget Assheton, *d* of 1st Baron Clitheroe, *qv*; three *s* one *d. Educ:* Eton; New Coll., Oxford. Green Howards, 1943-47 (Lieut seconded to Royal West African Frontier Force). BA Hons (Oxford) Modern History, 1949. Programme Assistant, BBC European Service, 1950-53. Contested (C) Keighley, 1955; MP (C) Keighley, 1959-64, Chelsea, 1966-Sept. 1974; Parliamentary Private Secretary: to Minister of Health, 1960-61; to Minister without Portfolio, 1962-64; to Lord President of the Council, 1970-72. Second Church Estates Commissioner, 1970-74; a Church Commissioner, 1976-. *Recreations:* shooting, walking, reading. *Heir: s* William Ralph Worsley, *b* 12 Sept. 1956. *Address:* Hovingham Hall, York YO6 4LU. *T:* Hovingham 206; 25 Flood Street, SW3. *T:* 01-352 9821. *Club:* Yorkshire (York).

WORSNOP, Bernard Lister, BSc, PhD, FInstP; *b* Bradford, 11 Nov. 1892; *s* of Julius Worsnop and Marie Aykroyd; *m* 1st, Nellie (*d* 1951), *d* of J. H. Wilkinson, Heaton, Bradford; one *s* one *d*; 2nd, Caryl Boyce Gale, *d* of late A. E. Gale, Farnham, Surrey. *Educ:* Carlton Sch., Bradford; King's Coll., London. BSc (1st Class Hons Physics), 1913; AKC 1914; Jelf Medallist, 1913; Layton Research Scholar, 1914; PhD 1927. Served in European War, 1915-19 (i/c X-ray Department, Military Hospital, Cosham, 1915-16; Sound Ranging in France, 1916-19 (Captain, RE); Lecturer in Physics, King's Coll., London, 1919; later Senior Lecturer and Sub-Dean of the Faculty of Science and Lecturer in Radiology, King's College; Head of Dept of Mathematics and Physics, The Polytechnic, Regent Street, 1933-37; Head of Quintin School, 1937-58. Major commanding LU OTC Survey Co., 1923-35; President of the Field Survey Association, 1930-31. *Publications:* Advanced Practical Physics (with H. T. Flint); X-Rays; originator and general editor of Methuen's Monographs on Physical Subjects; original papers in scientific journals. *Address:* Pennyfarthings, 11 Higher Woolbrook Park, Sidmouth, Devon. *T:* Sidmouth 2068.

WORSTHORNE, Peregrine Gerard; Associate Editor, Sunday Telegraph, since 1976; *b* 22 Dec. 1923; *s* of Col Koch de Gooreynd, OBE (who assumed surname of Worsthorne by deed poll, 1921), and of Baroness Norman, *qv*; *m* 1950, Claude Bertrand de Colasse; one *d. Educ:* Stowe; Peterhouse, Cambridge (BA); Magdalen Coll., Oxford. Commnd Oxf. and Bucks LI, 1942; attached Phantom, GHQ Liaison Regt, 1944-45. Sub-editor, Glasgow Herald, 1946; Editorial staff: Times, 1948-53; Daily Telegraph, 1953-61; Deputy Editor, Sunday Telegraph, 1961-76. *Publication:* The Socialist Myth, 1972. *Recreations:* tennis, reading. *Address:* 6 Kempson Road, SW6 4PU. *T:* 01-736 0572; Westerlies, Wivenhoe, Essex. *T:* Wivenhoe 2886. *Clubs:* Beefsteak, Garrick.
See also S. P. E. C. W. Towneley.

WORSWICK, George David Norman; Director, National Institute of Economic and Social Research, since 1965; *b* 18 Aug. 1916; *s* of Thomas Worswick, OBE, and Eveline (*née* Green); *m* 1940, Sylvia, *d* of A. E. Walsh, MBE; one *s* two *d* (and one *s* decd). *Educ:* St Paul's Sch.; New Coll., Oxford (Scholar). 1st class Hon. Mods (Maths), 1935; 1st class Final Hons (Maths), 1937; Dipl. in Economics and Political Science (Distinction), 1938. Research staff, Oxford Univ. Institute of Statistics, 1940-60; Fellow and Tutor in Economics, Magdalen Coll., Oxford, 1945-65 (Sen. Tutor, 1955-57; Vice-President, 1963-65; Emeritus Fellow, 1969). Member UN Technical Assistance Mission to Turkey, 1954. Vis. Prof. of Economics, MIT, 1962-63. Mem, SSRC, 1966-70. Pres., Sect. F, British Assoc., 1971. Hon. DSc City, 1975. *Publications:* Joint Editor: The British Economy 1945-50, 1952; The British Economy in the 1950's, 1962; (ed) The Free Trade Proposals, 1960; (jt) Profits in the British Economy 1909-1938, 1967; (ed) Uses of Economics, 1972; (ed jtly) The Medium Term, 1974; (ed) The Concept and Measurement of Involuntary Unemployment, 1976; articles in Oxford Economic Papers, etc. *Recreation:* squash. *Address:* 7 Highmore Road, SE3 7UA. *T:* 01-858 2238. *Club:* United Oxford & Cambridge University.

WORTH, Abbot of; see Farwell, Rt Rev. G. V.

WORTH, George Arthur, MBE; JP; Farmer and Landowner; b 3 May 1907; s of late Arthur Hovendon Worth; m 1935, Janet Maitland, d of late Air Chief Marshal Sir A. M. Longmore, GCB, DSO; two s two d. Educ: Marlborough Coll.; Sidney Sussex Coll., Cambridge. Served War of 1939-45, RAF. JP Parts of Holland, Lincs, 1939; High Sheriff of Lincolnshire, 1948-49; DL Lincs, 1950-73. Address: 5 Church Lane, Manton, Oakham, Leics.

WORTH, Irene, Hon. CBE 1975; actress; b 23 June 1916. Educ: University of California, Los Angeles (BE). Antoinette Perry Award for distinguished achievement in the Theatre, 1965. First appeared as Fenella in Escape Me Never, New York, 1942; debut on Broadway as Cecily Harden in The Two Mrs Carrolls, Booth Theatre, 1943. Studied for six months with Elsie Fogerty, 1944-45. Subsequently appeared frequently at Mercury, Bolton's, Q, Embassy, etc. Parts include: Anabelle Jones in Love Goes to Press, Duchess Theatre, 1946 (after Embassy); Ilona Szabo in The Play's the Thing, St James's, 1947 (after tour and Lyric, Hammersmith); Eileen Perry in Edward my Son, Lyric, 1948; Lady Fortrose in Home is Tomorrow, Cambridge Theatre, 1948; Olivia Raines in Champagne for Delilah, New, 1949; Celia Coplestone in The Cocktail Party, New, 1950 (after Edinburgh Festival, 1949; Henry Miller Theatre, New York, 1950); Desdemona in Othello, Old Vic, 1951; Helena in Midsummer Night's Dream, Old Vic, 1952; Catherine de Vausselles in The Other Heart, Old Vic, 1952; Lady Macbeth in Macbeth, Desdemona in Othello, Helena in Midsummer Night's Dream, Catherine de Vausselles in The Other Heart, Old Vic tour of S Africa, 1952; Portia in The Merchant of Venice, Old Vic, 1953; Helena in All's Well That Ends Well and Queen Margaret in Richard III, First Season Shakespeare Festival Theatre, Stratford, Ont, Canada, 1953; Frances Farrar in A Day By The Sea, Haymarket, 1953-54; Alcestis in A Life in the Sun, Edinburgh Festival, 1955; leading rôles in: The Queen and the Rebels, Haymarket, 1955; Hotel Paradiso, Winter Garden, 1956; Maria Stuart, Phœnix Theatre, NY, 1957, Old Vic, 1958; The Potting Shed, Globe Theatre, London, 1958; Rosalind in As You Like It, Shakespeare Festival Theatre, Stratford, Ont, 1959; Albertine Prine in Toys in the Attic, Hudson Theatre, New York, 1960 (NY Newspaper Guild Page One Award); Season at Royal Shakespeare Theatre, Stratford, 1962; Goneril in King Lear, Aldwych, 1962; Doctor Mathilde von Zahnd in The Physicists, Aldwych, 1963; Clodia Pulcher in The Ides of March, Haymarket, 1963; World tour of King Lear for Royal Shakespeare Company, 1964; Alice in Tiny Alice, Billy Rose Theatre, New York, 1965 (Tony award 1965), Aldwych, 1970; Hilde in A Song at Twilight, Anne in Shadows of the Evening, Anna-Mary in Come into the Garden Maud (Noël Coward Trilogy), Queen's, 1966 (Evening Standard Award); Hesione Hushabye in Heartbreak House, Chichester and Lyric, 1967 (Variety Club of GB Award, 1967); Jocasta in Seneca's Oedipus, National Theatre, 1968; Hedda in Hedda Gabler, Stratford, Ont, 1970; worked with internat. Co. for Theatre Res., Paris and Iran, 1971; Notes on a Love Affair, Globe, 1972; Madame Arkadina, The Seagull, Chichester, 1973; Hamlet, Ghosts, The Seagull, Greenwich, 1974; Sweet Bird of Youth, New York, 1975 (Tony Award, 1975; Jefferson Award, 1975); Misalliance, Lake Forest, Ill, 1976; The Childhood of Maxim Gorky, NY, 1977. Films: Order to Kill, 1957 (British Film Academy Award for Best Woman's Performance, 1958); The Scapegoat, 1958; King Lear (Goneril), 1970; Nicholas and Alexandra, 1971. Daily Mail National Television Award, 1953-54, and has subseq. appeared on Television and acted with CBC Television in NY and Canada. Whitbread Anglo-American Award for Outstanding Actress, 1967. Recreation: music.

WORTHINGTON, Edgar Barton, CBE 1967; MA, PhD; environmental consultant; b 13 Jan. 1905; s of Edgar Worthington and Amy E. Beale; m 1930, Stella Desmond Johnson; three d. Educ: Rugby; Gonville and Caius Coll., Cambridge. Expeditions to African Lakes, 1927-31; Balfour Student, 1930-33, and Demonstrator in Zoology, Cambridge Univ., 1933-37; Scientist for the African Research Survey, 1934-37; Mungo Park Medal, RSGS, 1939; Director of Laboratories and Secretary of Freshwater Biological Assoc., Windermere, 1937-46; Scientific Adviser to Middle East Supply Centre, 1943-45; Development Adviser, Uganda, 1946; Scientific Secretary to Colonial Research Council, 1946-49, to E Africa High Commission, 1950-51; Secretary-General to Scientific Council for Africa South of the Sahara, 1951-55; Deputy Director-General (Scientific) Nature Conservancy, 1957-65; Scientific Dir, Internat. Biological Programme, 1964-74; Pres., Cttee on Water Res. of Internat. Council of Scientific Unions, 1973-77. Order of Golden Ark (Netherlands), 1976. Publications: (with Stella Worthington) Inland Waters of Africa, 1933; Science in Africa, 1938; Middle East Science, 1946; Development Plan for Uganda, 1947; (with T. T. Macan) Life in Lakes and Rivers, 1951, rev. edn 1973; Science in the Development of Africa, 1958; (ed) Man-made Lakes: problems and environmental effects, 1973; Evolution of the IBP, 1975; (ed) Arid Land Irrigation: problems and environmental effects, 1976; official reports and papers in scientific journals. Recreations: field sports and farming. Address: Colin Godmans, Furner's Green, Uckfield, East Sussex. T: Chelwood Gate 322. Clubs: Athenæum, Farmers'.

WORTHINGTON, Air Vice-Marshal (Retired) Sir Geoffrey (Luis), KBE 1960 (CBE 1945); CB 1957; idc; psa; Director-General of Equipment, Air Ministry, 1958-61, retired; b 26 April 1903; s of late Commander H. E. F. Worthington, RN; m 1931, Margaret Joan, d of late Maj.-Gen. A. G. Stevenson, CB, CMG, DSO; two s one d. Educ: HMS Conway; Eastbourne Coll. RAF Coll., Cranwell, 1921. Joined RAF, 1922; resigned 1924; re-joined, 1926, in Stores Branch; RAF Staff Coll., 1934. Served War of 1939-45 (despatches, CBE): HQ Maintenance Comd, 1939-43; Air Cdre, 1943; HQ AEAF, 1944; SHAEF, 1944-45; Air Comd, Far East, 1945-47; Director of Equipment B, Air Ministry, 1948-49; idc 1950; Director of Equipment D, Air Ministry, 1951-53; AOC No 42 Group, Maintenance Comd, 1954-55; Air Vice-Marshal, 1956; AOC No 40 Group, 1955-58. Comdr US Legion of Merit, 1955. Recreations: sailing, golf. Address: Pear Tree House, Ship Road, Burnham-on-Crouch, Essex. T: Maldon 782388. Clubs: Royal Air Force; Royal Burnham Yacht.

WORTHINGTON, George Noel; a Recorder of the Crown Court since 1972; Solicitor; b 22 June 1923; s of late George Errol Worthington and Edith Margaret Boys Worthington; m 1954, Jacqueline Kemble Lightfoot, 2nd d of late G. L. S. Lightfoot and Mrs Lightfoot, Carlisle; two s one d. Educ: Rossall Sch., Lancashire. Served War of 1939-45 in Royal Armoured Corps, 1941-46. Admitted a solicitor, 1949. Recreation: gardening. Address: Albyfield, Wetheral, Carlisle, Cumbria. T: Wetheral 60359. Club: Cumberland County (Carlisle).

WORTLEY, Prof. Ben Atkinson, OBE 1946; QC 1969; LLD (Manchester), LLM (Leeds); Hon. Docteur de l'Univ. de Rennes (1955); Strasbourg (1965); membre de l'Institut de droit international, 1967 (associé 1956); Professor of Jurisprudence and International Law, University of Manchester, 1946-75, now Emeritus; Barrister of Gray's Inn, 1947; b 16 Nov. 1907; o s of late John Edward Wortley and late Mary Cicely (née King), Huddersfield; m 1935, Kathleen Mary Prynne; two s one d. Educ: King James's Grammar Sch., Almondbury; Leeds Univ.; France. Law Society Open Schol., 1925; 1st Class Hons LLB, 1928, and at Law Society's Final, 1929, also D. Reardon Prizeman. Practised full-time till 1931. Taught Law, London School Econ., 1931-33; Manchester Univ., 1933-34; Birmingham Univ., 1934-36; Manchester Univ., 1936-; visiting Prof. Tulane Univ., New Orleans, 1959. Ministry of Home Security, 1939-43; Instructor Commander RN (temp.), 1943-46. Board member: Inst. Advanced Legal Studies, 1947-77; International Inst. for Unification of Private Law, Rome; British Yearbook of International Law; Society of Public Teachers of Law (President, 1964-65). Member Royal Netherlands Academy, 1960; Commendatore (Italy), 1961; Correspondent Hellenic Inst. for International and Foreign Law, and of Belgian Society for Comparative Law. Representative of HM Government at International Confs at The Hague, 1951, 1956, 1960, 1964, and at New York, 1955 and 1958. Sometime Mem., Lord Chancellor's Cttee on Conflict of Laws. Hon. DCL Durham, 1975. Hon. Brother, de la Salle Order, 1973; KSS, 1975. Publications: lectures, 1939, 1947, 1954 and 1958, published by Hague Academy of International Law; ed, 1961-, 13 vols Schill lecture series (inc. EEC Law 1972); Expropriation in Public International Law, 1959; Jurisprudence, 1967; part editor, Dicey's Conflict of Laws, 1949; (ed) UN, The First Ten Years, 1957; (ed) Law of the Common Market, 1974. Recreations: languages, international. Address: 24 Gravel Lane, Wilmslow, Cheshire. T: Wilmslow 22810. Club: Athenæum.

WOTHERSPOON, Ralph; Writer and Journalist; b 1897; o s of George Wotherspoon, MA (sometime Vice-Master, King's College School) and Juliana Mary, d of Henry Norton, JP, Green Hill, Carmarthen, Wales; unmarried. Educ: Eastbourne Coll.; Merton Coll., Oxford. BA Distinction Honour School English Literature. War service, 1915-19, 5th Bn Queen's Royal West Surreys (TF) and Royal Garrison Artillery; War Service, 1940-41, AOER, Captain, General List; Embarkation Staff Officer Movement Control Southampton, Liverpool; invalided, Oct. 1941; Ministry of Supply, 1942; Ministry of Information, 1943; Regional Press Officer, London and SE Region, 1944-45; Member original Cherwell Editorial Staff, 1920-21; Editorial

Staff, George Newnes & Co. Ltd, 1923; Private Secretary to late Henry Arthur Jones, Dramatist, 1923; to Colonel Hon. Angus McDonnell, 1924; Vice-Chairman Kent Federation Junior Imperial League since inception 1928 until 1933; Secretary of Primrose League, 1935-40; as a writer has contributed extensively in prose and verse to leading humorous journals, magazines, newspapers, etc.; first wrote for Punch, 1924 (Woon, 1928); Member contrib. staff of services paper Blighty, 1939-45; Director, Smith and Whiley Theatrical Productions, 1948-61 (original backer of Agatha Christie's play, The Mousetrap, 1951). *Publications:* Ready-Made Rhymes, 1927; (with Aubrey Hammond) Jack and Jill, the Underground Fairy Tale, 1932-33; (with L. N. Jackson) Some Sports and Pastimes of the English, 1937; (with L. N. Jackson) numerous broadcasts from BBC West Regional, including serial sketches, The Life We Lead; one-act play, All in The Day's Work. *Recreations:* formerly playing, now watching Rugby football; golf, fishing, motoring, railways. *Address:* Charterhouse, EC1. *Clubs:* Royal Automobile, (Senior Member) Myrmidon, Mousetrap.

WOUK, Herman; author, US; *b* New York, 27 May 1915; *s* of Abraham Isaac Wouk and Esther Wouk (*née* Levine); *m* 1945, Betty Sarah Brown; two *s* (and one *s* decd). *Educ:* Townsend Harris High Sch.; Columbia Univ. (AB). Employed as a writer of comedians' scripts for radio programmes, 1935-41; Visiting Professor of English, Yeshiva Univ., 1952-58; Presidential consultative expert to the United States Treasury, 1941. Served United States Naval Reserve, 1942-46, Deck Officer (four campaign stars). Member Officers' Reserve Naval Services. Columbia University Medal for excellence, 1952. Trustee, College of the Virgin Islands, 1963-69. Hon. Doctor of Humane Letters, Yeshiva Univ., New York City, 1955; Hon. Doctor of Letters, Clark Univ., 1960. *Publications: novels:* Aurora Dawn (American Book of the Month), 1947; The City Boy, 1948; The Caine Mutiny (Pulitzer Prize), 1951; Marjorie Morningstar, 1955; Youngblood Hawke, 1962; Don't Stop The Carnival, 1965; The Winds of War, 1971; *plays:* The Traitor, 1949; The Caine Mutiny Court-Martial, 1953; Nature's Way, 1957; *non-fiction:* This Is My God, 1959, rev. edn 1973. *Address:* c/o Harold Matson Co. Inc., 22 East 40th Street, New York, NY 10016, USA. *Clubs:* Cosmos, Metropolitan, (Washington); Bohemian (San Francisco).

WRAIGHT, Sir John (Richard), KBE 1976; CMG 1962; HM Diplomatic Service, retired; company consultant and company director, since 1976; *b* 4 June 1916; *s* of late Richard George Wraight; *m* 1947, Marquita Elliott. Served War of 1939-45 with Honourable Artillery Company and RHA, Western Desert and Libya; Ministry of Economic Warfare Mission in the Middle East, Cairo, 1944. Economic Warfare Adviser, HQ Mediterranean Allied Air Forces, Italy, June-Dec. 1944. Foreign Office, 1945; Special Assistant to Chief of UNRRA Operations in Europe, 1946. Entered Foreign (subseq. Diplomatic) Service, 1947; British Embassy: Athens, 1948; Tel Aviv, 1950; Washington, 1953; Asst Head of Economic Relations Dept, Foreign Office, 1957; Counsellor (Commercial): Cairo, 1959; Brussels and Luxembourg, 1962 (UK Comr on Tripartite Commn for Restitution of Monetary Gold, Brussels, 1962-68); Minister and Consul-General, Milan, 1968-73; Ambassador to Switzerland, 1973-76. Commander of the Order of the Crown (Belgium), 1966. *Recreations:* music, travel, gardening. *Address:* 35 Jameson Street, W8 7SH. *Clubs:* Travellers'; Grande Société (Berne).

WRAN, Hon. Neville Kenneth, QC (NSW) 1968; MLA; Premier of New South Wales, since 1976. *Educ:* Fort Street Boys' High Sch., Sydney; Sydney Univ. (LLB). Solicitor before admission to Bar of NSW, 1957. Joined Australian Labor Party, 1954; Branch and Electorate Council positions; Mem., Central Exec., NSW Br. Elected to Legislative Council, 1970; Dep. Leader of Opposition, 1971; Leader, Legislative Council, 1972; MLA for Bass Hill, Nov. 1973; Leader of Opposition, Dec. 1973-76. Is especially interested in law reform, civil liberties, industrial relations, conservation, art and cultural matters. Member: NSW Legal and Constitutional Cttee; Federal Legal and Constitutional Cttee; NSW Bar Assoc. *Recreations:* reading, walking, swimming. *Address:* Parliament House, Sydney, NSW, Australia. *Club:* Sydney Labor (Hon Life Mem.).

WRANGHAM, Cuthbert Edward, CBE 1946; BA 1929; *b* 16 Dec. 1907; *yr s* of late W. G. Wrangham and late E. A. F. Wilberforce; *m* 1st, 1935, Teresa Jane, *er d* of late Ralph Cotton; three *s* two *d* ; 2nd, 1958, Jean Ursula Margaret Tunstall, *yr d* of late Lt-Col T. T. Behrens. *Educ:* Eton Coll.; King's Coll., Cambridge. Air Min. and Min. of Aircraft Production, 1939-45; Monopolies Commn, 1954-56; Chairman: Shelbourne Hotel Ltd, 1950-60; Power-Gas Corporation Ltd, 1960-61; Short Brothers & Harland Ltd, 1961-67; Doxford and Sunderland Ltd,

1969-71; Marine & General Mutual Life Assurance Soc., 1961-72; C. Tennant Sons & Co. Ltd, 1967-72 (Director, 1937). Hon. DL Wilberforce Coll., Ohio, 1957. *Address:* Rosemary House, Catterick, North Yorkshire. *T:* Old Catterick 1375. *Club:* English-Speaking Union.

WRANGHAM, Sir Geoffrey Walter, Kt 1958; Judge of High Court of Justice, Family Division (formerly Probate, Divorce and Admiralty Division), 1958-73; retired; *b* 16 June 1900; *s* of late W. G. Wrangham and late E. A. F. Wilberforce; *m* 1925, Mary (*d* 1933), *d* of late S. D. Winkworth; one *s* one *d* ; *m* 1947, Joan, *d* of late Col W. Boyle; one *s* one *d*. *Educ:* Eton Coll.; Balliol Coll., Oxford. Called to Bar, 1923; joined North-Eastern Circuit; Gresham Lecturer in Law, 1925-33; Practised in London, 1923-33, thereafter in Bradford; Recorder of York, 1941-50; Judge of County Courts, Circuit 20, 1950-57, Circuit 16, 1957-58; Chm., N Riding QS, 1946-58, Dep. Chm. 1958-71; Master of the Bench, Inner Temple, 1958. Served KOYLI and RAC (Lt-Col), 1940-45. *Publications:* Edited (with W. A. Macfarlane) 8th Edition Clerk and Lindsell on Torts, 18th edition Chitty on Contracts. *Address:* Butlesdon House, Low Buston, Warkworth, Northumberland. *T:* Warkworth 300.

WRATTEN, Donald Peter; Senior Director, Telecommunications Personnel, Post Office, since 1975; *b* 8 July 1925; *er s* of late Frederick George and Margaret Wratten; *m* 1947, Margaret Kathleen (*née* Marsh); one *s* one *d*. *Educ:* Morehall Elem. Sch. and Harvey Grammar Sch., Folkestone; London Sch. of Economics. Storehand, temp. clerk, meteorological asst (Air Min.), 1940-43; service with RAF Meteorological Wing, 1943-47. LSE, 1947-50. Joined Post Office, 1950; Private Sec. to Asst Postmaster Gen., 1955-56; seconded to Unilever Ltd, 1959; Private Sec. to Postmaster Gen., 1965-66; Head of Telecommunications Marketing Div., 1966-67; Director: Eastern Telecommunications Region, 1967-69; Exec. Dir, Giro and Remittance Services, 1969-74 (Sen. Dir, 1970-74); Sen. Dir Data Processing Service, 1974-75. Member: Court, Cranfield Inst. of Technology, 1976-; Business Educn Council, 1977-. *Recreations:* travel, topography, photography, consumer affairs, do-it-yourself. *Address:* 10 Homefield Road, Radlett, Herts. *T:* Radlett 4500. *Club:* Reform.

WRAXALL, 2nd Baron, *cr* 1928, of Clyst St George, Co. Devon; **George Richard Lawley Gibbs;** DL; *b* 16 May 1928 (for whom Queen Mary was sponsor); *er s* of 1st Baron and Hon. Ursula Mary Lawley, OBE 1945, RRC, *e d* of 6th Baron Wenlock; *S* father 1931. *Educ:* Eton; RMA Sandhurst. Coldstream Guards, 1948-53; Lieut North Somerset Yeomanry/44 Royal Tank Regt (TA), Dec. 1958; Captain, 1962; Major, 1965; retired 1967. Chairman: N Somerset Conservative Assoc., 1970-74; Avon County Scout Assoc., 1976-; Chm. Governors, St Katherine's Sch., Bristol. DL Avon, 1974. *Heir: b* Hon. Eustace Hubert Beilby Gibbs, *qv. Address:* Tyntesfield, Bristol. *T:* Flax Bourton 2923. *Clubs:* Royal Automobile, Cavalry and Guards.

WRAXALL, Sir Morville (William Lascelles), 8th Bt, *cr* 1813; on staff of a rubber company from 1947; *b* 11 June 1922; *o s* of Sir Charles Wraxall, 7th Bt and Marceline, *d* of O. Cauro, of Cauro, Corsica; *S* father 1951; *m* 1956, Irmgard Wilhelmina Maria Schnidrig, Basle, Switzerland; two *s* one *d*. *Educ:* St Mark's Coll., Alexandria, Egypt. RASC 1940-46 (Africa Star and clasp). *Recreations:* gardening, woodwork, stamp collecting. *Heir: s* Charles Frederick Lascelles Wraxall, *b* 17 Sept. 1961.

WRAY, Sir Kenneth O. R.; *see* Roberts-Wray.

WRAY, Martin Osterfield, CMG 1956; OBE 1954; *b* 14 June 1912; *s* of late C. N. O. Wray; *m* 1938, Lilian Joyce, *d* of late R. W. Playfair, Nairobi, Kenya; one *s* two *d*. *Educ:* St George's Sch., Harpenden; Wadham Coll., Oxford. Colonial Administrative Service in Uganda, 1935; Administrative Secretary, Zanzibar, 1949; Administrative Secretary to High Commissioner for Basutoland, the Bechuanaland Protectorate and Swaziland, 1952; Resident Commissioner, Bechuanaland Protectorate, 1955-59; Chief Secretary, Northern Rhodesia, 1959-62. *Address:* Prospect House, East Knoyle, Wilts. *Club:* Royal Commonwealth Society.

WRENBURY, 3rd Baron, *cr* 1915; **John Burton Buckley;** Partner, Thomson Snell and Passmore, since 1974; *b* 18 June 1927; *s* of 2nd Baron and Helen Malise, 2nd *d* of late His Honour John Cameron Graham of Ballewan, Stirlingshire; *S* father, 1940; *m* 1st, 1956, Carolyn Joan Maule (marr. diss., 1961), *o d* of Lt-Col Ian Burn-Murdoch, OBE, of Gartincaber, Doune, Perthshire; 2nd, 1961, Penelope Sara Frances, *o d* of Edward D. Fort, The White House, Sixpenny Handley, Dorset; one *s* two *d*. *Educ:* Eton Coll.; King's Coll., Cambridge. Deputy Legal Adviser to the National Trust, 1955-56; Partner, Freshfield's,

Solicitors, 1956-74. *Heir: s* Hon. William Edward Buckley, *b* 19 June 1966. *Address:* Oldcastle, Dallington, near Heathfield, East Sussex. *T:* Rushlake Green 400. *Club:* Oriental.

WREY, Sir (Castel) Richard Bourchier, 14th Bt, *cr* 1628; *b* 27 March 1903; *s* of late Edward Castel Wrey and Katharine Joan, *d* of Rev. John Dene; *S* uncle, 1948; *m* 1946, Alice Sybil, *d* of Dr Lubke, Durban, S Africa; two *s. Educ:* Oundle. Served War of 1939-45; 2nd Lieut, RASC (Supp. Res.), France, 1939-40 (invalided); joined RN as ordinary seaman, 1940; Lieut, RNVR, 1942. *Heir: s* George Richard Bourchier Wrey, *b* 2 Oct. 1948. *Address:* Hollamoor Farm, Tawstock, Barnstaple, N Devon.

WRIGGLESWORTH, Ian William; MP (Lab and Co-op) Teesside, Thornaby, since Feb. 1974; *b* Dec. 1939; *s* of Edward and Elsie Wrigglesworth; *m* Patricia Truscott; two *s. Educ:* Stockton Grammar Sch.; Stockton-Billingham Technical Coll; Coll. of St Mark and St John, Chelsea. Formerly: Personal Assistant to Gen. Sec., NUT; Head of Research and Information Dept of Co-operative Party; Press and Public Affairs Manager of National Giro. PPS to Mr Alec Lyon, Minister of State, Home Office, 1974; PPS to Rt Hon. Roy Jenkins, Home Secretary, 1974-76; Vice-Chairman: Labour, Economic, Finance and Taxation Assoc.; Parly Labour Party Economic Gp. *Address:* House of Commons, SW1. *Clubs:* Middlesbrough Labour; Acklam Garden City.

WRIGHT, Alan John; a Master of the Supreme Court, Supreme Court Taxing Office, since 1972; *b* 21 April 1925; *s* of late Rev. Henry George Wright, MA and Winifred Annie Wright; *m* 1952, Alma Beatrice Ridding; two *s* one *d. Educ:* St Olave's and St Saviour's Grammar Sch., Southwark; Keble Coll., Oxford. BA 1949, MA 1964. Served with RAF, India, Burma and China, 1943-46. Solicitor 1952; in private practice with Shaen Roscoe & Co., 1952-71; Legal Adviser to Trades Union Congress, 1955-71. *Recreations:* Germanic studies, walking, physical fitness training, travel, youth work, industrial law. *Address:* 21 Brockley Park, Forest Hill, SE23 1PT.

WRIGHT, Alec Michael John, CMG 1967; *b* Hong Kong, 19 Sept. 1912; *s* of Arthur Edgar Wright and Margery Hepworth Chapman; *m* 1948, Ethel Surtees; one *d. Educ:* Brentwood Sch. ARICS 1934; ARIBA 1937. Articled pupil followed by private practice in London. Joined Colonial Service, 1938; appointed Architect in Hong Kong, 1938. Commissioned Hong Kong Volunteer Defence Force, 1941; POW in Hong Kong, 1941-45. Chief Architect, Public Works Dept, Hong Kong, 1950; Asst Director of Public Works, 1956; Dep. Director, 1959; Director, 1963-69; Commissioner for Hong Kong in London, 1969-73. *Address:* 13 Montrose Court, Exhibition Road, SW7 2QG. *T:* 01-584 4293. *Club:* Hong Kong (Hong Kong).
See also Sir Denis Wright.

WRIGHT, (Arthur Robert) Donald; Appointments Secretary to the Archbishops of Canterbury and York, since 1975; *b* 20 June 1923; *y s* of late Charles North Wright; *m* 1948, Helen Muryell Buxton, *e d* of late Prof. Patrick Buxton, CMG, FRS; two *s* three *d. Educ:* Bryanston School; Queens' College, Cambridge. Commissioned in Royal Artillery and served in France, Germany and India, 1942-46 (despatches). Taught at: University Coll. Sch., 1948-50; The Hill School, Pennsylvania, 1950; Leighton Park School, 1950-52; Marlborough College (Housemaster), 1953-63; Headmaster, Shrewsbury Sch., 1963-75. Chm., Headmasters' Conf., 1971; Member: Health Educn Council, 1971-74; IBA Educn Adv. Council, 1972-74; Council, Bible Reading Fellowship, 1976-; Chm. Council, the William Temple Foundn, 1977-; Sec., Crown Appts Commn, 1977-. Governor: The Downs School, Colwall, 1973-; Benenden School, 1977-. *Address:* Fielden House, Little College Street, Westminster, SW1P 3SH; 11 Station Road, Haddenham, Aylesbury, Bucks. *Club:* Royal Commonwealth Society.

WRIGHT, Basil Charles; Film Producer; *b* 12 June 1907; *s* of Major Lawrence Wright, TD, and Gladys Marsden. *Educ:* Sherborne; Corpus Christi Coll., Cambridge. Mawson Schol., CCC, 1926; BA (Hons), Classics and Economics. Concerned with John Grierson and others in development of Documentary Film, 1929-; directed, among many films: Song of Ceylon (Gold Medal and Prix du Gouvernement, Brussels), 1935; (with Harry Watt) Night Mail, 1936; Waters of Time, 1951; (with Paul Rotha) World Without End, 1953; (with Gladys Wright) took film expedition to Greece and made The Immortal Land, 1957 (Council of Europe Award, 1959) and Greek Sculpture (with Michael Ayrton), 1959; A Place for Gold, 1960; Visiting Lectr on Film Art, Univ. of Calif, Los Angeles, 1962 and 1968; Senior Lectr in Film History, Nat. Film Sch., 1971-73. Producer, Crown Film Unit, 1945. Governor: Bryanston School, 1949-; British Film Institute, 1953; Fellow, British Film Academy,

1955; Council Mem., Roy. Coll. of Art, 1954-57. Gold Cross, Royal Order of King George I, Greece, 1963. *Publications:* The Use of the Film, 1948; The Long View, 1974. *Recreations:* opera, ballet, gardening. *Address:* Little Adam Farm, Frieth, Henley-on-Thames, Oxon. *Club:* Savile.

WRIGHT, Beatrice Frederika, (Lady Wright); *b* New Haven, Connecticut; *d* of Mr and Mrs F. Roland Clough; *m* 1st, 1932, John Rankin Rathbone (Flight Lieut, RAFVR, MP, killed in action, 1940); one *s* one *d*; 2nd, 1942, Paul Hervé Giraud Wright (*see* Sir Paul Wright); one *d. Educ:* Ethel Walker School, Simsbury, Conn; Radcliffe College, Oxford. MP (U) Bodmin Div. of Cornwall, 1941-45. *Address:* 3 Ormonde Gate, SW3 4EU.
See also J. R. Rathbone.

WRIGHT, Billy; see Wright, W. A.

WRIGHT, Claud William, CB 1969; Emeritus Fellow, Wolfson College, Oxford, since 1977; *b* 9 Jan. 1917; *s* of Horace Vipan Wright and Catherine Margaret Sales; *m* 1947, Alison Violet Readman; one *s* four *d. Educ:* Charterhouse; Christ Church, Oxford (MA). Assistant Principal, War Office, 1939; Private, Essex Regiment, 1940; 2nd Lieut, KRRC, 1940; War Office, rising to GSO2, 1942-45; Principal, War Office, 1944; Min. of Defence: Principal, 1947; Asst Sec., 1951; Asst Under-Sec. of State, 1961-68; Dep. Under-Sec. of State, 1968-71; Dep. Sec., DES, 1971-76. Mem. Cttee of Enquiry into conditions of service life for young servicemen, 1969-70; Chm., Cttee on Provincial Museums and Galleries, 1971-73. Lyell Fund, 1947, R. H. Worth Prize, 1958, Geological Society of London; Foulerton Award, Geologists Association, 1955; Stamford Raffles Award, Zoological Society of London, 1965. President, Geologists Assoc., 1956-58. Hon. Associate, British Museum (Nat. Hist.), 1973. *Publications:* (with W. J. Arkell *et al*) vol. on Ammonites, 1957, (with W. K. Spencer) on Starfish, 1966, in Treatise on Invertebrate Palaeontology; (with J. S. H. Collins) British Cretaceous Crabs, 1972. Papers in geological, palaeontological and archaeological journals. *Recreations:* palaeontology, natural history, Oriental ceramics, gardening, archæology. *Address:* Old Rectory, Seaborough, Beaminster, Dorset. *T:* Broadwindsor 426. *Club:* Athenæum.

WRIGHT, Sir Denis (Arthur Hepworth), GCMG 1971 (KCMG 1961; CMG 1954); HM Diplomatic Service, retired; Director: The Chartered Bank, since 1971; Shell Transport & Trading Co. Ltd, since 1971; Mitchell Cotts Group, since 1971; Standard Chartered Bank Ltd, since 1971; *b* 23 March 1911; *s* of late A. E. Wright, Hong Kong, and Margery Hepworth Chapman, York; *m* 1939, Iona Craig, Bolney, Sussex; no *c. Educ:* Brentwood School; St Edmund Hall, Oxford, Hon. Fellow 1972. Asst Advertising Manager to Gallaher & Co. (Tobacco Manufacturers), 1935-39. Employed from outbreak of war as Vice-Consul on economic warfare work at HM Consulate at Constantza (Roumania), 1939-41. Vice-Consul-in-charge of HM Consulate at Trebizond (Turkey), 1941-43; Acting-Consul-in-charge of HM Consulate, Mersin (Turkey), 1943-45; First Secretary (Commercial) to HM Embassy, Belgrade, 1946-48; Superintending Trade Consul at Chicago for Middle-Western Region of USA, 1949-51; Head of Economic Relations Department in the Foreign Office, 1951-53; appointed Chargé d'Affaires, Teheran, on resumption of diplomatic relations with Persia, Dec. 1953; Counsellor, HM Embassy, Teheran, 1954-55; Asst Under-Sec., FO, 1955-59; Ambassador to Ethiopia, 1959-62; Asst Under-Sec., FO, 1962; Ambassador to Iran, 1963-71. Governor, Oversea Service, Farnham Castle, 1972-; Mem. Council, British Inst. for Persian Studies, 1973-; Chm., Iran Soc., 1976. Hon. Fellow St Antony's Coll., Oxford, 1976. *Publication:* The English Amongst the Persians, 1977. *Address:* Duck Bottom, Haddenham, Aylesbury, Bucks. *Club:* Travellers'.
See also A. M. J. Wright.

WRIGHT, Desmond Garforth, QC 1974; *b* 13 July 1923; *s* of late Arthur Victor Wright and Doris Greensill; *m* 1952, Elizabeth Anna Bacon; one *s* one *d. Educ:* Gigglewick; Royal Naval Coll., Greenwich; Worcester Coll., Oxford (MA). Cholmondley Scholar of Lincoln's Inn. Served War of 1939-45: RNVR, 1942-46. Staff of Flag Officer Malaya Forward Area, 1946. Called to Bar, Lincoln's Inn, 1950. *Publication:* Wright on Walls, 1954. *Recreations:* cartology, conversation, skiing on snow. *Address:* 22 Old Buildings, Lincoln's Inn WC2A 3UJ. *T:* 01-405 2072. *Club:* RNVR.

WRIGHT, Donald; see Wright, A. R. D.

WRIGHT, Prof. Donald Arthur, MSc; DSc; FInstP; FRAS; Honorary Research Fellow in Archaeology, University of

Durham, since 1976; *b* Stoke-on-Trent, 29 March 1911; *m* 1937, Mary Kathleen Rimmer; one *s* one *d*. *Educ:* Orme School, Newcastle-under-Lyme; University of Birmingham. 1st Class Hons BSc 1932; MSc 1934; DSc Birmingham 1955. Research Physicist, GEC, Wembley, 1934-59; Head of Solid Physics Laboratory, Research Labs, GEC, Wembley, 1955-59; Prof. of Applied Physics, Univ. of Durham, 1960-76. Fellow Institute of Physics, 1946. Member of Board, Institute of Physics, 1957-64. Mem. of Council, Physical Society, 1955-58, Hon. Treasurer, 1958-60. *Publications:* Semiconductors, 1950 (revd edn 1965); Thermoelectric Cooling in Progress in Cryogenics, Vol. I, 1959; Thermoelectric Generation in Direct Generation of Electricity, 1965; many papers on electron emission and solid-state physics in learned journals. *Recreations:* tennis, music. *Address:* Museum of Archaeology, Fulling Mill, Durham; 16 St Mary's Close, Shincliffe, Durham. *T:* Durham 3408.

WRIGHT, Mrs Edmund Gordon; *see* Cross, H. M.

WRIGHT, (Edmund) Kenneth, MA, FCA; Chartered Accountant; Partner in Dearden and Co., 1940-76; *b* 10 Dec. 1909; *s* of late William Ameers Wright and late Martha Wright; *m* 1942, Daisy, *d* of late Rev. T. W. Thornton and Mrs Thornton; one *s* one *d*. *Educ:* preparatory schs in Southern Africa; Leighton Park Sch.; St Catharine's Coll., Cambridge (Engl. and Economics Triposes). ACA 1937, FCA 1945. London Ambulance Service, 1940-45. Chm., London and Dist Soc. of Chartered Accountants, 1957-58; Mem. Council, Inst. of Chartered Accountants, 1959-76 (Dep. Pres., 1972, Pres., 1973). Governor, Leighton Park Sch., 1949-. *Publications:* numerous books and papers on fiscal and accountancy subjects in national and professional press, including: The Development of an Accounting Practice, 1965; Professional Goodwill and Partnership Amenities, 1967; Financial Planning for Individuals, 1970, 2nd edn 1971; (with Malcolm Penney) Capital Transfer Tax Planning, 1975, 2nd edn 1976. *Recreations:* gardening, writing, civic amenities. *Address:* Old Orchard, Sevenoaks Road, Ightham, Kent. *T:* Borough Green 882374. *Clubs:* Reform, Gresham.

WRIGHT, Sir Edward (Maitland), Kt 1977; MA, DPhil; FRSE; Research Fellow, University of Aberdeen, since 1976; *b* 1906; *s* of M. T. Wright, Farnley, Leeds; *m* 1934, Elizabeth Phyllis, *d* of H. P. Harris, Bryn Mally Hall, N Wales; one *s*. *Educ:* Jesus Coll. and Christ Church, Oxford; Univ. of Göttingen. Master, Chard School, Somerset, 1923-26; Scholar, Jesus College, Oxford, 1926-30; Senior Scholar, Christ Church, 1930-33; Lecturer, King's College, London, 1932-33; Lecturer, Christ Church, 1933-35; Flt Lieut, RAFVR, 1941-43; Principal Scientific Officer, Air Ministry, 1943-45; Prof. of Mathematics, 1935-62, Vice-Principal, 1961-62, Principal and Vice-Chancellor, 1962-76, Univ. of Aberdeen. Member: Anderson Cttee on Grants to Students, 1958-60; Hale Cttee on Univ. Teaching Methods, 1961-64; Scottish Universities Entrance Bd, 1948-62 (Chm. 1955-62); Royal Commission on Medical Education, 1965-67. Vice-Pres., RUSI, 1969-72. Hon. LLD: St Andrews, 1963; Pennsylvania, 1975; Hon. DSc Strathclyde, 1974. Hon. Fellow, Jesus College, Oxford, 1963. *Publications:* Introduction to the Theory of Numbers (with Professor G. H. Hardy), 1938, 2nd edn 1945, 3rd edn 1954, 4th edn 1960; Mathematical papers in scientific journals. *Address:* 16 Primrosehill Avenue, Cults, Aberdeen. *T:* Aberdeen 861185. *Clubs:* Caledonian; University (Aberdeen); Royal Scottish Automobile (Glasgow).

WRIGHT, Eric David, CB 1975; Deputy Under-Secretary of State, Home Office, and Director-General, Prison Service, since 1973; *b* 12 June 1917; *s* of Charles Henry and Cecelia Wright; *m* 1944, Doris (*née* Nicholls); one *s*. *Educ:* Ealing County Grammar School. Joined War Office, 1935; Principal, 1945; seconded to Dept of the Army, Australia, 1951; Asst Secretary, 1955; Command Secretary, BAOR, 1955-58; Imperial Defence College, 1964; Asst Under-Sec. of State, MoD, 1965; on loan to Home Office, Police Dept, 1970-73. *Address:* c/o Home Office, Queen Anne's Gate, SW1H 9AT.

WRIGHT, Prof. Esmond; Director, Institute of United States Studies, and Professor of American History, London University, since 1971; *b* 5 Nov. 1915; *m* 1945, Olive Adamson. *Educ:* University of Durham (Open Entrance Schol.); Univ. of Virginia (Commonwealth Fund Fellow). War Service, 1940-46, mainly in Middle East; demobilised as Lt-Col, 1946. Glasgow Univ., 1946-67; Prof. of Modern History, 1957-67. MP (C) Glasgow, Pollok, March 1967-1970. Founder-Mem., British Association for American Studies (Chm., 1965-68). Dep-Chm., Border TV. Member: Marshall Aid Commemoration Commn; Exec. Cttee, AA (Hon. Treas., 1971-). FRHistS. *Publications:* A Short History of our own Times, 1951; George Washington and the American Revolution, 1957; The World Today, 1961, 4th edn 1978; Fabric of Freedom, 1961, 2nd edn 1978; (ed) Illustrated World History, 1964; Benjamin Franklin and American Independence, 1966; (ed) Causes and Consequences of the American Revolution, 1966; (ed) American Themes, 1967; American Profiles, 1967; (ed) Benjamin Franklin, a profile, 1970; A Time for Courage, 1971; A Tug of Loyalties, 1974; articles in periodicals. *Address:* 31 Tavistock Square, WC1. *T:* 01-387 5534. *Club:* Athenæum.

WRIGHT, Frank T. W.; *see* Wynyard-Wright.

WRIGHT, Frederick Matthew, OBE 1976 (MBE 1945); General Manager, British Railways, Western Region and Member of British Railways (Western) Board, 1972-76; *b* 26 June 1916; *s* of Thomas Bell Wright and Ethel Johnson; *m* 1940, Claire Agnes (*née* Cook); one *s* one *d*. *Educ:* Rutherford Coll., Newcastle upon Tyne. FCIT; FInstM. Joined LNER, 1933. Served with Royal Engrs in France, Madagascar, Africa and India, 1939-45. British Railways: posts in traffic depts, 1945-61; Eastern Region: Commercial Supt, Great Northern Line, 1961; Divisional Man., Doncaster, 1964; Asst Gen. Man., York, 1968; Mem., BR (Eastern) Bd, 1969; Dep. Gen. Man., York, 1970. Dorset County Dir, St John Ambulance Assoc., 1976-. OStJ 1975. *Recreations:* gardening, soccer, Rugby, cricket (critic). *Address:* 6 Chaucer Road, Canford Cliffs, Poole, Dorset BH13 7HB. *Club:* Army and Navy.

WRIGHT, Georg Henrik von, GCVO (Hon.); MA; Research Professor in the Academy of Finland, since 1961; *b* Helsingfors, 14 June 1916; *s* of Tor von Wright and Ragni Elisabeth Alfthan; *m* 1941, Maria Elisabeth von Troil, CVO (Hon.); one *s* one *d*. *Educ:* Svenska Normallyceum, Helsingfors; Helsingfors Univ. Helsingfors University: Lectr and Acting Prof. of Philosophy, 1943-46; Prof. of Philosophy, 1946-61 (also in Univ. of Cambridge, 1948-51); Prof. at Large, Cornell Univ., 1965-77; Chancellor of Abo Academy, 1968-77; Visiting Professor: Cornell Univ., 1954 and 1958; Univ. Calif., Los Angeles, 1963; Univ. Pittsburg, 1966; Univ. Karlsruhe, 1975; Lectures: Shearman Meml, University Coll., London, 1956; Gifford, Univ. of St Andrews, 1959-60; Tarner, Trinity Coll., Cambridge, 1969; Woodbridge, Columbia Univ., 1972. President: Internat. Union of History and Philosophy of Science, 1963-65; Acad. of Finland, 1968-69; Philosophical Soc. of Finland, 1962-73; Institut International de Philosophie, 1975-. Fellow: Finnish Soc. of Sciences (Pres., 1966-67); New Soc. of Letters, Lund; Royal Swedish Academy of Sciences; Royal Soc. of Letters, Lund; British Academy; Royal Swedish Academy of Letters, History and Antiquities; Finnish Acad. of Sciences; Royal Danish Acad. of Sciences and Letters; Hon. Foreign Mem., Amer. Acad. of Arts and Sciences. Sometime Fellow, Trinity College, Cambridge. Hon. degrees: Helsingfors Univ. (doctor of pol. sci.); Univ. of Liverpool (DLitt); Univ. of Lund (doctor of philosophy); Turku Univ. (doctor of philosophy). *Publications:* The Logical Problem of Induction, 1941, rev. edn 1957; Den logiska Empirismen, 1943; Über Wahrscheinlichkeit, 1945; A Treatise on Induction and Probability, 1951; An Essay in Modal Logic, 1951; Logical Studies, 1957; The Varieties of Goodness, 1963; The Logic of Preference, 1963; Norm and Action, 1963; An Essay in Deontic Logic, 1968; Time, Change, and Contradiction, 1969; Explanation and Understanding, 1971; Causality and Determinism, 1974. *Address:* 4 Skepparegatan, Helsingfors, Finland.

WRIGHT, George Paul; Chief Superintendent, Royal Signals and Radar Establishment, Ministry of Defence, Baldock, since 1976; *b* 27 April 1919; *s* of late George Maurice Wright, CBE, and of late Lois Dorothy Wright (*née* Norburn); *m* 1957, Jean Margaret Reid, *d* of Lt-Col Charles Alexander Reid Scott, DSO and Marjorie Reid Scott (*née* Mackintosh); one *s* one *d*. *Educ:* Bishops Stortford Coll.; Magdalen Coll., Oxford. BA 1948, MA 1951; FInstP. Admty Signal Estabt, 1939-45; Services Electronics Research Lab., 1945-57; Dept of Physical Research, Admty, 1957-63; Services Electronics Research Lab., 1963-76 (Dir, 1972-76). *Recreations:* music, sailing, gardening. *Address:* Little Hormead Bury, Buntingford, Herts. *T:* Great Hormead 260. *Clubs:* Athenæum, United Oxford & Cambridge University, Naval, Civil Service; Blackwater Sailing.

WRIGHT, Gerard, QC 1973; *b* 23 July 1929; *s* of Leo Henry and Catherine M. F. Wright; *m* 1950, Betty Mary Fenn; one *s* two *d*. *Educ:* Stonyhurst Coll.; Lincoln Coll., Oxford (BA, BCL). Served in Army, 1947-49, rank T/Captain. Called to Bar, Gray's Inn, 1954; Northern Circuit. KHS 1974. *Recreations:* skiing, sailing, squash. *Address:* Birdie Brow, Chobham Road, Sunningdale, Berks. *T:* Ascot 25906; 13 King's Bench Walk, Temple, EC4Y 7EN. *T:* 01-353 7804. *Club:* Racquet (Liverpool).

WRIGHT, Prof. H(enry) Myles; FRIBA; FRTPI; Lever Professor of Civic Design, University of Liverpool, 1954-75; now Emeritus Professor; University Planning Consultant, 1957-77; *b* 9 June 1908; *s* of H. T. Wright, Gosforth, Newcastle upon Tyne; *m* 1939, Catharine Noble, *y d* of Very Rev. H. N. Craig, Dean of Kildare; two *d. Educ:* Fettes College, Edinburgh (Foundationer); King's College, Newcastle upon Tyne; St John's College, Cambridge. Assistant in various private offices, 1930-35; Asst Editor, The Architects' Journal, and in private practice, 1935-40; Partner in firm of Sir William Holford, 1948-54; principally engaged on planning proposals for Cambridge and Corby New Town. Member British Caribbean Federal Capital Commn, 1956. *Publications:* The Planner's Notebook, 1948; Cambridge Planning Proposals, 1950, and Corby New Town (with Lord Holford), 1952; Land Use in an Urban Environment (Editor and contributor), 1961; The Dublin Region: Preliminary and Final Reports, 1965 and 1967; other technical publications. *Recreations:* walking, reading. *Address:* Beech House, Parkgate Road, Neston, Cheshire L64 9XE. *Club:* Kildare Street and University (Dublin).

WRIGHT, Prof. Jack Clifford, MA, BA; Professor of Sanskrit in the University of London, at the School of Oriental and African Studies since 1964; *b* 5 Dec. 1933; *s* of Jack and Dorothy Wright, Aberdeen; *m* 1958, Hazel Chisholm (*née* Strachan), Crathes, Banchory; one *s. Educ:* Robert Gordon's Coll., Aberdeen; Univ. of Aberdeen (MA Hons in French and German, 1955); University of Zürich; Univ. of London (BA Hons in Sanskrit, 1959). Lectr in Sanskrit, Sch. of Oriental and African Studies, Univ. of London, 1959-64. *Address:* School of Oriental and African Studies, University of London, WC1.

WRIGHT, Adm. Jerauld, DSM (US) (twice); Silver and Bronze Star Medals; Legion of Merit (US); USN retired; US Ambassador to Nationalist China, 1963-65; *b* Amherst, Mass., 4 June 1898; *s* of Gen. William Mason Wright and Marjorie R. (Jerauld) Wright; *m* 1938, Phyllis B. Thompson; one *s* one *d. Educ:* US Naval Academy. Ensign, USN, 1917; promoted through grades to Admiral, 1954, Executive Staff of US Naval Academy; operational staff appointments for N African, Sicilian and Italian landings; Mem., Gen. Mark Clark's Expedition to North Africa. Comdr, USS Santa Fe, Pacific, 1943-44; Comdr Amphibious Group Five, 1944-45; Comdr Cruiser Div. Six, 1945; Asst Chief of Naval Operations for Fleet Readiness, 1945-48; Comdr. Amphibious Force, US Atlantic Fleet, 1949-51; US Rep. NATO Standing Group, Washington, 1951-52; C-in-C US Naval Forces, E Atlantic and Medit., 1952-54; Supreme Allied Commander, Atlantic, and C-in-C Western Atlantic Area, NATO, 1954-60; C-in-C Atlantic (US Unified Command), and C-in-C Atlantic Fleet, 1954-60. Pres. US Naval Inst., 1959. Holds Hon. doctorates in Laws and Science. Awarded foreign decorations. *Address:* (Home) 2706 36th Street NW, Washington, DC 20007, USA. *Clubs:* Metropolitan, Alibi, Chevy Chase (Washington); Knickerbocker, Brooke (New York).

WRIGHT, Joe Booth; HM Diplomatic Service; Ambassador to Ivory Coast, Upper Volta and Niger, since 1975; *b* 24 Aug. 1920; *s* of Joe Booth Wright and Annie Elizabeth Wright; *m* 1st, 1945, Pat (*née* Beaumont); one *s* two *d*; 2nd, 1967, Patricia Maxine (*née* Nicholls). *Educ:* King Edward VI Grammar Sch., Retford; Univ. of London. BA Hons, French. GPO, 1939-47. Served War, HM Forces: RAOC, Intelligence Corps, 1941-46. Entered Foreign Office, 1947; FO, 1947-51; Vice-Consul, Jerusalem, 1951; Consul, Munich, 1952, and Basra, 1954; Dep. Consul, Tamsui, 1956; FO, 1959-64; Consul, Surabaya, 1964; Consul, Medan, 1965-67; First Sec. (Information), Nicosia, 1968; Head of Chancery and Consul, Tunis, 1968-71; Consul-General: Hanoi, 1971-72; Geneva, 1973-75. *Recreations:* cricket, film-going, music, writing. *Address:* c/o Foreign and Commonwealth Office, SW1. *Club:* Royal Over-Seas League.

WRIGHT, Captain John, DSC 1944; RN (retd); General Manager, HM Dockyard, Devonport, 1972-77; *b* 30 April 1921; *s* of Percy Robert and Lucy Ada Wright; *m* 1946, Ethel Lumley Sunderland; one *s* two *d. Educ:* Liverpool Univ. (Part I for BSc). MIEE; Silver Medal, City and Guilds. Served War: RNVR, 1942; 16th Destroyer Flotilla, 1942; HMS Birmingham, 1943; HMS Diadem, 1943. Devonport Gunnery Sch., 1946; HMS Collingwood, 1948; BJSM, USA, 1951; Admiralty Surface Weapons Estabt, 1952; HMS Cumberland, 1956; Naval Ordnance Div., 1958; British Naval Staff, USA, 1960; Polaris Technical Dept, 1964; HM Dockyard, Chatham, 1968; RN retd 1972. *Recreations:* fishing, gardening. *Address:* The Ferns, Seymour Road, Mannamead, Plymouth PL3 5AT. *T:* Plymouth 61635.

WRIGHT, Air Cdre John Allan Cecil C.; see Cecil-Wright.

WRIGHT, John Henry, CBE 1964; HM Diplomatic Service, retired; with Government Communications HQ, 1970-77; *b* 6 Dec. 1910; *s* of John Robert Wright and Margaret Leadbetter; *m* 1939, Joan Harvey; two *s. Educ:* Barrow Grammar Sch.; Trinity Coll., Cambridge. Vice-Consul, Genoa, 1934; Addis Ababa, 1937; Havana, 1939; 2nd Sec., Quito, 1943; 1st Sec., 1945; transf. to Foreign Office, 1948; 1st Sec. (Commercial), Helsinki, 1950; 1st Sec. (Commercial), Santiago, 1953; Counsellor, at Shanghai, of HM Chargé d'Affaires in China, 1958-60; Counsellor, temporarily employed in Foreign Office, Dec. 1960-61; HM Consul-General at Rotterdam, 1961-63; Ambassador to Honduras, 1963-69. *Recreations:* lawn tennis, walking, music. *Address:* Horse Inn House, Bourton-on-the-Hill, Moreton-in-Marsh, Glos. *Club:* United Oxford & Cambridge University.

WRIGHT, John Hurrell C.; see Collier-Wright.

WRIGHT, John Keith; Under Secretary and Deputy Director-General of Economic Planning, Ministry of Overseas Development (formerly Overseas Development Administration, FCO), since 1971; *b* 30 May 1928; *s* of late James Wright and of Elsie Wright, Walton-on-Thames, Surrey; *m* 1958, Thérèse Marie-Claire, *er d* of René Aubenas, Paris. *Educ:* Tiffins' Sch.; King's Coll., Cambridge (MA Hist., 1950; Dipl. in Economics, 1954; Gladstone Memorial Prize, 1954); Yale Univ. OEEC, Paris: Economics and Statistics Directorate, 1951-52; Agriculture and Food Directorate, 1954-56; UK Atomic Energy Authority, 1956-61; Chief Scientific Adviser's staff, MoD, 1961-66 (UK Delegn to 18 Nation Disarmament Conf., 1962-64); Sen. Econ. Adviser, CO, 1966-68; Head of Economists Dept and subseq. Dir (Economic), FCO, 1968-71. Chm., Economists' Panel, First Division Assoc., 1973-75. Has exhibited at Royal Academy. *Publications:* articles on economic subjects. *Recreations:* conversation, economic history, piano-playing, opera, motor cars. *Address:* 47 Brunswick Gardens, W8. *T:* 01-229 2106; Bowling Corner, Sandwich, Kent. *T:* Sandwich 2103. *Clubs:* Athenæum, Beefsteak.

WRIGHT, (John) Michael, QC 1974; a Recorder of the Crown Court, since 1974; *b* 26 Oct. 1932; *s* of Prof. John George Wright, DSc, MVSc, FRCVS, and Elsie Lloyd Razey; *m* 1959, Kathleen, *er d* of F. A. Meanwell; one *s* two *d. Educ:* King's Sch., Chester; Oriel Coll., Oxford. BA Jurisprudence 1956. Served Royal Artillery, 1951-53. Called to Bar, Lincoln's Inn, 1957; Mem. Bar Council, 1972-; Mem. Senate of Four Inns of Court, 1973-; Mem. Supreme Court Rules Cttee, 1973-74. *Recreations:* books, music. *Address:* 2 Crown Office Row, Temple, EC4Y 7HJ. *T:* 01-353 9337; White Friars, St Albans Road, Reigate, Surrey. *T:* Reigate 47792.

WRIGHT, Prof. John Nicholson; Professor of Logic and Metaphysics in the United College, the University of St Andrews, 1936-66, now Emeritus; Master of St Salvator's College in the University of St Andrews, 1959-66; Acting Master, 1966-67; retired; General Council Assessor, University Court, 1969-72; *b* 21 Aug. 1896; *e s* of John Nicholson Wright and Elizabeth Ann Humble; *m* 1923, Florencia Emilia Cowper (*d* 1966), Pacasmayo, Peru, and Canterbury, Kent; two *d. Educ:* Bede Collegiate School, Sunderland; Ryhope Grammar School; St Chad's College, University of Durham (scholar and prizeman). Served 4th Bn Durham Light Infantry, 1916-19. BA 1920, MA 1923. Assistant in Dept of Logic and Metaphysics, Univ. of St Andrews, 1920; Lecturer in Logic and Psychology, Univ. Coll., Dundee, 1924-36; Adviser of Studies in Arts, 1932; Dean of the Faculty of Arts, Univ. of St Andrews, 1937-50. Chairman of Regional Cttee for Adult Education, 1938-50; War Office Lecturer to HM Forces in Middle East, 1945 and 1947, Far East, 1950; Member of Advisory Committee on Education to the War Office, 1945; member Fulbright Commission, 1957. President, Mind Association, 1959. President Scottish Amateur Swimming Assoc., 1935, and on Selection Cttee for British Empire Games. Chairman Council of St Leonards and St Katharines Schools, 1952-67 (Hon. Vice-Pres.), 1969). Fellow, Morse College, Yale Univ., 1964. Hon. LLD St Andrews Univ., 1967. Order of Polonia Restituta, 1944; Norwegian Order of Freedom, 1947. *Publications:* articles and reviews in learned journals and on philosophy and logic in Chambers's Encyclopædia. *Recreations:* music, swimming. *Address:* 120 North Street, St Andrews, Fife. *T:* 5320. *Club:* Royal and Ancient Golf (St Andrews).

WRIGHT, Sir (John) Oliver, KCMG 1974 (CMG 1964); DSC 1944; HM Diplomatic Service; Ambassador to the Federal Republic of Germany, since 1975; *b* 6 March 1921; *m* 1942, Lillian Marjory Osborne; three *s. Educ:* Solihull School; Christ's College, Cambridge (MA). Served in RNVR, 1941-45. Joined

HM Diplomatic Service, Nov. 1945; served: New York, 1946-47; Bucharest, 1948-50; Singapore, 1950-51; Foreign Office, 1952-54; Berlin, 1954-56; Pretoria, 1957-58. Imperial Defence College, 1959. Asst Private Sec. to Sec. of State for Foreign Affairs, 1960; Counsellor and Private Sec., 1963; Private Sec. to the Prime Minister, 1964-66 (to Rt Hon. Sir Alec Douglas-Home, and subseq. to Rt Hon. Harold Wilson); Ambassador to Denmark, 1966-69; seconded to Home Office as UK Rep. to NI Govt, Aug. 1969-March 1970; Chief Clerk, HM Diplomatic Service, 1970-72; Dep. Under-Sec. of State, FCO, 1972-75. *Recreations:* theatre, gardening. *Address:* Burstow Hall, near Horley, Surrey. *T:* Horley 3494. *Club:* Travellers'.

WRIGHT, Judith, (Mrs J. P. McKinney); writer; *b* 31 May 1915; *d* of late Phillip Arundel Wright, CMG, and Ethel Mabel (*née* Bigg); *m* J. P. McKinney; one *d. Educ:* NSW Correspondence Sch.; New England Girls' Sch.; Sydney Univ. Secretarial work, 1938-42; Univ. Statistician (Univ. of Queensland), 1945-48. Creative Arts Fellow, ANU, 1974. Dr of Letters (Hon.): Univ. of Queensland, 1962; Univ. of New England, 1963; Univ. of Sydney, 1976; Monash Univ., 1977. Encyclopædia Britannica Writer's Award, 1965; Robert Frost Medallion, Fellowship of Australian Writers, 1975. FAHA 1970. *Publications: verse:* The Moving Image, 1946; Woman to Man, 1950; The Gateway, 1953; The Two Fires, 1955; Birds, 1960; Five Senses, 1963; The Other Half, 1966; Collected Poems, 1971; Alive, 1972; Fourth Quarter, 1976; *biographical novel:* The Generations of Men, 1955; *criticism:* Preoccupations in Australian Poetry, 1964; Charles Harpur, 1977; *anthologies:* The Oxford Book of Australian Verse, 1954; New Land New Language, 1956; *short stories:* The Nature of Love, 1966; *essays:* Because I Was Invited, 1975; *documentary prose:* The Coral Battleground; four books for children; also critical essays and monographs. *Recreation:* gardening. *Address:* c/o Post Office, Braidwood, NSW 2622, Australia.

WRIGHT, Kenneth; *see* Wright, E. K.

WRIGHT, Louis Booker; Hon. OBE 1968; historian, writer; consultant in history, National Geographic Society, since 1971; Director, Folger Shakespeare Library, 1948-68; *b* 1 March 1899; *s* of Thomas Fleming Wright and Lena Booker Wright; *m* 1925, Frances Black; one *s. Educ:* Wofford College; University of North Carolina. AB 1920, Wofford Coll.; MA 1924, PhD 1926, N Carolina. Service in US Army, 1918; newspaper corres. and editor, 1918-23; instructor and associate Prof. of Eng., University of North Carolina, 1926-32; visiting scholar, Huntington Library, 1931-32; member permanent research group, Huntington Library, also Chm., Cttee on Fellowships and Mem. Exec. Cttee, 1932-48; Vis. Professor: Univs of Michigan 1935, Washington 1942, Calif. at Los Angeles 1934-48; Pomona Coll., 1941-48; Calif. Inst. of Technology, 1932-48; Univ. of Minnesota, 1946; Indiana Univ. on the Patten Foundation, 1953. Chm. Advisory Bd, John Simon Guggenheim Memorial Foundation; Vice-Chm., Council on Library Resources, Inc.; Mem. Bd of Directors H. F. du Pont Winterthur Museum and Harry S. Truman Library Inst. for Nat. and Internat. Affairs. Trustee: Shakespeare Birthplace Trust; National Geographic Society. Hon. LittD: Wofford, 1941; Mills College, 1947; Princeton, 1948; Amherst, 1948; Occidental College, 1949; Bucknell, 1951; Franklin and Marshall, 1957; Colby Coll., 1959; Univ. of British Columbia, 1960; Leicester Univ., 1965; Hon. LLD: Tulane, 1950; George Washington, 1958; Chattanooga, 1959; Akron, 1961; St Andrews, 1961; Washington and Lee, 1964; Mercer, 1965; LHD: Northwestern, 1948; Univ. of N Carolina, 1950; Yale, 1954; Rockford Coll., 1956; Coe Coll., 1959; Georgetown Univ., 1961; California State Coll., 1966; Univ. of California, 1967; Brown Univ., 1968; Univ. of S Carolina, 1972; Lander Coll., 1974; Hon. DLitt, Birmingham, England, 1964. FRSA (Benjamin Franklin Medal, 1969); FRSL; FRHistS; Mem., Amer. Philosophical Soc. and other learned socs. Cosmos Club award for distinction in hist. and letters, 1973. *Publications:* Middle-Class Culture in Elizabethan England, 1935; Puritans in the South Seas, 1936; The First Gentlemen of Virginia, 1940; Religion and Empire, 1942; The First Americans in North Africa, 1945; The Atlantic Frontier, 1947; Culture on the Moving Frontier, 1955; The Cultural Life of the American Colonies, 1957; Shakespeare for Everyman, 1964; Everyday Life in Colonial America, 1965; The Dream of Prosperity in Colonial America, 1965; The History of the Thirteen Colonies, 1967; Everyday Life on the American Frontier, 1968; Gold, Glory and the Gospel, 1970; Barefoot in Arcadia: memories of a more innocent era, 1974; Tradition and the Founding Fathers, 1975; South Carolina: a Bicentennial History, 1976; Of Books and Men, 1976; The John Henry County Map of Virginia 1770, 1977. Edited: Letters of Robert Carter, 1940; The Secret Diary of William Byrd of Westover, 1709-12, 1941; Quebec to Carolina

in 1785-1786, 1943; An Essay Upon the Government of the English Plantation on the Continent of America, 1701, 1945; The History and Present State of Virginia, 1705 (by Robert Beverley), 1947; The Historie of Travell into Virginia Britania, 1612, (by William Strachey) 1953; The Folger Library General Reader's Shakespeare, 1957-68; William Byrd of Virginia: The London Diary 1717-1721, and Other Writings, 1958; The Elizabethans' America, 1965; The Prose Works of William Byrd of Westover, 1966; West and by North: North America seen through the eyes of its seafaring discoverers, 1971; The Moving Frontier, 1972. *Recreation:* fishing. *Address:* 3702 Leland Street, Chevy Chase, Md 20015, USA. *T:* 652-5509. *Clubs:* Cosmos (Washington); Century (New York).

WRIGHT, Prof. Margaret S.; *see* Scott Wright.

WRIGHT, Martin; Director, Howard League for Penal Reform, since 1971; *b* 24 April 1930; *s* of late Clifford Kent Wright and Rosalie Wright, Stoke Newington; *m* 1957, Louisa Mary Nicholls; three *s* two *d. Educ:* Repton; Jesus Coll., Oxford. Librarian, Inst. of Criminology, Cambridge, 1964-71. Mem. Council, The Cyrenians, 1969- (Chm., Cambridge Cyrene Community (formerly Cambridge Simon Community), 1965-71). ALA 1960. *Publication:* (ed) The Use of Criminological Literature, 1974. *Address:* 107 Palace Road, SW2. *T:* 01-671 8037.

WRIGHT, Michael Thomas; Editor, Country Life, since 1973; *b* 10 Dec. 1936; *o c* of Thomas Manning Wright and Hilda Evelyn Wright (*née* Whiting); *m* 1964, Jennifer Olga Angus, 2nd *d* of C. B. Angus, Singapore; two *s. Educ:* Bristol Grammar Sch.; Gonville and Caius Coll., Cambridge (MA); Trinity Coll., Dublin. Member, Honourable Society of Gray's Inn. Churchwarden, St Michael's Parish Church, Highgate. Judge, RICS/The Times Conservation Awards, 1976, 1977. Formerly: Financial Analyst, Ford Motor Co. Asst Sec., Town Planning Inst.; Editor, Town Planning Inst. Jl; Asst Editor, Country Life; Managing Editor, Journal of Royal Inst. of British Architects; Dep. Editor, Country Life. *Publications:* contrib. articles to: TPI Jl, RIBA Jl; Water Space; Country Life. *Recreations:* music, tennis, walking; participation in local amenity society work. *Address:* 7 Fitzwarren Gardens, Highgate, N19 3TR. *T:* 01-272 2971.

WRIGHT, Sir Oliver; *see* Wright, Sir J. O.

WRIGHT, Patrick Richard Henry; HM Diplomatic Service; Ambassador to Luxembourg, since 1977; *b* 28 June 1931; *s* of late Herbert H. S. Wright and of Rachel Wright (*née* Green), Chetwode, Bucks; *m* 1958, Virginia Anne Gaffney; two *s* one *d. Educ:* Marlborough; Merton Coll. (Postmaster), Oxford (MA). Served Royal Artillery, 1950-51; joined Diplomatic Service, 1955; Middle East Centre for Arabic Studies, 1956-57; Third Secretary, British Embassy, Beirut, 1958-60; Private Sec. to Ambassador and later First Sec., British Embassy, Washington, 1960-65; Private Sec. to Permanent Under-Sec., FO, 1965-67; First Sec. and Head of Chancery, Cairo, 1967-70; Dep. Political Resident, Bahrain, 1971-72; Head of Middle East Dept, FCO, 1972-74; Private Sec. (Overseas Affairs) to Prime Minister, 1974-77. *Recreations:* music, archaeology, walking. *Address:* 1 Well Lane, SW14. *T:* 01-876 4176. *Club:* United Oxford & Cambridge University.

WRIGHT, Sir Paul (Hervé Giraud), KCMG 1975 (CMG 1960); OBE 1952; HM Diplomatic Service, retired; Special Representative of the Secretary of State for Foreign and Commonwealth Affairs, since 1975; Hon. Secretary General, London Celebrations Committee for the Queen's Silver Jubilee, 1977; *b* 12 May 1915; *o s* of late Richard Hervé Giraud Wright; *m* 1942, Beatrice Frederika Rathbone (*see* Beatrice Wright), widow of Flt-Lt J. R. Rathbone, MP; one *d. Educ:* Westminster. Employed by John Lewis Partnership Ltd, 1933-39. Served HM Forces, War of 1939-45; Major, KRRC; HQ 21 Army Group, 1944-45 (despatches). Contested (L) NE Bethnal Green, 1945. Asst Dir, Public Relations, National Coal Bd, 1946-48; Dir, Public Relations, Festival of Britain, 1948-51. HM Foreign Service: Paris and New York, 1951-54; Foreign Office, 1954-56; The Hague, 1956-57; Head of Information, Policy Dept in FO, 1957-60; Cairo, 1960-61; UK Delegn to N Atlantic Council, 1961-64; Minister (Information), Washington, 1965-68, and Dir-Gen., British Inf. Services, NY, 1964-68; Ambassador to Congo (Kinshasa) and to Republic of Burundi, 1969-71; Ambassador to the Lebanon, 1971-75. *Address:* 3 Ormonde Gate, SW3 4EU. *Club:* Garrick.

WRIGHT, Peter Harold, VC 1944; late Company Sergeant-Major, Coldstream Guards; farmer; *b* 10 Aug. 1916, British; *m* 1946, Mollie Mary Hurren, Wenhaston; one *s* two *d. Educ:*

Brooke, Norfolk (elementary school). Left school at 14 and worked on father's farm up to the age of 20. Joined Coldstream Guards, 1936; sailed for Egypt, 1937. Served in Egypt, Palestine, Syria and throughout the Libyan campaign and North Africa, took part in the landing at Salerno, Italy, Sept. 1943; demobilised, 1945. *Address:* Poplar Farm, Helmingham, Stowmarket, Suffolk.

WRIGHT, Brig. Richard Eustace John G.; *see* Gerrard-Wright.

WRIGHT, Sir Richard (Michael) C.; *see* Cory-Wright.

WRIGHT, Robert Anthony Kent, QC 1973; *b* 7 Jan. 1922; *s* of Robert and Eva Wright; *m* 1956, Gillian Elizabeth Drummond Hancock. *Educ:* Hilton Coll., Natal, S Africa; St Paul's Sch., London; The Queen's Coll., Oxford (MA). Indian Army, 1942-46, Major. Oxford, 1946-48. Called to Bar, Lincoln's Inn, 1949. *Recreations:* music, sailing, golf, walking. *Address:* 24 Old Buildings, Lincoln's Inn, WC2A 3UJ. *T:* 01-242 5532. *Clubs:* National Liberal; Bosham Sailing (Bosham); Royal Wimbledon Golf (Wimbledon).

WRIGHT, Sir Robert (Brash), Kt 1976; DSO 1945; OBE 1944; FRCP, Consultant, FRCSE, FRCSGlas; Surgeon in Charge, Southern General Hospital, Glasgow, since 1953; *b* 1 March 1915; 2nd *s* of Dr Hugh P. Wright and Janet Brash; *m* 1946, Helen Tait; one *s* two *d*. *Educ:* Hamilton Acad.; Univ. of Glasgow (BSc 1934; MB, ChB Hons 1937; ChM 1953). FRCP 1970. FRCSE 1947, FRCSGlas 1962. RAMC, 1939-46. Asst Surg., Western Infirm., Glasgow, 1946-53. Pres., RCPSG, 1968-70; Member: GMC, 1970-; Scottish Council for Post Grad. Med. Educn, 1968. Hon. FRCS 1975; Hon. FRACS 1968. *Publications:* articles in med. and surg. jls. *Recreations:* gardening, walking and wondering. *Address:* 12A Grange Road, Bearsden, Glasgow G61 3PL. *Clubs:* Caledonian; Royal Scottish Automobile (Glasgow).

WRIGHT, Lt-Col Robert Ernest, CIE 1929; BA (Sen. Mod.), MD, MCh (Hon.), DPH (TCD), IMS retired; late Professor of Ophthalmology Medical College and Superintendent Government Ophthalmic Hospital, Madras, India; *b* 1884; *s* of R. Wright, JP, of Prumplestown, Carlow, Ireland; *m* 1930, Ruby Evelyn Sheldon, *d* of Dr S. T. Pruen, Cheltenham. *Educ:* Trinity College, Dublin. Graduated with Honours in 1906, taking Large Gold Medal and Senior Moderatorship in Natural Science; also Med. Travelling Prize; joined the IMS 1907; served in Burma with the Hpi-maw Expedition, 1910; Assistant Director Pasteur Institute of S India, 1912; served in Mesopotamia European War (despatches); brevet promotion to Major, 1915; Lieut-Col, 1927; retired, 1938; Member Internat. Council of Ophthalmology, 1929-39. Re-employed by W. D. as Ophth. Specialist, 1939-46. *Publications:* various papers in Medical Literature dealing chiefly Clinical Ophthalmology, biological and ophthalmological research. *Recreations:* shooting, fishing. *Address:* c/o Barclays Bank, Fleet, Hants. *Club:* East India, Sports and Public Schools.

WRIGHT, Very Rev. Ronald (William Vernon) Selby, CVO 1968; TD; DD; FRSE; FSA Scotland; JP; Minister Emeritus of the Canongate (The Kirk of Holyroodhouse), Edinburgh, and of Edinburgh Castle (Minister, 1936-77); Chaplain to: the Queen in Scotland, since 1961; The Queen's Bodyguard for Scotland, Royal Company of Archers, since 1973; *b* 12 June 1908; *s* of late Vernon O. Wright, ARCM, and late Anna Gilberta, *d* of Major R. E. Selby; unmarried. *Educ:* Edinburgh Academy; Melville Coll.; Edinburgh Univ. (MA; Hon. DD 1956); New Coll. Edinburgh. Warden, St Giles' Cathedral Boys' Club, 1927-36, and Canongate Boys' Club (formerly St Giles'), 1937-. Cadet Officer, The Royal Scots, 1927-31; Student-Asst at St Giles' Cathedral, 1929-36; Asst Minister of Glasgow Cathedral, 1936; Warden of first Scottish Public Schools' and Clubs' Camp, 1938; Chaplain to 7th/9th (Highlanders) Bn The Royal Scots, 1938-42 (France, 1940), 1947-49; Senior Chaplain to the Forces: 52nd (Lowland) Div., 1942-43; Edinburgh Garrison, 1943; Middle East Forces, 1943-44; NE London, 1944; 10th Indian Div., CMF, 1944-45 (despatches); Hon. SCF, 1945-. Special Preacher, Oxford Univ., 1944; Select Preacher, Cambridge Univ., 1947; Visiting Preacher: Aberdeen Univ., 1946, 1953, 1965, 1973; St Andrews Univ., 1951, 1956, 1967, 1973; Glasgow Univ., 1955, 1973; Edinburgh Univ., 1959; Birmingham Univ., 1959; Hull Univ., 1967; Dundee Univ., 1973. Chaplain to, the Lord High Comr, 1959, and 1960. Conducted numerous series of religious broadcasts for BBC as Radio Padre, toured for War Office and BBC all Home Comds in 1942 and 1943 and MEF, 1943-44; toured transit camps etc in Italy, Austria, S Germany, etc, 1945; toured, for Church of Scotland: India, 1972; for HM Forces: Hong Kong 1973; Singapore, 1973. Moderator, Presbytery of Edinburgh, 1963; Moderator, Gen. Assembly of the Church of

Scotland, 1972-73. Chm., Edinburgh and Leith Old People's Welfare Council, 1956-69; Extraordinary Dir, The Edinburgh Academy, 1973-; Hon. Chaplain: Fettes Coll., 1957-60; Loretto Sch., 1960- (Hon. Old Lorettonian, 1976); Edinburgh Acad., 1966-73; Merchant Co. of Edinburgh, 1973-; ChStJ 1976; Pres., Scottish Church Soc., 1971-74; Vice-President: Scottish Assoc. of Boys Clubs; Old Edinburgh Club; Hon. Pres. Scottish Churches FA; Patron, Lothian Amateur FA. Mem. Edinburgh Educn Cttee, 1960-70. Governor: Rannoch Sch.; St George's Sch. JP Edinburgh, 1963. Cross of St Mark, 1970. *Publications:* Asking Why (with A. W. Loos), 1939; The Average Man, 1942; Let's Ask the Padre, 1943; The Greater Victory, 1943; The Padre Presents, 1944; Small Talks, 1945; Whatever the Years, 1947; What Worries Me, 1950; Great Men, 1951; They Looked to Him, 1954; Our Club, 1954; The Kirk in the Canongate, 1956; The Selfsame Miracles, 1957; Our Club and Panmure House, 1958; Roses in December, 1960; The Seven Words, 1964; An Illustrated Guide to the Canongate, 1965; Take up God's Armour, 1967; The Seven Dwarfs, 1968; Haply I May Remember, 1970; In Christ We Are All One, 1972; Seven Sevens, 1977; edited and contributed to Asking Them Questions, 1936; A Scottish Camper's Prayer Book, 1936; I Attack, 1937; Asking Them Questions-Second Series, 1938; Front Line Religion, 1941; Soldiers Also Asked, 1943; Asking Them Questions-Third Series, 1950; Asking Them Questions (a Selection), 1953; The Beloved Captain: Essays by Donald Hankey, 1956; (with L. Menzies and R. A. Knox) St Margaret, Queen of Scotland, 1957; A Manual of Church Doctrine (with T. F. Torrance), 1960; Fathers of the Kirk, 1960; Asking Them Questions, a new series, 1972, 1973; contrib. to Chambers's Encyclopædia, etc. Editor, Scottish Forces' Magazine (quarterly), 1941-76. *Recreations:* trying to run a Boys' Club since 1927, camping, history of old Edinburgh. *Address:* The Queen's House, 36 Moray Place, Edinburgh EH3 6BX. *T:* 031-226 5566. *Clubs:* Athenæum; New, Puffins (Edinburgh).

WRIGHT, Sir Rowland (Sydney), Kt 1976; CBE 1970; Chairman, ICI Ltd, since 1975; *b* 4 Oct. 1915; *s* of late Sydney Henry Wright and Elsie May; *m* 1940, Kathleen Mary Hodgkinson, BA; two *s* one *d*. *Educ:* High Pavement Sch., Nottingham; UC Nottingham. BSc London; FRIC. Joined ICI Ltd, Dyestuffs Div., 1937; Production Dir, Imperial Chemical (Pharmaceuticals) Ltd, 1955-57; Production Dir, Dyestuffs Div., 1957-58; Research Dir, 1958-61; Jt Man. Dir, ICI Ltd Agricultural Div., 1961-63, Chm. 1964-65; Personnel Dir, ICI Ltd, 1966-70; Dep. Chm., ICI Ltd, 1971-75; Director: AE&CI Ltd, 1970- (Dep. Chm., 1971-75); Royal Insurance Co., 1973-; Barclays Bank Ltd, 1977-. Chm., Reorganisation Commn for Eggs, 1967-68; Past Mem. Council, Foundn for Management Educn; Mem. Council, Chemical Industries Assoc., 1968-73; Pres. Inst. of Manpower Studies, 1971-77, Hon. Pres., 1977-; Vice-Pres., Soc. of Chemical Industry, 1971-74; Mem., British Shippers' Council, 1975; Trustee, Civic Trust, 1975. Governor, London Graduate School of Business Studies. FRSA 1970; FBIM 1975; Mem., Royal Instn, 1971. *Recreations:* gardening, photography. *Address:* Imperial Chemical House, Millbank, SW1P 3JP. *T:* 01-834 4444.

WRIGHT, Roy Kilner; Senior Assistant Editor, Daily Mail, since 1977; *b* 12 March 1926; *s* of Ernest Wright and Louise Wright; *m* 1st (marr. diss.); two *d*; 2nd, 1969, Jane Barnicoat (*née* Selby). *Educ:* elementary sch., St Helens, Lancs. Jun. Reporter, St Helens Reporter, 1941; Army Service; Sub-Editor: Middlesbrough Gazette, 1947; Daily Express, Manchester, 1951; Daily Mirror, London, 1952; Features Editor, Daily Express, London; Dep. Editor, London Evening Standard; Dep. Editor, Daily Express, 1976, Editor, 1976-77; Dir, Beaverbrook Newspapers, 1976-77. *Address:* 50 Hurlingham Road, SW6. *T:* 01-736 0403. *Club:* Reform.

WRIGHT, Roy William, CBE 1970; MIEE; Director, since 1957, Deputy Chairman and Deputy Chief Executive, 1965-75, The Rio Tinto-Zinc Corporation; Director: Palabora Mining Co., Johannesburg, since 1963; Rio Tinto South Africa Ltd, Johannesburg, since 1960; Rio Algom Ltd, Toronto, since 1960; Lornex Mining Co., Vancouver, since 1970; Davy International Ltd, since 1976; A. P. V. Holdings Ltd, since 1976; *b* 10 Sept. 1914; *s* of late Arthur William Wright; *m* 1939, Mary Letitia, *d* of late Llewelyn Davies; two *d*. *Educ:* King Edward VI Sch., Chelmsford; Faraday House Coll., London. Served War of 1939-45, S African Navy and RN in S Atlantic, N Atlantic and Arctic; Lt-Comdr 1944. Joined Rio Tinto Co. Ltd, 1952; Man. Dir, Rio Tinto Canada, 1956; Dir, Rio Tinto Co. Ltd, 1957. Chairman: Process Plant Expert Cttee, Min. of Technology, 1968; Econ. Develt Cttee for Electronics Industry, NEDO, 1971-76. *Address:* Cobbers, Forest Row, East Sussex. *T:* Forest Row 2009. *Clubs:* Royal Automobile; Toronto (Toronto).

WRIGHT, Sewall; Professor Emeritus of Genetics, University of Wisconsin, since 1960; *b* 21 Dec. 1889; *s* of Philip Green Wright and Elizabeth Quincy Sewall; *m* 1921, Louise Lane Williams; two *s* one *d. Educ:* Lombard Coll.; University of Illinois; Harvard Univ. BS Lombard Coll., 1911; MS Illinois, 1912; ScD Harvard, 1915. Senior Animal Husbandman, US Dept of Agriculture, 1915-25; University of Chicago: Assoc. Professor of Zoology, 1926-29; Professor of Zoology, 1930-37; Ernest D. Burton Distinguished Service Professor, 1937-54; Leon J. Cole Professor of Genetics, University of Wisconsin, 1955-60; Hitchcock Professor, University of California, 1943; Fulbright Professor, University of Edinburgh, 1949-50. Hon. Member, Royal Society of Edinburgh; Foreign Member: Royal Society, London; Royal Danish Acad. of Sciences and Letters. Hon. ScD: Rochester, 1942; Yale, 1949; Harvard, 1951; Knox Coll., 1957; Western Reserve, 1958; Chicago, 1959; Illinois, 1961; Wisconsin, 1965; Hon. LLD, Michigan State, 1955. Nat. Medal of Science, 1966. *Publications:* Evolution and the Genetics of Populations, vol. 1, 1968, vol. 2, 1969, vols 3 and 4, 1977; numerous papers on genetics of characters of guinea pig, population genetics, theory of evolution and path analysis. *Recreation:* travel. *Address:* 3905 Council Crest, Madison, Wisconsin 53711, USA. *Club:* University (Madison).

WRIGHT, Shirley Edwin McEwan; industrial consultant; *b* 4 May 1915; *s* of Alfred Coningsby Wright and Elsie Derbyshire; *m* 1939, Dora Fentem; one *s* three *d. Educ:* Herbert Strutt Sch., Belper; Coll. of Technology, Manchester; Univ. of Sheffield. BEng, CEng, FIMechE. College Apprentice, Metropolitan Vickers, Manchester, 1936; joined MV Plant Engrg, 1937; joined ICI Explosives Div., 1938; Asst Chief Engr, ICI Nobel Div., 1955; Dir, Irvine Harbour Bd, 1956; Engrg Man., 1960 and Mem. Ayrshire Rivers Bd, 1962; Engrg and Techn Dir, ICI Nobel Div., 1965; Pres., Philippine Explosives Corp., 1970; Chief Exec., Livingston Develt Corp., 1972-77. *Publications:* Revision Engineering Codes, 1959; Ionising Radiation Hazards, 1961. *Recreations:* cricket, golf, swimming, gardening. *Address:* Hazeldene, West Kilbride, Ayrshire. *T:* West Kilbride 822659.

WRIGHT, Stanley Harris; Director: Lazard Bros & Co. Ltd, since 1972; Wilkinson Match Ltd, since 1974; *b* 9 April 1930; *er s* of John Charles Wright and Doris Wright; *m* 1st, 1957, Angela Vivien Smith (marr. diss. 1973); one *s*; 2nd, 1973, Alison Elizabeth Franks. *Educ:* Bolton Sch.; Merton Coll., Oxford (Postmaster); 1st cl. hons PPE. Asst Principal, BoT, 1952-55; 2nd Sec., UK Delegn to OEEC, Paris, 1955-57; Principal, HM Treasury, 1958-64; 1st Sec. (Financial), British Embassy, Washington, 1964-66; Asst Sec., HM Treasury, 1966-68; Lazard Bros & Co. Ltd, 1969 and 1970 (Man. Dir 1969); Under-Sec., HM Treasury, 1970-72. Mem. Layfield Cttee on Local Government Finance, 1974-76. Mem. Council, Westfield Coll., 1977-. *Recreations:* various. *Address:* 6 Holly Place, NW3. *Club:* Reform.

WRIGHT, Thomas Erskine, MA; Supernumerary Fellow, Queen's College, Oxford, since 1953; *b* 15 Sept. 1902; *s* of Rev. Thomas Wright, MA, Stirling, and Isabel Hamilton Ritchie; unmarried. *Educ:* Stirling High Sch.; Univ. of Glasgow; Balliol Coll., Oxford (Snell Exhibitioner and Hon. Scholar). 1st Class Hons in Classics, Univ. of Glasgow, 1924; Hertford and Craven Scholarships, Chancellor's Prize (Latin Prose), Ferguson Scholarship in Classics, 1925; 1st Class Hons Mods, Chancellor's Prize (Latin Verse), Ireland Scholarship, 1926; 1st Class Lit Hum, 1928. Official Fellow of the Queen's Coll., Oxford, and Praelector in Classics, 1928-48; became Tutor and Senior Tutor and held various other college offices. Professor of Humanity, Univ. of St Andrews, 1948-62, Dean of the Faculty of Arts, 1951-54; Member of the University Grants Cttee, 1954-63; Sec. and Treas., Carnegie Trust for Univs of Scotland, 1962-69. *Publications:* The Latin Contribution to a Liberal Education, 1949; contributions to Oxford Classical Dictionary, *Veterum Laudes,* Fifty Years of Classical Scholarship, and periodicals. *Address:* 10 Gladstone Place, Stirling. *T:* Stirling 2681. *Club:* Stirling and County (Stirling).

WRIGHT, Prof. William, MA; ScD; BSc, PhD, CEng, FInstCE, FInstnProdE; FIEI; FRSE; FTCD; Professor of Engineering, Trinity College, Dublin, since 1957; Director, Graduate School of Engineering Studies since 1963; Dean, Faculty of Mathematical and Engineering Sciences, since 1969; *b* 3 Dec. 1918; *s* of late Rev. James Wright, DD; *m* 1st, 1944, Mildred Anderson (*d* 1959), *d* of James Robertson, MA; two *s* one *d*; 2nd, Barbara Robinson, MA, PhD, LLB, FTCD, Chevalier de l'Ordre National du Mérite, *d* of W. Edward Robinson; one *s. Educ:* Inverness Royal Academy; George Watson's Coll.; Glasgow Univ. Civil Engineer with LMSR and Min. of Transport, 1935-39. Served War, 1939-46, Captain, Royal Engineers, Middle East, Italy and Germany. Consulting Engineer, 1946-49. Glasgow Univ., 1938-39 and 1946-49 (John Oliphant Bursar) 1st Class Hons Civil Engineering. Lecturer in Civil Engineering, Aberdeen Univ., 1949-54; Head of Dept of Civil Engineering, Southampton Univ., 1954-57. Mem. Council, Instn of Production Engineers, 1964; Pres., Instn of Engineers of Ireland, 1977-78. AMICE 1949; PhD Aberdeen, 1952; MICEI 1957; MICE 1958; MA Dublin, 1960; ScD Dublin, 1963. *Publications:* papers in learned journals in Britain and America. *Recreations:* fishing, mountaineering. *Address:* Les Trembles, 35 Palmerston Road, Rathmines, Dublin 6. *T:* Dublin 978619.

WRIGHT, William Alan, CIE 1945; AFC; *b* 27 Nov. 1895; *s* of Rev. Thomas Wright and Annie Pedley; *m* 1948, Elizabeth Ada, *d* of A. E. Garrott, Launceston, Tasmania; one *s* one *d. Educ:* Oundle. 2nd Lieut, Leicestershire Regt, Jan, 1915; joined the Royal Flying Corps, Sept. 1916; Captain about July 1917 (Chevalier of Crown of Belgium and Belgian Croix de Guerre); transferred to RAF on its formation (AFC); joined Indian Civil Service, 1921, and served in Burma, acting Judge Rangoon High Court in 1939; with Government of India, War Dept, 1942-45, as Deputy Secretary, and then as officiating Joint Secretary; Deputy Director of Civil Affairs, Burma, Brig. 1945; Judge Rangoon High Court, 1945-48. *Address:* Unit 3, 71 Robinson Road, Hawthorn, Victoria 3122, Australia.

WRIGHT, William Ambrose, (Billy Wright), CBE 1959; Head of Sport and Outside Broadcasts, ATV Network Ltd, since 1966; *b* 6 Feb. 1924; *m* 1958, Joy Beverley; two *d,* and one step *s. Educ:* Madeley Secondary Modern Sch. Professional Footballer; became Captain, Wolverhampton Wanderers Football Club; played for England 105 times; Captain of England 90 times; Manager of Arsenal Football Club, 1962-66. FA Cup Winners medal; 3 Football League Winners Medals. *Publications:* Captain of England; The World's my Football Pitch. *Recreations:* golf, cricket. *Address:* 87 Lyonsdown Road, New Barnet, Herts. *T:* 01-440 3181.

WRIGHT, Prof. William David, ARCS, DIC, DSc; Professor of Applied Optics, Imperial College of Science and Technology, 1951-73; *b* 6 July 1906; *s* of late William John Wright and Grace Elizabeth Ansell; *m* 1932, Dorothy Mary Hudson; two *s. Educ:* Southgate County Sch.; Imperial Coll. Research engineer at Westinghouse Electric and Manufacturing Co., Pittsburgh, USA, 1929-30; research and consultant physicist to Electric and Musical Industries, 1930-39. Lecturer and Reader in Technical Optics Section, Imperial Coll., 1931-51. Chm. Physical Soc. Colour Group, 1941-43; Vice-Pres., Physical Soc., 1948-50; Sec., International Commn for Optics, 1953-66; Chairman: Physical Soc. Optical Group, 1956-59; Colour Group (GB), 1973-75; Pres., International Colour Assoc., 1967-69. Hon. DSc City Univ., 1971. *Publications:* The Perception of Light, 1938; The Measurement of Colour, 4th edn, 1969; Researches on Normal and Defective Colour Vision, 1946; Photometry and the Eye, 1950; The Rays are not Coloured, 1967. About 80 original scientific papers, mainly dealing with colour and vision. *Address:* 19 Chalk Lane, Cockfosters, Barnet, Herts EN4 9HJ. *T:* 01-440 4181.

WRIGHT, Most Rev. William Lockridge, DD, DCL, LLD; *b* 8 Sept. 1904; *s* of Rev. Canon J. de Pencier Wright and Lucy Lockridge; *m* 1936, Margaret Clare, BA; two *s* two *d. Educ:* Queen's University, Kingston, Ontario; Trinity College, Toronto. LTh 1927. Curate St George's, Toronto, 1926-28; Incumbent St James', Tweed, 1928-32; Curate Christ's Church Cathedral, Hamilton, 1933-36; Rector St George's Church, Toronto, 1936-40; Rector St Luke's Cathedral, Sault Ste Marie, 1940-44; Dean St Luke's Cathedral, 1941-44; Bishop of Algoma, 1944; Archbishop of Algoma and Metropolitan of Ontario, 1955-74; Acting Primate of the Anglican Church of Canada, Aug. 1970-Jan. 1971. DD (juris dig.) 1941; DCL (Bishop's Univ. Lennoxville), 1953; DD (*hc*): Wycliffe Coll., Toronto, 1956; Huron Coll., 1957; Montreal Diocesan Coll., 1958; LLD (*hc*) Laurentian University of Sudbury, Ont, 1964. *Recreations:* ice hockey, rugby football. *Address:* Box 637, Sault Ste Marie, Ontario, Canada.

WRIGHTSON, Sir John (Garmondsway), 3rd Bt, *cr* 1900; TD 1948; DL; Hon. Treasurer, Smeatonian Society of Civil Engineers, since 1949; *b* 18 June 1911; *s* of 2nd Bt and Gwendolin Cotterill (*d* 1964), *d* of G. Harding Neame; *S* father, 1950; *m* 1939, Hon. Rosemary Dawson, *y d* of 1st Viscount Dawson, PC, GCVO, KCB, KCMG; one *s* three *d. Educ:* Eton. Late Major, Durham LI (TA). Served War of 1939-45, 6th Airborne Div., France and Germany (despatches). Chm., Head, Wrightson & Co., 1960-76, retired. Hon. Col, 7th Bn, The Light Infantry (V), T&AVR, 1975-. High Sheriff, Durham, 1959, DL 1960. Hon. DCL Durham, 1971. *Heir:* *s* Charles Mark Garmondsway Wrightson [*b* 18 Feb. 1951; *m* 1975, Stella

Virginia, *d* of late George Dean]. *Address:* Neasham Hall, near Darlington. *T:* Darlington 720333. *Club:* Carlton.
See also Oliver Wrightson.

WRIGHTSON, Oliver; a Recorder of the Crown Court, since 1972; *b* 28 May 1920; *y s* of Col Sir Thomas Garmondsway Wrightson, 2nd Bt, TD. *Educ:* Eton; Balliol Coll., Oxford. Called to Bar, Lincoln's Inn, 1950. *Recreations:* lawn tennis, music. *Address:* The Bridge House, Eryholme, Darlington, Yorks. *Club:* Northern Counties (Newcastle upon Tyne).
See also Sir John Wrightson, Bt.

WRIGLEY, Arthur Joseph, CBE 1965; MD (London) Gold Medal; FRCS; FRCOG; retired as Obstetric Physician, St Thomas' Hospital, London; *b* 5 May 1902; *er s* of late Canon Joseph Henry Wrigley, Clitheroe, Lancs; *m* 1930, Ann (*d* 1976), *d* of late Colonel J. W. Slater, CMG, Dunscar, Lancs; one *s* one *d. Educ:* Rossall Sch.; St Thomas' Hospital. Hon. FCOG S Africa. *Publications:* many medical. *Address:* Green Garth, Elm Grove, Alderley Edge, Cheshire SK9 7PD. *T:* Macclesfield 582194.

WRIGLEY, Dr Fred, CBE 1974; FPS; JP; Chairman: British Health-Care Export Council, since 1976; United Medical Company International, since 1977; *b* 2 Jan. 1909; *s* of Benjamin Wrigley and Mary Ellen Wrigley; *m* 1936, Catherine Margaret, *d* of Percy and Agnes M. Hogley; one *s* one *d. Educ:* Victoria Univ. of Manchester. MRCS, LRCP; DIH. FPS 1968 (for distinction in pharmacy). Dir of Clin. Res., Roche Prod. Ltd, 1945-52; Manager, CIBA Pharmaceuticals, Montreal, 1952-55; Wellcome Foundation Ltd: Gen. Sales Man., then various posts (sales and associated cos overseas), 1955-67; Dep. Chm., 1967-74; Dir, 1957-74; Chm., Wellcome (France), 1974; Pres., Wellcome Italia and other overseas cos, 1974; Chm., Calmic Ltd, 1960-74. Consultant Adviser, Commercial Policy and Exports, to Sec. of State for Health and Social Security, 1974-77. Adjunct Prof. of Econs, East Carolina Univ., NC, 1972-, Vis. Prof. of Internat. Business, 1973-. Assoc. of British Pharm. Industry: Mem. Council, 1958-60; Mem., Bd of Management, 1971-73; Chm., Scientific and Technical Cttee, 1972-73. Pres., Hunterian Soc., 1972-73 (Hon. Fellow 1973). Chm., Mid-Herts Hosp. Man. Cttee, 1964-68. Dir, British Exec. Service Overseas, 1972-75. Member: NW Metrop. Reg. Hosp. Bd, 1968-74; Med. Sch. Council, St Mary's Hosp., 1971-74; Council, Pharm. Soc. of GB, 1970-72. Governor: UCH, 1966-74; Marsden Hosp., 1974-75; Inveresk Res. Internat., 1974-77. Liveryman, Soc. of Apothecaries. Vice-Pres., Herts Scout Council (formerly Asst County Comr). First Hon. Mem., Pharm. Soc. of Nigeria, 1969; first Hon. Citizen, Greenville, NC, 1973. JP Welwyn Bench, Herts, 1968. *Publications:* medico-scientific in BMJ and Lancet. *Recreations:* fishing, cooking. *Address:* 2 Sherrards Park Road, Welwyn Garden City, Herts AL8 7JP. *T:* Welwyn Garden 22626. *Clubs:* Farmers', MCC.

WRIGLEY, Air Vice-Marshal Henry Bertram, CB 1962; CBE 1956; DL; Senior Technical Staff Officer, Royal Air Force Fighter Command, 1960-64, retired; *b* 24 Nov. 1909; *s* of Frederick William Wrigley and Anne Jeffreys, Seascale, Cumberland; *m* 1935, Audrey, *d* of C. S. Boryer, Portsmouth; one *d. Educ:* Whitehaven Grammar Sch.; RAF Coll., Cranwell. 33 Squadron, 1930; HMS Glorious 1931; HMS Eagle, 1933; long Signals Course, 1934; various signals appointments until 1937; RAF Signals Officer, HMS Glorious, 1938; served War of 1939-45, X Force, Norway, 1940; Fighter Command, 1940-43; HQ South East Asia, 1943-46; RAF Staff Coll., 1946; comd Northern Signals Area, 1946-50; jssc 1950; Inspector, Radio Services, 1950-52; Chief Signals Officer, 2nd TAF, 1952-54; Director of: Signals (I), Air Ministry, 1954-57; Guided Weapons (Air), Min. of Aviation, 1957-60. DL, Hertfordshire, 1966. *Recreation:* gardening. *Address:* Boonwood, Turpin's Chase, Oaklands Rise, Welwyn, Herts. *T:* Welwyn 5231. *Club:* Royal Air Force.

WRIGLEY, Mrs H. L.; *see* Baillie, Isobel.

WRIGLEY, Prof. Jack, CBE 1977; Professor of Education, University of Reading, since 1967; *b* 8 March 1923; *s* of Harry and Ethel Wrigley; *m* 1946, Edith Baron; two *s. Educ:* Oldham High Sch.; Manchester Univ. BSc, MEd (Manch.); PhD ((Queen's, Belfast). Asst Mathematics Teacher: Stretford Grammar Sch., 1946-47; Chadderton Grammar Sch., 1948-50; Research Asst, Manchester Univ., 1950-51; Lectr in Educn: Queen's Univ., Belfast, 1951-57; Univ. of London Inst. of Educn, 1957-62; Research Adviser, Curriculum Study Gp in Min. of Educn, 1962-63; Prof. of Educn, Univ. of Southampton, 1963-67; Dir of Studies, Schools Council, 1967-75. Member: Bullock Cttee on Teaching of Reading and other uses of English, 1972-74; Educational Research Board, SRC, 1975-; SSRC, 1976,

Chm. Educnl Res. Bd, 1976. *Publications:* (ed) The Dissemination of Curriculum Development, 1976; contrib. learned jls. *Recreations:* chess (Ulster Chess Champion, 1957), theatre, foreign travel. *Address:* 68 Grosvenor Road, Caversham, Reading, Berks RG4 0ES. *T:* Reading 471812.

WRIGLEY, Michael Harold, OBE 1971; HM Diplomatic Service; retired; *b* 30 July 1924; *e s* of Edward Whittaker Wrigley and Audrey Margaret Wrigley; *m* 1950, Anne Phillida Brewis; two *s* two *d. Educ:* Harrow; Worcester Coll., Oxford. Served War of 1939-45: Rifle Brigade, 1943-47. HM Diplomatic Service, 1950; served HM Embassies: Brussels, 1952-54; Bangkok, 1956-59; Office of Commissioner-Gen. for South-East Asia, Singapore, 1959-60; HM Embassy, Bangkok (again), 1961-64 and 1966-71; Counsellor, Kuala Lumpur, 1971-74; Counsellor, FCO, 1974-76. *Recreations:* shooting, racing. *Address:* Ganton Hall, Scarborough, N Yorks. *T:* Sherburn 223. *Clubs:* Turf; Royal Bangkok Sports (Bangkok).

WRISBERG, Lt-Gen. Sir (Frederick) George, KBE 1949 (CBE 1942); CB 1945; late Royal Regiment of Artillery; *b* 3 Jan. 1895; *s* of late Captain F. W. Wrisberg, Royal Artillery; *m* 1918, Margaret, *d* of late C. Ward, Swadlincote, Derbyshire; one *d.* 2nd Lieut, RA, 1916; served European War, 1916-17, in France and Belgium (wounded); Experimental Officer, Air Defence Experimental Establishment, 1929-33; Staff Captain, War Office, 1934-36; Deputy Assistant Director of Artillery, War Office, 1936-38; Assistant Director, 1938-40; Director Weapons Production, 1940-43; Director-General of Weapons and Instrument Production, Ministry of Supply, 1943-46; Controller of Supplies, Ministry of Supply, 1946-49; retired 1949. Colonel Commandant RA, 1950-60; Chairman, Linotype and Machinery Ltd, 1960-66. Comdr Legion of Merit, USA, 1947. *Address:* 5 Moorlands, Wilderness Road, Chislehurst, Kent. *T:* 01-467 1245. *Clubs:* Naval and Military; Chislehurst Golf.

WRIXON-BECHER, Major Sir William F.; *see* Becher.

WROTTESLEY, family name of **Baron Wrottesley.**

WROTTESLEY, 6th Baron *cr* 1838; **Clifton Hugh Lancelot de Verdon Wrottesley;** Bt 1642; *b* 10 Aug. 1968; *s* of Hon. Richard Francis Gerard Wrottesley (*d* 1970) (2nd *s* of 5th Baron) and of Georgina Anne, *er d* of Lt-Col Peter Thomas Clifton, *qv*; S grandfather, 1977. *Heir:* uncle Hon. Mark Wrottesley, *b* 21 June 1951. *Address:* Dummer House, Basingstoke, Hants.

WYATT, Vice-Admiral Sir (Arthur) Guy (Norris), KBE 1949; CB 1948; Retired; *b* 8 March 1893; *s* of late Arthur Norris Wyatt and May (*née* Reynolds); *m* 1922, Anne Christine, *d* of late Hon. James Hogue, Sydney, NSW; no *c. Educ:* Stubbington; RN Colleges, Osborne and Dartmouth. Joined Naval College, Osborne, 1906; Lieut., 1915; Comdr, 1929; Capt, 1936; Rear-Adm., 1945; Vice-Adm., 1948. Served European War, 1914-18; commanded HMTBD Beagle, 1918. Joined Royal Naval Surveying Service, 1918; surveys in Home Waters, Australia, New Zealand, East Africa, West Indies, Mediterranean, East Indies, Persian Gulf and Labrador. Served War of 1939-45, Admiralty, and in command of HMS Challenger, South East Asia and SW Pacific (despatches); Hydrographer of the Navy, 1945-50; retired list, 1948. *Recreations:* yacht cruising, fishing. *Address:* Holly Tree Orchard, Woodbridge, Tasmania 7162, Australia. *Clubs:* Royal Cruising; Tasmanian, Royal Yacht of Tasmania (Hobart).

WYATT, Arthur Hope; HM Diplomatic Service; Diplomatic Service Inspector, since 1977; *b* 12 Oct. 1929; *s* of Frank and Maggie Wyatt, Anderton, Lancs; *m* 1957, Barbara Yvonne, *d* of Major J. P. Flynn, late Indian Army; two *d. Educ:* Bolton School. Army, 1947-50; FO, 1950-52; 3rd Sec., Ankara, 1952-56; 2nd Sec., Phnom Penh, 1956-58; 2nd Sec., Ankara, 1958-61; FO, 1962-66; 1st Sec., Bonn, 1966-70; FCO, 1970-72; Counsellor and Head of Chancery, Lagos, 1972-75; Dep. High Comr, Valletta, 1975-76. *Recreations:* golf, football, bridge, stamp collecting. *Address:* c/o Foreign and Commonwealth Office, SW1A 2AH. *T:* 01-839 7010.

WYATT, David Joseph, CBE 1977; HM Diplomatic Service; Counsellor and Head of Chancery, Stockholm, since 1976; *b* 12 Aug. 1931; *s* of late Frederick Wyatt and of Lena (*née* Parr); *m* 1957, Annemarie Angst; two *s* one *d. Educ:* Leigh Grammar Sch. National Service, RAF, 1950-52. Entered Foreign Service, 1949; Berne, 1954; FO, 1957-61; Second Sec., Vienna, 1961; First Sec., Canberra, 1965; FCO, 1969-71; First Sec., Ottawa, 1971; Counsellor, 1974; seconded Northern Ireland Office, Belfast, 1974-76. *Address:* c/o Foreign and Commonwealth Office, SW1; British Embassy, Stockholm, Sweden.

WYATT, Gavin Edward, CMG 1965; Director, Projects Department, Europe, Middle East and North Africa Region, International Bank for Reconstruction and Development, 1975-76; *b* 12 Jan. 1914; *s* of Edward A. Wyatt and Blanche M. Muller; *m* 1950, Mary Mackinnon, *d* of John Macdonald, Oban; one *s* one *d*. *Educ:* Newton Abbot Grammar Sch. CEng, FIEE 1951; FIMechE 1962. Engineer and Manager, East African Power & Lighting Co. Ltd, Tanganyika and Kenya, 1939-57; Chief Exec. Officer and General Manager, Electricity Corp. of Nigeria, 1957-62; Man. Director, East Africa Power & Lighting Co. Ltd, 1962-64; World Bank: Engineer, 1965; Division Chief, 1969; Asst Dir, 1974; Dir, 1975. *Recreations:* gardening, sailing, farming. *Address:* Holne Bridge Lodge, Ashburton, South Devon.

WYATT, Vice-Admiral Sir Guy; *see* Wyatt, Vice-Admiral Sir A. G. N.

WYATT, Woodrow Lyle; Chairman, Horserace Totalisator Board, since 1976; *b* 4 July 1918; *y s* of late Robert Harvey Lyle Wyatt and Ethel Morgan; *m* 1957, Lady Moorea Hastings (marr. diss., 1966), *e d* of 15th Earl of Huntingdon, *q v*; one *s*; *m* 1966, Veronica, *widow* of Dr Laszlo Banszky; one *d*. *Educ:* Eastbourne Coll.; Worcester Coll., Oxford, MA. Served throughout War of 1939-45 (despatches for Normandy); Major, 1944. Founder and Editor, English Story, 1940-50; Editorial Staff, New Statesman and Nation, 1947-48; Weekly Columnist: Reynolds News, 1949-61; Daily Mirror, 1965-73; Sunday Mirror, 1973-. Began Panorama with Richard Dimbleby, 1955; under contract BBC TV, 1955-59; introduced non-heat-set web offset colour printing to England, 1962. MP (Lab), Aston Div. of Birmingham, 1945-55, Bosworth Div. of Leicester, 1959-70; Member of Parly Delegn to India, 1946; Personal Asst to Sir Stafford Cripps on Cabinet Mission to India, 1946; Parly Under-Sec. of State, and Financial Sec., War Office, May-Oct. 1951. Contested (Lab) Grantham Div. of Lincolnshire, 1955. Mem. Council, Zoological Soc. of London, 1968-71, 1973-77. *Publications:* The Jews at Home, 1950; Southwards from China, 1952; Into the Dangerous World, 1952; The Peril in Our Midst, 1956; Distinguished for Talent, 1958; Turn Again, Westminster, 1973; The Exploits of Mr Saucy Squirrel, 1976; The Further Exploits of Mr Saucy Squirrel, 1977; What's Left of the Labour Party?, 1977. *Address:* 19 Cavendish Avenue, NW8. *T:* 01-286 9020; Conock Old Manor, Devizes, Wilts. *T:* Chirton 214.

WYBURN, Prof. George McCreath; Regius Professor of Anatomy, Glasgow University, 1948-72; *b* 11 March 1903; *s* of Robert Wyburn, Solicitor; *m* 1935, Jean Sharp; four *s* two *d*. *Educ:* High Sch., Glasgow; University of Glasgow. Graduated from Glasgow Univ., 1925; appointed to staff of Anatomy Dept, University of Glasgow, 1930; Senior Lecturer, Anatomy Dept, 1935. *Publications:* scientific publications in Journal of Anatomy, Proc. and Trans. of Royal Society of Edinburgh, Journal of Endocrinology, Journal of Surgery, Journal of Obstetrics and Gynecology, etc. *Address:* 7 Woodvale Avenue, Bearsden, Glasgow G61 2JS. *Club:* Glasgow Golf.

WYETH, Andrew N.; artist; landscape painter; *b* 12 July 1917; *s* of Newell and Caroline Wyeth; *m* 1940, Betsy Merle James; two *s*. *Educ:* privately. First one man exhibn, William Macbeth Gall., NY, 1937; subsequent exhibitions include: Doll & Richards, Boston, 1938, 1940, 1942, 1944; Cornell Univ., 1938; Macbeth Gall., 1938, 1941, 1943, 1945; Art Inst. of Chicago, 1941; Museum of Modern Art, NYC, 1943; Dunn Internat. Exhibn, London, 1963; one man exhibns: M. Knoedler and Co., NYC, 1953, 1958; MIT, Cambridge, 1966; The White House, Washington DC, 1970; Tokyo, 1974; retrospective, Metropolitan Museum, NY, 1976. Member: Nat. Inst. of Arts and Letters (Gold Medal, 1965); Amer. Acad. of Arts and Sciences; Amer. Acad. of Arts and Letters (Medal of Merit, 1947); Académie des Beaux-Arts, 1977. Presidential Medal of Freedom, 1963; Einstein Award, 1967. Hon. AFD: Colby Coll., Maine, 1954; Harvard, 1955; Dickinson, 1958; Swarthmore, 1958; Nasson Coll., Maine, 1963; Temple Univ., 1963; Maryland, 1964; Delaware, 1964; Northwestern Univ., 1964; Hon. LHD Tufts, 1963. *Address:* Chadds Ford, Pa 19317, USA.

WYETH, Paul James Logan, RP 1958; RBA 1957; ARCA 1947; portrait painter and mural painter; *b* 1 Feb. 1920; *s* of Bob Logan (stage name), comedian; *m* 1948, Tina Vasilakon, Greece; two *d*. *Educ:* Kilburn Polytechnic. Willesden School of Art, 1931-33; Hammersmith School of Arts, 1933-39; RCA, 1939-40 and 1946-47. *Publications:* How to Paint in Oil Colours, 1955; How to Paint in Water-Colours, 1958. *Recreations:* reading, swimming. *Address:* 19 Burstock Road, Putney, SW15. *T:* 01-788 3284. *Club:* Chelsea Arts.

WYETH, Rex; solicitor; a Recorder of the Crown Court, since 1972; *b* 11 Aug. 1914; *s* of William James and Edith Emily Wyeth; *m* 1st, 1939, Leah Nichols (*d* 1943); 2nd, 1947, Gabriele Bopst (*d* 1969); one *d*. *Educ:* Tolworth Council Sch.; Surbiton County Sch. Solicitor's Clerk, 1931; qual. Solicitor, 1939; served with RAOC, 1940-46; admitted Solicitor, 1946; in private practice thereafter. *Recreations:* indifferent golf and worse bridge. *Address:* 8 Stone Buildings, Lincoln's Inn, WC2A 3TA. *T:* 01-242 7588. *Club:* Golfers'.

WYFOLD, 3rd Baron, *cr* 1919, of Accrington, **Hermon Robert Fleming Hermon-Hodge;** 3rd Bt, *cr* 1902; Director, Robert Fleming Holdings, and other companies; *b* 26 June 1915; *s* of 2nd Baron and Dorothy (*d* 1976), *e d* of late Robert Fleming, Joyce Grove, Oxford; *S* father, 1942. *Educ:* Eton; Le Rosey, Switzerland. Captain, Grenadier Guards (RARO), 1939-65. *Heir:* none. *Address:* Sarsden House, Churchill, Oxfordshire. *T:* Kingham 226. *Clubs:* Carlton, Pratt's; Metropolitan (New York).

WYKEHAM, Air Marshal Sir Peter, KCB 1965 (CB 1961); DSO 1943 and Bar 1944; OBE 1949; DFC 1940 and Bar 1941; AFC 1951; technical consultant, since 1969; *b* 13 Sept. 1915; *s* of Guy Vane and Audrey Irene Wykeham-Barnes; family changed name by Deed Poll, 1955, from Wykeham-Barnes to Wykeham; *m* 1949, Barbara, *d* of J. B. Priestley, *q v*; two *s* one *d*. *Educ:* RAF Halton. Commissioned, 1937; served with fighter sqns, 1937-43 (commanded Nos 73, 257 and 23 sqns); commanded fighter sectors and wings, 1943-45; Air Ministry, 1946-48; Test Pilot, 1948-51; seconded to US Air Force, Korea, 1950; commanded fighter stations, 1951-53; NATO, 1953-56; staff appointments, 1956-59; AOC No 38 Gp, RAF, 1960-62; Dir, Jt Warfare Staff, Min. of Defence, Aug. 1962-64. Comdr, FEAF, 1964-66; Dep. Chief of Air Staff, 1967-69. FRAeS 1968; Fellow, Guild of Air Pilots and Air Navigators; FBIM. Chevalier, Order of Dannebrog, 1945; US Air Medal, 1950. *Publications:* Fighter Command, 1960; Santos-Dumont, 1962. *Recreations:* sailing, writing. *Address:* South Bank, 112 Lower Ham Road, Kingston-on-Thames, Surrey. *Club:* Royal Automobile.

WYKES, James Cochrane, MA (Cantab); Television Adviser, Inner London Education Authority, since 1975; *b* 19 Oct. 1913; *m* 1938, Cecile Winifred Graham, *e d* of J. Graham Rankin; one *s* one *d*. *Educ:* Oundle Sch.; Clare Coll., Cambridge (Open Exhibn in Classics). 1st Class Hons, Classical Tripos, Part I, 1934; 2nd Class Hons Classical Tripos, Part II, 1935; Asst Master, Loretto Sch., 1935-51; Headmaster, St Bees Sch., 1951-63; Head of Educational Broadcasting, ATV Network, 1963-66; Dir of Television, ILEA, 1966-75. Chm., Nat. Educnl Closed Circuit Television Assoc., 1970-72. Served War of 1939-45: Black Watch (RHR), 1940-44. *Publication:* Caesar at Alexandria, 1951. *Recreations:* athletic sports, fishing, ornithology, music. *Address:* Cluanie, Crowsley Road, Shiplake-on-Thames, Oxon. *T:* Wargrave 3166. *Clubs:* Lansdowne, MCC.

WYLDBORE-SMITH, Maj.-Gen. Francis Brian, CB 1965; DSO 1943; OBE 1944; General Officer Commanding, 44th Division (TA) and Home Counties District, 1965-68; *b* 10 July 1913; *s* of Rev. W. R. Wyldbore-Smith and Mrs D. Wyldbore-Smith; *m* 1944, Hon. Molly Angela Cayzer, *d* of 1st Baron Rotherwick; one *s* four *d*. *Educ:* Wellington Coll.; RMA, Woolwich. Served Middle East, Italy, France and Germany, 1941-45; Military Adviser to CIGS, 1947-49; GSO1, 7 Armoured Div., 1951-53; Comd 15/19 King's Royal Hussars, 1954-56; IDC 1959; BGS Combat Development, 1959-62; Chief of Staff to Commander-in-Chief, Far East Command, 1962-64. Col, 15/19 Hussars, 1970-. Dir, Cons. Bd of Finance. *Recreations:* hunting, shooting. *Address:* Grantham House, Grantham, Lincs. *T:* Grantham 4705. *Clubs:* Buck's, Naval and Military.

WYLER, William; Legion of Merit (USA), 1945; Legion of Honour (France), 1948; Cavaliere Ufficiale (Italy); Film Producer and Director; *b* Mulhouse, Alsace, 1 July 1902; *s* of Leopold Wyler (Swiss) and Melanie Auerbach (German; Non-Arian); *m* 1st, 1934, Margaret Sullavan (marr. diss., 1936), actress; 2nd, 1938, Margaret Tallichet; one *s* three *d* (one *s* decd). *Educ:* Mulhouse, Alsace; Lausanne; Paris. Directed films since 1926; successes include: Counsellor-at-Law, 1934; The Good Fairy, 1935; These Three, 1936; Dodsworth, 1936; Dead End, 1937; Jezebel, 1937; The Letter, 1938; Wuthering Heights, 1939; The Little Foxes, 1940; Mrs Miniver, 1941 (Academy Award for directing and Best Picture); The Best Years of our Lives, 1946 (Acad. award for directing and Best Picture); The Heiress, 1948; Detective Story, 1951; Carrie, 1952; Roman Holiday, 1953; The Desperate House, 1955; Friendly Persuasion, 1956 (Golden Palm Leaf, Cannes, 1957); The Big Country, 1957; Ben Hur, 1959 (Academy Award for Directing and Best Picture); The Children's Hour, 1962; The Collector,

1965; How to Steal a Million, 1966; Funny Girl, 1968; The Liberation of Lord Byron Jones, 1970. Served 1942-45 as Major and Lt-Col in USAF, prod. and directed documentary films: The Memphis Belle, Thunderbolt; Air Medal (USA), 1943. *Recreations:* tennis, ski-ing. *Address:* 1121 Summit Drive, Beverly Hills, Calif 90210, USA.

WYLES, Lilian Mary Elizabeth, BEM 1949; retired (but lectures and broadcasts on police subjects and child welfare); *b* Bourne, Lincs, 1895; *d* of Joseph Wyles, brewer, and Julia Grylls Wyles, Bourne House, Bourne. *Educ:* Thanet Hall, Margate; privately. Joined Metropolitan Police, 1919; Sergeant, 1919; Inspector, 1922; transferred from Uniform Branch to CID, 1922; Chief Inspector, 1932. Organised Women's Branch of CID. Retired, 1949. *Publication:* A Woman at Scotland Yard (autobiography), 1952. *Recreations:* sailing, embroidery, cooking.

WYLIE, Rt. Hon. Lord; Norman Russell Wylie, PC 1970; VRD 1961; a Senator of the College of Justice in Scotland, since 1974; *b* 26 Oct. 1923; *o s* of late William Galloway Wylie and late Mrs Nellie Smart Wylie (*née* Russell), Elderslie, Renfrewshire; *m* 1963, Gillian Mary, *yr d* of late Dr R. E. Verney, Edinburgh; three *s. Educ:* Paisley Grammar Sch.; St Edmund Hall, Oxford (Hon. Fellow, 1975); Univs of Glasgow and Edinburgh. BA (Oxon) 1948; LLB (Glasgow) 1951. Admitted to Faculty of Advocates, 1952; QC (Scotland) 1964. Appointed Counsel to Air Ministry in Scotland, 1956; Advocate-Depute, 1959; Solicitor-General for Scotland, April-Oct. 1964. MP (C) Pentlands Div., Edinburgh, Oct. 1964-Feb. 1974; Lord Advocate, 1970-74. Served in Fleet Air Arm, 1942-46; subseq. RNR; Lt-Comdr, 1954. *Recreations:* shooting, sailing. *Address:* 30 Lauder Road, Edinburgh 9. *T:* 031-667 8377. *Clubs:* New (Edinburgh); Royal Highland Yacht.

WYLIE, Sir Campbell, Kt 1963; ED; QC; *b* NZ, 14 May 1905; *m* 1933, Leita Caroline Clark; no *c. Educ:* Auckland Grammar Sch.; Univ. of New Zealand. LLM 1st Class hons (Univ. of New Zealand), 1928; Barrister and Solicitor (New Zealand), 1928; Barrister-at-law, Inner Temple, 1950. Was in private practice, New Zealand, until 1940. War service, 1940-46 (despatches). Crown Counsel, Malaya, 1946; Senior Federal Counsel, 1950; Attorney-General: Barbados, 1951; British Guiana, 1955; The West Indies, 1956; Federal Justice, Supreme Court of The West Indies, 1959-62; Chief Justice, Unified Judiciary of Sarawak, N Borneo and Brunei, 1962-63; Chief Justice, High Court in Borneo, 1963-66; Law Revision Commissioner, Tonga, 1966-67; Chief Justice, Seychelles, 1967-69; Comr for Law Revision and Reform, Seychelles, 1970-71. QC 1952 (Barbados), 1955 (British Guiana). *Address:* 11 Boomerang Crescent, Isle of Sorrento, Surfers Paradise, Queensland 4217, Australia. *T:* 385532. *Club:* Union (Malta).

WYLIE, Rt. Hon. Norman Russell; *see* Wylie, Rt Hon. Lord.

WYLIE, William Derek, FRCP, FRCS, FFARCS; Senior Consultant Anaesthetist, St Thomas' Hospital, SE1, since 1966; Consultant Anaesthetist, The Royal Masonic Hospital, since 1959; Dean, St Thomas's Hospital Medical School, since 1974; Adviser in Anaesthetics to the Health Service Commissioner, since 1974; *b* 24 Oct. 1918; *s* of Edward and Mabel Wylie, Huddersfield; *m* 1945, Margaret Helen, 2nd *d* of F. W. Toms, Jersey, CI (formerly Dep. Inspector-Gen., Western Range, Indian Police); two *s* two *d. Educ:* Uppingham Sch.; Gonville and Caius Coll., Cambridge (MA; MB, BChir); St Thomas's Hosp. Med. Sch. MRCP 1945, FFARCS 1953, FRCP 1967, FRCS 1972. Resident posts at St Thomas' Hosp., 1943-45. Served RAFVR, 1945-47, Wing Comdr. Apptd Hon. Staff, St Thomas' Hosp., 1946; Consultant, 1948; Cons. Anaesthetist, The National Hosp. for Nervous Diseases, 1950-67. Examiner: FFARCS, 1959-72; FFARCSI, 1966-. Mem., Bd of Faculty of Anaesthetists, RCS, 1968-70 (Dean, 1967-69; Vice-Dean, 1965-66; Bernard Johnson Adviser in Postgraduate Studies, 1959-67); Mem. Council, RCS, 1967-69; FRSM (Mem. Council, 1962-72; Hon. Treas., 1964-70; Pres., Section of Anaesthetics, 1963); Mem., Bd of Governors, St Thomas' Hosp., 1969-74; elected Mem. Council, Med. Defence Union (Vice-Pres., 1962-). Jenny Hartmann Lectr, Basle Univ., 1961; Clover Lectr and Medallist, RCS(Eng), 1974. Hon. Citizen of Dallas, USA, 1963; Hon. FFARCSI, 1971. *Publications:* The Practical Management of Pain in Labour, 1953; A Practice of Anaesthesia, 3rd edn, 1972 (jtly with Dr H. C. Churchill-Davidson); papers in specialist and gen. med. jls. *Recreations:* reading, travel, philately. *Address:* 28 Copse Hill, Wimbledon, SW20 0HG. *T:* 01-946 5652. *Club:* Royal Automobile.

WYLLIE, Robert Lyon, CBE 1960; DL; JP; FCA; *b* 4 March 1897; *s* of Rev. Robert Howie Wyllie, MA, Dundee; *m* 1924, Anne, *d* of Thomas Rutherford, Harrington, Cumberland; two

d. Educ: Hermitage Sch., Helensburgh; Queen's Park Sch., Glasgow. Served European War, 1914-18, with Lothians and Border Horse (France). Chartered Accountant, 1920; FCA 1949. Dir, Ashley Accessories Ltd; Life Vice-President, Cumberland Development Council Ltd. Formerly Chairman: W Cumberland Industrial Develt Co. Ltd; W Cumberland Silk Mills Ltd; Cumberland Develt Council Ltd; Whitehaven & Dist Disablement Advisory Cttee, and Youth Employment Cttee; Vice-Chm. W Cumberland Hosp. Management Cttee; Hon. Treas., NW Div., YMCA. JP 1951; DL 1957, Cumbria, formerly Cumberland. OStJ 1976. *Recreation:* fishing. *Address:* The Cottage, Papcastle, Cockermouth, Cumbria. *T:* Cockermouth 823292.

WYMAN, John Bernard, MBE 1945; FFARCS; Consultant Anaesthetist, Westminster Hospital, since 1948; Dean, Westminster Medical School, since 1964 (Sub-Dean, 1959-64); *b* 24 May 1916; *s* of Louis Wyman and Bertha Wyman; *m* 1948, Joan Dorothea Beighton; three *s* one *d. Educ:* Davenant Foundn Sch., London; King's Coll., London; Westminster Med. Sch. MRCS, LRCP 1941; DA 1945; FFARCS 1953. Military Service, 1942-46: Major RAMC; N Africa, Italy and India. Cons. Anaesthetist, Woolwich War Memorial Hospital Hosp., 1946-64; formerly Hon. Anaesthetist, Italian Hosp. Hunterian Prof., RCS, 1953. Member: Bd of Governors, Westminster Hosp., 1959-74; Sch. Council, Westminster Med. Sch., 1959-; Croydon AHA, 1974-75; Kensington and Chelsea and Westminster AHA, 1975-. *Publications:* chapters in med. text books and papers in gen. and specialist jls on anaesthesia and med. educn. *Recreation:* gardening. *Address:* Chilling Street Cottage, Sharpthorne, Sussex. *T:* Sharpthorne 810281. *Club:* Savage.

WYN-HARRIS, Sir Percy, KCMG 1952 (CMG 1949); MBE 1941; MA (Cantab); *b* 24 Aug. 1903; *e s* of late Percy Martin Harris, JP, and Catherine Mary Davies; *m* 1st, 1932, Mary M. Macdonald (*d* 1976), *d* of late Ranald Macdonald, CBE, Christchurch, New Zealand; one *s*; 2nd, 1976, Mrs Julie Gunning-Scheltema, *widow* of late M. F. Gunning, MRINA. *Educ:* Gresham's Sch.; Caius Coll., Cambridge. Colonial Administrative Service, 1926; District Officer, Kenya, 1926-45; Settlement Officer (Kikuyu Land Claims), 1939-40; District Commissioner, Nyeri, 1941-43; Labour Liaison Officer, Kenya, 1943; Labour Comr, Kenya, 1944-46. Provincial Comr, Kenya, 1945; Chief Native Comr and Mem. for African Affairs on Executive Council, Kenya, 1947-49; Governor and C-in-C of the Gambia, 1949-58; Mem. Devlin Commn of Enquiry into disturbances in Nyasaland, 1959; Administrator, Northern Cameroons, for period of plebiscite under UN supervision, 1960-61; toured Canada, Australia, and New Zealand as Special Representative Overseas of the Duke of Edinburgh's Award, 1962-63. With E. E. Shipton, 2nd ascent of Mt Kenya, 1929; first visit to North Island, Lake Rudolf, 1931; Mem. of Mt Everest expedition, 1933, and took part in first assault with L. R. Wager, reaching height of approx. 28,000 ft; mem. Mt Everest Expedition, 1936. Circumnavigation of the world, 1962-69, in 12 ton Gunning Grundel Sloop. KStJ 1950. *Address:* Little Hawsted, Steep, Petersfield, Hants. *T:* Petersfield 3435. *Clubs:* Alpine, East India, Sports and Public Schools, Little Ship.

WYNDHAM, family name of **Baron Egremont and Leconfield.**

WYNDHAM, Sir Harold (Stanley), Kt 1969; CBE 1961; retired from Department of Education, New South Wales; *b* Forbes, NSW, Australia, 27 June 1903; *s* of late Stanley Charles Wyndham; *m* 1936, Beatrice Margaret, *d* of Rt. Rev. A. C. Grieve; three *s. Educ:* Fort Street Boys' High Sch.; Univ. of Sydney (MA Hons, Cl. I); Stanford Univ. (EdD). Lectr, Sydney Teachers' Coll., 1925-27 and 1934; Teacher, NSW Dept of Educn, 1928-32; Carnegie Fellow, Stanford, 1932-33; Head of Research and Guidance, NSW Dept of Educn, 1935-40; Inspector of Schools, 1940-41. Flt Lt (A&SD Br.), RAAF, 1942-43; Commonwealth Dept of Post-War Reconstruction, 1944-46 (Leader, Aust. Delegn, Constituent Meeting for UNESCO, London, 1945); Sec., NSW Dept of Educn, 1948-51; Dep. Dir-Gen. of Educn, 1951-52; Dir-Gen. and Permanent Head, Dept of Education, 1952-68, Macquarie Univ., Professorial Fellow, 1969-75, Hon. Professorial Fellow, 1976-. Mem. Aust. Delegn to: UNESCO, 1958 and 1966; Commonwealth Educn Conf., Oxford, 1959. Vis. Fellow to Canada, 1966; Fellow, Royal Inst. of Public Admin.; Fellow and Past-Pres., Aust. Coll. of Educn; Mem., Nat. Library Council of Australia, 1962-73; Chm., Soldiers' Children Educn Bd, Repatriation Dept, 1964-. *Publications:* Class Grouping in the Primary School, 1932; Ability Grouping, 1934; articles in a number of professional jls. *Recreations:* music, gardening. *Address:* 3 Amarna Parade, Roseville, NSW 2069, Australia. *T:* 406-4129. *Club:* University (Sydney).

WYNDHAM-QUIN, family name of **Earl of Dunraven**.

WYNDHAM-QUIN, Captain Hon. Valentine Maurice; RN (retired); *b* 1890; *yr s* of 5th Earl of Dunraven, CB, DSO; *u* and *Heir-Pres.* of 7th Earl of Dunraven and Mount-Earl, *qv*; *m* 1919, Marjorie Elizabeth (*d* 1969), *d* of late Rt Hon. E. G. Pretyman; three *d. Educ:* Eton; HMS Britannia. Served European War, 1914-19, in command of destroyers of the Patrol Flotillas, Grand Fleet and Harwich Force; retired 1934; returned to Active Service, 1939-44, in command of HM Ships in Home Waters, the South Atlantic and Mediterranean Fleet (despatches 4 times); Naval Attaché, Buenos Aires, 1944-47; retired 1948. Chairman, Royal National Life Boat Institution, 1964-68. *Recreations:* hunting and shooting. *Address:* 66 Cadogan Square, SW1. *T:* 01-584 1364. *Clubs:* White's; Royal Yacht Squadron (Cowes).
See also Baron Egremont, Marquess of Salisbury.

WYNDHAM WHITE, Sir Eric, KCMG 1968; *b* 26 Jan. 1913; *s* of Henry Wyndham White and Helen White (*née* Peppiatt); *m* 1947, Tina Gibson Thayer, Worcester, Mass, USA; two *d. Educ:* Westminster City Sch.; London Sch. of Economics, Univ. of London. LLB first class hons. Member of the Bar, Middle Temple, 1938; Asst Lectr, LSE, 1938-39; Mem. British delegs. Internat. Chamber of Commerce Congresses, Berlin, 1937, Copenhagen, 1939; Min. of Economic Warfare, 1939-41; First Sec., HM Embassy, Washington, 1942-45; Economic Counsellor, HM Embassy, Paris, 1945-46; Special Asst to European Director, UNRRA, 1945; Sec.-Gen., Emergency Economic Cttee for Europe (EECE), 1946; Exec. Sec. Prep. Cttee for ITO, then Sec.-Gen., UN Conf. on Internat. Trade and Employment (London, Geneva, Havana, 1946-48); Exec. Sec., GATT, 1948-65, Dir-Gen., 1965-68. Hon. Dr *rerum publicarum*, of Sch. of Economics, Business and Public Administration, St Gall (Switzerland), 1963; Hon. Dr Laws: Univ. California, Los Angeles, 1966; Dartmouth Coll., New Hampshire, 1968. *Publications:* numerous articles and addresses in various learned jls (legal and economic) in England and abroad. *Recreations:* gardening, ski-ing, music. *Address:* Case Postale 470, 1200 Geneva 3 Rive, Switzerland. *Club:* Reform.

WYNFORD, 8th Baron, *cr* 1829; **Robert Samuel Best**; MBE 1953; DL; Lt-Col Royal Welch Fusiliers; *b* 5 Jan. 1917; *e s* of 7th Baron and Evelyn (*d* 1929), *d* of late Maj.-Gen. Sir Edward S. May, KCB, CMG; *S* father, 1943; *m* 1941, Anne Daphne Mametz, *d* of late Maj.-Gen. J. R. Minshull Ford, CB, DSO, MC; one *s* two *d. Educ:* Eton; RMC, Sandhurst. 2nd Lieut, RWF, 1937; served BEF; GHQ Home Forces; North Africa (Croix de Guerre); Egypt; Italy; wounded, 1944; Instructor, Staff College, 1945-46; War Office, 1947-49; OC Depot, RWF, 1955-57; Instructor Joint Service Staff Coll., 1957-60; RARO 1960. DL Dorset, 1970. *Heir: s* Hon. John Philip Best, *b* 23 Nov. 1950. *Address:* Wynford House, Wynford Eagle, Dorchester, Dorset DT2 0ET. *TA* and *T:* Maiden Newton 241. *Club:* Army and Navy.

WYNN, family name of **Baron Newborough**.

WYNN, Arthur Henry Ashford; Adviser on Standards, Department of Trade and Industry (formerly Ministry of Technology), 1965-71; *b* 22 Jan. 1910; *s* of late Prof. William Henry Wynn, MD, MSc; *m* 1938, Margaret Patricia Moxon; three *s* one *d. Educ:* Oundle Sch.; Trinity Coll., Cambridge (Entrance Scholar, Nat. Science and Mathematics; MA). Barrister-at-Law, Lincoln's Inn, 1939; Director of Safety in Mines Research Establishment, Ministry of Fuel and Power, 1948-55; Scientific Member of National Coal Board, 1955-65; Member: Advisory Council on Research and Development, Ministry of Power, 1955-65; Safety in Mines Research Advisory Board, 1950-65; Exec. Cttee, British Standards Institution, 1966-71; Advisory Council on Calibration and Measurement, 1967-71; Chairman: Standing Joint Cttee on Metrication, 1966-69; Adv. Cttee on Legal Units of Measurement, 1969-71. *Publications:* (with Margaret Wynn): The Protection of Maternity and Infancy in Finland, 1974; The Right of Every Child to Health Care in France, 1974; Nutrition Counselling in Canada, 1975; Prevention of Handicap of Perinatal Origin in France, 1976; Prevention of Preterm Birth, 1977. *Address:* 9 View Road, N6. *T:* 01-348 1470.

WYNN, Sir (Owen) Watkin W.; *see* Williams-Wynn.

WYNN, Terence Bryan; Editor, Liberal News, and Head of Liberal Party Organisation's Press Office, since 1977; *b* 20 Nov. 1928; *o s* of late Bernard Wynn and Elsie Wynn (*née* Manges); unmarried. *Educ:* St Cuthbert's Grammar Sch., Newcastle upon Tyne. Started as jun. reporter with Hexham Courant, Northumberland, 1945; Blyth News, 1947-48; Shields Evening News, 1948-50; Sunderland Echo, 1950-53; Reporter with Daily Sketch, 1953-58; News Editor, Tyne Tees Television, 1958, then Head of News and Current Affairs, 1960-66; Editorial Planning, BBC Television News, 1966-67; Sen. Press and Information Officer with Land Commn, 1967-71; Sen. Inf. Officer, HM Customs and Excise, 1971-72; Editor, The Universe, 1972-77. Helped to found and first Editor of Roman Catholic monthly newspaper, Northern Cross. Chm., Catholic Writers' Guild, 1967-70 (Hon. Vice-Pres., 1970); Judge for British Television News Film of the Year Awards, 1961-64; Mem. Mass Media Commn, RC Bishops' Conf. of England and Wales. *Publication:* Walsingham, a modern mystery play, 1975. *Recreations:* reading, writing, talking. *Address:* (office) 11 Whitehall Place, SW1A 2HE; Bosco Villa, 30 Queen's Road, South Benfleet, Essex. *T:* South Benfleet 2033. *Club:* Press.

WYNN-WILLIAMS, George, MB, BS London; FRCS; FRCOG; Surgeon, Chelsea Hospital for Women; Consulting Obstetrician to City of Westminster; Consulting Gynæcologist, Chelsea Hospital for Women; Consulting Obstetric Surgeon, Queen Charlotte's Hospital; Consulting Gynæcologist to the Civil Service; Teacher in Gynæcology and Obstetrics, London University; *b* 10 Aug. 1912; *er s* of William Wynn-Williams, MRCS, LRCP, and Jane Anderson Brymer, Caernarvon, N Wales; *m* 1943, Penelope, *o d* of 1st and last Earl Jowitt of Stevenage, PC, and Lesley McIntyre; two *s* one *d. Educ:* Rossall; King's Coll.; Westminster Hospital. MRCS, LRCP 1937; MB, BS (London) 1938; MRCOG 1941; FRCS 1943; FRCOG 1967. Alfred Hughes Anatomy Prize, King's Coll.; Chadwick Prize in Clinical Surgery, Forensic Medicine and Public Health Prizes, Westminster Hospital. Various appointments 1937-41; Chief Asst and Surgical Registrar and Grade I Surgeon, EMS, 1941-45; Acting Obst. and Gynæcol. Registrar, Westminster Hosp., 1941-46; Surgeon-in-Charge, Mobile Surg. Team to Portsmouth and Southampton, June-Oct. 1944; Chief Asst, Chelsea Hosp. for Women, 1946-47; Obst. Registrar, Queen Charlotte's Hosp., 1946-50; Cons. Obstetrician, Borough of Tottenham; Cons. Gynæcologist, Weir Hosp. Surgical Tutor, Westminster Hosp., 1941-46; Obst. and Gynæcol. Tutor, Westminster Hosp., 1941-48; Lectr and Demonstrator to Postgrad. Students, Queen Charlotte's Hosp., 1946-50; Lectr to Postgrad. Students, Chelsea Women's Hosp., 1946-; Examiner, Central Midwives' Board; Recognized Lectr of London Univ.; Assoc. Examiner in Obst. and Gynæcol., Worshipful Co. of Apothecaries. Member: BMA; Soc. for Study of Fertility; The Pilgrims. FRSM. *Publications:* (jtly) Queen Charlotte's Text Book of Obstetrics; contributions to medical journals, including Human Artificial Insemination, in Hospital Medicine, 1973; Infertile Patients with Positive Immune Fluorescent Serum, 1976; Spermatazoal Antibodies treated with Condom Coitus, 1976. *Recreations:* tennis, shooting, fishing. *Address:* 48 Wimpole Street, W1M 7DG. *T:* 01-487 4866; 39 Hurlingham Court, SW6; The Hall, Wittersham, Isle of Oxney, Kent. *Clubs:* Hurlingham, Chelsea Arts, English-Speaking Union, Oriental; Rye Golf.

WYNNE, Prof. Charles Gorrie, FRS 1970; BA, PhD; Director of Optical Design Group, Imperial College, London, since 1960; Professor of Optical Design, University of London, since 1969; at present working at the Royal Greenwich Observatory, Herstmonceux Castle, Sussex; *b* 18 May 1911; *s* of C. H. and A. E. Wynne; *m* 1937, Jean Richardson; two *s* one *d. Educ:* Wyggeston Grammar Sch., Leicester; Exeter Coll., Oxford (Scholar). Optical Designer, Taylor Taylor & Hobson Ltd, 1935-43; Wray (Optical Works) Ltd, 1943-60, latterly Director. Hon. Sec. (business), Physical Soc., 1947-60; Hon. Sec., Inst. of Physics and Physical Soc., 1960-66. Editor, Optica Acta, 1954-65. *Publications:* scientific papers on aberration theory and optical instruments in Proc. Phys. Soc., Mon. Not. RAS, Astrophys. Jl, Optica Acta, etc. *Address:* Morar, Boreham Street, near Hailsham, Sussex. *T:* Herstmonceux 2234.

WYNNE, David; sculptor, since 1949; *b* Lyndhurst, Hants, 25 May 1926; *s* of Comdr Charles Edward Wynne and Mrs Millicent Wynne (*née* Beyts); *m* 1959, Gillian Mary Leslie Bennett (*née* Grant); two *s*, and one step *s* one step *d. Educ:* Stowe Sch.; Trinity Coll., Cambridge. FZS; FRSA. Served RN, 1944-47: minesweepers and aircraft carriers (Sub-Lieut RNVR). No formal art training. First exhibited at Leicester Galls, 1950, and at Royal Acad., 1952. One-man Exhibitions: Leicester Galls, 1955, 1959; Tooth's Gall., 1964, 1966; Temple Gall., 1964; Findlay Galls, New York, 1967, 1970, 1973; Covent Garden Gall., 1970, 1971; Fitzwilliam Museum, Cambridge, 1972; Pepsico World HQ, New York, 1976; also various mixed exhibns. Large works in public places: Magdalen Coll., Oxford; Malvern Girls' Coll.; Civic Centre, Newcastle upon Tyne; Lewis's, Hanley; Ely Cathedral; Birmingham Cath.; Church of St Paul, Ashford Hill, Berks; Ch. of St Thomas More, Bradford-on-Avon; Mission Ch., Portsmouth; London: Albert Bridge;

British Oxygen Co., Hammersmith; Cadogan Place Gardens and Cadogan Sq.; Crystal Palace Park; Guildhall; Longbow House; St Katharine-by-the-Tower; Taylor Woodrow; Wates Ltd, Norbury; USA: Ambassador Coll., Texas, and Ambassador Coll., Calif; Atlantic Richfield Oil Co., New Mexico; Lakeland Meml Hosp., Wis; First Fed. Savings, Mass; Pepsico World HQ, Purchase, NY; also Perth, WA. Bronze portrait heads include: Sir Thomas Beecham, 1956; Sir John Gielgud, 1962; Yehudi Menuhin, 1963; The Beatles, 1964; Kokoschka, 1965; Sir Alec Douglas-Home, 1966; Robert, Marquess of Salisbury, 1967; The Prince of Wales, 1969; Lord Baden-Powell, 1971; Virginia Wade, 1972; The Queen, 1973; King Hassan of Morocco, 1973; Air Chief Marshal Lord Dowding, 1974; The Begum Aga Khan, 1975; Pele, 1976; Lord Hailsham, 1977; Prince Michael of Kent, 1977. Designed: Common Market 50 pence piece of clasped hands, 1973; the Queen's Silver Jubilee Medal, 1977 (with new effigy of the Queen wearing St Edward's Crown). *Relevant publications:* T. S. R. Boase, The Sculpture of David Wynne 1949-1967, 1968; Graham Hughes, The Sculpture of David Wynne 1968-1974, 1974. *Recreations:* Active sports, poetry, music. *Address:* 12 South Side, SW19. *T:* 01-946 1514. *Clubs:* Hurlingham; Leander (Henley-on-Thames); 1st and 3rd Trinity Boat; St Moritz Tobogganing; The Royal Tennis Court (Hampton Court Palace).

WYNNE, Col J. F. W.; *see* Williams-Wynne.

WYNNE-EDWARDS, Vero Copner, CBE 1973; FRS 1970; MA, DSc, FRSC, FRSE; Regius Professor of Natural History, University of Aberdeen, 1946-74, Vice Principal, 1972-74; *b* 4 July 1906; 3rd *s* of late Rev. Canon John Rosindale Wynne-Edwards and Lilian Agnes Streatfeild; *m* 1929, Jeannie Campbell, *e d* of late Percy Morris, Devon County Architect; one *s* one *d. Educ:* Leeds Grammar Sch.; Rugby Sch.; New Coll., Oxford. 1st Class Hons in Natural Science (Zoology), Oxford, 1927; Senior Scholar of New Coll., 1927-29; Student Probationer, Marine Biological Laboratory, Plymouth, 1927-29; Assistant Lecturer in Zoology, Univ. of Bristol, 1929-30; Asst Prof. of Zoology, McGill Univ., Montreal, 1930-44; Associate Prof., 1944-46. Canadian representative, MacMillan Baffin Island expedition, 1937; Canadian Fisheries Research Board expeditions to Mackenzie River, 1944, and Yukon Territory, 1945; Baird Expedition to Central Baffin Island, 1950. Visiting Prof. of Conservation, University of Louisville, Kentucky, 1959, Commonwealth Universities Interchange Fellow New Zealand, 1962. Jt Editor, Journal of Applied Ecology, 1963-68. Member: Nature Conservancy, 1954-57; Red Deer Commn (Vice-Chm.), 1959-68; Royal Commn on Environmental Pollution, 1970-74; President: British Ornithologists' Union, 1965-70; Scottish Marine Biological Assoc., 1967-73; Section D, British Assoc., 1974; Chairman: NERC, 1968-71; Home Office and Scottish Office Adv. Cttees on Protection of Birds, 1970-; Scientific Authority for Animals, DoE, 1976-. For. Mem., Societas Scientiarum Fennica, 1965; Hon. Mem., British Ecological Soc., 1977. Hon. DUniv Stirling, 1974; Hon. LLD Aberdeen, 1976. Godman-Salvin Medal, British Ornithologists' Union, 1977; Neill Prize, RSE, 1977. *Publications:* Animal Dispersion in relation to social behaviour, 1962; scientific papers on ornithology (esp. oceanic birds), animal populations. *Recreation:* ski-ing. *Address:* Ravelston, William Street, Torphins, Via Banchory, Aberdeenshire AB3 4JR. *Club:* Naval and Military.

WYNNE-EYTON, Mrs Selena Frances, CBE 1943; *b* 21 Jan. 1898; *m* 1916, Wing Comdr S. Wynne-Eyton, DSO, AFC (whom she divorced 1932; he was killed flying, 1944); no *c. Educ:* Downe House, Kent (now Cold Ash, Newbury). Joined WAAF June 1939; posted to Air Ministry as Assistant Director, Sept. 1939; Commanding Officer of WAAF Officers' Sch., and later Senior WAAF Staff Officer at Technical Training Command, 1941; Senior WAAF Staff Officer, HQ, RAF, MEF, 1943-45; with Control Commission for Germany (British Element), 1945-50. *Address:* Marsh Cottage, Fingringhoe, near Colchester, Essex. *T:* Rowhedge 273.

WYNNE FINCH, Colonel John Charles; CBE 1956; MC; DL; HM Lieutenant of County of Denbigh, 1951-66; Member of Welsh Agricultural Land Sub-Commission, 1948, Chairman, 1953-63; Agricultural Land Commission, 1952, Deputy Chairman, 1953-63; *b* 31 Aug. 1891; *e s* of late Lieut-Colonel Charles Arthur Wynne Finch, Scots Guards, and Maud Emily, 2nd *d* of late Hon. Richard Charteris, 2nd *s* of 8th Earl of Wemyss; *m* 1914, Alice Mary Sybil (*d* 1970), 2nd *d* of late Rt Rev. Hon. Edward Carr Glyn and Lady Mary Glyn; one *s* two *d. Educ:* Eton; RMC, Sandhurst. Lord of the Manor of Hieraethog, Denbighshire; patron of 1 living; served European War, 1914-18 (MC). Commanded 3rd Battalion Coldstream Guards, 1932-36; retired pay, 1937. Served War of 1939-45. JP, Denbighshire;

then Caernarvonshire (later Gwynedd); DL, Gwynedd. High Sheriff of Denbighshire, 1949. President, Welsh Agricultural Society, 1962. Member, Nature Conservancy, 1957-63; Member, Nature Conservancy, Wales, 1957-66; Chairman, National Trust Cttee for Wales, 1957-69. KStJ 1966. *Address:* Voelas, Betws-y-Coed, Gwynedd LL24 0SU. *T:* Pentrefoelas 206.

WYNNE-JONES, family name of **Baron Wynne-Jones.**

WYNNE-JONES, Baron, *cr* 1964, of Abergele (Life Peer); **William Francis Kenrick Wynne-Jones;** Pro-Vice-Chancellor, 1965-68, Professor of Chemistry, Head of the School of Chemistry, 1956-68, University of Newcastle upon Tyne; Chancellor, Newcastle upon Tyne Polytechnic, since 1976; *b* 8 May 1903; *y s* of late Rev. T. J. Jones, Shaistaganj, India; *m* 1st, 1928, Ann Drummond (*d* 1969); two *d*; 2nd, 1972, Rusheen Preston, *d* of Mrs Neville Preston. *Educ:* Monkton Combe Sch., Bath; University College of Wales, Aberystwyth; Balliol Coll., Oxford. Research Asst and Lectr in Physical Chemistry, Univ. of Bristol; International Research Fellow, Univ. of Copenhagen; Lectr in Chemistry, Univ. of Reading; Leverhulme Research Fellow, Princeton Univ.; Prof. of Chemistry, University College, Dundee; Head of Chemistry Div., Royal Aircraft Establishment, Farnborough. Chm., Scientific and Technical Cttee, N Atlantic Assembly, 1973-77. Chm. of Governors, Newcastle upon Tyne Polytechnic, 1973-76. Coal Carbonisation Science Lectr and Medallist, 1972. Hon. DSc Bristol, 1968. *Publications:* articles in scientific journals. *Address:* Carlyle House, 16 Chelsea Embankment, SW3.

WYNNE-JONES, Tom Neville, CMG 1954; CBE 1950 (OBE 1943); Architect to the Ceylon University and Ceylon Army Cantonment, Panagode, Sri Lanka, 1953-71, retired; reemployed as Consultant Adviser and Documentator to Ministry of Buildings, to 1973; *b* 19 Nov. 1893; *m* 1920, Mabel (Phil) Phillips (*d* 1972). *Educ:* Technical Coll. and School of Arts and Crafts, Swansea. Articled pupil to Sir Charles Tamlyn Ruthen, OBE, 1909-14. War Service, France, 1914-18, commnd RE; Army of Occupation as DORE Abbeville, demobilised Nov. 1919. PWD Ceylon, 1920; Architect, various grades, to Chief Architect, 1932-53. FRIBA, CEng, FIStructE; FRSH (Life Mem.); FCIA (PP); FIE(PP) (Life Mem.). *Recreations:* settling down, reading, writing, sketching, still a student. *Address:* Long Sands, 15 Second Avenue, Frinton-on-Sea, Essex. *Clubs:* Rotary (Colombo) (longest and oldest member); Frinton-on-Sea Golf.

WYNNE MASON, Walter, CMG 1967; MC 1941; Director of External Relations and Records, Commonwealth War Graves Commission, 1956-70; *b* 21 March 1910; *y s* of late George and Eva Mason, Wellington, NZ; *m* 1945, Freda Miller, *d* of late Frederick and Lilian Miller, Woodford, Essex; two *s* one *d. Educ:* Scots Coll., NZ; Victoria University College, NZ (MA). NZ Govt Education Service 1934-39; served NZ Army, 1939-46; NZ War Histories, 1947-48; NZ Diplomatic Service, 1949-54; Chief, Middle East, Commonwealth War Graves Commission, 1954-56. *Publication:* Prisoners of War, 1954. *Recreations:* lawn tennis, theatre, music. *Address:* Keene House, Hillier Road, Guildford, Surrey. *T:* Guildford 72601. *Club:* Royal Automobile.

WYNTER, Sir Luther (Reginald), Kt 1977; CBE 1966 (OBE 1962, MBE 1950); MD; FICS; private medical practitioner, Antigua, since 1927; *b* 15 Sept. 1899; *s* of Thomas Nathaniel Wynter and Pauline Jane Wynter; *m* 1927, Arah Adner Busby. *Educ:* Wolmers High Sch., Jamaica; Coll. of City of Detroit, USA; Dalhousie Univ. (MD, CM); Moorfields Hosp. (DOMS). FICS (Ophthalmology) 1969. Gen. med. practitioner, Hamilton, Ont, Canada, 1925-27; actg govt radiologist, Antigua, 1937-51; ophthalmologist, Antigua, 1953-64, hon. consulting ophthalmologist, 1966-. Nominated Mem., Antigua Govt, 1956-66; Senator and Pres. of Senate, 1967-68 (often acting as Governor or Dep. to Governor). Hon. LLD: Univ. of the West Indies, 1972; Dalhousie, 1975. *Recreation:* learning to play bridge. *Address:* PO Box 154, St John's, Antigua, West Indies. *T:* (office) St John's 20255, (home) Hodges Bay 30021. *Clubs:* (Hon. Life Mem.) Mill Reef, (Hon. Mem.) Lions (Antigua).

WYNYARD-WRIGHT, Frank Trueman, MA; *b* 29 Jan. 1884; *s* of Rev. Frank Wynyard-Wright and Annie Grace Trueman; *m* Laura Kathleen Tweed (*d* 1964), Lincoln; one *s. Educ:* Rossall; Emmanuel Coll., Cambridge. Asst Master, Lexden House, Seaford; Headmaster, St Peter's Sch., Sheringham, for 10 years; Headmaster, Thames Nautical Training Coll., HMS Worcester; resigned, 1935. Served Malaya States Regt, 1914-18; world traveller, 1912-21. *Recreations:* photography, lecturing. *Address:* Grayshott Nursing Home, Boundary Road, Grayshott, Hindhead, Surrey. *T:* 4478. *Clubs:* Penn, Alpine.

WYSS, Sophie; Concert Singer; *b* 1897; 2nd *d* of Oscar and Helène Wyss, La Neuveille, Switzerland; *m* 1925, Captain Arnold Gyde; two *s. Educ:* Conservatoires de Genève et Bâle. Operatic debut, Geneva, 1922; recitals and chamber concerts for BBC, 1927-64; concerts throughout Great Britain, in Europe and in Australia. First performances include: Britten's Les Illuminations, Our Hunting Fathers; all Roberto Gerhard's vocal works; works of Lennox Berkeley, Alan Rawsthorne, Elizabeth Maconchy, Racine Fricker, Matyas Seiber, William Wordsworth and many other composers. Inspired many of these composers to write French as well as English songs and to re-arrange innumerable Folk songs into modern idiom. *Address:* 19 The Mall, Surbiton, Surrey.

Y

YAHYA KHAN, General Agha Muhammad, HPk (Hilal-i-Pakistan); HJ (Hilal-i-Jurat); President of Pakistan, and Chief Martial Law Administrator, 1969-71; *b* 4 Feb. 1917; *s* of Khan Bahadur Agha Saadat Ali Khan; *m* 1945, Begum Fakhira Yahya; one *s* one *d. Educ:* Indian Military Academy (King's Cadet). On commissioning, he was attached to 2nd Bn Worcester Regt and later to 3rd Bn Baluch Regt. War of 1939-45: 5 year tour of duty overseas with his Regt in Egypt, Sudan, Libya, Cyprus, Iraq, Italy, etc. Staff Coll., Quetta (grad. 1946); Lt-Col, 1947; Brig. 1951; Maj.-Gen. and CGS, 1957 (associated with modernisation of Army); GOC E Pakistan, Dec. 1962-Aug. 1964; commanded an infantry div. during War with India, 1965; became C-in-C of Army, Sept. 1966; President Ayub Khan called upon him to preserve the integrity of Pakistan, 24 March 1969. *Recreations:* golf, shooting, reading.

YAMEY, Prof. Basil Selig, CBE 1972; FBA 1977; Professor of Economics, University of London, since 1960; Member (part-time), Monopolies and Mergers Commission, since 1966; *b* 4 May 1919; *s* of Solomon and Leah Yamey; *m* 1948, Helen Bloch; one *s* one *d. Educ:* Tulbagh High Sch.; Univ. of Cape Town; LSE. Lectr in Commerce, Rhodes Univ., 1945; Senior Lectr in Commerce, Univ. of Cape Town, 1946; Lectr in Commerce, LSE, 1948; Associate Prof. of Commerce, McGill Univ., 1949; Reader in Economics, Univ. of London, 1950. Trustee, National Gallery, 1974-; Mem., Cinematograph Films Council, 1969-73. *Publications:* Economics of Resale Price Maintenance, 1954; (jt editor) Studies in History of Accounting, 1956; (with P. T. Bauer) Economics of Under-developed Countries, 1957; (jt editor) Capital, Saving and Credit in Peasant Societies, 1963; (with H. C. Edey and H. Thomson) Accounting in England and Scotland, 1543-1800, 1963; (with R. B. Stevens) The Restrictive Practices Court, 1965; (ed) Resale Price Maintenance, 1966; (with P. T. Bauer) Markets, Market Control and Marketing Reform: Selected Papers, 1968; (ed) Economics of Industrial Structure, 1973; (jt editor) Economics of Retailing, 1973; (jt editor) Debits, Credits, Finance and Profits, 1974; (with B. A. Goss) Economics of Futures Trading, 1976; articles on economics, economic history and law in learned journals. *Address:* 36 Hampstead Way, NW11. *T:* 01-455 5810.

YANG, Chen Ning; Einstein Professor and Director, Institute for Theoretical Physics, State University of New York at Stony Brook, New York, since 1966; *b* Hofei, China, 22 Sept. 1922; *s* of Professor and Mrs Ke-Chuan Yang; *m* 1950, Chih-Li Tu; two *s* one *d. Educ:* National Southwest Associated Univ., Kunming, China (BSc); University of Chicago (PhD). Institute for Advanced Study, Princeton, NJ: Member, 1949-55; Prof. of Physics, 1955-65; Hon. DSc: Princeton Univ., 1958; Polytechnic Inst. of Brooklyn, 1965; Univ. of Wroclaw, Poland, 1974; Gustavus Adolphus Coll., Minn., 1975. Nobel Prize in Physics, 1957. Einstein Award in Sciences, 1957. *Publications:* contrib. to Physical Review, Reviews of Modern Physics. *Address:* State University of New York at Stony Brook, New York 11790, USA.

YANG, Ti-Liang; Hon. Mr Justice Yang; Judge of the High Court, Hong Kong, since 1976; *b* 30 June 1929; *s* of Shao-nan Yang and Mrs Yang; *m* 1954, Eileen Barbara (*née* Tam); two *s. Educ:* UCL (LLB Hons). Called to the Bar, Gray's Inn, 1954. Magistrate, Hong Kong, 1956; Sen. Magistrate, 1963; District Judge, Dist Court, 1968; Puisne Judge, Supreme Court, 1975. *Publications:* contrib. Internat. and Comparative Law Qly. *Recreations:* philately, reading, walking, oriental ceramics, shooting. *Address:* Supreme Court, Hong Kong. *T:* Hong Kong 5-239728. *Clubs:* Hong Kong, Hong Kong Country, Rotary

Club of Hong Kong, Royal Hong Kong Jockey, Hong Kong Gun (Hong Kong).

YANKOV, Alexander; Ambassador and Permanent Representative of the People's Republic of Bulgaria to the UN; Deputy Minister for Foreign Affairs, Bulgaria; *b* 22 June 1924; *m* 1949, Eliza; one *s* one *d. Educ:* Sofia Univ. Law Sch.; Hague Acad. of Internat. Law. PhD Internat. Law. Prof. of Internat. Law, Sofia Univ. (Asst Prof. 1951-54, Associate Prof. 1958-64). Sec., Internat. Union of Students, Prague, 1954-57; Counsellor, Perm. Mission of Bulgaria to UN, mem. delegns to sessions of UN Gen. Assembly, 1965-68; Vice-Chm., UN Cttee on Peaceful Uses of Sea-bed, 1968-72; Ambassador of Bulgaria to Court of St James's, 1972-76. Mem., Perm. Court of Arbitration at The Hague, 1971; Mem. Court of Arbitration to Bulgarian Chamber of Commerce, 1970. Pres., 8th Session, IMCO, 1973; Head of Bulgarian Delegn, 3rd UN Conf. on Law of the Sea; Chm., 3rd Cttee, UN Conf. on Law of the Sea. Order 9 Sept. 1944, 1959; Order of Freedom of the People, 1960; Order of Cyril and Methodius, 1962; Order of People's Republic of Bulgaria, 1974 (all Bulgaria). *Publications:* The European Collective Security System, 1958; Reservations to Declarations of Acceptance of Compulsory Jurisdiction of International Court of Justice, 1961; The Peace Treaty with the Two German States and its Legal Effect, 1962; Principles of International Law as Applied in Treaty Practice of Bulgaria, 1964; The United Nations: Legal Status and International Personality, 1965; Exploration and Uses of the Sea-bed: a new legal framework, 1970; United Nations Declaration on Principles of Friendly Relations and Progressive Development of International Law, 1971; United Nations and Development of International Trade Law, 1971, etc. *Recreations:* theatre, swimming. *Address:* Bulgarian Mission to the UN, 11 East 84th Street, New York, NY 10028, USA.

YAPP, Sir Stanley Graham, Kt 1975; Leader, West Midlands County Council, 1973-77; Member, Birmingham City Council, later Birmingham District Council, 1961-77 (Leader, 1973); *s* of late William and of Elsie Yapp; *m* Carol Ann; one *s* one *d*. Member, West Midlands Economic Planning Council (Chm Transport Cttee); Member many bodies both local and national, inc.: Vice-Chm. LAMSAC; Member: Local Govt Trng Board; Nat. Jt Councils on pay and conditions; AMA; BR Adv. Bd, Midlands and N Western Reg., 1977-; Chm., West Midlands Planning Authorities Conf., 1973-75, Vice-Chm. 1975-. Governor, BFI, 1977-. *Publications:* contribs to Local Government Chronicle, Municipal Journal, Rating and Valuation. *Recreations:* astronomy, vintage public transport, brass-banding. *Address:* 12 Moreton Close, Harborne, Birmingham B32 2JN.

YARBOROUGH, 7th Earl of, *cr* 1837; **John Edward Pelham;** Baron Yarborough, Baron Worsley, 1794; Major Grenadier Guards, retired 1952; Vice Lord-Lieutenant (formerly Vice-Lieutenant), Lincolnshire, since 1964; JP; *b* 2 June 1920; *s* of 6th Earl of Yarborough; *S* father, 1966; *m* 1957, Mrs Ann Duffin, *d* of late John Herbert Upton, Ingmire Hall, Yorkshire; one *s* three *d. Educ:* Eton; Trinity College, Cambridge. Contested (C) Grimsby, 1955. President: Midland Area, British Legion, 1959-60, East Midland Area, 1960-62; Nat. Exec. Council, British Legion, 1962-73; Patron, E Midlands Area, 1974-. High Sheriff of Lincolnshire, 1964; Hon. Col, 440 Light AD Regt, RA (TA), 1965-69, Humber Regt, RA T&AVR, 1969-71; Dep. Hon. Col, 2nd Bn, Yorkshire Volunteers, 1971-72. JP, Parts of Lindsey, 1965. *Recreations:* shooting, sailing. *Heir: s* Lord Worsley, *qv. Address:* Brocklesby Park, Habrough, South Humberside DN37 8PL. *T:* Roxton 242. *Clubs:* Cavalry and Guards, Boodle's; Royal Yacht Squadron.

YARBURGH-BATESON; *see* de Yarburgh-Bateson, family name of Baron Deramore.

YARDE, Air Vice-Marshal Brian Courtenay, CVO 1953; CBE 1949; psa; *b* 5 September 1905; *s* of late John Edward Yarde, Crediton, Devon, and Bedford; *m* 1927, Marjorie, *d* of late W. Sydney Smith, Bedford; two *d. Educ:* Bedford School; RAF College, Cranwell (Sword of Honour), 1926. Served War of 1939-45 in France, Malaya, Middle East, UK (despatches thrice); Deputy Director of Bomber Operations, Air Ministry, 1945; Senior Director, RAF Staff College, 1946-47; Station Commander, Gatow, 1947-49 (Berlin Airlift); Provost Marshal and Chief of the Royal Air Force Police, 1951-53; Air Officer Commanding No. 62 Group, 1953-54. Air Commodore, 1951; Acting Air Vice-Marshal, 1954; Commandant-General of the Royal Air Force Regiment and Inspector of Ground Combat Training, 1954-57, retired. Chairman, Courtenay Caterers Ltd, Andover. Officer American Legion of Merit. *Address:* Wiremead, East Cholderton, Andover, Hants. *T:* Weyhill 2265.

YARDE-BULLER, family name of **Baron Churston.**

YARDLEY, Prof. David Charles Miller; Barber Professor of Law, University of Birmingham, since Oct. 1974; Barrister-at-Law; *b* 4 June 1929; *s* of Geoffrey Miller Yardley and Doris Woodward Yardley (*née* Jones); *m* 1954, Patricia Anne Tempest Olver; two *s* two *d. Educ:* The Old Hall Sch., Wellington; Ellesmere Coll., Shropshire; Univ. of Birmingham (LLB); Univ. of Oxford (MA, DPhil). Called to Bar, Gray's Inn, 1952. RAF Flying Officer (nat. service), 1949-51. Bigelow Teaching Fellow, Univ. of Chicago, 1953-54; Fellow and Tutor in Jurisprudence, St Edmund Hall, Oxford, 1953-74; CUF Lectr, Univ. of Oxford, 1954-74. Sen. Proctor, Univ. of Oxford, 1965-66; Visiting Prof. of Law, Univ. of Sydney, 1971. Constitutional Consultant, Govt of W Nigeria, 1956; Chm., Thames Valley Rent Tribunal, 1963-; Vice-Pres., Thames Valley Rent Assessment Panel, 1966-; Oxford City Councillor, 1966-74; Chm. of Governors, St Helen's Sch., Abingdon, 1967-; Chm., Oxford Area Nat. Ins. Local Appeal Tribunal, 1969-. *Publications:* Introduction to British Constitutional Law, 1960, 4th edn, 1974; A Source Book of English Administrative Law, 1963, 2nd edn, 1970; The Future of the Law, 1964; Geldart's Elements of English Law, 7th edn, 1966, 8th edn, 1975; Hanbury's English Courts of Law, 4th edn, 1967. *Recreations:* lawn tennis, squash racquets, theatre, cats. *Address:* 9 Belbroughton Road, Oxford OX2 6UZ. *T:* Oxford 54831.

YARMOUTH, Earl of; Henry Jocelyn Seymour; *b* 6 July 1958; *s* and *heir* of 8th Marquess of Hertford, *qv.*

YARNOLD, Rev. Edward John, SJ; DD; Tutor in Theology, Campion Hall, Oxford, since 1964 (Master, 1965-72; Senior Tutor, 1972-74); *b* 14 Jan. 1926; *s* of Edward Cabré Yarnold and Agnes (*née* Deakin). *Educ:* St Michael's Coll., Leeds; Campion Hall, Oxford; Heythrop College. MA Oxon; STL Rome. Taught classics at St Francis Xavier's Coll., Liverpool, 1954-57; ordained, 1960; taught classics at St Michael's Coll., Leeds, 1962-64. Sarum Lectr, Univ. of Oxford, 1972-73. Assoc. Gen. Sec., Ecumenical Soc. of Blessed Virgin Mary, 1975-; Mem., Anglican-Roman Catholic Internat. Commn, 1970-. *Publications:* The Theology of Original Sin, 1971; The Awe-Inspiring Rites of Initiation, 1972; The Second Gift, 1974; (with H. Chadwick) Truth and Authority, 1977; (ed jtly and contrib.) The Study of Liturgy, 1978; articles in learned jls. *Address:* Campion Hall, Oxford. *T:* Oxford 40861.

YARROW, Sir Eric Grant, 3rd Bt, *cr* 1916; MBE (mil.) 1946; DL; Chairman: Yarrow & Co. Ltd, since 1962; Yarrow (Shipbuilders) Ltd, since 1967; Yarrow Engineers (Glasgow) Ltd, since 1969; Yarrow-Admiralty Research Department Ltd, since 1969; Y-ARD (Australia) Pty Ltd, since 1968; Yarrow Africa Maritime Consultancy (Pty) Ltd, since 1969; Vice-Chairman, Water-tube Boilermakers' Association, since 1966; Director: Standard Life Assurance Co., since 1958; Yarrow (Africa) (Holdings) (Pty) Ltd, since 1949; Clydesdale Bank Ltd, since 1962 (Joint Deputy Chairman, since 1975); Croftinloan (Holdings) Ltd, since 1959; *b* 23 April 1920; *o s* of Sir Harold Yarrow, 2nd Bt and 1st wife, Eleanor Etheldreda (*d* 1934); *S* father, 1962; *m* 1st, 1951, Rosemary Ann (*d* 1957), *yr d* of H. T. Young, Roehampton, SW15; one *s*; 2nd, 1959, Annette Elizabeth Françoise (marr. diss. 1975), *d* of late A. J. E. Steven, Grianach, Ardgay, Ross-shire; three *s* (including twin *s*). *Educ:* Marlborough Coll.; Glasgow Univ. Served apprenticeship, G. & J. Weir Ltd. Served Burma, 1942-45; Major RE, 1945. Asst Manager Yarrow & Co., 1946; Dir, 1948; Man. Dir, 1958-67. Mem. Council, RINA, 1957-; Vice-Pres., 1965; Hon. Vice-Pres., 1972. Mem., General Cttee, Lloyd's Register of Shipping, 1960; Prime Warden, Worshipful Co. of Shipwrights, 1970; Deacon, Incorporation of Hammermen of Glasgow, 1961-62; Retired Mem. Council, Institution of Engineers & Shipbuilders in Scotland. Pres., Scottish Convalescent Home for Children, 1957-70; Mem. Exec. Cttee Princess Louise Scottish Hospital at Erskine. OStJ. DL Renfrewshire, 1970. *Recreations:* golf, shooting. *Heir: e s* Richard Grant Yarrow, *b* 21 March 1953. *Address:* Cloak, Kilmacolm, Renfrewshire PA13 4SD. *T:* Kilmacolm 2067. *Clubs:* Army and Navy; Royal Scottish Automobile.

YARWOOD, Dame Elizabeth (Ann), DBE 1969; JP; DL; *b* 25 Nov. 1900; *d* of Henry and Margaret Gaskell; *m* 1918, Vernon Yarwood; two *s. Educ:* Whitworth Street High Sch., Manchester. Councillor, Manchester City Council, 1938-74, Alderman, 1955-74; Lord Mayor of Manchester, 1967-68. Director: Manchester & Salford Co-operative Society Ltd, 1955; Manchester Ship Canal, 1964. Vice-Pres., Manchester County Girl Guides Assoc. Freeman of the City of Manchester, 1974. JP Manchester, 1945; DL Lancs, 1974. *Recreation:* reading. *Address:* 80 Yew Tree Lane, Manchester M23 0DR. *T:* 061-998 3179.

YATES, Anne; *see* Yates, E. A.

YATES, Lt-Gen. Sir David P.; *see* Peel Yates.

YATES, (Edith) Anne, (Mrs S. J. Yates), CBE 1972; Member: National Water Council, since 1973 (Chairman, Training Committee); Manpower Services Commission, 1974-76; English Tourist Board, since 1975; *b* 21 Dec. 1912; *d* of William Blakeman and Frances Dorothea (*née* Thacker); *m* 1935, Stanley James Yates; two *s* one *d. Educ:* Barrs' Hill Girls' Sch., Coventry. County Councillor, 1955, County Alderman, 1966, Notts; Chm., Notts CC, Feb. 1968-March 1974. Chairman: E Midlands Sports Council, 1972-77; Midlands Tourist Bd, 1971-76; Indep. Chm., Nat. Cttee on Recreation Management Trng, 1976-; Member: Sports Council, 1971-74; E Midlands Council of Sport and Recreation, 1977-. *Recreations:* reading, music, theatre. *Address:* Manor Close, Rolleston, Newark, Notts. *T:* Southwell 3362.

YATES, Dame Frances Amelia, DBE 1977 (OBE 1972); DLit; FBA 1967; Hon. Fellow, Warburg Institute since Oct. 1967; Reader in the History of the Renaissance, Warburg Institute, University of London, 1956-67; *b* 28 Nov. 1899; *d* of James Alfred Yates, Royal Corps of Naval Constructors, and Hannah Eliza Malpas. *Educ:* Laurel Bank School, Glasgow; Birkenhead High School; University College, London. BA London 1924 (First Cl. Hons in French), MA London 1926; DLit London 1965. Private research and writing, some teaching at N London Collegiate School, 1926-39; Ambulance Attendant, 1939-41. Warburg Inst., Univ. of London: Part-time Research Assistant, 1941-44; Lecturer and editor of publications, 1944-56. James Ford special lecture, Oxford, 1970; Northcliffe Lectr, UCL, 1974. FRSL 1943; Fellow, Soc. Humanities, Cornell Univ., 1968. Hon. Fellow, Lady Margaret Hall, Oxford, 1970. Hon. DLitt: Edinburgh, 1969; Oxford, 1970; East Anglia, 1971; Exeter, 1971. Hon. For. Mem., Amer. Acad. of Arts and Sciences, 1975. Rose Mary Crawshay Prize, British Acad., 1934; Senior Wolfson History Prize, 1973. *Publications:* John Florio, The Life of an Italian in Shakespeare's England, 1934; A Study of Love's Labour's Lost, 1936; The French Academies of the Sixteenth Century (Warburg Inst.), 1947; The Valois Tapestries (Warburg Inst.), 1959; Giordano Bruno and the Hermetic Tradition, 1964; The Art of Memory, 1966; Theatre of the World, 1969; The Rosicrucian Enlightenment, 1972; Astraea: the imperial theme in the sixteenth century, 1975; Shakespeare's Last Plays: a new approach, 1975; Elizabethan Neoplatonism Reconsidered: Spenser and Francesco Giorgi, 1977; many articles in Jl of Warburg and Courtauld Institutes and elsewhere. *Recreations:* reading, travel. *Address:* 5 Coverts Road, Claygate, Surrey; Warburg Institute, Woburn Square, WC1. *T:* 01-580 9663. *Club:* University Women's.

YATES, Frank, CBE 1963; ScD; FRS 1948; Computer Department, Rothamsted Experimental Station, since 1968 (formerly Head of Statistics Department and Agricultural Research Statistical Service, and Deputy Director); Senior Research Fellow, Mathematics Department, Imperial College, London University; *b* 1902; *s* of Percy and Edith Yates, Didsbury, Manchester; *m* Pauline (*d* 1976), *d* of Vladimir Shoubersky. *Educ:* Clifton; St John's Coll., Cambridge. Research Officer and Mathematical Adviser, Gold Coast Geodetic Survey, 1927-31; Rothamsted Experimental Station, 1931, Dept of Statistics, 1933, Agric. Res. Statistical Service, 1947, Dep. Dir, 1958; Scientific Adviser to various Mins, UNO, FAO, 1939-; Wing Comdr (Hon.) RAF, 1943-45; Mem. UN Sub-Commn on Statistical Sampling, 1947-52. Sen. Res. Fellow, Imperial Coll., 1969-74; Sen. Vis. Fellow, Imperial Coll., 1974-77. Pres., British Computer Society, 1960-61; Pres., Royal Statistical Society, 1967-68. Royal Medal of the Royal Society, 1966. *Publications:* Design and Analysis of Factorial Experiments, 1937; (with R. A. Fisher) Statistical Tables for Biological, Medical and Agricultural Research, 1938 (6th edn 1963); Sampling Methods for Censuses and Surveys, 1949 (3rd edn 1960); Experimental Design: Selected Papers, 1970. Numerous scientific papers. *Recreation:* mountaineering. *Address:* Stackyard, Rothamsted, Harpenden, Herts. *T:* Harpenden 2732. *Club:* Athenæum.

YATES, Ian Humphrey Nelson; General Manager and Chief Executive, The Press Association Ltd, since 1975; *b* 24 Jan. 1931; *s* of James Nelson Yates and Martha (*née* Nutter); *m* 1956, Daphne J. Hudson, MCSP; three *s. Educ:* Lancaster Royal Grammar Sch.; Canford Sch., Wimborne. Royal Scots Greys, Germany and ME (National Service Commn), 1951-53. Management Trainee, Westminster Press Ltd, 1953-58 (Westmorland Gazette, and Telegraph & Argus, Bradford); Asst to Man. Dir, King & Hutchings Ltd, Uxbridge, 1958-60; Bradford and District Newspapers: Asst Gen. Man., 1960; Gen.

Man., 1964; Man. Dir, 1969-75; Dir, Westminster Press Planning Div., 1969-75. President: Young Newspapermen's Assoc., 1966; Yorks Newspaper Soc., 1968. Member: Council, Newspaper Soc., 1970-75; Commonwealth Press Union, 1977-. *Recreations:* walking, reading, theatre. *Address:* Woodbury, 11 Holmwood Close, East Horsley, Surrey. *T:* East Horsley 3873.

YATES, Rt. Rev. John; *see* Gloucester, Bishop of.

YATES, Sir Thomas, Kt 1959; CBE 1951; retired as General Secretary, National Union of Seamen (1947-60) and Chairman of the TUC, (1957-58); Member, Southern Region Railway Board, 1963; *b* 25 Sept. 1896; *s* of William Yates, Sea View, Wallasey, Cheshire; *m* 1st, 1918, Lilian Grace (*d* 1960), *d* of William K. Church; three *s* one *d*; 2nd, 1962, Mrs Dorothy Kilpatrick. *Educ:* St Mary's Sch., Wallasey. Served European War, 1914-18, with Loyal North Lancashire Regiment. District Secretary for SW Coast, National Union of Seamen, 1940-41, and for Scottish Area, 1941-42, National Organiser, 1942-43, and Asst General-Secretary, 1943-47. Chm. of Merchant Seamen's War Memorial Soc.; Member: Seamen's Welfare Board; Merchant Navy Training Board; Management Cttee of Merchant Navy Comforts Trust; Coastal Advisory Cttee; Gen. Council of King George's Fund for Sailors; Exec. Council of Navy League; Shipping Defence Cttee; Personnel Training Cttee; National Maritime Board; International Labour Office Maritime Commission; Covent Garden Market Authority. Delegate for international seafarers to International Labour Office and World Health Organisation Joint Cttee; Representative of Trades Union Congress on Govt's Colonial Advisory Cttee and on various other Joint Bodies. *Address:* 9/84 Cronulla Street, Carlton, Sydney, NSW 2218, Australia.

YATES, William; MP (L) Holt, Victoria, Commonwealth Parliament, since 1975; Senior Partner, World Wide Industrial Consultants; *b* 15 September 1921; *er s* of late William Yates and of Mrs John T. Renshaw, Burrells, Appleby, Westmorland; *m* 1st, 1946, Hon. Rosemary (marr. diss. 1955), *yr d* of 1st Baron Elton; two *d* (one *s* decd); 2nd, 1957, Camilla, *d* of late E. W. D. Tennant, Orford House, Ugley, Bishop's Stortford; four *s*. *Educ:* Uppingham; Hertford Coll., Oxford. Served War, 1940-45, North Africa and Italy; Captain The Bays, 1945. Shropshire Yeomanry, 1956-67. Appointed Legal Officer to report on State lands in Department of Custodian's Office in Tripoli, Libya, 1951. MP (C) The Wrekin Division of Shropshire, 1955-66. Myron Taylor Lectures in International Affairs, Cornell Univ., USA, 1958 and 1966. Mem. Inst. of Internat. Affairs, Victoria. Mem. Liberal Party Parly Cttee for Defence and Foreign Affairs, 1975-. *Address:* Parliament House, Canberra, ACT 2600, Australia; 35 Robinson Street, Dandenong, Victoria 3175, Australia. *Clubs:* Cavalry and Guards, St Stephen's.

YATES-BELL, John Geoffrey, FRCS; retired; Consultant Urologist to King's College Hospital; *b* 6 Dec. 1902; *s* of John Bell, FRCVS, and Matilda Bell, London; *m* 1932, Winifred Frances Hordern (*née* Perryman); one *s* one *d*. *Educ:* St Dunstan's College; King's College, London. MB, BS London 1926; FRCS 1930. King's College Hospital: House Surgeon, 1926-28; Surgical Registrar, 1928-29; Junior Urological Surgeon, 1930; Hon. Urological Surgeon, 1937. Emeritus Urological Surgeon, Epsom and Leatherhead Hosps. President, Urological Section, RSM, 1952 (Vice-Pres. 1939); Fellow Internat. Soc. of Urology, 1934; Founder Member, British Assoc. of Urological Surgeons (Hon. Treas., 1954-56). *Publications:* Kidney and Ureter, Stone (British Surgical Practice), 1950; articles in British Jl of Urology, Jl of Urology, Medical Press, Lancet, etc. *Recreation:* lawn tennis. *Address:* Westane, Tyrrells Wood, Leatherhead, Surrey KT22 8QJ. *T:* Leatherhead 73170.

YEABSLEY, Sir Richard Ernest, Kt 1950; CBE 1943; FCA; *b* 16 May 1898; *m* 1923, Hilda Maude Willson; one *d*. *Educ:* Alperton School. Served European War, 3rd Bn (City of London Regiment) Royal Fusiliers, 1914-19. Independent member of Hosiery Working Party, 1945; Member: Committee to examine the organisation and methods of distribution of Building Materials, 1946; Committee to enquire into the resources of Minerals in the United Kingdom, 1946; Supreme Court Cttee on Practice and Procedure, 1947; Cttee on Resale Price Maintenance, 1947; Monopolies and Restrictive Practices Commn, 1949-56. Accountant Adviser to BoT, 1942-68; formerly Sen. Partner, Hill, Vellacott & Co., and Hill, Vellacott & Bailey, Chartered Accountants, retd March 1963; Pres. Society of Incorporated Accountants, 1956-57. *Address:* 9 Alverton Hall, West Cliff Road, Bournemouth. *T:* Bournemouth 766293. *Club:* Royal Automobile.

YELLOWLEES, Sir Henry, KCB 1975 (CB 1971); Chief Medical Officer, Department of Health and Social Security, Department of Education and Science and Home Office, since 1973; *b* 1919; *s* of late Henry Yellowlees, OBE, Psychiatrist of Bath. *Educ:* Stowe Sch.; University Coll., Oxford. MA, BM, BCh Oxon 1950. FRCP 1971 (MRCP 1966, LRCP 1950), MRCS Eng., FFCM 1972. Pilot, RAF, 1941-45. Resident Med. Officer, Mddx Hosp., London, 1951-54; Asst Senior Med. Officer, South West Regional Hosp. Bd, 1954-59; Dep. Sen. Admin. Med. Officer, North West Metropolitan Regional Hosp. Bd, 1959-63; Principal Med. Officer, Min. of Health, 1963-65 (seconded); Senior Principal Med. Officer, 1965-67 (established); Dep. Chief Med. Officer, 1967-72, 2nd Chief Med. Officer, 1972-73, Dept of Health and Social Security. Mem., Medical Research Council, 1974-. Hon. FRCP Glasgow, 1974; Hon. FRCPsych, 1977; Fellow Brit. Inst. of Management, 1974. *Address:* Alexander Fleming House, Elephant and Castle, SE1 6BY.

YEMM, Prof. Edmund William, BA, DPhil Oxon; Melville Wills Professor of Botany, University of Bristol, 1955-74; *b* 16 July 1909; *s* of William H. Yemm and Annie L. Brett; *m* 1935, Marie Solari; one *s* three *d*. *Educ:* Wyggeston School, Leicester; Queen's College, Oxford. Foundation, Schol., Queen's Coll., 1928; Christopher Welch Schol., 1931. Major, REME, 1942-45. Research Fellow, Queen's Coll., 1935-38; Lecturer, Univ. of Bristol, 1939-49; Reader in Botany, Univ. of Bristol, 1950-55; Pro-Vice-Chancellor, Bristol Univ., 1970-73. Fellowship, Rockefeller Foundation, 1954; Vis. Prof., Western Reserve Univ., 1966-67. *Publications:* scientific papers in Proc. Royal Soc., New Phytologist, Biochemical Jl, Jl of Ecology, Jl of Experimental Botany. *Recreations:* cricket, gardening; formerly football (Oxford Univ. Assoc. Football Blue, 1929-31). *Address:* The Wycke, 61 Long Ashton Road, Bristol BS18 9HW. *T:* Long Ashton 2258.

YENDELL, Rear-Adm. William John, CB 1957; RN, retired; *b* 29 Dec. 1903; *e s* of late Charles Yendell; *m* 1937, Monica Duncan; one *d*. *Educ:* RN Colleges Osborne and Dartmouth. Qualified Gunnery Officer, 1929; commanded HM Ships: Bittern, 1938; Shah, 1943-45; Glasgow, 1950; Superb, 1950. Director of Naval Ordnance, 1951-54; Assistant Chief of Naval Staff (Warfare), 1954-57. Naval ADC 1954-. Comdr, 1937; Captain, 1945. *Recreations:* painting and most games. *Address:* The Bell Cottage, Newtonmore, Inverness-shire. *T:* Newtonmore 344. *Club:* Royal Naval and Royal Albert Yacht (Portsmouth).

YEO, Douglas; Director, Shell Research Ltd, Biosciences Laboratory, Sittingbourne, Kent, since 1976; *b* 13 June 1925; *s* of Sydney and Hylda Yeo; *m* 1947, Joan Elisabeth Chell; two *d*. *Educ:* Secondary Sch., St Austell; University Coll., Exeter (BSc London). Expedn on locust control, Kenya, 1945. HMOCS, 1948-63; Tropical Pesticides Research Inst., Uganda and Tanzania, 1948-61 (Scientific Officer, 1948-51, Sen. Scientific Officer, 1951-57, Prin. Scientific Officer, 1957-61). Internat. African Migratory Locust Control Organisation, Mali: on secondment, 1958, 1960; Dir and Sec. Gen., 1961-63. Research Dir, Shell Research Ltd, Woodstock Agricultural Research Centre, 1963-69; Dir, 1969-76. *Publications:* papers in Bulletin Ent. Res., Bull. WHO Anti-Locust Bull., Quart. Jl Royal Met. Soc., Jl Sci. Fd. Agric., Plant Protection Confs, etc. Vis. Prof., Wye Coll. FIBiol. *Recreations:* sailing, fishing. *Address:* Brewster House, Doddington, near Sittingbourne, Kent. *T:* Doddington 207. *Club:* Royal Corinthian Yacht (Burnham on Crouch).

YEO, Kok Cheang, CMG 1956; MD; MB; BS; DPH; DTM&H; *b* 1 April 1903; *s* of Yeo Kim Hong; *m* Florence, *d* of late Sir Robert Ho-tung, KBE; one *s* two *d*. *Educ:* Hong Kong University; Cambridge University; London School of Hygiene and Tropical Medicine. MB, BS, Hong Kong 1925, MD, 1930; DTM&H (England) 1927; DPH, Cambridge, 1928. Assistant Medical Officer of Health, Hong Kong, 1928; Lecturer and Examiner in public health, Hong Kong University, 1936-37; Official JP 1938; Chinese Health Officer, senior grade, 1939-47; Deputy Director of Health Services, and Vice-Chairman of Urban Council, 1947-50; Deputy Director of Medical and Health Services, 1950-52; member of Legislative Council, Hong Kong, 1951-57; Director of Medical and Health Services, Hong Kong, 1952-58; Professor of Social Medicine, Hong Kong University, 1953-58; retd 1958. *Address:* Brendon Cottage, Station Road, Northiam, East Sussex TN31 6QL. *T:* Northiam 2269.

YERBURGH, family name of **Baron Alvingham.**

YERBY, Frank Garvin; Novelist; *b* 5 September 1916; *s* of Rufus Garvin Yerby and Wilhelmina Smythe; *m* 1956, Blanca Calle

Pérez; two s two d of former marriage. *Educ:* Haines Institute; Paine College; Fisk Univ.; Univ. of Chicago. Teacher, Florida Agricultural and Mechanical Coll., 1939; Southern Univ. (Baton Rouge, Louisiana), 1940-41; War work: laboratory technician, Ford Motor Company, Detroit, 1941-44; Ranger Aircraft, New York, 1944-45; writer since 1944; O. Henry Award for short story, 1944. *Publications:* The Foxes of Harrow, 1946; The Vixens, 1947; The Golden Hawk, 1948; Pride's Castle, 1949; Floodtide, 1950; A Woman Called Fancy, 1951; The Saracen Blade, 1952; The Devil's Laughter, 1953; Benton's Row, 1954; The Treasure of Pleasant Valley, 1955; Captain Rebel, 1956; Fairoaks, 1957; The Serpent and the Staff, 1958; Jarrett's Jade, 1959; Gillian, 1960; The Garfield Honor, 1961; Griffin's Way, 1962; The Old Gods Laugh, 1964; An Odor of Sanctity, 1965; Goat Song, 1967; Judas, My Brother, 1968; Speak Now, 1969; The Man from Dahomey, 1970; The Girl from Storyville, 1972; The Voyage Unplanned, 1974; Tobias and the Angel, 1975; A Rose for Ana María, 1976; Hail the Conquering Hero, 1977. *Recreations:* photography, painting. *Address:* c/o Wm Morris Agency, 1350 Avenue of the Americas, New York, NY 10019, USA. *Clubs:* Authors Guild (New York); Real Sociedad Hipica Española (Madrid).

YOCKLUNN, Sir John (Soong Chung), KCVO 1977; Kt 1975; National Librarian of Papua New Guinea, since 1975; *b* Canton, China, 5 May 1933; *s* of late Charles Soong Yocklunn and Wui Sin Yocklunn, formerly of W Australia. *Educ:* Northam High Sch., W Australia; Univ. of W Australia (BA); Aust. Nat. Univ. (BA); Univ. of Sheffield (MA). ALAA. Dept of the Treasury, Canberra, 1959-63; Nat. Library of Australia, Canberra, 1964-67; Librarian-in-Charge, Admin Coll. of Papua New Guinea, Port Moresby, 1967-69; Exec. Officer, Public Service Board of Papua New Guinea, 1969-70; Librarian, Admin Coll., 1970-72. Principal Private Sec. to Chief Minister, 1972-73; study in UK, under James Cook Bicentenary Schol., 1973-74; on return, given task of organising a national library. Vice-Pres., Pangu Pati, 1968-72; Nat. Campaign Manager for Pangu Pati for 1972 general elections in Papua New Guinea; Treasurer, Pangu Pati, 1973-77. Asst Dir, Visit of Prince of Wales to PNG, 1975; Dir, Visit of the Queen and Prince Philip to PNG, 1977. *Publications:* The Charles Barrett Collection of Books relating to Papua New Guinea, 1967, 2nd edn 1969; articles on librarianship and politics in various jls and encyclopedias. *Recreations:* book collecting, music, art. *Address:* PO Box 1821, Boroko, Papua New Guinea. *T:* (office) Port Moresby 271112; (home) Port Moresby 258898.

YOFFEY, Joseph Mendel, DSc, MD, FRCS; Visiting Professor, Hebrew University of Jerusalem, since 1969; Professor of Anatomy, University of Bristol, 1942-67, now Professor Emeritus; *b* 10 July 1902; *s* of Rabbi Israel Jacob Yoffey and Pere Jaffe; *m* 1940, Betty Gillis, LLB; three *d. Educ:* Manchester Grammar School; Univ. of Manchester. Leech Research Fellow, University of Manchester, 1926-27; Research Scholar, BMA, 1928-29; House Surgeon, Manchester Royal Infirmary, 1929-30; Asst Lectr in Anatomy, Univ. of Manchester, 1930; Senior Lectr in Anatomy, University College of South Wales and Monmouthshire, Cardiff; Hunterian Prof., RCS England, 1933 and 1940; Fellow of Rockefeller Foundn, 1937-39. Visiting Professor: Univ. of Washington, 1958; Univ. of Calif., San Francisco, 1967-68; John Curtin Sch. of Medical Research, ANU, 1968-69. John Hunter Triennial Medal, RCS, 1968. Hon. LLD Manchester, 1973. Knight First Class of the Order of the Dannebrog (Denmark), 1959. *Publications:* Quantitative Cellular Hæmatology, 1960; Bone Marrow Reactions, 1966; (with Dr F. C. Courtice) Lymphatics, Lymph and the Lymphomyeloid Complex, 1970; Bone Marrow in Hypoxia and Rebound, 1973; numerous scientific papers. *Recreations:* music, walking, modern Hebrew. *Address:* 1 Rehov Degania, Beth Hakerem, Jerusalem, Israel. *T:* Jerusalem 525738.

YONG NYUK LIN; MP (Singapore); *b* Seremban, Malaya, 24 June 1918; *s* of late Yong Thean Yong and Chen Shak Moi; *m* 1939, Kwa Geok Lan; two *d. Educ:* Raffles Coll., Singapore. Science Master, King George V Sch., Seremban, Malaya, 1938-41; with Overseas Assurance Corp., Singapore, 1941 (resigned, as Gen. Manager, 1958). Minister for Educn, 1959-63; Chm., Singapore Harbour Bd, 1961-62; Minister for: Health, 1963-68; Communications, 1968-75; Minister without Portfolio, 1975-76; High Comr in London, 1975-76. *Address:* 50 Oei Tiong Ham Park, Singapore 10.

YONGE, Sir (Charles) Maurice, Kt 1967; CBE 1954; FRS 1946; FRSE; DSc(Ed.); Hon. Fellow in Zoology, University of Edinburgh; *b* 9 Dec. 1899; *s* of John Arthur Yonge, MA, JP, and Sarah Edith Carr; *m* 1st, Martha Jane (*d* 1945), *d* of R. T. Lennox, Newmilns, Ayrshire; one *s* one *d*; 2nd, Phyllis Greenlaw, *d* of Dr D. M. M. Fraser, Eastry, Kent; one *s. Educ:*

Silcoates School, Wakefield; Edinburgh Univ. Baxter Natural Science Scholar, 1922-24; Carnegie Research Scholar, 1924-25. Temporary Asst Naturalist, Marine Biological Assoc., Plymouth, 1925-27; Balfour Student, Univ. of Cambridge, 1927-29; leader, Great Barrier Reef Expedition, 1928-29; Physiologist, Marine Biological Assoc., Plymouth, 1930-32; Prof. of Zoology, Univ. of Bristol, 1933-44; Regius Prof. of Zoology, Univ. of Glasgow, 1944-64, Research Fellow in Zoology, 1965-70. Visiting Prof., Univ. of California, 1949; Prather Lecturer, Harvard Univ., 1957; Visiting Prof., Univ. of Washington, 1959, 1969. Mem., Advisory Cttee on Fishery Research to the Development Commission, 1937-56; UK Representative, Pacific Science Council; Pres. and Chm. of Council, Scottish Marine Biological Assoc., 1944-67; Chairman: Supervisory Cttee, Brown Trout Lab., Pitlochry, 1949-59; Colonial Fisheries Adv. Cttee; Mem., Audio-Visual Aids Cttee of Univ. Grants Cttee; Mem., Natural Environment Research Council, 1965-70; Vice-Pres. and Hon. Mem. Marine Biological Assoc. UK; Vice-Pres. Royal Soc. of Edinburgh, 1953-56 (Makdougall-Brisbane Prize, 1957), Pres., 1970-73; Pres., Section D, British Assoc., 1961; Mem. Council, Royal Society, 1952-54, 1968-70. Hon. Life Fellow, Pacific Science Assoc.; Mem., Royal Danish Acad. of Science and Letters; Hon. Member: Malac. Soc. London; California Academy of Sciences; Royal Soc. of NZ. Hon. DSc: Bristol, 1959; Heriot-Watt, 1971; Manchester, 1975. Darwin Medal, Royal Society, 1968. *Publications:* (with F. S. Russell) The Seas, 1928, 4th edn 1975; A Year on the Great Barrier Reef, 1930; British Marine Life, 1944; The Sea Shore, 1949; (with J. Barrett) Guide to the Seashore, 1958; Oysters, 1960; (ed, with K. M. Wilbur) Physiology of Mollusca, vol. i, 1964, vol. ii, 1967; (with T. E. Thompson) Living Marine Molluscs, 1976; (ed, with F. S. Russell) Advances in Marine Biology; numerous scientific papers in standard scientific journals, since 1923. *Recreations:* travel, reading of history, woodwork. *Address:* 13 Cumin Place, Edinburgh EH9 2JX. *T:* 031-667 3678.

YOOL, Air Vice-Marshal William Munro, CB 1946; CBE 1941; RAF, retired list; *b* 26 May 1894. Director of Auxiliaries, Reserves and Air Cadets, Dec. 1951-54; Acting Air Vice-Marshal and AOA, Technical Training Command, 1944; formerly AOA, HQ, Mediterranean and Middle East; retd 1949. *Address:* Dawney Hill Cottage, Pirbright, Surrey GU24 0JB.

YORK, Archbishop of, since 1975; **Most Rev. and Rt. Hon. Stuart Yarworth Blanch,** PC 1975; *b* 1918; *s* of late William Edwin and of Elizabeth Blanch; *m* 1943, Brenda Gertrude, *d* of late William Arthur Coyte; one *s* four *d. Educ:* Alleyns Sch., Dulwich; Oxford (BA 1st cl. Theo. 1948, MA 1952). Employee of Law Fire Insurance Soc. Ltd, 1936-40; Navigator in RAF, 1940-46; St Catherine's Coll., Oxford, 1946-49 (Hon. Fellow, 1975); Curate of Highfield, Oxford, 1949-52; Vicar of Eynsham, Oxon, 1952-57; Tutor and Vice-Principal of Wycliffe Hall, Oxford, 1957-60 (Chm. 1967-); Oriel Canon of Rochester and Warden of Rochester Theological Coll., 1960-66; Bishop of Liverpool, 1966-75. Mem. Council, York Univ., 1976-. Hon. LLD Liverpool, 1975; Hon. DD Hull, 1977. *Publications:* The World Our Orphanage, 1972; For All Mankind, 1976. *Recreations:* squash, walking, music. *Address:* Bishopthorpe, York YO2 1QE. *Club:* Royal Commonwealth Society.

YORK, Dean of; see Jasper, Very Rev. R. C. D.

YORK, Archdeacon of; see Stanbridge, Ven. L. C.

YORK, Christopher, DL; *b* 27 July 1909; *s* of late Col Edward York; *m* 1934, Pauline Rosemary, *d* of late Sir Lionel Fletcher, CBE; one *s* three *d. Educ:* Eton; RMC Sandhurst. Joined The Royal Dragoons, India, 1930; retired, 1934, on to Supplementary Reserve; rejoined Regt, 1939, rank Major; joined Land Agents Soc., 1934, and passed examinations, acting as Land Agent until elected MP; MP (U) Harrogate Division, 1950-54 (Ripon Division of the West Riding, 1939-50); DL West Riding of Yorkshire, Later N Yorkshire, 1954; High Sheriff of Yorkshire, 1966. Hon. Fellow, Royal Veterinary Coll., 1971. *Recreation:* shooting. *Address:* South Park, Long Marston, York. *TA* and *T:* Rufforth 357. *Clubs:* Boodle's, Carlton; Yorkshire (York).

YORKE, family name of **Earl of Hardwicke.**

YORKE, Richard Michael, QC 1971; a Recorder of the Crown Court, since 1972; *b* 13 July 1930; *e s* of Gilbert Victor Yorke, Civil Engineer. *Educ:* Solihull Sch., Warwickshire; Balliol Coll., Oxford (MA). Commissioned 2nd Lt, RA, July 1949 (Prize of Honour, Best Officer Cadet); Lieut, Honourable Artillery Company, 1951; Captain, 1953. Asst to Sec., British Road Services, 1953-56. Called to Bar, Gray's Inn, 1956 (Lee Prizeman); started practice in Oct. 1956; joined Inner Temple,

1968; Barrister, Supreme Court of NSW and High Court of Australia, 1972; QC NSW 1974. Contested (C): Durham, 1966; Loughborough, Feb. and Oct. 1974. Pres., Civil Aviation Review Bd, 1972-75. Mem. Special Panel, Transport Tribunal, 1976. Voluntary Governor, Bart's Hospital, 1974. *Recreations:* ocean racing, flying, skiing. *Address:* Gray's Inn Chambers, Gray's Inn, WC1R 5JA. *T:* 01-242 5609. *Telex:* 23424 Saplegis; Selborne Chambers, 174 Philip Street, Sydney, NSW 2000. *T:* 25 2181; (home) 5 Cliveden Place, SW1W 8LA. *T:* 01-730 6054. *Clubs:* Cavalry and Guards, Royal Ocean Racing, St Stephen's; County (Durham); Northern Constitutional (Newcastle); Island Sailing (Cowes).

YORKSHIRE, EAST RIDING, Archdeacon of; *see* Snelgrove, Ven. D. G.

YORSTON, Sir (Robert) Keith, Kt 1969; CBE 1962 (OBE 1960); FCA, FASA, FCIS; Hon. FAIM; *b* 12 Feb. 1902; *s* of late R. Yorston, Shetland Is; *m* 1934, Gwendolen C., *d* of late F. A. Ridley; one *s* one *d. Educ:* Caulfield Public Sch.; Univ. of Melbourne (BCom). Principal, Aust. Accountancy Coll., Sydney, 1933-66. In practice as a Chartered Acct, in Sydney, 1933-70. Federal Pres., Australian-American Assoc., 1960, 1962-64, 1966-67, 1972; NSW Pres., Australian-American Assoc., 1957-63, 1965-74; Pres., Aust. Soc. of Accts, NSW, 1959. Rep. Australia at: Internat. Congress of Accts, 1957, 1962; Internat. Congress of Inst. of Management, 1957. Chm., NSW State Council Metropolitan Opera (New York) Auditions; Member: Australian Auditions Council, for Metropolitan Opera, New York; Council, Scots Coll., Bellevue Hill; Adjudicating Panel for best Annual Report in Australia (since inception of Annual Report Award); Bd, Scottish Hosp., Sydney. Mem. Adv. Bd, Presbyterian Foundation. Chairman: The Presbyterian Church (NSW) Property Trust, 1964-75; Council, Presbyterian Ladies Coll., Armidale. Annual Research Lecturer, Aust. Soc. of Accts: Univ. Sydney, 1951; Univ. WA, 1952; Univ. Tas, 1953; Univ. Melb., 1959; Edgar Sabine Memorial Lecture, Adelaide Univ., 1959; Guest Lectr, Jubilee Convention of NZ Soc. of Accts, 1960. *Publications:* (several books reproduced in other countries, such as UK, India and New Zealand; numerous standard text books (some jointly) on accounting, law and company practice (mostly with 2-6 edns) including: Australian Company Director, 1932; Australian Shareholders Guide, 1958, 3rd edn 1971; Australian Commercial Dictionary, 1945, 5th edn 1972; Limited Liability Companies in Australia, 1956; Twentieth Century Commerce and Book-keeping, 12th edn 1960; Costing Procedures, 1951, 5th edn 1976; Advanced Accounting, 1948, rev. 6th edn 1971; Elementary Accounting, 1952, 5th edn 1975; Company Law in New South Wales, 1947, 3rd edn 1968; Company Law in Victoria, 1955, 2nd edn 1959; Accounting Fundamentals, 1949, 6th edn 1966; Australian Mercantile Law, 1939, 14th edn 1971; Annual Reports of Companies, 1958; Australian Secretarial Practice, 1936, 5th edn 1965; Company Secretary's Guide (NSW), 1946, 2nd edn 1950; Company Secretary's Guide (Victoria), 1948, 2nd edn 1952; Company Secretary's Guide (Queensland), 1947; Company Law, 1962, 4th edn 1968; Proprietary and Private Companies in Australia, 1939, 2nd edn 1952. *Address:* 29 Trafalgar Avenue, Roseville, NSW 2069, Australia.

YOST, Charles Woodruff; Special Adviser, Aspen Institute, since 1976; Honorary Co-Chairman (formerly Counsellor), United Nations Association; *b* 6 Nov. 1907; *s* of Nicholas Doxtater and Gertrude (Cooper); *m* 1934, Irena Oldakowska; two *s* one *d. Educ:* Hotchkiss Sch.; Princeton Univ. (AB); Univ. of Paris. Entered US Foreign Service, 1930; served: Alexandria, 1930-32; Warsaw, 1932-33. Journalist, 1933-35. Dept of State, 1935-45; Asst to Chm., Dumbarton Oaks and San Francisco Confs, 1945; Sec.-Gen., US Delegn, Berlin Conf., 1945; Political Adviser to Comdg Gen., India-Burma Theatre, 1945; Chargé d'Affaires, Bangkok, 1946; Pol. Adviser to US Delegn to UN, 1946; Prague, 1947; Vienna, 1948-49; Pol. Adviser to US Delegn to UN, 1949; Dir, Office of Eastern European Affairs, 1949-50; Minister to Athens, 1950-53; Dep. High Comr for Austria, 1953-54; Laos: Minister, 1954, Ambassador, 1955-56; Minister in Paris, 1956-57; Ambassador to Syria, 1957, to Morocco, 1958-61; Dep. Rep. to UN Security Council, 1961-65; Career Ambassador, 1964; Dep. Perm. Rep. to UN, 1965-66; Senior Fellow, Council on Foreign Relations, 1966-69; Ambassador and Perm. Rep. of US to UN, 1969-71; Distinguished Lectr on Foreign Policy, Columbia Univ. Sch. of Internat. Affairs, 1971-73; Pres., Nat. Cttee on US-China Relations, 1973-75; Sen. Fellow, Brookings Instn, 1975-76. Hon. LLD: St Lawrence Univ., 1963; Princeton Univ., 1969. Rockefeller Public Service Award, 1964. *Publications:* Age of Triumph and Frustration, 1964; The Insecurity of Nations, 1968; The Conduct and Misconduct of Foreign Affairs, 1971. *Recreations:* swimming, riding, literature,

arts. *Address:* 2801 New Mexico Avenue, NW, Washington, DC 20036, USA. *Clubs:* Century, Princeton (New York); Cosmos (Washington).

YOUDE, Sir Edward, KCMG 1977 (CMG 1968); MBE 1949; HM Diplomatic Service; Ambassador to China, since 1974; *b* 19 June 1924; *m* 1951, Pamela Fitt; two *d. Educ:* Sch. of Oriental Studies, Univ. of London. RNVR, 1943-46. Joined Foreign Office, 1947. First Secretary: Washington, 1956-59; Peking, 1960-62; Foreign Office, 1962-65; Counsellor and Head of Chancery, UK Mission to UN, 1965-69; a Private Secretary to the Prime Minister, 1969-70; IDC, 1970-71; Head of Personnel Services Dept, FCO, 1971-73; Asst Under-Sec. of State, FCO, 1973-74. *Recreations:* walking, theatre, music. *Address:* c/o Foreign and Commonwealth Office, SW1.

YOUDS, Edward Ernest; His Honour Judge Youds; a Circuit Judge, Bedford, since 1972; *b* 21 Nov. 1910; *s* of late Edward Youds. *Educ:* Birkenhead Sch.; Magdalene Coll., Cambridge. BA, LLB (Hons) Cantab. Called to Bar, Gray's Inn, 1936. Practised on Northern Circuit as Barrister-at-law. Served 1940-45, France and Germany (despatches, 1945). Dep. Chm., Lancs County Sessions, 1961-66; County Court Judge, 1966-69; Puisne Judge, High Court, Uganda, 1969-72. *Address:* Bedford County Court, Silver Street, Bedford.

YOUELL, Rev. Canon George; a Residentiary Canon of Ely Cathedral since 1970, Vice-Dean and Treasurer, since 1973; *b* 23 Dec. 1910; *s* of late Herbert Youell, Beccles; *m* 1936, Gertrude Barron, *d* of late J. Irvine, West Hartlepool; two *s* three *d. Educ:* Beccles; St Michaels; Hartley Coll., Manchester; St Stephen's House, Oxford; Univ. of Keele (MA 1969). Ordained, 1933; Curate, St John's, Chester, 1933; Clerical Dir of Industrial Christian Fellowship, 1937; chaplain attached to 2nd Bn Grenadier Guards (BEF and Guards Armoured Div.), 1939; Sen. Chaplain to Forces: Nigeria, 1942; Woolwich and SE London, 1944; Nigeria and Gold Coast, 1945; Rector of Ightfield with Calverhall, Salop, 1947; Rural Dean of Leek, 1952-56; Vicar of Leek, 1952-61; Archdeacon of Stoke-upon-Trent, 1956-70; Vicar of Horton, Leek, 1968-70; Chaplain, Univ. of Keele, 1961-68; Hon. Canon, Lichfield Cathedral, 1967-70. *Publications:* Africa Marches, 1949; contributor on colonial and sociological affairs to the Guardian, 1947-51. *Recreation:* fell walking. *Address:* The Almonry, Ely, Cambs. *T:* Ely 2067. *Club:* Army and Navy.

YOUENS, Ven. Archdeacon John Ross, CB 1970; OBE 1959; MC 1946; Chaplain to the Queen since 1969; Treasurer, Corporation of the Sons of the Clergy, since 1976; *b* 29 Sept. 1914; *e s* of late Canon F. A. C. Youens; *m* 1940, Pamela Gordon Lincoln (*née* Chandler); one *s* (two *d* decd). *Educ:* Buxton Coll.; Kelham Theological Coll. Curate of Warsop, Notts, 1939-40. Commissioned RA Chaplains' Dept, 1940; Aldershot and SE Comd, 1940-42; Sen. Chaplain: 59 Inf. Div., 1942; Chatham, 1943; 2nd Army Troops, June 1944; Guards Armd Div., Nov. 1944-45; 3rd Inf. Div. in Egypt and Palestine, 1945-48; 7th Armd Div. in Germany, 1948-50; Aldershot, 1950-51; DACG, Egypt, 1951-53; Tripoli, 1953-54; Sen. Chaplain, RMA Sandhurst, 1955-58; DACG, Gibraltar, 1958-60; ACG War Office, 1960-61, Rhine Army, 1961-66; Chaplain General to the Forces, 1966-74; Hon. Archdeacon, 1974. Mem. Council, Keston Coll., Centre for the Study of Religion and Communism, 1975-. *Recreation:* golf. *Address:* Bulfigs, Hook Heath, Woking, Surrey GU22 0QE. *T:* Woking 68031. *Clubs:* Army and Navy, Cavalry and Guards (Hon. Mem.).

YOUENS, Sir Peter (William), Kt 1965; CMG 1962; OBE 1960; *b* 29 April 1916; 2nd *s* of late Canon F. A. C. Youens; *m* 1943, Diana Stephanie, *d* of Edward Hawkins, Southacre, Norfolk; two *d. Educ:* King Edward VII's School, Sheffield; Wadham College, Oxford. MA (Oxon), 1938. Joined Colonial Administrative Service; naval service, 1939-40. Sub-Lt, Cadet S. L., 1939; Asst Dist Comr, 1942; Dist Comr, 1948; Colony Comr and Member, Sierra Leone Legislative Council, 1950; Asst Sec., Nyasaland, 1951; Dep. Chief Sec., 1953-63; Secretary to the Prime Minister and to the Cabinet, Malawi, 1964-66 (Nyasaland, 1963-64); Mem., Nyasaland Legislative Council, 1954-61. Retired, 1966. Exec. Dir, Lonrho Ltd, 1966-69; Partner, John Tyzack & Partners Ltd, 1969-. *Address:* The Old Parsonage, Hurstborne Priors, Whitchurch, Hants. *Clubs:* East India, Devonshire, Sports and Public Schools; Vincent's (Oxford).

YOUNG, family name of **Baron Kennet,** and **Baroness Young.**

YOUNG; *see* Hughes-Young, family name of Baron St Helens.

YOUNG; see Mackworth-Young.

YOUNG, Baroness *cr* 1971 (Life Peer), of Farnworth in the County Palatine of Lancaster; **Janet Mary Young;** *b* 23 Oct. 1926; *d* of John Norman Leonard Baker and Phyllis Marguerite Baker (*née* Hancock); *m* 1950, Geoffrey Tyndale Young; three *d. Educ:* Dragon School Oxford, Headington School, and in America; St Anne's Coll., Oxford; MA (Politics, Philosophy and Economics). Baroness in Waiting (Govt Whip), 1972-73; Parly Under-Sec. of State, DoE, 1973-74. A Vice-Chm., Cons. Party Organisation, 1975-. Councillor Oxford City Council, 1957; Alderman, 1967-72; Leader of Conservative Group, 1967-72. Dir, UK Provident Instn, 1975-. Mem., BR Adv. Bd, Western Reg., 1977-. Hon. FIMunE. *Recreation:* music. *Address:* 23 Northmoor Road, Oxford OX2 6UR. *T:* Oxford 58295.

YOUNG, Prof. Alec David, OBE 1964; MA; FRS 1973; FRAeS; AFAIAA; Professor and Head of the Department of Aeronautical Engineering, Queen Mary College, London University, since 1954; Vice-Principal, Queen Mary College, 1966; *b* 15 Aug. 1913; *s* of Isaac Young and Katherine (*née* Freeman); *m* 1st, 1937, Dora Caplan (*d* 1970); two *s* one *d* ; 2nd, 1971, Rena Waldmann (*née* Szafer). *Educ:* Caius Coll., Cambridge. Wrangler, Mathematical Tripos, 1935. Research Student in Aeronautics, Cambridge, 1935-36; Mem. of staff, Aerodynamics Dept, Royal Aircraft Estab., 1936-46; College of Aeronautics: Senior Lectr and Dep. Head of Dept of Aerodynamics, 1946-50; Prof. and Head of Dept of Aerodynamics, 1950-54. Dean, Faculty of Engineering, Univ. of London, 1962-66; Mem. Senate, Univ. of London, 1970-. Mem. various Cttees of Aeronautical Research Council, Chm. of Council, 1968-71. Chm., Bd of Direction, Von Karman Institute for Fluid Dynamics, 1964; Mem., Advisory Bd, RAF Coll., Cranwell, 1966. Gold Medal, 1972, Royal Aeronautical Soc. (Past Chm., Aerodynamics Data Sheets Cttee); FRAeS, 1951. Ludwig Prandtl Ring, Deutsche Gesellschaft für Luft-und Raumfahrt, 1976. Commandeur de l'Ordre de Leopold, 1976. *Publications:* various, of Aeronautical Research Council, Coll. of Aeronautics Reports series; articles in Aeronautical Quarterly and Jl of Royal Aeronautical Soc., Quarterly Jl of Mechanics and Applied Mathematics, and Aircraft Engineering. Co-author of An Elementary Treatise on the Mechanics of Fluids, 1960, 2nd edn 1970. *Recreation:* drama. *Address:* 17 Regent Square, Bruce Road, Bow, E3 3HQ. *T:* 01-980 9355.

YOUNG, Maj.-Gen. Alexander, CB 1971; *b* 22 Feb. 1915; *s* of late Alexander and Mary M. K. G. Young, Edinburgh; *m* 1942, Joan Madeline, *d* of late John N. Stephens, London; one *s. Educ:* Daniel Stewart's Coll., Edinburgh. Served, BEF, 1940; WO, 1942-46; HQ, Caribbean Area, 1947-50; WO, 1950-52; HQ Middle East Comd, Egypt and Cyprus, 1954-57; Bt Lt-Col 1955; Comdr RAOC, 4 Inf. Div., 1957-59; HQ, BAOR, 1959-61; WO, 1961-64; Dep. Dir, Ordnance Services, Eastern Comd, 1964-65; Comd COD, Bicester, 1965-67; Comd UK Base Org., 1967-68; Dir of Ordnance Services, MoD, 1968-71. Col Comdt, RAOC, 1971-75. FBIM. *Recreations:* travel, golf. *Address:* Gaddons Cottage, Seaward Drive, West Wittering, Sussex. *T:* West Wittering 2118. *Club:* Army and Navy.

YOUNG, Alexander; free-lance concert and opera singer; Head of Department of Vocal Studies, Royal Northern College of Music, Manchester, since 1973; *b* London; *m* 1948, Jean Anne Prewett; one *s* one *d. Educ:* secondary; (scholar) Royal Coll. of Music, London; studied in London with late Prof. Pollmann, of Vienna State Academy. FRNCM 1977. Served War, HM Forces, 1941-46. Has regular engagements with the BBC and has sung in the USA, Canada, and most European countries, as well as frequently in Britain. First operatic rôle (tenor), as Scaramuccio in Strauss' Ariadne, Edin. Fest., with Glyndebourne Opera, 1950; parts at Glyndebourne, and began broadcasting for BBC, 1951 (subseq. incl. opera, oratorio, recitals, light music, etc). First appearances: with English Opera Group, world Première of Lennox Berkeley's opera, A Dinner Engagement, 1954; also appeared at Royal Festival Hall, several times with Sir Thomas Beecham, in Mozart Requiem; at Sadler's Wells Opera, as Eisenstein in Die Fledermaus, 1959, and subsequently in many roles such as: Ramiro in La Cenerentola; title role in Count Ory; Almaviva in The Barber of Seville; notable roles include: Tom in Stravinsky's Rake's Progress (which he created for British audiences); David in Die Meistersinger; title role in Mozart's Idomeneo. At Covent Garden sang in: Strauss's Arabella; Britten's A Midsummer Night's Dream. Oratorio roles include: Evangelist in Bach Passions; Elgar's Dream of Gerontius; Britten's War Requiem. Is regularly engaged by Welsh National Opera and Scottish Opera. Many commercial recordings, especially of Handel oratorios and operas, as well as The Rake's Progress conducted by the composer. Lieder recitals a speciality. *Recreation:* photography. *Address:* Royal Northern College of Music, 124 Oxford Road, Manchester M13 9RD.

YOUNG, Andrew; United States Ambassador to the United Nations, since 1977; *b* New Orleans, La, 12 March 1932; *s* of Andrew J. Young and Daisy Fuller; *m* 1954, Jean Childs; one *s* three *d. Educ:* Howard Univ., USA; Hartford Theological Seminary. Ordained, United Church of Christ, 1955; Pastor, Thomasville, Ga, 1955-57; Associate Dir for Youth Work, Nat. Council of Churches, 1957-61; Admin. Christian Educn Programme, United Church of Christ, 1961-64; Mem. Staff, Southern Christian Leadership Conf., 1961-70; Exec. Dir, 1964-70; Exec. Vice-Pres., 1967-70; Perm. Rep. to UN, 1977-. Chairman: Atlanta Community Relations Commn, 1970-72; Democratic voter registration drive, 1976; during 1960s organized voter registration and community develt programmes. Holds numerous hon. degrees and awards. *Address:* Permanent Mission of the United States to the United Nations, 799 United Nations Plaza, New York, NY 10017, USA.

YOUNG, Col Sir Arthur (Edwin), KBE 1971; Kt 1965; CMG 1953; CVO 1962; KPM 1952; Commissioner, City of London Police, 1950-71 (seconded 1969-70 as Chief Constable, Royal Ulster Constabulary); President, Greater London Scout County (Boy Scouts' Association), since 1972; *b* 1907; *s* of Edwin Young; *m* 1st, 1939, Ivy Ada (*d* 1956); one *s*; 2nd, 1957, Margaret Furnival Homan (*née* Dolphin), Sidmouth and Washington (*d* 1966); 3rd, 1970, Mrs Ileen Turner. *Educ:* Portsmouth Grammar Sch. Joined Portsmouth City Police, 1924. Chief Constable, Leamington 1938; Senior Assistant Chief Constable of Birmingham, 1941; Allied Control Commission for Italy (Public Safety), 1943-45; Chief Constable of Hertfordshire, 1945; Assistant Commissioner of Police of the Metropolis, May 1947. Visited the Gold Coast, 1951, to make recommendations to Govt on re-organisation of Gold Coast Police; Comr of Federation of Malaya Police, 1952; Comr of Kenya Police, 1954. Hon. Comr of Police, New York. Director, Police Extended Interviews, 1962-71; Chairman: Police Council for Great Britain, 1965-71; Council, Police Athletic Assoc., 1952-71; Life Saving Federation, 1968. Member: Advisory Council National Police Fund, 1950-71 (Chairman Educ. Committee); Board of Governors of the Police Coll. and Atlantic Coll., 1966-71; Vice-President, Police Mutual Assurance Soc., 1960-71. King Gustav VI of Sweden's medal of merit, for services to sport, 1962, 1977. Vice-Chairman, National Small-Bore Rifle Assoc., 1964. Officer (Brother) Order of St John. Holds many foreign decorations. *Recreation:* walking. *Address:* 22 Grand Court, Eastbourne BN21 4BU. *T:* Eastbourne 25905. *Club:* Athenæum.

YOUNG, Bertram Alfred; dramatic critic, since 1964, and arts editor, 1971-77, The Financial Times; *b* 20 Jan. 1912; *y* (twin) *s* of Bertram William Young and Dora Elizabeth Young (*née* Knight); unmarried. *Educ:* Highgate. Served with Artists Rifles, 1930-35, and Lancs Fusiliers, KAR and Staff, 1939-48; Asst Editor, Punch, 1949-62; Dramatic Critic, Punch, 1962-64. Mem., British Council Drama Adv. Cttee. *Publications:* Tooth and Claw, 1958; How to Avoid People, 1963; Bechuanaland, 1966; Cabinet Pudding, 1967; author of about 20 radio plays broadcast 1938-49. *Recreation:* music (consumer only). *Address:* 28 Elm Park Gardens, Chelsea, SW10 9NZ. *T:* 01-352 5423. *Club:* Garrick.

YOUNG, Air Vice-Marshal Brian Pashley, CB 1972; CBE 1960 (OBE 1944); Commandant General, Royal Air Force Regiment, and Inspector of Ground Defence, 1968-73, retired; *b* 5 May 1918; *s* of Kenneth Noel Young and Flora Elizabeth Young, Natal, S Africa; *m* 1942, Patricia Josephine, *d* of Thomas Edward Cole, Bedford; three *s* two *d. Educ:* Michaelhouse, Natal, SA; RAF Coll., Cranwell. Fighter Comd, UK and France, 1938-40 (wounded); Hosp., 1941-42; Coastal Comd, N Ire and Western Isles, 1942-43; Aden and Persian Gulf, 1944; Staff Coll., Haifa, 1945; Middle East, 1946-47; Air Min., 1948-50; Bomber Comd HQ No 1 Gp, Hemswell/Gaydon, 1951-57; HQ Bomber Comd, 1958-60; NATO, Fontainebleau, Asst Chief of Staff, Intelligence, 1960-62; IDC 1963; AOC, Central Reconnaisance Establt, 1964-67. *Recreations:* cricket, squash; Rep. RAF: athletics, 1939, Rugby, 1947-48. *Address:* 22 Highfield Road, Purley, Surrey. *T:* 01-660 7817. *Club:* Royal Air Force.

YOUNG, Sir Brian (Walter Mark), Kt 1976; MA; Director-General, Independent Broadcasting Authority (formerly Independent Television Authority), since 1970; *b* 23 Aug. 1922; *er s* of late Sir Mark Young, GCMG and late Josephine (*née* Price); *m* 1947, Fiona Marjorie, *o d* of late Allan, 16th Stewart of Appin, and of Mrs Stewart; one *s* two *d. Educ:* Eton; King's College, Cambridge. Served in RNVR, mainly in destroyers, 1941-45. First class hons in Part I, 1946, and Part II, 1947, of Classical Tripos; Porson Prize, 1946; Winchester Reading Prize, 1947; BA 1947; MA 1952. Assistant Master at Eton, 1947-52; Headmaster of Charterhouse, 1952-64; Dir, Nuffield Foundn,

1964-70. Member: Central Advisory Council for Education, 1956-59 (Crowther Report); Central Religious Adv. Cttee of BBC and ITA, 1960-64. *Publications:* Via Vertendi, 1952; Intelligent Reading (with P. D. R. Gardiner), 1964. *Address:* IBA, 70 Brompton Road, SW3 1EY.

YOUNG, Carmichael Aretas, MD, FRCP; Physician and Physician i/c Diabetic Clinic, St Mary's Hospital Teaching Group, London, W2, since 1948; Consultant in Chest Diseases, Ministry of Pensions, since 1948; *b* Adelaide, S Australia, 19 Aug. 1913; *e s* of Aretas Henry Young, Adelaide, SA and Isabelle Wilson, Parattah, Tas; *m* 1939, Marie, 2nd *d* of W. H. Lewry, Botley, Hants; three *s* one *d. Educ:* Carey Grammar Sch., Kew, Vic.; St Mary's Hosp. Medical Sch., Univ. of London. MRCS, LRCP 1936, FRCP 1950; MB, BS (London), 1936, MD 1940. House Phys. and House Surg., St Mary's Hosp., 1936-37; House Phys., Asst Resident MO, Brompton Hosp., 1938; Asst, Professorial Medical Unit, St Mary's, 1939; Phys., EMS, 1940-41; Medical Specialist 10th (Brit.) CCS, 1942-43 (despatches); No 1 Gen. Hosp., 1944; Lt-Col RAMC O i/c Medical Div. 43 Gen. Hosp., 1945; OC 43 Gen. Hosp., Beirut, 1946. Medical Registrar, Prince of Wales' Gen. Hosp., 1946-47; Sub-Dean, St Mary's Hosp. Medical School, 1952-53; Examiner: Soc. of Apothecaries, Medicine, 1964-70; Univ. London, Therapeutics, Medicine, 1957-62; Conj. Bd, Pathology, Medicine (Chm., 1970-71); Pro-Censor, 1973-74, Censor, 1974-75, RCP; Royal Soc. Med. Mem., Bd of Governors, St Mary's Hosp., 1958-61. Hon. Colonel No 4 Gen. Hosp. AER, 1961. *Publications:* History of the Otter Swimming Club, 1869-1969, 1969; short articles in medical jls. *Recreations:* swimming, water-polo, golf, reading. *Address:* 38 Devonshire Street, W1. *T:* 01-935 7883; 01-788 0490. *Clubs:* Royal Wimbledon Golf; Otter Swimming (Pres. 1964-67).

YOUNG, Rev. Canon (Cecil) Edwyn; Chaplain, The Queen's Chapel of the Savoy, and Chaplain of the Royal Victorian Order, since 1974; Chaplain to the Queen since 1972; *b* 29 April 1913; *er s* of Cecil Morgan Young and Doris Edith Virginia Young, Colombo, Ceylon; *m* 1944, Beatrice Mary, *e d* of Percy Montague Rees and Beatrice Rees; two *s* one *d. Educ:* Radley Coll.; Dorchester Missionary College. Curate, St Peter's, London Docks, 1936-41; Priest in Charge, St Francis, N Kensington, 1941-44; Rector of Broughton with Ripton Regis, 1944-47; Vicar of St Silas, Pentonville, 1947-53; Rector of Stepney, 1953-64, and Rural Dean of Stepney, 1959-64; Prebendary of St Paul's, 1959-64; Rector and Rural Dean of Liverpool, 1964-73; Canon Diocesan, 1965-73. Commissary, Diocese of North Queensland, 1959-, Canon to the Ordinary, 1974-. Chaplain: Worshipful Co. of Distillers, 1974-; Weavers' Co., 1977-; to Chm., Freight Forwarders Inst., 1974-. Pres., Sion College, 1963-64. *Publications:* No Fun Like Work, 1970; (contrib.) Father Groser, East End Priest, 1971. *Recreations:* meeting people; wild flowers; the theatre, especially music hall; watching cricket. *Address:* The Queen's Chapel of the Savoy, Strand, WC2; 18 Coombe Lane West, Kingston on Thames. *T:* 01-942 1196. *Clubs:* Greenroom, City Livery.

YOUNG, (Charles) Kenneth, FRSL; Political and Literary Adviser to Beaverbrook Newspapers since 1965, and formerly, Editor of the Yorkshire Post; *b* 27 Nov. 1916; *o s* of late Robert William Young, Iron Founder, Middlestown, Wakefield, and late Alice Jane Young (*née* Ramsden); *m* 1951, Phyllis, *d* of late Lt-Col J. A. Dicker; three *s* two *d. Educ:* Queen Elizabeth's Grammar Sch. (Junior Dept), Wakefield; Coatham Sch., Redcar; Leeds Univ. BA (1st Cl. Hons Eng. Lang. and Lit.), 1938. Served War of 1939-45. Royal Corps of Signals, 1940; Intelligence Corps, 1941 (Algeria, Italy, Greece); Foreign Office, 1944. BBC European Service, 1948; Daily Mirror, 1949; Daily Mail, 1950; Permanent Under-Sec. Dept, Cabinet Office, 1950; Daily Telegraph, 1952-60; Editor of The Yorkshire Post, 1960-64. FRSL 1964. Broadcaster: Editor, Television series, The Book Man, 1960. Governor, Welbeck College, 1963-73. *Publications:* D. H. Lawrence, 1952; John Dryden (critical biography), 1954; Ford Madox Ford, 1958; (ed) The Bed Post, 1962; (ed) The Second Bed Post, 1965; A. J. Balfour, authorised biography, 1963; Churchill and Beaverbrook: a study in friendship and politics, 1966; Rhodesia and Independence: a study in British colonial policy, 1967, 2nd edn 1969; Sir Compton Mackenzie, an essay, 1967; Music's Great Days in the Spas and Watering-places, 1968; The Greek Passion: a study in people and politics, 1969; Sir Alec Douglas-Home, 1970; Chapel, 1972; (ed) Diaries of Sir Robert Bruce Lockhart, vol. I, 1973, vol. II, 1978; H. G. Wells, an essay, 1974; Life of 6th Earl of Rosebery, 1974; Arnold Bennett, an essay, 1975; Baldwin: a biography, 1976; J. B. Priestley, an essay, 1978. *Recreations:* being with family, listening to music, talk. *Address:* 35 Central Parade, Herne Bay, Kent. *T:* Herne Bay 5419. *Clubs:* Beefsteak, Press.

YOUNG, Christopher Alwyne Jack, FRS 1972; *b* 7 March 1912; *s* of Henry George and Penelope Young; *m* 1946, Wendy Gladys Henniker Heaton, *d* of Peter Edward and Ellen Mary Tyson, Alnwick, Northumberland; no *c. Educ:* Colston's Sch.; St Edmund Hall, Oxford (BA, BSc). Cheltenham Coll., 1934-37; Sudan Govt Service, 1937-40; ICI Ltd, Billingham Div. (incl. TA and FIDO Projects), 1940-46. Dir, ICI Central Instrument Research Laboratory, 1946-71; Technical Dir, ICI Corporate Laboratory, 1971-73. Chairman: Instrumentation and Control Panel of Engineering Equipment Users' Assoc., 1949-58; Process Control Terminology Panel of BSI, 1949-59; Instrument Adv. Cttee of City and Guilds Inst., 1949-64; Process Control Engrg Cttee, BSI, 1971-. Governor, Battersea Polytechnic, 1956-66. Member: OEEC Mission to USA on Chemical Engrg, 1950; Inst. of Measurement and Control (formerly Soc. Inst. Tech.), Council, 1951-54, Pres., 1954-57; Scientific Instrument Research Assoc., Council, 1953-56. Chm., Control Advisory Cttee, 1965-67; UK Automation Council, R&D Cttee, 1957-59; Chm., Instrumentation and Control Adv. Cttee of Assoc. of British Chemical Manufrs, 1954-58; British Council Mission to USSR on Automation, 1959; Glazebrook Cttee, Nat. Phys. Laboratory, 1966-68; Fluids and Heat Cttee, Nat. Engrg Laboratory Steering Cttee, 1966-68; Univ. of Surrey, Council, 1966-72; Council for Nat. Academic Awards, Instrumentation and Systems Engrg Bd, 1967-; Hon. Fellow, Inst of Measurement and Control, 1973. Hon. DTech Univ. of Bradford, 1969. First Sir Harold Hartley Medal, 1969. *Publications:* Process Control, 1954; An Introduction to Process Control System Design, 1955; numerous papers on instrumentation and control. *Address:* Concord House, White Cross, Zeals, Warminster, Wilts BA12 6PH. *T:* Bourton (Dorset) 482.

YOUNG, Christopher Godfrey; a Recorder of the Crown Court, since 1975; *b* 9 Sept. 1932; *s* of the late Harold Godfrey Young, MB, ChB, and Gladys Mary Young; *m* 1969, Jeanetta Margaret, *d* of Halford and Dorothy Vaughan; one *s. Educ:* Bedford Sch.; King's Coll., Univ. of London (LLB Hons 1954). Called to the Bar, Gray's Inn, 1957; Midland and Oxford Circuit, 1959. Chm., Maidwell with Draughton Parish Council, 1973-76. *Recreations:* music, natural history, gardening. *Address:* School Farm House, Maidwell, Northants. *T:* Maidwell 682; 2 Crown Office Row, Temple, EC4. *T:* 01-353 1365. *Club:* Northampton and County (Northampton).

YOUNG, Colin, OBE 1976; Director, National Film School of Great Britain, since 1970; *b* 5 April 1927; *s* of Colin Young and Agnes Holmes Kerr Young; *m* 1960, Kristin Ohman; two *s. Educ:* Bellahouston Academy, Glasgow; Univs of Glasgow, St Andrews and California (Los Angeles). Theatre and film critic, Bon Accord, Aberdeen, 1951; cameraman, editor, writer, director, 1953-; producer, 1967-; UCLA (Motion Pictures): Instructor, 1956-59; Asst Prof., 1959-64; Assoc. Prof., 1964-68; Prof., 1968-70, Head, Motion Picture Div., Theater Arts Dept, UCLA, 1964-65; Chm., Dept of Theater Arts, 1965-70. Vice-Chm., 1972-76, Chm., 1976-, Edinburgh Film Festival; Governor, BFI, 1974-. Member: Arts Council Film Cttee, 1972-76; Public Media Panel, Nat. Endowment for Arts, Washington, 1972-77; Gen. Adv. Council, BBC, 1973-; Council of Management, BAFTA, 1974-; Exec. Cttee, Centre International de Liaison des Ecoles de Cinéma et de Télévision, 1974-. FBKS 1975. Chm., Cttee on Educational Policy, UCLA, 1968-69. Los Angeles Editor, Film Quarterly, 1958-68. *Publications:* various articles in collections of film essays (including Principles of Visual Anthropology, 1975), 1961-; experimental film essay for Unesco, 1963; ethnographic film essay for Unesco, 1966; contribs to Film Quarterly, Sight and Sound, Jl of Aesthetic Education, Jl of the Producers Guild of America, Kosmorama (Copenhagen), etc. *Address:* National Film School, Beaconsfield, Bucks. *Clubs:* Savile, Le Petit Club Français.

YOUNG, Rt. Rev. David Nigel de Lorentz; see Ripon, Bishop of.

YOUNG, Maj.-Gen. David Tod, CB 1977; DFC 1952; Director of Infantry, since 1977; *b* 17 May 1926; *s* of late William Young and Davina Tod Young; *m* 1950, Joyce Marian Melville; two *s. Educ:* George Watson's Coll., Edinburgh. Commissioned, The Royal Scots (The Royal Regt), 1945 (Col, 1975). Attached Glider Pilot Regt, 1949-52; Bt Lt-Col, 1964; Mil. Asst to Dep. Chief of Gen. Staff, MoD, 1964-67; commanded 1st Bn The Royal Scots (The Royal Regt), 1967-69; Col Gen. Staff, Staff Coll., 1969-70; Comdr, 12th Mechanized Bde, 1970-72; Dep. Mil. Sec., MoD, 1972-74; Comdr Land Forces, NI, 1975-77. *Recreations:* golf, shooting, spectator of sports. *Club:* Royal Scots (Edinburgh).

YOUNG, David Wright; MP (Lab) Bolton East, since Feb. 1974; teacher; *b* Greenock, Scotland, 12 Oct. 1928. *Educ:* Greenock

Academy; Glasgow Univ.; St Paul's Coll., Cheltenham. Head of History Dept; subseq. insurance executive. Joined Labour Party, 1955; contested: South Worcestershire, 1959; Banbury, 1965; Bath, 1970. Formerly Alderman, Nuneaton Borough Council; Councillor, Nuneaton District Council. Chm., Coventry East Labour Party, 1964-68. Member, Transport and General Workers Union; Member, Fabian Society. Is especially interested in comprehensive educn, defence, pensions, economics. *Recreations:* reading, motoring. *Address:* House of Commons, SW1A 0AA.

YOUNG, Dr Edith Isabella, CBE 1964; *b* 7 March 1904; *d* of William Ross Young and Margaret Ramsay Young (*née* Hill). *Educ:* High Sch., Stirling; Univ. of Glasgow. BSc 1924, MA (1st cl. Hons Mathematics and Natural Philosophy) 1925. HM Inspector of Schools, Scottish Educn Dept, 1935-64; HM Inspector, in charge of Dundee and Angus, 1946-52; HM Chief Inspector, Highland Div., 1952-64. UNESCO expert on the teaching of science in Yugoslavia, Oct. 1956-Feb. 1957; UK Deleg., UNESCO Conf., Belgrade, 1960; Mem. Council for Technical Educn and Trg for Overseas Countries, 1964-68 (Chm., Women's Gp); UK Deleg. to Commonwealth Conf. on Trg of Technicians in Huddersfield, 1966; Co-Chm., Women's Nat. Commn, 1971-73; Pres., British Fedn of Univ. Women, 1967-70. Chairman: Northern Regional Nurse Trng Cttee, 1967-; Inverness Hosp. Bd, 1968-74. Hon. LLD Southampton, 1967. *Recreations:* sundry. *Address:* 36 Broadstone Park, Inverness. *T:* Inverness 33216. *Clubs:* Royal Over-Seas League, University Women's.

YOUNG, Edward Preston, DSO 1944; DSC 1943; writer and freelance book designer; *b* 17 Nov. 1913; *m* 1st, 1945, Diana Lilian Graves (marr. diss.); two *d*; 2nd, 1956, Mary Reoch Cressall. *Educ:* Highgate Sch. Served War, 1940-45: RNVR; entered submarine service 1940 (despatches, DSC); first RNVR officer to command operational submarine, 1943 (DSO, Bar to DSC); temp. Commander RNVR, 1945. Man. Dir, Rainbird Publishing Gp Ltd, 1970-73. *Publications:* One of Our Submarines, 1952; Look at Lighthouses, 1961; The Fifth Passenger, 1962; Look at Submarines, 1964. *Recreation:* gardening. *Address:* c/o Barclays Bank Ltd, 19 Cumberland Place, W1. *Club:* Garrick.

YOUNG, Rev. Canon Edwyn; see Young, Rev. Canon C. E.

YOUNG, Eric Edgar; HM Diplomatic Service, retired; *b* 1 July 1912; *yr s* of late Frank E. Young, Dulwich; *m* 1938, Aurora Corral, San Sebastian, Spain; two *d*. *Educ:* Alleyn's Sch., Dulwich; Jesus Coll., Oxford. Served Army, 1940-46 (Major, RAC). Diplomatic (formerly Foreign) Service, 1946-70; Served at: Buenos Aires, 1946-49; Montevideo, 1950-52; Mexico City, 1952-55; FO, 1955-58; Rangoon, 1958-60; HM Consul, Tamsui (Formosa), 1960-62; FO, 1962-64; Adv. to Kenya Min. of Foreign Affairs, Nairobi, 1964-67; HM Consul-General, Paris, 1967-70. *Publications:* The Bowes Museum, Barnard Castle, Catalogue of Spanish and Italian Paintings, 1970; Bartolomé Bermejo: The Great Hispano-Flemish Master, 1975; contrib. to: Apollo, The Burlington Magazine, The Connoisseur, Archivo Español de Arte, Goya, Revista de Arte, Art Bulletin (NY), Museum Studies (Chicago), J. Paul Getty Museum Jl. *Recreation:* art history. *Address:* 19 Hyde Park Gardens Mews, W2 2NU.
See also Sir F. G. Young.

YOUNG, Eric William, BEng (Hons); MIMechE, MIEE; *b* 26 March 1896; 2nd *s* of Colonel C. A. Young, CB, CMG; *m* 1936, Mrs Olive Bruce. *Educ:* Epsom Coll.; Shrewsbury Sch.; Liverpool Univ. (BEng Hons, 1922). Served RE (T) (Lieut) 1913-19. Metropolitan Vickers Ltd, 1922-26; Technical Manager, Electrolux Ltd, 1926-39; Rootes Ltd: General Manager, Aero Engine Factories, 1939-45; Director and General Manager, Sunbeam Talbot Ltd, 1945-46; Director, Rootes Export Co. Ltd, 1946-47; Sales Director, Harry Ferguson Ltd, 1947-53; Managing Director, Eastern Hemisphere Division, Massey-Ferguson Ltd, 1953-56; Vice-Chm., Massey-Ferguson Holdings Ltd, 1956-65, Chm., 1965-70. *Recreations:* golf, gardening. *Address:* Childerstone, Liphook, Hampshire. *T:* Liphook 722125. *Clubs:* Bath; Liphook Golf.

YOUNG, Sir Frank (George), Kt 1973; FRS 1949; DSc, PhD (London), MA (Cantab), FRSM; CChem, FRIC; Sir William Dunn Professor of Biochemistry, University of Cambridge, 1949-75; now Professor Emeritus; Master of Darwin College, Cambridge, 1964-76, Hon. Fellow 1977; Hon. Fellow of Trinity Hall, Cambridge, since 1965 (Fellow, 1949-64); Fellow of University College, London; *b* 25 March 1908; *er s* of late Frank E. Young, Dulwich; *m* 1933, Ruth (MB, BS, DPM), *o d* of Thomas Turner, Beckenham, Kent; three *s* one *d. Educ:*

Alleyn's Sch., Dulwich; University Coll., London. Beit Memorial Fellow at University Coll., London, University of Aberdeen and University of Toronto, 1932-36; Member of Scientific Staff, Medical Research Council, 1936-42; Professor of Biochemistry, University of London, 1942-49. Vice Pres. and Hon. Mem., British Diabetic Assoc., 1948-; Member: Medical Res. Council, 1950-54; Commission on Higher Educ. for Africans in Central Africa, 1952; Inter-University Council for Higher Education Overseas, 1961-73; Commission on new Chinese University in Hong Kong, 1962-63; Medical Sub-Cttee, UGC, 1964-73; Board of Governors of United Cambridge Hospitals, 1964-68; Royal Commn on Medical Educn, 1965-68; Council, British Nutrition Foundn, 1967-; Council of Nestlé Foundn, Lausanne, 1970-. Trustee: of Kennedy Memorial Trust, 1964-76; Ciba Foundn, 1967-. President: European Assoc. for the Study of Diabetes, 1965-68, Hon. Mem., 1973; British Nutrition Foundn, 1970-76; Internat. Diabetes Fedn, 1970-73 (Hon. Pres., 1973-); Vice-Pres. and Mem. of Exec. Bd, Internat. Council of Scientific Unions, 1970-73. Chairman: Smith Kline and French Trustees (UK), 1963-77; Clinical Endocrinology Cttee (MRC), 1965-72; Adv. Cttee on Irradiation of Food (UK), 1967-; Executive Council, Ciba Foundation, 1967-77. Croonian Lecturer, Royal Society, 1962. Named lectureships held abroad: Renziehausen, Pittsburg, 1939; Sterling, Yale, 1939; Jacobæus, Oslo, 1948; Dohme, Johns Hopkins, 1950; Banting, Toronto, 1950; Banting, San Francisco, 1950; Richardson, Harvard, 1952; Hanna, Western Reserve, 1952; Woodward, Yale, 1958; Brailsford Robertson, Adelaide, 1960; Upjohn, Atlantic City, 1963. Hon. or corresp. member of many foreign medical and scientific bodies. Hon. FRCP. Hon. LLD Aberdeen; Hon. DSc Rhodesia; Doctor *hc*: Catholic University of Chile; Univ. Montpellier. *Publications:* scientific papers in Biochemical Journal and other scientific and medical journals on hormonal control of metabolism, diabetes mellitus, and related topics. *Address:* 11 Bentley Road, Cambridge CB2 2AW. *T:* Cambridge 52650. *Club:* Athenæum.
See also E. E. Young.

YOUNG, Frederick Trestrail Clive, CBE 1937; *b* 19 March 1887; *y s* of late James Young, Calcutta, and of late L. Z. Young, Rockmount, Helensburgh, Dunbartonshire; *m* 1920, Hope MacLellan Fulton, Findhorn, Helensburgh; two *s* one *d. Educ:* Merchiston Castle, Edinburgh (School Captain); Pembroke Coll., Cambridge. BA (Hons Classical Tripos, 1909); Sudan Political Service, 1910, District Commissioner; Commissioner Nomad (Beja) Administration, 1926; Assistant Civil Secretary, 1929-32; Governor: Kassala Province, 1932-34; Blue Nile Province, 1934-36; Retired, 1936; Order of Nile 4th class, 1920, 3rd class, 1930; King George V Jubilee Medal, 1935. *Recreations:* golf, tennis, sailing. *Address:* West Down House, Budleigh Salterton, Devon. *T:* Budleigh Salterton 2762. *Club:* Royal Commonwealth Society.

YOUNG, Frieda Margaret, OBE 1969; HM Diplomatic Service, retired; *b* 9 April 1913; *d* of Arthur Edward Young. *Educ:* Wyggeston Grammar Sch., Leicester; Wycombe Abbey Sch., Bucks; and in France and Germany. Home Office, 1937-39; Min. of Home Security, 1939-41; MOI 1941-44; Paris 1944-48; Tehran 1948-51; Vienna 1951-54; FO 1954-57; First Secretary and Consul, Reykjavik, 1957-59; Consul, Cleveland, 1959-62; FO 1962-65; Consul, Bergen, 1965-68; Consul-General, Rotterdam, 1968-73. *Recreations:* travel, photography, bird-watching. *Address:* 6 Lady Street, Lavenham, Suffolk. *Club:* Royal Commonwealth Society.

YOUNG, George Bell, CBE 1976; Managing Director, East Kilbride Development Corporation, since 1973 (and Stonehouse, 1973-77); *b* 17 June 1924; *s* of late George Bell Young and of Jemima Mackinlay; *m* 1946, Margaret Wylie Boyd (decd); one *s. Educ:* Queens Park, Glasgow. MIEx 1958; MInstM 1969; MBIM 1970. RNVR, 1942-45, Lieut (destroyers and mine-sweepers). Journalist and Feature Writer, Glasgow Herald, 1945-48; North of Scotland Hydro-Electric Board, 1948-52; London Sec. of Scottish Council (Development and Industry), 1952-68; Gen. Man., E Kilbride Develt Corp., 1968-73. Mem. Council, Nat. Trust for Scotland, 1974-; Dir, Royal Caledonian Schools, 1957-; Chm., East Kilbride and District National Savings Cttee, 1968-; Scottish Chm., British Heart Foundn, 1975-, and Mem., East Kilbride Cttee, 1970-; E Kilbride Cttee, Order of St John (OStJ 1973). FRSA 1970. *Recreations:* golf, fishing, beachcombing. *Address:* 4 Newlands Place, East Kilbride, Lanarkshire. *T:* East Kilbride 30094; Spindrift, 10 Ferry Row, Fairlie, Ayrshire. *Clubs:* Caledonian; Royal Scottish Automobile (Glasgow); Largs (Kelburn) Golf.

YOUNG, George Kennedy, CB 1960; CMG 1955; MBE 1945; *b* 8 April 1911; *s* of late George Stuart Young and Margaret Kennedy, Moffat, Dumfriesshire; *m* 1939, Géryke, *d* of late Dr

M. A. G. Harthoorn, Batavia, Dutch EI. *Educ:* Dumfries Acad.; Univs of St Andrews, Giessen, Dijon, Yale, MA (First Class Hons Mod. Langs) 1934; Commonwealth Fund Fellowship, 1934-36; MA (Political Science), Yale, 1936; Editorial staff The Glasgow Herald, 1936-38; British United Press, 1938-39. Served War of 1939-45; commissioned KOSB 1940 (despatches, E Africa, 1941); specially employed list, Italy and W Europe, 1943-45. Berlin correspondent, British United Press, 1946. Joined HM Foreign Service, 1946; Vienna, 1946; Economic Relations Dept, FO, 1949; British Middle East Office, 1951; Ministry of Defence, 1953-61; Under-Secretary, 1960. Kleinwort, Benson Ltd, 1961-76; Pres., Nuclear Fuel Finance SA, 1969-76. Medal of Freedom (Bronze Palm), 1945. *Publications:* Masters of Indecision, 1962; Merchant Banking, 1966; Finance and World Power, 1968; Who Goes Home?, 1969; Who is my Liege?, 1972. *Recreations:* music, reading, swimming, walking. *Address:* 37 Abbotsbury House, W14. *T:* 01-603 8432.

YOUNG, Sir George (Samuel Knatchbull), 6th Bt, *cr* 1813; MP (C) Ealing, Acton, since Feb. 1974; Economic Adviser, Post Office Corporation, 1969-74; *b* 16 July 1941; *s* of Sir George Young, 5th Bt, CMG, and Elisabeth (*née* Knatchbull-Hugessen); *S* father 1960; *m* 1964, Aurelia Nemon-Stuart, *er d* of Oscar Nemon, *qv,* and of Mrs Nemon-Stuart, Boar's Hill, Oxford; two *s* two *d*. *Educ:* Eton; Christ Church, Oxford (Open Exhibitioner); MA Oxon, MPhil Surrey. Economist, NEDO, 1966-67; Kobler Research Fellow, University of Surrey, 1967-69. Councillor, London Borough of Lambeth, 1968-71; Mem., GLC, for London Borough of Ealing, 1970-73. An Opposition Whip, 1976-. Chm., Acton Housing Assoc., 1972-. *Publications:* Accommodation Services in the UK 1970-1980, 1970; Tourism, Blessing or Blight?, 1973. *Recreations:* squash, bicycling. *Heir: s* George Horatio Young, *b* 11 Oct. 1966. *Address:* Formosa Place, Cookham, Berks SL6 9QT. *T:* Bourne End 25519.

YOUNG, Gerard Francis, CBE 1967; JP; CEng, FIMechE; HM Lord-Lieutenant for South Yorkshire, since 1974; Chairman, Tempered Group Ltd; *b* 5 May 1910; *s* of Smelter J. Young, MICE, and Edith, *d* of Sir John Aspinall, Pres. ICE and Pres. IMechE; *m* 1937, Diana Graham Murray, MA, JP, *d* of Charles Graham Murray, MD; two *s* three *d*. *Educ:* Ampleforth College. Engrg Apprentice, LNER, Doncaster. Entered family firm, The Tempered Spring Co. Ltd (later Tempered Group Ltd), 1930; Dir, 1936; Man. Dir, 1942; Chm., 1954-. Dir, 1958, Chm., 1967-, Sheffield Area Board, Sun Alliance & London Insurance Group; Dir, National Vulcan Engineering Group, 1962-. Member: Nat. Bd for Prices and Incomes, 1968-71; Top Salaries Review Body, 1971-74; Armed Forces Pay Review Body, 1971-74; Gen. Comr of Income Tax, 1947-74 (Chm., Don Div., 1968-74). Dir, Crucible Theatre Trust Ltd, 1967-75; Sec., Assoc. of Christian Communities in Sheffield, 1940-46; Chm., Radio Hallam Ltd, 1973-; Trustee: Sheffield Town Trust; J. G. Graves Charitable Fund; Freshgate Foundn, etc. Univ. of Sheffield: Mem. Council, 1943; Treas., 1947-51; Pro-Chancellor, 1951-67; Chm., 1956-67. Mem. Bd of Govs, United Sheffield Hosps, 1948-53 (Chm. of Finance Cttee, 1948-50); Chm., Royal Hosp., 1951-53. Master, Company of Cutlers in Hallamshire, 1961-62. JP Sheffield, 1950. High Sheriff of Hallamshire, 1973-74; DL West Riding of Yorks, 1974. Hon. LLD Sheffield, 1962. KStJ 1976; GCSG 1974. *Recreations:* variety in public work; tranquility at home. *Address:* 69 Carsick Hill Crescent, Sheffield S10 3LS. *T:* Sheffield 302834. *Clubs:* Junior Carlton; Sheffield (Sheffield).

YOUNG, Air Vice-Marshal Gordon, CBE 1963; retired; *b* 29 May 1919; *s* of late Robert Young, MBE, and late Emily Florence Young, Doncaster; *m* 1943, Pamela Doris Weatherstone-Smith; two *d. Educ:* Maltby Grammar School; Sheffield Univ. Served War of 1939-45, Flying Boat Ops S Atlantic and Western Approaches (despatches); Air Min., 1945-47; Asst Air Attaché, Moscow, 1949-52; OC No 204 Sqdn, 1954-55; RAF Staff Coll., 1956; OC Flying Wing, RAF St Mawgan, 1958-60; Asst Chief, Comdrs-in-Chief Mission to Soviet Forces in Germany, 1960-63; OC RAF Wyton, 1963-65; Air Attaché, Bonn, 1966-68; SASO Coastal Command, 1968-69; COS No 18 (M) Gp, 1969-71. *Recreation:* bird-watching (MBOU 1969). *Address:* Middle Hill, Ormsary Road, Lochgilphead, Argyll. *T:* Ardrishaig 455. *Club:* Royal Air Force.

YOUNG, Most Rev. Guilford; see Hobart, Archbishop of, (RC).

YOUNG, Maj.-Gen. Hugh A., CB 1946; CBE 1945; DSO 1944; CD 1954; Vice-President, Central Mortgage and Housing Corporation since 1947; *b* 3 April 1898; *s* of Andrew and Emily Young, Winnipeg; *m* 1927; one *s* one *d. Educ:* Winnipeg Collegiate; University of Manitoba (BSc Elec. Engineering, 1924). RC Signals, 1924; Staff Coll., Camberley, England, 1933-34; various General Staff appointments during the war;

commanded Inf. Bde, operations Normandy, 1944; QMG Canadian Army, 1944-47; retired, 1947. Dep. Minister of Department of Resources and Development, and Comr of NW Territories, Canada, 1950-53; Dep. Minister, Dept of Public Works, 1953-63. *Address:* Apt 104, Plaza Towers, 465 Richmond Road, Ottawa, Canada. *Clubs:* Rideau, Ottawa Country (Ottawa).

YOUNG, James Alexander, CB 1970; Permanent Secretary, Department of Agriculture for N Ireland, since 1966; *b* Co. Tyrone, 17 Oct. 1918; *s* of Percy James and Margaret Young; *m* 1945, Margaret Doreen Patterson; two *d. Educ:* Royal Sch., Dungannon, Co. Tyrone; Queen's Univ., Belfast (BAgr). Asst Agr. Adviser to UK High Commissioner in Ottawa, Canada, 1946-49; Principal, Loughry Agricultural Coll., Cookstown, Co. Tyrone, 1949-63; Asst Sec., Min. of Agriculture for N Ireland, 1963-66. Hon. LLD Belfast, 1974. *Recreations:* Rugby football, gardening, photography. *Address:* Westways, Manse Road, Newtownards, Co. Down, N Ireland. *T:* Newtownards 2029.

YOUNG, Jimmy; see Young, L. R.

YOUNG, John Allen, CBE 1975; Chairman and Managing Director, Young & Co.'s Brewery, since 1962; *b* 7 Aug. 1921; *e s* of late William Allen Young and of Joan Barrow Simonds; *m* 1951, Yvonne Lieutenant, Liège; one *s. Educ:* Nautical Coll., Pangbourne; Corpus Christi Coll., Cambridge (BA Hons Econs). Served War, 1939-45: Lt-Comdr (A) RNVR; comd 888 Naval Air Sqdn (despatches). Runciman Ltd, 1947; Moor Line, 1949; Young & Co.'s Brewery, 1954-. Director: Foster-Probyn Ltd; Cockburn & Campbell; Chm., RI Shipping Ltd. Gen. Comr of Taxes, 1965-. President: London Carthorse Parade Soc., 1957-68; Shire Horse Soc., 1963-64 (Treas., 1962-73); Greater London Horse Show, 1972-74; Battersea Scouts, 1974-. Member: Bd of Governors, Nat. Hosps for Nervous Diseases, 1972- (Chm. Finance, 1974-); Cttee of Management, Inst. of Neurology (Chm., Jt Res. Adv. Cttee, 1973-). *Recreations:* music, sailing. *Address:* Moonsbrook Cottage, Wisborough Green, West Sussex. *T:* Wisborough Green 355. *Clubs:* Anglo-Belgian; Royal Yacht Squadron (Cowes).

YOUNG, Major John Darling, JP; Lord-Lieutenant of Buckinghamshire, since 1969; *b* 4 Jan. 1910; *o s* of late Sir Frederick Young; *m* 1934, Nina (*d* 1974), *d* of late Lt-Col H. W. Harris; three *d. Educ:* Eton and Oxford (BA). Commissioned The Life Guards, 1932-46; Middle East and Italy, 1940-44. Member Bucks Agricultural Executive Cttee, 1947-58. DL 1958, High Sheriff, 1960, JP 1964, CC 1964-77, CA 1969-74, Buckinghamshire. KStJ 1969. *Recreation:* shooting. *Address:* Thornton Hall, Thornton, Milton Keynes MK17 0HB. *T:* Buckingham 3234; Lethem, Jedburgh, Roxburghshire. *T:* Camptown 208. *Clubs:* Turf, Cavalry and Guards.

YOUNG, Hon. Sir John (McIntosh), KCMG 1975; Hon. Mr Justice Young; Lieutenant-Governor of Victoria and Chief Justice of the Supreme Court of Victoria, Australia, since 1974; *b* Melbourne, 17 Dec. 1919; *s* of George David Young, Glasgow, and Kathleen Mildred Young, Melbourne; *m* 1951, Elisabeth Mary, *yr d* of late Dr Edward Wing Twining, Manchester; one *s* two *d. Educ:* Geelong Grammar Sch.; Brasenose Coll., Oxford (MA); Inner Temple; Univ. of Melbourne (LLB). Served War: Scots Guards, 1940-46 (Captain 1943); NW Europe (despatches), 1945. Admitted Victorian Bar, 1948; Associate to Mr Justice Dixon, High Court of Australia, 1948; practice as barrister, 1949-74; Hon. Sec., Victorian Bar Council, 1950-60; Lectr in Company Law, Univ. of Melbourne, 1957-61; Hon. Treas., Medico Legal Soc. of Vic., 1955-65 (Vice-Pres., 1966-68; Pres., 1968-69). QC (Vic.) 1961; admitted Tasmanian Bar, 1964, QC 1964; NSW Bar, 1968, QC 1968; Consultant, Faculty of Law, Monash Univ., 1968-74. Mem., Bd of Examiners for Barristers and Solicitors, 1969-72; Mem. Council, Geelong Grammar Sch., 1974; Pres., Victorian Council of Legal Educn and Victoria Law Foundn, 1974-. President: Victorian Br., Scout Assoc. of Australia, 1974-; St John Council for Victoria, 1975-. *Publications:* (co-author) Australian Company Law and Practice, 1965; articles in legal jls. *Recreations:* riding, golf. *Address:* 25 Alma Road, Camberwell, Victoria 3124, Australia. *T:* 822862. *Clubs:* Cavalry and Guards; Melbourne, Australian (Melbourne).

YOUNG, John Richard Dendy; Advocate of Supreme Court, South Africa, since 1971; *b* 4 Sept. 1907; 5th *s* of James Young and Evelyn Maud Hammond; *m* 1946, Patricia Maureen Mount; four *s* two *d. Educ:* Hankey, Cape Province, SA; Humansdorp, CP, SA; University, South Africa (External). Joined Public Service, S Rhodesia, 1926; resigned to practise at Bar, 1934; joined Military Forces, 1940; active service, North Africa, Sicily and Italy; commissioned in the field; demobilised, 1945. QC

1948; MP Southern Rhodesia, 1948-53; Member Federal Assembly, 1953-56; Judge of the High Court of Rhodesia, 1956-68; Chief Justice, Botswana, 1968-71. *Recreation:* tennis. *Address:* Onaway, Aboyne Road, Kenilworth, Cape, South Africa. *Club:* Salisbury (Rhodesia).

YOUNG, Sir John (William Roe), 5th Bt, *cr* 1821; Chairman, Mancunian Building Society, since 1975; *b* 28 June 1913; *e s of* Sir Cyril Roe Muston Young, 4th Bt, and Gertrude Annie, *d* of John Elliott, Braunton, N Devon; *S* father, 1955; *m* 1st, 1946, Joan Minnie Agnes Aldous (*d* 1958); one *s* one *d*; 2nd, 1960, Joy Maureen, *d* of A. G. Clarke. *Educ:* Elizabeth Coll., Guernsey, CI. Served with RNVR, 1941-45 (prisoner-of-war, Hong Kong). *Heir: s* John Kenyon Roe Young, *b* 23 April 1947. *Address:* c/o Standard Chartered Bank, 38 Bishopsgate, EC2; Mancunian Building Society, 22 Dickinson Street, Manchester M1 4LF. *Club:* Naval.

YOUNG, John Zachary, MA; FRS 1945; Professor of Anatomy, University College, London, 1945-74, now Emeritus, Hon. Fellow, 1975; *b* 18 March 1907; *s* of Philip Young and Constance Maria Lloyd. *Educ:* Wells House, Malvern Wells; Marlborough Coll.; Magdalen Coll., Oxford (Demy). Senior Demy, Magdalen Coll., 1929, Christopher Welch Scholar, 1928, Naples Biological Scholar, 1928, 1929; Fellow of Magdalen Coll., Oxford, 1931-45 (Hon. Fellow, 1975); University Demonstrator in Zoology and Comparative Anatomy, Oxford, 1933-45; Rockefeller Fellow, 1936. Fullerton Professor of Physiology, Royal Institution, 1958-61. Pres., Marine Biol Assoc., 1976-. Foreign Member: Amer. Acad. of Arts and Scis; Amer. Philosophical Soc.; Accademia dei Lincei. Hon. DSc: Bristol, 1965; McGill, 1967; Durham, 1969; Bath, 1973; Glasgow, 1975. Royal Medal, Royal Society, 1967. *Publications:* The Life of Vertebrates, 1950; Doubt and Certainty in Science, 1951; The Life of Mammals, 1957; A Model of the Brain, 1964 (lectures); The Memory System of the Brain, 1966; An Introduction to the Study of Man, 1971; The Anatomy of the Nervous System of *Octopus vulgaris*, 1971; scientific papers, mostly on the nervous system. *Address:* 166 Camden Road, NW1. *T:* 01-485 0498.

YOUNG, Kenneth; *see* Young, C. K.

YOUNG, Kenneth Middleton, CBE 1977; Member of Board (Personnel and Industrial Relations), Post Office Corporation, since 1972; *b* 1 Aug. 1931; *s* of Cyril W. D. Young and Gwladys Middleton Young; *m* 1958, Brenda May Thomas; one *s* one *d*. *Educ:* Neath Grammar Sch.; University Coll. of Wales, Aberystwyth; Coll. of Science and Technology, Univ. of Manchester. BA (Hons) 1952. Pilot Officer/Navigator, General Duties (Aircrew), RAF, 1952-54. Asst Personnel Manager, Elliott-Automation Ltd, 1955-59; Collective Agreements Manager, later Salary Administration Manager, Massey-Ferguson (UK) Ltd, 1959-64; Personnel Adviser, Aviation Div., Smiths Industries Ltd, 1964-66; Group Personnel Manager, General Electric Company Ltd, and Dir, GEC (Management) Ltd, 1966-71. Mem., Management Bd, Engineering Employers Fedn, 1971. MIPM. *Recreations:* photography; Chelsea Football Club. *Address:* Ingleton, Main Drive, Gerrards Cross, Bucks. *T:* Gerrards Cross 85422.

YOUNG, Leslie, DSc (London), PhD, FRIC; Professor of Biochemistry in the University of London, and Head of the Department of Biochemistry, St Thomas's Hospital Medical School, London, SE1, 1948-76, now Professor Emeritus; Hon. Consultant, St Thomas' Hospital; *b* 27 Feb. 1911; *o c* of John and Ethel Young; *m* 1939, Ruth Elliott; one *s*. *Educ:* Sir Joseph Williamson's Mathematical Sch., Rochester; Royal College of Science, London; University College, London. Sir Edward Frankland Prize and Medal of Royal Institute of Chemistry, 1932; Bayliss-Starling Memorial Scholar in Physiology, University Coll., London, 1933-34; Asst Lectr in Biochemistry, University College, London, 1934-35; Commonwealth Fund Fellow in Biochemistry at Washington Univ. Medical School and Yale Univ., USA, 1935-37; Lectr in Biochemistry, University Coll., London, 1937-39; Assoc. Prof. of Biochemistry, Univ. of Toronto, 1939-44; chemical warfare research for the Dept of Nat. Defence, Canada, 1940-46; Prof. of Biochemistry, Univ. of Toronto, 1944-47; Reader in Biochemistry, University Coll., London, 1947-48. Hon. Sec., The Biochemical Soc., 1950-53; Vice-Pres., The Royal Institute of Chemistry, 1964-66; Mem., Bd of Governors, St Thomas' Hosp., 1970-74; Chm. of Council, Queen Elizabeth Coll., London Univ., 1975-. *Publications:* (with G. A. Maw) The Metabolism of Sulphur Compounds, 1958; papers on chem. and biochem. subjects in various scientific journals. *Address:* 23 Oaklands Avenue, Esher, Surrey KT10 8HX. *T:* 01-398 1262. *Club:* Athenæum.

YOUNG, Leslie Ronald, (Jimmy Young); Presenter, Jimmy Young Programme, BBC Radio Two, since 1973 (Radio One, 1967-73); *b* 21 Sept.; *s* of Frederick George Young and Gertrude Woolford; *m* 1st, 1946, Wendy Wilkinson (marr. diss.); one *d*; 2nd, 1950, Sally Douglas (marr. diss.). *Educ:* East Dean Grammar Sch., Cinderford, Glos. RAF, 1939-46. First BBC radio broadcast, songs at piano, 1949; pianist, singer, bandleader, West End, London, 1950-51; first theatre appearance, Empire Theatre, Croydon, 1952; regular theatre appearances, 1952-; first radio broadcast introd. records, Flat Spin, 1953; BBC TV Bristol, Pocket Edition series, 1955; first introd. radio Housewives' Choice, 1955; BBC radio series, incl.: The Night is Young, 12 o'clock Spin, Younger Than Springtime, Saturday Special, Keep Young, Through Till Two, 1959-65; presented progs, Radio Luxembourg, 1960-68. BBC TV: series, Jimmy Young Asks, 1972; The World of Jimmy Young, 1973. First live direct BBC Broadcasts to Europe from Soviet Union, Jimmy Young Programme, 16 and 17 May 1977. ITV series: Whose Baby?, 1973; Jim's World, 1974. Hit Records: 1st, Too Young, 1951; Unchained Melody, The Man From Laramie, 1955 (1st Brit. singer to have 2 consec. no 1 hit records); Chain Gang, More, 1956; Miss You, 1963. Weekly Column, Daily Sketch, 1968-71. Variety Club of GB Award, Radio Personality of the Year, 1968. *Publications:* Jimmy Young Cookbook: No. 1, 1968; No. 2, 1969; No 3, 1970; No 4, 1972; (autobiog.) JY, 1973; contrib. magazines, incl. Punch, Woman's Own. *Recreation:* worrying. *Address:* MAM Agency Ltd, 24-25 New Bond Street, W1Y 9HD. *T:* 01-629 9255. *Clubs:* Wig and Pen; Wigan Rugby League Social.

YOUNG, Mark; General Secretary, British Air Line Pilots' Association, since 1974; *b* 7 June 1929; *s* of Arnold Young and Florence May (*née* Lambert); *m* 1952, Charlotte Maria (*née* Rigol); two *s* two *d*. *Educ:* Pendower Technical Sch., Newcastle upon Tyne. Electrician, 1944-61; Head of Res., ETU, 1961; National Officer, ETU, 1963-73. *Recreations:* flying, ballooning, golf, tennis. *Address:* 81 New Road, Harlington, Hayes, Mddx.

YOUNG, Mary Lavinia Bessie, OBE 1967; Matron of the Westminster Hospital, SW1, 1951-66, retired; Mayor of Shaftesbury, Dorset, 1971-72; *b* 15 Nov. 1911; *d* of late Bennett and Rosalind Young. *Educ:* Girls' High Sch., Shaftesbury, Dorset. SRN, RSCN, SCM. Belgrave Hospital for Sick Children, SW9, 1929-32; KCH, SE5, 1933-36; Chiswick and Ealing Maternity Hospital, 1937; private nursing, 1938. King's College Hospital: Night Sister, 1938-40; Home Sister, 1940-41; Sister, Private Patients' Wing, 1941-44. Asst Matron, Royal Hospital, Richmond Surrey, 1944-45; Asst and Dep. Matron, Westminster Hospital, SW1, 1945-51. *Recreation:* gardening. *Address:* St Martins, Angel Square, Shaftesbury, Dorset. *T:* Shaftesbury 2020.

YOUNG, Michael, BSc (Econ), MA, PhD; Director, Institute of Community Studies since 1953; Trustee, Dartington Hall, since 1942; *b* 9 Aug. 1915; father a musician, mother a writer; *m* 1st, 1945, Joan Lawson; two *s* one *d*; 2nd, 1960, Sasha Moorsom; one *s* one *d*. *Educ:* Dartington Hall Sch.; London Univ. Barrister, Gray's Inn. Dir of Political and Economic Planning, 1941-45; Sec., Research Dept, Lab. Party, 1945-51. Chairman: Social Science Research Council, 1965-68; Dartington Amenity Research Trust, 1967-; Internat. Extension Coll., 1970-; Nat. Consumer Council, 1975-77; Mutual Aid Centre, 1977-; Dir, Mauritius Coll. of the Air, 1972; Member: Central Adv. Council for Education, 1963-66; NEDC, 1975-; President: Consumer's Assoc, 1965- (Chm., 1956-65); National Extension Coll., 1971- (Chm., 1962-71); Adv. Centre for Educn, 1976- (Chm., 1959-76). Fellow, Churchill Coll., Cambridge, 1961-66; Vis. Prof. of Extension Educn, Ahmadu Bello Univ., Nigeria, 1974. Hon. LittD Sheffield, 1965; Hon. Dr Open Univ., 1973; Hon. DLitt Adelaide, 1974. *Publications:* Family and Kinship in East London (with Peter Willmott), 1957; The Rise of the Meritocracy, 1958; Family and Class in a London Suburb (with Peter Willmott), 1960; Innovation and Research in Education, 1965; Learning Begins at Home (with Patrick McGeeney), 1968; (ed) Forecasting and the Social Sciences, 1968; The Symmetrical Family (with Peter Willmott), 1973; (ed) The Poverty Report, 1974 and 1975. *Recreation:* painting. *Address:* 18 Victoria Park Square, E2. *Club:* Reform.

YOUNG, Sir Norman (Smith), Kt 1968; Chairman: Pipelines Authority of South Australia, since 1967; South Australian Brewing Co. Ltd; News Ltd; Elder Smith Goldsbrough Mort Ltd; director of other companies; *b* 24 July 1911; *s* of Thomas and Margaret Young; *m* 1936, Jean Fairbairn Sincock; two *s* one *d*. *Educ:* Norwood High Sch.; University of Adelaide. Member: Adelaide City Council, 1949-60; Municipal Tramways Trust, 1951-67 (Dep. Chairman); Royal Commn on Television, 1953-54; Bankruptcy Law Review Cttee, 1956-62. Fellow, Inst. of

Chartered Accountants, 1933; FASA, 1932; Associate in Commerce, University of Adelaide, 1930. *Publication:* Bankruptcy Practice in Australia, 1942. *Address:* 256 Stanley Street, North Adelaide, South Australia 5006, Australia. *T:* 2673688.

YOUNG, Brig. Peter, DSO 1942; MC 1942 and two Bars 1943; military historian; Captain-Generall, The Sealed Knot Society of Cavaliers and Roundheads, since 1968; *b* 28 July 1915; *s* of Dallas H. W. Young, MBE, and Irene Barbara Lushington Mellor; *m* 1950, Joan Duckworth; no *c. Educ:* Monmouth Sch.; Trinity Coll., Oxford. 2nd Lieut, Bedfordshire and Hertfordshire Regt, 1939. Served War of 1939-45: BEF Dunkirk (wounded), 1940; No 3 Commando, 1940; raids on Guernsey, 1940; Lofoten and Vaagso, 1941, Dieppe, 1942, Sicily and Italy, 1943; comd No 3 Commando, 1943-44; Normandy, 1944; Arakan, 1944-45; comd 1st Commando Bde, 1945-46. Commanded 9th Regt Arab Legion, 1953-56. Reader in Military History, Royal Military Acad., Sandhurst, 1959-69. Gen. Editor, Military Memoirs series, 1967-; Editor, Purnell's History of First World War, 1970-72; Editor in Chief, Orbis' World War II, 1972-74; Vice-President: Commando Assoc.; Naseby Preservation Soc.; Chm., Cheriton 1644 Assoc. FRHistS; FSA 1960; FRGS 1968. Order of El Istiqlal (Jordan) 3rd Class, 1954. *Publications:* Bedouin Command, 1956; Storm from the Sea, 1958; The Great Civil War (with late Lt-Col Alfred H. Burne, DSO), 1959; Cromwell, 1962; Hastings to Culloden (with John Adair), 1964; World War 1939-45, 1966; Edgehill, 1642: The Campaign and the Battle, 1967; The British Army, 1642-1970, 1967; The Israeli Campaign, 1967, 1967; (ed) Decisive Battles of the Second World War, 1967; Charge (with Lt-Col J. P. Lawford), 1967; (jt editor) The Civil War: Richard Atkyns and John Gwyn, 1967; Oliver Cromwell, 1968; Commando, 1969; Cropredy Bridge, 1644 (with Margaret Toynbee), 1970; Marston Moor, 1644, 1970; (ed with Lt-Col J. P. Lawford) History of the British Army, 1970; Chasseurs of the Guard, 1971; The Arab Legion, 1971; George Washington's Army, 1972; (ed) John Cruso, Militarie Instructions for the Cavallirie, 1972; Blücher's Army, 1973; Armies of the English Civil War, 1973; (with Lt-Col J. P. Lawford) Wellington's Masterpiece, 1973; (ed and contrib.) The War Game, 1973; (ed and contrib.) The Machinery of War, 1973; (with R. Holmes) The English Civil War, 1974; Atlas of the Second World War, 1974; (with M. Toynbee) Strangers in Oxford, 1974; (with W. Emberton) The Cavalier Army, 1974; (ed with Brig. M. Calvert) A Dictionary of Battles 1816-1976; numerous articles in Army Historical Research Journal and Encyclopædia. *Recreation:* equitation. *Address:* Flat 3, Twyning Manor, Tewkesbury, Glos. *Clubs:* Savage, The Sette of Odd Volumes.

YOUNG, Ven. Peter Claude; Archdeacon of Cornwall and Canon Residentiary of Truro Cathedral, since 1965; Examining Chaplain to Bishop of Truro, since 1965; *b* 21 July 1916; *s* of Rev. Thomas Young and of Mrs Ethel Ashton Young; *m* 1944, Marjorie Désirée Rose; two *s. Educ:* Exeter Sch.; Exeter Coll., Oxford; Wycliffe Hall, Oxford. BA 1938, BLitt 1940, MA 1942, Oxon. Asst Curate of Ottery St Mary, 1940-44; Asst Curate of Stoke Damerel, i/c of St Bartholomew's, Milehouse, Plymouth, 1944-47; Rector of Highweek, Newton Abbot, 1947-59; Vicar of Emmanuel, Plymouth, 1959-65. *Recreations:* motoring, fishing, reading. *Address:* Petherton, Kenwyn Road, Truro, Cornwall. *T:* Truro 2866.

YOUNG, Pierre Henry John, FRS 1974; Director of Advanced Engineering, Rolls Royce Ltd, since 1976; *b* 12 June 1926; *s* of late David Hunter Young and late Jeanne (*née* Barrus); *m* 1953, Lily Irène (*née* Cahn); one *s* one *d. Educ:* Lycée Condorcet,Paris; Westminster Sch.; Trinity Coll., Cambridge (BA). FRAeS, FIMechE. Joined Bristol Siddeley Engines Ltd, 1949; i/c Concorde Olympus 593 engine programme from 1962; Engrg Dir, Olympus 593, Rolls Royce Ltd, 1966-70, Techn. Dir 1970-73; Dep. Company Technical Dir, Rolls Royce (1971) Ltd, 1973-76. *Publications:* contrib. Jl RAeS. *Recreation:* mountain-walking. *Address:* 5 Rockleaze Avenue, Bristol BS9 1NG; PO Box 3, Filton, Bristol BS12 7QE.

YOUNG, Sir Richard (Dilworth), Kt 1970; BSc, FIMechE; FBIM; Director: Boosey & Hawkes Ltd, since 1977; Ingersoll Manufacturing Consultants SA, since 1976; Rugby Portland Cement Co., since 1968; Commonwealth Finance Development Corp. Ltd, since 1968; *b* 9 April 1914; *s* of Philip Young and Constance Maria Lloyd; *m* 1951, Jean Barbara Paterson Lockwood, *d* of F. G. Lockwood; four *s. Educ:* Bromsgrove; Bristol Univ. Joined Weldless Steel Tube Co. Ltd, 1934; served with various Tube Investments companies in production and engineering capacities until 1944; Representative of TI in S America and Man. Dir of Tubos Britanicos (Argentina) Ltda, 1945-50; Man. Dir of TI (Export) Ltd, 1950-53; Sales Dir of TI

Aluminium Ltd, 1953-56; Asst to Chm. of Tube Investments Ltd, 1957-60; Dir, 1958; Asst Man. Dir, 1959; Man. Dir, 1961-64; Alfred Herbert Ltd: Dep. Chm., 1965-66; Chm., 1966-74; Man. Dir, 1969-70; Dir, Ingersoll Milling Machine Co., USA, 1967-71. Member: Council BIM, 1960-65; Council, IMechE, 1969-76; Adv. Cttee on Scientific Manpower, 1962-65; SSRC, 1973-75; Council, Warwick Univ., 1966-; Central Adv. Council on Science and Technol., 1967-70; SRC Engineering Bd, 1974-76. *Address:* Bearley Manor, Bearley, near Stratford-on-Avon, Warwickshire. *T:* Snitterfield 220. *Club:* Athenæum.

YOUNG, Robert Henry; Consultant Orthopædic Surgeon, St George's Hospital, SW1, since 1946; Hon. Consultant, St Peter's Hospital, Chertsey, since 1939; *b* 6 Oct. 1903; *s* of James Allen Young and Constance Barrow Young; *m* 1st, 1929, Nancy Willcox; 2nd, 1961, Norma, *d* of Leslie Williams; two *s. Educ:* Sherborne Sch.; Emmanuel Coll., Cambridge; St Thomas' Hospital, SE1. *Publications:* numerous articles in leading medical journals. *Address:* 111 Harley Street, W1. *Club:* United Oxford & Cambridge University.

YOUNG, Robert S.; Play Producer and Adjudicator; retired; *b* near Manchester, 28 May 1891; *s* of late Alexander Young, Manchester, merchant, and Elizabeth Stevenson, both from Sligo, Ireland; *m* 1923, Doris Lillian Hill, Salisbury; no *c. Educ:* Manchester Grammar Sch. Travelled in South America, South Africa, seven years in New Zealand; invited to stand for NZ Parliament for Labour; joined NZ Forces when war broke out in 1914; saw service at Anzac and in France (twice wounded); after the war joined Sir Frank Benson on the stage, founded the County Players Repertory Theatre at Tonbridge, Kent. MP (Lab) Islington North, 1929-31; actively interested in Labour movement for past 60 years. *Publication:* Cricket on the Green. *Recreations:* lacrosse, keen cricketer. *Address:* Ham Cottage, Albourne Road, Hurstpierpoint, Hassocks, Sussex.

YOUNG, Roger William, MA; STh, FRSE; Principal of George Watson's College, Edinburgh, since 1958; *b* 15 Nov. 1923; *yr s* of Charles Bowden Young and Dr Ruth Young, *qv*; *m* 1950, Caroline Mary Christie; two *s* two *d. Educ:* Dragon Sch., Oxford; Westminster Sch. (King's Scholar); Christ Church, Oxford (Scholar). Served War of 1939-45, RNVR, 1942-45. Classical Mods, 1946, Lit Hum 1948. Resident Tutor, St Catharine's, Cumberland Lodge, Windsor, 1949-51; Asst Master, The Manchester Grammar Sch., 1951-58. 1st Class in Archbishop's examination in Theology (Lambeth Diploma), 1957. Participant, US State Dept Foreign Leader Program, 1964. Member: Edinburgh Marriage Guidance Council, 1960-75; Scottish Council of Christian Educn Movement, 1960- (Chm., 1961-67); Management Assoc., SE Scotland, 1965-; Educational Research Bd of SSRC, 1966-70; Court, Edinburgh Univ., 1967-76; Public Schools Commn, 1968-70; Consultative Cttee on the Curriculum, 1972-75; Adv. Cttee, Scottish Centre for Studies in Sch. Administration, 1972-75; Royal Soc. of Edinburgh Dining Club, 1972-; Scottish Adv. Cttee, Community Service Volunteers, 1973-; Edinburgh Festival Council, 1970-76; Hon. Sec., Headmasters' Assoc. of Scotland, 1968-72, Pres., 1972-74; Chm., HMC, 1976. Conducted Enquiry on Stirling Univ., 1974. *Publications:* Lines of Thought, 1958; Everybody's Business, 1968; Everybody's World, 1970; Report on the Policies and Running of Stirling University 1966-1973, 1974. *Recreations:* gardening, photography, climbing, golf. *Address:* 27 Merchiston Gardens, Edinburgh EH10 5DD. *T:* 031-337 6880.

YOUNG, Ruth, CBE 1941 (MBE 1928); MB, ChB; *b* 26 Jan. 1884; *d* of William B. Wilson, Flax Merchant, Dundee; *m* 1917, C. B. Young, sometime Reader in English, Delhi Univ.; two *s* one *d. Educ:* High Sch., Dundee; St Andrews Univ. BSc 1907, MB, ChB 1909; Postgraduate Study, Vienna and Dresden. Lecturer, Women's Christian Medical Coll., Ludhiana, Punjab, India, 1910-16; Professor of Surgery, Lady Hardinge Medical Coll., Delhi, 1916-17; voluntary work till 1925, chiefly in Maternity and Child Welfare; Personal Assistant to Chief Medical Officer, Women's Medical Service of India, 1925-31; Director, Maternity and Child Welfare Bureau, Indian Red Cross Society, 1931-35; Principal, Lady Hardinge Medical Coll., New Delhi, 1936-40; Rockefeller Fellowship to study Public Health Nursing in China, Japan, Canada and USA, 1934. In Ethiopia, to advise Ethiopian Women's Work Association on Welfare Work, 1943. Medical Adviser, Women's Foreign Mission, Church of Scotland, retired, 1951. Kaisar-i-Hind Gold Medal, 1936; Silver Jubilee and Coronation Medals. *Publications:* The Work of Medical Women in India (with Dr M. I. Balfour), 1929; The Science of Health, 1932; Handbook for Health Visitors (Indian Red Cross Society), 1933; numerous pamphlets on Maternity and Child Welfare, Health, etc., relating to India. *Recreation:* gardening. *Address:* 220

Bruntsfield Place, Edinburgh EH10 4DE. *T*: 031-229 3103.
See also Roger William Young.

YOUNG, Sir Stephen Stewart Templeton, 3rd Bt, *cr* 1945; solicitor; *b* 24 May 1947; *s* of Sir Alastair Young, 2nd Bt, and Dorothy Constance Marcelle (*d* 1964), *d* of late Lt-Col Charles Ernest Chambers, and *widow* of Lt J. H. Grayburn, VC, 43rd LI; *S* father, 1963; *m* 1974, Viola Margaret Nowell-Smith, *d* of Prof. P. H. Nowell-Smith, *qv* and Perilla Thyme (she *m* 2nd, Lord Roberthall, *qv*). *Educ:* Rugby; Trinity Coll., Oxford; Edinburgh Univ. Voluntary Service Overseas, Sudan, 1968-69. *Heir: uncle* Patrick Templeton Young [*b* 5 July 1925; *m* 1950, Jenny, *d* of Sir Walter Eric Bassett, *qv*; one *s* one *d*].

YOUNG, Maj.-Gen. Thomas, CB 1951; OBE 1945; retired, 1953; *b* 4 June 1893; *s* of William Fulton Young, Kilmarnock, and Euphemia Murray Wilson, Crosshouse; *m* 1922, Alison Rowe; no *c.* *Educ:* University of Glasgow. MB, ChB (Glasgow) 1915; MD 1951; DPH (Cambridge) (Dist. in Principles of Hygiene), 1924; Lieut, RAMC (SR) 1914; served European War, Dardanelles, MEF, EEF, 1915-22 (despatches twice); India, 1925-31 and 1934-39. Major, 1927; Lt-Col, 1941; Temp. Major, 1919 and 1924; Temp. Lt-Col, 1939; Temp. Col, 1941; Dep. Dir of Hygiene, BNAF and CMF, 1942-46 (despatches twice); Col, 1945; Comdt Army School of Hygiene, 1946; Brig., 1947; Dir of Medical Services, FARELF, 1948; Maj.-Gen., 1949; KHP, 1950; QHP, 1952-53. Dir, Army Health, 1949-53; retired, 1953. Col Comdt, RAMC, 1955-61. Legion of Merit (USA) Légionnaire, 1946; Médaille de la Reconnaissance Française, 1945. *Publications:* contributions to Journal of RAMC. *Recreation:* gardening. *Address:* Flat 25, Swallowfield Park, near Reading, Berks. *T:* Reading 882330.

YOUNG, Wayland; *see* Kennet, Baron.

YOUNG, Sir William, Kt 1975; CBE 1960; Chairman, Scottish Milk Marketing Board, since 1962; *b* 13 June 1905; *s* of John and Jessie Young; *m* 1937, Elizabeth Clelland Smith; one *s* one *d*. *Educ:* Kilmarnock Acad.; West of Scotland Agricultural Coll. Elected Pres., National Farmers' Union of Scotland, 1945. Mem., Scottish Milk Marketing Bd, 1943- (Vice-Chm. 1950, Chm. 1962); Chm., Royal Highland and Agricultural Soc. of Scotland, 1969 (Hon. Treas., 1973). FRAgSs. *Recreations:* curling, bowling. *Address:* Kyleholm, Skerrington Mains, Kilmarnock, Strathclyde, Scotland. *T:* Kilmarnock 26021.

YOUNG, William Hilary, CMG 1957; HM Diplomatic Service, retired; Ambassador to Colombia 1966-70; *b* 14 Jan. 1913; *s* of late Rev. Arthur John Christopher Young and Ethel Margaret (*née* Goodwin); *m* 1946, Barbara Gordon Richmond, *d* of Gordon Park Richmond; one *s* one *d.* *Educ:* Marlborough Coll.; Emmanuel Coll., Cambridge. Entered Consular Service, 1935; served HM Legation, Tehran, 1938-41; Foreign Office, 1941-45; 1st Secretary, 1945; Berlin (Political Division, Control Commission), 1945-48; HM Legation, Budapest, 1948-50; attached to IDC, 1951; Counsellor: UK High Commn, New Delhi, 1952-54; Foreign Office, 1954-57; Minister, Moscow, 1957-60; Senior Civilian Instructor, IDC, 1960-62; Minister, British Embassy, Pretoria and Cape Town, 1962-65; Fellow, Harvard University Center for Internat. Affairs, 1965-66. *Address:* Blackmoor, Four Elms, Edenbridge, Kent.

YOUNG, Sir William Neil, 10th Bt, *cr* 1769; stockbroker with Fielding Newson-Smith & Co.; *b* 22 Jan. 1941; *s* of Captain William Elliot Young, RAMC (killed in action 27 May 1942), and Mary, *d* of late Rev. John Macdonald; *S* grandfather, 1944; *m* 1965, Christine Veronica Morley, *o d* of R. B. Morley, Buenos Aires; one *s* one *d.* *Educ:* Wellington Coll.; Sandhurst. Captain, 16th/5th The Queen's Royal Lancers, retired 1970. *Recreations:* helicopter flying, ski-ing, sailing, tennis, shooting. *Heir: s* William Lawrence Elliot Young, *b* 26 May 1970. *Address:* 22 Elm Park Road, SW3.

YOUNG-HERRIES, Sir Michael Alexander Robert; *see* Herries.

YOUNGER, family name of Viscount Younger of Leckie.

YOUNGER OF LECKIE, 3rd Viscount, *cr* 1923; **Edward George Younger;** OBE 1940; 3rd Bt of Leckie, *cr* 1911; Lord-Lieutenant, Stirling and Falkirk (formerly of County of Stirling), since 1964; Colonel, Argyll and Sutherland Highlanders (TA); *b* 21 Nov. 1906; *er s* of 2nd Viscount and Maud (*d* 1957), *e d* of Sir John Gilmour, 1st Bt; *S* father 1946; *m* 1930, Evelyn Margaret, *e d* of late Alexander Logan McClure, KC; three *s* one *d.* *Educ:* Winchester; New Coll., Oxford. Served War of 1939-45 (OBE). *Heir: s* Hon. George (Kenneth Hotson) Younger, *qv.* *Address:* Leckie, Gargunnock, Stirling. *T:* Gargunnock 281. *Club:* New (Edinburgh).

YOUNGER, Maj.-Gen. Allan Elton, DSO 1944; OBE 1962; MA; Director-General, Royal United Services Institute for Defence Studies, since 1976; *b* 4 May 1919; *s* of late Brig. Arthur Allan Shakespear Younger, DSO, and late Marjorie Rhoda Younger (*née* Hall_iley); *m* 1942, Diana Lanyon; three *d. Educ:* Gresham's; RMA Woolwich; Christ's Coll., Cambridge. Commnd RE, 1939; France and Belgium, 1940; France, Holland and Germany, 1944-45; Burma, 1946-47; Malaya, 1948; Korea, 1950-51; RMA Sandhurst, 1954-57; Bt Lt-Col 1959; comd 36 Corps Engineer Regt in UK and Kenya, 1960-62; Instructor US Army Comd and Gen. Staff Coll., Fort Leavenworth, 1963-66; Programme Evaluation Gp, 1966-68; Chief Engr, Army Strategic Comd, 1968-69; COS, HQ Allied Forces Northern Europe, Oslo, 1970-72; Sen. Army Mem., Directing Staff, RCDS, 1972-75. Col Comdt, RE, 1974-. Silver Star (US), 1951. *Publications:* contribs to RUSI Jl, Military Review (USA). *Recreations:* ski-ing, writing. *Address:* Southern Haye, Heath Rise, Camberley, Surrey. *T:* Camberley 21214. *Club:* Army and Navy.

YOUNGER, Charles Frank Johnston, DSO 1944; TD 1952; Director, Bank of Scotland; a Vice-Chairman, Norwich Union Life and Fire Societies; Deputy Chairman: Scottish Union and National Insurance Co. Ltd; Maritime Insurance Co. Ltd; a Vice-President, The Brewers' Society; Member of Royal Company of Archers (Queen's Body Guard for Scotland); *b* 11 Dec. 1908; *s* of late Major Charles Arthur Johnston Younger, King's Dragoon Guards; *m* 1935, Joanna, *e d* of late Rev. John Kyrle Chatfield, BD, MA, LLB; one *d. Educ:* Royal Naval Coll., Dartmouth. Served Royal Navy, 1926-37. Served War of 1939-45 (despatches, DSO); RA (Field), 15th Scottish Division, 1939-41; 17th Indian Light Div., Burma, 1942-45; commanded 129th Lowland Field Regt, RA, 1942-45 and 278th Lowland Field Regt RA (TA), 1946-52 (Lt-Col). Joined William Younger & Co. Ltd, 1937, Dir 1945-73; Dir, Scottish & Newcastle Breweries Ltd, 1946-73. Chairman: Brewers' Soc., 1963-64 (Vice-Pres., 1965-); Scottish Union & National Insurance Co., 1954-57, 1966-68. UK deleg. to EFTA Brewing Ind. Council, 1964-73; Mem. Council, CBI, 1965-73. Mem., Worshipful Company of Brewers. Freeman of the City of London. *Recreations:* country pursuits. *Address:* Gledswood House, near Melrose, Roxburghshire. *T:* Melrose 2234; 6 Cadogan Gardens, SW3. *T:* 01-730 2048. *Clubs:* Boodle's, Pratt's.
See also Lord Irwin.

YOUNGER, Hon. George (Kenneth Hotson), TD 1964; DL; MP (C) Ayr, since 1964; *b* 22 Sept. 1931; *e s* and *heir* of 3rd Viscount Younger of Leckie, *qv*; *m* 1954, Diana Rhona, *er d* of Captain G. S. Tuck, RN, Little London, Chichester, Sussex; three *s* one *d. Educ:* Cargilfield Sch.; Edinburgh; Winchester Coll.; New Coll., Oxford. Commnd in Argyll and Sutherland Highlanders, 1950; served BAOR and Korea, 1951; 7th Bn Argyll and Sutherland Highlanders (TA), 1951-65; Hon. Col, 154 (Lowland) Transport Regt, RCT, T&AVR, 1977-. Director: George Younger & Son Ltd, 1958-68; J. G. Thomson & Co. Ltd, Leith, 1962-66; Maclachlans Ltd, 1968-70. Contested (U) North Lanarkshire, 1959; Unionist Candidate for Kinross and West Perthshire, 1963, but stood down in favour of Sir A. Douglas-Home. Scottish Conservative Whip, 1965-67; Parly Under-Sec. of State for Develt, Scottish Office, 1970-74; Minister of State for Defence, 1974. Chm., Conservative Party in Scotland, 1974-75 (Dep. Chm., 1967-70). Member of Queen's Body Guard for Scotland (Royal Company of Archers). DL Stirlingshire, 1968. *Recreations:* music, tennis, sailing, golf. *Address:* Easter Leckie, Gargunnock, Stirlingshire. *T:* Gargunnock 274. *Clubs:* Caledonian; Highland Brigade.

YOUNGER, Maj.-Gen. Sir John William, 3rd Bt *cr* 1911; CBE 1969 (MBE 1945); Director, Management and Support of Intelligence, 1972-76, retired; *b* 18 Nov. 1920; *s* of Sir William Robert Younger, 2nd Bt, and of Joan Gwendoline Johnstone (now Mrs Dennis Wheatley); *S* father, 1973; *m* 1st, 1948, Mrs Stella Jane Dodd (marr. diss. 1952), *d* of Rev. John George Lister; one *s* one *d.*; 2nd, 1953, Marcella Granito, Princess Pignatelli Di Belmonte, *d* of Prof. Avv. R. Scheggi. *Educ:* Canford Sch.; RMC Sandhurst. Served War 1939-45, Middle East (PoW) (MBE); 2nd Lt, Coldstream Gds, 1939; Lt Col 1959; AQMG, HQ London Dist, 1961-63; Col 1963; AAG, War Office, 1963-65; Brig. 1967; Dep. Dir, Army Staff Duties, MoD, 1967-70; Dir of Quartering (A), MoD, 1970-73; Maj.-Gen. 1971. *Recreations:* golf, photography, travel. *Heir: s* Julian William Richard Younger, *b* 10 Feb. 1950. *Address:* 23 Cadogan Square, SW1X 0HU. *Club:* Boodle's.

YOUNGER, Maj.-Gen. Ralph, CB 1957; CBE 1954; DSO 1945; MC 1941; JP; DL; *b* 12 July 1904; *s* of late William Younger, Ravenswood, Melrose; *m* 1938, Greta Mary, *d* of late A. W. Turnbull, Clifton, Maybank, Yeovil; one *s* one *d. Educ:*

Charterhouse, Trinity Coll., Cambridge. 2nd Lieut, 7th Hussars, 1926; served War of 1939-45 (MC, DSO), 7th Hussars, Western Desert, 1940-41; Burma, 1942; 3rd Carabiniers, India, 1942-43; Burma, 1944; Comdr 255 Ind. Tank Bde, Burma, 1945; Lieut-Colonel comdg Royal Scots Greys, 1947-48; Commander: 30 Lowland Armoured Bde, TA, 1949-50; 7th Armoured Bde, 1950-53; Royal Armoured Corps Centre, 1953-54; GOC North Midland District and Commander 49th Armoured Division, TA, 1954-57; retired, 1958. Colonel, 7th Queen's Own Hussars, 1952-58, of Queen's Own Hussars, 1958-62; Commandant, Army Cadet Force (Scotland), 1959-65; Chairman, T&AFA, Roxburgh, Berwick and Selkirk, 1966-68; Member Royal Company of Archers (Queen's Body Guard for Scotland); Col, The Royal Scots Dragoon Guards (Carabiniers and Greys), 1971-74. JP Roxburghshire, 1961; DL Roxburgh, 1962; Ettrick and Lauderdale, 1975. Joint Master Duke of Buccleuch's Foxhounds, 1960-66. *Recreations:* hunting, fishing, and shooting. *Address:* Ravenswood, Melrose, Roxburghshire. *T:* St Boswells 2219. *Clubs:* Cavalry and Guards, Army and Navy, MCC.

YOUNGER, Sir William McEwan, 1st Bt, *cr* 1964, of Fountainbridge; DSO 1942; DL; Chairman: Scottish & Newcastle Breweries Ltd, 1960-69 (Managing Director, 1960-67); The Second Scottish Investment Trust Company Ltd, 1965-75; *b* 6 Sept. 1905; *y s* of late William Younger, Ravenswood, Melrose; *m* 1936, Nora Elizabeth Balfour (marr. diss., 1967); one *d. Educ:* Winchester; Balliol Coll., Oxford. Served War of 1939-45 (despatches, DSO); Western Desert, 1941-43; Italy, 1943-45; Lt-Col, RA. Hon. Sec., Scottish Unionist Assoc., 1955-64; Chm., Conservative Party in Scotland, 1971-74. Mem. Queen's Body Guard for Scotland. Director: British Linen Bank, 1955-71; Scottish Television, 1964-71; Chm., Highland Tourist (Cairngorm Development) Ltd, 1966-. DL Midlothian, 1956. *Recreations:* mountaineering and fishing. *Heir:* none. *Address:* 29 Moray Place, Edinburgh. *T:* 031-225 8173. *Clubs:* Carlton, Alpine; New (Edinburgh).

YOUNGHUSBAND, Dame Eileen (Louise), DBE 1964 (CBE 1955; MBE 1946); JP; formerly Chairman Hammersmith Juvenile Court; *b* 1 Jan. 1902; *d* of late Sir Francis Younghusband, KCSI, KCIE. *Educ:* privately; London Univ. Social work in S and E London, 1924-29; JP 1933. Lecturer, London School of Economics, 1929-39 and 1944-57; Adviser, Nat. Institute for Social Work Training, 1961-67; Principal Officer for Employment and Training, Nat. Assoc. of Girls' Clubs, 1939-44; and Director of British Council Social Welfare Courses, 1942-44; Welfare investigation for Nat. Assistance Board, 1944; seconded from time to time to UNRRA and the United Nations, 1945-; co-opted member of McNair Cttee, 1943; member of departmental Cttee on Social Workers in the Mental Health Services, 1948; member Cttee of Enquiry into the Law and Practice Relating to Charitable Trusts; Member Cttee on the Probation Service, 1962; Chairman, Ministry of Health Working Party on Social Workers in the Health and Welfare Services, 1959; President, Internat. Assoc. of Schools of Social Work, 1961-68; member numerous Cttees for penal reform, child care, youth service, care of old people, family welfare, social studies, international social work, etc. LLD (*hc*): Univ. of British Columbia, 1955; Univ. of Nottingham, 1963; DLitt (*hc*) Univ. of Bradford, 1968; DUniv. York, 1968. Hon. DSocSci, Hong Kong Univ., 1972. Hon. Fellow LSE, 1961. René Sand Award, Internat. Council on Social Welfare, 1976. *Publications:* The Employment and Training of Social Workers (Carnegie UK Trust), 1946; Social Work in Britain (Carnegie UK Trust), 1951; Third International Survey of Training for Social Work (UN, NY, 1959); Social Work and Social Change (London), 1964. Numerous articles in social service publications. *Recreations:* gardening, reading and travel. *Address:* 24 Lansdowne Road, W11 3LL. *T:* 01-727 4613.

YOUNGSON, Prof. Alexander John; Director, Research School of Social Sciences, Australian National University, since 1974; *b* 28 Sept. 1918; *s* of Alexander Brown, MA, MB, ChB and Helen Youngson; *m* 1948, Elizabeth Gisborne Naylor; one *s* one *d. Educ:* Aberdeen Grammar Sch.; Aberdeen Univ. Pilot, Fleet Air Arm, 1940-45. MA Aberdeen Univ., 1947; Commonwealth Fellow, 1947-48. Lecturer, University of St Andrews, 1948-50; Lecturer, University of Cambridge, 1950-58; Prof. of Political Economy 1963-74, and Vice-Principal, 1971-74, Univ. of Edinburgh. Mem., Royal Fine Art Commn for Scotland, 1972-74. DLitt Aberdeen Univ., 1952. *Publications:* The American Economy, 1860-1940, 1951; Possibilities of Economic Progress, 1959; The British Economy, 1920-1957, 1960; The Making of Classical Edinburgh, 1966; Overhead Capital, 1967; After the Forty-Five, 1973; Beyond the Highland Line, 1974; contrib. to various journals devoted to economics and economic history. *Recreations:* gardening, fishing. *Address:* Box 4 PO, Canberra, ACT 2600, Australia.

YOUNSON, Maj.-Gen. Eric John, OBE 1952; BSc; CEng, MIEEE, MBIM, FRAeS, FRSA; Deputy Director, Scientific Instrument Manufacturers' Association of Great Britain, since 1974; Clerk to the Worshipful Company of Scientific Instrument Makers, since 1976; Secretary General, Comité des Industries de la Mesure Electrique et Electronique de la Communauté; *b* 1 March 1919; *o s* of late Ernest M. Younson, MLitt, BCom, Jarrow; *m* 1946, Jean Beaumont Carter, BA; three *d. Educ:* Jarrow Grammar Sch.; Univ. of Durham; Royal Military Coll. of Science. Served War of 1939-45: commissioned, RA, 1940; UK and NW Europe (despatches). Directing Staff, RMCS, 1953-55; Atomic Weapons Research Estab., 1957-58; Attaché (Washington) as rep. of Chief Scientific Adviser, 1958-61; Head of Defence Science 3, MoD, 1961-63; Dep. Dir of Artillery, 1964-66; Dir of Guided Weapons Trials and Ranges, Min. of Technology, 1967-69; Vice-Pres., Ordnance Board, 1970-72, Pres., 1972-73, retired 1973; Sen. Asst Dir, Central Bureau for Educnl Visits and Exchanges, 1973-74. *Publications:* articles on gunnery and scientific subjects in Service jls; occasional poetry. *Recreations:* photography, electronics. *Address:* SIMA House, 20 Peel Street, W8. *T:* 01-727 2614; 7 Pondwick Road, Harpenden, Herts. *T:* Harpenden 5892. *Club:* Army and Navy.

YOUSUF, Lt-Gen. Mohammed, Nishan-e-Liaqat; Ambassador of Pakistan to Portugal, since 1977, and to the Holy See, since 1972; *b* 14 Oct. 1908; *m* 1936, Zubeida Begum; four *s* two *d. Educ:* Royal Military Coll., Sandhurst. Attached for a year to York and Lancaster Regt; subsequently posted to 7th Light Cavalry. Served War of 1939-45, campaigns in Arakan and Assam. Later posted to 18th Cavalry. Supervised evacuation of refugees from across Indian borders, 1947; Member Pakistan Nationalisation Cttee; in comd Bde, Jan. 1948; Maj.-Gen., 1948; GOC East Pakistan, 1950-51; later Chief of General Staff, Pakistan Army; Lt-Gen., 1954; retired from Army, 1956. High Comr for Pakistan in Australia and New Zealand, 1956-59; High Comr for Pakistan in UK, 1959-63, and Ambassador to Ireland, 1962-63; Ambassador for Pakistan to Afghanistan, 1963-68; High Comr for Pakistan in UK, Oct. 1971; first Ambassador of Pakistan to London, Jan.-Aug. 1972; Ambassador to Switzerland, 1972-77. *Recreations:* polo and shooting. *Address:* Pakistan Embassy, Rua Pero da Alenquer no 12, Restelo, Lisbon, Portugal.

YOXALL, Harry Waldo, OBE 1966; MC 1916 and Bar 1917; JP; Chairman, The Condé Nast Publications Ltd, 1957-64; President, Periodical Proprietors' Association, 1956-59 (Vice-President, 1959-65); Vice-President, International Federation of the Periodical Press, 1960-65; *b* 4 June 1896; *o s* of late Sir James Yoxall, MA, MP, JP, and late Lady Yoxall, JP (*née* Coles); *m* 1918, Josephine Fairchild Baldwin (*d* 1970); one *s* one *d. Educ:* St Paul's Sch. (captain of the school); Balliol Coll., Oxford (scholar). Served KRRC, 1915-19; British Military Mission to US, 1917-18. Joined The Condé Nast Publications Inc., 1921; appointed Business Manager and Director, The Condé Nast Publications Ltd, 1924; Managing Director, 1934. Comr of Income Tax for Elmbridge Div. of Surrey, 1944-50. Chairman, General Periodicals' Council, Periodical Proprietors' Assoc., 1947-51. Member Council of Royal College of Art, 1951-54; a Governor of the Star and Garter Home for Disabled Sailors, Soldiers and Airmen, 1943-76, Vice-Pres., 1976- (Chairman, Finance Cttee, 1964-68). Chm., Internat. Wine and Food Soc., 1972-75, Vice-Pres., 1975-. JP Richmond, Surrey, 1941- (Past Chairman of Bench and of Juvenile Court). Grand Officier, Confrérie des Chavaliers du Tastevin, 1977. *Publications:* Modern Love, 1927; All Abroad, 1928; A Respectable Man, 1935; Journey into Faith, 1963; Forty Years in Management, 1964; A Fashion of Life, 1966; The Wines of Burgundy, 1968; Retirement a Pleasure, 1971; The Enjoyment of Wine, 1972. *Recreations:* wine, bridge, golf. *Address:* 10 Campden House Court, W8. *T:* 01-937 3847. *Clubs:* Savile, Saintsbury; Richmond Golf (Richmond, Surrey).

YPRES, 3rd Earl of, *cr* 1922; Viscount, *cr* 1916; of Ypres and of High Lake; **John Richard Charles Lambart French;** *b* 30 Dec. 1921; *o s* of 2nd Earl and Olivia Mary (*d* 1934), *d* of Maj.-Gen. Thomas John; *S* father, 1958; *m* 1st, 1943, Maureen Helena (marr. diss. 1972), *d* of Major H. John Kelly, US Foreign Service (retd), and of Mrs Kelly, Stow Bedon Hall, Attleborough, Norfolk; three *d*; 2nd, 1972, Deborah, *d* of R. Roberts, Liverpool; one *d. Educ:* Winchester; Trinity Coll., Dublin. Served War of 1939-45 as Captain, King's Royal Rifle Corps. *Heir:* none.

YUDKIN, John, MA, PhD, MD, BCh (Cambridge); BSc (London); FRCP, FRIC, FIBiol; Professor of Nutrition, University of London, at Queen Elizabeth College, 1954-71, Emeritus Professor, since 1971; *b* 8 August 1910; 3rd *s* of Louis and Sarah Yudkin, London; *m* 1933, Emily Himmelweit; three *s*.

Educ: Hackney Downs (formerly Grocers' Company) School, London; Chelsea Polytechnic; Christ's Coll., Cambridge; London Hospital. Research in Biochemical Laboratory, Cambridge, 1931-36; Research in Nutritional Laboratory, Cambridge, 1938-43; Benn Levy Research Student, 1933-35; Grocers' Company Research Scholar, 1938-39; Sir Halley Stewart Research Fellow, 1940-43; Dir of Medical Studies, Christ's Coll., Cambridge, 1940-43; Prof. of Physiology, Queen Elizabeth Coll., 1945-54; Fellow, Queen Elizabeth Coll., London, 1976. William Julius Mickle Fellow, 1961-62. *Publications:* This Slimming Business, 1958; The Complete Slimmer, 1964; Changing Food Habits, 1964; Our Changing Fare, 1966; Pure, White and Deadly, 1972; This Nutrition Business, 1976; numerous articles on biochemistry and nutrition in scientific and medical journals. *Address:* 16 Holly Walk, Hampstead, NW3. *T:* 01-794 3023.

YUKAWA, Prof. Hideki; Decoration of Cultural Merit (Japan), 1943; Director, Research Institute for Fundamental Physics, Kyoto University, Japan, 1953-70; Professor Emeritus, Kyoto and Osaka Universities; *b* 23 Jan. 1907; *s* of Takuji and Koyuki Ogawa; *m* 1932, Sumi Yukawa; two *s. Educ:* Kyoto University, Kyoto, Japan. Asst Prof., Osaka Univ., Japan, 1936-39; visited Europe and USA, 1939. Awarded Imperial Prize of Japan Acad., 1940; Member of Japan Acad., 1946-. Visiting Prof., Institute for Advanced Study, Princeton USA, 1948-49; Visiting Prof., Columbia Univ., USA, 1949-51; For. Associate, Nat. Acad. of Sciences, USA, 1949; Foreign Member: Royal Society, London, 1963; Academy of Science, USSR. Nobel Prize for Physics, 1949; Lomonosov Medal, 1964; Order Pour le Merite, W Germany, 1967. *Publications:* Introduction to Quantum Mechanics (in Japanese), 1947; Introduction to Theory of Elementary Particles (in Japanese), 1948; Editor of Progress of Theoretical Physics, (Kyoto, Japan) 1946-; Reference: Physical Review (USA); Reviews of Modern Physics (USA). *Address:* Yukawa Hall, Kyoto University, Kyoto, Japan; Izumikawa, Shimogamo, Sakyo-ku, Kyoto, Japan.

YUKAWA, Morio, Hon. GCVO; Grand Master of Ceremonies, Imperial Household, Tokyo, since 1972; *b* 23 Feb. 1908; *m* 1940, Teiko Kohiyama; two *s. Educ:* Tokyo Imperial Univ. (Law Dept). Joined Diplomatic Service, and apptd Attaché, London, 1933; Dir, Trade Bureau of Economic Stabilization Bd (Cabinet), 1950; Dir, Econ. Affairs Bureau (For. Min.), 1951; Counsellor, Paris, 1952; Dir, Internat. Co-op. Bureau (For. Min.), 1954; again Dir, Econ. Affairs Bureau, 1955; Ambassador to The Philippines, 1957-61; Dep. Vice-Minister (For. Min.), 1961-63; Ambassador to Belgium, 1963-68; concurrently Ambassador to Luxembourg and Chief of Japanese Mission to European Economic Community, 1964-68; Ambassador to Court of St James's, 1968-72. Holds foreign decorations, inc. Hon. GCVO 1971. *Publications:* articles and brochures, principally on historical subjects. *Recreations:* golf, theatre, history and biography. *Address:* Sanbancho Hilltop, 5-10 Sanbancho, Chiyoda-ku, Tokyo, Japan. *Clubs:* Tokyo, Nihon, Gakushikai (Tokyo); Hodogaya Country (Yokohama).

YUKON, Bishop of, since 1968; **Rt. Rev. John Timothy Frame,** DD; *b* 8 Dec. 1930; *m* ; three *d. Educ:* Univ. of Toronto. Burns Lake Mission, Dio. Caledonia, 1957; Hon. Canon of Caledonia, 1965. *Address:* PO Box 4247, Whitehorse, Yukon Y1A 3T3, Canada.

Z

ZAFRULLA KHAN, Hon. Chaudhri Sir Muhammad, KCSI 1937; Kt 1935; BA (Hons, Punjab), LLB (Hons, London); Hon. Bencher, Lincoln's Inn; Barrister-at-Law, Lincoln's Inn; President, International Court of Justice, 1970-73 (Member, 1954-61, 1964-73); *b* 6 Feb. 1893. *Educ:* Government College, Lahore; King's Coll. and Lincoln's Inn, London. Advocate, Sialkot, Punjab, 1914-16; practised in Lahore High Court, 1916-35; Editor, "Indian Cases", 1916-32. Member, Punjab Legislative Council, 1926-35; Deleg. Indian Round Table Confs, 1930, 1931 and 1932; Deleg. to Joint Select Cttee on Indian Parliamentary Reforms, 1933; Pres. All-India Muslim League, 1931; Mem. Viceroy's Exec. Council, 1935-41; Leader Indian Deleg to Session of Assembly of League of Nations, Dec. 1939; Agent-General to Government of India in China, 1942; Judge, Indian Fedl Court, Oct. 1941-June 1947; Constitutional Adviser to Nawab of Bhopal, June-Dec. 1947; Minister of Foreign Affairs and Commonwealth Relations, Pakistan, 1947-54;

Leader Pakistan Delegn: to Annual Sessions of Gen. Assembly of UN, 1947-54; to Security Council of UN, on India-Pakistan dispute, 1948-51; Permanent Rep. of Pakistan at UN, 1961-64; Pres., UN Gen. Assembly, 1962. Hon. LLD: Cantab; Columbia; Denver; California; Hon. FKC London; Hon. Fellow, LSE. *Publications:* Indian Cases; the Criminal Law Journal of India; Reprints of Punjab Criminal Rulings, Vol. IV; Fifteen Years' Digest; Islam: Its Meaning for Modern Man, 1962; (ed and trans.) The Quran, 1970. *Address:* 16 Gressenhall Road, SW18.

ZAHEDI, Ardeshir; Ambassador of Iran to the United States, 1960-62 and since 1973; Ambassador of Iran to Mexico, 1973-76; *b* Tehran, 16 Oct. 1928; *s* of General Fazlollah and Khadijeh Zahedi; *m* 1957, HIH Princess Shahnaz Pahlavi (marr. diss., 1964); one *d. Educ:* American Coll. of Beirut; Utah State Univ. (BS). Treasurer, Jt Iran-American Commn, and Asst to Dir of Point 4 Program, 1950; took part in revolution led by Gen. Zahedi which overthrew Mossadegh, 1953; Special Adviser to Prime Minister, 1953; Chamberlain to HIM the Shahanshah of Iran, 1954-59; Head of Iranian Students Program, 1959-60; Head of Mission representing Iran at 150th Anniv. Celebrations in Argentina, 1960; Ambassador of Iran to the Court of St James's, 1962-66; Foreign Minister of Iran, 1967-71. Represented Iranian Govt: at signing of Treaty banning Nuclear Tests, London, 1963; at Independence Celebrations, Bahamas, 1973. Hon. Doctorates: Utah State Univ., 1951; Chungang Univ. of Seoul, 1969; East Texas State, 1973; Kent State Univ., 1974; St Louis Univ., 1975. Holds decorations from Iran and 23 other countries incl. Iranian Taj with Grand Cordon First Class, 1975. *Recreations:* hunting, shooting. *Address:* Imperial Embassy of Iran, 3005 Massachusetts Avenue, Washington, DC, USA.

ZAHIRUDDIN bin Syed Hassan, Tan Sri Syed, PSM, SPMP, JMN, PJK; Governor of Malacca, since 1975; *b* 11 Oct. 1918; *m* 1949, Puan Sri Halimah, *d* of Hj. Mohd. Noh; five *s* five *d. Educ:* Malay Coll., Kuala Kangsar; Raffles Coll., Singapore (Dip.Arts). Passed Cambridge Sch. Cert. Malay Officer, Tanjong Malim, etc, 1945-47; Dep. Asst Dist Officer, 1948; Asst Dist Officer, 1951-54; 2nd Asst State Sec., Perak, 1955; Registrar of Titles and Asst State Sec. (Lands), Perak, 1956; Dist Officer, Batang Padang, Tapah, 1957; Dep. Sec., Public Services Commn, 1958; Principal Asst Sec. (Service), Fedn Estabt Office, Kuala Lumpur, 1960; State Sec., Perak, 1961; Permanent Sec.: Min. of Agric. and Co-operatives, Kuala Lumpur, 1963; Min. of Educn, Kuala Lumpur, 1966; Dir-Gen., Public Services Dept, Kuala Lumpur, 1969; retd, 1972. High Comr for Malaysia in London, 1974-75. Chm., Railway Services Commn, Kuala Lumpur, 1972-. Chairman: Special Cttee on Superannuation in the Public Services and Statutory Bodies; Bd of Governors, Malay Coll., Kuala Kangsar; Interim Council of Nat. Inst. of Technology; Central Bd. Vice-Pres., Subang Nat. Golf Club. Hon. GCVO 1974. *Recreation:* golf. *Address:* Governor's Residence, Malacca, Malaysia.

ZAIDI, Bashir Husain, Syed, CIE 1941; Padma Vibhushan 1976; Chairman, Associated Journals Ltd, since 1952; Member: Court Aligarh University; Executive Council, Meerut University; Director of several industrial concerns; *b* 1898; *s* of Syed Shaukat Husain Zaidi; *m* 1937, Qudsia Abdullah (*d* 1960); two *s* one *d. Educ:* St Stephen's College, Delhi; Cambridge University. Called to Bar, Lincoln's Inn, 1923; served Aligarh Univ., 1923-30; entered Rampur State service, 1930; Chief Minister Rampur State, UP, 1936-49; Member: Indian Constituent Assembly, 1947-49, Indian Parliament, 1950-52; Indian Delegation to Gen. Assembly of UN, 1951; Indian Parliament (Lok Sabha), 1952-57; (Rajya Sabha) 1964-70; Govt of India's Commn of Inquiry on Communal Disturbances, 1967-69. Vice-Chancellor, Aligarh Muslim University, 1956-62. Leader, Good Will Mission to 9 Afro-Asian countries, 1964; Leader Cultural Delegn to participate in Afghan Independence Week celebrations, 1965; Mem., Governing Body, Indian Council for Cultural Relations. Vice-Pres., Youth Hostels Assoc. of India. DLitt *hc* : Aligarh 1964; Kanpur, 1974. *Address:* Zaidi Villa, Jamianagar, New Delhi, India.

ZAIMIS, Prof. Eleanor, MD; FRCP; Professor of Pharmacology in University of London at the Royal Free Hospital School of Medicine, since 1958; *b* 16 June 1915; *d* of late Jean Christides and of Helen Christides; *m* 1st, 1938, Evanghelos Chrysafis, MD; 2nd, 1943, John Zaimis, RHN (marr. diss. 1957). *Educ:* Greek Gymnasium; Universities of Bucharest, Roumania and Athens, Greece. MB 1938, MD 1941, BScChem 1947, Athens. Assistant to Professor of Pharmacology, Athens University, 1938-47; Head of Dept of Health, Youth Centres, Municipality of Athens, 1940-45; Member of Greek Government's Penicillin and Streptomycin Cttee, 1945-47. British Council Scholar, 1947-48; MRC Fellow, 1948-50; Research Worker: Dept of Pharmacology, Bristol University, Oct.-Dec. 1947; Depts of

Chemistry and Physiology, Nat. Inst. for Med. Research, London, Jan.-Nov. 1948; Dept of Pharmacology, School of Pharmacy, London University, 1948-50. Lecturer in Pharmacology, School of Pharmacy, London University, 1950-54; Reader in Pharmacology, London University, Royal Free Hospital School of Medicine, 1954-58. Visiting Lecturer: Univ. of Rio de Janeiro, 1958; Internat. Anaesthesiology Centre, WHO, Copenhagen, 1959. Cameron Prize, Edinburgh, 1956; Gairdner Foundation International Award, Toronto, 1958; Hon. Member, Rome Acad. Medicine, 1965; Corresp. Mem., Academy of Athens, 1971. Cross of Commander, Greek Royal Order of Benevolence, 1962; N. P. Kravkov Pharmacology Medal, USSR Acad. of Med. Sciences, 1968. *Publications:* Textbook on Hygiene (Greek Academy's Prize, 1948); (ed) Nerve Growth Factor and its Antiserum, 1972; (ed) Neuromuscular Junction, Heffter's Handbook of Experimental Pharmacology, vol. 42, 1976; papers on pharmacological and physiological subjects in scientific journals. *Recreation:* motoring. *Address:* Department of Pharmacology, Royal Free Hospital School of Medicine, 8 Hunter Street, WC1N 1BP. *T:* 01-837 5385; Flat 3, Marsh Mills, Wargrave Road, Henley-on-Thames, Oxon.

ZANGWILL, Prof. Oliver Louis, FRS 1977; Professor of Experimental Psychology, University of Cambridge, since 1952; *b* 29 Oct. 1913; *yr s* of Israel Zangwill, author and dramatist, and Edith Ayrton Zangwill; *m* 1st, 1947, Joy Sylvia (marr. diss. 1976), *d* of late Thomas Moult; 2nd, 1976, Shirley Florence Tribe, BDS (Edin.). *Educ:* University College School, London; King's College, Cambridge (BA 1935, MA 1939). Natural Science Tripos, Part I, Class 2, 1934; Moral Science Tripos, Part II, Class 1, with special distinction, 1935. Research Student, Cambridge Psychological Laboratory, 1935-40; Psychologist, Brain Injuries Unit, Edinburgh 1940-45; Asst Director, Institute of Experimental Psychology, Oxford, 1945-52; Senior Lecturer in General Psychology, Univ. of Oxford, 1948-52. Visiting Psychologist, Nat. Hosp. for Nervous Diseases, Queen Square, London, 1947-; Hon. Consulting Psychologist to United Cambridge Hospitals, 1969-. Editor, Quart. Jl Exper. Psychology, 1958-66. President: Sect. J. Brit. Assoc. Adv. Sci., 1963; Experimental Psychology Soc., 1962-63; British Psychological Soc., 1974-75. Mem., Biological Research Board, Medical Research Council, 1962-66. Professorial Fellow, King's College, Cambridge, 1955-. Mem., Assoc. of British Neurologists, 1973. Hon. For. Mem., Soc. Française de Neurologie, 1971. Sir Frederic Bartlett Lectr, 1971. Kenneth Craik Award, St John's Coll., Cambridge, 1977-78. *Publications:* An Introduction to Modern Psychology, 1950; Cerebral Dominance and its relation to psychological function, 1960; (Jt Author and Jt Editor) Current Problems in Animal Behaviour, 1961; (Jt Author and Jt Editor) Amnesia, 1966, 2nd edn 1977; papers in psychological and medical journals. *Recreations:* reading, natural history. *Address:* Psychological Laboratory, Downing Street, Cambridge. *T:* Cambridge 51386.

ZANUCK, Darryl Francis; Chairman of the Board and Chief Executive Officer, 20th Century-Fox Film Corporation, 1969-71, Chairman Emeritus since 1971; *b* 5 Sept. 1902; *s* of Frank H. and Louise Torpin Norton Zanuck; *m* 1924, Virginia Ogelsby Fox; one *s* two *d*. *Educ:* Oakdale, Nebraska; Los Angeles, Calif. Served European War, 1917-18, with 37th Div.; with Warner Bros till 1933 (Producer of Little Caesar, Public Enemy, Five Star Final, I am a Fugitive from a Chain Gang, The Jazz Singer); joined Joseph M. Schenck in 20th Century Pictures (Producer of House of Rothschild, Les Misérables, Cardinal Richelieu and others). Amalgamated 20th Century with Fox, 1935, and became Vice-Pres., later President; first winner Irving Thalberg Memorial Trophy, again winner in 1944 and 1951. Supervised production training films for defence forces, Lt-Col 1941; Col 1942 (Legion of Merit). *Films:* with 20th Century-Fox include: Wilson, How Green was my Valley, This above all, The Purple Heart, Winged Victory, Grapes of Wrath, The Razor's Edge, Forever Amber, Gentleman's Agreement, The Snake Pit, Pinky, All About Eve. D. F. Zanuck Productions: Island in the Sun, The Sun Also Rises, 1957; The Roots of Heaven, 1958. Produced: Crack in the Mirror, 1959 (Paris); The Big Gamble, 1960 (France, Ireland, Africa); The Longest Day, 1962. Comdr Legion of Honour (France); Comdr of Order of Arts and Letters (France), 1968; Comdr in Order of Merit (Italy), 1969. *Recreations:* big-game hunting, polo, ski-ing. *Address:* c/o 20th Century-Fox Film Corporation, 444 West 56th Street, New York, NY 10019, USA.

ZARNECKI, Prof. George, CBE 1970; MA, PhD; FSA; FBA 1968; Professor of History of Art, University of London, since 1963 (Reader, 1959-63); Deputy Director, Courtauld Institute of Art, 1961-74; *b* 12 Sept. 1915; *m* 1945, Anne Leslie Frith; one *s* one *d*. *Educ:* Cracow Univ. MA Cracow Univ., 1938; PhD Univ.

of London, 1950. Junior Asst, Inst. of History of Art, Cracow Univ., 1936-39. Served war of 1939-45 as lance-corporal in Polish Army; in France, 1939-40 (Polish Cross of Valour and Croix de Guerre, 1940); prisoner of war, 1940-42; interned in Spain, 1942-43; in Polish Army in UK, 1943-45. On staff of Courtauld Institute of Art, Univ. of London, 1945-. Slade Professor of Fine Art, Univ. of Oxford, 1960-61. Vice-President: Soc. of Antiquaries of London, 1968-72; British Soc. of Master Glass Painters, 1976-; Member: Conservation Cttee, Council for Places of Worship, 1969-75; Royal Commn on Historical Monuments, 1971-; Arts Sub-Cttee of UGC, 1972-; Inst. for Advanced Study, Princeton, 1966. *Publications:* English Romanesque Sculpture 1066-1140, 1951; Later English Romanesque Sculpture 1140-1210, 1953; English Romanesque Lead Sculpture, 1957; Early Sculpture of Ely Cathedral, 1958; Gislebertus, sculpteur d'Autun, 1960 (English edn, 1961); Romanesque Sculpture at Lincoln Cathedral, 1964; La sculpture a Payerne, Lausanne, 1966; 1066 and Architectural Sculpture (Proceedings of Brit. Acad.), 1966; Romanik (Belser Stilgeschichte, VI), 1970 (English edn, Romanesque Art, 1971); The Monastic Achievement, 1972; (contrib.) Westminster Abbey, 1972; Art of the Medieval World, 1975; articles in archaeological journals. *Address:* 22 Essex Park, N3 1NE. *T:* 01-346 6497.

ZEALLEY, Christopher Bennett; Chairman, Consumers' Association, since 1976; Director since 1970 and Trustee since 1976, Dartington Hall Trust; *b* 5 May 1931; *s* of Sir Alec Zealley and Lady Zealley (*née* King); *m* 1966, Ann Elizabeth Sandwith; one *s* one *d*. *Educ:* Sherborne Sch.; King's Coll., Cambridge (MA Law). Commnd RNVR, 1953; ICI Ltd, 1955-66; IRC, 1967-70. Chairman: Public Interest Research Centre, 1972-; Social Audit Ltd, 1972-. Director: British United Trawlers Ltd; JT Group Ltd; Good Food Club Ltd (Chm.); Dartington Hall Ltd. Mem. Council, NACRO. *Recreation:* music. *Address:* Culverwood, Rattery, South Brent, Devon. *Club:* Naval.

ZEEMAN, Prof. Erik Christopher, FRS 1975; Professor, Director of Mathematics Research Centre, University of Warwick, since 1964; Senior Fellow, Science Research Council, since 1976; *b* 4 Feb. 1925; *s* of Christian Zeeman and Christine Zeeman (*née* Bushell); *m* 1960, Rosemary Gledhill; three *s* two *d*. *Educ:* Christ's Hospital; Christ's Coll., Cambridge (MA, PhD). Commonwealth Fellow, 1954; Fellow of Gonville and Caius Coll., Cambridge, 1953-64; Lectr, Cambridge Univ., 1955-64. Visiting Prof. at various institutes, incl.: IAS; Princeton; IHES, Paris; IMPA, Rio; also at various univs, incl.: California, Florida, Pisa. Hon. Dr, Strasbourg. *Publications:* numerous research papers on topology, dynamical systems, and applications to biology and the social sciences, in various mathematical and other jls. *Recreation:* family. *Address:* 40 Warwick New Road, Leamington Spa. *T:* Leamington 26997.

ZEFFIRELLI, G. Franco (Corsi); opera, film and theatrical producer and designer since 1949; *b* 12 February 1923. *Educ:* Florence. Designer: (in Italy): A Streetcar Named Desire; Troilus and Cressida; Three Sisters. Has produced and designed numerous operas at La Scala, Milan, 1952-, and in all the great cities of Italy, at world-famous festivals, and in UK and USA; *operas include:* Lucia di Lammermoor, Cavalleria Rusticana, and Pagliacci (Covent Garden, 1959, 1973); Falstaff (Covent Garden, 1961); L'Elisir D'Amore (Glyndebourne, 1961); Don Giovanni, and Alcina (Covent Garden, 1962); Tosca, Rigoletto (Covent Garden, 1964, 1966, 1973); Don Giovanni (Staatsoper-Wien, 1972); Otello (Metropolitan, NY, 1972); Antony and Cleopatra (Metropolitan, NY, 1973); Otello (La Scala, 1976); *stage:* Romeo and Juliet (Old Vic, 1960); Othello (Stratford-on-Avon), 1961; Amleto (National Theatre), 1964; After the Fall (Rome), 1964; Who's Afraid of Virginia Woolf (Paris), 1964, (Milan), 1965; La Lupa (Rome), 1965; Much Ado About Nothing (National Theatre), 1966; Black Comedy (Rome), 1967; A Delicate Balance (Rome), 1967; Saturday, Sunday, Monday (Nat. Theatre), 1973; *films:* The Taming of the Shrew, 1965-66; Florence, Days of Destruction, 1966; Romeo and Juliet, 1967; Brother Sun, Sister Moon, 1973; Jesus of Nazareth, 1977. Produced Beethoven's Missa Solemnis, San Pietro, Rome, 1971. *Address:* Via due Macelli 31, Rome.

ZEHETMAYR, John Walter Lloyd, VRD 1963; FIFor; Senior Officer for Wales and Conservator South Wales, Forestry Commission, since 1966; *b* 24 Dec. 1921; *s* of late Walter Zehetmayr and late Gladys Zehetmayr; *m* 1945, Isabell (Betty) Neill-Kennedy; two *s* one *d*. *Educ:* St Paul's, Kensington; Keble Coll., Oxford (MA). Served RNVR, 1942-46 (despatches); now Lt Cdr RNR retired. Forestry Commission: Silviculturist, 1948-56; Chief Work Study Officer, 1956-64; Conservator West Scotland, 1964-66. Mem. Prince of Wales' Cttee. *Publications:* Experiments in Tree Planting on Peat, 1954; Afforestation of

Upland Heaths, 1960. *Recreations:* garden, conservation, skiing. *Address:* The Haven, Augusta Road, Penarth, S Glam CF6 2RH.

ZEPLER, Eric Ernest; Emeritus Professor of Electronics, Southampton University (Professor, 1949-63); Research Fellow, Institute of Sound and Vibration, Southampton University, 1963-73; Past President British IRE; *b* 27 Jan. 1898; *s* of Dr med. M. Zepler and F. Guttfreundt; *m* 1926, Eleanor Fischer; one *s* one *d. Educ:* Realgymnasium Altena (Westphalia); Univ. Bonn, Berlin, Würzburg. Dr Phil., Würzburg, 1922. Research Engineer, Telefunken, 1925; Head of Design of Receivers and Direction Finders, Telefunken, 1932-35; came to England, 1935; Research Engineer, Marconi's Wireless Tel. Co. Ltd, 1936-40; Lecturer University Coll., Southampton, 1941; seconded to Cavendish Laboratory, 1943-46. Hon. DSc Southampton, 1977. *Publications:* The Technique of Radio Design, 1943; (contrib. 2 chapters) University Radio Conference Proceedings, 1944; Under the Spell of the Chess Problem, 1951; (co-editor with S. W. Punnett) Electronic Devices and Networks, 1963; Electronic Circuit Techniques, 1963; (with K. G. Nichols) Transients in Electronic Engineering, 1971; contrib. to Telefunken Zeitung, Wireless Engr. *Recreations:* music, chess, bridge. *Address:* 6 Saxholm Way, Southampton SO1 7GU. *T:* Southampton 768020.

ZETLAND, 3rd Marquess of; Lawrence Aldred Mervyn Dundas; Bt 1762; Baron Dundas, 1794; Earl of Zetland, 1838; Earl of Ronaldshay (UK), 1892; DL; Temporary Major Yorkshire Hussars (TA); *b* 12 Nov. 1908; *er s* of 2nd Marquess of Zetland, KG, PC, GCSI, GCIE, FBA, and Cicely, *d* of Colonel Mervyn Archdale; *S* father, 1961; *m* 1936, Penelope, *d* of late Col Ebenezer Pike, CBE, MC; three *s* one *d. Educ:* Harrow; Trinity Coll., Cambridge. ADC on Staff of Viceroy of India, 1930-31. DL, North Yorks, 1965. *Heir: s* Earl of Ronaldshay, *qv. Address:* Aske, Richmond, North Yorks DL10 5HJ. *T:* Richmond (Yorks) 3222; 59 Cadogan Place, SW1. *T:* 01-235 6542. *Club:* All England Lawn Tennis.

ZETTER, Paul Isaac; Chairman: Zetters Group Ltd, since 1972; Sports Aid Foundation Ltd, since 1976; *b* 9 July 1923; *s* of Simon Zetter and Esther Zetter; *m* 1954, Helen Lore Morgenstern; one *s* one *d. Educ:* City of London Sch. Army, 1941-46. Family business, 1946-; became public co., 1965. *Publication:* It Could Be Verse, 1976. *Recreations:* varied water sports, writing. *Address:* 86 Clerkenwell Road, EC1. *Club:* Royal Automobile.

ZETTERLING, Mai Elizabeth; Actress, films and stage, film director, writer; *b* 24 May 1925; *d* of Joel and Lina Zetterling; *m* 1st, 1944, Tutte Lemkow; one *s* one *d*; 2nd, 1958, David John Hughes (marr. diss. 1977). *Educ:* Stockholm, Sweden. Graduate of Royal Theatre School of Drama, Stockholm. First appeared as Cecilia in Midsummer Dream in the Workhouse, Blanche Theatre, Stockholm, Oct. 1941. Stage successes (all at Royal Theatre, Stockholm) include: Janet in St Mark's Eve; Agnes in The Beautiful People; Brigid in Shadow and Substance; Maria in Twelfth Night; Nerissa in Merchant of Venice; Electra in Les Mouches; Adela in House of Bernarda. First appearance in London, as Hedwig in The Wild Duck, St Martin's, Nov. 1948; subsequently Nina in The Seagull, Lyric, Hammersmith, and St James's, 1949; Eurydice in Point of Departure, Lyric, Hammersmith and Duke of York's, 1950; Karen in The Trap, Duke of York's, 1952; Nora Helmer in A Doll's House, Lyric, Hammersmith, 1953; Poppy in The Count of Clérambard, Garrick, 1955; Thérèse Tard in Restless Heart, St James's, 1957; Tekla in Creditors, Lyric, Hammersmith, 1959, etc. *Swedish films* include: Frenzy, Iris, Rain Follows Dew, Music in the Dark, A Doll's House, Swinging on a Rainbow. *English films* include: Frieda, The Bad Lord Byron, Quartet, Portrait from Life, Lost People, Blackmailed, Hell is Sold Out, Tall Headlines, Desperate moment, Faces in the Dark, Offbeat, The Main Attraction, and Only Two Can Play. *United States films* include: Knock on Wood, Prize of Gold, and Seven Waves Away. Director of documentary films for BBC; Dir and Prod and co-writer with David Hughes of short film The War Game; 1st Award at Venice for Narrative Shorts, 1963; Director: Swedish full-length films, Alskande Par, (Eng.) Loving Couples, 1965; Night Games, 1966 (and see *infra*); Dr Glas, 1968; Flickorna, 1968; The Girls, 1968; Writer and Director: Visions of Eight (Olympics film), USA, 1972; Vincent the Dutchman, (award 1973;) We Have Many Names (and actress), Sweden, 1975; The Moon is a Green Cheese, Sweden, 1976; The Native Squatter (for Canadian TV), Sweden, 1977. *Publications:* The Cat's Tale (with David Hughes), 1965; Night Games (novel), 1966; Shadow of the Sun (short stories), 1975; Bird of Passage (novel), 1976. *Recreations:* gardening, cooking, alchemy. *Address:* c/o Douglas Rae Management Ltd, 28 Charing Cross Road, W1.

ZHUKOV, Georgi Alexandrovich; Orders of: Lenin; Red Banner of Labour (2); Red Star; Joliot-Curie Medal; Columnist of Pravda, since 1962; Alternate Member, Central Committee, CPSU, since 1976; MP since 1962; Member, Foreign Relations Committee, USSR Supreme Soviet, since 1966; Chairman, Soviet-French parliamentary group, since 1966; Vice-President, Soviet Committee of Peace, since 1965, Member Presidium, World Peace Council, since 1974; Vice-President, Soviet-American Institute, since 1961; President, Society USSR-France, since 1958; Secretary, Moscow writing organization, since 1970; *b* 1908. *Educ:* Lomonosov Inst., Moscow. Corresp.: local papers in Lugansk, Kharkov, 1927-32; Komsomolskaya Pravda, 1932-46 (Mem. Editorial Bd) Pravda, 1946-47; Pravda in Paris, 1947-52; Foreign Editor of Pravda, 1952-57; Chairman, USSR Council of Ministers' State Committee for Cultural Relations with Foreign Countries, 1957-62. Mem., Central Auditing Cttee of CPSU, 1956-76, elected by XX, XXII, XXIII and XXIV Congresses of CPSU. Prizes: Lenin (for Journalism); Vorovsky; Union of Soviet Journalists; internat. organization of journalists. *Publications:* Border, 1938; Russians and Japan, 1945; Soldier's Life, 1946; American Notes (essays), 1947; The West After War, 1948; Three Months in Geneva, 1954; Taming Tigers, 1961; Japan, 1962; Meetings in Transcarpathia, 1962; One MIG from a Thousand, 1963; These Seventeen Years, 1963; Silent Art, 1964; The People of the Thirties, 1964; Vietnam, 1965; America, 1967; The People of the Forties, 1968, 2nd edn 1975; From Battle to Battle: letters from the ideological struggle front, 1970; Chilean Diary, 1970; The USA on the Threshold of the Seventies, 1970; The People in the War (about Vietnam), 1972; 33 Visas, 1972; Times of Great Changes, 1973; Alex and others, 1974; Poisoners, 1975; The War: the beginning and the end, 1975; Letters from Rambouillet, 1975; European Horizons, 1975; Thirty Conversations with TV viewers, 1977. *Address:* 24 Pravda Street, Moscow, USSR.

ZIEGLER, Henri Alexandre Léonard; Grand Officier, Légion d'Honneur; Croix de Guerre (1939-45); Rosette de la Résistance; Hon. CBE; Hon. CVO; Legion of Merit (US); French Aviation Executive; *b* Limoges, 18 Nov. 1906; *s* of Charles Ziegler and Alix Mousnier-Buisson; *m* 1932, Gillette Rizzi; three *s* one *d. Educ:* Collège Stanislas, Paris; Ecole Polytechnique (Grad.); Ecole Nationale Supérieure de l'Aéronautique. Officer-Pilot in French Air Force, 1928 (5000 hours); Tech. Officer, Min. of Aviation, 1929; Dep. Dir of Flight Test Centre, 1938; Foreign Missions: Gt Britain, USA, Germany, Poland, USSR. War of 1939-45: Dep. Buying Mission, USA, Dec. 1939; French Resistance, 1941-44; Col and Chief of Staff, Forces Françaises de l'Intérieur (London), 1944. Dir-Gen., Air France, 1946-54. Dir of Cabinet: of J. Chaban-Delmas (Min. of Public Works, Transport and Tourism), 1954; of Gen. Cormiglion-Molignier (Min. of Public Works), 1955-56; Admin. Dir-Gen., Ateliers d'aviation Louis Breguet, 1957-67. Pres. Dir-Gen.: Sud Aviation, 1968; Soc. Nationale Industrielle Aérospatiale, 1970-73; Pres., Airbus Industrie, 1970-74. Pres., Air Alpes, 1961-76; Pres., Forum Atomique Européen (FORATOM), 1956-60; Admin. Inst. du Transport Aérien, 1969; Pres., Union Syndicale des Industries Aérospatiales, 1971-74. Mem., Amicale des anciens des essais en vol. Hon. Fellow, Soc. of Experimental Test Pilots; Hon. FRAeS. *Recreation:* alpinism. *Address:* 55 boulevard Lannes, 75116 Paris, France. *Club:* Aéro-Club de France (Paris).

ZIEGLER, Philip Sandeman; Editorial Director, William Collins and Sons, since 1972; *b* 24 Dec. 1929; *s* of Major Colin Louis Ziegler, DSO, DL, and Mrs Dora Ziegler (*née* Barnwell); *m* 1st, 1960, Sarah Collins; one *s* one *d*; 2nd, 1971, Mary Clare Charrington; one *s. Educ:* Eton; New Coll., Oxford (1st Cl. Hons Jurisprudence; Chancellor's Essay Prize). Entered Foreign Service, 1952; served in Vientiane, Paris, Pretoria and Bogotá; resigned 1967; joined William Collins and Sons Ltd, 1967. *Publications:* Duchess of Dino, 1962; Addington, 1965; The Black Death, 1968; William IV, 1971; Omdurman, 1973; Melbourne, 1976 (W. H. Heinemann Award). *Address:* 22 Cottesmore Gardens, W8 5PR. *T:* 01-937 1903. *Club:* Travellers'.

ZIENKIEWICZ, Prof. Olgierd Cecil; Professor, and Head of Civil Engineering Department, University of Wales at Swansea, since 1961; *b* Caterham, 18 May 1921; *s* of Casimir Zienkiewicz and Edith Violet (*née* Penny); *m* 1952, Helen Jean (*née* Fleming), Toronto; two *s* one *d. Educ:* Katowice, Poland; Imperial Coll., London. BSc (Eng); ACGI; PhD; DIC; DSc (Eng); DipEng; FICE; FASCE. Consulting engrg, 1945-49; Lectr, Univ. of Edinburgh, 1949-57; Prof. of Structural Mechanics, Northwestern Univ., 1957-61. Hon. Founder Mem., GAMNI, France. Chairman: Cttee on Analysis and Design, Internat. Congress of Large Dams; Jt Computer Cttee, Instn of Civil Engineers. Mem. Council, ICE, 1972-75 (Chm., S Wales and Mon. Br.); Telford Premium, ICE, 1963-67. James Clayton Fund Prizes, IMechE, 1967, 1973. Hon. Dr, Lisbon, 1972; Hon. DSc NUI, 1975. General Editor, Internat. Jl Numerical Methods in Engineering; Member Editorial Board: Internat. Jl Solids and Structures; Internat. Jl Earthquakes and Structural Mechanics; Internat. Jl Rock Mechanics. *Publications:* Stress Analysis, 1965; Rock Mechanics, 1968; Finite Element Method, 1967, 3rd edn 1977; Optimum Design of Structures, 1973; Finite Elements in Fluids, 1975; numerous papers in Jl ICE, Jl Mech. Sci., Proc. Royal Soc., etc. *Recreations:* sailing, skin-diving. *Address:* 29 Somerset Road, Langland, Swansea. *T:* Swansea 68776. *Clubs:* Rotary (Mumbles); Bristol Channel Yacht, Mumbles Yacht.

ZIJLSTRA, Jelle; Central Banker; President, Netherlands Bank, since 1967; *b* 27 Aug. 1918; *s* of Ane Zijlstra and Pietje Postuma; *m* 1946, Hetty Bloksma; two *s* three *d*. *Educ:* Netherlands Sch. of Economics. Asst, Netherlands Sch. of Economics, 1945; Prof., Theoretical Economics, 1948-52; Prof., Public Finance, 1963-66, Free Univ. of Amsterdam; Minister of Economic Affairs, 1952-58; of Finance, 1959-1963; Prime Minister, 1966-67. Mem., Chm. Board, and Pres., BIS, 1967-; Governor, IMF, 1967-. *Publications:* Planned Economy, 1947; The Velocity of Money and its Significance for the Value of Money and for Monetary Equilibrium, 1948; Economic Order and Economic Policy, 1952. *Recreations:* sailing, ski-ing. *Address:* De Nederlandsche Bank NV, Westeinde 1, Amsterdam, Netherlands; Bavoylaan 14, Den Haag, Netherlands.

ZILKHA, Selim Khedoury; Chairman/Managing Director, Mothercare Ltd and associate companies, since 1961; *b* 7 April 1927; *s* of Khedoury Aboodi Zilkha and Louise (*née* Bashi); *m* (marr. diss.); one *s* one *d*. *Educ:* English Sch., Heliopolis, Egypt; Horace Mann Sch. for Boys, USA; Williams Coll., USA (BA Major Philos.). Chairman: Amerfin Co. Ltd, GB, 1955-68; Spirella Co. of Great Britain Ltd, 1957-62; Chm./Jt Man. Dir, Lewis & Burrows Ltd, 1961-64. Dir, Zilkha & Sons Inc., USA, 1947-. *Recreations:* bridge, backgammon, golf, tennis. *Address:* 74 Portland Place, W1. *T:* 01-580 3563. *Clubs:* Portland, Brooks's; Sunningdale Golf; Travellers' (Paris).

ZIMAN, Herbert David; Literary Editor of The Daily Telegraph, 1956-68; *b* Hampstead, 21 March 1902; *s* of late David Ziman, Reefton, New Zealand and Lena (*née* Cohen); *m* 1928, Jean Ritchie, *d* of late C. J. Macalister, MD, FRCP, TD, of Liverpool and Bourton-on-the-Water; two *d* (and one *s* decd). *Educ:* Rugby (Scholar and Senior Leaving Exhibitioner) and University College, Oxford (Senior Scholar). Leader-writer and Asst Literary Editor, Liverpool Daily Post, 1925-26; Film critic of Liverpool Daily Post, 1926-29, and of Glasgow Herald, 1927-29; Museum, Library and Archæological Correspondent, The Times, 1930-33; Leader-writer, Daily Telegraph, 1934-39, and 1946-55. Served in Artists' Rifles, Middlesex Regt and Intelligence Corps (GSO3 South-Eastern Command and Southern Command) and in Political Intelligence Dept, 1939-44. Daily Telegraph War Correspondent in France, Belgium, Holland and Germany with 1st Canadian, 2nd British and 1st US Armies, 1944-45. Special Correspondent of Daily Telegraph subsequently in Western Europe, Greece, Turkey, USSR, Israel, China, Uganda, Kenya, Congo, United States, Canada, Mexico, Chile and Brazil. Hon. Secretary, Friends of the National Libraries, 1931-37, Exec. Cttee FNL, 1937-; Council, Anglo-Belgian Union, 1957-. *Address:* 10 Eton Road, NW3. *T:* 01-722 5526. *Club:* Reform.

ZIMAN, Prof. John Michael, FRS 1967; Henry Overton Wills Professor of Physics and Director of the H. H. Wills Physics Laboratory, University of Bristol, since 1976; *b* 16 May 1925; *s* of late Solomon Netheim Ziman, ICS, retired, and Nellie Frances Ziman (*née* Gaster); *m* 1951, Rosemary Milnes Dixon; two adopted *s* two adopted *d*. *Educ:* Hamilton High Sch., NZ; Victoria University Coll., Wellington, NZ; Balliol Coll., Oxford. Junior Lectr in Mathematics, Oxford Univ., 1951-53; Pressed Steel Co. Ltd Research Fellow, Oxford Univ., 1953-54; Lectr in Physics, Cambridge Univ., 1954-64; Fellow of King's Coll., Cambridge, 1957-64; Editor of Cambridge Review, 1958-59; Tutor for Advanced Students, King's Coll., Cambridge, 1959-63; Prof. of Theoretical Physics, 1964-69, Melville Wills Prof. of Physics, 1969-76, Univ. of Bristol. Rutherford Memorial Lectr in India and Pakistan, 1968. Chm., Council for Science and Society; Mem., Scientific Council, Internat. Centre for Theoretical Physics, Trieste. *Publications:* Electrons and Phonons, 1960; Electrons in Metals, 1963; (with Jasper Rose) Camford Observed, 1964; Principles of the Theory of Solids, 1965; Public Knowledge, 1968; Elements of Advanced Quantum Theory, 1969; The Force of Knowledge, 1976; numerous articles in scientific jls. *Address:* H. H. Wills Physics Laboratory, Tyndall Avenue, Bristol BS8 1TL. *T:* 24161.

ZIMBALIST, Efrem; Violinist; Director of The Curtis Institute of Music, Philadelphia, 1941-68, retired; *b* Russia, 1889; *m* 1st, 1914, Alma Gluck, singer; one *s* one *d*; 2nd, 1943, Mary Louise Curtis Bok. Musical training Imperial School, St Petersburg, under Leopold Auer. Has concertized continuously since debut in 1907 in Berlin. Composer of works for orchestra: American Rhapsody; Concerto for violin and orchestra (1st performance with Philadelphia Orchestra, 1947); Landara (Opera Première, Acad. of Music, Phila, 1957); Concerto for piano and orchestra (1st perf. with New Orleans Symph. Orch., 1959); String Quartet in E minor; Violin Sonata; many minor works for voice, violin and piano. *Address:* 2255 Lindley Way, Reno, Nevada 89502, USA.

ZINN, Major William Victor, CEng, FICE, FIStructE; MEIC (Canada), MSCE (France); Principal of W. V. Zinn & Associates, International Consulting Civil and Structural Engineers, since 1934; *b* 7 July 1903; *s* of late Roman Reuben Zinn and Bertha Zinn (*née* Simon); *m* 1st, 1934, Laure (*d* 1960), *d* of Chaim and Fleur Modiano, London; one *s* one *d*; 2nd, 1963, Monica, *d* of late Alan Ribton-Turner and Josephine Ribton-Turner (*née* Carey). *Educ:* University College Sch. and University Coll., London. BSc(Eng), MConsE London. War Service, 14th Army Burma, Major RE (retd), 1939-45. Sen. Partner: Haigh Zinn & Associates, Haigh Zinn & Humphreys, and Airport Development Consultants; New Steelworks, Guest Keen & Nettlefolds, Cardiff, 1932-35; Consultant assisting UKAEA and Min. of Works on Atomic Power Stations at Harwell, Windscale, Capenhurst, Calder Hall, Chapel Cross and Dounreay, 1952-56. *Works:* London Hilton Hotel and Royal Garden Hotel; London Govt Offices: Min. of Transport, Min. of Housing, Min. of Works, Dept of Postmaster-Gen., Central Electricity Authority and Min. of Civil Aviation; County Halls: Devon, Gloucester, Norfolk, Lanarkshire, 1954-66; Housing Projects for UK Local Authorities, totalling over 53,000 dwellings, 1934-69; overseas: Princes Bldg and Mandarin Hotel, also Brit. Mil. Hosp., Hong Kong, 1965; Feasibility Reports for World Bank: Teesta Barrage, and Chandpur Irrigation Project (East Pakistan), 1960-62; Ceylon Water Supplies and Drainage for World Health Organisation of the UNO, 1968; development of new techniques for deep underground city excavations, 1960-66; Engineering Consultant for Livingston New Town, Scotland, 1968; Tsing Yi Bridge (2,000 ft), Hong Kong, 1973; underground car park, Houses of Parliament, Westminster, 1974. *Publications:* Economical Construction of Deep Basements, 1968; Detailing by Computer, 1969. *Address:* Longdene, Haslemere, Surrey.

ZINNEMANN, Fred; Film Director since 1934; *b* Austria, 29 April 1907; *s* of Dr Oskar Zinnemann, Physician and Anna F. Zinnemann; *m* 1936, Renée Bartlett; one *s*. *Educ:* Vienna Univ. (Law School). First film, The Wave (documentary) directed for Mexican Govt, 1934; initiated, with others, school of neo-realism in American cinema, directing among other films: The Seventh Cross, 1943; The Search, 1948; The Men, 1949; Teresa, 1950; High Noon, 1951; Member of the Wedding, 1952; From Here to Eternity, 1953. Later films include: Oklahoma!, 1956; The Nun's Story, 1959; The Sundowners, 1960; Behold a Pale Horse, 1964; A Man for All Seasons, 1966; The Day of the Jackal, 1973; Julia, 1977. Member: Amer. Film Inst.; Acad. of Motion Picture Arts; Directors' Guild of America. Awards include: Academy Award, Los Angeles, 1951, 1954, 1967; Film Critics' Award, NY, 1952, 1954, 1960, 1967; Golden Thistle Award, Edinburgh, 1965; Moscow Film Festival Award, 1967; D. W. Griffith Award, 1970. Gold Medal of City of Vienna, 1967. *Publication:* article on directing films, Encyclopædia Britannica. *Recreations:* mountain climbing, chamber music. *Address:* 37 Blomfield Road, W9. *T:* 01-289 0433. *Club:* Sierra (San Francisco).

ZOBEL de AYALA, Jaime; Philippine Ambassador to the Court of St James's and concurrently to Scandinavian countries, 1971-74; *b* 18 July 1934; *s* of Alfonso Zobel de Ayala and Carmen Pfitz y Herrero; *m* 1958, Beatriz Miranda; two *s* five *d*. *Educ:* La Salle, Madrid; Harvard Univ. (BA, Arch. Scis). Major, Philippine Air Force (Res.). Chm. of Board and Senior Vice-Pres., Ayala Corp. First Pres., Cultural Center of Philippines, 1969-70. Comendador de la Orden del Merito Civil, Spain, 1968; Knight of Grand Band, Liberia, 1972. *Recreation:* horseback riding. *Address:* Ayala Corporation, PO Box 259, Commercial Centre, Makati, Rizal, D-708, Philippines. *Clubs:* White's; Fox (Harvard).

ZOUCHE, 18th Baron, *cr* 1308, of Haryngworth; **James Assheton Frankland;** Bt 1660; served 15/19th the King's Royal Hussars, 1963-68; *b* 23 Feb. 1943; *s* of Major Hon. Sir Thomas William Assheton Frankland, 11th Bt, and Mrs Robert Pardoe (*d* 1972), *d* of late Capt. Hon. Edward Kay-Shuttleworth; *S* to father's Btcy 1944; S grandmother, 17th Baroness Zouche, 1965. *Educ:* Lycée Jaccard, Lausanne. *Heir: u* Hon. Roger Nathaniel Frankland [*b* 11 April 1909; *m* 1st, 1931 (marr. diss., 1947); two *s* ; 2nd, 1947, Olivia, *d* of Rev. Hon. Nigel Campbell and *widow* of Major S. J. R. Bucknill, Irish Guards]. *Address:* The Courthouse, Leck, by Carnforth, Lancs. *Club:* Cavalry and Guards.

ZSÖGÖD, Géza B. G.; *see* Grosschmid-Zsögöd, G. B.

ZUCKERMAN, family name of **Baron Zuckerman.**

ZUCKERMAN, Baron *cr* 1971 (Life Peer), of Burnham Thorpe, Norfolk; **Solly Zuckerman,** OM 1968; KCB 1964 (CB 1946); Kt 1956; FRS 1943; MA, MD, DSc; MRCS, FRCP; Chief Scientific Adviser to HM Government, 1964-71; Professor Emeritus, University of Birmingham; Professor Emeritus, University of East Anglia; Fellow of University College, London; *b* Cape Town, 1904; *m* 1939, Lady Joan Rufus Isaacs, *er* of 2nd Marquess of Reading, PC, GCMG, CBE, MC, TD, QC; one *s* one *d. Educ:* S African College Sch.; Univ. of Cape Town (Liberman Scholar); University Coll. Hosp., London (Goldsmid Exhibitioner). Demonstrator of Anatomy, Univ. of Cape Town, 1923-25; Union Research Scholar, 1925; Research Anatomist to the Zoological Soc. of London, and Demonstrator of Anatomy, University Coll., London, 1928-32; Research Associate and Rockefeller Research Fellow, Yale Univ., 1933-34; University Demonstrator and Lectr in Human Anatomy Dept, Oxford, 1934-45; Sands Cox Prof. of Anatomy, Univ. of Birmingham, 1943-68; Prof. at Large, Univ. of East Anglia, 1969-74. William Julius Mickle Fellow, Univ of London, 1935; Beit Memorial Research Fellow, 1934-37; Hunterian Prof., Royal Coll. of Surgeons, 1937; Agricultural Research Council, 1949-59; Chm., Defence Research Policy Cttee, 1960-64; Chm., Cttee on Scientific Manpower, 1950-64; Chm. Natural Resources (Techn.) Cttee, 1951-64; Dep. Chm. Advisory Council on Scientific Policy, 1948-64; Chief Scientific Adviser to the Sec. of State for Defence, 1960-66; Chm., Central Adv. Cttee for Science and Technology, 1965-70. Mem., Royal Commn on Environmental Pollution, 1970-74. Visitor, Bedford Coll., 1968-. Lectures: Gregynog, University Coll. of Wales, 1956; Mason, Univ. of Birmingham, 1957; Lees Knowles, Cambridge, 1965; Maurice Lubbock, Oxford, 1967; Maurice Bloch, Glasgow, 1969, Trueman Wood, RSA, 1969; TLS, 1971; Compton, MIT, 1972; Lord Hastings Meml, Norwich, 1972; Romanes, Oxford, 1975; Rhodes, S Africa, 1975. BBC Gen. Adv. Council, 1957-62. President: Zoological Soc., London, 1977- (Hon. Sec., 1955-77); Fauna Preservation Soc., 1974-; Hon. Mem. Acad. das Ciencias de Lisboa; Fellow Commoner, Christ's Coll., Cambridge. President: Parly and Scientific Cttee, 1973-76; Assoc. Learned and Professional Soc. Publishers, 1973-; British Indust. Biological Res. Assoc., 1973-77. Mem., WHO Adv. Cttee on Med. Research, 1974-. Dr (*hc*) Univ. of Bordeaux, 1961. Group Capt. (Hon.) RAF, 1943-46. Scientific Advisory posts, Combined Ops RAF, 1939-46. A Trustee of the British Museum (Natural History), 1967-. Hon. DSc: Univ. of Sussex, 1963; Jacksonville, 1964; Bradford, 1966; Hon. LLD Birmingham, 1970. Hon. Fellow RCS, 1964; Hon. FPS, 1975; FIBiol. Foreign Member: American Philosophical Soc.; Amer. Acad. of Arts and Sciences. Gold Medal, Zoolog. Soc. of London, 1971; Medal of Freedom with Silver Palm (US); Chevalier de la Légion d'Honneur (France). *Publications:* The Social Life of Monkeys and Apes, 1932; Functional Affinities of Man, Monkeys and Apes, 1933; A New System of Anatomy, 1961; Scientists and War, 1966; The Image of Technology, 1968; Beyond the Ivory Tower, 1970; (ed) The Ovary (Vols 1 and 2), 1961; (ed) The Zoological Society of London 1826-1976 and Beyond, 1977; contributions to scientific journals. *Address:* University of East Anglia, University Village, Norwich. *Clubs:* Beefsteak, Brooks's.

ZUKERMAN, Pinchas; concert violinist; *b* Tel Aviv, Israel, 16 July 1948; *s* of Jehuda and Miriam Zukerman; *m* 1968, Eugenia Rich, flautist; two *d* . *Educ:* Juilliard School of Music. Début, USA, 1969; Europe, 1970. Violin soloist with every major orchestra in USA and Europe; tours of USA, Europe, Israel, Scandinavia, Australia; extensive recordings. First prize, Leventritt Internat. Violin Competition, 1967. *Recreations:* tennis, horseback riding. *Address:* c/o Sheldon Gold, ICM Artists Ltd, 40 West 57th Street, New York, NY 10019, USA. *T:* (212) 556-5600.

ZULU, Rt. Rev. Alphaeus Hamilton; *b* 29 June 1905; *m* 1929, Miriam Adelaide Magwaza; one *s* six *d* . *Educ:* St Chad's Coll., Ladysmith (qual. teacher); Univ. of S Africa. BA (dist. Soc. Anthrop.) 1938; LTh 1940. Deacon, 1940; Priest, 1942. Curate of St Faith's Mission, Durban, 1940-52, Priest-in-charge, 1952-60; Suffragan Bishop of St John's, (formerly St John's, Kaffraria), 1960-66; Bishop of Zululand, 1966-75. Jt Pres.,

World Council of Churches, 1968-75. Hon. PhD Natal, 1974. *Recreation:* tennis. *Address:* PO Box 177, Edendale, Natal 4505, S Africa.

ZULUETA, Sir Philip Francis de, Kt 1963; Chairman, Antony Gibbs Holdings Ltd, since 1976 (Chief Executive, 1973-76); *b* 2 Jan. 1925; *o s* of late Professor Francis de Zulueta; *m* 1955, Hon. Marie-Louise, *e d* of 2nd Baron Windlesham; one *s* one *d. Educ:* Beaumont; New College, Oxford (Scholar). MA. Welsh Guards, NW Europe, 1943-47 (Capt., 1945). Foreign Service, 1949: Moscow, 1950-52; Private Sec. to successive Prime Ministers (Lord Avon, Mr Macmillan, Sir A. Douglas-Home), 1955-64. Asst Sec., HM Treasury, 1962. Resigned from Foreign Service and joined Philip Hill-Higginson, Erlangers, 1964; Director: Hill Samuel & Co., 1965-72; Tangyanika Concessions Ltd; Union Minière, and other cos. Member: Adv. Council, BBC, 1967-71; Franco-British Council, Exec. Cttee, Trilateral Commn. Kt of Honour and Devotion, SMO Malta, 1965. *Address:* 11 Vicarage Gardens, W8 4AH. *T:* 01-229 1177; Eastergate House, Eastergate, West Sussex PO20 6UT. *T:* Eastergate 2108. *Clubs:* Beefsteak, Pratt's, White's; Jockey (Paris).

ZUNTZ, Prof. Günther, FBA 1956; DrPhil (Marburg); Emeritus Professor, Manchester University; Professor of Hellenistic Greek, 1963-69; *b* 28 Jan. 1902; *s* of Dr Leo Zuntz and Edith (*née* Bähring); *m* 1947, M. A. Garratt; two *s* one *d. Educ:* Bismarck-Gymnasium, Berlin-Wilmersdorf; Berlin, Marburg, Göttingen and Graz Universities. Teacher, Odenwaldschule, 1924-26; Teacher, Marburg Gymnasium and Kassel Gymnasium, 1926-32; worked for Monumenta Musicae Byzantinae, in Copenhagen, 1935-39, in Oxford, 1939-47; Librarian, Mansfield College, Oxford, 1944-47; Senior Lecturer, Manchester University, 1947-55 (Reader, 1955-63). Korresp. Mitglied, Oesterreich. Akad. der Wissenschaften, 1974. *Publications:* Hölderlins Pindar-Übersetzung, 1928; (with C. Höeg) Prophetologium, i-vi, 1939-71; The Ancestry of the Harklean New Testament, 1945; The Text of the Epistles, 1953; The Political Plays of Euripides, 1955, corrected repr., 1963; The Transmission of Plays of Euripides, 1965; Persephone, 1971; Opuscula Selecta, 1972. Articles in many learned journals. *Recreation:* music. *Address:* Westbourne, 43 Manchester Road, Buxton, Derbyshire. *T:* Buxton 2805.